Peterson

How to Get Money for College 2014

PETERSON'S

About Peterson's

Peterson's provides the accurate, dependable, high-quality education content and guidance you need to succeed. No matter where you are on your academic or professional path, you can rely on Peterson's print and digital publications for the most up-to-date education exploration data, expert test-prep tools, and top-notch career success resources—everything you need to achieve your goals.

Visit us online at **www.petersonsbooks.com** and let Peterson's help you achieve your goals.

For more information, contact Peterson's, 3 Columbia Circle, Suite 205, Albany, NY 12203-5158; 800-338-3282 Ext. 54229; or find us on the World Wide Web at www.petersonspublishing.com.

Previous editions published as *How to Get Money for College* © 2009, 2010, 2011, 2012; *Peterson's College Money Handbook* © 1983, 1984, 1985, 1986, 1987, 1988, 1989, 1990, 1991, 1997, 1998, 1999, 2000, 2001, 2002, 2003, 2004, 2005, 2006, 2007, 2008; and as *Paying Less for College* © 1992, 1993, 1994, 1995, 1996

Bernadette Webster, Managing Editor; Jill C. Schwartz, Editor; Ken Britschge, Research Project Manager; Nicole Gallo, Research Associate; Phyllis Johnson, Software Engineer; Ray Golaszewski, Publishing Operations Manager; Linda M. Williams, Composition Manager

Peterson's makes reasonable efforts to obtain accurate, complete, and timely data from reliable sources. Nevertheless, Peterson's and the third-party data suppliers make no representation or warranty, either expressed or implied, as to the accuracy, timeliness, or completeness of the data or the results to be obtained from using the data, including, but not limited to, its quality, performance, merchantability, or fitness for a particular purpose, non-infringement or otherwise.

Neither Peterson's nor the third-party data suppliers warrant, guarantee, or make any representations that the results from using the data will be successful or will satisfy users' requirements. The entire risk to the results and performance is assumed by the user.

ISSN 1544-2330
ISBN: 978-0-7689-3757-2

Printed in the United States of America

10 9 8 7 6 5 4 3 2 1   15 14 13

Thirty-first Edition

By producing this book on recycled paper (40% post-consumer waste) 196 trees were saved.

Sustainability—Its Importance to Peterson's

What does sustainability mean to Peterson's? As a leading publisher, we are aware that our business has a direct impact on vital resources—most especially the trees that are used to make our books. Peterson's is proud that its products are certified to the Sustainable Forestry Initiative (SFI) chain-of-custody standard and that all of its books are printed on paper that is 40 percent post-consumer waste using vegetable-based ink.

Being a part of the Sustainable Forestry Initiative (SFI) means that all of out vendors—from paper suppliers to printers—have undergone rigorous audits to demonstrate that they are maintaining a sustainable environment.

Peterson's continuously strives to find new ways to incorporate sustainability throughout all aspects of its business.

Contents

A Note from the Peterson's Editors

The news media seem to constantly remind us that a college education is expensive. It certainly appears to be beyond the means of many Americans. The sticker price for four years at state-supported colleges can be more than $45,000, and private colleges and universities can cost more than $150,000. And these numbers continue to rise.

But there is good news. The system operates to provide the needed money so that most families and students are able to afford a college education while making only a reasonable financial sacrifice. However, because the college financial aid system is complex, finding the money is often easier said than done. That is why the process demands study, planning, calculation, flexibility, filling out forms, and meeting deadlines. Fortunately, for most people, it can produce positive results. There are many ways to manage college costs and many channels through which you can receive help. Be sure to take full advantage of the opportunities that have been opened up to students and their families by the many organizations, foundations, and businesses that have organized to help you with the burden of college expenses.

For nearly forty years, Peterson's has given students and parents the most comprehensive, up-to-date information on how to get their fair share of the financial aid pie. *Peterson's How to Get Money for College* is both a quick reference and a comprehensive resource that puts valuable information about college costs and financial aid opportunities at your fingertips.

- **The ABCs of Paying for College** provides insight into federal financial aid programs that are available, offers an overview of the financial aid landscape, walks you through the process of filing for aid, and provides proven tips on how to successfully navigate the financial aid process to obtain the federal, state, and institutional aid you deserve.

- The **Quick-Reference Chart** offers a snapshot comparison of the financial aid programs available at more than 2,500 four-year institutions across the country.

- The **Profiles of College Financial Aid Programs** provide unbiased financial aid data for each of the more than 2,500 four-year institutions listed.

- The **Appendix** lists the state scholarship and grant programs offered by all fifty states and the District of Columbia.

- The six **Indexes** included in the back of the book allow you to search for specific award programs based on a variety of criteria, including merit-based awards, athletic grants, ROTC programs, and much more.

Peterson's publishes a full line of books—financial aid, education exploration, test prep, and career preparation. Peterson's publications can be found at high school guidance offices, college libraries and career centers, and your local bookstore and library. Peterson's books are now also available as eBooks and online at www.petersonsbooks.com.

We welcome any comments or suggestions you may have about this publication. Your feedback will help us make educational dreams possible for you—and others like you.

The ABC's of Paying for College

A Guide to Financing Your Child's College Education

Don Betterton

Given the lifelong benefit of a college degree (college graduates are projected to earn in a lifetime $1 million more than those with only a high school diploma), higher education is a worthwhile investment. However, it is also an expensive one made even more difficult to manage by cost increases that have outpaced both inflation and gains in family income. The reality of higher education economics is that paying for a child's college education is an issue that shows no sign of getting easier.

Because of the high cost involved (even the most inexpensive four-year education at a public institution costs about $10,000 a year), good information about college budgets and strategies for reducing the "sticker price" is essential. You have made a good start by taking the time to read *Peterson's How to Get Money for College*. In the pages that follow, you will find valuable information about the four main sources of aid—federal, state, institutional, and private. Before you learn about the various programs, however, it will be helpful if you have an overview of how the college financial aid system operates and what long-range financing strategies are available.

FINANCIAL AID

Financial aid refers to money that is awarded to a student, usually in a "package" that consists of gift aid (commonly called a scholarship or grant), a student loan, and/or a campus job.

COLLEGE COSTS

The starting point for organizing a plan to pay for your child's college education is to make a good estimate of the yearly cost of attendance. You can use the **College Cost Worksheet** on the next page to do this.

To estimate your college costs for 2014–15, refer to the tuition and fees and room and board figures shown in the College **Costs At-a-Glance** chart. If your child will commute from your home, use $2,500 instead of the college's room and board charges and $900 for transportation. We have used $800 for books and $1,500 for personal expenses. Finally, estimate the cost of two round trips if your home is more than a few hundred miles from the college. Add the items to calculate the total budget. You should now have a reasonably good estimate of college costs for 2014–15. (To determine the costs for later years, adding 4 percent per year will probably give you a fairly accurate estimate.)

DO YOU QUALIFY FOR NEED-BASED AID?

The next step is to evaluate whether or not you are likely to qualify for financial aid based on need. This step is critical, since more than 90 percent of the yearly total of $128 billion in student aid is awarded only after a determination is made that the family lacks sufficient financial resources to pay the full cost of college on its own. To judge your chance of receiving need-based aid, it is necessary to estimate an Expected Family Contribution (EFC) according to a government formula known as the Federal Methodology (FM). The official Federal Student Aid Website provides a FAFSA4caster tool (similar to an EFC calculator) that helps you get a head start on the financial aid process, including getting an early estimate of your eligibility for federal aid. The tool will also allow you to transfer the information provided into the actual Free Application for Federal Student Aid (FAFSA) form when you are ready to complete it. You can find the tool at http://www.fafsa4caster.ed.gov/F4CApp/index/index.jsf.

APPLYING FOR NEED-BASED AID

Because the federal government provides about 67 percent of all aid awarded, the application, FAFSA, and need evaluation process is controlled by the U.S. Department of Education. In addition, nearly every state that offers student assistance uses the federal government's system to award its own aid. Furthermore, in addition to arranging for the payment of federal and state aid, many colleges use the FAFSA to award their own funds to eligible students. (Note: In addition to the FAFSA, some colleges also ask the family to complete the CSS/Financial Aid PROFILE® application.)

The FAFSA is your "passport" to receiving your share of the billions of dollars awarded annually in need-based aid. Even if you're uncertain as to whether or not you qualify for need-based aid, everyone who might need assistance in financing an education should pick up a FAFSA from the high school guidance office after mid-November 2013. This form will ask for 2013 financial data, and it should be filed after January 1, 2014, in time to meet the earliest college or state scholarship deadline. Within two to four weeks after you submit the form, you will receive a summary of the FAFSA

College Cost Worksheet

	College 1	College 2	College 3	Commuter College
Tuition and Fees	_____	_____	_____	_____
Room and Board	_____	_____	_____	$2,500
Books	$ 800	$ 800	$ 800	$ 750
Personal Expenses	$1,500	$1,500	$1,500	$1,500
Travel	_____	_____	_____	$ 900
Total Budget	_____	_____	_____	_____

information, called the Student Aid Report, or SAR. The SAR will give you the EFC and also allow you to make corrections to the data you submitted.

You can also apply for federal student aid via the Internet using FAFSA on the Web. FAFSA on the Web can be accessed at www.fafsa.ed.gov. Both the student and at least one parent should apply for a federal PIN number at www.pin.ed.gov. The PIN number serves as your electronic signature when applying for aid on the Web. (Note: Many colleges provide the option to apply for early decision or early action admission. If you apply for this before January 1, 2014, which is prior to when the FAFSA can be used, follow the college's instructions. Many colleges use either PROFILE or their own application form for early admission candidates.)

AWARDING AID

About the same time you receive the SAR, the colleges you list will receive your FAFSA information so they can calculate a financial aid award in a package that typically includes aid from at least one of the major sources—federal, state, college, or private. In addition, the award will probably consist of a combination of a scholarship, grant, loan, or campus job. These last two pieces—loan and job—are called self-help aid because they require effort on your child's part (that is, the aid must be either earned through work or paid back later). Scholarships or grants are outright gifts that have no such obligation.

It is important that you understand each part of the package. You'll want to know, for example, how much aid is a gift, the interest rate and repayment terms of the student loan, or how many hours per week the campus job requires. There should be an enclosure with the award letter that answers these questions. If not, make a list of your questions and call or visit the financial aid office.

Once you understand the terms of each item in the award letter, you should turn your attention to the "bottom line"— how much you will have to pay at each college where your child

is accepted. In addition to understanding the aid award, this means having a good estimate of the college budget so you can accurately calculate how much you and your child will have to contribute. (Often, an aid package does not cover the entire need.) Colleges differ in how much detail they include in their award notifications. Many colleges provide full information— types and amounts of aid, yearly costs, and the EFC for the parent and student shares. If these important items are missing or incomplete, you can do the work on your own. (See the **Comparing Financial Aid Awards and Family Contribution Worksheet** on this page.) For example, if the award letter only shows the college's direct charges—tuition, room, and board— you need to estimate indirect costs such as books, personal expenses, and travel. Then subtract the total aid awarded from the yearly cost to get the EFC. A portion of that amount may be your child's contribution (35 percent of student assets and 50 percent of student earnings over $2,200) and the remainder is the parental share. If you can afford this amount at your child's first-choice college, the financial aid system has worked well for you, and your child's college enrollment plans can go forward.

But if you think your EFC is too high, you should contact the college's financial aid office and ask whether additional aid is available. Many private high-cost colleges are willing to work with families to help make attendance at their institutions possible. Most colleges also allow applicants to appeal their financial aid awards, the budget used for you, or any of the elements used to determine the family contribution, especially if there are extenuating circumstances or if the information has changed since the application was submitted. Some colleges may also reconsider an award based on a "competitive appeal," the submission of a more favorable award letter from another college.

If your appeal is unsuccessful and there is still a gap between the expected family contribution and what you feel you can pay from income and savings, you are left with two choices. One option is for your child to attend a college where paying your share of the bill will not be a problem. (This assumes that an affordable option was included on your child's original list of colleges, a wise admission application strategy.)

Comparing Financial Aid Awards and Family Contribution Worksheet

	College 1	College 2	College 3
Cost of Attendance	_____	_____	_____
Aid Awarded	_____	_____	_____
Grant/Scholarship	_____	_____	_____
Loan	_____	_____	_____
Job	_____	_____	_____
Total Aid	_____	_____	_____
Expected Family Contribution	_____	_____	_____
Student Contribution	_____	_____	_____
Parent Contribution	_____	_____	_____

The second is to look into alternate methods of financing. At this stage, parental loans and tuition payment plans are the best financing options. A parental loan can bring the yearly cost down to a manageable level by spreading payments over a number of years. This is the type of financing that families use when purchasing a home or automobile. A tuition payment plan is essentially a short-term loan and allows you to pay the costs over ten to twelve months. It is an option for families who have the resources available but need help with managing their cash flow.

NON-NEED-BASED AID

Regardless of whether you might qualify for a need-based award, it is always worthwhile to look into merit, or non-need, scholarships from sources such as foundations, agencies, reli-gious groups, and service organizations. For a family that isn't eligible for need-based aid, merit scholarships are the only form of gift aid available. If your child later qualifies for a need-based award, a merit scholarship can be quite helpful in providing additional resources if the aid does not fully cover the costs. Even if the college meets 100 percent of need, a merit scholarship reduces the self-help (loan and job) portion of an award.

In searching for merit-based scholarships, keep in mind that there are relatively few awards (compared to those that are need-based), and most of them are highly competitive. Use the following checklist in your search.

- Take advantage of any scholarships for which your child is automatically eligible based on parents' employer benefits, military service, association or church membership, other affiliations, or student or parent attributes (ethnic back-

How Need Is Calculated and Aid Is Awarded

	College 1	College 2
Total Cost of Attendance	$10,000	$ 24,000
− Expected Family Contribution	− 5,500	− 5,500
= Financial Need	$ 4,500	$ 18,500
− Grant Aid Awarded	− 675	−14,575
− Campus Job (Work-Study) Awarded	− 1,400	− 1,300
− Student Loan Awarded	− 2,425	− 2,625
= Unmet Need	0	0

Note: Sometimes an institution is unable to meet all need. The amount of unmet need is called "the gap."

ground, nationality, and so on). Company or union tuition remissions are the most common examples of these awards.

- Look for other awards for which your child might be eligible based on the previous characteristics and affiliations but where there is a selection process and an application is required. Free computerized searches are available on the Internet. (You should not pay a fee for a scholarship search.) Peterson's free scholarship search can be accessed by logging on to www.petersons.com/finaid. Scholarship directories, such as *Peterson's Scholarships, Grants & Prizes*, which details more than 3,600 scholarship programs, and *Peterson's Best Scholarships for Best Students* are useful resources and can be found in bookstores, high school guidance offices, or public libraries and are also available as eBooks.

- See if your state has a merit scholarship program.

- Look into national scholarship competitions. High school guidance counselors usually know about these scholarships. Examples of these awards are the National Meritt Scholarship Program, the Coca-Cola Scholarship, Gates Millennium Scholars, Intel Science Talent Search, and the U.S. Senate Youth Program.

- ROTC (Reserve Officers' Training Corps) scholarships are offered by the Army, Navy, Air Force, and Marine Corps. A full ROTC scholarship covers tuition, fees, textbook costs and, in some cases, a stipend. Acceptance of an ROTC scholarship entails a commitment to take military science courses and to serve for a specific number of years as an officer in the sponsoring branch of the service. Competition is heavy, and preference may be given to students in certain fields of study, such as engineering, languages, science, and health professions. Application procedures vary by service. Contact an armed services recruiter or high school guidance counselor for further information.

- Investigate community scholarships. High school guidance counselors usually have a list of these awards, and announcements are published in local newspapers. Most common are awards given by service organizations like the American Legion, Rotary International, and the local women's club.

- If your child is strong academically or is very talented in fields such as athletics or performing/creative arts, you may want to consider colleges that offer their own merit awards to gifted students they wish to enroll. Refer to the Non-Need Scholarships for Undergraduates index.

In addition to merit scholarships, there are loan and job opportunities for students who do not qualify for need-based aid. Some of the organizations that sponsor scholarships—for example, the Air Force Aid Society—also provide loans.

Work opportunities during the academic year are another type of assistance that is not restricted to aid recipients. Many colleges will, after assigning jobs to students on aid, open campus positions to all students looking for work. In addition, there are usually off-campus employment opportunities available to everyone.

Note

A point of clarification about whether to put college savings in your name or your child's: If you are certain that your child will not be a candidate for need-based aid, there may be a tax advantage to accumulating money in his or her name. However, when it comes to maximizing aid eligibility, it is important to understand that student assets are assessed at a 20 percent rate and parental assets at about 5 percent. Therefore, if your college savings are in your child's name, it may be wise to reestablish title to these funds before applying for financial aid. You should contact your financial planner or accountant before making any modifications to your asset structure.

FINANCING YOUR CHILD'S COLLEGE EDUCATION

"Financing" means putting together resources to pay the balance due the college over and above payments from the primary sources of aid—grants, scholarships, student loans, and jobs. Financing strategies are important because the high cost of a college education today often requires a family, whether or not it receives aid, to think about stretching its college payment beyond the four-year period of enrollment. For high-cost colleges, it is not unreasonable to think about a 10-4-10 plan: ten years of saving; four years of paying college bills out of current income, savings, and borrowing; and ten years to repay a parental loan.

Savings

Although saving for college is always a good idea, many families are unclear about its advantages. Some families do not save because after normal living expenses have been covered, they do not have much money to set aside. An affordable but regular savings plan through a payroll deduction is usually the answer to the problem of spending your entire paycheck every month.

The second reason why saving for college is not a high priority is the belief that the financial aid system penalizes a family

What Is CSS/Financial Aid PROFILE®?

There are many complexities in the financial aid process: knowing which aid is merit-based and which aid is need-based; understanding the difference between grants, loans, and work-study; and determining whether funds are from federal, state, institutional, or private sources.

In addition, the aid application process itself can be confusing. It can involve more than the Free Application for Federal Student Aid (FAFSA) and the Federal Methodology (FM). Many colleges feel that the federal aid system (FAFSA and FM) does not collect or evaluate information thoroughly enough for them to award their own institutional funds. These colleges have made an arrangement with the College Scholarship Service, a branch of the College Board, to establish a separate application system.

The application is called the CSS/Financial Aid PROFILE®, and the need-analysis formula is referred to as the Institutional Methodology (IM). If you apply for financial aid at one of the colleges that uses PROFILE, the admission material will state that PROFILE is required in addition to the FAFSA. You should read the information carefully and file PROFILE to meet the earliest college deadline. Before you can receive PROFILE, however, you must register, either by phone or through the Web (https://profileonline.collegeboard.com/index.jsp), providing enough basic information so the PROFILE package can be designed specifically for you. The FAFSA is free, but there is a charge for PROFILE. As with the FAFSA, PROFILE can be submitted via the Internet.

In addition to the requirement by certain colleges that you submit both the FAFSA and PROFILE (when used, PROFILE is always in addition to the FAFSA; it does not replace it), you should understand that each system has its own method for analyzing a family's ability to pay for college. The main differences between PROFILE's Institutional Methodology and the FAFSA's Federal Methodology are:

- PROFILE includes equity in the family home as an asset; the FAFSA doesn't.

- PROFILE takes a broader look at assets not included on the FAFSA.

- PROFILE expects a minimum student contribution, usually in the form of summer earnings; the FAFSA has no such minimum.

- PROFILE may collect information on the noncustodial parent; the FAFSA does not.

- PROFILE allows for more professional judgment than the FAFSA. Medical expenses, private secondary school costs, and a variety of special circumstances are considered under PROFILE, subject to the discretion of the aid counselor on campus.

- PROFILE includes information on assets not reported on the FAFSA, including life insurance, annuities, retirement plans, etc.

To summarize: PROFILE's Institutional Methodology tends to be both more complete in its data collection and more rigorous in its analysis than the FAFSA's Federal Methodology. When IM results are compared to FM results for thousands of applicants, IM will usually come up with a somewhat higher expected parental contribution than FM.

Creditworthiness

If you will be borrowing to pay for your child's college education, making sure you qualify for a loan is critical. For the most part, that means your credit record must be free of default or delinquency. You can check your credit history with one or more of the following three major credit bureaus and clean up any adverse information that appears. The numbers below will offer specific information on what you need to provide to obtain a report. All of the credit bureaus accept credit report requests over their Web sites. You will usually be asked to provide your full name, phone number, social security number, birth date, and addresses for the last five years. You are entitled to a free report from each bureau.

Equifax Credit Information
P.O. Box 740241
Atlanta, GA 30374
800-685-1111
http://www.equifax.com

Trans Union
800-888-4213
http://www.transunion.com

Experian
888-397-3742
http://www.experian.com

by lowering aid eligibility. The Federal Methodology of need determination is very kind to families that save. In fact, savings are ignored completely for most families that earn less than $50,000. Savings in the form of home equity, retirement plans, and most annuities are excluded from the calculation. And even when savings are counted, a maximum of 5 percent of the total is expected each year. In other words, if a family has $40,000 in savings after an asset protection allowance is considered, the contribution is no greater than $2,000. Given the impact of compound interest it is easy to see that a long-term savings plan can make paying for college much easier.

A sensible savings plan is important because of the financial advantage of saving compared to borrowing. The amount of money students borrow for college is now greater than the amount they receive in grants and scholarships. With loans becoming so widespread, savings should be carefully considered as an alternative to borrowing. Your incentive for saving is that a dollar saved is a dollar not borrowed.

Borrowing

Once you've calculated your "bottom-line" parental contribution and determined that the amount is not affordable out of your current income and assets, the most likely alternative is borrowing. Beginning July 1, 2010, as a result of the Health Care and Education Reconciliation Act, federal student loans are no longer made by private lenders under the Federal Family Education Loan (FFEL) Program. Instead, all new federal student loans come directly from the U.S. Department of Education under the Direct Loan Program, which offers subsidized and unsubsidized (Stafford) loans for students, PLUS loans for parents and graduate/professional students, and consolidation loans for both students and parents. For additional information, go online to

https://studentloans.gov/myDirectLoan/index.action or call 800-4-FED-AID (toll-free).

For the Direct PLUS Loan, parents must complete a Direct PLUS Loan application and promissory note, contained in a single form that can be obtained from a school's financial aid office. The yearly limit on a PLUS Loan is equal to the student's cost of attendance minus any other financial aid the student receives. For example, if your cost of attendance is $6,000, and you receive $4,500 in other financial aid, your parents can borrow up to $1,500. PLUS loans carry fixed rates for loans made on or after July 1, 2006. The fixed interest rate for Direct PLUS loans is 7.9 percent. Interest is charged on a PLUS Loan from the date of the first disbursement until the loan is paid in full. A PLUS Loan made to the parent cannot be transferred to the student. The parent is responsible for repaying the PLUS Loan. For more details about PLUS Loans, visit www.direct.ed.gov/about.html.

MAKE FINANCIAL AID WORK FOR YOU

If you are like millions of families that benefit from financial aid, it is likely that your child's college plans can go forward without undue worry about the costs involved. The key is to understand the financial aid system and to follow the best path for your family. The result of good information and good planning should be that you will receive your fair share of the billions of dollars available each year and that the cost of college will not prevent your child from attending.

Don Betterton is a former Director of Undergraduate Financial Aid at Princeton University and a Certified College Planner (CCP).

Federal Financial Aid Programs

There are a number of sources of financial aid available to students: federal and state governments, private agencies, and the colleges themselves. In addition, there are three different forms of aid: grants, earnings, and loans.

The federal government is the single largest source of financial aid for students. In recent years, the U.S. Department of Education's student financial aid programs made more than $80 billion available in loans, grants, and other aid to 14 million students. At present, there are four federal grant programs—Federal Pell Grant, Federal Supplemental Educational Opportunity Grant (FSEOG), Teacher Education Assistance for College and Higher Education (TEACH) Grant, and Iraq and Afghanistan Service Grant. There are two federal loan programs: Federal Perkins Loan Program and the William D. Ford Federal Direct Loan Program. The federal government also has a job program, Federal Work-Study Program (FWS), which helps colleges provide employment for students. In addition to the student aid programs, there are also tuition tax credits and deductions. They are the American Opportunity Credit, the Lifetime Learning Credit, the Tuition and Fees Tax Deduction, and the Student Loan Interest Tax Deduction. Also, there is AmeriCorps. AmeriCorps will pay the interest that is accrued on qualified student loans for members who complete the service program.

The majority of federal higher education loans are made in the Direct Loan Program, which makes available two kinds of loans: loans to students and PLUS loans to parents or to graduate or professional students. These loans are either subsidized or unsubsidized. Subsidized loans are made on the basis of demonstrated student need, and the interest is paid by the government during the time the student is in school or deferment. For the unsubsidized (non-need-based) loans and PLUS loans, interest begins to accrue as funds are disbursed.

All new federal student loans come directly from the U.S. Department of Education under the Direct Loan Program. Students interested in receiving federal student aid should continue to complete a Free Application for Federal Student Aid (FAFSA) for each school year that they wish to be considered for aid. For more information about applying for federal student aid, call 800-4-FED-AID (800-433-3243)(toll-free) or visit www.fafsa.ed.gov.

FEDERAL PELL GRANT

The Federal Pell Grant is the largest grant program; more than 6 million students receive Pell Grants annually. This grant is intended to be the starting point of assistance for lower-income families. Eligibility for a Pell Grant is based on the Expected Family Contribution. The amount you receive will depend on your EFC and the cost of education at the college you will attend. The highest award depends on how much funding the program receives from the government. The maximum for 2014–15 is $5,645. Pell Grants range from $605 to $5,645. As of July 1, 2012, a student can not receive a Federal Pell Grant for more than 12 semesters or the equivalent. A student will receive notice when he/she is close to their limit.

FEDERAL SUPPLEMENTAL EDUCATIONAL OPPORTUNITY GRANT (FSEOG)

As its name implies, Federal Supplemental Educational Opportunity Grants provide additional need-based federal grant money to supplement the Federal Pell Grant Program. Each participating college is given funds to award to especially needy students. The maximum award is $4,000 per year, but the amount you receive depends on the college's awarding policy, the availability of FSEOG funds, the total cost of education, and the amount of other aid awarded.

FEDERAL WORK-STUDY PROGRAM (FWS)

This program provides jobs for students who demonstrate need. Salaries are paid by funds from the federal government as well as the college. Students work on an hourly basis on or off campus and must be paid at least the federal minimum wage. Students may earn only up to the amount awarded in the financial aid package.

FEDERAL PERKINS LOAN PROGRAM

This is a low-interest (5%) loan for students with exceptional financial need. Perkins Loans are made through the college's financial aid office with the college as the lender. Undergraduate students can borrow a maximum of $5,500 per year, and there is a cumulative limit of $27,500. The annual limit for graduate and professional-degree-seeking students is $8,000 with a total cumulative limit (including the $27,500) of $60,000. Borrowers may take up to ten years to repay the loan, beginning nine months after they graduate, leave school, or drop below half-time status. No interest accrues while they are in school, and, under certain conditions (e.g., they teach in low-income areas, work in law enforcement, are full-time nurses or medical technicians, serve as Peace Corps or VISTA volunteers, etc.), some or all of the loan can be cancelled. In addition, payments can be deferred under certain conditions such as unemployment.

FEDERAL DIRECT LOANS

A Direct Loan is borrowed directly from the U.S. Department of Education through the college's financial aid office.

The Unsubsidized Direct Loan Program carries a fixed 6.8 percent interest rate. The interest rate for Direct Subsidized Loans first disbursed between July 1, 2010, and June 30, 2011,

Federal Financial Aid Programs

Name of Program	Type of Program	Maximum Award Per Year
Federal Pell Grant	need-based grant	$5,645
Federal Supplemental Educational Opportunity Grant (FSEOG)	need-based grant	$4,000
Teacher Education Assistance for College and Higher Education (TEACH) Grants	need/merit	up to $4,000 a year (based on strict criteria being met)
Iraq and Afghanistan Service Grant	need/merit	$5,645 (based on strict criteria being met)
Federal Work-Study Program (FWS)	need-based part-time job	no maximum
Federal Perkins Loan Program	need-based loan	$5,500
Subsidized Federal Direct Loan	need-based grant student loan	$3,500 (first year)
Unsubsidized Federal Direct Loan	non-need based	$5,500 (first year, dependent student)

was 4.5 percent. For Direct Subsidized loans disbursed on or after July 1, 2011, and before June 30, 2013, the interest rate is fixed at 3.4 percent. Note: The interest rate on new loans for July 1, 2013 through July 1, 2014 was not available at the time of this book's publication.

The maximum amount dependent students may borrow in any one year is $5,500 for freshmen, $6,500 for sophomores, and $7,500 for juniors and seniors, with a maximum of $31,000 for the total undergraduate program (of which not more than $23,000 can be subsidized). The maximum amount independent students can borrow is $9,500 for freshmen (of which no more than $3,500 can be subsidized), $10,500 for sophomores (of which no more than $4,500 can be subsidized), and $12,500 for juniors and seniors (of which no more than $5,500 can be subsidized). Independent students can borrow up to $57,500 (of which no more than $23,000 can be subsidized) for the total undergraduate program. Borrowers may be charged a small origination fee, which is deducted from the loan proceeds. See the helpful, easy-to-read chart on the next page for maximum annual and total subsidized and unsubsidized loan limits.

To apply for a Federal Student Loan, you must first complete the FAFSA to determine eligibility for a subsidized loan and then complete a separate loan application that is submitted to the Department of Education. The Department of Education will send a master promissory for completion. The proceeds of the loan, less the origination fee, will be sent to the college to be either credited to your account or released to you directly.

Direct loans are processed by the financial aid office as part of the overall financial aid package.

Once the repayment period starts, borrowers of both subsidized and unsubsidized Federal Direct Loans have to pay a combination of interest and principal monthly for up to a 25-year period. There are a number of repayment options as well as opportunities to consolidate federal loans. There are also provisions for extended repayments, deferments, and repayment forbearance, if needed. Note: If you receive a Direct Subsidized Loan that is first disbursed between July 1, 2012, and July 1, 2014, you will be responsible for paying any interest that accrues during your grace period (first six months after graduation). If you choose not to pay the interest that accrues during your grace period, the interest will be added to your principal balance.

DIRECT PLUS LOANS

PLUS loans are for parents of dependent students to help families with the cost of education. There is no needs test to qualify. A Direct PLUS Loan has a fixed interest rate of 7.9 percent. There is no yearly limit; you can borrow up to the cost of your child's education, less other financial aid received. Repayment begins sixty days after the funds are disbursed. The origination fee is 4 percent and may be subtracted from the proceeds. Parent borrowers must generally have a good credit record to qualify.

Maximum Annual and Total Subsidized and Unsubsidized Loan Limits as of July 1, 2012.

Year	Dependent Students (except students whose parents are unable to obtain PLUS Loans)	Independent Students (and dependent undergraduate students whose parents are unable to obtain PLUS Loans)
First-Year Undergraduate	$5,500—No more than $3,500 of this amount may be in subsidized loans.	$9,500—No more than $3,500 of this amount may be in subsidized loans.
Second-Year Undergraduate	$6,500—No more than $4,500 of this amount may be in subsidized loans.	$10,500—No more than $4,500 of this amount may be in subsidized loans.
Third-Year and Beyond Undergraduate	$7,500 per year—No more than $5,500 of this amount may be in subsidized loans.	$12,500 per year—No more than $5,500 of this amount may be in subsidized loans.
Graduate or Professional Degree Students	Not Applicable	$20,500
Maximum Total Debt from Subsidized and Unsubsidized Loans	$31,000—No more than $23,000 of this amount may be in subsidized loans.	$57,500 for undergraduates—No more than $23,000 of this amount may be in subsidized loans. $138,500 for graduate or professional students—No more than $65,500 of this amount may be in subsidized loans. The graduate debt limit includes all federal loans received for undergraduate study.

Source: http://studentaid.ed.gov/types/loans/subsidized-unsubsidized

AMERICAN OPPORTUNITY CREDIT AND LIFETIME LEARNING CREDIT

Tuition tax credits allow families to reduce their tax bill by the out-of-pocket college tuition expense. Unlike a tax deduction, which is modified according to your tax bracket, a tax credit is a dollar-for-dollar reduction in taxes paid.

There are two programs: the American Opportunity Credit and the Lifetime Learning Credit. As is true of many federal programs, there are numerous rules and restrictions that apply. You should check with your tax preparer, financial adviser, or IRS Publication 970 for information about your own particular situation.

American Opportunity Credit

The American Opportunity Credit (formerly the Hope Credit) can be claimed for expenses for the first four years of postsecondary education. This is a change from the previous Hope Credit. The American Opportunity Credit includes expenses for course-related books, supplies, and equipment. It is a tax credit of up to $2,500 of the cost of qualifying tuition and expenses, and up to 40 percent of the credit is refundable (up to $1,000).

Eligibility also differs from the former Hope Credit. A taxpayer who pays qualified tuition and related expenses and whose federal income tax return has a modified adjusted gross income of $80,000 or less ($160,000 or less for joint filers) is eligible for the credit. The credit is reduced ratably if a taxpayer's modified adjusted gross income exceeds those amounts. A taxpayer whose modified adjusted gross income is greater than $90,000 ($180,000 for joint filers) cannot benefit from this credit.

For more information about the American Opportunity Tax Credit, go online to http://www.irs.gov/uac/American-Opportunity-Tax-Credit:-Questions-and-Answers.

Lifetime Learning Credit

The Lifetime Learning Credit is the counterpart of the American Opportunity Credit. The qualifying taxpayer can claim an annual tax credit of up to $2,000—20 percent of the first $10,000 of tuition. The credit is available for net tuition and fees, less grant aid. The total credit available is limited to $2,000 per year per taxpayer (or joint-filing couple). There is no limit on the number of years the lifetime learning credit can be claimed for each student. However, a taxpayer cannot claim both the American Opportunity Credit and Lifetime Learning Credit for the same student in one year. For more information, visit http://www.irs.gov/uac/Tax-Benefits-for-Education:-Information-Center.

TUITION AND FEES TAX DEDUCTION

The Tuition and Fees Tax Deduction could reduce taxable income by as much as $4,000. This deduction is taken as an adjustment to income, which means you can claim this deduction even if you do not itemize deductions on Schedule A of Form 1040. This deduction may benefit taxpayers who do not qualify for either the American Opportunity Credit or Lifetime Learning Credit.

Up to $4,000 may be deducted for tuition and fees required for enrollment or attendance at an eligible postsecondary institution. Personal living and family expenses, including room and board, insurance, medical, and transportation, are not deductible expenses.

The exact amount of the Tuition and Fees Tax Deduction depends on the amount of qualified tuition and related expenses paid for one's self, spouse, or dependents, and your Adjusted Gross Income. Consult the IRS or your tax preparer for more information.

STUDENT LOAN INTEREST TAX DEDUCTION

If you made student loan interest payments in 2012, you may be able to reduce your taxable income by up to $2,500. You should check with your lender with regards to the amount of interest you paid if you did not receive an IRS Form 1098-E and your tax preparer or IRS Publication 970 for additional information.

AMERICORPS

AmeriCorps is a national umbrella group of service programs for students. Participants work in a public or private nonprofit agency and provide service to the community in one of four priority areas: education, human services, the environment, and public safety. In exchange, they earn a stipend (for living expenses), health insurance coverage, and $4,725 per year for up to two years to apply toward college expenses. Many student-loan lenders will postpone the repayment of student loans during service in AmeriCorps, and AmeriCorps will pay the interest that is accrued on qualified student loans for members who complete the service program. Participants can work before, during, or after college and can use the funds to either pay current educational expenses or repay federal student loans. For more information, visit http://www.americorps.gov.

Inside the Federal Work-Study Program

I f you're like millions of other families with college-age youth you may have had that moment. It's the stomach-churning wrinkle in time when you realize that the gap between the amount of money you've saved for your child's college education and the cost of that dream university seems as insurmountable as crossing the ocean on a surfboard. Even as you fill out the Free Application for Federal Student Aid (FAFSA) and your child gets the award letter from the college, the sticker shock can be depressing. But there is glimmer of hope, and it's called the Federal Work-Study Program (FWS).

The federally-funded FWS, formerly known as the College Campus Work-Study Program, was a part of the anti-poverty legislation that swept the country in the 1960s. FWS partners with 3,400 institutions in the country to pay students to work on a college or university campus. Looking at the words "work study," may instill fear in some parent's hearts. They may think of nightmarish scenarios where their son or daughter spends so much time guarding the science building that they won't have time for their studies. This isn't necessarily true. There are several aspects to the federally supported work-study program that makes it an attractive option for students looking to lower their college bill.

WORK-STUDY CAN BE A VALUABLE EXPERIENCE

Last year, Congress allocated more than $1.1 billion to support about 768,000 students enrolled in the Federal Work-Study Program. The program pays participating institutions up to 75 percent of the costs of employing college students who are in need of financial aid. Students get their college bills reduced, and colleges receive help with labor. But there are some caveats.

Work-study options are not guaranteed, and there are only a limited number of spots available. Congress has already cut the work-study funding, and there were 160,000 fewer jobs available in 2010. Colleges and universities like that the FWS is federally subsidized, so they will offer this option as part of a financial aid package first because it saves them money. So send your FASFA as early as possible, especially if you want to beat out the millions of students who seek work-study jobs! Also, don't forget to indicate on your FASFA that you are interested in a work-study job.

In addition, it may be best to choose work-study over outside employment. You may believe that work is work, but when it comes to work-study jobs that sentiment is not true. Work-study jobs are usually better for students because the payment you receive is NOT counted against you when applying for financial aid. This could make a huge difference in how much aid you receive from your chosen institution.

WORK-STUDY JOBS—NOT ALWAYS "BORING"

Not all work-study jobs have to be through educational institutions. The program also funds jobs at a federal, state, or local public agency; a private nonprofit organization; or even a private for-profit organization. Check and see if your school has a partnership with an off-campus workplace. You might be able to find a work-study position in your field of study. This allows you to gain valuable experience and not just collect "man hours" while you pay down your college price tag.

Still, the type of job a student is privy to largely depends upon the intuition's work-study program. Some programs focus on interesting options such as janitorial services, cafeteria work, or even telemarketer. But with a little ingenuity, students can find a work-study assignment that fits their academic and financial need. For example, at Colorado College, a private school in Colorado Springs, work-study students can apply for jobs as diverse as stage manager for theater productions or work off campus at a nonprofit such as the Children's Literacy Center. To ensure you get a work-study position that fits your career goals, it's best to talk to officials at your institution early and often about available work-study options. For example, according to the U.S. Department of Education, a college must use 7 percent of its work-study funds to support students "working in community service jobs, including reading tutors for preschool age or elementary school children, mathematics tutors for students enrolled in elementary school through ninth grade, literacy tutors in a family literacy project performing family literacy activities, or emergency preparedness and response." When you talk to your institution's financial aid office you might mention your experience in any of these areas. This won't guarantee you a "better" work-study job, but it certainly can't hurt.

TAKE ANOTHER LOOK AT WORK-STUDY

With flexible hours, guaranteed pay and the ability to help your institution and community, the work-study option is an attractive way for students to pay for their college education. Do not over look its benefits. Indicate work-study on your FAFSA application, and apply early. Who knows? You could end up as a tennis racquet stringer at Colorado College. For more information about FWS, go to http://www2.ed.gov/programs/fws/index.html.

Analyzing Financial Aid Award Letters

Richard Woodland

You have just received the financial aid award letters. Now what? This is the time to do a detailed analysis of each college's offer to help you pay for your child's education. Remember, accepting financial aid is a family matter. More often than not, parents need to borrow money to send their dependent children to college. You need to clearly understand the types of aid you and your child are being offered. How much is "free" money in the form of grants and/or scholarships that does not have to be repaid? If your financial aid award package includes loans, what are the terms and conditions for these loans? A good tool to have with you is the federal government's most recent issue of *Funding Education Beyond High School: The Guide to Federal Student Aid,* available from the school's financial aid office or at http://www.fsapubs.gov. This publication is very helpful in explaining the federal grant and loan programs that are usually a part of the aid package.

Let's take a minute to explain what is meant by "financial aid award package." A college will offer an aid applicant a combination of aid types, "packaged" in the form of grants and scholarships, loans, and a work-study job, based on the information provided on the FAFSA and/or another application. Many schools use a priority filing date, which guarantees that all applications received by this date will be considered for the full range of institutional aid programs available. Late applicants (by even one day!) often are only awarded the basic aid programs from state and federal sources. *It is important to apply on time.*

EVALUATE EACH LETTER

As each award letter comes in, read it through carefully. The following are some critical points to consider:

- **Does the Cost of Attendance (COA) include all projected costs?** Each award letter should state the school's academic year COA. Tuition, fees, room, board, books, transportation, and personal expenses are what normally make up the COA. Does the award letter itemize all these components? Or does it omit some? This is crucial because this is what you will need to budget for. If you need additional information, be sure to contact the financial aid office. They will be glad to provide you with information or answer any questions you may have about their costs.

- **What is your Expected Family Contribution (EFC)?** Is the school's—not just the federal government's—EFC listed on the award letter? Some schools may require a higher EFC than you expected. Be aware that the EFC may increase or decrease each year depending on the information you provide on the renewal FAFSA or other financial aid application.

- **Is there unmet need?** Does the aid package cover the difference between the COA and the EFC? Not every school can cover your full need. If the aid package does not cover your full need, does the information with the award letter provide you with alternative loan options? If not, contact the financial aid office for more information.

- **Is the scholarship renewable for four years?** If your child is awarded a scholarship based on scholastic achievement or talent, you need to ask these questions: Is there a minimum grade point average he has to maintain? Can he switch majors but keep the scholarship? Does he need to participate in an "honors college" program to maintain the scholarship? If he needs to change to part-time status, will the award amount be prorated, or does he need to maintain full-time status? If it is an athletic or "special talent" scholarship, will he continue to receive the award if for some reason he cannot continue with the specific program? Renewal of scholarship funds is often the biggest misunderstanding between families and colleges. Be sure you clearly understand the terms and conditions of all grants and scholarships.

- **What will the college do to your child's award if she receives outside, noninstitutional scholarships?** Will the award be used to cover unmet need or reduce her student loans? Will the college reduce her institutional grants or scholarships? Or will they reduce her work-study award? (This is a good time to compare each school's policy on this matter.) Remember, your overall aid cannot total more than the COA, and many programs cannot exceed your financial need.

- **What are the interest rates of the loans that are offered?** Did another school offer you more than one loan and why? *Do not* sign the award letter until you understand your loan obligations. Again, *Funding Education Beyond High School: The Guide to Federal Student Aid* can be very helpful with this part of the analysis.

- **Is the school likely to cover the same expenses every year?** In particular, ask if grant or scholarship funds are normally reduced or increased after the freshman year, even if family income and EFC remain the same. Some colleges will *increase* the self-help (loan, job) percentage every year but not necessarily the free money.

- **If work-study was awarded, how many hours a week will your child be expected to work?** If you feel working that many hours will have a negative impact on your child's academic performance, you may want to request that the awarded job funds be changed to a loan. You must ask immediately because funds are limited. Many schools are flexible with these funds early in the process.

- **What happens if (or more likely, when) tuition increases?** Check with the financial aid office to find out what its policy is for renewing an aid package. If, for example, tuition increases by 5 percent each of the next three years and your EFC remains the same, what will happen to your scholarships, grants, and loans?

You can always appeal your award letter if you feel that your needs are not being met, if your family situation has changed, or if you have received a better award from a competitive school. You have the right to ask for a reconsideration of your award. (Do not use the word *negotiate*.) When asking for reconsideration, be sure to provide the aid officer with all relevant information.

COMPARE LETTERS

After you have received and reviewed all the award letters from the schools your child is considering, the next step is to compare them and determine which schools are offering the best aid packages. Following are three sample award letters and a sample spreadsheet that shows you how to analyze and compare each school's awards.

(Note: These award letters are simply for discussion purposes. They should not be considered to be representative award letters with an EFC of $9,550.)

Once you have entered all the information into a spreadsheet of your own and come up with the balances, here are some things to consider for each school:

- **How much is the balance?** Ideally, your balance should be $0, but look to see which school has the lowest balance amount.

- **What part of the aid package comes in the form of grants and scholarships?** It is important to note this because these awards (gift aid) do not have to be paid back.

- **Look at the loans.** Usually, the best financial deal contains more money in scholarships and less in loan dollars. Based on expected freshman-year borrowing, determine the debt burden at each school once your child graduates. You have to multiply the amount of your loan by four or five years, depending on how long it will take for your child to graduate.

UNIVERSITY A
FINANCIAL AID AWARD LETTER
2013-2014

Date: 4/21/13
ID#: 0000000009

Dear Jane Smith,
We are pleased to inform you that you are eligible to receive the financial assistance indictate in the area labled "Your Financial Aid."
We estimated your budget based on the following assumptions:

In-state resident and living on campus.

	FALL	SPRING	TOTAL
Tuition and Fees	$3,849	$3,849	$7,698
Room & Board	3,769	3,770	7,539
Books	420	420	840
Transportation	973	974	1,947
Personal expenses	369	369	738
Estimated Coast of Attendance	**$9,380**	**$9,382**	**$18,762**

Your Financial Aid

	FALL	SPRING	TOTAL
Federal Pell Grant	$1,950	$1,950	$3,900
Federal Direct Subsidized Loan	$1,750	$1,750	$3,500
State Grant	432	432	864
Total Financial Aid	**$4,132**	**$4,132**	**$8,264**
Unmet Need	**$5,248**	**$5,250**	**$10,498**

What to Do Next:
- Verify that accurate assumptions have been used to determine your awards.
- Carefully review and follow the instructions on the Data Changes Form.
- To reduce or decline all or part of your loans, you must complete and return the Data Changes Form.
- We will assume you fully accept the awards above unless you submit changes to us immediately.
- Return corrections and required documents promptly.
- Retain this letter for your records.

UNIVERSITY B
FINANCIAL AID AWARD LETTER
2013-2014

Date: 4/21/13
ID#: 0000000009

Dear Jane Smith,
We are pleased to inform you that you are eligible to receive the financial assistance indictate in the area labled "Your Financial Aid." We estimated your budget based on the following assumptions:

Nonresident and living on campus.

	FALL	SPRING	TOTAL
Tuition and Fees	$9,805	$9,085	$18,170
Room & Board	2,835	2,835	5,670
Books	410	410	820
Transportation	875	875	1,750
Personal Expenses	378	377	755
Estimated Coast of Attendance	**$13,583**	**$13,582**	**$27,165**

Your Financial Aid

	FALL	SPRING	TOTAL
Federal Pell Grant	$1,950	$1,950	$3,900
Federal SEOG Grant	225	225	450
Academic Excellence Scholarship	500	500	1,000
Federal Work-Study	1,050	1,050	2,100
Federal Perkins Loan Program	1,250	1,250	2,500
Subsidized Federal Stafford Student Loan	1,750	1,750	3,500
University Student Loan	2,000	2,000	4,000
Total Financial Aid	**$8,725**	**$8,725**	**$17,450**
Unmet Need	**$4,858**	**$4,857**	**$9,715**

What to Do Next:
- Verify that accurate assumptions have been used to determine your awards.
- Carefully review and follow the instructions on the Data Changes Form.
- To reduce or decline all or part of your loans, you must complete and return the Data Changes Form.
- We will assume you fully accept the awards above unless you submit changes to us immediately.
- Return corrections and required documents promptly.
- Retain this letter for your records.

UNIVERSITY C
FINANCIAL AID AWARD LETTER
2013-2014

Date: 4/21/13
ID#: 0000000009

Dear Jane Smith,

We are pleased to inform you that you are eligible to receive the financial assistance indictate in the area labled "Your Financial Aid." We estimated your budget based on the following assumptions:

Living on campus.

	FALL	SPRING	TOTAL
Tuition and Fees	$14,955	$14,955	$29,910
Room & Board	4,194	4,193	8,387
Books	450	450	900
Transportation	350	350	700
Personal Expenses	1,295	1,293	2,588
Estimated Coast of Attendance	**$21,244**	**$21,241**	**$42,485**

Your Financial Aid

	FALL	SPRING	TOTAL
Institutional Grant	$10,805	$10,805	$21,610
Federal Pell Grant	$1,950	$1,950	$3,900
Federal SEOG Grant	2,000	2,000	4,000
Federal Work-Study Program	1,713	1,712	3,425
Total Financial Aid	**$16,468**	**$16,467**	**$32,935**
Unmet Need	**$4,776**	**$4,774**	**$9,550**

What to Do Next:
- Verify that accurate assumptions have been used to determine your awards.
- Carefully review and follow the instructions on the Data Changes Form.
- To reduce or decline all or part of your loans, you must complete and return the Data Changes Form.
- We will assume you fully accept the awards above unless you submit changes to us immediately.
- Return corrections and required documents promptly.
- Retain this letter for your records.

Comparison Grid

	University A (State University)	University B (Nonresident State University)	University C (Private College)
Cost of Attendance	$18,762	$27,165	$42,485
Tuition and Fees	7,698	18,170	29,910
Room & Board	7,539	5,670	8,367
Books	840	820	900
Transportation	1,947	1,750	700
Personal Expenses	738	755	2,558
Grants and Scholarships	4,764	5,350	29,510
Loans	3,500	10,000	0
Work-Study	0	2,00	3,425
Expected Family Contribution	9,550	9,550	9,550
Balance	$948	$165	$0

Some things to notice:

- At all schools, the federal Pell Grant remains the same.
- The loan amounts varied greatly among these schools.
- Even though University C (a private college) has the highest "sticker price," the net cost is less than the state schools.
- University B is a state university, but you are classified as an out-of-state resident (or nonresident). Many Students in this situation find that the higher out-of-state costs combined with lower grant aid make this a costly decision.
- All schools assume that you will be residing in on-campus housing. But if you choose to commute to University A, you would save a substatial amount because you would not have the $7,539 room and board cost.

And remember that the loan amounts will probably increase each year. You also should take into consideration that you will have to borrow even more as the COA increases each year. To determine the best loan deal, consider:

—What are the terms of the loans?

—What are interest rates?

—Do you pay the yearly interest rate during enrollment or is the interest subsidized or paid by the government?

—Is any money due during enrollment or is it deferred until after graduation? Figuring out how much you will owe at each school at graduation will give you a clear picture of what your financial situation will be after graduation.

However, unless cost is your only concern, you shouldn't simply choose the school offering the lowest loan amounts. Many other factors need to be considered, such as academic and social environment. And you should never reject a school based solely on insufficient financial aid. Consult with an aid administrator to discuss possible alternatives.

Finally, if the college that costs the most is still the one your child wants to attend, there are a number of ways to find money to cover the gap between the aid package and your actual cost, including paying more than the EFC figure, increasing student borrowing, working more hours, and taking out a PLUS loan.

Richard Woodland is the former Director of Financial Aid at Rutgers University–Camden and the current Director of Student Services and Financial Assistance at the Curtis Institute of Music in Philadelphia, Pennsylvania.

Online Filing of FAFSA and CSS/Financial Aid PROFILE® Applications

Richard Woodland

Over the past few years, there have been major advancements in the way students apply both for admission to college and for financial aid. The two primary financial aid applications, the Free Application for Federal Student Aid (FAFSA) and the CSS/Financial Aid PROFILE® application from the College Scholarship Service offer direct, online applications. FAFSA on the Web and PROFILE are available in both English and Spanish.

WHY FILE ONLINE?

There are two reasons why it is a good idea to file online. First, the online environment prevents you from making many mistakes. For example, if there is a question that is required of all applicants, you cannot inadvertently skip it. If the application software thinks your answer may not be accurate, it will prompt you to check it before proceeding. The financial aid process can be complicated, and applying online greatly reduces the chance for error. The second reason is turnaround time. The online applications are processed in a matter of days, not weeks. Since time is an important factor when applying for financial aid, it is prudent to have your application processed as quickly as possible.

SOME COMMON CONCERNS ABOUT ONLINE FILING

Both the FASFA and PROFILE online applications have become much more user-friendly. You do not have to be a computer expert to use these programs. Both applications allow you to save your completed data and return later if you are interrupted or need to gather additional information. Both systems use secure encryption technology to protect your privacy. FASFA information is shared with other federal agencies as required as part of the application process, online or paper. FAFSA information is also sent to your state of legal residence for state aid purposes and to any college or program your child lists on the application. The information on the application is highly personal, and every precaution is taken to safeguard your privacy.

Now, let's discuss some specific issues related to each application.

THE FAFSA

The FAFSA is the universal application for all federal financial aid programs. It is the primary application used for most state and college financial aid programs. Before using the FAFSA online application, you need to secure an electronic signature, or Personal Identification Number (PIN). This is similar to the access codes used at ATM machines, online banking, etc. It is easy to obtain a PIN number. Simply go to www.pin.ed.gov and apply online. You will receive a reply via e-mail in about 48 hours. If your child is under 24 years of age, he or she and one parent will need a PIN number. If there is more than one child in college, a parent only needs one PIN number. However, each college applicant will need to have his or her own PIN.

The FASFA online application is not presented in the same format as the paper FAFSA. Although all of the questions are exactly the same, the order of some of the items on the online application has been rearranged to make it easier to complete and allow for some built-in skip-logic. You can easily obtain a copy of the electronic FAFSA by logging on to www.fafsa.ed.gov. Just click on "FAFSA on the Web Worksheet." Completing this first will make the online entry that much easier. There are a number of other worksheets available that can also make the process easier. You should print them out and decide which are applicable to your situation. Everyone should review Worksheets A, B, and C. If you have not completed your federal tax return, the Income Estimator worksheets are easy to use and can reduce much of the guesswork.

After completing the online FASFA, be sure to print a copy of the pages at the end of the process so that you have a copy of your answers and the confirmation number. Although lost applications are extremely rare, having this information will give you peace of mind. You can go online as often as you wish to check the status of your application.

THE CSS/FINANCIAL AID PROFILE®

The CSS/Financial Aid PROFILE® is a more comprehensive financial aid application that is used primarily at private, higher-cost colleges and universities to award nonfederal student aid funds. Many private scholarship programs also use the PROFILE. A complete list of colleges and programs that use the PROFILE can be found at https://profileonline.collegeboard.com/ index.jsp.

The PROFILE application fee is $25 for the application and initial school report and $16 for each additional school report. You must have a credit card, debit card, or checking account to use this service. (Note: A limited number of fee waivers are available for families with incomes below the poverty line. See the high school guidance officer for more information on the fee waiver program.)

Complete information on the online PROFILE application is available at www.collegeboard.com/profile. Although the customized PROFILE application is processed in about one week, you should allow for enough processing time (usually two to three weeks) to meet the earliest deadline established by the school or program.

WHAT HAPPENS NEXT?

Once you decide to apply online, the processors will only respond to you electronically. You will not receive any paper acknowledgments—all confirmations will be sent via e-mail. When it is time to reapply for aid in subsequent years (usually quite easy as most of the data are carried over from the pre-

vious application), all reminders will be sent to the e-mail address that is on file, so it is important to report any changes in your e-mail address.

It is easy to update the FAFSA following your initial application. For example, if you used estimated income information and now you have your federal tax return completed, you can simply return to www.fafsa.ed.gov and change your income figures. But be sure to go through the entire process and print out the updated confirmation page. In general, the PROFILE is a one-time application, filed well before tax season. Any updates are usually done directly through the schools.

Both processors offer helpful information, both in print and online. Check with your high school guidance office or local college financial aid office for additional assistance. If you need to call the FAFSA processor, the phone number is 800-4FED-AID (toll-free). You can contact PROFILE customer service via e-mail at help@cssprofile.org or by phone at 305-829-9793.

Richard Woodland is the former Director of Financial Aid at Rutgers University–Camden and the current Director of Student Services and Financial Assistance at the Curtis Institute of Music in Philadelphia, Pennsylvania.

Falsifying Information on Your FAFSA Could Bring Big Problems

With the cost of college rising each year and college graduates saddled with more than $1 trillion in debt to pay for their postsecondary studies, more and more families are desperate to secure payment-free options for higher education. Nothing illuminates this fact better than the meteoric rise in applications for financial aid through the annually Free Application for Federal Student Aid (FAFSA). In the 2004–05 academic year, more than 11 million students sent in FAFSA applications. Less than seven years later, that number doubled to more than 22 million. With more and more students applying for federal financial aid, there is, unfortunately, an increased temptation to commit fraud. Parents try to do whatever they can to lower their Expected Family Contribution (EFC), and sometimes this can lead to falsifying information. This is a big no-no, but that doesn't stop people from trying.

A quick search on Google, and you can find parents and students asking boldly, "Do people lying on their FAFSA really get caught?" or "How do I hide the fact that I have money from FAFSA?" Cheating on the FAFSA seems as intuitive as forgetting to report that second job you have to the Internal Revenue Service.

A 2010 report released by the Government Accountability Office, the Congress-created financial watchdog, found that fifteen for-profit universities encouraged fraud and/or engaged in deceptive marketing practices. The report stated that one college admission worker encouraged an undercover applicant to not report $250,000 in savings on the student's FAFSA. Another college representative told an undercover applicant to falsify the number of dependents he had from 0 to 3.

It all seems so deceptively easy—giving thousands of dollars in savings to a student's uncle temporarily to hide that asset; writing down grandma's address to gain in-state tuition rates; forgetting to mention your true immigration status; or the extreme example of one Alaskan woman who used a false identity. In that situation, after claiming she suffered from years of child abuse, the woman used an obscure federal law to secure a new identity to hide from her accused abuser. (The abuser she named was never charged with a crime.) She received a new social security number and card. But instead of living a new life in anonymity, she used her *old* identity to apply for federal student loans—a lot of them. Arrested and convicted, the woman was sentenced to five years in prison and ordered to pay back nearly $1 million.

The prospect of going to jail for filling out false information on your FAFSA application may not have crossed your mind, but it is certainly a possibility. Falsifying information—knowingly or unknowingly—is a federal crime. It is punishable by up to $20,000 in fines and up to five years in prison. And though there are books offering tantalizing options to "game," the federal student aid system—do not be tempted.

You do not want to start your college career by committing a crime against the government. It's just not worth it. Your FAFSA is checked against your IRS documents by professionals who do not want to take the chance that they will use their precious scarce financial aid resources to support students who really do not need it. Students who falsify information to get financial aid leave deserving cash-strapped students out in the cold. Fortunately, though, fraud in the federal aid system is low—a recent government study found that about 5 percent of applications contain false information.

Even if you do not intend to defraud the government, inaccurate information on your FAFSA can get you into trouble. It is critical that you fill the application out as accurately as possible. It may look like an innocuous document, but it amounts to a partnership between you and the federal government, and it is essential that partnership is based upon trust.

Here are some tips to avoid making mistakes on your FAFSA that could cost you financial aid or even your freedom:

- Accurately report your assets, address, dependents, income, and so on. It just doesn't make sense to lie. All that information is easily verifiable. Income includes wages, tips, social security payments, child support payments, and other untaxed income. But retirement income such as those in a 401K or IRA does not have to be reported. Check with your tax advisor when filling out your FAFSA application.

- Fill out your FAFSA completely. Mistakes can cost you time as you might have to reapply, and that will literally cost you money.

- Avoid books, consultants, and websites that promise to lower your EFC by questionable means. Trying to "game," the federal aid system is just going to cause you headaches.

College is expensive, and families are smart to try to lower that expense as much as possible. But planning, saving, and focusing on academic pursuits to garner scholarships and grants is a much better way of acquiring money for college than trying to put one over on the federal government. Being honest is always the best policy—especially when applying for federal financial aid.

Middle-Income Families: Making the Financial Aid Process Work

Richard Woodland

A report from the U.S. Department of Education's National Center for Education Statistics took a close look at how middle-income families finance a college education. The report, *Middle Income Undergraduates: Where They Enroll and How They Pay for Their Education,* was one of the first detailed studies of these families. Even though 31 percent of middle-income families have the entire cost of attendance covered by financial aid, there is widespread angst among middle-income families that, while they earn too much to qualify for grant assistance, they are financially unable to pay the spiraling costs of higher education.

For the purposes of the federal study, middle income is defined as those families with incomes between $35,000 and $70,000. The good news is that 52 percent of these families received grants, while the balance received loans. Other sources of aid, including work-study, also helped close the gap.

So how do these families do it? Is there a magic key that will open the door to significant amounts of grants and scholarships?

The report found some interesting trends. One way families can make college more affordable is by choosing a less expensive college. In fact, in this income group, 29 percent choose to enroll in low-to moderate-cost schools. These include schools where the total cost is less than $8,500 per year. In this sector, we find the community colleges and lower-priced state colleges and universities. But almost half of these middle-income families choose schools in the upper-level tier, with costs ranging from $8,500 to $16,000. The remaining 23 percent enrolled at the highest-tier schools, with costs above $16,000. Clearly, while cost is a factor, middle-income families are not limiting their choices based on costs alone.

The report shows that families pay these higher costs with a combination of family assets, current income, and long-term borrowing. This is often referred to as the "past-present-future" model of financing. In fact, just by looking at the Expected Family Contributions, it is clear that there is a significant gap in what families need and what the financial aid process can provide. Families are closing this gap by making the financial sacrifices necessary to pay the price at higher-cost schools, especially if they think their child is academically strong. The report concludes that parents are more likely to pay for a higher-priced education if their child scores high on the SAT.

The best place for middle-income families to start is with the high school guidance office. This office has information on financial aid and valuable leads on local scholarships. Most guidance officers report that there are far fewer applicants for these locally based scholarships than one would expect. So read the information they send home and check on the application process. A few of those $500–$1,000 scholarships can add up!

Plan to attend a financial aid awareness program. If your school does not offer one, contact your local college financial aid office and see when and where they will be speaking. You can get a lot of "inside" information on how the financial aid process works.

Next, be sure to file the correct applications for aid. Remember, each school can have a different set of requirements. For example, many higher-cost private colleges will require the CSS/Financial Aid PROFILE® application, filed in September or October of the senior year. Other schools may have their own institutional aid application. All schools will require the Free Application for Federal Student Aid (FAFSA). Watch the deadlines! It is imperative that you meet the school's published application deadline. Generally, schools are not flexible about this, so be sure to double-check the due date of all applications.

Finally, become a smart educational consumer. Peterson's has a wide range of resources available to help you understand the process. Be sure to also check your local library, bookstore, and of course, the Internet.

Once admitted to the various colleges and universities, you will receive an award notice outlining the aid you are eligible to receive. If you feel the offer is not sufficient, or if you have some unique financial circumstances, call the school's financial aid office to see if you can have your application reviewed again. The financial aid office is your best source for putting the pieces together and finding financial solutions.

The financial aid office will help you determine the "net price." This is the actual out-of-pocket cost that you will need to cover. Through a combination of student and parent loans, most families are able to meet these expenses with other forms of financial aid and family resources.

Many students help meet their educational expenses by working while in school. While this works for many students, research shows that too many hours spent away from your studies will negatively impact your academic success. Most experts feel that working 10 to 15 hours a week is optimal.

An overlooked source of aid is the tax credits given to middle-income families. Rather than extending eligibility for traditional sources of grant assistance to middle-income families, the federal tax system has built in a number of significant tax benefits, known as the American Opportunity Tax Credit (AOTC) and Lifetime Learning Tax Credit, for middle-income families. The AOTC was enacted in 2009 for 2009 and 2010. It was extended for two years as part of the Tax Relief, Unemployment Insurance Reauthorization, and Job Creation Act of 2010 and had been set to expire on December 31, 2012. This break is currently extended through the 2013–17 tax years. The maximum AOTC tax credit is $2,500 per student. This is real money in your pocket. You do not need to itemize your deductions to qualify for this tax credit.

A tool to help families get a handle on the ever-rising costs of college is to assume that you can pay one third of the "net charges" from savings, another third from available (non-retirement) assets, and the rest from parent borrowing. If any one of these "thirds" is not available, shift that amount to one of the other resources. However, if it looks like you will be financing most or all of the costs from future income (borrowing), it may be wise to consider a lower-cost college.

Millions of middle-income families send their children to colleges and universities every year. Only 8 percent attend the lowest-priced schools. By using the concept of past-present-future financing, institutional assistance, federal and state aid, meaningful targeted tax relief, and student earnings, you can afford even the highest-cost schools.

_____

Richard Woodland is the former Director of Financial Aid at Rutgers University–Camden and the current Director of Student Services and Financial Assistance at the Curtis Institute of Music in Philadelphia, Pennsylvania.

Parents' and Students' Common Questions Answered

Q *Are a student's chances of being admitted to a college reduced if the student applies for financial aid?*

A Generally no. Nearly all colleges have a policy of "need-blind" admissions, which means that a student's financial need is not taken into account in the admission decision. There are a few selective colleges, however, that do consider ability to pay before deciding whether or not to admit a student. Some colleges will mention this in their literature; others may not. The best advice is to apply for financial aid if the student needs assistance to attend college.

Q *Are parents penalized for saving money for college?*

A No. As a matter of fact, families that have made a concerted effort to save money for college are in a much better position than those that have not. For example, a student from a family that has saved money may not have to borrow as much. Furthermore, the "taxing rate" on savings is quite low—only about 5 percent of the parents' assets are assessed and neither the home equity nor retirement savings are included. For example, a single 40-year-old parent who saved $40,000 for college expenses will have about $1,900 counted as part of the parental contribution. Two parents, if the older one is 40 years old (a parent's age factors into the formulation), would have about $300 counted. (Note: The "taxing rate" for student assets is much higher—20 percent—compared to 5 percent for parents.)

Q *How does the financial aid system work in cases of divorce or separation? How are stepparents treated?*

A In cases of divorce or separation, the financial aid application(s) should be completed by the parent with whom the student lived for the longest period of time in the past twelve months (custodial parent). If the custodial parent has remarried, the stepparent is considered a family member and must complete the application along with the biological parent. If your family has any special circumstances, you should discuss these directly with the financial aid office. (Note: Colleges that award their own aid may ask the noncustodial biological parent to complete a separate aid application and a contribution will be calculated.)

Q *When are students considered independent of parental support in applying for financial aid?*

A The student must be at least 24 years of age in order to be considered independent. If younger than 24, the student must be married, be a graduate or professional student, have legal dependents other than a spouse, be an orphan or ward of the court, or be a veteran of the armed forces or on active military duty. However, in very unusual situations, students who can clearly document estrangement from their parents can appeal to the financial aid office for additional consideration.

Q *What can a family do if a job loss occurs?*

A Financial aid eligibility is based on the previous year's income. So the family's 2013 income would be reported to determine eligibility for the 2014–15 academic year. In that way, the family's income can be verified with an income tax return. But the previous year's income may not accurately reflect the current financial situation, particularly if a parent lost a job or retired. In these instances, the projected income for the coming year can be used instead. Families should discuss the situation directly with the financial aid office and be prepared to provide appropriate documentation.

Q *When my daughter first went to college, we applied for financial aid and were denied because our Expected Family Contribution was too high. Now, my son is a high school senior, and we will soon have two in college. Will we get the same results?*

A The results will definitely be different. Both your son and your daughter should apply. As described earlier, need-based financial aid is based on your Expected Family Contribution, or EFC. When you have two children in college, this amount is divided in half for each child.

Q *I've heard about the "middle-income squeeze" in regard to financial aid. What is it?*

A The so-called "middle-income squeeze" is the idea that low-income families qualify for aid, high-income families have adequate resources to pay for education, and those in the middle are not eligible for aid but do not have the ability to pay full college costs. There is no provision in the Federal Methodology that treats middle-income students differently than others (such as an income cutoff for eligibility). The Expected Family Contribution rises proportionately as income and assets increase. If a middle-income family does not qualify for aid, it is because the need analysis formula yields a contribution that exceeds college costs. But keep in mind that if a $65,000-income family does not qualify for grant aid at a public university with a $16,000 cost, the same family will likely be eligible for aid at a private college with a cost of $25,000 or more. Also, there are loan programs available to parents and students that are not based on need. Middle-income families should realize, however, that many of the grant programs funded by federal and state governments are directed at lower-income families. It is therefore likely that a larger share of an aid package for a middle-income student will consist of loans rather than grants.

Q *Given our financial condition, my daughter will be receiving financial aid. We will help out as much as we can, and, in fact, we ourselves will be borrowing. But I am concerned that she will have to take on a lot of loans in order to go to the college of her choice. Does she have any options?*

A She does. If offered a loan, she can decline all or part of it. One option is for her to ask in the financial aid office to have some of the loan changed to a work-study job. If this is not possible, she can find her own part-time work. Often there is an employment office on campus that can help her locate a job. In most cases, the more she works, the less she has to borrow. It is important to remember that the education loans offered to students have very attractive terms and conditions, with flexible repayment options. Students should look upon these loans as a long-term investment that will reap significant rewards.

Q *What are some easy ways to improve my chances of receiving aid?*

A When filling out your scholarship or financial aid application, it's important to remember that the smallest mistake could hurt your chances for landing free money, or even worse, it could disqualify you completely from an awards contest. Grants and scholarships are highly competitive, so it's a good idea to make a list of what's needed and make sure you have everything before submitting your application. If you are submitting an essay, have another pair of eyes look at it for any spelling and grammar errors. Keep a file on everything you're applying for so that you don't miss any elements of an application. Make sure you're using reputable sites to conduct your free scholarship searches. If you have to pay to apply for an award or look for scholarships, chances are you're being scammed. In a nutshell, the best advice is to follow all directions, and make sure that you meet all deadlines.

In addition, when filling out the FAFSA, it's important to pay close attention to the details, since any errors may delay the application process. These days, it's preferable to fill out the FAFSA online, since mailed forms can take weeks to process. If you're confused or concerned about something on the application, contact the Federal Student Aid Information Center at 1-800-4FED-AID; questions can also be asked through the FAFSA Web site. Your college's financial aid office should also be able to assist you. The FAFSA is available each year starting Jan. 1, and it's essential that you don't miss the deadline to apply. The sooner you apply, the sooner you'll know the kind of funding package you are likely to receive, and this will help you determine if you need to apply for any additional aid.

Q *Is it possible to change your financial aid package?*

A Yes. Most colleges have an appeal process. A request to change a need-based loan to a work-study job is usually approved if funds are available. A request to consider special financial circumstances may also be granted. At most colleges, a request for more grant money is rarely approved unless it is based on a change in the information reported. Applicants should speak with the financial aid office if they have concerns about their financial package. Some colleges may even respond to a competitive appeal, that is, a request to match another college's offer.

Q *The cost of attending college seems to be going up so much faster than the Consumer Price Index. Why is that, and how can I plan for my child's four years?*

A The cost of higher education cannot be compared to the Consumer Price Index (CPI). The CPI does not take into account most of the costs faced by colleges. For example, the dollars that universities spend on grants and scholarships have risen rapidly. Many universities have increased enrollment of students from less affluent families, further increasing the need for institutional financial aid. Colleges are expected to be on the cutting edge of technology, not only in research but also in the classroom and in the library. Many colleges have deferred needed maintenance and repairs that can now no longer be put off. In addition, there is market pressure to provide many expensive lifestyle amenities that were not expected ten years ago. In general, you can expect that college costs will rise at least 2 to 3 percent faster than inflation.

Q *I'm struggling with the idea that all students should apply to the college of their choice, regardless of cost, because financial aid will level the playing field. I feel I will be penalized because I have saved for college. My* son has been required to save half of his allowance since age six for his college education. Will that count against him when he applies for financial aid? It's difficult to explain to him that his college choices may be limited because of the responsible choices and sacrifices we have made as a family. What can we do to make the most of our situation?

A In general, it is always better to have planned ahead for college by saving. Families that have put away sufficient funds to pay for college will quickly realize that they have made the burden easier for themselves and their children. In today's college financing world, schools assume that paying for the cost of attendance is a ten-year commitment. So by saving when your child is young, you reap significant advantages from compound interest on the assets and reduce the need to borrow as much while in school. This should reduce the number of years after college that you will be burdened with loans. Families should spend the student's assets first, since the financial aid formulas count these more heavily than parental assets. Then, after the first year, you can explain to the college how you spent these assets, and why you might now need assistance. When looking at parental information, the income of the family is by far the most important component. Contrary to popular belief, parental assets play a minor role in the calculation of need. With this strategy, you have done the right thing, and in the long run, it should prove to be a wise financial plan.

Picking the right college also involves other factors. Students should select the colleges to which they are going to apply in two ways. First, and most important, is to look at colleges that meet your son's academic and lifestyle interests. Most experts will tell him to pick a few "reach" schools (i.e., schools where he is not sure he has the grades and scores required) and at least one or two academically "safe" schools. He should also select one or two financially "safe" schools that you are sure you can afford with either moderate or little financial aid. Most students do not get into all of their first-choice schools, and not everyone can afford the schools to which they are admitted. By working closely with the guidance office in high school and the admissions and financial aid offices at the college, you can maximize your options.

Q My son was awarded a $2,500 scholarship. This can be split and used for two years. When filling out the FAFSA, do we have to claim the full amount, or just the $1,250 he plans to use the first year?

A Congratulations to your son on the scholarship. Nowhere on the FAFSA should you report this scholarship. It is not considered income or an asset. However, once you choose a school to attend, you must notify the financial aid office for its advice on how to take the funds. But remember, do NOT report it on the FAFSA.

Q I will be receiving a scholarship from my local high school. How will this scholarship be treated in my financial aid award?

A Federal student aid regulations specify that all forms of aid must be included within the defined level of need. This means that additional aid, such as outside scholarships, must be combined with any need-based aid you receive; it may not be kept separate and used to reduce your family's contribution. If the college has not filled 100 percent of your need, it will usually allow outside scholarships to close the gap. Once your total need has been met, the college must reduce other aid and replace it with the outside award. Most colleges will allow you to use some, if not all, of an outside scholarship to replace self-help aid (loans and Federal Work-Study Program awards) rather than grant aid.

Q I know we're supposed to apply for financial aid as soon as possible after January 1. What if I don't have my W-2s yet and my tax return isn't done?

A The first financial aid application deadlines usually fall in early February. Most colleges use either March 1 or March 15 as their "priority filing date." Chances are you'll have your W-2 forms by then, but you won't have a completed tax return. If that is the case, complete the financial aid application using your best estimates. Then, when you receive the Student Aid Report (SAR), you can use your tax return to make corrections. Just be sure to check with each college for its deadline.

Q Is there enough aid available to make it worthwhile for me to consider colleges that are more expensive than I can afford?

A Definitely. More than $100 billion in aid is awarded to undergraduates every year. With more than half of all enrolled students qualifying for some type of assistance, this totals more than $5,500 per student. You should view financial aid as a large, national system of tuition discounts, some given according to a student's ability and talent, others based on what a student's family can afford to pay. If you qualify for need-based financial aid, you will essentially pay only your calculated family contribution, regardless of the cost of the college. You will not pay the "sticker price" (the cost of attendance listed in the college catalog) but a lower rate that is reduced by the amount of aid you receive. No college should be ruled out until after financial aid is considered. In addition, when deciding which college to attend, consider that the short-term cost of a college education is only one criterion. If the college meets your educational needs and you are convinced it can launch you on an exciting career, a significant up-front investment may turn out to be a bargain over the long run.

Q *If I don't qualify for need-based aid, what options are available?*

A You should try to put together your own aid package to help reduce your parents' share. There are three sources to look into. First, search for merit scholarships. Second, seek employment, during both the summer and the academic year. The student employment office should be able to help you find a campus job. Third, look into borrowing. Even if you don't qualify for the need-based loan programs, the unsubsidized Federal Direct Loan is available to all students. The terms and conditions are the same as the subsidized loan programs except that interest accrues while you are in college.

After you have contributed what you can through scholarships, employment, and loans, your parents will be faced with their share of the college bill. Many colleges have monthly payment plans that allow families to spread their payments over the academic year. If these monthly payments turn out to be more than your parents can afford, they can take out a parent loan. By borrowing from the college itself, from a commercial agency or lender, or through PLUS, your parents can extend the payments over a ten-year period or longer. Borrowing reduces the monthly obligation to its lowest level, but the total amount paid will be the highest due to principal and interest payments. Before making a decision on where to borrow parental loan funds, be sure to first check with the financial aid office to determine what is the best source of alternative funds.

How to Use This Guide

QUICK-REFERENCE CHART

The amount of aid available at colleges can vary greatly. "College Costs At-a-Glance" lists the percent of freshmen who applied for and received need-based gift aid and the percent of those whose need was fully met. Also listed are the average freshman financial aid package, the average cost after aid, and the average indebtedness upon graduation.

PROFILES OF COLLEGE FINANCIAL AID PROGRAMS

After the federal government, colleges provide the largest amount of financial aid to students. In addition, they control most of the money channeled to students from the federal government. The amount and makeup of your financial aid package will depend on the institution's particular circumstances and its decisions concerning your application. The main section of this book shows you the pattern and extent of each college's current awards. The profiles present detailed factual and statistical data for each school in a uniform format to enable easy, quick references and comparisons. Items that could not be collected in time for publication for specific institutions do not appear in those institutions' profiles. Colleges that supplied no data are listed by name and address only so that you do not overlook them in your search for colleges.

There is much anecdotal evidence that students and their families fail to apply for financial aid under the misconception that student aid goes only to poor families. Financial need in the context of college expenses is not the same as being needy in the broad social context. Middle-class families typically qualify for need-based financial aid; at expensive schools, even upper-middle income families can qualify for need-based financial aid. Peterson's encourages you to apply for financial aid whether or not you think that you will qualify.

To help you understand the definition and significance of each item, the following outline of the profile format explains what is covered in each section. The term college or colleges is frequently used throughout to refer to any institution of higher education, regardless of its official definition.

The College

The name of the college is the official name as it appears on the institution's charter. The city and state listed are the official location of the school. The subhead line shows tuition and required fees, as they were charged to the majority of full-time undergraduate students in the 2012–13 academic year. Any exceptions to the 2012–13 academic year are so noted. For a public institution, the tuition and fees shown are for state residents, and this is noted. If a college's annual expenses are expressed as a comprehensive fee (including full-time tuition, mandatory fees, and college room and board), this is noted, as

are any unusual definitions, such as tuition only. The average undergraduate aid package is the average total package of grant, loan, and work-study aid that was awarded to meet the officially defined financial need of full-time undergraduates enrolled in fall 2012 (or fall 2011) who applied for financial aid, were determined to have need, and then actually received financial aid. This information appears in more detail in each profile.

About the Institution

This paragraph gives the reader a brief introduction to a college. It contains the following elements:

Institutional Control

Private institutions are designated as *independent* (nonprofit), *independent/religious* (sponsored by or affiliated with a religious group or having a nondenominational or interdenominational religious orientation), or *proprietary* (profit-making). Public institutions are designated by their primary source of support, such as *federal, state, commonwealth* (Puerto Rico), *territory* (U.S. territories), *county, district* (an administrative unit of public education, often having boundaries different from those of units of local government), *state-and locally-supported* ("locally" refers to county, district, or city), *state-supported* (funded by the state), or *state-related* (funded primarily by the state but administered autonomously).

Type of Student Body

The categories are *men* (100 percent of student body), *coed-primarily men, women* (100 percent of student body), *coed-primarily women,* and *coed.* A few schools are designated as *undergraduate: women only, graduate: coed* or *undergraduate: men only, graduate: coed.*

Degrees Awarded

Associate, bachelor's (baccalaureate), *master's, doctoral* (doctorate), and *first professional* (in such fields as law and medicine). There are no institutions in this book that award the associate degree only. Many award the bachelor's as the highest degree.

Number of Undergraduate Majors

This shows the number of academic fields in which the institution offers associate and/or bachelor's degrees. The purpose of this is to give you an indication of the range of subjects available.

Enrollment

These figures are based on the actual number of full-time and part-time students enrolled in degree programs as of fall 2011. In most instances, they are designated as *total enrollment* (for the specific college or university) and *freshmen.* If the institution is a university and its total enrollment figure includes graduate students, a separate figure for *undergraduates* may be provided. If the profiled institution is a subunit of a university, the figures may be designated *total university enrollment* for the entire university and *total unit enrollment* for the specific subunit.

Methodology Used for Determining Need

Private colleges usually have larger financial aid programs, but public colleges usually have lower sticker prices, especially for in-state or local students. At a public college, your financial need will be less, and you will receive a smaller financial aid package. This note on whether a college uses federal (FAFSA) or institutional methodology (usually CSS/Financial Aid PRO-FILE®) will let you know whether you will have to complete one or two kinds of financial aid application forms. Federal Methodology is the needs-analysis formula used by the U.S. Department of Education to determine the Expected Family Contribution (EFC), which, when subtracted from the cost of attendance at an institution, determines the financial need of a student. There is no relative advantage or disadvantage to using one methodology over the other.

Undergraduate Expenses

If provided by the institution, the one-time application fee is listed. Costs are given for the 2013–14 academic year or for the 2012–13 academic year if 2013–14 figures were not yet available. (Peterson's collects information for freshmen specifically.) Annual expenses may be expressed as a comprehensive fee (including full-time tuition, mandatory fees, and college room and board) or may be given as separate figures for full-time tuition, fees, room and board, or room only. For public institutions where tuition differs according to state residence, separate figures are given for area or state residents and for nonresidents. Part-time tuition is expressed in terms of a per-unit rate (per credit, per semester hour, etc.), as specified by the institution.

The tuition structure at some institutions is complex. Freshmen and sophomores may be charged a different rate from that charged juniors and seniors, a professional or vocational division may have a different fee structure from the liberal arts division of the same institution, or part-time tuition may be prorated on a sliding scale according to the number of credit hours taken. Tuition and fees may vary according to academic program, campus/location, class time (day, evening, weekend), course/credit load, course level, degree level, reciprocity agreements, and student level. If tuition and fees differ for international students, the rate charged is listed.

Room and board charges are reported as a double occupancy and nineteen meals per week plan or the equivalent and may vary according to board plan selected, campus/location, gender, type of housing facility, or student level. If no college-owned or -operated housing facilities are offered, the phrase *college housing not available* will appear.

If a college offers a *guaranteed tuition* plan, it promises that the tuition rate of an entering student will not increase for the entire term of enrollment, from entrance to graduation. Other payment plans might include *tuition prepayment*, which allows an entering student to lock in the current tuition rate for the entire term of enrollment by paying the full amount in advance rather than year by year, and *installment* and *deferred payment*

plans, which allow students to delay the payment of the full tuition.

Guaranteed tuition and tuition prepayment help you to plan the total cost of education and can save you from the financial distress sometimes caused by tuition hikes. Colleges that offer such plans may also help you to arrange financing, which in the long run can cost less than the total of four years of increasing tuition rates. Deferred payment or installment payments may better fit your personal financial situation, especially if you do not qualify for financial aid and, due to other financial commitments, find that obtaining the entire amount due is burdensome. Carefully investigate these plans, however, to see what premium you may pay at the end to allow you to defer immediate payment.

Freshman Financial Aid

Usually, these are actual figures for the 2011–12 term, beginning in fall 2011; figures may also be estimated for the 2012–13 term. The particular term for which these data apply is indicated. The figures are for degree-seeking full-time freshman students. The first figure is the number of freshmen who applied for any kind of financial aid. The next figure is the percentage of those freshmen financial aid applicants who were determined to have financial need—that is, through the formal needs-assessment process, had a calculated expected family contribution that was less than the total college cost. The next figure is the percentage of this group of eligible freshmen who received any financial aid. The next figure is the percentage of this preceding group of eligible aid recipients whose need was fully met by financial aid. The *Average percent of need met* is the average percentage of financial need met for freshmen who received any need-based aid. The *Average financial aid package* is the average dollar amount awarded (need-based or non-need-based) to freshmen who applied for aid, were deemed eligible, and received any aid; awards used to reduce the expected family contribution are excluded from this average. The final line in most profiles is the percentage of freshmen who had no financial need but who received non-need-based aid other than athletic scholarships or special-group tuition benefits.

What do these data mean to you? If financial aid is important in your comparison of colleges, the relative percentage of students who received any aid, whose need was fully met, and the average percentage of need met have the most weight. These figures reflect the relative abundance of student aid available to the average eligible applicant. The average dollar amount of the aid package has real meaning, but only in relation to the college's expense; you will be especially interested in the difference between this figure and the costs figure, which is what the average student (in any given statistical group, there actually may be no average individual) will have to pay. Of course, if the financial aid package is largely loans rather than grants, you will have to pay this amount eventually. Relative differences in the figures of the number of students who apply for aid and who are deemed eligible can hinge on any number of factors: the relative sticker price of the college, the relative level of wealth of the students' families, the proportion of only children in college and students with siblings in college (families with two or more children in college are more likely to apply for aid and be considered eligible), or the relative sophistication in financial aid matters (or quality of college counseling they may have received) of the students and their families. While these may be interesting, they will not mean too much to most students and families. If you are among the unlucky (or, perhaps, lucky) families who do not qualify for need-based financial aid, the final sentence of this paragraph in the profile will be of interest because it reveals the relative policies that the college has in distributing merit-based aid to students who cannot demonstrate need.

Undergraduate Financial Aid

This is the parallel paragraph to the Freshman Financial Aid paragraph. The same definitions apply, except that the group being considered is degree-seeking full-time undergraduate students (including freshmen).

There are cases of students who chose a particular college because they received a really generous financial aid package in their freshman year and then had to scramble to pay the tuition bill in their later years. If a financial aid package is a key factor in the decision to attend a particular college, you want to be certain that the package offered to all undergraduates is not too far from that offered to freshmen. The key figures are those for the percentage of students who received any aid, the percentage of financial aid recipients whose need was fully met, the average percentage of need met, and the dollar figure of the average financial aid package. Generally, colleges assume that after the freshman year, students develop study habits and time-management skills that will allow them to take on part-time and summer employment without hurting their academic performance. So, the proportion of self-help aid (work-study and student loans) in the financial aid package tends to increase after the freshman year. This pattern, which is true of most colleges, can be verified in the freshman-undergraduate figures in the paragraph on Gift Aid (Need-Based).

Gift Aid (Need-Based)

Total amount is the total dollar figure in 2012–13 (estimated) or 2011–12 (actual) of need-based scholarships and grant (gift) aid awarded to degree-seeking full-time and part-time students that was used to meet financial need. The percentages of this aid from federal, state, institutional (college or university), and external (e.g., foundations, civic organizations, etc.) sources are shown. *Receiving aid* shows the percentages (and number, in parentheses) of freshmen and of all undergraduates who applied for aid, were considered eligible, and received any need-based gift aid. *Average award* is the average dollar amount of awards to freshmen and all undergraduates who applied for aid, were considered eligible, and received any need-based gift aid. *Scholarships, grants, and awards* cites major categories of need-based gift aid provided by the college; these include Federal Pell Grants, Federal Supplemental Educational Opportunity Grants (FSEOG), state scholarships, private scholarships, college/university gift aid from institutional funds, United Negro College Fund aid, Federal Nursing Scholarships, and others.

Scholarships and grants are gifts awarded to students that do not need to be repaid. These are preferable to loans, which have to be repaid, or work-study wages, which may take time away from studies and personal pursuits. The total amount of need-based gift aid has to be placed into the context of the total number of undergraduate students (shown in the About the Institution paragraph) and the relative expense of the institution. Filing the FAFSA automatically puts you in line to receive any available federal grants for which you may qualify. However, if the college being considered has a higher than usual proportion of gift aid coming from state, institutional, or external sources, be sure to check with the financial aid office to find out what these sources may be and how to apply for them. For almost all colleges, the percentage of freshmen receiving need-based gift aid will be higher than the percentage of all undergraduates receiving need-based gift aid. However, if you are dependent on need-based gift aid and the particular college under consideration shows a sharper drop from the freshman to undergraduate years than other colleges of a similar type, you might want to think about how this change will affect your ability to pay for later years at this college.

Gift Aid (Non-Need-Based)

Total amount is the total dollar figure in 2012–13 (estimated) or 2011–12 (actual) of non-need-based scholarships and grant (gift) aid awarded to degree-seeking full-time and part-time students. Non-need-based aid that was used to meet financial need is not included in this total. The percentages of this aid from federal, state, institutional (college or university), and external (e.g., National Merit Scholarships, civic, religious, fraternal organizations, etc.) sources are shown. *Receiving aid* shows the percentages (and number, in parentheses) of freshmen and of all undergraduates who were determined to have need and received non-need-based gift aid. *Average award* is the average dollar amount of awards to freshmen and all undergraduates determined to have no need but received non-need-based awards. *Scholarships, grants, and awards by category* cites the major categories in which non-need-based awards are available and the number of awards made in that category (in parentheses, the total dollar value of these awards). The categories listed are *Academic interests/achievement*, *Creative arts/performance*, *Special achievements/activities*, and *Special characteristics*. *Tuition waivers* indicate special categories of students (minority students, children of alumni, college employees or children of employees, adult students, and senior citizens) who may qualify for a full or partial waiver of tuition. *ROTC* indicates Army, Naval, and Air Force ROTC programs that are offered on campus; a program offered by arrangement on another campus is indicated by the word *cooperative*.

This section covers college-administered scholarships awarded to undergraduates on the basis of merit or personal attributes without regard to need. If you do not qualify for financial aid but nevertheless lack the resources to pay for college, non-need-based awards will be of special interest to you. Some personal characteristics are completely beyond an individual's control, and talents and achievements take a number of years to develop or attain. However, certain criteria for these awards, such as religious involvement, community service, and special academic interests can be attained in a relatively brief period of time. ROTC programs offer such benefits as tuition, the cost of textbooks, and living allowances. In return, you must fulfill a service obligation after graduating from college. Because they can be a significant help in paying for college, these programs have become quite competitive. Certain subject areas, such as nursing, health care, or the technical fields, are in stronger demand than others. Among the obligations to consider about ROTC are that you must spend a regular portion of your available time in military training programs and that ROTC entails a multiyear commitment after your graduation to serve as an officer in the armed services branch sponsoring the program.

Loans

The figures here represent loans that are part of the financial aid award package. *Student loans* represents the total dollar amount of loans from all sources to full-time and part-time degree-seeking undergraduates or their parents. *Average need-based loan* represents the percentage of these loans that goes to meet financial need, and the percentage that goes to pay the non-need portion (the expected family contribution) are indicated. The percentage of a past graduating class who borrowed through any loan program (except parent loans) while enrolled at the college is shown, as is the average dollar figure per-borrower of cumulative undergraduate indebtedness (this does not include loans from other institutions). *Parent loans* shows the total amount borrowed through parent loan programs as well as the percentages that were applied to the need-based and non-needbased portions of financial need. *Programs* indicates the major loan programs available to undergraduates. These include Direct Student Loans (subsidized and unsubsidized and PLUS), Perkins Loans, Federal Nursing Loans, state loans, college/university loans, and other types.

Note: As a result of the Health Care and Education Reconciliation Act, as of July 1, 2010, federal student loans are no longer made by private lenders under the Federal Family Education Loan (FFEL) Program. Instead, all new federal student loans come directly from the U.S. Department of Education under the Direct Loan Program. Any FFEL loans noted in this section of an institution's profile are no longer available.

Loans are forms of aid that must be repaid with interest. Most people will borrow money to pay college costs. The loans available through financial aid programs are offered at very favorable interest rates. In comparing colleges, the dollar amount of total indebtedness is a factor to be considered. Typically, this amount would increase proportionate to the tuition. However, if it does not, this could mean that the college provides relatively generous grant or work-study aid rather than loans in its financial aid package.

Work-Study

The total dollar amounts, number, and average dollar amount of *Federal work-study* (FWS) jobs appear first. The total dollar figure of *State or other work-study/employment*, if available, is shown, as is the percentage of those dollars that go to meet financial need. The number of part-time jobs available on campus to undergraduates, other than work-study, is shown last.

FWS is a federally funded program that enables students with demonstrated need to earn money by working on or off campus, usually in a nonprofit organization. FWS jobs are a special category of jobs that are open to students only through the financial aid office. Other kinds of part-time jobs are routinely available at most colleges and may vary widely. In comparing colleges, you may find characteristic differences in how the "self-help" amounts (loans and work-study) are apportioned.

Athletic Awards

The total dollar amount of athletic scholarships given by the college to undergraduate students, including percentages that are need-based and non-need-based, is indicated.

Applying for Financial Aid

Required financial aid forms include the FAFSA (Free Application for Federal Student Aid), the institution's own form, CSS/Financial Aid PROFILE, a state aid form, a noncustodial (divorced/separated) parent's statement, a business/farm supplement, and others. The college's financial aid application deadline is noted as the *Financial aid deadline* and is shown in one of three ways: as a specific date if it is an absolute deadline; noted as *continuous*, which means processing goes on without a deadline or until all available aid has been awarded; or as a date with the note *(priority)*, meaning that you are encouraged to apply before that date in order to have the best chance of obtaining aid. *Notification date* is listed as either a specific date or *continuous*. The date by which a reply to the college with the decision to accept or decline its financial aid package is listed as either a specific date or as a number of weeks from the date of notification.

Be prepared to check early with the colleges as to exactly which forms will be required. All colleges require the FAFSA for students applying for federal aid. In most cases, colleges have a limited amount of funds set aside to use as financial aid. It is possible that the first eligible students will get a larger share of what is available.

Contact

The name, title, address, telephone and fax numbers, and e-mail address of the person to contact for further information (student financial aid contact) are given at the end of the profile. You should feel free to write or call for any materials you need or if you have questions.

APPENDIX

This section lists more than 400 state-specific grants and loans. Award amounts, number of awards, eligibility requirements, application requirements, and deadlines are given for all programs.

INDEXES

Six indexes in the back of the book allow you to search for particular award programs based on the following criteria:

Non-Need Scholarships for Undergraduates

This index lists the colleges that report that they offer scholarships based on academic interests, abilities, achievements, or personal characteristics other than financial need. Specific categories appear in alphabetical order under the following broad groups:

- Academic Interests/Achievements
- Creative Arts/Performance
- Special Achievements/Activities
- Special Characteristics
- See the index for specific categories in each group.

Athletic Grants for Undergraduates

This index lists the colleges that report offering scholarships on the basis of athletic abilities.

Co-op Programs

This index lists colleges that report offering cooperative education programs. These are formal arrangements with off-campus employers that are designed to allow students to combine study and work, often in a position related to the student's field of study. Salaries typically are set at regular marketplace levels, and academic credit is often given.

ROTC Programs

This index lists colleges that offer Reserve Officers' Training Corps programs. The index is arranged by the branch of service that sponsors the program.

Tuition Waivers

This index lists colleges that report offering full or partial tuition waivers for certain categories of students. A majority of colleges offer tuition waivers to employees or children of employees.

Because this benefit is so common and the affected employees usually are aware of it, no separate index of schools offering this option is provided. However, this information is included in the individual college profiles.

Tuition Payment Alternatives

This index lists colleges that report offering tuition payment alternatives. These payment alternatives include deferred payment plans, guaranteed tuition plans, installment payment plans, and prepayment plans.

DATA COLLECTION PROCEDURES

The data contained in the college chart, profiles, and indexes were collected in winter and spring 2013 through *Peterson's Annual Survey of Undergraduate Financial Aid* and *Peterson's Annual Survey of Undergraduate Institutions*. Questionnaires were sent to the more than 2,100 institutions of higher education that are accredited in the United States and U.S. territories and offer full four-or five-year baccalaureate degrees via full-time on-campus programs of study. Officials at the colleges—usually financial aid or admission officers but sometimes registrars or institutional research staff members—completed and returned the forms. Peterson's has every reason to believe that the data presented in this book are accurate. However, students should always confirm costs and other facts with a specific school at the time of application, since colleges can and do change policies and fees whenever necessary.

The state aid data presented in Peterson's *How to Get Money for College* was submitted by state officials (usually the director of the state scholarship commission) to Peterson's in the spring of 2013. Because regulations for any government-sponsored program may be changed at any time, you should request written descriptive materials from the office administering a program in which you are interested.

CRITERIA FOR INCLUSION IN THIS BOOK

To be included in this guide, an institution must have full accreditation or be a candidate for accreditation (preaccreditation) status by an institutional or specialized accrediting body recognized by the U.S. Department of Education or the Council for Higher Education Accreditation (CHEA). Institutional accrediting bodies, which review each institution as a whole, include the six regional associations of schools and colleges (Middle States, New England, North Central, Northwest, Southern, and Western), each of which is responsible for a specified portion of the United States and its territories. Other institutional accrediting bodies are national in scope and accredit specific kinds of institutions (e.g., Bible colleges, independent colleges, and rabbinical and Talmudic schools). Program registration by the New York State Board of Regents is considered to be the equivalent of institutional accreditation, since the board requires that all programs offered by an institution meet its standards before recognition is granted. There are recognized specialized or professional accrediting bodies in more than forty different fields, each of which is authorized to accredit institutions or specific programs in its particular field. For specialized institutions that offer programs in one field only, we designate this to be the equivalent of institutional accreditation. A full explanation of the accrediting process and complete information on recognized, institutional (regional and national) and specialized accrediting bodies can be found online at www.chea.org or at www.ed.gov/admins/finaid/accred/index.html.

Quick -Reference Chart

College Costs At-a-Glance

To help shed some light on the typical patterns of financial aid offered by colleges, we have prepared the following chart. This chart can help you to better understand financial aid practices in general, form realistic expectations about the amounts of aid that might be provided by specific colleges or universities, and prepare for meaningful discussions with the financial aid officers at colleges being considered. The data appearing in the chart have been supplied by the schools themselves and are also shown in the individual college profiles.

Tuition and fees are based on the total of full-time tuition and mandatory fees for the 2013–14 academic year or for the 2012–13 academic year if 2013–14 figures are not available. More information about these costs, as well as the costs of room and board and the year for which they are current, can be found in the individual college profiles. For institutions that have two or more tuition rates for different categories of students or types of programs, the lowest rate is used in figuring the cost.

The colleges are listed alphabetically by state. An "NR" in any individual column indicates that the applicable data element was "Not Reported."

The chart is divided into eight columns of information for each college:

1. Institutional Control
Whether the school is independent (ind.), including independent, independent–religious, and proprietary, or public (pub.), including federal, state, commonwealth, territory, county, district, city, state, local, and state-related.

2. Tuition and Fees
Based on the total of full-time tuition and mandatory fees. An asterisk indicates that the school includes room and board in their mandatory fees.

3. Room and Board
If a school has room and board costs that vary according to the type of accommodation and meal plan, either the lowest figures are represented or the figures are for the most common room arrangement and a full meal plan. If a school has only housing arrangements, a dagger appears to the right of the number. An "NA" will appear in this column if no college-owned or -operated housing facilities are offered.

4. Percent of Eligible Freshmen Receiving Need-Based Gift Awards
Calculated by dividing the number of freshman students determined to have need who received need-based gift aid by the number of full-time freshmen.

5. Percent of Freshmen Whose Need Was Fully Met
Calculated by dividing the number of freshman students whose financial need was fully met by the number of freshmen with need.

6. Average Financial Aid Package for Freshmen
The average dollar amount from all sources, including *gift aid* (scholarships and grants) and *self-help* (jobs and loans), awarded to freshmen receiving aid. Note that this aid package may exceed tuition and fees if the average aid package included coverage of room and board expenses.

7. Average Net Cost After Aid
Average aid package subtracted from published costs (tuition, fees, room, and board) to produce what the average student will have to pay.

8. Average Indebtedness Upon Graduation
Average per-student indebtedness of graduating seniors.

Because personal situations vary widely, it is very important to note that an individual's aid package can be quite different from the averages. Moreover, the data shown for each school can fluctuate widely from year to year, depending on the number of applicants, the amount of need to be met, and the financial resources and policies of the college. Peterson's intent in presenting this chart is to provide you with useful facts and figures that can serve as general guidelines in the pursuit of financial aid. We caution you to use the data only as a jumping-off point for further investigation and analysis, not as a means to rank or select colleges.

After you have narrowed down the choice of colleges based on academic and personal criteria, we recommend that you carefully study this chart. From it, you can develop a list of questions for financial aid officers at the colleges under serious consideration. Here are just a few questions you might want to ask: About the Institution

- What are the specific types and sources of aid provided to freshmen at this school?

- What factors does this college consider in determining whether a financial aid applicant is qualified for its need-based aid programs?

- How does the college determine the combination of types of aid that make up an individual's package?

- How are non-need-based awards treated: as a part of the aid package or as a part of the parental/family contribution?

- Does this school "guarantee" financial aid and, if so, how is its policy implemented? Guaranteed aid means that, by policy, 100 percent of need is met for all students judged to have need. Implementation determines *how* need is met and varies widely from school to school. For example, grade point average may determine the apportioning of scholarship, loan, and work-study aid. Rules for freshmen may be different from those for upperclass students.

- To what degree is the admission process "need-blind"? Need-blind means that admission decisions are made without regard to the student's need for financial aid.

- What are the norms and practices for upperclass students? Peterson's chart presents information on *freshmen* financial aid only; however, the financial aid office should be able and willing to provide you with comparable figures for upperclass students. A college might offer a wonderful package for the freshman year, then leave students mostly on their own to fund the remaining three years. Or the school may provide a higher proportion of scholarship money for freshmen, then rebalance its aid packages to contain more self-help aid (loans and work-study) in upperclass years.

There is an assumption that, all other factors being equal, students who have settled into the pattern of college time management can handle more work-study hours than freshmen. Grade point average, tuition increases, changes in parental financial circumstances, and other factors may also affect the redistribution.

Michael Steidel is Director of Admission at Carnegie Mellon University.

College Costs At-a-Glance

	Institutional Control ind.=independent; pub.=public	Tuition and Fees	Room and Board	Percent of Eligible Freshmen Receiving Need-Based Gift Awards	Percent of Freshmen Whose Need Was Fully Met	Average Financial Aid Package for Freshmen	Average Net Cost After Aid	Average Indebtedness Upon Graduation
Alabama								
Alabama State University	pub.	$6312	$5366	87%	26%	$14,611	—	$29,795
Amridge University	ind.	$6000	NA	100%	NR	NR	NR	NR
Athens State University	pub.	$5340	NA	NR	NR	$12,815	—	NR
Auburn University	pub.	$9446	$10,606	86%	26%	$12,352	$7700	$24,903
Auburn University at Montgomery	pub.	$8150	$3270†	67%	23%	NR	NR	NR
Faulkner University	ind.	$17,380	$6650	87%	37%	$4950	$19,080	$9500
Heritage Christian University	ind.	$12,776	$5426	40%	40%	$11,050	$7152	$18,950
Huntingdon College	ind.	$22,500	$8250	100%	17%	$17,145	$13,605	$21,034
Jacksonville State University	pub.	$7950	$6300	52%	NR	$8630	$5620	NR
Samford University	ind.	$25,150	$8250	99%	23%	$17,254	$16,146	$25,252
Spring Hill College	ind.	$29,450	$11,296	98%	20%	$30,933	$9813	$30,356
Troy University	pub.	$9070	$7071	62%	NR	$3678	$12,463	NR
Tuskegee University	ind.	$18,900	$8450	85%	68%	$19,250	$8100	$28,575
The University of Alabama	pub.	$9200	$8650	79%	21%	$11,479	$6371	$27,639
The University of Alabama at Birmingham	pub.	$8400	$5400†	64%	16%	$10,124	$3676	$21,503
The University of Alabama in Huntsville	pub.	$8794	$8070	89%	17%	$10,839	$6025	$25,437
University of Mobile	ind.	$17,680	$8650	62%	19%	$16,908	$9422	$29,474
University of Montevallo	pub.	$9280	$5522	89%	17%	$8873	$5929	$24,723
University of North Alabama	pub.	$8148	$5678	74%	50%	$6752	$7074	$32,640
University of South Alabama	pub.	$7950	$7150	89%	14%	$9062	$6038	NR
The University of West Alabama	pub.	$7320	$5920	81%	2%	$9136	$4104	$27,815
Alaska								
Alaska Bible College	ind.	$9390	$5400	NR	NR	NR	NR	NR
Alaska Pacific University	ind.	$29,880	$9300	46%	NR	$11,861	$27,319	$12,119
University of Alaska Anchorage	pub.	$4950	$9780	88%	40%	$7681	$7049	$30,363
University of Alaska Fairbanks	pub.	$5580	$7200	88%	30%	$8812	$3968	$29,762
Arizona								
American Indian College of the Assemblies of God, Inc.	ind.	$16,040	$6202	NR	NR	NR	NR	NR
Arizona State University	pub.	$9724	$9094	95%	17%	$12,756	$6062	$18,615
Embry-Riddle Aeronautical University–Prescott	ind.	$31,034	$9550	100%	NR	$14,012	$26,572	NR
Northern Arizona University	pub.	$9271	$8784	67%	12%	$9835	$8220	$22,621
Prescott College	ind.	$28,019	$5900	98%	10%	$22,273	$11,646	$23,476
The University of Arizona	pub.	$10,035	$9714	95%	13%	$12,180	$7569	$22,269
Arkansas								
Arkansas State University	pub.	$7180	$7150	97%	35%	$10,100	$4230	$21,000
Arkansas Tech University	pub.	$6798	$5846	88%	8%	$8886	$3758	$22,649
Harding University	ind.	$15,240	$6192	99%	29%	$13,461	$7971	$32,752
Henderson State University	pub.	$6984	$5332	69%	3%	$11,705	$611	$6747
Hendrix College	ind.	$37,816	$10,620	100%	42%	$29,273	$19,163	$24,492
John Brown University	ind.	$22,734	$8262	92%	16%	$20,817	$10,179	$24,160
Lyon College	ind.	$23,594	$7560	100%	31%	$22,627	$8527	$17,179

NA = not applicable; NR = not reported; * = includes room and board; † = room only; — = not available.

College Costs At-a-Glance

	Institutional Control ind.=independent; pub.=public	Tuition and Fees	Room and Board	Percent of Eligible Freshmen Receiving Need-Based Gift Awards	Percent of Freshmen Whose Need Was Fully Met	Average Financial Aid Package for Freshmen	Average Net Cost After Aid	Average Indebtedness Upon Graduation
Ouachita Baptist University	ind.	$22,340	$6640	95%	30%	$19,418	$9562	$24,367
Philander Smith College	ind.	$11,910	$7600	99%	5%	$12,466	$7044	$37,450
Southern Arkansas University–Magnolia	pub.	$7346	$4974	74%	34%	$12,983	—	$13,120
University of Arkansas	pub.	$7553	$8672	85%	24%	$10,004	$6221	$24,647
Williams Baptist College	ind.	NR	NR	85%	NR	$14,862	—	$18,720
California								
Academy of Art University	ind.	$23,840	$13,400	69%	NR	$8936	$28,304	$46,726
Alliant International University	ind.	$16,930	$7340	100%	NR	$13,550	$10,720	NR
American Jewish University	ind.	$28,496	$14,082	100%	NR	$27,000	$15,578	$29,500
Azusa Pacific University	ind.	$31,076	$4242†	91%	3%	$19,088	$16,230	$23,070
Biola University	ind.	$31,004	$7912	99%	6%	$16,773	$22,143	$34,587
California Baptist University	ind.	$26,900	$8990	98%	9%	$16,593	$19,297	$33,807
California Christian College	ind.	$8010	$4200	100%	NR	$8794	$3416	$33,595
California College of the Arts	ind.	$40,334	$8000†	100%	6%	$26,584	$21,750	$36,300
California Institute of Integral Studies	ind.	NR	NA	NR	NR	NR	NR	$21,026
California Institute of Technology	ind.	$41,538	$12,507	100%	100%	$37,984	$16,061	$15,090
California Lutheran University	ind.	$34,360	$11,510	100%	17%	$23,880	$21,990	$26,610
California Maritime Academy	pub.	NR	NR	65%	NR	$19,729	—	$18,579
California Polytechnic State University, San Luis Obispo	pub.	$8523	$10,679	83%	6%	$9543	$9659	NR
California State Polytechnic University, Pomona	pub.	$6623	$11,615	79%	NR	$9567	$8671	$18,805
California State University, Bakersfield	pub.	$6709	$8787	100%	4%	$4156	$11,340	$10,101
California State University, Chico	pub.	$8906	$11,208	72%	13%	$12,538	$7576	NR
California State University, Dominguez Hills	pub.	$6095	$10,733	86%	2%	$5698	$11,130	$11,783
California State University, East Bay	pub.	$6309	$11,321	88%	2%	$11,357	$6273	$19,303
California State University, Fresno	pub.	$6274	$10,192	86%	13%	$11,194	$5272	$16,100
California State University, Fullerton	pub.	$6182	$12,096	82%	85%	$11,010	$7268	$14,983
California State University, Long Beach	pub.	$6240	$11,300	85%	75%	$12,507	$5033	NR
California State University, Los Angeles	pub.	$6335	$9728	90%	10%	$12,384	$3679	NR
California State University, Monterey Bay	pub.	$5963	$9498	79%	29%	$10,967	$4494	$18,349
California State University, Northridge	pub.	$6520	$12,404	84%	NR	$11,411	$7513	$17,198
California State University, Sacramento	pub.	$6620	$11,724	83%	5%	$10,804	$7540	$4456
California State University, San Bernardino	pub.	$12,021	$9972	86%	6%	$11,648	$10,345	$21,787
California State University, San Marcos	pub.	$7298	NR	90%	NR	$8397	—	$19,257
California State University, Stanislaus	pub.	$6584	$9056	80%	31%	$14,711	$929	NR
Chapman University	ind.	$43,573	$12,204	88%	10%	$32,039	$23,738	$29,371
Claremont McKenna College	ind.	$44,085	$13,980	100%	100%	$39,953	$18,112	$23,179
Concordia University	ind.	$29,630	$9050	100%	15%	$19,085	$19,595	$29,091
Dominican University of California	ind.	$39,050	$13,940	100%	4%	$28,131	$24,859	$39,125
Fresno Pacific University	ind.	NR	NR	81%	11%	$21,264	—	$21,993
Harvey Mudd College	ind.	$44,442	$14,471	96%	100%	$41,827	$17,086	$24,194
Hope International University	ind.	$26,050	$8600	83%	21%	$16,750	$17,900	$20,500
John Paul the Great Catholic University	ind.	NR	NR	100%	NR	NR	NR	NR

NA = not applicable; NR = not reported; * = includes room and board; † = room only; — = not available.

College Costs At-a-Glance

	Institutional Control ind.=independent; pub.=public	Tuition and Fees	Room and Board	Percent of Eligible Freshmen Receiving Need-Based Gift Awards	Percent of Freshmen Whose Need Was Fully Met	Average Financial Aid Package for Freshmen	Average Net Cost After Aid	Average Indebtedness Upon Graduation
Laguna College of Art & Design	ind.	NR	NA	85%	NR	$10,600	—	$38,000
La Sierra University	ind.	$28,314	$7380	100%	19%	$21,378	$14,316	$21,882
Loyola Marymount University	ind.	$38,900	$14,395	91%	15%	$23,356	$29,939	$34,629
The Master's College and Seminary	ind.	$29,480	$9360	98%	11%	$19,556	$19,284	$18,121
Menlo College	ind.	$37,100	$11,902	100%	11%	$29,239	$19,763	$25,753
Mills College	ind.	$41,494	$12,625	96%	20%	$38,795	$15,324	$27,021
Mount St. Mary's College	ind.	$33,852	$10,530	100%	6%	$28,106	$16,276	$34,998
National University	ind.	$14,670	NA	76%	2%	$4896	$9774	NR
Notre Dame de Namur University	ind.	$31,206	$12,152	99%	4%	$25,031	$18,327	$31,915
Occidental College	ind.	$46,270	$12,940	100%	100%	$38,084	$21,126	$28,723
Otis College of Art and Design	ind.	NR	NR	96%	7%	$22,594	—	$41,842
Pacific Union College	ind.	$26,850	$7485	100%	2%	$22,470	$11,865	$33,662
Pepperdine University	ind.	$42,772	$12,600	42%	33%	$40,014	$15,358	$30,101
Pitzer College	ind.	$43,402	$13,864	96%	100%	$41,456	$15,810	$20,900
Point Loma Nazarene University	ind.	$29,510	$9550	94%	17%	$19,970	$19,090	$31,851
Pomona College	ind.	$41,438	$13,526	100%	100%	$40,107	$14,857	$15,714
Saint Mary's College of California	ind.	$39,890	$13,660	99%	8%	$25,905	$27,645	$31,828
San Diego Christian College	ind.	$25,888	$9278	76%	16%	$16,232	$18,934	$23,868
San Diego State University	pub.	$6766	$13,812	68%	9%	$9000	$11,578	$17,600
San Francisco Art Institute	ind.	$36,618	$13,844	100%	NR	$16,960	$33,502	$29,541
San Francisco Conservatory of Music	ind.	$38,140	NR	100%	11%	$24,795	$13,345	$18,028
San Francisco State University	pub.	$6440	$11,576	74%	7%	$11,932	$6084	$20,493
San Jose State University	pub.	$13,704	$11,733	72%	61%	$16,334	$9103	$16,519
Santa Clara University	ind.	$40,572	$12,276	79%	38%	$26,310	$26,538	$28,672
Scripps College	ind.	$43,620	$13,468	100%	100%	$36,473	$20,615	$17,487
Simpson University	ind.	$23,300	$7500	85%	5%	$19,784	$11,016	$28,196
Soka University of America	ind.	$28,808	$10,916	100%	11%	$32,990	$6734	$22,387
Sonoma State University	pub.	$7396	$11,241	57%	9%	$11,900	$6737	$21,206
Stanford University	ind.	$42,690	$13,166	96%	92%	$41,894	$13,962	$18,833
Thomas Aquinas College	ind.	$24,500	$7950	99%	100%	$22,441	$10,009	$17,820
University of California, Berkeley	pub.	$12,874	$15,000	93%	44%	$21,767	$6107	$17,964
University of California, Davis	pub.	$15,727	NR	97%	14%	$21,420	—	$19,285
University of California, Irvine	pub.	$14,226	$11,735	97%	39%	$22,665	$3296	$19,828
University of California, Los Angeles	pub.	$12,692	$12,675	96%	25%	$22,560	$2807	$20,409
University of California, Merced	pub.	$13,070	$14,272	97%	38%	$24,674	$2668	$18,786
University of California, Riverside	pub.	$12,960	$13,200	97%	32%	$23,585	$2575	$20,613
University of California, San Diego	pub.	$13,234	$11,924	95%	41%	$22,041	$3117	$20,474
University of California, Santa Barbara	pub.	$15,036	$13,275	94%	23%	$23,996	$4315	$19,325
University of California, Santa Cruz	pub.	$13,417	$14,856	95%	21%	$24,719	$3554	$20,358
University of La Verne	ind.	$35,000	$11,910	93%	15%	$28,210	$18,700	$30,566
University of Redlands	ind.	$39,338	$11,924	99%	48%	$33,263	$17,999	$32,035
University of San Diego	ind.	$41,392	$11,910	98%	13%	$29,600	$23,702	$29,874

NA = not applicable; NR = not reported; * = includes room and board; † = room only; — = not available.

College Costs At-a-Glance

	Institutional Control ind.=independent; pub.=public	Tuition and Fees	Room and Board	Percent of Eligible Freshmen Receiving Need-Based Gift Awards	Percent of Freshmen Whose Need Was Fully Met	Average Financial Aid Package for Freshmen	Average Net Cost After Aid	Average Indebtedness Upon Graduation
University of the Pacific	ind.	$38,320	$12,038	99%	10%	$26,896	$23,462	NR
Westmont College	ind.	NR	NR	100%	21%	$26,504	—	$31,277
Whittier College	ind.	$40,096	$11,494	91%	12%	$30,802	$20,788	$25,212
William Jessup University	ind.	$22,900	$9070	100%	13%	$20,164	$11,806	$21,057
Woodbury University	ind.	$31,444	$9952	99%	4%	$20,798	$20,598	$37,856
Colorado								
Adams State University	pub.	$6448	$7900	96%	2%	$11,340	$3008	$27,785
The Colorado College	ind.	$41,942	$9728	97%	90%	$38,292	$13,378	$19,970
Colorado Mesa University	pub.	$6870	$9103	92%	13%	$7408	$8565	$24,714
Colorado Mountain College	pub.	$1860	$8164	NR	NR	NR	NR	NR
Colorado School of Mines	pub.	NR	NR	56%	22%	$12,239	—	$33,209
Colorado State University	pub.	$8649	$10,278	71%	36%	$16,131	$2796	$22,131
Fort Lewis College	pub.	$6923	$8590	64%	5%	$11,720	$3793	$19,811
Metropolitan State University of Denver	pub.	NR	NA	83%	1%	$6367	—	$31,427
Naropa University	ind.	$28,790	$8980	100%	7%	$33,234	$4536	$26,511
Nazarene Bible College	ind.	$10,800	NA	100%	NR	$7600	$3200	$31,757
Regis University	ind.	$32,424	$9380	98%	43%	$23,723	$18,081	$28,127
Rocky Mountain College of Art + Design	ind.	$27,648	NA	44%	13%	$20,855	$6793	$30,067
University of Colorado Boulder	pub.	$9482	$11,730	70%	62%	$12,944	$8268	$23,413
University of Colorado Colorado Springs	pub.	$8339	$8300	69%	6%	$6445	$10,194	$15,447
University of Colorado Denver	pub.	$7494	$10,410	85%	5%	$8120	$9784	$21,285
University of Denver	ind.	$40,707	$11,080	98%	32%	$30,905	$20,882	$30,268
University of Northern Colorado	pub.	$6514	$10,040	88%	44%	$6136	$10,418	NR
Western State Colorado University	pub.	$7343	$8792	100%	22%	$9280	$6855	$18,558
Connecticut								
Central Connecticut State University	pub.	$8321	$10,056	86%	2%	$8052	$10,325	$22,171
Eastern Connecticut State University	pub.	$9376	$11,168	80%	10%	$8586	$11,958	$26,168
Fairfield University	ind.	$41,690	$12,550	86%	12%	$27,725	$26,515	$28,507
Lyme Academy College of Fine Arts	ind.	$28,536	$10,800	NR	NR	$18,949	$20,387	$31,000
Post University	ind.	$27,450	$10,430	95%	15%	$20,135	$17,745	$16,499
Quinnipiac University	ind.	$39,330	$14,250	98%	12%	$23,867	$29,713	$42,730
Sacred Heart University	ind.	$34,030	$13,230	100%	12%	$18,087	$29,173	$42,779
Southern Connecticut State University	pub.	$8570	$10,641	69%	25%	$13,274	$5937	$23,663
Trinity College	ind.	$45,730	$11,800	97%	100%	$41,912	$15,618	$18,868
University of Bridgeport	ind.	$28,140	$12,050	86%	5%	$25,200	$14,990	$37,136
University of Connecticut	pub.	$12,022	$11,722	72%	10%	$12,086	$11,658	$24,373
University of Hartford	ind.	$33,358	$12,248	90%	30%	$16,846	$28,760	$28,933
University of New Haven	ind.	$32,750	$13,700	100%	10%	$20,276	$26,174	$42,217
University of Saint Joseph	ind.	$31,826	$13,598	100%	11%	$22,479	$22,945	NR
Wesleyan University	ind.	$45,628	$12,574	94%	100%	$42,088	$16,114	$20,966
Western Connecticut State University	pub.	$8893	$10,907	89%	3%	$7920	$11,880	$22,505
Yale University	ind.	$44,000	$13,500	100%	100%	$46,331	$11,169	$10,742

NA = not applicable; NR = not reported; * = includes room and board; † = room only; — = not available.

College Costs At-a-Glance

	Institutional Control ind.=independent; pub.=public	Tuition and Fees	Room and Board	Percent of Eligible Freshmen Receiving Need-Based Gift Awards	Percent of Freshmen Whose Need Was Fully Met	Average Financial Aid Package for Freshmen	Average Net Cost After Aid	Average Indebtedness Upon Graduation
Delaware								
University of Delaware	pub.	$11,682	$10,758	87%	48%	$14,427	$8013	$33,649
Wesley College	ind.	$22,392	$10,438	100%	NR	$14,765	$18,065	NR
District of Columbia								
American University	ind.	$39,499	$13,920	90%	38%	$30,402	$23,017	NR
The Catholic University of America	ind.	$36,820	$14,274	99%	44%	$25,293	$25,801	NR
Corcoran College of Art and Design	ind.	$31,130	$12,900	97%	NR	$26,896	$17,134	$46,596
Gallaudet University	ind.	$12,806	$10,790	100%	24%	$19,568	$4028	$10,347
Georgetown University	ind.	$43,070	$13,312	93%	100%	$37,569	$18,813	$25,540
The George Washington University	ind.	$47,335	$11,378	97%	58%	$38,163	$20,550	$33,398
Howard University	ind.	$22,883	$9342	58%	10%	$16,502	$15,723	$10,136
University of the District of Columbia	pub.	$7255	$6600	NR	NR	NR	NR	NR
Florida								
The Baptist College of Florida	ind.	$9400	$4138	100%	5%	$6511	$7027	$22,803
Barry University	ind.	$28,160	$11,988†	86%	6%	$23,891	$16,257	$38,634
Bethune-Cookman University	ind.	$14,410	$8548	97%	4%	$14,124	$8834	$22,175
Clearwater Christian College	ind.	$17,060	$8300	100%	3%	$12,253	$13,107	$22,321
Eckerd College	ind.	$37,362	$10,144	100%	16%	$29,923	$17,583	$33,957
Embry-Riddle Aeronautical University–Daytona	ind.	$31,334	$9550	100%	NR	$13,607	$27,277	NR
Embry-Riddle Aeronautical University–Worldwide	ind.	$7032	NA	79%	NR	$4266	$2766	NR
Flagler College	ind.	$15,340	$8350	99%	14%	$11,554	$12,136	$24,519
Florida Agricultural and Mechanical University	pub.	$5187	$8754	89%	26%	$13,285	$656	$29,702
Florida Atlantic University	pub.	$5986	$11,353	92%	12%	$10,044	$7295	$19,281
Florida Gulf Coast University	pub.	$4855	$9424	58%	9%	$8926	$5353	$27,308
Florida Institute of Technology	ind.	$36,020	$12,270	100%	40%	$32,855	$15,435	$38,953
Florida International University	pub.	$6417	$11,330	66%	7%	$6926	$10,821	$17,706
Florida National University	ind.	$13,230	NA	99%	NR	NR	NR	$8700
Florida Southern College	ind.	$27,200	$9100	100%	27%	$21,974	$14,326	$26,509
Florida State University	pub.	$6402	$9626	63%	67%	$9470	$6558	$22,405
Hodges University	ind.	$12,260	NA	89%	22%	$8400	$3860	$18,400
Jacksonville University	ind.	$59,800	$39,930	100%	37%	$24,934	$74,796	NR
Lynn University	ind.	$33,400	$10,900	79%	100%	$17,544	$26,756	$33,472
Millennia Atlantic University	ind.	NR	NR	78%	9%	$8500	—	NR
New College of Florida	pub.	$6783	$8856	100%	44%	$12,104	$3535	$16,640
Northwood University, Florida Campus	ind.	$22,130	$10,041	87%	25%	$22,610	$9561	$27,505
Nova Southeastern University	ind.	$24,500	$9516	99%	14%	$24,280	$9736	$31,137
Palm Beach Atlantic University	ind.	$25,532	$8350	100%	13%	$17,836	$16,046	$24,749
Ringling College of Art and Design	ind.	$35,300	$12,230	95%	2%	$16,254	$31,276	$48,515
Rollins College	ind.	$39,900	$12,470	100%	62%	$33,676	$18,694	$24,096
St. Thomas University	ind.	$25,110	$7140	77%	42%	NR	NR	NR
Stetson University	ind.	$36,644	$10,688	100%	25%	$33,011	$14,321	$32,750

NA = not applicable; NR = not reported; * = includes room and board; † = room only; — = not available.

College Costs At-a-Glance

	Institutional Control ind.=independent; pub.=public	Tuition and Fees	Room and Board	Percent of Eligible Freshmen Receiving Need-Based Gift Awards	Percent of Freshmen Whose Need Was Fully Met	Average Financial Aid Package for Freshmen	Average Net Cost After Aid	Average Indebtedness Upon Graduation
Trinity Baptist College	ind.	$9040	$5510	NR	NR	NR	NR	NR
Trinity College of Florida	ind.	$13,320	$6550	100%	NR	$9883	$9987	$5500
University of Central Florida	pub.	$6247	$9357	50%	17%	$6816	$8788	$20,086
University of Florida	pub.	$6143	$9370	67%	23%	$13,093	$2420	$19,636
University of Miami	ind.	$42,852	$12,314	99%	45%	$34,845	$20,321	$26,786
University of North Florida	pub.	$6235	$8190	57%	16%	$8650	$5775	$17,000
The University of Tampa	ind.	$25,222	$9116	75%	19%	$15,512	$18,826	$31,032
University of West Florida	pub.	$7022	$9210	78%	15%	$8846	$7386	NR
Webber International University	ind.	$20,418	$7900	100%	6%	$16,603	$11,715	NR
Georgia								
Armstrong Atlantic State University	pub.	$5844	$9770	52%	52%	$6500	$9114	$21,000
Berry College	ind.	$27,650	$9679	100%	24%	$24,755	$12,574	$20,611
Brenau University	ind.	$21,908	$10,884	99%	13%	$22,665	$10,127	$23,317
Clayton State University	pub.	$5916	$8862	89%	3%	$9431	$5347	$28,872
Columbus State University	pub.	$6592	$8542	69%	17%	$9017	$6117	$25,687
Covenant College	ind.	$28,270	$8040	99%	38%	$22,324	$13,986	$22,861
Emmanuel College	ind.	$15,700	$6440	100%	24%	$14,823	$7317	$22,228
Emory University	ind.	$42,980	$12,000	94%	81%	$35,945	$19,035	$27,737
Fort Valley State University	pub.	NR	NR	96%	4%	$14,568	—	$8263
Georgia College & State University	pub.	$8618	$9268	39%	NR	$7686	$10,200	$19,852
Georgia Institute of Technology	pub.	$10,098	$9236	94%	34%	$19,073	$261	$26,412
Georgia Southern University	pub.	$6724	$9290	88%	11%	$8548	$7466	$21,562
Georgia Southwestern State University	pub.	$5780	$7378	68%	13%	$9003	$4155	$26,294
Georgia State University	pub.	$9664	$11,546	72%	4%	$11,196	$10,014	$21,817
Kennesaw State University	pub.	$6486	$7966	83%	11%	$7590	$6862	$20,666
LaGrange College	ind.	$24,462	$10,178	100%	22%	$23,020	$11,620	$32,270
Life University	ind.	$11,978	$12,854	70%	NR	$8300	$16,532	$31,000
Mercer University	ind.	$32,466	$10,697	99%	27%	$30,748	$12,415	$31,488
Morehouse College	ind.	$24,744	$12,672	65%	8%	$13,450	$23,966	NR
Oglethorpe University	ind.	$31,280	$11,300	96%	14%	$28,042	$14,538	$22,692
Piedmont College	ind.	$20,730	$8530	100%	24%	$18,849	$10,411	$18,129
Savannah College of Art and Design	ind.	$32,405	$12,990	62%	12%	$28,283	$17,112	$37,776
Shorter University	ind.	NR	NR	100%	22%	$16,164	—	$19,625
Southern Polytechnic State University	pub.	$6678	$7280	46%	28%	$1999	$11,959	$22,250
Spelman College	ind.	$23,794	$11,541	98%	16%	$13,904	$21,431	$33,898
University of Georgia	pub.	$9842	$8970	97%	24%	$12,058	$6754	$19,621
University of North Georgia	pub.	$6570	$8430	59%	28%	$8021	$6979	$12,166
University of West Georgia	pub.	$6710	$7482	89%	23%	$9228	$4964	$18,603
Valdosta State University	pub.	$5792	$7070	88%	27%	$15,329	—	$23,826
Wesleyan College	ind.	$19,000	$8400	100%	16%	$17,583	$9817	$34,368
Young Harris College	ind.	$25,280	$9660	100%	29%	$19,132	$15,808	$25,158

NA = not applicable; NR = not reported; * = includes room and board; † = room only; — = not available.

College Costs At-a-Glance

	Institutional Control ind.=independent; pub.=public	Tuition and Fees	Room and Board	Percent of Eligible Freshmen Receiving Need-Based Gift Awards	Percent of Freshmen Whose Need Was Fully Met	Average Financial Aid Package for Freshmen	Average Net Cost After Aid	Average Indebtedness Upon Graduation
Hawaii								
Hawai`i Pacific University	ind.	$19,980	$13,230	52%	19%	$19,037	$14,173	$30,893
University of Hawaii at Hilo	pub.	$6496	NR	73%	24%	$9721	—	$13,035
University of Hawaii at Manoa	pub.	$9884	$10,029	98%	28%	$11,694	$8219	$21,405
University of Hawaii–West Oahu	pub.	$5592	NA	40%	NR	$4450	$1142	NR
Idaho								
Boise State University	pub.	$5884	$7174	81%	47%	$9867	$3191	$27,369
The College of Idaho	ind.	$23,000	$8646	100%	17%	$24,707	$6939	$27,008
Idaho State University	pub.	$6070	$5838	83%	7%	$8971	$2937	$24,602
Lewis-Clark State College	pub.	$5562	NR	75%	8%	$7347	—	NR
New Saint Andrews College	ind.	$11,200	NA	NR	NR	NR	NR	NR
Northwest Nazarene University	ind.	$26,550	$6400	100%	25%	$18,853	$14,097	$28,872
University of Idaho	pub.	$6212	$7682	75%	36%	$13,554	$340	$26,809
Illinois								
Augustana College	ind.	$34,614	$8784	99%	20%	$25,327	$18,071	$34,120
Aurora University	ind.	$20,720	$9542	81%	18%	$18,824	$11,438	$25,484
Benedictine University	ind.	$25,850	$8380	65%	NR	$19,662	$14,568	$19,560
Bradley University	ind.	$29,664	$9050	99%	20%	$18,274	$20,440	$26,109
Chicago State University	pub.	$9254	$8221	89%	1%	$16,490	$985	$37,834
DePaul University	ind.	$32,295	$11,717	83%	10%	$21,917	$22,095	$28,284
Dominican University	ind.	$28,690	$8818	100%	13%	$23,856	$13,652	$28,281
Eastern Illinois University	pub.	$10,930	$9174	71%	9%	$11,293	$8811	$28,575
East-West University	ind.	$19,020	$7641†	100%	NR	$13,770	$12,891	$3800
Elmhurst College	ind.	$32,945	$9112	99%	32%	$24,820	$17,237	$29,787
Eureka College	ind.	NR	NR	100%	13%	$16,529	—	$27,714
Greenville College	ind.	$22,920	$7576	100%	14%	$18,298	$12,198	$23,976
Illinois College	ind.	$26,500	$8500	100%	24%	$23,656	$11,344	$29,762
Illinois Institute of Technology	ind.	$38,512	NR	99%	15%	$34,526	$3986	$31,073
Illinois State University	pub.	$12,726	$9364	55%	4%	$7073	$15,017	$27,910
Illinois Wesleyan University	ind.	$37,954	$8838	98%	34%	$27,634	$19,158	$32,964
Knox College	ind.	$38,952	$8400	97%	35%	$30,376	$16,976	$27,542
Lake Forest College	ind.	$38,300	$9050	100%	16%	$32,000	$15,350	$30,801
Lakeview College of Nursing	ind.	NR	NA	NR	NR	NR	NR	$25,000
Lewis University	ind.	$26,780	$9530	100%	20%	$20,668	$15,642	$31,400
Loyola University Chicago	ind.	$35,503	$12,900	98%	12%	$30,940	$17,463	$36,328
MacMurray College	ind.	$21,400	$7650	100%	14%	$20,568	$8482	$36,658
McKendree University	ind.	$26,050	$8690	100%	20%	$21,182	$13,558	$23,005
Millikin University	ind.	$28,644	$8970	98%	29%	$24,330	$13,284	$29,871
Monmouth College	ind.	$31,500	$7600	100%	16%	$30,251	$8849	$31,578
National Louis University	ind.	NR	NA	100%	NR	$18,689	—	$29,900
North Central College	ind.	$31,071	$8883	100%	22%	$23,790	$16,164	$33,304

NA = not applicable; NR = not reported; * = includes room and board; † = room only; — = not available.

College Costs At-a-Glance

	Institutional Control ind.=independent; pub.=public	Tuition and Fees	Room and Board	Percent of Eligible Freshmen Receiving Need-Based Gift Awards	Percent of Freshmen Whose Need Was Fully Met	Average Financial Aid Package for Freshmen	Average Net Cost After Aid	Average Indebtedness Upon Graduation
Northeastern Illinois University	pub.	$9926	NA	92%	1%	$8090	$1836	$11,112
Northern Illinois University	pub.	$13,061	$10,648	97%	13%	$14,059	$9650	$30,521
Olivet Nazarene University	ind.	$28,090	$7900	100%	27%	$22,459	$13,531	$31,313
Principia College	ind.	$25,980	$10,500	100%	44%	$25,918	$10,562	NR
Quincy University	ind.	$25,834	$9880	100%	19%	$24,534	$11,180	$26,080
Resurrection University	ind.	$11,639	NA	NR	NR	NR	NR	NR
Robert Morris University Illinois	ind.	$22,800	$11,754	97%	5%	$14,940	$19,614	$30,133
Rockford College	ind.	$26,310	$7320	98%	9%	$17,322	$16,308	$22,245
Roosevelt University	ind.	$25,950	$12,100	83%	21%	$23,217	$14,833	NR
Saint Anthony College of Nursing	ind.	$20,286	NA	NR	NR	NR	NR	NR
Saint Francis Medical Center College of Nursing	ind.	$16,964	$3200†	NR	NR	NR	NR	NR
School of the Art Institute of Chicago	ind.	$39,020	$13,810	100%	7%	$31,035	$21,795	$39,914
Shimer College	ind.	$31,230	$10,626	100%	NR	$17,741	$24,115	$30,000
Southern Illinois University Carbondale	pub.	$11,528	$9126	76%	5%	$14,205	$6449	$32,652
Southern Illinois University Edwardsville	pub.	$9251	$8281	70%	29%	$11,620	$5912	$25,998
Trinity Christian College	ind.	$23,513	$8442	100%	12%	$17,373	$14,582	$28,124
Trinity College of Nursing and Health Sciences	ind.	$24,982	NA	NR	NR	NR	NR	$9500
University of Chicago	ind.	$44,574	$13,137	98%	100%	$38,524	$19,187	$22,663
University of Illinois at Chicago	pub.	$13,354	$10,882	85%	12%	$14,065	$10,171	$22,256
University of Illinois at Springfield	pub.	$11,132	$10,350	94%	17%	$12,194	$9288	$21,057
University of Illinois at Urbana–Champaign	pub.	$15,338	$10,636	81%	33%	$14,647	$11,327	$24,657
University of St. Francis	ind.	$26,824	$8268	66%	75%	$22,081	$13,011	$28,267
Western Illinois University	pub.	$9955	$8820	83%	25%	$10,146	$8629	$24,993
Wheaton College	ind.	$30,120	$8560	99%	15%	$22,466	$16,214	$24,067
Indiana								
Anderson University	ind.	$26,200	$9110	98%	36%	$20,972	$14,338	$32,363
Ball State University	pub.	$8980	$8870	63%	30%	$10,271	$7579	$27,373
Bethel College	ind.	$24,970	$7460	88%	14%	$20,242	$12,188	$24,207
Butler University	ind.	$33,138	$11,110	99%	15%	$23,604	$20,644	$35,210
Calumet College of Saint Joseph	ind.	$15,620	NA	69%	14%	$11,764	$3856	$23,000
Crossroads Bible College	ind.	$9980	$3400†	100%	100%	$6950	$6430	$9618
DePauw University	ind.	$38,750	$10,200	100%	29%	$31,834	$17,116	$26,570
Earlham College	ind.	$41,450	$8260	94%	44%	$37,079	$12,631	$26,089
Franklin College	ind.	$26,895	$7950	100%	11%	$18,468	$16,377	$34,160
Goshen College	ind.	$28,500	$9460	100%	20%	$20,488	$17,472	$21,953
Hanover College	ind.	$30,268	$9230	100%	24%	$23,921	$15,577	$27,626
Huntington University	ind.	$24,040	$8180	97%	8%	$19,818	$12,402	$31,149
Indiana State University	pub.	$8098	$8262	66%	12%	$9982	$6378	$24,484
Indiana Tech	ind.	$24,860	$9380	88%	30%	$17,420	$16,820	NR
Indiana University Bloomington	pub.	$10,033	$8853	81%	16%	$11,693	$7193	$28,769
Indiana University East	pub.	$6496	NA	91%	14%	$8200	—	$30,632
Indiana University Kokomo	pub.	$6541	NA	83%	4%	$6720	—	$26,217

NA = not applicable; NR = not reported; * = includes room and board; † = room only; — = not available.

College Costs At-a-Glance

	Institutional Control ind.=independent; pub.=public	Tuition and Fees	Room and Board	Percent of Eligible Freshmen Receiving Need-Based Gift Awards	Percent of Freshmen Whose Need Was Fully Met	Average Financial Aid Package for Freshmen	Average Net Cost After Aid	Average Indebtedness Upon Graduation
Indiana University Northwest	pub.	$6626	NA	83%	1%	$7106	—	$30,369
Indiana University–Purdue University Fort Wayne	pub.	$6876	$7210†	69%	3%	$8717	$5369	$26,498
Indiana University–Purdue University Indianapolis	pub.	$8605	$7944	82%	5%	$9507	$7042	$30,752
Indiana University South Bend	pub.	$6728	$6838†	86%	3%	$7279	$6287	$27,417
Indiana University Southeast	pub.	$6576	$6570†	86%	5%	$7308	$5838	$24,609
Indiana Wesleyan University	ind.	$23,628	$7560	99%	31%	$21,516	$9672	$22,940
Manchester University	ind.	$27,920	$9250	100%	26%	$24,401	$12,769	$29,039
Purdue University	pub.	$10,466	$9990	64%	44%	$12,668	$7788	$27,798
Purdue University Calumet	pub.	$6991	$7717	70%	13%	$4052	$10,656	$26,273
Purdue University North Central	pub.	$7045	NA	65%	3%	$6485	$560	$22,952
Rose-Hulman Institute of Technology	ind.	$39,078	$10,935	100%	15%	$28,031	$21,982	$44,965
Saint Joseph's College	ind.	$27,350	$8250	99%	23%	$24,409	$11,191	$30,963
Saint Mary-of-the-Woods College	ind.	$27,672	$9800	83%	77%	$24,813	$12,659	$18,742
Saint Mary's College	ind.	$33,280	$10,140	98%	28%	$27,047	$16,373	$31,891
Taylor University	ind.	$28,088	$7757	100%	22%	$19,318	$16,527	$26,003
Trine University	ind.	$28,850	$9500	88%	23%	$23,417	$14,933	$32,662
University of Evansville	ind.	$30,556	$10,010	100%	32%	$26,242	$14,324	$27,679
University of Indianapolis	ind.	$23,830	$9090	54%	11%	$16,536	$16,384	$32,495
University of Notre Dame	ind.	$42,971	$11,934	95%	100%	$38,664	$16,241	$29,480
University of Southern Indiana	pub.	$6325	$7502	78%	8%	$8226	$5601	$19,429
Valparaiso University	ind.	$32,250	$9164	100%	26%	$24,998	$16,416	$31,957
Wabash College	ind.	$35,650	$8510	99%	73%	$31,769	$12,391	$28,919
Iowa								
Allen College	ind.	$18,829	$7281	100%	NR	$9340	$16,770	NR
Briar Cliff University	ind.	$25,642	$7542	100%	86%	$21,124	$12,060	$29,487
Buena Vista University	ind.	$28,314	$8180	100%	48%	$31,954	$4540	NR
Central College	ind.	$30,700	$9980	100%	19%	$26,013	$14,667	$27,790
Clarke University	ind.	$28,000	$8400	100%	26%	$23,314	$13,086	$26,865
Coe College	ind.	$35,730	$7750	100%	15%	$29,271	$14,209	$29,500
Cornell College	ind.	$34,705	$7900	100%	22%	$32,040	$10,565	$27,227
Dordt College	ind.	$25,520	$7230	100%	31%	$21,689	$11,061	$21,859
Drake University	ind.	$30,880	$8700	99%	26%	$21,359	$18,221	$32,114
Graceland University	ind.	$23,530	$7890	100%	21%	$21,164	$10,256	$39,022
Grand View University	ind.	$22,708	$7264	90%	35%	$21,269	$8703	$33,464
Grinnell College	ind.	$41,004	$9614	99%	100%	$38,718	$11,900	$16,226
Iowa State University of Science and Technology	pub.	$7726	$7721	100%	37%	$12,000	$3447	$30,374
Iowa Wesleyan College	ind.	$24,300	$7980	100%	4%	$23,474	$8806	$32,666
Loras College	ind.	$28,165	$7650	83%	39%	$25,458	$10,357	$31,664
Luther College	ind.	$37,480	$6850	100%	37%	$29,605	$14,725	$35,619
Morningside College	ind.	$25,000	$7620	82%	28%	$25,717	$6903	$36,140
Mount Mercy University	ind.	$26,310	$8075	100%	19%	$18,386	$15,999	$28,900
St. Ambrose University	ind.	$26,740	$9016	99%	24%	$19,228	$16,528	$37,236

NA = not applicable; NR = not reported; * = includes room and board; † = room only; — = not available.

College Costs At-a-Glance

	Institutional Control ind.=independent; pub.=public	Tuition and Fees	Room and Board	Percent of Eligible Freshmen Receiving Need-Based Gift Awards	Percent of Freshmen Whose Need Was Fully Met	Average Financial Aid Package for Freshmen	Average Net Cost After Aid	Average Indebtedness Upon Graduation
Simpson College	ind.	$30,999	$7963	100%	28%	$29,667	$9295	$35,228
The University of Iowa	pub.	$8061	$9420	67%	29%	$12,603	$4878	$28,554
University of Northern Iowa	pub.	$7635	$7597	50%	19%	$7708	$7524	$23,575
Upper Iowa University	ind.	$24,400	$7510	65%	NR	$9041	$22,869	$27,361
Waldorf College	ind.	$20,316	$6856	87%	16%	$14,074	$13,098	$36,966
Wartburg College	ind.	$34,250	$4150†	100%	24%	$25,294	$13,106	$36,567
Kansas								
Benedictine College	ind.	$23,175	$8190	100%	24%	$18,948	$12,417	$26,980
Bethel College	ind.	$23,500	$7980	88%	41%	$21,548	$9932	$20,356
Emporia State University	pub.	$5272	$6629	97%	15%	$6686	$5215	$23,538
Fort Hays State University	pub.	NR	NR	95%	17%	$7218	—	$22,887
Kansas State University	pub.	$8047	$7450	59%	20%	$11,289	$4208	$25,147
McPherson College	ind.	$21,801	$7764	82%	20%	$20,412	$9153	$27,529
Pittsburg State University	pub.	$5494	$6758	68%	39%	$8367	$3885	$20,808
Southwestern College	ind.	$23,886	$6636	100%	12%	$19,016	$11,506	$34,056
The University of Kansas	pub.	$9678	$7258	66%	14%	$8933	$8003	$23,468
Washburn University	pub.	$5486	$6216	64%	16%	$9288	$2414	$17,995
Wichita State University	pub.	$6442	$6460	74%	72%	$4231	$8671	$21,068
Kentucky								
Asbury University	ind.	$26,076	$5962	99%	26%	$19,282	$12,756	$26,854
Bellarmine University	ind.	$33,180	$9770	100%	21%	$27,350	$15,600	$28,722
Berea College	ind.	NR	NR	100%	NR	$28,239	—	$7224
Campbellsville University	ind.	$22,196	$8200	100%	13%	$19,034	$11,362	$10,183
Centre College	ind.	$36,000	$9100	100%	34%	$27,404	$17,696	$25,500
Clear Creek Baptist Bible College	ind.	$5370	$3470	100%	12%	$7314	$1526	NR
Eastern Kentucky University	pub.	$7320	$7316	71%	40%	$10,074	$4562	$26,150
Georgetown College	ind.	$30,770	$7920	100%	38%	$26,977	$11,713	$26,730
Kentucky State University	pub.	$6858	$6580	92%	1%	$10,097	$3341	$39,623
Kentucky Wesleyan College	ind.	$21,200	$7500	100%	11%	$15,146	$13,554	NR
Lindsey Wilson College	ind.	$22,070	$8400	100%	21%	NR	NR	$27,542
Murray State University	pub.	$6840	$7638	92%	23%	$11,716	$2762	$20,644
Northern Kentucky University	pub.	$8064	$7430	58%	15%	$8544	$6950	$13,432
Thomas More College	ind.	$27,220	$7500	100%	21%	$20,662	$14,058	$32,650
Transylvania University	ind.	$29,865	$8750	100%	22%	$24,845	$13,770	$26,604
Union College	ind.	$20,800	$6650	100%	11%	$18,375	$9075	$18,843
University of Louisville	pub.	$9466	$7570	98%	25%	$11,720	$5316	$19,886
University of Pikeville	ind.	$17,050	$6700	100%	35%	$19,261	$4489	$24,954
University of the Cumberlands	ind.	$19,640	$7500	100%	12%	$19,519	$7621	$20,090
Western Kentucky University	pub.	$8472	$7320	70%	30%	$12,766	$3026	$26,110
Louisiana								
Centenary College of Louisiana	ind.	$29,500	$9336	100%	29%	$24,104	$14,732	$21,820

NA = not applicable; NR = not reported; * = includes room and board; † = room only; — = not available.

Peterson's How to Get Money for College 2014

College Costs At-a-Glance

	Institutional Control ind.=independent; pub.=public	Tuition and Fees	Room and Board	Percent of Eligible Freshmen Receiving Need-Based Gift Awards	Percent of Freshmen Whose Need Was Fully Met	Average Financial Aid Package for Freshmen	Average Net Cost After Aid	Average Indebtedness Upon Graduation
Dillard University	ind.	$14,850	$8686	100%	9%	$11,831	$11,705	$39,906
Louisiana College	ind.	$13,780	$4448	100%	20%	$10,927	$7301	NR
Louisiana State University and Agricultural and Mechanical College	pub.	$6989	$10,218	93%	27%	$12,600	$4607	$20,125
Louisiana Tech University	pub.	NR	NR	97%	20%	$8821	—	$18,555
Loyola University New Orleans	ind.	$36,610	$12,185	100%	15%	$30,148	$18,647	$23,178
Nicholls State University	pub.	$5679	$8560	96%	29%	$9311	$4928	$27,396
Northwestern State University of Louisiana	pub.	$5480	$7826	63%	5%	$11,115	$2191	$24,676
Saint Joseph Seminary College	ind.	$15,140	$13,040	NR	NR	NR	NR	NR
Southeastern Louisiana University	pub.	$5426	$6510	65%	33%	$8195	$3741	$19,661
Tulane University	ind.	$45,240	$11,547	99%	77%	$31,130	$25,657	$35,100
University of Louisiana at Lafayette	pub.	$5374	$8102	96%	12%	$8073	$5403	NR
University of New Orleans	pub.	$5922	$8310	74%	12%	$9030	$5202	$18,271
Xavier University of Louisiana	ind.	$18,700	$7600	70%	NR	$18,572	$7728	$25,566
Maine								
Bates College	ind.	$44,300	$12,935	98%	97%	$38,185	$19,050	$24,515
Bowdoin College	ind.	$44,118	$12,010	100%	100%	$40,879	$15,249	$22,755
Colby College	ind.	$55,700*	NR	100%	100%	$40,178	$15,522	$24,453
College of the Atlantic	ind.	$38,952	$9258	100%	47%	$33,696	$14,514	$22,473
Husson University	ind.	$15,130	$8256	98%	5%	$13,118	$10,268	$33,385
Maine Maritime Academy	pub.	$11,525	$9548	84%	11%	$8610	$12,463	$41,672
New England School of Communications	ind.	$14,104	$8306	76%	NR	NR	NR	$34,426
Unity College	ind.	$24,100	$8714	100%	10%	$18,123	$14,691	NR
University of Maine	pub.	$10,588	$8644	93%	14%	$15,867	$3365	$32,438
University of Maine at Augusta	pub.	$7448	NA	88%	3%	$8026	—	$24,353
University of Maine at Farmington	pub.	$9137	$8454	87%	7%	$10,735	$6856	$26,319
University of Maine at Fort Kent	pub.	$7575	$7400	83%	17%	$9829	$5146	$21,911
University of Maine at Presque Isle	pub.	$7435	$7422	94%	34%	$11,133	$3724	$18,052
University of New England	ind.	$31,870	$12,500	NR	NR	NR	NR	NR
University of Southern Maine	pub.	$8920	$9130	78%	7%	$9120	$8930	NR
Maryland								
Bowie State University	pub.	$6639	$9597	73%	76%	$8415	$7821	$25,972
Capitol College	ind.	NR	NR	91%	NR	$17,161	—	$34,609
Frostburg State University	pub.	$7728	$7990	69%	18%	$8783	$6935	$20,736
Goucher College	ind.	$39,084	$11,168	98%	13%	$30,410	$19,842	$29,135
Hood College	ind.	$32,300	$10,910	100%	21%	$24,575	$18,635	$28,121
The Johns Hopkins University	ind.	$45,970	$13,832	91%	97%	$37,917	$21,885	$23,092
Loyola University Maryland	ind.	$42,430	$12,120	87%	100%	$26,745	$27,805	$32,392
McDaniel College	ind.	$36,960	$8640	98%	25%	$29,516	$16,084	$31,919
Morgan State University	pub.	NR	NR	82%	6%	$20,994	—	$36,086
Mount St. Mary's University	ind.	$32,954	$11,018	100%	28%	$23,790	$20,182	$32,311
Notre Dame of Maryland University	ind.	$30,850	$10,150	100%	12%	$24,726	$16,274	$28,735

NA = not applicable; NR = not reported; * = includes room and board; † = room only; — = not available.

College Costs At-a-Glance

	Institutional Control ind.=independent; pub.=public	Tuition and Fees	Room and Board	Percent of Eligible Freshmen Receiving Need-Based Gift Awards	Percent of Freshmen Whose Need Was Fully Met	Average Financial Aid Package for Freshmen	Average Net Cost After Aid	Average Indebtedness Upon Graduation
Peabody Conservatory of The Johns Hopkins University	ind.	$38,915	$12,680	73%	18%	$18,100	$33,495	$33,961
St. John's College	ind.	$45,004	$10,644	99%	13%	$36,407	$19,241	$29,265
St. Mary's College of Maryland	pub.	$14,773	$11,305	79%	10%	$13,646	$12,432	$23,834
Salisbury University	pub.	$7700	$9120	88%	16%	$7143	$9677	$23,159
Stevenson University	ind.	$25,310	$11,894	99%	10%	$16,803	$20,401	$28,032
Towson University	pub.	$8132	$10,338	56%	13%	$9227	$9243	$23,812
University of Maryland, Baltimore County	pub.	$9764	$10,142	85%	21%	$10,915	$8991	$22,601
University of Maryland, College Park	pub.	$8909	$9893	62%	21%	$11,370	$7432	$25,276
University of Maryland Eastern Shore	pub.	$6998	$8374	78%	NR	$9594	$5778	$27,215
University of Maryland University College	pub.	$6384	NA	80%	3%	$5564	$820	NR
Washington Adventist University	ind.	$20,220	$7600	100%	20%	$10,442	$17,378	NR
Washington College	ind.	$39,944	$8824	100%	66%	$31,111	$17,657	$34,208
Massachusetts								
American International College	ind.	$29,158	$11,710	100%	16%	$24,081	$16,787	$33,170
Amherst College	ind.	$44,610	$11,650	100%	100%	$45,438	$10,822	$14,566
Anna Maria College	ind.	$30,456	$11,450	96%	19%	$22,355	$19,551	$49,206
Assumption College	ind.	$33,805	$10,590	100%	18%	$25,676	$18,719	$34,579
Babson College	ind.	$43,520	$14,142	92%	68%	$37,261	$20,401	$31,918
Bay Path College	ind.	$28,532	$11,440	100%	12%	$26,570	$13,402	$31,456
Becker College	ind.	$30,340	$11,050	NR	NR	NR	NR	$44,596
Bentley University	ind.	$39,628	$12,960	83%	44%	$31,077	$21,511	$30,375
Boston Architectural College	ind.	NR	NA	72%	3%	$9989	—	NR
Boston College	ind.	$43,878	$12,608	89%	100%	$34,302	$22,184	$20,975
Boston University	ind.	$42,994	$13,190	94%	54%	$37,655	$18,529	$36,150
Brandeis University	ind.	$44,294	$12,256	98%	98%	$37,391	$19,159	$27,906
Bridgewater State University	pub.	$8052	$10,700	86%	5%	$8632	$10,120	$30,189
Cambridge College	ind.	NR	NA	NR	NR	$3500	—	NR
Clark University	ind.	$39,550	$7470	99%	68%	$32,364	$14,656	$25,175
College of the Holy Cross	ind.	$44,272	$11,960	81%	100%	$33,492	$22,740	$26,567
Curry College	ind.	$33,465	$12,760	95%	6%	$23,406	$22,819	$41,876
Eastern Nazarene College	ind.	$26,884	$8300	100%	27%	$24,566	$10,618	NR
Emerson College	ind.	$35,730	$14,516	87%	39%	$19,193	$31,053	$22,844
Emmanuel College	ind.	$33,650	$12,990	82%	49%	$26,384	$20,256	NR
Endicott College	ind.	$28,166	$13,200	86%	9%	$18,969	$22,397	$36,198
Fisher College	ind.	$26,775	$13,924	95%	NR	NR	NR	NR
Framingham State University	pub.	$8080	$9540	94%	36%	$11,740	$5880	$22,975
Franklin W. Olin College of Engineering	ind.	$42,500	$15,000	70%	100%	$31,258	$26,242	$12,541
Gordon College	ind.	$33,230	$9430	100%	16%	$20,641	$22,019	$37,662
Hampshire College	ind.	$46,625	$12,030	100%	22%	$34,143	$24,512	$22,550
Harvard University	ind.	$40,866	$13,630	100%	100%	$46,301	$8195	$13,098
Lasell College	ind.	$29,000	$12,300	100%	21%	$21,097	$20,203	$39,559
Lesley University	ind.	$32,250	$14,000	98%	29%	$19,921	$26,329	$23,000

NA = not applicable; NR = not reported; * = includes room and board; † = room only; — = not available.

College Costs At-a-Glance

	Institutional Control ind.=independent; pub.=public	Tuition and Fees	Room and Board	Percent of Eligible Freshmen Receiving Need-Based Gift Awards	Percent of Freshmen Whose Need Was Fully Met	Average Financial Aid Package for Freshmen	Average Net Cost After Aid	Average Indebtedness Upon Graduation
Massachusetts College of Art and Design	pub.	$10,400	$12,150	70%	NR	$10,463	$12,087	$25,875
Massachusetts College of Liberal Arts	pub.	$8525	$9102	86%	73%	$14,397	$3230	$29,534
Massachusetts Institute of Technology	ind.	$42,050	$12,188	96%	100%	$37,979	$16,259	$20,794
Massachusetts Maritime Academy	pub.	NR	NR	NR	NR	NR	NR	$32,400
Merrimack College	ind.	$33,920	$11,690	100%	13%	$21,045	$24,565	NR
Mount Holyoke College	ind.	$41,456	$12,140	98%	100%	$31,846	$21,750	$22,691
Newbury College	ind.	$28,950	$12,900	100%	NR	$15,482	$26,368	$29,530
New England Conservatory of Music	ind.	$38,455	$12,350	100%	9%	$22,194	$28,611	$25,189
Nichols College	ind.	$31,740	$10,700	100%	6%	$21,400	$21,040	$30,890
Northeastern University	ind.	$39,736	$13,620	98%	36%	$29,409	$23,947	NR
Pine Manor College	ind.	$24,301	$12,750	100%	3%	$25,120	$11,931	$30,808
School of the Museum of Fine Arts, Boston	ind.	$38,028	$11,990	88%	3%	$17,937	$32,081	NR
Simmons College	ind.	$35,370	$13,400	100%	18%	$25,593	$23,177	NR
Smith College	ind.	$41,460	$13,860	96%	100%	$39,440	$15,880	$23,071
Stonehill College	ind.	$36,160	$13,810	83%	48%	$27,392	$22,578	$27,794
Suffolk University	ind.	$30,792	$14,730	95%	6%	$23,479	$22,043	$33,823
Tufts University	ind.	$46,598	$12,182	94%	100%	$35,033	$23,747	$23,068
University of Massachusetts Amherst	pub.	$13,415	$10,767	90%	13%	$13,920	$10,262	$27,945
University of Massachusetts Boston	pub.	$11,966	NA	92%	45%	$14,554	—	$25,499
University of Massachusetts Dartmouth	pub.	$11,681	NR	89%	38%	$14,665	—	$32,349
University of Massachusetts Lowell	pub.	$11,852	$10,282	91%	59%	$13,872	$8262	$29,212
Wellesley College	ind.	$43,554	$13,488	96%	100%	$39,937	$17,105	$14,189
Wentworth Institute of Technology	ind.	$27,950	$12,526	71%	31%	$18,897	$21,579	$24,747
Western New England University	ind.	$31,912	$12,144	100%	10%	$23,697	$20,359	NR
Westfield State University	pub.	$8297	$9233	64%	9%	$7807	$9723	$24,825
Wheaton College	ind.	$45,074	$11,500	93%	52%	$33,378	$23,196	$27,520
Wheelock College	ind.	$30,955	$12,800	100%	17%	$20,524	$23,231	$49,439
Williams College	ind.	$43,190	$11,370	100%	100%	$44,508	$10,052	$12,749
Worcester Polytechnic Institute	ind.	$42,778	$13,082	99%	46%	$31,426	$24,434	NR
Worcester State University	pub.	$8157	$10,500	92%	42%	$11,983	$6674	$20,449
Michigan								
Adrian College	ind.	$29,156	$8796	100%	6%	$25,275	$12,677	$30,645
Albion College	ind.	$34,194	$9690	100%	19%	$26,742	$17,142	$36,029
Alma College	ind.	$31,060	$8990	100%	13%	$28,721	$11,329	$31,297
Andrews University	ind.	$24,478	$7528	61%	21%	$25,487	$6519	$33,249
Calvin College	ind.	$28,250	$9335	100%	18%	$21,083	$16,502	$32,957
Central Michigan University	pub.	$10,950	$8368	83%	60%	$12,368	$6950	$31,520
Cleary University	ind.	NR	NA	94%	6%	$13,049	—	$32,259
Concordia University Ann Arbor	ind.	$22,464	$8298	100%	42%	$17,102	$13,660	$17,652
Cornerstone University	ind.	$24,168	$7910	100%	15%	$19,152	$12,926	$32,071
Davenport University	ind.	$13,022	$8434	NR	NR	NR	NR	NR
Eastern Michigan University	pub.	$9026	$8286	85%	1%	$9399	$7913	$25,133

NA = not applicable; NR = not reported; * = includes room and board; † = room only; — = not available.

College Costs At-a-Glance

	Institutional Control ind.=independent; pub.=public	Tuition and Fees	Room and Board	Percent of Eligible Freshmen Receiving Need-Based Gift Awards	Percent of Freshmen Whose Need Was Fully Met	Average Financial Aid Package for Freshmen	Average Net Cost After Aid	Average Indebtedness Upon Graduation
Ferris State University	pub.	$10,710	$8744	70%	18%	$11,530	$7924	$36,930
Grace Bible College	ind.	$15,300	$7000	95%	5%	$9849	$12,451	$21,527
Grand Valley State University	pub.	$10,078	$7920	87%	12%	$10,949	$7049	$28,728
Hillsdale College	ind.	$22,890	$9000	67%	37%	$13,638	$18,252	$25,502
Hope College	ind.	$28,720	$8810	86%	27%	$23,044	$14,486	$37,010
Kalamazoo College	ind.	$37,710	$8274	100%	46%	$32,931	$13,053	$27,845
Kettering University	ind.	$33,946	$6660	100%	12%	$22,475	$18,131	NR
Kuyper College	ind.	NR	NR	98%	7%	$17,611	—	$13,615
Lake Superior State University	pub.	$9715	$8481	75%	31%	$10,306	$7890	$28,500
Lawrence Technological University	ind.	$27,870	$8987	98%	26%	$21,168	$15,689	$41,529
Michigan State University	pub.	$13,800	$8476	59%	21%	$11,718	$10,558	$24,987
Michigan Technological University	pub.	$13,353	$8865	84%	21%	$14,114	$8104	$34,938
Northern Michigan University	pub.	$8710	$8404	61%	13%	$8833	$8281	$29,371
Northwood University, Michigan Campus	ind.	$20,996	$8770	91%	26%	$21,185	$8581	$32,457
Oakland University	pub.	$11,183	$8208	82%	7%	$12,885	$6506	$19,697
Olivet College	ind.	NR	NR	100%	30%	$16,353	—	$24,890
Saginaw Valley State University	pub.	$8120	$8190	90%	NR	NR	NR	NR
Spring Arbor University	ind.	$22,538	$7900	100%	22%	$22,408	$8030	$32,791
University of Michigan	pub.	$13,819	$9752	72%	77%	$18,230	$5341	$27,815
University of Michigan–Dearborn	pub.	$10,482	NA	76%	3%	$10,662	—	$23,437
University of Michigan–Flint	pub.	$9514	$7506	68%	5%	$10,187	$6833	$26,899
Western Michigan University	pub.	$9982	$8414	68%	24%	$15,353	$3043	$30,867
Minnesota								
Bemidji State University	pub.	$8106	$6970	70%	16%	$8525	$6551	NR
Bethany Lutheran College	ind.	$23,140	$7110	100%	14%	$20,012	$10,238	$31,884
Bethel University	ind.	$30,840	$8900	100%	18%	$21,583	$18,157	$32,483
Carleton College	ind.	$44,445	$11,553	100%	100%	$35,113	$20,885	$17,289
College of Saint Benedict	ind.	$36,218	$9271	98%	44%	$30,885	$14,604	$40,030
The College of St. Scholastica	ind.	$31,612	$8348	83%	29%	$23,647	$16,313	$39,918
Concordia College	ind.	$32,814	$7160	99%	21%	$25,220	$14,754	$38,075
Concordia University, St. Paul	ind.	$19,700	$7750	99%	15%	$25,898	$1552	$42,020
Crown College	ind.	$22,430	$7480	NR	NR	NR	NR	$33,239
Gustavus Adolphus College	ind.	$37,606	$8880	100%	30%	$31,279	$15,207	$28,124
Hamline University	ind.	$33,752	$8700	100%	20%	$25,467	$16,985	$40,472
Macalester College	ind.	$45,388	$10,068	100%	100%	$37,945	$17,511	$23,285
McNally Smith College of Music	ind.	$25,990	$5100	61%	NR	$7844	$23,246	NR
Minneapolis College of Art and Design	ind.	NR	NR	100%	7%	$21,672	—	$43,650
Minnesota State University Mankato	pub.	$8396	$7053	82%	37%	$9278	$6171	$29,587
Minnesota State University Moorhead	pub.	$7834	$6984	64%	NR	NR	NR	$25,124
Northwestern College	ind.	$26,960	$8210	98%	8%	$19,740	$15,430	$24,299
St. Catherine University	ind.	$33,276	$8288	100%	17%	$29,500	$12,064	$39,230
St. Cloud State University	pub.	$7439	$6994	73%	11%	$8445	$5988	$30,990

NA = not applicable; NR = not reported; * = includes room and board; † = room only; — = not available.

College Costs At-a-Glance

	Institutional Control ind.=independent; pub.=public	Tuition and Fees	Room and Board	Percent of Eligible Freshmen Receiving Need-Based Gift Awards	Percent of Freshmen Whose Need Was Fully Met	Average Financial Aid Package for Freshmen	Average Net Cost After Aid	Average Indebtedness Upon Graduation
Saint John's University	ind.	$35,486	$8639	99%	42%	$28,318	$15,807	$34,889
Saint Mary's University of Minnesota	ind.	$29,315	$7700	100%	18%	$24,135	$12,880	$35,134
St. Olaf College	ind.	$39,560	$9090	100%	100%	$35,190	$13,460	$27,637
University of Minnesota, Crookston	pub.	$11,455	$7018	95%	27%	$13,370	$5103	$27,608
University of Minnesota, Duluth	pub.	$12,748	$6732	91%	22%	$10,567	$8913	$31,711
University of Minnesota, Morris	pub.	$12,550	$7324	95%	42%	$15,592	$4282	$25,124
University of Minnesota, Twin Cities Campus	pub.	$13,459	$8000	85%	30%	$12,910	$8549	$29,702
University of St. Thomas	ind.	$33,787	$8778	99%	18%	$23,042	$19,523	$36,077
Winona State University	pub.	$8930	$7800	54%	12%	$6591	$10,139	$32,576
Mississippi								
Alcorn State University	pub.	$5724	$7999	95%	10%	$14,958	—	$29,001
Belhaven University	ind.	$19,200	$6890	68%	6%	$15,537	$10,553	$37,076
Blue Mountain College	ind.	$9230	$4000	98%	32%	$11,620	$1610	$23,107
Jackson State University	pub.	$5988	$6996	84%	6%	$13,118	—	NR
Millsaps College	ind.	$30,974	$10,826	100%	31%	$27,094	$14,706	$28,965
Mississippi College	ind.	$14,868	$7150	72%	29%	$15,930	$6088	$26,677
Mississippi State University	pub.	$6264	$8486	92%	30%	$13,045	$1705	$26,139
Mississippi University for Women	pub.	$5316	$5991	82%	40%	$10,180	$1127	$22,398
University of Mississippi	pub.	$6282	$9200	88%	14%	$9347	$6135	$23,986
University of Southern Mississippi	pub.	$6336	$6907	69%	32%	$10,446	$2797	$29,502
Missouri								
Central Methodist University	ind.	$20,590	NR	70%	18%	$17,813	$2777	$22,086
City Vision College	ind.	$6000	NR	100%	NR	$2220	$3780	NR
College of the Ozarks	ind.	$430	$5900	100%	18%	$18,943	—	$8915
Columbia College	ind.	$19,386	NR	65%	22%	$13,801	$5585	$11,726
Culver-Stockton College	ind.	$23,300	$7600	100%	22%	$21,281	$9619	$24,859
Drury University	ind.	$22,415	$8200	94%	87%	$7935	$22,680	$21,550
Evangel University	ind.	$19,050	$6640	98%	7%	$15,263	$10,427	$34,434
Kansas City Art Institute	ind.	$31,992	$9372	100%	15%	$23,950	$17,414	$26,660
Lincoln University	pub.	$6624	$4750	92%	3%	$9447	$1927	$27,910
Lindenwood University	ind.	$14,600	$7580	82%	89%	$9488	$12,692	NR
Maryville University of Saint Louis	ind.	$23,746	$9242	100%	20%	$19,570	$13,418	$21,835
Missouri Baptist University	ind.	$20,654	$8230	87%	13%	$20,926	$7958	$21,479
Missouri Southern State University	pub.	$5090	$5976	86%	8%	$9275	$1791	$20,005
Missouri State University	pub.	$6792	$6844	88%	14%	$8164	$5472	$20,545
Missouri University of Science and Technology	pub.	$9350	$8900	97%	24%	$11,773	$6477	$21,659
Missouri Valley College	ind.	NR	NR	100%	44%	$14,900	—	$23,200
Missouri Western State University	pub.	$6385	$6918	98%	12%	$7467	$5836	$22,287
Northwest Missouri State University	pub.	$7719	$8614	86%	47%	$9208	$7125	$23,400
Park University	ind.	$9900	$7151	78%	23%	$10,825	$6226	$21,558
Research College of Nursing	ind.	$29,840	$8460	NR	NR	NR	NR	NR
Rockhurst University	ind.	$29,840	$8060	76%	1%	$30,538	$7362	$20,003

NA = not applicable; NR = not reported; * = includes room and board; † = room only; — = not available.

College Costs At-a-Glance

	Institutional Control ind.=independent; pub.=public	Tuition and Fees	Room and Board	Percent of Eligible Freshmen Receiving Need-Based Gift Awards	Percent of Freshmen Whose Need Was Fully Met	Average Financial Aid Package for Freshmen	Average Net Cost After Aid	Average Indebtedness Upon Graduation
Saint Louis Christian College	ind.	$8215	$4000	100%	NR	$20,737	—	$22,586
St. Louis College of Pharmacy	ind.	$26,125	$9280	100%	14%	$14,617	$20,788	$119,711
Saint Louis University	ind.	$35,266	$9612	97%	18%	$26,900	$17,978	$36,797
Southeast Missouri State University	pub.	$6750	$8110	94%	16%	$8153	$6707	$24,398
Southwest Baptist University	ind.	$19,150	$6350	86%	20%	$16,742	$8758	NR
Stephens College	ind.	$27,210	$10,300	100%	NR	$22,765	$14,745	$22,293
Truman State University	pub.	$7216	$7504	99%	38%	$11,431	$3289	$22,922
University of Central Missouri	pub.	NR	NR	60%	16%	$8149	—	$23,766
University of Missouri–Kansas City	pub.	$9220	$11,428	96%	9%	$10,463	$10,185	$24,326
University of Missouri–St. Louis	pub.	$9474	$8830	88%	30%	$13,960	$4344	$24,377
Washington University in St. Louis	ind.	$44,841	$13,977	96%	100%	$35,508	$23,310	NR
Webster University	ind.	$23,010	$9950	90%	1%	$15,170	$17,790	$29,723
Westminster College	ind.	$20,850	$8450	100%	41%	$20,155	$9145	$26,723
William Jewell College	ind.	$31,100	$8020	100%	18%	$25,089	$14,031	$31,324
Montana								
Carroll College	ind.	$26,554	$8062	100%	19%	$18,801	$15,815	$28,005
Montana State University	pub.	$6749	$8070	78%	6%	$11,860	$2959	$27,320
Montana State University Billings	pub.	$5711	$6320	85%	4%	$8553	$3478	$27,178
Montana State University–Northern	pub.	$5070	$6275	92%	5%	$9054	$2291	$21,365
Montana Tech of The University of Montana	pub.	$6693	$7626	90%	42%	$9592	$4727	$25,360
Rocky Mountain College	ind.	$23,718	$7430	98%	19%	$19,420	$11,728	$30,948
University of Great Falls	ind.	$20,960	$6800	91%	7%	$17,228	$10,532	$25,690
The University of Montana	pub.	$6216	$7262	65%	12%	$8390	$5088	$29,126
The University of Montana Western	pub.	$4719	$6180	83%	6%	$2844	$8055	$22,683
Nebraska								
College of Saint Mary	ind.	$25,310	$6800	100%	20%	$20,350	$11,760	$31,522
Concordia University, Nebraska	ind.	$24,750	$6700	100%	28%	$18,987	$12,463	$27,222
Creighton University	ind.	$33,330	$9446	100%	31%	$29,251	$13,525	$36,333
Doane College	ind.	$25,080	$7140	99%	30%	$19,810	$12,410	$26,803
Hastings College	ind.	NR	NR	100%	26%	$17,548	—	$26,669
Nebraska Methodist College	ind.	$17,067	$6160†	85%	20%	$9553	$13,674	$39,753
Nebraska Wesleyan University	ind.	$27,240	$7550	100%	20%	$18,589	$16,201	$28,077
University of Nebraska at Kearney	pub.	$6506	$8038	66%	47%	$10,994	$3550	NR
University of Nebraska at Omaha	pub.	$6550	$8090	60%	30%	$8430	$6210	$25,145
University of Nebraska–Lincoln	pub.	$7896	$9122	81%	19%	$12,466	$4552	$23,280
Wayne State College	pub.	$5520	$5960	75%	40%	$8647	$2833	NR
Nevada								
Sierra Nevada College	ind.	$28,483	$11,772	100%	9%	$21,200	$19,055	$27,000
University of Nevada, Las Vegas	pub.	$6585	$10,524	82%	14%	$8872	$8237	$21,126
University of Nevada, Reno	pub.	$6365	$9518	61%	11%	$7895	$7988	$19,500

NA = not applicable; NR = not reported; * = includes room and board; † = room only; — = not available.

College Costs At-a-Glance

	Institutional Control ind.=independent; pub.=public	Tuition and Fees	Room and Board	Percent of Eligible Freshmen Receiving Need-Based Gift Awards	Percent of Freshmen Whose Need Was Fully Met	Average Financial Aid Package for Freshmen	Average Net Cost After Aid	Average Indebtedness Upon Graduation
New Hampshire								
College of Saint Mary Magdalen	ind.	NR	NR	100%	35%	$14,300	—	NR
Daniel Webster College	ind.	$15,090	$10,290	61%	6%	$5662	$19,718	$45,665
Dartmouth College	ind.	$45,212	$12,954	97%	100%	$45,587	$12,579	$17,825
Franklin Pierce University	ind.	$29,950	$11,260	100%	21%	$23,903	$17,307	$35,551
Keene State College	pub.	$12,776	$8762	73%	10%	$10,873	$10,665	$33,248
New England College	ind.	$31,744	$12,434	98%	13%	$26,502	$17,676	$33,797
Plymouth State University	pub.	$12,560	$9440	60%	12%	$8874	$13,126	$31,214
Saint Anselm College	ind.	$35,634	$12,690	100%	23%	$24,629	$23,695	$42,631
Thomas More College of Liberal Arts	ind.	NR	NR	100%	3%	$16,889	—	$20,107
University of New Hampshire	pub.	$16,422	$9764	69%	22%	$21,088	$5098	$35,168
University of New Hampshire at Manchester	pub.	$13,757	NA	51%	13%	$10,922	$2835	$25,411
New Jersey								
Bloomfield College	ind.	$25,050	$10,700	96%	2%	$23,844	$11,906	$20,467
Caldwell College	ind.	$29,000	$11,000	79%	9%	$22,700	$17,300	$21,209
The College of New Jersey	pub.	$14,378	$10,998	39%	15%	$11,034	$14,342	$33,889
College of Saint Elizabeth	ind.	$29,907	$12,254	NR	NR	NR	NR	NR
Drew University	ind.	$44,068	$11,944	NR	NR	NR	NR	$24,470
Felician College	ind.	$29,990	$11,650	81%	5%	$26,744	$14,896	$38,598
Georgian Court University	ind.	$26,740	$12,860	99%	22%	$26,431	$13,169	$36,114
Kean University	pub.	$10,601	$13,934	72%	3%	$9107	$15,428	$30,335
Monmouth University	ind.	$29,710	$10,802	42%	18%	$21,636	$18,876	$34,810
Montclair State University	pub.	$11,058	$13,443	97%	13%	$8461	$16,040	$28,070
New Jersey Institute of Technology	pub.	$14,740	$11,750	67%	2%	$12,163	$14,327	$34,867
Princeton University	ind.	$40,715	$13,080	100%	100%	$39,406	$14,389	$5096
Ramapo College of New Jersey	pub.	$13,144	$11,370	41%	14%	$12,742	$11,772	$30,053
The Richard Stockton College of New Jersey	pub.	$12,322	$10,796	54%	29%	$16,163	$6955	$34,287
Rider University	ind.	$33,420	$12,340	99%	16%	$25,177	$20,583	$32,718
Rowan University	pub.	$12,380	$10,972	49%	11%	$9315	$14,037	$35,027
Rutgers, The State University of New Jersey, Camden	pub.	$12,923	$11,206	80%	6%	$12,070	$12,059	$27,535
Rutgers, The State University of New Jersey, Newark	pub.	$12,590	$12,285	83%	98%	$13,097	$11,778	$24,837
Rutgers, The State University of New Jersey, New Brunswick	pub.	$13,073	$11,412	71%	8%	$12,992	$11,493	$26,656
Saint Peter's University	ind.	$32,230	$13,458	99%	12%	$28,057	$17,631	$32,218
New Mexico								
Eastern New Mexico University	pub.	$5776	$6090	96%	100%	$10,356	$1510	$14,821
New Mexico Highlands University	pub.	$3504	$5920	92%	1%	$1472	$7952	NR
New Mexico Institute of Mining and Technology	pub.	$5496	$6304	57%	24%	$11,261	$539	$18,834
New Mexico State University	pub.	$6040	$7182	98%	16%	$9442	$3780	$18,922
St. John's College	ind.	$45,004	$9994	86%	95%	$35,980	$19,018	$28,563
New York								
Adelphi University	ind.	$29,320	$11,900	68%	1%	$19,000	$22,220	$35,429

NA = not applicable; NR = not reported; * = includes room and board; † = room only; — = not available.

College Costs At-a-Glance

	Institutional Control ind.=independent; pub.=public	Tuition and Fees	Room and Board	Percent of Eligible Freshmen Receiving Need-Based Gift Awards	Percent of Freshmen Whose Need Was Fully Met	Average Financial Aid Package for Freshmen	Average Net Cost After Aid	Average Indebtedness Upon Graduation
Albany College of Pharmacy and Health Sciences	ind.	$27,630	$9760	99%	14%	$15,372	$22,018	$29,160
Alfred University	ind.	$28,774	$11,498	100%	11%	$25,728	$14,544	$34,494
Bard College	ind.	$46,370	$13,502	97%	58%	$39,829	$20,043	$24,913
Barnard College	ind.	$43,502	$13,810	97%	100%	$40,899	$16,413	$19,931
Baruch College of the City University of New York	pub.	$5430	$11,590†	36%	41%	$4694	$12,326	$4972
Binghamton University, State University of New York	pub.	$7645	$12,446	81%	12%	$10,590	$9501	$23,710
Brooklyn College of the City University of New York	pub.	$5884	NR	88%	81%	$7500	—	$12,200
Buffalo State College, State University of New York	pub.	$6694	$11,192	87%	16%	$9240	$8646	$16,900
Canisius College	ind.	$32,030	$11,820	100%	32%	$29,373	$14,477	$36,383
Cazenovia College	ind.	$28,022	$11,398	100%	8%	$27,421	$11,999	NR
City College of the City University of New York	pub.	$5131	NR	97%	66%	$8646	—	$16,944
Clarkson University	ind.	$40,610	$12,998	99%	15%	$39,187	$14,421	$27,866
Colgate University	ind.	$44,640	$11,075	100%	100%	$42,313	$13,402	$20,751
The College at Brockport, State University of New York	pub.	$7210	$11,386	77%	16%	$10,418	$8178	$27,844
The College of New Rochelle	ind.	$31,260	$11,690	89%	6%	$26,756	$16,194	$22,923
The College of Saint Rose	ind.	$27,684	$11,250	89%	18%	$17,580	$21,354	$34,919
College of Staten Island of the City University of New York	pub.	$5858	NR	96%	3%	$7804	—	NR
Columbia University	ind.	$47,346	$11,496	95%	100%	$43,087	$15,755	NR
Columbia University, School of General Studies	ind.	$45,699	$10,233	NR	NR	NR	NR	NR
Cooper Union for the Advancement of Science and Art	ind.	$40,250	$13,970	100%	63%	$37,500	$16,720	$15,864
Cornell University	ind.	$43,413	$13,678	98%	100%	$42,248	$14,843	$20,490
Dominican College	ind.	$23,970	$11,980	100%	11%	$17,762	$18,188	$17,930
D'Youville College	ind.	$22,240	$10,250	100%	30%	$17,496	$14,994	$33,411
Elmira College	ind.	$38,150	$11,800	100%	18%	$30,429	$19,521	$28,586
Eugene Lang College The New School for Liberal Arts	ind.	$38,570	$17,300	98%	11%	$29,230	$26,640	$34,455
Farmingdale State College	pub.	$7125	$11,860	88%	16%	$8587	$10,398	$18,867
Fashion Institute of Technology	pub.	$6358	$12,598	71%	11%	$13,266	$5690	$27,955
Hamilton College	ind.	$44,350	$11,270	100%	100%	$40,594	$15,026	$18,568
Hartwick College	ind.	$38,930	$10,485	98%	17%	$28,851	$20,564	$30,751
Hilbert College	ind.	$20,500	$8650	100%	13%	$14,807	$14,343	$16,608
Hobart and William Smith Colleges	ind.	$44,438	$11,261	98%	76%	$29,793	$25,906	$34,463
Hofstra University	ind.	$35,950	$12,370	98%	21%	$24,000	$24,320	NR
Houghton College	ind.	$27,728	$8012	100%	12%	$24,585	$11,155	$22,197
Hunter College of the City University of New York	pub.	$5829	$5500†	99%	19%	$6914	$4415	$11,000
Iona College	ind.	$32,770	$13,175	77%	17%	$21,088	$24,857	$31,960
Ithaca College	ind.	$37,000	$13,400	96%	57%	$31,780	$18,620	NR
John Jay College of Criminal Justice of the City University of New York	pub.	$5760	NA	85%	NR	$10,150	—	$11,890
The Juilliard School	ind.	$33,630	$12,770	96%	23%	$30,900	$15,500	$24,117
Keuka College	ind.	$26,320	$10,280	90%	1%	$22,711	$13,889	$19,845
The King's College	ind.	$29,240	$11,600†	100%	12%	$24,457	$16,383	$23,270
Le Moyne College	ind.	$30,460	$11,740	100%	25%	$22,089	$20,111	$34,532
LIM College	ind.	$23,645	$15,850†	77%	NR	$9404	$30,091	$35,400

NA = not applicable; NR = not reported; * = includes room and board; † = room only; — = not available.

College Costs At-a-Glance

	Institutional Control ind.=independent; pub.=public	Tuition and Fees	Room and Board	Percent of Eligible Freshmen Receiving Need-Based Gift Awards	Percent of Freshmen Whose Need Was Fully Met	Average Financial Aid Package for Freshmen	Average Net Cost After Aid	Average Indebtedness Upon Graduation
Long Island University–Brooklyn Campus	ind.	$30,790	$11,700	98%	4%	$19,313	$23,177	NR
Long Island University–C. W. Post Campus	ind.	$32,862	$12,240	69%	16%	$20,514	$24,588	NR
Manhattan College	ind.	$35,725	$13,080	99%	11%	$22,566	$26,239	$34,189
Manhattanville College	ind.	$35,370	$14,340	86%	23%	$32,453	$17,257	$36,384
Mannes College The New School for Music	ind.	$37,520	$17,300	100%	12%	$26,225	$28,595	$34,455
Marist College	ind.	$30,000	$12,600	75%	17%	$16,794	$25,806	$33,707
Marymount Manhattan College	ind.	$25,688	$14,430	100%	3%	$13,068	$27,050	$15,206
Medgar Evers College of the City University of New York	pub.	$5432	NA	97%	NR	$3908	$1524	NR
Mercy College	ind.	$17,556	$12,184	93%	2%	$15,080	$14,660	$24,138
Molloy College	ind.	$24,420	$12,080	98%	17%	$16,610	$19,890	$29,823
Mount Saint Mary College	ind.	$26,250	$13,290	100%	20%	$16,818	$22,722	$28,716
Nazareth College of Rochester	ind.	$27,222	$11,144	100%	30%	$23,507	$14,859	$30,500
New York City College of Technology of the City University of New York	pub.	$5769	NA	99%	10%	$8985	—	NR
New York Institute of Technology	ind.	$28,940	$11,650	72%	NR	$18,712	$21,878	NR
New York School of Interior Design	ind.	$27,894	$14,400†	100%	NR	$9557	$32,737	$35,502
New York University	ind.	$43,204	$16,133	97%	3%	$28,920	$30,417	$35,104
Niagara University	ind.	$27,230	$11,300	98%	50%	$25,251	$13,279	$32,114
Nyack College	ind.	$23,250	$8650	100%	17%	$19,138	$12,762	$32,003
Pace University	ind.	$36,564	$12,590	100%	8%	$30,563	$18,591	$35,895
Parsons The New School for Design	ind.	$40,140	$15,100	96%	25%	$25,252	$29,988	$32,715
Paul Smith's College	ind.	NR	NR	100%	13%	$22,576	—	$16,175
Polytechnic Institute of New York University	ind.	NR	NR	94%	43%	$29,625	—	$30,560
Purchase College, State University of New York	pub.	$7230	$11,566	83%	3%	$9124	$9672	$26,684
Queens College of the City University of New York	pub.	$5730	NR	77%	61%	$6450	—	$20,624
Rensselaer Polytechnic Institute	ind.	$44,475	$12,450	100%	37%	$34,436	$22,489	$31,000
Roberts Wesleyan College	ind.	$27,464	$9630	100%	18%	$23,246	$13,848	$33,528
Rochester Institute of Technology	ind.	$34,424	$11,740	95%	82%	$24,000	$22,164	NR
Russell Sage College	ind.	$28,000	$10,995	84%	NR	NR	NR	$27,907
Sage College of Albany	ind.	$28,000	$10,995	87%	NR	NR	NR	$28,971
St. Bonaventure University	ind.	$28,727	$10,704	100%	20%	$24,807	$14,624	$37,102
St. John Fisher College	ind.	$28,430	$10,940	100%	45%	$20,384	$18,986	$32,157
St. John's University	ind.	$35,520	$15,270	90%	12%	$27,045	$23,745	$29,199
St. Joseph's College, Long Island Campus	ind.	$20,125	NA	98%	30%	$12,118	$8007	$25,137
St. Joseph's College, New York	ind.	$20,115	NA	100%	16%	$15,145	$4970	$25,836
St. Lawrence University	ind.	$44,390	$11,435	98%	33%	$39,811	$16,014	$25,058
Sarah Lawrence College	ind.	$46,924	$9324†	98%	53%	$30,946	$25,302	$15,309
School of Visual Arts	ind.	$31,030	$16,200	72%	2%	$14,555	$32,675	$29,678
Siena College	ind.	$31,368	$12,495	99%	19%	$21,000	$22,863	$32,000
Skidmore College	ind.	$44,020	$11,744	96%	100%	$37,067	$18,697	$22,753
State University of New York at Fredonia	pub.	$7058	$11,100	78%	12%	$10,364	$7794	$27,431
State University of New York at New Paltz	pub.	NR	NR	50%	6%	$9493	—	$24,445

NA = not applicable; NR = not reported; * = includes room and board; † = room only; — = not available.

College Costs At-a-Glance

	Institutional Control ind.=independent; pub.=public	Tuition and Fees	Room and Board	Percent of Eligible Freshmen Receiving Need-Based Gift Awards	Percent of Freshmen Whose Need Was Fully Met	Average Financial Aid Package for Freshmen	Average Net Cost After Aid	Average Indebtedness Upon Graduation
State University of New York at Oswego	pub.	$6841	$12,510	89%	9%	$7887	$11,464	$27,004
State University of New York at Plattsburgh	pub.	$6808	$10,582	90%	23%	$12,018	$5372	$25,297
State University of New York College at Cortland	pub.	$6942	$11,430	70%	9%	$13,122	$5250	$27,534
State University of New York College at Geneseo	pub.	$7095	$10,960	94%	62%	$6006	$12,049	$21,000
State University of New York College at Old Westbury	pub.	$6624	$9700	96%	126%	$9074	$7250	$18,972
State University of New York College at Oneonta	pub.	$6887	$10,540	73%	4%	$8818	$8609	$15,373
State University of New York College at Potsdam	pub.	$6842	$10,180	94%	47%	$13,701	$3321	$20,734
State University of New York College of Agriculture and Technology at Cobleskill	pub.	$8262	$10,866	100%	2%	$8727	$10,401	$21,195
State University of New York College of Environmental Science and Forestry	pub.	$6593	$14,400	89%	87%	$13,000	$7993	$26,000
State University of New York College of Technology at Delhi	pub.	$7090	$10,346	86%	NR	NR	NR	NR
State University of New York Institute of Technology	pub.	$6764	$10,290	95%	100%	$10,338	$6716	NR
State University of New York Maritime College	pub.	$6782	$10,444	NR	NR	NR	NR	NR
Stony Brook University, State University of New York	pub.	$7560	$10,934	90%	17%	$11,359	$7135	$20,954
Syracuse University	ind.	$39,004	$13,692	91%	70%	$35,120	$17,576	$33,504
Union College	ind.	$46,785	$11,463	95%	99%	$36,912	$21,336	NR
University at Albany, State University of New York	pub.	$7563	$11,276	89%	7%	$9925	$8914	$24,126
University at Buffalo, the State University of New York	pub.	$7989	$11,310	99%	99%	$9505	$9794	$16,025
University of Rochester	ind.	$43,666	$12,618	100%	100%	$37,988	$18,296	$27,601
Utica College	ind.	NR	NR	100%	9%	$28,269	—	$42,303
Vassar College	ind.	$46,270	$10,800	100%	100%	$45,236	$11,834	$17,234
Villa Maria College of Buffalo	ind.	$18,010	NA	98%	12%	$10,528	$7482	$24,408
Wagner College	ind.	$39,220	$11,660	100%	25%	$26,233	$24,647	NR
Webb Institute	ind.	NR	$13,750	33%	NR	$4500	$9250	$4500
Wells College	ind.	$34,700	$11,900	100%	19%	$34,198	$12,402	$30,933
Yeshiva University	ind.	$37,600	$11,150	99%	29%	$32,031	$16,719	$22,705
North Carolina								
Appalachian State University	pub.	$5859	$7060	82%	28%	$8641	$4278	$20,016
Barton College	ind.	$24,180	$7940	100%	12%	$18,479	$13,641	NR
Belmont Abbey College	ind.	$27,622	$10,403	100%	11%	$20,368	$17,657	$21,004
Brevard College	ind.	$23,900	$8200	99%	14%	$20,145	$11,955	$29,002
Campbell University	ind.	NR	NR	74%	51%	$20,748	—	$24,820
Carolina Christian College	ind.	$7700	NA	100%	100%	$5500	$2200	$6500
Catawba College	ind.	$26,820	$9410	83%	14%	$22,102	$14,128	$31,966
Chowan University	ind.	$22,160	$7870	80%	19%	$16,402	$13,628	$38,932
Davidson College	ind.	$42,849	$11,834	95%	100%	$32,021	$22,662	$23,904
Duke University	ind.	NR	NR	95%	100%	$41,979	—	$19,506
East Carolina University	pub.	$5869	$8300	70%	9%	$9614	$4555	$25,983
Elizabeth City State University	pub.	$4428	$7213	100%	NR	NR	NR	NR
Elon University	ind.	$28,980	$9480	86%	NR	$16,094	$22,366	$28,183
Fayetteville State University	pub.	$5671	$6142	100%	20%	$10,828	$985	$23,147 *

NA = not applicable; NR = not reported; * = includes room and board; † = room only; — = not available.

College Costs At-a-Glance

	Institutional Control ind.=independent; pub.=public	Tuition and Fees	Room and Board	Percent of Eligible Freshmen Receiving Need-Based Gift Awards	Percent of Freshmen Whose Need Was Fully Met	Average Financial Aid Package for Freshmen	Average Net Cost After Aid	Average Indebtedness Upon Graduation
Gardner-Webb University	ind.	$24,640	$7940	79%	24%	$20,272	$12,308	$27,261
Guilford College	ind.	$32,470	$8800	92%	4%	$22,998	$18,272	$25,025
Johnson C. Smith University	ind.	$18,236	$7100	94%	5%	$16,757	$8579	$32,621
Lees-McRae College	ind.	$24,450	$8500	74%	NR	$16,270	$16,680	NR
Meredith College	ind.	$29,106	$8348	100%	18%	$21,961	$15,493	$33,945
Methodist University	ind.	NR	NR	91%	9%	$16,805	—	$29,809
Mid-Atlantic Christian University	ind.	$12,160	$7780	100%	NR	$9047	$10,893	$37,108
Montreat College	ind.	$22,784	$7494	99%	18%	$20,129	$10,149	$18,147
Mount Olive College	ind.	NR	NR	99%	14%	$14,333	—	$28,201
New Life Theological Seminary	ind.	NR	NA	100%	100%	$11,905	—	NR
North Carolina Agricultural and Technical State University	pub.	$5058	$7349	74%	5%	$14,094	—	$28,119
North Carolina Central University	pub.	$3244	$9923	84%	4%	$11,865	$1302	NR
North Carolina State University	pub.	$7788	$8414	95%	34%	$12,846	$3356	$22,626
Piedmont International University	ind.	$13,195	$6410	NR	NR	NR	NR	NR
Saint Augustine's College	ind.	$17,160	$7562	100%	57%	$6735	$17,987	$28,960
University of North Carolina at Asheville	pub.	$5866	$7584	95%	33%	$11,229	$2221	$17,696
The University of North Carolina at Chapel Hill	pub.	$7690	$9734	94%	78%	$15,939	$1485	$16,983
The University of North Carolina at Greensboro	pub.	$6229	$8948	62%	21%	$9665	$5512	$24,199
The University of North Carolina at Pembroke	pub.	$4857	$7010	94%	10%	$9121	$2746	$23,760
The University of North Carolina Wilmington	pub.	$5800	$8016	100%	27%	$8220	$5596	$25,821
Wake Forest University	ind.	$44,742	$12,000	84%	89%	$34,647	$22,095	$33,262
Warren Wilson College	ind.	$29,540	$8796	97%	16%	$26,074	$12,262	$23,239
Western Carolina University	pub.	$6479	$7477	98%	14%	$8551	$5405	$18,483
William Peace University	ind.	$23,900	$9141	100%	7%	$23,939	$9102	$33,147
North Dakota								
Mayville State University	pub.	$6193	$4854	89%	17%	$7996	$3051	$30,351
Minot State University	pub.	$5921	$4994	86%	100%	$7694	$3221	$25,117
University of Mary	ind.	$13,600	$6290	75%	48%	$11,870	$8020	$28,970
Valley City State University	pub.	$6324	$5480	98%	100%	$9962	$1842	$27,884
Ohio								
Antioch University Midwest	ind.	NR	NA	NR	NR	NR	NR	$40,000
Ashland University	ind.	$28,858	$9502	100%	NR	$26,270	$12,090	$36,058
Baldwin Wallace University	ind.	$27,060	$7520	100%	33%	$24,089	$10,491	$31,022
Bluffton University	ind.	$27,426	$9010	100%	49%	$26,015	$10,421	$37,879
Bowling Green State University	pub.	$10,513	$8064	93%	12%	$12,988	$5589	$31,262
Capital University	ind.	$31,364	$8460	98%	17%	$23,883	$15,941	$33,200
Case Western Reserve University	ind.	$40,490	$12,436	100%	67%	$33,989	$18,937	$37,610
Cedarville University	ind.	$25,496	$5540	85%	18%	$23,280	$7756	$28,251
Cincinnati Christian University	ind.	$15,266	$6672	95%	11%	$11,980	$9958	$32,280
Cleveland Institute of Art	ind.	$36,509	$12,132	100%	6%	$26,167	$22,474	$30,541
Cleveland Institute of Music	ind.	NR	NR	100%	10%	$28,807	—	$27,092
Cleveland State University	pub.	$9314	$11,848	87%	7%	$9344	$11,818	$23,436

NA = not applicable; NR = not reported; * = includes room and board; † = room only; — = not available.

College Costs At-a-Glance

	Institutional Control ind.=independent; pub.=public	Tuition and Fees	Room and Board	Percent of Eligible Freshmen Receiving Need-Based Gift Awards	Percent of Freshmen Whose Need Was Fully Met	Average Financial Aid Package for Freshmen	Average Net Cost After Aid	Average Indebtedness Upon Graduation
College of Mount St. Joseph	ind.	$25,800	$8080	98%	24%	$20,801	$13,079	NR
The College of Wooster	ind.	$39,810	$9590	98%	63%	$36,045	$13,355	$26,750
Columbus College of Art & Design	ind.	$28,524	$7490	100%	6%	$18,213	$17,801	$36,100
Defiance College	ind.	$27,360	$8850	89%	11%	$23,288	$12,922	$36,663
Denison University	ind.	$42,280	$10,360	100%	48%	$37,445	$15,195	NR
Heidelberg University	ind.	$24,582	$8974	100%	15%	$21,520	$12,036	$35,470
John Carroll University	ind.	$34,480	$10,040	99%	17%	$27,889	$16,631	$31,727
Kent State University	pub.	$9672	$9176	87%	39%	$9415	$9433	$31,954
Kent State University at Geauga	pub.	$5472	NA	66%	43%	$5987	—	NR
Kent State University at Stark	pub.	$5472	NA	79%	43%	$6601	—	NR
Kenyon College	ind.	$45,640	$11,170	98%	75%	$37,805	$19,005	$20,992
Lake Erie College	ind.	$27,368	$8336	100%	16%	$21,626	$14,078	$34,758
Lourdes University	ind.	$17,455	NR	82%	NR	$14,715	$2740	NR
Malone University	ind.	$25,678	$8656	100%	18%	$21,790	$12,544	$33,263
Marietta College	ind.	$30,940	$9560	98%	28%	$27,091	$13,409	$32,314
Mercy College of Ohio	ind.	NR	NR	83%	NR	$8858	—	$24,127
Miami University	pub.	$13,595	$10,596	68%	17%	$10,647	$13,544	$27,817
Mount Carmel College of Nursing	ind.	$11,365	$5000†	25%	NR	$7375	$8990	$8985
Mount Vernon Nazarene University	ind.	$23,690	$6980	96%	14%	$19,139	$11,531	$25,462
Oberlin College	ind.	NR	NR	64%	100%	$31,983	—	NR
The Ohio State University	pub.	$10,037	$10,392	86%	24%	$12,201	$8228	$26,409
Ohio University	pub.	$10,282	$10,010	77%	13%	$8562	$11,730	$27,060
Ohio University–Chillicothe	pub.	$4956	NA	87%	7%	$6668	—	$27,060
Ohio University–Eastern	pub.	NR	NA	86%	13%	$5978	—	$27,060
Ohio University–Lancaster	pub.	NR	NA	82%	13%	$6409	—	$27,060
Ohio University–Southern Campus	pub.	NR	NA	93%	7%	$6762	—	$27,060
Ohio University–Zanesville	pub.	$5104	NR	90%	21%	$6596	—	$27,060
Ohio Wesleyan University	ind.	$39,150	$10,310	100%	31%	$28,940	$20,520	$30,900
Pontifical College Josephinum	ind.	NR	NR	22%	33%	$10,817	—	$15,324
Tiffin University	ind.	$20,700	$9573	99%	10%	$17,482	$12,791	$30,119
The University of Akron	pub.	$9863	$9878	63%	8%	$7402	$12,339	$23,392
University of Cincinnati	pub.	$10,784	$10,170	41%	11%	$8656	$12,298	$30,078
University of Dayton	ind.	$33,400	$10,350	100%	34%	$22,850	$20,900	$40,628
University of Mount Union	ind.	$26,650	$8480	100%	13%	$21,041	$14,089	$33,568
University of Rio Grande	ind.	NR	NR	79%	73%	$5159	—	$22,633
The University of Toledo	pub.	$9275	$9738	98%	14%	$10,766	$8247	$30,421
Ursuline College	ind.	$26,760	$8900	100%	9%	$23,278	$12,382	$25,963
Wittenberg University	ind.	$38,030	$9736	100%	1%	$30,942	$16,824	$31,712
Wright State University	pub.	$8354	$8629	86%	12%	$9693	$7290	$28,349
Xavier University	ind.	$33,000	$10,740	97%	22%	$19,737	$24,003	$32,155
Youngstown State University	pub.	$7712	$8150	82%	9%	$8151	$7711	$24,209

NA = not applicable; NR = not reported; * = includes room and board; † = room only; — = not available.

College Costs At-a-Glance

	Institutional Control ind.=independent; pub.=public	Tuition and Fees	Room and Board	Percent of Eligible Freshmen Receiving Need-Based Gift Awards	Percent of Freshmen Whose Need Was Fully Met	Average Financial Aid Package for Freshmen	Average Net Cost After Aid	Average Indebtedness Upon Graduation
Oklahoma								
Cameron University	pub.	$4770	$3884	95%	5%	$8457	$197	$15,020
Hillsdale Free Will Baptist College	ind.	$10,880	$6470	79%	NR	$11,672	$5678	$22,313
Northeastern State University	pub.	$4857	$5914	94%	83%	$10,210	$561	$20,503
Northwestern Oklahoma State University	pub.	$5198	$3780	90%	NR	NR	NR	$14,975
Oklahoma Baptist University	ind.	$20,856	$6200	86%	30%	$20,451	$6605	$23,039
Oklahoma Christian University	ind.	$18,800	$6175	66%	47%	$21,347	$3628	$29,388
Oklahoma City University	ind.	$28,190	$9170	100%	27%	$21,838	$15,522	$25,557
Oklahoma State University	pub.	$7441	$6868	79%	17%	$12,558	$1751	$22,736
Oklahoma Wesleyan University	ind.	$21,140	$7240	96%	13%	$14,016	$14,364	$20,060
Oral Roberts University	ind.	$22,438	$9296	99%	37%	$15,320	$16,414	$34,555
Rogers State University	pub.	$5047	$6425	80%	4%	$8324	$3148	$19,019
Southeastern Oklahoma State University	pub.	$5060	$4970	72%	19%	$9566	$464	$15,605
University of Oklahoma	pub.	$7341	$8382	55%	85%	$11,837	$3886	$26,005
University of Science and Arts of Oklahoma	pub.	$5400	$5160	96%	11%	$9174	$1386	$18,378
University of Tulsa	ind.	$34,350	$10,476	37%	61%	$25,426	$19,400	$34,574
Oregon								
Concordia University	ind.	NR	NR	66%	9%	$17,175	—	$32,888
Corban University	ind.	$26,430	$8145	100%	10%	$19,626	$14,949	$23,853
Eastern Oregon University	pub.	NR	NR	69%	21%	$9590	—	$25,109
George Fox University	ind.	$30,230	$9360	94%	35%	$27,240	$12,350	$23,512
Lewis & Clark College	ind.	$41,928	$10,636	100%	24%	$32,748	$19,816	$25,134
Linfield College	ind.	$34,328	$9500	98%	33%	$28,193	$15,635	$29,751
Marylhurst University	ind.	NR	NA	100%	NR	$8939	—	$43,471
Northwest Christian University	ind.	$24,880	$7600	100%	19%	$19,140	$13,340	$32,045
Oregon College of Art & Craft	ind.	NR	NR	56%	6%	$18,439	—	$22,500
Oregon Institute of Technology	pub.	NR	NR	79%	43%	$6832	—	$28,546
Oregon State University	pub.	$8138	$10,563	87%	19%	$10,651	$8050	NR
Pacific University	ind.	$35,260	$9992	98%	17%	$27,564	$17,688	$30,880
Portland State University	pub.	$7653	$11,019	78%	23%	$12,894	$5778	$26,066
Reed College	ind.	$44,460	$11,460	82%	100%	$36,132	$19,788	$19,407
University of Oregon	pub.	$9310	$10,580	51%	13%	$9763	$10,127	$24,528
University of Portland	ind.	$35,260	$7290†	83%	9%	$25,780	$16,770	$27,544
Warner Pacific College	ind.	NR	NR	91%	7%	$16,122	—	$33,035
Western Oregon University	pub.	$8529	NR	87%	8%	$9480	—	$28,774
Willamette University	ind.	$40,874	$9820	99%	44%	$29,552	$21,142	$26,740
Pennsylvania								
Albright College	ind.	$36,660	$10,000	100%	11%	$29,826	$16,834	$27,051
Allegheny College	ind.	$37,610	$9540	100%	29%	$31,387	$15,763	NR
Arcadia University	ind.	$35,620	$12,150	100%	14%	$26,972	$20,798	$41,393
Baptist Bible College of Pennsylvania	ind.	$19,710	$7180	80%	4%	$14,442	$12,448	$23,677

NA = not applicable; NR = not reported; * = includes room and board; † = room only; — = not available.

College Costs At-a-Glance

	Institutional Control ind.=independent; pub.=public	Tuition and Fees	Room and Board	Percent of Eligible Freshmen Receiving Need-Based Gift Awards	Percent of Freshmen Whose Need Was Fully Met	Average Financial Aid Package for Freshmen	Average Net Cost After Aid	Average Indebtedness Upon Graduation
Bloomsburg University of Pennsylvania	pub.	$8343	$7498	60%	8%	$7274	$8567	$27,223
Bryn Mawr College	ind.	$42,246	$13,340	100%	100%	$41,074	$14,512	$23,579
Bucknell University	ind.	$46,902	$11,258	100%	95%	$28,500	$29,660	$21,163
Cabrini College	ind.	$29,000	NR	87%	18%	$23,503	$5497	$32,503
Cairn University	ind.	$22,455	$4625†	99%	17%	$17,659	$9421	$30,633
Carnegie Mellon University	ind.	$47,642	$11,990	95%	26%	$31,612	$28,020	$31,747
Cedar Crest College	ind.	$31,196	$9990	100%	10%	$26,840	$14,346	$31,933
Chatham University	ind.	$32,454	$9986	95%	7%	$29,723	$12,717	$40,297
Chestnut Hill College	ind.	$31,170	$9875	98%	10%	$20,920	$20,125	$10,688
Clarion University of Pennsylvania	pub.	$9141	$7186	81%	4%	$7680	$8647	$29,410
DeSales University	ind.	$30,150	$10,970	100%	20%	$23,660	$17,460	$28,875
Dickinson College	ind.	$44,551	$11,178	96%	84%	$34,269	$21,460	$25,574
Duquesne University	ind.	$30,034	$10,198	99%	23%	$22,813	$17,419	$25,228
Edinboro University of Pennsylvania	pub.	$8578	$7362	96%	3%	$7780	$8160	$23,633
Elizabethtown College	ind.	$38,200	$9400	100%	19%	$26,025	$21,575	NR
Franklin & Marshall College	ind.	$44,360	$11,750	98%	100%	$40,679	$15,431	$33,200
Gannon University	ind.	$27,546	$10,940	100%	17%	$21,970	$16,516	NR
Geneva College	ind.	$25,220	$9250	100%	15%	$19,168	$15,302	$26,883
Gettysburg College	ind.	$44,210	$10,560	97%	92%	$35,056	$19,714	$25,530
Grove City College	ind.	$14,880	$8108	100%	11%	$6405	$16,583	$28,767
Gwynedd-Mercy College	ind.	$28,340	$9850	100%	15%	$19,663	$18,527	$36,067
Harrisburg University of Science and Technology	ind.	$23,900	$6340†	99%	7%	$17,528	$12,712	$38,779
Haverford College	ind.	$43,702	$13,290	98%	100%	$41,352	$15,640	$14,171
Indiana University of Pennsylvania	pub.	$8672	$10,466	70%	6%	$9563	$9575	$35,229
Juniata College	ind.	$37,170	$10,200	100%	23%	$29,241	$18,129	$31,213
Keystone College	ind.	$21,200	$9800	100%	11%	$20,096	$10,904	$8675
King's College	ind.	$29,174	$11,020	100%	15%	$21,167	$19,027	$36,538
Kutztown University of Pennsylvania	pub.	$8596	$8890	64%	6%	$7326	$10,160	$30,831
Lafayette College	ind.	$43,970	$13,080	97%	81%	$37,641	$19,409	$26,717
Lancaster Bible College	ind.	NR	NR	100%	8%	$13,816	—	$20,668
La Roche College	ind.	$24,058	$9732	67%	29%	$26,024	$7766	$26,296
La Salle University	ind.	$36,650	$12,210	99%	13%	$26,648	$22,212	$37,225
Lebanon Valley College	ind.	$34,470	$9180	100%	17%	$25,471	$18,179	$34,561
Lehigh University	ind.	$42,220	$11,230	96%	48%	$36,189	$17,261	$31,122
Lock Haven University of Pennsylvania	pub.	$8564	$8016	66%	45%	$8662	$7918	$23,840
Lycoming College	ind.	$32,756	$9420	100%	22%	$27,893	$14,283	$35,990
Mansfield University of Pennsylvania	pub.	$8926	$8592	71%	34%	$8669	$8849	$34,174
Marywood University	ind.	$30,440	$13,566	95%	2%	$21,936	$22,070	$41,198
Mercyhurst University	ind.	$29,037	$10,104	100%	26%	$25,960	$13,181	$26,063
Messiah College	ind.	$30,470	$9070	99%	17%	$21,772	$17,768	$35,306
Millersville University of Pennsylvania	pub.	$8600	$9234	73%	10%	$7570	$10,264	$30,210
Misericordia University	ind.	$27,230	$11,190	100%	23%	$19,765	$18,655	NR

NA = not applicable; NR = not reported; * = includes room and board; † = room only; — = not available.

Peterson's How to Get Money for College 2014

College Costs At-a-Glance

	Institutional Control ind.=independent; pub.=public	Tuition and Fees	Room and Board	Percent of Eligible Freshmen Receiving Need-Based Gift Awards	Percent of Freshmen Whose Need Was Fully Met	Average Financial Aid Package for Freshmen	Average Net Cost After Aid	Average Indebtedness Upon Graduation
Moravian College	ind.	$34,484	$10,146	100%	11%	$26,847	$17,783	NR
Mount Aloysius College	ind.	NR	NR	100%	NR	$14,670	—	$33,793
Muhlenberg College	ind.	$41,510	$11,140	99%	87%	$26,110	$26,540	$25,858
Neumann University	ind.	$24,232	$11,070	100%	1%	$20,250	$15,052	$27,000
Peirce College	ind.	$16,500	NA	90%	NR	$7343	$9157	NR
Penn State Abington	pub.	$13,356	NR	83%	3%	$9830	$3526	$35,100
Penn State Altoona	pub.	$13,900	$9690	62%	5%	$8480	$15,110	$35,100
Penn State Berks	pub.	$13,900	$10,560	62%	4%	$8195	$16,265	$35,100
Penn State Erie, The Behrend College	pub.	$13,900	$9690	67%	4%	$8815	$14,775	$35,100
Penn State Harrisburg	pub.	$13,900	$11,000	62%	7%	$9202	$15,698	$35,100
Penn State Shenango	pub.	$13,244	NA	90%	1%	$11,264	$1980	$35,100
Penn State University Park	pub.	$16,444	$9690	48%	8%	$9481	$16,653	$35,100
Pennsylvania College of Technology	pub.	$14,370	$10,500	79%	NR	$14,358	$10,512	NR
Philadelphia University	ind.	$31,874	$10,178	100%	14%	$24,833	$17,219	$39,938
Point Park University	ind.	$25,190	$8000	100%	15%	$21,053	$12,137	$26,526
Robert Morris University	ind.	$24,064	$11,360	100%	11%	$21,703	$13,721	$41,093
Rosemont College	ind.	$30,950	$12,380	100%	12%	$28,011	$15,319	$22,597
Saint Charles Borromeo Seminary, Overbrook	ind.	$19,150	$12,060	67%	100%	$20,000	$11,210	$19,000
Saint Francis University	ind.	$28,878	$9900	54%	16%	$22,404	$16,374	$9677
Saint Joseph's University	ind.	$37,830	$12,800	98%	23%	$24,005	$26,625	NR
Seton Hill University	ind.	$29,450	$9944	100%	19%	$24,590	$14,804	$32,290
Shippensburg University of Pennsylvania	pub.	$9154	$7910	70%	11%	$7598	$9466	$27,661
Slippery Rock University of Pennsylvania	pub.	$8747	$9364	65%	13%	$8152	$9959	$28,959
Swarthmore College	ind.	$43,080	$12,670	100%	100%	$39,427	$16,323	$20,020
Temple University	pub.	$13,596	$10,276	85%	30%	$15,332	$8540	$33,500
Thiel College	ind.	$25,988	$10,120	100%	5%	$21,360	$14,748	$28,401
University of Pennsylvania	ind.	$43,738	$12,368	97%	100%	$40,582	$15,524	$21,190
University of Pittsburgh	pub.	$16,590	$9870	77%	13%	$15,810	$10,650	$33,662
University of Pittsburgh at Bradford	pub.	$12,810	$7960	95%	22%	$12,975	$7795	$35,810
University of Pittsburgh at Greensburg	pub.	$12,890	$8730	86%	12%	$10,716	$10,904	$33,095
University of Pittsburgh at Johnstown	pub.	$12,892	$8230	66%	12%	$12,754	$8368	$35,090
The University of Scranton	ind.	$37,456	$12,804	97%	11%	$21,694	$28,566	$38,560
University of the Sciences	ind.	NR	NR	100%	34%	$31,256	—	$10,620
Ursinus College	ind.	NR	NR	100%	21%	$32,460	—	$40,652
Valley Forge Christian College	ind.	NR	NR	99%	7%	$10,943	—	$36,136
Villanova University	ind.	$42,740	$11,370	93%	17%	$33,169	$20,941	$35,297
Washington & Jefferson College	ind.	$38,310	$9960	86%	17%	$28,300	$19,970	NR
Waynesburg University	ind.	$19,810	$8250	100%	31%	$15,863	$12,197	$29,000
West Chester University of Pennsylvania	pub.	$8620	$6786	47%	6%	$6137	$9269	$30,345
Westminster College	ind.	$31,410	$9570	100%	20%	$25,141	$15,839	$32,753
Widener University	ind.	$36,382	$12,248	76%	20%	$28,530	$20,100	$40,460
Wilkes University	ind.	$29,326	$12,034	99%	10%	$20,936	$20,424	$38,442

NA = not applicable; NR = not reported; * = includes room and board; † = room only; — = not available.

College Costs At-a-Glance

	Institutional Control ind.=independent; pub.=public	Tuition and Fees	Room and Board	Percent of Eligible Freshmen Receiving Need-Based Gift Awards	Percent of Freshmen Whose Need Was Fully Met	Average Financial Aid Package for Freshmen	Average Net Cost After Aid	Average Indebtedness Upon Graduation
Wilson College	ind.	NR	NR	NR	NR	NR	NR	$32,565
York College of Pennsylvania	ind.	$17,010	$9580	64%	26%	$11,676	$14,914	$35,297
Puerto Rico								
Carlos Albizu University	ind.	$6919	NA	NR	NR	NR	NR	NR
EDP University of Puerto Rico	ind.	$6240	NA	100%	NR	$5700	$540	$4256
EDP University of Puerto Rico–San Sebastian	ind.	$6120	NR	97%	NR	$5398	$722	$4729
Inter American University of Puerto Rico, Bayamón Campus	ind.	$5620	NR	91%	NR	$145	$5475	NR
Inter American University of Puerto Rico, Guayama Campus	ind.	$4562	NA	26%	NR	$115	$4447	NR
Inter American University of Puerto Rico, Ponce Campus	ind.	$4080	NA	NR	NR	NR	NR	NR
National University College	ind.	NR	NR	100%	NR	$5519	—	$4633
Polytechnic University of Puerto Rico	ind.	$7548	NA	100%	NR	$7249	$299	NR
Universidad Adventista de las Antillas	ind.	$5550	$2900	100%	NR	$2900	$5550	NR
Universidad del Turabo	ind.	$19,512	$8600	100%	NR	NR	NR	NR
Universidad Teolgica del Caribe	ind.	$4448	$2400	100%	NR	NR	NR	NR
University of Puerto Rico at Bayamón	pub.	$2212	NR	NR	NR	NR	NR	NR
Rhode Island								
Brown University	ind.	$43,758	$11,258	96%	100%	$40,523	$14,493	$23,521
Bryant University	ind.	$37,234	$13,664	78%	50%	$23,109	$27,789	$44,580
Providence College	ind.	$42,206	$12,440	98%	39%	$28,357	$26,289	$26,832
Rhode Island College	pub.	$7598	$9534	91%	19%	$9402	$7730	$23,110
Roger Williams University	ind.	$31,668	$14,120	58%	10%	$18,935	$26,853	$38,550
Salve Regina University	ind.	$33,950	$11,900	99%	11%	$22,520	$23,330	$39,996
University of Rhode Island	pub.	$12,450	NR	95%	70%	$15,701	—	$30,387
South Carolina								
Anderson University	ind.	$22,790	$8348	100%	33%	$19,479	$11,659	$27,187
Bob Jones University	ind.	$13,430	$5790	92%	NR	$10,500	$8720	NR
The Citadel, The Military College of South Carolina	pub.	$11,772	$6115	77%	21%	$12,803	$5084	$31,217
Clemson University	pub.	$13,076	$7552	40%	19%	$12,173	$8455	$31,172
Coastal Carolina University	pub.	$9760	$7700	51%	8%	$9363	$8097	$34,040
Coker College	ind.	$24,576	$7610	96%	27%	$20,903	$11,283	$32,842
College of Charleston	pub.	$9918	$10,461	72%	22%	$12,581	$7798	$32,880
Columbia International University	ind.	$18,740	$7096	74%	11%	$16,544	$9292	$25,638
Converse College	ind.	$28,276	$8854	100%	23%	$23,916	$13,214	$28,986
Francis Marion University	pub.	$9066	$6820	85%	NR	$11,035	$4851	$26,453
Furman University	ind.	$41,532	$10,509	100%	29%	$26,910	$25,131	$26,661
Limestone College	ind.	$22,080	$7800	100%	15%	$16,942	$12,938	$31,409
Medical University of South Carolina	pub.	$15,438	NA	NR	NR	NR	NR	NR
Newberry College	ind.	$23,800	$9000	99%	16%	$20,509	$12,291	$30,610
Presbyterian College	ind.	$32,680	$8750	100%	39%	$32,031	$9399	$25,425
University of South Carolina	pub.	$10,488	$8459	44%	30%	$12,340	$6607	$25,022
University of South Carolina Aiken	pub.	$9024	$6780	95%	27%	$10,817	$4987	$22,677

NA = not applicable; NR = not reported; * = includes room and board; † = room only; — = not available.

College Costs At-a-Glance	Institutional Control ind.=independent; pub.=public	Tuition and Fees	Room and Board	Percent of Eligible Freshmen Receiving Need-Based Gift Awards	Percent of Freshmen Whose Need Was Fully Met	Average Financial Aid Package for Freshmen	Average Net Cost After Aid	Average Indebtedness Upon Graduation
University of South Carolina Upstate	pub.	$9892	$7250	66%	13%	$11,180	$5962	$25,301
Winthrop University	pub.	$13,026	$7464	98%	18%	$13,298	$7192	$22,521
Wofford College	ind.	$35,515	$10,280	91%	43%	$27,554	$18,241	$22,118
South Dakota								
Augustana College	ind.	$27,780	$6626	100%	25%	$23,816	$10,590	$34,878
Dakota State University	pub.	$7950	$5235	62%	12%	$7498	$5687	$25,926
Dakota Wesleyan University	ind.	$21,750	$6800	100%	30%	$18,700	$9850	$29,526
Mount Marty College	ind.	$22,130	$6390	100%	48%	$24,523	$3997	$32,369
Northern State University	pub.	$7269	$6147	84%	25%	$9889	$3527	$27,153
South Dakota School of Mines and Technology	pub.	NR	NR	74%	44%	$13,258	—	$18,331
South Dakota State University	pub.	$7404	$5586	62%	85%	$8791	$4199	$22,735
The University of South Dakota	pub.	$7704	$6648	53%	55%	$5608	$8744	$25,033
Tennessee								
American Baptist College of American Baptist Theological Seminary	ind.	$9005	$2000†	82%	NR	$8273	$2732	$5469
Austin Peay State University	pub.	$6648	$7380	85%	NR	$10,397	$3631	$26,030
Belmont University	ind.	$26,130	$12,420	93%	14%	$14,354	$24,196	$31,079
Carson-Newman University	ind.	$22,652	$6406	100%	26%	$23,283	$5775	$23,859
Christian Brothers University	ind.	$27,284	$6140	99%	20%	$23,331	$10,093	$22,696
Fisk University	ind.	NR	NR	100%	37%	$14,181	—	$6147
Freed-Hardeman University	ind.	$20,468	$7296	100%	31%	$16,126	$11,638	$41,086
King College	ind.	$24,960	$8180	96%	16%	$20,662	$12,478	$10,892
Lane College	ind.	$8560	$6040	94%	2%	$5408	$9192	$12,348
Lee University	ind.	$13,750	$6762	96%	30%	$12,502	$8010	$27,882
LeMoyne-Owen College	ind.	NR	NR	99%	5%	$10,556	—	NR
Lipscomb University	ind.	$24,754	$9224	64%	23%	$19,642	$14,336	$15,155
Maryville College	ind.	$31,132	$9890	100%	19%	$30,575	$10,447	NR
Memphis College of Art	ind.	$26,250	$8000	100%	10%	$20,337	$13,913	NR
Middle Tennessee State University	pub.	$7210	$7532	67%	15%	$10,606	$4136	$22,039
Milligan College	ind.	$26,760	$5850	100%	30%	$20,655	$11,955	$27,687
Rhodes College	ind.	$38,092	$9504	99%	48%	$34,271	$13,325	$26,372
Sewanee: The University of the South	ind.	$35,756	$10,214	100%	64%	$33,849	$12,121	$23,721
Southern Adventist University	ind.	$19,124	$5584	100%	85%	$17,177	$7531	$34,114
Tennessee State University	pub.	NR	NR	86%	1%	$14,351	—	$30,477
Tennessee Technological University	pub.	$6724	$7642	52%	26%	$11,945	$2421	$6432
Tennessee Wesleyan College	ind.	NR	NR	100%	18%	$15,700	—	$27,011
Trevecca Nazarene University	ind.	$21,290	$7488	NR	NR	NR	NR	NR
Union University	ind.	$25,650	$8430	71%	26%	$22,414	$11,666	$26,936
University of Memphis	pub.	$8234	$6860	71%	23%	$9433	$5661	$22,214
The University of Tennessee	pub.	$9092	$8752	97%	27%	$12,866	$4978	$22,860
The University of Tennessee at Chattanooga	pub.	$7212	$8300	96%	25%	$8631	$6881	$19,836

NA = not applicable; NR = not reported; * = includes room and board; † = room only; — = not available.

College Costs At-a-Glance

	Institutional Control ind.=independent; pub.=public	Tuition and Fees	Room and Board	Percent of Eligible Freshmen Receiving Need-Based Gift Awards	Percent of Freshmen Whose Need Was Fully Met	Average Financial Aid Package for Freshmen	Average Net Cost After Aid	Average Indebtedness Upon Graduation
The University of Tennessee at Martin	pub.	$7049	$5593	69%	27%	$12,826	—	$12,436
Vanderbilt University	ind.	$42,118	$13,818	89%	100%	$44,416	$11,520	$17,349
Texas								
Abilene Christian University	ind.	$28,350	$8800	100%	30%	$20,221	$16,929	$39,705
Angelo State University	pub.	$7493	$8026	75%	14%	$10,212	$5307	$21,373
Baptist University of the Americas	ind.	$5280	$3380	NR	NR	NR	NR	NR
Baylor University	ind.	$36,137	$10,748	98%	13%	$23,498	$23,387	NR
The College of Saints John Fisher & Thomas More	ind.	$8000	$2000	100%	15%	$15,800	—	$5474
Concordia University Texas	ind.	$23,600	$8460	98%	15%	$16,922	$15,138	$30,587
Dallas Baptist University	ind.	$21,110	$6498	62%	55%	$16,121	$11,487	$18,943
East Texas Baptist University	ind.	$21,530	$6145	79%	12%	$16,107	$11,568	$23,458
Hardin-Simmons University	ind.	$23,460	$6792	68%	31%	$26,698	$3554	$40,972
Houston Baptist University	ind.	$27,930	$6500	100%	20%	$23,701	$10,729	NR
Howard Payne University	ind.	$23,200	$6800	86%	21%	$17,348	$12,652	$29,208
Lamar University	pub.	$9011	$7966	81%	NR	$6961	$10,016	$26,224
LeTourneau University	ind.	$24,540	$8940	100%	16%	$22,004	$11,476	$41,522
Lubbock Christian University	ind.	$17,760	$6674	99%	14%	$13,760	$10,674	$29,053
McMurry University	ind.	$23,305	$7460	90%	8%	$21,519	$9246	$38,921
Midwestern State University	pub.	$7238	$6350	92%	19%	$9990	$3598	$22,891
Northwood University, Texas Campus	ind.	$20,996	$9107	92%	17%	$23,720	$6383	$24,254
Rice University	ind.	$38,942	$13,000	100%	100%	$35,549	$16,393	$18,133
St. Edward's University	ind.	$33,720	$10,954	88%	11%	$25,537	$19,137	$34,314
Sam Houston State University	pub.	$8120	$8092	88%	9%	$10,152	$6060	$27,202
Schreiner University	ind.	$21,540	$10,062	100%	12%	$17,390	$14,212	$20,900
Southern Methodist University	ind.	$43,800	$13,955	71%	36%	$35,683	$22,072	$30,987
Southwestern University	ind.	$35,240	$11,010	100%	33%	$30,816	$15,434	$36,299
Stephen F. Austin State University	pub.	$7928	$8476	79%	8%	$10,747	$5657	$20,858
Tarleton State University	pub.	$6939	$7336	77%	39%	$7653	$6622	$15,548
Texas A&M International University	pub.	$6838	$6275	98%	4%	$9816	$3297	$17,644
Texas A&M University	pub.	$8506	$8400	98%	53%	$16,477	$429	$22,955
Texas A&M University–Commerce	pub.	$8376	$3627	98%	21%	$11,774	$229	$28,839
Texas A&M University–Corpus Christi	pub.	NR	NR	90%	10%	$8997	—	$24,168
Texas Christian University	ind.	$36,590	NR	98%	31%	$21,669	$14,921	$38,516
Texas College	ind.	$9686	$7000	98%	1%	$8767	$7919	$21,147
Texas Lutheran University	ind.	$24,990	$7340	100%	25%	$22,417	$9913	$37,145
Texas Southern University	pub.	$7646	$10,566	100%	100%	$17,500	$712	$39,197
Texas State University–San Marcos	pub.	$8772	$7070	86%	32%	$12,599	$3243	$23,575
Texas Tech University	pub.	$8942	$8275	83%	17%	$9907	$7310	$18,358
Texas Wesleyan University	ind.	$20,840	$7470	100%	15%	$13,598	$14,712	NR
Texas Woman's University	pub.	$6703	$6930	93%	15%	$9331	$4302	$25,155
Trinity University	ind.	$33,688	$10,496	100%	37%	$29,216	$14,968	$42,987
University of Dallas	ind.	$31,070	$9890	99%	18%	$26,613	$14,347	$31,466

NA = not applicable; NR = not reported; * = includes room and board; † = room only; — = not available.

College Costs At-a-Glance

	Institutional Control ind.=independent; pub.=public	Tuition and Fees	Room and Board	Percent of Eligible Freshmen Receiving Need-Based Gift Awards	Percent of Freshmen Whose Need Was Fully Met	Average Financial Aid Package for Freshmen	Average Net Cost After Aid	Average Indebtedness Upon Graduation
University of Houston	pub.	$9888	NR	94%	23%	$13,387	—	$16,582
University of Houston–Clear Lake	pub.	$6580	$8354†	NR	NR	NR	NR	NR
University of Mary Hardin-Baylor	ind.	$24,150	$6620	100%	7%	$17,429	$13,341	$34,655
University of North Texas	pub.	$9078	$7150	80%	23%	$12,113	$4115	NR
University of St. Thomas	ind.	$26,890	$7900	100%	15%	$19,110	$15,680	$33,936
The University of Texas at Arlington	pub.	$8878	$7708	77%	21%	$12,058	$4528	$22,137
The University of Texas at Austin	pub.	$9792	$10,946	94%	32%	$13,669	$7069	$26,097
The University of Texas at Brownsville	pub.	$5116	$6602	92%	NR	$6967	$4751	NR
The University of Texas at Dallas	pub.	$11,592	$9050	92%	33%	$14,694	$5948	$17,516
The University of Texas at El Paso	pub.	NR	NR	89%	14%	$12,874	—	$20,913
The University of Texas at San Antonio	pub.	$8419	$9693	94%	23%	$10,434	$7678	$25,140
The University of Texas of the Permian Basin	pub.	$6459	$7616	72%	20%	$10,500	$3575	$14,629
The University of Texas–Pan American	pub.	$5165	$5656	97%	6%	$10,125	$696	$15,257
University of the Incarnate Word	ind.	$23,690	$10,094	100%	28%	$18,353	$15,431	NR
Wayland Baptist University	ind.	$14,630	$4157	99%	7%	$11,665	$7122	$21,981
West Texas A&M University	pub.	$6790	$5000	90%	19%	$11,426	$364	$19,774
Utah								
Brigham Young University	ind.	$4710	$7200	64%	2%	$6486	$5424	$14,377
Dixie State College of Utah	pub.	$4709	$4348	92%	3%	$6379	$2678	$22,412
Neumont University	ind.	$23,100	$4230†	NR	NR	NR	NR	NR
Southern Utah University	pub.	$5576	$2878†	100%	9%	$8008	$446	$13,478
University of Utah	pub.	$7138	$7155	82%	14%	$14,194	$99	$20,796
Utah State University	pub.	$6183	$5620	86%	15%	$8137	$3666	$18,900
Utah Valley University	pub.	$4786	NA	86%	8%	$4126	$660	$14,288
Western Governors University	ind.	NR	NA	66%	12%	$6313	—	$35,327
Westminster College	ind.	$28,210	$7890	99%	22%	$23,150	$12,950	$28,323
Vermont								
Bennington College	ind.	$44,220	$12,770	99%	19%	$36,238	$20,752	$25,716
Burlington College	ind.	$22,410	$6870†	100%	NR	$16,520	$12,760	$39,107
Champlain College	ind.	$31,350	$13,500	93%	12%	$16,847	$28,003	NR
Green Mountain College	ind.	NR	NR	99%	5%	$27,661	—	$42,269
Johnson State College	pub.	$10,543	$9138	96%	10%	$15,524	$4157	NR
Marlboro College	ind.	$37,640	$9930	100%	NR	$29,719	$17,851	$20,051
Middlebury College	ind.	$43,731	$11,839	95%	95%	$38,670	$16,900	$17,246
Norwich University	ind.	$31,782	$10,976	100%	17%	$27,661	$15,097	$35,310
Saint Michael's College	ind.	$39,015	$9725	99%	31%	$26,539	$22,201	$33,054
Southern Vermont College	ind.	$21,275	$9943	85%	16%	$15,254	$15,964	$24,652
Sterling College	ind.	$28,760	$8332	93%	7%	$24,984	$12,108	$39,724
University of Vermont	pub.	$15,254	$10,094	98%	11%	$21,526	$3822	$27,588
Vermont Technical College	pub.	$12,544	$8786	90%	9%	$10,617	$10,713	$22,380

NA = not applicable; NR = not reported; * = includes room and board; † = room only; — = not available.

College Costs At-a-Glance

	Institutional Control ind.=independent; pub.=public	Tuition and Fees	Room and Board	Percent of Eligible Freshmen Receiving Need-Based Gift Awards	Percent of Freshmen Whose Need Was Fully Met	Average Financial Aid Package for Freshmen	Average Net Cost After Aid	Average Indebtedness Upon Graduation
Virginia								
Averett University	ind.	$25,950	$8370	100%	10%	$20,000	$14,320	$31,373
Bluefield College	ind.	$21,060	$7640	100%	17%	$16,297	$12,403	$20,934
Bridgewater College	ind.	$29,090	$10,790	100%	33%	$25,979	$13,901	$31,153
Christendom College	ind.	$22,720	$8280	81%	100%	$14,725	$16,275	$25,875
Christopher Newport University	pub.	$10,572	$9728	70%	15%	$8012	$12,288	$24,400
The College of William and Mary	pub.	$13,570	$9072	72%	22%	$14,812	$7830	$24,344
Emory & Henry College	ind.	$28,122	$9426	80%	44%	$26,482	$11,066	$29,510
Ferrum College	ind.	$27,425	$9130	89%	6%	$22,561	$13,994	$24,788
George Mason University	pub.	$9620	$9250	78%	8%	$11,987	$6883	$25,822
Hampden-Sydney College	ind.	$35,570	$11,166	100%	17%	$29,766	$16,970	$30,248
Hampton University	ind.	$20,724	$9230	98%	36%	$5707	$24,247	$9597
Hollins University	ind.	$32,075	$11,220	100%	24%	$29,987	$13,308	$31,104
James Madison University	pub.	$9176	$8873	53%	89%	$7604	$10,445	$22,792
Jefferson College of Health Sciences	ind.	NR	NR	99%	5%	$9895	—	$17,024
Liberty University	ind.	$20,892	$7976	100%	10%	$12,435	$16,433	$21,830
Longwood University	pub.	$10,890	$8448	86%	49%	$11,905	$7433	$26,439
Lynchburg College	ind.	$32,005	$8680	100%	18%	$25,181	$15,504	$33,353
Mary Baldwin College	ind.	$28,720	$8400	100%	9%	$24,373	$12,747	$27,642
Marymount University	ind.	$26,430	$11,550	45%	20%	$19,058	$18,922	$25,598
Norfolk State University	pub.	$6860	$8130	NR	NR	NR	NR	NR
Old Dominion University	pub.	$8450	$9066	70%	15%	$9925	$7591	$25,585
Radford University	pub.	$8590	$7881	63%	25%	$8601	$7870	$25,241
Randolph College	ind.	$31,540	$10,790	100%	18%	$27,128	$15,202	$33,737
Randolph-Macon College	ind.	$33,525	$10,400	100%	25%	$25,209	$18,716	$31,112
Regent University	ind.	$15,960	$8430	98%	9%	$11,634	$12,756	$45,326
Roanoke College	ind.	$36,472	$11,524	99%	21%	$28,401	$19,595	$33,004
Shenandoah University	ind.	$27,850	$9240	100%	19%	$19,000	$18,090	$27,000
Sweet Briar College	ind.	$32,325	$11,440	100%	18%	$26,448	$17,317	$23,596
University of Management and Technology	ind.	NR	NA	100%	100%	NR	NR	NR
University of Mary Washington	pub.	$9246	$10,238	45%	13%	$7700	$11,784	$21,000
University of Richmond	ind.	$45,320	$10,270	98%	94%	$41,347	$14,243	$21,825
University of Virginia	pub.	$12,458	$9717	84%	97%	$22,824	—	$21,591
The University of Virginia's College at Wise	pub.	$8509	$9440	97%	44%	$10,026	$7923	$15,033
Virginia Commonwealth University	pub.	$9885	$8748	79%	10%	$11,277	$7356	$28,889
Virginia Intermont College	ind.	$24,642	$7769	100%	16%	$19,642	$12,769	$18,335
Virginia Military Institute	pub.	$13,835	$7733	88%	48%	$14,050	$7518	$22,259
Virginia Polytechnic Institute and State University	pub.	$9187	$7406	69%	16%	$16,600	—	$25,759
Virginia State University	pub.	$7420	$9680	80%	34%	$11,696	$5404	$28,250
Virginia Union University	ind.	$14,630	$7672	95%	5%	$11,765	$10,537	$31,153
Virginia Wesleyan College	ind.	$32,182	$8508	100%	11%	$21,910	$18,780	$36,445
Washington and Lee University	ind.	$43,362	$9450	100%	100%	$44,349	$8463	$23,409

NA = not applicable; NR = not reported; * = includes room and board; † = room only; — = not available.

College Costs At-a-Glance

	Institutional Control ind.=independent; pub.=public	Tuition and Fees	Room and Board	Percent of Eligible Freshmen Receiving Need-Based Gift Awards	Percent of Freshmen Whose Need Was Fully Met	Average Financial Aid Package for Freshmen	Average Net Cost After Aid	Average Indebtedness Upon Graduation
Washington								
Bastyr University	ind.	$21,990	$7050†	NR	NR	NR	NR	NR
DigiPen Institute of Technology	ind.	$26,560	$10,441	100%	NR	$5500	$31,501	$47,500
Eastern Washington University	pub.	$7976	$8412	76%	27%	$12,975	$3413	$23,604
The Evergreen State College	pub.	$8395	$9240	66%	10%	$8012	$9623	$15,706
Gonzaga University	ind.	$33,652	$8730	100%	31%	$24,204	$18,178	$29,776
Northwest University	ind.	NR	NR	98%	14%	$19,612	—	$31,691
Pacific Lutheran University	ind.	$34,740	$10,100	100%	40%	$28,009	$16,831	$31,320
Saint Martin's University	ind.	$29,834	$9660	100%	22%	$23,893	$15,601	$34,235
Seattle Pacific University	ind.	$32,067	$9492	100%	6%	$28,411	$13,148	$28,263
Seattle University	ind.	$34,800	$10,296	89%	8%	$27,375	$17,721	$29,498
University of Puget Sound	ind.	$41,868	$10,780	100%	19%	$28,062	$24,586	$28,923
University of Washington	pub.	$11,305	NR	85%	23%	$17,000	—	$20,800
University of Washington, Bothell	pub.	NR	NR	90%	22%	$14,200	—	$18,559
University of Washington, Tacoma	pub.	$11,902	NR	88%	33%	$14,800	—	$20,700
Washington State University	pub.	$12,300	$10,524	65%	30%	$16,695	$6129	$23,433
Western Washington University	pub.	$8805	$9372	81%	20%	$13,143	$5034	$20,473
Whitman College	ind.	$42,106	$10,560	100%	52%	$31,278	$21,388	$16,797
Whitworth University	ind.	$34,346	$9364	100%	20%	$29,994	$13,716	$23,636
West Virginia								
Fairmont State University	pub.	$5804	$7686	88%	11%	$2727	$10,763	$24,060
Glenville State College	pub.	$5860	$8400	85%	11%	$12,781	$1479	$30,299
Marshall University	pub.	$5930	$8988	79%	31%	$9893	$5025	$26,727
Ohio Valley University	ind.	$18,750	$6900	100%	22%	$14,010	$11,640	$24,868
Shepherd University	pub.	$5834	$8424	68%	25%	$10,971	$3287	$23,940
University of Charleston	ind.	$25,700	$9000	85%	8%	$17,822	$16,878	NR
West Virginia University	pub.	$6090	$8782	54%	30%	$5361	$9511	$27,511
West Virginia University Institute of Technology	pub.	$5558	$8414	92%	33%	$6970	$7002	$13,184
West Virginia Wesleyan College	ind.	$26,794	$7740	100%	32%	$23,523	$11,011	$25,655
Wheeling Jesuit University	ind.	$25,640	$5000	66%	37%	$21,386	$9254	$30,516
Wisconsin								
Alverno College	ind.	$22,126	$7050	100%	NR	$17,696	$11,480	$41,405
Bellin College	ind.	NR	NA	NR	NR	NR	NR	$33,961
Beloit College	ind.	$50,250	$7256	100%	24%	$28,742	$28,764	$27,981
Cardinal Stritch University	ind.	$24,330	$7030	100%	14%	$21,627	$9733	$27,292
Carroll University	ind.	NR	NR	100%	22%	$19,700	—	$35,986
Concordia University Wisconsin	ind.	$23,970	$9050	98%	28%	$20,824	$12,196	$31,897
Edgewood College	ind.	$23,740	$8476	99%	7%	$20,477	$11,739	$23,464
Lakeland College	ind.	$21,242	$7340	98%	10%	$17,862	$10,720	$30,105
Lawrence University	ind.	$40,023	$8247	100%	37%	$31,608	$16,662	$30,724
Marian University	ind.	$23,440	$6140	100%	8%	$16,603	$12,977	$27,000

NA = not applicable; NR = not reported; * = includes room and board; † = room only; — = not available.

College Costs At-a-Glance

	Institutional Control ind.=independent; pub.=public	Tuition and Fees	Room and Board	Percent of Eligible Freshmen Receiving Need-Based Gift Awards	Percent of Freshmen Whose Need Was Fully Met	Average Financial Aid Package for Freshmen	Average Net Cost After Aid	Average Indebtedness Upon Graduation
Marquette University	ind.	$34,640	$10,730	99%	23%	$22,661	$22,709	$34,602
Milwaukee School of Engineering	ind.	$34,470	$8271	100%	10%	$23,772	$18,969	$38,038
Mount Mary College	ind.	$25,098	$7738	100%	15%	$23,232	$9604	$29,618
Northland College	ind.	$29,990	$7510	99%	17%	$32,590	$4910	$24,374
Northland International University	ind.	NR	NR	99%	7%	$9276	—	$11,482
Ripon College	ind.	$31,602	$8815	100%	17%	$27,046	$13,371	$31,216
St. Norbert College	ind.	$30,675	$7813	99%	25%	$25,330	$13,158	$31,331
University of Wisconsin–Eau Claire	pub.	$8691	$6300	80%	28%	$8707	$6284	$23,825
University of Wisconsin–Green Bay	pub.	$7648	$7076	62%	32%	$8339	$6385	$23,650
University of Wisconsin–La Crosse	pub.	$8754	$6000	42%	17%	$6735	$8019	$24,863
University of Wisconsin–Madison	pub.	$10,384	$8080	65%	29%	$12,279	$6185	$24,700
University of Wisconsin–Milwaukee	pub.	$9187	$7945	57%	18%	$7224	$9908	$32,371
University of Wisconsin–Parkside	pub.	$7287	$7082	74%	NR	NR	NR	NR
University of Wisconsin–River Falls	pub.	$7700	$6902	60%	1%	$6159	$8443	$25,557
University of Wisconsin–Stevens Point	pub.	$7505	$6538	53%	58%	$6571	$7472	$24,054
University of Wisconsin–Stout	pub.	$8944	$6054	35%	40%	$10,193	$4805	$29,879
University of Wisconsin–Superior	pub.	$7904	$5992	56%	25%	$11,422	$2474	$26,486
University of Wisconsin–Whitewater	pub.	$7528	$5736	60%	56%	$6926	$6338	$25,147
Wisconsin Lutheran College	ind.	$23,620	$8530	100%	14%	$20,605	$11,545	$25,368
Wyoming								
University of Wyoming	pub.	$4278	$9084	63%	26%	$9259	$4103	$21,241

NA = not applicable; NR = not reported; * = includes room and board; † = room only; — = not available.

Profiles of College
Financial Aid Programs

ABILENE CHRISTIAN UNIVERSITY
Abilene, TX

Tuition & fees: $28,350	Average undergraduate aid package: $17,821

ABOUT THE INSTITUTION Independent Church of Christ, coed. **Awards:** certificates, associate, bachelor's, master's, and doctoral degrees. 73 undergraduate majors. **Total enrollment:** 4,367. Undergraduates: 3,626. Freshmen: 957. Federal methodology is used as a basis for awarding need-based institutional aid.

UNDERGRADUATE EXPENSES for 2013–2014 Application fee: $50. **Comprehensive fee:** $37,150 includes full-time tuition ($28,350) and room and board ($8800). **College room only:** $3980. Full-time tuition and fees vary according to course load. Room and board charges vary according to board plan and housing facility. **Part-time tuition:** $950 per credit. Part-time tuition and fees vary according to course load. **Payment plan:** Tuition prepayment.

FRESHMAN FINANCIAL AID (Fall 2012, est.) 814 applied for aid; of those 82% were deemed to have need. 100% of freshmen with need received aid; of those 30% had need fully met. **Average percent of need met:** 74% (excluding resources awarded to replace EFC). **Average financial aid package:** $20,221 (excluding resources awarded to replace EFC). 30% of all full-time freshmen had no need and received non-need-based gift aid.

UNDERGRADUATE FINANCIAL AID (Fall 2012, est.) 2,663 applied for aid; of those 84% were deemed to have need. 100% of undergraduates with need received aid; of those 25% had need fully met. **Average percent of need met:** 66% (excluding resources awarded to replace EFC). **Average financial aid package:** $17,821 (excluding resources awarded to replace EFC). 32% of all full-time undergraduates had no need and received non-need-based gift aid.

GIFT AID (NEED-BASED) Total amount: $29,758,180 (13% federal, 9% state, 74% institutional, 4% external sources). **Receiving aid:** Freshmen: 70% (668); all full-time undergraduates: 65% (2,217). **Average award:** Freshmen: $16,418; Undergraduates: $14,259. **Scholarships, grants, and awards:** Federal Pell, FSEOG, state, private, college/university gift aid from institutional funds.

GIFT AID (NON-NEED-BASED) Total amount: $10,250,667 (97% institutional, 3% external sources). **Receiving aid:** Freshmen: 69% (664). Undergraduates: 61% (2,082). **Average award:** Freshmen: $10,955. Undergraduates: $8463. **Scholarships, grants, and awards by category:** Academic interests/achievement: agriculture, biological sciences, business, communication, education, English, foreign languages, general academic interests/achievements, mathematics, physical sciences, religion/biblical studies, social sciences. Creative arts/performance: art/fine arts, debating, journalism/publications, music, theater/drama. Special achievements/activities: cheerleading/drum major, leadership. Special characteristics: children of faculty/staff, ethnic background, first-generation college students, local/state students, members of minority groups, out-of-state students, previous college experience, relatives of clergy, religious affiliation. **Tuition waivers:** Full or partial for employees or children of employees.

LOANS Student loans: $24,605,799 (29% need-based, 71% non-need-based). 68% of past graduating class borrowed through all loan programs. Average indebtedness per student: $39,705. **Average need-based loan:** Freshmen: $3522. Undergraduates: $4464. **Parent loans:** $4,480,583 (100% non-need-based). **Programs:** Federal Direct (Subsidized and Unsubsidized Stafford, PLUS), Perkins, state.

WORK-STUDY Federal work-study: Total amount: $619,625; jobs available. **State or other work-study/employment:** Total amount: $525,230 (9% need-based, 91% non-need-based). Part-time jobs available.

ATHLETIC AWARDS Total amount: $3,459,659 (53% need-based, 47% non-need-based).

APPLYING FOR FINANCIAL AID Required financial aid form: FAFSA. **Financial aid deadline (priority):** 3/1. **Notification date:** Continuous beginning 4/1. Students must reply within 3 weeks of notification.

CONTACT Ed Kerestly, Director of Student Financial Services, Abilene Christian University, ACU Box 29007, Abilene, TX 79699-9007, 325-674-2130. E-mail: thedepot@acu.edu. Website: http://www.acu.edu/.

ABRAHAM BALDWIN AGRICULTURAL COLLEGE
Tifton, GA

ABOUT THE INSTITUTION State-supported, coed. 48 undergraduate majors.

GIFT AID (NEED-BASED) Scholarships, grants, and awards: Federal Pell, FSEOG, state, private, college/university gift aid from institutional funds, HOPE Scholarships.

LOANS Programs: Perkins, state.

APPLYING FOR FINANCIAL AID Required financial aid forms: FAFSA, institution's own form.

CONTACT Shawn Thomas, Director of Student Financial Services, Abraham Baldwin Agricultural College, 2802 Moore Highway, ABAC 23, Tifton, GA 31793-2601, 229-391-4910 or toll-free 800-733-3653. Fax: 229-391-4911. E-mail: finaid@abac.edu. Website: http://www.abac.edu/.

ACADEMY COLLEGE
Bloomington, MN

Tuition & fees: N/R	Average undergraduate aid package: N/A

ABOUT THE INSTITUTION Proprietary, coed. 25 undergraduate majors.

GIFT AID (NEED-BASED) Scholarships, grants, and awards: Federal Pell, FSEOG, state, private, college/university gift aid from institutional funds.

LOANS Programs: Federal Direct (Subsidized and Unsubsidized Stafford, PLUS), state, alternative loans.

APPLYING FOR FINANCIAL AID Required financial aid forms: FAFSA, institution's own form, state aid form. **Financial aid deadline:** Continuous. **Notification date:** Continuous.

CONTACT Kellye MacLeod, Director of Financial Aid, Academy College, 1101 East 78th Street, Bloomington, MN 55420, 952-851-0066 or toll-free 800-292-9149. Fax: 952-851-0094. E-mail: finaid@academycollege.edu. Website: http://www.academycollege.edu/.

ACADEMY OF ART UNIVERSITY
San Francisco, CA

Tuition & fees: $23,840	Average undergraduate aid package: $9183

ABOUT THE INSTITUTION Proprietary, coed. **Awards:** certificates, bachelor's, and master's degrees. 31 undergraduate majors. **Total enrollment:** 18,115. Undergraduates: 11,992. Freshmen: 1,240. Federal methodology is used as a basis for awarding need-based institutional aid.

UNDERGRADUATE EXPENSES for 2013–2014 Application fee: $100. **Comprehensive fee:** $37,240 includes full-time tuition ($23,550), mandatory fees ($290), and room and board ($13,400). Full-time tuition and fees vary according to course load. Room and board charges vary according to board plan and housing facility. **Part-time tuition:** $785 per credit. Part-time tuition and fees vary according to course load.

FRESHMAN FINANCIAL AID (Fall 2011) 636 applied for aid; of those 92% were deemed to have need. 98% of freshmen with need received aid; of those .2% had need fully met. **Average percent of need met:** 30% (excluding resources awarded to replace EFC). **Average financial aid package:** $8936 (excluding resources awarded to replace EFC). 1% of all full-time freshmen had no need and received non-need-based gift aid.

UNDERGRADUATE FINANCIAL AID (Fall 2011) 4,028 applied for aid; of those 91% were deemed to have need. 99% of undergraduates with need received aid. **Average percent of need met:** 35% (excluding resources awarded to replace EFC). **Average financial aid package:** $9183 (excluding resources awarded to replace EFC). 1% of all full-time undergraduates had no need and received non-need-based gift aid.

GIFT AID (NEED-BASED) Total amount: $24,285,716 (85% federal, 15% state). **Receiving aid:** Freshmen: 38% (395); all full-time undergraduates: 38% (2,513). **Average award:** Freshmen: $5379; Undergraduates: $5464. **Scholarships, grants, and awards:** Federal Pell, FSEOG, state.

GIFT AID (NON-NEED-BASED) Total amount: $16,735,271 (13% institutional, 87% external sources). **Receiving aid:** Freshmen: 12% (126). Undergraduates: 9% (580). **Average award:** Freshmen: $1110. Undergraduates: $3996.

LOANS Student loans: $125,943,197 (44% need-based, 56% non-need-based). 61% of past graduating class borrowed through all loan programs. Average indebtedness per student: $46,726. **Average need-based loan:** Freshmen: $3231. Undergrad-

uates: '$3936. **Parent loans:** $40,962,265 (100% non-need-based). **Programs:** Federal Direct (Subsidized and Unsubsidized Stafford, PLUS), alternative loans.
WORK-STUDY Federal work-study: Total amount: $398,152; 128 jobs averaging $3111.
ATHLETIC AWARDS Total amount: $3,532,348 (100% non-need-based).
APPLYING FOR FINANCIAL AID Required financial aid forms: FAFSA, institution's own form. **Financial aid deadline:** Continuous. **Notification date:** Continuous. Students must reply within 3 weeks of notification.
CONTACT Mr. Joe Vollaro, Executive Vice President of Financial Aid and Compliance, Academy of Art University, 79 New Montgomery Street, San Francisco, CA 94105-3410, 415-618-6528 or toll-free 800-544-ARTS. *Fax:* 415-618-6273. *E-mail:* jvollaro@academyart.edu.
Website: http://www.academyart.edu/.

ADAMS STATE UNIVERSITY
Alamosa, CO

Tuition & fees (CO res): $6448	Average undergraduate aid package: $12,079

ABOUT THE INSTITUTION State-supported, coed. **Awards:** associate, bachelor's, and master's degrees. 78 undergraduate majors. **Total enrollment:** 3,283. Undergraduates: 2,431. Freshmen: 514. Federal methodology is used as a basis for awarding need-based institutional aid.
UNDERGRADUATE EXPENSES for 2013-2014 Application fee: $30. **Tuition, state resident:** full-time $3816. **Tuition, nonresident:** full-time $14,784. **Required fees:** full-time $2632. Full-time tuition and fees vary according to course load. Part-time tuition and fees vary according to course load. **College room and board:** $7900. **Room only:** $4200. Room and board charges vary according to board plan and housing facility.
FRESHMAN FINANCIAL AID (Fall 2011) 551 applied for aid; of those 84% were deemed to have need. 97% of freshmen with need received aid; of those 2% had need fully met. **Average percent of need met:** 58% (excluding resources awarded to replace EFC). **Average financial aid package:** $11,340 (excluding resources awarded to replace EFC).
UNDERGRADUATE FINANCIAL AID (Fall 2011) 1,878 applied for aid; of those 87% were deemed to have need. 98% of undergraduates with need received aid; of those 1% had need fully met. **Average percent of need met:** 59% (excluding resources awarded to replace EFC). **Average financial aid package:** $12,079 (excluding resources awarded to replace EFC).
GIFT AID (NEED-BASED) Total amount: $12,583,540 (47% federal, 11% state, 31% institutional, 11% external sources). **Receiving aid:** Freshmen: 76% (433); all full-time undergraduates: 75% (1,513). **Average award:** Freshmen: $7717; Undergraduates: $7717. **Scholarships, grants, and awards:** Federal Pell, FSEOG, state, private, college/university gift aid from institutional funds.
GIFT AID (NON-NEED-BASED) Tuition waivers: Full or partial for employees or children of employees, senior citizens.
LOANS Student loans: $11,665,253 (42% need-based, 58% non-need-based). 75% of past graduating class borrowed through all loan programs. *Average indebtedness per student:* $27,785. **Average need-based loan:** Freshmen: $3016. Undergraduates: $3764. **Parent loans:** $1,282,891 (100% non-need-based). **Programs:** Federal Direct (Subsidized and Unsubsidized Stafford, PLUS), Perkins, alternative loans.
WORK-STUDY Federal work-study: Total amount: $239,614; 241 jobs averaging $993. **State or other work-study/employment:** Total amount: $447,450 (57% need-based, 43% non-need-based). 408 part-time jobs averaging $2025.
ATHLETIC AWARDS Total amount: $1,584,279 (100% need-based).
APPLYING FOR FINANCIAL AID Required financial aid form: FAFSA. **Financial aid deadline:** Continuous. **Notification date:** Continuous beginning 3/1.
CONTACT Phil Schroeder, Director of Student Financial Aid, Adams State University, 208 Edgemont Boulevard, Alamosa, CO 81102, 719-587-7306 or toll-free 800-824-6494. *Fax:* 719-587-7366.
Website: http://www.adams.edu/.

ADELPHI UNIVERSITY
Garden City, NY

Tuition & fees: $29,320	Average undergraduate aid package: $19,000

ABOUT THE INSTITUTION Independent, coed. **Awards:** certificates, associate, bachelor's, master's, and doctoral degrees. 47 undergraduate majors. **Total enrollment:** 7,859. Undergraduates: 5,103. Freshmen: 999. Federal methodology is used as a basis for awarding need-based institutional aid.
UNDERGRADUATE EXPENSES for 2013-2014 Application fee: $40. **Comprehensive fee:** $41,220 includes full-time tuition ($27,870), mandatory fees ($1450), and room and board ($11,900). **College room only:** $8420. Full-time tuition and fees vary according to course level, course load, location, program, and student level. Room and board charges vary according to board plan and housing facility. **Part-time tuition:** $860 per credit hour. Part-time tuition and fees vary according to course level, course load, location, program, and student level. **Payment plan:** Tuition prepayment.
FRESHMAN FINANCIAL AID (Fall 2012, est.) 880 applied for aid; of those 85% were deemed to have need. 97% of freshmen with need received aid; of those 1% had need fully met. **Average percent of need met:** 34% (excluding resources awarded to replace EFC). **Average financial aid package:** $19,000 (excluding resources awarded to replace EFC). 20% of all full-time freshmen had no need and received non-need-based gift aid.
UNDERGRADUATE FINANCIAL AID (Fall 2012, est.) 3,654 applied for aid; of those 90% were deemed to have need. 87% of undergraduates with need received aid; of those 1% had need fully met. **Average percent of need met:** 32% (excluding resources awarded to replace EFC). **Average financial aid package:** $19,000 (excluding resources awarded to replace EFC). 20% of all full-time undergraduates had no need and received non-need-based gift aid.
GIFT AID (NEED-BASED) Total amount: $38,858,624 (14% federal, 12% state, 74% institutional). **Receiving aid:** Freshmen: 50% (494); all full-time undergraduates: 44% (1,970). **Average award:** Freshmen: $6837; Undergraduates: $6685. **Scholarships, grants, and awards:** Federal Pell, FSEOG, state, private, college/university gift aid from institutional funds, United Negro College Fund, endowed and restricted scholarships and grants.
GIFT AID (NON-NEED-BASED) Total amount: $13,928,604 (95% institutional, 5% external sources). **Receiving aid:** Freshmen: 66% (661). Undergraduates: 57% (2,567). **Average award:** Freshmen: $13,967. Undergraduates: $11,471. **Scholarships, grants, and awards by category:** Academic interests/achievement: 3,527 awards ($33,064,801 total): business, communication, computer science, foreign languages, general academic interests/achievements, mathematics, physical sciences. Creative arts/performance: 111 awards ($849,625 total): art/fine arts, cinema/film/broadcasting, dance, music, performing arts, theater/drama. Special achievements/activities: 1,475 awards ($1,276,500 total): community service, general special achievements/activities, leadership, memberships. Special characteristics: 454 awards ($2,818,394 total): children and siblings of alumni, children of faculty/staff, veterans. **Tuition waivers:** Full or partial for children of alumni, employees or children of employees, senior citizens. **ROTC:** Army cooperative, Air Force cooperative.
LOANS Student loans: $27,042,871 (55% need-based, 45% non-need-based). 72% of past graduating class borrowed through all loan programs. *Average indebtedness per student:* $35,429. **Average need-based loan:** Freshmen: $4262. Undergraduates: $4581. **Parent loans:** $7,908,688 (86% need-based, 14% non-need-based). **Programs:** Federal Direct (Subsidized and Unsubsidized Stafford, PLUS), Perkins, Federal Nursing, New York HELP Program, private loans.
WORK-STUDY Federal work-study: Total amount: $1,700,863; 343 jobs averaging $1680. **State or other work-study/employment:** Total amount: $2,207,086 (100% non-need-based). 996 part-time jobs averaging $2216.
ATHLETIC AWARDS Total amount: $3,268,325 (57% need-based, 43% non-need-based).
APPLYING FOR FINANCIAL AID Required financial aid forms: FAFSA, state aid form. **Financial aid deadline (priority):** 3/1. **Notification date:** Continuous beginning 3/1.
CONTACT Ms. Sheryl Mihopulos, Director of Student Financial Services, Adelphi University, 1 South Avenue, PO Box 701, Garden City, NY 11530, 516-877-3365 or toll-free 800-ADELPHI. *Fax:* 516-877-3380. *E-mail:* mihopulos@adelphi.edu.
Website: http://www.adelphi.edu/.

ADRIAN COLLEGE
Adrian, MI

Tuition & fees: $29,156	Average undergraduate aid package: $24,428

ABOUT THE INSTITUTION Independent United Methodist Church, coed. *Awards:* associate, bachelor's, and master's degrees. 46 undergraduate majors. *Total enrollment:* 1,678. Undergraduates: 461. Freshmen: 461. Both federal and institutional methodology are used as a basis for awarding need-based institutional aid.

UNDERGRADUATE EXPENSES for 2013–2014 *Comprehensive fee:* $37,952 includes full-time tuition ($28,606), mandatory fees ($550), and room and board ($8796). *College room only:* $4226. Room and board charges vary according to board plan and housing facility.

FRESHMAN FINANCIAL AID (Fall 2012, est.) 545 applied for aid; of those 95% were deemed to have need. 100% of freshmen with need received aid; of those 6% had need fully met. *Average percent of need met:* 74% (excluding resources awarded to replace EFC). *Average financial aid package:* $25,275 (excluding resources awarded to replace EFC). 8% of all full-time freshmen had no need and received non-need-based gift aid.

UNDERGRADUATE FINANCIAL AID (Fall 2012, est.) 1,581 applied for aid; of those 95% were deemed to have need. 100% of undergraduates with need received aid; of those 8% had need fully met. *Average percent of need met:* 74% (excluding resources awarded to replace EFC). *Average financial aid package:* $24,428 (excluding resources awarded to replace EFC). 12% of all full-time undergraduates had no need and received non-need-based gift aid.

GIFT AID (NEED-BASED) *Total amount:* $29,062,724 (11% federal, 5% state, 81% institutional, 3% external sources). *Receiving aid:* Freshmen: 89% (518); all full-time undergraduates: 86% (1,489). *Average award:* Freshmen: $21,093; Undergraduates: $19,428. *Scholarships, grants, and awards:* Federal Pell, FSEOG, state, private, college/university gift aid from institutional funds.

GIFT AID (NON-NEED-BASED) *Total amount:* $3,338,247 (95% institutional, 5% external sources). *Receiving aid:* Freshmen: 4% (26). Undergraduates: 5% (86). *Average award:* Freshmen: $12,708. Undergraduates: $12,964. *Scholarships, grants, and awards by category:* Academic interests/achievement: 1,457 awards ($8,314,567 total): business, general academic interests/achievements. *Creative arts/performance:* 227 awards ($539,692 total): art/fine arts, music, theater/drama. *Special achievements/activities:* 35 awards ($74,250 total): religious involvement. *Special characteristics:* 305 awards ($4,017,139 total): children and siblings of alumni, children of faculty/staff, children of union members/company employees, first-generation college students, general special characteristics, international students, religious affiliation, veterans, veterans' children. *ROTC:* Army cooperative.

LOANS *Student loans:* $13,881,561 (79% need-based, 21% non-need-based). 75% of past graduating class borrowed through all loan programs. *Average indebtedness per student:* $30,645. *Average need-based loan:* Freshmen: $3108. Undergraduates: $4104. *Parent loans:* $3,341,624 (36% need-based, 64% non-need-based). *Programs:* Federal Direct (Subsidized and Unsubsidized Stafford, PLUS), Perkins.

WORK-STUDY *Federal work-study:* Total amount: $1,815,757; 1,155 jobs averaging $1800. *State or other work-study/employment:* Total amount: $105,300 (100% non-need-based). 72 part-time jobs averaging $1800.

APPLYING FOR FINANCIAL AID *Required financial aid form:* FAFSA. *Financial aid deadline (priority):* 3/1. *Notification date:* Continuous beginning 3/15. Students must reply by 5/1 or within 2 weeks of notification.

CONTACT Mr. Andrew Spohn, Director of Financial Aid, Adrian College, 110 South Madison Street, Adrian, MI 49221-2575, 517-265-5161 Ext. 4306 or toll-free 800-877-2246. *Fax:* 517-264-3394. *E-mail:* aspohn@adrian.edu. *Website:* http://www.adrian.edu/.

ADVENTIST UNIVERSITY OF HEALTH SCIENCES
Orlando, FL

Tuition & fees: N/R	Average undergraduate aid package: N/A

ABOUT THE INSTITUTION Independent, coed. *Awards:* associate, bachelor's, and master's degrees. 8 undergraduate majors. *Total enrollment:* 2,671. Undergraduates: 2,576. Freshmen: 96. Federal methodology is used as a basis for awarding need-based institutional aid.

GIFT AID (NEED-BASED) *Total amount:* $3,254,757 (89% federal, 6% state, 2% institutional, 3% external sources). *Scholarships, grants, and awards:* Federal Pell, FSEOG, state, private, college/university gift aid from institutional funds.

GIFT AID (NON-NEED-BASED) *Total amount:* $2,207,380 (58% state, 3% institutional, 39% external sources). *ROTC:* Air Force cooperative.

LOANS *Student loans:* $15,026,501 (34% need-based, 66% non-need-based). *Parent loans:* $564,830 (100% non-need-based). *Programs:* Federal Direct (Subsidized and Unsubsidized Stafford, PLUS), private loans.

APPLYING FOR FINANCIAL AID *Required financial aid forms:* FAFSA, institution's own form. *Financial aid deadline:* 7/22 (priority: 4/10). *Notification date:* Continuous. Students must reply within 2 weeks of notification.

CONTACT Starr Bender, Director of Financial Aid, Adventist University of Health Sciences, 671 Winyah Drive, Orlando, FL 32803, 407-303-6963 or toll-free 800-500-7747. *Fax:* 407-303-7680. *E-mail:* starr.bender@adu.edu. *Website:* http://www.adu.edu/.

AGNES SCOTT COLLEGE
Decatur, GA

ABOUT THE INSTITUTION Independent Presbyterian Church (U.S.A.), undergraduate: women only; graduate: coed. *Awards:* bachelor's degrees. 35 undergraduate majors. *Total enrollment:* 885. Undergraduates: 885. Freshmen: 232.

GIFT AID (NEED-BASED) *Scholarships, grants, and awards:* Federal Pell, FSEOG, state, private, college/university gift aid from institutional funds.

GIFT AID (NON-NEED-BASED) *Scholarships, grants, and awards by category:* Academic interests/achievement: general academic interests/achievements. *Creative arts/performance:* music. *Special achievements/activities:* community service, leadership. *Special characteristics:* adult students, children of educators, children of faculty/staff, international students, local/state students, religious affiliation, veterans, veterans' children.

LOANS *Programs:* Federal Direct (Subsidized and Unsubsidized Stafford, PLUS).

WORK-STUDY *Federal work-study:* Total amount: $658,057; 292 jobs averaging $2300. *State or other work-study/employment:* Total amount: $142,600 (2% need-based, 98% non-need-based). 61 part-time jobs averaging $2300.

APPLYING FOR FINANCIAL AID *Required financial aid forms:* FAFSA, federal income tax form(s).

CONTACT Patrick Bonones, Director of Financial Aid, Agnes Scott College, 141 East College Avenue, Decatur, GA 30030-3797, 404-471-6395 or toll-free 800-868-8602. *Fax:* 404-471-6159. *E-mail:* finaid@agnesscott.edu. *Website:* http://www.agnesscott.edu/.

AIB COLLEGE OF BUSINESS
Des Moines, IA

CONTACT Financial Aid Office, AIB College of Business, 2500 Fleur Drive, Des Moines, IA 50321-1799, 515-244-4221 or toll-free 800-444-1921. *Website:* http://www.aib.edu/.

ALABAMA AGRICULTURAL AND MECHANICAL UNIVERSITY
Huntsville, AL

ABOUT THE INSTITUTION State-supported, coed. 36 undergraduate majors.

GIFT AID (NEED-BASED) *Scholarships, grants, and awards:* Federal Pell, FSEOG, state, private, college/university gift aid from institutional funds.

GIFT AID (NON-NEED-BASED) *Scholarships, grants, and awards by category:* Academic interests/achievement: agriculture, biological sciences, engineering/technologies, general academic interests/achievements, health fields, mathematics, military science, physical sciences, social sciences. *Creative arts/performance:* art/fine arts, music.

LOANS *Programs:* Federal Direct (Subsidized and Unsubsidized Stafford, PLUS), Perkins, Sallie Mae Smart Option Loans.

WORK-STUDY *Federal work-study:* Total amount: $228,424; 81 jobs averaging $2820.

APPLYING FOR FINANCIAL AID *Required financial aid form:* FAFSA.

CONTACT Ms. Deborah Gordon, Financial Aid Officer, Alabama Agricultural and Mechanical University, PO BOX 907, Huntsville, AL 35762, 256-372-4853 or toll-free 800-553-0816. *Fax:* 256-372-5407. *E-mail:* deborah.gordon@aamu.edu. *Website:* http://www.aamu.edu/.

ALABAMA STATE UNIVERSITY
Montgomery, AL

Tuition & fees (AL res): $6312	Average undergraduate aid package: $17,887

ABOUT THE INSTITUTION State-supported, coed. *Awards:* certificates, bachelor's, master's, and doctoral degrees. 31 undergraduate majors. *Total enrollment:* 5,816. Undergraduates: 5,130. Freshmen: 1,414. Federal methodology is used as a basis for awarding need-based institutional aid.

UNDERGRADUATE EXPENSES for 2013–2014 *Application fee:* $25. *One-time required fee:* $150. *Tuition, state resident:* full-time $6312; part-time $263 per credit hour. *Tuition, nonresident:* full-time $12,624; part-time $526 per credit hour. *Required fees:* $213 per term. *College room and board:* $5366. Room and board charges vary according to board plan and housing facility.

FRESHMAN FINANCIAL AID (Fall 2012, est.) 1,426 applied for aid; of those 92% were deemed to have need. 95% of freshmen with need received aid; of those 26% had need fully met. *Average percent of need met:* 78% (excluding resources awarded to replace EFC). *Average financial aid package:* $14,611 (excluding resources awarded to replace EFC). 2% of all full-time freshmen had no need and received non-need-based gift aid.

UNDERGRADUATE FINANCIAL AID (Fall 2012, est.) 4,586 applied for aid; of those 100% were deemed to have need. 100% of undergraduates with need received aid; of those 39% had need fully met. *Average percent of need met:* 84% (excluding resources awarded to replace EFC). *Average financial aid package:* $17,887 (excluding resources awarded to replace EFC). 1% of all full-time undergraduates had no need and received non-need-based gift aid.

GIFT AID (NEED-BASED) *Total amount:* $25,066,615 (80% federal, 20% institutional). *Receiving aid:* Freshmen: 75% (1,083); all full-time undergraduates: 84% (3,941). *Average award:* Freshmen: $5382; Undergraduates: $4897. *Scholarships, grants, and awards:* Federal Pell, FSEOG, state, private, college/university gift aid from institutional funds, United Negro College Fund.

GIFT AID (NON-NEED-BASED) *Total amount:* $4,531,532 (4% federal, 61% state, 18% institutional, 17% external sources). *Receiving aid:* Freshmen: 28% (409). Undergraduates: 38% (1,782). *Average award:* Freshmen: $9062. Undergraduates: $9552. *Scholarships, grants, and awards by category:* Academic interests/achievement: general academic interests/achievements. Creative arts/performance: general creative arts/performance, music, theater/drama. Special achievements/activities: leadership. Special characteristics: general special characteristics, members of minority groups. *Tuition waivers:* Full or partial for employees or children of employees. *ROTC:* Army cooperative, Air Force.

LOANS *Student loans:* $35,762,970 (44% need-based, 56% non-need-based). 89% of past graduating class borrowed through all loan programs. *Average indebtedness per student:* $29,795. *Average need-based loan:* Freshmen: $3425. Undergraduates: $3791. *Parent loans:* $4,995,868 (80% need-based, 20% non-need-based). *Programs:* Federal Direct (Subsidized and Unsubsidized Stafford, PLUS), Perkins.

WORK-STUDY *Federal work-study:* Total amount: $1,505,000; jobs available. *State or other work-study/employment:* Total amount: $522,827 (100% non-need-based). Part-time jobs available.

ATHLETIC AWARDS Total amount: $3,573,597 (94% need-based, 6% non-need-based).

APPLYING FOR FINANCIAL AID *Required financial aid form:* FAFSA. *Financial aid deadline (priority):* 4/1. *Notification date:* Continuous beginning 5/1.

CONTACT Mrs. Dorenda A. Adams, Director of Financial Aid, Alabama State University, PO Box 271, Montgomery, AL 36101-0271, 334-229-4323 or toll-free 800-253-5037. *Fax:* 334-299-4924. *E-mail:* dadams@alasu.edu. *Website:* http://www.alasu.edu/.

ALASKA BIBLE COLLEGE
Glennallen, AK

Tuition & fees: $9390	Average undergraduate aid package: N/A

ABOUT THE INSTITUTION Independent nondenominational, coed. *Awards:* certificates, associate, and bachelor's degrees. 1 undergraduate major. *Total enrollment:* 34. Undergraduates: 34. Freshmen: 11. Institutional methodology is used as a basis for awarding need-based institutional aid.

UNDERGRADUATE EXPENSES for 2013–2014 *Application fee:* $35. *Comprehensive fee:* $14,790 includes full-time tuition ($9000), mandatory fees ($390), and room and board ($5400). Room and board charges vary according to housing facility. *Part-time tuition:* $375 per credit.

GIFT AID (NEED-BASED) *Total amount:* $121,485 (99% federal, 1% institutional). *Scholarships, grants, and awards:* Federal Pell, FSEOG, private, college/university gift aid from institutional funds.

GIFT AID (NON-NEED-BASED) *Total amount:* $83,055 (59% federal, 23% state, 5% institutional, 13% external sources). *Scholarships, grants, and awards by category:* Academic interests/achievement: general academic interests/achievements, religion/biblical studies. Creative arts/performance: music. Special achievements/activities: religious involvement. Special characteristics: children of faculty/staff, local/state students, married students, religious affiliation, spouses of current students. *Tuition waivers:* Full or partial for employees or children of employees.

LOANS *Programs:* state.

WORK-STUDY *State or other work-study/employment:* Total amount: $15,662 (100% need-based). Part-time jobs available.

APPLYING FOR FINANCIAL AID *Required financial aid form:* institution's own form. *Financial aid deadline:* 7/1. *Notification date:* 8/1. Students must reply within 2 weeks of notification.

CONTACT Jared Palmer, Financial Aid Coordinator, Alaska Bible College, PO Box 289, Glennallen, AK 99588-0289, 907-822-3201 Ext. 225 or toll-free 800-478-7884. *Fax:* 907-822-5027. *E-mail:* jpalmer@akbible.edu. *Website:* http://www.akbible.edu/.

ALASKA PACIFIC UNIVERSITY
Anchorage, AK

Tuition & fees: $29,880	Average undergraduate aid package: $11,770

ABOUT THE INSTITUTION Independent, coed. *Awards:* certificates, associate, bachelor's, master's, and doctoral degrees. 15 undergraduate majors. *Total enrollment:* 693. Undergraduates: 436. Freshmen: 29. Federal methodology is used as a basis for awarding need-based institutional aid.

UNDERGRADUATE EXPENSES for 2013–2014 *Application fee:* $25. *Comprehensive fee:* $39,180 includes full-time tuition ($29,700), mandatory fees ($180), and room and board ($9300). *College room only:* $4400. Full-time tuition and fees vary according to course load, degree level, program, and reciprocity agreements. Room and board charges vary according to board plan and housing facility. *Part-time tuition:* $1240 per semester hour. Part-time tuition and fees vary according to course load, degree level, and program.

FRESHMAN FINANCIAL AID (Fall 2012, est.) 28 applied for aid; of those 100% were deemed to have need. 100% of freshmen with need received aid. *Average percent of need met:* 79% (excluding resources awarded to replace EFC). *Average financial aid package:* $11,861 (excluding resources awarded to replace EFC).

UNDERGRADUATE FINANCIAL AID (Fall 2012, est.) 290 applied for aid; of those 70% were deemed to have need. 100% of undergraduates with need received aid. *Average percent of need met:* 78% (excluding resources awarded to replace EFC). *Average financial aid package:* $11,770 (excluding resources awarded to replace EFC). 30% of all full-time undergraduates had no need and received non-need-based gift aid.

GIFT AID (NEED-BASED) *Total amount:* $888,746 (53% federal, 3% state, 28% institutional, 16% external sources). *Receiving aid:* Freshmen: 46% (13); all full-time undergraduates: 44% (127). *Average award:* Freshmen: $2540; Undergraduates: $2190. *Scholarships, grants, and awards:* Federal Pell, FSEOG, state, private, college/university gift aid from institutional funds, Bureau of Indian Affairs Grants, Yellow Ribbon Grant Program, Native Alaskan Scholarships.

GIFT AID (NON-NEED-BASED) *Total amount:* $2,883,830 (90% institutional, 10% external sources). *Receiving aid:* Freshmen: 46% (13). Undergraduates: 63% (184). *Average award:* Undergraduates: $4500. *Scholarships, grants, and awards by category: Academic interests/achievement:* biological sciences, business, communication, education, general academic interests/achievements, health fields, humanities, mathematics, physical sciences, religion/biblical studies, social sciences. *Creative arts/performance:* art/fine arts, journalism/publications, music, theater/drama. *Special achievements/activities:* community service, general special achievements/activities, leadership, religious involvement. *Special characteristics:* children and siblings of alumni, children of faculty/staff, ethnic background, general special characteristics, international students, local/state students, members of minority groups, out-of-state students, previous college experience, religious affiliation. *Tuition waivers:* Full or partial for employees or children of employees. *ROTC:* Army cooperative, Air Force cooperative.

LOANS *Student loans:* $3,809,999 (22% need-based, 78% non-need-based). 76% of past graduating class borrowed through all loan programs. *Average indebtedness per student:* $12,119. *Average need-based loan:* Freshmen: $1772. Undergraduates: $2274. *Parent loans:* $349,537 (100% non-need-based). *Programs:* Federal Direct (Subsidized and Unsubsidized Stafford, PLUS), state, alternative loans.

WORK-STUDY *Federal work-study:* Total amount: $39,056; 35 jobs averaging $1116. *State or other work-study/employment:* Total amount: $80,800 (100% non-need-based). 29 part-time jobs averaging $3107.

APPLYING FOR FINANCIAL AID *Required financial aid form:* FAFSA. *Financial aid deadline (priority):* 4/15. *Notification date:* Continuous beginning 2/1. Students must reply by 2/1 or within 4 weeks of notification.

CONTACT Mr. Phong Moua, Director of Student Financial Services, Alaska Pacific University, 4101 University Drive, Grant Hall RM 125, Anchorage, AK 99508-4672, 907-564-8342 or toll-free 800-252-7528. *Fax:* 907-564-8372. *E-mail:* pmoua@alaskapacific.edu.
Website: http://www.alaskapacific.edu/.

ALBANY COLLEGE OF PHARMACY AND HEALTH SCIENCES
Albany, NY

Tuition & fees: $27,630	Average undergraduate aid package: $12,568

ABOUT THE INSTITUTION Independent, coed. *Awards:* bachelor's, master's, and doctoral degrees. 7 undergraduate majors. *Total enrollment:* 1,701. Undergraduates: 1,072. Freshmen: 247. Federal methodology is used as a basis for awarding need-based institutional aid.

UNDERGRADUATE EXPENSES for 2013–2014 *Application fee:* $75. *Comprehensive fee:* $37,390 includes full-time tuition ($26,900), mandatory fees ($730), and room and board ($9760). *College room only:* $6400. Full-time tuition and fees vary according to degree level, program, and student level. Room and board charges vary according to board plan, housing facility, and location. *Part-time tuition:* $900 per credit hour. Part-time tuition and fees vary according to degree level, program, and student level.

FRESHMAN FINANCIAL AID (Fall 2012, est.) 238 applied for aid; of those 90% were deemed to have need. 99% of freshmen with need received aid; of those 14% had need fully met. *Average percent of need met:* 55% (excluding resources awarded to replace EFC). *Average financial aid package:* $15,372 (excluding resources awarded to replace EFC). 12% of all full-time freshmen had no need and received non-need-based gift aid.

UNDERGRADUATE FINANCIAL AID (Fall 2012, est.) 999 applied for aid; of those 90% were deemed to have need. 98% of undergraduates with need received aid; of those 9% had need fully met. *Average percent of need met:* 39% (excluding resources awarded to replace EFC). *Average financial aid package:* $12,568 (excluding resources awarded to replace EFC). 11% of all full-time undergraduates had no need and received non-need-based gift aid.

GIFT AID (NEED-BASED) *Total amount:* $7,339,387 (15% federal, 11% state, 69% institutional, 5% external sources). *Receiving aid:* Freshmen: 83% (208); all full-time undergraduates: 70% (755). *Average award:* Freshmen: $12,120; Undergraduates: $9719. *Scholarships, grants, and awards:* Federal Pell, FSEOG, state, private, college/university gift aid from institutional funds.

GIFT AID (NON-NEED-BASED) *Total amount:* $1,377,652 (2% state, 89% institutional, 9% external sources). *Receiving aid:* Freshmen: 8% (20). Undergraduates: 5% (56). *Average award:* Freshmen: $10,146. Undergraduates: $8338. *Scholarships, grants, and awards by category: Academic interests/achievement:* general academic interests/achievements. *Tuition waivers:* Full or partial for employees or children of employees.

LOANS *Student loans:* $16,127,794 (78% need-based, 22% non-need-based). 61% of past graduating class borrowed through all loan programs. *Average indebtedness per student:* $29,160. *Average need-based loan:* Freshmen: $3826. Undergraduates: $4615. *Parent loans:* $3,457,024 (63% need-based, 37% non-need-based). *Programs:* Federal Direct (Subsidized and Unsubsidized Stafford, PLUS), Perkins, state, Health Professions Student Loans (HPSL).

WORK-STUDY *Federal work-study:* Total amount: $102,373; jobs available. *State or other work-study/employment:* Total amount: $11,520 (31% need-based, 69% non-need-based). Part-time jobs available.

ATHLETIC AWARDS Total amount: $500 (100% need-based).

APPLYING FOR FINANCIAL AID *Required financial aid forms:* FAFSA, CSS Financial Aid PROFILE. *Financial aid deadline:* 5/1 (priority: 2/1). *Notification date:* 3/15. Students must reply by 4/1 or within 2 weeks of notification.

CONTACT Kathleen Montague, Director of Financial Aid, Albany College of Pharmacy and Health Sciences, 106 New Scotland Avenue, Albany, NY 12208-3425, 518-694-7256 or toll-free 888-203-8010. *Fax:* 518-694-7322. *E-mail:* financial_aid@acphs.edu .
Website: http://www.acphs.edu/.

ALBANY STATE UNIVERSITY
Albany, GA

ABOUT THE INSTITUTION State-supported, coed. *Awards:* certificates, bachelor's, and master's degrees. 33 undergraduate majors. *Total enrollment:* 4,663. Undergraduates: 4,187. Freshmen: 1,062.

GIFT AID (NEED-BASED) *Scholarships, grants, and awards:* Federal Pell, FSEOG, state, private, college/university gift aid from institutional funds, Federal Nursing, Thurgood Marshall Scholarship Fund.

GIFT AID (NON-NEED-BASED) *Scholarships, grants, and awards by category: Academic interests/achievement:* biological sciences, computer science, education, general academic interests/achievements, health fields, mathematics, social sciences. *Creative arts/performance:* music.

LOANS *Programs:* Federal Direct (Subsidized and Unsubsidized Stafford, PLUS), Perkins, Federal Nursing, state.

WORK-STUDY *Federal work-study:* Total amount: $423,571; jobs available. *State or other work-study/employment:* Total amount: $383,000 (100% non-need-based). Part-time jobs available.

APPLYING FOR FINANCIAL AID *Required financial aid forms:* FAFSA, state aid form.

CONTACT Vickie Grant, Research Coordinator, Albany State University, 504 College Drive, Albany, GA 31705-2717, 912-430-2732 or toll-free 866-579-3498. *Fax:* 912-430-3936. *E-mail:* vickie.grant@asurams.edu.
Website: http://www.asurams.edu/.

ALBERTUS MAGNUS COLLEGE
New Haven, CT

CONTACT Andrew Foster, Director of Financial Aid, Albertus Magnus College, 700 Prospect Street, New Haven, CT 06511-1189, 203-773-8508 or toll-free 800-578-9160. *Fax:* 203-773-8972. *E-mail:* financial_aid@albertus.edu.
Website: http://www.albertus.edu/.

ALBION COLLEGE
Albion, MI

Tuition & fees: $34,194	Average undergraduate aid package: $26,466

ABOUT THE INSTITUTION Independent Methodist, coed. *Awards:* bachelor's degrees. 58 undergraduate majors. *Total enrollment:* 1,382. Undergraduates: 1,382. Freshmen: 360. Federal methodology is used as a basis for awarding need-based institutional aid.

UNDERGRADUATE EXPENSES for 2013–2014 *One-time required fee:* $185. *Comprehensive fee:* $43,884 includes full-time tuition ($33,600), mandatory fees ($594), and room and board ($9690). *College room only:* $4740. Full-time tuition and fees vary according to course load. Room and board charges vary according to board plan and housing facility. *Part-time tuition:* $1430 per credit hour. *Part-time fees:* $297 per term. Part-time tuition and fees vary according to course load.

FRESHMAN FINANCIAL AID (Fall 2012, est.) 310 applied for aid; of those 86% were deemed to have need. 100% of freshmen with need received aid; of those 19% had need fully met. *Average percent of need met:* 81% (excluding resources awarded to replace EFC). *Average financial aid package:* $26,742 (excluding resources awarded to replace EFC). 24% of all full-time freshmen had no need and received non-need-based gift aid.

UNDERGRADUATE FINANCIAL AID (Fall 2012, est.) 1,063 applied for aid; of those 89% were deemed to have need. 100% of undergraduates with need received aid; of those 20% had need fully met. *Average percent of need met:* 80% (excluding resources awarded to replace EFC). *Average financial aid package:* $26,466 (excluding resources awarded to replace EFC). 29% of all full-time undergraduates had no need and received non-need-based gift aid.

GIFT AID (NEED-BASED) *Total amount:* $19,990,931 (7% federal, 5% state, 86% institutional, 2% external sources). *Receiving aid:* Freshmen: 74% (268); all full-time undergraduates: 70% (948). *Average award:* Freshmen: $21,465; Undergraduates: $21,488. *Scholarships, grants, and awards:* Federal Pell, FSEOG, state, private, college/university gift aid from institutional funds.

GIFT AID (NON-NEED-BASED) *Total amount:* $6,808,258 (99% institutional, 1% external sources). *Receiving aid:* Freshmen: 66% (237). Undergraduates: 63% (857). *Average award:* Freshmen: $16,731. Undergraduates: $15,585. *Scholarships, grants, and awards by category:* Academic interests/achievement: 1,103 awards ($16,648,422 total): business, communication, general academic interests/achievements, mathematics. *Creative arts/performance:* 77 awards ($84,550 total): art/fine arts, dance, music, performing arts, theater/drama. *Special characteristics:* 153 awards ($233,550 total): children and siblings of alumni, relatives of clergy. *Tuition waivers:* Full or partial for employees or children of employees.

LOANS *Student loans:* $10,340,310 (41% need-based, 59% non-need-based). 62% of past graduating class borrowed through all loan programs. *Average indebtedness per student:* $36,029. *Average need-based loan:* Freshmen: $5392. Undergraduates: $5296. *Parent loans:* $2,702,100 (100% non-need-based). *Programs:* Federal Direct (Subsidized and Unsubsidized Stafford, PLUS), Perkins.

WORK-STUDY *Federal work-study:* Total amount: $454,516; 401 jobs averaging $1094.

APPLYING FOR FINANCIAL AID *Required financial aid form:* FAFSA. *Financial aid deadline (priority):* 3/1. *Notification date:* Continuous beginning 3/15.

CONTACT Ms. Ann Whitmer, Director of Financial Aid, Albion College, Kellogg Center Box 4670, Albion, MI 49224-1831, 517-629-0440 or toll-free 800-858-6770. *Fax:* 517-629-0581. *E-mail:* financialaid@albion.edu. *Website:* http://www.albion.edu/.

ALBRIGHT COLLEGE
Reading, PA

Tuition & fees: $36,660	Average undergraduate aid package: $27,673

ABOUT THE INSTITUTION Independent United Methodist Church, coed. *Awards:* certificates, bachelor's, and master's degrees. 42 undergraduate majors.

Total enrollment: 1,690. Undergraduates: 1,625. Freshmen: 410. Federal methodology is used as a basis for awarding need-based institutional aid.

UNDERGRADUATE EXPENSES for 2013–2014 *Application fee:* $25. *Comprehensive fee:* $46,660 includes full-time tuition ($35,860), mandatory fees ($800), and room and board ($10,000). *College room only:* $5550. Full-time tuition and fees vary according to degree level. Room and board charges vary according to board plan and housing facility. *Part-time tuition:* $4483 per course. Part-time tuition and fees vary according to degree level.

FRESHMAN FINANCIAL AID (Fall 2012, est.) 381 applied for aid; of those 94% were deemed to have need. 100% of freshmen with need received aid; of those 11% had need fully met. *Average percent of need met:* 78% (excluding resources awarded to replace EFC). *Average financial aid package:* $29,826 (excluding resources awarded to replace EFC). 6% of all full-time freshmen had no need and received non-need-based gift aid.

UNDERGRADUATE FINANCIAL AID (Fall 2012, est.) 1,452 applied for aid; of those 94% were deemed to have need. 100% of undergraduates with need received aid; of those 15% had need fully met. *Average percent of need met:* 76% (excluding resources awarded to replace EFC). *Average financial aid package:* $27,673 (excluding resources awarded to replace EFC). 8% of all full-time undergraduates had no need and received non-need-based gift aid.

GIFT AID (NEED-BASED) *Total amount:* $30,381,121 (12% federal, 7% state, 75% institutional, 6% external sources). *Receiving aid:* Freshmen: 87% (358); all full-time undergraduates: 86% (1,362). *Average award:* Freshmen: $24,441; Undergraduates: $22,306. *Scholarships, grants, and awards:* Federal Pell, FSEOG, state, private, college/university gift aid from institutional funds, Academic Competitiveness Grants, National SMART Grants.

GIFT AID (NON-NEED-BASED) *Total amount:* $2,829,467 (87% institutional, 13% external sources). *Receiving aid:* Freshmen: 6% (25). Undergraduates: 8% (132). *Average award:* Freshmen: $10,642. Undergraduates: $13,251. *Scholarships, grants, and awards by category:* Creative arts/performance: art/fine arts, journalism/publications, music, theater/drama. *Special achievements/activities:* general special achievements/activities, memberships, religious involvement. *Special characteristics:* children and siblings of alumni, ethnic background, siblings of current students. *Tuition waivers:* Full or partial for employees or children of employees, adult students, senior citizens. *ROTC:* Army cooperative.

LOANS *Student loans:* $14,254,732 (74% need-based, 26% non-need-based). 82% of past graduating class borrowed through all loan programs. *Average indebtedness per student:* $27,051. *Average need-based loan:* Freshmen: $4376. Undergraduates: $4633. *Parent loans:* $4,141,679 (43% need-based, 57% non-need-based). *Programs:* Federal Direct (Subsidized and Unsubsidized Stafford, PLUS), Perkins, private loans.

WORK-STUDY *Federal work-study:* Total amount: $1,661,184; jobs available. *State or other work-study/employment:* Total amount: $430,057 (14% need-based, 86% non-need-based). Part-time jobs available.

APPLYING FOR FINANCIAL AID *Required financial aid forms:* FAFSA, CSS Financial Aid PROFILE, state aid form. *Financial aid deadline:* Continuous. *Notification date:* Continuous beginning 3/15. Students must reply by 5/1 or within 2 weeks of notification.

CONTACT Chris Hanlon, Director of Financial Aid, Albright College, PO Box 15234, Reading, PA 19612-5234, 610-921-7515 or toll-free 800-252-1856. *Fax:* 610-921-7729. *E-mail:* chanlon@alb.edu. *Website:* http://www.albright.edu/.

ALCORN STATE UNIVERSITY
Alcorn State, MS

Tuition & fees (MS res): $5724	Average undergraduate aid package: $14,832

ABOUT THE INSTITUTION State-supported, coed. *Awards:* certificates, associate, bachelor's and master's degrees. 26 undergraduate majors. *Total enrollment:* 3,950. Undergraduates: 3,208. Freshmen: 581. Both federal and institutional methodology are used as a basis for awarding need-based institutional aid.

UNDERGRADUATE EXPENSES for 2013–2014 *Tuition, state resident:* full-time $5724; part-time $238 per credit hour. *Tuition, nonresident:* full-time $14,162; part-time $586 per credit hour. Full-time tuition and fees vary according to course load. Part-time tuition and fees vary according to course load. *College room and board:* $7999. Room and board charges vary according to housing facility.

FRESHMAN FINANCIAL AID (Fall 2012, est.) 563 applied for aid; of those 96% were deemed to have need. 100% of freshmen with need received aid; of those 10% had need fully met. *Average percent of need met:* 49% (excluding resources awarded to replace EFC). *Average financial aid package:* $14,958 (excluding resources awarded to replace EFC). 32% of all full-time freshmen had no need and received non-need-based gift aid.
UNDERGRADUATE FINANCIAL AID (Fall 2012, est.) 1,332 applied for aid; of those 98% were deemed to have need. 100% of undergraduates with need received aid; of those 8% had need fully met. *Average percent of need met:* 49% (excluding resources awarded to replace EFC). *Average financial aid package:* $14,832 (excluding resources awarded to replace EFC). 19% of all full-time undergraduates had no need and received non-need-based gift aid.
GIFT AID (NEED-BASED) *Total amount:* $18,242,947 (74% federal, 1% state, 25% institutional). *Receiving aid:* Freshmen: 91% (515); all full-time undergraduates: 42% (1,189). *Average award:* Freshmen: $5629; Undergraduates: $5405. *Scholarships, grants, and awards:* Federal Pell, FSEOG, state, private, college/university gift aid from institutional funds.
GIFT AID (NON-NEED-BASED) *Receiving aid:* Freshmen: 31% (174). Undergraduates: 10% (283). *Average award:* Freshmen: $7493. Undergraduates: $6930. *Scholarships, grants, and awards by category: Academic interests/achievement:* 177 awards ($1,448,525 total): general academic interests/achievements. *Creative arts/performance:* 156 awards ($833,773 total): music. *Special achievements/activities:* 2 awards ($33,858 total): leadership. *Special characteristics:* 63 awards ($180,326 total): children of faculty/staff. *Tuition waivers:* Full or partial for employees or children of employees. *ROTC:* Army.
LOANS *Student loans:* $33,119,904 (31% need-based, 69% non-need-based). 89% of past graduating class borrowed through all loan programs. *Average indebtedness per student:* $29,001. *Average need-based loan:* Freshmen: $3390. Undergraduates: $3791. *Parent loans:* $1,215,578 (100% non-need-based). *Programs:* Federal Direct (Subsidized and Unsubsidized Stafford, PLUS).
WORK-STUDY *Federal work-study:* Total amount: $523,180; 368 jobs averaging $1497.
ATHLETIC AWARDS Total amount: $2,340,836 (100% non-need-based).
APPLYING FOR FINANCIAL AID *Required financial aid forms:* FAFSA, institution's own form. *Financial aid deadline (priority):* 3/15. *Notification date:* Continuous beginning 4/1. Students must reply within 4 weeks of notification.
CONTACT Mrs. Juanita M. Russell, Director of Financial Aid, Alcorn State University, 1000 ASU Drive #28, Alcorn State, MS 39096-7500, 601-877-6190 or toll-free 800-222-6790. *Fax:* 601-877-6110. *E-mail:* juanita@alcorn.edu. *Website:* http://www.alcorn.edu/.

ALDERSON-BROADDUS COLLEGE
Philippi, WV

CONTACT Brian Weingart, Director of Financial Aid, Alderson-Broaddus College, College Hill Road, Philippi, WV 26416, 304-457-6354 or toll-free 800-263-1549. *Fax:* 304-457-6391.
Website: http://www.ab.edu/.

ALFRED UNIVERSITY
Alfred, NY

Tuition & fees: $28,774	Average undergraduate aid package: $23,774

ABOUT THE INSTITUTION Independent, coed. *Awards:* certificates, bachelor's, master's, and doctoral degrees. 41 undergraduate majors. *Total enrollment:* 2,362. Undergraduates: 1,935. Freshmen: 536. Both federal and institutional methodology are used as a basis for awarding need-based institutional aid.
UNDERGRADUATE EXPENSES for 2013–2014 *Application fee:* $50. *Comprehensive fee:* $40,272 includes full-time tuition ($27,824), mandatory fees ($950), and room and board ($11,498). Full-time tuition and fees vary according to program. Room and board charges vary according to board plan and housing facility. *Part-time tuition:* $902 per credit hour. *Part-time fees:* $160 per year. *Payment plan:* Tuition prepayment.

FRESHMAN FINANCIAL AID (Fall 2011) 528 applied for aid; of those 90% were deemed to have need. 100% of freshmen with need received aid; of those 11% had need fully met. *Average percent of need met:* 85% (excluding resources awarded to replace EFC). *Average financial aid package:* $25,728 (excluding resources awarded to replace EFC). 5% of all full-time freshmen had no need and received non-need-based gift aid.
UNDERGRADUATE FINANCIAL AID (Fall 2011) 1,700 applied for aid; of those 90% were deemed to have need. 100% of undergraduates with need received aid; of those 15% had need fully met. *Average percent of need met:* 83% (excluding resources awarded to replace EFC). *Average financial aid package:* $23,774 (excluding resources awarded to replace EFC). 7% of all full-time undergraduates had no need and received non-need-based gift aid.
GIFT AID (NEED-BASED) *Total amount:* $27,106,097 (14% federal, 9% state, 77% institutional). *Receiving aid:* Freshmen: 85% (475); all full-time undergraduates: 80% (1,512). *Average award:* Freshmen: $19,388; Undergraduates: $17,387. *Scholarships, grants, and awards:* Federal Pell, FSEOG, state, private, college/university gift aid from institutional funds.
GIFT AID (NON-NEED-BASED) *Total amount:* $2,542,105 (2% federal, 3% state, 76% institutional, 19% external sources). *Receiving aid:* Freshmen: 50% (278). Undergraduates: 44% (837). *Average award:* Freshmen: $7298. Undergraduates: $8290. *Scholarships, grants, and awards by category: Academic interests/achievement:* biological sciences, business, communication, education, engineering/technologies, English, foreign languages, general academic interests/achievements, humanities, international studies, mathematics, military science, physical sciences, pre-medicine, social sciences. *Creative arts/performance:* art/fine arts, creative writing, general creative arts/performance, performing arts. *Special achievements/activities:* leadership. *Special characteristics:* children of educators, children of faculty/staff, international students. *Tuition waivers:* Full or partial for employees or children of employees. *ROTC:* Army cooperative.
LOANS *Student loans:* $14,166,807 (54% need-based, 46% non-need-based). 85% of past graduating class borrowed through all loan programs. *Average indebtedness per student:* $34,494. *Average need-based loan:* Freshmen: $5033. Undergraduates: $5611. *Parent loans:* $3,889,938 (100% non-need-based). *Programs:* Federal Direct (Subsidized and Unsubsidized Stafford, PLUS), Perkins, college/university, alternative loans.
WORK-STUDY *Federal work-study:* Total amount: $1,966,584; jobs available.
APPLYING FOR FINANCIAL AID *Required financial aid forms:* FAFSA, institution's own form, state aid form, noncustodial (divorced/separated) parent's statement, business/farm supplement. *Financial aid deadline:* 3/15. *Notification date:* Continuous beginning 2/15. Students must reply by 5/1 or within 2 weeks of notification.
CONTACT Mr. Earl Pierce Jr., Director of Student Financial Aid, Alfred University, Alumni Hall, One Saxon Drive, Alfred, NY 14802-1205, 607-871-2159 or toll-free 800-541-9229. *Fax:* 607-871-2252. *E-mail:* pierce@alfred.edu. *Website:* http://www.alfred.edu/.

ALICE LLOYD COLLEGE
Pippa Passes, KY

ABOUT THE INSTITUTION Independent, coed. *Awards:* bachelor's degrees. 17 undergraduate majors. *Total enrollment:* 608. Undergraduates: 608. Freshmen: 200.
GIFT AID (NEED-BASED) *Scholarships, grants, and awards:* Federal Pell, FSEOG, state, private, college/university gift aid from institutional funds.
GIFT AID (NON-NEED-BASED) *Scholarships, grants, and awards by category: Special achievements/activities:* general special achievements/activities. *Special characteristics:* members of minority groups.
LOANS *Programs:* Federal Direct (Subsidized and Unsubsidized Stafford, PLUS), college/university, Bagby Loans (for freshmen).
WORK-STUDY *Federal work-study:* Total amount: $800,945; 342 jobs averaging $2320. *State or other work-study/employment:* Total amount: $474,920 (12% need-based, 88% non-need-based). 262 part-time jobs averaging $2320.
APPLYING FOR FINANCIAL AID *Required financial aid form:* FAFSA.
CONTACT Ms. Jacqueline Stewart, Director of Financial Aid, Alice Lloyd College, 100 Purpose Road, Pippa Passes, KY 41844, 606-368-6058 or toll-free 888-280-4252. *E-mail:* jacquelinestewart@alc.edu. *Website:* http://www.alc.edu/.

ALLEGHENY COLLEGE
Meadville, PA

Tuition & fees: $37,610	Average undergraduate aid package: $30,739

ABOUT THE INSTITUTION Independent, coed. **Awards:** bachelor's degrees. 47 undergraduate majors. **Total enrollment:** 2,123. Undergraduates: 2,123. Freshmen: 559. Federal methodology is used as a basis for awarding need-based institutional aid.

UNDERGRADUATE EXPENSES for 2013–2014 Application fee: $35. **Comprehensive fee:** $47,150 includes full-time tuition ($37,260), mandatory fees ($350), and room and board ($9540). **College room only:** $5020. Room and board charges vary according to board plan and housing facility. **Part-time tuition:** $1553 per credit hour. **Part-time fees:** $175 per term. Part-time tuition and fees vary according to course load.

FRESHMAN FINANCIAL AID (Fall 2012, est.) 514 applied for aid; of those 85% were deemed to have need. 100% of freshmen with need received aid; of those 29% had need fully met. **Average percent of need met:** 89% (excluding resources awarded to replace EFC). **Average financial aid package:** $31,387 (excluding resources awarded to replace EFC). 24% of all full-time freshmen had no need and received non-need-based gift aid.

UNDERGRADUATE FINANCIAL AID (Fall 2012, est.) 1,695 applied for aid; of those 89% were deemed to have need. 100% of undergraduates with need received aid; of those 31% had need fully met. **Average percent of need met:** 88% (excluding resources awarded to replace EFC). **Average financial aid package:** $30,739 (excluding resources awarded to replace EFC). 26% of all full-time undergraduates had no need and received non-need-based gift aid.

GIFT AID (NEED-BASED) Total amount: $34,697,638 (8% federal, 5% state, 84% institutional, 3% external sources). **Receiving aid:** Freshmen: 75% (439); all full-time undergraduates: 72% (1,505). **Average award:** Freshmen: $24,732; Undergraduates: $23,731. **Scholarships, grants, and awards:** Federal Pell, FSEOG, state, private, college/university gift aid from institutional funds, Veterans Education Benefits (GI Bill), Yellow Ribbon Grant Program.

GIFT AID (NON-NEED-BASED) Total amount: $9,755,927 (94% institutional, 6% external sources). **Receiving aid:** Freshmen: 12% (72). Undergraduates: 11% (237). **Average award:** Freshmen: $16,411. Undergraduates: $14,359. **Scholarships, grants, and awards by category:** Academic interests/achievement: 1,760 awards ($25,614,917 total): general academic interests/achievements. **Special characteristics:** 89 awards ($2,425,102 total): adult students, children of educators, children of faculty/staff, international students. **Tuition waivers:** Full or partial for employees or children of employees.

LOANS Student loans: $13,790,358 (45% need-based, 55% non-need-based). **Average need-based loan:** Freshmen: $4450. Undergraduates: $5009. **Parent loans:** $4,749,108 (100% non-need-based). **Programs:** Federal Direct (Subsidized and Unsubsidized Stafford, PLUS), Perkins, private loans.

WORK-STUDY Federal work-study: Total amount: $2,422,943; 1,232 jobs averaging $2000. **State or other work-study/employment:** Total amount: $473,135 (100% non-need-based). 109 part-time jobs averaging $4500.

APPLYING FOR FINANCIAL AID Required financial aid form: FAFSA. **Financial aid deadline (priority):** 2/15. **Notification date:** Continuous beginning 3/1. Students must reply by 5/1 or within 4 weeks of notification.

CONTACT Mr. Jonathan Boleratz, Interim Director of Financial Aid, Allegheny College, 520 North Main Street, Meadville, PA 16335, 800-835-7780 or toll-free 800-521-5293. Fax: 814-332-2349. E-mail: fao@allegheny.edu. Website: http://www.allegheny.edu/.

ALLEGHENY WESLEYAN COLLEGE
Salem, OH

CONTACT Esther Phelps, Financial Aid Director, Allegheny Wesleyan College, 2161 Woodsdale Road, Salem, OH 44460, 330-337-6403 Ext. 15 or toll-free 800-292-3153. Fax: 330-337-6255. Website: http://www.awc.edu/.

ALLEN COLLEGE
Waterloo, IA

Tuition & fees: $18,829	Average undergraduate aid package: $11,305

ABOUT THE INSTITUTION Independent, coed, primarily women. **Awards:** certificates, associate, bachelor's, master's, and doctoral degrees (liberal arts and general education courses offered at either University of North Iowa or Wartburg College). 4 undergraduate majors. **Total enrollment:** 551. Undergraduates: 385. Freshmen: 1. Federal methodology is used as a basis for awarding need-based institutional aid.

UNDERGRADUATE EXPENSES for 2013–2014 Application fee: $50. **Comprehensive fee:** $26,110 includes full-time tuition ($16,771), mandatory fees ($2058), and room and board ($7281). **College room only:** $3641. Full-time tuition and fees vary according to course load and program. **Part-time tuition:** $541 per credit. **Part-time fees:** $73 per credit. Part-time tuition and fees vary according to course load and program.

FRESHMAN FINANCIAL AID (Fall 2012, est.) 1 applied for aid; of those 100% were deemed to have need. 100% of freshmen with need received aid. **Average percent of need met:** 43% (excluding resources awarded to replace EFC). **Average financial aid package:** $9340 (excluding resources awarded to replace EFC).

UNDERGRADUATE FINANCIAL AID (Fall 2012, est.) 280 applied for aid; of those 92% were deemed to have need. 99% of undergraduates with need received aid; of those 3% had need fully met. **Average percent of need met:** 48% (excluding resources awarded to replace EFC). **Average financial aid package:** $11,305 (excluding resources awarded to replace EFC). 6% of all full-time undergraduates had no need and received non-need-based gift aid.

GIFT AID (NEED-BASED) Total amount: $1,732,102 (23% federal, 42% state, 22% institutional, 13% external sources). **Receiving aid:** Freshmen: 100% (1); all full-time undergraduates: 80% (225). **Average award:** Freshmen: $5840; Undergraduates: $6593. **Scholarships, grants, and awards:** Federal Pell, FSEOG, state, private, college/university gift aid from institutional funds, Federal Nursing, Scholarships for Disadvantaged Students (SDS).

GIFT AID (NON-NEED-BASED) Total amount: $42,450 (59% institutional, 41% external sources). **Average award:** Undergraduates: $1403. **Scholarships, grants, and awards by category:** Academic interests/achievement: health fields. **Special achievements/activities:** community service, general special achievements/activities, leadership. **Special characteristics:** 18 awards ($25,250 total): children of faculty/staff, general special characteristics, local/state students, members of minority groups, out-of-state students. **Tuition waivers:** Full or partial for employees or children of employees. **ROTC:** Army cooperative.

LOANS Student loans: $2,595,988 (73% need-based, 27% non-need-based). **Average need-based loan:** Freshmen: $3500. Undergraduates: $4827. **Parent loans:** $653,968 (42% need-based, 58% non-need-based). **Programs:** Federal Direct (Subsidized and Unsubsidized Stafford, PLUS), Perkins, Federal Nursing, state, college/university.

WORK-STUDY Federal work-study: Total amount: $32,470; 10 jobs averaging $3247.

APPLYING FOR FINANCIAL AID Required financial aid forms: FAFSA, institution's own form. **Financial aid deadline:** Continuous. **Notification date:** Continuous beginning 4/1. Students must reply within 2 weeks of notification.

CONTACT Kathie S. Aswegan, Financial Aid Coordinator, Allen College, Barrett Forum, 1825 Logan Avenue, Waterloo, IA 50703-1990, 319-226-2003. Fax: 319-226-2051. E-mail: kathie.aswegan@allencollege.edu. Website: http://www.allencollege.edu/.

ALLEN UNIVERSITY
Columbia, SC

CONTACT Ms. Donna Foster, Director of Financial Aid, Allen University, 1530 Harden Street, Columbia, SC 29204-1085, 803-376-5736 or toll-free 877-625-5368. E-mail: donnaf@allenuniversity.edu. Website: http://www.allenuniversity.edu/.

ALLIANT INTERNATIONAL UNIVERSITY
San Diego, CA

Tuition & fees: $16,930	Average undergraduate aid package: $13,650

ABOUT THE INSTITUTION Independent, coed. *Awards:* certificates, bachelor's, master's, and doctoral degrees. 4 undergraduate majors. *Total enrollment:* 3,554. Undergraduates: 132. Federal methodology is used as a basis for awarding need-based institutional aid.

UNDERGRADUATE EXPENSES for 2013–2014 *Application fee:* $45. *Comprehensive fee:* $24,270 includes full-time tuition ($16,740), mandatory fees ($190), and room and board ($7340). Full-time tuition and fees vary according to course load and location. Room and board charges vary according to board plan. *Part-time tuition:* $620 per unit. Part-time tuition and fees vary according to course load and location.

FRESHMAN FINANCIAL AID (Fall 2012, est.) 3 applied for aid; of those 100% were deemed to have need. 100% of freshmen with need received aid. *Average percent of need met:* 67% (excluding resources awarded to replace EFC). *Average financial aid package:* $13,550 (excluding resources awarded to replace EFC).

UNDERGRADUATE FINANCIAL AID (Fall 2012, est.) 77 applied for aid; of those 97% were deemed to have need. 100% of undergraduates with need received aid. *Average percent of need met:* 67% (excluding resources awarded to replace EFC). *Average financial aid package:* $13,650 (excluding resources awarded to replace EFC). 7% of all full-time undergraduates had no need and received non-need-based gift aid.

GIFT AID (NEED-BASED) *Total amount:* $494,897 (91% federal, 9% state). *Receiving aid:* Freshmen: 100% (3); all full-time undergraduates: 42% (55). *Average award:* Freshmen: $7550; Undergraduates: $6750. *Scholarships, grants, and awards:* Federal Pell, FSEOG, state, private, college/university gift aid from institutional funds.

GIFT AID (NON-NEED-BASED) *Total amount:* $23,776 (43% institutional, 57% external sources). *Receiving aid:* Freshmen: 100% (3). Undergraduates: 19% (25). *Average award:* Undergraduates: $4000. *Scholarships, grants, and awards by category:* Academic interests/achievement: 32 awards ($92,721 total): business, communication, computer science, education, English, foreign languages, general academic interests/achievements, humanities, international studies, social sciences. *Special achievements/activities:* community service, general special achievements/activities, leadership. *Special characteristics:* children and siblings of alumni, children of current students, children of faculty/staff, international students, local/state students, siblings of current students, spouses of current students, veterans. *Tuition waivers:* Full or partial for employees or children of employees.

LOANS *Student loans:* $972,020 (62% need-based, 38% non-need-based). *Average need-based loan:* Freshmen: $5500. Undergraduates: $5500. *Parent loans:* $57,799 (100% non-need-based). *Programs:* Federal Direct (Subsidized and Unsubsidized Stafford, PLUS), Perkins, alternative loans.

WORK-STUDY *Federal work-study:* Total amount: $51,325; 13 jobs averaging $4000. *State or other work-study/employment:* 2 part-time jobs averaging $3000.

APPLYING FOR FINANCIAL AID *Required financial aid form:* FAFSA. *Financial aid deadline (priority):* 3/2. *Notification date:* Continuous beginning 3/15. Students must reply within 3 weeks of notification.

CONTACT Deborah Spindler, Director of Financial Aid, Alliant International University, 10455 Pomerado Road, San Diego, CA 92131-1799, 858-635-4559 Ext. 4700 or toll-free 866-825-5426. *Fax:* 858-635-4848. *E-mail:* dspindler@alliant.edu. *Website:* http://www.alliant.edu/.

ALLIED AMERICAN UNIVERSITY
Laguna Hills, CA

CONTACT Financial Aid Office, Allied American University, 22952 Alcade Drive, Laguna Hills, CA 92653, 888-384-0849. *Website:* http://allied.edu/.

ALMA COLLEGE
Alma, MI

Tuition & fees: $31,060	Average undergraduate aid package: $26,245

ABOUT THE INSTITUTION Independent Presbyterian, coed. *Awards:* bachelor's degrees. 59 undergraduate majors. *Total enrollment:* 1,464. Undergraduates: 1,464. Freshmen: 427. Federal methodology is used as a basis for awarding need-based institutional aid.

UNDERGRADUATE EXPENSES for 2013–2014 *Application fee:* $25. *Comprehensive fee:* $40,050 includes full-time tuition ($30,700), mandatory fees ($360), and room and board ($8990). *College room only:* $4495. Room and board charges vary according to board plan and housing facility. *Part-time tuition:* $1000 per credit hour. Part-time tuition and fees vary according to course load.

FRESHMAN FINANCIAL AID (Fall 2012, est.) 425 applied for aid; of those 92% were deemed to have need. 100% of freshmen with need received aid; of those 13% had need fully met. *Average percent of need met:* 91% (excluding resources awarded to replace EFC). *Average financial aid package:* $28,721 (excluding resources awarded to replace EFC). 12% of all full-time freshmen had no need and received non-need-based gift aid.

UNDERGRADUATE FINANCIAL AID (Fall 2012, est.) 1,323 applied for aid; of those 89% were deemed to have need. 100% of undergraduates with need received aid; of those 13% had need fully met. *Average percent of need met:* 87% (excluding resources awarded to replace EFC). *Average financial aid package:* $26,245 (excluding resources awarded to replace EFC). 15% of all full-time undergraduates had no need and received non-need-based gift aid.

GIFT AID (NEED-BASED) *Total amount:* $22,451,357 (8% federal, 6% state, 85% institutional, 1% external sources). *Receiving aid:* Freshmen: 89% (389); all full-time undergraduates: 84% (1,182). *Average award:* Freshmen: $22,204; Undergraduates: $19,594. *Scholarships, grants, and awards:* Federal Pell, FSEOG, state, private, college/university gift aid from institutional funds.

GIFT AID (NON-NEED-BASED) *Total amount:* $3,940,820 (99% institutional, 1% external sources). *Receiving aid:* Freshmen: 11% (50). Undergraduates: 10% (148). *Average award:* Freshmen: $13,279. Undergraduates: $14,480. *Scholarships, grants, and awards by category:* Academic interests/achievement: 1,248 awards ($15,564,325 total): general academic interests/achievements. *Creative arts/performance:* 308 awards ($776,600 total): art/fine arts, dance, music, performing arts, theater/drama. *Special achievements/activities:* 13 awards ($12,000 total): religious involvement. *Special characteristics:* 187 awards ($175,050 total): children and siblings of alumni, children of current students. *Tuition waivers:* Full or partial for employees or children of employees. *ROTC:* Army cooperative.

LOANS *Student loans:* $10,944,927 (73% need-based, 27% non-need-based). 77% of past graduating class borrowed through all loan programs. *Average indebtedness per student:* $31,297. *Average need-based loan:* Freshmen: $3813. Undergraduates: $3980. *Parent loans:* $16,448,985 (29% need-based, 71% non-need-based). *Programs:* Federal Direct (Subsidized and Unsubsidized Stafford, PLUS), Perkins, college/university, alternative loans.

WORK-STUDY *Federal work-study:* Total amount: $632,595; 514 jobs averaging $1227.

APPLYING FOR FINANCIAL AID *Required financial aid form:* FAFSA. *Financial aid deadline (priority):* 3/1. *Notification date:* Continuous beginning 3/1. Students must reply within 3 weeks of notification.

CONTACT Mrs. Michelle L. McNier, Director of Student Financial Assistance, Alma College, 614 West Superior Street, Alma, MI 48801-1599, 989-463-7347 or toll-free 800-321-ALMA. *Fax:* 989-463-7993. *E-mail:* mcnierml@alma.edu. *Website:* http://www.alma.edu/.

ALVERNIA UNIVERSITY
Reading, PA

ABOUT THE INSTITUTION Independent Roman Catholic, coed. *Awards:* associate, bachelor's, master's, and doctoral degrees. 40 undergraduate majors. *Total enrollment:* 2,891. Undergraduates: 2,347. Freshmen: 412.

GIFT AID (NEED-BASED) *Scholarships, grants, and awards:* Federal Pell, FSEOG, state, private, college/university gift aid from institutional funds.

GIFT AID (NON-NEED-BASED) *Scholarships, grants, and awards by category:* Academic interests/achievement: general academic interests/achievements.

Special achievements/activities: community service, leadership, memberships, religious involvement. *Special characteristics:* children and siblings of alumni, children of faculty/staff, general special characteristics, local/state students, siblings of current students.
LOANS *Programs:* Federal Direct (Subsidized and Unsubsidized Stafford, PLUS), Perkins.
APPLYING FOR FINANCIAL AID *Required financial aid forms:* FAFSA, state aid form.
CONTACT Ms. Christine Saadi, Director of Student Financial Planning, Alvernia University, 400 Saint Bernardine Street, Reading, PA 19607-1799, 610-796-8213 or toll-free 888-ALVERNIA (in-state). *Fax:* 610-796-8336. *E-mail:* christine.saadi@alvernia.edu.
Website: http://www.alvernia.edu/.

ALVERNO COLLEGE
Milwaukee, WI

Tuition & fees: $22,126	Average undergraduate aid package: $15,791

ABOUT THE INSTITUTION Independent Roman Catholic, undergraduate: women only; graduate: coed. *Awards:* certificates, associate, bachelor's, and master's degrees (also offers weekend program with significant enrollment not reflected in profile). 42 undergraduate majors. *Total enrollment:* 2,522. Undergraduates: 1,932. Freshmen: 199. Federal methodology is used as a basis for awarding need-based institutional aid.
UNDERGRADUATE EXPENSES for 2013–2014 *Application fee:* $20. *Comprehensive fee:* $29,176 includes full-time tuition ($21,576), mandatory fees ($550), and room and board ($7050). Full-time tuition and fees vary according to program. Room and board charges vary according to board plan and housing facility. *Part-time tuition:* $899 per credit hour. Part-time tuition and fees vary according to program.
FRESHMAN FINANCIAL AID (Fall 2012, est.) 186 applied for aid; of those 97% were deemed to have need. 100% of freshmen with need received aid. *Average financial aid package:* $17,696 (excluding resources awarded to replace EFC). 4% of all full-time freshmen had no need and received non-need-based gift aid.
UNDERGRADUATE FINANCIAL AID (Fall 2012, est.) 1,338 applied for aid; of those 97% were deemed to have need. 100% of undergraduates with need received aid. *Average financial aid package:* $15,791 (excluding resources awarded to replace EFC). 6% of all full-time undergraduates had no need and received non-need-based gift aid.
GIFT AID (NEED-BASED) *Total amount:* $18,038,180 (29% federal, 14% state, 57% institutional). *Receiving aid:* Freshmen: 95% (181); all full-time undergraduates: 91% (1,275). *Average award:* Freshmen: $14,635; Undergraduates: $12,014. *Scholarships, grants, and awards:* Federal Pell, FSEOG, state, private, college/university gift aid from institutional funds.
GIFT AID (NON-NEED-BASED) *Total amount:* $923,279 (65% institutional, 35% external sources). *Receiving aid:* Freshmen: 91% (173). Undergraduates: 78% (1,088). *Average award:* Freshmen: $8600. Undergraduates: $6168. *Scholarships, grants, and awards by category:* Academic interests/achievement: 1,753 awards ($7,243,474 total): general academic interests/achievements. *Creative arts/performance:* 17 awards ($18,284 total): art/fine arts, music. *Special achievements/activities:* 3 awards ($63,478 total): community service. *Special characteristics:* 10 awards ($80,187 total): children of faculty/staff, international students. *Tuition waivers:* Full or partial for employees or children of employees. *ROTC:* Army cooperative, Air Force cooperative.
LOANS *Student loans:* $19,633,792 (39% need-based, 61% non-need-based). 92% of past graduating class borrowed through all loan programs. *Average indebtedness per student:* $41,405. *Average need-based loan:* Freshmen: $3362. Undergraduates: $4206. *Parent loans:* $657,405 (100% non-need-based). *Programs:* Federal Direct (Subsidized and Unsubsidized Stafford, PLUS), Perkins, state.
WORK-STUDY *Federal work-study:* Total amount: $263,614; 99 jobs averaging $2310. *State or other work-study/employment:* Total amount: $581,012 (100% non-need-based). Part-time jobs available.
APPLYING FOR FINANCIAL AID *Required financial aid forms:* FAFSA, institution's own form. *Financial aid deadline (priority):* 3/15. *Notification date:* Continuous beginning 3/15. Students must reply within 2 weeks of notification.

CONTACT Dan Goyette, Director of Financial Aid, Alverno College, 3400 South 43rd Street, PO Box 343922, Milwaukee, WI 53234-3922, 414-382-6046 or toll-free 800-933-3401. *Fax:* 414-382-6354. *E-mail:* dan.goyette@alverno.edu. *Website:* http://www.alverno.edu/.

AMERICAN ACADEMY OF ART
Chicago, IL

CONTACT Ms. Ione Fitzgerald, Director of Financial Aid, American Academy of Art, 332 South Michigan Avenue, Suite 300, Chicago, IL 60604, 312-461-0600 or toll-free 888-461-0600. *Fax:* 312-294-9570.
Website: http://www.aaart.edu/.

AMERICAN BAPTIST COLLEGE OF AMERICAN BAPTIST THEOLOGICAL SEMINARY
Nashville, TN

Tuition & fees: $9005	Average undergraduate aid package: $8273

ABOUT THE INSTITUTION Independent Baptist, coed. *Awards:* bachelor's degrees. *Total enrollment:* 122. Undergraduates: 109. Freshmen: 4. Federal methodology is used as a basis for awarding need-based institutional aid.
UNDERGRADUATE EXPENSES for 2013–2014 *Application fee:* $30. *Tuition:* full-time $8688.
FRESHMAN FINANCIAL AID (Fall 2011) 11 applied for aid; of those 100% were deemed to have need. 100% of freshmen with need received aid. *Average percent of need met:* 35% (excluding resources awarded to replace EFC). *Average financial aid package:* $8273 (excluding resources awarded to replace EFC).
UNDERGRADUATE FINANCIAL AID (Fall 2011) 77 applied for aid; of those 100% were deemed to have need. 100% of undergraduates with need received aid. *Average percent of need met:* 35% (excluding resources awarded to replace EFC). *Average financial aid package:* $8273 (excluding resources awarded to replace EFC).
GIFT AID (NEED-BASED) *Total amount:* $331,256 (94% federal, 6% state). *Receiving aid:* Freshmen: 75% (9); all full-time undergraduates: 68% (65). *Average award:* Freshmen: $4235; Undergraduates: $4235. *Scholarships, grants, and awards:* Federal Pell, FSEOG, state.
LOANS *Student loans:* $564,336 (100% need-based). 75% of past graduating class borrowed through all loan programs. *Average indebtedness per student:* $5469. *Average need-based loan:* Freshmen: $3971. Undergraduates: $3971. *Parent loans:* $7250 (100% need-based). *Programs:* Federal Direct (Subsidized and Unsubsidized Stafford, PLUS).
WORK-STUDY *Federal work-study:* Total amount: $6741; 25 jobs averaging $200.
APPLYING FOR FINANCIAL AID *Required financial aid form:* FAFSA. *Financial aid deadline:* 7/23 (priority: 1/2). *Notification date:* Continuous beginning 7/30. Students must reply by 8/15 or within 2 weeks of notification.
CONTACT Dr. Barbara Wilson, Financial Aid Consultant, American Baptist College of American Baptist Theological Seminary, 1800 Baptist World Center Drive, Nashville, TN 37207, 615-687-6903 Ext. 6903. *Fax:* 615-226-7855. *E-mail:* bwilson@abcnash.edu.
Website: http://www.abcnash.edu/.

AMERICAN INDIAN COLLEGE OF THE ASSEMBLIES OF GOD, INC.
Phoenix, AZ

Tuition & fees: $16,040   **Average undergraduate aid package: N/A**

ABOUT THE INSTITUTION Independent Assemblies of God, coed. 3 undergraduate majors. Federal methodology is used as a basis for awarding need-based institutional aid.

UNDERGRADUATE EXPENSES for 2013–2014 *Comprehensive fee:* $22,242 includes full-time tuition ($11,700), mandatory fees ($4340), and room and board ($6202). *College room only:* $3510. Full-time tuition and fees vary according to course load. Room and board charges vary according to housing facility. *Part-time tuition:* $390 per credit hour. Part-time tuition and fees vary according to course load.

GIFT AID (NEED-BASED) *Scholarships, grants, and awards:* Federal Pell, FSEOG, state, private, college/university gift aid from institutional funds.

GIFT AID (NON-NEED-BASED) *Scholarships, grants, and awards by category:* *Academic interests/achievement:* general academic interests/achievements. *Tuition waivers:* Full or partial for employees or children of employees.

WORK-STUDY Federal work-study jobs available.

APPLYING FOR FINANCIAL AID *Required financial aid form:* FAFSA. *Financial aid deadline (priority):* 4/1. *Notification date:* Continuous.

CONTACT Nadine Waldrop, Director of Student Financial Aid, American Indian College of the Assemblies of God, Inc., 10020 North Fifteenth Avenue, Phoenix, AZ 85021-2199, 602-944-3335 Ext. 223. *Fax:* 602-944-1952. *E-mail:* nwaldrop@aicag.edu. *Website:* http://www.aicag.edu/.

AMERICAN INTERCONTINENTAL UNIVERSITY ATLANTA
Atlanta, GA

CONTACT Financial Aid Office, American InterContinental University Atlanta, 6600 Peachtree-Dunwoody Road, 500 Embassy Row, Atlanta, GA 30328, 404-965-6500 or toll-free 800-353-1744. *Website:* http://www.aiuniv.edu/.

AMERICAN INTERCONTINENTAL UNIVERSITY HOUSTON
Houston, TX

CONTACT Financial Aid Office, American InterContinental University Houston, 9999 Richmond Avenue, Houston, TX 77042, 832-242-5788 or toll-free 888-607-9888. *Website:* http://www.aiuniv.edu/.

AMERICAN INTERCONTINENTAL UNIVERSITY ONLINE
Hoffman Estates, IL

CONTACT Financial Aid Office, American InterContinental University Online, 5550 Prairie Stone Parkway, Suite 400, Hoffman Estates, IL 60192, 847-851-5000 or toll-free 877-701-3800. *Website:* http://www.aiuniv.edu/.

AMERICAN INTERCONTINENTAL UNIVERSITY SOUTH FLORIDA
Weston, FL

CONTACT Financial Aid Office, American InterContinental University South Florida, 2250 North Commerce Parkway, Suite 100, Weston, FL 33326, 954-446-6100 or toll-free 888-603-4888. *Website:* http://www.aiuniv.edu/.

AMERICAN INTERNATIONAL COLLEGE
Springfield, MA

Tuition & fees: $29,158   **Average undergraduate aid package: $22,929**

ABOUT THE INSTITUTION Independent, coed. 42 undergraduate majors. Federal methodology is used as a basis for awarding need-based institutional aid.

UNDERGRADUATE EXPENSES for 2013–2014 *Comprehensive fee:* $40,868 includes full-time tuition ($29,158) and room and board ($11,710). Full-time tuition and fees vary according to program. Room and board charges vary according to board plan and housing facility. *Part-time tuition:* $601 per credit hour. *Part-time fees:* $30 per term. Part-time tuition and fees vary according to course load and program. *Payment plan:* Tuition prepayment.

FRESHMAN FINANCIAL AID (Fall 2012, est.) 288 applied for aid; of those 95% were deemed to have need. 100% of freshmen with need received aid; of those 16% had need fully met. *Average percent of need met:* 71% (excluding resources awarded to replace EFC). *Average financial aid package:* $24,081 (excluding resources awarded to replace EFC). 10% of all full-time freshmen had no need and received non-need-based gift aid.

UNDERGRADUATE FINANCIAL AID (Fall 2012, est.) 1,269 applied for aid; of those 95% were deemed to have need. 100% of undergraduates with need received aid; of those 13% had need fully met. *Average percent of need met:* 69% (excluding resources awarded to replace EFC). *Average financial aid package:* $22,929 (excluding resources awarded to replace EFC). 10% of all full-time undergraduates had no need and received non-need-based gift aid.

GIFT AID (NEED-BASED) *Total amount:* $20,670,190 (19% federal, 4% state, 75% institutional, 2% external sources). *Receiving aid:* Freshmen: 89% (274); all full-time undergraduates: 89% (1,207). *Average award:* Freshmen: $20,587; Undergraduates: $18,873. *Scholarships, grants, and awards:* Federal Pell, FSEOG, state, private, college/university gift aid from institutional funds.

GIFT AID (NON-NEED-BASED) *Total amount:* $2,281,515 (1% federal, 93% institutional, 6% external sources). *Receiving aid:* Freshmen: 14% (43). Undergraduates: 10% (140). *Average award:* Freshmen: $12,525. Undergraduates: $12,269. *Scholarships, grants, and awards by category:* *Academic interests/achievement:* general academic interests/achievements. *Special achievements/activities:* general special achievements/activities. *Special characteristics:* children of faculty/staff, children of public servants, first-generation college students, previous college experience. *Tuition waivers:* Full or partial for employees or children of employees.

LOANS *Student loans:* $13,268,138 (81% need-based, 19% non-need-based). 86% of past graduating class borrowed through all loan programs. *Average indebtedness per student:* $33,170. *Average need-based loan:* Freshmen: $3205. Undergraduates: $4174. *Parent loans:* $2,013,000 (66% need-based, 34% non-need-based). *Programs:* Federal Direct (Subsidized and Unsubsidized Stafford, PLUS), Perkins.

WORK-STUDY *Federal work-study:* Total amount: $282,702; jobs available. *State or other work-study/employment:* Total amount: $68,283 (100% need-based). Part-time jobs available.

ATHLETIC AWARDS Total amount: $4,840,036 (50% need-based, 50% non-need-based).

APPLYING FOR FINANCIAL AID *Required financial aid form:* FAFSA. *Financial aid deadline (priority):* 5/1. *Notification date:* Continuous beginning 2/15. Students must reply by 5/1 or within 2 weeks of notification.

CONTACT Ms. Sage Stachowiak, Director of Financial Aid, American International College, 1000 State Street, Springfield, MA 01109-3189, 413-205-3521 or toll-free 800-242-3142. *Fax:* 413-205-3912. *E-mail:* sage.stachowiak@aic.edu. *Website:* http://www.aic.edu/.

AMERICAN JEWISH UNIVERSITY
Bel Air, CA

Tuition & fees: $28,496	Average undergraduate aid package: $27,500

ABOUT THE INSTITUTION Independent Jewish, coed. **Awards:** bachelor's and master's degrees. 10 undergraduate majors. **Total enrollment:** 257. Undergraduates: 125. Freshmen: 13. Both federal and institutional methodology are used as a basis for awarding need-based institutional aid.

UNDERGRADUATE EXPENSES for 2013–2014 Application fee: $35. **Comprehensive fee:** $42,578 includes full-time tuition ($26,784), mandatory fees ($1712), and room and board ($14,082). **College room only:** $7098. Full-time tuition and fees vary according to course load and degree level. Room and board charges vary according to board plan and housing facility. **Part-time tuition:** $1116 per unit. Part-time tuition and fees vary according to course load and degree level.

FRESHMAN FINANCIAL AID (Fall 2011) 15 applied for aid; of those 100% were deemed to have need. 100% of freshmen with need received aid. **Average percent of need met:** 100% (excluding resources awarded to replace EFC). **Average financial aid package:** $27,000 (excluding resources awarded to replace EFC). 80% of all full-time freshmen had no need and received non-need-based gift aid.

UNDERGRADUATE FINANCIAL AID (Fall 2011) 129 applied for aid; of those 100% were deemed to have need. 100% of undergraduates with need received aid. **Average percent of need met:** 95% (excluding resources awarded to replace EFC). **Average financial aid package:** $27,500 (excluding resources awarded to replace EFC). 33% of all full-time undergraduates had no need and received non-need-based gift aid.

GIFT AID (NEED-BASED) Total amount: $315,905 (59% federal, 41% state). **Receiving aid:** Freshmen: 100% (15); all full-time undergraduates: 91% (129). **Average award:** Freshmen: $10,500; Undergraduates: $10,000. **Scholarships, grants, and awards:** Federal Pell, FSEOG, state, private, college/university gift aid from institutional funds.

GIFT AID (NON-NEED-BASED) Total amount: $883,839 (100% institutional). **Receiving aid:** Freshmen: 100% (15). Undergraduates: 91% (129). **Average award:** Freshmen: $2500. Undergraduates: $2500. **Scholarships, grants, and awards by category:** Academic interests/achievement: business, general academic interests/achievements, premedicine. Special achievements/activities: leadership. **Tuition waivers:** Full or partial for employees or children of employees.

LOANS Student loans: $529,595 (40% need-based, 60% non-need-based). 85% of past graduating class borrowed through all loan programs. Average indebtedness per student: $29,500. **Average need-based loan:** Freshmen: $3500. Undergraduates: $4500. **Parent loans:** $318,337 (100% non-need-based). **Programs:** Federal Direct (Subsidized and Unsubsidized Stafford, PLUS), alternative loans.

WORK-STUDY Federal work-study: Total amount: $32,851; 27 jobs averaging $889.

APPLYING FOR FINANCIAL AID Required financial aid forms: FAFSA, institution's own form, federal income tax form(s). **Financial aid deadline (priority):** 3/2. **Notification date:** Continuous beginning 3/15. Students must reply within 3 weeks of notification.

CONTACT Larisa Zadoyen, Director of Financial Aid, American Jewish University, 15600 Mulholland Drive, Bel Air, CA 90077-1599, 310-476-9777 Ext. 252 or toll-free 888-853-6763. *Fax:* 310-476-4613. *E-mail:* lzadoyen@ajula.edu. *Website:* http://www.ajula.edu/.

AMERICAN MUSICAL AND DRAMATIC ACADEMY, LOS ANGELES
Los Angeles, CA

CONTACT Financial Aid Office, American Musical and Dramatic Academy, Los Angeles, 6305 Yucca Street, Los Angeles, CA 90028, 323-469-3300 or toll-free 888-474-9444. *Website:* http://www.amda.edu/.

AMERICAN SENTINEL UNIVERSITY
Aurora, CO

CONTACT Financial Aid Office, American Sentinel University, 2260 South Xanadu Way, Suite 310, Aurora, CO 80014 or toll-free 800-729-2427. *Website:* http://www.americansentinel.edu/.

AMERICAN UNIVERSITY
Washington, DC

Tuition & fees: $39,499	Average undergraduate aid package: $27,138

ABOUT THE INSTITUTION Independent Methodist, coed. **Awards:** certificates, associate, bachelor's, master's, and doctoral degrees. 82 undergraduate majors. **Total enrollment:** 12,904. Undergraduates: 7,299. Freshmen: 1,597. Institutional methodology is used as a basis for awarding need-based institutional aid.

UNDERGRADUATE EXPENSES for 2013–2014 Application fee: $65. **Comprehensive fee:** $53,419 includes full-time tuition ($38,982), mandatory fees ($517), and room and board ($13,920). **College room only:** $9290. Full-time tuition and fees vary according to location. Room and board charges vary according to board plan, housing facility, and location. **Part-time tuition:** $1299 per credit hour. **Part-time fees:** $170 per term. Part-time tuition and fees vary according to course load and location. **Payment plan:** Tuition prepayment.

FRESHMAN FINANCIAL AID (Fall 2012, est.) 1,141 applied for aid; of those 75% were deemed to have need. 99% of freshmen with need received aid; of those 38% had need fully met. **Average percent of need met:** 85% (excluding resources awarded to replace EFC). **Average financial aid package:** $30,402 (excluding resources awarded to replace EFC). 15% of all full-time freshmen had no need and received non-need-based gift aid.

UNDERGRADUATE FINANCIAL AID (Fall 2012, est.) 4,243 applied for aid; of those 82% were deemed to have need. 98% of undergraduates with need received aid; of those 23% had need fully met. **Average percent of need met:** 72% (excluding resources awarded to replace EFC). **Average financial aid package:** $27,138 (excluding resources awarded to replace EFC). 14% of all full-time undergraduates had no need and received non-need-based gift aid.

GIFT AID (NEED-BASED) Total amount: $55,256,767 (10% federal, 81% institutional, 9% external sources). **Receiving aid:** Freshmen: 48% (765); all full-time undergraduates: 41% (2,686). **Average award:** Freshmen: $21,739; Undergraduates: $19,733. **Scholarships, grants, and awards:** Federal Pell, FSEOG, private, college/university gift aid from institutional funds.

GIFT AID (NON-NEED-BASED) Total amount: $36,203,462 (100% institutional). **Receiving aid:** Freshmen: 26% (410). Undergraduates: 20% (1,338). **Average award:** Freshmen: $14,560. Undergraduates: $17,504. **Scholarships, grants, and awards by category:** Academic interests/achievement: general academic interests/achievements. Creative arts/performance: general creative arts/performance. Special achievements/activities: general special achievements/activities, leadership, memberships. Special characteristics: adult students, children and siblings of alumni, children of faculty/staff, ethnic background, first-generation college students, local/state students, members of minority groups, previous college experience, relatives of clergy, spouses of current students. **Tuition waivers:** Full or partial for employees or children of employees. **ROTC:** Army cooperative, Air Force cooperative.

LOANS Student loans: $25,055,927 (60% need-based, 40% non-need-based). **Average need-based loan:** Freshmen: $4313. Undergraduates: $5052. **Parent loans:** $21,716,167 (100% non-need-based). **Programs:** Federal Direct (Subsidized and Unsubsidized Stafford, PLUS), Perkins, college/university.

WORK-STUDY Federal work-study: Total amount: $2,384,320; 1,407 jobs averaging $1663.

ATHLETIC AWARDS Total amount: $4,193,784 (100% non-need-based).

APPLYING FOR FINANCIAL AID Required financial aid forms: FAFSA, institution's own form. **Financial aid deadline:** 2/15. **Notification date:** 4/1. Students must reply by 5/1 or within 4 weeks of notification.

CONTACT Brian Lee Sang, Director of Financial Aid, American University, 4400 Massachusetts Avenue, NW, Washington, DC 20016-8001, 202-885-6500. *Fax:* 202-885-1025. *E-mail:* facounselor@american.edu. *Website:* http://www.american.edu/.

AMERICAN UNIVERSITY OF HEALTH SCIENCES
Signal Hill, CA

CONTACT Financial Aid Office, American University of Health Sciences, 1600 East Hill Street, Building #1, Signal Hill, CA 90755, 562-988-2278. *Website:* http://www.auhs.edu/.

AMERICAN UNIVERSITY OF PUERTO RICO
Bayamón, PR

CONTACT Mr. Yahaira Melendez, Financial Aid Director, American University of Puerto Rico, PO Box 2037, Bayamón, PR 00960-2037, 787-620-2040 Ext. 2031. *Fax:* 787-785-7377. *E-mail:* melendezy@aupr.edu. *Website:* http://www.aupr.edu/.

AMHERST COLLEGE
Amherst, MA

Tuition & fees: $44,610 — **Average undergraduate aid package: $44,888**

ABOUT THE INSTITUTION Independent, coed. *Awards:* bachelor's degrees. 38 undergraduate majors. *Total enrollment:* 1,817. Undergraduates: 1,817. Freshmen: 463. Institutional methodology is used as a basis for awarding need-based institutional aid.

UNDERGRADUATE EXPENSES for 2013–2014 *Application fee:* $60. *Comprehensive fee:* $56,260 includes full-time tuition ($43,860), mandatory fees ($750), and room and board ($11,650). *College room only:* $6310.

FRESHMAN FINANCIAL AID (Fall 2012, est.) 309 applied for aid; of those 85% were deemed to have need. 100% of freshmen with need received aid; of those 100% had need fully met. *Average percent of need met:* 100% (excluding resources awarded to replace EFC). *Average financial aid package:* $45,438 (excluding resources awarded to replace EFC).

UNDERGRADUATE FINANCIAL AID (Fall 2012, est.) 1,197 applied for aid; of those 89% were deemed to have need. 100% of undergraduates with need received aid; of those 100% had need fully met. *Average percent of need met:* 100% (excluding resources awarded to replace EFC). *Average financial aid package:* $44,888 (excluding resources awarded to replace EFC).

GIFT AID (NEED-BASED) *Total amount:* $46,495,423 (4% federal, 95% institutional, 1% external sources). *Receiving aid:* Freshmen: 56% (264); all full-time undergraduates: 55% (1,067). *Average award:* Freshmen: $43,576; Undergraduates: $43,424. *Scholarships, grants, and awards:* Federal Pell, FSEOG, state, private, college/university gift aid from institutional funds.

GIFT AID (NON-NEED-BASED) *Total amount:* $252,534 (100% external sources). *ROTC:* Army cooperative, Air Force cooperative.

LOANS *Student loans:* $1,910,556 (33% need-based, 67% non-need-based). 30% of past graduating class borrowed through all loan programs. *Average indebtedness per student:* $14,566. *Average need-based loan:* Freshmen: $2131. Undergraduates: $2898. *Parent loans:* $2,415,330 (100% non-need-based). *Programs:* Federal Direct (Subsidized and Unsubsidized Stafford, PLUS), Perkins, college/university.

WORK-STUDY *Federal work-study:* Total amount: $1,029,815; 616 jobs averaging $1672. *State or other work-study/employment:* Total amount: $411,517 (100% need-based). 245 part-time jobs averaging $1680.

APPLYING FOR FINANCIAL AID *Required financial aid forms:* FAFSA, CSS Financial Aid PROFILE, noncustodial (divorced/separated) parent's statement, business/farm supplement, federal income tax form(s), W-2 forms. *Financial aid deadline (priority):* 2/15. *Notification date:* 4/1. Students must reply by 5/1.

CONTACT Gail W. Holt, Dean of Financial Aid, Amherst College, B-5 Converse Hall, PO Box 5000, Amherst, MA 01002-5000, 413-542-2296. *Fax:* 413-542-2628. *E-mail:* finaid@amherst.edu. *Website:* http://www.amherst.edu/.

AMRIDGE UNIVERSITY
Montgomery, AL

Tuition & fees: $6000 — **Average undergraduate aid package: $9260**

ABOUT THE INSTITUTION Independent Church of Christ, coed. *Awards:* associate, bachelor's, master's, and doctoral degrees. 4 undergraduate majors. Federal methodology is used as a basis for awarding need-based institutional aid.

UNDERGRADUATE EXPENSES for 2013–2014 *Application fee:* $50. *Tuition:* full-time $6000; part-time $365 per semester hour. *Required fees:* $400 per term. Full-time tuition and fees vary according to course load and student level. Part-time tuition and fees vary according to course load and student level.

FRESHMAN FINANCIAL AID (Fall 2012, est.) 8 applied for aid; of those 100% were deemed to have need. 100% of freshmen with need received aid.

UNDERGRADUATE FINANCIAL AID (Fall 2012, est.) 364 applied for aid; of those 100% were deemed to have need. 100% of undergraduates with need received aid; of those 100% had need fully met. *Average percent of need met:* 90% (excluding resources awarded to replace EFC). *Average financial aid package:* $9260 (excluding resources awarded to replace EFC). 4% of all full-time undergraduates had no need and received non-need-based gift aid.

GIFT AID (NEED-BASED) *Total amount:* $1,883,866 (90% federal, 9% institutional, 1% external sources). *Receiving aid:* Freshmen: 100% (8); all full-time undergraduates: 81% (364). *Average award:* Undergraduates: $6831. *Scholarships, grants, and awards:* Federal Pell, FSEOG, state, private, college/university gift aid from institutional funds.

GIFT AID (NON-NEED-BASED) *Total amount:* $972,517 (100% institutional). *Receiving aid:* Freshmen: 100% (8). Undergraduates: 81% (364). *Average award:* Undergraduates: $4200. *Scholarships, grants, and awards by category:* Special achievements/activities: religious involvement. Special characteristics: 69 awards ($50,053 total): children of educators, children of faculty/staff, veterans. *Tuition waivers:* Full or partial for employees or children of employees.

LOANS *Student loans:* $9,036,963 (28% need-based, 72% non-need-based). *Average need-based loan:* Undergraduates: $8260. *Parent loans:* $10,000 (100% need-based). *Programs:* Federal Direct (Subsidized and Unsubsidized Stafford, PLUS).

WORK-STUDY Federal work-study jobs available.

APPLYING FOR FINANCIAL AID *Required financial aid forms:* FAFSA, institution's own form. *Financial aid deadline:* Continuous. *Notification date:* 8/31. Students must reply within 2 weeks of notification.

CONTACT Starr Fain, Director of Financial Aid, Amridge University, 1200 Taylor Road, Montgomery, AL 36117, 334-387-3877 Ext. 7523 or toll-free 888-790-8080. *Fax:* 334-387-3878. *E-mail:* starrfain@amridgeuniversity.edu. *Website:* http://www.amridgeuniversity.edu/.

ANDERSON UNIVERSITY
Anderson, IN

Tuition & fees: $26,200 — **Average undergraduate aid package: $20,419**

ABOUT THE INSTITUTION Independent Church of God, coed. *Awards:* associate, bachelor's, master's, and doctoral degrees. 65 undergraduate majors. *Total enrollment:* 2,516. Undergraduates: 2,034. Freshmen: 519. Federal methodology is used as a basis for awarding need-based institutional aid.

UNDERGRADUATE EXPENSES for 2013–2014 *Application fee:* $25. *Comprehensive fee:* $35,310 includes full-time tuition ($26,120), mandatory fees ($80), and room and board ($9110). *College room only:* $5830. Room and board charges vary according to board plan and housing facility. *Part-time tuition:* $1089 per semester hour. Part-time tuition and fees vary according to course load.

FRESHMAN FINANCIAL AID (Fall 2011) 460 applied for aid; of those 88% were deemed to have need. 100% of freshmen with need received aid; of those 36% had need fully met. *Average percent of need met:* 96% (excluding resources awarded to replace EFC). *Average financial aid package:* $20,972 (excluding resources awarded to replace EFC). 18% of all full-time freshmen had no need and received non-need-based gift aid.

UNDERGRADUATE FINANCIAL AID (Fall 2011) 1,752 applied for aid; of those 91% were deemed to have need. 100% of undergraduates with need received

aid; of those 42% had need fully met. *Average percent of need met:* 82% (excluding resources awarded to replace EFC). *Average financial aid package:* $20,419 (excluding resources awarded to replace EFC). 16% of all full-time undergraduates had no need and received non-need-based gift aid.

GIFT AID (NEED-BASED) *Total amount:* $21,501,666 (15% federal, 12% state, 68% institutional, 5% external sources). *Receiving aid:* Freshmen: 80% (398); all full-time undergraduates: 82% (1,567). *Average award:* Freshmen: $15,035; Undergraduates: $14,057. *Scholarships, grants, and awards:* Federal Pell, FSEOG, state, private, college/university gift aid from institutional funds.

GIFT AID (NON-NEED-BASED) *Total amount:* $4,774,089 (1% federal, 89% institutional, 10% external sources). *Receiving aid:* Freshmen: 26% (128). Undergraduates: 22% (424). *Average award:* Freshmen: $12,586. Undergraduates: $11,396. *Scholarships, grants, and awards by category: Academic interests/achievement:* general academic interests/achievements. *Creative arts/performance:* art/fine arts, music. *Special achievements/activities:* leadership. *Special characteristics:* adult students, children of faculty/staff, international students, relatives of clergy. *Tuition waivers:* Full or partial for employees or children of employees.

LOANS *Student loans:* $13,936,033 (79% need-based, 21% non-need-based). 79% of past graduating class borrowed through all loan programs. *Average indebtedness per student:* $32,363. *Average need-based loan:* Freshmen: $3637. Undergraduates: $4382. *Parent loans:* $4,691,794 (51% need-based, 49% non-need-based). *Programs:* Perkins.

WORK-STUDY *Federal work-study:* Total amount: $557,524; 1,011 jobs averaging $2611. *State or other work-study/employment:* Total amount: $997,140 (28% need-based, 72% non-need-based). Part-time jobs available.

APPLYING FOR FINANCIAL AID *Required financial aid form:* FAFSA. *Financial aid deadline (priority):* 3/1. *Notification date:* Continuous beginning 3/1.

CONTACT Mr. Kenneth Nieman, Director of Student Financial Services, Anderson University, 1100 East Fifth Street, Anderson, IN 46012-3495, 765-641-4180 or toll-free 800-428-6414. *Fax:* 765-641-3831. *E-mail:* kfnieman@anderson.edu. *Website:* http://www.anderson.edu/.

ANDERSON UNIVERSITY
Anderson, SC

Tuition & fees: $22,790	Average undergraduate aid package: $17,029

ABOUT THE INSTITUTION Independent Baptist, coed. *Awards:* bachelor's, master's, and doctoral degrees. 32 undergraduate majors. *Total enrollment:* 2,922. Undergraduates: 2,630. Freshmen: 538. Federal methodology is used as a basis for awarding need-based institutional aid.

UNDERGRADUATE EXPENSES for 2013–2014 *Application fee:* $25. *Comprehensive fee:* $31,138 includes full-time tuition ($20,820), mandatory fees ($1970), and room and board ($8348). *College room only:* $4316. Full-time tuition and fees vary according to course load and program. Room and board charges vary according to board plan and housing facility. *Part-time tuition:* $515 per credit hour. Part-time tuition and fees vary according to program.

FRESHMAN FINANCIAL AID (Fall 2012, est.) 520 applied for aid; of those 82% were deemed to have need. 100% of freshmen with need received aid; of those 33% had need fully met. *Average percent of need met:* 79% (excluding resources awarded to replace EFC). *Average financial aid package:* $19,479 (excluding resources awarded to replace EFC). 19% of all full-time freshmen had no need and received non-need-based gift aid.

UNDERGRADUATE FINANCIAL AID (Fall 2012, est.) 2,030 applied for aid; of those 88% were deemed to have need. 99% of undergraduates with need received aid; of those 26% had need fully met. *Average percent of need met:* 70% (excluding resources awarded to replace EFC). *Average financial aid package:* $17,029 (excluding resources awarded to replace EFC). 14% of all full-time undergraduates had no need and received non-need-based gift aid.

GIFT AID (NEED-BASED) *Total amount:* $22,746,527 (17% federal, 27% state, 54% institutional, 2% external sources). *Receiving aid:* Freshmen: 77% (424); all full-time undergraduates: 80% (1,727). *Average award:* Freshmen: $16,528; Undergraduates: $13,714. *Scholarships, grants, and awards:* Federal Pell, FSEOG, state, private, college/university gift aid from institutional funds.

GIFT AID (NON-NEED-BASED) *Total amount:* $6,382,497 (1% federal, 37% state, 60% institutional, 2% external sources). *Receiving aid:* Freshmen: 20% (113).

Undergraduates: 17% (370). *Average award:* Freshmen: $10,924. Undergraduates: $9971. *Scholarships, grants, and awards by category: Academic interests/achievement:* 2,189 awards ($12,575,537 total): business, education, general academic interests/achievements, religion/biblical studies. *Creative arts/performance:* 246 awards ($381,937 total): art/fine arts, music, performing arts, theater/drama. *Special achievements/activities:* 221 awards ($303,962 total): cheerleading/drum major, leadership, memberships. *Special characteristics:* 894 awards ($1,925,308 total): children of faculty/staff, general special characteristics, international students, members of minority groups, out-of-state students, religious affiliation. *Tuition waivers:* Full or partial for employees or children of employees. *ROTC:* Army cooperative, Air Force cooperative.

LOANS *Student loans:* $14,388,699 (77% need-based, 23% non-need-based). 73% of past graduating class borrowed through all loan programs. *Average indebtedness per student:* $27,187. *Average need-based loan:* Freshmen: $4304. Undergraduates: $4891. *Parent loans:* $1,618,137 (43% need-based, 57% non-need-based). *Programs:* Federal Direct (Subsidized and Unsubsidized Stafford, PLUS), Perkins, state, private loans.

WORK-STUDY *Federal work-study:* Total amount: $345,167; 204 jobs averaging $1898. *State or other work-study/employment:* Total amount: $144,744 (100% need-based). 296 part-time jobs averaging $489.

ATHLETIC AWARDS Total amount: $1,456,035 (61% need-based, 39% non-need-based).

APPLYING FOR FINANCIAL AID *Required financial aid form:* FAFSA. *Financial aid deadline:* 7/30 (priority: 3/1). *Notification date:* Continuous beginning 3/15. Students must reply within 2 weeks of notification.

CONTACT Michael Yohe, Director of Financial Aid Planning, Anderson University, 316 Boulevard, Anderson, SC 29621-4035, 864-231-2181 or toll-free 800-542-3594. *Fax:* 864-231-2008. *E-mail:* myohe@andersonuniversity.edu. *Website:* http://www.andersonuniversity.edu/.

ANDREWS UNIVERSITY
Berrien Springs, MI

Tuition & fees: $24,478	Average undergraduate aid package: $25,910

ABOUT THE INSTITUTION Independent Seventh-day Adventist, coed. *Awards:* certificates, associate, bachelor's, master's, and doctoral degrees. 64 undergraduate majors. *Total enrollment:* 1,634. Undergraduates: 1,917. Freshmen: 388. Federal methodology is used as a basis for awarding need-based institutional aid.

UNDERGRADUATE EXPENSES for 2013–2014 *Application fee:* $30. *Comprehensive fee:* $32,006 includes full-time tuition ($23,700), mandatory fees ($778), and room and board ($7528). *College room only:* $4008. Full-time tuition and fees vary according to course load. Room and board charges vary according to board plan. *Part-time tuition:* $988 per credit hour. Part-time tuition and fees vary according to course load.

FRESHMAN FINANCIAL AID (Fall 2012, est.) 295 applied for aid; of those 89% were deemed to have need. 100% of freshmen with need received aid; of those 21% had need fully met. *Average percent of need met:* 85% (excluding resources awarded to replace EFC). *Average financial aid package:* $25,487 (excluding resources awarded to replace EFC). 28% of all full-time freshmen had no need and received non-need-based gift aid.

UNDERGRADUATE FINANCIAL AID (Fall 2012, est.) 1,237 applied for aid; of those 92% were deemed to have need. 100% of undergraduates with need received aid; of those 14% had need fully met. *Average percent of need met:* 85% (excluding resources awarded to replace EFC). *Average financial aid package:* $25,910 (excluding resources awarded to replace EFC). 33% of all full-time undergraduates had no need and received non-need-based gift aid.

GIFT AID (NEED-BASED) *Total amount:* $22,936,190 (13% federal, 1% state, 69% institutional, 17% external sources). *Receiving aid:* Freshmen: 43% (160); all full-time undergraduates: 45% (790). *Average award:* Freshmen: $4676; Undergraduates: $5598. *Scholarships, grants, and awards:* Federal Pell, FSEOG, state, private, college/university gift aid from institutional funds.

GIFT AID (NON-NEED-BASED) *Receiving aid:* Freshmen: 71% (264). Undergraduates: 65% (1,133). *Average award:* Freshmen: $9252. Undergraduates: $8152. *Scholarships, grants, and awards by category: Academic interests/achievement:* 1,692 awards ($9,976,717 total): general academic interests/achievements. *Creative arts/performance:* 34 awards ($34,435 total): music. *Special achieve-*

ments/activities: 227 awards ($303,117 total): leadership, religious involvement. Special characteristics: 111 awards ($1,237,461 total): children of faculty/staff, general special characteristics, international students. Tuition waivers: Full or partial for employees or children of employees, senior citizens.

LOANS Student loans: $20,399,014 (35% need-based, 65% non-need-based). 62% of past graduating class borrowed through all loan programs. Average indebtedness per student: $33,249. Average need-based loan: Freshmen: $3373. Undergraduates: $4553. Parent loans: $3,987,585 (100% non-need-based). Programs: Federal Direct (Subsidized and Unsubsidized Stafford, PLUS), Perkins.

WORK-STUDY Federal work-study: Total amount: $829,651; 868 jobs averaging $956. State or other work-study/employment: Total amount: $1500 (100% need-based). 1 part-time job averaging $1500.

APPLYING FOR FINANCIAL AID Required financial aid forms: FAFSA, institution's own form. Financial aid deadline: Continuous. Notification date: Continuous.

CONTACT Cynthia Gammon, Assistant Director of Student Financial Services, Andrews University, Student Financial Services Administration Building, Berrien Springs, MI 49104, 800-253-2874. Fax: 269-471-3228. E-mail: sfs@andrews.edu. Website: http://www.andrews.edu/.

ANGELO STATE UNIVERSITY
San Angelo, TX

Tuition & fees (TX res): $7493	Average undergraduate aid package: $9695

ABOUT THE INSTITUTION State-supported, coed. Awards: bachelor's, master's, and doctoral degrees. 36 undergraduate majors. Total enrollment: 6,886. Undergraduates: 6,006. Freshmen: 1,402. Federal methodology is used as a basis for awarding need-based institutional aid.

UNDERGRADUATE EXPENSES for 2013–2014 Application fee: $35. Tuition, state resident: full-time $4994; part-time $166.58 per credit hour. Tuition, nonresident: full-time $15,524; part-time $517.58 per credit hour. Required fees: full-time $2499; $28 per credit hour or $631.25 per term. College room and board: $8026; Room only: $5298. Room and board charges vary according to board plan and housing facility.

FRESHMAN FINANCIAL AID (Fall 2011) 1,160 applied for aid; of those 82% were deemed to have need. 100% of freshmen with need received aid; of those 14% had need fully met. Average percent of need met: 75% (excluding resources awarded to replace EFC). Average financial aid package: $10,212 (excluding resources awarded to replace EFC). 15% of all full-time freshmen had no need and received non-need-based gift aid.

UNDERGRADUATE FINANCIAL AID (Fall 2011) 4,375 applied for aid; of those 85% were deemed to have need. 100% of undergraduates with need received aid; of those 12% had need fully met. Average percent of need met: 69% (excluding resources awarded to replace EFC). Average financial aid package: $9695 (excluding resources awarded to replace EFC). 13% of all full-time undergraduates had no need and received non-need-based gift aid.

GIFT AID (NEED-BASED) Total amount: $22,477,025 (77% federal, 23% state). Receiving aid: Freshmen: 58% (717); all full-time undergraduates: 60% (3,102). Average award: Freshmen: $3418; Undergraduates: $3045. Scholarships, grants, and awards: Federal Pell, FSEOG, state, private, college/university gift aid from institutional funds, Federal Nursing, Carr Academic Scholarships.

GIFT AID (NON-NEED-BASED) Total amount: $14,668,293 (3% state, 90% institutional, 7% external sources). Receiving aid: Freshmen: 55% (679). Undergraduates: 31% (1,609). Average award: Freshmen: $3786. Undergraduates: $3224. Scholarships, grants, and awards by category: Academic interests/achievement: agriculture, biological sciences, business, communication, computer science, education, English, foreign languages, general academic interests/achievements, humanities, international studies, mathematics, military science, physical sciences, pre-medicine, social sciences. Creative arts/performance: art/fine arts, dance, journalism/publications, music, performing arts, theater/drama. Special achievements/activities: cheerleading/drum major, general special achievements/activities, hobbies/interests, leadership, memberships, rodeo. Special characteristics: first-generation college students, local/state students. Tuition waivers: Full or partial for employees or children of employees, senior citizens. ROTC: Air Force.

LOANS Student loans: $66,825,803 (44% need-based, 56% non-need-based). 60% of past graduating class borrowed through all loan programs. Average indebtedness

per student: $21,373. Average need-based loan: Freshmen: $3357. Undergraduates: $4044. Parent loans: $28,057,132 (100% non-need-based). Programs: Federal Direct (Subsidized and Unsubsidized Stafford, PLUS), Perkins, Federal Nursing, state, college/university, alternative loans.

WORK-STUDY Federal work-study: Total amount: $19,210,044; jobs available. State or other work-study/employment: Total amount: $192,054 (100% need-based). Part-time jobs available.

ATHLETIC AWARDS Total amount: $1,357,684 (100% non-need-based).

APPLYING FOR FINANCIAL AID Required financial aid form: FAFSA. Financial aid deadline: Continuous. Notification date: Continuous beginning 4/1. Students must reply within 4 weeks of notification.

CONTACT Ms. Michelle Bennett, Director of Financial Aid, Angelo State University, ASU Station #11015, San Angelo, TX 76909-1015, 325-942-2246 or toll-free 800-946-8627. Fax: 325-942-2082. E-mail: michelle.bennett@angelo.edu. Website: http://www.angelo.edu/.

ANNA MARIA COLLEGE
Paxton, MA

Tuition & fees: $30,456	Average undergraduate aid package: $21,945

ABOUT THE INSTITUTION Independent Roman Catholic, coed. Awards: certificates, associate, bachelor's, and master's degrees. 57 undergraduate majors. Total enrollment: 1,456. Undergraduates: 1,017. Freshmen: 223. Federal methodology is used as a basis for awarding need-based institutional aid.

UNDERGRADUATE EXPENSES for 2013–2014 Application fee: $40. Comprehensive fee: $41,906 includes full-time tuition ($28,752), mandatory fees ($1704), and room and board ($11,450). Full-time tuition and fees vary according to course load and program. Room and board charges vary according to board plan and housing facility. Part-time tuition and fees vary according to class time, course load, and program.

FRESHMAN FINANCIAL AID (Fall 2012, est.) 196 applied for aid; of those 95% were deemed to have need. 100% of freshmen with need received aid; of those 19% had need fully met. Average percent of need met: 19% (excluding resources awarded to replace EFC). Average financial aid package: $22,355 (excluding resources awarded to replace EFC). 4% of all full-time freshmen had no need and received non-need-based gift aid.

UNDERGRADUATE FINANCIAL AID (Fall 2012, est.) 623 applied for aid; of those 92% were deemed to have need. 100% of undergraduates with need received aid; of those 22% had need fully met. Average percent of need met: 22% (excluding resources awarded to replace EFC). Average financial aid package: $21,945 (excluding resources awarded to replace EFC). 6% of all full-time undergraduates had no need and received non-need-based gift aid.

GIFT AID (NEED-BASED) Total amount: $6,520,227 (24% federal, 8% state, 68% institutional). Receiving aid: Freshmen: 73% (180); all full-time undergraduates: 64% (519). Average award: Freshmen: $9370; Undergraduates: $8646. Scholarships, grants, and awards: Federal Pell, FSEOG, state, private, college/university gift aid from institutional funds.

GIFT AID (NON-NEED-BASED) Total amount: $5,820,474 (97% institutional, 3% external sources). Receiving aid: Freshmen: 74% (182). Undergraduates: 68% (553). Average award: Freshmen: $7722. Undergraduates: $7171. Scholarships, grants, and awards by category: Academic interests/achievement: general academic interests/achievements. Creative arts/performance: music. Special achievements/activities: religious involvement. Special characteristics: children of faculty/staff, general special characteristics, local/state students, previous college experience. ROTC: Air Force cooperative.

LOANS Student loans: $8,308,582 (37% need-based, 63% non-need-based). 86% of past graduating class borrowed through all loan programs. Average indebtedness per student: $49,206. Average need-based loan: Freshmen: $3324. Undergraduates: $4263. Parent loans: $2,286,348 (100% non-need-based). Programs: Federal Direct (Subsidized and Unsubsidized Stafford, PLUS), Perkins, state.

WORK-STUDY Federal work-study: Total amount: $445,443; jobs available.

APPLYING FOR FINANCIAL AID Required financial aid form: FAFSA. Financial aid deadline (priority): 3/1. Notification date: Continuous beginning 3/15. Students must reply within 4 weeks of notification.

CONTACT Sandra J. Pereira, Director of Financial Aid, Anna Maria College, 50 Sunset Lane, Paxton, MA 01612-1198, 508-849-3363. *Fax:* 508-849-3229. *E-mail:* spereira@annamaria.edu.
Website: http://www.annamaria.edu/.

ANTIOCH UNIVERSITY MIDWEST
Yellow Springs, OH

Tuition & fees: N/R	Average undergraduate aid package: $8800

ABOUT THE INSTITUTION Independent, coed. *Awards:* certificates, bachelor's, and master's degrees. 11 undergraduate majors. *Total enrollment:* 364. Undergraduates: 116. Federal methodology is used as a basis for awarding need-based institutional aid.
UNDERGRADUATE FINANCIAL AID (Fall 2011) 35 applied for aid; of those 97% were deemed to have need. 100% of undergraduates with need received aid. *Average percent of need met:* 30% (excluding resources awarded to replace EFC). *Average financial aid package:* $8800 (excluding resources awarded to replace EFC).
GIFT AID (NEED-BASED) *Total amount:* $455,923 (81% federal, 17% state, 2% external sources). *Receiving aid:* All full-time undergraduates: 38% (25). *Average award:* Undergraduates: $5000. *Scholarships, grants, and awards:* Federal Pell, FSEOG, state.
GIFT AID (NON-NEED-BASED) *Total amount:* $4972 (100% external sources). *Scholarships, grants, and awards by category:* Academic interests/achievement: 9 awards ($12,472 total): education, health fields.
LOANS *Student loans:* $839,479 (42% need-based, 58% non-need-based). 63% of past graduating class borrowed through all loan programs. *Average indebtedness per student:* $40,000. *Average need-based loan:* Undergraduates: $7000. *Programs:* Federal Direct (Subsidized and Unsubsidized Stafford, PLUS), Perkins.
WORK-STUDY *Federal work-study:* Total amount: $77,040; 5 jobs averaging $7000.
APPLYING FOR FINANCIAL AID *Required financial aid forms:* FAFSA, institution's own form. *Financial aid deadline:* Continuous. *Notification date:* Continuous beginning 4/1.
CONTACT Djana Tomas, Financial Aid Coordinator, Antioch University Midwest, 900 Dayton Street, Yellow Springs, OH 45387, 937-769-1841. *Fax:* 937-769-1804. *E-mail:* dtomas@antioch.edu.
Website: http://midwest.antioch.edu/.

ANTIOCH UNIVERSITY SANTA BARBARA
Santa Barbara, CA

CONTACT Cecilia Schneider, Financial Aid Director, Antioch University Santa Barbara, 801 Garden Street, Santa Barbara, CA 93101-1580, 805-962-8179 Ext. 108 or toll-free 866-526-8462. *Fax:* 805-962-4786.
Website: http://www.antiochsb.edu/.

ANTIOCH UNIVERSITY SEATTLE
Seattle, WA

CONTACT Katy Stahl, Director of Financial Aid, Antioch University Seattle, 2326 Sixth Avenue, Seattle, WA 98121-1814, 206-268-4004 or toll-free 888-268-4477. *Fax:* 206-268-4242. *E-mail:* kstahl@antiochseattle.edu.
Website: http://www.antiochsea.edu/.

APEX SCHOOL OF THEOLOGY
Durham, NC

CONTACT Financial Aid Office, Apex School of Theology, 2945 South Miami Boulevard, Suite 114, Durham, NC 27703, 919-572-1625.
Website: http://www.apexsot.edu/.

APPALACHIAN BIBLE COLLEGE
Bradley, WV

ABOUT THE INSTITUTION Independent nondenominational, coed. *Awards:* certificates, diplomas, associate, bachelor's, and master's degrees. 2 undergraduate majors. *Total enrollment:* 302. Undergraduates: 286. Freshmen: 73.
GIFT AID (NEED-BASED) *Scholarships, grants, and awards:* Federal Pell, FSEOG, state, private, college/university gift aid from institutional funds.
GIFT AID (NON-NEED-BASED) *Scholarships, grants, and awards by category:* Academic interests/achievement: general academic interests/achievements, religion/biblical studies. Special achievements/activities: general special achievements/activities, religious involvement. Special characteristics: children and siblings of alumni, children of educators, children of faculty/staff, general special characteristics, international students, married students, relatives of clergy, religious affiliation, spouses of current students, veterans.
LOANS *Programs:* Federal Direct (Subsidized and Unsubsidized Stafford, PLUS).
WORK-STUDY *Federal work-study:* Total amount: $16,376; 26 jobs averaging $630. *State or other work-study/employment:* Part-time jobs available.
APPLYING FOR FINANCIAL AID *Required financial aid forms:* FAFSA, institution's own form.
CONTACT Deana Steinke, Director of Financial Aid, Appalachian Bible College, 161 College Drive, Mount Hope, WV 25880, 304-877-6428 Ext. 3247 or toll-free 800-678-9ABC. *Fax:* 304-877-5082. *E-mail:* deana.steinke@abc.edu.
Website: http://www.abc.edu/.

APPALACHIAN STATE UNIVERSITY
Boone, NC

Tuition & fees (NC res): $5859	Average undergraduate aid package: $9104

ABOUT THE INSTITUTION State-supported, coed. *Awards:* certificates, bachelor's, master's, and doctoral degrees. 89 undergraduate majors. *Total enrollment:* 17,589. Undergraduates: 15,712. Freshmen: 3,028. Federal methodology is used as a basis for awarding need-based institutional aid.
UNDERGRADUATE EXPENSES for 2013–2014 *Application fee:* $55. *Tuition, state resident:* full-time $3542; part-time $106.50 per credit hour. *Tuition, nonresident:* full-time $15,590; part-time $513.50 per credit hour. *Required fees:* full-time $2317; $13 per credit hour. Part-time tuition and fees vary according to course load. *College room and board:* $7060; *Room only:* $3900. Room and board charges vary according to board plan and housing facility.
FRESHMAN FINANCIAL AID (Fall 2012, est.) 1,575 applied for aid; of those 98% were deemed to have need. 93% of freshmen with need received aid; of those 28% had need fully met. *Average percent of need met:* 68% (excluding resources awarded to replace EFC). *Average financial aid package:* $8641 (excluding resources awarded to replace EFC). 2% of all full-time freshmen had no need and received non-need-based gift aid.
UNDERGRADUATE FINANCIAL AID (Fall 2012, est.) 7,574 applied for aid; of those 97% were deemed to have need. 95% of undergraduates with need received aid; of those 33% had need fully met. *Average percent of need met:* 70% (excluding resources awarded to replace EFC). *Average financial aid package:* $9104 (excluding resources awarded to replace EFC). 3% of all full-time undergraduates had no need and received non-need-based gift aid.
GIFT AID (NEED-BASED) *Total amount:* $41,095,440 (39% federal, 32% state, 24% institutional, 5% external sources). *Receiving aid:* Freshmen: 39% (1,172); all full-time undergraduates: 38% (5,594). *Average award:* Freshmen: $7710; Undergraduates: $7394. *Scholarships, grants, and awards:* Federal Pell, FSEOG, state, private, college/university gift aid from institutional funds.

GIFT AID (NON-NEED-BASED) *Total amount:* $2,325,781 (1% federal, 13% state, 45% institutional, 41% external sources). *Receiving aid:* Freshmen: 17% (501). Undergraduates: 17% (2,465). *Average award:* Freshmen: $2235. Undergraduates: $2510. *Scholarships, grants, and awards by category: Academic interests/achievement:* general academic interests/achievements. *Creative arts/performance:* general creative arts/performance. *Special achievements/activities:* general special achievements/activities. *Special characteristics:* first-generation college students, general special characteristics, handicapped students, members of minority groups, out-of-state students, veterans, veterans' children. *Tuition waivers:* Full or partial for employees or children of employees. *ROTC:* Army.

LOANS *Student loans:* $49,189,780 (77% need-based, 23% non-need-based). 54% of past graduating class borrowed through all loan programs. *Average indebtedness per student:* $20,016. *Average need-based loan:* Freshmen: $4850. Undergraduates: $5773. *Parent loans:* $23,402,247 (61% need-based, 39% non-need-based). *Programs:* Federal Direct (Subsidized and Unsubsidized Stafford, PLUS), Perkins.

WORK-STUDY *Federal work-study:* Total amount: $517,500; 306 jobs averaging $1685.

ATHLETIC AWARDS Total amount: $3,935,798 (51% need-based, 49% non-need-based).

APPLYING FOR FINANCIAL AID *Required financial aid form:* FAFSA. *Financial aid deadline:* Continuous. *Notification date:* Continuous beginning 4/1. Students must reply within 3 weeks of notification.

CONTACT Esther Manogin, Director of Student Financial Aid, Appalachian State University, John E. Thomas Hall, ASU Box 32059, Boone, NC 28608-2059, 828-262-2190. *Fax:* 828-262-2585. *E-mail:* manoginem@appstate.edu. *Website:* http://www.appstate.edu/.

AQUINAS COLLEGE
Grand Rapids, MI

ABOUT THE INSTITUTION Independent Roman Catholic, coed. *Awards:* associate, bachelor's, and master's degrees. 53 undergraduate majors. *Total enrollment:* 2,327. Undergraduates: 2,114. Freshmen: 376.

GIFT AID (NEED-BASED) *Scholarships, grants, and awards:* Federal Pell, FSEOG, state, private, college/university gift aid from institutional funds.

GIFT AID (NON-NEED-BASED) *Scholarships, grants, and awards by category: Academic interests/achievement:* general academic interests/achievements. *Special characteristics:* children and siblings of alumni, children of faculty/staff.

LOANS *Programs:* Federal Direct (Subsidized and Unsubsidized Stafford, PLUS), Perkins.

WORK-STUDY *Federal work-study:* Total amount: $150,000; jobs available. *State or other work-study/employment:* Total amount: $700,000 (50% need-based, 50% non-need-based). Part-time jobs available.

APPLYING FOR FINANCIAL AID *Required financial aid form:* FAFSA.

CONTACT David J. Steffee, Director of Financial Aid, Aquinas College, 1607 Robinson Road, Grand Rapids, MI 49506-1799, 616-459-8281 Ext. 5127 or toll-free 800-678-9593. *Fax:* 616-732-4547. *E-mail:* steffdav@aquinas.edu. *Website:* http://www.aquinas.edu/.

AQUINAS COLLEGE
Nashville, TN

CONTACT Mrs. Kylie Pruitt, Director of Financial Aid, Aquinas College, 4210 Harding Road, Nashville, TN 37205-2005, 615-297-7545 Ext. 431 or toll-free 800-649-9956. *Fax:* 615-279-3891. *E-mail:* pruittk@aquinascollege.edu. *Website:* http://www.aquinascollege.edu/.

ARCADIA UNIVERSITY
Glenside, PA

Tuition & fees: $35,620	Average undergraduate aid package: $25,768

ABOUT THE INSTITUTION Independent Presbyterian Church (U.S.A.), coed. *Awards:* certificates, bachelor's, master's, and doctoral degrees. 66 undergraduate majors. *Total enrollment:* 4,027. Undergraduates: 2,360. Freshmen: 680. Federal methodology is used as a basis for awarding need-based institutional aid.

UNDERGRADUATE EXPENSES for 2013–2014 *Application fee:* $30. *Comprehensive fee:* $47,770 includes full-time tuition ($34,960), mandatory fees ($660), and room and board ($12,150). Full-time tuition and fees vary according to course load, degree level, and program. Room and board charges vary according to board plan.

FRESHMAN FINANCIAL AID (Fall 2012, est.) 641 applied for aid; of those 93% were deemed to have need. 100% of freshmen with need received aid; of those 14% had need fully met. *Average percent of need met:* 72% (excluding resources awarded to replace EFC). *Average financial aid package:* $26,972 (excluding resources awarded to replace EFC). 11% of all full-time freshmen had no need and received non-need-based gift aid.

UNDERGRADUATE FINANCIAL AID (Fall 2012, est.) 1,941 applied for aid; of those 92% were deemed to have need. 100% of undergraduates with need received aid; of those 16% had need fully met. *Average percent of need met:* 63% (excluding resources awarded to replace EFC). *Average financial aid package:* $25,768 (excluding resources awarded to replace EFC). 13% of all full-time undergraduates had no need and received non-need-based gift aid.

GIFT AID (NEED-BASED) *Total amount:* $36,447,680 (9% federal, 89% institutional, 2% external sources). *Receiving aid:* Freshmen: 86% (593); all full-time undergraduates: 83% (1,784). *Average award:* Freshmen: $23,378; Undergraduates: $21,581. *Scholarships, grants, and awards:* Federal Pell, FSEOG, state, private, college/university gift aid from institutional funds, Academic Competitiveness Grants, National SMART Grants, TEACH Grants.

GIFT AID (NON-NEED-BASED) *Total amount:* $6,324,682 (1% state, 97% institutional, 2% external sources). *Receiving aid:* Freshmen: 9% (60). Undergraduates: 10% (205). *Average award:* Freshmen: $15,112. Undergraduates: $15,750. *Scholarships, grants, and awards by category: Academic interests/achievement:* 2,216 awards ($29,087,484 total): general academic interests/achievements. *Creative arts/performance:* applied art and design, art/fine arts, theater/drama. *Special achievements/activities:* 723 awards ($6,735,350 total): community service, general special achievements/activities, leadership, memberships. *Special characteristics:* 27 awards ($78,000 total): children and siblings of alumni, relatives of clergy, religious affiliation.

LOANS *Student loans:* $20,515,863 (70% need-based, 30% non-need-based). 83% of past graduating class borrowed through all loan programs. *Average indebtedness per student:* $41,393. *Average need-based loan:* Freshmen: $3236. Undergraduates: $4061. *Parent loans:* $5,757,910 (49% need-based, 51% non-need-based). *Programs:* Federal Direct (Subsidized and Unsubsidized Stafford, PLUS), Perkins.

WORK-STUDY *Federal work-study:* Total amount: $2,148,614; 1,257 jobs averaging $1656. *State or other work-study/employment:* Total amount: $322,718 (100% non-need-based). 190 part-time jobs averaging $1643.

APPLYING FOR FINANCIAL AID *Required financial aid forms:* FAFSA, institution's own form. *Financial aid deadline (priority):* 3/1. *Notification date:* Continuous beginning 3/1. Students must reply by 5/1.

CONTACT Holly Kirkpatrick, Director of Financial Aid, Arcadia University, 450 South Easton Road, Glenside, PA 19038, 215-572-4475 or toll-free 877-ARCADIA. *Fax:* 215-572-4049. *E-mail:* kirkpath@arcadia.edu. *Website:* http://www.arcadia.edu/.

ARGOSY UNIVERSITY, ATLANTA
Atlanta, GA

CONTACT Financial Aid Office, Argosy University, Atlanta, 980 Hammond Drive, Suite 100, Atlanta, GA 30328, 770-671-1200 or toll-free 888-671-4777. *Website:* http://www.argosy.edu/atlanta/.

ARGOSY UNIVERSITY, CHICAGO
Chicago, IL

CONTACT Financial Aid Office, Argosy University, Chicago, 225 North Michigan Avenue, Suite 1300, Chicago, IL 60601, 312-777-7600 or toll-free 800-626-4123. *Website:* http://www.argosy.edu/chicago/.

ARGOSY UNIVERSITY, DALLAS
Farmers Branch, TX

CONTACT Financial Aid Office, Argosy University, Dallas, 5001 Lyndon B. Johnson Freeway, Heritage Square, Farmers Branch, TX 75244, 214-890-9900 or toll-free 866-954-9900. *Website:* http://www.argosy.edu/dallas/.

ARGOSY UNIVERSITY, DENVER
Denver, CO

CONTACT Financial Aid Office, Argosy University, Denver, 7600 East Eastman Avenue, Denver, CO 80231, 303-923-4110 or toll-free 866-431-5981. *Website:* http://www.argosy.edu/denver/.

ARGOSY UNIVERSITY, HAWAII
Honolulu, HI

CONTACT Financial Aid Office, Argosy University, Hawaii, 400 ASB Tower, 1001 Bishop Street, Honolulu, HI 96813, 808-536-5555 or toll-free 888-323-2777. *Website:* http://www.argosy.edu/hawaii/.

ARGOSY UNIVERSITY, INLAND EMPIRE
Ontario, CA

CONTACT Financial Aid Office, Argosy University, Inland Empire, 3401 Centre Lake Drive, Suite 200, Ontario, CA 91761, 909-472-0800 or toll-free 866-217-9075. *Website:* http://www.argosy.edu/inland-empire/.

ARGOSY UNIVERSITY, NASHVILLE
Nashville, TN

CONTACT Financial Aid Office, Argosy University, Nashville, 100 Centerview Drive, Suite 225, Nashville, TN 37214, 615-525-2800 or toll-free 866-833-6598. *Website:* http://www.argosy.edu/nashville/.

ARGOSY UNIVERSITY, ORANGE COUNTY
Orange, CA

CONTACT Financial Aid Office, Argosy University, Orange County, 601 South Lewis Street, Orange, CA 92868, 714-338-6200 or toll-free 800-716-9598. *Website:* http://www.argosy.edu/locations/los-angeles-orange-county/.

ARGOSY UNIVERSITY, PHOENIX
Phoenix, AZ

CONTACT Financial Aid Office, Argosy University, Phoenix, 2233 West Dunlap Avenue, Phoenix, AZ 85021, 602-216-2600 or toll-free 866-216-2777. *Website:* http://www.argosy.edu/phoenix/.

ARGOSY UNIVERSITY, SALT LAKE CITY
Draper, UT

CONTACT Financial Aid Office, Argosy University, Salt Lake City, 121 West Election Road, Suite 300, Draper, UT 84020 or toll-free 888-639-4756. *Website:* http://www.argosy.edu/locations/salt-lake-city/.

ARGOSY UNIVERSITY, SAN DIEGO
San Diego, CA

CONTACT Financial Aid Office, Argosy University, San Diego, 1615 Murray Canyon Road, Suite 100, San Diego, CA 92108, 619-321-3000 or toll-free 866-505-0333. *Website:* http://www.argosy.edu/sandiego/.

ARGOSY UNIVERSITY, SAN FRANCISCO BAY AREA
Alameda, CA

CONTACT Financial Aid Office, Argosy University, San Francisco Bay Area, 1005 Atlantic Avenue, Alameda, CA 94501, 510-217-4700 or toll-free 866-215-2777. *Website:* http://www.argosy.edu/sanfrancisco/.

ARGOSY UNIVERSITY, SARASOTA
Sarasota, FL

CONTACT Financial Aid Office, Argosy University, Sarasota, 5250 17th Street, Sarasota, FL 34235, 941-379-0404 or toll-free 800-331-5995. *Website:* http://www.argosy.edu/sarasota/.

ARGOSY UNIVERSITY, SCHAUMBURG
Schaumburg, IL

CONTACT Financial Aid Office, Argosy University, Schaumburg, 999 North Plaza Drive, Suite 111, Schaumburg, IL 60173-5403, 847-969-4900 or toll-free 866-290-2777. *Website:* http://www.argosy.edu/schaumburg/.

ARGOSY UNIVERSITY, SEATTLE
Seattle, WA

CONTACT Financial Aid Office, Argosy University, Seattle, 2601-A Elliott Avenue, Seattle, WA 98121, 206-283-4500 or toll-free 866-283-2777. *Website:* http://www.argosy.edu/seattle/.

ARGOSY UNIVERSITY, TAMPA
Tampa, FL

CONTACT Financial Aid Office, Argosy University, Tampa, 1403 North Howard Avenue, Tampa, FL 33607, 813-393-5290 or toll-free 800-850-6488. *Website:* http://www.argosy.edu/tampa/.

ARGOSY UNIVERSITY, TWIN CITIES
Eagan, MN

CONTACT Financial Aid Office, Argosy University, Twin Cities, 1515 Central Parkway, Eagan, MN 55121, 651-846-2882 or toll-free 888-844-2004. *Website:* http://www.argosy.edu/twincities/.

ARGOSY UNIVERSITY, WASHINGTON DC
Arlington, VA

CONTACT Financial Aid Office, Argosy University, Washington DC, 1550 Wilson Boulevard, Suite 600, Arlington, VA 22209, 703-526-5800 or toll-free 866-703-2777. *Website:* http://www.argosy.edu/washingtondc/.

ARIZONA CHRISTIAN UNIVERSITY
Phoenix, AZ

CONTACT Ms. Jill Golike, Director of Financial Aid, Arizona Christian University, 2625 East Cactus Road, Phoenix, AZ 85032-7097, 602-489-5300 Ext. 115 or toll-free 800-247-2697. *Fax:* 800-971-3688. *E-mail:* jill.golike@arizonachristian.edu. *Website:* http://arizonachristian.edu/.

ARIZONA STATE UNIVERSITY
Tempe, AZ

Tuition & fees (AZ res): $9724	Average undergraduate aid package: $12,011

ABOUT THE INSTITUTION State-supported, coed. *Awards:* certificates, bachelor's, master's, and doctoral degrees (profile includes data for the West, Polytechnic and Downtown Phoenix campuses). 128 undergraduate majors. *Total enrollment:* 73,378. Undergraduates: 59,382. Freshmen: 9,265. Federal methodology is used as a basis for awarding need-based institutional aid.

UNDERGRADUATE EXPENSES for 2013–2014 *Application fee:* $50. *Tuition, state resident:* full-time $9208; part-time $658 per credit hour. *Tuition, nonresident:* full-time $22,461; part-time $936 per credit hour. *Required fees:* full-time $516; $154 per term. Full-time tuition and fees vary according to program. Part-time tuition and fees vary according to program. *College room and board:* $9094; *Room only:* $5998. Room and board charges vary according to board plan, housing facility, and location.

FRESHMAN FINANCIAL AID (Fall 2011) 7,312 applied for aid; of those 80% were deemed to have need. 100% of freshmen with need received aid; of those 17% had need fully met. *Average percent of need met:* 59% (excluding resources awarded to replace EFC). *Average financial aid package:* $12,756 (excluding resources awarded to replace EFC). 20% of all full-time freshmen had no need and received non-need-based gift aid.

UNDERGRADUATE FINANCIAL AID (Fall 2011) 37,125 applied for aid; of those 87% were deemed to have need. 100% of undergraduates with need received aid; of those 15% had need fully met. *Average percent of need met:* 56% (excluding resources awarded to replace EFC). *Average financial aid package:* $12,011 (excluding resources awarded to replace EFC). 12% of all full-time undergraduates had no need and received non-need-based gift aid.

GIFT AID (NEED-BASED) *Total amount:* $244,363,485 (44% federal, 49% institutional, 7% external sources). *Receiving aid:* Freshmen: 62% (5,594); all full-time undergraduates: 56% (28,361). *Average award:* Freshmen: $9323; Undergraduates: $8182. *Scholarships, grants, and awards:* Federal Pell, FSEOG, state, private, college/university gift aid from institutional funds, Federal Nursing.

GIFT AID (NON-NEED-BASED) *Total amount:* $75,360,409 (5% federal, 72% institutional, 23% external sources). *Receiving aid:* Freshmen: 6% (541). Undergraduates: 3% (1,637). *Average award:* Freshmen: $7505. Undergraduates: $7884. *Scholarships, grants, and awards by category:* Academic interests/achievement: general academic interests/achievements. Creative arts/performance: art/fine arts, dance, music, theater/drama. Special achievements/activities: leadership. Special characteristics: children of faculty/staff, international students, local/state students, out-of-state students. *Tuition waivers:* Full or partial for employees or children of employees. ROTC: Army, Naval, Air Force.

LOANS *Student loans:* $247,978,789 (80% need-based, 20% non-need-based). 55% of past graduating class borrowed through all loan programs. *Average indebtedness per student:* $18,615. *Average need-based loan:* Freshmen: $3125. Undergraduates: $4209. *Parent loans:* $93,064,852 (45% need-based, 55% non-need-based). *Programs:* Federal Direct (Subsidized and Unsubsidized Stafford, PLUS), Perkins, Federal Nursing, state, private loans.

WORK-STUDY *Federal work-study:* Total amount: $3,438,388; 1,363 jobs averaging $2526. *State or other work-study/employment:* Total amount: $23,035,960 (38% need-based, 62% non-need-based). 6,866 part-time jobs averaging $3354.

ATHLETIC AWARDS Total amount: $8,407,613 (42% need-based, 58% non-need-based).

APPLYING FOR FINANCIAL AID *Required financial aid form:* FAFSA. *Financial aid deadline (priority):* 3/1. *Notification date:* Continuous beginning 3/1.

CONTACT Financial Aid Office, Arizona State University, Box 870412, Tempe, AZ 85287-0412, 480-965-3355. *Fax:* 480-965-9484. *E-mail:* admissions@asu.edu. *Website:* http://www.asu.edu/.

ARKANSAS BAPTIST COLLEGE
Little Rock, AR

CONTACT Office of Financial Aid, Arkansas Baptist College, 1600 Bishop Street, Little Rock, AR 72202-6067, 501-374-7856. *Website:* http://www.arkansasbaptist.edu/.

ARKANSAS STATE UNIVERSITY
Jonesboro, AR

Tuition & fees (AR res): $7180	Average undergraduate aid package: $8500

ABOUT THE INSTITUTION State-supported, coed. *Awards:* certificates, associate, bachelor's, master's, and doctoral degrees. 75 undergraduate majors. *Total enrollment:* 13,877. Undergraduates: 10,168. Freshmen: 1,671. Both federal and institutional methodology are used as a basis for awarding need-based institutional aid.

UNDERGRADUATE EXPENSES for 2013–2014 *Application fee:* $15. *Tuition, state resident:* full-time $5430; part-time $181 per credit hour. *Tuition, nonresident:* full-time $10,860; part-time $362 per credit hour. *Required fees:* full-time $1750; $56 per credit hour or $25 per term. Full-time tuition and fees vary according to course load, location, and program. Part-time tuition and fees vary according to course load, location, and program. *College room and board:* $7150. Room and board charges vary according to board plan, housing facility, and student level.

FRESHMAN FINANCIAL AID (Fall 2012, est.) 1,549 applied for aid; of those 97% were deemed to have need. 100% of freshmen with need received aid; of those 35% had need fully met. *Average percent of need met:* 62% (excluding resources awarded to replace EFC). *Average financial aid package:* $10,100 (excluding resources awarded to replace EFC). 13% of all full-time freshmen had no need and received non-need-based gift aid.

UNDERGRADUATE FINANCIAL AID (Fall 2012, est.) 7,797 applied for aid; of those 88% were deemed to have need. 98% of undergraduates with need received aid;

of those 34% had need fully met. *Average percent of need met:* 45% (excluding resources awarded to replace EFC). *Average financial aid package:* $8500 (excluding resources awarded to replace EFC). 8% of all full-time undergraduates had no need and received non-need-based gift aid.
GIFT AID (NEED-BASED) *Total amount:* $65,500,000 (42% federal, 33% state, 22% institutional, 3% external sources). *Receiving aid:* Freshmen: 89% (1,450); all full-time undergraduates: 83% (6,529). *Average award:* Freshmen: $9900; Undergraduates: $8000. *Scholarships, grants, and awards:* Federal Pell, FSEOG, state, private, college/university gift aid from institutional funds.
GIFT AID (NON-NEED-BASED) *Receiving aid:* Freshmen: 38% (627). Undergraduates: 41% (3,213). *Average award:* Freshmen: $5000. Undergraduates: $5550. *Scholarships, grants, and awards by category: Academic interests/achievement:* 2,048 awards ($11,268,866 total): agriculture, area/ethnic studies, biological sciences, business, communication, computer science, education, engineering/technologies, English, general academic interests/achievements, health fields, humanities, library science, mathematics, military science, physical sciences, premedicine, social sciences. *Creative arts/performance:* 340 awards ($861,464 total): art/fine arts, cinema/film/broadcasting, debating, journalism/publications, music, performing arts, theater/drama. *Special achievements/activities:* 77 awards ($88,700 total): cheerleading/drum major, community service, general special achievements/activities, leadership. *Special characteristics:* 140 awards ($413,800 total): adult students, children and siblings of alumni, children of faculty/staff, ethnic background, first-generation college students, general special characteristics, handicapped students, local/state students, members of minority groups, out-of-state students, veterans, veterans' children. *Tuition waivers:* Full or partial for employees or children of employees, senior citizens. *ROTC:* Army.
LOANS *Student loans:* $62,000,000 (74% need-based, 26% non-need-based). 68% of past graduating class borrowed through all loan programs. *Average indebtedness per student:* $21,000. *Average need-based loan:* Freshmen: $5800. Undergraduates: $8000. *Programs:* Federal Direct (Subsidized and Unsubsidized Stafford, PLUS), Perkins.
WORK-STUDY *Federal work-study:* Total amount: $700,000; 155 jobs averaging $3179. *State or other work-study/employment:* Total amount: $2,500,000 (100% non-need-based). 310 part-time jobs averaging $3550.
ATHLETIC AWARDS Total amount: $5,100,000 (80% need-based, 20% non-need-based).
APPLYING FOR FINANCIAL AID *Required financial aid forms:* FAFSA, institution's own form. *Financial aid deadline:* 7/1 (priority: 2/15). *Notification date:* Continuous beginning 6/1. Students must reply within 2 weeks of notification.
CONTACT Mr. Terry Finney, Director of Financial Aid, Arkansas State University, PO Box 1620, State University, AR 72467, 870-972-2310 or toll-free 800-382-3030. *Fax:* 870-972-2794. *E-mail:* finaid@astate.edu.
Website: http://www.astate.edu/.

ARKANSAS TECH UNIVERSITY
Russellville, AR

Tuition & fees (AR res): $6798	Average undergraduate aid package: $9044

ABOUT THE INSTITUTION State-supported, coed. *Awards:* certificates, associate, bachelor's, and master's degrees. 67 undergraduate majors. *Total enrollment:* 10,950. Undergraduates: 10,089. Freshmen: 1,787. Federal methodology is used as a basis for awarding need-based institutional aid.
UNDERGRADUATE EXPENSES for 2013–2014 *Tuition, state resident:* full-time $5610; part-time $187 per credit hour. *Tuition, nonresident:* full-time $11,220; part-time $374 per credit hour. *Required fees:* full-time $1188; $20 per credit hour or $159 per term. Full-time tuition and fees vary according to course load and location. Part-time tuition and fees vary according to course load and location. *College room and board:* $5846; *Room only:* $3582. Room and board charges vary according to board plan, housing facility, and location.
FRESHMAN FINANCIAL AID (Fall 2011) 1,720 applied for aid; of those 67% were deemed to have need. 98% of freshmen with need received aid; of those 8% had need fully met. *Average percent of need met:* 66% (excluding resources awarded to replace EFC). *Average financial aid package:* $8886 (excluding resources awarded to replace EFC). 20% of all full-time freshmen had no need and received non-need-based gift aid.

UNDERGRADUATE FINANCIAL AID (Fall 2011) 6,418 applied for aid; of those 74% were deemed to have need. 99% of undergraduates with need received aid; of those 16% had need fully met. *Average percent of need met:* 68% (excluding resources awarded to replace EFC). *Average financial aid package:* $9044 (excluding resources awarded to replace EFC). 13% of all full-time undergraduates had no need and received non-need-based gift aid.
GIFT AID (NEED-BASED) *Total amount:* $22,604,663 (89% federal, 11% state). *Receiving aid:* Freshmen: 57% (997); all full-time undergraduates: 57% (4,004). *Average award:* Freshmen: $4115; Undergraduates: $4688. *Scholarships, grants, and awards:* Federal Pell, FSEOG, state, private.
GIFT AID (NON-NEED-BASED) *Total amount:* $25,131,050 (50% state, 42% institutional, 8% external sources). *Receiving aid:* Freshmen: 39% (687). Undergraduates: 27% (1,870). *Average award:* Freshmen: $5853. Undergraduates: $6606. *Scholarships, grants, and awards by category: Academic interests/achievement:* biological sciences, business, computer science, education, engineering/technologies, general academic interests/achievements, health fields, humanities, military science, physical sciences, social sciences. *Creative arts/performance:* cinema/film/broadcasting, creative writing, journalism/publications, theater/drama. *Special achievements/activities:* general special achievements/activities, hobbies/interests, junior miss, leadership, memberships. *Special characteristics:* children of faculty/staff, general special characteristics, out-of-state students, public servants. *Tuition waivers:* Full or partial for employees or children of employees, senior citizens. *ROTC:* Army cooperative.
LOANS *Student loans:* $38,257,337 (46% need-based, 54% non-need-based). 57% of past graduating class borrowed through all loan programs. *Average indebtedness per student:* $22,649. *Average need-based loan:* Freshmen: $2839. Undergraduates: $3696. *Parent loans:* $764,744 (100% non-need-based). *Programs:* Federal Direct (Subsidized and Unsubsidized Stafford, PLUS), Perkins.
WORK-STUDY *Federal work-study:* Total amount: $270,102; jobs available. *State or other work-study/employment:* Total amount: $428,188 (17% need-based, 83% non-need-based). Part-time jobs available.
ATHLETIC AWARDS Total amount: $1,192,595 (100% non-need-based).
APPLYING FOR FINANCIAL AID *Required financial aid forms:* FAFSA, institution's own form. *Financial aid deadline (priority):* 4/15. *Notification date:* Continuous beginning 5/1. Students must reply within 2 weeks of notification.
CONTACT Financial Aid Office, Arkansas Tech University, 1605 Coliseum Drive, Suite 117, Russellville, AR 72801, 479-968-0399 or toll-free 800-582-6953. *Fax:* 479-964-0857. *E-mail:* fa.help@atu.edu.
Website: http://www.atu.edu/.

ARLINGTON BAPTIST COLLEGE
Arlington, TX

CONTACT Mr. David B. Clogston Jr., Business Manager, Arlington Baptist College, 3001 West Division Street, Arlington, TX 76012-3425, 817-461-8741 Ext. 110. *Fax:* 817-274-1138.
Website: http://www.arlingtonbaptistcollege.edu/.

ARMSTRONG ATLANTIC STATE UNIVERSITY
Savannah, GA

Tuition & fees (GA res): $5844	Average undergraduate aid package: $7750

ABOUT THE INSTITUTION State-supported, coed. *Awards:* certificates, associate, bachelor's, master's, and doctoral degrees. 35 undergraduate majors. *Total enrollment:* 7,439. Undergraduates: 6,731. Freshmen: 1,065. Federal methodology is used as a basis for awarding need-based institutional aid.
UNDERGRADUATE EXPENSES for 2013–2014 *Application fee:* $25. *Tuition, state resident:* full-time $4512; part-time $150.40 per credit hour. *Tuition, nonresident:* full-time $16,416; part-time $547.02 per credit hour. *Required fees:* full-time $1332; $666 per term. Full-time tuition and fees vary according to course load, location, and program. Part-time tuition and fees vary

according to course load, location, and program. **College room and board:** $9770. **Room only:** $5908. Room and board charges vary according to board plan and housing facility.

FRESHMAN FINANCIAL AID (Fall 2011) 854 applied for aid; of those 80% were deemed to have need. 100% of freshmen with need received aid; of those 52% had need fully met. **Average percent of need met:** 82% (excluding resources awarded to replace EFC). **Average financial aid package:** $6500 (excluding resources awarded to replace EFC). 15% of all full-time freshmen had no need and received non-need-based gift aid.

UNDERGRADUATE FINANCIAL AID (Fall 2011) 4,721 applied for aid; of those 80% were deemed to have need. 100% of undergraduates with need received aid; of those 52% had need fully met. **Average percent of need met:** 82% (excluding resources awarded to replace EFC). **Average financial aid package:** $7750 (excluding resources awarded to replace EFC). 11% of all full-time undergraduates had no need and received non-need-based gift aid.

GIFT AID (NEED-BASED) Total amount: $13,035,926 (100% federal). **Receiving aid:** Freshmen: 33% (355); all full-time undergraduates: 33% (1,963). **Average award:** Freshmen: $4000; Undergraduates: $4000. **Scholarships, grants, and awards:** Federal Pell, FSEOG, state, private, college/university gift aid from institutional funds, Federal Nursing.

GIFT AID (NON-NEED-BASED) Total amount: $7,359,190 (78% state, 5% institutional, 17% external sources). **Receiving aid:** Freshmen: 7% (71). Undergraduates: 7% (392). **Average award:** Freshmen $3000. Undergraduates: $3000. **Scholarships, grants, and awards by category:** Academic interests/achievement: biological sciences, computer science, education, engineering/technologies, English, foreign languages, general academic interests/achievements, health fields, humanities, international studies, mathematics, military science, physical sciences. *Creative arts/performance:* art/fine arts, general creative arts/performance, music. *Special achievements/activities:* community service. *Special characteristics:* ethnic background, international students, religious affiliation. **Tuition waivers:** Full or partial for employees or children of employees, senior citizens. **ROTC:** Army, Naval cooperative.

LOANS Student loans: $35,289,176 (53% need-based, 47% non-need-based). 50% of past graduating class borrowed through all loan programs. **Average indebtedness per student:** $21,000. **Average need-based loan:** Freshmen: $4500. Undergraduates: $4500. **Parent loans:** $3,386,999 (100% non-need-based). **Programs:** Federal Direct (Subsidized and Unsubsidized Stafford, PLUS), state, college/university, alternative loans.

WORK-STUDY Federal work-study: Total amount: $252,188; 69 jobs averaging $3650. **State or other work-study/employment:** Total amount: $65,425 (100% non-need-based). Part-time jobs available.

ATHLETIC AWARDS Total amount: $1,053,157 (100% non-need-based).

APPLYING FOR FINANCIAL AID Required financial aid forms: FAFSA, scholarship application form. **Financial aid deadline (priority):** 3/15. **Notification date:** Continuous beginning 2/1. Students must reply by 4/15 or within 6 weeks of notification.

CONTACT Lee Ann Kirkland, Director of Financial Aid, Armstrong Atlantic State University, 11935 Abercorn Street, Savannah, GA 31419-1997, 912-344-2614 or toll-free 800-633-2349. *Fax:* 912-344-3448. *E-mail:* finaid@armstrong.edu. *Website:* http://www.armstrong.edu/.

ART ACADEMY OF CINCINNATI
Cincinnati, OH

CONTACT Ms. Karen Geiger, Director of Financial Aid, Art Academy of Cincinnati, 1212 Jackson Street, Cincinnati, OH 45202, 513-562-8773 or toll-free 800-323-5692. *Fax:* 513-562-8778. *E-mail:* financialaid@artacademy.edu. *Website:* http://www.artacademy.edu/.

ART CENTER COLLEGE OF DESIGN
Pasadena, CA

ABOUT THE INSTITUTION Independent, coed. **Awards:** bachelor's and master's degrees. 18 undergraduate majors. **Total enrollment:** 1,869. Undergraduates: 1,657. Freshmen: 159.

GIFT AID (NEED-BASED) Scholarships, grants, and awards: Federal Pell, FSEOG, state, private, college/university gift aid from institutional funds.

GIFT AID (NON-NEED-BASED) Scholarships, grants, and awards by category: Creative arts/performance: art/fine arts.

LOANS Programs: college/university, alternative loans.

WORK-STUDY Federal work-study: Total amount: $654,274; jobs available.

APPLYING FOR FINANCIAL AID Required financial aid form: FAFSA.

CONTACT Clema McKenzie, Director of Financial Aid, Art Center College of Design, 1700 Lida Street, Pasadena, CA 91103-1999, 626-396-2215. *Fax:* 626-683-8684. *Website:* http://www.artcenter.edu/.

THE ART INSTITUTE OF ATLANTA
Atlanta, GA

CONTACT Financial Aid Office, The Art Institute of Atlanta, 6600 Peachtree Dunwoody Road, NE, 100 Embassy Row, Atlanta, GA 30328, 770-394-8300 or toll-free 800-275-4242. *Website:* http://www.artinstitutes.edu/atlanta/.

THE ART INSTITUTE OF ATLANTA–DECATUR
Decatur, GA

CONTACT Financial Aid Office, The Art Institute of Atlanta–Decatur, One West Court Square, Suite 110, Decatur, GA 30030 or toll-free 866-856-6203. *Website:* http://www.artinstitutes.edu/decatur/.

THE ART INSTITUTE OF AUSTIN
Austin, TX

CONTACT Financial Aid Office, The Art Institute of Austin, 101 W. Louis Henna Boulevard, Suite 100, Austin, TX 78728, 512-691-1707 or toll-free 866-583-7952. *Website:* http://www.artinstitutes.edu/austin.

THE ART INSTITUTE OF CALIFORNIA–HOLLYWOOD, A CAMPUS OF ARGOSY UNIVERSITY
North Hollywood, CA

CONTACT Financial Aid Office, The Art Institute of California–Hollywood, a campus of Argosy University, 5250 Lankershim Boulevard, North Hollywood, CA 91601, 818-299-5100 or toll-free 877-468-6232.

THE ART INSTITUTE OF CALIFORNIA–INLAND EMPIRE, A CAMPUS OF ARGOSY UNIVERSITY
San Bernardino, CA

CONTACT Financial Aid Office, The Art Institute of California–Inland Empire, a campus of Argosy University, 674 East Brier Drive, San Bernardino, CA 92408, 909-915-2100 or toll-free 800-353-0812. *Website:* http://www.artinstitutes.edu/inlandempire/.

THE ART INSTITUTE OF CALIFORNIA–LOS ANGELES, A CAMPUS OF ARGOSY UNIVERSITY
Santa Monica, CA

CONTACT Financial Aid Office, The Art Institute of California–Los Angeles, a campus of Argosy University, 2900 31st Street, Santa Monica, CA 90405-3035, 310-752-4700 or toll-free 888-646-4610.
Website: http://www.artinstitutes.edu/losangeles/.

THE ART INSTITUTE OF CALIFORNIA–ORANGE COUNTY, A CAMPUS OF ARGOSY UNIVERSITY
Santa Ana, CA

CONTACT Financial Aid Office, The Art Institute of California–Orange County, a campus of Argosy University, 3601 West Sunflower Avenue, Santa Ana, CA 92704, 714-830-0200 or toll-free 888-549-3055.
Website: http://www.artinstitutes.edu/orangecounty/.

THE ART INSTITUTE OF CALIFORNIA–SACRAMENTO, A CAMPUS OF ARGOSY UNIVERSITY
Sacramento, CA

CONTACT Financial Aid Office, The Art Institute of California–Sacramento, a campus of Argosy University, 2850 Gateway Oaks Drive, Suite 100, Sacramento, CA 95833 or toll-free 800-477-1957.
Website: http://www.artinstitutes.edu/sacramento/.

THE ART INSTITUTE OF CALIFORNIA–SAN DIEGO, A CAMPUS OF ARGOSY UNIVERSITY
San Diego, CA

CONTACT Financial Aid Office, The Art Institute of California–San Diego, a campus of Argosy University, 10025 Mesa Rim Road, San Diego, CA 92121, 619-546-0602 or toll-free 866-275-2422.

THE ART INSTITUTE OF CALIFORNIA–SAN FRANCISCO, A CAMPUS OF ARGOSY UNIVERSITY
San Francisco, CA

CONTACT Financial Aid Office, The Art Institute of California–San Francisco, a campus of Argosy University, 1170 Market Street, San Francisco, CA 94102-4908, 415-865-0198 or toll-free 888-493-3261. *Fax:* 415-863-5831.

THE ART INSTITUTE OF CALIFORNIA–SILICON VALLEY, A CAMPUS OF ARGOSY UNIVERSITY
Sunnyvale, CA

CONTACT Financial Aid Office, The Art Institute of California–Silicon Valley, a campus of Argosy University, 1120 Kifer Road, Sunnyvale, CA 94086, 408-962-6400 or toll-free 866-583-7961.
Website: http://www.artinstitutes.edu/silicon-valley/.

THE ART INSTITUTE OF CHARLESTON
Charleston, SC

CONTACT Financial Aid Office, The Art Institute of Charleston, 24 North Market Street, Charleston, SC 29401, 843-727-3500 or toll-free 866-211-0107.
Website: http://www.artinstitutes.edu/charleston/.

THE ART INSTITUTE OF CHARLOTTE
Charlotte, NC

CONTACT Financial Aid Office, The Art Institute of Charlotte, Three LakePointe Plaza, 2110 Water Ridge Parkway, Charlotte, NC 28217, 704-357-8020 or toll-free 800-872-4417.
Website: http://www.artinstitutes.edu/charlotte/.

THE ART INSTITUTE OF COLORADO
Denver, CO

CONTACT Financial Aid Office, The Art Institute of Colorado, 1200 Lincoln Street, Denver, CO 80203, 303-837-0825 or toll-free 800-275-2420.
Website: http://www.artinstitutes.edu/denver/.

THE ART INSTITUTE OF DALLAS
Dallas, TX

CONTACT Financial Aid Office, The Art Institute of Dallas, 8080 Park Lane, Suite 100, Dallas, TX 75231-5993, 214-692-8080 or toll-free 800-275-4243.
Website: http://www.artinstitutes.edu/dallas/.

THE ART INSTITUTE OF FORT LAUDERDALE
Fort Lauderdale, FL

CONTACT Financial Aid Office, The Art Institute of Fort Lauderdale, 1799 Southeast 17th Street Causeway, Fort Lauderdale, FL 33316-3000, 954-527-1799 or toll-free 800-275-7603.

THE ART INSTITUTE OF FORT WORTH
Fort Worth, TX

CONTACT Financial Aid Office, The Art Institute of Fort Worth, 7000 Calmont Avenue, Suite 150, Fort Worth, TX 76116, 817-210-0808 or toll-free 888-422-9686. *Website:* http://www.artinstitutes.edu/fort-worth/.

THE ART INSTITUTE OF HOUSTON
Houston, TX

CONTACT Financial Aid Office, The Art Institute of Houston, 1900 Yorktown Street, Houston, TX 77056, 713-623-2040 or toll-free 800-275-4244.

THE ART INSTITUTE OF HOUSTON - NORTH
Houston, TX

CONTACT Financial Aid Office, The Art Institute of Houston - North, 10740 North Gessner Drive, Suite 190, Houston, TX 77064 or toll-free 866-830-4450. *Website:* http://www.artinstitutes.edu/houston-north/.

THE ART INSTITUTE OF INDIANAPOLIS
Indianapolis, IN

CONTACT Financial Aid Office, The Art Institute of Indianapolis, 3500 Depauw Boulevard, Suite 1010, Indianapolis, IN 46268, 317-613-4800 or toll-free 866-441-9031. *Website:* http://www.artinstitutes.edu/indianapolis/.

THE ART INSTITUTE OF JACKSONVILLE
Jacksonville, FL

CONTACT Financial Aid Office, The Art Institute of Jacksonville, 8775 Baypine Road, Jacksonville, FL 32256, 904-732-9393 or toll-free 800-924-1589. *Website:* http://www.artinstitutes.edu/jacksonville/.

THE ART INSTITUTE OF LAS VEGAS
Henderson, NV

CONTACT Financial Aid Office, The Art Institute of Las Vegas, 2350 Corporate Circle Drive, Henderson, NV 89074, 702-369-9944 or toll-free 800-833-2678. *Website:* http://www.artinstitutes.edu/lasvegas/.

THE ART INSTITUTE OF MICHIGAN
Novi, MI

CONTACT Financial Aid Office, The Art Institute of Michigan, 28125 Cabot Drive, Suite 120, Novi, MI 48377, 248-675-3800 or toll-free 800-479-0087. *Website:* http://www.artinstitutes.edu/detroit/.

THE ART INSTITUTE OF MICHIGAN–TROY
Troy, MI

CONTACT Financial Aid Office, The Art Institute of Michigan–Troy, 1414 East Maple Avenue, Suite 150, Troy, MI 48083, 248-837-3200 or toll-free 877-320-3275. *Website:* http://www.artinstitutes.edu/troy.

THE ART INSTITUTE OF PHILADELPHIA
Philadelphia, PA

CONTACT Financial Aid Office, The Art Institute of Philadelphia, 1622 Chestnut Street, Philadelphia, PA 19103, 215-567-7080 or toll-free 800-275-2474.

THE ART INSTITUTE OF PHOENIX
Phoenix, AZ

CONTACT Financial Aid Office, The Art Institute of Phoenix, 2233 West Dunlap Avenue, Phoenix, AZ 85021-2859, 602-331-7500 or toll-free 800-474-2479. *Website:* http://www.artinstitutes.edu/phoenix/.

THE ART INSTITUTE OF PITTSBURGH
Pittsburgh, PA

CONTACT Financial Aid Office, The Art Institute of Pittsburgh, 420 Boulevard of the Allies, Pittsburgh, PA 15219, 412-263-6600 or toll-free 800-275-2470.

THE ART INSTITUTE OF PORTLAND
Portland, OR

CONTACT Financial Aid Office, The Art Institute of Portland, 1122 NW Davis Street, Portland, OR 97209, 503-228-6528 or toll-free 888-228-6528. *Website:* http://www.artinstitutes.edu/portland/.

THE ART INSTITUTE OF RALEIGH-DURHAM
Durham, NC

CONTACT Financial Aid Office, The Art Institute of Raleigh-Durham, 410 Blackwell Street, Suite 200, Durham, NC 27701 or toll-free 888-245-9593. *Website:* http://www.artinstitutes.edu/raleigh-durham.

THE ART INSTITUTE OF ST. LOUIS
St. Charles, MO

CONTACT Financial Aid Office, The Art Institute of St. Louis, 1520 South Fifth Street, St. Charles, MO 63303, 636-688-3010. *Website:* http://www.artinstitutes.edu/st-louis/.

THE ART INSTITUTE OF SALT LAKE CITY
Draper, UT

CONTACT Financial Aid Office, The Art Institute of Salt Lake City, 121 West Election Road, Suite 100, Draper, UT 84020-9492 or toll-free 800-978-0096. *Website:* http://www.artinstitutes.edu/SaltLakeCity/.

THE ART INSTITUTE OF SAN ANTONIO
San Antonio, TX

CONTACT Financial Aid Office, The Art Institute of San Antonio, 1000 IH-10 West, Suite 200, San Antonio, TX 78230, 210-338-7320 or toll-free 888-222-0040. *Website:* http://www.artinstitutes.edu/san-antonio/.

THE ART INSTITUTE OF TAMPA
Tampa, FL

CONTACT Financial Aid Office, The Art Institute of Tampa, Parkside at Tampa Bay Park, 4401 North Himes Avenue, Suite 150, Tampa, FL 33614, 813-873-2112 or toll-free 866-703-3277. *Website:* http://www.artinstitutes.edu/tampa/.

THE ART INSTITUTE OF TENNESSEE–NASHVILLE
Nashville, TN

CONTACT Financial Aid Office, The Art Institute of Tennessee–Nashville, 100 Centerview Drive, Suite 250, Nashville, TN 37214, 615-874-1067 or toll-free 866-747-5770. *Website:* http://www.artinstitutes.edu/nashville/.

THE ART INSTITUTE OF TUCSON
Tucson, AZ

CONTACT Financial Aid Office, The Art Institute of Tucson, 5099 East Grant Road, Suite 100, Tucson, AZ 85712, 520-881-2900 or toll-free 866-690-8850. *Website:* http://www.artinstitutes.edu/tucson/.

THE ART INSTITUTE OF VIRGINIA BEACH
Virginia Beach, VA

CONTACT Financial Aid Office, The Art Institute of Virginia Beach, Two Columbus Center, 4500 Main Street, Suite 100, Virginia Beach, VA 23462, 757-493-6700 or toll-free 877-437-4428. *Website:* http://www.artinstitutes.edu/virginia-beach/.

THE ART INSTITUTE OF WASHINGTON
Arlington, VA

CONTACT Financial Aid Office, The Art Institute of Washington, 1820 North Fort Myer Drive, Arlington, VA 22209, 703-247-6849 or toll-free 877-303-3771. *Fax:* 703-247-6829.

THE ART INSTITUTE OF WASHINGTON–DULLES
Sterling, VA

CONTACT Financial Aid Office, The Art Institute of Washington–Dulles, The Corporate Office Park at Dulles Town Center, 21000 Atlantic Boulevard, Suite 100, Sterling, VA 20166, 571-449-4400 or toll-free 888-627-5008. *Website:* http://www.artinstitutes.edu/washington-dulles/.

THE ART INSTITUTE OF WISCONSIN
Milwaukee, WI

CONTACT Financial Aid Office, The Art Institute of Wisconsin, 320 East Buffalo Street, Suite 600, Milwaukee, WI 53202, 414-978-5000 or toll-free 877-285-4234. *Website:* http://www.artinstitutes.edu/milwaukee.

THE ART INSTITUTES INTERNATIONAL–KANSAS CITY
Lenexa, KS

CONTACT Financial Aid Office, The Art Institutes International–Kansas City, 8208 Melrose Drive, Lenexa, KS 66214 or toll-free 866-530-8508. *Website:* http://www.artinstitutes.edu/kansascity/.

THE ART INSTITUTES INTERNATIONAL MINNESOTA
Minneapolis, MN

CONTACT Financial Aid Office, The Art Institutes International Minnesota, 15 South 9th Street, Minneapolis, MN 55402, 612-332-3361 or toll-free 800-777-3643.

ASBURY UNIVERSITY
Wilmore, KY

Tuition & fees: $26,076	Average undergraduate aid package: $19,597

ABOUT THE INSTITUTION Independent nondenominational, coed. *Awards:* associate, bachelor's, and master's degrees. 46 undergraduate majors. *Total enrollment:* 1,765. Undergraduates: 1,529. Freshmen: 322. Both federal and institutional methodology are used as a basis for awarding need-based institutional aid.
UNDERGRADUATE EXPENSES for 2013–2014 *Comprehensive fee:* $32,038 includes full-time tuition ($25,894), mandatory fees ($182), and room and board ($5962). Full-time tuition and fees vary according to course load, location, and program. Room and board charges vary according to board plan, housing facility, and location. *Part-time tuition:* $996 per credit. Part-time tuition and fees vary according to course load, location, and program.
FRESHMAN FINANCIAL AID (Fall 2012, est.) 295 applied for aid; of those 83% were deemed to have need. 100% of freshmen with need received aid; of those 26%

had need fully met. *Average percent of need met:* 83% (excluding resources awarded to replace EFC). *Average financial aid package:* $19,282 (excluding resources awarded to replace EFC). 16% of all full-time freshmen had no need and received non-need-based gift aid.

UNDERGRADUATE FINANCIAL AID (Fall 2012, est.) 1,019 applied for aid; of those 87% were deemed to have need. 99% of undergraduates with need received aid; of those 23% had need fully met. *Average percent of need met:* 81% (excluding resources awarded to replace EFC). *Average financial aid package:* $19,597 (excluding resources awarded to replace EFC). 11% of all full-time undergraduates had no need and received non-need-based gift aid.

GIFT AID (NEED-BASED) *Total amount:* $4,962,951 (50% federal, 38% state, 12% external sources). *Receiving aid:* Freshmen: 79% (244); all full-time undergraduates: 77% (876). *Average award:* Freshmen: $12,812; Undergraduates: $12,669. *Scholarships, grants, and awards:* Federal Pell, FSEOG, state, private, college/university gift aid from institutional funds.

GIFT AID (NON-NEED-BASED) *Total amount:* $434,339 (18% federal, 48% state, 34% external sources). *Receiving aid:* Freshmen: 33% (103). Undergraduates: 28% (314). *Average award:* Freshmen: $9630. Undergraduates: $11,431. *Scholarships, grants, and awards by category:* Academic interests/achievement: general academic interests/achievements. *Creative arts/performance:* music. *Special achievements/activities:* leadership. *Special characteristics:* children and siblings of alumni, children of faculty/staff, ethnic background, international students, out-of-state students, relatives of clergy, siblings of current students. *Tuition waivers:* Full or partial for employees or children of employees, senior citizens. *ROTC:* Army cooperative, Air Force cooperative.

LOANS *Student loans:* $8,420,900 (89% need-based, 11% non-need-based). 75% of past graduating class borrowed through all loan programs. *Average indebtedness per student:* $26,854. *Average need-based loan:* Freshmen: $2982. Undergraduates: $4038. *Parent loans:* $1,170,215 (74% need-based, 26% non-need-based). *Programs:* Federal Direct (Subsidized and Unsubsidized Stafford, PLUS), Perkins, college/university, private loans.

WORK-STUDY *Federal work-study:* Total amount: $1,007,795; jobs available.

ATHLETIC AWARDS Total amount: $1,765,699 (70% need-based, 30% non-need-based).

APPLYING FOR FINANCIAL AID *Financial aid deadline:* Continuous. *Notification date:* Continuous beginning 1/31.

CONTACT Mr. Ronald Anderson, Director of Financial Aid, Asbury University, One Macklem Drive, Wilmore, KY 40390, 859-858-3511 Ext. 2195 or toll-free 800-888-1818. *Fax:* 859-858-3921. *E-mail:* ron.anderson@asbury.edu. *Website:* http://www.asbury.edu/.

ASHFORD UNIVERSITY
Clinton, IA

CONTACT Lisa Kramer, Director of Financial Aid, Ashford University, 400 North Bluff Boulevard, PO Box 2967, Clinton, IA 52733-2967, 563-242-4023 Ext. 1243 or toll-free 866-711-1700. *Fax:* 563-242-8684.
Website: http://www.ashford.edu/.

ASHLAND UNIVERSITY
Ashland, OH

Tuition & fees: $28,858	Average undergraduate aid package: $25,115

ABOUT THE INSTITUTION Independent Brethren Church, coed. *Awards:* certificates, diplomas, bachelor's, master's, and doctoral degrees. 66 undergraduate majors. *Total enrollment:* 6,491. Undergraduates: 3,146. Freshmen: 675. Federal methodology is used as a basis for awarding need-based institutional aid.

UNDERGRADUATE EXPENSES for 2013–2014 *Comprehensive fee:* $38,360 includes full-time tuition ($27,930), mandatory fees ($928), and room and board ($9502). *College room only:* $5172. Full-time tuition and fees vary according to location and program. Room and board charges vary according to board plan and housing facility. Part-time tuition and fees vary according to course load, location, and program.

FRESHMAN FINANCIAL AID (Fall 2012, est.) 468 applied for aid; of those 100% were deemed to have need. 100% of freshmen with need received aid. *Average financial aid package:* $26,270 (excluding resources awarded to replace EFC). 9% of all full-time freshmen had no need and received non-need-based gift aid.

UNDERGRADUATE FINANCIAL AID (Fall 2012, est.) 1,947 applied for aid; of those 100% were deemed to have need. 100% of undergraduates with need received aid. *Average financial aid package:* $25,115 (excluding resources awarded to replace EFC). 9% of all full-time undergraduates had no need and received non-need-based gift aid.

GIFT AID (NEED-BASED) *Total amount:* $31,120,449 (13% federal, 4% state, 82% institutional, 1% external sources). *Receiving aid:* Freshmen: 86% (468); all full-time undergraduates: 82% (1,946). *Average award:* Freshmen: $19,756; Undergraduates: $18,414. *Scholarships, grants, and awards:* Federal Pell, FSEOG, state, private, college/university gift aid from institutional funds.

GIFT AID (NON-NEED-BASED) *Total amount:* $3,277,602 (1% federal, 98% institutional, 1% external sources). *Receiving aid:* Freshmen: 76% (415). Undergraduates: 62% (1,466). *Average award:* Freshmen: $11,968. Undergraduates: $11,236. *Scholarships, grants, and awards by category:* Academic interests/achievement: 2,014 awards ($17,316,256 total): general academic interests/achievements, mathematics, physical sciences, social sciences. *Creative arts/performance:* 139 awards ($331,270 total): art/fine arts, music, theater/drama. *Special achievements/activities:* 63 awards ($71,600 total): cheerleading/drum major, leadership, religious involvement. *Special characteristics:* 439 awards ($3,357,323 total): children and siblings of alumni, children of faculty/staff, ethnic background, international students, members of minority groups, out-of-state students, relatives of clergy, religious affiliation, siblings of current students, veterans. *Tuition waivers:* Full or partial for children of alumni, employees or children of employees, senior citizens. *ROTC:* Army cooperative, Air Force cooperative.

LOANS *Student loans:* $13,423,463 (91% need-based, 9% non-need-based). 87% of past graduating class borrowed through all loan programs. *Average indebtedness per student:* $36,058. *Average need-based loan:* Freshmen: $3853. Undergraduates: $4648. *Parent loans:* $4,398,331 (96% need-based, 4% non-need-based). *Programs:* Federal Direct (Subsidized and Unsubsidized Stafford, PLUS), Perkins, college/university.

WORK-STUDY *Federal work-study:* Total amount: $3,611,878; 1,380 jobs averaging $2589.

ATHLETIC AWARDS Total amount: $4,116,798 (72% need-based, 28% non-need-based).

APPLYING FOR FINANCIAL AID *Required financial aid form:* FAFSA. *Financial aid deadline:* Continuous. *Notification date:* Continuous beginning 3/1.

CONTACT Mr. Stephen C. Howell, Director of Financial Aid, Ashland University, 401 College Avenue, Ashland, OH 44805-3702, 419-289-5944 or toll-free 800-882-1548. *Fax:* 419-289-5976. *E-mail:* showell@ashland.edu. *Website:* http://www.exploreashland.com/.

ASHWORTH COLLEGE
Norcross, GA

CONTACT Financial Aid Office, Ashworth College, 6625 The Corners Parkway, Suite 500, Norcross, GA 30092, 770-729-8400 or toll-free 800-957-5412. *Website:* http://www.ashworthcollege.edu/.

ASPEN UNIVERSITY
Denver, CO

CONTACT Jennifer Quinn, Director of Financial Aid, Aspen University, 720 South Colorado Bouleavrd #1150N, Denver, CO 80246, 800-441-4746. *Fax:* 303-336-1144. *E-mail:* jquinn@aspen.edu. *Website:* http://www.aspen.edu/.

ASSUMPTION COLLEGE
Worcester, MA

Tuition & fees: $33,805	Average undergraduate aid package: $24,802

ABOUT THE INSTITUTION Independent Roman Catholic, coed. *Awards:* certificates, bachelor's, and master's degrees. 44 undergraduate majors. *Total enrollment:* 2,588. Undergraduates: 2,056. Freshmen: 559. Federal methodology is used as a basis for awarding need-based institutional aid.

UNDERGRADUATE EXPENSES for 2013–2014 *Application fee:* $50. *Comprehensive fee:* $44,395 includes full-time tuition ($33,390), mandatory fees ($415), and room and board ($10,590). *College room only:* $6660. Full-time tuition and fees vary according to course load and reciprocity agreements. Room and board charges vary according to housing facility. *Part-time tuition:* $1113 per credit hour. Part-time tuition and fees vary according to course load.

FRESHMAN FINANCIAL AID (Fall 2012, est.) 516 applied for aid; of those 90% were deemed to have need. 100% of freshmen with need received aid; of those 18% had need fully met. *Average percent of need met:* 76% (excluding resources awarded to replace EFC). *Average financial aid package:* $25,676 (excluding resources awarded to replace EFC). 15% of all full-time freshmen had no need and received non-need-based gift aid.

UNDERGRADUATE FINANCIAL AID (Fall 2012, est.) 1,744 applied for aid; of those 91% were deemed to have need. 100% of undergraduates with need received aid; of those 19% had need fully met. *Average percent of need met:* 75% (excluding resources awarded to replace EFC). *Average financial aid package:* $24,802 (excluding resources awarded to replace EFC). 17% of all full-time undergraduates had no need and received non-need-based gift aid.

GIFT AID (NEED-BASED) *Total amount:* $29,018,339 (7% federal, 3% state, 88% institutional, 2% external sources). *Receiving aid:* Freshmen: 83% (462); all full-time undergraduates: 78% (1,585). *Average award:* Freshmen: $20,746; Undergraduates: $19,344. *Scholarships, grants, and awards:* Federal Pell, FSEOG, state, private, college/university gift aid from institutional funds, Academic Competitiveness Grants, National SMART Grants.

GIFT AID (NON-NEED-BASED) *Total amount:* $4,615,457 (97% institutional, 3% external sources). *Receiving aid:* Freshmen: 11% (64). Undergraduates: 9% (180). *Average award:* Freshmen: $11,424. Undergraduates: $10,808. *Scholarships, grants, and awards by category:* Academic interests/achievement: 1,505 awards ($16,925,200 total): general academic interests/achievements. *Special characteristics:* members of minority groups. *Tuition waivers:* Full or partial for employees or children of employees. *ROTC:* Army cooperative, Air Force cooperative.

LOANS *Student loans:* $16,886,122 (68% need-based, 32% non-need-based). 81% of past graduating class borrowed through all loan programs. *Average indebtedness per student:* $34,579. *Average need-based loan:* Freshmen: $3916. Undergraduates: $4887. *Parent loans:* $6,260,380 (36% need-based, 64% non-need-based). *Programs:* Federal Direct (Subsidized and Unsubsidized Stafford, PLUS), Perkins, state, college/university.

WORK-STUDY *Federal work-study:* Total amount: $675,770; 464 jobs averaging $1456.

ATHLETIC AWARDS Total amount: $2,082,397 (41% need-based, 59% non-need-based).

APPLYING FOR FINANCIAL AID *Required financial aid form:* FAFSA. *Financial aid deadline:* 2/15. *Notification date:* Continuous beginning 2/16. Students must reply by 5/1.

CONTACT William C. Smith, Director of Financial Aid, Assumption College, 500 Salisbury Street, Worcester, MA 01609-1296, 508-767-7157 or toll-free 866-477-7776. *Fax:* 508-767-7376. *E-mail:* fa@assumption.edu. *Website:* http://www.assumption.edu/.

ATHENS STATE UNIVERSITY
Athens, AL

Tuition & fees (AL res): $5340	Average undergraduate aid package: $12,815

ABOUT THE INSTITUTION State-supported, coed. *Awards:* certificates and bachelor's degrees. 36 undergraduate majors. *Total enrollment:* 3,415. Undergraduates: 3,415. Federal methodology is used as a basis for awarding need-based institutional aid.

UNDERGRADUATE EXPENSES for 2013–2014 *Application fee:* $30. *Tuition, state resident:* full-time $4590. *Tuition, nonresident:* full-time $9180. *Required fees:* full-time $750.

UNDERGRADUATE FINANCIAL AID (Fall 2011) 1,046 applied for aid; of those .1% were deemed to have need. 100% of undergraduates with need received aid. *Average financial aid package:* $12,815 (excluding resources awarded to replace EFC).

GIFT AID (NEED-BASED) *Total amount:* $5,200,254 (99% federal, 1% state). *Scholarships, grants, and awards:* Federal Pell, FSEOG, state, private, college/university gift aid from institutional funds.

GIFT AID (NON-NEED-BASED) *Total amount:* $169,392 (100% federal). *Receiving aid:* Undergraduates: 1. *Tuition waivers:* Full or partial for employees or children of employees, senior citizens.

LOANS *Student loans:* $13,738,784 (100% non-need-based). *Programs:* Federal Direct (Subsidized and Unsubsidized Stafford, PLUS), college/university.

WORK-STUDY *Federal work-study:* Total amount: $36,638; jobs available.

APPLYING FOR FINANCIAL AID *Required financial aid form:* FAFSA. *Financial aid deadline:* Continuous. *Notification date:* Continuous beginning 5/1. Students must reply within 2 weeks of notification.

CONTACT Renee Stanford, Financial Aid Officer, Athens State University, 300 North Beaty Street, Athens, AL 35611, 256-233-8122 or toll-free 800-522-0272. *Fax:* 256-233-8178. *E-mail:* finaid@athens.edu. *Website:* http://www.athens.edu/.

ATLANTIC UNIVERSITY COLLEGE
Guaynabo, PR

CONTACT Mrs. Velma Aponte, Financial Aid Coordinator, Atlantic University College, Calle Colton #9, Guaynabo, PR 00970, 787-720-1092. *E-mail:* atlaneco@coqui.net. *Website:* http://www.atlanticu.edu/.

AUBURN UNIVERSITY
Auburn University, AL

Tuition & fees (AL res): $9446	Average undergraduate aid package: $10,502

ABOUT THE INSTITUTION State-supported, coed. *Awards:* certificates, bachelor's, master's, and doctoral degrees. 137 undergraduate majors. *Total enrollment:* 25,134. Undergraduates: 20,175. Freshmen: 3,852. Federal methodology is used as a basis for awarding need-based institutional aid.

UNDERGRADUATE EXPENSES for 2013–2014 *Application fee:* $50. *Tuition, state resident:* full-time $7872; part-time $328 per semester hour. *Tuition, nonresident:* full-time $23,616; part-time $984 per semester hour. *Required fees:* full-time $1574; $787 per term. Full-time tuition and fees vary according to program and reciprocity agreements. Part-time tuition and fees vary according to course load, program, and reciprocity agreements. *College room and board:* $10,606; *Room only:* $5500. Room and board charges vary according to board plan and housing facility.

FRESHMAN FINANCIAL AID (Fall 2011) 2,606 applied for aid; of those 61% were deemed to have need. 100% of freshmen with need received aid; of those 26% had need fully met. *Average percent of need met:* 59% (excluding resources awarded to replace EFC). *Average financial aid package:* $12,352 (excluding resources awarded to replace EFC). 15% of all full-time freshmen had no need and received non-need-based gift aid.

UNDERGRADUATE FINANCIAL AID (Fall 2011) 11,837 applied for aid; of those 60% were deemed to have need. 100% of undergraduates with need received aid; of those 15% had need fully met. *Average percent of need met:* 48% (excluding resources awarded to replace EFC). *Average financial aid package:* $10,502 (excluding resources awarded to replace EFC). 9% of all full-time undergraduates had no need and received non-need-based gift aid.

GIFT AID (NEED-BASED) *Total amount:* $36,298,578 (41% federal, 3% state, 47% institutional, 9% external sources). *Receiving aid:* Freshmen: 32% (1,354); all full-time undergraduates: 28% (5,190). *Average award:* Freshmen: $7881; Undergraduates: $6735. *Scholarships, grants, and awards:* Federal Pell, FSEOG, state, private, college/university gift aid from institutional funds.

GIFT AID (NON-NEED-BASED) *Total amount:* $43,769,006 (1% federal, 7% state, 77% institutional, 15% external sources). *Receiving aid:* Freshmen: 7% (305). Undergraduates: 4% (671). *Average award:* Freshmen: $2885. Undergraduates: $2893. *Scholarships, grants, and awards by category:* Academic interests/achievement: agriculture, architecture, biological sciences, business, communication, computer science, education, engineering/technologies, English, foreign languages, general academic interests/achievements, health fields, home economics, humanities, mathematics, physical sciences, premedicine, social sciences. *Creative arts/performance:* applied art and design, art/fine arts, cinema/film/broadcasting, creative writing, journalism/publications, music, performing arts, theater/drama. *Special achievements/activities:* cheerleading/drum major, leadership, memberships. *Special characteristics:* children and siblings of alumni, children of faculty/staff, children of union members/company employees, ethnic background, local/state students, married students, out-of-state students. *Tuition waivers:* Full or partial for employees or children of employees. *ROTC:* Army, Naval, Air Force.

LOANS *Student loans:* $63,217,404 (74% need-based, 26% non-need-based). 45% of past graduating class borrowed through all loan programs. *Average indebtedness per student:* $24,903. *Average need-based loan:* Freshmen: $3503. Undergraduates: $4545. *Parent loans:* $26,845,364 (48% need-based, 52% non-need-based). *Programs:* Federal Direct (Subsidized and Unsubsidized Stafford, PLUS), Perkins, Federal Nursing, college/university.

WORK-STUDY *Federal work-study:* Total amount: $891,393; 223 jobs averaging $3862.

ATHLETIC AWARDS Total amount: $10,739,423 (3% need-based, 97% non-need-based).

APPLYING FOR FINANCIAL AID *Required financial aid form:* FAFSA. *Financial aid deadline (priority):* 3/1. *Notification date:* Continuous beginning 10/2. Students must reply by 5/1.

CONTACT Mr. Mike Reynolds, Director of Student Financial Services, Auburn University, 203 Mary Martin Hall, Auburn University, AL 36849, 334-844-4634 or toll-free 800-AUBURN9. *Fax:* 334-844-6085. *E-mail:* finaid7@auburn.edu. *Website:* http://www.auburn.edu/.

AUBURN UNIVERSITY AT MONTGOMERY
Montgomery, AL

Tuition & fees (AL res): $8150	Average undergraduate aid package: N/A

ABOUT THE INSTITUTION State-supported, coed. *Awards:* certificates, bachelor's, master's, and doctoral degrees. 30 undergraduate majors. *Total enrollment:* 4,989. Undergraduates: 4,225. Freshmen: 785. Federal methodology is used as a basis for awarding need-based institutional aid.

UNDERGRADUATE EXPENSES for 2013–2014 *Tuition, state resident:* full-time $7500; part-time $250 per credit hour. *Tuition, nonresident:* full-time $22,500; part-time $750 per credit hour. *Required fees:* full-time $650. Full-time tuition and fees vary according to course load. Part-time tuition and fees vary according to course load. *Room only:* $3270. Room and board charges vary according to housing facility.

FRESHMAN FINANCIAL AID (Fall 2012, est.) 487 applied for aid. of those 23% had need fully met.

UNDERGRADUATE FINANCIAL AID (Fall 2012, est.) 2,102 applied for aid. of those 22% had need fully met.

GIFT AID (NEED-BASED) *Total amount:* $9,757,563 (99% federal, 1% institutional). *Receiving aid:* Freshmen: 43% (302); all full-time undergraduates: 44% (1,280). *Average award:* Freshmen: $4744; Undergraduates: $4631. *Scholarships, grants, and awards:* Federal Pell, FSEOG, state, college/university gift aid from institutional funds.

GIFT AID (NON-NEED-BASED) *Total amount:* $3,513,460 (91% institutional, 9% external sources). *Scholarships, grants, and awards by category:* Academic interests/achievement: general academic interests/achievements. *Tuition waivers:* Full or partial for employees or children of employees. *ROTC:* Army, Air Force cooperative.

LOANS *Student loans:* $23,600,888 (45% need-based, 55% non-need-based). *Average need-based loan:* Freshmen: $3406. Undergraduates: $4110. *Parent loans:* $691,768 (100% non-need-based). *Programs:* Federal Direct (Subsidized and Unsubsidized Stafford, PLUS), Perkins.

WORK-STUDY *Federal work-study:* Total amount: $186,154; jobs available.

APPLYING FOR FINANCIAL AID *Required financial aid form:* FAFSA. *Financial aid deadline (priority):* 3/1. *Notification date:* Continuous. Students must reply within 2 weeks of notification.

CONTACT Mr. Anthony Richey, Senior Director of Financial Aid, Auburn University at Montgomery, PO Box 244023, Montgomery, AL 36124-4023, 334-244-3571 or toll-free 800-227-2649. *Fax:* 334-244-3913. *E-mail:* arichey@aum.edu. *Website:* http://www.aum.edu/.

AUGSBURG COLLEGE
Minneapolis, MN

CONTACT Mr. Paul L. Terrio, Director of Student Financial Services, Augsburg College, 2211 Riverside Avenue, Minneapolis, MN 55454-1351, 612-330-1049 or toll-free 800-788-5678. *Fax:* 612-330-1308. *E-mail:* terriop@augsburg.edu. *Website:* http://www.augsburg.edu/.

AUGUSTANA COLLEGE
Rock Island, IL

Tuition & fees: $34,614	Average undergraduate aid package: $24,211

ABOUT THE INSTITUTION Independent Evangelical Lutheran Church in America, coed. *Awards:* bachelor's degrees. 58 undergraduate majors. *Total enrollment:* 2,551. Undergraduates: 2,551. Freshmen: 656. Federal methodology is used as a basis for awarding need-based institutional aid.

UNDERGRADUATE EXPENSES for 2013–2014 *Application fee:* $30. *Comprehensive fee:* $43,398 includes full-time tuition ($34,614) and room and board ($8784). Full-time tuition and fees vary according to student level. Room and board charges vary according to board plan and housing facility. Part-time tuition and fees vary according to course load. *Payment plan:* Tuition prepayment.

FRESHMAN FINANCIAL AID (Fall 2011) 677 applied for aid; of those 84% were deemed to have need. 100% of freshmen with need received aid; of those 20% had need fully met. *Average percent of need met:* 86% (excluding resources awarded to replace EFC). *Average financial aid package:* $25,327 (excluding resources awarded to replace EFC). 19% of all full-time freshmen had no need and received non-need-based gift aid.

UNDERGRADUATE FINANCIAL AID (Fall 2011) 2,201 applied for aid; of those 86% were deemed to have need. 100% of undergraduates with need received aid; of those 22% had need fully met. *Average percent of need met:* 85% (excluding resources awarded to replace EFC). *Average financial aid package:* $24,211 (excluding resources awarded to replace EFC). 23% of all full-time undergraduates had no need and received non-need-based gift aid.

GIFT AID (NEED-BASED) *Total amount:* $34,158,276 (7% federal, 8% state, 84% institutional, 1% external sources). *Receiving aid:* Freshmen: 79% (560); all full-time undergraduates: 74% (1,857). *Average award:* Freshmen: $19,871; Undergraduates: $18,374. *Scholarships, grants, and awards:* Federal Pell, FSEOG, state, private, college/university gift aid from institutional funds.

GIFT AID (NON-NEED-BASED) *Total amount:* $10,420,469 (99% institutional, 1% external sources). *Receiving aid:* Freshmen: 11% (77). Undergraduates: 11% (279). *Average award:* Freshmen: $15,705. Undergraduates: $14,382. *Scholarships, grants, and awards by category:* Academic interests/achievement: 1,969 awards ($27,501,246 total): area/ethnic studies, biological sciences, business, communication, computer science, education, English, foreign languages, general academic interests/achievements, humanities, mathematics, physical sciences, religion/biblical studies, social sciences. *Creative arts/performance:* 371 awards ($937,977 total): art/fine arts, creative writing, debating, music, theater/drama. *Special characteristics:* 462 awards ($3,212,094 total): children and siblings of alumni, children of faculty/staff, ethnic background, international students, members of minority groups, religious affiliation, siblings of current students. *Tuition waivers:* Full or partial for employees or children of employees.

LOANS *Student loans:* $15,268,757 (72% need-based, 28% non-need-based). 71% of past graduating class borrowed through all loan programs. *Average indebtedness per student:* $34,120. *Average need-based loan:* Freshmen: $4031. Undergraduates: $4705. *Parent loans:* $5,677,712 (33% need-based, 67% non-need-based). *Programs:* Federal Direct (Subsidized and Unsubsidized Stafford, PLUS), Perkins. **WORK-STUDY** *Federal work-study:* Total amount: $3,015,831; 1,293 jobs averaging $2319. **APPLYING FOR FINANCIAL AID** *Required financial aid forms:* FAFSA, institution's own form. *Financial aid deadline (priority):* 3/1. *Notification date:* Continuous beginning 2/15. Students must reply by 5/1. **CONTACT** Sue Standley, Director of Financial Aid, Augustana College, 639 38th Street, Rock Island, IL 61201-2296, 309-794-7207 or toll-free 800-798-8100. *Fax:* 309-794-7174. *E-mail:* suestandley@augustana.edu. *Website:* http://www.augustana.edu/.

Programs: Federal Direct (Subsidized and Unsubsidized Stafford, PLUS), Perkins, Federal Nursing, college/university, private loans, Minnesota SELF Loans. **WORK-STUDY** *Federal work-study:* Total amount: $605,054; 372 jobs averaging $1604. *State or other work-study/employment:* Total amount: $128,746 (5% need-based, 95% non-need-based). 131 part-time jobs averaging $976. **ATHLETIC AWARDS** Total amount: $3,011,602 (38% need-based, 62% non-need-based). **APPLYING FOR FINANCIAL AID** *Required financial aid form:* FAFSA. *Financial aid deadline (priority):* 3/1. *Notification date:* Continuous beginning 4/1. Students must reply by 5/1 or within 3 weeks of notification. **CONTACT** Ms. Brenda L. Murtha, Director of Financial Aid, Augustana College, 2001 South Summit Avenue, Sioux Falls, SD 57197, 605-274-5216 or toll-free 800-727-2844. *Fax:* 605-274-5295. *E-mail:* brenda.murtha@augie.edu. *Website:* http://www.augie.edu/.

AUGUSTANA COLLEGE
Sioux Falls, SD

Tuition & fees: $27,780	Average undergraduate aid package: $22,001

ABOUT THE INSTITUTION Independent Evangelical Lutheran Church in America, coed. *Awards:* bachelor's and master's degrees. 64 undergraduate majors. *Total enrollment:* 1,839. Undergraduates: 1,771. Freshmen: 407. Federal methodology is used as a basis for awarding need-based institutional aid. **UNDERGRADUATE EXPENSES** for 2013–2014 *Comprehensive fee:* $34,406 includes full-time tuition ($27,380), mandatory fees ($400), and room and board ($6626). *College room only:* $3214. Full-time tuition and fees vary according to course load and degree level. Room and board charges vary according to board plan and housing facility. *Part-time tuition:* $420 per credit hour. Part-time tuition and fees vary according to course load and degree level. **FRESHMAN FINANCIAL AID (Fall 2012, est.)** 319 applied for aid; of those 82% were deemed to have need. 100% of freshmen with need received aid; of those 25% had need fully met. *Average percent of need met:* 96% (excluding resources awarded to replace EFC). *Average financial aid package:* $23,816 (excluding resources awarded to replace EFC). 34% of all full-time freshmen had no need and received non-need-based gift aid. **UNDERGRADUATE FINANCIAL AID (Fall 2012, est.)** 1,303 applied for aid; of those 86% were deemed to have need. 100% of undergraduates with need received aid; of those 20% had need fully met. *Average percent of need met:* 86% (excluding resources awarded to replace EFC). *Average financial aid package:* $22,001 (excluding resources awarded to replace EFC). 32% of all full-time undergraduates had no need and received non-need-based gift aid. **GIFT AID (NEED-BASED)** *Total amount:* $16,429,236 (13% federal, 82% institutional, 5% external sources). *Receiving aid:* Freshmen: 64% (260); all full-time undergraduates: 65% (1,115). *Average award:* Freshmen: $20,145; Undergraduates: $17,566. *Scholarships, grants, and awards:* Federal Pell, FSEOG, state, private, college/university gift aid from institutional funds, need-linked special talent scholarships, minority scholarships. **GIFT AID (NON-NEED-BASED)** *Total amount:* $8,217,357 (1% federal, 4% state, 91% institutional, 4% external sources). *Receiving aid:* Freshmen: 63% (256). Undergraduates: 64% (1,098). *Average award:* Freshmen: $14,693. Undergraduates: $12,769. *Scholarships, grants, and awards by category: Academic interests/achievement:* biological sciences, business, communication, computer science, education, English, foreign languages, general academic interests/achievements, health fields, humanities, international studies, mathematics, physical sciences, premedicine, religion/biblical studies, social sciences. *Creative arts/performance:* art/fine arts, creative writing, journalism/publications, music, performing arts, theater/drama. *Special achievements/activities:* general special achievements/activities, leadership. *Special characteristics:* children and siblings of alumni, children of current students, children of faculty/staff, ethnic background, international students, local/state students, members of minority groups, religious affiliation, siblings of current students, spouses of current students, veterans. *Tuition waivers:* Full or partial for employees or children of employees. *ROTC:* Army cooperative, Air Force cooperative. **LOANS** *Student loans:* $10,806,909 (63% need-based, 37% non-need-based). 79% of past graduating class borrowed through all loan programs. *Average indebtedness per student:* $34,878. *Average need-based loan:* Freshmen: $4283. Undergraduates: $4972. *Parent loans:* $1,205,782 (26% need-based, 74% non-need-based).

AURORA UNIVERSITY
Aurora, IL

Tuition & fees: $20,720	Average undergraduate aid package: $17,248

ABOUT THE INSTITUTION Independent, coed. *Awards:* certificates, bachelor's, master's, and doctoral degrees. 33 undergraduate majors. *Total enrollment:* 4,702. Undergraduates: 3,015. Freshmen: 525. Federal methodology is used as a basis for awarding need-based institutional aid. **UNDERGRADUATE EXPENSES** for 2013–2014 *Application fee:* $25. *Comprehensive fee:* $30,262 includes full-time tuition ($20,500), mandatory fees ($220), and room and board ($9542). Full-time tuition and fees vary according to location. Room and board charges vary according to board plan, housing facility, and location. *Part-time tuition:* $590 per semester hour. Part-time tuition and fees vary according to course load, location, and program. **FRESHMAN FINANCIAL AID (Fall 2012, est.)** 507 applied for aid; of those 89% were deemed to have need. 100% of freshmen with need received aid; of those 18% had need fully met. *Average percent of need met:* 84% (excluding resources awarded to replace EFC). *Average financial aid package:* $18,824 (excluding resources awarded to replace EFC). 14% of all full-time freshmen had no need and received non-need-based gift aid. **UNDERGRADUATE FINANCIAL AID (Fall 2012, est.)** 2,345 applied for aid; of those 90% were deemed to have need. 100% of undergraduates with need received aid; of those 21% had need fully met. *Average percent of need met:* 83% (excluding resources awarded to replace EFC). *Average financial aid package:* $17,248 (excluding resources awarded to replace EFC). 17% of all full-time undergraduates had no need and received non-need-based gift aid. **GIFT AID (NEED-BASED)** *Total amount:* $11,369,435 (41% federal, 35% state, 24% institutional). *Receiving aid:* Freshmen: 70% (365); all full-time undergraduates: 66% (1,725). *Average award:* Freshmen: $7803; Undergraduates: $6537. *Scholarships, grants, and awards:* Federal Pell, FSEOG, state, private, college/university gift aid from institutional funds. **GIFT AID (NON-NEED-BASED)** *Total amount:* $18,946,458 (3% federal, 96% institutional, 1% external sources). *Receiving aid:* Freshmen: 85% (446). Undergraduates: 75% (1,971). *Average award:* Freshmen: $9070. Undergraduates: $7766. *Scholarships, grants, and awards by category: Academic interests/achievement:* 2,353 awards ($16,868,569 total): business, education, general academic interests/achievements. *Creative arts/performance:* 61 awards ($86,350 total): art/fine arts, music, theater/drama. *Special achievements/activities:* 158 awards ($299,215 total): general special achievements/activities, religious involvement. *Special characteristics:* 378 awards ($833,832 total): children and siblings of alumni, children of faculty/staff, out-of-state students, parents of current students, religious affiliation, siblings of current students, veterans, veterans' children. *Tuition waivers:* Full or partial for employees or children of employees, senior citizens. *ROTC:* Army cooperative. **LOANS** *Student loans:* $15,910,642 (45% need-based, 55% non-need-based). 82% of past graduating class borrowed through all loan programs. *Average indebtedness per student:* $25,484. *Average need-based loan:* Freshmen: $3310. Undergraduates: $4418. *Parent loans:* $1,766,088 (100% non-need-based). *Programs:* Federal Direct (Subsidized and Unsubsidized Stafford, PLUS), Perkins, college/university, alternative loans.

WORK-STUDY *Federal work-study:* Total amount: $2,061,511; 1,266 jobs averaging $1572. *State or other work-study/employment:* Total amount: $301,242 (100% non-need-based). 28 part-time jobs averaging $8759.

APPLYING FOR FINANCIAL AID *Required financial aid form:* FAFSA. *Financial aid deadline (priority):* 1/1. *Notification date:* Continuous beginning 3/1. Students must reply by 5/1 or within 3 weeks of notification.

CONTACT Mrs. Heather McKane, Dean of Student Financial Services, Aurora University, 347 South Gladstone Avenue, Aurora, IL 60506-4892, 630-844-6190 or toll-free 800-742-5281. *Fax:* 630-844-6191. *E-mail:* finaid@aurora.edu. *Website:* http://www.aurora.edu/.

AUSTIN COLLEGE
Sherman, TX

ABOUT THE INSTITUTION Independent Presbyterian, coed. *Awards:* bachelor's and master's degrees. 27 undergraduate majors. *Total enrollment:* 1,353. Undergraduates: 1,329. Freshmen: 359.

GIFT AID (NEED-BASED) *Scholarships, grants, and awards:* Federal Pell, FSEOG, state, private, college/university gift aid from institutional funds.

GIFT AID (NON-NEED-BASED) *Scholarships, grants, and awards by category:* Academic interests/achievement: biological sciences, business, communication, education, engineering/technologies, English, foreign languages, general academic interests/achievements, health fields, humanities, international studies, physical sciences, premedicine, religion/biblical studies, social sciences. *Creative arts/performance:* art/fine arts, music, theater/drama. *Special achievements/activities:* community service, general special achievements/activities, leadership, religious involvement. *Special characteristics:* children of faculty/staff, first-generation college students, handicapped students, international students, local/state students, relatives of clergy, veterans.

LOANS *Programs:* Federal Direct (Subsidized and Unsubsidized Stafford, PLUS), Perkins, state, private loans.

WORK-STUDY *Federal work-study:* Total amount: $621,489; jobs available. *State or other work-study/employment:* Total amount: $154,350 (8% need-based, 92% non-need-based). Part-time jobs available.

APPLYING FOR FINANCIAL AID *Required financial aid form:* FAFSA.

CONTACT Mrs. Laurie Coulter, Assistant Vice President for Institutional Enrollment and Executive Director of Financial Aid, Austin College, 900 North Grand Avenue, Sherman, TX 75090, 903-813-2900 or toll-free 800-596-4276 (in-state), 800-526-4276 (out-of-state). *Fax:* 903-813-3198. *E-mail:* finaid@austincollege.edu. *Website:* http://www.austincollege.edu/.

AUSTIN GRADUATE SCHOOL OF THEOLOGY
Austin, TX

ABOUT THE INSTITUTION Independent Church of Christ, coed. 1 undergraduate major.

GIFT AID (NEED-BASED) *Scholarships, grants, and awards:* Federal Pell, FSEOG, college/university gift aid from institutional funds.

GIFT AID (NON-NEED-BASED) *Scholarships, grants, and awards by category:* Academic interests/achievement: religion/biblical studies. *Special achievements/activities:* religious involvement.

LOANS *Programs:* Federal Direct (Subsidized and Unsubsidized Stafford, PLUS).

WORK-STUDY *Federal work-study:* Total amount: $7000; 7 jobs averaging $1000.

APPLYING FOR FINANCIAL AID *Required financial aid forms:* FAFSA, institution's own form.

CONTACT David Arthur, Director of Financial Aid, Austin Graduate School of Theology, 7640 Guadalupe Street, Austin, TX 78752, 512-476-2772 Ext. 105 or toll-free 866-AUS-GRAD. *Fax:* 512-476-3919. *E-mail:* darthur@austingrad.edu. *Website:* http://www.austingrad.edu/.

AUSTIN PEAY STATE UNIVERSITY
Clarksville, TN

Tuition & fees (TN res): $6648	Average undergraduate aid package: $9517

ABOUT THE INSTITUTION State-supported, coed. *Awards:* certificates, associate, bachelor's, and master's degrees. 34 undergraduate majors. *Total enrollment:* 10,597. Undergraduates: 9,735. Freshmen: 1,522. Federal methodology is used as a basis for awarding need-based institutional aid.

UNDERGRADUATE EXPENSES for 2013–2014 *Application fee:* $15. *One-time required fee:* $75. *Tuition, state resident:* full-time $5424; part-time $226 per credit hour. *Tuition, nonresident:* full-time $19,512; part-time $813 per credit hour. *Required fees:* full-time $1224. Full-time tuition and fees vary according to location and program. Part-time tuition and fees vary according to location and program. *College room and board:* $7380; *Room only:* $4600. Room and board charges vary according to board plan and housing facility.

FRESHMAN FINANCIAL AID (Fall 2011) 1,237 applied for aid; of those 86% were deemed to have need. 99% of freshmen with need received aid. *Average financial aid package:* $10,397 (excluding resources awarded to replace EFC). 12% of all full-time freshmen had no need and received non-need-based gift aid.

UNDERGRADUATE FINANCIAL AID (Fall 2011) 6,562 applied for aid; of those 88% were deemed to have need. 98% of undergraduates with need received aid. *Average financial aid package:* $9517 (excluding resources awarded to replace EFC). 8% of all full-time undergraduates had no need and received non-need-based gift aid.

GIFT AID (NEED-BASED) *Total amount:* $28,431,193 (86% federal, 14% state). *Receiving aid:* Freshmen: 69% (884); all full-time undergraduates: 71% (5,046). *Average award:* Freshmen: $7108; Undergraduates: $7357. *Scholarships, grants, and awards:* Federal Pell, FSEOG, state, private, college/university gift aid from institutional funds.

GIFT AID (NON-NEED-BASED) *Total amount:* $20,124,270 (48% state, 9% institutional, 43% external sources). *Receiving aid:* Freshmen: 65% (831). Undergraduates: 40% (2,844). *Average award:* Freshmen: $4512. Undergraduates: $4307. *Scholarships, grants, and awards by category:* Academic interests/achievement: 390 awards ($1,078,759 total): agriculture, biological sciences, business, communication, computer science, education, English, foreign languages, general academic interests/achievements, health fields, humanities, international studies, mathematics, military science, physical sciences, social sciences. *Creative arts/performance:* 384 awards ($364,745 total): art/fine arts, creative writing, debating, journalism/publications, music, performing arts, theater/drama. *Special achievements/activities:* 160 awards ($111,290 total): general special achievements/activities, leadership, memberships. *Special characteristics:* 62 awards ($110,898 total): children of educators, children of faculty/staff, ethnic background, general special characteristics, members of minority groups, veterans. *Tuition waivers:* Full or partial for employees or children of employees, senior citizens. *ROTC:* Army, Air Force cooperative.

LOANS *Student loans:* $43,136,971 (46% need-based, 54% non-need-based). 59% of past graduating class borrowed through all loan programs. *Average indebtedness per student:* $26,030. *Average need-based loan:* Freshmen: $3094. Undergraduates: $3835. *Parent loans:* $3,710,885 (100% non-need-based). *Programs:* Federal Direct (Subsidized and Unsubsidized Stafford, PLUS), Perkins.

WORK-STUDY *Federal work-study:* Total amount: $712,483; 171 jobs averaging $2219. *State or other work-study/employment:* Total amount: $717,995 (100% non-need-based). 420 part-time jobs averaging $1710.

ATHLETIC AWARDS Total amount: $2,691,580 (100% non-need-based).

APPLYING FOR FINANCIAL AID *Required financial aid form:* FAFSA. *Financial aid deadline (priority):* 2/11. *Notification date:* Continuous beginning 4/6.

CONTACT Ms. Donna Price, Director of Student Financial Aid, Austin Peay State University, PO Box 4546, Clarksville, TN 37044, 931-221-7907 or toll-free 800-844-2778. *Fax:* 931-221-6329. *E-mail:* priced@apsu.edu. *Website:* http://www.apsu.edu/.

AVE MARIA UNIVERSITY
Ave Maria, FL

CONTACT Anne Hart, Financial Aid Director, Ave Maria University, 5050 Ave Maria Boulevard, Ave Maria, FL 34142, 239-280-1669 or toll-free 877-283-8648. *Fax:* 239-280-2566. *E-mail:* amufinancialaid@avemaria.edu. *Website:* http://www.avemaria.edu/.

AVERETT UNIVERSITY
Danville, VA

Tuition & fees: $25,950	Average undergraduate aid package: $20,339

ABOUT THE INSTITUTION Independent Baptist General Association of Virginia, coed. *Awards:* associate, bachelor's, and master's degrees. 43 undergraduate majors. *Total enrollment:* 914. Undergraduates: 892. Freshmen: 257. Federal methodology is used as a basis for awarding need-based institutional aid.

UNDERGRADUATE EXPENSES for 2013–2014 *Comprehensive fee:* $34,320 includes full-time tuition ($25,950) and room and board ($8370). *College room only:* $5650. Full-time tuition and fees vary according to course load, degree level, location, and program. Room and board charges vary according to board plan and housing facility. *Part-time tuition:* $1080 per credit hour. Part-time tuition and fees vary according to course load, degree level, location, and program.

FRESHMAN FINANCIAL AID (Fall 2012, est.) 239 applied for aid; of those 93% were deemed to have need. 100% of freshmen with need received aid; of those 10% had need fully met. *Average percent of need met:* 71% (excluding resources awarded to replace EFC). *Average financial aid package:* $20,000 (excluding resources awarded to replace EFC). 16% of all full-time freshmen had no need and received non-need-based gift aid.

UNDERGRADUATE FINANCIAL AID (Fall 2012, est.) 786 applied for aid; of those 94% were deemed to have need. 100% of undergraduates with need received aid; of those 15% had need fully met. *Average percent of need met:* 74% (excluding resources awarded to replace EFC). *Average financial aid package:* $20,339 (excluding resources awarded to replace EFC). 18% of all full-time undergraduates had no need and received non-need-based gift aid.

GIFT AID (NEED-BASED) *Total amount:* $12,074,710 (16% federal, 12% state, 64% institutional, 8% external sources). *Receiving aid:* Freshmen: 87% (223); all full-time undergraduates: 81% (732). *Average award:* Freshmen: $16,576; Undergraduates: $16,458. *Scholarships, grants, and awards:* Federal Pell, FSEOG, state, private, college/university gift aid from institutional funds.

GIFT AID (NON-NEED-BASED) *Total amount:* $2,490,480 (11% state, 80% institutional, 9% external sources). *Receiving aid:* Freshmen: 8% (20). Undergraduates: 9% (81). *Average award:* Freshmen: $12,010. Undergraduates: $11,035. *Scholarships, grants, and awards by category:* Academic interests/ achievement: 258 awards ($469,253 total): biological sciences, business, education, engineering/technologies, English, foreign languages, general academic interests/ achievements, health fields, home economics, humanities, mathematics, physical sciences, premedicine, religion/biblical studies. *Creative arts/performance:* 11 awards ($13,346 total): art/fine arts, journalism/publications, music, theater/drama. *Special achievements/activities:* 64 awards ($108,771 total): general special achievements/ activities, leadership, memberships, religious involvement. *Special characteristics:* 132 awards ($145,900 total): adult students, children and siblings of alumni, children of union members/company employees, first-generation college students, general special characteristics, international students, local/state students, out-of-state students, relatives of clergy, religious affiliation. *Tuition waivers:* Full or partial for employees or children of employees, senior citizens.

LOANS *Student loans:* $6,285,293 (83% need-based, 17% non-need-based). 73% of past graduating class borrowed through all loan programs. *Average indebtedness per student:* $31,373. *Average need-based loan:* Freshmen: $3787. Undergraduates: $4654. *Parent loans:* $1,928,501 (37% need-based, 63% non-need-based). *Programs:* Federal Direct (Subsidized and Unsubsidized Stafford, PLUS), Perkins, state, alternative loans.

WORK-STUDY *Federal work-study:* Total amount: $96,981; 142 jobs averaging $902.

APPLYING FOR FINANCIAL AID *Required financial aid forms:* FAFSA, state aid form. *Financial aid deadline (priority):* 4/1. *Notification date:* Continuous. Students must reply within 2 weeks of notification.

CONTACT Carl Bradsher, Dean of Financial Assistance, Averett University, 420 West Main Street, Danville, VA 24541-3692, 434-791-5646 or toll-free 800-AVERETT. *Fax:* 434-791-5647. *E-mail:* carl.bradsher@averett.edu. *Website:* http://www.averett.edu/.

AVILA UNIVERSITY
Kansas City, MO

CONTACT Nancy Merz, Director of Financial Aid, Avila University, 11901 Wornall Road, Kansas City, MO 64145, 816-501-3782 or toll-free 800-GO-AVILA. *Fax:* 816-501-2462. *E-mail:* nancy.merz@avila.edu. *Website:* http://www.avila.edu/.

AZUSA PACIFIC UNIVERSITY
Azusa, CA

Tuition & fees: $31,076	Average undergraduate aid package: $18,005

ABOUT THE INSTITUTION Independent nondenominational, coed. *Awards:* certificates, bachelor's, master's, and doctoral degrees. 36 undergraduate majors. *Total enrollment:* 10,184. Undergraduates: 6,224. Freshmen: 1,250. Federal methodology is used as a basis for awarding need-based institutional aid.

UNDERGRADUATE EXPENSES for 2013–2014 *Application fee:* $45. *Tuition:* full-time $30,236; part-time $1261 per credit. Room and board charges vary according to board plan and housing facility.

FRESHMAN FINANCIAL AID (Fall 2011) 989 applied for aid; of those 91% were deemed to have need. 100% of freshmen with need received aid; of those 3% had need fully met. *Average percent of need met:* 65% (excluding resources awarded to replace EFC). *Average financial aid package:* $19,088 (excluding resources awarded to replace EFC). 17% of all full-time freshmen had no need and received non-need-based gift aid.

UNDERGRADUATE FINANCIAL AID (Fall 2011) 4,366 applied for aid; of those 85% were deemed to have need. 100% of undergraduates with need received aid; of those 4% had need fully met. *Average percent of need met:* 63% (excluding resources awarded to replace EFC). *Average financial aid package:* $18,005 (excluding resources awarded to replace EFC). 19% of all full-time undergraduates had no need and received non-need-based gift aid.

GIFT AID (NEED-BASED) *Total amount:* $55,830,970 (12% federal, 18% state, 66% institutional, 4% external sources). *Receiving aid:* Freshmen: 70% (826); all full-time undergraduates: 61% (3,142). *Average award:* Freshmen: $9705; Undergraduates: $9824. *Scholarships, grants, and awards:* Federal Pell, FSEOG, state, private, college/university gift aid from institutional funds, Federal Nursing.

GIFT AID (NON-NEED-BASED) *Total amount:* $9,267,212 (89% institutional, 11% external sources). *Receiving aid:* Freshmen: 65% (764). Undergraduates: 59% (3,014). *Average award:* Freshmen: $7680. Undergraduates: $7670. *Scholarships, grants, and awards by category:* Academic interests/achievement: general academic interests/achievements. *Creative arts/performance:* general creative arts/performance. *Special achievements/activities:* leadership. *Special characteristics:* members of minority groups, religious affiliation. *ROTC:* Army, Air Force cooperative.

LOANS *Student loans:* $29,806,138 (85% need-based, 15% non-need-based). 78% of past graduating class borrowed through all loan programs. *Average indebtedness per student:* $23,070. *Average need-based loan:* Freshmen: $3585. Undergraduates: $4586. *Parent loans:* $14,423,891 (55% need-based, 45% non-need-based). *Programs:* Federal Direct (Subsidized and Unsubsidized Stafford, PLUS), Perkins, Federal Nursing.

WORK-STUDY *Federal work-study:* Total amount: $1,090,995; 1,172 jobs averaging $931.

ATHLETIC AWARDS Total amount: $3,338,197 (69% need-based, 31% non-need-based).

APPLYING FOR FINANCIAL AID *Required financial aid forms:* FAFSA, institution's own form. *Financial aid deadline:* 7/1 (priority: 3/2). *Notification date:* Continuous beginning 3/1. Students must reply within 3 weeks of notification.

CONTACT Todd Ross, Interim Director of Student Financial Services, Azusa Pacific University, 901 East Alosta Avenue, PO Box 7000, Azusa, CA 91702-7000, 626-812-3009 or toll-free 800-TALK-APU. *E-mail:* tross@apu.edu. *Website:* http://www.apu.edu/.

BABSON COLLEGE
Wellesley, MA

Tuition & fees: $43,520	Average undergraduate aid package: $34,782

ABOUT THE INSTITUTION Independent, coed. *Awards:* certificates, bachelor's, and master's degrees. 24 undergraduate majors. *Total enrollment:* 3,250. Undergraduates: 2,015. Freshmen: 470. Both federal and institutional methodology are used as a basis for awarding need-based institutional aid.

UNDERGRADUATE EXPENSES for 2013–2014 *Application fee:* $75. *Comprehensive fee:* $57,662 includes full-time tuition ($43,520) and room and board ($14,142). *College room only:* $9126. Room and board charges vary according to board plan and housing facility.

FRESHMAN FINANCIAL AID (Fall 2012, est.) 260 applied for aid; of those 78% were deemed to have need. 100% of freshmen with need received aid; of those 68% had need fully met. *Average percent of need met:* 96% (excluding resources awarded to replace EFC). *Average financial aid package:* $37,261 (excluding resources awarded to replace EFC). 5% of all full-time freshmen had no need and received non-need-based gift aid.

UNDERGRADUATE FINANCIAL AID (Fall 2012, est.) 960 applied for aid; of those 92% were deemed to have need. 100% of undergraduates with need received aid; of those 37% had need fully met. *Average percent of need met:* 95% (excluding resources awarded to replace EFC). *Average financial aid package:* $34,782 (excluding resources awarded to replace EFC). 7% of all full-time undergraduates had no need and received non-need-based gift aid.

GIFT AID (NEED-BASED) *Total amount:* $25,790,000 (7% federal, 1% state, 92% institutional). *Receiving aid:* Freshmen: 40% (186); all full-time undergraduates: 41% (836). *Average award:* Freshmen: $32,063; Undergraduates: $29,177. *Scholarships, grants, and awards:* Federal Pell, FSEOG, state, college/university gift aid from institutional funds.

GIFT AID (NON-NEED-BASED) *Total amount:* $3,185,000 (84% institutional, 16% external sources). *Receiving aid:* Freshmen: 2% (8). Undergraduates: 4% (87). *Average award:* Freshmen: $24,752. Undergraduates: $24,000. *Scholarships, grants, and awards by category: Academic interests/achievement:* general academic interests/achievements. *Special achievements/activities:* leadership. *Special characteristics:* veterans. *Tuition waivers:* Full or partial for employees or children of employees. *ROTC:* Army cooperative, Naval cooperative, Air Force cooperative.

LOANS *Student loans:* $7,553,000 (48% need-based, 52% non-need-based). 48% of past graduating class borrowed through all loan programs. *Average indebtedness per student:* $31,918. *Average need-based loan:* Freshmen: $3445. Undergraduates: $4072. *Parent loans:* $3,510,000 (100% non-need-based). *Programs:* Federal Direct (Subsidized and Unsubsidized Stafford, PLUS), Perkins, state.

WORK-STUDY *Federal work-study:* Total amount: $1,355,000; jobs available. *State or other work-study/employment:* Part-time jobs available.

APPLYING FOR FINANCIAL AID *Required financial aid forms:* FAFSA, CSS Financial Aid PROFILE, noncustodial (divorced/separated) parent's statement, business/farm supplement, federal income tax form(s), W-2 forms, verification worksheet. *Financial aid deadline:* 2/15. *Notification date:* 4/1. Students must reply by 5/1.

CONTACT Ms. Melissa Shaak, Director of Student Financial Services, Babson College, Hollister Hall, Third Floor, Babson Park, MA 02457-0310, 781-239-4219 or toll-free 800-488-3696. *Fax:* 781-239-5510. *E-mail:* shaak@babson.edu. *Website:* http://www.babson.edu/.

BACONE COLLEGE
Muskogee, OK

ABOUT THE INSTITUTION Independent American Baptist Churches in the U.S.A., coed. 26 undergraduate majors.

GIFT AID (NEED-BASED) *Scholarships, grants, and awards:* Federal Pell, FSEOG, state, private, college/university gift aid from institutional funds.

WORK-STUDY Federal work-study jobs available.

APPLYING FOR FINANCIAL AID *Required financial aid forms:* FAFSA, institution's own form.

CONTACT Mrs. Kathye Watson, Office of Financial Aid, Bacone College, 2299 Old Bacone Road, Muskogee, OK 74403-1597, 918-781-7294 or toll-free 888-682-5514 Ext. 7340. *Fax:* 918-781-7416. *E-mail:* financialaid@bacone.edu. *Website:* http://www.bacone.edu/.

BAIS BINYOMIN ACADEMY
Stamford, CT

CONTACT Financial Aid Office, Bais Binyomin Academy, 132 Prospect Street, Stamford, CT 06901-1202, 203-325-4351.

BAKER COLLEGE OF ALLEN PARK
Allen Park, MI

CONTACT Financial Aid Office, Baker College of Allen Park, 4500 Enterprise Drive, Allen Park, MI 48101, 313-425-3700 or toll-free 800-767-4120. *Website:* http://www.baker.edu/.

BAKER COLLEGE OF AUBURN HILLS
Auburn Hills, MI

CONTACT Financial Aid Office, Baker College of Auburn Hills, 1500 University Drive, Auburn Hills, MI 48326-1586, 248-340-0600 or toll-free 888-429-0410. *Website:* http://www.baker.edu/.

BAKER COLLEGE OF CADILLAC
Cadillac, MI

CONTACT Financial Aid Office, Baker College of Cadillac, 9600 East 13th Street, Cadillac, MI 49601, 231-876-3100 or toll-free 888-313-3463. *Website:* http://www.baker.edu/.

BAKER COLLEGE OF CLINTON TOWNSHIP
Clinton Township, MI

CONTACT Financial Aid Office, Baker College of Clinton Township, 34950 Little Mack Avenue, Clinton Township, MI 48035-4701, 586-791-6610 or toll-free 888-272-2842. *Website:* http://www.baker.edu/.

BAKER COLLEGE OF FLINT
Flint, MI

CONTACT Financial Aid Office, Baker College of Flint, 1050 West Bristol Road, Flint, MI 48507-5508, 810-767-7600 or toll-free 800-964-4299. *Website:* http://www.baker.edu/.

BAKER COLLEGE OF JACKSON
Jackson, MI

CONTACT Financial Aid Office, Baker College of Jackson, 2800 Springport Road, Jackson, MI 49202, 517-789-6123 or toll-free 888-343-3683. *Website:* http://www.baker.edu/.

BAKER COLLEGE OF MUSKEGON
Muskegon, MI

CONTACT Financial Aid Office, Baker College of Muskegon, 1903 Marquette Avenue, Muskegon, MI 49442-3497, 231-777-5200 or toll-free 800-937-0337. *Website:* http://www.baker.edu/.

BAKER COLLEGE OF OWOSSO
Owosso, MI

CONTACT Financial Aid Office, Baker College of Owosso, 1020 South Washington Street, Owosso, MI 48867-4400, 989-729-3300 or toll-free 800-879-3797. *Website:* http://www.baker.edu/.

BAKER COLLEGE OF PORT HURON
Port Huron, MI

CONTACT Financial Aid Office, Baker College of Port Huron, 3403 Lapeer Road, Port Huron, MI 48060-2597, 810-985-7000 or toll-free 888-262-2442. *Website:* http://www.baker.edu/.

BAKER UNIVERSITY
Baldwin City, KS

CONTACT Mrs. Jeanne Mott, Financial Aid Director, Baker University, Box 65, Baldwin City, KS 66006-0065, 785-594-4595 or toll-free 800-873-4282. *Fax:* 785-594-8358. *Website:* http://www.bakeru.edu/.

BALDWIN WALLACE UNIVERSITY
Berea, OH

Tuition & fees: $27,060	Average undergraduate aid package: $21,205

ABOUT THE INSTITUTION Independent Methodist, coed. *Awards:* certificates, bachelor's, and master's degrees. 73 undergraduate majors. *Total enrollment:* 4,173. Undergraduates: 3,512. Freshmen: 712. Federal methodology is used as a basis for awarding need-based institutional aid.
UNDERGRADUATE EXPENSES for 2013–2014 Application fee: $25. **Comprehensive fee:** $34,580 includes full-time tuition ($27,060) and room and board ($7520). *College room only:* $4340. Full-time tuition and fees vary according to class time, course level, course load, degree level, program, and reciprocity agreements. Room and board charges vary according to housing facility. *Part-time tuition:* $840 per semester hour. Part-time tuition and fees vary according to class time, course level, course load, degree level, program, and reciprocity agreements.
FRESHMAN FINANCIAL AID (Fall 2012, est.) 688 applied for aid; of those 88% were deemed to have need. 100% of freshmen with need received aid; of those 33% had need fully met. *Average percent of need met:* 89% (excluding resources awarded to replace EFC). *Average financial aid package:* $24,089 (excluding resources awarded to replace EFC). 15% of all full-time freshmen had no need and received non-need-based gift aid.

UNDERGRADUATE FINANCIAL AID (Fall 2012, est.) 2,701 applied for aid; of those 89% were deemed to have need. 100% of undergraduates with need received aid; of those 34% had need fully met. *Average percent of need met:* 85% (excluding resources awarded to replace EFC). *Average financial aid package:* $21,205 (excluding resources awarded to replace EFC). 17% of all full-time undergraduates had no need and received non-need-based gift aid.
GIFT AID (NEED-BASED) Total amount: $36,047,647 (14% federal, 5% state, 80% institutional, 1% external sources). *Receiving aid:* Freshmen: 85% (604); all full-time undergraduates: 80% (2,416). *Average award:* Freshmen: $18,455; Undergraduates: $16,134. *Scholarships, grants, and awards:* Federal Pell, FSEOG, state, private, college/university gift aid from institutional funds.
GIFT AID (NON-NEED-BASED) Total amount: $6,666,721 (1% state, 97% institutional, 2% external sources). *Receiving aid:* Freshmen: 11% (79). Undergraduates: 7% (218). *Average award:* Freshmen: $11,215. Undergraduates: $10,327. *Scholarships, grants, and awards by category:* Academic interests/achievement: 2,099 awards ($16,828,979 total): general academic interests/achievements. *Creative arts/performance:* 245 awards ($794,078 total): music. *Special achievements/activities:* leadership. *Special characteristics:* 868 awards ($1,912,125 total): children and siblings of alumni, members of minority groups, religious affiliation, siblings of current students. *Tuition waivers:* Full or partial for children of alumni, employees or children of employees. *ROTC:* Army cooperative, Air Force cooperative.
LOANS Student loans: $18,335,004 (61% need-based, 39% non-need-based). 83% of past graduating class borrowed through all loan programs. *Average indebtedness per student:* $31,022. *Average need-based loan:* Freshmen: $3530. Undergraduates: $4557. *Parent loans:* $22,119,452 (61% need-based, 39% non-need-based). *Programs:* Federal Direct (Subsidized and Unsubsidized Stafford, PLUS), Perkins.
WORK-STUDY Federal work-study: Total amount: $466,000; 875 jobs averaging $969. *State or other work-study/employment:* Total amount: $1,125,000 (62% need-based, 38% non-need-based). 351 part-time jobs averaging $700.
APPLYING FOR FINANCIAL AID Required financial aid form: FAFSA. *Financial aid deadline:* 9/1 (priority: 5/1). *Notification date:* Continuous beginning 2/14.
CONTACT Dr. George L. Rolleston, Director of Financial Aid, Baldwin Wallace University, 275 Eastland Road, Berea, OH 44017-2088, 440-826-2108 or toll-free 877-BW-APPLY. *Fax:* 440-826-8048. *E-mail:* grollest@bw.edu. *Website:* http://www.bw.edu/.

BALL STATE UNIVERSITY
Muncie, IN

Tuition & fees (IN res): $8980	Average undergraduate aid package: $10,255

ABOUT THE INSTITUTION State-supported, coed. *Awards:* certificates, associate, bachelor's, master's, and doctoral degrees. 85 undergraduate majors. *Total enrollment:* 21,053. Undergraduates: 16,652. Freshmen: 3,556. Federal methodology is used as a basis for awarding need-based institutional aid.
UNDERGRADUATE EXPENSES for 2013–2014 Application fee: $55. *Tuition, state resident:* full-time $8318; part-time $270 per credit hour. *Tuition, nonresident:* full-time $22,988; part-time $906 per credit hour. *Required fees:* full-time $662. Full-time tuition and fees vary according to course load, program, and reciprocity agreements. Part-time tuition and fees vary according to course load and reciprocity agreements. *College room and board:* $8870. Room and board charges vary according to board plan and housing facility.
FRESHMAN FINANCIAL AID (Fall 2012, est.) 3,316 applied for aid; of those 76% were deemed to have need. 100% of freshmen with need received aid; of those 30% had need fully met. *Average percent of need met:* 65% (excluding resources awarded to replace EFC). *Average financial aid package:* $10,271 (excluding resources awarded to replace EFC). 8% of all full-time freshmen had no need and received non-need-based gift aid.
UNDERGRADUATE FINANCIAL AID (Fall 2012, est.) 13,112 applied for aid; of those 79% were deemed to have need. 99% of undergraduates with need received aid; of those 31% had need fully met. *Average percent of need met:* 65% (excluding resources awarded to replace EFC). *Average financial aid package:* $10,255 (excluding resources awarded to replace EFC). 9% of all full-time undergraduates had no need and received non-need-based gift aid.

GIFT AID (NEED-BASED) *Total amount:* $36,703,822 (63% federal, 26% state, 11% institutional). *Receiving aid:* Freshmen: 45% (1,605); all full-time undergraduates: 40% (6,122). *Average award:* Freshmen: $5638; Undergraduates: $6027. *Scholarships, grants, and awards:* Federal Pell, FSEOG, state, private, college/university gift aid from institutional funds.

GIFT AID (NON-NEED-BASED) *Total amount:* $39,272,366 (4% federal, 26% state, 56% institutional, 14% external sources). *Receiving aid:* Freshmen: 29% (1,022). Undergraduates: 23% (3,567). *Average award:* Freshmen: $7514. Undergraduates: $7166. *Scholarships, grants, and awards by category: Academic interests/achievement:* 3,782 awards ($13,840,781 total): architecture, biological sciences, business, communication, education, engineering/technologies, English, foreign languages, general academic interests/achievements, health fields, humanities, international studies, mathematics, military science, physical sciences, social sciences. *Creative arts/performance:* 136 awards ($99,186 total): art/fine arts, cinema/film/broadcasting, dance, debating, general creative arts/performance, journalism/publications, music, performing arts, theater/drama. *Special achievements/activities:* 177 awards ($1,314,895 total): community service, general special achievements/activities, leadership. *Special characteristics:* 1,518 awards ($12,761,656 total): adult students, children and siblings of alumni, children of faculty/staff, ethnic background, general special characteristics, international students, local/state students, members of minority groups, out-of-state students, veterans, veterans' children. *Tuition waivers:* Full or partial for employees or children of employees, senior citizens. *ROTC:* Army.

LOANS *Student loans:* $98,920,231 (42% need-based, 58% non-need-based). 72% of past graduating class borrowed through all loan programs. *Average indebtedness per student:* $27,373. *Average need-based loan:* Freshmen: $3526. Undergraduates: $4300. *Parent loans:* $57,844,210 (100% non-need-based). *Programs:* Federal Direct (Subsidized and Unsubsidized Stafford, PLUS), Perkins.

WORK-STUDY *Federal work-study:* Total amount: $2,137,900; 512 jobs averaging $2253. *State or other work-study/employment:* Total amount: $7,955,722 (100% non-need-based). Part-time jobs available.

ATHLETIC AWARDS Total amount: $5,940,646 (100% non-need-based).

APPLYING FOR FINANCIAL AID *Required financial aid form:* FAFSA. *Financial aid deadline (priority):* 3/10. *Notification date:* Continuous beginning 4/1.

CONTACT Dr. John McPherson, Director of Scholarships and Financial Aid, Ball State University, Lucina Hall, Room 245, Muncie, IN 47306-1099, 800-227-4017 or toll-free 800-482-4BSU. *Fax:* 765-285-4247. *E-mail:* finaid@bsu.edu. *Website:* http://www.bsu.edu/.

fully met. *Average percent of need met:* 64% (excluding resources awarded to replace EFC). *Average financial aid package:* $14,442 (excluding resources awarded to replace EFC). 18% of all full-time freshmen had no need and received non-need-based gift aid.

UNDERGRADUATE FINANCIAL AID (Fall 2011) 492 applied for aid; of those 92% were deemed to have need. 100% of undergraduates with need received aid; of those 7% had need fully met. *Average percent of need met:* 64% (excluding resources awarded to replace EFC). *Average financial aid package:* $13,779 (excluding resources awarded to replace EFC). 14% of all full-time undergraduates had no need and received non-need-based gift aid.

GIFT AID (NEED-BASED) *Total amount:* $1,957,178 (66% federal, 23% state, 11% institutional). *Receiving aid:* Freshmen: 68% (71); all full-time undergraduates: 62% (326). *Average award:* Freshmen: $7104; Undergraduates: $5813. *Scholarships, grants, and awards:* Federal Pell, FSEOG, state, private, college/university gift aid from institutional funds.

GIFT AID (NON-NEED-BASED) *Total amount:* $2,795,538 (91% institutional, 9% external sources). *Receiving aid:* Freshmen: 82% (86). Undergraduates: 79% (420). *Average award:* Freshmen: $5317. Undergraduates: $4644. *Scholarships, grants, and awards by category: Academic interests/achievement:* 418 awards ($1,693,613 total): education, general academic interests/achievements, religion/biblical studies. *Creative arts/performance:* 16 awards ($27,642 total): general creative arts/performance, music. *Special achievements/activities:* 125 awards ($225,000 total): general special achievements/activities, leadership, religious involvement. *Special characteristics:* 47 awards ($285,123 total): children of faculty/staff, general special characteristics, married students. *Tuition waivers:* Full or partial for employees or children of employees. *ROTC:* Army cooperative, Naval cooperative, Air Force cooperative.

LOANS *Student loans:* $3,745,275 (100% need-based). 81% of past graduating class borrowed through all loan programs. *Average indebtedness per student:* $23,677. *Average need-based loan:* Freshmen: $3414. Undergraduates: $4341. *Parent loans:* $730,622 (100% non-need-based). *Programs:* Federal Direct (Subsidized and Unsubsidized Stafford, PLUS), alternative loans.

WORK-STUDY *Federal work-study:* Total amount: $97,284; 65 jobs averaging $1497. *State or other work-study/employment:* Part-time jobs available.

APPLYING FOR FINANCIAL AID *Required financial aid form:* FAFSA. *Financial aid deadline (priority):* 5/1. *Notification date:* Continuous beginning 2/1.

CONTACT Mr. Steven E. Brown, Director of Student Financial Services, Baptist Bible College of Pennsylvania, 538 Venard Road, Clarks Summit, PA 18411, 570-586-2400 Ext. 9206 or toll-free 800-451-7664. *Fax:* 570-587-8045. *E-mail:* sbrown@bbc.edu. *Website:* http://www.bbc.edu/.

BAPTIST BIBLE COLLEGE
Springfield, MO

CONTACT Bob Kotulski, Director of Financial Aid, Baptist Bible College, 628 East Kearney, Springfield, MO 65803-3498, 417-268-6036 or toll-free 800-228-5754. *Fax:* 417-268-6694.
Website: http://www.gobbc.edu/.

BAPTIST BIBLE COLLEGE OF PENNSYLVANIA
Clarks Summit, PA

Tuition & fees: $19,710	Average undergraduate aid package: $13,779

ABOUT THE INSTITUTION Independent Baptist, coed. *Awards:* certificates, associate, bachelor's, master's, and doctoral degrees. 28 undergraduate majors. *Total enrollment:* 1,001. Undergraduates: 722. Freshmen: 115. Federal methodology is used as a basis for awarding need-based institutional aid.

UNDERGRADUATE EXPENSES for 2013–2014 *Application fee:* $40. *Comprehensive fee:* $26,890 includes full-time tuition ($18,420), mandatory fees ($1290), and room and board ($7180). *College room only:* $2560. Room and board charges vary according to board plan. *Part-time tuition:* $614 per credit. *Part-time fees:* $43 per credit.

FRESHMAN FINANCIAL AID (Fall 2011) 98 applied for aid; of those 91% were deemed to have need. 100% of freshmen with need received aid; of those 4% had need

THE BAPTIST COLLEGE OF FLORIDA
Graceville, FL

Tuition & fees: $9400	Average undergraduate aid package: $7444

ABOUT THE INSTITUTION Independent Southern Baptist, coed. *Awards:* associate, bachelor's, and master's degrees. 9 undergraduate majors. *Total enrollment:* 606. Undergraduates: 596. Freshmen: 63. Federal methodology is used as a basis for awarding need-based institutional aid.

UNDERGRADUATE EXPENSES for 2013–2014 *Application fee:* $25. *Comprehensive fee:* $13,538 includes full-time tuition ($9000), mandatory fees ($400), and room and board ($4138). Room and board charges vary according to board plan and housing facility. *Part-time tuition:* $300 per credit hour.

FRESHMAN FINANCIAL AID (Fall 2012, est.) 165 applied for aid; of those 41% were deemed to have need. 60% of freshmen with need received aid; of those 5% had need fully met. *Average percent of need met:* 30% (excluding resources awarded to replace EFC). *Average financial aid package:* $6511 (excluding resources awarded to replace EFC). 1% of all full-time freshmen had no need and received non-need-based gift aid.

UNDERGRADUATE FINANCIAL AID (Fall 2012, est.) 738 applied for aid; of those 67% were deemed to have need. 77% of undergraduates with need received aid; of those 5% had need fully met. *Average percent of need met:* 36% (excluding resources awarded to replace EFC). *Average financial aid package:* $7444 (excluding resources awarded to replace EFC). 1% of all full-time undergraduates had no need and received non-need-based gift aid.

GIFT AID (NEED-BASED) *Total amount:* $1,999,024 (65% federal, 18% state, 4% institutional, 13% external sources). *Receiving aid:* Freshmen: 25% (41); all full-time undergraduates: 33% (359). *Average award:* Freshmen: $5100; Undergraduates: $5177. *Scholarships, grants, and awards:* Federal Pell, FSEOG, state, private, college/university gift aid from institutional funds.
GIFT AID (NON-NEED-BASED) *Total amount:* $145,449 (39% state, 15% institutional, 46% external sources). *Receiving aid:* Freshmen: 1% (1). Undergraduates: 1% (9). *Average award:* Freshmen: $1000. Undergraduates: $1750. *Scholarships, grants, and awards by category:* Academic interests/achievement: 240 awards ($216,860 total): education, religion/biblical studies. *Creative arts/performance:* 2 awards ($330 total): music. *Special characteristics:* 241 awards ($219,348 total): children with a deceased or disabled parent, religious affiliation, spouses of current students. *Tuition waivers:* Full or partial for employees or children of employees.
LOANS *Student loans:* $1,816,919 (85% need-based, 15% non-need-based). 6% of past graduating class borrowed through all loan programs. *Average indebtedness per student:* $22,803. *Average need-based loan:* Freshmen: $2489. Undergraduates: $3488. *Parent loans:* $79,606 (46% need-based, 54% non-need-based). *Programs:* Federal Direct (Subsidized and Unsubsidized Stafford, PLUS).
WORK-STUDY *Federal work-study:* Total amount: $50,738; 22 jobs averaging $2306.
APPLYING FOR FINANCIAL AID *Required financial aid forms:* FAFSA, institution's own form, state aid form, business/farm supplement, student authorization form. *Financial aid deadline:* 4/15 (priority: 4/1). *Notification date:* Continuous beginning 6/15. Students must reply within 4 weeks of notification.
CONTACT Stephanie E. Powell, Director of Financial Aid, The Baptist College of Florida, 5400 College Drive, Graceville, FL 32440-3306, 850-263-3261 Ext. 461 or toll-free 800-328-2660 Ext. 460. *Fax:* 850-263-2141. *E-mail:* finaid@baptistcollege.edu. *Website:* http://www.baptistcollege.edu/.

BAPTIST COLLEGE OF HEALTH SCIENCES
Memphis, TN

CONTACT Leanne Smith, Financial Aid Officer, Baptist College of Health Sciences, 1003 Monroe Avenue, Memphis, TN 38104, 901-227-6805 or toll-free 866-575-2247. *Fax:* 901-227-4311. *E-mail:* leanne.smith@bchs.edu. *Website:* http://www.bchs.edu/.

BAPTIST MISSIONARY ASSOCIATION THEOLOGICAL SEMINARY
Jacksonville, TX

CONTACT Dr. Philip Attebery, Dean/Registrar, Baptist Missionary Association Theological Seminary, 1530 East Pine Street, Jacksonville, TX 75766-5407, 903-586-2501 or toll-free 800-259-5673. *Fax:* 903-586-0378. *E-mail:* bmatsem@bmats.edu. *Website:* http://www.bmats.edu/.

BAPTIST UNIVERSITY OF THE AMERICAS
San Antonio, TX

Tuition & fees: $5280	Average undergraduate aid package: N/A

ABOUT THE INSTITUTION Independent Baptist, coed. *Awards:* certificates, diplomas, associate, and bachelor's degrees (associate degree in Cross-Cultural Studies). 4 undergraduate majors. *Total enrollment:* 175. Undergraduates: 27. Freshmen: 27. Both federal and institutional methodology are used as a basis for awarding need-based institutional aid.
UNDERGRADUATE EXPENSES for 2013–2014 *Application fee:* $25. *Comprehensive fee:* $8660 includes full-time tuition ($4800), mandatory fees ($480), and

room and board ($3380). *College room only:* $2500. *Part-time tuition:* $200 per credit. *Part-time fees:* $20 per hour.
GIFT AID (NEED-BASED) *Scholarships, grants, and awards:* Federal Pell, FSEOG, private, college/university gift aid from institutional funds.
GIFT AID (NON-NEED-BASED) *Scholarships, grants, and awards by category:* Academic interests/achievement: business, humanities, religion/biblical studies. *Tuition waivers:* Full or partial for employees or children of employees.
WORK-STUDY *Federal work-study:* 2 jobs averaging $5268. *State or other work-study/employment:* 72 part-time jobs averaging $2877.
APPLYING FOR FINANCIAL AID *Required financial aid forms:* FAFSA, institution's own form. *Notification date:* Continuous.
CONTACT Mrs. Araceli G. Acosta, Financial Aid Administrator, Baptist University of the Americas, 8019 South Pan Am Expressway, San Antonio, TX 78224, 210-924-4338 Ext. 214 or toll-free 800-721-1396. *Fax:* 210-924-2701. *E-mail:* araceli.acosta@bua.edu.
Website: http://www.bua.edu/.

BARCLAY COLLEGE
Haviland, KS

CONTACT Christina Foster, Financial Aid Coordinator, Barclay College, 607 North Kingman, Haviland, KS 67059, 800-862-0226. *Fax:* 620-862-5403. *E-mail:* financialaid@barclaycollege.edu.
Website: http://www.barclaycollege.edu/.

BARD COLLEGE
Annandale-on-Hudson, NY

Tuition & fees: $46,370	Average undergraduate aid package: $36,279

ABOUT THE INSTITUTION Independent, coed. *Awards:* bachelor's, master's, and doctoral degrees. 78 undergraduate majors. *Total enrollment:* 2,322. Undergraduates: 2,051. Freshmen: 537. Both federal and institutional methodology are used as a basis for awarding need-based institutional aid.
UNDERGRADUATE EXPENSES for 2013–2014 *Application fee:* $50. *One-time required fee:* $1574. *Comprehensive fee:* $59,872 includes full-time tuition ($45,730), mandatory fees ($640), and room and board ($13,502). Full-time tuition and fees vary according to degree level. *Part-time tuition:* $1429 per credit hour. Part-time tuition and fees vary according to degree level. *Payment plan:* Tuition prepayment.
FRESHMAN FINANCIAL AID (Fall 2012, est.) 394 applied for aid; of those 96% were deemed to have need. 100% of freshmen with need received aid; of those 58% had need fully met. *Average percent of need met:* 88% (excluding resources awarded to replace EFC). *Average financial aid package:* $39,829 (excluding resources awarded to replace EFC). 1% of all full-time freshmen had no need and received non-need-based gift aid.
UNDERGRADUATE FINANCIAL AID (Fall 2012, est.) 1,374 applied for aid; of those 97% were deemed to have need. 100% of undergraduates with need received aid; of those 49% had need fully met. *Average percent of need met:* 80% (excluding resources awarded to replace EFC). *Average financial aid package:* $36,279 (excluding resources awarded to replace EFC). 1% of all full-time undergraduates had no need and received non-need-based gift aid.
GIFT AID (NEED-BASED) *Total amount:* $40,118,862 (5% federal, 2% state, 92% institutional, 1% external sources). *Receiving aid:* Freshmen: 68% (367); all full-time undergraduates: 64% (1,248). *Average award:* Freshmen: $34,385; Undergraduates: $31,912. *Scholarships, grants, and awards:* Federal Pell, FSEOG, state, private, college/university gift aid from institutional funds.
GIFT AID (NON-NEED-BASED) *Total amount:* $358,176 (100% institutional). *Average award:* Freshmen: $16,800. Undergraduates: $17,030. *Scholarships, grants, and awards by category:* Academic interests/achievement: biological sciences, computer science, mathematics, physical sciences. *Special achievements/activities:* 1 award ($5000 total): leadership. *Special characteristics:* 1 award ($44,176 total): children of educators, children of faculty/staff. *Tuition waivers:* Full or partial for employees or children of employees.

LOANS *Student loans:* $7,549,745 (96% need-based, 4% non-need-based). 49% of past graduating class borrowed through all loan programs. *Average indebtedness per student:* $24,913. *Average need-based loan:* Freshmen: $5253. Undergraduates: $5746. *Parent loans:* $4,303,952 (93% need-based, 7% non-need-based). *Programs:* Federal Direct (Subsidized and Unsubsidized Stafford, PLUS), Perkins, college/university loans from institutional funds (international students only).
WORK-STUDY *Federal work-study:* Total amount: $1,282,325; 806 jobs averaging $1565. *State or other work-study/employment:* Total amount: $41,250 (100% need-based). 82 part-time jobs averaging $1650.
APPLYING FOR FINANCIAL AID *Required financial aid forms:* FAFSA, CSS Financial Aid PROFILE, state aid form, noncustodial (divorced/separated) parent's statement, business/farm supplement. *Financial aid deadline:* 2/15 (priority: 2/1). *Notification date:* 4/1. Students must reply by 5/1 or within 2 weeks of notification.
CONTACT Denise Ann Ackerman, Director of Financial Aid, Bard College, Annandale Road, Annandale-on-Hudson, NY 12504, 845-758-7525. *Fax:* 845-758-7336. *E-mail:* finaid@bard.edu.
Website: http://www.bard.edu/.

BARD COLLEGE AT SIMON'S ROCK
Great Barrington, MA

ABOUT THE INSTITUTION Independent, coed. *Awards:* associate and bachelor's degrees. 44 undergraduate majors. *Total enrollment:* 350. Undergraduates: 350. Freshmen: 118.
GIFT AID (NEED-BASED) *Scholarships, grants, and awards:* Federal Pell, FSEOG, state, private, college/university gift aid from institutional funds.
GIFT AID (NON-NEED-BASED) *Scholarships, grants, and awards by category:* Academic interests/achievement: general academic interests/achievements. *Special characteristics:* children and siblings of alumni, children of faculty/staff, local/state students, members of minority groups.
LOANS *Programs:* Federal Direct (Subsidized and Unsubsidized Stafford, PLUS), Perkins.
WORK-STUDY *Federal work-study:* Total amount: $159,000; 156 jobs averaging $1000.
APPLYING FOR FINANCIAL AID *Required financial aid forms:* FAFSA, CSS Financial Aid PROFILE, noncustodial (divorced/separated) parent's statement.
CONTACT Ms. Ann Murtagh Gitto, Director of Financial Aid, Bard College at Simon's Rock, 84 Alford Road, Great Barrington, MA 01230-9702, 413-528-7297 or toll-free 800-235-7186. *Fax:* 413-528-7339. *E-mail:* agitto@simons-rock.edu.
Website: http://www.simons-rock.edu/.

BARNARD COLLEGE
New York, NY

Tuition & fees: $43,502	Average undergraduate aid package: $41,408

ABOUT THE INSTITUTION Independent, women only. *Awards:* bachelor's degrees. 48 undergraduate majors. *Total enrollment:* 2,445. Undergraduates: 2,445. Freshmen: 612. Both federal and institutional methodology are used as a basis for awarding need-based institutional aid.
UNDERGRADUATE EXPENSES for 2013–2014 *Application fee:* $55. *Comprehensive fee:* $57,312 includes full-time tuition ($41,850), mandatory fees ($1652), and room and board ($13,810). *College room only:* $8240. Room and board charges vary according to board plan and housing facility. *Payment plan:* Tuition prepayment.
FRESHMAN FINANCIAL AID (Fall 2012, est.) 318 applied for aid; of those 75% were deemed to have need. 100% of freshmen with need received aid; of those 100% had need fully met. *Average percent of need met:* 100% (excluding resources awarded to replace EFC). *Average financial aid package:* $40,899 (excluding resources awarded to replace EFC).
UNDERGRADUATE FINANCIAL AID (Fall 2012, est.) 1,107 applied for aid; of those 87% were deemed to have need. 100% of undergraduates with need received aid; of those 100% had need fully met. *Average percent of need met:* 100% (excluding resources awarded to replace EFC). *Average financial aid package:* $41,408 (excluding resources awarded to replace EFC).

GIFT AID (NEED-BASED) *Total amount:* $34,159,619 (6% federal, 4% state, 87% institutional, 3% external sources). *Receiving aid:* Freshmen: 39% (231); all full-time undergraduates: 38% (932). *Average award:* Freshmen: $42,306; Undergraduates: $42,572. *Scholarships, grants, and awards:* Federal Pell, FSEOG, state, private, college/university gift aid from institutional funds.
GIFT AID (NON-NEED-BASED) *Total amount:* $533,934 (4% state, 96% external sources). *Tuition waivers:* Full or partial for employees or children of employees. *ROTC:* Air Force cooperative.
LOANS *Student loans:* $4,647,211 (74% need-based, 26% non-need-based). 46% of past graduating class borrowed through all loan programs. *Average indebtedness per student:* $19,931. *Average need-based loan:* Freshmen: $3450. Undergraduates: $4547. *Parent loans:* $4,833,647 (100% non-need-based). *Programs:* Federal Direct (Subsidized and Unsubsidized Stafford, PLUS), Perkins, state, college/university.
WORK-STUDY *Federal work-study:* Total amount: $385,850; 191 jobs averaging $2020. *State or other work-study/employment:* Total amount: $1,180,398 (90% need-based, 10% non-need-based). 527 part-time jobs averaging $2013.
APPLYING FOR FINANCIAL AID *Required financial aid forms:* FAFSA, CSS Financial Aid PROFILE, state aid form, noncustodial (divorced/separated) parent's statement, federal income tax form(s). *Financial aid deadline:* 2/15. *Notification date:* 3/31. Students must reply by 5/1.
CONTACT Nanette DiLauro, Director of Financial Aid, Barnard College, 3009 Broadway, New York, NY 10027-6598, 212-854-2154. *Fax:* 212-854-2902. *E-mail:* finaid@barnard.edu.
Website: http://www.barnard.edu/.

BARRY UNIVERSITY
Miami Shores, FL

Tuition & fees: $28,160	Average undergraduate aid package: $19,074

ABOUT THE INSTITUTION Independent Roman Catholic, coed. *Awards:* certificates, bachelor's, master's, and doctoral degrees. 58 undergraduate majors. *Total enrollment:* 9,070. Undergraduates: 4,619. Freshmen: 625. Federal methodology is used as a basis for awarding need-based institutional aid.
UNDERGRADUATE EXPENSES for 2013–2014 *Application fee:* $30. *Tuition:* full-time $28,160. Part-time tuition and fees vary according to course load. Room and board charges vary according to board plan.
FRESHMAN FINANCIAL AID (Fall 2012, est.) 561 applied for aid; of those 97% were deemed to have need. 100% of freshmen with need received aid; of those 6% had need fully met. *Average percent of need met:* 64% (excluding resources awarded to replace EFC). *Average financial aid package:* $23,891 (excluding resources awarded to replace EFC). 2% of all full-time freshmen had no need and received non-need-based gift aid.
UNDERGRADUATE FINANCIAL AID (Fall 2012, est.) 3,352 applied for aid; of those 96% were deemed to have need. 99% of undergraduates with need received aid; of those 5% had need fully met. *Average percent of need met:* 52% (excluding resources awarded to replace EFC). *Average financial aid package:* $19,074 (excluding resources awarded to replace EFC). 2% of all full-time undergraduates had no need and received non-need-based gift aid.
GIFT AID (NEED-BASED) *Total amount:* $18,376,442 (56% federal, 7% state, 37% institutional). *Receiving aid:* Freshmen: 75% (465); all full-time undergraduates: 66% (2,507). *Average award:* Freshmen: $9130; Undergraduates: $7083. *Scholarships, grants, and awards:* Federal Pell, FSEOG, state, private, college/university gift aid from institutional funds, Federal Nursing.
GIFT AID (NON-NEED-BASED) *Total amount:* $29,894,128 (16% state, 83% institutional, 1% external sources). *Receiving aid:* Freshmen: 86% (533). Undergraduates: 81% (3,095). *Average award:* Freshmen: $12,729; Undergraduates: $10,293. *ROTC:* Army cooperative, Air Force cooperative.
LOANS *Student loans:* $33,428,062 (42% need-based, 58% non-need-based). 71% of past graduating class borrowed through all loan programs. *Average indebtedness per student:* $38,634. *Average need-based loan:* Freshmen: $3187. Undergraduates: $4644. *Parent loans:* $3,583,387 (100% non-need-based). *Programs:* Perkins, Federal Nursing, college/university, alternative loans.
WORK-STUDY *Federal work-study:* Total amount: $907,790; jobs available. *State or other work-study/employment:* Total amount: $414,016 (100% non-need-based). Part-time jobs available.
ATHLETIC AWARDS Total amount: $2,807,146 (100% non-need-based).

APPLYING FOR FINANCIAL AID *Required financial aid form:* FAFSA. *Financial aid deadline:* Continuous. *Notification date:* Continuous beginning 1/25.

CONTACT Mr. Dart Humeston, Assistant Dean of Enrollment Services and Director of Financial Aid, Barry University, 11300 Northeast Second Avenue, Miami Shores, FL 33161-6695, 305-899-3673 or toll-free 800-695-2279. *E-mail:* finaid@mail.barry.edu. *Website:* http://www.barry.edu/.

BARTON COLLEGE
Wilson, NC

Tuition & fees: $24,180	Average undergraduate aid package: $16,043

ABOUT THE INSTITUTION Independent Christian Church (Disciples of Christ), coed. *Awards:* bachelor's and master's degrees. 33 undergraduate majors. *Total enrollment:* 1,106. Undergraduates: 1,094. Freshmen: 202. Federal methodology is used as a basis for awarding need-based institutional aid.

UNDERGRADUATE EXPENSES for 2013–2014 *Application fee:* $25. *Comprehensive fee:* $32,120 includes full-time tuition ($22,278), mandatory fees ($1902), and room and board ($7940). *College room only:* $3600. Full-time tuition and fees vary according to class time, course load, and program. Room and board charges vary according to board plan and housing facility. *Part-time tuition:* $941 per credit hour. Part-time tuition and fees vary according to class time, course load, and program.

FRESHMAN FINANCIAL AID (Fall 2012, est.) 195 applied for aid; of those 93% were deemed to have need. 100% of freshmen with need received aid; of those 12% had need fully met. *Average percent of need met:* 61% (excluding resources awarded to replace EFC). *Average financial aid package:* $18,479 (excluding resources awarded to replace EFC). 10% of all full-time freshmen had no need and received non-need-based gift aid.

UNDERGRADUATE FINANCIAL AID (Fall 2012, est.) 1,061 applied for aid; of those 94% were deemed to have need. 98% of undergraduates with need received aid; of those 8% had need fully met. *Average percent of need met:* 56% (excluding resources awarded to replace EFC). *Average financial aid package:* $16,043 (excluding resources awarded to replace EFC). 9% of all full-time undergraduates had no need and received non-need-based gift aid.

GIFT AID (NEED-BASED) *Total amount:* $10,954,940 (23% federal, 23% state, 52% institutional, 2% external sources). *Receiving aid:* Freshmen: 78% (181); all full-time undergraduates: 82% (938). *Average award:* Freshmen: $15,597; Undergraduates: $12,738. *Scholarships, grants, and awards:* Federal Pell, FSEOG, state, private, college/university gift aid from institutional funds.

GIFT AID (NON-NEED-BASED) *Total amount:* $943,359 (1% federal, 4% state, 92% institutional, 3% external sources). *Receiving aid:* Freshmen: 7% (17). Undergraduates: 5% (56). *Average award:* Freshmen: $13,414. Undergraduates: $11,838. *Scholarships, grants, and awards by category:* Academic interests/achievement: biological sciences, business, communication, computer science, education, English, general academic interests/achievements, health fields, humanities, international studies, mathematics, physical sciences, religion/biblical studies, social sciences. Creative arts/performance: art/fine arts, music, theater/drama. Special achievements/activities: general special achievements/activities, leadership, religious involvement. Special characteristics: adult students, children and siblings of alumni, children of faculty/staff, international students, local/state students, relatives of clergy, religious affiliation, siblings of current students, veterans. *Tuition waivers:* Full or partial for children of alumni, employees or children of employees, adult students, senior citizens.

LOANS *Student loans:* $8,066,691 (88% need-based, 12% non-need-based). *Average need-based loan:* Freshmen: $3034. Undergraduates: $4188. *Parent loans:* $1,909,735 (57% need-based, 43% non-need-based). *Programs:* Perkins, alternative loans.

WORK-STUDY *Federal work-study:* Total amount: $237,523; jobs available. *State or other work-study/employment:* Part-time jobs available.

ATHLETIC AWARDS Total amount: $1,375,125 (60% need-based, 40% non-need-based).

APPLYING FOR FINANCIAL AID *Required financial aid form:* FAFSA. *Financial aid deadline (priority):* 4/1. *Notification date:* Continuous. Students must reply by 5/1 or within 2 weeks of notification.

CONTACT Mrs. Bridget Ellis, Director of Financial Aid, Barton College, Box 5000, Wilson, NC 27893, 252-399-6371 or toll-free 800-345-4973. *Fax:* 252-399-6572. *E-mail:* aid@barton.edu. *Website:* http://www.barton.edu/.

BARUCH COLLEGE OF THE CITY UNIVERSITY OF NEW YORK
New York, NY

Tuition & fees (NY res): $5430	Average undergraduate aid package: $4686

ABOUT THE INSTITUTION State and locally supported, coed. *Awards:* certificates, bachelor's, and master's degrees. 41 undergraduate majors. *Total enrollment:* 18,055. Undergraduates: 14,266. Freshmen: 1,311. Federal methodology is used as a basis for awarding need-based institutional aid.

UNDERGRADUATE EXPENSES for 2013–2014 *Application fee:* $65. *Tuition, state resident:* full-time $5430. *Tuition, nonresident:* full-time $14,550. Full-time tuition and fees vary according to course load. Part-time tuition and fees vary according to course load. *Room only:* $11,590. Room and board charges vary according to housing facility.

FRESHMAN FINANCIAL AID (Fall 2012, est.) 1,101 applied for aid; of those 79% were deemed to have need. 53% of freshmen with need received aid; of those 41% had need fully met. *Average percent of need met:* 41% (excluding resources awarded to replace EFC). *Average financial aid package:* $4694 (excluding resources awarded to replace EFC). 17% of all full-time freshmen had no need and received non-need-based gift aid.

UNDERGRADUATE FINANCIAL AID (Fall 2012, est.) 7,745 applied for aid; of those 80% were deemed to have need. 84% of undergraduates with need received aid; of those 30% had need fully met. *Average percent of need met:* 30% (excluding resources awarded to replace EFC). *Average financial aid package:* $4686 (excluding resources awarded to replace EFC). 23% of all full-time undergraduates had no need and received non-need-based gift aid.

GIFT AID (NEED-BASED) *Total amount:* $56,596,846 (51% federal, 44% state, 4% institutional, 1% external sources). *Receiving aid:* Freshmen: 14% (164); all full-time undergraduates: 25% (2,529). *Average award:* Freshmen: $5024; Undergraduates: $5016. *Scholarships, grants, and awards:* Federal Pell, FSEOG, state, college/university gift aid from institutional funds.

GIFT AID (NON-NEED-BASED) *Receiving aid:* Freshmen: 25% (293). Undergraduates: 32% (3,258). *Average award:* Freshmen: $2802. Undergraduates: $3300. *Scholarships, grants, and awards by category:* Academic interests/achievement: general academic interests/achievements. *Tuition waivers:* Full or partial for employees or children of employees, senior citizens. *ROTC:* Army cooperative.

LOANS *Student loans:* $26,167,354 (34% need-based, 66% non-need-based). 21% of past graduating class borrowed through all loan programs. *Average indebtedness per student:* $4972. *Average need-based loan:* Freshmen: $3204. Undergraduates: $3686. *Parent loans:* $484,288 (100% non-need-based). *Programs:* Federal Direct (Subsidized and Unsubsidized Stafford, PLUS), Perkins.

WORK-STUDY *Federal work-study:* Total amount: $3,729,472; 2,484 jobs averaging $1470. *State or other work-study/employment:* Total amount: $118,581 (100% need-based). 67 part-time jobs averaging $1640.

APPLYING FOR FINANCIAL AID *Required financial aid forms:* FAFSA, state aid form. *Financial aid deadline (priority):* 4/15. *Notification date:* Continuous beginning 4/21. Students must reply by 6/1 or within 2 weeks of notification.

CONTACT Ms. Elizabeth Riquez, Financial Aid Services, Baruch College of the City University of New York, One Bernard Baruch Way, Box H-880, New York, NY 10010-5585, 646-312-1399. *Fax:* 646-312-1361. *E-mail:* elizabeth.riquez@baruch.cuny.edu. *Website:* http://www.baruch.cuny.edu/.

BASTYR UNIVERSITY
Kenmore, WA

Tuition & fees: $21,990	Average undergraduate aid package: $17,052

ABOUT THE INSTITUTION Independent, coed. **Awards:** certificates, bachelor's, master's, and doctoral degrees. 7 undergraduate majors. **Total enrollment:** 1,028. Undergraduates: 221. Federal methodology is used as a basis for awarding need-based institutional aid.

UNDERGRADUATE EXPENSES for 2013–2014 **Application fee:** $60. **Tuition:** full-time $21,090; part-time $590 per credit hour. Full-time tuition and fees vary according to course load and program. Part-time tuition and fees vary according to course load and program. Room and board charges vary according to housing facility.

UNDERGRADUATE FINANCIAL AID (Fall 2011) 186 applied for aid; of those 99% were deemed to have need. 99% of undergraduates with need received aid. **Average percent of need met:** 42% (excluding resources awarded to replace EFC). **Average financial aid package:** $17,052 (excluding resources awarded to replace EFC).

GIFT AID (NEED-BASED) Total amount: $1,012,096 (49% federal, 34% state, 12% institutional, 5% external sources). **Receiving aid:** All full-time undergraduates: 70% (148). **Average award:** Undergraduates: $11,425. **Scholarships, grants, and awards:** Federal Pell, FSEOG, state, private, college/university gift aid from institutional funds.

GIFT AID (NON-NEED-BASED) Scholarships, grants, and awards by category: Academic interests/achievement: health fields. **Tuition waivers:** Full or partial for employees or children of employees.

LOANS Student loans: $5,189,539 (72% need-based, 28% non-need-based). **Average need-based loan:** Undergraduates: $8569. **Parent loans:** $253,173 (80% need-based, 20% non-need-based). **Programs:** Federal Direct (Subsidized and Unsubsidized Stafford, PLUS), Perkins.

WORK-STUDY Federal work-study: Total amount: $45,774; 109 jobs averaging $1500. **State or other work-study/employment:** Total amount: $24,259 (100% need-based). 38 part-time jobs averaging $1500.

APPLYING FOR FINANCIAL AID Required financial aid forms: FAFSA, institution's own form. **Financial aid deadline (priority):** 4/15. **Notification date:** Continuous beginning 3/1. Students must reply within 2 weeks of notification.

CONTACT Danette Carter, Director of Financial Aid, Bastyr University, 14500 Juanita Drive NE, Kenmore, WA 98028-4966, 425-602-3083. Fax: 425-602-3094. E-mail: finaid@bastyr.edu.
Website: http://www.bastyr.edu/.

BATES COLLEGE
Lewiston, ME

Tuition & fees: $44,300	Average undergraduate aid package: $38,887

ABOUT THE INSTITUTION Independent, coed. **Awards:** bachelor's degrees. 35 undergraduate majors. **Total enrollment:** 1,753. Undergraduates: 1,753. Freshmen: 503. Institutional methodology is used as a basis for awarding need-based institutional aid.

UNDERGRADUATE EXPENSES for 2013–2014 **Application fee:** $60. **Comprehensive fee:** $57,235 includes full-time tuition ($44,040), mandatory fees ($260), and room and board ($12,935). **Payment plan:** Tuition prepayment.

FRESHMAN FINANCIAL AID (Fall 2012, est.) 258 applied for aid; of those 87% were deemed to have need. 93% of freshmen with need received aid; of those 97% had need fully met. **Average percent of need met:** 100% (excluding resources awarded to replace EFC). **Average financial aid package:** $38,185 (excluding resources awarded to replace EFC).

UNDERGRADUATE FINANCIAL AID (Fall 2012, est.) 872 applied for aid; of those 92% were deemed to have need. 93% of undergraduates with need received aid; of those 97% had need fully met. **Average percent of need met:** 100% (excluding resources awarded to replace EFC). **Average financial aid package:** $38,887 (excluding resources awarded to replace EFC).

GIFT AID (NEED-BASED) Total amount: $26,177,797 (4% federal, 95% institutional, 1% external sources). **Receiving aid:** Freshmen: 41% (205); all full-time under-

graduates: 41% (726). **Average award:** Freshmen: $36,387; Undergraduates: $36,058. **Scholarships, grants, and awards:** Federal Pell, FSEOG, state, private, college/university gift aid from institutional funds.

GIFT AID (NON-NEED-BASED) Total amount: $289,077 (100% external sources). **Tuition waivers:** Full or partial for employees or children of employees.

LOANS Student loans: $2,956,867 (51% need-based, 49% non-need-based). 40% of past graduating class borrowed through all loan programs. **Average indebtedness per student:** $24,515. **Average need-based loan:** Freshmen: $3446. Undergraduates: $3523. **Parent loans:** $1,428,932 (100% non-need-based). **Programs:** Federal Direct (Subsidized and Unsubsidized Stafford, PLUS), Perkins, state.

WORK-STUDY Federal work-study: Total amount: $800,015; 438 jobs averaging $1826. **State or other work-study/employment:** Total amount: $442,700 (100% need-based). 251 part-time jobs averaging $1764.

APPLYING FOR FINANCIAL AID Required financial aid forms: FAFSA, CSS Financial Aid PROFILE, noncustodial (divorced/separated) parent's statement. **Financial aid deadline:** 2/15. **Notification date:** 4/1. Students must reply by 5/1.

CONTACT Ms. Wendy G. Glass, Director of Student Financial Services, Bates College, 44 Mountain Avenue, Lewiston, ME 04240, 207-786-6096. Fax: 207-786-8350. E-mail: wglass@bates.edu.
Website: http://www.bates.edu/.

BAUDER COLLEGE
Atlanta, GA

CONTACT Financial Aid Office, Bauder College, 384 Northyards Boulevard NW, Suites 190 and 400, Atlanta, GA 30313, 404-237-7573 or toll-free 800-935-1857. Website: http://atlanta.bauder.edu/.

BAYAMÓN CENTRAL UNIVERSITY
Bayamón, PR

CONTACT Financial Aid Director, Bayamón Central University, PO Box 1725, Bayamón, PR 00960-1725, 787-786-3030 Ext. 2115. Fax: 787-785-4365. Website: http://www.ucb.edu.pr/.

BAYLOR UNIVERSITY
Waco, TX

Tuition & fees: $36,137	Average undergraduate aid package: $23,851

ABOUT THE INSTITUTION Independent Baptist, coed. **Awards:** certificates, bachelor's, master's, and doctoral degrees. 124 undergraduate majors. **Total enrollment:** 15,364. Undergraduates: 12,918. Freshmen: 3,254. Federal methodology is used as a basis for awarding need-based institutional aid.

UNDERGRADUATE EXPENSES for 2013–2014 **Application fee:** $50. **Comprehensive fee:** $46,885 includes full-time tuition ($32,574), mandatory fees ($3563), and room and board ($10,748). **College room only:** $5312. Room and board charges vary according to board plan and housing facility. **Part-time tuition:** $1357 per semester hour. **Part-time fees:** $142 per semester hour.

FRESHMAN FINANCIAL AID (Fall 2012, est.) 2,485 applied for aid; of those 80% were deemed to have need. 100% of freshmen with need received aid; of those 13% had need fully met. **Average percent of need met:** 63% (excluding resources awarded to replace EFC). **Average financial aid package:** $23,498 (excluding resources awarded to replace EFC). 34% of all full-time freshmen had no need and received non-need-based gift aid.

UNDERGRADUATE FINANCIAL AID (Fall 2012, est.) 8,522 applied for aid; of those 86% were deemed to have need. 100% of undergraduates with need received aid; of those 13% had need fully met. **Average percent of need met:** 62% (excluding resources awarded to replace EFC). **Average financial aid package:** $23,851 (excluding resources awarded to replace EFC). 32% of all full-time undergraduates had no need and received non-need-based gift aid.

GIFT AID (NEED-BASED) Total amount: $123,051,961 (10% federal, 7% state, 80% institutional, 3% external sources). **Receiving aid:** Freshmen: 60% (1,943); all

full-time undergraduates: 55% (6,971). *Average award:* Freshmen: $18,473; Undergraduates: $18,172. *Scholarships, grants, and awards:* Federal Pell, FSEOG, state, college/university gift aid from institutional funds.
GIFT AID (NON-NEED-BASED) *Total amount:* $51,618,625 (98% institutional, 2% external sources). *Receiving aid:* Freshmen: 59% (1,913). Undergraduates: 52% (6,546). *Average award:* Freshmen: $12,851. Undergraduates: $12,130. *Scholarships, grants, and awards by category:* Academic interests/achievement: 11,360 awards ($102,738,434 total): business, communication, computer science, education, engineering/technologies, English, foreign languages, general academic interests/achievements, health fields, home economics, humanities, international studies, mathematics, military science, physical sciences, premedicine, religion/biblical studies, social sciences. *Creative arts/performance:* 460 awards ($2,340,410 total): art/fine arts, cinema/film/broadcasting, debating, journalism/publications, music, theater/drama. *Special achievements/activities:* 302 awards ($5,201,515 total): community service, leadership, religious involvement. *Special characteristics:* 225 awards ($5,100,281 total): children of faculty/staff. *Tuition waivers:* Full or partial for employees or children of employees. *ROTC:* Army, Air Force.
LOANS *Student loans:* $78,448,874 (72% need-based, 28% non-need-based). *Average need-based loan:* Freshmen: $2765. Undergraduates: $3782. *Parent loans:* $24,499,394 (44% need-based, 56% non-need-based). *Programs:* Federal Direct (Subsidized and Unsubsidized Stafford, PLUS), Perkins, Federal Nursing, state, private loans.
WORK-STUDY *Federal work-study:* Total amount: $15,069,378; 5,311 jobs averaging $2837. *State or other work-study/employment:* Part-time jobs available.
ATHLETIC AWARDS Total amount: $10,587,075 (46% need-based, 54% non-need-based).
APPLYING FOR FINANCIAL AID *Required financial aid forms:* FAFSA, state residency affirmation (TX residents only). *Financial aid deadline (priority):* 3/1. *Notification date:* Continuous beginning 3/1. Students must reply by 5/1 or within 2 weeks of notification.
CONTACT Office of Admission Services, Baylor University, PO Box 97056, Waco, TX 76798-7056, 254-710-3435 or toll-free 800-BAYLORU. *Fax:* 254-710-3436. *E-mail:* admissions@baylor.edu.
Website: http://www.baylor.edu/.

BAY PATH COLLEGE
Longmeadow, MA

Tuition & fees: $28,532	Average undergraduate aid package: $22,819

ABOUT THE INSTITUTION Independent, undergraduate: women only; graduate: coed. *Awards:* certificates, associate, bachelor's, and master's degrees. 18 undergraduate majors. *Total enrollment:* 2,370. Undergraduates: 1,558. Freshmen: 155. Federal methodology is used as a basis for awarding need-based institutional aid.
UNDERGRADUATE EXPENSES for 2013–2014 *Application fee:* $25. *Comprehensive fee:* $39,972 includes full-time tuition ($28,532) and room and board ($11,440). Room and board charges vary according to board plan. *Part-time tuition:* $480 per credit. Part-time tuition and fees vary according to course load.
FRESHMAN FINANCIAL AID (Fall 2012, est.) 149 applied for aid; of those 98% were deemed to have need. 100% of freshmen with need received aid; of those 12% had need fully met. *Average percent of need met:* 79% (excluding resources awarded to replace EFC). *Average financial aid package:* $26,570 (excluding resources awarded to replace EFC). 5% of all full-time freshmen had no need and received non-need-based gift aid.
UNDERGRADUATE FINANCIAL AID (Fall 2012, est.) 619 applied for aid; of those 94% were deemed to have need. 100% of undergraduates with need received aid; of those 8% had need fully met. *Average percent of need met:* 66% (excluding resources awarded to replace EFC). *Average financial aid package:* $22,819 (excluding resources awarded to replace EFC). 9% of all full-time undergraduates had no need and received non-need-based gift aid.
GIFT AID (NEED-BASED) *Total amount:* $10,174,822 (16% federal, 4% state, 79% institutional, 1% external sources). *Receiving aid:* Freshmen: 94% (146); all full-time undergraduates: 91% (579). *Average award:* Freshmen: $20,473; Undergraduates: $17,432. *Scholarships, grants, and awards:* Federal Pell, FSEOG, state, private, college/university gift aid from institutional funds.
GIFT AID (NON-NEED-BASED) *Total amount:* $818,812 (98% institutional, 2% external sources). *Receiving aid:* Freshmen: 8% (13). Undergraduates: 5% (31).

Average award: Freshmen: $14,653. Undergraduates: $12,028. *Scholarships, grants, and awards by category:* Academic interests/achievement: general academic interests/achievements. *Special characteristics:* adult students, children of faculty/staff, children with a deceased or disabled parent, general special characteristics, international students, siblings of current students. *Tuition waivers:* Full or partial for employees or children of employees. *ROTC:* Army cooperative, Air Force cooperative.
LOANS *Student loans:* $5,055,034 (57% need-based, 43% non-need-based). 91% of past graduating class borrowed through all loan programs. *Average indebtedness per student:* $31,456. *Average need-based loan:* Freshmen: $5396. Undergraduates: $5267. *Parent loans:* $1,240,019 (46% need-based, 54% non-need-based). *Programs:* Federal Direct (Subsidized and Unsubsidized Stafford, PLUS), Perkins.
WORK-STUDY *Federal work-study:* Total amount: $482,085; 201 jobs averaging $2400. *State or other work-study/employment:* Total amount: $178,867 (100% need-based). Part-time jobs available.
APPLYING FOR FINANCIAL AID *Required financial aid form:* FAFSA. *Financial aid deadline (priority):* 3/1. *Notification date:* Continuous beginning 3/1. Students must reply within 2 weeks of notification.
CONTACT Stephanie King, Director of Student Financial Services, Bay Path College, 588 Longmeadow Street, Longmeadow, MA 01106-2292, 413-565-1345 or toll-free 800-782-7284 Ext. 1331. *Fax:* 413-565-1101. *E-mail:* pbrand@baypath.edu. *Website:* http://www.baypath.edu/.

BEACON COLLEGE
Leesburg, FL

CONTACT Financial Aid Office, Beacon College, 105 East Main Street, Leesburg, FL 34748, 352-787-7660.
Website: http://www.beaconcollege.edu/.

BECKER COLLEGE
Worcester, MA

Tuition & fees: $30,340	Average undergraduate aid package: N/A

ABOUT THE INSTITUTION Independent, coed. *Awards:* associate and bachelor's degrees (also includes Leicester, MA small town campus). 26 undergraduate majors. *Total enrollment:* 1,826. Undergraduates: 1,826. Freshmen: 381. Federal methodology is used as a basis for awarding need-based institutional aid.
UNDERGRADUATE EXPENSES for 2013–2014 *Comprehensive fee:* $41,390 includes full-time tuition ($28,900), mandatory fees ($1440), and room and board ($11,050). Full-time tuition and fees vary according to class time, course load, and program. Room and board charges vary according to board plan and housing facility. *Part-time tuition:* $1200 per credit hour. Part-time tuition and fees vary according to class time, course load, and program.
GIFT AID (NEED-BASED) *Scholarships, grants, and awards:* Federal Pell, FSEOG, state, private, college/university gift aid from institutional funds.
GIFT AID (NON-NEED-BASED) *Scholarships, grants, and awards by category:* Academic interests/achievement: general academic interests/achievements. *Special achievements/activities:* general special achievements/activities, leadership. *Special characteristics:* children of faculty/staff, siblings of current students, twins. *Tuition waivers:* Full or partial for employees or children of employees, senior citizens. *ROTC:* Army cooperative.
LOANS *Student loans:* 95% of past graduating class borrowed through all loan programs. *Average indebtedness per student:* $44,596. *Programs:* Federal Direct (Subsidized and Unsubsidized Stafford, PLUS), state, alternative loans.
WORK-STUDY Federal work-study jobs available.
APPLYING FOR FINANCIAL AID *Required financial aid form:* FAFSA. *Financial aid deadline (priority):* 3/1. *Notification date:* Continuous beginning 3/15. Students must reply within 2 weeks of notification.
CONTACT Mr. Heather Ruland, Director of Financial Aid, Becker College, 61 Sever Street, Worcester, MA 01615-0071, 508-373-9430 or toll-free 877-5BECKER. *Fax:* 508-890-1511. *E-mail:* financialaid@becker.edu.
Website: http://www.becker.edu/.

BEIS MEDRASH HEICHAL DOVID
Far Rockaway, NY

CONTACT Financial Aid Office, Beis Medrash Heichal Dovid, 257 Beach 17th Street, Far Rockaway, NY 11691, 718-868-2300.

BELHAVEN UNIVERSITY
Jackson, MS

Tuition & fees: $19,200	Average undergraduate aid package: $11,062

ABOUT THE INSTITUTION Independent Presbyterian, coed. **Awards:** certificates, associate, bachelor's, and master's degrees. 29 undergraduate majors. **Total enrollment:** 3,519. Undergraduates: 2,545. Freshmen: 296. Federal methodology is used as a basis for awarding need-based institutional aid.
UNDERGRADUATE EXPENSES for 2013–2014 Application fee: $25. **Comprehensive fee:** $26,090 includes full-time tuition ($19,200) and room and board ($6890). Room and board charges vary according to housing facility. **Part-time tuition:** $375 per credit. Part-time tuition and fees vary according to course load.
FRESHMAN FINANCIAL AID (Fall 2012, est.) 221 applied for aid; of those 91% were deemed to have need. 98% of freshmen with need received aid; of those 6% had need fully met. **Average percent of need met:** 57% (excluding resources awarded to replace EFC). **Average financial aid package:** $15,537 (excluding resources awarded to replace EFC). 19% of all full-time freshmen had no need and received non-need-based gift aid.
UNDERGRADUATE FINANCIAL AID (Fall 2012, est.) 1,089 applied for aid; of those 94% were deemed to have need. 98% of undergraduates with need received aid; of those 10% had need fully met. **Average percent of need met:** 60% (excluding resources awarded to replace EFC). **Average financial aid package:** $11,062 (excluding resources awarded to replace EFC). 17% of all full-time undergraduates had no need and received non-need-based gift aid.
GIFT AID (NEED-BASED) Total amount: $4,541,493 (86% federal, 2% state, 7% institutional, 5% external sources). **Receiving aid:** Freshmen: 48% (134); all full-time undergraduates: 57% (693). **Average award:** Freshmen: $3594; Undergraduates: $3595. **Scholarships, grants, and awards:** Federal Pell, FSEOG, state, private, college/university gift aid from institutional funds.
GIFT AID (NON-NEED-BASED) Total amount: $5,987,247 (3% state, 97% institutional). **Receiving aid:** Freshmen: 69% (193). Undergraduates: 78% (951). **Average award:** Freshmen: $4100. Undergraduates: $3600. **Scholarships, grants, and awards by category: Academic interests/achievement:** biological sciences, business, communication, education, English, foreign languages, general academic interests/achievements, humanities, international studies, mathematics, premedicine, religion/biblical studies, social sciences. **Creative arts/performance:** applied art and design, art/fine arts, creative writing, dance, journalism/publications, music, performing arts, theater/drama. **Special achievements/activities:** cheerleading/drum major, general special achievements/activities, junior miss, leadership. **Special characteristics:** children of faculty/staff, general special characteristics, international students, local/state students. **Tuition waivers:** Full or partial for employees or children of employees. **ROTC:** Army cooperative, Air Force cooperative.
LOANS Student loans: $12,051,313 (42% need-based, 58% non-need-based). 93% of past graduating class borrowed through all loan programs. **Average indebtedness per student:** $37,076. **Average need-based loan:** Freshmen: $2907. Undergraduates: $3723. **Parent loans:** $828,333 (100% need-based). **Programs:** Federal Direct (Subsidized and Unsubsidized Stafford, PLUS), Perkins.
WORK-STUDY Federal work-study: Total amount: $327,002; jobs available. **State or other work-study/employment:** Total amount: $31,824 (100% need-based). Part-time jobs available.
ATHLETIC AWARDS Total amount: $2,693,258 (100% non-need-based).
APPLYING FOR FINANCIAL AID Required financial aid form: FAFSA. **Financial aid deadline (priority):** 2/1. **Notification date:** Continuous.
CONTACT Mr. Tawesia Colyer, Director of Student Financial Planning, Belhaven University, 1500 Peachtree Street, Jackson, MS 39202-1789, 601-968-8890 or toll-free 800-960-5940. **E-mail:** tcolyer@belhaven.edu. **Website:** http://www.belhaven.edu/.

BELLARMINE UNIVERSITY
Louisville, KY

Tuition & fees: $33,180	Average undergraduate aid package: $26,374

ABOUT THE INSTITUTION Independent Roman Catholic, coed. **Awards:** certificates, bachelor's, master's, and doctoral degrees. 38 undergraduate majors. **Total enrollment:** 3,602. Undergraduates: 2,730. Freshmen: 607. Both federal and institutional methodology are used as a basis for awarding need-based institutional aid.
UNDERGRADUATE EXPENSES for 2013–2014 Application fee: $25. **Comprehensive fee:** $42,950 includes full-time tuition ($31,900), mandatory fees ($1280), and room and board ($9770). **College room only:** $5990. Room and board charges vary according to board plan and housing facility. **Part-time tuition:** $755 per credit hour.
FRESHMAN FINANCIAL AID (Fall 2012, est.) 569 applied for aid; of those 89% were deemed to have need. 100% of freshmen with need received aid; of those 21% had need fully met. **Average percent of need met:** 76% (excluding resources awarded to replace EFC). **Average financial aid package:** $27,350 (excluding resources awarded to replace EFC). 16% of all full-time freshmen had no need and received non-need-based gift aid.
UNDERGRADUATE FINANCIAL AID (Fall 2012, est.) 1,962 applied for aid; of those 92% were deemed to have need. 96% of undergraduates with need received aid; of those 19% had need fully met. **Average percent of need met:** 73% (excluding resources awarded to replace EFC). **Average financial aid package:** $26,374 (excluding resources awarded to replace EFC). 21% of all full-time undergraduates had no need and received non-need-based gift aid.
GIFT AID (NEED-BASED) Total amount: $37,004,588 (7% federal, 12% state, 79% institutional, 2% external sources). **Receiving aid:** Freshmen: 84% (507); all full-time undergraduates: 75% (1,724). **Average award:** Freshmen: $20,704; Undergraduates: $19,713. **Scholarships, grants, and awards:** Federal Pell, FSEOG, state, private, college/university gift aid from institutional funds.
GIFT AID (NON-NEED-BASED) Total amount: $10,540,105 (6% state, 92% institutional, 2% external sources). **Receiving aid:** Freshmen: 25% (153). Undergraduates: 22% (516). **Average award:** Freshmen: $20,404. Undergraduates: $18,457. **Scholarships, grants, and awards by category: Academic interests/achievement:** biological sciences, business, education, general academic interests/achievements, health fields. **Creative arts/performance:** art/fine arts, music. **Special achievements/activities:** cheerleading/drum major, community service, general special achievements/activities, leadership, religious involvement. **Special characteristics:** adult students, children and siblings of alumni, children of faculty/staff, ethnic background, international students, local/state students, members of minority groups, out-of-state students, previous college experience, religious affiliation. **Tuition waivers:** Full or partial for employees or children of employees, senior citizens. **ROTC:** Army cooperative, Air Force cooperative.
LOANS Student loans: $14,116,568 (81% need-based, 19% non-need-based). 69% of past graduating class borrowed through all loan programs. **Average indebtedness per student:** $28,722. **Average need-based loan:** Freshmen: $3391. Undergraduates: $4329. **Parent loans:** $2,835,161 (50% need-based, 50% non-need-based). **Programs:** Federal Direct (Subsidized and Unsubsidized Stafford, PLUS).
WORK-STUDY Federal work-study: Total amount: $446,940; 251 jobs averaging $1688. **State or other work-study/employment:** Total amount: $98,650 (67% need-based, 33% non-need-based). Part-time jobs available.
ATHLETIC AWARDS Total amount: $2,520,807 (41% need-based, 59% non-need-based).
APPLYING FOR FINANCIAL AID Required financial aid form: FAFSA. **Financial aid deadline (priority):** 3/1. **Notification date:** Continuous beginning 3/15. Students must reply by 5/1.
CONTACT Ms. Heather Boutell, Director of Financial Aid, Bellarmine University, 2001 Newburg Road, Louisville, KY 40205-0671, 502-452-8124 or toll-free 800-274-4723 Ext. 8131. **Fax:** 502-452-8002. **E-mail:** hboutell@bellarmine.edu. **Website:** http://www.bellarmine.edu/.

BELLEVUE UNIVERSITY
Bellevue, NE

CONTACT Mr. Jon Dotterer, Director of Financial Aid, Bellevue University, 1000 Galvin Road South, Bellevue, NE 68005, 402-293-3762 or toll-free 800-756-7920. *Fax:* 402-293-2062.
Website: http://www.bellevue.edu/.

BELLIN COLLEGE
Green Bay, WI

Tuition & fees: N/R	Average undergraduate aid package: $21,230

ABOUT THE INSTITUTION Independent, coed, primarily women. 1 undergraduate major. Federal methodology is used as a basis for awarding need-based institutional aid.
UNDERGRADUATE FINANCIAL AID (Fall 2012, est.) 122 applied for aid; of those 96% were deemed to have need. 100% of undergraduates with need received aid; of those 2% had need fully met. *Average percent of need met:* 67% (excluding resources awarded to replace EFC). *Average financial aid package:* $21,230 (excluding resources awarded to replace EFC). 1% of all full-time undergraduates had no need and received non-need-based gift aid.
GIFT AID (NEED-BASED) *Total amount:* $815,724 (26% federal, 17% state, 44% institutional, 13% external sources). *Receiving aid:* All full-time undergraduates: 52% (114). *Average award:* Undergraduates: $5448. *Scholarships, grants, and awards:* Federal Pell, FSEOG, state, private, college/university gift aid from institutional funds.
GIFT AID (NON-NEED-BASED) *Average award:* Undergraduates: $857. *Scholarships, grants, and awards by category:* Academic interests/achievement: 18 awards ($47,321 total): general academic interests/achievements.
LOANS *Student loans:* $2,731,826 (88% need-based, 12% non-need-based). 88% of past graduating class borrowed through all loan programs. *Average indebtedness per student:* $33,961. *Average need-based loan:* Undergraduates: $4979. *Parent loans:* $314,972 (69% need-based, 31% non-need-based). *Programs:* Federal Direct (Subsidized and Unsubsidized Stafford, PLUS), state, private loans.
WORK-STUDY Federal work-study jobs available.
APPLYING FOR FINANCIAL AID *Required financial aid form:* FAFSA. *Financial aid deadline (priority):* 3/1. *Notification date:* 4/1. Students must reply within 2 weeks of notification.
CONTACT Mrs. Lena C. Goodman, Director of Financial Aid, Bellin College, 3201 Eaton Road, Green Bay, WI 54311, 920-433-6638 or toll-free 800-236-8707. *Fax:* 920-433-1922. *E-mail:* lena.goodman@bellincollege.edu.
Website: http://www.bellincollege.edu/.

BELMONT ABBEY COLLEGE
Belmont, NC

Tuition & fees: $27,622	Average undergraduate aid package: $15,085

ABOUT THE INSTITUTION Independent Roman Catholic, coed. *Awards:* bachelor's degrees. 11 undergraduate majors. *Total enrollment:* 1,706. Undergraduates: 1,706. Freshmen: 303. Federal methodology is used as a basis for awarding need-based institutional aid.
UNDERGRADUATE EXPENSES for 2013–2014 *Application fee:* $35. *One-time required fee:* $400. *Comprehensive fee:* $38,025 includes full-time tuition ($27,622) and room and board ($10,403). *College room only:* $6137. Full-time tuition and fees vary according to class time, course load, location, program, and reciprocity agreements. Room and board charges vary according to board plan, housing facility, and location. *Part-time tuition:* $921 per credit hour. Part-time tuition and fees vary according to class time, course load, location, and reciprocity agreements.
FRESHMAN FINANCIAL AID (Fall 2011) 112 applied for aid; of those 84% were deemed to have need. 100% of freshmen with need received aid; of those 11% had need fully met. *Average percent of need met:* 67% (excluding resources awarded

to replace EFC). *Average financial aid package:* $20,368 (excluding resources awarded to replace EFC). 7% of all full-time freshmen had no need and received non-need-based gift aid.
UNDERGRADUATE FINANCIAL AID (Fall 2011) 1,124 applied for aid; of those 93% were deemed to have need. 100% of undergraduates with need received aid; of those 7% had need fully met. *Average percent of need met:* 54% (excluding resources awarded to replace EFC). *Average financial aid package:* $15,085 (excluding resources awarded to replace EFC). 10% of all full-time undergraduates had no need and received non-need-based gift aid.
GIFT AID (NEED-BASED) *Total amount:* $10,818,039 (27% federal, 20% state, 50% institutional, 3% external sources). *Receiving aid:* Freshmen: 35% (94); all full-time undergraduates: 66% (1,037). *Average award:* Freshmen: $17,418; Undergraduates: $10,867. *Scholarships, grants, and awards:* Federal Pell, FSEOG, state, private, college/university gift aid from institutional funds.
GIFT AID (NON-NEED-BASED) *Total amount:* $2,471,089 (5% state, 92% institutional, 3% external sources). *Receiving aid:* Freshmen: 3% (8). Undergraduates: 3% (54). *Average award:* Freshmen: $13,542. Undergraduates: $12,734. *Scholarships, grants, and awards by category:* Academic interests/achievement: 534 awards ($5,428,443 total): general academic interests/achievements. Creative arts/performance: 6 awards ($12,000 total): theater/drama. *Special characteristics:* 14 awards ($277,620 total): children of faculty/staff. *Tuition waivers:* Full or partial for employees or children of employees, senior citizens. *ROTC:* Army cooperative, Air Force cooperative.
LOANS *Student loans:* $9,509,236 (45% need-based, 55% non-need-based). 81% of past graduating class borrowed through all loan programs. *Average indebtedness per student:* $21,004. *Average need-based loan:* Freshmen: $3235. Undergraduates: $4484. *Parent loans:* $3,095,120 (38% need-based, 62% non-need-based). *Programs:* Federal Direct (Subsidized and Unsubsidized Stafford, PLUS),
WORK-STUDY *Federal work-study:* Total amount: $109,405; 109 jobs averaging $2000.
ATHLETIC AWARDS Total amount: $1,094,699 (55% need-based, 45% non-need-based).
APPLYING FOR FINANCIAL AID *Required financial aid form:* FAFSA. *Financial aid deadline (priority):* 4/1. *Notification date:* Continuous beginning 3/15. Students must reply within 2 weeks of notification.
CONTACT Ms. Julie Hodge, Associate Director of Financial Aid, Belmont Abbey College, 100 Belmont Mt. Holly Road, Belmont, NC 28012-1802, 704-461-6718 or toll-free 888-BAC-0110. *Fax:* 704-461-6882. *E-mail:* juliehodge@bac.edu.
Website: http://www.belmontabbeycollege.edu/.

BELMONT UNIVERSITY
Nashville, TN

Tuition & fees: $26,130	Average undergraduate aid package: $13,648

ABOUT THE INSTITUTION Independent Christian, coed. *Awards:* certificates, bachelor's, master's, and doctoral degrees. 94 undergraduate majors. *Total enrollment:* 6,665. Undergraduates: 5,289. Freshmen: 1,254. Federal methodology is used as a basis for awarding need-based institutional aid.
UNDERGRADUATE EXPENSES for 2013–2014 *Application fee:* $50. *Comprehensive fee:* $38,550 includes full-time tuition ($24,900), mandatory fees ($1230), and room and board ($12,420). *College room only:* $8200. Full-time tuition and fees vary according to class time, course load, and location. Room and board charges vary according to board plan, housing facility, and location. *Part-time tuition:* $950 per credit hour. *Part-time fees:* $840 per year. Part-time tuition and fees vary according to course load.
FRESHMAN FINANCIAL AID (Fall 2012, est.) 997 applied for aid; of those 69% were deemed to have need. 100% of freshmen with need received aid; of those 14% had need fully met. *Average percent of need met:* 53% (excluding resources awarded to replace EFC). *Average financial aid package:* $14,354 (excluding resources awarded to replace EFC). 22% of all full-time freshmen had no need and received non-need-based gift aid.
UNDERGRADUATE FINANCIAL AID (Fall 2012, est.) 3,492 applied for aid; of those 78% were deemed to have need. 100% of undergraduates with need received aid; of those 11% had need fully met. *Average percent of need met:* 47% (excluding resources awarded to replace EFC). *Average financial aid package:*

$13,648 (excluding resources awarded to replace EFC). 17% of all full-time undergraduates had no need and received non-need-based gift aid.
GIFT AID (NEED-BASED) *Total amount:* $15,260,568 (24% federal, 3% state, 66% institutional, 7% external sources). *Receiving aid:* Freshmen: 51% (641); all full-time undergraduates: 48% (2,330). *Average award:* Freshmen: $11,868; Undergraduates: $10,988. *Scholarships, grants, and awards:* Federal Pell, FSEOG, state, private, college/university gift aid from institutional funds.
GIFT AID (NON-NEED-BASED) *Total amount:* $15,497,782 (30% state, 70% institutional). *Receiving aid:* Freshmen: 6% (76). Undergraduates: 4% (203). *Average award:* Freshmen: $7674. Undergraduates: $7541. *Scholarships, grants, and awards by category: Academic interests/achievement:* general academic interests/achievements, religion/biblical studies. *Creative arts/performance:* music. *Special characteristics:* children of faculty/staff. *Tuition waivers:* Full or partial for employees or children of employees, senior citizens. *ROTC:* Army cooperative, Naval cooperative, Air Force cooperative.
LOANS *Student loans:* $11,138,143 (68% need-based, 32% non-need-based). 52% of past graduating class borrowed through all loan programs. *Average indebtedness per student:* $31,079. *Average need-based loan:* Freshmen: $3518. Undergraduates: $4438. *Parent loans:* $10,117,297 (100% non-need-based). *Programs:* Federal Direct (PLUS), Perkins, college/university.
WORK-STUDY *Federal work-study:* Total amount: $773,000; jobs available.
ATHLETIC AWARDS Total amount: $4,031,061 (100% non-need-based).
APPLYING FOR FINANCIAL AID *Required financial aid form:* FAFSA. *Financial aid deadline (priority):* 3/1. *Notification date:* Continuous beginning 3/15. Students must reply by 5/1 or within 2 weeks of notification.
CONTACT Mrs. Pat Smedley, Director of Student Financial Services, Belmont University, 1900 Belmont Boulevard, Nashville, TN 37212-3757, 615-460-6403. *E-mail:* pat.smedley@belmont.edu. *Website:* http://www.belmont.edu/.

BELOIT COLLEGE
Beloit, WI

Tuition & fees: $50,250	Average undergraduate aid package: $28,565

ABOUT THE INSTITUTION Independent, coed. *Awards:* bachelor's degrees. 54 undergraduate majors. *Total enrollment:* 1,359. Undergraduates: 1,359. Freshmen: 311. Both federal and institutional methodology are used as a basis for awarding need-based institutional aid.
UNDERGRADUATE EXPENSES for 2013–2014 *Comprehensive fee:* $57,506 includes full-time tuition ($49,970), mandatory fees ($280), and room and board ($7256). *College room only:* $4256. Room and board charges vary according to board plan.
FRESHMAN FINANCIAL AID (Fall 2012, est.) 255 applied for aid; of those 87% were deemed to have need. 100% of freshmen with need received aid; of those 24% had need fully met. *Average percent of need met:* 87% (excluding resources awarded to replace EFC). *Average financial aid package:* $28,742 (excluding resources awarded to replace EFC). 23% of all full-time freshmen had no need and received non-need-based gift aid.
UNDERGRADUATE FINANCIAL AID (Fall 2012, est.) 979 applied for aid; of those 87% were deemed to have need. 100% of undergraduates with need received aid; of those 20% had need fully met. *Average percent of need met:* 88% (excluding resources awarded to replace EFC). *Average financial aid package:* $28,565 (excluding resources awarded to replace EFC). 28% of all full-time undergraduates had no need and received non-need-based gift aid.
GIFT AID (NEED-BASED) *Total amount:* $20,293,383 (6% federal, 2% state, 91% institutional, 1% external sources). *Receiving aid:* Freshmen: 72% (223); all full-time undergraduates: 67% (847). *Average award:* Freshmen: $24,974; Undergraduates: $23,784. *Scholarships, grants, and awards:* Federal Pell, FSEOG, state, private, college/university gift aid from institutional funds.
GIFT AID (NON-NEED-BASED) *Total amount:* $6,910,031 (98% institutional, 2% external sources). *Receiving aid:* Freshmen: 14% (44). Undergraduates: 12% (153). *Average award:* Freshmen: $17,592. Undergraduates: $15,975. *Scholarships, grants, and awards by category: Academic interests/achievement:* general academic interests/achievements. *Creative arts/performance:* music. *Special achievements/activities:* community service, general special achievements/activities,

leadership. *Special characteristics:* members of minority groups, siblings of current students. *Tuition waivers:* Full or partial for employees or children of employees.
LOANS *Student loans:* $7,510,120 (63% need-based, 37% non-need-based). 57% of past graduating class borrowed through all loan programs. *Average indebtedness per student:* $27,981. *Average need-based loan:* Freshmen: $3256. Undergraduates: $4757. *Parent loans:* $1,532,305 (20% need-based, 80% non-need-based). *Programs:* Federal Direct (Subsidized and Unsubsidized Stafford, PLUS), Perkins, college/university.
WORK-STUDY *Federal work-study:* Total amount: $810,467; jobs available. *State or other work-study/employment:* Total amount: $232,778 (7% need-based, 93% non-need-based). Part-time jobs available.
APPLYING FOR FINANCIAL AID *Required financial aid forms:* FAFSA, institution's own form. *Financial aid deadline (priority):* 3/1. *Notification date:* Continuous beginning 3/1. Students must reply by 5/1.
CONTACT Mr. Jon Urish, Senior Associate Director of Admissions and Financial Aid, Beloit College, 700 College Street, Beloit, WI 53511-5596, 608-363-2663 or toll-free 800-9-BELOIT. *Fax:* 608-363-2075. *E-mail:* urishj@beloit.edu. *Website:* http://www.beloit.edu/.

BEMIDJI STATE UNIVERSITY
Bemidji, MN

Tuition & fees (MN res): $8106	Average undergraduate aid package: $9240

ABOUT THE INSTITUTION State-supported, coed. *Awards:* certificates, associate, bachelor's, and master's degrees. 70 undergraduate majors. *Total enrollment:* 5,017. Undergraduates: 4,744. Freshmen: 772. Federal methodology is used as a basis for awarding need-based institutional aid.
UNDERGRADUATE EXPENSES for 2013–2014 *Application fee:* $20. *Tuition, state resident:* full-time $7146. *Tuition, nonresident:* full-time $7146. *Required fees:* full-time $960. Full-time tuition and fees vary according to course load, location, program, and reciprocity agreements. Part-time tuition and fees vary according to course load, location, program, and reciprocity agreements. *College room and board:* $6970. Room and board charges vary according to board plan and housing facility.
FRESHMAN FINANCIAL AID (Fall 2012, est.) 541 applied for aid; of those 70% were deemed to have need. 100% of freshmen with need received aid; of those 16% had need fully met. *Average percent of need met:* 64% (excluding resources awarded to replace EFC). *Average financial aid package:* $8525 (excluding resources awarded to replace EFC). 24% of all full-time freshmen had no need and received non-need-based gift aid.
UNDERGRADUATE FINANCIAL AID (Fall 2012, est.) 2,847 applied for aid; of those 80% were deemed to have need. 100% of undergraduates with need received aid; of those 18% had need fully met. *Average percent of need met:* 66% (excluding resources awarded to replace EFC). *Average financial aid package:* $9240 (excluding resources awarded to replace EFC). 16% of all full-time undergraduates had no need and received non-need-based gift aid.
GIFT AID (NEED-BASED) *Total amount:* $11,175,458 (66% federal, 32% state, 1% institutional, 1% external sources). *Receiving aid:* Freshmen: 43% (268); all full-time undergraduates: 48% (1,670). *Average award:* Freshmen: $5516; Undergraduates: $5472. *Scholarships, grants, and awards:* Federal Pell, FSEOG, state, private, college/university gift aid from institutional funds.
GIFT AID (NON-NEED-BASED) *Total amount:* $5,067,011 (13% federal, 10% state, 59% institutional, 18% external sources). *Receiving aid:* Freshmen: 52% (324). Undergraduates: 54% (1,872). *Average award:* Freshmen: $9809. Undergraduates: $10,304. *Scholarships, grants, and awards by category: Academic interests/achievement:* general academic interests/achievements. *Creative arts/performance:* 39 awards ($95,480 total): general creative arts/performance. *Special characteristics:* 162 awards ($386,851 total): children and siblings of alumni, children of faculty/staff, international students, out-of-state students. *Tuition waivers:* Full or partial for employees or children of employees, senior citizens.
LOANS *Student loans:* $25,517,180 (40% need-based, 60% non-need-based). *Average need-based loan:* Freshmen: $3454. Undergraduates: $4033. *Parent loans:* $721,749 (100% non-need-based). *Programs:* Federal Direct (Subsidized and Unsubsidized Stafford, PLUS), Perkins, state, alternative loans.

WORK-STUDY *Federal work-study:* Total amount: $704,844; 234 jobs averaging $1245. *State or other work-study/employment:* Total amount: $653,172 (100% need-based). 185 part-time jobs averaging $1583.

ATHLETIC AWARDS Total amount: $1,236,262 (100% non-need-based).

APPLYING FOR FINANCIAL AID *Required financial aid forms:* FAFSA, institution's own form. *Financial aid deadline (priority):* 3/31. *Notification date:* Continuous beginning 6/15.

CONTACT Financial Aid Office, Bemidji State University, 1500 Birchmont Drive NE #14, Bemidji, MN 56601-2699, 218-755-2034 or toll-free 800-475-2001. *Fax:* 218-755-4361. *E-mail:* financialaid@bemidjistate.edu.
Website: http://www.bemidjistate.edu/.

BENEDICT COLLEGE
Columbia, SC

Tuition & fees: $18,286	Average undergraduate aid package: N/A

ABOUT THE INSTITUTION Independent Baptist, coed. 32 undergraduate majors. Both federal and institutional methodology are used as a basis for awarding need-based institutional aid.

UNDERGRADUATE EXPENSES for 2013–2014 *Comprehensive fee:* $26,390 includes full-time tuition ($16,354), mandatory fees ($1932), and room and board ($8104). *Part-time tuition:* $515 per credit hour. *Part-time fees:* $60 per credit hour. Part-time tuition and fees vary according to course load.

GIFT AID (NEED-BASED) *Scholarships, grants, and awards:* Federal Pell, FSEOG, state, private, TEACH Grants.

GIFT AID (NON-NEED-BASED) *Scholarships, grants, and awards by category:* Academic interests/achievement: general academic interests/achievements. Creative arts/performance: general creative arts/performance, music. *Tuition waivers:* Full or partial for employees or children of employees.

LOANS *Programs:* Federal Direct (Subsidized and Unsubsidized Stafford, PLUS), Perkins, state, college/university.

APPLYING FOR FINANCIAL AID *Required financial aid form:* FAFSA. *Financial aid deadline (priority):* 4/15. *Notification date:* Continuous.

CONTACT Mrs. Bichevia Green, Associate Director of Financial Aid, Benedict College, 1600 Harden Street, Columbia, SC 29204, 803-705-4418 or toll-free 800-868-6598. *Fax:* 803-705-6629. *E-mail:* greenb@benedict.edu.
Website: http://www.benedict.edu/.

BENEDICTINE COLLEGE
Atchison, KS

Tuition & fees: $23,175	Average undergraduate aid package: $18,831

ABOUT THE INSTITUTION Independent Roman Catholic, coed. *Awards:* bachelor's and master's degrees. 38 undergraduate majors. *Total enrollment:* 2,149. Undergraduates: 2,086. Freshmen: 488. Both federal and institutional methodology are used as a basis for awarding need-based institutional aid.

UNDERGRADUATE EXPENSES for 2013–2014 *Application fee:* $50. *Comprehensive fee:* $31,365 includes full-time tuition ($22,550), mandatory fees ($625), and room and board ($8190). *College room only:* $4540. Full-time tuition and fees vary according to course load and degree level. Room and board charges vary according to board plan and housing facility. Part-time tuition and fees vary according to course load and degree level.

FRESHMAN FINANCIAL AID (Fall 2012, est.) 429 applied for aid; of those 86% were deemed to have need. 100% of freshmen with need received aid; of those 24% had need fully met. *Average percent of need met:* 75% (excluding resources awarded to replace EFC). *Average financial aid package:* $18,948 (excluding resources awarded to replace EFC). 18% of all full-time freshmen had no need and received non-need-based gift aid.

UNDERGRADUATE FINANCIAL AID (Fall 2012, est.) 1,436 applied for aid; of those 87% were deemed to have need. 100% of undergraduates with need received aid; of those 21% had need fully met. *Average percent of need met:* 76% (excluding resources awarded to replace EFC). *Average financial aid package:*

$18,831 (excluding resources awarded to replace EFC). 19% of all full-time undergraduates had no need and received non-need-based gift aid.

GIFT AID (NEED-BASED) *Total amount:* $11,960,541 (18% federal, 6% state, 72% institutional, 4% external sources). *Receiving aid:* Freshmen: 76% (371); all full-time undergraduates: 73% (1,247). *Average award:* Freshmen: $15,283; Undergraduates: $14,222. *Scholarships, grants, and awards:* Federal Pell, FSEOG, state, private, college/university gift aid from institutional funds.

GIFT AID (NON-NEED-BASED) *Total amount:* $3,640,185 (96% institutional, 4% external sources). *Receiving aid:* Freshmen: 12% (60). Undergraduates: 10% (164). *Average award:* Freshmen: $10,012. Undergraduates: $9688. *Scholarships, grants, and awards by category:* Academic interests/achievement: general academic interests/achievements. Creative arts/performance: music, theater/drama. Special achievements/activities: general special achievements/activities. Special characteristics: children of educators, ethnic background, general special characteristics, international students, local/state students, members of minority groups, out-of-state students, religious affiliation, veterans' children. *Tuition waivers:* Full or partial for employees or children of employees, senior citizens. *ROTC:* Army cooperative.

LOANS *Student loans:* $8,858,257 (76% need-based, 24% non-need-based). 79% of past graduating class borrowed through all loan programs. *Average indebtedness per student:* $26,980. *Average need-based loan:* Freshmen: $3724. Undergraduates: $4646. *Parent loans:* $4,393,453 (36% need-based, 64% non-need-based). *Programs:* Perkins, alternative loans.

WORK-STUDY *Federal work-study:* Total amount: $643,679; 347 jobs averaging $1314. *State or other work-study/employment:* Part-time jobs available.

ATHLETIC AWARDS Total amount: $7,649,469 (69% need-based, 31% non-need-based).

APPLYING FOR FINANCIAL AID *Required financial aid form:* FAFSA. *Financial aid deadline (priority):* 3/15. *Notification date:* Continuous beginning 3/1. Students must reply within 2 weeks of notification.

CONTACT Mr. Tony Tanking, Director of Financial Aid, Benedictine College, 1020 North Second Street, Atchison, KS 66002-1499, 913-360-7484 or toll-free 800-467-5340. *Fax:* 913-367-5462. *E-mail:* ttanking@benedictine.edu.
Website: http://www.benedictine.edu/.

BENEDICTINE UNIVERSITY
Lisle, IL

Tuition & fees: $25,850	Average undergraduate aid package: $16,870

ABOUT THE INSTITUTION Independent Roman Catholic, coed. *Awards:* certificates, associate, bachelor's, master's, and doctoral degrees. 51 undergraduate majors. *Total enrollment:* 6,516. Undergraduates: 3,724. Freshmen: 612. Federal methodology is used as a basis for awarding need-based institutional aid.

UNDERGRADUATE EXPENSES for 2013–2014 *Application fee:* $40. *Comprehensive fee:* $34,230 includes full-time tuition ($24,850), mandatory fees ($1000), and room and board ($8380). *College room only:* $5860. Full-time tuition and fees vary according to class time, degree level, and location. Room and board charges vary according to board plan, housing facility, and location. *Part-time tuition:* $830 per credit hour. *Part-time fees:* $15 per credit hour. Part-time tuition and fees vary according to class time and degree level.

FRESHMAN FINANCIAL AID (Fall 2012, est.) 539 applied for aid; of those 91% were deemed to have need. 100% of freshmen with need received aid. *Average financial aid package:* $19,662 (excluding resources awarded to replace EFC). 9% of all full-time freshmen had no need and received non-need-based gift aid.

UNDERGRADUATE FINANCIAL AID (Fall 2012, est.) 2,408 applied for aid; of those 93% were deemed to have need. 99% of undergraduates with need received aid. *Average financial aid package:* $16,870 (excluding resources awarded to replace EFC). 11% of all full-time undergraduates had no need and received non-need-based gift aid.

GIFT AID (NEED-BASED) *Total amount:* $10,525,215 (54% federal, 41% state, 5% institutional). *Receiving aid:* Freshmen: 54% (319); all full-time undergraduates: 49% (1,423). *Average award:* Freshmen: $7899; Undergraduates: $7229. *Scholarships, grants, and awards:* Federal Pell, FSEOG, state, private, college/university gift aid from institutional funds.

GIFT AID (NON-NEED-BASED) *Total amount:* $21,533,763 (98% institutional, 2% external sources). *Receiving aid:* Freshmen: 80% (475). Undergraduates: 63% (1,836). *Average award:* Freshmen: $10,696. Undergraduates: $9799. *Schol-*

arships, grants, and awards by category: *Academic interests/achievement:* 2,135 awards ($14,667,374 total): general academic interests/achievements. *Creative arts/performance:* 15 awards ($39,850 total): music. *Special achievements/activities:* 1,862 awards ($2,013,098 total): community service, general special achievements/activities, leadership, memberships. *Special characteristics:* 1,506 awards ($3,836,523 total): children and siblings of alumni, children of faculty/staff, general special characteristics, international students, out-of-state students, relatives of clergy, siblings of current students, veterans, veterans' children. *Tuition waivers:* Full or partial for employees or children of employees. *ROTC:* Army cooperative.

LOANS *Student loans:* $19,802,309 (55% need-based, 45% non-need-based). 77% of past graduating class borrowed through all loan programs. *Average indebtedness per student:* $19,560. *Average need-based loan:* Freshmen: $3723. Undergraduates: $4478. *Parent loans:* $3,527,704 (100% non-need-based). *Programs:* Federal Direct (Subsidized and Unsubsidized Stafford, PLUS), Perkins, alternative loans.

WORK-STUDY *Federal work-study:* Total amount: $300,000; 215 jobs averaging $1264. *State or other work-study/employment:* Part-time jobs available.

APPLYING FOR FINANCIAL AID *Required financial aid form:* FAFSA. *Financial aid deadline:* Continuous. *Notification date:* Continuous beginning 2/15. Students must reply within 2 weeks of notification.

CONTACT Diane Battistella, Senior Associate Dean of Financial Aid, Benedictine University, 5700 College Road, Lisle, IL 60532, 630-829-6415 or toll-free 888-829-6363 (out-of-state). *Fax:* 630-829-6101. *E-mail:* dbattistella@ben.edu. *Website:* http://www.ben.edu/.

BENNETT COLLEGE
Greensboro, NC

ABOUT THE INSTITUTION Independent United Methodist, women only. *Awards:* bachelor's degrees. 18 undergraduate majors. *Total enrollment:* 736. Undergraduates: 736. Freshmen: 158.

GIFT AID (NEED-BASED) *Scholarships, grants, and awards:* Federal Pell, FSEOG, state, private, college/university gift aid from institutional funds, United Negro College Fund, United Methodist Church Scholarships.

GIFT AID (NON-NEED-BASED) *Scholarships, grants, and awards by category: Academic interests/achievement:* general academic interests/achievements. *Special achievements/activities:* general special achievements/activities. *Special characteristics:* children of faculty/staff, relatives of clergy, religious affiliation.

LOANS *Programs:* Federal Direct (Subsidized and Unsubsidized Stafford), Perkins.

WORK-STUDY *Federal work-study:* Total amount: $140,512; jobs available.

APPLYING FOR FINANCIAL AID *Required financial aid forms:* FAFSA, institution's own form, state aid form.

CONTACT Ms. Keisha Ragsdale, Director of Financial Aid, Bennett College, 900 East Washington Street, Greensboro, NC 27401, 336-370-8678 or toll-free 800-413-5323. *Fax:* 336-517-2204. *E-mail:* kragsdale@bennett.edu. *Website:* http://www.bennett.edu/.

BENNINGTON COLLEGE
Bennington, VT

Tuition & fees: $44,220	Average undergraduate aid package: $35,822

ABOUT THE INSTITUTION Independent, coed. *Awards:* certificates, bachelor's, and master's degrees. 104 undergraduate majors. *Total enrollment:* 826. Undergraduates: 688. Freshmen: 197. Both federal and institutional methodology are used as a basis for awarding need-based institutional aid.

UNDERGRADUATE EXPENSES for 2013–2014 *Application fee:* $60. *Comprehensive fee:* $56,990 includes full-time tuition ($43,070), mandatory fees ($1150), and room and board ($12,770). *College room only:* $6850. *Part-time tuition:* $1440 per credit hour.

FRESHMAN FINANCIAL AID (Fall 2012, est.) 154 applied for aid; of those 77% were deemed to have need. 100% of freshmen with need received aid; of those 19% had need fully met. *Average percent of need met:* 82% (excluding resources awarded to replace EFC). *Average financial aid package:* $36,238 (excluding resources awarded to replace EFC). 34% of all full-time freshmen had no need and received non-need-based gift aid.

UNDERGRADUATE FINANCIAL AID (Fall 2012, est.) 522 applied for aid; of those 85% were deemed to have need. 99% of undergraduates with need received aid; of those 12% had need fully met. *Average percent of need met:* 80% (excluding resources awarded to replace EFC). *Average financial aid package:* $35,822 (excluding resources awarded to replace EFC). 26% of all full-time undergraduates had no need and received non-need-based gift aid.

GIFT AID (NEED-BASED) *Total amount:* $13,375,972 (6% federal, 92% institutional, 2% external sources). *Receiving aid:* Freshmen: 59% (117); all full-time undergraduates: 63% (434). *Average award:* Freshmen: $32,396; Undergraduates: $30,716. *Scholarships, grants, and awards:* Federal Pell, FSEOG, state, private, college/university gift aid from institutional funds.

GIFT AID (NON-NEED-BASED) *Total amount:* $3,408,801 (96% institutional, 4% external sources). *Receiving aid:* Freshmen: 10% (19). Undergraduates: 5% (33). *Average award:* Freshmen: $17,368. Undergraduates: $17,121. *Scholarships, grants, and awards by category: Academic interests/achievement:* 488 awards ($5,939,404 total): general academic interests/achievements. *Special characteristics:* 9 awards ($259,803 total): children of educators, children of faculty/staff, veterans, veterans' children. *Tuition waivers:* Full or partial for employees or children of employees.

LOANS *Student loans:* $3,222,727 (78% need-based, 22% non-need-based). 68% of past graduating class borrowed through all loan programs. *Average indebtedness per student:* $25,716. *Average need-based loan:* Freshmen: $3103. Undergraduates: $4156. *Parent loans:* $1,674,546 (36% need-based, 64% non-need-based). *Programs:* Federal Direct (Subsidized and Unsubsidized Stafford, PLUS), college/university.

WORK-STUDY *Federal work-study:* Total amount: $723,325; 363 jobs averaging $2300. *State or other work-study/employment:* Total amount: $96,600 (100% non-need-based). 41 part-time jobs averaging $2300.

APPLYING FOR FINANCIAL AID *Required financial aid forms:* FAFSA, institution's own form, CSS Financial Aid PROFILE, noncustodial (divorced/separated) parent's statement, federal income tax form(s), W-2 forms. *Financial aid deadline:* 2/15 (priority: 2/1). *Notification date:* 4/1. Students must reply by 5/1 or within 2 weeks of notification.

CONTACT Meg Woolmington, Director of Financial Aid, Bennington College, One College Drive, Bennington, VT 05201, 802-440-4325 or toll-free 800-833-6845. *Fax:* 802-440-4880. *E-mail:* finaid@bennington.edu. *Website:* http://www.bennington.edu/.

BENTLEY UNIVERSITY
Waltham, MA

Tuition & fees: $39,628	Average undergraduate aid package: $31,152

ABOUT THE INSTITUTION Independent, coed. *Awards:* certificates, associate, bachelor's, master's, and doctoral degrees. 21 undergraduate majors. *Total enrollment:* 5,565. Undergraduates: 4,228. Freshmen: 911. Both federal and institutional methodology are used as a basis for awarding need-based institutional aid.

UNDERGRADUATE EXPENSES for 2013–2014 *Application fee:* $50. *Comprehensive fee:* $52,588 includes full-time tuition ($38,130), mandatory fees ($1498), and room and board ($12,960). *College room only:* $7790. Room and board charges vary according to board plan and housing facility. *Part-time tuition:* $1932 per course. *Part-time fees:* $45 per term. Part-time tuition and fees vary according to class time and course load.

FRESHMAN FINANCIAL AID (Fall 2012, est.) 617 applied for aid; of those 69% were deemed to have need. 99% of freshmen with need received aid; of those 44% had need fully met. *Average percent of need met:* 96% (excluding resources awarded to replace EFC). *Average financial aid package:* $31,077 (excluding resources awarded to replace EFC). 19% of all full-time freshmen had no need and received non-need-based gift aid.

UNDERGRADUATE FINANCIAL AID (Fall 2012, est.) 2,496 applied for aid; of those 78% were deemed to have need. 99% of undergraduates with need received aid; of those 45% had need fully met. *Average percent of need met:* 95% (excluding resources awarded to replace EFC). *Average financial aid package:* $31,152 (excluding resources awarded to replace EFC). 16% of all full-time undergraduates had no need and received non-need-based gift aid.

GIFT AID (NEED-BASED) *Total amount:* $38,716,232 (8% federal, 3% state, 89% institutional). *Receiving aid:* Freshmen: 38% (347); all full-time undergraduates:

40% (1,653). *Average award:* Freshmen: $23,988; Undergraduates: $23,737. *Scholarships, grants, and awards:* Federal Pell, FSEOG, state, private, college/university gift aid from institutional funds.

GIFT AID (NON-NEED-BASED) *Total amount:* $20,721,300 (95% institutional, 5% external sources). *Receiving aid:* Freshmen: 20% (178). Undergraduates: 15% (603). *Average award:* Freshmen: $16,709. Undergraduates: $15,803. *Scholarships, grants, and awards by category: Academic interests/achievement:* 1,307 awards ($22,982,844 total): general academic interests/achievements. *Special achievements/activities:* 16 awards ($120,000 total): community service. *Special characteristics:* 34 awards ($438,481 total): international students, members of minority groups. *Tuition waivers:* Full or partial for employees or children of employees. *ROTC:* Army cooperative, Air Force cooperative.

LOANS *Student loans:* $18,649,927 (51% need-based, 49% non-need-based). 59% of past graduating class borrowed through all loan programs. *Average indebtedness per student:* $30,375. *Average need-based loan:* Freshmen: $3833. Undergraduates: $5055. *Parent loans:* $9,055,407 (100% non-need-based). *Programs:* Federal Direct (Subsidized and Unsubsidized Stafford, PLUS), Perkins, state.

WORK-STUDY *Federal work-study:* Total amount: $1,784,059; 950 jobs averaging $1494. *State or other work-study/employment:* Total amount: $1,123,050 (100% non-need-based). 644 part-time jobs averaging $1458.

ATHLETIC AWARDS Total amount: $2,186,334 (33% need-based, 67% non-need-based).

APPLYING FOR FINANCIAL AID *Required financial aid forms:* FAFSA, CSS Financial Aid PROFILE, noncustodial (divorced/separated) parent's statement, business/farm supplement, federal income tax form(s). *Financial aid deadline:* 2/1. *Notification date:* 3/15.

CONTACT Donna Kendall, Executive Director of Enrollment Management and Financial Assistance, Bentley University, 175 Forest Street, Waltham, MA 02452-4705, 781-891-3441 or toll-free 800-523-2354. *Fax:* 781-891-2448. *E-mail:* finaid@bentley.edu.
Website: http://www.bentley.edu/.

BEREA COLLEGE
Berea, KY

Tuition & fees: N/R	Average undergraduate aid package: $27,666

ABOUT THE INSTITUTION Independent, coed. *Awards:* bachelor's degrees. 38 undergraduate majors. *Total enrollment:* 1,658. Undergraduates: 1,658. Freshmen: 391. Federal methodology is used as a basis for awarding need-based institutional aid.

FRESHMAN FINANCIAL AID (Fall 2012, est.) 391 applied for aid; of those 100% were deemed to have need. 100% of freshmen with need received aid. *Average percent of need met:* 100% (excluding resources awarded to replace EFC). *Average financial aid package:* $28,239 (excluding resources awarded to replace EFC).

UNDERGRADUATE FINANCIAL AID (Fall 2012, est.) 1,604 applied for aid; of those 100% were deemed to have need. 100% of undergraduates with need received aid. *Average percent of need met:* 100% (excluding resources awarded to replace EFC). *Average financial aid package:* $27,666 (excluding resources awarded to replace EFC).

GIFT AID (NEED-BASED) *Total amount:* $41,011,953 (16% federal, 8% state, 75% institutional, 1% external sources). *Receiving aid:* Freshmen: 100% (391); all full-time undergraduates: 100% (1,604). *Average award:* Freshmen: $28,163; Undergraduates: $25,569. *Scholarships, grants, and awards:* Federal Pell, FSEOG, state, private, college/university gift aid from institutional funds.

LOANS *Student loans:* $890,698 (100% need-based). 72% of past graduating class borrowed through all loan programs. *Average indebtedness per student:* $7224. *Average need-based loan:* Freshmen: $748. Undergraduates: $1289. *Parent loans:* $1172 (100% need-based). *Programs:* Federal Direct (Subsidized and Unsubsidized Stafford, PLUS), Perkins, college/university.

WORK-STUDY *Federal work-study:* Total amount: $2,538,203; jobs available. *State or other work-study/employment:* Total amount: $446,466 (100% need-based). Part-time jobs available.

APPLYING FOR FINANCIAL AID *Required financial aid form:* FAFSA. *Financial aid deadline (priority):* 2/1. *Notification date:* Continuous beginning 3/1. Students must reply by 5/1.

CONTACT Nancy Melton, Director of Student Financial Aid Services, Berea College, CPO 2172, Berea, KY 40404, 859-985-3313 or toll-free 800-326-5948. *Fax:* 859-985-3914. *E-mail:* meltonn@berea.edu.
Website: http://www.berea.edu/.

BERGIN UNIVERSITY OF CANINE STUDIES
Rohnert Park, CA

CONTACT Financial Aid Office, Bergin University of Canine Studies, 5860 Labath Avenue, Rohnert Park, CA 94928, 707-545-3647.
Website: http://www.berginu.edu/.

BERKELEY COLLEGE
Woodland Park, NJ

Tuition & fees: N/R	Average undergraduate aid package: N/A

ABOUT THE INSTITUTION Proprietary, coed. 13 undergraduate majors.

GIFT AID (NEED-BASED) *Scholarships, grants, and awards:* Federal Pell, state, private.

LOANS *Programs:* alternative loans.

APPLYING FOR FINANCIAL AID *Required financial aid form:* state income tax form(s). *Financial aid deadline (priority):* 5/1. *Notification date:* Continuous. Students must reply within 4 weeks of notification.

CONTACT Office of Financial Aid, Berkeley College, 44 Rifle Camp Road, Woodland Park, NJ 07424-3353, 800-446-5400. *E-mail:* financialaid@berkeleycollege.edu.
Website: http://www.berkeleycollege.edu/.

BERKELEY COLLEGE–NEW YORK CITY CAMPUS
New York, NY

Tuition & fees: N/R	Average undergraduate aid package: N/A

ABOUT THE INSTITUTION Proprietary, coed. 10 undergraduate majors.

GIFT AID (NEED-BASED) *Scholarships, grants, and awards:* Federal Pell, FSEOG, state, private.

LOANS *Programs:* Federal Direct (Subsidized and Unsubsidized Stafford), alternative loans.

APPLYING FOR FINANCIAL AID *Required financial aid form:* state income tax form(s). *Notification date:* Continuous.

CONTACT Office of Financial Aid, Berkeley College–New York City Campus, 3 East 43rd Street, New York, NY 10017, 800-446-5400. *E-mail:* financialaid@berkeleycollege.edu.
Website: http://www.berkeleycollege.edu/.

BERKLEE COLLEGE OF MUSIC
Boston, MA

ABOUT THE INSTITUTION Independent, coed. *Awards:* diplomas, bachelor's, and master's degrees. 13 undergraduate majors. *Total enrollment:* 4,521. Undergraduates: 4,447. Freshmen: 778.

GIFT AID (NEED-BASED) *Scholarships, grants, and awards:* Federal Pell, FSEOG, state, private, college/university gift aid from institutional funds, Academic Competitiveness Grants.

GIFT AID (NON-NEED-BASED) *Scholarships, grants, and awards by category: Academic interests/achievement:* education, engineering/technologies, general academic interests/achievements. *Creative arts/performance:* music. *Special characteristics:* children of faculty/staff.

LOANS *Programs:* Federal Direct (Subsidized and Unsubsidized Stafford, PLUS), Perkins, state.
WORK-STUDY *Federal work-study:* Total amount: $333,539; jobs available. *State or other work-study/employment:* Total amount: $3,885,456 (100% non-need-based). Part-time jobs available.
APPLYING FOR FINANCIAL AID *Required financial aid form:* FAFSA.
CONTACT Office of Financial Aid, Berklee College of Music, 1140 Boylston Street, Boston, MA 02215-3693, 617-747-2274 or toll-free 800-BERKLEE. *Fax:* 617-747-2073. *E-mail:* financialaid@berklee.edu.
Website: http://www.berklee.edu/.

BERRY COLLEGE
Mount Berry, GA

Tuition & fees: $27,650	Average undergraduate aid package: $23,802

ABOUT THE INSTITUTION Independent interdenominational, coed. *Awards:* bachelor's and master's degrees. 36 undergraduate majors. *Total enrollment:* 2,166. Undergraduates: 2,041. Freshmen: 618. Federal methodology is used as a basis for awarding need-based institutional aid.
UNDERGRADUATE EXPENSES for 2013–2014 *Application fee:* $50. *Comprehensive fee:* $37,329 includes full-time tuition ($27,450), mandatory fees ($200), and room and board ($9679). *College room only:* $5456. Room and board charges vary according to board plan and housing facility. *Part-time tuition:* $915 per credit hour.
FRESHMAN FINANCIAL AID (Fall 2012, est.) 578 applied for aid; of those 83% were deemed to have need. 100% of freshmen with need received aid; of those 24% had need fully met. *Average percent of need met:* 84% (excluding resources awarded to replace EFC). *Average financial aid package:* $24,755 (excluding resources awarded to replace EFC). 23% of all full-time freshmen had no need and received non-need-based gift aid.
UNDERGRADUATE FINANCIAL AID (Fall 2012, est.) 1,734 applied for aid; of those 84% were deemed to have need. 100% of undergraduates with need received aid; of those 26% had need fully met. *Average percent of need met:* 83% (excluding resources awarded to replace EFC). *Average financial aid package:* $23,802 (excluding resources awarded to replace EFC). 26% of all full-time undergraduates had no need and received non-need-based gift aid.
GIFT AID (NEED-BASED) *Total amount:* $27,000,451 (10% federal, 11% state, 77% institutional, 2% external sources). *Receiving aid:* Freshmen: 77% (478); all full-time undergraduates: 73% (1,457). *Average award:* Freshmen: $19,759; Undergraduates: $18,578. *Scholarships, grants, and awards:* Federal Pell, FSEOG, state, private, college/university gift aid from institutional funds.
GIFT AID (NON-NEED-BASED) *Total amount:* $9,111,447 (19% state, 76% institutional, 5% external sources). *Receiving aid:* Freshmen: 15% (90). Undergraduates: 14% (275). *Average award:* Freshmen: $10,392. Undergraduates: $11,355. *Scholarships, grants, and awards by category:* Academic interests/achievement: agriculture, business, communication, education, English, general academic interests/achievements, humanities, religion/biblical studies. Creative arts/performance: art/fine arts, debating, journalism/publications, music, theater/drama. Special achievements/activities: community service, leadership, religious involvement. Special characteristics: adult students, children of faculty/staff, ethnic background, first-generation college students, international students, local/state students, members of minority groups, out-of-state students, veterans, veterans' children. *Tuition waivers:* Full or partial for employees or children of employees, senior citizens.
LOANS *Student loans:* $12,511,479 (64% need-based, 36% non-need-based). 76% of past graduating class borrowed through all loan programs. *Average indebtedness per student:* $20,611. *Average need-based loan:* Freshmen: $4269. Undergraduates: $4803. *Parent loans:* $3,153,316 (32% need-based, 68% non-need-based). *Programs:* Federal Direct (Subsidized and Unsubsidized Stafford, PLUS), Perkins, state, college/university.
WORK-STUDY *Federal work-study:* Total amount: $1,964,770; 560 jobs averaging $3508. *State or other work-study/employment:* Total amount: $8,054,400 (2% need-based, 98% non-need-based). 2,132 part-time jobs averaging $3778.
APPLYING FOR FINANCIAL AID *Required financial aid forms:* FAFSA, state aid form. *Financial aid deadline (priority):* 3/1. *Notification date:* Continuous beginning 2/15. Students must reply by 5/1.

CONTACT Mrs. Marcia McConnell, Director of Financial Aid, Berry College, 2277 Martha Berry Highway, NW, Mount Berry, GA 30149-5007, 706-236-1714 or toll-free 800-237-7942. *Fax:* 706-290-2160. *E-mail:* financialaid@berry.edu.
Website: http://www.berry.edu/.

BETHANY COLLEGE
Lindsborg, KS

ABOUT THE INSTITUTION Independent Lutheran, coed. *Awards:* bachelor's degrees. 44 undergraduate majors. *Total enrollment:* 626. Undergraduates: 626. Freshmen: 149.
GIFT AID (NEED-BASED) *Scholarships, grants, and awards:* Federal Pell, FSEOG, state, private, college/university gift aid from institutional funds, Academic Competitiveness Grants, National SMART Grants, TEACH Grants.
GIFT AID (NON-NEED-BASED) *Scholarships, grants, and awards by category:* Academic interests/achievement: general academic interests/achievements. Creative arts/performance: art/fine arts, music, theater/drama. Special achievements/activities: cheerleading/drum major. Special characteristics: adult students, children and siblings of alumni, religious affiliation, siblings of current students.
LOANS *Programs:* Federal Direct (Subsidized and Unsubsidized Stafford, PLUS), Perkins, college/university.
WORK-STUDY *Federal work-study:* Total amount: $504,656; 381 jobs averaging $1342. *State or other work-study/employment:* Part-time jobs available.
APPLYING FOR FINANCIAL AID *Required financial aid form:* FAFSA.
CONTACT Ms. Amber Maneth, Office of Financial Aid, Bethany College, 335 East Swensson, Lindsborg, KS 67456-1897, 785-227-3311 Ext. 8248 or toll-free 800-826-2281. *Fax:* 785-227-2004. *E-mail:* manetha@bethanylb.edu.
Website: http://www.bethanylb.edu/.

BETHANY COLLEGE
Bethany, WV

CONTACT Sheila Nelson-Hensley, Director of Financial Aid, Bethany College, PO Box 488, Bethany, WV 26032, 304-829-7141 or toll-free 800-922-7611. *Fax:* 304-829-7142. *E-mail:* admission@bethanywv.edu.
Website: http://www.bethanywv.edu/.

BETHANY LUTHERAN COLLEGE
Mankato, MN

Tuition & fees: $23,140	Average undergraduate aid package: $18,694

ABOUT THE INSTITUTION Independent Lutheran, coed. *Awards:* bachelor's degrees. 25 undergraduate majors. *Total enrollment:* 600. Undergraduates: 600. Freshmen: 137. Federal methodology is used as a basis for awarding need-based institutional aid.
UNDERGRADUATE EXPENSES for 2013–2014 *One-time required fee:* $130. *Comprehensive fee:* $30,250 includes full-time tuition ($22,810), mandatory fees ($330), and room and board ($7110). *College room only:* $3310. Room and board charges vary according to board plan and housing facility. *Part-time tuition:* $960 per credit. *Part-time fees:* $165 per term. Part-time tuition and fees vary according to course load.
FRESHMAN FINANCIAL AID (Fall 2011) 153 applied for aid; of those 88% were deemed to have need. 100% of freshmen with need received aid; of those 14% had need fully met. *Average percent of need met:* 84% (excluding resources awarded to replace EFC). *Average financial aid package:* $20,012 (excluding resources awarded to replace EFC). 14% of all full-time freshmen had no need and received non-need-based gift aid.
UNDERGRADUATE FINANCIAL AID (Fall 2011) 559 applied for aid; of those 90% were deemed to have need. 100% of undergraduates with need received aid; of those 14% had need fully met. *Average percent of need met:* 81% (excluding resources awarded to replace EFC). *Average financial aid package:* $18,694

(excluding resources awarded to replace EFC). 13% of all full-time undergraduates had no need and received non-need-based gift aid.

GIFT AID (NEED-BASED) *Total amount:* $6,208,644 (17% federal, 12% state, 68% institutional, 3% external sources). *Receiving aid:* Freshmen: 83% (134); all full-time undergraduates: 84% (505). *Average award:* Freshmen: $15,084; Undergraduates: $13,352. *Scholarships, grants, and awards:* Federal Pell, FSEOG, state, private, college/university gift aid from institutional funds.

GIFT AID (NON-NEED-BASED) *Total amount:* $674,131 (86% institutional, 14% external sources). *Receiving aid:* Freshmen: 4% (7). Undergraduates: 6% (37). *Average award:* Freshmen: $7461. Undergraduates: $6292. *Scholarships, grants, and awards by category: Creative arts/performance:* 77 awards ($148,000 total): art/fine arts, debating, journalism/publications, music, theater/drama. *Special characteristics:* 14 awards ($247,830 total): children of faculty/staff. *Tuition waivers:* Full or partial for employees or children of employees, senior citizens. **ROTC:** Army cooperative.

LOANS *Student loans:* $4,572,526 (71% need-based, 29% non-need-based). 94% of past graduating class borrowed through all loan programs. *Average indebtedness per student:* $31,884. *Average need-based loan:* Freshmen: $5261. Undergraduates: $5621. *Parent loans:* $379,358 (26% need-based, 74% non-need-based). *Programs:* Federal Direct (Subsidized and Unsubsidized Stafford, PLUS), Perkins, state, alternative loans.

WORK-STUDY *Federal work-study:* Total amount: $40,927; 25 jobs averaging $1637. *State or other work-study employment:* Total amount: $219,268 (63% need-based, 37% non-need-based). 267 part-time jobs averaging $821.

APPLYING FOR FINANCIAL AID *Required financial aid forms:* FAFSA, institution's own form, business/farm supplement, federal income tax form(s), W-2 forms. *Financial aid deadline (priority):* 4/15. *Notification date:* Continuous beginning 3/1. Students must reply within 4 weeks of notification.

CONTACT Financial Aid Office, Bethany Lutheran College, 700 Luther Drive, Mankato, MN 56001-6163, 507-344-7328 or toll-free 800-944-3066. *Fax:* 507-344-7376. *E-mail:* finaid@blc.edu. *Website:* http://www.blc.edu/.

BETHEL COLLEGE
Mishawaka, IN

Tuition & fees: $24,970	Average undergraduate aid package: $16,405

ABOUT THE INSTITUTION Independent Missionary Church, coed. *Awards:* associate, bachelor's, and master's degrees. 52 undergraduate majors. *Total enrollment:* 1,963. Undergraduates: 1,801. Freshmen: 233. Federal methodology is used as a basis for awarding need-based institutional aid.

UNDERGRADUATE EXPENSES for 2013–2014 *Application fee:* $25. *Comprehensive fee:* $32,430 includes full-time tuition ($24,620), mandatory fees ($350), and room and board ($7460). *College room only:* $3560. Full-time tuition and fees vary according to program. Room and board charges vary according to board plan and housing facility. *Part-time tuition:* $782 per credit. Part-time tuition and fees vary according to program.

FRESHMAN FINANCIAL AID (Fall 2012, est.) 221 applied for aid; of those 90% were deemed to have need. 100% of freshmen with need received aid; of those 14% had need fully met. *Average percent of need met:* 71% (excluding resources awarded to replace EFC). *Average financial aid package:* $20,242 (excluding resources awarded to replace EFC). 11% of all full-time freshmen had no need and received non-need-based gift aid.

UNDERGRADUATE FINANCIAL AID (Fall 2012, est.) 1,332 applied for aid; of those 93% were deemed to have need. 100% of undergraduates with need received aid; of those 14% had need fully met. *Average percent of need met:* 66% (excluding resources awarded to replace EFC). *Average financial aid package:* $16,405 (excluding resources awarded to replace EFC). 9% of all full-time undergraduates had no need and received non-need-based gift aid.

GIFT AID (NEED-BASED) *Receiving aid:* Freshmen: 78% (176); all full-time undergraduates: 71% (1,003). *Average award:* Freshmen: $8680; Undergraduates: $7754. *Scholarships, grants, and awards:* Federal Pell, FSEOG, state, private, college/university gift aid from institutional funds, Federal Nursing.

GIFT AID (NON-NEED-BASED) *Receiving aid:* Freshmen: 77% (175). Undergraduates: 60% (849). *Average award:* Freshmen: $8338. Undergraduates: $8067. *Scholarships, grants, and awards by category: Academic interests/*

achievement: 757 awards ($4,117,000 total): biological sciences, business, communication, education, English, general academic interests/achievements, health fields, mathematics, physical sciences, premedicine, religion/biblical studies, social sciences. *Creative arts/performance:* 84 awards ($198,800 total): art/fine arts, journalism/publications, music, theater/drama. *Special achievements/activities:* 49 awards ($138,874 total): cheerleading/drum major, general special achievements/activities, leadership, religious involvement. *Special characteristics:* 640 awards ($1,943,000 total): adult students, children of faculty/staff, international students, members of minority groups, relatives of clergy, religious affiliation, siblings of current students, spouses of current students. *Tuition waivers:* Full or partial for employees or children of employees. **ROTC:** Army cooperative, Air Force cooperative.

LOANS *Student loans:* 82% of past graduating class borrowed through all loan programs. *Average indebtedness per student:* $24,207. *Average need-based loan:* Freshmen: $3626. Undergraduates: $4473. *Programs:* Federal Direct (Subsidized and Unsubsidized Stafford, PLUS), Perkins, Federal Nursing, college/university.

WORK-STUDY *Federal work-study:* 53 jobs averaging $2536.

APPLYING FOR FINANCIAL AID *Required financial aid forms:* FAFSA, institution's own form. *Financial aid deadline:* 3/10 (priority: 3/1). *Notification date:* Continuous beginning 4/1.

CONTACT Mr. Guy A. Fisher, Director of Financial Aid, Bethel College, 1001 Bethel Circle, Mishawaka, IN 46545-5591, 574-257-3316 or toll-free 800-422-4101. *Fax:* 574-807-7122. *E-mail:* fisherg@bethelcollege.edu. *Website:* http://www.bethelcollege.edu/.

BETHEL COLLEGE
North Newton, KS

Tuition & fees: $23,500	Average undergraduate aid package: $22,638

ABOUT THE INSTITUTION Independent Mennonite Church USA, coed. *Awards:* certificates and bachelor's degrees. 17 undergraduate majors. *Total enrollment:* 472. Undergraduates: 472. Freshmen: 101. Federal methodology is used as a basis for awarding need-based institutional aid.

UNDERGRADUATE EXPENSES for 2013–2014 *Application fee:* $20. *One-time required fee:* $200. *Comprehensive fee:* $31,480 includes full-time tuition ($23,500) and room and board ($7980). *College room only:* $4310.

FRESHMAN FINANCIAL AID (Fall 2011) 121 applied for aid; of those 98% were deemed to have need. 100% of freshmen with need received aid; of those 41% had need fully met. *Average percent of need met:* 90% (excluding resources awarded to replace EFC). *Average financial aid package:* $21,548 (excluding resources awarded to replace EFC). 4% of all full-time freshmen had no need and received non-need-based gift aid.

UNDERGRADUATE FINANCIAL AID (Fall 2011) 442 applied for aid; of those 95% were deemed to have need. 100% of undergraduates with need received aid; of those 41% had need fully met. *Average percent of need met:* 92% (excluding resources awarded to replace EFC). *Average financial aid package:* $22,638 (excluding resources awarded to replace EFC). 14% of all full-time undergraduates had no need and received non-need-based gift aid.

GIFT AID (NEED-BASED) *Total amount:* $1,515,824 (62% federal, 29% state, 9% institutional). *Receiving aid:* Freshmen: 83% (105); all full-time undergraduates: 73% (362). *Average award:* Freshmen: $4275; Undergraduates: $5065. *Scholarships, grants, and awards:* Federal Pell, FSEOG, state, college/university gift aid from institutional funds.

GIFT AID (NON-NEED-BASED) *Total amount:* $4,421,079 (89% institutional, 11% external sources). *Receiving aid:* Freshmen: 94% (119). Undergraduates: 83% (414). *Average award:* Freshmen: $10,093. Undergraduates: $8984. *Scholarships, grants, and awards by category: Academic interests/achievement:* biological sciences, communication, general academic interests/achievements, social sciences. *Creative arts/performance:* art/fine arts, debating, music, theater/drama. *Special achievements/activities:* cheerleading/drum major. *Special characteristics:* children and siblings of alumni, children of current students, children of faculty/staff, ethnic background, general special characteristics, international students, local/state students, previous college experience, relatives of clergy, religious affiliation, siblings of current students, spouses of current students.

LOANS *Student loans:* $3,189,388 (100% need-based). 78% of past graduating class borrowed through all loan programs. *Average indebtedness per student:* $20,356. *Average need-based loan:* Freshmen: $7082. Undergraduates: $8088.

Parent loans: $622,724 (100% non-need-based). *Programs:* Federal Direct (Subsidized and Unsubsidized Stafford, PLUS), Perkins.
WORK-STUDY *Federal work-study:* Total amount: $494,051; jobs available. *State or other work-study/employment:* Part-time jobs available.
ATHLETIC AWARDS Total amount: $928,953 (100% non-need-based).
APPLYING FOR FINANCIAL AID *Required financial aid form:* FAFSA. *Financial aid deadline (priority):* 4/1. *Notification date:* Continuous beginning 2/1. Students must reply by 5/1 or within 2 weeks of notification.
CONTACT Mr. Tony Graber, Director of Financial Aid, Bethel College, 300 East 27th Street, North Newton, KS 67117, 316-284-5232 or toll-free 800-522-1887 Ext. 230. *Fax:* 316-284-5845. *E-mail:* tgraber@bethelks.edu.
Website: http://www.bethelks.edu/.

BETHEL COLLEGE
Hampton, VA

CONTACT Financial Aid Office, Bethel College, 1705 Todds Lane, Hampton, VA 23666, 757-826-1426.
Website: http://bethel-college.com/.

BETHEL UNIVERSITY
St. Paul, MN

Tuition & fees: $30,840	Average undergraduate aid package: $21,159

ABOUT THE INSTITUTION Independent Baptist General Conference, coed. *Awards:* certificates, associate, bachelor's, master's, and doctoral degrees. 54 undergraduate majors. *Total enrollment:* 5,326. Undergraduates: 3,467. Freshmen: 659. Federal methodology is used as a basis for awarding need-based institutional aid.
UNDERGRADUATE EXPENSES for 2013–2014 *Comprehensive fee:* $39,740 includes full-time tuition ($30,700), mandatory fees ($140), and room and board ($8900). *College room only:* $5100. Room and board charges vary according to board plan. *Part-time tuition:* $1280 per credit. Part-time tuition and fees vary according to course load. *Payment plan:* Tuition prepayment.
FRESHMAN FINANCIAL AID (Fall 2011) 632 applied for aid; of those 84% were deemed to have need. 100% of freshmen with need received aid; of those 18% had need fully met. *Average percent of need met:* 76% (excluding resources awarded to replace EFC). *Average financial aid package:* $21,583 (excluding resources awarded to replace EFC). 21% of all full-time freshmen had no need and received non-need-based gift aid.
UNDERGRADUATE FINANCIAL AID (Fall 2011) 2,342 applied for aid; of those 87% were deemed to have need. 100% of undergraduates with need received aid; of those 17% had need fully met. *Average percent of need met:* 74% (excluding resources awarded to replace EFC). *Average financial aid package:* $21,159 (excluding resources awarded to replace EFC). 21% of all full-time undergraduates had no need and received non-need-based gift aid.
GIFT AID (NEED-BASED) *Total amount:* $30,546,754 (13% federal, 9% state, 75% institutional, 3% external sources). *Receiving aid:* Freshmen: 78% (529); all full-time undergraduates: 76% (2,037). *Average award:* Freshmen: $16,682; Undergraduates: $15,466. *Scholarships, grants, and awards:* Federal Pell, FSEOG, state, private, college/university gift aid from institutional funds.
GIFT AID (NON-NEED-BASED) *Total amount:* $5,605,404 (7% federal, 88% institutional, 5% external sources). *Receiving aid:* Freshmen: 10% (69). Undergraduates: 8% (203). *Average award:* Freshmen: $9908. Undergraduates: $8352. *Scholarships, grants, and awards by category:* Academic interests/achievement: 1,895 awards ($10,210,875 total): general academic interests/achievements. *Creative arts/performance:* 131 awards ($300,325 total): art/fine arts, debating, music, theater/drama. *Special achievements/activities:* community service, junior miss, leadership, religious involvement. *Special characteristics:* children and siblings of alumni, children of faculty/staff, ethnic background, international students, members of minority groups, out-of-state students, relatives of clergy, religious affiliation. *Tuition waivers:* Full or partial for employees or children of employees. *ROTC:* Army cooperative, Air Force cooperative.
LOANS *Student loans:* $20,242,362 (73% need-based, 27% non-need-based). 76% of past graduating class borrowed through all loan programs. *Average indebtedness*

per student: $32,483. *Average need-based loan:* Freshmen: $3811. Undergraduates: $4364. *Parent loans:* $4,437,992 (40% need-based, 60% non-need-based). *Programs:* Federal Direct (Subsidized and Unsubsidized Stafford, PLUS), Perkins, state, alternative loans.
WORK-STUDY *Federal work-study:* Total amount: $629,277; 350 jobs averaging $2500. *State or other work-study/employment:* Total amount: $2,492,548 (45% need-based, 55% non-need-based). 1,500 part-time jobs averaging $2500.
APPLYING FOR FINANCIAL AID *Required financial aid forms:* FAFSA, institution's own form. *Financial aid deadline (priority):* 4/15. *Notification date:* Continuous beginning 3/1.
CONTACT Mr. Jeffrey D. Olson, Director of Financial Aid, Bethel University, 3900 Bethel Drive, St. Paul, MN 55112-6999, 651-638-6241 or toll-free 800-255-8706 Ext. 6242. *Fax:* 651-635-1491. *E-mail:* finaid@bethel.edu.
Website: http://www.bethel.edu/.

BETHEL UNIVERSITY
McKenzie, TN

CONTACT Laura Bateman, Office of Financial Aid, Bethel University, 325 Cherry Avenue, McKenzie, TN 38201, 901-352-4007. *Fax:* 901-352-4069.
Website: http://www.bethelu.edu/.

BETHESDA UNIVERSITY OF CALIFORNIA
Anaheim, CA

CONTACT Ms. Grace Choi, Financial Aid Administrator, Bethesda University of California, 730 North Euclid Street, Anaheim, CA 92801, 714-683-1413. *Fax:* 714-517-1948. *E-mail:* financialaid@bcu.edu.
Website: http://www.buc.edu/.

BETH HAMEDRASH SHAAREI YOSHER INSTITUTE
Brooklyn, NY

CONTACT Financial Aid Office, Beth HaMedrash Shaarei Yosher Institute, 4102-10 16th Avenue, Brooklyn, NY 11204, 718-854-2290.

BETH HATALMUD RABBINICAL COLLEGE
Brooklyn, NY

CONTACT Financial Aid Office, Beth Hatalmud Rabbinical College, 2127 82nd Street, Brooklyn, NY 11204, 718-259-2525.

BETH MEDRASH GOVOHA
Lakewood, NJ

CONTACT Financial Aid Office, Beth Medrash Govoha, 617 Sixth Street, Lakewood, NJ 08701-2797, 732-367-1060.

BETHUNE-COOKMAN UNIVERSITY
Daytona Beach, FL

Tuition & fees: $14,410	Average undergraduate aid package: $13,786

ABOUT THE INSTITUTION Independent Methodist, coed. *Awards:* bachelor's and master's degrees. 38 undergraduate majors. *Total enrollment:* 3,543. Undergraduates: 3,486. Freshmen: 899. Federal methodology is used as a basis for awarding need-based institutional aid.

UNDERGRADUATE EXPENSES for 2013–2014 *Application fee:* $25. *Comprehensive fee:* $22,958 includes full-time tuition ($14,410) and room and board ($8548). Full-time tuition and fees vary according to course load and degree level. Room and board charges vary according to housing facility. *Part-time tuition:* $600 per credit hour. Part-time tuition and fees vary according to course load and degree level.

FRESHMAN FINANCIAL AID (Fall 2012, est.) 947 applied for aid; of those 98% were deemed to have need. 100% of freshmen with need received aid; of those 4% had need fully met. *Average percent of need met:* 53% (excluding resources awarded to replace EFC). *Average financial aid package:* $14,124 (excluding resources awarded to replace EFC). 1% of all full-time freshmen had no need and received non-need-based gift aid.

UNDERGRADUATE FINANCIAL AID (Fall 2012, est.) 3,279 applied for aid; of those 98% were deemed to have need. 100% of undergraduates with need received aid; of those 4% had need fully met. *Average percent of need met:* 48% (excluding resources awarded to replace EFC). *Average financial aid package:* $13,786 (excluding resources awarded to replace EFC). 1% of all full-time undergraduates had no need and received non-need-based gift aid.

GIFT AID (NEED-BASED) *Total amount:* $27,962,303 (50% federal, 20% state, 26% institutional, 4% external sources). *Receiving aid:* Freshmen: 95% (900); all full-time undergraduates: 95% (3,114). *Average award:* Freshmen: $10,886; Undergraduates: $9893. *Scholarships, grants, and awards:* Federal Pell, FSEOG, state, private, college/university gift aid from institutional funds, United Negro College Fund.

GIFT AID (NON-NEED-BASED) *Total amount:* $750,846 (26% state, 68% institutional, 6% external sources). *Receiving aid:* Freshmen: 3% (29). Undergraduates: 3% (91). *Average award:* Freshmen: $10,724. Undergraduates: $11,062. *Scholarships, grants, and awards by category:* Academic interests/achievement: 192 awards ($1,811,923 total): general academic interests/achievements. *Tuition waivers:* Full or partial for employees or children of employees. *ROTC:* Army cooperative, Air Force cooperative.

LOANS *Student loans:* $28,719,283 (95% need-based, 5% non-need-based). 96% of past graduating class borrowed through all loan programs. *Average indebtedness per student:* $22,175. *Average need-based loan:* Freshmen: $3691. Undergraduates: $4331. *Parent loans:* $5,221,194 (82% need-based, 18% non-need-based). *Programs:* Federal Direct (Subsidized and Unsubsidized Stafford, PLUS), alternative loans.

WORK-STUDY *Federal work-study:* Total amount: $516,912; 295 jobs averaging $1808. *State or other work-study/employment:* 140 part-time jobs averaging $2200.

ATHLETIC AWARDS Total amount: $3,466,062 (88% need-based, 12% non-need-based).

APPLYING FOR FINANCIAL AID *Required financial aid form:* FAFSA. *Financial aid deadline (priority):* 4/1. *Notification date:* Continuous beginning 4/1. Students must reply within 3 weeks of notification.

CONTACT Mr. Calvin Davis, Director of Financial Aid, Bethune-Cookman University, 640 Mary McLeod Bethune Boulevard, Daytona Beach, FL 32114-3099, 386-481-2781 or toll-free 800-448-0228. *Fax:* 386-481-2621. *E-mail:* davisca@cookman.edu.
Website: http://www.cookman.edu/.

BEULAH HEIGHTS UNIVERSITY
Atlanta, GA

CONTACT Ms. Patricia Banks, Director of Financial Aid, Beulah Heights University, 892 Berne Street, SE, Atlanta, GA 30316, 404-627-2681 or toll-free 888-777-BHBC. *Fax:* 404-627-0702. *E-mail:* pat.banks@beulah.org.
Website: http://www.beulah.org/.

BINGHAMTON UNIVERSITY, STATE UNIVERSITY OF NEW YORK
Binghamton, NY

Tuition & fees (NY res): $7645	Average undergraduate aid package: $11,783

ABOUT THE INSTITUTION State-supported, coed. *Awards:* certificates, bachelor's, master's, and doctoral degrees. 75 undergraduate majors. *Total enrollment:* 15,308. Undergraduates: 12,356. Freshmen: 2,664. Federal methodology is used as a basis for awarding need-based institutional aid.

UNDERGRADUATE EXPENSES for 2013–2014 *Application fee:* $50. *Tuition, state resident:* full-time $5570; part-time $232 per credit hour. *Tuition, nonresident:* full-time $14,720; part-time $613 per credit hour. *Required fees:* full-time $2075; $84.42 per credit hour or $24.50 per term. Full-time tuition and fees vary according to program. Part-time tuition and fees vary according to course load and program. *College room and board:* $12,446. Room and board charges vary according to board plan and housing facility.

FRESHMAN FINANCIAL AID (Fall 2012, est.) 2,061 applied for aid; of those 57% were deemed to have need. 100% of freshmen with need received aid; of those 12% had need fully met. *Average percent of need met:* 66% (excluding resources awarded to replace EFC). *Average financial aid package:* $10,590 (excluding resources awarded to replace EFC). 1% of all full-time freshmen had no need and received non-need-based gift aid.

UNDERGRADUATE FINANCIAL AID (Fall 2012, est.) 8,109 applied for aid; of those 70% were deemed to have need. 100% of undergraduates with need received aid; of those 20% had need fully met. *Average percent of need met:* 74% (excluding resources awarded to replace EFC). *Average financial aid package:* $11,783 (excluding resources awarded to replace EFC). 2% of all full-time undergraduates had no need and received non-need-based gift aid.

GIFT AID (NEED-BASED) *Total amount:* $34,374,809 (46% federal, 46% state, 5% institutional, 3% external sources). *Receiving aid:* Freshmen: 37% (953); all full-time undergraduates: 39% (4,683). *Average award:* Freshmen: $7706; Undergraduates: $7230. *Scholarships, grants, and awards:* Federal Pell, FSEOG, state, private, college/university gift aid from institutional funds.

GIFT AID (NON-NEED-BASED) *Total amount:* $1,893,068 (46% state, 16% institutional, 38% external sources). *Receiving aid:* Freshmen: 6% (164). Undergraduates: 5% (581). *Average award:* Freshmen: $3439. Undergraduates: $6709. *Scholarships, grants, and awards by category:* Academic interests/achievement: 215 awards ($356,000 total): area/ethnic studies, biological sciences, business, computer science, education, engineering/technologies, English, foreign languages, general academic interests/achievements, health fields, humanities, international studies, mathematics, physical sciences, premedicine, social sciences. *Creative arts/performance:* 15 awards ($14,000 total): art/fine arts, cinema/film/broadcasting, creative writing, dance, general creative arts/performance, journalism/publications, music, performing arts, theater/drama. *Special achievements/activities:* 399 awards ($436,923 total): community service, general special achievements/activities, leadership. *Special characteristics:* 85 awards ($175,000 total): adult students, children of faculty/staff, ethnic background, first-generation college students, handicapped students, international students, local/state students, married students, members of minority groups, out-of-state students. *ROTC:* Army cooperative, Air Force cooperative.

LOANS *Student loans:* $75,485,161 (73% need-based, 27% non-need-based). 53% of past graduating class borrowed through all loan programs. *Average indebtedness per student:* $23,710. *Average need-based loan:* Freshmen: $4141. Undergraduates: $5482. *Parent loans:* $13,370,884 (68% need-based, 32% non-need-based). *Programs:* Federal Direct (Subsidized and Unsubsidized Stafford, PLUS), Perkins, Federal Nursing, college/university.

WORK-STUDY *Federal work-study:* Total amount: $596,666; 353 jobs averaging $1417.

ATHLETIC AWARDS Total amount: $3,840,906 (100% non-need-based).

APPLYING FOR FINANCIAL AID *Required financial aid forms:* FAFSA, state aid form. *Financial aid deadline (priority):* 2/1. *Notification date:* Continuous beginning 3/4. Students must reply within 2 weeks of notification.

CONTACT Mr. Dennis Chavez, Director of Student Financial Aid and Student Records, Binghamton University, State University of New York, PO Box 6000, Binghamton, NY 13902-6000, 607-777-2428. *Fax:* 607-777-6897. *E-mail:* finaid@binghamton.edu.
Website: http://www.binghamton.edu/.

BIOLA UNIVERSITY
La Mirada, CA

Tuition & fees: $31,004	Average undergraduate aid package: $17,348

ABOUT THE INSTITUTION Independent interdenominational, coed. *Awards:* certificates, bachelor's, master's, and doctoral degrees. 78 undergraduate majors. *Total enrollment:* 1,965. Undergraduates: 8,674. Freshmen: 930. Both federal and institutional methodology are used as a basis for awarding need-based institutional aid.

UNDERGRADUATE EXPENSES for 2013–2014 *Application fee:* $45. *Comprehensive fee:* $38,916 includes full-time tuition ($31,004) and room and board ($7912). *College room only:* $4732. Full-time tuition and fees vary according to course load. Room and board charges vary according to board plan, housing facility, and location. *Part-time tuition:* $1292 per unit. Part-time tuition and fees vary according to course load.

FRESHMAN FINANCIAL AID (Fall 2011) 803 applied for aid; of those 80% were deemed to have need. 99% of freshmen with need received aid; of those 6% had need fully met. *Average percent of need met:* 50% (excluding resources awarded to replace EFC). *Average financial aid package:* $16,773 (excluding resources awarded to replace EFC). 22% of all full-time freshmen had no need and received non-need-based gift aid.

UNDERGRADUATE FINANCIAL AID (Fall 2011) 3,200 applied for aid; of those 87% were deemed to have need. 99% of undergraduates with need received aid; of those 5% had need fully met. *Average percent of need met:* 50% (excluding resources awarded to replace EFC). *Average financial aid package:* $17,348 (excluding resources awarded to replace EFC). 20% of all full-time undergraduates had no need and received non-need-based gift aid.

GIFT AID (NEED-BASED) *Total amount:* $33,518,036 (17% federal, 21% state, 62% institutional). *Receiving aid:* Freshmen: 68% (625); all full-time undergraduates: 67% (2,657). *Average award:* Freshmen: $12,990; Undergraduates: $12,496. *Scholarships, grants, and awards:* Federal Pell, FSEOG, state, private, college/university gift aid from institutional funds.

GIFT AID (NON-NEED-BASED) *Total amount:* $4,967,291 (100% institutional). *Receiving aid:* Freshmen: 2% (22). Undergraduates: 2% (68). *Average award:* Freshmen: $6523. Undergraduates: $6009. *Scholarships, grants, and awards by category:* Academic interests/achievement: biological sciences, communication, general academic interests/achievements. Creative arts/performance: art/fine arts, cinema/film/broadcasting, journalism/publications, music, theater/drama. Special achievements/activities: community service, leadership. Special characteristics: adult students, children and siblings of alumni, children of faculty/staff, ethnic background, international students, relatives of clergy. *ROTC:* Army cooperative, Air Force cooperative.

LOANS *Student loans:* $25,509,174 (80% need-based, 20% non-need-based). 73% of past graduating class borrowed through all loan programs. *Average indebtedness per student:* $34,587. *Average need-based loan:* Freshmen: $2752. Undergraduates: $3509. *Parent loans:* $5,873,448 (100% non-need-based). *Programs:* Federal Direct (Subsidized and Unsubsidized Stafford, PLUS), Perkins, Federal Nursing, college/university, alternative loans.

WORK-STUDY *Federal work-study:* Total amount: $552,596; 501 jobs averaging $1106.

ATHLETIC AWARDS Total amount: $1,760,828 (63% need-based, 37% non-need-based).

APPLYING FOR FINANCIAL AID *Required financial aid forms:* FAFSA, state aid form. *Financial aid deadline (priority):* 3/1. *Notification date:* Continuous beginning 3/1.

CONTACT Jonathan Choy, Office of Financial Aid, Biola University, 13800 Biola Avenue, La Mirada, CA 90639-0001, 562-903-4742 or toll-free 800-652-4652. *Fax:* 562-906-4541. *E-mail:* finaid@biola.edu. *Website:* http://www.biola.edu/.

BIRMINGHAM-SOUTHERN COLLEGE
Birmingham, AL

CONTACT Financial Aid Office, Birmingham-Southern College, 900 Arkadelphia Road, Birmingham, AL 35254, 205-226-4688 or toll-free 800-523-5793. *Fax:* 205-226-3082. *E-mail:* finaid@bsc.edu. *Website:* http://www.bsc.edu/.

BIRTHINGWAY COLLEGE OF MIDWIFERY
Portland, OR

CONTACT Financial Aid Office, Birthingway College of Midwifery, 12113 SE Foster Road, Portland, OR 97299, 503-760-3131. *Website:* http://www.birthingway.edu/.

BLACKBURN COLLEGE
Carlinville, IL

CONTACT Mrs. Jane Kelsey, Financial Aid Administrator, Blackburn College, 700 College Avenue, Carlinville, IL 62626-1498, 217-854-3231 Ext. 4227 or toll-free 800-233-3550. *Fax:* 217-854-3731. *Website:* http://www.blackburn.edu/.

BLACK HILLS STATE UNIVERSITY
Spearfish, SD

CONTACT Ms. Deb Henriksen, Director of Financial Aid, Black Hills State University, 1200 University Street, Spearfish, SD 57799-9670, 605-642-6581 or toll-free 800-255-2478. *Fax:* 605-642-6913. *E-mail:* deb.henriksen@bhsu.edu. *Website:* http://www.bhsu.edu/.

BLESSING-RIEMAN COLLEGE OF NURSING
Quincy, IL

CONTACT Mrs. Misty McBee, Financial Aid Coordinator, Blessing-Rieman College of Nursing, Broadway at 11th Street, PO Box 7005, Quincy, IL 62301, 217-223-8400 Ext. 6993 or toll-free 800-877-9140 Ext. 6964. *Fax:* 217-223-1781. *E-mail:* mmcbee@brcn.edu. *Website:* http://www.brcn.edu/.

BLOOMFIELD COLLEGE
Bloomfield, NJ

Tuition & fees: $25,050	Average undergraduate aid package: $22,693

ABOUT THE INSTITUTION Independent Presbyterian Church (U.S.A.), coed. *Awards:* certificates, bachelor's, and master's degrees. 20 undergraduate majors. *Total enrollment:* 2,045. Undergraduates: 2,036. Freshmen: 382. Federal methodology is used as a basis for awarding need-based institutional aid.

UNDERGRADUATE EXPENSES for 2013–2014 *Application fee:* $40. *Comprehensive fee:* $35,750 includes full-time tuition ($23,850), mandatory fees ($1200), and room and board ($10,700). *College room only:* $5350. Room and board charges vary according to housing facility. *Part-time tuition:* $2980 per course. Part-time tuition and fees vary according to course load.

FRESHMAN FINANCIAL AID (Fall 2012, est.) 368 applied for aid; of those 99% were deemed to have need. 100% of freshmen with need received aid; of those 2% had need fully met. *Average percent of need met:* 56% (excluding resources awarded to replace EFC). *Average financial aid package:* $23,844 (excluding resources awarded to replace EFC). 1% of all full-time freshmen had no need and received non-need-based gift aid.

UNDERGRADUATE FINANCIAL AID (Fall 2012, est.) 1,711 applied for aid; of those 94% were deemed to have need. 100% of undergraduates with need received aid; of those 2% had need fully met. *Average percent of need met:* 56% (excluding resources awarded to replace EFC). *Average financial aid package:* $22,693

(excluding resources awarded to replace EFC). 4% of all full-time undergraduates had no need and received non-need-based gift aid.

GIFT AID (NEED-BASED) *Total amount:* $26,094,501 (25% federal, 40% state, 35% institutional). *Receiving aid:* Freshmen: 93% (348); all full-time undergraduates: 89% (1,540). *Average award:* Freshmen: $17,965; Undergraduates: $15,904. *Scholarships, grants, and awards:* Federal Pell, FSEOG, state, private, college/university gift aid from institutional funds.

GIFT AID (NON-NEED-BASED) *Total amount:* $4,358,284 (1% state, 97% institutional, 2% external sources). *Receiving aid:* Freshmen: 35% (129). Undergraduates: 35% (615). *Average award:* Freshmen: $7500. Undergraduates: $14,329. *Scholarships, grants, and awards by category:* Academic interests/achievement: 418 awards ($2,345,519 total): biological sciences, business, computer science, education, English, general academic interests/achievements, health fields, humanities, mathematics, physical sciences, religion/biblical studies, social sciences. *Creative arts/performance:* 1 award ($1500 total): applied art and design, art/fine arts, cinema/film/broadcasting, general creative arts/performance, performing arts, theater/drama. *Special achievements/activities:* 282 awards ($2,290,922 total): community service, general special achievements/activities, leadership. *Special characteristics:* 65 awards ($721,387 total): adult students, children and siblings of alumni, children of current students, general special characteristics, international students, out-of-state students, siblings of current students, spouses of current students. *Tuition waivers:* Full or partial for employees or children of employees, senior citizens. *ROTC:* Army cooperative.

LOANS *Student loans:* $14,176,993 (50% need-based, 50% non-need-based). 92% of past graduating class borrowed through all loan programs. *Average indebtedness per student:* $20,467. *Average need-based loan:* Freshmen: $3460. Undergraduates: $4197. *Parent loans:* $1,754,714 (100% non-need-based). *Programs:* Federal Direct (Subsidized and Unsubsidized Stafford, PLUS).

WORK-STUDY *Federal work-study:* Total amount: $1,093,322; 484 jobs averaging $2170. *State or other work-study/employment:* Part-time jobs available.

ATHLETIC AWARDS Total amount: $1,516,016 (100% non-need-based).

APPLYING FOR FINANCIAL AID *Required financial aid form:* FAFSA. *Financial aid deadline:* 6/1 (priority: 3/15). *Notification date:* Continuous beginning 2/15. Students must reply within 2 weeks of notification.

CONTACT Ms. Jamie Shahin, Acting Director of Financial Aid, Bloomfield College, 467 Franklin Street, Bloomfield, NJ 07003-9981, 973-748-9000 Ext. 1213 or toll-free 800-848-4555 Ext. 230. *Fax:* 973-748-9735. *E-mail:* jamie_shahin@bloomfield.edu. *Website:* http://www.bloomfield.edu/.

BLOOMSBURG UNIVERSITY OF PENNSYLVANIA
Bloomsburg, PA

Tuition & fees (PA res): $8343	Average undergraduate aid package: $8391

ABOUT THE INSTITUTION State-supported, coed. *Awards:* certificates, bachelor's, master's, and doctoral degrees. 40 undergraduate majors. *Total enrollment:* 9,950. Undergraduates: 9,201. Freshmen: 1,924. Federal methodology is used as a basis for awarding need-based institutional aid.

UNDERGRADUATE EXPENSES for 2013–2014 *Application fee:* $35. *Tuition, state resident:* full-time $6428; part-time $268 per credit. *Tuition, nonresident:* full-time $16,070; part-time $670 per credit. *Required fees:* full-time $1915; $70.25 per credit or $55 per term. Full-time tuition and fees vary according to course load and location. Part-time tuition and fees vary according to course load and location. *College room and board:* $7498; *Room only:* $4598. Room and board charges vary according to board plan and housing facility.

FRESHMAN FINANCIAL AID (Fall 2012, est.) 1,740 applied for aid; of those 73% were deemed to have need. 97% of freshmen with need received aid; of those 8% had need fully met. *Average percent of need met:* 48% (excluding resources awarded to replace EFC). *Average financial aid package:* $7274 (excluding resources awarded to replace EFC). 2% of all full-time freshmen had no need and received non-need-based gift aid.

UNDERGRADUATE FINANCIAL AID (Fall 2012, est.) 7,421 applied for aid; of those 75% were deemed to have need. 98% of undergraduates with need received aid; of those 13% had need fully met. *Average percent of need met:* 56% (excluding resources awarded to replace EFC). *Average financial aid package:* $8391

(excluding resources awarded to replace EFC). 2% of all full-time undergraduates had no need and received non-need-based gift aid.

GIFT AID (NEED-BASED) *Total amount:* $19,807,481 (59% federal, 39% state, 2% institutional). *Receiving aid:* Freshmen: 39% (746); all full-time undergraduates: 39% (3,359). *Average award:* Freshmen: $5911; Undergraduates: $5474. *Scholarships, grants, and awards:* Federal Pell, FSEOG, state, private, college/university gift aid from institutional funds.

GIFT AID (NON-NEED-BASED) *Total amount:* $2,317,664 (12% state, 34% institutional, 54% external sources). *Receiving aid:* Freshmen: 14% (272). Undergraduates: 9% (779). *Average award:* Freshmen: $1699. Undergraduates: $1553. *Scholarships, grants, and awards by category:* Academic interests/achievement: 465 awards ($689,559 total): biological sciences, business, communication, computer science, education, English, foreign languages, general academic interests/achievements, health fields, humanities, international studies, mathematics, physical sciences, religion/biblical studies, social sciences. *Special characteristics:* 265 awards ($995,223 total): children of faculty/staff, international students. *Tuition waivers:* Full or partial for minority students, employees or children of employees, senior citizens. *ROTC:* Army, Air Force cooperative.

LOANS *Student loans:* $57,302,313 (39% need-based, 61% non-need-based). 71% of past graduating class borrowed through all loan programs. *Average indebtedness per student:* $27,223. *Average need-based loan:* Freshmen: $3359. Undergraduates: $4224. *Parent loans:* $9,804,651 (100% non-need-based). *Programs:* Federal Direct (Subsidized and Unsubsidized Stafford, PLUS), Perkins, state, alternative loans.

WORK-STUDY *Federal work-study:* Total amount: $1,671,757; 669 jobs averaging $2475. *State or other work-study/employment:* Total amount: $4,321,903 (100% non-need-based). 1,143 part-time jobs averaging $3724.

ATHLETIC AWARDS Total amount: $482,300 (100% non-need-based).

APPLYING FOR FINANCIAL AID *Required financial aid form:* FAFSA. *Financial aid deadline (priority):* 3/15. *Notification date:* Continuous beginning 4/1.

CONTACT Mr. John J. Bieryla, Director of Financial Aid, Bloomsburg University of Pennsylvania, 119 Warren Student Services Center, 400 East 2nd Street, Bloomsburg, PA 17815-1301, 570-389-4279. *Fax:* 570-389-4795. *E-mail:* stfinaid@bloomu.edu. *Website:* http://www.bloomu.edu/.

BLUEFIELD COLLEGE
Bluefield, VA

Tuition & fees: $21,060	Average undergraduate aid package: $14,060

ABOUT THE INSTITUTION Independent Southern Baptist, coed. *Awards:* bachelor's degrees. 41 undergraduate majors. *Total enrollment:* 828. Undergraduates: 828. Freshmen: 144. Federal methodology is used as a basis for awarding need-based institutional aid.

UNDERGRADUATE EXPENSES for 2013–2014 *Comprehensive fee:* $28,700 includes full-time tuition ($21,060) and room and board ($7640). *College room only:* $2990. Full-time tuition and fees vary according to course load and program. Room and board charges vary according to housing facility. *Part-time tuition:* $880 per credit. Part-time tuition and fees vary according to course load and program.

FRESHMAN FINANCIAL AID (Fall 2012, est.) 136 applied for aid; of those 93% were deemed to have need. 100% of freshmen with need received aid; of those 17% had need fully met. *Average percent of need met:* 69% (excluding resources awarded to replace EFC). *Average financial aid package:* $16,297 (excluding resources awarded to replace EFC). 12% of all full-time freshmen had no need and received non-need-based gift aid.

UNDERGRADUATE FINANCIAL AID (Fall 2012, est.) 677 applied for aid; of those 95% were deemed to have need. 99% of undergraduates with need received aid; of those 14% had need fully met. *Average percent of need met:* 58% (excluding resources awarded to replace EFC). *Average financial aid package:* $14,060 (excluding resources awarded to replace EFC). 8% of all full-time undergraduates had no need and received non-need-based gift aid.

GIFT AID (NEED-BASED) *Total amount:* $5,074,780 (31% federal, 21% state, 38% institutional, 10% external sources). *Receiving aid:* Freshmen: 86% (127); all full-time undergraduates: 85% (621). *Average award:* Freshmen: $13,167; Undergraduates: $10,273. *Scholarships, grants, and awards:* Federal Pell, FSEOG, state, private, college/university gift aid from institutional funds.

GIFT AID (NON-NEED-BASED) *Total amount:* $688,680 (32% state, 57% institutional, 11% external sources). *Receiving aid:* Freshmen: 11% (17). Undergraduates: 7% (52). *Average award:* Freshmen: $3902. Undergraduates: $5239. *Scholarships, grants, and awards by category: Academic interests/achievement:* 19 awards ($349,755 total): general academic interests/achievements. *Creative arts/performance:* 70 awards ($186,050 total): art/fine arts, music, performing arts, theater/drama. *Special achievements/activities:* 13 awards ($28,800 total): cheerleading/drum major. *Special characteristics:* 163 awards ($343,902 total): adult students, children of faculty/staff, ethnic background, first-generation college students, general special characteristics, local/state students, members of minority groups, out-of-state students, religious affiliation, veterans, veterans' children. *Tuition waivers:* Full or partial for employees or children of employees, senior citizens.

LOANS *Student loans:* $5,382,496 (85% need-based, 15% non-need-based). 83% of past graduating class borrowed through all loan programs. *Average indebtedness per student:* $20,934. *Average need-based loan:* Freshmen: $3691. Undergraduates: $4727. *Parent loans:* $1,118,162 (40% need-based, 60% non-need-based). *Programs:* Federal Direct (Subsidized and Unsubsidized Stafford, PLUS), alternative loans.

WORK-STUDY *Federal work-study:* Total amount: $61,750; 79 jobs averaging $782.

ATHLETIC AWARDS Total amount: $1,641,379 (79% need-based, 21% non-need-based).

APPLYING FOR FINANCIAL AID *Required financial aid forms:* FAFSA, state aid form. *Financial aid deadline (priority):* 6/1. *Notification date:* Continuous. Students must reply by 8/24.

CONTACT Ms. Carly Jean Kestner, Director of Financial Aid, Bluefield College, 3000 College Drive, Bluefield, VA 24605, 276-326-4215 or toll-free 800-872-0175. *Fax:* 276-326-4356. *E-mail:* ckestner@bluefield.edu. *Website:* http://www.bluefield.edu/.

BLUEFIELD STATE COLLEGE
Bluefield, WV

Tuition & fees: N/R	Average undergraduate aid package: $3539

ABOUT THE INSTITUTION State-supported, coed. *Awards:* associate and bachelor's degrees. 17 undergraduate majors. *Total enrollment:* 1,935. Undergraduates: 1,935. Freshmen: 307. Federal methodology is used as a basis for awarding need-based institutional aid.

UNDERGRADUATE EXPENSES for 2013–2014 *Tuition, area resident:* part-time $217 per credit hour. *Tuition, state resident:* part-time $314 per credit hour. *Tuition, nonresident:* part-time $414 per credit hour.

FRESHMAN FINANCIAL AID (Fall 2012, est.) 278 applied for aid; of those 84% were deemed to have need. 100% of freshmen with need received aid; of those 8% had need fully met. *Average percent of need met:* 67% (excluding resources awarded to replace EFC). *Average financial aid package:* $3243 (excluding resources awarded to replace EFC). 11% of all full-time freshmen had no need and received non-need-based gift aid.

UNDERGRADUATE FINANCIAL AID (Fall 2012, est.) 1,426 applied for aid; of those 90% were deemed to have need. 99% of undergraduates with need received aid; of those 16% had need fully met. *Average percent of need met:* 69% (excluding resources awarded to replace EFC). *Average financial aid package:* $3539 (excluding resources awarded to replace EFC). 5% of all full-time undergraduates had no need and received non-need-based gift aid.

GIFT AID (NEED-BASED) *Total amount:* $7,108,644 (79% federal, 21% state). *Receiving aid:* Freshmen: 73% (219); all full-time undergraduates: 74% (1,168). *Average award:* Freshmen: $3721; Undergraduates: $3638. *Scholarships, grants, and awards:* Federal Pell, FSEOG, state.

GIFT AID (NON-NEED-BASED) *Total amount:* $1,473,045 (37% state, 22% institutional, 41% external sources). *Receiving aid:* Freshmen: 25% (75). Undergraduates: 14% (215). *Average award:* Freshmen: $1108. Undergraduates: $1207. *Scholarships, grants, and awards by category: Academic interests/achievement:* engineering/technologies, general academic interests/achievements. *Special achievements/activities:* cheerleading/drum major, general special achievements/activities, junior miss, leadership. *Special characteristics:* general special characteristics. *Tuition waivers:* Full or partial for adult students, senior citizens.

LOANS *Student loans:* $8,581,975 (46% need-based, 54% non-need-based). 72% of past graduating class borrowed through all loan programs. *Average indebtedness per student:* $24,999. *Average need-based loan:* Freshmen: $3706. Undergraduates: $4232. *Parent loans:* $103,920 (100% non-need-based). *Programs:* Federal Direct (Subsidized and Unsubsidized Stafford, PLUS), Perkins.

WORK-STUDY *Federal work-study:* Total amount: $186,810; jobs available. *State or other work-study/employment:* Total amount: $220,000 (100% non-need-based). Part-time jobs available.

ATHLETIC AWARDS Total amount: $337,932 (100% need-based).

APPLYING FOR FINANCIAL AID *Required financial aid forms:* FAFSA, institution's own form. *Financial aid deadline (priority):* 3/1. *Notification date:* 6/1.

CONTACT Mr. Tom Ilse, Director of Financial Aid, Bluefield State College, 219 Rock Street, Bluefield, WV 24701-2198, 304-327-4020 or toll-free 800-344-8892 Ext. 4065 (in-state), 800-654-7798 Ext. 4065 (out-of-state). *Fax:* 304-325-7747. *E-mail:* tilse@bluefieldstate.edu. *Website:* http://www.bluefieldstate.edu/.

BLUE MOUNTAIN COLLEGE
Blue Mountain, MS

Tuition & fees: $9230	Average undergraduate aid package: $9636

ABOUT THE INSTITUTION Independent Southern Baptist, coed. *Awards:* bachelor's and master's degrees. 22 undergraduate majors. *Total enrollment:* 513. Undergraduates: 502. Freshmen: 69. Federal methodology is used as a basis for awarding need-based institutional aid.

UNDERGRADUATE EXPENSES for 2013–2014 *Application fee:* $10. *Comprehensive fee:* $13,230 includes full-time tuition ($8250), mandatory fees ($980), and room and board ($4000). Full-time tuition and fees vary according to course load and degree level. Room and board charges vary according to board plan. *Part-time tuition:* $275 per semester hour. *Part-time fees:* $365 per term. Part-time tuition and fees vary according to course load and degree level.

FRESHMAN FINANCIAL AID (Fall 2012, est.) 67 applied for aid; of those 79% were deemed to have need. 100% of freshmen with need received aid; of those 32% had need fully met. *Average percent of need met:* 76% (excluding resources awarded to replace EFC). *Average financial aid package:* $11,620 (excluding resources awarded to replace EFC). 6% of all full-time freshmen had no need and received non-need-based gift aid.

UNDERGRADUATE FINANCIAL AID (Fall 2012, est.) 484 applied for aid; of those 95% were deemed to have need. 100% of undergraduates with need received aid; of those 82% had need fully met. *Average percent of need met:* 45% (excluding resources awarded to replace EFC). *Average financial aid package:* $9636 (excluding resources awarded to replace EFC). 51% of all full-time undergraduates had no need and received non-need-based gift aid.

GIFT AID (NEED-BASED) *Total amount:* $2,118,152 (52% federal, 11% state, 32% institutional, 5% external sources). *Receiving aid:* Freshmen: 73% (52); all full-time undergraduates: 76% (375). *Average award:* Freshmen: $11,750; Undergraduates: $4173. *Scholarships, grants, and awards:* Federal Pell, FSEOG, state, private, college/university gift aid from institutional funds.

GIFT AID (NON-NEED-BASED) *Total amount:* $282,265 (3% federal, 97% institutional). *Receiving aid:* Freshmen: 34% (24). Undergraduates: 93% (458). *Average award:* Freshmen: $925. *Scholarships, grants, and awards by category: Academic interests/achievement:* biological sciences, business, education, English, general academic interests/achievements, health fields, humanities, library science, mathematics, physical sciences, premedicine, religion/biblical studies, social sciences. *Creative arts/performance:* art/fine arts, music, theater/drama. *Special achievements/activities:* general special achievements/activities, leadership, memberships, religious involvement. *Special characteristics:* children and siblings of alumni, children of current students, children of faculty/staff, married students, parents of current students, religious affiliation, siblings of current students, spouses of current students, twins. *Tuition waivers:* Full or partial for employees or children of employees.

LOANS *Student loans:* $1,781,270 (52% need-based, 48% non-need-based). 69% of past graduating class borrowed through all loan programs. *Average indebtedness per student:* $23,107. *Average need-based loan:* Freshmen: $2755. Undergraduates: $4490. *Parent loans:* $86,359 (100% non-need-based). *Programs:* Federal Direct (Subsidized and Unsubsidized Stafford, PLUS), Perkins.

WORK-STUDY *Federal work-study:* Total amount: $51,474; 56 jobs averaging $507. *State or other work-study/employment:* Total amount: $54,323 (100% non-need-based). 55 part-time jobs averaging $406.
ATHLETIC AWARDS Total amount: $904,329 (100% non-need-based).
APPLYING FOR FINANCIAL AID *Required financial aid forms:* FAFSA, state aid form. *Financial aid deadline (priority):* 3/1. *Notification date:* Continuous beginning 4/1. Students must reply within 2 weeks of notification.
CONTACT Mrs. Michelle L. Hall, Director of Financial Aid, Blue Mountain College, PO Box 160, Blue Mountain, MS 38610-0160, 662-685-4771 Ext. 141 or toll-free 800-235-0136. *Fax:* 662-685-4776. *E-mail:* financialaid@bmc.edu.
Website: http://www.bmc.edu/.

BLUFFTON UNIVERSITY
Bluffton, OH

Tuition & fees: $27,426	Average undergraduate aid package: $24,591

ABOUT THE INSTITUTION Independent Mennonite, coed. *Awards:* bachelor's and master's degrees. 38 undergraduate majors. *Total enrollment:* 1,198. Undergraduates: 1,077. Freshmen: 239. Both federal and institutional methodology are used as a basis for awarding need-based institutional aid.
UNDERGRADUATE EXPENSES for 2013–2014 *Application fee:* $20. *Comprehensive fee:* $36,436 includes full-time tuition ($26,976), mandatory fees ($450), and room and board ($9010). Full-time tuition and fees vary according to course load and reciprocity agreements. Room and board charges vary according to board plan and housing facility. *Part-time tuition:* $1124 per credit hour. *Part-time fees:* $113 per term. Part-time tuition and fees vary according to course load.
FRESHMAN FINANCIAL AID (Fall 2012, est.) 233 applied for aid; of those 93% were deemed to have need. 100% of freshmen with need received aid; of those 49% had need fully met. *Average percent of need met:* 92% (excluding resources awarded to replace EFC). *Average financial aid package:* $26,015 (excluding resources awarded to replace EFC). 9% of all full-time freshmen had no need and received non-need-based gift aid.
UNDERGRADUATE FINANCIAL AID (Fall 2012, est.) 708 applied for aid; of those 94% were deemed to have need. 100% of undergraduates with need received aid; of those 42% had need fully met. *Average percent of need met:* 88% (excluding resources awarded to replace EFC). *Average financial aid package:* $24,591 (excluding resources awarded to replace EFC). 10% of all full-time undergraduates had no need and received non-need-based gift aid.
GIFT AID (NEED-BASED) *Total amount:* $11,233,977 (17% federal, 5% state, 74% institutional, 4% external sources). *Receiving aid:* Freshmen: 91% (217); all full-time undergraduates: 80% (667). *Average award:* Freshmen: $19,998; Undergraduates: $17,939. *Scholarships, grants, and awards:* Federal Pell, FSEOG, state, private, college/university gift aid from institutional funds.
GIFT AID (NON-NEED-BASED) *Total amount:* $2,183,021 (90% institutional, 10% external sources). *Receiving aid:* Freshmen: 8% (18). Undergraduates: 6% (47). *Average award:* Freshmen: $12,820. Undergraduates: $13,071. *Scholarships, grants, and awards by category:* Academic interests/achievement: 515 awards ($5,480,681 total): general academic interests/achievements. Creative arts/performance: 51 awards ($66,000 total): art/fine arts, music. Special characteristics: 359 awards ($1,166,265 total): children of faculty/staff, international students, members of minority groups, out-of-state students, religious affiliation. *Tuition waivers:* Full or partial for employees or children of employees.
LOANS *Student loans:* $7,920,364 (94% need-based, 6% non-need-based). 85% of past graduating class borrowed through all loan programs. *Average indebtedness per student:* $37,879. *Average need-based loan:* Freshmen: $4369. Undergraduates: $4832. *Parent loans:* $1,926,816 (69% need-based, 31% non-need-based). *Programs:* Federal Direct (Subsidized and Unsubsidized Stafford, PLUS), Perkins, alternative loans.
WORK-STUDY *Federal work-study:* Total amount: $1,255,320; 557 jobs averaging $2225. *State or other work-study/employment:* Total amount: $417,375 (49% need-based, 51% non-need-based). 182 part-time jobs averaging $2265.
APPLYING FOR FINANCIAL AID *Required financial aid form:* FAFSA. *Financial aid deadline:* 10/1 (priority: 5/1). *Notification date:* Continuous beginning 3/1. Students must reply within 3 weeks of notification.

CONTACT Lawrence Matthews, Director of Financial Aid, Bluffton University, 1 University Drive, Bluffton, OH 45817-2104, 419-358-3266 or toll-free 800-488-3257. *Fax:* 419-358-3073. *E-mail:* matthewsl@bluffton.edu.
Website: http://www.bluffton.edu/.

BOB JONES UNIVERSITY
Greenville, SC

Tuition & fees: $13,430	Average undergraduate aid package: $12,000

ABOUT THE INSTITUTION Independent Christian, coed. *Awards:* certificates, associate, bachelor's, master's, and doctoral degrees. 50 undergraduate majors. *Total enrollment:* 3,469. Undergraduates: 2,976. Freshmen: 695. Federal methodology is used as a basis for awarding need-based institutional aid.
UNDERGRADUATE EXPENSES for 2013–2014 *Comprehensive fee:* $19,220 includes full-time tuition ($12,820), mandatory fees ($610), and room and board ($5790). Full-time tuition and fees vary according to program. *Part-time tuition:* $624 per credit hour. Part-time tuition and fees vary according to program.
FRESHMAN FINANCIAL AID (Fall 2011) 536 applied for aid; of those 90% were deemed to have need. 96% of freshmen with need received aid. *Average percent of need met:* 46% (excluding resources awarded to replace EFC). *Average financial aid package:* $10,500 (excluding resources awarded to replace EFC).
UNDERGRADUATE FINANCIAL AID (Fall 2011) 2,210 applied for aid; of those 93% were deemed to have need. 96% of undergraduates with need received aid. *Average percent of need met:* 46% (excluding resources awarded to replace EFC). *Average financial aid package:* $12,000 (excluding resources awarded to replace EFC).
GIFT AID (NEED-BASED) *Total amount:* $13,950,000 (35% federal, 28% state, 27% institutional, 10% external sources). *Receiving aid:* Freshmen: 61% (423); all full-time undergraduates: 62% (1,729). *Average award:* Freshmen: $6500; Undergraduates: $6500. *Scholarships, grants, and awards:* Federal Pell, FSEOG, state, private, college/university gift aid from institutional funds.
GIFT AID (NON-NEED-BASED) *Receiving aid:* Freshmen: 5% (34). Undergraduates: 9% (240). *Tuition waivers:* Full or partial for employees or children of employees, senior citizens.
LOANS *Student loans:* $9,200,000 (100% need-based). *Average need-based loan:* Freshmen: $32,950. Undergraduates: $3936. *Parent loans:* $1,700,000 (100% non-need-based). *Programs:* Federal Direct (Subsidized and Unsubsidized Stafford, PLUS), college/university.
WORK-STUDY Federal work-study jobs available. *State or other work-study/employment:* Total amount: $3,800,000 (100% non-need-based). Part-time jobs available.
APPLYING FOR FINANCIAL AID *Required financial aid form:* FAFSA. *Financial aid deadline:* Continuous. *Notification date:* Continuous.
CONTACT Office of Financial Aid, Bob Jones University, 1700 Wade Hampton Boulevard, Greenville, SC 29614, 864-242-5100 Ext. 3040 or toll-free 800-BJANDME. *E-mail:* finaid@bju.edu.
Website: http://www.bju.edu/.

BOISE BIBLE COLLEGE
Boise, ID

CONTACT Beth Turner, Financial Aid Counselor, Boise Bible College, 8695 West Marigold Street, Boise, ID 83714-1220, 208-376-7731 Ext. 12 or toll-free 800-893-7755. *Fax:* 208-376-7743. *E-mail:* betht@boisebible.edu.
Website: http://www.boisebible.edu/.

BOISE STATE UNIVERSITY
Boise, ID

Tuition & fees (ID res): $5884	Average undergraduate aid package: $9738

ABOUT THE INSTITUTION State-supported, coed. *Awards:* certificates, associate, bachelor's, master's, and doctoral degrees. 89 undergraduate majors. *Total enrollment:* 22,674. Undergraduates: 19,653. Freshmen: 2,373. Federal methodology is used as a basis for awarding need-based institutional aid.

UNDERGRADUATE EXPENSES for 2013–2014 *Application fee:* $50. *Tuition, state resident:* full-time $3990; part-time $239 per credit hour. *Tuition, nonresident:* full-time $15,430; part-time $331 per credit hour. *Required fees:* full-time $1894; $92 per credit hour or $92 per credit hour. Full-time tuition and fees vary according to reciprocity agreements. *College room and board:* $7174; *Room only:* $3674. Room and board charges vary according to board plan and housing facility.

FRESHMAN FINANCIAL AID (Fall 2012, est.) 1,494 applied for aid; of those 94% were deemed to have need. 100% of freshmen with need received aid; of those 47% had need fully met. *Average percent of need met:* 16% (excluding resources awarded to replace EFC). *Average financial aid package:* $9867 (excluding resources awarded to replace EFC). 20% of all full-time freshmen had no need and received non-need-based gift aid.

UNDERGRADUATE FINANCIAL AID (Fall 2012, est.) 8,647 applied for aid; of those 90% were deemed to have need. 100% of undergraduates with need received aid; of those 35% had need fully met. *Average percent of need met:* 20% (excluding resources awarded to replace EFC). *Average financial aid package:* $9738 (excluding resources awarded to replace EFC). 7% of all full-time undergraduates had no need and received non-need-based gift aid.

GIFT AID (NEED-BASED) *Total amount:* $37,973,291 (82% federal, 3% state, 11% institutional, 4% external sources). *Receiving aid:* Freshmen: 51% (1,141); all full-time undergraduates: 47% (6,004). *Average award:* Freshmen: $4580; Undergraduates: $4867. *Scholarships, grants, and awards:* Federal Pell, FSEOG, state, private, college/university gift aid from institutional funds, Leveraging Educational Assistance Program (LEAP).

GIFT AID (NON-NEED-BASED) *Total amount:* $1,765,659 (9% federal, 13% state, 55% institutional, 23% external sources). *Receiving aid:* Freshmen: 9% (208). Undergraduates: 4% (449). *Average award:* Freshmen: $1157. Undergraduates: $1317. *Scholarships, grants, and awards by category:* Academic interests/achievement: 2,136 awards ($4,298,166 total): biological sciences, business, communication, computer science, education, engineering/technologies, English, foreign languages, general academic interests/achievements, health fields, humanities, international studies, mathematics, military science, physical sciences, premedicine, social sciences. *Creative arts/performance:* 332 awards ($455,104 total): art/fine arts, dance, debating, general creative arts/performance, journalism/publications, music, performing arts, theater/drama. *Special achievements/activities:* 121 awards ($149,295 total): cheerleading/drum major, community service, leadership, rodeo. *Special characteristics:* 1,886 awards ($2,123,884 total): ethnic background, first-generation college students, general special characteristics, handicapped students, international students, local/state students, members of minority groups, out-of-state students, previous college experience, spouses of current students, veterans, veterans' children. *Tuition waivers:* Full or partial for employees or children of employees, senior citizens. *ROTC:* Army.

LOANS *Student loans:* $88,553,183 (75% need-based, 25% non-need-based). 64% of past graduating class borrowed through all loan programs. *Average indebtedness per student:* $27,369. *Average need-based loan:* Freshmen: $5029. Undergraduates: $7000. *Parent loans:* $4,143,079 (38% need-based, 62% non-need-based). *Programs:* Federal Direct (Subsidized and Unsubsidized Stafford, PLUS), Perkins, state, college/university, Alaska Loans.

WORK-STUDY *Federal work-study:* Total amount: $2,419,564; 310 jobs averaging $1921. *State or other work-study/employment:* Total amount: $2,753,031 (100% need-based). 256 part-time jobs averaging $2194.

ATHLETIC AWARDS Total amount: $2,799,931 (63% need-based, 37% non-need-based).

APPLYING FOR FINANCIAL AID *Required financial aid form:* FAFSA. *Financial aid deadline:* 6/30 (priority: 2/15). *Notification date:* Continuous beginning 3/15. Students must reply by 6/1 or within 4 weeks of notification.

CONTACT Office of Financial Aid and Scholarships, Boise State University, Administration Building, Room 123, Boise, ID 83725-1315, 208-426-1664 or toll-free 800-824-7017. *Fax:* 208-426-1305. *E-mail:* faquest@boisestate.edu. *Website:* http://www.boisestate.edu/.

BON SECOURS MEMORIAL COLLEGE OF NURSING
Richmond, VA

CONTACT Financial Aid Office, Bon Secours Memorial College of Nursing, 8550 Magellan Parkway, Suite 1100, Richmond, VA 23227-1149, 804-627-5300 or toll-free 866-238-7414.
Website: http://www.bsmcon.edu/.

BORICUA COLLEGE
New York, NY

CONTACT Ms. Rosalia Cruz, Financial Aid Administrator, Boricua College, 3755 Broadway, New York, NY 10032-1560, 212-694-1000 Ext. 611. *Fax:* 212-694-1015. *E-mail:* rcruz@boricuacollege.edu.
Website: http://www.boricuacollege.edu/.

BOSTON ARCHITECTURAL COLLEGE
Boston, MA

Tuition & fees: N/R	Average undergraduate aid package: $9921

ABOUT THE INSTITUTION Independent, coed. *Awards:* certificates, bachelor's, and master's degrees. 4 undergraduate majors. *Total enrollment:* 920. Undergraduates: 466. Freshmen: 20. Federal methodology is used as a basis for awarding need-based institutional aid.

FRESHMAN FINANCIAL AID (Fall 2011) 67 applied for aid; of those 93% were deemed to have need. 52% of freshmen with need received aid; of those 3% had need fully met. *Average percent of need met:* 18% (excluding resources awarded to replace EFC). *Average financial aid package:* $9989 (excluding resources awarded to replace EFC).

UNDERGRADUATE FINANCIAL AID (Fall 2011) 264 applied for aid; of those 95% were deemed to have need. 67% of undergraduates with need received aid; of those 1% had need fully met. *Average percent of need met:* 25% (excluding resources awarded to replace EFC). *Average financial aid package:* $9921 (excluding resources awarded to replace EFC).

GIFT AID (NEED-BASED) *Total amount:* $2,261,698 (38% federal, 2% state, 50% institutional, 10% external sources). *Receiving aid:* Freshmen: 34% (23); all full-time undergraduates: 51% (136). *Average award:* Freshmen: $6479; Undergraduates: $5813. *Scholarships, grants, and awards:* Federal Pell, FSEOG, state, college/university gift aid from institutional funds.

GIFT AID (NON-NEED-BASED) *Total amount:* $44,798 (98% institutional, 2% external sources). *Scholarships, grants, and awards by category:* Academic interests/achievement: architecture, general academic interests/achievements. *Special achievements/activities:* leadership.

LOANS *Student loans:* $4,293,638 (91% need-based, 9% non-need-based). *Average need-based loan:* Freshmen: $5656. Undergraduates: $5410. *Parent loans:* $1,230,182 (100% non-need-based). *Programs:* Federal Direct (Subsidized and Unsubsidized Stafford, PLUS), state.

WORK-STUDY *Federal work-study:* Total amount: $83,137; jobs available.

APPLYING FOR FINANCIAL AID *Required financial aid form:* FAFSA. *Financial aid deadline (priority):* 4/15. *Notification date:* Continuous beginning 4/1. Students must reply within 2 weeks of notification.

CONTACT Mr. James Ryan, Dean of Enrollment and Student Financial Services, Boston Architectural College, 100 Massachusetts Avenue, 3rd Floor, Boston, MA 02115, 617-585-0125 or toll-free 877-585-0100. *Fax:* 617-585-0131. *E-mail:* james.ryan@the-bac.edu.
Website: http://www.the-bac.edu/.

BOSTON BAPTIST COLLEGE
Boston, MA

CONTACT Financial Aid Office, Boston Baptist College, 950 Metropolitan Avenue, Boston, MA 02136, 617-364-3510 or toll-free 888-235-2014. *Website:* http://www.boston.edu/.

BOSTON COLLEGE
Chestnut Hill, MA

Tuition & fees: $43,878	Average undergraduate aid package: $34,578

ABOUT THE INSTITUTION Independent Roman Catholic (Jesuit), coed. *Awards:* certificates, bachelor's, master's, and doctoral degrees (also offers continuing education program with significant enrollment not reflected in profile). 50 undergraduate majors. *Total enrollment:* 13,783. Undergraduates: 9,110. Freshmen: 2,405. Institutional methodology is used as a basis for awarding need-based institutional aid.

UNDERGRADUATE EXPENSES for 2013–2014 *Application fee:* $70. *One-time required fee:* $458. *Comprehensive fee:* $56,486 includes full-time tuition ($43,140), mandatory fees ($738), and room and board ($12,608). *College room only:* $7790. Room and board charges vary according to housing facility.

FRESHMAN FINANCIAL AID (Fall 2011) 1,098 applied for aid; of those 82% were deemed to have need. 100% of freshmen with need received aid; of those 100% had need fully met. *Average percent of need met:* 100% (excluding resources awarded to replace EFC). *Average financial aid package:* $34,302 (excluding resources awarded to replace EFC). 1% of all full-time freshmen had no need and received non-need-based gift aid.

UNDERGRADUATE FINANCIAL AID (Fall 2011) 4,435 applied for aid; of those 87% were deemed to have need. 100% of undergraduates with need received aid; of those 100% had need fully met. *Average percent of need met:* 100% (excluding resources awarded to replace EFC). *Average financial aid package:* $34,578 (excluding resources awarded to replace EFC). 2% of all full-time undergraduates had no need and received non-need-based gift aid.

GIFT AID (NEED-BASED) *Total amount:* $98,563,946 (7% federal, 1% state, 89% institutional, 3% external sources). *Receiving aid:* Freshmen: 38% (793); all full-time undergraduates: 38% (3,448). *Average award:* Freshmen: $29,414; Undergraduates: $28,586. *Scholarships, grants, and awards:* Federal Pell, FSEOG, state, private, college/university gift aid from institutional funds.

GIFT AID (NON-NEED-BASED) *Total amount:* $6,898,603 (25% federal, 47% institutional, 28% external sources). *Receiving aid:* Freshmen: 1% (20). Undergraduates: 1% (78). *Average award:* Freshmen: $19,490. Undergraduates: $15,634. *Scholarships, grants, and awards by category:* Academic interests/achievement: 99 awards ($2,617,790 total): general academic interests/achievements, military science. *Tuition waivers:* Full or partial for employees or children of employees. *ROTC:* Army cooperative, Naval cooperative, Air Force cooperative.

LOANS *Student loans:* $23,625,684 (82% need-based, 18% non-need-based). 52% of past graduating class borrowed through all loan programs. *Average indebtedness per student:* $20,975. *Average need-based loan:* Freshmen: $4364. Undergraduates: $5403. *Parent loans:* $33,764,877 (100% non-need-based). *Programs:* Perkins, Federal Nursing, state.

WORK-STUDY *Federal work-study:* Total amount: $7,635,853; 3,156 jobs averaging $2143.

ATHLETIC AWARDS Total amount: $14,435,797 (14% need-based, 86% non-need-based).

APPLYING FOR FINANCIAL AID *Required financial aid forms:* FAFSA, CSS Financial Aid PROFILE, business/farm supplement, federal income tax form(s), W-2 forms. *Financial aid deadline (priority):* 2/1. *Notification date:* 4/1. Students must reply by 5/1.

CONTACT Office of Student Services, Boston College, Lyons Hall, 140 Commonwealth Avenue, Chestnut Hill, MA 02467, 617-552-3300 or toll-free 800-360-2522. *Fax:* 617-552-4889. *E-mail:* studentservices@bc.edu. *Website:* http://www.bc.edu/.

THE BOSTON CONSERVATORY
Boston, MA

CONTACT Jessica Raine, Financial Aid Assistant, The Boston Conservatory, 8 The Fenway, Boston, MA 02215, 617-912-9147. *Fax:* 617-536-1496. *E-mail:* jraine@bostonconservatory.edu. *Website:* http://www.bostonconservatory.edu/.

BOSTON UNIVERSITY
Boston, MA

Tuition & fees: $42,994	Average undergraduate aid package: $37,038

ABOUT THE INSTITUTION Independent, coed. *Awards:* certificates, bachelor's, master's, and doctoral degrees. 110 undergraduate majors. *Total enrollment:* 32,603. Undergraduates: 18,306. Freshmen: 3,877. Both federal and institutional methodology are used as a basis for awarding need-based institutional aid.

UNDERGRADUATE EXPENSES for 2013–2014 *Application fee:* $80. *Comprehensive fee:* $56,184 includes full-time tuition ($42,400), mandatory fees ($594), and room and board ($13,190). *College room only:* $8600. Full-time tuition and fees vary according to class time. Room and board charges vary according to board plan and housing facility. *Part-time tuition:* $1325 per credit hour. *Part-time fees:* $40 per term. Part-time tuition and fees vary according to class time and course load. *Payment plan:* Tuition prepayment.

FRESHMAN FINANCIAL AID (Fall 2012, est.) 2,160 applied for aid; of those 83% were deemed to have need. 100% of freshmen with need received aid; of those 54% had need fully met. *Average percent of need met:* 92% (excluding resources awarded to replace EFC). *Average financial aid package:* $37,655 (excluding resources awarded to replace EFC). 6% of all full-time freshmen had no need and received non-need-based gift aid.

UNDERGRADUATE FINANCIAL AID (Fall 2012, est.) 7,741 applied for aid; of those 92% were deemed to have need. 100% of undergraduates with need received aid; of those 46% had need fully met. *Average percent of need met:* 89% (excluding resources awarded to replace EFC). *Average financial aid package:* $37,038 (excluding resources awarded to replace EFC). 7% of all full-time undergraduates had no need and received non-need-based gift aid.

GIFT AID (NEED-BASED) *Total amount:* $185,264,080 (8% federal, 1% state, 88% institutional, 3% external sources). *Receiving aid:* Freshmen: 43% (1,682); all full-time undergraduates: 42% (6,771). *Average award:* Freshmen: $26,464; Undergraduates: $25,047. *Scholarships, grants, and awards:* Federal Pell, FSEOG, state, private, college/university gift aid from institutional funds.

GIFT AID (NON-NEED-BASED) *Total amount:* $28,923,096 (8% federal, 65% institutional, 27% external sources). *Receiving aid:* Freshmen: 17% (653). Undergraduates: 11% (1,753). *Average award:* Freshmen: $22,043. Undergraduates: $22,631. *Scholarships, grants, and awards by category:* Academic interests/achievement: 1,375 awards ($20,707,454 total): education, engineering/technologies, foreign languages, general academic interests/achievements. *Creative arts/performance:* 222 awards ($1,844,838 total): art/fine arts, music, theater/drama. *Special achievements/activities:* 55 awards ($1,364,160 total): general special achievements/activities, leadership, memberships. *Special characteristics:* 395 awards ($6,247,398 total): children and siblings of alumni, local/state students, relatives of clergy, religious affiliation. *Tuition waivers:* Full or partial for employees or children of employees. *ROTC:* Army, Naval, Air Force.

LOANS *Student loans:* $86,644,018 (70% need-based, 30% non-need-based). 59% of past graduating class borrowed through all loan programs. *Average indebtedness per student:* $36,150. *Average need-based loan:* Freshmen: $6521. Undergraduates: $7631. *Parent loans:* $37,277,668 (45% need-based, 55% non-need-based). *Programs:* Federal Direct (Subsidized and Unsubsidized Stafford, PLUS), Perkins, state, alternative loans.

WORK-STUDY *Federal work-study:* Total amount: $6,249,360; 3,238 jobs averaging $1930. *State or other work-study/employment:* Total amount: $3,157,543 (54% need-based, 46% non-need-based). 129 part-time jobs averaging $13,114.

ATHLETIC AWARDS Total amount: $13,129,659 (22% need-based, 78% non-need-based).

APPLYING FOR FINANCIAL AID *Required financial aid forms:* FAFSA, CSS Financial Aid PROFILE. *Financial aid deadline:* 2/15. *Notification date:*

Continuous beginning 3/15. Students must reply by 5/1 or within 2 weeks of notification.

CONTACT Julie Wickstrom, Director of Financial Assistance, Boston University, 881 Commonwealth Avenue, Boston, MA 02215, 617-353-4176. *Fax:* 617-353-8200. *E-mail:* finaid@bu.edu.
Website: http://www.bu.edu/.

BOWDOIN COLLEGE
Brunswick, ME

Tuition & fees: $44,118	Average undergraduate aid package: $38,283

ABOUT THE INSTITUTION Independent, coed. *Awards:* bachelor's degrees (SAT or ACT considered if submitted. Test scores are required for home-schooled applicants). 42 undergraduate majors. *Total enrollment:* 1,839. Undergraduates: 1,839. Freshmen: 492. Institutional methodology is used as a basis for awarding need-based institutional aid.

UNDERGRADUATE EXPENSES for 2013–2014 *Application fee:* $60. *Comprehensive fee:* $56,128 includes full-time tuition ($43,676), mandatory fees ($442), and room and board ($12,010). *College room only:* $5620. Room and board charges vary according to board plan.

FRESHMAN FINANCIAL AID (Fall 2012, est.) 291 applied for aid; of those 81% were deemed to have need. 100% of freshmen with need received aid; of those 100% had need fully met. *Average percent of need met:* 100% (excluding resources awarded to replace EFC). *Average financial aid package:* $40,879 (excluding resources awarded to replace EFC). 2% of all full-time freshmen had no need and received non-need-based gift aid.

UNDERGRADUATE FINANCIAL AID (Fall 2012, est.) 975 applied for aid; of those 88% were deemed to have need. 100% of undergraduates with need received aid; of those 100% had need fully met. *Average percent of need met:* 100% (excluding resources awarded to replace EFC). *Average financial aid package:* $38,283 (excluding resources awarded to replace EFC). 5% of all full-time undergraduates had no need and received non-need-based gift aid.

GIFT AID (NEED-BASED) *Total amount:* $31,523,558 (5% federal, 92% institutional, 3% external sources). *Receiving aid:* Freshmen: 48% (237); all full-time undergraduates: 47% (857). *Average award:* Freshmen: $39,204; Undergraduates: $36,492. *Scholarships, grants, and awards:* Federal Pell, FSEOG, state, private, college/university gift aid from institutional funds.

GIFT AID (NON-NEED-BASED) *Total amount:* $964,035 (9% institutional, 91% external sources). *Average award:* Freshmen: $1000. Undergraduates: $1000. *Scholarships, grants, and awards by category: Academic interests/achievement:* 86 awards ($86,000 total): general academic interests/achievements. *Special achievements/activities:* leadership. *Special characteristics:* children of faculty/staff. *Tuition waivers:* Full or partial for employees or children of employees.

LOANS *Student loans:* 35% of past graduating class borrowed through all loan programs. *Average indebtedness per student:* $22,755. *Programs:* Federal Direct (Subsidized and Unsubsidized Stafford), Perkins, state.

WORK-STUDY *Federal work-study:* Total amount: $531,258; 327 jobs averaging $1625. *State or other work-study/employment:* Total amount: $720,012 (100% need-based). 432 part-time jobs averaging $1667.

APPLYING FOR FINANCIAL AID *Required financial aid forms:* FAFSA, CSS Financial Aid PROFILE, noncustodial (divorced/separated) parent's statement, business/farm supplement. *Financial aid deadline:* 2/15. *Notification date:* 4/5. Students must reply by 5/1 or within 1 week of notification.

CONTACT Mr. Michael D. Bartini, Director of Student Aid, Bowdoin College, 5300 College Station, Brunswick, ME 04011-8444, 207-725-3146. *Fax:* 207-725-3864. *E-mail:* mbartini@bowdoin.edu.
Website: http://www.bowdoin.edu/.

BOWIE STATE UNIVERSITY
Bowie, MD

Tuition & fees (MD res): $6639	Average undergraduate aid package: $8413

ABOUT THE INSTITUTION State-supported, coed. *Awards:* certificates, bachelor's, master's, and doctoral degrees. 29 undergraduate majors. *Total enrollment:* 5,421. Undergraduates: 4,283. Freshmen: 484. Federal methodology is used as a basis for awarding need-based institutional aid.

UNDERGRADUATE EXPENSES for 2013–2014 *Application fee:* $40. *Tuition, state resident:* full-time $4683; part-time $207 per credit hour. *Tuition, nonresident:* full-time $15,239; part-time $641 per credit hour. *Required fees:* full-time $1956; $86.96 per credit hour. Part-time tuition and fees vary according to course load. *College room and board:* $9597. Room and board charges vary according to board plan and housing facility.

FRESHMAN FINANCIAL AID (Fall 2012, est.) 339 applied for aid; of those 100% were deemed to have need. 100% of freshmen with need received aid; of those 76% had need fully met. *Average percent of need met:* 47% (excluding resources awarded to replace EFC). *Average financial aid package:* $8415 (excluding resources awarded to replace EFC). 2% of all full-time freshmen had no need and received non-need-based gift aid.

UNDERGRADUATE FINANCIAL AID (Fall 2012, est.) 2,551 applied for aid; of those 100% were deemed to have need. 100% of undergraduates with need received aid; of those 43% had need fully met. *Average percent of need met:* 46% (excluding resources awarded to replace EFC). *Average financial aid package:* $8413 (excluding resources awarded to replace EFC). 1% of all full-time undergraduates had no need and received non-need-based gift aid.

GIFT AID (NEED-BASED) *Total amount:* $16,669,516 (53% federal, 25% state, 21% institutional, 1% external sources). *Receiving aid:* Freshmen: 57% (248); all full-time undergraduates: 63% (1,925). *Average award:* Freshmen: $7601; Undergraduates: $6618. *Scholarships, grants, and awards:* Federal Pell, FSEOG, state, private, college/university gift aid from institutional funds, United Negro College Fund, Federal Nursing.

GIFT AID (NON-NEED-BASED) *Total amount:* $658,321 (1% federal, 8% state, 83% institutional, 8% external sources). *Receiving aid:* Freshmen: 65% (284). Undergraduates: 67% (2,067). *Average award:* Freshmen: $366. Undergraduates: $94. *Scholarships, grants, and awards by category: Academic interests/achievement:* biological sciences, business, communication, computer science, engineering/technologies, mathematics, military science. *Creative arts/performance:* 117 awards ($256,648 total): applied art and design, art/fine arts, general creative arts/performance, music. *Special achievements/activities:* 338 awards ($1,894,320 total). *Special characteristics:* first-generation college students. *Tuition waivers:* Full or partial for employees or children of employees, senior citizens. *ROTC:* Army.

LOANS *Student loans:* $22,119,008 (83% need-based, 17% non-need-based). 82% of past graduating class borrowed through all loan programs. *Average indebtedness per student:* $25,972. *Average need-based loan:* Freshmen: $3268. Undergraduates: $4023. *Parent loans:* $2,393,799 (38% need-based, 62% non-need-based). *Programs:* Federal Direct (Subsidized and Unsubsidized Stafford, PLUS), Perkins, Federal Nursing, state, college/university.

WORK-STUDY *Federal work-study:* Total amount: $114,204; 45 jobs averaging $2538.

ATHLETIC AWARDS Total amount: $782,326 (65% need-based, 35% non-need-based).

APPLYING FOR FINANCIAL AID *Required financial aid forms:* FAFSA, institution's own form. *Financial aid deadline (priority):* 3/1. *Notification date:* Continuous beginning 4/1. Students must reply within 2 weeks of notification.

CONTACT Deborah Stanley, Director of Financial Aid, Bowie State University, 14000 Jericho Park Road, Bowie, MD 20715, 301-860-3543 or toll-free 877-772-6943. *Fax:* 301-860-3549. *E-mail:* dstanley@bowiestate.edu.
Website: http://www.bowiestate.edu/.

BOWLING GREEN STATE UNIVERSITY
Bowling Green, OH

Tuition & fees (OH res): $10,513	Average undergraduate aid package: $13,285

ABOUT THE INSTITUTION State-supported, coed. *Awards:* certificates, bachelor's, master's, and doctoral degrees. 199 undergraduate majors. *Total enrollment:* 17,286. Undergraduates: 14,815. Freshmen: 3,621. Federal methodology is used as a basis for awarding need-based institutional aid.

UNDERGRADUATE EXPENSES for 2013–2014 *Application fee:* $45. *Tuition, state resident:* full-time $8913; part-time $371.40 per credit hour. *Tuition, nonresident:* full-time $16,222; part-time $676.40 per credit hour. *Required fees:* full-time $1600; $66 per credit hour. Full-time tuition and fees vary according to course load and location. Part-time tuition and fees vary according to course load and location. *College room and board:* $8064. Room and board charges vary according to board plan and housing facility.

FRESHMAN FINANCIAL AID (Fall 2012, est.) 3,211 applied for aid; of those 80% were deemed to have need. 100% of freshmen with need received aid; of those 12% had need fully met. *Average percent of need met:* 75% (excluding resources awarded to replace EFC). *Average financial aid package:* $12,988 (excluding resources awarded to replace EFC). 21% of all full-time freshmen had no need and received non-need-based gift aid.

UNDERGRADUATE FINANCIAL AID (Fall 2012, est.) 11,212 applied for aid; of those 84% were deemed to have need. 100% of undergraduates with need received aid; of those 13% had need fully met. *Average percent of need met:* 75% (excluding resources awarded to replace EFC). *Average financial aid package:* $13,285 (excluding resources awarded to replace EFC). 17% of all full-time undergraduates had no need and received non-need-based gift aid.

GIFT AID (NEED-BASED) *Total amount:* $48,004,461 (44% federal, 7% state, 44% institutional, 5% external sources). *Receiving aid:* Freshmen: 66% (2,369); all full-time undergraduates: 58% (7,899). *Average award:* Freshmen: $6056; Undergraduates: $5948. *Scholarships, grants, and awards:* Federal Pell, FSEOG, state, private, college/university gift aid from institutional funds.

GIFT AID (NON-NEED-BASED) *Total amount:* $12,497,227 (1% federal, 6% state, 87% institutional, 6% external sources). *Receiving aid:* Freshmen: 5% (180). Undergraduates: 5% (636). *Average award:* Freshmen: $3629. Undergraduates: $4012. *Scholarships, grants, and awards by category:* Academic interests/achievement: biological sciences, business, communication, computer science, education, engineering/technologies, English, foreign languages, general academic interests/achievements, health fields, home economics, humanities, international studies, mathematics, military science, physical sciences, social sciences. *Creative arts/performance:* art/fine arts, cinema/film/broadcasting, creative writing, dance, debating, journalism/publications, music, performing arts, theater/drama. *Special achievements/activities:* general special achievements/activities, leadership. *Special characteristics:* children and siblings of alumni, children of faculty/staff, general special characteristics, international students, members of minority groups. *Tuition waivers:* Full or partial for employees or children of employees, senior citizens. *ROTC:* Army, Air Force.

LOANS *Student loans:* $84,718,390 (75% need-based, 25% non-need-based). 80% of past graduating class borrowed through all loan programs. *Average indebtedness per student:* $31,262. *Average need-based loan:* Freshmen: $6383. Undergraduates: $7303. *Parent loans:* $30,493,895 (41% need-based, 59% non-need-based). *Programs:* Federal Direct (Subsidized and Unsubsidized Stafford, PLUS), Perkins, Federal Nursing, state, college/university, alternative loans.

WORK-STUDY *Federal work-study:* Total amount: $718,593; 512 jobs averaging $1930.

ATHLETIC AWARDS Total amount: $5,421,264 (38% need-based, 62% non-need-based).

APPLYING FOR FINANCIAL AID *Required financial aid form:* FAFSA. *Financial aid deadline:* Continuous. *Notification date:* Continuous beginning 4/15. Students must reply within 3 weeks of notification.

CONTACT Eric Bucks, Associate Director of Student Financial Aid, Bowling Green State University, 231 Administration Building, Bowling Green, OH 43403, 419-372-2651. *Fax:* 419-372-0404. *Website:* http://www.bgsu.edu/.

BRADLEY UNIVERSITY
Peoria, IL

Tuition & fees: $29,664	Average undergraduate aid package: $18,951

ABOUT THE INSTITUTION Independent, coed. *Awards:* certificates, bachelor's, master's, and doctoral degrees. 104 undergraduate majors. *Total enrollment:* 5,451. Undergraduates: 4,872. Freshmen: 1,016. Federal methodology is used as a basis for awarding need-based institutional aid.

UNDERGRADUATE EXPENSES for 2013–2014 *Application fee:* $35. *One-time required fee:* $200. *Comprehensive fee:* $38,714 includes full-time tuition ($29,320), mandatory fees ($344), and room and board ($9050). *College room only:* $5250. Full-time tuition and fees vary according to course load and program. Room and board charges vary according to board plan. *Part-time tuition:* $740 per credit. Part-time tuition and fees vary according to course load and program.

FRESHMAN FINANCIAL AID (Fall 2012, est.) 963 applied for aid; of those 72% were deemed to have need. 100% of freshmen with need received aid; of those 20% had need fully met. *Average percent of need met:* 69% (excluding resources awarded to replace EFC). *Average financial aid package:* $18,274 (excluding resources awarded to replace EFC). 15% of all full-time freshmen had no need and received non-need-based gift aid.

UNDERGRADUATE FINANCIAL AID (Fall 2012, est.) 3,849 applied for aid; of those 86% were deemed to have need. 97% of undergraduates with need received aid; of those 16% had need fully met. *Average percent of need met:* 68% (excluding resources awarded to replace EFC). *Average financial aid package:* $18,951 (excluding resources awarded to replace EFC). 20% of all full-time undergraduates had no need and received non-need-based gift aid.

GIFT AID (NEED-BASED) *Total amount:* $52,360,447 (11% federal, 12% state, 74% institutional, 3% external sources). *Receiving aid:* Freshmen: 68% (691); all full-time undergraduates: 69% (3,129). *Average award:* Freshmen: $15,021; Undergraduates: $14,351. *Scholarships, grants, and awards:* Federal Pell, FSEOG, state, private, college/university gift aid from institutional funds.

GIFT AID (NON-NEED-BASED) *Total amount:* $6,935,109 (95% institutional, 5% external sources). *Receiving aid:* Freshmen: 11% (111). Undergraduates: 7% (330). *Average award:* Freshmen: $8478. Undergraduates: $7744. *Scholarships, grants, and awards by category:* Academic interests/achievement: general academic interests/achievements. *Creative arts/performance:* art/fine arts, music, theater/drama. *Special achievements/activities:* community service, leadership. *Special characteristics:* children and siblings of alumni, children of faculty/staff. *Tuition waivers:* Full or partial for employees or children of employees, senior citizens. *ROTC:* Army.

LOANS *Student loans:* $23,398,535 (56% need-based, 44% non-need-based). 73% of past graduating class borrowed through all loan programs. *Average indebtedness per student:* $26,109. *Average need-based loan:* Freshmen: $4171. Undergraduates: $5874. *Parent loans:* $12,599,398 (41% need-based, 59% non-need-based). *Programs:* Federal Direct (Subsidized and Unsubsidized Stafford, PLUS), Perkins, Federal Nursing.

WORK-STUDY *Federal work-study:* Total amount: $607,844; jobs available.

ATHLETIC AWARDS Total amount: $3,435,446 (40% need-based, 60% non-need-based).

APPLYING FOR FINANCIAL AID *Required financial aid form:* FAFSA. *Financial aid deadline (priority):* 3/1. *Notification date:* Continuous beginning 3/1.

CONTACT Mr. David L. Pardieck, Director of Financial Assistance, Bradley University, 1501 West Bradley Avenue, Peoria, IL 61625-0002, 309-677-3089 or toll-free 800-447-6460. *E-mail:* dlp@bradley.edu. *Website:* http://www.bradley.edu/.

BRANDEIS UNIVERSITY
Waltham, MA

Tuition & fees: $44,294	Average undergraduate aid package: $33,633

ABOUT THE INSTITUTION Independent, coed. *Awards:* certificates, bachelor's, master's, and doctoral degrees. 43 undergraduate majors. *Total* *enrollment:* 5,808. Undergraduates: 3,588. Freshmen: 820. Institutional methodology is used as a basis for awarding need-based institutional aid.

UNDERGRADUATE EXPENSES for 2013–2014 *Application fee:* $65. *Comprehensive fee:* $56,550 includes full-time tuition ($42,682), mandatory fees ($1612), and room and board ($12,256). *College room only:* $6812. Full-time tuition and fees vary according to student level. Room and board charges vary according to board plan and housing facility. Part-time tuition and fees vary according to course load. *Payment plan:* Tuition prepayment.

FRESHMAN FINANCIAL AID (Fall 2011) 596 applied for aid; of those 82% were deemed to have need. 99% of freshmen with need received aid; of those 98% had need fully met. *Average percent of need met:* 95% (excluding resources awarded to replace EFC). *Average financial aid package:* $37,391 (excluding resources awarded to replace EFC). 1% of all full-time freshmen had no need and received non-need-based gift aid.

UNDERGRADUATE FINANCIAL AID (Fall 2011) 2,115 applied for aid; of those 86% were deemed to have need. 99% of undergraduates with need received aid; of those 47% had need fully met. *Average percent of need met:* 90% (excluding resources awarded to replace EFC). *Average financial aid package:* $33,633 (excluding resources awarded to replace EFC). 7% of all full-time undergraduates had no need and received non-need-based gift aid.

GIFT AID (NEED-BASED) *Total amount:* $52,813,276 (8% federal, 1% state, 89% institutional, 2% external sources). *Receiving aid:* Freshmen: 55% (472); all full-time undergraduates: 50% (1,742). *Average award:* Freshmen: $35,353; Undergraduates: $30,179. *Scholarships, grants, and awards:* Federal Pell, FSEOG, state, private, college/university gift aid from institutional funds.

GIFT AID (NON-NEED-BASED) *Total amount:* $7,125,355 (1% federal, 83% institutional, 16% external sources). *Receiving aid:* Freshmen: 4% (33). Undergraduates: 4% (132). *Average award:* Freshmen: $4702. Undergraduates: $21,351. *Tuition waivers:* Full or partial for employees or children of employees. *ROTC:* Army cooperative, Air Force cooperative.

LOANS *Student loans:* $14,628,063 (63% need-based, 37% non-need-based). 56% of past graduating class borrowed through all loan programs. *Average indebtedness per student:* $27,906. *Average need-based loan:* Freshmen: $2437. Undergraduates: $4156. *Parent loans:* $6,420,134 (16% need-based, 84% non-need-based). *Programs:* Federal Direct (Subsidized and Unsubsidized Stafford, PLUS), Perkins, state, college/university.

WORK-STUDY *Federal work-study:* Total amount: $1,162,942; jobs available. *State or other work-study/employment:* Total amount: $747,970 (21% need-based, 79% non-need-based). Part-time jobs available.

APPLYING FOR FINANCIAL AID *Required financial aid forms:* FAFSA, CSS Financial Aid PROFILE, state aid form, noncustodial (divorced/separated) parent's statement. *Financial aid deadline:* 2/1. *Notification date:* 4/1. Students must reply by 5/1.

CONTACT Nicole Bonanni, Assistant Director for Student Services, Office of Student Financial Services, Brandeis University, Usdan Student Center, 415 South Street, Waltham, MA 02454-9110, 781-736-3700 or toll-free 800-622-0622 (out-of-state). *Fax:* 781-736-3719. *E-mail:* sfs@brandeis.edu. *Website:* http://www.brandeis.edu/.

BRANDMAN UNIVERSITY
Irvine, CA

CONTACT Financial Aid Office, Brandman University, 16355 Laguna Canyon Road, Irvine, CA 92618, 949-753-4774 or toll-free 800-746-0082. *Website:* http://www.brandman.edu/irvine/.

BRENAU UNIVERSITY
Gainesville, GA

Tuition & fees: $21,908	Average undergraduate aid package: $19,555

ABOUT THE INSTITUTION Independent, women only. *Awards:* associate, bachelor's, and master's degrees (also offers coed evening and weekend programs with significant enrollment not reflected in profile). 31 undergraduate majors. *Total enrollment:* 864. Undergraduates: 802. Freshmen: 175. Federal methodology is used as a basis for awarding need-based institutional aid.

UNDERGRADUATE EXPENSES for 2013–2014 *Application fee:* $35. *Comprehensive fee:* $32,792 includes full-time tuition ($21,908) and room and board ($10,884). Full-time tuition and fees vary according to location and program. Part-time tuition and fees vary according to course load, location, and program.

FRESHMAN FINANCIAL AID (Fall 2012, est.) 158 applied for aid; of those 90% were deemed to have need. 100% of freshmen with need received aid; of those 13% had need fully met. *Average percent of need met:* 75% (excluding resources awarded to replace EFC). *Average financial aid package:* $22,665 (excluding resources awarded to replace EFC). 8% of all full-time freshmen had no need and received non-need-based gift aid.

UNDERGRADUATE FINANCIAL AID (Fall 2012, est.) 612 applied for aid; of those 93% were deemed to have need. 100% of undergraduates with need received aid; of those 15% had need fully met. *Average percent of need met:* 68% (excluding resources awarded to replace EFC). *Average financial aid package:* $19,555 (excluding resources awarded to replace EFC). 6% of all full-time undergraduates had no need and received non-need-based gift aid.

GIFT AID (NEED-BASED) *Total amount:* $9,343,778 (18% federal, 15% state, 66% institutional, 1% external sources). *Receiving aid:* Freshmen: 83% (141); all full-time undergraduates: 81% (566). *Average award:* Freshmen: $18,436; Undergraduates: $15,490. *Scholarships, grants, and awards:* Federal Pell, FSEOG, private, college/university gift aid from institutional funds.

GIFT AID (NON-NEED-BASED) *Total amount:* $754,734 (16% state, 83% institutional, 1% external sources). *Receiving aid:* Freshmen: 5% (8). Undergraduates: 6% (44). *Average award:* Freshmen: $13,376. Undergraduates: $12,930. *Scholarships, grants, and awards by category: Academic interests/achievement:* biological sciences, business, communication, education, English, general academic interests/achievements, health fields, humanities. *Creative arts/performance:* applied art and design, art/fine arts, cinema/film/broadcasting, creative writing, dance, journalism/publications, music, performing arts, theater/drama. *Special achievements/activities:* cheerleading/drum major, community service, general special achievements/activities, leadership. *Special characteristics:* children of faculty/staff, first-generation college students, general special characteristics, international students. *Tuition waivers:* Full or partial for employees or children of employees.

LOANS *Student loans:* $5,119,662 (91% need-based, 9% non-need-based). 89% of past graduating class borrowed through all loan programs. *Average indebtedness per student:* $23,317. *Average need-based loan:* Freshmen: $3639. Undergraduates: $4667. *Parent loans:* $418,526 (38% need-based, 62% non-need-based). *Programs:* Federal Direct (Subsidized and Unsubsidized Stafford, PLUS), Perkins, Federal Nursing, state.

WORK-STUDY *Federal work-study:* Total amount: $224,964; 112 jobs averaging $1993.

ATHLETIC AWARDS Total amount: $1,315,205 (84% need-based, 16% non-need-based).

APPLYING FOR FINANCIAL AID *Required financial aid forms:* FAFSA, state aid form. *Financial aid deadline (priority):* 4/1. *Notification date:* Continuous beginning 3/1.

CONTACT Mrs. Pam Barrett, Associate Vice President and Director of Financial Aid, Brenau University, 500 Washington Street, SE, Gainesville, GA 30501-3697, 770-534-6176 or toll-free 800-252-5119. *Fax:* 770-538-4306. *E-mail:* pbarrett@brenau.edu. *Website:* http://www.brenau.edu/.

BRESCIA UNIVERSITY
Owensboro, KY

CONTACT Mr. Britton Hibbitt, Administrative Assistant to Financial Aid, Brescia University, 717 Frederica Street, Owensboro, KY 42301-3023, 270-686-4253 or toll-free 877-273-7242. *Fax:* 270-686-4253. *E-mail:* financial.aid@brescia.edu. *Website:* http://www.brescia.edu/.

BREVARD COLLEGE
Brevard, NC

Tuition & fees: $23,900	Average undergraduate aid package: $19,367

ABOUT THE INSTITUTION Independent United Methodist, coed. *Awards:* bachelor's degrees. 21 undergraduate majors. *Total enrollment:* 633. Undergraduates: 633. Freshmen: 220. Federal methodology is used as a basis for awarding need-based institutional aid.

UNDERGRADUATE EXPENSES for 2013–2014 *Application fee:* $30. *Comprehensive fee:* $32,100 includes full-time tuition ($23,900) and room and board ($8200). Full-time tuition and fees vary according to course load. Room and board charges vary according to board plan and housing facility. *Part-time tuition:* $850 per credit hour. Part-time tuition and fees vary according to course load.

FRESHMAN FINANCIAL AID (Fall 2011) 165 applied for aid; of those 90% were deemed to have need. 100% of freshmen with need received aid; of those 14% had need fully met. *Average percent of need met:* 73% (excluding resources awarded to replace EFC). *Average financial aid package:* $20,145 (excluding resources awarded to replace EFC). 21% of all full-time freshmen had no need and received non-need-based gift aid.

UNDERGRADUATE FINANCIAL AID (Fall 2011) 493 applied for aid; of those 87% were deemed to have need. 100% of undergraduates with need received aid; of those 16% had need fully met. *Average percent of need met:* 73% (excluding resources awarded to replace EFC). *Average financial aid package:* $19,367 (excluding resources awarded to replace EFC). 30% of all full-time undergraduates had no need and received non-need-based gift aid.

GIFT AID (NEED-BASED) *Total amount:* $5,584,230 (22% federal, 17% state, 59% institutional, 2% external sources). *Receiving aid:* Freshmen: 78% (148); all full-time undergraduates: 70% (430). *Average award:* Freshmen: $16,655; Undergraduates: $15,928. *Scholarships, grants, and awards:* Federal Pell, FSEOG, state, private, college/university gift aid from institutional funds.

GIFT AID (NON-NEED-BASED) *Total amount:* $1,556,294 (6% state, 75% institutional, 19% external sources). *Receiving aid:* Freshmen: 9% (17). Undergraduates: 8% (46). *Average award:* Freshmen: $6379. Undergraduates: $5241. *Scholarships, grants, and awards by category:* Academic interests/achievement: general academic interests/achievements. *Creative arts/performance:* art/fine arts, music, theater/drama. *Special achievements/activities:* cheerleading/drum major, community service, general special achievements/activities, leadership. *Special characteristics:* children of faculty/staff, international students, local/state students, previous college experience, veterans' children. *Tuition waivers:* Full or partial for employees or children of employees, senior citizens.

LOANS *Student loans:* $2,030,102 (62% need-based, 38% non-need-based). 52% of past graduating class borrowed through all loan programs. *Average indebtedness per student:* $29,002. *Average need-based loan:* Freshmen: $2786. Undergraduates: $3532. *Parent loans:* $1,157,127 (39% need-based, 61% non-need-based). *Programs:* Federal Direct (Subsidized and Unsubsidized Stafford, PLUS), Perkins.

WORK-STUDY *Federal work-study:* Total amount: $44,900; 66 jobs averaging $1430. *State or other work-study/employment:* Total amount: $61,400 (19% need-based, 81% non-need-based). Part-time jobs available.

ATHLETIC AWARDS Total amount: $709,546 (17% need-based, 83% non-need-based).

APPLYING FOR FINANCIAL AID *Required financial aid form:* FAFSA. *Financial aid deadline (priority):* 2/1. *Notification date:* Continuous beginning 2/1. Students must reply by 5/1 or within 4 weeks of notification.

CONTACT Ms. Beth Pocock, Director of Financial Aid, Brevard College, 1 Brevard College Drive, Brevard, NC 28712, 828-884-8287 or toll-free 800-527-9090. *Fax:* 828-884-3790. *E-mail:* finaid@brevard.edu. *Website:* http://www.brevard.edu/.

BREWTON-PARKER COLLEGE
Mt. Vernon, GA

CONTACT Mrs. Shannon Mullins, Executive Director of Financial Aid, Brewton-Parker College, PO Box 197, Mt. Vernon, GA 30445-0197, 800-342-1087 Ext. 213 or toll-free 800-342-1087. *Fax:* 912-583-3598. *E-mail:* smullins@bpc.edu. *Website:* http://www.bpc.edu/.

BRIARCLIFFE COLLEGE
Bethpage, NY

CONTACT Johanna Kelly, Financial Aid Director, Briarcliffe College, 1055 Stewart Avenue, Bethpage, NY 11714, 516-918-3600 or toll-free 888-349-4999 (in-state), 888-348-4999 (out-of-state). *Website:* http://www.briarcliffe.edu/.

BRIAR CLIFF UNIVERSITY
Sioux City, IA

Tuition & fees: $25,642	Average undergraduate aid package: $19,220

ABOUT THE INSTITUTION Independent Roman Catholic, coed. *Awards:* certificates, associate, bachelor's, and master's degrees. 29 undergraduate majors. *Total enrollment:* 1,185. Undergraduates: 1,088. Freshmen: 237. Federal methodology is used as a basis for awarding need-based institutional aid.

UNDERGRADUATE EXPENSES for 2013–2014 *Application fee:* $20. *Comprehensive fee:* $33,184 includes full-time tuition ($24,520), mandatory fees ($1122), and room and board ($7542). Room and board charges vary according to board plan and housing facility. *Part-time tuition:* $810 per hour.

FRESHMAN FINANCIAL AID (Fall 2011) 227 applied for aid; of those 94% were deemed to have need. 100% of freshmen with need received aid; of those 86% had need fully met. *Average percent of need met:* 86% (excluding resources awarded to replace EFC). *Average financial aid package:* $21,124 (excluding resources awarded to replace EFC). 11% of all full-time freshmen had no need and received non-need-based gift aid.

UNDERGRADUATE FINANCIAL AID (Fall 2011) 833 applied for aid; of those 87% were deemed to have need. 100% of undergraduates with need received aid; of those 79% had need fully met. *Average percent of need met:* 79% (excluding resources awarded to replace EFC). *Average financial aid package:* $19,220 (excluding resources awarded to replace EFC). 17% of all full-time undergraduates had no need and received non-need-based gift aid.

GIFT AID (NEED-BASED) *Total amount:* $8,728,985 (24% federal, 15% state, 58% institutional, 3% external sources). *Receiving aid:* Freshmen: 90% (213); all full-time undergraduates: 85% (724). *Average award:* Freshmen: $7240; Undergraduates: $7155. *Scholarships, grants, and awards:* Federal Pell, FSEOG, state, private, college/university gift aid from institutional funds.

GIFT AID (NON-NEED-BASED) *Total amount:* $1,794,095 (3% state, 94% institutional, 3% external sources). *Receiving aid:* Freshmen: 90% (213). Undergraduates: 85% (724). *Average award:* Freshmen: $6400. Undergraduates: $6752. *Scholarships, grants, and awards by category:* Academic interests/achievement: 577 awards ($3,660,955 total): biological sciences, business, communication, computer science, education, English, foreign languages, general academic interests/achievements, health fields, humanities, mathematics, physical sciences, religion/biblical studies, social sciences. *Creative arts/performance:* 72 awards ($233,146 total): art/fine arts, music, theater/drama. *Special achievements/activities:* 224 awards ($217,000 total): leadership, religious involvement. *Special characteristics:* 57 awards ($55,000 total): children and siblings of alumni, first-generation college students, international students, members of minority groups. *Tuition waivers:* Full or partial for employees or children of employees, adult students, senior citizens. *ROTC:* Army cooperative.

LOANS *Student loans:* $6,499,846 (64% need-based, 36% non-need-based). 86% of past graduating class borrowed through all loan programs. *Average indebtedness per student:* $29,487. *Average need-based loan:* Freshmen: $3940. Undergraduates: $4825. *Parent loans:* $938,017 (88% need-based, 12% non-need-based). *Programs:* Federal Direct (Subsidized and Unsubsidized Stafford, PLUS), Perkins, alternative loans, partnership loans, Minnesota SELF Loans.

WORK-STUDY *Federal work-study:* Total amount: $225,391; 237 jobs averaging $1500. *State or other work-study/employment:* Total amount: $340,000 (100% non-need-based). 183 part-time jobs averaging $1500.

ATHLETIC AWARDS Total amount: $2,387,526 (81% need-based, 19% non-need-based).

APPLYING FOR FINANCIAL AID *Required financial aid forms:* FAFSA, federal income tax form(s). *Financial aid deadline:* 3/15. *Notification date:* Continuous beginning 3/15. Students must reply within 4 weeks of notification.

CONTACT Brian K. Eben, Office of Student Financial Aid, Briar Cliff University, 3303 Rebecca Street, PO Box 2100, Sioux City, IA 51104-2100, 712-279-5239 or toll-free 800-662-3303. *Fax:* 712-279-1632.
Website: http://www.briarcliff.edu/.

BRIDGEWATER COLLEGE
Bridgewater, VA

Tuition & fees: $29,090	Average undergraduate aid package: $23,927

ABOUT THE INSTITUTION Independent Church of the Brethren, coed. *Awards:* bachelor's degrees. 31 undergraduate majors. *Total enrollment:* 1,760. Undergraduates: 1,760. Freshmen: 552. Federal methodology is used as a basis for awarding need-based institutional aid.

UNDERGRADUATE EXPENSES for 2013–2014 *Application fee:* $30. *Comprehensive fee:* $39,880 includes full-time tuition ($28,500), mandatory fees ($590), and room and board ($10,790). *College room only:* $5490. Room and board charges vary according to housing facility. *Part-time tuition:* $980 per credit hour. *Part-time fees:* $40 per term.

FRESHMAN FINANCIAL AID (Fall 2012, est.) 515 applied for aid; of those 92% were deemed to have need. 100% of freshmen with need received aid; of those 33% had need fully met. *Average percent of need met:* 85% (excluding resources awarded to replace EFC). *Average financial aid package:* $25,979 (excluding resources awarded to replace EFC). 14% of all full-time freshmen had no need and received non-need-based gift aid.

UNDERGRADUATE FINANCIAL AID (Fall 2012, est.) 1,562 applied for aid; of those 93% were deemed to have need. 100% of undergraduates with need received aid; of those 29% had need fully met. *Average percent of need met:* 83% (excluding resources awarded to replace EFC). *Average financial aid package:* $23,927 (excluding resources awarded to replace EFC). 17% of all full-time undergraduates had no need and received non-need-based gift aid.

GIFT AID (NEED-BASED) *Total amount:* $24,957,533 (8% federal, 13% state, 78% institutional, 1% external sources). *Receiving aid:* Freshmen: 86% (472); all full-time undergraduates: 83% (1,446). *Average award:* Freshmen: $23,178; Undergraduates: $20,482. *Scholarships, grants, and awards:* Federal Pell, FSEOG, state, private, college/university gift aid from institutional funds.

GIFT AID (NON-NEED-BASED) *Total amount:* $9,664,219 (6% state, 91% institutional, 3% external sources). *Receiving aid:* Freshmen: 84% (464). Undergraduates: 80% (1,401). *Average award:* Freshmen: $17,101. Undergraduates: $14,907. *Scholarships, grants, and awards by category: Academic interests/ achievement:* 1,481 awards ($21,988,738 total): general academic interests/achievements. *Creative arts/performance:* 36 awards ($73,776 total): music. *Special characteristics:* 391 awards ($1,740,392 total): children of educators, children of faculty/staff, international students, members of minority groups, previous college experience, religious affiliation. *Tuition waivers:* Full or partial for employees or children of employees, senior citizens.

LOANS *Student loans:* $11,447,401 (60% need-based, 40% non-need-based). 78% of past graduating class borrowed through all loan programs. *Average indebtedness per student:* $31,153. *Average need-based loan:* Freshmen: $3727. Undergraduates: $4607. *Parent loans:* $3,625,374 (9% need-based, 91% non-need-based). *Programs:* Federal Direct (Subsidized and Unsubsidized Stafford, PLUS), Perkins.

WORK-STUDY *Federal work-study:* Total amount: $382,121; 278 jobs averaging $1174. *State or other work-study/employment:* Total amount: $112,118 (100% non-need-based). 157 part-time jobs averaging $751.

APPLYING FOR FINANCIAL AID *Required financial aid forms:* FAFSA, state aid form. *Financial aid deadline (priority):* 3/1. *Notification date:* Continuous beginning 3/21. Students must reply within 2 weeks of notification.

CONTACT Mr. Scott Morrison, Director of Financial Aid, Bridgewater College, 402 East College Street, Bridgewater, VA 22812-1599, 540-828-5377 or toll-free 800-759-8328. *Fax:* 540-828-5671. *E-mail:* smorriso@bridgewater.edu.
Website: http://www.bridgewater.edu/.

BRIDGEWATER STATE UNIVERSITY
Bridgewater, MA

Tuition & fees (MA res): $8052	Average undergraduate aid package: $10,368

ABOUT THE INSTITUTION State-supported, coed. *Awards:* certificates, bachelor's, and master's degrees. 80 undergraduate majors. *Total enrollment:* 11,417. Undergraduates: 9,684. Freshmen: 1,454. Federal methodology is used as a basis for awarding need-based institutional aid.

UNDERGRADUATE EXPENSES for 2013–2014 *Application fee:* $40. *Tuition, state resident:* full-time $910; part-time $38 per credit hour. *Tuition, nonresident:* full-time $7050; part-time $294 per credit hour. *Required fees:* full-time $7142; $292.21 per credit hour. Full-time tuition and fees vary according to class time. *College room and board:* $10,700; *Room only:* $7000. Room and board charges vary according to board plan and housing facility.

FRESHMAN FINANCIAL AID (Fall 2011) 1,421 applied for aid; of those 74% were deemed to have need. 99% of freshmen with need received aid; of those 5% had need fully met. *Average financial aid package:* $8632 (excluding resources awarded to replace EFC). 1% of all full-time freshmen had no need and received non-need-based gift aid.

UNDERGRADUATE FINANCIAL AID (Fall 2011) 7,601 applied for aid; of those 66% were deemed to have need. 99% of undergraduates with need received aid; of those 7% had need fully met. *Average financial aid package:* $10,368 (excluding resources awarded to replace EFC). 1% of all full-time undergraduates had no need and received non-need-based gift aid.

GIFT AID (NEED-BASED) *Total amount:* $18,092,946 (65% federal, 18% state, 17% institutional). *Receiving aid:* Freshmen: 62% (900); all full-time undergraduates: 49% (3,866). *Average award:* Freshmen: $4493; Undergraduates: $4146. *Scholarships, grants, and awards:* Federal Pell, FSEOG, state, private, college/university gift aid from institutional funds.

GIFT AID (NON-NEED-BASED) *Total amount:* $5,948,279 (4% federal, 18% state, 8% institutional, 70% external sources). *Receiving aid:* Freshmen: 20% (292). Undergraduates: 10% (774). *Average award:* Freshmen: $6915. Undergraduates: $5278. *Scholarships, grants, and awards by category: Academic interests/ achievement:* general academic interests/achievements. *Special characteristics:* local/ state students, members of minority groups. *Tuition waivers:* Full or partial for employees or children of employees, senior citizens. *ROTC:* Army cooperative, Air Force cooperative.

LOANS *Student loans:* $58,442,834 (42% need-based, 58% non-need-based). 85% of past graduating class borrowed through all loan programs. *Average indebtedness per student:* $30,189. *Average need-based loan:* Freshmen: $3501. Undergraduates: $3997. *Parent loans:* $6,595,753 (100% non-need-based). *Programs:* Federal Direct (Subsidized and Unsubsidized Stafford, PLUS), Perkins, state, private loans.

WORK-STUDY *Federal work-study:* Total amount: $899,768; 526 jobs averaging $1710.

APPLYING FOR FINANCIAL AID *Required financial aid form:* FAFSA. *Financial aid deadline (priority):* 3/1. *Notification date:* Continuous beginning 3/30.

CONTACT Office of Financial Aid, Bridgewater State University, Tillinghast Hall, Room 100, 45 School Street, Bridgewater, MA 02325-0001, 508-531-1341. *Fax:* 508-531-1728. *E-mail:* finaid@bridgew.edu.
Website: http://www.bridgew.edu/.

BRIGHAM YOUNG UNIVERSITY
Provo, UT

Tuition & fees: $4710	Average undergraduate aid package: $7178

ABOUT THE INSTITUTION Independent The Church of Jesus Christ of Latter-day Saints, coed. *Awards:* bachelor's, master's, and doctoral degrees. 102 undergraduate majors. *Total enrollment:* 34,409. Undergraduates: 31,060. Freshmen: 5,525. Both federal and institutional methodology are used as a basis for awarding need-based institutional aid.

UNDERGRADUATE EXPENSES for 2013–2014 *Application fee:* $35. *Comprehensive fee:* $11,910 includes full-time tuition ($4710) and room and board ($7200). Room and board charges vary according to board plan, housing facility, and location. **Part-time tuition:** $242 per credit hour. Part-time tuition and fees vary according to course load.

FRESHMAN FINANCIAL AID (Fall 2011) 2,536 applied for aid; of those 72% were deemed to have need. 92% of freshmen with need received aid; of those 2% had need fully met. **Average percent of need met:** 29% (excluding resources awarded to replace EFC). **Average financial aid package:** $6486 (excluding resources awarded to replace EFC). 33% of all full-time freshmen had no need and received non-need-based gift aid.

UNDERGRADUATE FINANCIAL AID (Fall 2011) 14,898 applied for aid; of those 87% were deemed to have need. 95% of undergraduates with need received aid; of those 2% had need fully met. **Average percent of need met:** 34% (excluding resources awarded to replace EFC). **Average financial aid package:** $7178 (excluding resources awarded to replace EFC). 24% of all full-time undergraduates had no need and received non-need-based gift aid.

GIFT AID (NEED-BASED) Total amount: $52,519,431 (86% federal, 14% institutional). **Receiving aid:** Freshmen: 19% (1,071); all full-time undergraduates: 37% (10,501). **Average award:** Freshmen: $4515; Undergraduates: $4603. **Scholarships, grants, and awards:** Federal Pell, private, college/university gift aid from institutional funds.

GIFT AID (NON-NEED-BASED) Total amount: $52,098,399 (84% institutional, 16% external sources). **Receiving aid:** Freshmen: 27% (1,510). Undergraduates: 24% (6,754). **Average award:** Freshmen: $3641. Undergraduates: $3649. **Scholarships, grants, and awards by category:** Academic interests/achievement: general academic interests/achievements. Creative arts/performance: art/fine arts, music, theater/drama. Special achievements/activities: leadership, religious involvement. Special characteristics: local/state students, members of minority groups, religious affiliation. **Tuition waivers:** Full or partial for employees or children of employees. **ROTC:** Army, Air Force.

LOANS Student loans: $37,719,110 (58% need-based, 42% non-need-based). 31% of past graduating class borrowed through all loan programs. **Average indebtedness per student:** $14,377. **Average need-based loan:** Freshmen: $3249. Undergraduates: $4254. **Parent loans:** $1,288,902 (100% non-need-based). **Programs:** Federal Direct (Subsidized and Unsubsidized Stafford, PLUS).

WORK-STUDY State or other work-study/employment: Part-time jobs available.

ATHLETIC AWARDS Total amount: $4,380,287 (100% non-need-based).

APPLYING FOR FINANCIAL AID Required financial aid form: FAFSA. **Financial aid deadline (priority):** 4/15. **Notification date:** Continuous beginning 4/1.

CONTACT Stephen E. Hill, Director of Financial Aid, Brigham Young University, C-144 ASB, Provo, UT 84602, 801-422-4104. Fax: 801-422-0234.
Website: http://www.byu.edu/.

BRIGHAM YOUNG UNIVERSITY–HAWAII
Laie, HI

CONTACT Mr. Wes Duke, Director of Financial Aid, Brigham Young University–Hawaii, BYUH #1980, 55-220 Kulanui Street, Laie, HI 96762, 808-293-3530. Fax: 808-293-3349. E-mail: duekw@byuh.edu.
Website: http://www.byuh.edu/.

BRIGHAM YOUNG UNIVERSITY–IDAHO
Rexburg, ID

CONTACT Financial Aid Office, Brigham Young University–Idaho, Rexburg, ID 83460, 208-496-2011.
Website: http://www.byui.edu/.

BROADVIEW UNIVERSITY–BOISE
Meridian, ID

Tuition & fees: $15,948 — **Average undergraduate aid package: N/A**

ABOUT THE INSTITUTION Proprietary, coed. **Awards:** diplomas, associate, and bachelor's degrees. 12 undergraduate majors. Both federal and institutional methodology are used as a basis for awarding need-based institutional aid.

UNDERGRADUATE EXPENSES for 2013–2014 Application fee: $50. **Tuition:** full-time $14,400; part-time $435 per credit. **Required fees:** full-time $1548; $43 per credit. Full-time tuition and fees vary according to course level, course load, degree level, location, and program. Part-time tuition and fees vary according to course level, course load, degree level, location, and program.

GIFT AID (NEED-BASED) Scholarships, grants, and awards: Federal Pell, FSEOG, private, college/university gift aid from institutional funds.

GIFT AID (NON-NEED-BASED) Scholarships, grants, and awards by category: Academic interests/achievement: business, computer science, engineering/technologies, health fields. Special achievements/activities: community service. Special characteristics: children of faculty/staff, veterans, veterans' children. **Tuition waivers:** Full or partial for employees or children of employees.

LOANS Programs: Federal Direct (Subsidized and Unsubsidized Stafford, PLUS), college/university, alternative loans.

APPLYING FOR FINANCIAL AID Required financial aid forms: FAFSA, institution's own form. **Financial aid deadline:** Continuous. **Notification date:** Continuous beginning 1/2. Students must reply within 2 weeks of notification.

CONTACT Office of Financial Aid, Broadview University–Boise, 2750 East Gala Court, Meridian, ID 83642, 208-577-2900 or toll-free 877-572-5757. Fax: 208-577-2901.
Website: http://www.broadviewuniversity.edu/.

BROADVIEW UNIVERSITY–LAYTON
Layton, UT

Tuition & fees: $15,948 — **Average undergraduate aid package: N/A**

ABOUT THE INSTITUTION Proprietary, coed. **Awards:** diplomas, associate, and bachelor's degrees. 12 undergraduate majors. **Total enrollment:** 434. Undergraduates: 434. Freshmen: 58. Both federal and institutional methodology are used as a basis for awarding need-based institutional aid.

UNDERGRADUATE EXPENSES for 2013–2014 Application fee: $50. **Tuition:** full-time $14,400; part-time $435 per credit. **Required fees:** full-time $1548; $43 per credit. Full-time tuition and fees vary according to course load, degree level, location, and program. Part-time tuition and fees vary according to course load, degree level, location, and program.

GIFT AID (NEED-BASED) Scholarships, grants, and awards: Federal Pell, FSEOG, private, college/university gift aid from institutional funds.

GIFT AID (NON-NEED-BASED) Scholarships, grants, and awards by category: Academic interests/achievement: business, computer science, engineering/technologies, health fields. Special achievements/activities: community service. Special characteristics: children of faculty/staff, veterans, veterans' children. **Tuition waivers:** Full or partial for employees or children of employees.

LOANS Programs: Federal Direct (Subsidized and Unsubsidized Stafford, PLUS), college/university, alternative loans.

APPLYING FOR FINANCIAL AID Required financial aid forms: FAFSA, institution's own form. **Financial aid deadline:** Continuous. **Notification date:** Continuous beginning 1/2. Students must reply within 2 weeks of notification.

CONTACT Office of Financial Aid, Broadview University–Layton, 869 West Hill Field Road, Layton, UT 84041, 801-660-6000 or toll-free 866-253-7744. Fax: 801-669-6001.
Website: http://www.broadviewuniversity.edu/.

BROADVIEW UNIVERSITY–OREM
Orem, UT

Tuition & fees: $15,948	Average undergraduate aid package: N/A

ABOUT THE INSTITUTION Proprietary, coed. **Awards:** diplomas, associate, and bachelor's degrees. 12 undergraduate majors. **Total enrollment:** 285. Undergraduates: 285. Freshmen: 59. Both federal and institutional methodology are used as a basis for awarding need-based institutional aid.

UNDERGRADUATE EXPENSES for 2013–2014 **Application fee:** $50. **Tuition:** full-time $14,400; part-time $435 per credit. **Required fees:** full-time $1548; $43 per credit. Full-time tuition and fees vary according to course level, course load, degree level, location, and program. Part-time tuition and fees vary according to course level, course load, degree level, location, and program.

GIFT AID (NEED-BASED) Scholarships, grants, and awards: Federal Pell, FSEOG, private, college/university gift aid from institutional funds.

GIFT AID (NON-NEED-BASED) Scholarships, grants, and awards by category: Academic interests/achievement: business, computer science, engineering/technologies, health fields. Special achievements/activities: community service. Special characteristics: children of faculty/staff, veterans, veterans' children. **Tuition waivers:** Full or partial for employees or children of employees.

LOANS Programs: Federal Direct (Subsidized and Unsubsidized Stafford, PLUS), college/university, alternative loans.

APPLYING FOR FINANCIAL AID Required financial aid forms: FAFSA, institution's own form. **Financial aid deadline:** Continuous. **Notification date:** Continuous beginning 1/2. Students must reply within 2 weeks of notification.

CONTACT Office of Financial Aid, Broadview University–Orem, 898 North 1200 West, Orem, UT 84057, 801-822-5800 or toll-free 877-822-5838. Fax: 801-822-5801. Website: http://www.broadviewuniversity.edu/.

BROADVIEW UNIVERSITY–SALT LAKE CITY
Salt Lake City, UT

Tuition & fees: $15,948	Average undergraduate aid package: N/A

ABOUT THE INSTITUTION Proprietary, coed. **Awards:** associate and bachelor's degrees. 7 undergraduate majors. **Total enrollment:** 34. Undergraduates: 34. Freshmen: 16. Both federal and institutional methodology are used as a basis for awarding need-based institutional aid.

UNDERGRADUATE EXPENSES for 2013–2014 **Application fee:** $50. **Tuition:** full-time $14,400; part-time $460 per credit. **Required fees:** full-time $1548; $43 per credit. Full-time tuition and fees vary according to course level, course load, degree level, location, and program. Part-time tuition and fees vary according to course level, course load, degree level, location, and program.

GIFT AID (NEED-BASED) Scholarships, grants, and awards: Federal Pell, FSEOG, private, college/university gift aid from institutional funds.

GIFT AID (NON-NEED-BASED) Scholarships, grants, and awards by category: Special achievements/activities: community service. Special characteristics: children of faculty/staff, veterans, veterans' children. **Tuition waivers:** Full or partial for employees or children of employees.

LOANS Programs: Federal Direct (Subsidized and Unsubsidized Stafford, PLUS), college/university, alternative loans.

APPLYING FOR FINANCIAL AID Required financial aid forms: FAFSA, institution's own form. **Financial aid deadline:** Continuous. **Notification date:** Continuous beginning 1/2. Students must reply within 2 weeks of notification.

CONTACT Office of Financial Aid, Broadview University–Salt Lake City, 240 East Morris Avenue, Salt Lake City, UT 84115, 801-300-4300 or toll-free 877-801-8889. Fax: 801-300-4301. Website: http://www.broadviewuniversity.edu/.

BROADVIEW UNIVERSITY–WEST JORDAN
West Jordan, UT

Tuition & fees: $15,948	Average undergraduate aid package: N/A

ABOUT THE INSTITUTION Proprietary, coed. **Awards:** diplomas, associate, bachelor's, and master's degrees. 15 undergraduate majors. **Total enrollment:** 702. Undergraduates: 701. Freshmen: 110. Both federal and institutional methodology are used as a basis for awarding need-based institutional aid.

UNDERGRADUATE EXPENSES for 2013–2014 **Application fee:** $50. **Tuition:** full-time $14,400; part-time $460 per credit. **Required fees:** full-time $1548; $43 per credit. Full-time tuition and fees vary according to course level, course load, degree level, location, and program. Part-time tuition and fees vary according to course level, course load, degree level, location, and program.

GIFT AID (NEED-BASED) Scholarships, grants, and awards: Federal Pell, FSEOG, private, college/university gift aid from institutional funds.

GIFT AID (NON-NEED-BASED) Scholarships, grants, and awards by category: Academic interests/achievement: business, computer science, engineering/technologies, health fields. Special achievements/activities: community service. Special characteristics: children of faculty/staff, veterans, veterans' children. **Tuition waivers:** Full or partial for employees or children of employees.

LOANS Programs: Federal Direct (Subsidized and Unsubsidized Stafford, PLUS), college/university, alternative loans.

APPLYING FOR FINANCIAL AID Required financial aid forms: FAFSA, institution's own form. **Financial aid deadline:** Continuous. **Notification date:** Continuous beginning 1/2. Students must reply within 2 weeks of notification.

CONTACT Office of Financial Aid, Broadview University–West Jordan, 1902 West 7800 South, West Jordan, UT 84088, 801-304-4224 or toll-free 866-304-4224. Fax: 801-304-4229. Website: http://www.broadviewuniversity.edu/.

BROOKLINE COLLEGE
Phoenix, AZ

CONTACT Financial Aid Office, Brookline College, 2445 West Dunlap Avenue, Suite 100, Phoenix, AZ 85021, 602-242-6265 or toll-free 800-793-2428. Website: http://brooklinecollege.edu/.

BROOKLINE COLLEGE
Tempe, AZ

CONTACT Financial Aid Office, Brookline College, 1140-1150 South Priest Drive, Tempe, AZ 85281, 480-545-8755 or toll-free 888-886-2428. Website: http://brooklinecollege.edu/.

BROOKLINE COLLEGE
Tucson, AZ

CONTACT Financial Aid Office, Brookline College, 5441 East 22nd Street, Suite 125, Tucson, AZ 85711, 520-748-9799 or toll-free 888-292-2428. Website: http://brooklinecollege.edu/.

BROOKLINE COLLEGE
Albuquerque, NM

CONTACT Financial Aid Office, Brookline College, 4201 Central Avenue NW, Suite J, Albuquerque, NM 87105-1649, 505-880-2877 or toll-free 888-660-2428. Website: http://brooklinecollege.edu/.

BROOKLYN COLLEGE OF THE CITY UNIVERSITY OF NEW YORK
Brooklyn, NY

Tuition & fees (NY res): $5884	Average undergraduate aid package: $7500

ABOUT THE INSTITUTION State and locally supported, coed. 76 undergraduate majors. Federal methodology is used as a basis for awarding need-based institutional aid.

UNDERGRADUATE EXPENSES for 2013–2014 Tuition, state resident: full-time $5430. **Tuition, nonresident:** full-time $14,550. **Required fees:** full-time $454.

FRESHMAN FINANCIAL AID (Fall 2012, est.) 1,013 applied for aid; of those 83% were deemed to have need. 94% of freshmen with need received aid; of those 81% had need fully met. **Average percent of need met:** 94% (excluding resources awarded to replace EFC). **Average financial aid package:** $7500 (excluding resources awarded to replace EFC). 22% of all full-time freshmen had no need and received non-need-based gift aid.

UNDERGRADUATE FINANCIAL AID (Fall 2012, est.) 8,998 applied for aid; of those 87% were deemed to have need. 89% of undergraduates with need received aid; of those 76% had need fully met. **Average percent of need met:** 95% (excluding resources awarded to replace EFC). **Average financial aid package:** $7500 (excluding resources awarded to replace EFC). 11% of all full-time undergraduates had no need and received non-need-based gift aid.

GIFT AID (NEED-BASED) Total amount: $52,556,630 (57% federal, 43% state). **Receiving aid:** Freshmen: 61% (690); all full-time undergraduates: 74% (6,831). **Average award:** Freshmen: $3300; Undergraduates: $3300. **Scholarships, grants, and awards:** Federal Pell, FSEOG, state, private, college/university gift aid from institutional funds.

GIFT AID (NON-NEED-BASED) Total amount: $1,252,748 (4% federal, 3% state, 88% institutional, 5% external sources). **Receiving aid:** Freshmen: 25% (288). Undergraduates: 22% (2,005). **Average award:** Freshmen: $3500. Undergraduates: $3500. **Scholarships, grants, and awards by category:** Academic interests/achievement: 209 awards ($630,000 total): general academic interests/achievements. Creative arts/performance: 16 awards ($32,000 total): general creative arts/performance.

LOANS Student loans: $31,315,475 (98% need-based, 2% non-need-based). 48% of past graduating class borrowed through all loan programs. **Average indebtedness per student:** $12,200. **Average need-based loan:** Freshmen: $3200. Undergraduates: $3200. **Parent loans:** $404,049 (100% need-based). **Programs:** Federal Direct (Subsidized and Unsubsidized Stafford, PLUS), Perkins.

WORK-STUDY Federal work-study: Total amount: $3,336,592; 1,350 jobs averaging $1400. **State or other work-study/employment:** Total amount: $123,915 (100% need-based). Part-time jobs available.

APPLYING FOR FINANCIAL AID Required financial aid forms: FAFSA, state aid form. **Financial aid deadline:** 5/1. **Notification date:** Continuous beginning 5/15.

CONTACT Mr. Ahad Farhang, Director of Financial Aid, Brooklyn College of the City University of New York, 2900 Bedford Avenue, Brooklyn, NY 11210-2889, 718-951-5669. Fax: 718-951-4778. E-mail: afarhang@brooklyn.cuny.edu. Website: http://www.brooklyn.cuny.edu/.

BROOKS INSTITUTE
Santa Barbara, CA

Tuition & fees: N/R	Average undergraduate aid package: N/A

ABOUT THE INSTITUTION Proprietary, coed. 4 undergraduate majors. Federal methodology is used as a basis for awarding need-based institutional aid.

GIFT AID (NEED-BASED) Scholarships, grants, and awards: Federal Pell, FSEOG, state, private, college/university gift aid from institutional funds, Veterans Education Benefits (GI Bill), Yellow Ribbon Grant Program.

GIFT AID (NON-NEED-BASED) Scholarships, grants, and awards by category: Creative arts/performance: applied art and design, art/fine arts, cinema/film/broadcasting, journalism/publications. Special achievements/activities: general special achievements/activities.

LOANS Programs: Federal Direct (Subsidized and Unsubsidized Stafford, PLUS), alternative loans.
WORK-STUDY Federal work-study jobs available.
APPLYING FOR FINANCIAL AID Required financial aid forms: FAFSA, institution's own form. **Financial aid deadline:** Continuous. **Notification date:** Continuous. Students must reply within 4 weeks of notification.
CONTACT Stacey Eymann, Student Finance Manager, Brooks Institute, 27 East Cota Street, Santa Barbara, CA 93101, 888-304-3456 Ext. 7631 or toll-free 888-276-4999. Fax: 805-679-6920. E-mail: seymann@brooks.edu. Website: http://www.brooks.edu/.

BROWN MACKIE COLLEGE–BIRMINGHAM
Birmingham, AL

CONTACT Financial Aid Office, Brown Mackie College–Birmingham, 105 Vulcan Road, Suite 400, Birmingham, AL 35209, 205-299-4699 or toll-free 888-299-4699. Website: http://www.brownmackie.edu/birmingham.

BROWN MACKIE COLLEGE–DALLAS/FT. WORTH
Bedford, TX

CONTACT Financial Aid Office, Brown Mackie College–Dallas/Ft. Worth, 2200 North Highway 121, Suite 270, Bedford, TX 76021, 817-799-0500. Website: http://www.brownmackie.edu/dallas/.

BROWN MACKIE COLLEGE–SAN ANTONIO
San Antonio, TX

CONTACT Financial Aid Office, Brown Mackie College–San Antonio, 4715 Fredericksburg Road, Suite 100, San Antonio, TX 78229, 210-460-1714 or toll-free 877-460-1714. Website: http://www.brownmackie.edu/san-antonio.

BROWN UNIVERSITY
Providence, RI

Tuition & fees: $43,758	Average undergraduate aid package: $39,526

ABOUT THE INSTITUTION Independent, coed. **Awards:** bachelor's, master's, and doctoral degrees. 76 undergraduate majors. **Total enrollment:** 8,885. Undergraduates: 6,435. Freshmen: 1,536. Both federal and institutional methodology are used as a basis for awarding need-based institutional aid.

UNDERGRADUATE EXPENSES for 2013–2014 Application fee: $75. **Comprehensive fee:** $55,016 includes full-time tuition ($42,808), mandatory fees ($950), and room and board ($11,258). **College room only:** $6974. Room and board charges vary according to board plan.

FRESHMAN FINANCIAL AID (Fall 2012, est.) 856 applied for aid; of those 87% were deemed to have need. 100% of freshmen with need received aid; of those 100% had need fully met. **Average percent of need met:** 100% (excluding resources awarded to replace EFC). **Average financial aid package:** $40,523 (excluding resources awarded to replace EFC).

UNDERGRADUATE FINANCIAL AID (Fall 2012, est.) 2,943 applied for aid; of those 92% were deemed to have need. 100% of undergraduates with need received aid; of those 100% had need fully met. **Average percent of need met:** 100% (excluding resources awarded to replace EFC). **Average financial aid package:**

$39,526 (excluding resources awarded to replace EFC). 1% of all full-time undergraduates had no need and received non-need-based gift aid.

GIFT AID (NEED-BASED) *Total amount:* $98,816,275 (5% federal, 90% institutional, 5% external sources). *Receiving aid:* Freshmen: 47% (716); all full-time undergraduates: 42% (2,565). *Average award:* Freshmen: $38,050; Undergraduates: $36,541. *Scholarships, grants, and awards:* Federal Pell, FSEOG, state, private, college/university gift aid from institutional funds.

GIFT AID (NON-NEED-BASED) *Total amount:* $4,008,512 (1% institutional, 99% external sources). *Average award:* Undergraduates: $9615. *Scholarships, grants, and awards by category: Special characteristics:* 20 awards ($179,656 total): veterans, veterans' children. *Tuition waivers:* Full or partial for employees or children of employees. *ROTC:* Army cooperative.

LOANS *Student loans:* $11,660,488 (72% need-based, 28% non-need-based). 37% of past graduating class borrowed through all loan programs. *Average indebtedness per student:* $23,521. *Average need-based loan:* Freshmen: $4853. Undergraduates: $5579. *Parent loans:* $8,857,192 (1% need-based, 99% non-need-based). *Programs:* Federal Direct (Subsidized and Unsubsidized Stafford, PLUS), Perkins, college/university.

WORK-STUDY *Federal work-study:* Total amount: $3,538,075; 1,544 jobs averaging $2288. *State or other work-study/employment:* Total amount: $868,676 (100% need-based). 367 part-time jobs averaging $2354.

APPLYING FOR FINANCIAL AID *Required financial aid forms:* FAFSA, CSS Financial Aid PROFILE, noncustodial (divorced/separated) parent's statement. *Financial aid deadline:* 3/1. *Notification date:* 4/1. Students must reply by 5/1.

CONTACT Office of Financial Aid, Brown University, PO Box 1827, Providence, RI 02912, 401-863-2721. *Fax:* 401-863-7575. *E-mail:* financial_aid@brown.edu. *Website:* http://www.brown.edu/.

BRYAN COLLEGE
Dayton, TN

CONTACT Rick Taphorn, Director of Financial Aid, Bryan College, PO Box 7000, Dayton, TN 37321-7000, 423-775-7339 or toll-free 800-277-9522. *Fax:* 423-775-7300. *E-mail:* finaid@bryan.edu. *Website:* http://www.bryan.edu/.

BRYANT & STRATTON COLLEGE
Cleveland, OH

CONTACT Bill Davenport, Financial Aid Supervisor, Bryant & Stratton College, 1700 East 13th Street, Cleveland, OH 44114-3203, 216-771-1700. *Fax:* 216-771-7787. *Website:* http://www.bryantstratton.edu/.

BRYANT & STRATTON COLLEGE - WAUWATOSA CAMPUS
Wauwatosa, WI

CONTACT Financial Aid Office, Bryant & Stratton College - Wauwatosa Campus, 10950 W. Potter Road, Wauwatosa, WI 53226, 414-302-7000. *Website:* http://www.bryantstratton.edu/.

BRYANT UNIVERSITY
Smithfield, RI

Tuition & fees: $37,234	Average undergraduate aid package: $22,549

ABOUT THE INSTITUTION Independent, coed. *Awards:* bachelor's and master's degrees. 39 undergraduate majors. *Total enrollment:* 3,418. Undergraduates: 3,180. Freshmen: 772. Federal methodology is used as a basis for awarding need-based institutional aid.

UNDERGRADUATE EXPENSES for 2013–2014 *Application fee:* $50. *Comprehensive fee:* $50,898 includes full-time tuition ($36,872), mandatory fees ($362), and room and board ($13,664). *College room only:* $8020. Room and board charges vary according to board plan and housing facility. *Part-time tuition:* $806.89 per credit hour. Part-time tuition and fees vary according to course load.

FRESHMAN FINANCIAL AID (Fall 2012, est.) 599 applied for aid; of those 87% were deemed to have need. 100% of freshmen with need received aid; of those 50% had need fully met. *Average percent of need met:* 52% (excluding resources awarded to replace EFC). *Average financial aid package:* $23,109 (excluding resources awarded to replace EFC). 17% of all full-time freshmen had no need and received non-need-based gift aid.

UNDERGRADUATE FINANCIAL AID (Fall 2012, est.) 2,240 applied for aid; of those 89% were deemed to have need. 100% of undergraduates with need received aid; of those 50% had need fully met. *Average percent of need met:* 53% (excluding resources awarded to replace EFC). *Average financial aid package:* $22,549 (excluding resources awarded to replace EFC). 13% of all full-time undergraduates had no need and received non-need-based gift aid.

GIFT AID (NEED-BASED) *Total amount:* $26,245,445 (9% federal, 1% state, 89% institutional, 1% external sources). *Receiving aid:* Freshmen: 52% (405); all full-time undergraduates: 55% (1,699). *Average award:* Freshmen: $11,816; Undergraduates: $12,758. *Scholarships, grants, and awards:* Federal Pell, FSEOG, state, private, college/university gift aid from institutional funds.

GIFT AID (NON-NEED-BASED) *Total amount:* $17,189,438 (99% institutional, 1% external sources). *Receiving aid:* Freshmen: 43% (334). Undergraduates: 25% (777). *Average award:* Freshmen: $12,412. Undergraduates: $12,781. *Scholarships, grants, and awards by category: Academic interests/achievement:* 1,043 awards ($13,493,825 total): general academic interests/achievements. *Special characteristics:* 217 awards ($3,855,799 total): international students, members of minority groups, siblings of current students. *Tuition waivers:* Full or partial for employees or children of employees. *ROTC:* Army.

LOANS *Student loans:* $22,501,767 (38% need-based, 62% non-need-based). 88% of past graduating class borrowed through all loan programs. *Average indebtedness per student:* $44,580. *Average need-based loan:* Freshmen: $3862. Undergraduates: $5044. *Parent loans:* $7,851,819 (32% need-based, 68% non-need-based). *Programs:* Federal Direct (Subsidized and Unsubsidized Stafford, PLUS), Perkins, private loans.

WORK-STUDY *Federal work-study:* Total amount: $311,074; jobs available. *State or other work-study/employment:* Total amount: $1,436,100 (29% need-based, 71% non-need-based). Part-time jobs available.

ATHLETIC AWARDS Total amount: $5,443,774 (42% need-based, 58% non-need-based).

APPLYING FOR FINANCIAL AID *Required financial aid form:* FAFSA. *Financial aid deadline (priority):* 2/15. *Notification date:* 3/24. Students must reply by 5/1.

CONTACT Mr. John B. Canning, Director of Financial Aid, Bryant University, 1150 Douglas Pike, Smithfield, RI 02917-1284, 401-232-6020 or toll-free 800-622-7001. *Fax:* 401-232-6293. *E-mail:* jcanning@bryant.edu. *Website:* http://www.bryant.edu/.

BRYN ATHYN COLLEGE OF THE NEW CHURCH
Bryn Athyn, PA

CONTACT Wendy Cooper, Associate Director of Financial Aid, Bryn Athyn College of the New Church, Box 717, Bryn Athyn, PA 19009, 267-502-2630 or toll-free 800-767-9552. *Fax:* 267-502-4866. *E-mail:* financialaid@brynathyn.edu. *Website:* http://www.brynathyn.edu/.

BRYN MAWR COLLEGE
Bryn Mawr, PA

Tuition & fees: $42,246	Average undergraduate aid package: $40,897

ABOUT THE INSTITUTION Independent, undergraduate: women only; graduate: coed. *Awards:* certificates, bachelor's, master's, and doctoral degrees. 33 undergraduate majors. *Total enrollment:* 1,774. Undergraduates: 1,322. Freshmen: 365. Institutional methodology is used as a basis for awarding need-based institutional aid.

UNDERGRADUATE EXPENSES for 2013–2014 *Application fee:* $50. *Comprehensive fee:* $55,586 includes full-time tuition ($41,260), mandatory fees ($986), and room and board ($13,340). *College room only:* $7620. *Part-time tuition:* $5160 per course.

FRESHMAN FINANCIAL AID (Fall 2012, est.) 235 applied for aid; of those 79% were deemed to have need. 100% of freshmen with need received aid; of those 100% had need fully met. *Average percent of need met:* 100% (excluding resources awarded to replace EFC). *Average financial aid package:* $41,074 (excluding resources awarded to replace EFC). 24% of all full-time freshmen had no need and received non-need-based gift aid.

UNDERGRADUATE FINANCIAL AID (Fall 2012, est.) 845 applied for aid; of those 85% were deemed to have need. 99% of undergraduates with need received aid; of those 100% had need fully met. *Average percent of need met:* 100% (excluding resources awarded to replace EFC). *Average financial aid package:* $40,897 (excluding resources awarded to replace EFC). 16% of all full-time undergraduates had no need and received non-need-based gift aid.

GIFT AID (NEED-BASED) *Total amount:* $25,574,111 (5% federal, 1% state, 93% institutional, 1% external sources). *Receiving aid:* Freshmen: 51% (186); all full-time undergraduates: 55% (717). *Average award:* Freshmen: $35,239; Undergraduates: $35,342. *Scholarships, grants, and awards:* Federal Pell, FSEOG, state, college/university gift aid from institutional funds.

GIFT AID (NON-NEED-BASED) *Total amount:* $3,695,461 (1% state, 95% institutional, 4% external sources). *Receiving aid:* Freshmen: 3% (11). Undergraduates: 2% (21). *Average award:* Freshmen: $11,970. Undergraduates: $15,794. *Scholarships, grants, and awards by category:* Academic interests/achievement: general academic interests/achievements. Special achievements/activities: leadership. *ROTC:* Air Force cooperative.

LOANS *Student loans:* $4,701,532 (60% need-based, 40% non-need-based). 52% of past graduating class borrowed through all loan programs. *Average indebtedness per student:* $23,579. *Average need-based loan:* Freshmen: $4828. Undergraduates: $4818. *Parent loans:* $1,528,008 (100% non-need-based). *Programs:* Federal Direct (Subsidized and Unsubsidized Stafford, PLUS), Perkins.

WORK-STUDY *Federal work-study:* Total amount: $1,027,345; jobs available. *State or other work-study/employment:* Total amount: $350,638 (100% need-based). Part-time jobs available.

APPLYING FOR FINANCIAL AID *Required financial aid forms:* FAFSA, CSS Financial Aid PROFILE. *Financial aid deadline:* 3/1. *Notification date:* Continuous. Students must reply by 5/1.

CONTACT Ethel M. Desmarais, Director of Student Financial Services, Bryn Mawr College, 101 North Merion Avenue, Bryn Mawr, PA 19010-2899, 610-526-7922 or toll-free 800-BMC-1885. *Fax:* 610-526-5249. *E-mail:* edesmara@brynmawr.edu. *Website:* http://www.brynmawr.edu/.

BUCKNELL UNIVERSITY
Lewisburg, PA

Tuition & fees: $46,902	Average undergraduate aid package: $27,000

ABOUT THE INSTITUTION Independent, coed. *Awards:* bachelor's and master's degrees. 59 undergraduate majors. *Total enrollment:* 3,618. Undergraduates: 3,536. Freshmen: 918. Both federal and institutional methodology are used as a basis for awarding need-based institutional aid.

UNDERGRADUATE EXPENSES for 2013–2014 *Application fee:* $60. *Comprehensive fee:* $58,160 includes full-time tuition ($46,646), mandatory fees ($256), and room and board ($11,258). *College room only:* $6622. Room and board charges vary according to board plan and housing facility. *Part-time tuition:* $5121 per course. *Payment plan:* Tuition prepayment.

FRESHMAN FINANCIAL AID (Fall 2012, est.) 481 applied for aid; of those 84% were deemed to have need. 100% of freshmen with need received aid; of those 95% had need fully met. *Average percent of need met:* 95% (excluding resources awarded to replace EFC). *Average financial aid package:* $28,500 (excluding resources awarded to replace EFC). 6% of all full-time freshmen had no need and received non-need-based gift aid.

UNDERGRADUATE FINANCIAL AID (Fall 2012, est.) 1,847 applied for aid; of those 86% were deemed to have need. 100% of undergraduates with need received aid; of those 95% had need fully met. *Average percent of need met:* 95% (excluding resources awarded to replace EFC). *Average financial aid package:* $27,000 (excluding resources awarded to replace EFC). 6% of all full-time undergraduates had no need and received non-need-based gift aid.

GIFT AID (NEED-BASED) *Total amount:* $48,522,140 (3% federal, 2% state, 92% institutional, 3% external sources). *Receiving aid:* Freshmen: 44% (402); all full-time undergraduates: 44% (1,533). *Average award:* Freshmen: $24,649; Undergraduates: $23,150. *Scholarships, grants, and awards:* Federal Pell, FSEOG, state, private, college/university gift aid from institutional funds.

GIFT AID (NON-NEED-BASED) *Total amount:* $2,500,000 (100% institutional). *Receiving aid:* Freshmen: 6% (57). Undergraduates: 6% (203). *Average award:* Freshmen: $14,855. Undergraduates: $13,562. *Scholarships, grants, and awards by category:* Academic interests/achievement: 107 awards ($1,305,640 total): business, engineering/technologies, general academic interests/achievements, mathematics, physical sciences. Creative arts/performance: 127 awards ($793,500 total): art/fine arts, creative writing, dance, music, performing arts, theater/drama. Special achievements/activities: 115 awards ($5,104,056 total): general special achievements/activities, leadership. *Tuition waivers:* Full or partial for employees or children of employees. *ROTC:* Army.

LOANS *Student loans:* $11,334,383 (100% need-based). 55% of past graduating class borrowed through all loan programs. *Average indebtedness per student:* $21,163. *Average need-based loan:* Freshmen: $3456. Undergraduates: $4816. *Parent loans:* $7,753,534 (100% non-need-based). *Programs:* Federal Direct (Subsidized and Unsubsidized Stafford, PLUS), Perkins.

WORK-STUDY *Federal work-study:* Total amount: $600,000; 600 jobs averaging $1500. *State or other work-study/employment:* Total amount: $50,000 (100% need-based). 50 part-time jobs averaging $1500.

ATHLETIC AWARDS Total amount: $773,490 (100% non-need-based).

APPLYING FOR FINANCIAL AID *Required financial aid forms:* FAFSA, CSS Financial Aid PROFILE, noncustodial (divorced/separated) parent's statement. *Financial aid deadline:* 1/15. *Notification date:* 4/1. Students must reply by 5/1.

CONTACT Andrea Leithner Stauffer, Director of Financial Aid, Bucknell University, One Dent Drive, Lewisburg, PA 17837, 570-577-1331. *Fax:* 570-577-1481. *E-mail:* finaid@bucknell.edu. *Website:* http://www.bucknell.edu/.

BUENA VISTA UNIVERSITY
Storm Lake, IA

Tuition & fees: $28,314	Average undergraduate aid package: $30,793

ABOUT THE INSTITUTION Independent Presbyterian Church (U.S.A.), coed. *Awards:* bachelor's and master's degrees. 59 undergraduate majors. *Total enrollment:* 971. Undergraduates: 913. Freshmen: 228. Federal methodology is used as a basis for awarding need-based institutional aid.

UNDERGRADUATE EXPENSES for 2013–2014 *Comprehensive fee:* $36,494 includes full-time tuition ($28,314) and room and board ($8180). Full-time tuition and fees vary according to location. Room and board charges vary according to board plan. Part-time tuition and fees vary according to location. *Payment plan:* Guaranteed tuition.

FRESHMAN FINANCIAL AID (Fall 2012, est.) 217 applied for aid; of those 91% were deemed to have need. 100% of freshmen with need received aid; of those 48% had need fully met. *Average percent of need met:* 86% (excluding resources awarded to replace EFC). *Average financial aid package:* $31,954 (excluding resources awarded to replace EFC). 3% of all full-time freshmen had no need and received non-need-based gift aid.

UNDERGRADUATE FINANCIAL AID (Fall 2012, est.) 810 applied for aid; of those 92% were deemed to have need. 100% of undergraduates with need received aid; of those 47% had need fully met. **Average percent of need met:** 83% (excluding resources awarded to replace EFC). **Average financial aid package:** $30,793 (excluding resources awarded to replace EFC). 3% of all full-time undergraduates had no need and received non-need-based gift aid.
GIFT AID (NEED-BASED) Total amount: $15,385,981 (13% federal, 11% state, 76% institutional). **Receiving aid:** Freshmen: 86% (197); all full-time undergraduates: 83% (733). **Average award:** Freshmen: $20,131; Undergraduates: $18,894. **Scholarships, grants, and awards:** Federal Pell, FSEOG, state, private, college/university gift aid from institutional funds.
GIFT AID (NON-NEED-BASED) Total amount: $1,754,967 (3% state, 84% institutional, 13% external sources). **Receiving aid:** Freshmen: 46% (104). Undergraduates: 27% (241). **Average award:** Freshmen: $16,907. Undergraduates: $11,269. **Scholarships, grants, and awards by category:** Academic interests/achievement: biological sciences, business, computer science, education, general academic interests/achievements, humanities, international studies, mathematics. Creative arts/performance: art/fine arts, music, theater/drama. Special achievements/activities: general special achievements/activities, leadership. Special characteristics: children of faculty/staff, ethnic background, international students, out-of-state students, religious affiliation, siblings of current students. Tuition waivers: Full or partial for employees or children of employees. ROTC: Army.
LOANS Student loans: $7,658,839 (43% need-based, 57% non-need-based). **Average need-based loan:** Freshmen: $5187. Undergraduates: $5223. **Parent loans:** $1,008,321 (100% non-need-based). **Programs:** Federal Direct (Subsidized and Unsubsidized Stafford, PLUS), Perkins, college/university.
WORK-STUDY Federal work-study: Total amount: $437,025; 365 jobs averaging $1145. **State or other work-study/employment:** Total amount: $207,630 (100% non-need-based). 252 part-time jobs averaging $1655.
APPLYING FOR FINANCIAL AID Required financial aid form: FAFSA. **Financial aid deadline (priority):** 6/1. **Notification date:** Continuous beginning 2/1.
CONTACT Mrs. Leanne Valentine, Director of Financial Assistance, Buena Vista University, 610 West Fourth Street, Storm Lake, IA 50588, 712-749-2164 or toll-free 800-383-9600. Fax: 712-749-1451. E-mail: valentinel@bvu.edu. Website: http://www.bvu.edu/.

BUFFALO STATE COLLEGE, STATE UNIVERSITY OF NEW YORK
Buffalo, NY

Tuition & fees (NY res): $6694	Average undergraduate aid package: $8832

ABOUT THE INSTITUTION State-supported, coed. **Awards:** certificates, bachelor's, and master's degrees. 79 undergraduate majors. **Total enrollment:** 11,214. Undergraduates: 9,731. Federal methodology is used as a basis for awarding need-based institutional aid.
UNDERGRADUATE EXPENSES for 2013–2014 Application fee: $40. **Tuition, state resident:** full-time $5570. **Tuition, nonresident:** full-time $14,820. **Required fees:** full-time $1124. Part-time tuition and fees vary according to course load. **College room and board:** $11,192; **Room only:** $6592. Room and board charges vary according to board plan, housing facility, and student level.
FRESHMAN FINANCIAL AID (Fall 2012, est.) 1,219 applied for aid; of those 90% were deemed to have need. 92% of freshmen with need received aid; of those 16% had need fully met. **Average percent of need met:** 16% (excluding resources awarded to replace EFC). **Average financial aid package:** $9240 (excluding resources awarded to replace EFC). 17% of all full-time freshmen had no need and received non-need-based gift aid.
UNDERGRADUATE FINANCIAL AID (Fall 2012, est.) 7,421 applied for aid; of those 100% were deemed to have need. 86% of undergraduates with need received aid; of those 22% had need fully met. **Average percent of need met:** 22% (excluding resources awarded to replace EFC). **Average financial aid package:** $8832 (excluding resources awarded to replace EFC). 11% of all full-time undergraduates had no need and received non-need-based gift aid.
GIFT AID (NEED-BASED) Total amount: $35,095,566 (56% federal, 44% state). **Receiving aid:** Freshmen: 67% (884); all full-time undergraduates: 64% (5,546).

Average award: Freshmen: $6916; Undergraduates: $5966. **Scholarships, grants, and awards:** Federal Pell, FSEOG, state, private.
GIFT AID (NON-NEED-BASED) Total amount: $2,824,157 (15% federal, 1% state, 47% institutional, 37% external sources). **Receiving aid:** Freshmen: 17% (221). Undergraduates: 11% (922). **Average award:** Freshmen: $2252. Undergraduates: $2611. **Scholarships, grants, and awards by category:** Academic interests/achievement: 494 awards ($887,224 total): general academic interests/achievements. Creative arts/performance: general creative arts/performance. Special achievements/activities: general special achievements/activities. Tuition waivers: Full or partial for employees or children of employees. ROTC: Army cooperative.
LOANS Student loans: $47,433,291 (50% need-based, 50% non-need-based). 55% of past graduating class borrowed through all loan programs. Average indebtedness per student: $16,900. **Average need-based loan:** Freshmen: $3794. Undergraduates: $4292. **Parent loans:** $4,762,796 (67% need-based, 33% non-need-based). **Programs:** Federal Direct (Subsidized and Unsubsidized Stafford, PLUS), Perkins.
WORK-STUDY Federal work-study: Total amount: $410,774; 312 jobs averaging $2505. **State or other work-study/employment:** Total amount: $781,882 (100% non-need-based). 346 part-time jobs averaging $2786.
APPLYING FOR FINANCIAL AID Required financial aid form: FAFSA. **Financial aid deadline:** 5/1 (priority: 3/1). **Notification date:** Continuous beginning 5/1.
CONTACT Connie F. Cooke, Director of Financial Aid, Buffalo State College, State University of New York, 1300 Elmwood Avenue, Buffalo, NY 14222-1095, 716-878-4902. Fax: 716-878-4903. E-mail: finaid@buffalostate.edu. Website: http://www.buffalostate.edu/.

BURLINGTON COLLEGE
Burlington, VT

Tuition & fees: $22,410	Average undergraduate aid package: $14,460

ABOUT THE INSTITUTION Independent, coed. **Awards:** certificates, associate, bachelor's, and master's degrees. 18 undergraduate majors. **Total enrollment:** 187. Undergraduates: 185. Freshmen: 37. Federal methodology is used as a basis for awarding need-based institutional aid.
UNDERGRADUATE EXPENSES for 2013–2014 Application fee: $50. **Tuition:** full-time $22,410. Full-time tuition and fees vary according to course load and program. Part-time tuition and fees vary according to course load and program. Room and board charges vary according to housing facility.
FRESHMAN FINANCIAL AID (Fall 2012, est.) 33 applied for aid; of those 85% were deemed to have need. 100% of freshmen with need received aid. **Average percent of need met:** 53% (excluding resources awarded to replace EFC). **Average financial aid package:** $16,520 (excluding resources awarded to replace EFC).
UNDERGRADUATE FINANCIAL AID (Fall 2012, est.) 147 applied for aid; of those 93% were deemed to have need. 96% of undergraduates with need received aid. **Average percent of need met:** 47% (excluding resources awarded to replace EFC). **Average financial aid package:** $14,460 (excluding resources awarded to replace EFC). 1% of all full-time undergraduates had no need and received non-need-based gift aid.
GIFT AID (NEED-BASED) Total amount: $1,345,205 (38% federal, 20% state, 36% institutional, 6% external sources). **Receiving aid:** Freshmen: 78% (28); all full-time undergraduates: 79% (131). **Average award:** Freshmen: $10,954; Undergraduates: $9164. **Scholarships, grants, and awards:** Federal Pell, FSEOG, state, private, college/university gift aid from institutional funds.
GIFT AID (NON-NEED-BASED) Total amount: $19,464 (100% institutional). **Average award:** Undergraduates: $5250. **Scholarships, grants, and awards by category:** Academic interests/achievement: general academic interests/achievements. Special achievements/activities: community service, general special achievements/activities, leadership. Tuition waivers: Full or partial for employees or children of employees.
LOANS Student loans: $1,519,878 (94% need-based, 6% non-need-based). 86% of past graduating class borrowed through all loan programs. Average indebtedness per student: $39,107. **Average need-based loan:** Freshmen: $4711. Undergraduates: $5078. **Parent loans:** $448,700 (80% need-based, 20% non-need-based). **Programs:** Federal Direct (Subsidized and Unsubsidized Stafford, PLUS), Perkins.

WORK-STUDY *Federal work-study:* Total amount: $93,530; jobs available. *State or other work-study/employment:* Total amount: $9000 (100% non-need-based). Part-time jobs available.
APPLYING FOR FINANCIAL AID *Required financial aid form:* FAFSA. *Financial aid deadline:* Continuous. *Notification date:* Continuous beginning 2/15.
CONTACT Ms. Lindy Walsh, Director of Financial Aid, Burlington College, 351 North Avenue, Burlington, VT 05401, 802-862-9616 or toll-free 800-862-9616. *Fax:* 802-846-3072. *E-mail:* lwalsh@burlington.edu.
Website: http://www.burlington.edu/.

BUTLER UNIVERSITY
Indianapolis, IN

Tuition & fees: $33,138	Average undergraduate aid package: $22,467

ABOUT THE INSTITUTION Independent, coed. *Awards:* associate, bachelor's, master's, and doctoral degrees. 55 undergraduate majors. *Total enrollment:* 4,771. Undergraduates: 4,020. Freshmen: 1,101. Federal methodology is used as a basis for awarding need-based institutional aid.
UNDERGRADUATE EXPENSES for 2013–2014 *Application fee:* $35. *One-time required fee:* $288. *Comprehensive fee:* $44,248 includes full-time tuition ($32,280), mandatory fees ($858), and room and board ($11,110). *College room only:* $5370. Full-time tuition and fees vary according to course load, degree level, and program. Room and board charges vary according to housing facility. Part-time tuition and fees vary according to course load, degree level, and program.
FRESHMAN FINANCIAL AID (Fall 2012, est.) 1,059 applied for aid; of those 71% were deemed to have need. 100% of freshmen with need received aid; of those 15% had need fully met. *Average percent of need met:* 74% (excluding resources awarded to replace EFC). *Average financial aid package:* $23,604 (excluding resources awarded to replace EFC). 26% of all full-time freshmen had no need and received non-need-based gift aid.
UNDERGRADUATE FINANCIAL AID (Fall 2012, est.) 3,793 applied for aid; of those 73% were deemed to have need. 100% of undergraduates with need received aid; of those 16% had need fully met. *Average percent of need met:* 72% (excluding resources awarded to replace EFC). *Average financial aid package:* $22,467 (excluding resources awarded to replace EFC). 22% of all full-time undergraduates had no need and received non-need-based gift aid.
GIFT AID (NEED-BASED) *Total amount:* $47,121,885 (7% federal, 6% state, 79% institutional, 8% external sources). *Receiving aid:* Freshmen: 67% (738); all full-time undergraduates: 64% (2,659). *Average award:* Freshmen: $19,179; Undergraduates: $18,179. *Scholarships, grants, and awards:* Federal Pell, FSEOG, state, private, college/university gift aid from institutional funds.
GIFT AID (NON-NEED-BASED) *Total amount:* $12,806,890 (82% institutional, 18% external sources). *Receiving aid:* Freshmen: 10% (106). Undergraduates: 8% (350). *Average award:* Freshmen: $11,666. Undergraduates: $11,459. *Scholarships, grants, and awards by category:* Academic interests/achievement: biological sciences, business, communication, computer science, education, engineering/technologies, English, foreign languages, general academic interests/achievements, health fields, humanities, international studies, mathematics, physical sciences, premedicine, religion/biblical studies, social sciences. *Creative arts/performance:* applied art and design, art/fine arts, cinema/film/broadcasting, dance, journalism/publications, music, performing arts, theater/drama. *Tuition waivers:* Full or partial for employees or children of employees. *ROTC:* Army, Air Force cooperative.
LOANS *Student loans:* $32,064,396 (71% need-based, 29% non-need-based). 64% of past graduating class borrowed through all loan programs. *Average indebtedness per student:* $35,210. *Average need-based loan:* Freshmen: $4076. Undergraduates: $4861. *Parent loans:* $6,864,402 (35% need-based, 65% non-need-based). *Programs:* Federal Direct (Subsidized and Unsubsidized Stafford, PLUS), Perkins.
WORK-STUDY *Federal work-study:* Total amount: $363,281; 287 jobs averaging $975.
ATHLETIC AWARDS Total amount: $4,300,596 (29% need-based, 71% non-need-based).
APPLYING FOR FINANCIAL AID *Required financial aid form:* FAFSA. *Financial aid deadline (priority):* 3/1. *Notification date:* 3/15. Students must reply within 3 weeks of notification.

CONTACT Mrs. Leslie Middleton, Associate Director of Financial Aid, Butler University, 4600 Sunset Avenue, Indianapolis, IN 46208-3485, 317-940-8200 or toll-free 888-940-8100. *Fax:* 317-940-8250. *E-mail:* lmmiddle@butler.edu.
Website: http://www.butler.edu/.

CABARRUS COLLEGE OF HEALTH SCIENCES
Concord, NC

Tuition & fees: N/R	Average undergraduate aid package: N/A

ABOUT THE INSTITUTION Independent, coed. 6 undergraduate majors. Federal methodology is used as a basis for awarding need-based institutional aid.
GIFT AID (NEED-BASED) *Scholarships, grants, and awards:* Federal Pell, FSEOG, state, private, college/university gift aid from institutional funds.
GIFT AID (NON-NEED-BASED) *Scholarships, grants, and awards by category:* Special characteristics: first-generation college students.
LOANS *Programs:* state.
APPLYING FOR FINANCIAL AID *Required financial aid form:* FAFSA. *Financial aid deadline (priority):* 4/15. *Notification date:* Continuous beginning 7/1. Students must reply within 2 weeks of notification.
CONTACT Valerie Richard, Director of Financial Aid, Cabarrus College of Health Sciences, 401 Medical Park Drive, Concord, NC 28025, 704-403-3507. *Fax:* 704-403-2077. *E-mail:* valerie.richard@cabarruscollege.edu.
Website: http://www.cabarruscollege.edu/.

CABRINI COLLEGE
Radnor, PA

Tuition & fees: $29,000	Average undergraduate aid package: $20,553

ABOUT THE INSTITUTION Independent Roman Catholic, coed. *Awards:* bachelor's and master's degrees. 35 undergraduate majors. *Total enrollment:* 2,801. Undergraduates: 1,405. Freshmen: 385. Federal methodology is used as a basis for awarding need-based institutional aid.
UNDERGRADUATE EXPENSES for 2013–2014 *Application fee:* $35. *Tuition:* full-time $28,090. Part-time tuition and fees vary according to course load. Room and board charges vary according to board plan and housing facility.
FRESHMAN FINANCIAL AID (Fall 2012, est.) 364 applied for aid; of those 90% were deemed to have need. 100% of freshmen with need received aid; of those 18% had need fully met. *Average percent of need met:* 56% (excluding resources awarded to replace EFC). *Average financial aid package:* $23,503 (excluding resources awarded to replace EFC). 16% of all full-time freshmen had no need and received non-need-based gift aid.
UNDERGRADUATE FINANCIAL AID (Fall 2012, est.) 1,117 applied for aid; of those 91% were deemed to have need. 100% of undergraduates with need received aid; of those 29% had need fully met. *Average percent of need met:* 58% (excluding resources awarded to replace EFC). *Average financial aid package:* $20,553 (excluding resources awarded to replace EFC). 22% of all full-time undergraduates had no need and received non-need-based gift aid.
GIFT AID (NEED-BASED) *Total amount:* $18,226,669 (12% federal, 7% state, 79% institutional, 2% external sources). *Receiving aid:* Freshmen: 74% (285); all full-time undergraduates: 59% (772). *Average award:* Freshmen: $10,299; Undergraduates: $10,591. *Scholarships, grants, and awards:* Federal Pell, FSEOG, state, private, college/university gift aid from institutional funds.
GIFT AID (NON-NEED-BASED) *Total amount:* $2,887,480 (1% state, 99% institutional). *Receiving aid:* Freshmen: 85% (326). Undergraduates: 78% (1,008). *Average award:* Freshmen: $9650. Undergraduates: $10,876. *Scholarships, grants, and awards by category:* Academic interests/achievement: 1,248 awards ($16,758,957 total): general academic interests/achievements. *Special characteristics:* 351 awards ($436,700 total): children and siblings of alumni, out-of-state students, siblings of current students. *Tuition waivers:* Full or partial for children of alumni, employees or children of employees, senior citizens. *ROTC:* Army cooperative, Air Force cooperative.

LOANS *Student loans:* $10,595,839 (67% need-based, 33% non-need-based). 78% of past graduating class borrowed through all loan programs. *Average indebtedness per student:* $32,503. *Average need-based loan:* Freshmen: $3203. Undergraduates: $3876. *Parent loans:* $3,297,680 (92% need-based, 8% non-need-based). *Programs:* Federal Direct (Subsidized and Unsubsidized Stafford, PLUS), Perkins.

WORK-STUDY *Federal work-study:* Total amount: $414,502; 287 jobs averaging $1446.

APPLYING FOR FINANCIAL AID *Required financial aid form:* FAFSA. *Financial aid deadline (priority):* 2/15. *Notification date:* Continuous beginning 3/1.

CONTACT Mrs. Michelle Taylor, Director of Financial Aid, Cabrini College, 610 King of Prussia Road, Grace Hall, First Floor, Radnor, PA 19087-3698, 610-902-8424 or toll-free 800-848-1003. *Fax:* 610-902-8426. *E-mail:* michelle.rose.taylor@cabrini.edu. *Website:* http://www.cabrini.edu/.

CAIRN UNIVERSITY
Langhorne, PA

Tuition & fees: $22,455	Average undergraduate aid package: $17,074

ABOUT THE INSTITUTION Independent nondenominational, coed. *Awards:* certificates, bachelor's, and master's degrees. 11 undergraduate majors. *Total enrollment:* 1,200. Undergraduates: 952. Freshmen: 173. Federal methodology is used as a basis for awarding need-based institutional aid.

UNDERGRADUATE EXPENSES for 2013–2014 *Application fee:* $25. *Tuition:* full-time $22,250; part-time $660 per credit. Full-time tuition and fees vary according to course load and location. Part-time tuition and fees vary according to course load and location. Room and board charges vary according to board plan and location.

FRESHMAN FINANCIAL AID (Fall 2012, est.) 160 applied for aid; of those 90% were deemed to have need. 100% of freshmen with need received aid; of those 17% had need fully met. *Average percent of need met:* 75% (excluding resources awarded to replace EFC). *Average financial aid package:* $17,659 (excluding resources awarded to replace EFC). 15% of all full-time freshmen had no need and received non-need-based gift aid.

UNDERGRADUATE FINANCIAL AID (Fall 2012, est.) 772 applied for aid; of those 93% were deemed to have need. 100% of undergraduates with need received aid; of those 11% had need fully met. *Average percent of need met:* 70% (excluding resources awarded to replace EFC). *Average financial aid package:* $17,074 (excluding resources awarded to replace EFC). 13% of all full-time undergraduates had no need and received non-need-based gift aid.

GIFT AID (NEED-BASED) *Total amount:* $8,780,310 (20% federal, 10% state, 69% institutional, 1% external sources). *Receiving aid:* Freshmen: 83% (142); all full-time undergraduates: 80% (701). *Average award:* Freshmen: $13,969; Undergraduates: $12,557. *Scholarships, grants, and awards:* Federal Pell, FSEOG, state, private, college/university gift aid from institutional funds.

GIFT AID (NON-NEED-BASED) *Total amount:* $1,062,796 (98% institutional, 2% external sources). *Receiving aid:* Freshmen: 12% (20). Undergraduates: 6% (56). *Average award:* Freshmen: $8933. Undergraduates: $7665. *Scholarships, grants, and awards by category:* Academic interests/achievement: general academic interests/achievements. Creative arts/performance: music. Special achievements/activities: general special achievements/activities. Special characteristics: children of faculty/staff, relatives of clergy. *Tuition waivers:* Full or partial for employees or children of employees. *ROTC:* Air Force cooperative.

LOANS *Student loans:* $7,097,535 (80% need-based, 20% non-need-based). 82% of past graduating class borrowed through all loan programs. *Average indebtedness per student:* $30,633. *Average need-based loan:* Freshmen: $4128. Undergraduates: $4949. *Parent loans:* $744,587 (46% need-based, 54% non-need-based). *Programs:* Federal Direct (Subsidized and Unsubsidized Stafford, PLUS).

WORK-STUDY *Federal work-study:* Total amount: $100,401; jobs available.

APPLYING FOR FINANCIAL AID *Required financial aid form:* FAFSA. *Financial aid deadline:* Continuous. *Notification date:* Continuous beginning 2/15. Students must reply within 2 weeks of notification.

CONTACT Mr. Stephen Cassel, Director of Financial Aid, Cairn University, 200 Manor Avenue, Langhorne, PA 19047-2990, 215-702-4243 or toll-free 800-RUN-2-PBU. *Fax:* 215-702-4248. *E-mail:* scassel@cairn.edu. *Website:* http://cairn.edu/.

CALDWELL COLLEGE
Caldwell, NJ

Tuition & fees: $29,000	Average undergraduate aid package: $19,089

ABOUT THE INSTITUTION Independent Roman Catholic, coed. *Awards:* certificates, bachelor's, master's, and doctoral degrees. 27 undergraduate majors. *Total enrollment:* 2,213. Undergraduates: 1,591. Freshmen: 292. Both federal and institutional methodology are used as a basis for awarding need-based institutional aid.

UNDERGRADUATE EXPENSES for 2013–2014 *Application fee:* $40. *Comprehensive fee:* $40,000 includes full-time tuition ($27,900), mandatory fees ($1100), and room and board ($11,000). Full-time tuition and fees vary according to course load and location. Room and board charges vary according to housing facility. *Part-time tuition:* $738 per credit hour. *Part-time fees:* $150 per semester hour. Part-time tuition and fees vary according to course load and location.

FRESHMAN FINANCIAL AID (Fall 2012, est.) 279 applied for aid; of those 100% were deemed to have need. 97% of freshmen with need received aid; of those 9% had need fully met. *Average percent of need met:* 74% (excluding resources awarded to replace EFC). *Average financial aid package:* $22,700 (excluding resources awarded to replace EFC). 4% of all full-time freshmen had no need and received non-need-based gift aid.

UNDERGRADUATE FINANCIAL AID (Fall 2012, est.) 1,254 applied for aid; of those 92% were deemed to have need. 99% of undergraduates with need received aid; of those 10% had need fully met. *Average percent of need met:* 72% (excluding resources awarded to replace EFC). *Average financial aid package:* $19,089 (excluding resources awarded to replace EFC). 4% of all full-time undergraduates had no need and received non-need-based gift aid.

GIFT AID (NEED-BASED) *Total amount:* $11,292,791 (24% federal, 37% state, 39% institutional). *Receiving aid:* Freshmen: 73% (212); all full-time undergraduates: 70% (884). *Average award:* Freshmen: $16,960; Undergraduates: $12,661. *Scholarships, grants, and awards:* Federal Pell, FSEOG, state, private, college/university gift aid from institutional funds.

GIFT AID (NON-NEED-BASED) *Total amount:* $7,625,142 (98% institutional, 2% external sources). *Receiving aid:* Freshmen: 52% (151). Undergraduates: 48% (604). *Average award:* Freshmen: $15,658. Undergraduates: $10,019. *Scholarships, grants, and awards by category:* Academic interests/achievement: 596 awards ($6,987,641 total): biological sciences, general academic interests/achievements, health fields. Creative arts/performance: 39 awards ($76,800 total): art/fine arts, music. Special achievements/activities: 167 awards ($337,391 total): community service, general special achievements/activities, religious involvement. Special characteristics: 98 awards ($520,401 total): children of current students, children of faculty/staff, general special characteristics, parents of current students, public servants, relatives of clergy, religious affiliation, siblings of current students, spouses of current students, twins, veterans. *Tuition waivers:* Full or partial for children of alumni, employees or children of employees, adult students, senior citizens. *ROTC:* Army cooperative.

LOANS *Student loans:* $9,439,168 (39% need-based, 61% non-need-based). 89% of past graduating class borrowed through all loan programs. *Average indebtedness per student:* $21,209. *Average need-based loan:* Freshmen: $3222. Undergraduates: $3784. *Parent loans:* $2,640,736 (100% non-need-based). *Programs:* Federal Direct (Subsidized and Unsubsidized Stafford, PLUS), state, private loans.

WORK-STUDY *Federal work-study:* Total amount: $212,055; 152 jobs averaging $1395. *State or other work-study/employment:* Total amount: $510,300 (100% non-need-based). 143 part-time jobs averaging $3569.

ATHLETIC AWARDS Total amount: $1,110,530 (100% non-need-based).

APPLYING FOR FINANCIAL AID *Required financial aid forms:* FAFSA, state aid form. *Financial aid deadline:* Continuous. *Notification date:* Continuous beginning 2/15. Students must reply within 4 weeks of notification.

CONTACT Mr. Hayato Suzuki, Director of Financial Aid, Caldwell College, 120 Bloomfield Avenue, Caldwell, NJ 07006, 973-618-3221. *Fax:* 973-618-3650. *E-mail:* financialaid@caldwell.edu. *Website:* http://www.caldwell.edu/.

CALIFORNIA BAPTIST UNIVERSITY
Riverside, CA

Tuition & fees: $26,900	Average undergraduate aid package: $15,926

ABOUT THE INSTITUTION Independent Southern Baptist, coed. *Awards:* bachelor's and master's degrees. 66 undergraduate majors. *Total enrollment:* 6,031. Undergraduates: 4,954. Freshmen: 909. Federal methodology is used as a basis for awarding need-based institutional aid.

UNDERGRADUATE EXPENSES for 2013–2014 *Application fee:* $45. *Comprehensive fee:* $35,890 includes full-time tuition ($25,090), mandatory fees ($1810), and room and board ($8990). *College room only:* $4560. Full-time tuition and fees vary according to course load, location, and program. Room and board charges vary according to board plan and housing facility. *Part-time tuition:* $5790 per year. *Part-time fees:* $350 per year. Part-time tuition and fees vary according to course load, location, and program.

FRESHMAN FINANCIAL AID (Fall 2012, est.) 697 applied for aid; of those 80% were deemed to have need. 100% of freshmen with need received aid; of those 9% had need fully met. *Average percent of need met:* 55% (excluding resources awarded to replace EFC). *Average financial aid package:* $16,593 (excluding resources awarded to replace EFC). 5% of all full-time freshmen had no need and received non-need-based gift aid.

UNDERGRADUATE FINANCIAL AID (Fall 2012, est.) 3,787 applied for aid; of those 77% were deemed to have need. 99% of undergraduates with need received aid; of those 9% had need fully met. *Average percent of need met:* 54% (excluding resources awarded to replace EFC). *Average financial aid package:* $15,926 (excluding resources awarded to replace EFC). 4% of all full-time undergraduates had no need and received non-need-based gift aid.

GIFT AID (NEED-BASED) *Total amount:* $44,806,037 (23% federal, 25% state, 51% institutional, 1% external sources). *Receiving aid:* Freshmen: 64% (548); all full-time undergraduates: 67% (2,879). *Average award:* Freshmen: $13,871; Undergraduates: $12,462. *Scholarships, grants, and awards:* Federal Pell, FSEOG, state, private, college/university gift aid from institutional funds.

GIFT AID (NON-NEED-BASED) *Total amount:* $1,132,722 (98% institutional, 2% external sources). *Receiving aid:* Freshmen: 42% (359). Undergraduates: 41% (1,752). *Average award:* Freshmen: $6437. Undergraduates: $6194. *Scholarships, grants, and awards by category:* Academic interests/achievement: general academic interests/achievements, religion/biblical studies. Creative arts/performance: art/fine arts, music, theater/drama. Special achievements/activities: cheerleading/drum major. Special characteristics: adult students, children of faculty/staff, international students, relatives of clergy, religious affiliation, siblings of current students, veterans. *Tuition waivers:* Full or partial for employees or children of employees. *ROTC:* Army, Air Force cooperative.

LOANS *Student loans:* $44,623,537 (94% need-based, 6% non-need-based). 82% of past graduating class borrowed through all loan programs. *Average indebtedness per student:* $33,807. *Average need-based loan:* Freshmen: $3475. Undergraduates: $4489. *Parent loans:* $9,446,094 (87% need-based, 13% non-need-based). *Programs:* Federal Direct (Subsidized and Unsubsidized Stafford, PLUS), Perkins, alternative loans.

WORK-STUDY *Federal work-study:* Total amount: $250,000; jobs available.

ATHLETIC AWARDS Total amount: $4,373,876 (93% need-based, 7% non-need-based).

APPLYING FOR FINANCIAL AID *Required financial aid forms:* FAFSA, state aid form. *Financial aid deadline (priority):* 3/2. *Notification date:* Continuous beginning 3/2. Students must reply by 6/1.

CONTACT Ms. Rebecca Sanchez, Financial Aid Director, California Baptist University, 8432 Magnolia Avenue, Riverside, CA 92504-3297, 951-343-4236 or toll-free 877-228-8866. *Fax:* 951-343-4518. *E-mail:* rsanchez@calbaptist.edu. *Website:* http://www.calbaptist.edu/.

CALIFORNIA CHRISTIAN COLLEGE
Fresno, CA

Tuition & fees: $8010	Average undergraduate aid package: $9049

ABOUT THE INSTITUTION Independent Free Will Baptist, coed. *Awards:* associate and bachelor's degrees. 1 undergraduate major. *Total enrollment:* 20. Undergraduates: 20. Freshmen: 5. Federal methodology is used as a basis for awarding need-based institutional aid.

UNDERGRADUATE EXPENSES for 2013–2014 *Application fee:* $40. *Comprehensive fee:* $12,210 includes full-time tuition ($7440), mandatory fees ($570), and room and board ($4200). *Part-time tuition:* $310 per credit hour.

FRESHMAN FINANCIAL AID (Fall 2011) 8 applied for aid; of those 100% were deemed to have need. 100% of freshmen with need received aid. *Average percent of need met:* 52% (excluding resources awarded to replace EFC). *Average financial aid package:* $8794 (excluding resources awarded to replace EFC).

UNDERGRADUATE FINANCIAL AID (Fall 2011) 23 applied for aid; of those 96% were deemed to have need. 100% of undergraduates with need received aid; of those 5% had need fully met. *Average percent of need met:* 52% (excluding resources awarded to replace EFC). *Average financial aid package:* $9049 (excluding resources awarded to replace EFC).

GIFT AID (NEED-BASED) *Total amount:* $127,007 (89% federal, 7% state, 4% external sources). *Receiving aid:* Freshmen: 100% (8); all full-time undergraduates: 91% (21). *Average award:* Freshmen: $4838; Undergraduates: $4600. *Scholarships, grants, and awards:* Federal Pell, FSEOG, state, private, college/university gift aid from institutional funds.

LOANS *Student loans:* $123,026 (100% need-based). 100% of past graduating class borrowed through all loan programs. *Average indebtedness per student:* $33,595. *Average need-based loan:* Freshmen: $3500. Undergraduates: $3484. *Programs:* Federal Direct (Subsidized and Unsubsidized Stafford, PLUS).

WORK-STUDY *Federal work-study:* Total amount: $11,534; 10 jobs averaging $1153.

APPLYING FOR FINANCIAL AID *Required financial aid forms:* FAFSA, institution's own form, Cal Grant forms, GPA verification form (CA residents only). *Financial aid deadline (priority):* 3/2. *Notification date:* 8/15.

CONTACT Mindy Scroggins, Financial Aid Coordinator, California Christian College, 4881 East University Avenue, Fresno, CA 93703, 559-251-4215 Ext. 5580. *Fax:* 559-251-4231. *E-mail:* financialaid@calchristiancollege.edu. *Website:* http://www.calchristiancollege.edu/.

CALIFORNIA COAST UNIVERSITY
Santa Ana, CA

CONTACT Financial Aid Office, California Coast University, 925 North Spurgeon Street, Santa Ana, CA 92701, 714-547-9625 or toll-free 888-CCU-UNIV. *Website:* http://www.calcoast.edu/.

CALIFORNIA COLLEGE
San Diego, CA

Tuition & fees: N/R	Average undergraduate aid package: N/A

ABOUT THE INSTITUTION Proprietary, coed. 9 undergraduate majors. Federal methodology is used as a basis for awarding need-based institutional aid.

GIFT AID (NEED-BASED) *Scholarships, grants, and awards:* Federal Pell, FSEOG, state.

LOANS *Programs:* Federal Direct (Subsidized and Unsubsidized Stafford, PLUS).

APPLYING FOR FINANCIAL AID *Required financial aid forms:* FAFSA, institution's own form. *Financial aid deadline:* Continuous. *Notification date:* Continuous.

CONTACT Raul Rivera, Senior Financial Aid Officer, California College, 6602 Convoy Court, #100, San Diego, CA 92111, 619-680-4430 Ext. 1507 or toll-free 800-622-3188. *Fax:* 619-695-5793. *E-mail:* raul.rivera@cc-sd.edu. *Website:* http://www.cc-sd.edu/.

CALIFORNIA COLLEGE OF THE ARTS
San Francisco, CA

Tuition & fees: $40,334	Average undergraduate aid package: $25,533

ABOUT THE INSTITUTION Independent, coed. *Awards:* certificates, bachelor's, and master's degrees. 22 undergraduate majors. *Total enrollment:* 1,932. Undergraduates: 1,465. Freshmen: 233. Federal methodology is used as a basis for awarding need-based institutional aid.

UNDERGRADUATE EXPENSES for 2013–2014 *Application fee:* $60. *Tuition:* full-time $39,984; part-time $1666 per unit. Full-time tuition and fees vary according to degree level. Part-time tuition and fees vary according to course load and degree level. Room and board charges vary according to housing facility.

FRESHMAN FINANCIAL AID (Fall 2012, est.) 151 applied for aid; of those 89% were deemed to have need. 100% of freshmen with need received aid; of those 6% had need fully met. *Average percent of need met:* 64% (excluding resources awarded to replace EFC). *Average financial aid package:* $26,584 (excluding resources awarded to replace EFC). 21% of all full-time freshmen had no need and received non-need-based gift aid.

UNDERGRADUATE FINANCIAL AID (Fall 2012, est.) 916 applied for aid; of those 93% were deemed to have need. 100% of undergraduates with need received aid; of those 4% had need fully met. *Average percent of need met:* 58% (excluding resources awarded to replace EFC). *Average financial aid package:* $25,533 (excluding resources awarded to replace EFC). 16% of all full-time undergraduates had no need and received non-need-based gift aid.

GIFT AID (NEED-BASED) *Total amount:* $18,462,397 (13% federal, 10% state, 72% institutional, 5% external sources). *Receiving aid:* Freshmen: 58% (134); all full-time undergraduates: 62% (848). *Average award:* Freshmen: $22,962; Undergraduates: $20,474. *Scholarships, grants, and awards:* Federal Pell, FSEOG, state, private, college/university gift aid from institutional funds.

GIFT AID (NON-NEED-BASED) *Total amount:* $2,137,122 (97% institutional, 3% external sources). *Receiving aid:* Freshmen: 48% (111). Undergraduates: 35% (475). *Average award:* Freshmen: $8900. Undergraduates: $8635. *Scholarships, grants, and awards by category: Academic interests/achievement:* general academic interests/achievements. *Tuition waivers:* Full or partial for employees or children of employees.

LOANS *Student loans:* $10,489,251 (93% need-based, 7% non-need-based). 64% of past graduating class borrowed through all loan programs. *Average indebtedness per student:* $36,300. *Average need-based loan:* Freshmen: $3613. Undergraduates: $5035. *Parent loans:* $2,666,085 (73% need-based, 27% non-need-based). *Programs:* Federal Direct (Subsidized and Unsubsidized Stafford, PLUS), Perkins, private loans.

WORK-STUDY *Federal work-study:* Total amount: $390,768; 806 jobs averaging $3019. *State or other work-study/employment:* Total amount: $634,886 (100% non-need-based). 99 part-time jobs averaging $2916.

APPLYING FOR FINANCIAL AID *Required financial aid form:* FAFSA. *Financial aid deadline (priority):* 3/1. *Notification date:* Continuous beginning 4/1. Students must reply by 5/1 or within 3 weeks of notification.

CONTACT Office of Financial Aid, California College of the Arts, 1111 Eighth Street, San Francisco, CA 94107, 415-703-9528 or toll-free 800-447-1ART. *Fax:* 415-551-9261. *E-mail:* finaid@cca.edu. *Website:* http://www.cca.edu/.

CALIFORNIA INSTITUTE OF INTEGRAL STUDIES
San Francisco, CA

Tuition & fees: N/R	Average undergraduate aid package: $6200

ABOUT THE INSTITUTION Independent, coed. 1 undergraduate major. Federal methodology is used as a basis for awarding need-based institutional aid.

UNDERGRADUATE FINANCIAL AID (Fall 2011) 80 applied for aid; of those 94% were deemed to have need. 100% of undergraduates with need received aid; of those 3% had need fully met. *Average percent of need met:* 10% (excluding resources awarded to replace EFC). *Average financial aid package:* $6200

(excluding resources awarded to replace EFC). 2% of all full-time undergraduates had no need and received non-need-based gift aid.

GIFT AID (NEED-BASED) *Total amount:* $532,403 (54% federal, 8% state, 37% institutional, 1% external sources). *Receiving aid:* All full-time undergraduates: 65% (55). *Average award:* Undergraduates: $5400. *Scholarships, grants, and awards:* Federal Pell, FSEOG, state, private, college/university gift aid from institutional funds, Workforce Investment Act Grants, Yellow Ribbon Grant Program.

GIFT AID (NON-NEED-BASED) *Total amount:* $6095 (98% institutional, 2% external sources). *Receiving aid:* Undergraduates: 2% (2). *Average award:* Undergraduates: $2100. *Scholarships, grants, and awards by category: Creative arts/performance:* 1 award ($15,000 total): creative writing. *Special achievements/activities:* 1 award ($15,000 total): community service, leadership. *Special characteristics:* 17 awards ($3000 total): ethnic background, international students, public servants, veterans, veterans' children.

LOANS *Student loans:* $1,543,507 (96% need-based, 4% non-need-based). 83% of past graduating class borrowed through all loan programs. *Average indebtedness per student:* $21,026. *Average need-based loan:* Undergraduates: $5500. *Parent loans:* $29,422 (61% need-based, 39% non-need-based). *Programs:* Federal Direct (Subsidized and Unsubsidized Stafford, PLUS), private loans.

WORK-STUDY *Federal work-study:* Total amount: $6000; 2 jobs averaging $6000.

APPLYING FOR FINANCIAL AID *Financial aid deadline (priority):* 4/15. *Notification date:* Continuous. Students must reply within 4 weeks of notification.

CONTACT Financial Aid Office, California Institute of Integral Studies, 1453 Mission Street, San Francisco, CA 94103, 415-575-6122. *Fax:* 415-575-1268. *E-mail:* finaid@ciis.edu. *Website:* http://www.ciis.edu/.

CALIFORNIA INSTITUTE OF TECHNOLOGY
Pasadena, CA

Tuition & fees: $41,538	Average undergraduate aid package: $38,756

ABOUT THE INSTITUTION Independent, coed. *Awards:* certificates, bachelor's, master's, and doctoral degrees. 25 undergraduate majors. *Total enrollment:* 2,243. Undergraduates: 997. Freshmen: 264. Both federal and institutional methodology are used as a basis for awarding need-based institutional aid.

UNDERGRADUATE EXPENSES for 2013–2014 *Application fee:* $65. *One-time required fee:* $500. *Comprehensive fee:* $54,045 includes full-time tuition ($39,990), mandatory fees ($1548), and room and board ($12,507). *College room only:* $7035. Full-time tuition and fees vary according to course load. *Part-time tuition:* $1111 per credit hour. Part-time tuition and fees vary according to course load.

FRESHMAN FINANCIAL AID (Fall 2012, est.) 216 applied for aid; of those 75% were deemed to have need. 100% of freshmen with need received aid; of those 100% had need fully met. *Average percent of need met:* 100% (excluding resources awarded to replace EFC). *Average financial aid package:* $37,984 (excluding resources awarded to replace EFC).

UNDERGRADUATE FINANCIAL AID (Fall 2012, est.) 609 applied for aid; of those 86% were deemed to have need. 100% of undergraduates with need received aid; of those 100% had need fully met. *Average percent of need met:* 100% (excluding resources awarded to replace EFC). *Average financial aid package:* $38,756 (excluding resources awarded to replace EFC). 1% of all full-time undergraduates had no need and received non-need-based gift aid.

GIFT AID (NEED-BASED) *Total amount:* $17,140,040 (4% federal, 94% institutional, 2% external sources). *Receiving aid:* Freshmen: 62% (163); all full-time undergraduates: 52% (522). *Average award:* Freshmen: $34,931; Undergraduates: $34,831. *Scholarships, grants, and awards:* Federal Pell, FSEOG, state, private, college/university gift aid from institutional funds.

GIFT AID (NON-NEED-BASED) *Total amount:* $438,159 (13% institutional, 87% external sources). *Receiving aid:* Freshmen: 1% (2). Undergraduates: 3% (30). *Average award:* Undergraduates: $56,382. *Scholarships, grants, and awards by category: Academic interests/achievement:* 1 award ($56,382 total): general academic interests/achievements. *Tuition waivers:* Full or partial for employees or children of employees. *ROTC:* Army cooperative, Air Force cooperative.

LOANS *Student loans:* $1,473,684 (96% need-based, 4% non-need-based). 44% of past graduating class borrowed through all loan programs. *Average indebtedness per student:* $15,090. *Average need-based loan:* Freshmen: $4147. Undergraduates: $3978. *Parent loans:* $423,345 (47% need-based, 53% non-need-based). *Programs:* Federal Direct (Subsidized and Unsubsidized Stafford, PLUS), Perkins, college/university.

WORK-STUDY *Federal work-study:* Total amount: $881,881; 288 jobs averaging $3062. *State or other work-study/employment:* Total amount: $150,800 (93% need-based, 7% non-need-based). 58 part-time jobs averaging $2600.

APPLYING FOR FINANCIAL AID *Required financial aid forms:* FAFSA, institution's own form, CSS Financial Aid PROFILE, state aid form, noncustodial (divorced/separated) parent's statement, business/farm supplement. *Financial aid deadline (priority):* 2/1. *Notification date:* Continuous beginning 3/30. Students must reply by 5/1 or within 2 weeks of notification.

CONTACT Don Crewell, Director of Financial Aid, California Institute of Technology, 1200 East California Boulevard, MC 20-90, Pasadena, CA 91125-3405, 626-395-6280. *Fax:* 626-564-8136. *E-mail:* dcrewell@caltech.edu. *Website:* http://www.caltech.edu/.

CALIFORNIA INSTITUTE OF THE ARTS
Valencia, CA

CONTACT Ms. Bobbi Heuer, Director of Financial Aid, California Institute of the Arts, 24700 McBean Parkway, Valencia, CA 91355-2340, 661-253-7869 or toll-free 800-545-2787. *Fax:* 661-287-3816. *E-mail:* bheuer@calarts.edu. *Website:* http://www.calarts.edu/.

CALIFORNIA INTERCONTINENTAL UNIVERSITY
Diamond Bar, CA

CONTACT Financial Aid Office, California Intercontinental University, 1470 Valley Vista Drive, Suite 150, Diamond Bar, CA 91765, 909-396-6090 or toll-free 866-687-2258. *Website:* http://caluniversity.edu/.

CALIFORNIA LUTHERAN UNIVERSITY
Thousand Oaks, CA

Tuition & fees: $34,360	Average undergraduate aid package: $22,740

ABOUT THE INSTITUTION Independent Lutheran, coed. *Awards:* certificates, bachelor's, master's, and doctoral degrees. 53 undergraduate majors. *Total enrollment:* 4,103. Undergraduates: 2,713. Freshmen: 502. Federal methodology is used as a basis for awarding need-based institutional aid.

UNDERGRADUATE EXPENSES for 2013–2014 *Application fee:* $45. *Comprehensive fee:* $45,870 includes full-time tuition ($33,910), mandatory fees ($450), and room and board ($11,510). *College room only:* $6220. Room and board charges vary according to board plan. *Part-time tuition:* $1090 per credit hour. *Part-time fees:* $225 per term.

FRESHMAN FINANCIAL AID (Fall 2012, est.) 463 applied for aid; of those 84% were deemed to have need. 100% of freshmen with need received aid; of those 17% had need fully met. *Average percent of need met:* 70% (excluding resources awarded to replace EFC). *Average financial aid package:* $23,880 (excluding resources awarded to replace EFC). 28% of all full-time freshmen had no need and received non-need-based gift aid.

UNDERGRADUATE FINANCIAL AID (Fall 2012, est.) 1,952 applied for aid; of those 90% were deemed to have need. 100% of undergraduates with need received aid; of those 11% had need fully met. *Average percent of need met:* 65% (excluding resources awarded to replace EFC). *Average financial aid package:*

$22,740 (excluding resources awarded to replace EFC). 26% of all full-time undergraduates had no need and received non-need-based gift aid.

GIFT AID (NEED-BASED) *Total amount:* $32,640,206 (9% federal, 14% state, 76% institutional, 1% external sources). *Receiving aid:* Freshmen: 69% (387); all full-time undergraduates: 67% (1,729). *Average award:* Freshmen: $20,870; Undergraduates: $18,880. *Scholarships, grants, and awards:* Federal Pell, FSEOG, state, private, college/university gift aid from institutional funds.

GIFT AID (NON-NEED-BASED) *Receiving aid:* Freshmen: 3% (15). Undergraduates: 2% (62). *Average award:* Freshmen: $14,400. Undergraduates: $13,020. *Scholarships, grants, and awards by category:* Academic interests/achievement: biological sciences, business, communication, computer science, education, English, foreign languages, general academic interests/achievements, humanities, international studies, mathematics, physical sciences, religion/biblical studies, social sciences. *Creative arts/performance:* art/fine arts, creative writing, journalism/publications, music, performing arts, theater/drama. *Special achievements/activities:* community service, general special achievements/activities, leadership, religious involvement. *Special characteristics:* adult students, children and siblings of alumni, children of faculty/staff, international students, relatives of clergy, religious affiliation, veterans, veterans' children. *ROTC:* Army cooperative, Air Force cooperative.

LOANS *Student loans:* $13,296,565 (94% need-based, 6% non-need-based). 76% of past graduating class borrowed through all loan programs. *Average indebtedness per student:* $26,610. *Average need-based loan:* Freshmen: $3500. Undergraduates: $4680. *Parent loans:* $9,238,242 (87% need-based, 13% non-need-based). *Programs:* Federal Direct (Subsidized and Unsubsidized Stafford, PLUS), Perkins.

WORK-STUDY *Federal work-study:* Total amount: $500,000; 301 jobs averaging $2500.

APPLYING FOR FINANCIAL AID *Required financial aid forms:* FAFSA, Cal Grant forms, GPA verification form (CA residents only). *Financial aid deadline (priority):* 3/1. *Notification date:* Continuous beginning 3/15. Students must reply by 5/1 or within 2 weeks of notification.

CONTACT Susan Arias, Director of Financial Aid, California Lutheran University, 60 West Olsen Road, Thousand Oaks, CA 91360-2787, 805-493-3115 or toll-free 877-258-3678. *Fax:* 805-493-3114. *E-mail:* arias@callutheran.edu. *Website:* http://www.callutheran.edu/.

CALIFORNIA MARITIME ACADEMY
Vallejo, CA

Tuition & fees: N/R	Average undergraduate aid package: $20,970

ABOUT THE INSTITUTION State-supported, coed. *Awards:* bachelor's and master's degrees. 4 undergraduate majors. *Total enrollment:* 863. Undergraduates: 863. Freshmen: 145. Federal methodology is used as a basis for awarding need-based institutional aid.

FRESHMAN FINANCIAL AID (Fall 2012, est.) 286 applied for aid; of those 80% were deemed to have need. 98% of freshmen with need received aid; of those .4% had need fully met. *Average percent of need met:* 80% (excluding resources awarded to replace EFC). *Average financial aid package:* $19,729 (excluding resources awarded to replace EFC).

UNDERGRADUATE FINANCIAL AID (Fall 2012, est.) 723 applied for aid; of those 80% were deemed to have need. 99% of undergraduates with need received aid; of those 44% had need fully met. *Average percent of need met:* 86% (excluding resources awarded to replace EFC). *Average financial aid package:* $20,970 (excluding resources awarded to replace EFC). 1% of all full-time undergraduates had no need and received non-need-based gift aid.

GIFT AID (NEED-BASED) *Total amount:* $4,583,506 (41% federal, 14% state, 41% institutional, 4% external sources). *Receiving aid:* Freshmen: 45% (144); all full-time undergraduates: 52% (452). *Average award:* Freshmen: $8878; Undergraduates: $7261. *Scholarships, grants, and awards:* Federal Pell, FSEOG, state, private, college/university gift aid from institutional funds.

GIFT AID (NON-NEED-BASED) *Total amount:* $32,700 (100% external sources). *Average award:* Undergraduates: $2500. *Scholarships, grants, and awards by category:* Academic interests/achievement: 36 awards ($100,000 total): general academic interests/achievements. *ROTC:* Naval cooperative.

LOANS *Student loans:* $5,823,682 (86% need-based, 14% non-need-based). 65% of past graduating class borrowed through all loan programs. *Average indebtedness per student:* $18,579. *Average need-based loan:* Freshmen: $4424. Undergrad-

CALIFORNIA MARITIME ACADEMY

uates: $3673. **Parent loans:** $4,414,221 (61% need-based, 39% non-need-based). **Programs:** Federal Direct (Subsidized and Unsubsidized Stafford, PLUS), Perkins.

WORK-STUDY *Federal work-study:* Total amount: $34,108; 19 jobs averaging $1795.

ATHLETIC AWARDS Total amount: $60,000 (78% need-based, 22% non-need-based).

APPLYING FOR FINANCIAL AID *Required financial aid forms:* FAFSA, state aid form. *Financial aid deadline (priority):* 3/2. *Notification date:* Continuous beginning 4/15. Students must reply by 6/1.

CONTACT Nicole Hill, Director of Financial Aid, California Maritime Academy, 200 Maritime Academy Drive, Vallejo, CA 94590-0644, 707-654-1275 or toll-free 800-561-1945. *Fax:* 707-654-1007. *E-mail:* finaid@csum.edu. *Website:* http://www.csum.edu/.

CALIFORNIA MIRAMAR UNIVERSITY
San Diego, CA

CONTACT Financial Aid Office, California Miramar University, 9750 Miramar Road, Suite 180, San Diego, CA 92126, 858-653-3000 or toll-free 877-570-5678. *Website:* http://www.calmu.edu/.

CALIFORNIA NATIONAL UNIVERSITY FOR ADVANCED STUDIES
Northridge, CA

CONTACT Office of Academic Affairs, California National University for Advanced Studies, 16909 Parthenia Street, North Hills, CA 91343, 800-782-2422. *Website:* http://www.cnuas.edu/.

CALIFORNIA POLYTECHNIC STATE UNIVERSITY, SAN LUIS OBISPO
San Luis Obispo, CA

Tuition & fees (CA res): $8523	Average undergraduate aid package: $10,101

ABOUT THE INSTITUTION State-supported, coed. *Awards:* bachelor's and master's degrees. 63 undergraduate majors. *Total enrollment:* 18,679. Undergraduates: 17,680. Freshmen: 3,701. Federal methodology is used as a basis for awarding need-based institutional aid.

UNDERGRADUATE EXPENSES for 2013–2014 *Application fee:* $55. *Tuition, state resident:* full-time $5472. *Tuition, nonresident:* full-time $16,632; part-time $248 per unit. *Required fees:* full-time $3051. Full-time tuition and fees vary according to course load, degree level, and program. Part-time tuition and fees vary according to course load, degree level, and program. *College room and board:* $10,679; *Room only:* $6123. Room and board charges vary according to housing facility.

FRESHMAN FINANCIAL AID (Fall 2011) 3,418 applied for aid; of those 55% were deemed to have need. 89% of freshmen with need received aid; of those 6% had need fully met. *Average percent of need met:* 58% (excluding resources awarded to replace EFC). *Average financial aid package:* $9543 (excluding resources awarded to replace EFC). 9% of all full-time freshmen had no need and received non-need-based gift aid.

UNDERGRADUATE FINANCIAL AID (Fall 2011) 10,309 applied for aid; of those 70% were deemed to have need. 91% of undergraduates with need received aid; of those 5% had need fully met. *Average percent of need met:* 60% (excluding resources awarded to replace EFC). *Average financial aid package:* $10,101 (excluding resources awarded to replace EFC). 5% of all full-time undergraduates had no need and received non-need-based gift aid.

GIFT AID (NEED-BASED) *Total amount:* $43,871,311 (35% federal, 53% state, 6% institutional, 6% external sources). *Receiving aid:* Freshmen: 32% (1,371); all full-time undergraduates: 30% (5,020). *Average award:* Freshmen: $3370; Undergrad-

uates: $3605. *Scholarships, grants, and awards:* Federal Pell, FSEOG, state, private, college/university gift aid from institutional funds, TEACH Grants.

GIFT AID (NON-NEED-BASED) *Total amount:* $4,377,548 (55% institutional, 45% external sources). *Receiving aid:* Freshmen: 1% (53). Undergraduates: 1% (118). *Average award:* Freshmen: $1948. Undergraduates: $2416. *Scholarships, grants, and awards by category:* Academic interests/achievement: agriculture, architecture, biological sciences, business, communication, computer science, education, engineering/technologies, English, foreign languages, general academic interests/achievements, health fields, home economics, humanities, international studies, library science, mathematics, military science, physical sciences, social sciences. *Creative arts/performance:* applied art and design, art/fine arts, cinema/film/broadcasting, creative writing, dance, debating, general creative arts/performance, journalism/publications, music, performing arts, theater/drama. *Special achievements/activities:* community service, leadership, rodeo. *Special characteristics:* children and siblings of alumni, general special characteristics, local/state students. *Tuition waivers:* Full or partial for employees or children of employees. *ROTC:* Army.

LOANS *Student loans:* $42,122,521 (68% need-based, 32% non-need-based). *Average need-based loan:* Freshmen: $3188. Undergraduates: $3794. *Parent loans:* $29,326,323 (23% need-based, 77% non-need-based). *Programs:* Federal Direct (Subsidized and Unsubsidized Stafford, PLUS), Perkins, college/university, alternative loans.

WORK-STUDY *Federal work-study:* Total amount: $900,716; jobs available.

ATHLETIC AWARDS Total amount: $3,693,627 (32% need-based, 68% non-need-based).

APPLYING FOR FINANCIAL AID *Required financial aid form:* FAFSA. *Financial aid deadline (priority):* 3/2. *Notification date:* Continuous beginning 4/1.

CONTACT Lois Kelly, Director of Financial Aid, California Polytechnic State University, San Luis Obispo, Financial Aid Office, Administration Building, Room 212, San Luis Obispo, CA 93407, 805-756-2927. *Fax:* 805-756-7243. *E-mail:* financialaid@calpoly.edu. *Website:* http://www.calpoly.edu/.

CALIFORNIA STATE POLYTECHNIC UNIVERSITY, POMONA
Pomona, CA

Tuition & fees (CA res): $6623	Average undergraduate aid package: $10,005

ABOUT THE INSTITUTION State-supported, coed. *Awards:* bachelor's, master's, and doctoral degrees. 52 undergraduate majors. *Total enrollment:* 22,156. Undergraduates: 20,542. Freshmen: 3,120. Federal methodology is used as a basis for awarding need-based institutional aid.

UNDERGRADUATE EXPENSES for 2013–2014 *Application fee:* $55. *Tuition, state resident:* full-time $5970. *Tuition, nonresident:* full-time $17,130. *Required fees:* full-time $653; $248 per credit. Full-time tuition and fees vary according to course load, degree level, and program. Part-time tuition and fees vary according to course load, degree level, and program. *College room and board:* $11,615; *Room only:* $6921. Room and board charges vary according to board plan and housing facility.

FRESHMAN FINANCIAL AID (Fall 2012, est.) 2,620 applied for aid; of those 78% were deemed to have need. 91% of freshmen with need received aid; of those .4% had need fully met. *Average percent of need met:* 58% (excluding resources awarded to replace EFC). *Average financial aid package:* $9567 (excluding resources awarded to replace EFC). 1% of all full-time freshmen had no need and received non-need-based gift aid.

UNDERGRADUATE FINANCIAL AID (Fall 2012, est.) 13,503 applied for aid; of those 87% were deemed to have need. 93% of undergraduates with need received aid; of those 1% had need fully met. *Average percent of need met:* 54% (excluding resources awarded to replace EFC). *Average financial aid package:* $10,005 (excluding resources awarded to replace EFC). 1% of all full-time undergraduates had no need and received non-need-based gift aid.

GIFT AID (NEED-BASED) *Total amount:* $109,705,374 (51% federal, 49% state). *Receiving aid:* Freshmen: 49% (1,464); all full-time undergraduates: 51% (8,978). *Average award:* Freshmen: $9004; Undergraduates: $8772. *Scholarships, grants, and awards:* Federal Pell, FSEOG, state, private, college/university gift aid from institutional funds.

GIFT AID (NON-NEED-BASED) *Total amount:* $1,885,570 (6% state, 14% institutional, 80% external sources). *Receiving aid:* Freshmen: 5% (157). Undergraduates: 4% (791). *Average award:* Freshmen: $2000. Undergraduates: $2791. *Scholarships, grants, and awards by category:* Academic interests/achievement: agriculture, architecture, biological sciences, business, computer science, education, engineering/technologies, general academic interests/achievements, humanities, mathematics, physical sciences, social sciences. *Special achievements/activities:* hobbies/interests, leadership. *Special characteristics:* children and siblings of alumni, children of current students, members of minority groups. *Tuition waivers:* Full or partial for employees or children of employees. *ROTC:* Army.

LOANS *Student loans:* $59,393,834 (54% need-based, 46% non-need-based). 45% of past graduating class borrowed through all loan programs. *Average indebtedness per student:* $18,805. *Average need-based loan:* Freshmen: $3539. Undergraduates: $4525. *Parent loans:* $2,969,280 (100% non-need-based). *Programs:* Perkins, college/university, alternative loans.

WORK-STUDY *Federal work-study:* Total amount: $883,593; 323 jobs averaging $2736.

ATHLETIC AWARDS Total amount: $631,331 (100% non-need-based).

APPLYING FOR FINANCIAL AID *Required financial aid form:* FAFSA. *Financial aid deadline:* Continuous. *Notification date:* Continuous beginning 4/1. Students must reply within 6 weeks of notification.

CONTACT Diana Minor, Director of Financial Aid and Scholarships, California State Polytechnic University, Pomona, 3801 West Temple Avenue, Pomona, CA 91768-2557, 909-869-3704. *Fax:* 909-869-4757. *E-mail:* dyminor@csupomona.edu. *Website:* http://www.csupomona.edu/.

CALIFORNIA STATE UNIVERSITY, BAKERSFIELD
Bakersfield, CA

Tuition & fees (CA res): $6709	Average undergraduate aid package: $4175

ABOUT THE INSTITUTION State-supported, coed. *Awards:* bachelor's and master's degrees. 30 undergraduate majors. *Total enrollment:* 8,002. Undergraduates: 6,737. Freshmen: 1,060. Federal methodology is used as a basis for awarding need-based institutional aid.

UNDERGRADUATE EXPENSES for 2013–2014 *Tuition, state resident:* full-time $5472. *Tuition, nonresident:* full-time $16,632. *Required fees:* full-time $1237. Full-time tuition and fees vary according to course load, degree level, and reciprocity agreements. Part-time tuition and fees vary according to course load, degree level, and reciprocity agreements. *College room and board:* $8787. Room and board charges vary according to board plan.

FRESHMAN FINANCIAL AID (Fall 2011) 1,340 applied for aid; of those 76% were deemed to have need. 62% of freshmen with need received aid; of those 4% had need fully met. *Average percent of need met:* 72% (excluding resources awarded to replace EFC). *Average financial aid package:* $4156 (excluding resources awarded to replace EFC).

UNDERGRADUATE FINANCIAL AID (Fall 2011) 3,411 applied for aid; of those 93% were deemed to have need. 86% of undergraduates with need received aid; of those 3% had need fully met. *Average percent of need met:* 72% (excluding resources awarded to replace EFC). *Average financial aid package:* $4175 (excluding resources awarded to replace EFC).

GIFT AID (NEED-BASED) *Total amount:* $44,493,460 (44% federal, 53% state, 1% institutional, 2% external sources). *Receiving aid:* Freshmen: 28% (627); all full-time undergraduates: 42% (2,719). *Average award:* Freshmen: $8322; Undergraduates: $3255. *Scholarships, grants, and awards:* Federal Pell, FSEOG, state, private, college/university gift aid from institutional funds, Federal Nursing.

GIFT AID (NON-NEED-BASED) *Total amount:* $6472 (100% state). *Receiving aid:* Freshmen: 3% (74). Undergraduates: 4% (243). *Scholarships, grants, and awards by category:* Academic interests/achievement: agriculture, architecture, biological sciences, business, communication, education, foreign languages, general academic interests/achievements, health fields, humanities, mathematics, physical sciences, premedicine, religion/biblical studies, social sciences. *Creative arts/performance:* art/fine arts, dance, music, theater/drama. *Special achievements/activities:* community service, general special achievements/activities, leadership. *Special characteristics:* children of faculty/staff, children of union members/company

employees, ethnic background, first-generation college students, local/state students, veterans.

LOANS *Student loans:* $21,208,950 (100% need-based). 86% of past graduating class borrowed through all loan programs. *Average indebtedness per student:* $10,101. *Average need-based loan:* Freshmen: $1114. Undergraduates: $1463. *Parent loans:* $281,524 (100% need-based). *Programs:* Federal Direct (Subsidized and Unsubsidized Stafford, PLUS), Perkins, Federal Nursing, college/university.

WORK-STUDY *Federal work-study:* Total amount: $266,983; jobs available.

ATHLETIC AWARDS Total amount: $1,737,680 (100% need-based).

APPLYING FOR FINANCIAL AID *Required financial aid forms:* FAFSA, state aid form. *Financial aid deadline:* Continuous. *Notification date:* Continuous beginning 4/15. Students must reply within 3 weeks of notification.

CONTACT Dr. Ron Radney, Director of Financial Aid and Scholarships, California State University, Bakersfield, 9001 Stockdale Highway, Bakersfield, CA 93311-1022, 661-654-3271 or toll-free 800-788-2782. *Fax:* 661-654-6800. *E-mail:* rradney@csub.edu. *Website:* http://www.csub.edu/.

CALIFORNIA STATE UNIVERSITY CHANNEL ISLANDS
Camarillo, CA

CONTACT Financial Aid Office, California State University Channel Islands, One University Drive, Camarillo, CA 93012, 805-437-8400. *Website:* http://www.csuci.edu/.

CALIFORNIA STATE UNIVERSITY, CHICO
Chico, CA

Tuition & fees (CA res): $8906	Average undergraduate aid package: $11,501

ABOUT THE INSTITUTION State-supported, coed. *Awards:* certificates, bachelor's, and master's degrees. 115 undergraduate majors. *Total enrollment:* 16,470. Undergraduates: 15,316. Freshmen: 2,714. Federal methodology is used as a basis for awarding need-based institutional aid.

UNDERGRADUATE EXPENSES for 2013–2014 *Application fee:* $55. *Tuition, state resident:* full-time $7438. *Tuition, nonresident:* full-time $18,598. *Required fees:* full-time $1468. Full-time tuition and fees vary according to degree level. Part-time tuition and fees vary according to course load and degree level. *College room and board:* $11,208. Room and board charges vary according to board plan and housing facility.

FRESHMAN FINANCIAL AID (Fall 2011) 1,984 applied for aid; of those 75% were deemed to have need. 93% of freshmen with need received aid; of those 13% had need fully met. *Average percent of need met:* 80% (excluding resources awarded to replace EFC). *Average financial aid package:* $12,538 (excluding resources awarded to replace EFC). 2% of all full-time freshmen had no need and received non-need-based gift aid.

UNDERGRADUATE FINANCIAL AID (Fall 2011) 9,927 applied for aid; of those 84% were deemed to have need. 96% of undergraduates with need received aid; of those 14% had need fully met. *Average percent of need met:* 84% (excluding resources awarded to replace EFC). *Average financial aid package:* $11,501 (excluding resources awarded to replace EFC). 1% of all full-time undergraduates had no need and received non-need-based gift aid.

GIFT AID (NEED-BASED) *Total amount:* $59,129,099 (46% federal, 54% state). *Receiving aid:* Freshmen: 41% (992); all full-time undergraduates: 43% (6,057). *Average award:* Freshmen: $10,449; Undergraduates: $9374. *Scholarships, grants, and awards:* Federal Pell, FSEOG, state, private, college/university gift aid from institutional funds, United Negro College Fund.

GIFT AID (NON-NEED-BASED) *Total amount:* $2,817,515 (2% state, 40% institutional, 58% external sources). *Receiving aid:* Freshmen: 13% (317). Undergraduates: 8% (1,146). *Average award:* Freshmen: $2111. Undergraduates: $2595. *Scholarships, grants, and awards by category:* Academic interests/achievement: agriculture, area/ethnic studies, biological sciences, business, communication, computer science, education, engineering/technologies, English, foreign languages, general academic interests/achievements, health fields, humanities, international studies, mathematics, physical sciences, social sciences. *Creative arts/performance:* applied art and design, art/fine arts, cinema/film/broadcasting, creative writing, dance, debating, general creative arts/performance, journalism/publications, music, performing arts, theater/drama. *Special achievements/activities:* community service, general special achievements/activities, hobbies/interests, leadership, memberships. *Special characteristics:* adult students, children of faculty/staff, ethnic background, first-generation college students, handicapped students, international students, local/state students, married students, members of minority groups, out-of-state students. *Tuition waivers:* Full or partial for employees or children of employees, senior citizens.

LOANS *Student loans:* $44,315,678 (60% need-based, 40% non-need-based). *Average need-based loan:* Freshmen: $3510. Undergraduates: $4427. *Parent loans:* $4,779,331 (100% non-need-based). *Programs:* Federal Direct (Subsidized and Unsubsidized Stafford, PLUS), Perkins, college/university.

WORK-STUDY *Federal work-study:* Total amount: $10,129,526; jobs available.

ATHLETIC AWARDS Total amount: $589,311 (65% need-based, 35% non-need-based).

APPLYING FOR FINANCIAL AID *Required financial aid forms:* FAFSA, institution's own form. *Financial aid deadline:* Continuous. *Notification date:* Continuous beginning 3/2.

CONTACT Dan Reed, Director of Financial Aid and Scholarships, California State University, Chico, 400 West First Street, Student Services Center, Room 250, Chico, CA 95929-0705, 530-898-6451 or toll-free 800-542-4426 (out-of-state). *Fax:* 530-898-6883. *E-mail:* finaid@csuchico.edu.
Website: http://www.csuchico.edu/.

CALIFORNIA STATE UNIVERSITY, DOMINGUEZ HILLS
Carson, CA

Tuition & fees (CA res): $6095	Average undergraduate aid package: $6687

ABOUT THE INSTITUTION State-supported, coed. *Awards:* certificates, bachelor's, and master's degrees. 68 undergraduate majors. *Total enrollment:* 13,933. Undergraduates: 11,427. Freshmen: 1,214. Federal methodology is used as a basis for awarding need-based institutional aid.

UNDERGRADUATE EXPENSES for 2013–2014 *Application fee:* $55. *Tuition, state resident:* full-time $5472. *Tuition, nonresident:* full-time $16,632; part-time $372 per credit. *Required fees:* full-time $623. *College room and board:* $10,733. Room and board charges vary according to housing facility.

FRESHMAN FINANCIAL AID (Fall 2012, est.) 1,080 applied for aid; of those 92% were deemed to have need. 100% of freshmen with need received aid; of those 2% had need fully met. *Average percent of need met:* 37% (excluding resources awarded to replace EFC). *Average financial aid package:* $5698 (excluding resources awarded to replace EFC). 4% of all full-time freshmen had no need and received non-need-based gift aid.

UNDERGRADUATE FINANCIAL AID (Fall 2012, est.) 6,038 applied for aid; of those 97% were deemed to have need. 98% of undergraduates with need received aid; of those 2% had need fully met. *Average percent of need met:* 36% (excluding resources awarded to replace EFC). *Average financial aid package:* $6687 (excluding resources awarded to replace EFC). 2% of all full-time undergraduates had no need and received non-need-based gift aid.

GIFT AID (NEED-BASED) *Total amount:* $34,260,379 (45% federal, 53% state, 1% institutional, 1% external sources). *Receiving aid:* Freshmen: 76% (850); all full-time undergraduates: 63% (4,922). *Average award:* Freshmen: $5216; Undergraduates: $5038. *Scholarships, grants, and awards:* Federal Pell, FSEOG, state, private, college/university gift aid from institutional funds.

GIFT AID (NON-NEED-BASED) *Total amount:* $36,901 (74% institutional, 26% external sources). *Receiving aid:* Freshmen: 22% (252). Undergraduates: 26% (2,061). *Average award:* Freshmen: $3960. Undergraduates: $4373. *Tuition waivers:* Full or partial for employees or children of employees, senior citizens. *ROTC:* Army, Air Force cooperative.

LOANS *Student loans:* $19,186,856 (96% need-based, 4% non-need-based). 54% of past graduating class borrowed through all loan programs. *Average indebtedness per student:* $11,783. *Average need-based loan:* Freshmen: $1704. Undergrad-

uates: $2400. *Parent loans:* $390,006 (58% need-based, 42% non-need-based). *Programs:* Federal Direct (Subsidized and Unsubsidized Stafford, PLUS), Perkins, college/university.

WORK-STUDY *Federal work-study:* Total amount: $258,703; 139 jobs averaging $1861.

ATHLETIC AWARDS Total amount: $228,322 (81% need-based, 19% non-need-based).

APPLYING FOR FINANCIAL AID *Required financial aid form:* FAFSA. *Financial aid deadline:* 5/16 (priority: 3/2). *Notification date:* Continuous beginning 3/15. Students must reply within 2 weeks of notification.

CONTACT Mrs. Delores S. Lee, Director of Financial Aid, California State University, Dominguez Hills, 1000 East Victoria Street, Carson, CA 90747-0001, 310-243-3189. *Fax:* 310-516-4498. *E-mail:* dslee@csudh.edu.
Website: http://www.csudh.edu/.

CALIFORNIA STATE UNIVERSITY, EAST BAY
Hayward, CA

Tuition & fees (CA res): $6309	Average undergraduate aid package: $11,342

ABOUT THE INSTITUTION State-supported, coed. *Awards:* certificates, bachelor's, master's, and doctoral degrees. 90 undergraduate majors. *Total enrollment:* 13,851. Undergraduates: 11,450. Freshmen: 1,572. Federal methodology is used as a basis for awarding need-based institutional aid.

UNDERGRADUATE EXPENSES for 2013–2014 *Application fee:* $55. *Tuition, state resident:* full-time $5472. *Tuition, nonresident:* full-time $16,632. *Required fees:* full-time $837. *College room and board:* $11,321.

FRESHMAN FINANCIAL AID (Fall 2012, est.) 881 applied for aid; of those 95% were deemed to have need. 99% of freshmen with need received aid; of those 2% had need fully met. *Average percent of need met:* 57% (excluding resources awarded to replace EFC). *Average financial aid package:* $11,357 (excluding resources awarded to replace EFC).

UNDERGRADUATE FINANCIAL AID (Fall 2012, est.) 6,459 applied for aid; of those 98% were deemed to have need. 98% of undergraduates with need received aid; of those 2% had need fully met. *Average percent of need met:* 54% (excluding resources awarded to replace EFC). *Average financial aid package:* $11,342 (excluding resources awarded to replace EFC).

GIFT AID (NEED-BASED) *Total amount:* $54,888,587 (42% federal, 56% state, 1% institutional, 1% external sources). *Receiving aid:* Freshmen: 60% (726); all full-time undergraduates: 50% (5,256). *Average award:* Freshmen: $9794; Undergraduates: $9618. *Scholarships, grants, and awards:* Federal Pell, FSEOG, state, private, college/university gift aid from institutional funds.

GIFT AID (NON-NEED-BASED) *Scholarships, grants, and awards by category:* Academic interests/achievement: general academic interests/achievements. *Creative arts/performance:* music.

LOANS *Student loans:* $33,933,712 (90% need-based, 10% non-need-based). 43% of past graduating class borrowed through all loan programs. *Average indebtedness per student:* $19,303. *Average need-based loan:* Freshmen: $5525. Undergraduates: $7083. *Parent loans:* $4,253,024 (38% need-based, 62% non-need-based). *Programs:* Federal Direct (Subsidized and Unsubsidized Stafford, PLUS), Perkins, college/university.

WORK-STUDY *Federal work-study:* Total amount: $1,945,838; jobs available.

ATHLETIC AWARDS Total amount: $544,528 (100% need-based).

APPLYING FOR FINANCIAL AID *Required financial aid form:* FAFSA. *Financial aid deadline (priority):* 3/2. *Notification date:* Continuous beginning 3/31. Students must reply within 4 weeks of notification.

CONTACT Office of Financial Aid, California State University, East Bay, 25800 Carlos Bee Boulevard, Hayward, CA 94542-3028, 510-885-2784. *Fax:* 510-885-2161. *E-mail:* finaid@csueastbay.edu.
Website: http://www.csueastbay.edu/.

CALIFORNIA STATE UNIVERSITY, FRESNO
Fresno, CA

Tuition & fees (CA res): $6274	Average undergraduate aid package: $11,897

ABOUT THE INSTITUTION State-supported, coed. *Awards:* certificates, bachelor's, master's, and doctoral degrees. 87 undergraduate majors. *Total enrollment:* 22,565. Undergraduates: 19,719. Freshmen: 3,060. Federal methodology is used as a basis for awarding need-based institutional aid.

UNDERGRADUATE EXPENSES for 2013–2014 *Application fee:* $55. *Tuition, state resident:* full-time $6274. *Tuition, nonresident:* full-time $14,400; part-time $372 per credit hour. *College room and board:* $10,192. Room and board charges vary according to board plan.

FRESHMAN FINANCIAL AID (Fall 2012, est.) 2,656 applied for aid; of those 89% were deemed to have need. 97% of freshmen with need received aid; of those 13% had need fully met. *Average percent of need met:* 69% (excluding resources awarded to replace EFC). *Average financial aid package:* $11,194 (excluding resources awarded to replace EFC). 2% of all full-time freshmen had no need and received non-need-based gift aid.

UNDERGRADUATE FINANCIAL AID (Fall 2012, est.) 13,863 applied for aid; of those 93% were deemed to have need. 97% of undergraduates with need received aid; of those 13% had need fully met. *Average percent of need met:* 69% (excluding resources awarded to replace EFC). *Average financial aid package:* $11,897 (excluding resources awarded to replace EFC). 1% of all full-time undergraduates had no need and received non-need-based gift aid.

GIFT AID (NEED-BASED) Total amount: $116,358,781 (44% federal, 56% state). *Receiving aid:* Freshmen: 65% (1,977); all full-time undergraduates: 61% (10,441). *Average award:* Freshmen: $10,378; Undergraduates: $9968. *Scholarships, grants, and awards:* Federal Pell, FSEOG, state, private, college/university gift aid from institutional funds.

GIFT AID (NON-NEED-BASED) Total amount: $5,307,006 (65% institutional, 35% external sources). *Receiving aid:* Freshmen: 12% (370). Undergraduates: 9% (1,485). *Average award:* Freshmen: $3421. Undergraduates: $3930. *Scholarships, grants, and awards by category: Academic interests/achievement:* 989 awards ($2,788,042 total): agriculture, area/ethnic studies, biological sciences, business, communication, education, engineering/technologies, English, foreign languages, general academic interests/achievements, health fields, humanities, mathematics, physical sciences, social sciences. *Creative arts/performance:* 195 awards ($190,858 total): art/fine arts, journalism/publications, music, theater/drama. *Special achievements/activities:* 25 awards ($32,250 total): community service, leadership. *Special characteristics:* 3 awards ($2259 total): handicapped students, local/state students. *ROTC:* Army, Air Force.

LOANS Student loans: $83,345,706 (57% need-based, 43% non-need-based). 71% of past graduating class borrowed through all loan programs. *Average indebtedness per student:* $16,100. *Average need-based loan:* Freshmen: $3114. Undergraduates: $4202. *Parent loans:* $1,640,661 (100% non-need-based). *Programs:* Federal Direct (Subsidized and Unsubsidized Stafford, PLUS), Perkins, Federal Nursing, college/university, alternative loans.

WORK-STUDY Federal work-study: Total amount: $922,324; 240 jobs averaging $3009.

ATHLETIC AWARDS Total amount: $4,551,259 (100% non-need-based).

APPLYING FOR FINANCIAL AID Required financial aid form: FAFSA. *Financial aid deadline (priority):* 3/2. *Notification date:* Continuous beginning 4/1. Students must reply within 3 weeks of notification.

CONTACT Bernard Ogden, Director of Financial Aid, California State University, Fresno, 5150 North Maple Avenue, JA64, Fresno, CA 93740, 559-278-2182. *Fax:* 559-278-4833. *E-mail:* bogden@csufresno.edu. *Website:* http://www.csufresno.edu/.

CALIFORNIA STATE UNIVERSITY, FULLERTON
Fullerton, CA

Tuition & fees (CA res): $6182	Average undergraduate aid package: $11,273

ABOUT THE INSTITUTION State-supported, coed. *Awards:* certificates, bachelor's, master's, and doctoral degrees. 71 undergraduate majors. *Total enrollment:* 37,677. Undergraduates: 32,379. Freshmen: 4,526. Federal methodology is used as a basis for awarding need-based institutional aid.

UNDERGRADUATE EXPENSES for 2013–2014 *Application fee:* $55. *Tuition, state resident:* full time $0. *Tuition, nonresident:* full-time $11,160; part-time $372 per unit. *Required fees:* full-time $6182; $1945. Full-time tuition and fees vary according to course load. Part-time tuition and fees vary according to course load. *College room and board:* $12,096. Room and board charges vary according to board plan and housing facility.

FRESHMAN FINANCIAL AID (Fall 2012, est.) 3,795 applied for aid; of those 72% were deemed to have need. 99% of freshmen with need received aid; of those 85% had need fully met. *Average percent of need met:* 57% (excluding resources awarded to replace EFC). *Average financial aid package:* $11,010 (excluding resources awarded to replace EFC). 9% of all full-time freshmen had no need and received non-need-based gift aid.

UNDERGRADUATE FINANCIAL AID (Fall 2012, est.) 19,555 applied for aid; of those 81% were deemed to have need. 99% of undergraduates with need received aid; of those 86% had need fully met. *Average percent of need met:* 67% (excluding resources awarded to replace EFC). *Average financial aid package:* $11,273 (excluding resources awarded to replace EFC). 6% of all full-time undergraduates had no need and received non-need-based gift aid.

GIFT AID (NEED-BASED) Total amount: $141,882,308 (41% federal, 57% state, 1% institutional, 1% external sources). *Receiving aid:* Freshmen: 50% (2,198); all full-time undergraduates: 48% (12,504). *Average award:* Freshmen: $6635; Undergraduates: $7071. *Scholarships, grants, and awards:* Federal Pell, FSEOG, state, private, college/university gift aid from institutional funds, Federal Nursing.

GIFT AID (NON-NEED-BASED) Total amount: $436,503 (37% institutional, 63% external sources). *Receiving aid:* Freshmen: 9% (381). Undergraduates: 6% (1,483). *Average award:* Freshmen: $7301. Undergraduates: $7826. *Scholarships, grants, and awards by category: Academic interests/achievement:* 1,896 awards ($2,838,765 total): area/ethnic studies, biological sciences, business, communication, computer science, education, engineering/technologies, English, foreign languages, general academic interests/achievements, health fields, humanities, mathematics, military science, physical sciences, religion/biblical studies, social sciences. *Creative arts/performance:* 268 awards ($173,151 total): art/fine arts, cinema/film/broadcasting, dance, journalism/publications, music, performing arts, theater/drama. *Special achievements/activities:* 227 awards ($236,450 total): general special achievements/activities, leadership. *Special characteristics:* 116 awards ($494,695 total): general special characteristics. *Tuition waivers:* Full or partial for employees or children of employees, senior citizens. *ROTC:* Army.

LOANS Student loans: $82,164,282 (84% need-based, 16% non-need-based). 42% of past graduating class borrowed through all loan programs. *Average indebtedness per student:* $14,983. *Average need-based loan:* Freshmen: $5756. Undergraduates: $6758. *Parent loans:* $5,105,986 (68% need-based, 32% non-need-based). *Programs:* Federal Direct (Subsidized and Unsubsidized Stafford, PLUS), Perkins, college/university, private loans.

WORK-STUDY Federal work-study: Total amount: $832,941; 215 jobs averaging $3303.

ATHLETIC AWARDS Total amount: $2,573,748 (88% need-based, 12% non-need-based).

APPLYING FOR FINANCIAL AID Required financial aid form: FAFSA. *Financial aid deadline (priority):* 3/2. *Notification date:* Continuous beginning 4/22. Students must reply within 4 weeks of notification.

CONTACT Ms. Cecilia Schouwe, Director of Financial Aid, California State University, Fullerton, 800 North State College Boulevard, Fullerton, CA 92831-3599, 657-278-3128. *Fax:* 657-278-7090. *E-mail:* cschouwe@fullerton.edu. *Website:* http://www.fullerton.edu/.

CALIFORNIA STATE UNIVERSITY, LONG BEACH

Long Beach, CA

Tuition & fees (CA res): $6240	Average undergraduate aid package: $13,678

ABOUT THE INSTITUTION State-supported, coed. **Awards:** certificates, bachelor's, master's, and doctoral degrees. 148 undergraduate majors. **Total enrollment:** 36,279. Undergraduates: 30,931. Freshmen: 4,276. Federal methodology is used as a basis for awarding need-based institutional aid.

UNDERGRADUATE EXPENSES for 2013–2014 Application fee: $55. **Tuition, state resident:** full-time $0. **Tuition, nonresident:** full-time $11,160; part-time $372 per unit. **Required fees:** full-time $6240. Full-time tuition and fees vary according to degree level and program. Part-time tuition and fees vary according to course load, degree level, and program. **College room and board:** $11,300. Room and board charges vary according to board plan.

FRESHMAN FINANCIAL AID (Fall 2012, est.) 3,559 applied for aid; of those 84% were deemed to have need. 91% of freshmen with need received aid; of those 75% had need fully met. **Average percent of need met:** 81% (excluding resources awarded to replace EFC). **Average financial aid package:** $12,507 (excluding resources awarded to replace EFC).

UNDERGRADUATE FINANCIAL AID (Fall 2012, est.) 20,755 applied for aid; of those 93% were deemed to have need. 91% of undergraduates with need received aid; of those 54% had need fully met. **Average percent of need met:** 83% (excluding resources awarded to replace EFC). **Average financial aid package:** $13,678 (excluding resources awarded to replace EFC).

GIFT AID (NEED-BASED) Total amount: $154,967,000 (42% federal, 54% state, 3% institutional, 1% external sources). **Receiving aid:** Freshmen: 56% (2,310); all full-time undergraduates: 59% (14,565). **Average award:** Freshmen: $7982; Undergraduates: $6554. **Scholarships, grants, and awards:** Federal Pell, FSEOG, state, private, college/university gift aid from institutional funds.

GIFT AID (NON-NEED-BASED) Total amount: $24,000 (100% federal). **Receiving aid:** Freshmen: 8% (319). Undergraduates: 10% (2,396). **Tuition waivers:** Full or partial for employees or children of employees, senior citizens. **ROTC:** Army.

LOANS Student loans: $105,000,000 (61% need-based, 39% non-need-based). 39% of past graduating class borrowed through all loan programs. **Average need-based loan:** Freshmen: $2918. Undergraduates: $3721. **Parent loans:** $3,300,000 (100% non-need-based). **Programs:** Federal Direct (Subsidized and Unsubsidized Stafford, PLUS), Perkins.

WORK-STUDY Federal work-study: Total amount: $1,212,000; jobs available.

ATHLETIC AWARDS Total amount: $2,300,000 (100% non-need-based).

APPLYING FOR FINANCIAL AID Required financial aid form: FAFSA. **Financial aid deadline (priority):** 3/2. **Notification date:** 4/1. Students must reply within 4 weeks of notification.

CONTACT Nicolas Valdivia, Office of Financial Aid, California State University, Long Beach, 1250 Bellflower Boulevard, Long Beach, CA 90840, 562-985-8403. *Website:* http://www.csulb.edu/.

CALIFORNIA STATE UNIVERSITY, LOS ANGELES

Los Angeles, CA

Tuition & fees (CA res): $6335	Average undergraduate aid package: $13,186

ABOUT THE INSTITUTION State-supported, coed. **Awards:** bachelor's, master's, and doctoral degrees. 62 undergraduate majors. **Total enrollment:** 21,755. Undergraduates: 18,074. Freshmen: 2,908. Federal methodology is used as a basis for awarding need-based institutional aid.

UNDERGRADUATE EXPENSES for 2013–2014 Application fee: $55. **Tuition, state resident:** full-time $0. **Tuition, nonresident:** full-time $15,263; part-time $248 per unit. **Required fees:** full-time $6335. Full-time tuition and fees vary according to course level and course load. Part-time tuition and fees vary

according to course level and course load. **College room and board:** $9728; **Room only:** $5895. Room and board charges vary according to housing facility.

FRESHMAN FINANCIAL AID (Fall 2011) 1,893 applied for aid; of those 94% were deemed to have need. 98% of freshmen with need received aid; of those 10% had need fully met. **Average percent of need met:** 77% (excluding resources awarded to replace EFC). **Average financial aid package:** $12,384 (excluding resources awarded to replace EFC). 1% of all full-time freshmen had no need and received non-need-based gift aid.

UNDERGRADUATE FINANCIAL AID (Fall 2011) 12,055 applied for aid; of those 97% were deemed to have need. 98% of undergraduates with need received aid; of those 16% had need fully met. **Average percent of need met:** 77% (excluding resources awarded to replace EFC). **Average financial aid package:** $13,186 (excluding resources awarded to replace EFC). 1% of all full-time undergraduates had no need and received non-need-based gift aid.

GIFT AID (NEED-BASED) Total amount: $115,088,393 (46% federal, 52% state, 2% institutional). **Receiving aid:** Freshmen: 66% (1,564); all full-time undergraduates: 71% (10,219). **Average award:** Freshmen: $14,748; Undergraduates: $12,369. **Scholarships, grants, and awards:** Federal Pell, FSEOG, state, private, college/university gift aid from institutional funds.

GIFT AID (NON-NEED-BASED) Total amount: $230,213 (100% institutional). **Average award:** Freshmen: $1932. Undergraduates: $4422. **Scholarships, grants, and awards by category:** Academic interests/achievement: biological sciences, business, communication, computer science, education, engineering/technologies, English, foreign languages, general academic interests/achievements, health fields, mathematics, physical sciences, social sciences. Creative arts/performance: art/fine arts, general creative arts/performance, journalism/publications, music, theater/drama. Special achievements/activities: community service, general special achievements/activities. Special characteristics: general special characteristics. **Tuition waivers:** Full or partial for employees or children of employees. **ROTC:** Army cooperative, Air Force cooperative.

LOANS Student loans: $45,722,081 (96% need-based, 4% non-need-based). **Average need-based loan:** Freshmen: $4012. Undergraduates: $5516. **Parent loans:** $717,177 (75% need-based, 25% non-need-based). **Programs:** Federal Direct (Subsidized and Unsubsidized Stafford), Perkins, Federal Nursing, state.

WORK-STUDY Federal work-study: Total amount: $744,038; jobs available.

ATHLETIC AWARDS Total amount: $830,801 (50% need-based, 50% non-need-based).

APPLYING FOR FINANCIAL AID Required financial aid form: FAFSA. **Financial aid deadline (priority):** 3/2. **Notification date:** Continuous beginning 4/1.

CONTACT Tamie L. Nguyen, Director of Financial Aid, California State University, Los Angeles, 5151 State University Drive, Los Angeles, CA 90032, 323-343-6260. *Fax:* 323-343-3166. *E-mail:* tnguyen10@cslanet.calstatela.edu. *Website:* http://www.calstatela.edu/.

CALIFORNIA STATE UNIVERSITY, MONTEREY BAY

Seaside, CA

Tuition & fees (CA res): $5963	Average undergraduate aid package: $10,319

ABOUT THE INSTITUTION State-supported, coed. **Awards:** bachelor's and master's degrees. 23 undergraduate majors. **Total enrollment:** 5,609. Undergraduates: 5,194. Freshmen: 902. Federal methodology is used as a basis for awarding need-based institutional aid.

UNDERGRADUATE EXPENSES for 2013–2014 Application fee: $55. **Tuition, state resident:** full-time $0. **Tuition, nonresident:** full-time $11,160; part-time $372 per credit hour. **Required fees:** full-time $5963. Full-time tuition and fees vary according to course load and degree level. Part-time tuition and fees vary according to course load and degree level. **College room and board:** $9498. Room and board charges vary according to board plan and housing facility.

FRESHMAN FINANCIAL AID (Fall 2012, est.) 806 applied for aid; of those 79% were deemed to have need. 95% of freshmen with need received aid; of those 29% had need fully met. **Average percent of need met:** 78% (excluding resources awarded to replace EFC). **Average financial aid package:** $10,967 (excluding resources awarded to replace EFC). 1% of all full-time freshmen had no need and received non-need-based gift aid.

UNDERGRADUATE FINANCIAL AID (Fall 2012, est.) 3,831 applied for aid; of those 85% were deemed to have need. 94% of undergraduates with need received aid; of those 31% had need fully met. *Average percent of need met:* 74% (excluding resources awarded to replace EFC). *Average financial aid package:* $10,319 (excluding resources awarded to replace EFC). 1% of all full-time undergraduates had no need and received non-need-based gift aid.

GIFT AID (NEED-BASED) Total amount: $22,703,946 (49% federal, 48% state, 3% institutional). *Receiving aid:* Freshmen: 54% (482); all full-time undergraduates: 51% (2,481). *Average award:* Freshmen: $10,385; Undergraduates: $8922. *Scholarships, grants, and awards:* Federal Pell, FSEOG, state, private, college/university gift aid from institutional funds.

GIFT AID (NON-NEED-BASED) Total amount: $375,261 (21% institutional, 79% external sources). *Receiving aid:* Freshmen: 10% (88). Undergraduates: 5% (263). *Average award:* Freshmen: $6285. Undergraduates: $1584. *Scholarships, grants, and awards by category: Academic interests/achievement:* business, general academic interests/achievements. *Special achievements/activities:* leadership. *Special characteristics:* children and siblings of alumni, general special characteristics, local/state students. *Tuition waivers:* Full or partial for employees or children of employees, senior citizens.

LOANS Student loans: $17,625,831 (53% need-based, 47% non-need-based). 78% of past graduating class borrowed through all loan programs. *Average indebtedness per student:* $18,349. *Average need-based loan:* Freshmen: $3316. Undergraduates: $4277. *Parent loans:* $2,099,354 (100% non-need-based). *Programs:* Federal Direct (Subsidized and Unsubsidized Stafford, PLUS), Perkins.

WORK-STUDY Federal work-study: Total amount: $110,653; jobs available. *State or other work-study/employment:* Part-time jobs available.

ATHLETIC AWARDS Total amount: $469,348 (100% non-need-based).

APPLYING FOR FINANCIAL AID Required financial aid forms: FAFSA, state aid form. *Financial aid deadline:* 6/1 (priority: 3/2). *Notification date:* Continuous beginning 4/1.

CONTACT Office of Financial Aid, California State University, Monterey Bay, 100 Campus Center, Building 47, Seaside, CA 93955-8001, 831-582-5100. *Fax:* 831-582-3782.
Website: http://www.csumb.edu/.

CALIFORNIA STATE UNIVERSITY, NORTHRIDGE
Northridge, CA

Tuition & fees (CA res): $6520	Average undergraduate aid package: $18,189

ABOUT THE INSTITUTION State-supported, coed. *Awards:* bachelor's and master's degrees. 59 undergraduate majors. *Total enrollment:* 36,164. Undergraduates: 31,119. Freshmen: 4,149. Federal methodology is used as a basis for awarding need-based institutional aid.

UNDERGRADUATE EXPENSES for 2013-2014 Application fee: $55. *Tuition, state resident:* full-time $0. *Tuition, nonresident:* full-time $11,160; part-time $372 per credit hour. *Required fees:* full-time $6520. *College room and board:* $12,404. Room and board charges vary according to board plan and housing facility.

FRESHMAN FINANCIAL AID (Fall 2011) 4,372 applied for aid; of those 91% were deemed to have need. 100% of freshmen with need received aid. *Average financial aid package:* $11,411 (excluding resources awarded to replace EFC). 2% of all full-time freshmen had no need and received non-need-based gift aid.

UNDERGRADUATE FINANCIAL AID (Fall 2011) 19,138 applied for aid; of those 95% were deemed to have need. 100% of undergraduates with need received aid. *Average financial aid package:* $18,189 (excluding resources awarded to replace EFC). 4% of all full-time undergraduates had no need and received non-need-based gift aid.

GIFT AID (NEED-BASED) Total amount: $157,652,002 (45% federal, 54% state, 1% institutional). *Receiving aid:* Freshmen: 65% (3,339); all full-time undergraduates: 59% (14,880). *Average award:* Freshmen: $10,570; Undergraduates: $15,051. *Scholarships, grants, and awards:* Federal Pell, FSEOG, state, private, college/university gift aid from institutional funds.

GIFT AID (NON-NEED-BASED) Total amount: $2,172,776 (58% institutional, 42% external sources). *Receiving aid:* Freshmen: 2% (124). Undergraduates: 4%

(940). *Average award:* Freshmen: $1509. Undergraduates: $1608. *Scholarships, grants, and awards by category: Academic interests/achievement:* business, communication, computer science, education, engineering/technologies, English, general academic interests/achievements, mathematics, social sciences. *Creative arts/performance:* journalism/publications, music. *Special achievements/activities:* leadership. *Tuition waivers:* Full or partial for employees or children of employees, senior citizens. *ROTC:* Army cooperative, Air Force cooperative.

LOANS Student loans: $86,869,571 (58% need-based, 42% non-need-based). 46% of past graduating class borrowed through all loan programs. *Average indebtedness per student:* $17,198. *Average need-based loan:* Freshmen: $4781. Undergraduates: $6076. *Parent loans:* $2,907,804 (100% non-need-based). *Programs:* Perkins.

WORK-STUDY Federal work-study: Total amount: $1,596,595; jobs available.

ATHLETIC AWARDS Total amount: $1,838,497 (100% non-need-based).

APPLYING FOR FINANCIAL AID Required financial aid form: FAFSA. *Financial aid deadline (priority):* 3/2. *Notification date:* Continuous beginning 4/1.

CONTACT Lili Vidal, Director of Financial Aid and Scholarships, California State University, Northridge, 18111 Nordhoff Street, Northridge, CA 91330-8307, 818-677-4085. *Fax:* 818-677-6787. *E-mail:* financial.aid@csun.edu.
Website: http://www.csun.edu/.

CALIFORNIA STATE UNIVERSITY, SACRAMENTO
Sacramento, CA

Tuition & fees (CA res): $6620	Average undergraduate aid package: $10,925

ABOUT THE INSTITUTION State-supported, coed. *Awards:* bachelor's, master's, and doctoral degrees. 55 undergraduate majors. *Total enrollment:* 28,016. Undergraduates: 24,701. Freshmen: 2,912. Federal methodology is used as a basis for awarding need-based institutional aid.

UNDERGRADUATE EXPENSES for 2013-2014 Application fee: $55. *Tuition, state resident:* full-time $5472. *Tuition, nonresident:* full-time $16,632. *Required fees:* full-time $1148. *College room and board:* $11,724. Room and board charges vary according to board plan and housing facility.

FRESHMAN FINANCIAL AID (Fall 2011) 2,500 applied for aid; of those 86% were deemed to have need. 92% of freshmen with need received aid; of those 5% had need fully met. *Average percent of need met:* 60% (excluding resources awarded to replace EFC). *Average financial aid package:* $10,804 (excluding resources awarded to replace EFC). 1% of all full-time freshmen had no need and received non-need-based gift aid.

UNDERGRADUATE FINANCIAL AID (Fall 2011) 16,147 applied for aid; of those 92% were deemed to have need. 94% of undergraduates with need received aid; of those 4% had need fully met. *Average percent of need met:* 58% (excluding resources awarded to replace EFC). *Average financial aid package:* $10,925 (excluding resources awarded to replace EFC). 1% of all full-time undergraduates had no need and received non-need-based gift aid.

GIFT AID (NEED-BASED) Total amount: $129,963,306 (43% federal, 57% state). *Receiving aid:* Freshmen: 59% (1,650); all full-time undergraduates: 57% (11,617). *Average award:* Freshmen: $10,504; Undergraduates: $9608. *Scholarships, grants, and awards:* Federal Pell, FSEOG, state, private, college/university gift aid from institutional funds, Federal Nursing.

GIFT AID (NON-NEED-BASED) Total amount: $3,767,420 (5% federal, 1% state, 16% institutional, 78% external sources). *Receiving aid:* Freshmen: 11% (316). Undergraduates: 5% (993). *Average award:* Freshmen: $500. Undergraduates: $927. *ROTC:* Army, Air Force.

LOANS Student loans: $102,474,429 (56% need-based, 44% non-need-based). 43% of past graduating class borrowed through all loan programs. *Average indebtedness per student:* $4456. *Average need-based loan:* Freshmen: $3367. Undergraduates: $4476. *Parent loans:* $11,695,661 (100% non-need-based). *Programs:* Federal Direct (Subsidized and Unsubsidized Stafford, PLUS), Perkins, Federal Nursing, college/university.

WORK-STUDY Federal work-study: Total amount: $772,530; jobs available. *State or other work-study/employment:* Total amount: $172,733 (100% need-based). Part-time jobs available.

ATHLETIC AWARDS Total amount: $3,921,300 (100% need-based).
APPLYING FOR FINANCIAL AID *Required financial aid form:* FAFSA. *Financial aid deadline:* Continuous. *Notification date:* Continuous beginning 4/27.

CONTACT Rachel Mason, Financial Aid Advisor, California State University, Sacramento, 6000 J Street, Sacramento, CA 95819-6044, 916-278-6554. *Fax:* 916-278-6082.
Website: http://www.csus.edu/.

CALIFORNIA STATE UNIVERSITY, SAN BERNARDINO
San Bernardino, CA

Tuition & fees (CA res): $12,021	Average undergraduate aid package: $11,702

ABOUT THE INSTITUTION State-supported, coed. *Awards:* bachelor's, master's, and doctoral degrees. 52 undergraduate majors. *Total enrollment:* 18,234. Undergraduates: 15,885. Freshmen: 2,448. Federal methodology is used as a basis for awarding need-based institutional aid.
UNDERGRADUATE EXPENSES for 2013–2014 *Application fee:* $55. *Tuition, state resident:* full-time $5472. *Tuition, nonresident:* full-time $11,160. *Required fees:* full-time $6549. Part-time tuition and fees vary according to course load. *College room and board:* $9972. Room and board charges vary according to board plan and housing facility.
FRESHMAN FINANCIAL AID (Fall 2012, est.) 1,813 applied for aid; of those 91% were deemed to have need. 98% of freshmen with need received aid; of those 6% had need fully met. *Average percent of need met:* 69% (excluding resources awarded to replace EFC). *Average financial aid package:* $11,648 (excluding resources awarded to replace EFC). 1% of all full-time freshmen had no need and received non-need-based gift aid.
UNDERGRADUATE FINANCIAL AID (Fall 2012, est.) 12,606 applied for aid; of those 90% were deemed to have need. 98% of undergraduates with need received aid; of those 9% had need fully met. *Average percent of need met:* 68% (excluding resources awarded to replace EFC). *Average financial aid package:* $11,702 (excluding resources awarded to replace EFC). 1% of all full-time undergraduates had no need and received non-need-based gift aid.
GIFT AID (NEED-BASED) *Total amount:* $95,509,987 (45% federal, 54% state, 1% institutional). *Receiving aid:* Freshmen: 69% (1,381); all full-time undergraduates: 67% (9,460). *Average award:* Freshmen: $10,377; Undergraduates: $9414. *Scholarships, grants, and awards:* Federal Pell, FSEOG, state, private, college/university gift aid from institutional funds.
GIFT AID (NON-NEED-BASED) *Total amount:* $913,173 (37% institutional, 63% external sources). *Receiving aid:* Freshmen: 7% (136). Undergraduates: 6% (785). *Average award:* Freshmen: $4713. Undergraduates: $3242. *Scholarships, grants, and awards by category: Academic interests/achievement:* 301 awards ($1,447,103 total): biological sciences, business, computer science, education, foreign languages, general academic interests/achievements, health fields, international studies, mathematics, physical sciences, social sciences. *Creative arts/performance:* 31 awards ($38,304 total): art/fine arts, general creative arts/performance, journalism/publications, music, theater/drama. *Special achievements/activities:* community service, general special achievements/activities, hobbies/interests, memberships. *Special characteristics:* 7 awards ($38,304 total): children of public servants, children with a deceased or disabled parent, first-generation college students, handicapped students, veterans, veterans' children. *Tuition waivers:* Full or partial for employees or children of employees, senior citizens. *ROTC:* Army, Air Force.
LOANS *Student loans:* $42,167,428 (94% need-based, 6% non-need-based). 61% of past graduating class borrowed through all loan programs. *Average indebtedness per student:* $21,787. *Average need-based loan:* Freshmen: $3373. Undergraduates: $4075. *Parent loans:* $27,368,797 (100% non-need-based). *Programs:* Federal Direct (Subsidized and Unsubsidized Stafford, PLUS), Perkins.
WORK-STUDY *Federal work-study:* Total amount: $1,201,816; 314 jobs averaging $3795.
ATHLETIC AWARDS Total amount: $496,093 (100% non-need-based).
APPLYING FOR FINANCIAL AID *Required financial aid forms:* FAFSA, state aid form. *Financial aid deadline (priority):* 3/2. *Notification date:* Continuous beginning 4/1.

CONTACT Ms. Roseanna Ruiz, Director of Financial Aid, California State University, San Bernardino, 5500 University Parkway, San Bernardino, CA 92407-2397, 909-537-5227. *Fax:* 909-537-4024.
Website: http://www.csusb.edu/.

CALIFORNIA STATE UNIVERSITY, SAN MARCOS
San Marcos, CA

Tuition & fees (CA res): $7298	Average undergraduate aid package: $8373

ABOUT THE INSTITUTION State-supported, coed. *Awards:* bachelor's and master's degrees. 23 undergraduate majors. *Total enrollment:* 10,363. Undergraduates: 9,928. Freshmen: 1,783. Federal methodology is used as a basis for awarding need-based institutional aid.
UNDERGRADUATE EXPENSES for 2013–2014 *Application fee:* $55. *Tuition, state resident:* full-time $0. *Tuition, nonresident:* full-time $11,762; part-time $372 per unit. *Required fees:* full-time $7298; $2251 per term. Part-time tuition and fees vary according to course load. Room and board charges vary according to housing facility.
FRESHMAN FINANCIAL AID (Fall 2011) 991 applied for aid; of those 78% were deemed to have need. 83% of freshmen with need received aid. *Average financial aid package:* $8397 (excluding resources awarded to replace EFC). 2% of all full-time freshmen had no need and received non-need-based gift aid.
UNDERGRADUATE FINANCIAL AID (Fall 2011) 4,426 applied for aid; of those 90% were deemed to have need. 91% of undergraduates with need received aid. *Average financial aid package:* $8373 (excluding resources awarded to replace EFC). 1% of all full-time undergraduates had no need and received non-need-based gift aid.
GIFT AID (NEED-BASED) *Total amount:* $32,535,099 (46% federal, 49% state, 2% institutional, 3% external sources). *Receiving aid:* Freshmen: 43% (578); all full-time undergraduates: 42% (2,833). *Average award:* Freshmen: $8050; Undergraduates: $8373. *Scholarships, grants, and awards:* Federal Pell, FSEOG, state, private, college/university gift aid from institutional funds.
GIFT AID (NON-NEED-BASED) *Receiving aid:* Freshmen: 10% (141). Undergraduates: 6% (388). *Average award:* Freshmen: $1021. Undergraduates: $1841. *Scholarships, grants, and awards by category: Academic interests/achievement:* general academic interests/achievements, mathematics. *Special achievements/activities:* leadership. *Special characteristics:* local/state students. *Tuition waivers:* Full or partial for employees or children of employees, senior citizens. *ROTC:* Army cooperative, Naval cooperative, Air Force cooperative.
LOANS *Student loans:* $31,970,026 (53% need-based, 47% non-need-based). 63% of past graduating class borrowed through all loan programs. *Average indebtedness per student:* $19,257. *Average need-based loan:* Freshmen: $3121. Undergraduates: $4167. *Parent loans:* $933,730 (100% non-need-based). *Programs:* Federal Direct (Subsidized and Unsubsidized Stafford, PLUS), Perkins, college/university.
WORK-STUDY *Federal work-study:* Total amount: $297,924; 145 jobs averaging $2055.
ATHLETIC AWARDS Total amount: $165,083 (100% non-need-based).
APPLYING FOR FINANCIAL AID *Required financial aid form:* FAFSA. *Financial aid deadline (priority):* 3/2. *Notification date:* 4/16.

CONTACT Financial Aid and Scholarships Office, California State University, San Marcos, 333 South Twin Oaks Valley Road, San Marcos, CA 92096-0001, 760-750-4850. *Fax:* 760-750-3047. *E-mail:* finaid@csusm.edu.
Website: http://www.csusm.edu/.

CALIFORNIA STATE UNIVERSITY, STANISLAUS
Turlock, CA

Tuition & fees (CA res): $6584	Average undergraduate aid package: $14,722

ABOUT THE INSTITUTION State-supported, coed. **Awards:** certificates, bachelor's, master's, and doctoral degrees. 50 undergraduate majors. **Total enrollment:** 8,882. Undergraduates: 7,621. Freshmen: 1,109. Federal methodology is used as a basis for awarding need-based institutional aid.

UNDERGRADUATE EXPENSES for 2013–2014 Application fee: $55. **Tuition, state resident:** full-time $5472. **Tuition, nonresident:** full-time $16,632. **Required fees:** full-time $1112. Full-time tuition and fees vary according to course load and reciprocity agreements. Part-time tuition and fees vary according to course load and reciprocity agreements. **College room and board:** $9056. Room and board charges vary according to board plan and housing facility.

FRESHMAN FINANCIAL AID (Fall 2012, est.) 920 applied for aid; of those 93% were deemed to have need. 97% of freshmen with need received aid; of those 31% had need fully met. **Average percent of need met:** 73% (excluding resources awarded to replace EFC). **Average financial aid package:** $14,711 (excluding resources awarded to replace EFC). 1% of all full-time freshmen had no need and received non-need-based gift aid.

UNDERGRADUATE FINANCIAL AID (Fall 2012, est.) 5,235 applied for aid; of those 95% were deemed to have need. 98% of undergraduates with need received aid; of those 19% had need fully met. **Average percent of need met:** 70% (excluding resources awarded to replace EFC). **Average financial aid package:** $14,722 (excluding resources awarded to replace EFC). 1% of all full-time undergraduates had no need and received non-need-based gift aid.

GIFT AID (NEED-BASED) Total amount: $47,777,015 (42% federal, 28% state, 30% institutional). **Receiving aid:** Freshmen: 62% (668); all full-time undergraduates: 72% (4,521). **Average award:** Freshmen: $10,365; Undergraduates: $9343. **Scholarships, grants, and awards:** Federal Pell, FSEOG, state, private, college/university gift aid from institutional funds.

GIFT AID (NON-NEED-BASED) Total amount: $952,085 (2% federal, 41% institutional, 57% external sources). **Receiving aid:** Freshmen: 3% (31). Undergraduates: 3% (165). **Average award:** Freshmen: $2000. Undergraduates: $1976. **Scholarships, grants, and awards by category:** Academic interests/achievement: 145 awards ($198,012 total): agriculture, area/ethnic studies, biological sciences, business, communication, computer science, education, English, foreign languages, general academic interests/achievements, health fields, humanities, international studies, mathematics, physical sciences, premedicine, social sciences. Creative arts/performance: 44 awards ($48,675 total): art/fine arts, music. Special achievements/activities: 107 awards ($356,880 total): community service, general special achievements/activities, leadership, memberships. Special characteristics: 43 awards ($79,750 total): children of faculty/staff, first-generation college students, general special characteristics, local/state students.

LOANS Student loans: $24,420,442 (52% need-based, 48% non-need-based). **Average need-based loan:** Freshmen: $3186. Undergraduates: $5135. **Parent loans:** $2,004,550 (100% non-need-based). **Programs:** Federal Direct (Subsidized and Unsubsidized Stafford, PLUS), Perkins, private loans.

WORK-STUDY Federal work-study: Total amount: $489,593; 148 jobs averaging $3433. **State or other work-study/employment:** Part-time jobs available.

ATHLETIC AWARDS Total amount: $639,016 (100% non-need-based).

APPLYING FOR FINANCIAL AID Required financial aid forms: FAFSA, state aid form. **Financial aid deadline (priority):** 3/2. **Notification date:** Continuous beginning 3/15. Students must reply within 3 weeks of notification.

CONTACT Ms. Noelia Gonzalez, Director of Financial Aid and Scholarships, California State University, Stanislaus, One University Circle, Turlock, CA 95382, 209-667-3337 or toll-free 800-300-7420. Fax: 209-664-7064. E-mail: ngonzalez4@csustan.edu.
Website: http://www.csustan.edu/.

CALIFORNIA UNIVERSITY OF MANAGEMENT AND SCIENCES
Anaheim, CA

CONTACT Financial Aid Office, California University of Management and Sciences, 721 North Euclid Street, Anaheim, CA 92801, 714-533-3946.
Website: http://www.calums.edu/.

CALIFORNIA UNIVERSITY OF PENNSYLVANIA
California, PA

ABOUT THE INSTITUTION State-supported, coed. **Awards:** certificates, associate, bachelor's, and master's degrees. 44 undergraduate majors. **Total enrollment:** 8,608. Undergraduates: 6,683. Freshmen: 960.

GIFT AID (NEED-BASED) Scholarships, grants, and awards: Federal Pell, FSEOG, state, private, college/university gift aid from institutional funds, Academic Competitiveness Grants, National SMART Grants.

GIFT AID (NON-NEED-BASED) Scholarships, grants, and awards by category: Academic interests/achievement: general academic interests/achievements. Creative arts/performance: general creative arts/performance. Special achievements/activities: general special achievements/activities. Special characteristics: ethnic background, international students, members of minority groups, veterans.

LOANS Programs: Federal Direct (Subsidized and Unsubsidized Stafford, PLUS), Perkins, college/university.

WORK-STUDY Federal work-study: Total amount: $513,375; jobs available. **State or other work-study/employment:** Total amount: $1,904,840 (100% non-need-based). Part-time jobs available.

APPLYING FOR FINANCIAL AID Required financial aid form: FAFSA.

CONTACT Office of Financial Aid, California University of Pennsylvania, 250 University Avenue, California, PA 15419-1394, 724-938-4415 or toll-free 888-412-0479.
Website: http://www.calu.edu/.

CALUMET COLLEGE OF SAINT JOSEPH
Whiting, IN

Tuition & fees: $15,620	Average undergraduate aid package: $12,760

ABOUT THE INSTITUTION Independent Roman Catholic, coed. **Awards:** certificates, associate, bachelor's, and master's degrees. 17 undergraduate majors. **Total enrollment:** 1,030. Undergraduates: 867. Freshmen: 134. Both federal and institutional methodology are used as a basis for awarding need-based institutional aid.

UNDERGRADUATE EXPENSES for 2013–2014 Tuition: full-time $15,420; part-time $490 per credit. **Required fees:** full-time $200; $100 per term. Full-time tuition and fees vary according to course load and program. Part-time tuition and fees vary according to course load and program.

FRESHMAN FINANCIAL AID (Fall 2011) 105 applied for aid; of those 92% were deemed to have need. 98% of freshmen with need received aid; of those 14% had need fully met. **Average percent of need met:** 66% (excluding resources awarded to replace EFC). **Average financial aid package:** $11,764 (excluding resources awarded to replace EFC). 3% of all full-time freshmen had no need and received non-need-based gift aid.

UNDERGRADUATE FINANCIAL AID (Fall 2011) 444 applied for aid; of those 92% were deemed to have need. 100% of undergraduates with need received aid; of those 13% had need fully met. **Average percent of need met:** 67% (excluding resources awarded to replace EFC). **Average financial aid package:** $12,760 (excluding resources awarded to replace EFC). 3% of all full-time undergraduates had no need and received non-need-based gift aid.

GIFT AID (NEED-BASED) Total amount: $3,437,705 (56% federal, 25% state, 18% institutional, 1% external sources). **Receiving aid:** Freshmen: 62% (66); all full-time undergraduates: 66% (300). *Average award:* Freshmen: $8458; Undergraduates: $8071. *Scholarships, grants, and awards:* Federal Pell, FSEOG, state, private, college/university gift aid from institutional funds, United Negro College Fund.

GIFT AID (NON-NEED-BASED) *Total amount:* $636,719 (46% institutional, 54% external sources). *Receiving aid:* Freshmen: 25% (27). Undergraduates: 22% (103). *Average award:* Freshmen: $4667. Undergraduates: $2962. *Scholarships, grants, and awards by category: Academic interests/achievement:* 59 awards ($130,449 total): general academic interests/achievements. *Creative arts/performance:* art/fine arts, theater/drama. *Special achievements/activities:* 31 awards ($44,800 total): leadership. *Special characteristics:* 60 awards ($120,462 total): children and siblings of alumni, children of faculty/staff, general special characteristics, previous college experience. *Tuition waivers:* Full or partial for children of alumni, employees or children of employees, senior citizens.

LOANS *Student loans:* $4,676,596 (44% need-based, 56% non-need-based). 64% of past graduating class borrowed through all loan programs. *Average indebtedness per student:* $23,000. *Average need-based loan:* Freshmen: $1627. Undergraduates: $2094. *Parent loans:* $197,144 (100% non-need-based). *Programs:* Federal Direct (Subsidized and Unsubsidized Stafford, PLUS).

WORK-STUDY *Federal work-study:* Total amount: $63,991; 29 jobs averaging $2207. *State or other work-study/employment:* Part-time jobs available.

ATHLETIC AWARDS Total amount: $1,078,162 (100% non-need-based).

APPLYING FOR FINANCIAL AID *Required financial aid form:* FAFSA. *Financial aid deadline (priority):* 3/1. *Notification date:* Continuous beginning 4/1.

CONTACT Gina Pirtle, Director of Financial Aid and Business Office Operations, Calumet College of Saint Joseph, 2400 New York Avenue, Whiting, IN 46394, 219-473-4379 or toll-free 877-700-9100. *E-mail:* gpirtle@ccsj.edu. *Website:* http://www.ccsj.edu/.

CALVARY BIBLE COLLEGE AND THEOLOGICAL SEMINARY
Kansas City, MO

Tuition & fees: $10,116	Average undergraduate aid package: N/A

ABOUT THE INSTITUTION Independent nondenominational, coed. *Awards:* certificates, diplomas, associate, bachelor's, and master's degrees. 35 undergraduate majors. *Total enrollment:* 337. Undergraduates: 283. Freshmen: 33. Both federal and institutional methodology are used as a basis for awarding need-based institutional aid.

UNDERGRADUATE EXPENSES for 2013–2014 *Application fee:* $25. *Comprehensive fee:* $15,116 includes full-time tuition ($9300), mandatory fees ($816), and room and board ($5000). Room and board charges vary according to housing facility. *Part-time tuition:* $310 per credit. *Part-time fees:* $29 per credit; $120 per term. *Payment plan:* Guaranteed tuition.

GIFT AID (NEED-BASED) *Scholarships, grants, and awards:* Federal Pell, FSEOG, private, college/university gift aid from institutional funds.

GIFT AID (NON-NEED-BASED) *Scholarships, grants, and awards by category: Academic interests/achievement:* general academic interests/achievements. *Creative arts/performance:* general creative arts/performance. *Special achievements/activities:* general special achievements/activities, religious involvement. *Special characteristics:* children and siblings of alumni, children of educators, children of faculty/staff, relatives of clergy, religious affiliation, siblings of current students, spouses of current students. *Tuition waivers:* Full or partial for employees or children of employees. **ROTC:** Army cooperative.

LOANS *Programs:* Federal Direct (Subsidized and Unsubsidized Stafford, PLUS).

APPLYING FOR FINANCIAL AID *Required financial aid forms:* FAFSA, institution's own form. *Financial aid deadline:* 4/1 (priority: 3/1). *Notification date:* Continuous beginning 5/1.

CONTACT Mr. Robert Crank, Director of Financial Aid, Calvary Bible College and Theological Seminary, 15800 Calvary Road, Kansas City, MO 64147-1341, 816-322-0110 Ext. 1323 or toll-free 800-326-3960. *Fax:* 816-331-4474. *E-mail:* finaid@calvary.edu. *Website:* http://www.calvary.edu/.

CALVIN COLLEGE
Grand Rapids, MI

Tuition & fees: $28,250	Average undergraduate aid package: $19,642

ABOUT THE INSTITUTION Independent Christian Reformed, coed. *Awards:* bachelor's and master's degrees. 105 undergraduate majors. *Total enrollment:* 4,008. Undergraduates: 3,930. Freshmen: 977. Both federal and institutional methodology are used as a basis for awarding need-based institutional aid.

UNDERGRADUATE EXPENSES for 2013–2014 *Application fee:* $35. *Comprehensive fee:* $37,585 includes full-time tuition ($28,025), mandatory fees ($225), and room and board ($9335). Full-time tuition and fees vary according to degree level and program. Room and board charges vary according to board plan and housing facility. *Part-time tuition:* $670 per credit hour. Part-time tuition and fees vary according to course load and degree level. *Payment plan:* Tuition prepayment.

FRESHMAN FINANCIAL AID (Fall 2012, est.) 861 applied for aid; of those 74% were deemed to have need. 100% of freshmen with need received aid; of those 18% had need fully met. *Average percent of need met:* 74% (excluding resources awarded to replace EFC). *Average financial aid package:* $21,083 (excluding resources awarded to replace EFC). 32% of all full-time freshmen had no need and received non-need-based gift aid.

UNDERGRADUATE FINANCIAL AID (Fall 2012, est.) 3,114 applied for aid; of those 78% were deemed to have need. 100% of undergraduates with need received aid; of those 16% had need fully met. *Average percent of need met:* 70% (excluding resources awarded to replace EFC). *Average financial aid package:* $19,642 (excluding resources awarded to replace EFC). 30% of all full-time undergraduates had no need and received non-need-based gift aid.

GIFT AID (NEED-BASED) *Total amount:* $32,188,376 (13% federal, 5% state, 79% institutional, 3% external sources). *Receiving aid:* Freshmen: 65% (637); all full-time undergraduates: 64% (2,402). *Average award:* Freshmen: $14,671; Undergraduates: $12,967. *Scholarships, grants, and awards:* Federal Pell, FSEOG, state, private, college/university gift aid from institutional funds.

GIFT AID (NON-NEED-BASED) *Total amount:* $11,298,971 (96% institutional, 4% external sources). *Receiving aid:* Freshmen: 7% (68). Undergraduates: 6% (231). *Average award:* Freshmen: $8354. Undergraduates: $6573. *Scholarships, grants, and awards by category: Academic interests/achievement:* $17,500,000 total: architecture, area/ethnic studies, biological sciences, business, communication, computer science, education, engineering/technologies, English, foreign languages, general academic interests/achievements, health fields, humanities, international studies, mathematics, physical sciences, premedicine, religion/biblical studies, social sciences. *Creative arts/performance:* $250,000 total: art/fine arts, music, performing arts, theater/drama. *Special achievements/activities:* $75,000 total: community service, leadership, religious involvement. *Special characteristics:* $7,500,000 total: adult students, children and siblings of alumni, children of faculty/staff, children of union members/company employees, children of workers in trades, children with a deceased or disabled parent, ethnic background, first-generation college students, handicapped students, international students, members of minority groups, out-of-state students, religious affiliation, twins. *Tuition waivers:* Full or partial for employees or children of employees. **ROTC:** Army cooperative.

LOANS *Student loans:* $24,023,321 (74% need-based, 26% non-need-based). 63% of past graduating class borrowed through all loan programs. *Average indebtedness per student:* $32,957. *Average need-based loan:* Freshmen: $4900. Undergraduates: $6740. *Parent loans:* $2,884,080 (50% need-based, 50% non-need-based). *Programs:* Federal Direct (Subsidized and Unsubsidized Stafford, PLUS), Perkins, state, college/university, alternative loans.

WORK-STUDY *Federal work-study:* Total amount: $1,916,300; 1,241 jobs averaging $1544. *State or other work-study/employment:* Total amount: $1,482,994 (17% need-based, 83% non-need-based). 977 part-time jobs averaging $1518.

APPLYING FOR FINANCIAL AID *Required financial aid form:* FAFSA. *Financial aid deadline (priority):* 2/15. *Notification date:* Continuous beginning 3/15.

CONTACT Mr. Craig Heerema, Financial Aid Administrator, Calvin College, Spoelhof Center 263, Grand Rapids, MI 49546, 616-526-6134 or toll-free 800-688-0122. *Fax:* 616-526-6883. *E-mail:* cheerema@calvin.edu. *Website:* http://www.calvin.edu/.

CAMBRIDGE COLLEGE
Cambridge, MA

Tuition & fees: N/R	Average undergraduate aid package: $8094

ABOUT THE INSTITUTION Independent, coed. *Awards:* certificates, bachelor's, master's, and doctoral degrees. 4 undergraduate majors. *Total enrollment:* 3,757. Undergraduates: 1,090. Freshmen: 68. Federal methodology is used as a basis for awarding need-based institutional aid.

FRESHMAN FINANCIAL AID (Fall 2011) 3 applied for aid; of those 33% were deemed to have need. 100% of freshmen with need received aid. *Average financial aid package:* $3500 (excluding resources awarded to replace EFC).

UNDERGRADUATE FINANCIAL AID (Fall 2011) 219 applied for aid; of those 95% were deemed to have need. 98% of undergraduates with need received aid. *Average financial aid package:* $8094 (excluding resources awarded to replace EFC).

GIFT AID (NEED-BASED) *Total amount:* $1,845,103 (100% federal). *Receiving aid:* All full-time undergraduates: 1% (3). *Average award:* Undergraduates: $4912. *Scholarships, grants, and awards:* Federal Pell, FSEOG, state, private, college/university gift aid from institutional funds.

LOANS *Average need-based loan:* Freshmen: $3500. Undergraduates: $4302. *Programs:* Federal Direct (Subsidized Stafford, PLUS).

WORK-STUDY Federal work-study jobs available.

APPLYING FOR FINANCIAL AID *Required financial aid forms:* FAFSA, institution's own form. *Financial aid deadline:* Continuous. *Notification date:* Continuous.

CONTACT Dr. Frank Lauder, Director of Financial Aid, Cambridge College, 1000 Massachusetts Avenue, Cambridge, MA 02138, 617-868-1000 Ext. 1440 or toll-free 800-877-4723. *Fax:* 617-349-3561. *E-mail:* francis.lauder@cambridgecollege.edu. *Website:* http://www.cambridgecollege.edu/.

CAMERON UNIVERSITY
Lawton, OK

Tuition & fees (OK res): $4770	Average undergraduate aid package: $8936

ABOUT THE INSTITUTION State-supported, coed. *Awards:* certificates, associate, bachelor's, and master's degrees. 38 undergraduate majors. *Total enrollment:* 6,112. Undergraduates: 5,567. Freshmen: 921. Federal methodology is used as a basis for awarding need-based institutional aid.

UNDERGRADUATE EXPENSES for 2013–2014 *Application fee:* $15. *Tuition, state resident:* full-time $3225; part-time $107.50 per credit hour. *Tuition, nonresident:* full-time $10,200; part-time $340 per credit hour. *Required fees:* full-time $1545; $51.50 per credit hour. Full-time tuition and fees vary according to course load, location, and program. Part-time tuition and fees vary according to course load, location, and program. *College room and board:* $3884; *Room only:* $1504. Room and board charges vary according to board plan and housing facility.

FRESHMAN FINANCIAL AID (Fall 2011) 925 applied for aid; of those 83% were deemed to have need. 91% of freshmen with need received aid; of those 5% had need fully met. *Average percent of need met:* 55% (excluding resources awarded to replace EFC). *Average financial aid package:* $8457 (excluding resources awarded to replace EFC). 4% of all full-time freshmen had no need and received non-need-based gift aid.

UNDERGRADUATE FINANCIAL AID (Fall 2011) 3,006 applied for aid; of those 88% were deemed to have need. 87% of undergraduates with need received aid; of those 4% had need fully met. *Average percent of need met:* 56% (excluding resources awarded to replace EFC). *Average financial aid package:* $8936 (excluding resources awarded to replace EFC). 6% of all full-time undergraduates had no need and received non-need-based gift aid.

GIFT AID (NEED-BASED) *Total amount:* $15,610,856 (81% federal, 15% state, 2% institutional, 2% external sources). *Receiving aid:* Freshmen: 60% (662); all full-time undergraduates: 56% (2,191). *Average award:* Freshmen: $5571; Undergraduates: $5456. *Scholarships, grants, and awards:* Federal Pell, FSEOG, state, private, college/university gift aid from institutional funds.

GIFT AID (NON-NEED-BASED) *Total amount:* $1,206,239 (14% state, 29% institutional, 57% external sources). *Receiving aid:* Freshmen: 16% (179). Undergraduates: 14% (554). *Average award:* Freshmen: $1043. Undergraduates: $1154. *Scholarships, grants, and awards by category: Academic interests/achievement:* agriculture, biological sciences, business, communication, computer science, education, engineering/technologies, English, foreign languages, general academic interests/achievements, health fields, mathematics, military science, physical sciences, social sciences. *Creative arts/performance:* art/fine arts, cinema/film/broadcasting, creative writing, debating, journalism/publications, music, performing arts, theater/drama. *Special achievements/activities:* cheerleading/drum major, general special achievements/activities, leadership. *Special characteristics:* international students, members of minority groups, out-of-state students. *Tuition waivers:* Full or partial for employees or children of employees. *ROTC:* Army.

LOANS *Student loans:* $16,281,183 (47% need-based, 53% non-need-based). 36% of past graduating class borrowed through all loan programs. *Average indebtedness per student:* $15,020. *Average need-based loan:* Freshmen: $2973. Undergraduates: $3691. *Parent loans:* $97,627 (100% non-need-based). *Programs:* Federal Direct (Subsidized and Unsubsidized Stafford, PLUS).

WORK-STUDY *Federal work-study:* Total amount: $149,090; 78 jobs averaging $1899. *State or other work-study/employment:* Total amount: $1,190,912 (100% non-need-based). 245 part-time jobs averaging $4716.

ATHLETIC AWARDS Total amount: $632,540 (100% non-need-based).

APPLYING FOR FINANCIAL AID *Required financial aid form:* FAFSA. *Financial aid deadline:* Continuous. *Notification date:* Continuous beginning 4/1. Students must reply by 8/1 or within 2 weeks of notification.

CONTACT Mr. Donald Hall, Director of Financial Aid, Cameron University, 2800 West Gore Boulevard, Lawton, OK 73505-6377, 580-581-2293 or toll-free 888-454-7600. *Fax:* 580-581-2556. *E-mail:* dhall@cameron.edu. *Website:* http://www.cameron.edu/.

CAMPBELLSVILLE UNIVERSITY
Campbellsville, KY

Tuition & fees: $22,196	Average undergraduate aid package: $15,848

ABOUT THE INSTITUTION Independent Kentucky Baptist Convention, coed. *Awards:* certificates, associate, bachelor's, and master's degrees. 56 undergraduate majors. *Total enrollment:* 3,664. Undergraduates: 3,132. Freshmen: 579. Federal methodology is used as a basis for awarding need-based institutional aid.

UNDERGRADUATE EXPENSES for 2013–2014 *Application fee:* $20. *Comprehensive fee:* $30,396 includes full-time tuition ($21,696), mandatory fees ($500), and room and board ($8200). Room and board charges vary according to housing facility. *Part-time tuition:* $904 per credit hour.

FRESHMAN FINANCIAL AID (Fall 2011) 449 applied for aid; of those 95% were deemed to have need. 99% of freshmen with need received aid; of those 13% had need fully met. *Average percent of need met:* 75% (excluding resources awarded to replace EFC). *Average financial aid package:* $19,034 (excluding resources awarded to replace EFC). 5% of all full-time freshmen had no need and received non-need-based gift aid.

UNDERGRADUATE FINANCIAL AID (Fall 2011) 1,655 applied for aid; of those 95% were deemed to have need. 99% of undergraduates with need received aid; of those 12% had need fully met. *Average percent of need met:* 70% (excluding resources awarded to replace EFC). *Average financial aid package:* $15,848 (excluding resources awarded to replace EFC). 6% of all full-time undergraduates had no need and received non-need-based gift aid.

GIFT AID (NEED-BASED) *Total amount:* $20,899,984 (25% federal, 22% state, 47% institutional, 6% external sources). *Receiving aid:* Freshmen: 82% (425); all full-time undergraduates: 87% (1,545). *Average award:* Freshmen: $16,276; Undergraduates: $12,914. *Scholarships, grants, and awards:* Federal Pell, FSEOG, state, college/university gift aid from institutional funds.

GIFT AID (NON-NEED-BASED) *Total amount:* $1,517,131 (17% state, 63% institutional, 20% external sources). *Receiving aid:* Freshmen: 8% (43). Undergraduates: 8% (139). *Average award:* Freshmen: $10,356. Undergraduates: $7147. *Scholarships, grants, and awards by category: Academic interests/achievement:* 535 awards ($3,287,075 total): biological sciences, business, communication, computer science, education, English, general academic interests/achievements, health fields, humanities, mathematics, physical sciences, premedicine, religion/biblical studies, social sciences. *Creative arts/performance:* 175 awards ($546,147 total): art/fine arts, journalism/publications, music, theater/drama. *Special achievements/activities:* 285 awards ($646,147 total): cheerleading/drum major, junior miss, leadership, religious involvement. *Special characteristics:* 195 awards ($1,036,485 total): adult students, children of educators, children of faculty/staff, international students, relatives of clergy, religious affiliation, veterans. *Tuition waivers:* Full or partial for employees or children of employees, adult students, senior citizens. *ROTC:* Army cooperative.

LOANS *Student loans:* $10,804,660 (86% need-based, 14% non-need-based). 58% of past graduating class borrowed through all loan programs. *Average indebtedness per student:* $10,183. *Average need-based loan:* Freshmen: $2849. Undergraduates: $3649. *Parent loans:* $1,576,784 (56% need-based, 44% non-need-based). *Programs:* Federal Direct (Subsidized and Unsubsidized Stafford, PLUS), Perkins, college/university.

WORK-STUDY *Federal work-study:* Total amount: $478,252; 375 jobs averaging $1675. *State or other work-study/employment:* Total amount: $64,573 (71% need-based, 29% non-need-based). 32 part-time jobs averaging $1650.

ATHLETIC AWARDS Total amount: $2,800,036 (60% need-based, 40% non-need-based).

APPLYING FOR FINANCIAL AID *Required financial aid form:* FAFSA. *Financial aid deadline (priority):* 3/1. *Notification date:* Continuous beginning 3/15. Students must reply within 3 weeks of notification.

CONTACT Mr. Aaron Gabehart, Financial Aid Counselor, Campbellsville University, 1 University Drive, Campbellsville, KY 42718, 270-789-5305 or toll-free 800-264-6014. *Fax:* 270-789-5060. *E-mail:* finaid@campbellsville.edu. *Website:* http://www.campbellsville.edu/.

CAMPBELL UNIVERSITY
Buies Creek, NC

Tuition & fees: N/R	Average undergraduate aid package: $17,627

ABOUT THE INSTITUTION Independent North Carolina Baptist State Convention, coed. 85 undergraduate majors. Federal methodology is used as a basis for awarding need-based institutional aid.

FRESHMAN FINANCIAL AID (Fall 2011) 820 applied for aid; of those 91% were deemed to have need. 100% of freshmen with need received aid; of those 51% had need fully met. *Average percent of need met:* 80% (excluding resources awarded to replace EFC). *Average financial aid package:* $20,748 (excluding resources awarded to replace EFC). 8% of all full-time freshmen had no need and received non-need-based gift aid.

UNDERGRADUATE FINANCIAL AID (Fall 2011) 3,919 applied for aid; of those 81% were deemed to have need. 100% of undergraduates with need received aid; of those 26% had need fully met. *Average percent of need met:* 80% (excluding resources awarded to replace EFC). *Average financial aid package:* $17,627 (excluding resources awarded to replace EFC). 11% of all full-time undergraduates had no need and received non-need-based gift aid.

GIFT AID (NEED-BASED) *Total amount:* $33,748,362 (22% federal, 15% state, 59% institutional, 4% external sources). *Receiving aid:* Freshmen: 63% (550); all full-time undergraduates: 45% (2,062). *Average award:* Freshmen: $6157; Undergraduates: $5632. *Scholarships, grants, and awards:* Federal Pell, FSEOG, state, private, college/university gift aid from institutional funds.

GIFT AID (NON-NEED-BASED) *Total amount:* $10,145,346 (50% state, 46% institutional, 4% external sources). *Receiving aid:* Freshmen: 85% (737). Undergraduates: 68% (3,083). *Average award:* Freshmen: $12,202. Undergraduates: $19,002. *Scholarships, grants, and awards by category: Academic interests/achievement:* 2,465 awards ($22,450,919 total): general academic interests/achievements. *Creative arts/performance:* 57 awards ($67,250 total): art/fine arts, creative writing, journalism/publications, music, theater/drama. *Special achievements/activities:* 29 awards ($102,100 total): cheerleading/drum major, religious involvement. *Special characteristics:* 67 awards ($947,095 total): children of faculty/staff.

LOANS *Student loans:* $28,821,929 (90% need-based, 10% non-need-based). 75% of past graduating class borrowed through all loan programs. *Average indebtedness per student:* $24,820. *Average need-based loan:* Freshmen: $3314. Undergraduates: $6335. *Parent loans:* $35,487,025 (90% need-based, 10% non-need-based). *Programs:* Federal Direct (Subsidized and Unsubsidized Stafford, PLUS), Perkins, state.

WORK-STUDY *Federal work-study:* Total amount: $1,390,725; 983 jobs averaging $1416. *State or other work-study/employment:* Total amount: $665,279 (100% non-need-based). 710 part-time jobs averaging $1135.

ATHLETIC AWARDS Total amount: $4,262,891 (62% need-based, 38% non-need-based).

APPLYING FOR FINANCIAL AID *Required financial aid form:* FAFSA. *Financial aid deadline (priority):* 2/15. *Notification date:* Continuous. Students must reply within 2 weeks of notification.

CONTACT Financial Aid Office, Campbell University, PO Box 36, Buies Creek, NC 27506, 910-893-1310 or toll-free 800-334-4111. *Fax:* 910-814-5788. *Website:* http://www.campbell.edu/.

CANISIUS COLLEGE
Buffalo, NY

Tuition & fees: $32,030	Average undergraduate aid package: $27,009

ABOUT THE INSTITUTION Independent Roman Catholic (Jesuit), coed. *Awards:* certificates, associate, bachelor's, and master's degrees. 112 undergraduate majors. *Total enrollment:* 4,908. Undergraduates: 3,280. Freshmen: 713. Federal methodology is used as a basis for awarding need-based institutional aid.

UNDERGRADUATE EXPENSES for 2013–2014 *Application fee:* $40. *Comprehensive fee:* $43,850 includes full-time tuition ($30,780), mandatory fees ($1250), and room and board ($11,820). *College room only:* $6940. Full-time tuition and fees vary according to course load and degree level. Room and board charges vary according to board plan and housing facility. *Part-time tuition:* $879 per credit. *Part-time fees:* $20.50 per credit hour; $63 per credit. Part-time tuition and fees vary according to course load and degree level.

FRESHMAN FINANCIAL AID (Fall 2012, est.) 660 applied for aid; of those 93% were deemed to have need. 100% of freshmen with need received aid; of those 32% had need fully met. *Average percent of need met:* 85% (excluding resources awarded to replace EFC). *Average financial aid package:* $29,373 (excluding resources awarded to replace EFC). 14% of all full-time freshmen had no need and received non-need-based gift aid.

UNDERGRADUATE FINANCIAL AID (Fall 2012, est.) 2,451 applied for aid; of those 94% were deemed to have need. 100% of undergraduates with need received aid; of those 26% had need fully met. *Average percent of need met:* 81% (excluding resources awarded to replace EFC). *Average financial aid package:* $27,009 (excluding resources awarded to replace EFC). 19% of all full-time undergraduates had no need and received non-need-based gift aid.

GIFT AID (NEED-BASED) *Total amount:* $45,232,243 (11% federal, 8% state, 81% institutional). *Receiving aid:* Freshmen: 86% (610); all full-time undergraduates: 77% (2,272). *Average award:* Freshmen: $22,566; Undergraduates: $20,666. *Scholarships, grants, and awards:* Federal Pell, FSEOG, state, private, college/university gift aid from institutional funds.

GIFT AID (NON-NEED-BASED) *Total amount:* $4,077,470 (1% state, 98% institutional, 1% external sources). *Receiving aid:* Freshmen: 19% (135). Undergraduates: 15% (435). *Average award:* Freshmen: $15,448. Undergraduates: $15,361. *Scholarships, grants, and awards by category: Academic interests/achievement:* 2,245 awards ($27,653,568 total): general academic interests/achievements. *Creative arts/performance:* 91 awards ($176,000 total): art/fine arts, dance, music. *Special achievements/activities:* 3 awards ($15,696 total): religious involvement. *Special characteristics:* 471 awards ($3,683,962 total): children and siblings of alumni, children of educators, children of faculty/staff, international students, religious affiliation. *Tuition waivers:* Full or partial for employees or children of employees. *ROTC:* Army.

LOANS *Student loans:* $17,641,016 (75% need-based, 25% non-need-based). 72% of past graduating class borrowed through all loan programs. *Average indebtedness per student:* $36,383. *Average need-based loan:* Freshmen: $3682. Undergraduates: $4363. *Parent loans:* $8,638,748 (28% need-based, 72% non-need-based). *Programs:* Federal Direct (Subsidized and Unsubsidized Stafford, PLUS), Perkins.

WORK-STUDY *Federal work-study:* Total amount: $988,091; 556 jobs averaging $1777. *State or other work-study/employment:* Total amount: $35,752 (84% need-based, 16% non-need-based). Part-time jobs available.

ATHLETIC AWARDS Total amount: $1,952,267 (61% need-based, 39% non-need-based).

APPLYING FOR FINANCIAL AID *Required financial aid forms:* FAFSA, state aid form. *Financial aid deadline (priority):* 2/15. *Notification date:* Continuous beginning 3/15. Students must reply by 5/1.
CONTACT Mr. Curtis Gaume, Director of Student Financial Aid, Canisius College, 2001 Main Street, Buffalo, NY 14208-1098, 716-888-2300 or toll-free 800-843-1517. *Fax:* 716-888-2377. *E-mail:* gaume@canisius.edu.
Website: http://www.canisius.edu/.

CAPELLA UNIVERSITY
Minneapolis, MN

CONTACT University Services, Capella University, 222 South Ninth Street, Minneapolis, MN 55402, 888-227-3552 or toll-free 866-283-7921.
Website: http://www.capella.edu/.

CAPITAL UNIVERSITY
Columbus, OH

Tuition & fees: $31,364	Average undergraduate aid package: $22,845

ABOUT THE INSTITUTION Independent Evangelical Lutheran Church in America, coed. *Awards:* bachelor's, master's, and doctoral degrees. 60 undergraduate majors. *Total enrollment:* 3,584. Undergraduates: 2,720. Freshmen: 670. Federal methodology is used as a basis for awarding need-based institutional aid.
UNDERGRADUATE EXPENSES for 2013–2014 *Application fee:* $25. *Comprehensive fee:* $39,824 includes full-time tuition ($31,364) and room and board ($8460). Full-time tuition and fees vary according to course load. Room and board charges vary according to board plan and housing facility. *Part-time tuition:* $1045 per credit hour. Part-time tuition and fees vary according to course load.
FRESHMAN FINANCIAL AID (Fall 2011) 600 applied for aid; of those 93% were deemed to have need. 100% of freshmen with need received aid; of those 17% had need fully met. *Average percent of need met:* 76% (excluding resources awarded to replace EFC). *Average financial aid package:* $23,883 (excluding resources awarded to replace EFC). 11% of all full-time freshmen had no need and received non-need-based gift aid.
UNDERGRADUATE FINANCIAL AID (Fall 2011) 2,103 applied for aid; of those 93% were deemed to have need. 100% of undergraduates with need received aid; of those 17% had need fully met. *Average percent of need met:* 76% (excluding resources awarded to replace EFC). *Average financial aid package:* $22,845 (excluding resources awarded to replace EFC). 6% of all full-time undergraduates had no need and received non-need-based gift aid.
GIFT AID (NEED-BASED) *Total amount:* $39,694,265 (10% federal, 2% state, 88% institutional). *Receiving aid:* Freshmen: 87% (543); all full-time undergraduates: 79% (1,843). *Average award:* Freshmen: $18,701; Undergraduates: $17,683. *Scholarships, grants, and awards:* Federal Pell, FSEOG, state, private, college/university gift aid from institutional funds, Federal Nursing.
GIFT AID (NON-NEED-BASED) *Total amount:* $1,992,839 (3% institutional, 97% external sources). *Receiving aid:* Freshmen: 86% (540). Undergraduates: 78% (1,841). *Average award:* Freshmen: $16,697. Undergraduates: $16,387. *Scholarships, grants, and awards by category:* Academic interests/achievement: general academic interests/achievements. Creative arts/performance: music, performing arts. Special achievements/activities: hobbies/interests, leadership, religious involvement. Special characteristics: children and siblings of alumni, children of faculty/staff, ethnic background, international students, members of minority groups, out-of-state students, relatives of clergy, religious affiliation, siblings of current students. *Tuition waivers:* Full or partial for employees or children of employees, senior citizens. *ROTC:* Army, Air Force cooperative.
LOANS *Student loans:* $19,734,877 (42% need-based, 58% non-need-based). 79% of past graduating class borrowed through all loan programs. *Average indebtedness per student:* $33,200. *Average need-based loan:* Freshmen: $3753. Undergraduates: $4355. *Parent loans:* $8,428,999 (100% non-need-based). *Programs:* Federal Direct (Subsidized and Unsubsidized Stafford, PLUS), Perkins, Federal Nursing, college/university.
WORK-STUDY *Federal work-study:* Total amount: $518,974; jobs available. *State or other work-study/employment:* Part-time jobs available.

APPLYING FOR FINANCIAL AID *Required financial aid form:* FAFSA. *Financial aid deadline (priority):* 3/1. *Notification date:* Continuous beginning 3/25. Students must reply by 5/1.
CONTACT Ms. Susan Kannenwischer, Office of Financial Aid, Capital University, 1 College and Main Street, Columbus, OH 43209-2394, 614-236-6511 or toll-free 866-544-6175. *Fax:* 614-236-6926. *E-mail:* finaid@capital.edu.
Website: http://www.capital.edu/.

CAPITOL COLLEGE
Laurel, MD

Tuition & fees: N/R	Average undergraduate aid package: $13,929

ABOUT THE INSTITUTION Independent, coed. 13 undergraduate majors. Federal methodology is used as a basis for awarding need-based institutional aid.
FRESHMAN FINANCIAL AID (Fall 2011) 60 applied for aid; of those 93% were deemed to have need. 100% of freshmen with need received aid. *Average percent of need met:* 50% (excluding resources awarded to replace EFC). *Average financial aid package:* $17,161 (excluding resources awarded to replace EFC). 5% of all full-time freshmen had no need and received non-need-based gift aid.
UNDERGRADUATE FINANCIAL AID (Fall 2011) 317 applied for aid; of those 73% were deemed to have need. 100% of undergraduates with need received aid; of those 9% had need fully met. *Average percent of need met:* 47% (excluding resources awarded to replace EFC). *Average financial aid package:* $13,929 (excluding resources awarded to replace EFC). 3% of all full-time undergraduates had no need and received non-need-based gift aid.
GIFT AID (NEED-BASED) *Total amount:* $1,116,966 (60% federal, 30% state, 7% institutional, 3% external sources). *Receiving aid:* Freshmen: 69% (51); all full-time undergraduates: 70% (227). *Average award:* Freshmen: $3509; Undergraduates: $4153. *Scholarships, grants, and awards:* Federal Pell, FSEOG, state, private, college/university gift aid from institutional funds.
GIFT AID (NON-NEED-BASED) *Total amount:* $1,746,476 (100% institutional). *Receiving aid:* Freshmen: 62% (46). Undergraduates: 70% (227). *Average award:* Freshmen: $5500. Undergraduates: $5864. *Scholarships, grants, and awards by category:* Academic interests/achievement: general academic interests/achievements.
LOANS *Student loans:* $2,006,215 (100% need-based). 100% of past graduating class borrowed through all loan programs. *Average indebtedness per student:* $34,609. *Average need-based loan:* Freshmen: $3085. Undergraduates: $3597. *Parent loans:* $241,989 (100% need-based). *Programs:* Federal Direct (Subsidized and Unsubsidized Stafford, PLUS), Perkins.
WORK-STUDY *Federal work-study:* Total amount: $61,699; 39 jobs averaging $1647. *State or other work-study/employment:* Total amount: $75,275 (100% need-based). 67 part-time jobs averaging $1124.
APPLYING FOR FINANCIAL AID *Required financial aid form:* FAFSA. *Financial aid deadline:* Continuous. *Notification date:* Continuous. Students must reply within 3 weeks of notification.
CONTACT Suzanne Thompson, Director of Financial Aid, Capitol College, 11301 Springfield Road, Laurel, MD 20708-9759, 301-369-2800 Ext. 3037 or toll-free 800-950-1992. *Fax:* 301-369-2328. *E-mail:* sthompson@capitol-college.edu.
Website: http://www.capitol-college.edu/.

CARDINAL STRITCH UNIVERSITY
Milwaukee, WI

Tuition & fees: $24,330	Average undergraduate aid package: $11,172

ABOUT THE INSTITUTION Independent Roman Catholic, coed. *Awards:* certificates, associate, bachelor's, master's, and doctoral degrees. 42 undergraduate majors. *Total enrollment:* 4,641. Undergraduates: 2,782. Freshmen: 161. Federal methodology is used as a basis for awarding need-based institutional aid.
UNDERGRADUATE EXPENSES for 2013–2014 *Comprehensive fee:* $31,360 includes full-time tuition ($23,680), mandatory fees ($650), and room and board ($7030). *College room only:* $1900. Full-time tuition and fees vary according

to degree level and program. Room and board charges vary according to board plan. *Part-time tuition:* $740 per credit hour. *Part-time fees:* $460 per year. Part-time tuition and fees vary according to course load, degree level, and program.

FRESHMAN FINANCIAL AID (Fall 2012, est.) 148 applied for aid; of those 97% were deemed to have need. 100% of freshmen with need received aid; of those 14% had need fully met. *Average percent of need met:* 72% (excluding resources awarded to replace EFC). *Average financial aid package:* $21,627 (excluding resources awarded to replace EFC). 9% of all full-time freshmen had no need and received non-need-based gift aid.

UNDERGRADUATE FINANCIAL AID (Fall 2012, est.) 2,184 applied for aid; of those 87% were deemed to have need. 98% of undergraduates with need received aid; of those 5% had need fully met. *Average percent of need met:* 42% (excluding resources awarded to replace EFC). *Average financial aid package:* $11,172 (excluding resources awarded to replace EFC). 5% of all full-time undergraduates had no need and received non-need-based gift aid.

GIFT AID (NEED-BASED) *Total amount:* $12,957,999 (35% federal, 9% state, 54% institutional, 2% external sources). *Receiving aid:* Freshmen: 91% (144); all full-time undergraduates: 58% (1,444). *Average award:* Freshmen: $17,411; Undergraduates: $8754. *Scholarships, grants, and awards:* Federal Pell, FSEOG, state, private, college/university gift aid from institutional funds.

GIFT AID (NON-NEED-BASED) *Total amount:* $1,827,437 (9% federal, 86% institutional, 5% external sources). *Receiving aid:* Freshmen: 8% (13). Undergraduates: 2% (51). *Average award:* Freshmen: $12,919. Undergraduates: $10,971. *Scholarships, grants, and awards by category: Academic interests/ achievement:* general academic interests/achievements. *Creative arts/performance:* art/fine arts, music, theater/drama. *Special achievements/activities:* community service. *Special characteristics:* children and siblings of alumni, children of current students, religious affiliation, siblings of current students, spouses of current students. *Tuition waivers:* Full or partial for employees or children of employees.

LOANS *Student loans:* $17,983,182 (90% need-based, 10% non-need-based). 87% of past graduating class borrowed through all loan programs. *Average indebtedness per student:* $27,292. *Average need-based loan:* Freshmen: $3123. Undergraduates: $3954. *Parent loans:* $663,741 (51% need-based, 49% non-need-based). *Programs:* Federal Direct (Subsidized and Unsubsidized Stafford, PLUS), Perkins, state.

WORK-STUDY *Federal work-study:* Total amount: $906,518; jobs available. *State or other work-study/employment:* Total amount: $938,439 (78% need-based, 22% non-need-based). Part-time jobs available.

ATHLETIC AWARDS Total amount: $580,559 (67% need-based, 33% non-need-based).

APPLYING FOR FINANCIAL AID *Required financial aid forms:* FAFSA, institution's own form. *Financial aid deadline:* Continuous. *Notification date:* Continuous beginning 3/1. Students must reply within 2 weeks of notification.

CONTACT Financial Aid Office, Cardinal Stritch University, 6801 North Yates Road, Milwaukee, WI 53217-3985, 414-410-4000 or toll-free 800-347-8822 Ext. 4040. *Website:* http://www.stritch.edu/.

CAREER POINT COLLEGE
San Antonio, TX

CONTACT Financial Aid Office, Career Point College, 4522 Fredericksburg Road, San Antonio, TX 78201, 210-732-3000.
Website: http://www.careerpointcollege.edu/.

CARIBBEAN UNIVERSITY
Bayamón, PR

CONTACT Financial Aid Office, Caribbean University, Box 493, Bayamón, PR 00960-0493, 787-780-0070.
Website: http://www.caribbean.edu/.

CARLETON COLLEGE
Northfield, MN

Tuition & fees: $44,445	Average undergraduate aid package: $37,454

ABOUT THE INSTITUTION Independent, coed. *Awards:* bachelor's degrees. 39 undergraduate majors. *Total enrollment:* 2,055. Undergraduates: 2,055. Freshmen: 528. Both federal and institutional methodology are used as a basis for awarding need-based institutional aid.

UNDERGRADUATE EXPENSES for 2013–2014 *Application fee:* $30. *Comprehensive fee:* $55,998 includes full-time tuition ($44,184), mandatory fees ($261), and room and board ($11,553). *College room only:* $6069. Room and board charges vary according to board plan. *Payment plan:* Tuition prepayment.

FRESHMAN FINANCIAL AID (Fall 2011) 380 applied for aid; of those 77% were deemed to have need. 100% of freshmen with need received aid; of those 100% had need fully met. *Average percent of need met:* 100% (excluding resources awarded to replace EFC). *Average financial aid package:* $35,113 (excluding resources awarded to replace EFC). 7% of all full-time freshmen had no need and received non-need-based gift aid.

UNDERGRADUATE FINANCIAL AID (Fall 2011) 1,716 applied for aid; of those 66% were deemed to have need. 100% of undergraduates with need received aid; of those 100% had need fully met. *Average percent of need met:* 100% (excluding resources awarded to replace EFC). *Average financial aid package:* $37,454 (excluding resources awarded to replace EFC). 6% of all full-time undergraduates had no need and received non-need-based gift aid.

GIFT AID (NEED-BASED) *Total amount:* $33,458,027 (3% federal, 1% state, 92% institutional, 4% external sources). *Receiving aid:* Freshmen: 56% (294); all full-time undergraduates: 56% (1,134). *Average award:* Freshmen: $31,445; Undergraduates: $31,320. *Scholarships, grants, and awards:* Federal Pell, FSEOG, state, private, college/university gift aid from institutional funds.

GIFT AID (NON-NEED-BASED) *Total amount:* $1,113,852 (30% institutional, 70% external sources). *Receiving aid:* Freshmen: 10% (53). Undergraduates: 10% (201). *Average award:* Freshmen: $2054. Undergraduates: $2622. *Scholarships, grants, and awards by category: Academic interests/achievement:* 221 awards ($329,696 total): general academic interests/achievements. *Creative arts/performance:* 4 awards ($3120 total): music. *Tuition waivers:* Full or partial for employees or children of employees.

LOANS *Student loans:* $4,811,513 (95% need-based, 5% non-need-based). 40% of past graduating class borrowed through all loan programs. *Average indebtedness per student:* $17,289. *Average need-based loan:* Freshmen: $4138. Undergraduates: $4690. *Parent loans:* $1,435,463 (89% need-based, 11% non-need-based). *Programs:* Federal Direct (Subsidized and Unsubsidized Stafford, PLUS), Perkins, state, college/university.

WORK-STUDY *Federal work-study:* Total amount: $912,251; 357 jobs averaging $2555. *State or other work-study/employment:* Total amount: $3,354,085 (57% need-based, 43% non-need-based). 1,326 part-time jobs averaging $2503.

APPLYING FOR FINANCIAL AID *Required financial aid forms:* FAFSA, CSS Financial Aid PROFILE, noncustodial (divorced/separated) parent's statement. *Financial aid deadline:* 2/15. *Notification date:* 4/1. Students must reply by 5/1 or within 2 weeks of notification.

CONTACT Mr. Rodney M. Oto, Director of Student Financial Services, Carleton College, One North College Street, Northfield, MN 55057-4001, 507-222-4138 or toll-free 800-995-2275. *Fax:* 507-222-4269.
Website: http://www.carleton.edu/.

CARLOS ALBIZU UNIVERSITY
San Juan, PR

Tuition & fees: $6919	Average undergraduate aid package: $5204

ABOUT THE INSTITUTION Independent, coed, primarily women. *Awards:* bachelor's, master's, and doctoral degrees. 3 undergraduate majors. *Total enrollment:* 930. Undergraduates: 162. Federal methodology is used as a basis for awarding need-based institutional aid.

UNDERGRADUATE EXPENSES for 2013–2014 *Tuition:* full-time $5940; part-time $165 per credit. *Required fees:* full-time $979; $333 per term.

UNDERGRADUATE FINANCIAL AID (Fall 2012, est.) 54 applied for aid; of those 100% were deemed to have need. 100% of undergraduates with need received aid. *Average percent of need met:* 48% (excluding resources awarded to replace EFC). *Average financial aid package:* $5204 (excluding resources awarded to replace EFC).

GIFT AID (NEED-BASED) *Total amount:* $193,854 (89% federal, 6% state, 5% external sources). *Receiving aid:* All full-time undergraduates: 55% (39). *Average award:* Undergraduates: $2388. *Scholarships, grants, and awards:* Federal Pell, FSEOG, state, college/university gift aid from institutional funds.

GIFT AID (NON-NEED-BASED) *Scholarships, grants, and awards by category:* Academic interests/achievement: social sciences. *Tuition waivers:* Full or partial for employees or children of employees.

LOANS *Student loans:* $224,339 (23% need-based, 77% non-need-based). *Average need-based loan:* Undergraduates: $4890. *Programs:* Federal Direct (Subsidized and Unsubsidized Stafford, PLUS).

WORK-STUDY *Federal work-study:* Total amount: $8384; 6 jobs averaging $1397.

APPLYING FOR FINANCIAL AID *Notification date:* Continuous.

CONTACT Mrs. Doris J. Quero, Director, Carlos Albizu University, PO Box 9023711, San Juan, PR 00901, 787-725-6500 Ext. 1529. *Fax:* 787-721-4008. *E-mail:* dquero@albizu.edu.
Website: http://www.albizu.edu/.

CARLOS ALBIZU UNIVERSITY, MIAMI CAMPUS
Miami, FL

CONTACT Maria V. Chavez, Senior Financial Aid Officer, Carlos Albizu University, Miami Campus, 2173 Northwest 99th Avenue, Miami, FL 33172, 305-593-1223 Ext. 153 or toll-free 888-GO-TO-CAU (in-state), 800-GO-TO-CAU (out-of-state). *Fax:* 305-593-8902. *E-mail:* mchavez@albizu.edu.
Website: http://www.mia.albizu.edu/.

CARLOW UNIVERSITY
Pittsburgh, PA

CONTACT Ms. Natalie Wilson, Director of Financial Aid, Carlow University, 3333 Fifth Avenue, Pittsburgh, PA 15213-3165, 412-578-6171 or toll-free 800-333-CARLOW.
Website: http://www.carlow.edu/.

CARNEGIE MELLON UNIVERSITY
Pittsburgh, PA

Tuition & fees: $47,642	Average undergraduate aid package: $32,077

ABOUT THE INSTITUTION Independent, coed. *Awards:* certificates, bachelor's, master's, and doctoral degrees. 74 undergraduate majors. *Total enrollment:* 12,569. Undergraduates: 6,279. Freshmen: 1,408. Both federal and institutional methodology are used as a basis for awarding need-based institutional aid.

UNDERGRADUATE EXPENSES for 2013–2014 *Application fee:* $70. *Comprehensive fee:* $59,632 includes full-time tuition ($46,670), mandatory fees ($972), and room and board ($11,990). *College room only:* $7070. Full-time tuition and fees vary according to student level. Room and board charges vary according to board plan and housing facility. Part-time tuition and fees vary according to student level.

FRESHMAN FINANCIAL AID (Fall 2012, est.) 984 applied for aid; of those 76% were deemed to have need. 99% of freshmen with need received aid; of those 26% had need fully met. *Average percent of need met:* 83% (excluding resources awarded to replace EFC). *Average financial aid package:* $31,612 (excluding resources awarded to replace EFC). 8% of all full-time freshmen had no need and received non-need-based gift aid.

UNDERGRADUATE FINANCIAL AID (Fall 2012, est.) 3,413 applied for aid; of those 84% were deemed to have need. 98% of undergraduates with need received aid; of those 29% had need fully met. *Average percent of need met:* 83% (excluding resources awarded to replace EFC). *Average financial aid package:* $32,077 (excluding resources awarded to replace EFC). 7% of all full-time undergraduates had no need and received non-need-based gift aid.

GIFT AID (NEED-BASED) *Total amount:* $71,015,858 (8% federal, 1% state, 88% institutional, 3% external sources). *Receiving aid:* Freshmen: 50% (707); all full-time undergraduates: 44% (2,694). *Average award:* Freshmen: $26,048; Undergraduates: $26,305. *Scholarships, grants, and awards:* Federal Pell, FSEOG, state, private, college/university gift aid from institutional funds.

GIFT AID (NON-NEED-BASED) *Total amount:* $10,508,409 (86% institutional, 14% external sources). *Receiving aid:* Freshmen: 18% (257). Undergraduates: 18% (1,081). *Average award:* Freshmen: $7295. Undergraduates: $9040. *Scholarships, grants, and awards by category:* Academic interests/achievement: general academic interests/achievements. Creative arts/performance: art/fine arts, music. Special achievements/activities: leadership. Special characteristics: local/state students, members of minority groups, out-of-state students. *ROTC:* Army, Naval, Air Force.

LOANS *Student loans:* $23,060,628 (87% need-based, 13% non-need-based). 45% of past graduating class borrowed through all loan programs. *Average indebtedness per student:* $31,747. *Average need-based loan:* Freshmen: $4842. Undergraduates: $5721. *Parent loans:* $7,274,936 (22% need-based, 78% non-need-based). *Programs:* Federal Direct (Subsidized and Unsubsidized Stafford, PLUS), Perkins.

WORK-STUDY *Federal work-study:* Total amount: $5,433,838; jobs available. *State or other work-study/employment:* Part-time jobs available.

APPLYING FOR FINANCIAL AID *Required financial aid forms:* FAFSA, institution's own form, federal income tax form(s). *Financial aid deadline (priority):* 2/15. *Notification date:* 3/15.

CONTACT Office of Enrollment Services, Carnegie Mellon University, 5000 Forbes Avenue, Pittsburgh, PA 15213-3890, 412-268-8186. *Fax:* 412-268-8084. *E-mail:* thehub@andrew.cmu.edu.
Website: http://www.cmu.edu/.

CAROLINA CHRISTIAN COLLEGE
Winston-Salem, NC

Tuition & fees: $7700	Average undergraduate aid package: $9500

ABOUT THE INSTITUTION Independent nondenominational, coed. *Awards:* associate, bachelor's, and master's degrees. 1 undergraduate major. *Total enrollment:* 78. Undergraduates: 70. Freshmen: 9. Federal methodology is used as a basis for awarding need-based institutional aid.

UNDERGRADUATE EXPENSES for 2013–2014 *Application fee:* $50. *Tuition:* full-time $7500; part-time $937.50 per course.

FRESHMAN FINANCIAL AID (Fall 2012, est.) 5 applied for aid; of those 100% were deemed to have need. 100% of freshmen with need received aid; of those 100% had need fully met. *Average percent of need met:* 100% (excluding resources awarded to replace EFC). *Average financial aid package:* $5500 (excluding resources awarded to replace EFC).

UNDERGRADUATE FINANCIAL AID (Fall 2012, est.) 74 applied for aid; of those 96% were deemed to have need. 97% of undergraduates with need received aid; of those 59% had need fully met. *Average percent of need met:* 95% (excluding resources awarded to replace EFC). *Average financial aid package:* $9500 (excluding resources awarded to replace EFC).

GIFT AID (NEED-BASED) *Total amount:* $9000 (56% federal, 44% institutional). *Receiving aid:* Freshmen: 100% (5); all full-time undergraduates: 55% (41). *Average award:* Freshmen: $750; Undergraduates: $1500. *Scholarships, grants, and awards:* Federal Pell, FSEOG.

GIFT AID (NON-NEED-BASED) *Average award:* Undergraduates: $3500. *Tuition waivers:* Full or partial for employees or children of employees.

LOANS *Student loans:* $280,000 (100% need-based). 90% of past graduating class borrowed through all loan programs. *Average indebtedness per student:* $6500. *Programs:* Federal Direct (Subsidized and Unsubsidized Stafford, PLUS).

APPLYING FOR FINANCIAL AID *Required financial aid form:* FAFSA. *Financial aid deadline:* Continuous. *Notification date:* Continuous.

CONTACT LaTanya V. Lucas, Academic Dean, Carolina Christian College, 4209 Indiana Avenue, Winston Salem, NC 27105, 336-744-0900 Ext. 106. *E-mail:* latanya@carolina.edu.
Website: http://www.carolina.edu/.

CAROLINA COLLEGE OF BIBLICAL STUDIES
Fayetteville, NC

CONTACT Financial Aid Office, Carolina College of Biblical Studies, 817 South McPherson Church Road, Fayetteville, NC 28303, 910-323-5614.
Website: http://carolinabiblecollege.org/.

CARROLL COLLEGE
Helena, MT

Tuition & fees: $26,554	Average undergraduate aid package: $18,415

ABOUT THE INSTITUTION Independent Roman Catholic, coed. *Awards:* associate and bachelor's degrees. 50 undergraduate majors. *Total enrollment:* 1,464. Undergraduates: 1,464. Freshmen: 383. Federal methodology is used as a basis for awarding need-based institutional aid.
UNDERGRADUATE EXPENSES for 2013–2014 *Application fee:* $35. *Comprehensive fee:* $34,616 includes full-time tuition ($26,004), mandatory fees ($550), and room and board ($8062). *College room only:* $4292. Full-time tuition and fees vary according to course load. Room and board charges vary according to board plan and housing facility. *Part-time tuition:* $1094 per credit hour. *Part-time fees:* $137.50 per term. Part-time tuition and fees vary according to course load.
FRESHMAN FINANCIAL AID (Fall 2011) 286 applied for aid; of those 80% were deemed to have need. 100% of freshmen with need received aid; of those 19% had need fully met. *Average percent of need met:* 75% (excluding resources awarded to replace EFC). *Average financial aid package:* $18,801 (excluding resources awarded to replace EFC). 33% of all full-time freshmen had no need and received non-need-based gift aid.
UNDERGRADUATE FINANCIAL AID (Fall 2011) 1,012 applied for aid; of those 87% were deemed to have need. 100% of undergraduates with need received aid; of those 13% had need fully met. *Average percent of need met:* 69% (excluding resources awarded to replace EFC). *Average financial aid package:* $18,415 (excluding resources awarded to replace EFC). 31% of all full-time undergraduates had no need and received non-need-based gift aid.
GIFT AID (NEED-BASED) *Total amount:* $11,314,943 (17% federal, 76% institutional, 7% external sources). *Receiving aid:* Freshmen: 67% (229); all full-time undergraduates: 65% (864). *Average award:* Freshmen: $14,979; Undergraduates: $13,760. *Scholarships, grants, and awards:* Federal Pell, FSEOG, state, private, college/university gift aid from institutional funds.
GIFT AID (NON-NEED-BASED) *Total amount:* $5,504,520 (13% federal, 75% institutional, 12% external sources). *Receiving aid:* Freshmen: 12% (42). Undergraduates: 8% (107). *Average award:* Freshmen: $12,208. Undergraduates: $10,304. *Scholarships, grants, and awards by category:* Academic interests/achievement: 1,189 awards ($10,776,375 total): general academic interests/achievements. Creative arts/performance: 81 awards ($107,974 total): art/fine arts, creative writing, debating, music, performing arts, theater/drama. Special achievements/activities: 69 awards ($92,712 total): cheerleading/drum major, general special achievements/activities, leadership, religious involvement. Special characteristics: 176 awards ($1,098,745 total): children of faculty/staff, children of union members/company employees, international students, religious affiliation, siblings of current students, spouses of current students, veterans. *Tuition waivers:* Full or partial for employees or children of employees, senior citizens. *ROTC:* Army.
LOANS *Student loans:* $6,647,236 (79% need-based, 21% non-need-based). 69% of past graduating class borrowed through all loan programs. *Average indebtedness per student:* $28,005. *Average need-based loan:* Freshmen: $3166. Undergraduates: $1470. *Parent loans:* $2,189,204 (45% need-based, 55% non-need-based). *Programs:* Federal Direct (Subsidized and Unsubsidized Stafford, PLUS), Perkins, private loans.

WORK-STUDY *Federal work-study:* Total amount: $350,683; 226 jobs averaging $2087. *State or other work-study/employment:* Part-time jobs available.
ATHLETIC AWARDS Total amount: $1,838,791 (47% need-based, 53% non-need-based).
APPLYING FOR FINANCIAL AID *Required financial aid form:* FAFSA. *Financial aid deadline (priority):* 3/1. *Notification date:* Continuous. Students must reply within 2 weeks of notification.
CONTACT Ms. Janet Riis, Director of Financial Aid, Carroll College, 1601 North Benton Avenue, Helena, MT 59625-0002, 406-447-5423 or toll-free 800-992-3648. *Fax:* 406-447-4533. *E-mail:* jriis@carroll.edu.
Website: http://www.carroll.edu/.

CARROLL UNIVERSITY
Waukesha, WI

Tuition & fees: N/R	Average undergraduate aid package: $19,779

ABOUT THE INSTITUTION Independent Presbyterian, coed. 77 undergraduate majors. Federal methodology is used as a basis for awarding need-based institutional aid.
FRESHMAN FINANCIAL AID (Fall 2012, est.) 703 applied for aid; of those 89% were deemed to have need. 100% of freshmen with need received aid; of those 22% had need fully met. *Average percent of need met:* 100% (excluding resources awarded to replace EFC). *Average financial aid package:* $19,700 (excluding resources awarded to replace EFC). 14% of all full-time freshmen had no need and received non-need-based gift aid.
UNDERGRADUATE FINANCIAL AID (Fall 2012, est.) 2,573 applied for aid; of those 88% were deemed to have need. 100% of undergraduates with need received aid; of those 26% had need fully met. *Average percent of need met:* 100% (excluding resources awarded to replace EFC). *Average financial aid package:* $19,779 (excluding resources awarded to replace EFC). 19% of all full-time undergraduates had no need and received non-need-based gift aid.
GIFT AID (NEED-BASED) *Total amount:* $37,146,948 (12% federal, 7% state, 79% institutional, 2% external sources). *Receiving aid:* Freshmen: 86% (626); all full-time undergraduates: 81% (2,277). *Average award:* Freshmen: $15,161; Undergraduates: $14,594. *Scholarships, grants, and awards:* Federal Pell, FSEOG, state, private, college/university gift aid from institutional funds.
GIFT AID (NON-NEED-BASED) *Total amount:* $9,861,111 (1% federal, 99% institutional). *Receiving aid:* Freshmen: 9% (65). Undergraduates: 10% (293). *Average award:* Freshmen: $10,982. Undergraduates: $11,074. *Scholarships, grants, and awards by category:* Academic interests/achievement: 2,346 awards ($23,930,745 total): biological sciences, business, computer science, education, general academic interests/achievements, health fields, humanities, international studies, mathematics, physical sciences, premedicine, social sciences. Creative arts/performance: 93 awards ($143,150 total): art/fine arts, journalism/publications, music, performing arts, theater/drama. Special achievements/activities: 993 awards ($520,051 total): general special achievements/activities, junior miss, leadership, memberships, religious involvement. Special characteristics: 1,268 awards ($1,603,458 total): adult students, children and siblings of alumni, children of current students, children of faculty/staff, general special characteristics, international students, siblings of current students, spouses of current students.
LOANS *Student loans:* $26,809,014 (40% need-based, 60% non-need-based). 89% of past graduating class borrowed through all loan programs. *Average indebtedness per student:* $35,986. *Average need-based loan:* Freshmen: $3155. Undergraduates: $4184. *Parent loans:* $4,249,394 (75% need-based, 25% non-need-based). *Programs:* Federal Direct (Subsidized and Unsubsidized Stafford, PLUS), Perkins, state, college/university.
WORK-STUDY *Federal work-study:* Total amount: $3,364,240; 1,097 jobs averaging $2242. *State or other work-study/employment:* Total amount: $2,374,084 (100% non-need-based). 940 part-time jobs averaging $2259.
APPLYING FOR FINANCIAL AID *Required financial aid form:* FAFSA. *Financial aid deadline:* Continuous. *Notification date:* Continuous beginning 2/15. Students must reply by 5/1 or within 2 weeks of notification.
CONTACT Dawn Scott, Director of Financial Aid, Carroll University, 100 North East Avenue, Waukesha, WI 53186-5593, 262-524-7297 or toll-free 800-CARROLL. *Fax:* 262-951-3037. *E-mail:* dscott@carrollu.edu.
Website: http://www.carrollu.edu/.

CARSON-NEWMAN UNIVERSITY
Jefferson City, TN

Tuition & fees: $22,652	Average undergraduate aid package: $13,257

ABOUT THE INSTITUTION Independent Southern Baptist, coed. **Awards:** associate, bachelor's, and master's degrees. 66 undergraduate majors. **Total enrollment:** 1,967. Undergraduates: 1,646. Freshmen: 453. Federal methodology is used as a basis for awarding need-based institutional aid.

UNDERGRADUATE EXPENSES for 2013–2014 Application fee: $25. **Comprehensive fee:** $29,058 includes full-time tuition ($21,660), mandatory fees ($992), and room and board ($6406). Full-time tuition and fees vary according to class time and course load. Room and board charges vary according to board plan, gender, and housing facility. **Part-time tuition:** $900 per credit hour.

FRESHMAN FINANCIAL AID (Fall 2012, est.) 453 applied for aid; of those 90% were deemed to have need. 100% of freshmen with need received aid; of those 26% had need fully met. **Average percent of need met:** 85% (excluding resources awarded to replace EFC). **Average financial aid package:** $23,283 (excluding resources awarded to replace EFC). 9% of all full-time freshmen had no need and received non-need-based gift aid.

UNDERGRADUATE FINANCIAL AID (Fall 2012, est.) 1,478 applied for aid; of those 88% were deemed to have need. 100% of undergraduates with need received aid; of those 25% had need fully met. **Average percent of need met:** 79% (excluding resources awarded to replace EFC). **Average financial aid package:** $13,257 (excluding resources awarded to replace EFC). 13% of all full-time undergraduates had no need and received non-need-based gift aid.

GIFT AID (NEED-BASED) Total amount: $19,531,276 (16% federal, 20% state, 61% institutional, 3% external sources). **Receiving aid:** Freshmen: 90% (407); all full-time undergraduates: 82% (1,291). **Average award:** Freshmen: $18,035; Undergraduates: $15,067. **Scholarships, grants, and awards:** Federal Pell, FSEOG, state, private, college/university gift aid from institutional funds.

GIFT AID (NON-NEED-BASED) Total amount: $2,240,403 (19% state, 76% institutional, 5% external sources). **Receiving aid:** Freshmen: 88% (398). Undergraduates: 80% (1,260). **Average award:** Freshmen: $12,048. Undergraduates: $10,490. **Scholarships, grants, and awards by category:** Academic interests/achievement: biological sciences, business, education, general academic interests/achievements, home economics, mathematics, military science, religion/biblical studies. Creative arts/performance: art/fine arts, debating, journalism/publications, music. **Special achievements/activities:** leadership, memberships. **Special characteristics:** children and siblings of alumni, members of minority groups, relatives of clergy, siblings of current students. **Tuition waivers:** Full or partial for employees or children of employees, senior citizens. **ROTC:** Army, Air Force cooperative.

LOANS Student loans: $10,809,117 (93% need-based, 7% non-need-based). 70% of past graduating class borrowed through all loan programs. **Average indebtedness per student:** $23,859. **Average need-based loan:** Freshmen: $3330. Undergraduates: $3852. **Parent loans:** $1,514,778 (93% need-based, 7% non-need-based). **Programs:** Perkins, state, college/university, alternative loans.

WORK-STUDY Federal work-study: Total amount: $499,075; 274 jobs averaging $1821. **State or other work-study/employment:** Total amount: $10,700 (67% need-based, 33% non-need-based). 8 part-time jobs averaging $1338.

ATHLETIC AWARDS Total amount: $2,125,491 (71% need-based, 29% non-need-based).

APPLYING FOR FINANCIAL AID Required financial aid forms: FAFSA, institution's own form. **Financial aid deadline (priority):** 4/1. **Notification date:** Continuous. Students must reply within 2 weeks of notification.

CONTACT Danette Seale, Director of Financial Aid, Carson-Newman University, 1646 Russell Avenue, Jefferson City, TN 37760, 865-471-3247 or toll-free 800-678-9061. Fax: 865-471-3502. E-mail: dseale@cn.edu. Website: http://www.cn.edu/.

CARTHAGE COLLEGE
Kenosha, WI

CONTACT Vatistas Vatistas, Director of Financial Aid, Carthage College, 2001 Alford Park Drive, Kenosha, WI 53140, 262-551-6001 or toll-free 800-351-4058. Fax: 262-551-5762. E-mail: vvatistas@carthage.edu. Website: http://www.carthage.edu/.

CASE WESTERN RESERVE UNIVERSITY
Cleveland, OH

Tuition & fees: $40,490	Average undergraduate aid package: $33,214

ABOUT THE INSTITUTION Independent, coed. **Awards:** certificates, bachelor's, master's, and doctoral degrees. 66 undergraduate majors. **Total enrollment:** 10,026. Undergraduates: 4,386. Freshmen: 1,372. Federal methodology is used as a basis for awarding need-based institutional aid.

UNDERGRADUATE EXPENSES for 2013–2014 One-time required fee: $465. **Comprehensive fee:** $52,926 includes full-time tuition ($40,120), mandatory fees ($370), and room and board ($12,436). **College room only:** $7140. Room and board charges vary according to board plan, housing facility, and student level. **Part-time tuition:** $1672 per credit hour. Part-time tuition and fees vary according to course load.

FRESHMAN FINANCIAL AID (Fall 2012, est.) 1,082 applied for aid; of those 79% were deemed to have need. 100% of freshmen with need received aid; of those 67% had need fully met. **Average percent of need met:** 88% (excluding resources awarded to replace EFC). **Average financial aid package:** $33,989 (excluding resources awarded to replace EFC). 25% of all full-time freshmen had no need and received non-need-based gift aid.

UNDERGRADUATE FINANCIAL AID (Fall 2012, est.) 3,090 applied for aid; of those 87% were deemed to have need. 100% of undergraduates with need received aid; of those 47% had need fully met. **Average percent of need met:** 82% (excluding resources awarded to replace EFC). **Average financial aid package:** $33,214 (excluding resources awarded to replace EFC). 22% of all full-time undergraduates had no need and received non-need-based gift aid.

GIFT AID (NEED-BASED) Total amount: $68,470,335 (7% federal, 2% state, 88% institutional, 3% external sources). **Receiving aid:** Freshmen: 62% (853); all full-time undergraduates: 64% (2,643). **Average award:** Freshmen: $29,174; Undergraduates: $27,174. **Scholarships, grants, and awards:** Federal Pell, FSEOG, state, private, college/university gift aid from institutional funds.

GIFT AID (NON-NEED-BASED) Total amount: $24,689,747 (94% institutional, 6% external sources). **Receiving aid:** Freshmen: 42% (574). Undergraduates: 28% (1,156). **Average award:** Freshmen: $23,372. Undergraduates: $21,117. **Scholarships, grants, and awards by category:** Academic interests/achievement: 2,587 awards ($49,731,936 total): biological sciences, business, communication, computer science, education, engineering/technologies, English, foreign languages, general academic interests/achievements, health fields, humanities, international studies, mathematics, physical sciences, premedicine, religion/biblical studies, social sciences. Creative arts/performance: 38 awards ($747,510 total): art/fine arts, creative writing, dance, general creative arts/performance, music, performing arts, theater/drama. Special achievements/activities: 72 awards ($154,750 total): leadership. Special characteristics: 199 awards ($5,637,167 total): children of faculty/staff. **Tuition waivers:** Full or partial for employees or children of employees. **ROTC:** Army, Air Force cooperative.

LOANS Student loans: $21,136,253 (77% need-based, 23% non-need-based). 52% of past graduating class borrowed through all loan programs. **Average indebtedness per student:** $37,610. **Average need-based loan:** Freshmen: $3868. Undergraduates: $4906. **Parent loans:** $11,609,929 (65% need-based, 35% non-need-based). **Programs:** Federal Direct (Subsidized and Unsubsidized Stafford, PLUS), Perkins, Federal Nursing, college/university, alternative loans.

WORK-STUDY Federal work-study: Total amount: $4,074,462; 1,711 jobs averaging $2297.

APPLYING FOR FINANCIAL AID Required financial aid forms: FAFSA, institution's own form, CSS Financial Aid PROFILE. **Financial aid deadline (pri-**

ority): 2/15. **Notification date:** Continuous beginning 3/15. Students must reply by 5/1 or within 2 weeks of notification.
CONTACT Mrs. Venus M. Puliafico, Director of University Financial Aid, Case Western Reserve University, 2049 Martin Luther King Jr. Drive, Cleveland, OH 44106-7049, 216-368-4530. *Fax:* 216-368-5054. *E-mail:* vxp4@case.edu. *Website:* http://www.case.edu/.

CASTLETON STATE COLLEGE
Castleton, VT

CONTACT Kathleen O'Meara, Director of Financial Aid, Castleton State College, Castleton, VT 05735, 802-468-1292 or toll-free 800-639-8521. *Fax:* 802-468-5237. *E-mail:* kathy.omeara@castleton.edu. *Website:* http://www.castleton.edu/.

CATAWBA COLLEGE
Salisbury, NC

Tuition & fees: $26,820	Average undergraduate aid package: $19,761

ABOUT THE INSTITUTION Independent United Church of Christ, coed. **Awards:** bachelor's and master's degrees. 37 undergraduate majors. **Total enrollment:** 1,293. Undergraduates: 1,279. Freshmen: 296. Federal methodology is used as a basis for awarding need-based institutional aid.
UNDERGRADUATE EXPENSES for 2013–2014 Application fee: $25. **Comprehensive fee:** $36,230 includes full-time tuition ($26,820) and room and board ($9410). Full-time tuition and fees vary according to class time and course load. **Part-time tuition:** $680 per credit hour. **Part-time fees:** $50 per term. Part-time tuition and fees vary according to class time and course load.
FRESHMAN FINANCIAL AID (Fall 2011) 286 applied for aid; of those 91% were deemed to have need. 100% of freshmen with need received aid; of those 14% had need fully met. **Average financial aid package:** $22,102 (excluding resources awarded to replace EFC). 13% of all full-time freshmen had no need and received non-need-based gift aid.
UNDERGRADUATE FINANCIAL AID (Fall 2011) 1,108 applied for aid; of those 92% were deemed to have need. 98% of undergraduates with need received aid; of those 15% had need fully met. **Average financial aid package:** $19,761 (excluding resources awarded to replace EFC). 12% of all full-time undergraduates had no need and received non-need-based gift aid.
GIFT AID (NEED-BASED) Total amount: $5,790,776 (42% federal, 24% state, 25% institutional, 9% external sources). **Receiving aid:** Freshmen: 71% (216); all full-time undergraduates: 67% (826). **Average award:** Freshmen: $7506; Undergraduates: $6324. **Scholarships, grants, and awards:** Federal Pell, FSEOG, state, private, college/university gift aid from institutional funds.
GIFT AID (NON-NEED-BASED) Total amount: $9,682,113 (16% state, 84% institutional). **Receiving aid:** Freshmen: 85% (260). Undergraduates: 81% (994). **Average award:** Freshmen: $8327. Undergraduates: $8472. **Scholarships, grants, and awards by category:** Academic interests/achievement: education, general academic interests/achievements. Creative arts/performance: music, theater/drama. Special achievements/activities: general special achievements/activities, leadership. Special characteristics: local/state students. **Tuition waivers:** Full or partial for employees or children of employees. **ROTC:** Army cooperative, Air Force cooperative.
LOANS Student loans: $6,799,889 (56% need-based, 44% non-need-based). 86% of past graduating class borrowed through all loan programs. *Average indebtedness per student:* $31,966. **Average need-based loan:** Freshmen: $3996. Undergraduates: $4477. **Parent loans:** $2,093,792 (100% non-need-based). **Programs:** Federal Direct (Subsidized and Unsubsidized Stafford, PLUS), Perkins, state, college/university, alternative loans, TERI Loans, Nellie Mae Loans, Advantage Loans.
WORK-STUDY Federal work-study: Total amount: $201,253; jobs available. **State or other work-study/employment:** Total amount: $470,185 (100% need-based). Part-time jobs available.
ATHLETIC AWARDS Total amount: $2,776,849 (100% non-need-based).

APPLYING FOR FINANCIAL AID Required financial aid form: FAFSA. **Financial aid deadline (priority):** 3/15. **Notification date:** Continuous beginning 2/15. Students must reply within 2 weeks of notification.
CONTACT Dawn Snook, Director of Financial Aid, Catawba College, 2300 West Innes Street, Salisbury, NC 28144-2488, 704-637-4416 or toll-free 800-CATAWBA. *Fax:* 704-637-4252. *E-mail:* dasnook@catawba.edu. *Website:* http://www.catawba.edu/.

THE CATHOLIC UNIVERSITY OF AMERICA
Washington, DC

Tuition & fees: $36,820	Average undergraduate aid package: $22,879

ABOUT THE INSTITUTION Independent Roman Catholic Church, coed. **Awards:** certificates, associate, bachelor's, master's, and doctoral degrees. 60 undergraduate majors. **Total enrollment:** 6,838. Undergraduates: 3,694. Freshmen: 884. Federal methodology is used as a basis for awarding need-based institutional aid.
UNDERGRADUATE EXPENSES for 2013–2014 Application fee: $55. **One-time required fee:** $425. **Comprehensive fee:** $51,094 includes full-time tuition ($36,320), mandatory fees ($500), and room and board ($14,274). **College room only:** $8876. Full-time tuition and fees vary according to program. Room and board charges vary according to board plan and housing facility. **Part-time tuition:** $1420 per credit hour. **Part-time fees:** $290 per year. Part-time tuition and fees vary according to course load and program.
FRESHMAN FINANCIAL AID (Fall 2012, est.) 699 applied for aid; of those 82% were deemed to have need. 100% of freshmen with need received aid; of those 44% had need fully met. **Average percent of need met:** 81% (excluding resources awarded to replace EFC). **Average financial aid package:** $25,293 (excluding resources awarded to replace EFC). 28% of all full-time freshmen had no need and received non-need-based gift aid.
UNDERGRADUATE FINANCIAL AID (Fall 2012, est.) 2,373 applied for aid; of those 87% were deemed to have need. 100% of undergraduates with need received aid; of those 42% had need fully met. **Average percent of need met:** 77% (excluding resources awarded to replace EFC). **Average financial aid package:** $22,879 (excluding resources awarded to replace EFC). 28% of all full-time undergraduates had no need and received non-need-based gift aid.
GIFT AID (NEED-BASED) Total amount: $38,670,944 (6% federal, 93% institutional, 1% external sources). **Receiving aid:** Freshmen: 65% (569); all full-time undergraduates: 59% (2,018). **Average award:** Freshmen: $21,661; Undergraduates: $19,076. **Scholarships, grants, and awards:** Federal Pell, FSEOG, state, private, college/university gift aid from institutional funds.
GIFT AID (NON-NEED-BASED) Total amount: $13,237,595 (99% institutional, 1% external sources). **Average award:** Freshmen: $14,057. Undergraduates: $13,666. **Scholarships, grants, and awards by category:** Academic interests/achievement: general academic interests/achievements. Creative arts/performance: music, theater/drama. Special characteristics: children and siblings of alumni, children of faculty/staff, religious affiliation, siblings of current students, twins, veterans, veterans' children. **Tuition waivers:** Full or partial for employees or children of employees. **ROTC:** Army cooperative, Naval cooperative, Air Force cooperative.
LOANS Student loans: $20,629,097 (90% need-based, 10% non-need-based). **Average need-based loan:** Freshmen: $3887. Undergraduates: $4680. **Parent loans:** $11,771,310 (90% need-based, 10% non-need-based). **Programs:** Federal Direct (Subsidized and Unsubsidized Stafford, PLUS), Perkins, Federal Nursing, commercial loans.
WORK-STUDY Federal work-study: Total amount: $546,800; 289 jobs averaging $1892.
APPLYING FOR FINANCIAL AID Required financial aid form: FAFSA. **Financial aid deadline:** 4/10 (priority: 2/15). **Notification date:** Continuous beginning 4/1. Students must reply by 5/1 or within 2 weeks of notification.
CONTACT Mr. Joseph Dobrota, Director of Financial Aid, The Catholic University of America, 620 Michigan Avenue, NE, Washington, DC 20064, 202-319-5307 or toll-free 800-673-2772. *Fax:* 202-319-5573. *E-mail:* dobrota@cua.edu. *Website:* http://www.cua.edu/.

CAZENOVIA COLLEGE
Cazenovia, NY

Tuition & fees: $28,022	Average undergraduate aid package: $26,117

ABOUT THE INSTITUTION Independent, coed. 21 undergraduate majors. Federal methodology is used as a basis for awarding need-based institutional aid.

UNDERGRADUATE EXPENSES for 2013–2014 *Comprehensive fee:* $39,420 includes full-time tuition ($27,550), mandatory fees ($472), and room and board ($11,398). Full-time tuition and fees vary according to class time, course load, and program. Room and board charges vary according to board plan and housing facility. *Part-time tuition:* $585 per credit hour. Part-time tuition and fees vary according to class time and course load.

FRESHMAN FINANCIAL AID (Fall 2012, est.) 261 applied for aid; of those 95% were deemed to have need. 100% of freshmen with need received aid; of those 8% had need fully met. *Average percent of need met:* 79% (excluding resources awarded to replace EFC). *Average financial aid package:* $27,421 (excluding resources awarded to replace EFC). 6% of all full-time freshmen had no need and received non-need-based gift aid.

UNDERGRADUATE FINANCIAL AID (Fall 2012, est.) 845 applied for aid; of those 94% were deemed to have need. 100% of undergraduates with need received aid; of those 10% had need fully met. *Average percent of need met:* 78% (excluding resources awarded to replace EFC). *Average financial aid package:* $26,117 (excluding resources awarded to replace EFC). 8% of all full-time undergraduates had no need and received non-need-based gift aid.

GIFT AID (NEED-BASED) *Total amount:* $17,100,080 (13% federal, 9% state, 77% institutional, 1% external sources). *Receiving aid:* Freshmen: 93% (249); all full-time undergraduates: 89% (791). *Average award:* Freshmen: $12,147; Undergraduates: $13,623. *Scholarships, grants, and awards:* Federal Pell, FSEOG, state, private, college/university gift aid from institutional funds.

GIFT AID (NON-NEED-BASED) *Total amount:* $1,622,492 (2% state, 95% institutional, 3% external sources). *Receiving aid:* Freshmen: 16% (43). Undergraduates: 8% (75). *Average award:* Freshmen: $17,965. Undergraduates: $13,997. *Scholarships, grants, and awards by category: Academic interests/achievement:* general academic interests/achievements. *Tuition waivers:* Full or partial for employees or children of employees.

LOANS *Student loans:* $7,585,676 (76% need-based, 24% non-need-based). 82% of past graduating class borrowed through all loan programs. *Average need-based loan:* Freshmen: $3452. Undergraduates: $4311. *Parent loans:* $2,639,002 (50% need-based, 50% non-need-based). *Programs:* Federal Direct (Subsidized and Unsubsidized Stafford, PLUS).

WORK-STUDY *Federal work-study:* Total amount: $331,250; jobs available.

APPLYING FOR FINANCIAL AID *Required financial aid forms:* FAFSA, state aid form. *Financial aid deadline (priority):* 3/1. *Notification date:* Continuous. Students must reply by 5/1 or within 2 weeks of notification.

CONTACT Christine L. Mandel, Director of Financial Aid, Cazenovia College, 3 Sullivan Street, Cazenovia, NY 13035, 315-655-7887 or toll-free 800-654-3210. *Fax:* 315-655-7219. *E-mail:* finaid@cazenovia.edu. *Website:* http://www.cazenovia.edu/.

CEDAR CREST COLLEGE
Allentown, PA

Tuition & fees: $31,196	Average undergraduate aid package: $24,153

ABOUT THE INSTITUTION Independent United Church of Christ, coed, primarily women. *Awards:* certificates, bachelor's, and master's degrees. 41 undergraduate majors. *Total enrollment:* 1,567. Undergraduates: 1,359. Freshmen: 145. Federal methodology is used as a basis for awarding need-based institutional aid.

UNDERGRADUATE EXPENSES for 2013–2014 *Comprehensive fee:* $41,186 includes full-time tuition ($31,196) and room and board ($9990). *College room only:* $5160. Full-time tuition and fees vary according to class time, course load, and program. Room and board charges vary according to board plan and housing facility. Part-time tuition and fees vary according to class time, course load, and program.

FRESHMAN FINANCIAL AID (Fall 2012, est.) 141 applied for aid; of those 95% were deemed to have need. 100% of freshmen with need received aid; of those 10% had need fully met. *Average percent of need met:* 79% (excluding resources awarded to replace EFC). *Average financial aid package:* $26,840 (excluding resources awarded to replace EFC). 8% of all full-time freshmen had no need and received non-need-based gift aid.

UNDERGRADUATE FINANCIAL AID (Fall 2012, est.) 531 applied for aid; of those 96% were deemed to have need. 100% of undergraduates with need received aid; of those 9% had need fully met. *Average percent of need met:* 74% (excluding resources awarded to replace EFC). *Average financial aid package:* $24,153 (excluding resources awarded to replace EFC). 6% of all full-time undergraduates had no need and received non-need-based gift aid.

GIFT AID (NEED-BASED) *Total amount:* $10,211,666 (13% federal, 10% state, 72% institutional, 5% external sources). *Receiving aid:* Freshmen: 92% (134); all full-time undergraduates: 93% (508). *Average award:* Freshmen: $23,477; Undergraduates: $19,819. *Scholarships, grants, and awards:* Federal Pell, FSEOG, state, private, college/university gift aid from institutional funds, Federal Nursing.

GIFT AID (NON-NEED-BASED) *Total amount:* $583,648 (1% state, 89% institutional, 10% external sources). *Receiving aid:* Freshmen: 8% (12). Undergraduates: 1% (3). *Average award:* Freshmen: $13,545. Undergraduates: $10,893. *Scholarships, grants, and awards by category: Academic interests/achievement:* business, communication, English, general academic interests/achievements. *Creative arts/performance:* art/fine arts, dance, performing arts, theater/drama. *Special achievements/activities:* community service, general special achievements/activities, junior miss, leadership, memberships, religious involvement. *Special characteristics:* adult students, children and siblings of alumni, general special characteristics, previous college experience, relatives of clergy, siblings of current students. *Tuition waivers:* Full or partial for children of alumni, employees or children of employees. *ROTC:* Army cooperative.

LOANS *Student loans:* $5,374,058 (81% need-based, 19% non-need-based). 92% of past graduating class borrowed through all loan programs. *Average indebtedness per student:* $31,933. *Average need-based loan:* Freshmen: $3497. Undergraduates: $4476. *Parent loans:* $1,542,977 (43% need-based, 57% non-need-based). *Programs:* Federal Direct (Subsidized and Unsubsidized Stafford, PLUS), Perkins, Federal Nursing.

WORK-STUDY *Federal work-study:* Total amount: $121,434; jobs available. *State or other work-study/employment:* Total amount: $94,800 (76% need-based, 24% non-need-based). Part-time jobs available.

APPLYING FOR FINANCIAL AID *Required financial aid form:* FAFSA. *Financial aid deadline (priority):* 5/1. *Notification date:* Continuous beginning 9/15.

CONTACT Ms. Valerie D. Kreiser, Director of Student Financial Services, Cedar Crest College, 212 Blaney Hall, 100 College Drive, Allentown, PA 18104-6196, 610-606-4666 Ext. 3314 or toll-free 800-360-1222. *Fax:* 610-606-4653. *E-mail:* financialservices@cedarcrest.edu. *Website:* http://www.cedarcrest.edu/.

CEDARVILLE UNIVERSITY
Cedarville, OH

Tuition & fees: $25,496	Average undergraduate aid package: $23,356

ABOUT THE INSTITUTION Independent Baptist, coed. *Awards:* certificates, bachelor's, master's, and doctoral degrees. 76 undergraduate majors. *Total enrollment:* 3,380. Undergraduates: 3,220. Freshmen: 832. Federal methodology is used as a basis for awarding need-based institutional aid.

UNDERGRADUATE EXPENSES for 2013–2014 *Application fee:* $30. *Comprehensive fee:* $31,036 includes full-time tuition ($25,496) and room and board ($5540). *College room only:* $3140. Room and board charges vary according to board plan. *Part-time tuition:* $965 per credit. Part-time tuition and fees vary according to course load.

FRESHMAN FINANCIAL AID (Fall 2011) 814 applied for aid; of those 82% were deemed to have need. 100% of freshmen with need received aid; of those 18% had need fully met. *Average percent of need met:* 31% (excluding resources awarded to replace EFC). *Average financial aid package:* $23,280 (excluding resources awarded to replace EFC). 19% of all full-time freshmen had no need and received non-need-based gift aid.

UNDERGRADUATE FINANCIAL AID (Fall 2011) 2,353 applied for aid; of those 85% were deemed to have need. 100% of undergraduates with need received aid; of those 16% had need fully met. *Average percent of need met:* 36% (excluding resources awarded to replace EFC). *Average financial aid package:* $23,356 (excluding resources awarded to replace EFC). 17% of all full-time undergraduates had no need and received non-need-based gift aid.

GIFT AID (NEED-BASED) *Total amount:* $8,717,869 (32% federal, 4% state, 63% institutional, 1% external sources). *Receiving aid:* Freshmen: 61% (570); all full-time undergraduates: 57% (1,674). *Average award:* Freshmen: $3689; Undergraduates: $4078. *Scholarships, grants, and awards:* Federal Pell, FSEOG, state, private, college/university gift aid from institutional funds, Federal Nursing.

GIFT AID (NON-NEED-BASED) *Total amount:* $21,027,733 (1% federal, 77% institutional, 22% external sources). *Receiving aid:* Freshmen: 60% (552). Undergraduates: 55% (1,627). *Average award:* Freshmen: $18,636. Undergraduates: $18,113. *Scholarships, grants, and awards by category:* Academic interests/achievement: 643 awards ($2,740,210 total): general academic interests/achievements. Creative arts/performance: 43 awards ($113,525 total): debating, music. Special achievements/activities: 34 awards ($592,850 total): leadership. Special characteristics: 203 awards ($2,908,809 total): children and siblings of alumni, children of faculty/staff, ethnic background, general special characteristics, religious affiliation, veterans. *Tuition waivers:* Full or partial for employees or children of employees, senior citizens. *ROTC:* Army cooperative, Air Force cooperative.

LOANS *Student loans:* $10,864,341 (68% need-based, 32% non-need-based). 69% of past graduating class borrowed through all loan programs. *Average indebtedness per student:* $28,251. *Average need-based loan:* Freshmen: $4716. Undergraduates: $5869. *Parent loans:* $15,208,215 (100% non-need-based). *Programs:* Federal Direct (Subsidized and Unsubsidized Stafford, PLUS), Perkins, Federal Nursing, college/university.

WORK-STUDY *Federal work-study:* Total amount: $384,209; 479 jobs averaging $802. *State or other work-study/employment:* Total amount: $1,737,674 (100% non-need-based). 1,608 part-time jobs averaging $1046.

ATHLETIC AWARDS Total amount: $1,088,409 (100% non-need-based).

APPLYING FOR FINANCIAL AID *Required financial aid form:* FAFSA. *Financial aid deadline (priority):* 3/1. *Notification date:* Continuous beginning 3/1. Students must reply within 4 weeks of notification.

CONTACT Mr. Russell Kim Jenerette, Executive Director of Financial Aid, Cedarville University, 251 North Main Street, Cedarville, OH 45314-0601, 937-766-7866 Ext. 3640 or toll-free 800-CEDARVILLE. *E-mail:* kimjenerette@cedarville.edu. *Website:* http://www.cedarville.edu/.

CENTENARY COLLEGE
Hackettstown, NJ

ABOUT THE INSTITUTION Independent United Methodist Church, coed. *Awards:* certificates, associate, bachelor's, and master's degrees. 27 undergraduate majors. *Total enrollment:* 2,644. Undergraduates: 1,915. Freshmen: 306.

GIFT AID (NEED-BASED) *Scholarships, grants, and awards:* Federal Pell, FSEOG, state, private, college/university gift aid from institutional funds.

GIFT AID (NON-NEED-BASED) *Scholarships, grants, and awards by category:* Academic interests/achievement: general academic interests/achievements. Special achievements/activities: leadership. Special characteristics: children and siblings of alumni, children of faculty/staff, ethnic background, general special characteristics, local/state students, out-of-state students, previous college experience, religious affiliation, siblings of current students.

LOANS *Programs:* Federal Direct (Subsidized and Unsubsidized Stafford, PLUS), Perkins, state, NJ Class loans.

APPLYING FOR FINANCIAL AID *Required financial aid form:* FAFSA.

CONTACT Michelle Burwell, Associate Director of Financial Aid, Centenary College, 400 Jefferson Street, Hackettstown, NJ 07840-2100, 908-852-1400 Ext. 2240 or toll-free 800-236-8679. *Fax:* 908-813-2632. *E-mail:* burwellm@centenarycollege.edu. *Website:* http://www.centenarycollege.edu/.

CENTENARY COLLEGE OF LOUISIANA
Shreveport, LA

Tuition & fees: $29,500	Average undergraduate aid package: $29,507

ABOUT THE INSTITUTION Independent United Methodist, coed. *Awards:* bachelor's and master's degrees. 29 undergraduate majors. *Total enrollment:* 776. Undergraduates: 698. Freshmen: 158. Federal methodology is used as a basis for awarding need-based institutional aid.

UNDERGRADUATE EXPENSES for 2013–2014 *Application fee:* $30. *Comprehensive fee:* $38,836 includes full-time tuition ($29,500) and room and board ($9336). *College room only:* $4816. Full-time tuition and fees vary according to degree level. Room and board charges vary according to board plan and housing facility. *Part-time tuition:* $880 per credit hour. Part-time tuition and fees vary according to course load, degree level, and program.

FRESHMAN FINANCIAL AID (Fall 2012, est.) 151 applied for aid; of those 79% were deemed to have need. 100% of freshmen with need received aid; of those 29% had need fully met. *Average percent of need met:* 77% (excluding resources awarded to replace EFC). *Average financial aid package:* $24,104 (excluding resources awarded to replace EFC). 25% of all full-time freshmen had no need and received non-need-based gift aid.

UNDERGRADUATE FINANCIAL AID (Fall 2012, est.) 481 applied for aid; of those 80% were deemed to have need. 100% of undergraduates with need received aid; of those 20% had need fully met. *Average percent of need met:* 74% (excluding resources awarded to replace EFC). *Average financial aid package:* $29,507 (excluding resources awarded to replace EFC). 23% of all full-time undergraduates had no need and received non-need-based gift aid.

GIFT AID (NEED-BASED) *Total amount:* $9,641,265 (12% federal, 11% state, 76% institutional, 1% external sources). *Receiving aid:* Freshmen: 75% (119); all full-time undergraduates: 57% (386). *Average award:* Freshmen: $20,939; Undergraduates: $25,230. *Scholarships, grants, and awards:* Federal Pell, FSEOG, state, private, college/university gift aid from institutional funds.

GIFT AID (NON-NEED-BASED) *Total amount:* $3,089,394 (10% state, 89% institutional, 1% external sources). *Receiving aid:* Freshmen: 20% (32). Undergraduates: 11% (76). *Average award:* Freshmen: $13,437. Undergraduates: $13,568. *Scholarships, grants, and awards by category:* Academic interests/achievement: 706 awards ($6,945,727 total): biological sciences, business, communication, education, engineering/technologies, English, foreign languages, general academic interests/achievements, health fields, humanities, mathematics, physical sciences, premedicine, religion/biblical studies, social sciences. Creative arts/performance: 136 awards ($321,701 total): art/fine arts, dance, general creative arts/performance, music, performing arts, theater/drama. Special achievements/activities: 62 awards ($81,067 total): community service, general special achievements/activities, hobbies/interests, religious involvement. Special characteristics: 148 awards ($669,389 total): children and siblings of alumni, children of educators, children of faculty/staff, ethnic background, first-generation college students, general special characteristics, international students, local/state students, members of minority groups, out-of-state students, relatives of clergy, religious affiliation, siblings of current students. *Tuition waivers:* Full or partial for employees or children of employees.

LOANS *Student loans:* $2,854,962 (50% need-based, 50% non-need-based). 50% of past graduating class borrowed through all loan programs. *Average indebtedness per student:* $21,820. *Average need-based loan:* Freshmen: $3418. Undergraduates: $5423. *Parent loans:* $1,264,913 (89% need-based, 11% non-need-based). *Programs:* Federal Direct (Subsidized and Unsubsidized Stafford, PLUS), Perkins.

WORK-STUDY *Federal work-study:* Total amount: $328,600; 170 jobs averaging $1933. *State or other work-study/employment:* Total amount: $40,150 (100% non-need-based). 33 part-time jobs averaging $1217.

APPLYING FOR FINANCIAL AID *Required financial aid form:* FAFSA. *Financial aid deadline (priority):* 2/15. *Notification date:* Continuous beginning 3/15. Students must reply by 5/1.

CONTACT Mrs. Lynette Viskozki, Director of Financial Aid, Centenary College of Louisiana, PO Box 41188, Shreveport, LA 71134-1188, 318-869-5137 or toll-free 800-234-4448. *Fax:* 318-841-7266. *E-mail:* lviskozk@centenary.edu. *Website:* http://www.centenary.edu/.

CENTRAL BAPTIST COLLEGE
Conway, AR

CONTACT Christi Bell, Financial Aid Director, Central Baptist College, 1501 College Avenue, Conway, AR 72032-6470, 800-205-6872 Ext. 185 or toll-free 800-205-6872. *Fax:* 501-329-2941. *E-mail:* financialaid@cbc.edu. *Website:* http://www.cbc.edu/.

CENTRAL BIBLE COLLEGE
Springfield, MO

CONTACT Rick Woolverton, Director of Financial Aid, Central Bible College, 3000 North Grant, Springfield, MO 65803-1096, 417-833-2551 or toll-free 800-831-4222. *Fax:* 417-833-2168. *Website:* http://www.cbcag.edu/.

CENTRAL CHRISTIAN COLLEGE OF KANSAS
McPherson, KS

CONTACT Mike Reimer, Financial Aid Director, Central Christian College of Kansas, 1200 South Main, PO Box 1403, McPherson, KS 67460, 620-241-0723 Ext. 333 or toll-free 800-835-0078. *Fax:* 620-241-6032. *E-mail:* miker@centralchristian.edu. *Website:* http://www.centralchristian.edu/.

CENTRAL CHRISTIAN COLLEGE OF THE BIBLE
Moberly, MO

Tuition & fees: N/R | Average undergraduate aid package: N/A

ABOUT THE INSTITUTION Independent Christian Churches and Churches of Christ, coed. 2 undergraduate majors. Institutional methodology is used as a basis for awarding need-based institutional aid.
FRESHMAN FINANCIAL AID (Fall 2012, est.) 53 applied for aid.
UNDERGRADUATE FINANCIAL AID (Fall 2012, est.) 309 applied for aid.
GIFT AID (NEED-BASED) *Total amount:* $893,766 (100% federal). *Scholarships, grants, and awards:* Federal Pell, FSEOG, private, college/university gift aid from institutional funds.
GIFT AID (NON-NEED-BASED) *Total amount:* $2,819,521 (95% institutional, 5% external sources). *Scholarships, grants, and awards by category:* Academic interests/achievement: religion/biblical studies.
LOANS *Student loans:* $1,075,644 (100% need-based). *Parent loans:* $19,250 (100% non-need-based). *Programs:* Federal Direct (Subsidized and Unsubsidized Stafford, PLUS), alternative loans.
WORK-STUDY *Federal work-study:* Total amount: $14,191; jobs available.
APPLYING FOR FINANCIAL AID *Required financial aid form:* FAFSA. *Financial aid deadline:* Continuous. *Notification date:* Continuous beginning 4/1. Students must reply by 6/15 or within 4 weeks of notification.
CONTACT Rhonda J. Dunham, Financial Aid Director, Central Christian College of the Bible, 911 East Urbandale Drive, Moberly, MO 65270-1997, 660-263-3900 Ext. 121 or toll-free 888-263-3900. *Fax:* 660-263-3936. *E-mail:* rdunham@cccb.edu. *Website:* http://www.cccb.edu/.

CENTRAL COLLEGE
Pella, IA

Tuition & fees: $30,700 | Average undergraduate aid package: $24,093

ABOUT THE INSTITUTION Independent Reformed Church in America, coed. *Awards:* bachelor's degrees. 37 undergraduate majors. *Total enrollment:* 1,486. Undergraduates: 1,486. Freshmen: 320. Federal methodology is used as a basis for awarding need-based institutional aid.
UNDERGRADUATE EXPENSES for 2013-2014 *Application fee:* $25. *Comprehensive fee:* $40,680 includes full-time tuition ($30,700) and room and board ($9980). *College room only:* $4892. Room and board charges vary according to board plan. *Part-time tuition:* $1279 per credit. Part-time tuition and fees vary according to course load.
FRESHMAN FINANCIAL AID (Fall 2012, est.) 308 applied for aid; of those 93% were deemed to have need. 100% of freshmen with need received aid; of those 19% had need fully met. *Average percent of need met:* 81% (excluding resources awarded to replace EFC). *Average financial aid package:* $26,013 (excluding resources awarded to replace EFC). 11% of all full-time freshmen had no need and received non-need-based gift aid.
UNDERGRADUATE FINANCIAL AID (Fall 2012, est.) 1,274 applied for aid; of those 93% were deemed to have need. 100% of undergraduates with need received aid; of those 18% had need fully met. *Average percent of need met:* 77% (excluding resources awarded to replace EFC). *Average financial aid package:* $24,093 (excluding resources awarded to replace EFC). 16% of all full-time undergraduates had no need and received non-need-based gift aid.
GIFT AID (NEED-BASED) *Total amount:* $21,626,704 (8% federal, 11% state, 79% institutional, 2% external sources). *Receiving aid:* Freshmen: 89% (285); all full-time undergraduates: 84% (1,183). *Average award:* Freshmen: $22,609; Undergraduates: $18,374. *Scholarships, grants, and awards:* Federal Pell, FSEOG, state, private, college/university gift aid from institutional funds.
GIFT AID (NON-NEED-BASED) *Total amount:* $4,368,717 (14% federal, 83% institutional, 3% external sources). *Receiving aid:* Freshmen: 22% (70). Undergraduates: 9% (120). *Average award:* Freshmen: $15,409. Undergraduates: $14,260. *Scholarships, grants, and awards by category: Academic interests/achievement:* biological sciences, business, communication, computer science, education, foreign languages, general academic interests/achievements, health fields, humanities, international studies, mathematics, physical sciences, premedicine, religion/biblical studies, social sciences. *Creative arts/performance:* art/fine arts, creative writing, music, theater/drama. *Special achievements/activities:* community service, religious involvement. *Special characteristics:* children and siblings of alumni, children of current students, children of faculty/staff, general special characteristics, handicapped students, international students, local/state students, members of minority groups, out-of-state students, previous college experience, religious affiliation, siblings of current students, twins, veterans, veterans' children. *Tuition waivers:* Full or partial for employees or children of employees.
LOANS *Student loans:* $11,192,202 (67% need-based, 33% non-need-based). 85% of past graduating class borrowed through all loan programs. *Average indebtedness per student:* $27,790. *Average need-based loan:* Freshmen: $2704. Undergraduates: $4413. *Parent loans:* $3,140,086 (38% need-based, 62% non-need-based). *Programs:* Federal Direct (Subsidized and Unsubsidized Stafford, PLUS), Perkins, college/university, alternative loans.
WORK-STUDY *Federal work-study:* Total amount: $909,075; jobs available. *State or other work-study/employment:* Total amount: $773,946 (40% need-based, 60% non-need-based). Part-time jobs available.
APPLYING FOR FINANCIAL AID *Required financial aid form:* FAFSA. *Financial aid deadline (priority):* 3/15. *Notification date:* Continuous beginning 3/15. Students must reply by 5/1 or within 2 weeks of notification.
CONTACT Wayne Dille, Director of Financial Aid, Central College, 812 University Street, Campus Box 5800, Pella, IA 50219-1999, 641-628-5336 or toll-free 877-462-3687. *Fax:* 641-628-7199. *E-mail:* dillew@central.edu. *Website:* http://www.central.edu/.

CENTRAL CONNECTICUT STATE UNIVERSITY
New Britain, CT

Tuition & fees (CT res): $8321	Average undergraduate aid package: $7866

ABOUT THE INSTITUTION State-supported, coed. **Awards:** certificates, bachelor's, master's, and doctoral degrees. 52 undergraduate majors. **Total enrollment:** 12,521. Undergraduates: 10,092. Freshmen: 1,387. Federal methodology is used as a basis for awarding need-based institutional aid.

UNDERGRADUATE EXPENSES for 2013–2014 Application fee: $50. **Tuition, state resident:** full-time $4285; part-time $179 per credit. **Tuition, non-resident:** full-time $13,866; part-time $182 per credit. **Required fees:** full-time $4036; $218 per credit or $223 per credit. Full-time tuition and fees vary according to course level, course load, program, and reciprocity agreements. Part-time tuition and fees vary according to course level, course load, and program. **College room and board:** $10,056; **Room only:** $5850. Room and board charges vary according to board plan.

FRESHMAN FINANCIAL AID (Fall 2012, est.) 1,174 applied for aid; of those 76% were deemed to have need. 98% of freshmen with need received aid; of those 2% had need fully met. **Average percent of need met:** 71% (excluding resources awarded to replace EFC). **Average financial aid package:** $8052 (excluding resources awarded to replace EFC). 3% of all full-time freshmen had no need and received non-need-based gift aid.

UNDERGRADUATE FINANCIAL AID (Fall 2012, est.) 7,259 applied for aid; of those 79% were deemed to have need. 92% of undergraduates with need received aid; of those 3% had need fully met. **Average percent of need met:** 61% (excluding resources awarded to replace EFC). **Average financial aid package:** $7866 (excluding resources awarded to replace EFC). 1% of all full-time undergraduates had no need and received non-need-based gift aid.

GIFT AID (NEED-BASED) Total amount: $23,382,624 (62% federal, 15% state, 23% institutional). **Receiving aid:** Freshmen: 56% (756); all full-time undergraduates: 54% (4,220). **Average award:** Freshmen: $4574; Undergraduates: $3740. **Scholarships, grants, and awards:** Federal Pell, FSEOG, state, college/university gift aid from institutional funds.

GIFT AID (NON-NEED-BASED) Total amount: $2,999,268 (70% institutional, 30% external sources). **Receiving aid:** Freshmen: 12% (166). Undergraduates: 12% (934). **Average award:** Freshmen: $3144. Undergraduates: $3425. **Scholarships, grants, and awards by category:** Academic interests/achievement: general academic interests/achievements. **Special characteristics:** members of minority groups. **Tuition waivers:** Full or partial for employees or children of employees, senior citizens. **ROTC:** Army cooperative, Air Force cooperative.

LOANS Student loans: $56,947,090 (39% need-based, 61% non-need-based). 54% of past graduating class borrowed through all loan programs. **Average indebtedness per student:** $22,171. **Average need-based loan:** Freshmen: $3634. Undergraduates: $4303. **Programs:** Federal Direct (Subsidized and Unsubsidized Stafford, PLUS), Perkins.

WORK-STUDY Federal work-study: Total amount: $365,100; jobs available. **State or other work-study/employment:** Total amount: $2,317,897 (100% non-need-based). Part-time jobs available.

ATHLETIC AWARDS Total amount: $3,426,160 (100% non-need-based).

APPLYING FOR FINANCIAL AID Required financial aid form: FAFSA. **Financial aid deadline:** 9/15 (priority: 3/1). **Notification date:** Continuous beginning 3/30. Students must reply within 2 weeks of notification.

CONTACT Mr. Dennis Williams, Associate Director of Financial Aid, Central Connecticut State University, Davidson Hall, Room 221, New Britain, CT 06050-4010, 860-832-2200. Fax: 860-832-3330. E-mail: finaid@ccsu.edu. Website: http://www.ccsu.edu/.

CENTRAL METHODIST UNIVERSITY
Fayette, MO

Tuition & fees: $20,590	Average undergraduate aid package: $17,098

ABOUT THE INSTITUTION Independent Methodist, coed. **Awards:** associate and bachelor's degrees. 47 undergraduate majors. **Total enrollment:** 1,173. Undergraduates: 1,173. Freshmen: 302. Federal methodology is used as a basis for awarding need-based institutional aid.

UNDERGRADUATE EXPENSES for 2013–2014 Application fee: $20. **Tuition:** full-time $20,590; part-time $190 per credit hour. Full-time tuition and fees vary according to location. Part-time tuition and fees vary according to course load and location. Room and board charges vary according to board plan and housing facility.

FRESHMAN FINANCIAL AID (Fall 2011) 273 applied for aid; of those 93% were deemed to have need. 100% of freshmen with need received aid; of those 18% had need fully met. **Average percent of need met:** 27% (excluding resources awarded to replace EFC). **Average financial aid package:** $17,813 (excluding resources awarded to replace EFC). 15% of all full-time freshmen had no need and received non-need-based gift aid.

UNDERGRADUATE FINANCIAL AID (Fall 2011) 999 applied for aid; of those 94% were deemed to have need. 100% of undergraduates with need received aid; of those 17% had need fully met. **Average percent of need met:** 29% (excluding resources awarded to replace EFC). **Average financial aid package:** $17,098 (excluding resources awarded to replace EFC). 17% of all full-time undergraduates had no need and received non-need-based gift aid.

GIFT AID (NEED-BASED) Total amount: $3,319,337 (68% federal, 32% state). **Receiving aid:** Freshmen: 59% (176); all full-time undergraduates: 57% (652). **Average award:** Freshmen: $5030; Undergraduates: $4990. **Scholarships, grants, and awards:** Federal Pell, FSEOG, state, private, college/university gift aid from institutional funds.

GIFT AID (NON-NEED-BASED) Total amount: $531,084 (3% state, 97% external sources). **Receiving aid:** Freshmen: 85% (252). Undergraduates: 82% (939). **Average award:** Freshmen: $8871. Undergraduates: $11,267. **Scholarships, grants, and awards by category:** Academic interests/achievement: biological sciences, business, communication, computer science, education, English, foreign languages, general academic interests/achievements, health fields, humanities, mathematics, physical sciences, premedicine, religion/biblical studies, social sciences. Creative arts/performance: music, theater/drama. **Special achievements/activities:** cheerleading/drum major, leadership, religious involvement. **Special characteristics:** children and siblings of alumni, children of faculty/staff, general special characteristics, international students, relatives of clergy, religious affiliation, siblings of current students, spouses of current students. **Tuition waivers:** Full or partial for children of alumni, employees or children of employees. **ROTC:** Army cooperative, Air Force cooperative.

LOANS Student loans: $5,886,732 (51% need-based, 49% non-need-based). 73% of past graduating class borrowed through all loan programs. **Average indebtedness per student:** $22,086. **Average need-based loan:** Freshmen: $3467. Undergraduates: $4185. **Parent loans:** $1,288,991 (100% non-need-based). **Programs:** Federal Direct (Subsidized and Unsubsidized Stafford, PLUS), Perkins.

WORK-STUDY Federal work-study: Total amount: $167,870; jobs available. **State or other work-study/employment:** Total amount: $577,807 (100% non-need-based). Part-time jobs available.

ATHLETIC AWARDS Total amount: $2,355,100 (100% non-need-based).

APPLYING FOR FINANCIAL AID Required financial aid form: FAFSA. **Financial aid deadline (priority):** 3/15. **Notification date:** Continuous beginning 1/1.

CONTACT Mrs. Kristen M. Gibbs, Director of Financial Assistance, Central Methodist University, 411 Central Methodist Square, Fayette, MO 65248-1198, 660-248-6244 or toll-free 888-CMU-1854 (in-state), 877-CMU-1854 (out-of-state). Fax: 660-248-6288. E-mail: kgibbs@centralmethodist.edu. Website: http://www.centralmethodist.edu/.

CENTRAL MICHIGAN UNIVERSITY
Mount Pleasant, MI

Tuition & fees (MI res): $10,950	Average undergraduate aid package: $11,867

ABOUT THE INSTITUTION State-supported, coed. *Awards:* certificates, bachelor's, master's, and doctoral degrees. 100 undergraduate majors. *Total enrollment:* 27,626. Undergraduates: 21,332. Freshmen: 3,417. Federal methodology is used as a basis for awarding need-based institutional aid.

UNDERGRADUATE EXPENSES for 2013–2014 *Application fee:* $35. *Tuition, state resident:* full-time $10,950; part-time $365 per credit hour. *Tuition, nonresident:* full-time $23,670; part-time $789 per credit hour. Full-time tuition and fees vary according to location. Part-time tuition and fees vary according to location. *College room and board:* $8368; *Room only:* $4184. Room and board charges vary according to board plan, housing facility, location, and student level.

FRESHMAN FINANCIAL AID (Fall 2012, est.) 3,399 applied for aid; of those 76% were deemed to have need. 96% of freshmen with need received aid; of those 60% had need fully met. *Average percent of need met:* 86% (excluding resources awarded to replace EFC). *Average financial aid package:* $12,368 (excluding resources awarded to replace EFC). 12% of all full-time freshmen had no need and received non-need-based gift aid.

UNDERGRADUATE FINANCIAL AID (Fall 2012, est.) 14,712 applied for aid; of those 78% were deemed to have need. 98% of undergraduates with need received aid; of those 59% had need fully met. *Average percent of need met:* 85% (excluding resources awarded to replace EFC). *Average financial aid package:* $11,867 (excluding resources awarded to replace EFC). 8% of all full-time undergraduates had no need and received non-need-based gift aid.

GIFT AID (NEED-BASED) *Total amount:* $51,210,126 (52% federal, 3% state, 42% institutional, 3% external sources). *Receiving aid:* Freshmen: 54% (2,059); all full-time undergraduates: 47% (8,773). *Average award:* Freshmen: $8013; Undergraduates: $5869. *Scholarships, grants, and awards:* Federal Pell, FSEOG, state, private, college/university gift aid from institutional funds, United Negro College Fund.

GIFT AID (NON-NEED-BASED) *Total amount:* $9,181,083 (1% federal, 79% institutional, 20% external sources). *Receiving aid:* Freshmen: 9% (329). Undergraduates: 3% (537). *Average award:* Freshmen: $4759. Undergraduates: $4045. *Scholarships, grants, and awards by category:* Academic interests/achievement: 4,420 awards ($15,850,166 total): biological sciences, business, communication, computer science, education, engineering/technologies, English, foreign languages, general academic interests/achievements, health fields, home economics, humanities, international studies, mathematics, military science, physical sciences, premedicine, religion/biblical studies, social sciences. Creative arts/performance: 169 awards ($333,706 total): applied art and design, art/fine arts, cinema/film/broadcasting, creative writing, dance, general creative arts/performance, journalism/publications, music, performing arts, theater/drama. Special achievements/activities: 732 awards ($5,988,932 total): general special achievements/activities, leadership. Special characteristics: 211 awards ($1,339,111 total): children and siblings of alumni, children of faculty/staff, ethnic background, international students, local/state students, out-of-state students. *Tuition waivers:* Full or partial for children of alumni, employees or children of employees, senior citizens. *ROTC:* Army, Air Force cooperative.

LOANS *Student loans:* $107,380,706 (69% need-based, 31% non-need-based). 75% of past graduating class borrowed through all loan programs. *Average indebtedness per student:* $31,520. *Average need-based loan:* Freshmen: $5565. Undergraduates: $6791. *Parent loans:* $32,743,724 (26% need-based, 74% non-need-based). *Programs:* Federal Direct (Subsidized and Unsubsidized Stafford, PLUS), Perkins, alternative loans.

WORK-STUDY *Federal work-study:* Total amount: $1,246,486; 902 jobs averaging $1382. *State or other work-study/employment:* Total amount: $10,655,586 (23% need-based, 77% non-need-based). 4,302 part-time jobs averaging $2477.

ATHLETIC AWARDS Total amount: $4,715,908 (35% need-based, 65% non-need-based).

APPLYING FOR FINANCIAL AID *Required financial aid form:* FAFSA. *Financial aid deadline (priority):* 3/1. *Notification date:* Continuous beginning 3/25.

CONTACT Mr. Kirk M. Yats, Director of Scholarships and Financial Aid, Central Michigan University, Mount Pleasant, MI 48859, 989-774-3674 or toll-free 888-292-5366. *Fax:* 989-774-3634. *E-mail:* cmuosfa@cmich.edu. *Website:* http://www.cmich.edu/.

CENTRAL PENN COLLEGE
Summerdale, PA

CONTACT Kathy Shepard, Financial Aid Director, Central Penn College, College Hill and Valley Roads, Summerdale, PA 17093, 717-728-2261 or toll-free 800-759-2727. *Fax:* 717-728-2350. *E-mail:* financial-aid@centralpenn.edu. *Website:* http://www.centralpenn.edu/.

CENTRAL STATE UNIVERSITY
Wilberforce, OH

CONTACT Jean Hurst, Interim Director of Student Financial Aid, Central State University, PO Box 1004, Wilberforce, OH 45384, 937-376-6579 or toll-free 800-388-CSUI (in-state), 800-388-2781 (out-of-state). *Fax:* 937-376-6519. *E-mail:* jhurst@centralstate.edu. *Website:* http://www.centralstate.edu/.

CENTRAL WASHINGTON UNIVERSITY
Ellensburg, WA

ABOUT THE INSTITUTION State-supported, coed. *Awards:* certificates, bachelor's, and master's degrees. 73 undergraduate majors. *Total enrollment:* 11,320. Undergraduates: 10,770. Freshmen: 1,383.

GIFT AID (NEED-BASED) *Scholarships, grants, and awards:* Federal Pell, FSEOG, state, private, college/university gift aid from institutional funds.

GIFT AID (NON-NEED-BASED) *Scholarships, grants, and awards by category:* Academic interests/achievement: general academic interests/achievements. Creative arts/performance: art/fine arts, general creative arts/performance. Special achievements/activities: leadership. Special characteristics: children and siblings of alumni, local/state students, members of minority groups, religious affiliation.

LOANS *Programs:* Federal Direct (Subsidized and Unsubsidized Stafford, PLUS), Perkins, college/university.

APPLYING FOR FINANCIAL AID *Required financial aid form:* FAFSA.

CONTACT Ms. Agnes Canedo, Director of Financial Aid, Central Washington University, 400 East University Way, Ellensburg, WA 98926-7495, 509-963-3049 or toll-free 866-298-4968. *Fax:* 509-963-1788. *E-mail:* canedoa@cwu.edu. *Website:* http://www.cwu.edu/.

CENTRAL YESHIVA TOMCHEI TMIMIM-LUBAVITCH
Brooklyn, NY

CONTACT Rabbi Moshe M. Gluckowsky, Director of Financial Aid , Central Yeshiva Tomchei Tmimim-Lubavitch, 841-853 Ocean Parkway, Brooklyn, NY 11230, 718-859-2277.

CENTRE COLLEGE
Danville, KY

Tuition & fees: $36,000	Average undergraduate aid package: $26,961

ABOUT THE INSTITUTION Independent Presbyterian Church (U.S.A.), coed. *Awards:* bachelor's degrees. 27 undergraduate majors. *Total enrollment:* 1,344. Undergraduates: 1,344. Freshmen: 351. Both federal and institutional methodology are used as a basis for awarding need-based institutional aid.

UNDERGRADUATE EXPENSES for 2013–2014 *Application fee:* $40. *Comprehensive fee:* $45,100 includes full-time tuition ($36,000) and room and board ($9100). *College room only:* $4550. Room and board charges vary according to board plan. *Part-time tuition:* $1300 per credit.

FRESHMAN FINANCIAL AID (Fall 2012, est.) 284 applied for aid; of those 79% were deemed to have need. 100% of freshmen with need received aid; of those 34% had need fully met. *Average percent of need met:* 86% (excluding resources awarded to replace EFC). *Average financial aid package:* $27,404 (excluding resources awarded to replace EFC). 33% of all full-time freshmen had no need and received non-need-based gift aid.

UNDERGRADUATE FINANCIAL AID (Fall 2012, est.) 1,000 applied for aid; of those 84% were deemed to have need. 100% of undergraduates with need received aid; of those 28% had need fully met. *Average percent of need met:* 84% (excluding resources awarded to replace EFC). *Average financial aid package:* $26,961 (excluding resources awarded to replace EFC). 33% of all full-time undergraduates had no need and received non-need-based gift aid.

GIFT AID (NEED-BASED) *Total amount:* $19,901,173 (4% federal, 12% state, 82% institutional, 2% external sources). *Receiving aid:* Freshmen: 64% (223); all full-time undergraduates: 63% (841). *Average award:* Freshmen: $24,790; Undergraduates: $23,643. *Scholarships, grants, and awards:* Federal Pell, FSEOG, state, private, college/university gift aid from institutional funds.

GIFT AID (NON-NEED-BASED) *Total amount:* $7,737,082 (7% state, 91% institutional, 2% external sources). *Average award:* Freshmen: $16,036. Undergraduates: $17,231. *Scholarships, grants, and awards by category: Academic interests/achievement:* 1,089 awards ($14,986,250 total): foreign languages, general academic interests/achievements. *Creative arts/performance:* 109 awards ($423,750 total): music, theater/drama. *Special achievements/activities:* 30 awards ($67,500 total): community service. *Special characteristics:* 205 awards ($2,052,347 total): children and siblings of alumni, children of faculty/staff, ethnic background, first-generation college students. *Tuition waivers:* Full or partial for employees or children of employees, adult students, senior citizens. *ROTC:* Army cooperative, Air Force cooperative.

LOANS *Student loans:* $4,998,399 (60% need-based, 40% non-need-based). 52% of past graduating class borrowed through all loan programs. *Average indebtedness per student:* $25,500. *Average need-based loan:* Freshmen: $3479. Undergraduates: $4600. *Parent loans:* $1,690,354 (100% non-need-based). *Programs:* Federal Direct (Subsidized and Unsubsidized Stafford, PLUS), Perkins, college/university.

WORK-STUDY *Federal work-study:* Total amount: $573,060; 369 jobs averaging $1535. *State or other work-study/employment:* Total amount: $5580 (100% non-need-based). 2 part-time jobs averaging $2790.

APPLYING FOR FINANCIAL AID *Required financial aid forms:* FAFSA, institution's own form. *Financial aid deadline:* 1/31. *Notification date:* 4/1. Students must reply by 5/1.

CONTACT Ms. Elaine Larson, Director of Student Financial Planning, Centre College, 600 West Walnut Street, Danville, KY 40422-1394, 859-238-5365 or toll-free 800-423-6236. *Fax:* 859-238-8719. *E-mail:* finaid@centre.edu. *Website:* http://www.centre.edu/.

CHADRON STATE COLLEGE
Chadron, NE

CONTACT Ms. Sherry Douglas, Director of Financial Aid, Chadron State College, 1000 Main Street, Chadron, NE 69337, 308-432-6230 or toll-free 800-242-3766. *Fax:* 308-432-6229. *E-mail:* finaid@csc.edu. *Website:* http://www.csc.edu/.

CHAMBERLAIN COLLEGE OF NURSING
Phoenix, AZ

CONTACT Financial Aid Office, Chamberlain College of Nursing, 2149 West Dunlap Avenue, Phoenix, AZ 85021, 602-331-2720 or toll-free 888-556-8CCN. *Website:* http://www.chamberlain.edu/.

CHAMBERLAIN COLLEGE OF NURSING
Jacksonville, FL

CONTACT Financial Aid Office, Chamberlain College of Nursing, 5200 Belfort Road, Jacksonville, FL 32256-6040, 904-251-8100 or toll-free 888-556-8CCN. *Website:* http://www.chamberlain.edu/.

CHAMBERLAIN COLLEGE OF NURSING
Miramar, FL

CONTACT Financial Aid Office, Chamberlain College of Nursing, 2300 SW 145th Avenue, Miramar, FL 33027, 954-885-3510. *Website:* http://www.chamberlain.edu/.

CHAMBERLAIN COLLEGE OF NURSING
Atlanta, GA

CONTACT Financial Aid Office, Chamberlain College of Nursing, 5775 Peachtree-Dunwoody Road, NE, Suite A100, Atlanta, GA 30342, 404-250-8500. *Website:* http://www.chamberlain.edu/.

CHAMBERLAIN COLLEGE OF NURSING
Addison, IL

CONTACT Financial Aid Office, Chamberlain College of Nursing, 1221 N. Swift Road, Addison, IL 60101-6106, 630-953-3680 or toll-free 888-556-8CCN. *Website:* http://www.chamberlain.edu/.

CHAMBERLAIN COLLEGE OF NURSING
Chicago, IL

CONTACT Financial Aid Office, Chamberlain College of Nursing, 3300 N. Campbell Avenue, Chicago, IL 60618, 773-961-3000 or toll-free 888-556-8CCN. *Website:* http://www.chamberlain.edu/.

CHAMBERLAIN COLLEGE OF NURSING
Indianapolis, IN

CONTACT Financial Aid Office, Chamberlain College of Nursing, 9100 Keystone Crossing, Suite 600, Indianapolis, IN 46240, 317-816-7335. *Website:* http://www.chamberlain.edu/.

CHAMBERLAIN COLLEGE OF NURSING
St. Louis, MO

Tuition & fees: $16,960	Average undergraduate aid package: N/A

ABOUT THE INSTITUTION Proprietary, coed. *Awards:* bachelor's degrees. 1 undergraduate major. *Total enrollment:* 540. Undergraduates: 540. Freshmen: 9. Both federal and institutional methodology are used as a basis for awarding need-based institutional aid.

UNDERGRADUATE EXPENSES for 2013–2014 *Application fee:* $95. *Tuition:* full-time $16,360; part-time $665 per credit hour.

GIFT AID (NEED-BASED) *Scholarships, grants, and awards:* Federal Pell, FSEOG, private, college/university gift aid from institutional funds.

GIFT AID (NON-NEED-BASED) *Scholarships, grants, and awards by category:* Academic interests/achievement: general academic interests/achievements, health fields.

LOANS *Programs:* Federal Direct (Subsidized and Unsubsidized Stafford, PLUS).

APPLYING FOR FINANCIAL AID *Required financial aid forms:* FAFSA, institution's own form. *Financial aid deadline (priority):* 4/1. *Notification date:* Continuous. Students must reply within 2 weeks of notification.

CONTACT Financial Aid Counselor, Chamberlain College of Nursing, 11830 Westline Industrial Drive, Suite 106, St. Louis, MO 63146, 314-991-6200 or toll-free 888-556-8CCN.
Website: http://www.chamberlain.edu/.

CHAMBERLAIN COLLEGE OF NURSING
Cleveland, OH

CONTACT Financial Aid Office, Chamberlain College of Nursing, 6700 Euclid Avenue, Suite 201, Cleveland, OH 44103, 216-361-6005.
Website: http://www.chamberlain.edu/.

CHAMBERLAIN COLLEGE OF NURSING
Columbus, OH

CONTACT Financial Aid Office, Chamberlain College of Nursing, 1350 Alum Creek Drive, Columbus, OH 43209, 614-252-8890 or toll-free 888-556-8CCN.
Website: http://www.chamberlain.edu/.

CHAMBERLAIN COLLEGE OF NURSING
Houston, TX

CONTACT Financial Aid Office, Chamberlain College of Nursing, 10025 Equity Drive, Houston, TX 77041, 713-277-9800.
Website: http://www.chamberlain.edu/.

CHAMBERLAIN COLLEGE OF NURSING
Arlington, VA

CONTACT Financial Aid Office, Chamberlain College of Nursing, 2450 Crystal Drive, Arlington, VA 22202, 703-416-7300 or toll-free 888-556-8CCN.
Website: http://www.chamberlain.edu/.

CHAMINADE UNIVERSITY OF HONOLULU
Honolulu, HI

ABOUT THE INSTITUTION Independent Roman Catholic, coed. *Awards:* certificates, associate, bachelor's, and master's degrees. 23 undergraduate majors. *Total enrollment:* 2,144. Undergraduates: 1,372. Freshmen: 235.

GIFT AID (NEED-BASED) *Scholarships, grants, and awards:* Federal Pell, FSEOG, state, private, college/university gift aid from institutional funds.

GIFT AID (NON-NEED-BASED) *Scholarships, grants, and awards by category:* Academic interests/achievement: general academic interests/achievements.

LOANS *Programs:* Federal Direct (Subsidized and Unsubsidized Stafford, PLUS), Perkins, alternative loans.

WORK-STUDY Federal work-study jobs available.

APPLYING FOR FINANCIAL AID *Required financial aid form:* FAFSA.

CONTACT Amy Takiguchi, Director of Financial Aid, Chaminade University of Honolulu, 3140 Waialae Avenue, Honolulu, HI 96816-1578, 808-735-4780 or toll-free 800-735-3733. *Fax:* 808-739-8362. *E-mail:* finaid@chaminade.edu.
Website: http://www.chaminade.edu/.

CHAMPLAIN COLLEGE
Burlington, VT

Tuition & fees: $31,350	Average undergraduate aid package: $15,215

ABOUT THE INSTITUTION Independent, coed. *Awards:* certificates, associate, bachelor's, and master's degrees. 37 undergraduate majors. *Total enrollment:* 3,233. Undergraduates: 2,793. Freshmen: 601. Federal methodology is used as a basis for awarding need-based institutional aid.

UNDERGRADUATE EXPENSES for 2013–2014 *Comprehensive fee:* $44,850 includes full-time tuition ($31,250), mandatory fees ($100), and room and board ($13,500). *Part-time tuition:* $1240 per credit hour.

FRESHMAN FINANCIAL AID (Fall 2011) 345 applied for aid; of those 78% were deemed to have need. 100% of freshmen with need received aid; of those 12% had need fully met. *Average percent of need met:* 61% (excluding resources awarded to replace EFC). *Average financial aid package:* $16,847 (excluding resources awarded to replace EFC). 12% of all full-time freshmen had no need and received non-need-based gift aid.

UNDERGRADUATE FINANCIAL AID (Fall 2011) 1,750 applied for aid; of those 81% were deemed to have need. 100% of undergraduates with need received aid; of those 7% had need fully met. *Average percent of need met:* 53% (excluding resources awarded to replace EFC). *Average financial aid package:* $15,215 (excluding resources awarded to replace EFC). 12% of all full-time undergraduates had no need and received non-need-based gift aid.

GIFT AID (NEED-BASED) *Total amount:* $16,882,741 (22% federal, 9% state, 59% institutional, 10% external sources). *Receiving aid:* Freshmen: 51% (249); all full-time undergraduates: 54% (1,163). *Average award:* Freshmen: $8442; Undergraduates: $8031. *Scholarships, grants, and awards:* Federal Pell, FSEOG, state, private, college/university gift aid from institutional funds.

GIFT AID (NON-NEED-BASED) *Total amount:* $1,434,910 (100% institutional). *Receiving aid:* Freshmen: 35% (170). Undergraduates: 43% (930). *Average award:* Freshmen: $7204. Undergraduates: $4752. *Scholarships, grants, and awards by category:* Academic interests/achievement: business, communication, computer science, education, engineering/technologies, general academic interests/achievements, health fields, social sciences. *Special characteristics:* first-generation college students, general special characteristics, international students, members of minority groups. *Tuition waivers:* Full or partial for employees or children of employees. *ROTC:* Army cooperative.

LOANS *Student loans:* $11,938,905 (100% need-based). *Average need-based loan:* Freshmen: $3944. Undergraduates: $4606. *Parent loans:* $12,007,581 (100% need-based). *Programs:* Federal Direct (Subsidized and Unsubsidized Stafford, PLUS), Perkins, state.

WORK-STUDY *Federal work-study:* Total amount: $1,111,179; jobs available.

APPLYING FOR FINANCIAL AID *Required financial aid form:* FAFSA. *Financial aid deadline:* 2/15. *Notification date:* 3/30.

CONTACT Kristi Jovell, Director of Financial Aid, Champlain College, 163 South Willard Street, Burlington, VT 05401, 802-860-2777 or toll-free 800-570-5858. *Fax:* 802-860-2775. *E-mail:* kjovell@champlain.edu. *Website:* http://www.champlain.edu/.

CHANCELLOR UNIVERSITY
Cleveland, OH

CONTACT Eric Damon, Director of Financial Aid, Chancellor University, 3921 Chester Avenue, Cleveland, OH 44114, 216-361-2734 or toll-free 888-316-9377. *Fax:* 216-361-9096. *Website:* http://www.chancelloru.edu/.

CHAPMAN UNIVERSITY
Orange, CA

Tuition & fees: $43,573	Average undergraduate aid package: $30,655

ABOUT THE INSTITUTION Independent Christian Church (Disciples of Christ), coed. *Awards:* certificates, bachelor's, master's, and doctoral degrees. 49 undergraduate majors. *Total enrollment:* 7,566. Undergraduates: 5,677. Freshmen: 1,278. Both federal and institutional methodology are used as a basis for awarding need-based institutional aid.

UNDERGRADUATE EXPENSES for 2013–2014 *Application fee:* $65. *Comprehensive fee:* $55,777 includes full-time tuition ($42,890), mandatory fees ($683), and room and board ($12,204). *College room only:* $8238. Room and board charges vary according to board plan and housing facility. *Part-time tuition:* $1330 per credit. *Payment plan:* Tuition prepayment.

FRESHMAN FINANCIAL AID (Fall 2012, est.) 974 applied for aid; of those 80% were deemed to have need. 100% of freshmen with need received aid; of those 10% had need fully met. *Average percent of need met:* 10% (excluding resources awarded to replace EFC). *Average financial aid package:* $32,039 (excluding resources awarded to replace EFC). 25% of all full-time freshmen had no need and received non-need-based gift aid.

UNDERGRADUATE FINANCIAL AID (Fall 2012, est.) 3,730 applied for aid; of those 88% were deemed to have need. 99% of undergraduates with need received aid; of those 10% had need fully met. *Average percent of need met:* 10% (excluding resources awarded to replace EFC). *Average financial aid package:* $30,655 (excluding resources awarded to replace EFC). 25% of all full-time undergraduates had no need and received non-need-based gift aid.

GIFT AID (NEED-BASED) *Total amount:* $78,375,179 (6% federal, 8% state, 85% institutional, 1% external sources). *Receiving aid:* Freshmen: 61% (685); all full-time undergraduates: 61% (2,821). *Average award:* Freshmen: $12,400; Undergraduates: $15,331. *Scholarships, grants, and awards:* Federal Pell, FSEOG, state, private, college/university gift aid from institutional funds.

GIFT AID (NON-NEED-BASED) *Total amount:* $20,132,691 (98% institutional, 2% external sources). *Receiving aid:* Freshmen: 54% (604). Undergraduates: 46% (2,131). *Average award:* Freshmen: $18,033. Undergraduates: $17,053. *Scholarships, grants, and awards by category:* Academic interests/achievement: 2,982 awards ($50,106,194 total): biological sciences, general academic interests/achievements, physical sciences. *Creative arts/performance:* 315 awards ($988,178 total): art/fine arts, cinema/film/broadcasting, creative writing, dance, music, performing arts, theater/drama. *Special characteristics:* 52 awards ($51,650 total): children and siblings of alumni. *Tuition waivers:* Full or partial for employees or children of employees. *ROTC:* Army cooperative, Air Force cooperative.

LOANS *Student loans:* $32,104,466 (88% need-based, 12% non-need-based). 73% of past graduating class borrowed through all loan programs. *Average indebtedness per student:* $29,371. *Average need-based loan:* Freshmen: $3557. Undergraduates: $4266. *Parent loans:* $25,193,107 (86% need-based, 14% non-need-based). *Programs:* Federal Direct (Subsidized and Unsubsidized Stafford), Perkins.

WORK-STUDY *Federal work-study:* Total amount: $8,293,717; 2,853 jobs averaging $2907.

APPLYING FOR FINANCIAL AID *Required financial aid forms:* FAFSA, state aid form. *Financial aid deadline (priority):* 3/2. *Notification date:* Continuous beginning 3/15. Students must reply within 3 weeks of notification.

CONTACT Mr. Jack Millis, Director of Financial Aid, Chapman University, One University Drive, Orange, CA 92866, 714-562-6049 or toll-free 888-CUAPPLY. *Fax:* 714-997-6743. *E-mail:* millis@chapman.edu. *Website:* http://www.chapman.edu/.

CHARLES DREW UNIVERSITY OF MEDICINE AND SCIENCE
Los Angeles, CA

CONTACT Financial Aid Office, Charles Drew University of Medicine and Science, 1731 East 120th Street, Los Angeles, CA 90059, 323-563-4824. *Fax:* 323-569-0597. *Website:* http://www.cdrewu.edu/.

CHARLESTON SOUTHERN UNIVERSITY
Charleston, SC

CONTACT Mr. Jim Rhoden, Director of Admissions, Charleston Southern University, PO Box 118087, 9200 University Boulevard, Charleston, SC 29423-8087, 843-863-7050 or toll-free 800-947-7474. *Fax:* 843-863-7070. *Website:* http://www.charlestonsouthern.edu/.

CHARTER OAK STATE COLLEGE
New Britain, CT

CONTACT Velma Walters, Director, Financial Aid, Charter Oak State College, 55 Paul J. Manafort Drive, New Britain, CT 06053-2142, 860-832-3872. *Fax:* 860-832-3999. *E-mail:* sfa@charteroak.edu. *Website:* http://www.charteroak.edu/.

CHATHAM UNIVERSITY
Pittsburgh, PA

Tuition & fees: $32,454	Average undergraduate aid package: $29,133

ABOUT THE INSTITUTION Independent, undergraduate: women only; graduate: coed. *Awards:* certificates, bachelor's, master's, and doctoral degrees. 41 undergraduate majors. *Total enrollment:* 2,178. Undergraduates: 922. Freshmen: 117. Both federal and institutional methodology are used as a basis for awarding need-based institutional aid.

UNDERGRADUATE EXPENSES for 2013–2014 *Application fee:* $35. *Comprehensive fee:* $42,440 includes full-time tuition ($31,294), mandatory fees ($1160), and room and board ($9986). *College room only:* $5061. Room and board charges vary according to board plan and housing facility. *Part-time tuition:* $759 per credit. Part-time tuition and fees vary according to course load.

FRESHMAN FINANCIAL AID (Fall 2012, est.) 110 applied for aid; of those 86% were deemed to have need. 100% of freshmen with need received aid; of those 7% had need fully met. *Average percent of need met:* 71% (excluding resources awarded to replace EFC). *Average financial aid package:* $29,723 (excluding resources awarded to replace EFC). 3% of all full-time freshmen had no need and received non-need-based gift aid.

UNDERGRADUATE FINANCIAL AID (Fall 2012, est.) 553 applied for aid; of those 96% were deemed to have need. 100% of undergraduates with need received aid; of those 10% had need fully met. *Average percent of need met:* 67% (excluding resources awarded to replace EFC). *Average financial aid package:* $29,133 (excluding resources awarded to replace EFC). 9% of all full-time undergraduates had no need and received non-need-based gift aid.

GIFT AID (NEED-BASED) *Total amount:* $9,807,073 (13% federal, 9% state, 74% institutional, 4% external sources). *Receiving aid:* Freshmen: 77% (90); all full-time undergraduates: 84% (500). *Average award:* Freshmen: $10,043; Undergrad-

uates: $8189. **Scholarships, grants, and awards:** Federal Pell, FSEOG, state, private, college/university gift aid from institutional funds.
GIFT AID (NON-NEED-BASED) Total amount: $1,967,669 (92% institutional, 8% external sources). **Receiving aid:** Freshmen: 77% (90). Undergraduates: 89% (532). **Average award:** Freshmen: $9000. Undergraduates: $11,670. **Scholarships, grants, and awards by category:** Academic interests/achievement: 603 awards ($6,724,723 total): general academic interests/achievements. Creative arts/performance: 30 awards ($59,700 total): applied art and design, art/fine arts, music. Special achievements/activities: 328 awards ($958,250 total): leadership. Special characteristics: 22 awards ($38,000 total): children and siblings of alumni, siblings of current students. **Tuition waivers:** Full or partial for employees or children of employees.
ROTC: Army cooperative, Naval cooperative, Air Force cooperative.
LOANS Student loans: $3,747,783 (52% need-based, 48% non-need-based). 76% of past graduating class borrowed through all loan programs. Average indebtedness per student: $40,297. **Average need-based loan:** Freshmen: $3794. Undergraduates: $4557. **Parent loans:** $992,774 (75% need-based, 25% non-need-based). **Programs:** Federal Direct (Subsidized and Unsubsidized Stafford, PLUS), Perkins.
WORK-STUDY Federal work-study: Total amount: $309,200; 147 jobs averaging $2103. **State or other work-study/employment:** Total amount: $55,000 (100% non-need-based). Part-time jobs available.
APPLYING FOR FINANCIAL AID Required financial aid form: FAFSA. **Financial aid deadline:** Continuous. **Notification date:** Continuous beginning 3/1. Students must reply by 5/1.
CONTACT Dr. Jennifer Burns, Director of Financial Aid, Chatham University, Woodland Road, Pittsburgh, PA 15232-2826, 412-365-1849 or toll-free 800-837-1290. Fax: 412-365-1643. E-mail: jburns@chatham.edu.
Website: http://www.chatham.edu/.

CHESTNUT HILL COLLEGE
Philadelphia, PA

Tuition & fees: $31,170	Average undergraduate aid package: $21,349

ABOUT THE INSTITUTION Independent Roman Catholic, coed. **Awards:** certificates, associate, bachelor's, master's, and doctoral degrees (profile includes figures from both traditional and accelerated (part-time) programs). 38 undergraduate majors. **Total enrollment:** 2,301. Undergraduates: 1,581. Freshmen: 211. Federal methodology is used as a basis for awarding need-based institutional aid.
UNDERGRADUATE EXPENSES for 2013–2014 Application fee: $35. **Comprehensive fee:** $41,045 includes full-time tuition ($31,000), mandatory fees ($170), and room and board ($9875). Room and board charges vary according to housing facility. **Part-time tuition:** $665 per credit hour.
FRESHMAN FINANCIAL AID (Fall 2012, est.) 201 applied for aid; of those 94% were deemed to have need. 98% of freshmen with need received aid; of those 10% had need fully met. **Average percent of need met:** 64% (excluding resources awarded to replace EFC). **Average financial aid package:** $20,920 (excluding resources awarded to replace EFC). 6% of all full-time freshmen had no need and received non-need-based gift aid.
UNDERGRADUATE FINANCIAL AID (Fall 2012, est.) 1,089 applied for aid; of those 93% were deemed to have need. 100% of undergraduates with need received aid; of those 11% had need fully met. **Average percent of need met:** 68% (excluding resources awarded to replace EFC). **Average financial aid package:** $21,349 (excluding resources awarded to replace EFC). 5% of all full-time undergraduates had no need and received non-need-based gift aid.
GIFT AID (NEED-BASED) Total amount: $13,865,635 (22% federal, 10% state, 67% institutional, 1% external sources). **Receiving aid:** Freshmen: 86% (180); all full-time undergraduates: 77% (960). **Average award:** Freshmen: $16,788; Undergraduates: $14,291. **Scholarships, grants, and awards:** Federal Pell, FSEOG, state, private, college/university gift aid from institutional funds.
GIFT AID (NON-NEED-BASED) Total amount: $3,123,266 (100% institutional). **Receiving aid:** Undergraduates: 2% (31). **Average award:** Freshmen: $11,125. Undergraduates: $12,546. **Scholarships, grants, and awards by category:** Academic interests/achievement: 780 awards ($8,459,422 total): general academic interests/achievements. Creative arts/performance: music. **Tuition waivers:** Full or partial for employees or children of employees, senior citizens.

LOANS Student loans: $10,484,832 (79% need-based, 21% non-need-based). 80% of past graduating class borrowed through all loan programs. Average indebtedness per student: $10,688. **Average need-based loan:** Freshmen: $3343. Undergraduates: $4398. **Parent loans:** $1,351,804 (34% need-based, 66% non-need-based). **Programs:** Federal Direct (Subsidized and Unsubsidized Stafford, PLUS), Perkins.
WORK-STUDY Federal work-study: Total amount: $155,811; 334 jobs averaging $1000. **State or other work-study/employment:** 92 part-time jobs averaging $1000.
ATHLETIC AWARDS Total amount: $1,127,559 (90% need-based, 10% non-need-based).
APPLYING FOR FINANCIAL AID Required financial aid form: FAFSA. **Financial aid deadline:** Continuous. **Notification date:** Continuous beginning 2/15.
CONTACT Ms. Kristina Wilhelm-Nelson, Acting Director of Financial Aid, Chestnut Hill College, 9601 Germantown Avenue, Philadelphia, PA 19118-2693, 215-248-7192 or toll-free 800-248-0052. Fax: 215-248-7217. E-mail: wilhelmk@chc.edu.
Website: http://www.chc.edu/.

CHEYNEY UNIVERSITY OF PENNSYLVANIA
Cheyney, PA

CONTACT Mr. James Brown, Director of Financial Aid, Cheyney University of Pennsylvania, 1837 University Circle, Cheyney, PA 19319, 610-399-2302 or toll-free 800-CHEYNEY. Fax: 610-399-2411. E-mail: jbrown@cheyney.edu.
Website: http://www.cheyney.edu/.

CHICAGO STATE UNIVERSITY
Chicago, IL

Tuition & fees (IL res): $9254	Average undergraduate aid package: $16,129

ABOUT THE INSTITUTION State-supported, coed. **Awards:** certificates, bachelor's, master's, and doctoral degrees. 34 undergraduate majors. **Total enrollment:** 6,107. Undergraduates: 4,618. Freshmen: 323. Both federal and institutional methodology are used as a basis for awarding need-based institutional aid.
UNDERGRADUATE EXPENSES for 2013–2014 Application fee: $25. **Tuition, state resident:** full-time $6840. **Tuition, nonresident:** full-time $13,606. **Required fees:** full-time $2414. **College room and board:** $8221. **Payment plans:** Guaranteed tuition, tuition prepayment.
FRESHMAN FINANCIAL AID (Fall 2012, est.) 289 applied for aid; of those 100% were deemed to have need. 100% of freshmen with need received aid; of those 1% had need fully met. **Average percent of need met:** 64% (excluding resources awarded to replace EFC). **Average financial aid package:** $16,490 (excluding resources awarded to replace EFC). 1% of all full-time freshmen had no need and received non-need-based gift aid.
UNDERGRADUATE FINANCIAL AID (Fall 2012, est.) 2,865 applied for aid; of those 100% were deemed to have need. 100% of undergraduates with need received aid; of those 1% had need fully met. **Average percent of need met:** 59% (excluding resources awarded to replace EFC). **Average financial aid package:** $16,129 (excluding resources awarded to replace EFC). 1% of all full-time undergraduates had no need and received non-need-based gift aid.
GIFT AID (NEED-BASED) Total amount: $23,503,256 (67% federal, 32% state, 1% institutional). **Receiving aid:** Freshmen: 87% (258); all full-time undergraduates: 88% (2,547). **Average award:** Freshmen: $7400; Undergraduates: $7056. **Scholarships, grants, and awards:** Federal Pell, FSEOG, state, private, college/university gift aid from institutional funds, Federal Nursing.
GIFT AID (NON-NEED-BASED) Total amount: $186,186 (25% federal, 69% state, 6% institutional). **Receiving aid:** Freshmen: 1% (3). Undergraduates: 3% (87). **Average award:** Freshmen: $4764. Undergraduates: $6425. **Scholarships, grants, and awards by category:** Academic interests/achievement: general academic interests/achievements, physical sciences. Creative arts/performance: art/fine arts, journalism/publications, music. Special achievements/activities: leadership. **ROTC:** Army, Naval cooperative, Air Force cooperative.

LOANS *Student loans:* $35,974,198 (100% need-based). 26% of past graduating class borrowed through all loan programs. *Average indebtedness per student:* $37,834. *Average need-based loan:* Freshmen: $3137. Undergraduates: $4124. *Parent loans:* $3,710,404 (100% need-based). *Programs:* Federal Direct (Subsidized and Unsubsidized Stafford, PLUS), Perkins, Federal Nursing.

WORK-STUDY *Federal work-study:* Total amount: $402,323; jobs available. *State or other work-study/employment:* Part-time jobs available.

ATHLETIC AWARDS Total amount: $1,305,547 (77% need-based, 23% non-need-based).

APPLYING FOR FINANCIAL AID *Required financial aid form:* FAFSA. *Financial aid deadline:* 6/30 (priority: 1/15). *Notification date:* Continuous beginning 4/1. Students must reply within 16 weeks of notification.

CONTACT Ms. Cheri Sidney, Interim Director of Student Financial Aid, Chicago State University, 9501 South Martin Luther King Drive, Chicago, IL 60628, 773-995-3534.
Website: http://www.csu.edu/.

CHOWAN UNIVERSITY
Murfreesboro, NC

Tuition & fees: $22,160	Average undergraduate aid package: $16,142

ABOUT THE INSTITUTION Independent Baptist, coed. *Awards:* associate, bachelor's, and master's degrees. 50 undergraduate majors. *Total enrollment:* 1,316. Undergraduates: 1,308. Freshmen: 516. Federal methodology is used as a basis for awarding need-based institutional aid.

UNDERGRADUATE EXPENSES for 2013–2014 *Application fee:* $20. *Comprehensive fee:* $30,030 includes full-time tuition ($22,160) and room and board ($7870). *College room only:* $3900. Full-time tuition and fees vary according to class time, course load, and program. Room and board charges vary according to board plan and housing facility. Part-time tuition and fees vary according to class time and program.

FRESHMAN FINANCIAL AID (Fall 2012, est.) 657 applied for aid; of those 98% were deemed to have need. 100% of freshmen with need received aid; of those 19% had need fully met. *Average percent of need met:* 83% (excluding resources awarded to replace EFC). *Average financial aid package:* $16,402 (excluding resources awarded to replace EFC). 4% of all full-time freshmen had no need and received non-need-based gift aid.

UNDERGRADUATE FINANCIAL AID (Fall 2012, est.) 1,338 applied for aid; of those 97% were deemed to have need. 100% of undergraduates with need received aid; of those 19% had need fully met. *Average percent of need met:* 77% (excluding resources awarded to replace EFC). *Average financial aid package:* $16,142 (excluding resources awarded to replace EFC). 6% of all full-time undergraduates had no need and received non-need-based gift aid.

GIFT AID (NEED-BASED) *Total amount:* $15,302,117 (27% federal, 13% state, 59% institutional, 1% external sources). *Receiving aid:* Freshmen: 74% (513); all full-time undergraduates: 69% (1,003). *Average award:* Freshmen: $9684; Undergraduates: $8447. *Scholarships, grants, and awards:* Federal Pell, FSEOG, state, private, college/university gift aid from institutional funds.

GIFT AID (NON-NEED-BASED) *Total amount:* $560,661 (8% state, 42% institutional, 50% external sources). *Receiving aid:* Freshmen: 10% (70). Undergraduates: 11% (159). *Average award:* Freshmen: $5594. Undergraduates: $7562. *Scholarships, grants, and awards by category:* Academic interests/achievement: 1,374 awards ($10,774,252 total): general academic interests/achievements. *Creative arts/performance:* 26 awards ($66,977 total): music. *Special achievements/activities:* 400 awards ($974,956 total): leadership. *Special characteristics:* 370 awards ($928,552 total): children of educators, children of faculty/staff, children of public servants, children of union members/company employees, first-generation college students, general special characteristics, handicapped students, international students, local/state students, out-of-state students, public servants, relatives of clergy, religious affiliation, veterans, veterans' children. *Tuition waivers:* Full or partial for employees or children of employees, senior citizens.

LOANS *Student loans:* $10,813,676 (98% need-based, 2% non-need-based). 95% of past graduating class borrowed through all loan programs. *Average indebtedness per student:* $38,932. *Average need-based loan:* Freshmen: $3198. Undergraduates: $3759. *Parent loans:* $2,459,543 (92% need-based, 8% non-need-based). *Programs:* Federal Direct (Subsidized and Unsubsidized Stafford, PLUS), Perkins, state, alternative loans.

WORK-STUDY *Federal work-study:* Total amount: $456,518; 292 jobs averaging $1563. *State or other work-study/employment:* Total amount: $263,765 (100% non-need-based). 218 part-time jobs averaging $1209.

ATHLETIC AWARDS Total amount: $1,507,421 (96% need-based, 4% non-need-based).

APPLYING FOR FINANCIAL AID *Required financial aid form:* FAFSA. *Financial aid deadline (priority):* 5/1. *Notification date:* Continuous beginning 4/1. Students must reply within 2 weeks of notification.

CONTACT Mrs. Sharon W. Rose, Director of Financial Aid, Chowan University, One University Place, Murfreesboro, NC 27855, 252-398-1229 or toll-free 888-4-CHOWAN. *Fax:* 252-398-6513. *E-mail:* roses1@chowan.edu.
Website: http://www.chowan.edu/.

CHRISTENDOM COLLEGE
Front Royal, VA

Tuition & fees: $22,720	Average undergraduate aid package: $15,535

ABOUT THE INSTITUTION Independent Roman Catholic, coed. *Awards:* associate, bachelor's, and master's degrees. 7 undergraduate majors. *Total enrollment:* 453. Undergraduates: 388. Freshmen: 104. Institutional methodology is used as a basis for awarding need-based institutional aid.

UNDERGRADUATE EXPENSES for 2013–2014 *Application fee:* $25. *Comprehensive fee:* $31,000 includes full-time tuition ($22,050), mandatory fees ($670), and room and board ($8280).

FRESHMAN FINANCIAL AID (Fall 2012, est.) 84 applied for aid; of those 86% were deemed to have need. 100% of freshmen with need received aid; of those 100% had need fully met. *Average percent of need met:* 90% (excluding resources awarded to replace EFC). *Average financial aid package:* $14,725 (excluding resources awarded to replace EFC). 25% of all full-time freshmen had no need and received non-need-based gift aid.

UNDERGRADUATE FINANCIAL AID (Fall 2012, est.) 238 applied for aid; of those 89% were deemed to have need. 100% of undergraduates with need received aid; of those 100% had need fully met. *Average percent of need met:* 90% (excluding resources awarded to replace EFC). *Average financial aid package:* $15,535 (excluding resources awarded to replace EFC). 23% of all full-time undergraduates had no need and received non-need-based gift aid.

GIFT AID (NEED-BASED) *Total amount:* $1,857,090 (100% institutional). *Receiving aid:* Freshmen: 56% (58); all full-time undergraduates: 54% (206). *Average award:* Freshmen: $6270; Undergraduates: $7545. *Scholarships, grants, and awards:* private, college/university gift aid from institutional funds.

GIFT AID (NON-NEED-BASED) *Total amount:* $663,430 (93% institutional, 7% external sources). *Receiving aid:* Freshmen: 19% (20). Undergraduates: 16% (61). *Average award:* Freshmen: $7290. Undergraduates: $7175. *Scholarships, grants, and awards by category:* Academic interests/achievement: 147 awards ($919,980 total): general academic interests/achievements. *Tuition waivers:* Full or partial for employees or children of employees.

LOANS *Student loans:* $1,923,918 (68% need-based, 32% non-need-based). 60% of past graduating class borrowed through all loan programs. *Average indebtedness per student:* $25,875. *Average need-based loan:* Freshmen: $6540. Undergraduates: $6550. *Programs:* college/university.

WORK-STUDY *State or other work-study/employment:* Total amount: $287,100 (100% need-based). 145 part-time jobs averaging $1980.

APPLYING FOR FINANCIAL AID *Required financial aid form:* institution's own form. *Financial aid deadline (priority):* 4/1. *Notification date:* Continuous beginning 3/1. Students must reply within 4 weeks of notification.

CONTACT Ms. Alisa Polk, Financial Aid Officer, Christendom College, 134 Christendom Drive, Front Royal, VA 22630-5103, 800-877-5456 Ext. 1214 or toll-free 800-877-5456. *Fax:* 540-636-1655. *E-mail:* apolk@christendom.edu.
Website: http://www.christendom.edu/.

CHRISTIAN BROTHERS UNIVERSITY
Memphis, TN

Tuition & fees: $27,284	Average undergraduate aid package: $20,450

ABOUT THE INSTITUTION Independent Roman Catholic, coed. **Awards:** certificates, bachelor's, and master's degrees. 37 undergraduate majors. **Total enrollment:** 1,598. Undergraduates: 1,237. Freshmen: 255. Federal methodology is used as a basis for awarding need-based institutional aid.

UNDERGRADUATE EXPENSES for 2013–2014 Application fee: $25. **Comprehensive fee:** $33,424 includes full-time tuition ($26,694), mandatory fees ($590), and room and board ($6140). Full-time tuition and fees vary according to class time and program. Room and board charges vary according to board plan and housing facility. **Part-time tuition:** $936 per credit hour. **Part-time fees:** $115 per term. Part-time tuition and fees vary according to class time, course load, and program.

FRESHMAN FINANCIAL AID (Fall 2011) 306 applied for aid; of those 85% were deemed to have need. 100% of freshmen with need received aid; of those 20% had need fully met. **Average percent of need met:** 79% (excluding resources awarded to replace EFC). **Average financial aid package:** $23,331 (excluding resources awarded to replace EFC). 25% of all full-time freshmen had no need and received non-need-based gift aid.

UNDERGRADUATE FINANCIAL AID (Fall 2011) 1,185 applied for aid; of those 81% were deemed to have need. 100% of undergraduates with need received aid; of those 21% had need fully met. **Average percent of need met:** 75% (excluding resources awarded to replace EFC). **Average financial aid package:** $20,450 (excluding resources awarded to replace EFC). 29% of all full-time undergraduates had no need and received non-need-based gift aid.

GIFT AID (NEED-BASED) Total amount: $15,611,660 (19% federal, 19% state, 60% institutional, 2% external sources). **Receiving aid:** Freshmen: 84% (257); all full-time undergraduates: 79% (943). **Average award:** Freshmen: $18,338; Undergraduates: $15,206. **Scholarships, grants, and awards:** Federal Pell, FSEOG, state, private, college/university gift aid from institutional funds.

GIFT AID (NON-NEED-BASED) Total amount: $4,158,117 (10% state, 78% institutional, 12% external sources). **Receiving aid:** Freshmen: 41% (127). Undergraduates: 42% (500). **Average award:** Freshmen: $6876. Undergraduates: $6781. **Scholarships, grants, and awards by category:** Academic interests/achievement: engineering/technologies, general academic interests/achievements, health fields. Creative arts/performance: general creative arts/performance, performing arts. Special achievements/activities: general special achievements/activities, leadership. Special characteristics: children and siblings of alumni, general special characteristics, religious affiliation, veterans, veterans' children. **ROTC:** Army cooperative, Naval cooperative, Air Force cooperative.

LOANS Student loans: $7,030,663 (81% need-based, 19% non-need-based). 64% of past graduating class borrowed through all loan programs. Average indebtedness per student: $22,696. **Average need-based loan:** Freshmen: $3459. Undergraduates: $4492. **Parent loans:** $978,084 (46% need-based, 54% non-need-based). **Programs:** Federal Direct (Subsidized and Unsubsidized Stafford, PLUS), Perkins, college/university, alternative loans.

WORK-STUDY Federal work-study: Total amount: $108,021; 171 jobs averaging $632. **State or other work-study/employment:** Total amount: $117,135 (44% need-based, 56% non-need-based). 159 part-time jobs averaging $737.

ATHLETIC AWARDS Total amount: $1,380,761 (34% need-based, 66% non-need-based).

APPLYING FOR FINANCIAL AID Required financial aid form: FAFSA. **Financial aid deadline (priority):** 2/15. **Notification date:** Continuous beginning 2/28. Students must reply by 5/1 or within 2 weeks of notification.

CONTACT Ms. Cynthia Stanley, Acting Director of Student Financial Assistance, Christian Brothers University, 650 East Parkway South, Memphis, TN 38104, 901-321-3305 or toll-free 877-321-4CBU. Fax: 901-321-3327. E-mail: cynthia.stanley@cbu.edu. Website: http://www.cbu.edu/.

CHRISTIAN LIFE COLLEGE
Mount Prospect, IL

CONTACT Jeanna Wilson, Office of Financial Aid, Christian Life College, 400 East Gregory Street, Mt. Prospect, IL 60056, 847-259-1840. Fax: 847-259-3888. Website: http://www.christianlifecollege.edu/.

CHRISTOPHER NEWPORT UNIVERSITY
Newport News, VA

Tuition & fees (VA res): $10,572	Average undergraduate aid package: $8064

ABOUT THE INSTITUTION State-supported, coed. **Awards:** bachelor's and master's degrees. 36 undergraduate majors. **Total enrollment:** 5,186. Undergraduates: 5,046. Freshmen: 1,376. Federal methodology is used as a basis for awarding need-based institutional aid.

UNDERGRADUATE EXPENSES for 2013–2014 Application fee: $50. **Tuition, state resident:** full-time $6210; part-time $258 per credit hour. **Tuition, nonresident:** full-time $15,364; part-time $641 per credit hour. **Required fees:** full-time $4362; $181 per credit hour. Full-time tuition and fees vary according to course load. Part-time tuition and fees vary according to course load. **College room and board:** $9728; **Room only:** $6358. Room and board charges vary according to board plan and housing facility.

FRESHMAN FINANCIAL AID (Fall 2012, est.) 1,167 applied for aid; of those 56% were deemed to have need. 98% of freshmen with need received aid; of those 15% had need fully met. **Average percent of need met:** 68% (excluding resources awarded to replace EFC). **Average financial aid package:** $8012 (excluding resources awarded to replace EFC). 18% of all full-time freshmen had no need and received non-need-based gift aid.

UNDERGRADUATE FINANCIAL AID (Fall 2012, est.) 3,877 applied for aid; of those 57% were deemed to have need. 99% of undergraduates with need received aid; of those 16% had need fully met. **Average percent of need met:** 67% (excluding resources awarded to replace EFC). **Average financial aid package:** $8064 (excluding resources awarded to replace EFC). 13% of all full-time undergraduates had no need and received non-need-based gift aid.

GIFT AID (NEED-BASED) Total amount: $8,545,252 (41% federal, 51% state, 8% institutional). **Receiving aid:** Freshmen: 33% (455); all full-time undergraduates: 30% (1,501). **Average award:** Freshmen: $5742; Undergraduates: $5418. **Scholarships, grants, and awards:** Federal Pell, FSEOG, state, private, college/university gift aid from institutional funds.

GIFT AID (NON-NEED-BASED) Total amount: $2,967,830 (69% institutional, 31% external sources). **Receiving aid:** Freshmen: 23% (315). Undergraduates: 14% (707). **Average award:** Freshmen: $1592. Undergraduates: $1698. **Scholarships, grants, and awards by category:** Academic interests/achievement: biological sciences, business, communication, computer science, education, engineering/technologies, English, foreign languages, general academic interests/achievements, humanities, mathematics, military science, religion/biblical studies. Creative arts/performance: art/fine arts, music, theater/drama. Special achievements/activities: general special achievements/activities, leadership. Special characteristics: local/state students. **Tuition waivers:** Full or partial for employees or children of employees, senior citizens. **ROTC:** Army.

LOANS Student loans: $24,146,119 (34% need-based, 66% non-need-based). 51% of past graduating class borrowed through all loan programs. Average indebtedness per student: $24,400. **Average need-based loan:** Freshmen: $3189. Undergraduates: $4070. **Parent loans:** $6,095,690 (100% non-need-based). **Programs:** Federal Direct (Subsidized and Unsubsidized Stafford, PLUS).

WORK-STUDY Federal work-study: Total amount: $113,500; 96 jobs averaging $1045. **State or other work-study/employment:** 1,762 part-time jobs averaging $1177.

APPLYING FOR FINANCIAL AID Required financial aid form: FAFSA. **Financial aid deadline (priority):** 3/1. **Notification date:** Continuous beginning 3/1. Students must reply within 3 weeks of notification.

CONTACT Clara Johnson, Director of Financial Aid, Christopher Newport University, 1 Avenue of the Arts, Newport News, VA 23606, 757-594-7170 or toll-free 800-333-4268. *Fax:* 757-594-7113. *E-mail:* clara.johnson@cnu.edu. *Website:* http://www.cnu.edu/.

CINCINNATI CHRISTIAN UNIVERSITY
Cincinnati, OH

Tuition & fees: $15,266	Average undergraduate aid package: $11,279

ABOUT THE INSTITUTION Independent Church of Christ, coed. *Awards:* associate, bachelor's, and master's degrees. 12 undergraduate majors. *Total enrollment:* 923, Undergraduates: 677. Federal methodology is used as a basis for awarding need-based institutional aid.

UNDERGRADUATE EXPENSES for 2013–2014 *Application fee:* $40. *Comprehensive fee:* $21,938 includes full-time tuition ($14,766), mandatory fees ($500), and room and board ($6672). *College room only:* $2820. Full-time tuition and fees vary according to course load and student level. Room and board charges vary according to board plan, housing facility, and student level. *Part-time tuition:* $600 per credit. *Part-time fees:* $500 per year. Part-time tuition and fees vary according to course load and student level.

UNDERGRADUATE FINANCIAL AID (Fall 2011) 555 applied for aid; of those 93% were deemed to have need. 100% of undergraduates with need received aid; of those 8% had need fully met. *Average percent of need met:* 50% (excluding resources awarded to replace EFC). *Average financial aid package:* $11,279 (excluding resources awarded to replace EFC). 9% of all full-time undergraduates had no need and received non-need-based gift aid.

GIFT AID (NEED-BASED) *Total amount:* $3,589,330 (37% federal, 8% state, 47% institutional, 8% external sources). *Receiving aid:* Entering class: 80% (97); all full-time undergraduates: 77% (470). *Average award:* Freshmen: $9270; Undergraduates: $7893. *Scholarships, grants, and awards:* Federal Pell, FSEOG, state, private, college/university gift aid from institutional funds.

GIFT AID (NON-NEED-BASED) *Total amount:* $507,162 (74% institutional, 26% external sources). *Receiving aid:* Freshmen: 7% (9). Undergraduates: 5% (29). *Average award:* Freshmen: $6098. Undergraduates: $5145. *Scholarships, grants, and awards by category: Academic interests/achievement:* education, general academic interests/achievements, religion/biblical studies. *Creative arts/performance:* music. *Special achievements/activities:* general special achievements/activities, leadership, religious involvement. *Special characteristics:* children of faculty/staff, international students, married students, members of minority groups, parents of current students, siblings of current students. *Tuition waivers:* Full or partial for employees or children of employees.

LOANS *Student loans:* $4,699,143 (84% need-based, 16% non-need-based). 75% of past graduating class borrowed through all loan programs. *Average indebtedness per student:* $32,280. *Average need-based loan:* Freshmen: $2897. Undergraduates: $3916. *Parent loans:* $911,647 (54% need-based, 46% non-need-based). *Programs:* Federal Direct (Subsidized and Unsubsidized Stafford, PLUS), college/university, private loans.

WORK-STUDY *Federal work-study:* Total amount: $226,013; 235 jobs averaging $1555.

ATHLETIC AWARDS Total amount: $362,227 (78% need-based, 22% non-need-based).

APPLYING FOR FINANCIAL AID *Required financial aid form:* FAFSA. *Financial aid deadline (priority):* 3/1. *Notification date:* Continuous beginning 4/1. Students must reply by 8/1.

CONTACT Marcella Farmer, Associate Director of Financial Aid, Cincinnati Christian University, 2700 Glenway Avenue, Cincinnati, OH 45204-1799, 513-244-8130 or toll-free 800-949-4228 (in-state), 800-949-4CCU (out-of-state). *Fax:* 513-244-8453. *E-mail:* financialaid@ccuniversity.edu. *Website:* http://www.ccuniversity.edu/.

CINCINNATI COLLEGE OF MORTUARY SCIENCE
Cincinnati, OH

CONTACT Ms. Pat Leon, Financial Aid Officer, Cincinnati College of Mortuary Science, 645 West North Bend Road, Cincinnati, OH 45224-1428, 513-761-2020 or toll-free 888-377-8433. *Website:* http://www.ccms.edu/.

THE CITADEL, THE MILITARY COLLEGE OF SOUTH CAROLINA
Charleston, SC

Tuition & fees (SC res): $11,772	Average undergraduate aid package: $14,436

ABOUT THE INSTITUTION State-supported, coed, primarily men. *Awards:* certificates, bachelor's, and master's degrees. 17 undergraduate majors. *Total enrollment:* 3,499. Undergraduates: 2,629. Freshmen: 676. Federal methodology is used as a basis for awarding need-based institutional aid.

UNDERGRADUATE EXPENSES for 2013–2014 *Application fee:* $40. *Tuition, state resident:* full-time $10,523; part-time $410 per credit. *Tuition, nonresident:* full-time $28,776; part-time $743 per credit. *Required fees:* full-time $1249. *College room and board:* $6115.

FRESHMAN FINANCIAL AID (Fall 2012, est.) 574 applied for aid; of those 74% were deemed to have need. 97% of freshmen with need received aid; of those 21% had need fully met. *Average percent of need met:* 54% (excluding resources awarded to replace EFC). *Average financial aid package:* $12,803 (excluding resources awarded to replace EFC). 19% of all full-time freshmen had no need and received non-need-based gift aid.

UNDERGRADUATE FINANCIAL AID (Fall 2012, est.) 1,792 applied for aid; of those 79% were deemed to have need. 97% of undergraduates with need received aid; of those 25% had need fully met. *Average percent of need met:* 62% (excluding resources awarded to replace EFC). *Average financial aid package:* $14,436 (excluding resources awarded to replace EFC). 19% of all full-time undergraduates had no need and received non-need-based gift aid.

GIFT AID (NEED-BASED) *Total amount:* $12,624,519 (22% federal, 15% state, 28% institutional, 35% external sources). *Receiving aid:* Freshmen: 47% (318); all full-time undergraduates: 44% (1,074). *Average award:* Freshmen: $13,268; Undergraduates: $14,157. *Scholarships, grants, and awards:* Federal Pell, FSEOG, state, private, college/university gift aid from institutional funds.

GIFT AID (NON-NEED-BASED) *Total amount:* $6,355,681 (21% state, 37% institutional, 42% external sources). *Receiving aid:* Freshmen: 8% (57). Undergraduates: 9% (219). *Average award:* Freshmen: $8844. Undergraduates: $13,984. *Scholarships, grants, and awards by category: Academic interests/achievement:* biological sciences, business, engineering/technologies, general academic interests/achievements, humanities, military science, religion/biblical studies. *Creative arts/performance:* journalism/publications, music. *Special achievements/activities:* community service, leadership, religious involvement. *Special characteristics:* children and siblings of alumni, children with a deceased or disabled parent, local/state students, out-of-state students. *Tuition waivers:* Full or partial for employees or children of employees, senior citizens. *ROTC:* Army, Naval, Air Force.

LOANS *Student loans:* $9,226,802 (85% need-based, 15% non-need-based). 52% of past graduating class borrowed through all loan programs. *Average indebtedness per student:* $31,217. *Average need-based loan:* Freshmen: $3372. Undergraduates: $4322. *Parent loans:* $12,061,356 (81% need-based, 19% non-need-based). *Programs:* Federal Direct (Subsidized and Unsubsidized Stafford, PLUS), Perkins, state.

WORK-STUDY *Federal work-study:* Total amount: $120,843; 83 jobs averaging $1500.

ATHLETIC AWARDS Total amount: $5,061,829 (48% need-based, 52% non-need-based).

APPLYING FOR FINANCIAL AID *Required financial aid form:* FAFSA. *Financial aid deadline (priority):* 2/28. *Notification date:* 3/15. Students must reply within 2 weeks of notification.

CONTACT Lt. Col. Hank M. Fuller, Director of Financial Aid and Scholarships, The Citadel, The Military College of South Carolina, 171 Moultrie Street, Charleston, SC 29409, 843-953-5187 or toll-free 800-868-1842. *Fax:* 843-953-6759. *E-mail:* hank.fuller@citadel.edu.
Website: http://www.citadel.edu/.

CITY COLLEGE OF THE CITY UNIVERSITY OF NEW YORK
New York, NY

Tuition & fees (NY res): $5131	Average undergraduate aid package: $8978

ABOUT THE INSTITUTION State and locally supported, coed. *Awards:* certificates, bachelor's, master's, and doctoral degrees. 67 undergraduate majors. *Total enrollment:* 16,161. Undergraduates: 13,113. Freshmen: 1,397. Federal methodology is used as a basis for awarding need-based institutional aid.
UNDERGRADUATE EXPENSES for 2013–2014 Application fee: $65. *Tuition, state resident:* full-time $5131. *Tuition, nonresident:* full-time $13,800. Full-time tuition and fees vary according to course load and program. Part-time tuition and fees vary according to course load and program. Room and board charges vary according to housing facility.
FRESHMAN FINANCIAL AID (Fall 2011) 1,218 applied for aid; of those 90% were deemed to have need. 94% of freshmen with need received aid; of those 66% had need fully met. *Average percent of need met:* 83% (excluding resources awarded to replace EFC). *Average financial aid package:* $8646 (excluding resources awarded to replace EFC). 14% of all full-time freshmen had no need and received non-need-based gift aid.
UNDERGRADUATE FINANCIAL AID (Fall 2011) 8,872 applied for aid; of those 98% were deemed to have need. 97% of undergraduates with need received aid; of those 82% had need fully met. *Average percent of need met:* 82% (excluding resources awarded to replace EFC). *Average financial aid package:* $8978 (excluding resources awarded to replace EFC). 8% of all full-time undergraduates had no need and received non-need-based gift aid.
GIFT AID (NEED-BASED) Total amount: $52,079,000 (58% federal, 35% state, 6% institutional, 1% external sources). *Receiving aid:* Freshmen: 72% (1,001); all full-time undergraduates: 87% (8,220). *Average award:* Freshmen: $7942; Undergraduates: $7801. *Scholarships, grants, and awards:* Federal Pell, FSEOG, state, private, college/university gift aid from institutional funds.
GIFT AID (NON-NEED-BASED) Total amount: $3,956,000 (9% state, 72% institutional, 19% external sources). *Receiving aid:* Freshmen: 42% (589). Undergraduates: 10% (982). *Average award:* Freshmen: $2900. Undergraduates: $4085. *Scholarships, grants, and awards by category: Academic interests/achievement:* architecture, area/ethnic studies, biological sciences, communication, computer science, education, engineering/technologies, English, foreign languages, general academic interests/achievements, humanities, international studies, mathematics, premedicine, social sciences. *Creative arts/performance:* applied art and design, art/fine arts, cinema/film/broadcasting, creative writing, general creative arts/performance, music, performing arts. *Special achievements/activities:* community service, general special achievements/activities, leadership. *Special characteristics:* children and siblings of alumni, local/state students. *Tuition waivers:* Full or partial for senior citizens. **ROTC:** Army.
LOANS Student loans: $27,207,000 (95% need-based, 5% non-need-based). 22% of past graduating class borrowed through all loan programs. *Average indebtedness per student:* $16,944. *Average need-based loan:* Freshmen: $2002. Undergraduates: $4115. *Parent loans:* $931,080 (22% need-based, 78% non-need-based). *Programs:* Federal Direct (Subsidized and Unsubsidized Stafford, PLUS), Perkins.
WORK-STUDY Federal work-study: Total amount: $4,732,000; jobs available. *State or other work-study/employment:* Part-time jobs available.
APPLYING FOR FINANCIAL AID Required financial aid forms: FAFSA, state aid form. *Financial aid deadline (priority):* 3/15. *Notification date:* Continuous beginning 4/1.
CONTACT Thelma Mason, Director of Financial Aid, City College of the City University of New York, 160 Convent Avenue, Wille Administration Building, Room 104, New York, NY 10031, 212-650-5816. *Fax:* 212-650-5829. *E-mail:* tmason@ccny.cuny.edu.
Website: http://www.ccny.cuny.edu/.

CITY UNIVERSITY OF SEATTLE
Bellevue, WA

CONTACT Ms. Jean L. Roberts, Director of Student Financial Services, City University of Seattle, 11900 Northeast 1st Street, Bellevue, WA 98005, 425-709-5251 or toll-free 888-42-CITYU. *Fax:* 425-709-5263. *E-mail:* jroberts@cityu.edu.
Website: http://www.cityu.edu/.

CITY VISION COLLEGE
Kansas City, MO

Tuition & fees: $6000	Average undergraduate aid package: $2770

ABOUT THE INSTITUTION Independent Christian, coed. *Awards:* certificates and bachelor's degrees. 3 undergraduate majors. *Total enrollment:* 63. Undergraduates: 63. Entering class: 29. Both federal and institutional methodology are used as a basis for awarding need-based institutional aid.
UNDERGRADUATE EXPENSES for 2013–2014 Application fee: $25. *One-time required fee:* $25. *Tuition:* full-time $6000; part-time $3000 per year. Full-time tuition and fees vary according to course load. Part-time tuition and fees vary according to course load.
UNDERGRADUATE FINANCIAL AID (Fall 2011) 22 applied for aid; of those 100% were deemed to have need. 100% of undergraduates with need received aid. *Average percent of need met:* 100% (excluding resources awarded to replace EFC). *Average financial aid package:* $2770 (excluding resources awarded to replace EFC).
GIFT AID (NEED-BASED) Total amount: $64,568 (100% federal). *Receiving aid:* Entering class: 100% (1); all full-time undergraduates: 32% (22). *Average award:* Freshmen: $2220; Undergraduates: $2770. *Scholarships, grants, and awards:* Federal Pell.
GIFT AID (NON-NEED-BASED) Total amount: $550 (100% institutional). *Receiving aid:* Undergraduates: 1% (1). *Tuition waivers:* Full or partial for employees or children of employees.
LOANS Programs: Federal Direct (Subsidized and Unsubsidized Stafford), private loans.
APPLYING FOR FINANCIAL AID Required financial aid forms: FAFSA, institution's own form, CSS Financial Aid PROFILE. *Financial aid deadline:* Continuous. *Notification date:* Continuous.
CONTACT Miss Rachael A. Jarboe, Financial Aid and Technical Support Administrator, City Vision College, 31 Torrey Street, Dorchester, MA 02124, 816-960-2008 Ext. 2. *Fax:* 617-825-0213. *E-mail:* rjarboe@cityvision.edu.
Website: http://www.cityvision.edu/.

CLAFLIN UNIVERSITY
Orangeburg, SC

CONTACT Ms. Yolanda Frazier, Interim Director of Financial Aid, Claflin University, Tingly Hall, Suite 12, 400 Magnolia Street, Orangeburg, SC 29115, 803-535-5720 or toll-free 800-922-1276. *Fax:* 803-535-5383. *E-mail:* yfrazier@claflin.edu.
Website: http://www.claflin.edu/.

CLAREMONT MCKENNA COLLEGE
Claremont, CA

Tuition & fees: $44,085	Average undergraduate aid package: $39,332

ABOUT THE INSTITUTION Independent, coed. *Awards:* bachelor's and master's degrees. 32 undergraduate majors. *Total enrollment:* 1,295. Undergraduates: 1,264. Freshmen: 291. Both federal and institutional methodology are used as a basis for awarding need-based institutional aid.

UNDERGRADUATE EXPENSES for 2013–2014 *Application fee:* $60. *Comprehensive fee:* $58,065 includes full-time tuition ($43,840), mandatory fees ($245), and room and board ($13,980). *College room only:* $7380. Full-time tuition and fees vary according to course load. Room and board charges vary according to board plan and housing facility. *Part-time tuition:* $7306.67 per course. Part-time tuition and fees vary according to course load.
FRESHMAN FINANCIAL AID (Fall 2012, est.) 158 applied for aid; of those 84% were deemed to have need. 100% of freshmen with need received aid; of those 100% had need fully met. *Average percent of need met:* 100% (excluding resources awarded to replace EFC). *Average financial aid package:* $39,953 (excluding resources awarded to replace EFC). 4% of all full-time freshmen had no need and received non-need-based gift aid.
UNDERGRADUATE FINANCIAL AID (Fall 2012, est.) 575 applied for aid; of those 90% were deemed to have need. 100% of undergraduates with need received aid; of those 100% had need fully met. *Average percent of need met:* 100% (excluding resources awarded to replace EFC). *Average financial aid package:* $39,332 (excluding resources awarded to replace EFC). 6% of all full-time undergraduates had no need and received non-need-based gift aid.
GIFT AID (NEED-BASED) *Total amount:* $19,599,027 (4% federal, 4% state, 90% institutional, 2% external sources). *Receiving aid:* Freshmen: 46% (133); all full-time undergraduates: 41% (518). *Average award:* Freshmen: $38,393; Undergraduates: $37,778. *Scholarships, grants, and awards:* Federal Pell, FSEOG, state, private, college/university gift aid from institutional funds.
GIFT AID (NON-NEED-BASED) *Total amount:* $2,164,783 (53% institutional, 47% external sources). *Receiving aid:* Freshmen: 5% (14). Undergraduates: 4% (48). *Average award:* Freshmen: $20,395. Undergraduates: $16,256. *Scholarships, grants, and awards by category: Academic interests/achievement:* general academic interests/achievements, military science. *Special achievements/activities:* leadership. *Tuition waivers:* Full or partial for employees or children of employees. *ROTC:* Army, Air Force cooperative.
LOANS *Student loans:* $2,123,244 (100% non-need-based). 31% of past graduating class borrowed through all loan programs. *Average indebtedness per student:* $23,179. *Parent loans:* $1,030,129 (100% non-need-based). *Programs:* Federal Direct (Subsidized and Unsubsidized Stafford, PLUS), Perkins, college/university.
WORK-STUDY *Federal work-study:* Total amount: $660,430; jobs available. *State or other work-study/employment:* Total amount: $137,491 (100% need-based). Part-time jobs available.
APPLYING FOR FINANCIAL AID *Required financial aid forms:* FAFSA, CSS Financial Aid PROFILE, state aid form, noncustodial (divorced/separated) parent's statement, business/farm supplement. *Financial aid deadline:* 2/1 (priority: 2/1). *Notification date:* 4/1. Students must reply by 5/1.
CONTACT Ms. Georgette R. DeVeres, Associate Vice President of Admission and Dean of Admission and Financial Aid, Claremont McKenna College, Kravis Center, 888 Columbia Avenue, Claremont, CA 91711, 909-621-8356. *Fax:* 909-607-0661. *E-mail:* gdeveres@cmc.edu.
Website: http://www.claremontmckenna.edu/.

CLARION UNIVERSITY OF PENNSYLVANIA
Clarion, PA

Tuition & fees (PA res): $9141	Average undergraduate aid package: $8044

ABOUT THE INSTITUTION State-supported, coed. *Awards:* certificates, associate, bachelor's, and master's degrees. 51 undergraduate majors. *Total enrollment:* 6,520. Undergraduates: 5,518. Freshmen: 1,132. Federal methodology is used as a basis for awarding need-based institutional aid.
UNDERGRADUATE EXPENSES for 2013–2014 *Application fee:* $30. *Tuition, state resident:* full-time $9141. *Tuition, nonresident:* full-time $12,861. Full-time tuition and fees vary according to course level and course load. Part-time tuition and fees vary according to course level and course load. *College room and board:* $7186. Room and board charges vary according to board plan, housing facility, and location.
FRESHMAN FINANCIAL AID (Fall 2011) 1,145 applied for aid; of those 86% were deemed to have need. 98% of freshmen with need received aid; of those 4% had need fully met. *Average percent of need met:* 53% (excluding resources awarded to replace EFC). *Average financial aid package:* $7680 (excluding resources

awarded to replace EFC). 4% of all full-time freshmen had no need and received non-need-based gift aid.
UNDERGRADUATE FINANCIAL AID (Fall 2011) 4,566 applied for aid; of those 88% were deemed to have need. 98% of undergraduates with need received aid; of those 6% had need fully met. *Average percent of need met:* 55% (excluding resources awarded to replace EFC). *Average financial aid package:* $8044 (excluding resources awarded to replace EFC). 3% of all full-time undergraduates had no need and received non-need-based gift aid.
GIFT AID (NEED-BASED) *Total amount:* $17,310,146 (53% federal, 41% state, 6% institutional). *Receiving aid:* Freshmen: 65% (780); all full-time undergraduates: 60% (2,991). *Average award:* Freshmen: $5712; Undergraduates: $5459. *Scholarships, grants, and awards:* Federal Pell, FSEOG, state, private, college/university gift aid from institutional funds, United Negro College Fund.
GIFT AID (NON-NEED-BASED) *Total amount:* $1,021,549 (2% state, 98% external sources). *Receiving aid:* Freshmen: 25% (304). Undergraduates: 19% (948). *Average award:* Freshmen: $1701. Undergraduates: $1936. *Scholarships, grants, and awards by category: Academic interests/achievement:* general academic interests/achievements. *Creative arts/performance:* art/fine arts, general creative arts/performance. *Special achievements/activities:* leadership. *Special characteristics:* children and siblings of alumni, local/state students, members of minority groups. *Tuition waivers:* Full or partial for employees or children of employees, senior citizens. *ROTC:* Army cooperative.
LOANS *Student loans:* $33,218,848 (44% need-based, 56% non-need-based). 81% of past graduating class borrowed through all loan programs. *Average indebtedness per student:* $29,410. *Average need-based loan:* Freshmen: $3195. Undergraduates: $3994. *Parent loans:* $6,776,014 (100% non-need-based). *Programs:* Federal Direct (Subsidized and Unsubsidized Stafford, PLUS), Perkins, private loans.
WORK-STUDY *Federal work-study:* Total amount: $234,949; jobs available. *State or other work-study/employment:* Total amount: $1,147,103 (100% non-need-based). Part-time jobs available.
ATHLETIC AWARDS Total amount: $587,990 (100% non-need-based).
APPLYING FOR FINANCIAL AID *Required financial aid forms:* FAFSA, state aid form. *Financial aid deadline (priority):* 5/1. *Notification date:* Continuous beginning 3/30.
CONTACT Director of Financial Aid, Clarion University of Pennsylvania, 104 Egbert Hall, Clarion, PA 16214, 814-393-2315 or toll-free 800-672-7171. *Fax:* 814-393-2520. *E-mail:* aidoffice@clarion.edu.
Website: http://www.clarion.edu/.

CLARK ATLANTA UNIVERSITY
Atlanta, GA

CONTACT Office of Financial Aid, Clark Atlanta University, 223 James P. Brawley Drive, Atlanta, GA 30314, 404-880-8992 or toll-free 800-688-3228. *Fax:* 404-880-8070. *E-mail:* studentfinancialaid@cau.edu.
Website: http://www.cau.edu/.

CLARKE UNIVERSITY
Dubuque, IA

Tuition & fees: $28,000	Average undergraduate aid package: $21,509

ABOUT THE INSTITUTION Independent Roman Catholic, coed. *Awards:* associate, bachelor's, master's, and doctoral degrees. 30 undergraduate majors. *Total enrollment:* 1,191. Undergraduates: 967. Freshmen: 155. Federal methodology is used as a basis for awarding need-based institutional aid.
UNDERGRADUATE EXPENSES for 2013–2014 *Application fee:* $25. *Comprehensive fee:* $36,400 includes full-time tuition ($27,100), mandatory fees ($900), and room and board ($8400). *College room only:* $4100. Room and board charges vary according to housing facility. *Part-time tuition:* $690 per credit.
FRESHMAN FINANCIAL AID (Fall 2012, est.) 152 applied for aid; of those 90% were deemed to have need. 100% of freshmen with need received aid; of those 26% had need fully met. *Average percent of need met:* 74% (excluding resources awarded to replace EFC). *Average financial aid package:* $23,314 (excluding

resources awarded to replace EFC). 12% of all full-time freshmen had no need and received non-need-based gift aid.

UNDERGRADUATE FINANCIAL AID (Fall 2012, est.) 749 applied for aid; of those 94% were deemed to have need. 100% of undergraduates with need received aid; of those 19% had need fully met. *Average percent of need met:* 68% (excluding resources awarded to replace EFC). *Average financial aid package:* $21,509 (excluding resources awarded to replace EFC). 11% of all full-time undergraduates had no need and received non-need-based gift aid.

GIFT AID (NEED-BASED) *Total amount:* $9,243,661 (18% federal, 14% state, 67% institutional, 1% external sources). *Receiving aid:* Freshmen: 87% (137); all full-time undergraduates: 87% (694). *Average award:* Freshmen: $19,704; Undergraduates: $17,141. *Scholarships, grants, and awards:* Federal Pell, FSEOG, state, private, college/university gift aid from institutional funds.

GIFT AID (NON-NEED-BASED) *Total amount:* $621,589 (98% institutional, 2% external sources). *Receiving aid:* Freshmen: 85% (134). Undergraduates: 80% (639). *Average award:* Freshmen: $15,089. Undergraduates: $15,913. *Scholarships, grants, and awards by category: Academic interests/achievement:* 701 awards ($4,104,520 total): computer science, foreign languages, general academic interests/achievements. *Creative arts/performance:* 57 awards ($168,875 total): art/fine arts, music, theater/drama. *Special achievements/activities:* 109 awards ($136,225 total): community service, leadership. *Special characteristics:* 211 awards ($593,285 total): children and siblings of alumni, children of faculty/staff, local/state students, relatives of clergy, religious affiliation, siblings of current students, spouses of current students. *Tuition waivers:* Full or partial for children of alumni, employees or children of employees, adult students, senior citizens. *ROTC:* Army cooperative.

LOANS *Student loans:* $8,987,222 (36% need-based, 64% non-need-based). 89% of past graduating class borrowed through all loan programs. *Average indebtedness per student:* $26,865. *Average need-based loan:* Freshmen: $3279. Undergraduates: $4494. *Parent loans:* $1,193,383 (89% need-based, 11% non-need-based). *Programs:* Federal Direct (Subsidized and Unsubsidized Stafford, PLUS), Perkins, Federal Nursing, college/university, private loans.

WORK-STUDY *Federal work-study:* Total amount: $423,900; 311 jobs averaging $1316.

ATHLETIC AWARDS Total amount: $1,694,791 (100% non-need-based).

APPLYING FOR FINANCIAL AID *Financial aid deadline (priority):* 4/15. *Notification date:* Continuous beginning 3/1. Students must reply by 5/1 or within 2 weeks of notification.

CONTACT Amy Norton, Director of Financial Aid, Clarke University, 1550 Clarke Drive, Dubuque, IA 52001-3198, 563-588-6327 or toll-free 800-383-2345. *Fax:* 563-584-8605. *E-mail:* amy.norton@clarke.edu. *Website:* http://www.clarke.edu/.

CLARKSON COLLEGE
Omaha, NE

CONTACT Pam Shelton, Director of Financial Aid, Clarkson College, 101 South 42nd Street, Omaha, NE 68131-2739, 402-552-2749 or toll-free 800-647-5500. *Fax:* 402-552-6165. *E-mail:* shelton@clarksoncollege.edu. *Website:* http://www.clarksoncollege.edu/.

CLARKSON UNIVERSITY
Potsdam, NY

Tuition & fees: $40,610	Average undergraduate aid package: $36,967

ABOUT THE INSTITUTION Independent, coed. *Awards:* bachelor's, master's, and doctoral degrees. 35 undergraduate majors. *Total enrollment:* 3,604. Undergraduates: 3,072. Freshmen: 778. Federal methodology is used as a basis for awarding need-based institutional aid.

UNDERGRADUATE EXPENSES for 2013–2014 *Application fee:* $50. *Comprehensive fee:* $53,608 includes full-time tuition ($39,770), mandatory fees ($840), and room and board ($12,998). *College room only:* $6886. Full-time tuition and fees vary according to course load. Room and board charges vary according to board

---

plan and housing facility. *Part-time tuition:* $1324 per credit. Part-time tuition and fees vary according to course load. *Payment plan:* Tuition prepayment.

FRESHMAN FINANCIAL AID (Fall 2012, est.) 722 applied for aid; of those 94% were deemed to have need. 100% of freshmen with need received aid; of those 15% had need fully met. *Average percent of need met:* 90% (excluding resources awarded to replace EFC). *Average financial aid package:* $39,187 (excluding resources awarded to replace EFC). 12% of all full-time freshmen had no need and received non-need-based gift aid.

UNDERGRADUATE FINANCIAL AID (Fall 2012, est.) 2,725 applied for aid; of those 95% were deemed to have need. 100% of undergraduates with need received aid; of those 17% had need fully met. *Average percent of need met:* 89% (excluding resources awarded to replace EFC). *Average financial aid package:* $36,967 (excluding resources awarded to replace EFC). 13% of all full-time undergraduates had no need and received non-need-based gift aid.

GIFT AID (NEED-BASED) *Total amount:* $68,770,899 (8% federal, 4% state, 87% institutional, 1% external sources). *Receiving aid:* Freshmen: 87% (676); all full-time undergraduates: 86% (2,573). *Average award:* Freshmen: $29,869; Undergraduates: $26,790. *Scholarships, grants, and awards:* Federal Pell, FSEOG, state, private, college/university gift aid from institutional funds, Higher Education Opportunity Program (HEOP).

GIFT AID (NON-NEED-BASED) *Total amount:* $8,474,113 (12% federal, 1% state, 84% institutional, 3% external sources). *Receiving aid:* Freshmen: 10% (74). Undergraduates: 8% (248). *Average award:* Freshmen: $18,807. Undergraduates: $15,548. *Scholarships, grants, and awards by category: Academic interests/achievement:* 2,297 awards ($22,666,998 total): biological sciences, business, communication, computer science, engineering/technologies, general academic interests/achievements, humanities, mathematics, military science, physical sciences, social sciences. *Special achievements/activities:* 891 awards ($6,332,750 total): general special achievements/activities, leadership. *Special characteristics:* 838 awards ($2,526,406 total): children and siblings of alumni, children of faculty/staff, general special characteristics, international students, local/state students, members of minority groups, veterans. *Tuition waivers:* Full or partial for employees or children of employees. *ROTC:* Army, Air Force.

LOANS *Student loans:* $22,870,627 (77% need-based, 23% non-need-based). 80% of past graduating class borrowed through all loan programs. *Average indebtedness per student:* $27,866. *Average need-based loan:* Freshmen: $3848. Undergraduates: $4685. *Parent loans:* $8,977,694 (51% need-based, 49% non-need-based). *Programs:* Federal Direct (Subsidized and Unsubsidized Stafford, PLUS), Perkins, college/university, private loans.

WORK-STUDY *Federal work-study:* Total amount: $471,624; 1,919 jobs averaging $1600. *State or other work-study/employment:* Total amount: $476,774 (66% need-based, 34% non-need-based). 71 part-time jobs averaging $9587.

ATHLETIC AWARDS Total amount: $1,719,942 (9% need-based, 91% non-need-based).

APPLYING FOR FINANCIAL AID *Required financial aid forms:* FAFSA, state aid form. *Financial aid deadline:* 3/1 (priority: 2/15). *Notification date:* Continuous beginning 3/18. Students must reply by 5/1 or within 2 weeks of notification.

CONTACT Mrs. Pamela A. Nichols, Director of Financial Aid, Clarkson University, 8 Clarkson Avenue, Box 5615, Potsdam, NY 13699, 315-268-6413 or toll-free 800-527-6577. *Fax:* 315-268-3899. *E-mail:* pnichols@clarkson.edu. *Website:* http://www.clarkson.edu/.

CLARK UNIVERSITY
Worcester, MA

Tuition & fees: $39,550	Average undergraduate aid package: $32,364

ABOUT THE INSTITUTION Independent, coed. *Awards:* certificates, bachelor's, master's, and doctoral degrees. 48 undergraduate majors. *Total enrollment:* 3,503. Undergraduates: 2,352. Freshmen: 594. Institutional methodology is used as a basis for awarding need-based institutional aid.

UNDERGRADUATE EXPENSES for 2013–2014 *Application fee:* $55. *Comprehensive fee:* $47,020 includes full-time tuition ($39,200), mandatory fees ($350), and room and board ($7470). *College room only:* $4170. Room and board charges vary according to board plan and housing facility. *Part-time tuition:* $1225 per credit hour. *Part-time fees:* $1225 per credit hour. *Payment plan:* Tuition prepayment.

FRESHMAN FINANCIAL AID (Fall 2012, est.) 424 applied for aid; of those 80% were deemed to have need. 99% of freshmen with need received aid; of those 68% had need fully met. *Average percent of need met:* 95% (excluding resources awarded to replace EFC). *Average financial aid package:* $32,364 (excluding resources awarded to replace EFC). 30% of all full-time freshmen had no need and received non-need-based gift aid.

UNDERGRADUATE FINANCIAL AID (Fall 2012, est.) 1,613 applied for aid; of those 80% were deemed to have need. 99% of undergraduates with need received aid; of those 68% had need fully met. *Average percent of need met:* 95% (excluding resources awarded to replace EFC). *Average financial aid package:* $32,364 (excluding resources awarded to replace EFC). 30% of all full-time undergraduates had no need and received non-need-based gift aid.

GIFT AID (NEED-BASED) *Total amount:* $27,885,814 (10% federal, 1% state, 87% institutional, 2% external sources). *Receiving aid:* Freshmen: 57% (335); all full-time undergraduates: 57% (1,274). *Average award:* Freshmen: $25,010; Undergraduates: $25,010. *Scholarships, grants, and awards:* Federal Pell, FSEOG, state, college/university gift aid from institutional funds.

GIFT AID (NON-NEED-BASED) *Total amount:* $10,798,871 (100% institutional). *Receiving aid:* Freshmen: 19% (113). Undergraduates: 19% (430). *Average award:* Freshmen: $15,601. Undergraduates: $15,601. *Scholarships, grants, and awards by category:* Academic interests/achievement: general academic interests/achievements. Special achievements/activities: community service, general special achievements/activities. *Tuition waivers:* Full or partial for employees or children of employees. *ROTC:* Army cooperative, Naval cooperative, Air Force cooperative.

LOANS *Student loans:* $10,448,931 (63% need-based, 37% non-need-based). 91% of past graduating class borrowed through all loan programs. *Average indebtedness per student:* $25,175. *Average need-based loan:* Freshmen: $3778. Undergraduates: $3778. *Parent loans:* $3,733,583 (9% need-based, 91% non-need-based). *Programs:* Federal Direct (Subsidized and Unsubsidized Stafford, PLUS), Perkins, state.

WORK-STUDY *Federal work-study:* Total amount: $1,435,040; 1,000 jobs averaging $2000.

APPLYING FOR FINANCIAL AID *Required financial aid forms:* FAFSA, CSS Financial Aid PROFILE, noncustodial (divorced/separated) parent's statement. *Financial aid deadline:* 2/1. *Notification date:* 3/31. Students must reply by 5/1.

CONTACT Ms. Mary Ellen Severance, Director of Financial Assistance, Clark University, 950 Main Street, Worcester, MA 01610-1477, 508-793-7478 or toll-free 800-GO-CLARK. *Fax:* 508-793-8802. *E-mail:* finaid@clarku.edu. *Website:* http://www.clarku.edu/.

CLAYTON STATE UNIVERSITY
Morrow, GA

Tuition & fees (GA res): $5916	Average undergraduate aid package: $9145

ABOUT THE INSTITUTION State-supported, coed. *Awards:* certificates, associate, bachelor's, and master's degrees. 37 undergraduate majors. *Total enrollment:* 7,140. Undergraduates: 6,808. Freshmen: 612. Federal methodology is used as a basis for awarding need-based institutional aid.

UNDERGRADUATE EXPENSES for 2013–2014 *Application fee:* $40. *Tuition, state resident:* full-time $4512; part-time $150.40 per credit hour. *Tuition, nonresident:* full-time $16,416; part-time $547.20 per credit hour. *Required fees:* full-time $1404; $702 per term. Full-time tuition and fees vary according to course load. Part-time tuition and fees vary according to course load. *College room and board:* $8862; *Room only:* $5574. Room and board charges vary according to board plan and housing facility.

FRESHMAN FINANCIAL AID (Fall 2012, est.) 451 applied for aid; of those 93% were deemed to have need. 100% of freshmen with need received aid; of those 3% had need fully met. *Average percent of need met:* 51% (excluding resources awarded to replace EFC). *Average financial aid package:* $9431 (excluding resources awarded to replace EFC). 1% of all full-time freshmen had no need and received non-need-based gift aid.

UNDERGRADUATE FINANCIAL AID (Fall 2012, est.) 3,574 applied for aid; of those 95% were deemed to have need. 100% of undergraduates with need received aid; of those 3% had need fully met. *Average percent of need met:* 45% (excluding resources awarded to replace EFC). *Average financial aid package:* $9145

(excluding resources awarded to replace EFC). 1% of all full-time undergraduates had no need and received non-need-based gift aid.

GIFT AID (NEED-BASED) *Total amount:* $22,620,106 (82% federal, 16% state, 1% institutional, 1% external sources). *Receiving aid:* Freshmen: 78% (374); all full-time undergraduates: 73% (2,818). *Average award:* Freshmen: $6759; Undergraduates: $5807. *Scholarships, grants, and awards:* Federal Pell, FSEOG, state, private, college/university gift aid from institutional funds, Federal Nursing.

GIFT AID (NON-NEED-BASED) *Total amount:* $492,689 (85% state, 11% institutional, 4% external sources). *Receiving aid:* Freshmen: 4% (20). Undergraduates: 2% (94). *Average award:* Freshmen: $2375. Undergraduates: $1749. *Tuition waivers:* Full or partial for employees or children of employees, senior citizens. *ROTC:* Army, Naval cooperative, Air Force cooperative.

LOANS *Student loans:* $54,764,912 (94% need-based, 6% non-need-based). 71% of past graduating class borrowed through all loan programs. *Average indebtedness per student:* $28,872. *Average need-based loan:* Freshmen: $3442. Undergraduates: $4410. *Parent loans:* $13,219,904 (66% need-based, 34% non-need-based). *Programs:* Federal Direct (Subsidized and Unsubsidized Stafford, PLUS), state.

WORK-STUDY *Federal work-study:* Total amount: $253,533; 41 jobs averaging $6225.

ATHLETIC AWARDS Total amount: $777,134 (36% need-based, 64% non-need-based).

APPLYING FOR FINANCIAL AID *Required financial aid form:* FAFSA. *Financial aid deadline (priority):* 7/15. *Notification date:* Continuous beginning 4/15.

CONTACT Patricia Barton, Director of Financial Aid, Clayton State University, 2000 Clayton State Boulevard, Morrow, GA 30260, 678-466-4181. *Fax:* 678-466-4189. *E-mail:* financialaid@mail.clayton.edu. *Website:* http://www.clayton.edu/.

CLEAR CREEK BAPTIST BIBLE COLLEGE
Pineville, KY

Tuition & fees: $5370	Average undergraduate aid package: $6823

ABOUT THE INSTITUTION Independent Southern Baptist, coed, primarily men. *Awards:* certificates, diplomas, associate, and bachelor's degrees. 2 undergraduate majors. *Total enrollment:* 172. Undergraduates: 172. Institutional methodology is used as a basis for awarding need-based institutional aid.

UNDERGRADUATE EXPENSES for 2013–2014 *Application fee:* $50. *Comprehensive fee:* $8840 includes full-time tuition ($5220), mandatory fees ($150), and room and board ($3470). *College room only:* $1870.

FRESHMAN FINANCIAL AID (Fall 2012, est.) 8 applied for aid; of those 100% were deemed to have need. 100% of freshmen with need received aid; of those 12% had need fully met. *Average percent of need met:* 73% (excluding resources awarded to replace EFC). *Average financial aid package:* $7314 (excluding resources awarded to replace EFC). 25% of all full-time freshmen had no need and received non-need-based gift aid.

UNDERGRADUATE FINANCIAL AID (Fall 2012, est.) 111 applied for aid; of those 96% were deemed to have need. 100% of undergraduates with need received aid; of those 2% had need fully met. *Average percent of need met:* 68% (excluding resources awarded to replace EFC). *Average financial aid package:* $6823 (excluding resources awarded to replace EFC). 14% of all full-time undergraduates had no need and received non-need-based gift aid.

GIFT AID (NEED-BASED) *Total amount:* $720,572 (74% federal, 16% institutional, 10% external sources). *Receiving aid:* Freshmen: 100% (8); all full-time undergraduates: 86% (107). *Average award:* Freshmen: $7314; Undergraduates: $6823. *Scholarships, grants, and awards:* Federal Pell, FSEOG, state, private, college/university gift aid from institutional funds.

GIFT AID (NON-NEED-BASED) *Total amount:* $60,976 (42% federal, 58% institutional). *Receiving aid:* Freshmen: 38% (3). Undergraduates: 38% (47). *Average award:* Freshmen: $2824. Undergraduates: $3042. *Scholarships, grants, and awards by category:* Academic interests/achievement: 6 awards ($1885 total): general academic interests/achievements. Creative arts/performance: 6 awards ($1200 total): music. Special characteristics: 2 awards ($1108 total): handicapped students, international students.

LOANS *Student loans:* $18,400 (100% non-need-based).

WORK-STUDY *Federal work-study:* Total amount: $38,082; 35 jobs averaging $1088.

APPLYING FOR FINANCIAL AID *Required financial aid forms:* FAFSA, institution's own form. *Financial aid deadline:* Continuous. *Notification date:* Continuous beginning 6/1.

CONTACT Mr. Sam Risner, Director of Financial Aid, Clear Creek Baptist Bible College, 300 Clear Creek Road, Pineville, KY 40977-9754, 606-337-3196 Ext. 142. *Fax:* 606-337-1631. *E-mail:* srisner@ccbbc.edu. *Website:* http://www.ccbbc.edu/.

CLEARWATER CHRISTIAN COLLEGE
Clearwater, FL

Tuition & fees: $17,060	Average undergraduate aid package: $12,655

ABOUT THE INSTITUTION Independent nondenominational, coed. *Awards:* certificates, associate, bachelor's, and master's degrees. 22 undergraduate majors. *Total enrollment:* 498. Undergraduates: 485. Freshmen: 115. Federal methodology is used as a basis for awarding need-based institutional aid.

UNDERGRADUATE EXPENSES for 2013–2014 *Application fee:* $35. *Comprehensive fee:* $25,360 includes full-time tuition ($17,060) and room and board ($8300). *College room only:* $5050. Full-time tuition and fees vary according to student level. Room and board charges vary according to board plan. *Payment plan:* Guaranteed tuition.

FRESHMAN FINANCIAL AID (Fall 2012, est.) 95 applied for aid; of those 91% were deemed to have need. 100% of freshmen with need received aid; of those 3% had need fully met. *Average percent of need met:* 51% (excluding resources awarded to replace EFC). *Average financial aid package:* $12,253 (excluding resources awarded to replace EFC). 19% of all full-time freshmen had no need and received non-need-based gift aid.

UNDERGRADUATE FINANCIAL AID (Fall 2012, est.) 444 applied for aid; of those 86% were deemed to have need. 100% of undergraduates with need received aid; of those 8% had need fully met. *Average percent of need met:* 53% (excluding resources awarded to replace EFC). *Average financial aid package:* $12,655 (excluding resources awarded to replace EFC). 21% of all full-time undergraduates had no need and received non-need-based gift aid.

GIFT AID (NEED-BASED) *Total amount:* $3,811,820 (25% federal, 19% state, 47% institutional, 9% external sources). *Receiving aid:* Freshmen: 78% (86); all full-time undergraduates: 78% (379). *Average award:* Freshmen: $9383; Undergraduates: $9641. *Scholarships, grants, and awards:* Federal Pell, FSEOG, state, private, college/university gift aid from institutional funds.

GIFT AID (NON-NEED-BASED) *Total amount:* $727,419 (22% state, 60% institutional, 18% external sources). *Receiving aid:* Freshmen: 2% (2). Undergraduates: 5% (24). *Average award:* Freshmen: $4227. Undergraduates: $3835. *Scholarships, grants, and awards by category:* Academic interests/achievement: business, education, general academic interests/achievements, premedicine, religion/biblical studies. Creative arts/performance: 42 awards ($63,500 total): music. Special achievements/activities: 20 awards ($80,000 total): leadership. Special characteristics: children and siblings of alumni, ethnic background, religious affiliation, siblings of current students. *Tuition waivers:* Full or partial for employees or children of employees. *ROTC:* Army cooperative, Naval cooperative, Air Force cooperative.

LOANS *Student loans:* $1,992,614 (86% need-based, 14% non-need-based). 67% of past graduating class borrowed through all loan programs. *Average indebtedness per student:* $22,321. *Average need-based loan:* Freshmen: $4330. Undergraduates: $4779. *Parent loans:* $343,105 (45% need-based, 55% non-need-based). *Programs:* Federal Direct (Subsidized and Unsubsidized Stafford, PLUS), state, alternative loans.

WORK-STUDY *Federal work-study:* Total amount: $26,596; jobs available. *State or other work-study/employment:* Total amount: $15,885 (100% need-based). Part-time jobs available.

APPLYING FOR FINANCIAL AID *Required financial aid forms:* FAFSA, state aid form. *Financial aid deadline:* Continuous. *Notification date:* Continuous beginning 3/1.

CONTACT Mr. Ryan McNamara, Director of Financial Aid, Clearwater Christian College, 3400 Gulf-to-Bay Boulevard, Clearwater, FL 33759-4595, 727-726-1153 Ext. 214 or toll-free 800-348-4463. *Fax:* 727-723-8566. *E-mail:* ryanmcnamara@clearwater.edu. *Website:* http://www.clearwater.edu/.

CLEARY UNIVERSITY
Ann Arbor, MI

Tuition & fees: N/R	Average undergraduate aid package: $14,209

ABOUT THE INSTITUTION Independent, coed. *Awards:* certificates, associate, bachelor's, and master's degrees. 9 undergraduate majors. *Total enrollment:* 704. Undergraduates: 618. Freshmen: 30. Federal methodology is used as a basis for awarding need-based institutional aid.

FRESHMAN FINANCIAL AID (Fall 2011) 32 applied for aid; of those 100% were deemed to have need. 100% of freshmen with need received aid; of those 6% had need fully met. *Average percent of need met:* 42% (excluding resources awarded to replace EFC). *Average financial aid package:* $13,049 (excluding resources awarded to replace EFC). 10% of all full-time freshmen had no need and received non-need-based gift aid.

UNDERGRADUATE FINANCIAL AID (Fall 2011) 249 applied for aid; of those 100% were deemed to have need. 100% of undergraduates with need received aid; of those 4% had need fully met. *Average percent of need met:* 41% (excluding resources awarded to replace EFC). *Average financial aid package:* $14,209 (excluding resources awarded to replace EFC). 10% of all full-time undergraduates had no need and received non-need-based gift aid.

GIFT AID (NEED-BASED) *Total amount:* $1,164,516 (72% federal, 23% state, 4% institutional, 1% external sources). *Receiving aid:* Freshmen: 71% (30); all full-time undergraduates: 70% (230). *Average award:* Freshmen: $1107; Undergraduates: $1300. *Scholarships, grants, and awards:* Federal Pell, FSEOG, state, private, college/university gift aid from institutional funds.

GIFT AID (NON-NEED-BASED) *Total amount:* $205,326 (100% institutional). *Receiving aid:* Freshmen: 19% (8). Undergraduates: 16% (52). *Average award:* Freshmen: $1814. Undergraduates: $2678. *Scholarships, grants, and awards by category:* Academic interests/achievement: 259 awards: business, computer science, general academic interests/achievements. Special characteristics: children of faculty/staff, veterans.

LOANS *Student loans:* $3,920,808 (43% need-based, 57% non-need-based). 81% of past graduating class borrowed through all loan programs. *Average indebtedness per student:* $32,259. *Average need-based loan:* Freshmen: $1309. *Parent loans:* $100,210 (100% non-need-based). *Programs:* Federal Direct (Subsidized and Unsubsidized Stafford, PLUS).

WORK-STUDY *Federal work-study:* Total amount: $33,423; 18 jobs averaging $2475. *State or other work-study/employment:* Part-time jobs available.

APPLYING FOR FINANCIAL AID *Required financial aid form:* FAFSA. *Financial aid deadline (priority):* 3/1. *Notification date:* Continuous beginning 4/1. Students must reply by 7/1 or within 2 weeks of notification.

CONTACT Vesta Smith-Campbell, Director of Financial Aid, Cleary University, 3750 Cleary Drive, Howell, MI 48843, 800-589-1979 Ext. 2234 or toll-free 800-686-1883. *Fax:* 517-552-8022. *E-mail:* vscampbell@cleary.edu. *Website:* http://www.cleary.edu/.

CLEMSON UNIVERSITY
Clemson, SC

Tuition & fees (SC res): $13,076	Average undergraduate aid package: $9578

ABOUT THE INSTITUTION State-supported, coed. *Awards:* certificates, bachelor's, master's, and doctoral degrees. 75 undergraduate majors. *Total enrollment:* 20,768. Undergraduates: 16,562. Freshmen: 3,463. Federal methodology is used as a basis for awarding need-based institutional aid.

UNDERGRADUATE EXPENSES for 2013–2014 *Application fee:* $70. *Tuition, state resident:* full-time $13,076. *Tuition, nonresident:* full-time

$29,720. Full-time tuition and fees vary according to course load, location, and program. Part-time tuition and fees vary according to program. **College room and board:** $7552. Room and board charges vary according to board plan, housing facility, and location.

FRESHMAN FINANCIAL AID (Fall 2012, est.) 2,678 applied for aid; of those 68% were deemed to have need. 99% of freshmen with need received aid; of those 19% had need fully met. **Average percent of need met:** 66% (excluding resources awarded to replace EFC). **Average financial aid package:** $12,173 (excluding resources awarded to replace EFC). 25% of all full-time freshmen had no need and received non-need-based gift aid.

UNDERGRADUATE FINANCIAL AID (Fall 2012, est.) 11,655 applied for aid; of those 78% were deemed to have need. 94% of undergraduates with need received aid; of those 11% had need fully met. **Average percent of need met:** 50% (excluding resources awarded to replace EFC). **Average financial aid package:** $9578 (excluding resources awarded to replace EFC). 21% of all full-time undergraduates had no need and received non-need-based gift aid.

GIFT AID (NEED-BASED) Total amount: $55,168,619 (24% federal, 43% state, 25% institutional, 8% external sources). **Receiving aid:** Freshmen: 21% (712); all full-time undergraduates: 22% (3,404). **Average award:** Freshmen: $4530; Undergraduates: $4256. **Scholarships, grants, and awards:** Federal Pell, FSEOG, state, private, college/university gift aid from institutional funds.

GIFT AID (NON-NEED-BASED) Total amount: $44,684,191 (52% state, 36% institutional, 12% external sources). **Receiving aid:** Freshmen: 51% (1,770). Undergraduates: 31% (4,867). **Average award:** Freshmen: $7017. Undergraduates: $5950. **Scholarships, grants, and awards by category:** Academic interests/achievement: agriculture, architecture, biological sciences, business, communication, computer science, education, engineering/technologies, English, foreign languages, general academic interests/achievements, health fields, humanities, international studies, mathematics, military science, physical sciences, premedicine, social sciences. Creative arts/performance: applied art and design, art/fine arts, performing arts, theater/drama. Special achievements/activities: community service, general special achievements/activities, leadership. Special characteristics: children of faculty/staff, ethnic background, local/state students, members of minority groups, veterans. **Tuition waivers:** Full or partial for senior citizens. **ROTC:** Army, Air Force.

LOANS Student loans: $85,423,748 (30% need-based, 70% non-need-based). 45% of past graduating class borrowed through all loan programs. **Average indebtedness per student:** $31,172. **Average need-based loan:** Freshmen: $3577. Undergraduates: $4372. **Parent loans:** $17,419,382 (78% need-based, 22% non-need-based). **Programs:** Federal Direct (Subsidized and Unsubsidized Stafford, PLUS), Perkins, state, college/university, private loans.

WORK-STUDY Federal work-study: Total amount: $1,661,954; 715 jobs averaging $2322. **State or other work-study/employment:** Total amount: $8,000,000 (100% non-need-based). 2,162 part-time jobs averaging $3700.

ATHLETIC AWARDS Total amount: $5,987,347 (20% need-based, 80% non-need-based).

APPLYING FOR FINANCIAL AID Required financial aid form: FAFSA. **Financial aid deadline (priority):** 3/1. **Notification date:** 4/1. Students must reply by 5/1.

CONTACT Mr. Chuck Knepfle, Director of Financial Aid, Clemson University, G01 Sikes Hall, Clemson, SC 29634-5123, 864-656-2280. *Fax:* 864-656-1831. *E-mail:* finaid@clemson.edu. *Website:* http://www.clemson.edu/.

CLEVELAND INSTITUTE OF ART
Cleveland, OH

Tuition & fees: $36,509	Average undergraduate aid package: $25,519

ABOUT THE INSTITUTION Independent, coed. **Awards:** bachelor's degrees. 15 undergraduate majors. **Total enrollment:** 556. Undergraduates: 556. Freshmen: 138. Federal methodology is used as a basis for awarding need-based institutional aid.

UNDERGRADUATE EXPENSES for 2013–2014 Application fee: $30. **Comprehensive fee:** $48,641 includes full-time tuition ($34,270), mandatory fees ($2239), and room and board ($12,132). **College room only:** $6912. Full-time tuition and fees vary according to program, reciprocity agreements, and student level. Room and board charges vary according to board plan. **Part-time tuition:** $1430 per credit. **Part-time fees:** $150 per credit; $115 per term. Part-time tuition and fees vary according to course load, program, reciprocity agreements, and student level.

FRESHMAN FINANCIAL AID (Fall 2012, est.) 127 applied for aid; of those 93% were deemed to have need. 100% of freshmen with need received aid; of those 6% had need fully met. **Average percent of need met:** 62% (excluding resources awarded to replace EFC). **Average financial aid package:** $26,167 (excluding resources awarded to replace EFC). 14% of all full-time freshmen had no need and received non-need-based gift aid.

UNDERGRADUATE FINANCIAL AID (Fall 2012, est.) 498 applied for aid; of those 95% were deemed to have need. 100% of undergraduates with need received aid; of those 6% had need fully met. **Average percent of need met:** 62% (excluding resources awarded to replace EFC). **Average financial aid package:** $25,519 (excluding resources awarded to replace EFC). 12% of all full-time undergraduates had no need and received non-need-based gift aid.

GIFT AID (NEED-BASED) Total amount: $9,367,021 (13% federal, 4% state, 81% institutional, 2% external sources). **Receiving aid:** Freshmen: 73% (118); all full-time undergraduates: 86% (473). **Average award:** Freshmen: $20,750; Undergraduates: $19,868. **Scholarships, grants, and awards:** Federal Pell, FSEOG, state, private, college/university gift aid from institutional funds.

GIFT AID (NON-NEED-BASED) Total amount: $968,383 (100% institutional). **Receiving aid:** Freshmen: 2% (4). Undergraduates: 4% (21). **Average award:** Freshmen: $12,630. Undergraduates: $13,135. **Scholarships, grants, and awards by category:** Creative arts/performance: 492 awards ($5,682,713 total): art/fine arts. **Tuition waivers:** Full or partial for employees or children of employees.

LOANS Student loans: $5,365,792 (87% need-based, 13% non-need-based). 81% of past graduating class borrowed through all loan programs. **Average indebtedness per student:** $30,541. **Average need-based loan:** Freshmen: $4496. Undergraduates: $4728. **Parent loans:** $1,766,022 (73% need-based, 27% non-need-based). **Programs:** Federal Direct (Subsidized and Unsubsidized Stafford, PLUS), Perkins.

WORK-STUDY Federal work-study: Total amount: $572,755; 338 jobs averaging $1979.

APPLYING FOR FINANCIAL AID Required financial aid form: FAFSA. **Financial aid deadline (priority):** 3/15. **Notification date:** Continuous beginning 3/1. Students must reply by 5/1 or within 3 weeks of notification.

CONTACT Mr. Martin Joseph Carney Jr., Director of Financial Aid, Cleveland Institute of Art, 11141 East Boulevard, Cleveland, OH 44106-1700, 216-421-7425 or toll-free 800-223-4700. *Fax:* 216-754-3634. *E-mail:* financialaid@cia.edu. *Website:* http://www.cia.edu/.

CLEVELAND INSTITUTE OF MUSIC
Cleveland, OH

Tuition & fees: N/R	Average undergraduate aid package: $29,214

ABOUT THE INSTITUTION Independent, coed. 3 undergraduate majors. Federal methodology is used as a basis for awarding need-based institutional aid.

FRESHMAN FINANCIAL AID (Fall 2012, est.) 56 applied for aid; of those 86% were deemed to have need. 100% of freshmen with need received aid; of those 10% had need fully met. **Average percent of need met:** 68% (excluding resources awarded to replace EFC). **Average financial aid package:** $28,807 (excluding resources awarded to replace EFC). 15% of all full-time freshmen had no need and received non-need-based gift aid.

UNDERGRADUATE FINANCIAL AID (Fall 2012, est.) 193 applied for aid; of those 81% were deemed to have need. 100% of undergraduates with need received aid; of those 9% had need fully met. **Average percent of need met:** 67% (excluding resources awarded to replace EFC). **Average financial aid package:** $29,214 (excluding resources awarded to replace EFC). 36% of all full-time undergraduates had no need and received non-need-based gift aid.

GIFT AID (NEED-BASED) Total amount: $3,722,323 (6% federal, 92% institutional, 2% external sources). **Receiving aid:** Freshmen: 67% (48); all full-time undergraduates: 57% (157). **Average award:** Freshmen: $24,746; Undergraduates: $23,863. **Scholarships, grants, and awards:** Federal Pell, FSEOG, state, private, college/university gift aid from institutional funds.

GIFT AID (NON-NEED-BASED) Total amount: $2,063,579 (94% institutional, 6% external sources). **Receiving aid:** Freshmen: 7% (5). Undergraduates: 5% (13). **Average award:** Freshmen: $19,709. Undergraduates: $18,644. **Scholarships, grants, and awards by category:** Creative arts/performance: 245 awards ($5,328,925 total): music. **Special characteristics:** 1 award ($24,180 total): children of faculty/staff.

LOANS *Student loans:* $1,082,620 (85% need-based, 15% non-need-based). 62% of past graduating class borrowed through all loan programs. *Average indebtedness per student:* $27,092. *Average need-based loan:* Freshmen: $3877. Undergraduates: $5299. *Parent loans:* $1,090,656 (53% need-based, 47% non-need-based). *Programs:* Federal Direct (Subsidized and Unsubsidized Stafford, PLUS), Perkins, college/university, private loans.

WORK-STUDY *Federal work-study:* Total amount: $152,763; 73 jobs averaging $2052. *State or other work-study/employment:* Total amount: $48,125 (19% need-based, 81% non-need-based). 23 part-time jobs averaging $2092.

APPLYING FOR FINANCIAL AID *Required financial aid forms:* FAFSA, CSS Financial Aid PROFILE. *Financial aid deadline (priority):* 2/15. *Notification date:* 4/1. Students must reply by 5/1.

CONTACT Ms. Kristie Gripp, Director of Financial Aid, Cleveland Institute of Music, 11021 East Boulevard, Cleveland, OH 44106-1776, 216-795-3192. *Fax:* 216-707-4519. *E-mail:* kxg26@case.edu. *Website:* http://www.cim.edu/.

CLEVELAND STATE UNIVERSITY
Cleveland, OH

Tuition & fees (OH res): $9314	Average undergraduate aid package: $8821

ABOUT THE INSTITUTION State-supported, coed. *Awards:* certificates, bachelor's, master's, and doctoral degrees. 78 undergraduate majors. *Total enrollment:* 17,525. Undergraduates: 12,038. Freshmen: 1,588. Federal methodology is used as a basis for awarding need-based institutional aid.

UNDERGRADUATE EXPENSES for 2013–2014 *Application fee:* $30. *Tuition, state resident:* full-time $9264; part-time $386 per credit hour. *Tuition, nonresident:* full-time $12,386; part-time $516 per credit hour. *Required fees:* full-time $50; $25 per term. Full-time tuition and fees vary according to course load, degree level, and program. Part-time tuition and fees vary according to course load, degree level, and program. *College room and board:* $11,848; *Room only:* $7648. Room and board charges vary according to board plan and housing facility.

FRESHMAN FINANCIAL AID (Fall 2012, est.) 1,334 applied for aid; of those 90% were deemed to have need. 99% of freshmen with need received aid; of those 7% had need fully met. *Average percent of need met:* 48% (excluding resources awarded to replace EFC). *Average financial aid package:* $9344 (excluding resources awarded to replace EFC). 5% of all full-time freshmen had no need and received non-need-based gift aid.

UNDERGRADUATE FINANCIAL AID (Fall 2012, est.) 7,157 applied for aid; of those 92% were deemed to have need. 98% of undergraduates with need received aid; of those 6% had need fully met. *Average percent of need met:* 45% (excluding resources awarded to replace EFC). *Average financial aid package:* $8821 (excluding resources awarded to replace EFC). 5% of all full-time undergraduates had no need and received non-need-based gift aid.

GIFT AID (NEED-BASED) *Total amount:* $33,640,563 (68% federal, 11% state, 15% institutional, 6% external sources). *Receiving aid:* Freshmen: 68% (1,043); all full-time undergraduates: 61% (5,176). *Average award:* Freshmen: $6853; Undergraduates: $6090. *Scholarships, grants, and awards:* Federal Pell, FSEOG, state, private, college/university gift aid from institutional funds.

GIFT AID (NON-NEED-BASED) *Total amount:* $2,921,923 (2% federal, 6% state, 80% institutional, 12% external sources). *Receiving aid:* Freshmen: 3% (50). Undergraduates: 2% (168). *Average award:* Freshmen: $5298. Undergraduates: $5013. *Scholarships, grants, and awards by category:* Academic interests/achievement: biological sciences, business, communication, computer science, education, engineering/technologies, English, general academic interests/achievements, health fields, humanities, mathematics, physical sciences, premedicine, social sciences. *Creative arts/performance:* art/fine arts, creative writing, dance, journalism/publications, music, performing arts, theater/drama. *Special achievements/activities:* cheerleading/drum major. *Special characteristics:* children of faculty/staff, general special characteristics, out-of-state students. *Tuition waivers:* Full or partial for employees or children of employees, senior citizens. *ROTC:* Army cooperative, Air Force cooperative.

LOANS *Student loans:* $64,471,615 (88% need-based, 12% non-need-based). 57% of past graduating class borrowed through all loan programs. *Average indebtedness per student:* $23,436. *Average need-based loan:* Freshmen: $3321. Undergrad-

uates: $4240. *Parent loans:* $2,523,996 (52% need-based, 48% non-need-based). *Programs:* Federal Direct (Subsidized and Unsubsidized Stafford, PLUS), Perkins, state, alternative loans.

WORK-STUDY *Federal work-study:* Total amount: $1,699,772; 416 jobs averaging $3697. *State or other work-study/employment:* Part-time jobs available.

ATHLETIC AWARDS Total amount: $2,610,354 (37% need-based, 63% non-need-based).

APPLYING FOR FINANCIAL AID *Required financial aid form:* FAFSA. *Financial aid deadline (priority):* 2/15. *Notification date:* Continuous beginning 3/15. Students must reply within 4 weeks of notification.

CONTACT Financial Aid Office, Cleveland State University, 1621 Euclid Avenue, Cleveland, OH 44115, 216-687-5594 or toll-free 888-CSU-OHIO. *E-mail:* campus411@csuohio.edu. *Website:* http://www.csuohio.edu/.

COASTAL CAROLINA UNIVERSITY
Conway, SC

Tuition & fees (SC res): $9760	Average undergraduate aid package: $9283

ABOUT THE INSTITUTION State-supported, coed. *Awards:* certificates, bachelor's, and master's degrees. 40 undergraduate majors. *Total enrollment:* 9,335. Undergraduates: 8,746. Freshmen: 2,206. Federal methodology is used as a basis for awarding need-based institutional aid.

UNDERGRADUATE EXPENSES for 2013–2014 *Application fee:* $45. *Tuition, state resident:* full-time $9680; part-time $407 per credit hour. *Tuition, nonresident:* full-time $21,970; part-time $920 per credit hour. *Required fees:* full-time $80. Full-time tuition and fees vary according to course load and degree level. Part-time tuition and fees vary according to course load and degree level. *College room and board:* $7700; *Room only:* $5000. Room and board charges vary according to board plan and housing facility.

FRESHMAN FINANCIAL AID (Fall 2011) 1,948 applied for aid; of those 82% were deemed to have need. 98% of freshmen with need received aid; of those 8% had need fully met. *Average percent of need met:* 48% (excluding resources awarded to replace EFC). *Average financial aid package:* $9363 (excluding resources awarded to replace EFC). 16% of all full-time freshmen had no need and received non-need-based gift aid.

UNDERGRADUATE FINANCIAL AID (Fall 2011) 6,741 applied for aid; of those 84% were deemed to have need. 99% of undergraduates with need received aid; of those 9% had need fully met. *Average percent of need met:* 47% (excluding resources awarded to replace EFC). *Average financial aid package:* $9283 (excluding resources awarded to replace EFC). 15% of all full-time undergraduates had no need and received non-need-based gift aid.

GIFT AID (NEED-BASED) *Total amount:* $14,940,877 (93% federal, 7% state). *Receiving aid:* Freshmen: 38% (810); all full-time undergraduates: 40% (3,089). *Average award:* Freshmen: $4794; Undergraduates: $4661. *Scholarships, grants, and awards:* Federal Pell, FSEOG, state, private, college/university gift aid from institutional funds, Academic Competitiveness Grants, National SMART Grants.

GIFT AID (NON-NEED-BASED) *Total amount:* $12,388,519 (68% state, 20% institutional, 12% external sources). *Receiving aid:* Freshmen: 32% (683). Undergraduates: 21% (1,663). *Average award:* Freshmen: $12,764. Undergraduates: $12,396. *Scholarships, grants, and awards by category:* Academic interests/achievement: 2,061 awards ($5,592,677 total): biological sciences, business, education, general academic interests/achievements, humanities, mathematics. *Creative arts/performance:* 68 awards ($61,824 total): art/fine arts, music, theater/drama. *Special achievements/activities:* 28 awards ($27,900 total): cheerleading/drum major. *Special characteristics:* 1,441 awards ($4,077,451 total): general special characteristics, international students, local/state students, out-of-state students, veterans' children. *Tuition waivers:* Full or partial for employees or children of employees, senior citizens. *ROTC:* Army.

LOANS *Student loans:* $56,416,487 (35% need-based, 65% non-need-based). 72% of past graduating class borrowed through all loan programs. *Average indebtedness per student:* $34,040. *Average need-based loan:* Freshmen: $7987. Undergraduates: $8176. *Parent loans:* $19,026,504 (100% non-need-based). *Programs:* Federal Direct (Subsidized and Unsubsidized Stafford, PLUS), Perkins, state.

WORK-STUDY *Federal work-study:* Total amount: $323,327; 140 jobs averaging $2242. *State or other work-study/employment:* Total amount: $2,462,849 (100% non-need-based). 1,022 part-time jobs averaging $2410.

ATHLETIC AWARDS Total amount: $3,767,749 (100% non-need-based).

APPLYING FOR FINANCIAL AID *Required financial aid form:* FAFSA. *Financial aid deadline (priority):* 3/1. *Notification date:* Continuous beginning 3/1. Students must reply by 5/15.

CONTACT Mrs. Dawn H. Hitchcock, Interim Co-Director of Financial Aid and Scholarships, Coastal Carolina University, PO Box 261954, Conway, SC 29528-6054, 843-349-2190 or toll-free 800-277-7000. *Fax:* 843-349-2347. *E-mail:* dawn@ coastal.edu.

Website: http://www.coastal.edu/.

COE COLLEGE
Cedar Rapids, IA

Tuition & fees: $35,730	Average undergraduate aid package: $27,104

ABOUT THE INSTITUTION Independent Presbyterian Church, coed. *Awards:* bachelor's and master's degrees. 66 undergraduate majors. *Total enrollment:* 1,367. Undergraduates: 1,364. Freshmen: 364. Federal methodology is used as a basis for awarding need-based institutional aid.

UNDERGRADUATE EXPENSES for 2013–2014 *Application fee:* $30. *Comprehensive fee:* $43,480 includes full-time tuition ($35,400), mandatory fees ($330), and room and board ($7750). *College room only:* $3450. Room and board charges vary according to housing facility. *Part-time tuition:* $4035 per course. Part-time tuition and fees vary according to course load.

FRESHMAN FINANCIAL AID (Fall 2011) 334 applied for aid; of those 94% were deemed to have need. 100% of freshmen with need received aid; of those 15% had need fully met. *Average percent of need met:* 84% (excluding resources awarded to replace EFC). *Average financial aid package:* $29,271 (excluding resources awarded to replace EFC). 11% of all full-time freshmen had no need and received non-need-based gift aid.

UNDERGRADUATE FINANCIAL AID (Fall 2011) 1,149 applied for aid; of those 91% were deemed to have need. 100% of undergraduates with need received aid; of those 19% had need fully met. *Average percent of need met:* 80% (excluding resources awarded to replace EFC). *Average financial aid package:* $27,104 (excluding resources awarded to replace EFC). 18% of all full-time undergraduates had no need and received non-need-based gift aid.

GIFT AID (NEED-BASED) *Total amount:* $22,990,856 (9% federal, 7% state, 81% institutional, 3% external sources). *Receiving aid:* Freshmen: 87% (313); all full-time undergraduates: 80% (1,044). *Average award:* Freshmen: $24,234; Undergraduates: $22,297. *Scholarships, grants, and awards:* Federal Pell, FSEOG, state, private, college/university gift aid from institutional funds, Federal Nursing, ROTC Scholarships.

GIFT AID (NON-NEED-BASED) *Total amount:* $5,989,166 (5% federal, 90% institutional, 5% external sources). *Receiving aid:* Freshmen: 11% (38). Undergraduates: 11% (147). *Average award:* Freshmen: $18,514. Undergraduates: $18,489. *Scholarships, grants, and awards by category: Academic interests/achievement:* 1,561 awards ($16,500,731 total): biological sciences, business, English, foreign languages, general academic interests/achievements, mathematics, physical sciences, premedicine. *Creative arts/performance:* 58 awards ($410,390 total): art/fine arts, creative writing, music, performing arts, theater/drama. *Special achievements/activities:* 7 awards ($6000 total): community service. *Special characteristics:* 320 awards ($2,819,333 total): adult students, children and siblings of alumni, children of educators, children of faculty/staff, ethnic background, general special characteristics, international students, members of minority groups, religious affiliation, siblings of current students, veterans, veterans' children. *Tuition waivers:* Full or partial for employees or children of employees, adult students, senior citizens. *ROTC:* Army, Air Force cooperative.

LOANS *Student loans:* $8,543,773 (77% need-based, 23% non-need-based). 80% of past graduating class borrowed through all loan programs. *Average indebtedness per student:* $29,500. *Average need-based loan:* Freshmen: $4785. Undergraduates: $5061. *Parent loans:* $2,526,248 (32% need-based, 68% non-need-based). *Programs:* Federal Direct (Subsidized and Unsubsidized Stafford, PLUS), Perkins, college/university.

WORK-STUDY *Federal work-study:* Total amount: $672,260; 523 jobs averaging $1656. *State or other work-study/employment:* Total amount: $328,700 (16% need-based, 84% non-need-based). 228 part-time jobs averaging $1421.

APPLYING FOR FINANCIAL AID *Required financial aid form:* FAFSA. *Financial aid deadline (priority):* 3/1. *Notification date:* Continuous beginning 3/15. Students must reply by 5/1 or within 2 weeks of notification.

CONTACT Ms. Barbara Hoffman, Director of Financial Aid, Coe College, 1220 First Avenue, NE, Cedar Rapids, IA 52402-5070, 319-399-8540 or toll-free 877-225-5263. *Fax:* 319-399-8886.

Website: http://www.coe.edu/.

COGSWELL POLYTECHNICAL COLLEGE
Sunnyvale, CA

ABOUT THE INSTITUTION Independent, coed, primarily men. *Awards:* bachelor's and master's degrees. 8 undergraduate majors. *Total enrollment:* 11. Undergraduates: 392. Freshmen: 62.

GIFT AID (NEED-BASED) *Scholarships, grants, and awards:* Federal Pell, FSEOG, state, private, college/university gift aid from institutional funds.

LOANS *Programs:* Federal Direct (Subsidized and Unsubsidized Stafford, PLUS), private loans.

WORK-STUDY *Federal work-study:* Total amount: $21,356; 14 jobs averaging $1900.

APPLYING FOR FINANCIAL AID *Required financial aid forms:* FAFSA, state aid form.

CONTACT Lisa Mandy, Director of Financial Aid, Cogswell Polytechnical College, 1175 Bordeaux Drive, Sunnyvale, CA 94089, 408-498-5107 or toll-free 800-264-7955. *Fax:* 408-747-0765. *E-mail:* lmandy@cogswell.edu.

Website: http://www.cogswell.edu/.

COKER COLLEGE
Hartsville, SC

Tuition & fees: $24,576	Average undergraduate aid package: $17,576

ABOUT THE INSTITUTION Independent, coed. *Awards:* bachelor's and master's degrees (also offers evening program with significant enrollment not reflected in profile). 41 undergraduate majors. *Total enrollment:* 1,163. Undergraduates: 1,155. Freshmen: 198. Both federal and institutional methodology are used as a basis for awarding need-based institutional aid.

UNDERGRADUATE EXPENSES for 2013–2014 *Application fee:* $25. *Comprehensive fee:* $32,186 includes full-time tuition ($24,576) and room and board ($7610). *College room only:* $3620. Full-time tuition and fees vary according to course load, location, and program. Room and board charges vary according to board plan and housing facility. Part-time tuition and fees vary according to course load, location, and program.

FRESHMAN FINANCIAL AID (Fall 2011) 197 applied for aid; of those 93% were deemed to have need. 100% of freshmen with need received aid; of those 27% had need fully met. *Average percent of need met:* 99% (excluding resources awarded to replace EFC). *Average financial aid package:* $20,903 (excluding resources awarded to replace EFC). 9% of all full-time freshmen had no need and received non-need-based gift aid.

UNDERGRADUATE FINANCIAL AID (Fall 2011) 924 applied for aid; of those 95% were deemed to have need. 100% of undergraduates with need received aid; of those 18% had need fully met. *Average percent of need met:* 96% (excluding resources awarded to replace EFC). *Average financial aid package:* $17,576 (excluding resources awarded to replace EFC). 5% of all full-time undergraduates had no need and received non-need-based gift aid.

GIFT AID (NEED-BASED) *Total amount:* $10,284,106 (72% federal, 15% state, 11% institutional, 2% external sources). *Receiving aid:* Freshmen: 84% (176); all full-time undergraduates: 89% (864). *Average award:* Freshmen: $6489; Undergraduates: $6536. *Scholarships, grants, and awards:* Federal Pell, FSEOG, state, private, college/university gift aid from institutional funds.

GIFT AID (NON-NEED-BASED) *Total amount:* $7,867,018 (5% federal, 19% state, 74% institutional, 2% external sources). *Receiving aid:* Freshmen: 84% (175). Undergraduates: 62% (605). *Average award:* Freshmen: $5375. Undergraduates: $5272. *Scholarships, grants, and awards by category: Academic interests/achievement:* 322 awards ($2,259,309 total): general academic interests/achievements. *Creative arts/performance:* 51 awards ($71,369 total): art/fine arts, creative writing, dance, general creative arts/performance, music, theater/drama. *Special achievements/activities:* 9 awards ($3750 total): leadership. *Special characteristics:* 55 awards ($369,866 total): children and siblings of alumni, children of faculty/staff, international students, previous college experience. *Tuition waivers:* Full or partial for employees or children of employees.

LOANS *Student loans:* $9,661,675 (42% need-based, 58% non-need-based). 89% of past graduating class borrowed through all loan programs. *Average indebtedness per student:* $32,842. *Average need-based loan:* Freshmen: $3552. Undergraduates: $4517. *Parent loans:* $741,394 (100% non-need-based). *Programs:* Federal Direct (Subsidized and Unsubsidized Stafford, PLUS), Perkins, state, private loans.

WORK-STUDY *Federal work-study:* Total amount: $69,529; 82 jobs averaging $848. *State or other work-study/employment:* Total amount: $3064 (100% non-need-based). Part-time jobs available.

ATHLETIC AWARDS Total amount: $1,236,236 (100% non-need-based).

APPLYING FOR FINANCIAL AID *Required financial aid form:* FAFSA. *Financial aid deadline:* 6/1 (priority: 4/1). *Notification date:* Continuous beginning 3/1. Students must reply by 5/1 or within 3 weeks of notification.

CONTACT Betty Williams, Director of Financial Aid, Coker College, 300 East College Avenue, Hartsville, SC 29550, 843-383-8055 or toll-free 800-950-1908. *Fax:* 843-383-8056. *E-mail:* bwilliams@coker.edu.
Website: http://www.coker.edu/.

THE COLBURN SCHOOL CONSERVATORY OF MUSIC
Los Angeles, CA

CONTACT Ms. Kathleen Tesar, Associate Dean, The Colburn School Conservatory of Music, 200 South Grand Avenue, Los Angeles, CA 90012, 213-621-4534. *Fax:* 213-625-0371. *E-mail:* admissions@colburnschool.edu.
Website: http://www.colburnschool.edu/.

COLBY COLLEGE
Waterville, ME

Comprehensive fee: $55,700	Average undergraduate aid package: $38,613

ABOUT THE INSTITUTION Independent, coed. *Awards:* bachelor's degrees. 46 undergraduate majors. *Total enrollment:* 1,863. Undergraduates: 1,863. Freshmen: 493. Both federal and institutional methodology are used as a basis for awarding need-based institutional aid.

UNDERGRADUATE EXPENSES for 2013–2014 *Comprehensive fee:* $55,700. Room and board charges vary according to housing facility. Part-time tuition and fees vary according to course load.

FRESHMAN FINANCIAL AID (Fall 2012, est.) 264 applied for aid; of those 73% were deemed to have need. 100% of freshmen with need received aid; of those 100% had need fully met. *Average percent of need met:* 100% (excluding resources awarded to replace EFC). *Average financial aid package:* $40,178 (excluding resources awarded to replace EFC). 1% of all full-time freshmen had no need and received non-need-based gift aid.

UNDERGRADUATE FINANCIAL AID (Fall 2012, est.) 886 applied for aid; of those 79% were deemed to have need. 100% of undergraduates with need received aid; of those 99% had need fully met. *Average percent of need met:* 100% (excluding resources awarded to replace EFC). *Average financial aid package:* $38,613 (excluding resources awarded to replace EFC). 2% of all full-time undergraduates had no need and received non-need-based gift aid.

GIFT AID (NEED-BASED) *Total amount:* $25,867,225 (7% federal, 92% institutional, 1% external sources). *Receiving aid:* Freshmen: 39% (193); all full-time undergraduates: 37% (694). *Average award:* Freshmen: $38,716; Undergraduates:

$36,924. *Scholarships, grants, and awards:* Federal Pell, FSEOG, state, private, college/university gift aid from institutional funds, Academic Competitiveness Grants, National SMART Grants, Colby National Merit Scholarships.

GIFT AID (NON-NEED-BASED) *Total amount:* $268,854 (68% institutional, 32% external sources). *Receiving aid:* Freshmen: 1% (3). Undergraduates: 1% (15). *Average award:* Freshmen: $500. Undergraduates: $3754. *Scholarships, grants, and awards by category: Academic interests/achievement:* 31 awards ($10,100 total): general academic interests/achievements. *Special characteristics:* 14 awards ($171,775 total): general special characteristics. *Tuition waivers:* Full or partial for employees or children of employees. *ROTC:* Army cooperative.

LOANS *Student loans:* $2,295,373 (100% non-need-based). 34% of past graduating class borrowed through all loan programs. *Average indebtedness per student:* $24,453. *Average need-based loan:* Undergraduates: $811. *Parent loans:* $1,865,431 (100% non-need-based). *Programs:* Federal Direct (Subsidized and Unsubsidized Stafford, PLUS), Perkins, state, alternative loans.

WORK-STUDY *Federal work-study:* Total amount: $712,452; 409 jobs averaging $1697. *State or other work-study/employment:* Total amount: $265,805 (100% need-based). 147 part-time jobs averaging $1768.

APPLYING FOR FINANCIAL AID *Required financial aid forms:* FAFSA, CSS Financial Aid PROFILE, federal income tax form(s). *Financial aid deadline:* 2/1. *Notification date:* 4/1. Students must reply by 5/1.

CONTACT Ms. Melissa Rose, Director of Financial Aid, Colby College, 4850 Mayflower Hill, Waterville, ME 04901-8848, 207-859-4832 or toll-free 800-723-3032. *Fax:* 207-859-4828. *E-mail:* finaid@colby.edu.
Website: http://www.colby.edu/.

COLBY-SAWYER COLLEGE
New London, NH

ABOUT THE INSTITUTION Independent, coed. 20 undergraduate majors.

GIFT AID (NEED-BASED) *Scholarships, grants, and awards:* Federal Pell, FSEOG, state, private, college/university gift aid from institutional funds.

GIFT AID (NON-NEED-BASED) *Scholarships, grants, and awards by category: Academic interests/achievement:* general academic interests/achievements. *Creative arts/performance:* applied art and design, art/fine arts, creative writing. *Special achievements/activities:* community service, leadership. *Special characteristics:* children of faculty/staff.

LOANS *Programs:* Federal Direct (Subsidized and Unsubsidized Stafford, PLUS), Perkins.

APPLYING FOR FINANCIAL AID *Required financial aid form:* FAFSA.

CONTACT Mr. Ted Craigie, Director of Financial Aid, Colby-Sawyer College, 541 Main Street, New London, NH 03257-7835, 603-526-3717 or toll-free 800-272-1015. *Fax:* 603-526-3737. *E-mail:* cscfinaid@colby-sawyer.edu.
Website: http://www.colby-sawyer.edu/.

COLEGIO UNIVERSITARIO DE SAN JUAN
San Juan, PR

CONTACT Financial Aid Office, Colegio Universitario de San Juan, 180 Jose R Oliver Street, Tres Monjitas Industrial Park, San Juan, PR 00918, 787-250-7111.
Website: http://www.cunisanjuan.edu/.

COLEMAN UNIVERSITY
San Diego, CA

CONTACT Financial Aid Office, Coleman University, 8888 Balboa Avenue, San Diego, CA 92123, 858-499-0202 or toll-free 800-430-2030. *Fax:* 858-499-0233. *E-mail:* faoffice@coleman.edu.
Website: http://www.coleman.edu/.

COLGATE UNIVERSITY
Hamilton, NY

Tuition & fees: $44,640	Average undergraduate aid package: $42,522

ABOUT THE INSTITUTION Independent, coed. *Awards:* bachelor's and master's degrees. 51 undergraduate majors. *Total enrollment:* 2,865. Undergraduates: 2,850. Freshmen: 756. Institutional methodology is used as a basis for awarding need-based institutional aid.

UNDERGRADUATE EXPENSES for 2013–2014 *Application fee:* $60. *One-time required fee:* $50. *Comprehensive fee:* $55,715 includes full-time tuition ($44,330), mandatory fees ($310), and room and board ($11,075). *College room only:* $5345. Full-time tuition and fees vary according to course load. Room and board charges vary according to board plan and housing facility. *Part-time tuition:* $5541.25 per course. Part-time tuition and fees vary according to course load. *Payment plan:* Tuition prepayment.

FRESHMAN FINANCIAL AID (Fall 2012, est.) 312 applied for aid; of those 81% were deemed to have need. 100% of freshmen with need received aid; of those 100% had need fully met. *Average percent of need met:* 100% (excluding resources awarded to replace EFC). *Average financial aid package:* $42,313 (excluding resources awarded to replace EFC).

UNDERGRADUATE FINANCIAL AID (Fall 2012, est.) 1,145 applied for aid; of those 89% were deemed to have need. 100% of undergraduates with need received aid; of those 100% had need fully met. *Average percent of need met:* 100% (excluding resources awarded to replace EFC). *Average financial aid package:* $42,522 (excluding resources awarded to replace EFC).

GIFT AID (NEED-BASED) *Total amount:* $38,833,957 (4% federal, 2% state, 92% institutional, 2% external sources). *Receiving aid:* Freshmen: 33% (252); all full-time undergraduates: 35% (1,009). *Average award:* Freshmen: $38,421; Undergraduates: $38,288. *Scholarships, grants, and awards:* Federal Pell, FSEOG, state, college/university gift aid from institutional funds.

GIFT AID (NON-NEED-BASED) *Total amount:* $793,911 (10% institutional, 90% external sources). *Tuition waivers:* Full or partial for employees or children of employees. *ROTC:* Army cooperative.

LOANS *Student loans:* $6,045,436 (41% need-based, 59% non-need-based). 34% of past graduating class borrowed through all loan programs. *Average indebtedness per student:* $20,751. *Average need-based loan:* Freshmen: $1802. Undergraduates: $3861. *Parent loans:* $4,218,801 (100% non-need-based). *Programs:* Federal Direct (Subsidized and Unsubsidized Stafford, PLUS), Perkins.

WORK-STUDY *Federal work-study:* Total amount: $1,133,234; 539 jobs averaging $2080. *State or other work-study/employment:* Total amount: $505,358 (98% need-based, 2% non-need-based). 283 part-time jobs averaging $1811.

ATHLETIC AWARDS Total amount: $6,697,715 (100% non-need-based).

APPLYING FOR FINANCIAL AID *Required financial aid forms:* CSS Financial Aid PROFILE, noncustodial (divorced/separated) parent's statement. *Financial aid deadline:* 1/15. *Notification date:* 4/1. Students must reply by 5/1 or within 2 weeks of notification.

CONTACT Office of Financial Aid, Colgate University, 13 Oak Drive, Hamilton, NY 13346, 315-228-7431. *Fax:* 315-228-7050. *E-mail:* finaid@colgate.edu. *Website:* http://www.colgate.edu/.

THE COLLEGE AT BROCKPORT, STATE UNIVERSITY OF NEW YORK
Brockport, NY

Tuition & fees (NY res): $7210	Average undergraduate aid package: $9821

ABOUT THE INSTITUTION State-supported, coed. *Awards:* certificates, bachelor's, and master's degrees. 107 undergraduate majors. *Total enrollment:* 8,271. Undergraduates: 7,133. Freshmen: 1,084. Federal methodology is used as a basis for awarding need-based institutional aid.

UNDERGRADUATE EXPENSES for 2013–2014 *Application fee:* $50. *Tuition, state resident:* full-time $5870. *Tuition, nonresident:* full-time $14,820. *Required fees:* full-time $1340. Part-time tuition and fees vary according to course load. *College room and board:* $11,386. Room and board charges vary according to board plan and housing facility.

FRESHMAN FINANCIAL AID (Fall 2012, est.) 923 applied for aid; of those 76% were deemed to have need. 99% of freshmen with need received aid; of those 16% had need fully met. *Average percent of need met:* 73% (excluding resources awarded to replace EFC). *Average financial aid package:* $10,418 (excluding resources awarded to replace EFC). 8% of all full-time freshmen had no need and received non-need-based gift aid.

UNDERGRADUATE FINANCIAL AID (Fall 2012, est.) 4,808 applied for aid; of those 82% were deemed to have need. 99% of undergraduates with need received aid; of those 11% had need fully met. *Average percent of need met:* 69% (excluding resources awarded to replace EFC). *Average financial aid package:* $9821 (excluding resources awarded to replace EFC). 3% of all full-time undergraduates had no need and received non-need-based gift aid.

GIFT AID (NEED-BASED) *Total amount:* $19,486,454 (61% federal, 38% state, 1% external sources). *Receiving aid:* Freshmen: 54% (534); all full-time undergraduates: 59% (3,156). *Average award:* Freshmen: $5802; Undergraduates: $5357. *Scholarships, grants, and awards:* Federal Pell, FSEOG, state, private, college/university gift aid from institutional funds.

GIFT AID (NON-NEED-BASED) *Total amount:* $4,979,705 (15% federal, 7% state, 57% institutional, 21% external sources). *Receiving aid:* Freshmen: 27% (266). Undergraduates: 16% (849). *Average award:* Freshmen: $4086. Undergraduates: $4350. *Scholarships, grants, and awards by category:* Academic interests/achievement: 1,052 awards ($3,105,155 total): biological sciences, business, communication, computer science, education, English, foreign languages, general academic interests/achievements, health fields, humanities, international studies, mathematics, military science, physical sciences, premedicine, social sciences. *Creative arts/performance:* 39 awards ($36,800 total): art/fine arts, cinema/film/broadcasting, creative writing, dance, general creative arts/performance, journalism/publications, music, performing arts, theater/drama. *Special achievements/activities:* 33 awards ($32,178 total): community service, general special achievements/activities, hobbies/interests, leadership, religious involvement. *Special characteristics:* 35 awards ($54,600 total): children and siblings of alumni, ethnic background, first-generation college students, general special characteristics, international students, local/state students, married students, members of minority groups, out-of-state students, previous college experience, religious affiliation, veterans. *Tuition waivers:* Full or partial for employees or children of employees, senior citizens. *ROTC:* Army, Naval cooperative, Air Force cooperative.

LOANS *Student loans:* $42,657,654 (47% need-based, 53% non-need-based). 82% of past graduating class borrowed through all loan programs. *Average indebtedness per student:* $27,844. *Average need-based loan:* Freshmen: $4495. Undergraduates: $4927. *Parent loans:* $4,271,790 (100% non-need-based). *Programs:* Federal Direct (Subsidized and Unsubsidized Stafford, PLUS), Perkins, Federal Nursing, alternative loans.

WORK-STUDY *Federal work-study:* Total amount: $1,100,157; 531 jobs averaging $2072. *State or other work-study/employment:* Total amount: $2,248,237 (100% non-need-based). 1,580 part-time jobs averaging $1423.

APPLYING FOR FINANCIAL AID *Required financial aid forms:* FAFSA, state aid form. *Financial aid deadline (priority):* 3/15. *Notification date:* Continuous beginning 2/15. Students must reply by 5/1.

CONTACT Mr. J. Scott Atkinson, Director of Enrollment Services, The College at Brockport, State University of New York, 350 New Campus Drive, Brockport, NY 14420-2937, 585-395-2501. *Fax:* 585-395-5445. *E-mail:* satkinso@brockport.edu. *Website:* http://www.brockport.edu/.

COLLEGE FOR CREATIVE STUDIES
Detroit, MI

ABOUT THE INSTITUTION Independent, coed. *Awards:* certificates, bachelor's, and master's degrees. 10 undergraduate majors. *Total enrollment:* 1,441. Undergraduates: 1,386. Freshmen: 305.

GIFT AID (NEED-BASED) *Scholarships, grants, and awards:* Federal Pell, FSEOG, state, private, college/university gift aid from institutional funds.

GIFT AID (NON-NEED-BASED) *Scholarships, grants, and awards by category:* Academic interests/achievement: general academic interests/achievements. Creative arts/performance: applied art and design, art/fine arts.

LOANS *Programs:* Federal Direct (Subsidized and Unsubsidized Stafford, PLUS), private loans.

APPLYING FOR FINANCIAL AID *Required financial aid form:* FAFSA.

CONTACT Office of Financial Aid, College for Creative Studies, 201 East Kirby, Detroit, MI 48202-4034, 313-664-7495 or toll-free 800-952-ARTS. *Fax:* 313-872-1521. *E-mail:* finaid@collegeforcreativestudies.edu. *Website:* http://www.collegeforcreativestudies.edu/.

COLLEGE OF BIBLICAL STUDIES– HOUSTON
Houston, TX

Tuition & fees: N/R	Average undergraduate aid package: N/A

ABOUT THE INSTITUTION Independent nondenominational, coed. *Awards:* certificates, associate, and bachelor's degrees. 2 undergraduate majors. *Total enrollment:* 643. Undergraduates: 643. Federal methodology is used as a basis for awarding need-based institutional aid.

GIFT AID (NEED-BASED) *Scholarships, grants, and awards:* college/university gift aid from institutional funds.

APPLYING FOR FINANCIAL AID *Required financial aid form:* FAFSA. *Financial aid deadline:* 8/5. *Notification date:* Continuous.

CONTACT Roshanna Hardison, Director of Student Financial Services, College of Biblical Studies–Houston, 7000 Regency Square Boulevard, Houston, TX 77036, 832-252-0728. *E-mail:* roshanna.hardison@cbshouston.edu. *Website:* http://www.cbshouston.edu/.

COLLEGE OF CHARLESTON
Charleston, SC

Tuition & fees (SC res): $9918	Average undergraduate aid package: $12,724

ABOUT THE INSTITUTION State-supported, coed. *Awards:* certificates, bachelor's, and master's degrees (also offers graduate degree programs through University of Charleston, South Carolina). 48 undergraduate majors. *Total enrollment:* 11,723. Undergraduates: 10,506. Freshmen: 2,138. Federal methodology is used as a basis for awarding need-based institutional aid.

UNDERGRADUATE EXPENSES for 2013–2014 *Application fee:* $50. *Tuition, state resident:* full-time $9918; part-time $413 per semester hour. *Tuition, nonresident:* full-time $25,304; part-time $1054 per semester hour. Full-time tuition and fees vary according to degree level. Part-time tuition and fees vary according to course load and degree level. *College room and board:* $10,461; *Room only:* $7111. Room and board charges vary according to board plan and housing facility.

FRESHMAN FINANCIAL AID (Fall 2012, est.) 1,577 applied for aid; of those 69% were deemed to have need. 94% of freshmen with need received aid; of those 22% had need fully met. *Average percent of need met:* 57% (excluding resources awarded to replace EFC). *Average financial aid package:* $12,581 (excluding resources awarded to replace EFC). 23% of all full-time freshmen had no need and received non-need-based gift aid.

UNDERGRADUATE FINANCIAL AID (Fall 2012, est.) 6,090 applied for aid; of those 77% were deemed to have need. 96% of undergraduates with need received aid; of those 20% had need fully met. *Average percent of need met:* 57% (excluding resources awarded to replace EFC). *Average financial aid package:* $12,724 (excluding resources awarded to replace EFC). 18% of all full-time undergraduates had no need and received non-need-based gift aid.

GIFT AID (NEED-BASED) *Total amount:* $25,335,973 (42% federal, 31% state, 23% institutional, 4% external sources). *Receiving aid:* Freshmen: 35% (738); all full-time undergraduates: 32% (3,116). *Average award:* Freshmen: $3275; Undergraduates: $3030. *Scholarships, grants, and awards:* Federal Pell, FSEOG, state, private, college/university gift aid from institutional funds.

GIFT AID (NON-NEED-BASED) *Total amount:* $18,506,590 (55% state, 40% institutional, 5% external sources). *Receiving aid:* Freshmen: 34% (726). Undergraduates: 20% (1,901). *Average award:* Freshmen: $10,468. Undergraduates: $10,788. *Scholarships, grants, and awards by category:* Academic interests/achievement: biological sciences, business, communication, computer science, education, engineering/technologies, English, foreign languages, general academic interests/

achievements, health fields, humanities, mathematics, physical sciences, premedicine, social sciences. *Creative arts/performance:* art/fine arts, music, performing arts, theater/drama. *Special characteristics:* general special characteristics. *Tuition waivers:* Full or partial for senior citizens. *ROTC:* Air Force cooperative.

LOANS *Student loans:* $37,514,921 (68% need-based, 32% non-need-based). 48% of past graduating class borrowed through all loan programs. *Average indebtedness per student:* $32,880. *Average need-based loan:* Freshmen: $2954. Undergraduates: $3578. *Parent loans:* $25,255,693 (56% need-based, 44% non-need-based). *Programs:* Federal Direct (Subsidized and Unsubsidized Stafford, PLUS), Perkins.

WORK-STUDY *Federal work-study:* Total amount: $261,877; jobs available. *State or other work-study/employment:* Part-time jobs available.

ATHLETIC AWARDS Total amount: $3,890,696 (23% need-based, 77% non-need-based).

APPLYING FOR FINANCIAL AID *Required financial aid form:* FAFSA. *Financial aid deadline (priority):* 3/15. *Notification date:* Continuous beginning 4/10. Students must reply within 8 weeks of notification.

CONTACT Mr. Don Griggs, Director of Financial Aid, College of Charleston, 66 George Street, Charleston, SC 29424, 843-953-5540. *Fax:* 843-953-7192. *Website:* http://www.cofc.edu/.

COLLEGE OF COASTAL GEORGIA
Brunswick, GA

CONTACT Financial Aid Office, College of Coastal Georgia, One College Drive, Brunswick, GA 31520, 912-264-7235 or toll-free 800-675-7235. *Website:* http://www.ccga.edu/.

THE COLLEGE OF IDAHO
Caldwell, ID

Tuition & fees: $23,000	Average undergraduate aid package: $23,706

ABOUT THE INSTITUTION Independent, coed. *Awards:* bachelor's and master's degrees. 36 undergraduate majors. *Total enrollment:* 1,059. Undergraduates: 1,042. Freshmen: 292. Federal methodology is used as a basis for awarding need-based institutional aid.

UNDERGRADUATE EXPENSES for 2013–2014 *One-time required fee:* $355. *Comprehensive fee:* $31,646 includes full-time tuition ($22,600), mandatory fees ($400), and room and board ($8646). Room and board charges vary according to board plan and housing facility. *Part-time tuition:* $940 per credit. Part-time tuition and fees vary according to course load.

FRESHMAN FINANCIAL AID (Fall 2012, est.) 212 applied for aid; of those 100% were deemed to have need. 100% of freshmen with need received aid; of those 17% had need fully met. *Average percent of need met:* 94% (excluding resources awarded to replace EFC). *Average financial aid package:* $24,707 (excluding resources awarded to replace EFC). 18% of all full-time freshmen had no need and received non-need-based gift aid.

UNDERGRADUATE FINANCIAL AID (Fall 2012, est.) 707 applied for aid; of those 100% were deemed to have need. 100% of undergraduates with need received aid; of those 17% had need fully met. *Average percent of need met:* 93% (excluding resources awarded to replace EFC). *Average financial aid package:* $23,706 (excluding resources awarded to replace EFC). 21% of all full-time undergraduates had no need and received non-need-based gift aid.

GIFT AID (NEED-BASED) *Total amount:* $5,204,698 (36% federal, 39% institutional, 25% external sources). *Receiving aid:* Freshmen: 74% (212); all full-time undergraduates: 71% (707). *Average award:* Freshmen: $7630; Undergraduates: $7240. *Scholarships, grants, and awards:* Federal Pell, FSEOG, state, private, college/university gift aid from institutional funds.

GIFT AID (NON-NEED-BASED) *Total amount:* $9,580,442 (2% state, 95% institutional, 3% external sources). *Receiving aid:* Freshmen: 74% (212). Undergraduates: 71% (707). *Average award:* Freshmen: $13,304. Undergraduates: $12,358. *Scholarships, grants, and awards by category:* Academic interests/achievement: 871 awards ($5,915,059 total): biological sciences, business, education, English, foreign languages, general academic interests/achievements, humanities, mathematics, physical sciences, premedicine, religion/biblical studies, social sciences. *Creative* arts/performance: 168 awards ($320,424 total): art/fine arts, debating, music, performing arts, theater/drama. *Special achievements/activities:* 4 awards ($11,732 total): leadership. *Special characteristics:* 257 awards ($1,184,528 total): children and siblings of alumni, children of educators, children of faculty/staff, first-generation college students, international students, local/state students, married students, members of minority groups, out-of-state students, siblings of current students, veterans' children. *Tuition waivers:* Full or partial for employees or children of employees. *ROTC:* Army cooperative.

LOANS *Student loans:* $5,224,863 (49% need-based, 51% non-need-based). 55% of past graduating class borrowed through all loan programs. *Average indebtedness per student:* $27,008. *Average need-based loan:* Freshmen: $3831. Undergraduates: $4561. *Parent loans:* $740,391 (100% non-need-based). *Programs:* Federal Direct (Subsidized and Unsubsidized Stafford, PLUS), Perkins, private loans.

WORK-STUDY *Federal work-study:* Total amount: $115,700; 151 jobs averaging $800. *State or other work-study/employment:* Total amount: $33,065 (100% need-based). 46 part-time jobs averaging $800.

ATHLETIC AWARDS Total amount: $1,112,085 (100% non-need-based).

APPLYING FOR FINANCIAL AID *Required financial aid forms:* FAFSA, institution's own form. *Financial aid deadline (priority):* 2/15. *Notification date:* Continuous. Students must reply within 3 weeks of notification.

CONTACT Juanitta M. Pearson, Director of Financial Aid Services, The College of Idaho, 2112 Cleveland Boulevard, Caldwell, ID 83605, 208-459-5307 or toll-free 800-244-3246. *Fax:* 208-459-5844. *E-mail:* jpearson@collegeofidaho.edu. *Website:* http://www.collegeofidaho.edu/.

COLLEGE OF MOUNT ST. JOSEPH
Cincinnati, OH

Tuition & fees: $25,800	Average undergraduate aid package: $18,744

ABOUT THE INSTITUTION Independent Roman Catholic, coed. *Awards:* certificates, associate, bachelor's, master's, and doctoral degrees. 36 undergraduate majors. *Total enrollment:* 2,294. Undergraduates: 1,840. Freshmen: 281. Federal methodology is used as a basis for awarding need-based institutional aid.

UNDERGRADUATE EXPENSES for 2013–2014 *Application fee:* $25. *One-time required fee:* $200. *Comprehensive fee:* $33,880 includes full-time tuition ($24,900), mandatory fees ($900), and room and board ($8080). *College room only:* $3990. Full-time tuition and fees vary according to course load and reciprocity agreements. Room and board charges vary according to board plan and housing facility. *Part-time tuition:* $500 per credit hour. Part-time tuition and fees vary according to course load and reciprocity agreements.

FRESHMAN FINANCIAL AID (Fall 2012, est.) 249 applied for aid; of those 91% were deemed to have need. 100% of freshmen with need received aid; of those 24% had need fully met. *Average percent of need met:* 84% (excluding resources awarded to replace EFC). *Average financial aid package:* $20,801 (excluding resources awarded to replace EFC). 16% of all full-time freshmen had no need and received non-need-based gift aid.

UNDERGRADUATE FINANCIAL AID (Fall 2012, est.) 1,082 applied for aid; of those 89% were deemed to have need. 100% of undergraduates with need received aid; of those 21% had need fully met. *Average percent of need met:* 76% (excluding resources awarded to replace EFC). *Average financial aid package:* $18,744 (excluding resources awarded to replace EFC). 18% of all full-time undergraduates had no need and received non-need-based gift aid.

GIFT AID (NEED-BASED) *Total amount:* $14,269,985 (24% federal, 6% state, 68% institutional, 2% external sources). *Receiving aid:* Freshmen: 81% (222); all full-time undergraduates: 77% (938). *Average award:* Freshmen: $15,735; Undergraduates: $14,102. *Scholarships, grants, and awards:* Federal Pell, FSEOG, state, private, college/university gift aid from institutional funds.

GIFT AID (NON-NEED-BASED) *Total amount:* $2,372,255 (12% federal, 87% institutional, 1% external sources). *Receiving aid:* Freshmen: 9% (24). Undergraduates: 8% (101). *Average award:* Freshmen: $10,619. Undergraduates: $10,341. *Scholarships, grants, and awards by category:* Academic interests/achievement: 212 awards ($2,209,367 total): general academic interests/achievements. Creative arts/performance: 10 awards ($17,000 total): art/fine arts, music. Special achievements/activities: 16 awards ($38,000 total): community service, leadership. Special characteristics: 31 awards ($725,803 total): adult students, children and siblings of alumni, children of faculty/staff. *Tuition waivers:* Full or partial for employees or

children of employees, senior citizens. *ROTC:* Army cooperative, Air Force cooperative.

LOANS *Student loans:* $10,861,390 (93% need-based, 7% non-need-based). *Average need-based loan:* Freshmen: $4042. Undergraduates: $4569. *Parent loans:* $2,332,731 (87% need-based, 13% non-need-based). *Programs:* Perkins, Federal Nursing, state.

WORK-STUDY *Federal work-study:* Total amount: $133,400; 32 jobs averaging $1425. *State or other work-study/employment:* Total amount: $434,900 (98% need-based, 2% non-need-based). 109 part-time jobs averaging $1482.

APPLYING FOR FINANCIAL AID *Required financial aid form:* FAFSA. *Financial aid deadline (priority):* 3/1. *Notification date:* Continuous beginning 1/31. Students must reply by 5/1 or within 4 weeks of notification.

CONTACT Ms. Kathryn Kelly, Director of Student Administrative Services, College of Mount St. Joseph, 5701 Delhi Road, Cincinnati, OH 45233-1670, 513-244-4418 or toll-free 800-654-9314. *Fax:* 513-244-4201. *E-mail:* kathy_kelly@mail.msj.edu. *Website:* http://www.msj.edu/.

COLLEGE OF MOUNT SAINT VINCENT
Riverdale, NY

CONTACT Ms. Monica Simotas, Director of Financial Aid, College of Mount Saint Vincent, 6301 Riverdale Avenue, Riverdale, NY 10471, 718-405-3290 or toll-free 800-665-CMSV. *Fax:* 718-405-3490. *E-mail:* msimotas@mountsaintvincent.edu. *Website:* http://www.mountsaintvincent.edu/.

THE COLLEGE OF NEW JERSEY
Ewing, NJ

Tuition & fees (NJ res): $14,378	Average undergraduate aid package: $10,647

ABOUT THE INSTITUTION State-supported, coed. *Awards:* certificates, bachelor's, and master's degrees. 48 undergraduate majors. *Total enrollment:* 7,270. Undergraduates: 6,545. Freshmen: 1,363. Federal methodology is used as a basis for awarding need-based institutional aid.

UNDERGRADUATE EXPENSES for 2013–2014 *Application fee:* $75. *Tuition, state resident:* full-time $10,102; part-time $358 per credit hour. *Tuition, nonresident:* full-time $20,254; part-time $716.87 per credit hour. *Required fees:* full-time $4276; $170.29 per credit hour. Part-time tuition and fees vary according to course load. *College room and board:* $10,998; *Room only:* $8006. Room and board charges vary according to board plan.

FRESHMAN FINANCIAL AID (Fall 2012, est.) 1,189 applied for aid; of those 66% were deemed to have need. 95% of freshmen with need received aid; of those 15% had need fully met. *Average percent of need met:* 45% (excluding resources awarded to replace EFC). *Average financial aid package:* $11,034 (excluding resources awarded to replace EFC). 15% of all full-time freshmen had no need and received non-need-based gift aid.

UNDERGRADUATE FINANCIAL AID (Fall 2012, est.) 4,643 applied for aid; of those 73% were deemed to have need. 96% of undergraduates with need received aid; of those 14% had need fully met. *Average percent of need met:* 47% (excluding resources awarded to replace EFC). *Average financial aid package:* $10,647 (excluding resources awarded to replace EFC). 10% of all full-time undergraduates had no need and received non-need-based gift aid.

GIFT AID (NEED-BASED) *Total amount:* $21,637,917 (24% federal, 31% state, 38% institutional, 7% external sources). *Receiving aid:* Freshmen: 21% (288); all full-time undergraduates: 21% (1,342). *Average award:* Freshmen: $14,369; Undergraduates: $11,219. *Scholarships, grants, and awards:* Federal Pell, FSEOG, state, private, college/university gift aid from institutional funds, Federal Nursing.

GIFT AID (NON-NEED-BASED) *Total amount:* $5,596,679 (1% federal, 2% state, 84% institutional, 13% external sources). *Receiving aid:* Freshmen: 27% (364). Undergraduates: 21% (1,315). *Average award:* Freshmen: $5798. Undergraduates: $4609. *Scholarships, grants, and awards by category:* Academic interests/achievement: general academic interests/achievements. Creative arts/performance: art/fine arts, music. Special characteristics: children with a deceased or disabled parent, members of minority groups. *Tuition waivers:* Full or partial for employees or children of employees, senior citizens. *ROTC:* Army cooperative, Air Force cooperative.

LOANS *Student loans:* $33,816,317 (79% need-based, 21% non-need-based). 60% of past graduating class borrowed through all loan programs. *Average indebtedness per student:* $33,889. *Average need-based loan:* Freshmen: $3600. Undergraduates: $4603. *Parent loans:* $4,286,907 (80% need-based, 20% non-need-based). *Programs:* Federal Direct (Subsidized and Unsubsidized Stafford, PLUS), Perkins, Federal Nursing.

WORK-STUDY *Federal work-study:* Total amount: $132,160; jobs available.

APPLYING FOR FINANCIAL AID *Required financial aid form:* FAFSA. *Financial aid deadline (priority):* 3/1. *Notification date:* Continuous beginning 6/1. Students must reply within 2 weeks of notification.

CONTACT Mr. Wilbert Casaine, Director of Financial Aid, The College of New Jersey, PO Box 7718, Ewing, NJ 08628, 609-771-2602. *Fax:* 609-637-5154. *E-mail:* casainew@tcnj.edu.
Website: http://www.tcnj.edu/.

THE COLLEGE OF NEW ROCHELLE
New Rochelle, NY

Tuition & fees: $31,260	Average undergraduate aid package: $22,319

ABOUT THE INSTITUTION Independent, coed, primarily women. *Awards:* certificates, bachelor's, and master's degrees (also offers a non-traditional adult program with significant enrollment not reflected in profile). 35 undergraduate majors. *Total enrollment:* 1,670. Undergraduates: 840. Freshmen: 84. Federal methodology is used as a basis for awarding need-based institutional aid.

UNDERGRADUATE EXPENSES for 2013–2014 *Application fee:* $35. *Comprehensive fee:* $42,950 includes full-time tuition ($30,210), mandatory fees ($1050), and room and board ($11,690). Full-time tuition and fees vary according to course load, location, and program. Room and board charges vary according to housing facility. *Part-time tuition:* $896 per credit. *Part-time fees:* $450 per term. Part-time tuition and fees vary according to course load, location, and program.

FRESHMAN FINANCIAL AID (Fall 2011) 108 applied for aid; of those 96% were deemed to have need. 100% of freshmen with need received aid; of those 6% had need fully met. *Average percent of need met:* 76% (excluding resources awarded to replace EFC). *Average financial aid package:* $26,756 (excluding resources awarded to replace EFC). 4% of all full-time freshmen had no need and received non-need-based gift aid.

UNDERGRADUATE FINANCIAL AID (Fall 2011) 535 applied for aid; of those 95% were deemed to have need. 100% of undergraduates with need received aid; of those 2% had need fully met. *Average percent of need met:* 64% (excluding resources awarded to replace EFC). *Average financial aid package:* $22,319 (excluding resources awarded to replace EFC). 5% of all full-time undergraduates had no need and received non-need-based gift aid.

GIFT AID (NEED-BASED) *Total amount:* $9,305,655 (21% federal, 10% state, 68% institutional, 1% external sources). *Receiving aid:* Freshmen: 86% (93); all full-time undergraduates: 83% (446). *Average award:* Freshmen: $12,109; Undergraduates: $10,056. *Scholarships, grants, and awards:* Federal Pell, FSEOG, state, private, college/university gift aid from institutional funds.

GIFT AID (NON-NEED-BASED) *Total amount:* $369,496 (100% institutional). *Receiving aid:* Freshmen: 95% (103). Undergraduates: 80% (431). *Average award:* Freshmen: $11,875. Undergraduates: $14,044. *Scholarships, grants, and awards by category:* Academic interests/achievement: 260 awards ($2,985,000 total): area/ethnic studies, biological sciences, business, communication, education, English, foreign languages, general academic interests/achievements, health fields, humanities, mathematics, physical sciences, premedicine, religion/biblical studies, social sciences. *Creative arts/performance:* 50 awards ($358,200 total): applied art and design, art/fine arts, cinema/film/broadcasting, creative writing, dance, debating, general creative arts/performance, journalism/publications, music, performing arts, theater/drama. *Special achievements/activities:* 87 awards ($92,750 total): community service, general special achievements/activities, hobbies/interests, leadership, memberships, religious involvement. *Special characteristics:* 60 awards ($275,865 total): children and siblings of alumni, children of faculty/staff, children of union members/company employees, children of workers in trades, general special characteristics, out-of-state students, parents of current students, previous college experience, siblings of current students, spouses of current students, spouses of deceased or disabled public servants, veterans,

veterans' children. *Tuition waivers:* Full or partial for employees or children of employees.

LOANS *Student loans:* $5,241,876 (54% need-based, 46% non-need-based). 89% of past graduating class borrowed through all loan programs. *Average indebtedness per student:* $22,923. *Average need-based loan:* Freshmen: $4696. Undergraduates: $5586. *Parent loans:* $541,134 (97% need-based, 3% non-need-based). *Programs:* Federal Direct (Subsidized and Unsubsidized Stafford, PLUS), Perkins, Federal Nursing.

WORK-STUDY *Federal work-study:* Total amount: $988,781; 391 jobs averaging $2529. *State or other work-study/employment:* Part-time jobs available.

APPLYING FOR FINANCIAL AID *Required financial aid forms:* FAFSA, institution's own form, federal income tax form(s). *Financial aid deadline:* Continuous. *Notification date:* Continuous beginning 1/1. Students must reply within 2 weeks of notification.

CONTACT Anne Pelak, Director of Financial Aid, The College of New Rochelle, 29 Castle Place, New Rochelle, NY 10805-2339, 914-654-5225 or toll-free 800-933-5923. *Fax:* 914-654-5420. *E-mail:* apelak@cnr.edu.
Website: http://www.cnr.edu/.

COLLEGE OF SAINT BENEDICT
Saint Joseph, MN

Tuition & fees: $36,218	Average undergraduate aid package: $28,920

ABOUT THE INSTITUTION Independent Roman Catholic, women only. *Awards:* bachelor's degrees (coordinate with Saint John's University for men). 50 undergraduate majors. *Total enrollment:* 2,070. Undergraduates: 2,070. Freshmen: 490. Federal methodology is used as a basis for awarding need-based institutional aid.

UNDERGRADUATE EXPENSES for 2013–2014 *Comprehensive fee:* $45,489 includes full-time tuition ($35,298), mandatory fees ($920), and room and board ($9271). *College room only:* $4463. Room and board charges vary according to board plan and housing facility. *Part-time tuition:* $1471 per semester hour. Part-time tuition and fees vary according to course load.

FRESHMAN FINANCIAL AID (Fall 2012, est.) 415 applied for aid; of those 85% were deemed to have need. 100% of freshmen with need received aid; of those 44% had need fully met. *Average percent of need met:* 90% (excluding resources awarded to replace EFC). *Average financial aid package:* $30,885 (excluding resources awarded to replace EFC). 23% of all full-time freshmen had no need and received non-need-based gift aid.

UNDERGRADUATE FINANCIAL AID (Fall 2012, est.) 1,590 applied for aid; of those 89% were deemed to have need. 100% of undergraduates with need received aid; of those 35% had need fully met. *Average percent of need met:* 86% (excluding resources awarded to replace EFC). *Average financial aid package:* $28,920 (excluding resources awarded to replace EFC). 25% of all full-time undergraduates had no need and received non-need-based gift aid.

GIFT AID (NEED-BASED) *Total amount:* $30,732,055 (8% federal, 7% state, 82% institutional, 3% external sources). *Receiving aid:* Freshmen: 71% (347); all full-time undergraduates: 67% (1,362). *Average award:* Freshmen: $24,394; Undergraduates: $22,145. *Scholarships, grants, and awards:* Federal Pell, FSEOG, state, college/university gift aid from institutional funds.

GIFT AID (NON-NEED-BASED) *Total amount:* $9,884,230 (1% federal, 95% institutional, 4% external sources). *Receiving aid:* Freshmen: 70% (342). Undergraduates: 65% (1,310). *Average award:* Freshmen: $15,133. Undergraduates: $13,827. *Scholarships, grants, and awards by category:* Academic interests/achievement: 1,825 awards ($22,911,823 total): computer science, engineering/technologies, general academic interests/achievements, mathematics, military science, physical sciences. *Creative arts/performance:* 228 awards ($502,537 total): art/fine arts, music, theater/drama. *Special characteristics:* 442 awards ($2,918,437 total): international students, out-of-state students. *Tuition waivers:* Full or partial for employees or children of employees. *ROTC:* Army cooperative.

LOANS *Student loans:* $15,898,944 (91% need-based, 9% non-need-based). 74% of past graduating class borrowed through all loan programs. *Average indebtedness per student:* $40,030. *Average need-based loan:* Freshmen: $4289. Undergraduates: $5097. *Parent loans:* $1,421,385 (89% need-based, 11% non-need-based). *Programs:* Federal Direct (Subsidized and Unsubsidized Stafford, PLUS), Perkins, state, private loans.

WORK-STUDY *Federal work-study:* Total amount: $1,544,133; 632 jobs averaging $2507. *State or other work-study/employment:* Total amount: $2,092,372 (69% need-based, 31% non-need-based). 884 part-time jobs averaging $2503.

APPLYING FOR FINANCIAL AID *Required financial aid forms:* FAFSA, institution's own form. *Financial aid deadline (priority):* 3/15. *Notification date:* Continuous beginning 3/15. Students must reply by 5/1.

CONTACT Mr. Stuart Perry, Executive Director of Financial Aid, College of Saint Benedict, 37 South College Avenue, Saint Joseph, MN 56374-2099, 320-363-5388 or toll-free 800-544-1489. *Fax:* 320-363-6090. *E-mail:* sperry@csbsju.edu. *Website:* http://www.csbsju.edu/.

COLLEGE OF SAINT ELIZABETH
Morristown, NJ

Tuition & fees: $29,907 | Average undergraduate aid package: N/A

ABOUT THE INSTITUTION Independent Roman Catholic, coed, primarily women. *Awards:* certificates, bachelor's, master's, and doctoral degrees (also offers coed adult undergraduate degree program and coed graduate programs). 28 undergraduate majors. *Total enrollment:* 1,687. Undergraduates: 1,079. Freshmen: 146. Both federal and institutional methodology are used as a basis for awarding need-based institutional aid.

UNDERGRADUATE EXPENSES for 2013–2014 *Application fee:* $35. *Comprehensive fee:* $42,161 includes full-time tuition ($28,026), mandatory fees ($1881), and room and board ($12,254). Full-time tuition and fees vary according to class time and location. Room and board charges vary according to board plan. *Part-time tuition:* $806 per credit hour. Part-time tuition and fees vary according to class time, course load, location, program, and reciprocity agreements.

GIFT AID (NEED-BASED) *Total amount:* $7,815,983 (23% federal, 39% state, 37% institutional, 1% external sources). *Scholarships, grants, and awards:* Federal Pell, FSEOG, state, private, college/university gift aid from institutional funds.

GIFT AID (NON-NEED-BASED) *Total amount:* $4,575,217 (1% state, 99% institutional). *Scholarships, grants, and awards by category:* Academic interests/achievement: general academic interests/achievements. Special achievements/activities: community service, leadership. Special characteristics: adult students, children and siblings of alumni. *Tuition waivers:* Full or partial for children of alumni, employees or children of employees, senior citizens.

LOANS *Student loans:* $4,822,239 (54% need-based, 46% non-need-based). *Programs:* Perkins.

WORK-STUDY *Federal work-study:* Total amount: $120,777; 519 jobs averaging $227.

APPLYING FOR FINANCIAL AID *Required financial aid form:* FAFSA. *Financial aid deadline:* Continuous. *Notification date:* Continuous beginning 11/15. Students must reply by 5/1 or within 2 weeks of notification.

CONTACT Debra Wulff, Director of Financial Aid, College of Saint Elizabeth, 2 Convent Road, Morristown, NJ 07960-6989, 973-290-4492 or toll-free 800-210-7900. *E-mail:* dwulff@cse.edu. *Website:* http://www.cse.edu/.

COLLEGE OF ST. JOSEPH
Rutland, VT

ABOUT THE INSTITUTION Independent Roman Catholic, coed. *Awards:* certificates, associate, bachelor's, and master's degrees. 13 undergraduate majors. *Total enrollment:* 377. Undergraduates: 237. Freshmen: 44.

GIFT AID (NEED-BASED) *Scholarships, grants, and awards:* Federal Pell, FSEOG, state, private, college/university gift aid from institutional funds.

GIFT AID (NON-NEED-BASED) *Scholarships, grants, and awards by category:* Academic interests/achievement: general academic interests/achievements. Creative arts/performance: music. Special achievements/activities: leadership. Special characteristics: general special characteristics, local/state students, previous college experience, religious affiliation, veterans.

LOANS *Programs:* Federal Direct (Subsidized and Unsubsidized Stafford, PLUS), Perkins.

WORK-STUDY *Federal work-study:* Total amount: $47,137; 42 jobs averaging $1121. *State or other work-study/employment:* Total amount: $31,214 (95% need-based, 5% non-need-based). 40 part-time jobs averaging $780.

APPLYING FOR FINANCIAL AID *Required financial aid forms:* FAFSA, institution's own form.

CONTACT Julie Rosmus, Director of Financial Aid, College of St. Joseph, 71 Clement Road, Rutland, VT 05701-3899, 802-773-5900 Ext. 3274 or toll-free 877-270-9998. *Fax:* 802-776-5275. *E-mail:* jrosmus@csj.edu. *Website:* http://www.csj.edu/.

COLLEGE OF SAINT MARY
Omaha, NE

Tuition & fees: $25,310 | Average undergraduate aid package: $17,850

ABOUT THE INSTITUTION Independent Roman Catholic, women only. *Awards:* certificates, associate, bachelor's, master's, and doctoral degrees. 22 undergraduate majors. *Total enrollment:* 1,037. Undergraduates: 782. Freshmen: 91. Federal methodology is used as a basis for awarding need-based institutional aid.

UNDERGRADUATE EXPENSES for 2013–2014 *Application fee:* $30. *Comprehensive fee:* $32,110 includes full-time tuition ($24,830), mandatory fees ($480), and room and board ($6800). Full-time tuition and fees vary according to location and program. *Part-time tuition:* $825 per credit. *Part-time fees:* $16 per credit. Part-time tuition and fees vary according to class time, course load, location, and program.

FRESHMAN FINANCIAL AID (Fall 2012, est.) 76 applied for aid; of those 87% were deemed to have need. 100% of freshmen with need received aid; of those 20% had need fully met. *Average percent of need met:* 77% (excluding resources awarded to replace EFC). *Average financial aid package:* $20,350 (excluding resources awarded to replace EFC). 13% of all full-time freshmen had no need and received non-need-based gift aid.

UNDERGRADUATE FINANCIAL AID (Fall 2012, est.) 631 applied for aid; of those 94% were deemed to have need. 100% of undergraduates with need received aid; of those 8% had need fully met. *Average percent of need met:* 61% (excluding resources awarded to replace EFC). *Average financial aid package:* $17,850 (excluding resources awarded to replace EFC). 6% of all full-time undergraduates had no need and received non-need-based gift aid.

GIFT AID (NEED-BASED) *Total amount:* $6,631,272 (25% federal, 3% state, 67% institutional, 5% external sources). *Receiving aid:* Freshmen: 87% (66); all full-time undergraduates: 90% (570). *Average award:* Freshmen: $16,721; Undergraduates: $12,160. *Scholarships, grants, and awards:* Federal Pell, FSEOG, state, private, college/university gift aid from institutional funds, Federal Nursing.

GIFT AID (NON-NEED-BASED) *Total amount:* $493,693 (1% federal, 83% institutional, 16% external sources). *Receiving aid:* Freshmen: 14% (11). Undergraduates: 5% (34). *Average award:* Freshmen: $11,010. Undergraduates: $7904. *Scholarships, grants, and awards by category:* Academic interests/achievement: 644 awards ($2,199,196 total): biological sciences, education, general academic interests/achievements, mathematics. Creative arts/performance: 8 awards ($10,000 total): art/fine arts, debating, music. Special achievements/activities: 333 awards ($380,500 total): community service, general special achievements/activities, leadership, religious involvement. Special characteristics: 160 awards ($214,110 total): children of faculty/staff, first-generation college students, general special characteristics, international students. *Tuition waivers:* Full or partial for employees or children of employees, senior citizens. *ROTC:* Army cooperative, Air Force cooperative.

LOANS *Student loans:* $6,750,432 (88% need-based, 12% non-need-based). 77% of past graduating class borrowed through all loan programs. *Average indebtedness per student:* $31,522. *Average need-based loan:* Freshmen: $3741. Undergraduates: $6047. *Parent loans:* $921,433 (47% need-based, 53% non-need-based). *Programs:* Federal Direct (Subsidized and Unsubsidized Stafford, PLUS), Perkins, Federal Nursing.

WORK-STUDY *Federal work-study:* Total amount: $279,965; 161 jobs averaging $1739. *State or other work-study/employment:* Total amount: $64,800 (77% need-based, 23% non-need-based). 10 part-time jobs averaging $7160.

ATHLETIC AWARDS Total amount: $573,292 (75% need-based, 25% non-need-based).

APPLYING FOR FINANCIAL AID *Required financial aid form:* FAFSA. *Financial aid deadline (priority):* 3/15. *Notification date:* Continuous beginning 3/15. Students must reply within 2 weeks of notification.

CONTACT Beth Sisk, Director of Financial Aid and the Express Center, College of Saint Mary, 7000 Mercy Road, Omaha, NE 68106, 402-399-2362 or toll-free 800-926-5534. *Fax:* 402-399-2480. *E-mail:* finaid@csm.edu. *Website:* http://www.csm.edu/.

COLLEGE OF SAINT MARY MAGDALEN
Warner, NH

Tuition & fees: N/R	Average undergraduate aid package: $12,675

ABOUT THE INSTITUTION Independent Roman Catholic, coed. 1 undergraduate major. Institutional methodology is used as a basis for awarding need-based institutional aid.
FRESHMAN FINANCIAL AID (Fall 2012, est.) 26 applied for aid; of those 100% were deemed to have need. 100% of freshmen with need received aid; of those 35% had need fully met. *Average percent of need met:* 36% (excluding resources awarded to replace EFC). *Average financial aid package:* $14,300 (excluding resources awarded to replace EFC). 22% of all full-time freshmen had no need and received non-need-based gift aid.
UNDERGRADUATE FINANCIAL AID (Fall 2012, est.) 59 applied for aid; of those 100% were deemed to have need. 100% of undergraduates with need received aid; of those 37% had need fully met. *Average percent of need met:* 36% (excluding resources awarded to replace EFC). *Average financial aid package:* $12,675 (excluding resources awarded to replace EFC). 14% of all full-time undergraduates had no need and received non-need-based gift aid.
GIFT AID (NEED-BASED) Total amount: $570,442 (100% institutional). *Receiving aid:* Freshmen: 96% (26); all full-time undergraduates: 91% (59). *Average award:* Freshmen: $9087; Undergraduates: $9669. *Scholarships, grants, and awards:* private, college/university gift aid from institutional funds.
GIFT AID (NON-NEED-BASED) Total amount: $181,902 (98% institutional, 2% external sources). *Receiving aid:* Freshmen: 96% (26). Undergraduates: 54% (35). *Average award:* Freshmen: $6833. Undergraduates: $3667. *Scholarships, grants, and awards by category:* Academic interests/achievement: 35 awards ($177,402 total): English, foreign languages, general academic interests/achievements, humanities, religion/biblical studies.
LOANS Student loans: $204,170 (100% need-based). 71% of past graduating class borrowed through all loan programs. *Programs:* alternative loans.
APPLYING FOR FINANCIAL AID *Required financial aid forms:* institution's own form, business/farm supplement, federal income tax form(s). *Financial aid deadline:* Continuous. *Notification date:* Continuous beginning 2/1. Students must reply within 4 weeks of notification.
CONTACT Marie A. Lasher, Financial Aid Director, College of Saint Mary Magdalen, 511 Kearsarge Mountain Road, Warner, NH 03278, 603-456-2656 Ext. 136 or toll-free 877-498-1723. *Fax:* 603-456-2660. *E-mail:* babson@magdalen.edu. *Website:* http://www.magdalen.edu/.

THE COLLEGE OF SAINT ROSE
Albany, NY

Tuition & fees: $27,684	Average undergraduate aid package: $16,599

ABOUT THE INSTITUTION Independent, coed. *Awards:* certificates, bachelor's, and master's degrees. 50 undergraduate majors. *Total enrollment:* 4,698. Undergraduates: 2,881. Freshmen: 590. Federal methodology is used as a basis for awarding need-based institutional aid.
UNDERGRADUATE EXPENSES for 2013–2014 *Application fee:* $40. *Comprehensive fee:* $38,934 includes full-time tuition ($26,750), mandatory fees ($934), and room and board ($11,250). *College room only:* $5630. Full-time tuition and fees vary according to class time and course load. Room and board charges vary according to board plan and housing facility. *Part-time tuition:* $894 per credit hour. *Part-time fees:* $30 per credit hour; $78 per semester hour. Part-time tuition and fees vary according to class time and course load.

FRESHMAN FINANCIAL AID (Fall 2011) 579 applied for aid; of those 90% were deemed to have need. 100% of freshmen with need received aid; of those 18% had need fully met. *Average percent of need met:* 83% (excluding resources awarded to replace EFC). *Average financial aid package:* $17,580 (excluding resources awarded to replace EFC). 11% of all full-time freshmen had no need and received non-need-based gift aid.
UNDERGRADUATE FINANCIAL AID (Fall 2011) 2,554 applied for aid; of those 90% were deemed to have need. 99% of undergraduates with need received aid; of those 16% had need fully met. *Average percent of need met:* 80% (excluding resources awarded to replace EFC). *Average financial aid package:* $16,599 (excluding resources awarded to replace EFC). 12% of all full-time undergraduates had no need and received non-need-based gift aid.
GIFT AID (NEED-BASED) Total amount: $18,841,969 (26% federal, 19% state, 54% institutional, 1% external sources). *Receiving aid:* Freshmen: 78% (463); all full-time undergraduates: 73% (2,018). *Average award:* Freshmen: $14,694; Undergraduates: $12,673. *Scholarships, grants, and awards:* Federal Pell, FSEOG, state, private, college/university gift aid from institutional funds.
GIFT AID (NON-NEED-BASED) Total amount: $15,717,889 (1% federal, 97% institutional, 2% external sources). *Receiving aid:* Freshmen: 71% (422). Undergraduates: 60% (1,670). *Average award:* Freshmen: $11,711. Undergraduates: $9683. *Scholarships, grants, and awards by category:* Academic interests/achievement: business, communication, education, engineering/technologies, English, foreign languages, general academic interests/achievements, humanities, mathematics, premedicine, social sciences. *Creative arts/performance:* art/fine arts, music. *Special achievements/activities:* community service. *Special characteristics:* adult students, children and siblings of alumni, children of faculty/staff, children of union members/company employees, ethnic background, general special characteristics, members of minority groups, out-of-state students, siblings of current students, twins. *Tuition waivers:* Full or partial for employees or children of employees. *ROTC:* Army cooperative, Naval cooperative, Air Force cooperative.
LOANS Student loans: $16,419,396 (55% need-based, 45% non-need-based). 85% of past graduating class borrowed through all loan programs. *Average indebtedness per student:* $34,919. *Average need-based loan:* Freshmen: $3229. Undergraduates: $4107. *Parent loans:* $7,565,182 (99% need-based, 1% non-need-based). *Programs:* Federal Direct (Subsidized and Unsubsidized Stafford, PLUS), Perkins.
WORK-STUDY *Federal work-study:* Total amount: $378,613; jobs available. *State or other work-study/employment:* Total amount: $8444 (100% non-need-based). Part-time jobs available.
ATHLETIC AWARDS Total amount: $2,272,342 (91% need-based, 9% non-need-based).
APPLYING FOR FINANCIAL AID *Required financial aid forms:* FAFSA, state aid form. *Financial aid deadline:* 4/1 (priority: 2/1). *Notification date:* Continuous beginning 3/1. Students must reply by 5/1 or within 2 weeks of notification.
CONTACT Steven Dwire, Assistant Vice President of Financial Aid and Enrollment Management, The College of Saint Rose, 432 Western Avenue, Albertus Hall, Room 206, Albany, NY 12203-1419, 518-458-4915 or toll-free 800-637-8556. *Fax:* 518-454-2802. *E-mail:* finaid@strose.edu. *Website:* http://www.strose.edu/.

THE COLLEGE OF ST. SCHOLASTICA
Duluth, MN

Tuition & fees: $31,612	Average undergraduate aid package: $20,491

ABOUT THE INSTITUTION Independent Roman Catholic Church, coed. *Awards:* certificates, bachelor's, master's, and doctoral degrees. 36 undergraduate majors. *Total enrollment:* 4,144. Undergraduates: 2,877. Freshmen: 475. Federal methodology is used as a basis for awarding need-based institutional aid.
UNDERGRADUATE EXPENSES for 2013–2014 *Comprehensive fee:* $39,960 includes full-time tuition ($31,416), mandatory fees ($196), and room and board ($8348). *College room only:* $4644. Full-time tuition and fees vary according to class time and program. Room and board charges vary according to board plan and housing facility. *Part-time tuition:* $981 per credit. Part-time tuition and fees vary according to class time, course load, and program.
FRESHMAN FINANCIAL AID (Fall 2012, est.) 434 applied for aid; of those 88% were deemed to have need. 100% of freshmen with need received aid; of those 29% had need fully met. *Average percent of need met:* 75% (excluding resources

awarded to replace EFC). **Average financial aid package:** $23,647 (excluding resources awarded to replace EFC). 9% of all full-time freshmen had no need and received non-need-based gift aid.

UNDERGRADUATE FINANCIAL AID (Fall 2012, est.) 2,142 applied for aid; of those 92% were deemed to have need. 99% of undergraduates with need received aid; of those 21% had need fully met. **Average percent of need met:** 69% (excluding resources awarded to replace EFC). **Average financial aid package:** $20,491 (excluding resources awarded to replace EFC). 6% of all full-time undergraduates had no need and received non-need-based gift aid.

GIFT AID (NEED-BASED) Total amount: $11,260,409 (36% federal, 27% state, 37% institutional). **Receiving aid:** Freshmen: 67% (318); all full-time undergraduates: 64% (1,577). **Average award:** Freshmen: $7345; Undergraduates: $6830. **Scholarships, grants, and awards:** Federal Pell, FSEOG, state, private, college/university gift aid from institutional funds.

GIFT AID (NON-NEED-BASED) Total amount: $26,416,223 (2% federal, 95% institutional, 3% external sources). **Receiving aid:** Freshmen: 78% (371). Undergraduates: 64% (1,582). **Average award:** Freshmen: $12,717. Undergraduates: $11,928. **Scholarships, grants, and awards by category:** Academic interests/achievement: general academic interests/achievements. Creative arts/performance: music. Special characteristics: children and siblings of alumni, children of faculty/staff, ethnic background, handicapped students, international students, members of minority groups, previous college experience, religious affiliation, siblings of current students, spouses of current students. **Tuition waivers:** Full or partial for employees or children of employees, senior citizens. **ROTC:** Air Force cooperative.

LOANS Student loans: $25,163,638 (30% need-based, 70% non-need-based). 75% of past graduating class borrowed through all loan programs. **Average indebtedness per student:** $39,918. **Average need-based loan:** Freshmen: $3435. Undergraduates: $4569. **Parent loans:** $2,452,792 (100% non-need-based). **Programs:** Federal Direct (Subsidized and Unsubsidized Stafford, PLUS), Perkins, Federal Nursing, state, private loans.

WORK-STUDY Federal work-study: Total amount: $434,506; jobs available. **State or other work-study/employment:** Total amount: $1,647,693 (16% need-based, 84% non-need-based). Part-time jobs available.

APPLYING FOR FINANCIAL AID Required financial aid form: FAFSA. **Financial aid deadline (priority):** 3/1. **Notification date:** Continuous beginning 5/1. Students must reply by 5/1 or within 2 weeks of notification.

CONTACT Mr. Jon P. Erickson, Director of Financial Aid, The College of St. Scholastica, 1200 Kenwood Avenue, Duluth, MN 55811-4199, 218-723-6725 or toll-free 800-249-6412. Fax: 218-733-2229. E-mail: jerickso@css.edu. Website: http://www.css.edu/.

THE COLLEGE OF SAINTS JOHN FISHER & THOMAS MORE
Fort Worth, TX

Tuition & fees: $8000	Average undergraduate aid package: $15,800

ABOUT THE INSTITUTION Independent Roman Catholic Church, coed. **Awards:** associate and bachelor's degrees. 1 undergraduate major. **Total enrollment:** 21. Undergraduates: 21. Freshmen: 13. Institutional methodology is used as a basis for awarding need-based institutional aid.

UNDERGRADUATE EXPENSES for 2013–2014 Application fee: $25. **Comprehensive fee:** $10,000 includes full-time tuition ($8000) and room and board ($2000).

FRESHMAN FINANCIAL AID (Fall 2012, est.) 13 applied for aid; of those 100% were deemed to have need. 100% of freshmen with need received aid; of those 15% had need fully met. **Average percent of need met:** 88% (excluding resources awarded to replace EFC). **Average financial aid package:** $15,800 (excluding resources awarded to replace EFC).

UNDERGRADUATE FINANCIAL AID (Fall 2012, est.) 20 applied for aid; of those 100% were deemed to have need. 100% of undergraduates with need received aid; of those 30% had need fully met. **Average percent of need met:** 88% (excluding resources awarded to replace EFC). **Average financial aid package:** $15,800 (excluding resources awarded to replace EFC).

GIFT AID (NEED-BASED) Total amount: $312,225 (100% institutional). **Receiving aid:** Freshmen: 100% (13); all full-time undergraduates: 100% (20).

Average award: Freshmen: $15,800; Undergraduates: $15,800. **Scholarships, grants, and awards:** college/university gift aid from institutional funds. **GIFT AID (NON-NEED-BASED) ROTC:** Army cooperative. **LOANS Student loans:** 17% of past graduating class borrowed through all loan programs. **Average indebtedness per student:** $5474. **APPLYING FOR FINANCIAL AID Required financial aid form:** institution's own form. **Financial aid deadline:** 6/15. **Notification date:** 7/1. Students must reply by 7/15 or within 2 weeks of notification. **CONTACT** Mr. Peter M. Capani, Director of Enrollment Management, The College of Saints John Fisher & Thomas More, 3020 Lubbock Avenue, Fort Worth, TX 76109, 817-923-8459 Ext. 1. E-mail: peter.capani@fishermore.edu. Website: http://www.fishermore.edu/.

COLLEGE OF STATEN ISLAND OF THE CITY UNIVERSITY OF NEW YORK
Staten Island, NY

Tuition & fees (NY res): $5858	Average undergraduate aid package: $8074

ABOUT THE INSTITUTION State and locally supported, coed. **Awards:** certificates, associate, bachelor's, master's, and doctoral degrees. 41 undergraduate majors. **Total enrollment:** 14,321. Undergraduates: 13,364. Freshmen: 2,556. Federal methodology is used as a basis for awarding need-based institutional aid.

UNDERGRADUATE EXPENSES for 2013–2014 Application fee: $65. **Tuition, state resident:** full-time $5430; part-time $230 per credit. **Tuition, non-resident:** full-time $14,550; part-time $485 per credit. **Required fees:** full-time $428; $128 per term.

FRESHMAN FINANCIAL AID (Fall 2012, est.) 2,098 applied for aid; of those 77% were deemed to have need. 93% of freshmen with need received aid; of those 3% had need fully met. **Average percent of need met:** 58% (excluding resources awarded to replace EFC). **Average financial aid package:** $7804 (excluding resources awarded to replace EFC). 6% of all full-time freshmen had no need and received non-need-based gift aid.

UNDERGRADUATE FINANCIAL AID (Fall 2012, est.) 7,775 applied for aid; of those 85% were deemed to have need. 96% of undergraduates with need received aid; of those 2% had need fully met. **Average percent of need met:** 55% (excluding resources awarded to replace EFC). **Average financial aid package:** $8074 (excluding resources awarded to replace EFC). 3% of all full-time undergraduates had no need and received non-need-based gift aid.

GIFT AID (NEED-BASED) Total amount: $49,035,171 (58% federal, 37% state, 5% external sources). **Receiving aid:** Freshmen: 60% (1,439); all full-time undergraduates: 61% (6,006). **Average award:** Freshmen: $7517; Undergraduates: $7244. **Scholarships, grants, and awards:** Federal Pell, FSEOG, state, private, college/university gift aid from institutional funds, United Negro College Fund, Federal Nursing.

GIFT AID (NON-NEED-BASED) Total amount: $1,359,989 (23% federal, 34% state, 43% external sources). **Receiving aid:** Freshmen: 50% (1,201). Undergraduates: 51% (5,051). **Average award:** Freshmen: $1499. Undergraduates: $1703. **Scholarships, grants, and awards by category:** Academic interests/achievement: architecture, area/ethnic studies, biological sciences, business, communication, computer science, education, engineering/technologies, English, foreign languages, general academic interests/achievements, health fields, home economics, humanities, international studies, library science, mathematics, physical sciences, premedicine, social sciences. Creative arts/performance: applied art and design, art/fine arts, cinema/film/broadcasting, creative writing, dance, debating, general creative arts/performance, journalism/publications, music, performing arts, theater/drama. Special achievements/activities: community service, general special achievements/activities, hobbies/interests, leadership. Special characteristics: 12 awards ($25,300 total): adult students, children and siblings of alumni, children of faculty/staff, children with a deceased or disabled parent, ethnic background, first-generation college students, general special characteristics, handicapped students, international students, local/state students, members of minority groups, previous college experience, public servants, spouses of deceased or disabled public servants, veterans, veterans' children. **Tuition waivers:** Full or partial for employees or children of employees, senior citizens.

LOANS Student loans: $10,371,502 (100% need-based). **Average need-based loan:** Freshmen: $2823. Undergraduates: $4751. **Programs:** Federal Direct (Subsidized and Unsubsidized Stafford, PLUS), Perkins.

WORK-STUDY *Federal work-study:* Total amount: $1,095,200; 350 jobs averaging $1400. *State or other work-study/employment:* Total amount: $2250 (100% non-need-based). Part-time jobs available.
APPLYING FOR FINANCIAL AID *Required financial aid forms:* FAFSA, state aid form. *Financial aid deadline (priority):* 3/30. *Notification date:* Continuous beginning 6/1.
CONTACT Mr. Philippe Marius, Director of Financial Aid, College of Staten Island of the City University of New York, 2800 Victory Boulevard, 2A-401A, Staten Island, NY 10314-6600, 718-982-2030. *Fax:* 718-982-2037. *E-mail:* financialaid@csi.cuny.edu. *Website:* http://www.csi.cuny.edu/.

COLLEGE OF THE ATLANTIC
Bar Harbor, ME

Tuition & fees: $38,952 — Average undergraduate aid package: $35,359

ABOUT THE INSTITUTION Independent, coed. *Awards:* bachelor's and master's degrees. 42 undergraduate majors. *Total enrollment:* 340. Undergraduates: 330. Freshmen: 73. Both federal and institutional methodology are used as a basis for awarding need-based institutional aid.
UNDERGRADUATE EXPENSES for 2013–2014 *Application fee:* $50. *Comprehensive fee:* $48,210 includes full-time tuition ($38,403), mandatory fees ($549), and room and board ($9258). *College room only:* $5952. Full-time tuition and fees vary according to course load. Room and board charges vary according to board plan. *Part-time tuition:* $4267 per credit. *Part-time fees:* $183 per term. Part-time tuition and fees vary according to course load.
FRESHMAN FINANCIAL AID (Fall 2012, est.) 67 applied for aid; of those 99% were deemed to have need. 100% of freshmen with need received aid; of those 47% had need fully met. *Average percent of need met:* 94% (excluding resources awarded to replace EFC). *Average financial aid package:* $33,696 (excluding resources awarded to replace EFC). 7% of all full-time freshmen had no need and received non-need-based gift aid.
UNDERGRADUATE FINANCIAL AID (Fall 2012, est.) 272 applied for aid; of those 97% were deemed to have need. 100% of undergraduates with need received aid; of those 51% had need fully met. *Average percent of need met:* 95% (excluding resources awarded to replace EFC). *Average financial aid package:* $35,359 (excluding resources awarded to replace EFC). 7% of all full-time undergraduates had no need and received non-need-based gift aid.
GIFT AID (NEED-BASED) *Total amount:* $8,129,015 (6% federal, 1% state, 92% institutional, 1% external sources). *Receiving aid:* Freshmen: 90% (66); all full-time undergraduates: 84% (259). *Average award:* Freshmen: $28,542; Undergraduates: $30,483. *Scholarships, grants, and awards:* Federal Pell, FSEOG, state, private, college/university gift aid from institutional funds.
GIFT AID (NON-NEED-BASED) *Total amount:* $149,900 (98% institutional, 2% external sources). *Receiving aid:* Undergraduates: 1% (3). *Average award:* Freshmen: $6800. Undergraduates: $5996. *Scholarships, grants, and awards by category:* Academic interests/achievement: 24 awards ($147,400 total): general academic interests/achievements. *Tuition waivers:* Full or partial for employees or children of employees.
LOANS *Student loans:* $1,374,401 (62% need-based, 38% non-need-based). 56% of past graduating class borrowed through all loan programs. *Average indebtedness per student:* $22,473. *Average need-based loan:* Freshmen: $4048. Undergraduates: $4620. *Parent loans:* $313,643 (100% non-need-based). *Programs:* Federal Direct (Subsidized and Unsubsidized Stafford, PLUS), Perkins.
WORK-STUDY *Federal work-study:* Total amount: $651,157; 210 jobs averaging $2511. *State or other work-study/employment:* Total amount: $125,599 (99% need-based, 1% non-need-based). 53 part-time jobs averaging $2336.
APPLYING FOR FINANCIAL AID *Required financial aid forms:* FAFSA, institution's own form, noncustodial (divorced/separated) parent's statement. *Financial aid deadline (priority):* 2/15. *Notification date:* 4/1. Students must reply by 5/1 or within 2 weeks of notification.
CONTACT Bruce Hazam, Director of Financial Aid, College of the Atlantic, 105 Eden Street, Bar Harbor, ME 04609-1198, 207-801-5645 or toll-free 800-528-0025. *Fax:* 207-288-4126. *E-mail:* bhazam@coa.edu. *Website:* http://www.coa.edu/.

COLLEGE OF THE HOLY CROSS
Worcester, MA

Tuition & fees: $44,272 — Average undergraduate aid package: $33,123

ABOUT THE INSTITUTION Independent Roman Catholic (Jesuit), coed. *Awards:* bachelor's degrees (standardized tests are optional for admission to the College of Holy Cross). 34 undergraduate majors. *Total enrollment:* 2,926. Undergraduates: 2,926. Freshmen: 763. Both federal and institutional methodology are used as a basis for awarding need-based institutional aid.
UNDERGRADUATE EXPENSES for 2013–2014 *Application fee:* $60. *Comprehensive fee:* $56,232 includes full-time tuition ($43,660), mandatory fees ($612), and room and board ($11,960). *College room only:* $6450. Room and board charges vary according to housing facility.
FRESHMAN FINANCIAL AID (Fall 2012, est.) 574 applied for aid; of those 87% were deemed to have need. 94% of freshmen with need received aid; of those 100% had need fully met. *Average percent of need met:* 100% (excluding resources awarded to replace EFC). *Average financial aid package:* $33,492 (excluding resources awarded to replace EFC). 1% of all full-time freshmen had no need and received non-need-based gift aid.
UNDERGRADUATE FINANCIAL AID (Fall 2012, est.) 1,892 applied for aid; of those 93% were deemed to have need. 96% of undergraduates with need received aid; of those 100% had need fully met. *Average percent of need met:* 100% (excluding resources awarded to replace EFC). *Average financial aid package:* $33,123 (excluding resources awarded to replace EFC). 1% of all full-time undergraduates had no need and received non-need-based gift aid.
GIFT AID (NEED-BASED) *Total amount:* $34,148,592 (7% federal, 2% state, 91% institutional). *Receiving aid:* Freshmen: 50% (382); all full-time undergraduates: 47% (1,367). *Average award:* Freshmen: $30,733; Undergraduates: $30,191. *Scholarships, grants, and awards:* Federal Pell, FSEOG, state, private, college/university gift aid from institutional funds.
GIFT AID (NON-NEED-BASED) *Total amount:* $4,195,018 (56% institutional, 44% external sources). *Receiving aid:* Freshmen: 1% (8). Undergraduates: 1% (28). *Average award:* Freshmen: $16,560. Undergraduates: $28,625. *Scholarships, grants, and awards by category:* Academic interests/achievement: 34 awards ($979,687 total): general academic interests/achievements, humanities, military science. Creative arts/performance: 5 awards ($214,000 total): music. Special characteristics: 31 awards ($1,326,800 total): children of faculty/staff. *Tuition waivers:* Full or partial for employees or children of employees. *ROTC:* Army cooperative, Naval, Air Force cooperative.
LOANS *Student loans:* $13,202,336 (83% need-based, 17% non-need-based). 55% of past graduating class borrowed through all loan programs. *Average indebtedness per student:* $26,567. *Average need-based loan:* Freshmen: $5138. Undergraduates: $5492. *Parent loans:* $8,412,805 (100% non-need-based). *Programs:* Federal Direct (Subsidized and Unsubsidized Stafford, PLUS), Perkins, MEFA Loans.
WORK-STUDY *Federal work-study:* Total amount: $1,795,572; 1,108 jobs averaging $1638.
ATHLETIC AWARDS Total amount: $8,566,078 (65% need-based, 35% non-need-based).
APPLYING FOR FINANCIAL AID *Required financial aid forms:* FAFSA, CSS Financial Aid PROFILE, noncustodial (divorced/separated) parent's statement, business/farm supplement, federal income tax form(s). *Financial aid deadline:* 2/1. *Notification date:* 4/1. Students must reply by 5/1.
CONTACT Ms. Lynne Myers, Director of Financial Aid, College of the Holy Cross, One College Street, Worcester, MA 01610-2395, 508-793-2265 or toll-free 800-442-2421. *Fax:* 508-793-2527. *Website:* http://www.holycross.edu/.

COLLEGE OF THE OZARKS
Point Lookout, MO

Tuition & fees: $430 — Average undergraduate aid package: $18,398

ABOUT THE INSTITUTION Independent Presbyterian, coed. *Awards:* bachelor's degrees. 63 undergraduate majors. *Total enrollment:* 1,379. Undergrad-

uates: 1,379. Freshmen: 245. Federal methodology is used as a basis for awarding need-based institutional aid.

UNDERGRADUATE EXPENSES for 2013–2014 *College room only:* $2900. *Part-time tuition:* $295 per credit. Part-time tuition and fees vary according to course load. Each student participates in the on-campus work program for 15 hours per week and two forty-hour work weeks. Earnings from participation in the work program, plus any federal and/or state aid for which students qualify, plus a College of the Ozarks Cost of Education Scholarship combine to meet each students full tuition charge.

FRESHMAN FINANCIAL AID (Fall 2012, est.) 250 applied for aid; of those 99% were deemed to have need. 100% of freshmen with need received aid; of those 18% had need fully met. *Average percent of need met:* 83% (excluding resources awarded to replace EFC). *Average financial aid package:* $18,943 (excluding resources awarded to replace EFC). 6% of all full-time freshmen had no need and received non-need-based gift aid.

UNDERGRADUATE FINANCIAL AID (Fall 2012, est.) 1,323 applied for aid; of those 97% were deemed to have need. 100% of undergraduates with need received aid; of those 28% had need fully met. *Average percent of need met:* 85% (excluding resources awarded to replace EFC). *Average financial aid package:* $18,398 (excluding resources awarded to replace EFC). 6% of all full-time undergraduates had no need and received non-need-based gift aid.

GIFT AID (NEED-BASED) *Total amount:* $19,488,976 (18% federal, 6% state, 74% institutional, 2% external sources). *Receiving aid:* Freshmen: 94% (247); all full-time undergraduates: 94% (1,282). *Average award:* Freshmen: $15,521; Undergraduates: $15,295. *Scholarships, grants, and awards:* Federal Pell, FSEOG, state, private, college/university gift aid from institutional funds.

GIFT AID (NON-NEED-BASED) *Total amount:* $1,987,941 (97% institutional, 3% external sources). *Receiving aid:* Freshmen: 10% (27). Undergraduates: 12% (164). *Average award:* Freshmen: $13,660. Undergraduates: $13,919. *ROTC:* Army.

LOANS *Student loans:* $252,005 (69% need-based, 31% non-need-based). 11% of past graduating class borrowed through all loan programs. *Average indebtedness per student:* $8915.

WORK-STUDY *Federal work-study:* Total amount: $3,426,620; 996 jobs averaging $3694. *State or other work-study/employment:* Total amount: $1,842,920 (29% need-based, 71% non-need-based). 524 part-time jobs averaging $3643.

ATHLETIC AWARDS Total amount: $271,525 (50% need-based, 50% non-need-based).

APPLYING FOR FINANCIAL AID *Required financial aid form:* FAFSA. *Financial aid deadline (priority):* 2/15. *Notification date:* 7/1.

CONTACT Mrs. Kyla R. McCarty, Director of Financial Aid, College of the Ozarks, PO Box 17, Point Lookout, MO 65726, 417-690-3290 or toll-free 800-222-0525. *Fax:* 417-690-3286. *E-mail:* mccarty@cofo.edu. *Website:* http://www.cofo.edu/.

THE COLLEGE OF WILLIAM AND MARY
Williamsburg, VA

Tuition & fees (VA res): $13,570	Average undergraduate aid package: $16,407

ABOUT THE INSTITUTION State-supported, coed. *Awards:* certificates, bachelor's, master's, and doctoral degrees. 41 undergraduate majors. *Total enrollment:* 8,258. Undergraduates: 6,171. Freshmen: 1,467. Federal methodology is used as a basis for awarding need-based institutional aid.

UNDERGRADUATE EXPENSES for 2013–2014 *Application fee:* $70. *Tuition, state resident:* full-time $13,570. *Tuition, nonresident:* full-time $37,344. *College room and board:* $9072; *Room only:* $5790. Room and board charges vary according to board plan and housing facility.

FRESHMAN FINANCIAL AID (Fall 2011) 944 applied for aid; of those 52% were deemed to have need. 93% of freshmen with need received aid; of those 22% had need fully met. *Average percent of need met:* 73% (excluding resources awarded to replace EFC). *Average financial aid package:* $14,812 (excluding resources awarded to replace EFC). 3% of all full-time freshmen had no need and received non-need-based gift aid.

UNDERGRADUATE FINANCIAL AID (Fall 2011) 3,092 applied for aid; of those 67% were deemed to have need. 96% of undergraduates with need received aid;

of those 25% had need fully met. *Average percent of need met:* 75% (excluding resources awarded to replace EFC). *Average financial aid package:* $16,407 (excluding resources awarded to replace EFC). 5% of all full-time undergraduates had no need and received non-need-based gift aid.

GIFT AID (NEED-BASED) *Total amount:* $22,333,759 (13% federal, 13% state, 69% institutional, 5% external sources). *Receiving aid:* Freshmen: 22% (328); all full-time undergraduates: 26% (1,563). *Average award:* Freshmen: $13,037; Undergraduates: $12,849. *Scholarships, grants, and awards:* Federal Pell, FSEOG, state, private, college/university gift aid from institutional funds.

GIFT AID (NON-NEED-BASED) *Total amount:* $2,789,504 (8% federal, 57% institutional, 35% external sources). *Receiving aid:* Freshmen: 14% (205). Undergraduates: 11% (652). *Average award:* Freshmen: $6948. Undergraduates: $6050. *Scholarships, grants, and awards by category:* Academic interests/ achievement: 16 awards ($331,329 total): general academic interests/achievements. Creative arts/performance: 48 awards ($46,106 total): music, theater/drama. Special characteristics: 167 awards ($2,096,396 total): general special characteristics. *Tuition waivers:* Full or partial for senior citizens. *ROTC:* Army.

LOANS *Student loans:* $15,320,779 (40% need-based, 60% non-need-based). 41% of past graduating class borrowed through all loan programs. *Average indebtedness per student:* $24,344. *Average need-based loan:* Freshmen: $3185. Undergraduates: $4483. *Parent loans:* $7,284,223 (45% need-based, 55% non-need-based). *Programs:* Federal Direct (Subsidized and Unsubsidized Stafford, PLUS), Perkins.

WORK-STUDY *Federal work-study:* Total amount: $167,490; 144 jobs averaging $1163.

ATHLETIC AWARDS Total amount: $6,641,081 (16% need-based, 84% non-need-based).

APPLYING FOR FINANCIAL AID *Required financial aid forms:* FAFSA, CSS Financial Aid PROFILE. *Financial aid deadline (priority):* 3/15. *Notification date:* Continuous beginning 3/15. Students must reply by 5/1 or within 2 weeks of notification.

CONTACT Mr. Edward P. Irish, Director of Financial Aid, The College of William and Mary, PO Box 8795, Williamsburg, VA 23187, 757-221-2425. *Fax:* 757-221-2515. *E-mail:* epiris@wm.edu. *Website:* http://www.wm.edu/.

THE COLLEGE OF WOOSTER
Wooster, OH

Tuition & fees: $39,810	Average undergraduate aid package: $35,763

ABOUT THE INSTITUTION Independent Presbyterian Church (U.S.A.), coed. *Awards:* bachelor's degrees. 46 undergraduate majors. *Total enrollment:* 2,080. Undergraduates: 2,080. Freshmen: 573. Both federal and institutional methodology are used as a basis for awarding need-based institutional aid.

UNDERGRADUATE EXPENSES for 2013–2014 *Application fee:* $40. *Comprehensive fee:* $49,400 includes full-time tuition ($39,500), mandatory fees ($310), and room and board ($9590). *College room only:* $4440. Full-time tuition and fees vary according to course load. Room and board charges vary according to board plan and housing facility. *Part-time tuition:* $1230 per credit. Part-time tuition and fees vary according to course load.

FRESHMAN FINANCIAL AID (Fall 2012, est.) 435 applied for aid; of those 86% were deemed to have need. 100% of freshmen with need received aid; of those 63% had need fully met. *Average percent of need met:* 95% (excluding resources awarded to replace EFC). *Average financial aid package:* $36,045 (excluding resources awarded to replace EFC). 33% of all full-time freshmen had no need and received non-need-based gift aid.

UNDERGRADUATE FINANCIAL AID (Fall 2012, est.) 1,345 applied for aid; of those 89% were deemed to have need. 100% of undergraduates with need received aid; of those 60% had need fully met. *Average percent of need met:* 94% (excluding resources awarded to replace EFC). *Average financial aid package:* $35,763 (excluding resources awarded to replace EFC). 38% of all full-time undergraduates had no need and received non-need-based gift aid.

GIFT AID (NEED-BASED) *Total amount:* $32,214,365 (6% federal, 1% state, 91% institutional, 2% external sources). *Receiving aid:* Freshmen: 65% (370); all full-time undergraduates: 58% (1,180). *Average award:* Freshmen: $28,247; Undergraduates: $27,300. *Scholarships, grants, and awards:* Federal Pell, FSEOG, state, private, college/university gift aid from institutional funds.

GIFT AID (NON-NEED-BASED) *Total amount:* $15,218,666 (97% institutional, 3% external sources). *Receiving aid:* Freshmen: 9% (49). Undergraduates: 7% (134). *Average award:* Freshmen: $17,410. Undergraduates: $18,482. *Scholarships, grants, and awards by category:* Academic interests/achievement: 1,526 awards ($24,163,381 total): general academic interests/achievements. *Creative arts/performance:* 126 awards ($528,452 total): dance, music, theater/drama. *Special achievements/activities:* 243 awards ($1,536,751 total): community service, religious involvement. *Special characteristics:* 187 awards ($5,152,325 total): children of educators, children of faculty/staff, members of minority groups. *Tuition waivers:* Full or partial for employees or children of employees.
LOANS *Student loans:* $9,210,208 (67% need-based, 33% non-need-based). 49% of past graduating class borrowed through all loan programs. *Average indebtedness per student:* $26,750. *Average need-based loan:* Freshmen: $5072. Undergraduates: $6142. *Parent loans:* $4,203,015 (22% need-based, 78% non-need-based). *Programs:* Federal Direct (Subsidized and Unsubsidized Stafford, PLUS), Perkins.
WORK-STUDY *Federal work-study:* Total amount: $1,472,381; 886 jobs averaging $1662. *State or other work-study/employment:* Total amount: $136,000 (100% non-need-based). 68 part-time jobs averaging $2000.
APPLYING FOR FINANCIAL AID *Required financial aid forms:* FAFSA, institution's own form. *Financial aid deadline (priority):* 2/15. *Notification date:* Continuous beginning 2/15. Students must reply by 5/1.
CONTACT Mr. Joseph Winge, Director of Financial Aid, The College of Wooster, Pearl House, 804 Beall Avenue, Wooster, OH 44691, 800-877-3688 or toll-free 800-877-9905. *Fax:* 330-263-2634. *E-mail:* financialaid@wooster.edu. *Website:* http://www.wooster.edu/.

COLORADO CHRISTIAN UNIVERSITY
Lakewood, CO

CONTACT Mr. Steve Woodburn, Director of Financial Aid, Colorado Christian University, 180 South Garrison Street, Lakewood, CO 80226-7499, 303-963-3230 or toll-free 800-44-FAITH. *Fax:* 303-963-3231. *E-mail:* sfs@ccu.edu. *Website:* http://www.ccu.edu/.

THE COLORADO COLLEGE
Colorado Springs, CO

Tuition & fees: $41,942	Average undergraduate aid package: $37,319

ABOUT THE INSTITUTION Independent, coed. *Awards:* bachelor's and master's degrees (master's degree in education only). 48 undergraduate majors. *Total enrollment:* 2,026. Undergraduates: 2,008. Freshmen: 510. Both federal and institutional methodology are used as a basis for awarding need-based institutional aid.
UNDERGRADUATE EXPENSES for 2013–2014 *Application fee:* $60. *One-time required fee:* $150. *Comprehensive fee:* $51,670 includes full-time tuition ($41,742), mandatory fees ($200), and room and board ($9728). *College room only:* $5496. Room and board charges vary according to board plan and housing facility. *Part-time tuition:* $6957 per course. Part-time tuition and fees vary according to course load.
FRESHMAN FINANCIAL AID (Fall 2011) 235 applied for aid; of those 83% were deemed to have need. 100% of freshmen with need received aid; of those 90% had need fully met. *Average percent of need met:* 99% (excluding resources awarded to replace EFC). *Average financial aid package:* $38,292 (excluding resources awarded to replace EFC). 8% of all full-time freshmen had no need and received non-need-based gift aid.
UNDERGRADUATE FINANCIAL AID (Fall 2011) 737 applied for aid; of those 94% were deemed to have need. 100% of undergraduates with need received aid; of those 83% had need fully met. *Average percent of need met:* 99% (excluding resources awarded to replace EFC). *Average financial aid package:* $37,319 (excluding resources awarded to replace EFC). 6% of all full-time undergraduates had no need and received non-need-based gift aid.
GIFT AID (NEED-BASED) *Total amount:* $22,451,045 (6% federal, 1% state, 91% institutional, 2% external sources). *Receiving aid:* Freshmen: 39% (190); all full-time undergraduates: 34% (688). *Average award:* Freshmen: $31,141; Undergraduates: $29,708. *Scholarships, grants, and awards:* Federal Pell, FSEOG, state, private, college/university gift aid from institutional funds.
GIFT AID (NON-NEED-BASED) *Total amount:* $3,890,484 (67% institutional, 33% external sources). *Receiving aid:* Freshmen: 29% (142). Undergraduates: 18% (368). *Average award:* Freshmen: $7999. Undergraduates: $7854. *Scholarships, grants, and awards by category:* Academic interests/achievement: 143 awards ($1,403,823 total): biological sciences, general academic interests/achievements, mathematics, physical sciences. *Special characteristics:* 27 awards ($701,819 total): children of faculty/staff, international students. *Tuition waivers:* Full or partial for employees or children of employees. *ROTC:* Army cooperative.
LOANS *Student loans:* $4,151,465 (66% need-based, 34% non-need-based). 32% of past graduating class borrowed through all loan programs. *Average indebtedness per student:* $19,970. *Average need-based loan:* Freshmen: $3978. Undergraduates: $4273. *Parent loans:* $2,416,218 (11% need-based, 89% non-need-based). *Programs:* Federal Direct (Subsidized and Unsubsidized Stafford, PLUS), Perkins.
WORK-STUDY *Federal work-study:* Total amount: $429,345; 340 jobs averaging $1771. *State or other work-study/employment:* Total amount: $267,637 (90% need-based, 10% non-need-based). 110 part-time jobs averaging $1728.
ATHLETIC AWARDS Total amount: $1,488,427 (12% need-based, 88% non-need-based).
APPLYING FOR FINANCIAL AID *Required financial aid forms:* FAFSA, CSS Financial Aid PROFILE, noncustodial (divorced/separated) parent's statement, federal income tax form(s), W-2 forms. *Financial aid deadline:* 2/15. *Notification date:* 3/20. Students must reply by 5/1.
CONTACT Mr. James M. Swanson, Director of Financial Aid, The Colorado College, 14 East Cache La Poudre Street, Colorado Springs, CO 80903-3294, 719-389-6651 or toll-free 800-542-7214. *Fax:* 719-389-6173. *E-mail:* financialaid@coloradocollege.edu. *Website:* http://www.coloradocollege.edu/.

COLORADO HEIGHTS UNIVERSITY
Denver, CO

CONTACT Financial Aid Office, Colorado Heights University, 3001 South Federal Boulevard, Denver, CO 80236, 303-936-4200. *Website:* http://www.chu.edu/.

COLORADO MESA UNIVERSITY
Grand Junction, CO

Tuition & fees (CO res): $6870	Average undergraduate aid package: $7857

ABOUT THE INSTITUTION State-supported, coed. *Awards:* certificates, associate, bachelor's, master's, and doctoral degrees. 44 undergraduate majors. *Total enrollment:* 9,482. Undergraduates: 10,393. Freshmen: 3,094. Federal methodology is used as a basis for awarding need-based institutional aid.
UNDERGRADUATE EXPENSES for 2013–2014 *Application fee:* $30. *Tuition, state resident:* full-time $6102; part-time $203.41 per credit hour. *Tuition, nonresident:* full-time $16,280; part-time $542.69 per credit hour. *Required fees:* full-time $768; $25.61 per credit hour. Full-time tuition and fees vary according to course load. Part-time tuition and fees vary according to course load. *College room and board:* $9103. Room and board charges vary according to board plan and housing facility.
FRESHMAN FINANCIAL AID (Fall 2011) 1,787 applied for aid; of those 81% were deemed to have need. 99% of freshmen with need received aid; of those 13% had need fully met. *Average percent of need met:* 56% (excluding resources awarded to replace EFC). *Average financial aid package:* $7408 (excluding resources awarded to replace EFC). 6% of all full-time freshmen had no need and received non-need-based gift aid.
UNDERGRADUATE FINANCIAL AID (Fall 2011) 5,563 applied for aid; of those 85% were deemed to have need. 99% of undergraduates with need received aid; of those 12% had need fully met. *Average percent of need met:* 56% (excluding resources awarded to replace EFC). *Average financial aid package:* $7857 (excluding resources awarded to replace EFC). 4% of all full-time undergraduates had no need and received non-need-based gift aid.

GIFT AID (NEED-BASED) *Total amount:* $22,438,613 (70% federal, 14% state, 9% institutional, 7% external sources). *Receiving aid:* Freshmen: 65% (1,308); all full-time undergraduates: 64% (4,261). *Average award:* Freshmen: $4943; Undergraduates: $4787. *Scholarships, grants, and awards:* Federal Pell, FSEOG, state, private, college/university gift aid from institutional funds.

GIFT AID (NON-NEED-BASED) *Total amount:* $3,235,393 (29% federal, 44% institutional, 27% external sources). *Receiving aid:* Freshmen: 4% (90). Undergraduates: 3% (201). *Average award:* Freshmen: $2595. Undergraduates: $2230. *Scholarships, grants, and awards by category:* Academic interests/achievement: biological sciences, business, communication, computer science, education, engineering/technologies, English, foreign languages, general academic interests/achievements, health fields, humanities, mathematics, physical sciences, social sciences. *Creative arts/performance:* art/fine arts, creative writing, dance, journalism/publications, music, performing arts, theater/drama. *Special achievements/activities:* general special achievements/activities, hobbies/interests, leadership. *Special characteristics:* adult students, first-generation college students, international students, local/state students, members of minority groups, out-of-state students. *Tuition waivers:* Full or partial for employees or children of employees.

LOANS *Student loans:* $39,521,024 (89% need-based, 11% non-need-based). 69% of past graduating class borrowed through all loan programs. *Average indebtedness per student:* $24,714. *Average need-based loan:* Freshmen: $3142. Undergraduates: $3727. *Parent loans:* $12,119,538 (66% need-based, 34% non-need-based). *Programs:* Federal Direct (Subsidized and Unsubsidized Stafford), Perkins.

WORK-STUDY *Federal work-study:* Total amount: $356,733; jobs available. *State or other work-study/employment:* Total amount: $3,800,882 (28% need-based, 72% non-need-based). Part-time jobs available.

ATHLETIC AWARDS Total amount: $1,248,222 (50% need-based, 50% non-need-based).

APPLYING FOR FINANCIAL AID *Required financial aid form:* FAFSA. *Financial aid deadline:* Continuous. *Notification date:* Continuous beginning 3/1. Students must reply within 2 weeks of notification.

CONTACT Mr. Curt Martin, Director of Financial Aid, Colorado Mesa University, 1100 North Avenue, Grand Junction, CO 81501-3122, 970-248-1065 or toll-free 800-982-MESA. *Fax:* 970-248-1191. *E-mail:* cumartin@coloradomesa.edu. *Website:* http://www.coloradomesa.edu/.

COLORADO MOUNTAIN COLLEGE
Glenwood Springs, CO

Tuition & fees (area res): $1860	Average undergraduate aid package: N/A

ABOUT THE INSTITUTION District-supported, coed. *Awards:* certificates, associate, and bachelor's degrees. 26 undergraduate majors. *Total enrollment:* 2,465. Undergraduates: 2,465. Federal methodology is used as a basis for awarding need-based institutional aid.

UNDERGRADUATE EXPENSES for 2013–2014 *Tuition, area resident:* full-time $1680; part-time $56 per credit. *Tuition, state resident:* full-time $2850; part-time $95 per credit. *Tuition, nonresident:* full-time $9970; part-time $299 per credit. *Required fees:* full-time $180. Full-time tuition and fees vary according to course level. Part-time tuition and fees vary according to course level. *College room and board:* $8164.

FRESHMAN FINANCIAL AID (Fall 2011) 34% of all full-time freshmen had no need and received non-need-based gift aid.

UNDERGRADUATE FINANCIAL AID (Fall 2011) 14% of all full-time undergraduates had no need and received non-need-based gift aid.

GIFT AID (NEED-BASED) *Total amount:* $3,795,368 (92% federal, 8% state). *Scholarships, grants, and awards:* Federal Pell, FSEOG, state, private, college/university gift aid from institutional funds.

GIFT AID (NON-NEED-BASED) *Total amount:* $1,601,375 (78% federal, 22% institutional). *Average award:* Freshmen: $1451. Undergraduates: $1269. *Scholarships, grants, and awards by category:* Special characteristics: local/state students. *Tuition waivers:* Full or partial for senior citizens.

LOANS *Student loans:* $2,723,730 (55% need-based, 45% non-need-based). *Parent loans:* $237,072 (100% non-need-based). *Programs:* Federal Direct (Subsidized and Unsubsidized Stafford, PLUS), Perkins, Federal Nursing, state.

WORK-STUDY *Federal work-study:* Total amount: $48,822; jobs available. *State or other work-study/employment:* Total amount: $77,663 (84% need-based, 16% non-need-based). Part-time jobs available.

APPLYING FOR FINANCIAL AID *Required financial aid form:* FAFSA. *Financial aid deadline (priority):* 3/31. *Notification date:* Continuous.

CONTACT Rita Bayless, Director of Financial Aid, Colorado Mountain College, 802 Grand Avenue, Glenwood Springs, CO 81601, 970-947-8338 or toll-free 800-621-8559. *E-mail:* rbayless@coloradomtn.edu. *Website:* http://www.coloradomtn.edu/.

COLORADO MOUNTAIN COLLEGE, ALPINE CAMPUS
Steamboat Springs, CO

CONTACT Financial Aid Office, Colorado Mountain College, Alpine Campus, 1330 Bob Adams Drive, Steamboat Springs, CO 80487, 970-870-4444 or toll-free 800-621-8559. *Website:* http://www.coloradomtn.edu/.

COLORADO MOUNTAIN COLLEGE, TIMBERLINE CAMPUS
Leadville, CO

CONTACT Financial Aid Office, Colorado Mountain College, Timberline Campus, 901 South Highway 24, Leadville, CO 80461, 719-486-2015 or toll-free 800-621-8559. *Website:* http://www.coloradomtn.edu/.

COLORADO SCHOOL OF MINES
Golden, CO

Tuition & fees: N/R	Average undergraduate aid package: $12,214

ABOUT THE INSTITUTION State-supported, coed. *Awards:* certificates, bachelor's, master's, and doctoral degrees. 17 undergraduate majors. *Total enrollment:* 5,632. Undergraduates: 4,169. Freshmen: 949. Federal methodology is used as a basis for awarding need-based institutional aid.

FRESHMAN FINANCIAL AID (Fall 2011) 742 applied for aid; of those 67% were deemed to have need. 100% of freshmen with need received aid; of those 22% had need fully met. *Average percent of need met:* 62% (excluding resources awarded to replace EFC). *Average financial aid package:* $12,239 (excluding resources awarded to replace EFC). 25% of all full-time freshmen had no need and received non-need-based gift aid.

UNDERGRADUATE FINANCIAL AID (Fall 2011) 2,622 applied for aid; of those 76% were deemed to have need. 100% of undergraduates with need received aid; of those 20% had need fully met. *Average percent of need met:* 61% (excluding resources awarded to replace EFC). *Average financial aid package:* $12,214 (excluding resources awarded to replace EFC). 22% of all full-time undergraduates had no need and received non-need-based gift aid.

GIFT AID (NEED-BASED) *Total amount:* $15,442,407 (21% federal, 5% state, 58% institutional, 16% external sources). *Receiving aid:* Freshmen: 32% (277); all full-time undergraduates: 33% (1,205). *Average award:* Freshmen: $4495; Undergraduates: $5859. *Scholarships, grants, and awards:* Federal Pell, FSEOG, state, private, college/university gift aid from institutional funds.

GIFT AID (NON-NEED-BASED) *Total amount:* $5,893,594 (85% institutional, 15% external sources). *Receiving aid:* Freshmen: 43% (380). Undergraduates: 34% (1,255). *Average award:* Freshmen: $8112. Undergraduates: $6032. *Scholarships, grants, and awards by category:* Academic interests/achievement: business, computer science, engineering/technologies, general academic interests/achievements, mathematics, military science, physical sciences. *ROTC:* Army, Air Force.

LOANS *Student loans:* $24,212,624 (46% need-based, 54% non-need-based). 51% of past graduating class borrowed through all loan programs. *Average indebtedness per student:* $33,209. *Average need-based loan:* Freshmen: $3411. Undergraduates: $4614. *Parent loans:* $8,617,261 (55% need-based, 45% non-need-based). *Programs:* Federal Direct (Subsidized and Unsubsidized Stafford, PLUS), Perkins, college/university.

WORK-STUDY *Federal work-study:* Total amount: $430,097; 193 jobs averaging $1065. *State or other work-study/employment:* Total amount: $2,432,374 (65% need-based, 35% non-need-based). 1,234 part-time jobs averaging $1987.
ATHLETIC AWARDS Total amount: $1,922,028 (50% need-based, 50% non-need-based).
APPLYING FOR FINANCIAL AID *Required financial aid form:* FAFSA. *Financial aid deadline (priority):* 3/1. *Notification date:* Continuous beginning 3/1.
CONTACT Jill Robertson, Director of Financial Aid, Colorado School of Mines, 1600 Maple Street, Golden, CO 80401-1887, 303-273-3220 or toll-free 800-446-9488 Ext. 3220. *Fax:* 303-384-2252. *E-mail:* finaid@mines.edu.
Website: http://www.mines.edu/.

COLORADO STATE UNIVERSITY
Fort Collins, CO

Tuition & fees (CO res): $8649	Average undergraduate aid package: $15,195

ABOUT THE INSTITUTION State-supported, coed. *Awards:* bachelor's, master's, and doctoral degrees. 119 undergraduate majors. *Total enrollment:* 30,647. Undergraduates: 23,479. Freshmen: 4,544. Federal methodology is used as a basis for awarding need-based institutional aid.
UNDERGRADUATE EXPENSES for 2013–2014 *Application fee:* $50. *Tuition, state resident:* full-time $6875; part-time $312.20 per credit hour. *Tuition, nonresident:* full-time $22,667; part-time $1133 per credit hour. *Required fees:* full-time $1774; $29.84 per credit hour or $149.22 per term. Full-time tuition and fees vary according to course load, program, and student level. Part-time tuition and fees vary according to course load, program, and student level. *College room and board:* $10,278; *Room only:* $4720. Room and board charges vary according to board plan and housing facility.
FRESHMAN FINANCIAL AID (Fall 2011) 3,636 applied for aid; of those 67% were deemed to have need. 100% of freshmen with need received aid; of those 36% had need fully met. *Average percent of need met:* 71% (excluding resources awarded to replace EFC). *Average financial aid package:* $16,131 (excluding resources awarded to replace EFC). 13% of all full-time freshmen had no need and received non-need-based gift aid.
UNDERGRADUATE FINANCIAL AID (Fall 2011) 15,032 applied for aid; of those 74% were deemed to have need. 100% of undergraduates with need received aid; of those 18% had need fully met. *Average percent of need met:* 69% (excluding resources awarded to replace EFC). *Average financial aid package:* $15,195 (excluding resources awarded to replace EFC). 11% of all full-time undergraduates had no need and received non-need-based gift aid.
GIFT AID (NEED-BASED) *Total amount:* $60,419,334 (38% federal, 8% state, 45% institutional, 9% external sources). *Receiving aid:* Freshmen: 39% (1,721); all full-time undergraduates: 37% (7,623). *Average award:* Freshmen: $12,167; Undergraduates: $9360. *Scholarships, grants, and awards:* Federal Pell, FSEOG, state, private, college/university gift aid from institutional funds.
GIFT AID (NON-NEED-BASED) *Total amount:* $11,573,660 (1% state, 83% institutional, 16% external sources). *Average award:* Freshmen: $3918. Undergraduates: $4306. *Scholarships, grants, and awards by category:* Academic interests/achievement: 13,640 awards ($32,577,457 total): general academic interests/achievements. Creative arts/performance: 458 awards ($499,550 total): art/fine arts, creative writing, dance, music, theater/drama. Special achievements/activities: 138 awards ($380,338 total): general special achievements/activities. Special characteristics: children of faculty/staff, first-generation college students, international students. Tuition waivers: Full or partial for employees or children of employees. ROTC: Army, Air Force.
LOANS *Student loans:* $85,136,897 (79% need-based, 21% non-need-based). 48% of past graduating class borrowed through all loan programs. *Average indebtedness per student:* $22,131. *Average need-based loan:* Freshmen: $5246. Undergraduates: $6925. *Parent loans:* $41,803,507 (67% need-based, 33% non-need-based). *Programs:* Federal Direct (Subsidized and Unsubsidized Stafford, PLUS), Perkins, alternative loans.
WORK-STUDY *Federal work-study:* Total amount: $883,178; 454 jobs averaging $1983. *State or other work-study/employment:* Total amount: $2,213,227 (78% need-based, 22% non-need-based). 1,198 part-time jobs averaging $1860.

ATHLETIC AWARDS Total amount: $6,312,979 (28% need-based, 72% non-need-based).
APPLYING FOR FINANCIAL AID *Required financial aid form:* FAFSA. *Financial aid deadline (priority):* 3/1. *Notification date:* Continuous beginning 3/1.
CONTACT Student Financial Services Office, Colorado State University, Room 103, Centennial Hall, Fort Collins, CO 80523-8024, 970-491-6321. *E-mail:* sfs@colostate.edu.
Website: http://www.colostate.edu/.

COLORADO STATE UNIVERSITY– PUEBLO
Pueblo, CO

ABOUT THE INSTITUTION State-supported, coed. 27 undergraduate majors.
GIFT AID (NEED-BASED) *Scholarships, grants, and awards:* Federal Pell, FSEOG, state, private, college/university gift aid from institutional funds, TEACH Grants.
GIFT AID (NON-NEED-BASED) *Scholarships, grants, and awards by category:* Academic interests/achievement: biological sciences, business, communication, computer science, education, engineering/technologies, English, foreign languages, general academic interests/achievements, health fields, mathematics, physical sciences, premedicine, social sciences. Creative arts/performance: applied art and design, art/fine arts, cinema/film/broadcasting, journalism/publications, music. Special achievements/activities: community service, general special achievements/activities, leadership. Special characteristics: children and siblings of alumni, children of faculty/staff, ethnic background, first-generation college students, general special characteristics, handicapped students, international students, out-of-state students.
LOANS *Programs:* Federal Direct (Subsidized and Unsubsidized Stafford, PLUS), Perkins, Federal Nursing.
WORK-STUDY *Federal work-study:* Total amount: $479,117; 236 jobs averaging $2030. *State or other work-study/employment:* Total amount: $742,316 (62% need-based, 38% non-need-based). 329 part-time jobs averaging $2256.
APPLYING FOR FINANCIAL AID *Required financial aid forms:* FAFSA, institution's own form.
CONTACT Sean McGivney, Director of Student Financial Services, Colorado State University–Pueblo, 2200 Bonforte Boulevard, Pueblo, CO 81001-4901, 719-549-2753. *Fax:* 719-549-2088.
Website: http://www.colostate-pueblo.edu/.

COLORADO TECHNICAL UNIVERSITY COLORADO SPRINGS
Colorado Springs, CO

CONTACT Jacqueline Harris, Senior Director of Student Finance Services, Colorado Technical University Colorado Springs, 4435 North Chestnut Street, Colorado Springs, CO 80907-3896, 719-598-0200 or toll-free 866-942-6555. *Fax:* 719-598-3740. *Website:* http://www.coloradotech.edu/.

COLORADO TECHNICAL UNIVERSITY DENVER SOUTH
Aurora, CO

CONTACT Ms. Natalie Dietsch, Financial Aid Manager, Colorado Technical University Denver South, 5775 Denver Tech Center Boulevard, Suite 100, Greenwood Village, CO 80111, 303-694-6600 or toll-free 888-309-6555. *Fax:* 303-694-6673. *Website:* http://www.coloradotech.edu/.

COLORADO TECHNICAL UNIVERSITY NORTH KANSAS CITY

North Kansas City, MO

CONTACT Financial Aid Office, Colorado Technical University North Kansas City, 520 East 19th Avenue, North Kansas City, MO 64116, 816-472-7400. *Website:* http://kc.coloradotech.edu/.

COLORADO TECHNICAL UNIVERSITY SIOUX FALLS

Sioux Falls, SD

CONTACT Vikki Van Hull, Financial Aid Officer, Colorado Technical University Sioux Falls, 3901 West 59th Street, Sioux Falls, SD 57108, 605-361-0200 Ext. 140. *Fax:* 605-361-5954. *E-mail:* vvanhull@sf.coloradotech.edu. *Website:* http://www.coloradotech.edu/Sioux-Falls.

COLUMBIA CENTRO UNIVERSITARIO

Caguas, PR

CONTACT Financial Aid Officer, Columbia Centro Universitario, Carr 183, Km 1.7, PO Box 8517, Caguas, PR 00726, 787-743-4041 Ext. 244. *Fax:* 787-744-7031. *Website:* http://www.columbiaco.edu/.

COLUMBIA CENTRO UNIVERSITARIO

Yauco, PR

CONTACT Financial Aid Office, Columbia Centro Universitario, Calle Betances #3, Box 3062, Yauco, PR 00698, 787-856-0945. *Website:* http://www.columbiaco.edu/.

COLUMBIA COLLEGE

Columbia, MO

Tuition & fees: $19,386	Average undergraduate aid package: $11,081

ABOUT THE INSTITUTION Independent Christian Church (Disciples of Christ), coed. *Awards:* associate, bachelor's, and master's degrees (offers continuing education program with significant enrollment not reflected in profile). 40 undergraduate majors. *Total enrollment:* 1,193. Undergraduates: 953. Freshmen: 148. Federal methodology is used as a basis for awarding need-based institutional aid.

UNDERGRADUATE EXPENSES for 2013–2014 *Application fee:* $35. *Tuition:* full-time $19,386; part-time $417 per credit hour. Full-time tuition and fees vary according to class time, course load, degree level, and program. Part-time tuition and fees vary according to class time, course load, degree level, and location. Room and board charges vary according to board plan and housing facility. *Payment plan:* Guaranteed tuition.

FRESHMAN FINANCIAL AID (Fall 2011) 98 applied for aid; of those 87% were deemed to have need. 85% of freshmen with need received aid; of those 22% had need fully met. *Average percent of need met:* 61% (excluding resources awarded to replace EFC). *Average financial aid package:* $13,801 (excluding resources awarded to replace EFC). 7% of all full-time freshmen had no need and received non-need-based gift aid.

UNDERGRADUATE FINANCIAL AID (Fall 2011) 552 applied for aid; of those 91% were deemed to have need. 90% of undergraduates with need received aid; of those 13% had need fully met. *Average percent of need met:* 56% (excluding resources awarded to replace EFC). *Average financial aid package:* $11,081 (excluding resources awarded to replace EFC). 4% of all full-time undergraduates had no need and received non-need-based gift aid.

GIFT AID (NEED-BASED) *Total amount:* $1,624,345 (79% federal, 16% state, 5% institutional). *Receiving aid:* Freshmen: 32% (47); all full-time undergraduates: 41% (325). *Average award:* Freshmen: $3712; Undergraduates: $4026. *Scholarships, grants, and awards:* Federal Pell, FSEOG, state, private.

GIFT AID (NON-NEED-BASED) *Total amount:* $3,390,373 (1% state, 94% institutional, 5% external sources). *Receiving aid:* Freshmen: 26% (39). Undergraduates: 27% (213). *Average award:* Freshmen: $7774. Undergraduates: $9034. *Scholarships, grants, and awards by category: Academic interests/achievement:* 345 awards ($2,925,374 total): biological sciences, business, education, English, general academic interests/achievements, humanities, mathematics, physical sciences, religion/biblical studies, social sciences. *Creative arts/performance:* 11 awards ($26,000 total): art/fine arts, creative writing, music. *Special achievements/activities:* 139 awards ($1,164,726 total): leadership. *Special characteristics:* 180 awards ($953,226 total): children and siblings of alumni, children of current students, children of educators, children of faculty/staff, first-generation college students, local/state students, parents of current students, previous college experience, religious affiliation, siblings of current students, spouses of current students, veterans. *Tuition waivers:* Full or partial for children of alumni, employees or children of employees, senior citizens. *ROTC:* Army cooperative, Naval cooperative, Air Force cooperative.

LOANS *Student loans:* $4,182,776 (43% need-based, 57% non-need-based). 53% of past graduating class borrowed through all loan programs. *Average indebtedness per student:* $11,726. *Average need-based loan:* Freshmen: $3306. Undergraduates: $4297. *Parent loans:* $478,199 (100% non-need-based). *Programs:* Federal Direct (Subsidized and Unsubsidized Stafford, PLUS).

WORK-STUDY *Federal work-study:* Total amount: $324,701; 139 jobs averaging $2336. *State or other work-study/employment:* Total amount: $358,296 (100% non-need-based). 171 part-time jobs averaging $1960.

ATHLETIC AWARDS Total amount: $1,132,899 (100% non-need-based).

APPLYING FOR FINANCIAL AID *Required financial aid form:* FAFSA. *Financial aid deadline (priority):* 3/1. *Notification date:* Continuous beginning 3/1.

CONTACT Sharon Abernathy, Director of Financial Aid, Columbia College, 1001 Rogers Street, Columbia, MO 65216-0002, 573-875-7360 or toll-free 800-231-2391. *Fax:* 573-875-7452. *E-mail:* saabernathy@ccis.edu. *Website:* http://www.ccis.edu/.

COLUMBIA COLLEGE

Columbia, SC

CONTACT Anita Kaminer Elliott, Director of Financial Aid, Columbia College, 1301 Columbia College Drive, Columbia, SC 29203-5998, 803-786-3612 or toll-free 800-277-1301. *Fax:* 803-786-3560. *Website:* http://www.columbiasc.edu/.

COLUMBIA COLLEGE CHICAGO

Chicago, IL

CONTACT Ms. Jennifer Waters, Executive Director of Student Financial Services, Columbia College Chicago, 600 South Michigan Avenue, Chicago, IL 60605-1996, 312-369-7831. *Fax:* 312-986-7008. *E-mail:* jwaters@colum.edu. *Website:* http://www.colum.edu/.

COLUMBIA COLLEGE HOLLYWOOD

Tarzana, CA

CONTACT Mr. Jan Hastings, Financial Aid Administrator, Columbia College Hollywood, 18618 Oxnard Street, Tarzana, CA 91356, 818-401-1030 or toll-free 800-785-0585. *Fax:* 818-345-8660. *E-mail:* finaid@columbiacollege.edu. *Website:* http://www.columbiacollege.edu/.

COLUMBIA INTERNATIONAL UNIVERSITY
Columbia, SC

Tuition & fees: $18,740	Average undergraduate aid package: $15,846

ABOUT THE INSTITUTION Independent nondenominational, coed. **Awards:** certificates, associate, bachelor's, master's, and doctoral degrees. 19 undergraduate majors. **Total enrollment:** 953. Undergraduates: 534. Freshmen: 106. Federal methodology is used as a basis for awarding need-based institutional aid.

UNDERGRADUATE EXPENSES for 2013–2014 Application fee: $45. **One-time required fee:** $825. **Comprehensive fee:** $25,836 includes full-time tuition ($18,200), mandatory fees ($540), and room and board ($7096). **College room only:** $3548. Full-time tuition and fees vary according to course load, program, and reciprocity agreements. Room and board charges vary according to board plan and housing facility. **Part-time tuition:** $750 per credit hour. **Part-time fees:** $10 per credit; $120 per term. Part-time tuition and fees vary according to course load, program, and reciprocity agreements.

FRESHMAN FINANCIAL AID (Fall 2011) 91 applied for aid; of those 99% were deemed to have need. 100% of freshmen with need received aid; of those 11% had need fully met. **Average percent of need met:** 71% (excluding resources awarded to replace EFC). **Average financial aid package:** $16,544 (excluding resources awarded to replace EFC). 10% of all full-time freshmen had no need and received non-need-based gift aid.

UNDERGRADUATE FINANCIAL AID (Fall 2011) 541 applied for aid; of those 86% were deemed to have need. 100% of undergraduates with need received aid; of those 10% had need fully met. **Average percent of need met:** 61% (excluding resources awarded to replace EFC). **Average financial aid package:** $15,846 (excluding resources awarded to replace EFC). 6% of all full-time undergraduates had no need and received non-need-based gift aid.

GIFT AID (NEED-BASED) Total amount: $5,064,125 (26% federal, 22% state, 49% institutional, 3% external sources). **Receiving aid:** Freshmen: 63% (67); all full-time undergraduates: 69% (386). **Average award:** Freshmen: $9510; Undergraduates: $9836. **Scholarships, grants, and awards:** Federal Pell, FSEOG, state, private, college/university gift aid from institutional funds.

GIFT AID (NON-NEED-BASED) Total amount: $1,471,287 (7% state, 90% institutional, 3% external sources). **Receiving aid:** Freshmen: 79% (84). Undergraduates: 74% (411). **Average award:** Freshmen: $6083. Undergraduates: $6792. **Scholarships, grants, and awards by category:** Academic interests/achievement: 367 awards ($1,317,033 total): business, communication, education, English, general academic interests/achievements, international studies, religion/biblical studies. Creative arts/performance: music. Special achievements/activities: 35 awards ($277,415 total): general special achievements/activities, leadership, religious involvement. Special characteristics: 235 awards ($672,229 total): children and siblings of alumni, children of faculty/staff, ethnic background, international students, local/state students, members of minority groups, relatives of clergy, religious affiliation, spouses of current students, veterans, veterans' children. **Tuition waivers:** Full or partial for employees or children of employees.

LOANS Student loans: $2,504,925 (56% need-based, 44% non-need-based). 59% of past graduating class borrowed through all loan programs. Average indebtedness per student: $25,638. **Average need-based loan:** Freshmen: $3484. Undergraduates: $4416. **Parent loans:** $495,531 (100% non-need-based). **Programs:** Federal Direct (Subsidized and Unsubsidized Stafford, PLUS).

WORK-STUDY Federal work-study: Total amount: $204,697; 133 jobs averaging $2000. **State or other work-study/employment:** Total amount: $236,786 (66% need-based, 34% non-need-based). 105 part-time jobs averaging $2000.

APPLYING FOR FINANCIAL AID Required financial aid forms: FAFSA, institution's own form, state aid form. **Financial aid deadline (priority):** 4/15. **Notification date:** Continuous beginning 3/1. Students must reply within 2 weeks of notification.

CONTACT Mrs. Melissa Chambers, Financial Aid Office Manager, Columbia International University, 7435 Monticello Road, Columbia, SC 29203, 800-777-2227 Ext. 5036 or toll-free 800-777-2227 Ext. 5024. Fax: 803-223-2505. E-mail: mchambers@ciu.edu. Website: http://www.ciu.edu/.

COLUMBIA UNIVERSITY
New York, NY

Tuition & fees: $47,346	Average undergraduate aid package: $42,716

ABOUT THE INSTITUTION Independent, coed. **Awards:** bachelor's, master's, and doctoral degrees. 78 undergraduate majors. **Total enrollment:** 6,068. Undergraduates: 6,068. Freshmen: 1,415. Both federal and institutional methodology are used as a basis for awarding need-based institutional aid.

UNDERGRADUATE EXPENSES for 2013–2014 Application fee: $80. **One-time required fee:** $511. **Comprehensive fee:** $58,842 includes full-time tuition ($45,028), mandatory fees ($2318), and room and board ($11,496).

FRESHMAN FINANCIAL AID (Fall 2012, est.) 882 applied for aid; of those 82% were deemed to have need. 100% of freshmen with need received aid; of those 100% had need fully met. **Average percent of need met:** 100% (excluding resources awarded to replace EFC). **Average financial aid package:** $43,087 (excluding resources awarded to replace EFC).

UNDERGRADUATE FINANCIAL AID (Fall 2012, est.) 3,324 applied for aid; of those 95% were deemed to have need. 100% of undergraduates with need received aid; of those 100% had need fully met. **Average percent of need met:** 100% (excluding resources awarded to replace EFC). **Average financial aid package:** $42,716 (excluding resources awarded to replace EFC).

GIFT AID (NEED-BASED) Total amount: $124,990,620 (5% federal, 1% state, 92% institutional, 2% external sources). **Receiving aid:** Freshmen: 49% (691); all full-time undergraduates: 50% (3,028). **Average award:** Freshmen: $42,785; Undergraduates: $42,716. **Scholarships, grants, and awards:** Federal Pell, FSEOG, state, private, college/university gift aid from institutional funds.

GIFT AID (NON-NEED-BASED) Total amount: $674,717 (6% federal, 1% state, 93% external sources). **Receiving aid:** Freshmen: 5. Undergraduates: 18. **Tuition waivers:** Full or partial for employees or children of employees. **ROTC:** Army cooperative, Naval, Air Force cooperative.

LOANS Student loans: $6,973,428 (44% need-based, 56% non-need-based). **Average need-based loan:** Freshmen: $2346. Undergraduates: $3620. **Parent loans:** $6,570,552 (6% need-based, 94% non-need-based). **Programs:** Perkins, alternative loans.

WORK-STUDY Federal work-study: Total amount: $4,943,322; jobs available. **State or other work-study/employment:** Total amount: $2,133,513 (72% need-based, 28% non-need-based). Part-time jobs available.

APPLYING FOR FINANCIAL AID Required financial aid forms: FAFSA, CSS Financial Aid PROFILE, noncustodial (divorced/separated) parent's statement, federal income tax form(s). **Financial aid deadline:** 3/1. **Notification date:** 4/1. Students must reply by 5/1.

CONTACT Kathryn Tuman, Executive Director of Financial Aid, Columbia University, 100 Hamilton Hall, MC 2802, 1130 Amsterdam Avenue, New York, NY 10027, 212-854-3711. Fax: 212-854-5353. E-mail: kat56@columbia.edu. Website: http://www.columbia.edu/.

COLUMBIA UNIVERSITY, SCHOOL OF GENERAL STUDIES
New York, NY

Tuition & fees: $45,699	Average undergraduate aid package: N/A

ABOUT THE INSTITUTION Independent, coed. **Awards:** certificates and bachelor's degrees. 79 undergraduate majors. **Total enrollment:** 1,632. Undergraduates: 1,632. Freshmen: 119. Both federal and institutional methodology are used as a basis for awarding need-based institutional aid.

UNDERGRADUATE EXPENSES for 2013–2014 Application fee: $80. **Comprehensive fee:** $55,932 includes full-time tuition ($43,620), mandatory fees ($2079), and room and board ($10,233). **College room only:** $5823. Full-time tuition and fees vary according to course load, program, and student level. Room and board charges vary according to board plan and housing facility. **Part-time tuition:** $1454 per credit hour. Part-time tuition and fees vary according to course load, program, and student level. **Payment plan:** Tuition prepayment.

COLUMBIA UNIVERSITY, SCHOOL OF GENERAL STUDIES

GIFT AID (NEED-BASED) Total amount: $16,462,907 (24% federal, 3% state, 69% institutional, 4% external sources). **Scholarships, grants, and awards:** Federal Pell, FSEOG, state, private, college/university gift aid from institutional funds.
GIFT AID (NON-NEED-BASED) Total amount: $1,284,927 (99% institutional, 1% external sources). **Scholarships, grants, and awards by category:** Academic interests/achievement: general academic interests/achievements. **Tuition waivers:** Full or partial for employees or children of employees. **ROTC:** Army cooperative, Naval, Air Force cooperative.
LOANS Student loans: $17,345,036 (94% need-based, 6% non-need-based). **Parent loans:** $692,144 (77% need-based, 23% non-need-based). **Programs:** Perkins, college/university.
WORK-STUDY Federal work-study: Total amount: $690,501; jobs available.
APPLYING FOR FINANCIAL AID Required financial aid forms: FAFSA, institution's own form. **Financial aid deadline:** 6/1 (priority: 6/1). **Notification date:** Continuous. Students must reply within 3 weeks of notification.
CONTACT Mr. Skip Bailey, Director of Educational Financing, Columbia University, School of General Studies, 408 Lewisohn Hall, 2970 Broadway, New York, NY 10027, 212-854-2772 or toll-free 800-895-1169. Fax: 212-854-6316. E-mail: gs_financial_aid@columbia.edu. Website: http://www.gs.columbia.edu/.

COLUMBUS COLLEGE OF ART & DESIGN
Columbus, OH

Tuition & fees: $28,524	Average undergraduate aid package: $18,296

ABOUT THE INSTITUTION Independent, coed. **Awards:** bachelor's and master's degrees. 7 undergraduate majors. **Total enrollment:** 1,400. Undergraduates: 1,375. Freshmen: 260. Federal methodology is used as a basis for awarding need-based institutional aid.
UNDERGRADUATE EXPENSES for 2013–2014 Application fee: $30. **Comprehensive fee:** $36,014 includes full-time tuition ($27,504), mandatory fees ($1020), and room and board ($7490). Full-time tuition and fees vary according to course load. Room and board charges vary according to board plan, housing facility, and student level. **Part-time tuition:** $1146 per credit hour. **Part-time fees:** $180 per semester hour. Part-time tuition and fees vary according to course load.
FRESHMAN FINANCIAL AID (Fall 2012, est.) 260 applied for aid; of those 93% were deemed to have need. 97% of freshmen with need received aid; of those 6% had need fully met. **Average percent of need met:** 49% (excluding resources awarded to replace EFC). **Average financial aid package:** $18,213 (excluding resources awarded to replace EFC). 15% of all full-time freshmen had no need and received non-need-based gift aid.
UNDERGRADUATE FINANCIAL AID (Fall 2012, est.) 1,218 applied for aid; of those 93% were deemed to have need. 98% of undergraduates with need received aid; of those 9% had need fully met. **Average percent of need met:** 52% (excluding resources awarded to replace EFC). **Average financial aid package:** $18,296 (excluding resources awarded to replace EFC). 15% of all full-time undergraduates had no need and received non-need-based gift aid.
GIFT AID (NEED-BASED) Total amount: $14,215,671 (17% federal, 5% state, 77% institutional, 1% external sources). **Receiving aid:** Freshmen: 80% (233); all full-time undergraduates: 81% (1,101). **Average award:** Freshmen: $14,108; Undergraduates: $12,773. **Scholarships, grants, and awards:** Federal Pell, FSEOG, state, private, college/university gift aid from institutional funds.
GIFT AID (NON-NEED-BASED) Total amount: $2,338,132 (99% institutional, 1% external sources). **Receiving aid:** Freshmen: 2% (5). Undergraduates: 3% (43). **Average award:** Freshmen: $10,011. Undergraduates: $10,071. **Scholarships, grants, and awards by category:** Creative arts/performance: art/fine arts. **Special characteristics:** children of educators, children of faculty/staff, local/state students. **Tuition waivers:** Full or partial for children of alumni, employees or children of employees.
LOANS Student loans: $10,558,028 (82% need-based, 18% non-need-based). 87% of past graduating class borrowed through all loan programs. Average indebtedness per student: $36,100. **Average need-based loan:** Freshmen: $4756. Undergraduates: $6092. **Parent loans:** $6,206,671 (77% need-based, 23% non-need-based). **Programs:** Federal Direct (Subsidized and Unsubsidized Stafford, PLUS), Perkins, state.

WORK-STUDY Federal work-study: Total amount: $483,901; 187 jobs averaging $3465. **State or other work-study/employment:** 210 part-time jobs averaging $3465.
APPLYING FOR FINANCIAL AID Required financial aid forms: FAFSA, institution's own form, federal income tax form(s), verification worksheet. **Financial aid deadline (priority):** 3/1. **Notification date:** 3/15. Students must reply within 2 weeks of notification.
CONTACT Mrs. Anna Marie Schofield, Director of Financial Aid, Columbus College of Art & Design, 60 Cleveland Avenue, Columbus, OH 43215-1758, 614-224-9101 Ext. 3274 or toll-free 877-997-2223. Fax: 614-222-4034. E-mail: aschofield@ccad.edu. Website: http://www.ccad.edu/.

COLUMBUS STATE UNIVERSITY
Columbus, GA

Tuition & fees (GA res): $6592	Average undergraduate aid package: $8997

ABOUT THE INSTITUTION State-supported, coed. **Awards:** certificates, associate, bachelor's, master's, and doctoral degrees. 40 undergraduate majors. **Total enrollment:** 8,239. Undergraduates: 7,025. Freshmen: 1,159. Federal methodology is used as a basis for awarding need-based institutional aid.
UNDERGRADUATE EXPENSES for 2013–2014 Application fee: $40. **Tuition, state resident:** full-time $4852; part-time $161.74 per semester hour. **Tuition, nonresident:** full-time $17,128; part-time $570.94 per semester hour. **Required fees:** full-time $1740; $870 per term. **College room and board:** $8542. Room and board charges vary according to board plan.
FRESHMAN FINANCIAL AID (Fall 2012, est.) 982 applied for aid; of those 81% were deemed to have need. 100% of freshmen with need received aid; of those 17% had need fully met. **Average percent of need met:** 71% (excluding resources awarded to replace EFC). **Average financial aid package:** $9017 (excluding resources awarded to replace EFC). 6% of all full-time freshmen had no need and received non-need-based gift aid.
UNDERGRADUATE FINANCIAL AID (Fall 2012, est.) 4,215 applied for aid; of those 84% were deemed to have need. 100% of undergraduates with need received aid; of those 18% had need fully met. **Average percent of need met:** 73% (excluding resources awarded to replace EFC). **Average financial aid package:** $8997 (excluding resources awarded to replace EFC). 5% of all full-time undergraduates had no need and received non-need-based gift aid.
GIFT AID (NEED-BASED) Total amount: $14,843,281 (99% federal, 1% external sources). **Receiving aid:** Freshmen: 52% (547); all full-time undergraduates: 52% (2,544). **Average award:** Freshmen: $4803; Undergraduates: $4727. **Scholarships, grants, and awards:** Federal Pell, FSEOG, state, private, college/university gift aid from institutional funds.
GIFT AID (NON-NEED-BASED) Total amount: $9,272,835 (1% federal, 84% state, 8% institutional, 7% external sources). **Receiving aid:** Freshmen: 42% (446). Undergraduates: 27% (1,304). **Average award:** Freshmen: $2098. Undergraduates: $1638. **Scholarships, grants, and awards by category:** Academic interests/achievement: biological sciences, business, communication, computer science, education, English, general academic interests/achievements, health fields, humanities, international studies, mathematics, military science, physical sciences. Creative arts/performance: art/fine arts, dance, music, performing arts, theater/drama. Special achievements/activities: cheerleading/drum major, community service, general special achievements/activities, leadership. **ROTC:** Army.
LOANS Student loans: $36,454,579 (45% need-based, 55% non-need-based). 67% of past graduating class borrowed through all loan programs. Average indebtedness per student: $25,687. **Average need-based loan:** Freshmen: $3319. Undergraduates: $4106. **Parent loans:** $1,297,472 (100% non-need-based). **Programs:** Federal Direct (Subsidized and Unsubsidized Stafford, PLUS), Perkins, Federal Nursing, state, college/university.
WORK-STUDY Federal work-study: Total amount: $468,982; jobs available.
ATHLETIC AWARDS Total amount: $1,105,854 (100% non-need-based).
APPLYING FOR FINANCIAL AID Required financial aid form: FAFSA. **Financial aid deadline (priority):** 5/1. **Notification date:** Continuous beginning 5/1.

CONTACT Ms. Patricia Garrett, Associate Director of Financial Aid, Columbus State University, 4225 University Avenue, Columbus, GA 31907-5645, 706-507-8800 or toll-free 866-264-2035. *Fax:* 706-568-2230. *E-mail:* garrett_patricia2@columbusstate.edu. *Website:* http://www.columbusstate.edu/.

CONCEPTION SEMINARY COLLEGE
Conception, MO

CONTACT Br. Justin Hernandez, PhD, Financial Aid Director, Conception Seminary College, PO Box 502, Conception, MO 64433-0502, 660-944-2851. *Fax:* 660-944-2829. *E-mail:* justin@conception.edu. *Website:* http://www.conception.edu/.

CONCORDIA COLLEGE
Moorhead, MN

Tuition & fees: $32,814	Average undergraduate aid package: $24,124

ABOUT THE INSTITUTION Independent Evangelical Lutheran Church in America, coed. *Awards:* bachelor's and master's degrees. 57 undergraduate majors. *Total enrollment:* 2,631. Undergraduates: 2,603. Freshmen: 633. Federal methodology is used as a basis for awarding need-based institutional aid.

UNDERGRADUATE EXPENSES for 2013–2014 *Application fee:* $20. *Comprehensive fee:* $39,974 includes full-time tuition ($32,600), mandatory fees ($214), and room and board ($7160). *College room only:* $3090. Full-time tuition and fees vary according to course load and degree level. Room and board charges vary according to board plan and housing facility. *Part-time tuition:* $1280 per contact hour. Part-time tuition and fees vary according to course load and degree level.

FRESHMAN FINANCIAL AID (Fall 2011) 672 applied for aid; of those 86% were deemed to have need. 100% of freshmen with need received aid; of those 21% had need fully met. *Average percent of need met:* 92% (excluding resources awarded to replace EFC). *Average financial aid package:* $25,220 (excluding resources awarded to replace EFC). 19% of all full-time freshmen had no need and received non-need-based gift aid.

UNDERGRADUATE FINANCIAL AID (Fall 2011) 2,266 applied for aid; of those 88% were deemed to have need. 100% of undergraduates with need received aid; of those 16% had need fully met. *Average percent of need met:* 88% (excluding resources awarded to replace EFC). *Average financial aid package:* $24,124 (excluding resources awarded to replace EFC). 22% of all full-time undergraduates had no need and received non-need-based gift aid.

GIFT AID (NEED-BASED) *Total amount:* $31,656,197 (12% federal, 8% state, 77% institutional, 3% external sources). *Receiving aid:* Freshmen: 79% (569); all full-time undergraduates: 73% (1,960). *Average award:* Freshmen: $18,449; Undergraduates: $16,144. *Scholarships, grants, and awards:* Federal Pell, FSEOG, state, private, college/university gift aid from institutional funds.

GIFT AID (NON-NEED-BASED) *Total amount:* $8,397,374 (5% federal, 90% institutional, 5% external sources). *Receiving aid:* Freshmen: 11% (81). Undergraduates: 8% (222). *Average award:* Freshmen: $11,914. Undergraduates: $10,920. *Scholarships, grants, and awards by category:* Academic interests/achievement: 2,427 awards ($22,503,211 total): general academic interests/achievements. Creative arts/performance: 298 awards ($715,361 total): art/fine arts, debating, music, theater/drama. Special characteristics: 93 awards ($1,134,578 total): international students. *Tuition waivers:* Full or partial for employees or children of employees. *ROTC:* Army cooperative, Air Force cooperative.

LOANS *Student loans:* $20,927,406 (62% need-based, 38% non-need-based). 80% of past graduating class borrowed through all loan programs. *Average indebtedness per student:* $38,075. *Average need-based loan:* Freshmen: $6909. Undergraduates: $8026. *Parent loans:* $2,606,768 (26% need-based, 74% non-need-based). *Programs:* Federal Direct (Subsidized and Unsubsidized Stafford, PLUS), Perkins, state, college/university, private loans.

WORK-STUDY *Federal work-study:* Total amount: $2,749,337; 1,549 jobs averaging $1775. *State or other work-study/employment:* Total amount: $2,296,950 (12% need-based, 88% non-need-based). 1,011 part-time jobs averaging $2719.

APPLYING FOR FINANCIAL AID *Required financial aid form:* FAFSA. *Financial aid deadline:* Continuous. *Notification date:* Continuous beginning 3/15. Students must reply within 6 weeks of notification.

CONTACT Mr. Eric Addington, Director of Financial Aid, Concordia College, 901 South 8th Street, Moorhead, MN 56562, 218-299-3010 or toll-free 800-699-9897. *Fax:* 218-299-3025. *E-mail:* eaddingt@cord.edu. *Website:* http://www.concordiacollege.edu/.

CONCORDIA COLLEGE ALABAMA
Selma, AL

CONTACT Mrs. T. H. Bridges, Financial Aid Office, Concordia College Alabama, 1804 Green Street, Selma, AL 36701, 334-874-5700. *Fax:* 334-874-3728. *E-mail:* tbridges@concordiaselma.edu. *Website:* http://www.ccal.edu/.

CONCORDIA COLLEGE–NEW YORK
Bronxville, NY

CONTACT Janice Spikereit, Director of Financial Aid, Concordia College–New York, 171 White Plains Road, Bronxville, NY 10708, 914-337-9300 Ext. 2146 or toll-free 800-YES-COLLEGE. *Fax:* 914-395-4500. *E-mail:* financialaid@concordia-ny.edu. *Website:* http://www.concordia-ny.edu/.

CONCORDIA UNIVERSITY
Irvine, CA

Tuition & fees: $29,630	Average undergraduate aid package: $17,606

ABOUT THE INSTITUTION Independent Lutheran Church–Missouri Synod, coed. *Awards:* associate, bachelor's, and master's degrees (associate's degree for international students only). 27 undergraduate majors. *Total enrollment:* 3,519. Undergraduates: 1,738. Freshmen: 301. Federal methodology is used as a basis for awarding need-based institutional aid.

UNDERGRADUATE EXPENSES for 2013–2014 *Application fee:* $50. *Comprehensive fee:* $38,680 includes full-time tuition ($29,000), mandatory fees ($630), and room and board ($9050). *College room only:* $5100. Full-time tuition and fees vary according to course load. Room and board charges vary according to board plan and housing facility. *Part-time tuition:* $900 per unit. *Part-time fees:* $315 per term. Part-time tuition and fees vary according to course load.

FRESHMAN FINANCIAL AID (Fall 2012, est.) 278 applied for aid; of those 81% were deemed to have need. 100% of freshmen with need received aid; of those 15% had need fully met. *Average percent of need met:* 68% (excluding resources awarded to replace EFC). *Average financial aid package:* $19,085 (excluding resources awarded to replace EFC). 17% of all full-time freshmen had no need and received non-need-based gift aid.

UNDERGRADUATE FINANCIAL AID (Fall 2012, est.) 1,296 applied for aid; of those 85% were deemed to have need. 100% of undergraduates with need received aid; of those 13% had need fully met. *Average percent of need met:* 60% (excluding resources awarded to replace EFC). *Average financial aid package:* $17,606 (excluding resources awarded to replace EFC). 15% of all full-time undergraduates had no need and received non-need-based gift aid.

GIFT AID (NEED-BASED) *Total amount:* $12,306,806 (17% federal, 20% state, 63% institutional). *Receiving aid:* Freshmen: 75% (225); all full-time undergraduates: 65% (1,014). *Average award:* Freshmen: $15,415; Undergraduates: $14,255. *Scholarships, grants, and awards:* Federal Pell, FSEOG, state, private, college/university gift aid from institutional funds.

GIFT AID (NON-NEED-BASED) *Total amount:* $2,572,139 (100% institutional). *Receiving aid:* Freshmen: 9% (27). Undergraduates: 6% (94). *Average award:* Freshmen: $7673. Undergraduates: $7578. *Scholarships, grants, and awards by category:* Academic interests/achievement: 1,091 awards ($6,213,544 total): general academic interests/achievements. Creative arts/performance: 209

awards ($771,000 total): debating, music, theater/drama. *Special characteristics:* 259 awards ($1,050,775 total): children of faculty/staff, first-generation college students, religious affiliation. *Tuition waivers:* Full or partial for employees or children of employees.

LOANS *Student loans:* $10,941,885 (38% need-based, 62% non-need-based). 67% of past graduating class borrowed through all loan programs. *Average indebtedness per student:* $29,091. *Average need-based loan:* Freshmen: $3414. Undergraduates: $4542. *Parent loans:* $3,721,599 (100% non-need-based). *Programs:* Federal Direct (Subsidized and Unsubsidized Stafford, PLUS), private loans.

WORK-STUDY *Federal work-study:* Total amount: $95,600; 43 jobs averaging $2305. *State or other work-study/employment:* Part-time jobs available.

ATHLETIC AWARDS Total amount: $3,797,488 (60% need-based, 40% non-need-based).

APPLYING FOR FINANCIAL AID *Required financial aid forms:* FAFSA, state aid form, department scholarship application form. *Financial aid deadline:* 3/2 (priority: 3/2). *Notification date:* Continuous beginning 3/15. Students must reply within 4 weeks of notification.

CONTACT Lori McDonald, Director of Financial Aid, Concordia University, 1530 Concordia West, Irvine, CA 92612-3299, 949-214-3074 or toll-free 800-229-1200. *Fax:* 949-214-3500. *E-mail:* lori.mcdonald@cui.edu. *Website:* http://www.cui.edu/.

CONCORDIA UNIVERSITY
Portland, OR

Tuition & fees: N/R	Average undergraduate aid package: $17,414

ABOUT THE INSTITUTION Independent Lutheran Church–Missouri Synod, coed. *Awards:* certificates, associate, bachelor's, and master's degrees. 33 undergraduate majors. *Total enrollment:* 3,111. Undergraduates: 1,369. Freshmen: 247. Federal methodology is used as a basis for awarding need-based institutional aid.

FRESHMAN FINANCIAL AID (Fall 2011) 202 applied for aid; of those 84% were deemed to have need. 100% of freshmen with need received aid; of those 9% had need fully met. *Average financial aid package:* $17,175 (excluding resources awarded to replace EFC). 19% of all full-time freshmen had no need and received non-need-based gift aid.

UNDERGRADUATE FINANCIAL AID (Fall 2011) 999 applied for aid; of those 91% were deemed to have need. 100% of undergraduates with need received aid; of those 6% had need fully met. *Average financial aid package:* $17,414 (excluding resources awarded to replace EFC). 12% of all full-time undergraduates had no need and received non-need-based gift aid.

GIFT AID (NEED-BASED) *Total amount:* $4,569,496 (49% federal, 4% state, 47% institutional). *Receiving aid:* Freshmen: 53% (112); all full-time undergraduates: 63% (668). *Average award:* Freshmen: $6016; Undergraduates: $5826. *Scholarships, grants, and awards:* Federal Pell, FSEOG, state, private, college/university gift aid from institutional funds.

GIFT AID (NON-NEED-BASED) *Total amount:* $7,695,293 (90% institutional, 10% external sources). *Receiving aid:* Freshmen: 80% (168). Undergraduates: 75% (802). *Average award:* Freshmen: $7146. Undergraduates: $7683. *Scholarships, grants, and awards by category:* Academic interests/achievement: general academic interests/achievements, religion/biblical studies. *Creative arts/performance:* music. *Special achievements/activities:* leadership, religious involvement. *Special characteristics:* children of faculty/staff, relatives of clergy, religious affiliation. *ROTC:* Air Force cooperative.

LOANS *Student loans:* $9,267,099 (42% need-based, 58% non-need-based). 80% of past graduating class borrowed through all loan programs. *Average indebtedness per student:* $32,888. *Average need-based loan:* Freshmen: $3305. Undergraduates: $4814. *Parent loans:* $3,393,165 (100% non-need-based). *Programs:* Perkins, alternative loans.

WORK-STUDY *Federal work-study:* Total amount: $107,669; jobs available. *State or other work-study/employment:* Total amount: $402,651 (100% non-need-based). Part-time jobs available.

ATHLETIC AWARDS Total amount: $1,866,715 (100% non-need-based).

APPLYING FOR FINANCIAL AID *Required financial aid form:* FAFSA. *Financial aid deadline:* Continuous. *Notification date:* Continuous beginning 3/15. Students must reply by 5/1 or within 2 weeks of notification.

CONTACT Mr. Robert Clarke, Director of Financial Aid, Concordia University, 2811 Northeast Holman Street, Portland, OR 97211-6099, 503-493-6555 or toll-free 800-321-9371. *Fax:* 503-280-8661. *E-mail:* jcullen@cu-portland.edu. *Website:* http://www.cu-portland.edu/.

CONCORDIA UNIVERSITY ANN ARBOR
Ann Arbor, MI

Tuition & fees: $22,464	Average undergraduate aid package: $16,822

ABOUT THE INSTITUTION Independent Lutheran Church–Missouri Synod, coed. *Awards:* certificates, associate, bachelor's, and master's degrees. 35 undergraduate majors. *Total enrollment:* 711. Undergraduates: 509. Freshmen: 169. Federal methodology is used as a basis for awarding need-based institutional aid.

**UNDERGRADUATE EXPENSES for 2013–2014 *Application fee:* $25. *Comprehensive fee:* $30,762 includes full-time tuition ($22,464) and room and board ($8298). Full-time tuition and fees vary according to location and program. Room and board charges vary according to housing facility. *Part-time tuition:* $936 per credit hour. Part-time tuition and fees vary according to course load, location, and program.

FRESHMAN FINANCIAL AID (Fall 2012, est.) 108 applied for aid; of those 78% were deemed to have need. 100% of freshmen with need received aid; of those 42% had need fully met. *Average percent of need met:* 81% (excluding resources awarded to replace EFC). *Average financial aid package:* $17,102 (excluding resources awarded to replace EFC). 22% of all full-time freshmen had no need and received non-need-based gift aid.

UNDERGRADUATE FINANCIAL AID (Fall 2012, est.) 403 applied for aid; of those 87% were deemed to have need. 100% of undergraduates with need received aid; of those 27% had need fully met. *Average percent of need met:* 77% (excluding resources awarded to replace EFC). *Average financial aid package:* $16,822 (excluding resources awarded to replace EFC). 17% of all full-time undergraduates had no need and received non-need-based gift aid.

GIFT AID (NEED-BASED) *Total amount:* $3,509,281 (23% federal, 6% state, 65% institutional, 6% external sources). *Receiving aid:* Freshmen: 67% (84); all full-time undergraduates: 73% (351). *Average award:* Freshmen: $12,784; Undergraduates: $11,351. *Scholarships, grants, and awards:* Federal Pell, FSEOG, state, private, college/university gift aid from institutional funds.

GIFT AID (NON-NEED-BASED) *Total amount:* $735,549 (85% institutional, 15% external sources). *Receiving aid:* Freshmen: 12% (15). Undergraduates: 12% (57). *Average award:* Freshmen: $7786. Undergraduates: $6955. *Scholarships, grants, and awards by category:* Academic interests/achievement: $1,789,664 total: business, education, general academic interests/achievements, religion/biblical studies. *Creative arts/performance:* $266,814 total: art/fine arts, music, performing arts, theater/drama. *Special characteristics:* $563,782 total: children and siblings of alumni, children of faculty/staff, ethnic background, general special characteristics, out-of-state students, religious affiliation, siblings of current students. *Tuition waivers:* Full or partial for employees or children of employees. *ROTC:* Army cooperative, Air Force cooperative.

LOANS *Student loans:* $2,866,209 (70% need-based, 30% non-need-based). 96% of past graduating class borrowed through all loan programs. *Average indebtedness per student:* $17,652. *Average need-based loan:* Freshmen: $3984. Undergraduates: $4496. *Parent loans:* $789,644 (27% need-based, 73% non-need-based). *Programs:* Federal Direct (Subsidized and Unsubsidized Stafford, PLUS), Perkins.

WORK-STUDY *Federal work-study:* Total amount: $75,000; 121 jobs averaging $609. *State or other work-study/employment:* Total amount: $78,685 (16% need-based, 84% non-need-based). 73 part-time jobs averaging $1009.

ATHLETIC AWARDS Total amount: $979,523 (61% need-based, 39% non-need-based).

APPLYING FOR FINANCIAL AID *Required financial aid form:* FAFSA. *Financial aid deadline (priority):* 3/15. *Notification date:* Continuous beginning 2/1. Students must reply by 5/1 or within 4 weeks of notification.

CONTACT Mr. Steven P. Taylor, Financial Aid Office, Concordia University Ann Arbor, 4090 Geddes Road, Ann Arbor, MI 48105-2797, 734-995-7408 or toll-free 877-995-7520 (in-state), 877-955-7520 (out-of-state). *Fax:* 734-995-4610. *E-mail:* taylos@cuaa.edu. *Website:* http://www.cuaa.edu/.

CONCORDIA UNIVERSITY CHICAGO
River Forest, IL

ABOUT THE INSTITUTION Independent Lutheran Church–Missouri Synod, coed. *Awards:* certificates, bachelor's, master's, and doctoral degrees. 61 undergraduate majors. *Total enrollment:* 5,454. Undergraduates: 1,515. Freshmen: 318.
GIFT AID (NEED-BASED) *Scholarships, grants, and awards:* Federal Pell, FSEOG, state, private, college/university gift aid from institutional funds.
GIFT AID (NON-NEED-BASED) *Scholarships, grants, and awards by category:* Academic interests/achievement: biological sciences, business, communication, computer science, education, English, foreign languages, general academic interests/achievements, mathematics, religion/biblical studies. *Creative arts/performance:* art/fine arts, music. *Special characteristics:* children and siblings of alumni, children of faculty/staff, international students, religious affiliation.
LOANS *Programs:* Federal Direct (Subsidized and Unsubsidized Stafford, PLUS), Perkins.
APPLYING FOR FINANCIAL AID *Required financial aid form:* FAFSA.
CONTACT Aida Asencio-Pinto, Director of Student Financial Planning, Concordia University Chicago, 7400 Augusta Street, River Forest, IL 60305-1499, 708-209-3113 or toll-free 800-285-2668. *Fax:* 708-488-4102. *E-mail:* aida.asencio-pinto@cuchicago.edu.
Website: http://www.cuchicago.edu/.

CONCORDIA UNIVERSITY, NEBRASKA
Seward, NE

Tuition & fees: $24,750	Average undergraduate aid package: $18,594

ABOUT THE INSTITUTION Independent Lutheran Church–Missouri Synod, coed. *Awards:* certificates, bachelor's, and master's degrees. 73 undergraduate majors. *Total enrollment:* 2,091. Undergraduates: 1,481. Freshmen: 296. Federal methodology is used as a basis for awarding need-based institutional aid.
UNDERGRADUATE EXPENSES for 2013–2014 *Comprehensive fee:* $31,450 includes full-time tuition ($24,500), mandatory fees ($250), and room and board ($6700). *College room only:* $2750. Room and board charges vary according to board plan and housing facility. *Part-time tuition:* $765 per credit hour.
FRESHMAN FINANCIAL AID (Fall 2012, est.) 272 applied for aid; of those 89% were deemed to have need. 100% of freshmen with need received aid; of those 28% had need fully met. *Average percent of need met:* 78% (excluding resources awarded to replace EFC). *Average financial aid package:* $18,987 (excluding resources awarded to replace EFC). 6% of all full-time freshmen had no need and received non-need-based gift aid.
UNDERGRADUATE FINANCIAL AID (Fall 2012, est.) 1,011 applied for aid; of those 87% were deemed to have need. 100% of undergraduates with need received aid; of those 25% had need fully met. *Average percent of need met:* 77% (excluding resources awarded to replace EFC). *Average financial aid package:* $18,594 (excluding resources awarded to replace EFC). 10% of all full-time undergraduates had no need and received non-need-based gift aid.
GIFT AID (NEED-BASED) *Total amount:* $10,968,624 (13% federal, 1% state, 71% institutional, 15% external sources). *Receiving aid:* Freshmen: 82% (243); all full-time undergraduates: 76% (882). *Average award:* Freshmen: $15,144; Undergraduates: $14,340. *Scholarships, grants, and awards:* Federal Pell, FSEOG, state, private, college/university gift aid from institutional funds.
GIFT AID (NON-NEED-BASED) *Total amount:* $3,164,012 (100% institutional). *Receiving aid:* Freshmen: 14% (41). Undergraduates: 12% (138). *Average award:* Freshmen: $9580. Undergraduates: $11,370. *Scholarships, grants, and awards by category:* Academic interests/achievement: biological sciences, business, communication, computer science, education, English, general academic interests/achievements, health fields, humanities, mathematics, physical sciences, premedicine, religion/biblical studies, social sciences. *Creative arts/performance:* applied art and design, art/fine arts, dance, debating, music, theater/drama. *Special characteristics:* children and siblings of alumni, children of educators, children of faculty/staff, international students, local/state students, members of minority groups, religious affiliation, veterans, veterans' children. *Tuition waivers:* Full or partial for employees or children of employees. *ROTC:* Army cooperative, Air Force cooperative.

LOANS *Student loans:* $6,160,148 (46% need-based, 54% non-need-based). 78% of past graduating class borrowed through all loan programs. *Average indebtedness per student:* $27,222. *Average need-based loan:* Freshmen: $3675. Undergraduates: $4555. *Parent loans:* $2,096,056 (100% non-need-based). *Programs:* Federal Direct (Subsidized and Unsubsidized Stafford, PLUS), Perkins.
WORK-STUDY *Federal work-study:* Total amount: $101,788; 70 jobs averaging $1454.
ATHLETIC AWARDS Total amount: $2,643,069 (74% need-based, 26% non-need-based).
APPLYING FOR FINANCIAL AID *Required financial aid form:* FAFSA. *Financial aid deadline (priority):* 3/1. *Notification date:* Continuous beginning 3/1. Students must reply within 4 weeks of notification.
CONTACT Mr. Aaron W. Roberts, Director of Undergraduate Recruitment, Concordia University, Nebraska, 800 North Columbia Avenue, Seward, NE 68434-1556, 800-535-5494. *Fax:* 402-643-4073. *E-mail:* admiss@cune.edu. *Website:* http://www.cune.edu/.

CONCORDIA UNIVERSITY, ST. PAUL
St. Paul, MN

Tuition & fees: $19,700	Average undergraduate aid package: $22,531

ABOUT THE INSTITUTION Independent Lutheran Church–Missouri Synod, coed. *Awards:* certificates, associate, bachelor's, and master's degrees. 51 undergraduate majors. *Total enrollment:* 3,013. Undergraduates: 1,824. Freshmen: 181. Federal methodology is used as a basis for awarding need-based institutional aid.
UNDERGRADUATE EXPENSES for 2013–2014 *Application fee:* $30. *Comprehensive fee:* $27,450 includes full-time tuition ($19,700) and room and board ($7750). Full-time tuition and fees vary according to program. Room and board charges vary according to board plan and housing facility. *Part-time tuition:* $635 per credit. Part-time tuition and fees vary according to course load and program.
FRESHMAN FINANCIAL AID (Fall 2012, est.) 176 applied for aid; of those 92% were deemed to have need. 100% of freshmen with need received aid; of those 15% had need fully met. *Average percent of need met:* 79% (excluding resources awarded to replace EFC). *Average financial aid package:* $25,898 (excluding resources awarded to replace EFC). 4% of all full-time freshmen had no need and received non-need-based gift aid.
UNDERGRADUATE FINANCIAL AID (Fall 2012, est.) 858 applied for aid; of those 92% were deemed to have need. 99% of undergraduates with need received aid; of those 17% had need fully met. *Average percent of need met:* 72% (excluding resources awarded to replace EFC). *Average financial aid package:* $22,531 (excluding resources awarded to replace EFC). 8% of all full-time undergraduates had no need and received non-need-based gift aid.
GIFT AID (NEED-BASED) *Total amount:* $17,203,919 (18% federal, 11% state, 69% institutional, 2% external sources). *Receiving aid:* Freshmen: 89% (161); all full-time undergraduates: 82% (754). *Average award:* Freshmen: $21,183; Undergraduates: $17,791. *Scholarships, grants, and awards:* Federal Pell, FSEOG, state, private, college/university gift aid from institutional funds.
GIFT AID (NON-NEED-BASED) *Total amount:* $1,426,863 (1% state, 99% institutional). *Receiving aid:* Freshmen: 8% (14). Undergraduates: 10% (90). *Average award:* Freshmen: $13,100. Undergraduates: $9737. *Scholarships, grants, and awards by category:* Academic interests/achievement: general academic interests/achievements, mathematics, physical sciences, religion/biblical studies. *Creative arts/performance:* art/fine arts, music, theater/drama. *Special characteristics:* children of faculty/staff, religious affiliation, veterans, veterans' children. *Tuition waivers:* Full or partial for employees or children of employees. *ROTC:* Army cooperative, Air Force cooperative.
LOANS *Student loans:* $13,223,697 (92% need-based, 8% non-need-based). 87% of past graduating class borrowed through all loan programs. *Average indebtedness per student:* $42,020. *Average need-based loan:* Freshmen: $3940. Undergraduates: $4773. *Parent loans:* $1,573,829 (85% need-based, 15% non-need-based). *Programs:* Federal Direct (Subsidized and Unsubsidized Stafford, PLUS), Perkins, state, private loans.
WORK-STUDY *Federal work-study:* Total amount: $401,071; jobs available. *State or other work-study/employment:* Total amount: $483,454 (100% need-based). Part-time jobs available.

ATHLETIC AWARDS Total amount: $2,825,537 (84% need-based, 16% non-need-based).

APPLYING FOR FINANCIAL AID *Required financial aid forms:* FAFSA, institution's own form. *Financial aid deadline (priority):* 5/1. *Notification date:* Continuous beginning 3/1. Students must reply within 3 weeks of notification.

CONTACT Ms. Jeanie Peck, Financial Aid Director, Concordia University, St. Paul, 1282 Concordia Avenue, St. Paul, MN 55104-5494, 651-603-6300 or toll-free 800-333-4705. *Fax:* 651-603-6298. *E-mail:* finaid@csp.edu. *Website:* http://www.csp.edu/.

CONCORDIA UNIVERSITY TEXAS
Austin, TX

Tuition & fees: $23,600	Average undergraduate aid package: $17,946

ABOUT THE INSTITUTION Independent Lutheran Church–Missouri Synod, coed. *Awards:* certificates, associate, bachelor's, and master's degrees. 24 undergraduate majors. *Total enrollment:* 2,584. Undergraduates: 1,591. Freshmen: 259. Federal methodology is used as a basis for awarding need-based institutional aid.

UNDERGRADUATE EXPENSES for 2013–2014 *Application fee:* $25. *Comprehensive fee:* $32,060 includes full-time tuition ($23,600) and room and board ($8460). Full-time tuition and fees vary according to course load, degree level, and program. Room and board charges vary according to board plan. Part-time tuition and fees vary according to course load, degree level, and program.

FRESHMAN FINANCIAL AID (Fall 2012, est.) 211 applied for aid; of those 86% were deemed to have need. 99% of freshmen with need received aid; of those 15% had need fully met. *Average percent of need met:* 68% (excluding resources awarded to replace EFC). *Average financial aid package:* $16,922 (excluding resources awarded to replace EFC). 19% of all full-time freshmen had no need and received non-need-based gift aid.

UNDERGRADUATE FINANCIAL AID (Fall 2012, est.) 955 applied for aid; of those 88% were deemed to have need. 100% of undergraduates with need received aid; of those 15% had need fully met. *Average percent of need met:* 72% (excluding resources awarded to replace EFC). *Average financial aid package:* $17,946 (excluding resources awarded to replace EFC). 18% of all full-time undergraduates had no need and received non-need-based gift aid.

GIFT AID (NEED-BASED) *Total amount:* $12,325,689 (20% federal, 18% state, 61% institutional, 1% external sources). *Receiving aid:* Freshmen: 76% (177); all full-time undergraduates: 71% (799). *Average award:* Freshmen: $13,694; Undergraduates: $13,802. *Scholarships, grants, and awards:* Federal Pell, FSEOG, state, private, college/university gift aid from institutional funds.

GIFT AID (NON-NEED-BASED) *Total amount:* $2,478,734 (1% federal, 99% institutional). *Receiving aid:* Freshmen: 10% (24). Undergraduates: 8% (86). *Average award:* Freshmen: $10,486. Undergraduates: $9671. *Scholarships, grants, and awards by category:* Academic interests/achievement: biological sciences, business, communication, computer science, education, English, foreign languages, general academic interests/achievements, health fields, international studies, mathematics, physical sciences, religion/biblical studies, social sciences. *Creative arts/performance:* music. *Special achievements/activities:* junior miss, leadership, religious involvement. *Special characteristics:* adult students, children and siblings of alumni, children of faculty/staff, religious affiliation, veterans, veterans' children. *Tuition waivers:* Full or partial for employees or children of employees. *ROTC:* Army cooperative, Air Force cooperative.

LOANS *Student loans:* $9,259,951 (47% need-based, 53% non-need-based). 77% of past graduating class borrowed through all loan programs. *Average indebtedness per student:* $30,587. *Average need-based loan:* Freshmen: $3573. Undergraduates: $4738. *Parent loans:* $2,030,634 (100% non-need-based). *Programs:* Federal Direct (Subsidized and Unsubsidized Stafford, PLUS), state.

WORK-STUDY *Federal work-study:* Total amount: $147,928; 104 jobs averaging $1577. *State or other work-study/employment:* Total amount: $25,218 (100% need-based). 12 part-time jobs averaging $2102.

APPLYING FOR FINANCIAL AID *Required financial aid forms:* FAFSA, institution's own form. *Financial aid deadline:* Continuous. *Notification date:* Continuous beginning 2/15. Students must reply within 2 weeks of notification.

CONTACT Russell Jeffrey, Director of Student Financial Services, Concordia University Texas, 11400 Concordia University Drive, Austin, TX 78726, 512-313-4672 or toll-free 800-865-4282. *Fax:* 512-313-1670. *E-mail:* russell.jeffrey@concordia.edu. *Website:* http://www.concordia.edu/.

CONCORDIA UNIVERSITY WISCONSIN
Mequon, WI

Tuition & fees: $23,970	Average undergraduate aid package: $17,777

ABOUT THE INSTITUTION Independent Lutheran Church–Missouri Synod, coed. *Awards:* certificates, associate, bachelor's, master's, and doctoral degrees. 73 undergraduate majors. *Total enrollment:* 7,751. Undergraduates: 4,419. Freshmen: 610. Federal methodology is used as a basis for awarding need-based institutional aid.

UNDERGRADUATE EXPENSES for 2013–2014 *Application fee:* $35. *Comprehensive fee:* $33,020 includes full-time tuition ($23,970) and room and board ($9050). Full-time tuition and fees vary according to program. Room and board charges vary according to board plan. Part-time tuition and fees vary according to program.

FRESHMAN FINANCIAL AID (Fall 2012, est.) 564 applied for aid; of those 89% were deemed to have need. 100% of freshmen with need received aid; of those 28% had need fully met. *Average percent of need met:* 79% (excluding resources awarded to replace EFC). *Average financial aid package:* $20,824 (excluding resources awarded to replace EFC). 14% of all full-time freshmen had no need and received non-need-based gift aid.

UNDERGRADUATE FINANCIAL AID (Fall 2012, est.) 2,486 applied for aid; of those 91% were deemed to have need. 100% of undergraduates with need received aid; of those 21% had need fully met. *Average percent of need met:* 68% (excluding resources awarded to replace EFC). *Average financial aid package:* $17,777 (excluding resources awarded to replace EFC). 11% of all full-time undergraduates had no need and received non-need-based gift aid.

GIFT AID (NEED-BASED) *Total amount:* $26,986,819 (22% federal, 6% state, 67% institutional, 5% external sources). *Receiving aid:* Freshmen: 83% (491); all full-time undergraduates: 79% (2,109). *Average award:* Freshmen: $14,335; Undergraduates: $11,787. *Scholarships, grants, and awards:* Federal Pell, FSEOG, state, private, college/university gift aid from institutional funds.

GIFT AID (NON-NEED-BASED) *Total amount:* $4,975,307 (100% institutional). *Receiving aid:* Freshmen: 19% (115). Undergraduates: 11% (306). *Average award:* Freshmen: $10,421. Undergraduates: $9561. *Scholarships, grants, and awards by category:* Academic interests/achievement: 341 awards ($3,958,685 total): religion/biblical studies. *Creative arts/performance:* 102 awards ($163,192 total): music. *Special characteristics:* 353 awards ($631,359 total): out-of-state students.

LOANS *Student loans:* $26,924,820 (53% need-based, 47% non-need-based). 80% of past graduating class borrowed through all loan programs. *Average indebtedness per student:* $31,897. *Average need-based loan:* Freshmen: $5374. Undergraduates: $6031. *Parent loans:* $3,163,864 (100% non-need-based). *Programs:* Federal Direct (Subsidized and Unsubsidized Stafford, PLUS), state.

WORK-STUDY *Federal work-study:* Total amount: $1,528,279; 261 jobs averaging $1703.

APPLYING FOR FINANCIAL AID *Required financial aid form:* FAFSA. *Financial aid deadline (priority):* 3/15. *Notification date:* Continuous beginning 1/21. Students must reply within 3 weeks of notification.

CONTACT Mr. Steven P. Taylor, Director of Financial Aid, Concordia University Wisconsin, 12800 North Lake Shore Drive, Mequon, WI 53097-2402, 262-243-4392 or toll-free 888-628-9472. *Fax:* 262-243-2992. *E-mail:* steve.taylor@cuw.edu. *Website:* http://www.cuw.edu/.

CONCORD UNIVERSITY
Athens, WV

ABOUT THE INSTITUTION State-supported, coed. *Awards:* associate, bachelor's, and master's degrees. 38 undergraduate majors. *Total enrollment:* 2,888. Undergraduates: 2,652. Freshmen: 573.

GIFT AID (NEED-BASED) *Scholarships, grants, and awards:* Federal Pell, FSEOG, state, private, college/university gift aid from institutional funds.

GIFT AID (NON-NEED-BASED) *Scholarships, grants, and awards by category:* Academic interests/achievement: business, communication, education, English, general academic interests/achievements, mathematics, physical sciences, premedicine, social sciences. *Creative arts/performance:* art/fine arts, journalism/publications, music, theater/drama. *Special achievements/activities:* community service, general special achievements/activities, leadership. *Special characteristics:* children of faculty/ staff, veterans, veterans' children.

LOANS *Programs:* Federal Direct (Subsidized and Unsubsidized Stafford, PLUS), Perkins.

WORK-STUDY *Federal work-study:* Total amount: $300,810; 209 jobs averaging $1428.

APPLYING FOR FINANCIAL AID *Required financial aid forms:* FAFSA, institution's own form, state aid form, verification worksheet.

CONTACT Debra Turner, Director of Financial Aid, Concord University, PO Box 1000, Athens, WV 24712-1000, 304-384-6069 or toll-free 888-384-5249. *Fax:* 304-384-3084. *E-mail:* turner@concord.edu. *Website:* http://www.concord.edu/.

CONNECTICUT COLLEGE
New London, CT

ABOUT THE INSTITUTION Independent, coed. *Awards:* bachelor's and master's degrees. 48 undergraduate majors. *Total enrollment:* 1,933. Undergraduates: 1,926. Freshmen: 503.

GIFT AID (NEED-BASED) *Scholarships, grants, and awards:* Federal Pell, FSEOG, state, college/university gift aid from institutional funds.

LOANS *Programs:* Federal Direct (Subsidized and Unsubsidized Stafford, PLUS), Perkins.

APPLYING FOR FINANCIAL AID *Required financial aid forms:* FAFSA, CSS Financial Aid PROFILE, noncustodial (divorced/separated) parent's statement, business/farm supplement.

CONTACT Ms. Elaine Solinga, Director of Financial Aid Services, Connecticut College, 270 Mohegan Avenue, New London, CT 06320-4196, 860-439-2058. *Fax:* 860-439-5357. *E-mail:* finaid@conncoll.edu. *Website:* http://www.connecticutcollege.edu/.

CONSERVATORY OF MUSIC OF PUERTO RICO
San Juan, PR

ABOUT THE INSTITUTION Commonwealth-supported, coed. 7 undergraduate majors.

GIFT AID (NEED-BASED) *Scholarships, grants, and awards:* Federal Pell, FSEOG, state, private, college/university gift aid from institutional funds.

GIFT AID (NON-NEED-BASED) *Scholarships, grants, and awards by category:* Creative arts/performance: music.

APPLYING FOR FINANCIAL AID *Required financial aid forms:* FAFSA, institution's own form.

CONTACT Mr. Michael Rajaballey, Director of Financial Aid, Conservatory of Music of Puerto Rico, 951 Ave. Ponce de Leon, Miramar, San Juan, PR 00907, 787-751-0160 Ext. 231. *Fax:* 787-763-3886. *E-mail:* mrajaballey@cmpr.gobierno.pr. *Website:* http://www.cmpr.edu/.

CONVERSE COLLEGE
Spartanburg, SC

Tuition & fees: $28,276	Average undergraduate aid package: $23,249

ABOUT THE INSTITUTION Independent, undergraduate: women only; graduate: coed. *Awards:* certificates, bachelor's, and master's degrees. 47 undergraduate majors. *Total enrollment:* 1,221. Undergraduates: 690. Freshmen: 186. Federal methodology is used as a basis for awarding need-based institutional aid.

UNDERGRADUATE EXPENSES for 2013–2014 *Comprehensive fee:* $37,130 includes full-time tuition ($28,276) and room and board ($8854). Full-time tuition and fees vary according to course load and program. Room and board charges

vary according to board plan, housing facility, and student level. *Part-time tuition:* $850 per credit hour. Part-time tuition and fees vary according to program.

FRESHMAN FINANCIAL AID (Fall 2012, est.) 175 applied for aid; of those 90% were deemed to have need. 100% of freshmen with need received aid; of those 23% had need fully met. *Average percent of need met:* 77% (excluding resources awarded to replace EFC). *Average financial aid package:* $23,916 (excluding resources awarded to replace EFC). 14% of all full-time freshmen had no need and received non-need-based gift aid.

UNDERGRADUATE FINANCIAL AID (Fall 2012, est.) 590 applied for aid; of those 94% were deemed to have need. 100% of undergraduates with need received aid; of those 21% had need fully met. *Average percent of need met:* 76% (excluding resources awarded to replace EFC). *Average financial aid package:* $23,249 (excluding resources awarded to replace EFC). 12% of all full-time undergraduates had no need and received non-need-based gift aid.

GIFT AID (NEED-BASED) *Total amount:* $10,174,470 (14% federal, 20% state, 65% institutional, 1% external sources). *Receiving aid:* Freshmen: 86% (158); all full-time undergraduates: 89% (546). *Average award:* Freshmen: $20,717; Undergraduates: $19,470. *Scholarships, grants, and awards:* Federal Pell, FSEOG, state, private, college/university gift aid from institutional funds.

GIFT AID (NON-NEED-BASED) *Total amount:* $1,841,182 (26% state, 72% institutional, 2% external sources). *Receiving aid:* Freshmen: 15% (28). Undergraduates: 15% (93). *Average award:* Freshmen: $13,105. Undergraduates: $14,597. *Scholarships, grants, and awards by category:* Academic interests/ achievement: 608 awards ($6,803,034 total): general academic interests/achievements. Creative arts/performance: 211 awards ($536,485 total): applied art and design, general creative arts/performance, music, theater/drama. *Special characteristics:* 17 awards ($58,428 total): children and siblings of alumni, children of faculty/staff. *Tuition waivers:* Full or partial for employees or children of employees. *ROTC:* Army cooperative.

LOANS *Student loans:* $4,896,942 (80% need-based, 20% non-need-based). 75% of past graduating class borrowed through all loan programs. *Average indebtedness per student:* $28,986. *Average need-based loan:* Freshmen: $3763. Undergraduates: $4996. *Parent loans:* $1,015,905 (47% need-based, 53% non-need-based). *Programs:* Federal Direct (Subsidized and Unsubsidized Stafford, PLUS), Perkins, state.

WORK-STUDY *Federal work-study:* Total amount: $107,750; 88 jobs averaging $1511. *State or other work-study/employment:* 60 part-time jobs averaging $1000.

ATHLETIC AWARDS Total amount: $801,437 (60% need-based, 40% non-need-based).

APPLYING FOR FINANCIAL AID *Required financial aid form:* FAFSA. *Financial aid deadline (priority):* 3/15. *Notification date:* Continuous beginning 3/1. Students must reply by 5/1 or within 2 weeks of notification.

CONTACT Ms. Margaret P. Collins, Director of Financial Assistance, Converse College, 580 East Main Street, Spartanburg, SC 29302-0006, 864-596-9019 or toll-free 800-766-1125. *Fax:* 864-596-9749. *E-mail:* peggy.collins@converse.edu. *Website:* http://www.converse.edu/.

COOPER UNION FOR THE ADVANCEMENT OF SCIENCE AND ART
New York, NY

Tuition & fees: $40,250	Average undergraduate aid package: $37,500

ABOUT THE INSTITUTION Independent, coed. *Awards:* certificates, bachelor's, and master's degrees (also offers master's program primarily made up of currently-enrolled students). 8 undergraduate majors. *Total enrollment:* 991. Undergraduates: 927. Freshmen: 201. Both federal and institutional methodology are used as a basis for awarding need-based institutional aid.

UNDERGRADUATE EXPENSES for 2013–2014 *Application fee:* $65. *Comprehensive fee:* $54,220 includes full-time tuition ($38,550), mandatory fees ($1700), and room and board ($13,970). *College room only:* $9970. Room and board charges vary according to board plan and housing facility. All international students are assessed a fee of $1,910/year. Please note: All of our undergraduate students (including international) specifically for the 2012-2013 school year are offered a full-tuition scholarship valued at $38.550.

FRESHMAN FINANCIAL AID (Fall 2011) 120 applied for aid; of those 50% were deemed to have need. 100% of freshmen with need received aid; of those 63% had need fully met. *Average percent of need met:* 92% (excluding resources awarded to replace EFC). *Average financial aid package:* $37,500 (excluding resources awarded to replace EFC). 70% of all full-time freshmen had no need and received non-need-based gift aid.

UNDERGRADUATE FINANCIAL AID (Fall 2011) 406 applied for aid; of those 72% were deemed to have need. 100% of undergraduates with need received aid; of those 44% had need fully met. *Average percent of need met:* 91% (excluding resources awarded to replace EFC). *Average financial aid package:* $37,500 (excluding resources awarded to replace EFC). 67% of all full-time undergraduates had no need and received non-need-based gift aid.

GIFT AID (NEED-BASED) *Total amount:* $1,924,452 (42% federal, 16% state, 30% institutional, 12% external sources). *Receiving aid:* Freshmen: 30% (60); all full-time undergraduates: 33% (291). *Average award:* Freshmen: $42,754; Undergraduates: $43,208. *Scholarships, grants, and awards:* Federal Pell, FSEOG, state, private, college/university gift aid from institutional funds.

GIFT AID (NON-NEED-BASED) *Total amount:* $32,676,142 (100% institutional). *Receiving aid:* Freshmen: 30% (60). Undergraduates: 33% (291). *Average award:* Freshmen: $37,500. Undergraduates: $37,500. *Scholarships, grants, and awards by category:* Academic interests/achievement: 583 awards ($21,862,500 total): architecture, engineering/technologies. Creative arts/performance: 272 awards ($10,200,000 total): art/fine arts.

LOANS *Student loans:* $1,096,065 (86% need-based, 14% non-need-based). 23% of past graduating class borrowed through all loan programs. *Average indebtedness per student:* $15,864. *Average need-based loan:* Freshmen: $3291. Undergraduates: $3887. *Parent loans:* $169,600 (40% need-based, 60% non-need-based). *Programs:* Federal Direct (Subsidized and Unsubsidized Stafford, PLUS), Perkins, college/university.

WORK-STUDY *Federal work-study:* Total amount: $47,063; 54 jobs averaging $872. *State or other work-study/employment:* Total amount: $812,412 (32% need-based, 68% non-need-based). 505 part-time jobs averaging $1619.

APPLYING FOR FINANCIAL AID *Required financial aid forms:* FAFSA, CSS Financial Aid PROFILE. *Financial aid deadline:* 6/1 (priority: 4/15). *Notification date:* 6/1. Students must reply by 6/30 or within 2 weeks of notification.

CONTACT Ms. Mary Ruokonen, Director of Financial Aid, Cooper Union for the Advancement of Science and Art, 30 Cooper Square, New York, NY 10003-7120, 212-353-4130. *Fax:* 212-353-4343. *E-mail:* ruokon@cooper.edu. *Website:* http://www.cooper.edu/.

COPPIN STATE UNIVERSITY
Baltimore, MD

CONTACT Mr. Mose Cartier, Director of Financial Aid, Coppin State University, 2500 West North Avenue, Baltimore, MD 21216-3698, 410-951-3647 or toll-free 800-635-3674. *Fax:* 410-951-3637. *E-mail:* ftayree@coppin.edu. *Website:* http://www.coppin.edu/.

CORBAN UNIVERSITY
Salem, OR

Tuition & fees: $26,430	Average undergraduate aid package: $19,467

ABOUT THE INSTITUTION Independent Christian, coed. *Awards:* certificates, associate, bachelor's, master's, and doctoral degrees. 48 undergraduate majors. *Total enrollment:* 1,160. Undergraduates: 954. Freshmen: 218. Federal methodology is used as a basis for awarding need-based institutional aid.

UNDERGRADUATE EXPENSES for 2013–2014 *Application fee:* $35. *One-time required fee:* $100. *Comprehensive fee:* $34,575 includes full-time tuition ($25,975), mandatory fees ($455), and room and board ($8145). *College room only:* $2375. Full-time tuition and fees vary according to course level, degree level, program, and reciprocity agreements. Room and board charges vary according to board plan. *Part-time tuition:* $1082 per credit hour. Part-time tuition and fees vary

according to course level, course load, degree level, program, and reciprocity agreements.

FRESHMAN FINANCIAL AID (Fall 2012, est.) 175 applied for aid; of those 92% were deemed to have need. 100% of freshmen with need received aid; of those 10% had need fully met. *Average percent of need met:* 63% (excluding resources awarded to replace EFC). *Average financial aid package:* $19,626 (excluding resources awarded to replace EFC). 16% of all full-time freshmen had no need and received non-need-based gift aid.

UNDERGRADUATE FINANCIAL AID (Fall 2012, est.) 740 applied for aid; of those 95% were deemed to have need. 100% of undergraduates with need received aid; of those 11% had need fully met. *Average percent of need met:* 64% (excluding resources awarded to replace EFC). *Average financial aid package:* $19,467 (excluding resources awarded to replace EFC). 12% of all full-time undergraduates had no need and received non-need-based gift aid.

GIFT AID (NEED-BASED) *Total amount:* $9,048,459 (18% federal, 3% state, 73% institutional, 6% external sources). *Receiving aid:* Freshmen: 74% (161); all full-time undergraduates: 86% (704). *Average award:* Freshmen: $16,774; Undergraduates: $15,974. *Scholarships, grants, and awards:* Federal Pell, FSEOG, state, private, college/university gift aid from institutional funds.

GIFT AID (NON-NEED-BASED) *Total amount:* $933,812 (4% federal, 89% institutional, 7% external sources). *Receiving aid:* Freshmen: 5% (11). Undergraduates: 6% (46). *Average award:* Freshmen: $7516. Undergraduates: $7487. *Scholarships, grants, and awards by category:* Academic interests/achievement: general academic interests/achievements. Creative arts/performance: music, performing arts. Special achievements/activities: general special achievements/activities, hobbies/interests, leadership, memberships, religious involvement. Special characteristics: children of faculty/staff, international students, relatives of clergy, siblings of current students. *Tuition waivers:* Full or partial for employees or children of employees, senior citizens. *ROTC:* Army cooperative, Air Force cooperative.

LOANS *Student loans:* $4,962,758 (83% need-based, 17% non-need-based). 80% of past graduating class borrowed through all loan programs. *Average indebtedness per student:* $23,853. *Average need-based loan:* Freshmen: $3702. Undergraduates: $4498. *Parent loans:* $1,087,933 (68% need-based, 32% non-need-based). *Programs:* Federal Direct (Subsidized and Unsubsidized Stafford, PLUS), Perkins, state.

WORK-STUDY *Federal work-study:* Total amount: $361,366; 200 jobs averaging $1806.

ATHLETIC AWARDS Total amount: $1,510,928 (83% need-based, 17% non-need-based).

APPLYING FOR FINANCIAL AID *Required financial aid form:* FAFSA. *Financial aid deadline (priority):* 2/15. *Notification date:* Continuous beginning 3/1.

CONTACT Nathan Warthan, Director of Financial Aid, Corban University, 5000 Deer Park Drive, SE, Salem, OR 97301-9392, 503-375-7006 or toll-free 800-845-3005. *Fax:* 503-585-4316. *E-mail:* financialaid@corban.edu. *Website:* http://www.corban.edu/.

CORCORAN COLLEGE OF ART AND DESIGN
Washington, DC

Tuition & fees: $31,130	Average undergraduate aid package: $12,339

ABOUT THE INSTITUTION Independent, coed. *Awards:* certificates, associate, bachelor's, and master's degrees. 8 undergraduate majors. *Total enrollment:* 640. Undergraduates: 386. Freshmen: 49. Federal methodology is used as a basis for awarding need-based institutional aid.

UNDERGRADUATE EXPENSES for 2013–2014 *Application fee:* $45. *Comprehensive fee:* $44,030 includes full-time tuition ($30,930), mandatory fees ($200), and room and board ($12,900). *College room only:* $10,400. Part-time tuition and fees vary according to course load and degree level.

FRESHMAN FINANCIAL AID (Fall 2012, est.) 33 applied for aid; of those 100% were deemed to have need. 100% of freshmen with need received aid. *Average percent of need met:* 54% (excluding resources awarded to replace EFC). *Average financial aid package:* $26,896 (excluding resources awarded to replace EFC). 13% of all full-time freshmen had no need and received non-need-based gift aid.

UNDERGRADUATE FINANCIAL AID (Fall 2012, est.) 206 applied for aid; of those 100% were deemed to have need. 100% of undergraduates with need received aid. **Average percent of need met:** 25% (excluding resources awarded to replace EFC). **Average financial aid package:** $12,339 (excluding resources awarded to replace EFC). 19% of all full-time undergraduates had no need and received non-need-based gift aid.

GIFT AID (NEED-BASED) Total amount: $623,658 (86% federal, 3% state, 11% institutional). **Receiving aid:** Freshmen: 84% (32); all full-time undergraduates: 68% (206). **Average award:** Freshmen: $12,620; Undergraduates: $10,988. **Scholarships, grants, and awards:** Federal Pell, FSEOG, state, college/university gift aid from institutional funds.

GIFT AID (NON-NEED-BASED) Total amount: $346,603 (2% state, 94% institutional, 4% external sources). **Receiving aid:** Freshmen: 76% (29). Undergraduates: 68% (204). **Average award:** Freshmen: $7200. Undergraduates: $7465. **Scholarships, grants, and awards by category:** Academic interests/achievement: general academic interests/achievements. Creative arts/performance: applied art and design. **Tuition waivers:** Full or partial for employees or children of employees.

LOANS Student loans: $2,385,639 (39% need-based, 61% non-need-based). 82% of past graduating class borrowed through all loan programs. Average indebtedness per student: $46,596. **Average need-based loan:** Freshmen: $3845. Undergraduates: $4715. **Parent loans:** $893,442 (100% non-need-based). **Programs:** Federal Direct (Subsidized and Unsubsidized Stafford, PLUS), Perkins.

WORK-STUDY Federal work-study: Total amount: $112,759; 53 jobs averaging $2127.

APPLYING FOR FINANCIAL AID Required financial aid form: FAFSA. **Financial aid deadline:** Continuous. **Notification date:** Continuous beginning 3/1. Students must reply within 2 weeks of notification.

CONTACT Diane Morris, Director of Financial Aid, Corcoran College of Art and Design, 500 17th Street, NW, Washington, DC 20006-4804, 202-639-1816 or toll-free 888-CORCORAN. Fax: 202-737-6921. E-mail: dmorris@corcoran.org. Website: http://www.corcoran.edu/.

CORNELL COLLEGE
Mount Vernon, IA

Tuition & fees: $34,705	Average undergraduate aid package: $30,087

ABOUT THE INSTITUTION Independent Methodist, coed. **Awards:** bachelor's degrees. 47 undergraduate majors. **Total enrollment:** 1,180. Undergraduates: 1,180. Freshmen: 302. Federal methodology is used as a basis for awarding need-based institutional aid.

UNDERGRADUATE EXPENSES for 2013–2014 Application fee: $30. **Comprehensive fee:** $42,605 includes full-time tuition ($34,480), mandatory fees ($225), and room and board ($7900). **College room only:** $3700. Room and board charges vary according to board plan and housing facility. **Part-time tuition:** $2586 per course. **Part-time fees:** $113 per year. Part-time tuition and fees vary according to course load and reciprocity agreements.

FRESHMAN FINANCIAL AID (Fall 2012, est.) 260 applied for aid; of those 91% were deemed to have need. 100% of freshmen with need received aid; of those 22% had need fully met. **Average percent of need met:** 89% (excluding resources awarded to replace EFC). **Average financial aid package:** $32,040 (excluding resources awarded to replace EFC). 13% of all full-time freshmen had no need and received non-need-based gift aid.

UNDERGRADUATE FINANCIAL AID (Fall 2012, est.) 964 applied for aid; of those 91% were deemed to have need. 100% of undergraduates with need received aid; of those 17% had need fully met. **Average percent of need met:** 84% (excluding resources awarded to replace EFC). **Average financial aid package:** $30,087 (excluding resources awarded to replace EFC). 19% of all full-time undergraduates had no need and received non-need-based gift aid.

GIFT AID (NEED-BASED) Total amount: $20,234,828 (9% federal, 2% state, 86% institutional, 3% external sources). **Receiving aid:** Freshmen: 78% (236); all full-time undergraduates: 75% (877). **Average award:** Freshmen: $24,096; Undergraduates: $20,435. **Scholarships, grants, and awards:** Federal Pell, FSEOG, state, private, college/university gift aid from institutional funds, TEACH Grants.

GIFT AID (NON-NEED-BASED) Total amount: $3,298,063 (98% institutional, 2% external sources). **Receiving aid:** Freshmen: 72% (217). Undergraduates: 66% (772). **Average award:** Freshmen: $12,094. Undergraduates: $11,535. **Scholar-**

ships, grants, and awards by category: Academic interests/achievement: 524 awards ($6,483,160 total): general academic interests/achievements. Creative arts/performance: 124 awards ($577,000 total): art/fine arts, music, performing arts, theater/drama. Special achievements/activities: 267 awards ($1,471,970 total): community service, leadership, religious involvement. Special characteristics: 210 awards ($3,244,293 total): children of educators, children of faculty/staff, ethnic background, international students, local/state students, members of minority groups, relatives of clergy, religious affiliation. **Tuition waivers:** Full or partial for employees or children of employees.

LOANS Student loans: $6,886,268 (52% need-based, 48% non-need-based). 81% of past graduating class borrowed through all loan programs. Average indebtedness per student: $27,227. **Average need-based loan:** Freshmen: $3976. Undergraduates: $4775. **Parent loans:** $2,631,148 (100% non-need-based). **Programs:** Federal Direct (Subsidized and Unsubsidized Stafford, PLUS), Perkins, state, college/university, United Methodist Student Loans.

WORK-STUDY Federal work-study: Total amount: $681,747; 585 jobs averaging $1165.

APPLYING FOR FINANCIAL AID Required financial aid form: FAFSA. **Financial aid deadline:** 3/1. **Notification date:** Continuous beginning 3/1. Students must reply by 5/1 or within 2 weeks of notification.

CONTACT Ms. Cindi P. Reints, Director of Financial Assistance, Cornell College, Peter Paul Luce Admission Center, 600 First Street West, Mount Vernon, IA 52314-1098, 319-895-4216 or toll-free 800-747-1112. Fax: 319-895-4106. E-mail: creints@cornellcollege.edu. Website: http://www.cornellcollege.edu/.

CORNELL UNIVERSITY
Ithaca, NY

Tuition & fees: $43,413	Average undergraduate aid package: $40,942

ABOUT THE INSTITUTION Independent, coed. **Awards:** bachelor's, master's, and doctoral degrees. 81 undergraduate majors. **Total enrollment:** 21,131. Undergraduates: 14,167. Freshmen: 3,307. Institutional methodology is used as a basis for awarding need-based institutional aid.

UNDERGRADUATE EXPENSES for 2013–2014 Application fee: $75. **Comprehensive fee:** $57,091 includes full-time tuition ($43,185), mandatory fees ($228), and room and board ($13,678). **College room only:** $8112. Full-time tuition and fees vary according to degree level. Room and board charges vary according to board plan and housing facility.

FRESHMAN FINANCIAL AID (Fall 2012, est.) 1,907 applied for aid; of those 80% were deemed to have need. 100% of freshmen with need received aid; of those 100% had need fully met. **Average percent of need met:** 100% (excluding resources awarded to replace EFC). **Average financial aid package:** $42,248 (excluding resources awarded to replace EFC).

UNDERGRADUATE FINANCIAL AID (Fall 2012, est.) 8,035 applied for aid; of those 88% were deemed to have need. 100% of undergraduates with need received aid; of those 100% had need fully met. **Average percent of need met:** 100% (excluding resources awarded to replace EFC). **Average financial aid package:** $40,942 (excluding resources awarded to replace EFC).

GIFT AID (NEED-BASED) Total amount: $245,978,511 (6% federal, 2% state, 89% institutional, 3% external sources). **Receiving aid:** Freshmen: 47% (1,502); all full-time undergraduates: 48% (6,877). **Average award:** Freshmen: $37,941; Undergraduates: $35,752. **Scholarships, grants, and awards:** Federal Pell, FSEOG, state, private, college/university gift aid from institutional funds.

GIFT AID (NON-NEED-BASED) Tuition waivers: Full or partial for employees or children of employees. **ROTC:** Army, Naval, Air Force.

LOANS Student loans: $26,003,571 (100% need-based). 45% of past graduating class borrowed through all loan programs. Average indebtedness per student: $20,490. **Average need-based loan:** Freshmen: $2757. Undergraduates: $3549. **Parent loans:** $8,466,877 (100% need-based). **Programs:** Federal Direct (Subsidized and Unsubsidized Stafford, PLUS), Perkins, college/university.

WORK-STUDY Federal work-study: Total amount: $9,414,637; 5,213 jobs averaging $1800. **State or other work-study/employment:** Total amount: $1,980,015 (100% need-based). 1,338 part-time jobs averaging $1540.

APPLYING FOR FINANCIAL AID Required financial aid forms: FAFSA, institution's own form, CSS Financial Aid PROFILE, noncustodial (divorced/separated)

parent's statement, business/farm supplement, federal income tax form(s). *Financial aid deadline:* 2/15. *Notification date:* 4/1. Students must reply by 5/1.
CONTACT Mr. Thomas Keane, Director of Financial Aid and Student Employment, Cornell University, 203 Day Hall, Ithaca, NY 14853-2488, 607-255-5145. *Website:* http://www.cornell.edu/.

CORNERSTONE UNIVERSITY
Grand Rapids, MI

Tuition & fees: $24,168	Average undergraduate aid package: $18,938

ABOUT THE INSTITUTION Independent nondenominational, coed. *Awards:* diplomas, associate, bachelor's, and master's degrees. 42 undergraduate majors. *Total enrollment:* 2,747. Undergraduates: 2,125. Freshmen: 343. Federal methodology is used as a basis for awarding need-based institutional aid.
UNDERGRADUATE EXPENSES for 2013–2014 *Application fee:* $25. *Comprehensive fee:* $32,078 includes full-time tuition ($23,598), mandatory fees ($570), and room and board ($7910). Full-time tuition and fees vary according to course load and reciprocity agreements. Room and board charges vary according to board plan and housing facility. *Part-time tuition:* $905 per credit. *Part-time fees:* $185 per term. Part-time tuition and fees vary according to course load.
FRESHMAN FINANCIAL AID (Fall 2012, est.) 309 applied for aid; of those 92% were deemed to have need. 100% of freshmen with need received aid; of those 15% had need fully met. *Average percent of need met:* 71% (excluding resources awarded to replace EFC). *Average financial aid package:* $19,152 (excluding resources awarded to replace EFC). 11% of all full-time freshmen had no need and received non-need-based gift aid.
UNDERGRADUATE FINANCIAL AID (Fall 2012, est.) 1,118 applied for aid; of those 92% were deemed to have need. 100% of undergraduates with need received aid; of those 15% had need fully met. *Average percent of need met:* 69% (excluding resources awarded to replace EFC). *Average financial aid package:* $18,938 (excluding resources awarded to replace EFC). 11% of all full-time undergraduates had no need and received non-need-based gift aid.
GIFT AID (NEED-BASED) *Total amount:* $13,784,705 (16% federal, 8% state, 74% institutional, 2% external sources). *Receiving aid:* Freshmen: 86% (282); all full-time undergraduates: 84% (1,028). *Average award:* Freshmen: $15,665; Undergraduates: $14,649. *Scholarships, grants, and awards:* Federal Pell, FSEOG, state, private, college/university gift aid from institutional funds.
GIFT AID (NON-NEED-BASED) *Total amount:* $1,723,857 (98% institutional, 2% external sources). *Receiving aid:* Freshmen: 9% (29). Undergraduates: 8% (103). *Average award:* Freshmen: $9882. Undergraduates: $8441. *Scholarships, grants, and awards by category:* Academic interests/achievement: business, communication, computer science, education, English, foreign languages, general academic interests/achievements, humanities, mathematics, physical sciences, religion/biblical studies, social sciences. Creative arts/performance: music. Special achievements/activities: leadership. Special characteristics: children of faculty/staff. Tuition waivers: Full or partial for employees or children of employees. ROTC: Army cooperative.
LOANS *Student loans:* $7,499,875 (49% need-based, 51% non-need-based). 88% of past graduating class borrowed through all loan programs. *Average indebtedness per student:* $32,071. *Average need-based loan:* Freshmen: $3426. Undergraduates: $4652. *Parent loans:* $1,087,233 (100% non-need-based). *Programs:* Federal Direct (Subsidized and Unsubsidized Stafford, PLUS), Perkins.
WORK-STUDY *Federal work-study:* Total amount: $348,500; 242 jobs averaging $1213.
ATHLETIC AWARDS Total amount: $1,406,653 (66% need-based, 34% non-need-based).
APPLYING FOR FINANCIAL AID *Required financial aid form:* FAFSA. *Financial aid deadline:* Continuous. *Notification date:* Continuous beginning 3/1. Students must reply within 4 weeks of notification.
CONTACT Mrs. Carol S. Carpenter, Director of Student Financial Services, Cornerstone University, 1001 East Beltline Avenue, NE, Grand Rapids, MI 49525-5897, 616-222-1424 or toll-free 800-787-9778. *Fax:* 616-222-1400. *E-mail:* carol.carpenter@cornerstone.edu.
Website: http://www.cornerstone.edu/.

CORNISH COLLEGE OF THE ARTS
Seattle, WA

CONTACT Sharron Starling, Office of Admissions, Cornish College of the Arts, 1000 Lenora Street, Seattle, WA 98121, 206-726-5017 or toll-free 800-726-ARTS. *Fax:* 206-720-1011. *E-mail:* admissions@cornish.edu.
Website: http://www.cornish.edu/.

COVENANT COLLEGE
Lookout Mountain, GA

Tuition & fees: $28,270	Average undergraduate aid package: $22,443

ABOUT THE INSTITUTION Independent Presbyterian Church in America, coed. *Awards:* associate, bachelor's, and master's degrees (master's degree in education only). 27 undergraduate majors. *Total enrollment:* 1,135. Undergraduates: 1,065. Freshmen: 268. Federal methodology is used as a basis for awarding need-based institutional aid.
UNDERGRADUATE EXPENSES for 2013–2014 *Application fee:* $35. *Comprehensive fee:* $36,310 includes full-time tuition ($27,500), mandatory fees ($770), and room and board ($8040). Full-time tuition and fees vary according to course load. *Part-time tuition:* $1150 per credit hour. Part-time tuition and fees vary according to course load.
FRESHMAN FINANCIAL AID (Fall 2011) 234 applied for aid; of those 82% were deemed to have need. 100% of freshmen with need received aid; of those 38% had need fully met. *Average percent of need met:* 85% (excluding resources awarded to replace EFC). *Average financial aid package:* $22,324 (excluding resources awarded to replace EFC). 25% of all full-time freshmen had no need and received non-need-based gift aid.
UNDERGRADUATE FINANCIAL AID (Fall 2011) 712 applied for aid; of those 87% were deemed to have need. 100% of undergraduates with need received aid; of those 38% had need fully met. *Average percent of need met:* 83% (excluding resources awarded to replace EFC). *Average financial aid package:* $22,443 (excluding resources awarded to replace EFC). 27% of all full-time undergraduates had no need and received non-need-based gift aid.
GIFT AID (NEED-BASED) *Total amount:* $11,109,593 (11% federal, 4% state, 81% institutional, 4% external sources). *Receiving aid:* Freshmen: 67% (191); all full-time undergraduates: 63% (610). *Average award:* Freshmen: $16,347; Undergraduates: $16,030. *Scholarships, grants, and awards:* Federal Pell, FSEOG, state, private, college/university gift aid from institutional funds.
GIFT AID (NON-NEED-BASED) *Total amount:* $3,247,897 (6% state, 85% institutional, 9% external sources). *Average award:* Freshmen: $11,230. Undergraduates: $10,449. *Scholarships, grants, and awards by category:* Academic interests/achievement: general academic interests/achievements. Creative arts/performance: music. Special achievements/activities: leadership. Special characteristics: children of faculty/staff, international students, members of minority groups, religious affiliation. Tuition waivers: Full or partial for employees or children of employees, senior citizens. ROTC: Army cooperative.
LOANS *Student loans:* $4,028,829 (92% need-based, 8% non-need-based). 66% of past graduating class borrowed through all loan programs. *Average indebtedness per student:* $22,861. *Average need-based loan:* Freshmen: $5484. Undergraduates: $6221. *Parent loans:* $1,122,023 (86% need-based, 14% non-need-based). *Programs:* Perkins, state, college/university.
WORK-STUDY *Federal work-study:* Total amount: $299,544; jobs available. *State or other work-study/employment:* Total amount: $909,002 (88% need-based, 12% non-need-based). Part-time jobs available.
APPLYING FOR FINANCIAL AID *Required financial aid forms:* FAFSA, state aid form. *Financial aid deadline:* Continuous. *Notification date:* Continuous beginning 2/1. Students must reply within 3 weeks of notification.
CONTACT Mrs. Margaret Stewart, Assistant Director of Financial Aid, Covenant College, 14049 Scenic Highway, Lookout Mountain, GA 30750, 706-419-1152 or toll-free 888-451-2683. *Fax:* 706-820-2820. *E-mail:* margaret.stewart@covenant.edu.
Website: http://www.covenant.edu/.

COX COLLEGE
Springfield, MO

Tuition & fees: N/R	Average undergraduate aid package: N/A

ABOUT THE INSTITUTION Independent, coed, primarily women. 1 undergraduate major. Federal methodology is used as a basis for awarding need-based institutional aid.

GIFT AID (NEED-BASED) *Total amount:* $1,917,183 (73% federal, 14% state, 11% institutional, 2% external sources). *Scholarships, grants, and awards:* Federal Pell, FSEOG, state, private, college/university gift aid from institutional funds, United Negro College Fund, Federal Nursing.

LOANS *Student loans:* $5,887,740 (100% need-based). *Parent loans:* $63,048 (100% need-based). *Programs:* Federal Direct (Subsidized and Unsubsidized Stafford, PLUS).

WORK-STUDY *Federal work-study:* Total amount: $13,615; 7 jobs averaging $1945.

APPLYING FOR FINANCIAL AID *Required financial aid forms:* FAFSA, institution's own form. *Financial aid deadline (priority):* 4/1. *Notification date:* Continuous beginning 6/1.

CONTACT Victoria L. Jacobson, Financial Aid Counselor, Cox College, 1423 North Jefferson Avenue, Springfield, MO 65802, 417-269-3458 or toll-free 866-898-5355 (in-state). *Fax:* 417-269-3586. *E-mail:* victoria.jacobson@coxcollege.edu. *Website:* http://www.coxcollege.edu/.

CREATIVE CENTER
Omaha, NE

CONTACT Financial Aid Office, Creative Center, 10850 Emmet Street, Omaha, NE 68164, 402-898-1000 or toll-free 888-898-1789 (out-of-state). *Website:* http://www.creativecenter.edu/.

CREIGHTON UNIVERSITY
Omaha, NE

Tuition & fees: $33,330	Average undergraduate aid package: $27,505

ABOUT THE INSTITUTION Independent Roman Catholic (Jesuit), coed. *Awards:* certificates, diplomas, associate, bachelor's, master's, and doctoral degrees. 58 undergraduate majors. *Total enrollment:* 7,736. Undergraduates: 4,032. Freshmen: 945. Federal methodology is used as a basis for awarding need-based institutional aid.

UNDERGRADUATE EXPENSES for 2013–2014 *Application fee:* $40. *Comprehensive fee:* $42,776 includes full-time tuition ($31,856), mandatory fees ($1474), and room and board ($9446). *College room only:* $5350. Full-time tuition and fees vary according to course load and degree level. Room and board charges vary according to board plan and housing facility. *Part-time tuition:* $996 per credit hour. *Part-time fees:* $184 per degree program. Part-time tuition and fees vary according to course load and degree level.

FRESHMAN FINANCIAL AID (Fall 2012, est.) 768 applied for aid; of those 77% were deemed to have need. 100% of freshmen with need received aid; of those 31% had need fully met. *Average percent of need met:* 88% (excluding resources awarded to replace EFC). *Average financial aid package:* $29,251 (excluding resources awarded to replace EFC). 31% of all full-time freshmen had no need and received non-need-based gift aid.

UNDERGRADUATE FINANCIAL AID (Fall 2012, est.) 2,679 applied for aid; of those 84% were deemed to have need. 99% of undergraduates with need received aid; of those 25% had need fully met. *Average percent of need met:* 83% (excluding resources awarded to replace EFC). *Average financial aid package:* $27,505 (excluding resources awarded to replace EFC). 33% of all full-time undergraduates had no need and received non-need-based gift aid.

GIFT AID (NEED-BASED) *Total amount:* $42,068,459 (8% federal, 1% state, 87% institutional, 4% external sources). *Receiving aid:* Freshmen: 63% (593); all full-time undergraduates: 58% (2,214). *Average award:* Freshmen: $22,896; Undergraduates: $21,524. *Scholarships, grants, and awards:* Federal Pell, FSEOG, state, private, college/university gift aid from institutional funds, Federal Nursing.

GIFT AID (NON-NEED-BASED) *Total amount:* $16,271,814 (98% institutional, 2% external sources). *Receiving aid:* Freshmen: 59% (560). Undergraduates: 44% (1,694). *Average award:* Freshmen: $15,107. Undergraduates: $15,118. *Scholarships, grants, and awards by category: Academic interests/achievement:* business, education, general academic interests/achievements, military science. *Creative arts/performance:* art/fine arts, creative writing, dance, debating, journalism/publications, music, performing arts, theater/drama. *Special achievements/activities:* leadership. *Special characteristics:* children of faculty/staff, first-generation college students, local/state students, members of minority groups, religious affiliation, siblings of current students. *Tuition waivers:* Full or partial for employees or children of employees, adult students. *ROTC:* Army, Air Force cooperative.

LOANS *Student loans:* $25,045,146 (40% need-based, 60% non-need-based). 61% of past graduating class borrowed through all loan programs. *Average indebtedness per student:* $36,333. *Average need-based loan:* Freshmen: $4850. Undergraduates: $5683. *Parent loans:* $4,857,944 (100% non-need-based). *Programs:* Federal Direct (Subsidized and Unsubsidized Stafford, PLUS), Perkins, Federal Nursing, college/university.

WORK-STUDY *Federal work-study:* Total amount: $1,771,121; jobs available.

ATHLETIC AWARDS Total amount: $3,711,976 (32% need-based, 68% non-need-based).

APPLYING FOR FINANCIAL AID *Required financial aid forms:* FAFSA, institution's own form. *Financial aid deadline (priority):* 3/1. *Notification date:* Continuous beginning 3/15. Students must reply by 5/1 or within 4 weeks of notification.

CONTACT Sarah Trausch, Assistant Director of Financial Aid, Creighton University, 2500 California Plaza, Omaha, NE 68178, 402-280-2731 or toll-free 800-282-5835. *Fax:* 402-280-2895. *E-mail:* sarahtrausch@creighton.edu. *Website:* http://www.creighton.edu/.

THE CRISWELL COLLEGE
Dallas, TX

CONTACT Ester Waggoner, Financial Aid Director, The Criswell College, 4010 Gaston Avenue, Dallas, TX 75246, 800-899-0012. *Fax:* 214-818-1310. *E-mail:* ewaggoner@criswell.edu. *Website:* http://www.criswell.edu/.

CROSSROADS BIBLE COLLEGE
Indianapolis, IN

Tuition & fees: $9980	Average undergraduate aid package: $7945

ABOUT THE INSTITUTION Independent Baptist, coed. *Awards:* certificates, associate, and bachelor's degrees. 8 undergraduate majors. *Total enrollment:* 232. Undergraduates: 232. Freshmen: 27. Institutional methodology is used as a basis for awarding need-based institutional aid.

UNDERGRADUATE EXPENSES for 2013–2014 *Application fee:* $10. *Tuition:* full-time $9480; part-time $395 per credit hour. *Required fees:* full-time $500; $250 per term.

FRESHMAN FINANCIAL AID (Fall 2011) 19 applied for aid; of those 100% were deemed to have need. 100% of freshmen with need received aid; of those 100% had need fully met. *Average percent of need met:* 84% (excluding resources awarded to replace EFC). *Average financial aid package:* $6950 (excluding resources awarded to replace EFC).

UNDERGRADUATE FINANCIAL AID (Fall 2011) 133 applied for aid; of those 100% were deemed to have need. 100% of undergraduates with need received aid; of those 98% had need fully met. *Average percent of need met:* 98% (excluding resources awarded to replace EFC). *Average financial aid package:* $7945 (excluding resources awarded to replace EFC).

GIFT AID (NEED-BASED) *Total amount:* $1,273,787 (58% federal, 34% state, 8% institutional). *Receiving aid:* Freshmen: 83% (19); all full-time undergraduates: 91% (133). *Average award:* Freshmen: $4667; Undergraduates: $5662. *Scholarships, grants, and awards: Federal Pell, FSEOG, state, college/university gift aid from institutional funds.

GIFT AID (NON-NEED-BASED) Receiving aid: Freshmen: 9% (2). Undergraduates: 1% (2). **Scholarships, grants, and awards by category:** Academic interests/achievement: religion/biblical studies. Special achievements/activities: religious involvement. Special characteristics: 13 awards ($54,202 total): children of faculty/staff, married students, siblings of current students, spouses of current students. **Tuition waivers:** Full or partial for employees or children of employees.

LOANS Student loans: $1,403,241 (100% need-based). 84% of past graduating class borrowed through all loan programs. Average indebtedness per student: $9618. **Average need-based loan:** Freshmen: $3500. Undergraduates: $5500. **Parent loans:** $8230 (100% need-based). **Programs:** Federal Direct (Subsidized and Unsubsidized Stafford, PLUS).

WORK-STUDY Federal work-study: Total amount: $26,958; 14 jobs averaging $1509.

APPLYING FOR FINANCIAL AID Required financial aid forms: FAFSA, institution's own form. **Financial aid deadline:** 6/30 (priority: 5/31). **Notification date:** 7/31. Students must reply within 2 weeks of notification.

CONTACT Mrs. Phyllis Dodson, Senior Director of Financial Aid, Crossroads Bible College, 601 North Shortridge Road, Indianapolis, IN 46219, 317-789-8250 or toll-free 800-822-3119. Fax: 317-789-8253. E-mail: pdodson@crossroads.edu. Website: http://www.crossroads.edu/.

CROSSROADS COLLEGE
Rochester, MN

CONTACT Polly Kellogg-Bradley, Director of Financial Aid, Crossroads College, 920 Mayowood Road SW, Rochester, MN 55902, 507-288-4563 or toll-free 800-456-7651. Fax: 507-288-9046. E-mail: financialaid@crossroadscollege.edu. Website: http://www.crossroadscollege.edu/.

CROWN COLLEGE
St. Bonifacius, MN

Tuition & fees: $22,430	Average undergraduate aid package: N/A

ABOUT THE INSTITUTION Independent The Christian and Missionary Alliance, coed. **Awards:** certificates, associate, bachelor's, and master's degrees. 34 undergraduate majors. **Total enrollment:** 1,269. Undergraduates: 1,088. Freshmen: 185. Federal methodology is used as a basis for awarding need-based institutional aid.

UNDERGRADUATE EXPENSES for 2013–2014 **Application fee:** $20. **Comprehensive fee:** $29,910 includes full-time tuition ($22,430) and room and board ($7480). **College room only:** $3890. Full-time tuition and fees vary according to course load and program. Room and board charges vary according to board plan and housing facility. **Part-time tuition:** $950 per credit. Part-time tuition and fees vary according to course load and program.

GIFT AID (NEED-BASED) Total amount: $17,332,823 (27% federal, 10% state, 61% institutional, 2% external sources). **Scholarships, grants, and awards:** Federal Pell, FSEOG, state, private, college/university gift aid from institutional funds.

GIFT AID (NON-NEED-BASED) Total amount: $4,492,902 (8% federal, 2% state, 87% institutional, 3% external sources). **Scholarships, grants, and awards by category:** Academic interests/achievement: general academic interests/achievements. Creative arts/performance: music. Special achievements/activities: leadership. Special characteristics: children and siblings of alumni, children of faculty/staff, international students, members of minority groups, relatives of clergy, siblings of current students. **Tuition waivers:** Full or partial for employees or children of employees. **ROTC:** Army cooperative.

LOANS Student loans: $13,984,389 (83% need-based, 17% non-need-based). 79% of past graduating class borrowed through all loan programs. Average indebtedness per student: $33,239. **Parent loans:** $686,541 (61% need-based, 39% non-need-based). **Programs:** Federal Direct (Subsidized and Unsubsidized Stafford, PLUS), Perkins, state, SELF Loans, CitiAssist Loans, Sallie Mae Signature Loans, alternative loans.

WORK-STUDY Federal work-study: Total amount: $129,395; jobs available. **State or other work-study/employment:** Total amount: $68,400 (88% need-based, 12% non-need-based). Part-time jobs available.

APPLYING FOR FINANCIAL AID Required financial aid form: FAFSA. **Financial aid deadline:** 8/1 (priority: 4/15). **Notification date:** Continuous. Students must reply by 4/1 or within 3 weeks of notification.

CONTACT Mrs. Shannon Schaaf, Director of Financial Aid, Crown College, 8700 College View Drive, St. Bonifacius, MN 55375-9001, 952-446-4175 or toll-free 800-68-CROWN. Fax: 952-446-4178. E-mail: finaid@crown.edu. Website: http://www.crown.edu/.

THE CULINARY INSTITUTE OF AMERICA
Hyde Park, NY

CONTACT Kathleen Gailor, Director of Financial Aid, The Culinary Institute of America, 1946 Campus Drive, Hyde Park, NY 12538-1499, 845-451-1243 or toll-free 800-CULINARY. Fax: 845-905-4030. E-mail: finaid@culinary.edu. Website: http://www.ciachef.edu/.

CULINARY INSTITUTE OF VIRGINIA
Norfolk, VA

CONTACT Ms. Lynn Robinson, Director of Financial Aid, Culinary Institute of Virginia, 8 Abbott Park Place, Providence, RI 02903, 401-598-4648 or toll-free 866-619-CHEF. Fax: 401-598-1040. E-mail: fp@jwu.edu. Website: http://www.chefva.com/.

CULVER-STOCKTON COLLEGE
Canton, MO

Tuition & fees: $23,300	Average undergraduate aid package: $20,614

ABOUT THE INSTITUTION Independent Christian Church (Disciples of Christ), coed. **Awards:** bachelor's degrees. 34 undergraduate majors. **Total enrollment:** 769. Undergraduates: 769. Freshmen: 217. Federal methodology is used as a basis for awarding need-based institutional aid.

UNDERGRADUATE EXPENSES for 2013–2014 **One-time required fee:** $200. **Comprehensive fee:** $30,900 includes full-time tuition ($23,000), mandatory fees ($300), and room and board ($7600). **College room only:** $3400. Room and board charges vary according to board plan and housing facility. **Part-time tuition:** $540 per credit hour. **Part-time fees:** $12.50 per credit hour.

FRESHMAN FINANCIAL AID (Fall 2012, est.) 214 applied for aid; of those 94% were deemed to have need. 100% of freshmen with need received aid; of those 22% had need fully met. **Average percent of need met:** 78% (excluding resources awarded to replace EFC). **Average financial aid package:** $21,281 (excluding resources awarded to replace EFC). 7% of all full-time freshmen had no need and received non-need-based gift aid.

UNDERGRADUATE FINANCIAL AID (Fall 2012, est.) 654 applied for aid; of those 94% were deemed to have need. 100% of undergraduates with need received aid; of those 19% had need fully met. **Average percent of need met:** 77% (excluding resources awarded to replace EFC). **Average financial aid package:** $20,614 (excluding resources awarded to replace EFC). 10% of all full-time undergraduates had no need and received non-need-based gift aid.

GIFT AID (NEED-BASED) Total amount: $8,164,871 (21% federal, 7% state, 70% institutional, 2% external sources). **Receiving aid:** Freshmen: 93% (202); all full-time undergraduates: 90% (615). **Average award:** Freshmen: $18,126; Undergraduates: $16,903. **Scholarships, grants, and awards:** Federal Pell, FSEOG, state, private, college/university gift aid from institutional funds.

GIFT AID (NON-NEED-BASED) Total amount: $965,479 (1% federal, 1% state, 93% institutional, 5% external sources). **Receiving aid:** Freshmen: 14% (31). Undergraduates: 11% (76). **Average award:** Freshmen: $7433. Undergraduates: $10,282. **Scholarships, grants, and awards by category:** Academic interests/achievement: 687 awards ($4,982,032 total): general academic interests/achievements. Creative arts/performance: 100 awards ($366,837 total): art/fine arts, debating, music, theater/drama. *Special achievements/activities:* 60 awards ($149,450 total): cheerleading/drum major, general special achievements/activities, leadership. *Special characteristics:* 81 awards ($518,826 total): children and siblings of alumni, children of faculty/staff, international students, local/state students, religious affiliation, veterans, veterans' children. *Tuition waivers:* Full or partial for employees or children of employees, senior citizens.

LOANS *Student loans:* $5,290,458 (76% need-based, 24% non-need-based). 85% of past graduating class borrowed through all loan programs. *Average indebtedness per student:* $24,859. *Average need-based loan:* Freshmen: $3487. Undergraduates: $4150. *Parent loans:* $1,027,546 (36% need-based, 64% non-need-based). *Programs:* Federal Direct (Subsidized and Unsubsidized Stafford, PLUS), Perkins, Federal Nursing, state, college/university.

WORK-STUDY *Federal work-study:* Total amount: $82,247; 81 jobs averaging $1015. *State or other work-study/employment:* Total amount: $308,857 (52% need-based, 48% non-need-based). 276 part-time jobs averaging $1115.

ATHLETIC AWARDS Total amount: $2,655,023 (83% need-based, 17% non-need-based).

APPLYING FOR FINANCIAL AID *Required financial aid form:* FAFSA. *Financial aid deadline:* 6/1 (priority: 3/1). *Notification date:* Continuous. Students must reply within 2 weeks of notification.

CONTACT Ms. Tina M. Wiseman, Director of Financial Aid, Culver-Stockton College, One College Hill, Canton, MO 63435, 573-288-6307 Ext. 6306 or toll-free 800-537-1883. *Fax:* 573-288-6308. *E-mail:* twiseman@culver.edu. *Website:* http://www.culver.edu/.

CUMBERLAND UNIVERSITY
Lebanon, TN

CONTACT Ms. Beatrice LaChance, Director of Student Financial Services, Cumberland University, One Cumberland Square, Lebanon, TN 37087-3554, 615-444-2562 Ext. 1244 or toll-free 800-467-0562. *Fax:* 615-443-8424. *E-mail:* lvaughan@cumberland.edu. *Website:* http://www.cumberland.edu/.

CURRY COLLEGE
Milton, MA

Tuition & fees: $33,465	Average undergraduate aid package: $21,860

ABOUT THE INSTITUTION Independent, coed. *Awards:* certificates, bachelor's, and master's degrees. 28 undergraduate majors. *Total enrollment:* 3,040. Undergraduates: 2,769. Freshmen: 584. Federal methodology is used as a basis for awarding need-based institutional aid.

UNDERGRADUATE EXPENSES for 2013–2014 *Application fee:* $50. *One-time required fee:* $290. *Comprehensive fee:* $46,225 includes full-time tuition ($31,900), mandatory fees ($1565), and room and board ($12,760). *College room only:* $7160. Full-time tuition and fees vary according to class time and location. Room and board charges vary according to board plan and housing facility. *Part-time tuition:* $1063 per credit hour. Part-time tuition and fees vary according to class time, course load, and location.

FRESHMAN FINANCIAL AID (Fall 2012, est.) 457 applied for aid; of those 100% were deemed to have need. 100% of freshmen with need received aid; of those 6% had need fully met. *Average percent of need met:* 67% (excluding resources awarded to replace EFC). *Average financial aid package:* $23,406 (excluding resources awarded to replace EFC). 13% of all full-time freshmen had no need and received non-need-based gift aid.

UNDERGRADUATE FINANCIAL AID (Fall 2012, est.) 1,483 applied for aid; of those 100% were deemed to have need. 100% of undergraduates with need received aid; of those 6% had need fully met. *Average percent of need met:* 67% (excluding resources awarded to replace EFC). *Average financial aid package:* $21,860 (excluding resources awarded to replace EFC). 10% of all full-time undergraduates had no need and received non-need-based gift aid.

GIFT AID (NEED-BASED) *Total amount:* $24,308,973 (13% federal, 3% state, 81% institutional, 3% external sources). *Receiving aid:* Freshmen: 75% (432); all full-time undergraduates: 68% (1,360). *Average award:* Freshmen: $15,108; Undergrad-

uates: $13,856. *Scholarships, grants, and awards:* Federal Pell, FSEOG, state, private, college/university gift aid from institutional funds.

GIFT AID (NON-NEED-BASED) *Total amount:* $1,588,834 (9% federal, 79% institutional, 12% external sources). *Receiving aid:* Freshmen: 2% (11). Undergraduates: 1% (28). *Average award:* Freshmen: $5416. Undergraduates: $5607. *Scholarships, grants, and awards by category: Academic interests/achievement:* 746 awards ($3,547,500 total): general academic interests/achievements. *Tuition waivers:* Full or partial for children of alumni, employees or children of employees. **ROTC:** Army cooperative.

LOANS *Student loans:* $20,025,896 (35% need-based, 65% non-need-based). 79% of past graduating class borrowed through all loan programs. *Average indebtedness per student:* $41,876. *Average need-based loan:* Freshmen: $3599. Undergraduates: $4435. *Parent loans:* $9,208,507 (100% non-need-based). *Programs:* Federal Direct (Subsidized and Unsubsidized Stafford, PLUS), Perkins, state.

WORK-STUDY *Federal work-study:* Total amount: $1,591,780; 832 jobs averaging $1851.

APPLYING FOR FINANCIAL AID *Required financial aid form:* FAFSA. *Financial aid deadline (priority):* 3/1. *Notification date:* Continuous beginning 3/1.

CONTACT Linda Brennan, Director of Financial Aid, Curry College, 1071 Blue Hill Avenue, Milton, MA 02186-2395, 617-333-2354 or toll-free 800-669-0686. *Fax:* 617-333-2915. *E-mail:* Fin-aid@curry.edu. *Website:* http://www.curry.edu/.

CURTIS INSTITUTE OF MUSIC
Philadelphia, PA

CONTACT Richard Woodland, Director of Student Financial Assistance, Curtis Institute of Music, 1726 Locust Street, Philadelphia, PA 19103-6107, 215-717-3143. *E-mail:* richard.woodland@curtis.edu. *Website:* http://www.curtis.edu/.

DAEMEN COLLEGE
Amherst, NY

CONTACT Mr. Jeffrey Pagano, Director of Financial Aid, Daemen College, 4380 Main Street, Amherst, NY 14226-3592, 716-839-8254 or toll-free 800-462-7652. *Fax:* 716-839-8378. *E-mail:* jpagano@daemen.edu. *Website:* http://www.daemen.edu/.

DAKOTA STATE UNIVERSITY
Madison, SD

Tuition & fees (SD res): $7950	Average undergraduate aid package: $7784

ABOUT THE INSTITUTION State-supported, coed. *Awards:* certificates, associate, bachelor's, master's, and doctoral degrees. 29 undergraduate majors. *Total enrollment:* 3,110. Undergraduates: 2,872. Freshmen: 313. Federal methodology is used as a basis for awarding need-based institutional aid.

UNDERGRADUATE EXPENSES for 2013–2014 *Application fee:* $20. *Tuition, state resident:* full-time $3726; part-time $124 per credit hour. *Tuition, nonresident:* full-time $5591; part-time $186 per credit hour. *Required fees:* full-time $4224. Full-time tuition and fees vary according to location and reciprocity agreements. Part-time tuition and fees vary according to location and reciprocity agreements. *College room and board:* $5235; *Room only:* $2770. Room and board charges vary according to board plan and housing facility.

FRESHMAN FINANCIAL AID (Fall 2011) 275 applied for aid; of those 83% were deemed to have need. 100% of freshmen with need received aid; of those 12% had need fully met. *Average percent of need met:* 78% (excluding resources awarded to replace EFC). *Average financial aid package:* $7498 (excluding resources awarded to replace EFC). 9% of all full-time freshmen had no need and received non-need-based gift aid.

UNDERGRADUATE FINANCIAL AID (Fall 2011) 1,054 applied for aid; of those 85% were deemed to have need. 100% of undergraduates with need received aid; of those 12% had need fully met. *Average percent of need met:* 77% (excluding resources awarded to replace EFC). *Average financial aid package:* $7784 (excluding resources awarded to replace EFC). 7% of all full-time undergraduates had no need and received non-need-based gift aid.

GIFT AID (NEED-BASED) *Total amount:* $3,509,730 (78% federal, 3% state, 10% institutional, 9% external sources). *Receiving aid:* Freshmen: 48% (141); all full-time undergraduates: 43% (531). *Average award:* Freshmen: $4453; Undergraduates: $4532. *Scholarships, grants, and awards:* Federal Pell, FSEOG, state, private, college/university gift aid from institutional funds, Agency Assistance (Veterans Benefits/Department of Labor).

GIFT AID (NON-NEED-BASED) *Total amount:* $351,628 (9% federal, 14% state, 40% institutional, 37% external sources). *Receiving aid:* Freshmen: 51% (152). Undergraduates: 31% (376). *Average award:* Freshmen: $2394. Undergraduates: $3291. *Scholarships, grants, and awards by category: Academic interests/achievement:* 324 awards ($395,600 total): business, communication, computer science, education, English, general academic interests/achievements, mathematics. *Creative arts/performance:* 9 awards ($2150 total): music. *Tuition waivers:* Full or partial for employees or children of employees, senior citizens. *ROTC:* Air Force cooperative.

LOANS *Student loans:* $9,362,931 (71% need-based, 29% non-need-based). 79% of past graduating class borrowed through all loan programs. *Average indebtedness per student:* $25,926. *Average need-based loan:* Freshmen: $3293. Undergraduates: $3931. *Parent loans:* $870,128 (71% need-based, 29% non-need-based). *Programs:* Federal Direct (Subsidized and Unsubsidized Stafford, PLUS), Perkins, alternative loans.

WORK-STUDY *Federal work-study:* Total amount: $278,743; 149 jobs averaging $1780. *State or other work-study/employment:* Total amount: $97,554 (100% non-need-based). 20 part-time jobs averaging $4878.

ATHLETIC AWARDS Total amount: $235,323 (71% need-based, 29% non-need-based).

APPLYING FOR FINANCIAL AID *Required financial aid forms:* FAFSA, institutional scholarship application form. *Financial aid deadline (priority):* 3/1. *Notification date:* Continuous beginning 4/1. Students must reply within 2 weeks of notification.

CONTACT Denise Grayson, Financial Aid Director, Dakota State University, 103 Heston Hall, 820 North Washington Avenue, Madison, SD 57042-1799, 605-256-5158 or toll-free 888-DSU-9988. *Fax:* 605-256-5020. *E-mail:* fa@dsu.edu. *Website:* http://www.dsu.edu/.

DAKOTA WESLEYAN UNIVERSITY
Mitchell, SD

Tuition & fees: $21,750	Average undergraduate aid package: $18,000

ABOUT THE INSTITUTION Independent United Methodist, coed. *Awards:* associate, bachelor's, and master's degrees. 46 undergraduate majors. *Total enrollment:* 836. Undergraduates: 758. Freshmen: 202. Federal methodology is used as a basis for awarding need-based institutional aid.

UNDERGRADUATE EXPENSES for 2013–2014 *Application fee:* $25. *Comprehensive fee:* $28,550 includes full-time tuition ($21,750) and room and board ($6800). *College room only:* $2900. Room and board charges vary according to board plan and housing facility.

FRESHMAN FINANCIAL AID (Fall 2012, est.) 192 applied for aid; of those 89% were deemed to have need. 100% of freshmen with need received aid; of those 30% had need fully met. *Average percent of need met:* 81% (excluding resources awarded to replace EFC). *Average financial aid package:* $18,700 (excluding resources awarded to replace EFC). 12% of all full-time freshmen had no need and received non-need-based gift aid.

UNDERGRADUATE FINANCIAL AID (Fall 2012, est.) 649 applied for aid; of those 93% were deemed to have need. 100% of undergraduates with need received aid; of those 20% had need fully met. *Average percent of need met:* 74% (excluding resources awarded to replace EFC). *Average financial aid package:* $18,000 (excluding resources awarded to replace EFC). 12% of all full-time undergraduates had no need and received non-need-based gift aid.

GIFT AID (NEED-BASED) *Total amount:* $6,991,491 (21% federal, 2% state, 74% institutional, 3% external sources). *Receiving aid:* Freshmen: 87% (171); all full-time undergraduates: 86% (596). *Average award:* Freshmen: $14,800; Undergraduates: $13,400. *Scholarships, grants, and awards:* Federal Pell, FSEOG, state, college/university gift aid from institutional funds.

GIFT AID (NON-NEED-BASED) *Total amount:* $1,145,130 (1% federal, 4% state, 88% institutional, 7% external sources). *Receiving aid:* Freshmen: 18% (36). Undergraduates: 12% (81). *Average award:* Freshmen: $11,643. Undergraduates: $9326. *Scholarships, grants, and awards by category: Academic interests/achievement:* 671 awards ($5,909,987 total): biological sciences, business, education, general academic interests/achievements, health fields, mathematics, premedicine. *Creative arts/performance:* 28 awards ($52,425 total): music, theater/drama. *Special achievements/activities:* 373 awards ($1,418,184 total): cheerleading/drum major, general special achievements/activities. *Special characteristics:* 78 awards ($217,972 total): children of faculty/staff, religious affiliation. *Tuition waivers:* Full or partial for senior citizens. *ROTC:* Army.

LOANS *Student loans:* $5,811,832 (85% need-based, 15% non-need-based). 82% of past graduating class borrowed through all loan programs. *Average indebtedness per student:* $29,526. *Average need-based loan:* Freshmen: $3400. Undergraduates: $3900. *Parent loans:* $559,957 (53% need-based, 47% non-need-based). *Programs:* Federal Direct (Subsidized and Unsubsidized Stafford, PLUS), Perkins, private loans, United Methodist Student Loans (for members of Methodist Church).

WORK-STUDY *Federal work-study:* Total amount: $104,099; 93 jobs averaging $1400. *State or other work-study/employment:* Part-time jobs available.

ATHLETIC AWARDS Total amount: $1,407,934 (70% need-based, 30% non-need-based).

APPLYING FOR FINANCIAL AID *Financial aid deadline (priority):* 4/1. *Notification date:* Continuous beginning 3/1. Students must reply within 2 weeks of notification.

CONTACT Kristy O'Kief, Director of Financial Aid, Dakota Wesleyan University, 1200 West University Avenue, Mitchell, SD 57301, 605-995-2656 or toll-free 800-333-8506. *Fax:* 605-995-2638. *E-mail:* krokief@dwu.edu. *Website:* http://www.dwu.edu/.

DALLAS BAPTIST UNIVERSITY
Dallas, TX

Tuition & fees: $21,110	Average undergraduate aid package: $15,939

ABOUT THE INSTITUTION Independent Baptist General Convention of Texas, coed. *Awards:* certificates, associate, bachelor's, master's, and doctoral degrees. 44 undergraduate majors. *Total enrollment:* 5,622. Undergraduates: 3,513. Freshmen: 492. Federal methodology is used as a basis for awarding need-based institutional aid.

UNDERGRADUATE EXPENSES for 2013–2014 *Application fee:* $25. *Comprehensive fee:* $27,608 includes full-time tuition ($20,910), mandatory fees ($200), and room and board ($6498). *College room only:* $2590. Room and board charges vary according to board plan and housing facility. *Part-time tuition:* $697 per credit hour. *Part-time fees:* $100 per term.

FRESHMAN FINANCIAL AID (Fall 2012, est.) 461 applied for aid; of those 77% were deemed to have need. 99% of freshmen with need received aid; of those 55% had need fully met. *Average percent of need met:* 71% (excluding resources awarded to replace EFC). *Average financial aid package:* $16,121 (excluding resources awarded to replace EFC). 20% of all full-time freshmen had no need and received non-need-based gift aid.

UNDERGRADUATE FINANCIAL AID (Fall 2012, est.) 1,999 applied for aid; of those 81% were deemed to have need. 98% of undergraduates with need received aid; of those 43% had need fully met. *Average percent of need met:* 64% (excluding resources awarded to replace EFC). *Average financial aid package:* $15,939 (excluding resources awarded to replace EFC). 17% of all full-time undergraduates had no need and received non-need-based gift aid.

GIFT AID (NEED-BASED) *Total amount:* $6,979,787 (59% federal, 41% state). *Receiving aid:* Freshmen: 45% (219); all full-time undergraduates: 43% (1,038). *Average award:* Freshmen: $3634; Undergraduates: $3698. *Scholarships, grants, and awards:* Federal Pell, FSEOG, state, private, college/university gift aid from institutional funds.

GIFT AID (NON-NEED-BASED) *Total amount:* $15,122,234 (87% institutional, 13% external sources). *Receiving aid:* Freshmen: 68% (333). Undergraduates: 57% (1,374). *Average award:* Freshmen: $7724. Undergraduates: $7991. *Scholarships, grants, and awards by category: Academic interests/achievement:* 1,301 awards ($3,051,808 total): biological sciences, business, communication, computer science, education, English, general academic interests/achievements, humanities, mathematics, physical sciences, premedicine, religion/biblical studies, social sciences. *Creative arts/performance:* 87 awards ($245,700 total): art/fine arts, music. *Special achievements/activities:* 1,648 awards ($6,600,162 total): community service, general special achievements/activities, leadership, memberships, religious involvement. *Special characteristics:* 321 awards ($980,661 total): children of faculty/staff, general special characteristics, relatives of clergy, religious affiliation, veterans, veterans' children. *Tuition waivers:* Full or partial for employees or children of employees. *ROTC:* Army cooperative, Air Force cooperative.

LOANS *Student loans:* $17,684,478 (36% need-based, 64% non-need-based). 72% of past graduating class borrowed through all loan programs. *Average indebtedness per student:* $18,943. *Average need-based loan:* Freshmen: $3350. Undergraduates: $4139. *Parent loans:* $6,962,355 (100% non-need-based). *Programs:* Federal Direct (Subsidized and Unsubsidized Stafford, PLUS), state.

WORK-STUDY *Federal work-study:* Total amount: $324,505; 88 jobs averaging $2673. *State or other work-study/employment:* Total amount: $32,700 (100% need-based). 22 part-time jobs averaging $1477.

ATHLETIC AWARDS Total amount: $1,715,879 (100% non-need-based).

APPLYING FOR FINANCIAL AID *Required financial aid forms:* FAFSA, institution's own form. *Financial aid deadline:* Continuous. *Notification date:* Continuous beginning 2/1.

CONTACT Mr. Lee Ferguson, Director of Financial Aid, Dallas Baptist University, 3000 Mountain Creek Parkway, Dallas, TX 75211-9299, 214-333-5363 or toll-free 800-460-1328. *Fax:* 214-333-5586. *E-mail:* lee@dbu.edu. *Website:* http://www.dbu.edu/.

DALLAS CHRISTIAN COLLEGE
Dallas, TX

CONTACT Robin L. Walker, Director of Student Financial Aid, Dallas Christian College, 2700 Christian Parkway, Dallas, TX 75234-7299, 972-241-3371 Ext. 105 or toll-free 800-688-1029. *Fax:* 972-241-8021. *E-mail:* finaid@dallas.edu. *Website:* http://www.dallas.edu/.

DALTON STATE COLLEGE
Dalton, GA

ABOUT THE INSTITUTION State-supported, coed. *Awards:* certificates, associate, and bachelor's degrees. 39 undergraduate majors. *Total enrollment:* 5,047. Undergraduates: 5,047. Freshmen: 926.

GIFT AID (NEED-BASED) *Scholarships, grants, and awards:* Federal Pell, FSEOG, state, private.

GIFT AID (NON-NEED-BASED) *Scholarships, grants, and awards by category: Academic interests/achievement:* biological sciences, business, computer science, education, engineering/technologies, English, general academic interests/achievements, health fields, humanities, social sciences. *Special achievements/activities:* community service, hobbies/interests, leadership, memberships. *Special characteristics:* adult students, children of faculty/staff, local/state students, members of minority groups, out-of-state students.

LOANS *Programs:* state.

APPLYING FOR FINANCIAL AID *Required financial aid form:* FAFSA.

CONTACT Holly Woods, Assistant Director of Financial Aid, Dalton State College, 650 College Drive, Dalton, GA 30720, 706-272-4545 or toll-free 800-829-4436. *Fax:* 706-272-2458. *E-mail:* finaid@daltonstate.edu. *Website:* http://www.daltonstate.edu/.

DANIEL WEBSTER COLLEGE
Nashua, NH

Tuition & fees: $15,090	Average undergraduate aid package: $9044

ABOUT THE INSTITUTION Independent, coed. *Awards:* bachelor's and master's degrees. 13 undergraduate majors. *Total enrollment:* 621. Undergraduates: 603. Freshmen: 145. Federal methodology is used as a basis for awarding need-based institutional aid.

UNDERGRADUATE EXPENSES for 2013–2014 *Comprehensive fee:* $25,380 includes full-time tuition ($15,090) and room and board ($10,290). *College room only:* $5050. Full-time tuition and fees vary according to course load. Room and board charges vary according to board plan and housing facility. *Part-time tuition:* $503 per credit. Part-time tuition and fees vary according to course load.

FRESHMAN FINANCIAL AID (Fall 2012, est.) 134 applied for aid; of those 84% were deemed to have need. 96% of freshmen with need received aid; of those 6% had need fully met. *Average percent of need met:* 38% (excluding resources awarded to replace EFC). *Average financial aid package:* $5662 (excluding resources awarded to replace EFC).

UNDERGRADUATE FINANCIAL AID (Fall 2012, est.) 464 applied for aid; of those 86% were deemed to have need. 96% of undergraduates with need received aid; of those 3% had need fully met. *Average percent of need met:* 60% (excluding resources awarded to replace EFC). *Average financial aid package:* $9044 (excluding resources awarded to replace EFC). 1% of all full-time undergraduates had no need and received non-need-based gift aid.

GIFT AID (NEED-BASED) *Total amount:* $1,261,224 (76% federal, 2% state, 16% institutional, 6% external sources). *Receiving aid:* Freshmen: 46% (66); all full-time undergraduates: 46% (252). *Average award:* Freshmen: $3183; Undergraduates: $4300. *Scholarships, grants, and awards:* Federal Pell, FSEOG, state, private.

GIFT AID (NON-NEED-BASED) *Total amount:* $754,370 (100% institutional). *Receiving aid:* Undergraduates: 12% (66). *Average award:* Undergraduates: $8229. *Scholarships, grants, and awards by category: Academic interests/achievement:* 70 awards ($581,100 total): business, computer science, engineering/technologies, general academic interests/achievements. *Special achievements/activities:* 1 award ($27,940 total): leadership. *Tuition waivers:* Full or partial for employees or children of employees. *ROTC:* Army cooperative, Air Force cooperative.

LOANS *Student loans:* $4,899,955 (35% need-based, 65% non-need-based). 84% of past graduating class borrowed through all loan programs. *Average indebtedness per student:* $45,665. *Average need-based loan:* Freshmen: $3403. Undergraduates: $4257. *Parent loans:* $3,246,735 (100% non-need-based). *Programs:* Federal Direct (Subsidized and Unsubsidized Stafford, PLUS), alternative loans.

WORK-STUDY *Federal work-study:* Total amount: $121,163; jobs available.

APPLYING FOR FINANCIAL AID *Required financial aid forms:* FAFSA, institution's own form. *Financial aid deadline (priority):* 3/1. *Notification date:* Continuous beginning 3/15. Students must reply within 2 weeks of notification.

CONTACT Darla Ammidown, Director of Financial Aid , Daniel Webster College, 20 University Drive, Nashua, NH 03063-1300, 603-577-6533 or toll-free 800-325-6876. *Fax:* 603-577-6593. *E-mail:* dammidown@dwc.edu. *Website:* http://www.dwc.edu/.

DARKEI NOAM RABBINICAL COLLEGE
Brooklyn, NY

CONTACT Ms. Rivi Horowitz, Director of Financial Aid, Darkei Noam Rabbinical College, 2822 Avenue J, Brooklyn, NY 11219, 718-338-6464.

DARTMOUTH COLLEGE
Hanover, NH

Tuition & fees: $45,212	Average undergraduate aid package: $43,412

ABOUT THE INSTITUTION Independent, coed. *Awards:* bachelor's, master's, and doctoral degrees. 60 undergraduate majors. *Total enrollment:* 6,277. Undergraduates: 4,193. Freshmen: 1,095. Both federal and institutional methodology are used as a basis for awarding need-based institutional aid.

UNDERGRADUATE EXPENSES for 2013–2014 *Application fee:* $80. *Comprehensive fee:* $58,166 includes full-time tuition ($43,782), mandatory fees ($1430), and room and board ($12,954). *College room only:* $7755. Full-time tuition and fees vary according to student level. Room and board charges vary according to board plan. *Payment plan:* Tuition prepayment.

FRESHMAN FINANCIAL AID (Fall 2012, est.) 632 applied for aid; of those 82% were deemed to have need. 100% of freshmen with need received aid; of those 100% had need fully met. *Average percent of need met:* 100% (excluding resources awarded to replace EFC). *Average financial aid package:* $45,587 (excluding resources awarded to replace EFC).

UNDERGRADUATE FINANCIAL AID (Fall 2012, est.) 2,403 applied for aid; of those 88% were deemed to have need. 100% of undergraduates with need received aid; of those 100% had need fully met. *Average percent of need met:* 100% (excluding resources awarded to replace EFC). *Average financial aid package:* $43,412 (excluding resources awarded to replace EFC).

GIFT AID (NEED-BASED) *Total amount:* $82,355,110 (5% federal, 92% institutional, 3% external sources). *Receiving aid:* Freshmen: 46% (504); all full-time undergraduates: 50% (2,038). *Average award:* Freshmen: $41,436; Undergraduates: $40,342. *Scholarships, grants, and awards:* Federal Pell, FSEOG, state, private, college/university gift aid from institutional funds.

GIFT AID (NON-NEED-BASED) *Total amount:* $1,368,029 (12% federal, 88% external sources). *ROTC:* Army cooperative.

LOANS *Student loans:* $9,807,110 (59% need-based, 41% non-need-based). 46% of past graduating class borrowed through all loan programs. *Average indebtedness per student:* $17,825. *Average need-based loan:* Freshmen: $4115. Undergraduates: $3764. *Parent loans:* $3,882,380 (100% non-need-based). *Programs:* Federal Direct (Subsidized and Unsubsidized Stafford, PLUS), Perkins, Federal Nursing, state, college/university.

WORK-STUDY *Federal work-study:* Total amount: $2,527,665; 1,176 jobs averaging $2150. *State or other work-study/employment:* Total amount: $1,199,118 (100% need-based). Part-time jobs available.

APPLYING FOR FINANCIAL AID *Required financial aid forms:* FAFSA, CSS Financial Aid PROFILE, noncustodial (divorced/separated) parent's statement, business/farm supplement, federal income tax form(s), W-2 forms. *Financial aid deadline:* 2/1. *Notification date:* 4/2. Students must reply by 5/1.

CONTACT Ms. Virginia S. Hazen, Director of Financial Aid, Dartmouth College, 6024 McNutt Hall, Hanover, NH 03755, 603-646-2451. *Fax:* 603-646-1414. *E-mail:* virginia.s.hazen@dartmouth.edu. *Website:* http://www.dartmouth.edu/.

DAVENPORT UNIVERSITY
Grand Rapids, MI

Tuition & fees: $13,022	Average undergraduate aid package: N/A

ABOUT THE INSTITUTION Independent, coed. *Awards:* certificates, diplomas, associate, bachelor's, and master's degrees. 21 undergraduate majors. *Total enrollment:* 11,304. Undergraduates: 8,882. Freshmen: 728. Federal methodology is used as a basis for awarding need-based institutional aid.

UNDERGRADUATE EXPENSES for 2013–2014 *Application fee:* $25. *Comprehensive fee:* $21,456 includes full-time tuition ($12,672), mandatory fees ($350), and room and board ($8434). Full-time tuition and fees vary according to location and program. Room and board charges vary according to board plan and housing facility. *Part-time tuition:* $528 per credit hour. Part-time tuition and fees vary according to location and program.

GIFT AID (NEED-BASED) *Total amount:* $1,360,754 (78% federal, 22% state). *Scholarships, grants, and awards:* Federal Pell, FSEOG, state, private, college/university gift aid from institutional funds.

GIFT AID (NON-NEED-BASED) *Total amount:* $2,118,566 (100% institutional). *Scholarships, grants, and awards by category:* Academic interests/achievement: general academic interests/achievements. *Special achievements/activities:* memberships. *Tuition waivers:* Full or partial for employees or children of employees.

LOANS *Student loans:* $3,163,951 (100% need-based). *Programs:* private loans.

WORK-STUDY Federal work-study jobs available. *State or other work-study/employment:* Part-time jobs available.

APPLYING FOR FINANCIAL AID *Required financial aid form:* FAFSA. *Financial aid deadline (priority):* 3/1. *Notification date:* 3/1.

CONTACT David DeBoer, Executive Director of Financial Aid, Davenport University, 6191 Kraft Avenue SE, Grand Rapids, MI 49512, 616-732-1132 or toll-free 800-925-3884 (in-state), 866-925-3884 (out-of-state). *Fax:* 616-732-1167. *E-mail:* david.debore@davenport.edu. *Website:* http://www.davenport.edu/.

DAVIDSON COLLEGE
Davidson, NC

Tuition & fees: $42,849	Average undergraduate aid package: $34,121

ABOUT THE INSTITUTION Independent Presbyterian, coed. *Awards:* bachelor's degrees. 24 undergraduate majors. *Total enrollment:* 1,790. Undergraduates: 1,790. Freshmen: 490. Both federal and institutional methodology are used as a basis for awarding need-based institutional aid.

UNDERGRADUATE EXPENSES for 2013–2014 *Application fee:* $50. *Comprehensive fee:* $54,683 includes full-time tuition ($42,425), mandatory fees ($424), and room and board ($11,834). *College room only:* $6249. Room and board charges vary according to board plan.

FRESHMAN FINANCIAL AID (Fall 2011) 285 applied for aid; of those 80% were deemed to have need. 100% of freshmen with need received aid; of those 100% had need fully met. *Average percent of need met:* 100% (excluding resources awarded to replace EFC). *Average financial aid package:* $32,021 (excluding resources awarded to replace EFC). 5% of all full-time freshmen had no need and received non-need-based gift aid.

UNDERGRADUATE FINANCIAL AID (Fall 2011) 876 applied for aid; of those 95% were deemed to have need. 100% of undergraduates with need received aid; of those 100% had need fully met. *Average percent of need met:* 100% (excluding resources awarded to replace EFC). *Average financial aid package:* $34,121 (excluding resources awarded to replace EFC). 6% of all full-time undergraduates had no need and received non-need-based gift aid.

GIFT AID (NEED-BASED) *Total amount:* $23,309,387 (5% federal, 2% state, 93% institutional). *Receiving aid:* Freshmen: 44% (215); all full-time undergraduates: 46% (802). *Average award:* Freshmen: $30,683; Undergraduates: $29,064. *Scholarships, grants, and awards:* Federal Pell, FSEOG, state, private, college/university gift aid from institutional funds, need-linked special talent scholarships.

GIFT AID (NON-NEED-BASED) *Total amount:* $7,245,784 (8% federal, 9% state, 64% institutional, 19% external sources). *Receiving aid:* Freshmen: 10% (50). Undergraduates: 9% (152). *Average award:* Freshmen: $21,484. Undergraduates: $21,747. *Scholarships, grants, and awards by category:* Academic interests/achievement: biological sciences, business, education, foreign languages, general academic interests/achievements, international studies, mathematics, physical sciences, premedicine, religion/biblical studies, social sciences. *Creative arts/performance:* art/fine arts, creative writing, music, performing arts, theater/drama. *Special achievements/activities:* community service, general special achievements/activities, leadership, religious involvement. *Special characteristics:* general special characteristics, local/state students, out-of-state students, relatives of clergy. *Tuition waivers:* Full or partial for employees or children of employees. *ROTC:* Army, Air Force cooperative.

LOANS *Student loans:* $3,007,024 (26% need-based, 74% non-need-based). 22% of past graduating class borrowed through all loan programs. *Average indebtedness per student:* $23,904. *Average need-based loan:* Freshmen: $2802. Undergraduates: $3303. *Parent loans:* $2,526,687 (100% non-need-based). *Programs:* Federal Direct (Subsidized and Unsubsidized Stafford, PLUS), alternative loans.

WORK-STUDY *Federal work-study:* Total amount: $464,474; 302 jobs averaging $1538. *State or other work-study/employment:* Total amount: $232,179 (100% need-based). 137 part-time jobs averaging $1695.

ATHLETIC AWARDS Total amount: $2,945,839 (100% non-need-based).

APPLYING FOR FINANCIAL AID *Required financial aid forms:* FAFSA, CSS Financial Aid PROFILE, noncustodial (divorced/separated) parent's statement, business/farm supplement, federal income tax form(s), W-2 forms. *Financial aid deadline:* 3/1. *Notification date:* 4/2. Students must reply by 5/1.

CONTACT Mr. David R. Gelinas, Director of Financial Aid, Davidson College, 413 North Main Street, PO Box 7157, Davidson, NC 28035-7157, 704-894-2232 or toll-free 800-768-0380. *Fax:* 704-894-2845. *E-mail:* dagelinas@davidson.edu. *Website:* http://www.davidson.edu/.

DAVIS & ELKINS COLLEGE
Elkins, WV

CONTACT Susan M. George, Director of Financial Planning, Davis & Elkins College, 100 Campus Drive, Elkins, WV 26241-3996, 304-637-1373 or toll-free 800-624-3157. *Fax:* 304-637-1986. *E-mail:* ssw@davisandelkins.edu. *Website:* http://www.dewv.edu/.

DAVIS COLLEGE
Johnson City, NY

CONTACT Stephanie D. Baker, Financial Aid Director, Davis College, 400 Riverside Drive, Johnson City, NY 13790, 607-729-1581 Ext. 401 or toll-free 877-949-3248. *Fax:* 607-770-6886. *E-mail:* financialaid@davisny.edu. *Website:* http://www.davisny.edu/.

DAYMAR INSTITUTE
Clarksville, TN

CONTACT Financial Aid Office, Daymar Institute, 1860 Wilma Rudolph Boulevard, Clarksville, TN 37040, 931-552-7600. *Website:* http://www.daymarinstitute.edu/.

DAYMAR INSTITUTE
Murfreesboro, TN

CONTACT Financial Aid Office, Daymar Institute, 415 Golden Bear Court, Murfreesboro, TN 37128. *Website:* http://www.daymarinstitute.edu/.

DEFIANCE COLLEGE
Defiance, OH

Tuition & fees: $27,360	Average undergraduate aid package: $22,903

ABOUT THE INSTITUTION Independent United Church of Christ, coed. *Awards:* associate, bachelor's, and master's degrees. 32 undergraduate majors. *Total enrollment:* 1,021. Undergraduates: 932. Freshmen: 241. Federal methodology is used as a basis for awarding need-based institutional aid.

UNDERGRADUATE EXPENSES for 2013–2014 *Application fee:* $25. *Comprehensive fee:* $36,210 includes full-time tuition ($26,740), mandatory fees ($620), and room and board ($8850). Full-time tuition and fees vary according to program. Room and board charges vary according to board plan and housing facility. Part-time tuition and fees vary according to course load.

FRESHMAN FINANCIAL AID (Fall 2012, est.) 220 applied for aid; of those 93% were deemed to have need. 100% of freshmen with need received aid; of those 11% had need fully met. *Average percent of need met:* 72% (excluding resources awarded to replace EFC). *Average financial aid package:* $23,288 (excluding resources awarded to replace EFC). 13% of all full-time freshmen had no need and received non-need-based gift aid.

UNDERGRADUATE FINANCIAL AID (Fall 2012, est.) 696 applied for aid; of those 96% were deemed to have need. 100% of undergraduates with need received aid; of those 11% had need fully met. *Average percent of need met:* 72% (excluding resources awarded to replace EFC). *Average financial aid package:* $22,903 (excluding resources awarded to replace EFC). 9% of all full-time undergraduates had no need and received non-need-based gift aid.

GIFT AID (NEED-BASED) *Total amount:* $9,468,075 (20% federal, 5% state, 73% institutional, 2% external sources). *Receiving aid:* Freshmen: 77% (182); all full-time undergraduates: 75% (548). *Average award:* Freshmen: $9532; Undergraduates: $7845. *Scholarships, grants, and awards:* Federal Pell, FSEOG, state, private, college/university gift aid from institutional funds.

GIFT AID (NON-NEED-BASED) *Total amount:* $2,788,278 (11% federal, 83% institutional, 6% external sources). *Receiving aid:* Freshmen: 87% (205). Undergraduates: 90% (661). *Average award:* Freshmen: $15,467. Undergraduates: $13,416. *Scholarships, grants, and awards by category: Academic interests/achievement:* 716 awards ($6,189,756 total): biological sciences, business, communication, computer science, education, English, general academic interests/achievements, health fields, humanities, international studies, mathematics, physical sciences, premedicine, religion/biblical studies, social sciences. *Creative arts/performance:* 7 awards ($4500 total): applied art and design, art/fine arts, music. *Special achievements/activities:* 97 awards ($191,000 total): community service, general special achievements/activities, leadership, religious involvement. *Special characteristics:* 173 awards ($811,415 total): children and siblings of alumni, children of faculty/staff, international students, members of minority groups, out-of-state students, religious affiliation, veterans, veterans' children. *Tuition waivers:* Full or partial for employees or children of employees, senior citizens.

LOANS *Student loans:* $7,839,727 (63% need-based, 37% non-need-based). 91% of past graduating class borrowed through all loan programs. *Average indebtedness per student:* $36,663. *Average need-based loan:* Freshmen: $3543. Undergraduates: $4534. *Parent loans:* $1,519,837 (38% need-based, 62% non-need-based). *Programs:* Federal Direct (Subsidized and Unsubsidized Stafford, PLUS), Perkins, alternative loans.

WORK-STUDY *Federal work-study:* Total amount: $1,347,672; 553 jobs averaging $2437. *State or other work-study/employment:* Total amount: $98,400 (100% non-need-based). 41 part-time jobs averaging $2400.

APPLYING FOR FINANCIAL AID *Required financial aid form:* FAFSA. *Financial aid deadline (priority):* 4/1. *Notification date:* Continuous beginning 2/15. Students must reply by 5/1 or within 2 weeks of notification.

CONTACT Amy Francis, Director of Financial Aid, Defiance College, 701 North Clinton Street, Defiance, OH 43512-1610, 419-783-2376 or toll-free 800-520-4632. *Fax:* 419-783-2579. *E-mail:* afrancis@defiance.edu. *Website:* http://www.defiance.edu/.

DELAWARE STATE UNIVERSITY
Dover, DE

ABOUT THE INSTITUTION State-supported, coed. *Awards:* bachelor's, master's, and doctoral degrees. 137 undergraduate majors. *Total enrollment:* 4,178. Undergraduates: 3,744. Freshmen: 1,086.

GIFT AID (NEED-BASED) *Scholarships, grants, and awards:* Federal Pell, FSEOG, state, Federal Nursing.

GIFT AID (NON-NEED-BASED) *Scholarships, grants, and awards by category: Academic interests/achievement:* general academic interests/achievements. *Creative arts/performance:* music. *Special achievements/activities:* general special achievements/activities. *Special characteristics:* out-of-state students.

LOANS *Programs:* Perkins, Federal Nursing.

WORK-STUDY *Federal work-study:* Total amount: $197,227; jobs available. *State or other work-study/employment:* Part-time jobs available.

APPLYING FOR FINANCIAL AID *Required financial aid form:* FAFSA.

CONTACT Janet Lynn Iocono, Executive Director of Student Financial Services, Delaware State University, 1200 North DuPont Highway, Dover, DE 19901-2277, 302-857-6250 or toll-free 800-845-2544. *E-mail:* jiocono@desu.edu. *Website:* http://www.desu.edu/.

DELAWARE VALLEY COLLEGE
Doylestown, PA

ABOUT THE INSTITUTION Independent, coed. *Awards:* certificates, associate, bachelor's, and master's degrees. 29 undergraduate majors. *Total enrollment:* 2,253. Undergraduates: 1,983. Freshmen: 424.

GIFT AID (NEED-BASED) *Scholarships, grants, and awards:* Federal Pell, FSEOG, state, private, college/university gift aid from institutional funds.

GIFT AID (NON-NEED-BASED) *Scholarships, grants, and awards by category:* *Academic interests/achievement:* general academic interests/achievements. *Creative arts/performance:* general creative arts/performance. *Special characteristics:* children and siblings of alumni.

LOANS *Programs:* Federal Direct (Subsidized and Unsubsidized Stafford, PLUS), Perkins, alternative loans.

WORK-STUDY *Federal work-study:* Total amount: $176,179; jobs available. *State or other work-study/employment:* Total amount: $709,743 (89% need-based, 11% non-need-based). Part-time jobs available.

APPLYING FOR FINANCIAL AID *Required financial aid forms:* FAFSA, state aid form.

CONTACT Ms. Joan Hock, Director of Student Financial Aid, Delaware Valley College, 700 East Butler Avenue, Doylestown, PA 18901-2697, 215-489-2975 or toll-free 800-2DELVAL. *E-mail:* finaid@devalcol.edu. *Website:* http://www.delval.edu/.

DELTA STATE UNIVERSITY
Cleveland, MS

ABOUT THE INSTITUTION State-supported, coed. *Awards:* certificates, bachelor's, master's, and doctoral degrees. 38 undergraduate majors. *Total enrollment:* 4,763. Undergraduates: 2,756. Freshmen: 384.

GIFT AID (NEED-BASED) *Scholarships, grants, and awards:* Federal Pell, FSEOG, state, private, college/university gift aid from institutional funds.

GIFT AID (NON-NEED-BASED) *Scholarships, grants, and awards by category:* *Academic interests/achievement:* biological sciences, business, computer science, education, English, foreign languages, general academic interests/achievements, health fields, humanities, mathematics, physical sciences, premedicine, social sciences. *Creative arts/performance:* art/fine arts, creative writing, journalism/publications, music, performing arts. *Special achievements/activities:* cheerleading/drum major, general special achievements/activities, leadership, memberships. *Special characteristics:* children and siblings of alumni, children of faculty/staff, general special characteristics, out-of-state students.

LOANS *Programs:* Federal Direct (Subsidized and Unsubsidized Stafford, PLUS), Perkins.

APPLYING FOR FINANCIAL AID *Required financial aid forms:* FAFSA, institution's own form.

CONTACT Ms. Ann Margaret Mullins, Director of Student Financial Assistance, Delta State University, Kent Wyatt Hall 144, Highway 8 West, Cleveland, MS 38733-0001, 662-846-4670 or toll-free 800-468-6378. *Fax:* 662-846-4683. *E-mail:* amullins@deltastate.edu. *Website:* http://www.deltastate.edu/.

DENISON UNIVERSITY
Granville, OH

Tuition & fees: $42,280	Average undergraduate aid package: $36,688

ABOUT THE INSTITUTION Independent, coed. *Awards:* bachelor's degrees. 38 undergraduate majors. *Total enrollment:* 2,275. Undergraduates: 2,275. Freshmen: 623. Federal methodology is used as a basis for awarding need-based institutional aid.

UNDERGRADUATE EXPENSES for 2013–2014 *Application fee:* $40. *Comprehensive fee:* $52,640 includes full-time tuition ($41,380), mandatory fees ($900), and room and board ($10,360). *College room only:* $5700. Room and board charges vary according to board plan and housing facility. *Part-time tuition:* $1290 per credit. *Part-time fees:* $660 per term. Part-time tuition and fees vary according to course load.

FRESHMAN FINANCIAL AID (Fall 2012, est.) 436 applied for aid; of those 81% were deemed to have need. 100% of freshmen with need received aid; of those 48% had need fully met. *Average percent of need met:* 97% (excluding resources awarded to replace EFC). *Average financial aid package:* $37,445 (excluding resources awarded to replace EFC). 40% of all full-time freshmen had no need and received non-need-based gift aid.

UNDERGRADUATE FINANCIAL AID (Fall 2012, est.) 1,384 applied for aid; of those 86% were deemed to have need. 100% of undergraduates with need received aid; of those 28% had need fully met. *Average percent of need met:* 96% (excluding resources awarded to replace EFC). *Average financial aid package:* $36,688 (excluding resources awarded to replace EFC). 44% of all full-time undergraduates had no need and received non-need-based gift aid.

GIFT AID (NEED-BASED) *Total amount:* $20,146,478 (10% federal, 1% state, 86% institutional, 3% external sources). *Receiving aid:* Freshmen: 56% (354); all full-time undergraduates: 52% (1,190). *Average award:* Freshmen: $32,388; Undergraduates: $30,749. *Scholarships, grants, and awards:* Federal Pell, FSEOG, state, private, college/university gift aid from institutional funds.

GIFT AID (NON-NEED-BASED) *Total amount:* $33,998,323 (100% institutional). *Receiving aid:* Freshmen: 53% (331). Undergraduates: 47% (1,076). *Average award:* Freshmen: $18,241. Undergraduates: $16,450. *Scholarships, grants, and awards by category:* *Academic interests/achievement:* 66 awards ($215,607 total): biological sciences, English, foreign languages, mathematics, physical sciences. *Creative arts/performance:* 70 awards ($325,009 total). *Special characteristics:* 25 awards ($662,126 total): children of faculty/staff, veterans. *Tuition waivers:* Full or partial for employees or children of employees. *ROTC:* Army cooperative.

LOANS *Student loans:* $8,080,629 (100% need-based). *Average need-based loan:* Freshmen: $3748. Undergraduates: $4626. *Parent loans:* $3,708,340 (100% non-need-based). *Programs:* Federal Direct (Subsidized and Unsubsidized Stafford, PLUS), Perkins, college/university.

WORK-STUDY *Federal work-study:* Total amount: $1,209,268; 488 jobs averaging $2550. *State or other work-study/employment:* Part-time jobs available.

APPLYING FOR FINANCIAL AID *Required financial aid form:* FAFSA. *Financial aid deadline (priority):* 3/15. *Notification date:* Continuous beginning 3/28. Students must reply within 2 weeks of notification.

CONTACT Ms. Nancy Hoover, Director of Financial Aid, Denison University, PO Box M, Granville, OH 43023-0613, 740-587-6279 or toll-free 800-DENISON. *Fax:* 740-587-5706. *E-mail:* hoover@denison.edu. *Website:* http://www.denison.edu/.

DENVER SCHOOL OF NURSING
Denver, CO

CONTACT Financial Aid Office, Denver School of Nursing, 1401 19th Street, Denver, CO 80202, 303-292-0015 or toll-free 888-479-5550. *Website:* http://www.denverschoolofnursing.edu/.

DEPAUL UNIVERSITY
Chicago, IL

Tuition & fees: $32,295	Average undergraduate aid package: $20,150

ABOUT THE INSTITUTION Independent Roman Catholic, coed. *Awards:* certificates, bachelor's, master's, and doctoral degrees. 106 undergraduate majors. *Total enrollment:* 24,966. Undergraduates: 16,498. Freshmen: 2,593. Federal methodology is used as a basis for awarding need-based institutional aid.

UNDERGRADUATE EXPENSES for 2013–2014 *Application fee:* $40. *Comprehensive fee:* $44,012 includes full-time tuition ($31,650), mandatory fees ($645), and room and board ($11,717). *College room only:* $8486. Full-time tuition and fees vary according to course load and program. Room and board charges vary according to board plan, housing facility, and location. *Part-time tuition:* $530 per credit hour. Part-time tuition and fees vary according to course load and program.

FRESHMAN FINANCIAL AID (Fall 2011) 2,085 applied for aid; of those 86% were deemed to have need. 99% of freshmen with need received aid; of those 10% had need fully met. *Average percent of need met:* 66% (excluding resources awarded to replace EFC). *Average financial aid package:* $21,917 (excluding resources

awarded to replace EFC). 21% of all full-time freshmen had no need and received non-need-based gift aid.

UNDERGRADUATE FINANCIAL AID (Fall 2011) 10,592 applied for aid; of those 91% were deemed to have need. 98% of undergraduates with need received aid; of those 8% had need fully met. *Average percent of need met:* 60% (excluding resources awarded to replace EFC). *Average financial aid package:* $20,150 (excluding resources awarded to replace EFC). 11% of all full-time undergraduates had no need and received non-need-based gift aid.
GIFT AID (NEED-BASED) *Total amount:* $113,400,000 (27% federal, 19% state, 54% institutional). *Receiving aid:* Freshmen: 60% (1,467); all full-time under-graduates: 60% (7,992). *Average award:* Freshmen: $12,012; Undergraduates: $13,213. *Scholarships, grants, and awards:* Federal Pell, FSEOG, state, private, college/university gift aid from institutional funds, Academic Competitiveness Grants, National SMART Grants, TEACH Grants.
GIFT AID (NON-NEED-BASED) *Total amount:* $56,600,000 (97% institutional, 3% external sources). *Receiving aid:* Freshmen: 63% (1,537). Undergraduates: 35% (4,697). *Average award:* Freshmen: $9370. Undergraduates: $9262. *Scholarships, grants, and awards by category:* Academic interests/achievement: general academic interests/achievements. Creative arts/performance: art/fine arts, music, performing arts, theater/drama. Special achievements/activities: community service, leadership. Special characteristics: children of faculty/staff, local/state students. *Tuition waivers:* Full or partial for employees or children of employees. *ROTC:* Army.
LOANS *Student loans:* $90,000,000 (46% need-based, 54% non-need-based). 63% of past graduating class borrowed through all loan programs. *Average indebtedness per student:* $28,284. *Average need-based loan:* Freshmen: $3466. Undergraduates: $4578. *Parent loans:* $56,000 (100% non-need-based). *Programs:* Federal Direct (Subsidized and Unsubsidized Stafford, PLUS), Perkins, private loans.
WORK-STUDY *Federal work-study:* Total amount: $1,700,000; jobs available. *State or other work-study/employment:* Total amount: $7,000,000 (60% need-based, 40% non-need-based). Part-time jobs available.
ATHLETIC AWARDS Total amount: $4,800,000 (100% non-need-based).
APPLYING FOR FINANCIAL AID *Required financial aid form:* FAFSA. *Financial aid deadline (priority):* 2/15. *Notification date:* Continuous beginning 3/15. Students must reply by 5/1 or within 4 weeks of notification.
CONTACT Christopher Rone, Associate Director of Financial Aid, DePaul University, 1 East Jackson Boulevard, Chicago, IL 60604-2287, 773-325-7815 or toll-free 800-4DE-PAUL (out-of-state). *Fax:* 773-325-7746. *Website:* http://www.depaul.edu/.

DEPAUW UNIVERSITY
Greencastle, IN

Tuition & fees: $38,750	Average undergraduate aid package: $31,812

ABOUT THE INSTITUTION Independent United Methodist Church, coed. *Awards:* bachelor's degrees. 45 undergraduate majors. *Total enrollment:* 2,336. Undergraduates: 2,336. Freshmen: 578. Both federal and institutional methodology are used as a basis for awarding need-based institutional aid.
UNDERGRADUATE EXPENSES for 2013–2014 *Application fee:* $40. *Comprehensive fee:* $48,950 includes full-time tuition ($38,280), mandatory fees ($470), and room and board ($10,200). Room and board charges vary according to board plan. *Part-time tuition:* $1196.25 per credit hour.
FRESHMAN FINANCIAL AID (Fall 2012, est.) 462 applied for aid; of those 80% were deemed to have need. 100% of freshmen with need received aid; of those 29% had need fully met. *Average percent of need met:* 87% (excluding resources awarded to replace EFC). *Average financial aid package:* $31,834 (excluding resources awarded to replace EFC). 43% of all full-time freshmen had no need and received non-need-based gift aid.
UNDERGRADUATE FINANCIAL AID (Fall 2012, est.) 1,472 applied for aid; of those 86% were deemed to have need. 100% of undergraduates with need received aid; of those 28% had need fully met. *Average percent of need met:* 88% (excluding resources awarded to replace EFC). *Average financial aid package:* $31,812 (excluding resources awarded to replace EFC). 44% of all full-time undergraduates had no need and received non-need-based gift aid.
GIFT AID (NEED-BASED) *Total amount:* $34,635,698 (6% federal, 3% state, 83% institutional, 8% external sources). *Receiving aid:* Freshmen: 63% (367); all full-

time undergraduates: 55% (1,257). *Average award:* Freshmen: $28,438; Undergraduates: $27,534. *Scholarships, grants, and awards:* Federal Pell, FSEOG, state, private, college/university gift aid from institutional funds.
GIFT AID (NON-NEED-BASED) *Total amount:* $19,903,461 (93% institutional, 7% external sources). *Receiving aid:* Freshmen: 15% (88). Undergraduates: 11% (247). *Average award:* Freshmen: $15,218. Undergraduates: $16,722. *Scholarships, grants, and awards by category:* Academic interests/achievement: general academic interests/achievements. Special achievements/activities: community service. Special characteristics: children and siblings of alumni. *Tuition waivers:* Full or partial for employees or children of employees. *ROTC:* Army cooperative, Air Force cooperative.
LOANS *Student loans:* $10,908,318 (59% need-based, 41% non-need-based). 54% of past graduating class borrowed through all loan programs. *Average indebtedness per student:* $26,570. *Average need-based loan:* Freshmen: $3685. Undergraduates: $4320. *Parent loans:* $4,117,359 (31% need-based, 69% non-need-based). *Programs:* Federal Direct (Subsidized and Unsubsidized Stafford, PLUS), Perkins, college/university.
WORK-STUDY *Federal work-study:* Total amount: $917,396; jobs available. *State or other work-study/employment:* Total amount: $693,437 (44% need-based, 56% non-need-based). Part-time jobs available.
APPLYING FOR FINANCIAL AID *Required financial aid forms:* FAFSA, CSS Financial Aid PROFILE. *Financial aid deadline:* 3/1 (priority: 2/15). *Notification date:* 3/15. Students must reply by 5/1.
CONTACT Craig Slaughter, Director of Financial Aid, DePauw University, 200 East Seminary, Greencastle, IN 46135-0037, 765-658-4030 or toll-free 800-447-2495. *Fax:* 765-658-4137. *E-mail:* financialaid@depauw.edu. *Website:* http://www.depauw.edu/.

DESALES UNIVERSITY
Center Valley, PA

Tuition & fees: $30,150	Average undergraduate aid package: $19,577

ABOUT THE INSTITUTION Independent Roman Catholic, coed. *Awards:* certificates, bachelor's, master's, and doctoral degrees. 42 undergraduate majors. *Total enrollment:* 3,255. Undergraduates: 2,468. Freshmen: 389. Federal methodology is used as a basis for awarding need-based institutional aid.
UNDERGRADUATE EXPENSES for 2013–2014 *Comprehensive fee:* $41,120 includes full-time tuition ($29,000), mandatory fees ($1150), and room and board ($10,970). Full-time tuition and fees vary according to course load, degree level, and program. Room and board charges vary according to board plan and housing facility. *Part-time tuition:* $1210 per credit hour. Part-time tuition and fees vary according to course load, degree level, and program.
FRESHMAN FINANCIAL AID (Fall 2012, est.) 369 applied for aid; of those 88% were deemed to have need. 100% of freshmen with need received aid; of those 20% had need fully met. *Average percent of need met:* 72% (excluding resources awarded to replace EFC). *Average financial aid package:* $23,660 (excluding resources awarded to replace EFC). 16% of all full-time freshmen had no need and received non-need-based gift aid.
UNDERGRADUATE FINANCIAL AID (Fall 2012, est.) 1,585 applied for aid; of those 91% were deemed to have need. 98% of undergraduates with need received aid; of those 18% had need fully met. *Average percent of need met:* 69% (excluding resources awarded to replace EFC). *Average financial aid package:* $19,577 (excluding resources awarded to replace EFC). 15% of all full-time undergraduates had no need and received non-need-based gift aid.
GIFT AID (NEED-BASED) *Total amount:* $22,387,245 (13% federal, 9% state, 77% institutional, 1% external sources). *Receiving aid:* Freshmen: 84% (325); all full-time undergraduates: 75% (1,359). *Average award:* Freshmen: $18,552; Undergraduates: $16,572. *Scholarships, grants, and awards:* Federal Pell, FSEOG, state, private, college/university gift aid from institutional funds.
GIFT AID (NON-NEED-BASED) *Total amount:* $3,325,153 (2% federal, 95% institutional, 3% external sources). *Receiving aid:* Freshmen: 71% (277). Undergraduates: 68% (1,242). *Average award:* Freshmen: $10,436. Undergraduates: $10,653. *Scholarships, grants, and awards by category:* Academic interests/achievement: 1,411 awards ($7,038,347 total): biological sciences, business, communication, computer science, education, English, foreign languages, general academic interests/achievements, health fields, humanities, mathematics, physical sciences, pre-

medicine, religion/biblical studies, social sciences. *Creative arts/performance:* 187 awards ($323,289 total): cinema/film/broadcasting, dance, performing arts, theater/drama. *Special achievements/activities:* 8 awards ($13,000 total): community service. *Tuition waivers:* Full or partial for employees or children of employees, adult students, senior citizens. *ROTC:* Army cooperative.

LOANS *Student loans:* $18,470,676 (76% need-based, 24% non-need-based). 79% of past graduating class borrowed through all loan programs. *Average indebtedness per student:* $28,875. *Average need-based loan:* Freshmen: $3377. Undergraduates: $4492. *Parent loans:* $3,526,638 (44% need-based, 56% non-need-based). *Programs:* Federal Direct (Subsidized and Unsubsidized Stafford, PLUS), Perkins, Federal Nursing.

WORK-STUDY *Federal work-study:* Total amount: $944,406; 530 jobs averaging $1942. *State or other work-study/employment:* Total amount: $483,400 (3% need-based, 97% non-need-based). 275 part-time jobs averaging $1995.

APPLYING FOR FINANCIAL AID *Required financial aid forms:* FAFSA, state aid form, PHEAA form (PA residents only). *Financial aid deadline:* 5/1 (priority: 2/15). *Notification date:* Continuous beginning 2/15. Students must reply by 5/1 or within 2 weeks of notification.

CONTACT Mrs. Joyce Farmer, Director of Financial Aid, DeSales University, 2755 Station Avenue, Center Valley, PA 18034-9568, 610-282-1100 Ext. 1208. *Fax:* 610-282-0131. *E-mail:* joyce.farmer@desales.edu.
Website: http://www.desales.edu/.

DESIGN INSTITUTE OF SAN DIEGO
San Diego, CA

CONTACT Financial Aid Office, Design Institute of San Diego, 8555 Commerce Avenue, San Diego, CA 92121, 858-566-1200 or toll-free 800-619-4337.
Website: http://www.disd.edu/.

DEVRY COLLEGE OF NEW YORK
New York, NY

CONTACT Elvira Senese, Dean of Student Finance, DeVry College of New York, 30-20 Thomson Avenue, Long Island City, NY 11101, 718-472-2728 or toll-free 866-338-7941. *Fax:* 718-269-4284.
Website: http://www.devry.edu/.

DEVRY UNIVERSITY
Mesa, AZ

CONTACT Financial Aid Office, DeVry University, 1201 South Alma School Road, Mesa, AZ 85210-2011, 480-827-1511 or toll-free 866-338-7941.
Website: http://www.devry.edu/.

DEVRY UNIVERSITY
Phoenix, AZ

Tuition & fees: $16,156	Average undergraduate aid package: N/A

ABOUT THE INSTITUTION Proprietary, coed. *Awards:* certificates, associate, bachelor's, and master's degrees. 13 undergraduate majors. *Total enrollment:* 1,318. Undergraduates: 1,111. Freshmen: 98. Federal methodology is used as a basis for awarding need-based institutional aid.

UNDERGRADUATE EXPENSES for 2013–2014 *Application fee:* $40. *Tuition:* full-time $16,076; part-time $609 per credit hour.

GIFT AID (NEED-BASED) *Scholarships, grants, and awards:* Federal Pell, FSEOG, state, private, college/university gift aid from institutional funds.

LOANS *Programs:* Federal Direct (Subsidized and Unsubsidized Stafford, PLUS), Perkins.

APPLYING FOR FINANCIAL AID *Required financial aid form:* FAFSA. *Financial aid deadline:* Continuous. *Notification date:* Continuous.

CONTACT Student Finance Office, DeVry University, 2149 West Dunlap Avenue, Phoenix, AZ 85021-2995, 602-749-4545 or toll-free 866-338-7941.
Website: http://www.devry.edu/.

DEVRY UNIVERSITY
Alhambra, CA

CONTACT Financial Aid Office, DeVry University, Unit 100, Building A-11, First Floor, 1000 South Fremont Avenue, Alhambra, CA 91803, 626-293-4300 or toll-free 866-338-7941.
Website: http://www.devry.edu/.

DEVRY UNIVERSITY
Anaheim, CA

CONTACT Financial Aid Office, DeVry University, 1900 South State College Boulevard, Suite 150, Anaheim, CA 92806-6136, 714-935-3200 or toll-free 866-338-7941.
Website: http://www.devry.edu/.

DEVRY UNIVERSITY
Bakersfield, CA

CONTACT Financial Aid Office, DeVry University, 3000 Ming Avenue, Bakersfield, CA 93304-4136, 661-833-7120 or toll-free 866-338-7941.
Website: http://www.devry.edu/.

DEVRY UNIVERSITY
Daly City, CA

CONTACT Financial Aid Office, DeVry University, 2001 Junipero Serra Boulevard, Suite 161, Daly City, CA 94014-3899, 650-991-3520 or toll-free 866-338-7941.
Website: http://www.devry.edu/.

DEVRY UNIVERSITY
Elk Grove, CA

CONTACT Financial Aid Office, DeVry University, Sacramento Center, 2216 Kausen Drive, Elk Grove, CA 95758, 916-478-2847 or toll-free 866-338-7941.
Website: http://www.devry.edu/.

DEVRY UNIVERSITY
Fremont, CA

CONTACT Kim Kane, Director of Student Finance, DeVry University, 6600 Dumbarton Circle, Fremont, CA 94555, 510-574-1100 or toll-free 866-338-7941. *Fax:* 510-742-0868.
Website: http://www.devry.edu/.

DEVRY UNIVERSITY
Irvine, CA

CONTACT Financial Aid Office, DeVry University, 430 Exchange, Suite 250, Irvine, CA 92602-1303, 949-752-5631 or toll-free 866-338-7941. *Website:* http://www.devry.edu/.

DEVRY UNIVERSITY
Long Beach, CA

CONTACT Kathy Odom, Director of Financial Aid, DeVry University, 3880 Kilroy Airport Way, Long Beach, CA 90806, 562-427-0861 or toll-free 866-338-7941. *Fax:* 562-989-1578. *Website:* http://www.devry.edu/.

DEVRY UNIVERSITY
Oakland, CA

CONTACT Financial Aid Office, DeVry University, 505 14th Street, Oakland, CA 94612, 866-473-3879 or toll-free 866-338-7941. *Website:* http://www.devry.edu/.

DEVRY UNIVERSITY
Palmdale, CA

CONTACT Ann Logan, Dean of Student Finance, DeVry University, 22801 Roscoe Boulevard, West Hills, CA 91304, 818-932-3001 or toll-free 866-338-7941. *Fax:* 818-932-3131. *Website:* http://www.devry.edu/.

DEVRY UNIVERSITY
Pomona, CA

Tuition & fees: $16,156	Average undergraduate aid package: N/A

ABOUT THE INSTITUTION Proprietary, coed. *Awards:* certificates, associate, bachelor's, and master's degrees. 15 undergraduate majors. *Total enrollment:* 2,637. Undergraduates: 2,323. Freshmen: 151. Federal methodology is used as a basis for awarding need-based institutional aid.

UNDERGRADUATE EXPENSES for 2013–2014 *Application fee:* $40. *Tuition:* full-time $16,076; part-time $609 per credit hour.

GIFT AID (NEED-BASED) *Scholarships, grants, and awards:* Federal Pell, FSEOG, state, private, college/university gift aid from institutional funds.

LOANS *Programs:* Federal Direct (Subsidized and Unsubsidized Stafford, PLUS), Perkins.

APPLYING FOR FINANCIAL AID *Required financial aid form:* FAFSA. *Financial aid deadline:* Continuous. *Notification date:* Continuous.

CONTACT Student Finance Office, DeVry University, 901 Corporate Center Drive, Pomona, CA 91768-2642, 909-622-8866 or toll-free 866-338-7941. *Website:* http://www.devry.edu/.

DEVRY UNIVERSITY
San Diego, CA

CONTACT Financial Aid Office, DeVry University, 2655 Camino Del Rio North, Suite 201, San Diego, CA 92108-1633, 619-683-2446 or toll-free 866-338-7941. *Website:* http://www.devry.edu/.

DEVRY UNIVERSITY
Sherman Oaks, CA

CONTACT Financial Aid Office, DeVry University, 15301 Ventura Boulevard, D-100, Sherman Oaks, CA 91403, 888-610-0800 or toll-free 866-338-7941. *Website:* http://www.devry.edu/.

DEVRY UNIVERSITY
Colorado Springs, CO

CONTACT Carol Oppman, Director of Financial Aid, DeVry University, 225 South Union Boulevard, Colorado Springs, CO 80910, 719-632-3000 or toll-free 866-338-7941. *Fax:* 719-632-1909. *Website:* http://www.devry.edu/.

DEVRY UNIVERSITY
Westminster, CO

CONTACT Office of Financial Aid, DeVry University, 1870 West 122nd Avenue, Westminster, CO 80234-2010, 303-280-7400 or toll-free 866-338-7941. *Website:* http://www.devry.edu/.

DEVRY UNIVERSITY
Jacksonville, FL

CONTACT Financial Aid Office, DeVry University, 5200 Belfort Road, Jacksonville, FL 32256-6040. *Website:* http://www.devry.edu/locations/campuses/loc_jacksonville.jsp.

DEVRY UNIVERSITY
Miami, FL

CONTACT Financial Aid Office, DeVry University, 8700 West Flagler Street, Suite 100, Miami, FL 33174-2535, 305-229-4833 or toll-free 866-338-7941. *Website:* http://www.devry.edu/.

DEVRY UNIVERSITY
Miramar, FL

CONTACT Office of Financial Aid, DeVry University, 2300 Southwest 145th Avenue, Miramar, FL 33027, 954-499-9700 or toll-free 866-338-7941. *Website:* http://www.devry.edu/.

DEVRY UNIVERSITY
Orlando, FL

CONTACT Estrella Velazquez-Domenech, Director of Student Finance, DeVry University, 4000 Millenia Boulevard, Orlando, FL 32839, 407-345-2816 or toll-free 866-338-7941. *Fax:* 407-355-4855. *Website:* http://www.devry.edu/.

DEVRY UNIVERSITY
Tampa, FL

CONTACT Financial Aid Office, DeVry University, 3030 North Rocky Point Drive West, Suite 100, Tampa, FL 33607-5901, 813-288-8994 or toll-free 866-338-7941. *Website:* http://www.devry.edu/.

DEVRY UNIVERSITY
Alpharetta, GA

CONTACT David Pickett, Assistant Director of Financial Aid, DeVry University, 2555 Northwinds Parkway, Alpharetta, GA 30004, 770-521-4900 or toll-free 866-338-7941. *Fax:* 770-664-8024. *Website:* http://www.devry.edu/.

DEVRY UNIVERSITY
Decatur, GA

Tuition & fees: $16,156	Average undergraduate aid package: N/A

ABOUT THE INSTITUTION Proprietary, coed. *Awards:* certificates, associate, bachelor's, and master's degrees. 16 undergraduate majors. *Total enrollment:* 2,554. Undergraduates: 2,240. Freshmen: 140. Federal methodology is used as a basis for awarding need-based institutional aid.

UNDERGRADUATE EXPENSES for 2013–2014 *Application fee:* $40. *Tuition:* full-time $16,076; part-time $609 per credit hour.

GIFT AID (NEED-BASED) *Scholarships, grants, and awards:* Federal Pell, FSEOG, state, private, college/university gift aid from institutional funds.

LOANS *Programs:* Federal Direct (Subsidized and Unsubsidized Stafford, PLUS), Perkins.

APPLYING FOR FINANCIAL AID *Required financial aid form:* FAFSA. *Financial aid deadline:* Continuous. *Notification date:* Continuous.

CONTACT Student Finance Office, DeVry University, 1 West Court Square, Suite 100, Decatur, GA 30030-2556, 404-270-2702 or toll-free 866-338-7941. *Website:* http://www.devry.edu/.

DEVRY UNIVERSITY
Duluth, GA

CONTACT Financial Aid Office, DeVry University, 3505 Koger Boulevard, Suite 170, Duluth, GA 30096-7671, 678-380-9780 or toll-free 866-338-7941. *Website:* http://www.devry.edu/.

DEVRY UNIVERSITY
Addison, IL

CONTACT Sejal Amin, Director of Student Finance, DeVry University, 1221 North Swift Road, Addison, IL 60101-6106, 630-953-1300 or toll-free 866-338-7941. *Website:* http://www.devry.edu/.

DEVRY UNIVERSITY
Chicago, IL

CONTACT Milena Dobrina, Director of Financial Aid, DeVry University, 3300 North Campbell Avenue, Chicago, IL 60618-5994, 773-929-8500 or toll-free 866-338-7941. *Fax:* 773-348-1780. *Website:* http://www.devry.edu/.

DEVRY UNIVERSITY
Downers Grove, IL

CONTACT Financial Aid Office, DeVry University, 3005 Highland Parkway, Downers Grove, IL 60515, 630-515-3000 or toll-free 866-338-7941. *Website:* http://www.devry.edu/.

DEVRY UNIVERSITY
Elgin, IL

CONTACT Financial Aid Office, DeVry University, Randall Point, 2250 Point Boulevard, Suite 250, Elgin, IL 60123, 847-649-3980 or toll-free 866-338-7941. *Website:* http://www.devry.edu/.

DEVRY UNIVERSITY
Gurnee, IL

CONTACT Financial Aid Office, DeVry University, 1075 Tri-State Parkway, Suite 800, Gurnee, IL 60031-9126, 847-855-2649 or toll-free 866-338-7941. *Website:* http://www.devry.edu/.

DEVRY UNIVERSITY
Naperville, IL

CONTACT Financial Aid Office, DeVry University, 2056 Westings Avenue, Suite 40, Naperville, IL 60563-2361, 630-428-9086 or toll-free 866-338-7941. *Website:* http://www.devry.edu/.

DEVRY UNIVERSITY
Tinley Park, IL

CONTACT Director of Student Finance, DeVry University, 18624 West Creek Drive, Tinley Park, IL 60477, 708-342-3300 or toll-free 866-338-7941. *Fax:* 708-342-3120. *Website:* http://www.devry.edu/.

DEVRY UNIVERSITY
Indianapolis, IN

CONTACT Financial Aid Office, DeVry University, 9100 Keystone Crossing, Suite 350, Indianapolis, IN 46240-2158, 317-581-8854 or toll-free 866-338-7941. *Website:* http://www.devry.edu/.

DEVRY UNIVERSITY
Merrillville, IN

CONTACT Financial Aid Office, DeVry University, Twin Towers, 1000 East 80th Place, Suite 222 Mall, Merrillville, IN 46410-5673, 219-736-7440 or toll-free 866-338-7941. *Website:* http://www.devry.edu/.

DEVRY UNIVERSITY
Louisville, KY

CONTACT Financial Aid Office, DeVry University, 10172 Linn Station Road, Suite 300, Louisville, KY 40223 or toll-free 866-338-7941.
Website: http://www.devry.edu/.

DEVRY UNIVERSITY
Bethesda, MD

CONTACT Financial Aid Office, DeVry University, 4550 Montgomery Avenue, Suite 100 North, Bethesda, MD 20814-3304, 301-652-8477 or toll-free 866-338-7941.
Website: http://www.devry.edu/.

DEVRY UNIVERSITY
Southfield, MI

CONTACT Mr. Stephen Haworth, Regulatory Compliance Specialist, DeVry University, 26999 Central Park Boulevard, Suite 125, Southfield, MI 48076, 630-706-3172 or toll-free 866-338-7941. *Fax:* 630-574-1991. *E-mail:* shaworth@devry.com.
Website: http://www.devry.edu/.

DEVRY UNIVERSITY
Edina, MN

CONTACT Financial Aid Office, DeVry University, 7700 France Avenue South, Suite 575, Edina, MN 55435, 952-838-1860 or toll-free 866-338-7941.
Website: http://www.devry.edu/.

DEVRY UNIVERSITY
Kansas City, MO

CONTACT Maureen Kelly, Senior Associate Director of Financial Aid, DeVry University, 11224 Holmes Street, Kansas City, MO 64131-3698, 816-941-0430 or toll-free 866-338-7941.
Website: http://www.devry.edu/.

DEVRY UNIVERSITY
Kansas City, MO

CONTACT Financial Aid Office, DeVry University, City Center Square, 1100 Main Street, Suite 118, Kansas City, MO 64105-2112, 816-221-1300 or toll-free 866-338-7941.
Website: http://www.devry.edu/.

DEVRY UNIVERSITY
St. Louis, MO

CONTACT Financial Aid Office, DeVry University, 1801 Park 270 Drive, Suite 260, St. Louis, MO 63146-4020, 314-542-4222 or toll-free 866-338-7941.
Website: http://www.devry.edu/.

DEVRY UNIVERSITY
Henderson, NV

CONTACT Financial Aid Office, DeVry University, 2490 Paseo Verde Parkway, Henderson, NV 89074-7120, 702-933-9700 or toll-free 866-338-7941.
Website: http://www.devry.edu/.

DEVRY UNIVERSITY
North Brunswick, NJ

Tuition & fees: $16,156 | **Average undergraduate aid package: N/A**

ABOUT THE INSTITUTION Proprietary, coed. *Awards:* associate, bachelor's, and master's degrees. 9 undergraduate majors. *Total enrollment:* 1,414. Undergraduates: 1,213. Freshmen: 113. Federal methodology is used as a basis for awarding need-based institutional aid.
UNDERGRADUATE EXPENSES for 2013–2014 *Application fee:* $40. *Tuition:* full-time $16,076; part-time $609 per credit hour.
GIFT AID (NEED-BASED) *Scholarships, grants, and awards:* Federal Pell, FSEOG, state, private, college/university gift aid from institutional funds.
LOANS *Programs:* Federal Direct (Subsidized and Unsubsidized Stafford, PLUS), Perkins.
APPLYING FOR FINANCIAL AID *Notification date:* Continuous.
CONTACT Student Finance Office, DeVry University, 630 U.S. Highway 1, North Brunswick, NJ 08902, 732-729-3777 or toll-free 866-338-7941.
Website: http://www.devry.edu/.

DEVRY UNIVERSITY
Paramus, NJ

CONTACT Financial Aid Office, DeVry University, 35 Plaza, 81 East State Route 4, Suite 102, Paramus, NJ 07652, 201-556-2840 or toll-free 866-338-7941.
Website: http://www.devry.edu/.

DEVRY UNIVERSITY
Charlotte, NC

CONTACT Financial Aid Office, DeVry University, 2015 Ayrsley Town Boulevard, Suite 109, Charlotte, NC 28273-4068, 704-362-2345 or toll-free 866-338-7941.
Website: http://www.devry.edu/.

DEVRY UNIVERSITY
Columbus, OH

Tuition & fees: $16,156 | **Average undergraduate aid package: N/A**

ABOUT THE INSTITUTION Proprietary, coed. *Awards:* certificates, associate, bachelor's, and master's degrees. 9 undergraduate majors. *Total enrollment:* 2,476. Undergraduates: 2,198. Freshmen: 185. Federal methodology is used as a basis for awarding need-based institutional aid.
UNDERGRADUATE EXPENSES for 2013–2014 *Application fee:* $40. *Tuition:* full-time $16,076; part-time $609 per credit hour.
GIFT AID (NEED-BASED) *Scholarships, grants, and awards:* Federal Pell, FSEOG, state, private, college/university gift aid from institutional funds.
GIFT AID (NON-NEED-BASED) *ROTC:* Army.
LOANS *Programs:* Federal Direct (Subsidized and Unsubsidized Stafford, PLUS), Perkins.
APPLYING FOR FINANCIAL AID *Required financial aid form:* FAFSA. *Financial aid deadline:* Continuous. *Notification date:* Continuous.

CONTACT Student Finance Office, DeVry University, 1350 Alum Creek Drive, Columbus, OH 43209-2705, 614-253-7291 or toll-free 866-338-7941. *Fax:* 614-252-4108.
Website: http://www.devry.edu/.

DEVRY UNIVERSITY
Columbus, OH

CONTACT Financial Aid Office, DeVry University, 8800 Lyra Drive, Columbus, OH 43240, 614-854-7500 or toll-free 866-338-7941.
Website: http://www.devry.edu/.

DEVRY UNIVERSITY
Seven Hills, OH

CONTACT Financial Aid Office, DeVry University, The Genesis Building, 6000 Lombardo Center, Suite 200, Seven Hills, OH 44131, 216-328-8754 or toll-free 866-338-7941.
Website: http://www.devry.edu/.

DEVRY UNIVERSITY
Oklahoma City, OK

CONTACT Financial Aid Office, DeVry University, Lakepointe Towers, 4013 Northwest Expressway Street, Suite 100, Oklahoma City, OK 73116, 405-767-9516 or toll-free 866-338-7941.
Website: http://www.devry.edu/.

DEVRY UNIVERSITY
Portland, OR

CONTACT Financial Aid Office, DeVry University, 9755 Southwest Barnes Road, Suite 150, Portland, OR 97225-6651, 503-296-7468 or toll-free 866-338-7941.
Website: http://www.devry.edu/.

DEVRY UNIVERSITY
Fort Washington, PA

CONTACT Financial Aid Office, DeVry University, 1140 Virginia Drive, Fort Washington, PA 19034, 215-591-5700 or toll-free 866-338-7941.
Website: http://www.devry.edu/.

DEVRY UNIVERSITY
King of Prussia, PA

CONTACT Financial Aid Office, DeVry University, 150 Allendale Road, Buillding 3, Suite 3201, King of Prussia, PA 19406-2926, 610-205-3130 or toll-free 866-338-7941.
Website: http://www.devry.edu/.

DEVRY UNIVERSITY
Philadelphia, PA

CONTACT Financial Aid Office, DeVry University, Philadelphia Downtown Center, 1800 JFK Boulevard, Suite 104, Philadelphia, PA 19103-7421 or toll-free 866-338-7941.
Website: http://www.devry.edu/.

DEVRY UNIVERSITY
Pittsburgh, PA

CONTACT Financial Aid Office, DeVry University, FreeMarkets Center, 210 Sixth Avenue, Suite 200, Pittsburgh, PA 15222-2606, 412-642-9072 or toll-free 866-338-7941.
Website: http://www.devry.edu/.

DEVRY UNIVERSITY
Memphis, TN

CONTACT Financial Aid Office, DeVry University, 6401 Poplar Avenue, Suite 600, Memphis, TN 38119, 901-537-2560 or toll-free 866-338-7941.
Website: http://www.devry.edu/.

DEVRY UNIVERSITY
Nashville, TN

CONTACT Financial Aid Office, DeVry University, 3343 Perimeter Hill Drive, Suite 200, Nashville, TN 37211-4147, 615-445-3456 or toll-free 866-338-7941.
Website: http://www.devry.edu/.

DEVRY UNIVERSITY
Houston, TX

CONTACT Financial Aid Office, DeVry University, 11125 Equity Drive, Houston, TX 77041, 713-973-3100 or toll-free 866-338-7941.
Website: http://www.devry.edu/.

DEVRY UNIVERSITY
Irving, TX

Tuition & fees: $16,156	Average undergraduate aid package: N/A

ABOUT THE INSTITUTION Proprietary, coed. *Awards:* certificates, associate, bachelor's, and master's degrees. 12 undergraduate majors. *Total enrollment:* 1,220. Undergraduates: 926. Freshmen: 64. Federal methodology is used as a basis for awarding need-based institutional aid.

UNDERGRADUATE EXPENSES for 2013–2014 *Application fee:* $40. *Tuition:* full-time $16,076; part-time $609 per credit hour.

GIFT AID (NEED-BASED) *Scholarships, grants, and awards:* Federal Pell, FSEOG, state, private, college/university gift aid from institutional funds.

LOANS *Programs:* Federal Direct (Subsidized and Unsubsidized Stafford, PLUS), Perkins.

APPLYING FOR FINANCIAL AID *Required financial aid form:* FAFSA. *Financial aid deadline:* Continuous. *Notification date:* Continuous.

CONTACT Student Finance Office, DeVry University, 4800 Regent Boulevard, Irving, TX 75063-2440, 972-929-9310 or toll-free 866-338-7941.
Website: http://www.devry.edu/.

DEVRY UNIVERSITY
Richardson, TX

CONTACT Financial Aid Office, DeVry University, Richardson Center, 2201 North Central Expressway, Richardson, TX 75080, 972-792-7450 or toll-free 866-338-7941.
Website: http://www.devry.edu/.

DEVRY UNIVERSITY
Sandy, UT

CONTACT Financial Aid Office, DeVry University, 9350 South 150 E, Suite 420, Sandy, UT 84070, 801-565-5110 or toll-free 866-338-7941. *Website:* http://www.devry.edu/.

DEVRY UNIVERSITY
Arlington, VA

CONTACT Roberta McDevitt, Director of Student Finance, DeVry University, 2341 Jefferson Davis Highway, Arlington, VA 22202, 866-338-7932 or toll-free 866-338-7941. *Fax:* 703-414-4040. *Website:* http://www.devry.edu/.

DEVRY UNIVERSITY
Chesapeake, VA

CONTACT Financial Aid Office, DeVry University, 1317 Executive Boulevard, Suite 100, Chesapeake, VA 23320-3671, 757-382-5680 or toll-free 866-338-7941. *Website:* http://www.devry.edu/.

DEVRY UNIVERSITY
Manassas, VA

CONTACT Financial Aid Office, DeVry University, 10432 Balls Ford Road, Suite 130, Manassas, VA 20109-3173, 703-396-6611 or toll-free 866-338-7941. *Website:* http://www.devry.edu/.

DEVRY UNIVERSITY
Bellevue, WA

CONTACT Financial Aid Office, DeVry University, 600 108th Avenue NE, Suite 230, Bellevue, WA 98004-5110, 425-455-2242 or toll-free 866-338-7941. *Website:* http://www.devry.edu/.

DEVRY UNIVERSITY
Federal Way, WA

CONTACT Diane Rooney, Assistant Director of Student Finance, DeVry University, 3600 South 344th Way, Federal Way, WA 98001, 253-943-2800 or toll-free 866-338-7941. *Fax:* 253-943-5503. *Website:* http://www.devry.edu/.

DEVRY UNIVERSITY
Milwaukee, WI

CONTACT Financial Aid Office, DeVry University, 411 East Wisconsin Avenue, Suite 300, Milwaukee, WI 53202, 414-278-7677 or toll-free 866-338-7941. *Website:* http://www.devry.edu/.

DEVRY UNIVERSITY
Waukesha, WI

CONTACT Financial Aid Office, DeVry University, N14 W23833 Stone Ridge Drive, Suite 450, Waukesha, WI 53188-1157, 262-347-2911 or toll-free 866-338-7941. *Website:* http://www.devry.edu/.

DEVRY UNIVERSITY ONLINE
Addison, IL

CONTACT Financial Aid Office, DeVry University Online, 1221 North Swift Road, Addison, IL 60101-6106 or toll-free 866-338-7941. *Website:* http://www.devry.edu/.

DICKINSON COLLEGE
Carlisle, PA

Tuition & fees: $44,551	Average undergraduate aid package: $36,221

ABOUT THE INSTITUTION Independent, coed. *Awards:* bachelor's degrees. 42 undergraduate majors. *Total enrollment:* 2,386. Undergraduates: 2,386. Freshmen: 602. Both federal and institutional methodology are used as a basis for awarding need-based institutional aid.

UNDERGRADUATE EXPENSES for 2013–2014 *Application fee:* $65. *One-time required fee:* $25. *Comprehensive fee:* $55,729 includes full-time tuition ($44,101), mandatory fees ($450), and room and board ($11,178). *College room only:* $5765. Room and board charges vary according to board plan and housing facility. *Part-time tuition:* $5515 per course. *Part-time fees:* $56 per course.

FRESHMAN FINANCIAL AID (Fall 2012, est.) 417 applied for aid; of those 82% were deemed to have need. 98% of freshmen with need received aid; of those 84% had need fully met. *Average percent of need met:* 99% (excluding resources awarded to replace EFC). *Average financial aid package:* $34,269 (excluding resources awarded to replace EFC). 13% of all full-time freshmen had no need and received non-need-based gift aid.

UNDERGRADUATE FINANCIAL AID (Fall 2012, est.) 1,472 applied for aid; of those 90% were deemed to have need. 99% of undergraduates with need received aid; of those 69% had need fully met. *Average percent of need met:* 96% (excluding resources awarded to replace EFC). *Average financial aid package:* $36,221 (excluding resources awarded to replace EFC). 12% of all full-time undergraduates had no need and received non-need-based gift aid.

GIFT AID (NEED-BASED) *Total amount:* $38,183,264 (5% federal, 1% state, 92% institutional, 2% external sources). *Receiving aid:* Freshmen: 54% (322); all full-time undergraduates: 54% (1,269). *Average award:* Freshmen: $29,030; Undergraduates: $30,004. *Scholarships, grants, and awards:* Federal Pell, FSEOG, state, private, college/university gift aid from institutional funds.

GIFT AID (NON-NEED-BASED) *Total amount:* $5,249,459 (21% federal, 68% institutional, 11% external sources). *Receiving aid:* Freshmen: 6% (38). Undergraduates: 4% (100). *Average award:* Freshmen: $10,770. Undergraduates: $11,084. *Scholarships, grants, and awards by category: Academic interests/achievement:* 679 awards ($8,092,911 total): general academic interests/achievements, military science. *Special characteristics:* 31 awards ($1,078,885 total): children and siblings of alumni, children of faculty/staff. *Tuition waivers:* Full or partial for employees or children of employees, senior citizens. *ROTC:* Army.

LOANS *Student loans:* $9,350,517 (69% need-based, 31% non-need-based). 53% of past graduating class borrowed through all loan programs. *Average indebtedness per student:* $25,574. *Average need-based loan:* Freshmen: $4634. Undergraduates: $5487. *Parent loans:* $3,983,381 (18% need-based, 82% non-need-based). *Programs:* Federal Direct (Subsidized and Unsubsidized Stafford, PLUS), Perkins, college/university.

WORK-STUDY *Federal work-study:* Total amount: $2,005,106; 925 jobs averaging $2248. *State or other work-study/employment:* Total amount: $593,223 (74% need-based, 26% non-need-based). 179 part-time jobs averaging $3535.

APPLYING FOR FINANCIAL AID *Required financial aid forms:* FAFSA, CSS Financial Aid PROFILE, state aid form, noncustodial (divorced/separated) parent's statement. *Financial aid deadline:* 2/1 (priority: 11/15). *Notification date:* 3/20. Students must reply by 5/1 or within 2 weeks of notification.

CONTACT Rick A. Heckman, Director of Financial Aid, Dickinson College, PO Box 1773, Carlisle, PA 17013-2896, 717-245-1308 or toll-free 800-644-1773. *Fax:* 717-245-1972. *E-mail:* finaid@dickinson.edu.
Website: http://www.dickinson.edu/.

DICKINSON STATE UNIVERSITY
Dickinson, ND

ABOUT THE INSTITUTION State-supported, coed. *Awards:* certificates, associate, and bachelor's degrees. 43 undergraduate majors. *Total enrollment:* 2,668. Undergraduates: 2,668. Freshmen: 369.

GIFT AID (NEED-BASED) *Scholarships, grants, and awards:* Federal Pell, FSEOG, state, college/university gift aid from institutional funds, National Guard tuition waivers, staff waivers.

GIFT AID (NON-NEED-BASED) *Scholarships, grants, and awards by category:* Academic interests/achievement: agriculture, biological sciences, business, communication, computer science, education, English, foreign languages, general academic interests/achievements, health fields, humanities, mathematics, physical sciences, premedicine, social sciences. *Creative arts/performance:* art/fine arts, creative writing, journalism/publications, music, theater/drama. *Special achievements/activities:* cheerleading/drum major, leadership, rodeo. *Special characteristics:* children of faculty/staff, children with a deceased or disabled parent, ethnic background, general special characteristics, international students, members of minority groups, veterans, veterans' children.

LOANS *Programs:* Perkins, Federal Nursing, state, college/university, Alaska Loans, alternative loans.

WORK-STUDY *Federal work-study:* Total amount: $184,976; jobs available. *State or other work-study/employment:* Part-time jobs available.

APPLYING FOR FINANCIAL AID *Required financial aid form:* FAFSA.

CONTACT Ms. Sandy Klein, Director of Financial Aid, Dickinson State University, 291 Campus Drive, Dickinson, ND 58601-4896, 701-483-2371 or toll-free 800-279-4295. *Fax:* 701-483-2720. *E-mail:* sandy.klein@dickinsonstate.edu.
Website: http://www.dickinsonstate.edu/.

DIGIPEN INSTITUTE OF TECHNOLOGY
Redmond, WA

Tuition & fees: $26,560	Average undergraduate aid package: $7000

ABOUT THE INSTITUTION Proprietary, coed. *Awards:* bachelor's and master's degrees. 5 undergraduate majors. *Total enrollment:* 1,041. Undergraduates: 884. Federal methodology is used as a basis for awarding need-based institutional aid.

UNDERGRADUATE EXPENSES for 2013–2014 *Application fee:* $35. *One-time required fee:* $150. *Comprehensive fee:* $37,001 includes full-time tuition ($26,400), mandatory fees ($160), and room and board ($10,441). Full-time tuition and fees vary according to course load and program. Room and board charges vary according to board plan and housing facility. *Part-time tuition:* $15,460 per year. Part-time tuition and fees vary according to course load and program.

FRESHMAN FINANCIAL AID (Fall 2011) 7 applied for aid; of those 100% were deemed to have need. 100% of freshmen with need received aid. *Average financial aid package:* $5500 (excluding resources awarded to replace EFC). 16% of all full-time freshmen had no need and received non-need-based gift aid.

UNDERGRADUATE FINANCIAL AID (Fall 2011) 11 applied for aid; of those 91% were deemed to have need. 100% of undergraduates with need received aid. *Average financial aid package:* $7000 (excluding resources awarded to replace EFC). 7% of all full-time undergraduates had no need and received non-need-based gift aid.

GIFT AID (NEED-BASED) *Total amount:* $4,210,299 (89% federal, 9% state, 1% institutional, 1% external sources). *Receiving aid:* Freshmen: 5% (7); all full-time undergraduates: 1% (10). *Average award:* Freshmen: $3042; Undergraduates: $3345. *Scholarships, grants, and awards:* Federal Pell, state, private, college/university gift aid from institutional funds.

GIFT AID (NON-NEED-BASED) *Total amount:* $2,725,500 (91% federal, 7% institutional, 2% external sources). *Average award:* Freshmen: $2852. Undergraduates: $2050. *Scholarships, grants, and awards by category:* Academic interests/achievement: 63 awards ($191,084 total): computer science. *Special achievements/activities:* 4 awards ($5500 total): general special achievements/activities. *Special characteristics:* 19 awards ($75,829 total): ethnic background, members of minority groups, veterans. *Tuition waivers:* Full or partial for employees or children of employees.

LOANS *Student loans:* $1,706,232 (100% non-need-based). 17% of past graduating class borrowed through all loan programs. *Average indebtedness per student:* $47,500. *Average need-based loan:* Freshmen: $3909. Undergraduates: $3981. *Parent loans:* $4,957,849 (100% non-need-based). *Programs:* Federal Direct (Subsidized and Unsubsidized Stafford, PLUS), private loans.

WORK-STUDY Federal work-study jobs available. *State or other work-study/employment:* Part-time jobs available.

APPLYING FOR FINANCIAL AID *Required financial aid forms:* FAFSA, institution's own form. *Financial aid deadline:* Continuous. *Notification date:* Continuous beginning 1/1. Students must reply within 2 weeks of notification.

CONTACT Mrs. Kimberly King, Director of Financial Aid, DigiPen Institute of Technology, 9931 Willows Road, Redmond, WA 98052, 425-895-4446. *Fax:* 425-558-0378. *E-mail:* kimking@digipen.edu.
Website: http://www.digipen.edu/.

DILLARD UNIVERSITY
New Orleans, LA

Tuition & fees: $14,850	Average undergraduate aid package: $12,705

ABOUT THE INSTITUTION Independent interdenominational, coed. *Awards:* bachelor's degrees. 24 undergraduate majors. *Total enrollment:* 1,307. Undergraduates: 1,307. Freshmen: 351. Federal methodology is used as a basis for awarding need-based institutional aid.

UNDERGRADUATE EXPENSES for 2013–2014 *Application fee:* $30. *Comprehensive fee:* $23,536 includes full-time tuition ($13,650), mandatory fees ($1200), and room and board ($8686). *College room only:* $5690. Room and board charges vary according to housing facility and student level. Part-time tuition and fees vary according to course load.

FRESHMAN FINANCIAL AID (Fall 2011) 420 applied for aid; of those 96% were deemed to have need. 100% of freshmen with need received aid; of those 9% had need fully met. *Average percent of need met:* 57% (excluding resources awarded to replace EFC). *Average financial aid package:* $11,831 (excluding resources awarded to replace EFC). 6% of all full-time freshmen had no need and received non-need-based gift aid.

UNDERGRADUATE FINANCIAL AID (Fall 2011) 1,324 applied for aid; of those 97% were deemed to have need. 99% of undergraduates with need received aid; of those 7% had need fully met. *Average percent of need met:* 56% (excluding resources awarded to replace EFC). *Average financial aid package:* $12,705 (excluding resources awarded to replace EFC). 4% of all full-time undergraduates had no need and received non-need-based gift aid.

GIFT AID (NEED-BASED) *Total amount:* $10,676,125 (47% federal, 7% state, 27% institutional, 19% external sources). *Receiving aid:* Freshmen: 87% (398); all full-time undergraduates: 89% (1,222). *Average award:* Freshmen: $8692; Undergraduates: $8990. *Scholarships, grants, and awards:* Federal Pell, FSEOG, state, private, college/university gift aid from institutional funds, United Negro College Fund.

GIFT AID (NON-NEED-BASED) *Total amount:* $819,588 (1% federal, 6% state, 67% institutional, 26% external sources). *Receiving aid:* Freshmen: 5% (24). Undergraduates: 5% (72). *Average award:* Freshmen: $6635. Undergraduates: $8870. *Scholarships, grants, and awards by category:* Academic interests/achievement: 587 awards ($2,967,444 total): general academic interests/achievements. *Creative arts/performance:* 27 awards ($92,750 total): art/fine arts, music, theater/drama. *Special characteristics:* 27 awards ($181,282 total): children of faculty/staff. *Tuition waivers:* Full or partial for employees or children of employees. *ROTC:* Army cooperative, Air Force cooperative.

LOANS *Student loans:* $9,955,188 (93% need-based, 7% non-need-based). 98% of past graduating class borrowed through all loan programs. *Average indebtedness per student:* $39,906. *Average need-based loan:* Freshmen: $3375. Undergraduates: $4109. *Parent loans:* $2,669,473 (79% need-based, 21% non-need-based). *Pro-*

grams: Federal Direct (Subsidized and Unsubsidized Stafford, PLUS), Perkins, Federal Nursing, alternative loans.

WORK-STUDY *Federal work-study:* Total amount: $292,818; 257 jobs averaging $1189.

ATHLETIC AWARDS Total amount: $492,791 (77% need-based, 23% non-need-based).

APPLYING FOR FINANCIAL AID *Required financial aid forms:* FAFSA, institution's own form. *Financial aid deadline (priority):* 3/1. *Notification date:* Continuous beginning 3/15. Students must reply within 4 weeks of notification.

CONTACT Mr. Theodis Wright, Director of Financial Aid and Scholarships, Dillard University, 2601 Gentilly Boulevard, New Orleans, LA 70122-3097, 504-816-4677 or toll-free 800-216-8094. *Fax:* 504-816-5456. *E-mail:* twright@dillard.edu. *Website:* http://www.dillard.edu/.

DIXIE STATE COLLEGE OF UTAH
St. George, UT

Tuition & fees (UT res): $4709	Average undergraduate aid package: $7279

ABOUT THE INSTITUTION State-supported, coed. *Awards:* certificates, diplomas, associate, and bachelor's degrees. 34 undergraduate majors. *Total enrollment:* 9,044. Undergraduates: 9,044. Freshmen: 1,957. Federal methodology is used as a basis for awarding need-based institutional aid.

UNDERGRADUATE EXPENSES for 2013–2014 *Application fee:* $35. *Tuition, state resident:* full-time $4089; part-time $144.54 per credit hour. *Tuition, nonresident:* full-time $11,721; part-time $462.53 per credit hour. *Required fees:* full-time $620; $310 per term. Full-time tuition and fees vary according to course load. Part-time tuition and fees vary according to course load. *College room and board:* $4348; *Room only:* $1550. Room and board charges vary according to board plan and housing facility.

FRESHMAN FINANCIAL AID (Fall 2011) 1,202 applied for aid; of those 91% were deemed to have need. 97% of freshmen with need received aid; of those 3% had need fully met. *Average percent of need met:* 34% (excluding resources awarded to replace EFC). *Average financial aid package:* $6379 (excluding resources awarded to replace EFC). 18% of all full-time freshmen had no need and received non-need-based gift aid.

UNDERGRADUATE FINANCIAL AID (Fall 2011) 4,364 applied for aid; of those 92% were deemed to have need. 97% of undergraduates with need received aid; of those 2% had need fully met. *Average percent of need met:* 35% (excluding resources awarded to replace EFC). *Average financial aid package:* $7279 (excluding resources awarded to replace EFC). 11% of all full-time undergraduates had no need and received non-need-based gift aid.

GIFT AID (NEED-BASED) *Total amount:* $21,536,292 (84% federal, 7% state, 5% institutional, 4% external sources). *Receiving aid:* Freshmen: 63% (978); all full-time undergraduates: 66% (3,563). *Average award:* Freshmen: $5096; Undergraduates: $5234. *Scholarships, grants, and awards:* Federal Pell, FSEOG, state, private, college/university gift aid from institutional funds.

GIFT AID (NON-NEED-BASED) *Receiving aid:* Freshmen: 29% (451). Undergraduates: 22% (1,204). *Average award:* Freshmen: $2252. Undergraduates: $2206. *Tuition waivers:* Full or partial for children of alumni, employees or children of employees, senior citizens. *ROTC:* Army.

LOANS *Student loans:* $25,446,929 (50% need-based, 50% non-need-based). 52% of past graduating class borrowed through all loan programs. *Average indebtedness per student:* $22,412. *Average need-based loan:* Freshmen: $3010. Undergraduates: $3818. *Parent loans:* $1,360,152 (100% non-need-based). *Programs:* Federal Direct (Subsidized and Unsubsidized Stafford, PLUS), Perkins.

WORK-STUDY *Federal work-study:* Total amount: $400,372; jobs available. *State or other work-study/employment:* Total amount: $201,281 (100% need-based). Part-time jobs available.

ATHLETIC AWARDS Total amount: $1,275,765 (100% need-based).

APPLYING FOR FINANCIAL AID *Required financial aid forms:* FAFSA, institution's own form. *Financial aid deadline:* 6/30 (priority: 5/1). *Notification date:* Continuous beginning 3/1. Students must reply within 2 weeks of notification.

CONTACT J. D. Robertson, Director of Financial Aid, Dixie State College of Utah, 225 South 700 East, St. George, UT 84770, 435-652-7575. *Fax:* 435-656-4087. *E-mail:* finaid@dixie.edu. *Website:* http://www.dixie.edu/.

DOANE COLLEGE
Crete, NE

Tuition & fees: $25,080	Average undergraduate aid package: $19,073

ABOUT THE INSTITUTION Independent United Church of Christ, coed. *Awards:* certificates, bachelor's, and master's degrees (non-traditional undergraduate programs and graduate programs offered at Lincoln campus). 40 undergraduate majors. *Total enrollment:* 1,149. Undergraduates: 1,149. Freshmen: 337. Both federal and institutional methodology are used as a basis for awarding need-based institutional aid.

UNDERGRADUATE EXPENSES for 2013–2014 *Comprehensive fee:* $32,220 includes full-time tuition ($24,460), mandatory fees ($620), and room and board ($7140). Full-time tuition and fees vary according to location. Room and board charges vary according to board plan, housing facility, and location. *Part-time tuition:* $815 per credit hour. Part-time tuition and fees vary according to course load and location.

FRESHMAN FINANCIAL AID (Fall 2012, est.) 323 applied for aid; of those 87% were deemed to have need. 100% of freshmen with need received aid; of those 30% had need fully met. *Average percent of need met:* 88% (excluding resources awarded to replace EFC). *Average financial aid package:* $19,810 (excluding resources awarded to replace EFC). 7% of all full-time freshmen had no need and received non-need-based gift aid.

UNDERGRADUATE FINANCIAL AID (Fall 2012, est.) 1,014 applied for aid; of those 100% were deemed to have need. 100% of undergraduates with need received aid; of those 26% had need fully met. *Average percent of need met:* 83% (excluding resources awarded to replace EFC). *Average financial aid package:* $19,073 (excluding resources awarded to replace EFC). 7% of all full-time undergraduates had no need and received non-need-based gift aid.

GIFT AID (NEED-BASED) *Total amount:* $4,962,068 (34% federal, 8% state, 46% institutional, 12% external sources). *Receiving aid:* Freshmen: 82% (278); all full-time undergraduates: 78% (885). *Average award:* Freshmen: $15,982; Undergraduates: $14,569. *Scholarships, grants, and awards:* Federal Pell, FSEOG, state, private, college/university gift aid from institutional funds.

GIFT AID (NON-NEED-BASED) *Total amount:* $6,649,468 (4% federal, 96% institutional). *Receiving aid:* Freshmen: 17% (57). Undergraduates: 11% (128). *Average award:* Freshmen: $10,627. Undergraduates: $11,128. *Scholarships, grants, and awards by category:* Academic interests/achievement: general academic interests/achievements. Creative arts/performance: art/fine arts, debating, music, performing arts, theater/drama. Special characteristics: children and siblings of alumni, children of faculty/staff, religious affiliation, siblings of current students. *Tuition waivers:* Full or partial for employees or children of employees, senior citizens. *ROTC:* Army cooperative, Air Force cooperative.

LOANS *Student loans:* $6,673,983 (49% need-based, 51% non-need-based). 80% of past graduating class borrowed through all loan programs. *Average indebtedness per student:* $26,803. *Average need-based loan:* Freshmen: $3437. Undergraduates: $4379. *Parent loans:* $2,947,393 (100% non-need-based). *Programs:* Federal Direct (Subsidized and Unsubsidized Stafford, PLUS), Perkins.

WORK-STUDY *Federal work-study:* Total amount: $537,900; jobs available. *State or other work-study/employment:* Total amount: $340,657 (100% non-need-based). Part-time jobs available.

ATHLETIC AWARDS Total amount: $4,072,576 (59% need-based, 41% non-need-based).

APPLYING FOR FINANCIAL AID *Required financial aid form:* FAFSA. *Financial aid deadline:* Continuous. *Notification date:* Continuous beginning 3/1. Students must reply within 2 weeks of notification.

CONTACT Peggy Tvrdy, Director of Financial Aid, Doane College, 1014 Boswell Avenue, Crete, NE 68333-2430, 402-826-8260 or toll-free 800-333-6263. *Fax:* 402-826-8600. *E-mail:* peggy.tvrdy@doane.edu. *Website:* http://www.doane.edu/.

DOMINICAN COLLEGE
Orangeburg, NY

Tuition & fees: $23,970	Average undergraduate aid package: $15,358

ABOUT THE INSTITUTION Independent, coed. *Awards:* certificates, associate, bachelor's, master's, and doctoral degrees. 35 undergraduate majors. *Total enrollment:* 2,051. Undergraduates: 1,595. Freshmen: 293. Federal methodology is used as a basis for awarding need-based institutional aid.

UNDERGRADUATE EXPENSES for 2013–2014 *Application fee:* $35. *Comprehensive fee:* $35,950 includes full-time tuition ($23,200), mandatory fees ($770), and room and board ($11,980). Full-time tuition and fees vary according to degree level. Room and board charges vary according to board plan and housing facility. *Part-time tuition:* $700 per credit hour. Part-time tuition and fees vary according to degree level and program.

FRESHMAN FINANCIAL AID (Fall 2012, est.) 289 applied for aid; of those 92% were deemed to have need. 100% of freshmen with need received aid; of those 11% had need fully met. *Average percent of need met:* 61% (excluding resources awarded to replace EFC). *Average financial aid package:* $17,762 (excluding resources awarded to replace EFC). 14% of all full-time freshmen had no need and received non-need-based gift aid.

UNDERGRADUATE FINANCIAL AID (Fall 2012, est.) 1,296 applied for aid; of those 92% were deemed to have need. 99% of undergraduates with need received aid; of those 10% had need fully met. *Average percent of need met:* 56% (excluding resources awarded to replace EFC). *Average financial aid package:* $15,358 (excluding resources awarded to replace EFC). 10% of all full-time undergraduates had no need and received non-need-based gift aid.

GIFT AID (NEED-BASED) *Total amount:* $14,780,302 (21% federal, 11% state, 67% institutional, 1% external sources). *Receiving aid:* Freshmen: 91% (266); all full-time undergraduates: 82% (1,114). *Average award:* Freshmen: $14,615; Undergraduates: $12,358. *Scholarships, grants, and awards:* Federal Pell, FSEOG, state, private, college/university gift aid from institutional funds.

GIFT AID (NON-NEED-BASED) *Total amount:* $380,710 (10% state, 69% institutional, 21% external sources). *Receiving aid:* Freshmen: 8% (22). Undergraduates: 6% (86). *Average award:* Freshmen: $6730. Undergraduates: $7041. *Scholarships, grants, and awards by category:* Academic interests/achievement: education, general academic interests/achievements, health fields. *Special characteristics:* children of faculty/staff, general special characteristics, relatives of clergy. *Tuition waivers:* Full or partial for employees or children of employees, senior citizens.

LOANS *Student loans:* $21,320,960 (61% need-based, 39% non-need-based). 95% of past graduating class borrowed through all loan programs. *Average indebtedness per student:* $17,930. *Average need-based loan:* Freshmen: $3259. Undergraduates: $4033. *Parent loans:* $6,054,940 (73% need-based, 27% non-need-based). *Programs:* Perkins, Federal Nursing.

WORK-STUDY *Federal work-study:* Total amount: $336,750; 262 jobs averaging $2000. *State or other work-study/employment:* Total amount: $290,780 (72% need-based, 28% non-need-based). Part-time jobs available.

ATHLETIC AWARDS Total amount: $1,532,775 (60% need-based, 40% non-need-based).

APPLYING FOR FINANCIAL AID *Required financial aid forms:* FAFSA, state aid form. *Financial aid deadline (priority):* 2/15. *Notification date:* Continuous beginning 2/15. Students must reply within 4 weeks of notification.

CONTACT Dr. Stacy Salinas, Director of Financial Aid, Dominican College, 470 Western Highway, Orangeburg, NY 10962-1210, 845-848-7818 or toll-free 866-432-4636. *Fax:* 845-359-4317. *E-mail:* stacy.salinas@dc.edu. *Website:* http://www.dc.edu/.

DOMINICAN UNIVERSITY
River Forest, IL

Tuition & fees: $28,690	Average undergraduate aid package: $20,810

ABOUT THE INSTITUTION Independent Roman Catholic, coed. *Awards:* certificates, bachelor's, master's, and doctoral degrees. 64 undergraduate majors. *Total enrollment:* 3,589. Undergraduates: 1,995. Freshmen: 406. Federal methodology is used as a basis for awarding need-based institutional aid.

UNDERGRADUATE EXPENSES for 2013–2014 *Application fee:* $25. *One-time required fee:* $250. *Comprehensive fee:* $37,508 includes full-time tuition ($28,440), mandatory fees ($250), and room and board ($8818). Full-time tuition and fees vary according to course load. Room and board charges vary according to board plan and housing facility. *Part-time tuition:* $948 per credit hour. *Part-time fees:* $40. Part-time tuition and fees vary according to course load.

FRESHMAN FINANCIAL AID (Fall 2012, est.) 388 applied for aid; of those 96% were deemed to have need. 100% of freshmen with need received aid; of those 13% had need fully met. *Average percent of need met:* 78% (excluding resources awarded to replace EFC). *Average financial aid package:* $23,856 (excluding resources awarded to replace EFC). 7% of all full-time freshmen had no need and received non-need-based gift aid.

UNDERGRADUATE FINANCIAL AID (Fall 2012, est.) 1,632 applied for aid; of those 94% were deemed to have need. 100% of undergraduates with need received aid; of those 11% had need fully met. *Average percent of need met:* 70% (excluding resources awarded to replace EFC). *Average financial aid package:* $20,810 (excluding resources awarded to replace EFC). 7% of all full-time undergraduates had no need and received non-need-based gift aid.

GIFT AID (NEED-BASED) *Total amount:* $20,938,220 (19% federal, 18% state, 62% institutional, 1% external sources). *Receiving aid:* Freshmen: 92% (371); all full-time undergraduates: 86% (1,463). *Average award:* Freshmen: $20,637; Undergraduates: $17,633. *Scholarships, grants, and awards:* Federal Pell, FSEOG, state, private, college/university gift aid from institutional funds.

GIFT AID (NON-NEED-BASED) *Total amount:* $1,413,232 (3% federal, 1% state, 92% institutional, 4% external sources). *Receiving aid:* Freshmen: 10% (41). Undergraduates: 7% (124). *Average award:* Freshmen: $8750. Undergraduates: $8317. *Scholarships, grants, and awards by category:* Academic interests/achievement: 1,653 awards ($19,990,843 total): general academic interests/achievements. Creative arts/performance: 3 awards ($22,500 total): applied art and design, art/fine arts. *Special characteristics:* 224 awards ($568,170 total): children and siblings of alumni, children of faculty/staff, siblings of current students. *Tuition waivers:* Full or partial for employees or children of employees.

LOANS *Student loans:* $12,045,922 (83% need-based, 17% non-need-based). 84% of past graduating class borrowed through all loan programs. *Average indebtedness per student:* $28,281. *Average need-based loan:* Freshmen: $3232. Undergraduates: $4224. *Parent loans:* $1,536,201 (38% need-based, 62% non-need-based). *Programs:* Federal Direct (Subsidized and Unsubsidized Stafford, PLUS).

WORK-STUDY *Federal work-study:* Total amount: $500,841; 365 jobs averaging $2500. *State or other work-study/employment:* Total amount: $370,075 (38% need-based, 62% non-need-based). 157 part-time jobs averaging $2500.

APPLYING FOR FINANCIAL AID *Required financial aid form:* FAFSA. *Financial aid deadline (priority):* 3/1. *Notification date:* Continuous beginning 2/15. Students must reply within 2 weeks of notification.

CONTACT Marie von Ebers, Director of Financial Aid, Dominican University, 7900 West Division Street, River Forest, IL 60305-1099, 708-524-6950 or toll-free 800-828-8475. *Fax:* 708-366-6478. *E-mail:* vonebers@dom.edu. *Website:* http://www.dom.edu/.

DOMINICAN UNIVERSITY OF CALIFORNIA
San Rafael, CA

Tuition & fees: $39,050	Average undergraduate aid package: $25,198

ABOUT THE INSTITUTION Independent Roman Catholic Church, coed. *Awards:* certificates, bachelor's, and master's degrees. 23 undergraduate majors. *Total enrollment:* 2,278. Undergraduates: 1,662. Freshmen: 279. Federal methodology is used as a basis for awarding need-based institutional aid.

UNDERGRADUATE EXPENSES for 2013–2014 *Application fee:* $40. *Comprehensive fee:* $52,990 includes full-time tuition ($38,600), mandatory fees ($450), and room and board ($13,940). *College room only:* $7880. Full-time tuition and fees vary according to course load. Room and board charges vary according to board plan. *Part-time tuition:* $1560 per credit. *Part-time fees:* $150 per term.

FRESHMAN FINANCIAL AID (Fall 2011) 251 applied for aid; of those 92% were deemed to have need. 100% of freshmen with need received aid; of those 4% had need fully met. *Average percent of need met:* 67% (excluding resources awarded to replace EFC). *Average financial aid package:* $28,131 (excluding resources awarded to replace EFC). 15% of all full-time freshmen had no need and received non-need-based gift aid.

UNDERGRADUATE FINANCIAL AID (Fall 2011) 1,181 applied for aid; of those 92% were deemed to have need. 100% of undergraduates with need received aid; of those 4% had need fully met. *Average percent of need met:* 61% (excluding resources awarded to replace EFC). *Average financial aid package:* $25,198 (excluding resources awarded to replace EFC). 16% of all full-time undergraduates had no need and received non-need-based gift aid.

GIFT AID (NEED-BASED) *Total amount:* $22,083,053 (10% federal, 13% state, 76% institutional, 1% external sources). *Receiving aid:* Freshmen: 82% (230); all full-time undergraduates: 82% (1,078). *Average award:* Freshmen: $24,067; Undergraduates: $20,882. *Scholarships, grants, and awards:* Federal Pell, FSEOG, state, private, college/university gift aid from institutional funds, Scholarships for Disadvantaged Students (SDS).

GIFT AID (NON-NEED-BASED) *Total amount:* $2,950,266 (96% institutional, 4% external sources). *Receiving aid:* Freshmen: 6% (17). Undergraduates: 4% (52). *Average award:* Freshmen: $13,354. Undergraduates: $11,639. *Scholarships, grants, and awards by category:* Academic interests/achievement: general academic interests/achievements. Creative arts/performance: music. Special achievements/activities: community service, leadership. Special characteristics: adult students, children and siblings of alumni, children of faculty/staff, international students, members of minority groups, veterans, veterans' children. *Tuition waivers:* Full or partial for employees or children of employees.

LOANS *Student loans:* $12,546,653 (79% need-based, 21% non-need-based). 89% of past graduating class borrowed through all loan programs. *Average indebtedness per student:* $39,125. *Average need-based loan:* Freshmen: $3831. Undergraduates: $4608. *Parent loans:* $5,656,410 (57% need-based, 43% non-need-based). *Programs:* Federal Direct (Subsidized and Unsubsidized Stafford, PLUS), Perkins, private loans.

WORK-STUDY *Federal work-study:* Total amount: $321,046; jobs available. *State or other work-study/employment:* Total amount: $181,867 (100% non-need-based). Part-time jobs available.

ATHLETIC AWARDS Total amount: $682,975 (76% need-based, 24% non-need-based).

APPLYING FOR FINANCIAL AID *Required financial aid forms:* FAFSA, institution's own form. *Financial aid deadline (priority):* 3/2. *Notification date:* Continuous beginning 3/15. Students must reply within 2 weeks of notification.

CONTACT Ms. Shanon Little, Director of Financial Aid, Dominican University of California, 50 Acacia Avenue, San Rafael, CA 94901-2298, 415-257-1302 or toll-free 888-323-6763. Fax: 415-485-3294. E-mail: shanon.little@dominican.edu. Website: http://www.dominican.edu/.

DORDT COLLEGE
Sioux Center, IA

Tuition & fees: $25,520	Average undergraduate aid package: $20,194

ABOUT THE INSTITUTION Independent Christian Reformed, coed. *Awards:* associate, bachelor's, and master's degrees. 85 undergraduate majors. *Total enrollment:* 1,400. Undergraduates: 1,379. Freshmen: 342. Federal methodology is used as a basis for awarding need-based institutional aid.

UNDERGRADUATE EXPENSES for 2013–2014 *Comprehensive fee:* $32,750 includes full-time tuition ($25,100), mandatory fees ($420), and room and board ($7230). *College room only:* $3700. Full-time tuition and fees vary according to course load. Room and board charges vary according to board plan and housing facility. *Part-time tuition:* $960 per quarter hour.

FRESHMAN FINANCIAL AID (Fall 2012, est.) 297 applied for aid; of those 85% were deemed to have need. 100% of freshmen with need received aid; of those 31% had need fully met. *Average percent of need met:* 80% (excluding resources awarded to replace EFC). *Average financial aid package:* $21,689 (excluding resources awarded to replace EFC). 20% of all full-time freshmen had no need and received non-need-based gift aid.

UNDERGRADUATE FINANCIAL AID (Fall 2012, est.) 980 applied for aid; of those 88% were deemed to have need. 100% of undergraduates with need received aid; of those 28% had need fully met. *Average percent of need met:* 78%

(excluding resources awarded to replace EFC). *Average financial aid package:* $20,194 (excluding resources awarded to replace EFC). 19% of all full-time undergraduates had no need and received non-need-based gift aid.

GIFT AID (NEED-BASED) *Total amount:* $14,500,890 (13% federal, 8% state, 72% institutional, 7% external sources). *Receiving aid:* Freshmen: 74% (251); all full-time undergraduates: 74% (862). *Average award:* Freshmen: $15,042; Undergraduates: $13,426. *Scholarships, grants, and awards:* Federal Pell, FSEOG, state, private, college/university gift aid from institutional funds.

GIFT AID (NON-NEED-BASED) *Total amount:* $2,333,077 (93% institutional, 7% external sources). *Receiving aid:* Freshmen: 13% (46). Undergraduates: 10% (114). *Average award:* Freshmen: $17,434. Undergraduates: $17,166. *Scholarships, grants, and awards by category:* Academic interests/achievement: agriculture, biological sciences, business, communication, computer science, education, engineering/technologies, English, foreign languages, general academic interests/achievements, humanities, mathematics, physical sciences, premedicine, religion/biblical studies, social sciences. Creative arts/performance: journalism/publications, music, theater/drama. Special achievements/activities: general special achievements/activities, leadership. Special characteristics: children and siblings of alumni, children of faculty/staff, general special characteristics, handicapped students, international students, local/state students, members of minority groups, out-of-state students, religious affiliation. *Tuition waivers:* Full or partial for employees or children of employees, senior citizens.

LOANS *Student loans:* $9,999,141 (91% need-based, 9% non-need-based). 81% of past graduating class borrowed through all loan programs. *Average indebtedness per student:* $21,859. *Average need-based loan:* Freshmen: $5260. Undergraduates: $5297. *Parent loans:* $5,893,655 (87% need-based, 13% non-need-based). *Programs:* Federal Direct (Subsidized and Unsubsidized Stafford, PLUS), Perkins, state, college/university, alternative loans.

WORK-STUDY *Federal work-study:* Total amount: $688,440; 446 jobs averaging $1500. *State or other work-study/employment:* Total amount: $1,125,340 (76% need-based, 24% non-need-based). 497 part-time jobs averaging $1500.

ATHLETIC AWARDS Total amount: $1,986,125 (78% need-based, 22% non-need-based).

APPLYING FOR FINANCIAL AID *Required financial aid forms:* FAFSA, institution's own form. *Financial aid deadline (priority):* 4/1. *Notification date:* Continuous beginning 3/1. Students must reply within 3 weeks of notification.

CONTACT Mr. Michael Epema, Director of Financial Aid, Dordt College, 498 4th Avenue NE, Sioux Center, IA 51250-1697, 712-722-6087 Ext. 6082 or toll-free 800-343-6738. Fax: 712-722-6035. E-mail: michael.epema@dordt.edu. Website: http://www.dordt.edu/.

DOWLING COLLEGE
Oakdale, NY

ABOUT THE INSTITUTION Independent, coed. *Awards:* certificates, bachelor's, master's, and doctoral degrees. 50 undergraduate majors. *Total enrollment:* 4,416. Undergraduates: 2,883. Freshmen: 358.

GIFT AID (NEED-BASED) *Scholarships, grants, and awards:* Federal Pell, FSEOG, state, private, college/university gift aid from institutional funds.

GIFT AID (NON-NEED-BASED) *Scholarships, grants, and awards by category:* Academic interests/achievement: business, education, general academic interests/achievements, mathematics, social sciences. Special achievements/activities: general special achievements/activities. Special characteristics: adult students, children and siblings of alumni, children of educators, children of faculty/staff, children of public servants, children of union members/company employees, children of workers in trades, ethnic background, first-generation college students, general special characteristics, local/state students, members of minority groups, previous college experience, public servants, siblings of current students, twins, veterans.

LOANS *Programs:* Federal Direct (Subsidized and Unsubsidized Stafford, PLUS), Perkins, state, private loans.

APPLYING FOR FINANCIAL AID *Required financial aid forms:* FAFSA, state aid form.

CONTACT Ms. Denise Scalzo, Director of Student Financial Services, Dowling College, 150 Idle Hour Boulevard, Oakdale, NY 11769-1999, 631-244-3159 or toll-free 800-DOWLING. E-mail: scalzod@dowling.edu. Website: http://www.dowling.edu/.

DRAKE UNIVERSITY
Des Moines, IA

Tuition & fees: $30,880	Average undergraduate aid package: $21,650

ABOUT THE INSTITUTION Independent, coed. *Awards:* certificates, bachelor's, master's, and doctoral degrees. 66 undergraduate majors. *Total enrollment:* 5,270. Undergraduates: 3,365. Freshmen: 848. Federal methodology is used as a basis for awarding need-based institutional aid.

UNDERGRADUATE EXPENSES for 2013–2014 *Application fee:* $25. *Comprehensive fee:* $39,580 includes full-time tuition ($30,734), mandatory fees ($146), and room and board ($8700). *College room only:* $4470. Full-time tuition and fees vary according to course load, program, and student level. Room and board charges vary according to board plan. *Part-time tuition:* $610 per hour. Part-time tuition and fees vary according to class time and program.

FRESHMAN FINANCIAL AID (Fall 2012, est.) 713 applied for aid; of those 80% were deemed to have need. 100% of freshmen with need received aid; of those 26% had need fully met. *Average percent of need met:* 74% (excluding resources awarded to replace EFC). *Average financial aid package:* $21,359 (excluding resources awarded to replace EFC). 27% of all full-time freshmen had no need and received non-need-based gift aid.

UNDERGRADUATE FINANCIAL AID (Fall 2012, est.) 2,341 applied for aid; of those 83% were deemed to have need. 100% of undergraduates with need received aid; of those 26% had need fully met. *Average percent of need met:* 75% (excluding resources awarded to replace EFC). *Average financial aid package:* $21,650 (excluding resources awarded to replace EFC). 32% of all full-time undergraduates had no need and received non-need-based gift aid.

GIFT AID (NEED-BASED) *Total amount:* $28,282,377 (12% federal, 5% state, 80% institutional, 3% external sources). *Receiving aid:* Freshmen: 66% (562); all full-time undergraduates: 60% (1,898). *Average award:* Freshmen: $15,215; Undergraduates: $14,719. *Scholarships, grants, and awards:* Federal Pell, FSEOG, state, private, college/university gift aid from institutional funds.

GIFT AID (NON-NEED-BASED) *Total amount:* $15,087,201 (2% federal, 95% institutional, 3% external sources). *Receiving aid:* Freshmen: 12% (104). Undergraduates: 10% (302). *Average award:* Freshmen: $11,692. Undergraduates: $11,607. *Scholarships, grants, and awards by category:* Academic interests/achievement: 2,510 awards ($26,512,757 total): general academic interests/achievements. Creative arts/performance: 309 awards ($1,481,023 total): art/fine arts, music, theater/drama. Special characteristics: 238 awards ($355,764 total): children and siblings of alumni, international students. *Tuition waivers:* Full or partial for children of alumni, employees or children of employees, senior citizens. *ROTC:* Army, Air Force cooperative.

LOANS *Student loans:* $28,952,281 (47% need-based, 53% non-need-based). 65% of past graduating class borrowed through all loan programs. *Average indebtedness per student:* $32,114. *Average need-based loan:* Freshmen: $3098. Undergraduates: $4554. *Parent loans:* $41,452,151 (21% need-based, 79% non-need-based). *Programs:* Federal Direct (Subsidized and Unsubsidized Stafford, PLUS), Perkins, college/university, Federal Health Professions Loans.

WORK-STUDY *Federal work-study:* Total amount: $3,024,122; 1,616 jobs averaging $1871.

ATHLETIC AWARDS Total amount: $3,973,778 (33% need-based, 67% non-need-based).

APPLYING FOR FINANCIAL AID *Required financial aid form:* FAFSA. *Financial aid deadline:* Continuous. *Notification date:* Continuous beginning 3/1. Students must reply by 5/1 or within 3 weeks of notification.

CONTACT Office of Student Financial Planning, Drake University, 2507 University Avenue, Des Moines, IA 50311-4516, 800-443-7253 Ext. 2905 or toll-free 800-44-DRAKE Ext. 3181. *Fax:* 515-271-4042. *E-mail:* financialaid@drake.edu. *Website:* http://www.drake.edu/.

DREW UNIVERSITY
Madison, NJ

Tuition & fees: $44,068	Average undergraduate aid package: $30,732

ABOUT THE INSTITUTION Independent United Methodist Church, coed. *Awards:* certificates, master's, and doctoral degrees. 42 undergraduate majors. *Total enrollment:* 2,447. Undergraduates: 1,640. Freshmen: 363. Federal methodology is used as a basis for awarding need-based institutional aid.

UNDERGRADUATE EXPENSES for 2013–2014 *Application fee:* $60. *Comprehensive fee:* $56,012 includes full-time tuition ($42,936), mandatory fees ($1132), and room and board ($11,944). *College room only:* $7684. Full-time tuition and fees vary according to course load. Room and board charges vary according to board plan and housing facility. *Part-time tuition:* $1789 per credit hour. Part-time tuition and fees vary according to course load. *Payment plan:* Tuition prepayment.

UNDERGRADUATE FINANCIAL AID (Fall 2011) 1,248 applied for aid; of those 90% were deemed to have need. 100% of undergraduates with need received aid; of those 11% had need fully met. *Average percent of need met:* 72% (excluding resources awarded to replace EFC). *Average financial aid package:* $30,732 (excluding resources awarded to replace EFC). 26% of all full-time undergraduates had no need and received non-need-based gift aid.

GIFT AID (NEED-BASED) *Total amount:* $29,041,364 (8% federal, 10% state, 80% institutional, 2% external sources). *Receiving aid:* All full-time undergraduates: 68% (1,120). *Average award:* Undergraduates: $25,930. *Scholarships, grants, and awards:* Federal Pell, FSEOG, state, private, college/university gift aid from institutional funds.

GIFT AID (NON-NEED-BASED) *Total amount:* $6,094,535 (94% institutional, 6% external sources). *Receiving aid:* Undergraduates: 5% (83). *Average award:* Undergraduates: $11,778. *Scholarships, grants, and awards by category:* Academic interests/achievement: general academic interests/achievements. Creative arts/performance: general creative arts/performance. Special characteristics: members of minority groups. *Tuition waivers:* Full or partial for employees or children of employees, senior citizens.

LOANS *Student loans:* $7,521,692 (58% need-based, 42% non-need-based). 66% of past graduating class borrowed through all loan programs. *Average indebtedness per student:* $24,470. *Average need-based loan:* Undergraduates: $4740. *Parent loans:* $8,654,200 (54% need-based, 46% non-need-based). *Programs:* Federal Direct (Subsidized and Unsubsidized Stafford, PLUS), Perkins, state.

WORK-STUDY *Federal work-study:* Total amount: $308,607; jobs available. *State or other work-study/employment:* Total amount: $363,069 (84% need-based, 16% non-need-based). Part-time jobs available.

APPLYING FOR FINANCIAL AID *Required financial aid form:* FAFSA. *Financial aid deadline:* 2/15. *Notification date:* 3/30. Students must reply by 5/1.

CONTACT Renee Volak, Director of Financial Assistance, Drew University, 36 Madison Avenue, Madison, NJ 07940-1493, 973-408-3112. *Fax:* 973-408-3188. *E-mail:* finaid@drew.edu. *Website:* http://www.drew.edu/.

DREXEL UNIVERSITY
Philadelphia, PA

CONTACT Helen Gourousis, Director of Financial Aid, Drexel University, 3141 Chestnut Street, Philadelphia, PA 19104-2875, 215-895-5928 or toll-free 800-2-DREXEL. *Fax:* 215-895-6903. *E-mail:* gouroush@drexel.edu. *Website:* http://www.drexel.edu/.

DRURY UNIVERSITY
Springfield, MO

Tuition & fees: $22,415	Average undergraduate aid package: $8465

ABOUT THE INSTITUTION Independent, coed. *Awards:* bachelor's and master's degrees (also offers evening program with significant enrollment not reflected in profile). 45 undergraduate majors. *Total enrollment:* 2,060. Undergraduates: 1,607. Freshmen: 364. Federal methodology is used as a basis for awarding need-based institutional aid.

UNDERGRADUATE EXPENSES for 2013–2014 *Application fee:* $25. *One-time required fee:* $150. *Comprehensive fee:* $30,615 includes full-time tuition ($21,700), mandatory fees ($715), and room and board ($8200). Full-time tuition and fees vary according to class time. Room and board charges vary according to board plan and housing facility. Part-time tuition and fees vary according to class time. *Payment plan:* Tuition prepayment.

FRESHMAN FINANCIAL AID (Fall 2012, est.) 346 applied for aid; of those 88% were deemed to have need. 100% of freshmen with need received aid; of those 87% had need fully met. *Average percent of need met:* 81% (excluding resources awarded to replace EFC). *Average financial aid package:* $7935 (excluding resources awarded to replace EFC). 4% of all full-time freshmen had no need and received non-need-based gift aid.

UNDERGRADUATE FINANCIAL AID (Fall 2012, est.) 1,562 applied for aid; of those 98% were deemed to have need. 100% of undergraduates with need received aid; of those 94% had need fully met. *Average percent of need met:* 83% (excluding resources awarded to replace EFC). *Average financial aid package:* $8465 (excluding resources awarded to replace EFC). 4% of all full-time undergraduates had no need and received non-need-based gift aid.

GIFT AID (NEED-BASED) *Total amount:* $17,081,391 (31% federal, 6% state, 60% institutional, 3% external sources). *Receiving aid:* Freshmen: 79% (287); all full-time undergraduates: 94% (1,514). *Average award:* Freshmen: $6255; Undergraduates: $7075. *Scholarships, grants, and awards:* Federal Pell, FSEOG, state, private, college/university gift aid from institutional funds.

GIFT AID (NON-NEED-BASED) *Total amount:* $3,636,248 (6% state, 90% institutional, 4% external sources). *Receiving aid:* Freshmen: 77% (279). Undergraduates: 91% (1,464). *Average award:* Freshmen: $4075. Undergraduates: $4684. *Scholarships, grants, and awards by category:* Academic interests/achievement: 1,464 awards ($6,409,441 total): architecture, biological sciences, business, communication, computer science, education, English, foreign languages, general academic interests/achievements, health fields, humanities, mathematics, physical sciences, premedicine, social sciences. *Creative arts/performance:* 216 awards ($489,510 total): art/fine arts, creative writing, debating, music, theater/drama. *Special achievements/activities:* 174 awards ($168,500 total): cheerleading/drum major, leadership, religious involvement. *Special characteristics:* 178 awards ($564,885 total): children and siblings of alumni, children of faculty/staff, ethnic background, international students, members of minority groups, relatives of clergy, religious affiliation, veterans. *Tuition waivers:* Full or partial for minority students, children of alumni, employees or children of employees. *ROTC:* Army cooperative.

LOANS *Student loans:* $22,055,459 (91% need-based, 9% non-need-based). 68% of past graduating class borrowed through all loan programs. *Average indebtedness per student:* $21,550. *Average need-based loan:* Freshmen: $4500. Undergraduates: $6500. *Parent loans:* $2,223,364 (100% need-based). *Programs:* Federal Direct (Subsidized and Unsubsidized Stafford, PLUS), Perkins.

WORK-STUDY *Federal work-study:* Total amount: $334,462; 332 jobs averaging $2500. *State or other work-study/employment:* Total amount: $187,500 (100% non-need-based). Part-time jobs available.

ATHLETIC AWARDS Total amount: $2,874,752 (17% need-based, 83% non-need-based).

APPLYING FOR FINANCIAL AID *Required financial aid forms:* FAFSA, institution's own form. *Financial aid deadline (priority):* 2/15. *Notification date:* Continuous beginning 3/1. Students must reply by 3/1 or within 2 weeks of notification.

CONTACT Ms. Annette Avery, Director of Financial Aid, Drury University, 900 North Benton Avenue, Springfield, MO 65802-3791, 417-873-7312 or toll-free 800-922-2274. *Fax:* 417-873-6906. *E-mail:* aavery@drury.edu. *Website:* http://www.drury.edu/.

DUKE UNIVERSITY
Durham, NC

Tuition & fees: N/R	Average undergraduate aid package: $42,391

ABOUT THE INSTITUTION Independent United Methodist Church, coed. 45 undergraduate majors. Both federal and institutional methodology are used as a basis for awarding need-based institutional aid.

FRESHMAN FINANCIAL AID (Fall 2012, est.) 948 applied for aid; of those 84% were deemed to have need. 100% of freshmen with need received aid; of those 100% had need fully met. *Average percent of need met:* 100% (excluding resources awarded to replace EFC). *Average financial aid package:* $41,979 (excluding resources awarded to replace EFC). 4% of all full-time freshmen had no need and received non-need-based gift aid.

UNDERGRADUATE FINANCIAL AID (Fall 2012, est.) 3,387 applied for aid; of those 90% were deemed to have need. 100% of undergraduates with need received aid; of those 100% had need fully met. *Average percent of need met:* 100% (excluding resources awarded to replace EFC). *Average financial aid package:* $42,391 (excluding resources awarded to replace EFC). 4% of all full-time undergraduates had no need and received non-need-based gift aid.

GIFT AID (NEED-BASED) *Total amount:* $109,842,397 (4% federal, 1% state, 91% institutional, 4% external sources). *Receiving aid:* Freshmen: 45% (761); all full-time undergraduates: 43% (2,886). *Average award:* Freshmen: $37,533; Undergraduates: $37,507. *Scholarships, grants, and awards:* Federal Pell, FSEOG, state, private, college/university gift aid from institutional funds.

GIFT AID (NON-NEED-BASED) *Total amount:* $13,281,439 (71% institutional, 29% external sources). *Receiving aid:* Freshmen: 5% (78). Undergraduates: 3% (201). *Average award:* Freshmen: $54,947. Undergraduates: $54,637. *Scholarships, grants, and awards by category:* Academic interests/achievement: 128 awards ($7,037,498 total): general academic interests/achievements, mathematics. *Creative arts/performance:* creative writing. *Special achievements/activities:* 86 awards ($4,673,006 total): general special achievements/activities, leadership. *Special characteristics:* 51 awards ($2,805,158 total): children and siblings of alumni, ethnic background, local/state students.

LOANS *Student loans:* $14,706,377 (83% need-based, 17% non-need-based). 39% of past graduating class borrowed through all loan programs. *Average indebtedness per student:* $19,506. *Average need-based loan:* Freshmen: $3502. Undergraduates: $3657. *Parent loans:* $7,555,732 (69% need-based, 31% non-need-based). *Programs:* Federal Direct (Subsidized and Unsubsidized Stafford, PLUS), Perkins, college/university, alternative loans.

WORK-STUDY *Federal work-study:* Total amount: $3,877,045; 2,079 jobs averaging $1864. *State or other work-study/employment:* Total amount: $1,568,682 (63% need-based, 37% non-need-based). 583 part-time jobs averaging $1685.

ATHLETIC AWARDS Total amount: $15,097,742 (23% need-based, 77% non-need-based).

APPLYING FOR FINANCIAL AID *Required financial aid forms:* FAFSA, CSS Financial Aid PROFILE, noncustodial (divorced/separated) parent's statement, business/farm supplement, federal income tax form(s), W-2 forms. *Financial aid deadline:* 3/1. *Notification date:* 4/1. Students must reply by 5/1.

CONTACT Alison Rabil, Director of Financial Aid, Duke University, 2127 Campus Drive Annex, Box 90397, Durham, NC 27708-0397, 919-684-6225. *Fax:* 919-660-9811. *E-mail:* finaid@duke.edu. *Website:* http://www.duke.edu/.

DUNLAP-STONE UNIVERSITY
Phoenix, AZ

ABOUT THE INSTITUTION Proprietary, coed. 1 undergraduate major.

CONTACT Office of the Bursar, Dunlap-Stone University, 19820 North 7th Street, Suite #100, Phoenix, AZ 85024, 800-474-8013. *E-mail:* info@expandglobal.com. *Website:* http://www.dunlap-stone.edu/.

DUQUESNE UNIVERSITY
Pittsburgh, PA

Tuition & fees: $30,034	Average undergraduate aid package: $22,520

ABOUT THE INSTITUTION Independent Roman Catholic, coed. *Awards:* certificates, bachelor's, master's, and doctoral degrees. 71 undergraduate majors. *Total enrollment:* 9,956. Undergraduates: 5,832. Freshmen: 1,526. Federal methodology is used as a basis for awarding need-based institutional aid.

UNDERGRADUATE EXPENSES for 2013–2014 *Application fee:* $50. *Comprehensive fee:* $40,232 includes full-time tuition ($27,668), mandatory fees ($2366), and room and board ($10,198). *College room only:* $5562. Full-time tuition and fees vary according to program. Room and board charges vary according to board plan and housing facility. *Part-time tuition:* $902 per credit. *Part-time fees:* $92 per credit. Part-time tuition and fees vary according to program.

FRESHMAN FINANCIAL AID (Fall 2011) 1,193 applied for aid; of those 83% were deemed to have need. 100% of freshmen with need received aid; of those 23% had need fully met. *Average percent of need met:* 89% (excluding resources awarded to replace EFC). *Average financial aid package:* $22,813 (excluding resources awarded to replace EFC). 24% of all full-time freshmen had no need and received non-need-based gift aid.

UNDERGRADUATE FINANCIAL AID (Fall 2011) 4,586 applied for aid; of those 85% were deemed to have need. 100% of undergraduates with need received aid; of those 25% had need fully met. *Average percent of need met:* 78% (excluding resources awarded to replace EFC). *Average financial aid package:* $22,520 (excluding resources awarded to replace EFC). 24% of all full-time undergraduates had no need and received non-need-based gift aid.

GIFT AID (NEED-BASED) *Total amount:* $56,300,047 (9% federal, 10% state, 76% institutional, 5% external sources). *Receiving aid:* Freshmen: 74% (981); all full-time undergraduates: 70% (3,827). *Average award:* Freshmen: $16,383; Undergraduates: $15,343. *Scholarships, grants, and awards:* Federal Pell, FSEOG, state, private, college/university gift aid from institutional funds, United Negro College Fund.

GIFT AID (NON-NEED-BASED) *Total amount:* $12,825,548 (1% state, 93% institutional, 6% external sources). *Receiving aid:* Freshmen: 73% (970). Undergraduates: 66% (3,591). *Average award:* Freshmen: $10,216. Undergraduates: $8990. *Scholarships, grants, and awards by category:* Academic interests/achievement: 5,074 awards ($41,072,067 total): general academic interests/achievements. Creative arts/performance: 234 awards ($1,650,883 total): dance, music. Special characteristics: 1,176 awards ($11,412,738 total): children and siblings of alumni, children of faculty/staff, ethnic background, general special characteristics, international students, members of minority groups, relatives of clergy, religious affiliation. *Tuition waivers:* Full or partial for employees or children of employees, senior citizens. *ROTC:* Army, Naval cooperative, Air Force cooperative.

LOANS *Student loans:* $46,683,000 (89% need-based, 11% non-need-based). 80% of past graduating class borrowed through all loan programs. *Average indebtedness per student:* $25,228. *Average need-based loan:* Freshmen: $3726. Undergraduates: $3081. *Parent loans:* $16,094,330 (90% need-based, 10% non-need-based). *Programs:* Federal Direct (Subsidized and Unsubsidized Stafford, PLUS), Perkins, Federal Nursing, private loans.

WORK-STUDY *Federal work-study:* Total amount: $8,649,510; 3,332 jobs averaging $2913.

ATHLETIC AWARDS Total amount: $5,810,823 (63% need-based, 37% non-need-based).

APPLYING FOR FINANCIAL AID *Required financial aid forms:* FAFSA, institution's own form. *Financial aid deadline:* 5/1. *Notification date:* Continuous beginning 3/1. Students must reply by 5/1 or within 3 weeks of notification.

CONTACT Mr. Richard C. Esposito, Director of Financial Aid, Duquesne University, 600 Forbes Avenue, Pittsburgh, PA 15282-0299, 412-396-6607 or toll-free 800-456-0590. *Fax:* 412-396-5284. *E-mail:* esposito@duq.edu. *Website:* http://www.duq.edu/.

D'YOUVILLE COLLEGE
Buffalo, NY

Tuition & fees: $22,240	Average undergraduate aid package: $17,124

ABOUT THE INSTITUTION Independent, coed. 24 undergraduate majors. Federal methodology is used as a basis for awarding need-based institutional aid.

UNDERGRADUATE EXPENSES for 2013–2014 *Comprehensive fee:* $32,490 includes full-time tuition ($21,930), mandatory fees ($310), and room and board ($10,250). Full-time tuition and fees vary according to course load, degree level, and program. Room and board charges vary according to board plan and housing facility. *Part-time tuition:* $680 per credit hour. *Part-time fees:* $3 per credit hour; $55 per term. Part-time tuition and fees vary according to course load, degree level, and program. *Payment plan:* Guaranteed tuition.

FRESHMAN FINANCIAL AID (Fall 2012, est.) 227 applied for aid; of those 87% were deemed to have need. 100% of freshmen with need received aid; of those 30% had need fully met. *Average percent of need met:* 76% (excluding resources awarded to replace EFC). *Average financial aid package:* $17,496 (excluding resources awarded to replace EFC). 10% of all full-time freshmen had no need and received non-need-based gift aid.

UNDERGRADUATE FINANCIAL AID (Fall 2012, est.) 898 applied for aid; of those 89% were deemed to have need. 100% of undergraduates with need received aid; of those 24% had need fully met. *Average percent of need met:* 70% (excluding resources awarded to replace EFC). *Average financial aid package:* $17,124 (excluding resources awarded to replace EFC). 9% of all full-time undergraduates had no need and received non-need-based gift aid.

GIFT AID (NEED-BASED) *Total amount:* $9,060,653 (18% federal, 13% state, 67% institutional, 2% external sources). *Receiving aid:* Freshmen: 76% (198); all full-time undergraduates: 82% (781). *Average award:* Freshmen: $13,998; Undergraduates: $13,351. *Scholarships, grants, and awards:* Federal Pell, FSEOG, state, private, college/university gift aid from institutional funds.

GIFT AID (NON-NEED-BASED) *Total amount:* $1,042,617 (2% state, 95% institutional, 3% external sources). *Receiving aid:* Freshmen: 10% (27). Undergraduates: 9% (86). *Average award:* Freshmen: $8661. Undergraduates: $8758. *Scholarships, grants, and awards by category:* Academic interests/achievement: biological sciences, business, education, English, general academic interests/achievements, health fields, humanities, international studies, mathematics, premedicine, social sciences. Special characteristics: children and siblings of alumni, children of faculty/staff, veterans. *Tuition waivers:* Full or partial for children of alumni, employees or children of employees, senior citizens.

LOANS *Student loans:* $7,801,527 (74% need-based, 26% non-need-based). 85% of past graduating class borrowed through all loan programs. *Average indebtedness per student:* $33,411. *Average need-based loan:* Freshmen: $3549. Undergraduates: $4286. *Parent loans:* $784,010 (51% need-based, 49% non-need-based). *Programs:* Federal Direct (Subsidized and Unsubsidized Stafford, PLUS), Perkins, Federal Nursing, college/university.

WORK-STUDY *Federal work-study:* Total amount: $234,565; 267 jobs averaging $1500. *State or other work-study/employment:* Total amount: $127,363 (100% non-need-based). 169 part-time jobs averaging $750.

APPLYING FOR FINANCIAL AID *Required financial aid forms:* FAFSA, state aid form. *Financial aid deadline (priority):* 2/15. *Notification date:* Continuous beginning 3/15. Students must reply within 2 weeks of notification.

CONTACT Ms. Lorraine A. Metz, Director of Financial Aid, D'Youville College, 320 Porter Avenue, Buffalo, NY 14201-1084, 716-829-7500 or toll-free 800-777-3921. *Fax:* 716-829-7779. *E-mail:* metzla@dyc.edu. *Website:* http://www.dyc.edu/.

EARLHAM COLLEGE
Richmond, IN

Tuition & fees: $41,450	Average undergraduate aid package: $36,001

ABOUT THE INSTITUTION Independent Society of Friends, coed. *Awards:* bachelor's and master's degrees. 36 undergraduate majors. *Total enrollment:* 1,211. Undergraduates: 1,087. Freshmen: 286. Federal methodology is used as a basis for awarding need-based institutional aid.

UNDERGRADUATE EXPENSES for 2013–2014 *Comprehensive fee:* $49,710 includes full-time tuition ($40,600), mandatory fees ($850), and room and board ($8260). *College room only:* $4190. Room and board charges vary according to board plan. *Part-time tuition:* $1353 per credit. *Payment plan:* Tuition pre-payment.

FRESHMAN FINANCIAL AID (Fall 2011) 162 applied for aid; of those 89% were deemed to have need. 100% of freshmen with need received aid; of those 44% had need fully met. *Average percent of need met:* 96% (excluding resources awarded to replace EFC). *Average financial aid package:* $37,079 (excluding resources awarded to replace EFC). 13% of all full-time freshmen had no need and received non-need-based gift aid.

UNDERGRADUATE FINANCIAL AID (Fall 2011) 719 applied for aid; of those 92% were deemed to have need. 100% of undergraduates with need received aid; of those 45% had need fully met. *Average percent of need met:* 96% (excluding resources awarded to replace EFC). *Average financial aid package:* $36,001 (excluding resources awarded to replace EFC). 16% of all full-time undergraduates had no need and received non-need-based gift aid.

GIFT AID (NEED-BASED) *Total amount:* $23,989,761 (7% federal, 2% state, 90% institutional, 1% external sources). *Receiving aid:* Freshmen: 58% (136); all full-time undergraduates: 60% (621). *Average award:* Freshmen: $22,882; Undergraduates: $21,544. *Scholarships, grants, and awards:* Federal Pell, FSEOG, state, private, college/university gift aid from institutional funds.

GIFT AID (NON-NEED-BASED) *Total amount:* $1,858,072 (79% institutional, 21% external sources). *Receiving aid:* Freshmen: 32% (75). Undergraduates: 37% (385). *Average award:* Freshmen: $9214. Undergraduates: $8204. *Scholarships, grants, and awards by category: Academic interests/achievement:* general academic interests/achievements. *Special achievements/activities:* religious involvement. *Special characteristics:* ethnic background. *Tuition waivers:* Full or partial for employees or children of employees.

LOANS *Student loans:* $3,992,335 (85% need-based, 15% non-need-based). 58% of past graduating class borrowed through all loan programs. *Average indebtedness per student:* $26,089. *Average need-based loan:* Freshmen: $4170. Undergraduates: $5043. *Parent loans:* $1,101,379 (30% need-based, 70% non-need-based). *Programs:* Federal Direct (Subsidized and Unsubsidized Stafford, PLUS), Perkins, college/university.

WORK-STUDY *Federal work-study:* Total amount: $892,819; jobs available. *State or other work-study/employment:* Total amount: $637,682 (4% need-based, 96% non-need-based). Part-time jobs available.

APPLYING FOR FINANCIAL AID *Required financial aid form:* FAFSA. *Financial aid deadline:* 3/1. *Notification date:* Continuous beginning 2/15. Students must reply by 5/1 or within 3 weeks of notification.

CONTACT Mr. Robert W. Arnold, Director of Financial Aid, Earlham College, National Road West, Richmond, IN 47374-4095, 765-983-1217 or toll-free 800-327-5426. *Fax:* 765-983-1299. *E-mail:* boba@earlham.edu.
Website: http://www.earlham.edu/.

resources awarded to replace EFC). 2% of all full-time freshmen had no need and received non-need-based gift aid.

UNDERGRADUATE FINANCIAL AID (Fall 2012, est.) 13,387 applied for aid; of those 82% were deemed to have need. 97% of undergraduates with need received aid; of those 9% had need fully met. *Average percent of need met:* 66% (excluding resources awarded to replace EFC). *Average financial aid package:* $9718 (excluding resources awarded to replace EFC). 3% of all full-time undergraduates had no need and received non-need-based gift aid.

GIFT AID (NEED-BASED) *Total amount:* $66,146,730 (45% federal, 27% state, 27% institutional, 1% external sources). *Receiving aid:* Freshmen: 42% (1,677); all full-time undergraduates: 42% (7,716). *Average award:* Freshmen: $8031; Undergraduates: $7529. *Scholarships, grants, and awards:* Federal Pell, FSEOG, state, private, college/university gift aid from institutional funds, Federal Nursing.

GIFT AID (NON-NEED-BASED) *Total amount:* $4,600,972 (18% state, 35% institutional, 47% external sources). *Receiving aid:* Freshmen: 5% (206). Undergraduates: 6% (1,042). *Average award:* Freshmen: $4532. Undergraduates: $3467. *Scholarships, grants, and awards by category: Academic interests/achievement:* biological sciences, business, communication, education, engineering/technologies, English, foreign languages, general academic interests/achievements, health fields, home economics, humanities, international studies, mathematics, military science, physical sciences. *Creative arts/performance:* applied art and design, art/fine arts, dance, music, performing arts. *Special characteristics:* adult students, children and siblings of alumni, children of faculty/staff, ethnic background, general special characteristics, handicapped students. *Tuition waivers:* Full or partial for employees or children of employees, senior citizens. *ROTC:* Army, Air Force.

LOANS *Student loans:* $102,496,622 (96% need-based, 4% non-need-based). 65% of past graduating class borrowed through all loan programs. *Average indebtedness per student:* $25,983. *Average need-based loan:* Freshmen: $3452. Undergraduates: $4053. *Parent loans:* $15,126,407 (100% need-based). *Programs:* Federal Direct (Subsidized and Unsubsidized Stafford, PLUS), Perkins, Federal Nursing, state.

WORK-STUDY *Federal work-study:* Total amount: $1,303,279; 445 jobs averaging $2510. *State or other work-study/employment:* 1,213 part-time jobs averaging $1100.

ATHLETIC AWARDS Total amount: $5,551,224 (44% need-based, 56% non-need-based).

APPLYING FOR FINANCIAL AID *Required financial aid forms:* FAFSA, scholarship application form. *Financial aid deadline (priority):* 3/1. *Notification date:* 4/1. Students must reply within 8 weeks of notification.

CONTACT Ms. Julie Poorman, Director of Financial Aid, East Carolina University, East 5th Street, Greenville, NC 27858-4353, 252-328-6610. *Fax:* 252-328-4347. *E-mail:* poormanj@ecu.edu.
Website: http://www.ecu.edu/.

EAST CAROLINA UNIVERSITY
Greenville, NC

Tuition & fees (NC res): $5869	Average undergraduate aid package: $9718

ABOUT THE INSTITUTION State-supported, coed. *Awards:* certificates, bachelor's, master's, and doctoral degrees. 90 undergraduate majors. *Total enrollment:* 26,947. Undergraduates: 21,298. Freshmen: 4,015. Federal methodology is used as a basis for awarding need-based institutional aid.

UNDERGRADUATE EXPENSES for 2013–2014 *Application fee:* $70. *Tuition, state resident:* full-time $3758; part-time $469.75 per course. *Tuition, nonresident:* full-time $17,572; part-time $2196 per course. *Required fees:* full-time $2111; $263.88 per course. Full-time tuition and fees vary according to location. Part-time tuition and fees vary according to course load and location. *College room and board:* $8300; *Room only:* $4774. Room and board charges vary according to board plan and housing facility.

FRESHMAN FINANCIAL AID (Fall 2012, est.) 3,301 applied for aid; of those 75% were deemed to have need. 96% of freshmen with need received aid; of those 9% had need fully met. *Average percent of need met:* 66% (excluding resources awarded to replace EFC). *Average financial aid package:* $9614 (excluding

EAST CENTRAL UNIVERSITY
Ada, OK

CONTACT Marcia Carter, Director of Financial Aid, East Central University, 1100 East 14th, Ada, OK 74820-6899, 580-332-8000 Ext. 242. *Fax:* 580-436-5612. *Website:* http://www.ecok.edu/.

EASTERN CONNECTICUT STATE UNIVERSITY
Willimantic, CT

Tuition & fees (area res): $9376	Average undergraduate aid package: $8202

ABOUT THE INSTITUTION State-supported, coed. *Awards:* associate, bachelor's, and master's degrees. 29 undergraduate majors. *Total enrollment:* 5,440. Undergraduates: 5,258. Freshmen: 1,015. Federal methodology is used as a basis for awarding need-based institutional aid.

UNDERGRADUATE EXPENSES for 2013–2014 *Application fee:* $50. *Tuition, area resident:* full-time $4510. *Tuition, state resident:* full-time $4510. *Tuition, nonresident:* full-time $14,594. *Required fees:* full-time $4866. Full-time tuition and fees vary according to reciprocity agreements. *College room and board:* $11,168; *Room only:* $6392. Room and board charges vary according to board plan.

FRESHMAN FINANCIAL AID (Fall 2011) 840 applied for aid; of those 72% were deemed to have need. 97% of freshmen with need received aid; of those 10% had need fully met. *Average percent of need met:* 62% (excluding resources awarded to replace EFC). *Average financial aid package:* $8586 (excluding resources awarded to replace EFC). 2% of all full-time freshmen had no need and received non-need-based gift aid.

UNDERGRADUATE FINANCIAL AID (Fall 2011) 3,587 applied for aid; of those 78% were deemed to have need. 96% of undergraduates with need received aid; of those 7% had need fully met. *Average percent of need met:* 57% (excluding resources awarded to replace EFC). *Average financial aid package:* $8202 (excluding resources awarded to replace EFC). 2% of all full-time undergraduates had no need and received non-need-based gift aid.

GIFT AID (NEED-BASED) *Total amount:* $11,781,937 (48% federal, 15% state, 34% institutional, 3% external sources). *Receiving aid:* Freshmen: 51% (472); all full-time undergraduates: 43% (1,907). *Average award:* Freshmen: $6491; Undergraduates: $5764. *Scholarships, grants, and awards:* Federal Pell, FSEOG, state, private, college/university gift aid from institutional funds.

GIFT AID (NON-NEED-BASED) *Total amount:* $763,884 (8% state, 63% institutional, 29% external sources). *Receiving aid:* Freshmen: 1% (5). Undergraduates: 1% (26). *Average award:* Freshmen: $3386. Undergraduates: $2588. *Scholarships, grants, and awards by category:* Academic interests/achievement: area/ethnic studies, biological sciences, business, communication, computer science, education, English, foreign languages, general academic interests/achievements, humanities, mathematics, physical sciences, social sciences. *Special achievements/activities:* community service, general special achievements/activities, leadership, memberships. *Special characteristics:* children of faculty/staff, children of union members/company employees, general special characteristics, international students, local/state students, members of minority groups, previous college experience, veterans. *ROTC:* Army cooperative, Air Force cooperative.

LOANS *Student loans:* $26,819,262 (75% need-based, 25% non-need-based). 75% of past graduating class borrowed through all loan programs. *Average indebtedness per student:* $26,168. *Average need-based loan:* Freshmen: $3391. Undergraduates: $4264. *Parent loans:* $4,328,753 (59% need-based, 41% non-need-based). *Programs:* Federal Direct (Subsidized and Unsubsidized Stafford, PLUS), Perkins, alternative loans.

WORK-STUDY *Federal work-study:* Total amount: $137,217; 81 jobs averaging $1694. *State or other work-study/employment:* Total amount: $71,107 (92% need-based, 8% non-need-based). 38 part-time jobs averaging $1871.

APPLYING FOR FINANCIAL AID *Required financial aid form:* FAFSA. *Financial aid deadline (priority):* 3/15. *Notification date:* Continuous. Students must reply within 2 weeks of notification.

CONTACT Patrick Kelly, Financial Aid Office, Eastern Connecticut State University, 83 Windham Street, Willimantic, CT 06226-2295, 860-465-5205. *Fax:* 860-465-2811. *E-mail:* financialaid@easternct.edu. *Website:* http://www.easternct.edu/.

EASTERN ILLINOIS UNIVERSITY
Charleston, IL

Tuition & fees (IL res): $10,930	Average undergraduate aid package: $10,231

ABOUT THE INSTITUTION State-supported, coed. *Awards:* certificates, bachelor's, and master's degrees. 45 undergraduate majors. *Total enrollment:* 10,417. Undergraduates: 8,975. Freshmen: 1,295. Federal methodology is used as a basis for awarding need-based institutional aid.

UNDERGRADUATE EXPENSES for 2013–2014 *Application fee:* $30. *Tuition, state resident:* full-time $8370; part-time $279 per credit hour. *Tuition, nonresident:* full-time $25,110; part-time $837 per credit hour. *Required fees:* full-time $2560; $92 per credit hour. Full-time tuition and fees vary according to course load and student level. Part-time tuition and fees vary according to course load and student level. *College room and board:* $9174. Room and board charges vary according to board plan and housing facility. *Payment plan:* Guaranteed tuition.

FRESHMAN FINANCIAL AID (Fall 2012, est.) 1,183 applied for aid; of those 77% were deemed to have need. 99% of freshmen with need received aid; of those 9% had need fully met. *Average percent of need met:* 66% (excluding resources awarded to replace EFC). *Average financial aid package:* $11,293 (excluding

resources awarded to replace EFC). 13% of all full-time freshmen had no need and received non-need-based gift aid.

UNDERGRADUATE FINANCIAL AID (Fall 2012, est.) 6,895 applied for aid; of those 77% were deemed to have need. 99% of undergraduates with need received aid; of those 8% had need fully met. *Average percent of need met:* 60% (excluding resources awarded to replace EFC). *Average financial aid package:* $10,231 (excluding resources awarded to replace EFC). 4% of all full-time undergraduates had no need and received non-need-based gift aid.

GIFT AID (NEED-BASED) *Total amount:* $31,709,877 (46% federal, 35% state, 14% institutional, 5% external sources). *Receiving aid:* Freshmen: 52% (634); all full-time undergraduates: 45% (3,563). *Average award:* Freshmen: $3479; Undergraduates: $3594. *Scholarships, grants, and awards:* Federal Pell, FSEOG, state, private, college/university gift aid from institutional funds.

GIFT AID (NON-NEED-BASED) *Total amount:* $2,652,338 (7% federal, 32% state, 35% institutional, 26% external sources). *Receiving aid:* Freshmen: 39% (475). Undergraduates: 18% (1,379). *Average award:* Freshmen: $3083. Undergraduates: $4002. *Tuition waivers:* Full or partial for employees or children of employees, senior citizens. *ROTC:* Army.

LOANS *Student loans:* $53,953,234 (89% need-based, 11% non-need-based). 72% of past graduating class borrowed through all loan programs. *Average indebtedness per student:* $28,575. *Average need-based loan:* Freshmen: $3045. Undergraduates: $4194. *Parent loans:* $11,501,196 (74% need-based, 26% non-need-based). *Programs:* Federal Direct (Subsidized and Unsubsidized Stafford, PLUS), Perkins, college/university.

WORK-STUDY *Federal work-study:* Total amount: $560,830; 294 jobs averaging $991. *State or other work-study/employment:* 2,680 part-time jobs averaging $1440.

ATHLETIC AWARDS Total amount: $3,315,331 (45% need-based, 55% non-need-based).

APPLYING FOR FINANCIAL AID *Required financial aid form:* FAFSA. *Financial aid deadline (priority):* 3/1. *Notification date:* Continuous beginning 3/1. Students must reply within 2 weeks of notification.

CONTACT Jerry Donna, Director of Financial Aid, Eastern Illinois University, 600 Lincoln Avenue, Charleston, IL 61920-3099, 217-581-3713 or toll-free 877-581-2348 (in-state), 800-252-5711 (out-of-state). *Fax:* 217-581-6422. *E-mail:* finaid@eiu.edu. *Website:* http://www.eiu.edu/.

EASTERN KENTUCKY UNIVERSITY
Richmond, KY

Tuition & fees (KY res): $7320	Average undergraduate aid package: $9932

ABOUT THE INSTITUTION State-supported, coed. *Awards:* certificates, associate, bachelor's, master's, and doctoral degrees. 111 undergraduate majors. *Total enrollment:* 16,062. Undergraduates: 13,902. Freshmen: 2,421. Federal methodology is used as a basis for awarding need-based institutional aid.

UNDERGRADUATE EXPENSES for 2013–2014 *Application fee:* $30. *Tuition, state resident:* full-time $7320; part-time $305 per credit hour. *Tuition, nonresident:* full-time $16,464; part-time $686 per credit hour. Part-time tuition and fees vary according to course load. *College room and board:* $7316. Room and board charges vary according to board plan and housing facility.

FRESHMAN FINANCIAL AID (Fall 2012, est.) 2,047 applied for aid; of those 83% were deemed to have need. 99% of freshmen with need received aid; of those 40% had need fully met. *Average percent of need met:* 84% (excluding resources awarded to replace EFC). *Average financial aid package:* $10,074 (excluding resources awarded to replace EFC). 10% of all full-time freshmen had no need and received non-need-based gift aid.

UNDERGRADUATE FINANCIAL AID (Fall 2012, est.) 9,368 applied for aid; of those 85% were deemed to have need. 97% of undergraduates with need received aid; of those 39% had need fully met. *Average percent of need met:* 85% (excluding resources awarded to replace EFC). *Average financial aid package:* $9932 (excluding resources awarded to replace EFC). 11% of all full-time undergraduates had no need and received non-need-based gift aid.

GIFT AID (NEED-BASED) *Total amount:* $44,934,807 (57% federal, 29% state, 12% institutional, 2% external sources). *Receiving aid:* Freshmen: 52% (1,187); all full-time undergraduates: 48% (5,394). *Average award:* Freshmen: $5758; Undergraduates: $5736. *Scholarships, grants, and awards:* Federal Pell, FSEOG, state, private, college/university gift aid from institutional funds.

GIFT AID (NON-NEED-BASED) *Total amount:* $5,879,513 (48% state, 46% institutional, 6% external sources). *Receiving aid:* Freshmen: 65% (1,485). Undergraduates: 38% (4,234). *Average award:* Freshmen: $5279. Undergraduates: $5743. *Scholarships, grants, and awards by category: Academic interests/achievement:* 2,210 awards ($10,454,835 total): general academic interests/achievements. *Creative arts/performance:* 135 awards ($389,510 total): music. *Special achievements/activities:* 28 awards ($22,800 total): cheerleading/drum major. *Special characteristics:* 457 awards ($1,722,826 total): children and siblings of alumni, children of faculty/staff, members of minority groups. *ROTC:* Army, Air Force cooperative.
LOANS *Student loans:* $67,313,249 (87% need-based, 13% non-need-based). 71% of past graduating class borrowed through all loan programs. *Average indebtedness per student:* $26,150. *Average need-based loan:* Freshmen: $2822. Undergraduates: $3806. *Parent loans:* $25,074,880 (69% need-based, 31% non-need-based). *Programs:* Federal Direct (Subsidized and Unsubsidized Stafford, PLUS), Perkins, college/university.
WORK-STUDY *Federal work-study:* Total amount: $3,413,892; 1,200 jobs averaging $1800. *State or other work-study/employment:* Total amount: $3,624,853 (100% non-need-based). 1,200 part-time jobs averaging $1800.
ATHLETIC AWARDS Total amount: $3,734,657 (41% need-based, 59% non-need-based).
APPLYING FOR FINANCIAL AID *Required financial aid form:* FAFSA. *Financial aid deadline (priority):* 2/1. *Notification date:* Continuous beginning 4/1.
CONTACT Office of Financial Aid, Eastern Kentucky University, 521 Lancaster Avenue, SSB CPO 59, Richmond, KY 40475-3102, 859-622-2361 or toll-free 800-465-9191. *Fax:* 859-622-2019. *E-mail:* finaid@eku.edu.
Website: http://www.eku.edu/.

EASTERN MENNONITE UNIVERSITY
Harrisonburg, VA

CONTACT Ms. Renee Leap, Assistant Director of Financial Assistance, Eastern Mennonite University, 1200 Park Road, Harrisonburg, VA 22802-2462, 540-432-4138 or toll-free 800-368-2665. *Fax:* 540-432-4081. *E-mail:* leapr@emu.edu.
Website: http://www.emu.edu/.

EASTERN MICHIGAN UNIVERSITY
Ypsilanti, MI

Tuition & fees (MI res): $9026	Average undergraduate aid package: $8751

ABOUT THE INSTITUTION State-supported, coed. *Awards:* certificates, bachelor's, master's, and doctoral degrees. 128 undergraduate majors. *Total enrollment:* 23,502. Undergraduates: 18,914. Freshmen: 2,646. Federal methodology is used as a basis for awarding need-based institutional aid.
UNDERGRADUATE EXPENSES for 2013–2014 *Application fee:* $30. *One-time required fee:* $300. *Tuition, state resident:* full-time $7701; part-time $256.70 per credit hour. *Tuition, nonresident:* full-time $22,683; part-time $756.10 per credit hour. *Required fees:* full-time $1325; $40.90 per credit hour or $48.20 per term. Full-time tuition and fees vary according to course level and reciprocity agreements. Part-time tuition and fees vary according to course level and reciprocity agreements. *College room and board:* $8286; *Room only:* $3952. Room and board charges vary according to board plan, housing facility, and location.
FRESHMAN FINANCIAL AID (Fall 2011) 1,895 applied for aid; of those 84% were deemed to have need. 98% of freshmen with need received aid; of those 1% had need fully met. *Average percent of need met:* 70% (excluding resources awarded to replace EFC). *Average financial aid package:* $9399 (excluding resources awarded to replace EFC). 18% of all full-time freshmen had no need and received non-need-based gift aid.
UNDERGRADUATE FINANCIAL AID (Fall 2011) 10,505 applied for aid; of those 88% were deemed to have need. 99% of undergraduates with need received aid; of those 1% had need fully met. *Average percent of need met:* 64% (excluding resources awarded to replace EFC). *Average financial aid package:* $8751 (excluding resources awarded to replace EFC). 11% of all full-time undergraduates had no need and received non-need-based gift aid.

GIFT AID (NEED-BASED) *Total amount:* $41,103,166 (87% federal, 1% state, 12% institutional). *Receiving aid:* Freshmen: 63% (1,335); all full-time undergraduates: 58% (7,430). *Average award:* Freshmen: $4399; Undergraduates: $4348. *Scholarships, grants, and awards:* Federal Pell, FSEOG, state, private, college/university gift aid from institutional funds.
GIFT AID (NON-NEED-BASED) *Total amount:* $19,023,365 (1% state, 92% institutional, 7% external sources). *Receiving aid:* Freshmen: 45% (951). Undergraduates: 26% (3,383). *Average award:* Freshmen: $4524. Undergraduates: $4559. *Scholarships, grants, and awards by category: Academic interests/achievement:* 2,494 awards ($6,396,502 total): agriculture, architecture, biological sciences, business, communication, computer science, education, engineering/technologies, English, foreign languages, general academic interests/achievements, health fields, home economics, humanities, mathematics, physical sciences, religion/biblical studies, social sciences. *Creative arts/performance:* 111 awards ($123,287 total): applied art and design, art/fine arts, cinema/film/broadcasting, creative writing, dance, debating, general creative arts/performance, music, performing arts, theater/drama. *Special achievements/activities:* 130 awards ($130,427 total): general special achievements/activities, leadership, memberships, religious involvement. *Special characteristics:* 347 awards ($3,961,509 total): children and siblings of alumni, ethnic background, international students, members of minority groups, out-of-state students, previous college experience, religious affiliation. *Tuition waivers:* Full or partial for employees or children of employees. *ROTC:* Army, Naval cooperative, Air Force cooperative.
LOANS *Student loans:* $142,273,140 (44% need-based, 56% non-need-based). 68% of past graduating class borrowed through all loan programs. *Average indebtedness per student:* $25,133. *Average need-based loan:* Freshmen: $3220. Undergraduates: $4116. *Parent loans:* $14,324,350 (100% non-need-based). *Programs:* Federal Direct (Subsidized and Unsubsidized Stafford, PLUS), Perkins, private loans.
WORK-STUDY *Federal work-study:* Total amount: $1,304,169; 808 jobs averaging $1474. *State or other work-study/employment:* Part-time jobs available.
ATHLETIC AWARDS Total amount: $6,657,427 (100% non-need-based).
APPLYING FOR FINANCIAL AID *Required financial aid form:* FAFSA. *Financial aid deadline:* Continuous. *Notification date:* Continuous beginning 3/1.
CONTACT Cynthia Van Pelt, Director of Financial Aid, Eastern Michigan University, 403 Pierce Hall, Ypsilanti, MI 48197, 734-487-1048 or toll-free 800-GO TO EMU. *Fax:* 734-487-0174. *E-mail:* cvanpelt@emich.edu.
Website: http://www.emich.edu/.

EASTERN NAZARENE COLLEGE
Quincy, MA

Tuition & fees: $26,884	Average undergraduate aid package: $23,272

ABOUT THE INSTITUTION Independent Church of the Nazarene, coed. *Awards:* certificates, associate, bachelor's, and master's degrees. 106 undergraduate majors. *Total enrollment:* 1,036. Undergraduates: 862. Freshmen: 172. Federal methodology is used as a basis for awarding need-based institutional aid.
UNDERGRADUATE EXPENSES for 2013–2014 *Comprehensive fee:* $35,184 includes full-time tuition ($25,944), mandatory fees ($940), and room and board ($8300). Full-time tuition and fees vary according to class time, course load, degree level, location, program, and reciprocity agreements. Room and board charges vary according to board plan and housing facility. *Part-time tuition:* $1081 per credit. *Part-time fees:* $350 per term. Part-time tuition and fees vary according to class time, degree level, location, program, and reciprocity agreements.
FRESHMAN FINANCIAL AID (Fall 2012, est.) 158 applied for aid; of those 91% were deemed to have need. 100% of freshmen with need received aid; of those 27% had need fully met. *Average percent of need met:* 73% (excluding resources awarded to replace EFC). *Average financial aid package:* $24,566 (excluding resources awarded to replace EFC). 10% of all full-time freshmen had no need and received non-need-based gift aid.
UNDERGRADUATE FINANCIAL AID (Fall 2012, est.) 526 applied for aid; of those 85% were deemed to have need. 100% of undergraduates with need received aid; of those 27% had need fully met. *Average percent of need met:* 72% (excluding resources awarded to replace EFC). *Average financial aid package:* $23,272 (excluding resources awarded to replace EFC). 10% of all full-time undergraduates had no need and received non-need-based gift aid.

GIFT AID (NEED-BASED) *Total amount:* $6,989,882 (23% federal, 4% state, 71% institutional, 2% external sources). *Receiving aid:* Freshmen: 83% (143); all full-time undergraduates: 61% (412). *Average award:* Freshmen: $14,192; Undergraduates: $11,847. *Scholarships, grants, and awards:* Federal Pell, FSEOG, state, private, college/university gift aid from institutional funds, United Negro College Fund.

GIFT AID (NON-NEED-BASED) *Total amount:* $1,210,567 (2% federal, 2% state, 92% institutional, 4% external sources). *Receiving aid:* Freshmen: 5% (8). Undergraduates: 5% (32). *Average award:* Freshmen: $11,147. Undergraduates: $11,001. *Scholarships, grants, and awards by category: Academic interests/ achievement:* general academic interests/achievements. *Special achievements/activities:* hobbies/interests, leadership, religious involvement. *Special characteristics:* children and siblings of alumni, children of faculty/staff, international students, religious affiliation, veterans. *Tuition waivers:* Full or partial for employees or children of employees. *ROTC:* Army cooperative, Naval cooperative, Air Force cooperative.

LOANS *Student loans:* $5,034,774 (82% need-based, 18% non-need-based). *Average need-based loan:* Freshmen: $5925. Undergraduates: $8724. *Parent loans:* $1,992,647 (77% need-based, 23% non-need-based). *Programs:* Federal Direct (Subsidized and Unsubsidized Stafford, PLUS), Perkins, state, alternative loans.

WORK-STUDY *Federal work-study:* Total amount: $72,933; jobs available. *State or other work-study/employment:* Part-time jobs available.

APPLYING FOR FINANCIAL AID *Required financial aid forms:* FAFSA, institution's own form. *Financial aid deadline (priority):* 7/1. *Notification date:* Continuous beginning 1/15. Students must reply within 2 weeks of notification.

CONTACT Lerick Fanfanx, Director of Financial Aid, Eastern Nazarene College, 23 East Elm Avenue, Quincy, MA 02170, 617-745-3869 or toll-free 800-88-ENC88. *Fax:* 617-745-3992. *E-mail:* lerick.fanfanx@enc .edu. *Website:* http://www.enc.edu/.

neering/technologies, English, foreign languages, general academic interests/achievements, health fields, home economics, humanities, mathematics, military science, physical sciences, premedicine, religion/biblical studies, social sciences. *Creative arts/ performance:* applied art and design, art/fine arts, cinema/film/broadcasting, creative writing, dance, debating, general creative arts/performance, journalism/publications, music, performing arts, theater/drama. *Special achievements/activities:* community service, general special achievements/activities, hobbies/interests, leadership, memberships, rodeo. *Special characteristics:* children and siblings of alumni, ethnic background, first-generation college students, general special characteristics, international students, members of minority groups, out-of-state students, veterans. *Tuition waivers:* Full or partial for employees or children of employees, senior citizens.

LOANS *Student loans:* $18,527,535 (32% need-based, 68% non-need-based). 94% of past graduating class borrowed through all loan programs. *Average indebtedness per student:* $14,821. *Average need-based loan:* Freshmen: $3382. Undergraduates: $4130. *Parent loans:* $80,820 (100% non-need-based). *Programs:* Federal Direct (Subsidized and Unsubsidized Stafford, PLUS), Perkins, state, college/university.

WORK-STUDY *Federal work-study:* Total amount: $1,461,382; jobs available. *State or other work-study/employment:* Total amount: $322,653 (100% need-based). Part-time jobs available.

ATHLETIC AWARDS Total amount: $999,044 (100% non-need-based).

APPLYING FOR FINANCIAL AID *Required financial aid form:* FAFSA. *Financial aid deadline:* Continuous. *Notification date:* Continuous beginning 3/1.

CONTACT Mr. Brent Small, Director of Financial Aid, Eastern New Mexico University, Station 20, 1500 South Avenue K, Portales, NM 88130, 575-562-2194 or toll-free 800-367-3668. *Fax:* 575-562-2198. *E-mail:* brent.small@enmu.edu. *Website:* http://www.enmu.edu/.

EASTERN NEW MEXICO UNIVERSITY
Portales, NM

Tuition & fees (NM res): $5776	Average undergraduate aid package: $11,015

ABOUT THE INSTITUTION State-supported, coed. *Awards:* associate, bachelor's, and master's degrees. 52 undergraduate majors. *Total enrollment:* 5,814. Undergraduates: 4,586. Freshmen: 709. Federal methodology is used as a basis for awarding need-based institutional aid.

UNDERGRADUATE EXPENSES for 2013–2014 *One-time required fee:* $120. *Tuition, state resident:* full-time $4350; part-time $121.85 per credit hour. *Tuition, nonresident:* full-time $9860; part-time $351.45 per credit hour. *Required fees:* full-time $1426; $59.40 per credit hour. Full-time tuition and fees vary according to course load and reciprocity agreements. Part-time tuition and fees vary according to course load. *College room and board:* $6090; *Room only:* $2930. Room and board charges vary according to gender, housing facility, location, and student level.

FRESHMAN FINANCIAL AID (Fall 2011) 434 applied for aid; of those 100% were deemed to have need. 100% of freshmen with need received aid; of those 100% had need fully met. *Average percent of need met:* 42% (excluding resources awarded to replace EFC). *Average financial aid package:* $10,356 (excluding resources awarded to replace EFC). 18% of all full-time freshmen had no need and received non-need-based gift aid.

UNDERGRADUATE FINANCIAL AID (Fall 2011) 1,635 applied for aid; of those 100% were deemed to have need. 99% of undergraduates with need received aid; of those 100% had need fully met. *Average percent of need met:* 44% (excluding resources awarded to replace EFC). *Average financial aid package:* $11,015 (excluding resources awarded to replace EFC). 8% of all full-time undergraduates had no need and received non-need-based gift aid.

GIFT AID (NEED-BASED) *Total amount:* $13,591,898 (77% federal, 23% state). *Receiving aid:* Freshmen: 59% (415); all full-time undergraduates: 55% (1,570). *Average award:* Freshmen: $4736; Undergraduates: $4575. *Scholarships, grants, and awards:* Federal Pell, FSEOG, state, private, college/university gift aid from institutional funds.

GIFT AID (NON-NEED-BASED) *Total amount:* $2,471,807 (74% institutional, 26% external sources). *Receiving aid:* Freshmen: 53% (374). Undergraduates: 34% (975). *Average award:* Freshmen: $3539. Undergraduates: $4213. *Scholarships, grants, and awards by category: Academic interests/achievement:* agriculture, biological sciences, business, communication, computer science, education, engi-

EASTERN OREGON UNIVERSITY
La Grande, OR

Tuition & fees: N/R	Average undergraduate aid package: $9860

ABOUT THE INSTITUTION State-supported, coed. *Awards:* certificates, associate, bachelor's, and master's degrees. 22 undergraduate majors. *Total enrollment:* 4,298. Undergraduates: 3,900. Freshmen: 385. Federal methodology is used as a basis for awarding need-based institutional aid.

FRESHMAN FINANCIAL AID (Fall 2012, est.) 348 applied for aid; of those 85% were deemed to have need. 100% of freshmen with need received aid; of those 21% had need fully met. *Average percent of need met:* 45% (excluding resources awarded to replace EFC). *Average financial aid package:* $9590 (excluding resources awarded to replace EFC). 2% of all full-time freshmen had no need and received non-need-based gift aid.

UNDERGRADUATE FINANCIAL AID (Fall 2012, est.) 2,084 applied for aid; of those 90% were deemed to have need. 99% of undergraduates with need received aid; of those 10% had need fully met. *Average percent of need met:* 50% (excluding resources awarded to replace EFC). *Average financial aid package:* $9860 (excluding resources awarded to replace EFC). 1% of all full-time undergraduates had no need and received non-need-based gift aid.

GIFT AID (NEED-BASED) *Total amount:* $10,434,338 (88% federal, 11% state, 1% institutional). *Receiving aid:* Freshmen: 53% (203); all full-time undergraduates: 60% (1,408). *Average award:* Freshmen: $5204; Undergraduates: $5495. *Scholarships, grants, and awards:* Federal Pell, FSEOG, state, private, college/university gift aid from institutional funds.

GIFT AID (NON-NEED-BASED) *Total amount:* $952,092 (28% institutional, 72% external sources). *Receiving aid:* Freshmen: 8% (30). Undergraduates: 5% (126). *Average award:* Freshmen: $2244. Undergraduates: $1579. *Scholarships, grants, and awards by category: Academic interests/achievement:* general academic interests/achievements. *Creative arts/performance:* art/fine arts, general creative arts/performance. *Special achievements/activities:* leadership. *Special characteristics:* local/state students, members of minority groups. *ROTC:* Army.

LOANS *Student loans:* $24,050,317 (45% need-based, 55% non-need-based). 72% of past graduating class borrowed through all loan programs. *Average indebtedness per student:* $25,109. *Average need-based loan:* Freshmen: $3332. Undergraduates: $4552. *Parent loans:* $5,802,663 (100% non-need-based). *Programs:* Federal Direct (Subsidized and Unsubsidized Stafford, PLUS), Perkins.

WORK-STUDY *Federal work-study:* Total amount: $354,736; jobs available.

APPLYING FOR FINANCIAL AID *Required financial aid form:* FAFSA. *Financial aid deadline (priority):* 1/1. *Notification date:* Continuous beginning 4/1. Students must reply within 4 weeks of notification.

CONTACT Financial Aid Office, Eastern Oregon University, One University Boulevard, Inlow Hall, Room 201, La Grande, OR 97850-2899, 541-962-3550 or toll-free 800-452-8639. *Fax:* 541-962-3661. *E-mail:* fao@eou.edu. *Website:* http://www.eou.edu/.

EASTERN UNIVERSITY
St. Davids, PA

ABOUT THE INSTITUTION Independent Christian, coed. *Awards:* associate, bachelor's, master's, and doctoral degrees. 35 undergraduate majors. *Total enrollment:* 4,263. Undergraduates: 2,701. Freshmen: 459.

GIFT AID (NEED-BASED) *Scholarships, grants, and awards:* Federal Pell, FSEOG, state, private, college/university gift aid from institutional funds, United Negro College Fund.

GIFT AID (NON-NEED-BASED) *Scholarships, grants, and awards by category: Academic interests/achievement:* general academic interests/achievements. *Creative arts/performance:* dance, music. *Special achievements/activities:* community service, leadership, memberships. *Special characteristics:* children and siblings of alumni.

LOANS *Programs:* Federal Direct (Subsidized and Unsubsidized Stafford, PLUS), Perkins, alternative loans.

APPLYING FOR FINANCIAL AID *Required financial aid form:* FAFSA.

CONTACT Office of Student Financial Aid, Eastern University, 1300 Eagle Road, St. Davids, PA 19087-3696, 610-225-5102 or toll-free 800-452-0996. *Fax:* 610-225-5651. *E-mail:* finaid@eastern.edu. *Website:* http://www.eastern.edu/.

EASTERN WASHINGTON UNIVERSITY
Cheney, WA

Tuition & fees (WA res): $7976	Average undergraduate aid package: $13,333

ABOUT THE INSTITUTION State-supported, coed. *Awards:* certificates, bachelor's, master's, and doctoral degrees. 93 undergraduate majors. *Total enrollment:* 12,587. Undergraduates: 11,360. Freshmen: 1,572. Federal methodology is used as a basis for awarding need-based institutional aid.

UNDERGRADUATE EXPENSES for 2013–2014 *Tuition, state resident:* full-time $7425; part-time $247.50 per credit. *Tuition, nonresident:* full-time $18,168; part-time $605.60 per credit. *Required fees:* full-time $551; $551 per year. Full-time tuition and fees vary according to program and reciprocity agreements. Part-time tuition and fees vary according to program and reciprocity agreements. *College room and board:* $8412; *Room only:* $4500. Room and board charges vary according to board plan and housing facility.

FRESHMAN FINANCIAL AID (Fall 2011) 1,285 applied for aid; of those 77% were deemed to have need. 98% of freshmen with need received aid; of those 27% had need fully met. *Average percent of need met:* 86% (excluding resources awarded to replace EFC). *Average financial aid package:* $12,975 (excluding resources awarded to replace EFC). 11% of all full-time freshmen had no need and received non-need-based gift aid.

UNDERGRADUATE FINANCIAL AID (Fall 2011) 7,397 applied for aid; of those 84% were deemed to have need. 98% of undergraduates with need received aid; of those 24% had need fully met. *Average percent of need met:* 63% (excluding resources awarded to replace EFC). *Average financial aid package:* $13,333 (excluding resources awarded to replace EFC). 5% of all full-time undergraduates had no need and received non-need-based gift aid.

GIFT AID (NEED-BASED) *Total amount:* $37,023,949 (50% federal, 38% state, 7% institutional, 5% external sources). *Receiving aid:* Freshmen: 50% (733); all full-time undergraduates: 49% (4,580). *Average award:* Freshmen: $7455; Undergraduates: $7345. *Scholarships, grants, and awards:* Federal Pell, FSEOG, state, private, college/university gift aid from institutional funds.

GIFT AID (NON-NEED-BASED) *Total amount:* $530,855 (14% institutional, 86% external sources). *Receiving aid:* Freshmen: 20% (293). Undergraduates: 10% (900). *Average award:* Freshmen: $3007. Undergraduates: $3528. *Scholarships, grants, and awards by category: Academic interests/achievement:* 1,077 awards: area/ethnic studies, biological sciences, business, communication, computer science, education, engineering/technologies, English, foreign languages, general academic interests/achievements, health fields, humanities, international studies, mathematics, military science, physical sciences, premedicine, social sciences. *Creative arts/performance:* 80 awards: art/fine arts, cinema/film/broadcasting, creative writing, journalism/publications, music, theater/drama. *Special characteristics:* 668 awards: adult students, children and siblings of alumni, children of union members/company employees, ethnic background, first-generation college students, handicapped students, local/state students, married students, spouses of deceased or disabled public servants, veterans, veterans' children. *ROTC:* Army.

LOANS *Student loans:* $45,791,685 (85% need-based, 15% non-need-based). 56% of past graduating class borrowed through all loan programs. *Average indebtedness per student:* $23,604. *Average need-based loan:* Freshmen: $3164. Undergraduates: $4162. *Parent loans:* $11,164,057 (63% need-based, 37% non-need-based). *Programs:* Federal Direct (Subsidized and Unsubsidized Stafford, PLUS), Perkins.

WORK-STUDY *Federal work-study:* Total amount: $316,142; 162 jobs averaging $2042. *State or other work-study/employment:* Total amount: $569,582 (100% need-based). 277 part-time jobs averaging $2151.

ATHLETIC AWARDS Total amount: $2,058,732 (47% need-based, 53% non-need-based).

APPLYING FOR FINANCIAL AID *Required financial aid form:* FAFSA. *Financial aid deadline (priority):* 2/15. *Notification date:* Continuous beginning 4/15. Students must reply within 4 weeks of notification.

CONTACT Mr. Bruce DeFrates, Director of Financial Aid and Scholarships, Eastern Washington University, 102 Sutton Hall, Cheney, WA 99004-2447, 509-359-2314. *Fax:* 509-359-4330. *E-mail:* bdefrates@ewu.edu. *Website:* http://www.ewu.edu/.

EAST STROUDSBURG UNIVERSITY OF PENNSYLVANIA
East Stroudsburg, PA

ABOUT THE INSTITUTION State-supported, coed. *Awards:* associate, bachelor's, and master's degrees. 49 undergraduate majors. *Total enrollment:* 7,353. Undergraduates: 6,656. Freshmen: 1,412.

GIFT AID (NEED-BASED) *Scholarships, grants, and awards:* Federal Pell, FSEOG, state, private, college/university gift aid from institutional funds.

GIFT AID (NON-NEED-BASED) *Scholarships, grants, and awards by category: Academic interests/achievement:* biological sciences, business, communication, computer science, education, English, foreign languages, general academic interests/achievements, health fields, mathematics, physical sciences, social sciences. *Creative arts/performance:* applied art and design, art/fine arts, music, theater/drama. *Special achievements/activities:* general special achievements/activities, leadership. *Special characteristics:* adult students, children and siblings of alumni, handicapped students, international students, local/state students, members of minority groups.

LOANS *Programs:* Federal Direct (Subsidized and Unsubsidized Stafford, PLUS), Perkins.

APPLYING FOR FINANCIAL AID *Required financial aid form:* FAFSA.

CONTACT Kizzy Morris, Registrar and Director of Enrollment Services, East Stroudsburg University of Pennsylvania, 200 Prospect Street, East Stroudsburg, PA 18301-2999, 570-422-2820 or toll-free 877-230-5547. *Fax:* 570-422-2849. *Website:* http://www.esu.edu/.

EAST TENNESSEE STATE UNIVERSITY
Johnson City, TN

ABOUT THE INSTITUTION State-supported, coed. *Awards:* certificates, bachelor's, master's, and doctoral degrees. 49 undergraduate majors. *Total enrollment:* 15,133. Undergraduates: 12,267. Freshmen: 2,082.

GIFT AID (NEED-BASED) *Scholarships, grants, and awards:* Federal Pell, FSEOG, state, private, college/university gift aid from institutional funds, Federal Nursing.

GIFT AID (NON-NEED-BASED) *Scholarships, grants, and awards by category:* *Academic interests/achievement:* biological sciences, business, computer science, education, engineering/technologies, English, general academic interests/achievements, health fields, mathematics, military science, social sciences. *Creative arts/performance:* art/fine arts, journalism/publications, music, theater/drama. *Special achievements/activities:* leadership, memberships. *Special characteristics:* children of union members/company employees, members of minority groups.

LOANS *Programs:* Federal Direct (Subsidized and Unsubsidized Stafford, PLUS), Perkins, Federal Nursing, state, college/university.

WORK-STUDY *Federal work-study:* Total amount: $632,514; jobs available. *State or other work-study/employment:* Total amount: $497,956 (100% need-based). Part-time jobs available.

APPLYING FOR FINANCIAL AID *Required financial aid form:* FAFSA.

CONTACT Margaret L. Miller, Director of Financial Aid, East Tennessee State University, PO Box 70722, Johnson City, TN 37614, 423-439-4300 or toll-free 800-462-3878. *Fax:* 423-439-5855. *E-mail:* finaid@etsu.edu.
Website: http://www.etsu.edu/.

EAST TEXAS BAPTIST UNIVERSITY
Marshall, TX

Tuition & fees: $21,530	Average undergraduate aid package: $15,408

ABOUT THE INSTITUTION Independent Baptist, coed. *Awards:* certificates, bachelor's, and master's degrees. 42 undergraduate majors. *Total enrollment:* 1,290. Undergraduates: 1,241. Freshmen: 350. Federal methodology is used as a basis for awarding need-based institutional aid.

UNDERGRADUATE EXPENSES for 2013–2014 *Application fee:* $25. *Comprehensive fee:* $27,675 includes full-time tuition ($20,670), mandatory fees ($860), and room and board ($6145). *College room only:* $2540. Room and board charges vary according to board plan and housing facility. *Part-time tuition:* $689 per credit hour. *Part-time fees:* $35 per credit hour.

FRESHMAN FINANCIAL AID (Fall 2011) 319 applied for aid; of those 91% were deemed to have need. 100% of freshmen with need received aid; of those 12% had need fully met. *Average percent of need met:* 37% (excluding resources awarded to replace EFC). *Average financial aid package:* $16,107 (excluding resources awarded to replace EFC). 12% of all full-time freshmen had no need and received non-need-based gift aid.

UNDERGRADUATE FINANCIAL AID (Fall 2011) 1,028 applied for aid; of those 91% were deemed to have need. 100% of undergraduates with need received aid; of those 15% had need fully met. *Average percent of need met:* 40% (excluding resources awarded to replace EFC). *Average financial aid package:* $15,408 (excluding resources awarded to replace EFC). 9% of all full-time undergraduates had no need and received non-need-based gift aid.

GIFT AID (NEED-BASED) *Total amount:* $3,693,132 (67% federal, 33% state). *Receiving aid:* Freshmen: 70% (231); all full-time undergraduates: 66% (707). *Average award:* Freshmen: $6066; Undergraduates: $5696. *Scholarships, grants, and awards:* Federal Pell, FSEOG, state, private, college/university gift aid from institutional funds, Federal Nursing.

GIFT AID (NON-NEED-BASED) *Total amount:* $8,943,162 (1% state, 95% institutional, 4% external sources). *Receiving aid:* Freshmen: 88% (289). Undergraduates: 83% (893). *Average award:* Freshmen: $7542. Undergraduates: $8975. *Scholarships, grants, and awards by category:* *Academic interests/achievement:* 853 awards ($3,837,316 total): biological sciences, business, communication, education, English, general academic interests/achievements, health fields, humanities, mathematics, physical sciences, religion/biblical studies, social sciences. *Creative arts/performance:* 92 awards ($268,162 total): music, theater/drama. *Special achievements/activities:* 700 awards ($1,644,034 total): general special achievements/activities, leadership, religious involvement. *Special characteristics:* 139 awards ($500,687 total): children and siblings of alumni, children of faculty/staff, general special characteristics, international students, religious affiliation. *Tuition waivers:* Full or partial for employees or children of employees.

LOANS *Student loans:* $7,431,305 (42% need-based, 58% non-need-based). 84% of past graduating class borrowed through all loan programs. *Average indebtedness*

per student: $23,458. *Average need-based loan:* Freshmen: $3121. Undergraduates: $3958. *Parent loans:* $1,162,923 (100% non-need-based). *Programs:* Federal Direct (Subsidized and Unsubsidized Stafford, PLUS), Perkins, state.

WORK-STUDY *Federal work-study:* Total amount: $141,359; 133 jobs averaging $962. *State or other work-study/employment:* Total amount: $352,247 (5% need-based, 95% non-need-based). 302 part-time jobs averaging $1195.

APPLYING FOR FINANCIAL AID *Required financial aid forms:* FAFSA, institution's own form. *Financial aid deadline (priority):* 6/1. *Notification date:* Continuous.

CONTACT Tommy Young, Director of Financial Aid, East Texas Baptist University, One Tiger Drive, Marshall, TX 75670-1498, 903-923-2137 or toll-free 800-804-ETBU. *Fax:* 903-934-8120. *E-mail:* tyoung@etbu.edu.
Website: http://www.etbu.edu/.

EAST-WEST UNIVERSITY
Chicago, IL

Tuition & fees: $19,020	Average undergraduate aid package: N/A

ABOUT THE INSTITUTION Independent, coed. *Awards:* certificates, associate, and bachelor's degrees. 7 undergraduate majors. *Total enrollment:* 755. Undergraduates: 755. Freshmen: 260. Federal methodology is used as a basis for awarding need-based institutional aid.

UNDERGRADUATE EXPENSES for 2013–2014 *Application fee:* $40. *Tuition:* full-time $17,550.

FRESHMAN FINANCIAL AID (Fall 2011) 688 applied for aid; of those 100% were deemed to have need. 100% of freshmen with need received aid. *Average financial aid package:* $13,770 (excluding resources awarded to replace EFC).

GIFT AID (NEED-BASED) *Total amount:* $5,535,054 (54% federal, 31% state, 15% institutional). *Receiving aid:* Freshmen: 100% (688). *Average award:* Freshmen: $3500. *Scholarships, grants, and awards:* Federal Pell, FSEOG, state, college/university gift aid from institutional funds.

GIFT AID (NON-NEED-BASED) *Scholarships, grants, and awards by category:* *Academic interests/achievement:* general academic interests/achievements.

LOANS *Student loans:* $3,710,846 (100% need-based). 65% of past graduating class borrowed through all loan programs. *Average indebtedness per student:* $3800. *Parent loans:* $16,073 (100% need-based). *Programs:* Federal Direct (Subsidized and Unsubsidized Stafford, PLUS).

WORK-STUDY *Federal work-study:* Total amount: $75,915; 38 jobs averaging $2000.

APPLYING FOR FINANCIAL AID *Required financial aid form:* FAFSA. *Financial aid deadline (priority):* 3/1. *Notification date:* Continuous beginning 1/31. Students must reply by 5/15 or within 4 weeks of notification.

CONTACT Cesar Campos, Director of Financial Aid, East-West University, 816 South Michigan Avenue, Chicago, IL 60605-2103, 312-939-0111 Ext. 1806. *Fax:* 312-939-0083. *E-mail:* elizabth@eastwest.edu.
Website: http://www.eastwest.edu/.

ECCLESIA COLLEGE
Springdale, AR

CONTACT Financial Aid Office, Ecclesia College, 9653 Nations Drive, Springdale, AR 72762, 479-248-7236.
Website: http://www.ecollege.edu/.

ECKERD COLLEGE
St. Petersburg, FL

Tuition & fees: $37,362	Average undergraduate aid package: $26,201

ABOUT THE INSTITUTION Independent Presbyterian, coed. *Awards:* bachelor's degrees. 36 undergraduate majors. *Total enrollment:* 1,893. Undergrad-

uates: 1,893. Freshmen: 532. Federal methodology is used as a basis for awarding need-based institutional aid.

UNDERGRADUATE EXPENSES for 2013–2014 *Application fee:* $40. *Comprehensive fee:* $47,506 includes full-time tuition ($37,046), mandatory fees ($316), and room and board ($10,144). *College room only:* $5106. Room and board charges vary according to board plan and housing facility. *Part-time tuition:* $4361 per course.

FRESHMAN FINANCIAL AID (Fall 2012, est.) 428 applied for aid; of those 82% were deemed to have need. 100% of freshmen with need received aid; of those 16% had need fully met. *Average percent of need met:* 87% (excluding resources awarded to replace EFC). *Average financial aid package:* $29,923 (excluding resources awarded to replace EFC). 29% of all full-time freshmen had no need and received non-need-based gift aid.

UNDERGRADUATE FINANCIAL AID (Fall 2012, est.) 1,318 applied for aid; of those 82% were deemed to have need. 100% of undergraduates with need received aid; of those 18% had need fully met. *Average percent of need met:* 86% (excluding resources awarded to replace EFC). *Average financial aid package:* $26,201 (excluding resources awarded to replace EFC). 33% of all full-time undergraduates had no need and received non-need-based gift aid.

GIFT AID (NEED-BASED) *Total amount:* $20,536,290 (9% federal, 5% state, 84% institutional, 2% external sources). *Receiving aid:* Freshmen: 66% (349); all full-time undergraduates: 58% (1,076). *Average award:* Freshmen: $20,946; Undergraduates: $19,732. *Scholarships, grants, and awards:* Federal Pell, FSEOG, state, college/university gift aid from institutional funds.

GIFT AID (NON-NEED-BASED) *Total amount:* $9,358,665 (4% state, 93% institutional, 3% external sources). *Receiving aid:* Freshmen: 8% (44). Undergraduates: 8% (139). *Average award:* Freshmen: $14,190. Undergraduates: $12,706. *Scholarships, grants, and awards by category:* Academic interests/achievement: general academic interests/achievements. Creative arts/performance: art/fine arts, creative writing, music, theater/drama. Special characteristics: children of faculty/staff, international students, local/state students, religious affiliation. *Tuition waivers:* Full or partial for employees or children of employees. *ROTC:* Army cooperative, Air Force cooperative.

LOANS *Student loans:* $9,320,088 (82% need-based, 18% non-need-based). 58% of past graduating class borrowed through all loan programs. *Average indebtedness per student:* $33,957. *Average need-based loan:* Freshmen: $3939. Undergraduates: $4672. *Parent loans:* $4,531,374 (37% need-based, 63% non-need-based). *Programs:* Federal Direct (Subsidized and Unsubsidized Stafford, PLUS), Perkins, college/university.

WORK-STUDY *Federal work-study:* Total amount: $1,360,740; jobs available. *State or other work-study/employment:* Total amount: $40,000 (100% non-need-based). Part-time jobs available.

ATHLETIC AWARDS Total amount: $1,394,865 (33% need-based, 67% non-need-based).

APPLYING FOR FINANCIAL AID *Required financial aid form:* FAFSA. *Financial aid deadline (priority):* 3/1. *Notification date:* Continuous beginning 2/20. Students must reply by 5/1.

CONTACT Dr. Pat Garrett Watkins, Director of Financial Aid, Eckerd College, 4200 54th Avenue, South, St. Petersburg, FL 33711, 727-864-8334 or toll-free 800-456-9009. *Fax:* 727-866-2304. *E-mail:* watkinpe@eckerd.edu. *Website:* http://www.eckerd.edu/.

ECPI COLLEGE OF TECHNOLOGY
Raleigh, NC

CONTACT Financial Aid Office, ECPI College of Technology, 4101 Doie Cope Road, Raleigh, NC 27613, 919-571-0057 or toll-free 800-986-1200. *Website:* http://www.ecpi.edu/.

ECPI COLLEGE OF TECHNOLOGY
Glen Allen, VA

CONTACT Financial Aid Office, ECPI College of Technology, 4305 Cox Road, Glen Allen, VA 23060, 804-934-0100 or toll-free 800-986-1200. *Website:* http://www.ecpi.edu/.

ECPI COLLEGE OF TECHNOLOGY
Manassas, VA

CONTACT Financial Aid Office, ECPI College of Technology, 10021 Balls Ford Road, Manassas, VA 20109, 703-330-5300 or toll-free 866-708-6172. *Website:* http://www.ecpi.edu/.

ECPI COLLEGE OF TECHNOLOGY
Newport News, VA

CONTACT Financial Aid Office, ECPI College of Technology, 1001 Omni Boulevard, #100, Newport News, VA 23606, 757-838-9191 or toll-free 866-499-0335. *Website:* http://www.ecpi.edu/.

ECPI COLLEGE OF TECHNOLOGY
Virginia Beach, VA

ABOUT THE INSTITUTION Proprietary, coed. 28 undergraduate majors.

GIFT AID (NEED-BASED) *Scholarships, grants, and awards:* Federal Pell, FSEOG, state, private, college/university gift aid from institutional funds.

GIFT AID (NON-NEED-BASED) *Scholarships, grants, and awards by category:* Academic interests/achievement: business, computer science, engineering/technologies, health fields. Special achievements/activities: community service, general special achievements/activities. Special characteristics: adult students, children and siblings of alumni, children of current students, children of faculty/staff, general special characteristics, parents of current students, veterans, veterans' children.

LOANS *Programs:* Federal Direct (Subsidized and Unsubsidized Stafford, PLUS), Perkins, college/university, private loans.

APPLYING FOR FINANCIAL AID *Required financial aid forms:* FAFSA, institution's own form.

CONTACT Mrs. Kathi Turner, Director of Financial Aid, ECPI College of Technology, 5555 Greenwich Road, Suite 300, Virginia Beach, VA 23462, 757-490-9090 or toll-free 866-499-0336. *Fax:* 757-671-8661. *E-mail:* kturner@ecpi.edu. *Website:* http://www.ecpi.edu/.

EDGEWOOD COLLEGE
Madison, WI

Tuition & fees: $23,740	Average undergraduate aid package: $17,858

ABOUT THE INSTITUTION Independent Roman Catholic, coed, primarily women. *Awards:* bachelor's, master's, and doctoral degrees. 49 undergraduate majors. *Total enrollment:* 3,064. Undergraduates: 2,028. Freshmen: 342. Federal methodology is used as a basis for awarding need-based institutional aid.

UNDERGRADUATE EXPENSES for 2013–2014 *Application fee:* $25. *Comprehensive fee:* $32,216 includes full-time tuition ($23,740) and room and board ($8476). Full-time tuition and fees vary according to degree level. Room and board charges vary according to housing facility. *Part-time tuition:* $747 per credit. Part-time tuition and fees vary according to course load and degree level.

FRESHMAN FINANCIAL AID (Fall 2011) 263 applied for aid; of those 92% were deemed to have need. 100% of freshmen with need received aid; of those 7% had need fully met. *Average percent of need met:* 77% (excluding resources awarded to replace EFC). *Average financial aid package:* $20,477 (excluding resources awarded to replace EFC). 16% of all full-time freshmen had no need and received non-need-based gift aid.

UNDERGRADUATE FINANCIAL AID (Fall 2011) 1,454 applied for aid; of those 92% were deemed to have need. 100% of undergraduates with need received aid; of those 9% had need fully met. *Average percent of need met:* 71% (excluding resources awarded to replace EFC). *Average financial aid package:* $17,858 (excluding resources awarded to replace EFC). 14% of all full-time undergraduates had no need and received non-need-based gift aid.

GIFT AID (NEED-BASED) Total amount: $15,513,298 (22% federal, 12% state, 56% institutional, 10% external sources). **Receiving aid:** Freshmen: 81% (239); all full-time undergraduates: 71% (1,237). **Average award:** Freshmen: $15,611; Undergraduates: $12,225. **Scholarships, grants, and awards:** Federal Pell, FSEOG, state, private, college/university gift aid from institutional funds.

GIFT AID (NON-NEED-BASED) Total amount: $2,080,375 (5% federal, 63% institutional, 32% external sources). **Receiving aid:** Freshmen: 2% (7). Undergraduates: 3% (58). **Average award:** Freshmen: $6608. Undergraduates: $4790. **Scholarships, grants, and awards by category:** Academic interests/achievement: 1,181 awards ($4,809,375 total): area/ethnic studies, foreign languages, general academic interests/achievements. Creative arts/performance: 119 awards ($186,750 total): art/fine arts, creative writing, music, performing arts, theater/drama. Special achievements/activities: 53 awards ($284,944 total): community service. Special characteristics: 67 awards ($610,375 total): children of faculty/staff. **Tuition waivers:** Full or partial for employees or children of employees. **ROTC:** Army cooperative, Naval cooperative, Air Force cooperative.

LOANS Student loans: $14,789,707 (78% need-based, 22% non-need-based). 75% of past graduating class borrowed through all loan programs. *Average indebtedness per student:* $23,464. **Average need-based loan:** Freshmen: $3619. Undergraduates: $5328. **Parent loans:** $1,643,337 (47% need-based, 53% non-need-based). **Programs:** Federal Direct (Subsidized and Unsubsidized Stafford, PLUS), Perkins, state.

WORK-STUDY Federal work-study: Total amount: $913,477; 433 jobs averaging $2027. **State or other work-study/employment:** Total amount: $2,113,538 (52% need-based, 48% non-need-based). 737 part-time jobs averaging $1961.

APPLYING FOR FINANCIAL AID Required financial aid form: FAFSA. **Financial aid deadline (priority):** 3/1. **Notification date:** Continuous beginning 3/15.

CONTACT Ms. Kari J. Gribble, Director of Financial Aid and Edgewood Central, Edgewood College, 1000 Edgewood College Drive, Madison, WI 53711-1997, 608-663-4300 or toll-free 800-444-4861 Ext. 2294. *E-mail:* ecentral@edgewood.edu. *Website:* http://www.edgewood.edu/.

GIFT AID (NON-NEED-BASED) Total amount: $2,736,221 (4% federal, 12% state, 46% institutional, 38% external sources). **Receiving aid:** Freshmen: 38% (560). Undergraduates: 31% (1,886). **Average award:** Freshmen: $3193. Undergraduates: $2213. **Scholarships, grants, and awards by category:** Academic interests/achievement: biological sciences, business, communication, computer science, education, engineering/technologies, English, foreign languages, general academic interests/achievements, health fields, humanities, mathematics, military science, physical sciences, premedicine, religion/biblical studies, social sciences. Creative arts/performance: art/fine arts, cinema/film/broadcasting, journalism/publications, music. Special achievements/activities: general special achievements/activities. Special characteristics: adult students, children and siblings of alumni, children of faculty/staff, children of union members/company employees, children with a deceased or disabled parent, first-generation college students, general special characteristics, handicapped students, international students, local/state students, members of minority groups, out-of-state students, religious affiliation, veterans, veterans' children. **Tuition waivers:** Full or partial for minority students, employees or children of employees, senior citizens. **ROTC:** Army.

LOANS Student loans: $42,026,110 (43% need-based, 57% non-need-based). 46% of past graduating class borrowed through all loan programs. *Average indebtedness per student:* $23,633. **Average need-based loan:** Freshmen: $3063. Undergraduates: $3841. **Parent loans:** $7,541,011 (100% non-need-based). **Programs:** Federal Direct (Subsidized and Unsubsidized Stafford, PLUS), Perkins, Federal Nursing.

WORK-STUDY Federal work-study: Total amount: $423,543; 347 jobs averaging $1505. **State or other work-study/employment:** Total amount: $1,343,181 (4% need-based, 96% non-need-based). 648 part-time jobs averaging $1829.

ATHLETIC AWARDS Total amount: $976,703 (100% non-need-based).

APPLYING FOR FINANCIAL AID Required financial aid forms: FAFSA; state aid form. **Financial aid deadline (priority):** 3/15. **Notification date:** Continuous beginning 4/1. Students must reply within 2 weeks of notification.

CONTACT Ms. Alyssa Dobson, Interim Director of Financial Aid, Edinboro University of Pennsylvania, Hamilton Hall, Edinboro, PA 16444, 814-732-5555 Ext. 474 or toll-free 888-846-2676. *Fax:* 814-732-2129. *E-mail:* finaid@edinboro.edu. *Website:* http://www.edinboro.edu/.

EDINBORO UNIVERSITY OF PENNSYLVANIA
Edinboro, PA

Tuition & fees (PA res): $8578	Average undergraduate aid package: $8407

ABOUT THE INSTITUTION State-supported, coed. **Awards:** certificates, associate, bachelor's, and master's degrees. 47 undergraduate majors. **Total enrollment:** 7,462. Undergraduates: 6,090. Freshmen: 1,235. Federal methodology is used as a basis for awarding need-based institutional aid.

UNDERGRADUATE EXPENSES for 2013–2014 Application fee: $30. **Tuition, state resident:** full-time $6428; part-time $268 per credit. **Tuition, nonresident:** full-time $9642; part-time $402 per credit. **Required fees:** full-time $2150; $90 per credit. Part-time tuition and fees vary according to course load. **College room and board:** $7362; **Room only:** $5200. Room and board charges vary according to board plan.

FRESHMAN FINANCIAL AID (Fall 2011) 1,402 applied for aid; of those 90% were deemed to have need. 98% of freshmen with need received aid; of those 3% had need fully met. **Average percent of need met:** 47% (excluding resources awarded to replace EFC). **Average financial aid package:** $7780 (excluding resources awarded to replace EFC). 1% of all full-time freshmen had no need and received non-need-based gift aid.

UNDERGRADUATE FINANCIAL AID (Fall 2011) 5,468 applied for aid; of those 90% were deemed to have need. 98% of undergraduates with need received aid; of those 4% had need fully met. **Average percent of need met:** 48% (excluding resources awarded to replace EFC). **Average financial aid package:** $8407 (excluding resources awarded to replace EFC). 1% of all full-time undergraduates had no need and received non-need-based gift aid.

GIFT AID (NEED-BASED) Total amount: $20,756,940 (61% federal, 37% state, 2% institutional). **Receiving aid:** Freshmen: 80% (1,180); all full-time undergraduates: 77% (4,660). **Average award:** Freshmen: $4261; Undergraduates: $4148. **Scholarships, grants, and awards:** Federal Pell, FSEOG, state, private, college/university gift aid from institutional funds.

EDP UNIVERSITY OF PUERTO RICO
Hato Rey, PR

Tuition & fees: $6240	Average undergraduate aid package: $5587

ABOUT THE INSTITUTION Proprietary, coed. **Awards:** certificates, associate, bachelor's, and master's degrees. 13 undergraduate majors. **Total enrollment:** 1,198. Undergraduates: 1,141. Freshmen: 107. Federal methodology is used as a basis for awarding need-based institutional aid.

UNDERGRADUATE EXPENSES for 2013–2014 Application fee: $15. **Tuition:** full-time $5400; part-time $170 per credit hour. **Required fees:** full-time $840; $170 per credit hour or $420 per credit hour. Full-time tuition and fees vary according to course load and program. Part-time tuition and fees vary according to course load and program.

FRESHMAN FINANCIAL AID (Fall 2011) 71 applied for aid; of those 100% were deemed to have need. 100% of freshmen with need received aid. **Average percent of need met:** 95% (excluding resources awarded to replace EFC). **Average financial aid package:** $5700 (excluding resources awarded to replace EFC).

UNDERGRADUATE FINANCIAL AID (Fall 2011) 1,028 applied for aid; of those 100% were deemed to have need. 100% of undergraduates with need received aid. **Average percent of need met:** 90% (excluding resources awarded to replace EFC). **Average financial aid package:** $5587 (excluding resources awarded to replace EFC).

GIFT AID (NEED-BASED) Total amount: $1,924,391 (96% federal, 3% state, 1% external sources). **Receiving aid:** Freshmen: 95% (71); all full-time undergraduates: 90% (1,028). **Average award:** Freshmen: $5434; Undergraduates: $5416. **Scholarships, grants, and awards:** Federal Pell, FSEOG, state.

GIFT AID (NON-NEED-BASED) Receiving aid: Undergraduates: 5% (60). **Scholarships, grants, and awards by category:** Special characteristics: veterans, veterans' children. **Tuition waivers:** Full or partial for employees or children of employees.

LOANS Student loans: $229,767 (100% need-based). 1% of past graduating class borrowed through all loan programs. *Average indebtedness per student:* $4256.

Average need-based loan: Freshmen: $2096. Undergraduates: $3137. **Programs:** Federal Direct (Subsidized and Unsubsidized Stafford, PLUS).

WORK-STUDY *Federal work-study:* Total amount: $69,013; 35 jobs averaging $1972.

APPLYING FOR FINANCIAL AID *Required financial aid form:* FAFSA. *Financial aid deadline:* Continuous. *Notification date:* Continuous beginning 8/15.

CONTACT Yaitzaenid Gonzalez, Financial Aid Administrator, EDP University of Puerto Rico, PO Box 192303, San Juan, PR 00919-2303, 787-765-3560 Ext. 253. *Fax:* 787-777-0025. *E-mail:* ygonzalez@edpcollege.edu. *Website:* http://www.edpuniversity.edu/.

EDP UNIVERSITY OF PUERTO RICO–SAN SEBASTIAN
San Sebastian, PR

Tuition & fees: $6120	Average undergraduate aid package: $6052

ABOUT THE INSTITUTION Proprietary, coed. **Awards:** associate and bachelor's degrees. 9 undergraduate majors. **Total enrollment:** 881. Undergraduates: 881. Freshmen: 217. Federal methodology is used as a basis for awarding need-based institutional aid.

UNDERGRADUATE EXPENSES for 2013–2014 **Application fee:** $15. *Tuition:* full-time $5400; part-time $156 per credit hour. *Required fees:* full-time $720; $156 per credit hour or $360 per term. Full-time tuition and fees vary according to course load and program. Part-time tuition and fees vary according to course load and program.

FRESHMAN FINANCIAL AID (Fall 2011) 182 applied for aid; of those 100% were deemed to have need. 100% of freshmen with need received aid. *Average percent of need met:* 92% (excluding resources awarded to replace EFC). *Average financial aid package:* $5398 (excluding resources awarded to replace EFC).

UNDERGRADUATE FINANCIAL AID (Fall 2011) 1,019 applied for aid; of those 100% were deemed to have need. 100% of undergraduates with need received aid. *Average percent of need met:* 95% (excluding resources awarded to replace EFC). *Average financial aid package:* $6052 (excluding resources awarded to replace EFC).

GIFT AID (NEED-BASED) *Total amount:* $4,553,149 (97% federal, 3% state). *Receiving aid:* Freshmen: 92% (177); all full-time undergraduates: 90% (965). *Average award:* Freshmen: $5272; Undergraduates: $5299. **Scholarships, grants, and awards:** Federal Pell, FSEOG, state.

GIFT AID (NON-NEED-BASED) *Receiving aid:* Undergraduates: 2% (25). **Scholarships, grants, and awards by category:** *Special characteristics:* veterans, veterans' children. *Tuition waivers:* Full or partial for employees or children of employees.

LOANS *Student loans:* $1,731,784 (100% need-based). 1% of past graduating class borrowed through all loan programs. *Average indebtedness per student:* $4729. *Average need-based loan:* Freshmen: $3485. Undergraduates: $3607. **Programs:** Federal Direct (Subsidized and Unsubsidized Stafford, PLUS).

WORK-STUDY *Federal work-study:* Total amount: $59,439; 43 jobs averaging $1382.

APPLYING FOR FINANCIAL AID *Required financial aid form:* FAFSA. *Financial aid deadline:* Continuous. *Notification date:* Continuous beginning 8/15.

CONTACT Mrs. Yaitzaenid Gonzalez, Financial Aid Administrator, EDP University of Puerto Rico–San Sebastian, PO Box 192303, San Juan , PR 00919, 787-765-3560 Ext. 253. *Fax:* 787-777-0025. *E-mail:* ygonzalez@edpcollege.edu. *Website:* http://www.edpuniversity.edu/.

EDWARD WATERS COLLEGE
Jacksonville, FL

CONTACT Gabriel Mbomeh, Director of Financial Aid, Edward Waters College, 1658 Kings Road, Jacksonville, FL 32209-6199, 904-366-2528 or toll-free 888-898-3191. *Website:* http://www.ewc.edu/.

ELIZABETH CITY STATE UNIVERSITY
Elizabeth City, NC

Tuition & fees (NC res): $4428	Average undergraduate aid package: N/A

ABOUT THE INSTITUTION State-supported, coed. **Awards:** bachelor's and master's degrees. 35 undergraduate majors. **Total enrollment:** 2,878. Undergraduates: 2,760. Freshmen: 472. Federal methodology is used as a basis for awarding need-based institutional aid.

UNDERGRADUATE EXPENSES for 2013–2014 **Application fee:** $30. *Tuition, area resident:* part-time $347 per credit hour. *Tuition, state resident:* full-time $2776. *Tuition, nonresident:* full-time $13,633; part-time $1704.11 per credit hour. *Required fees:* full-time $1652. *College room and board:* $7213; *Room only:* $4440. Room and board charges vary according to housing facility.

FRESHMAN FINANCIAL AID (Fall 2011) 359 applied for aid; of those 100% were deemed to have need. 100% of freshmen with need received aid.

UNDERGRADUATE FINANCIAL AID (Fall 2011) 2,836 applied for aid; of those 93% were deemed to have need. 100% of undergraduates with need received aid.

GIFT AID (NEED-BASED) *Total amount:* $15,546,419 (64% federal, 29% state, 6% institutional, 1% external sources). *Receiving aid:* Freshmen: 93% (359); all full-time undergraduates: 93% (2,643). *Average award:* Undergraduates: $5882. **Scholarships, grants, and awards:** Federal Pell, FSEOG, state, private, college/university gift aid from institutional funds, United Negro College Fund.

GIFT AID (NON-NEED-BASED) *Total amount:* $281,146 (100% institutional). **Scholarships, grants, and awards by category:** *Academic interests/achievement:* computer science, education, general academic interests/achievements, mathematics, military science. *Creative arts/performance:* music, performing arts. *Special characteristics:* ethnic background, handicapped students, international students, members of minority groups, veterans, veterans' children. *ROTC:* Army.

LOANS *Student loans:* $13,604,195 (59% need-based, 41% non-need-based). *Average need-based loan:* Undergraduates: $3633. *Parent loans:* $1,513,661 (100% need-based). **Programs:** Federal Direct (Subsidized and Unsubsidized Stafford, PLUS), Perkins.

WORK-STUDY *Federal work-study:* Total amount: $316,497; jobs available.

ATHLETIC AWARDS Total amount: $526,533 (100% need-based).

APPLYING FOR FINANCIAL AID *Required financial aid form:* FAFSA. *Financial aid deadline (priority):* 3/15. *Notification date:* Continuous beginning 4/1.

CONTACT LaTonya M. Gregory, Assistant Director of Financial Aid, Elizabeth City State University, 1704 Weeksville Road, Campus Box 914, Elizabeth City, NC 27909-7806, 252-335-3285 or toll-free 800-347-3278. *Fax:* 252-335-3716. *Website:* http://www.ecsu.edu/.

ELIZABETHTOWN COLLEGE
Elizabethtown, PA

Tuition & fees: $38,200	Average undergraduate aid package: $25,493

ABOUT THE INSTITUTION Independent Church of the Brethren, coed. **Awards:** bachelor's and master's degrees. 47 undergraduate majors. **Total enrollment:** 1,911. Undergraduates: 1,885. Freshmen: 505. Both federal and institutional methodology are used as a basis for awarding need-based institutional aid.

UNDERGRADUATE EXPENSES for 2013–2014 **Application fee:** $30. **Comprehensive fee:** $47,600 includes full-time tuition ($38,200) and room and board ($9400). **College room only:** $4650. Full-time tuition and fees vary according to course load. Room and board charges vary according to board plan and housing facility. *Part-time tuition:* $925 per credit hour. *Part-time fees:* $525. Part-time tuition and fees vary according to course load.

FRESHMAN FINANCIAL AID (Fall 2012, est.) 441 applied for aid; of those 91% were deemed to have need. 100% of freshmen with need received aid; of those 19% had need fully met. *Average percent of need met:* 81% (excluding resources awarded to replace EFC). *Average financial aid package:* $26,025 (excluding resources awarded to replace EFC). 18% of all full-time freshmen had no need and received non-need-based gift aid.

UNDERGRADUATE FINANCIAL AID (Fall 2012, est.) 1,565 applied for aid; of those 91% were deemed to have need. 100% of undergraduates with need received aid; of those 18% had need fully met. *Average percent of need met:* 78% (excluding resources awarded to replace EFC). *Average financial aid package:* $25,493 (excluding resources awarded to replace EFC). 21% of all full-time undergraduates had no need and received non-need-based gift aid.

GIFT AID (NEED-BASED) *Total amount:* $29,801,139 (6% federal, 6% state, 80% institutional, 8% external sources). *Receiving aid:* Freshmen: 79% (401); all full-time undergraduates: 77% (1,422). *Average award:* Freshmen: $22,198; Undergraduates: $20,942. *Scholarships, grants, and awards:* Federal Pell, FSEOG, state, private, college/university gift aid from institutional funds.

GIFT AID (NON-NEED-BASED) *Total amount:* $8,933,422 (83% institutional, 17% external sources). *Receiving aid:* Freshmen: 12% (61). Undergraduates: 11% (206). *Average award:* Freshmen: $18,537. Undergraduates: $16,032. *Scholarships, grants, and awards by category: Academic interests/achievement:* biological sciences, business, communication, computer science, education, engineering/technologies, English, foreign languages, general academic interests/achievements, health fields, humanities, international studies, mathematics, physical sciences, premedicine, religion/biblical studies, social sciences. *Creative arts/performance:* art/fine arts, music, performing arts, theater/drama. *Special achievements/activities:* religious involvement. *Special characteristics:* children of faculty/staff, international students, local/state students, members of minority groups, religious affiliation, siblings of current students. *Tuition waivers:* Full or partial for employees or children of employees.

LOANS *Student loans:* $13,188,978 (68% need-based, 32% non-need-based). *Average need-based loan:* Freshmen: $3546. Undergraduates: $4433. *Parent loans:* $6,455,416 (33% need-based, 67% non-need-based). *Programs:* Federal Direct (Subsidized and Unsubsidized Stafford, PLUS), Perkins.

WORK-STUDY *Federal work-study:* Total amount: $1,261,553; 968 jobs averaging $1325.

APPLYING FOR FINANCIAL AID *Required financial aid forms:* FAFSA, institution's own form, state aid form, federal income tax form(s), W-2 forms. *Financial aid deadline (priority):* 3/15. *Notification date:* Continuous beginning 3/1. Students must reply by 5/1 or within 2 weeks of notification.

CONTACT Ms. Elizabeth K. McCloud, Director of Financial Aid, Elizabethtown College, 1 Alpha Drive, Elizabethtown, PA 17022-2298, 717-361-1404. *Fax:* 717-361-1514. *E-mail:* mcclouek@etown.edu. *Website:* http://www.etown.edu/.

ELLIS UNIVERSITY
Chicago, IL

CONTACT Financial Aid Office, Ellis University, 111 North Canal Street, Suite 380, Chicago, IL 60606-7204 or toll-free 877-355-4762. *Website:* http://www.ellis.edu/.

ELMHURST COLLEGE
Elmhurst, IL

Tuition & fees: $32,945	Average undergraduate aid package: $21,775

ABOUT THE INSTITUTION Independent United Church of Christ, coed. *Awards:* bachelor's and master's degrees. 68 undergraduate majors. *Total enrollment:* 3,298. Undergraduates: 3,052. Freshmen: 560. Federal methodology is used as a basis for awarding need-based institutional aid.

UNDERGRADUATE EXPENSES for 2013–2014 *Comprehensive fee:* $42,057 includes full-time tuition ($32,720), mandatory fees ($225), and room and

board ($9112). *College room only:* $5520. Room and board charges vary according to board plan and housing facility. *Part-time tuition:* $993 per semester hour. Part-time tuition and fees vary according to course load.

FRESHMAN FINANCIAL AID (Fall 2012, est.) 517 applied for aid; of those 87% were deemed to have need. 100% of freshmen with need received aid; of those 32% had need fully met. *Average percent of need met:* 80% (excluding resources awarded to replace EFC). *Average financial aid package:* $24,820 (excluding resources awarded to replace EFC). 11% of all full-time freshmen had no need and received non-need-based gift aid.

UNDERGRADUATE FINANCIAL AID (Fall 2012, est.) 2,761 applied for aid; of those 81% were deemed to have need. 100% of undergraduates with need received aid; of those 40% had need fully met. *Average percent of need met:* 73% (excluding resources awarded to replace EFC). *Average financial aid package:* $21,775 (excluding resources awarded to replace EFC). 16% of all full-time undergraduates had no need and received non-need-based gift aid.

GIFT AID (NEED-BASED) *Total amount:* $39,461,867 (10% federal, 11% state, 78% institutional, 1% external sources). *Receiving aid:* Freshmen: 80% (446); all full-time undergraduates: 74% (2,226). *Average award:* Freshmen: $21,699; Undergraduates: $19,165. *Scholarships, grants, and awards:* Federal Pell, FSEOG, state, private, college/university gift aid from institutional funds.

GIFT AID (NON-NEED-BASED) *Total amount:* $10,061,669 (99% institutional, 1% external sources). *Receiving aid:* Freshmen: 31% (173). Undergraduates: 26% (775). *Average award:* Freshmen: $15,556. Undergraduates: $13,219. *Scholarships, grants, and awards by category: Academic interests/achievement:* 1,881 awards ($23,430,467 total): biological sciences, business, communication, computer science, education, English, foreign languages, general academic interests/achievements, health fields, humanities, international studies, mathematics, physical sciences, premedicine, religion/biblical studies, social sciences. *Creative arts/performance:* 167 awards ($1,525,719 total): art/fine arts, music, theater/drama. *Special characteristics:* 899 awards ($3,600,608 total): children and siblings of alumni, children of current students, children with a deceased or disabled parent, ethnic background, members of minority groups, religious affiliation, siblings of current students, spouses of current students, veterans, veterans' children. *Tuition waivers:* Full or partial for employees or children of employees, senior citizens. *ROTC:* Army cooperative, Air Force cooperative.

LOANS *Student loans:* $15,845,395 (47% need-based, 53% non-need-based). 70% of past graduating class borrowed through all loan programs. *Average indebtedness per student:* $29,787. *Average need-based loan:* Freshmen: $3687. Undergraduates: $4394. *Parent loans:* $4,863,951 (42% need-based, 58% non-need-based). *Programs:* Federal Direct (Subsidized and Unsubsidized Stafford, PLUS), Perkins, alternative loans.

WORK-STUDY *Federal work-study:* Total amount: $347,296; 396 jobs averaging $877. *State or other work-study/employment:* Total amount: $581,334 (100% non-need-based). 361 part-time jobs averaging $1610.

APPLYING FOR FINANCIAL AID *Required financial aid form:* FAFSA. *Financial aid deadline (priority):* 3/1. *Notification date:* Continuous beginning 3/1. Students must reply within 3 weeks of notification.

CONTACT Ruth A. Pusich, Director of Financial Aid, Elmhurst College, Goebel Hall 106A, 190 Prospect Avenue, Elmhurst, IL 60126-3296, 630-617-3080 or toll-free 800-697-1871. *Fax:* 630-617-5188. *E-mail:* ruthp@elmhurst.edu. *Website:* http://www.elmhurst.edu/.

ELMIRA COLLEGE
Elmira, NY

Tuition & fees: $38,150	Average undergraduate aid package: $29,374

ABOUT THE INSTITUTION Independent, coed. *Awards:* associate, bachelor's, and master's degrees. 61 undergraduate majors. *Total enrollment:* 1,533. Undergraduates: 1,386. Freshmen: 356. Federal methodology is used as a basis for awarding need-based institutional aid.

UNDERGRADUATE EXPENSES for 2013–2014 *Application fee:* $50. *Comprehensive fee:* $49,950 includes full-time tuition ($36,600), mandatory fees ($1550), and room and board ($11,800). *College room only:* $6300. Room and board charges vary according to housing facility. Part-time tuition and fees vary according to course load and degree level. *Payment plan:* Tuition prepayment.

FRESHMAN FINANCIAL AID (Fall 2012, est.) 322 applied for aid; of those 93% were deemed to have need. 100% of freshmen with need received aid; of those 18%

had need fully met. **Average percent of need met:** 77% (excluding resources awarded to replace EFC). **Average financial aid package:** $30,429 (excluding resources awarded to replace EFC). 15% of all full-time freshmen had no need and received non-need-based gift aid.

UNDERGRADUATE FINANCIAL AID (Fall 2012, est.) 1,037 applied for aid; of those 94% were deemed to have need. 100% of undergraduates with need received aid; of those 16% had need fully met. **Average percent of need met:** 76% (excluding resources awarded to replace EFC). **Average financial aid package:** $29,374 (excluding resources awarded to replace EFC). 17% of all full-time undergraduates had no need and received non-need-based gift aid.

GIFT AID (NEED-BASED) Total amount: $24,183,082 (6% federal, 4% state, 87% institutional, 3% external sources). **Receiving aid:** Freshmen: 84% (300); all full-time undergraduates: 81% (975). **Average award:** Freshmen: $27,361; Undergraduates: $25,512. **Scholarships, grants, and awards:** Federal Pell, FSEOG, state, private, college/university gift aid from institutional funds.

GIFT AID (NON-NEED-BASED) Total amount: $6,156,781 (1% federal, 1% state, 90% institutional, 8% external sources). **Receiving aid:** Freshmen: 13% (48). Undergraduates: 10% (122). **Average award:** Freshmen: $26,083. Undergraduates: $23,117. **Scholarships, grants, and awards by category:** Academic interests/achievement: 777 awards ($16,256,462 total): general academic interests/achievements. Special achievements/activities: 92 awards ($895,000 total): leadership. Special characteristics: 513 awards ($3,054,784 total): children of faculty/staff, international students, local/state students, out-of-state students, previous college experience, siblings of current students, veterans. **Tuition waivers:** Full or partial for employees or children of employees. **ROTC:** Army, Air Force cooperative.

LOANS Student loans: $9,159,651 (72% need-based, 28% non-need-based). 80% of past graduating class borrowed through all loan programs. **Average indebtedness per student:** $28,586. **Average need-based loan:** Freshmen: $3529. Undergraduates: $4220. **Parent loans:** $4,717,301 (47% need-based, 53% non-need-based). **Programs:** Federal Direct (Subsidized and Unsubsidized Stafford, PLUS), Perkins, college/university.

WORK-STUDY Federal work-study: Total amount: $346,643; 298 jobs averaging $1200. **State or other work-study/employment:** Total amount: $272,820 (36% need-based, 64% non-need-based). 224 part-time jobs averaging $1200.

APPLYING FOR FINANCIAL AID Required financial aid forms: FAFSA, state aid form. **Financial aid deadline (priority):** 2/1. **Notification date:** Continuous beginning 2/1. Students must reply by 5/1 or within 3 weeks of notification.

CONTACT Kathleen L. Cohen, Dean of Financial Aid, Elmira College, One Park Place, Elmira, NY 14901-2099, 607-735-1728 or toll-free 800-935-6472. *Fax:* 607-735-1718. *E-mail:* kcohen@elmira.edu.
Website: http://www.elmira.edu/.

ELMS COLLEGE
Chicopee, MA

CONTACT Ms. April Arcouette, Assistant Director of Student Financial Aid Services, Elms College, 291 Springfield Street, Chicopee, MA 01013-2839, 413-265-2249 or toll-free 800-255-ELMS. *Fax:* 413-265-2671. *E-mail:* arcouettea@elms.edu.
Website: http://www.elms.edu/.

ELON UNIVERSITY
Elon, NC

Tuition & fees: $28,980	Average undergraduate aid package: $17,378

ABOUT THE INSTITUTION Independent United Church of Christ, coed. **Awards:** bachelor's, master's, and doctoral degrees. 60 undergraduate majors. **Total enrollment:** 6,029. Undergraduates: 5,357. Freshmen: 1,425. Institutional methodology is used as a basis for awarding need-based institutional aid.

UNDERGRADUATE EXPENSES for 2013–2014 Application fee: $50. **Comprehensive fee:** $38,460 includes full-time tuition ($28,633), mandatory fees ($347), and room and board ($9480). **College room only:** $4690. Room and board charges vary according to board plan and housing facility. **Part-time tuition:** $898 per hour. Part-time tuition and fees vary according to course load.

FRESHMAN FINANCIAL AID (Fall 2012, est.) 839 applied for aid; of those 61% were deemed to have need. 99% of freshmen with need received aid. **Average percent of need met:** 62% (excluding resources awarded to replace EFC). **Average financial aid package:** $16,094 (excluding resources awarded to replace EFC). 22% of all full-time freshmen had no need and received non-need-based gift aid.

UNDERGRADUATE FINANCIAL AID (Fall 2012, est.) 2,563 applied for aid; of those 72% were deemed to have need. 99% of undergraduates with need received aid. **Average percent of need met:** 63% (excluding resources awarded to replace EFC). **Average financial aid package:** $17,378 (excluding resources awarded to replace EFC). 21% of all full-time undergraduates had no need and received non-need-based gift aid.

GIFT AID (NEED-BASED) Total amount: $18,679,381 (12% federal, 9% state, 77% institutional, 2% external sources). **Receiving aid:** Freshmen: 31% (433); all full-time undergraduates: 32% (1,643). **Average award:** Freshmen: $12,349; Undergraduates: $13,628. **Scholarships, grants, and awards:** Federal Pell, FSEOG, state, private, college/university gift aid from institutional funds.

GIFT AID (NON-NEED-BASED) Total amount: $7,454,205 (2% state, 94% institutional, 4% external sources). **Receiving aid:** Freshmen: 17% (246). Undergraduates: 16% (853). **Average award:** Freshmen: $6114. Undergraduates: $5882. **Scholarships, grants, and awards by category:** Academic interests/achievement: 1,927 awards ($8,776,079 total): biological sciences, business, communication, computer science, education, engineering/technologies, general academic interests/achievements, mathematics, military science, physical sciences, premedicine, religion/biblical studies, social sciences. Creative arts/performance: 96 awards ($250,480 total): art/fine arts, journalism/publications, music, performing arts, theater/drama. Special achievements/activities: 41 awards ($71,322 total): community service, general special achievements/activities, leadership, religious involvement. Special characteristics: 110 awards ($1,447,476 total): adult students, children of faculty/staff, ethnic background, first-generation college students, international students, members of minority groups, relatives of clergy. **Tuition waivers:** Full or partial for employees or children of employees. **ROTC:** Army, Air Force cooperative.

LOANS Student loans: $16,465,354 (69% need-based, 31% non-need-based). 44% of past graduating class borrowed through all loan programs. **Average indebtedness per student:** $28,183. **Average need-based loan:** Freshmen: $3380. Undergraduates: $4402. **Parent loans:** $9,725,697 (54% need-based, 46% non-need-based). **Programs:** Federal Direct (Subsidized and Unsubsidized Stafford, PLUS), state, college/university, alternative loans.

WORK-STUDY Federal work-study: Total amount: $3,025,027; 1,308 jobs averaging $2306.

ATHLETIC AWARDS Total amount: $7,227,914 (32% need-based, 68% non-need-based).

APPLYING FOR FINANCIAL AID Required financial aid forms: FAFSA, institution's own form, CSS Financial Aid PROFILE. **Financial aid deadline (priority):** 3/15. **Notification date:** 3/30.

CONTACT Patrick Murphy, PhD, Director of Financial Planning, Elon University, 2725 Campus Box, Elon, NC 27244, 336-278-7640 or toll-free 800-334-8448. *Fax:* 336-278-7639. *E-mail:* finaid@elon.edu.
Website: http://www.elon.edu/.

EMBRY-RIDDLE AERONAUTICAL UNIVERSITY–DAYTONA
Daytona Beach, FL

Tuition & fees: $31,334	Average undergraduate aid package: $12,778

ABOUT THE INSTITUTION Independent, coed. **Awards:** associate, bachelor's, master's, and doctoral degrees. 22 undergraduate majors. **Total enrollment:** 5,120. Undergraduates: 4,534. Freshmen: 941. Federal methodology is used as a basis for awarding need-based institutional aid.

UNDERGRADUATE EXPENSES for 2013–2014 Application fee: $50. **Comprehensive fee:** $40,884 includes full-time tuition ($30,120), mandatory fees ($1214), and room and board ($9550). **College room only:** $5600. Room and board charges vary according to board plan and housing facility. **Part-time tuition:** $1255 per credit hour.

FRESHMAN FINANCIAL AID (Fall 2012, est.) 860 applied for aid; of those 98% were deemed to have need. 100% of freshmen with need received aid. *Average financial aid package:* $13,607 (excluding resources awarded to replace EFC).
UNDERGRADUATE FINANCIAL AID (Fall 2012, est.) 3,557 applied for aid; of those 95% were deemed to have need. 100% of undergraduates with need received aid. *Average financial aid package:* $12,778 (excluding resources awarded to replace EFC).
GIFT AID (NEED-BASED) *Total amount:* $40,684,475 (16% federal, 7% state, 57% institutional, 20% external sources). *Receiving aid:* Freshmen: 90% (845); all full-time undergraduates: 80% (3,386). *Average award:* Freshmen: $11,603; Undergraduates: $10,461. *Scholarships, grants, and awards:* Federal Pell, FSEOG, state, private, college/university gift aid from institutional funds.
GIFT AID (NON-NEED-BASED) *Scholarships, grants, and awards by category:* Academic interests/achievement: general academic interests/achievements. *Special achievements/activities:* leadership. *Special characteristics:* children and siblings of alumni, children of faculty/staff, members of minority groups. *Tuition waivers:* Full or partial for employees or children of employees. *ROTC:* Army, Naval, Air Force.
LOANS *Student loans:* $35,406,089 (100% need-based). *Average need-based loan:* Freshmen: $3691. Undergraduates: $4487. *Parent loans:* $24,380,573 (100% need-based). *Programs:* Federal Direct (Subsidized and Unsubsidized Stafford, PLUS), Perkins, college/university.
WORK-STUDY *Federal work-study:* Total amount: $261,842; jobs available. *State or other work-study/employment:* Total amount: $2,947,497 (100% need-based). Part-time jobs available.
ATHLETIC AWARDS Total amount: $2,889,030 (100% need-based).
APPLYING FOR FINANCIAL AID *Required financial aid form:* FAFSA. *Financial aid deadline:* Continuous. *Notification date:* Continuous.
CONTACT Barbara Dryden, Director of Financial Aid, Embry-Riddle Aeronautical University–Daytona, 600 South Clyde Morris Boulevard, Daytona Beach, FL 32114-3900, 800-943-6279 or toll-free 800-862-2416. *Fax:* 386-226-6307. *E-mail:* dbfinaid@erau.edu.
Website: http://www.embryriddle.edu/.

EMBRY-RIDDLE AERONAUTICAL UNIVERSITY–PRESCOTT
Prescott, AZ

Tuition & fees: $31,034	Average undergraduate aid package: $16,233

ABOUT THE INSTITUTION Independent, coed. *Awards:* bachelor's and master's degrees. 14 undergraduate majors. *Total enrollment:* 1,724. Undergraduates: 1,678. Freshmen: 375. Federal methodology is used as a basis for awarding need-based institutional aid.
UNDERGRADUATE EXPENSES for 2013–2014 *Application fee:* $50. *Comprehensive fee:* $40,584 includes full-time tuition ($30,120), mandatory fees ($914), and room and board ($9550). *College room only:* $5600. Room and board charges vary according to board plan and housing facility. *Part-time tuition:* $1255 per credit hour.
FRESHMAN FINANCIAL AID (Fall 2012, est.) 365 applied for aid; of those 96% were deemed to have need. 96% of freshmen with need received aid. *Average financial aid package:* $14,012 (excluding resources awarded to replace EFC).
UNDERGRADUATE FINANCIAL AID (Fall 2012, est.) 1,472 applied for aid; of those 98% were deemed to have need. 100% of undergraduates with need received aid. *Average financial aid package:* $16,233 (excluding resources awarded to replace EFC).
GIFT AID (NEED-BASED) *Total amount:* $18,259,511 (11% federal, 70% institutional, 19% external sources). *Receiving aid:* Freshmen: 89% (334); all full-time undergraduates: 88% (1,380). *Average award:* Freshmen: $10,894; Undergraduates: $10,760. *Scholarships, grants, and awards:* Federal Pell, FSEOG, state, private, college/university gift aid from institutional funds.
GIFT AID (NON-NEED-BASED) *Scholarships, grants, and awards by category:* Academic interests/achievement: general academic interests/achievements. *Special achievements/activities:* leadership. *Special characteristics:* children and siblings of alumni, children of faculty/staff. *Tuition waivers:* Full or partial for employees or children of employees. *ROTC:* Army, Air Force.

LOANS *Student loans:* $12,593,730 (100% need-based). *Average need-based loan:* Freshmen: $3349. Undergraduates: $4547. *Parent loans:* $8,523,426 (100% need-based). *Programs:* Federal Direct (Subsidized and Unsubsidized Stafford, PLUS), college/university.
WORK-STUDY *Federal work-study:* Total amount: $62,162; jobs available. *State or other work-study/employment:* Part-time jobs available.
ATHLETIC AWARDS Total amount: $1,110,357 (100% need-based).
APPLYING FOR FINANCIAL AID *Required financial aid form:* FAFSA. *Financial aid deadline (priority):* 3/1. *Notification date:* Continuous beginning 3/1. Students must reply within 4 weeks of notification.
CONTACT Mr. Dan Lupin, Director of Financial Aid, Embry-Riddle Aeronautical University–Prescott, 3700 Willow Creek Road, Prescott, AZ 86301-3720, 800-888-3728. *Fax:* 928-777-3893. *E-mail:* prfinaid@erau.edu.
Website: http://www.embryriddle.edu/.

EMBRY-RIDDLE AERONAUTICAL UNIVERSITY–WORLDWIDE
Daytona Beach, FL

Tuition & fees: $7032	Average undergraduate aid package: $4933

ABOUT THE INSTITUTION Independent, coed. *Awards:* certificates, associate, bachelor's, master's, and doctoral degrees (programs offered at 100 military bases worldwide). 4 undergraduate majors. *Total enrollment:* 16,482. Undergraduates: 11,117. Freshmen: 338. Federal methodology is used as a basis for awarding need-based institutional aid.
UNDERGRADUATE EXPENSES for 2013–2014 *Application fee:* $50. *Tuition:* full-time $7032; part-time $305 per credit. Full-time tuition and fees vary according to program and reciprocity agreements. Part-time tuition and fees vary according to program and reciprocity agreements.
FRESHMAN FINANCIAL AID (Fall 2012, est.) 14 applied for aid; of those 100% were deemed to have need. 100% of freshmen with need received aid. *Average financial aid package:* $4266 (excluding resources awarded to replace EFC).
UNDERGRADUATE FINANCIAL AID (Fall 2012, est.) 1,259 applied for aid; of those 99% were deemed to have need. 100% of undergraduates with need received aid. *Average financial aid package:* $4933 (excluding resources awarded to replace EFC).
GIFT AID (NEED-BASED) *Total amount:* $6,416,538 (85% federal, 4% state, 10% institutional, 1% external sources). *Receiving aid:* Freshmen: 23% (11); all full-time undergraduates: 25% (705). *Average award:* Freshmen: $3987; Undergraduates: $4204. *Scholarships, grants, and awards:* Federal Pell, state, private, college/university gift aid from institutional funds.
GIFT AID (NON-NEED-BASED) *Scholarships, grants, and awards by category:* Academic interests/achievement: general academic interests/achievements. *Special achievements/activities:* leadership. *Special characteristics:* children of faculty/staff. *Tuition waivers:* Full or partial for employees or children of employees.
LOANS *Student loans:* $15,116,331 (100% need-based). *Average need-based loan:* Freshmen: $2993. Undergraduates: $4458. *Parent loans:* $37,895 (100% need-based). *Programs:* Federal Direct (Subsidized and Unsubsidized Stafford, PLUS).
APPLYING FOR FINANCIAL AID *Required financial aid form:* FAFSA. *Financial aid deadline:* Continuous. *Notification date:* Continuous beginning 3/1. Students must reply within 4 weeks of notification.
CONTACT Ms. Dagmar Bowen, Director of Financial Aid, Embry-Riddle Aeronautical University–Worldwide, 600 South Clyde Morris Boulevard, Daytona Beach, FL 32114-3900, 866-567-7202 or toll-free 800-522-6787. *Fax:* 386-226-6915. *E-mail:* wwfinaid@erau.edu.
Website: http://www.embryriddle.edu/.

EMERSON COLLEGE
Boston, MA

Tuition & fees: $35,730	Average undergraduate aid package: $18,643

ABOUT THE INSTITUTION Independent, coed. *Awards:* certificates, bachelor's, master's, and doctoral degrees. 28 undergraduate majors. *Total enrollment:* 4,513. Undergraduates: 3,675. Freshmen: 866. Both federal and institutional methodology are used as a basis for awarding need-based institutional aid.

UNDERGRADUATE EXPENSES for 2013–2014 *Application fee:* $65. *Comprehensive fee:* $50,246 includes full-time tuition ($35,072), mandatory fees ($658), and room and board ($14,516). Room and board charges vary according to board plan.

FRESHMAN FINANCIAL AID (Fall 2011) 671 applied for aid; of those 84% were deemed to have need. 100% of freshmen with need received aid; of those 39% had need fully met. *Average percent of need met:* 75% (excluding resources awarded to replace EFC). *Average financial aid package:* $19,193 (excluding resources awarded to replace EFC). 4% of all full-time freshmen had no need and received non-need-based gift aid.

UNDERGRADUATE FINANCIAL AID (Fall 2011) 2,329 applied for aid; of those 87% were deemed to have need. 100% of undergraduates with need received aid; of those 44% had need fully met. *Average percent of need met:* 72% (excluding resources awarded to replace EFC). *Average financial aid package:* $18,643 (excluding resources awarded to replace EFC). 6% of all full-time undergraduates had no need and received non-need-based gift aid.

GIFT AID (NEED-BASED) *Total amount:* $28,260,685 (10% federal, 1% state, 84% institutional, 5% external sources). *Receiving aid:* Freshmen: 57% (492); all full-time undergraduates: 49% (1,749). *Average award:* Freshmen: $17,589; Undergraduates: $16,237. *Scholarships, grants, and awards:* Federal Pell, FSEOG, state, private, college/university gift aid from institutional funds.

GIFT AID (NON-NEED-BASED) *Total amount:* $2,474,473 (93% institutional, 7% external sources). *Receiving aid:* Freshmen: 2% (21). Undergraduates: 2% (61). *Average award:* Freshmen: $13,627. Undergraduates: $13,825. *Scholarships, grants, and awards by category:* Academic interests/achievement: 354 awards ($5,026,698 total): general academic interests/achievements. Creative arts/performance: 23 awards ($259,625 total): performing arts. Special achievements/activities: 10 awards ($45,000 total): leadership. Special characteristics: 113 awards ($355,159 total): general special characteristics. *Tuition waivers:* Full or partial for employees or children of employees.

LOANS Student loans: $24,843,804 (69% need-based, 31% non-need-based). 64% of past graduating class borrowed through all loan programs. *Average indebtedness per student:* $22,844. *Average need-based loan:* Freshmen: $3736. Undergraduates: $4407. *Parent loans:* $11,983,882 (46% need-based, 54% non-need-based). *Programs:* Perkins, state.

WORK-STUDY *Federal work-study:* Total amount: $485,359; 462 jobs averaging $2000. *State or other work-study/employment:* Total amount: $654,220 (47% need-based, 53% non-need-based). 56 part-time jobs averaging $11,683.

APPLYING FOR FINANCIAL AID *Required financial aid forms:* FAFSA, CSS Financial Aid PROFILE, noncustodial (divorced/separated) parent's statement, business/farm supplement. *Financial aid deadline (priority):* 3/1. *Notification date:* 4/1. Students must reply by 5/1 or within 3 weeks of notification.

CONTACT Ruthanne Madsen, Associate Vice President for Enrollment and Student Financial Services, Emerson College, 120 Boylston Street, Boston, MA 02116-4624, 617-824-8655. *Fax:* 617-824-8619. *E-mail:* finaid@emerson.edu.
Website: http://www.emerson.edu/.

UNDERGRADUATE EXPENSES for 2013–2014 *Application fee:* $25. *Comprehensive fee:* $22,140 includes full-time tuition ($15,700) and room and board ($6440). Room and board charges vary according to housing facility. *Part-time tuition:* $630 per credit hour.

FRESHMAN FINANCIAL AID (Fall 2012, est.) 174 applied for aid; of those 92% were deemed to have need. 100% of freshmen with need received aid; of those 24% had need fully met. *Average percent of need met:* 75% (excluding resources awarded to replace EFC). *Average financial aid package:* $14,823 (excluding resources awarded to replace EFC). 13% of all full-time freshmen had no need and received non-need-based gift aid.

UNDERGRADUATE FINANCIAL AID (Fall 2012, est.) 629 applied for aid; of those 90% were deemed to have need. 100% of undergraduates with need received aid; of those 17% had need fully met. *Average percent of need met:* 68% (excluding resources awarded to replace EFC). *Average financial aid package:* $14,500 (excluding resources awarded to replace EFC). 14% of all full-time undergraduates had no need and received non-need-based gift aid.

GIFT AID (NEED-BASED) *Total amount:* $4,887,989 (38% federal, 18% state, 41% institutional, 3% external sources). *Receiving aid:* Freshmen: 83% (160); all full-time undergraduates: 81% (564). *Average award:* Freshmen: $11,684; Undergraduates: $10,673. *Scholarships, grants, and awards:* Federal Pell, FSEOG, state, college/university gift aid from institutional funds.

GIFT AID (NON-NEED-BASED) *Total amount:* $896,221 (30% state, 61% institutional, 9% external sources). *Receiving aid:* Freshmen: 12% (24). Undergraduates: 8% (55). *Average award:* Freshmen: $4491. Undergraduates: $4982. *Scholarships, grants, and awards by category:* Academic interests/achievement: 387 awards ($1,324,333 total): business, communication, education, English, general academic interests/achievements, health fields, religion/biblical studies. Creative arts/performance: 38 awards ($53,527 total): applied art and design, art/fine arts, creative writing, dance, general creative arts/performance, journalism/publications, music, performing arts, theater/drama. Special achievements/activities: 18 awards ($85,180 total): cheerleading/drum major, general special achievements/activities, hobbies/interests, leadership, memberships, religious involvement. Special characteristics: 672 awards ($645,999 total): adult students, children of current students, children of educators, children of faculty/staff, first-generation college students, general special characteristics, international students, local/state students, married students, parents of current students, relatives of clergy, religious affiliation, siblings of current students, spouses of current students, twins. *Tuition waivers:* Full or partial for employees or children of employees, senior citizens.

LOANS Student loans: $3,859,768 (84% need-based, 16% non-need-based). 84% of past graduating class borrowed through all loan programs. *Average indebtedness per student:* $22,228. *Average need-based loan:* Freshmen: $2907. Undergraduates: $3560. *Parent loans:* $850,294 (41% need-based, 59% non-need-based). *Programs:* Federal Direct (Subsidized and Unsubsidized Stafford, PLUS), state.

WORK-STUDY *Federal work-study:* Total amount: $524,427; 318 jobs averaging $1649. *State or other work-study/employment:* Total amount: $151,015 (100% non-need-based). 135 part-time jobs averaging $1118.

ATHLETIC AWARDS Total amount: $1,803,104 (59% need-based, 41% non-need-based).

APPLYING FOR FINANCIAL AID *Required financial aid forms:* FAFSA, institution's own form, state aid form. *Financial aid deadline:* 6/15 (priority: 5/1). *Notification date:* Continuous beginning 3/1. Students must reply within 2 weeks of notification.

CONTACT Mrs. Niki Stinson, Assistant Director of Financial Aid, Emmanuel College, PO Box 129, Franklin Springs, GA 30639-0129, 706-245-2871 or toll-free 800-860-8800. *Fax:* 706-245-2846. *E-mail:* nstinson@ec.edu.
Website: http://www.ec.edu/.

EMMANUEL COLLEGE
Franklin Springs, GA

Tuition & fees: $15,700	Average undergraduate aid package: $14,500

ABOUT THE INSTITUTION Independent Pentecostal Holiness Church, coed. *Awards:* associate and bachelor's degrees. 23 undergraduate majors. *Total enrollment:* 806. Undergraduates: 806. Freshmen: 188. Federal methodology is used as a basis for awarding need-based institutional aid.

EMMANUEL COLLEGE
Boston, MA

Tuition & fees: $33,650	Average undergraduate aid package: $26,204

ABOUT THE INSTITUTION Independent Roman Catholic, coed. *Awards:* certificates, bachelor's, and master's degrees. 34 undergraduate majors. *Total enrollment:* 2,488. Undergraduates: 2,198. Freshmen: 553. Federal methodology is used as a basis for awarding need-based institutional aid.

UNDERGRADUATE EXPENSES for 2013–2014 *Application fee:* $60. *One-time required fee:* $225. *Comprehensive fee:* $46,640 includes full-time tuition ($33,450), mandatory fees ($200), and room and board ($12,990). Full-time tuition and fees vary according to course load, degree level, and program. Room and board charges vary according to housing facility. Part-time tuition and fees vary according to program.

FRESHMAN FINANCIAL AID (Fall 2012, est.) 517 applied for aid; of those 92% were deemed to have need. 100% of freshmen with need received aid; of those 49% had need fully met. *Average percent of need met:* 78% (excluding resources awarded to replace EFC). *Average financial aid package:* $26,384 (excluding resources awarded to replace EFC). 13% of all full-time freshmen had no need and received non-need-based gift aid.

UNDERGRADUATE FINANCIAL AID (Fall 2012, est.) 1,631 applied for aid; of those 92% were deemed to have need. 99% of undergraduates with need received aid; of those 58% had need fully met. *Average percent of need met:* 74% (excluding resources awarded to replace EFC). *Average financial aid package:* $26,204 (excluding resources awarded to replace EFC). 15% of all full-time undergraduates had no need and received non-need-based gift aid.

GIFT AID (NEED-BASED) *Total amount:* $27,263,418 (9% federal, 3% state, 84% institutional, 4% external sources). *Receiving aid:* Freshmen: 71% (390); all full-time undergraduates: 70% (1,271). *Average award:* Freshmen: $19,694; Undergraduates: $18,336. *Scholarships, grants, and awards:* Federal Pell, FSEOG, state, private, college/university gift aid from institutional funds.

GIFT AID (NON-NEED-BASED) *Total amount:* $3,083,018 (7% federal, 93% institutional). *Receiving aid:* Freshmen: 42% (233). Undergraduates: 47% (864). *Average award:* Freshmen: $10,074. Undergraduates: $10,978. *Scholarships, grants, and awards by category: Academic interests/achievement:* biological sciences, education, engineering/technologies, foreign languages, general academic interests/achievements, health fields, humanities, mathematics, physical sciences, religion/biblical studies, social sciences. *Creative arts/performance:* general creative arts/performance. *Special achievements/activities:* community service, leadership. *Special characteristics:* children and siblings of alumni, children of educators, children of faculty/staff, children of union members/company employees, ethnic background, general special characteristics, handicapped students, international students, local/state students, religious affiliation, siblings of current students. *Tuition waivers:* Full or partial for employees or children of employees. *ROTC:* Army cooperative, Air Force cooperative.

LOANS *Student loans:* $15,274,175 (94% need-based, 6% non-need-based). *Average need-based loan:* Freshmen: $3677. Undergraduates: $4747. *Parent loans:* $8,456,680 (100% non-need-based). *Programs:* Federal Direct (Subsidized and Unsubsidized Stafford, PLUS), Perkins, state.

WORK-STUDY *Federal work-study:* Total amount: $151,084; jobs available. *State or other work-study/employment:* Total amount: $1,121,148 (100% non-need-based). Part-time jobs available.

APPLYING FOR FINANCIAL AID *Required financial aid forms:* FAFSA, institution's own form. *Financial aid deadline (priority):* 2/15. *Notification date:* Continuous beginning 3/1.

CONTACT Jennifer Porter, Associate Vice President for Student Financial Services, Emmanuel College, 400 The Fenway, Boston, MA 02115, 617-735-9938. *Fax:* 617-735-9939. *E-mail:* financialservices@emmanuel.edu. *Website:* http://www.emmanuel.edu/.

EMMAUS BIBLE COLLEGE
Dubuque, IA

CONTACT Steve Seeman, Financial Aid Director, Emmaus Bible College, 2570 Asbury Road, Dubuque, IA 52001-3097, 800-397-2425 Ext. 1309 or toll-free 800-397-2425. *Fax:* 563-588-1216. *E-mail:* financialaid@emmaus.edu. *Website:* http://www.emmaus.edu/.

EMORY & HENRY COLLEGE
Emory, VA

Tuition & fees: $28,122	Average undergraduate aid package: $25,588

ABOUT THE INSTITUTION Independent United Methodist, coed. *Awards:* diplomas, bachelor's, and master's degrees. 26 undergraduate majors. *Total enrollment:* 945. Undergraduates: 897. Freshmen: 246. Federal methodology is used as a basis for awarding need-based institutional aid.

UNDERGRADUATE EXPENSES for 2013–2014 *Comprehensive fee:* $37,548 includes full-time tuition ($28,122) and room and board ($9426). *College room only:* $4782. Full-time tuition and fees vary according to course load, degree level, and location. Room and board charges vary according to board plan, housing facility, and location. *Part-time tuition:* $1125 per credit hour. Part-time tuition and fees vary according to course load, degree level, and location.

FRESHMAN FINANCIAL AID (Fall 2012, est.) 227 applied for aid; of those 90% were deemed to have need. 100% of freshmen with need received aid; of those 44% had need fully met. *Average percent of need met:* 90% (excluding resources awarded to replace EFC). *Average financial aid package:* $26,482 (excluding resources awarded to replace EFC). 14% of all full-time freshmen had no need and received non-need-based gift aid.

UNDERGRADUATE FINANCIAL AID (Fall 2012, est.) 789 applied for aid; of those 93% were deemed to have need. 100% of undergraduates with need received aid; of those 34% had need fully met. *Average percent of need met:* 88% (excluding resources awarded to replace EFC). *Average financial aid package:* $25,588 (excluding resources awarded to replace EFC). 15% of all full-time undergraduates had no need and received non-need-based gift aid.

GIFT AID (NEED-BASED) *Total amount:* $15,010,646 (10% federal, 8% state, 80% institutional, 2% external sources). *Receiving aid:* Freshmen: 67% (165); all full-time undergraduates: 73% (635). *Average award:* Freshmen: $24,654; Undergraduates: $22,596. *Scholarships, grants, and awards:* Federal Pell, FSEOG, state, private, college/university gift aid from institutional funds.

GIFT AID (NON-NEED-BASED) *Total amount:* $3,053,232 (12% state, 85% institutional, 3% external sources). *Receiving aid:* Freshmen: 16% (40). Undergraduates: 11% (92). *Average award:* Freshmen: $14,775. Undergraduates: $14,308. *Scholarships, grants, and awards by category: Academic interests/achievement:* 832 awards ($9,854,226 total): general academic interests/achievements, premedicine, religion/biblical studies. *Creative arts/performance:* 53 awards ($79,853 total): art/fine arts, journalism/publications, music, theater/drama. *Special characteristics:* 318 awards ($997,106 total): children of educators, children of faculty/staff, out-of-state students. *Tuition waivers:* Full or partial for employees or children of employees.

LOANS *Student loans:* $5,132,643 (84% need-based, 16% non-need-based). 79% of past graduating class borrowed through all loan programs. *Average indebtedness per student:* $29,510. *Average need-based loan:* Freshmen: $3540. Undergraduates: $4508. *Parent loans:* $2,626,055 (35% need-based, 65% non-need-based). *Programs:* Federal Direct (Subsidized and Unsubsidized Stafford, PLUS), Perkins.

WORK-STUDY *Federal work-study:* Total amount: $102,850; 151 jobs averaging $1119.

APPLYING FOR FINANCIAL AID *Required financial aid forms:* FAFSA, state aid form. *Financial aid deadline (priority):* 4/1. *Notification date:* Continuous beginning 3/1. Students must reply within 2 weeks of notification.

CONTACT Ms. Scarlett C. Blevins, Financial Aid Officer, Emory & Henry College, PO Box 947, Emory, VA 24327-0010, 276-944-6115 or toll-free 800-848-5493. *Fax:* 276-944-6884. *E-mail:* scblevins@ehc.edu. *Website:* http://www.ehc.edu/.

EMORY UNIVERSITY
Atlanta, GA

Tuition & fees: $42,980	Average undergraduate aid package: $37,552

ABOUT THE INSTITUTION Independent Methodist, coed. *Awards:* certificates, associate, bachelor's, master's, and doctoral degrees (enrollment figures include Emory University, Oxford College; application data for main campus only). 58 undergraduate majors. *Total enrollment:* 13,893. Undergraduates: 7,441. Freshmen: 1,780. Both federal and institutional methodology are used as a basis for awarding need-based institutional aid.

UNDERGRADUATE EXPENSES for 2013–2014 *Application fee:* $50. *Comprehensive fee:* $54,980 includes full-time tuition ($42,400), mandatory fees ($580), and room and board ($12,000). *College room only:* $7200. Full-time tuition and fees vary according to degree level and location. Room and board charges vary according to board plan, housing facility, location, and student level. *Part-time tuition:* $1766 per credit hour.

FRESHMAN FINANCIAL AID (Fall 2012, est.) 681 applied for aid; of those 88% were deemed to have need. 100% of freshmen with need received aid; of those 81% had need fully met. *Average percent of need met:* 94% (excluding resources awarded to replace EFC). *Average financial aid package:* $35,945 (excluding resources awarded to replace EFC). 4% of all full-time freshmen had no need and received non-need-based gift aid.

UNDERGRADUATE FINANCIAL AID (Fall 2012, est.) 2,956 applied for aid; of those 92% were deemed to have need. 100% of undergraduates with need received aid; of those 79% had need fully met. *Average percent of need met:* 95% (excluding resources awarded to replace EFC). *Average financial aid package:* $37,552 (excluding resources awarded to replace EFC). 6% of all full-time undergraduates had no need and received non-need-based gift aid.

GIFT AID (NEED-BASED) *Total amount:* $87,277,480 (8% federal, 2% state, 88% institutional, 2% external sources). *Receiving aid:* Freshmen: 41% (561); all full-time undergraduates: 46% (2,575). *Average award:* Freshmen: $33,148; Undergraduates: $33,833. *Scholarships, grants, and awards:* Federal Pell, FSEOG, private, college/university gift aid from institutional funds.

GIFT AID (NON-NEED-BASED) *Total amount:* $11,704,767 (18% state, 71% institutional, 11% external sources). *Receiving aid:* Freshmen: 14% (190). Undergraduates: 13% (728). *Average award:* Freshmen: $17,850. Undergraduates: $21,047. *Scholarships, grants, and awards by category: Academic interests/achievement:* business, general academic interests/achievements, humanities, physical sciences. *Creative arts/performance:* art/fine arts, cinema/film/broadcasting, debating, music, theater/drama. *Special achievements/activities:* leadership. *Special characteristics:* children of faculty/staff, local/state students, religious affiliation, veterans, veterans' children. *Tuition waivers:* Full or partial for employees or children of employees. *ROTC:* Army cooperative, Naval cooperative, Air Force cooperative.

LOANS *Student loans:* $17,509,082 (56% need-based, 44% non-need-based). 45% of past graduating class borrowed through all loan programs. *Average indebtedness per student:* $27,737. *Average need-based loan:* Freshmen: $4169. Undergraduates: $5228. *Parent loans:* $4,477,319 (100% non-need-based). *Programs:* Federal Direct (Subsidized and Unsubsidized Stafford, PLUS), Perkins, Federal Nursing, state, college/university, alternative loans.

WORK-STUDY *Federal work-study:* Total amount: $5,006,788; jobs available. *State or other work-study/employment:* Total amount: $691,200 (22% need-based, 78% non-need-based). Part-time jobs available.

APPLYING FOR FINANCIAL AID *Required financial aid forms:* FAFSA, CSS Financial Aid PROFILE, noncustodial (divorced/separated) parent's statement. *Financial aid deadline:* 3/1 (priority: 2/15). *Notification date:* 4/1. Students must reply by 5/1.

CONTACT Dean Bentley, Director of Financial Aid, Emory University, Boisfeuillet Jones Center Suite 300, 200 Dowman Drive, Atlanta, GA 30322-1960, 404-727-6039 or toll-free 800-727-6036. *Fax:* 404-727-6709. *E-mail:* finaid1@emory.edu. *Website:* http://www.emory.edu/.

vary according to course load, degree level, and location. *College room and board:* $6629; *Room only:* $3438. Room and board charges vary according to board plan, housing facility, and location.

FRESHMAN FINANCIAL AID (Fall 2012, est.) 541 applied for aid; of those 75% were deemed to have need. 100% of freshmen with need received aid; of those 15% had need fully met. *Average percent of need met:* 67% (excluding resources awarded to replace EFC). *Average financial aid package:* $6686 (excluding resources awarded to replace EFC). 22% of all full-time freshmen had no need and received non-need-based gift aid.

UNDERGRADUATE FINANCIAL AID (Fall 2012, est.) 2,603 applied for aid; of those 82% were deemed to have need. 100% of undergraduates with need received aid; of those 14% had need fully met. *Average percent of need met:* 65% (excluding resources awarded to replace EFC). *Average financial aid package:* $6600 (excluding resources awarded to replace EFC). 13% of all full-time undergraduates had no need and received non-need-based gift aid.

GIFT AID (NEED-BASED) *Total amount:* $9,521,114 (69% federal, 7% state, 13% institutional, 11% external sources). *Receiving aid:* Freshmen: 66% (394); all full-time undergraduates: 55% (1,817). *Average award:* Freshmen: $5696; Undergraduates: $5215. *Scholarships, grants, and awards:* Federal Pell, FSEOG, state, private, college/university gift aid from institutional funds, Jones Foundation Grants.

GIFT AID (NON-NEED-BASED) *Total amount:* $2,098,673 (1% federal, 2% state, 35% institutional, 62% external sources). *Receiving aid:* Freshmen: 5% (30). Undergraduates: 2% (73). *Average award:* Freshmen: $1876. Undergraduates: $1647. *Scholarships, grants, and awards by category: Academic interests/achievement:* 1,240 awards ($1,735,443 total): biological sciences, business, communication, computer science, education, engineering/technologies, English, foreign languages, general academic interests/achievements, health fields, humanities, library science, mathematics, physical sciences, premedicine, social sciences. *Creative arts/performance:* 119 awards ($86,891 total): art/fine arts, creative writing, debating, music, theater/drama. *Special achievements/activities:* 30 awards ($16,330 total): leadership, memberships. *Special characteristics:* 23 awards ($13,574 total): children and siblings of alumni, children of faculty/staff, children of union members/company employees, handicapped students, international students, members of minority groups, religious affiliation, veterans, veterans' children. *Tuition waivers:* Full or partial for employees or children of employees, senior citizens.

LOANS *Student loans:* $17,466,912 (73% need-based, 27% non-need-based). 68% of past graduating class borrowed through all loan programs. *Average indebtedness per student:* $23,538. *Average need-based loan:* Freshmen: $5292. Undergraduates: $6481. *Parent loans:* $5,505,277 (18% need-based, 82% non-need-based). *Programs:* Perkins, alternative loans, Alaska Loans.

WORK-STUDY *Federal work-study:* Total amount: $474,595; 241 jobs averaging $1933. *State or other work-study/employment:* Total amount: $18,977 (92% need-based, 8% non-need-based). 11 part-time jobs averaging $1682.

ATHLETIC AWARDS Total amount: $1,194,274 (47% need-based, 53% non-need-based).

APPLYING FOR FINANCIAL AID *Required financial aid forms:* FAFSA, state aid form. *Financial aid deadline (priority):* 3/15. *Notification date:* Continuous. Students must reply within 2 weeks of notification.

CONTACT Elaine Henrie, Director of Financial Aid, Emporia State University, 1200 Commercial Street, Emporia, KS 66801-5087, 620-341-5457 or toll-free 877-GOTOESU (in-state), 877-468-6378 (out-of-state). *Fax:* 620-341-6088. *E-mail:* ehenrie@emporia.edu. *Website:* http://www.emporia.edu/.

EMPORIA STATE UNIVERSITY
Emporia, KS

Tuition & fees (KS res): $5272	Average undergraduate aid package: $6600

ABOUT THE INSTITUTION State-supported, coed. *Awards:* certificates, bachelor's, master's, and doctoral degrees. 35 undergraduate majors. *Total enrollment:* 5,867. Undergraduates: 3,771. Freshmen: 621. Federal methodology is used as a basis for awarding need-based institutional aid.

UNDERGRADUATE EXPENSES for 2013–2014 *Application fee:* $30. *Tuition, state resident:* full-time $4102; part-time $137 per credit hour. *Tuition, nonresident:* full-time $15,156; part-time $505 per credit hour. *Required fees:* full-time $1170; $70 per credit hour or $70 per credit hour. Full-time tuition and fees vary according to course load, degree level, and location. Part-time tuition and fees

ENDICOTT COLLEGE
Beverly, MA

Tuition & fees: $28,166	Average undergraduate aid package: $19,525

ABOUT THE INSTITUTION Independent, coed. *Awards:* certificates, associate, bachelor's, master's, and doctoral degrees. 24 undergraduate majors. *Total enrollment:* 4,625. Undergraduates: 2,762. Freshmen: 645. Federal methodology is used as a basis for awarding need-based institutional aid.

UNDERGRADUATE EXPENSES for 2013–2014 *Application fee:* $50. *Comprehensive fee:* $41,366 includes full-time tuition ($27,666), mandatory fees ($500), and room and board ($13,200). *College room only:* $9100. Room and board charges vary according to board plan and housing facility. *Payment plan:* Tuition pre-payment.

FRESHMAN FINANCIAL AID (Fall 2012, est.) 608 applied for aid; of those 78% were deemed to have need. 100% of freshmen with need received aid; of those 9% had need fully met. *Average percent of need met:* 61% (excluding resources awarded to replace EFC). *Average financial aid package:* $18,969 (excluding resources awarded to replace EFC). 17% of all full-time freshmen had no need and received non-need-based gift aid.

UNDERGRADUATE FINANCIAL AID (Fall 2012, est.) 2,114 applied for aid; of those 75% were deemed to have need. 99% of undergraduates with need received aid; of those 11% had need fully met. *Average percent of need met:* 63% (excluding resources awarded to replace EFC). *Average financial aid package:* $19,525 (excluding resources awarded to replace EFC). 17% of all full-time undergraduates had no need and received non-need-based gift aid.

GIFT AID (NEED-BASED) *Total amount:* $20,044,104 (9% federal, 2% state, 89% institutional). *Receiving aid:* Freshmen: 63% (405); all full-time undergraduates: 55% (1,326). *Average award:* Freshmen: $10,534; Undergraduates: $10,563. *Scholarships, grants, and awards:* Federal Pell, FSEOG, state, private, college/university gift aid from institutional funds.

GIFT AID (NON-NEED-BASED) *Total amount:* $3,826,641 (88% institutional, 12% external sources). *Receiving aid:* Freshmen: 48% (309). Undergraduates: 40% (956). *Average award:* Freshmen: $7855. Undergraduates: $7749. *Scholarships, grants, and awards by category: Academic interests/achievement:* 1,131 awards ($8,381,408 total): business, education, general academic interests/achievements, health fields. *Creative arts/performance:* 2 awards ($2250 total): art/fine arts, music, performing arts. *Special achievements/activities:* 8 awards ($13,700 total): community service, general special achievements/activities, leadership, religious involvement. *Special characteristics:* 139 awards ($772,782 total): children and siblings of alumni, children of educators, general special characteristics, international students, local/state students, religious affiliation. *Tuition waivers:* Full or partial for employees or children of employees. *ROTC:* Army cooperative.

LOANS *Student loans:* $18,539,203 (35% need-based, 65% non-need-based). 73% of past graduating class borrowed through all loan programs. *Average indebtedness per student:* $36,198. *Average need-based loan:* Freshmen: $3685. Undergraduates: $4556. *Parent loans:* $5,339,013 (100% non-need-based). *Programs:* Federal Direct (Subsidized and Unsubsidized Stafford, PLUS), Perkins.

WORK-STUDY *Federal work-study:* Total amount: $1,200,335; 619 jobs averaging $2000.

APPLYING FOR FINANCIAL AID *Required financial aid forms:* FAFSA, institution's own form. *Financial aid deadline (priority):* 3/15. *Notification date:* Continuous beginning 3/1. Students must reply within 2 weeks of notification.

CONTACT Ms. Marcia Toomey, Director of Financial Aid, Endicott College, 376 Hale Street, Beverly, MA 01915-2096, 978-232-2060 or toll-free 800-325-1114. *Fax:* 978-232-2085. *E-mail:* mtoomey@endicott.edu.
Website: http://www.endicott.edu/.

EPIC BIBLE COLLEGE
Sacramento, CA

CONTACT Financial Aid Office, Epic Bible College, 5225 Hillsdale Boulevard, Sacramento, CA 95842, 916-348-4689.
Website: http://epic.edu/.

ERSKINE COLLEGE
Due West, SC

CONTACT Mrs. Becky Pressley, Director of Financial Aid, Erskine College, PO Box 337, Due West, SC 29639, 864-379-8832 or toll-free 800-241-8721. *Fax:* 864-379-2172. *E-mail:* pressley@erskine.edu.
Website: http://www.erskine.edu/.

ESCUELA DE ARTES PLASTICAS DE PUERTO RICO
San Juan, PR

CONTACT Mr. Alfred Diaz Melendez, Financial Aid Administrator, Escuela de Artes Plasticas de Puerto Rico, PO Box 9021112, San Juan, PR 00902-1112, 787-725-8120 Ext. 317. *Fax:* 787-725-3798. *E-mail:* adiaz@eap.edu.
Website: http://www.eap.edu/.

EUGENE LANG COLLEGE THE NEW SCHOOL FOR LIBERAL ARTS
New York, NY

Tuition & fees: $38,570	Average undergraduate aid package: $28,480

ABOUT THE INSTITUTION Independent, coed. *Awards:* bachelor's degrees. 23 undergraduate majors. *Total enrollment:* 1,457. Undergraduates: 290. Freshmen: 290. Federal methodology is used as a basis for awarding need-based institutional aid.

UNDERGRADUATE EXPENSES for 2013–2014 *Application fee:* $50. *Comprehensive fee:* $55,870 includes full-time tuition ($37,710), mandatory fees ($860), and room and board ($17,300). *College room only:* $13,900. *Part-time tuition:* $1280 per credit hour.

FRESHMAN FINANCIAL AID (Fall 2011) 149 applied for aid; of those 87% were deemed to have need. 95% of freshmen with need received aid; of those 11% had need fully met. *Average percent of need met:* 66% (excluding resources awarded to replace EFC). *Average financial aid package:* $29,230 (excluding resources awarded to replace EFC). 6% of all full-time freshmen had no need and received non-need-based gift aid.

UNDERGRADUATE FINANCIAL AID (Fall 2011) 926 applied for aid; of those 91% were deemed to have need. 93% of undergraduates with need received aid; of those 13% had need fully met. *Average percent of need met:* 64% (excluding resources awarded to replace EFC). *Average financial aid package:* $28,480 (excluding resources awarded to replace EFC). 4% of all full-time undergraduates had no need and received non-need-based gift aid.

GIFT AID (NEED-BASED) *Total amount:* $16,479,605 (11% federal, 2% state, 84% institutional, 3% external sources). *Receiving aid:* Freshmen: 46% (121); all full-time undergraduates: 54% (752). *Average award:* Freshmen: $22,285; Undergraduates: $21,630. *Scholarships, grants, and awards:* Federal Pell, FSEOG, state, private, college/university gift aid from institutional funds.

GIFT AID (NON-NEED-BASED) *Total amount:* $1,416,909 (87% institutional, 13% external sources). *Receiving aid:* Freshmen: 6% (16). Undergraduates: 4% (51). *Average award:* Freshmen: $11,980. Undergraduates: $7475. *Scholarships, grants, and awards by category: Academic interests/achievement:* general academic interests/achievements. *Special achievements/activities:* general special achievements/activities, leadership. *Special characteristics:* local/state students, members of minority groups.

LOANS *Student loans:* $6,966,926 (95% need-based, 5% non-need-based). 44% of past graduating class borrowed through all loan programs. *Average indebtedness per student:* $34,455. *Average need-based loan:* Freshmen: $8190. Undergraduates: $9620. *Parent loans:* $3,668,310 (91% need-based, 9% non-need-based). *Programs:* Federal Direct (Subsidized and Unsubsidized Stafford, PLUS), Perkins.

WORK-STUDY *Federal work-study:* Total amount: $304,620; jobs available. *State or other work-study/employment:* Part-time jobs available.

APPLYING FOR FINANCIAL AID *Required financial aid forms:* FAFSA, state aid form. *Financial aid deadline:* Continuous. *Notification date:* Continuous beginning 4/1. Students must reply within 4 weeks of notification.

CONTACT Office of Student Financial Services, Eugene Lang College The New School for Liberal Arts, 72 Fifth Avenue, New York, NY 10011, 212-229-8930 or toll-free 800-292-3040. *E-mail:* sfs@newschool.edu.
Website: http://www.newschool.edu/lang.

EUREKA COLLEGE
Eureka, IL

Tuition & fees: N/R	Average undergraduate aid package: $14,279

ABOUT THE INSTITUTION Independent Christian Church (Disciples of Christ), coed. 35 undergraduate majors. Both federal and institutional methodology are used as a basis for awarding need-based institutional aid.
FRESHMAN FINANCIAL AID (Fall 2012, est.) 149 applied for aid; of those 85% were deemed to have need. 100% of freshmen with need received aid; of those 13% had need fully met. *Average percent of need met:* 76% (excluding resources awarded to replace EFC). *Average financial aid package:* $16,529 (excluding resources awarded to replace EFC). 19% of all full-time freshmen had no need and received non-need-based gift aid.
UNDERGRADUATE FINANCIAL AID (Fall 2012, est.) 667 applied for aid; of those 87% were deemed to have need. 100% of undergraduates with need received aid; of those 13% had need fully met. *Average percent of need met:* 67% (excluding resources awarded to replace EFC). *Average financial aid package:* $14,279 (excluding resources awarded to replace EFC). 19% of all full-time undergraduates had no need and received non-need-based gift aid.
GIFT AID (NEED-BASED) *Total amount:* $5,500,885 (23% federal, 25% state, 50% institutional, 2% external sources). *Receiving aid:* Freshmen: 81% (127); all full-time undergraduates: 77% (580). *Average award:* Freshmen: $12,100; Undergraduates: $9547. *Scholarships, grants, and awards:* Federal Pell, FSEOG, state, private, college/university gift aid from institutional funds.
GIFT AID (NON-NEED-BASED) *Total amount:* $723,003 (99% institutional, 1% external sources). *Average award:* Freshmen: $9198. Undergraduates: $5259. *Scholarships, grants, and awards by category:* Academic interests/achievement: 688 awards ($2,873,564 total): general academic interests/achievements. Creative arts/performance: 163 awards ($158,250 total): art/fine arts, music, performing arts, theater/drama. Special achievements/activities: 54 awards ($492,880 total): community service, leadership, religious involvement. Special characteristics: 118 awards ($294,268 total): children and siblings of alumni, children of faculty/staff, relatives of clergy, religious affiliation, siblings of current students.
LOANS *Student loans:* $5,441,714 (93% need-based, 7% non-need-based). 76% of past graduating class borrowed through all loan programs. *Average indebtedness per student:* $27,714. *Average need-based loan:* Freshmen: $3763. Undergraduates: $4576. *Parent loans:* $803,516 (81% need-based, 19% non-need-based). *Programs:* Federal Direct (Subsidized and Unsubsidized Stafford, PLUS), Perkins, college/university, alternative loans.
WORK-STUDY *Federal work-study:* Total amount: $73,907; 114 jobs averaging $648. *State or other work-study/employment:* Total amount: $251,763 (100% non-need-based). 100 part-time jobs averaging $2518.
APPLYING FOR FINANCIAL AID *Required financial aid form:* FAFSA. *Financial aid deadline (priority):* 3/1. *Notification date:* Continuous beginning 3/1. Students must reply within 2 weeks of notification.
CONTACT Ms. Ellen Rigsby, Assistant Dean and Director of Financial Aid, Eureka College, 300 East College Avenue, Eureka, IL 61530, 309-467-6311 or toll-free 888-4-EUREKA. Fax: 309-467-6897. E-mail: eraid@eureka.edu.
Website: http://www.eureka.edu/.

EVANGEL UNIVERSITY
Springfield, MO

Tuition & fees: $19,050	Average undergraduate aid package: $14,057

ABOUT THE INSTITUTION Independent Assemblies of God, coed. *Awards:* associate, bachelor's, and master's degrees. 48 undergraduate majors. *Total enrollment:* 2,079. Undergraduates: 1,879. Freshmen: 384. Federal methodology is used as a basis for awarding need-based institutional aid.
UNDERGRADUATE EXPENSES for 2013–2014 *Application fee:* $25. *Comprehensive fee:* $25,690 includes full-time tuition ($17,930), mandatory fees ($1120), and room and board ($6640). *College room only:* $3430. Full-time tuition and fees vary according to course load. Room and board charges vary according to board plan. *Part-time tuition:* $747 per credit hour. Part-time tuition and fees vary according to course load.
FRESHMAN FINANCIAL AID (Fall 2011) 398 applied for aid; of those 92% were deemed to have need. 100% of freshmen with need received aid; of those 7% had need fully met. *Average percent of need met:* 62% (excluding resources awarded to replace EFC). *Average financial aid package:* $15,263 (excluding resources awarded to replace EFC). 8% of all full-time freshmen had no need and received non-need-based gift aid.
UNDERGRADUATE FINANCIAL AID (Fall 2011) 1,642 applied for aid; of those 90% were deemed to have need. 100% of undergraduates with need received aid; of those 9% had need fully met. *Average percent of need met:* 60% (excluding resources awarded to replace EFC). *Average financial aid package:* $14,057 (excluding resources awarded to replace EFC). 8% of all full-time undergraduates had no need and received non-need-based gift aid.
GIFT AID (NEED-BASED) *Total amount:* $10,092,125 (37% federal, 1% state, 51% institutional, 11% external sources). *Receiving aid:* Freshmen: 88% (359); all full-time undergraduates: 75% (1,416). *Average award:* Freshmen: $10,468; Undergraduates: $8980. *Scholarships, grants, and awards:* Federal Pell, FSEOG, state, private, college/university gift aid from institutional funds.
GIFT AID (NON-NEED-BASED) *Total amount:* $926,956 (76% institutional, 24% external sources). *Receiving aid:* Freshmen: 3% (14). Undergraduates: 4% (79). *Average award:* Freshmen: $4155. Undergraduates: $3938. *Scholarships, grants, and awards by category:* Academic interests/achievement: 783 awards ($2,420,402 total): biological sciences, business, communication, computer science, education, engineering/technologies, English, foreign languages, general academic interests/achievements, health fields, humanities, international studies, mathematics, physical sciences, premedicine, religion/biblical studies, social sciences. Creative arts/performance: 150 awards ($290,015 total): art/fine arts, debating, music, theater/drama. Special achievements/activities: 215 awards ($198,332 total): cheerleading/drum major, general special achievements/activities, leadership, religious involvement. Special characteristics: 382 awards ($2,176,278 total): adult students, children and siblings of alumni, children of educators, children of faculty/staff, general special characteristics, out-of-state students, relatives of clergy, religious affiliation. *Tuition waivers:* Full or partial for employees or children of employees. *ROTC:* Army cooperative.
LOANS *Student loans:* $15,502,891 (82% need-based, 18% non-need-based). 79% of past graduating class borrowed through all loan programs. *Average indebtedness per student:* $34,434. *Average need-based loan:* Freshmen: $3933. Undergraduates: $4640. *Parent loans:* $3,205,241 (63% need-based, 37% non-need-based). *Programs:* Federal Direct (Subsidized and Unsubsidized Stafford, PLUS), Perkins, college/university.
WORK-STUDY *Federal work-study:* Total amount: $1,460,936; 1,135 jobs averaging $1825. *State or other work-study/employment:* Total amount: $195,380 (74% need-based, 26% non-need-based). 88 part-time jobs averaging $1244.
ATHLETIC AWARDS Total amount: $2,022,154 (74% need-based, 26% non-need-based).
APPLYING FOR FINANCIAL AID *Required financial aid form:* FAFSA. *Financial aid deadline (priority):* 3/1. *Notification date:* Continuous beginning 3/1. Students must reply within 4 weeks of notification.
CONTACT Mrs. Dorynda Carpenter, Director of Student Financial Services, Evangel University, 1111 North Glenstone Avenue, Springfield, MO 65802-2191, 417-865-2811 Ext. 7302 or toll-free 800-382-6435. Fax: 417-575-5478. E-mail: carpenterd@evangel.edu.
Website: http://www.evangel.edu/.

EVEREST UNIVERSITY
Jacksonville, FL

CONTACT Financial Aid Office, Everest University, 8226 Phillips Highway, Jacksonville, FL 32256, 904-731-4949 or toll-free 888-741-4270.
Website: http://www.everest.edu/.

EVEREST UNIVERSITY
Lakeland, FL

CONTACT Brian Jones, Senior Finance Officer, Everest University, Office of Financial Aid, 995 East Memorial Boulevard, Lakeland, FL 33801, 863-686-1444 Ext. 118 or toll-free 888-741-4270. *Fax:* 863-682-1077.
Website: http://www.everest.edu/.

EVEREST UNIVERSITY
Largo, FL

CONTACT Mr. Will Scott, Director of Student Finance, Everest University, 1199 East Bay Drive, Largo, FL 33770, 727-725-2688 Ext. 166 or toll-free 888-741-4270. *Fax:* 727-373-4408. *E-mail:* wscott@cci.edu.
Website: http://www.everest.edu/.

EVEREST UNIVERSITY
Melbourne, FL

CONTACT Ida C. Liska, Director of Student Finance, Everest University, 2401 North Harbor City Boulevard, Melbourne, FL 32935-6657, 321-253-2929 Ext. 142. *E-mail:* iliska@cci.edu.
Website: http://www.everest.edu/.

EVEREST UNIVERSITY
Orlando, FL

CONTACT Ms. Linda Kaisrlik, Director of Student Finance, Everest University, 5421 Diplomat Circle, Orlando, FL 32810-5674, 407-628-5870 Ext. 118 or toll-free 800-628-5870.
Website: http://www.everest.edu/.

EVEREST UNIVERSITY
Orlando, FL

CONTACT Sherri Williams, Director of Financial Aid, Everest University, 2411 Sand Lake Road, Orlando, FL 32809, 407-851-2525 or toll-free 888-741-4270 (in-state), 888-471-4270 (out-of-state).
Website: http://www.everest.edu/.

EVEREST UNIVERSITY
Pompano Beach, FL

CONTACT Sharon Scheible, Director of Student Financial Aid, Everest University, 1040 Bayview Drive, Fort Lauderdale, FL 33304-2522, 954-568-1600 Ext. 52. *Fax:* 954-564-5283. *E-mail:* scheible@cci.edu.
Website: http://www.everest.edu/.

EVEREST UNIVERSITY
Tampa, FL

CONTACT Mr. Rod Kirkwood, Financial Aid Director, Everest University, 3319 West Hillsborough Avenue, Tampa, FL 33614, 813-879-6000 Ext. 145. *Fax:* 813-871-2483. *E-mail:* rkirkwoo@cci.edu.
Website: http://www.everest.edu/.

EVEREST UNIVERSITY
Tampa, FL

CONTACT Ms. Ginger Waymire, Director of Financial Aid, Everest University, 3924 Coconut Palm Drive, Tampa, FL 33619, 813-621-0041 Ext. 118 or toll-free 888-741-4270. *Fax:* 813-621-6283. *E-mail:* gwaymire@cci.edu.
Website: http://www.everest.edu/.

EVERGLADES UNIVERSITY
Altamonte Springs, FL

CONTACT Financial Aid Office, Everglades University, 887 East Altamonte Drive, Altamonte Springs, FL 32701, 407-277-0311 or toll-free 866-289-1078.
Website: http://www.evergladesuniversity.edu/.

EVERGLADES UNIVERSITY
Boca Raton, FL

CONTACT Seeta Singh Moonilal, Financial Aid Director, Everglades University, 5002 T Rex Avenue, Suite 100, Boca Raton, FL 33431, 561-912-1211 or toll-free 888-772-6077. *Fax:* 561-912-1191. *E-mail:* seetasm@evergladesuniversity.edu.
Website: http://www.evergladesuniversity.edu/.

EVERGLADES UNIVERSITY
Sarasota, FL

CONTACT Financial Aid Office, Everglades University, 6001 Lake Osprey Drive #110, Sarasota, FL 34240, 941-907-2262 or toll-free 866-907-2262.
Website: http://www.evergladesuniversity.edu/.

THE EVERGREEN STATE COLLEGE
Olympia, WA

Tuition & fees (WA res): $8395	Average undergraduate aid package: $8790

ABOUT THE INSTITUTION State-supported, coed. *Awards:* bachelor's and master's degrees. 41 undergraduate majors. *Total enrollment:* 4,509. Undergraduates: 4,193. Freshmen: 534. Federal methodology is used as a basis for awarding need-based institutional aid.

UNDERGRADUATE EXPENSES for 2013–2014 *Application fee:* $50. *Tuition, state resident:* full-time $7812; part-time $260.40 per credit hour. *Tuition, nonresident:* full-time $18,978; part-time $632.60 per credit hour. *Required fees:* full-time $583; $7.85 per credit hour or $3 per term. Full-time tuition and fees vary according to course load, location, and program. Part-time tuition and fees vary according to course load, location, and program. *College room and board:* $9240; *Room only:* $6150. Room and board charges vary according to board plan, housing facility, location, and student level.

FRESHMAN FINANCIAL AID (Fall 2011) 425 applied for aid; of those 78% were deemed to have need. 95% of freshmen with need received aid; of those 10% had need fully met. *Average percent of need met:* 84% (excluding resources awarded to replace EFC). *Average financial aid package:* $8012 (excluding resources awarded to replace EFC). 1% of all full-time freshmen had no need and received non-need-based gift aid.

UNDERGRADUATE FINANCIAL AID (Fall 2011) 3,070 applied for aid; of those 88% were deemed to have need. 95% of undergraduates with need received aid; of those 9% had need fully met. *Average percent of need met:* 67% (excluding resources awarded to replace EFC). *Average financial aid package:* $8790 (excluding resources awarded to replace EFC). 1% of all full-time undergraduates had no need and received non-need-based gift aid.

GIFT AID (NEED-BASED) *Total amount:* $18,667,152 (47% federal, 42% state, 9% institutional, 2% external sources). *Receiving aid:* Freshmen: 39% (210); all full-

time undergraduates: 52% (2,123). **Average award:** Freshmen: $7466; Undergraduates: $9174. **Scholarships, grants, and awards:** Federal Pell, FSEOG, state, private, college/university gift aid from institutional funds.
GIFT AID (NON-NEED-BASED) Total amount: $169,112 (3% state, 45% institutional, 52% external sources). **Receiving aid:** Freshmen: 9% (48). Undergraduates: 7% (276). **Average award:** Freshmen: $6164. Undergraduates: $5673. **Scholarships, grants, and awards by category:** *Academic interests/achievement:* general academic interests/achievements. *Creative arts/performance:* applied art and design, art/fine arts, creative writing. *Special achievements/activities:* community service, general special achievements/activities. *Special characteristics:* adult students, first-generation college students, local/state students, veterans, veterans' children. *Tuition waivers:* Full or partial for employees or children of employees, senior citizens.
LOANS Student loans: $17,270,825 (92% need-based, 8% non-need-based). 48% of past graduating class borrowed through all loan programs. *Average indebtedness per student:* $15,706. **Average need-based loan:** Freshmen: $3149. Undergraduates: $4209. **Parent loans:** $4,503,804 (73% need-based, 27% non-need-based). **Programs:** Federal Direct (Subsidized and Unsubsidized Stafford, PLUS), Perkins, college/university.
WORK-STUDY Federal work-study: Total amount: $329,364; jobs available. *State or other work-study/employment:* Total amount: $587,021 (100% need-based). Part-time jobs available.
ATHLETIC AWARDS Total amount: $163,599 (81% need-based, 19% non-need-based).
APPLYING FOR FINANCIAL AID Required financial aid forms: FAFSA, institution's own form. **Financial aid deadline (priority):** 3/1. **Notification date:** Continuous beginning 4/1. Students must reply within 6 weeks of notification.
CONTACT Financial Aid Office, The Evergreen State College, 2700 Evergreen Parkway NW, Olympia, WA 98505, 360-867-6205. *Fax:* 360-866-6576. *E-mail:* finaid@evergreen.edu.
Website: http://www.evergreen.edu/.

EXCELSIOR COLLEGE
Albany, NY

Tuition & fees: N/R	Average undergraduate aid package: N/A

ABOUT THE INSTITUTION Independent, coed. **Awards:** certificates, associate, bachelor's, and master's degrees (offers only external degree programs). 40 undergraduate majors. **Total enrollment:** 37,194. Undergraduates: 35,302. Federal methodology is used as a basis for awarding need-based institutional aid.
UNDERGRADUATE EXPENSES for 2013–2014 Application fee: $80. **Tuition:** part-time $390 per credit hour.
GIFT AID (NEED-BASED) Total amount: $3,412,754 (75% federal, 7% state, 12% institutional, 6% external sources). **Scholarships, grants, and awards:** Federal Pell, FSEOG, state, private, college/university gift aid from institutional funds, Federal Nursing, Veterans Education Benefits (GI Bill).
GIFT AID (NON-NEED-BASED) Tuition waivers: Full or partial for employees or children of employees.
LOANS Student loans: $8,336,521 (100% need-based). **Parent loans:** $6485 (100% non-need-based). **Programs:** Federal Direct (Subsidized and Unsubsidized Stafford, PLUS), Federal Nursing.
APPLYING FOR FINANCIAL AID Notification date: Continuous.
CONTACT Donna L. Cooper, Director of Financial Aid, Excelsior College, 7 Columbia Circle, Albany, NY 12203-5159, 518-464-8500 or toll-free 888-647-2388. *Fax:* 518-464-8777.
Website: http://www.excelsior.edu/.

EX'PRESSION COLLEGE FOR DIGITAL ARTS
Emeryville, CA

CONTACT Financial Aid Office, Ex'pression College for Digital Arts, 6601 Shellmound Street, Emeryville, CA 94608, 510-654-2934 or toll-free 877-833-8800. *Website:* http://www.expression.edu/.

FAIRFIELD UNIVERSITY
Fairfield, CT

Tuition & fees: $41,690	Average undergraduate aid package: $29,491

ABOUT THE INSTITUTION Independent Roman Catholic (Jesuit), coed. **Awards:** certificates, bachelor's, master's, and doctoral degrees. 45 undergraduate majors. **Total enrollment:** 4,999. Undergraduates: 3,879. Freshmen: 990. Both federal and institutional methodology are used as a basis for awarding need-based institutional aid.
UNDERGRADUATE EXPENSES for 2013–2014 Application fee: $60. **One-time required fee:** $230. **Comprehensive fee:** $54,240 includes full-time tuition ($41,090), mandatory fees ($600), and room and board ($12,550). **College room only:** $7690. Room and board charges vary according to board plan and housing facility. **Part-time tuition:** $700 per credit hour. **Part-time fees:** $60 per term. Part-time tuition and fees vary according to course load.
FRESHMAN FINANCIAL AID (Fall 2012, est.) 766 applied for aid; of those 70% were deemed to have need. 100% of freshmen with need received aid; of those 12% had need fully met. **Average percent of need met:** 88% (excluding resources awarded to replace EFC). **Average financial aid package:** $27,725 (excluding resources awarded to replace EFC). 32% of all full-time freshmen had no need and received non-need-based gift aid.
UNDERGRADUATE FINANCIAL AID (Fall 2012, est.) 2,414 applied for aid; of those 76% were deemed to have need. 100% of undergraduates with need received aid; of those 13% had need fully met. **Average percent of need met:** 88% (excluding resources awarded to replace EFC). **Average financial aid package:** $29,491 (excluding resources awarded to replace EFC). 21% of all full-time undergraduates had no need and received non-need-based gift aid.
GIFT AID (NEED-BASED) Total amount: $34,788,242 (9% federal, 5% state, 86% institutional). **Receiving aid:** Freshmen: 47% (461); all full-time undergraduates: 48% (1,666). **Average award:** Freshmen: $15,122; Undergraduates: $19,098. **Scholarships, grants, and awards:** Federal Pell, FSEOG, state, private, college/university gift aid from institutional funds.
GIFT AID (NON-NEED-BASED) Total amount: $19,559,617 (97% institutional, 3% external sources). **Receiving aid:** Freshmen: 46% (452). Undergraduates: 29% (1,008). **Average award:** Freshmen: $13,148. Undergraduates: $16,105. **Scholarships, grants, and awards by category:** *Academic interests/achievement:* 715 awards ($7,906,074 total): general academic interests/achievements. *Creative arts/performance:* 32 awards ($31,495 total): general creative arts/performance. *Special achievements/activities:* 8 awards ($42,000 total): general special achievements/activities, leadership. *Special characteristics:* 166 awards ($2,599,288 total): children and siblings of alumni, children of faculty/staff, ethnic background, first-generation college students, veterans. *Tuition waivers:* Full or partial for employees or children of employees. *ROTC:* Army cooperative, Air Force cooperative.
LOANS Student loans: $21,114,611 (49% need-based, 51% non-need-based). 67% of past graduating class borrowed through all loan programs. *Average indebtedness per student:* $28,507. **Average need-based loan:** Freshmen: $4179. Undergraduates: $4839. **Parent loans:** $8,121,693 (100% non-need-based). **Programs:** Federal Direct (Subsidized and Unsubsidized Stafford, PLUS), Perkins, Federal Nursing, alternative loans.
WORK-STUDY Federal work-study: Total amount: $439,080; 422 jobs averaging $997.
ATHLETIC AWARDS Total amount: $5,693,695 (100% non-need-based).
APPLYING FOR FINANCIAL AID Required financial aid forms: FAFSA, CSS Financial Aid PROFILE, noncustodial (divorced/separated) parent's statement, business/farm supplement. **Financial aid deadline:** 2/15. **Notification date:** 4/1. Students must reply by 5/1.

CONTACT Diana DeVellis, Office of Financial Aid, Fairfield University, 1073 North Benson Road, Fairfield, CT 06824-5195, 203-254-4125. *Fax:* 203-254-4008. *E-mail:* finaid@fairfield.edu. *Website:* http://www.fairfield.edu/.

FAIRLEIGH DICKINSON UNIVERSITY, COLLEGE AT FLORHAM
Madison, NJ

CONTACT Financial Aid Office, Fairleigh Dickinson University, College at Florham, 285 Madison Avenue, Madison, NJ 07940-1099, 973-443-8700 or toll-free 800-338-8803. *Website:* http://www.fdu.edu/.

FAIRLEIGH DICKINSON UNIVERSITY, METROPOLITAN CAMPUS
Teaneck, NJ

CONTACT Financial Aid Office, Fairleigh Dickinson University, Metropolitan Campus, 100 River Road, Teaneck, NJ 07666-1914, 201-692-2363 or toll-free 800-338-8803. *Website:* http://www.fdu.edu/.

FAIRMONT STATE UNIVERSITY
Fairmont, WV

Tuition & fees (WV res): $5804	Average undergraduate aid package: $3115

ABOUT THE INSTITUTION State-supported, coed. *Awards:* certificates, associate, bachelor's, and master's degrees. 42 undergraduate majors. *Total enrollment:* 4,451. Undergraduates: 4,112. Freshmen: 739. Federal methodology is used as a basis for awarding need-based institutional aid.

UNDERGRADUATE EXPENSES for 2013–2014 *Tuition, state resident:* full-time $5804; part-time $243 per credit hour. *Tuition, nonresident:* full-time $12,240; part-time $510 per credit hour. Full-time tuition and fees vary according to location. Part-time tuition and fees vary according to course load and location. *College room and board:* $7686; *Room only:* $4186. Room and board charges vary according to board plan and housing facility.

FRESHMAN FINANCIAL AID (Fall 2011) 706 applied for aid; of those 77% were deemed to have need. 98% of freshmen with need received aid; of those 11% had need fully met. *Average percent of need met:* 71% (excluding resources awarded to replace EFC). *Average financial aid package:* $2727 (excluding resources awarded to replace EFC). 12% of all full-time freshmen had no need and received non-need-based gift aid.

UNDERGRADUATE FINANCIAL AID (Fall 2011) 3,309 applied for aid; of those 84% were deemed to have need. 97% of undergraduates with need received aid; of those 6% had need fully met. *Average percent of need met:* 65% (excluding resources awarded to replace EFC). *Average financial aid package:* $3115 (excluding resources awarded to replace EFC). 7% of all full-time undergraduates had no need and received non-need-based gift aid.

GIFT AID (NEED-BASED) *Total amount:* $14,657,927 (59% federal, 37% state, 4% institutional). *Receiving aid:* Freshmen: 64% (469); all full-time undergraduates: 63% (2,302). *Average award:* Freshmen: $6181; Undergraduates: $5750. *Scholarships, grants, and awards:* Federal Pell, FSEOG, state, private, college/university gift aid from institutional funds.

GIFT AID (NON-NEED-BASED) *Total amount:* $659,595 (3% state, 32% institutional, 65% external sources). *Receiving aid:* Freshmen: 23% (172). Undergraduates: 15% (531). *Average award:* Freshmen: $5338. Undergraduates: $5264. *Scholarships, grants, and awards by category: Academic interests/achievement:* 548 awards ($2,068,322 total): architecture, biological sciences, business, computer science, education, engineering/technologies, English, general academic interests/achievements, health fields, humanities, international studies, mathematics, physical sciences, social sciences. *Creative arts/performance:* 604 awards ($2,640,372

total): art/fine arts, creative writing, debating, general creative arts/performance, journalism/publications, music, theater/drama. *Special achievements/activities:* 106 awards ($103,959 total): cheerleading/drum major, general special achievements/activities, leadership. *Special characteristics:* 29 awards ($35,240 total): adult students, children and siblings of alumni, children of faculty/staff, ethnic background, first-generation college students, general special characteristics, handicapped students, international students, local/state students, members of minority groups, out-of-state students, previous college experience, veterans, veterans' children. *Tuition waivers:* Full or partial for employees or children of employees. *ROTC:* Army, Air Force cooperative.

LOANS *Student loans:* $11,701,149 (7% need-based, 93% non-need-based). 71% of past graduating class borrowed through all loan programs. *Average indebtedness per student:* $24,060. *Average need-based loan:* Freshmen: $2970. Undergraduates: $3812. *Parent loans:* $837,354 (100% non-need-based). *Programs:* Federal Direct (Subsidized and Unsubsidized Stafford, PLUS), Perkins.

WORK-STUDY *Federal work-study:* Total amount: $200,807; 119 jobs averaging $1687. *State or other work-study/employment:* Total amount: $552,950 (100% non-need-based). 275 part-time jobs averaging $2011.

ATHLETIC AWARDS Total amount: $1,219,498 (71% need-based, 29% non-need-based).

APPLYING FOR FINANCIAL AID *Required financial aid form:* FAFSA. *Financial aid deadline (priority):* 3/1. *Notification date:* Continuous beginning 4/1. Students must reply within 2 weeks of notification.

CONTACT Cynthia K. Hudok, Director of Financial Aid and Scholarships, Fairmont State University, 1201 Locust Avenue, Fairmont, WV 26554, 304-367-4892 or toll-free 800-641-5678. *Fax:* 304-367-4584. *E-mail:* financialaid@fairmontstate.edu. *Website:* http://www.fairmontstate.edu/.

FAITH BAPTIST BIBLE COLLEGE AND THEOLOGICAL SEMINARY
Ankeny, IA

CONTACT Mr. Breck Appell, Director of Financial Assistance, Faith Baptist Bible College and Theological Seminary, 1900 Northwest 4th Street, Ankeny, IA 50021-2152, 515-964-0601 or toll-free 888-FAITH 4U. *Fax:* 515-964-1638. *Website:* http://www.faith.edu/.

FAITH THEOLOGICAL SEMINARY
Baltimore, MD

CONTACT Financial Aid Office, Faith Theological Seminary, 529 Walker Avenue, Baltimore, MD 21212, 410-323-6211. *Website:* http://www.faiththeological.org/.

FAMILY OF FAITH COLLEGE
Shawnee, OK

CONTACT Financial Aid Office, Family of Faith College, 30 Kinville, Shawnee, OK 74802, 405-273-5331. *Website:* http://www.familyoffaithcollege.edu/.

FARMINGDALE STATE COLLEGE
Farmingdale, NY

Tuition & fees (NY res): $7125	Average undergraduate aid package: $8502

ABOUT THE INSTITUTION State-supported, coed. *Awards:* certificates, associate, and bachelor's degrees. 43 undergraduate majors. *Total enrollment:* 7,889. Undergraduates: 7,889. Freshmen: 1,190. Federal methodology is used as a basis for awarding need-based institutional aid.

UNDERGRADUATE EXPENSES for 2013–2014 *Application fee:* $50. *Tuition, area resident:* part-time $245 per credit. *Tuition, state resident:* full-

time $5870; part-time $245 per credit. **Tuition, nonresident:** full-time $15,320; part-time $638 per credit. **Required fees:** full-time $1255. Part-time tuition and fees vary according to course load. **College room and board:** $11,860; **Room only:** $7260. Room and board charges vary according to board plan and housing facility.
FRESHMAN FINANCIAL AID (Fall 2012, est.) 919 applied for aid; of those 71% were deemed to have need. 100% of freshmen with need received aid; of those 16% had need fully met. **Average percent of need met:** 69% (excluding resources awarded to replace EFC). **Average financial aid package:** $8587 (excluding resources awarded to replace EFC). 1% of all full-time freshmen had no need and received non-need-based gift aid.
UNDERGRADUATE FINANCIAL AID (Fall 2012, est.) 3,884 applied for aid; of those 78% were deemed to have need. 100% of undergraduates with need received aid; of those 10% had need fully met. **Average percent of need met:** 65% (excluding resources awarded to replace EFC). **Average financial aid package:** $8502 (excluding resources awarded to replace EFC). 1% of all full-time undergraduates had no need and received non-need-based gift aid.
GIFT AID (NEED-BASED) Total amount: $17,006,147 (55% federal, 45% state). **Receiving aid:** Freshmen: 49% (571); all full-time undergraduates: 46% (2,594). **Average award:** Freshmen: $6274; Undergraduates: $5990. **Scholarships, grants, and awards:** Federal Pell, FSEOG, state, college/university gift aid from institutional funds, Federal Nursing.
GIFT AID (NON-NEED-BASED) Total amount: $464,894 (38% state, 23% Institutional, 39% external sources). **Receiving aid:** Freshmen: 3% (31). Undergraduates: 3% (147). **Average award:** Freshmen: $1450. Undergraduates: $1046. **Scholarships, grants, and awards by category:** Academic interests/achievement: general academic interests/achievements, health fields. Special achievements/activities: general special achievements/activities. Special characteristics: children and siblings of alumni, general special characteristics. ROTC: Army cooperative, Naval cooperative, Air Force cooperative.
LOANS Student loans: $23,803,859 (42% need-based, 58% non-need-based). 43% of past graduating class borrowed through all loan programs. **Average indebtedness per student:** $18,867. **Average need-based loan:** Freshmen: $3284. Undergraduates: $3978. **Parent loans:** $1,036,435 (100% non-need-based). **Programs:** Federal Direct (Subsidized and Unsubsidized Stafford, PLUS), Perkins, alternative loans.
WORK-STUDY Federal work-study: Total amount: $1,017,309; 386 jobs averaging $2636.
APPLYING FOR FINANCIAL AID Required financial aid forms: FAFSA, institution's own form, state aid form. **Financial aid deadline (priority):** 4/1. **Notification date:** Continuous beginning 4/1.
CONTACT Office of Financial Aid, Farmingdale State College, 2350 Broadhollow Road, Route 110, Farmingdale, NY 11735, 631-420-2328 or toll-free 877-4-FARMINGDALE. Fax: 631-420-3662. Website: http://www.farmingdale.edu/.

FASHION INSTITUTE OF TECHNOLOGY
New York, NY

Tuition & fees (NY res): $6358	Average undergraduate aid package: $13,912

ABOUT THE INSTITUTION State and locally supported, coed, primarily women. **Awards:** certificates, associate, bachelor's, and master's degrees. 20 undergraduate majors. **Total enrollment:** 10,052. Undergraduates: 9,848. Freshmen: 1,233. Federal methodology is used as a basis for awarding need-based institutional aid.
UNDERGRADUATE EXPENSES for 2013–2014 Application fee: $50. **Tuition, state resident:** full-time $5768; part-time $240 per credit hour. **Tuition, nonresident:** full-time $15,430; part-time $643 per credit hour. **Required fees:** full-time $590; $7.50 per credit hour or $170 per term. Full-time tuition and fees vary according to degree level. Part-time tuition and fees vary according to degree level. **College room and board:** $12,598. Room and board charges vary according to board plan and housing facility.
FRESHMAN FINANCIAL AID (Fall 2011) 953 applied for aid; of those 69% were deemed to have need. 98% of freshmen with need received aid; of those 11% had need fully met. **Average percent of need met:** 75% (excluding resources awarded to replace EFC). **Average financial aid package:** $13,266 (excluding resources awarded to replace EFC).

UNDERGRADUATE FINANCIAL AID (Fall 2011) 5,128 applied for aid; of those 77% were deemed to have need. 98% of undergraduates with need received aid; of those 10% had need fully met. **Average percent of need met:** 72% (excluding resources awarded to replace EFC). **Average financial aid package:** $13,912 (excluding resources awarded to replace EFC). 1% of all full-time undergraduates had no need and received non-need-based gift aid.
GIFT AID (NEED-BASED) Total amount: $16,155,506 (62% federal, 26% state, 7% institutional, 5% external sources). **Receiving aid:** Freshmen: 38% (460); all full-time undergraduates: 37% (2,821). **Average award:** Freshmen: $5344; Undergraduates: $5199. **Scholarships, grants, and awards:** Federal Pell, FSEOG, state, private, college/university gift aid from institutional funds.
GIFT AID (NON-NEED-BASED) Total amount: $78,000 (100% institutional). **Receiving aid:** Freshmen: 1% (15). Undergraduates: 1% (56). **Average award:** Undergraduates: $1950. **Scholarships, grants, and awards by category:** Creative arts/performance: applied art and design. **Tuition waivers:** Full or partial for employees or children of employees, senior citizens.
LOANS Student loans: $31,011,481 (39% need-based, 61% non-need-based). 54% of past graduating class borrowed through all loan programs. **Average indebtedness per student:** $27,955. **Average need-based loan:** Freshmen: $3373. Undergraduates: $4323. **Parent loans:** $7,932,258 (100% need-based). **Programs:** Federal Direct (Subsidized and Unsubsidized Stafford, PLUS), Perkins, alternative loans.
WORK-STUDY Federal work-study: Total amount: $289,419; jobs available.
APPLYING FOR FINANCIAL AID Required financial aid forms: FAFSA, state aid form. **Financial aid deadline (priority):** 2/15. **Notification date:** Continuous beginning 4/15. Students must reply within 2 weeks of notification.
CONTACT Financial Aid Office, Fashion Institute of Technology, Seventh Avenue at 27th Street, New York, NY 10001-5992, 212-217-3560. Website: http://www.fitnyc.edu/.

FAULKNER UNIVERSITY
Montgomery, AL

Tuition & fees: $17,380	Average undergraduate aid package: $5600

ABOUT THE INSTITUTION Independent Church of Christ, coed. **Awards:** associate, bachelor's, master's, and doctoral degrees. 29 undergraduate majors. **Total enrollment:** 3,327. Undergraduates: 2,763. Freshmen: 388. Federal methodology is used as a basis for awarding need-based institutional aid.
UNDERGRADUATE EXPENSES for 2013–2014 Application fee: $25. **Comprehensive fee:** $24,030 includes full-time tuition ($15,730), mandatory fees ($1650), and room and board ($6650). **College room only:** $3250. Full-time tuition and fees vary according to class time, course load, degree level, location, and program. Room and board charges vary according to board plan and housing facility. **Part-time tuition:** $530 per semester hour. **Part-time fees:** $415 per semester hour. Part-time tuition and fees vary according to class time, degree level, and location.
FRESHMAN FINANCIAL AID (Fall 2011) 256 applied for aid; of those 85% were deemed to have need. 92% of freshmen with need received aid; of those 37% had need fully met. **Average percent of need met:** 56% (excluding resources awarded to replace EFC). **Average financial aid package:** $4950 (excluding resources awarded to replace EFC). 15% of all full-time freshmen had no need and received non-need-based gift aid.
UNDERGRADUATE FINANCIAL AID (Fall 2011) 1,748 applied for aid; of those 85% were deemed to have need. 92% of undergraduates with need received aid; of those 37% had need fully met. **Average percent of need met:** 60% (excluding resources awarded to replace EFC). **Average financial aid package:** $5600 (excluding resources awarded to replace EFC). 15% of all full-time undergraduates had no need and received non-need-based gift aid.
GIFT AID (NEED-BASED) Total amount: $8,759,362 (100% federal). **Receiving aid:** Freshmen: 56% (174); all full-time undergraduates: 58% (1,189). **Average award:** Freshmen: $4000; Undergraduates: $5100. **Scholarships, grants, and awards:** Federal Pell, FSEOG, state, private, college/university gift aid from institutional funds.
GIFT AID (NON-NEED-BASED) Total amount: $4,076,832 (12% state, 84% institutional, 4% external sources). **Receiving aid:** Freshmen: 35% (109). Undergraduates: 36% (738). **Average award:** Freshmen: $1500. Undergraduates: $1700. **Scholarships, grants, and awards by category:** Academic interests/achievement: general academic interests/achievements, religion/biblical studies. Cre-

ative arts/performance: journalism/publications, music, theater/drama. *Special achievements/activities:* cheerleading/drum major, leadership, religious involvement. *Special characteristics:* adult students, children and siblings of alumni, children of faculty/staff, local/state students, out-of-state students, relatives of clergy, religious affiliation, siblings of current students. *Tuition waivers:* Full or partial for employees or children of employees, adult students, senior citizens. *ROTC:* Army cooperative, Air Force cooperative.

LOANS *Student loans:* $21,471,063 (48% need-based, 52% non-need-based). 85% of past graduating class borrowed through all loan programs. *Average indebtedness per student:* $9500. *Average need-based loan:* Freshmen: $2700. Undergraduates: $5000. *Parent loans:* $1,384,356 (100% non-need-based). *Programs:* Federal Direct (Subsidized and Unsubsidized Stafford, PLUS), Perkins.

WORK-STUDY *Federal work-study:* Total amount: $257,886; jobs available. *State or other work-study/employment:* Total amount: $800 (100% non-need-based). Part-time jobs available.

ATHLETIC AWARDS Total amount: $2,970,859 (100% non-need-based).

APPLYING FOR FINANCIAL AID *Required financial aid forms:* FAFSA, institution's own form; state aid form. *Financial aid deadline (priority):* 3/1. *Notification date:* 6/1. Students must reply by 8/1.

CONTACT Mr. William G. Jackson II, Director of Financial Aid, Faulkner University, 5345 Atlanta Highway, Montgomery, AL 36109-3398, 334-386-7195 or toll-free 800-879-9816. *Fax:* 334-386-7201. *E-mail:* faid@faulkner.edu. *Website:* http://www.faulkner.edu/.

FAYETTEVILLE STATE UNIVERSITY
Fayetteville, NC

Tuition & fees (NC res): $5671	Average undergraduate aid package: $9978

ABOUT THE INSTITUTION State-supported, coed. *Awards:* bachelor's, master's, and doctoral degrees. 41 undergraduate majors. *Total enrollment:* 6,060. Undergraduates: 5,287. Freshmen: 612. Federal methodology is used as a basis for awarding need-based institutional aid.

UNDERGRADUATE EXPENSES for 2013–2014 *Application fee:* $35. *Tuition, state resident:* full-time $2585. *Tuition, nonresident:* full-time $13,289. *Required fees:* full-time $3086. Full-time tuition and fees vary according to course level, course load, degree level, location, and program. Part-time tuition and fees vary according to course level, course load, degree level, location, and program. *College room and board:* $6142; *Room only:* $3392. Room and board charges vary according to board plan and housing facility.

FRESHMAN FINANCIAL AID (Fall 2012, est.) 665 applied for aid; of those 94% were deemed to have need. 98% of freshmen with need received aid; of those 20% had need fully met. *Average percent of need met:* 83% (excluding resources awarded to replace EFC). *Average financial aid package:* $10,828 (excluding resources awarded to replace EFC). 1% of all full-time freshmen had no need and received non-need-based gift aid.

UNDERGRADUATE FINANCIAL AID (Fall 2012, est.) 3,654 applied for aid; of those 94% were deemed to have need. 98% of undergraduates with need received aid; of those 17% had need fully met. *Average percent of need met:* 75% (excluding resources awarded to replace EFC). *Average financial aid package:* $9978 (excluding resources awarded to replace EFC). 1% of all full-time undergraduates had no need and received non-need-based gift aid.

GIFT AID (NEED-BASED) *Total amount:* $22,952,268 (64% federal, 19% state, 15% institutional, 2% external sources). *Receiving aid:* Freshmen: 88% (608); all full-time undergraduates: 84% (3,272). *Average award:* Freshmen: $7601; Undergraduates: $6276. *Scholarships, grants, and awards:* Federal Pell, FSEOG, state, private, college/university gift aid from institutional funds, United Negro College Fund, Federal Nursing.

GIFT AID (NON-NEED-BASED) *Total amount:* $12,622 (20% state, 80% institutional). *Receiving aid:* Freshmen: 5% (33). Undergraduates: 10% (403). *Average award:* Freshmen: $1000. Undergraduates: $1340. *Scholarships, grants, and awards by category:* Academic interests/achievement: general academic interests/achievements. *Creative arts/performance:* music. *Special characteristics:* local/state students. *Tuition waivers:* Full or partial for employees or children of employees, senior citizens. *ROTC:* Army cooperative, Air Force.

LOANS *Student loans:* $30,502,370 (94% need-based, 6% non-need-based). 87% of past graduating class borrowed through all loan programs. *Average indebtedness*

per student: $23,147. *Average need-based loan:* Freshmen: $3355. Undergraduates: $4125. *Parent loans:* $370,104 (66% need-based, 34% non-need-based). *Programs:* Federal Direct (Subsidized and Unsubsidized Stafford, PLUS), Perkins.

WORK-STUDY *Federal work-study:* Total amount: $383,246; jobs available. *State or other work-study/employment:* Part-time jobs available.

ATHLETIC AWARDS Total amount: $742,289 (100% need-based).

APPLYING FOR FINANCIAL AID *Required financial aid forms:* FAFSA, federal income tax form(s), W-2 forms. *Financial aid deadline:* 3/1. *Notification date:* Continuous beginning 4/1.

CONTACT Mr. Keith Townsend, Administrative Assistant, Fayetteville-State University, 1200 Murchison Road, Fayetteville, NC 28301-4298, 910-672-1327 or toll-free 800-222-2594. *Fax:* 910-672-1423. *E-mail:* ktownse7@uncfsu.edu. *Website:* http://www.uncfsu.edu/.

FELICIAN COLLEGE
Lodi, NJ

Tuition & fees: $29,990	Average undergraduate aid package: $23,662

ABOUT THE INSTITUTION Independent Roman Catholic, coed. *Awards:* certificates, associate, bachelor's, master's, and doctoral degrees. 31 undergraduate majors. *Total enrollment:* 2,109. Undergraduates: 1,775. Freshmen: 229. Federal methodology is used as a basis for awarding need-based institutional aid.

UNDERGRADUATE EXPENSES for 2013–2014 *Application fee:* $30. *Comprehensive fee:* $41,640 includes full-time tuition ($28,360), mandatory fees ($1630), and room and board ($11,650). Full-time tuition and fees vary according to program. Room and board charges vary according to housing facility. *Part-time tuition:* $935 per credit hour. Part-time tuition and fees vary according to course load and program.

FRESHMAN FINANCIAL AID (Fall 2012, est.) 225 applied for aid; of those 98% were deemed to have need. 100% of freshmen with need received aid; of those 5% had need fully met. *Average percent of need met:* 69% (excluding resources awarded to replace EFC). *Average financial aid package:* $26,744 (excluding resources awarded to replace EFC). 2% of all full-time freshmen had no need and received non-need-based gift aid.

UNDERGRADUATE FINANCIAL AID (Fall 2012, est.) 1,334 applied for aid; of those 96% were deemed to have need. 99% of undergraduates with need received aid; of those 5% had need fully met. *Average percent of need met:* 65% (excluding resources awarded to replace EFC). *Average financial aid package:* $23,662 (excluding resources awarded to replace EFC). 3% of all full-time undergraduates had no need and received non-need-based gift aid.

GIFT AID (NEED-BASED) *Total amount:* $20,935,332 (21% federal, 29% state, 49% institutional, 1% external sources). *Receiving aid:* Freshmen: 78% (178); all full-time undergraduates: 59% (871). *Average award:* Freshmen: $16,573; Undergraduates: $12,202. *Scholarships, grants, and awards:* Federal Pell, FSEOG, state, private, college/university gift aid from institutional funds.

GIFT AID (NON-NEED-BASED) *Total amount:* $2,099,328 (9% federal, 90% institutional, 1% external sources). *Receiving aid:* Freshmen: 82% (188). Undergraduates: 59% (875). *Average award:* Freshmen: $7875. Undergraduates: $11,324. *Scholarships, grants, and awards by category:* Academic interests/achievement: 964 awards ($11,709,132 total): business, education, English, general academic interests/achievements, health fields, religion/biblical studies. *Special characteristics:* 11 awards ($186,473 total): children of faculty/staff, siblings of current students. *Tuition waivers:* Full or partial for employees or children of employees.

LOANS *Student loans:* $13,102,196 (83% need-based, 17% non-need-based). 80% of past graduating class borrowed through all loan programs. *Average indebtedness per student:* $38,598. *Average need-based loan:* Freshmen: $3307. Undergraduates: $4131. *Parent loans:* $2,911,661 (69% need-based, 31% non-need-based). *Programs:* state.

WORK-STUDY Federal work-study jobs available. *State or other work-study/employment:* Part-time jobs available.

ATHLETIC AWARDS Total amount: $1,981,294 (55% need-based, 45% non-need-based).

APPLYING FOR FINANCIAL AID *Required financial aid form:* FAFSA. *Financial aid deadline:* Continuous. *Notification date:* Continuous beginning 4/1.

CONTACT Ms. Janet Mariano-Merli, Financial Aid Director, Felician College, 262 South Main Street, Lodi, NJ 07644, 201-559-6040. *Fax:* 201-559-6025. *E-mail:* merlij@felician.edu.
Website: http://www.felician.edu/.

CONTACT Nancy Wencl, Assistant Director of Financial Aid, Ferris State University, 1201 South State Street, Big Rapids, MI 49307-2020, 231-591-2100 or toll-free 800-433-7747. *Fax:* 231-591-2950. *E-mail:* wencln@ferris.edu.
Website: http://www.ferris.edu/.

FERRIS STATE UNIVERSITY
Big Rapids, MI

Tuition & fees (MI res): $10,710	Average undergraduate aid package: $10,495

ABOUT THE INSTITUTION State-supported, coed. *Awards:* certificates, associate, bachelor's, master's, and doctoral degrees (associate degree). 118 undergraduate majors. *Total enrollment:* 14,533. Undergraduates: 13,261. Freshmen: 2,139. Federal methodology is used as a basis for awarding need-based institutional aid.

UNDERGRADUATE EXPENSES for 2013–2014 *Application fee:* $30. *One-time required fee:* $162. *Tuition, state resident:* full-time $10,710; part-time $357 per credit hour. *Tuition, nonresident:* full-time $16,080; part-time $536 per credit hour. Full-time tuition and fees vary according to location and program. Part-time tuition and fees vary according to location. *College room and board:* $8744. Room and board charges vary according to board plan and housing facility.

FRESHMAN FINANCIAL AID (Fall 2012, est.) 1,953 applied for aid; of those 84% were deemed to have need. 99% of freshmen with need received aid; of those 18% had need fully met. *Average percent of need met:* 67% (excluding resources awarded to replace EFC). *Average financial aid package:* $11,530 (excluding resources awarded to replace EFC). 14% of all full-time freshmen had no need and received non-need-based gift aid.

UNDERGRADUATE FINANCIAL AID (Fall 2012, est.) 8,526 applied for aid; of those 82% were deemed to have need. 99% of undergraduates with need received aid; of those 13% had need fully met. *Average percent of need met:* 61% (excluding resources awarded to replace EFC). *Average financial aid package:* $10,495 (excluding resources awarded to replace EFC). 10% of all full-time undergraduates had no need and received non-need-based gift aid.

GIFT AID (NEED-BASED) *Total amount:* $28,363,640 (88% federal, 2% state, 10% institutional). *Receiving aid:* Freshmen: 55% (1,137); all full-time undergraduates: 53% (4,866). *Average award:* Freshmen: $4555; Undergraduates: $4645. *Scholarships, grants, and awards:* Federal Pell, FSEOG, state, private, college/university gift aid from institutional funds.

GIFT AID (NON-NEED-BASED) *Total amount:* $26,378,785 (3% federal, 28% state, 58% institutional, 11% external sources). *Receiving aid:* Freshmen: 60% (1,254). Undergraduates: 40% (3,692). *Average award:* Freshmen: $4660. Undergraduates: $4465. *Scholarships, grants, and awards by category:* Academic interests/achievement: 4,394 awards ($10,653,231 total): agriculture, architecture, biological sciences, business, communication, computer science, education, engineering/technologies, general academic interests/achievements, health fields, mathematics. *Creative arts/performance:* 647 awards ($2,031,213 total): applied art and design, art/fine arts, debating, general creative arts/performance, journalism/publications, music, theater/drama. *Special achievements/activities:* 115 awards ($30,182 total): general special achievements/activities, memberships. *Special characteristics:* 160 awards ($140,575 total): adult students, children and siblings of alumni, ethnic background, general special characteristics, international students, local/state students, members of minority groups, previous college experience, veterans. *Tuition waivers:* Full or partial for employees or children of employees. *ROTC:* Army cooperative.

LOANS *Student loans:* $80,706,105 (43% need-based, 57% non-need-based). 81% of past graduating class borrowed through all loan programs. *Average indebtedness per student:* $36,930. *Average need-based loan:* Freshmen: $3730. Undergraduates: $4560. *Parent loans:* $9,428,380 (100% non-need-based). *Programs:* Federal Direct (Subsidized and Unsubsidized Stafford, PLUS), Perkins, Federal Nursing, college/university, alternative loans.

WORK-STUDY *Federal work-study:* Total amount: $1,126,555; 481 jobs averaging $2293. *State or other work-study/employment:* Total amount: $2,299,805 (100% non-need-based). 270 part-time jobs averaging $1610.

ATHLETIC AWARDS Total amount: $1,891,595 (100% non-need-based).

APPLYING FOR FINANCIAL AID *Required financial aid form:* FAFSA. *Financial aid deadline (priority):* 2/15. *Notification date:* Continuous beginning 4/1. Students must reply within 3 weeks of notification.

FERRUM COLLEGE
Ferrum, VA

Tuition & fees: $27,425	Average undergraduate aid package: $38,937

ABOUT THE INSTITUTION Independent United Methodist, coed. *Awards:* bachelor's degrees. 31 undergraduate majors. *Total enrollment:* 1,510. Undergraduates: 1,510. Freshmen: 550. Both federal and institutional methodology are used as a basis for awarding need-based institutional aid.

UNDERGRADUATE EXPENSES for 2013–2014 *Application fee:* $25. *Comprehensive fee:* $36,555 includes full-time tuition ($27,310), mandatory fees ($115), and room and board ($9130). *Part-time tuition:* $545 per credit hour.

FRESHMAN FINANCIAL AID (Fall 2011) 543 applied for aid; of those 98% were deemed to have need. 100% of freshmen with need received aid; of those 6% had need fully met. *Average percent of need met:* 37% (excluding resources awarded to replace EFC). *Average financial aid package:* $22,561 (excluding resources awarded to replace EFC). 1% of all full-time freshmen had no need and received non-need-based gift aid.

UNDERGRADUATE FINANCIAL AID (Fall 2011) 1,452 applied for aid; of those 98% were deemed to have need. 100% of undergraduates with need received aid; of those 25% had need fully met. *Average percent of need met:* 80% (excluding resources awarded to replace EFC). *Average financial aid package:* $38,937 (excluding resources awarded to replace EFC). 3% of all full-time undergraduates had no need and received non-need-based gift aid.

GIFT AID (NEED-BASED) *Total amount:* $10,651,768 (35% federal, 1% state, 54% institutional, 10% external sources). *Receiving aid:* Freshmen: 82% (473); all full-time undergraduates: 74% (1,111). *Average award:* Freshmen: $10,490; Undergraduates: $16,418. *Scholarships, grants, and awards:* Federal Pell, FSEOG, state, private, college/university gift aid from institutional funds.

GIFT AID (NON-NEED-BASED) *Total amount:* $13,750,985 (22% state, 74% institutional, 4% external sources). *Receiving aid:* Freshmen: 92% (531). Undergraduates: 94% (1,405). *Average award:* Freshmen: $10,823. Undergraduates: $16,287. *Scholarships, grants, and awards by category:* Academic interests/achievement: general academic interests/achievements. *Special achievements/activities:* general special achievements/activities, religious involvement. *Special characteristics:* children of faculty/staff, international students, local/state students, relatives of clergy, religious affiliation.

LOANS *Student loans:* $10,344,907 (45% need-based, 55% non-need-based). 97% of past graduating class borrowed through all loan programs. *Average indebtedness per student:* $24,788. *Average need-based loan:* Freshmen: $2858. Undergraduates: $6795. *Parent loans:* $6,499,797 (100% non-need-based). *Programs:* Federal Direct (Subsidized and Unsubsidized Stafford, PLUS), Perkins.

WORK-STUDY *Federal work-study:* Total amount: $1,976,633; 1,021 jobs averaging $2207.

APPLYING FOR FINANCIAL AID *Required financial aid forms:* FAFSA, state aid form. *Financial aid deadline (priority):* 3/1. *Notification date:* Continuous beginning 1/15.

CONTACT Heather Hollandsworth, Director of Financial Aid, Ferrum College, PO Box 1000, Ferrum, VA 24088-9001, 540-365-4282 or toll-free 800-868-9797. *Fax:* 540-365-4266. *E-mail:* hhollandsworth@ferrum.edu.
Website: http://www.ferrum.edu/.

FINLANDIA UNIVERSITY
Hancock, MI

Tuition & fees: N/R	Average undergraduate aid package: N/A

ABOUT THE INSTITUTION Independent Evangelical Lutheran Church in America, coed. 15 undergraduate majors. Federal methodology is used as a basis for awarding need-based institutional aid.

GIFT AID (NEED-BASED) *Scholarships, grants, and awards:* Federal Pell, FSEOG, state, private, college/university gift aid from institutional funds.

GIFT AID (NON-NEED-BASED) *Scholarships, grants, and awards by category:* Academic interests/achievement: general academic interests/achievements. *Creative arts/performance:* art/fine arts, general creative arts/performance. *Special achievements/activities:* community service, general special achievements/activities, leadership, religious involvement. *Special characteristics:* children of current students, children of faculty/staff, first-generation college students, international students, religious affiliation, siblings of current students, spouses of current students, twins.

LOANS *Programs:* Federal Direct (Subsidized and Unsubsidized Stafford, PLUS), private loans.

APPLYING FOR FINANCIAL AID *Required financial aid form:* FAFSA. *Financial aid deadline (priority):* 3/1. *Notification date:* Continuous beginning 3/1. Students must reply within 3 weeks of notification.

CONTACT Sandra Turnquist, Director of Financial Aid, Finlandia University, 601 Quincy Street, Hancock, MI 49930, 906-487-7240 or toll-free 877-202-5491. *Fax:* 906-487-7383. *E-mail:* sandra.turnquist@finlandia.edu. *Website:* http://www.finlandia.edu/.

FISHER COLLEGE
Boston, MA

Tuition & fees: $26,775	Average undergraduate aid package: N/A

ABOUT THE INSTITUTION Independent, coed. *Awards:* certificates, associate, and bachelor's degrees. 25 undergraduate majors. *Total enrollment:* 1,751. Undergraduates: 1,751. Freshmen: 349. Federal methodology is used as a basis for awarding need-based institutional aid.

UNDERGRADUATE EXPENSES for 2013–2014 *Application fee:* $50. *Comprehensive fee:* $40,699 includes full-time tuition ($25,780), mandatory fees ($995), and room and board ($13,924). Room and board charges vary according to housing facility. *Part-time tuition:* $300 per credit.

FRESHMAN FINANCIAL AID (Fall 2012, est.) 305 applied for aid; of those 79% were deemed to have need. 100% of freshmen with need received aid.

UNDERGRADUATE FINANCIAL AID (Fall 2012, est.) 1,047 applied for aid; of those 84% were deemed to have need. 100% of undergraduates with need received aid.

GIFT AID (NEED-BASED) *Total amount:* $13,859,883 (62% federal, 2% state, 36% institutional). *Receiving aid:* Freshmen: 55% (229); all full-time undergraduates: 61% (697). *Scholarships, grants, and awards:* FSEOG, state, private, college/university gift aid from institutional funds.

GIFT AID (NON-NEED-BASED) *Total amount:* $4,994,706 (35% federal, 64% institutional, 1% external sources). *Receiving aid:* Freshmen: 57% (237). Undergraduates: 51% (575). *Scholarships, grants, and awards by category:* Academic interests/achievement: general academic interests/achievements. *ROTC:* Army cooperative.

LOANS *Student loans:* $5,810,947 (50% need-based, 50% non-need-based). 71% of past graduating class borrowed through all loan programs. *Parent loans:* $1,730,087 (100% non-need-based). *Programs:* Federal Direct (Subsidized and Unsubsidized Stafford, PLUS), Perkins, state.

WORK-STUDY *Federal work-study:* Total amount: $61,800; jobs available.

APPLYING FOR FINANCIAL AID *Required financial aid form:* FAFSA. *Financial aid deadline:* Continuous. *Notification date:* Continuous.

CONTACT Colleen Woods, Director of Financial Aid, Fisher College, 1 Arlington Street, Third Floor, Boston, MA 02116, 617-236-5470. *E-mail:* cwoods@fisher.edu. *Website:* http://www.fisher.edu/.

FISK UNIVERSITY
Nashville, TN

Tuition & fees: N/R	Average undergraduate aid package: $12,920

ABOUT THE INSTITUTION Independent United Church of Christ, coed. 20 undergraduate majors. Both federal and institutional methodology are used as a basis for awarding need-based institutional aid.

FRESHMAN FINANCIAL AID (Fall 2011) 181 applied for aid; of those 98% were deemed to have need. 100% of freshmen with need received aid; of those 37% had need fully met. *Average percent of need met:* 85% (excluding resources awarded to replace EFC). *Average financial aid package:* $14,181 (excluding resources awarded to replace EFC).

UNDERGRADUATE FINANCIAL AID (Fall 2011) 554 applied for aid; of those 90% were deemed to have need. 100% of undergraduates with need received aid; of those 32% had need fully met. *Average percent of need met:* 75% (excluding resources awarded to replace EFC). *Average financial aid package:* $12,920 (excluding resources awarded to replace EFC).

GIFT AID (NEED-BASED) *Total amount:* $8,022,037 (23% federal, 7% state, 67% institutional, 3% external sources). *Receiving aid:* Freshmen: 98% (177); all full-time undergraduates: 90% (499). *Average award:* Freshmen: $11,486; Undergraduates: $10,417. *Scholarships, grants, and awards:* Federal Pell, FSEOG, state, private, college/university gift aid from institutional funds, United Negro College Fund.

LOANS *Student loans:* $3,024,964 (100% need-based). 49% of past graduating class borrowed through all loan programs. *Average indebtedness per student:* $6147. *Average need-based loan:* Freshmen: $2904. Undergraduates: $3780. *Parent loans:* $1,073,428 (100% need-based). *Programs:* Federal Direct (Subsidized and Unsubsidized Stafford, PLUS), Perkins.

WORK-STUDY *Federal work-study:* Total amount: $234,120; jobs available.

APPLYING FOR FINANCIAL AID *Required financial aid form:* FAFSA. *Financial aid deadline:* 6/1 (priority: 3/1). *Notification date:* Continuous beginning 4/1. Students must reply within 2 weeks of notification.

CONTACT Mary Chambliss, Director of Financial Aid, Fisk University, 1000 17th Avenue North, Nashville, TN 37208-3051, 615-329-8735 or toll-free 888-702-0022. *E-mail:* mchambliss@fisk.edu. *Website:* http://www.fisk.edu/.

FITCHBURG STATE UNIVERSITY
Fitchburg, MA

CONTACT Office of Financial Aid, Fitchburg State University, 160 Pearl Street, Fitchburg, MA 01420, 978-665-3454 or toll-free 800-705-9692. *Fax:* 978-665-3556. *E-mail:* finaid@fitchburgstate.edu. *Website:* http://www.fitchburgstate.edu/.

FIVE TOWNS COLLEGE
Dix Hills, NY

CONTACT Ms. Mary Venezia, Financial Aid Director, Five Towns College, 305 North Service Road, Dix Hills, NY 11746-6055, 631-656-2113. *Fax:* 631-656-2191. *E-mail:* mvenezia@ftc.edu. *Website:* http://www.ftc.edu/.

FLAGLER COLLEGE
St. Augustine, FL

Tuition & fees: $15,340	Average undergraduate aid package: $11,033

ABOUT THE INSTITUTION Independent, coed. *Awards:* bachelor's degrees. 25 undergraduate majors. *Total enrollment:* 2,847. Undergraduates: 2,847. Freshmen: 646. Federal methodology is used as a basis for awarding need-based institutional aid.

UNDERGRADUATE EXPENSES for 2013–2014 *Application fee:* $40. *Comprehensive fee:* $23,690 includes full-time tuition ($15,340) and room and board ($8350). *College room only:* $4070. Room and board charges vary according to board plan and housing facility. *Part-time tuition:* $510 per credit hour.

FRESHMAN FINANCIAL AID (Fall 2012, est.) 520 applied for aid; of those 73% were deemed to have need. 100% of freshmen with need received aid; of those 14% had need fully met. *Average percent of need met:* 78% (excluding resources awarded to replace EFC). *Average financial aid package:* $11,554 (excluding resources awarded to replace EFC). 1% of all full-time freshmen had no need and received non-need-based gift aid.

UNDERGRADUATE FINANCIAL AID (Fall 2012, est.) 2,373 applied for aid; of those 75% were deemed to have need. 100% of undergraduates with need received aid; of those 17% had need fully met. *Average percent of need met:* 79% (excluding resources awarded to replace EFC). *Average financial aid package:* $11,033 (excluding resources awarded to replace EFC). 3% of all full-time undergraduates had no need and received non-need-based gift aid.

GIFT AID (NEED-BASED) *Total amount:* $11,393,876 (33% federal, 35% state, 30% institutional, 2% external sources). *Receiving aid:* Freshmen: 62% (376); all full-time undergraduates: 63% (1,686). *Average award:* Freshmen: $5421; Undergraduates: $4650. *Scholarships, grants, and awards:* Federal Pell, FSEOG, state, private, college/university gift aid from institutional funds.

GIFT AID (NON-NEED-BASED) *Total amount:* $1,821,405 (1% federal, 76% state, 18% institutional, 5% external sources). *Receiving aid:* Freshmen: 5% (28). Undergraduates: 5% (144). *Average award:* Freshmen: $4100. Undergraduates: $2990. *Scholarships, grants, and awards by category:* Academic interests/achievement: 62 awards ($114,225 total): business, communication, education, English, foreign languages, general academic interests/achievements, humanities, religion/biblical studies, social sciences. *Creative arts/performance:* 8 awards ($36,850 total): applied art and design, art/fine arts, cinema/film/broadcasting, performing arts, theater/drama. *Special achievements/activities:* 96 awards ($170,520 total): general special achievements/activities, leadership, memberships, religious involvement. *Special characteristics:* 200 awards ($705,602 total): children of educators, children of faculty/staff, ethnic background, first-generation college students, general special characteristics, local/state students, members of minority groups, out-of-state students. *Tuition waivers:* Full or partial for employees or children of employees.

LOANS *Student loans:* $18,432,000 (63% need-based, 37% non-need-based). 68% of past graduating class borrowed through all loan programs. *Average indebtedness per student:* $24,519. *Average need-based loan:* Freshmen: $3159. Undergraduates: $4122. *Parent loans:* $2,674,244 (38% need-based, 62% non-need-based). *Programs:* Federal Direct (Subsidized and Unsubsidized Stafford, PLUS), Perkins.

WORK-STUDY *Federal work-study:* Total amount: $278,723; 285 jobs averaging $1111. *State or other work-study/employment:* Total amount: $54,700 (6% need-based, 94% non-need-based). 54 part-time jobs averaging $1164.

ATHLETIC AWARDS Total amount: $1,271,952 (56% need-based, 44% non-need-based).

APPLYING FOR FINANCIAL AID *Required financial aid forms:* FAFSA, institution's own form. *Financial aid deadline (priority):* 4/1. *Notification date:* Continuous beginning 2/15. Students must reply within 2 weeks of notification.

CONTACT Office of Financial Aid, Flagler College, PO Box 1027, St. Augustine, FL 32085-1027, 904-819-6225 or toll-free 800-304-4208. *Fax:* 904-819-6453. *E-mail:* financialaid@flagler.edu. *Website:* http://www.flagler.edu/.

UNDERGRADUATE FINANCIAL AID (Fall 2011) 9,766 applied for aid; of those 89% were deemed to have need. 100% of undergraduates with need received aid; of those 23% had need fully met. *Average percent of need met:* 74% (excluding resources awarded to replace EFC). *Average financial aid package:* $12,521 (excluding resources awarded to replace EFC). 1% of all full-time undergraduates had no need and received non-need-based gift aid.

GIFT AID (NEED-BASED) *Total amount:* $47,329,628 (75% federal, 7% state, 18% institutional). *Receiving aid:* Freshmen: 79% (1,525); all full-time undergraduates: 76% (7,732). *Average award:* Freshmen: $7017; Undergraduates: $5738. *Scholarships, grants, and awards:* Federal Pell, FSEOG, state, private, college/university gift aid from institutional funds, United Negro College Fund.

GIFT AID (NON-NEED-BASED) *Total amount:* $10,833,910 (53% state, 19% institutional, 28% external sources). *Receiving aid:* Freshmen: 44% (848). Undergraduates: 25% (2,529). *Average award:* Freshmen: $5029. Undergraduates: $3608. *Scholarships, grants, and awards by category:* Academic interests/achievement: agriculture, architecture, area/ethnic studies, biological sciences, business, communication, computer science, education, engineering/technologies, English, foreign languages, general academic interests/achievements, health fields, humanities, mathematics, military science, physical sciences, premedicine, social sciences. *Creative arts/performance:* applied art and design, art/fine arts, cinema/film/broadcasting, creative writing, dance, journalism/publications, music, performing arts, theater/drama. *Special achievements/activities:* cheerleading/drum major, community service, general special achievements/activities, leadership. *Special characteristics:* 720 awards ($4,077,077 total): ethnic background, first-generation college students, general special characteristics, local/state students, out-of-state students. *Tuition waivers:* Full or partial for employees or children of employees, senior citizens. *ROTC:* Army, Naval, Air Force cooperative.

LOANS *Student loans:* $61,340,827 (48% need-based, 52% non-need-based). 85% of past graduating class borrowed through all loan programs. *Average indebtedness per student:* $29,702. *Average need-based loan:* Freshmen: $3390. Undergraduates: $3903. *Parent loans:* $13,046,808 (100% non-need-based). *Programs:* Federal Direct (Subsidized and Unsubsidized Stafford, PLUS), Perkins, private loans.

WORK-STUDY *Federal work-study:* Total amount: $544,133; 233 jobs averaging $2300.

ATHLETIC AWARDS Total amount: $2,078,387 (100% non-need-based).

APPLYING FOR FINANCIAL AID *Required financial aid form:* FAFSA. *Financial aid deadline:* Continuous. *Notification date:* Continuous beginning 4/15.

CONTACT Ms. Lisa A. Stewart, Director of Financial Aid, Florida Agricultural and Mechanical University, 101 Foote-Hilyer Administration Center, Tallahassee, FL 32307, 850-599-3730 or toll-free 866-642-1198. *Website:* http://www.famu.edu/.

FLORIDA AGRICULTURAL AND MECHANICAL UNIVERSITY
Tallahassee, FL

Tuition & fees (FL res): $5187	Average undergraduate aid package: $12,521

ABOUT THE INSTITUTION State-supported, coed. *Awards:* certificates, associate, bachelor's, master's, and doctoral degrees. 53 undergraduate majors. *Total enrollment:* 12,057. Undergraduates: 10,053. Freshmen: 1,518. Federal methodology is used as a basis for awarding need-based institutional aid.

UNDERGRADUATE EXPENSES for 2013–2014 *Application fee:* $30. *Tuition, state resident:* full-time $4929; part-time $164.29 per credit. *Tuition, nonresident:* full-time $16,869; part-time $562.31 per credit. *Required fees:* full-time $258; $129 per term. *College room and board:* $8754; *Room only:* $4928. Room and board charges vary according to board plan and housing facility. *Payment plan:* Tuition prepayment.

FRESHMAN FINANCIAL AID (Fall 2011) 1,917 applied for aid; of those 89% were deemed to have need. 100% of freshmen with need received aid; of those 26% had need fully met. *Average percent of need met:* 78% (excluding resources awarded to replace EFC). *Average financial aid package:* $13,285 (excluding resources awarded to replace EFC). 1% of all full-time freshmen had no need and received non-need-based gift aid.

FLORIDA ATLANTIC UNIVERSITY
Boca Raton, FL

Tuition & fees (FL res): $5986	Average undergraduate aid package: $10,684

ABOUT THE INSTITUTION State-supported, coed. *Awards:* certificates, associate, bachelor's, master's, and doctoral degrees. 65 undergraduate majors. *Total enrollment:* 30,038. Undergraduates: 24,823. Freshmen: 3,237. Federal methodology is used as a basis for awarding need-based institutional aid.

UNDERGRADUATE EXPENSES for 2013–2014 *Application fee:* $30. *Tuition, state resident:* full-time $5986; part-time $199.54 per credit hour. *Tuition, nonresident:* full-time $21,543; part-time $718.09 per credit hour. Full-time tuition and fees vary according to course load. Part-time tuition and fees vary according to course load. *College room and board:* $11,353. Room and board charges vary according to board plan and housing facility. *Payment plan:* Tuition prepayment.

FRESHMAN FINANCIAL AID (Fall 2012, est.) 2,780 applied for aid; of those 70% were deemed to have need. 99% of freshmen with need received aid; of those 12% had need fully met. *Average percent of need met:* 65% (excluding resources awarded to replace EFC). *Average financial aid package:* $10,044 (excluding resources awarded to replace EFC). 3% of all full-time freshmen had no need and received non-need-based gift aid.

UNDERGRADUATE FINANCIAL AID (Fall 2012, est.) 13,008 applied for aid; of those 79% were deemed to have need. 98% of undergraduates with need received

aid; of those 14% had need fully met. *Average percent of need met:* 66% (excluding resources awarded to replace EFC). *Average financial aid package:* $10,684 (excluding resources awarded to replace EFC). 2% of all full-time undergraduates had no need and received non-need-based gift aid.

GIFT AID (NEED-BASED) *Total amount:* $68,418,503 (64% federal, 19% state, 14% institutional, 3% external sources). *Receiving aid:* Freshmen: 58% (1,770); all full-time undergraduates: 58% (8,887). *Average award:* Freshmen: $6078; Undergraduates: $5871. *Scholarships, grants, and awards:* Federal Pell, FSEOG, state, private, college/university gift aid from institutional funds, Federal Nursing.

GIFT AID (NON-NEED-BASED) *Total amount:* $6,217,117 (73% state, 14% institutional, 13% external sources). *Receiving aid:* Freshmen: 5% (144). Undergraduates: 3% (456). *Average award:* Freshmen: $2275. Undergraduates: $2502. *Scholarships, grants, and awards by category: Academic interests/achievement:* business, engineering/technologies, general academic interests/achievements, physical sciences, social sciences. *Creative arts/performance:* music, performing arts. *Tuition waivers:* Full or partial for employees or children of employees, senior citizens. *ROTC:* Army, Air Force cooperative.

LOANS *Student loans:* $103,252,445 (76% need-based, 24% non-need-based). 46% of past graduating class borrowed through all loan programs. *Average indebtedness per student:* $19,281. *Average need-based loan:* Freshmen: $5305. Undergraduates: $6777. *Parent loans:* $3,147,421 (39% need-based, 61% non-need-based). *Programs:* Federal Direct (Subsidized and Unsubsidized Stafford, PLUS), Perkins, college/university.

WORK-STUDY *Federal work-study:* Total amount: $597,688; 187 jobs averaging $2373. *State or other work-study/employment:* Total amount: $9963 (100% need-based). 3 part-time jobs averaging $3298.

ATHLETIC AWARDS Total amount: $3,401,035 (43% need-based, 57% non-need-based).

APPLYING FOR FINANCIAL AID *Required financial aid form:* FAFSA. *Financial aid deadline (priority):* 3/1. *Notification date:* Continuous beginning 5/1. Students must reply within 3 weeks of notification.

CONTACT Tracy Boulukos, Director of Student Financial Aid, Florida Atlantic University, 777 Glades Road, Boca Raton, FL 33431-0991, 561-297-3528. *E-mail:* tbouluko@fau.edu. *Website:* http://www.fau.edu/.

FLORIDA CHRISTIAN COLLEGE
Kissimmee, FL

CONTACT Ms. Sandra Peppard, Director of Student Financial Aid, Florida Christian College, 1011 Bill Beck Boulevard, Kissimmee, FL 34744-5301, 407-847-8966 Ext. 365 or toll-free 888-GO-TO-FCC. *Fax:* 407-847-3925. *E-mail:* sandi.peppard@fcc.edu. *Website:* http://www.fcc.edu/.

FLORIDA COLLEGE
Temple Terrace, FL

ABOUT THE INSTITUTION Independent, coed. *Awards:* associate and bachelor's degrees. 10 undergraduate majors. *Total enrollment:* 532. Undergraduates: 532. Freshmen: 182.

GIFT AID (NEED-BASED) *Scholarships, grants, and awards:* Federal Pell, FSEOG, state, private, college/university gift aid from institutional funds.

GIFT AID (NON-NEED-BASED) *Scholarships, grants, and awards by category: Academic interests/achievement:* business, education, general academic interests/achievements, religion/biblical studies. *Creative arts/performance:* music. *Special achievements/activities:* general special achievements/activities. *Special characteristics:* children of faculty/staff.

LOANS *Programs:* Federal Direct (Subsidized and Unsubsidized Stafford, PLUS), Perkins.

APPLYING FOR FINANCIAL AID *Required financial aid form:* FAFSA.

CONTACT Lisa McClister, Director of Financial Aid, Florida College, 119 North Glen Arven Avenue, Temple Terrace, FL 33617, 813-988-5131 Ext. 131. *Fax:* 813-899-6772. *E-mail:* mcclisterl@floridacollege.edu. *Website:* http://www.floridacollege.edu/.

FLORIDA GULF COAST UNIVERSITY
Fort Myers, FL

Tuition & fees (FL res): $4855	Average undergraduate aid package: $9088

ABOUT THE INSTITUTION State-supported, coed. *Awards:* certificates, associate, bachelor's, master's, and doctoral degrees. 42 undergraduate majors. *Total enrollment:* 13,471. Undergraduates: 12,155. Freshmen: 2,776. Federal methodology is used as a basis for awarding need-based institutional aid.

UNDERGRADUATE EXPENSES for 2013-2014 *Application fee:* $30. *Tuition, state resident:* full-time $4855. *Tuition, nonresident:* full-time $20,090. Full-time tuition and fees vary according to course load. Part-time tuition and fees vary according to course load. *College room and board:* $9424. Room and board charges vary according to board plan.

FRESHMAN FINANCIAL AID (Fall 2011) 2,167 applied for aid; of those 64% were deemed to have need. 100% of freshmen with need received aid; of those 9% had need fully met. *Average percent of need met:* 18% (excluding resources awarded to replace EFC). *Average financial aid package:* $8926 (excluding resources awarded to replace EFC). 4% of all full-time freshmen had no need and received non-need-based gift aid.

UNDERGRADUATE FINANCIAL AID (Fall 2011) 7,217 applied for aid; of those 67% were deemed to have need. 100% of undergraduates with need received aid; of those 9% had need fully met. *Average percent of need met:* 19% (excluding resources awarded to replace EFC). *Average financial aid package:* $9088 (excluding resources awarded to replace EFC). 3% of all full-time undergraduates had no need and received non-need-based gift aid.

GIFT AID (NEED-BASED) *Total amount:* $25,015,067 (60% federal, 25% state, 12% institutional, 3% external sources). *Receiving aid:* Freshmen: 31% (798); all full-time undergraduates: 33% (2,999). *Average award:* Freshmen: $4998; Undergraduates: $5035. *Scholarships, grants, and awards:* Federal Pell, FSEOG, state, private, college/university gift aid from institutional funds.

GIFT AID (NON-NEED-BASED) *Total amount:* $4,909,236 (71% state, 21% institutional, 8% external sources). *Receiving aid:* Freshmen: 43% (1,086). Undergraduates: 21% (1,928). *Average award:* Freshmen: $3427. Undergraduates: $3796. *Scholarships, grants, and awards by category: Academic interests/achievement:* biological sciences, business, education, engineering/technologies, general academic interests/achievements, health fields, humanities, mathematics, physical sciences, religion/biblical studies, social sciences. *Creative arts/performance:* art/fine arts, music. *Special achievements/activities:* community service, leadership. *Special characteristics:* adult students, ethnic background, handicapped students, international students, local/state students, members of minority groups, out-of-state students.

LOANS *Student loans:* $35,590,626 (79% need-based, 21% non-need-based). 42% of past graduating class borrowed through all loan programs. *Average indebtedness per student:* $27,308. *Average need-based loan:* Freshmen: $6573. Undergraduates: $7132. *Programs:* Federal Direct (Subsidized and Unsubsidized Stafford, PLUS).

WORK-STUDY *Federal work-study:* Total amount: $371,368; jobs available. *State or other work-study/employment:* Total amount: $1,910,786 (100% need-based). Part-time jobs available.

ATHLETIC AWARDS Total amount: $687,558 (100% non-need-based).

APPLYING FOR FINANCIAL AID *Required financial aid forms:* FAFSA, institution's own form, state aid form. *Financial aid deadline:* 6/30 (priority: 3/1). *Notification date:* Continuous.

CONTACT Jorge Lopez-Rosado, Director of Student Financial Services, Florida Gulf Coast University, 10501 FGCU Boulevard South, Fort Myers, FL 33965, 239-590-1210 or toll-free 888-889-1095. *Fax:* 239-590-7923. *E-mail:* faso@fgcu.edu. *Website:* http://www.fgcu.edu/.

FLORIDA INSTITUTE OF TECHNOLOGY
Melbourne, FL

Tuition & fees: $36,020	Average undergraduate aid package: $32,459

ABOUT THE INSTITUTION Independent, coed. *Awards:* certificates, bachelor's, master's, and doctoral degrees. 53 undergraduate majors. *Total enrollment:* 5,384. Undergraduates: 2,978. Freshmen: 756. Federal methodology is used as a basis for awarding need-based institutional aid.

UNDERGRADUATE EXPENSES for 2013–2014 *Comprehensive fee:* $48,290 includes full-time tuition ($35,460), mandatory fees ($560), and room and board ($12,270). *College room only:* $7150. Full-time tuition and fees vary according to course load, program, and student level. Room and board charges vary according to board plan and housing facility. *Part-time tuition:* $1025 per credit hour.

FRESHMAN FINANCIAL AID (Fall 2012, est.) 544 applied for aid; of those 88% were deemed to have need. 100% of freshmen with need received aid; of those 40% had need fully met. *Average percent of need met:* 86% (excluding resources awarded to replace EFC). *Average financial aid package:* $32,855 (excluding resources awarded to replace EFC). 27% of all full-time freshmen had no need and received non-need-based gift aid.

UNDERGRADUATE FINANCIAL AID (Fall 2012, est.) 1,797 applied for aid; of those 89% were deemed to have need. 100% of undergraduates with need received aid; of those 32% had need fully met. *Average percent of need met:* 83% (excluding resources awarded to replace EFC). *Average financial aid package:* $32,459 (excluding resources awarded to replace EFC). 24% of all full-time undergraduates had no need and received non-need-based gift aid.

GIFT AID (NEED-BASED) *Total amount:* $33,286,314 (16% federal, 12% state, 70% institutional, 2% external sources). *Receiving aid:* Freshmen: 63% (476); all full-time undergraduates: 58% (1,598). *Average award:* Freshmen: $21,560; Undergraduates: $21,384. *Scholarships, grants, and awards:* Federal Pell, FSEOG, state, private, college/university gift aid from institutional funds.

GIFT AID (NON-NEED-BASED) *Total amount:* $10,412,845 (9% federal, 4% state, 86% institutional, 1% external sources). *Receiving aid:* Freshmen: 63% (476). Undergraduates: 56% (1,557). *Average award:* Freshmen: $13,696. Undergraduates: $12,038. *Scholarships, grants, and awards by category:* Academic interests/achievement: 1,782 awards ($20,763,108 total): general academic interests/achievements, military science. *Creative arts/performance:* 34 awards ($32,000 total): music. *Special achievements/activities:* 98 awards ($1,054,750 total): cheerleading/drum major, hobbies/interests, leadership, memberships. *Special characteristics:* 1,205 awards ($3,492,087 total): children and siblings of alumni, children of faculty/staff, general special characteristics, international students, previous college experience, siblings of current students. *Tuition waivers:* Full or partial for employees or children of employees, senior citizens. *ROTC:* Army.

LOANS *Student loans:* $13,577,641 (95% need-based, 5% non-need-based). 61% of past graduating class borrowed through all loan programs. *Average indebtedness per student:* $38,953. *Average need-based loan:* Freshmen: $3488. Undergraduates: $4977. *Parent loans:* $9,626,106 (95% need-based, 5% non-need-based). *Programs:* Federal Direct (Subsidized and Unsubsidized Stafford), Perkins, state, college/university.

WORK-STUDY *Federal work-study:* Total amount: $1,329,683; 690 jobs averaging $1930. *State or other work-study/employment:* Total amount: $29,270 (100% need-based). 11 part-time jobs averaging $2661.

ATHLETIC AWARDS Total amount: $4,012,901 (58% need-based, 42% non-need-based).

APPLYING FOR FINANCIAL AID *Required financial aid forms:* FAFSA, state aid form. *Financial aid deadline (priority):* 3/1. *Notification date:* Continuous beginning 2/15. Students must reply by 5/1 or within 4 weeks of notification.

CONTACT Office of Financial Aid, Florida Institute of Technology, 150 West University Boulevard, Melbourne, FL 32901-6975, 321-674-8070 or toll-free 800-888-4348. *Fax:* 321-724-2778. *E-mail:* finaid@fit.edu. *Website:* http://www.fit.edu/.

FLORIDA INTERNATIONAL UNIVERSITY
Miami, FL

Tuition & fees (FL res): $6417	Average undergraduate aid package: $7960

ABOUT THE INSTITUTION State-supported, coed. *Awards:* certificates, bachelor's, master's, and doctoral degrees. 63 undergraduate majors. *Total enrollment:* 46,261. Undergraduates: 37,468. Freshmen: 4,345. Federal methodology is used as a basis for awarding need-based institutional aid.

UNDERGRADUATE EXPENSES for 2013–2014 *Application fee:* $30. *Tuition, state resident:* full-time $6050; part-time $201.66 per credit hour. *Tuition, nonresident:* full-time $18,449; part-time $614.96 per credit hour. *Required fees:* full-time $367. Full-time tuition and fees vary according to course load. Part-time tuition and fees vary according to course load. *College room and board:* $11,330. Room and board charges vary according to board plan and housing facility.

FRESHMAN FINANCIAL AID (Fall 2011) 3,163 applied for aid; of those 98% were deemed to have need. 98% of freshmen with need received aid; of those 7% had need fully met. *Average percent of need met:* 18% (excluding resources awarded to replace EFC). *Average financial aid package:* $6926 (excluding resources awarded to replace EFC). 33% of all full-time freshmen had no need and received non-need-based gift aid.

UNDERGRADUATE FINANCIAL AID (Fall 2011) 16,384 applied for aid; of those 97% were deemed to have need. 98% of undergraduates with need received aid; of those 9% had need fully met. *Average percent of need met:* 17% (excluding resources awarded to replace EFC). *Average financial aid package:* $7960 (excluding resources awarded to replace EFC). 9% of all full-time undergraduates had no need and received non-need-based gift aid.

GIFT AID (NEED-BASED) *Total amount:* $103,775,839 (76% federal, 8% state, 16% institutional). *Receiving aid:* Freshmen: 48% (2,007); all full-time undergraduates: 50% (11,325). *Average award:* Freshmen: $5760; Undergraduates: $5750. *Scholarships, grants, and awards:* Federal Pell, FSEOG, state, private, college/university gift aid from institutional funds.

GIFT AID (NON-NEED-BASED) *Total amount:* $39,398,428 (10% federal, 50% state, 33% institutional, 7% external sources). *Receiving aid:* Freshmen: 63% (2,633). Undergraduates: 37% (8,526). *Average award:* Freshmen: $527. Undergraduates: $455. *Scholarships, grants, and awards by category:* Academic interests/achievement: 2,677 awards ($4,305,900 total): architecture, biological sciences, business, communication, computer science, education, engineering/technologies, English, foreign languages, general academic interests/achievements, health fields, humanities, mathematics, physical sciences, social sciences. *Creative arts/performance:* 107 awards ($222,029 total): art/fine arts, dance, journalism/publications, music, performing arts, theater/drama. *Special characteristics:* 1,154 awards ($1,278,105 total): first-generation college students, veterans, veterans' children. *Tuition waivers:* Full or partial for employees or children of employees, senior citizens. *ROTC:* Army, Air Force.

LOANS *Student loans:* $239,511,068 (47% need-based, 53% non-need-based). 46% of past graduating class borrowed through all loan programs. *Average indebtedness per student:* $17,706. *Average need-based loan:* Freshmen: $7655. Undergraduates: $9284. *Parent loans:* $2,359,079 (100% non-need-based). *Programs:* Federal Direct (Subsidized and Unsubsidized Stafford, PLUS), Perkins, college/university.

WORK-STUDY *Federal work-study:* Total amount: $2,517,686; 627 jobs averaging $4424. *State or other work-study/employment:* Total amount: $81,993 (100% need-based). 24 part-time jobs averaging $3678.

ATHLETIC AWARDS Total amount: $5,238,746 (2% need-based, 98% non-need-based).

APPLYING FOR FINANCIAL AID *Required financial aid form:* FAFSA. *Financial aid deadline:* 5/15 (priority: 3/1). *Notification date:* Continuous beginning 2/15. Students must reply within 4 weeks of notification.

CONTACT Francisco Valines, Director of Financial Aid, Florida International University, 11200 SW 8th Street, PC 125, Miami, FL 33199, 305-348-7272. *Fax:* 305-348-2346. *E-mail:* francisco.valines@fiu.edu. *Website:* http://www.fiu.edu/.

FLORIDA MEMORIAL UNIVERSITY
Miami-Dade, FL

CONTACT Brian Phillip, Director of Financial Aid, Florida Memorial University, 15800 Northwest 42nd Avenue, Miami, FL 33054, 305-626-3745 or toll-free 800-822-1362. *Fax:* 305-626-3106. *Website:* http://www.fmuniv.edu/.

FLORIDA NATIONAL UNIVERSITY
Hialeah, FL

Tuition & fees: $13,230	Average undergraduate aid package: N/A

ABOUT THE INSTITUTION Proprietary, coed. *Awards:* certificates, diplomas, associate, bachelor's, and master's degrees. 45 undergraduate majors. *Total enrollment:* 2,506. Undergraduates: 2,487. Freshmen: 592. Federal methodology is used as a basis for awarding need-based institutional aid.
UNDERGRADUATE EXPENSES for 2013–2014 *Tuition:* full-time $12,600; part-time $525 per credit. *Payment plans:* Guaranteed tuition, tuition prepayment.
FRESHMAN FINANCIAL AID (Fall 2011) 513 applied for aid; of those 99% were deemed to have need. 100% of freshmen with need received aid.
UNDERGRADUATE FINANCIAL AID (Fall 2011) 1,223 applied for aid; of those 99% were deemed to have need. 100% of undergraduates with need received aid.
GIFT AID (NEED-BASED) *Total amount:* $16,521,902 (97% federal, 2% state, 1% institutional). *Receiving aid:* Freshmen: 93% (502); all full-time undergraduates: 93% (1,198). *Average award:* Freshmen: $5460; Undergraduates: $5460. *Scholarships, grants, and awards:* Federal Pell, FSEOG, state, private, college/university gift aid from institutional funds.
GIFT AID (NON-NEED-BASED) *Receiving aid:* Freshmen: 93% (502). Undergraduates: 93% (1,198). *Tuition waivers:* Full or partial for employees or children of employees.
LOANS *Student loans:* $20,737,116 (100% need-based). 95% of past graduating class borrowed through all loan programs. *Average indebtedness per student:* $8700. *Parent loans:* $1,449,378 (100% need-based). *Programs:* Federal Direct (Subsidized and Unsubsidized Stafford, PLUS), Perkins.
WORK-STUDY *Federal work-study:* Total amount: $135,097; 15 jobs averaging $8300. *State or other work-study/employment:* Part-time jobs available.
APPLYING FOR FINANCIAL AID *Required financial aid form:* FAFSA. *Financial aid deadline:* Continuous. *Notification date:* Continuous.
CONTACT Mr. Omar Sanchez, Director of Financial Aid, Florida National University, 4425 West Jose Regueiro (20th) Avenue, Hialeah, FL 33012, 305-821-3333 Ext. 1003. *Fax:* 305-362-0595. *E-mail:* omarsnc@fnu.edu. *Website:* http://www.fnu.edu/.

FLORIDA SOUTHERN COLLEGE
Lakeland, FL

Tuition & fees: $27,200	Average undergraduate aid package: $21,210

ABOUT THE INSTITUTION Independent United Methodist Church, coed. *Awards:* bachelor's and master's degrees. 53 undergraduate majors. *Total enrollment:* 2,238. Undergraduates: 2,040. Freshmen: 537. Federal methodology is used as a basis for awarding need-based institutional aid.
UNDERGRADUATE EXPENSES for 2013–2014 *Application fee:* $30. *Comprehensive fee:* $36,300 includes full-time tuition ($26,600), mandatory fees ($600), and room and board ($9100). *College room only:* $5000. Full-time tuition and fees vary according to student level. Room and board charges vary according to board plan and housing facility. *Part-time tuition:* $780 per semester hour. Part-time tuition and fees vary according to class time.
FRESHMAN FINANCIAL AID (Fall 2012, est.) 492 applied for aid; of those 80% were deemed to have need. 100% of freshmen with need received aid; of those 27% had need fully met. *Average percent of need met:* 75% (excluding resources awarded to replace EFC). *Average financial aid package:* $21,974 (excluding resources awarded to replace EFC). 26% of all full-time freshmen had no need and received non-need-based gift aid.
UNDERGRADUATE FINANCIAL AID (Fall 2012, est.) 1,756 applied for aid; of those 83% were deemed to have need. 100% of undergraduates with need received aid; of those 24% had need fully met. *Average percent of need met:* 72% (excluding resources awarded to replace EFC). *Average financial aid package:* $21,210 (excluding resources awarded to replace EFC). 24% of all full-time undergraduates had no need and received non-need-based gift aid.
GIFT AID (NEED-BASED) *Total amount:* $26,977,885 (12% federal, 15% state, 61% institutional, 12% external sources). *Receiving aid:* Freshmen: 73% (392); all full-time undergraduates: 72% (1,436). *Average award:* Freshmen: $17,981; Undergraduates: $15,632. *Scholarships, grants, and awards:* Federal Pell, FSEOG, state, private, college/university gift aid from institutional funds, Federal Nursing.
GIFT AID (NON-NEED-BASED) *Total amount:* $5,737,074 (12% state, 75% institutional, 13% external sources). *Receiving aid:* Freshmen: 50% (271). Undergraduates: 52% (1,024). *Average award:* Freshmen: $12,001. Undergraduates: $13,038. *Scholarships, grants, and awards by category:* Academic interests/achievement: agriculture, biological sciences, business, communication, education, general academic interests/achievements, health fields, physical sciences, religion/biblical studies, social sciences. Creative arts/performance: art/fine arts, music, theater/drama. Special achievements/activities: community service, general special achievements/activities, leadership. Special characteristics: children and siblings of alumni, children of faculty/staff, general special characteristics, local/state students, out-of-state students, relatives of clergy, religious affiliation, siblings of current students. *Tuition waivers:* Full or partial for children of alumni, employees or children of employees. *ROTC:* Army, Air Force cooperative.
LOANS *Student loans:* $18,464,116 (85% need-based, 15% non-need-based). 63% of past graduating class borrowed through all loan programs. *Average indebtedness per student:* $26,509. *Average need-based loan:* Freshmen: $3475. Undergraduates: $4624. *Parent loans:* $8,723,735 (78% need-based, 22% non-need-based). *Programs:* Federal Direct (Subsidized and Unsubsidized Stafford, PLUS), Perkins.
WORK-STUDY *Federal work-study:* Total amount: $203,498; 139 jobs averaging $1500. *State or other work-study/employment:* Total amount: $937,935 (82% need-based, 18% non-need-based). 358 part-time jobs averaging $2142.
ATHLETIC AWARDS Total amount: $2,802,158 (68% need-based, 32% non-need-based).
APPLYING FOR FINANCIAL AID *Required financial aid forms:* FAFSA, institution's own form. *Financial aid deadline:* 7/1 (priority: 3/1). *Notification date:* Continuous beginning 3/1. Students must reply within 3 weeks of notification.
CONTACT Mr. William L. Healy, Director of Financial Aid, Florida Southern College, 111 Lake Hollingsworth Drive, Lakeland, FL 33801-5698, 863-680-4140 or toll-free 800-274-4131. *Fax:* 863-680-4567. *E-mail:* whealy@flsouthern.edu. *Website:* http://www.flsouthern.edu/.

FLORIDA STATE UNIVERSITY
Tallahassee, FL

Tuition & fees (FL res): $6402	Average undergraduate aid package: $9850

ABOUT THE INSTITUTION State-supported, coed. *Awards:* certificates, associate, bachelor's, master's, and doctoral degrees. 49 undergraduate majors. *Total enrollment:* 40,695. Undergraduates: 32,171. Freshmen: 5,712. Federal methodology is used as a basis for awarding need-based institutional aid.
UNDERGRADUATE EXPENSES for 2013–2014 *Application fee:* $30. *Tuition, state resident:* full-time $3397; part-time $113.24 per credit hour. *Tuition, nonresident:* full-time $18,564; part-time $618.79 per credit hour. *Required fees:* full-time $3005; $98.85 per credit hour or $20 per term. Full-time tuition and fees vary according to course load, degree level, and location. Part-time tuition and fees vary according to course load, degree level, and location. *College room and board:* $9626; *Room only:* $5694. Room and board charges vary according to board plan and housing facility. *Payment plan:* Tuition prepayment.
FRESHMAN FINANCIAL AID (Fall 2012, est.) 5,349 applied for aid; of those 46% were deemed to have need. 100% of freshmen with need received aid; of those 67% had need fully met. *Average percent of need met:* 64% (excluding resources awarded to replace EFC). *Average financial aid package:* $9470 (excluding resources awarded to replace EFC). 8% of all full-time freshmen had no need and received non-need-based gift aid.

UNDERGRADUATE FINANCIAL AID (Fall 2012, est.) 24,347 applied for aid; of those 48% were deemed to have need. 100% of undergraduates with need received aid; of those 66% had need fully met. **Average percent of need met:** 67% (excluding resources awarded to replace EFC). **Average financial aid package:** $9850 (excluding resources awarded to replace EFC). 7% of all full-time undergraduates had no need and received non-need-based gift aid.

GIFT AID (NEED-BASED) Total amount: $91,096,393 (50% federal, 28% state, 20% institutional, 2% external sources). **Receiving aid:** Freshmen: 29% (1,548); all full-time undergraduates: 29% (7,131). **Average award:** Freshmen: $3866; Undergraduates: $3912. **Scholarships, grants, and awards:** Federal Pell, FSEOG, state, private, college/university gift aid from institutional funds, Academic Competitiveness Grants, National SMART Grants.

GIFT AID (NON-NEED-BASED) Total amount: $36,426,124 (75% state, 18% institutional, 7% external sources). **Receiving aid:** Freshmen: 43% (2,324). Undergraduates: 38% (9,285). **Average award:** Freshmen: $2295. Undergraduates: $2335. **Scholarships, grants, and awards by category:** Academic interests/achievement: general academic interests/achievements. Creative arts/performance: cinema/film/broadcasting, dance, music, theater/drama. Special characteristics: local/state students. **Tuition waivers:** Full or partial for employees or children of employees, senior citizens. **ROTC:** Army, Naval cooperative, Air Force.

LOANS Student loans: $127,201,993 (54% need-based, 46% non-need-based). 51% of past graduating class borrowed through all loan programs. **Average indebtedness per student:** $22,405. **Average need-based loan:** Freshmen: $3014. Undergraduates: $3960. **Parent loans:** $8,676,293 (29% need-based, 71% non-need-based). **Programs:** Federal Direct (Subsidized and Unsubsidized Stafford, PLUS), Perkins, college/university.

WORK-STUDY Federal work-study: Total amount: $1,603,000; 852 jobs averaging $1200. **State or other work-study/employment:** Total amount: $54,680 (100% need-based). 29 part-time jobs averaging $1200.

ATHLETIC AWARDS Total amount: $2,275,345 (5% need-based, 95% non-need-based).

APPLYING FOR FINANCIAL AID Required financial aid form: FAFSA. **Financial aid deadline:** Continuous. **Notification date:** Continuous beginning 3/1.

CONTACT Darryl Marshall, Director of Financial Aid, Florida State University, University Center A4400, Tallahassee, FL 32306-2430, 850-644-5716. Fax: 850-644-6404. E-mail: ofacs@admin.fsu.edu.
Website: http://www.fsu.edu/.

FLORIDA TECH UNIVERSITY ONLINE
Tampa, FL

CONTACT Financial Aid Office, Florida Tech University Online, 9417 Princess Palm Avenue, Tampa, FL 33619, 855-300-1469.
Website: http://floridatechonline.com/.

FONTBONNE UNIVERSITY
St. Louis, MO

CONTACT Financial Aid Office, Fontbonne University, 6800 Wydown Boulevard, St. Louis, MO 63105-3098, 314-889-1414 or toll-free 800-205-5862. Fax: 314-889-1451.
Website: http://www.fontbonne.edu/.

FORDHAM UNIVERSITY
New York, NY

ABOUT THE INSTITUTION Independent Roman Catholic (Jesuit), coed. **Awards:** certificates, bachelor's, master's, and doctoral degrees (branch locations at Rose Hill and Lincoln Center). 98 undergraduate majors. **Total enrollment:** 15,170. Undergraduates: 8,325. Freshmen: 1,882.

GIFT AID (NEED-BASED) Scholarships, grants, and awards: Federal Pell, FSEOG, state, private, college/university gift aid from institutional funds.

GIFT AID (NON-NEED-BASED) Scholarships, grants, and awards by category: Academic interests/achievement: biological sciences, business, communication, foreign languages, general academic interests/achievements. Creative arts/performance: dance, music. Special achievements/activities: general special achievements/activities. Special characteristics: adult students, children and siblings of alumni, children of faculty/staff, children with a deceased or disabled parent, handicapped students.

LOANS Programs: Perkins.

APPLYING FOR FINANCIAL AID Required financial aid forms: FAFSA, CSS Financial Aid PROFILE, noncustodial (divorced/separated) parent's statement, business/farm supplement.

CONTACT Angela Van Dekker, Assistant Vice President of Student Financial Services, Fordham University, 441 East Fordham Road, Thebaud Hall, Room 208, New York, NY 10458, 718-817-3804 or toll-free 800-FORDHAM. Fax: 718-817-3817. E-mail: avandekker@fordham.edu.
Website: http://www.fordham.edu/.

FORT HAYS STATE UNIVERSITY
Hays, KS

Tuition & fees: N/R	Average undergraduate aid package: $7013

ABOUT THE INSTITUTION State-supported, coed. **Awards:** certificates, associate, bachelor's, and master's degrees. 66 undergraduate majors. **Total enrollment:** 12,802. Undergraduates: 11,158. Freshmen: 1,017. Federal methodology is used as a basis for awarding need-based institutional aid.

FRESHMAN FINANCIAL AID (Fall 2011) 804 applied for aid; of those 80% were deemed to have need. 97% of freshmen with need received aid; of those 17% had need fully met. **Average percent of need met:** 60% (excluding resources awarded to replace EFC). **Average financial aid package:** $7218 (excluding resources awarded to replace EFC). 30% of all full-time freshmen had no need and received non-need-based gift aid.

UNDERGRADUATE FINANCIAL AID (Fall 2011) 4,774 applied for aid; of those 85% were deemed to have need. 98% of undergraduates with need received aid; of those 10% had need fully met. **Average percent of need met:** 56% (excluding resources awarded to replace EFC). **Average financial aid package:** $7013 (excluding resources awarded to replace EFC). 19% of all full-time undergraduates had no need and received non-need-based gift aid.

GIFT AID (NEED-BASED) Total amount: $15,657,161 (78% federal, 5% state, 8% institutional, 9% external sources). **Receiving aid:** Freshmen: 52% (593); all full-time undergraduates: 59% (3,469). **Average award:** Freshmen: $5091; Undergraduates: $4258. **Scholarships, grants, and awards:** Federal Pell, FSEOG, state, private, college/university gift aid from institutional funds.

GIFT AID (NON-NEED-BASED) Total amount: $2,581,327 (1% federal, 31% institutional, 68% external sources). **Receiving aid:** Freshmen: 5% (61). Undergraduates: 2% (137). **Average award:** Freshmen: $929. Undergraduates: $693. **Scholarships, grants, and awards by category:** Academic interests/achievement: agriculture, area/ethnic studies, biological sciences, business, communication, computer science, education, engineering/technologies, English, foreign languages, general academic interests/achievements, health fields, home economics, humanities, international studies, mathematics, military science, physical sciences, premedicine, religion/biblical studies, social sciences. Creative arts/performance: applied art and design, art/fine arts, cinema/film/broadcasting, creative writing, dance, debating, general creative arts/performance, journalism/publications, music, performing arts, theater/drama. Special achievements/activities: cheerleading/drum major, leadership, rodeo. Special characteristics: adult students, children and siblings of alumni, children of faculty/staff, general special characteristics, international students, spouses of current students, veterans, veterans' children.

LOANS Student loans: $31,577,992 (77% need-based, 23% non-need-based). 72% of past graduating class borrowed through all loan programs. **Average indebtedness per student:** $22,887. **Average need-based loan:** Freshmen: $2800. Undergraduates: $3719. **Parent loans:** $2,138,471 (26% need-based, 74% non-need-based). **Programs:** Federal Direct (Subsidized and Unsubsidized Stafford, PLUS), Perkins, college/university.

WORK-STUDY Federal work-study: Total amount: $656,272; 232 jobs averaging $3155. **State or other work-study/employment:** Total amount: $79,866 (59% need-based, 41% non-need-based). 315 part-time jobs averaging $2187.

ATHLETIC AWARDS Total amount: $1,745,555 (55% need-based, 45% non-need-based).
APPLYING FOR FINANCIAL AID *Required financial aid forms:* FAFSA, state aid form. *Financial aid deadline (priority):* 3/1. *Notification date:* Continuous beginning 3/15. Students must reply within 2 weeks of notification.
CONTACT Craig Karlin, Director of Financial Assistance, Fort Hays State University, Custer Hall, Room 306, 600 Park Street, Hays, KS 67601, 785-628-4408 or toll-free 800-628-FHSU. *Fax:* 785-628-4014. *E-mail:* finaid@fhsu.edu.
Website: http://www.fhsu.edu/.

FORT LEWIS COLLEGE
Durango, CO

Tuition & fees (CO res): $6923	Average undergraduate aid package: $12,120

ABOUT THE INSTITUTION State-supported, coed. *Awards:* bachelor's degrees. 62 undergraduate majors. *Total enrollment:* 3,891. Undergraduates: 3,891. Freshmen: 857. Federal methodology is used as a basis for awarding need-based institutional aid.
UNDERGRADUATE EXPENSES for 2013–2014 *Application fee:* $40. *Tuition, state resident:* full-time $5232; part-time $218 per credit hour. *Tuition, nonresident:* full-time $16,072; part-time $670 per credit hour. *Required fees:* full-time $1691. Full-time tuition and fees vary according to course load and reciprocity agreements. Part-time tuition and fees vary according to course load and reciprocity agreements. *College room and board:* $8590; *Room only:* $4270. Room and board charges vary according to board plan and housing facility.
FRESHMAN FINANCIAL AID (Fall 2011) 610 applied for aid; of those 79% were deemed to have need. 100% of freshmen with need received aid; of those 5% had need fully met. *Average percent of need met:* 98% (excluding resources awarded to replace EFC). *Average financial aid package:* $11,720 (excluding resources awarded to replace EFC). 25% of all full-time freshmen had no need and received non-need-based gift aid.
UNDERGRADUATE FINANCIAL AID (Fall 2011) 2,521 applied for aid; of those 83% were deemed to have need. 99% of undergraduates with need received aid; of those 5% had need fully met. *Average percent of need met:* 90% (excluding resources awarded to replace EFC). *Average financial aid package:* $12,120 (excluding resources awarded to replace EFC). 19% of all full-time undergraduates had no need and received non-need-based gift aid.
GIFT AID (NEED-BASED) *Total amount:* $11,871,889 (55% federal, 6% state, 33% institutional, 6% external sources). *Receiving aid:* Freshmen: 40% (307); all full-time undergraduates: 44% (1,488). *Average award:* Freshmen: $4469; Undergraduates: $4920. *Scholarships, grants, and awards:* Federal Pell, FSEOG, state, private, college/university gift aid from institutional funds, United Negro College Fund.
GIFT AID (NON-NEED-BASED) *Total amount:* $2,232,499 (89% institutional, 11% external sources). *Receiving aid:* Freshmen: 46% (353). Undergraduates: 38% (1,279). *Average award:* Freshmen: $2822. Undergraduates: $3152. *Scholarships, grants, and awards by category: Academic interests/achievement:* agriculture, area/ethnic studies, biological sciences, business, communication, computer science, education, English, general academic interests/achievements, humanities, mathematics, physical sciences, social sciences. *Creative arts/performance:* art/fine arts, music, performing arts, theater/drama. *Special achievements/activities:* general special achievements/activities, leadership. *Special characteristics:* children and siblings of alumni, children of faculty/staff, ethnic background, first-generation college students, general special characteristics, handicapped students, international students, local/state students, out-of-state students, veterans' children. *Tuition waivers:* Full or partial for minority students, employees or children of employees.
LOANS *Student loans:* $11,692,645 (87% need-based, 13% non-need-based). 57% of past graduating class borrowed through all loan programs. *Average indebtedness per student:* $19,811. *Average need-based loan:* Freshmen: $303. Undergraduates: $3828. *Parent loans:* $3,682,952 (73% need-based, 27% non-need-based). *Programs:* Federal Direct (Subsidized and Unsubsidized Stafford, PLUS), Perkins.
WORK-STUDY *Federal work-study:* Total amount: $209,934; jobs available. *State or other work-study/employment:* Total amount: $749,308 (30% need-based, 70% non-need-based). Part-time jobs available.
ATHLETIC AWARDS Total amount: $1,569,224 (48% need-based, 52% non-need-based).

APPLYING FOR FINANCIAL AID *Required financial aid form:* FAFSA. *Financial aid deadline (priority):* 2/15. *Notification date:* Continuous beginning 3/1.
CONTACT Ms. Tracey Piccoli, Director of Financial Aid, Fort Lewis College, 1000 Rim Drive, 101 Miller Student Services Building, Durango, CO 81301, 800-352-7512 or toll-free 877-FLC-COLO. *Fax:* 970-247-7108. *E-mail:* finaid_off@fortlewis.edu. *Website:* http://www.fortlewis.edu/.

FORT VALLEY STATE UNIVERSITY
Fort Valley, GA

Tuition & fees: N/R	Average undergraduate aid package: $14,568

ABOUT THE INSTITUTION State-supported, coed. 35 undergraduate majors. Federal methodology is used as a basis for awarding need-based institutional aid.
FRESHMAN FINANCIAL AID (Fall 2012, est.) 610 applied for aid; of those 94% were deemed to have need. 95% of freshmen with need received aid; of those 4% had need fully met. *Average percent of need met:* 45% (excluding resources awarded to replace EFC). *Average financial aid package:* $14,568 (excluding resources awarded to replace EFC).
UNDERGRADUATE FINANCIAL AID (Fall 2012, est.) 2,940 applied for aid; of those 100% were deemed to have need. 97% of undergraduates with need received aid; of those 3% had need fully met. *Average percent of need met:* 45% (excluding resources awarded to replace EFC). *Average financial aid package:* $14,568 (excluding resources awarded to replace EFC).
GIFT AID (NEED-BASED) *Total amount:* $16,586,267 (100% federal). *Receiving aid:* Freshmen: 85% (519); all full-time undergraduates: 81% (2,373). *Average award:* Freshmen: $7437; Undergraduates: $7437. *Scholarships, grants, and awards:* Federal Pell, FSEOG, state, private, college/university gift aid from institutional funds.
GIFT AID (NON-NEED-BASED) *Total amount:* $3,244,652 (10% federal, 76% state, 7% institutional, 7% external sources). *Receiving aid:* Freshmen: 70% (427). Undergraduates: 70% (2,058). *Scholarships, grants, and awards by category: Academic interests/achievement:* agriculture, business, general academic interests/achievements, home economics, military science, premedicine, social sciences. *Creative arts/performance:* journalism/publications, music. *Special achievements/activities:* general special achievements/activities. *Special characteristics:* handicapped students, international students, out-of-state students.
LOANS *Student loans:* $40,333,398 (39% need-based, 61% non-need-based). 88% of past graduating class borrowed through all loan programs. *Average indebtedness per student:* $8263. *Average need-based loan:* Freshmen: $5550. Undergraduates: $5550. *Parent loans:* $2,315,748 (100% non-need-based). *Programs:* Federal Direct (Subsidized and Unsubsidized Stafford, PLUS), Perkins.
WORK-STUDY *Federal work-study:* Total amount: $229,350; 153 jobs averaging $1500.
ATHLETIC AWARDS Total amount: $687,950 (100% non-need-based).
APPLYING FOR FINANCIAL AID *Required financial aid form:* FAFSA. *Financial aid deadline (priority):* 3/1. *Notification date:* Continuous beginning 4/15.
CONTACT Lakeshia Sanders, Office of Financial Aid, Fort Valley State University, 1005 State University Drive, Fort Valley, GA 31030, 478-825-6182 or toll-free 877-462-3878. *Fax:* 478-825-6976. *Website:* http://www.fvsu.edu/.

FRAMINGHAM STATE UNIVERSITY
Framingham, MA

Tuition & fees (MA res): $8080	Average undergraduate aid package: $11,197

ABOUT THE INSTITUTION State-supported, coed. *Awards:* certificates, bachelor's, and master's degrees. 24 undergraduate majors. *Total enrollment:* 6,506. Undergraduates: 4,490. Freshmen: 826. Federal methodology is used as a basis for awarding need-based institutional aid.

UNDERGRADUATE EXPENSES for 2013–2014 *Application fee:* $45. *Tuition, state resident:* full-time $970; part-time $162 per course. *Tuition, nonresident:* full-time $7050; part-time $1175 per course. *Required fees:* full-time $7110; $1250 per course. Full-time tuition and fees vary according to class time. Part-time tuition and fees vary according to class time and course load. *College room and board:* $9540; *Room only:* $6380. Room and board charges vary according to board plan and housing facility. *Payment plan:* Tuition prepayment.

FRESHMAN FINANCIAL AID (Fall 2012, est.) 750 applied for aid; of those 76% were deemed to have need. 100% of freshmen with need received aid; of those 36% had need fully met. *Average percent of need met:* 80% (excluding resources awarded to replace EFC). *Average financial aid package:* $11,740 (excluding resources awarded to replace EFC). 18% of all full-time freshmen had no need and received non-need-based gift aid.

UNDERGRADUATE FINANCIAL AID (Fall 2012, est.) 3,087 applied for aid; of those 77% were deemed to have need. 100% of undergraduates with need received aid; of those 36% had need fully met. *Average percent of need met:* 78% (excluding resources awarded to replace EFC). *Average financial aid package:* $11,197 (excluding resources awarded to replace EFC). 9% of all full-time undergraduates had no need and received non-need-based gift aid.

GIFT AID (NEED-BASED) *Total amount:* $9,552,274 (52% federal, 29% state, 17% institutional, 2% external sources). *Receiving aid:* Freshmen: 65% (535); all full-time undergraduates: 50% (1,892). *Average award:* Freshmen: $5277; Undergraduates: $5107. *Scholarships, grants, and awards:* Federal Pell, FSEOG, state, private, college/university gift aid from institutional funds.

GIFT AID (NON-NEED-BASED) *Total amount:* $545,264 (7% state, 81% institutional, 12% external sources). *Receiving aid:* Freshmen: 2% (13). Undergraduates: 1% (32). *Average award:* Freshmen: $732. Undergraduates: $863. *Scholarships, grants, and awards by category: Academic interests/achievement:* biological sciences, education, engineering/technologies, English, general academic interests/achievements, home economics, mathematics, physical sciences. *Special characteristics:* children of faculty/staff, children of public servants, children of union members/company employees, veterans. *Tuition waivers:* Full or partial for employees or children of employees, senior citizens.

LOANS *Student loans:* $20,815,675 (40% need-based, 60% non-need-based). 70% of past graduating class borrowed through all loan programs. *Average indebtedness per student:* $22,975. *Average need-based loan:* Freshmen: $5950. Undergraduates: $5786. *Parent loans:* $3,155,789 (50% need-based, 50% non-need-based). *Programs:* Federal Direct (Subsidized and Unsubsidized Stafford, PLUS), Perkins, state.

WORK-STUDY *Federal work-study:* Total amount: $110,000; 98 jobs averaging $1122. *State or other work-study/employment:* Total amount: $50,000 (100% need-based). 53 part-time jobs averaging $1132.

APPLYING FOR FINANCIAL AID *Required financial aid form:* FAFSA. *Financial aid deadline (priority):* 3/1. *Notification date:* Continuous beginning 3/15. Students must reply by 5/1 or within 2 weeks of notification.

CONTACT Office of Financial Aid, Framingham State University, 100 State Street, PO Box 9101, Framingham, MA 01701-9101, 508-626-4534. *Fax:* 508-626-4598. *Website:* http://www.framingham.edu/.

FRANCISCAN UNIVERSITY OF STEUBENVILLE
Steubenville, OH

ABOUT THE INSTITUTION Independent Roman Catholic, coed. *Awards:* associate, bachelor's, and master's degrees. 32 undergraduate majors. *Total enrollment:* 2,823. Undergraduates: 2,131. Freshmen: 449.

GIFT AID (NEED-BASED) *Scholarships, grants, and awards:* Federal Pell, FSEOG, state, private, college/university gift aid from institutional funds.

GIFT AID (NON-NEED-BASED) *Scholarships, grants, and awards by category: Academic interests/achievement:* general academic interests/achievements. *Special achievements/activities:* religious involvement. *Special characteristics:* children of faculty/staff, international students, local/state students, religious affiliation, siblings of current students.

LOANS *Programs:* Federal Direct (Subsidized and Unsubsidized Stafford, PLUS), Perkins, Federal Nursing.

WORK-STUDY *Federal work-study:* Total amount: $126,439; jobs available. *State or other work-study/employment:* Total amount: $1,021,799 (86% need-based, 14% non-need-based). Part-time jobs available.

APPLYING FOR FINANCIAL AID *Required financial aid form:* FAFSA.

CONTACT John Herrmann, Director of Student Financial Services, Franciscan University of Steubenville, 1235 University Boulevard, Steubenville, OH 43952-1763, 740-284-5215 or toll-free 800-783-6220. *Fax:* 740-284-5469. *E-mail:* jherrmann@franciscan.edu. *Website:* http://www.franciscan.edu/.

FRANCIS MARION UNIVERSITY
Florence, SC

Tuition & fees (SC res): $9066	Average undergraduate aid package: $9953

ABOUT THE INSTITUTION State-supported, coed. *Awards:* certificates, bachelor's, and master's degrees. 31 undergraduate majors. *Total enrollment:* 4,093. Undergraduates: 3,780. Freshmen: 814. Federal methodology is used as a basis for awarding need-based institutional aid.

UNDERGRADUATE EXPENSES for 2013–2014 *Application fee:* $32. *Tuition, state resident:* full-time $8708; part-time $435.40 per credit hour. *Tuition, nonresident:* full-time $17,416; part-time $870.80 per credit hour. *Required fees:* full-time $358. Full-time tuition and fees vary according to program. Part-time tuition and fees vary according to course load and program. *College room and board:* $6820; *Room only:* $3842. Room and board charges vary according to board plan and housing facility.

FRESHMAN FINANCIAL AID (Fall 2011) 652 applied for aid; of those 94% were deemed to have need. 100% of freshmen with need received aid. *Average financial aid package:* $11,035 (excluding resources awarded to replace EFC). 2% of all full-time freshmen had no need and received non-need-based gift aid.

UNDERGRADUATE FINANCIAL AID (Fall 2011) 2,926 applied for aid; of those 95% were deemed to have need. 100% of undergraduates with need received aid. *Average financial aid package:* $9953 (excluding resources awarded to replace EFC). 1% of all full-time undergraduates had no need and received non-need-based gift aid.

GIFT AID (NEED-BASED) *Total amount:* $10,156,229 (93% federal, 7% state). *Receiving aid:* Freshmen: 64% (521); all full-time undergraduates: 67% (2,229). *Average award:* Freshmen: $4749; Undergraduates: $4454. *Scholarships, grants, and awards:* Federal Pell, FSEOG, state, private, Academic Competitiveness Grants, National SMART Grants.

GIFT AID (NON-NEED-BASED) *Total amount:* $7,792,046 (83% state, 13% institutional, 4% external sources). *Receiving aid:* Freshmen: 66% (535). Undergraduates: 46% (1,523). *Average award:* Freshmen: $2068. Undergraduates: $1922. *Scholarships, grants, and awards by category: Academic interests/achievement:* biological sciences, business, computer science, education, English, general academic interests/achievements, health fields, humanities, mathematics, pre-medicine, social sciences. *Creative arts/performance:* art/fine arts, music, theater/drama. *Special achievements/activities:* cheerleading/drum major. *Special characteristics:* adult students, children and siblings of alumni, children of faculty/staff, children of union members/company employees, handicapped students, international students, out-of-state students, spouses of deceased or disabled public servants, veterans, veterans' children. *Tuition waivers:* Full or partial for employees or children of employees, senior citizens. *ROTC:* Army.

LOANS *Student loans:* $22,676,065 (44% need-based, 56% non-need-based). *Average indebtedness per student:* $26,453. *Average need-based loan:* Freshmen: $3325. Undergraduates: $4187. *Parent loans:* $2,192,584 (100% non-need-based). *Programs:* Federal Direct (Subsidized and Unsubsidized Stafford, PLUS), state.

WORK-STUDY *Federal work-study:* Total amount: $91,552; jobs available. *State or other work-study/employment:* Total amount: $843,016 (100% non-need-based). Part-time jobs available.

ATHLETIC AWARDS Total amount: $737,205 (100% non-need-based).

APPLYING FOR FINANCIAL AID *Required financial aid form:* FAFSA. *Financial aid deadline:* 6/30 (priority: 3/1). *Notification date:* Continuous beginning 1/30.

CONTACT Miss Kim Ellisor, Director of Financial Assistance, Francis Marion University, PO Box 100547, Florence, SC 29502-0547, 843-661-1190 or toll-free 800-368-7551.
Website: http://www.fmarion.edu/.

FRANKLIN & MARSHALL COLLEGE
Lancaster, PA

Tuition & fees: $44,360	Average undergraduate aid package: $38,286

ABOUT THE INSTITUTION Independent, coed. *Awards:* bachelor's degrees. 40 undergraduate majors. *Total enrollment:* 2,365. Undergraduates: 2,365. Freshmen: 599. Both federal and institutional methodology are used as a basis for awarding need-based institutional aid.

UNDERGRADUATE EXPENSES for 2013–2014 *Application fee:* $60. *One-time required fee:* $200. *Comprehensive fee:* $56,110 includes full-time tuition ($44,260), mandatory fees ($100), and room and board ($11,750). *College room only:* $7330. Room and board charges vary according to board plan and housing facility. *Part-time tuition:* $5533 per course.

FRESHMAN FINANCIAL AID (Fall 2012, est.) 389 applied for aid; of those 82% were deemed to have need. 100% of freshmen with need received aid; of those 100% had need fully met. *Average percent of need met:* 100% (excluding resources awarded to replace EFC). *Average financial aid package:* $40,679 (excluding resources awarded to replace EFC). 1% of all full-time freshmen had no need and received non-need-based gift aid.

UNDERGRADUATE FINANCIAL AID (Fall 2012, est.) 1,373 applied for aid; of those 85% were deemed to have need. 100% of undergraduates with need received aid; of those 100% had need fully met. *Average percent of need met:* 100% (excluding resources awarded to replace EFC). *Average financial aid package:* $38,286 (excluding resources awarded to replace EFC). 4% of all full-time undergraduates had no need and received non-need-based gift aid.

GIFT AID (NEED-BASED) *Total amount:* $37,901,183 (4% federal, 2% state, 92% institutional, 2% external sources). *Receiving aid:* Freshmen: 52% (313); all full-time undergraduates: 45% (1,110). *Average award:* Freshmen: $36,703; Undergraduates: $34,145. *Scholarships, grants, and awards:* Federal Pell, FSEOG, state, private, college/university gift aid from institutional funds.

GIFT AID (NON-NEED-BASED) *Total amount:* $2,968,012 (7% federal, 59% institutional, 34% external sources). *Receiving aid:* Freshmen: 18% (105). Undergraduates: 10% (257). *Average award:* Freshmen: $2500. Undergraduates: $14,372. *Scholarships, grants, and awards by category:* Creative arts/performance: music. *Tuition waivers:* Full or partial for employees or children of employees. *ROTC:* Army cooperative.

LOANS *Student loans:* $9,491,855 (54% need-based, 46% non-need-based). 49% of past graduating class borrowed through all loan programs. *Average indebtedness per student:* $33,200. *Average need-based loan:* Freshmen: $3166. Undergraduates: $4261. *Parent loans:* $4,474,679 (3% need-based, 97% non-need-based). *Programs:* Federal Direct (Subsidized and Unsubsidized Stafford, PLUS), Perkins, college/university.

WORK-STUDY *Federal work-study:* Total amount: $1,585,119; jobs available. *State or other work-study/employment:* Total amount: $332,350 (100% need-based). Part-time jobs available.

APPLYING FOR FINANCIAL AID *Required financial aid forms:* FAFSA, CSS Financial Aid PROFILE, state aid form, noncustodial (divorced/separated) parent's statement, business/farm supplement, federal income tax form(s), W-2 forms. *Financial aid deadline:* 2/15. *Notification date:* 4/1. Students must reply by 5/1.

CONTACT Mr. Clarke Paine, Director of Financial Aid, Franklin & Marshall College, PO Box 3003, Lancaster, PA 17604-3003, 717-291-3991 or toll-free 877-678-9111. *Fax:* 717-291-4462. *E-mail:* clarke.paine@fandm.edu.
Website: http://www.fandm.edu/.

FRANKLIN COLLEGE
Franklin, IN

Tuition & fees: $26,895	Average undergraduate aid package: $20,017

ABOUT THE INSTITUTION Independent American Baptist Churches in the U.S.A., coed. *Awards:* bachelor's degrees. 32 undergraduate majors. *Total enrollment:* 1,053. Undergraduates: 1,053. Freshmen: 286. Federal methodology is used as a basis for awarding need-based institutional aid.

UNDERGRADUATE EXPENSES for 2013–2014 *Application fee:* $30. *One-time required fee:* $380. *Comprehensive fee:* $34,845 includes full-time tuition ($26,710), mandatory fees ($185), and room and board ($7950). *College room only:* $4720. Room and board charges vary according to board plan. *Part-time tuition:* $380 per credit.

FRESHMAN FINANCIAL AID (Fall 2011) 264 applied for aid; of those 90% were deemed to have need. 100% of freshmen with need received aid; of those 11% had need fully met. *Average percent of need met:* 70% (excluding resources awarded to replace EFC). *Average financial aid package:* $18,468 (excluding resources awarded to replace EFC). 14% of all full-time freshmen had no need and received non-need-based gift aid.

UNDERGRADUATE FINANCIAL AID (Fall 2011) 971 applied for aid; of those 91% were deemed to have need. 100% of undergraduates with need received aid; of those 12% had need fully met. *Average percent of need met:* 74% (excluding resources awarded to replace EFC). *Average financial aid package:* $20,017 (excluding resources awarded to replace EFC). 13% of all full-time undergraduates had no need and received non-need-based gift aid.

GIFT AID (NEED-BASED) *Total amount:* $13,501,906 (13% federal, 16% state, 66% institutional, 5% external sources). *Receiving aid:* Freshmen: 86% (237); all full-time undergraduates: 86% (878). *Average award:* Freshmen: $15,521; Undergraduates: $15,833. *Scholarships, grants, and awards:* Federal Pell, FSEOG, state, private, college/university gift aid from institutional funds.

GIFT AID (NON-NEED-BASED) *Total amount:* $1,996,715 (2% state, 85% institutional, 13% external sources). *Receiving aid:* Freshmen: 9% (25). Undergraduates: 9% (96). *Average award:* Freshmen: $10,090. Undergraduates: $10,037. *Scholarships, grants, and awards by category:* Academic interests/achievement: general academic interests/achievements. *Creative arts/performance:* art/fine arts, journalism/publications, music, performing arts, theater/drama. *Special characteristics:* children and siblings of alumni, children of faculty/staff, ethnic background, members of minority groups, out-of-state students, religious affiliation, siblings of current students. *Tuition waivers:* Full or partial for employees or children of employees, senior citizens. *ROTC:* Army cooperative.

LOANS *Student loans:* $8,139,425 (75% need-based, 25% non-need-based). 92% of past graduating class borrowed through all loan programs. *Average indebtedness per student:* $34,160. *Average need-based loan:* Freshmen: $3148. Undergraduates: $4562. *Parent loans:* $2,261,806 (49% need-based, 51% non-need-based). *Programs:* Federal Direct (Subsidized and Unsubsidized Stafford, PLUS), Perkins, college/university.

WORK-STUDY *Federal work-study:* Total amount: $212,607; jobs available. *State or other work-study/employment:* Total amount: $8000 (43% need-based, 57% non-need-based). Part-time jobs available.

APPLYING FOR FINANCIAL AID *Required financial aid forms:* FAFSA, institution's own form. *Financial aid deadline (priority):* 3/10. *Notification date:* Continuous beginning 3/1. Students must reply by 5/1 or within 4 weeks of notification.

CONTACT Elizabeth Sappenfield, Director of Financial Aid, Franklin College, 101 Branigin Boulevard, Franklin, IN 46131-2598, 317-738-8075 or toll-free 800-852-0232. *Fax:* 317-738-8072. *E-mail:* finaid@franklincollege.edu.
Website: http://www.franklincollege.edu/.

FRANKLIN PIERCE UNIVERSITY
Rindge, NH

Tuition & fees: $29,950	Average undergraduate aid package: $24,077

ABOUT THE INSTITUTION Independent, coed. *Awards:* certificates, associate, bachelor's, master's, and doctoral degrees (profile does not reflect significant enrollment at 6 continuing education sites; master's degree is only offered at these sites). 45 undergraduate majors. **Total enrollment:** 2,267. Undergraduates: 1,737. Freshmen: 538. Federal methodology is used as a basis for awarding need-based institutional aid.

UNDERGRADUATE EXPENSES for 2013–2014 Application fee: $40. **Comprehensive fee:** $41,210 includes full-time tuition ($28,250), mandatory fees ($1700), and room and board ($11,260). **College room only:** $6634. Full-time tuition and fees vary according to course load, degree level, location, and program. Room and board charges vary according to board plan, housing facility, and student level. **Part-time tuition:** $945 per credit hour. Part-time tuition and fees vary according to course load, degree level, location, and program.

FRESHMAN FINANCIAL AID (Fall 2012, est.) 498 applied for aid; of those 91% were deemed to have need. 100% of freshmen with need received aid; of those 21% had need fully met. **Average percent of need met:** 75% (excluding resources awarded to replace EFC). **Average financial aid package:** $23,903 (excluding resources awarded to replace EFC). 15% of all full-time freshmen had no need and received non-need-based gift aid.

UNDERGRADUATE FINANCIAL AID (Fall 2012, est.) 1,234 applied for aid; of those 91% were deemed to have need. 100% of undergraduates with need received aid; of those 20% had need fully met. **Average percent of need met:** 75% (excluding resources awarded to replace EFC). **Average financial aid package:** $24,077 (excluding resources awarded to replace EFC). 15% of all full-time undergraduates had no need and received non-need-based gift aid.

GIFT AID (NEED-BASED) Total amount: $19,232,269 (9% federal, 1% state, 89% institutional, 1% external sources). **Receiving aid:** Freshmen: 84% (451); all full-time undergraduates: 80% (1,123). **Average award:** Freshmen: $19,782; Undergraduates: $19,218. **Scholarships, grants, and awards:** Federal Pell, FSEOG, state, private, college/university gift aid from institutional funds.

GIFT AID (NON-NEED-BASED) Total amount: $373,951 (100% institutional). **Receiving aid:** Freshmen: 13% (72). Undergraduates: 11% (160). **Average award:** Freshmen: $13,552. Undergraduates: $12,604. **Scholarships, grants, and awards by category:** Academic interests/achievement: communication, general academic interests/achievements. Creative arts/performance: performing arts, theater/drama. Special achievements/activities: general special achievements/activities, leadership. Special characteristics: adult students, children and siblings of alumni, children of current students, children of educators, children of faculty/staff, general special characteristics, international students, local/state students, married students, parents of current students, siblings of current students, spouses of current students. **Tuition waivers:** Full or partial for employees or children of employees, senior citizens. **ROTC:** Army cooperative, Air Force cooperative.

LOANS Student loans: $10,741,092 (73% need-based, 27% non-need-based). 80% of past graduating class borrowed through all loan programs. Average indebtedness per student: $35,551. **Average need-based loan:** Freshmen: $3870. Undergraduates: $4800. **Parent loans:** $5,829,617 (41% need-based, 59% non-need-based). **Programs:** Federal Direct (Subsidized and Unsubsidized Stafford, PLUS), Perkins.

WORK-STUDY Federal work-study: Total amount: $250,000; 804 jobs averaging $1429. **State or other work-study/employment:** Total amount: $975,000 (100% need-based). Part-time jobs available.

ATHLETIC AWARDS Total amount: $1,638,412 (46% need-based, 54% non-need-based).

APPLYING FOR FINANCIAL AID Required financial aid form: FAFSA. **Financial aid deadline (priority):** 3/1. **Notification date:** Continuous beginning 3/1.

CONTACT Kenneth Ferreira, Executive Director of Student Financial Services, Franklin Pierce University, 40 University Drive, Rindge, NH 03461-0060, 603-899-4180 or toll-free 800-437-0048. Fax: 603-899-4372. E-mail: ferreirak@franklinpierce.edu. Website: http://www.franklinpierce.edu/.

FRANKLIN UNIVERSITY
Columbus, OH

CONTACT Ms. Marlowe Collier, Financial Aid Assistant, Franklin University, 201 South Grant Avenue, Columbus, OH 43215-5399, 614-797-4700 or toll-free 877-341-6300. Fax: 614-220-8931. E-mail: finaid@franklin.edu. Website: http://www.franklin.edu/.

FRANKLIN W. OLIN COLLEGE OF ENGINEERING
Needham, MA

Tuition & fees: $42,500	Average undergraduate aid package: $33,543

ABOUT THE INSTITUTION Independent, coed. **Awards:** bachelor's degrees. 3 undergraduate majors. **Total enrollment:** 355. Undergraduates: 355. Freshmen: 81. Federal methodology is used as a basis for awarding need-based institutional aid.

UNDERGRADUATE EXPENSES for 2013–2014 Application fee: $80. **One-time required fee:** $2656. **Comprehensive fee:** $57,500 includes full-time tuition ($42,000), mandatory fees ($500), and room and board ($15,000). **College room only:** $9000. **Part-time tuition:** $1400 per credit.

FRESHMAN FINANCIAL AID (Fall 2012, est.) 62 applied for aid; of those 69% were deemed to have need. 100% of freshmen with need received aid; of those 100% had need fully met. **Average percent of need met:** 100% (excluding resources awarded to replace EFC). **Average financial aid package:** $31,258 (excluding resources awarded to replace EFC). 47% of all full-time freshmen had no need and received non-need-based gift aid.

UNDERGRADUATE FINANCIAL AID (Fall 2012, est.) 177 applied for aid; of those 76% were deemed to have need. 100% of undergraduates with need received aid; of those 100% had need fully met. **Average percent of need met:** 100% (excluding resources awarded to replace EFC). **Average financial aid package:** $33,543 (excluding resources awarded to replace EFC). 61% of all full-time undergraduates had no need and received non-need-based gift aid.

GIFT AID (NEED-BASED) Total amount: $4,676,836 (2% federal, 96% institutional, 2% external sources). **Receiving aid:** Freshmen: 37% (30); all full-time undergraduates: 28% (95). **Average award:** Freshmen: $20,160; Undergraduates: $17,058. **Scholarships, grants, and awards:** Federal Pell, FSEOG, state, private, college/university gift aid from institutional funds, Academic Competitiveness Grants, National SMART Grants, National Merit Scholarships.

GIFT AID (NON-NEED-BASED) Total amount: $5,934,239 (99% institutional, 1% external sources). **Receiving aid:** Freshmen: 53% (43). Undergraduates: 39% (135). **Average award:** Freshmen: $20,000. Undergraduates: $25,390. **Scholarships, grants, and awards by category:** Academic interests/achievement: general academic interests/achievements.

LOANS Student loans: $616,122 (38% need-based, 62% non-need-based). 18% of past graduating class borrowed through all loan programs. Average indebtedness per student: $12,541. **Average need-based loan:** Freshmen: $2832. Undergraduates: $3178. **Parent loans:** $131,458 (100% non-need-based). **Programs:** Federal Direct (Subsidized and Unsubsidized Stafford, PLUS).

APPLYING FOR FINANCIAL AID Required financial aid form: FAFSA. **Financial aid deadline:** 2/15. **Notification date:** Continuous beginning 3/25. Students must reply by 5/1.

CONTACT Ms. Jean Ricker, Manager of Financial Aid, Franklin W. Olin College of Engineering, CC300, Needham, MA 02492, 781-292-2343. E-mail: jean.ricker@olin.edu. Website: http://www.olin.edu/.

FREED-HARDEMAN UNIVERSITY
Henderson, TN

Tuition & fees: $20,468	Average undergraduate aid package: $16,249

ABOUT THE INSTITUTION Independent Church of Christ, coed. **Awards:** certificates, associate, bachelor's, master's, and doctoral degrees. 54 undergraduate majors. **Total enrollment:** 1,904. Undergraduates: 1,449. Freshmen: 321. Federal methodology is used as a basis for awarding need-based institutional aid.

UNDERGRADUATE EXPENSES for 2013–2014 Comprehensive fee: $27,764 includes full-time tuition ($20,468) and room and board ($7296). **College room only:** $3980. Room and board charges vary according to board plan and housing facility. **Part-time tuition:** $642 per credit hour.

FRESHMAN FINANCIAL AID (Fall 2012, est.) 280 applied for aid; of those 84% were deemed to have need. 100% of freshmen with need received aid; of those 31%

had need fully met. *Average percent of need met:* 60% (excluding resources awarded to replace EFC). *Average financial aid package:* $16,126 (excluding resources awarded to replace EFC). 17% of all full-time freshmen had no need and received non-need-based gift aid.

UNDERGRADUATE FINANCIAL AID (Fall 2012, est.) 1,221 applied for aid; of those 88% were deemed to have need. 100% of undergraduates with need received aid; of those 23% had need fully met. *Average percent of need met:* 65% (excluding resources awarded to replace EFC). *Average financial aid package:* $16,249 (excluding resources awarded to replace EFC). 14% of all full-time undergraduates had no need and received non-need-based gift aid.

GIFT AID (NEED-BASED) *Total amount:* $11,576,434 (22% federal, 16% state, 59% institutional, 3% external sources). *Receiving aid:* Freshmen: 74% (236); all full-time undergraduates: 81% (1,047). *Average award:* Freshmen: $13,084; Undergraduates: $12,433. *Scholarships, grants, and awards:* Federal Pell, FSEOG, state, private, college/university gift aid from institutional funds, Academic Competitiveness Grants, TEACH Grants.

GIFT AID (NON-NEED-BASED) *Total amount:* $2,985,046 (2% federal, 24% state, 67% institutional, 7% external sources). *Receiving aid:* Freshmen: 17% (55). Undergraduates: 15% (188). *Average award:* Freshmen: $10,362. Undergraduates: $8625. *Tuition waivers:* Full or partial for employees or children of employees.

LOANS *Student loans:* $8,346,366 (75% need-based, 25% non-need-based). 78% of past graduating class borrowed through all loan programs. *Average indebtedness per student:* $41,086. *Average need-based loan:* Freshmen: $2795. Undergraduates: $3730. *Parent loans:* $4,206,760 (45% need-based, 55% non-need-based). *Programs:* Federal Direct (Subsidized and Unsubsidized Stafford, PLUS), Perkins, alternative loans.

WORK-STUDY *Federal work-study:* Total amount: $1,163,016; jobs available. *State or other work-study/employment:* Total amount: $4300 (100% need-based). Part-time jobs available.

ATHLETIC AWARDS Total amount: $1,823,709 (57% need-based, 43% non-need-based).

APPLYING FOR FINANCIAL AID *Required financial aid forms:* FAFSA, institution's own form. *Financial aid deadline:* Continuous. *Notification date:* Continuous beginning 3/1.

CONTACT Mrs. Summer Judd, Director of Financial Aid, Freed-Hardeman University, 158 East Main Street, Henderson, TN 38340-2399, 731-989-6662 or toll-free 800-FHU-FHU-1. *Fax:* 731-989-6775. *E-mail:* sjudd@fhu.edu. *Website:* http://www.fhu.edu/.

FRESNO PACIFIC UNIVERSITY
Fresno, CA

Tuition & fees: N/R	Average undergraduate aid package: $14,778

ABOUT THE INSTITUTION Independent Mennonite Brethren Church, coed. 42 undergraduate majors. Federal methodology is used as a basis for awarding need-based institutional aid.

FRESHMAN FINANCIAL AID (Fall 2012, est.) 236 applied for aid; of those 94% were deemed to have need. 100% of freshmen with need received aid; of those 11% had need fully met. *Average percent of need met:* 72% (excluding resources awarded to replace EFC). *Average financial aid package:* $21,264 (excluding resources awarded to replace EFC). 11% of all full-time freshmen had no need and received non-need-based gift aid.

UNDERGRADUATE FINANCIAL AID (Fall 2012, est.) 1,968 applied for aid; of those 95% were deemed to have need. 99% of undergraduates with need received aid; of those 6% had need fully met. *Average percent of need met:* 55% (excluding resources awarded to replace EFC). *Average financial aid package:* $14,778 (excluding resources awarded to replace EFC). 8% of all full-time undergraduates had no need and received non-need-based gift aid.

GIFT AID (NEED-BASED) *Receiving aid:* Freshmen: 71% (180); all full-time undergraduates: 70% (1,512). *Average award:* Freshmen: $11,181; Undergraduates: $8001. *Scholarships, grants, and awards:* Federal Pell, FSEOG, state, private, college/university gift aid from institutional funds.

GIFT AID (NON-NEED-BASED) *Receiving aid:* Freshmen: 86% (218). Undergraduates: 45% (961). *Average award:* Freshmen: $10,555. Undergraduates: $9329. *Scholarships, grants, and awards by category: Academic interests/achievement:* business, general academic interests/achievements, humanities, social sciences. *Creative arts/performance:* music, performing arts, theater/drama. *Special*

characteristics: children of faculty/staff, members of minority groups, relatives of clergy, religious affiliation, spouses of current students.

LOANS *Student loans:* 75% of past graduating class borrowed through all loan programs. *Average indebtedness per student:* $21,993. *Average need-based loan:* Freshmen: $3380. Undergraduates: $4460. *Programs:* Federal Direct (Subsidized and Unsubsidized Stafford, PLUS), Perkins.

WORK-STUDY Federal work-study jobs available.

APPLYING FOR FINANCIAL AID *Required financial aid forms:* FAFSA, institution's own form. *Financial aid deadline (priority):* 3/2. *Notification date:* Continuous beginning 3/2. Students must reply by 7/30 or within 3 weeks of notification.

CONTACT April Powell, Director of Financial Aid, Fresno Pacific University, 1717 South Chestnut Avenue, #2004, Fresno, CA 93702, 559-453-2041 or toll-free 800-660-6089. *Fax:* 559-453-5595. *E-mail:* sfs@fresno.edu. *Website:* http://www.fresno.edu/.

FRIENDS UNIVERSITY
Wichita, KS

CONTACT Brandon Pierce, Director of Financial Aid, Friends University, 2100 University Street, Wichita, KS 67213, 316-295-5658 or toll-free 800-794-6945. *Fax:* 316-295-5703. *E-mail:* piercb@friends.edu. *Website:* http://www.friends.edu/.

FROSTBURG STATE UNIVERSITY
Frostburg, MD

Tuition & fees (MD res): $7728	Average undergraduate aid package: $8855

ABOUT THE INSTITUTION State-supported, coed. *Awards:* certificates, bachelor's, master's, and doctoral degrees. 46 undergraduate majors. *Total enrollment:* 5,421. Undergraduates: 4,631. Freshmen: 814. Federal methodology is used as a basis for awarding need-based institutional aid.

UNDERGRADUATE EXPENSES for 2013-2014 *Application fee:* $30. *Tuition, state resident:* full-time $5630; part-time $233 per credit. *Tuition, nonresident:* full-time $16,278; part-time $457 per credit. *Required fees:* full-time $2098; $96 per credit or $25 per term. Full-time tuition and fees vary according to location. Part-time tuition and fees vary according to course load and location. *College room and board:* $7990; *Room only:* $3762. Room and board charges vary according to board plan and housing facility.

FRESHMAN FINANCIAL AID (Fall 2012, est.) 709 applied for aid; of those 71% were deemed to have need. 100% of freshmen with need received aid; of those 18% had need fully met. *Average percent of need met:* 62% (excluding resources awarded to replace EFC). *Average financial aid package:* $8783 (excluding resources awarded to replace EFC). 20% of all full-time freshmen had no need and received non-need-based gift aid.

UNDERGRADUATE FINANCIAL AID (Fall 2012, est.) 3,616 applied for aid; of those 74% were deemed to have need. 100% of undergraduates with need received aid; of those 15% had need fully met. *Average percent of need met:* 62% (excluding resources awarded to replace EFC). *Average financial aid package:* $8855 (excluding resources awarded to replace EFC). 17% of all full-time undergraduates had no need and received non-need-based gift aid.

GIFT AID (NEED-BASED) *Total amount:* $12,896,206 (56% federal, 23% state, 16% institutional, 5% external sources). *Receiving aid:* Freshmen: 41% (345); all full-time undergraduates: 43% (1,871). *Average award:* Freshmen: $6952; Undergraduates: $6388. *Scholarships, grants, and awards:* Federal Pell, FSEOG, state, private, college/university gift aid from institutional funds.

GIFT AID (NON-NEED-BASED) *Total amount:* $3,794,320 (1% federal, 14% state, 67% institutional, 18% external sources). *Receiving aid:* Freshmen: 20% (168). Undergraduates: 17% (755). *Average award:* Freshmen: $3016. Undergraduates: $3100. *Scholarships, grants, and awards by category: Academic interests/achievement:* biological sciences, business, communication, computer science, education, engineering/technologies, English, foreign languages, general academic interests/achievements, health fields, humanities, international studies, mathematics, physical sciences, premedicine, social sciences. *Creative arts/performance:* art/fine arts, creative writing, journalism/publications, music, performing arts, theater/drama. *Special achievements/activities:* community service, leadership. *Special characteristics:* adult students, children of union members/company employees, international students, local/ state students, out-of-state students, veterans, veterans' children. *Tuition waivers:* Full or partial for employees or children of employees, senior citizens.

LOANS *Student loans:* $27,277,560 (38% need-based, 62% non-need-based). 68% of past graduating class borrowed through all loan programs. *Average indebtedness per student:* $20,736. *Average need-based loan:* Freshmen: $3138. Undergraduates: $4010. *Parent loans:* $3,610,779 (100% non-need-based). *Programs:* Federal Direct (Subsidized and Unsubsidized Stafford, PLUS), Perkins.

WORK-STUDY *Federal work-study:* Total amount: $93,371; 147 jobs averaging $635. *State or other work-study/employment:* Part-time jobs available.

APPLYING FOR FINANCIAL AID *Required financial aid form:* FAFSA. *Financial aid deadline (priority):* 3/1. *Notification date:* Continuous beginning 3/15. Students must reply within 3 weeks of notification.

CONTACT Mrs. Angela Hovatter, Director of Financial Aid, Frostburg State University, 114 Pullen Hall, Frostburg, MD 21532-1099, 301-687-4301. *Fax:* 301-687-7074. *E-mail:* ahovatter@frostburg.edu. *Website:* http://www.frostburg.edu/.

FULL SAIL UNIVERSITY
Winter Park, FL

CONTACT Financial Aid Office, Full Sail University, 3300 University Boulevard, Winter Park, FL 32792, 800-575-1142 or toll-free 800-226-7625. *Website:* http://www.fullsail.edu/.

FURMAN UNIVERSITY
Greenville, SC

Tuition & fees: $41,532	Average undergraduate aid package: $30,492

ABOUT THE INSTITUTION Independent, coed. *Awards:* bachelor's and master's degrees. 50 undergraduate majors. *Total enrollment:* 2,915. Undergraduates: 2,753. Freshmen: 695. Both federal and institutional methodology are used as a basis for awarding need-based institutional aid.

UNDERGRADUATE EXPENSES for 2013–2014 *Application fee:* $50. *Comprehensive fee:* $52,041 includes full-time tuition ($41,152), mandatory fees ($380), and room and board ($10,509). *College room only:* $5704. Room and board charges vary according to board plan and housing facility. *Part-time tuition:* $1286 per credit. Part-time tuition and fees vary according to course load.

FRESHMAN FINANCIAL AID (Fall 2012, est.) 466 applied for aid; of those 61% were deemed to have need. 100% of freshmen with need received aid; of those 29% had need fully met. *Average percent of need met:* 64% (excluding resources awarded to replace EFC). *Average financial aid package:* $26,910 (excluding resources awarded to replace EFC). 35% of all full-time freshmen had no need and received non-need-based gift aid.

UNDERGRADUATE FINANCIAL AID (Fall 2012, est.) 1,397 applied for aid; of those 74% were deemed to have need. 100% of undergraduates with need received aid; of those 31% had need fully met. *Average percent of need met:* 73% (excluding resources awarded to replace EFC). *Average financial aid package:* $30,492 (excluding resources awarded to replace EFC). 36% of all full-time undergraduates had no need and received non-need-based gift aid.

GIFT AID (NEED-BASED) *Total amount:* $27,633,113 (7% federal, 4% state, 86% institutional, 3% external sources). *Receiving aid:* Freshmen: 41% (282); all full-time undergraduates: 38% (1,012). *Average award:* Freshmen: $21,093; Undergraduates: $24,227. *Scholarships, grants, and awards:* Federal Pell, FSEOG, state, private, college/university gift aid from institutional funds.

GIFT AID (NON-NEED-BASED) *Total amount:* $19,084,172 (20% state, 73% institutional, 7% external sources). *Receiving aid:* Freshmen: 40% (281). Undergraduates: 38% (1,012). *Average award:* Freshmen: $13,697. Undergraduates: $16,049. *Scholarships, grants, and awards by category:* Academic interests/ achievement: area/ethnic studies, biological sciences, business, communication, computer science, education, engineering/technologies, English, foreign languages, general academic interests/achievements, health fields, humanities, international studies, math-

ematics, military science, physical sciences, premedicine, religion/biblical studies, social sciences. *Creative arts/performance:* art/fine arts, creative writing, music, theater/ drama. *Special achievements/activities:* community service, leadership, religious involvement. *Special characteristics:* children of faculty/staff, ethnic background, international students, local/state students, relatives of clergy, religious affiliation, veterans. *Tuition waivers:* Full or partial for employees or children of employees. *ROTC:* Army.

LOANS *Student loans:* $8,000,431 (39% need-based, 61% non-need-based). 43% of past graduating class borrowed through all loan programs. *Average indebtedness per student:* $26,661. *Average need-based loan:* Freshmen: $4038. Undergraduates: $4826. *Parent loans:* $4,070,819 (57% need-based, 43% non-need-based). *Programs:* Federal Direct (Subsidized and Unsubsidized Stafford, PLUS), Perkins, state, alternative loans.

WORK-STUDY *Federal work-study:* Total amount: $900,773; 609 jobs averaging $1462.

ATHLETIC AWARDS Total amount: $9,079,584 (50% need-based, 50% non-need-based).

APPLYING FOR FINANCIAL AID *Required financial aid forms:* FAFSA, CSS Financial Aid PROFILE, state aid form. *Financial aid deadline:* 1/15. *Notification date:* 4/2. Students must reply by 5/1 or within 2 weeks of notification.

CONTACT Mr. Forrest Stuart, Associate Vice President of Financial Aid, Furman University, 3300 Poinsett Highway, Greenville, SC 29613, 864-294-2204. *Fax:* 864-294-3127. *E-mail:* forrest.stuart@furman.edu. *Website:* http://www.furman.edu/.

GALLAUDET UNIVERSITY
Washington, DC

Tuition & fees: $12,806	Average undergraduate aid package: $19,287

ABOUT THE INSTITUTION Independent, coed. *Awards:* certificates, bachelor's, master's, and doctoral degrees (undergraduate programs are open primarily to the students with hearing-impairments). 22 undergraduate majors. *Total enrollment:* 1,546. Undergraduates: 1,118. Freshmen: 201. Federal methodology is used as a basis for awarding need-based institutional aid.

UNDERGRADUATE EXPENSES for 2013–2014 *Application fee:* $50. *Comprehensive fee:* $23,596 includes full-time tuition ($12,430), mandatory fees ($376), and room and board ($10,790). *College room only:* $5960. Full-time tuition and fees vary according to degree level. Room and board charges vary according to board plan. *Part-time tuition:* $621.50 per credit hour. Part-time tuition and fees vary according to degree level.

FRESHMAN FINANCIAL AID (Fall 2012, est.) 154 applied for aid; of those 91% were deemed to have need. 100% of freshmen with need received aid; of those 24% had need fully met. *Average percent of need met:* 77% (excluding resources awarded to replace EFC). *Average financial aid package:* $19,568 (excluding resources awarded to replace EFC). 7% of all full-time freshmen had no need and received non-need-based gift aid.

UNDERGRADUATE FINANCIAL AID (Fall 2012, est.) 940 applied for aid; of those 92% were deemed to have need. 98% of undergraduates with need received aid; of those 27% had need fully met. *Average percent of need met:* 76% (excluding resources awarded to replace EFC). *Average financial aid package:* $19,287 (excluding resources awarded to replace EFC). 4% of all full-time undergraduates had no need and received non-need-based gift aid.

GIFT AID (NEED-BASED) *Total amount:* $14,592,991 (18% federal, 53% state, 28% institutional, 1% external sources). *Receiving aid:* Freshmen: 78% (140); all full-time undergraduates: 75% (839). *Average award:* Freshmen: $17,952; Undergraduates: $17,124. *Scholarships, grants, and awards:* Federal Pell, FSEOG, state, private, college/university gift aid from institutional funds.

GIFT AID (NON-NEED-BASED) *Total amount:* $747,870 (69% state, 29% institutional, 2% external sources). *Receiving aid:* Freshmen: 18% (32). Undergraduates: 18% (197). *Average award:* Freshmen: $17,079. Undergraduates: $16,569. *Scholarships, grants, and awards by category:* Academic interests/ achievement: general academic interests/achievements. *Special achievements/activities:* leadership. *Special characteristics:* members of minority groups. *Tuition waivers:* Full or partial for employees or children of employees.

LOANS *Student loans:* $2,882,173 (96% need-based, 4% non-need-based). 58% of past graduating class borrowed through all loan programs. *Average indebtedness per*

student: $10,347. **Average need-based loan:** Freshmen: $3225. Undergraduates: $4034. **Parent loans:** $358,401 (70% need-based, 30% non-need-based). **Programs:** Federal Direct (Subsidized and Unsubsidized Stafford, PLUS), Perkins.
WORK-STUDY Federal work-study: Total amount: $31,199; 20 jobs averaging $1560.
APPLYING FOR FINANCIAL AID Required financial aid forms: FAFSA, institution's own form. **Financial aid deadline:** Continuous. **Notification date:** Continuous beginning 3/1.
CONTACT Janel Grossinger, Director of Financial Aid, Gallaudet University, Chapel Hall, Room G-02, 800 Florida Avenue, NE, Washington, DC 20002, 202-651-5290 or toll-free 800-995-0550. Fax: 202-651-5740. E-mail: financial.aid@gallaudet.edu. Website: http://www.gallaudet.edu/.

GANNON UNIVERSITY
Erie, PA

Tuition & fees: $27,546	Average undergraduate aid package: $21,641

ABOUT THE INSTITUTION Independent Roman Catholic, coed. **Awards:** certificates, bachelor's, master's, and doctoral degrees. 62 undergraduate majors. **Total enrollment:** 4,008. Undergraduates: 3,008. Freshmen: 629. Federal methodology is used as a basis for awarding need-based institutional aid.
UNDERGRADUATE EXPENSES for 2013–2014 Application fee: $25. **Comprehensive fee:** $38,486 includes full-time tuition ($27,000), mandatory fees ($546), and room and board ($10,940). **College room only:** $5740. Full-time tuition and fees vary according to class time, course load, and program. Room and board charges vary according to board plan and housing facility. **Part-time tuition:** $650 per credit hour. **Part-time fees:** $18 per credit hour. Part-time tuition and fees vary according to class time, course load, and program.
FRESHMAN FINANCIAL AID (Fall 2012, est.) 611 applied for aid; of those 85% were deemed to have need. 100% of freshmen with need received aid; of those 17% had need fully met. **Average percent of need met:** 73% (excluding resources awarded to replace EFC). **Average financial aid package:** $21,970 (excluding resources awarded to replace EFC). 13% of all full-time freshmen had no need and received non-need-based gift aid.
UNDERGRADUATE FINANCIAL AID (Fall 2012, est.) 2,284 applied for aid; of those 91% were deemed to have need. 100% of undergraduates with need received aid; of those 22% had need fully met. **Average percent of need met:** 71% (excluding resources awarded to replace EFC). **Average financial aid package:** $21,641 (excluding resources awarded to replace EFC). 15% of all full-time undergraduates had no need and received non-need-based gift aid.
GIFT AID (NEED-BASED) Total amount: $33,738,705 (12% federal, 11% state, 72% institutional, 5% external sources). **Receiving aid:** Freshmen: 84% (519); all full-time undergraduates: 81% (2,049). **Average award:** Freshmen: $18,390; Undergraduates: $17,346. **Scholarships, grants, and awards:** Federal Pell, FSEOG, state, private, college/university gift aid from institutional funds.
GIFT AID (NON-NEED-BASED) Total amount: $5,724,311 (73% institutional, 27% external sources). **Receiving aid:** Freshmen: 11% (66). Undergraduates: 10% (257). **Average award:** Freshmen: $12,543. Undergraduates: $10,877. **Scholarships, grants, and awards by category:** Academic interests/achievement: 1,081 awards ($11,365,051 total): biological sciences, business, education, engineering/technologies, English, foreign languages, general academic interests/achievements, humanities, international studies, mathematics, premedicine, religion/biblical studies, social sciences. Creative arts/performance: 76 awards ($134,750 total): music, performing arts, theater/drama. Special achievements/activities: 689 awards ($1,183,550 total): community service, leadership. Special characteristics: 966 awards ($2,024,962 total): adult students, ethnic background, international students, members of minority groups, religious affiliation, veterans. **Tuition waivers:** Full or partial for employees or children of employees, senior citizens. **ROTC:** Army.
LOANS Student loans: $19,028,553 (69% need-based, 31% non-need-based). 78% of past graduating class borrowed through all loan programs. **Average need-based loan:** Freshmen: $3572. Undergraduates: $4504. **Parent loans:** $4,090,647 (82% need-based, 18% non-need-based). **Programs:** Federal Direct (Subsidized and Unsubsidized Stafford, PLUS), Perkins, Federal Nursing.
WORK-STUDY Federal work-study: Total amount: $816,442; 514 jobs averaging $2300. **State or other work-study/employment:** Total amount: $243,800 (100% non-need-based). 160 part-time jobs averaging $2300.

ATHLETIC AWARDS Total amount: $3,245,255 (70% need-based, 30% non-need-based).
APPLYING FOR FINANCIAL AID Required financial aid form: FAFSA. **Financial aid deadline (priority):** 3/15. **Notification date:** Continuous beginning 11/1.
CONTACT Ms. Sharon Krahe, Director of Financial Aid, Gannon University, 109 University Square, Erie, PA 16541, 814-871-7670 or toll-free 800-GANNONU. Fax: 814-871-5826. E-mail: krahe001@gannon.edu. Website: http://www.gannon.edu/.

GARDNER-WEBB UNIVERSITY
Boiling Springs, NC

Tuition & fees: $24,640	Average undergraduate aid package: $19,032

ABOUT THE INSTITUTION Independent Baptist, coed. **Awards:** certificates, associate, bachelor's, master's, and doctoral degrees. 66 undergraduate majors. **Total enrollment:** 4,854. Undergraduates: 2,677. Freshmen: 493. Federal methodology is used as a basis for awarding need-based institutional aid.
UNDERGRADUATE EXPENSES for 2013–2014 Application fee: $40. **One-time required fee:** $100. **Comprehensive fee:** $32,580 includes full-time tuition ($24,250), mandatory fees ($390), and room and board ($7940). **College room only:** $4080. Full-time tuition and fees vary according to degree level. Room and board charges vary according to board plan and housing facility. **Part-time tuition:** $387 per credit hour. Part-time tuition and fees vary according to course load.
FRESHMAN FINANCIAL AID (Fall 2012, est.) 461 applied for aid; of those 89% were deemed to have need. 100% of freshmen with need received aid; of those 24% had need fully met. **Average percent of need met:** 78% (excluding resources awarded to replace EFC). **Average financial aid package:** $20,272 (excluding resources awarded to replace EFC). 16% of all full-time freshmen had no need and received non-need-based gift aid.
UNDERGRADUATE FINANCIAL AID (Fall 2012, est.) 1,394 applied for aid; of those 89% were deemed to have need. 100% of undergraduates with need received aid; of those 22% had need fully met. **Average percent of need met:** 74% (excluding resources awarded to replace EFC). **Average financial aid package:** $19,032 (excluding resources awarded to replace EFC). 17% of all full-time undergraduates had no need and received non-need-based gift aid.
GIFT AID (NEED-BASED) Total amount: $15,403,062 (18% federal, 21% state, 58% institutional, 3% external sources). **Receiving aid:** Freshmen: 65% (322); all full-time undergraduates: 63% (965). **Average award:** Freshmen: $7076; Undergraduates: $7091. **Scholarships, grants, and awards:** Federal Pell, FSEOG, state, private, college/university gift aid from institutional funds.
GIFT AID (NON-NEED-BASED) Total amount: $2,365,244 (98% institutional, 2% external sources). **Receiving aid:** Freshmen: 83% (407). Undergraduates: 71% (1,099). **Average award:** Freshmen: $10,857. Undergraduates: $9202. **Scholarships, grants, and awards by category:** Academic interests/achievement: biological sciences, business, communication, computer science, education, English, foreign languages, general academic interests/achievements, health fields, humanities, mathematics, physical sciences, premedicine, religion/biblical studies, social sciences. Creative arts/performance: art/fine arts, music, theater/drama. Special achievements/activities: cheerleading/drum major, religious involvement. Special characteristics: children of faculty/staff, handicapped students, local/state students, members of minority groups, out-of-state students, previous college experience, relatives of clergy. **Tuition waivers:** Full or partial for employees or children of employees. **ROTC:** Army, Air Force cooperative.
LOANS Student loans: $9,566,575 (94% need-based, 6% non-need-based). 73% of past graduating class borrowed through all loan programs. **Average indebtedness per student:** $27,261. **Average need-based loan:** Freshmen: $3255. Undergraduates: $4248. **Parent loans:** $3,522,833 (84% need-based, 16% non-need-based). **Programs:** Federal Direct (Subsidized and Unsubsidized Stafford, PLUS), Perkins, state, alternative loans.
WORK-STUDY Federal work-study: Total amount: $298,379; 210 jobs averaging $1421. **State or other work-study/employment:** Total amount: $30,285 (77% need-based, 23% non-need-based). 23 part-time jobs averaging $1317.
ATHLETIC AWARDS Total amount: $5,897,812 (65% need-based, 35% non-need-based).

APPLYING FOR FINANCIAL AID *Required financial aid forms:* FAFSA, state aid form. *Financial aid deadline (priority):* 3/15. *Notification date:* 3/1. Students must reply within 2 weeks of notification.

CONTACT Summer Nance, Assistant Vice President of Financial Planning, Gardner-Webb University, PO Box 955, Boiling Springs, NC 28017, 704-406-4243 or toll-free 800-253-6472. *Fax:* 704-406-4102.
Website: http://www.gardner-webb.edu/.

GENEVA COLLEGE
Beaver Falls, PA

Tuition & fees: $25,220	Average undergraduate aid package: $19,077

ABOUT THE INSTITUTION Independent Reformed Presbyterian Church of North America, coed. *Awards:* associate, bachelor's, and master's degrees (also offers non-traditional programs in Philadelphia and western Pennsylvania with significant enrollment not reflected in profile). 35 undergraduate majors. *Total enrollment:* 1,646. Undergraduates: 1,342. Freshmen: 340. Federal methodology is used as a basis for awarding need-based institutional aid.

UNDERGRADUATE EXPENSES for 2013–2014 *Application fee:* $40. *Comprehensive fee:* $34,470 includes full-time tuition ($25,220) and room and board ($9250). Full-time tuition and fees vary according to course load. Room and board charges vary according to board plan. *Part-time tuition:* $850 per credit. Part-time tuition and fees vary according to course load.

FRESHMAN FINANCIAL AID (Fall 2012, est.) 350 applied for aid; of those 91% were deemed to have need. 100% of freshmen with need received aid; of those 15% had need fully met. *Average percent of need met:* 75% (excluding resources awarded to replace EFC). *Average financial aid package:* $19,168 (excluding resources awarded to replace EFC). 9% of all full-time freshmen had no need and received non-need-based gift aid.

UNDERGRADUATE FINANCIAL AID (Fall 2012, est.) 1,275 applied for aid; of those 92% were deemed to have need. 100% of undergraduates with need received aid; of those 17% had need fully met. *Average percent of need met:* 75% (excluding resources awarded to replace EFC). *Average financial aid package:* $19,077 (excluding resources awarded to replace EFC). 14% of all full-time undergraduates had no need and received non-need-based gift aid.

GIFT AID (NEED-BASED) *Total amount:* $16,269,214 (15% federal, 12% state, 70% institutional, 3% external sources). *Receiving aid:* Freshmen: 90% (319); all full-time undergraduates: 83% (1,162). *Average award:* Freshmen: $15,551; Undergraduates: $14,897. *Scholarships, grants, and awards:* Federal Pell, FSEOG, state, private, college/university gift aid from institutional funds.

GIFT AID (NON-NEED-BASED) *Total amount:* $2,457,920 (4% federal, 2% state, 90% institutional, 4% external sources). *Receiving aid:* Freshmen: 9% (32). Undergraduates: 8% (116). *Average award:* Freshmen: $9657. Undergraduates: $9510. *Scholarships, grants, and awards by category: Academic interests/achievement:* engineering/technologies, general academic interests/achievements, religion/biblical studies. *Creative arts/performance:* music. *Special characteristics:* children of faculty/staff, religious affiliation. *Tuition waivers:* Full or partial for employees or children of employees. *ROTC:* Army cooperative.

LOANS *Student loans:* $9,082,780 (76% need-based, 24% non-need-based). 93% of past graduating class borrowed through all loan programs. *Average indebtedness per student:* $26,883. *Average need-based loan:* Freshmen: $3202. Undergraduates: $4076. *Parent loans:* $1,892,731 (40% need-based, 60% non-need-based). *Programs:* Federal Direct (Subsidized and Unsubsidized Stafford, PLUS), Perkins.

WORK-STUDY *Federal work-study:* Total amount: $240,000; 260 jobs averaging $2000.

APPLYING FOR FINANCIAL AID *Required financial aid form:* FAFSA. *Financial aid deadline (priority):* 3/15. *Notification date:* Continuous beginning 3/1. Students must reply within 4 weeks of notification.

CONTACT Mr. Steven Bell, Director of Financial Aid, Geneva College, 3200 College Avenue, Beaver Falls, PA 15010-3599, 724-847-6530 or toll-free 800-847-8255. *Fax:* 724-847-6776. *E-mail:* financialaid@geneva.edu.
Website: http://www.geneva.edu/.

GEORGE FOX UNIVERSITY
Newberg, OR

Tuition & fees: $30,230	Average undergraduate aid package: $26,429

ABOUT THE INSTITUTION Independent Friends, coed. *Awards:* certificates, bachelor's, master's, and doctoral degrees. 46 undergraduate majors. *Total enrollment:* 3,484. Undergraduates: 2,184. Freshmen: 422. Federal methodology is used as a basis for awarding need-based institutional aid.

UNDERGRADUATE EXPENSES for 2013–2014 *Application fee:* $40. *Comprehensive fee:* $39,590 includes full-time tuition ($29,900), mandatory fees ($330), and room and board ($9360). *College room only:* $5460. Room and board charges vary according to board plan. *Part-time tuition:* $905 per semester hour. Part-time tuition and fees vary according to course load.

FRESHMAN FINANCIAL AID (Fall 2012, est.) 384 applied for aid; of those 89% were deemed to have need. 100% of freshmen with need received aid; of those 35% had need fully met. *Average percent of need met:* 85% (excluding resources awarded to replace EFC). *Average financial aid package:* $27,240 (excluding resources awarded to replace EFC). 8% of all full-time freshmen had no need and received non-need-based gift aid.

UNDERGRADUATE FINANCIAL AID (Fall 2012, est.) 1,651 applied for aid; of those 92% were deemed to have need. 99% of undergraduates with need received aid; of those 33% had need fully met. *Average percent of need met:* 85% (excluding resources awarded to replace EFC). *Average financial aid package:* $26,429 (excluding resources awarded to replace EFC). 6% of all full-time undergraduates had no need and received non-need-based gift aid.

GIFT AID (NEED-BASED) *Total amount:* $25,040,345 (5% federal, 2% state, 89% institutional, 4% external sources). *Receiving aid:* Freshmen: 77% (323); all full-time undergraduates: 73% (1,408). *Average award:* Freshmen: $10,116; Undergraduates: $9787. *Scholarships, grants, and awards:* Federal Pell, FSEOG, state, private, college/university gift aid from institutional funds, Academic Competitiveness Grants, National SMART Grants, TEACH Grants.

GIFT AID (NON-NEED-BASED) *Total amount:* $1,550,484 (92% institutional, 8% external sources). *Receiving aid:* Freshmen: 65% (275). Undergraduates: 63% (1,213). *Average award:* Freshmen: $10,329. Undergraduates: $8812. *Scholarships, grants, and awards by category: Academic interests/achievement:* biological sciences, business, communication, computer science, education, engineering/technologies, English, foreign languages, general academic interests/achievements, health fields, home economics, humanities, international studies, mathematics, physical sciences, religion/biblical studies, social sciences. *Creative arts/performance:* art/fine arts, cinema/film/broadcasting, debating, music, theater/drama. *Special achievements/activities:* leadership, religious involvement. *Special characteristics:* children and siblings of alumni, children of faculty/staff, ethnic background, international students, members of minority groups, out-of-state students, relatives of clergy, religious affiliation. *Tuition waivers:* Full or partial for employees or children of employees, senior citizens. *ROTC:* Air Force cooperative.

LOANS *Student loans:* $10,565,837 (87% need-based, 13% non-need-based). 79% of past graduating class borrowed through all loan programs. *Average indebtedness per student:* $23,512. *Average need-based loan:* Freshmen: $2986. Undergraduates: $3633. *Parent loans:* $399,839 (8% need-based, 92% non-need-based). *Programs:* Federal Direct (Subsidized and Unsubsidized Stafford, PLUS), Perkins, alternative loans.

WORK-STUDY *Federal work-study:* Total amount: $318,366; jobs available. *State or other work-study/employment:* Total amount: $2,358,986 (92% need-based, 8% non-need-based). Part-time jobs available.

APPLYING FOR FINANCIAL AID *Required financial aid forms:* FAFSA, state aid form. *Financial aid deadline (priority):* 2/1. *Notification date:* Continuous beginning 3/1. Students must reply within 6 weeks of notification.

CONTACT James Oshiro, Director of Financial Aid, George Fox University, 414 North Meridian Street, Newberg, OR 97132-2697, 503-554-2290 or toll-free 800-765-4369. *Fax:* 503-554-3880. *E-mail:* sfs@georgefox.edu.
Website: http://www.georgefox.edu/.

GEORGE MASON UNIVERSITY
Fairfax, VA

Tuition & fees (VA res): $9620	Average undergraduate aid package: $11,790

ABOUT THE INSTITUTION State-supported, coed. *Awards:* certificates, bachelor's, master's, and doctoral degrees. 63 undergraduate majors. *Total enrollment:* 32,961. Undergraduates: 20,653. Freshmen: 2,694. Federal methodology is used as a basis for awarding need-based institutional aid.

UNDERGRADUATE EXPENSES for 2013–2014 *Application fee:* $60. *One-time required fee:* $180. *Tuition, state resident:* full-time $7010; part-time $292.08 per credit hour. *Tuition, nonresident:* full-time $25,154; part-time $1048.08 per credit hour. *Required fees:* full-time $2610; $108.75 per credit hour. Full-time tuition and fees vary according to course load. Part-time tuition and fees vary according to course load. *College room and board:* $9250; *Room only:* $5510. Room and board charges vary according to board plan and housing facility.

FRESHMAN FINANCIAL AID (Fall 2011) 2,160 applied for aid; of those 67% were deemed to have need. 94% of freshmen with need received aid; of those 8% had need fully met. *Average percent of need met:* 62% (excluding resources awarded to replace EFC). *Average financial aid package:* $11,987 (excluding resources awarded to replace EFC). 5% of all full-time freshmen had no need and received non-need-based gift aid.

UNDERGRADUATE FINANCIAL AID (Fall 2011) 10,825 applied for aid; of those 79% were deemed to have need. 96% of undergraduates with need received aid; of those 7% had need fully met. *Average percent of need met:* 60% (excluding resources awarded to replace EFC). *Average financial aid package:* $11,790 (excluding resources awarded to replace EFC). 4% of all full-time undergraduates had no need and received non-need-based gift aid.

GIFT AID (NEED-BASED) *Total amount:* $42,644,060 (56% federal, 36% state, 8% institutional). *Receiving aid:* Freshmen: 40% (1,065); all full-time undergraduates: 39% (6,358). *Average award:* Freshmen: $6644; Undergraduates: $6294. *Scholarships, grants, and awards:* Federal Pell, FSEOG, state, private, college/university gift aid from institutional funds.

GIFT AID (NON-NEED-BASED) *Total amount:* $9,079,704 (74% institutional, 26% external sources). *Receiving aid:* Freshmen: 17% (452). Undergraduates: 9% (1,388). *Average award:* Freshmen: $5654. Undergraduates: $5407. *Scholarships, grants, and awards by category:* Academic interests/achievement: 1,763 awards ($6,658,586 total): general academic interests/achievements. *Creative arts/performance:* general creative arts/performance. *Special characteristics:* general special characteristics. *Tuition waivers:* Full or partial for employees or children of employees, senior citizens. *ROTC:* Army, Air Force cooperative.

LOANS *Student loans:* $78,886,614 (73% need-based, 27% non-need-based). 57% of past graduating class borrowed through all loan programs. *Average indebtedness per student:* $25,822. *Average need-based loan:* Freshmen: $3273. Undergraduates: $4330. *Parent loans:* $16,826,419 (45% need-based, 55% non-need-based). *Programs:* Federal Direct (Subsidized and Unsubsidized Stafford, PLUS), Perkins, Federal Nursing.

WORK-STUDY *Federal work-study:* Total amount: $782,282; 333 jobs averaging $2284.

ATHLETIC AWARDS Total amount: $4,479,480 (100% non-need-based).

APPLYING FOR FINANCIAL AID *Required financial aid form:* FAFSA. *Financial aid deadline (priority):* 3/1. *Notification date:* Continuous beginning 4/1. Students must reply within 2 weeks of notification.

CONTACT Heidi Granger, Office of Student Financial Aid, George Mason University, Mail Stop 3B5, Fairfax, VA 22030-4444, 703-993-2353. *Fax:* 703-993-2350. *E-mail:* finaid@gmu.edu. *Website:* http://www.gmu.edu/.

GEORGETOWN COLLEGE
Georgetown, KY

Tuition & fees: $30,770	Average undergraduate aid package: $26,633

ABOUT THE INSTITUTION Independent Baptist Church, coed. *Awards:* bachelor's and master's degrees. 34 undergraduate majors. *Total enrollment:* 1,543. Undergraduates: 1,116. Freshmen: 237. Federal methodology is used as a basis for awarding need-based institutional aid.

UNDERGRADUATE EXPENSES for 2013–2014 *Application fee:* $30. *Comprehensive fee:* $38,690 includes full-time tuition ($30,770) and room and board ($7920). *College room only:* $3820. Full-time tuition and fees vary according to course load and degree level. Room and board charges vary according to board plan and housing facility. *Part-time tuition:* $1270 per credit hour. Part-time tuition and fees vary according to degree level.

FRESHMAN FINANCIAL AID (Fall 2012, est.) 219 applied for aid; of those 93% were deemed to have need. 100% of freshmen with need received aid; of those 38% had need fully met. *Average percent of need met:* 84% (excluding resources awarded to replace EFC). *Average financial aid package:* $26,977 (excluding resources awarded to replace EFC). 14% of all full-time freshmen had no need and received non-need-based gift aid.

UNDERGRADUATE FINANCIAL AID (Fall 2012, est.) 951 applied for aid; of those 93% were deemed to have need. 100% of undergraduates with need received aid; of those 49% had need fully met. *Average percent of need met:* 84% (excluding resources awarded to replace EFC). *Average financial aid package:* $26,633 (excluding resources awarded to replace EFC). 17% of all full-time undergraduates had no need and received non-need-based gift aid.

GIFT AID (NEED-BASED) *Total amount:* $17,991,685 (10% federal, 16% state, 72% institutional, 2% external sources). *Receiving aid:* Freshmen: 86% (204); all full-time undergraduates: 82% (889). *Average award:* Freshmen: $17,038; Undergraduates: $18,640. *Scholarships, grants, and awards:* Federal Pell, FSEOG, state, private, college/university gift aid from institutional funds.

GIFT AID (NON-NEED-BASED) *Total amount:* $3,087,631 (1% federal, 7% state, 91% institutional, 1% external sources). *Receiving aid:* Freshmen: 14% (33). Undergraduates: 18% (196). *Average award:* Freshmen: $13,807. Undergraduates: $14,958. *Scholarships, grants, and awards by category:* Academic interests/achievement: general academic interests/achievements. *Creative arts/performance:* art/fine arts, music, performing arts, theater/drama. *Special achievements/activities:* junior miss, leadership, religious involvement. *Special characteristics:* children and siblings of alumni, children of faculty/staff, local/state students, out-of-state students, relatives of clergy, religious affiliation. *Tuition waivers:* Full or partial for employees or children of employees. *ROTC:* Army cooperative, Air Force cooperative.

LOANS *Student loans:* $6,769,351 (96% need-based, 4% non-need-based). 63% of past graduating class borrowed through all loan programs. *Average indebtedness per student:* $26,730. *Average need-based loan:* Freshmen: $3810. Undergraduates: $4724. *Parent loans:* $1,670,111 (94% need-based, 6% non-need-based). *Programs:* Federal Direct (Subsidized and Unsubsidized Stafford, PLUS), Perkins, college/university.

WORK-STUDY *Federal work-study:* Total amount: $525,080; 561 jobs averaging $936.

ATHLETIC AWARDS Total amount: $2,333,480 (83% need-based, 17% non-need-based).

APPLYING FOR FINANCIAL AID *Required financial aid forms:* FAFSA, institution's own form. *Financial aid deadline:* 3/15 (priority: 2/1). *Notification date:* 3/1. Students must reply by 5/1.

CONTACT Tiffany Hornberger, Director of Student Financial Planning, Georgetown College, 400 East College Street, Georgetown, KY 40324-1696, 502-863-8027 or toll-free 800-788-9985. *Fax:* 502-868-7733. *E-mail:* financialaid@georgetowncollege.edu. *Website:* http://www.georgetowncollege.edu/.

GEORGETOWN UNIVERSITY
Washington, DC

Tuition & fees: $43,070	Average undergraduate aid package: $38,601

ABOUT THE INSTITUTION Independent Roman Catholic (Jesuit), coed. *Awards:* certificates, bachelor's, master's, and doctoral degrees. 48 undergraduate majors. *Total enrollment:* 17,357. Undergraduates: 7,552. Freshmen: 1,570. Both federal and institutional methodology are used as a basis for awarding need-based institutional aid.

UNDERGRADUATE EXPENSES for 2013–2014 *Application fee:* $70. *Comprehensive fee:* $56,382 includes full-time tuition ($42,360), mandatory fees ($710), and room and board ($13,312). Full-time tuition and fees vary according to course load and program. Room and board charges vary according to board plan and housing facility. Part-time tuition and fees vary according to course load and program.

FRESHMAN FINANCIAL AID (Fall 2012, est.) 1,165 applied for aid; of those 57% were deemed to have need. 95% of freshmen with need received aid; of those 100% had need fully met. **Average percent of need met:** 100% (excluding resources awarded to replace EFC). **Average financial aid package:** $37,569 (excluding resources awarded to replace EFC).
UNDERGRADUATE FINANCIAL AID (Fall 2012, est.) 4,123 applied for aid; of those 70% were deemed to have need. 97% of undergraduates with need received aid; of those 100% had need fully met. **Average percent of need met:** 100% (excluding resources awarded to replace EFC). **Average financial aid package:** $38,601 (excluding resources awarded to replace EFC).
GIFT AID (NEED-BASED) Total amount: $95,074,000 (6% federal, 90% institutional, 4% external sources). **Receiving aid:** Freshmen: 37% (582); all full-time undergraduates: 36% (2,588). **Average award:** Freshmen: $35,404; Undergraduates: $34,307. **Scholarships, grants, and awards:** Federal Pell, FSEOG, state, private, college/university gift aid from institutional funds.
GIFT AID (NON-NEED-BASED) Total amount: $3,252,000 (34% federal, 4% institutional, 62% external sources). **Receiving aid:** Freshmen: 16% (250). Undergraduates: 11% (800). **Scholarships, grants, and awards by category:** Special characteristics: 167 awards ($4,169,798 total): children of faculty/staff. **ROTC:** Army, Naval cooperative, Air Force cooperative.
LOANS Student loans: $19,525,000 (47% need-based, 53% non-need-based). 40% of past graduating class borrowed through all loan programs. **Average indebtedness per student:** $25,540. **Average need-based loan:** Freshmen: $3180. Undergraduates: $4555. **Parent loans:** $9,300,000 (100% non-need-based). **Programs:** Federal Direct (Subsidized and Unsubsidized Stafford, PLUS), Perkins, Federal Nursing, alternative loans.
WORK-STUDY Federal work-study: Total amount: $6,600,000; 1,884 jobs averaging $2880.
ATHLETIC AWARDS Total amount: $7,200,000 (25% need-based, 75% non-need-based).
APPLYING FOR FINANCIAL AID Required financial aid forms: FAFSA, CSS Financial Aid PROFILE, business/farm supplement. **Financial aid deadline:** 2/1. **Notification date:** 4/1. Students must reply by 5/1 or within 2 weeks of notification.
CONTACT Ms. Patricia A. McWade, Dean of Student Financial Services, Georgetown University, 37th and O Street, NW, Box 1252, Washington, DC 20057, 202-687-4547. Fax: 202-687-6542. E-mail: mcwadep@georgetown.edu.
Website: http://www.georgetown.edu/.

THE GEORGE WASHINGTON UNIVERSITY
Washington, DC

Tuition & fees: $47,335	Average undergraduate aid package: $39,207

ABOUT THE INSTITUTION Independent, coed. **Awards:** certificates, associate, bachelor's, master's, and doctoral degrees. 81 undergraduate majors. **Total enrollment:** 25,653. Undergraduates: 10,464. Freshmen: 2,387. Federal methodology is used as a basis for awarding need-based institutional aid.
UNDERGRADUATE EXPENSES for 2013–2014 Application fee: $75. **Comprehensive fee:** $58,713 includes full-time tuition ($47,290), mandatory fees ($45), and room and board ($11,378). Full-time tuition and fees vary according to student level. Room and board charges vary according to housing facility. **Part-time tuition:** $1315.25 per credit hour. **Part-time fees:** $1.75 per credit hour. Part-time tuition and fees vary according to course load. **Payment plan:** Guaranteed tuition.
FRESHMAN FINANCIAL AID (Fall 2011) 1,422 applied for aid; of those 78% were deemed to have need. 96% of freshmen with need received aid; of those 58% had need fully met. **Average percent of need met:** 90% (excluding resources awarded to replace EFC). **Average financial aid package:** $38,163 (excluding resources awarded to replace EFC). 19% of all full-time freshmen had no need and received non-need-based gift aid.
UNDERGRADUATE FINANCIAL AID (Fall 2011) 5,399 applied for aid; of those 93% were deemed to have need. 97% of undergraduates with need received aid; of those 58% had need fully met. **Average percent of need met:** 88% (excluding resources awarded to replace EFC). **Average financial aid package:** $39,207 (excluding resources awarded to replace EFC). 16% of all full-time undergraduates had no need and received non-need-based gift aid.

GIFT AID (NEED-BASED) Total amount: $137,072,085 (5% federal, 95% institutional). **Receiving aid:** Freshmen: 46% (1,030); all full-time undergraduates: 47% (4,585). **Average award:** Freshmen: $25,532; Undergraduates: $26,244. **Scholarships, grants, and awards:** Federal Pell, FSEOG, state, college/university gift aid from institutional funds.
GIFT AID (NON-NEED-BASED) Total amount: $19,985,572 (100% institutional). **Receiving aid:** Freshmen: 21% (475). Undergraduates: 13% (1,252). **Average award:** Freshmen: $17,407. Undergraduates: $17,517. **Scholarships, grants, and awards by category:** Academic interests/achievement: general academic interests/achievements. Creative arts/performance: general creative arts/performance. **Tuition waivers:** Full or partial for employees or children of employees. **ROTC:** Army cooperative, Naval, Air Force cooperative.
LOANS Student loans: $38,134,802 (80% need-based, 20% non-need-based). 47% of past graduating class borrowed through all loan programs. **Average indebtedness per student:** $33,398. **Average need-based loan:** Freshmen: $4854. Undergraduates: $5920. **Parent loans:** $21,347,112 (32% need-based, 68% non-need-based). **Programs:** Perkins.
WORK-STUDY Federal work-study: Total amount: $6,414,562; jobs available.
ATHLETIC AWARDS Total amount: $7,046,114 (28% need-based; 72% non-need-based).
APPLYING FOR FINANCIAL AID Required financial aid forms: FAFSA, CSS Financial Aid PROFILE. **Financial aid deadline:** 2/1. **Notification date:** Continuous beginning 3/24. Students must reply by 5/1.
CONTACT Dan Small, Executive Director of Student Financial Assistance, The George Washington University, 2121 I Street, NW, Rice Hall, Suite 301, Washington, DC 21044, 202-994-6620. Fax: 202-994-0906. E-mail: finaid@gwu.edu.
Website: http://www.gwu.edu/.

GEORGIA COLLEGE & STATE UNIVERSITY
Milledgeville, GA

Tuition & fees (GA res): $8618	Average undergraduate aid package: $7648

ABOUT THE INSTITUTION State-supported, coed. **Awards:** certificates, bachelor's, master's, and doctoral degrees. 39 undergraduate majors. **Total enrollment:** 6,444. Undergraduates: 5,568. Freshmen: 1,311. Federal methodology is used as a basis for awarding need-based institutional aid.
UNDERGRADUATE EXPENSES for 2013–2014 Application fee: $40. **Tuition, state resident:** full-time $6634. **Tuition, nonresident:** full-time $24,098. **Required fees:** full-time $1984; $992 per term. Full-time tuition and fees vary according to course load, location, and program. Part-time tuition and fees vary according to course load, location, and program. **College room and board:** $9268; **Room only:** $5268. Room and board charges vary according to board plan, housing facility, and location.
FRESHMAN FINANCIAL AID (Fall 2012, est.) 1,078 applied for aid; of those 51% were deemed to have need. 99% of freshmen with need received aid. **Average percent of need met:** 24% (excluding resources awarded to replace EFC). **Average financial aid package:** $7686 (excluding resources awarded to replace EFC). 1% of all full-time freshmen had no need and received non-need-based gift aid.
UNDERGRADUATE FINANCIAL AID (Fall 2012, est.) 4,869 applied for aid; of those 54% were deemed to have need. 97% of undergraduates with need received aid. **Average percent of need met:** 27% (excluding resources awarded to replace EFC). **Average financial aid package:** $7648 (excluding resources awarded to replace EFC). 1% of all full-time undergraduates had no need and received non-need-based gift aid.
GIFT AID (NEED-BASED) Total amount: $5,358,000 (97% federal, 3% institutional). **Receiving aid:** Freshmen: 19% (213); all full-time undergraduates: 22% (1,107). **Average award:** Freshmen: $4173; Undergraduates: $4163. **Scholarships, grants, and awards:** Federal Pell, FSEOG, state, college/university gift aid from institutional funds.
GIFT AID (NON-NEED-BASED) Total amount: $20,306,000 (94% state, 3% institutional, 3% external sources). **Receiving aid:** Freshmen: 46% (508). Undergraduates: 37% (1,875). **Average award:** Freshmen: $1909. Undergraduates: $1461. **Scholarships, grants, and awards by category:** Academic interests/achievement: biological sciences, business, computer science, education, humanities,

international studies, physical sciences, social sciences. *Creative arts/performance:* art/fine arts, journalism/publications, music. *Special achievements/activities:* general special achievements/activities. *Special characteristics:* adult students, children of faculty/staff, general special characteristics, local/state students, out-of-state students, public servants. *Tuition waivers:* Full or partial for employees or children of employees, senior citizens. *ROTC:* Army cooperative.

LOANS *Student loans:* $31,000,000 (39% need-based, 61% non-need-based). 57% of past graduating class borrowed through all loan programs. *Average indebtedness per student:* $19,852. *Average need-based loan:* Freshmen: $3282. Undergraduates: $3306. *Parent loans:* $3,400,000 (100% non-need-based). *Programs:* Federal Direct (Subsidized and Unsubsidized Stafford, PLUS), Perkins.

WORK-STUDY *Federal work-study:* Total amount: $203,000; jobs available.

ATHLETIC AWARDS Total amount: $648,000 (100% non-need-based).

APPLYING FOR FINANCIAL AID *Required financial aid form:* FAFSA. *Financial aid deadline (priority):* 3/1. *Notification date:* Continuous beginning 3/1. Students must reply within 2 weeks of notification.

CONTACT Ms. Cathy Crawley, Director of Financial Aid, Georgia College & State University, Campus Box 30, Milledgeville, GA 31061, 478-445-5149 or toll-free 800-342-0471 (in-state). *Fax:* 478-445-0729. *E-mail:* cathy.crawley@gcsu.edu. *Website:* http://www.gcsu.edu/.

GEORGIA GWINNETT COLLEGE
Lawrenceville, GA

CONTACT Financial Aid Office, Georgia Gwinnett College, 1000 University Center Lane, Lawrenceville, GA 60043, 678-407-5000 or toll-free 877-704-4422. *Website:* http://www.ggc.edu/.

GEORGIA INSTITUTE OF TECHNOLOGY
Atlanta, GA

Tuition & fees (GA res): $10,098	Average undergraduate aid package: $18,030

ABOUT THE INSTITUTION State-supported, coed. *Awards:* bachelor's, master's, and doctoral degrees. 34 undergraduate majors. *Total enrollment:* 21,557. Undergraduates: 14,527. Freshmen: 3,044. Federal methodology is used as a basis for awarding need-based institutional aid.

UNDERGRADUATE EXPENSES for 2013–2014 *Application fee:* $65. *Tuition, state resident:* full-time $7718; part-time $2293 per term. *Tuition, nonresident:* full-time $27,022; part-time $8017 per term. *Required fees:* full-time $2380; $1190 per term or $1190 per term. Part-time tuition and fees vary according to course load. *College room and board:* $9236; *Room only:* $5574. Room and board charges vary according to board plan and housing facility.

FRESHMAN FINANCIAL AID (Fall 2011) 2,169 applied for aid; of those 57% were deemed to have need. 96% of freshmen with need received aid; of those 34% had need fully met. *Average percent of need met:* 65% (excluding resources awarded to replace EFC). *Average financial aid package:* $19,073 (excluding resources awarded to replace EFC). 8% of all full-time freshmen had no need and received non-need-based gift aid.

UNDERGRADUATE FINANCIAL AID (Fall 2011) 8,452 applied for aid; of those 69% were deemed to have need. 96% of undergraduates with need received aid; of those 22% had need fully met. *Average percent of need met:* 62% (excluding resources awarded to replace EFC). *Average financial aid package:* $18,030 (excluding resources awarded to replace EFC). 6% of all full-time undergraduates had no need and received non-need-based gift aid.

GIFT AID (NEED-BASED) *Total amount:* $43,608,090 (27% federal, 43% state, 26% institutional, 4% external sources). *Receiving aid:* Freshmen: 42% (1,125); all full-time undergraduates: 39% (4,962). *Average award:* Freshmen: $10,437; Undergraduates: $8896. *Scholarships, grants, and awards:* Federal Pell, FSEOG, state, private, college/university gift aid from institutional funds, United Negro College Fund.

GIFT AID (NON-NEED-BASED) *Total amount:* $23,615,260 (80% state, 14% institutional, 6% external sources). *Receiving aid:* Freshmen: 35% (946). Undergraduates: 29% (3,635). *Average award:* Freshmen: $4372. Undergraduates: $4487. *Scholarships, grants, and awards by category: Academic interests/*

achievement: 2,345 awards ($12,097,652 total): architecture, biological sciences, computer science, engineering/technologies, general academic interests/achievements, physical sciences. *Special achievements/activities:* 445 awards ($682,825 total): cheerleading/drum major, general special achievements/activities, leadership. *Special characteristics:* 5,665 awards ($37,070,255 total): local/state students, members of minority groups. *Tuition waivers:* Full or partial for employees or children of employees. *ROTC:* Army, Naval, Air Force.

LOANS *Student loans:* $42,654,246 (82% need-based, 18% non-need-based). 44% of past graduating class borrowed through all loan programs. *Average indebtedness per student:* $26,412. *Average need-based loan:* Freshmen: $3835. Undergraduates: $4785. *Parent loans:* $23,709,201 (77% need-based, 23% non-need-based). *Programs:* Federal Direct (Subsidized and Unsubsidized Stafford, PLUS), Perkins, state, college/university.

WORK-STUDY *Federal work-study:* Total amount: $747,413; 388 jobs averaging $2539.

ATHLETIC AWARDS Total amount: $5,552,813 (47% need-based, 53% non-need-based).

APPLYING FOR FINANCIAL AID *Required financial aid forms:* FAFSA, institution's own form. *Financial aid deadline:* 2/15 (priority: 2/15). *Notification date:* 4/1. Students must reply by 5/1.

CONTACT Ms. Marie Mons, Director of Student Financial Planning and Services, Georgia Institute of Technology, 225 North Avenue, NW, Atlanta, GA 30332-0460, 404-894-4160. *Fax:* 404-894-7412. *E-mail:* marie.mons@finaid.gatech.edu. *Website:* http://www.gatech.edu/.

GEORGIAN COURT UNIVERSITY
Lakewood, NJ

Tuition & fees: $26,740	Average undergraduate aid package: $23,485

ABOUT THE INSTITUTION Independent Roman Catholic, coed, primarily women. *Awards:* certificates, bachelor's, and master's degrees. 30 undergraduate majors. *Total enrollment:* 2,555. Undergraduates: 1,772. Freshmen: 244. Federal methodology is used as a basis for awarding need-based institutional aid.

UNDERGRADUATE EXPENSES for 2013–2014 *Application fee:* $40. *Comprehensive fee:* $39,600 includes full-time tuition ($26,740) and room and board ($12,860). Part-time tuition and fees vary according to location.

FRESHMAN FINANCIAL AID (Fall 2012, est.) 155 applied for aid; of those 95% were deemed to have need. 100% of freshmen with need received aid; of those 22% had need fully met. *Average percent of need met:* 81% (excluding resources awarded to replace EFC). *Average financial aid package:* $26,431 (excluding resources awarded to replace EFC). 7% of all full-time freshmen had no need and received non-need-based gift aid.

UNDERGRADUATE FINANCIAL AID (Fall 2012, est.) 1,130 applied for aid; of those 93% were deemed to have need. 100% of undergraduates with need received aid; of those 26% had need fully met. *Average percent of need met:* 80% (excluding resources awarded to replace EFC). *Average financial aid package:* $23,485 (excluding resources awarded to replace EFC). 8% of all full-time undergraduates had no need and received non-need-based gift aid.

GIFT AID (NEED-BASED) *Total amount:* $16,056,549 (20% federal, 26% state, 54% institutional). *Receiving aid:* Freshmen: 91% (145); all full-time undergraduates: 80% (1,000). *Average award:* Freshmen: $19,642; Undergraduates: $15,107. *Scholarships, grants, and awards:* Federal Pell, FSEOG, state, private, college/university gift aid from institutional funds.

GIFT AID (NON-NEED-BASED) *Total amount:* $1,356,177 (100% institutional). *Receiving aid:* Freshmen: 6% (9). Undergraduates: 4% (54). *Average award:* Freshmen: $11,726. Undergraduates: $9943. *Scholarships, grants, and awards by category: Academic interests/achievement:* biological sciences, business, English, foreign languages, general academic interests/achievements, mathematics, physical sciences. *Creative arts/performance:* art/fine arts, creative writing, music. *Special achievements/activities:* general special achievements/activities. *Special characteristics:* children of faculty/staff, religious affiliation, spouses of current students, veterans. *Tuition waivers:* Full or partial for employees or children of employees.

LOANS *Student loans:* $10,904,438 (77% need-based, 23% non-need-based). 87% of past graduating class borrowed through all loan programs. *Average indebtedness per student:* $36,114. *Average need-based loan:* Freshmen: $4838. Undergrad-

uates: $7133. **Parent loans:** $703,669 (49% need-based, 51% non-need-based). **Programs:** Federal Direct (Subsidized and Unsubsidized Stafford, PLUS), state.
WORK-STUDY *Federal work-study:* Total amount: $187,668; jobs available. *State or other work-study/employment:* Total amount: $12,000 (100% non-need-based). Part-time jobs available.
ATHLETIC AWARDS Total amount: $938,934 (72% need-based, 28% non-need-based).
APPLYING FOR FINANCIAL AID *Required financial aid form:* FAFSA. *Financial aid deadline:* 8/1 (priority: 4/15). *Notification date:* Continuous beginning 2/1. Students must reply within 2 weeks of notification.
CONTACT Judith Schneider, Interim Director of Financial Aid, Georgian Court University, 900 Lakewood Avenue, Lakewood, NJ 08701-2697, 732-987-2258 or toll-free 800-458-8422. *Fax:* 732-987-2023. *E-mail:* financialaid@georgian.edu. *Website:* http://www.georgian.edu/.

GEORGIA REGENTS UNIVERSITY
Augusta, GA

ABOUT THE INSTITUTION State-supported, coed. *Awards:* certificates, associate, bachelor's, master's, and doctoral degrees. 36 undergraduate majors.
GIFT AID (NEED-BASED) *Scholarships, grants, and awards:* Federal Pell, FSEOG, state, private, college/university gift aid from institutional funds, Federal Nursing.
GIFT AID (NON-NEED-BASED) *Scholarships, grants, and awards by category:* Academic interests/achievement: health fields. Special characteristics: religious affiliation.
LOANS *Programs:* Federal Direct (Subsidized and Unsubsidized Stafford, PLUS), Perkins, Federal Nursing, state, college/university.
WORK-STUDY *Federal work-study:* Total amount: $72,000; jobs available.
APPLYING FOR FINANCIAL AID *Required financial aid forms:* FAFSA, institution's own form, state aid form.
CONTACT Beth Welsh, Director of Business Services, Georgia Regents University, 2013 Administration Building, Augusta, GA 30912-7320, 706-721-4901 or toll-free 800-519-3388. *Fax:* 706-721-9407. *E-mail:* osfa@georgiahealth.edu. *Website:* http://www.gru.edu/.

GEORGIA SOUTHERN UNIVERSITY
Statesboro, GA

Tuition & fees (GA res): $6724	Average undergraduate aid package: $8598

ABOUT THE INSTITUTION State-supported, coed. *Awards:* certificates, bachelor's, master's, and doctoral degrees. 80 undergraduate majors. *Total enrollment:* 20,574. Undergraduates: 17,993. Freshmen: 3,604. Federal methodology is used as a basis for awarding need-based institutional aid.
UNDERGRADUATE EXPENSES for 2013–2014 *Application fee:* $30. *Tuition, state resident:* full-time $4852; part-time $162 per credit hour. *Tuition, nonresident:* full-time $17,128; part-time $571 per credit hour. *Required fees:* full-time $1872; $936 per term. Full-time tuition and fees vary according to degree level, location, and program. Part-time tuition and fees vary according to course load, degree level, location, and program. *College room and board:* $9290; *Room only:* $5582. Room and board charges vary according to board plan and housing facility.
FRESHMAN FINANCIAL AID (Fall 2011) 3,295 applied for aid; of those 70% were deemed to have need. 98% of freshmen with need received aid; of those 11% had need fully met. *Average percent of need met:* 53% (excluding resources awarded to replace EFC). *Average financial aid package:* $8548 (excluding resources awarded to replace EFC). 2% of all full-time freshmen had no need and received non-need-based gift aid.
UNDERGRADUATE FINANCIAL AID (Fall 2011) 13,935 applied for aid; of those 75% were deemed to have need. 98% of undergraduates with need received aid; of those 8% had need fully met. *Average percent of need met:* 49% (excluding resources awarded to replace EFC). *Average financial aid package:* $8598 (excluding resources awarded to replace EFC). 2% of all full-time undergraduates had no need and received non-need-based gift aid.

GIFT AID (NEED-BASED) *Total amount:* $49,708,834 (57% federal, 39% state, 2% institutional, 2% external sources). *Receiving aid:* Freshmen: 57% (2,016); all full-time undergraduates: 54% (8,476). *Average award:* Freshmen: $6410; Undergraduates: $5876. *Scholarships, grants, and awards:* Federal Pell, FSEOG, state, private, college/university gift aid from institutional funds, Hope Scholarships, TEACH Grants.
GIFT AID (NON-NEED-BASED) *Total amount:* $10,551,387 (90% state, 6% institutional, 4% external sources). *Receiving aid:* Freshmen: 1% (47). Undergraduates: 1% (120). *Average award:* Freshmen: $2095. Undergraduates: $1867. *Scholarships, grants, and awards by category:* Academic interests/achievement: 787 awards ($1,252,213 total): biological sciences, business, communication, computer science, education, engineering/technologies, English, foreign languages, general academic interests/achievements, health fields, humanities, international studies, mathematics, military science, social sciences. Creative arts/performance: 59 awards ($61,300 total): art/fine arts, cinema/film/broadcasting, general creative arts/performance, music, theater/drama. Special achievements/activities: 165 awards ($189,300 total): cheerleading/drum major, community service, junior miss, leadership, memberships, religious involvement. Special characteristics: 28 awards ($118,162 total): adult students, children and siblings of alumni, children of public servants, first-generation college students, handicapped students, married students, members of minority groups, religious affiliation. *Tuition waivers:* Full or partial for employees or children of employees, senior citizens. *ROTC:* Army.
LOANS *Student loans:* $76,639,150 (81% need-based, 19% non-need-based). 68% of past graduating class borrowed through all loan programs. *Average indebtedness per student:* $21,562. *Average need-based loan:* Freshmen: $3428. Undergraduates: $4296. *Parent loans:* $13,695,768 (74% need-based, 26% non-need-based). *Programs:* Federal Direct (Subsidized and Unsubsidized Stafford, PLUS), Perkins, state, alternative loans.
WORK-STUDY *Federal work-study:* Total amount: $399,484; 216 jobs averaging $1849.
ATHLETIC AWARDS Total amount: $2,980,558 (53% need-based, 47% non-need-based).
APPLYING FOR FINANCIAL AID *Required financial aid form:* FAFSA. *Financial aid deadline (priority):* 4/20. *Notification date:* Continuous beginning 4/20.
CONTACT Mrs. Elise Boyett, Associate Director of Financial Aid, Georgia Southern University, PO Box 8065, Statesboro, GA 30460-8065, 912-478-5413. *Fax:* 912-478-0573. *E-mail:* eboyett@georgiasouthern.edu. *Website:* http://www.georgiasouthern.edu/.

GEORGIA SOUTHWESTERN STATE UNIVERSITY
Americus, GA

Tuition & fees (GA res): $5780	Average undergraduate aid package: $8799

ABOUT THE INSTITUTION State-supported, coed. *Awards:* certificates, bachelor's, and master's degrees. 25 undergraduate majors. *Total enrollment:* 2,973. Undergraduates: 2,749. Freshmen: 400. Federal methodology is used as a basis for awarding need-based institutional aid.
UNDERGRADUATE EXPENSES for 2013–2014 *Application fee:* $25. *Tuition, state resident:* full-time $4512. *Tuition, nonresident:* full-time $16,416. *Required fees:* full-time $1268. Full-time tuition and fees vary according to course load. Part-time tuition and fees vary according to course load. *College room and board:* $7378; *Room only:* $4620. Room and board charges vary according to board plan and housing facility.
FRESHMAN FINANCIAL AID (Fall 2012, est.) 346 applied for aid; of those 79% were deemed to have need. 99% of freshmen with need received aid; of those 13% had need fully met. *Average percent of need met:* 62% (excluding resources awarded to replace EFC). *Average financial aid package:* $9003 (excluding resources awarded to replace EFC). 7% of all full-time freshmen had no need and received non-need-based gift aid.
UNDERGRADUATE FINANCIAL AID (Fall 2012, est.) 1,725 applied for aid; of those 86% were deemed to have need. 99% of undergraduates with need received aid; of those 10% had need fully met. *Average percent of need met:* 59% (excluding resources awarded to replace EFC). *Average financial aid package:* $8799

(excluding resources awarded to replace EFC). 4% of all full-time undergraduates had no need and received non-need-based gift aid.

GIFT AID (NEED-BASED) Total amount: $5,888,645 (100% federal). **Receiving aid:** Freshmen: 50% (187); all full-time undergraduates: 52% (1,019). **Average award:** Freshmen: $4435; Undergraduates: $4538. **Scholarships, grants, and awards:** Federal Pell, FSEOG, state, private, college/university gift aid from institutional funds.

GIFT AID (NON-NEED-BASED) Total amount: $3,239,017 (80% state, 14% institutional, 6% external sources). **Receiving aid:** Freshmen: 51% (189). Undergraduates: 30% (592). **Average award:** Freshmen: $1804. Undergraduates: $1883. **Scholarships, grants, and awards by category:** Academic interests/achievement: general academic interests/achievements. Creative arts/performance: art/fine arts, music. Special achievements/activities: leadership.

LOANS Student loans: $15,212,540 (45% need-based, 55% non-need-based). 61% of past graduating class borrowed through all loan programs. Average indebtedness per student: $26,294. **Average need-based loan:** Freshmen: $3275. Undergraduates: $4182. **Parent loans:** $286,023 (100% non-need-based). **Programs:** Federal Direct (Subsidized and Unsubsidized Stafford, PLUS), Perkins, state, college/university.

WORK-STUDY Federal work-study: Total amount: $149,007; 70 jobs averaging $2129. **State or other work-study/employment:** Part-time jobs available.

ATHLETIC AWARDS Total amount: $528,317 (100% non-need-based).

APPLYING FOR FINANCIAL AID Required financial aid forms: FAFSA, institution's own form, state aid form. **Financial aid deadline:** 6/15 (priority: 4/15). **Notification date:** Continuous beginning 5/1. Students must reply within 8 weeks of notification.

CONTACT Angela Bryant, Director of Financial Aid, Georgia Southwestern State University, 800 Georgia Southwestern State University Drive, Americus, GA 31709-4693, 229-928-1378 or toll-free 800-338-0082. Fax: 229-931-2061. Website: http://www.gsw.edu/.

GEORGIA STATE UNIVERSITY
Atlanta, GA

Tuition & fees (GA res): $9664	Average undergraduate aid package: $9815

ABOUT THE INSTITUTION State-supported, coed. **Awards:** certificates, bachelor's, master's, and doctoral degrees. 50 undergraduate majors. **Total enrollment:** 32,092. Undergraduates: 24,665. Freshmen: 3,201. Federal methodology is used as a basis for awarding need-based institutional aid.

UNDERGRADUATE EXPENSES for 2013–2014 Application fee: $60. **Tuition, state resident:** full-time $7536; part-time $251.20 per credit hour. **Tuition, nonresident:** full-time $25,746; part-time $858.20 per credit hour. **Required fees:** full-time $2128; $1064 per term. Part-time tuition and fees vary according to course load. **College room and board:** $11,546; **Room only:** $7956. Room and board charges vary according to housing facility.

FRESHMAN FINANCIAL AID (Fall 2011) 2,552 applied for aid; of those 83% were deemed to have need. 98% of freshmen with need received aid; of those 4% had need fully met. **Average percent of need met:** 70% (excluding resources awarded to replace EFC). **Average financial aid package:** $11,196 (excluding resources awarded to replace EFC). 13% of all full-time freshmen had no need and received non-need-based gift aid.

UNDERGRADUATE FINANCIAL AID (Fall 2011) 15,048 applied for aid; of those 88% were deemed to have need. 98% of undergraduates with need received aid; of those 4% had need fully met. **Average percent of need met:** 61% (excluding resources awarded to replace EFC). **Average financial aid package:** $9815 (excluding resources awarded to replace EFC). 4% of all full-time undergraduates had no need and received non-need-based gift aid.

GIFT AID (NEED-BASED) Total amount: $50,863,443 (99% federal, 1% institutional). **Receiving aid:** Freshmen: 56% (1,509); all full-time undergraduates: 55% (9,646). **Average award:** Freshmen: $4779; Undergraduates: $4413. **Scholarships, grants, and awards:** Federal Pell, FSEOG, state, private, college/university gift aid from institutional funds, United Negro College Fund.

GIFT AID (NON-NEED-BASED) Total amount: $51,056,464 (91% state, 6% institutional, 3% external sources). **Receiving aid:** Freshmen: 63% (1,702). Undergraduates: 38% (6,567). **Average award:** Freshmen: $757. Undergraduates: $1129. **Tuition waivers:** Full or partial for employees or children of employees, senior citizens. **ROTC:** Army, Naval cooperative, Air Force cooperative.

LOANS Student loans: $114,446,410 (47% need-based, 53% non-need-based). 70% of past graduating class borrowed through all loan programs. Average indebtedness per student: $21,817. **Average need-based loan:** Freshmen: $3405. Undergraduates: $4317. **Parent loans:** $10,295,400 (100% non-need-based). **Programs:** Federal Direct (Subsidized and Unsubsidized Stafford, PLUS), Perkins, Federal Nursing, state.

WORK-STUDY Federal work-study: Total amount: $710,777; jobs available. **State or other work-study/employment:** Total amount: $485,552 (100% need-based). Part-time jobs available.

ATHLETIC AWARDS Total amount: $5,842,452 (100% non-need-based).

APPLYING FOR FINANCIAL AID Required financial aid form: FAFSA. **Financial aid deadline:** 4/1 (priority: 4/1). **Notification date:** Continuous beginning 3/1. Students must reply by 4/1 or within 3 weeks of notification.

CONTACT Louis Scott, Office of Financial Aid, Georgia State University, PO Box 4040, Atlanta, GA 30302, 404-413-2600. Fax: 404-413-2102. E-mail: onestopshop@gsu.edu. Website: http://www.gsu.edu/.

GETTYSBURG COLLEGE
Gettysburg, PA

Tuition & fees: $44,210	Average undergraduate aid package: $33,215

ABOUT THE INSTITUTION Independent Evangelical Lutheran Church in America, coed. **Awards:** bachelor's degrees. 82 undergraduate majors. **Total enrollment:** 2,597. Undergraduates: 2,597. Freshmen: 769. Both federal and institutional methodology are used as a basis for awarding need-based institutional aid.

UNDERGRADUATE EXPENSES for 2013–2014 Application fee: $60. **Comprehensive fee:** $54,770 includes full-time tuition ($44,210) and room and board ($10,560). Room and board charges vary according to board plan and housing facility.

FRESHMAN FINANCIAL AID (Fall 2012, est.) 541 applied for aid; of those 81% were deemed to have need. 97% of freshmen with need received aid; of those 92% had need fully met. **Average percent of need met:** 94% (excluding resources awarded to replace EFC). **Average financial aid package:** $35,056 (excluding resources awarded to replace EFC). 13% of all full-time freshmen had no need and received non-need-based gift aid.

UNDERGRADUATE FINANCIAL AID (Fall 2012, est.) 1,804 applied for aid; of those 87% were deemed to have need. 97% of undergraduates with need received aid; of those 94% had need fully met. **Average percent of need met:** 95% (excluding resources awarded to replace EFC). **Average financial aid package:** $33,215 (excluding resources awarded to replace EFC). 13% of all full-time undergraduates had no need and received non-need-based gift aid.

GIFT AID (NEED-BASED) Total amount: $45,324,184 (3% federal, 2% state, 93% institutional, 2% external sources). **Receiving aid:** Freshmen: 54% (415); all full-time undergraduates: 53% (1,481). **Average award:** Freshmen: $29,881; Undergraduates: $27,550. **Scholarships, grants, and awards:** Federal Pell, FSEOG, state, private, college/university gift aid from institutional funds, Academic Competitiveness Grants, National SMART Grants.

GIFT AID (NON-NEED-BASED) Total amount: $6,052,544 (7% federal, 86% institutional, 7% external sources). **Receiving aid:** Freshmen: 31% (238). Undergraduates: 28% (781). **Average award:** Freshmen: $13,222. Undergraduates: $13,444. **Scholarships, grants, and awards by category:** Academic interests/achievement: general academic interests/achievements. Creative arts/performance: music. **ROTC:** Army cooperative.

LOANS Student loans: $10,787,390 (58% need-based, 42% non-need-based). 58% of past graduating class borrowed through all loan programs. Average indebtedness per student: $25,530. **Average need-based loan:** Freshmen: $4238. Undergraduates: $5392. **Parent loans:** $6,470,858 (100% non-need-based). **Programs:** Federal Direct (Subsidized and Unsubsidized Stafford, PLUS), Perkins, college/university.

WORK-STUDY Federal work-study: Total amount: $368,195; 549 jobs averaging $670. **State or other work-study/employment:** Total amount: $1,249,319 (100% non-need-based). 804 part-time jobs averaging $1553.

APPLYING FOR FINANCIAL AID Required financial aid forms: FAFSA, CSS Financial Aid PROFILE, business/farm supplement, federal income tax form(s), verification worksheet. **Financial aid deadline:** 2/15. **Notification date:** 3/27. Students must reply by 5/1.

CONTACT Christina Gormley, Director of Financial Aid, Gettysburg College, 300 North Washington Street, Gettysburg, PA 17325, 717-337-6620 or toll-free 800-431-0803. *Fax:* 717-337-8555. *E-mail:* finaid@gettysburg.edu.
Website: http://www.gettysburg.edu/.

GLOBE STATE COLLEGE

GLENVILLE STATE COLLEGE
Glenville, WV

Tuition & fees (WV res): $5860	Average undergraduate aid package: $13,117

ABOUT THE INSTITUTION State-supported, coed. *Awards:* associate and bachelor's degrees. 32 undergraduate majors. *Total enrollment:* 1,857. Undergraduates: 1,857. Freshmen: 355. Federal methodology is used as a basis for awarding need-based institutional aid.

UNDERGRADUATE EXPENSES for 2013–2014 *Application fee:* $20. *Tuition, state resident:* full-time $5860; part-time $244 per credit hour. *Tuition, nonresident:* full-time $13,824; part-time $576 per credit hour. *Required fees:* $244 per credit hour. Full-time tuition and fees vary according to course load. *College room and board:* $8400; *Room only:* $4830. Room and board charges vary according to board plan and housing facility.

FRESHMAN FINANCIAL AID (Fall 2012, est.) 327 applied for aid; of those 90% were deemed to have need. 99% of freshmen with need received aid; of those 11% had need fully met. *Average percent of need met:* 70% (excluding resources awarded to replace EFC). *Average financial aid package:* $12,781 (excluding resources awarded to replace EFC). 5% of all full-time freshmen had no need and received non-need-based gift aid.

UNDERGRADUATE FINANCIAL AID (Fall 2012, est.) 1,117 applied for aid; of those 90% were deemed to have need. 99% of undergraduates with need received aid; of those 19% had need fully met. *Average percent of need met:* 74% (excluding resources awarded to replace EFC). *Average financial aid package:* $13,117 (excluding resources awarded to replace EFC). 5% of all full-time undergraduates had no need and received non-need-based gift aid.

GIFT AID (NEED-BASED) *Total amount:* $4,823,998 (70% federal, 30% state). *Receiving aid:* Freshmen: 73% (247); all full-time undergraduates: 68% (837). *Average award:* Freshmen: $6228; Undergraduates: $5632. *Scholarships, grants, and awards:* Federal Pell, FSEOG, state, private, college/university gift aid from institutional funds.

GIFT AID (NON-NEED-BASED) *Total amount:* $1,681,816 (53% state, 29% institutional, 18% external sources). *Receiving aid:* Freshmen: 55% (187). Undergraduates: 46% (566). *Average award:* Freshmen: $2266. Undergraduates: $2349. *Scholarships, grants, and awards by category: Academic interests/achievement:* 221 awards ($283,743 total): biological sciences, business, education, English, general academic interests/achievements, mathematics, social sciences. *Creative arts/performance:* 32 awards ($38,444 total): journalism/publications, music. *Special achievements/activities:* 6 awards ($2000 total): cheerleading/drum major. *Special characteristics:* 160 awards ($313,446 total): children of faculty/staff, first-generation college students, out-of-state students, veterans, veterans' children. *Tuition waivers:* Full or partial for employees or children of employees, senior citizens. *ROTC:* Army.

LOANS *Student loans:* $6,894,828 (45% need-based, 55% non-need-based). 84% of past graduating class borrowed through all loan programs. *Average indebtedness per student:* $30,299. *Average need-based loan:* Freshmen: $3231. Undergraduates: $3928. *Parent loans:* $440,693 (100% non-need-based). *Programs:* Federal Direct (Subsidized and Unsubsidized Stafford, PLUS), private loans.

WORK-STUDY *Federal work-study:* Total amount: $137,056; 131 jobs averaging $1046. *State or other work-study/employment:* Total amount: $617,486 (100% non-need-based). 308 part-time jobs averaging $2004.

ATHLETIC AWARDS Total amount: $1,355,584 (100% non-need-based).

APPLYING FOR FINANCIAL AID *Required financial aid form:* FAFSA. *Financial aid deadline (priority):* 2/1. *Notification date:* Continuous beginning 3/1. Students must reply within 3 weeks of notification.

CONTACT Ms. Karen Lay, Director of Financial Aid, Glenville State College, 200 High Street, Glenville, WV 26351-1200, 304-462-4103 Ext. 5 or toll-free 800-924-2010. *Fax:* 304-462-4407. *E-mail:* karen.lay@glenville.edu.
Website: http://www.glenville.edu/.

GLOBE INSTITUTE OF TECHNOLOGY
New York, NY

CONTACT Office of Admissions, Globe Institute of Technology, 291 Broadway, 2nd Floor, New York, NY 10007, 212-349-4330 or toll-free 888-51-GLOBE (in-state), 800-51-GLOBE (out-of-state). *Fax:* 212-227-5920. *E-mail:* admission@globe.edu.
Website: http://www.globe.edu/.

GLOBE UNIVERSITY–APPLETON
Grand Chute, WI

Tuition & fees: $16,848	Average undergraduate aid package: N/A

ABOUT THE INSTITUTION Proprietary, coed. *Awards:* diplomas, associate, and bachelor's degrees. 11 undergraduate majors. *Total enrollment:* 47. Undergraduates: 47. Freshmen: 24. Both federal and institutional methodology are used as a basis for awarding need-based institutional aid.

UNDERGRADUATE EXPENSES for 2013–2014 *Application fee:* $50. *Tuition:* full-time $15,300; part-time $460 per credit. *Required fees:* full-time $1548; $43 per credit. Full-time tuition and fees vary according to course load, degree level, location, and program. Part-time tuition and fees vary according to course load, degree level, location, and program.

GIFT AID (NEED-BASED) *Scholarships, grants, and awards:* Federal Pell, FSEOG, private, college/university gift aid from institutional funds.

GIFT AID (NON-NEED-BASED) *Scholarships, grants, and awards by category: Academic interests/achievement:* business, computer science, engineering/technologies, health fields. *Special achievements/activities:* community service. *Special characteristics:* children of faculty/staff, veterans, veterans' children. *Tuition waivers:* Full or partial for employees or children of employees.

LOANS *Programs:* Federal Direct (Subsidized and Unsubsidized Stafford, PLUS), college/university, alternative loans.

APPLYING FOR FINANCIAL AID *Required financial aid forms:* FAFSA, institution's own form. *Financial aid deadline:* Continuous. *Notification date:* Continuous beginning 1/2. Students must reply within 2 weeks of notification.

CONTACT Office of Financial Aid, Globe University–Appleton, 5045 West Grande Market Drive, Grand Chute, MN 54913, 920-384-1100. *Fax:* 920-364-1101.
Website: http://www.globeuniversity.edu/.

GLOBE UNIVERSITY–EAU CLAIRE
Eau Claire, WI

Tuition & fees: $16,848	Average undergraduate aid package: N/A

ABOUT THE INSTITUTION Proprietary, coed. *Awards:* diplomas, associate, and bachelor's degrees. 12 undergraduate majors. *Total enrollment:* 719. Undergraduates: 719. Freshmen: 99. Both federal and institutional methodology are used as a basis for awarding need-based institutional aid.

UNDERGRADUATE EXPENSES for 2013–2014 *Application fee:* $50. *Tuition:* full-time $15,300; part-time $460 per credit. *Required fees:* full-time $1548; $43 per credit. Full-time tuition and fees vary according to course load, degree level, location, and program. Part-time tuition and fees vary according to course load, degree level, location, and program.

GIFT AID (NEED-BASED) *Scholarships, grants, and awards:* Federal Pell, FSEOG, private, college/university gift aid from institutional funds.

GIFT AID (NON-NEED-BASED) *Scholarships, grants, and awards by category: Academic interests/achievement:* business, computer science, engineering/technologies, health fields. *Special achievements/activities:* community service. *Special characteristics:* children of faculty/staff, veterans, veterans' children. *Tuition waivers:* Full or partial for employees or children of employees.

LOANS *Programs:* Federal Direct (Subsidized and Unsubsidized Stafford, PLUS), college/university, alternative loans.

APPLYING FOR FINANCIAL AID *Required financial aid forms:* FAFSA, institution's own form. *Financial aid deadline:* Continuous. *Notification date:* Continuous beginning 1/2. Students must reply within 2 weeks of notification.

CONTACT Office of Financial Aid, Globe University–Eau Claire, 4955 Bullis Farm Road, Eau Claire, WI 54701-5168, 715-855-6600 or toll-free 877-303-6060 (in-state), 377-303-6060 (out-of-state). *Fax:* 715-855-6601.
Website: http://www.globeuniversity.edu/.

GLOBE UNIVERSITY–GREEN BAY
Bellevue, WI

Tuition & fees: $16,848	Average undergraduate aid package: N/A

ABOUT THE INSTITUTION Proprietary, coed. *Awards:* diplomas, associate, and bachelor's degrees. 11 undergraduate majors. *Total enrollment:* 215. Undergraduates: 215. Freshmen: 91. Both federal and institutional methodology are used as a basis for awarding need-based institutional aid.
UNDERGRADUATE EXPENSES for 2013–2014 *Application fee:* $50. *Tuition:* full-time $15,300; part-time $460 per credit. Full-time tuition and fees vary according to course load, degree level, location, and program. Part-time tuition and fees vary according to course load, degree level, location, and program.
GIFT AID (NEED-BASED) *Scholarships, grants, and awards:* Federal Pell, FSEOG, private, college/university gift aid from institutional funds.
GIFT AID (NON-NEED-BASED) *Scholarships, grants, and awards by category:* Academic interests/achievement: business, computer science, engineering/technologies, health fields. *Special achievements/activities:* community service. *Special characteristics:* children of faculty/staff, veterans, veterans' children. *Tuition waivers:* Full or partial for employees or children of employees.
LOANS *Programs:* Federal Direct (Subsidized and Unsubsidized Stafford, PLUS), college/university, alternative loans.
APPLYING FOR FINANCIAL AID *Required financial aid forms:* FAFSA, institution's own form. *Financial aid deadline:* Continuous. *Notification date:* Continuous beginning 1/2. Students must reply within 2 weeks of notification.
CONTACT Office of Financial Aid, Globe University–Green Bay, 2620 Development Drive, Bellevue, WI 54311, 920-264-1600. *Fax:* 920-264-1601.
Website: http://www.globeuniversity.edu/.

GLOBE UNIVERSITY–LA CROSSE
Onalaska, WI

Tuition & fees: $16,848	Average undergraduate aid package: N/A

ABOUT THE INSTITUTION Proprietary, coed. *Awards:* diplomas, associate, and bachelor's degrees. 12 undergraduate majors. *Total enrollment:* 534. Undergraduates: 534. Freshmen: 123. Both federal and institutional methodology are used as a basis for awarding need-based institutional aid.
UNDERGRADUATE EXPENSES for 2013–2014 *Application fee:* $50. *Tuition:* full-time $15,300; part-time $460 per credit. *Required fees:* full-time $1548; $43 per credit. Full-time tuition and fees vary according to course load, degree level, location, and program. Part-time tuition and fees vary according to course load, degree level, location, and program.
GIFT AID (NEED-BASED) *Scholarships, grants, and awards:* Federal Pell, FSEOG, private, college/university gift aid from institutional funds.
GIFT AID (NON-NEED-BASED) *Scholarships, grants, and awards by category:* Academic interests/achievement: business, computer science, engineering/technologies, health fields. *Special achievements/activities:* community service. *Special characteristics:* children of faculty/staff, veterans, veterans' children. *Tuition waivers:* Full or partial for employees or children of employees.
LOANS *Programs:* Federal Direct (Subsidized and Unsubsidized Stafford, PLUS), college/university, alternative loans.
APPLYING FOR FINANCIAL AID *Required financial aid forms:* FAFSA, institution's own form. *Financial aid deadline:* Continuous. *Notification date:* Continuous beginning 1/2. Students must reply within 2 weeks of notification.
CONTACT Office of Financial Aid, Globe University–La Crosse, 2651 Midwest Drive, Onalaska, WI 54650, 608-779-2600. *Fax:* 608-779-2601.
Website: http://www.globeuniversity.edu/.

GLOBE UNIVERSITY–MADISON EAST
Madison, WI

Tuition & fees: $16,848	Average undergraduate aid package: N/A

ABOUT THE INSTITUTION Proprietary, coed. *Awards:* diplomas, associate, and bachelor's degrees. 14 undergraduate majors. *Total enrollment:* 290. Undergraduates: 290. Freshmen: 81. Both federal and institutional methodology are used as a basis for awarding need-based institutional aid.
UNDERGRADUATE EXPENSES for 2013–2014 *Application fee:* $50. *Tuition:* full-time $15,300; part-time $460 per credit. *Required fees:* full-time $1548; $43 per credit. Full-time tuition and fees vary according to course load, degree level, location, and program. Part-time tuition and fees vary according to course load, degree level, location, and program.
GIFT AID (NEED-BASED) *Scholarships, grants, and awards:* Federal Pell, FSEOG, private, college/university gift aid from institutional funds.
GIFT AID (NON-NEED-BASED) *Scholarships, grants, and awards by category:* Academic interests/achievement: business, computer science, engineering/technologies, health fields. *Special achievements/activities:* community service. *Special characteristics:* children of faculty/staff, veterans, veterans' children. *Tuition waivers:* Full or partial for employees or children of employees.
LOANS *Programs:* Federal Direct (Subsidized and Unsubsidized Stafford, PLUS), college/university, alternative loans.
APPLYING FOR FINANCIAL AID *Required financial aid forms:* FAFSA, institution's own form. *Financial aid deadline:* Continuous. *Notification date:* Continuous beginning 1/2. Students must reply within 2 weeks of notification.
CONTACT Office of Financial Aid, Globe University–Madison East, 4901 Eastpark Boulevard, Madison, WI 53718, 608-216-9400. *Fax:* 608-216-9401.
Website: http://www.globeuniversity.edu/.

GLOBE UNIVERSITY–MADISON WEST
Middleton, WI

Tuition & fees: $16,848	Average undergraduate aid package: N/A

ABOUT THE INSTITUTION Proprietary, coed. *Awards:* diplomas, associate, and bachelor's degrees. 14 undergraduate majors. *Total enrollment:* 338. Undergraduates: 338. Freshmen: 86. Both federal and institutional methodology are used as a basis for awarding need-based institutional aid.
UNDERGRADUATE EXPENSES for 2013–2014 *Application fee:* $50. *Tuition:* full-time $15,300; part-time $460 per credit. Full-time tuition and fees vary according to course load, degree level, location, and program. Part-time tuition and fees vary according to course load, degree level, location, and program.
GIFT AID (NEED-BASED) *Scholarships, grants, and awards:* Federal Pell, FSEOG, private, college/university gift aid from institutional funds.
GIFT AID (NON-NEED-BASED) *Scholarships, grants, and awards by category:* Academic interests/achievement: business, computer science, engineering/technologies, health fields. *Special achievements/activities:* community service. *Special characteristics:* children of faculty/staff, veterans, veterans' children. *Tuition waivers:* Full or partial for employees or children of employees.
LOANS *Programs:* Federal Direct (Subsidized and Unsubsidized Stafford, PLUS), college/university, alternative loans.
APPLYING FOR FINANCIAL AID *Required financial aid forms:* FAFSA, institution's own form. *Financial aid deadline:* Continuous. *Notification date:* Continuous beginning 1/2. Students must reply within 2 weeks of notification.
CONTACT Office of Financial Aid, Globe University–Madison West, 1345 Deming Way, Middleton, WI 53562, 608-830-6900. *Fax:* 608-830-6901.
Website: http://www.globeuniversity.edu/.

GLOBE UNIVERSITY–MINNEAPOLIS
Minneapolis, MN

Tuition & fees: $16,848	Average undergraduate aid package: N/A

ABOUT THE INSTITUTION Proprietary, coed. *Awards:* diplomas, associate, bachelor's, master's, and doctoral degrees. 8 undergraduate majors. *Total enrollment:* 247. Undergraduates: 188. Freshmen: 27. Both federal and institutional methodology are used as a basis for awarding need-based institutional aid.

UNDERGRADUATE EXPENSES for 2013–2014 *Application fee:* $50. *Tuition:* full-time $15,300; part-time $460 per credit. *Required fees:* full-time $1548; $43 per credit. Full-time tuition and fees vary according to course load, degree level, location, and program. Part-time tuition and fees vary according to course load, degree level, location, and program.

GIFT AID (NEED-BASED) *Scholarships, grants, and awards:* Federal Pell, FSEOG, state, private, college/university gift aid from institutional funds.

GIFT AID (NON-NEED-BASED) *Scholarships, grants, and awards by category:* Academic interests/achievement: business, computer science, engineering/technologies, health fields. *Special achievements/activities:* community service. *Special characteristics:* children of faculty/staff, veterans, veterans' children. *Tuition waivers:* Full or partial for employees or children of employees.

LOANS *Programs:* Federal Direct (Subsidized and Unsubsidized Stafford, PLUS), state, college/university, alternative loans.

APPLYING FOR FINANCIAL AID *Required financial aid forms:* FAFSA, institution's own form, state aid form. *Financial aid deadline:* Continuous. *Notification date:* Continuous beginning 1/2. Students must reply within 2 weeks of notification.

CONTACT Office of Financial Aid, Globe University–Minneapolis, 80 South 8th Street, Suite 51, Minneapolis, MN 55402, 612-455-3000. *Fax:* 612-455-3001. *Website:* http://www.globeuniversity.edu/.

GLOBE UNIVERSITY–SIOUX FALLS
Sioux Falls, SD

Tuition & fees: $16,848	Average undergraduate aid package: N/A

ABOUT THE INSTITUTION Proprietary, coed. *Awards:* diplomas, associate, and bachelor's degrees. 10 undergraduate majors. *Total enrollment:* 368. Undergraduates: 368. Freshmen: 65. Both federal and institutional methodology are used as a basis for awarding need-based institutional aid.

UNDERGRADUATE EXPENSES for 2013–2014 *Application fee:* $50. *Tuition:* full-time $15,300; part-time $460 per credit. *Required fees:* full-time $1548; $43 per credit. Full-time tuition and fees vary according to course level, course load, degree level, location, and program. Part-time tuition and fees vary according to course level, course load, degree level, location, and program.

GIFT AID (NEED-BASED) *Scholarships, grants, and awards:* Federal Pell, FSEOG, private, college/university gift aid from institutional funds.

GIFT AID (NON-NEED-BASED) *Scholarships, grants, and awards by category:* Academic interests/achievement: business, computer science, engineering/technologies, health fields. *Special achievements/activities:* community service. *Special characteristics:* children of faculty/staff, veterans, veterans' children. *Tuition waivers:* Full or partial for employees or children of employees.

LOANS *Programs:* Federal Direct (Subsidized and Unsubsidized Stafford, PLUS), college/university, alternative loans.

APPLYING FOR FINANCIAL AID *Required financial aid forms:* FAFSA, institution's own form. *Financial aid deadline:* Continuous. *Notification date:* Continuous beginning 1/2. Students must reply within 2 weeks of notification.

CONTACT Office of Financial Aid, Globe University–Sioux Falls, 5101 South Broadband Lane, Sioux Falls, SD, 57108-2208, 605-977-0705 or toll-free 866-437-0705. *Fax:* 605-977-0784. *Website:* http://www.globeuniversity.edu/.

GLOBE UNIVERSITY–WAUSAU
Rothschild, WI

Tuition & fees: $16,848	Average undergraduate aid package: N/A

ABOUT THE INSTITUTION Proprietary, coed. *Awards:* diplomas, associate, and bachelor's degrees. 12 undergraduate majors. *Total enrollment:* 365. Undergraduates: 365. Freshmen: 114. Both federal and institutional methodology are used as a basis for awarding need-based institutional aid.

UNDERGRADUATE EXPENSES for 2013–2014 *Application fee:* $50. *Tuition:* full-time $15,300; part-time $460 per credit. *Required fees:* full-time $1548; $43 per credit. Full-time tuition and fees vary according to course load, degree level, location, and program. Part-time tuition and fees vary according to course load, degree level, location, and program.

GIFT AID (NEED-BASED) *Scholarships, grants, and awards:* Federal Pell, FSEOG, private, college/university gift aid from institutional funds.

GIFT AID (NON-NEED-BASED) *Scholarships, grants, and awards by category:* Academic interests/achievement: business, computer science, engineering/technologies, health fields. *Special achievements/activities:* community service. *Special characteristics:* children of faculty/staff, veterans, veterans' children. *Tuition waivers:* Full or partial for employees or children of employees.

LOANS *Programs:* Federal Direct (Subsidized and Unsubsidized Stafford, PLUS), college/university, alternative loans.

APPLYING FOR FINANCIAL AID *Required financial aid forms:* FAFSA, institution's own form. *Financial aid deadline:* Continuous. *Notification date:* Continuous beginning 1/2. Students must reply within 2 weeks of notification.

CONTACT Office of Financial Aid, Globe University–Wausau, 1480 Country Road XX, Rothschild, WI 54474, 715-301-1300. *Fax:* 715-301-1301. *Website:* http://www.globeuniversity.edu/.

GLOBE UNIVERSITY–WOODBURY
Woodbury, MN

Tuition & fees: $16,848	Average undergraduate aid package: N/A

ABOUT THE INSTITUTION Proprietary, coed. *Awards:* diplomas, associate, bachelor's, master's, and doctoral degrees. 18 undergraduate majors. *Total enrollment:* 1,542. Undergraduates: 1,499. Freshmen: 171. Both federal and institutional methodology are used as a basis for awarding need-based institutional aid.

UNDERGRADUATE EXPENSES for 2013–2014 *Application fee:* $50. *Tuition:* full-time $15,300; part-time $460 per credit. *Required fees:* full-time $1548; $43 per credit. Full-time tuition and fees vary according to course level, course load, degree level, location, and program. Part-time tuition and fees vary according to course level, course load, degree level, location, and program.

GIFT AID (NEED-BASED) *Scholarships, grants, and awards:* Federal Pell, FSEOG, state, private, college/university gift aid from institutional funds.

GIFT AID (NON-NEED-BASED) *Scholarships, grants, and awards by category:* Academic interests/achievement: business, computer science, engineering/technologies, health fields. *Special achievements/activities:* community service. *Special characteristics:* children of faculty/staff, veterans, veterans' children. *Tuition waivers:* Full or partial for employees or children of employees.

LOANS *Programs:* Federal Direct (Subsidized and Unsubsidized Stafford, PLUS), state, college/university, alternative loans.

APPLYING FOR FINANCIAL AID *Required financial aid forms:* FAFSA, institution's own form, state aid form. *Financial aid deadline:* Continuous. *Notification date:* Continuous beginning 1/4. Students must reply within 2 weeks of notification.

CONTACT Office of Financial Aid, Globe University–Woodbury, 8089 Globe Drive, Woodbury, MN 55125, 651-730-5100 or toll-free 800-231-0660. *Fax:* 651-730-5151. *Website:* http://www.globeuniversity.edu/.

GODDARD COLLEGE
Plainfield, VT

ABOUT THE INSTITUTION Independent, coed. **Awards:** bachelor's and master's degrees. 23 undergraduate majors. **Total enrollment:** 703. Undergraduates: 244. Freshmen: 7.

GIFT AID (NEED-BASED) *Scholarships, grants, and awards:* Federal Pell, FSEOG, state, private, college/university gift aid from institutional funds.

LOANS *Programs:* Federal Direct (Subsidized and Unsubsidized Stafford, PLUS), Perkins.

APPLYING FOR FINANCIAL AID *Required financial aid form:* FAFSA.

CONTACT Shannon Trainor, Assistant Director of Financial Aid, Goddard College, 123 Pitkin Road, Plainfield, VT 05667, 802-454-8311 Ext. 303 or toll-free 800-906-8312. *Fax:* 802-322-1000. *E-mail:* shannon.trainor@goddard.edu. *Website:* http://www.goddard.edu/.

GOD'S BIBLE SCHOOL AND COLLEGE
Cincinnati, OH

CONTACT Mrs. Lori Waggoner, Financial Aid Director, God's Bible School and College, 1810 Young Street, Cincinnati, OH 45202-6899, 513-721-7944 Ext. 205 or toll-free 800-486-4637. *Fax:* 513-721-1357. *E-mail:* lwaggoner@gbs.edu. *Website:* http://www.gbs.edu/.

GOLDEN GATE UNIVERSITY
San Francisco, CA

ABOUT THE INSTITUTION Independent, coed. 8 undergraduate majors.

GIFT AID (NEED-BASED) *Scholarships, grants, and awards:* Federal Pell, FSEOG, state, private, college/university gift aid from institutional funds.

GIFT AID (NON-NEED-BASED) *Scholarships, grants, and awards by category:* Academic interests/achievement: business, computer science, general academic interests/achievements, international studies. *Special achievements/activities:* community service, leadership. *Special characteristics:* adult students, children and siblings of alumni, children of faculty/staff, first-generation college students, general special characteristics, international students, members of minority groups, previous college experience, veterans.

LOANS *Programs:* Federal Direct (Subsidized and Unsubsidized Stafford, PLUS), Perkins.

WORK-STUDY *Federal work-study:* Total amount: $50,000; 26 jobs averaging $5000.

APPLYING FOR FINANCIAL AID *Required financial aid forms:* FAFSA, institution's own form.

CONTACT Kathleen Kelly, Associate Director of Financial Services, Golden Gate University, 536 Mission Street, San Francisco, CA 94105-2968, 415-442-7297 or toll-free 800-448-3381. *Fax:* 415-442-7819. *E-mail:* kwalsh@ggu.edu. *Website:* http://www.ggu.edu/.

GOLDEY-BEACOM COLLEGE
Wilmington, DE

Tuition & fees: $22,140	Average undergraduate aid package: N/A

ABOUT THE INSTITUTION Independent, coed. **Awards:** certificates, associate, bachelor's, and master's degrees. 18 undergraduate majors. **Total enrollment:** 1,352. Undergraduates: 625. Freshmen: 96. Federal methodology is used as a basis for awarding need-based institutional aid.

UNDERGRADUATE EXPENSES for 2013–2014 *Tuition:* full-time $21,840; part-time $728 per credit. *Required fees:* full-time $300; $10 per credit. Full-time tuition and fees vary according to course load. Part-time tuition and fees vary according to course load. Room and board charges vary according to housing facility.

GIFT AID (NEED-BASED) *Scholarships, grants, and awards:* Federal Pell, FSEOG, state, private, college/university gift aid from institutional funds.

GIFT AID (NON-NEED-BASED) *Scholarships, grants, and awards by category:* Academic interests/achievement: business, English, social sciences. **Tuition waivers:** Full or partial for children of alumni, employees or children of employees.

LOANS *Programs:* Federal Direct (Subsidized and Unsubsidized Stafford, PLUS), Perkins.

APPLYING FOR FINANCIAL AID *Required financial aid form:* FAFSA. **Financial aid deadline (priority):** 4/1. **Notification date:** Continuous beginning 10/1. Students must reply within 2 weeks of notification.

CONTACT Jane H. Lysle, Dean of Enrollment Management, Goldey-Beacom College, 4701 Limestone Road, Wilmington, DE 19808-1999, 302-225-6274 or toll-free 800-833-4877. *Fax:* 302-998-8631. *E-mail:* lyslej@gbc.edu. *Website:* http://www.gbc.edu/.

GOLDFARB SCHOOL OF NURSING AT BARNES-JEWISH COLLEGE
St. Louis, MO

ABOUT THE INSTITUTION Independent, coed, primarily women. **Awards:** certificates, bachelor's, master's, and doctoral degrees. 1 undergraduate major. **Total enrollment:** 838. Undergraduates: 637.

GIFT AID (NEED-BASED) *Scholarships, grants, and awards:* Federal Pell, FSEOG, state, private, college/university gift aid from institutional funds.

GIFT AID (NON-NEED-BASED) *Scholarships, grants, and awards by category:* Academic interests/achievement: general academic interests/achievements.

LOANS *Programs:* Federal Direct (Subsidized and Unsubsidized Stafford, PLUS).

WORK-STUDY *Federal work-study:* Total amount: $23,000; jobs available.

APPLYING FOR FINANCIAL AID *Required financial aid forms:* FAFSA, institution's own form.

CONTACT Jason Crowe, Director of Financial Aid, Goldfarb School of Nursing at Barnes-Jewish College, 4483 Duncan, St. Louis, MO 63110-1091, 314-454-7770 or toll-free 800-832-9009. *E-mail:* jcrowe@bjc.org. *Website:* http://www.barnesjewishcollege.edu/.

GONZAGA UNIVERSITY
Spokane, WA

Tuition & fees: $33,652	Average undergraduate aid package: $23,755

ABOUT THE INSTITUTION Independent Roman Catholic, coed. **Awards:** certificates, bachelor's, master's, and doctoral degrees. 53 undergraduate majors. **Total enrollment:** 7,781. Undergraduates: 4,906. Freshmen: 1,096. Federal methodology is used as a basis for awarding need-based institutional aid.

UNDERGRADUATE EXPENSES for 2013–2014 *Application fee:* $50. **Comprehensive fee:** $42,382 includes full-time tuition ($33,160), mandatory fees ($492), and room and board ($8730). **College room only:** $4580. Full-time tuition and fees vary according to course load, location, program, reciprocity agreements, and student level. Room and board charges vary according to board plan and housing facility. **Part-time tuition:** $885 per credit hour. Part-time tuition and fees vary according to course load, location, program, reciprocity agreements, and student level.

FRESHMAN FINANCIAL AID (Fall 2012, est.) 986 applied for aid; of those 71% were deemed to have need. 100% of freshmen with need received aid; of those 31% had need fully met. **Average percent of need met:** 83% (excluding resources awarded to replace EFC). **Average financial aid package:** $24,204 (excluding resources awarded to replace EFC). 35% of all full-time freshmen had no need and received non-need-based gift aid.

UNDERGRADUATE FINANCIAL AID (Fall 2012, est.) 3,512 applied for aid; of those 79% were deemed to have need. 100% of undergraduates with need received aid; of those 24% had need fully met. **Average percent of need met:** 77% (excluding resources awarded to replace EFC). **Average financial aid package:** $23,755 (excluding resources awarded to replace EFC). 37% of all full-time undergraduates had no need and received non-need-based gift aid.

GIFT AID (NEED-BASED) *Total amount:* $41,654,443 (10% federal, 7% state, 82% institutional, 1% external sources). *Receiving aid:* Freshmen: 62% (702); all full-time undergraduates: 58% (2,746). *Average award:* Freshmen: $18,680; Undergraduates: $17,880. **Scholarships, grants, and awards:** Federal Pell, FSEOG, state, private, college/university gift aid from institutional funds, United Negro College Fund, Federal Nursing.

GIFT AID (NON-NEED-BASED) Total amount: $27,797,838 (94% institutional, 6% external sources). **Receiving aid:** Freshmen: 15% (172). Undergraduates: 11% (509). **Average award:** Freshmen: $10,754. Undergraduates: $11,384. **Scholarships, grants, and awards by category:** Academic interests/achievement: 184 awards ($536,257 total): business, engineering/technologies, military science. Creative arts/performance: 88 awards ($176,000 total): debating, music. Special achievements/activities: 144 awards ($470,250 total): leadership, memberships. Special characteristics: 410 awards ($3,437,088 total): children and siblings of alumni, children of faculty/staff, international students, members of minority groups, siblings of current students. **Tuition waivers:** Full or partial for employees or children of employees. **ROTC:** Army.

LOANS Student loans: $29,565,614 (80% need-based, 20% non-need-based). 66% of past graduating class borrowed through all loan programs. Average indebtedness per student: $29,776. **Average need-based loan:** Freshmen: $4365. Undergraduates: $5351. **Parent loans:** $7,300,019 (75% need-based, 25% non-need-based). **Programs:** Federal Direct (Subsidized and Unsubsidized Stafford, PLUS), Perkins, Federal Nursing, state, college/university.

WORK-STUDY Federal work-study: Total amount: $1,362,026; 411 jobs averaging $1,224,122. **State or other work-study/employment:** Total amount: $1,538,558 (100% need-based). 476 part-time jobs averaging $3807.

ATHLETIC AWARDS Total amount: $3,719,937 (21% need-based, 79% non-need-based).

APPLYING FOR FINANCIAL AID Required financial aid form: FAFSA. **Financial aid deadline (priority):** 2/1. **Notification date:** Continuous beginning 3/1. Students must reply by 5/1 or within 3 weeks of notification.

CONTACT James White, Dean of Student Financial Services, Gonzaga University, 502 East Boone Avenue, Spokane, WA 99258-0072, 509-313-6568 or toll-free 800-322-2584 Ext. 6572. Fax: 509-313-5816. E-mail: whitej@gonzaga.edu. Website: http://www.gonzaga.edu/.

GORDON COLLEGE
Wenham, MA

Tuition & fees: $33,230	Average undergraduate aid package: $19,992

ABOUT THE INSTITUTION Independent nondenominational, coed. **Awards:** bachelor's and master's degrees. 33 undergraduate majors. **Total enrollment:** 1,909. Undergraduates: 1,580. Freshmen: 465. Federal methodology is used as a basis for awarding need-based institutional aid.

UNDERGRADUATE EXPENSES for 2013–2014 Application fee: $50. **Comprehensive fee:** $42,660 includes full-time tuition ($31,820), mandatory fees ($1410), and room and board ($9430). **College room only:** $6250. Full-time tuition and fees vary according to course load and program. Room and board charges vary according to board plan and housing facility. **Part-time tuition:** $1125 per credit. Part-time tuition and fees vary according to course load and program.

FRESHMAN FINANCIAL AID (Fall 2012, est.) 421 applied for aid; of those 86% were deemed to have need. 100% of freshmen with need received aid; of those 16% had need fully met. **Average percent of need met:** 68% (excluding resources awarded to replace EFC). **Average financial aid package:** $20,641 (excluding resources awarded to replace EFC). 24% of all full-time freshmen had no need and received non-need-based gift aid.

UNDERGRADUATE FINANCIAL AID (Fall 2012, est.) 1,309 applied for aid; of those 88% were deemed to have need. 100% of undergraduates with need received aid; of those 16% had need fully met. **Average percent of need met:** 68% (excluding resources awarded to replace EFC). **Average financial aid package:** $19,992 (excluding resources awarded to replace EFC). 24% of all full-time undergraduates had no need and received non-need-based gift aid.

GIFT AID (NEED-BASED) Total amount: $17,649,973 (9% federal, 2% state, 77% institutional, 12% external sources). **Receiving aid:** Freshmen: 73% (364); all full-time undergraduates: 72% (1,146). **Average award:** Freshmen: $16,749; Undergraduates: $15,295. **Scholarships, grants, and awards:** Federal Pell, FSEOG, state, private, college/university gift aid from institutional funds.

GIFT AID (NON-NEED-BASED) Total amount: $5,780,028 (84% institutional, 16% external sources). **Receiving aid:** Freshmen: 9% (46). Undergraduates: 7%

(119). **Average award:** Freshmen: $11,098. Undergraduates: $11,629. **Scholarships, grants, and awards by category:** Academic interests/achievement: 1,032 awards ($9,875,521 total): general academic interests/achievements. Creative arts/performance: 95 awards ($222,200 total): art/fine arts, music, theater/drama. Special achievements/activities: 216 awards ($1,543,308 total): leadership. Special characteristics: 216 awards ($121,410 total): children and siblings of alumni, relatives of clergy. **Tuition waivers:** Full or partial for employees or children of employees. **ROTC:** Army cooperative.

LOANS Student loans: $12,547,570 (71% need-based, 29% non-need-based). 85% of past graduating class borrowed through all loan programs. Average indebtedness per student: $37,662. **Average need-based loan:** Freshmen: $3654. Undergraduates: $4586. **Parent loans:** $3,402,734 (49% need-based, 51% non-need-based). **Programs:** Federal Direct (Subsidized and Unsubsidized Stafford, PLUS), Perkins, state.

WORK-STUDY Federal work-study: Total amount: $257,542; 766 jobs averaging $1536.

APPLYING FOR FINANCIAL AID Required financial aid form: FAFSA. **Financial aid deadline (priority):** 3/1. **Notification date:** Continuous beginning 2/15. Students must reply by 5/1 or within 2 weeks of notification.

CONTACT Daniel O'Connell, Director of Student Financial Services, Gordon College, 255 Grapevine Road, Wenham, MA 01984-1899, 978-867-4246 or toll-free 866-464-6736. Fax: 978-867-4657. E-mail: daniel.oconnell@gordon.edu. Website: http://www.gordon.edu/.

GOSHEN COLLEGE
Goshen, IN

Tuition & fees: $28,500	Average undergraduate aid package: $19,900

ABOUT THE INSTITUTION Independent Mennonite, coed. **Awards:** certificates, bachelor's, and master's degrees. 32 undergraduate majors. **Total enrollment:** 928. Undergraduates: 884. Freshmen: 168. Federal methodology is used as a basis for awarding need-based institutional aid.

UNDERGRADUATE EXPENSES for 2013–2014 Application fee: $25. **Comprehensive fee:** $37,960 includes full-time tuition ($28,500) and room and board ($9460). **College room only:** $5060. Full-time tuition and fees vary according to degree level and program. Room and board charges vary according to board plan and housing facility. **Part-time tuition:** $1190 per credit hour. Part-time tuition and fees vary according to course load, degree level, and program.

FRESHMAN FINANCIAL AID (Fall 2011) 146 applied for aid; of those 88% were deemed to have need. 100% of freshmen with need received aid; of those 20% had need fully met. **Average percent of need met:** 81% (excluding resources awarded to replace EFC). **Average financial aid package:** $20,488 (excluding resources awarded to replace EFC). 31% of all full-time freshmen had no need and received non-need-based gift aid.

UNDERGRADUATE FINANCIAL AID (Fall 2011) 731 applied for aid; of those 91% were deemed to have need. 100% of undergraduates with need received aid; of those 12% had need fully met. **Average percent of need met:** 80% (excluding resources awarded to replace EFC). **Average financial aid package:** $19,900 (excluding resources awarded to replace EFC). 23% of all full-time undergraduates had no need and received non-need-based gift aid.

GIFT AID (NEED-BASED) Total amount: $9,099,898 (15% federal, 9% state, 60% institutional, 16% external sources). **Receiving aid:** Freshmen: 67% (128); all full-time undergraduates: 72% (636). **Average award:** Freshmen: $17,553; Undergraduates: $16,306. **Scholarships, grants, and awards:** Federal Pell, FSEOG, state, private, college/university gift aid from institutional funds.

GIFT AID (NON-NEED-BASED) Total amount: $3,065,024 (78% institutional, 22% external sources). **Receiving aid:** Freshmen: 14% (26). Undergraduates: 9% (76). **Average award:** Freshmen: $12,579. Undergraduates: $11,206. **Scholarships, grants, and awards by category:** Academic interests/achievement: 15 awards ($85,000 total): business, communication, education, general academic interests/achievements. Creative arts/performance: music, theater/drama. Special achievements/activities: 1 award ($3000 total): community service, junior miss. Special characteristics: children of educators, children of faculty/staff, international students, members of minority groups. **Tuition waivers:** Full or partial for employees or children of employees.

LOANS *Student loans:* $4,695,262 (78% need-based, 22% non-need-based). 72% of past graduating class borrowed through all loan programs. *Average indebtedness per student:* $21,953. *Average need-based loan:* Freshmen: $3789. Undergraduates: $4875. *Parent loans:* $644,920 (39% need-based, 61% non-need-based). *Programs:* Federal Direct (Subsidized and Unsubsidized Stafford, PLUS), Perkins, Federal Nursing.

WORK-STUDY *Federal work-study:* Total amount: $159,880; jobs available. *State or other work-study/employment:* Total amount: $97,300 (100% non-need-based). Part-time jobs available.

ATHLETIC AWARDS Total amount: $1,064,886 (67% need-based, 33% non-need-based).

APPLYING FOR FINANCIAL AID *Required financial aid forms:* FAFSA, institution's own form. *Financial aid deadline (priority):* 3/15. *Notification date:* Continuous beginning 3/1. Students must reply by 5/1 or within 2 weeks of notification.

CONTACT Mrs. Judy S. Moore, Director of Enrollment, Goshen College, 1700 South Main Street, Goshen, IN 46526-4794, 574-535-7525 or toll-free 800-348-7422. *Fax:* 574-535-7654. *E-mail:* judysm@goshen.edu.

Website: http://www.goshen.edu/.

GOUCHER COLLEGE
Baltimore, MD

Tuition & fees: $39,084	Average undergraduate aid package: $28,225

ABOUT THE INSTITUTION Independent, coed. *Awards:* certificates, bachelor's, and master's degrees. 34 undergraduate majors. *Total enrollment:* 2,254. Undergraduates: 1,484. Freshmen: 410. Both federal and institutional methodology are used as a basis for awarding need-based institutional aid.

UNDERGRADUATE EXPENSES for 2013–2014 *Application fee:* $55. *Comprehensive fee:* $50,252 includes full-time tuition ($38,462), mandatory fees ($622), and room and board ($11,168). *College room only:* $6664. Room and board charges vary according to board plan and housing facility. *Part-time tuition:* $1282 per credit hour. *Payment plan:* Tuition prepayment.

FRESHMAN FINANCIAL AID (Fall 2012, est.) 341 applied for aid; of those 85% were deemed to have need. 100% of freshmen with need received aid; of those 13% had need fully met. *Average percent of need met:* 81% (excluding resources awarded to replace EFC). *Average financial aid package:* $30,410 (excluding resources awarded to replace EFC). 19% of all full-time freshmen had no need and received non-need-based gift aid.

UNDERGRADUATE FINANCIAL AID (Fall 2012, est.) 1,039 applied for aid; of those 88% were deemed to have need. 100% of undergraduates with need received aid; of those 11% had need fully met. *Average percent of need met:* 76% (excluding resources awarded to replace EFC). *Average financial aid package:* $28,225 (excluding resources awarded to replace EFC). 19% of all full-time undergraduates had no need and received non-need-based gift aid.

GIFT AID (NEED-BASED) *Total amount:* $21,956,832 (7% federal, 4% state, 85% institutional, 4% external sources). *Receiving aid:* Freshmen: 70% (285); all full-time undergraduates: 61% (883). *Average award:* Freshmen: $27,204; Undergraduates: $24,804. *Scholarships, grants, and awards:* Federal Pell, FSEOG, state, private, college/university gift aid from institutional funds.

GIFT AID (NON-NEED-BASED) *Total amount:* $4,788,583 (90% institutional, 10% external sources). *Receiving aid:* Freshmen: 8% (31). Undergraduates: 5% (77). *Average award:* Freshmen: $13,867. Undergraduates: $14,301. *Scholarships, grants, and awards by category:* Creative arts/performance: 24 awards ($175,000 total): art/fine arts, dance, music, performing arts, theater/drama. *Tuition waivers:* Full or partial for employees or children of employees. *ROTC:* Army cooperative, Air Force cooperative.

LOANS *Student loans:* $7,584,650 (72% need-based, 28% non-need-based). 43% of past graduating class borrowed through all loan programs. *Average indebtedness per student:* $29,135. *Average need-based loan:* Freshmen: $3237. Undergraduates: $4102. *Parent loans:* $3,191,803 (35% need-based, 65% non-need-based). *Programs:* Federal Direct (Subsidized and Unsubsidized Stafford, PLUS), Perkins, college/university.

WORK-STUDY *Federal work-study:* Total amount: $574,476; 436 jobs averaging $1041. *State or other work-study/employment:* Part-time jobs available.

APPLYING FOR FINANCIAL AID *Required financial aid forms:* FAFSA, CSS Financial Aid PROFILE. *Financial aid deadline (priority):* 2/1. *Notification date:* 4/1. Students must reply by 5/1 or within 2 weeks of notification.

CONTACT Stephanie Bender, Director of Student Financial Aid, Goucher College, 1021 Dulaney Valley Road, Baltimore, MD 21204-2794, 410-337-6141 or toll-free 800-468-2437. *Fax:* 410-337-6504.

Website: http://www.goucher.edu/.

GOVERNORS STATE UNIVERSITY
University Park, IL

ABOUT THE INSTITUTION State-supported, coed. *Awards:* certificates, bachelor's, master's, and doctoral degrees. 24 undergraduate majors. *Total enrollment:* 5,609. Undergraduates: 3,178.

GIFT AID (NEED-BASED) *Scholarships, grants, and awards:* Federal Pell, FSEOG, state, college/university gift aid from institutional funds.

GIFT AID (NON-NEED-BASED) *Scholarships, grants, and awards by category:* Academic interests/achievement: biological sciences, business, communication, education, English, general academic interests/achievements, health fields, mathematics, physical sciences, social sciences. Creative arts/performance: general creative arts/performance. Special achievements/activities: general special achievements/activities. Special characteristics: children of educators, children of public servants, members of minority groups, veterans.

LOANS *Programs:* Federal Direct (Subsidized and Unsubsidized Stafford, PLUS), Perkins.

APPLYING FOR FINANCIAL AID *Required financial aid form:* FAFSA.

CONTACT Brenda Moore, Financial Aid Counselor, Governors State University, One University Parkway, University Park, IL 60466-0975, 708-534-4480 or toll-free 800-GSU-8GSU. *E-mail:* bmoore@govst.edu.

Website: http://www.govst.edu/.

GRACE BIBLE COLLEGE
Grand Rapids, MI

Tuition & fees: $15,300	Average undergraduate aid package: $9582

ABOUT THE INSTITUTION Independent Grace Gospel Fellowship, coed. 18 undergraduate majors. Federal methodology is used as a basis for awarding need-based institutional aid.

UNDERGRADUATE EXPENSES for 2013–2014 *Comprehensive fee:* $22,300 includes full-time tuition ($15,300) and room and board ($7000). Room and board charges vary according to board plan and housing facility. Part-time tuition and fees vary according to course load.

FRESHMAN FINANCIAL AID (Fall 2011) 90 applied for aid; of those 94% were deemed to have need. 100% of freshmen with need received aid; of those 5% had need fully met. *Average percent of need met:* 60% (excluding resources awarded to replace EFC). *Average financial aid package:* $9849 (excluding resources awarded to replace EFC). 8% of all full-time freshmen had no need and received non-need-based gift aid.

UNDERGRADUATE FINANCIAL AID (Fall 2011) 321 applied for aid; of those 93% were deemed to have need. 100% of undergraduates with need received aid; of those 6% had need fully met. *Average percent of need met:* 63% (excluding resources awarded to replace EFC). *Average financial aid package:* $9582 (excluding resources awarded to replace EFC). 6% of all full-time undergraduates had no need and received non-need-based gift aid.

GIFT AID (NEED-BASED) *Total amount:* $2,092,443 (48% federal, 11% state, 38% institutional, 3% external sources). *Receiving aid:* Freshmen: 87% (81); all full-time undergraduates: 81% (274). *Average award:* Freshmen: $4438; Undergraduates: $4217. *Scholarships, grants, and awards:* Federal Pell, FSEOG, state, private, college/university gift aid from institutional funds.

GIFT AID (NON-NEED-BASED) *Receiving aid:* Freshmen: 67% (62). Undergraduates: 55% (187). *Average award:* Freshmen: $4636. Undergraduates: $3718. *Scholarships, grants, and awards by category:* Academic interests/achievement: 182 awards ($445,147 total): general academic interests/achievements. Creative arts/performance: 24 awards ($26,400 total): music. Special characteristics: 127 awards ($299,253 total): children of faculty/staff, general special characteristics,

relatives of clergy. *Tuition waivers:* Full or partial for employees or children of employees.
LOANS *Student loans:* $2,004,534 (52% need-based, 48% non-need-based). 59% of past graduating class borrowed through all loan programs. *Average indebtedness per student:* $21,527. *Average need-based loan:* Freshmen: $3002. Undergraduates: $3551. *Parent loans:* $311,968 (100% non-need-based). *Programs:* Federal Direct (Subsidized and Unsubsidized Stafford, PLUS).
WORK-STUDY *Federal work-study:* Total amount: $24,581; 76 jobs averaging $323. *State or other work-study/employment:* Part-time jobs available.
APPLYING FOR FINANCIAL AID *Required financial aid form:* FAFSA. *Financial aid deadline (priority):* 2/28. *Notification date:* Continuous beginning 5/15. Students must reply within 2 weeks of notification.
CONTACT Mr. Kurt Postma, Director of Financial Aid, Grace Bible College, 1011 Aldon Street, SW, Grand Rapids, MI 49509-1921, 616-538-2330 or toll-free 800-968-1887. *Fax:* 616-538-0599. *E-mail:* kpostma@gbcol.edu.
Website: http://www.gbcol.edu/.

GRACE COLLEGE
Winona Lake, IN

CONTACT Charlette Sauders, Director of Financial Aid, Grace College, 200 Seminary Drive, Winona Lake, IN 46590-1294, 574-372-5100 Ext. 6161 or toll-free 800-54-GRACE. *Fax:* 574-372-5144. *E-mail:* charlette.sauders@grace.edu.
Website: http://www.grace.edu/.

GRACE COLLEGE OF DIVINITY
Fayetteville, NC

CONTACT Financial Aid Office, Grace College of Divinity, 5117 Cliffdale Road, Fayetteville, NC 28314, 910-221-2224.
Website: http://www.gcdivinity.org/.

GRACELAND UNIVERSITY
Lamoni, IA

Tuition & fees: $23,530	Average undergraduate aid package: $18,973

ABOUT THE INSTITUTION Independent Community of Christ, coed. *Awards:* certificates, bachelor's, master's, and doctoral degrees. 45 undergraduate majors. *Total enrollment:* 2,318. Undergraduates: 1,515. Freshmen: 260. Federal methodology is used as a basis for awarding need-based institutional aid.
UNDERGRADUATE EXPENSES for 2013–2014 *Comprehensive fee:* $31,420 includes full-time tuition ($23,180), mandatory fees ($350), and room and board ($7890). Full-time tuition and fees vary according to course load. Room and board charges vary according to board plan, housing facility, and location. *Part-time tuition:* $725 per credit. Part-time tuition and fees vary according to course load.
FRESHMAN FINANCIAL AID (Fall 2012, est.) 216 applied for aid; of those 77% were deemed to have need. 97% of freshmen with need received aid; of those 21% had need fully met. *Average percent of need met:* 79% (excluding resources awarded to replace EFC). *Average financial aid package:* $21,164 (excluding resources awarded to replace EFC). 19% of all full-time freshmen had no need and received non-need-based gift aid.
UNDERGRADUATE FINANCIAL AID (Fall 2012, est.) 1,053 applied for aid; of those 75% were deemed to have need. 97% of undergraduates with need received aid; of those 14% had need fully met. *Average percent of need met:* 72% (excluding resources awarded to replace EFC). *Average financial aid package:* $18,973 (excluding resources awarded to replace EFC). 27% of all full-time undergraduates had no need and received non-need-based gift aid.
GIFT AID (NEED-BASED) *Total amount:* $10,622,964 (28% federal, 6% state, 64% institutional, 2% external sources). *Receiving aid:* Freshmen: 67% (162); all full-time undergraduates: 59% (733). *Average award:* Freshmen: $17,541; Undergraduates: $14,979. *Scholarships, grants, and awards:* Federal Pell, FSEOG, state, private, college/university gift aid from institutional funds.

GIFT AID (NON-NEED-BASED) *Total amount:* $3,355,016 (1% federal, 95% institutional, 4% external sources). *Receiving aid:* Freshmen: 23% (56). Undergraduates: 18% (221). *Average award:* Freshmen: $11,629. Undergraduates: $11,028. *Scholarships, grants, and awards by category: Academic interests/achievement:* computer science, engineering/technologies, English, general academic interests/achievements, physical sciences. *Creative arts/performance:* 11 awards ($295,166 total): applied art and design, creative writing, dance, music, theater/drama. *Special achievements/activities:* 10 awards ($241,650 total): cheerleading/drum major, general special achievements/activities, leadership, religious involvement. *Special characteristics:* children and siblings of alumni, children of faculty/staff, first-generation college students, general special characteristics, international students, local/state students, members of minority groups, religious affiliation. *Tuition waivers:* Full or partial for employees or children of employees, senior citizens.
LOANS *Student loans:* $9,361,450 (78% need-based, 22% non-need-based). 85% of past graduating class borrowed through all loan programs. *Average indebtedness per student:* $39,022. *Average need-based loan:* Freshmen: $4151. Undergraduates: $4963. *Parent loans:* $4,457,625 (85% need-based, 15% non-need-based). *Programs:* Federal Direct (Subsidized and Unsubsidized Stafford, PLUS), Perkins, state, college/university.
WORK-STUDY *Federal work-study:* Total amount: $325,730; 186 jobs averaging $1522. *State or other work-study/employment:* Total amount: $527,449 (14% need-based, 86% non-need-based). 375 part-time jobs averaging $1490.
ATHLETIC AWARDS Total amount: $2,685,703 (55% need-based, 45% non-need-based).
APPLYING FOR FINANCIAL AID *Required financial aid form:* FAFSA. *Financial aid deadline:* Continuous. *Notification date:* Continuous beginning 2/1. Students must reply within 2 weeks of notification.
CONTACT Talia Brown, Interim Director of Financial Aid, Graceland University, 1 University Place, Lamoni, IA 50140, 641-784-5136 or toll-free 866-GRACELAND. *Fax:* 641-784-5020. *E-mail:* financialaidservices@graceland.edu.
Website: http://www.graceland.edu/.

GRACE UNIVERSITY
Omaha, NE

CONTACT Marcy Pierce, Director of Financial Aid, Grace University, 1311 South Ninth Street, Omaha, NE 68108-3629, 402-449-2810 or toll-free 800-383-1422. *Fax:* 402-449-2921. *E-mail:* gufinaid@graceu.edu.
Website: http://www.graceuniversity.edu/.

GRAMBLING STATE UNIVERSITY
Grambling, LA

CONTACT Assistant Director of Student Financial Aid and Scholarships, Grambling State University, PO Box 629, Grambling, LA 71245, 318-274-6415 or toll-free 800-569-4714. *Fax:* 318-274-3358.
Website: http://www.gram.edu/.

GRAND CANYON UNIVERSITY
Phoenix, AZ

CONTACT Director of Financial Aid, Grand Canyon University, 3300 West Camelback Road, PO Box 11097, Phoenix, AZ 85017-3030, 800-800-9776 Ext. 2885 or toll-free 800-800-9776. *Fax:* 602-589-2044.
Website: http://www.gcu.edu/.

GRAND VALLEY STATE UNIVERSITY
Allendale, MI

Tuition & fees (MI res): $10,078	Average undergraduate aid package: $9226

ABOUT THE INSTITUTION State-supported, coed. *Awards:* certificates, bachelor's, master's, and doctoral degrees. 105 undergraduate majors. *Total enrollment:* 24,654. Undergraduates: 21,317. Freshmen: 3,966. Federal methodology is used as a basis for awarding need-based institutional aid.

UNDERGRADUATE EXPENSES for 2013–2014 *Application fee:* $30. *Tuition, state resident:* full-time $10,078; part-time $420 per credit hour. *Tuition, nonresident:* full-time $14,568; part-time $607 per credit hour. Full-time tuition and fees vary according to course level, degree level, program, and student level. Part-time tuition and fees vary according to course level, course load, degree level, program, and student level. *College room and board:* $7920; *Room only:* $5400. Room and board charges vary according to board plan, housing facility, and location.

FRESHMAN FINANCIAL AID (Fall 2012, est.) 3,581 applied for aid; of those 75% were deemed to have need. 99% of freshmen with need received aid; of those 12% had need fully met. *Average percent of need met:* 72% (excluding resources awarded to replace EFC). *Average financial aid package:* $10,949 (excluding resources awarded to replace EFC). 14% of all full-time freshmen had no need and received non-need-based gift aid.

UNDERGRADUATE FINANCIAL AID (Fall 2012, est.) 15,412 applied for aid; of those 80% were deemed to have need. 99% of undergraduates with need received aid; of those 11% had need fully met. *Average percent of need met:* 60% (excluding resources awarded to replace EFC). *Average financial aid package:* $9226 (excluding resources awarded to replace EFC). 12% of all full-time undergraduates had no need and received non-need-based gift aid.

GIFT AID (NEED-BASED) *Total amount:* $59,901,029 (53% federal, 43% institutional, 4% external sources). *Receiving aid:* Freshmen: 59% (2,308); all full-time undergraduates: 51% (9,500). *Average award:* Freshmen: $7469; Undergraduates: $6133. *Scholarships, grants, and awards:* Federal Pell, FSEOG, state, private, college/university gift aid from institutional funds.

GIFT AID (NON-NEED-BASED) *Total amount:* $7,059,468 (1% federal, 88% institutional, 11% external sources). *Receiving aid:* Freshmen: 2% (88). Undergraduates: 1% (257). *Average award:* Freshmen: $2362. Undergraduates: $2440. *Scholarships, grants, and awards by category: Academic interests/achievement:* business, communication, computer science, education, engineering/technologies, English, foreign languages, general academic interests/achievements, health fields, humanities, international studies, mathematics, physical sciences, premedicine, social sciences. *Creative arts/performance:* applied art and design, art/fine arts, cinema/film/broadcasting, dance, journalism/publications, music, theater/drama. *Special characteristics:* adult students, children and siblings of alumni, children of faculty/staff, children of union members/company employees, children of workers in trades, general special characteristics, handicapped students, international students, local/state students, out-of-state students, public servants, spouses of deceased or disabled public servants, veterans, veterans' children. *Tuition waivers:* Full or partial for employees or children of employees.

LOANS *Student loans:* $123,419,337 (43% need-based, 57% non-need-based). 72% of past graduating class borrowed through all loan programs. *Average indebtedness per student:* $28,728. *Average need-based loan:* Freshmen: $3867. Undergraduates: $4486. *Parent loans:* $71,213,463 (100% non-need-based). *Programs:* Federal Direct (Subsidized and Unsubsidized Stafford, PLUS), Perkins, Federal Nursing.

WORK-STUDY *Federal work-study:* Total amount: $5,929,125; 2,041 jobs averaging $2905. *State or other work-study/employment:* Part-time jobs available.

ATHLETIC AWARDS Total amount: $2,665,622 (45% need-based, 55% non-need-based).

APPLYING FOR FINANCIAL AID *Required financial aid form:* FAFSA. *Financial aid deadline (priority):* 3/1. *Notification date:* 3/10. Students must reply by 5/1 or within 4 weeks of notification.

CONTACT Michelle Rhodes, Office of Financial Aid, Grand Valley State University, 100 Student Services Building, Allendale, MI 49401, 616-331-3234 or toll-free 800-748-0246. *Fax:* 616-331-3180. *E-mail:* rhodesmi@gvsu.edu. *Website:* http://www.gvsu.edu/.

GRAND VIEW UNIVERSITY
Des Moines, IA

Tuition & fees: $22,708	Average undergraduate aid package: $17,334

ABOUT THE INSTITUTION Independent Evangelical Lutheran Church in America, coed. *Awards:* certificates, bachelor's, and master's degrees. 30 undergraduate majors. *Total enrollment:* 2,232. Undergraduates: 2,195. Freshmen: 292. Federal methodology is used as a basis for awarding need-based institutional aid.

UNDERGRADUATE EXPENSES for 2013–2014 *Comprehensive fee:* $29,972 includes full-time tuition ($22,208), mandatory fees ($500), and room and board ($7264). Full-time tuition and fees vary according to class time and course load. Room and board charges vary according to board plan and housing facility. *Part-time tuition:* $553 per credit hour. Part-time tuition and fees vary according to class time and course load.

FRESHMAN FINANCIAL AID (Fall 2012, est.) 281 applied for aid; of those 89% were deemed to have need. 100% of freshmen with need received aid; of those 35% had need fully met. *Average percent of need met:* 90% (excluding resources awarded to replace EFC). *Average financial aid package:* $21,269 (excluding resources awarded to replace EFC). 14% of all full-time freshmen had no need and received non-need-based gift aid.

UNDERGRADUATE FINANCIAL AID (Fall 2012, est.) 1,632 applied for aid; of those 91% were deemed to have need. 100% of undergraduates with need received aid; of those 25% had need fully met. *Average percent of need met:* 78% (excluding resources awarded to replace EFC). *Average financial aid package:* $17,334 (excluding resources awarded to replace EFC). 13% of all full-time undergraduates had no need and received non-need-based gift aid.

GIFT AID (NEED-BASED) *Total amount:* $15,794,811 (26% federal, 24% state, 48% institutional, 2% external sources). *Receiving aid:* Freshmen: 77% (226); all full-time undergraduates: 77% (1,367). *Average award:* Freshmen: $16,335; Undergraduates: $12,983. *Scholarships, grants, and awards:* Federal Pell, FSEOG, state, private, college/university gift aid from institutional funds, Federal Nursing.

GIFT AID (NON-NEED-BASED) *Total amount:* $1,768,534 (1% federal, 3% state, 86% institutional, 10% external sources). *Receiving aid:* Freshmen: 19% (55). Undergraduates: 9% (152). *Average award:* Freshmen: $8442. Undergraduates: $6810. *Scholarships, grants, and awards by category: Academic interests/achievement:* 1,709 awards ($7,910,453 total): general academic interests/achievements. *Creative arts/performance:* 95 awards ($114,850 total): art/fine arts, dance, music, theater/drama. *Special achievements/activities:* 31 awards ($30,380 total): cheerleading/drum major, community service, junior miss, religious involvement. *Special characteristics:* 129 awards ($731,084 total): children and siblings of alumni, children of educators, children of faculty/staff, veterans. *Tuition waivers:* Full or partial for children of alumni, employees or children of employees, senior citizens. *ROTC:* Army cooperative, Air Force cooperative.

LOANS *Student loans:* $22,462,861 (63% need-based, 37% non-need-based). 90% of past graduating class borrowed through all loan programs. *Average indebtedness per student:* $33,464. *Average need-based loan:* Freshmen: $3222. Undergraduates: $4052. *Parent loans:* $2,216,597 (7% need-based, 93% non-need-based). *Programs:* Federal Direct (Subsidized and Unsubsidized Stafford, PLUS), Perkins, college/university, private loans.

WORK-STUDY *Federal work-study:* Total amount: $536,429; 396 jobs averaging $1353. *State or other work-study/employment:* Total amount: $2250 (100% non-need-based). 1 part-time job averaging $2250.

ATHLETIC AWARDS Total amount: $3,114,277 (71% need-based, 29% non-need-based).

APPLYING FOR FINANCIAL AID *Financial aid deadline (priority):* 3/1. *Notification date:* Continuous beginning 3/10. Students must reply by 5/1 or within 3 weeks of notification.

CONTACT Michele Dunne, Director of Financial Aid, Grand View University, 1200 Grandview Avenue, Des Moines, IA 50316-1599, 515-263-2820 or toll-free 800-444-6083. *Fax:* 515-263-6191. *E-mail:* mdunne@grandview.edu. *Website:* http://www.grandview.edu/.

GRANTHAM UNIVERSITY
Kansas City, MO

CONTACT Financial Aid Office, Grantham University, 7200 Northwest 86th Street, Suite M, Kansas City, MO 64153 or toll-free 800-955-2527.
Website: http://www.grantham.edu/.

GREAT LAKES CHRISTIAN COLLEGE
Lansing, MI

CONTACT Financial Aid Officer, Great Lakes Christian College, 6211 West Willow Highway, Lansing, MI 48917-1299, 517-321-0242 or toll-free 800-YES-GLCC.
Website: http://www.glcc.edu/.

GREEN MOUNTAIN COLLEGE
Poultney, VT

Tuition & fees: N/R	Average undergraduate aid package: $23,458

ABOUT THE INSTITUTION Independent, coed. 20 undergraduate majors. Federal methodology is used as a basis for awarding need-based institutional aid.
FRESHMAN FINANCIAL AID (Fall 2012, est.) 157 applied for aid; of those 93% were deemed to have need. 100% of freshmen with need received aid; of those 5% had need fully met. *Average percent of need met:* 76% (excluding resources awarded to replace EFC). *Average financial aid package:* $27,661 (excluding resources awarded to replace EFC). 16% of all full-time freshmen had no need and received non-need-based gift aid.
UNDERGRADUATE FINANCIAL AID (Fall 2012, est.) 520 applied for aid; of those 93% were deemed to have need. 100% of undergraduates with need received aid; of those 11% had need fully met. *Average percent of need met:* 67% (excluding resources awarded to replace EFC). *Average financial aid package:* $23,458 (excluding resources awarded to replace EFC). 18% of all full-time undergraduates had no need and received non-need-based gift aid.
GIFT AID (NEED-BASED) *Total amount:* $9,250,725 (17% federal, 2% state, 79% institutional, 2% external sources). *Receiving aid:* Freshmen: 79% (144); all full-time undergraduates: 77% (481). *Average award:* Freshmen: $24,799; Undergraduates: $19,712. *Scholarships, grants, and awards:* Federal Pell, FSEOG, state, private, college/university gift aid from institutional funds.
GIFT AID (NON-NEED-BASED) *Total amount:* $1,609,422 (98% institutional, 2% external sources). *Receiving aid:* Freshmen: 3% (5). Undergraduates: 5% (34). *Average award:* Freshmen: $13,706. Undergraduates: $13,191. *Scholarships, grants, and awards by category: Academic interests/achievement:* 237 awards ($1,446,875 total): general academic interests/achievements. *Creative arts/performance:* 61 awards ($138,000 total): art/fine arts, creative writing, music, performing arts, theater/drama. *Special achievements/activities:* 283 awards ($1,064,817 total): community service, general special achievements/activities, leadership, religious involvement. *Special characteristics:* 32 awards ($337,917 total): children and siblings of alumni, children of current students, international students, parents of current students, relatives of clergy, religious affiliation, siblings of current students.
LOANS *Student loans:* $4,325,367 (77% need-based, 23% non-need-based). 79% of past graduating class borrowed through all loan programs. *Average indebtedness per student:* $42,269. *Average need-based loan:* Freshmen: $2775. Undergraduates: $3753. *Parent loans:* $1,179,453 (47% need-based, 53% non-need-based). *Programs:* Federal Direct (Subsidized and Unsubsidized Stafford, PLUS), private loans.
WORK-STUDY *Federal work-study:* Total amount: $211,247; 188 jobs averaging $1700. *State or other work-study/employment:* Total amount: $148,998 (55% need-based, 45% non-need-based). 122 part-time jobs averaging $1700.
APPLYING FOR FINANCIAL AID *Required financial aid form:* FAFSA. *Financial aid deadline (priority):* 3/1. *Notification date:* Continuous. Students must reply by 5/1 or within 4 weeks of notification.

CONTACT Wendy J. Ellis, Director of Student Financial Services, Green Mountain College, One Brennan Circle, Poultney, VT 05764-1199, 800-776-6675 Ext. 8209 or toll-free 800-776-6675. *Fax:* 802-287-8096. *E-mail:* ellisw@greenmtn.edu. *Website:* http://www.greenmtn.edu/.

GREENSBORO COLLEGE
Greensboro, NC

CONTACT Dawn VanArsdale Young, Director of Financial Aid, Greensboro College, 815 West Market Street, Greensboro, NC 27401-1875, 336-272-7102 Ext. 408 or toll-free 800-346-8226. *Fax:* 336-271-6634. *E-mail:* dvanarsdale@reensgborocollege.edu. *Website:* http://www.greensboro.edu/.

GREENVILLE COLLEGE
Greenville, IL

Tuition & fees: $22,920	Average undergraduate aid package: $17,499

ABOUT THE INSTITUTION Independent Free Methodist, coed. *Awards:* bachelor's and master's degrees. 54 undergraduate majors. *Total enrollment:* 1,463. Undergraduates: 1,224. Freshmen: 262. Federal methodology is used as a basis for awarding need-based institutional aid.
UNDERGRADUATE EXPENSES for 2013–2014 *Comprehensive fee:* $30,496 includes full-time tuition ($22,750), mandatory fees ($170), and room and board ($7576). *College room only:* $3664. Full-time tuition and fees vary according to degree level. Room and board charges vary according to housing facility. *Part-time tuition:* $482 per credit hour. Part-time tuition and fees vary according to course load and degree level.
FRESHMAN FINANCIAL AID (Fall 2012, est.) 242 applied for aid; of those 90% were deemed to have need. 100% of freshmen with need received aid; of those 14% had need fully met. *Average percent of need met:* 76% (excluding resources awarded to replace EFC). *Average financial aid package:* $18,298 (excluding resources awarded to replace EFC). 16% of all full-time freshmen had no need and received non-need-based gift aid.
UNDERGRADUATE FINANCIAL AID (Fall 2012, est.) 1,018 applied for aid; of those 92% were deemed to have need. 100% of undergraduates with need received aid; of those 11% had need fully met. *Average percent of need met:* 71% (excluding resources awarded to replace EFC). *Average financial aid package:* $17,499 (excluding resources awarded to replace EFC). 13% of all full-time undergraduates had no need and received non-need-based gift aid.
GIFT AID (NEED-BASED) *Total amount:* $12,474,103 (16% federal, 12% state, 69% institutional, 3% external sources). *Receiving aid:* Freshmen: 84% (219); all full-time undergraduates: 83% (906). *Average award:* Freshmen: $15,131; Undergraduates: $13,673. *Scholarships, grants, and awards:* Federal Pell, FSEOG, state, private, college/university gift aid from institutional funds.
GIFT AID (NON-NEED-BASED) *Total amount:* $1,421,489 (92% institutional, 8% external sources). *Receiving aid:* Freshmen: 10% (26). Undergraduates: 6% (68). *Average award:* Freshmen: $6881. Undergraduates: $7106. *Scholarships, grants, and awards by category: Academic interests/achievement:* biological sciences, business, education, engineering/technologies, general academic interests/achievements, mathematics, physical sciences, religion/biblical studies. *Creative arts/performance:* applied art and design, art/fine arts, music, performing arts. *Special achievements/activities:* leadership, memberships, religious involvement. *Special characteristics:* children and siblings of alumni, children of faculty/staff, international students, local/state students, out-of-state students, relatives of clergy, religious affiliation, siblings of current students. *Tuition waivers:* Full or partial for employees or children of employees, senior citizens.
LOANS *Student loans:* $7,780,821 (82% need-based, 18% non-need-based). 94% of past graduating class borrowed through all loan programs. *Average indebtedness per student:* $23,976. *Average need-based loan:* Freshmen: $3516. Undergraduates: $4346. *Parent loans:* $2,029,013 (29% need-based, 71% non-need-based). *Programs:* Federal Direct (Subsidized and Unsubsidized Stafford, PLUS), Perkins, college/university.
WORK-STUDY *Federal work-study:* Total amount: $383,308; jobs available. *State or other work-study/employment:* Part-time jobs available.

APPLYING FOR FINANCIAL AID *Required financial aid form:* FAFSA. *Financial aid deadline (priority):* 3/1. *Notification date:* Continuous beginning 3/1. Students must reply within 3 weeks of notification.

CONTACT Marilae Latham, Director of Financial Aid, Greenville College, 315 East College Avenue, Greenville, IL 62246-0159, 618-664-7110 or toll-free 800-345-4440. *Fax:* 618-664-7198. *E-mail:* marilae.latham@greenville.edu. *Website:* http://www.greenville.edu/.

GRINNELL COLLEGE
Grinnell, IA

Tuition & fees: $41,004	Average undergraduate aid package: $38,306

ABOUT THE INSTITUTION Independent, coed. *Awards:* bachelor's degrees. 27 undergraduate majors. *Total enrollment:* 1,674. Undergraduates: 1,674. Freshmen: 444. Both federal and institutional methodology are used as a basis for awarding need-based institutional aid.

UNDERGRADUATE EXPENSES for 2013–2014 *Application fee:* $30. *Comprehensive fee:* $50,618 includes full-time tuition ($40,628), mandatory fees ($376), and room and board ($9614). *College room only:* $4504. Room and board charges vary according to board plan and housing facility. *Part-time tuition:* $1270 per credit hour.

FRESHMAN FINANCIAL AID (Fall 2012, est.) 377 applied for aid; of those 88% were deemed to have need. 100% of freshmen with need received aid; of those 100% had need fully met. *Average percent of need met:* 100% (excluding resources awarded to replace EFC). *Average financial aid package:* $38,718 (excluding resources awarded to replace EFC). 13% of all full-time freshmen had no need and received non-need-based gift aid.

UNDERGRADUATE FINANCIAL AID (Fall 2012, est.) 1,250 applied for aid; of those 93% were deemed to have need. 100% of undergraduates with need received aid; of those 100% had need fully met. *Average percent of need met:* 100% (excluding resources awarded to replace EFC). *Average financial aid package:* $38,306 (excluding resources awarded to replace EFC). 14% of all full-time undergraduates had no need and received non-need-based gift aid.

GIFT AID (NEED-BASED) *Total amount:* $37,902,439 (4% federal, 1% state, 93% institutional, 2% external sources). *Receiving aid:* Freshmen: 74% (329); all full-time undergraduates: 71% (1,149). *Average award:* Freshmen: $32,267; Undergraduates: $32,984. *Scholarships, grants, and awards:* Federal Pell, FSEOG, state, private, college/university gift aid from institutional funds.

GIFT AID (NON-NEED-BASED) *Total amount:* $4,439,067 (82% institutional, 18% external sources). *Receiving aid:* Freshmen: 15% (67). Undergraduates: 6% (102). *Average award:* Freshmen: $15,791. Undergraduates: $13,626. *Scholarships, grants, and awards by category:* Academic interests/achievement: general academic interests/achievements. *Tuition waivers:* Full or partial for employees or children of employees.

LOANS *Student loans:* $3,335,091 (84% need-based, 16% non-need-based). 55% of past graduating class borrowed through all loan programs. *Average indebtedness per student:* $16,226. *Average need-based loan:* Freshmen: $4008. Undergraduates: $3484. *Programs:* Federal Direct (Subsidized and Unsubsidized Stafford, PLUS), Perkins, state.

WORK-STUDY *Federal work-study:* Total amount: $1,367,808; 591 jobs averaging $1200. *State or other work-study/employment:* Total amount: $882,055 (42% need-based, 58% non-need-based). 334 part-time jobs averaging $1364.

APPLYING FOR FINANCIAL AID *Required financial aid forms:* FAFSA, institution's own form, noncustodial (divorced/separated) parent's statement. *Financial aid deadline:* 2/1 (priority: 2/1). *Notification date:* 4/1. Students must reply by 5/1.

CONTACT Mr. Arnold Woods, Director of Student Financial Aid, Grinnell College, 1103 Park Street, Grinnell, IA 50112-1690, 641-269-3250 or toll-free 800-247-0113. *Fax:* 641-269-4937. *E-mail:* woods@grinnell.edu. *Website:* http://www.grinnell.edu/.

GROVE CITY COLLEGE
Grove City, PA

Tuition & fees: $14,880	Average undergraduate aid package: $6122

ABOUT THE INSTITUTION Independent Presbyterian, coed. *Awards:* bachelor's degrees. 40 undergraduate majors. *Total enrollment:* 2,506. Undergraduates: 2,506. Freshmen: 670. Institutional methodology is used as a basis for awarding need-based institutional aid.

UNDERGRADUATE EXPENSES for 2013–2014 *Application fee:* $50. *Comprehensive fee:* $22,988 includes full-time tuition ($14,880) and room and board ($8108). Full-time tuition and fees vary according to course load. Room and board charges vary according to housing facility. *Part-time tuition:* $465 per credit.

FRESHMAN FINANCIAL AID (Fall 2012, est.) 419 applied for aid; of those 72% were deemed to have need. 99% of freshmen with need received aid; of those 11% had need fully met. *Average percent of need met:* 51% (excluding resources awarded to replace EFC). *Average financial aid package:* $6405 (excluding resources awarded to replace EFC). 6% of all full-time freshmen had no need and received non-need-based gift aid.

UNDERGRADUATE FINANCIAL AID (Fall 2012, est.) 1,321 applied for aid; of those 81% were deemed to have need. 95% of undergraduates with need received aid; of those 8% had need fully met. *Average percent of need met:* 46% (excluding resources awarded to replace EFC). *Average financial aid package:* $6122 (excluding resources awarded to replace EFC). 12% of all full-time undergraduates had no need and received non-need-based gift aid.

GIFT AID (NEED-BASED) *Total amount:* $6,130,523 (16% state, 77% institutional, 7% external sources). *Receiving aid:* Freshmen: 44% (295); all full-time undergraduates: 40% (977). *Average award:* Freshmen: $6405; Undergraduates: $6122. *Scholarships, grants, and awards:* state, private, college/university gift aid from institutional funds.

GIFT AID (NON-NEED-BASED) *Total amount:* $1,386,927 (5% state, 50% institutional, 45% external sources). *Receiving aid:* Freshmen: 5% (32). Undergraduates: 3% (82). *Average award:* Freshmen: $2941. Undergraduates: $2034. *Scholarships, grants, and awards by category:* Academic interests/achievement: 528 awards ($849,346 total): biological sciences, business, communication, education, engineering/technologies, English, foreign languages, general academic interests/achievements, mathematics, physical sciences, religion/biblical studies, social sciences. Creative arts/performance: 7 awards ($9200 total): creative writing, music. Special achievements/activities: 23 awards ($70,727 total): general special achievements/activities, leadership, memberships, religious involvement. Special characteristics: 19 awards ($52,100 total): ethnic background, general special characteristics, handicapped students, members of minority groups. *Tuition waivers:* Full or partial for employees or children of employees. *ROTC:* Army cooperative.

LOANS *Student loans:* $12,360,197 (36% need-based, 64% non-need-based). 60% of past graduating class borrowed through all loan programs. *Average indebtedness per student:* $28,767. *Programs:* state, private loans.

APPLYING FOR FINANCIAL AID *Required financial aid form:* institution's own form. *Financial aid deadline:* 4/15. *Notification date:* Continuous beginning 3/18. Students must reply by 5/1.

CONTACT Thomas G. Ball, Director of Financial Aid, Grove City College, 100 Campus Drive, Grove City, PA 16127-2104, 724-458-3300. *Fax:* 724-450-4040. *E-mail:* financialaid@gcc.edu. *Website:* http://www.gcc.edu/.

GUILFORD COLLEGE
Greensboro, NC

Tuition & fees: $32,470	Average undergraduate aid package: $17,587

ABOUT THE INSTITUTION Independent Society of Friends, coed. *Awards:* certificates and bachelor's degrees. 39 undergraduate majors. *Total enrollment:* 2,462. Undergraduates: 2,462. Freshmen: 322. Federal methodology is used as a basis for awarding need-based institutional aid.

UNDERGRADUATE EXPENSES for 2013–2014 *Application fee:* $25. *Comprehensive fee:* $41,270 includes full-time tuition ($32,090), mandatory fees ($380), and room and board ($8800). Room and board charges vary according to board plan and housing facility. Part-time tuition and fees vary according to course load.

FRESHMAN FINANCIAL AID (Fall 2012, est.) 276 applied for aid; of those 93% were deemed to have need. 96% of freshmen with need received aid; of those 4% had need fully met. *Average financial aid package:* $22,998 (excluding resources awarded to replace EFC). 23% of all full-time freshmen had no need and received non-need-based gift aid.

UNDERGRADUATE FINANCIAL AID (Fall 2012, est.) 1,781 applied for aid; of those 90% were deemed to have need. 93% of undergraduates with need received aid; of those 5% had need fully met. *Average financial aid package:* $17,587 (excluding resources awarded to replace EFC). 10% of all full-time undergraduates had no need and received non-need-based gift aid.

GIFT AID (NEED-BASED) *Total amount:* $23,853,405 (22% federal, 9% state, 64% institutional, 5% external sources). *Receiving aid:* Freshmen: 76% (229); all full-time undergraduates: 78% (1,476). *Average award:* Freshmen: $20,643; Undergraduates: $18,681. *Scholarships, grants, and awards:* Federal Pell, FSEOG, state, private, college/university gift aid from institutional funds.

GIFT AID (NON-NEED-BASED) *Total amount:* $2,753,736 (91% institutional, 9% external sources). *Receiving aid:* Freshmen: 40% (121). Undergraduates: 54% (1,030). *Average award:* Freshmen: $13,444. Undergraduates: $12,594. *Scholarships, grants, and awards by category: Academic interests/achievement:* biological sciences, general academic interests/achievements. *Creative arts/performance:* music, theater/drama. *Special achievements/activities:* religious involvement. *Special characteristics:* 16 awards ($439,770 total): children of faculty/staff, first-generation college students, local/state students. *Tuition waivers:* Full or partial for employees or children of employees.

LOANS *Student loans:* $14,530,251 (91% need-based, 9% non-need-based). 75% of past graduating class borrowed through all loan programs. *Average indebtedness per student:* $25,025. *Average need-based loan:* Freshmen: $7851. Undergraduates: $7240. *Parent loans:* $2,078,500 (100% need-based). *Programs:* Perkins, college/university.

WORK-STUDY *Federal work-study:* Total amount: $397,874; 235 jobs averaging $1620. *State or other work-study/employment:* Total amount: $408,751 (100% need-based). 270 part-time jobs averaging $1463.

APPLYING FOR FINANCIAL AID *Required financial aid forms:* FAFSA, noncustodial (divorced/separated) parent's statement, business/farm supplement. *Financial aid deadline (priority):* 3/1. *Notification date:* Continuous. Students must reply within 2 weeks of notification.

CONTACT Mr. Paul J. Coscia, Director of Student Financial Services, Guilford College, 5800 West Friendly Avenue, Greensboro, NC 27410, 336-316-2395 or toll-free 800-992-7759. *Fax:* 336-316-2942. *E-mail:* pcoscia@guilford.edu. *Website:* http://www.guilford.edu/.

GUSTAVUS ADOLPHUS COLLEGE
St. Peter, MN

Tuition & fees: $37,606	Average undergraduate aid package: $29,160

ABOUT THE INSTITUTION Independent Evangelical Lutheran Church in America, coed. *Awards:* bachelor's degrees. 67 undergraduate majors. *Total enrollment:* 2,524. Undergraduates: 2,524. Freshmen: 678. Both federal and institutional methodology are used as a basis for awarding need-based institutional aid.

UNDERGRADUATE EXPENSES for 2013–2014 *One-time required fee:* $450. *Comprehensive fee:* $46,486 includes full-time tuition ($37,210), mandatory fees ($396), and room and board ($8880). *College room only:* $5710. Room and board charges vary according to board plan and housing facility. *Part-time tuition:* $5080 per course. *Payment plan:* Tuition prepayment.

FRESHMAN FINANCIAL AID (Fall 2011) 631 applied for aid; of those 90% were deemed to have need. 99% of freshmen with need received aid; of those 30% had need fully met. *Average percent of need met:* 91% (excluding resources awarded to replace EFC). *Average financial aid package:* $31,279 (excluding resources awarded to replace EFC). 23% of all full-time freshmen had no need and received non-need-based gift aid.

UNDERGRADUATE FINANCIAL AID (Fall 2011) 1,980 applied for aid; of those 90% were deemed to have need. 100% of undergraduates with need received aid; of those 22% had need fully met. *Average percent of need met:* 86% (excluding resources awarded to replace EFC). *Average financial aid package:*

$29,160 (excluding resources awarded to replace EFC). 27% of all full-time undergraduates had no need and received non-need-based gift aid.

GIFT AID (NEED-BASED) *Total amount:* $13,830,480 (6% federal, 6% state, 85% institutional, 3% external sources). *Receiving aid:* Freshmen: 77% (562); all full-time undergraduates: 71% (1,734). *Average award:* Freshmen: $26,577; Undergraduates: $24,018. *Scholarships, grants, and awards:* Federal Pell, FSEOG, state, private, college/university gift aid from institutional funds.

GIFT AID (NON-NEED-BASED) *Total amount:* $3,250,865 (93% institutional, 7% external sources). *Receiving aid:* Freshmen: 11% (84). Undergraduates: 7% (175). *Average award:* Freshmen: $14,192. Undergraduates: $12,711. *Scholarships, grants, and awards by category: Academic interests/achievement:* general academic interests/achievements. *Creative arts/performance:* art/fine arts, dance, debating, music, theater/drama. *Special achievements/activities:* junior miss. *Special characteristics:* children and siblings of alumni, ethnic background, first-generation college students, international students, members of minority groups, out-of-state students, siblings of current students. *ROTC:* Army cooperative.

LOANS *Student loans:* $4,302,030 (41% need-based, 59% non-need-based). 71% of past graduating class borrowed through all loan programs. *Average indebtedness per student:* $28,124. *Average need-based loan:* Freshmen: $3128. Undergraduates: $3661. *Parent loans:* $1,021,468 (78% need-based, 22% non-need-based). *Programs:* Federal Direct (Subsidized and Unsubsidized Stafford, PLUS), Perkins, state.

WORK-STUDY *Federal work-study:* Total amount: $771,125; 883 jobs averaging $4388. *State or other work-study/employment:* Total amount: $184,756 (76% need-based, 24% non-need-based). 427 part-time jobs averaging $2815.

APPLYING FOR FINANCIAL AID *Required financial aid form:* FAFSA. *Financial aid deadline:* 4/15 (priority: 2/15). *Notification date:* Continuous beginning 1/20. Students must reply by 5/1 or within 2 weeks of notification.

CONTACT Mr. Doug Minter, Dean of Financial Aid, Gustavus Adolphus College, 800 West College Avenue, St. Peter, MN 56082-1498, 507-933-7527 or toll-free 800-GUSTAVU(S). *Fax:* 507-933-7727. *E-mail:* finaid@gustavus.edu. *Website:* http://www.gustavus.edu/.

GUTENBERG COLLEGE
Eugene, OR

CONTACT Financial Aid Office, Gutenberg College, 1883 University Street, Eugene, OR 97403, 541-683-5141. *Website:* http://www.gutenberg.edu/.

GWYNEDD-MERCY COLLEGE
Gwynedd Valley, PA

Tuition & fees: $28,340	Average undergraduate aid package: $18,628

ABOUT THE INSTITUTION Independent Roman Catholic, coed. *Awards:* certificates, associate, bachelor's, and master's degrees. 32 undergraduate majors. *Total enrollment:* 2,710. Undergraduates: 2,347. Freshmen: 298. Federal methodology is used as a basis for awarding need-based institutional aid.

UNDERGRADUATE EXPENSES for 2013–2014 *Application fee:* $25. *Comprehensive fee:* $38,190 includes full-time tuition ($27,740), mandatory fees ($600), and room and board ($9850). Full-time tuition and fees vary according to program. Room and board charges vary according to board plan and housing facility. *Part-time tuition:* $600 per credit hour. Part-time tuition and fees vary according to program.

FRESHMAN FINANCIAL AID (Fall 2012, est.) 238 applied for aid; of those 91% were deemed to have need. 100% of freshmen with need received aid; of those 15% had need fully met. *Average percent of need met:* 70% (excluding resources awarded to replace EFC). *Average financial aid package:* $19,663 (excluding resources awarded to replace EFC). 10% of all full-time freshmen had no need and received non-need-based gift aid.

UNDERGRADUATE FINANCIAL AID (Fall 2012, est.) 1,390 applied for aid; of those 87% were deemed to have need. 99% of undergraduates with need received aid; of those 17% had need fully met. *Average percent of need met:* 65% (excluding resources awarded to replace EFC). *Average financial aid package:* $18,628

(excluding resources awarded to replace EFC). 11% of all full-time undergraduates had no need and received non-need-based gift aid.

GIFT AID (NEED-BASED) *Total amount:* $19,178,408 (17% federal, 11% state, 65% institutional, 7% external sources). *Receiving aid:* Freshmen: 83% (216); all full-time undergraduates: 70% (1,178). *Average award:* Freshmen: $16,199; Undergraduates: $15,288. *Scholarships, grants, and awards:* Federal Pell, FSEOG, state, private, college/university gift aid from institutional funds.

GIFT AID (NON-NEED-BASED) *Total amount:* $3,030,621 (4% federal, 1% state, 82% institutional, 13% external sources). *Receiving aid:* Freshmen: 9% (24). Undergraduates: 8% (142). *Average award:* Freshmen: $10,786. Undergraduates: $10,165. *Scholarships, grants, and awards by category:* Academic interests/achievement: general academic interests/achievements. *Special achievements/activities:* general special achievements/activities. *Special characteristics:* children and siblings of alumni, siblings of current students. *Tuition waivers:* Full or partial for employees or children of employees.

LOANS *Student loans:* $15,915,939 (71% need-based, 29% non-need-based). 91% of past graduating class borrowed through all loan programs. *Average indebtedness per student:* $36,067. *Average need-based loan:* Freshmen: $3365. Undergraduates: $4073. *Parent loans:* $2,286,430 (33% need-based, 67% non-need-based). *Programs:* Federal Direct (Subsidized and Unsubsidized Stafford, PLUS), Perkins, Federal Nursing, alternative loans.

WORK-STUDY *Federal work-study:* Total amount: $292,451; jobs available. *State or other work-study/employment:* Total amount: $7200 (100% need-based). Part-time jobs available.

APPLYING FOR FINANCIAL AID *Required financial aid forms:* FAFSA, institution's own form. *Financial aid deadline:* 5/1 (priority: 3/15). *Notification date:* Continuous beginning 2/15. Students must reply by 5/1 or within 2 weeks of notification.

CONTACT Mrs. Elizabeth R. Howard, Director of Student Financial Aid, Gwynedd-Mercy College, PO Box 901, Gwynedd Valley, PA 19437-0901, 215-646-7300 Ext. 483 or toll-free 800-DIAL-GMC. *Fax:* 215-641-5556. *E-mail:* howard.e@gmc.edu. *Website:* http://www.gmc.edu/.

HAMILTON COLLEGE
Clinton, NY

Tuition & fees: $44,350	Average undergraduate aid package: $39,386

ABOUT THE INSTITUTION Independent, coed. *Awards:* bachelor's degrees. 43 undergraduate majors. *Total enrollment:* 1,884. Undergraduates: 1,884. Freshmen: 469. Both federal and institutional methodology are used as a basis for awarding need-based institutional aid.

UNDERGRADUATE EXPENSES for 2013–2014 *Application fee:* $60. *Comprehensive fee:* $55,620 includes full-time tuition ($43,910), mandatory fees ($440), and room and board ($11,270). *College room only:* $6160. Room and board charges vary according to board plan. *Part-time tuition:* $5488.75 per course.

FRESHMAN FINANCIAL AID (Fall 2012, est.) 309 applied for aid; of those 82% were deemed to have need. 100% of freshmen with need received aid; of those 100% had need fully met. *Average percent of need met:* 100% (excluding resources awarded to replace EFC). *Average financial aid package:* $40,594 (excluding resources awarded to replace EFC).

UNDERGRADUATE FINANCIAL AID (Fall 2012, est.) 1,154 applied for aid; of those 75% were deemed to have need. 100% of undergraduates with need received aid; of those 100% had need fully met. *Average percent of need met:* 100% (excluding resources awarded to replace EFC). *Average financial aid package:* $39,386 (excluding resources awarded to replace EFC). 1% of all full-time undergraduates had no need and received non-need-based gift aid.

GIFT AID (NEED-BASED) *Total amount:* $30,357,795 (4% federal, 3% state, 91% institutional, 2% external sources). *Receiving aid:* Freshmen: 54% (254); all full-time undergraduates: 46% (868). *Average award:* Freshmen: $37,569; Undergraduates: $35,441. *Scholarships, grants, and awards:* Federal Pell, FSEOG, state, private, college/university gift aid from institutional funds.

GIFT AID (NON-NEED-BASED) *Total amount:* $904,166 (2% state, 54% institutional, 44% external sources). *Average award:* Undergraduates: $37,808. *Tuition waivers:* Full or partial for employees or children of employees. *ROTC:* Army cooperative, Air Force cooperative.

LOANS *Student loans:* $2,543,046 (100% need-based). 39% of past graduating class borrowed through all loan programs. *Average indebtedness per student:* $18,568. *Average need-based loan:* Freshmen: $2931. Undergraduates: $3880. *Programs:* Federal Direct (Subsidized and Unsubsidized Stafford, PLUS), Perkins, college/university.

WORK-STUDY *Federal work-study:* Total amount: $838,306; 556 jobs averaging $1508. *State or other work-study/employment:* Total amount: $105,600 (100% need-based). 58 part-time jobs averaging $1821.

APPLYING FOR FINANCIAL AID *Required financial aid forms:* FAFSA, institution's own form, CSS Financial Aid PROFILE, state aid form, noncustodial (divorced/separated) parent's statement, business/farm supplement. *Financial aid deadline:* 2/15 (priority: 2/15). *Notification date:* 4/1. Students must reply by 5/1.

CONTACT Office of Financial Aid, Hamilton College, 198 College Hill Road, Clinton, NY 13323, 315-859-4434 or toll-free 800-843-2655. *Fax:* 315-859-4962. *E-mail:* finaid@hamilton.edu. *Website:* http://www.hamilton.edu/.

HAMILTON TECHNICAL COLLEGE
Davenport, IA

CONTACT Ms. Lisa Boyd, Executive Vice President/Director of Financial Aid, Hamilton Technical College, 1011 East 53rd Street, Davenport, IA 52807-2653, 563-386-3570 Ext. 33 or toll-free 866-966-4825. *Fax:* 563-386-6756. *Website:* http://www.hamiltontechcollege.edu/.

HAMLINE UNIVERSITY
St. Paul, MN

Tuition & fees: $33,752	Average undergraduate aid package: $22,368

ABOUT THE INSTITUTION Independent United Methodist Church, coed. *Awards:* certificates, bachelor's, master's, and doctoral degrees. 50 undergraduate majors. *Total enrollment:* 4,683. Undergraduates: 2,140. Freshmen: 541. Federal methodology is used as a basis for awarding need-based institutional aid.

UNDERGRADUATE EXPENSES for 2013–2014 *Comprehensive fee:* $42,452 includes full-time tuition ($33,236), mandatory fees ($516), and room and board ($8700). *College room only:* $4500. Room and board charges vary according to board plan and housing facility. *Part-time tuition:* $1040 per credit. *Part-time fees:* $444 per year. Part-time tuition and fees vary according to course load.

FRESHMAN FINANCIAL AID (Fall 2012, est.) 509 applied for aid; of those 94% were deemed to have need. 100% of freshmen with need received aid; of those 20% had need fully met. *Average percent of need met:* 85% (excluding resources awarded to replace EFC). *Average financial aid package:* $25,467 (excluding resources awarded to replace EFC). 11% of all full-time freshmen had no need and received non-need-based gift aid.

UNDERGRADUATE FINANCIAL AID (Fall 2012, est.) 1,783 applied for aid; of those 94% were deemed to have need. 100% of undergraduates with need received aid; of those 15% had need fully met. *Average percent of need met:* 78% (excluding resources awarded to replace EFC). *Average financial aid package:* $22,368 (excluding resources awarded to replace EFC). 10% of all full-time undergraduates had no need and received non-need-based gift aid.

GIFT AID (NEED-BASED) *Total amount:* $32,288,180 (11% federal, 10% state, 77% institutional, 2% external sources). *Receiving aid:* Freshmen: 88% (476); all full-time undergraduates: 85% (1,671). *Average award:* Freshmen: $21,803; Undergraduates: $19,659. *Scholarships, grants, and awards:* Federal Pell, FSEOG, state, private, college/university gift aid from institutional funds, Academic Competitiveness Grants, National SMART Grants, TEACH Grants, United Methodist Scholarships.

GIFT AID (NON-NEED-BASED) *Total amount:* $1,665,418 (88% institutional, 12% external sources). *Receiving aid:* Freshmen: 13% (73). Undergraduates: 9% (183). *Average award:* Freshmen: $14,636. Undergraduates: $11,840. *Scholarships, grants, and awards by category:* Academic interests/achievement: 1,422 awards ($16,887,332 total): biological sciences, business, communication, education, English, foreign languages, general academic interests/achievements, health fields, humanities, international studies, mathematics, physical sciences, premedicine, religion/biblical studies, social sciences. *Creative arts/performance:* 118 awards ($419,411 total): art/fine arts, creative writing, general creative arts/performance, journalism/publications, music, performing arts, theater/drama. *Special achievements/activities:* 241 awards ($735,325 total): community service, general special achievements/activities, leadership, memberships. *Special characteristics:* 277 awards ($1,240,617 total): children and siblings of alumni, ethnic background, general special characteristics, handicapped students, international students, local/state students, members of minority groups, previous college experience, relatives of clergy, religious affiliation, veterans. *Tuition waivers:* Full or partial for employees or children of employees. **ROTC:** Army cooperative, Air Force cooperative.

LOANS *Student loans:* $14,431,456 (79% need-based, 21% non-need-based). 77% of past graduating class borrowed through all loan programs. *Average indebtedness per student:* $40,472. *Average need-based loan:* Freshmen: $3960. Undergraduates: $4664. *Parent loans:* $4,057,935 (39% need-based, 61% non-need-based). *Programs:* Federal Direct (Subsidized and Unsubsidized Stafford, PLUS), Perkins, state, alternative loans, United Methodist Student Loans.

WORK-STUDY *Federal work-study:* Total amount: $1,112,095; 472 jobs averaging $2356. *State or other work-study/employment:* Total amount: $2,090,251 (64% need-based, 36% non-need-based). 885 part-time jobs averaging $2362.

APPLYING FOR FINANCIAL AID *Required financial aid form:* FAFSA. *Financial aid deadline (priority):* 3/15. *Notification date:* Continuous beginning 3/15. Students must reply by 5/1 or within 2 weeks of notification.

CONTACT Ms. Lynette Wahl, Office of Financial Aid, Hamline University, 1536 Hewitt Avenue, MS C1915, St. Paul, MN 55104, 651-523-3000 or toll-free 800-753-9753. *Fax:* 651-523-2585. *E-mail:* finaid@hamline.edu. *Website:* http://www.hamline.edu/.

HAMPDEN-SYDNEY COLLEGE
Hampden-Sydney, VA

Tuition & fees: $35,570	Average undergraduate aid package: $28,572

ABOUT THE INSTITUTION Independent Presbyterian Church (U.S.A.), men only. *Awards:* bachelor's degrees. 28 undergraduate majors. *Total enrollment:* 1,080. Undergraduates: 1,080. Freshmen: 342. Both federal and institutional methodology are used as a basis for awarding need-based institutional aid.

UNDERGRADUATE EXPENSES for 2013–2014 *Application fee:* $30. *Comprehensive fee:* $46,736 includes full-time tuition ($34,498), mandatory fees ($1072), and room and board ($11,166). Room and board charges vary according to board plan and housing facility.

FRESHMAN FINANCIAL AID (Fall 2012, est.) 288 applied for aid; of those 78% were deemed to have need. 100% of freshmen with need received aid; of those 17% had need fully met. *Average percent of need met:* 83% (excluding resources awarded to replace EFC). *Average financial aid package:* $29,766 (excluding resources awarded to replace EFC). 35% of all full-time freshmen had no need and received non-need-based gift aid.

UNDERGRADUATE FINANCIAL AID (Fall 2012, est.) 786 applied for aid; of those 84% were deemed to have need. 100% of undergraduates with need received aid; of those 19% had need fully met. *Average percent of need met:* 81% (excluding resources awarded to replace EFC). *Average financial aid package:* $28,572 (excluding resources awarded to replace EFC). 38% of all full-time undergraduates had no need and received non-need-based gift aid.

GIFT AID (NEED-BASED) *Total amount:* $15,513,946 (6% federal, 8% state, 84% institutional, 2% external sources). *Receiving aid:* Freshmen: 66% (226); all full-time undergraduates: 61% (656). *Average award:* Freshmen: $25,230; Undergraduates: $23,649. *Scholarships, grants, and awards:* Federal Pell, FSEOG, state, private, college/university gift aid from institutional funds.

GIFT AID (NON-NEED-BASED) *Total amount:* $6,661,619 (13% state, 83% institutional, 4% external sources). *Receiving aid:* Freshmen: 8% (26). Undergraduates: 8% (82). *Average award:* Freshmen: $13,708. Undergraduates: $12,527. *Scholarships, grants, and awards by category: Academic interests/achievement:* biological sciences, education, general academic interests/achievements, health fields, international studies, premedicine, religion/biblical studies. *Creative arts/performance:* music. *Special achievements/activities:* general special achievements/activities, leadership. *Special characteristics:* children of educators, children of faculty/staff, ethnic background, international students, members of minority groups, out-of-state students, religious affiliation, veterans, veterans' children. *Tuition waivers:* Full or partial for employees or children of employees. **ROTC:** Army cooperative.

LOANS *Student loans:* $5,885,554 (67% need-based, 33% non-need-based). 55% of past graduating class borrowed through all loan programs. *Average indebtedness per student:* $30,248. *Average need-based loan:* Freshmen: $4318. Undergraduates: $5242. *Parent loans:* $4,464,790 (28% need-based, 72% non-need-based). *Programs:* Federal Direct (Subsidized and Unsubsidized Stafford, PLUS), Perkins, college/university.

WORK-STUDY *Federal work-study:* Total amount: $362,295; 255 jobs averaging $1372.

APPLYING FOR FINANCIAL AID *Required financial aid forms:* FAFSA, state aid form. *Financial aid deadline (priority):* 3/1. *Notification date:* 3/15. Students must reply by 5/1 or within 2 weeks of notification.

CONTACT Mrs. Zita Marie Barree, Director of Financial Aid, Hampden-Sydney College, PO Box 726, Hampden-Sydney, VA 23943-0726, 434-223-6119 or toll-free 800-755-0733. *Fax:* 434-223-6075. *E-mail:* hsfinaid@hsc.edu. *Website:* http://www.hsc.edu/.

HAMPSHIRE COLLEGE
Amherst, MA

Tuition & fees: $46,625	Average undergraduate aid package: $35,849

ABOUT THE INSTITUTION Independent, coed. *Awards:* bachelor's degrees. 57 undergraduate majors. *Total enrollment:* 1,461. Undergraduates: 1,484. Freshmen: 366. Institutional methodology is used as a basis for awarding need-based institutional aid.

UNDERGRADUATE EXPENSES for 2013–2014 *Application fee:* $60. *Comprehensive fee:* $58,655 includes full-time tuition ($45,100), mandatory fees ($1525), and room and board ($12,030). *College room only:* $7680. Room and board charges vary according to board plan.

FRESHMAN FINANCIAL AID (Fall 2012, est.) 275 applied for aid; of those 70% were deemed to have need. 100% of freshmen with need received aid; of those 22% had need fully met. *Average percent of need met:* 87% (excluding resources awarded to replace EFC). *Average financial aid package:* $34,143 (excluding resources awarded to replace EFC). 35% of all full-time freshmen had no need and received non-need-based gift aid.

UNDERGRADUATE FINANCIAL AID (Fall 2012, est.) 1,035 applied for aid; of those 84% were deemed to have need. 100% of undergraduates with need received aid; of those 69% had need fully met. *Average percent of need met:* 91% (excluding resources awarded to replace EFC). *Average financial aid package:* $35,849 (excluding resources awarded to replace EFC). 20% of all full-time undergraduates had no need and received non-need-based gift aid.

GIFT AID (NEED-BASED) *Total amount:* $26,268,825 (7% federal, 92% institutional, 1% external sources). *Receiving aid:* Freshmen: 55% (192); all full-time undergraduates: 61% (870). *Average award:* Freshmen: $29,118; Undergraduates: $29,910. *Scholarships, grants, and awards:* Federal Pell, FSEOG, state, private, college/university gift aid from institutional funds.

GIFT AID (NON-NEED-BASED) *Total amount:* $2,795,028 (1% federal, 96% institutional, 3% external sources). *Receiving aid:* Freshmen: 44% (155). Undergraduates: 33% (474). *Average award:* Freshmen: $9649. Undergraduates: $8913. *Scholarships, grants, and awards by category: Academic interests/achievement:* 273 awards ($2,371,272 total): biological sciences, English, general academic interests/achievements, humanities, international studies, mathematics, physical sciences, social sciences. *Creative arts/performance:* creative writing. *Special achievements/activities:* 2 awards ($12,000 total): community service, leadership. *Special characteristics:* children of faculty/staff. *Tuition waivers:* Full or partial for employees or children of employees. **ROTC:** Army cooperative.

LOANS *Student loans:* $4,935,748 (96% need-based, 4% non-need-based). 55% of past graduating class borrowed through all loan programs. *Average indebtedness per student:* $22,550. *Average need-based loan:* Freshmen: $2671. Undergraduates: $3536. *Parent loans:* $3,736,324 (84% need-based, 16% non-need-based). *Programs:* Federal Direct (Subsidized and Unsubsidized Stafford, PLUS), Perkins.

WORK-STUDY *Federal work-study:* Total amount: $1,837,391; 800 jobs averaging $2264. *State or other work-study/employment:* Total amount: $383,838 (68% need-based, 32% non-need-based). 137 part-time jobs averaging $2217.

APPLYING FOR FINANCIAL AID *Required financial aid forms:* FAFSA, CSS Financial Aid PROFILE, noncustodial (divorced/separated) parent's statement.

Financial aid deadline (priority): 2/1. *Notification date:* 4/1. Students must reply by 5/1 or within 2 weeks of notification.
CONTACT Ms. Jennifer Garratt Lawton, Director of Financial Aid, Hampshire College, 893 West Street, Amherst, MA 01002, 413-559-5484 or toll-free 877-937-4267. *Fax:* 413-559-5585. *E-mail:* financialaid@hampshire.edu. *Website:* http://www.hampshire.edu/.

HAMPTON UNIVERSITY
Hampton, VA

Tuition & fees: $20,724	Average undergraduate aid package: $5269

ABOUT THE INSTITUTION Independent, coed. *Awards:* certificates, associate, bachelor's, master's, and doctoral degrees. 77 undergraduate majors. *Total enrollment:* 4,754. Undergraduates: 3,851. Freshmen: 866. Federal methodology is used as a basis for awarding need-based institutional aid.
UNDERGRADUATE EXPENSES for 2013–2014 *Application fee:* $35. *Comprehensive fee:* $29,954 includes full-time tuition ($18,618), mandatory fees ($2106), and room and board ($9230). *College room only:* $4800. Full-time tuition and fees vary according to course load, degree level, location, and program. Room and board charges vary according to board plan, housing facility, and location. *Part-time tuition:* $472 per credit. Part-time tuition and fees vary according to course load and location.
FRESHMAN FINANCIAL AID (Fall 2012, est.) 569 applied for aid; of those 82% were deemed to have need. 94% of freshmen with need received aid; of those 36% had need fully met. *Average percent of need met:* 37% (excluding resources awarded to replace EFC). *Average financial aid package:* $5707 (excluding resources awarded to replace EFC). 9% of all full-time freshmen had no need and received non-need-based gift aid.
UNDERGRADUATE FINANCIAL AID (Fall 2012, est.) 2,160 applied for aid; of those 84% were deemed to have need. 95% of undergraduates with need received aid; of those 43% had need fully met. *Average percent of need met:* 43% (excluding resources awarded to replace EFC). *Average financial aid package:* $5269 (excluding resources awarded to replace EFC). 4% of all full-time undergraduates had no need and received non-need-based gift aid.
GIFT AID (NEED-BASED) *Total amount:* $8,630,521 (79% federal, 17% state, 2% institutional, 2% external sources). *Receiving aid:* Freshmen: 58% (426); all full-time undergraduates: 53% (1,695). *Average award:* Freshmen: $6231; Undergraduates: $4899. *Scholarships, grants, and awards:* Federal Pell, FSEOG, state, private, college/university gift aid from institutional funds, Federal Nursing.
GIFT AID (NON-NEED-BASED) *Total amount:* $13,434,210 (5% state, 66% institutional, 29% external sources). *Receiving aid:* Freshmen: 43% (318). Undergraduates: 24% (780). *Average award:* Freshmen: $11,761. Undergraduates: $12,546. *Scholarships, grants, and awards by category: Academic interests/achievement:* 383 awards ($5,025,020 total): architecture, biological sciences, business, communication, computer science, education, engineering/technologies, general academic interests/achievements, health fields, physical sciences. *Creative arts/performance:* 75 awards ($238,430 total): music. *Special achievements/activities:* 80 awards ($238,430 total): leadership. *Special characteristics:* 987 awards ($3,998,902 total): adult students, children of faculty/staff, international students, members of minority groups, veterans, veterans' children. *Tuition waivers:* Full or partial for employees or children of employees. *ROTC:* Army, Naval.
LOANS *Student loans:* $24,195,457 (93% need-based, 7% non-need-based). 98% of past graduating class borrowed through all loan programs. *Average indebtedness per student:* $9597. *Average need-based loan:* Freshmen: $4400. Undergraduates: $3611. *Parent loans:* $20,632,928 (85% need-based, 15% non-need-based). *Programs:* Federal Direct (Subsidized and Unsubsidized Stafford, PLUS), Perkins, Federal Nursing, college/university, private loans.
WORK-STUDY *Federal work-study:* Total amount: $337,820; 270 jobs averaging $1386. *State or other work-study/employment:* Total amount: $120,831 (100% non-need-based). 434 part-time jobs averaging $4995.
ATHLETIC AWARDS Total amount: $2,988,264 (93% need-based, 7% non-need-based).
APPLYING FOR FINANCIAL AID *Required financial aid forms:* FAFSA, Virginia Tuition Assistance Grant forms (VA residents only). *Financial aid deadline:* 4/15 (priority: 2/15). *Notification date:* Continuous beginning 4/15. Students must reply within 2 weeks of notification.

CONTACT Martin Miles, Director of Financial Aid, Hampton University, 2nd Floor, Whipple Barn, Hampton, VA 23668, 757-727-5332 or toll-free 800-624-3328. *Fax:* 757-728-6567. *E-mail:* martin.miles@hamptonu.edu. *Website:* http://www.hamptonu.edu/.

HANNIBAL-LAGRANGE UNIVERSITY
Hannibal, MO

CONTACT Brice Baumgardner, Director of Financial Aid, Hannibal-LaGrange University, 2800 Palmyra Road, Hannibal, MO 63401-1940, 573-629-3279 Ext. 3279 or toll-free 800-HLG-1119. *Fax:* 573-248-0954. *E-mail:* bbaumgardner@hlg.edu. *Website:* http://www.hlg.edu/.

HANOVER COLLEGE
Hanover, IN

Tuition & fees: $30,268	Average undergraduate aid package: $25,527

ABOUT THE INSTITUTION Independent Presbyterian, coed. *Awards:* bachelor's degrees. 29 undergraduate majors. *Total enrollment:* 1,123. Undergraduates: 1,123. Freshmen: 372. Federal methodology is used as a basis for awarding need-based institutional aid.
UNDERGRADUATE EXPENSES for 2013–2014 *Application fee:* $40. *One-time required fee:* $250. *Comprehensive fee:* $39,498 includes full-time tuition ($29,668), mandatory fees ($600), and room and board ($9230). *College room only:* $4588. Full-time tuition and fees vary according to reciprocity agreements. Room and board charges vary according to housing facility and location. *Part-time tuition:* $3296 per unit. Part-time tuition and fees vary according to course load and reciprocity agreements.
FRESHMAN FINANCIAL AID (Fall 2011) 345 applied for aid; of those 89% were deemed to have need. 100% of freshmen with need received aid; of those 24% had need fully met. *Average percent of need met:* 78% (excluding resources awarded to replace EFC). *Average financial aid package:* $23,921 (excluding resources awarded to replace EFC). 15% of all full-time freshmen had no need and received non-need-based gift aid.
UNDERGRADUATE FINANCIAL AID (Fall 2011) 1,007 applied for aid; of those 91% were deemed to have need. 100% of undergraduates with need received aid; of those 21% had need fully met. *Average percent of need met:* 81% (excluding resources awarded to replace EFC). *Average financial aid package:* $25,527 (excluding resources awarded to replace EFC). 18% of all full-time undergraduates had no need and received non-need-based gift aid.
GIFT AID (NEED-BASED) *Total amount:* $18,611,802 (9% federal, 8% state, 79% institutional, 4% external sources). *Receiving aid:* Freshmen: 83% (308); all full-time undergraduates: 81% (912). *Average award:* Freshmen: $20,027; Undergraduates: $20,938. *Scholarships, grants, and awards:* Federal Pell, FSEOG, state, private, college/university gift aid from institutional funds.
GIFT AID (NON-NEED-BASED) *Total amount:* $3,884,949 (95% institutional, 5% external sources). *Receiving aid:* Freshmen: 14% (53). Undergraduates: 11% (122). *Average award:* Freshmen: $15,586. Undergraduates: $15,202. *Scholarships, grants, and awards by category: Academic interests/achievement:* general academic interests/achievements. *Creative arts/performance:* art/fine arts, music, theater/drama. *Special characteristics:* children and siblings of alumni, children of faculty/staff, international students, members of minority groups, out-of-state students, religious affiliation, siblings of current students. *Tuition waivers:* Full or partial for employees or children of employees, senior citizens.
LOANS *Student loans:* $7,586,081 (71% need-based, 29% non-need-based). 82% of past graduating class borrowed through all loan programs. *Average indebtedness per student:* $27,626. *Average need-based loan:* Freshmen: $3450. Undergraduates: $4601. *Parent loans:* $3,329,637 (36% need-based, 64% non-need-based). *Programs:* Federal Direct (Subsidized and Unsubsidized Stafford, PLUS), college/university.
WORK-STUDY *Federal work-study:* Total amount: $596,223; 356 jobs averaging $1675.

APPLYING FOR FINANCIAL AID *Required financial aid form:* FAFSA. *Financial aid deadline (priority):* 3/1. *Notification date:* Continuous beginning 3/1. Students must reply by 5/1.
CONTACT Richard A. Nash, Director of Financial Aid, Hanover College, PO Box 108, Hanover, IN 47243-0108, 800-213-2178 Ext. 7029 or toll-free 800-213-2178. *Fax:* 812-866-7284. *E-mail:* finaid@hanover.edu.
Website: http://www.hanover.edu/.

APPLYING FOR FINANCIAL AID *Required financial aid form:* FAFSA. *Financial aid deadline (priority):* 4/15. *Notification date:* Continuous. Students must reply within 2 weeks of notification.
CONTACT Dr. Jonathan C. Roberts, Director of Student Financial Services, Harding University, PO Box 12282, Searcy, AR 72149-2282, 501-279-4257 or toll-free 800-477-4407. *Fax:* 501-279-4129. *E-mail:* jroberts@harding.edu.
Website: http://www.harding.edu/.

HARDING UNIVERSITY
Searcy, AR

Tuition & fees: $15,240	Average undergraduate aid package: $13,114

ABOUT THE INSTITUTION Independent Church of Christ, coed. *Awards:* certificates, bachelor's, master's, and doctoral degrees. 85 undergraduate majors. *Total enrollment:* 6,672. Undergraduates: 4,293. Freshmen: 1,022. Federal methodology is used as a basis for awarding need-based institutional aid.
UNDERGRADUATE EXPENSES for 2013–2014 *Application fee:* $40. *Comprehensive fee:* $21,432 includes full-time tuition ($14,790), mandatory fees ($450), and room and board ($6192). *College room only:* $3094. Full-time tuition and fees vary according to course load. Room and board charges vary according to board plan and housing facility. *Part-time tuition:* $493 per credit hour. *Part-time fees:* $25 per credit hour. Part-time tuition and fees vary according to course load. *Payment plan:* Tuition prepayment.
FRESHMAN FINANCIAL AID (Fall 2011) 884 applied for aid; of those 71% were deemed to have need. 100% of freshmen with need received aid; of those 29% had need fully met. *Average percent of need met:* 77% (excluding resources awarded to replace EFC). *Average financial aid package:* $13,461 (excluding resources awarded to replace EFC). 23% of all full-time freshmen had no need and received non-need-based gift aid.
UNDERGRADUATE FINANCIAL AID (Fall 2011) 3,136 applied for aid; of those 78% were deemed to have need. 99% of undergraduates with need received aid; of those 26% had need fully met. *Average percent of need met:* 71% (excluding resources awarded to replace EFC). *Average financial aid package:* $13,114 (excluding resources awarded to replace EFC). 32% of all full-time undergraduates had no need and received non-need-based gift aid.
GIFT AID (NEED-BASED) *Total amount:* $18,449,514 (28% federal, 12% state, 57% institutional, 3% external sources). *Receiving aid:* Freshmen: 61% (618); all full-time undergraduates: 55% (2,218). *Average award:* Freshmen: $9151; Undergraduates: $8510. *Scholarships, grants, and awards:* Federal Pell, FSEOG, state, private, college/university gift aid from institutional funds.
GIFT AID (NON-NEED-BASED) *Total amount:* $12,274,321 (1% federal, 11% state, 85% institutional, 3% external sources). *Receiving aid:* Freshmen: 13% (131). Undergraduates: 10% (423). *Average award:* Freshmen: $6076. Undergraduates: $7136. *Scholarships, grants, and awards by category: Academic interests/achievement:* 4,099 awards ($17,966,705 total): communication, computer science, engineering/technologies, English, general academic interests/achievements, health fields, religion/biblical studies. *Creative arts/performance:* 203 awards ($213,141 total): art/fine arts, cinema/film/broadcasting, debating, general creative arts/performance, journalism/publications, music. *Special achievements/activities:* 106 awards ($78,558 total): cheerleading/drum major, general special achievements/activities, leadership, religious involvement. *Special characteristics:* 567 awards ($3,275,583 total): children of faculty/staff, children with a deceased or disabled parent, general special characteristics, international students, relatives of clergy, siblings of current students. *Tuition waivers:* Full or partial for employees or children of employees, senior citizens.
LOANS *Student loans:* $21,355,831 (79% need-based, 21% non-need-based). 63% of past graduating class borrowed through all loan programs. *Average indebtedness per student:* $32,752. *Average need-based loan:* Freshmen: $4393. Undergraduates: $4853. *Parent loans:* $5,340,856 (66% need-based, 34% non-need-based). *Programs:* Federal Direct (Subsidized and Unsubsidized Stafford, PLUS), Perkins, Federal Nursing, state, college/university.
WORK-STUDY *Federal work-study:* Total amount: $431,404; 424 jobs averaging $807. *State or other work-study/employment:* Total amount: $2,344,356 (56% need-based, 44% non-need-based). 1,398 part-time jobs averaging $1677.
ATHLETIC AWARDS Total amount: $2,002,687 (40% need-based, 60% non-need-based).

HARDIN-SIMMONS UNIVERSITY
Abilene, TX

Tuition & fees: $23,460	Average undergraduate aid package: $20,933

ABOUT THE INSTITUTION Independent Baptist, coed. *Awards:* certificates, bachelor's, master's, and doctoral degrees. 73 undergraduate majors. *Total enrollment:* 2,301. Undergraduates: 1,853. Freshmen: 395. Federal methodology is used as a basis for awarding need-based institutional aid.
UNDERGRADUATE EXPENSES for 2013–2014 *Application fee:* $50. *Comprehensive fee:* $30,252 includes full-time tuition ($22,350), mandatory fees ($1110), and room and board ($6792). *College room only:* $3400. Full-time tuition and fees vary according to program. Room and board charges vary according to board plan and housing facility. *Part-time tuition:* $745 per credit hour. *Part-time fees:* $200 per term. Part-time tuition and fees vary according to course load and program. *Payment plan:* Guaranteed tuition.
FRESHMAN FINANCIAL AID (Fall 2012, est.) 390 applied for aid; of those 76% were deemed to have need. 100% of freshmen with need received aid; of those 31% had need fully met. *Average percent of need met:* 78% (excluding resources awarded to replace EFC). *Average financial aid package:* $26,698 (excluding resources awarded to replace EFC). 24% of all full-time freshmen had no need and received non-need-based gift aid.
UNDERGRADUATE FINANCIAL AID (Fall 2012, est.) 1,578 applied for aid; of those 73% were deemed to have need. 100% of undergraduates with need received aid; of those 21% had need fully met. *Average percent of need met:* 69% (excluding resources awarded to replace EFC). *Average financial aid package:* $20,933 (excluding resources awarded to replace EFC). 27% of all full-time undergraduates had no need and received non-need-based gift aid.
GIFT AID (NEED-BASED) *Total amount:* $4,560,279 (60% federal, 40% state). *Receiving aid:* Freshmen: 51% (203); all full-time undergraduates: 50% (805). *Average award:* Freshmen: $7200; Undergraduates: $7157. *Scholarships, grants, and awards:* Federal Pell, FSEOG, state, private, college/university gift aid from institutional funds, TEACH Grants.
GIFT AID (NON-NEED-BASED) *Total amount:* $13,759,961 (96% institutional, 4% external sources). *Receiving aid:* Freshmen: 69% (274). Undergraduates: 64% (1,034). *Average award:* Freshmen: $11,150. Undergraduates: $9039. *Scholarships, grants, and awards by category: Academic interests/achievement:* 1,809 awards ($12,731,698 total): biological sciences, business, communication, computer science, education, English, foreign languages, general academic interests/achievements, health fields, humanities, mathematics, physical sciences, premedicine, religion/biblical studies, social sciences. *Creative arts/performance:* applied art and design, art/fine arts, creative writing, journalism/publications, music, performing arts, theater/drama. *Special achievements/activities:* general special achievements/activities. *Special characteristics:* children and siblings of alumni, children of educators, children of faculty/staff, ethnic background, general special characteristics, handicapped students, out-of-state students, public servants, relatives of clergy, religious affiliation, siblings of current students, veterans, veterans' children. *Tuition waivers:* Full or partial for employees or children of employees.
LOANS *Student loans:* $18,256,867 (29% need-based, 71% non-need-based). 71% of past graduating class borrowed through all loan programs. *Average indebtedness per student:* $40,972. *Average need-based loan:* Freshmen: $3141. Undergraduates: $4495. *Parent loans:* $3,624,429 (100% non-need-based). *Programs:* Federal Direct (Subsidized and Unsubsidized Stafford, PLUS), Perkins, Federal Nursing, state, college/university.
WORK-STUDY *Federal work-study:* Total amount: $152,214; 165 jobs averaging $2400. *State or other work-study/employment:* Total amount: $18,048 (100% need-based). 91 part-time jobs averaging $2400.

APPLYING FOR FINANCIAL AID *Required financial aid form:* FAFSA. *Financial aid deadline (priority):* 3/1. *Notification date:* Continuous beginning 2/1. Students must reply within 2 weeks of notification.
CONTACT Mrs. Bridget Moore, Director of Financial Aid and Scholarships, Hardin-Simmons University, Box 16050, Abilene, TX 79698, 325-670-1482 or toll-free 877-464-7889. *Fax:* 325-670-5822. *E-mail:* bnmoore@hsutx.edu.
Website: http://www.hsutx.edu/.

HARRINGTON COLLEGE OF DESIGN
Chicago, IL

CONTACT Ms. Renee Darosky, Director of Financial Aid, Harrington College of Design, 410 South Michigan Avenue, Chicago, IL 60605-1496, 312-939-4975 or toll-free 866-590-4423 (in-state), 877-939-4975 (out-of-state). *Fax:* 312-697-8058. *E-mail:* financialaid@interiordesign.edu.
Website: http://www.harrington.edu/.

HARRISBURG UNIVERSITY OF SCIENCE AND TECHNOLOGY
Harrisburg, PA

Tuition & fees: $23,900	Average undergraduate aid package: $17,502

ABOUT THE INSTITUTION Independent, coed. *Awards:* certificates, bachelor's, and master's degrees. 5 undergraduate majors. *Total enrollment:* 322. Undergraduates: 223. Freshmen: 91. Federal methodology is used as a basis for awarding need-based institutional aid.
UNDERGRADUATE EXPENSES for 2013–2014 *Tuition:* full-time $23,900; part-time $1000 per credit hour. Full-time tuition and fees vary according to degree level. Part-time tuition and fees vary according to course load and degree level. Room and board charges vary according to housing facility.
FRESHMAN FINANCIAL AID (Fall 2012, est.) 135 applied for aid; of those 96% were deemed to have need. 100% of freshmen with need received aid; of those 7% had need fully met. *Average percent of need met:* 58% (excluding resources awarded to replace EFC). *Average financial aid package:* $17,528 (excluding resources awarded to replace EFC). 3% of all full-time freshmen had no need and received non-need-based gift aid.
UNDERGRADUATE FINANCIAL AID (Fall 2012, est.) 267 applied for aid; of those 94% were deemed to have need. 100% of undergraduates with need received aid; of those 5% had need fully met. *Average percent of need met:* 57% (excluding resources awarded to replace EFC). *Average financial aid package:* $17,502 (excluding resources awarded to replace EFC). 5% of all full-time undergraduates had no need and received non-need-based gift aid.
GIFT AID (NEED-BASED) *Total amount:* $2,255,335 (31% federal, 20% state, 49% institutional). *Receiving aid:* Freshmen: 85% (128); all full-time undergraduates: 89% (250). *Average award:* Freshmen: $13,675; Undergraduates: $13,330. *Scholarships, grants, and awards:* Federal Pell, FSEOG, state, private, college/university gift aid from institutional funds.
GIFT AID (NON-NEED-BASED) *Total amount:* $1,348,707 (18% federal, 3% state, 70% institutional, 9% external sources). *Receiving aid:* Freshmen: 6% (9). Undergraduates: 5% (13). *Average award:* Freshmen: $15,450. Undergraduates: $10,473. *Scholarships, grants, and awards by category:* Academic interests/achievement: biological sciences, business, computer science, physical sciences.
LOANS *Student loans:* $1,706,974 (43% need-based, 57% non-need-based). 84% of past graduating class borrowed through all loan programs. *Average indebtedness per student:* $38,779. *Average need-based loan:* Freshmen: $4727. Undergraduates: $5075. *Parent loans:* $966,594 (57% need-based, 43% non-need-based). *Programs:* Federal Direct (Subsidized and Unsubsidized Stafford, PLUS).
WORK-STUDY *Federal work-study:* Total amount: $14,930; 16 jobs averaging $1500.
APPLYING FOR FINANCIAL AID *Required financial aid form:* FAFSA. *Financial aid deadline:* Continuous. *Notification date:* Continuous. Students must reply within 2 weeks of notification.

CONTACT Mr. Vince P. Frank, Director of Financial Aid Services, Harrisburg University of Science and Technology, 326 Market Street, Harrisburg, PA 17101-2208, 717-901-5115 or toll-free 866-HBG-UNIV. *Fax:* 717-901-3115. *E-mail:* vfrank@harrisburgu.edu.
Website: http://www.HarrisburgU.edu/.

HARRISON COLLEGE
Indianapolis, IN

CONTACT Financial Aid Office, Harrison College, 550 East Washington Street, Indianapolis, IN 46204, 317-264-5656 or toll-free 888-544-4422.
Website: http://www.harrison.edu/.

HARRISON COLLEGE
Grove City, OH

CONTACT Financial Aid Office, Harrison College, 3880 Jackpot Road, Grove City, OH 43123, 614-539-8800 or toll-free 888-544-4422.
Website: http://www.harrison.edu/.

HARRIS-STOWE STATE UNIVERSITY
St. Louis, MO

CONTACT Regina Blackshear, Director of Financial Aid, Harris-Stowe State University, 3026 Laclede Avenue, St. Louis, MO 63103-2136, 314-340-3502. *Fax:* 314-340-3503.
Website: http://www.hssu.edu/.

HARTWICK COLLEGE
Oneonta, NY

Tuition & fees: $38,930	Average undergraduate aid package: $28,530

ABOUT THE INSTITUTION Independent, coed. *Awards:* bachelor's degrees. 33 undergraduate majors. *Total enrollment:* 1,558. Undergraduates: 1,558. Freshmen: 447. Federal methodology is used as a basis for awarding need-based institutional aid.
UNDERGRADUATE EXPENSES for 2013–2014 *One-time required fee:* $400. *Comprehensive fee:* $49,415 includes full-time tuition ($38,120), mandatory fees ($810), and room and board ($10,485). *College room only:* $5515. Room and board charges vary according to board plan and housing facility. *Part-time tuition:* $1217 per credit.
FRESHMAN FINANCIAL AID (Fall 2012, est.) 393 applied for aid; of those 95% were deemed to have need. 100% of freshmen with need received aid; of those 17% had need fully met. *Average percent of need met:* 78% (excluding resources awarded to replace EFC). *Average financial aid package:* $28,851 (excluding resources awarded to replace EFC). 16% of all full-time freshmen had no need and received non-need-based gift aid.
UNDERGRADUATE FINANCIAL AID (Fall 2012, est.) 1,278 applied for aid; of those 94% were deemed to have need. 100% of undergraduates with need received aid; of those 14% had need fully met. *Average percent of need met:* 78% (excluding resources awarded to replace EFC). *Average financial aid package:* $28,530 (excluding resources awarded to replace EFC). 18% of all full-time undergraduates had no need and received non-need-based gift aid.
GIFT AID (NEED-BASED) *Total amount:* $25,674,376 (9% federal, 6% state, 82% institutional, 3% external sources). *Receiving aid:* Freshmen: 82% (366); all full-time undergraduates: 77% (1,150). *Average award:* Freshmen: $19,628; Undergraduates: $18,977. *Scholarships, grants, and awards:* Federal Pell, FSEOG, state, private, college/university gift aid from institutional funds.
GIFT AID (NON-NEED-BASED) *Total amount:* $5,784,981 (94% institutional, 6% external sources). *Receiving aid:* Freshmen: 2% (8). Undergraduates: 3% (46). *Average award:* Freshmen: $18,133. Undergraduates: $16,384. *Scholarships,*

grants, and awards by category: *Creative arts/performance:* 8 awards ($25,500 total): art/fine arts, music. *Special characteristics:* 151 awards ($2,149,227 total): children and siblings of alumni, children of faculty/staff, international students, siblings of current students, veterans. **Tuition waivers:** Full or partial for employees or children of employees.

LOANS *Student loans:* $12,827,859 (78% need-based, 22% non-need-based). 72% of past graduating class borrowed through all loan programs. *Average indebtedness per student:* $30,751. *Average need-based loan:* Freshmen: $4085. Undergraduates: $4617. *Parent loans:* $17,075,896 (37% need-based, 63% non-need-based). *Programs:* Federal Direct (Subsidized and Unsubsidized Stafford, PLUS), Perkins, Federal Nursing, college/university, alternative loans.

WORK-STUDY *Federal work-study:* Total amount: $1,684,663; 898 jobs averaging $1670.

ATHLETIC AWARDS Total amount: $777,602 (21% need-based, 79% non-need-based).

APPLYING FOR FINANCIAL AID *Required financial aid form:* FAFSA. *Financial aid deadline:* Continuous. *Notification date:* Continuous beginning 10/15. Students must reply by 5/1 or within 2 weeks of notification.

CONTACT Mrs. Melissa Allen, Director of Financial Aid, Hartwick College, One Hartwick Drive, Oneonta, NY 13820, 607-431-4130 or toll-free 888-HARTWICK. *Fax:* 607-431-4006. *E-mail:* allenm@hartwick.edu. *Website:* http://www.hartwick.edu/.

HARVARD UNIVERSITY
Cambridge, MA

Tuition & fees: $40,866	Average undergraduate aid package: $45,561

ABOUT THE INSTITUTION Independent, coed. *Awards:* bachelor's, master's, and doctoral degrees. 43 undergraduate majors. *Total enrollment:* 10,573. Undergraduates: 6,676. Freshmen: 1,657. Institutional methodology is used as a basis for awarding need-based institutional aid.

UNDERGRADUATE EXPENSES for 2013–2014 *Application fee:* $75. *Comprehensive fee:* $54,496 includes full-time tuition ($37,576), mandatory fees ($3290), and room and board ($13,630). *College room only:* $8366. *Payment plan:* Tuition prepayment.

FRESHMAN FINANCIAL AID (Fall 2012, est.) 1,120 applied for aid; of those 87% were deemed to have need. 100% of freshmen with need received aid; of those 100% had need fully met. *Average percent of need met:* 100% (excluding resources awarded to replace EFC). *Average financial aid package:* $46,301 (excluding resources awarded to replace EFC).

UNDERGRADUATE FINANCIAL AID (Fall 2012, est.) 4,327 applied for aid; of those 93% were deemed to have need. 100% of undergraduates with need received aid; of those 100% had need fully met. *Average percent of need met:* 100% (excluding resources awarded to replace EFC). *Average financial aid package:* $45,561 (excluding resources awarded to replace EFC).

GIFT AID (NEED-BASED) *Total amount:* $170,663,986 (5% federal, 92% institutional, 3% external sources). *Receiving aid:* Freshmen: 75% (970); all full-time undergraduates: 84% (4,019). *Average award:* Freshmen: $44,206; Undergraduates: $42,464. *Scholarships, grants, and awards:* Federal Pell, FSEOG, state, private, college/university gift aid from institutional funds.

GIFT AID (NON-NEED-BASED) *Total amount:* $4,519,980 (14% federal, 4% institutional, 82% external sources). *ROTC:* Army cooperative, Naval, Air Force cooperative.

LOANS *Student loans:* $5,849,875 (76% need-based, 24% non-need-based). 25% of past graduating class borrowed through all loan programs. *Average indebtedness per student:* $13,098. *Average need-based loan:* Freshmen: $5329. Undergraduates: $5656. *Parent loans:* $5,798,843 (100% non-need-based). *Programs:* Federal Direct (Subsidized and Unsubsidized Stafford, PLUS), Perkins, state, college/university.

WORK-STUDY *Federal work-study:* Total amount: $2,762,667; 1,042 jobs averaging $2832. *State or other work-study/employment:* Total amount: $6,248,067 (89% need-based, 11% non-need-based). 2,185 part-time jobs averaging $2859.

APPLYING FOR FINANCIAL AID *Required financial aid forms:* FAFSA, CSS Financial Aid PROFILE, noncustodial (divorced/separated) parent's statement, business/farm supplement, federal income tax form(s). *Financial aid deadline (priority):* 2/1. *Notification date:* 4/1. Students must reply by 5/1 or within 2 weeks of notification.

CONTACT Financial Aid Office, Harvard University, 86 Brattle Street, Cambridge, MA 02138, 617-495-1581. *Fax:* 617-496-0256. *Website:* http://www.harvard.edu/.

HARVEY MUDD COLLEGE
Claremont, CA

Tuition & fees: $44,442	Average undergraduate aid package: $37,184

ABOUT THE INSTITUTION Independent, coed. *Awards:* bachelor's degrees. 7 undergraduate majors. *Total enrollment:* 783. Undergraduates: 783. Freshmen: 198. Both federal and Institutional methodology are used as a basis for awarding need-based institutional aid.

UNDERGRADUATE EXPENSES for 2013–2014 *Application fee:* $70. *One-time required fee:* $100. *Comprehensive fee:* $58,913 includes full-time tuition ($44,159), mandatory fees ($283), and room and board ($14,471). *College room only:* $7763. Room and board charges vary according to board plan.

FRESHMAN FINANCIAL AID (Fall 2012, est.) 134 applied for aid; of those 78% were deemed to have need. 100% of freshmen with need received aid; of those 100% had need fully met. *Average percent of need met:* 100% (excluding resources awarded to replace EFC). *Average financial aid package:* $41,827 (excluding resources awarded to replace EFC). 18% of all full-time freshmen had no need and received non-need-based gift aid.

UNDERGRADUATE FINANCIAL AID (Fall 2012, est.) 468 applied for aid; of those 86% were deemed to have need. 100% of undergraduates with need received aid; of those 100% had need fully met. *Average percent of need met:* 100% (excluding resources awarded to replace EFC). *Average financial aid package:* $37,184 (excluding resources awarded to replace EFC). 19% of all full-time undergraduates had no need and received non-need-based gift aid.

GIFT AID (NEED-BASED) *Total amount:* $13,120,511 (5% federal, 3% state, 88% institutional, 4% external sources). *Receiving aid:* Freshmen: 51% (101); all full-time undergraduates: 50% (390). *Average award:* Freshmen: $39,016; Undergraduates: $32,612. *Scholarships, grants, and awards:* Federal Pell, FSEOG, state, private, college/university gift aid from institutional funds.

GIFT AID (NON-NEED-BASED) *Total amount:* $1,953,016 (86% institutional, 14% external sources). *Receiving aid:* Freshmen: 22% (43). Undergraduates: 21% (164). *Average award:* Freshmen: $7883. Undergraduates: $10,305. *Scholarships, grants, and awards by category:* Academic interests/achievement: general academic interests/achievements. *Special characteristics:* international students. *Tuition waivers:* Full or partial for employees or children of employees. *ROTC:* Army cooperative, Air Force.

LOANS *Student loans:* $2,519,203 (88% need-based, 12% non-need-based). 48% of past graduating class borrowed through all loan programs. *Average indebtedness per student:* $24,194. *Average need-based loan:* Freshmen: $3747. Undergraduates: $5011. *Parent loans:* $1,338,849 (72% need-based, 28% non-need-based). *Programs:* Federal Direct (Subsidized and Unsubsidized Stafford, PLUS), Perkins, state, college/university, alternative loans.

WORK-STUDY *Federal work-study:* Total amount: $545,462; jobs available. *State or other work-study/employment:* Total amount: $149,577 (69% need-based, 31% non-need-based). Part-time jobs available.

APPLYING FOR FINANCIAL AID *Required financial aid forms:* FAFSA, CSS Financial Aid PROFILE, state aid form, noncustodial (divorced/separated) parent's statement, business/farm supplement. *Financial aid deadline:* 2/1. *Notification date:* 4/1. Students must reply by 5/1.

CONTACT Mrs. Gilma Lopez, Director of Financial Aid, Harvey Mudd College, 301 Platt Boulevard, Claremont, CA 91711-5994, 909-621-8055. *Fax:* 909-607-7046. *E-mail:* financial_aid@hmc.edu. *Website:* http://www.hmc.edu/.

HASKELL INDIAN NATIONS UNIVERSITY
Lawrence, KS

CONTACT Reta Brewer, Director of Financial Aid, Haskell Indian Nations University, 155 Indian Avenue, Box 5027, Lawrence, KS 66046-4800, 785-749-8468. *Fax:* 785-832-6617.
Website: http://www.haskell.edu/.

HASTINGS COLLEGE
Hastings, NE

Tuition & fees: N/R	Average undergraduate aid package: $18,269

ABOUT THE INSTITUTION Independent Presbyterian, coed. 81 undergraduate majors. Federal methodology is used as a basis for awarding need-based institutional aid.
FRESHMAN FINANCIAL AID (Fall 2011) 300 applied for aid; of those 83% were deemed to have need. 100% of freshmen with need received aid; of those 26% had need fully met. *Average percent of need met:* 75% (excluding resources awarded to replace EFC). *Average financial aid package:* $17,548 (excluding resources awarded to replace EFC). 22% of all full-time freshmen had no need and received non-need-based gift aid.
UNDERGRADUATE FINANCIAL AID (Fall 2011) 1,009 applied for aid; of those 87% were deemed to have need. 100% of undergraduates with need received aid; of those 22% had need fully met. *Average percent of need met:* 75% (excluding resources awarded to replace EFC). *Average financial aid package:* $18,269 (excluding resources awarded to replace EFC). 24% of all full-time undergraduates had no need and received non-need-based gift aid.
GIFT AID (NEED-BASED) Total amount: $10,349,995 (16% federal, 2% state, 74% institutional, 8% external sources). *Receiving aid:* Freshmen: 77% (247); all full-time undergraduates: 74% (873). *Average award:* Freshmen: $14,611; Undergraduates: $14,393. *Scholarships, grants, and awards:* Federal Pell, FSEOG, state, private, college/university gift aid from institutional funds.
GIFT AID (NON-NEED-BASED) Total amount: $3,912,597 (1% federal, 86% institutional, 13% external sources). *Receiving aid:* Freshmen: 17% (54). Undergraduates: 12% (137). *Average award:* Freshmen: $11,461. Undergraduates: $10,488. *Scholarships, grants, and awards by category: Academic interests/achievement:* communication, general academic interests/achievements, religion/biblical studies. *Creative arts/performance:* art/fine arts, dance, debating, journalism/publications, music, performing arts, theater/drama. *Special achievements/activities:* cheerleading/drum major, rodeo. *Special characteristics:* adult students, children and siblings of alumni, children of educators, children of faculty/staff, international students, religious affiliation, siblings of current students, spouses of current students.
LOANS Student loans: $6,350,637 (74% need-based, 26% non-need-based). 76% of past graduating class borrowed through all loan programs. *Average indebtedness per student:* $26,669. *Average need-based loan:* Freshmen: $3898. Undergraduates: $4724. *Parent loans:* $2,483,722 (42% need-based, 58% non-need-based). *Programs:* Federal Direct (Subsidized and Unsubsidized Stafford, PLUS), Perkins, college/university.
WORK-STUDY Federal work-study: Total amount: $47,130; 80 jobs averaging $670. *State or other work-study/employment:* Total amount: $170,715 (37% need-based, 63% non-need-based). Part-time jobs available.
ATHLETIC AWARDS Total amount: $3,100,016 (74% need-based, 26% non-need-based).
APPLYING FOR FINANCIAL AID Required financial aid forms: FAFSA, institution's own form. *Financial aid deadline:* 9/1 (priority: 5/1). *Notification date:* Continuous beginning 2/15. Students must reply within 2 weeks of notification.
CONTACT Ms. Terri Lynn Graham, Director of Student Financial Aid, Hastings College, 710 North Turner Avenue, Hastings, NE 68901, 402-461-7431 or toll-free 800-532-7642. *Fax:* 402-461-7714. *E-mail:* tgraham@hastings.edu.
Website: http://www.hastings.edu/.

HAVERFORD COLLEGE
Haverford, PA

Tuition & fees: $43,702	Average undergraduate aid package: $40,321

ABOUT THE INSTITUTION Independent, coed. *Awards:* bachelor's degrees. 38 undergraduate majors. *Total enrollment:* 1,205. Undergraduates: 1,205. Freshmen: 323. Institutional methodology is used as a basis for awarding need-based institutional aid.
UNDERGRADUATE EXPENSES for 2013–2014 Application fee: $60. *One-time required fee:* $210. *Comprehensive fee:* $56,992 includes full-time tuition ($43,310), mandatory fees ($392), and room and board ($13,290). *College room only:* $7570. *Payment plan:* Tuition prepayment.
FRESHMAN FINANCIAL AID (Fall 2012, est.) 173 applied for aid; of those 96% were deemed to have need. 100% of freshmen with need received aid; of those 100% had need fully met. *Average percent of need met:* 100% (excluding resources awarded to replace EFC). *Average financial aid package:* $41,352 (excluding resources awarded to replace EFC).
UNDERGRADUATE FINANCIAL AID (Fall 2012, est.) 620 applied for aid; of those 97% were deemed to have need. 100% of undergraduates with need received aid; of those 100% had need fully met. *Average percent of need met:* 100% (excluding resources awarded to replace EFC). *Average financial aid package:* $40,321 (excluding resources awarded to replace EFC).
GIFT AID (NEED-BASED) Total amount: $23,272,937 (4% federal, 1% state, 93% institutional, 2% external sources). *Receiving aid:* Freshmen: 50% (162); all full-time undergraduates: 48% (582). *Average award:* Freshmen: $39,317; Undergraduates: $39,702. *Scholarships, grants, and awards:* Federal Pell, FSEOG, state, college/university gift aid from institutional funds.
GIFT AID (NON-NEED-BASED) Tuition waivers: Full or partial for employees or children of employees.
LOANS Student loans: $1,291,057 (42% need-based, 58% non-need-based). 33% of past graduating class borrowed through all loan programs. *Average indebtedness per student:* $14,171. *Average need-based loan:* Freshmen: $832. Undergraduates: $955. *Parent loans:* $1,446,742 (100% non-need-based). *Programs:* Federal Direct (Subsidized and Unsubsidized Stafford, PLUS), Perkins.
WORK-STUDY Federal work-study: Total amount: $279,269; jobs available. *State or other work-study/employment:* Total amount: $600,175 (27% need-based, 73% non-need-based). Part-time jobs available.
APPLYING FOR FINANCIAL AID Required financial aid forms: FAFSA, CSS Financial Aid PROFILE, noncustodial (divorced/separated) parent's statement, business/farm supplement. *Financial aid deadline:* 2/1. *Notification date:* 4/1. Students must reply by 5/1 or within 2 weeks of notification.
CONTACT Mr. David J. Hoy, Director of Financial Aid, Haverford College, 370 Lancaster Avenue, Haverford, PA 19041-1392, 610-896-1350. *Fax:* 610-896-1338. *E-mail:* finaid@haverford.edu.
Website: http://www.haverford.edu/.

HAWAII PACIFIC UNIVERSITY
Honolulu, HI

Tuition & fees: $19,980	Average undergraduate aid package: $17,384

ABOUT THE INSTITUTION Independent, coed. *Awards:* certificates, associate, bachelor's, and master's degrees. 67 undergraduate majors. *Total enrollment:* 7,463. Undergraduates: 6,168. Freshmen: 475. Federal methodology is used as a basis for awarding need-based institutional aid.
UNDERGRADUATE EXPENSES for 2013–2014 Application fee: $50. *Comprehensive fee:* $33,210 includes full-time tuition ($19,980) and room and board ($13,230). Full-time tuition and fees vary according to course level, course load, degree level, location, program, and student level. Room and board charges vary according to housing facility. Part-time tuition and fees vary according to course level, course load, degree level, location, program, and student level.
FRESHMAN FINANCIAL AID (Fall 2012, est.) 437 applied for aid; of those 74% were deemed to have need. 100% of freshmen with need received aid; of those 19% had need fully met. *Average percent of need met:* 78% (excluding resources awarded to replace EFC). *Average financial aid package:* $19,037 (excluding

resources awarded to replace EFC). 6% of all full-time freshmen had no need and received non-need-based gift aid.

UNDERGRADUATE FINANCIAL AID (Fall 2012, est.) 2,802 applied for aid; of those 70% were deemed to have need. 99% of undergraduates with need received aid; of those 17% had need fully met. *Average percent of need met:* 72% (excluding resources awarded to replace EFC). *Average financial aid package:* $17,384 (excluding resources awarded to replace EFC). 4% of all full-time undergraduates had no need and received non-need-based gift aid.

GIFT AID (NEED-BASED) *Total amount:* $6,239,769 (94% federal, 6% institutional). *Receiving aid:* Freshmen: 36% (168); all full-time undergraduates: 29% (1,087). *Average award:* Freshmen: $1964; Undergraduates: $1989. *Scholarships, grants, and awards:* Federal Pell, FSEOG, state, private, college/university gift aid from institutional funds, Federal Nursing.

GIFT AID (NON-NEED-BASED) *Total amount:* $12,530,226 (92% institutional, 8% external sources). *Receiving aid:* Freshmen: 6% (26). Undergraduates: 5% (196). *Average award:* Freshmen: $260. Undergraduates: $1019. *Scholarships, grants, and awards by category:* Academic interests/achievement: biological sciences, business, communication, general academic interests/achievements, health fields, social sciences. Creative arts/performance: dance, journalism/publications, music. Special achievements/activities: cheerleading/drum major, community service, hobbies/interests, junior miss, leadership, memberships, religious involvement. Special characteristics: ethnic background, international students, local/state students, out-of-state students, previous college experience, relatives of clergy, religious affiliation. *Tuition waivers:* Full or partial for employees or children of employees. *ROTC:* Army cooperative, Air Force cooperative.

LOANS *Student loans:* $23,724,675 (34% need-based, 66% non-need-based). 50% of past graduating class borrowed through all loan programs. *Average indebtedness per student:* $30,893. *Average need-based loan:* Freshmen: $5096. Undergraduates: $5969. *Parent loans:* $8,467,629 (100% non-need-based). *Programs:* Federal Direct (Subsidized and Unsubsidized Stafford, PLUS), Perkins, Federal Nursing.

WORK-STUDY *Federal work-study:* Total amount: $327,360; 316 jobs averaging $3000.

ATHLETIC AWARDS Total amount: $1,775,392 (100% non-need-based).

APPLYING FOR FINANCIAL AID *Required financial aid form:* FAFSA. *Financial aid deadline (priority):* 3/1. *Notification date:* Continuous beginning 3/15. Students must reply within 3 weeks of notification.

CONTACT Adam Hatch, Director of Financial Aid, Hawaii Pacific University, 1164 Bishop Street, Suite 201, Honolulu, HI 96813-2785, 808-544-0253 or toll-free 866-225-5478. *Fax:* 808-544-0884. *E-mail:* financialaid@hpu.edu. *Website:* http://www.hpu.edu/.

FRESHMAN FINANCIAL AID (Fall 2012, est.) 326 applied for aid; of those 94% were deemed to have need. 100% of freshmen with need received aid; of those 15% had need fully met. *Average percent of need met:* 80% (excluding resources awarded to replace EFC). *Average financial aid package:* $21,520 (excluding resources awarded to replace EFC). 8% of all full-time freshmen had no need and received non-need-based gift aid.

UNDERGRADUATE FINANCIAL AID (Fall 2012, est.) 962 applied for aid; of those 94% were deemed to have need. 100% of undergraduates with need received aid; of those 20% had need fully met. *Average percent of need met:* 79% (excluding resources awarded to replace EFC). *Average financial aid package:* $20,773 (excluding resources awarded to replace EFC). 9% of all full-time undergraduates had no need and received non-need-based gift aid.

GIFT AID (NEED-BASED) *Total amount:* $13,725,576 (15% federal, 5% state, 78% institutional, 2% external sources). *Receiving aid:* Freshmen: 89% (307); all full-time undergraduates: 88% (909). *Average award:* Freshmen: $16,642; Undergraduates: $15,457. *Scholarships, grants, and awards:* Federal Pell, FSEOG, state, private, college/university gift aid from institutional funds.

GIFT AID (NON-NEED-BASED) *Total amount:* $1,082,544 (99% institutional, 1% external sources). *Receiving aid:* Freshmen: 79% (274). Undergraduates: 62% (638). *Average award:* Freshmen: $11,830. Undergraduates: $11,913. *Scholarships, grants, and awards by category:* Academic interests/achievement: general academic interests/achievements. Creative arts/performance: music, performing arts. Special characteristics: children of faculty/staff, international students, out-of-state students, relatives of clergy, religious affiliation. *Tuition waivers:* Full or partial for employees or children of employees. *ROTC:* Army cooperative, Air Force cooperative.

LOANS *Student loans:* $6,981,686 (97% need-based, 3% non-need-based). 86% of past graduating class borrowed through all loan programs. *Average indebtedness per student:* $35,470. *Average need-based loan:* Freshmen: $4037. Undergraduates: $4715. *Parent loans:* $2,044,831 (95% need-based, 5% non-need-based). *Programs:* Federal Direct (Subsidized and Unsubsidized Stafford, PLUS), Perkins.

WORK-STUDY *Federal work-study:* Total amount: $1,109,670; jobs available. *State or other work-study/employment:* Total amount: $170,750 (82% need-based, 18% non-need-based). Part-time jobs available.

APPLYING FOR FINANCIAL AID *Required financial aid form:* FAFSA. *Financial aid deadline:* Continuous. *Notification date:* Continuous beginning 3/1. Students must reply by 5/1.

CONTACT Ms. Juli L. Weininger, Director of Financial Aid, Heidelberg University, 310 East Market Street, Tiffin, OH 44883-2462, 419-448-2293 or toll-free 800-434-3352. *Fax:* 419-448-2296. *Website:* http://www.heidelberg.edu/.

HEBREW THEOLOGICAL COLLEGE
Skokie, IL

CONTACT Ms. Rhoda Morris, Financial Aid Administrator , Hebrew Theological College, 7135 Carpenter Road, Skokie, IL 60077-3263, 847-982-2500. *Fax:* 847-674-6381. *Website:* http://www.htc.edu/.

HELLENIC COLLEGE
Brookline, MA

CONTACT Gregory Floor, Director of Admissions/Financial Aid, Hellenic College, 50 Goddard Avenue, Brookline, MA 02146-7496, 617-731-3500 Ext. 1285 or toll-free 866-424-2338. *Fax:* 617-850-1465. *E-mail:* gfloor@hchc.edu. *Website:* http://www.hchc.edu/.

HEIDELBERG UNIVERSITY
Tiffin, OH

Tuition & fees: $24,582	Average undergraduate aid package: $20,773

ABOUT THE INSTITUTION Independent United Church of Christ, coed. *Awards:* bachelor's and master's degrees. 49 undergraduate majors. *Total enrollment:* 1,317. Undergraduates: 1,113. Freshmen: 282. Federal methodology is used as a basis for awarding need-based institutional aid.

UNDERGRADUATE EXPENSES for 2013–2014 *Application fee:* $25. *Comprehensive fee:* $33,556 includes full-time tuition ($24,000), mandatory fees ($582), and room and board ($8974). *College room only:* $4248. Full-time tuition and fees vary according to course load, degree level, and location. Room and board charges vary according to housing facility and location. Part-time tuition and fees vary according to course load, degree level, and location.

HENDERSON STATE UNIVERSITY
Arkadelphia, AR

Tuition & fees (AR res): $6984	Average undergraduate aid package: $11,019

ABOUT THE INSTITUTION State-supported, coed. *Awards:* certificates, bachelor's, and master's degrees. 37 undergraduate majors. *Total enrollment:* 3,771. Undergraduates: 3,363. Freshmen: 781. Federal methodology is used as a basis for awarding need-based institutional aid.

UNDERGRADUATE EXPENSES for 2013–2014 *Tuition, state resident:* full-time $5880; part-time $196 per credit hour. *Tuition, nonresident:* full-time $11,760; part-time $392 per credit hour. *Required fees:* full-time $1104. Full-time tuition and fees vary according to course load, degree level, and student level. Part-time tuition and fees vary according to course load, degree level, and student level.

College room and board: $5332. Room and board charges vary according to board plan and housing facility.

FRESHMAN FINANCIAL AID (Fall 2012, est.) 753 applied for aid; of those 85% were deemed to have need. 100% of freshmen with need received aid; of those 3% had need fully met. **Average percent of need met:** 92% (excluding resources awarded to replace EFC). **Average financial aid package:** $11,705 (excluding resources awarded to replace EFC). 52% of all full-time freshmen had no need and received non-need-based gift aid.

UNDERGRADUATE FINANCIAL AID (Fall 2012, est.) 2,992 applied for aid; of those 86% were deemed to have need. 98% of undergraduates with need received aid; of those 4% had need fully met. **Average percent of need met:** 84% (excluding resources awarded to replace EFC). **Average financial aid package:** $11,019 (excluding resources awarded to replace EFC). 40% of all full-time undergraduates had no need and received non-need-based gift aid.

GIFT AID (NEED-BASED) Total amount: $8,349,270 (96% federal, 4% state). **Receiving aid:** Freshmen: 57% (439); all full-time undergraduates: 55% (1,773). **Average award:** Freshmen: $4587; Undergraduates: $4360. **Scholarships, grants, and awards:** Federal Pell, FSEOG, state, private.

GIFT AID (NON-NEED-BASED) Total amount: $13,137,780 (4% federal, 48% state, 38% institutional, 10% external sources). **Receiving aid:** Freshmen: 72% (558). Undergraduates: 56% (1,809). **Average award:** Freshmen: $5231. Undergraduates: $5404. **Scholarships, grants, and awards by category:** Academic interests/achievement: biological sciences, education, general academic interests/achievements, international studies, mathematics. Creative arts/performance: art/fine arts, cinema/film/broadcasting, dance, debating, journalism/publications, music, performing arts, theater/drama. Special achievements/activities: cheerleading/drum major, general special achievements/activities, leadership. Special characteristics: children and siblings of alumni, children of faculty/staff, international students, out-of-state students. **Tuition waivers:** Full or partial for children of alumni, employees or children of employees, senior citizens. **ROTC:** Army cooperative.

LOANS Student loans: $16,833,069 (38% need-based, 62% non-need-based). 36% of past graduating class borrowed through all loan programs. **Average indebtedness per student:** $6747. **Average need-based loan:** Freshmen: $2792. Undergraduates: $3619. **Parent loans:** $481,298 (100% non-need-based). **Programs:** Federal Direct (Subsidized and Unsubsidized Stafford, PLUS), Perkins.

WORK-STUDY Federal work-study: Total amount: $254,213; jobs available. **State or other work-study/employment:** Total amount: $275,196 (100% non-need-based). Part-time jobs available.

ATHLETIC AWARDS Total amount: $1,314,013 (100% non-need-based).

APPLYING FOR FINANCIAL AID Required financial aid form: FAFSA. **Financial aid deadline (priority):** 6/1. **Notification date:** Continuous beginning 4/15.

CONTACT Ms. Vicki Taylor, Director of Financial Aid, Henderson State University, 1100 Henderson Street, HSU Box 7812, Arkadelphia, AR 71999-0001, 870-230-5138 or toll-free 800-228-7333. Fax: 870-230-5481. E-mail: taylorv@hsu.edu. Website: http://www.hsu.edu/.

HENDRIX COLLEGE
Conway, AR

Tuition & fees: $37,816	Average undergraduate aid package: $28,189

ABOUT THE INSTITUTION Independent United Methodist, coed. **Awards:** bachelor's and master's degrees. 31 undergraduate majors. **Total enrollment:** 1,388. Undergraduates: 1,373. Freshmen: 369. Federal methodology is used as a basis for awarding need-based institutional aid.

UNDERGRADUATE EXPENSES for 2013–2014 Application fee: $40. **Comprehensive fee:** $48,436 includes full-time tuition ($37,516), mandatory fees ($300), and room and board ($10,620). **College room only:** $5480. Full-time tuition and fees vary according to course load and student level. Room and board charges vary according to board plan and housing facility. Part-time tuition and fees vary according to course load and student level.

FRESHMAN FINANCIAL AID (Fall 2012, est.) 315 applied for aid; of those 78% were deemed to have need. 100% of freshmen with need received aid; of those 42% had need fully met. **Average percent of need met:** 85% (excluding resources awarded to replace EFC). **Average financial aid package:** $29,273 (excluding resources awarded to replace EFC). 31% of all full-time freshmen had no need and received non-need-based gift aid.

UNDERGRADUATE FINANCIAL AID (Fall 2012, est.) 1,071 applied for aid; of those 76% were deemed to have need. 100% of undergraduates with need received aid; of those 41% had need fully met. **Average percent of need met:** 83% (excluding resources awarded to replace EFC). **Average financial aid package:** $28,189 (excluding resources awarded to replace EFC). 39% of all full-time undergraduates had no need and received non-need-based gift aid.

GIFT AID (NEED-BASED) Total amount: $19,113,644 (6% federal, 7% state, 85% institutional, 2% external sources). **Receiving aid:** Freshmen: 66% (245); all full-time undergraduates: 60% (813). **Average award:** Freshmen: $26,065; Undergraduates: $24,498. **Scholarships, grants, and awards:** Federal Pell, FSEOG, state, private, college/university gift aid from institutional funds.

GIFT AID (NON-NEED-BASED) Total amount: $15,542,004 (14% state, 84% institutional, 2% external sources). **Receiving aid:** Freshmen: 25% (93). Undergraduates: 20% (275). **Average award:** Freshmen: $22,394. Undergraduates: $21,174. **Scholarships, grants, and awards by category:** Academic interests/achievement: $17,690,277 total: general academic interests/achievements. Creative arts/performance: $228,750 total: art/fine arts, dance, music, theater/drama. Special achievements/activities: $4,763,150 total: community service, general special achievements/activities, leadership, religious involvement. Special characteristics: $1,893,513 total: children of educators, children of faculty/staff, international students, previous college experience, relatives of clergy. **Tuition waivers:** Full or partial for employees or children of employees. **ROTC:** Army cooperative.

LOANS Student loans: $4,927,318 (64% need-based, 36% non-need-based). 52% of past graduating class borrowed through all loan programs. **Average indebtedness per student:** $24,492. **Average need-based loan:** Freshmen: $3692. Undergraduates: $4252. **Parent loans:** $2,077,644 (33% need-based, 67% non-need-based). **Programs:** Federal Direct (Subsidized and Unsubsidized Stafford, PLUS), Perkins, United Methodist Student Loans.

WORK-STUDY Federal work-study: Total amount: $739,818; 504 jobs averaging $1421. **State or other work-study/employment:** Total amount: $340,096 (9% need-based, 91% non-need-based). 301 part-time jobs averaging $1407.

APPLYING FOR FINANCIAL AID Required financial aid forms: FAFSA, state aid form. **Financial aid deadline (priority):** 3/1. **Notification date:** Continuous beginning 3/1. Students must reply by 5/1.

CONTACT Ms. Kristina Burford, Director of Financial Aid, Hendrix College, 1600 Washington Avenue, Conway, AR 72032, 501-450-1368 or toll-free 800-277-9017. Fax: 501-450-3871. E-mail: burford@hendrix.edu. Website: http://www.hendrix.edu/.

HENLEY-PUTNAM UNIVERSITY
Santa Clara, CA

CONTACT Financial Aid Office, Henley-Putnam University, 2804 Mission College Boulevard, Suite 240, Santa Clara, CA 95054, 408-453-9900 or toll-free 88-852-8746 (in-state), 888-852-8746 (out-of-state). Website: http://www.henley-putnam.edu/.

HERITAGE BIBLE COLLEGE
Dunn, NC

CONTACT Mrs. Laurie Minard, Director of Financial Aid, Heritage Bible College, Box 1628, Dunn, NC 28335, 800-297-6351 Ext. 226 or toll-free 800-297-6351. Fax: 910-892-1809. E-mail: lminard@heritagebiblecollege.edu. Website: http://www.heritagebiblecollege.edu/.

HERITAGE CHRISTIAN UNIVERSITY
Florence, AL

Tuition & fees: $12,776	Average undergraduate aid package: $13,500

ABOUT THE INSTITUTION Independent Church of Christ, coed, primarily men. **Awards:** associate, bachelor's, and master's degrees. 1 undergraduate major. **Total**

enrollment: 88. Undergraduates: 63. Freshmen: 8. Federal methodology is used as a basis for awarding need-based institutional aid.

UNDERGRADUATE EXPENSES for 2013–2014 *Application fee:* $25. *One-time required fee:* $300. *Comprehensive fee:* $18,202 includes full-time tuition ($11,936), mandatory fees ($840), and room and board ($5426). *College room only:* $3000. Room and board charges vary according to housing facility. *Part-time tuition:* $373 per credit hour. *Part-time fees:* $35 per credit hour.

FRESHMAN FINANCIAL AID (Fall 2011) 5 applied for aid; of those 100% were deemed to have need. 100% of freshmen with need received aid; of those 40% had need fully met. *Average percent of need met:* 100% (excluding resources awarded to replace EFC). *Average financial aid package:* $11,050 (excluding resources awarded to replace EFC).

UNDERGRADUATE FINANCIAL AID (Fall 2011) 21 applied for aid; of those 100% were deemed to have need. 100% of undergraduates with need received aid; of those 29% had need fully met. *Average percent of need met:* 93% (excluding resources awarded to replace EFC). *Average financial aid package:* $13,500 (excluding resources awarded to replace EFC).

GIFT AID (NEED-BASED) *Total amount:* $204,972 (49% federal, 51% institutional). *Receiving aid:* Freshmen: 40% (2); all full-time undergraduates: 54% (14). *Average award:* Freshmen: $7550; Undergraduates: $6550. *Scholarships, grants, and awards:* Federal Pell, FSEOG, private, college/university gift aid from institutional funds.

GIFT AID (NON-NEED-BASED) *Total amount:* $25,425 (100% institutional). *Receiving aid:* Freshmen: 80% (4). Undergraduates: 81% (21). *Scholarships, grants, and awards by category: Academic interests/achievement:* $43,365 total: general academic interests/achievements, international studies, religion/biblical studies. *Special achievements/activities:* $34,298 total: religious involvement. *Special characteristics:* $23,142 total: children and siblings of alumni, children of educators, children of faculty/staff, international students, married students, relatives of clergy, spouses of current students. *Tuition waivers:* Full or partial for employees or children of employees.

LOANS *Student loans:* $221,337 (54% need-based, 46% non-need-based). 81% of past graduating class borrowed through all loan programs. *Average indebtedness per student:* $18,950. *Average need-based loan:* Freshmen: $3500. Undergraduates: $4500. *Parent loans:* $5850 (100% need-based). *Programs:* Federal Direct (Subsidized and Unsubsidized Stafford, PLUS), college/university.

WORK-STUDY *Federal work-study:* Total amount: $6580; 8 jobs averaging $1500.

APPLYING FOR FINANCIAL AID *Required financial aid forms:* FAFSA, IRS tax return transcript (if selected for verification). *Financial aid deadline (priority):* 6/1. *Notification date:* Continuous beginning 7/15. Students must reply within 2 weeks of notification.

CONTACT Mechelle R. Thompson, Associate Director of Financial Aid, Heritage Christian University, PO Box HCU, Florence, AL 35630, 800-367-3565 Ext. 303 or toll-free 800-367-3565. *Fax:* 256-716-8021. *E-mail:* mthompson@hcu.edu. *Website:* http://www.hcu.edu/.

HERITAGE UNIVERSITY
Toppenish, WA

CONTACT Mr. Norberto Espindola, Director of Enrollment Management Services, Heritage University, 3240 Fort Road, Toppenish, WA 98948-9599, 509-865-8500 or toll-free 888-272-6190. *Fax:* 509-865-8659. *E-mail:* financial_aid@heritage.edu. *Website:* http://www.heritage.edu/.

HERZING UNIVERSITY
Birmingham, AL

CONTACT Financial Aid Office, Herzing University, 280 West Valley Avenue, Birmingham, AL 35209, 205-916-2800 or toll-free 800-596-0724. *Website:* http://www.herzing.edu/birmingham/.

HERZING UNIVERSITY
Winter Park, FL

CONTACT Financial Aid Office, Herzing University, 1595 South Semoran Boulevard, Winter Park, FL 32792, 407-478-0500 or toll-free 800-596-0724. *Website:* http://www.herzing.edu/.

HERZING UNIVERSITY
Atlanta, GA

CONTACT Financial Aid Office, Herzing University, 3393 Peachtree Road, Suite 1003, Atlanta, GA 30326, 404-816-4533 or toll-free 800-596-0724. *Website:* http://www.herzing.edu/atlanta/.

HERZING UNIVERSITY
Kenner, LA

CONTACT Financial Aid Office, Herzing University, 2500 Williams Boulevard, Kenner, LA 70062, 504-733-0074 or toll-free 800-596-0724. *Website:* http://www.herzing.edu/.

HERZING UNIVERSITY
Brookfield, WI

CONTACT Financial Aid Office, Herzing University, 555 South Executive Drive, Brookfield, WI 53005, 262-649-1710 or toll-free 800-596-0724. *Website:* http://www.herzing.edu/brookfield.

HERZING UNIVERSITY
Kenosha, WI

CONTACT Financial Aid Office, Herzing University, 4006 Washington Road, Kenosha, WI 53144, 866—724-9144 or toll-free 800-596-0724. *Website:* http://www.herzing.edu/kenosha.

HERZING UNIVERSITY
Madison, WI

CONTACT Financial Aid Office, Herzing University, 5218 East Terrace Drive, Madison, WI 53718, 608-249-6611 or toll-free 800-596-0724. *Website:* http://www.herzing.edu/madison/.

HERZING UNIVERSITY ONLINE
Milwaukee, WI

CONTACT Financial Aid Office, Herzing University Online, 525 North 6th Street, Milwaukee, WI 53203, 866-508-0748. *Website:* http://www.herzingonline.edu/.

HICKEY COLLEGE
St. Louis, MO

CONTACT Financial Aid Office, Hickey College, 940 West Port Plaza, Suite 101, St. Louis, MO 63146, 314-434-2212 or toll-free 800-777-1544. *Website:* http://www.hickeycollege.edu/.

HIGH POINT UNIVERSITY
High Point, NC

ABOUT THE INSTITUTION Independent United Methodist, coed. *Awards:* certificates, bachelor's, master's, and doctoral degrees. 43 undergraduate majors. *Total enrollment:* 4,263. Undergraduates: 4,070. Freshmen: 1,257.
GIFT AID (NEED-BASED) *Scholarships, grants, and awards:* Federal Pell, FSEOG, state, private, college/university gift aid from institutional funds.
GIFT AID (NON-NEED-BASED) *Scholarships, grants, and awards by category:* Academic interests/achievement: biological sciences, business, education, English, foreign languages, general academic interests/achievements, humanities, international studies, mathematics, physical sciences, premedicine, religion/biblical studies. Creative arts/performance: art/fine arts, music. Special achievements/activities: general special achievements/activities. Special characteristics: relatives of clergy.
LOANS *Programs:* Federal Direct (Subsidized and Unsubsidized Stafford, PLUS), Perkins.
WORK-STUDY *Federal work-study:* Total amount: $239,851; 252 jobs averaging $952. *State or other work-study/employment:* Part-time jobs available.
APPLYING FOR FINANCIAL AID *Required financial aid forms:* FAFSA, state aid form.
CONTACT Mr. Ron Elmore, Director of Student Financial Planning, High Point University, Box 3232, University Station, 833 Montlieu Avenue, High Point, NC 27262, 336-841-9128 or toll-free 800-345-6993. *Fax:* 336-884-0221. *E-mail:* relmore@highpoint.edu. *Website:* http://www.highpoint.edu/.

HILBERT COLLEGE
Hamburg, NY

Tuition & fees: $20,500	Average undergraduate aid package: $13,118

ABOUT THE INSTITUTION Independent, coed. *Awards:* associate, bachelor's, and master's degrees. 18 undergraduate majors. *Total enrollment:* 1,075. Undergraduates: 1,033. Freshmen: 182. Federal methodology is used as a basis for awarding need-based institutional aid.
UNDERGRADUATE EXPENSES for 2013–2014 *Application fee:* $25. *One-time required fee:* $50. *Comprehensive fee:* $29,150 includes full-time tuition ($19,900), mandatory fees ($600), and room and board ($8650). *College room only:* $4450. Full-time tuition and fees vary according to course load. Room and board charges vary according to board plan and housing facility. *Part-time tuition:* $485 per credit. *Part-time fees:* $13 per credit; $55 per term. Part-time tuition and fees vary according to course load.
FRESHMAN FINANCIAL AID (Fall 2012, est.) 176 applied for aid; of those 91% were deemed to have need. 99% of freshmen with need received aid; of those 13% had need fully met. *Average percent of need met:* 70% (excluding resources awarded to replace EFC). *Average financial aid package:* $14,807 (excluding resources awarded to replace EFC). 10% of all full-time freshmen had no need and received non-need-based gift aid.
UNDERGRADUATE FINANCIAL AID (Fall 2012, est.) 912 applied for aid; of those 90% were deemed to have need. 100% of undergraduates with need received aid; of those 18% had need fully met. *Average percent of need met:* 68% (excluding resources awarded to replace EFC). *Average financial aid package:* $13,118 (excluding resources awarded to replace EFC). 9% of all full-time undergraduates had no need and received non-need-based gift aid.
GIFT AID (NEED-BASED) *Total amount:* $7,412,900 (28% federal, 19% state, 44% institutional, 9% external sources). *Receiving aid:* Freshmen: 88% (159); all full-time undergraduates: 86% (799). *Average award:* Freshmen: $11,130; Undergraduates: $9081. *Scholarships, grants, and awards:* Federal Pell, FSEOG, state, private, college/university gift aid from institutional funds.
GIFT AID (NON-NEED-BASED) *Total amount:* $497,130 (4% state, 73% institutional, 23% external sources). *Receiving aid:* Freshmen: 4% (7). Undergraduates: 4% (37). *Average award:* Freshmen: $3633. Undergraduates: $3516. *Scholarships, grants, and awards by category:* Academic interests/achievement: 352 awards ($1,296,250 total): general academic interests/achievements. Special achievements/activities: 44 awards ($63,000 total): leadership. Special characteristics: 144 awards ($160,750 total): children and siblings of alumni, members of minority groups, siblings of current students. *Tuition waivers:* Full or partial for minority students, children of alumni, employees or children of employees, adult students, senior citizens. *ROTC:* Army cooperative.
LOANS *Student loans:* $7,461,086 (77% need-based, 23% non-need-based). 85% of past graduating class borrowed through all loan programs. *Average indebtedness per student:* $16,608. *Average need-based loan:* Freshmen: $4030. Undergraduates: $4706. *Parent loans:* $1,195,017 (40% need-based, 60% non-need-based). *Programs:* Federal Direct (Subsidized and Unsubsidized Stafford, PLUS), Perkins.
WORK-STUDY *Federal work-study:* Total amount: $101,915; 61 jobs averaging $1671.
APPLYING FOR FINANCIAL AID *Required financial aid forms:* FAFSA, state aid form. *Financial aid deadline (priority):* 3/1. *Notification date:* Continuous beginning 3/1. Students must reply within 2 weeks of notification.
CONTACT Beverly Chudy, Director of Financial Aid, Hilbert College, 5200 South Park Avenue, Hamburg, NY 14075-1597, 716-649-7900 Ext. 207 or toll-free 800-649-8003. *Fax:* 716-649-1152. *E-mail:* bchudy@hilbert.edu. *Website:* http://www.hilbert.edu/.

HILLSDALE COLLEGE
Hillsdale, MI

Tuition & fees: $22,890	Average undergraduate aid package: $18,298

ABOUT THE INSTITUTION Independent, coed. *Awards:* bachelor's, master's, and doctoral degrees. 42 undergraduate majors. *Total enrollment:* 1,447. Undergraduates: 1,434. Freshmen: 388. Both federal and institutional methodology are used as a basis for awarding need-based institutional aid.
UNDERGRADUATE EXPENSES for 2013–2014 *Comprehensive fee:* $31,890 includes full-time tuition ($22,250), mandatory fees ($640), and room and board ($9000). *College room only:* $4460. Room and board charges vary according to board plan. *Part-time tuition:* $880 per credit. *Payment plan:* Tuition prepayment.
FRESHMAN FINANCIAL AID (Fall 2012, est.) 286 applied for aid; of those 63% were deemed to have need. 96% of freshmen with need received aid; of those 37% had need fully met. *Average percent of need met:* 65% (excluding resources awarded to replace EFC). *Average financial aid package:* $13,638 (excluding resources awarded to replace EFC). 47% of all full-time freshmen had no need and received non-need-based gift aid.
UNDERGRADUATE FINANCIAL AID (Fall 2012, est.) 858 applied for aid; of those 70% were deemed to have need. 95% of undergraduates with need received aid; of those 42% had need fully met. *Average percent of need met:* 70% (excluding resources awarded to replace EFC). *Average financial aid package:* $18,298 (excluding resources awarded to replace EFC). 49% of all full-time undergraduates had no need and received non-need-based gift aid.
GIFT AID (NEED-BASED) *Total amount:* $3,443,365 (100% institutional). *Receiving aid:* Freshmen: 32% (117); all full-time undergraduates: 29% (405). *Average award:* Freshmen: $7324; Undergraduates: $7958. *Scholarships, grants, and awards:* private, college/university gift aid from institutional funds.
GIFT AID (NON-NEED-BASED) *Total amount:* $16,166,246 (91% institutional, 9% external sources). *Receiving aid:* Freshmen: 44% (159). Undergraduates: 37% (522). *Average award:* Freshmen: $4658. Undergraduates: $5268. *Scholarships, grants, and awards by category:* Academic interests/achievement: biological sciences, business, education, English, foreign languages, general academic interests/achievements, health fields, humanities, international studies, mathematics, physical sciences, premedicine, religion/biblical studies, social sciences. Creative arts/performance: art/fine arts, debating, journalism/publications, music, theater/drama. Special achievements/activities: community service, general special achievements/activities, leadership. Special characteristics: children of faculty/staff, international stu-

dents. *Tuition waivers:* Full or partial for children of alumni, employees or children of employees.

LOANS *Student loans:* $5,435,694 (54% need-based, 46% non-need-based). 55% of past graduating class borrowed through all loan programs. *Average indebtedness per student:* $25,502. *Average need-based loan:* Freshmen: $5854. Undergraduates: $6189. *Programs:* college/university, alternative loans.

ATHLETIC AWARDS Total amount: $2,654,765 (100% non-need-based).

APPLYING FOR FINANCIAL AID *Required financial aid forms:* institution's own form, noncustodial (divorced/separated) parent's statement, business/farm supplement. *Financial aid deadline:* 4/1 (priority: 2/1). *Notification date:* Continuous beginning 1/20. Students must reply by 5/1 or within 3 weeks of notification.

CONTACT Mr. Rich Moeggengberg, Director of Student Financial Aid, Hillsdale College, 33 East College Street, Hillsdale, MI 49242-1298, 517-607-2550. *Fax:* 517-607-2298. *E-mail:* rich.moeggenbeng@hillsdale.edu.
Website: http://www.hillsdale.edu/.

HILLSDALE FREE WILL BAPTIST COLLEGE
Moore, OK

Tuition & fees: $10,880	Average undergraduate aid package: $11,749

ABOUT THE INSTITUTION Independent Free Will Baptist, coed. *Awards:* associate, bachelor's, and master's degrees. 24 undergraduate majors. *Total enrollment:* 225. Undergraduates: 202. Freshmen: 53. Both federal and institutional methodology are used as a basis for awarding need-based institutional aid.

UNDERGRADUATE EXPENSES for 2013–2014 *Application fee:* $20. *Comprehensive fee:* $17,350 includes full-time tuition ($9000), mandatory fees ($1880), and room and board ($6470). *College room only:* $3020. Full-time tuition and fees vary according to course load. Room and board charges vary according to board plan and housing facility. *Part-time tuition:* $375 per credit. Part-time tuition and fees vary according to course load.

FRESHMAN FINANCIAL AID (Fall 2011) 52 applied for aid; of those 73% were deemed to have need. 100% of freshmen with need received aid. *Average percent of need met:* 50% (excluding resources awarded to replace EFC). *Average financial aid package:* $11,672 (excluding resources awarded to replace EFC). 11% of all full-time freshmen had no need and received non-need-based gift aid.

UNDERGRADUATE FINANCIAL AID (Fall 2011) 179 applied for aid; of those 86% were deemed to have need. 100% of undergraduates with need received aid. *Average percent of need met:* 50% (excluding resources awarded to replace EFC). *Average financial aid package:* $11,749 (excluding resources awarded to replace EFC). 11% of all full-time undergraduates had no need and received non-need-based gift aid.

GIFT AID (NEED-BASED) *Total amount:* $775,455 (67% federal, 28% state, 5% institutional). *Receiving aid:* Freshmen: 54% (30); all full-time undergraduates: 59% (116). *Average award:* Freshmen: $6510; Undergraduates: $6174. *Scholarships, grants, and awards:* Federal Pell, FSEOG, state, private, college/university gift aid from institutional funds, Bureau of Indian Affairs Grants.

GIFT AID (NON-NEED-BASED) *Total amount:* $507,464 (79% institutional, 21% external sources). *Receiving aid:* Freshmen: 54% (30). Undergraduates: 60% (117). *Average award:* Freshmen: $1998. Undergraduates: $2611. *Scholarships, grants, and awards by category:* Academic interests/achievement: $303,000 total: business, education, English, general academic interests/achievements, mathematics, religion/biblical studies. *Creative arts/performance:* $9410 total: music. *Special achievements/activities:* $22,000 total: religious involvement. *Special characteristics:* $113,370 total: children and siblings of alumni, children of educators, children of faculty/staff, general special characteristics, relatives of clergy, religious affiliation. *Tuition waivers:* Full or partial for children of alumni, employees or children of employees, senior citizens.

LOANS *Student loans:* $966,000 (52% need-based, 48% non-need-based). 80% of past graduating class borrowed through all loan programs. *Average indebtedness per student:* $22,313. *Average need-based loan:* Freshmen: $3500. Undergraduates: $3911. *Parent loans:* $70,743 (79% need-based, 21% non-need-based). *Programs:* Federal Direct (Subsidized and Unsubsidized Stafford, PLUS), Perkins.

WORK-STUDY *Federal work-study:* Total amount: $47,713; 49 jobs averaging $1015.

APPLYING FOR FINANCIAL AID *Required financial aid forms:* FAFSA, institution's own form. *Financial aid deadline (priority):* 6/30. *Notification date:* Continuous beginning 4/1. Students must reply within 4 weeks of notification.

CONTACT Denise Conklin, Director of Financial Aid, Hillsdale Free Will Baptist College, PO Box 7208, Moore, OK 73153-1208, 405-912-9012. *Fax:* 405-912-9050. *E-mail:* dconklin@hc.edu.
Website: http://www.hc.edu/.

HIRAM COLLEGE
Hiram, OH

CONTACT Ann Marie Gruber, Associate Director of Financial Aid, Hiram College, Box 67, Hiram, OH 44234-0067, 330-569-5107 or toll-free 800-362-5280. *Fax:* 330-569-5499.
Website: http://www.hiram.edu/.

HOBART AND WILLIAM SMITH COLLEGES
Geneva, NY

Tuition & fees: $44,438	Average undergraduate aid package: $30,891

ABOUT THE INSTITUTION Independent, coed. *Awards:* certificates, bachelor's, and master's degrees. 47 undergraduate majors. *Total enrollment:* 2,300. Undergraduates: 2,292. Freshmen: 600. Both federal and institutional methodology are used as a basis for awarding need-based institutional aid.

UNDERGRADUATE EXPENSES for 2013–2014 *Application fee:* $45. *Comprehensive fee:* $55,699 includes full-time tuition ($43,484), mandatory fees ($954), and room and board ($11,261). Room and board charges vary according to board plan. *Payment plan:* Tuition prepayment.

FRESHMAN FINANCIAL AID (Fall 2011) 502 applied for aid; of those 84% were deemed to have need. 99% of freshmen with need received aid; of those 76% had need fully met. *Average percent of need met:* 79% (excluding resources awarded to replace EFC). *Average financial aid package:* $29,793 (excluding resources awarded to replace EFC). 23% of all full-time freshmen had no need and received non-need-based gift aid.

UNDERGRADUATE FINANCIAL AID (Fall 2011) 1,636 applied for aid; of those 86% were deemed to have need. 99% of undergraduates with need received aid; of those 60% had need fully met. *Average percent of need met:* 79% (excluding resources awarded to replace EFC). *Average financial aid package:* $30,891 (excluding resources awarded to replace EFC). 23% of all full-time undergraduates had no need and received non-need-based gift aid.

GIFT AID (NEED-BASED) *Total amount:* $36,900,220 (7% federal, 4% state, 84% institutional, 5% external sources). *Receiving aid:* Freshmen: 70% (412); all full-time undergraduates: 71% (1,374). *Average award:* Freshmen: $26,869; Undergraduates: $26,852. *Scholarships, grants, and awards:* Federal Pell, FSEOG, state, private, college/university gift aid from institutional funds.

GIFT AID (NON-NEED-BASED) *Total amount:* $9,505,059 (1% state, 86% institutional, 13% external sources). *Receiving aid:* Freshmen: 17% (101). Undergraduates: 11% (220). *Average award:* Freshmen: $15,572. Undergraduates: $15,339. *Scholarships, grants, and awards by category:* Academic interests/achievement: 128 awards ($2,000,000 total): general academic interests/achievements, premedicine. *Creative arts/performance:* 19 awards ($180,500 total): art/fine arts, creative writing, dance, music, performing arts. *Special achievements/activities:* 15 awards ($176,114 total): leadership. *Tuition waivers:* Full or partial for employees or children of employees. *ROTC:* Army cooperative, Air Force cooperative.

LOANS *Student loans:* $11,264,584 (66% need-based, 34% non-need-based). 59% of past graduating class borrowed through all loan programs. *Average indebtedness per student:* $34,463. *Average need-based loan:* Freshmen: $3448. Undergraduates: $3933. *Parent loans:* $6,685,047 (31% need-based, 69% non-need-based). *Programs:* Federal Direct (Subsidized and Unsubsidized Stafford, PLUS), Perkins, college/university.

WORK-STUDY *Federal work-study:* Total amount: $1,900,426; 1,030 jobs averaging $1845. *State or other work-study/employment:* Total amount: $1,265,367 (12% need-based, 88% non-need-based). 519 part-time jobs averaging $1921.

APPLYING FOR FINANCIAL AID *Required financial aid forms:* FAFSA, CSS Financial Aid PROFILE, state aid form, noncustodial (divorced/separated) parent's statement, federal income tax form(s). *Financial aid deadline:* 2/15 (priority: 2/15). *Notification date:* 4/1. Students must reply by 5/1.

CONTACT Beth Nepa, Director of Financial Aid, Hobart and William Smith Colleges, Demarest Hall, 300 Pulteney Street, Geneva, NY 14456-3397, 315-781-3315 or toll-free 800-852-2256. *Fax:* 315-781-4048. *E-mail:* nepa@hws.edu. *Website:* http://www.hws.edu/.

HOBE SOUND BIBLE COLLEGE
Hobe Sound, FL

CONTACT Director of Financial Aid, Hobe Sound Bible College, PO Box 1065, Hobe Sound, FL 33475-1065, 561-546-5534. *Fax:* 561-545-1422. *Website:* http://www.hsbc.edu/.

HODGES UNIVERSITY
Naples, FL

Tuition & fees: $12,260	Average undergraduate aid package: $9350

ABOUT THE INSTITUTION Independent, coed. *Awards:* certificates, associate, bachelor's, and master's degrees. 8 undergraduate majors. *Total enrollment:* 2,255. Undergraduates: 2,067. Freshmen: 201. Federal methodology is used as a basis for awarding need-based institutional aid.

UNDERGRADUATE EXPENSES for 2013–2014 *Application fee:* $20. *Tuition:* full-time $11,760.

FRESHMAN FINANCIAL AID (Fall 2012, est.) 159 applied for aid; of those 92% were deemed to have need. 100% of freshmen with need received aid; of those 22% had need fully met. *Average percent of need met:* 68% (excluding resources awarded to replace EFC). *Average financial aid package:* $8400 (excluding resources awarded to replace EFC). 8% of all full-time freshmen had no need and received non-need-based gift aid.

UNDERGRADUATE FINANCIAL AID (Fall 2012, est.) 1,342 applied for aid; of those 90% were deemed to have need. 100% of undergraduates with need received aid; of those 23% had need fully met. *Average percent of need met:* 77% (excluding resources awarded to replace EFC). *Average financial aid package:* $9350 (excluding resources awarded to replace EFC). 4% of all full-time undergraduates had no need and received non-need-based gift aid.

GIFT AID (NEED-BASED) *Total amount:* $10,577,321 (98% federal, 2% state). *Receiving aid:* Freshmen: 79% (130); all full-time undergraduates: 80% (1,125). *Average award:* Freshmen: $2825. *Scholarships, grants, and awards:* Federal Pell, FSEOG, state, private, college/university gift aid from institutional funds.

GIFT AID (NON-NEED-BASED) *Total amount:* $4,527,434 (59% state, 36% institutional, 5% external sources). *Receiving aid:* Freshmen: 37% (61). Undergraduates: 63% (890). *Average award:* Freshmen: $375. Undergraduates: $230. *Scholarships, grants, and awards by category:* Special achievements/activities: general special achievements/activities. *Tuition waivers:* Full or partial for employees or children of employees.

LOANS *Student loans:* $23,000,000 (43% need-based, 57% non-need-based). 84% of past graduating class borrowed through all loan programs. *Average indebtedness per student:* $18,400. *Average need-based loan:* Freshmen: $2830. Undergraduates: $2830. *Parent loans:* $125,000 (100% need-based).

WORK-STUDY *Federal work-study:* Total amount: $230,000; 67 jobs averaging $3432.

APPLYING FOR FINANCIAL AID *Required financial aid form:* FAFSA. *Financial aid deadline:* Continuous. *Notification date:* Continuous.

CONTACT Mr. Joe Gilchrist, Vice President of Student Financial Services, Hodges University, 2655 Northbrooke Drive, Naples, FL 34119, 239-598-6116 or toll-free 800-466-8017. *Fax:* 239-598-6257. *E-mail:* jgilchrist@hodges.edu. *Website:* http://www.hodges.edu/.

HOFSTRA UNIVERSITY
Hempstead, NY

Tuition & fees: $35,950	Average undergraduate aid package: $23,000

ABOUT THE INSTITUTION Independent, coed. *Awards:* certificates, bachelor's, master's, and doctoral degrees. 129 undergraduate majors. *Total enrollment:* 11,023. Undergraduates: 6,893. Freshmen: 1,488. Federal methodology is used as a basis for awarding need-based institutional aid.

UNDERGRADUATE EXPENSES for 2013–2014 *Application fee:* $70. *Comprehensive fee:* $48,320 includes full-time tuition ($34,900), mandatory fees ($1050), and room and board ($12,370). *College room only:* $8450. Full-time tuition and fees vary according to course load and program. Room and board charges vary according to board plan and housing facility. *Part-time tuition:* $1100 per credit hour. *Part-time fees:* $145 per term. Part-time tuition and fees vary according to course load and program. *Payment plan:* Guaranteed tuition.

FRESHMAN FINANCIAL AID (Fall 2012, est.) 1,274 applied for aid; of those 85% were deemed to have need. 100% of freshmen with need received aid; of those 21% had need fully met. *Average percent of need met:* 67% (excluding resources awarded to replace EFC). *Average financial aid package:* $24,000 (excluding resources awarded to replace EFC). 21% of all full-time freshmen had no need and received non-need-based gift aid.

UNDERGRADUATE FINANCIAL AID (Fall 2012, est.) 5,028 applied for aid; of those 85% were deemed to have need. 99% of undergraduates with need received aid; of those 20% had need fully met. *Average percent of need met:* 59% (excluding resources awarded to replace EFC). *Average financial aid package:* $23,000 (excluding resources awarded to replace EFC). 20% of all full-time undergraduates had no need and received non-need-based gift aid.

GIFT AID (NEED-BASED) *Total amount:* $57,940,000 (13% federal, 7% state, 78% institutional, 2% external sources). *Receiving aid:* Freshmen: 71% (1,060); all full-time undergraduates: 62% (3,941). *Average award:* Freshmen: $17,000; Undergraduates: $15,000. *Scholarships, grants, and awards:* Federal Pell, FSEOG, state, private, college/university gift aid from institutional funds.

GIFT AID (NON-NEED-BASED) *Total amount:* $20,780,000 (1% federal, 1% state, 94% institutional, 4% external sources). *Receiving aid:* Freshmen: 11% (164). Undergraduates: 8% (486). *Average award:* Freshmen: $13,000. Undergraduates: $12,000. *Scholarships, grants, and awards by category:* Academic interests/achievement: 5,884 awards ($51,457,518 total): communication, engineering/technologies, general academic interests/achievements. Creative arts/performance: 260 awards ($611,163 total): applied art and design, art/fine arts, cinema/film/broadcasting, dance, journalism/publications, music, performing arts, theater/drama. Special achievements/activities: 260 awards ($5,894,720 total): general special achievements/activities, leadership. Special characteristics: 399 awards ($8,435,240 total): children and siblings of alumni, children of union members/company employees, general special characteristics, handicapped students, public servants, veterans. *Tuition waivers:* Full or partial for employees or children of employees, senior citizens. *ROTC:* Army.

LOANS *Student loans:* $50,000,000 (71% need-based, 29% non-need-based). 67% of past graduating class borrowed through all loan programs. *Average need-based loan:* Freshmen: $4000. Undergraduates: $5000. *Parent loans:* $33,300,000 (54% need-based, 46% non-need-based). *Programs:* Federal Direct (Subsidized and Unsubsidized Stafford, PLUS), Perkins, state, college/university.

WORK-STUDY *Federal work-study:* Total amount: $5,100,000; 1,726 jobs averaging $2973. *State or other work-study/employment:* Total amount: $4,300,000 (28% need-based, 72% non-need-based). 1,522 part-time jobs averaging $2852.

ATHLETIC AWARDS Total amount: $5,860,000 (56% need-based, 44% non-need-based).

APPLYING FOR FINANCIAL AID *Required financial aid forms:* FAFSA, state aid form. *Financial aid deadline (priority):* 2/15. *Notification date:* Continuous beginning 3/1. Students must reply by 5/1 or within 2 weeks of notification.

CONTACT Sandra Filbry, Director of Financial Aid, Hofstra University, 126 Hofstra University, Hempstead, NY 11549, 516-463-4335 or toll-free 800-HOFSTRA. *Fax:* 516-463-4936. *E-mail:* sandra.a.filbry@hofstra.edu. *Website:* http://www.hofstra.edu/.

HOLLINS UNIVERSITY
Roanoke, VA

Tuition & fees: $32,075	Average undergraduate aid package: $27,277

ABOUT THE INSTITUTION Independent, undergraduate: women only; graduate: coed. *Awards:* certificates, bachelor's, and master's degrees. 27 undergraduate majors. *Total enrollment:* 794. Undergraduates: 613. Freshmen: 128. Federal methodology is used as a basis for awarding need-based institutional aid.

UNDERGRADUATE EXPENSES for 2013–2014 *Application fee:* $40. *Comprehensive fee:* $43,295 includes full-time tuition ($31,490), mandatory fees ($585), and room and board ($11,220). *College room only:* $6700. *Part-time tuition:* $986 per credit hour. *Part-time fees:* $148.75 per term. *Payment plan:* Tuition prepayment.

FRESHMAN FINANCIAL AID (Fall 2012, est.) 114 applied for aid; of those 83% were deemed to have need. 100% of freshmen with need received aid; of those 24% had need fully met. *Average percent of need met:* 84% (excluding resources awarded to replace EFC). *Average financial aid package:* $29,987 (excluding resources awarded to replace EFC). 25% of all full-time freshmen had no need and received non-need-based gift aid.

UNDERGRADUATE FINANCIAL AID (Fall 2012, est.) 502 applied for aid; of those 89% were deemed to have need. 100% of undergraduates with need received aid; of those 19% had need fully met. *Average percent of need met:* 78% (excluding resources awarded to replace EFC). *Average financial aid package:* $27,277 (excluding resources awarded to replace EFC). 23% of all full-time undergraduates had no need and received non-need-based gift aid.

GIFT AID (NEED-BASED) *Total amount:* $9,769,063 (11% federal, 7% state, 81% institutional, 1% external sources). *Receiving aid:* Freshmen: 75% (95); all full-time undergraduates: 76% (445). *Average award:* Freshmen: $24,287; Undergraduates: $21,032. *Scholarships, grants, and awards:* Federal Pell, FSEOG, state, private, college/university gift aid from institutional funds.

GIFT AID (NON-NEED-BASED) *Total amount:* $2,702,590 (7% state, 93% institutional). *Receiving aid:* Freshmen: 75% (95). Undergraduates: 74% (434). *Average award:* Freshmen: $19,509. Undergraduates: $18,613. *Scholarships, grants, and awards by category: Academic interests/achievement:* general academic interests/achievements. *Creative arts/performance:* art/fine arts, creative writing, dance, music. *Special achievements/activities:* community service, general special achievements/activities, hobbies/interests, leadership. *Special characteristics:* adult students, children and siblings of alumni, children of faculty/staff, international students, local/state students, out-of-state students, previous college experience, veterans. *Tuition waivers:* Full or partial for employees or children of employees.

LOANS *Student loans:* $4,249,224 (84% need-based, 16% non-need-based). 77% of past graduating class borrowed through all loan programs. *Average indebtedness per student:* $31,104. *Average need-based loan:* Freshmen: $3889. Undergraduates: $4915. *Parent loans:* $1,327,961 (93% need-based, 7% non-need-based). *Programs:* Federal Direct (Subsidized and Unsubsidized Stafford, PLUS), Perkins, college/university.

WORK-STUDY *Federal work-study:* Total amount: $251,301; jobs available. *State or other work-study/employment:* Total amount: $300,499 (58% need-based, 42% non-need-based). Part-time jobs available.

APPLYING FOR FINANCIAL AID *Required financial aid forms:* FAFSA, state aid form. *Financial aid deadline (priority):* 2/15. *Notification date:* Continuous beginning 3/1. Students must reply by 5/1.

CONTACT Ms. MaryJean Corriss, Director of Scholarships and Financial Assistance, Hollins University, PO Box 9718, Roanoke, VA 24020-1688, 540-362-6332 or toll-free 800-456-9595. *Fax:* 540-362-6093. *E-mail:* corrissmj@hollins.edu. *Website:* http://www.hollins.edu/.

HOLY CROSS COLLEGE
Notre Dame, IN

CONTACT Robert Benjamin, Director of Financial Aid, Holy Cross College, PO Box 308, Notre Dame, IN 46556, 574-239-8362. *E-mail:* rbenjamin@hcc-nd.edu. *Website:* http://www.hcc-nd.edu/.

HOLY FAMILY UNIVERSITY
Philadelphia, PA

ABOUT THE INSTITUTION Independent Roman Catholic, coed. *Awards:* certificates, associate, bachelor's, master's, and doctoral degrees. 32 undergraduate majors. *Total enrollment:* 3,094. Undergraduates: 2,139. Freshmen: 312.

GIFT AID (NEED-BASED) *Scholarships, grants, and awards:* Federal Pell, FSEOG, state, private, college/university gift aid from institutional funds.

GIFT AID (NON-NEED-BASED) *Scholarships, grants, and awards by category: Academic interests/achievement:* general academic interests/achievements.

LOANS *Programs:* Federal Direct (Subsidized and Unsubsidized Stafford, PLUS), Perkins, Federal Nursing.

WORK-STUDY *Federal work-study:* Total amount: $376,199; 291 jobs averaging $1252.

APPLYING FOR FINANCIAL AID *Required financial aid form:* FAFSA.

CONTACT Financial Aid Office, Holy Family University, 9801 Frankford Avenue, Philadelphia, PA 19114-2094, 215-637-7700 Ext. 3233. *Fax:* 215-599-1694. *E-mail:* finaid@holyfamily.edu. *Website:* http://www.holyfamily.edu/.

HOLY NAMES UNIVERSITY
Oakland, CA

CONTACT Christina Miller, Director of Financial Aid, Holy Names University, 3500 Mountain Boulevard, Oakland, CA 94619-1699, 510-436-1327 or toll-free 800-430-1321. *Fax:* 510-436-1199. *E-mail:* miller@hnu.edu. *Website:* http://www.hnu.edu/.

HOOD COLLEGE
Frederick, MD

Tuition & fees: $32,300	Average undergraduate aid package: $25,598

ABOUT THE INSTITUTION Independent, coed. *Awards:* certificates, bachelor's, and master's degrees (also offers adult program with significant enrollment not reflected in profile). 30 undergraduate majors. *Total enrollment:* 2,422. Undergraduates: 1,434. Freshmen: 271. Federal methodology is used as a basis for awarding need-based institutional aid.

UNDERGRADUATE EXPENSES for 2013–2014 *Application fee:* $35. *Comprehensive fee:* $43,210 includes full-time tuition ($31,840), mandatory fees ($460), and room and board ($10,910). *College room only:* $5700. Room and board charges vary according to board plan and housing facility. *Part-time tuition:* $920 per credit hour. *Part-time fees:* $150 per term.

FRESHMAN FINANCIAL AID (Fall 2012, est.) 240 applied for aid; of those 88% were deemed to have need. 100% of freshmen with need received aid; of those 21% had need fully met. *Average percent of need met:* 75% (excluding resources awarded to replace EFC). *Average financial aid package:* $24,575 (excluding resources awarded to replace EFC). 20% of all full-time freshmen had no need and received non-need-based gift aid.

UNDERGRADUATE FINANCIAL AID (Fall 2012, est.) 1,141 applied for aid; of those 93% were deemed to have need. 100% of undergraduates with need received aid; of those 16% had need fully met. *Average percent of need met:* 76% (excluding resources awarded to replace EFC). *Average financial aid package:* $25,598 (excluding resources awarded to replace EFC). 14% of all full-time undergraduates had no need and received non-need-based gift aid.

GIFT AID (NEED-BASED) *Total amount:* $22,726,377 (9% federal, 6% state, 82% institutional, 3% external sources). *Receiving aid:* Freshmen: 78% (210); all full-time undergraduates: 84% (1,063). *Average award:* Freshmen: $21,590; Undergraduates: $21,551. *Scholarships, grants, and awards:* Federal Pell, FSEOG, state, private, college/university gift aid from institutional funds.

GIFT AID (NON-NEED-BASED) *Total amount:* $3,636,765 (1% state, 87% institutional, 12% external sources). *Receiving aid:* Freshmen: 13% (36). Undergraduates: 10% (123). *Average award:* Freshmen: $16,542. Undergraduates: $14,658. *Scholarships, grants, and awards by category: Academic interests/*

achievement: 1,099 awards ($10,927,311 total): general academic interests/achievements. *Creative arts/performance:* 17 awards ($8847 total): music. *Special characteristics:* 111 awards ($920,870 total): children and siblings of alumni, children of faculty/staff, international students, siblings of current students. *Tuition waivers:* Full or partial for employees or children of employees. *ROTC:* Army.
LOANS *Student loans:* $8,752,680 (79% need-based, 21% non-need-based). 75% of past graduating class borrowed through all loan programs. *Average indebtedness per student:* $28,121. *Average need-based loan:* Freshmen: $3151. Undergraduates: $4320. *Parent loans:* $3,015,465 (36% need-based, 64% non-need-based). *Programs:* Federal Direct (Subsidized and Unsubsidized Stafford, PLUS), Perkins.
WORK-STUDY *Federal work-study:* Total amount: $486,967; 372 jobs averaging $2000. *State or other work-study/employment:* Total amount: $81,800 (21% need-based, 79% non-need-based). 49 part-time jobs averaging $2000.
APPLYING FOR FINANCIAL AID *Required financial aid forms:* FAFSA, institution's own form. *Financial aid deadline (priority):* 2/15. *Notification date:* Continuous beginning 3/1. Students must reply by 5/1 or within 4 weeks of notification.
CONTACT Ms. Carol A. Schroyer, Director of Financial Aid, Hood College, 401 Rosemont Avenue, Frederick, MD 21701-8575, 301-696-3411 or toll-free 800-922-1599. *Fax:* 301-696-3812. *E-mail:* schroyer@hood.edu.
Website: http://www.hood.edu/.

HOPE COLLEGE
Holland, MI

Tuition & fees: $28,720	Average undergraduate aid package: $22,197

ABOUT THE INSTITUTION Independent Reformed Church in America, coed. *Awards:* bachelor's degrees. 76 undergraduate majors. *Total enrollment:* 3,343. Undergraduates: 3,343. Freshmen: 889. Federal methodology is used as a basis for awarding need-based institutional aid.
UNDERGRADUATE EXPENSES for 2013–2014 *Application fee:* $50. *Comprehensive fee:* $37,530 includes full-time tuition ($28,550), mandatory fees ($170), and room and board ($8810). *College room only:* $4040. Room and board charges vary according to board plan.
FRESHMAN FINANCIAL AID (Fall 2012, est.) 772 applied for aid; of those 79% were deemed to have need. 100% of freshmen with need received aid; of those 27% had need fully met. *Average percent of need met:* 79% (excluding resources awarded to replace EFC). *Average financial aid package:* $23,044 (excluding resources awarded to replace EFC). 24% of all full-time freshmen had no need and received non-need-based gift aid.
UNDERGRADUATE FINANCIAL AID (Fall 2012, est.) 2,385 applied for aid; of those 83% were deemed to have need. 99% of undergraduates with need received aid; of those 27% had need fully met. *Average percent of need met:* 78% (excluding resources awarded to replace EFC). *Average financial aid package:* $22,197 (excluding resources awarded to replace EFC). 25% of all full-time undergraduates had no need and received non-need-based gift aid.
GIFT AID (NEED-BASED) *Total amount:* $26,472,875 (11% federal, 7% state, 81% institutional, 1% external sources). *Receiving aid:* Freshmen: 58% (526); all full-time undergraduates: 53% (1,667). *Average award:* Freshmen: $18,259; Undergraduates: $16,796. *Scholarships, grants, and awards:* Federal Pell, FSEOG, state, private, college/university gift aid from institutional funds.
GIFT AID (NON-NEED-BASED) *Total amount:* $10,264,672 (5% federal, 84% institutional, 11% external sources). *Receiving aid:* Freshmen: 50% (453). Undergraduates: 43% (1,347). *Average award:* Freshmen: $8287. Undergraduates: $7919. *Scholarships, grants, and awards by category:* Academic interests/achievement: 2,059 awards ($13,430,473 total): general academic interests/achievements. *Creative arts/performance:* 158 awards ($422,102 total): art/fine arts, creative writing, dance, music, theater/drama. *Special characteristics:* 102 awards ($1,571,370 total): ethnic background. *Tuition waivers:* Full or partial for employees or children of employees. *ROTC:* Army cooperative.
LOANS *Student loans:* $15,918,642 (45% need-based, 55% non-need-based). 65% of past graduating class borrowed through all loan programs. *Average indebtedness per student:* $37,010. *Average need-based loan:* Freshmen: $3940. Undergraduates: $4706. *Parent loans:* $4,865,502 (100% non-need-based). *Programs:* Federal Direct (Subsidized and Unsubsidized Stafford, PLUS), Perkins.

WORK-STUDY *Federal work-study:* Total amount: $309,054; 240 jobs averaging $1425. *State or other work-study/employment:* Total amount: $1,890,384 (58% need-based, 42% non-need-based). 516 part-time jobs averaging $793.
APPLYING FOR FINANCIAL AID *Required financial aid forms:* FAFSA, institution's own form. *Financial aid deadline (priority):* 3/1. *Notification date:* Continuous beginning 3/15. Students must reply within 2 weeks of notification.
CONTACT Ms. Jill Nutt, Director of Financial Aid, Hope College, 141 East 12th Street, Holland, MI 49422-9000, 616-395-7765 or toll-free 800-968-7850. *Fax:* 616-395-7160. *E-mail:* hooyman@hope.edu.
Website: http://www.hope.edu/.

HOPE INTERNATIONAL UNIVERSITY
Fullerton, CA

Tuition & fees: $26,050	Average undergraduate aid package: $12,110

ABOUT THE INSTITUTION Independent Christian Churches and Churches of Christ, coed. *Awards:* certificates, associate, bachelor's, and master's degrees. 19 undergraduate majors. *Total enrollment:* 1,652. Undergraduates: 1,167. Freshmen: 286. Federal methodology is used as a basis for awarding need-based institutional aid.
UNDERGRADUATE EXPENSES for 2013–2014 *Application fee:* $40. *One-time required fee:* $160. *Comprehensive fee:* $34,650 includes full-time tuition ($25,550), mandatory fees ($500), and room and board ($8600). *College room only:* $4610. Full-time tuition and fees vary according to course level, course load, degree level, location, program, and reciprocity agreements. Room and board charges vary according to board plan and student level. *Part-time tuition:* $1075 per unit. *Part-time fees:* $500 per year. Part-time tuition and fees vary according to course level, course load, degree level, location, program, and reciprocity agreements.
FRESHMAN FINANCIAL AID (Fall 2012, est.) 109 applied for aid; of those 84% were deemed to have need. 100% of freshmen with need received aid; of those 21% had need fully met. *Average percent of need met:* 45% (excluding resources awarded to replace EFC). *Average financial aid package:* $16,750 (excluding resources awarded to replace EFC). 3% of all full-time freshmen had no need and received non-need-based gift aid.
UNDERGRADUATE FINANCIAL AID (Fall 2012, est.) 620 applied for aid; of those 96% were deemed to have need. 100% of undergraduates with need received aid; of those 16% had need fully met. *Average percent of need met:* 38% (excluding resources awarded to replace EFC). *Average financial aid package:* $12,110 (excluding resources awarded to replace EFC). 3% of all full-time undergraduates had no need and received non-need-based gift aid.
GIFT AID (NEED-BASED) *Total amount:* $3,965,981 (52% federal, 34% state, 14% institutional). *Receiving aid:* Freshmen: 68% (76); all full-time undergraduates: 60% (466). *Average award:* Freshmen: $11,294; Undergraduates: $8339. *Scholarships, grants, and awards:* Federal Pell, FSEOG, state, private, college/university gift aid from institutional funds.
GIFT AID (NON-NEED-BASED) *Total amount:* $2,407,264 (97% institutional, 3% external sources). *Receiving aid:* Freshmen: 74% (82). Undergraduates: 51% (399). *Average award:* Freshmen: $11,333. Undergraduates: $7550. *Scholarships, grants, and awards by category:* Academic interests/achievement: business, general academic interests/achievements. *Special achievements/activities:* leadership. *Special characteristics:* children of faculty/staff, international students, spouses of current students. *Tuition waivers:* Full or partial for employees or children of employees. *ROTC:* Army cooperative.
LOANS *Student loans:* $5,957,174 (48% need-based, 52% non-need-based). 70% of past graduating class borrowed through all loan programs. *Average indebtedness per student:* $20,500. *Average need-based loan:* Freshmen: $3500. Undergraduates: $4661. *Parent loans:* $1,297,894 (100% non-need-based). *Programs:* Federal Direct (Subsidized and Unsubsidized Stafford, PLUS), Perkins.
WORK-STUDY *Federal work-study:* Total amount: $69,000; 28 jobs averaging $2000. *State or other work-study/employment:* Part-time jobs available.
ATHLETIC AWARDS Total amount: $1,916,398 (100% non-need-based).
APPLYING FOR FINANCIAL AID *Required financial aid forms:* FAFSA, institution's own form. *Financial aid deadline (priority):* 3/2. *Notification date:* Continuous beginning 4/1. Students must reply within 2 weeks of notification.

CONTACT Mrs. Shannon O'Shields, Director of Student Financial Aid, Hope International University, 2500 East Nutwood Avenue, Fullerton, CA 92831, 714-879-3901 Ext. 2207 or toll-free 866-722-HOPE. *Fax:* 714-681-7421. *E-mail:* soshields@hiu.edu.
Website: http://www.hiu.edu/.

HORIZON COLLEGE SAN DIEGO
San Diego, CA

CONTACT Financial Aid Office, Horizon College San Diego, 5331 Mt. Alifan Drive, San Diego, CA 92111, 858-695-8587.
Website: http://www.horizoncollege.org/.

HOUGHTON COLLEGE
Houghton, NY

Tuition & fees: $27,728	Average undergraduate aid package: $22,532

ABOUT THE INSTITUTION Independent Wesleyan, coed. *Awards:* associate, bachelor's, and master's degrees. 64 undergraduate majors. *Total enrollment:* 1,165. Undergraduates: 1,147. Freshmen: 234. Federal methodology is used as a basis for awarding need-based institutional aid.
UNDERGRADUATE EXPENSES for 2013–2014 *Application fee:* $40. *Comprehensive fee:* $35,740 includes full-time tuition ($27,578), mandatory fees ($150), and room and board ($8012). *College room only:* $4298. Room and board charges vary according to board plan, gender, housing facility, and student level. *Part-time tuition:* $1159 per credit hour.
FRESHMAN FINANCIAL AID (Fall 2012, est.) 213 applied for aid; of those 93% were deemed to have need. 100% of freshmen with need received aid; of those 12% had need fully met. *Average percent of need met:* 80% (excluding resources awarded to replace EFC). *Average financial aid package:* $24,585 (excluding resources awarded to replace EFC). 14% of all full-time freshmen had no need and received non-need-based gift aid.
UNDERGRADUATE FINANCIAL AID (Fall 2012, est.) 928 applied for aid; of those 94% were deemed to have need. 100% of undergraduates with need received aid; of those 13% had need fully met. *Average percent of need met:* 78% (excluding resources awarded to replace EFC). *Average financial aid package:* $22,532 (excluding resources awarded to replace EFC). 16% of all full-time undergraduates had no need and received non-need-based gift aid.
GIFT AID (NEED-BASED) *Total amount:* $12,896,488 (14% federal, 8% state, 74% institutional, 4% external sources). *Receiving aid:* Freshmen: 85% (198); all full-time undergraduates: 80% (862). *Average award:* Freshmen: $18,668; Undergraduates: $16,494. *Scholarships, grants, and awards:* Federal Pell, FSEOG, state, private, college/university gift aid from institutional funds.
GIFT AID (NON-NEED-BASED) *Total amount:* $2,415,897 (1% state, 88% institutional, 11% external sources). *Receiving aid:* Freshmen: 9% (20). Undergraduates: 8% (85). *Average award:* Freshmen: $12,007. Undergraduates: $10,775. *Scholarships, grants, and awards by category:* Academic interests/achievement: 649 awards ($5,860,436 total): general academic interests/achievements. Creative arts/performance: 96 awards ($249,534 total): art/fine arts, music, performing arts. Special achievements/activities: 101 awards ($200,912 total): general special achievements/activities, leadership. Special characteristics: 667 awards ($3,312,906 total): adult students, children and siblings of alumni, children of faculty/staff, general special characteristics, international students, local/state students, relatives of clergy, religious affiliation, siblings of current students, veterans. *Tuition waivers:* Full or partial for employees or children of employees. *ROTC:* Army cooperative.
LOANS *Student loans:* $7,848,964 (78% need-based, 22% non-need-based). 79% of past graduating class borrowed through all loan programs. *Average indebtedness per student:* $22,197. *Average need-based loan:* Freshmen: $4831. Undergraduates: $5394. *Parent loans:* $1,251,856 (47% need-based, 53% non-need-based). *Programs:* Federal Direct (Subsidized and Unsubsidized Stafford, PLUS), Perkins, alternative loans.

WORK-STUDY *Federal work-study:* Total amount: $1,228,646; 614 jobs averaging $1905. *State or other work-study/employment:* Total amount: $8400 (100% non-need-based). 4 part-time jobs averaging $2100.
APPLYING FOR FINANCIAL AID *Required financial aid forms:* FAFSA, state aid form. *Financial aid deadline (priority):* 3/1. *Notification date:* Continuous beginning 3/15. Students must reply by 5/1 or within 4 weeks of notification.
CONTACT Mrs. Marianne Loper, Director of Financial Aid, Houghton College, One Willard Avenue, Houghton, NY 14744, 585-567-9328 or toll-free 800-777-2556. *Fax:* 585-567-9610. *E-mail:* marianne.loper@houghton.edu.
Website: http://www.houghton.edu/.

HOUSTON BAPTIST UNIVERSITY
Houston, TX

Tuition & fees: $27,930	Average undergraduate aid package: $23,847

ABOUT THE INSTITUTION Independent Baptist, coed. *Awards:* bachelor's and master's degrees. 59 undergraduate majors. *Total enrollment:* 2,589. Undergraduates: 2,052. Freshmen: 518. Federal methodology is used as a basis for awarding need-based institutional aid.
UNDERGRADUATE EXPENSES for 2013–2014 *Comprehensive fee:* $34,430 includes full-time tuition ($26,280), mandatory fees ($1650), and room and board ($6500). *College room only:* $3550. Room and board charges vary according to board plan and housing facility. *Part-time tuition:* $1100 per credit hour. *Part-time fees:* $825 per term. Part-time tuition and fees vary according to course load.
FRESHMAN FINANCIAL AID (Fall 2012, est.) 441 applied for aid; of those 94% were deemed to have need. 100% of freshmen with need received aid; of those 20% had need fully met. *Average percent of need met:* 72% (excluding resources awarded to replace EFC). *Average financial aid package:* $23,701 (excluding resources awarded to replace EFC). 19% of all full-time freshmen had no need and received non-need-based gift aid.
UNDERGRADUATE FINANCIAL AID (Fall 2012, est.) 1,489 applied for aid; of those 95% were deemed to have need. 100% of undergraduates with need received aid; of those 18% had need fully met. *Average percent of need met:* 70% (excluding resources awarded to replace EFC). *Average financial aid package:* $23,847 (excluding resources awarded to replace EFC). 22% of all full-time undergraduates had no need and received non-need-based gift aid.
GIFT AID (NEED-BASED) *Total amount:* $20,797,244 (20% federal, 9% state, 69% institutional, 2% external sources). *Receiving aid:* Freshmen: 80% (413); all full-time undergraduates: 76% (1,410). *Average award:* Freshmen: $16,042; Undergraduates: $15,553. *Scholarships, grants, and awards:* Federal Pell, FSEOG, state, private, college/university gift aid from institutional funds.
GIFT AID (NON-NEED-BASED) *Total amount:* $4,523,539 (98% institutional, 2% external sources). *Receiving aid:* Freshmen: 79% (407). Undergraduates: 74% (1,386). *Average award:* Freshmen: $12,448. Undergraduates: $9320. *Scholarships, grants, and awards by category:* Academic interests/achievement: 2,464 awards ($14,961,654 total): general academic interests/achievements, health fields, religion/biblical studies. Creative arts/performance: 65 awards ($150,150 total): art/fine arts, music. Special achievements/activities: 128 awards ($172,705 total): cheerleading/drum major, community service, leadership, religious involvement. Special characteristics: 49 awards ($255,544 total): children of faculty/staff, relatives of clergy. *Tuition waivers:* Full or partial for employees or children of employees. *ROTC:* Army cooperative, Naval cooperative, Air Force cooperative.
LOANS *Student loans:* $14,829,800 (74% need-based, 26% non-need-based). *Average need-based loan:* Freshmen: $4599. Undergraduates: $4565. *Parent loans:* $4,577,716 (7% need-based, 93% non-need-based). *Programs:* Federal Direct (Subsidized and Unsubsidized Stafford, PLUS).
WORK-STUDY *Federal work-study:* Total amount: $2,696,707; 936 jobs averaging $2881. *State or other work-study/employment:* Part-time jobs available.
ATHLETIC AWARDS Total amount: $4,746,537 (39% need-based, 61% non-need-based).
APPLYING FOR FINANCIAL AID *Required financial aid form:* FAFSA. *Financial aid deadline:* 4/15 (priority: 3/1). *Notification date:* Continuous beginning 3/10.

CONTACT Veronica Jene Gabbard, Senior Director of Financial Aid and Scholarships, Houston Baptist University, 7502 Fondren Road, Houston, TX 77074-3298, 281-649-3747 or toll-free 800-696-3210. *Fax:* 281-649-3298. *E-mail:* financialaid@hbu.edu.
Website: http://www.hbu.edu/.

HOWARD PAYNE UNIVERSITY
Brownwood, TX

Tuition & fees: $23,200	Average undergraduate aid package: $16,468

ABOUT THE INSTITUTION Independent Baptist General Convention of Texas, coed. *Awards:* certificates, associate, bachelor's, and master's degrees. 83 undergraduate majors. *Total enrollment:* 1,130. Undergraduates: 1,091. Freshmen: 299. Federal methodology is used as a basis for awarding need-based institutional aid.
UNDERGRADUATE EXPENSES for 2013–2014 *Comprehensive fee:* $30,000 includes full-time tuition ($21,800), mandatory fees ($1400), and room and board ($6800). Full-time tuition and fees vary according to course load, location, and program. Room and board charges vary according to board plan and housing facility. *Part-time tuition:* $700 per credit hour. Part-time tuition and fees vary according to location and program.
FRESHMAN FINANCIAL AID (Fall 2012, est.) 284 applied for aid; of those 92% were deemed to have need. 100% of freshmen with need received aid; of those 21% had need fully met. *Average percent of need met:* 78% (excluding resources awarded to replace EFC). *Average financial aid package:* $17,348 (excluding resources awarded to replace EFC). 12% of all full-time freshmen had no need and received non-need-based gift aid.
UNDERGRADUATE FINANCIAL AID (Fall 2012, est.) 847 applied for aid; of those 92% were deemed to have need. 100% of undergraduates with need received aid; of those 21% had need fully met. *Average percent of need met:* 74% (excluding resources awarded to replace EFC). *Average financial aid package:* $16,468 (excluding resources awarded to replace EFC). 15% of all full-time undergraduates had no need and received non-need-based gift aid.
GIFT AID (NEED-BASED) Total amount: $9,176,788 (21% federal, 12% state, 63% institutional, 4% external sources). *Receiving aid:* Freshmen: 76% (226); all full-time undergraduates: 74% (686). *Average award:* Freshmen: $15,529; Undergraduates: $13,104. *Scholarships, grants, and awards:* Federal Pell, FSEOG, state, private, college/university gift aid from institutional funds.
GIFT AID (NON-NEED-BASED) Total amount: $2,964,561 (94% institutional, 6% external sources). *Receiving aid:* Freshmen: 16% (48). Undergraduates: 13% (121). *Average award:* Freshmen: $11,253. Undergraduates: $9674. *Scholarships, grants, and awards by category:* Academic interests/achievement: biological sciences, business, communication, education, English, general academic interests/achievements, mathematics, physical sciences, premedicine, religion/biblical studies, social sciences. *Creative arts/performance:* art/fine arts, music, theater/drama. *Special achievements/activities:* community service, leadership, religious involvement. *Special characteristics:* children and siblings of alumni, children of faculty/staff, local/state students, relatives of clergy, religious affiliation. *Tuition waivers:* Full or partial for employees or children of employees.
LOANS Student loans: $6,123,423 (63% need-based, 37% non-need-based). 70% of past graduating class borrowed through all loan programs. *Average indebtedness per student:* $29,208. *Average need-based loan:* Freshmen: $3024. Undergraduates: $3877. *Parent loans:* $1,359,626 (32% need-based, 68% non-need-based). *Programs:* Federal Direct (Subsidized and Unsubsidized Stafford, PLUS), Perkins, state.
WORK-STUDY Federal work-study: Total amount: $125,736; 104 jobs averaging $1248. *State or other work-study/employment:* Total amount: $7685 (100% need-based). 8 part-time jobs averaging $960.
APPLYING FOR FINANCIAL AID *Required financial aid forms:* FAFSA, institution's own form. *Financial aid deadline (priority):* 3/15. *Notification date:* Continuous beginning 2/1. Students must reply within 2 weeks of notification.
CONTACT Glenda Huff, Director of Financial Aid, Howard Payne University, 1000 Fisk Avenue, Brownwood, TX 76801, 325-649-8014 or toll-free 800-880-4478. *Fax:* 325-649-8973. *E-mail:* ghuff@hputx.edu.
Website: http://www.hputx.edu/.

HOWARD UNIVERSITY
Washington, DC

Tuition & fees: $22,883	Average undergraduate aid package: $13,581

ABOUT THE INSTITUTION Independent, coed. 64 undergraduate majors. Federal methodology is used as a basis for awarding need-based institutional aid.
UNDERGRADUATE EXPENSES for 2013–2014 *Comprehensive fee:* $32,225 includes full-time tuition ($21,450), mandatory fees ($1433), and room and board ($9342). *College room only:* $5388. Full-time tuition and fees vary according to course load. Room and board charges vary according to board plan and housing facility. Part-time tuition and fees vary according to course load.
FRESHMAN FINANCIAL AID (Fall 2012, est.) 1,281 applied for aid; of those 89% were deemed to have need. 98% of freshmen with need received aid; of those 10% had need fully met. *Average percent of need met:* 74% (excluding resources awarded to replace EFC). *Average financial aid package:* $16,502 (excluding resources awarded to replace EFC).
UNDERGRADUATE FINANCIAL AID (Fall 2012, est.) 5,628 applied for aid; of those 90% were deemed to have need. 98% of undergraduates with need received aid; of those 8% had need fully met. *Average percent of need met:* 76% (excluding resources awarded to replace EFC). *Average financial aid package:* $13,581 (excluding resources awarded to replace EFC).
GIFT AID (NEED-BASED) Total amount: $26,634,402 (53% federal, 47% institutional). *Receiving aid:* Freshmen: 48% (643); all full-time undergraduates: 49% (2,984). *Average award:* Freshmen: $6240; Undergraduates: $4769. *Scholarships, grants, and awards:* Federal Pell, FSEOG, state, private, college/university gift aid from institutional funds, Federal Nursing.
GIFT AID (NON-NEED-BASED) Total amount: $37,108,222 (4% federal, 96% institutional). *Receiving aid:* Freshmen: 38% (501). Undergraduates: 37% (2,247). *Scholarships, grants, and awards by category:* Academic interests/achievement: architecture, biological sciences, business, communication, computer science, education, engineering/technologies, English, foreign languages, health fields, humanities, international studies, mathematics, military science, physical sciences, premedicine, religion/biblical studies, social sciences. *Creative arts/performance:* applied art and design, art/fine arts, cinema/film/broadcasting, dance, journalism/publications, music, performing arts, theater/drama. *Special achievements/activities:* cheerleading/drum major, general special achievements/activities, leadership, memberships, religious involvement. *Special characteristics:* adult students, ethnic background, first-generation college students, handicapped students, international students, local/state students, married students, members of minority groups, previous college experience, religious affiliation.
LOANS Student loans: $47,531,819 (40% need-based, 60% non-need-based). 91% of past graduating class borrowed through all loan programs. *Average indebtedness per student:* $10,136. *Average need-based loan:* Freshmen: $3675. Undergraduates: $4426. *Parent loans:* $35,820,707 (100% non-need-based). *Programs:* Federal Direct (Subsidized and Unsubsidized Stafford, PLUS), Perkins, Federal Nursing, district, college/university.
WORK-STUDY Federal work-study: Total amount: $724,872; 245 jobs averaging $2959. *State or other work-study/employment:* Total amount: $618,348 (100% non-need-based). 195 part-time jobs averaging $3171.
ATHLETIC AWARDS Total amount: $6,644,338 (100% non-need-based).
APPLYING FOR FINANCIAL AID *Required financial aid form:* FAFSA. *Financial aid deadline:* 8/15 (priority: 2/1). *Notification date:* Continuous beginning 4/1. Students must reply by 6/1 or within 1 week of notification.
CONTACT Miss Precious Smith, Assistant Director of Financial Aid and Scholarships, Howard University, 2400 Sixth Street, NW, Washington, DC 20059-0002, 202-806-2850 or toll-free 800-822-6363. *Fax:* 202-806-2818. *E-mail:* precious.smith@howard.edu.
Website: http://www.howard.edu/.

HULT INTERNATIONAL BUSINESS SCHOOL
Cambridge, MA

CONTACT Financial Aid Office, Hult International Business School, One Education Street, Cambridge, MA 02141, 617-746-1990.
Website: http://www.hult.edu/.

HUMBOLDT STATE UNIVERSITY
Arcata, CA

ABOUT THE INSTITUTION State-supported, coed. *Awards:* certificates, bachelor's, and master's degrees. 67 undergraduate majors. *Total enrollment:* 8,116. Undergraduates: 7,597. Freshmen: 1,237.

GIFT AID (NEED-BASED) *Scholarships, grants, and awards:* Federal Pell, FSEOG, state, private, college/university gift aid from institutional funds.

GIFT AID (NON-NEED-BASED) *Scholarships, grants, and awards by category: Academic interests/achievement:* general academic interests/achievements.

LOANS *Programs:* Federal Direct (Subsidized and Unsubsidized Stafford, PLUS), Perkins.

APPLYING FOR FINANCIAL AID *Required financial aid form:* FAFSA.

CONTACT Kim Coughlin-Lamphear, Director of Financial Aid, Humboldt State University, 1 Harpst Street, Arcata, CA 95521-8299, 707-826-4321 or toll-free 866-850-9556. *E-mail:* coughlin@humboldt.edu.
Website: http://www.humboldt.edu/.

HUMPHREYS COLLEGE
Stockton, CA

CONTACT Rita Franco, Director of Financial Aid, Humphreys College, 6650 Inglewood Avenue, Stockton, CA 95207-3896, 209-478-0800. *Fax:* 209-235-2983. *Website:* http://www.humphreys.edu/.

HUNTER COLLEGE OF THE CITY UNIVERSITY OF NEW YORK
New York, NY

Tuition & fees (NY res): $5829	Average undergraduate aid package: $6122

ABOUT THE INSTITUTION State and locally supported, coed. *Awards:* certificates, bachelor's, master's, and doctoral degrees. 63 undergraduate majors. *Total enrollment:* 23,007. Undergraduates: 16,708. Freshmen: 1,971. Federal methodology is used as a basis for awarding need-based institutional aid.

UNDERGRADUATE EXPENSES for 2013–2014 *Application fee:* $65. *Tuition, state resident:* full-time $5430; part-time $230 per credit. *Tuition, nonresident:* full-time $14,550; part-time $485 per credit. *Required fees:* full-time $399; $183.50. Full-time tuition and fees vary according to degree level and program. Part-time tuition and fees vary according to degree level and program. *Room only:* $5500.

FRESHMAN FINANCIAL AID (Fall 2011) 1,809 applied for aid; of those 81% were deemed to have need. 95% of freshmen with need received aid; of those 19% had need fully met. *Average percent of need met:* 78% (excluding resources awarded to replace EFC). *Average financial aid package:* $6914 (excluding resources awarded to replace EFC). 8% of all full-time freshmen had no need and received non-need-based gift aid.

UNDERGRADUATE FINANCIAL AID (Fall 2011) 8,845 applied for aid; of those 86% were deemed to have need. 96% of undergraduates with need received aid; of those 18% had need fully met. *Average percent of need met:* 76% (excluding resources awarded to replace EFC). *Average financial aid package:* $6122 (excluding resources awarded to replace EFC). 5% of all full-time undergraduates had no need and received non-need-based gift aid.

GIFT AID (NEED-BASED) *Total amount:* $37,732,040 (60% federal, 35% state, 5% institutional). *Receiving aid:* Freshmen: 65% (1,382); all full-time undergraduates: 66% (7,245). *Average award:* Freshmen: $5094; Undergraduates: $5080. *Scholarships, grants, and awards:* Federal Pell, FSEOG, state, private, college/university gift aid from institutional funds.

GIFT AID (NON-NEED-BASED) *Total amount:* $3,374,729 (73% institutional, 27% external sources). *Receiving aid:* Freshmen: 54% (1,140). Undergraduates: 54% (5,953). *Average award:* Freshmen: $2460. Undergraduates: $3421. *Scholarships, grants, and awards by category: Academic interests/achievement:* general academic interests/achievements.

LOANS *Student loans:* $10,572,521 (52% need-based, 48% non-need-based). 62% of past graduating class borrowed through all loan programs. *Average indebtedness per student:* $11,000. *Average need-based loan:* Freshmen: $4177. Undergraduates: $5331. *Parent loans:* $720,375 (100% need-based). *Programs:* Federal Direct (Subsidized and Unsubsidized Stafford, PLUS), Perkins.

WORK-STUDY *Federal work-study:* Total amount: $962,846; jobs available. *State or other work-study/employment:* Part-time jobs available.

APPLYING FOR FINANCIAL AID *Required financial aid forms:* FAFSA, state aid form. *Financial aid deadline (priority):* 4/1. *Notification date:* Continuous beginning 5/15.

CONTACT Aristalia Cortorreal Diaz, Director of Financial Aid, Hunter College of the City University of New York, 695 Park Avenue, New York, NY 10065-5085, 212-772-4400. *Fax:* 212-650-3666. *E-mail:* aristalia@hunter.cuny.edu. *Website:* http://www.hunter.cuny.edu/.

HUNTINGDON COLLEGE
Montgomery, AL

Tuition & fees: $22,500	Average undergraduate aid package: $16,177

ABOUT THE INSTITUTION Independent United Methodist, coed. *Awards:* bachelor's degrees. 32 undergraduate majors. *Total enrollment:* 1,118. Undergraduates: 1,118. Freshmen: 276. Both federal and institutional methodology are used as a basis for awarding need-based institutional aid.

UNDERGRADUATE EXPENSES for 2013–2014 *Comprehensive fee:* $30,750 includes full-time tuition ($21,500), mandatory fees ($1000), and room and board ($8250). Full-time tuition and fees vary according to course load, program, and student level. Room and board charges vary according to housing facility. *Part-time tuition:* $900 per credit hour. Part-time tuition and fees vary according to course load and program. *Payment plan:* Guaranteed tuition.

FRESHMAN FINANCIAL AID (Fall 2012, est.) 255 applied for aid; of those 91% were deemed to have need. 100% of freshmen with need received aid; of those 17% had need fully met. *Average percent of need met:* 66% (excluding resources awarded to replace EFC). *Average financial aid package:* $17,145 (excluding resources awarded to replace EFC). 15% of all full-time freshmen had no need and received non-need-based gift aid.

UNDERGRADUATE FINANCIAL AID (Fall 2012, est.) 783 applied for aid; of those 89% were deemed to have need. 100% of undergraduates with need received aid; of those 19% had need fully met. *Average percent of need met:* 68% (excluding resources awarded to replace EFC). *Average financial aid package:* $16,177 (excluding resources awarded to replace EFC). 21% of all full-time undergraduates had no need and received non-need-based gift aid.

GIFT AID (NEED-BASED) *Total amount:* $9,150,975 (24% federal, 2% state, 68% institutional, 6% external sources). *Receiving aid:* Freshmen: 85% (232); all full-time undergraduates: 75% (681). *Average award:* Freshmen: $14,195; Undergraduates: $13,015. *Scholarships, grants, and awards:* Federal Pell, FSEOG, state, private, college/university gift aid from institutional funds.

GIFT AID (NON-NEED-BASED) *Total amount:* $2,742,723 (1% federal, 1% state, 83% institutional, 15% external sources). *Receiving aid:* Freshmen: 11% (31). Undergraduates: 10% (94). *Average award:* Freshmen: $10,148. Undergraduates: $9808. *Scholarships, grants, and awards by category: Academic interests/achievement:* 265 awards ($2,489,599 total): biological sciences, computer science, general academic interests/achievements, mathematics. *Creative arts/performance:* 11 awards ($94,990 total): dance, music, performing arts. *Special achievements/activities:* 31 awards ($195,720 total): cheerleading/drum major, community service, junior miss. *Special characteristics:* 412 awards ($3,484,592 total): children and siblings of alumni, children of faculty/staff, children of workers in trades, international students, local/state students, religious affiliation, spouses of current students, veterans, veterans' children. *Tuition waivers:* Full or partial for children of alumni, employees or children of employees. *ROTC:* Army cooperative, Air Force cooperative.

LOANS *Student loans:* $6,874,624 (77% need-based, 23% non-need-based). 69% of past graduating class borrowed through all loan programs. *Average indebtedness per student:* $21,034. *Average need-based loan:* Freshmen: $3359. Undergraduates: $4047. *Parent loans:* $1,257,695 (31% need-based, 69% non-need-based). *Programs:* Federal Direct (Subsidized and Unsubsidized Stafford, PLUS), Perkins.

WORK-STUDY *Federal work-study:* Total amount: $165,397; 200 jobs averaging $1142. *State or other work-study/employment:* Part-time jobs available.

APPLYING FOR FINANCIAL AID *Required financial aid forms:* FAFSA, institution's own form, state aid form. *Financial aid deadline:* Continuous. *Notification date:* Continuous beginning 3/1. Students must reply by 5/1 or within 2 weeks of notification.

CONTACT Ms. Belinda Goris Duett, Director of Financial Aid, Huntingdon College, 1500 East Fairview Avenue, Montgomery, AL 36106-2148, 334-833-4519 or toll-free 800-763-0313. *Fax:* 334-833-4235. *E-mail:* bduett@huntingdon.edu. *Website:* http://www.huntingdon.edu/.

HUNTINGTON UNIVERSITY
Huntington, IN

Tuition & fees: $24,040	Average undergraduate aid package: $16,801

ABOUT THE INSTITUTION Independent Church of the United Brethren in Christ, coed. *Awards:* associate, bachelor's, and master's degrees. 76 undergraduate majors. *Total enrollment:* 1,189. Undergraduates: 1,134. Freshmen: 239. Both federal and institutional methodology are used as a basis for awarding need-based institutional aid.

UNDERGRADUATE EXPENSES for 2013–2014 *Application fee:* $20. *Comprehensive fee:* $32,220 includes full-time tuition ($23,300), mandatory fees ($740), and room and board ($8180). Full-time tuition and fees vary according to course load, degree level, and program. Room and board charges vary according to board plan. *Part-time tuition:* $700 per credit. Part-time tuition and fees vary according to course load, degree level, and program.

FRESHMAN FINANCIAL AID (Fall 2012, est.) 217 applied for aid; of those 93% were deemed to have need. 100% of freshmen with need received aid; of those 8% had need fully met. *Average percent of need met:* 75% (excluding resources awarded to replace EFC). *Average financial aid package:* $19,818 (excluding resources awarded to replace EFC). 8% of all full-time freshmen had no need and received non-need-based gift aid.

UNDERGRADUATE FINANCIAL AID (Fall 2012, est.) 907 applied for aid; of those 92% were deemed to have need. 99% of undergraduates with need received aid; of those 9% had need fully met. *Average percent of need met:* 68% (excluding resources awarded to replace EFC). *Average financial aid package:* $16,801 (excluding resources awarded to replace EFC). 14% of all full-time undergraduates had no need and received non-need-based gift aid.

GIFT AID (NEED-BASED) *Total amount:* $9,780,521 (17% federal, 12% state, 68% institutional, 3% external sources). *Receiving aid:* Freshmen: 82% (194); all full-time undergraduates: 75% (767). *Average award:* Freshmen: $17,131; Undergraduates: $13,973. *Scholarships, grants, and awards:* Federal Pell, FSEOG, state, private, college/university gift aid from institutional funds.

GIFT AID (NON-NEED-BASED) *Total amount:* $677,793 (94% institutional, 6% external sources). *Receiving aid:* Freshmen: 11% (27). Undergraduates: 11% (110). *Average award:* Freshmen: $9210. Undergraduates: $10,201. *Scholarships, grants, and awards by category:* Academic interests/achievement: biological sciences, business, communication, computer science, education, English, general academic interests/achievements, health fields, mathematics. *Creative arts/performance:* applied art and design, art/fine arts, cinema/film/broadcasting, creative writing, journalism/publications, music, theater/drama. *Special achievements/activities:* cheerleading/drum major, religious involvement. *Special characteristics:* children and siblings of alumni, children of current students, children of faculty/staff, ethnic background, international students, local/state students, parents of current students, previous college experience, relatives of clergy, religious affiliation, siblings of current students, spouses of current students, veterans, veterans' children. *Tuition waivers:* Full or partial for minority students, children of alumni, employees or children of employees.

LOANS *Student loans:* $7,437,384 (80% need-based, 20% non-need-based). 66% of past graduating class borrowed through all loan programs. *Average indebtedness per student:* $31,149. *Average need-based loan:* Freshmen: $3727. Undergraduates: $4728. *Parent loans:* $1,341,258 (48% need-based, 52% non-need-based). *Programs:* Federal Direct (Subsidized and Unsubsidized Stafford, PLUS), Perkins.

WORK-STUDY *Federal work-study:* Total amount: $200,000; 86 jobs averaging $1875.

ATHLETIC AWARDS Total amount: $1,243,780 (60% need-based, 40% non-need-based).

APPLYING FOR FINANCIAL AID *Required financial aid form:* FAFSA. *Financial aid deadline (priority):* 3/1. *Notification date:* Continuous beginning 2/1. Students must reply by 5/1 or within 2 weeks of notification.

CONTACT Mrs. Sharon Woods, Director of Financial Aid, Huntington University, 2303 College Avenue, Huntington, IN 46750, 260-359-4014 or toll-free 800-642-6493. *Fax:* 260-358-3699. *E-mail:* finaid@huntington.edu. *Website:* http://www.huntington.edu/.

HUSSON UNIVERSITY
Bangor, ME

Tuition & fees: $15,130	Average undergraduate aid package: $12,322

ABOUT THE INSTITUTION Independent, coed. *Awards:* certificates, associate, bachelor's, master's, and doctoral degrees. 34 undergraduate majors. *Total enrollment:* 3,077. Undergraduates: 2,409. Freshmen: 368. Federal methodology is used as a basis for awarding need-based institutional aid.

UNDERGRADUATE EXPENSES for 2013–2014 *Application fee:* $40. *Comprehensive fee:* $23,386 includes full-time tuition ($14,760), mandatory fees ($370), and room and board ($8256). *College room only:* $4102. Full-time tuition and fees vary according to class time. Room and board charges vary according to board plan and housing facility. *Part-time tuition:* $492 per credit. *Part-time fees:* $370 per year. Part-time tuition and fees vary according to class time and course load. *Payment plan:* Tuition prepayment.

FRESHMAN FINANCIAL AID (Fall 2012, est.) 372 applied for aid; of those 89% were deemed to have need. 98% of freshmen with need received aid; of those 5% had need fully met. *Average percent of need met:* 59% (excluding resources awarded to replace EFC). *Average financial aid package:* $13,118 (excluding resources awarded to replace EFC). 10% of all full-time freshmen had no need and received non-need-based gift aid.

UNDERGRADUATE FINANCIAL AID (Fall 2012, est.) 1,827 applied for aid; of those 90% were deemed to have need. 99% of undergraduates with need received aid; of those 6% had need fully met. *Average percent of need met:* 59% (excluding resources awarded to replace EFC). *Average financial aid package:* $12,322 (excluding resources awarded to replace EFC). 7% of all full-time undergraduates had no need and received non-need-based gift aid.

GIFT AID (NEED-BASED) *Total amount:* $12,828,241 (45% federal, 8% state, 41% institutional, 6% external sources). *Receiving aid:* Freshmen: 81% (320); all full-time undergraduates: 82% (1,525). *Average award:* Freshmen: $9417; Undergraduates: $8130. *Scholarships, grants, and awards:* Federal Pell, FSEOG, state, private, college/university gift aid from institutional funds.

GIFT AID (NON-NEED-BASED) *Total amount:* $605,371 (76% institutional, 24% external sources). *Receiving aid:* Freshmen: 2% (7). Undergraduates: 2% (35). *Average award:* Freshmen: $2786. Undergraduates: $2691. *Scholarships, grants, and awards by category:* Academic interests/achievement: business, computer science, education, general academic interests/achievements, health fields. *Special achievements/activities:* general special achievements/activities, leadership. *Special characteristics:* children of union members/company employees. *Tuition waivers:* Full or partial for employees or children of employees, senior citizens. *ROTC:* Army, Naval cooperative.

LOANS *Student loans:* $16,267,042 (80% need-based, 20% non-need-based). 85% of past graduating class borrowed through all loan programs. *Average indebtedness per student:* $33,385. *Average need-based loan:* Freshmen: $3135. Undergraduates: $4085. *Parent loans:* $1,674,233 (40% need-based, 60% non-need-based). *Programs:* Federal Direct (Subsidized and Unsubsidized Stafford, PLUS), Perkins, state, alternative loans.

WORK-STUDY *Federal work-study:* Total amount: $1,397,597; 1,000 jobs averaging $1300.

APPLYING FOR FINANCIAL AID *Required financial aid form:* FAFSA. *Financial aid deadline (priority):* 4/15. *Notification date:* Continuous. Students must reply by 5/1 or within 2 weeks of notification.

CONTACT Linda B. Hill, Director of Financial Aid, Husson University, One College Circle, Bangor, ME 04401, 207-941-7156 or toll-free 800-4-HUSSON. *Fax:* 207-973-1038. *E-mail:* conantl@husson.edu. *Website:* http://www.husson.edu/.

HUSTON-TILLOTSON UNIVERSITY
Austin, TX

CONTACT Antonio Holloway, Director of Financial Aid, Huston-Tillotson University, 900 Chicon Street, Austin, TX 78702, 512-505-3031. *Fax:* 512-505-3192. *E-mail:* aholloway@htu.edu. *Website:* http://www.htu.edu/.

IDAHO STATE UNIVERSITY
Pocatello, ID

Tuition & fees (ID res): $6070	Average undergraduate aid package: $9238

ABOUT THE INSTITUTION State-supported, coed. **Awards:** certificates, associate, bachelor's, master's, and doctoral degrees. 94 undergraduate majors. **Total enrollment:** 14,209. Undergraduates: 12,143. Freshmen: 1,705. Federal methodology is used as a basis for awarding need-based institutional aid.

UNDERGRADUATE EXPENSES for 2013–2014 Application fee: $40. **One-time required fee:** $40. **Tuition, state resident:** full-time $4418; part-time $304 per credit hour. **Tuition, nonresident:** full-time $16,218; part-time $494 per credit hour. **Required fees:** full-time $1652. Full-time tuition and fees vary according to course load, program, and reciprocity agreements. Part-time tuition and fees vary according to course load and reciprocity agreements. **College room and board:** $5838; **Room only:** $2520. Room and board charges vary according to board plan and housing facility.

FRESHMAN FINANCIAL AID (Fall 2011) 1,316 applied for aid; of those 84% were deemed to have need. 100% of freshmen with need received aid; of those 7% had need fully met. **Average percent of need met:** 50% (excluding resources awarded to replace EFC). **Average financial aid package:** $8971 (excluding resources awarded to replace EFC). 7% of all full-time freshmen had no need and received non-need-based gift aid.

UNDERGRADUATE FINANCIAL AID (Fall 2011) 6,523 applied for aid; of those 91% were deemed to have need. 99% of undergraduates with need received aid; of those 3% had need fully met. **Average percent of need met:** 48% (excluding resources awarded to replace EFC). **Average financial aid package:** $9238 (excluding resources awarded to replace EFC). 4% of all full-time undergraduates had no need and received non-need-based gift aid.

GIFT AID (NEED-BASED) Total amount: $27,932,767 (88% federal, 2% state, 7% institutional, 3% external sources). **Receiving aid:** Freshmen: 59% (910); all full-time undergraduates: 64% (4,885). **Average award:** Freshmen: $4559; Undergraduates: $4488. **Scholarships, grants, and awards:** Federal Pell, FSEOG, state, private, college/university gift aid from institutional funds, Federal Nursing.

GIFT AID (NON-NEED-BASED) Total amount: $1,806,553 (1% federal, 13% state, 68% institutional, 18% external sources). **Receiving aid:** Freshmen: 37% (571). Undergraduates: 18% (1,411). **Average award:** Freshmen: $2586. Undergraduates: $2363. **Scholarships, grants, and awards by category:** Academic interests/achievement: biological sciences, business, communication, computer science, education, engineering/technologies, English, foreign languages, general academic interests/achievements, health fields, home economics, humanities, international studies, mathematics, military science, physical sciences, premedicine, religion/biblical studies, social sciences. Creative arts/performance: art/fine arts, dance, debating, music, performing arts, theater/drama. Special achievements/activities: cheerleading/drum major, general special achievements/activities, junior miss, leadership, memberships, rodeo. Special characteristics: children and siblings of alumni, children of faculty/staff, ethnic background, first-generation college students, general special characteristics, handicapped students, international students, local/state students, members of minority groups, out-of-state students, previous college experience. Tuition waivers: Full or partial for employees or children of employees, senior citizens. ROTC: Army.

LOANS Student loans: $49,267,849 (98% need-based, 2% non-need-based). 64% of past graduating class borrowed through all loan programs. Average indebtedness per student: $24,602. **Average need-based loan:** Freshmen: $3100. Undergraduates: $3879. **Parent loans:** $847,159 (79% need-based, 21% non-need-based). **Programs:** Federal Direct (Subsidized and Unsubsidized Stafford, PLUS), Perkins, Federal Nursing.

WORK-STUDY Federal work-study: Total amount: $591,167; jobs available. **State or other work-study/employment:** Total amount: $400,088 (100% need-based). Part-time jobs available.

ATHLETIC AWARDS Total amount: $1,931,638 (35% need-based, 65% non-need-based).

APPLYING FOR FINANCIAL AID Required financial aid form: FAFSA. **Financial aid deadline (priority):** 3/1. **Notification date:** Continuous beginning 4/1.

CONTACT Mr. Kent Larson, Director of Financial Aid, Idaho State University, 921 South 8th Avenue, Stop 8077, Pocatello, ID 83209, 208-282-2981. *Fax:* 208-282-4755. *E-mail:* larskent@isu.edu. *Website:* http://www.isu.edu/.

ILLINOIS COLLEGE
Jacksonville, IL

Tuition & fees: $26,500	Average undergraduate aid package: $23,156

ABOUT THE INSTITUTION Independent interdenominational, coed. **Awards:** bachelor's and master's degrees. 44 undergraduate majors. **Total enrollment:** 987. Undergraduates: 970. Freshmen: 285. Federal methodology is used as a basis for awarding need-based institutional aid.

UNDERGRADUATE EXPENSES for 2013–2014 Comprehensive fee: $35,000 includes full-time tuition ($26,000), mandatory fees ($500), and room and board ($8500). **College room only:** $4600. Room and board charges vary according to board plan and housing facility. **Part-time tuition:** $800 per semester hour. **Part-time fees:** $125 per term.

FRESHMAN FINANCIAL AID (Fall 2012, est.) 252 applied for aid; of those 92% were deemed to have need. 100% of freshmen with need received aid; of those 24% had need fully met. **Average percent of need met:** 87% (excluding resources awarded to replace EFC). **Average financial aid package:** $23,656 (excluding resources awarded to replace EFC). 14% of all full-time freshmen had no need and received non-need-based gift aid.

UNDERGRADUATE FINANCIAL AID (Fall 2012, est.) 863 applied for aid; of those 91% were deemed to have need. 100% of undergraduates with need received aid; of those 22% had need fully met. **Average percent of need met:** 87% (excluding resources awarded to replace EFC). **Average financial aid package:** $23,156 (excluding resources awarded to replace EFC). 18% of all full-time undergraduates had no need and received non-need-based gift aid.

GIFT AID (NEED-BASED) Total amount: $14,012,017 (10% federal, 11% state, 77% institutional, 2% external sources). **Receiving aid:** Freshmen: 86% (231); all full-time undergraduates: 82% (783). **Average award:** Freshmen: $18,932; Undergraduates: $17,895. **Scholarships, grants, and awards:** Federal Pell, FSEOG, state, private, college/university gift aid from institutional funds.

GIFT AID (NON-NEED-BASED) Total amount: $3,134,427 (96% institutional, 4% external sources). **Receiving aid:** Freshmen: 13% (34). Undergraduates: 11% (102). **Average award:** Freshmen: $16,231. Undergraduates: $13,684. **Scholarships, grants, and awards by category:** Academic interests/achievement: general academic interests/achievements. Creative arts/performance: art/fine arts, music, theater/drama. Special characteristics: children of faculty/staff, international students, previous college experience. Tuition waivers: Full or partial for employees or children of employees.

LOANS Student loans: $7,006,006 (69% need-based, 31% non-need-based). 79% of past graduating class borrowed through all loan programs. Average indebtedness per student: $29,762. **Average need-based loan:** Freshmen: $4271. Undergraduates: $4904. **Parent loans:** $1,245,778 (25% need-based, 75% non-need-based). **Programs:** Federal Direct (Subsidized and Unsubsidized Stafford, PLUS), Perkins.

WORK-STUDY Federal work-study: Total amount: $814,296; 556 jobs averaging $1911. **State or other work-study/employment:** Part-time jobs available.

APPLYING FOR FINANCIAL AID Required financial aid form: FAFSA. **Financial aid deadline (priority):** 3/1. **Notification date:** Continuous beginning 3/1. Students must reply within 2 weeks of notification.

CONTACT Kate Taylor, Director of Financial Aid, Illinois College, 1101 West College Avenue, Jacksonville, IL 62650-2299, 217-245-3037 or toll-free 866-464-5265. *Fax:* 217-245-3274. *E-mail:* kataylor@ic.edu. *Website:* http://www.ic.edu/.

THE ILLINOIS INSTITUTE OF ART–CHICAGO
Chicago, IL

CONTACT Financial Aid Office, The Illinois Institute of Art–Chicago, 350 North Orleans Street, Suite 136, Chicago, IL 60654-1593, 800-351-3450.

THE ILLINOIS INSTITUTE OF ART–SCHAUMBURG
Schaumburg, IL

CONTACT Financial Aid Office, The Illinois Institute of Art–Schaumburg, 1000 North Plaza Drive, Suite 100, Schaumburg, IL 60173, 847-619-3450 or toll-free 800-314-3450.
Website: http://www.artinstitutes.edu/schaumburg/.

THE ILLINOIS INSTITUTE OF ART–TINLEY PARK
Tinley Park, IL

CONTACT Financial Aid Office, The Illinois Institute of Art–Tinley Park, 18670 Graphic Drive, Tinley Park, IL 60477, 708-781-4201 or toll-free 877-342-3298.
Website: http://www.artinstitutes.edu/tinleypark.

ILLINOIS INSTITUTE OF TECHNOLOGY
Chicago, IL

Tuition & fees: $38,512 | **Average undergraduate aid package: $32,667**

ABOUT THE INSTITUTION Independent, coed. *Awards:* bachelor's, master's, and doctoral degrees. 32 undergraduate majors. *Total enrollment:* 7,684. Undergraduates: 2,801. Freshmen: 408. Federal methodology is used as a basis for awarding need-based institutional aid.
UNDERGRADUATE EXPENSES for 2013–2014 Tuition: full-time $38,512; part-time $1204 per credit. Full-time tuition and fees vary according to student level. Part-time tuition and fees vary according to course load and student level. Room and board charges vary according to board plan and housing facility.
FRESHMAN FINANCIAL AID (Fall 2012, est.) 306 applied for aid; of those 92% were deemed to have need. 100% of freshmen with need received aid; of those 15% had need fully met. *Average percent of need met:* 83% (excluding resources awarded to replace EFC). *Average financial aid package:* $34,526 (excluding resources awarded to replace EFC). 30% of all full-time freshmen had no need and received non-need-based gift aid.
UNDERGRADUATE FINANCIAL AID (Fall 2012, est.) 1,656 applied for aid; of those 95% were deemed to have need. 100% of undergraduates with need received aid; of those 14% had need fully met. *Average percent of need met:* 78% (excluding resources awarded to replace EFC). *Average financial aid package:* $32,667 (excluding resources awarded to replace EFC). 36% of all full-time undergraduates had no need and received non-need-based gift aid.
GIFT AID (NEED-BASED) Total amount: $41,907,030 (11% federal, 7% state, 81% institutional, 1% external sources). *Receiving aid:* Freshmen: 69% (279); all full-time undergraduates: 60% (1,553). *Average award:* Freshmen: $28,407; Undergraduates: $26,620. *Scholarships, grants, and awards:* Federal Pell, FSEOG, state, private, college/university gift aid from institutional funds.
GIFT AID (NON-NEED-BASED) Total amount: $21,543,551 (4% federal, 95% institutional, 1% external sources). *Receiving aid:* Freshmen: 10% (41). Undergraduates: 7% (173). *Average award:* Freshmen: $23,077. Undergraduates: $19,440. *Scholarships, grants, and awards by category: Academic interests/achievement:* architecture, business, engineering/technologies, foreign languages, general academic interests/achievements, health fields. *Special achievements/activities:*

community service, general special achievements/activities, hobbies/interests, leadership, memberships. *Special characteristics:* children and siblings of alumni, children of faculty/staff, children of public servants, ethnic background, general special characteristics, international students, local/state students, members of minority groups, previous college experience, veterans, veterans' children. *Tuition waivers:* Full or partial for employees or children of employees. *ROTC:* Army, Naval, Air Force.
LOANS Student loans: $11,857,546 (84% need-based, 16% non-need-based). 65% of past graduating class borrowed through all loan programs. *Average indebtedness per student:* $31,073. *Average need-based loan:* Freshmen: $3878. Undergraduates: $4959. *Parent loans:* $3,382,980 (51% need-based, 49% non-need-based). *Programs:* Perkins.
WORK-STUDY Federal work-study: Total amount: $1,956,415; jobs available. *State or other work-study/employment:* Part-time jobs available.
ATHLETIC AWARDS Total amount: $753,252 (29% need-based, 71% non-need-based).
APPLYING FOR FINANCIAL AID Required financial aid form: FAFSA. *Financial aid deadline (priority):* 4/15. *Notification date:* Continuous beginning 3/1.
CONTACT Abby McGrath, Director of Financial Aid, Illinois Institute of Technology, 3300 South Federal Street, Chicago, IL 60616, 312-567-5730 or toll-free 866-472-3448. *Fax:* 312-567-3982. *E-mail:* finaid@iit.edu.
Website: http://www.iit.edu/.

ILLINOIS STATE UNIVERSITY
Normal, IL

Tuition & fees (IL res): $12,726 | **Average undergraduate aid package: $7364**

ABOUT THE INSTITUTION State-supported, coed. *Awards:* certificates, bachelor's, master's, and doctoral degrees. 65 undergraduate majors. *Total enrollment:* 20,706. Undergraduates: 18,257. Freshmen: 3,088. Federal methodology is used as a basis for awarding need-based institutional aid.
UNDERGRADUATE EXPENSES for 2013–2014 Application fee: $40. *Tuition, state resident:* full-time $12,726. *Tuition, nonresident:* full-time $20,887. Full-time tuition and fees vary according to course load and degree level. Part-time tuition and fees vary according to course load and degree level. *College room and board:* $9364. Room and board charges vary according to board plan, housing facility, and location. *Payment plan:* Guaranteed tuition.
FRESHMAN FINANCIAL AID (Fall 2011) 2,680 applied for aid; of those 78% were deemed to have need. 100% of freshmen with need received aid; of those 4% had need fully met. *Average percent of need met:* 75% (excluding resources awarded to replace EFC). *Average financial aid package:* $7073 (excluding resources awarded to replace EFC). 1% of all full-time freshmen had no need and received non-need-based gift aid.
UNDERGRADUATE FINANCIAL AID (Fall 2011) 13,511 applied for aid; of those 78% were deemed to have need. 100% of undergraduates with need received aid; of those 6% had need fully met. *Average percent of need met:* 75% (excluding resources awarded to replace EFC). *Average financial aid package:* $7364 (excluding resources awarded to replace EFC). 2% of all full-time undergraduates had no need and received non-need-based gift aid.
GIFT AID (NEED-BASED) Total amount: $51,246,241 (38% federal, 39% state, 20% institutional, 3% external sources). *Receiving aid:* Freshmen: 37% (1,134); all full-time undergraduates: 34% (5,788). *Average award:* Freshmen: $9268; Undergraduates: $8605. *Scholarships, grants, and awards:* Federal Pell, FSEOG, state, private, college/university gift aid from institutional funds, Federal Nursing.
GIFT AID (NON-NEED-BASED) Total amount: $6,107,723 (8% federal, 56% state, 25% institutional, 11% external sources). *Receiving aid:* Freshmen: 7% (217). Undergraduates: 7% (1,241). *Average award:* Freshmen: $1779. Undergraduates: $2221. *Scholarships, grants, and awards by category: Academic interests/achievement:* 718 awards ($1,675,047 total): agriculture, biological sciences, business, communication, computer science, education, engineering/technologies, English, foreign languages, general academic interests/achievements, health fields, home economics, humanities, international studies, library science, mathematics, military science, physical sciences, premedicine, social sciences. *Creative arts/performance:* 167 awards ($413,775 total): applied art and design, art/fine arts, cinema/film/broadcasting, creative writing, debating, general creative arts/performance, music, performing arts, theater/drama. *Special achievements/activities:* 1 award ($1500 total): community service, leadership. *Special characteristics:* 347 awards ($1,340,849 total):

children of faculty/staff, children of union members/company employees, children with a deceased or disabled parent, first-generation college students, general special characteristics, members of minority groups, previous college experience. *Tuition waivers:* Full or partial for minority students, employees or children of employees, senior citizens. *ROTC:* Army.
LOANS *Student loans:* $89,736,084 (67% need-based, 33% non-need-based). 67% of past graduating class borrowed through all loan programs. *Average indebtedness per student:* $27,910. *Average need-based loan:* Freshmen: $3329. Undergraduates: $3854. *Parent loans:* $33,694,928 (39% need-based, 61% non-need-based). *Programs:* Federal Direct (Subsidized and Unsubsidized Stafford, PLUS), Perkins, Federal Nursing.
WORK-STUDY *Federal work-study:* Total amount: $556,164; 372 jobs averaging $1980. *State or other work-study/employment:* Total amount: $62,765 (46% need-based, 54% non-need-based). 56 part-time jobs averaging $1529.
ATHLETIC AWARDS Total amount: $2,563,161 (34% need-based, 66% non-need-based).
APPLYING FOR FINANCIAL AID *Required financial aid form:* FAFSA. *Financial aid deadline (priority):* 3/1. *Notification date:* Continuous beginning 4/1.
CONTACT Mr. David Krueger, Assistant Director of Financial Aid, Illinois State University, Campus Box 2320, Normal, IL 61790-2320, 309-438-2231 or toll-free 800-366-2478. *Fax:* 309-438-3755. *E-mail:* financialaid@illinoisstate.edu.
Website: http://www.illinoisstate.edu/.

ILLINOIS WESLEYAN UNIVERSITY
Bloomington, IL

Tuition & fees: $37,954	Average undergraduate aid package: $26,643

ABOUT THE INSTITUTION Independent, coed. *Awards:* bachelor's degrees. 48 undergraduate majors. *Total enrollment:* 2,013. Undergraduates: 2,013. Freshmen: 490. Both federal and institutional methodology are used as a basis for awarding need-based institutional aid.
UNDERGRADUATE EXPENSES for 2013–2014 *Comprehensive fee:* $46,792 includes full-time tuition ($37,774), mandatory fees ($180), and room and board ($8838). *College room only:* $5584. *Part-time tuition:* $1180 per credit hour.
FRESHMAN FINANCIAL AID (Fall 2012, est.) 442 applied for aid; of those 79% were deemed to have need. 100% of freshmen with need received aid; of those 34% had need fully met. *Average percent of need met:* 86% (excluding resources awarded to replace EFC). *Average financial aid package:* $27,634 (excluding resources awarded to replace EFC). 27% of all full-time freshmen had no need and received non-need-based gift aid.
UNDERGRADUATE FINANCIAL AID (Fall 2012, est.) 1,580 applied for aid; of those 82% were deemed to have need. 100% of undergraduates with need received aid; of those 39% had need fully met. *Average percent of need met:* 87% (excluding resources awarded to replace EFC). *Average financial aid package:* $26,643 (excluding resources awarded to replace EFC). 30% of all full-time undergraduates had no need and received non-need-based gift aid.
GIFT AID (NEED-BASED) *Total amount:* $26,291,014 (7% federal, 7% state, 84% institutional, 2% external sources). *Receiving aid:* Freshmen: 70% (342); all full-time undergraduates: 64% (1,284). *Average award:* Freshmen: $22,782; Undergraduates: $20,554. *Scholarships, grants, and awards:* Federal Pell, FSEOG, state, private, college/university gift aid from institutional funds.
GIFT AID (NON-NEED-BASED) *Total amount:* $8,978,302 (100% institutional). *Receiving aid:* Freshmen: 10% (47). Undergraduates: 7% (134). *Average award:* Freshmen: $15,192. Undergraduates: $13,661. *Scholarships, grants, and awards by category: Academic interests/achievement:* general academic interests/achievements. *Creative arts/performance:* general creative arts/performance, music, theater/drama. *Special characteristics:* children of faculty/staff, general special characteristics, international students. *ROTC:* Army cooperative.
LOANS *Student loans:* $11,285,811 (49% need-based, 51% non-need-based). 70% of past graduating class borrowed through all loan programs. *Average indebtedness per student:* $32,964. *Average need-based loan:* Freshmen: $4292. Undergraduates: $5346. *Parent loans:* $4,013,565 (100% non-need-based). *Programs:* Federal Direct (Subsidized and Unsubsidized Stafford, PLUS), Perkins, Federal Nursing, college/university.

WORK-STUDY *Federal work-study:* Total amount: $347,592; jobs available. *State or other work-study/employment:* Total amount: $1,748,014 (86% need-based, 14% non-need-based). Part-time jobs available.
APPLYING FOR FINANCIAL AID *Required financial aid forms:* FAFSA, institution's own form. *Financial aid deadline (priority):* 3/1. *Notification date:* Continuous beginning 3/1. Students must reply by 5/1.
CONTACT Mr. Scott Seibring, Director of Financial Aid, Illinois Wesleyan University, 1312 North Park Street, PO Box 2900, Bloomington, IL 61702-2900, 309-556-3393 or toll-free 800-332-2498. *Fax:* 309-556-3833. *E-mail:* seibring@iwu.edu.
Website: http://www.iwu.edu/.

IMMACULATA UNIVERSITY
Immaculata, PA

CONTACT Mr. Peter Lysionek, Director of Student Financial Aid, Immaculata University, 1145 King Road, Box 500, Immaculata, PA 19345, 610-647-4400 Ext. 3026 or toll-free 877-428-6329. *Fax:* 610-640-0836. *E-mail:* plysionek@immaculata.edu.
Website: http://www.immaculata.edu/.

INDEPENDENCE UNIVERSITY
Salt Lake City, UT

CONTACT Financial Aid Director, Independence University, 2423 Hoover Avenue, National City, CA 91950-6605, 619-477-4800 or toll-free 800-972-5149. *Fax:* 619-477-5202.
Website: http://www.independence.edu/.

INDIANA STATE UNIVERSITY
Terre Haute, IN

Tuition & fees (IN res): $8098	Average undergraduate aid package: $9735

ABOUT THE INSTITUTION State-supported, coed. *Awards:* certificates, associate, bachelor's, master's, and doctoral degrees. 69 undergraduate majors. *Total enrollment:* 12,114. Undergraduates: 10,076. Freshmen: 2,664. Federal methodology is used as a basis for awarding need-based institutional aid.
UNDERGRADUATE EXPENSES for 2013–2014 *Application fee:* $25. *Tuition, state resident:* full-time $7898; part-time $286 per credit hour. *Tuition, nonresident:* full-time $17,444; part-time $617 per credit hour. *Required fees:* full-time $200; $100 per term. Part-time tuition and fees vary according to course load. *College room and board:* $8262. Room and board charges vary according to board plan, housing facility, and student level.
FRESHMAN FINANCIAL AID (Fall 2011) 2,364 applied for aid; of those 85% were deemed to have need. 98% of freshmen with need received aid; of those 12% had need fully met. *Average percent of need met:* 82% (excluding resources awarded to replace EFC). *Average financial aid package:* $9982 (excluding resources awarded to replace EFC). 10% of all full-time freshmen had no need and received non-need-based gift aid.
UNDERGRADUATE FINANCIAL AID (Fall 2011) 7,198 applied for aid; of those 84% were deemed to have need. 96% of undergraduates with need received aid; of those 11% had need fully met. *Average percent of need met:* 81% (excluding resources awarded to replace EFC). *Average financial aid package:* $9735 (excluding resources awarded to replace EFC). 10% of all full-time undergraduates had no need and received non-need-based gift aid.
GIFT AID (NEED-BASED) *Total amount:* $24,232,778 (69% federal, 26% state, 4% institutional, 1% external sources). *Receiving aid:* Freshmen: 52% (1,303); all full-time undergraduates: 46% (3,793). *Average award:* Freshmen: $6237; Undergraduates: $6095. *Scholarships, grants, and awards:* Federal Pell, FSEOG, state, private, college/university gift aid from institutional funds.
GIFT AID (NON-NEED-BASED) *Total amount:* $17,923,204 (38% state, 50% institutional, 12% external sources). *Receiving aid:* Freshmen: 57% (1,430). Undergraduates: 38% (3,130). *Average award:* Freshmen: $3093. Undergraduates: $3694.

Scholarships, grants, and awards by category: Academic interests/achievement: 2,658 awards ($4,304,775 total): general academic interests/achievements, premedicine. *Creative arts/performance:* 90 awards ($226,000 total): art/fine arts, performing arts. *Special characteristics:* 425 awards ($986,890 total): children and siblings of alumni, children of faculty/staff, members of minority groups, previous college experience, veterans. *Tuition waivers:* Full or partial for employees or children of employees, senior citizens. *ROTC:* Army, Air Force.

LOANS *Student loans:* $42,257,508 (45% need-based, 55% non-need-based). 71% of past graduating class borrowed through all loan programs. *Average indebtedness per student:* $24,484. *Average need-based loan:* Freshmen: $3242. Undergraduates: $3842. *Parent loans:* $10,752,396 (100% non-need-based). *Programs:* Federal Direct (Subsidized and Unsubsidized Stafford, PLUS), Perkins, alternative loans.

WORK-STUDY *Federal work-study:* Total amount: $500,287; 1,092 jobs averaging $2207. *State or other work-study/employment:* Part-time jobs available.

ATHLETIC AWARDS Total amount: $3,715,738 (100% non-need-based).

APPLYING FOR FINANCIAL AID *Required financial aid form:* FAFSA. *Financial aid deadline (priority):* 3/1. *Notification date:* Continuous beginning 4/1.

CONTACT Crystal Baker, Director of Student Financial Aid, Indiana State University, 150 Tirey Hall, Terre Haute, IN 47809-1401, 812-237-2215 or toll-free 800-468-6478. *Fax:* 812-237-4330. *E-mail:* isu-finaid@indstate.edu. *Website:* http://www.indstate.edu/.

INDIANA TECH
Fort Wayne, IN

Tuition & fees: $24,860	Average undergraduate aid package: $17,433

ABOUT THE INSTITUTION Independent, coed. *Awards:* associate, bachelor's, master's, and doctoral degrees. 35 undergraduate majors. *Total enrollment:* 4,912. Undergraduates: 4,470. Freshmen: 593. Federal methodology is used as a basis for awarding need-based institutional aid.

UNDERGRADUATE EXPENSES for 2013–2014 *Application fee:* $50. *Comprehensive fee:* $34,240 includes full-time tuition ($24,450), mandatory fees ($410), and room and board ($9380). Full-time tuition and fees vary according to class time, course load, and program. Room and board charges vary according to housing facility. *Part-time tuition:* $480 per credit hour. Part-time tuition and fees vary according to class time, course load, and program.

FRESHMAN FINANCIAL AID (Fall 2011) 342 applied for aid; of those 92% were deemed to have need. 96% of freshmen with need received aid; of those 30% had need fully met. *Average financial aid package:* $17,420 (excluding resources awarded to replace EFC). 1% of all full-time freshmen had no need and received non-need-based gift aid.

UNDERGRADUATE FINANCIAL AID (Fall 2011) 2,433 applied for aid; of those 96% were deemed to have need. 97% of undergraduates with need received aid; of those 37% had need fully met. *Average financial aid package:* $17,433 (excluding resources awarded to replace EFC). 1% of all full-time undergraduates had no need and received non-need-based gift aid.

GIFT AID (NEED-BASED) *Total amount:* $21,162,204 (62% federal, 35% state, 3% external sources). *Receiving aid:* Freshmen: 55% (265); all full-time undergraduates: 55% (1,768). *Average award:* Freshmen: $7349; Undergraduates: $7179. *Scholarships, grants, and awards:* Federal Pell, FSEOG, state, private, college/university gift aid from institutional funds.

GIFT AID (NON-NEED-BASED) *Total amount:* $257,349 (100% external sources). *Receiving aid:* Freshmen: 18% (88). Undergraduates: 19% (609). *Average award:* Freshmen: $9000. Undergraduates: $8722. *Scholarships, grants, and awards by category:* Academic interests/achievement: 887 awards ($4,629,933 total): business, computer science, engineering/technologies, general academic interests/achievements. *Special characteristics:* 103 awards ($751,043 total): children of faculty/staff, siblings of current students. *Tuition waivers:* Full or partial for employees or children of employees. *ROTC:* Army cooperative.

LOANS *Student loans:* $36,054,009 (42% need-based, 58% non-need-based). 69% of past graduating class borrowed through all loan programs. *Average need-based loan:* Freshmen: $99. Undergraduates: $640. *Parent loans:* $1,717,578 (100% non-need-based). *Programs:* Federal Direct (Subsidized and Unsubsidized Stafford, PLUS), Perkins.

WORK-STUDY *Federal work-study:* Total amount: $149,785; 103 jobs averaging $1488. *State or other work-study/employment:* Part-time jobs available.

ATHLETIC AWARDS Total amount: $5,126,787 (100% non-need-based).

APPLYING FOR FINANCIAL AID *Required financial aid form:* FAFSA. *Financial aid deadline (priority):* 3/1. *Notification date:* Continuous beginning 2/1. Students must reply within 2 weeks of notification.

CONTACT Ms. Julie Applegate, Financial Aid Counselor, Indiana Tech, 1600 East Washington Boulevard, Fort Wayne, IN 46803-1297, 800-937-2448 Ext. 2334 or toll-free 800-937-2448. *Fax:* 219-422-1578. *E-mail:* financialaid@indianatech.edu. *Website:* http://www.indianatech.edu/.

INDIANA UNIVERSITY BLOOMINGTON
Bloomington, IN

Tuition & fees (IN res): $10,033	Average undergraduate aid package: $11,366

ABOUT THE INSTITUTION State-supported, coed. *Awards:* certificates, bachelor's, master's, and doctoral degrees. 100 undergraduate majors. *Total enrollment:* 42,133. Undergraduates: 32,371. Freshmen: 7,192. Federal methodology is used as a basis for awarding need-based institutional aid.

UNDERGRADUATE EXPENSES for 2013–2014 *Application fee:* $55. *Tuition, state resident:* full-time $8750; part-time $273.40 per credit hour. *Tuition, nonresident:* full-time $30,200; part-time $943.75 per credit hour. *Required fees:* full-time $1283. Full-time tuition and fees vary according to location and program. Part-time tuition and fees vary according to course load, location, and program. *College room and board:* $8853; *Room only:* $5853. Room and board charges vary according to board plan and housing facility.

FRESHMAN FINANCIAL AID (Fall 2011) 5,158 applied for aid; of those 67% were deemed to have need. 95% of freshmen with need received aid; of those 16% had need fully met. *Average percent of need met:* 88% (excluding resources awarded to replace EFC). *Average financial aid package:* $11,693 (excluding resources awarded to replace EFC). 17% of all full-time freshmen had no need and received non-need-based gift aid.

UNDERGRADUATE FINANCIAL AID (Fall 2011) 19,119 applied for aid; of those 75% were deemed to have need. 96% of undergraduates with need received aid; of those 12% had need fully met. *Average percent of need met:* 88% (excluding resources awarded to replace EFC). *Average financial aid package:* $11,366 (excluding resources awarded to replace EFC). 18% of all full-time undergraduates had no need and received non-need-based gift aid.

GIFT AID (NEED-BASED) *Total amount:* $101,984,680 (29% federal, 26% state, 40% institutional, 5% external sources). *Receiving aid:* Freshmen: 36% (2,694); all full-time undergraduates: 34% (10,589). *Average award:* Freshmen: $10,920; Undergraduates: $9866. *Scholarships, grants, and awards:* Federal Pell, FSEOG, state, private, college/university gift aid from institutional funds.

GIFT AID (NON-NEED-BASED) *Total amount:* $54,929,456 (1% federal, 3% state, 83% institutional, 13% external sources). *Receiving aid:* Freshmen: 7% (488). Undergraduates: 5% (1,417). *Average award:* Freshmen: $8074. Undergraduates: $7351. *Tuition waivers:* Full or partial for employees or children of employees. *ROTC:* Army, Air Force.

LOANS *Student loans:* $113,289,026 (63% need-based, 37% non-need-based). 52% of past graduating class borrowed through all loan programs. *Average indebtedness per student:* $28,769. *Average need-based loan:* Freshmen: $3200. Undergraduates: $4449. *Parent loans:* $43,610,730 (38% need-based, 62% non-need-based). *Programs:* Federal Direct (Subsidized and Unsubsidized Stafford, PLUS), Perkins, college/university.

WORK-STUDY *Federal work-study:* Total amount: $897,920; jobs available. *State or other work-study/employment:* Total amount: $58,628 (54% need-based, 46% non-need-based). Part-time jobs available.

ATHLETIC AWARDS Total amount: $10,442,892 (31% need-based, 69% non-need-based).

APPLYING FOR FINANCIAL AID *Required financial aid form:* FAFSA. *Financial aid deadline (priority):* 3/10. *Notification date:* Continuous beginning 4/1.

INDIANA UNIVERSITY EAST
Richmond, IN

Tuition & fees (IN res): $6496	Average undergraduate aid package: $8506

ABOUT THE INSTITUTION State-supported, coed. *Awards:* certificates, bachelor's, and master's degrees. 23 undergraduate majors. *Total enrollment:* 4,186. Undergraduates: 4,052. Freshmen: 383. Federal methodology is used as a basis for awarding need-based institutional aid.

UNDERGRADUATE EXPENSES for 2013–2014 *Application fee:* $35. *Tuition, state resident:* full-time $5964; part-time $198.79 per credit hour. *Tuition, nonresident:* full-time $16,894; part-time $563.12 per credit hour. *Required fees:* full-time $532. Full-time tuition and fees vary according to course load, location, program, and reciprocity agreements. Part-time tuition and fees vary according to course load, location, program, and reciprocity agreements.

FRESHMAN FINANCIAL AID (Fall 2011) 379 applied for aid; of those 84% were deemed to have need. 98% of freshmen with need received aid; of those 14% had need fully met. *Average percent of need met:* 97% (excluding resources awarded to replace EFC). *Average financial aid package:* $8200 (excluding resources awarded to replace EFC). 5% of all full-time freshmen had no need and received non-need-based gift aid.

UNDERGRADUATE FINANCIAL AID (Fall 2011) 1,774 applied for aid; of those 89% were deemed to have need. 97% of undergraduates with need received aid; of those 7% had need fully met. *Average percent of need met:* 95% (excluding resources awarded to replace EFC). *Average financial aid package:* $8506 (excluding resources awarded to replace EFC). 4% of all full-time undergraduates had no need and received non-need-based gift aid.

GIFT AID (NEED-BASED) *Total amount:* $9,590,213 (65% federal, 27% state, 5% institutional, 3% external sources). *Receiving aid:* Freshmen: 72% (284); all full-time undergraduates: 70% (1,321). *Average award:* Freshmen: $6689; Undergraduates: $6273. *Scholarships, grants, and awards:* Federal Pell, FSEOG, state, private, college/university gift aid from institutional funds.

GIFT AID (NON-NEED-BASED) *Total amount:* $451,160 (10% federal, 12% state, 41% institutional, 37% external sources). *Receiving aid:* Freshmen: 7% (27). Undergraduates: 3% (55). *Average award:* Freshmen: $2146. Undergraduates: $1968. *Tuition waivers:* Full or partial for employees or children of employees.

LOANS *Student loans:* $13,654,423 (83% need-based, 17% non-need-based). 81% of past graduating class borrowed through all loan programs. *Average indebtedness per student:* $30,632. *Average need-based loan:* Freshmen: $2811. Undergraduates: $3800. *Parent loans:* $136,724 (33% need-based, 67% non-need-based). *Programs:* Federal Direct (Subsidized and Unsubsidized Stafford, PLUS), Perkins, college/university.

WORK-STUDY *Federal work-study:* Total amount: $93,602; jobs available.

ATHLETIC AWARDS Total amount: $217,527 (70% need-based, 30% non-need-based).

APPLYING FOR FINANCIAL AID *Required financial aid forms:* FAFSA, institution's own form. *Financial aid deadline (priority):* 3/10. *Notification date:* Continuous beginning 5/1. Students must reply within 2 weeks of notification.

INDIANA UNIVERSITY KOKOMO
Kokomo, IN

Tuition & fees (IN res): $6541	Average undergraduate aid package: $7708

ABOUT THE INSTITUTION State-supported, coed. *Awards:* certificates, associate, bachelor's, and master's degrees. 31 undergraduate majors. *Total enrollment:* 3,719. Undergraduates: 3,581. Freshmen: 450. Federal methodology is used as a basis for awarding need-based institutional aid.

UNDERGRADUATE EXPENSES for 2013–2014 *Application fee:* $35. *Tuition, state resident:* full-time $5949; part-time $198.31 per credit hour. *Tuition, nonresident:* full-time $16,894; part-time $563.12 per credit hour. *Required fees:* full-time $592. Full-time tuition and fees vary according to course load, location, and program. Part-time tuition and fees vary according to course load, location, and program.

FRESHMAN FINANCIAL AID (Fall 2011) 355 applied for aid; of those 81% were deemed to have need. 98% of freshmen with need received aid; of those 4% had need fully met. *Average percent of need met:* 92% (excluding resources awarded to replace EFC). *Average financial aid package:* $6720 (excluding resources awarded to replace EFC). 6% of all full-time freshmen had no need and received non-need-based gift aid.

UNDERGRADUATE FINANCIAL AID (Fall 2011) 1,589 applied for aid; of those 85% were deemed to have need. 97% of undergraduates with need received aid; of those 3% had need fully met. *Average percent of need met:* 92% (excluding resources awarded to replace EFC). *Average financial aid package:* $7708 (excluding resources awarded to replace EFC). 4% of all full-time undergraduates had no need and received non-need-based gift aid.

GIFT AID (NEED-BASED) *Total amount:* $7,672,433 (60% federal, 32% state, 4% institutional, 4% external sources). *Receiving aid:* Freshmen: 60% (233); all full-time undergraduates: 61% (1,076). *Average award:* Freshmen: $5913; Undergraduates: $5970. *Scholarships, grants, and awards:* Federal Pell, FSEOG, state, private, college/university gift aid from institutional funds.

GIFT AID (NON-NEED-BASED) *Total amount:* $502,073 (16% federal, 28% state, 25% institutional, 31% external sources). *Receiving aid:* Freshmen: 2% (9). Undergraduates: 2% (30). *Average award:* Freshmen: $1467. Undergraduates: $1531. *Tuition waivers:* Full or partial for employees or children of employees. *ROTC:* Army.

LOANS *Student loans:* $10,558,942 (77% need-based, 23% non-need-based). 73% of past graduating class borrowed through all loan programs. *Average indebtedness per student:* $26,217. *Average need-based loan:* Freshmen: $2784. Undergraduates: $3650. *Parent loans:* $60,757 (24% need-based, 76% non-need-based). *Programs:* Federal Direct (Subsidized and Unsubsidized Stafford, PLUS), Perkins, Federal Nursing, college/university.

WORK-STUDY *Federal work-study:* Total amount: $91,204; jobs available. *State or other work-study/employment:* Total amount: $2038 (100% need-based). Part-time jobs available.

APPLYING FOR FINANCIAL AID *Required financial aid form:* FAFSA. *Financial aid deadline (priority):* 3/10. *Notification date:* Continuous beginning 5/1. Students must reply within 4 weeks of notification.

INDIANA UNIVERSITY NORTHWEST
Gary, IN

Tuition & fees (IN res): $6626	Average undergraduate aid package: $8382

ABOUT THE INSTITUTION State-supported, coed. *Awards:* certificates, associate, bachelor's, and master's degrees. 42 undergraduate majors. *Total enrollment:* 6,184. Undergraduates: 5,636. Freshmen: 743. Federal methodology is used as a basis for awarding need-based institutional aid.

UNDERGRADUATE EXPENSES for 2013–2014 *Application fee:* $35. *Tuition, state resident:* full-time $6043; part-time $201.44 per credit hour. *Tuition, nonresident:* full-time $16,894; part-time $563.12 per credit hour. *Required fees:* full-time $583. Full-time tuition and fees vary according to course load, location, and program. Part-time tuition and fees vary according to course load, location, and program.

FRESHMAN FINANCIAL AID (Fall 2011) 659 applied for aid; of those 91% were deemed to have need. 95% of freshmen with need received aid; of those 1% had need fully met. *Average percent of need met:* 91% (excluding resources awarded to replace EFC). *Average financial aid package:* $7106 (excluding resources awarded to replace EFC). 4% of all full-time freshmen had no need and received non-need-based gift aid.

UNDERGRADUATE FINANCIAL AID (Fall 2011) 2,843 applied for aid; of those 91% were deemed to have need. 95% of undergraduates with need received aid; of those 2% had need fully met. *Average percent of need met:* 90% (excluding resources awarded to replace EFC). *Average financial aid package:* $8382 (excluding resources awarded to replace EFC). 3% of all full-time undergraduates had no need and received non-need-based gift aid.

GIFT AID (NEED-BASED) *Total amount:* $15,109,993 (66% federal, 27% state, 4% institutional, 3% external sources). *Receiving aid:* Freshmen: 63% (478); all full-time undergraduates: 61% (2,007). *Average award:* Freshmen: $6007; Undergraduates: $6361. *Scholarships, grants, and awards:* Federal Pell, FSEOG, state, private, college/university gift aid from institutional funds, Federal Nursing.

GIFT AID (NON-NEED-BASED) *Total amount:* $783,751 (8% federal, 8% state, 71% institutional, 13% external sources). *Receiving aid:* Freshmen: 1% (4). Undergraduates: 1% (20). *Average award:* Freshmen: $3754. Undergraduates: $4097. *Tuition waivers:* Full or partial for employees or children of employees. *ROTC:* Army.

LOANS *Student loans:* $23,972,616 (89% need-based, 11% non-need-based). 73% of past graduating class borrowed through all loan programs. *Average indebtedness per student:* $30,369. *Average need-based loan:* Freshmen: $3130. Undergraduates: $3904. *Parent loans:* $162,506 (37% need-based, 63% non-need-based). *Programs:* Federal Direct (Subsidized and Unsubsidized Stafford, PLUS), Perkins, college/university.

WORK-STUDY *Federal work-study:* Total amount: $202,017; jobs available.

ATHLETIC AWARDS Total amount: $45,825 (81% need-based, 19% non-need-based).

APPLYING FOR FINANCIAL AID *Required financial aid form:* FAFSA. *Financial aid deadline (priority):* 3/10. *Notification date:* Continuous beginning 4/15. Students must reply within 2 weeks of notification.

CONTACT Harold Burtley, Director of Scholarships and Financial Aid, Indiana University Northwest, 3400 Broadway, Hawthorn Hall, Room 111, Gary, IN 46408, 219-980-6778 or toll-free 800-968-7486. *Fax:* 219-981-5622. *E-mail:* finaidnw@iun.edu.
Website: http://www.iun.edu/.

to replace EFC). *Average financial aid package:* $9563 (excluding resources awarded to replace EFC). 2% of all full-time freshmen had no need and received non-need-based gift aid.

UNDERGRADUATE FINANCIAL AID (Fall 2011) 10,488 applied for aid; of those 84% were deemed to have need. 98% of undergraduates with need received aid; of those 5% had need fully met. *Average percent of need met:* 57% (excluding resources awarded to replace EFC). *Average financial aid package:* $9083 (excluding resources awarded to replace EFC). 2% of all full-time undergraduates had no need and received non-need-based gift aid.

GIFT AID (NEED-BASED) *Total amount:* $34,864,312 (59% federal, 41% state). *Receiving aid:* Freshmen: 50% (1,444); all full-time undergraduates: 50% (6,117). *Average award:* Freshmen: $5897; Undergraduates: $5547. *Scholarships, grants, and awards:* Federal Pell, FSEOG, state, private, college/university gift aid from institutional funds, United Negro College Fund.

GIFT AID (NON-NEED-BASED) *Total amount:* $3,880,839 (25% institutional, 75% external sources). *Receiving aid:* Freshmen: 21% (614). Undergraduates: 14% (1,673). *Average award:* Freshmen: $1496. Undergraduates: $1640. *Scholarships, grants, and awards by category: Academic interests/achievement:* 1,258 awards ($2,949,753 total): area/ethnic studies, biological sciences, business, communication, computer science, education, engineering/technologies, English, foreign languages, general academic interests/achievements, health fields, home economics, humanities, international studies, mathematics, physical sciences, premedicine, social sciences. *Creative arts/performance:* applied art and design, art/fine arts, dance, general creative arts/performance, journalism/publications, music, performing arts, theater/drama. *Special achievements/activities:* community service, general special achievements/activities, hobbies/interests, leadership. *Special characteristics:* 1,203 awards ($7,307,790 total): adult students, children of faculty/staff, ethnic background, international students. *Tuition waivers:* Full or partial for employees or children of employees, senior citizens. *ROTC:* Army.

LOANS *Student loans:* $79,667,742 (42% need-based, 58% non-need-based). 83% of past graduating class borrowed through all loan programs. *Average indebtedness per student:* $35,229. *Average need-based loan:* Freshmen: $3545. Undergraduates: $4146. *Parent loans:* $16,471,510 (100% non-need-based). *Programs:* Perkins, private loans.

WORK-STUDY *Federal work-study:* Total amount: $5,316,902; 1,003 jobs averaging $2063. *State or other work-study/employment:* Total amount: $1,135,533 (100% non-need-based). 1,650 part-time jobs averaging $2625.

ATHLETIC AWARDS Total amount: $1,096,739 (100% non-need-based).

APPLYING FOR FINANCIAL AID *Required financial aid form:* FAFSA. *Financial aid deadline:* 4/25. *Notification date:* Continuous.

CONTACT Mrs. Stacy Hopkins, Director of Financial Aid, Indiana University of Pennsylvania, 213 Clark Hall, Indiana, PA 15705, 724-357-2218 or toll-free 800-442-6830. *Fax:* 724-357-2094. *E-mail:* mccarthy@iup.edu.
Website: http://www.iup.edu/.

INDIANA UNIVERSITY OF PENNSYLVANIA
Indiana, PA

Tuition & fees (PA res): $8672	Average undergraduate aid package: $9083

ABOUT THE INSTITUTION State-supported, coed. *Awards:* certificates, associate, bachelor's, master's, and doctoral degrees. 69 undergraduate majors. *Total enrollment:* 15,379. Undergraduates: 13,058. Freshmen: 2,934. Federal methodology is used as a basis for awarding need-based institutional aid.

UNDERGRADUATE EXPENSES for 2013–2014 *Application fee:* $50. *Tuition, state resident:* full-time $6428; part-time $268 per credit hour. *Tuition, nonresident:* full-time $16,070; part-time $670 per credit hour. *Required fees:* full-time $2244; $52 per credit hour or $203 per term. Full-time tuition and fees vary according to course load and reciprocity agreements. Part-time tuition and fees vary according to course load and reciprocity agreements. *College room and board:* $10,466; *Room only:* $7740. Room and board charges vary according to board plan, housing facility, and location.

FRESHMAN FINANCIAL AID (Fall 2011) 2,683 applied for aid; of those 79% were deemed to have need. 98% of freshmen with need received aid; of those 6% had need fully met. *Average percent of need met:* 60% (excluding resources awarded

INDIANA UNIVERSITY–PURDUE UNIVERSITY FORT WAYNE
Fort Wayne, IN

Tuition & fees (IN res): $6876	Average undergraduate aid package: $9283

ABOUT THE INSTITUTION State-supported, coed. *Awards:* certificates, associate, bachelor's, and master's degrees. 103 undergraduate majors. *Total enrollment:* 13,771. Undergraduates: 13,117. Freshmen: 1,629. Federal methodology is used as a basis for awarding need-based institutional aid.

UNDERGRADUATE EXPENSES for 2013–2014 *Application fee:* $50. *Tuition, state resident:* full-time $6001; part-time $222.25 per credit hour. *Tuition, nonresident:* full-time $15,640; part-time $579.25 per credit hour. *Required fees:* full-time $875; $32.40 per credit hour. Full-time tuition and fees vary according to course load. Part-time tuition and fees vary according to course load. *Room only:* $7210. Room and board charges vary according to housing facility.

FRESHMAN FINANCIAL AID (Fall 2011) 1,704 applied for aid; of those 86% were deemed to have need. 95% of freshmen with need received aid; of those 3% had need fully met. *Average percent of need met:* 45% (excluding resources awarded to replace EFC). *Average financial aid package:* $8717 (excluding resources awarded to replace EFC). 1% of all full-time freshmen had no need and received non-need-based gift aid.

UNDERGRADUATE FINANCIAL AID (Fall 2011) 7,574 applied for aid; of those 89% were deemed to have need. 96% of undergraduates with need received aid; of those 4% had need fully met. **Average percent of need met:** 46% (excluding resources awarded to replace EFC). **Average financial aid package:** $9283 (excluding resources awarded to replace EFC). 1% of all full-time undergraduates had no need and received non-need-based gift aid.

GIFT AID (NEED-BASED) **Total amount:** $35,167,008 (61% federal, 33% state, 3% institutional, 3% external sources). **Receiving aid:** Freshmen: 51% (948); all full-time undergraduates: 53% (4,521). **Average award:** Freshmen: $5601; Undergraduates: $5831. **Scholarships, grants, and awards:** Federal Pell, FSEOG, state, private, college/university gift aid from institutional funds.

GIFT AID (NON-NEED-BASED) **Total amount:** $960,650 (22% state, 40% institutional, 38% external sources). **Receiving aid:** Freshmen: 25% (470). Undergraduates: 17% (1,446). **Average award:** Freshmen: $4001. Undergraduates: $2892. **Scholarships, grants, and awards by category:** Academic interests/achievement: general academic interests/achievements. Creative arts/performance: art/fine arts, music, theater/drama. Special achievements/activities: leadership. Special characteristics: children and siblings of alumni, local/state students. **Tuition waivers:** Full or partial for employees or children of employees, senior citizens. **ROTC:** Army.

LOANS **Student loans:** $52,741,355 (98% need-based, 2% non-need-based). 73% of past graduating class borrowed through all loan programs. Average indebtedness per student: $26,498. **Average need-based loan:** Freshmen: $3154. Undergraduates: $3784. **Parent loans:** $2,738,507 (97% need-based, 3% non-need-based). **Programs:** Federal Direct (Subsidized and Unsubsidized Stafford, PLUS), Perkins.

WORK-STUDY **Federal work-study:** Total amount: $362,985; 969 jobs averaging $3000.

ATHLETIC AWARDS Total amount: $2,072,241 (38% need-based, 62% non-need-based).

APPLYING FOR FINANCIAL AID **Required financial aid form:** FAFSA. **Financial aid deadline (priority):** 3/10. **Notification date:** Continuous beginning 4/1. Students must reply within 3 weeks of notification.

CONTACT Mr. Gerald Curd, Interim Director of Financial Aid, Indiana University–Purdue University Fort Wayne, 2101 East Coliseum Boulevard, Fort Wayne, IN 46805-1499, 260-481-6243 or toll-free 800-324-4739. E-mail: finaid@ipfw.edu. Website: http://www.ipfw.edu/.

INDIANA UNIVERSITY–PURDUE UNIVERSITY INDIANAPOLIS
Indianapolis, IN

Tuition & fees (IN res): $8605	Average undergraduate aid package: $9465

ABOUT THE INSTITUTION State-supported, coed. **Awards:** certificates, associate, bachelor's, master's, and doctoral degrees. 89 undergraduate majors. **Total enrollment:** 30,451. Undergraduates: 22,271. Freshmen: 3,279. Federal methodology is used as a basis for awarding need-based institutional aid.

UNDERGRADUATE EXPENSES for 2013–2014 **Application fee:** $50. **Tuition, state resident:** full-time $7623; part-time $254.10 per credit hour. **Tuition, nonresident:** full-time $28,080; part-time $936 per credit hour. **Required fees:** full-time $982. Full-time tuition and fees vary according to course load, location, and program. Part-time tuition and fees vary according to course load, location, and program. **College room and board:** $7944. Room and board charges vary according to housing facility.

FRESHMAN FINANCIAL AID (Fall 2011) 2,518 applied for aid; of those 83% were deemed to have need. 97% of freshmen with need received aid; of those 5% had need fully met. **Average percent of need met:** 90% (excluding resources awarded to replace EFC). **Average financial aid package:** $9507 (excluding resources awarded to replace EFC). 7% of all full-time freshmen had no need and received non-need-based gift aid.

UNDERGRADUATE FINANCIAL AID (Fall 2011) 13,390 applied for aid; of those 87% were deemed to have need. 97% of undergraduates with need received aid; of those 4% had need fully met. **Average percent of need met:** 90% (excluding resources awarded to replace EFC). **Average financial aid package:** $9465 (excluding resources awarded to replace EFC). 5% of all full-time undergraduates had no need and received non-need-based gift aid.

GIFT AID (NEED-BASED) **Total amount:** $70,816,571 (52% federal, 31% state, 14% institutional, 3% external sources). **Receiving aid:** Freshmen: 60% (1,675); all full-time undergraduates: 56% (8,846). **Average award:** Freshmen: $8193; Undergraduates: $7361. **Scholarships, grants, and awards:** Federal Pell, FSEOG, state, private, college/university gift aid from institutional funds.

GIFT AID (NON-NEED-BASED) **Total amount:** $13,409,388 (8% federal, 7% state, 39% institutional, 46% external sources). **Receiving aid:** Freshmen: 3% (98). Undergraduates: 2% (356). **Average award:** Freshmen: $6060. Undergraduates: $5022. **Scholarships, grants, and awards by category:** Academic interests/achievement: general academic interests/achievements. **Tuition waivers:** Full or partial for employees or children of employees. **ROTC:** Army, Air Force cooperative.

LOANS **Student loans:** $104,306,721 (81% need-based, 19% non-need-based). 74% of past graduating class borrowed through all loan programs. Average indebtedness per student: $30,752. **Average need-based loan:** Freshmen: $3409. Undergraduates: $4220. **Parent loans:** $6,671,838 (36% need-based, 64% non-need-based). **Programs:** Federal Direct (Subsidized and Unsubsidized Stafford, PLUS), Perkins, Federal Nursing, college/university.

WORK-STUDY **Federal work-study:** Total amount: $1,267,816; jobs available. **State or other work-study/employment:** Total amount: $56,398 (60% need-based, 40% non-need-based). Part-time jobs available.

ATHLETIC AWARDS Total amount: $1,967,258 (43% need-based, 57% non-need-based).

APPLYING FOR FINANCIAL AID **Required financial aid form:** FAFSA. **Financial aid deadline (priority):** 3/10. **Notification date:** Continuous beginning 4/1.

CONTACT Marvin Smith, Director of Student Financial Services, Indiana University–Purdue University Indianapolis, 420 University Boulevard, CE 250, Indianapolis, IN 46202-5145, 317-274-4162. Fax: 317-274-3664. E-mail: finaid@iupui.edu. Website: http://www.iupui.edu/.

INDIANA UNIVERSITY SOUTH BEND
South Bend, IN

Tuition & fees (IN res): $6728	Average undergraduate aid package: $8536

ABOUT THE INSTITUTION State-supported, coed. **Awards:** certificates, diplomas, associate, bachelor's, and master's degrees. 57 undergraduate majors. **Total enrollment:** 8,490. Undergraduates: 7,860. Freshmen: 950. Federal methodology is used as a basis for awarding need-based institutional aid.

UNDERGRADUATE EXPENSES for 2013–2014 **Application fee:** $35. **Tuition, state resident:** full-time $6138; part-time $204.61 per credit hour. **Tuition, nonresident:** full-time $16,894; part-time $563.12 per credit hour. **Required fees:** full-time $590. Full-time tuition and fees vary according to course load, location, and program. Part-time tuition and fees vary according to course load, location, and program. **Room only:** $6838. Room and board charges vary according to housing facility.

FRESHMAN FINANCIAL AID (Fall 2011) 800 applied for aid; of those 87% were deemed to have need. 97% of freshmen with need received aid; of those 3% had need fully met. **Average percent of need met:** 92% (excluding resources awarded to replace EFC). **Average financial aid package:** $7279 (excluding resources awarded to replace EFC). 1% of all full-time freshmen had no need and received non-need-based gift aid.

UNDERGRADUATE FINANCIAL AID (Fall 2011) 3,775 applied for aid; of those 89% were deemed to have need. 97% of undergraduates with need received aid; of those 2% had need fully met. **Average percent of need met:** 92% (excluding resources awarded to replace EFC). **Average financial aid package:** $8536 (excluding resources awarded to replace EFC). 2% of all full-time undergraduates had no need and received non-need-based gift aid.

GIFT AID (NEED-BASED) **Total amount:** $20,440,209 (61% federal, 30% state, 6% institutional, 3% external sources). **Receiving aid:** Freshmen: 66% (582); all full-time undergraduates: 63% (2,688). **Average award:** Freshmen: $5901; Undergraduates: $6572. **Scholarships, grants, and awards:** Federal Pell, FSEOG, state, private, college/university gift aid from institutional funds.

GIFT AID (NON-NEED-BASED) **Total amount:** $1,372,514 (12% federal, 7% state, 39% institutional, 42% external sources). **Receiving aid:** Freshmen: 2% (18). Undergraduates: 1% (53). **Average award:** Freshmen: $7382. Undergraduates:

$5516. *Tuition waivers:* Full or partial for employees or children of employees. *ROTC:* Army cooperative, Naval cooperative, Air Force cooperative. **LOANS** *Student loans:* $26,906,740 (86% need-based, 14% non-need-based). 75% of past graduating class borrowed through all loan programs. *Average indebtedness per student:* $27,417. *Average need-based loan:* Freshmen: $2946. Undergraduates: $3891. *Parent loans:* $592,358 (34% need-based, 66% non-need-based). *Programs:* Federal Direct (Subsidized and Unsubsidized Stafford, PLUS), Perkins, state. **WORK-STUDY** *Federal work-study:* Total amount: $249,584; jobs available. *State or other work-study/employment:* Total amount: $8039 (100% need-based). Part-time jobs available. **ATHLETIC AWARDS** Total amount: $242,689 (72% need-based, 28% non-need-based). **APPLYING FOR FINANCIAL AID** *Required financial aid forms:* FAFSA, institution's own form. *Financial aid deadline (priority):* 3/10. *Notification date:* Continuous beginning 5/1. **CONTACT** Cathy Buckman, Interim Director of Financial Aid, Indiana University South Bend, 1700 Mishawaka Avenue, PO Box 7111, Building 157, South Bend, IN 46634-7111, 574-520-4357 or toll-free 877-GO-2-IUSB. *Fax:* 574-520-5561. *E-mail:* sbfinaid@iusb.edu. *Website:* http://www.iusb.edu/.

INDIANA UNIVERSITY SOUTHEAST
New Albany, IN

Tuition & fees (IN res): $6576	Average undergraduate aid package: $7802

ABOUT THE INSTITUTION State-supported, coed. *Awards:* certificates, associate, bachelor's, and master's degrees. 38 undergraduate majors. *Total enrollment:* 6,904. Undergraduates: 6,203. Freshmen: 917. Federal methodology is used as a basis for awarding need-based institutional aid. **UNDERGRADUATE EXPENSES** for 2013–2014 *Application fee:* $35. *Tuition, state resident:* full-time $5960; part-time $198.65 per credit hour. *Tuition, nonresident:* full-time $16,894; part-time $563.12 per credit hour. *Required fees:* full-time $616. Full-time tuition and fees vary according to course load, location, program, and reciprocity agreements. Part-time tuition and fees vary according to course load, location, program, and reciprocity agreements. *Room only:* $6570. Room and board charges vary according to board plan and housing facility. **FRESHMAN FINANCIAL AID (Fall 2011)** 801 applied for aid; of those 79% were deemed to have need. 97% of freshmen with need received aid; of those 5% had need fully met. *Average percent of need met:* 92% (excluding resources awarded to replace EFC). *Average financial aid package:* $7308 (excluding resources awarded to replace EFC). 7% of all full-time freshmen had no need and received non-need-based gift aid. **UNDERGRADUATE FINANCIAL AID (Fall 2011)** 3,426 applied for aid; of those 83% were deemed to have need. 96% of undergraduates with need received aid; of those 3% had need fully met. *Average percent of need met:* 93% (excluding resources awarded to replace EFC). *Average financial aid package:* $7802 (excluding resources awarded to replace EFC). 4% of all full-time undergraduates had no need and received non-need-based gift aid. **GIFT AID (NEED-BASED)** *Total amount:* $15,743,805 (61% federal, 27% state, 7% institutional, 5% external sources). *Receiving aid:* Freshmen: 59% (526); all full-time undergraduates: 55% (2,251). *Average award:* Freshmen: $6203; Undergraduates: $6007. *Scholarships, grants, and awards:* Federal Pell, FSEOG, state, private, college/university gift aid from institutional funds. **GIFT AID (NON-NEED-BASED)** *Total amount:* $1,309,793 (2% federal, 15% state, 29% institutional, 54% external sources). *Receiving aid:* Freshmen: 2% (22). Undergraduates: 1% (51). *Average award:* Freshmen: $1380. Undergraduates: $1968. *Tuition waivers:* Full or partial for employees or children of employees. *ROTC:* Army cooperative, Air Force cooperative. **LOANS** *Student loans:* $21,087,590 (78% need-based, 22% non-need-based). 64% of past graduating class borrowed through all loan programs. *Average indebtedness per student:* $24,609. *Average need-based loan:* Freshmen: $2969. Undergraduates: $3813. *Parent loans:* $544,255 (33% need-based, 67% non-need-based). *Programs:* Federal Direct (Subsidized and Unsubsidized Stafford, PLUS), Perkins, college/university.

WORK-STUDY *Federal work-study:* Total amount: $288,555; jobs available. *State or other work-study/employment:* Total amount: $8796 (73% need-based, 27% non-need-based). Part-time jobs available. **ATHLETIC AWARDS** Total amount: $101,720 (67% need-based, 33% non-need-based). **APPLYING FOR FINANCIAL AID** *Required financial aid form:* FAFSA. *Financial aid deadline (priority):* 3/10. *Notification date:* Continuous beginning 5/1. Students must reply within 3 weeks of notification. **CONTACT** Brittany Hubbard, Director of Financial Aid, Indiana University Southeast, University Center, South Room 105, New Albany, IN 47150, 812-941-2246 or toll-free 800-852-8835. *Fax:* 812-941-2546. *E-mail:* financialaid@ius.edu. *Website:* http://www.ius.edu/.

INDIANA WESLEYAN UNIVERSITY
Marion, IN

Tuition & fees: $23,628	Average undergraduate aid package: $21,404

ABOUT THE INSTITUTION Independent Wesleyan, coed. *Awards:* certificates, associate, bachelor's, master's, and doctoral degrees (also offers adult program with significant enrollment not reflected in profile). 86 undergraduate majors. *Total enrollment:* 95. Undergraduates: 2,999. Freshmen: 725. Both federal and institutional methodology are used as a basis for awarding need-based institutional aid. **UNDERGRADUATE EXPENSES** for 2013–2014 *Application fee:* $25. *Comprehensive fee:* $31,188 includes full-time tuition ($23,628) and room and board ($7560). Full-time tuition and fees vary according to course load and degree level. Room and board charges vary according to board plan. *Part-time tuition:* $662 per credit hour. Part-time tuition and fees vary according to course load and degree level. **FRESHMAN FINANCIAL AID (Fall 2011)** 744 applied for aid; of those 85% were deemed to have need. 100% of freshmen with need received aid; of those 31% had need fully met. *Average percent of need met:* 83% (excluding resources awarded to replace EFC). *Average financial aid package:* $21,516 (excluding resources awarded to replace EFC). 13% of all full-time freshmen had no need and received non-need-based gift aid. **UNDERGRADUATE FINANCIAL AID (Fall 2011)** 2,832 applied for aid; of those 83% were deemed to have need. 100% of undergraduates with need received aid; of those 36% had need fully met. *Average percent of need met:* 80% (excluding resources awarded to replace EFC). *Average financial aid package:* $21,404 (excluding resources awarded to replace EFC). 13% of all full-time undergraduates had no need and received non-need-based gift aid. **GIFT AID (NEED-BASED)** *Total amount:* $32,272,712 (13% federal, 6% state, 73% institutional, 8% external sources). *Receiving aid:* Freshmen: 83% (626); all full-time undergraduates: 78% (2,304). *Average award:* Freshmen: $13,192; Undergraduates: $12,739. *Scholarships, grants, and awards:* Federal Pell, FSEOG, state, private, college/university gift aid from institutional funds. **GIFT AID (NON-NEED-BASED)** *Total amount:* $3,585,857 (13% federal, 6% state, 73% institutional, 8% external sources). *Receiving aid:* Freshmen: 10% (76). Undergraduates: 10% (282). *Average award:* Freshmen: $4617. Undergraduates: $4459. *Scholarships, grants, and awards by category:* Academic interests/achievement: biological sciences, business, communication, computer science, education, English, foreign languages, general academic interests/achievements, health fields, international studies, mathematics, physical sciences, premedicine, religion/biblical studies, social sciences. *Creative arts/performance:* art/fine arts, music, theater/drama. *Special achievements/activities:* cheerleading/drum major, community service, hobbies/interests, religious involvement. *Special characteristics:* children and siblings of alumni, children of faculty/staff, relatives of clergy, religious affiliation, siblings of current students, veterans. *Tuition waivers:* Full or partial for employees or children of employees. *ROTC:* Army. **LOANS** *Student loans:* $18,648,460 (75% need-based, 25% non-need-based). 78% of past graduating class borrowed through all loan programs. *Average indebtedness per student:* $22,940. *Average need-based loan:* Freshmen: $5082. Undergraduates: $6479. *Parent loans:* $5,172,110 (60% need-based, 40% non-need-based). *Programs:* Federal Direct (Subsidized and Unsubsidized Stafford, PLUS), Perkins, college/university. **WORK-STUDY** *Federal work-study:* Total amount: $1,406,868; jobs available. **ATHLETIC AWARDS** Total amount: $1,461,923 (60% need-based, 40% non-need-based).

APPLYING FOR FINANCIAL AID *Required financial aid form:* FAFSA. *Financial aid deadline (priority):* 3/10. *Notification date:* Continuous beginning 2/15.

CONTACT Financial Aid Office, Indiana Wesleyan University, 4201 South Washington Street, Marion, IN 46953-4999, 765-677-2116 or toll-free 866-468-6498. *Fax:* 765-677-2809. *E-mail:* finaid@indwes.edu. *Website:* http://www.indwes.edu/.

INDIAN RIVER STATE COLLEGE
Fort Pierce, FL

CONTACT Mary Lewis, Director of Financial Aid, Indian River State College, W Building, Main Campus, Fort Pierce, FL 34981, 772-462-7450 or toll-free 866-792-4772. *E-mail:* financialaid-info@irsc.edu. *Website:* http://www.irsc.edu/.

INSTE BIBLE COLLEGE
Ankeny, IA

CONTACT Financial Aid Office, INSTE Bible College, 2302 SW 3rd Street, Ankeny, IA 50023, 515-289-9200. *Website:* http://www.inste.edu/.

INSTITUTE OF AMERICAN INDIAN ARTS
Santa Fe, NM

ABOUT THE INSTITUTION Federally supported, coed. *Awards:* associate, bachelor's, and master's degrees. 5 undergraduate majors. *Total enrollment:* 414.

GIFT AID (NEED-BASED) *Scholarships, grants, and awards:* Federal Pell, FSEOG, state, private, college/university gift aid from institutional funds, Bureau of Indian Affairs Grants.

GIFT AID (NON-NEED-BASED) *Scholarships, grants, and awards by category: Academic interests/achievement:* business. *Creative arts/performance:* art/fine arts, creative writing, general creative arts/performance, performing arts. *Special characteristics:* veterans, veterans' children.

WORK-STUDY *Federal work-study:* Total amount: $14,888; 2 jobs averaging $2300. *State or other work-study/employment:* Total amount: $44,867 (45% need-based, 55% non-need-based). 3 part-time jobs averaging $2300.

APPLYING FOR FINANCIAL AID *Required financial aid forms:* FAFSA, institution's own form.

CONTACT Lala M. Gallegos, Director of Financial Aid, Institute of American Indian Arts, 83 Avan Nu Po Road, Santa Fe, NM 87508, 505-424-5724. *Fax:* 505-424-0909. *E-mail:* lgallegos@iaia.edu. *Website:* http://www.iaia.edu/.

INTER AMERICAN UNIVERSITY OF PUERTO RICO, AGUADILLA CAMPUS
Aguadilla, PR

CONTACT Mr. Juan Gonzalez, Director of Financial Aid , Inter American University of Puerto Rico, Aguadilla Campus, PO Box 20000, Aguadilla, PR 00605, 787-891-0925 Ext. 2108. *Fax:* 787-882-3020. *Website:* http://www.aguadilla.inter.edu/.

INTER AMERICAN UNIVERSITY OF PUERTO RICO, ARECIBO CAMPUS
Arecibo, PR

CONTACT Ramón O. de Jesús, Financial Aid Director, Inter American University of Puerto Rico, Arecibo Campus, PO Box 4050, Arecibo, PR 00614-4050, 787-878-5475 Ext. 2275. *Fax:* 787-880-1624. *Website:* http://www.arecibo.inter.edu/.

INTER AMERICAN UNIVERSITY OF PUERTO RICO, BARRANQUITAS CAMPUS
Barranquitas, PR

Tuition & fees: N/R   Average undergraduate aid package: N/A

ABOUT THE INSTITUTION Independent, coed. 21 undergraduate majors. Federal methodology is used as a basis for awarding need-based institutional aid.

GIFT AID (NEED-BASED) *Scholarships, grants, and awards:* Federal Pell, FSEOG, state, private, college/university gift aid from institutional funds.

GIFT AID (NON-NEED-BASED) *Scholarships, grants, and awards by category: Special characteristics:* adult students, veterans.

LOANS *Programs:* Federal Direct (Subsidized Stafford), Perkins.

APPLYING FOR FINANCIAL AID *Required financial aid forms:* FAFSA, institution's own form. *Financial aid deadline (priority):* 4/30. *Notification date:* Continuous.

CONTACT Mr. Eduardo Fontanez Colon, Financial Aid Officer, Inter American University of Puerto Rico, Barranquitas Campus, Box 517, Barranquitas, PR 00794, 787-857-3600 Ext. 2049. *Fax:* 787-857-2244. *Website:* http://www.br.inter.edu/.

INTER AMERICAN UNIVERSITY OF PUERTO RICO, BAYAMÓN CAMPUS
Bayamón, PR

Tuition & fees: $5620   Average undergraduate aid package: $935

ABOUT THE INSTITUTION Independent, coed. *Awards:* certificates, associate, bachelor's, and master's degrees. 45 undergraduate majors. *Total enrollment:* 4,915. Undergraduates: 4,782. Freshmen: 943. Federal methodology is used as a basis for awarding need-based institutional aid.

UNDERGRADUATE EXPENSES for 2013–2014 *Tuition:* full-time $5100; part-time $260 per semester hour. Full-time tuition and fees vary according to course load and program. Part-time tuition and fees vary according to course load and program.

FRESHMAN FINANCIAL AID (Fall 2011) 1,112 applied for aid; of those 98% were deemed to have need. 49% of freshmen with need received aid; of those .4% had need fully met. *Average percent of need met:* 1% (excluding resources awarded to replace EFC). *Average financial aid package:* $145 (excluding resources awarded to replace EFC).

UNDERGRADUATE FINANCIAL AID (Fall 2011) 2,858 applied for aid; of those 97% were deemed to have need. 61% of undergraduates with need received aid; of those .4% had need fully met. *Average percent of need met:* 7% (excluding resources awarded to replace EFC). *Average financial aid package:* $935 (excluding resources awarded to replace EFC).

GIFT AID (NEED-BASED) *Total amount:* $899,319 (5% federal, 35% state, 60% institutional). *Receiving aid:* Freshmen: 43% (491); all full-time undergraduates: 44% (1,313). *Average award:* Freshmen: $125; Undergraduates: $345. *Scholarships, grants, and awards:* Federal Pell, state, college/university gift aid from institutional funds.

GIFT AID (NON-NEED-BASED) *ROTC:* Army cooperative.

LOANS *Student loans:* $1,831,263 (100% need-based). *Average need-based loan:* Freshmen: $94. Undergraduates: $1446. *Parent loans:* $9600 (100% need-based). *Programs:* Perkins.
WORK-STUDY *Federal work-study:* Total amount: $222,348; jobs available.
ATHLETIC AWARDS Total amount: $31,020 (100% need-based).
APPLYING FOR FINANCIAL AID *Required financial aid form:* FAFSA. *Notification date:* Continuous.
CONTACT Mr. Hector L. Vargas, Interim Director of Students Services, Inter American University of Puerto Rico, Bayamón Campus, 500 Dr. John Will Harris Road, Bayamon, PR 00957, 787-279-1912 Ext. 2025. *E-mail:* hvargas@bayamon.inter.edu.
Website: http://www.bc.inter.edu/.

INTER AMERICAN UNIVERSITY OF PUERTO RICO, FAJARDO CAMPUS
Fajardo, PR

CONTACT Financial Aid Director, Inter American University of Puerto Rico, Fajardo Campus, Call Box 700003, Fajardo, PR 00738-7003, 787-863-2390 Ext. 2208.
Website: http://www.fajardo.inter.edu/.

INTER AMERICAN UNIVERSITY OF PUERTO RICO, GUAYAMA CAMPUS
Guayama, PR

Tuition & fees: $4562	Average undergraduate aid package: $2394

ABOUT THE INSTITUTION Independent, coed. 14 undergraduate majors. Federal methodology is used as a basis for awarding need-based institutional aid.
UNDERGRADUATE EXPENSES for 2013–2014 *Tuition:* full-time $4080.
FRESHMAN FINANCIAL AID (Fall 2012, est.) 164 applied for aid; of those 99% were deemed to have need. 43% of freshmen with need received aid. *Average percent of need met:* 1% (excluding resources awarded to replace EFC). *Average financial aid package:* $115 (excluding resources awarded to replace EFC).
UNDERGRADUATE FINANCIAL AID (Fall 2012, est.) 1,519 applied for aid; of those 100% were deemed to have need. 67% of undergraduates with need received aid; of those .1% had need fully met. *Average percent of need met:* 18% (excluding resources awarded to replace EFC). *Average financial aid package:* $2394 (excluding resources awarded to replace EFC).
GIFT AID (NEED-BASED) *Total amount:* $431,626 (2% federal, 40% state, 58% institutional). *Receiving aid:* Freshmen: 11% (18); all full-time undergraduates: 23% (347). *Average award:* Freshmen: $19; Undergraduates: $714. *Scholarships, grants, and awards:* Federal Pell, FSEOG, state, college/university gift aid from institutional funds.
GIFT AID (NON-NEED-BASED) *Tuition waivers:* Full or partial for employees or children of employees.
LOANS *Student loans:* $5,243,106 (100% need-based). *Average need-based loan:* Freshmen: $128. Undergraduates: $2538. *Parent loans:* $162,514 (100% need-based). *Programs:* Federal Direct (Subsidized and Unsubsidized Stafford, PLUS), Perkins.
WORK-STUDY *Federal work-study:* Total amount: $107,025; jobs available.
ATHLETIC AWARDS Total amount: $24,700 (100% need-based).
APPLYING FOR FINANCIAL AID *Required financial aid form:* FAFSA. *Financial aid deadline:* Continuous. *Notification date:* Continuous beginning 7/1. Students must reply within 5 weeks of notification.
CONTACT Senor Jose A. Vechini, Director of Financial Aid Office, Inter American University of Puerto Rico, Guayama Campus, Call Box 10004, Guayama, PR 00785, 787-864-2222 Ext. 2206. *Fax:* 787-864-8232. *E-mail:* javechi@inter.edu.
Website: http://www.guayama.inter.edu/.

INTER AMERICAN UNIVERSITY OF PUERTO RICO, METROPOLITAN CAMPUS
San Juan, PR

CONTACT Mrs. Luz M. Medina, Acting Director of Financial Aid, Inter American University of Puerto Rico, Metropolitan Campus, PO Box 191293, San Juan, PR 00919-1293, 787-758-2891. *Fax:* 787-250-0782.
Website: http://metro.inter.edu/.

INTER AMERICAN UNIVERSITY OF PUERTO RICO, PONCE CAMPUS
Mercedita, PR

Tuition & fees: $4080	Average undergraduate aid package: N/A

ABOUT THE INSTITUTION Independent, coed. *Awards:* associate, bachelor's, and master's degrees. 45 undergraduate majors. *Total enrollment:* 5,983. Undergraduates: 5,575. Freshmen: 950. Both federal and institutional methodology are used as a basis for awarding need-based institutional aid.
UNDERGRADUATE EXPENSES for 2013–2014 *Tuition:* full-time $4080; part-time $170 per credit. *Required fees:* $426 per semester hour. Full-time tuition and fees vary according to course load and program. Part-time tuition and fees vary according to course load and program.
GIFT AID (NEED-BASED) *Total amount:* $29,013,304 (89% federal, 4% state, 7% institutional). *Scholarships, grants, and awards:* Federal Pell, FSEOG, state, college/university gift aid from institutional funds, Federal Nursing.
LOANS *Student loans:* $3,210,123 (100% need-based). *Parent loans:* $127,926 (100% need-based). *Programs:* Federal Direct (Subsidized and Unsubsidized Stafford, PLUS), Perkins.
WORK-STUDY *Federal work-study:* Total amount: $542,175; jobs available.
ATHLETIC AWARDS Total amount: $172,315 (100% need-based).
APPLYING FOR FINANCIAL AID *Required financial aid form:* FAFSA. *Financial aid deadline:* Continuous. *Notification date:* Continuous.
CONTACT Debra Martinez, Financial Aid Officer, Inter American University of Puerto Rico, Ponce Campus, 104 Turpeaux Industrial Park, Mercedita, PR 00715-2201, 787-284-1912 Ext. 2161. *Fax:* 787-841-0103. *E-mail:* dmartinez@ponce.inter.edu.
Website: http://www.ponce.inter.edu/.

INTER AMERICAN UNIVERSITY OF PUERTO RICO, SAN GERMÁN CAMPUS
San Germán, PR

CONTACT Ms. Maria I. Lugo, Financial Aid Director, Inter American University of Puerto Rico, San Germán Campus, PO Box 5100, San German, PR 00683-5008, 787-264-1912 Ext. 7252. *Fax:* 787-892-6350.
Website: http://www.sg.inter.edu/.

INTERIOR DESIGNERS INSTITUTE
Newport Beach, CA .

CONTACT Office of Financial Aid, Interior Designers Institute, 1061 Camelback Road, Newport Beach, CA 92660, 949-675-4451.
Website: http://www.idi.edu/.

INTERNATIONAL ACADEMY OF DESIGN & TECHNOLOGY
Tampa, FL

CONTACT Financial Aid Office, International Academy of Design & Technology, 5225 Memorial Highway, Tampa, FL 33634-7350, 813-881-0007 or toll-free 888-315-6111. *Fax:* 813-881-3440.
Website: http://www.academy.edu/.

INTERNATIONAL ACADEMY OF DESIGN & TECHNOLOGY
Chicago, IL

CONTACT Barbara Williams, Financial Aid Director, International Academy of Design & Technology, 1 North State Street, Suite 400, Chicago, IL 60602, 312-980-9200 or toll-free 877-458-6111. *Fax:* 312-541-3929.
Website: http://www.iadtchicago.edu/.

INTERNATIONAL BAPTIST COLLEGE
Chandler, AZ

CONTACT Financial Aid Office, International Baptist College, 2211 West Germann Road, Chandler, AZ 85286, 480-838-7070 Ext. 268 or toll-free 800-422-4858. *Fax:* 480-838-5432. *E-mail:* financialaid@ibconline.edu.
Website: http://www.ibcs.edu/.

INTERNATIONAL BUSINESS COLLEGE
Fort Wayne, IN

CONTACT Financial Aid Office, International Business College, 5699 Coventry Lane, Fort Wayne, IN 46804, 219-459-4500 or toll-free 800-589-6363.
Website: http://www.ibcfortwayne.edu/.

IONA COLLEGE
New Rochelle, NY

Tuition & fees: $32,770	Average undergraduate aid package: $20,179

ABOUT THE INSTITUTION Independent Roman Catholic Church, coed. *Awards:* certificates, bachelor's, and master's degrees. 50 undergraduate majors. *Total enrollment:* 4,241. Undergraduates: 3,462. Freshmen: 722. Federal methodology is used as a basis for awarding need-based institutional aid.
UNDERGRADUATE EXPENSES for 2013–2014 *Application fee:* $50. *Comprehensive fee:* $45,945 includes full-time tuition ($30,670), mandatory fees ($2100), and room and board ($13,175). Room and board charges vary according to housing facility. *Part-time tuition:* $1020 per credit. *Part-time fees:* $520 per term. Part-time tuition and fees vary according to course load.
FRESHMAN FINANCIAL AID (Fall 2012, est.) 718 applied for aid; of those 85% were deemed to have need. 100% of freshmen with need received aid; of those 17% had need fully met. *Average percent of need met:* 26% (excluding resources awarded to replace EFC). *Average financial aid package:* $21,088 (excluding resources awarded to replace EFC). 15% of all full-time freshmen had no need and received non-need-based gift aid.
UNDERGRADUATE FINANCIAL AID (Fall 2012, est.) 2,859 applied for aid; of those 82% were deemed to have need. 99% of undergraduates with need received aid; of those 19% had need fully met. *Average percent of need met:* 28% (excluding resources awarded to replace EFC). *Average financial aid package:* $20,179 (excluding resources awarded to replace EFC). 17% of all full-time undergraduates had no need and received non-need-based gift aid.

GIFT AID (NEED-BASED) *Total amount:* $34,225,676 (12% federal, 9% state, 76% institutional, 3% external sources). *Receiving aid:* Freshmen: 65% (466); all full-time undergraduates: 56% (1,633). *Average award:* Freshmen: $6659; Undergraduates: $6432. *Scholarships, grants, and awards:* Federal Pell, FSEOG, state, private, college/university gift aid from institutional funds.
GIFT AID (NON-NEED-BASED) *Total amount:* $6,863,945 (2% state, 95% institutional, 3% external sources). *Receiving aid:* Freshmen: 82% (593). Undergraduates: 77% (2,263). *Average award:* Freshmen: $15,776. Undergraduates: $13,711. *Scholarships, grants, and awards by category: Academic interests/achievement:* 2,497 awards ($22,580,755 total): biological sciences, business, communication, computer science, education, English, foreign languages, general academic interests/achievements, humanities, mathematics, religion/biblical studies. *Creative arts/performance:* 30 awards ($97,500 total): music. *Special achievements/activities:* 6 awards ($74,928 total): community service. *Special characteristics:* 354 awards ($990,474 total): children and siblings of alumni, children of faculty/staff, relatives of clergy, religious affiliation, siblings of current students. *Tuition waivers:* Full or partial for children of alumni, employees or children of employees. *ROTC:* Army cooperative, Air Force cooperative.
LOANS *Student loans:* $18,755,504 (71% need-based, 29% non-need-based). 71% of past graduating class borrowed through all loan programs. *Average indebtedness per student:* $31,960. *Average need-based loan:* Freshmen: $2042. Undergraduates: $2708. *Parent loans:* $9,940,096 (45% need-based, 55% non-need-based). *Programs:* Federal Direct (Subsidized and Unsubsidized Stafford, PLUS), Perkins.
WORK-STUDY *Federal work-study:* Total amount: $434,084; 465 jobs averaging $1278. *State or other work-study/employment:* Total amount: $315,000 (100% non-need-based). 299 part-time jobs averaging $1261.
ATHLETIC AWARDS Total amount: $3,553,981 (59% need-based, 41% non-need-based).
APPLYING FOR FINANCIAL AID *Required financial aid forms:* FAFSA, state aid form. *Financial aid deadline:* 4/15. *Notification date:* Continuous beginning 3/1. Students must reply by 5/1 or within 2 weeks of notification.
CONTACT Mary Grant, Director of Financial Aid, Iona College, 715 North Avenue, New Rochelle, NY 10801-1890, 914-633-2676 or toll-free 800-231-IONA. *Fax:* 914-633-2486. *E-mail:* mgrant@iona.edu.
Website: http://www.iona.edu/.

IOWA STATE UNIVERSITY OF SCIENCE AND TECHNOLOGY
Ames, IA

Tuition & fees (IA res): $7726	Average undergraduate aid package: $11,821

ABOUT THE INSTITUTION State-supported, coed. *Awards:* certificates, bachelor's, master's, and doctoral degrees. 115 undergraduate majors. *Total enrollment:* 30,748. Undergraduates: 25,555. Freshmen: 5,366. Federal methodology is used as a basis for awarding need-based institutional aid.
UNDERGRADUATE EXPENSES for 2013–2014 *Application fee:* $40. *Tuition, state resident:* full-time $6648; part-time $277 per semester hour. *Tuition, nonresident:* full-time $18,760; part-time $782 per semester hour. *Required fees:* full-time $1078. Full-time tuition and fees vary according to class time, degree level, and program. Part-time tuition and fees vary according to class time, course load, degree level, and program. *College room and board:* $7721; *Room only:* $4093. Room and board charges vary according to board plan and housing facility.
FRESHMAN FINANCIAL AID (Fall 2011) 4,280 applied for aid; of those 68% were deemed to have need. 99% of freshmen with need received aid; of those 37% had need fully met. *Average percent of need met:* 84% (excluding resources awarded to replace EFC). *Average financial aid package:* $12,000 (excluding resources awarded to replace EFC). 31% of all full-time freshmen had no need and received non-need-based gift aid.
UNDERGRADUATE FINANCIAL AID (Fall 2011) 17,621 applied for aid; of those 72% were deemed to have need. 99% of undergraduates with need received aid; of those 37% had need fully met. *Average percent of need met:* 82% (excluding resources awarded to replace EFC). *Average financial aid package:* $11,821 (excluding resources awarded to replace EFC). 29% of all full-time undergraduates had no need and received non-need-based gift aid.

GIFT AID (NEED-BASED) *Total amount:* $78,896,274 (34% federal, 3% state, 58% institutional, 5% external sources). *Receiving aid:* Freshmen: 57% (2,848); all full-time undergraduates: 54% (12,390). *Average award:* Freshmen: $7846; Undergraduates: $6602. *Scholarships, grants, and awards:* Federal Pell, FSEOG, state, college/university gift aid from institutional funds.

GIFT AID (NON-NEED-BASED) *Total amount:* $28,700,499 (6% federal, 2% state, 70% institutional, 22% external sources). *Receiving aid:* Freshmen: 28% (1,394). Undergraduates: 27% (6,130). *Average award:* Freshmen: $3112. Undergraduates: $2664. *Scholarships, grants, and awards by category: Academic interests/achievement:* agriculture, architecture, area/ethnic studies, biological sciences, business, communication, computer science, education, engineering/technologies, English, foreign languages, general academic interests/achievements, health fields, home economics, humanities, international studies, library science, mathematics, military science, physical sciences, premedicine, social sciences. *Creative arts/performance:* applied art and design, art/fine arts, journalism/publications, music, theater/drama. *Special achievements/activities:* community service, general special achievements/activities, leadership, rodeo. *Special characteristics:* adult students, children and siblings of alumni, ethnic background, first-generation college students, general special characteristics, international students, local/state students, members of minority groups, out-of-state students. *ROTC:* Army, Naval, Air Force.

LOANS *Student loans:* $112,746,327 (62% need-based, 38% non-need-based). 65% of past graduating class borrowed through all loan programs. *Average indebtedness per student:* $30,374. *Average need-based loan:* Freshmen: $3349. Undergraduates: $4437. *Parent loans:* $29,251,890 (23% need-based, 77% non-need-based). *Programs:* Federal Direct (Subsidized and Unsubsidized Stafford, PLUS), Perkins, college/university, private loans.

WORK-STUDY *Federal work-study:* Total amount: $1,581,313; jobs available. *State or other work-study/employment:* Total amount: $1,387,438 (100% need-based). Part-time jobs available.

ATHLETIC AWARDS Total amount: $6,409,830 (54% need-based, 46% non-need-based).

APPLYING FOR FINANCIAL AID *Required financial aid form:* FAFSA. *Financial aid deadline (priority):* 3/1. *Notification date:* Continuous beginning 4/1. Students must reply by 5/1.

CONTACT Ms. Roberta Johnson, Director of Financial Aid, Iowa State University of Science and Technology, 0210 Beardshear Hall, Ames, IA 50011, 515-294-2223 or toll-free 800-262-3810. *Fax:* 515-294-3622. *E-mail:* rljohns@iastate.edu. *Website:* http://www.iastate.edu/.

IOWA WESLEYAN COLLEGE
Mount Pleasant, IA

Tuition & fees: $24,300	Average undergraduate aid package: $20,538

ABOUT THE INSTITUTION Independent United Methodist, coed. *Awards:* bachelor's degrees. 44 undergraduate majors. *Total enrollment:* 650. Undergraduates: 650. Freshmen: 111. Federal methodology is used as a basis for awarding need-based institutional aid.

UNDERGRADUATE EXPENSES for 2013–2014 *Application fee:* $20. *Comprehensive fee:* $32,280 includes full-time tuition ($24,300) and room and board ($7980). *College room only:* $3140. Room and board charges vary according to board plan and housing facility. *Part-time tuition:* $610 per credit hour. Part-time tuition and fees vary according to class time, course load, and location.

FRESHMAN FINANCIAL AID (Fall 2011) 105 applied for aid; of those 85% were deemed to have need. 100% of freshmen with need received aid; of those 4% had need fully met. *Average percent of need met:* 78% (excluding resources awarded to replace EFC). *Average financial aid package:* $23,474 (excluding resources awarded to replace EFC). 2% of all full-time freshmen had no need and received non-need-based gift aid.

UNDERGRADUATE FINANCIAL AID (Fall 2011) 529 applied for aid; of those 87% were deemed to have need. 100% of undergraduates with need received aid; of those 8% had need fully met. *Average percent of need met:* 73% (excluding resources awarded to replace EFC). *Average financial aid package:* $20,538 (excluding resources awarded to replace EFC). 11% of all full-time undergraduates had no need and received non-need-based gift aid.

GIFT AID (NEED-BASED) *Total amount:* $5,610,675 (27% federal, 13% state, 57% institutional, 3% external sources). *Receiving aid:* Freshmen: 79% (89); all full-time undergraduates: 78% (462). *Average award:* Freshmen: $17,878; Undergraduates:

$14,975. *Scholarships, grants, and awards:* Federal Pell, FSEOG, state, private, college/university gift aid from institutional funds.

GIFT AID (NON-NEED-BASED) *Total amount:* $20,616 (100% federal). *Average award:* Freshmen: $8750. Undergraduates: $8311. *Scholarships, grants, and awards by category: Academic interests/achievement:* 363 awards ($1,922,022 total): business, education, English, general academic interests/achievements, health fields, social sciences. *Creative arts/performance:* 42 awards ($84,902 total): art/fine arts, music. *Special characteristics:* 67 awards ($500,790 total): children of faculty/staff, international students. *Tuition waivers:* Full or partial for employees or children of employees.

LOANS *Student loans:* $4,739,802 (45% need-based, 55% non-need-based). 92% of past graduating class borrowed through all loan programs. *Average indebtedness per student:* $32,666. *Average need-based loan:* Freshmen: $3774. Undergraduates: $4380. *Parent loans:* $815,055 (100% need-based). *Programs:* Federal Direct (Subsidized and Unsubsidized Stafford, PLUS), Perkins, alternative loans.

WORK-STUDY *Federal work-study:* Total amount: $146,117; 115 jobs averaging $2000.

ATHLETIC AWARDS Total amount: $2,334,421 (100% need-based).

APPLYING FOR FINANCIAL AID *Required financial aid form:* FAFSA. *Financial aid deadline (priority):* 4/1. *Notification date:* Continuous beginning 3/15.

CONTACT Renae Armentrout, Director of Financial Aid, Iowa Wesleyan College, 601 North Main Street, Mount Pleasant, IA 52641-1398, 319-385-6242 or toll-free 800-582-2383. *Fax:* 319-385-6203. *E-mail:* rarmentrout@iwc.edu. *Website:* http://www.iwc.edu/.

ITHACA COLLEGE
Ithaca, NY

Tuition & fees: $37,000	Average undergraduate aid package: $30,772

ABOUT THE INSTITUTION Independent, coed. *Awards:* certificates, bachelor's, master's, and doctoral degrees. 102 undergraduate majors. *Total enrollment:* 6,760. Undergraduates: 6,276. Freshmen: 1,625. Institutional methodology is used as a basis for awarding need-based institutional aid.

UNDERGRADUATE EXPENSES for 2013–2014 *Application fee:* $60. *Comprehensive fee:* $50,400 includes full-time tuition ($37,000) and room and board ($13,400). *College room only:* $7200. Room and board charges vary according to board plan and housing facility. *Part-time tuition:* $1232 per credit hour.

FRESHMAN FINANCIAL AID (Fall 2012, est.) 1,372 applied for aid; of those 83% were deemed to have need. 100% of freshmen with need received aid; of those 57% had need fully met. *Average percent of need met:* 89% (excluding resources awarded to replace EFC). *Average financial aid package:* $31,780 (excluding resources awarded to replace EFC). 18% of all full-time freshmen had no need and received non-need-based gift aid.

UNDERGRADUATE FINANCIAL AID (Fall 2012, est.) 4,888 applied for aid; of those 87% were deemed to have need. 100% of undergraduates with need received aid; of those 45% had need fully met. *Average percent of need met:* 86% (excluding resources awarded to replace EFC). *Average financial aid package:* $30,772 (excluding resources awarded to replace EFC). 19% of all full-time undergraduates had no need and received non-need-based gift aid.

GIFT AID (NEED-BASED) *Total amount:* $88,281,913 (7% federal, 4% state, 87% institutional, 2% external sources). *Receiving aid:* Freshmen: 69% (1,087); all full-time undergraduates: 68% (4,152). *Average award:* Freshmen: $22,576; Undergraduates: $21,169. *Scholarships, grants, and awards:* Federal Pell, FSEOG, state, private, college/university gift aid from institutional funds.

GIFT AID (NON-NEED-BASED) *Total amount:* $18,025,085 (3% federal, 1% state, 90% institutional, 6% external sources). *Receiving aid:* Freshmen: 22% (350). Undergraduates: 15% (899). *Average award:* Freshmen: $10,967. Undergraduates: $10,666. *Scholarships, grants, and awards by category: Academic interests/achievement:* 3,945 awards ($39,066,023 total): communication, general academic interests/achievements. *Creative arts/performance:* 125 awards ($439,039 total): cinema/film/broadcasting, dance, journalism/publications, music, performing arts, theater/drama. *Special achievements/activities:* 274 awards ($1,575,607 total): leadership. *Special characteristics:* 698 awards ($4,435,592 total): children and siblings of alumni, children of faculty/staff, general special characteristics, members of minority groups, siblings of current students. *Tuition waivers:* Full or partial for children of alumni, employees or children of employees. **ROTC:** Army cooperative, Air Force cooperative.

LOANS *Student loans:* $33,155,019 (77% need-based, 23% non-need-based). *Average need-based loan:* Freshmen: $5346. Undergraduates: $6469. *Parent loans:* $30,914,107 (36% need-based, 64% non-need-based). *Programs:* Federal Direct (Subsidized and Unsubsidized Stafford, PLUS), Perkins, alternative loans.

WORK-STUDY *Federal work-study:* Total amount: $1,500,000; 3,332 jobs averaging $2350. *State or other work-study/employment:* Total amount: $11,488,525 (72% need-based, 28% non-need-based). 1,580 part-time jobs averaging $2398.

APPLYING FOR FINANCIAL AID *Required financial aid forms:* FAFSA, CSS Financial Aid PROFILE. *Financial aid deadline (priority):* 2/1. *Notification date:* Continuous beginning 2/15.

CONTACT Ms. Lisa Hoskey, Director of Student Financial Services, Ithaca College, 953 Danby Road, Ithaca, NY 14850-7002, 800-429-4275 or toll-free 800-429-4274. *Fax:* 607-274-1895. *E-mail:* finaid@ithaca.edu. *Website:* http://www.ithaca.edu/.

ITT TECHNICAL INSTITUTE
Tempe, AZ

CONTACT Financial Aid Office, ITT Technical Institute, 5005 S. Wendler Drive, Tempe, AZ 85282, 602-437-7500 or toll-free 800-879-4881. *Website:* http://www.itt-tech.edu/.

ITT TECHNICAL INSTITUTE
Clovis, CA

CONTACT Financial Aid Office, ITT Technical Institute, 362 N. Clovis Avenue, Clovis, CA 93612, 559-325-5400 or toll-free 800-564-9771. *Website:* http://www.itt-tech.edu/.

ITT TECHNICAL INSTITUTE
Concord, CA

CONTACT Financial Aid Office, ITT Technical Institute, 1140 Galaxy Way, Suite 400, Concord, CA 94520, 925-674-8200 or toll-free 800-211-7062. *Website:* http://www.itt-tech.edu/.

ITT TECHNICAL INSTITUTE
Corona, CA

CONTACT Financial Aid Office, ITT Technical Institute, 4160 Temescal Canyon Road, Suite 100, Corona, CA 92883, 951-277-5400 or toll-free 877-764-9661. *Website:* http://www.itt-tech.edu/.

ITT TECHNICAL INSTITUTE
Deerfield Beach, FL

CONTACT Financial Aid Office, ITT Technical Institute, 700 W. Hillsboro Boulevard, Suite 100, Building 1, Deerfield Beach, FL 33441, 954-360-4701 or toll-free 877-243-8548. *Website:* http://www.itt-tech.edu/.

ITT TECHNICAL INSTITUTE
West Palm Beach, FL

CONTACT Financial Aid Office, ITT Technical Institute, 1756 N. Congress Avenue, West Palm Beach, FL 33409, 561-233-4900 or toll-free 877-236-8164. *Website:* http://www.itt-tech.edu/.

ITT TECHNICAL INSTITUTE
Springfield, IL

CONTACT Financial Aid Office, ITT Technical Institute, 2501 Wabash Avenue, Springfield, IL 62704, 217-547-5700 or toll-free 877-263-2374. *Website:* http://www.itt-tech.edu/.

ITT TECHNICAL INSTITUTE
Indianapolis, IN

CONTACT Financial Aid Office, ITT Technical Institute, 2525 N. Shadeland Avenue, Suite 103, Indianapolis, IN 46219, 317-351-3800 or toll-free 877-264-1057. *Website:* http://www.itt-tech.edu/.

ITT TECHNICAL INSTITUTE
Indianapolis, IN

CONTACT Financial Aid Office, ITT Technical Institute, 9511 Angola Court, Indianapolis, IN 46268-1119, 317-875-8640 or toll-free 800-937-4488. *Website:* http://www.itt-tech.edu/.

ITT TECHNICAL INSTITUTE
South Bend, IN

CONTACT Financial Aid Office, ITT Technical Institute, 17390 Dugdale Drive, Suite 100, South Bend, IN 46635, 574-247-8300 or toll-free 877-474-1926. *Website:* http://www.itt-tech.edu/.

ITT TECHNICAL INSTITUTE
Overland Park, KS

CONTACT Financial Aid Office, ITT Technical Institute, 7600 West 119th Street, Suite 100, Overland Park, KS 66213, 913-253-1300 or toll-free 877-327-9026. *Website:* http://www.itt-tech.edu/.

ITT TECHNICAL INSTITUTE
Wichita, KS

CONTACT Financial Aid Office, ITT Technical Institute, 8111 E. 32nd Street North, Suite 103, Wichita, KS 67226, 316-609-4100 or toll-free 877-207-1047. *Website:* http://www.itt-tech.edu/.

ITT TECHNICAL INSTITUTE
Lexington, KY

CONTACT Financial Aid Office, ITT Technical Institute, 2473 Fortune Drive, Suite 180, Lexington, KY 40509, 859-246-3300 or toll-free 800-519-8151.
Website: http://www.itt-tech.edu/.

ITT TECHNICAL INSTITUTE
Hanover, MD

CONTACT Financial Aid Office, ITT Technical Institute, 7030 Dorsey Road, Suite 100, Hanover, MD 21076, 410-694-4700 or toll-free 877-243-6993.
Website: http://www.itt-tech.edu/.

ITT TECHNICAL INSTITUTE
Grand Rapids, MI

CONTACT Financial Aid Office, ITT Technical Institute, 3518 Plainfield Avenue NE, Grand Rapids, MI 49525, 616-365-4800 or toll-free 877-264-1715.
Website: http://www.itt-tech.edu/.

ITT TECHNICAL INSTITUTE
Southfield, MI

CONTACT Financial Aid Office, ITT Technical Institute, 26700 Lahser Road, Suite 100, Southfield, MI 48033, 248-603-6100 or toll-free 877-363-3221.
Website: http://www.itt-tech.edu/.

ITT TECHNICAL INSTITUTE
Madison, MS

CONTACT Financial Aid Office, ITT Technical Institute, 382 Galleria Parkway, Suite 100, Madison, MS 39110, 601-607-4500 or toll-free 800-209-2521.
Website: http://www.itt-tech.edu/.

ITT TECHNICAL INSTITUTE
Springfield, MO

CONTACT Financial Aid Office, ITT Technical Institute, 3216 South National Avenue, Springfield, MO 65807, 417-877-4800 or toll-free 877-219-4387.
Website: http://www.itt-tech.edu/.

ITT TECHNICAL INSTITUTE
Charlotte, NC

CONTACT Financial Aid Office, ITT Technical Institute, 10926 David Taylor Drive, Suite 100, Charlotte, NC 28262, 704-548-2300 or toll-free 877-243-7685.
Website: http://www.itt-tech.edu/.

ITT TECHNICAL INSTITUTE
Durham, NC

CONTACT Financial Aid Office, ITT Technical Institute, 3518 Westgate Drive, Suite 150, Durham, NC 27707, 919-401-1400 or toll-free 877-452-8662.
Website: http://www.itt-tech.edu/.

ITT TECHNICAL INSTITUTE
Oklahoma City, OK

CONTACT Financial Aid Office, ITT Technical Institute, 50 Penn Place Office Tower, 1900 Northwest Expressway, Suite 305R, Oklahoma City, OK 73118, 405-810-4100 or toll-free 800-518-1612.
Website: http://www.itt-tech.edu/.

ITT TECHNICAL INSTITUTE
Salem, OR

CONTACT Financial Aid Office, ITT Technical Institute, 4825 Commercial Street SE, Suite 100, Salem, OR 97302-2177, 503-576-2300 or toll-free 877-273-7397.
Website: http://www.itt-tech.edu/.

ITT TECHNICAL INSTITUTE
Germantown, WI

CONTACT Financial Aid Office, ITT Technical Institute, W177 N9886 Rivercrest Drive, Suite 200, Germantown, WI 53022, 262-257-7100 or toll-free 877-213-8538.
Website: http://www.itt-tech.edu/.

JACKSON STATE UNIVERSITY
Jackson, MS

Tuition & fees (MS res): $5988	Average undergraduate aid package: $10,770

ABOUT THE INSTITUTION State-supported, coed. 42 undergraduate majors. Federal methodology is used as a basis for awarding need-based institutional aid.

UNDERGRADUATE EXPENSES for 2013–2014 *Tuition, state resident:* full-time $5988. *Tuition, nonresident:* full-time $14,676. Full-time tuition and fees vary according to course load. Part-time tuition and fees vary according to course load. *College room and board:* $6996; *Room only:* $4214. Room and board charges vary according to board plan and housing facility.

FRESHMAN FINANCIAL AID (Fall 2011) 612 applied for aid; of those 96% were deemed to have need. 100% of freshmen with need received aid; of those 6% had need fully met. *Average percent of need met:* 58% (excluding resources awarded to replace EFC). *Average financial aid package:* $13,118 (excluding resources awarded to replace EFC). 50% of all full-time freshmen had no need and received non-need-based gift aid.

UNDERGRADUATE FINANCIAL AID (Fall 2011) 5,059 applied for aid; of those 96% were deemed to have need. 100% of undergraduates with need received aid; of those 6% had need fully met. *Average percent of need met:* 54% (excluding resources awarded to replace EFC). *Average financial aid package:* $10,770 (excluding resources awarded to replace EFC). 24% of all full-time undergraduates had no need and received non-need-based gift aid.

GIFT AID (NEED-BASED) *Total amount:* $25,565,728 (100% federal). *Receiving aid:* Freshmen: 79% (498); all full-time undergraduates: 75% (3,954). *Average award:* Freshmen: $5248; Undergraduates: $4981. *Scholarships, grants, and awards:* Federal Pell, FSEOG, state, private, college/university gift aid from institutional funds.

GIFT AID (NON-NEED-BASED) *Total amount:* $20,510,109 (12% state, 81% institutional, 7% external sources). *Receiving aid:* Freshmen: 56% (351). Undergraduates: 32% (1,702). *Average award:* Freshmen: $8706. Undergraduates: $7325. *Scholarships, grants, and awards by category:* Academic interests/achievement: general academic interests/achievements. Creative arts/performance: music. Special achievements/activities: leadership. Special characteristics: children of faculty/staff.

LOANS *Student loans:* $81,292,998 (28% need-based, 72% non-need-based). *Average need-based loan:* Freshmen: $3315. Undergraduates: $4161. *Parent loans:* $2,194,669 (100% non-need-based). *Programs:* Federal Direct (Subsidized and Unsubsidized Stafford, PLUS), Perkins.

WORK-STUDY *Federal work-study:* Total amount: $2,321,750; jobs available.

APPLYING FOR FINANCIAL AID *Required financial aid forms:* FAFSA, institution's own form, state aid form. *Financial aid deadline (priority):* 4/15. *Notification date:* Continuous beginning 5/1.

CONTACT Mrs. B. J. Moncure, Director of Financial Aid, Jackson State University, 1400 J.R. Lynch Street, PO Box 17065, Jackson, MS 39217, 601-979-2227 or toll-free 800-848-6817. *Fax:* 601-979-2237.
Website: http://www.jsums.edu/.

JACKSONVILLE STATE UNIVERSITY
Jacksonville, AL

Tuition & fees (AL res): $7950	Average undergraduate aid package: $8643

ABOUT THE INSTITUTION State-supported, coed. *Awards:* certificates, bachelor's, master's, and doctoral degrees. 58 undergraduate majors. *Total enrollment:* 9,161. Undergraduates: 7,991. Freshmen: 1,332. Federal methodology is used as a basis for awarding need-based institutional aid.
UNDERGRADUATE EXPENSES for 2013–2014 *Application fee:* $30. *Tuition, state resident:* full-time $7950. *Tuition, nonresident:* full-time $15,900. *College room and board:* $6300; *Room only:* $3550. Room and board charges vary according to board plan and housing facility.
FRESHMAN FINANCIAL AID (Fall 2011) 1,310 applied for aid; of those 98% were deemed to have need. 100% of freshmen with need received aid. *Average financial aid package:* $8630 (excluding resources awarded to replace EFC).
UNDERGRADUATE FINANCIAL AID (Fall 2011) 5,377 applied for aid; of those 98% were deemed to have need. 100% of undergraduates with need received aid. *Average financial aid package:* $8643 (excluding resources awarded to replace EFC).
GIFT AID (NEED-BASED) *Total amount:* $28,486,135 (59% federal, 1% state, 37% institutional, 3% external sources). *Receiving aid:* Freshmen: 48% (666); all full-time undergraduates: 52% (3,218). *Average award:* Freshmen: $4578; Undergraduates: $4415. *Scholarships, grants, and awards:* Federal Pell, FSEOG, state, private, college/university gift aid from institutional funds.
GIFT AID (NON-NEED-BASED) *Receiving aid:* Freshmen: 54% (750). Undergraduates: 33% (2,047). *Scholarships, grants, and awards by category:* Academic interests/achievement: biological sciences, business, communication, computer science, education, English, health fields, home economics, humanities, mathematics, military science, physical sciences, social sciences. *Creative arts/performance:* art/fine arts, journalism/publications, music, theater/drama. *Special achievements/activities:* general special achievements/activities. *Tuition waivers:* Full or partial for employees or children of employees. *ROTC:* Army.
LOANS *Student loans:* $49,375,056 (50% need-based, 50% non-need-based). *Average need-based loan:* Freshmen: $1000. Undergraduates: $970. *Parent loans:* $2,674,233 (100% non-need-based). *Programs:* Federal Direct (Subsidized and Unsubsidized Stafford, PLUS), state, college/university.
WORK-STUDY *Federal work-study:* Total amount: $363,185; 161 jobs averaging $1235. *State or other work-study/employment:* Total amount: $1,243,777 (100% non-need-based). Part-time jobs available.
ATHLETIC AWARDS Total amount: $4,937,640 (100% non-need-based).
APPLYING FOR FINANCIAL AID *Required financial aid forms:* FAFSA, institution's own form. *Financial aid deadline (priority):* 3/15. *Notification date:* Continuous beginning 4/15. Students must reply within 2 weeks of notification.
CONTACT Ms. Vickie Adams, Director of Financial Aid, Jacksonville State University, 700 Pelham Road North, Jacksonville, AL 36265-9982, 256-782-5006 Ext. 8399 or toll-free 800-231-5291. *Fax:* 256-782-5476. *E-mail:* finaid@jsu.edu.
Website: http://www.jsu.edu/.

JACKSONVILLE UNIVERSITY
Jacksonville, FL

Tuition & fees: $59,800	Average undergraduate aid package: $21,276

ABOUT THE INSTITUTION Independent, coed. *Awards:* certificates, bachelor's, master's, and doctoral degrees. 60 undergraduate majors. *Total enrollment:* 3,936. Undergraduates: 3,319. Freshmen: 495. Federal methodology is used as a basis for awarding need-based institutional aid.
UNDERGRADUATE EXPENSES for 2013–2014 *Application fee:* $30. *Comprehensive fee:* $99,730 includes full-time tuition ($29,900), mandatory fees ($29,900), and room and board ($39,930). *College room only:* $6190. Room and board charges vary according to board plan and housing facility. *Part-time tuition:* $498 per credit hour. *Part-time fees:* $498 per credit hour.
FRESHMAN FINANCIAL AID (Fall 2012, est.) 494 applied for aid; of those 84% were deemed to have need. 100% of freshmen with need received aid; of those 37% had need fully met. *Average percent of need met:* 83% (excluding resources awarded to replace EFC). *Average financial aid package:* $24,934 (excluding resources awarded to replace EFC). 12% of all full-time freshmen had no need and received non-need-based gift aid.
UNDERGRADUATE FINANCIAL AID (Fall 2012, est.) 2,093 applied for aid; of those 77% were deemed to have need. 100% of undergraduates with need received aid; of those 34% had need fully met. *Average percent of need met:* 77% (excluding resources awarded to replace EFC). *Average financial aid package:* $21,276 (excluding resources awarded to replace EFC). 17% of all full-time undergraduates had no need and received non-need-based gift aid.
GIFT AID (NEED-BASED) *Total amount:* $24,179,739 (18% federal, 14% state, 68% institutional). *Receiving aid:* Freshmen: 84% (416); all full-time undergraduates: 75% (1,615). *Average award:* Freshmen: $19,501; Undergraduates: $15,502. *Scholarships, grants, and awards:* Federal Pell, FSEOG, state, private, college/university gift aid from institutional funds.
GIFT AID (NON-NEED-BASED) *Total amount:* $3,730,158 (12% state, 88% institutional). *Receiving aid:* Freshmen: 16% (78). Undergraduates: 22% (478). *Average award:* Freshmen: $14,182. Undergraduates: $8706. *Scholarships, grants, and awards by category:* Academic interests/achievement: general academic interests/achievements. *Creative arts/performance:* art/fine arts, general creative arts/performance, music, theater/drama. *Special achievements/activities:* general special achievements/activities, leadership. *Special characteristics:* children of educators, children of faculty/staff, international students. *Tuition waivers:* Full or partial for employees or children of employees. *ROTC:* Army, Naval.
LOANS *Student loans:* $18,544,366 (86% need-based, 14% non-need-based). *Average need-based loan:* Freshmen: $2439. Undergraduates: $301. *Parent loans:* $3,240,465 (89% need-based, 11% non-need-based). *Programs:* Federal Direct (Subsidized and Unsubsidized Stafford, PLUS), Perkins.
WORK-STUDY *Federal work-study:* Total amount: $259,110; 218 jobs averaging $1187.
ATHLETIC AWARDS Total amount: $3,848,444 (65% need-based, 35% non-need-based).
APPLYING FOR FINANCIAL AID *Required financial aid forms:* FAFSA, institution's own form, proof of medical insurance coverage and waiver form. *Financial aid deadline (priority):* 3/31. *Notification date:* Continuous beginning 2/20.
CONTACT Breanne Simkin, Director of Financial Aid, Jacksonville University, 2800 University Boulevard North, Jacksonville, FL 32211, 904-256-7243 or toll-free 800-225-2027. *Fax:* 904-256-7148. *E-mail:* bsimkin@ju.edu.
Website: http://www.ju.edu/.

JAMES MADISON UNIVERSITY
Harrisonburg, VA

Tuition & fees (VA res): $9176	Average undergraduate aid package: $9240

ABOUT THE INSTITUTION State-supported, coed. *Awards:* certificates, bachelor's, master's, and doctoral degrees (also offers specialist in education degree). 48 undergraduate majors. *Total enrollment:* 19,722. Undergraduates: 17,900.

Freshmen: 4,029. Federal methodology is used as a basis for awarding need-based institutional aid.

UNDERGRADUATE EXPENSES for 2013–2014 *Application fee:* $50. *Tuition, area resident:* part-time $169 per credit hour. *Tuition, state resident:* full-time $5104. *Tuition, nonresident:* full-time $19,582; part-time $633 per credit hour. *Required fees:* full-time $4072. *College room and board:* $8873; *Room only:* $4451. Room and board charges vary according to board plan. *Payment plan:* Tuition prepayment.

FRESHMAN FINANCIAL AID (Fall 2012, est.) 3,123 applied for aid; of those 60% were deemed to have need. 87% of freshmen with need received aid; of those 89% had need fully met. *Average percent of need met:* 41% (excluding resources awarded to replace EFC). *Average financial aid package:* $7604 (excluding resources awarded to replace EFC). 3% of all full-time freshmen had no need and received non-need-based gift aid.

UNDERGRADUATE FINANCIAL AID (Fall 2012, est.) 10,026 applied for aid; of those 68% were deemed to have need. 91% of undergraduates with need received aid; of those 75% had need fully met. *Average percent of need met:* 46% (excluding resources awarded to replace EFC). *Average financial aid package:* $9240 (excluding resources awarded to replace EFC). 1% of all full-time undergraduates had no need and received non-need-based gift aid.

GIFT AID (NEED-BASED) *Total amount:* $29,752,382 (34% federal, 24% state, 32% institutional, 10% external sources). *Receiving aid:* Freshmen: 20% (867); all full-time undergraduates: 17% (2,944). *Average award:* Freshmen: $7556; Undergraduates: $7405. *Scholarships, grants, and awards:* Federal Pell, FSEOG, state, private, college/university gift aid from institutional funds.

GIFT AID (NON-NEED-BASED) *Total amount:* $4,412,502 (3% state, 83% institutional, 14% external sources). *Receiving aid:* Freshmen: 4% (163). Undergraduates: 3% (563). *Average award:* Freshmen: $3537. Undergraduates: $3126. *Scholarships, grants, and awards by category: Academic interests/achievement:* architecture, biological sciences, business, computer science, education, engineering/technologies, English, general academic interests/achievements, health fields, humanities, international studies, mathematics, military science, physical sciences, premedicine, religion/biblical studies, social sciences. *Creative arts/performance:* art/fine arts, cinema/film/broadcasting, dance, journalism/publications, music, theater/drama. *Special achievements/activities:* cheerleading/drum major, general special achievements/activities, leadership. *Special characteristics:* children and siblings of alumni, children of faculty/staff, handicapped students, international students, local/state students, members of minority groups, out-of-state students, siblings of current students. *Tuition waivers:* Full or partial for employees or children of employees. *ROTC:* Army, Air Force cooperative.

LOANS *Student loans:* $56,689,832 (39% need-based, 61% non-need-based). 54% of past graduating class borrowed through all loan programs. *Average indebtedness per student:* $22,792. *Average need-based loan:* Freshmen: $3624. Undergraduates: $4628. *Programs:* Federal Direct (Subsidized and Unsubsidized Stafford, PLUS), Perkins.

WORK-STUDY *Federal work-study:* Total amount: $472,500; jobs available. *State or other work-study/employment:* Total amount: $6,568,800 (100% non-need-based). Part-time jobs available.

ATHLETIC AWARDS Total amount: $5,889,747 (100% non-need-based).

APPLYING FOR FINANCIAL AID *Required financial aid form:* FAFSA. *Financial aid deadline (priority):* 3/1. *Notification date:* Continuous beginning 4/1. Students must reply within 4 weeks of notification.

CONTACT Lisa L. Tumer, Director of Financial Aid and Scholarships, James Madison University, 800 South Main Street, MSC 3519, Harrisonburg, VA 22807, 540-568-7820. *Fax:* 540-568-7994. *E-mail:* fin_aid@jmu.edu. *Website:* http://www.jmu.edu/.

JAMESTOWN COLLEGE
Jamestown, ND

ABOUT THE INSTITUTION Independent Presbyterian, coed. *Awards:* bachelor's and master's degrees. 44 undergraduate majors. *Total enrollment:* 945. Undergraduates: 939. Freshmen: 223.

GIFT AID (NEED-BASED) *Scholarships, grants, and awards:* Federal Pell, FSEOG, state, private, college/university gift aid from institutional funds, Federal Nursing.

GIFT AID (NON-NEED-BASED) *Scholarships, grants, and awards by category: Academic interests/achievement:* general academic interests/achievements, physical sciences. *Creative arts/performance:* art/fine arts, music, theater/drama.

Special achievements/activities: community service, leadership. *Special characteristics:* children of faculty/staff, general special characteristics, international students, relatives of clergy, religious affiliation, siblings of current students, spouses of current students, veterans.

LOANS *Programs:* Federal Direct (Subsidized and Unsubsidized Stafford, PLUS), Perkins, alternative loans.

WORK-STUDY *Federal work-study:* Total amount: $221,888; 243 jobs averaging $913. *State or other work-study/employment:* Total amount: $57,201 (100% non-need-based). 73 part-time jobs averaging $784.

APPLYING FOR FINANCIAL AID *Required financial aid form:* FAFSA.

CONTACT Margery Michael, Director of Financial Aid, Jamestown College, 6085 College Lane, Jamestown, ND 58405, 701-252-3467 Ext. 5568 or toll-free 800-336-2554. *Fax:* 701-253-4318. *E-mail:* mmichael@jc.edu. *Website:* http://www.jc.edu/.

JARVIS CHRISTIAN COLLEGE
Hawkins, TX

ABOUT THE INSTITUTION Independent Christian Church (Disciples of Christ), coed. *Awards:* bachelor's degrees. 16 undergraduate majors. *Total enrollment:* 603. Undergraduates: 603. Freshmen: 177.

GIFT AID (NEED-BASED) *Scholarships, grants, and awards:* Federal Pell, FSEOG, state, private, college/university gift aid from institutional funds, United Negro College Fund.

GIFT AID (NON-NEED-BASED) *Scholarships, grants, and awards by category: Academic interests/achievement:* education, general academic interests/achievements. *Special characteristics:* religious affiliation.

LOANS *Programs:* Federal Direct (Subsidized and Unsubsidized Stafford, PLUS), Perkins.

WORK-STUDY *Federal work-study:* Total amount: $229,229; 149 jobs averaging $1538. *State or other work-study/employment:* Total amount: $4631 (100% need-based). 2 part-time jobs averaging $2315.

APPLYING FOR FINANCIAL AID *Required financial aid form:* FAFSA.

CONTACT Alice Copeland, Director of Financial Aid, Jarvis Christian College, PO Box 1470, Hawkins, TX 75765, 903-730-4890 Ext. 2402. *Fax:* 903-730-4891. *E-mail:* alice.copeland@jarvis.edu. *Website:* http://www.jarvis.edu/.

JEFFERSON COLLEGE OF HEALTH SCIENCES
Roanoke, VA

Tuition & fees: N/R	Average undergraduate aid package: $12,422

ABOUT THE INSTITUTION Independent, coed. 11 undergraduate majors. Federal methodology is used as a basis for awarding need-based institutional aid.

FRESHMAN FINANCIAL AID (Fall 2011) 294 applied for aid; of those 63% were deemed to have need. 62% of freshmen with need received aid; of those 5% had need fully met. *Average percent of need met:* 38% (excluding resources awarded to replace EFC). *Average financial aid package:* $9895 (excluding resources awarded to replace EFC). 1% of all full-time freshmen had no need and received non-need-based gift aid.

UNDERGRADUATE FINANCIAL AID (Fall 2011) 1,427 applied for aid; of those 74% were deemed to have need. 78% of undergraduates with need received aid; of those 8% had need fully met. *Average percent of need met:* 47% (excluding resources awarded to replace EFC). *Average financial aid package:* $12,422 (excluding resources awarded to replace EFC). 3% of all full-time undergraduates had no need and received non-need-based gift aid.

GIFT AID (NEED-BASED) *Total amount:* $7,314,775 (29% federal, 22% state, 35% institutional, 14% external sources). *Receiving aid:* Freshmen: 15% (114); all full-time undergraduates: 41% (807). *Average award:* Freshmen: $7879; Undergraduates: $8533. *Scholarships, grants, and awards:* Federal Pell, FSEOG, state, private, college/university gift aid from institutional funds.

GIFT AID (NON-NEED-BASED) *Total amount:* $994,444 (21% state, 23% institutional, 56% external sources). *Receiving aid:* Freshmen: 1% (5). Undergraduates: 2% (34). *Average award:* Freshmen: $4090. Undergraduates: $3378. *Scholarships, grants, and awards by category: Academic interests/achievement:* 748 awards ($2,141,304 total): biological sciences, health fields. *Special characteristics:* 650 awards ($1,519,058 total): local/state students.

LOANS *Student loans:* $6,764,031 (88% need-based, 12% non-need-based). 60% of past graduating class borrowed through all loan programs. *Average indebtedness per student:* $17,024. *Average need-based loan:* Freshmen: $3817. Undergraduates: $4988. *Parent loans:* $1,128,772 (67% need-based, 33% non-need-based). *Programs:* Federal Direct (Subsidized and Unsubsidized Stafford, PLUS), alternative loans.

WORK-STUDY *Federal work-study:* Total amount: $82,705; 129 jobs averaging $736. *State or other work-study/employment:* Total amount: $122,264 (87% need-based, 13% non-need-based). 116 part-time jobs averaging $1137.

APPLYING FOR FINANCIAL AID *Required financial aid forms:* FAFSA, state aid form. *Financial aid deadline (priority):* 5/1. *Notification date:* Continuous beginning 5/1.

CONTACT Debra A. Johnson, Director of Financial Aid, Jefferson College of Health Sciences, 101 Elm Avenue SE, Roanoke, VA 24013-2222, 540-985-8492 or toll-free 888-985-8483. *Fax:* 540-224-6916. *E-mail:* djohnson@jchs.edu. *Website:* http://www.jchs.edu/.

THE JEWISH THEOLOGICAL SEMINARY
New York, NY

CONTACT Linda Levine, Registrar/Director of Financial Aid, The Jewish Theological Seminary, 3080 Broadway, New York, NY 10027-4649, 212-678-8007. *Fax:* 212-678-8947. *E-mail:* financialaid@jtsa.edu. *Website:* http://www.jtsa.edu/.

JOHN BROWN UNIVERSITY
Siloam Springs, AR

Tuition & fees: $22,734	Average undergraduate aid package: $19,072

ABOUT THE INSTITUTION Independent interdenominational, coed. *Awards:* associate, bachelor's, and master's degrees. 87 undergraduate majors. *Total enrollment:* 2,215. Undergraduates: 1,779. Freshmen: 318. Federal methodology is used as a basis for awarding need-based institutional aid.

UNDERGRADUATE EXPENSES for 2013–2014 *Application fee:* $25. *Comprehensive fee:* $30,996 includes full-time tuition ($21,736), mandatory fees ($998), and room and board ($8262). Full-time tuition and fees vary according to course load. Room and board charges vary according to board plan and housing facility. *Part-time tuition:* $694 per credit. Part-time tuition and fees vary according to course load.

FRESHMAN FINANCIAL AID (Fall 2012, est.) 266 applied for aid; of those 85% were deemed to have need. 100% of freshmen with need received aid; of those 16% had need fully met. *Average percent of need met:* 76% (excluding resources awarded to replace EFC). *Average financial aid package:* $20,817 (excluding resources awarded to replace EFC). 27% of all full-time freshmen had no need and received non-need-based gift aid.

UNDERGRADUATE FINANCIAL AID (Fall 2012, est.) 1,033 applied for aid; of those 87% were deemed to have need. 100% of undergraduates with need received aid; of those 16% had need fully met. *Average percent of need met:* 83% (excluding resources awarded to replace EFC). *Average financial aid package:* $19,072 (excluding resources awarded to replace EFC). 27% of all full-time undergraduates had no need and received non-need-based gift aid.

GIFT AID (NEED-BASED) *Total amount:* $12,045,567 (16% federal, 10% state, 72% institutional, 2% external sources). *Receiving aid:* Freshmen: 65% (207); all full-time undergraduates: 65% (831). *Average award:* Freshmen: $16,350; Undergraduates: $14,709. *Scholarships, grants, and awards:* Federal Pell, FSEOG, state, private, college/university gift aid from institutional funds.

GIFT AID (NON-NEED-BASED) *Total amount:* $7,417,841 (5% state, 67% institutional, 28% external sources). *Receiving aid:* Freshmen: 65% (207). Undergraduates: 65% (831). *Average award:* Freshmen: $13,998. Undergraduates:

$13,752. *Scholarships, grants, and awards by category: Academic interests/achievement:* general academic interests/achievements. *Creative arts/performance:* art/fine arts, journalism/publications, music, theater/drama. *Tuition waivers:* Full or partial for employees or children of employees. *ROTC:* Army cooperative, Air Force cooperative.

LOANS *Student loans:* $5,481,568 (61% need-based, 39% non-need-based). 57% of past graduating class borrowed through all loan programs. *Average indebtedness per student:* $24,160. *Average need-based loan:* Freshmen: $3301. Undergraduates: $3231. *Parent loans:* $1,302,572 (11% need-based, 89% non-need-based). *Programs:* Federal Direct (Subsidized and Unsubsidized Stafford, PLUS), Perkins, college/university.

WORK-STUDY *Federal work-study:* Total amount: $802,400; jobs available. *State or other work-study/employment:* Total amount: $359,250 (64% need-based, 36% non-need-based). Part-time jobs available.

ATHLETIC AWARDS Total amount: $1,803,200 (43% need-based, 57% non-need-based).

APPLYING FOR FINANCIAL AID *Required financial aid forms:* FAFSA, state aid form. *Financial aid deadline (priority):* 3/1. *Notification date:* Continuous beginning 3/1. Students must reply by 5/1 or within 2 weeks of notification.

CONTACT Mr. Kim Eldridge, Director of Student Financial Aid, John Brown University, 2000 West University Street, Siloam Springs, AR 72761-2121, 479-524-7424 or toll-free 877-JBU-INFO. *Fax:* 479-524-7405. *E-mail:* keldridg@jbu.edu. *Website:* http://www.jbu.edu/.

JOHN CARROLL UNIVERSITY
University Heights, OH

Tuition & fees: $34,480	Average undergraduate aid package: $26,574

ABOUT THE INSTITUTION Independent Roman Catholic (Jesuit), coed. *Awards:* certificates, bachelor's, and master's degrees. 53 undergraduate majors. *Total enrollment:* 3,583. Undergraduates: 2,949. Freshmen: 681. Federal methodology is used as a basis for awarding need-based institutional aid.

UNDERGRADUATE EXPENSES for 2013–2014 *One-time required fee:* $325. *Comprehensive fee:* $44,520 includes full-time tuition ($33,330), mandatory fees ($1150), and room and board ($10,040). Room and board charges vary according to board plan and housing facility. *Part-time tuition:* $1016 per credit. Part-time tuition and fees vary according to course load.

FRESHMAN FINANCIAL AID (Fall 2012, est.) 637 applied for aid; of those 81% were deemed to have need. 100% of freshmen with need received aid; of those 17% had need fully met. *Average percent of need met:* 81% (excluding resources awarded to replace EFC). *Average financial aid package:* $27,889 (excluding resources awarded to replace EFC). 23% of all full-time freshmen had no need and received non-need-based gift aid.

UNDERGRADUATE FINANCIAL AID (Fall 2012, est.) 2,510 applied for aid; of those 87% were deemed to have need. 100% of undergraduates with need received aid; of those 16% had need fully met. *Average percent of need met:* 78% (excluding resources awarded to replace EFC). *Average financial aid package:* $26,574 (excluding resources awarded to replace EFC). 20% of all full-time undergraduates had no need and received non-need-based gift aid.

GIFT AID (NEED-BASED) *Total amount:* $25,172,984 (14% federal, 5% state, 80% institutional, 1% external sources). *Receiving aid:* Freshmen: 75% (513); all full-time undergraduates: 57% (1,624). *Average award:* Freshmen: $23,065; Undergraduates: $21,571. *Scholarships, grants, and awards:* Federal Pell, FSEOG, state, private, college/university gift aid from institutional funds.

GIFT AID (NON-NEED-BASED) *Total amount:* $28,672,819 (98% institutional, 2% external sources). *Receiving aid:* Freshmen: 76% (517). Undergraduates: 57% (1,630). *Average award:* Freshmen: $15,167. Undergraduates: $13,828. *Scholarships, grants, and awards by category: Academic interests/achievement:* biological sciences, business, communication, computer science, education, English, foreign languages, health fields, mathematics, military science, physical sciences, pre-medicine, religion/biblical studies, social sciences. *Special achievements/activities:* community service, leadership. *Special characteristics:* children of educators, children of faculty/staff, local/state students, veterans, veterans' children. *Tuition waivers:* Full or partial for employees or children of employees, senior citizens. *ROTC:* Army.

LOANS *Student loans:* $17,749,530 (71% need-based, 29% non-need-based). 77% of past graduating class borrowed through all loan programs. *Average indebtedness*

per student: $31,727. **Average need-based loan:** Freshmen: $2976. Undergraduates: $4164. **Parent loans:** $4,665,422 (48% need-based, 52% non-need-based). **Programs:** Federal Direct (Subsidized and Unsubsidized Stafford, PLUS), Perkins.
WORK-STUDY *Federal work-study:* Total amount: $719,883; jobs available. *State or other work-study/employment:* Total amount: $1,300,476 (42% need-based, 58% non-need-based). Part-time jobs available.
APPLYING FOR FINANCIAL AID *Required financial aid form:* FAFSA. *Financial aid deadline:* 3/15 (priority: 2/15). **Notification date:** Continuous beginning 2/15. Students must reply by 5/1 or within 4 weeks of notification.
CONTACT Ms. Claudia A. Wenzel, Director of Financial Aid, John Carroll University, 20700 North Park Boulevard, University Heights, OH 44118-4581, 216-397-4248 or toll-free 888-335-6800. *Fax:* 216-397-3098. *E-mail:* jcuofa@jcu.edu. *Website:* http://www.jcu.edu/.

JOHN F. KENNEDY UNIVERSITY
Pleasant Hill, CA

CONTACT Mindy Bergeron, Director of Financial Aid, John F. Kennedy University, 100 Ellinwood Way, Pleasant Hill, CA 94523, 925-969-3385 or toll-free 800-696-JFKU. *Fax:* 925-969-3390. *E-mail:* bergeron@jfku.edu. *Website:* http://www.jfku.edu/.

JOHN JAY COLLEGE OF CRIMINAL JUSTICE OF THE CITY UNIVERSITY OF NEW YORK
New York, NY

Tuition & fees (NY res): $5760	Average undergraduate aid package: $10,150

ABOUT THE INSTITUTION State and locally supported, coed. **Awards:** certificates, associate, bachelor's, and master's degrees. 17 undergraduate majors. **Total enrollment:** 14,996. Undergraduates: 13,167. Freshmen: 1,908. Federal methodology is used as a basis for awarding need-based institutional aid.
UNDERGRADUATE EXPENSES for 2013–2014 *Application fee:* $65. *Tuition, state resident:* full-time $5430. *Tuition, nonresident:* full-time $14,550. *Required fees:* full-time $330. Full-time tuition and fees vary according to course load and program. Part-time tuition and fees vary according to course load and program.
FRESHMAN FINANCIAL AID (Fall 2011) 2,774 applied for aid; of those 89% were deemed to have need. 87% of freshmen with need received aid. *Average percent of need met:* 85% (excluding resources awarded to replace EFC). *Average financial aid package:* $10,150 (excluding resources awarded to replace EFC).
UNDERGRADUATE FINANCIAL AID (Fall 2011) 8,662 applied for aid; of those 85% were deemed to have need. 92% of undergraduates with need received aid. *Average percent of need met:* 85% (excluding resources awarded to replace EFC). *Average financial aid package:* $10,150 (excluding resources awarded to replace EFC).
GIFT AID (NEED-BASED) *Total amount:* $48,580,957 (69% federal, 30% state, 1% institutional). *Receiving aid:* Freshmen: 59% (1,829); all full-time undergraduates: 68% (6,711). *Average award:* Freshmen: $3175; Undergraduates: $3175. **Scholarships, grants, and awards:** Federal Pell, FSEOG, state, college/university gift aid from institutional funds.
GIFT AID (NON-NEED-BASED) *Receiving aid:* Freshmen: 6% (200). Undergraduates: 2% (196). **Scholarships, grants, and awards by category:** Academic interests/achievement: general academic interests/achievements. **Tuition waivers:** Full or partial for senior citizens.
LOANS *Student loans:* $30,088,600 (100% need-based). 20% of past graduating class borrowed through all loan programs. *Average indebtedness per student:* $11,890. *Average need-based loan:* Freshmen: $3500. Undergraduates: $3500. **Programs:** Federal Direct (Subsidized and Unsubsidized Stafford, PLUS), Perkins.
WORK-STUDY *Federal work-study:* Total amount: $715,779; jobs available. *State or other work-study/employment:* Part-time jobs available.

APPLYING FOR FINANCIAL AID *Required financial aid forms:* FAFSA, state aid form. *Financial aid deadline:* Continuous. **Notification date:** 4/1. Students must reply within 2 weeks of notification.
CONTACT Sylvia Lopez-Crespo, Director of Financial Aid, John Jay College of Criminal Justice of the City University of New York, 445 West 59th Street, New York, NY 10019-1093, 212-237-8897 or toll-free 877-JOHNJAY. *Fax:* 212-237-8936. *E-mail:* slopez@jjay.cuny.edu. *Website:* http://www.jjay.cuny.edu/.

JOHN PAUL THE GREAT CATHOLIC UNIVERSITY
San Diego, CA

Tuition & fees: N/R	Average undergraduate aid package: N/A

ABOUT THE INSTITUTION Independent religious, coed. Both federal and institutional methodology are used as a basis for awarding need-based institutional aid.
FRESHMAN FINANCIAL AID (Fall 2011) 28 applied for aid; of those 100% were deemed to have need. 100% of freshmen with need received aid.
UNDERGRADUATE FINANCIAL AID (Fall 2011) 102 applied for aid; of those 100% were deemed to have need. 100% of undergraduates with need received aid.
GIFT AID (NEED-BASED) *Total amount:* $230,046 (13% federal, 87% institutional). *Receiving aid:* Freshmen: 93% (28); all full-time undergraduates: 78% (102). **Scholarships, grants, and awards:** Federal Pell, private, college/university gift aid from institutional funds.
LOANS *Student loans:* $182,019 (28% need-based, 72% non-need-based). **Parent loans:** $31,812 (100% non-need-based). **Programs:** Federal Direct (Subsidized and Unsubsidized Stafford, PLUS), private loans.
APPLYING FOR FINANCIAL AID *Required financial aid form:* FAFSA. *Financial aid deadline:* Continuous. **Notification date:** Continuous beginning 1/15. Students must reply by 5/1 or within 4 weeks of notification.
CONTACT Lisa Williams, Director of Financial Aid, John Paul the Great Catholic University, 10174 Old Grove Road, Suite 200, San Diego, CA 92131, 858-653-6740 Ext. 1303. *Fax:* 858-653-3791. *E-mail:* lwilliams@jpcatholic.com. *Website:* http://www.jpcatholic.com/.

THE JOHNS HOPKINS UNIVERSITY
Baltimore, MD

Tuition & fees: $45,970	Average undergraduate aid package: $36,312

ABOUT THE INSTITUTION Independent, coed. **Awards:** certificates, diplomas, bachelor's, master's, and doctoral degrees. 65 undergraduate majors. **Total enrollment:** 7,221. Undergraduates: 5,192. Freshmen: 1,330. Institutional methodology is used as a basis for awarding need-based institutional aid.
UNDERGRADUATE EXPENSES for 2013–2014 *Application fee:* $70. **Comprehensive fee:** $59,802 includes full-time tuition ($45,470), mandatory fees ($500), and room and board ($13,832). *College room only:* $7920. Room and board charges vary according to board plan and housing facility. *Part-time tuition:* $1515 per credit hour.
FRESHMAN FINANCIAL AID (Fall 2012, est.) 851 applied for aid; of those 79% were deemed to have need. 100% of freshmen with need received aid; of those 97% had need fully met. *Average percent of need met:* 99% (excluding resources awarded to replace EFC). *Average financial aid package:* $37,917 (excluding resources awarded to replace EFC). 1% of all full-time freshmen had no need and received non-need-based gift aid.
UNDERGRADUATE FINANCIAL AID (Fall 2012, est.) 2,532 applied for aid; of those 91% were deemed to have need. 100% of undergraduates with need received aid; of those 99% had need fully met. *Average percent of need met:* 99% (excluding resources awarded to replace EFC). *Average financial aid package:* $36,312 (excluding resources awarded to replace EFC). 1% of all full-time undergraduates had no need and received non-need-based gift aid.
GIFT AID (NEED-BASED) *Total amount:* $71,076,967 (6% federal, 92% institutional, 2% external sources). *Receiving aid:* Freshmen: 46% (608); all full-time undergraduates: 41% (2,114). *Average award:* Freshmen: $36,882; Undergraduates:

$33,476. *Scholarships, grants, and awards:* Federal Pell, FSEOG, state, private, college/university gift aid from institutional funds.
GIFT AID (NON-NEED-BASED) *Total amount:* $4,431,066 (27% federal, 2% state, 58% institutional, 13% external sources). *Receiving aid:* Freshmen: 4% (58). Undergraduates: 4% (195). *Average award:* Freshmen: $33,435. Undergraduates: $30,898. *Scholarships, grants, and awards by category: Academic interests/ achievement:* 68 awards ($1,965,720 total): engineering/technologies, general academic interests/achievements. *Special characteristics:* 98 awards ($3,465,913 total): children of faculty/staff, local/state students. *Tuition waivers:* Full or partial for employees or children of employees. *ROTC:* Army, Air Force cooperative.
LOANS *Student loans:* $12,724,333 (60% need-based, 40% non-need-based). 49% of past graduating class borrowed through all loan programs. *Average indebtedness per student:* $23,092. *Average need-based loan:* Freshmen: $3332. Undergraduates: $4242. *Parent loans:* $9,564,760 (11% need-based, 89% non-need-based). *Programs:* Federal Direct (Subsidized and Unsubsidized Stafford, PLUS), Perkins, college/university.
WORK-STUDY *Federal work-study:* Total amount: $4,223,093; 1,839 jobs averaging $2296.
ATHLETIC AWARDS Total amount: $1,463,182 (12% need-based, 88% non-need-based).
APPLYING FOR FINANCIAL AID *Required financial aid forms:* FAFSA, CSS Financial Aid PROFILE, noncustodial (divorced/separated) parent's statement, business/farm supplement, federal income tax form(s). *Financial aid deadline:* 3/1. *Notification date:* 4/1. Students must reply by 5/1 or within 2 weeks of notification.
CONTACT Mr. Tom McDermott, Director of Student Financial Services, The Johns Hopkins University, 146 Garland Hall, Baltimore, MD 21218, 410-516-8028. *Fax:* 410-516-6015. *E-mail:* tmcderm1@jhu.edu.
Website: http://www.jhu.edu/.

JOHNSON & WALES UNIVERSITY
Denver, CO

CONTACT Ms. Lynn Robinson, Executive Director of Student Financial Services, Johnson & Wales University, 8 Abbott Park Place, Providence, RI 02903, 401-598-4648 or toll-free 877-598-3368. *Fax:* 401-598-1040. *E-mail:* fp@jwu.edu.
Website: http://www.jwu.edu/denver/.

JOHNSON & WALES UNIVERSITY
North Miami, FL

CONTACT Ms. Lynn Robinson, Executive Director of Student Financial Services, Johnson & Wales University, 8 Abbott Park Place, Providence, RI 02903, 401-598-4648 or toll-free 866-598-3567. *Fax:* 401-598-1040. *E-mail:* fp@jwu.edu.
Website: http://www.jwu.edu/northmiami/.

JOHNSON & WALES UNIVERSITY
Providence, RI

CONTACT Ms. Lynn Robinson, Executive Director of Student Financial Services, Johnson & Wales University, 8 Abbott Park Place, Providence, RI 02903, 401-598-4648 or toll-free 800-342-5598. *Fax:* 401-598-1040. *E-mail:* fp@jwu.edu.
Website: http://www.jwu.edu/providence/.

JOHNSON & WALES UNIVERSITY - CHARLOTTE CAMPUS
Charlotte, NC

CONTACT Ms. Lynn Robinson, Executive Director of Student Financial Services, Johnson & Wales University - Charlotte Campus, 8 Abbott Park Place, Providence, RI 02903, 401-598-1648 or toll-free 866-598-2427. *Fax:* 401-598-4751. *E-mail:* fp@jwu.edu.
Website: http://www.jwu.edu/charlotte/.

JOHNSON C. SMITH UNIVERSITY
Charlotte, NC

Tuition & fees: $18,236	Average undergraduate aid package: $15,437

ABOUT THE INSTITUTION Independent, coed. *Awards:* bachelor's degrees. 25 undergraduate majors. *Total enrollment:* 1,669. Undergraduates: 1,669. Freshmen: 386. Federal methodology is used as a basis for awarding need-based institutional aid.
UNDERGRADUATE EXPENSES for 2013–2014 *Application fee:* $25. *Comprehensive fee:* $25,336 includes full-time tuition ($15,466), mandatory fees ($2770), and room and board ($7100). *College room only:* $4086. Full-time tuition and fees vary according to course load. Room and board charges vary according to board plan and housing facility. *Part-time tuition:* $418 per credit hour. *Part-time fees:* $292 per term. Part-time tuition and fees vary according to course load.
FRESHMAN FINANCIAL AID (Fall 2012, est.) 324 applied for aid; of those 98% were deemed to have need. 100% of freshmen with need received aid; of those 5% had need fully met. *Average percent of need met:* 57% (excluding resources awarded to replace EFC). *Average financial aid package:* $16,757 (excluding resources awarded to replace EFC). 14% of all full-time freshmen had no need and received non-need-based gift aid.
UNDERGRADUATE FINANCIAL AID (Fall 2012, est.) 1,450 applied for aid; of those 98% were deemed to have need. 100% of undergraduates with need received aid; of those 5% had need fully met. *Average percent of need met:* 55% (excluding resources awarded to replace EFC). *Average financial aid package:* $15,437 (excluding resources awarded to replace EFC). 7% of all full-time undergraduates had no need and received non-need-based gift aid.
GIFT AID (NEED-BASED) *Total amount:* $13,461,706 (46% federal, 17% state, 33% institutional, 4% external sources). *Receiving aid:* Freshmen: 77% (298); all full-time undergraduates: 82% (1,318). *Average award:* Freshmen: $13,324; Undergraduates: $11,103. *Scholarships, grants, and awards:* Federal Pell, FSEOG, state, private, college/university gift aid from institutional funds, United Negro College Fund.
GIFT AID (NON-NEED-BASED) *Total amount:* $2,462,025 (2% state, 97% institutional, 1% external sources). *Receiving aid:* Freshmen: 4% (14). Undergraduates: 4% (63). *Average award:* Freshmen: $16,441. Undergraduates: $19,783. *Scholarships, grants, and awards by category: Academic interests/ achievement:* general academic interests/achievements. *Creative arts/performance:* music. *Special achievements/activities:* general special achievements/activities. *Special characteristics:* children of faculty/staff, ethnic background, general special characteristics, siblings of current students. *Tuition waivers:* Full or partial for children of alumni, employees or children of employees. *ROTC:* Army, Air Force cooperative.
LOANS *Student loans:* $13,685,115 (95% need-based, 5% non-need-based). 93% of past graduating class borrowed through all loan programs. *Average indebtedness per student:* $32,621. *Average need-based loan:* Freshmen: $4095. Undergraduates: $4723. *Parent loans:* $2,735,552 (73% need-based, 27% non-need-based). *Programs:* Perkins, alternative loans.
WORK-STUDY *Federal work-study:* Total amount: $577,000; 287 jobs averaging $2017. *State or other work-study/employment:* Total amount: $314,584 (77% need-based, 23% non-need-based). Part-time jobs available.
ATHLETIC AWARDS Total amount: $1,930,286 (74% need-based, 26% non-need-based).
APPLYING FOR FINANCIAL AID *Required financial aid forms:* FAFSA, state aid form. *Financial aid deadline (priority):* 3/1. *Notification date:* Continuous beginning 3/1. Students must reply within 2 weeks of notification.

CONTACT Office of Financial Aid, Johnson C. Smith University, 100 Beatties Ford Road, Charlotte, NC 28216, 704-378-1498 or toll-free 800-782-7303. *Fax:* 704-378-1292.
Website: http://www.jcsu.edu/.

JOHNSON STATE COLLEGE
Johnson, VT

Tuition & fees (VT res): $10,543	Average undergraduate aid package: $15,170

ABOUT THE INSTITUTION State-supported, coed. *Awards:* certificates, associate, bachelor's, and master's degrees. 58 undergraduate majors. *Total enrollment:* 1,882. Undergraduates: 1,647. Freshmen: 241. Federal methodology is used as a basis for awarding need-based institutional aid.

UNDERGRADUATE EXPENSES for 2013–2014 *Application fee:* $40. *Tuition, state resident:* full-time $9312; part-time $372 per credit. *Tuition, non-resident:* full-time $20,976; part-time $832 per credit. *Required fees:* full-time $1231. Full-time tuition and fees vary according to course load. Part-time tuition and fees vary according to course load. *College room and board:* $9138; *Room only:* $5442. Room and board charges vary according to board plan.

FRESHMAN FINANCIAL AID (Fall 2012, est.) 220 applied for aid; of those 84% were deemed to have need. 100% of freshmen with need received aid; of those 10% had need fully met. *Average percent of need met:* 83% (excluding resources awarded to replace EFC). *Average financial aid package:* $15,524 (excluding resources awarded to replace EFC). 11% of all full-time freshmen had no need and received non-need-based gift aid.

UNDERGRADUATE FINANCIAL AID (Fall 2012, est.) 932 applied for aid; of those 91% were deemed to have need. 100% of undergraduates with need received aid; of those 9% had need fully met. *Average percent of need met:* 80% (excluding resources awarded to replace EFC). *Average financial aid package:* $15,170 (excluding resources awarded to replace EFC). 5% of all full-time undergraduates had no need and received non-need-based gift aid.

GIFT AID (NEED-BASED) *Total amount:* $6,733,675 (51% federal, 15% state, 27% institutional, 7% external sources). *Receiving aid:* Freshmen: 75% (177); all full-time undergraduates: 73% (773). *Average award:* Freshmen: $9207; Undergraduates: $7544. *Scholarships, grants, and awards:* Federal Pell, FSEOG, state, private, college/university gift aid from institutional funds.

GIFT AID (NON-NEED-BASED) *Total amount:* $421,710 (1% state, 88% institutional, 11% external sources). *Receiving aid:* Freshmen: 5% (12). Undergraduates: 3% (29). *Average award:* Freshmen: $6187. Undergraduates: $5788. *Scholarships, grants, and awards by category: Academic interests/achievement:* business, education, general academic interests/achievements, mathematics. *Creative arts/performance:* art/fine arts, dance, music, performing arts, theater/drama. *Special achievements/activities:* community service, general special achievements/activities, leadership, memberships. *Special characteristics:* general special characteristics, international students, local/state students, members of minority groups. *Tuition waivers:* Full or partial for employees or children of employees. *ROTC:* Army cooperative.

LOANS *Student loans:* $10,311,809 (82% need-based, 18% non-need-based). *Average need-based loan:* Freshmen: $6922. Undergraduates: $8446. *Parent loans:* $1,337,194 (39% need-based, 61% non-need-based). *Programs:* Federal Direct (Subsidized and Unsubsidized Stafford, PLUS), Perkins.

WORK-STUDY *Federal work-study:* Total amount: $505,409; jobs available.

APPLYING FOR FINANCIAL AID *Required financial aid form:* FAFSA. *Financial aid deadline (priority):* 3/1. *Notification date:* Continuous beginning 4/1. Students must reply within 3 weeks of notification.

CONTACT Ms. Kimberly Goodell, Financial Aid Officer, Johnson State College, 337 College Hill, Johnson, VT 05656-9405, 802-635-2356 or toll-free 800-635-2356. *Fax:* 802-635-1463. *E-mail:* goodellk@badger.jsc.vsc.edu.
Website: http://www.jsc.edu/.

JOHNSON UNIVERSITY
Knoxville, TN

CONTACT Mr. Lawrence Rector, CPA, Financial Aid Director, Johnson University, 7900 Johnson Drive, Knoxville, TN 37998, 865-251-2303 Ext. 2316 or toll-free 800-827-2122. *Fax:* 865-251-2337. *E-mail:* lrector@jbc.edu.
Website: http://www.johnsonu.edu/.

JONES COLLEGE
Jacksonville, FL

CONTACT Mrs. Becky Davis, Director of Financial Assistance, Jones College, 5353 Arlington Expressway, Jacksonville, FL 32211-5540, 904-743-1122 or toll-free 800-631-4056. *Fax:* 904-743-4446.
Website: http://www.jones.edu/.

JONES INTERNATIONAL UNIVERSITY
Centennial, CO

CONTACT Mr. Tim Lehmann, Financial Aid Director, Jones International University, 9697 East Mineral Avenue, Centennial , CO 80112, 800-811-5663. *E-mail:* financialaid@international.edu.
Website: http://www.jiu.edu/.

JOSE MARIA VARGAS UNIVERSITY
Pembroke Pines, FL

CONTACT Financial Aid Office, Jose Maria Vargas University, 8300 South Palm Drive, Pembroke Pines, FL 33025, 954-322-4446.
Website: http://www.jmvu.edu/.

JUDSON COLLEGE
Marion, AL

CONTACT Mrs. Doris A. Wilson, Director of Financial Aid, Judson College, 302 Bibb Street, Marion, AL 36756, 334-683-5157 or toll-free 800-447-9472. *Fax:* 334-683-5282. *E-mail:* dwilson@judson.edu.
Website: http://www.judson.edu/.

JUDSON UNIVERSITY
Elgin, IL

CONTACT Roberto Santizo, Director of Financial Aid, Judson University, 1151 North State Street, Elgin, IL 60123-1498, 847-628-2532 or toll-free 800-879-5376. *Fax:* 847-628-2533. *E-mail:* rsantizo@judsonu.edu.
Website: http://www.judsonu.edu/.

THE JUILLIARD SCHOOL
New York, NY

Tuition & fees: $33,630	Average undergraduate aid package: $30,300

ABOUT THE INSTITUTION Independent, coed. *Awards:* certificates, diplomas, bachelor's, master's, and doctoral degrees. 4 undergraduate majors. *Total enrollment:* 1,009. Undergraduates: 684. Freshmen: 101. Federal methodology is used as a basis for awarding need-based institutional aid.

UNDERGRADUATE EXPENSES for 2013–2014 *Application fee:* $110. *Comprehensive fee:* $46,400 includes full-time tuition ($33,630) and room and board ($12,770).

FRESHMAN FINANCIAL AID (Fall 2011) 103 applied for aid; of those 79% were deemed to have need. 100% of freshmen with need received aid; of those 23% had need fully met. *Average percent of need met:* 78% (excluding resources awarded to replace EFC). *Average financial aid package:* $30,900 (excluding resources awarded to replace EFC). 6% of all full-time freshmen had no need and received non-need-based gift aid.

UNDERGRADUATE FINANCIAL AID (Fall 2011) 454 applied for aid; of those 87% were deemed to have need. 100% of undergraduates with need received aid; of those 22% had need fully met. *Average percent of need met:* 74% (excluding resources awarded to replace EFC). *Average financial aid package:* $30,300 (excluding resources awarded to replace EFC). 7% of all full-time undergraduates had no need and received non-need-based gift aid.

GIFT AID (NEED-BASED) *Total amount:* $9,567,908 (5% federal, 1% state, 91% institutional, 3% external sources). *Receiving aid:* Freshmen: 72% (78); all full-time undergraduates: 74% (378). *Average award:* Freshmen: $26,259; Undergraduates: $25,311. *Scholarships, grants, and awards:* Federal Pell, FSEOG, state, college/university gift aid from institutional funds.

GIFT AID (NON-NEED-BASED) *Total amount:* $594,155 (1% state, 98% institutional, 1% external sources). *Average award:* Freshmen: $10,285. Undergraduates: $17,187. *Scholarships, grants, and awards by category: Creative arts/performance:* dance, music, performing arts, theater/drama.

LOANS *Student loans:* $2,136,150 (94% need-based, 6% non-need-based). 70% of past graduating class borrowed through all loan programs. *Average indebtedness per student:* $24,117. *Average need-based loan:* Freshmen: $3456. Undergraduates: $4991. *Parent loans:* $822,571 (89% need-based, 11% non-need-based). *Programs:* Federal Direct (Subsidized and Unsubsidized Stafford, PLUS), Perkins.

WORK-STUDY *Federal work-study:* Total amount: $548,379; jobs available. *State or other work-study/employment:* Total amount: $703,430 (78% need-based, 22% non-need-based). Part-time jobs available.

APPLYING FOR FINANCIAL AID *Required financial aid forms:* FAFSA, institution's own form. *Financial aid deadline:* 3/1. *Notification date:* 4/1. Students must reply by 5/1.

CONTACT Tina Gonzalez, Director of Financial Aid, The Juilliard School, 60 Lincoln Center Plaza, New York, NY 10023, 212-799-5000 Ext. 211. *Fax:* 212-769-6420. *E-mail:* financialaid@juilliard.edu. *Website:* http://www.juilliard.edu/.

JUNIATA COLLEGE
Huntingdon, PA

Tuition & fees: $37,170	Average undergraduate aid package: $28,211

ABOUT THE INSTITUTION Independent Church of the Brethren, coed. *Awards:* bachelor's and master's degrees. 80 undergraduate majors. *Total enrollment:* 1,565. Undergraduates: 1,558. Freshmen: 402. Federal methodology is used as a basis for awarding need-based institutional aid.

UNDERGRADUATE EXPENSES for 2013–2014 *Application fee:* $30. *Comprehensive fee:* $47,370 includes full-time tuition ($36,410), mandatory fees ($760), and room and board ($10,200). *College room only:* $5380. Full-time tuition and fees vary according to course load and program. Room and board charges vary according to board plan. *Part-time tuition:* $1500 per credit hour.

FRESHMAN FINANCIAL AID (Fall 2012, est.) 350 applied for aid; of those 85% were deemed to have need. 100% of freshmen with need received aid; of those 23% had need fully met. *Average percent of need met:* 86% (excluding resources awarded to replace EFC). *Average financial aid package:* $29,241 (excluding resources awarded to replace EFC). 27% of all full-time freshmen had no need and received non-need-based gift aid.

UNDERGRADUATE FINANCIAL AID (Fall 2012, est.) 1,177 applied for aid; of those 89% were deemed to have need. 98% of undergraduates with need received aid; of those 19% had need fully met. *Average percent of need met:* 81% (excluding resources awarded to replace EFC). *Average financial aid package:* $28,211 (excluding resources awarded to replace EFC). 28% of all full-time undergraduates had no need and received non-need-based gift aid.

GIFT AID (NEED-BASED) *Total amount:* $23,221,256 (6% federal, 7% state, 85% institutional, 2% external sources). *Receiving aid:* Freshmen: 72% (296); all full-time undergraduates: 70% (1,030). *Average award:* Freshmen: $24,589; Undergraduates: $22,544. *Scholarships, grants, and awards:* Federal Pell, FSEOG, state, private, college/university gift aid from institutional funds.

GIFT AID (NON-NEED-BASED) *Total amount:* $7,625,978 (99% institutional, 1% external sources). *Receiving aid:* Freshmen: 10% (43). Undergraduates: 9% (129). *Average award:* Freshmen: $16,401. Undergraduates: $16,122. *Scholarships, grants, and awards by category: Academic interests/achievement:* biological sciences, business, communication, computer science, education, foreign languages, general academic interests/achievements, health fields, humanities, international studies, mathematics, physical sciences, premedicine, social sciences. *Creative arts/performance:* art/fine arts, music, performing arts, theater/drama. *Special achievements/activities:* community service, general special achievements/activities, leadership. *Special characteristics:* children of faculty/staff, ethnic background, international students, local/state students. *Tuition waivers:* Full or partial for employees or children of employees, senior citizens.

LOANS *Student loans:* $8,859,206 (68% need-based, 32% non-need-based). 72% of past graduating class borrowed through all loan programs. *Average indebtedness per student:* $31,213. *Average need-based loan:* Freshmen: $4093. Undergraduates: $5021. *Parent loans:* $15,848,498 (6% need-based, 94% non-need-based). *Programs:* Federal Direct (Subsidized and Unsubsidized Stafford, PLUS), Perkins, college/university.

WORK-STUDY *Federal work-study:* Total amount: $1,080,818; 340 jobs averaging $567. *State or other work-study/employment:* Total amount: $1,503,322 (16% need-based, 84% non-need-based). 368 part-time jobs averaging $965.

APPLYING FOR FINANCIAL AID *Required financial aid form:* FAFSA. *Financial aid deadline (priority):* 3/1. *Notification date:* Continuous. Students must reply by 5/1 or within 2 weeks of notification.

CONTACT Shane Himes, Director of Student Financial Planning, Juniata College, 1700 Moore Street, Huntingdon, PA 16652-2119, 814-641-3140 or toll-free 877-JUNIATA. *Fax:* 814-641-5311. *E-mail:* himess@juniata.edu. *Website:* http://www.juniata.edu/.

KALAMAZOO COLLEGE
Kalamazoo, MI

Tuition & fees: $37,710	Average undergraduate aid package: $31,025

ABOUT THE INSTITUTION Independent American Baptist Churches in the U.S.A., coed. *Awards:* bachelor's degrees. 24 undergraduate majors. *Total enrollment:* 1,379. Undergraduates: 1,379. Freshmen: 334. Both federal and institutional methodology are used as a basis for awarding need-based institutional aid.

UNDERGRADUATE EXPENSES for 2013–2014 *Application fee:* $40. *Comprehensive fee:* $45,984 includes full-time tuition ($37,392), mandatory fees ($318), and room and board ($8274). *College room only:* $4035. Room and board charges vary according to board plan.

FRESHMAN FINANCIAL AID (Fall 2012, est.) 260 applied for aid; of those 84% were deemed to have need. 100% of freshmen with need received aid; of those 46% had need fully met. *Average percent of need met:* 91% (excluding resources awarded to replace EFC). *Average financial aid package:* $32,931 (excluding resources awarded to replace EFC). 30% of all full-time freshmen had no need and received non-need-based gift aid.

UNDERGRADUATE FINANCIAL AID (Fall 2012, est.) 901 applied for aid; of those 88% were deemed to have need. 100% of undergraduates with need received aid; of those 37% had need fully met. *Average percent of need met:* 86% (excluding resources awarded to replace EFC). *Average financial aid package:* $31,025 (excluding resources awarded to replace EFC). 33% of all full-time undergraduates had no need and received non-need-based gift aid.

GIFT AID (NEED-BASED) *Total amount:* $18,897,769 (8% federal, 3% state, 87% institutional, 2% external sources). *Receiving aid:* Freshmen: 65% (217); all full-time undergraduates: 59% (783). *Average award:* Freshmen: $25,717; Undergraduates: $23,909. *Scholarships, grants, and awards:* Federal Pell, FSEOG, state, private, college/university gift aid from institutional funds.

GIFT AID (NON-NEED-BASED) *Total amount:* $9,221,294 (83% institutional, 17% external sources). *Receiving aid:* Freshmen: 63% (211). Undergraduates: 55% (740). *Average award:* Freshmen: $16,483. Undergraduates: $13,467. *Scholarships, grants, and awards by category: Academic interests/achievement: general academic interests/achievements. Special characteristics: children and siblings of alumni. Tuition waivers: Full or partial for employees or children of employees. ROTC: Army cooperative.

LOANS Student loans: $7,054,944 (49% need-based, 51% non-need-based). 53% of past graduating class borrowed through all loan programs. Average indebtedness per student: $27,845. Average need-based loan: Freshmen: $3991. Undergraduates: $4954. Parent loans: $2,003,967 (100% non-need-based). Programs: Federal Direct (Subsidized and Unsubsidized Stafford, PLUS), Perkins.

WORK-STUDY Federal work-study: Total amount: $593,933; 550 jobs averaging $2440. State or other work-study/employment: Total amount: $176,036 (100% need-based). Part-time jobs available.

APPLYING FOR FINANCIAL AID Required financial aid forms: FAFSA, institution's own form. Financial aid deadline (priority): 2/15. Notification date: Continuous beginning 3/22. Students must reply by 5/1.

CONTACT Marian Stowers, Director of Financial Aid, Kalamazoo College, 1200 Academy Street, Kalamazoo, MI 49006-3295, 269-337-7192 or toll-free 800-253-3602. Fax: 269-337-7390.

Website: http://www.kzoo.edu/.

KANSAS CITY ART INSTITUTE
Kansas City, MO

Tuition & fees: $31,992	Average undergraduate aid package: $22,050

ABOUT THE INSTITUTION Independent, coed. Awards: bachelor's degrees. 13 undergraduate majors. Total enrollment: 777. Undergraduates: 777. Freshmen: 196. Federal methodology is used as a basis for awarding need-based institutional aid.

UNDERGRADUATE EXPENSES for 2013–2014 Application fee: $35. Comprehensive fee: $41,364 includes full-time tuition ($31,992) and room and board ($9372).

FRESHMAN FINANCIAL AID (Fall 2012, est.) 156 applied for aid; of those 96% were deemed to have need. 100% of freshmen with need received aid; of those 15% had need fully met. Average percent of need met: 68% (excluding resources awarded to replace EFC). Average financial aid package: $23,950 (excluding resources awarded to replace EFC). 14% of all full-time freshmen had no need and received non-need-based gift aid.

UNDERGRADUATE FINANCIAL AID (Fall 2012, est.) 780 applied for aid; of those 96% were deemed to have need. 100% of undergraduates with need received aid; of those 11% had need fully met. Average percent of need met: 64% (excluding resources awarded to replace EFC). Average financial aid package: $22,050 (excluding resources awarded to replace EFC). 15% of all full-time undergraduates had no need and received non-need-based gift aid.

GIFT AID (NEED-BASED) Total amount: $13,343,446 (14% federal, 2% state, 79% institutional, 5% external sources). Receiving aid: Freshmen: 86% (150); all full-time undergraduates: 91% (745). Average award: Freshmen: $19,704; Undergraduates: $17,504. Scholarships, grants, and awards: Federal Pell, FSEOG, state, private, college/university gift aid from institutional funds.

GIFT AID (NON-NEED-BASED) Total amount: $2,145,754 (1% state, 89% institutional, 10% external sources). Receiving aid: Freshmen: 14% (25). Undergraduates: 10% (80). Average award: Freshmen: $13,565. Undergraduates: $13,052. Scholarships, grants, and awards by category: Creative arts/performance: art/fine arts.

LOANS Student loans: $4,980,072 (56% need-based, 44% non-need-based). 86% of past graduating class borrowed through all loan programs. Average indebtedness per student: $26,660. Average need-based loan: Freshmen: $3851. Undergraduates: $4579. Parent loans: $1,647,752 (100% non-need-based). Programs: Federal Direct (Subsidized and Unsubsidized Stafford, PLUS), Perkins, alternative loans.

WORK-STUDY Federal work-study: Total amount: $111,200; 140 jobs averaging $1205. State or other work-study/employment: Total amount: $214,923 (40% need-based, 60% non-need-based). 200 part-time jobs averaging $1000.

APPLYING FOR FINANCIAL AID Required financial aid form: FAFSA. Financial aid deadline (priority): 3/15. Notification date: Continuous beginning 3/15. Students must reply within 2 weeks of notification.

CONTACT Mrs. Darchelle Renee Webster, Financial Aid Director, Kansas City Art Institute, 4415 Warwick Boulevard, Kansas City, MO 64111-1874, 816-802-3337 or toll-free 800-522-5224. Fax: 816-802-3453. E-mail: financialaid@kcai.edu. Website: http://www.kcai.edu/.

KANSAS STATE UNIVERSITY
Manhattan, KS

Tuition & fees (KS res): $8047	Average undergraduate aid package: $11,182

ABOUT THE INSTITUTION State-supported, coed. Awards: certificates, associate, bachelor's, master's, and doctoral degrees. 81 undergraduate majors. Total enrollment: 24,378. Undergraduates: 19,853. Freshmen: 3,874. Federal methodology is used as a basis for awarding need-based institutional aid.

UNDERGRADUATE EXPENSES for 2013–2014 Application fee: $30. Tuition, state resident: full-time $7317. Tuition, nonresident: full-time $19,416. Required fees: full-time $730. Full-time tuition and fees vary according to course load, degree level, location, program, and reciprocity agreements. Part-time tuition and fees vary according to course load, degree level, location, program, and reciprocity agreements. College room and board: $7450. Room and board charges vary according to board plan, housing facility, and location.

FRESHMAN FINANCIAL AID (Fall 2011) 2,720 applied for aid; of those 70% were deemed to have need. 98% of freshmen with need received aid; of those 20% had need fully met. Average percent of need met: 81% (excluding resources awarded to replace EFC). Average financial aid package: $11,289 (excluding resources awarded to replace EFC). 15% of all full-time freshmen had no need and received non-need-based gift aid.

UNDERGRADUATE FINANCIAL AID (Fall 2011) 11,815 applied for aid; of those 77% were deemed to have need. 97% of undergraduates with need received aid; of those 18% had need fully met. Average percent of need met: 81% (excluding resources awarded to replace EFC). Average financial aid package: $11,182 (excluding resources awarded to replace EFC). 6% of all full-time undergraduates had no need and received non-need-based gift aid.

GIFT AID (NEED-BASED) Total amount: $42,685,335 (45% federal, 7% state, 40% institutional, 8% external sources). Receiving aid: Freshmen: 31% (1,106); all full-time undergraduates: 31% (5,399). Average award: Freshmen: $4433; Undergraduates: $4143. Scholarships, grants, and awards: Federal Pell, FSEOG, state, private, college/university gift aid from institutional funds.

GIFT AID (NON-NEED-BASED) Total amount: $75,925,152 (98% institutional, 2% external sources). Receiving aid: Freshmen: 38% (1,335). Undergraduates: 24% (4,093). Average award: Freshmen: $4017. Undergraduates: $3497. Tuition waivers: Full or partial for employees or children of employees. ROTC: Army, Air Force.

LOANS Student loans: $72,625,166 (73% need-based, 27% non-need-based). 61% of past graduating class borrowed through all loan programs. Average indebtedness per student: $25,147. Average need-based loan: Freshmen: $3293. Undergraduates: $4188. Parent loans: $25,080,239 (28% need-based, 72% non-need-based). Programs: Federal Direct (Subsidized and Unsubsidized Stafford, PLUS), Perkins, college/university.

WORK-STUDY Federal work-study: Total amount: $1,621,690; jobs available. State or other work-study/employment: Total amount: $131,056 (86% need-based, 14% non-need-based). Part-time jobs available.

ATHLETIC AWARDS Total amount: $4,342,420 (91% need-based, 9% non-need-based).

APPLYING FOR FINANCIAL AID Required financial aid form: FAFSA. Financial aid deadline (priority): 3/1. Notification date: Continuous beginning 4/1. Students must reply within 2 weeks of notification.

CONTACT Mr. Larry Moeder, Director of Admissions and Student Financial Assistance, Kansas State University, 104 Fairchild Hall, Manhattan, KS 66506, 785-532-6420 or toll-free 800-432-8270. E-mail: larrym@ksu.edu. Website: http://www.k-state.edu/.

KANSAS WESLEYAN UNIVERSITY
Salina, KS

CONTACT Mrs. Glenna Alexander, Director of Financial Assistance, Kansas Wesleyan University, 100 East Claflin, Salina, KS 67401-6196, 785-827-5541 Ext. 1130 or toll-free 800-874-1154 Ext. 1285. *Fax:* 785-827-0927. *E-mail:* kglennaa@acck.edu. *Website:* http://www.kwu.edu/.

KAPLAN UNIVERSITY, DAVENPORT CAMPUS
Davenport, IA

CONTACT Financial Aid Office, Kaplan University, Davenport Campus, 1801 East Kimberly Road, Suite 1, Davenport, IA 52807-2095, 563-355-3500 or toll-free 866-527-5268 (in-state), 800-527-5268 (out-of-state). *Website:* http://www.davenport.kaplanuniversity.edu/.

KAPLAN UNIVERSITY, MASON CITY CAMPUS
Mason City, IA

CONTACT Financial Aid Office, Kaplan University, Mason City Campus, 2570 4th Street, SW, Mason City, IA 50401, 641-423-2530 or toll-free 866-527-5268 (in-state), 800-527-5268 (out-of-state). *Website:* http://masoncity.kaplanuniversity.edu/.

KEAN UNIVERSITY
Union, NJ

Tuition & fees (NJ res): $10,601	Average undergraduate aid package: $9623

ABOUT THE INSTITUTION State-supported, coed. *Awards:* certificates, bachelor's, master's, and doctoral degrees. 48 undergraduate majors. *Total enrollment:* 15,391. Undergraduates: 12,895. Freshmen: 1,410. Federal methodology is used as a basis for awarding need-based institutional aid.
UNDERGRADUATE EXPENSES for 2013–2014 *Application fee:* $75. *Tuition, state resident:* full-time $6925; part-time $270 per credit. *Tuition, nonresident:* full-time $12,967; part-time $457 per credit. *Required fees:* full-time $3676; $135 per credit. Part-time tuition and fees vary according to course load. *College room and board:* $13,934; *Room only:* $10,804. Room and board charges vary according to board plan, housing facility, and student level.
FRESHMAN FINANCIAL AID (Fall 2012, est.) 1,188 applied for aid; of those 86% were deemed to have need. 92% of freshmen with need received aid; of those 3% had need fully met. *Average percent of need met:* 79% (excluding resources awarded to replace EFC). *Average financial aid package:* $9107 (excluding resources awarded to replace EFC). 2% of all full-time freshmen had no need and received non-need-based gift aid.
UNDERGRADUATE FINANCIAL AID (Fall 2012, est.) 8,061 applied for aid; of those 87% were deemed to have need. 95% of undergraduates with need received aid; of those 8% had need fully met. *Average percent of need met:* 82% (excluding resources awarded to replace EFC). *Average financial aid package:* $9623 (excluding resources awarded to replace EFC). 1% of all full-time undergraduates had no need and received non-need-based gift aid.
GIFT AID (NEED-BASED) *Total amount:* $36,877,257 (61% federal, 35% state, 3% institutional, 1% external sources). *Receiving aid:* Freshmen: 49% (678); all full-time undergraduates: 47% (4,671). *Average award:* Freshmen: $7579; Undergraduates: $7267. *Scholarships, grants, and awards:* Federal Pell, FSEOG, state, private, college/university gift aid from institutional funds.
GIFT AID (NON-NEED-BASED) *Total amount:* $282,485 (16% state, 84% institutional). *Receiving aid:* Freshmen: 10% (136). Undergraduates: 7% (685). *Average award:* Freshmen: $3101. Undergraduates: $3583. *Scholarships, grants,*

and awards by category: Academic interests/achievement: area/ethnic studies, biological sciences, business, communication, computer science, education, engineering/technologies, English, foreign languages, general academic interests/achievements, health fields, humanities, international studies, mathematics, physical sciences, social sciences. *Creative arts/performance:* applied art and design, art/fine arts, cinema/film/broadcasting, general creative arts/performance, music, performing arts, theater/drama. *Special achievements/activities:* general special achievements/activities. *Special characteristics:* general special characteristics. *Tuition waivers:* Full or partial for employees or children of employees, senior citizens. *ROTC:* Army cooperative, Air Force cooperative.
LOANS *Student loans:* $68,347,995 (43% need-based, 57% non-need-based). 71% of past graduating class borrowed through all loan programs. *Average indebtedness per student:* $30,335. *Average need-based loan:* Freshmen: $3515. Undergraduates: $4495. *Parent loans:* $5,850,184 (100% non-need-based). *Programs:* Federal Direct (Subsidized and Unsubsidized Stafford, PLUS), Perkins.
WORK-STUDY *Federal work-study:* Total amount: $385,771; 229 jobs averaging $1844.
APPLYING FOR FINANCIAL AID *Required financial aid form:* FAFSA. *Financial aid deadline (priority):* 4/17. *Notification date:* Continuous beginning 3/1. Students must reply by 5/1.
CONTACT Ms. Sherrell Watson-Hall, Associate Director of Financial Aid, Kean University, 1000 Morris Avenue, Union, NJ 07083, 908-737-3220. *Fax:* 908-737-3200. *E-mail:* finaid@kean.edu. *Website:* http://www.kean.edu/.

KEENE STATE COLLEGE
Keene, NH

Tuition & fees (NH res): $12,776	Average undergraduate aid package: $10,272

ABOUT THE INSTITUTION State-supported, coed. *Awards:* certificates, bachelor's, and master's degrees. 76 undergraduate majors. *Total enrollment:* 5,060. Undergraduates: 4,933. Freshmen: 1,186. Federal methodology is used as a basis for awarding need-based institutional aid.
UNDERGRADUATE EXPENSES for 2013–2014 *Application fee:* $50. *Tuition, state resident:* full-time $10,410; part-time $440 per credit hour. *Tuition, nonresident:* full-time $17,310; part-time $720 per credit hour. *Required fees:* full-time $2366; $94 per credit hour. Part-time tuition and fees vary according to course load. *College room and board:* $8762. Room and board charges vary according to board plan and housing facility.
FRESHMAN FINANCIAL AID (Fall 2011) 1,158 applied for aid; of those 75% were deemed to have need. 98% of freshmen with need received aid; of those 10% had need fully met. *Average percent of need met:* 65% (excluding resources awarded to replace EFC). *Average financial aid package:* $10,873 (excluding resources awarded to replace EFC). 9% of all full-time freshmen had no need and received non-need-based gift aid.
UNDERGRADUATE FINANCIAL AID (Fall 2011) 4,015 applied for aid; of those 78% were deemed to have need. 99% of undergraduates with need received aid; of those 12% had need fully met. *Average percent of need met:* 65% (excluding resources awarded to replace EFC). *Average financial aid package:* $10,272 (excluding resources awarded to replace EFC). 7% of all full-time undergraduates had no need and received non-need-based gift aid.
GIFT AID (NEED-BASED) *Total amount:* $13,741,179 (35% federal, 1% state, 55% institutional, 9% external sources). *Receiving aid:* Freshmen: 49% (620); all full-time undergraduates: 46% (2,199). *Average award:* Freshmen: $6682; Undergraduates: $5926. *Scholarships, grants, and awards:* Federal Pell, FSEOG, state, private, college/university gift aid from institutional funds.
GIFT AID (NON-NEED-BASED) *Total amount:* $3,808,376 (74% institutional, 26% external sources). *Receiving aid:* Freshmen: 19% (244). Undergraduates: 16% (760). *Average award:* Freshmen: $2091. Undergraduates: $2654. *Scholarships, grants, and awards by category:* Academic interests/achievement: 745 awards ($1,532,032 total): general academic interests/achievements. *Creative arts/performance:* 22 awards ($66,000 total): applied art and design, art/fine arts, cinema/film/broadcasting, dance, general creative arts/performance, music, theater/drama. *Special achievements/activities:* 76 awards ($134,438 total): general special achievements/activities, leadership. *Tuition waivers:* Full or partial for employees or children of employees, senior citizens. *ROTC:* Army cooperative, Air Force cooperative.

LOANS *Student loans:* $35,412,401 (35% need-based, 65% non-need-based). 80% of past graduating class borrowed through all loan programs. *Average indebtedness per student:* $33,248. *Average need-based loan:* Freshmen: $3873. Undergraduates: $4392. *Parent loans:* $10,622,612 (100% non-need-based). **Programs:** Perkins, college/university.

WORK-STUDY *Federal work-study:* Total amount: $3,292,410; 1,492 jobs averaging $2207. *State or other work-study/employment:* Total amount: $805,929 (100% non-need-based). 688 part-time jobs averaging $1171.

APPLYING FOR FINANCIAL AID *Required financial aid form:* FAFSA. *Financial aid deadline:* 3/1. *Notification date:* Continuous. Students must reply within 4 weeks of notification.

CONTACT Ms. Patricia Blodgett, Director of Financial Aid, Keene State College, 229 Main Street, Keene, NH 03435-2606, 603-358-2280 or toll-free 800-KSC-1909. *Fax:* 603-358-2794. *E-mail:* pblodget@keene.edu. *Website:* http://www.keene.edu/.

KEHILATH YAKOV RABBINICAL SEMINARY
Ossining, NY

CONTACT Financial Aid Office, Kehilath Yakov Rabbinical Seminary, 206 Wilson Street, Brooklyn, NY 11211-7207, 718-963-1212.

KEISER UNIVERSITY
Fort Lauderdale, FL

CONTACT Judy Martin, Financial Aid Director, Keiser University, 1500 NW 49 Street, Fort Lauderdale, FL 33309, 954-776-4456 or toll-free 888-534-7379. *Fax:* 954-749-4456. *E-mail:* judym@keiseruniversity.edu. *Website:* http://www.keiseruniversity.edu/.

KEISER UNIVERSITY
Fort Myers, FL

CONTACT Financial Aid Office, Keiser University, 9100 Forum Corporate Parkway, Fort Myers, FL 33905, 239-277-1336. *Website:* http://www.keiseruniversity.edu/.

KENDALL COLLEGE
Chicago, IL

ABOUT THE INSTITUTION Proprietary, coed. 23 undergraduate majors.

GIFT AID (NEED-BASED) *Scholarships, grants, and awards:* Federal Pell, FSEOG, state, private, college/university gift aid from institutional funds.

GIFT AID (NON-NEED-BASED) *Scholarships, grants, and awards by category:* Academic interests/achievement: business, education, general academic interests/achievements. *Special characteristics:* children of faculty/staff, international students, out-of-state students, veterans, veterans' children.

LOANS *Programs:* Federal Direct (Subsidized and Unsubsidized Stafford, PLUS), Perkins, alternative loans.

APPLYING FOR FINANCIAL AID *Required financial aid form:* FAFSA.

CONTACT Chris Miller, Director of Financial Aid, Kendall College, 900 N. North Branch Street, Chicago, IL 60642, 312-752-2428 or toll-free 888-90-KENDALL. *Fax:* 312-752-2267. *Website:* http://www.kendall.edu/.

KENNESAW STATE UNIVERSITY
Kennesaw, GA

Tuition & fees (GA res): $6486	Average undergraduate aid package: $7309

ABOUT THE INSTITUTION State-supported, coed. *Awards:* certificates, bachelor's, master's, and doctoral degrees. 50 undergraduate majors. *Total enrollment:* 24,604. Undergraduates: 22,684. Freshmen: 3,088. Federal methodology is used as a basis for awarding need-based institutional aid.

UNDERGRADUATE EXPENSES for 2013–2014 *Application fee:* $40. *Tuition, state resident:* full-time $4852; part-time $162 per credit hour. *Tuition, nonresident:* full-time $17,128; part-time $571 per credit hour. *Required fees:* full-time $1634; $817 per term. Part-time tuition and fees vary according to course load. *College room and board:* $7966. Room and board charges vary according to board plan and housing facility.

FRESHMAN FINANCIAL AID (Fall 2012, est.) 2,755 applied for aid; of those 77% were deemed to have need. 96% of freshmen with need received aid; of those 11% had need fully met. *Average percent of need met:* 77% (excluding resources awarded to replace EFC). *Average financial aid package:* $7590 (excluding resources awarded to replace EFC). 1% of all full-time freshmen had no need and received non-need-based gift aid.

UNDERGRADUATE FINANCIAL AID (Fall 2012, est.) 13,937 applied for aid; of those 85% were deemed to have need. 96% of undergraduates with need received aid; of those 17% had need fully met. *Average percent of need met:* 65% (excluding resources awarded to replace EFC). *Average financial aid package:* $7309 (excluding resources awarded to replace EFC). 1% of all full-time undergraduates had no need and received non-need-based gift aid.

GIFT AID (NEED-BASED) *Total amount:* $35,931,750 (97% federal, 2% state, 1% institutional). *Receiving aid:* Freshmen: 55% (1,696); all full-time undergraduates: 60% (10,250). *Average award:* Freshmen: $5269; Undergraduates: $6121. *Scholarships, grants, and awards:* Federal Pell, FSEOG, state, private, college/university gift aid from institutional funds.

GIFT AID (NON-NEED-BASED) *Total amount:* $26,192,018 (96% state, 4% institutional). *Receiving aid:* Freshmen: 47% (1,438). Undergraduates: 29% (4,847). *Average award:* Freshmen: $1496. Undergraduates: $1295. *Scholarships, grants, and awards by category:* Academic interests/achievement: biological sciences, business, communication, computer science, education, English, foreign languages, general academic interests/achievements, health fields, humanities, international studies, mathematics, physical sciences, premedicine, social sciences. *Creative arts/performance:* music, performing arts, theater/drama. *Special achievements/activities:* community service, leadership, memberships. *Special characteristics:* children and siblings of alumni, children of union members/company employees, children of workers in trades, ethnic background, general special characteristics, handicapped students, international students, local/state students, members of minority groups, religious affiliation, veterans' children. *Tuition waivers:* Full or partial for employees or children of employees, senior citizens. *ROTC:* Army cooperative, Air Force cooperative.

LOANS *Student loans:* $91,111,497 (47% need-based, 53% non-need-based). 57% of past graduating class borrowed through all loan programs. *Average indebtedness per student:* $20,666. *Average need-based loan:* Freshmen: $2089. Undergraduates: $3293. *Parent loans:* $5,143,750 (100% non-need-based). *Programs:* Federal Direct (Subsidized and Unsubsidized Stafford, PLUS), Perkins.

WORK-STUDY *Federal work-study:* Total amount: $511,528; 200 jobs averaging $2557. *State or other work-study/employment:* Total amount: $1112 (100% need-based). Part-time jobs available.

ATHLETIC AWARDS Total amount: $878,571 (100% non-need-based).

APPLYING FOR FINANCIAL AID *Required financial aid form:* FAFSA. *Financial aid deadline (priority):* 4/1. *Notification date:* Continuous beginning 4/1.

CONTACT Mr. Ron H. Day, Director of Student Financial Aid, Kennesaw State University, 1000 Chastain Road, Kennesaw, GA 30144-5591, 770-423-6021. *Fax:* 770-423-6708. *E-mail:* finaid@kennesaw.edu. *Website:* http://www.kennesaw.edu/.

KENT STATE UNIVERSITY
Kent, OH

Tuition & fees (OH res): $9672	Average undergraduate aid package: $9082

ABOUT THE INSTITUTION State-supported, coed. *Awards:* certificates, associate, bachelor's, master's, and doctoral degrees. 93 undergraduate majors. *Total enrollment:* 28,172. Undergraduates: 22,436. Freshmen: 4,124. Federal methodology is used as a basis for awarding need-based institutional aid.

UNDERGRADUATE EXPENSES for 2013–2014 *Application fee:* $40. *Tuition, state resident:* full-time $9672. *Tuition, nonresident:* full-time $17,632. Full-time tuition and fees vary according to course load. Part-time tuition and fees vary according to course load. *College room and board:* $9176. Room and board charges vary according to board plan and housing facility.

FRESHMAN FINANCIAL AID (Fall 2012, est.) 3,587 applied for aid; of those 83% were deemed to have need. 100% of freshmen with need received aid; of those 39% had need fully met. *Average percent of need met:* 53% (excluding resources awarded to replace EFC). *Average financial aid package:* $9415 (excluding resources awarded to replace EFC). 16% of all full-time freshmen had no need and received non-need-based gift aid.

UNDERGRADUATE FINANCIAL AID (Fall 2012, est.) 14,474 applied for aid; of those 87% were deemed to have need. 100% of undergraduates with need received aid; of those 36% had need fully met. *Average percent of need met:* 50% (excluding resources awarded to replace EFC). *Average financial aid package:* $9082 (excluding resources awarded to replace EFC). 12% of all full-time undergraduates had no need and received non-need-based gift aid.

GIFT AID (NEED-BASED) *Total amount:* $60,804,041 (51% federal, 7% state, 37% institutional, 5% external sources). *Receiving aid:* Freshmen: 64% (2,604); all full-time undergraduates: 52% (9,719). *Average award:* Freshmen: $6217; Undergraduates: $5604. *Scholarships, grants, and awards:* Federal Pell, FSEOG, state, private, college/university gift aid from institutional funds.

GIFT AID (NON-NEED-BASED) *Total amount:* $13,842,649 (13% federal, 10% state, 73% institutional, 4% external sources). *Receiving aid:* Freshmen: 19% (788). Undergraduates: 11% (1,987). *Average award:* Freshmen: $4295. Undergraduates: $4235. *Scholarships, grants, and awards by category:* Academic interests/achievement: architecture, area/ethnic studies, biological sciences, business, communication, computer science, education, engineering/technologies, English, foreign languages, general academic interests/achievements, health fields, humanities, international studies, library science, mathematics, military science, physical sciences, premedicine, religion/biblical studies, social sciences. Creative arts/performance: applied art and design, art/fine arts, cinema/film/broadcasting, creative writing, dance, general creative arts/performance, journalism/publications, music, performing arts, theater/drama. Special achievements/activities: community service, general special achievements/activities, leadership. Special characteristics: adult students, children and siblings of alumni, children of faculty/staff, children of union members/company employees, ethnic background, first-generation college students, handicapped students, international students, local/state students, members of minority groups, out-of-state students, previous college experience. *Tuition waivers:* Full or partial for employees or children of employees, senior citizens. ROTC: Army, Air Force.

LOANS *Student loans:* $121,580,301 (43% need-based, 57% non-need-based). 76% of past graduating class borrowed through all loan programs. *Average indebtedness per student:* $31,954. *Average need-based loan:* Freshmen: $3711. Undergraduates: $4327. *Parent loans:* $33,876,859 (18% need-based, 82% non-need-based). *Programs:* Federal Direct (Subsidized and Unsubsidized Stafford, PLUS), Perkins, Federal Nursing, state, college/university, alternative loans.

WORK-STUDY *Federal work-study:* Total amount: $1,164,227; 358 jobs averaging $2942.

ATHLETIC AWARDS Total amount: $5,741,401 (57% need-based, 43% non-need-based).

APPLYING FOR FINANCIAL AID *Required financial aid form:* FAFSA. *Financial aid deadline (priority):* 3/1. *Notification date:* 3/15. Students must reply within 2 weeks of notification.

CONTACT Mark A. Evans, Director of Student Financial Aid, Kent State University, 103 Schwartz Center, Kent, OH 44242-0001, 330-672-2972 or toll-free 800-988-KENT. *Fax:* 330-672-4014. *E-mail:* mevans@kent.edu. *Website:* http://www.kent.edu/.

KENT STATE UNIVERSITY AT GEAUGA
Burton, OH

Tuition & fees (OH res): $5472	Average undergraduate aid package: $6824

ABOUT THE INSTITUTION State-supported, coed. *Awards:* certificates, associate, and bachelor's degrees. 12 undergraduate majors. *Total enrollment:* 2,535. Undergraduates: 2,533. Freshmen: 271. Federal methodology is used as a basis for awarding need-based institutional aid.

UNDERGRADUATE EXPENSES for 2013–2014 *Application fee:* $30. *Tuition, state resident:* full-time $5472. *Tuition, nonresident:* full-time $13,432. Full-time tuition and fees vary according to course level and course load. Part-time tuition and fees vary according to course level and course load.

FRESHMAN FINANCIAL AID (Fall 2012, est.) 188 applied for aid; of those 87% were deemed to have need. 99% of freshmen with need received aid; of those 43% had need fully met. *Average percent of need met:* 46% (excluding resources awarded to replace EFC). *Average financial aid package:* $5987 (excluding resources awarded to replace EFC). 2% of all full-time freshmen had no need and received non-need-based gift aid.

UNDERGRADUATE FINANCIAL AID (Fall 2012, est.) 578 applied for aid; of those 90% were deemed to have need. 99% of undergraduates with need received aid; of those 29% had need fully met. *Average percent of need met:* 45% (excluding resources awarded to replace EFC). *Average financial aid package:* $6824 (excluding resources awarded to replace EFC). 1% of all full-time undergraduates had no need and received non-need-based gift aid.

GIFT AID (NEED-BASED) *Total amount:* $2,528,170 (97% federal, 1% institutional, 2% external sources). *Receiving aid:* Freshmen: 46% (107); all full-time undergraduates: 50% (365). *Average award:* Freshmen: $4321; Undergraduates: $4425. *Scholarships, grants, and awards:* Federal Pell, FSEOG, state, private, college/university gift aid from institutional funds.

GIFT AID (NON-NEED-BASED) *Total amount:* $71,811 (70% federal, 15% state, 11% institutional, 4% external sources). *Receiving aid:* Freshmen: 2% (5). Undergraduates: 2% (17). *Average award:* Freshmen: $505. Undergraduates: $503. *Tuition waivers:* Full or partial for employees or children of employees, senior citizens. ROTC: Army cooperative, Air Force cooperative.

LOANS *Student loans:* $7,138,818 (44% need-based, 56% non-need-based). *Average need-based loan:* Freshmen: $3319. Undergraduates: $3777. *Parent loans:* $163,338 (14% need-based, 86% non-need-based). *Programs:* Federal Direct (Subsidized and Unsubsidized Stafford, PLUS), Perkins, Federal Nursing, state, college/university, alternative loans.

WORK-STUDY *Federal work-study:* Total amount: $26,766; jobs available.

APPLYING FOR FINANCIAL AID *Required financial aid form:* FAFSA. *Financial aid deadline (priority):* 3/1. *Notification date:* 3/15. Students must reply within 2 weeks of notification.

CONTACT Donna Holcomb, Financial Aid Advisor, Kent State University at Geauga, 14111 Claridon-Troy Road, Burton, OH 44021, 440-834-3737. *Fax:* 440-834-8846. *E-mail:* dholcomb@kent.edu. *Website:* http://www.geauga.kent.edu/.

KENT STATE UNIVERSITY AT STARK
Canton, OH

Tuition & fees (OH res): $5472	Average undergraduate aid package: $7272

ABOUT THE INSTITUTION State-supported, coed. *Awards:* certificates, associate, bachelor's, and master's degrees. 19 undergraduate majors. *Total enrollment:* 4,864. Undergraduates: 4,816. Freshmen: 682. Federal methodology is used as a basis for awarding need-based institutional aid.

UNDERGRADUATE EXPENSES for 2013–2014 *Application fee:* $30. *Tuition, state resident:* full-time $5472. *Tuition, nonresident:* full-time $13,432. Full-time tuition and fees vary according to course level and course load. Part-time tuition and fees vary according to course level and course load.

FRESHMAN FINANCIAL AID (Fall 2012, est.) 518 applied for aid; of those 86% were deemed to have need. 100% of freshmen with need received aid; of those 43%

had need fully met. *Average percent of need met:* 51% (excluding resources awarded to replace EFC). *Average financial aid package:* $6601 (excluding resources awarded to replace EFC). 5% of all full-time freshmen had no need and received non-need-based gift aid.

UNDERGRADUATE FINANCIAL AID (Fall 2012, est.) 2,291 applied for aid; of those 90% were deemed to have need. 100% of undergraduates with need received aid; of those 30% had need fully met. *Average percent of need met:* 49% (excluding resources awarded to replace EFC). *Average financial aid package:* $7272 (excluding resources awarded to replace EFC). 2% of all full-time undergraduates had no need and received non-need-based gift aid.

GIFT AID (NEED-BASED) *Total amount:* $9,568,702 (95% federal, 3% institutional, 2% external sources). *Receiving aid:* Freshmen: 60% (349); all full-time undergraduates: 60% (1,598). *Average award:* Freshmen: $4228; Undergraduates: $4375. *Scholarships, grants, and awards:* Federal Pell, FSEOG, state, private, college/university gift aid from institutional funds.

GIFT AID (NON-NEED-BASED) *Total amount:* $673,374 (37% federal, 20% state, 39% institutional, 4% external sources). *Receiving aid:* Freshmen: 8% (45). Undergraduates: 5% (132). *Average award:* Freshmen: $2535. Undergraduates: $2851. *Tuition waivers:* Full or partial for employees or children of employees, senior citizens. *ROTC:* Army cooperative, Naval cooperative, Air Force cooperative.

LOANS *Student loans:* $22,525,191 (46% need-based, 54% non-need-based). *Average need-based loan:* Freshmen: $3362. Undergraduates: $3933. *Parent loans:* $525,889 (8% need-based, 92% non-need-based). *Programs:* Federal Direct (Subsidized and Unsubsidized Stafford, PLUS), Perkins, Federal Nursing, state, college/university, alternative loans.

WORK-STUDY *Federal work-study:* Total amount: $111,750; jobs available.

APPLYING FOR FINANCIAL AID *Required financial aid form:* FAFSA. *Financial aid deadline (priority):* 3/1. *Notification date:* 3/15. Students must reply within 2 weeks of notification.

CONTACT Gail Pukys, Assistant Director for Enrollment Management for Financial Aid, Kent State University at Stark, 134 Main Hall, North Canton, OH 44720, 330-244-3257. *Fax:* 330-499-0301. *E-mail:* gpukys@kent.edu. *Website:* http://www.stark.kent.edu/.

KENTUCKY CHRISTIAN UNIVERSITY
Grayson, KY

CONTACT Mrs. Jennie M. Bender, Director of Financial Aid, Kentucky Christian University, 100 Academic Parkway, Grayson, KY 41143-2205, 606-474-3226 or toll-free 800-522-3181. *Fax:* 606-474-3155. *E-mail:* jbender@kcu.edu. *Website:* http://www.kcu.edu/.

KENTUCKY MOUNTAIN BIBLE COLLEGE
Vancleve, KY

CONTACT Mrs. Rosita Marshall, Director of Financial Aid, Kentucky Mountain Bible College, PO Box 10, Vancleve, KY 41385-0010, 800-879-KMBC Ext. 175 or toll-free 800-879-KMBC. *Fax:* 800-659-4324. *E-mail:* finaid@kmbc.edu. *Website:* http://www.kmbc.edu/.

KENTUCKY STATE UNIVERSITY
Frankfort, KY

Tuition & fees (KY res): $6858	Average undergraduate aid package: $10,279

ABOUT THE INSTITUTION State-related, coed. *Awards:* associate, bachelor's, and master's degrees. 25 undergraduate majors. *Total enrollment:* 2,524. Undergraduates: 2,296. Freshmen: 323. Federal methodology is used as a basis for awarding need-based institutional aid.

UNDERGRADUATE EXPENSES for 2013–2014 *Application fee:* $30. *Tuition, state resident:* full-time $6108; part-time $229 per credit hour. *Tuition,*

nonresident: full-time $15,708; part-time $585 per credit hour. *Required fees:* full-time $750; $25 per credit hour. Full-time tuition and fees vary according to course load. Part-time tuition and fees vary according to course load. *College room and board:* $6580; *Room only:* $3340. Room and board charges vary according to board plan and housing facility.

FRESHMAN FINANCIAL AID (Fall 2012, est.) 314 applied for aid; of those 100% were deemed to have need. 92% of freshmen with need received aid; of those 1% had need fully met. *Average percent of need met:* 43% (excluding resources awarded to replace EFC). *Average financial aid package:* $10,097 (excluding resources awarded to replace EFC).

UNDERGRADUATE FINANCIAL AID (Fall 2012, est.) 1,621 applied for aid; of those 100% were deemed to have need. 95% of undergraduates with need received aid; of those 2% had need fully met. *Average percent of need met:* 45% (excluding resources awarded to replace EFC). *Average financial aid package:* $10,279 (excluding resources awarded to replace EFC). 1% of all full-time undergraduates had no need and received non-need-based gift aid.

GIFT AID (NEED-BASED) *Total amount:* $10,312,312 (62% federal, 7% state, 29% institutional, 2% external sources). *Receiving aid:* Freshmen: 83% (267); all full-time undergraduates: 78% (1,374). *Average award:* Freshmen: $6866; Undergraduates: $6898. *Scholarships, grants, and awards:* Federal Pell, FSEOG, state, college/university gift aid from institutional funds, TEACH Grants.

GIFT AID (NON-NEED-BASED) *Total amount:* $113,100 (17% state, 82% institutional, 1% external sources). *Receiving aid:* Freshmen: 1. Undergraduates: 7. *Average award:* Undergraduates: $2013. *Scholarships, grants, and awards by category:* Academic interests/achievement: agriculture, general academic interests/achievements, health fields. Creative arts/performance: art/fine arts, music, performing arts. Special achievements/activities: cheerleading/drum major, general special achievements/activities. Special characteristics: adult students, children of faculty/staff, children with a deceased or disabled parent, ethnic background, general special characteristics, local/state students. *Tuition waivers:* Full or partial for children of alumni, employees or children of employees, senior citizens. *ROTC:* Army cooperative, Air Force cooperative.

LOANS *Student loans:* $13,736,570 (100% need-based). 26% of past graduating class borrowed through all loan programs. *Average indebtedness per student:* $39,623. *Average need-based loan:* Freshmen: $3466. Undergraduates: $4019. *Parent loans:* $1,278,088 (100% need-based). *Programs:* Federal Direct (Subsidized and Unsubsidized Stafford, PLUS), alternative loans.

WORK-STUDY *Federal work-study:* Total amount: $354,600; 205 jobs averaging $1730.

ATHLETIC AWARDS Total amount: $951,339 (100% need-based).

APPLYING FOR FINANCIAL AID *Required financial aid form:* FAFSA. *Financial aid deadline (priority):* 4/15. *Notification date:* Continuous beginning 3/15. Students must reply within 2 weeks of notification.

CONTACT Ms. Victoria Owens, Director of Financial Aid, Kentucky State University, 400 East Main Street, Frankfort, KY 40601, 502-597-6033. *Fax:* 502-597-5950. *E-mail:* victoria.owens@kysu.edu. *Website:* http://www.kysu.edu/.

KENTUCKY WESLEYAN COLLEGE
Owensboro, KY

Tuition & fees: $21,200	Average undergraduate aid package: $15,970

ABOUT THE INSTITUTION Independent Methodist, coed. *Awards:* bachelor's degrees. 39 undergraduate majors. *Total enrollment:* 678. Undergraduates: 678. Freshmen: 158. Federal methodology is used as a basis for awarding need-based institutional aid.

UNDERGRADUATE EXPENSES for 2013–2014 *Comprehensive fee:* $28,700 includes full-time tuition ($20,600), mandatory fees ($600), and room and board ($7500). Full-time tuition and fees vary according to course load. Room and board charges vary according to board plan and housing facility. *Part-time tuition:* $585 per credit. Part-time tuition and fees vary according to course load.

FRESHMAN FINANCIAL AID (Fall 2011) 188 applied for aid; of those 93% were deemed to have need. 99% of freshmen with need received aid; of those 11% had need fully met. *Average percent of need met:* 63% (excluding resources awarded to replace EFC). *Average financial aid package:* $15,146 (excluding resources awarded to replace EFC). 9% of all full-time freshmen had no need and received non-need-based gift aid.

UNDERGRADUATE FINANCIAL AID (Fall 2011) 702 applied for aid; of those 93% were deemed to have need. 99% of undergraduates with need received aid; of those 16% had need fully met. *Average percent of need met:* 69% (excluding resources awarded to replace EFC). *Average financial aid package:* $15,970 (excluding resources awarded to replace EFC). 12% of all full-time undergraduates had no need and received non-need-based gift aid.
GIFT AID (NEED-BASED) *Total amount:* $8,279,286 (20% federal, 19% state, 56% institutional, 5% external sources). *Receiving aid:* Freshmen: 89% (172); all full-time undergraduates: 85% (641). *Average award:* Freshmen: $12,408; Undergraduates: $12,886. *Scholarships, grants, and awards:* Federal Pell, FSEOG, state, private, college/university gift aid from institutional funds.
GIFT AID (NON-NEED-BASED) *Total amount:* $1,403,938 (2% federal, 9% state, 80% institutional, 9% external sources). *Receiving aid:* Freshmen: 7% (13). Undergraduates: 10% (73). *Average award:* Freshmen: $9804. Undergraduates: $9561. *Scholarships, grants, and awards by category: Academic interests/achievement:* 612 awards ($3,795,747 total): general academic interests/achievements. *Creative arts/performance:* 50 awards ($138,370 total): art/fine arts, creative writing, general creative arts/performance, music, performing arts. *Special achievements/activities:* 10 awards ($15,590 total): general special achievements/activities, junior miss. *Special characteristics:* 126 awards ($173,715 total): children of faculty/staff, general special characteristics, out-of-state students, relatives of clergy, religious affiliation, veterans. *Tuition waivers:* Full or partial for children of alumni, employees or children of employees, senior citizens. *ROTC:* Army cooperative.
LOANS *Student loans:* $3,908,866 (80% need-based, 20% non-need-based). *Average need-based loan:* Freshmen: $3230. Undergraduates: $3930. *Parent loans:* $742,578 (54% need-based, 46% non-need-based). *Programs:* Federal Direct (Subsidized and Unsubsidized Stafford, PLUS), Perkins, alternative loans.
WORK-STUDY *Federal work-study:* Total amount: $143,621; 117 jobs averaging $1427. *State or other work-study/employment:* Part-time jobs available.
APPLYING FOR FINANCIAL AID *Required financial aid form:* FAFSA. *Financial aid deadline:* 3/15. *Notification date:* Continuous. Students must reply within 2 weeks of notification.
CONTACT Mrs. Samantha Hays, Director of Financial Aid, Kentucky Wesleyan College, 3000 Frederica Street, Owensboro, KY 42301, 270-852-3130 or toll-free 800-999-0592 (in-state), 800-990-0592 (out-of-state). *Fax:* 270-852-3133. *E-mail:* shays@kwc.edu.
Website: http://www.kwc.edu/.

KENYON COLLEGE
Gambier, OH

Tuition & fees: $45,640	Average undergraduate aid package: $37,283

ABOUT THE INSTITUTION Independent, coed. *Awards:* bachelor's degrees. 29 undergraduate majors. *Total enrollment:* 1,667. Undergraduates: 1,667. Freshmen: 446. Both federal and institutional methodology are used as a basis for awarding need-based institutional aid.
UNDERGRADUATE EXPENSES for 2013–2014 *Application fee:* $50. *Comprehensive fee:* $56,810 includes full-time tuition ($43,900), mandatory fees ($1740), and room and board ($11,170).
FRESHMAN FINANCIAL AID (Fall 2012, est.) 257 applied for aid; of those 74% were deemed to have need. 99% of freshmen with need received aid; of those 75% had need fully met. *Average percent of need met:* 96% (excluding resources awarded to replace EFC). *Average financial aid package:* $37,805 (excluding resources awarded to replace EFC). 14% of all full-time freshmen had no need and received non-need-based gift aid.
UNDERGRADUATE FINANCIAL AID (Fall 2012, est.) 870 applied for aid; of those 83% were deemed to have need. 99% of undergraduates with need received aid; of those 65% had need fully met. *Average percent of need met:* 95% (excluding resources awarded to replace EFC). *Average financial aid package:* $37,283 (excluding resources awarded to replace EFC). 12% of all full-time undergraduates had no need and received non-need-based gift aid.
GIFT AID (NEED-BASED) *Total amount:* $23,903,017 (4% federal, 92% institutional, 4% external sources). *Receiving aid:* Freshmen: 42% (185); all full-time undergraduates: 38% (698). *Average award:* Freshmen: $36,339; Undergraduates: $34,245. *Scholarships, grants, and awards:* Federal Pell, FSEOG, state, private, college/university gift aid from institutional funds.

GIFT AID (NON-NEED-BASED) *Total amount:* $4,525,419 (1% federal, 72% institutional, 27% external sources). *Receiving aid:* Freshmen: 8% (36). Undergraduates: 7% (120). *Average award:* Freshmen: $12,640. Undergraduates: $12,094. *Scholarships, grants, and awards by category: Academic interests/achievement:* 307 awards ($3,596,500 total): general academic interests/achievements. *Creative arts/performance:* 13 awards ($150,000 total): art/fine arts, creative writing, music. *Special characteristics:* 51 awards ($817,130 total): ethnic background, first-generation college students. *Tuition waivers:* Full or partial for employees or children of employees.
LOANS *Student loans:* $4,756,008 (58% need-based, 42% non-need-based). 41% of past graduating class borrowed through all loan programs. *Average indebtedness per student:* $20,992. *Average need-based loan:* Freshmen: $2911. Undergraduates: $4119. *Parent loans:* $1,892,886 (5% need-based, 95% non-need-based). *Programs:* Federal Direct (Subsidized and Unsubsidized Stafford, PLUS), Perkins, college/university.
WORK-STUDY *Federal work-study:* Total amount: $193,841; 199 jobs averaging $1360. *State or other work-study/employment:* Total amount: $472,248 (59% need-based, 41% non-need-based). 128 part-time jobs averaging $1366.
APPLYING FOR FINANCIAL AID *Required financial aid forms:* FAFSA, CSS Financial Aid PROFILE, noncustodial (divorced/separated) parent's statement, federal income tax form(s). *Financial aid deadline (priority):* 2/15. *Notification date:* 4/1. Students must reply by 5/1.
CONTACT Mr. Craig Daugherty, Director of Financial Aid, Kenyon College, Stephens Hall, Gambier, OH 43022-9623, 740-427-5430 or toll-free 800-848-2468. *Fax:* 740-427-5240. *E-mail:* daugherty@kenyon.edu.
Website: http://www.kenyon.edu/.

KETTERING COLLEGE
Kettering, OH

CONTACT Financial Aid Office, Kettering College, 3737 Southern Boulevard, Kettering, OH 45429-1299, 937-395-8601 or toll-free 800-433-5262.
Website: http://www.kc.edu/.

KETTERING UNIVERSITY
Flint, MI

Tuition & fees: $33,946	Average undergraduate aid package: $20,987

ABOUT THE INSTITUTION Independent, coed, primarily men. *Awards:* bachelor's and master's degrees. 14 undergraduate majors. *Total enrollment:* 2,079. Undergraduates: 1,745. Freshmen: 329. Federal methodology is used as a basis for awarding need-based institutional aid.
UNDERGRADUATE EXPENSES for 2013–2014 *Application fee:* $35. *Comprehensive fee:* $40,606 includes full-time tuition ($33,946) and room and board ($6660). *College room only:* $4150. *Part-time tuition:* $1132 per credit. *Payment plan:* Guaranteed tuition.
FRESHMAN FINANCIAL AID (Fall 2012, est.) 372 applied for aid; of those 95% were deemed to have need. 100% of freshmen with need received aid; of those 12% had need fully met. *Average percent of need met:* 65% (excluding resources awarded to replace EFC). *Average financial aid package:* $22,475 (excluding resources awarded to replace EFC). 19% of all full-time freshmen had no need and received non-need-based gift aid.
UNDERGRADUATE FINANCIAL AID (Fall 2012, est.) 1,300 applied for aid; of those 95% were deemed to have need. 100% of undergraduates with need received aid; of those 14% had need fully met. *Average percent of need met:* 63% (excluding resources awarded to replace EFC). *Average financial aid package:* $20,987 (excluding resources awarded to replace EFC). 24% of all full-time undergraduates had no need and received non-need-based gift aid.
GIFT AID (NEED-BASED) *Total amount:* $17,607,074 (12% federal, 6% state, 80% institutional, 2% external sources). *Receiving aid:* Freshmen: 95% (353); all full-time undergraduates: 77% (1,220). *Average award:* Freshmen: $17,421; Undergraduates: $15,267. *Scholarships, grants, and awards:* Federal Pell, FSEOG, state, private.

GIFT AID (NON-NEED-BASED) Total amount: $5,330,774 (96% institutional, 4% external sources). **Receiving aid:** Freshmen: 32% (120). Undergraduates: 22% (351). **Average award:** Freshmen: $14,893. Undergraduates: $12,325. **Scholarships, grants, and awards by category:** Academic interests/achievement: business, computer science, engineering/technologies, general academic interests/achievements, mathematics, physical sciences. Special achievements/activities: general special achievements/activities, leadership, memberships. Special characteristics: children of faculty/staff, local/state students, members of minority groups, siblings of current students. **Tuition waivers:** Full or partial for employees or children of employees.

LOANS Student loans: $13,658,720 (80% need-based, 20% non-need-based). **Average need-based loan:** Freshmen: $3442. Undergraduates: $4388. **Parent loans:** $2,138,000 (84% need-based, 16% non-need-based). **Programs:** Federal Direct (Subsidized and Unsubsidized Stafford, PLUS).

WORK-STUDY Federal work-study: Total amount: $1,325,128; jobs available.

APPLYING FOR FINANCIAL AID Required financial aid form: FAFSA. **Financial aid deadline:** Continuous. **Notification date:** Continuous beginning 2/15.

CONTACT Diane Bice, Director of Financial Aid, Kettering University, 1700 University Avenue, Flint, MI 48504-4898, 800-955-4464 Ext. 7859 or toll-free 800-955-4464 Ext. 7865 (in-state), 800-955-4464 (out-of-state). Fax: 810-762-9807. E-mail: finaid@kettering.edu. Website: http://www.kettering.edu/.

KEUKA COLLEGE
Keuka Park, NY

Tuition & fees: $26,320	Average undergraduate aid package: $17,472

ABOUT THE INSTITUTION Independent American Baptist Churches in the U.S.A., coed. **Awards:** bachelor's and master's degrees. 34 undergraduate majors. **Total enrollment:** 2,083. Undergraduates: 1,874. Freshmen: 244. Federal methodology is used as a basis for awarding need-based institutional aid.

UNDERGRADUATE EXPENSES for 2013–2014 Application fee: $30. **Comprehensive fee:** $36,600 includes full-time tuition ($25,530), mandatory fees ($790), and room and board ($10,280). **College room only:** $4880. Full-time tuition and fees vary according to degree level and program. Room and board charges vary according to board plan and housing facility. **Part-time tuition:** $850 per credit hour. **Part-time fees:** $700 per year. Part-time tuition and fees vary according to program.

FRESHMAN FINANCIAL AID (Fall 2012, est.) 224 applied for aid; of those 100% were deemed to have need. 100% of freshmen with need received aid; of those 1% had need fully met. **Average percent of need met:** 70% (excluding resources awarded to replace EFC). **Average financial aid package:** $22,711 (excluding resources awarded to replace EFC). 4% of all full-time freshmen had no need and received non-need-based gift aid.

UNDERGRADUATE FINANCIAL AID (Fall 2012, est.) 1,301 applied for aid; of those 100% were deemed to have need. 100% of undergraduates with need received aid; of those 3% had need fully met. **Average percent of need met:** 68% (excluding resources awarded to replace EFC). **Average financial aid package:** $17,472 (excluding resources awarded to replace EFC). 4% of all full-time undergraduates had no need and received non-need-based gift aid.

GIFT AID (NEED-BASED) Total amount: $17,030,965 (22% federal, 13% state, 64% institutional, 1% external sources). **Receiving aid:** Freshmen: 82% (201); all full-time undergraduates: 65% (1,007). **Average award:** Freshmen: $9181; Undergraduates: $8906. **Scholarships, grants, and awards:** Federal Pell, FSEOG, state, college/university gift aid from institutional funds.

GIFT AID (NON-NEED-BASED) Total amount: $1,705,788 (24% federal, 10% state, 63% institutional, 3% external sources). **Receiving aid:** Freshmen: 80% (197). Undergraduates: 57% (874). **Average award:** Freshmen: $11,678. Undergraduates: $11,967. **Scholarships, grants, and awards by category:** Academic interests/achievement: general academic interests/achievements, international studies. Special achievements/activities: community service, general special achievements/activities, leadership. Special characteristics: children and siblings of alumni, children of faculty/staff, international students, siblings of current students. **Tuition waivers:** Full or partial for employees or children of employees.

LOANS Student loans: $15,160,563 (84% need-based, 16% non-need-based). Average indebtedness per student: $19,845. **Average need-based loan:** Freshmen: $3263. Undergraduates: $4259. **Parent loans:** $2,195,241 (65% need-based, 35% non-need-based). **Programs:** Perkins.

WORK-STUDY Federal work-study: Total amount: $366,278; jobs available. **State or other work-study/employment:** Total amount: $122,985 (23% need-based, 77% non-need-based). Part-time jobs available.

APPLYING FOR FINANCIAL AID Required financial aid form: FAFSA. **Financial aid deadline:** Continuous. **Notification date:** Continuous beginning 3/1. Students must reply by 5/1 or within 2 weeks of notification.

CONTACT Jennifer Bates, Director of Financial Aid, Keuka College, 141 Central Avenue, Keuka Park, NY 14478-0098, 315-279-5232 or toll-free 800-33-KEUKA. Fax: 315-536-5327. E-mail: jbates@keuka.edu. Website: http://www.keuka.edu/.

KEYSTONE COLLEGE
La Plume, PA

Tuition & fees: $21,200	Average undergraduate aid package: $18,353

ABOUT THE INSTITUTION Independent, coed. **Awards:** certificates, associate, and bachelor's degrees. 47 undergraduate majors. **Total enrollment:** 1,683. Undergraduates: 1,670. Freshmen: 363. Federal methodology is used as a basis for awarding need-based institutional aid.

UNDERGRADUATE EXPENSES for 2013–2014 Application fee: $30. **One-time required fee:** $500. **Comprehensive fee:** $31,000 includes full-time tuition ($20,300), mandatory fees ($900), and room and board ($9800). **College room only:** $4950. Room and board charges vary according to board plan and housing facility. **Part-time tuition:** $400 per credit. **Part-time fees:** $225 per term. Part-time tuition and fees vary according to course load.

FRESHMAN FINANCIAL AID (Fall 2011) 346 applied for aid; of those 97% were deemed to have need. 100% of freshmen with need received aid; of those 11% had need fully met. **Average percent of need met:** 76% (excluding resources awarded to replace EFC). **Average financial aid package:** $20,096 (excluding resources awarded to replace EFC). 7% of all full-time freshmen had no need and received non-need-based gift aid.

UNDERGRADUATE FINANCIAL AID (Fall 2011) 1,253 applied for aid; of those 96% were deemed to have need. 100% of undergraduates with need received aid; of those 12% had need fully met. **Average percent of need met:** 72% (excluding resources awarded to replace EFC). **Average financial aid package:** $18,353 (excluding resources awarded to replace EFC). 9% of all full-time undergraduates had no need and received non-need-based gift aid.

GIFT AID (NEED-BASED) Total amount: $10,054,517 (33% federal, 24% state, 42% institutional, 1% external sources). **Receiving aid:** Freshmen: 92% (334); all full-time undergraduates: 85% (1,188). **Average award:** Freshmen: $15,921; Undergraduates: $13,837. **Scholarships, grants, and awards:** Federal Pell, FSEOG, state, private, college/university gift aid from institutional funds.

GIFT AID (NON-NEED-BASED) Total amount: $6,878,732 (100% institutional). **Receiving aid:** Freshmen: 70% (254). Undergraduates: 62% (865). **Average award:** Freshmen: $9738. Undergraduates: $7147. **Scholarships, grants, and awards by category:** Academic interests/achievement: 65 awards ($152,615 total): agriculture, computer science, health fields. Special characteristics: 50 awards ($35,520 total): children and siblings of alumni, international students, siblings of current students. **Tuition waivers:** Full or partial for employees or children of employees, senior citizens. **ROTC:** Army cooperative, Air Force cooperative.

LOANS Student loans: $10,441,912 (44% need-based, 56% non-need-based). 92% of past graduating class borrowed through all loan programs. Average indebtedness per student: $8675. **Average need-based loan:** Freshmen: $3258. Undergraduates: $3946. **Parent loans:** $3,300,250 (45% need-based, 55% non-need-based). **Programs:** Federal Direct (Subsidized and Unsubsidized Stafford, PLUS), Perkins, alternative loans.

WORK-STUDY Federal work-study: Total amount: $131,179; 456 jobs averaging $1433. **State or other work-study/employment:** Total amount: $85,000 (100% non-need-based). 171 part-time jobs averaging $1437.

APPLYING FOR FINANCIAL AID Required financial aid forms: FAFSA, state aid form. **Financial aid deadline:** 5/1 (priority: 4/1). **Notification date:** 3/1. Students must reply within 3 weeks of notification.

CONTACT Mr. Brian T. Weber, Director of Financial Assistance and Planning, Keystone College, One College Green, La Plume, PA 18440, 570-945-8130 or toll-free 877-4-COLLEGE. *Fax:* 570-945-8134. *E-mail:* brian.weber@keystone.edu. *Website:* http://www.keystone.edu/.

KING COLLEGE
Bristol, TN

Tuition & fees: $24,960	Average undergraduate aid package: $15,356

ABOUT THE INSTITUTION Independent Presbyterian Church (U.S.A.), coed. *Awards:* certificates, bachelor's, and master's degrees. 61 undergraduate majors. *Total enrollment:* 2,342. Undergraduates: 1,963. Freshmen: 214. Federal methodology is used as a basis for awarding need-based institutional aid.

UNDERGRADUATE EXPENSES for 2013–2014 *Application fee:* $20. *Comprehensive fee:* $33,140 includes full-time tuition ($23,608), mandatory fees ($1352), and room and board ($8180). *College room only:* $4108. Full-time tuition and fees vary according to course load and program. Room and board charges vary according to board plan. *Part-time tuition:* $600 per credit hour. Part-time tuition and fees vary according to course load and program.

FRESHMAN FINANCIAL AID (Fall 2011) 228 applied for aid; of those 90% were deemed to have need. 100% of freshmen with need received aid; of those 16% had need fully met. *Average percent of need met:* 74% (excluding resources awarded to replace EFC). *Average financial aid package:* $20,662 (excluding resources awarded to replace EFC). 13% of all full-time freshmen had no need and received non-need-based gift aid.

UNDERGRADUATE FINANCIAL AID (Fall 2011) 1,622 applied for aid; of those 91% were deemed to have need. 100% of undergraduates with need received aid; of those 16% had need fully met. *Average percent of need met:* 69% (excluding resources awarded to replace EFC). *Average financial aid package:* $15,356 (excluding resources awarded to replace EFC). 6% of all full-time undergraduates had no need and received non-need-based gift aid.

GIFT AID (NEED-BASED) *Total amount:* $14,448,230 (27% federal, 11% state, 58% institutional, 4% external sources). *Receiving aid:* Freshmen: 78% (195); all full-time undergraduates: 70% (1,250). *Average award:* Freshmen: $18,066; Undergraduates: $12,802. *Scholarships, grants, and awards:* Federal Pell, FSEOG, state, private, college/university gift aid from institutional funds.

GIFT AID (NON-NEED-BASED) *Total amount:* $1,513,584 (1% federal, 17% state, 72% institutional, 10% external sources). *Receiving aid:* Freshmen: 10% (25). Undergraduates: 6% (115). *Average award:* Freshmen: $9224. Undergraduates: $8673. *Scholarships, grants, and awards by category: Academic interests/achievement:* general academic interests/achievements. *Creative arts/performance:* music, performing arts, theater/drama. *Special achievements/activities:* general special achievements/activities. *Special characteristics:* children of faculty/staff, members of minority groups, relatives of clergy. *Tuition waivers:* Full or partial for employees or children of employees, senior citizens. *ROTC:* Army cooperative.

LOANS *Student loans:* $15,699,460 (78% need-based, 22% non-need-based). 95% of past graduating class borrowed through all loan programs. *Average indebtedness per student:* $10,892. *Average need-based loan:* Freshmen: $3800. Undergraduates: $4772. *Parent loans:* $3,825,318 (10% need-based, 90% non-need-based). *Programs:* Federal Direct (Subsidized and Unsubsidized Stafford, PLUS), Perkins, college/university.

WORK-STUDY *Federal work-study:* Total amount: $79,599; 86 jobs averaging $1563. *State or other work-study/employment:* 144 part-time jobs averaging $1296.

ATHLETIC AWARDS Total amount: $2,448,939 (66% need-based, 34% non-need-based).

APPLYING FOR FINANCIAL AID *Required financial aid form:* FAFSA. *Financial aid deadline (priority):* 3/1. *Notification date:* Continuous beginning 3/1. Students must reply within 2 weeks of notification.

CONTACT John C. McCarroll, Director of Financial Aid, King College, 1350 King College Road, Bristol, TN 37620-2699, 423-652-4728 or toll-free 800-362-0014. *Fax:* 423-652-6039. *E-mail:* nmbeverly@king.edu. *Website:* http://www.king.edu/.

THE KING'S COLLEGE
New York, NY

Tuition & fees: $29,240	Average undergraduate aid package: $24,333

ABOUT THE INSTITUTION Independent nondenominational, coed. *Awards:* bachelor's degrees. 2 undergraduate majors. *Total enrollment:* 582. Undergraduates: 581. Freshmen: 203. Federal methodology is used as a basis for awarding need-based institutional aid.

UNDERGRADUATE EXPENSES for 2013–2014 *Application fee:* $30. *Tuition:* full-time $28,890; part-time $1203.75 per credit hour. *Required fees:* full-time $350; $175 per term. Full-time tuition and fees vary according to course load. Part-time tuition and fees vary according to course load. Room and board charges vary according to location.

FRESHMAN FINANCIAL AID (Fall 2011) 147 applied for aid; of those 93% were deemed to have need. 100% of freshmen with need received aid; of those 12% had need fully met. *Average percent of need met:* 62% (excluding resources awarded to replace EFC). *Average financial aid package:* $24,457 (excluding resources awarded to replace EFC). 15% of all full-time freshmen had no need and received non-need-based gift aid.

UNDERGRADUATE FINANCIAL AID (Fall 2011) 387 applied for aid; of those 95% were deemed to have need. 100% of undergraduates with need received aid; of those 11% had need fully met. *Average percent of need met:* 64% (excluding resources awarded to replace EFC). *Average financial aid package:* $24,333 (excluding resources awarded to replace EFC). 18% of all full-time undergraduates had no need and received non-need-based gift aid.

GIFT AID (NEED-BASED) *Total amount:* $7,541,465 (9% federal, 87% institutional, 4% external sources). *Receiving aid:* Freshmen: 84% (136); all full-time undergraduates: 81% (369). *Average award:* Freshmen: $21,592; Undergraduates: $20,315. *Scholarships, grants, and awards:* Federal Pell, FSEOG, state, private, college/university gift aid from institutional funds.

GIFT AID (NON-NEED-BASED) *Total amount:* $1,515,969 (90% institutional, 10% external sources). *Receiving aid:* Freshmen: 7% (12). Undergraduates: 7% (31). *Average award:* Freshmen: $15,760. Undergraduates: $14,311. *Scholarships, grants, and awards by category: Academic interests/achievement:* 448 awards ($5,748,852 total): general academic interests/achievements. *Tuition waivers:* Full or partial for employees or children of employees.

LOANS *Student loans:* $2,630,161 (82% need-based, 18% non-need-based). 67% of past graduating class borrowed through all loan programs. *Average indebtedness per student:* $23,270. *Average need-based loan:* Freshmen: $4017. Undergraduates: $5238. *Parent loans:* $999,708 (64% need-based, 36% non-need-based). *Programs:* Federal Direct (Subsidized and Unsubsidized Stafford, PLUS).

APPLYING FOR FINANCIAL AID *Required financial aid form:* FAFSA. *Financial aid deadline (priority):* 3/15. *Notification date:* Continuous beginning 2/1.

CONTACT Anna Peters, Director of Financial Aid, The King's College, 52 Broadway, 5th Floor, New York, NY 10004, 212-659-7281 or toll-free 888-969-7200 Ext. 3610. *Fax:* 212-659-3613. *E-mail:* apeters@tkc.edu. *Website:* http://www.tkc.edu/.

KING'S COLLEGE
Wilkes-Barre, PA

Tuition & fees: $29,174	Average undergraduate aid package: $21,336

ABOUT THE INSTITUTION Independent Roman Catholic, coed. *Awards:* certificates, associate, bachelor's, and master's degrees. 39 undergraduate majors. *Total enrollment:* 2,494. Undergraduates: 2,218. Freshmen: 514. Federal methodology is used as a basis for awarding need-based institutional aid.

UNDERGRADUATE EXPENSES for 2013–2014 *Application fee:* $30. *Comprehensive fee:* $40,194 includes full-time tuition ($29,174) and room and board ($11,020). *College room only:* $5380. Room and board charges vary according to board plan. *Part-time tuition:* $530 per credit hour.

FRESHMAN FINANCIAL AID (Fall 2012, est.) 495 applied for aid; of those 95% were deemed to have need. 100% of freshmen with need received aid; of those 15%

had need fully met. *Average percent of need met:* 71% (excluding resources awarded to replace EFC). *Average financial aid package:* $21,167 (excluding resources awarded to replace EFC). 8% of all full-time freshmen had no need and received non-need-based gift aid.

UNDERGRADUATE FINANCIAL AID (Fall 2012, est.) 1,817 applied for aid; of those 92% were deemed to have need. 99% of undergraduates with need received aid; of those 16% had need fully met. *Average percent of need met:* 73% (excluding resources awarded to replace EFC). *Average financial aid package:* $21,336 (excluding resources awarded to replace EFC). 14% of all full-time undergraduates had no need and received non-need-based gift aid.

GIFT AID (NEED-BASED) *Total amount:* $27,746,809 (11% federal, 11% state, 77% institutional, 1% external sources). *Receiving aid:* Freshmen: 91% (468); all full-time undergraduates: 84% (1,658). *Average award:* Freshmen: $16,842; Undergraduates: $16,188. *Scholarships, grants, and awards:* Federal Pell, FSEOG, state, private, college/university gift aid from institutional funds.

GIFT AID (NON-NEED-BASED) *Total amount:* $4,859,015 (9% federal, 90% institutional, 1% external sources). *Receiving aid:* Freshmen: 11% (56). Undergraduates: 10% (197). *Average award:* Freshmen: $11,738. Undergraduates: $12,668. *Scholarships, grants, and awards by category: Academic interests/achievement:* 1,480 awards ($16,494,196 total): biological sciences, business, communication, computer science, education, English, foreign languages, general academic interests/achievements, health fields, humanities, mathematics, physical sciences, premedicine, religion/biblical studies, social sciences. *Special achievements/activities:* 1,652 awards ($4,417,439 total): community service, general special achievements/activities, leadership. *Special characteristics:* 331 awards ($2,312,048 total): children and siblings of alumni, children of educators, children of faculty/staff, international students, members of minority groups, relatives of clergy, siblings of current students, veterans. *Tuition waivers:* Full or partial for employees or children of employees, senior citizens. *ROTC:* Army, Air Force cooperative.

LOANS *Student loans:* $15,255,998 (74% need-based, 26% non-need-based). 82% of past graduating class borrowed through all loan programs. *Average indebtedness per student:* $36,538. *Average need-based loan:* Freshmen: $3720. Undergraduates: $4518. *Parent loans:* $4,358,719 (44% need-based, 56% non-need-based). *Programs:* Federal Direct (Subsidized and Unsubsidized Stafford, PLUS), Perkins, private loans.

WORK-STUDY *Federal work-study:* Total amount: $280,736; 427 jobs averaging $657. *State or other work-study/employment:* Total amount: $360,616 (19% need-based, 81% non-need-based). 168 part-time jobs averaging $2146.

APPLYING FOR FINANCIAL AID *Required financial aid forms:* FAFSA, institution's own form. *Financial aid deadline (priority):* 2/15. *Notification date:* Continuous beginning 3/1. Students must reply by 5/1 or within 2 weeks of notification.

CONTACT Ms. Donna Cerza, Director of Financial Aid, King's College, 133 North River Street, Wilkes-Barre, PA 18711-0801, 570-208-5868 or toll-free 888-KINGSPA. *Fax:* 570-208-6015. *E-mail:* finaid@kings.edu. *Website:* http://www.kings.edu/.

KING'S UNIVERSITY
Van Nuys, CA

CONTACT Mr. Norman V. Stoppenbrink Jr., Financial Aid Officer, King's University, 14800 Sherman Way, Los Angeles, CA 91405, 818-779-8040 Ext. 8278 or toll-free 888-779-8040. *Fax:* 818-779-8251. *E-mail:* financialaid@kingsuniversity.edu. *Website:* http://kingsuniversity.edu/.

KNOX COLLEGE
Galesburg, IL

Tuition & fees: $38,952	Average undergraduate aid package: $28,374

ABOUT THE INSTITUTION Independent, coed. *Awards:* bachelor's degrees. 39 undergraduate majors. *Total enrollment:* 1,430. Undergraduates: 1,430. Freshmen: 377. Both federal and institutional methodology are used as a basis for awarding need-based institutional aid.

UNDERGRADUATE EXPENSES for 2013–2014 *Application fee:* $40. *Comprehensive fee:* $47,352 includes full-time tuition ($38,286), mandatory fees ($666), and room and board ($8400). *College room only:* $4206. Full-time tuition and fees vary according to course load. Room and board charges vary according to housing facility. Part-time tuition and fees vary according to course load.

FRESHMAN FINANCIAL AID (Fall 2012, est.) 353 applied for aid; of those 86% were deemed to have need. 100% of freshmen with need received aid; of those 35% had need fully met. *Average percent of need met:* 90% (excluding resources awarded to replace EFC). *Average financial aid package:* $30,376 (excluding resources awarded to replace EFC). 19% of all full-time freshmen had no need and received non-need-based gift aid.

UNDERGRADUATE FINANCIAL AID (Fall 2012, est.) 1,199 applied for aid; of those 91% were deemed to have need. 99% of undergraduates with need received aid; of those 28% had need fully met. *Average percent of need met:* 87% (excluding resources awarded to replace EFC). *Average financial aid package:* $28,374 (excluding resources awarded to replace EFC). 22% of all full-time undergraduates had no need and received non-need-based gift aid.

GIFT AID (NEED-BASED) *Total amount:* $24,877,763 (8% federal, 4% state, 86% institutional, 2% external sources). *Receiving aid:* Freshmen: 78% (295); all full-time undergraduates: 76% (1,061). *Average award:* Freshmen: $24,762; Undergraduates: $22,949. *Scholarships, grants, and awards:* Federal Pell, FSEOG, state, private, college/university gift aid from institutional funds.

GIFT AID (NON-NEED-BASED) *Total amount:* $3,709,574 (97% institutional, 3% external sources). *Receiving aid:* Freshmen: 19% (71). Undergraduates: 12% (174). *Average award:* Freshmen: $14,942. Undergraduates: $12,870. *Scholarships, grants, and awards by category: Academic interests/achievement:* general academic interests/achievements, mathematics. *Creative arts/performance:* art/fine arts, creative writing, dance, music, theater/drama. *Special achievements/activities:* community service. *Tuition waivers:* Full or partial for employees or children of employees.

LOANS *Student loans:* $8,094,177 (55% need-based, 45% non-need-based). 64% of past graduating class borrowed through all loan programs. *Average indebtedness per student:* $27,542. *Average need-based loan:* Freshmen: $2978. Undergraduates: $5252. *Parent loans:* $1,953,860 (100% non-need-based). *Programs:* Federal Direct (Subsidized and Unsubsidized Stafford, PLUS), Perkins, college/university, private loans.

WORK-STUDY *Federal work-study:* Total amount: $1,507,404; jobs available. *State or other work-study/employment:* Total amount: $261,084 (100% need-based). Part-time jobs available.

APPLYING FOR FINANCIAL AID *Required financial aid forms:* FAFSA, institution's own form. *Financial aid deadline (priority):* 2/1. *Notification date:* Continuous beginning 3/1. Students must reply by 5/1 or within 2 weeks of notification.

CONTACT Ms. Ann M. Brill, Director of Financial Aid, Knox College, 2 East South Street, Galesburg, IL 61401, 309-341-7149 or toll-free 800-678-KNOX. *Fax:* 309-341-7453. *E-mail:* abrill@knox.edu. *Website:* http://www.knox.edu/.

KUTZTOWN UNIVERSITY OF PENNSYLVANIA
Kutztown, PA

Tuition & fees (PA res): $8596	Average undergraduate aid package: $7743

ABOUT THE INSTITUTION State-supported, coed. *Awards:* certificates, bachelor's, and master's degrees. 46 undergraduate majors. *Total enrollment:* 9,804. Undergraduates: 9,135. Freshmen: 1,997. Federal methodology is used as a basis for awarding need-based institutional aid.

UNDERGRADUATE EXPENSES for 2013–2014 *Application fee:* $35. *One-time required fee:* $238. *Tuition, state resident:* full-time $6428; part-time $268 per credit hour. *Tuition, nonresident:* full-time $16,070; part-time $670 per credit hour. *Required fees:* full-time $2168; $90.43 per credit hour. Part-time tuition and fees vary according to course load. *College room and board:* $8890; *Room only:* $5552. Room and board charges vary according to board plan and housing facility.

FRESHMAN FINANCIAL AID (Fall 2011) 1,856 applied for aid; of those 80% were deemed to have need. 97% of freshmen with need received aid; of those 6% had need fully met. *Average percent of need met:* 45% (excluding resources awarded to replace EFC). *Average financial aid package:* $7326 (excluding resources awarded to replace EFC). 1% of all full-time freshmen had no need and received non-need-based gift aid.

UNDERGRADUATE FINANCIAL AID (Fall 2011) 7,325 applied for aid; of those 83% were deemed to have need. 97% of undergraduates with need received aid; of those 8% had need fully met. *Average percent of need met:* 50% (excluding resources awarded to replace EFC). *Average financial aid package:* $7743 (excluding resources awarded to replace EFC). 1% of all full-time undergraduates had no need and received non-need-based gift aid.

GIFT AID (NEED-BASED) *Total amount:* $21,613,883 (53% federal, 41% state, 2% institutional, 4% external sources). *Receiving aid:* Freshmen: 45% (919); all full-time undergraduates: 43% (3,683). *Average award:* Freshmen: $5453; Undergraduates: $5191. *Scholarships, grants, and awards:* Federal Pell, FSEOG, state, private, college/university gift aid from institutional funds.

GIFT AID (NON-NEED-BASED) *Total amount:* $433,374 (1% federal, 21% state, 18% institutional, 60% external sources). *Receiving aid:* Freshmen: 5% (103). Undergraduates: 6% (502). *Average award:* Freshmen: $793. Undergraduates: $866. *Scholarships, grants, and awards by category: Academic interests/achievement:* biological sciences, business, communication, computer science, education, English, foreign languages, general academic interests/achievements, humanities, international studies, library science, mathematics, physical sciences. *Creative arts/performance:* applied art and design, art/fine arts, dance, music. *Special achievements/activities:* community service, general special achievements/activities, leadership, religious involvement. *Special characteristics:* children of faculty/staff, children of union members/company employees, first-generation college students, handicapped students, local/state students. *Tuition waivers:* Full or partial for employees or children of employees, senior citizens. *ROTC:* Army cooperative.

LOANS *Student loans:* $59,644,839 (84% need-based, 16% non-need-based). 81% of past graduating class borrowed through all loan programs. *Average indebtedness per student:* $30,831. *Average need-based loan:* Freshmen: $3269. Undergraduates: $4026. *Parent loans:* $13,124,698 (81% need-based, 19% non-need-based). *Programs:* Perkins.

WORK-STUDY *Federal work-study:* Total amount: $327,045; jobs available.

ATHLETIC AWARDS Total amount: $583,577 (67% need-based, 33% non-need-based).

APPLYING FOR FINANCIAL AID *Required financial aid form:* FAFSA. *Financial aid deadline (priority):* 2/15. *Notification date:* Continuous beginning 3/30. Students must reply by 5/1 or within 4 weeks of notification.

CONTACT Mr. Bernard McCree, Director of Financial Aid, Kutztown University of Pennsylvania, 209 Stratton Administration Center, Kutztown, PA 19530-0730, 610-683-4032 or toll-free 877-628-1915. *Fax:* 610-683-1380. *E-mail:* mccree@kutztown.edu. *Website:* http://www.kutztown.edu/.

KUYPER COLLEGE
Grand Rapids, MI

Tuition & fees: N/R	Average undergraduate aid package: $13,714

ABOUT THE INSTITUTION Independent Christian, coed. *Awards:* certificates, associate, and bachelor's degrees. 26 undergraduate majors. *Total enrollment:* 314. Undergraduates: 312. Freshmen: 46. Federal methodology is used as a basis for awarding need-based institutional aid.

FRESHMAN FINANCIAL AID (Fall 2012, est.) 66 applied for aid; of those 92% were deemed to have need. 98% of freshmen with need received aid; of those 7% had need fully met. *Average percent of need met:* 68% (excluding resources awarded to replace EFC). *Average financial aid package:* $17,611 (excluding resources awarded to replace EFC). 8% of all full-time freshmen had no need and received non-need-based gift aid.

UNDERGRADUATE FINANCIAL AID (Fall 2012, est.) 266 applied for aid; of those 95% were deemed to have need. 100% of undergraduates with need received aid; of those 10% had need fully met. *Average percent of need met:* 70% (excluding resources awarded to replace EFC). *Average financial aid package:* $13,714 (excluding resources awarded to replace EFC). 7% of all full-time undergraduates had no need and received non-need-based gift aid.

GIFT AID (NEED-BASED) *Total amount:* $2,353,540 (33% federal, 12% state, 53% institutional, 2% external sources). *Receiving aid:* Freshmen: 89% (59); all full-time undergraduates: 93% (252). *Average award:* Freshmen: $10,821; Undergraduates: $11,755. *Scholarships, grants, and awards:* Federal Pell, FSEOG, state, private, college/university gift aid from institutional funds.

GIFT AID (NON-NEED-BASED) *Total amount:* $68,105 (99% institutional, 1% external sources). *Average award:* Freshmen: $5016. Undergraduates: $5773. *Scholarships, grants, and awards by category: Academic interests/achievement:* 140 awards ($414,300 total): general academic interests/achievements. *Creative arts/performance:* 8 awards ($4510 total): music. *Special achievements/activities:* 8 awards ($15,500 total): leadership, religious involvement. *Special characteristics:* 58 awards ($304,568 total): children of faculty/staff, international students, members of minority groups. *ROTC:* Army cooperative.

LOANS *Student loans:* $1,876,453 (96% need-based, 4% non-need-based). 79% of past graduating class borrowed through all loan programs. *Average indebtedness per student:* $13,615. *Average need-based loan:* Freshmen: $3098. Undergraduates: $3395. *Parent loans:* $211,604 (98% need-based, 2% non-need-based). *Programs:* Federal Direct (Subsidized and Unsubsidized Stafford, PLUS), alternative loans.

WORK-STUDY *Federal work-study:* Total amount: $25,082; 12 jobs averaging $2487. *State or other work-study/employment:* Total amount: $290,000 (100% non-need-based). 110 part-time jobs averaging $2636.

APPLYING FOR FINANCIAL AID *Required financial aid form:* FAFSA. *Financial aid deadline (priority):* 3/1. *Notification date:* Continuous beginning 3/20. Students must reply within 2 weeks of notification.

CONTACT Ms. Agnes Russell, Director of Financial Aid, Kuyper College, 3333 East Beltline NE, Grand Rapids, MI 49525-9749, 616-222-3000 Ext. 656. *Fax:* 616-222-3045. *E-mail:* arussell@kuyper.edu. *Website:* http://www.kuyper.edu/.

LAFAYETTE COLLEGE
Easton, PA

Tuition & fees: $43,970	Average undergraduate aid package: $38,323

ABOUT THE INSTITUTION Independent Presbyterian Church (U.S.A.), coed. *Awards:* bachelor's degrees. 37 undergraduate majors. *Total enrollment:* 2,488. Undergraduates: 2,488. Freshmen: 629. Institutional methodology is used as a basis for awarding need-based institutional aid.

UNDERGRADUATE EXPENSES for 2013–2014 *One-time required fee:* $700. *Comprehensive fee:* $57,050 includes full-time tuition ($43,580), mandatory fees ($390), and room and board ($13,080). *College room only:* $8090. Full-time tuition and fees vary according to course load. Room and board charges vary according to board plan, housing facility, and student level. *Part-time tuition:* $5450 per course. Part-time tuition and fees vary according to course load. *Payment plan:* Tuition prepayment.

FRESHMAN FINANCIAL AID (Fall 2011) 401 applied for aid; of those 65% were deemed to have need. 100% of freshmen with need received aid; of those 81% had need fully met. *Average percent of need met:* 98% (excluding resources awarded to replace EFC). *Average financial aid package:* $37,641 (excluding resources awarded to replace EFC). 7% of all full-time freshmen had no need and received non-need-based gift aid.

UNDERGRADUATE FINANCIAL AID (Fall 2011) 1,402 applied for aid; of those 72% were deemed to have need. 100% of undergraduates with need received aid; of those 86% had need fully met. *Average percent of need met:* 98% (excluding resources awarded to replace EFC). *Average financial aid package:* $38,323 (excluding resources awarded to replace EFC). 7% of all full-time undergraduates had no need and received non-need-based gift aid.

GIFT AID (NEED-BASED) *Total amount:* $32,133,644 (4% federal, 2% state, 93% institutional, 1% external sources). *Receiving aid:* Freshmen: 40% (252); all full-time undergraduates: 40% (978). *Average award:* Freshmen: $33,213; Undergraduates: $32,709. *Scholarships, grants, and awards:* Federal Pell, FSEOG, state, private, college/university gift aid from institutional funds.

GIFT AID (NON-NEED-BASED) *Total amount:* $5,524,112 (80% institutional, 20% external sources). *Receiving aid:* Freshmen: 11% (72). Undergraduates: 10% (234). *Average award:* Freshmen: $19,252. Undergraduates: $20,842. *Scholarships, grants, and awards by category: Academic interests/achievement:*

general academic interests/achievements. *Creative arts/performance:* applied art and design, art/fine arts, cinema/film/broadcasting, creative writing, dance, general creative arts/performance, music, performing arts, theater/drama. *Tuition waivers:* Full or partial for employees or children of employees. *ROTC:* Army cooperative.

LOANS *Student loans:* $9,822,964 (45% need-based, 55% non-need-based). 56% of past graduating class borrowed through all loan programs. *Average indebtedness per student:* $26,717. *Average need-based loan:* Freshmen: $3587. Undergraduates: $4326. *Parent loans:* $4,117,860 (1% need-based, 99% non-need-based). *Programs:* Federal Direct (Subsidized and Unsubsidized Stafford, PLUS), Perkins, college/university.

WORK-STUDY *Federal work-study:* Total amount: $802,685; jobs available. *State or other work-study/employment:* Total amount: $1,163,853 (44% need-based, 56% non-need-based). Part-time jobs available.

ATHLETIC AWARDS Total amount: $2,048,717 (5% need-based, 95% non-need-based).

APPLYING FOR FINANCIAL AID *Required financial aid forms:* FAFSA, CSS Financial Aid PROFILE, noncustodial (divorced/separated) parent's statement, federal income tax form(s). *Financial aid deadline:* 3/1 (priority: 1/15). *Notification date:* 4/1. Students must reply by 5/1.

CONTACT Ms. Arlina DeNardo, Director of Financial Aid, Lafayette College, 107 Markle Hall, Easton, PA 18042-1777, 610-330-5055. *Fax:* 610-330-5758. *E-mail:* denardoa@lafayette.edu.
Website: http://www.lafayette.edu/.

LAGRANGE COLLEGE
LaGrange, GA

Tuition & fees: $24,462	Average undergraduate aid package: $21,894

ABOUT THE INSTITUTION Independent United Methodist, coed. *Awards:* certificates, bachelor's, and master's degrees. 26 undergraduate majors. *Total enrollment:* 902. Undergraduates: 834. Freshmen: 198. Federal methodology is used as a basis for awarding need-based institutional aid.

UNDERGRADUATE EXPENSES for 2013–2014 *Application fee:* $30. *Comprehensive fee:* $34,640 includes full-time tuition ($24,302), mandatory fees ($160), and room and board ($10,178). *College room only:* $5816. Full-time tuition and fees vary according to class time, course load, degree level, and program. Room and board charges vary according to board plan and housing facility. *Part-time tuition:* $1000 per semester hour. Part-time tuition and fees vary according to class time, course load, degree level, and program.

FRESHMAN FINANCIAL AID (Fall 2012, est.) 192 applied for aid; of those 93% were deemed to have need. 100% of freshmen with need received aid; of those 22% had need fully met. *Average percent of need met:* 79% (excluding resources awarded to replace EFC). *Average financial aid package:* $23,020 (excluding resources awarded to replace EFC). 10% of all full-time freshmen had no need and received non-need-based gift aid.

UNDERGRADUATE FINANCIAL AID (Fall 2012, est.) 715 applied for aid; of those 92% were deemed to have need. 100% of undergraduates with need received aid; of those 21% had need fully met. *Average percent of need met:* 73% (excluding resources awarded to replace EFC). *Average financial aid package:* $21,894 (excluding resources awarded to replace EFC). 11% of all full-time undergraduates had no need and received non-need-based gift aid.

GIFT AID (NEED-BASED) *Receiving aid:* Freshmen: 90% (178); all full-time undergraduates: 85% (657). *Average award:* Freshmen: $19,625; Undergraduates: $17,778. *Scholarships, grants, and awards:* Federal Pell, FSEOG, private, college/university gift aid from institutional funds.

GIFT AID (NON-NEED-BASED) *Receiving aid:* Freshmen: 15% (30). Undergraduates: 13% (99). *Average award:* Freshmen: $10,116. Undergraduates: $10,424. *Scholarships, grants, and awards by category:* Academic interests/achievement: education, general academic interests/achievements, health fields. Creative arts/performance: music, theater/drama. Special achievements/activities: leadership. Special characteristics: children of faculty/staff, ethnic background, first-generation college students, relatives of clergy, religious affiliation. *Tuition waivers:* Full or partial for employees or children of employees, senior citizens.

LOANS *Student loans:* 73% of past graduating class borrowed through all loan programs. *Average indebtedness per student:* $32,270. *Average need-based loan:*

Freshmen: $3666. Undergraduates: $4441. *Programs:* Federal Direct (Subsidized and Unsubsidized Stafford, PLUS), Perkins.

WORK-STUDY Federal work-study jobs available. *State or other work-study/employment:* Part-time jobs available.

APPLYING FOR FINANCIAL AID *Required financial aid forms:* FAFSA, state aid form. *Financial aid deadline (priority):* 3/1. *Notification date:* Continuous beginning 3/15. Students must reply within 4 weeks of notification.

CONTACT Michelle Reeves, Assistant Director, LaGrange College, 601 Broad Street, LaGrange, GA 30240-2999, 888-253-9918 or toll-free 800-593-2885. *Fax:* 706-880-8348. *E-mail:* mreeves@lagrange.edu.
Website: http://www.lagrange.edu/.

LAGUNA COLLEGE OF ART & DESIGN
Laguna Beach, CA

Tuition & fees: N/R	Average undergraduate aid package: $11,601

ABOUT THE INSTITUTION Independent, coed. 12 undergraduate majors. Federal methodology is used as a basis for awarding need-based institutional aid.

FRESHMAN FINANCIAL AID (Fall 2012, est.) 68 applied for aid; of those 96% were deemed to have need. 100% of freshmen with need received aid. *Average percent of need met:* 71% (excluding resources awarded to replace EFC). *Average financial aid package:* $10,600 (excluding resources awarded to replace EFC). 3% of all full-time freshmen had no need and received non-need-based gift aid.

UNDERGRADUATE FINANCIAL AID (Fall 2012, est.) 434 applied for aid; of those 91% were deemed to have need. 100% of undergraduates with need received aid; of those 1% had need fully met. *Average percent of need met:* 82% (excluding resources awarded to replace EFC). *Average financial aid package:* $11,601 (excluding resources awarded to replace EFC). 2% of all full-time undergraduates had no need and received non-need-based gift aid.

GIFT AID (NEED-BASED) *Total amount:* $1,607,092 (49% federal, 44% state, 6% institutional, 1% external sources). *Receiving aid:* Freshmen: 77% (55); all full-time undergraduates: 83% (379). *Average award:* Freshmen: $6000; Undergraduates: $5500. *Scholarships, grants, and awards:* Federal Pell, FSEOG, state, private, college/university gift aid from institutional funds.

GIFT AID (NON-NEED-BASED) *Total amount:* $2,174,074 (100% institutional). *Receiving aid:* Freshmen: 92% (65). Undergraduates: 86% (395). *Average award:* Freshmen: $4500. Undergraduates: $4500. *Scholarships, grants, and awards by category:* Academic interests/achievement: general academic interests/achievements. Creative arts/performance: applied art and design, art/fine arts.

LOANS *Student loans:* $3,193,352 (38% need-based, 62% non-need-based). 90% of past graduating class borrowed through all loan programs. *Average indebtedness per student:* $38,000. *Average need-based loan:* Freshmen: $4000. Undergraduates: $5500. *Parent loans:* $2,250,478 (100% need-based). *Programs:* Federal Direct (Subsidized and Unsubsidized Stafford, PLUS).

WORK-STUDY *Federal work-study:* Total amount: $45,000; 21 jobs averaging $2000.

APPLYING FOR FINANCIAL AID *Required financial aid form:* FAFSA. *Financial aid deadline:* Continuous. *Notification date:* Continuous beginning 2/15.

CONTACT Christopher Brown, Director of Admissions and Financial Aid, Laguna College of Art & Design, 2222 Laguna Canyon Road, Laguna Beach, CA 92651-1136, 949-376-6000 or toll-free 800-255-0762. *Fax:* 949-715-4084. *E-mail:* cbrown@lcad.edu.
Website: http://www.lcad.edu/.

LAKE ERIE COLLEGE
Painesville, OH

Tuition & fees: $27,368	Average undergraduate aid package: $20,606

ABOUT THE INSTITUTION Independent, coed. *Awards:* certificates, bachelor's, and master's degrees. 35 undergraduate majors. *Total enrollment:* 1,199.

Undergraduates: 1,032. Freshmen: 275. Federal methodology is used as a basis for awarding need-based institutional aid.

UNDERGRADUATE EXPENSES for 2013–2014 *Application fee:* $30. *One-time required fee:* $350. *Comprehensive fee:* $35,704 includes full-time tuition ($25,976), mandatory fees ($1392), and room and board ($8336). *College room only:* $4054. Full-time tuition and fees vary according to course load, degree level, and program. Room and board charges vary according to board plan. *Part-time tuition:* $688 per credit hour. *Part-time fees:* $51 per credit hour. Part-time tuition and fees vary according to course load, degree level, and program.

FRESHMAN FINANCIAL AID (Fall 2012, est.) 240 applied for aid; of those 91% were deemed to have need. 100% of freshmen with need received aid; of those 16% had need fully met. *Average percent of need met:* 75% (excluding resources awarded to replace EFC). *Average financial aid package:* $21,626 (excluding resources awarded to replace EFC). 1% of all full-time freshmen had no need and received non-need-based gift aid.

UNDERGRADUATE FINANCIAL AID (Fall 2012, est.) 808 applied for aid; of those 93% were deemed to have need. 100% of undergraduates with need received aid; of those 17% had need fully met. *Average percent of need met:* 72% (excluding resources awarded to replace EFC). *Average financial aid package:* $20,606 (excluding resources awarded to replace EFC). 1% of all full-time undergraduates had no need and received non-need-based gift aid.

GIFT AID (NEED-BASED) *Total amount:* $12,660,573 (13% federal, 4% state, 4% institutional, 79% external sources). *Receiving aid:* Freshmen: 83% (218); all full-time undergraduates: 83% (751). *Average award:* Freshmen: $18,645; Undergraduates: $16,822. *Scholarships, grants, and awards:* Federal Pell, FSEOG, state, private, college/university gift aid from institutional funds.

GIFT AID (NON-NEED-BASED) *Total amount:* $3,014,371 (2% institutional, 98% external sources). *Receiving aid:* Freshmen: 10% (27). Undergraduates: 10% (92). *Average award:* Freshmen: $2000. Undergraduates: $7355. *Scholarships, grants, and awards by category: Academic interests/achievement:* biological sciences, business, communication, education, English, foreign languages, general academic interests/achievements, humanities, international studies, mathematics, physical sciences, social sciences. *Creative arts/performance:* art/fine arts, dance, general creative arts/performance, music, performing arts, theater/drama. *Special achievements/activities:* community service, general special achievements/activities, hobbies/interests. *Special characteristics:* children of faculty/staff, twins, veterans, veterans' children. *Tuition waivers:* Full or partial for employees or children of employees, senior citizens.

LOANS *Student loans:* $7,076,391 (75% need-based, 25% non-need-based). 90% of past graduating class borrowed through all loan programs. *Average indebtedness per student:* $34,758. *Average need-based loan:* Freshmen: $3141. Undergraduates: $4162. *Parent loans:* $1,188,952 (55% need-based, 45% non-need-based). *Programs:* Federal Direct (Subsidized and Unsubsidized Stafford, PLUS), Perkins.

WORK-STUDY *Federal work-study:* Total amount: $118,249; jobs available.

ATHLETIC AWARDS Total amount: $3,762,662 (69% need-based, 31% non-need-based).

APPLYING FOR FINANCIAL AID *Required financial aid form:* FAFSA. *Financial aid deadline:* Continuous. *Notification date:* Continuous beginning 2/15. Students must reply by 5/1 or within 4 weeks of notification.

CONTACT Patricia Pangonis, Director of Financial Aid, Lake Erie College, 391 West Washington Street, Painesville, OH 44077-3389, 440-375-7102 or toll-free 800-916-0904. *Fax:* 440-375-7103. *E-mail:* finaid@lec.edu. *Website:* http://www.lec.edu/.

LAKE FOREST COLLEGE
Lake Forest, IL

Tuition & fees: $38,300	Average undergraduate aid package: $31,000

ABOUT THE INSTITUTION Independent, coed. *Awards:* certificates, bachelor's, and master's degrees. 32 undergraduate majors. *Total enrollment:* 1,516. Undergraduates: 1,497. Freshmen: 406. Both federal and institutional methodology are used as a basis for awarding need-based institutional aid.

UNDERGRADUATE EXPENSES for 2013–2014 *Comprehensive fee:* $47,350 includes full-time tuition ($37,660), mandatory fees ($640), and room and board ($9050). *College room only:* $4440.

FRESHMAN FINANCIAL AID (Fall 2012, est.) 352 applied for aid; of those 89% were deemed to have need. 100% of freshmen with need received aid; of those 16% had need fully met. *Average percent of need met:* 84% (excluding resources awarded to replace EFC). *Average financial aid package:* $32,000 (excluding resources awarded to replace EFC). 23% of all full-time freshmen had no need and received non-need-based gift aid.

UNDERGRADUATE FINANCIAL AID (Fall 2012, est.) 1,288 applied for aid; of those 94% were deemed to have need. 100% of undergraduates with need received aid; of those 28% had need fully met. *Average percent of need met:* 84% (excluding resources awarded to replace EFC). *Average financial aid package:* $31,000 (excluding resources awarded to replace EFC). 18% of all full-time undergraduates had no need and received non-need-based gift aid.

GIFT AID (NEED-BASED) *Total amount:* $32,770,432 (8% federal, 6% state, 81% institutional, 5% external sources). *Receiving aid:* Freshmen: 75% (314); all full-time undergraduates: 79% (1,207). *Average award:* Freshmen: $28,175; Undergraduates: $27,650. *Scholarships, grants, and awards:* Federal Pell, FSEOG, state, private, college/university gift aid from institutional funds.

GIFT AID (NON-NEED-BASED) *Total amount:* $4,467,352 (98% institutional, 2% external sources). *Average award:* Freshmen: $17,043. Undergraduates: $15,850. *Scholarships, grants, and awards by category: Academic interests/achievement:* biological sciences, computer science, English, foreign languages, general academic interests/achievements, mathematics, physical sciences, social sciences. *Creative arts/performance:* art/fine arts, creative writing, music, theater/drama. *Special achievements/activities:* leadership. *Special characteristics:* children and siblings of alumni, local/state students, previous college experience.

LOANS *Student loans:* $4,689,232 (89% need-based, 11% non-need-based). 66% of past graduating class borrowed through all loan programs. *Average indebtedness per student:* $30,801. *Average need-based loan:* Freshmen: $3989. Undergraduates: $5039. *Parent loans:* $2,242,617 (93% need-based, 7% non-need-based). *Programs:* Federal Direct (Subsidized and Unsubsidized Stafford, PLUS), Perkins, private loans.

WORK-STUDY *Federal work-study:* Total amount: $1,039,250; jobs available. *State or other work-study/employment:* Part-time jobs available.

APPLYING FOR FINANCIAL AID *Required financial aid forms:* FAFSA, institution's own form. *Financial aid deadline:* 5/1 (priority: 3/1). *Notification date:* Continuous beginning 3/1. Students must reply by 5/1 or within 3 weeks of notification.

CONTACT Mr. Jerry Cebrzynski, Director of Financial Aid, Lake Forest College, 555 North Sheridan Road, Lake Forest, IL 60045-2399, 847-735-5104 or toll-free 800-828-4751. *Fax:* 847-735-6271. *E-mail:* cebrzynski@lakeforest.edu. *Website:* http://www.lakeforest.edu/.

LAKELAND COLLEGE
Sheboygan, WI

Tuition & fees: $21,242	Average undergraduate aid package: $13,003

ABOUT THE INSTITUTION Independent United Church of Christ, coed. *Awards:* bachelor's and master's degrees. 30 undergraduate majors. *Total enrollment:* 3,749. Undergraduates: 2,964. Freshmen: 216. Federal methodology is used as a basis for awarding need-based institutional aid.

UNDERGRADUATE EXPENSES for 2013–2014 *Comprehensive fee:* $28,582 includes full-time tuition ($21,242) and room and board ($7340). Full-time tuition and fees vary according to degree level. Room and board charges vary according to board plan and housing facility. Part-time tuition and fees vary according to class time, course load, degree level, and location. *Payment plans:* Guaranteed tuition, tuition prepayment.

FRESHMAN FINANCIAL AID (Fall 2012, est.) 229 applied for aid; of those 90% were deemed to have need. 98% of freshmen with need received aid; of those 10% had need fully met. *Average percent of need met:* 74% (excluding resources awarded to replace EFC). *Average financial aid package:* $17,862 (excluding resources awarded to replace EFC). 16% of all full-time freshmen had no need and received non-need-based gift aid.

UNDERGRADUATE FINANCIAL AID (Fall 2012, est.) 1,411 applied for aid; of those 90% were deemed to have need. 99% of undergraduates with need received aid; of those 9% had need fully met. *Average percent of need met:* 63% (excluding resources awarded to replace EFC). *Average financial aid package:* $13,003

(excluding resources awarded to replace EFC). 9% of all full-time undergraduates had no need and received non-need-based gift aid.

GIFT AID (NEED-BASED) *Total amount:* $11,189,960 (28% federal, 10% state, 58% institutional, 4% external sources). *Receiving aid:* Freshmen: 72% (197); all full-time undergraduates: 71% (1,086). *Average award:* Freshmen: $13,795; Undergraduates: $9895. *Scholarships, grants, and awards:* Federal Pell, FSEOG, state, private, college/university gift aid from institutional funds, Academic Competitiveness Grants, National SMART Grants.

GIFT AID (NON-NEED-BASED) *Total amount:* $1,350,139 (91% institutional, 9% external sources). *Receiving aid:* Freshmen: 7% (20). Undergraduates: 4% (62). *Average award:* Freshmen: $6142. Undergraduates: $7433. *Scholarships, grants, and awards by category:* Academic interests/achievement: 589 awards ($3,985,288 total): biological sciences, business, engineering/technologies, English, general academic interests/achievements, physical sciences, religion/biblical studies. Creative arts/performance: 85 awards ($171,500 total): art/fine arts, creative writing, dance, debating, journalism/publications, music, performing arts. Special achievements/activities: community service, leadership, religious involvement. Special characteristics: 248 awards ($278,225 total): children and siblings of alumni, children of faculty/staff, out-of-state students, religious affiliation, siblings of current students. *Tuition waivers:* Full or partial for employees or children of employees, senior citizens.

LOANS *Student loans:* $14,466,879 (85% need-based, 15% non-need-based). 86% of past graduating class borrowed through all loan programs. *Average indebtedness per student:* $30,105. *Average need-based loan:* Freshmen: $3505. Undergraduates: $4150. *Parent loans:* $802,876 (46% need-based, 54% non-need-based). *Programs:* Federal Direct (Subsidized and Unsubsidized Stafford, PLUS), Perkins, alternative loans.

WORK-STUDY *Federal work-study:* Total amount: $738,996; 425 jobs averaging $2500. *State or other work-study/employment:* Total amount: $310,353 (18% need-based, 82% non-need-based). 100 part-time jobs averaging $2500.

APPLYING FOR FINANCIAL AID *Required financial aid forms:* FAFSA, institution's own form. *Financial aid deadline:* 7/1 (priority: 3/15). *Notification date:* Continuous beginning 3/1. Students must reply within 2 weeks of notification.

CONTACT Ms. Patty Taylor, Director of Financial Aid, Lakeland College, PO Box 359, Sheboygan, WI 53082-0359, 920-565-1214 or toll-free 800-569-2166. *Fax:* 920-565-1470.

Website: http://www.lakeland.edu/.

LAKE SUPERIOR STATE UNIVERSITY
Sault Sainte Marie, MI

Tuition & fees (MI res): $9715	Average undergraduate aid package: $9347

ABOUT THE INSTITUTION State-supported, coed. *Awards:* certificates, associate, bachelor's, and master's degrees. 57 undergraduate majors. *Total enrollment:* 2,530. Undergraduates: 2,523. Freshmen: 442. Both federal and institutional methodology are used as a basis for awarding need-based institutional aid.

UNDERGRADUATE EXPENSES for 2013–2014 *Application fee:* $25. *One-time required fee:* $125. *Tuition, state resident:* full-time $9540; part-time $397.50 per credit hour. *Tuition, nonresident:* full-time $14,310; part-time $596.25 per credit hour. *Required fees:* full-time $175. Full-time tuition and fees vary according to program and reciprocity agreements. Part-time tuition and fees vary according to course load, location, program, and reciprocity agreements. *College room and board:* $8481. Room and board charges vary according to board plan and housing facility.

FRESHMAN FINANCIAL AID (Fall 2011) 412 applied for aid; of those 87% were deemed to have need. 100% of freshmen with need received aid; of those 31% had need fully met. *Average percent of need met:* 67% (excluding resources awarded to replace EFC). *Average financial aid package:* $10,306 (excluding resources awarded to replace EFC). 16% of all full-time freshmen had no need and received non-need-based gift aid.

UNDERGRADUATE FINANCIAL AID (Fall 2011) 1,762 applied for aid; of those 87% were deemed to have need. 100% of undergraduates with need received aid; of those 25% had need fully met. *Average percent of need met:* 61% (excluding resources awarded to replace EFC). *Average financial aid package:* $9347 (excluding resources awarded to replace EFC). 13% of all full-time undergraduates had no need and received non-need-based gift aid.

GIFT AID (NEED-BASED) *Total amount:* $7,246,482 (67% federal, 24% state, 7% institutional, 2% external sources). *Receiving aid:* Freshmen: 55% (269); all full-time undergraduates: 51% (1,150). *Average award:* Freshmen: $6771; Undergraduates: $5548. *Scholarships, grants, and awards:* Federal Pell, FSEOG, state, private, college/university gift aid from institutional funds, Federal Nursing, Academic Competitiveness Grants, National SMART Grants.

GIFT AID (NON-NEED-BASED) *Total amount:* $3,314,263 (1% state, 83% institutional, 16% external sources). *Receiving aid:* Freshmen: 45% (218). Undergraduates: 27% (614). *Average award:* Freshmen: $4191. Undergraduates: $3515. *Scholarships, grants, and awards by category:* Academic interests/achievement: general academic interests/achievements. *Tuition waivers:* Full or partial for minority students, children of alumni, employees or children of employees, senior citizens.

LOANS *Student loans:* $13,643,830 (100% need-based). 76% of past graduating class borrowed through all loan programs. *Average indebtedness per student:* $28,500. *Average need-based loan:* Freshmen: $3118. Undergraduates: $4171. *Parent loans:* $3,141,967 (100% need-based). *Programs:* Federal Direct (Subsidized and Unsubsidized Stafford, PLUS), Perkins, Federal Nursing, alternative loans.

WORK-STUDY *Federal work-study:* Total amount: $341,354; jobs available. *State or other work-study/employment:* Total amount: $31,750 (100% need-based). Part-time jobs available.

ATHLETIC AWARDS Total amount: $1,214,284 (100% non-need-based).

APPLYING FOR FINANCIAL AID *Required financial aid form:* FAFSA. *Financial aid deadline (priority):* 3/1. *Notification date:* Continuous. Students must reply within 3 weeks of notification.

CONTACT Deborah Faust, Director of Financial Aid, Lake Superior State University, 650 West Easterday Avenue, Sault Sainte Marie, MI 49783, 906-635-2678 or toll-free 888-800-LSSU Ext. 2231. *Fax:* 906-635-6669. *E-mail:* finaid@lssu.edu.

Website: http://www.lssu.edu/.

LAKEVIEW COLLEGE OF NURSING
Danville, IL

Tuition & fees: N/R	Average undergraduate aid package: $18,200

ABOUT THE INSTITUTION Independent, coed. 1 undergraduate major. Federal methodology is used as a basis for awarding need-based institutional aid.

UNDERGRADUATE FINANCIAL AID (Fall 2012, est.) 419 applied for aid; of those 95% were deemed to have need. 100% of undergraduates with need received aid; of those 82% had need fully met. *Average percent of need met:* 76% (excluding resources awarded to replace EFC). *Average financial aid package:* $18,200 (excluding resources awarded to replace EFC).

GIFT AID (NEED-BASED) *Total amount:* $472,899 (44% federal, 56% state). *Receiving aid:* All full-time undergraduates: 81% (398). *Average award:* Undergraduates: $2200. *Scholarships, grants, and awards:* Federal Pell, state, private, college/university gift aid from institutional funds.

GIFT AID (NON-NEED-BASED) *Total amount:* $155,000 (52% institutional, 48% external sources). *Receiving aid:* Undergraduates: 26% (126). *Scholarships, grants, and awards by category:* Academic interests/achievement: health fields.

LOANS *Student loans:* $2,494,161 (100% need-based). 87% of past graduating class borrowed through all loan programs. *Average indebtedness per student:* $25,000. *Average need-based loan:* Undergraduates: $5500. *Parent loans:* $432,000 (100% non-need-based). *Programs:* Federal Direct (Subsidized and Unsubsidized Stafford, PLUS).

APPLYING FOR FINANCIAL AID *Financial aid deadline:* Continuous. *Notification date:* Continuous beginning 4/1. Students must reply within 4 weeks of notification.

CONTACT Ms. Janet Ingargiola, Director of Financial Aid, Lakeview College of Nursing, 903 North Logan Avenue, Danville, IL 61832, 217-709-0930. *Fax:* 217-709-0956. *E-mail:* jingarg@lakeviewcol.edu.

Website: http://www.lakeviewcol.edu/.

LAMAR UNIVERSITY
Beaumont, TX

Tuition & fees (TX res): $9011	Average undergraduate aid package: $7045

ABOUT THE INSTITUTION State-supported, coed. *Awards:* associate, bachelor's, master's, and doctoral degrees. 102 undergraduate majors. *Total enrollment:* 14,288. Undergraduates: 9,800. Freshmen: 1,698. Federal methodology is used as a basis for awarding need-based institutional aid.

UNDERGRADUATE EXPENSES for 2013–2014 *Tuition, state resident:* full-time $6240; part-time $208 per credit hour. *Tuition, nonresident:* full-time $18,270; part-time $609 per credit hour. *Required fees:* full-time $2771. Full-time tuition and fees vary according to course load. Part-time tuition and fees vary according to course load. *College room and board:* $7966; *Room only:* $5098. Room and board charges vary according to board plan.

FRESHMAN FINANCIAL AID (Fall 2011) 1,391 applied for aid; of those 83% were deemed to have need. 97% of freshmen with need received aid. *Average percent of need met:* 35% (excluding resources awarded to replace EFC). *Average financial aid package:* $6961 (excluding resources awarded to replace EFC). 15% of all full-time freshmen had no need and received non-need-based gift aid.

UNDERGRADUATE FINANCIAL AID (Fall 2011) 5,720 applied for aid; of those 84% were deemed to have need. 97% of undergraduates with need received aid. *Average percent of need met:* 37% (excluding resources awarded to replace EFC). *Average financial aid package:* $7045 (excluding resources awarded to replace EFC). 18% of all full-time undergraduates had no need and received non-need-based gift aid.

GIFT AID (NEED-BASED) *Total amount:* $24,938,920 (75% federal, 24% state, 1% institutional). *Receiving aid:* Freshmen: 56% (914); all full-time undergraduates: 51% (3,743). *Average award:* Freshmen: $4030; Undergraduates: $4432. *Scholarships, grants, and awards:* Federal Pell, FSEOG, state, private, college/university gift aid from institutional funds, United Negro College Fund.

GIFT AID (NON-NEED-BASED) *Total amount:* $63,859,535 (53% state, 45% institutional, 2% external sources). *Receiving aid:* Freshmen: 50% (810). Undergraduates: 39% (2,898). *Average award:* Freshmen: $2198. Undergraduates: $2772. *Scholarships, grants, and awards by category: Academic interests/achievement:* general academic interests/achievements. *Creative arts/performance:* general creative arts/performance. *Special achievements/activities:* general special achievements/activities. *Tuition waivers:* Full or partial for employees or children of employees, senior citizens.

LOANS *Student loans:* $39,762,380 (44% need-based, 56% non-need-based). 33% of past graduating class borrowed through all loan programs. *Average indebtedness per student:* $26,224. *Average need-based loan:* Freshmen: $2804. Undergraduates: $3790. *Parent loans:* $2,369,737 (100% non-need-based). *Programs:* Federal Direct (Subsidized and Unsubsidized Stafford, PLUS), Perkins, Federal Nursing, state.

WORK-STUDY *Federal work-study:* Total amount: $293,863; jobs available. *State or other work-study/employment:* Total amount: $90,220 (100% need-based). Part-time jobs available.

ATHLETIC AWARDS Total amount: $4,015,476 (100% non-need-based).

APPLYING FOR FINANCIAL AID *Required financial aid forms:* FAFSA, institution's own form. *Financial aid deadline (priority):* 3/31. *Notification date:* Continuous beginning 5/15. Students must reply within 2 weeks of notification.

CONTACT Financial Aid Department, Lamar University, PO Box 10042, Beaumont, TX 77710, 409-880-8450. *Fax:* 409-880-8934. *E-mail:* financialaid@lamar.edu. *Website:* http://www.lamar.edu/.

LANCASTER BIBLE COLLEGE
Lancaster, PA

Tuition & fees: N/R	Average undergraduate aid package: $14,096

ABOUT THE INSTITUTION Independent nondenominational, coed. 17 undergraduate majors. Federal methodology is used as a basis for awarding need-based institutional aid.

FRESHMAN FINANCIAL AID (Fall 2012, est.) 125 applied for aid; of those 94% were deemed to have need. 100% of freshmen with need received aid; of those 8% had

need fully met. *Average percent of need met:* 68% (excluding resources awarded to replace EFC). *Average financial aid package:* $13,816 (excluding resources awarded to replace EFC). 13% of all full-time freshmen had no need and received non-need-based gift aid.

UNDERGRADUATE FINANCIAL AID (Fall 2012, est.) 595 applied for aid; of those 92% were deemed to have need. 100% of undergraduates with need received aid; of those 8% had need fully met. *Average percent of need met:* 68% (excluding resources awarded to replace EFC). *Average financial aid package:* $14,096 (excluding resources awarded to replace EFC). 18% of all full-time undergraduates had no need and received non-need-based gift aid.

GIFT AID (NEED-BASED) *Total amount:* $5,366,885 (31% federal, 19% state, 46% institutional, 4% external sources). *Receiving aid:* Freshmen: 87% (117); all full-time undergraduates: 79% (525). *Average award:* Freshmen: $9327; Undergraduates: $9463. *Scholarships, grants, and awards:* Federal Pell, FSEOG, state, private, college/university gift aid from institutional funds, Office of Vocational Rehabilitation Awards, Blindness and Visual Services Awards.

GIFT AID (NON-NEED-BASED) *Total amount:* $586,534 (97% institutional, 3% external sources). *Receiving aid:* Freshmen: 82% (111). Undergraduates: 69% (458). *Average award:* Freshmen: $5824. Undergraduates: $5161. *Scholarships, grants, and awards by category: Academic interests/achievement:* 415 awards ($1,231,000 total): general academic interests/achievements. *Creative arts/performance:* 62 awards ($128,075 total): general creative arts/performance, music. *Special achievements/activities:* 103 awards ($122,250 total): general special achievements/activities, leadership, religious involvement. *Special characteristics:* 299 awards ($940,422 total): adult students, children and siblings of alumni, children of current students, children of faculty/staff, international students, married students, previous college experience, relatives of clergy, religious affiliation, siblings of current students, spouses of current students.

LOANS *Student loans:* $4,912,415 (80% need-based, 20% non-need-based). 18% of past graduating class borrowed through all loan programs. *Average indebtedness per student:* $20,668. *Average need-based loan:* Freshmen: $3201. Undergraduates: $4206. *Parent loans:* $677,715 (50% need-based, 50% non-need-based). *Programs:* Federal Direct (Subsidized and Unsubsidized Stafford, PLUS), Perkins, state, alternative loans.

WORK-STUDY *Federal work-study:* Total amount: $101,504; 65 jobs averaging $1562.

APPLYING FOR FINANCIAL AID *Required financial aid forms:* FAFSA, state aid form. *Financial aid deadline (priority):* 5/1. *Notification date:* Continuous beginning 3/1. Students must reply within 3 weeks of notification.

CONTACT Karen Fox, Director of Financial Aid, Lancaster Bible College, 901 Eden Road, Lancaster, PA 17601, 717-560-8254 Ext. 5352 or toll-free 800-544-7335. *Fax:* 717-560-8216. *E-mail:* kfox@lbc.edu. *Website:* http://www.lbc.edu/.

LANDER UNIVERSITY
Greenwood, SC

CONTACT Director of Financial Aid, Lander University, 320 Stanley Avenue, Greenwood, SC 29649, 864-388-8340 or toll-free 888-452-6337. *Fax:* 864-388-8811. *E-mail:* fhardin@lander.edu. *Website:* http://www.lander.edu/.

LANE COLLEGE
Jackson, TN

Tuition & fees: $8560	Average undergraduate aid package: $4422

ABOUT THE INSTITUTION Independent Christian Methodist Episcopal Church, coed. *Awards:* bachelor's degrees. 16 undergraduate majors. *Total enrollment:* 1,512. Undergraduates: 1,512. Freshmen: 325. Federal methodology is used as a basis for awarding need-based institutional aid.

UNDERGRADUATE EXPENSES for 2013–2014 *Comprehensive fee:* $14,600 includes full-time tuition ($7860), mandatory fees ($700), and room and board ($6040). Full-time tuition and fees vary according to course load. *Part-time tuition:*

$330 per credit hour. *Part-time fees:* $700 per year. Part-time tuition and fees vary according to course load.

FRESHMAN FINANCIAL AID (Fall 2012, est.) 324 applied for aid; of those 99% were deemed to have need. 100% of freshmen with need received aid; of those 2% had need fully met. *Average percent of need met:* 57% (excluding resources awarded to replace EFC). *Average financial aid package:* $5408 (excluding resources awarded to replace EFC). 1% of all full-time freshmen had no need and received non-need-based gift aid.

UNDERGRADUATE FINANCIAL AID (Fall 2012, est.) 1,470 applied for aid; of those 98% were deemed to have need. 100% of undergraduates with need received aid; of those 2% had need fully met. *Average percent of need met:* 55% (excluding resources awarded to replace EFC). *Average financial aid package:* $4422 (excluding resources awarded to replace EFC). 1% of all full-time undergraduates had no need and received non-need-based gift aid.

GIFT AID (NEED-BASED) *Total amount:* $10,368,070 (74% federal, 20% state, 3% institutional, 3% external sources). *Receiving aid:* Freshmen: 93% (303); all full-time undergraduates: 95% (1,412). *Average award:* Freshmen: $3733; Undergraduates: $3677. *Scholarships, grants, and awards:* Federal Pell, FSEOG, state, private, college/university gift aid from institutional funds, United Negro College Fund.

GIFT AID (NON-NEED-BASED) *Total amount:* $59,801 (38% state, 32% institutional, 30% external sources). *Receiving aid:* Freshmen: 1. Undergraduates: 5. *Average award:* Freshmen: $2119. Undergraduates: $1773. *Tuition waivers:* Full or partial for employees or children of employees, adult students.

LOANS *Student loans:* $10,623,418 (94% need-based, 6% non-need-based). 82% of past graduating class borrowed through all loan programs. *Average indebtedness per student:* $12,348. *Average need-based loan:* Freshmen: $1715. Undergraduates: $2049. *Parent loans:* $347,025 (89% need-based, 11% non-need-based). *Programs:* Federal Direct (Subsidized and Unsubsidized Stafford, PLUS).

WORK-STUDY *Federal work-study:* Total amount: $231,920; jobs available.

ATHLETIC AWARDS Total amount: $348,573 (94% need-based, 6% non-need-based).

APPLYING FOR FINANCIAL AID *Required financial aid form:* FAFSA. *Financial aid deadline (priority):* 4/1. *Notification date:* Continuous beginning 4/15. Students must reply within 2 weeks of notification.

CONTACT Mr. Tony Calhoun, Director of Financial Aid, Lane College, 545 Lane Avenue, Jackson, TN 38301, 731-426-7558 or toll-free 800-960-7533. *Fax:* 731-426-7652. *E-mail:* tcalhoun@lanecollege.edu. *Website:* http://www.lanecollege.edu/.

LANGSTON UNIVERSITY
Langston, OK

CONTACT Linda Morris, Associate Director of Financial Aid, Langston University, Gandy Hall, Langston, OK 73050, 405-466-3287. *Fax:* 405-466-2986. *E-mail:* lfmorris@lunet.edu. *Website:* http://www.langston.edu/.

LA ROCHE COLLEGE
Pittsburgh, PA

Tuition & fees: $24,058	Average undergraduate aid package: $24,869

ABOUT THE INSTITUTION Independent Roman Catholic Church, coed. *Awards:* certificates, associate, bachelor's, and master's degrees. 35 undergraduate majors. *Total enrollment:* 1,465. Undergraduates: 1,345. Freshmen: 249. Federal methodology is used as a basis for awarding need-based institutional aid.

UNDERGRADUATE EXPENSES for 2013–2014 *Application fee:* $50. *Comprehensive fee:* $33,790 includes full-time tuition ($23,328), mandatory fees ($730), and room and board ($9732). *College room only:* $6160. Full-time tuition and fees vary according to student level. Room and board charges vary according to board plan and housing facility. *Part-time tuition:* $595 per credit hour.

FRESHMAN FINANCIAL AID (Fall 2012, est.) 207 applied for aid; of those 88% were deemed to have need. 99% of freshmen with need received aid; of those 29% had need fully met. *Average percent of need met:* 92% (excluding resources awarded to replace EFC). *Average financial aid package:* $26,024 (excluding resources

awarded to replace EFC). 4% of all full-time freshmen had no need and received non-need-based gift aid.

UNDERGRADUATE FINANCIAL AID (Fall 2012, est.) 905 applied for aid; of those 95% were deemed to have need. 100% of undergraduates with need received aid; of those 33% had need fully met. *Average percent of need met:* 94% (excluding resources awarded to replace EFC). *Average financial aid package:* $24,869 (excluding resources awarded to replace EFC). 5% of all full-time undergraduates had no need and received non-need-based gift aid.

GIFT AID (NEED-BASED) *Total amount:* $4,547,425 (44% federal, 37% state, 19% institutional). *Receiving aid:* Freshmen: 49% (121); all full-time undergraduates: 57% (628). *Average award:* Freshmen: $7500; Undergraduates: $7778. *Scholarships, grants, and awards:* Federal Pell, FSEOG, state, private, college/university gift aid from institutional funds.

GIFT AID (NON-NEED-BASED) *Total amount:* $9,582,214 (93% institutional, 7% external sources). *Receiving aid:* Freshmen: 72% (179). Undergraduates: 78% (862). *Average award:* Freshmen: $12,795. Undergraduates: $16,799. *Scholarships, grants, and awards by category:* Academic interests/achievement: 976 awards ($7,700,096 total): general academic interests/achievements. *Tuition waivers:* Full or partial for employees or children of employees, senior citizens. *ROTC:* Army cooperative, Air Force cooperative.

LOANS *Student loans:* $3,423,484 (100% need-based). 78% of past graduating class borrowed through all loan programs. *Average indebtedness per student:* $26,296. *Average need-based loan:* Freshmen: $3464. Undergraduates: $4642. *Parent loans:* $1,649,772 (100% non-need-based). *Programs:* Federal Direct (Subsidized and Unsubsidized Stafford, PLUS), Perkins, state.

WORK-STUDY *Federal work-study:* Total amount: $264,575; 169 jobs averaging $1402.

APPLYING FOR FINANCIAL AID *Required financial aid form:* FAFSA. *Financial aid deadline (priority):* 5/1. *Notification date:* Continuous beginning 3/1. Students must reply within 2 weeks of notification.

CONTACT Mrs. Sharon Platt, Director of Financial Aid, La Roche College, 9000 Babcock Boulevard, Pittsburgh, PA 15237-5898, 412-536-1125 or toll-free 800-838-4LRC. *Fax:* 412-536-1072. *E-mail:* sharon.platt@laroche.edu. *Website:* http://www.laroche.edu/.

LA SALLE UNIVERSITY
Philadelphia, PA

Tuition & fees: $36,650	Average undergraduate aid package: $25,451

ABOUT THE INSTITUTION Independent Roman Catholic, coed. *Awards:* certificates, associate, bachelor's, master's, and doctoral degrees. 62 undergraduate majors. *Total enrollment:* 6,580. Undergraduates: 4,516. Freshmen: 926. Federal methodology is used as a basis for awarding need-based institutional aid.

UNDERGRADUATE EXPENSES for 2013–2014 *Application fee:* $35. *One-time required fee:* $150. *Comprehensive fee:* $48,860 includes full-time tuition ($36,250), mandatory fees ($400), and room and board ($12,210). *College room only:* $6430. Full-time tuition and fees vary according to course load and program. Room and board charges vary according to board plan and housing facility. *Part-time tuition:* $500 per credit hour. *Part-time fees:* $125 per term. Part-time tuition and fees vary according to course load and program.

FRESHMAN FINANCIAL AID (Fall 2011) 891 applied for aid; of those 94% were deemed to have need. 100% of freshmen with need received aid; of those 13% had need fully met. *Average percent of need met:* 74% (excluding resources awarded to replace EFC). *Average financial aid package:* $26,648 (excluding resources awarded to replace EFC). 12% of all full-time freshmen had no need and received non-need-based gift aid.

UNDERGRADUATE FINANCIAL AID (Fall 2011) 3,039 applied for aid; of those 93% were deemed to have need. 100% of undergraduates with need received aid; of those 16% had need fully met. *Average percent of need met:* 74% (excluding resources awarded to replace EFC). *Average financial aid package:* $25,451 (excluding resources awarded to replace EFC). 17% of all full-time undergraduates had no need and received non-need-based gift aid.

GIFT AID (NEED-BASED) *Total amount:* $56,049,363 (14% federal, 8% state, 74% institutional, 4% external sources). *Receiving aid:* Freshmen: 86% (825); all full-time undergraduates: 79% (2,763). *Average award:* Freshmen: $21,359; Undergraduates: $19,593. *Scholarships, grants, and awards:* Federal Pell, FSEOG, state, private, college/university gift aid from institutional funds.

GIFT AID (NON-NEED-BASED) *Total amount:* $11,048,780 (94% institutional, 6% external sources). *Receiving aid:* Freshmen: 8% (79). Undergraduates: 7% (259). *Average award:* Freshmen: $15,114. Undergraduates: $14,496. *Scholarships, grants, and awards by category:* Academic interests/achievement: 3,188 awards ($39,617,959 total): general academic interests/achievements. *Special achievements/activities:* 19 awards ($190,000 total): community service. *Special characteristics:* 83 awards ($2,453,088 total): children of faculty/staff, relatives of clergy, veterans. *Tuition waivers:* Full or partial for employees or children of employees. **ROTC:** Army cooperative, Air Force cooperative.

LOANS *Student loans:* $37,058,272 (69% need-based, 31% non-need-based). 77% of past graduating class borrowed through all loan programs. *Average indebtedness per student:* $37,225. *Average need-based loan:* Freshmen: $3748. Undergraduates: $4761. *Parent loans:* $8,277,433 (45% need-based, 55% non-need-based). *Programs:* Federal Direct (Subsidized and Unsubsidized Stafford, PLUS), Perkins.

WORK-STUDY *Federal work-study:* Total amount: $499,313; 377 jobs averaging $1324.

ATHLETIC AWARDS Total amount: $4,742,541 (49% need-based, 51% non-need-based).

APPLYING FOR FINANCIAL AID *Required financial aid form:* FAFSA. *Financial aid deadline (priority):* 2/15. *Notification date:* Continuous beginning 3/15. Students must reply by 5/1 or within 2 weeks of notification.

CONTACT Michael Wisniewski, Director of Student Financial Services, La Salle University, 1900 West Olney Avenue, Philadelphia, PA 19141-1199, 215-951-1070 or toll-free 800-328-1910. *Fax:* 215-951-5098.
Website: http://www.lasalle.edu/.

LASELL COLLEGE
Newton, MA

Tuition & fees: $29,000	Average undergraduate aid package: $20,448

ABOUT THE INSTITUTION Independent, coed. *Awards:* bachelor's and master's degrees. 40 undergraduate majors. *Total enrollment:* 325. Undergraduates: 1,655. Freshmen: 558. Federal methodology is used as a basis for awarding need-based institutional aid.

UNDERGRADUATE EXPENSES for 2013–2014 *Application fee:* $40. *Comprehensive fee:* $41,300 includes full-time tuition ($27,800), mandatory fees ($1200), and room and board ($12,300). Full-time tuition and fees vary according to program. Room and board charges vary according to board plan. *Part-time tuition:* $940 per credit hour. *Part-time fees:* $300 per term. Part-time tuition and fees vary according to course load and program.

FRESHMAN FINANCIAL AID (Fall 2011) 342 applied for aid; of those 91% were deemed to have need. 100% of freshmen with need received aid; of those 21% had need fully met. *Average percent of need met:* 65% (excluding resources awarded to replace EFC). *Average financial aid package:* $21,097 (excluding resources awarded to replace EFC). 15% of all full-time freshmen had no need and received non-need-based gift aid.

UNDERGRADUATE FINANCIAL AID (Fall 2011) 1,345 applied for aid; of those 91% were deemed to have need. 100% of undergraduates with need received aid; of those 24% had need fully met. *Average percent of need met:* 66% (excluding resources awarded to replace EFC). *Average financial aid package:* $20,448 (excluding resources awarded to replace EFC). 17% of all full-time undergraduates had no need and received non-need-based gift aid.

GIFT AID (NEED-BASED) *Total amount:* $19,030,246 (12% federal, 4% state, 83% institutional, 1% external sources). *Receiving aid:* Freshmen: 83% (310); all full-time undergraduates: 81% (1,217). *Average award:* Freshmen: $18,390; Undergraduates: $16,616. *Scholarships, grants, and awards:* Federal Pell, FSEOG, state, private, college/university gift aid from institutional funds.

GIFT AID (NON-NEED-BASED) *Total amount:* $2,847,075 (94% institutional, 6% external sources). *Receiving aid:* Freshmen: 15% (55). Undergraduates: 8% (116). *Average award:* Freshmen: $9684. Undergraduates: $8607. *Scholarships, grants, and awards by category:* Academic interests/achievement: general academic interests/achievements. *Special achievements/activities:* community service, general special achievements/activities, leadership. *Special characteristics:* children and siblings of alumni, children of faculty/staff, siblings of current students, veterans, veterans' children. *Tuition waivers:* Full or partial for children of alumni, employees or children of employees.

LOANS *Student loans:* $12,621,237 (86% need-based, 14% non-need-based). 85% of past graduating class borrowed through all loan programs. *Average indebtedness per student:* $39,559. *Average need-based loan:* Freshmen: $3400. Undergraduates: $4400. *Parent loans:* $5,660,928 (67% need-based, 33% non-need-based). *Programs:* Federal Direct (Subsidized and Unsubsidized Stafford, PLUS), Perkins.

WORK-STUDY Federal work-study jobs available.

APPLYING FOR FINANCIAL AID *Required financial aid forms:* FAFSA, institution's own form. *Financial aid deadline (priority):* 3/1. *Notification date:* Continuous beginning 2/15. Students must reply by 5/1 or within 2 weeks of notification.

CONTACT Michele R. Kosboth, Director of Student Financial Planning, Lasell College, 1844 Commonwealth Avenue, Newton, MA 02466-2709, 617-243-2227 or toll-free 888-LASELL-4. *Fax:* 617-243-2326. *E-mail:* finaid@lasell.edu.
Website: http://www.lasell.edu/.

LA SIERRA UNIVERSITY
Riverside, CA

Tuition & fees: $28,314	Average undergraduate aid package: $18,930

ABOUT THE INSTITUTION Independent Seventh-day Adventist, coed. *Awards:* certificates, bachelor's, master's, and doctoral degrees. 35 undergraduate majors. *Total enrollment:* 2,393. Undergraduates: 2,048. Freshmen: 506. Federal methodology is used as a basis for awarding need-based institutional aid.

UNDERGRADUATE EXPENSES for 2013–2014 *Application fee:* $30. *Comprehensive fee:* $35,694 includes full-time tuition ($27,180), mandatory fees ($1134), and room and board ($7380). Full-time tuition and fees vary according to course load, degree level, and location. Room and board charges vary according to board plan and housing facility. *Part-time tuition:* $755 per quarter hour. Part-time tuition and fees vary according to course load, degree level, and location.

FRESHMAN FINANCIAL AID (Fall 2012, est.) 460 applied for aid; of those 92% were deemed to have need. 100% of freshmen with need received aid; of those 19% had need fully met. *Average percent of need met:* 62% (excluding resources awarded to replace EFC). *Average financial aid package:* $21,378 (excluding resources awarded to replace EFC). 5% of all full-time freshmen had no need and received non-need-based gift aid.

UNDERGRADUATE FINANCIAL AID (Fall 2012, est.) 1,582 applied for aid; of those 92% were deemed to have need. 100% of undergraduates with need received aid; of those 20% had need fully met. *Average percent of need met:* 58% (excluding resources awarded to replace EFC). *Average financial aid package:* $18,930 (excluding resources awarded to replace EFC). 5% of all full-time undergraduates had no need and received non-need-based gift aid.

GIFT AID (NEED-BASED) *Total amount:* $11,395,646 (42% federal, 46% state, 12% institutional). *Receiving aid:* Freshmen: 85% (421); all full-time undergraduates: 78% (1,446). *Average award:* Freshmen: $18,717; Undergraduates: $16,612. *Scholarships, grants, and awards:* Federal Pell, FSEOG, state, private, college/university gift aid from institutional funds.

GIFT AID (NON-NEED-BASED) *Total amount:* $10,210,642 (95% institutional, 5% external sources). *Receiving aid:* Freshmen: 8% (39). Undergraduates: 6% (115). *Average award:* Freshmen: $10,813. Undergraduates: $7316. *Scholarships, grants, and awards by category:* Academic interests/achievement: general academic interests/achievements. *Creative arts/performance:* music, theater/drama. *Special achievements/activities:* leadership. *Special characteristics:* adult students, children of faculty/staff, relatives of clergy, religious affiliation, siblings of current students. *Tuition waivers:* Full or partial for employees or children of employees.

LOANS *Student loans:* $11,254,279 (53% need-based, 47% non-need-based). 47% of past graduating class borrowed through all loan programs. *Average indebtedness per student:* $21,882. *Average need-based loan:* Freshmen: $3239. Undergraduates: $4529. *Parent loans:* $3,745,658 (100% non-need-based). *Programs:* Federal Direct (Subsidized and Unsubsidized Stafford, PLUS), Perkins, state.

WORK-STUDY *Federal work-study:* Total amount: $1,264,332; jobs available.

ATHLETIC AWARDS Total amount: $143,827 (100% non-need-based).

APPLYING FOR FINANCIAL AID *Required financial aid forms:* FAFSA, state aid form. *Financial aid deadline:* 8/15 (priority: 3/2). *Notification date:* Continuous beginning 4/15. Students must reply by 8/5 or within 2 weeks of notification.

CONTACT Mrs. Esther Kinzer, Financial Aid Office, La Sierra University, 4500 Riverwalk Parkway, Riverside, CA 92515, 951-785-2935 or toll-free 800-874-5587. *Fax:* 951-785-2942. *E-mail:* sfs@lasierra.edu. *Website:* http://www.lasierra.edu/.

LAUREL UNIVERSITY
High Point, NC

ABOUT THE INSTITUTION Independent interdenominational, coed. *Awards:* certificates, associate, bachelor's, master's, and doctoral degrees. 10 undergraduate majors. *Total enrollment:* 353. Undergraduates: 278. Freshmen: 39.

GIFT AID (NEED-BASED) *Scholarships, grants, and awards:* Federal Pell, FSEOG, state, private, college/university gift aid from institutional funds.

GIFT AID (NON-NEED-BASED) *Scholarships, grants, and awards by category:* Academic interests/achievement: education, general academic interests/achievements, religion/biblical studies. *Special achievements/activities:* religious involvement. *Special characteristics:* children of faculty/staff, general special characteristics, married students, spouses of current students.

LOANS *Programs:* Federal Direct (Subsidized and Unsubsidized Stafford, PLUS).

WORK-STUDY *Federal work-study:* Total amount: $6250; 3 jobs averaging $2500. *State or other work-study/employment:* Part-time jobs available.

APPLYING FOR FINANCIAL AID *Required financial aid forms:* FAFSA, institution's own form.

CONTACT Mrs. Shirley P. Carter, Director of Financial Aid, Laurel University, 1215 Eastchester Drive, High Point, NC 27265, 336-887-3000 or toll-free 855-LaurelU. *Fax:* 336-889-2261. *E-mail:* scarter@laureluniversity.edu. *Website:* http://www.laureluniversity.edu/.

LAWRENCE TECHNOLOGICAL UNIVERSITY
Southfield, MI

Tuition & fees: $27,870	Average undergraduate aid package: $21,796

ABOUT THE INSTITUTION Independent, coed. *Awards:* certificates, associate, bachelor's, master's, and doctoral degrees. 49 undergraduate majors. *Total enrollment:* 4,154. Undergraduates: 3,065. Freshmen: 341. Federal methodology is used as a basis for awarding need-based institutional aid.

UNDERGRADUATE EXPENSES for 2013–2014 *Application fee:* $30. *Comprehensive fee:* $36,857 includes full-time tuition ($27,300), mandatory fees ($570), and room and board ($8987). *College room only:* $4959. Full-time tuition and fees vary according to course level, degree level, location, program, and student level. Room and board charges vary according to board plan and housing facility. *Part-time tuition:* $910 per credit hour. *Part-time fees:* $285 per term. Part-time tuition and fees vary according to course level, degree level, location, program, and student level.

FRESHMAN FINANCIAL AID (Fall 2011) 234 applied for aid; of those 81% were deemed to have need. 100% of freshmen with need received aid; of those 26% had need fully met. *Average percent of need met:* 72% (excluding resources awarded to replace EFC). *Average financial aid package:* $21,168 (excluding resources awarded to replace EFC). 14% of all full-time freshmen had no need and received non-need-based gift aid.

UNDERGRADUATE FINANCIAL AID (Fall 2011) 1,243 applied for aid; of those 79% were deemed to have need. 99% of undergraduates with need received aid; of those 15% had need fully met. *Average percent of need met:* 66% (excluding resources awarded to replace EFC). *Average financial aid package:* $21,796 (excluding resources awarded to replace EFC). 14% of all full-time undergraduates had no need and received non-need-based gift aid.

GIFT AID (NEED-BASED) *Total amount:* $13,531,314 (21% federal, 10% state, 68% institutional, 1% external sources). *Receiving aid:* Freshmen: 74% (187); all full-time undergraduates: 65% (933). *Average award:* Freshmen: $14,050; Undergraduates: $12,631. *Scholarships, grants, and awards:* Federal Pell, FSEOG, state, private, college/university gift aid from institutional funds, Michigan National Guard and ROTC Scholarships.

GIFT AID (NON-NEED-BASED) *Total amount:* $2,318,824 (1% state, 98% institutional, 1% external sources). *Receiving aid:* Freshmen: 61% (154). Undergrad-

uates: 48% (691). *Average award:* Freshmen: $12,596. Undergraduates: $10,381. *Scholarships, grants, and awards by category:* Academic interests/achievement: 2,449 awards ($12,140,635 total): architecture, business, computer science, education, engineering/technologies, general academic interests/achievements, humanities, international studies, mathematics, military science, physical sciences. *Special characteristics:* 66 awards ($915,327 total): children of faculty/staff, members of minority groups. *Tuition waivers:* Full or partial for employees or children of employees. *ROTC:* Air Force cooperative.

LOANS *Student loans:* $9,369,073 (97% need-based, 3% non-need-based). 75% of past graduating class borrowed through all loan programs. *Average indebtedness per student:* $41,529. *Average need-based loan:* Freshmen: $6079. Undergraduates: $8292. *Parent loans:* $5,338,146 (95% need-based, 5% non-need-based). *Programs:* Federal Direct (Subsidized and Unsubsidized Stafford, PLUS), Perkins, state, college/university, alternative loans.

WORK-STUDY *Federal work-study:* Total amount: $851,130; 61 jobs averaging $2380. *State or other work-study/employment:* Part-time jobs available.

ATHLETIC AWARDS Total amount: $38,305 (100% non-need-based).

APPLYING FOR FINANCIAL AID *Required financial aid form:* FAFSA. *Financial aid deadline (priority):* 4/1. *Notification date:* Continuous beginning 4/1. Students must reply within 2 weeks of notification.

CONTACT Mrs. Dee King, Interim Director of Financial Aid, Lawrence Technological University, 21000 West Ten Mile Road, Southfield, MI 48075-1058, 248-204-2127 or toll-free 800-225-5588. *Fax:* 248-204-2128. *E-mail:* mmartin@ltu.edu. *Website:* http://www.ltu.edu/.

LAWRENCE UNIVERSITY
Appleton, WI

Tuition & fees: $40,023	Average undergraduate aid package: $31,400

ABOUT THE INSTITUTION Independent, coed. *Awards:* bachelor's degrees. 59 undergraduate majors. *Total enrollment:* 1,525. Undergraduates: 1,525. Freshmen: 412. Institutional methodology is used as a basis for awarding need-based institutional aid.

UNDERGRADUATE EXPENSES for 2013–2014 *Application fee:* $40. *Comprehensive fee:* $48,270 includes full-time tuition ($39,732), mandatory fees ($291), and room and board ($8247). *College room only:* $3858. Room and board charges vary according to board plan. *Payment plan:* Tuition prepayment.

FRESHMAN FINANCIAL AID (Fall 2012, est.) 336 applied for aid; of those 83% were deemed to have need. 100% of freshmen with need received aid; of those 37% had need fully met. *Average percent of need met:* 88% (excluding resources awarded to replace EFC). *Average financial aid package:* $31,608 (excluding resources awarded to replace EFC). 29% of all full-time freshmen had no need and received non-need-based gift aid.

UNDERGRADUATE FINANCIAL AID (Fall 2012, est.) 1,060 applied for aid; of those 86% were deemed to have need. 100% of undergraduates with need received aid; of those 33% had need fully met. *Average percent of need met:* 88% (excluding resources awarded to replace EFC). *Average financial aid package:* $31,400 (excluding resources awarded to replace EFC). 32% of all full-time undergraduates had no need and received non-need-based gift aid.

GIFT AID (NEED-BASED) *Total amount:* $22,305,778 (8% federal, 3% state, 87% institutional, 2% external sources). *Receiving aid:* Freshmen: 69% (278); all full-time undergraduates: 62% (889). *Average award:* Freshmen: $26,494; Undergraduates: $24,461. *Scholarships, grants, and awards:* Federal Pell, FSEOG, state, private, college/university gift aid from institutional funds.

GIFT AID (NON-NEED-BASED) *Total amount:* $6,590,964 (96% institutional, 4% external sources). *Receiving aid:* Freshmen: 2% (7). Undergraduates: 2% (31). *Average award:* Freshmen: $17,324. Undergraduates: $13,829. *Scholarships, grants, and awards by category:* Academic interests/achievement: 670 awards ($7,647,796 total): general academic interests/achievements. *Creative arts/performance:* 124 awards ($1,250,791 total): music. *Special achievements/activities:* 398 awards ($1,305,681 total): community service, general special achievements/activities. *Special characteristics:* 233 awards ($4,220,729 total): children and siblings of alumni, ethnic background, international students, siblings of current students, veterans, veterans' children. *Tuition waivers:* Full or partial for employees or children of employees.

LOANS *Student loans:* $7,378,526 (52% need-based, 48% non-need-based). 65% of past graduating class borrowed through all loan programs. *Average indebtedness per student:* $30,724. *Average need-based loan:* Freshmen: $4663. Undergraduates: $5476. *Parent loans:* $1,850,867 (100% non-need-based). *Programs:* Federal Direct (Subsidized and Unsubsidized Stafford, PLUS), Perkins, private loans.
WORK-STUDY *Federal work-study:* Total amount: $1,531,065; 639 jobs averaging $2347. *State or other work-study/employment:* Total amount: $565,930 (100% non-need-based). 255 part-time jobs averaging $2134.
APPLYING FOR FINANCIAL AID *Required financial aid forms:* FAFSA, institution's own form, noncustodial (divorced/separated) parent's statement, federal income tax form(s). *Financial aid deadline (priority):* 3/1. *Notification date:* Continuous beginning 3/1. Students must reply by 5/1.
CONTACT Mrs. Sara Beth Holman, Director of Financial Aid, Lawrence University, 711 East Boldt Way, Appleton, WI 54911, 920-832-6583 or toll-free 800-227-0982. *Fax:* 920-832-6582. *E-mail:* sara.b.holman@lawrence.edu. *Website:* http://www.lawrence.edu/.

LEBANON VALLEY COLLEGE
Annville, PA

Tuition & fees: $34,470	Average undergraduate aid package: $24,546

ABOUT THE INSTITUTION Independent United Methodist, coed. *Awards:* certificates, associate, bachelor's, master's, and doctoral degrees. 36 undergraduate majors. *Total enrollment:* 1,984. Undergraduates: 1,744. Freshmen: 404. Federal methodology is used as a basis for awarding need-based institutional aid.
UNDERGRADUATE EXPENSES for 2013–2014 *Application fee:* $30. *Comprehensive fee:* $43,650 includes full-time tuition ($33,670), mandatory fees ($800), and room and board ($9180). *College room only:* $4480. Room and board charges vary according to board plan and housing facility. *Part-time tuition:* $575 per credit. Part-time tuition and fees vary according to class time and degree level. *Payment plan:* Tuition prepayment.
FRESHMAN FINANCIAL AID (Fall 2012, est.) 381 applied for aid; of those 92% were deemed to have need. 100% of freshmen with need received aid; of those 17% had need fully met. *Average percent of need met:* 75% (excluding resources awarded to replace EFC). *Average financial aid package:* $25,471 (excluding resources awarded to replace EFC). 14% of all full-time freshmen had no need and received non-need-based gift aid.
UNDERGRADUATE FINANCIAL AID (Fall 2012, est.) 1,479 applied for aid; of those 100% were deemed to have need. 100% of undergraduates with need received aid; of those 26% had need fully met. *Average percent of need met:* 79% (excluding resources awarded to replace EFC). *Average financial aid package:* $24,546 (excluding resources awarded to replace EFC). 13% of all full-time undergraduates had no need and received non-need-based gift aid.
GIFT AID (NEED-BASED) *Total amount:* $23,474,108 (7% federal, 9% state, 84% institutional). *Receiving aid:* Freshmen: 87% (351); all full-time undergraduates: 84% (1,358). *Average award:* Freshmen: $22,325; Undergraduates: $21,751. *Scholarships, grants, and awards:* Federal Pell, FSEOG, state, private, college/university gift aid from institutional funds, TEACH Grants.
GIFT AID (NON-NEED-BASED) *Total amount:* $5,032,672 (1% federal, 1% state, 81% institutional, 17% external sources). *Receiving aid:* Freshmen: 7% (28). Undergraduates: 14% (222). *Average award:* Freshmen: $14,396. Undergraduates: $14,149. *Scholarships, grants, and awards by category: Academic interests/achievement:* 1,152 awards ($16,591,045 total): biological sciences, English, general academic interests/achievements, mathematics, physical sciences, religion/biblical studies, social sciences. *Creative arts/performance:* 42 awards ($80,770 total): music. *Special achievements/activities:* 80 awards ($40,900 total): general special achievements/activities. *Special characteristics:* 238 awards ($1,839,777 total): children and siblings of alumni, children of faculty/staff, ethnic background, international students, veterans. *Tuition waivers:* Full or partial for employees or children of employees, senior citizens.
LOANS *Student loans:* $13,665,762 (39% need-based, 61% non-need-based). 84% of past graduating class borrowed through all loan programs. *Average indebtedness per student:* $34,561. *Average need-based loan:* Freshmen: $3715. Undergraduates: $4459. *Parent loans:* $6,719,693 (100% non-need-based). *Programs:* Federal Direct (Subsidized and Unsubsidized Stafford, PLUS), Perkins.

WORK-STUDY *Federal work-study:* Total amount: $1,553,950; 1,020 jobs averaging $1483.
APPLYING FOR FINANCIAL AID *Required financial aid form:* FAFSA. *Financial aid deadline (priority):* 3/1. *Notification date:* Continuous beginning 3/1. Students must reply by 5/1 or within 2 weeks of notification.
CONTACT Mrs. Kendra M. Feigert, Director of Financial Aid, Lebanon Valley College, 101 North College Avenue, Annville, PA 17003, 866-582-4236 or toll-free 866-LVC-4ADM. *Fax:* 717-867-6027. *E-mail:* feigert@lvc.edu. *Website:* http://www.lvc.edu/.

LEES-MCRAE COLLEGE
Banner Elk, NC

Tuition & fees: $24,450	Average undergraduate aid package: $13,523

ABOUT THE INSTITUTION Independent Presbyterian Church (U.S.A.), coed. *Awards:* bachelor's degrees. 18 undergraduate majors. *Total enrollment:* 837. Undergraduates: 837. Freshmen: 182. Both federal and institutional methodology are used as a basis for awarding need-based institutional aid.
UNDERGRADUATE EXPENSES for 2013–2014 *Application fee:* $35. *Comprehensive fee:* $32,950 includes full-time tuition ($23,950), mandatory fees ($500), and room and board ($8500). Full-time tuition and fees vary according to course load, location, and reciprocity agreements. Room and board charges vary according to housing facility. *Part-time tuition:* $650 per credit hour. *Part-time fees:* $650 per credit hour. Part-time tuition and fees vary according to course load, location, and reciprocity agreements.
FRESHMAN FINANCIAL AID (Fall 2012, est.) 161 applied for aid; of those 88% were deemed to have need. 100% of freshmen with need received aid. *Average percent of need met:* 74% (excluding resources awarded to replace EFC). *Average financial aid package:* $16,270 (excluding resources awarded to replace EFC). 17% of all full-time freshmen had no need and received non-need-based gift aid.
UNDERGRADUATE FINANCIAL AID (Fall 2012, est.) 658 applied for aid; of those 96% were deemed to have need. 100% of undergraduates with need received aid; of those .5% had need fully met. *Average percent of need met:* 75% (excluding resources awarded to replace EFC). *Average financial aid package:* $13,523 (excluding resources awarded to replace EFC). 18% of all full-time undergraduates had no need and received non-need-based gift aid.
GIFT AID (NEED-BASED) *Total amount:* $12,355,403 (15% federal, 9% state, 75% institutional, 1% external sources). *Receiving aid:* Freshmen: 58% (105); all full-time undergraduates: 66% (545). *Average award:* Freshmen: $8700; Undergraduates: $8840. *Scholarships, grants, and awards:* Federal Pell, FSEOG, state, private, college/university gift aid from institutional funds.
GIFT AID (NON-NEED-BASED) *Receiving aid:* Freshmen: 77% (141). Undergraduates: 76% (629). *Average award:* Freshmen: $9440. Undergraduates: $9500. *Scholarships, grants, and awards by category: Academic interests/achievement:* biological sciences, education, general academic interests/achievements, mathematics. *Creative arts/performance:* dance, journalism/publications, performing arts, theater/drama. *Special achievements/activities:* cheerleading/drum major, general special achievements/activities. *Special characteristics:* children of educators, children of faculty/staff, children with a deceased or disabled parent, international students, local/state students, previous college experience, relatives of clergy, religious affiliation, veterans. *Tuition waivers:* Full or partial for employees or children of employees.
LOANS *Student loans:* $4,950,132 (100% need-based). *Average need-based loan:* Freshmen: $3500. Undergraduates: $5000. *Parent loans:* $1,153,152 (100% need-based). *Programs:* Federal Direct (Subsidized and Unsubsidized Stafford, PLUS), Perkins, state.
WORK-STUDY *Federal work-study:* Total amount: $217,470; jobs available. *State or other work-study/employment:* Total amount: $32,000 (100% need-based). Part-time jobs available.
ATHLETIC AWARDS Total amount: $1,502,747 (100% need-based).
APPLYING FOR FINANCIAL AID *Required financial aid forms:* FAFSA, state aid form. *Financial aid deadline (priority):* 4/15. *Notification date:* Continuous beginning 3/1. Students must reply within 2 weeks of notification.
CONTACT Cathy Shell, Director of Financial Aid, Lees-McRae College, PO Box 128, Banner Elk, NC 28604-0128, 828-898-8740 or toll-free 800-280-4562. *Fax:* 828-898-8746. *E-mail:* shell@lmc.edu. *Website:* http://www.lmc.edu/.

LEE UNIVERSITY
Cleveland, TN

Tuition & fees: $13,750 | **Average undergraduate aid package: $10,358**

ABOUT THE INSTITUTION Independent Church of God, coed. *Awards:* certificates, bachelor's, and master's degrees. 66 undergraduate majors. *Total enrollment:* 4,954. Undergraduates: 4,565. Freshmen: 860. Federal methodology is used as a basis for awarding need-based institutional aid.

UNDERGRADUATE EXPENSES for 2013–2014 *Comprehensive fee:* $20,512 includes full-time tuition ($13,200), mandatory fees ($550), and room and board ($6762). *College room only:* $3502. Full-time tuition and fees vary according to course load, location, and program. Room and board charges vary according to board plan and housing facility. *Part-time tuition:* $550 per credit hour. *Part-time fees:* $550 per credit hour. Part-time tuition and fees vary according to course load, location, and program.

FRESHMAN FINANCIAL AID (Fall 2011) 735 applied for aid; of those 77% were deemed to have need. 99% of freshmen with need received aid; of those 30% had need fully met. *Average percent of need met:* 68% (excluding resources awarded to replace EFC). *Average financial aid package:* $12,502 (excluding resources awarded to replace EFC). 21% of all full-time freshmen had no need and received non-need-based gift aid.

UNDERGRADUATE FINANCIAL AID (Fall 2011) 3,248 applied for aid; of those 84% were deemed to have need. 99% of undergraduates with need received aid; of those 14% had need fully met. *Average percent of need met:* 49% (excluding resources awarded to replace EFC). *Average financial aid package:* $10,358 (excluding resources awarded to replace EFC). 13% of all full-time undergraduates had no need and received non-need-based gift aid.

GIFT AID (NEED-BASED) *Total amount:* $18,672,187 (43% federal, 21% state, 34% institutional, 2% external sources). *Receiving aid:* Freshmen: 64% (542); all full-time undergraduates: 64% (2,438). *Average award:* Freshmen: $10,814; Undergraduates: $8020. *Scholarships, grants, and awards:* Federal Pell, FSEOG, state, private, college/university gift aid from institutional funds.

GIFT AID (NON-NEED-BASED) *Total amount:* $6,327,908 (26% state, 70% institutional, 4% external sources). *Receiving aid:* Freshmen: 16% (132). Undergraduates: 7% (277). *Average award:* Freshmen: $9913. Undergraduates: $7241. *Scholarships, grants, and awards by category:* Academic interests/achievement: biological sciences, business, communication, education, general academic interests/achievements, religion/biblical studies. *Creative arts/performance:* music, theater/drama. *Special achievements/activities:* cheerleading/drum major, leadership, religious involvement. *Special characteristics:* children of faculty/staff, local/state students, siblings of current students, spouses of current students. *Tuition waivers:* Full or partial for employees or children of employees, senior citizens.

LOANS *Student loans:* $19,746,060 (82% need-based, 18% non-need-based). 64% of past graduating class borrowed through all loan programs. *Average indebtedness per student:* $27,882. *Average need-based loan:* Freshmen: $3486. Undergraduates: $4118. *Parent loans:* $2,687,289 (44% need-based, 56% non-need-based). *Programs:* Federal Direct (Subsidized and Unsubsidized Stafford, PLUS), Perkins, college/university.

WORK-STUDY *Federal work-study:* Total amount: $418,946; 243 jobs averaging $1715. *State or other work-study/employment:* Total amount: $1,266,600 (100% non-need-based). 624 part-time jobs averaging $1450.

ATHLETIC AWARDS Total amount: $1,938,401 (39% need-based, 61% non-need-based).

APPLYING FOR FINANCIAL AID *Required financial aid form:* FAFSA. *Financial aid deadline (priority):* 3/15. *Notification date:* Continuous beginning 2/1. Students must reply within 3 weeks of notification.

CONTACT Mrs. Marian Dill, Director of Student Financial Aid, Lee University, 1120 North Ocoee Street, Cleveland, TN 37311, 423-614-8300 or toll-free 800-533-9930. *Fax:* 423-614-8308. *E-mail:* finaid@leeuniversity.edu. *Website:* http://www.leeuniversity.edu/.

LEHIGH UNIVERSITY
Bethlehem, PA

Tuition & fees: $42,220 | **Average undergraduate aid package: $36,771**

ABOUT THE INSTITUTION Independent, coed. *Awards:* certificates, bachelor's, master's, and doctoral degrees. 68 undergraduate majors. *Total enrollment:* 7,080. Undergraduates: 4,883. Freshmen: 1,217. Both federal and institutional methodology are used as a basis for awarding need-based institutional aid.

UNDERGRADUATE EXPENSES for 2013–2014 *Application fee:* $70. *Comprehensive fee:* $53,450 includes full-time tuition ($41,920), mandatory fees ($300), and room and board ($11,230). *College room only:* $6450. Room and board charges vary according to board plan and housing facility. *Part-time tuition:* $1750 per credit hour. *Payment plan:* Tuition prepayment.

FRESHMAN FINANCIAL AID (Fall 2012, est.) 820 applied for aid; of those 65% were deemed to have need. 100% of freshmen with need received aid; of those 48% had need fully met. *Average percent of need met:* 94% (excluding resources awarded to replace EFC). *Average financial aid package:* $36,189 (excluding resources awarded to replace EFC). 7% of all full-time freshmen had no need and received non-need-based gift aid.

UNDERGRADUATE FINANCIAL AID (Fall 2012, est.) 2,798 applied for aid; of those 75% were deemed to have need. 100% of undergraduates with need received aid; of those 70% had need fully met. *Average percent of need met:* 95% (excluding resources awarded to replace EFC). *Average financial aid package:* $36,771 (excluding resources awarded to replace EFC). 6% of all full-time undergraduates had no need and received non-need-based gift aid.

GIFT AID (NEED-BASED) *Total amount:* $59,091,761 (6% federal, 2% state, 92% institutional). *Receiving aid:* Freshmen: 42% (517); all full-time undergraduates: 42% (2,039). *Average award:* Freshmen: $31,494; Undergraduates: $30,904. *Scholarships, grants, and awards:* Federal Pell, FSEOG, state, private, college/university gift aid from institutional funds, United Negro College Fund.

GIFT AID (NON-NEED-BASED) *Total amount:* $6,200,386 (52% institutional, 48% external sources). *Receiving aid:* Freshmen: 4% (46). Undergraduates: 4% (209). *Average award:* Freshmen: $11,550. Undergraduates: $10,259. *Scholarships, grants, and awards by category:* Academic interests/achievement: 356 awards ($3,892,628 total): business, communication, engineering/technologies, general academic interests/achievements, international studies, military science. *Creative arts/performance:* 65 awards ($118,040 total): general creative arts/performance, journalism/publications, music, performing arts, theater/drama. *Special achievements/activities:* 8 awards ($10,500 total): general special achievements/activities. *Special characteristics:* 95 awards ($3,697,064 total): children of faculty/staff, members of minority groups. *Tuition waivers:* Full or partial for employees or children of employees. *ROTC:* Army.

LOANS *Student loans:* $24,479,428 (41% need-based, 59% non-need-based). 54% of past graduating class borrowed through all loan programs. *Average indebtedness per student:* $31,122. *Average need-based loan:* Freshmen: $3887. Undergraduates: $4603. *Parent loans:* $6,780,114 (100% non-need-based). *Programs:* Federal Direct (Subsidized and Unsubsidized Stafford, PLUS), Perkins, college/university, private loans.

WORK-STUDY *Federal work-study:* Total amount: $2,730,554; 1,349 jobs averaging $1750. *State or other work-study/employment:* Total amount: $927,604 (7% need-based, 93% non-need-based). 33 part-time jobs averaging $1811.

ATHLETIC AWARDS Total amount: $6,611,594 (44% need-based, 56% non-need-based).

APPLYING FOR FINANCIAL AID *Required financial aid forms:* FAFSA, CSS Financial Aid PROFILE, noncustodial (divorced/separated) parent's statement, business/farm supplement. *Financial aid deadline:* 2/15. *Notification date:* 3/30. Students must reply by 5/1 or within 3 weeks of notification.

CONTACT Jennifer Mertz, Director of Financial Aid, Lehigh University, 218 West Packer Avenue, Bethlehem, PA 18015-3094, 610-758-3181. *Fax:* 610-758-6211. *E-mail:* jlm207@lehigh.edu. *Website:* http://www.lehigh.edu/.

LEHMAN COLLEGE OF THE CITY UNIVERSITY OF NEW YORK
Bronx, NY

Tuition & fees (NY res): $5808	Average undergraduate aid package: N/A

ABOUT THE INSTITUTION State and locally supported, coed. **Awards:** certificates, bachelor's, and master's degrees. 52 undergraduate majors. **Total enrollment:** 11,862. Undergraduates: 9,577. Freshmen: 551. Federal methodology is used as a basis for awarding need-based institutional aid.

UNDERGRADUATE EXPENSES for 2013–2014 Application fee: $65. **Tuition, state resident:** full-time $5430; part-time $230 per credit. **Tuition, non-resident:** full-time $11,640; part-time $485 per credit. **Required fees:** full-time $378. **Room only:** $8085.

GIFT AID (NEED-BASED) Scholarships, grants, and awards: Federal Pell, FSEOG, state, college/university gift aid from institutional funds.

GIFT AID (NON-NEED-BASED) ROTC: Army cooperative.

LOANS Programs: Federal Direct (Subsidized and Unsubsidized Stafford, PLUS), Perkins.

APPLYING FOR FINANCIAL AID Required financial aid forms: FAFSA, state aid form. **Financial aid deadline:** Continuous. **Notification date:** Continuous beginning 3/1.

CONTACT David Martinez, Director of Financial Aid, Lehman College of the City University of New York, 250 Bedford Park Boulevard West, Bronx, NY 10468-1589, 718-960-8545 or toll-free 877-LEHMAN1. Fax: 718-960-8328. E-mail: idmlc@cunyvm.cuny.edu.
Website: http://www.lehman.cuny.edu/.

LE MOYNE COLLEGE
Syracuse, NY

Tuition & fees: $30,460	Average undergraduate aid package: $21,106

ABOUT THE INSTITUTION Independent Roman Catholic (Jesuit), coed. **Awards:** certificates, bachelor's, and master's degrees. 52 undergraduate majors. **Total enrollment:** 3,339. Undergraduates: 2,749. Freshmen: 521. Both federal and institutional methodology are used as a basis for awarding need-based institutional aid.

UNDERGRADUATE EXPENSES for 2013–2014 Application fee: $35. **Comprehensive fee:** $42,200 includes full-time tuition ($29,470), mandatory fees ($990), and room and board ($11,740). **College room only:** $7430. Room and board charges vary according to board plan and housing facility. **Part-time tuition:** $618 per credit hour. Part-time tuition and fees vary according to class time and course load.

FRESHMAN FINANCIAL AID (Fall 2011) 598 applied for aid; of those 92% were deemed to have need. 100% of freshmen with need received aid; of those 25% had need fully met. **Average percent of need met:** 77% (excluding resources awarded to replace EFC). **Average financial aid package:** $22,089 (excluding resources awarded to replace EFC). 11% of all full-time freshmen had no need and received non-need-based gift aid.

UNDERGRADUATE FINANCIAL AID (Fall 2011) 2,173 applied for aid; of those 93% were deemed to have need. 100% of undergraduates with need received aid; of those 21% had need fully met. **Average percent of need met:** 74% (excluding resources awarded to replace EFC). **Average financial aid package:** $21,106 (excluding resources awarded to replace EFC). 8% of all full-time undergraduates had no need and received non-need-based gift aid.

GIFT AID (NEED-BASED) Total amount: $32,901,923 (12% federal, 9% state, 76% institutional, 3% external sources). **Receiving aid:** Freshmen: 87% (553); all full-time undergraduates: 84% (2,019). **Average award:** Freshmen: $18,064; Undergraduates: $16,543. **Scholarships, grants, and awards:** Federal Pell, FSEOG, state, private, college/university gift aid from institutional funds.

GIFT AID (NON-NEED-BASED) Total amount: $3,771,566 (88% institutional, 12% external sources). **Receiving aid:** Freshmen: 14% (87). Undergraduates: 11% (256). **Average award:** Freshmen: $6003. Undergraduates: $5895. **Scholarships, grants, and awards by category:** Academic interests/achievement: 377 awards ($6,186,720 total): general academic interests/achievements. Creative arts/perfor-

mance: 16 awards ($1930 total): music. **Special achievements/activities:** 631 awards ($6,274,105 total): leadership. **Special characteristics:** 125 awards ($772,300 total): children and siblings of alumni, members of minority groups. **Tuition waivers:** Full or partial for employees or children of employees. **ROTC:** Army cooperative, Air Force cooperative.

LOANS Student loans: $15,216,309 (94% need-based, 6% non-need-based). 85% of past graduating class borrowed through all loan programs. Average indebtedness per student: $34,532. **Average need-based loan:** Freshmen: $3781. Undergraduates: $4521. **Parent loans:** $6,423,367 (96% need-based, 4% non-need-based). **Programs:** Federal Direct (Subsidized and Unsubsidized Stafford, PLUS), Perkins.

WORK-STUDY Federal work-study: Total amount: $397,268; 396 jobs averaging $950. **State or other work-study/employment:** 375 part-time jobs averaging $1000.

ATHLETIC AWARDS Total amount: $1,520,719 (62% need-based, 38% non-need-based).

APPLYING FOR FINANCIAL AID Required financial aid forms: FAFSA, institution's own form, state aid form. **Financial aid deadline (priority):** 2/1. **Notification date:** 3/15. Students must reply by 5/1 or within 2 weeks of notification.

CONTACT Mr. William C. Cheetham, Director of Financial Aid, Le Moyne College, 1419 Salt Springs Road, Syracuse, NY 13214-1301, 315-445-4400 or toll-free 800-333-4733. Fax: 315-445-4182. E-mail: cheethwc@lemoyne.edu.
Website: http://www.lemoyne.edu/.

LEMOYNE-OWEN COLLEGE
Memphis, TN

Tuition & fees: N/R	Average undergraduate aid package: $10,527

ABOUT THE INSTITUTION Independent United Church of Christ, coed. 22 undergraduate majors. Federal methodology is used as a basis for awarding need-based institutional aid.

FRESHMAN FINANCIAL AID (Fall 2012, est.) 167 applied for aid; of those 98% were deemed to have need. 99% of freshmen with need received aid; of those 5% had need fully met. **Average percent of need met:** 61% (excluding resources awarded to replace EFC). **Average financial aid package:** $10,556 (excluding resources awarded to replace EFC). 2% of all full-time freshmen had no need and received non-need-based gift aid.

UNDERGRADUATE FINANCIAL AID (Fall 2012, est.) 902 applied for aid; of those 98% were deemed to have need. 99% of undergraduates with need received aid; of those 3% had need fully met. **Average percent of need met:** 57% (excluding resources awarded to replace EFC). **Average financial aid package:** $10,527 (excluding resources awarded to replace EFC). 1% of all full-time undergraduates had no need and received non-need-based gift aid.

GIFT AID (NEED-BASED) Total amount: $5,707,963 (66% federal, 21% state, 7% institutional, 6% external sources). **Receiving aid:** Freshmen: 91% (159); all full-time undergraduates: 90% (826). **Average award:** Freshmen: $7525; Undergraduates: $7029. **Scholarships, grants, and awards:** Federal Pell, FSEOG, state, private, college/university gift aid from institutional funds, United Negro College Fund.

GIFT AID (NON-NEED-BASED) Total amount: $172,035 (10% state, 70% institutional, 20% external sources). **Receiving aid:** Freshmen: 3% (6). Undergraduates: 2% (15). **Average award:** Freshmen: $11,072. Undergraduates: $13,210. **Scholarships, grants, and awards by category:** Academic interests/achievement: 69 awards ($404,727 total): general academic interests/achievements. Creative arts/performance: 23 awards ($69,879 total): journalism/publications, music. **Special characteristics:** 21 awards ($59,535 total): children of faculty/staff.

LOANS Student loans: $6,547,239 (96% need-based, 4% non-need-based). **Average need-based loan:** Freshmen: $3235. Undergraduates: $3983. **Parent loans:** $97,514 (68% need-based, 32% non-need-based). **Programs:** Federal Direct (Subsidized and Unsubsidized Stafford, PLUS).

WORK-STUDY Federal work-study: Total amount: $210,334; 140 jobs averaging $1623.

ATHLETIC AWARDS Total amount: $346,958 (73% need-based, 27% non-need-based).

APPLYING FOR FINANCIAL AID Required financial aid forms: FAFSA, institution's own form. **Financial aid deadline (priority):** 4/1. **Notification date:** Continuous beginning 5/1. Students must reply within 2 weeks of notification.

CONTACT Office of Student Financial Services, LeMoyne-Owen College, 807 Walker Avenue, Memphis, TN 38126-6595, 901-435-1552 Ext. 1555 or toll-free 800-737-7778. *Fax:* 901-435-1574. *Website:* http://www.loc.edu/.

LENOIR-RHYNE UNIVERSITY
Hickory, NC

ABOUT THE INSTITUTION Independent Lutheran, coed. *Awards:* certificates, bachelor's, and master's degrees. 72 undergraduate majors. *Total enrollment:* 1,860. Undergraduates: 1,595. Freshmen: 400.

GIFT AID (NEED-BASED) *Scholarships, grants, and awards:* Federal Pell, FSEOG, state, private, college/university gift aid from institutional funds.

GIFT AID (NON-NEED-BASED) *Scholarships, grants, and awards by category:* Academic interests/achievement: general academic interests/achievements. Creative arts/performance: music. Special achievements/activities: cheerleading/drum major, leadership. Special characteristics: children and siblings of alumni, children of faculty/staff, ethnic background, local/state students, members of minority groups, relatives of clergy, religious affiliation, siblings of current students.

LOANS *Programs:* Federal Direct (Subsidized and Unsubsidized Stafford, PLUS), Perkins, state.

WORK-STUDY *Federal work-study:* Total amount: $226,667; jobs available. *State or other work-study/employment:* Part-time jobs available.

APPLYING FOR FINANCIAL AID *Required financial aid forms:* FAFSA, state aid form.

CONTACT Nick Jenkins, Financial Aid Counselor, Lenoir-Rhyne University, PO Box 7227, Hickory, NC 28603, 828-328-7301 or toll-free 800-277-5721. *Fax:* 828-328-7039. *E-mail:* finaid@lr.edu. *Website:* http://www.lr.edu/.

LESLEY UNIVERSITY
Cambridge, MA

Tuition & fees: $32,250	Average undergraduate aid package: $21,300

ABOUT THE INSTITUTION Independent, coed. *Awards:* certificates, associate, bachelor's, master's, and doctoral degrees. 22 undergraduate majors. *Total enrollment:* 5,528. Undergraduates: 1,568. Freshmen: 335. Both federal and institutional methodology are used as a basis for awarding need-based institutional aid.

UNDERGRADUATE EXPENSES for 2013–2014 *Application fee:* $50. *Comprehensive fee:* $46,250 includes full-time tuition ($32,000), mandatory fees ($250), and room and board ($14,000). *College room only:* $8550. Full-time tuition and fees vary according to class time, course level, course load, degree level, location, program, reciprocity agreements, and student level. Room and board charges vary according to housing facility. *Part-time tuition:* $1310 per credit hour.

FRESHMAN FINANCIAL AID (Fall 2012, est.) 318 applied for aid; of those 91% were deemed to have need. 100% of freshmen with need received aid; of those 29% had need fully met. *Average percent of need met:* 72% (excluding resources awarded to replace EFC). *Average financial aid package:* $19,921 (excluding resources awarded to replace EFC). 19% of all full-time freshmen had no need and received non-need-based gift aid.

UNDERGRADUATE FINANCIAL AID (Fall 2012, est.) 1,470 applied for aid; of those 76% were deemed to have need. 100% of undergraduates with need received aid; of those 10% had need fully met. *Average percent of need met:* 70% (excluding resources awarded to replace EFC). *Average financial aid package:* $21,300 (excluding resources awarded to replace EFC). 8% of all full-time undergraduates had no need and received non-need-based gift aid.

GIFT AID (NEED-BASED) *Total amount:* $17,333,104 (12% federal, 1% state, 79% institutional, 8% external sources). *Receiving aid:* Freshmen: 84% (282); all full-time undergraduates: 66% (1,020). *Average award:* Freshmen: $13,000; Undergraduates: $13,631. *Scholarships, grants, and awards:* Federal Pell, FSEOG, state, private, college/university gift aid from institutional funds.

GIFT AID (NON-NEED-BASED) *Total amount:* $4,310,545 (100% institutional). *Receiving aid:* Freshmen: 28% (93). Undergraduates: 62% (959). *Average award:* Freshmen: $12,520. Undergraduates: $11,080. *Scholarships, grants, and*

awards by category: Academic interests/achievement: general academic interests/achievements. Creative arts/performance: art/fine arts. Special achievements/activities: general special achievements/activities. Special characteristics: ethnic background, local/state students, members of minority groups. *Tuition waivers:* Full or partial for employees or children of employees.

LOANS *Student loans:* $13,057,485 (34% need-based, 66% non-need-based). 90% of past graduating class borrowed through all loan programs. *Average indebtedness per student:* $23,000. *Average need-based loan:* Freshmen: $3698. Undergraduates: $4639. *Parent loans:* $2,356,325 (100% non-need-based). *Programs:* Federal Direct (Subsidized and Unsubsidized Stafford, PLUS), Perkins, state.

WORK-STUDY *Federal work-study:* Total amount: $450,000; jobs available. *State or other work-study/employment:* Part-time jobs available.

APPLYING FOR FINANCIAL AID *Required financial aid forms:* FAFSA, institution's own form. *Financial aid deadline (priority):* 3/15. *Notification date:* Continuous beginning 3/15.

CONTACT Scott A. Jewell, Director of Student Financial Services, Lesley University, 29 Everett Street, Cambridge, MA 02138-2790, 617-349-8714 or toll-free 800-999-1959 Ext. 8800. *Fax:* 617-349-8717. *E-mail:* sjewell@lesley.edu. *Website:* http://www.lesley.edu/.

LETOURNEAU UNIVERSITY
Longview, TX

Tuition & fees: $24,540	Average undergraduate aid package: $18,555

ABOUT THE INSTITUTION Independent nondenominational, coed. *Awards:* associate, bachelor's, and master's degrees. 42 undergraduate majors. *Total enrollment:* 2,843. Undergraduates: 2,450. Freshmen: 362. Federal methodology is used as a basis for awarding need-based institutional aid.

UNDERGRADUATE EXPENSES for 2013–2014 *Application fee:* $35. *Comprehensive fee:* $33,480 includes full-time tuition ($24,050), mandatory fees ($490), and room and board ($8940). Room and board charges vary according to board plan. *Part-time tuition:* $959 per credit hour. Part-time tuition and fees vary according to course load.

FRESHMAN FINANCIAL AID (Fall 2012, est.) 288 applied for aid; of those 84% were deemed to have need. 100% of freshmen with need received aid; of those 16% had need fully met. *Average percent of need met:* 77% (excluding resources awarded to replace EFC). *Average financial aid package:* $22,004 (excluding resources awarded to replace EFC). 24% of all full-time freshmen had no need and received non-need-based gift aid.

UNDERGRADUATE FINANCIAL AID (Fall 2012, est.) 1,161 applied for aid; of those 91% were deemed to have need. 99% of undergraduates with need received aid; of those 12% had need fully met. *Average percent of need met:* 63% (excluding resources awarded to replace EFC). *Average financial aid package:* $18,555 (excluding resources awarded to replace EFC). 16% of all full-time undergraduates had no need and received non-need-based gift aid.

GIFT AID (NEED-BASED) *Total amount:* $15,993,966 (28% federal, 11% state, 57% institutional, 4% external sources). *Receiving aid:* Freshmen: 76% (243); all full-time undergraduates: 77% (1,019). *Average award:* Freshmen: $17,961; Undergraduates: $13,868. *Scholarships, grants, and awards:* Federal Pell, FSEOG, state, private, college/university gift aid from institutional funds, United Negro College Fund.

GIFT AID (NON-NEED-BASED) *Total amount:* $2,566,726 (92% institutional, 8% external sources). *Receiving aid:* Freshmen: 9% (30). Undergraduates: 6% (83). *Average award:* Freshmen: $4039. Undergraduates: $9312. *Scholarships, grants, and awards by category:* Academic interests/achievement: general academic interests/achievements. Special achievements/activities: leadership. Special characteristics: children and siblings of alumni, local/state students, members of minority groups, religious affiliation. *Tuition waivers:* Full or partial for employees or children of employees.

LOANS *Student loans:* $16,423,084 (87% need-based, 13% non-need-based). 78% of past graduating class borrowed through all loan programs. *Average indebtedness per student:* $41,522. *Average need-based loan:* Freshmen: $3601. Undergraduates: $4570. *Parent loans:* $2,032,113 (62% need-based, 38% non-need-based). *Programs:* Federal Direct (Subsidized and Unsubsidized Stafford, PLUS), Perkins, state.

WORK-STUDY *Federal work-study:* Total amount: $497,998; jobs available. *State or other work-study/employment:* Total amount: $32,282 (100% need-based). Part-time jobs available.

APPLYING FOR FINANCIAL AID *Required financial aid form:* FAFSA. *Financial aid deadline (priority):* 2/1. *Notification date:* Continuous beginning 3/1. Students must reply within 2 weeks of notification.

CONTACT Financial Aid Office, LeTourneau University, PO Box 7001, Longview, TX 75607, 903-233-4312 or toll-free 800-759-8811. *Fax:* 903-233-4301. *E-mail:* finaid@letu.edu.

Website: http://www.letu.edu/.

LEWIS & CLARK COLLEGE
Portland, OR

Tuition & fees: $41,928 — Average undergraduate aid package: $33,842

ABOUT THE INSTITUTION Independent, coed. **Awards:** certificates, bachelor's, master's, and doctoral degrees. 27 undergraduate majors. **Total enrollment:** 3,703. Undergraduates: 2,150. Freshmen: 554. Both federal and institutional methodology are used as a basis for awarding need-based institutional aid.

UNDERGRADUATE EXPENSES for 2013–2014 Application fee: $50. **Comprehensive fee:** $52,564 includes full-time tuition ($41,568), mandatory fees ($360), and room and board ($10,636). **College room only:** $5722. Room and board charges vary according to board plan and housing facility. **Part-time tuition:** $1999 per credit hour.

FRESHMAN FINANCIAL AID (Fall 2012, est.) 445 applied for aid; of those 78% were deemed to have need. 100% of freshmen with need received aid; of those 24% had need fully met. **Average percent of need met:** 83% (excluding resources awarded to replace EFC). **Average financial aid package:** $32,748 (excluding resources awarded to replace EFC). 21% of all full-time freshmen had no need and received non-need-based gift aid.

UNDERGRADUATE FINANCIAL AID (Fall 2012, est.) 1,416 applied for aid; of those 89% were deemed to have need. 100% of undergraduates with need received aid; of those 28% had need fully met. **Average percent of need met:** 86% (excluding resources awarded to replace EFC). **Average financial aid package:** $33,842 (excluding resources awarded to replace EFC). 16% of all full-time undergraduates had no need and received non-need-based gift aid.

GIFT AID (NEED-BASED) Total amount: $31,407,330 (7% federal, 88% institutional, 5% external sources). **Receiving aid:** Freshmen: 63% (347); all full-time undergraduates: 62% (1,258). **Average award:** Freshmen: $26,945; Undergraduates: $26,301. **Scholarships, grants, and awards:** Federal Pell, FSEOG, state, private, college/university gift aid from institutional funds.

GIFT AID (NON-NEED-BASED) Total amount: $6,930,176 (98% institutional, 2% external sources). **Receiving aid:** Freshmen: 4% (21). Undergraduates: 3% (54). **Average award:** Freshmen: $11,869. Undergraduates: $12,666. **Scholarships, grants, and awards by category:** *Academic interests/achievement:* general academic interests/achievements. *Creative arts/performance:* debating, music. *Special achievements/activities:* community service, leadership. *Special characteristics:* children of faculty/staff. **Tuition waivers:** Full or partial for employees or children of employees.

LOANS Student loans: $8,003,625 (71% need-based, 29% non-need-based). 50% of past graduating class borrowed through all loan programs. *Average indebtedness per student:* $25,134. **Average need-based loan:** Freshmen: $4401, Undergraduates: $5250. **Parent loans:** $2,825,779 (3% need-based, 97% non-need-based). **Programs:** Federal Direct (Subsidized and Unsubsidized Stafford, PLUS), Perkins.

WORK-STUDY *Federal work-study:* Total amount: $2,488,235; jobs available. *State or other work-study/employment:* Total amount: $315,760 (100% non-need-based). Part-time jobs available.

APPLYING FOR FINANCIAL AID *Required financial aid forms:* FAFSA, CSS Financial Aid PROFILE. *Financial aid deadline (priority):* 2/15. *Notification date:* Continuous beginning 3/1. Students must reply by 5/1.

CONTACT Anastacia Dillon, Director of Financial Aid, Lewis & Clark College, Templeton Campus Center, MSC 56, Portland, OR 97219-7899, 503-768-7090 or toll-free 800-444-4111. *Fax:* 503-768-7074. *E-mail:* fao@lclark.edu.

Website: http://www.lclark.edu/.

LEWIS-CLARK STATE COLLEGE
Lewiston, ID

Tuition & fees (ID res): $5562 — Average undergraduate aid package: $8172

ABOUT THE INSTITUTION State-supported, coed. **Awards:** certificates, associate, and bachelor's degrees. 50 undergraduate majors. **Total enrollment:** 4,525. Undergraduates: 4,525. Freshmen: 515. Federal methodology is used as a basis for awarding need-based institutional aid.

UNDERGRADUATE EXPENSES for 2013–2014 Application fee: $35. **Tuition, state resident:** full-time $5562. **Tuition, nonresident:** full-time $15,476. Full-time tuition and fees vary according to course load and reciprocity agreements. Room and board charges vary according to board plan and housing facility.

FRESHMAN FINANCIAL AID (Fall 2011) 540 applied for aid; of those 85% were deemed to have need. 97% of freshmen with need received aid; of those 8% had need fully met. **Average percent of need met:** 8% (excluding resources awarded to replace EFC). **Average financial aid package:** $7347 (excluding resources awarded to replace EFC). 11% of all full-time freshmen had no need and received non-need-based gift aid.

UNDERGRADUATE FINANCIAL AID (Fall 2011) 2,348 applied for aid; of those 89% were deemed to have need. 98% of undergraduates with need received aid; of those 17% had need fully met. **Average percent of need met:** 17% (excluding resources awarded to replace EFC). **Average financial aid package:** $8172 (excluding resources awarded to replace EFC). 6% of all full-time undergraduates had no need and received non-need-based gift aid.

GIFT AID (NEED-BASED) Total amount: $9,032,715 (89% federal, 1% state, 5% institutional, 5% external sources). **Receiving aid:** Freshmen: 58% (337); all full-time undergraduates: 60% (1,630). **Average award:** Freshmen: $3978; Undergraduates: $4328. **Scholarships, grants, and awards:** Federal Pell, FSEOG, state, private, college/university gift aid from institutional funds.

GIFT AID (NON-NEED-BASED) Total amount: $670,546 (34% state, 51% institutional, 15% external sources). **Receiving aid:** Freshmen: 31% (179). Undergraduates: 13% (344). **Average award:** Freshmen: $1398. Undergraduates: $2130. *Scholarships, grants, and awards by category:* *Academic interests/achievement:* 71 awards ($125,011 total): biological sciences, business, education, English, general academic interests/achievements, health fields, humanities, mathematics, physical sciences, social sciences. *Creative arts/performance:* 13 awards ($26,782 total): art/fine arts, creative writing, debating, music, theater/drama. *Special achievements/activities:* 289 awards ($265,384 total): community service, general special achievements/activities, junior miss, leadership, rodeo. *Special characteristics:* 332 awards ($837,305 total): children and siblings of alumni, ethnic background, first-generation college students, general special characteristics, members of minority groups, out-of-state students, previous college experience. **Tuition waivers:** Full or partial for employees or children of employees, senior citizens. **ROTC:** Army cooperative, Naval cooperative, Air Force cooperative.

LOANS Student loans: $18,179,607 (47% need-based, 53% non-need-based). 61% of past graduating class borrowed through all loan programs. **Average need-based loan:** Freshmen: $2886. Undergraduates: $3783. **Parent loans:** $419,846 (100% non-need-based). **Programs:** Federal Direct (Subsidized and Unsubsidized Stafford, PLUS), Perkins, Federal Nursing.

WORK-STUDY *Federal work-study:* Total amount: $125,622; 91 jobs averaging $1380. *State or other work-study/employment:* Total amount: $135,544 (75% need-based, 25% non-need-based). 89 part-time jobs averaging $1412.

ATHLETIC AWARDS Total amount: $1,625,743 (100% non-need-based).

APPLYING FOR FINANCIAL AID *Required financial aid form:* FAFSA. *Financial aid deadline (priority):* 3/1. *Notification date:* Continuous beginning 4/15. Students must reply within 2 weeks of notification.

CONTACT Ms. Laura Hughes, Director of Financial Aid, Lewis-Clark State College, 500 8th Avenue, Lewiston, ID 83501-2698, 208-792-2224 or toll-free 800-933-5272. *Fax:* 208-792-2063. *E-mail:* lhughes@lcsc.edu.

Website: http://www.lcsc.edu/.

LEWIS UNIVERSITY
Romeoville, IL

Tuition & fees: $26,780	Average undergraduate aid package: $18,333

ABOUT THE INSTITUTION Independent Roman Catholic Church, coed. *Awards:* certificates, associate, bachelor's, master's, and doctoral degrees. 72 undergraduate majors. *Total enrollment:* 6,539. Undergraduates: 4,579. Freshmen: 673. Federal methodology is used as a basis for awarding need-based institutional aid.

UNDERGRADUATE EXPENSES for 2013–2014 *Application fee:* $40. *Comprehensive fee:* $36,310 includes full-time tuition ($26,780) and room and board ($9530). *College room only:* $6160. Full-time tuition and fees vary according to course load and program. Room and board charges vary according to board plan and housing facility. *Part-time tuition:* $780 per credit. *Part-time fees:* $780 per credit. Part-time tuition and fees vary according to course load and program.

FRESHMAN FINANCIAL AID (Fall 2012, est.) 641 applied for aid; of those 87% were deemed to have need. 100% of freshmen with need received aid; of those 20% had need fully met. *Average percent of need met:* 79% (excluding resources awarded to replace EFC). *Average financial aid package:* $20,668 (excluding resources awarded to replace EFC). 15% of all full-time freshmen had no need and received non-need-based gift aid.

UNDERGRADUATE FINANCIAL AID (Fall 2012, est.) 3,128 applied for aid; of those 90% were deemed to have need. 100% of undergraduates with need received aid; of those 19% had need fully met. *Average percent of need met:* 73% (excluding resources awarded to replace EFC). *Average financial aid package:* $18,333 (excluding resources awarded to replace EFC). 15% of all full-time undergraduates had no need and received non-need-based gift aid.

GIFT AID (NEED-BASED) *Total amount:* $32,342,506 (19% federal, 18% state, 62% institutional, 1% external sources). *Receiving aid:* Freshmen: 83% (558); all full-time undergraduates: 73% (2,631). *Average award:* Freshmen: $14,933; Undergraduates: $12,713. *Scholarships, grants, and awards:* Federal Pell, FSEOG, state, private, college/university gift aid from institutional funds, Federal Nursing.

GIFT AID (NON-NEED-BASED) *Total amount:* $6,402,933 (9% federal, 89% institutional, 2% external sources). *Receiving aid:* Freshmen: 10% (68). Undergraduates: 8% (291). *Average award:* Freshmen: $10,125. Undergraduates: $8735. *Scholarships, grants, and awards by category: Academic interests/achievement:* general academic interests/achievements. *Creative arts/performance:* art/fine arts, music, theater/drama. *Special achievements/activities:* cheerleading/drum major, community service, general special achievements/activities, memberships. *Special characteristics:* children and siblings of alumni, children of faculty/staff, religious affiliation, veterans, veterans' children. *Tuition waivers:* Full or partial for children of alumni, employees or children of employees, adult students. *ROTC:* Army cooperative, Air Force cooperative.

LOANS *Student loans:* $29,301,901 (75% need-based, 25% non-need-based). 82% of past graduating class borrowed through all loan programs. *Average indebtedness per student:* $31,400. *Average need-based loan:* Freshmen: $3409. Undergraduates: $4432. *Parent loans:* $7,388,772 (38% need-based, 62% non-need-based). *Programs:* Federal Direct (Subsidized and Unsubsidized Stafford, PLUS), Perkins.

WORK-STUDY *Federal work-study:* Total amount: $5,977,482; 1,833 jobs averaging $3261. *State or other work-study/employment:* Total amount: $646,990 (30% need-based, 70% non-need-based). 205 part-time jobs averaging $3156.

ATHLETIC AWARDS Total amount: $2,840,893 (48% need-based, 52% non-need-based).

APPLYING FOR FINANCIAL AID *Required financial aid form:* FAFSA. *Financial aid deadline:* 5/1. *Notification date:* Continuous beginning 2/1. Students must reply by 5/1 or within 2 weeks of notification.

CONTACT Ms. Janeen Decharinte, Director of Financial Aid, Lewis University, One University Parkway, Romeoville, IL 60446, 815-836-5263 or toll-free 800-897-9000. *Fax:* 815-836-5135. *E-mail:* decharja@lewisu.edu. *Website:* http://www.lewisu.edu/.

LEXINGTON COLLEGE
Chicago, IL

CONTACT Maria Lebron, Director of Financial Aid, Lexington College, 310 South Peoria Street, Suite 512, Chicago, IL 60607, 312-226-6294 Ext. 227. *Fax:* 312-226-6405. *E-mail:* finaid@lexingtoncollege.edu. *Website:* http://www.lexingtoncollege.edu/.

LIBERTY UNIVERSITY
Lynchburg, VA

Tuition & fees: $20,892	Average undergraduate aid package: $12,985

ABOUT THE INSTITUTION Independent nondenominational, coed. *Awards:* certificates, associate, bachelor's, master's, and doctoral degrees (also offers external degree program with significant enrollment not reflected in profile). 60 undergraduate majors. *Total enrollment:* 12,645. Undergraduates: 11,581. Freshmen: 2,629. Federal methodology is used as a basis for awarding need-based institutional aid.

UNDERGRADUATE EXPENSES for 2013–2014 *Application fee:* $40. *Comprehensive fee:* $28,868 includes full-time tuition ($19,486), mandatory fees ($1406), and room and board ($7976). Full-time tuition and fees vary according to course load. Room and board charges vary according to housing facility. *Part-time tuition:* $650 per credit hour. *Part-time fees:* $1550 per year. Part-time tuition and fees vary according to course load.

FRESHMAN FINANCIAL AID (Fall 2012, est.) 2,470 applied for aid; of those 79% were deemed to have need. 100% of freshmen with need received aid; of those 10% had need fully met. *Average percent of need met:* 56% (excluding resources awarded to replace EFC). *Average financial aid package:* $12,435 (excluding resources awarded to replace EFC). 7% of all full-time freshmen had no need and received non-need-based gift aid.

UNDERGRADUATE FINANCIAL AID (Fall 2012, est.) 10,198 applied for aid; of those 81% were deemed to have need. 100% of undergraduates with need received aid; of those 11% had need fully met. *Average percent of need met:* 58% (excluding resources awarded to replace EFC). *Average financial aid package:* $12,985 (excluding resources awarded to replace EFC). 7% of all full-time undergraduates had no need and received non-need-based gift aid.

GIFT AID (NEED-BASED) *Total amount:* $74,119,665 (21% federal, 8% state, 68% institutional, 3% external sources). *Receiving aid:* Freshmen: 74% (1,950); all full-time undergraduates: 73% (8,102). *Average award:* Freshmen: $9498; Undergraduates: $9065. *Scholarships, grants, and awards:* Federal Pell, FSEOG, state, private, college/university gift aid from institutional funds.

GIFT AID (NON-NEED-BASED) *Total amount:* $22,777,865 (1% federal, 11% state, 85% institutional, 3% external sources). *Receiving aid:* Freshmen: 12% (320). Undergraduates: 13% (1,483). *Average award:* Freshmen: $6813. Undergraduates: $7987. *Scholarships, grants, and awards by category: Academic interests/achievement:* biological sciences, business, communication, computer science, education, engineering/technologies, English, general academic interests/achievements, mathematics, premedicine, religion/biblical studies. *Creative arts/performance:* cinema/film/broadcasting, debating, journalism/publications, music, performing arts. *Special achievements/activities:* cheerleading/drum major, leadership. *Special characteristics:* children of faculty/staff, international students, local/state students, religious affiliation, veterans. *Tuition waivers:* Full or partial for employees or children of employees. *ROTC:* Army, Air Force cooperative.

LOANS *Student loans:* $62,295,470 (82% need-based, 18% non-need-based). 64% of past graduating class borrowed through all loan programs. *Average indebtedness per student:* $21,830. *Average need-based loan:* Freshmen: $3244. Undergraduates: $4169. *Parent loans:* $15,165,950 (77% need-based, 23% non-need-based). *Programs:* Federal Direct (Subsidized and Unsubsidized Stafford, PLUS), state, college/university, Canadian federal and provincial loans.

WORK-STUDY *Federal work-study:* Total amount: $1,678,939; jobs available. *State or other work-study/employment:* Part-time jobs available.

ATHLETIC AWARDS Total amount: $5,535,888 (63% need-based, 37% non-need-based).

APPLYING FOR FINANCIAL AID *Required financial aid forms:* FAFSA, state aid form. *Financial aid deadline:* 3/1. *Notification date:* Continuous beginning 3/15. Students must reply within 3 weeks of notification.

CONTACT Robert Ritz, Vice President of Financial Aid, Liberty University, 1971 University Boulevard, Lynchburg, VA 24502, 434-582-2270 or toll-free 800-543-5317. *Fax:* 434-582-2053. *E-mail:* financialaid@liberty.edu. *Website:* http://www.liberty.edu/.

LIFE PACIFIC COLLEGE
San Dimas, CA

CONTACT Mrs. Becky Huyck, Director of Financial Aid, Life Pacific College, 1100 Covina Boulevard, San Dimas, CA 91773-3298, 909-599-5433 Ext. 319 or toll-free 877-886-5433 Ext. 314. *Fax:* 909-599-6690. *E-mail:* bhuyck@lifepacific.edu. *Website:* http://www.lifepacific.edu/.

LIFE UNIVERSITY
Marietta, GA

Tuition & fees: $11,978	Average undergraduate aid package: $10,500

ABOUT THE INSTITUTION Independent, coed. *Awards:* associate, bachelor's, master's, and doctoral degrees. 5 undergraduate majors. *Total enrollment:* 2,655. Undergraduates: 843. Freshmen: 39. Federal methodology is used as a basis for awarding need-based institutional aid.

UNDERGRADUATE EXPENSES for 2013–2014 *Application fee:* $50. *Comprehensive fee:* $24,832 includes full-time tuition ($11,231), mandatory fees ($747), and room and board ($12,854). Full-time tuition and fees vary according to course load. *Part-time tuition:* $191 per credit hour. *Part-time fees:* $249 per term. Part-time tuition and fees vary according to course load.

FRESHMAN FINANCIAL AID (Fall 2012, est.) 31 applied for aid; of those 97% were deemed to have need. 100% of freshmen with need received aid. *Average percent of need met:* 25% (excluding resources awarded to replace EFC). *Average financial aid package:* $8300 (excluding resources awarded to replace EFC).

UNDERGRADUATE FINANCIAL AID (Fall 2012, est.) 459 applied for aid; of those 96% were deemed to have need. 98% of undergraduates with need received aid. *Average percent of need met:* 32% (excluding resources awarded to replace EFC). *Average financial aid package:* $10,500 (excluding resources awarded to replace EFC).

GIFT AID (NEED-BASED) *Total amount:* $2,287,000 (100% federal). *Receiving aid:* Freshmen: 60% (21); all full-time undergraduates: 54% (287). *Average award:* Freshmen: $5000; Undergraduates: $5300. *Scholarships, grants, and awards:* Federal Pell, FSEOG, state, private, college/university gift aid from institutional funds.

GIFT AID (NON-NEED-BASED) *Total amount:* $402,000 (79% state, 15% institutional, 6% external sources). *Receiving aid:* Freshmen: 51% (18). Undergraduates: 47% (247). *Scholarships, grants, and awards by category:* Academic interests/achievement: 35 awards ($225,000 total): general academic interests/achievements. *Special achievements/activities:* 221 awards ($700,000 total): general special achievements/activities. *Special characteristics:* 15 awards ($51,700 total): general special characteristics, international students. *Tuition waivers:* Full or partial for employees or children of employees.

LOANS *Student loans:* $4,409,000 (39% need-based, 61% non-need-based). 74% of past graduating class borrowed through all loan programs. *Average indebtedness per student:* $31,000. *Average need-based loan:* Freshmen: $3400. Undergraduates: $5300. *Parent loans:* $645,000 (100% need-based). *Programs:* Federal Direct (Subsidized and Unsubsidized Stafford, PLUS), Perkins, state, college/university, alternative loans.

WORK-STUDY *Federal work-study:* Total amount: $106,000; 125 jobs averaging $2000. *State or other work-study/employment:* Part-time jobs available.

ATHLETIC AWARDS Total amount: $357,000 (100% non-need-based).

APPLYING FOR FINANCIAL AID *Required financial aid forms:* FAFSA, institution's own form. *Financial aid deadline (priority):* 3/1. *Notification date:* Continuous beginning 5/1.

CONTACT Melissa Waters, Director of Financial Aid, Life University, 1269 Barclay Circle, Marietta, GA 30060, 770-426-2901 or toll-free 800-543-3202. *Fax:* 770-426-2926. *E-mail:* finaid@life.edu. *Website:* http://www.life.edu/.

LIM COLLEGE
New York, NY

Tuition & fees: $23,645	Average undergraduate aid package: $19,376

ABOUT THE INSTITUTION Proprietary, coed, primarily women. *Awards:* certificates, associate, bachelor's, and master's degrees. 4 undergraduate majors. *Total enrollment:* 1,552. Undergraduates: 1,477. Freshmen: 255. Federal methodology is used as a basis for awarding need-based institutional aid.

UNDERGRADUATE EXPENSES for 2013–2014 *Application fee:* $40. *Tuition:* full-time $23,070; part-time $770 per credit. *Required fees:* full-time $575; $338 per term.

FRESHMAN FINANCIAL AID (Fall 2012, est.) 255 applied for aid; of those 69% were deemed to have need. 100% of freshmen with need received aid. *Average financial aid package:* $9404 (excluding resources awarded to replace EFC). 12% of all full-time freshmen had no need and received non-need-based gift aid.

UNDERGRADUATE FINANCIAL AID (Fall 2012, est.) 1,391 applied for aid; of those 64% were deemed to have need. 100% of undergraduates with need received aid. *Average financial aid package:* $19,376 (excluding resources awarded to replace EFC). 16% of all full-time undergraduates had no need and received non-need-based gift aid.

GIFT AID (NEED-BASED) *Total amount:* $23,238,981 (75% federal, 2% state, 21% institutional, 2% external sources). *Receiving aid:* Freshmen: 52% (134); all full-time undergraduates: 51% (706). *Average award:* Freshmen: $6702; Undergraduates: $13,810. *Scholarships, grants, and awards:* Federal Pell, FSEOG, state, private, college/university gift aid from institutional funds.

GIFT AID (NON-NEED-BASED) *Total amount:* $1,756,925 (47% federal, 2% state, 49% institutional, 2% external sources). *Receiving aid:* Freshmen: 12% (32). Undergraduates: 17% (239). *Average award:* Freshmen: $3628. Undergraduates: $3840. *Scholarships, grants, and awards by category:* Academic interests/achievement: 226 awards ($867,874 total): general academic interests/achievements. *Special achievements/activities:* memberships. *Special characteristics:* local/state students.

LOANS *Student loans:* $14,147,548 (94% need-based, 6% non-need-based). 73% of past graduating class borrowed through all loan programs. *Average indebtedness per student:* $35,400. *Average need-based loan:* Freshmen: $4424. Undergraduates: $8870. *Parent loans:* $18,000,849 (91% need-based, 9% non-need-based). *Programs:* Federal Direct (Subsidized and Unsubsidized Stafford, PLUS), state.

WORK-STUDY Federal work-study jobs available.

APPLYING FOR FINANCIAL AID *Required financial aid forms:* FAFSA, state aid form. *Financial aid deadline (priority):* 4/1. *Notification date:* Continuous beginning 2/15. Students must reply by 5/1 or within 2 weeks of notification.

CONTACT Mr. Christopher Barto, Dean of Student Financial Services, LIM College, 12 East 53rd Street, New York, NY 10022-5268, 212-752-1530 or toll-free 800-677-1323. *Fax:* 212-317-8602. *E-mail:* cbarto@limcollege.edu. *Website:* http://www.limcollege.edu/.

LIMESTONE COLLEGE
Gaffney, SC

Tuition & fees: $22,080	Average undergraduate aid package: $16,498

ABOUT THE INSTITUTION Independent, coed. *Awards:* associate, bachelor's, and master's degrees. 50 undergraduate majors. *Total enrollment:* 937. Undergraduates: 902. Freshmen: 245. Federal methodology is used as a basis for awarding need-based institutional aid.

UNDERGRADUATE EXPENSES for 2013–2014 *Application fee:* $25. *Comprehensive fee:* $29,880 includes full-time tuition ($22,080) and room and board

($7800). *College room only:* $3900. Full-time tuition and fees vary according to class time and course load. Room and board charges vary according to housing facility. *Part-time tuition:* $920 per semester hour. Part-time tuition and fees vary according to class time.

FRESHMAN FINANCIAL AID (Fall 2012, est.) 222 applied for aid; of those 92% were deemed to have need. 100% of freshmen with need received aid; of those 15% had need fully met. *Average percent of need met:* 63% (excluding resources awarded to replace EFC). *Average financial aid package:* $16,942 (excluding resources awarded to replace EFC). 8% of all full-time freshmen had no need and received non-need-based gift aid.

UNDERGRADUATE FINANCIAL AID (Fall 2012, est.) 777 applied for aid; of those 94% were deemed to have need. 100% of undergraduates with need received aid; of those 14% had need fully met. *Average percent of need met:* 62% (excluding resources awarded to replace EFC). *Average financial aid package:* $16,498 (excluding resources awarded to replace EFC). 7% of all full-time undergraduates had no need and received non-need-based gift aid.

GIFT AID (NEED-BASED) *Total amount:* $7,724,103 (27% federal, 17% state, 53% institutional, 3% external sources). *Receiving aid:* Freshmen: 92% (205); all full-time undergraduates: 93% (726). *Average award:* Freshmen: $14,065; Undergraduates: $12,970. *Scholarships, grants, and awards:* Federal Pell, FSEOG, state, private, college/university gift aid from institutional funds.

GIFT AID (NON-NEED-BASED) *Total amount:* $637,023 (20% state, 63% institutional, 17% external sources). *Receiving aid:* Freshmen: 13% (29). Undergraduates: 11% (85). *Average award:* Freshmen: $6705. Undergraduates: $5401. *Scholarships, grants, and awards by category: Academic interests/achievement:* $1,949,678 total: biological sciences, business, communication, computer science, education, English, general academic interests/achievements, health fields, humanities, mathematics, physical sciences, premedicine, religion/biblical studies, social sciences. *Creative arts/performance:* $86,750 total: art/fine arts, music, performing arts, theater/drama. *Special achievements/activities:* $724,924 total: cheerleading/drum major, general special achievements/activities, leadership, religious involvement. *Special characteristics:* $1,023,999 total: children of faculty/staff, local/state students, out-of-state students, previous college experience, siblings of current students. *Tuition waivers:* Full or partial for employees or children of employees. *ROTC:* Army cooperative.

LOANS *Student loans:* $5,754,397 (84% need-based, 16% non-need-based). 90% of past graduating class borrowed through all loan programs. *Average indebtedness per student:* $31,409. *Average need-based loan:* Freshmen: $3306. Undergraduates: $3962. *Parent loans:* $1,395,946 (54% need-based, 46% non-need-based). *Programs:* Federal Direct (Subsidized and Unsubsidized Stafford, PLUS), Perkins.

WORK-STUDY *Federal work-study:* Total amount: $163,000; 126 jobs averaging $1413. *State or other work-study/employment:* Total amount: $1,023,591 (6% need-based, 94% non-need-based). 111 part-time jobs averaging $862.

ATHLETIC AWARDS Total amount: $1,976,045 (81% need-based, 19% non-need-based).

APPLYING FOR FINANCIAL AID *Required financial aid form:* FAFSA. *Financial aid deadline (priority):* 2/1. *Notification date:* Continuous beginning 1/15. Students must reply within 3 weeks of notification.

CONTACT Mr. Bobby Greer, Director of Financial Aid, Limestone College, 1115 College Drive, Gaffney, SC 29340-3799, 864-488-4567 or toll-free 800-795-7151. *Fax:* 864-487-8706. *E-mail:* bgreer@limestone.edu. *Website:* http://www.limestone.edu/.

LINCOLN CHRISTIAN UNIVERSITY
Lincoln, IL

ABOUT THE INSTITUTION Independent Christian Churches and Churches of Christ, coed. *Awards:* certificates, associate, bachelor's, master's, and doctoral degrees. 16 undergraduate majors. *Total enrollment:* 1,071. Undergraduates: 679. Freshmen: 100.

GIFT AID (NEED-BASED) *Scholarships, grants, and awards:* Federal Pell, FSEOG, state, private, college/university gift aid from institutional funds.

GIFT AID (NON-NEED-BASED) *Scholarships, grants, and awards by category: Academic interests/achievement:* general academic interests/achievements. *Special characteristics:* children of faculty/staff.

LOANS *Programs:* Federal Direct (Subsidized and Unsubsidized Stafford, PLUS), Perkins, alternative loans.

APPLYING FOR FINANCIAL AID *Required financial aid form:* FAFSA.

CONTACT Nancy Siddens, Director of Financial Aid, Lincoln Christian University, 100 Campus View Drive, Lincoln, IL 62656, 217-732-3168 Ext. 2250 or toll-free 888-522-5228. *Fax:* 217-732-4199. *E-mail:* finaid@lincolnchristian.edu. *Website:* http://www.lincolnchristian.edu/.

LINCOLN COLLEGE–NORMAL
Normal, IL

CONTACT Financial Aid Office, Lincoln College–Normal, 715 West Raab Road, Normal, IL 61761, 309-452-0500 or toll-free 800-569-0558. *Website:* http://www.lincolncollege.edu/normal/.

LINCOLN COLLEGE OF NEW ENGLAND
Southington, CT

CONTACT Financial Aid Office, Lincoln College of New England, 2279 Mount Vernon Road, Southington, CT 06489-1057, 860-628-4751 or toll-free 800-825-0087. *Website:* http://www.lincolncollegene.edu/.

LINCOLN CULINARY INSTITUTE
West Palm Beach, FL

CONTACT Financial Aid Office, Lincoln Culinary Institute, 2410 Metrocentre Boulevard, West Palm Beach, FL 33407, 561-842-8324. *Website:* http://www.lincolnedu.com/campus/west-palm-beach-culinary-fl.

LINCOLN MEMORIAL UNIVERSITY
Harrogate, TN

ABOUT THE INSTITUTION Independent, coed. *Awards:* certificates, associate, bachelor's, master's, and doctoral degrees. 43 undergraduate majors. *Total enrollment:* 4,338. Undergraduates: 1,851. Freshmen: 253.

GIFT AID (NEED-BASED) *Scholarships, grants, and awards:* Federal Pell, FSEOG, state, private, college/university gift aid from institutional funds.

GIFT AID (NON-NEED-BASED) *Scholarships, grants, and awards by category: Academic interests/achievement:* general academic interests/achievements. *Creative arts/performance:* music. *Special achievements/activities:* cheerleading/drum major. *Special characteristics:* children and siblings of alumni, children of faculty/staff, local/state students, members of minority groups.

LOANS *Programs:* Federal Direct (Subsidized and Unsubsidized Stafford, PLUS), Perkins, Federal Nursing.

APPLYING FOR FINANCIAL AID *Required financial aid form:* FAFSA.

CONTACT Bryan Erslan, Director of Financial Aid, Lincoln Memorial University, 6965 Cumberland Gap Parkway, Harrogate, TN 37752-1901, 423-869-6465 or toll-free 800-325-0900. *Fax:* 423-869-6347. *E-mail:* bryan.erslan@lmunet.edu. *Website:* http://www.lmunet.edu/.

LINCOLN UNIVERSITY
Oakland, CA

CONTACT Financial Aid Office, Lincoln University, 401 15th Street, Oakland, CA 94612, 510-628-8010 or toll-free 888-810-9998. *Website:* http://www.lincolnuca.edu/.

LINCOLN UNIVERSITY
Jefferson City, MO

Tuition & fees (MO res): $6624	Average undergraduate aid package: $9876

ABOUT THE INSTITUTION State-supported, coed. *Awards:* certificates, associate, bachelor's, and master's degrees. 46 undergraduate majors. *Total enrollment:* 3,205. Undergraduates: 3,013. Freshmen: 449. Federal methodology is used as a basis for awarding need-based institutional aid.

UNDERGRADUATE EXPENSES for 2013–2014 *Application fee:* $20. *Tuition, state resident:* full-time $6150; part-time $205 per credit hour. *Tuition, nonresident:* full-time $12,150; part-time $405 per credit hour. *Required fees:* full-time $474; $16.75 per credit hour or $36. Full-time tuition and fees vary according to location and reciprocity agreements. Part-time tuition and fees vary according to location and reciprocity agreements. *College room and board:* $4750; *Room only:* $2626. Room and board charges vary according to board plan and housing facility.

FRESHMAN FINANCIAL AID (Fall 2012, est.) 409 applied for aid; of those 94% were deemed to have need. 100% of freshmen with need received aid; of those 3% had need fully met. *Average percent of need met:* 59% (excluding resources awarded to replace EFC). *Average financial aid package:* $9447 (excluding resources awarded to replace EFC). 1% of all full-time freshmen had no need and received non-need-based gift aid.

UNDERGRADUATE FINANCIAL AID (Fall 2012, est.) 1,719 applied for aid; of those 90% were deemed to have need. 100% of undergraduates with need received aid; of those 4% had need fully met. *Average percent of need met:* 58% (excluding resources awarded to replace EFC). *Average financial aid package:* $9876 (excluding resources awarded to replace EFC). 1% of all full-time undergraduates had no need and received non-need-based gift aid.

GIFT AID (NEED-BASED) *Total amount:* $8,954,739 (76% federal, 7% state, 11% institutional, 6% external sources). *Receiving aid:* Freshmen: 83% (351); all full-time undergraduates: 73% (1,371). *Average award:* Freshmen: $5740; Undergraduates: $5467. *Scholarships, grants, and awards:* Federal Pell, FSEOG, state, private, college/university gift aid from institutional funds.

GIFT AID (NON-NEED-BASED) *Total amount:* $654,108 (14% federal, 1% state, 22% institutional, 63% external sources). *Receiving aid:* Freshmen: 2% (8). Undergraduates: 2% (33). *Average award:* Freshmen: $2000. Undergraduates: $2000. *Scholarships, grants, and awards by category:* Academic interests/achievement: 183 awards ($795,068 total): agriculture, general academic interests/achievements, military science. Creative arts/performance: 94 awards ($192,044 total): art/fine arts, journalism/publications, music, performing arts, theater/drama. Special achievements/activities: 17 awards ($10,136 total): cheerleading/drum major. Special characteristics: 237 awards ($593,032 total): adult students, children of faculty/staff, international students, out-of-state students. *Tuition waivers:* Full or partial for employees or children of employees. *ROTC:* Army, Naval cooperative, Air Force cooperative.

LOANS *Student loans:* $15,342,682 (40% need-based, 60% non-need-based). 70% of past graduating class borrowed through all loan programs. *Average indebtedness per student:* $27,910. *Average need-based loan:* Freshmen: $3409. Undergraduates: $4128. *Parent loans:* $715,120 (100% non-need-based). *Programs:* Federal Direct (Subsidized and Unsubsidized Stafford, PLUS), private loans.

WORK-STUDY *Federal work-study:* Total amount: $196,423; 125 jobs averaging $1490. *State or other work-study/employment:* Total amount: $578,572 (100% non-need-based). 188 part-time jobs averaging $3078.

ATHLETIC AWARDS Total amount: $1,160,820 (100% need-based).

APPLYING FOR FINANCIAL AID *Required financial aid forms:* FAFSA, institution's own form. *Financial aid deadline (priority):* 3/1. *Notification date:* Continuous beginning 3/15. Students must reply within 2 weeks of notification.

CONTACT Mr. Alfred Robinson, Director of Financial Aid, Lincoln University, 820 Chestnut Street, Jefferson City, MO 65102-0029, 573-681-6156 or toll-free 800-521-5052. *Fax:* 573-681-5871. *E-mail:* robinsona@lincolnu.edu. *Website:* http://www.lincolnu.edu/.

LINCOLN UNIVERSITY
Lincoln University, PA

ABOUT THE INSTITUTION State-related, coed. *Awards:* bachelor's and master's degrees. 47 undergraduate majors. *Total enrollment:* 2,101. Undergraduates: 1,678. Freshmen: 448.

GIFT AID (NEED-BASED) *Scholarships, grants, and awards:* Federal Pell, FSEOG, state, private, college/university gift aid from institutional funds, United Negro College Fund.

GIFT AID (NON-NEED-BASED) *Scholarships, grants, and awards by category:* Academic interests/achievement: biological sciences, business, communication, computer science, education, English, general academic interests/achievements, humanities, mathematics, physical sciences, social sciences. Creative arts/performance: music. Special achievements/activities: general special achievements/activities. Special characteristics: children and siblings of alumni, children of faculty/staff, international students.

LOANS *Programs:* Perkins.

WORK-STUDY Federal work-study jobs available.

APPLYING FOR FINANCIAL AID *Required financial aid form:* FAFSA.

CONTACT Thelma Ross, Director of Financial Aid, Lincoln University, PO Box 179, Lincoln University, PA 19352, 484-365-7583 or toll-free 800-790-0191. *Fax:* 484-365-8198. *E-mail:* tross@lincoln.edu. *Website:* http://www.lincoln.edu/.

LINDENWOOD UNIVERSITY
St. Charles, MO

Tuition & fees: $14,600	Average undergraduate aid package: $9093

ABOUT THE INSTITUTION Independent Presbyterian, coed. *Awards:* certificates, bachelor's, master's, and doctoral degrees. 100 undergraduate majors. *Total enrollment:* 11,903. Undergraduates: 8,296. Freshmen: 1,351. Both federal and institutional methodology are used as a basis for awarding need-based institutional aid.

UNDERGRADUATE EXPENSES for 2013–2014 *Application fee:* $30. *Comprehensive fee:* $22,180 includes full-time tuition ($14,250), mandatory fees ($350), and room and board ($7580). *College room only:* $4180. Full-time tuition and fees vary according to program. *Part-time tuition:* $412 per credit hour. Part-time tuition and fees vary according to course load.

FRESHMAN FINANCIAL AID (Fall 2012, est.) 905 applied for aid; of those 80% were deemed to have need. 100% of freshmen with need received aid; of those 89% had need fully met. *Average percent of need met:* 86% (excluding resources awarded to replace EFC). *Average financial aid package:* $9488 (excluding resources awarded to replace EFC). 43% of all full-time freshmen had no need and received non-need-based gift aid.

UNDERGRADUATE FINANCIAL AID (Fall 2012, est.) 5,148 applied for aid; of those 77% were deemed to have need. 100% of undergraduates with need received aid; of those 75% had need fully met. *Average percent of need met:* 90% (excluding resources awarded to replace EFC). *Average financial aid package:* $9093 (excluding resources awarded to replace EFC). 30% of all full-time undergraduates had no need and received non-need-based gift aid.

GIFT AID (NEED-BASED) *Total amount:* $36,090,000 (37% federal, 12% state, 51% institutional). *Receiving aid:* Freshmen: 46% (594); all full-time undergraduates: 51% (3,768). *Average award:* Freshmen: $7010; Undergraduates: $4819. *Scholarships, grants, and awards:* Federal Pell, FSEOG, state, private, college/university gift aid from institutional funds.

GIFT AID (NON-NEED-BASED) *Total amount:* $11,425,000 (1% federal, 1% state, 95% institutional, 3% external sources). *Receiving aid:* Freshmen: 26% (332). Undergraduates: 30% (2,188). *Average award:* Freshmen: $3498. Undergraduates: $3319. *Scholarships, grants, and awards by category:* Academic interests/achievement: biological sciences, business, communication, computer science, education, engineering/technologies, English, foreign languages, general academic interests/achievements, health fields, humanities, international studies, library science, mathematics, military science, physical sciences, premedicine, religion/biblical studies, social sciences. Creative arts/performance: applied art and design, art/fine arts, cinema/film/broadcasting, dance, debating, general creative arts/performance, music, performing arts, theater/drama. Special achievements/activities: cheerleading/drum major, com-

munity service, general special achievements/activities, junior miss, leadership. *Special characteristics:* children and siblings of alumni, children of faculty/staff, public servants, veterans, veterans' children. *Tuition waivers:* Full or partial for employees or children of employees, senior citizens. *ROTC:* Army.
LOANS *Student loans:* $46,000,000 (46% need-based, 54% non-need-based). *Average need-based loan:* Freshmen: $4234. Undergraduates: $4579. *Parent loans:* $3,800,000 (100% non-need-based). *Programs:* Federal Direct (Subsidized and Unsubsidized Stafford, PLUS).
WORK-STUDY *Federal work-study:* Total amount: $398,775; 166 jobs averaging $2400. *State or other work-study/employment:* Total amount: $7,900,000 (61% need-based, 39% non-need-based). Part-time jobs available.
ATHLETIC AWARDS Total amount: $3,900,000 (100% non-need-based).
APPLYING FOR FINANCIAL AID *Required financial aid form:* FAFSA. *Financial aid deadline (priority):* 4/1. *Notification date:* Continuous. Students must reply within 2 weeks of notification.
CONTACT Lori Bode, Director of Financial Aid, Lindenwood University, 209 South Kingshighway, St. Charles, MO 63301-1695, 636-949-4925. *Fax:* 636-949-4924. *E-mail:* lbode@lindenwood.edu.
Website: http://www.lindenwood.edu/.

LINDENWOOD UNIVERSITY– BELLEVILLE
Belleville, IL

CONTACT Financial Aid Office, Lindenwood University–Belleville, 2600 West Main Street, Belleville, IL 62226, 618-239-6000.
Website: http://belleville.lindenwood.edu/.

LINDSEY WILSON COLLEGE
Columbia, KY

Tuition & fees: $22,070	Average undergraduate aid package: N/A

ABOUT THE INSTITUTION Independent United Methodist, coed. *Awards:* associate, bachelor's, and master's degrees. 34 undergraduate majors. *Total enrollment:* 2,677. Undergraduates: 2,217. Freshmen: 526. Federal methodology is used as a basis for awarding need-based institutional aid.
UNDERGRADUATE EXPENSES for 2013–2014 *Comprehensive fee:* $30,470 includes full-time tuition ($21,840), mandatory fees ($230), and room and board ($8400). *College room only:* $3100. Full-time tuition and fees vary according to location. *Part-time tuition:* $910 per credit hour. Part-time tuition and fees vary according to location.
FRESHMAN FINANCIAL AID (Fall 2012, est.) 516 applied for aid; of those 97% were deemed to have need. 100% of freshmen with need received aid; of those 21% had need fully met.
UNDERGRADUATE FINANCIAL AID (Fall 2012, est.) 2,092 applied for aid; of those 95% were deemed to have need. 100% of undergraduates with need received aid; of those 22% had need fully met.
GIFT AID (NEED-BASED) *Total amount:* $29,420,089 (20% federal, 22% state, 56% institutional, 2% external sources). *Receiving aid:* Freshmen: 96% (496); all full-time undergraduates: 93% (1,961). *Scholarships, grants, and awards:* Federal Pell, FSEOG, state, private, college/university gift aid from institutional funds.
GIFT AID (NON-NEED-BASED) *Scholarships, grants, and awards by category:* Academic interests/achievement: biological sciences, business, education, English, general academic interests/achievements, mathematics, premedicine, religion/biblical studies. *Creative arts/performance:* applied art and design, music. *Special achievements/activities:* cheerleading/drum major, general special achievements/activities, junior miss, leadership, religious involvement. *Special characteristics:* children and siblings of alumni, children of faculty/staff, relatives of clergy, religious affiliation. *Tuition waivers:* Full or partial for employees or children of employees, senior citizens.
LOANS *Student loans:* $10,224,867 (100% need-based). 83% of past graduating class borrowed through all loan programs. *Average indebtedness per student:* $27,542. *Parent loans:* $661,544 (100% need-based). *Programs:* Federal Direct (Subsidized and Unsubsidized Stafford, PLUS), Perkins, college/university.

WORK-STUDY *Federal work-study:* Total amount: $620,733; 290 jobs averaging $2140. *State or other work-study/employment:* Total amount: $41,250 (100% need-based). 20 part-time jobs averaging $2063.
ATHLETIC AWARDS Total amount: $2,352,012 (100% need-based).
APPLYING FOR FINANCIAL AID *Required financial aid form:* FAFSA. *Financial aid deadline (priority):* 4/1. *Notification date:* Continuous beginning 4/15. Students must reply within 2 weeks of notification.
CONTACT Ms. Marilyn D. Radford, Director of Student Financial Services, Lindsey Wilson College, 210 Lindsey Wilson Street, Columbia, KY 42728, 270-384-8022 or toll-free 800-264-0138. *Fax:* 270-384-8591. *E-mail:* radfordm@lindsey.edu.
Website: http://www.lindsey.edu/.

LINFIELD COLLEGE
McMinnville, OR

Tuition & fees: $34,328	Average undergraduate aid package: $27,068

ABOUT THE INSTITUTION Independent American Baptist Churches in the USA, coed. *Awards:* bachelor's degrees. 43 undergraduate majors. *Total enrollment:* 1,663. Undergraduates: 1,663. Freshmen: 443. Federal methodology is used as a basis for awarding need-based institutional aid.
UNDERGRADUATE EXPENSES for 2013–2014 *Comprehensive fee:* $43,828 includes full-time tuition ($34,000), mandatory fees ($328), and room and board ($9500). *College room only:* $5180. Full-time tuition and fees vary according to location. Room and board charges vary according to board plan, housing facility, and location. *Part-time tuition:* $1059 per semester hour. Part-time tuition and fees vary according to course load and location.
FRESHMAN FINANCIAL AID (Fall 2012, est.) 399 applied for aid; of those 85% were deemed to have need. 100% of freshmen with need received aid; of those 33% had need fully met. *Average percent of need met:* 86% (excluding resources awarded to replace EFC). *Average financial aid package:* $28,193 (excluding resources awarded to replace EFC). 21% of all full-time freshmen had no need and received non-need-based gift aid.
UNDERGRADUATE FINANCIAL AID (Fall 2012, est.) 1,337 applied for aid; of those 87% were deemed to have need. 100% of undergraduates with need received aid; of those 29% had need fully met. *Average percent of need met:* 82% (excluding resources awarded to replace EFC). *Average financial aid package:* $27,068 (excluding resources awarded to replace EFC). 21% of all full-time undergraduates had no need and received non-need-based gift aid.
GIFT AID (NEED-BASED) *Total amount:* $23,049,495 (9% federal, 2% state, 84% institutional, 5% external sources). *Receiving aid:* Freshmen: 75% (332); all full-time undergraduates: 72% (1,140). *Average award:* Freshmen: $24,481; Undergraduates: $20,409. *Scholarships, grants, and awards:* Federal Pell, FSEOG, state, private, college/university gift aid from institutional funds.
GIFT AID (NON-NEED-BASED) *Total amount:* $5,846,151 (97% institutional, 3% external sources). *Receiving aid:* Freshmen: 76% (337). Undergraduates: 72% (1,140). *Average award:* Freshmen: $14,052. Undergraduates: $14,337. *Scholarships, grants, and awards by category:* Academic interests/achievement: 1,105 awards ($12,869,963 total): general academic interests/achievements. *Creative arts/performance:* 53 awards ($103,500 total): debating, music, theater/drama. *Special achievements/activities:* 58 awards ($95,750 total): community service, leadership. *Special characteristics:* 45 awards ($1,459,410 total): children of faculty/staff. *Tuition waivers:* Full or partial for employees or children of employees, senior citizens. *ROTC:* Air Force cooperative.
LOANS *Student loans:* $9,411,469 (67% need-based, 33% non-need-based). 72% of past graduating class borrowed through all loan programs. *Average indebtedness per student:* $29,751. *Average need-based loan:* Freshmen: $3848. Undergraduates: $4607. *Parent loans:* $3,633,526 (36% need-based, 64% non-need-based). *Programs:* Federal Direct (Subsidized and Unsubsidized Stafford, PLUS), Perkins, private loans.
WORK-STUDY *Federal work-study:* Total amount: $2,033,305; 531 jobs averaging $2427. *State or other work-study/employment:* Total amount: $1,521,714 (5% need-based, 95% non-need-based). 398 part-time jobs averaging $2234.
APPLYING FOR FINANCIAL AID *Required financial aid form:* FAFSA. *Financial aid deadline (priority):* 2/1. *Notification date:* 4/1. Students must reply by 5/1 or within 2 weeks of notification.

CONTACT Ms. Keri Burke, Director of Financial Aid, Linfield College, 900 Southeast Baker Street, A484, McMinnville, OR 97128-6894, 503-883-2269 or toll-free 800-640-2287. Fax: 503-883-2486. E-mail: finaid@linfield.edu. Website: http://www.linfield.edu/.

LIPSCOMB UNIVERSITY
Nashville, TN

Tuition & fees: $24,754	Average undergraduate aid package: $20,467

ABOUT THE INSTITUTION Independent Church of Christ, coed. **Awards:** certificates, associate, bachelor's, master's, and doctoral degrees. 102 undergraduate majors. **Total enrollment:** 4,254. Undergraduates: 2,740. Freshmen: 675. Both federal and institutional methodology are used as a basis for awarding need-based institutional aid.

UNDERGRADUATE EXPENSES for 2013–2014 Application fee: $50. **Comprehensive fee:** $33,978 includes full-time tuition ($22,978), mandatory fees ($1776), and room and board ($9224). **College room only:** $5184. Full-time tuition and fees vary according to course load. Room and board charges vary according to board plan and housing facility. **Part-time tuition:** $960 per hour. **Part-time fees:** $75 per credit hour. Part-time tuition and fees vary according to course load.

FRESHMAN FINANCIAL AID (Fall 2012, est.) 669 applied for aid; of those 67% were deemed to have need. 100% of freshmen with need received aid; of those 23% had need fully met. **Average percent of need met:** 63% (excluding resources awarded to replace EFC). **Average financial aid package:** $19,642 (excluding resources awarded to replace EFC). 33% of all full-time freshmen had no need and received non-need-based gift aid.

UNDERGRADUATE FINANCIAL AID (Fall 2012, est.) 2,374 applied for aid; of those 72% were deemed to have need. 100% of undergraduates with need received aid; of those 28% had need fully met. **Average percent of need met:** 63% (excluding resources awarded to replace EFC). **Average financial aid package:** $20,467 (excluding resources awarded to replace EFC). 24% of all full-time undergraduates had no need and received non-need-based gift aid.

GIFT AID (NEED-BASED) Total amount: $22,117,023 (16% federal, 20% state, 56% institutional, 8% external sources). **Receiving aid:** Freshmen: 43% (288); all full-time undergraduates: 43% (1,071). **Average award:** Freshmen: $4744; Undergraduates: $5509. **Scholarships, grants, and awards:** Federal Pell, FSEOG, state, private, college/university gift aid from institutional funds.

GIFT AID (NON-NEED-BASED) Total amount: $6,355,778 (16% state, 80% institutional, 4% external sources). **Receiving aid:** Freshmen: 67% (446). Undergraduates: 55% (1,376). **Average award:** Freshmen: $10,406. Undergraduates: $11,640. **Scholarships, grants, and awards by category:** Academic interests/achievement: biological sciences, business, communication, education, engineering/technologies, English, general academic interests/achievements, home economics, mathematics, premedicine, religion/biblical studies. Creative arts/performance: art/fine arts, journalism/publications, music, theater/drama. Special achievements/activities: cheerleading/drum major, community service, general special achievements/activities, leadership, religious involvement. Special characteristics: adult students, children and siblings of alumni, children of educators, children of faculty/staff, children with a deceased or disabled parent, international students, members of minority groups, relatives of clergy. **Tuition waivers:** Full or partial for employees or children of employees, adult students. **ROTC:** Army cooperative, Air Force cooperative.

LOANS Student loans: $12,068,219 (91% need-based, 9% non-need-based). 56% of past graduating class borrowed through all loan programs. **Average indebtedness per student:** $15,155. **Average need-based loan:** Freshmen: $3827. Undergraduates: $5548. **Parent loans:** $4,433,632 (82% need-based, 18% non-need-based). **Programs:** Federal Direct (Subsidized and Unsubsidized Stafford, PLUS), Perkins.

WORK-STUDY Federal work-study: Total amount: $531,611; 224 jobs averaging $1334.

ATHLETIC AWARDS Total amount: $3,732,485 (68% need-based, 32% non-need-based).

APPLYING FOR FINANCIAL AID Required financial aid form: FAFSA. **Financial aid deadline (priority):** 1/31. **Notification date:** Continuous beginning 1/31.

CONTACT Ms. Tiffany Summers, Director of Financial Aid, Lipscomb University, One University Park Drive, Nashville, TN 37204-3951, 615-966-1791 or toll-free 877-582-4766. Fax: 615-966-7640. E-mail: tiffany.summers@lipscomb.edu. Website: http://www.lipscomb.edu/.

LIVINGSTONE COLLEGE
Salisbury, NC

CONTACT Mrs. Terry Jefferies, Financial Aid Director, Livingstone College, 701 West Monroe Street, Price Building, Salisbury, NC 28144-5298, 704-216-6069 or toll-free 800-835-3435. Fax: 704-216-6319. E-mail: tjefferies@livingstone.edu. Website: http://www.livingstone.edu/.

LOCK HAVEN UNIVERSITY OF PENNSYLVANIA
Lock Haven, PA

Tuition & fees (PA res): $8564	Average undergraduate aid package: $8662

ABOUT THE INSTITUTION State-supported, coed. **Awards:** associate, bachelor's, and master's degrees. 47 undergraduate majors. **Total enrollment:** 5,328. Undergraduates: 4,969. Freshmen: 1,155. Federal methodology is used as a basis for awarding need-based institutional aid.

UNDERGRADUATE EXPENSES for 2013–2014 Application fee: $25. **One-time required fee:** $25. **Tuition, state resident:** full-time $6428. **Tuition, nonresident:** full-time $14,070. **Required fees:** full-time $2136. Full-time tuition and fees vary according to course load and location. Part-time tuition and fees vary according to course load and location. **College room and board:** $8016; **Room only:** $4712. Room and board charges vary according to board plan and housing facility.

FRESHMAN FINANCIAL AID (Fall 2012, est.) 1,105 applied for aid; of those 77% were deemed to have need. 100% of freshmen with need received aid; of those 45% had need fully met. **Average percent of need met:** 75% (excluding resources awarded to replace EFC). **Average financial aid package:** $8662 (excluding resources awarded to replace EFC). 1% of all full-time freshmen had no need and received non-need-based gift aid.

UNDERGRADUATE FINANCIAL AID (Fall 2012, est.) 4,327 applied for aid; of those 77% were deemed to have need. 100% of undergraduates with need received aid; of those 55% had need fully met. **Average percent of need met:** 75% (excluding resources awarded to replace EFC). **Average financial aid package:** $8662 (excluding resources awarded to replace EFC). 2% of all full-time undergraduates had no need and received non-need-based gift aid.

GIFT AID (NEED-BASED) Total amount: $15,003,688 (55% federal, 41% state, 1% institutional, 3% external sources). **Receiving aid:** Freshmen: 49% (561); all full-time undergraduates: 48% (2,198). **Average award:** Freshmen: $7622; Undergraduates: $7622. **Scholarships, grants, and awards:** Federal Pell, FSEOG, state, private, college/university gift aid from institutional funds.

GIFT AID (NON-NEED-BASED) Total amount: $947,471 (1% state, 19% institutional, 80% external sources). **Receiving aid:** Freshmen: 4% (46). Undergraduates: 5% (213). **Average award:** Freshmen: $2192. Undergraduates: $1129. **Scholarships, grants, and awards by category:** Academic interests/achievement: biological sciences, business, communication, computer science, education, English, foreign languages, general academic interests/achievements, health fields, international studies, library science, mathematics, physical sciences, premedicine, social sciences. Creative arts/performance: art/fine arts, journalism/publications, music, performing arts. Special achievements/activities: community service, leadership, memberships. Special characteristics: adult students, ethnic background, local/state students, married students, members of minority groups, previous college experience. **Tuition waivers:** Full or partial for minority students, employees or children of employees, senior citizens. **ROTC:** Army.

LOANS Student loans: $37,189,890 (37% need-based, 63% non-need-based). 85% of past graduating class borrowed through all loan programs. **Average indebtedness per student:** $23,840. **Average need-based loan:** Freshmen: $3542. Undergrad-

uates: $4241. *Parent loans:* $5,085,139 (100% non-need-based). *Programs:* Federal Direct (Subsidized and Unsubsidized Stafford, PLUS), Perkins, college/university.
WORK-STUDY *Federal work-study:* Total amount: $300,646; 269 jobs averaging $1044. *State or other work-study/employment:* Total amount: $899,354 (100% non-need-based). 731 part-time jobs averaging $1257.
ATHLETIC AWARDS Total amount: $602,502 (100% non-need-based).
APPLYING FOR FINANCIAL AID *Required financial aid forms:* FAFSA, state aid form. *Financial aid deadline:* 3/15. *Notification date:* Continuous beginning 4/10. Students must reply by 5/1 or within 2 weeks of notification.
CONTACT Heidi Hunter-Goldsworthy, Director of Financial Aid, Lock Haven University of Pennsylvania, Russell Hall 118, Lock Haven, PA 17745-2390, 570-484-2344 or toll-free 800-332-8900 (in-state), 800-233-8978 (out-of-state). *Fax:* 570-484-2918. *E-mail:* hgh4845@lhup.edu.
Website: http://www.lhup.edu/.

LOGAN UNIVERSITY–COLLEGE OF CHIROPRACTIC
Chesterfield, MO

CONTACT Linda K. Haman, Director of Financial Aid, Logan University–College of Chiropractic, 1851 Schoettler Road, PO Box 1065, Chesterfield, MO 63006-1065, 636-227-2100 Ext. 141 or toll-free 800-533-9210.
Website: http://www.logan.edu/.

LOMA LINDA UNIVERSITY
Loma Linda, CA

CONTACT Verdell Schaefer, Director of Financial Aid, Loma Linda University, 11139 Anderson Street, Loma Linda, CA 92350, 909-558-4509 or toll-free 800-422-4558. *Fax:* 909-558-4879. *E-mail:* finaid@univ.llu.edu.
Website: http://www.llu.edu/.

LONG ISLAND UNIVERSITY–BROOKLYN CAMPUS
Brooklyn, NY

Tuition & fees: $30,790	Average undergraduate aid package: $16,826

ABOUT THE INSTITUTION Independent, coed. *Awards:* certificates, associate, bachelor's, master's, and doctoral degrees. 63 undergraduate majors. *Total enrollment:* 8,567. Undergraduates: 5,109. Freshmen: 917. Federal methodology is used as a basis for awarding need-based institutional aid.
UNDERGRADUATE EXPENSES for 2013–2014 *Application fee:* $40. *Comprehensive fee:* $42,490 includes full-time tuition ($29,220), mandatory fees ($1570), and room and board ($11,700). *College room only:* $7220. Full-time tuition and fees vary according to program. Room and board charges vary according to board plan and housing facility. Part-time tuition and fees vary according to program.
FRESHMAN FINANCIAL AID (Fall 2012, est.) 878 applied for aid; of those 94% were deemed to have need. 98% of freshmen with need received aid; of those 4% had need fully met. *Average percent of need met:* 55% (excluding resources awarded to replace EFC). *Average financial aid package:* $19,313 (excluding resources awarded to replace EFC). 6% of all full-time freshmen had no need and received non-need-based gift aid.
UNDERGRADUATE FINANCIAL AID (Fall 2012, est.) 4,042 applied for aid; of those 96% were deemed to have need. 98% of undergraduates with need received aid; of those 5% had need fully met. *Average percent of need met:* 49% (excluding resources awarded to replace EFC). *Average financial aid package:* $16,826 (excluding resources awarded to replace EFC). 5% of all full-time undergraduates had no need and received non-need-based gift aid.
GIFT AID (NEED-BASED) *Total amount:* $31,793,031 (45% federal, 25% state, 30% institutional). *Receiving aid:* Freshmen: 88% (792); all full-time undergraduates: 79% (3,376). *Average award:* Freshmen: $11,393; Undergraduates: $8767. *Schol-*

arships, grants, and awards: Federal Pell, FSEOG, state, private, college/university gift aid from institutional funds, Scholarships for Disadvantaged Students (Nursing and Pharmacy).
GIFT AID (NON-NEED-BASED) *Total amount:* $20,333,794 (100% institutional). *Receiving aid:* Freshmen: 78% (707). Undergraduates: 83% (3,567). *Average award:* Freshmen: $6797. Undergraduates: $6418. *Scholarships, grants, and awards by category: Academic interests/achievement:* communication, education, general academic interests/achievements, health fields. *Creative arts/performance:* art/fine arts, cinema/film/broadcasting, dance, music, theater/drama. *Special achievements/activities:* cheerleading/drum major, general special achievements/activities, leadership. *Special characteristics:* children and siblings of alumni, children of faculty/staff, ethnic background, first-generation college students, general special characteristics, international students. *Tuition waivers:* Full or partial for employees or children of employees.
LOANS *Student loans:* $33,273,151 (40% need-based, 60% non-need-based). *Average need-based loan:* Freshmen: $3394. Undergraduates: $4098. *Parent loans:* $134,119,418 (100% non-need-based). *Programs:* Federal Direct (Subsidized and Unsubsidized Stafford, PLUS), Perkins, alternative loans, Health Professions Student Loans (HPSL).
WORK-STUDY *Federal work-study:* Total amount: $700,790; jobs available. *State or other work-study/employment:* Part-time jobs available.
ATHLETIC AWARDS Total amount: $6,038,633 (100% non-need-based).
APPLYING FOR FINANCIAL AID *Required financial aid forms:* FAFSA, state aid form. *Financial aid deadline:* Continuous. *Notification date:* Continuous beginning 4/1. Students must reply within 4 weeks of notification.
CONTACT Ms. Margaret Nelson, Associate Dean of Financial Services, Long Island University–Brooklyn Campus, 1 University Plaza, Brooklyn, NY 11201-8423, 718-488-1037 or toll-free 800-LIU-PLAN. *Fax:* 718-488-3343.
Website: http://www.liu.edu/.

LONG ISLAND UNIVERSITY–C. W. POST CAMPUS
Brookville, NY

Tuition & fees: $32,862	Average undergraduate aid package: $18,808

ABOUT THE INSTITUTION Independent, coed. *Awards:* certificates, associate, bachelor's, master's, and doctoral degrees. 85 undergraduate majors. *Total enrollment:* 11,012. Undergraduates: 8,315. Freshmen: 980. Federal methodology is used as a basis for awarding need-based institutional aid.
UNDERGRADUATE EXPENSES for 2013–2014 *Application fee:* $40. *Comprehensive fee:* $45,102 includes full-time tuition ($31,202), mandatory fees ($1660), and room and board ($12,240). *College room only:* $7680. Room and board charges vary according to board plan and housing facility.
FRESHMAN FINANCIAL AID (Fall 2012, est.) 866 applied for aid; of those 86% were deemed to have need. 99% of freshmen with need received aid; of those 16% had need fully met. *Average percent of need met:* 57% (excluding resources awarded to replace EFC). *Average financial aid package:* $20,514 (excluding resources awarded to replace EFC). 15% of all full-time freshmen had no need and received non-need-based gift aid.
UNDERGRADUATE FINANCIAL AID (Fall 2012, est.) 3,292 applied for aid; of those 87% were deemed to have need. 99% of undergraduates with need received aid; of those 12% had need fully met. *Average percent of need met:* 55% (excluding resources awarded to replace EFC). *Average financial aid package:* $18,808 (excluding resources awarded to replace EFC). 12% of all full-time undergraduates had no need and received non-need-based gift aid.
GIFT AID (NEED-BASED) *Total amount:* $17,000,470 (35% federal, 26% state, 39% institutional). *Receiving aid:* Freshmen: 53% (509); all full-time undergraduates: 52% (2,047). *Average award:* Freshmen: $8348; Undergraduates: $7848. *Scholarships, grants, and awards:* Federal Pell, FSEOG, state, private, college/university gift aid from institutional funds.
GIFT AID (NON-NEED-BASED) *Total amount:* $29,915,836 (100% institutional). *Receiving aid:* Freshmen: 57% (550). Undergraduates: 47% (1,862). *Average award:* Freshmen: $14,286. Undergraduates: $12,196. *Scholarships, grants, and awards by category: Academic interests/achievement:* biological sciences, business, computer science, education, general academic interests/achievements, health fields, mathematics. *Creative arts/performance:* art/fine arts, cinema/film/broadcasting,

dance, journalism/publications, music, theater/drama. *Special achievements/activities:* leadership. *Special characteristics:* adult students, children and siblings of alumni, children of faculty/staff, international students, siblings of current students. *Tuition waivers:* Full or partial for employees or children of employees. *ROTC:* Army cooperative.

LOANS *Student loans:* $23,262,182 (36% need-based, 64% non-need-based). *Average need-based loan:* Freshmen: $4004. Undergraduates: $4607. *Parent loans:* $14,763,876 (100% non-need-based). *Programs:* Federal Direct (Subsidized and Unsubsidized Stafford, PLUS), Perkins.

WORK-STUDY *Federal work-study:* Total amount: $1,164,200; jobs available. *State or other work-study/employment:* Part-time jobs available.

ATHLETIC AWARDS Total amount: $5,061,272 (100% non-need-based).

APPLYING FOR FINANCIAL AID *Required financial aid forms:* FAFSA, state aid form. *Financial aid deadline:* 3/15. *Notification date:* Continuous beginning 3/15. Students must reply by 5/1 or within 2 weeks of notification.

CONTACT Ms. Joanne Graziano, Office of Financial Assistance, Long Island University–C. W. Post Campus, 720 Northern Boulevard, Brookville, NY 11548-1300, 516-299-2323 or toll-free 800-LIU-PLAN. *Fax:* 516-299-3833. *E-mail:* post-sfs@liu.edu.
Website: http://www.liu.edu/.

LONGWOOD UNIVERSITY
Farmville, VA

Tuition & fees (VA res): $10,890	Average undergraduate aid package: $12,213

ABOUT THE INSTITUTION State-supported, coed. *Awards:* certificates, bachelor's, and master's degrees. 25 undergraduate majors. *Total enrollment:* 4,834. Undergraduates: 4,355. Freshmen: 976. Federal methodology is used as a basis for awarding need-based institutional aid.

UNDERGRADUATE EXPENSES for 2013–2014 *Application fee:* $50. *Tuition, state resident:* full-time $6120; part-time $204 per credit hour. *Tuition, nonresident:* full-time $17,760; part-time $592 per credit hour. *Required fees:* full-time $4770; $159 per credit hour. Full-time tuition and fees vary according to course load. Part-time tuition and fees vary according to course load. *College room and board:* $8448; *Room only:* $5524. Room and board charges vary according to board plan, housing facility, and location.

FRESHMAN FINANCIAL AID (Fall 2011) 840 applied for aid; of those 69% were deemed to have need. 98% of freshmen with need received aid; of those 49% had need fully met. *Average percent of need met:* 80% (excluding resources awarded to replace EFC). *Average financial aid package:* $11,905 (excluding resources awarded to replace EFC). 2% of all full-time freshmen had no need and received non-need-based gift aid.

UNDERGRADUATE FINANCIAL AID (Fall 2011) 3,050 applied for aid; of those 74% were deemed to have need. 98% of undergraduates with need received aid; of those 50% had need fully met. *Average percent of need met:* 80% (excluding resources awarded to replace EFC). *Average financial aid package:* $12,213 (excluding resources awarded to replace EFC). 4% of all full-time undergraduates had no need and received non-need-based gift aid.

GIFT AID (NEED-BASED) *Total amount:* $11,435,719 (33% federal, 37% state, 25% institutional, 5% external sources). *Receiving aid:* Freshmen: 47% (487); all full-time undergraduates: 43% (1,780). *Average award:* Freshmen: $6387; Undergraduates: $6311. *Scholarships, grants, and awards:* Federal Pell, FSEOG, state, private, college/university gift aid from institutional funds.

GIFT AID (NON-NEED-BASED) *Total amount:* $1,264,791 (8% state, 65% institutional, 27% external sources). *Receiving aid:* Freshmen: 1% (12). Undergraduates: 1% (51). *Average award:* Freshmen: $3252. Undergraduates: $4221. *Scholarships, grants, and awards by category:* Academic interests/achievement: biological sciences, business, computer science, education, English, general academic interests/achievements, humanities, international studies, mathematics, military science, social sciences. Creative arts/performance: art/fine arts, music, theater/drama. *Special achievements/activities:* community service, leadership, memberships. *Special characteristics:* children and siblings of alumni, general special characteristics, local/state students. *Tuition waivers:* Full or partial for employees or children of employees, senior citizens. *ROTC:* Army.

LOANS *Student loans:* $18,786,027 (64% need-based, 36% non-need-based). 64% of past graduating class borrowed through all loan programs. *Average indebtedness*

per student: $26,439. *Average need-based loan:* Freshmen: $7015. Undergraduates: $7703. *Parent loans:* $11,749,806 (23% need-based, 77% non-need-based). *Programs:* Federal Direct (Subsidized and Unsubsidized Stafford, PLUS), Perkins, private loans.

WORK-STUDY *Federal work-study:* Total amount: $415,377; 293 jobs averaging $1420. *State or other work-study/employment:* 475 part-time jobs averaging $1300.

ATHLETIC AWARDS Total amount: $2,292,327 (33% need-based, 67% non-need-based).

APPLYING FOR FINANCIAL AID *Required financial aid form:* FAFSA. *Financial aid deadline (priority):* 3/1. *Notification date:* Continuous beginning 4/1. Students must reply within 4 weeks of notification.

CONTACT Caroline Gibbs, Financial Aid Counselor, Longwood University, 201 High Street, Farmville, VA 23909, 434-395-2949 or toll-free 800-281-4677. *Fax:* 434-395-2829. *E-mail:* gibbsca@longwood.edu.
Website: http://www.longwood.edu/.

LORAS COLLEGE
Dubuque, IA

Tuition & fees: $28,165	Average undergraduate aid package: $25,794

ABOUT THE INSTITUTION Independent Roman Catholic, coed. *Awards:* associate, bachelor's, and master's degrees. 52 undergraduate majors. *Total enrollment:* 1,555. Undergraduates: 1,514. Freshmen: 361. Federal methodology is used as a basis for awarding need-based institutional aid.

UNDERGRADUATE EXPENSES for 2013–2014 *Application fee:* $25. *Comprehensive fee:* $35,815 includes full-time tuition ($26,813), mandatory fees ($1352), and room and board ($7650). *College room only:* $3875. Full-time tuition and fees vary according to course load and degree level. Room and board charges vary according to board plan and housing facility. *Part-time tuition:* $559 per credit hour.

FRESHMAN FINANCIAL AID (Fall 2012, est.) 349 applied for aid; of those 88% were deemed to have need. 100% of freshmen with need received aid; of those 39% had need fully met. *Average percent of need met:* 88% (excluding resources awarded to replace EFC). *Average financial aid package:* $25,458 (excluding resources awarded to replace EFC). 18% of all full-time freshmen had no need and received non-need-based gift aid.

UNDERGRADUATE FINANCIAL AID (Fall 2012, est.) 1,322 applied for aid; of those 89% were deemed to have need. 97% of undergraduates with need received aid; of those 57% had need fully met. *Average percent of need met:* 84% (excluding resources awarded to replace EFC). *Average financial aid package:* $25,794 (excluding resources awarded to replace EFC). 40% of all full-time undergraduates had no need and received non-need-based gift aid.

GIFT AID (NEED-BASED) *Total amount:* $15,688,070 (9% federal, 7% state, 84% institutional). *Receiving aid:* Freshmen: 68% (255); all full-time undergraduates: 60% (865). *Average award:* Freshmen: $18,894; Undergraduates: $18,379. *Scholarships, grants, and awards:* Federal Pell, FSEOG, state, private, college/university gift aid from institutional funds.

GIFT AID (NON-NEED-BASED) *Total amount:* $7,712,559 (1% federal, 96% institutional, 3% external sources). *Receiving aid:* Freshmen: 14% (53). Undergraduates: 22% (316). *Average award:* Freshmen: $12,507. Undergraduates: $11,761. *Scholarships, grants, and awards by category:* Academic interests/achievement: 1,950 awards ($23,800,000 total): engineering/technologies, general academic interests/achievements, physical sciences. Creative arts/performance: 120 awards ($150,000 total): music. *Tuition waivers:* Full or partial for employees or children of employees. *ROTC:* Army cooperative.

LOANS *Student loans:* $8,380,387 (52% need-based, 48% non-need-based). 82% of past graduating class borrowed through all loan programs. *Average indebtedness per student:* $31,664. *Average need-based loan:* Freshmen: $4098. Undergraduates: $5052. *Parent loans:* $2,177,280 (40% need-based, 60% non-need-based). *Programs:* Federal Direct (Subsidized and Unsubsidized Stafford, PLUS), Perkins, college/university.

WORK-STUDY *Federal work-study:* Total amount: $199,781; 578 jobs averaging $1920. *State or other work-study/employment:* Total amount: $397,780 (100% non-need-based). 250 part-time jobs averaging $1591.

APPLYING FOR FINANCIAL AID *Required financial aid form:* FAFSA. *Financial aid deadline (priority):* 4/15. *Notification date:* Continuous beginning 3/1. Students must reply within 3 weeks of notification.

CONTACT Ms. Julie A. Dunn, Director of Financial Planning, Loras College, 1450 Alta Vista Street, Dubuque, IA 52004-0178, 563-588-7136 or toll-free 800-245-6727. *Fax:* 563-588-7119. *E-mail:* julie.dunn@loras.edu. *Website:* http://www.loras.edu/.

LOUISIANA COLLEGE
Pineville, LA

Tuition & fees: $13,780	Average undergraduate aid package: $11,049

ABOUT THE INSTITUTION Independent Southern Baptist, coed. *Awards:* associate, bachelor's, and master's degrees. 56 undergraduate majors. *Total enrollment:* 1,557. Undergraduates: 1,153. Freshmen: 461. Federal methodology is used as a basis for awarding need-based institutional aid.

UNDERGRADUATE EXPENSES for 2013–2014 *Application fee:* $25. *Comprehensive fee:* $18,228 includes full-time tuition ($12,150), mandatory fees ($1630), and room and board ($4448). Full-time tuition and fees vary according to course load. Room and board charges vary according to board plan and housing facility. *Part-time tuition:* $405 per credit hour. Part-time tuition and fees vary according to course load.

FRESHMAN FINANCIAL AID (Fall 2012, est.) 326 applied for aid; of those 70% were deemed to have need. 97% of freshmen with need received aid; of those 20% had need fully met. *Average percent of need met:* 67% (excluding resources awarded to replace EFC). *Average financial aid package:* $10,927 (excluding resources awarded to replace EFC). 28% of all full-time freshmen had no need and received non-need-based gift aid.

UNDERGRADUATE FINANCIAL AID (Fall 2012, est.) 1,186 applied for aid; of those 76% were deemed to have need. 98% of undergraduates with need received aid; of those 21% had need fully met. *Average percent of need met:* 64% (excluding resources awarded to replace EFC). *Average financial aid package:* $11,049 (excluding resources awarded to replace EFC). 21% of all full-time undergraduates had no need and received non-need-based gift aid.

GIFT AID (NEED-BASED) *Total amount:* $10,013,888 (22% federal, 21% state, 53% institutional, 4% external sources). *Receiving aid:* Freshmen: 60% (222); all full-time undergraduates: 67% (844). *Average award:* Freshmen: $8792; Undergraduates: $8842. *Scholarships, grants, and awards:* Federal Pell, FSEOG, state, private, college/university gift aid from institutional funds, Leveraging Educational Assistance Program (LEAP).

GIFT AID (NON-NEED-BASED) *Total amount:* $125,500 (100% federal). *Average award:* Freshmen: $4287. Undergraduates: $5032. *Scholarships, grants, and awards by category:* Academic interests/achievement: business, general academic interests/achievements, health fields, religion/biblical studies. *Creative arts/performance:* music, performing arts, theater/drama. *Special achievements/activities:* leadership. *Special characteristics:* children of faculty/staff. *ROTC:* Army.

LOANS *Student loans:* $5,848,075 (94% need-based, 6% non-need-based). 49% of past graduating class borrowed through all loan programs. *Average need-based loan:* Freshmen: $2542. Undergraduates: $3168. *Parent loans:* $343,221 (100% need-based). *Programs:* Federal Direct (Subsidized and Unsubsidized Stafford, PLUS), college/university.

WORK-STUDY *Federal work-study:* Total amount: $321,735; jobs available.

APPLYING FOR FINANCIAL AID *Required financial aid forms:* FAFSA, institution's own form. *Financial aid deadline (priority):* 5/1. *Notification date:* Continuous. Students must reply by 5/1 or within 2 weeks of notification.

CONTACT Eric Gossett, Director of Financial Aid, Louisiana College, 1140 College Drive, Pineville, LA 71359-0001, 318-487-7387 or toll-free 800-487-1906. *Fax:* 318-487-7449. *E-mail:* gossett@lacollege.edu. *Website:* http://www.lacollege.edu/.

LOUISIANA STATE UNIVERSITY AND AGRICULTURAL AND MECHANICAL COLLEGE
Baton Rouge, LA

Tuition & fees (LA res): $6989	Average undergraduate aid package: $13,772

ABOUT THE INSTITUTION State-supported, coed. *Awards:* certificates, bachelor's, master's, and doctoral degrees. 67 undergraduate majors. *Total enrollment:* 30,225. Undergraduates: 24,626. Freshmen: 5,725. Federal methodology is used as a basis for awarding need-based institutional aid.

UNDERGRADUATE EXPENSES for 2013–2014 *Application fee:* $40. *Tuition, state resident:* full-time $5193. *Tuition, nonresident:* full-time $20,469. *Required fees:* full-time $1796. Part-time tuition and fees vary according to course load. *College room and board:* $10,218; *Room only:* $6600. Room and board charges vary according to board plan and housing facility.

FRESHMAN FINANCIAL AID (Fall 2011) 3,437 applied for aid; of those 68% were deemed to have need. 100% of freshmen with need received aid; of those 27% had need fully met. *Average percent of need met:* 72% (excluding resources awarded to replace EFC). *Average financial aid package:* $12,600 (excluding resources awarded to replace EFC). 16% of all full-time freshmen had no need and received non-need-based gift aid.

UNDERGRADUATE FINANCIAL AID (Fall 2011) 11,945 applied for aid; of those 73% were deemed to have need. 100% of undergraduates with need received aid; of those 24% had need fully met. *Average percent of need met:* 70% (excluding resources awarded to replace EFC). *Average financial aid package:* $13,772 (excluding resources awarded to replace EFC). 15% of all full-time undergraduates had no need and received non-need-based gift aid.

GIFT AID (NEED-BASED) *Total amount:* $66,848,938 (34% federal, 32% state, 32% institutional, 2% external sources). *Receiving aid:* Freshmen: 41% (2,186); all full-time undergraduates: 35% (7,650). *Average award:* Freshmen: $8782; Undergraduates: $9036. *Scholarships, grants, and awards:* Federal Pell, FSEOG, state, private, college/university gift aid from institutional funds.

GIFT AID (NON-NEED-BASED) *Total amount:* $64,421,956 (3% federal, 59% state, 34% institutional, 4% external sources). *Receiving aid:* Freshmen: 2% (100). Undergraduates: 1% (243). *Average award:* Freshmen: $3073. Undergraduates: $6101. *Scholarships, grants, and awards by category:* Academic interests/achievement: 953 awards ($1,258,000 total): agriculture, architecture, biological sciences, business, communication, computer science, education, engineering/technologies, English, foreign languages, general academic interests/achievements, home economics, humanities, mathematics, military science, physical sciences, premedicine. *Creative arts/performance:* 163 awards ($817,800 total): applied art and design, journalism/publications, music, performing arts, theater/drama. *Special characteristics:* 369 awards ($3,265,000 total): children with a deceased or disabled parent, general special characteristics. *Tuition waivers:* Full or partial for employees or children of employees. *ROTC:* Army, Naval cooperative, Air Force.

LOANS *Student loans:* $57,226,904 (70% need-based, 30% non-need-based). 39% of past graduating class borrowed through all loan programs. *Average indebtedness per student:* $20,125. *Average need-based loan:* Freshmen: $4715. Undergraduates: $6130. *Parent loans:* $22,351,283 (39% need-based, 61% non-need-based). *Programs:* Federal Direct (Subsidized and Unsubsidized Stafford, PLUS), Perkins, college/university.

WORK-STUDY *Federal work-study:* Total amount: $1,038,784; 550 jobs averaging $1400. *State or other work-study/employment:* Total amount: $15,761,037 (24% need-based, 76% non-need-based). 4,597 part-time jobs averaging $2600.

ATHLETIC AWARDS Total amount: $8,997,601 (39% need-based, 61% non-need-based).

APPLYING FOR FINANCIAL AID *Required financial aid forms:* FAFSA, institution's own form. *Financial aid deadline (priority):* 4/1. *Notification date:* Continuous beginning 12/15. Students must reply by 5/1.

CONTACT Ms. Amy Marix, Associate Director of Undergraduate Admissions and Student Aid, Louisiana State University and Agricultural and Mechanical College, 1146 Pleasant Hall, Baton Rouge, LA 70803-3103, 225-578-3113. *Fax:* 225-578-6300. *E-mail:* financialaid@lsu.edu. *Website:* http://www.lsu.edu/.

LOUISIANA STATE UNIVERSITY AT ALEXANDRIA
Alexandria, LA

CONTACT Financial Aid Office, Louisiana State University at Alexandria, 8100 Highway 71 South, Alexandria, LA 71302-9121, 318-445-3672 or toll-free 888-473-6417.
Website: http://www.lsua.edu/.

LOUISIANA STATE UNIVERSITY HEALTH SCIENCES CENTER
New Orleans, LA

CONTACT Mr. Patrick Gorman, Director of Financial Aid, Louisiana State University Health Sciences Center, 433 Bolivar Street, New Orleans, LA 70112, 504-568-4821. *Fax:* 504-599-1390.
Website: http://www.lsuhsc.edu/.

LOUISIANA STATE UNIVERSITY IN SHREVEPORT
Shreveport, LA

CONTACT Office of Student Financial Aid, Louisiana State University in Shreveport, One University Place, Shreveport, LA 71115-2399, 318-797-5363 or toll-free 800-229-5957. *Fax:* 318-797-5366.
Website: http://www.lsus.edu/.

LOUISIANA TECH UNIVERSITY
Ruston, LA

Tuition & fees: N/R	Average undergraduate aid package: $9197

ABOUT THE INSTITUTION State-supported, coed. *Awards:* certificates, associate, bachelor's, master's, and doctoral degrees. 79 undergraduate majors. *Total enrollment:* 11,304. Undergraduates: 8,958. Freshmen: 1,306. Institutional methodology is used as a basis for awarding need-based institutional aid.
FRESHMAN FINANCIAL AID (Fall 2012, est.) 805 applied for aid; of those 70% were deemed to have need. 98% of freshmen with need received aid; of those 20% had need fully met. *Average percent of need met:* 26% (excluding resources awarded to replace EFC). *Average financial aid package:* $8821 (excluding resources awarded to replace EFC). 62% of all full-time freshmen had no need and received non-need-based gift aid.
UNDERGRADUATE FINANCIAL AID (Fall 2012, est.) 4,743 applied for aid; of those 72% were deemed to have need. 98% of undergraduates with need received aid; of those 19% had need fully met. *Average percent of need met:* 48% (excluding resources awarded to replace EFC). *Average financial aid package:* $9197 (excluding resources awarded to replace EFC). 20% of all full-time undergraduates had no need and received non-need-based gift aid.
GIFT AID (NEED-BASED) *Total amount:* $19,749,442 (42% federal, 40% state, 16% institutional, 2% external sources). *Receiving aid:* Freshmen: 42% (528); all full-time undergraduates: 40% (3,026). *Average award:* Freshmen: $7537; Undergraduates: $7411. *Scholarships, grants, and awards:* Federal Pell, FSEOG, state, private, college/university gift aid from institutional funds.
GIFT AID (NON-NEED-BASED) *Total amount:* $10,977,502 (54% state, 39% institutional, 7% external sources). *Receiving aid:* Freshmen: 8% (96). Undergraduates: 7% (529). *Average award:* Freshmen: $1436. Undergraduates: $2127. *Scholarships, grants, and awards by category:* Academic interests/achievement: agriculture, architecture, biological sciences, business, computer science, education, engineering/technologies, English, foreign languages, general academic interests/achievements, health fields, home economics, international studies, mathematics, military science, physical sciences, social sciences. *Creative arts/performance:* applied art and design, art/fine arts, creative writing, debating, general creative arts/performance, journalism/publications, music, performing arts, theater/drama. *Special achievements/activities:* cheerleading/drum major, junior miss. *Special characteristics:* children and siblings of alumni, children of faculty/staff, children of public servants, handicapped students, international students, members of minority groups, out-of-state students, spouses of deceased or disabled public servants, veterans, veterans' children. *ROTC:* Army cooperative, Air Force.
LOANS *Student loans:* $18,766,381 (71% need-based, 29% non-need-based). 55% of past graduating class borrowed through all loan programs. *Average indebtedness per student:* $18,555. *Average need-based loan:* Freshmen: $2735. Undergraduates: $3712. *Parent loans:* $4,173,464 (29% need-based, 71% non-need-based). *Programs:* Federal Direct (Subsidized and Unsubsidized Stafford, PLUS), Perkins.
WORK-STUDY *Federal work-study:* Total amount: $620,130; 237 jobs averaging $2661. *State or other work-study/employment:* 918 part-time jobs averaging $2116.
ATHLETIC AWARDS Total amount: $2,326,359 (48% need-based, 52% non-need-based).
APPLYING FOR FINANCIAL AID *Required financial aid forms:* FAFSA, institution's own form. *Financial aid deadline (priority):* 4/15. *Notification date:* Continuous beginning 4/15. Students must reply within 3 weeks of notification.
CONTACT Office of Financial Aid, Louisiana Tech University, PO Box 7925, Ruston, LA 71272, 318-257-2641 or toll-free 800-528-3241. *Fax:* 318-257-2628. *E-mail:* techaid@latech.edu.
Website: http://www.latech.edu/.

LOURDES UNIVERSITY
Sylvania, OH

Tuition & fees: $17,455	Average undergraduate aid package: $12,127

ABOUT THE INSTITUTION Independent Roman Catholic, coed. *Awards:* certificates, associate, bachelor's, and master's degrees. 26 undergraduate majors. *Total enrollment:* 2,460. Undergraduates: 2,118. Freshmen: 264. Both federal and institutional methodology are used as a basis for awarding need-based institutional aid.
UNDERGRADUATE EXPENSES for 2013–2014 *Application fee:* $25. *Tuition:* full-time $17,455; part-time $582 per credit. Full-time tuition and fees vary according to course load and location. Part-time tuition and fees vary according to course load and location. Room and board charges vary according to board plan and housing facility.
FRESHMAN FINANCIAL AID (Fall 2012, est.) 253 applied for aid; of those 86% were deemed to have need. 100% of freshmen with need received aid. *Average financial aid package:* $14,715 (excluding resources awarded to replace EFC).
UNDERGRADUATE FINANCIAL AID (Fall 2012, est.) 1,219 applied for aid; of those 88% were deemed to have need. 100% of undergraduates with need received aid. *Average financial aid package:* $12,127 (excluding resources awarded to replace EFC).
GIFT AID (NEED-BASED) *Total amount:* $9,749,525 (49% federal, 16% state, 34% institutional, 1% external sources). *Receiving aid:* Freshmen: 70% (178); all full-time undergraduates: 66% (835). *Average award:* Freshmen: $6042; Undergraduates: $6180. *Scholarships, grants, and awards:* Federal Pell, FSEOG, state, private, college/university gift aid from institutional funds.
GIFT AID (NON-NEED-BASED) *Receiving aid:* Freshmen: 79% (201). Undergraduates: 56% (706). *Scholarships, grants, and awards by category:* Academic interests/achievement: 660 awards ($2,558,331 total): general academic interests/achievements. *Creative arts/performance:* art/fine arts, theater/drama. *Special achievements/activities:* general special achievements/activities, leadership. *Special characteristics:* adult students, ethnic background, local/state students, members of minority groups, out-of-state students, previous college experience, religious affiliation. *Tuition waivers:* Full or partial for employees or children of employees, senior citizens. *ROTC:* Army cooperative, Air Force cooperative.
LOANS *Student loans:* $14,106,214 (100% need-based). *Average need-based loan:* Freshmen: $3414. Undergraduates: $3928. *Parent loans:* $1,645,072 (100% need-based). *Programs:* Federal Direct (Subsidized and Unsubsidized Stafford, PLUS), Perkins, state, college/university, alternative loans.

WORK-STUDY *Federal work-study:* Total amount: $175,384; 100 jobs averaging $1754. *State or other work-study/employment:* Total amount: $215,000 (100% need-based). 230 part-time jobs averaging $935.
ATHLETIC AWARDS Total amount: $601,650 (100% need-based).
APPLYING FOR FINANCIAL AID *Required financial aid form:* FAFSA. *Financial aid deadline (priority):* 3/1. *Notification date:* Continuous beginning 3/1. Students must reply within 4 weeks of notification.
CONTACT Denise McClusky, Director of Financial Aid, Lourdes University, 6832 Convent Boulevard, Sylvania, OH 43560-2898, 419-824-3732 or toll-free 800-878-3210. *Fax:* 419-517-8866. *E-mail:* finaid@lourdes.edu.
Website: http://www.lourdes.edu/.

LOYOLA MARYMOUNT UNIVERSITY
Los Angeles, CA

Tuition & fees: $38,900	Average undergraduate aid package: $26,246

ABOUT THE INSTITUTION Independent Roman Catholic, coed. *Awards:* certificates, bachelor's, master's, and doctoral degrees. 49 undergraduate majors. *Total enrollment:* 9,492. Undergraduates: 6,085. Freshmen: 1,278. Both federal and institutional methodology are used as a basis for awarding need-based institutional aid.
UNDERGRADUATE EXPENSES for 2013–2014 *Application fee:* $60. *One-time required fee:* $225. *Comprehensive fee:* $53,295 includes full-time tuition ($38,212), mandatory fees ($688), and room and board ($14,395). *College room only:* $9995. Full-time tuition and fees vary according to reciprocity agreements. Room and board charges vary according to board plan and housing facility. *Part-time tuition:* $1594 per credit hour. *Part-time fees:* $8 per credit hour; $64 per term. Part-time tuition and fees vary according to course load.
FRESHMAN FINANCIAL AID (Fall 2011) 1,016 applied for aid; of those 75% were deemed to have need. 98% of freshmen with need received aid; of those 15% had need fully met. *Average percent of need met:* 63% (excluding resources awarded to replace EFC). *Average financial aid package:* $23,356 (excluding resources awarded to replace EFC). 23% of all full-time freshmen had no need and received non-need-based gift aid.
UNDERGRADUATE FINANCIAL AID (Fall 2011) 4,374 applied for aid; of those 78% were deemed to have need. 99% of undergraduates with need received aid; of those 16% had need fully met. *Average percent of need met:* 65% (excluding resources awarded to replace EFC). *Average financial aid package:* $26,246 (excluding resources awarded to replace EFC). 19% of all full-time undergraduates had no need and received non-need-based gift aid.
GIFT AID (NEED-BASED) *Total amount:* $58,868,452 (11% federal, 13% state, 75% institutional, 1% external sources). *Receiving aid:* Freshmen: 53% (683); all full-time undergraduates: 53% (3,100). *Average award:* Freshmen: $18,065; Undergraduates: $18,962. *Scholarships, grants, and awards:* Federal Pell, FSEOG, state, private, college/university gift aid from institutional funds.
GIFT AID (NON-NEED-BASED) *Total amount:* $13,832,957 (90% institutional, 10% external sources). *Receiving aid:* Freshmen: 7% (92). Undergraduates: 6% (359). *Average award:* Freshmen: $8178. Undergraduates: $9584. *Scholarships, grants, and awards by category:* Academic interests/achievement: 2,700 awards ($27,394,143 total): biological sciences, business, communication, education, engineering/technologies, English, foreign languages, general academic interests/achievements, humanities, international studies, mathematics, physical sciences, religion/biblical studies, social sciences. Creative arts/performance: 48 awards ($234,481 total): applied art and design, art/fine arts, cinema/film/broadcasting, creative writing, general creative arts/performance, journalism/publications, music, performing arts, theater/drama. Special achievements/activities: 148 awards ($1,540,063 total): community service, general special achievements/activities, leadership, memberships, religious involvement. Special characteristics: 377 awards ($6,257,294 total): adult students, children and siblings of alumni, children of faculty/staff, ethnic background, first-generation college students, general special characteristics, handicapped students, international students, local/state students, members of minority groups, out-of-state students, previous college experience, religious affiliation, veterans. *Tuition waivers:* Full or partial for employees or children of employees. *ROTC:* Army cooperative, Naval cooperative, Air Force.
LOANS *Student loans:* $27,500,509 (77% need-based, 23% non-need-based). 57% of past graduating class borrowed through all loan programs. *Average indebtedness per student:* $34,629. *Average need-based loan:* Freshmen: $4252. Undergraduates: $5461. *Parent loans:* $23,610,788 (49% need-based, 51% non-need-based).

Programs: Federal Direct (Subsidized and Unsubsidized Stafford, PLUS), Perkins, college/university.
WORK-STUDY *Federal work-study:* Total amount: $3,207,529; 1,651 jobs averaging $1943. *State or other work-study/employment:* Total amount: $5,857,381 (41% need-based, 59% non-need-based). 2,183 part-time jobs averaging $2683.
ATHLETIC AWARDS Total amount: $7,257,089 (51% need-based, 49% non-need-based).
APPLYING FOR FINANCIAL AID *Required financial aid form:* FAFSA. *Financial aid deadline:* 7/30 (priority: 2/1). *Notification date:* Continuous beginning 3/15. Students must reply by 5/1 or within 4 weeks of notification.
CONTACT Mrs. Catherine Graham, Director of Financial Aid, Loyola Marymount University, One LMU Drive, Suite 200, Los Angeles, CA 90045-8350, 310-338-2753 or toll-free 800-LMU-INFO. *Fax:* 310-338-2793. *E-mail:* finaid@lmu.edu.
Website: http://www.lmu.edu/.

LOYOLA UNIVERSITY CHICAGO
Chicago, IL

Tuition & fees: $35,503	Average undergraduate aid package: $29,572

ABOUT THE INSTITUTION Independent Roman Catholic (Jesuit), coed. *Awards:* certificates, bachelor's, master's, and doctoral degrees (also offers adult part-time program with significant enrollment not reflected in profile). 77 undergraduate majors. *Total enrollment:* 15,720. Undergraduates: 9,723. Freshmen: 2,003. Federal methodology is used as a basis for awarding need-based institutional aid.
UNDERGRADUATE EXPENSES for 2013–2014 *Comprehensive fee:* $48,403 includes full-time tuition ($34,343), mandatory fees ($1160), and room and board ($12,900). *College room only:* $8114. Full-time tuition and fees vary according to location, program, and student level. Room and board charges vary according to board plan, housing facility, and location. *Part-time tuition:* $690 per credit. *Part-time fees:* $158 per term. Part-time tuition and fees vary according to course load.
FRESHMAN FINANCIAL AID (Fall 2012, est.) 1,752 applied for aid; of those 85% were deemed to have need. 100% of freshmen with need received aid; of those 12% had need fully met. *Average percent of need met:* 82% (excluding resources awarded to replace EFC). *Average financial aid package:* $30,940 (excluding resources awarded to replace EFC). 22% of all full-time freshmen had no need and received non-need-based gift aid.
UNDERGRADUATE FINANCIAL AID (Fall 2012, est.) 7,190 applied for aid; of those 90% were deemed to have need. 99% of undergraduates with need received aid; of those 10% had need fully met. *Average percent of need met:* 79% (excluding resources awarded to replace EFC). *Average financial aid package:* $29,572 (excluding resources awarded to replace EFC). 18% of all full-time undergraduates had no need and received non-need-based gift aid.
GIFT AID (NEED-BASED) *Total amount:* $113,233,702 (14% federal, 9% state, 75% institutional, 2% external sources). *Receiving aid:* Freshmen: 73% (1,459); all full-time undergraduates: 70% (6,138). *Average award:* Freshmen: $20,193; Undergraduates: $18,304. *Scholarships, grants, and awards:* Federal Pell, FSEOG, state, private, college/university gift aid from institutional funds.
GIFT AID (NON-NEED-BASED) *Total amount:* $21,198,266 (4% federal, 91% institutional, 5% external sources). *Receiving aid:* Freshmen: 7% (139). Undergraduates: 5% (455). *Average award:* Freshmen: $12,355. Undergraduates: $10,775. *Scholarships, grants, and awards by category:* Academic interests/achievement: 5,053 awards ($53,264,691 total): general academic interests/achievements. Creative arts/performance: 35 awards ($120,500 total): art/fine arts, debating, journalism/publications, music, theater/drama. Special achievements/activities: 423 awards ($2,628,954 total): community service, general special achievements/activities, leadership, memberships. Special characteristics: 1,260 awards ($3,391,228 total): adult students, general special characteristics, religious affiliation. *Tuition waivers:* Full or partial for employees or children of employees, senior citizens. *ROTC:* Army cooperative, Naval cooperative, Air Force cooperative.
LOANS *Student loans:* $62,902,285 (80% need-based, 20% non-need-based). 72% of past graduating class borrowed through all loan programs. *Average indebtedness per student:* $36,328. *Average need-based loan:* Freshmen: $3824. Undergraduates: $4736. *Parent loans:* $30,754,495 (49% need-based, 51% non-need-based).
Programs: Federal Direct (Subsidized and Unsubsidized Stafford, PLUS), Perkins, Federal Nursing.

WORK-STUDY *Federal work-study:* Total amount: $11,496,171; 5,148 jobs averaging $2131.
ATHLETIC AWARDS Total amount: $4,382,189 (40% need-based, 60% non-need-based).
APPLYING FOR FINANCIAL AID *Required financial aid form:* FAFSA. *Financial aid deadline:* Continuous. *Notification date:* Continuous beginning 2/15. Students must reply within 3 weeks of notification.
CONTACT Mr. Edward Moore, Director of Scholarships, Loyola University Chicago, 6525 North Sheridan Road, Chicago, IL 60660, 773-508-7704 or toll-free 800-262-2373. *Fax:* 773-508-3397. *E-mail:* lufinaid@luc.edu. *Website:* http://www.luc.edu/.

LOYOLA UNIVERSITY MARYLAND
Baltimore, MD

Tuition & fees: $42,430	Average undergraduate aid package: $26,915

ABOUT THE INSTITUTION Independent Roman Catholic (Jesuit), coed. *Awards:* certificates, bachelor's, master's, and doctoral degrees. 35 undergraduate majors. *Total enrollment:* 5,978. Undergraduates: 3,917. Freshmen: 1,072. Institutional methodology is used as a basis for awarding need-based institutional aid.
UNDERGRADUATE EXPENSES for 2013–2014 *Application fee:* $50. *One-time required fee:* $165. *Comprehensive fee:* $54,550 includes full-time tuition ($41,030), mandatory fees ($1400), and room and board ($12,120). *College room only:* $9120. Full-time tuition and fees vary according to course load. Room and board charges vary according to housing facility. *Part-time tuition:* $665 per credit. *Part-time fees:* $25 per term. Part-time tuition and fees vary according to course load.
FRESHMAN FINANCIAL AID (Fall 2011) 838 applied for aid; of those 80% were deemed to have need. 100% of freshmen with need received aid; of those 100% had need fully met. *Average percent of need met:* 100% (excluding resources awarded to replace EFC). *Average financial aid package:* $26,745 (excluding resources awarded to replace EFC). 7% of all full-time freshmen had no need and received non-need-based gift aid.
UNDERGRADUATE FINANCIAL AID (Fall 2011) 2,645 applied for aid; of those 84% were deemed to have need. 100% of undergraduates with need received aid; of those 99% had need fully met. *Average percent of need met:* 98% (excluding resources awarded to replace EFC). *Average financial aid package:* $26,915 (excluding resources awarded to replace EFC). 9% of all full-time undergraduates had no need and received non-need-based gift aid.
GIFT AID (NEED-BASED) *Total amount:* $45,814,783 (6% federal, 1% state, 91% institutional, 2% external sources). *Receiving aid:* Freshmen: 54% (582); all full-time undergraduates: 51% (1,947). *Average award:* Freshmen: $20,680; Undergraduates: $20,270. *Scholarships, grants, and awards:* Federal Pell, FSEOG, state, private, college/university gift aid from institutional funds.
GIFT AID (NON-NEED-BASED) *Total amount:* $7,294,064 (17% federal, 1% state, 76% institutional, 6% external sources). *Receiving aid:* Freshmen: 6% (65). Undergraduates: 4% (170). *Average award:* Freshmen: $15,320. Undergraduates: $15,140. *Scholarships, grants, and awards by category:* Academic interests/achievement: general academic interests/achievements. *Tuition waivers:* Full or partial for employees or children of employees. *ROTC:* Army, Air Force cooperative.
LOANS *Student loans:* $20,626,238 (48% need-based, 52% non-need-based). 63% of past graduating class borrowed through all loan programs. *Average indebtedness per student:* $32,392. *Average need-based loan:* Freshmen: $4425. Undergraduates: $5105. *Parent loans:* $16,945,124 (100% non-need-based). *Programs:* Federal Direct (Subsidized and Unsubsidized Stafford, PLUS), Perkins, college/university.
WORK-STUDY *Federal work-study:* Total amount: $1,847,803; jobs available. *State or other work-study/employment:* Total amount: $992,050 (61% need-based, 39% non-need-based). Part-time jobs available.
ATHLETIC AWARDS Total amount: $5,318,611 (31% need-based, 69% non-need-based).
APPLYING FOR FINANCIAL AID *Required financial aid forms:* FAFSA, CSS Financial Aid PROFILE, noncustodial (divorced/separated) parent's statement. *Financial aid deadline:* 2/15. *Notification date:* 4/1. Students must reply by 5/1.

CONTACT Mr. Mark L. Lindenmeyer, Director of Financial Aid, Loyola University Maryland, 4501 North Charles Street, Baltimore, MD 21210-2699, 410-617-2576 or toll-free 800-221-9107. *Fax:* 410-617-5149. *E-mail:* lindenmeyer@loyola.edu. *Website:* http://www.loyola.edu/.

LOYOLA UNIVERSITY NEW ORLEANS
New Orleans, LA

Tuition & fees: $36,610	Average undergraduate aid package: $26,626

ABOUT THE INSTITUTION Independent Roman Catholic (Jesuit), coed. *Awards:* certificates, bachelor's, master's, and doctoral degrees. 47 undergraduate majors. *Total enrollment:* 4,933. Undergraduates: 3,200. Freshmen: 870. Federal methodology is used as a basis for awarding need-based institutional aid.
UNDERGRADUATE EXPENSES for 2013–2014 *Application fee:* $20. *Comprehensive fee:* $48,795 includes full-time tuition ($35,504), mandatory fees ($1106), and room and board ($12,185). *College room only:* $7250. Room and board charges vary according to board plan and housing facility. *Part-time tuition:* $1012 per credit.
FRESHMAN FINANCIAL AID (Fall 2012, est.) 739 applied for aid; of those 86% were deemed to have need. 100% of freshmen with need received aid; of those 15% had need fully met. *Average percent of need met:* 79% (excluding resources awarded to replace EFC). *Average financial aid package:* $30,148 (excluding resources awarded to replace EFC). 23% of all full-time freshmen had no need and received non-need-based gift aid.
UNDERGRADUATE FINANCIAL AID (Fall 2012, est.) 2,257 applied for aid; of those 88% were deemed to have need. 100% of undergraduates with need received aid; of those 16% had need fully met. *Average percent of need met:* 72% (excluding resources awarded to replace EFC). *Average financial aid package:* $26,626 (excluding resources awarded to replace EFC). 29% of all full-time undergraduates had no need and received non-need-based gift aid.
GIFT AID (NEED-BASED) *Total amount:* $43,290,174 (10% federal, 6% state, 80% institutional, 4% external sources). *Receiving aid:* Freshmen: 76% (638); all full-time undergraduates: 69% (1,976). *Average award:* Freshmen: $26,199; Undergraduates: $22,391. *Scholarships, grants, and awards:* Federal Pell, FSEOG, private, college/university gift aid from institutional funds.
GIFT AID (NON-NEED-BASED) *Total amount:* $16,471,427 (6% state, 90% institutional, 4% external sources). *Receiving aid:* Freshmen: 8% (66). Undergraduates: 8% (241). *Average award:* Freshmen: $14,633. Undergraduates: $15,158. *Scholarships, grants, and awards by category:* Academic interests/achievement: general academic interests/achievements. *Creative arts/performance:* general creative arts/performance. *Special characteristics:* children of faculty/staff. *Tuition waivers:* Full or partial for employees or children of employees, senior citizens. *ROTC:* Army cooperative, Naval cooperative, Air Force cooperative.
LOANS *Student loans:* $14,751,137 (79% need-based, 21% non-need-based). 66% of past graduating class borrowed through all loan programs. *Average indebtedness per student:* $23,178. *Average need-based loan:* Freshmen: $3303. Undergraduates: $4208. *Parent loans:* $4,871,961 (43% need-based, 57% non-need-based). *Programs:* Perkins.
WORK-STUDY *Federal work-study:* Total amount: $1,979,683; jobs available.
ATHLETIC AWARDS Total amount: $1,035,504 (38% need-based, 62% non-need-based).
APPLYING FOR FINANCIAL AID *Required financial aid form:* FAFSA. *Financial aid deadline:* 6/1 (priority: 2/15). *Notification date:* 3/1. Students must reply by 5/1 or within 2 weeks of notification.
CONTACT Ms. Catherine M. Simoneaux, Director of Scholarships and Financial Aid, Loyola University New Orleans, 6363 St. Charles Avenue, Box 206, New Orleans, LA 70118-6195, 504-865-3231 or toll-free 800-4-LOYOLA. *Fax:* 504-865-3233. *E-mail:* finaid@loyno.edu. *Website:* http://www.loyno.edu/.

LUBBOCK CHRISTIAN UNIVERSITY
Lubbock, TX

Tuition & fees: $17,760	Average undergraduate aid package: $13,738

ABOUT THE INSTITUTION Independent Church of Christ, coed. *Awards:* bachelor's and master's degrees. 56 undergraduate majors. *Total enrollment:* 2,135. Undergraduates: 1,640. Freshmen: 315. Federal methodology is used as a basis for awarding need-based institutional aid.

UNDERGRADUATE EXPENSES for 2013–2014 *Application fee:* $25. *Comprehensive fee:* $24,434 includes full-time tuition ($16,350), mandatory fees ($1410), and room and board ($6674). Full-time tuition and fees vary according to degree level and program. Room and board charges vary according to board plan and housing facility. *Part-time tuition:* $525 per semester hour. *Part-time fees:* $540 per term. Part-time tuition and fees vary according to course load, degree level, and program.

FRESHMAN FINANCIAL AID (Fall 2012, est.) 216 applied for aid; of those 85% were deemed to have need. 100% of freshmen with need received aid; of those 14% had need fully met. *Average percent of need met:* 70% (excluding resources awarded to replace EFC). *Average financial aid package:* $13,760 (excluding resources awarded to replace EFC). 12% of all full-time freshmen had no need and received non-need-based gift aid.

UNDERGRADUATE FINANCIAL AID (Fall 2012, est.) 1,139 applied for aid; of those 86% were deemed to have need. 100% of undergraduates with need received aid; of those 9% had need fully met. *Average percent of need met:* 64% (excluding resources awarded to replace EFC). *Average financial aid package:* $13,738 (excluding resources awarded to replace EFC). 15% of all full-time undergraduates had no need and received non-need-based gift aid.

GIFT AID (NEED-BASED) *Total amount:* $7,350,408 (35% federal, 22% state, 32% institutional, 11% external sources). *Receiving aid:* Freshmen: 48% (182); all full-time undergraduates: 70% (930). *Average award:* Freshmen: $9652; Undergraduates: $9371. *Scholarships, grants, and awards:* Federal Pell, FSEOG, state, college/university gift aid from institutional funds.

GIFT AID (NON-NEED-BASED) *Total amount:* $1,357,500 (1% federal, 77% institutional, 22% external sources). *Receiving aid:* Freshmen: 7% (25). Undergraduates: 6% (82). *Average award:* Freshmen: $4203. Undergraduates: $4707. *Scholarships, grants, and awards by category:* Academic interests/achievement: agriculture, business, communication, computer science, education, English, foreign languages, general academic interests/achievements, humanities, physical sciences, religion/biblical studies, social sciences. *Creative arts/performance:* art/fine arts, journalism/publications, music, performing arts, theater/drama. *Special achievements/activities:* 36 awards ($30,750 total): cheerleading/drum major, leadership. *Special characteristics:* 31 awards ($397,395 total): children of faculty/staff, general special characteristics. *Tuition waivers:* Full or partial for employees or children of employees. *ROTC:* Army cooperative, Air Force cooperative.

LOANS *Student loans:* $11,730,844 (77% need-based, 23% non-need-based). 77% of past graduating class borrowed through all loan programs. *Average indebtedness per student:* $29,053. *Average need-based loan:* Freshmen: $3826. Undergraduates: $4418. *Parent loans:* $3,060,906 (37% need-based, 63% non-need-based). *Programs:* Federal Direct (Subsidized and Unsubsidized Stafford, PLUS), Perkins, state.

WORK-STUDY *Federal work-study:* Total amount: $893,949; 715 jobs averaging $1797. *State or other work-study/employment:* Total amount: $19,327 (49% need-based, 51% non-need-based). 64 part-time jobs averaging $302.

ATHLETIC AWARDS Total amount: $2,065,637 (49% need-based, 51% non-need-based).

APPLYING FOR FINANCIAL AID *Required financial aid forms:* FAFSA, institution's own form. *Financial aid deadline (priority):* 6/1. *Notification date:* Continuous beginning 3/1.

CONTACT Mrs. Amy Hardesty, Director of Financial Aid, Lubbock Christian University, 5601 19th Street, Lubbock, TX 79407, 806-720-7176 or toll-free 800-933-7601. *Fax:* 806-720-7185. *E-mail:* amy.hardesty@lcu.edu. *Website:* http://www.lcu.edu/.

LUTHER COLLEGE
Decorah, IA

Tuition & fees: $37,480	Average undergraduate aid package: $27,771

ABOUT THE INSTITUTION Independent Evangelical Lutheran Church in America, coed. *Awards:* bachelor's degrees. 39 undergraduate majors. *Total enrollment:* 2,473. Undergraduates: 2,473. Freshmen: 645. Federal methodology is used as a basis for awarding need-based institutional aid.

UNDERGRADUATE EXPENSES for 2013–2014 *Application fee:* $25. *Comprehensive fee:* $44,330 includes full-time tuition ($37,330), mandatory fees ($150), and room and board ($6850). *College room only:* $3240. Full-time tuition and fees vary according to course load. Room and board charges vary according to board plan and housing facility. *Part-time tuition:* $1334 per credit hour. Part-time tuition and fees vary according to course load.

FRESHMAN FINANCIAL AID (Fall 2012, est.) 545 applied for aid; of those 85% were deemed to have need. 100% of freshmen with need received aid; of those 37% had need fully met. *Average percent of need met:* 90% (excluding resources awarded to replace EFC). *Average financial aid package:* $29,605 (excluding resources awarded to replace EFC). 13% of all full-time freshmen had no need and received non-need-based gift aid.

UNDERGRADUATE FINANCIAL AID (Fall 2012, est.) 1,964 applied for aid; of those 86% were deemed to have need. 100% of undergraduates with need received aid; of those 30% had need fully met. *Average percent of need met:* 86% (excluding resources awarded to replace EFC). *Average financial aid package:* $27,771 (excluding resources awarded to replace EFC). 11% of all full-time undergraduates had no need and received non-need-based gift aid.

GIFT AID (NEED-BASED) *Total amount:* $35,456,190 (7% federal, 4% state, 86% institutional, 3% external sources). *Receiving aid:* Freshmen: 72% (463); all full-time undergraduates: 71% (1,693). *Average award:* Freshmen: $22,284; Undergraduates: $20,503. *Scholarships, grants, and awards:* Federal Pell, FSEOG, state, private, college/university gift aid from institutional funds.

GIFT AID (NON-NEED-BASED) *Total amount:* $13,238,841 (82% institutional, 18% external sources). *Receiving aid:* Freshmen: 15% (98). Undergraduates: 12% (292). *Average award:* Freshmen: $17,406. Undergraduates: $14,833. *Scholarships, grants, and awards by category:* Academic interests/achievement: 1,973 awards ($24,671,031 total): general academic interests/achievements. *Creative arts/performance:* 805 awards ($2,430,719 total): music. *Special characteristics:* 650 awards ($1,155,268 total): children and siblings of alumni, members of minority groups, religious affiliation. *Tuition waivers:* Full or partial for employees or children of employees.

LOANS *Student loans:* $12,052,358 (77% need-based, 23% non-need-based). 78% of past graduating class borrowed through all loan programs. *Average indebtedness per student:* $35,619. *Average need-based loan:* Freshmen: $4799. Undergraduates: $4840. *Parent loans:* $5,667,207 (31% need-based, 69% non-need-based). *Programs:* Federal Direct (Subsidized and Unsubsidized Stafford, PLUS), Perkins, college/university.

WORK-STUDY *Federal work-study:* Total amount: $2,502,783; 1,066 jobs averaging $1988. *State or other work-study/employment:* Total amount: $2,173,400 (15% need-based, 85% non-need-based). 1,110 part-time jobs averaging $1678.

APPLYING FOR FINANCIAL AID *Required financial aid forms:* FAFSA, institution's own form. *Financial aid deadline (priority):* 3/1. *Notification date:* Continuous beginning 3/15. Students must reply by 5/1.

CONTACT Ms. Janice Cordell, Director of Financial Aid, Luther College, 700 College Drive, Decorah, IA 52101-1045, 563-387-1018 or toll-free 800-458-8437. *Fax:* 563-387-2241. *E-mail:* cordellj@luther.edu. *Website:* http://www.luther.edu/.

LUTHER RICE UNIVERSITY
Lithonia, GA

CONTACT Gary W. Cook, Director of Financial Aid, Luther Rice University, 3038 Evans Mill Road, Lithonia, GA 30038-2418, 770-484-1204 Ext. 241 or toll-free 800-442-1577. *Fax:* 678-990-5388. *E-mail:* gcook@lru.edu. *Website:* http://www.lru.edu/.

LYCOMING COLLEGE
Williamsport, PA

Tuition & fees: $32,756	Average undergraduate aid package: $27,007

ABOUT THE INSTITUTION Independent United Methodist, coed. **Awards:** bachelor's degrees. 39 undergraduate majors. **Total enrollment:** 1,365. Undergraduates: 1,365. Freshmen: 321. Federal methodology is used as a basis for awarding need-based institutional aid.

UNDERGRADUATE EXPENSES for 2013–2014 Application fee: $35. **One-time required fee:** $225. **Comprehensive fee:** $42,176 includes full-time tuition ($32,096), mandatory fees ($660), and room and board ($9420). Room and board charges vary according to board plan and housing facility. **Part-time tuition:** $1003 per contact hour. Part-time tuition and fees vary according to course load.

FRESHMAN FINANCIAL AID (Fall 2012, est.) 295 applied for aid; of those 89% were deemed to have need. 100% of freshmen with need received aid; of those 22% had need fully met. **Average percent of need met:** 78% (excluding resources awarded to replace EFC). **Average financial aid package:** $27,893 (excluding resources awarded to replace EFC). 17% of all full-time freshmen had no need and received non-need-based gift aid.

UNDERGRADUATE FINANCIAL AID (Fall 2012, est.) 1,205 applied for aid; of those 93% were deemed to have need. 100% of undergraduates with need received aid; of those 28% had need fully met. **Average percent of need met:** 77% (excluding resources awarded to replace EFC). **Average financial aid package:** $27,007 (excluding resources awarded to replace EFC). 15% of all full-time undergraduates had no need and received non-need-based gift aid.

GIFT AID (NEED-BASED) Total amount: $24,092,594 (8% federal, 8% state, 82% institutional, 2% external sources). **Receiving aid:** Freshmen: 82% (264); all full-time undergraduates: 84% (1,117). **Average award:** Freshmen: $22,426; Undergraduates: $21,559. **Scholarships, grants, and awards:** Federal Pell, FSEOG, state, private, college/university gift aid from institutional funds.

GIFT AID (NON-NEED-BASED) Total amount: $3,422,362 (93% institutional, 7% external sources). **Receiving aid:** Freshmen: 13% (41). Undergraduates: 9% (123). **Average award:** Freshmen: $16,263. Undergraduates: $15,868. **Scholarships, grants, and awards by category:** Academic interests/achievement: 1,080 awards ($14,185,333 total): biological sciences, business, communication, computer science, education, English, foreign languages, general academic interests/achievements, health fields, humanities, international studies, mathematics, physical sciences, premedicine, religion/biblical studies, social sciences. Creative arts/performance: 131 awards ($308,750 total): art/fine arts, creative writing, music, theater/drama. Special achievements/activities: 40 awards ($199,350 total): community service, general special achievements/activities, leadership. Special characteristics: 53 awards ($1,161,530 total): children of educators, children of faculty/staff, relatives of clergy. **Tuition waivers:** Full or partial for employees or children of employees. **ROTC:** Army cooperative.

LOANS Student loans: $10,364,243 (74% need-based, 26% non-need-based). 85% of past graduating class borrowed through all loan programs. **Average indebtedness per student:** $35,990. **Average need-based loan:** Freshmen: $3701. Undergraduates: $4680. **Parent loans:** $4,099,876 (37% need-based, 63% non-need-based). **Programs:** Federal Direct (Subsidized and Unsubsidized Stafford, PLUS), Perkins, college/university.

WORK-STUDY Federal work-study: Total amount: $189,542; 306 jobs averaging $619.

APPLYING FOR FINANCIAL AID Required financial aid forms: FAFSA, institution's own form, state aid form. **Financial aid deadline (priority):** 3/1. **Notification date:** Continuous beginning 3/1. Students must reply by 5/1.

CONTACT Mr. James S. Lakis, Director of Financial Aid, Lycoming College, 700 College Place, Williamsport, PA 17701-5192, 570-321-4040 or toll-free 800-345-3920 Ext. 4026. Fax: 570-321-4993. E-mail: lakis@lycoming.edu. Website: http://www.lycoming.edu/.

LYME ACADEMY COLLEGE OF FINE ARTS
Old Lyme, CT

Tuition & fees: $28,536	Average undergraduate aid package: $18,021

ABOUT THE INSTITUTION Independent, coed. **Awards:** certificates and bachelor's degrees. 4 undergraduate majors. **Total enrollment:** 85. Undergraduates: 83. Freshmen: 19. Federal methodology is used as a basis for awarding need-based institutional aid.

UNDERGRADUATE EXPENSES for 2013–2014 Application fee: $55. **Comprehensive fee:** $39,336 includes full-time tuition ($26,904), mandatory fees ($1632), and room and board ($10,800). **College room only:** $7200. **Part-time tuition:** $1121 per credit. **Part-time fees:** $68 per credit. Part-time tuition and fees vary according to course load.

FRESHMAN FINANCIAL AID (Fall 2012, est.) 15 applied for aid; of those 100% were deemed to have need. 100% of freshmen with need received aid. **Average financial aid package:** $18,949 (excluding resources awarded to replace EFC). 20% of all full-time freshmen had no need and received non-need-based gift aid.

UNDERGRADUATE FINANCIAL AID (Fall 2012, est.) 69 applied for aid; of those 100% were deemed to have need. 100% of undergraduates with need received aid. **Average financial aid package:** $18,021 (excluding resources awarded to replace EFC). 22% of all full-time undergraduates had no need and received non-need-based gift aid.

GIFT AID (NEED-BASED) Total amount: $918,173 (17% federal, 5% state, 70% institutional, 8% external sources). **Average award:** Freshmen: $8485; Undergraduates: $8125. **Scholarships, grants, and awards:** Federal Pell, FSEOG, state, private, college/university gift aid from institutional funds.

GIFT AID (NON-NEED-BASED) Average award: Freshmen: $8000. Undergraduates: $6000. **Scholarships, grants, and awards by category:** Creative arts/performance: art/fine arts. **Tuition waivers:** Full or partial for employees or children of employees.

LOANS Student loans: $379,981 (52% need-based, 48% non-need-based). 65% of past graduating class borrowed through all loan programs. **Average indebtedness per student:** $31,000. **Average need-based loan:** Freshmen: $3500. Undergraduates: $4700. **Parent loans:** $110,782 (100% need-based). **Programs:** Federal Direct (Subsidized and Unsubsidized Stafford, PLUS), CHESLA alternative loans.

WORK-STUDY Federal work-study: Total amount: $5666; 9 jobs averaging $839. **State or other work-study/employment:** Total amount: $3000 (100% need-based). 2 part-time jobs averaging $1345.

APPLYING FOR FINANCIAL AID Required financial aid form: FAFSA. **Financial aid deadline (priority):** 2/15. **Notification date:** Continuous beginning 3/1. Students must reply by 5/1 or within 2 weeks of notification.

CONTACT Mr. Stephen Podeszwa, Director of Financial Aid, Lyme Academy College of Fine Arts, 84 Lyme Street, Old Lyme, CT 06371, 860-434-3571 Ext. 114. Fax: 860-434-8725. E-mail: spodeszwa@lymeacademy.edu. Website: http://www.lymeacademy.edu/.

LYNCHBURG COLLEGE
Lynchburg, VA

Tuition & fees: $32,005	Average undergraduate aid package: $23,045

ABOUT THE INSTITUTION Independent Christian Church (Disciples of Christ), coed. **Awards:** certificates, bachelor's, master's, and doctoral degrees. 37 undergraduate majors. **Total enrollment:** 2,756. Undergraduates: 2,211. Freshmen: 517. Federal methodology is used as a basis for awarding need-based institutional aid.

UNDERGRADUATE EXPENSES for 2013–2014 Application fee: $30. **Comprehensive fee:** $40,685 includes full-time tuition ($31,060), mandatory fees ($945), and room and board ($8680). **College room only:** $4360. Room and board charges vary according to board plan and housing facility. **Part-time tuition:** $430 per credit hour. **Part-time fees:** $5.10 per credit hour. Part-time tuition and fees vary according to course load. **Payment plan:** Tuition prepayment.

FRESHMAN FINANCIAL AID (Fall 2012, est.) 484 applied for aid; of those 86% were deemed to have need. 100% of freshmen with need received aid; of those 18% had need fully met. *Average percent of need met:* 82% (excluding resources awarded to replace EFC). *Average financial aid package:* $25,181 (excluding resources awarded to replace EFC). 18% of all full-time freshmen had no need and received non-need-based gift aid.

UNDERGRADUATE FINANCIAL AID (Fall 2012, est.) 1,762 applied for aid; of those 89% were deemed to have need. 100% of undergraduates with need received aid; of those 18% had need fully met. *Average percent of need met:* 77% (excluding resources awarded to replace EFC). *Average financial aid package:* $23,045 (excluding resources awarded to replace EFC). 21% of all full-time undergraduates had no need and received non-need-based gift aid.

GIFT AID (NEED-BASED) *Total amount:* $29,739,775 (10% federal, 9% state, 78% institutional, 3% external sources). *Receiving aid:* Freshmen: 80% (416); all full-time undergraduates: 75% (1,566). *Average award:* Freshmen: $21,291; Undergraduates: $19,268. *Scholarships, grants, and awards:* Federal Pell, FSEOG, state, private, college/university gift aid from institutional funds.

GIFT AID (NON-NEED-BASED) *Total amount:* $2,150,681 (1% federal, 46% state, 27% institutional, 26% external sources). *Receiving aid:* Freshmen: 10% (51). Undergraduates: 9% (187). *Average award:* Freshmen: $11,663. Undergraduates: $11,183. *Scholarships, grants, and awards by category:* Academic interests/achievement: general academic interests/achievements. Creative arts/performance: art/fine arts, music, theater/drama. *Tuition waivers:* Full or partial for employees or children of employees, adult students, senior citizens.

LOANS *Student loans:* $14,885,385 (63% need-based, 37% non-need-based). 74% of past graduating class borrowed through all loan programs. *Average indebtedness per student:* $33,353. *Average need-based loan:* Freshmen: $3607. Undergraduates: $3644. *Parent loans:* $4,403,393 (55% need-based, 45% non-need-based). *Programs:* Federal Direct (Subsidized and Unsubsidized Stafford, PLUS), Perkins.

WORK-STUDY *Federal work-study:* Total amount: $225,653; 431 jobs averaging $1267. *State or other work-study/employment:* Total amount: $576,575 (30% need-based, 70% non-need-based). 300 part-time jobs averaging $1700.

APPLYING FOR FINANCIAL AID *Required financial aid forms:* FAFSA, state aid form. *Financial aid deadline (priority):* 3/5. *Notification date:* Continuous beginning 3/5. Students must reply by 5/1 or within 2 weeks of notification.

CONTACT Mrs. Michelle Davis, Director of Financial Aid, Lynchburg College, 1501 Lakeside Drive, Lynchburg, VA 24501-3199, 434-544-8228 or toll-free 800-426-8101. *Fax:* 434-544-8653.

Website: http://www.lynchburg.edu/.

LYNDON STATE COLLEGE
Lyndonville, VT

CONTACT Student Services Consultant, Lyndon State College, 1001 College Road, Lyndonville, VT 05851, 802-626-6396 or toll-free 800-225-1998. *Fax:* 802-626-9770. *E-mail:* financialaid@lyndonstate.edu.

Website: http://www.lyndonstate.edu/.

LYNN UNIVERSITY
Boca Raton, FL

Tuition & fees: $33,400	Average undergraduate aid package: $19,097

ABOUT THE INSTITUTION Independent, coed. *Awards:* certificates, bachelor's, master's, and doctoral degrees. 35 undergraduate majors. *Total enrollment:* 2,097. Undergraduates: 1,657. Freshmen: 409. Federal methodology is used as a basis for awarding need-based institutional aid.

UNDERGRADUATE EXPENSES for 2013–2014 *Application fee:* $45. *Comprehensive fee:* $44,300 includes full-time tuition ($31,900), mandatory fees ($1500), and room and board ($10,900). Full-time tuition and fees vary according to reciprocity agreements. Room and board charges vary according to board plan and housing facility. *Part-time tuition:* $925 per credit. Part-time tuition and fees vary according to class time and course load.

FRESHMAN FINANCIAL AID (Fall 2012, est.) 324 applied for aid; of those 57% were deemed to have need. 99% of freshmen with need received aid; of those 100%

had need fully met. *Average percent of need met:* 50% (excluding resources awarded to replace EFC). *Average financial aid package:* $17,544 (excluding resources awarded to replace EFC). 23% of all full-time freshmen had no need and received non-need-based gift aid.

UNDERGRADUATE FINANCIAL AID (Fall 2012, est.) 1,117 applied for aid; of those 59% were deemed to have need. 99% of undergraduates with need received aid; of those 100% had need fully met. *Average percent of need met:* 52% (excluding resources awarded to replace EFC). *Average financial aid package:* $19,097 (excluding resources awarded to replace EFC). 18% of all full-time undergraduates had no need and received non-need-based gift aid.

GIFT AID (NEED-BASED) *Total amount:* $7,075,910 (22% federal, 12% state, 65% institutional, 1% external sources). *Receiving aid:* Freshmen: 33% (144); all full-time undergraduates: 35% (524). *Average award:* Freshmen: $10,108; Undergraduates: $10,250. *Scholarships, grants, and awards:* Federal Pell, FSEOG, state, private, college/university gift aid from institutional funds.

GIFT AID (NON-NEED-BASED) *Total amount:* $3,064,457 (4% state, 94% institutional, 2% external sources). *Receiving aid:* Freshmen: 37% (158). Undergraduates: 38% (570). *Average award:* Freshmen: $10,639. Undergraduates: $11,387. *Scholarships, grants, and awards by category:* Academic interests/achievement: 581 awards ($5,506,746 total): business, communication, general academic interests/achievements, international studies. Creative arts/performance: music. Special achievements/activities: 2 awards ($20,000 total): leadership. Special characteristics: 301 awards ($2,034,180 total): children and siblings of alumni, children of educators, children of faculty/staff, out-of-state students, siblings of current students. *Tuition waivers:* Full or partial for employees or children of employees. *ROTC:* Air Force cooperative.

LOANS *Student loans:* $4,974,603 (89% need-based, 11% non-need-based). 35% of past graduating class borrowed through all loan programs. *Average indebtedness per student:* $33,472. *Average need-based loan:* Freshmen: $4012. Undergraduates: $4920. *Parent loans:* $4,225,308 (90% need-based, 10% non-need-based). *Programs:* Federal Direct (Subsidized and Unsubsidized Stafford, PLUS), Perkins, state, college/university.

WORK-STUDY *Federal work-study:* Total amount: $166,449; 82 jobs averaging $2030. *State or other work-study/employment:* Total amount: $275,504 (63% need-based, 37% non-need-based). 37 part-time jobs averaging $7446.

ATHLETIC AWARDS Total amount: $2,868,870 (60% need-based, 40% non-need-based).

APPLYING FOR FINANCIAL AID *Required financial aid form:* FAFSA. *Financial aid deadline (priority):* 3/1. *Notification date:* Continuous beginning 2/1. Students must reply within 2 weeks of notification.

CONTACT Mrs. Chan Park, Director of Student Financial Assistance, Lynn University, 3601 North Military Trail, Boca Raton, FL 33431-5598, 561-237-7186 or toll-free 800-888-5966. *Fax:* 561-237-7189. *E-mail:* cpark@lynn.edu. *Website:* http://www.lynn.edu/.

LYON COLLEGE
Batesville, AR

Tuition & fees: $23,594	Average undergraduate aid package: $21,897

ABOUT THE INSTITUTION Independent Presbyterian, coed. *Awards:* bachelor's degrees. 16 undergraduate majors. *Total enrollment:* 600. Undergraduates: 600. Freshmen: 160. Federal methodology is used as a basis for awarding need-based institutional aid.

UNDERGRADUATE EXPENSES for 2013–2014 *Application fee:* $25. *Comprehensive fee:* $31,154 includes full-time tuition ($23,370), mandatory fees ($224), and room and board ($7560). Room and board charges vary according to board plan and housing facility. *Part-time tuition:* $780 per credit hour.

FRESHMAN FINANCIAL AID (Fall 2012, est.) 142 applied for aid; of those 89% were deemed to have need. 100% of freshmen with need received aid; of those 31% had need fully met. *Average percent of need met:* 86% (excluding resources awarded to replace EFC). *Average financial aid package:* $22,627 (excluding resources awarded to replace EFC). 9% of all full-time freshmen had no need and received non-need-based gift aid.

UNDERGRADUATE FINANCIAL AID (Fall 2012, est.) 506 applied for aid; of those 89% were deemed to have need. 100% of undergraduates with need received aid; of those 24% had need fully met. *Average percent of need met:* 81% (excluding resources awarded to replace EFC). *Average financial aid package:*

$21,897 (excluding resources awarded to replace EFC). 12% of all full-time undergraduates had no need and received non-need-based gift aid.
GIFT AID (NEED-BASED) *Total amount:* $6,741,035 (18% federal, 16% state, 61% institutional, 5% external sources). *Receiving aid:* Freshmen: 81% (127); all full-time undergraduates: 78% (452). *Average award:* Freshmen: $19,909; Undergraduates: $18,274. *Scholarships, grants, and awards:* Federal Pell, FSEOG, state, private, college/university gift aid from institutional funds.
GIFT AID (NON-NEED-BASED) *Total amount:* $1,901,231 (1% federal, 30% state, 61% institutional, 8% external sources). *Receiving aid:* Freshmen: 24% (37). Undergraduates: 18% (102). *Average award:* Freshmen: $13,416. Undergraduates: $13,164. *Scholarships, grants, and awards by category:* Academic interests/achievement: 329 awards ($3,594,857 total): business, general academic interests/achievements. Creative arts/performance: 25 awards ($144,250 total): art/fine arts, music, theater/drama. Special achievements/activities: 12 awards ($105,406 total): cheerleading/drum major, general special achievements/activities. Special characteristics: 19 awards ($222,890 total): children of faculty/staff, ethnic background, first-generation college students, local/state students, members of minority groups, religious affiliation. *Tuition waivers:* Full or partial for employees or children of employees.
LOANS *Student loans:* $2,936,791 (79% need-based, 21% non-need-based). 72% of past graduating class borrowed through all loan programs. *Average indebtedness per student:* $17,179. *Average need-based loan:* Freshmen: $3279. Undergraduates: $4506. *Parent loans:* $374,850 (31% need-based, 69% non-need-based). *Programs:* Federal Direct (Subsidized and Unsubsidized Stafford, PLUS), Perkins.
WORK-STUDY *Federal work-study:* Total amount: $120,925; 157 jobs averaging $921. *State or other work-study/employment:* Total amount: $4000 (100% non-need-based). 4 part-time jobs averaging $1000.
ATHLETIC AWARDS Total amount: $2,466,623 (55% need-based, 45% non-need-based).
APPLYING FOR FINANCIAL AID *Required financial aid form:* FAFSA. *Financial aid deadline (priority):* 3/15. *Notification date:* Continuous beginning 9/1. Students must reply by 8/15.
CONTACT Mr. Tommy Tucker, Director of Student Assistance, Lyon College, 2300 Highland Road, Batesville, AR 72501, 870-307-7257 or toll-free 800-423-2542. *Fax:* 870-307-7542. *E-mail:* financialaid@lyon.edu.
Website: http://www.lyon.edu/.

MACALESTER COLLEGE
St. Paul, MN

Tuition & fees: $45,388	Average undergraduate aid package: $37,519

ABOUT THE INSTITUTION Independent Presbyterian, coed. *Awards:* bachelor's degrees. 35 undergraduate majors. *Total enrollment:* 2,070. Undergraduates: 2,070. Freshmen: 534. Both federal and institutional methodology are used as a basis for awarding need-based institutional aid.
UNDERGRADUATE EXPENSES for 2013–2014 *Application fee:* $40. *Comprehensive fee:* $55,456 includes full-time tuition ($45,167), mandatory fees ($221), and room and board ($10,068). *College room only:* $5412. Full-time tuition and fees vary according to course load. Room and board charges vary according to board plan and housing facility. *Part-time tuition:* $1411 per credit. Part-time tuition and fees vary according to course load.
FRESHMAN FINANCIAL AID (Fall 2012, est.) 439 applied for aid; of those 90% were deemed to have need. 100% of freshmen with need received aid; of those 100% had need fully met. *Average percent of need met:* 100% (excluding resources awarded to replace EFC). *Average financial aid package:* $37,945 (excluding resources awarded to replace EFC). 4% of all full-time freshmen had no need and received non-need-based gift aid.
UNDERGRADUATE FINANCIAL AID (Fall 2012, est.) 1,619 applied for aid; of those 90% were deemed to have need. 100% of undergraduates with need received aid; of those 100% had need fully met. *Average percent of need met:* 100% (excluding resources awarded to replace EFC). *Average financial aid package:* $37,519 (excluding resources awarded to replace EFC). 5% of all full-time undergraduates had no need and received non-need-based gift aid.
GIFT AID (NEED-BASED) *Total amount:* $47,052,112 (4% federal, 1% state, 93% institutional, 2% external sources). *Receiving aid:* Freshmen: 74% (395); all full-time undergraduates: 72% (1,457). *Average award:* Freshmen: $33,450; Undergrad-

uates: $31,864. *Scholarships, grants, and awards:* Federal Pell, FSEOG, state, private, college/university gift aid from institutional funds.
GIFT AID (NON-NEED-BASED) *Total amount:* $1,254,141 (75% institutional, 25% external sources). *Receiving aid:* Freshmen: 7% (36). Undergraduates: 4% (83). *Average award:* Freshmen: $10,425. Undergraduates: $9729. *Scholarships, grants, and awards by category:* Academic interests/achievement: general academic interests/achievements. Special characteristics: ethnic background. *Tuition waivers:* Full or partial for employees or children of employees. *ROTC:* Army cooperative, Naval cooperative, Air Force cooperative.
LOANS *Student loans:* $8,067,721 (93% need-based, 7% non-need-based). 60% of past graduating class borrowed through all loan programs. *Average indebtedness per student:* $23,285. *Average need-based loan:* Freshmen: $3436. Undergraduates: $4197. *Parent loans:* $1,351,084 (100% non-need-based). *Programs:* Federal Direct (Subsidized and Unsubsidized Stafford, PLUS), Perkins, state.
WORK-STUDY *Federal work-study:* Total amount: $500,972; jobs available. *State or other work-study/employment:* Total amount: $2,806,305 (96% need-based, 4% non-need-based). Part-time jobs available.
APPLYING FOR FINANCIAL AID *Required financial aid forms:* FAFSA, CSS Financial Aid PROFILE, noncustodial (divorced/separated) parent's statement, federal income tax form(s). *Financial aid deadline:* 3/1 (priority: 2/8). *Notification date:* 4/1. Students must reply by 5/1.
CONTACT Financial Aid Office, Macalester College, 1600 Grand Avenue, St. Paul, MN 55105, 651-696-6214 or toll-free 800-231-7974. *Fax:* 651-696-6866. *E-mail:* finaid@macalester.edu.
Website: http://www.macalester.edu/.

MACHZIKEI HADATH RABBINICAL COLLEGE
Brooklyn, NY

CONTACT Rabbi Baruch Rozmarin, Director of Financial Aid, Machzikei Hadath Rabbinical College, 5407 16th Avenue, Brooklyn, NY 11204-1805, 718-854-8777.

MACMURRAY COLLEGE
Jacksonville, IL

Tuition & fees: $21,400	Average undergraduate aid package: $18,624

ABOUT THE INSTITUTION Independent United Methodist, coed. 30 undergraduate majors. Federal methodology is used as a basis for awarding need-based institutional aid.
UNDERGRADUATE EXPENSES for 2013–2014 *Comprehensive fee:* $29,050 includes full-time tuition ($20,900), mandatory fees ($500), and room and board ($7650). Full-time tuition and fees vary according to course load. Room and board charges vary according to housing facility. *Part-time tuition:* $693 per credit hour. *Part-time fees:* $30 per credit hour. Part-time tuition and fees vary according to course load.
FRESHMAN FINANCIAL AID (Fall 2012, est.) 139 applied for aid; of those 96% were deemed to have need. 100% of freshmen with need received aid; of those 14% had need fully met. *Average percent of need met:* 80% (excluding resources awarded to replace EFC). *Average financial aid package:* $20,568 (excluding resources awarded to replace EFC). 8% of all full-time freshmen had no need and received non-need-based gift aid.
UNDERGRADUATE FINANCIAL AID (Fall 2012, est.) 549 applied for aid; of those 96% were deemed to have need. 100% of undergraduates with need received aid; of those 12% had need fully met. *Average percent of need met:* 75% (excluding resources awarded to replace EFC). *Average financial aid package:* $18,624 (excluding resources awarded to replace EFC). 6% of all full-time undergraduates had no need and received non-need-based gift aid.
GIFT AID (NEED-BASED) *Total amount:* $6,740,580 (25% federal, 18% state, 55% institutional, 2% external sources). *Receiving aid:* Freshmen: 92% (133); all full-time undergraduates: 91% (515). *Average award:* Freshmen: $14,618; Undergraduates: $12,922. *Scholarships, grants, and awards:* Federal Pell, FSEOG, state, private, college/university gift aid from institutional funds.

GIFT AID (NON-NEED-BASED) *Total amount:* $384,290 (96% institutional, 4% external sources). *Receiving aid:* Freshmen: 8% (12). Undergraduates: 6% (33). *Average award:* Freshmen: $7327. Undergraduates: $7238. *Scholarships, grants, and awards by category:* Academic interests/achievement: 439 awards ($2,228,556 total): general academic interests/achievements. *Special achievements/activities:* 25 awards ($91,520 total): leadership, memberships, religious involvement. *Special characteristics:* 33 awards ($77,013 total): children and siblings of alumni, children of faculty/staff, siblings of current students, veterans. *Tuition waivers:* Full or partial for children of alumni, employees or children of employees, adult students, senior citizens.

LOANS *Student loans:* $5,675,777 (81% need-based, 19% non-need-based). 87% of past graduating class borrowed through all loan programs. *Average indebtedness per student:* $36,658. *Average need-based loan:* Freshmen: $5122. Undergraduates: $5151. *Parent loans:* $644,978 (52% need-based, 48% non-need-based). *Programs:* Federal Direct (Subsidized and Unsubsidized Stafford, PLUS), Perkins.

WORK-STUDY *Federal work-study:* Total amount: $629,132; 348 jobs averaging $1532.

APPLYING FOR FINANCIAL AID *Required financial aid form:* FAFSA. *Financial aid deadline (priority):* 3/1. *Notification date:* Continuous beginning 3/1. Students must reply within 2 weeks of notification.

CONTACT Mrs. Laci N. Engelbrecht, Director of Financial Aid, MacMurray College, 447 East College Avenue, Jacksonville, IL 62650, 217-479-7041 or toll-free 800-252-7485. *Fax:* 217-291-0702. *E-mail:* financialaid@mac.edu. *Website:* http://www.mac.edu/.

MADONNA UNIVERSITY
Livonia, MI

CONTACT Cathy Durham, Financial Aid Secretary, Madonna University, 36600 Schoolcraft Road, Livonia, MI 48150-1173, 734-432-5663 or toll-free 800-852-4951. *Fax:* 734-432-5344. *E-mail:* finaid@madonna.edu. *Website:* http://www.madonna.edu/.

MAHARISHI UNIVERSITY OF MANAGEMENT
Fairfield, IA

CONTACT Mr. Bill Christensen, Director of Financial Aid, Maharishi University of Management, 1000 North 4th Street, DB 1127, Fairfield, IA 52557-1127, 641-472-1156 or toll-free 800-369-6480. *Fax:* 641-472-1133. *E-mail:* bchrist@mum.edu. *Website:* http://www.mum.edu/.

MAINE COLLEGE OF ART
Portland, ME

CONTACT Adrienne J. Amari, Director of Financial Aid, Maine College of Art, 522 Congress Street, Portland, ME 04101-3987, 207-775-3052 Ext. 5073 or toll-free 800-699-1509. *Fax:* 207-772-5069. *E-mail:* aamari@meca.edu. *Website:* http://www.meca.edu/.

MAINE MARITIME ACADEMY
Castine, ME

Tuition & fees (ME res): $11,525	Average undergraduate aid package: $9455

ABOUT THE INSTITUTION State-supported, coed, primarily men. *Awards:* associate, bachelor's, and master's degrees. 11 undergraduate majors. *Total enrollment:* 1,013. Undergraduates: 993. Freshmen: 320. Federal methodology is used as a basis for awarding need-based institutional aid.

UNDERGRADUATE EXPENSES for 2013–2014 *Tuition, state resident:* full-time $8800; part-time $334 per credit. *Tuition, nonresident:* full-time $18,800; part-time $645 per credit. *Required fees:* full-time $2725. Full-time tuition and fees vary according to course load and program. Part-time tuition and fees vary according to course load and program. *College room and board:* $9548; *Room only:* $3628. Room and board charges vary according to board plan.

FRESHMAN FINANCIAL AID (Fall 2012, est.) 201 applied for aid; of those 90% were deemed to have need. 98% of freshmen with need received aid; of those 11% had need fully met. *Average percent of need met:* 41% (excluding resources awarded to replace EFC). *Average financial aid package:* $8610 (excluding resources awarded to replace EFC). 2% of all full-time freshmen had no need and received non-need-based gift aid.

UNDERGRADUATE FINANCIAL AID (Fall 2012, est.) 849 applied for aid; of those 88% were deemed to have need. 99% of undergraduates with need received aid; of those 11% had need fully met. *Average percent of need met:* 47% (excluding resources awarded to replace EFC). *Average financial aid package:* $9455 (excluding resources awarded to replace EFC). 4% of all full-time undergraduates had no need and received non-need-based gift aid.

GIFT AID (NEED-BASED) *Total amount:* $2,949,252 (43% federal, 13% state, 22% institutional, 22% external sources). *Receiving aid:* Freshmen: 75% (150); all full-time undergraduates: 66% (562). *Average award:* Freshmen: $5879; Undergraduates: $6296. *Scholarships, grants, and awards:* Federal Pell, FSEOG, state, private, college/university gift aid from institutional funds.

GIFT AID (NON-NEED-BASED) *Total amount:* $999,347 (2% state, 80% institutional, 18% external sources). *Receiving aid:* Freshmen: 4% (9). Undergraduates: 4% (30). *Average award:* Freshmen: $4900. Undergraduates: $4001. *Scholarships, grants, and awards by category:* Academic interests/achievement: 182 awards ($637,247 total): biological sciences, business, engineering/technologies, general academic interests/achievements. *Special characteristics:* 7 awards ($61,600 total): children of faculty/staff. *ROTC:* Army cooperative, Naval.

LOANS *Student loans:* $9,881,293 (72% need-based, 28% non-need-based). 80% of past graduating class borrowed through all loan programs. *Average indebtedness per student:* $41,672. *Average need-based loan:* Freshmen: $3470. Undergraduates: $4770. *Parent loans:* $2,288,499 (46% need-based, 54% non-need-based). *Programs:* Federal Direct (Subsidized and Unsubsidized Stafford, PLUS), Perkins, college/university, alternative loans.

WORK-STUDY *Federal work-study:* Total amount: $106,092; 342 jobs averaging $788.

APPLYING FOR FINANCIAL AID *Required financial aid form:* FAFSA. *Financial aid deadline (priority):* 4/1. *Notification date:* Continuous beginning 4/1. Students must reply within 4 weeks of notification.

CONTACT Mrs. Kathy S. Heath, Director of Financial Aid, Maine Maritime Academy, Pleasant Street, Castine, ME 04420, 207-326-2205 or toll-free 800-464-6565 (in-state), 800-227-8465 (out-of-state). *Fax:* 207-326-2515. *E-mail:* bbayle@mma.edu. *Website:* http://www.mainemaritime.edu/.

MALONE UNIVERSITY
Canton, OH

Tuition & fees: $25,678	Average undergraduate aid package: $19,284

ABOUT THE INSTITUTION Independent Evangelical Friends Church–Eastern Region, coed. *Awards:* certificates, bachelor's, and master's degrees. 45 undergraduate majors. *Total enrollment:* 2,373. Undergraduates: 1,897. Freshmen: 353. Federal methodology is used as a basis for awarding need-based institutional aid.

UNDERGRADUATE EXPENSES for 2013–2014 *Application fee:* $20. *Comprehensive fee:* $34,334 includes full-time tuition ($24,934), mandatory fees ($744), and room and board ($8656). *College room only:* $4412. Room and board charges vary according to board plan. *Part-time tuition:* $445 per hour. Part-time tuition and fees vary according to course load.

FRESHMAN FINANCIAL AID (Fall 2012, est.) 336 applied for aid; of those 96% were deemed to have need. 100% of freshmen with need received aid; of those 18% had need fully met. *Average percent of need met:* 79% (excluding resources awarded to replace EFC). *Average financial aid package:* $21,790 (excluding resources awarded to replace EFC). 9% of all full-time freshmen had no need and received non-need-based gift aid.

UNDERGRADUATE FINANCIAL AID (Fall 2012, est.) 1,400 applied for aid; of those 95% were deemed to have need. 100% of undergraduates with need received

aid; of those 15% had need fully met. *Average percent of need met:* 72% (excluding resources awarded to replace EFC). *Average financial aid package:* $19,284 (excluding resources awarded to replace EFC). 11% of all full-time undergraduates had no need and received non-need-based gift aid.

GIFT AID (NEED-BASED) *Total amount:* $17,866,365 (19% federal, 6% state, 72% institutional, 3% external sources). *Receiving aid:* Freshmen: 92% (323); all full-time undergraduates: 79% (1,312). *Average award:* Freshmen: $18,204; Undergraduates: $15,450. *Scholarships, grants, and awards:* Federal Pell, FSEOG, state, private, college/university gift aid from institutional funds.

GIFT AID (NON-NEED-BASED) *Total amount:* $2,231,003 (2% federal, 92% institutional, 6% external sources). *Receiving aid:* Freshmen: 12% (41). Undergraduates: 7% (122). *Average award:* Freshmen: $9394. Undergraduates: $9167. *Scholarships, grants, and awards by category:* Academic interests/achievement: 1,409 awards ($10,174,630 total): biological sciences, business, communication, computer science, education, English, foreign languages, general academic interests/achievements, health fields, humanities, international studies, mathematics, physical sciences, premedicine, religion/biblical studies, social sciences. Creative arts/performance: 64 awards ($116,900 total): debating, journalism/publications, music, theater/drama. Special achievements/activities: 84 awards ($214,500 total): community service, general special achievements/activities, leadership, religious involvement. Special characteristics: 76 awards ($1,174,409 total): children and siblings of alumni, children of faculty/staff, general special characteristics, international students, parents of current students, relatives of clergy, religious affiliation, siblings of current students, spouses of current students, veterans. *Tuition waivers:* Full or partial for employees or children of employees, senior citizens. *ROTC:* Army cooperative, Air Force cooperative.

LOANS *Student loans:* $11,427,443 (81% need-based, 19% non-need-based). 79% of past graduating class borrowed through all loan programs. *Average indebtedness per student:* $33,263. *Average need-based loan:* Freshmen: $3592. Undergraduates: $4366. *Parent loans:* $2,513,843 (43% need-based, 57% non-need-based). *Programs:* Federal Direct (Subsidized and Unsubsidized Stafford, PLUS), Perkins, state, college/university, alternative loans.

WORK-STUDY *Federal work-study:* Total amount: $543,064; 337 jobs averaging $1970.

ATHLETIC AWARDS Total amount: $3,134,447 (67% need-based, 33% non-need-based).

APPLYING FOR FINANCIAL AID *Required financial aid form:* FAFSA. *Financial aid deadline:* 7/31 (priority: 3/1). *Notification date:* Continuous beginning 3/1. Students must reply within 2 weeks of notification.

CONTACT Mrs. Pamela Pustay, Director of Financial Aid, Malone University, 2600 Cleveland Avenue NW, Canton, OH 44709, 330-471-8161 or toll-free 800-521-1146. *Fax:* 330-471-8652. *E-mail:* ppustay@malone.edu. *Website:* http://www.malone.edu/.

MANCHESTER UNIVERSITY
North Manchester, IN

Tuition & fees: $27,920	Average undergraduate aid package: $24,423

ABOUT THE INSTITUTION Independent Church of the Brethren, coed. *Awards:* certificates, associate, bachelor's, master's, and doctoral degrees. 85 undergraduate majors. *Total enrollment:* 1,345. Undergraduates: 1,257. Freshmen: 372. Federal methodology is used as a basis for awarding need-based institutional aid.

UNDERGRADUATE EXPENSES for 2013–2014 *Application fee:* $25. *One-time required fee:* $250. *Comprehensive fee:* $37,170 includes full-time tuition ($27,000), mandatory fees ($920), and room and board ($9250). *College room only:* $5500. Room and board charges vary according to board plan and housing facility. *Part-time tuition:* $700 per credit hour. *Part-time fees:* $25. Part-time tuition and fees vary according to course load.

FRESHMAN FINANCIAL AID (Fall 2012, est.) 359 applied for aid; of those 94% were deemed to have need. 100% of freshmen with need received aid; of those 26% had need fully met. *Average financial aid package:* $24,401 (excluding resources awarded to replace EFC). 7% of all full-time freshmen had no need and received non-need-based gift aid.

UNDERGRADUATE FINANCIAL AID (Fall 2012, est.) 1,139 applied for aid; of those 94% were deemed to have need. 100% of undergraduates with need received aid; of those 24% had need fully met. *Average financial aid package:* $24,423

(excluding resources awarded to replace EFC). 6% of all full-time undergraduates had no need and received non-need-based gift aid.

GIFT AID (NEED-BASED) *Total amount:* $21,905,680 (8% federal, 10% state, 78% institutional, 4% external sources). *Receiving aid:* Freshmen: 91% (338); all full-time undergraduates: 87% (1,068). *Average award:* Freshmen: $20,173; Undergraduates: $19,591. *Scholarships, grants, and awards:* Federal Pell, FSEOG, state, private, college/university gift aid from institutional funds.

GIFT AID (NON-NEED-BASED) *Total amount:* $1,172,199 (95% institutional, 5% external sources). *Receiving aid:* Freshmen: 6% (22). Undergraduates: 4% (53). *Average award:* Freshmen: $15,158. Undergraduates: $14,241. *Scholarships, grants, and awards by category:* Academic interests/achievement: business, English, foreign languages, general academic interests/achievements, humanities. Creative arts/performance: music, theater/drama. Special achievements/activities: leadership. Special characteristics: children and siblings of alumni, ethnic background, international students, local/state students, members of minority groups, previous college experience, religious affiliation. *Tuition waivers:* Full or partial for employees or children of employees.

LOANS *Student loans:* 85% of past graduating class borrowed through all loan programs. *Average indebtedness per student:* $29,039. *Average need-based loan:* Freshmen: $3381. Undergraduates: $4218. *Parent loans:* $9,458,813 (57% need-based, 43% non-need-based). *Programs:* Federal Direct (Subsidized and Unsubsidized Stafford, PLUS), Perkins.

WORK-STUDY *Federal work-study:* Total amount: $1,383,867; jobs available. *State or other work-study/employment:* Part-time jobs available.

APPLYING FOR FINANCIAL AID *Required financial aid form:* FAFSA. *Financial aid deadline (priority):* 3/1. *Notification date:* Continuous beginning 3/15. Students must reply by 5/1 or within 3 weeks of notification.

CONTACT Mrs. Sherri Shockey, Director of Student Financial Services, Manchester University, 604 East College Avenue, North Manchester, IN 46962-1225, 260-982-5066 or toll-free 800-852-3648. *Fax:* 260-982-5043. *E-mail:* slshockey@manchester.edu. *Website:* http://www.manchester.edu/.

MANHATTAN CHRISTIAN COLLEGE
Manhattan, KS

CONTACT Mrs. Margaret Carlisle, Director of Financial Aid, Manhattan Christian College, 1415 Anderson Avenue, Manhattan, KS 66502-4081, 785-539-3571 or toll-free 877-246-4622. *E-mail:* carlisle@mccks.edu. *Website:* http://www.mccks.edu/.

MANHATTAN COLLEGE
Riverdale, NY

Tuition & fees: $35,725	Average undergraduate aid package: $20,131

ABOUT THE INSTITUTION Independent Roman Catholic Church, coed. *Awards:* certificates, bachelor's, and master's degrees. 43 undergraduate majors. *Total enrollment:* 3,800. Undergraduates: 3,351. Freshmen: 842. Federal methodology is used as a basis for awarding need-based institutional aid.

UNDERGRADUATE EXPENSES for 2013–2014 *Application fee:* $60. *Comprehensive fee:* $48,805 includes full-time tuition ($33,000), mandatory fees ($2725), and room and board ($13,080). Full-time tuition and fees vary according to course load, program, and student level. Room and board charges vary according to board plan. Part-time tuition and fees vary according to course load.

FRESHMAN FINANCIAL AID (Fall 2012, est.) 747 applied for aid; of those 85% were deemed to have need. 99% of freshmen with need received aid; of those 11% had need fully met. *Average percent of need met:* 69% (excluding resources awarded to replace EFC). *Average financial aid package:* $22,566 (excluding resources awarded to replace EFC). 15% of all full-time freshmen had no need and received non-need-based gift aid.

UNDERGRADUATE FINANCIAL AID (Fall 2012, est.) 2,605 applied for aid; of those 87% were deemed to have need. 99% of undergraduates with need received aid; of those 12% had need fully met. *Average percent of need met:* 67% (excluding resources awarded to replace EFC). *Average financial aid package:* $20,131

(excluding resources awarded to replace EFC). 16% of all full-time undergraduates had no need and received non-need-based gift aid.

GIFT AID (NEED-BASED) *Total amount:* $35,902,356 (12% federal, 9% state, 78% institutional, 1% external sources). *Receiving aid:* Freshmen: 74% (627); all full-time undergraduates: 81% (2,200). *Average award:* Freshmen: $18,589; Undergraduates: $16,015. *Scholarships, grants, and awards:* Federal Pell, FSEOG, state, private, college/university gift aid from institutional funds.

GIFT AID (NON-NEED-BASED) *Total amount:* $4,502,688 (4% state, 94% institutional, 2% external sources). *Receiving aid:* Freshmen: 5% (41). Undergraduates: 5% (124). *Average award:* Freshmen: $10,650. Undergraduates: $9875. *Scholarships, grants, and awards by category: Academic interests/ achievement:* biological sciences, business, computer science, foreign languages, general academic interests/achievements, mathematics, military science. *Creative arts/ performance:* music. *Special achievements/activities:* community service, leadership. *Special characteristics:* children of faculty/staff. *Tuition waivers:* Full or partial for employees or children of employees. *ROTC:* Army cooperative, Air Force.

LOANS *Student loans:* $20,156,896 (90% need-based, 10% non-need-based). 73% of past graduating class borrowed through all loan programs. *Average indebtedness per student:* $34,189. *Average need-based loan:* Freshmen: $2756. Undergraduates: $4428. *Parent loans:* $7,777,273 (91% need-based, 9% non-need-based). *Programs:* Federal Direct (Subsidized and Unsubsidized Stafford, PLUS), Perkins.

WORK-STUDY *Federal work-study:* Total amount: $600,000; jobs available. *State or other work-study/employment:* Total amount: $285,000 (100% non-need-based). Part-time jobs available.

ATHLETIC AWARDS Total amount: $4,242,113 (50% need-based, 50% non-need-based).

APPLYING FOR FINANCIAL AID *Required financial aid forms:* FAFSA, institution's own form, state aid form. *Financial aid deadline (priority):* 3/1. *Notification date:* 4/1. Students must reply by 5/1.

CONTACT Mr. Edward Keough, Director of Student Financial Services, Manhattan College, 4513 Manhattan College Parkway, Riverdale, NY 10471, 718-862-7100 or toll-free 800-622-9235. *Fax:* 718-862-8027. *E-mail:* finaid@manhattan.edu. *Website:* http://www.manhattan.edu/.

MANHATTAN SCHOOL OF MUSIC
New York, NY

CONTACT Ms. Amy Anderson, Assistant Dean for Enrollment Management, Manhattan School of Music, 120 Claremont Avenue, New York, NY 10027-4698, 212-749-2802 Ext. 4501. *Fax:* 212-749-3025. *E-mail:* aanderson@msmnyc.edu. *Website:* http://www.msmnyc.edu/.

MANHATTANVILLE COLLEGE
Purchase, NY

Tuition & fees: $35,370	Average undergraduate aid package: $35,732

ABOUT THE INSTITUTION Independent, coed. *Awards:* certificates, bachelor's, master's, and doctoral degrees. 40 undergraduate majors. *Total enrollment:* 3,019. Undergraduates: 1,767. Freshmen: 535. Federal methodology is used as a basis for awarding need-based institutional aid.

UNDERGRADUATE EXPENSES for 2013–2014 *Application fee:* $75. *Comprehensive fee:* $49,710 includes full-time tuition ($34,020), mandatory fees ($1350), and room and board ($14,340). *College room only:* $8680. Room and board charges vary according to board plan. *Part-time tuition:* $790 per credit. *Part-time fees:* $60 per term. Part-time tuition and fees vary according to program.

FRESHMAN FINANCIAL AID (Fall 2012, est.) 455 applied for aid; of those 100% were deemed to have need. 100% of freshmen with need received aid; of those 23% had need fully met. *Average percent of need met:* 72% (excluding resources awarded to replace EFC). *Average financial aid package:* $32,453 (excluding resources awarded to replace EFC). 2% of all full-time freshmen had no need and received non-need-based gift aid.

UNDERGRADUATE FINANCIAL AID (Fall 2012, est.) 1,345 applied for aid; of those 100% were deemed to have need. 100% of undergraduates with need received aid; of those 8% had need fully met. *Average percent of need met:* 73% (excluding

resources awarded to replace EFC). *Average financial aid package:* $35,732 (excluding resources awarded to replace EFC). 4% of all full-time undergraduates had no need and received non-need-based gift aid.

GIFT AID (NEED-BASED) *Total amount:* $16,468,536 (17% federal, 10% state, 73% institutional). *Receiving aid:* Freshmen: 74% (392); all full-time undergraduates: 73% (1,203). *Average award:* Freshmen: $8803; Undergraduates: $12,762. *Scholarships, grants, and awards:* Federal Pell, FSEOG, state, private, college/university gift aid from institutional funds.

GIFT AID (NON-NEED-BASED) *Total amount:* $23,804,484 (100% institutional). *Receiving aid:* Freshmen: 61% (324). Undergraduates: 59% (969). *Average award:* Freshmen: $11,841. Undergraduates: $16,665. *Scholarships, grants, and awards by category: Academic interests/achievement:* general academic interests/ achievements, mathematics. *Creative arts/performance:* dance, performing arts. *Special achievements/activities:* community service, leadership. *Special characteristics:* general special characteristics, previous college experience. *Tuition waivers:* Full or partial for employees or children of employees, senior citizens.

LOANS *Student loans:* $12,547,801 (81% need-based, 19% non-need-based). 69% of past graduating class borrowed through all loan programs. *Average indebtedness per student:* $36,384. *Average need-based loan:* Freshmen: $2582. Undergraduates: $3375. *Parent loans:* $3,723,620 (100% non-need-based). *Programs:* Federal Direct (Subsidized and Unsubsidized Stafford), Perkins.

WORK-STUDY Federal work-study jobs available. *State or other work-study/ employment:* Total amount: $325,200 (100% non-need-based). Part-time jobs available.

APPLYING FOR FINANCIAL AID *Required financial aid forms:* FAFSA, state aid form. *Financial aid deadline (priority):* 3/1. *Notification date:* Continuous. Students must reply by 5/1 or within 2 weeks of notification.

CONTACT Mr. Robert Gilmore, Director of Financial Aid, Manhattanville College, 2900 Purchase Street, Purchase, NY 10577-2132, 914-323-5357 or toll-free 800-328-4553. *Fax:* 914-323-5382. *E-mail:* financialaid@mville.edu. *Website:* http://www.manhattanville.edu/.

MANNES COLLEGE THE NEW SCHOOL FOR MUSIC
New York, NY

Tuition & fees: $37,520	Average undergraduate aid package: $23,700

ABOUT THE INSTITUTION Independent, coed. *Awards:* certificates, diplomas, bachelor's, and master's degrees. 7 undergraduate majors. *Total enrollment:* 381. Undergraduates: 39. Freshmen: 39. Federal methodology is used as a basis for awarding need-based institutional aid.

UNDERGRADUATE EXPENSES for 2013–2014 *Application fee:* $100. *Comprehensive fee:* $54,820 includes full-time tuition ($36,660), mandatory fees ($860), and room and board ($17,300). *College room only:* $13,900. *Part-time tuition:* $1200 per credit hour.

FRESHMAN FINANCIAL AID (Fall 2011) 12 applied for aid; of those 83% were deemed to have need. 80% of freshmen with need received aid; of those 12% had need fully met. *Average percent of need met:* 60% (excluding resources awarded to replace EFC). *Average financial aid package:* $26,225 (excluding resources awarded to replace EFC). 2% of all full-time freshmen had no need and received non-need-based gift aid.

UNDERGRADUATE FINANCIAL AID (Fall 2011) 55 applied for aid; of those 87% were deemed to have need. 92% of undergraduates with need received aid; of those 20% had need fully met. *Average percent of need met:* 59% (excluding resources awarded to replace EFC). *Average financial aid package:* $23,700 (excluding resources awarded to replace EFC). 3% of all full-time undergraduates had no need and received non-need-based gift aid.

GIFT AID (NEED-BASED) *Total amount:* $664,744 (17% federal, 3% state, 72% institutional, 8% external sources). *Receiving aid:* Freshmen: 17% (8); all full-time undergraduates: 25% (44). *Average award:* Freshmen: $18,280; Undergraduates: $16,515. *Scholarships, grants, and awards:* Federal Pell, FSEOG, state, college/ university gift aid from institutional funds.

GIFT AID (NON-NEED-BASED) *Total amount:* $1,006,038 (96% institutional, 4% external sources). *Receiving aid:* Freshmen: 2% (1). Undergraduates: 2% (3). *Average award:* Freshmen: $13,480. Undergraduates: $15,850. *Scholarships, grants, and awards by category: Academic interests/achievement:* general academic interests/achievements. *Creative arts/performance:* music, performing arts. *Special achievements/activities:* leadership. *Special characteristics:* international students, local/state students, members of minority groups.

LOANS *Student loans:* $362,222 (94% need-based, 6% non-need-based). 42% of past graduating class borrowed through all loan programs. *Average indebtedness per student:* $34,455. *Average need-based loan:* Freshmen: $7945. Undergraduates: $9260. *Parent loans:* $212,361 (93% need-based, 7% non-need-based). *Programs:* Federal Direct (Subsidized and Unsubsidized Stafford, PLUS), Perkins.

WORK-STUDY *Federal work-study:* Total amount: $4310; jobs available.

APPLYING FOR FINANCIAL AID *Required financial aid forms:* FAFSA, state aid form. *Financial aid deadline:* Continuous. *Notification date:* Continuous beginning 4/1. Students must reply within 4 weeks of notification.

CONTACT Office of Student Financial Services, Mannes College The New School for Music, 72 Fifth Avenue, New York, NY 10024-4402, 212-229-8930 or toll-free 800-292-3040. *Fax:* 212-229-5919. *E-mail:* sfs@newschool.edu.
Website: http://www.mannes.edu/.

MANSFIELD UNIVERSITY OF PENNSYLVANIA
Mansfield, PA

Tuition & fees (PA res): $8926	Average undergraduate aid package: $9260

ABOUT THE INSTITUTION State-supported, coed. *Awards:* associate, bachelor's, and master's degrees. 67 undergraduate majors. *Total enrollment:* 3,131. Undergraduates: 2,824. Freshmen: 595. Federal methodology is used as a basis for awarding need-based institutional aid.

UNDERGRADUATE EXPENSES for 2013–2014 *Application fee:* $25. *Tuition, state resident:* full-time $6428; part-time $268 per credit hour. *Tuition, nonresident:* full-time $16,070; part-time $670 per credit hour. *Required fees:* full-time $2498. Part-time tuition and fees vary according to course load. *College room and board:* $8592; *Room only:* $5780. Room and board charges vary according to board plan and housing facility.

FRESHMAN FINANCIAL AID (Fall 2011) 578 applied for aid; of those 91% were deemed to have need. 100% of freshmen with need received aid; of those 34% had need fully met. *Average percent of need met:* 46% (excluding resources awarded to replace EFC). *Average financial aid package:* $8669 (excluding resources awarded to replace EFC). 5% of all full-time freshmen had no need and received non-need-based gift aid.

UNDERGRADUATE FINANCIAL AID (Fall 2011) 2,409 applied for aid; of those 90% were deemed to have need. 100% of undergraduates with need received aid; of those 36% had need fully met. *Average percent of need met:* 47% (excluding resources awarded to replace EFC). *Average financial aid package:* $9260 (excluding resources awarded to replace EFC). 3% of all full-time undergraduates had no need and received non-need-based gift aid.

GIFT AID (NEED-BASED) *Total amount:* $9,553,544 (59% federal, 35% state, 5% institutional, 1% external sources). *Receiving aid:* Freshmen: 60% (373); all full-time undergraduates: 59% (1,558). *Average award:* Freshmen: $6584; Undergraduates: $6256. *Scholarships, grants, and awards:* Federal Pell, FSEOG, state, private, college/university gift aid from institutional funds.

GIFT AID (NON-NEED-BASED) *Total amount:* $1,057,303 (3% federal, 1% state, 55% institutional, 41% external sources). *Receiving aid:* Freshmen: 32% (200). Undergraduates: 17% (460). *Average award:* Freshmen: $2112. Undergraduates: $1990. *Scholarships, grants, and awards by category:* Academic interests/achievement: biological sciences, communication, education, general academic interests/achievements, health fields, mathematics, physical sciences. Creative arts/performance: art/fine arts, journalism/publications, music. Special achievements/activities: leadership. *Tuition waivers:* Full or partial for employees or children of employees, senior citizens. *ROTC:* Army cooperative.

LOANS *Student loans:* $20,688,474 (45% need-based, 55% non-need-based). 87% of past graduating class borrowed through all loan programs. *Average indebtedness per student:* $34,174. *Average need-based loan:* Freshmen: $3722. Undergraduates: $4567. *Parent loans:* $4,215,357 (100% non-need-based). *Programs:* Federal Direct (Subsidized and Unsubsidized Stafford, PLUS), Perkins.

WORK-STUDY *Federal work-study:* Total amount: $178,537; jobs available. *State or other work-study/employment:* Total amount: $1,042,273 (100% non-need-based). Part-time jobs available.

ATHLETIC AWARDS Total amount: $350,629 (100% non-need-based).

APPLYING FOR FINANCIAL AID *Required financial aid form:* FAFSA. *Financial aid deadline:* Continuous. *Notification date:* Continuous beginning 3/15.

CONTACT Ms. Darcie Stephens, Director of Financial Aid, Mansfield University of Pennsylvania, 224 South Hall, Mansfield, PA 16933, 570-662-4854 or toll-free 800-577-6826. *Fax:* 570-662-4136.
Website: http://www.mansfield.edu/.

MAPLE SPRINGS BAPTIST BIBLE COLLEGE AND SEMINARY
Capitol Heights, MD

CONTACT Ms. Fannie G. Thompson, Director of Business Affairs, Maple Springs Baptist Bible College and Seminary, 4130 Belt Road, Capitol Heights, MD 20743, 301-736-3631. *Fax:* 301-735-6507.
Website: http://www.msbbcs.edu/.

MARANATHA BAPTIST BIBLE COLLEGE
Watertown, WI

ABOUT THE INSTITUTION Independent Baptist, coed. *Awards:* certificates, associate, bachelor's, and master's degrees. 31 undergraduate majors. *Total enrollment:* 983. Undergraduates: 887. Freshmen: 188.

GIFT AID (NEED-BASED) *Scholarships, grants, and awards:* Federal Pell, FSEOG, state, private, college/university gift aid from institutional funds.

GIFT AID (NON-NEED-BASED) *Scholarships, grants, and awards by category:* Academic interests/achievement: business, general academic interests/achievements, religion/biblical studies. Creative arts/performance: music. Special characteristics: children and siblings of alumni, children of educators, children of faculty/staff, relatives of clergy, spouses of current students.

LOANS *Programs:* Federal Direct (Subsidized and Unsubsidized Stafford, PLUS), state, alternative loans.

WORK-STUDY *State or other work-study/employment:* Part-time jobs available.

APPLYING FOR FINANCIAL AID *Required financial aid form:* FAFSA.

CONTACT Mr. Bruce Roth, Associate Director of Financial Aid, Maranatha Baptist Bible College, 745 West Main Street, Watertown, WI 53094, 920-206-2318 or toll-free 800-622-2947. *Fax:* 920-261-9109. *E-mail:* financialaid@mbbc.edu.
Website: http://www.mbbc.edu/.

MARIA COLLEGE
Albany, NY

CONTACT Financial Aid Office, Maria College, 700 New Scotland Avenue, Albany, NY 12208-1798, 518-438-3111.
Website: http://www.mariacollege.edu/.

MARIAN UNIVERSITY
Indianapolis, IN

CONTACT Mr. John E. Shelton, Dean of Financial Aid, Marian University, 3200 Cold Spring Road, Indianapolis, IN 46222-1997, 317-955-6040 or toll-free 800-772-7264 (in-state). *Fax:* 317-955-6424. *E-mail:* jshelton@marian.edu.
Website: http://www.marian.edu/.

MARIAN UNIVERSITY
Fond du Lac, WI

Tuition & fees: $23,440	Average undergraduate aid package: $16,013

ABOUT THE INSTITUTION Independent Roman Catholic, coed. **Awards:** certificates, bachelor's, master's, and doctoral degrees. 46 undergraduate majors. **Total enrollment:** 2,306. Undergraduates: 1,798. Freshmen: 283. Federal methodology is used as a basis for awarding need-based institutional aid.

UNDERGRADUATE EXPENSES for 2013–2014 *Application fee:* $20. *One-time required fee:* $100. *Comprehensive fee:* $29,580 includes full-time tuition ($23,090), mandatory fees ($350), and room and board ($6140). *College room only:* $3690. Full-time tuition and fees vary according to course load and program. Room and board charges vary according to board plan. *Part-time tuition:* $350 per credit hour. Part-time tuition and fees vary according to course load and program.

FRESHMAN FINANCIAL AID (Fall 2011) 320 applied for aid; of those 90% were deemed to have need. 100% of freshmen with need received aid; of those 8% had need fully met. *Average percent of need met:* 71% (excluding resources awarded to replace EFC). *Average financial aid package:* $16,603 (excluding resources awarded to replace EFC). 10% of all full-time freshmen had no need and received non-need-based gift aid.

UNDERGRADUATE FINANCIAL AID (Fall 2011) 1,436 applied for aid; of those 92% were deemed to have need. 100% of undergraduates with need received aid; of those 10% had need fully met. *Average percent of need met:* 71% (excluding resources awarded to replace EFC). *Average financial aid package:* $16,013 (excluding resources awarded to replace EFC). 8% of all full-time undergraduates had no need and received non-need-based gift aid.

GIFT AID (NEED-BASED) Total amount: $15,965,446 (21% federal, 13% state, 65% institutional, 1% external sources). *Receiving aid:* Freshmen: 90% (288); all full-time undergraduates: 84% (1,261). *Average award:* Freshmen: $13,471; Undergraduates: $11,754. *Scholarships, grants, and awards:* Federal Pell, FSEOG, state, private, college/university gift aid from institutional funds, endowed and restricted scholarships and grants.

GIFT AID (NON-NEED-BASED) Total amount: $754,303 (95% institutional, 5% external sources). *Receiving aid:* Freshmen: 82% (264). Undergraduates: 71% (1,062). *Average award:* Freshmen: $6960. Undergraduates: $4990. *Scholarships, grants, and awards by category:* Academic interests/achievement: 1,597 awards ($6,249,578 total): general academic interests/achievements. Creative arts/performance: 16 awards ($25,850 total): music. Special characteristics: 165 awards ($568,316 total): children of faculty/staff, children of union members/company employees, children with a deceased or disabled parent, local/state students, out-of-state students, siblings of current students, veterans. *Tuition waivers:* Full or partial for employees or children of employees, senior citizens. *ROTC:* Army.

LOANS Student loans: $12,011,863 (81% need-based, 19% non-need-based). 83% of past graduating class borrowed through all loan programs. *Average indebtedness per student:* $27,000. *Average need-based loan:* Freshmen: $5205. Undergraduates: $6610. *Parent loans:* $2,137,394 (56% need-based, 44% non-need-based). *Programs:* Federal Direct (Subsidized and Unsubsidized Stafford, PLUS), Perkins, Federal Nursing.

WORK-STUDY Federal work-study: Total amount: $93,328; 173 jobs averaging $540. *State or other work-study/employment:* Total amount: $623,416 (100% non-need-based). 387 part-time jobs averaging $1611.

APPLYING FOR FINANCIAL AID Required financial aid forms: FAFSA, institution's own form. *Financial aid deadline (priority):* 3/1. *Notification date:* Continuous beginning 3/1. Students must reply within 4 weeks of notification.

CONTACT Ms. Pam Warren, Associate Director of Financial Aid, Marian University, 45 South National Avenue, Fond du Lac, WI 54935-4699, 920-923-7614 or toll-free 800-2-MARIAN. *Fax:* 920-923-8767. *E-mail:* pwarren@marianuniversity.edu. *Website:* http://www.marianuniversity.edu/.

MARIETTA COLLEGE
Marietta, OH

Tuition & fees: $30,940	Average undergraduate aid package: $25,790

ABOUT THE INSTITUTION Independent, coed. **Awards:** certificates, associate, bachelor's, and master's degrees. 44 undergraduate majors. **Total enrollment:** 1,622. Undergraduates: 1,487. Freshmen: 393. Federal methodology is used as a basis for awarding need-based institutional aid.

UNDERGRADUATE EXPENSES for 2013–2014 *Application fee:* $25. *Comprehensive fee:* $40,500 includes full-time tuition ($30,090), mandatory fees ($850), and room and board ($9560). *College room only:* $5500. *Part-time tuition:* $990 per credit.

FRESHMAN FINANCIAL AID (Fall 2012, est.) 389 applied for aid; of those 87% were deemed to have need. 100% of freshmen with need received aid; of those 28% had need fully met. *Average percent of need met:* 88% (excluding resources awarded to replace EFC). *Average financial aid package:* $27,091 (excluding resources awarded to replace EFC). 12% of all full-time freshmen had no need and received non-need-based gift aid.

UNDERGRADUATE FINANCIAL AID (Fall 2012, est.) 1,183 applied for aid; of those 92% were deemed to have need. 97% of undergraduates with need received aid; of those 31% had need fully met. *Average percent of need met:* 87% (excluding resources awarded to replace EFC). *Average financial aid package:* $25,790 (excluding resources awarded to replace EFC). 17% of all full-time undergraduates had no need and received non-need-based gift aid.

GIFT AID (NEED-BASED) Total amount: $19,611,039 (11% federal, 3% state, 86% institutional). *Receiving aid:* Freshmen: 84% (333); all full-time undergraduates: 74% (1,051). *Average award:* Freshmen: $17,978; Undergraduates: $16,083. *Scholarships, grants, and awards:* Federal Pell, FSEOG, state, private, college/university gift aid from institutional funds.

GIFT AID (NON-NEED-BASED) Total amount: $3,787,194 (1% state, 87% institutional, 12% external sources). *Receiving aid:* Freshmen: 61% (241). Undergraduates: 65% (926). *Average award:* Freshmen: $11,708. Undergraduates: $10,749. *Scholarships, grants, and awards by category:* Academic interests/achievement: 562 awards ($7,662,692 total): general academic interests/achievements, physical sciences. Creative arts/performance: 65 awards ($189,250 total): art/fine arts, music, performing arts, theater/drama. Special characteristics: 211 awards ($909,500 total): children and siblings of alumni, ethnic background, members of minority groups.

LOANS Student loans: $9,334,424 (55% need-based, 45% non-need-based). 83% of past graduating class borrowed through all loan programs. *Average indebtedness per student:* $32,314. *Average need-based loan:* Freshmen: $3705. Undergraduates: $4733. *Parent loans:* $2,738,514 (100% non-need-based). *Programs:* Federal Direct (Subsidized and Unsubsidized Stafford, PLUS), Perkins.

WORK-STUDY Federal work-study: Total amount: $1,701,047; 869 jobs averaging $1957.

APPLYING FOR FINANCIAL AID Required financial aid form: FAFSA. *Financial aid deadline (priority):* 3/1. *Notification date:* 3/15. Students must reply by 5/1 or within 2 weeks of notification.

CONTACT Mr. Kevin Lamb, Director of Financial Aid, Marietta College, 215 Fifth Street, Marietta, OH 45750-4000, 740-376-4712 or toll-free 800-331-7896. *Fax:* 740-376-4990. *E-mail:* finaid@marietta.edu. *Website:* http://www.marietta.edu/.

MARIST COLLEGE
Poughkeepsie, NY

Tuition & fees: $30,000	Average undergraduate aid package: $17,754

ABOUT THE INSTITUTION Independent, coed. **Awards:** certificates, bachelor's, and master's degrees. 48 undergraduate majors. **Total enrollment:** 6,377. Undergraduates: 5,560. Freshmen: 1,098. Federal methodology is used as a basis for awarding need-based institutional aid.

UNDERGRADUATE EXPENSES for 2013–2014 *Application fee:* $50. *One-time required fee:* $90. *Comprehensive fee:* $42,600 includes full-time tuition ($29,500), mandatory fees ($500), and room and board ($12,600). *College room only:* $8100. Full-time tuition and fees vary according to course load and location.

Room and board charges vary according to board plan, housing facility, and location. *Part-time tuition:* $634 per credit hour. *Part-time fees:* $40 per term. Part-time tuition and fees vary according to course load.

FRESHMAN FINANCIAL AID (Fall 2012, est.) 911 applied for aid; of those 74% were deemed to have need. 100% of freshmen with need received aid; of those 17% had need fully met. *Average financial aid package:* $16,794 (excluding resources awarded to replace EFC). 25% of all full-time freshmen had no need and received non-need-based gift aid.

UNDERGRADUATE FINANCIAL AID (Fall 2012, est.) 3,495 applied for aid; of those 81% were deemed to have need. 100% of undergraduates with need received aid; of those 16% had need fully met. *Average financial aid package:* $17,754 (excluding resources awarded to replace EFC). 23% of all full-time undergraduates had no need and received non-need-based gift aid.

GIFT AID (NEED-BASED) *Total amount:* $31,403,276 (11% federal, 6% state, 81% institutional, 2% external sources). *Receiving aid:* Freshmen: 46% (506); all full-time undergraduates: 41% (1,944). *Average award:* Freshmen: $14,233; Undergraduates: $14,182. *Scholarships, grants, and awards:* Federal Pell, FSEOG, state, private, college/university gift aid from institutional funds.

GIFT AID (NON-NEED-BASED) *Total amount:* $9,458,152 (6% federal, 2% state, 89% institutional, 3% external sources). *Receiving aid:* Freshmen: 39% (430). Undergraduates: 48% (2,301). *Average award:* Freshmen: $7698. Undergraduates: $7400. *Scholarships, grants, and awards by category:* Academic interests/achievement: 2,950 awards ($21,951,338 total): general academic interests/achievements. Creative arts/performance: 61 awards ($135,000 total): debating, music. Special characteristics: local/state students. *Tuition waivers:* Full or partial for employees or children of employees, adult students. *ROTC:* Army.

LOANS *Student loans:* $29,232,587 (78% need-based, 22% non-need-based). 73% of past graduating class borrowed through all loan programs. *Average indebtedness per student:* $33,707. *Average need-based loan:* Freshmen: $3898. Undergraduates: $4811. *Parent loans:* $9,834,718 (71% need-based, 29% non-need-based). *Programs:* Federal Direct (Subsidized and Unsubsidized Stafford, PLUS), Perkins, alternative loans.

WORK-STUDY *Federal work-study:* Total amount: $3,344,077; 1,370 jobs averaging $2441. *State or other work-study/employment:* Total amount: $1,035,975 (100% non-need-based). 701 part-time jobs averaging $1478.

ATHLETIC AWARDS Total amount: $3,532,810 (55% need-based, 45% non-need-based).

APPLYING FOR FINANCIAL AID *Required financial aid forms:* FAFSA, institution's own form. *Financial aid deadline:* 5/1 (priority: 2/15). *Notification date:* Continuous beginning 4/1. Students must reply by 5/1 or within 2 weeks of notification.

CONTACT Joseph R. Weglarz, Executive Director of Student Financial Services, Marist College, 3399 North Road, Poughkeepsie, NY 12601, 845-575-3230 or toll-free 800-436-5483. *Fax:* 845-575-3099. *E-mail:* joseph.weglarz@marist.edu. *Website:* http://www.marist.edu/.

MARLBORO COLLEGE
Marlboro, VT

Tuition & fees: $37,640	Average undergraduate aid package: $29,090

ABOUT THE INSTITUTION Independent, coed. *Awards:* bachelor's and master's degrees. 75 undergraduate majors. *Total enrollment:* 267. Undergraduates: 267. Freshmen: 59. Federal methodology is used as a basis for awarding need-based institutional aid.

UNDERGRADUATE EXPENSES for 2013–2014 *Application fee:* $50. *Comprehensive fee:* $47,570 includes full-time tuition ($36,300), mandatory fees ($1340), and room and board ($9930). *College room only:* $5470. Full-time tuition and fees vary according to program. *Part-time tuition:* $1210 per credit. *Part-time fees:* $210 per year. Part-time tuition and fees vary according to course load and program.

FRESHMAN FINANCIAL AID (Fall 2012, est.) 44 applied for aid; of those 91% were deemed to have need. 100% of freshmen with need received aid. *Average percent of need met:* 80% (excluding resources awarded to replace EFC). *Average financial aid package:* $29,719 (excluding resources awarded to replace EFC). 14% of all full-time freshmen had no need and received non-need-based gift aid.

UNDERGRADUATE FINANCIAL AID (Fall 2012, est.) 185 applied for aid; of those 96% were deemed to have need. 99% of undergraduates with need received aid. *Average percent of need met:* 75% (excluding resources awarded to replace EFC). *Average financial aid package:* $29,090 (excluding resources awarded to replace EFC). 18% of all full-time undergraduates had no need and received non-need-based gift aid.

GIFT AID (NEED-BASED) *Total amount:* $4,406,294 (9% federal, 1% state, 90% institutional). *Receiving aid:* Freshmen: 82% (40); all full-time undergraduates: 75% (176). *Average award:* Freshmen: $24,667; Undergraduates: $22,908. *Scholarships, grants, and awards:* Federal Pell, FSEOG, state, private, college/university gift aid from institutional funds.

GIFT AID (NON-NEED-BASED) *Total amount:* $89,803 (100% external sources). *Receiving aid:* Freshmen: 69% (34). Undergraduates: 68% (159). *Average award:* Freshmen: $8286. Undergraduates: $11,211. *Scholarships, grants, and awards by category:* Academic interests/achievement: general academic interests/achievements. Special achievements/activities: leadership. *Tuition waivers:* Full or partial for employees or children of employees, senior citizens.

LOANS *Student loans:* $1,506,502 (100% need-based). 71% of past graduating class borrowed through all loan programs. *Average indebtedness per student:* $20,051. *Average need-based loan:* Freshmen: $3454. Undergraduates: $4490. *Parent loans:* $561,196 (100% need-based). *Programs:* Federal Direct (Subsidized and Unsubsidized Stafford, PLUS).

WORK-STUDY *Federal work-study:* Total amount: $326,825; jobs available. *State or other work-study/employment:* Part-time jobs available.

APPLYING FOR FINANCIAL AID *Required financial aid form:* FAFSA. *Financial aid deadline (priority):* 3/1. *Notification date:* Continuous beginning 3/1. Students must reply by 5/1 or within 2 weeks of notification.

CONTACT Cathy S. Fuller, Associate Director of Financial Aid, Marlboro College, PO Box A, 2582 South Road, Marlboro, VT 05344-0300, 802-258-9237 or toll-free 800-343-0049. *Fax:* 802-258-9300. *E-mail:* finaid@marlboro.edu. *Website:* http://www.marlboro.edu/.

MARQUETTE UNIVERSITY
Milwaukee, WI

Tuition & fees: $34,640	Average undergraduate aid package: $22,236

ABOUT THE INSTITUTION Independent Roman Catholic (Jesuit), coed. *Awards:* certificates, bachelor's, master's, and doctoral degrees. 63 undergraduate majors. *Total enrollment:* 11,749. Undergraduates: 8,293. Freshmen: 1,928. Federal methodology is used as a basis for awarding need-based institutional aid.

UNDERGRADUATE EXPENSES for 2013–2014 *Application fee:* $30. *Comprehensive fee:* $45,370 includes full-time tuition ($34,200), mandatory fees ($440), and room and board ($10,730). *College room only:* $6900. Full-time tuition and fees vary according to course load and program. Room and board charges vary according to housing facility. *Part-time tuition:* $995 per credit. Part-time tuition and fees vary according to program.

FRESHMAN FINANCIAL AID (Fall 2012, est.) 1,570 applied for aid; of those 77% were deemed to have need. 100% of freshmen with need received aid; of those 23% had need fully met. *Average percent of need met:* 73% (excluding resources awarded to replace EFC). *Average financial aid package:* $22,661 (excluding resources awarded to replace EFC). 36% of all full-time freshmen had no need and received non-need-based gift aid.

UNDERGRADUATE FINANCIAL AID (Fall 2012, est.) 5,912 applied for aid; of those 81% were deemed to have need. 100% of undergraduates with need received aid; of those 23% had need fully met. *Average percent of need met:* 74% (excluding resources awarded to replace EFC). *Average financial aid package:* $22,236 (excluding resources awarded to replace EFC). 36% of all full-time undergraduates had no need and received non-need-based gift aid.

GIFT AID (NEED-BASED) *Total amount:* $74,324,814 (9% federal, 4% state, 81% institutional, 6% external sources). *Receiving aid:* Freshmen: 62% (1,187); all full-time undergraduates: 59% (4,706). *Average award:* Freshmen: $17,629; Undergraduates: $15,934. *Scholarships, grants, and awards:* Federal Pell, FSEOG, state, private, college/university gift aid from institutional funds.

GIFT AID (NON-NEED-BASED) *Total amount:* $32,471,488 (89% institutional, 11% external sources). *Receiving aid:* Freshmen: 8% (162). Undergraduates: 7% (543). *Average award:* Freshmen: $9775. Undergraduates: $9306. *Scholar-*

ships, grants, and awards by category: *Academic interests/achievement:* 6,831 awards ($58,779,077 total): biological sciences, business, communication, education, engineering/technologies, English, foreign languages, general academic interests/achievements, health fields, mathematics, physical sciences. *Creative arts/performance:* 12 awards ($9750 total): theater/drama. *Special characteristics:* 157 awards ($4,815,838 total): children of faculty/staff. **Tuition waivers:** Full or partial for employees or children of employees, senior citizens. *ROTC:* Army, Naval, Air Force.
LOANS *Student loans:* $47,892,867 (75% need-based, 25% non-need-based). 65% of past graduating class borrowed through all loan programs. *Average indebtedness per student:* $34,602. *Average need-based loan:* Freshmen: $4153. Undergraduates: $5363. *Parent loans:* $21,362,076 (36% need-based, 64% non-need-based). *Programs:* Federal Direct (Subsidized and Unsubsidized Stafford, PLUS), Perkins, Federal Nursing, state, college/university.
WORK-STUDY *Federal work-study:* Total amount: $4,404,416; jobs available. *State or other work-study/employment:* Part-time jobs available.
ATHLETIC AWARDS Total amount: $4,658,249 (30% need-based, 70% non-need-based).
APPLYING FOR FINANCIAL AID *Required financial aid form:* FAFSA. *Financial aid deadline:* Continuous. *Notification date:* Continuous beginning 3/20. Students must reply by 5/1 or within 3 weeks of notification.
CONTACT Susan Teerink, Director of Financial Aid, Marquette University, PO Box 1881, Milwaukee, WI 53201-1881, 414-288-4000 or toll-free 800-222-6544. *Fax:* 414-288-1718. *E-mail:* financialaid@marquette.edu.
Website: http://www.marquette.edu/.

MARSHALL UNIVERSITY
Huntington, WV

Tuition & fees (WV res): $5930	Average undergraduate aid package: $9438

ABOUT THE INSTITUTION State-supported, coed. *Awards:* certificates, associate, bachelor's, master's, and doctoral degrees. 53 undergraduate majors. *Total enrollment:* 13,708. Undergraduates: 9,885. Freshmen: 1,908. Federal methodology is used as a basis for awarding need-based institutional aid.
UNDERGRADUATE EXPENSES for 2013–2014 *Application fee:* $30. *Tuition, state resident:* full-time $4860; part-time $202.75 per credit hour. *Tuition, nonresident:* full-time $12,860; part-time $536 per credit hour. *Required fees:* full-time $1070. Full-time tuition and fees vary according to degree level, location, program, and reciprocity agreements. Part-time tuition and fees vary according to course load, degree level, location, program, and reciprocity agreements. *College room and board:* $8988; *Room only:* $5570. Room and board charges vary according to board plan and housing facility.
FRESHMAN FINANCIAL AID (Fall 2012, est.) 1,819 applied for aid; of those 75% were deemed to have need. 99% of freshmen with need received aid; of those 31% had need fully met. *Average percent of need met:* 51% (excluding resources awarded to replace EFC). *Average financial aid package:* $9893 (excluding resources awarded to replace EFC). 18% of all full-time freshmen had no need and received non-need-based gift aid.
UNDERGRADUATE FINANCIAL AID (Fall 2012, est.) 7,485 applied for aid; of those 80% were deemed to have need. 98% of undergraduates with need received aid; of those 30% had need fully met. *Average percent of need met:* 51% (excluding resources awarded to replace EFC). *Average financial aid package:* $9438 (excluding resources awarded to replace EFC). 13% of all full-time undergraduates had no need and received non-need-based gift aid.
GIFT AID (NEED-BASED) *Total amount:* $27,182,358 (69% federal, 30% state, 1% institutional). *Receiving aid:* Freshmen: 56% (1,065); all full-time undergraduates: 53% (4,534). *Average award:* Freshmen: $5961; Undergraduates: $5635. *Scholarships, grants, and awards:* Federal Pell, FSEOG, state, private, college/university gift aid from institutional funds, Federal Nursing.
GIFT AID (NON-NEED-BASED) *Total amount:* $13,899,509 (63% state, 23% institutional, 14% external sources). *Receiving aid:* Freshmen: 38% (729). Undergraduates: 24% (2,035). *Average award:* Freshmen: $6169. Undergraduates: $6406. *Scholarships, grants, and awards by category:* Academic interests/achievement: general academic interests/achievements. *Creative arts/performance:* art/fine arts, general creative arts/performance. *Special characteristics:* children and siblings of alumni, children of faculty/staff, local/state students, members of minority groups. *Tuition waivers:* Full or partial for employees or children of employees, senior citizens. *ROTC:* Army.
LOANS *Student loans:* $42,109,982 (93% need-based, 7% non-need-based). 62% of past graduating class borrowed through all loan programs. *Average indebtedness per student:* $26,727. *Average need-based loan:* Freshmen: $5928. Undergraduates: $7109. *Parent loans:* $3,337,054 (100% non-need-based). *Programs:* Federal Direct (Subsidized and Unsubsidized Stafford, PLUS), Perkins, Federal Nursing.
WORK-STUDY *Federal work-study:* Total amount: $461,851; jobs available. *State or other work-study/employment:* Part-time jobs available.
ATHLETIC AWARDS Total amount: $4,926,576 (100% non-need-based).
APPLYING FOR FINANCIAL AID *Required financial aid forms:* FAFSA, state aid form. *Financial aid deadline (priority):* 3/1. *Notification date:* 5/1.
CONTACT Ms. Kathy Bialk, Director of Student Financial Aid, Marshall University, One John Marshall Drive, Huntington, WV 25755, 304-696-2280 or toll-free 800-642-3499. *Fax:* 304-696-3242. *E-mail:* bialkk@marshall.edu.
Website: http://www.marshall.edu/.

MARS HILL COLLEGE
Mars Hill, NC

CONTACT Amanda Randolph, Director of Financial Aid, Mars Hill College, PO Box 370, Mars Hill, NC 28754, 828-689-1123 or toll-free 866-MHC-4-YOU. *Fax:* 828-689-1300. *E-mail:* arandolph@mhc.edu.
Website: http://www.mhc.edu/.

MARTIN LUTHER COLLEGE
New Ulm, MN

ABOUT THE INSTITUTION Independent Wisconsin Evangelical Lutheran Synod, coed. *Awards:* certificates, diplomas, bachelor's, and master's degrees. 6 undergraduate majors. *Total enrollment:* 799. Undergraduates: 742. Freshmen: 179.
GIFT AID (NEED-BASED) *Scholarships, grants, and awards:* Federal Pell, FSEOG, state, private, college/university gift aid from institutional funds.
GIFT AID (NON-NEED-BASED) *Scholarships, grants, and awards by category:* Academic interests/achievement: general academic interests/achievements. *Creative arts/performance:* music.
LOANS *Programs:* Federal Direct (Subsidized and Unsubsidized Stafford, PLUS), Perkins, state, college/university, alternative loans.
APPLYING FOR FINANCIAL AID *Required financial aid forms:* FAFSA, institution's own form.
CONTACT Mr. Gene Slettedahl, Director of Financial Aid, Martin Luther College, 1995 Luther Court, New Ulm, MN 56073, 507-354-8221 or toll-free 877-MLC-1995. *Fax:* 507-354-8225. *E-mail:* slettega@mlc-wels.edu.
Website: http://www.mlc-wels.edu/.

MARTIN METHODIST COLLEGE
Pulaski, TN

CONTACT Ms. Anita Beecham, Financial Aid Assistant, Martin Methodist College, 433 West Madison Street, Pulaski, TN 38478-2716, 931-363-9808 or toll-free 800-467-1273. *Fax:* 931-363-9818. *E-mail:* abeecham@martinmethodist.edu.
Website: http://www.martinmethodist.edu/.

MARTIN UNIVERSITY
Indianapolis, IN

CONTACT Berdia Marshall, Director of Financial Aid, Martin University, 2171 Avondale Place, Indianapolis, IN 46218-3867, 317-543-3670. *Fax:* 317-543-4790. *E-mail:* bmarshall@martin.edu.
Website: http://www.martin.edu/.

MARY BALDWIN COLLEGE
Staunton, VA

Tuition & fees: $28,720	Average undergraduate aid package: $20,147

ABOUT THE INSTITUTION Independent, coed, primarily women. *Awards:* certificates, bachelor's, and master's degrees. 34 undergraduate majors. *Total enrollment:* 1,804. Undergraduates: 1,526. Freshmen: 245. Federal methodology is used as a basis for awarding need-based institutional aid.

UNDERGRADUATE EXPENSES for 2013–2014 *Application fee:* $35. *One-time required fee:* $100. *Comprehensive fee:* $37,120 includes full-time tuition ($28,360), mandatory fees ($360), and room and board ($8400). *College room only:* $5360. Full-time tuition and fees vary according to degree level. Room and board charges vary according to housing facility. *Part-time tuition:* $427 per semester hour. *Part-time fees:* $427 per semester hour. Part-time tuition and fees vary according to degree level.

FRESHMAN FINANCIAL AID (Fall 2012, est.) 243 applied for aid; of those 94% were deemed to have need. 100% of freshmen with need received aid; of those 9% had need fully met. *Average percent of need met:* 72% (excluding resources awarded to replace EFC). *Average financial aid package:* $24,373 (excluding resources awarded to replace EFC). 15% of all full-time freshmen had no need and received non-need-based gift aid.

UNDERGRADUATE FINANCIAL AID (Fall 2012, est.) 944 applied for aid; of those 93% were deemed to have need. 100% of undergraduates with need received aid; of those 12% had need fully met. *Average percent of need met:* 69% (excluding resources awarded to replace EFC). *Average financial aid package:* $20,147 (excluding resources awarded to replace EFC). 10% of all full-time undergraduates had no need and received non-need-based gift aid.

GIFT AID (NEED-BASED) *Total amount:* $14,108,198 (22% federal, 12% state, 61% institutional, 5% external sources). *Receiving aid:* Freshmen: 80% (229); all full-time undergraduates: 84% (865). *Average award:* Freshmen: $20,664; Undergraduates: $15,944. *Scholarships, grants, and awards:* Federal Pell, FSEOG, state, private, college/university gift aid from institutional funds.

GIFT AID (NON-NEED-BASED) *Total amount:* $2,010,912 (11% state, 77% institutional, 12% external sources). *Receiving aid:* Freshmen: 4% (12). Undergraduates: 6% (61). *Average award:* Freshmen: $13,093. Undergraduates: $12,874. *Scholarships, grants, and awards by category: Academic interests/achievement:* 715 awards ($7,566,939 total): general academic interests/achievements. *Special achievements/activities:* 50 awards ($132,328 total): leadership. *Special characteristics:* 37 awards ($385,892 total): children of educators, children of faculty/staff. *Tuition waivers:* Full or partial for employees or children of employees. *ROTC:* Army, Naval cooperative, Air Force cooperative.

LOANS *Student loans:* $10,198,345 (86% need-based, 14% non-need-based). 91% of past graduating class borrowed through all loan programs. *Average indebtedness per student:* $27,642. *Average need-based loan:* Freshmen: $3780. Undergraduates: $4352. *Parent loans:* $2,289,682 (43% need-based, 57% non-need-based). *Programs:* Perkins, alternative loans.

WORK-STUDY *Federal work-study:* Total amount: $429,557; 302 jobs averaging $1255. *State or other work-study/employment:* Total amount: $112,735 (39% need-based, 61% non-need-based). 79 part-time jobs averaging $1577.

APPLYING FOR FINANCIAL AID *Required financial aid forms:* FAFSA, state aid form (VA residents only). *Financial aid deadline:* Continuous. *Notification date:* Continuous beginning 3/15. Students must reply within 3 weeks of notification.

CONTACT Mrs. Robin Dietrich, Director of Financial Aid, Mary Baldwin College, PO Box 1500, Staunton, VA 24402, 540-887-7025 or toll-free 800-468-2262. *Fax:* 540-887-7229. *E-mail:* rdietric@mbc.edu. *Website:* http://www.mbc.edu/.

MARYGROVE COLLEGE
Detroit, MI

CONTACT Mr. Donald Hurt, Director of Financial Aid, Marygrove College, 8425 West McNichols Road, Detroit, MI 48221-2599, 313-862-8000 Ext. 436 or toll-free 866-313-1297. *Website:* http://www.marygrove.edu/.

MARYLAND INSTITUTE COLLEGE OF ART
Baltimore, MD

CONTACT Ms. Diane Prengaman, Associate Vice President for Financial Aid, Maryland Institute College of Art, 1300 Mount Royal Avenue, Baltimore, MD 21217, 410-225-2285. *Fax:* 410-225-2337. *E-mail:* dprengam@mica.edu. *Website:* http://www.mica.edu/.

MARYLHURST UNIVERSITY
Marylhurst, OR

Tuition & fees: N/R	Average undergraduate aid package: $13,577

ABOUT THE INSTITUTION Independent Roman Catholic, coed, primarily women. *Awards:* certificates, bachelor's, and master's degrees. 20 undergraduate majors. *Total enrollment:* 1,722. Undergraduates: 839. Freshmen: 15. Federal methodology is used as a basis for awarding need-based institutional aid.

FRESHMAN FINANCIAL AID (Fall 2012, est.) 3 applied for aid; of those 100% were deemed to have need. 100% of freshmen with need received aid. *Average percent of need met:* 44% (excluding resources awarded to replace EFC). *Average financial aid package:* $8939 (excluding resources awarded to replace EFC).

UNDERGRADUATE FINANCIAL AID (Fall 2012, est.) 186 applied for aid; of those 96% were deemed to have need. 100% of undergraduates with need received aid; of those 3% had need fully met. *Average percent of need met:* 48% (excluding resources awarded to replace EFC). *Average financial aid package:* $13,577 (excluding resources awarded to replace EFC). 1% of all full-time undergraduates had no need and received non-need-based gift aid.

GIFT AID (NEED-BASED) *Total amount:* $2,783,194 (50% federal, 5% state, 34% institutional, 11% external sources). *Receiving aid:* Freshmen: 75% (3); all full-time undergraduates: 60% (172). *Average award:* Freshmen: $5856; Undergraduates: $8879. *Scholarships, grants, and awards:* Federal Pell, FSEOG, state, private, college/university gift aid from institutional funds, United Negro College Fund.

GIFT AID (NON-NEED-BASED) *Total amount:* $185,969 (95% institutional, 5% external sources). *Receiving aid:* Undergraduates: 1. *Average award:* Undergraduates: $5756.

LOANS *Student loans:* $5,669,843 (89% need-based, 11% non-need-based). 93% of past graduating class borrowed through all loan programs. *Average indebtedness per student:* $43,471. *Average need-based loan:* Freshmen: $2799. Undergraduates: $4821. *Parent loans:* $137,568 (54% need-based, 46% non-need-based). *Programs:* Federal Direct (Subsidized and Unsubsidized Stafford, PLUS), Perkins.

WORK-STUDY *Federal work-study:* Total amount: $158,815; 52 jobs averaging $3640.

APPLYING FOR FINANCIAL AID *Required financial aid forms:* FAFSA, institution's own form. *Financial aid deadline:* Continuous. *Notification date:* Continuous beginning 4/1. Students must reply within 8 weeks of notification.

CONTACT Tracy Reisinger, Office of Financial Aid, Marylhurst University, 17600 Pacific Highway, PO Box 261, Marylhurst, OR 97036, 503-699-6253 or toll-free 800-634-9982. *Fax:* 503-635-6585. *E-mail:* treisinger@marylhurst.edu. *Website:* http://www.marylhurst.edu/.

MARYMOUNT COLLEGE, PALOS VERDES, CALIFORNIA
Rancho Palos Verdes, CA

CONTACT Financial Aid Office, Marymount College, Palos Verdes, California, 30800 Palos Verdes Drive East, Rancho Palos Verdes, CA 90275-6299, 310-377-5501. *Website:* http://www.marymountpv.edu/.

MARYMOUNT MANHATTAN COLLEGE
New York, NY

Tuition & fees: $25,688	Average undergraduate aid package: $12,510

ABOUT THE INSTITUTION Independent, coed. *Awards:* certificates, associate, and bachelor's degrees. 22 undergraduate majors. *Total enrollment:* 1,908. Undergraduates: 1,908. Freshmen: 462. Both federal and institutional methodology are used as a basis for awarding need-based institutional aid.

UNDERGRADUATE EXPENSES for 2013–2014 *Application fee:* $60. *Comprehensive fee:* $40,118 includes full-time tuition ($24,482), mandatory fees ($1206), and room and board ($14,430). *College room only:* $11,930. *Part-time tuition:* $816 per credit hour.

FRESHMAN FINANCIAL AID (Fall 2011) 347 applied for aid; of those 88% were deemed to have need. 100% of freshmen with need received aid; of those 3% had need fully met. *Average percent of need met:* 54% (excluding resources awarded to replace EFC). *Average financial aid package:* $13,068 (excluding resources awarded to replace EFC). 2% of all full-time freshmen had no need and received non-need-based gift aid.

UNDERGRADUATE FINANCIAL AID (Fall 2011) 1,382 applied for aid; of those 81% were deemed to have need. 100% of undergraduates with need received aid; of those 8% had need fully met. *Average percent of need met:* 51% (excluding resources awarded to replace EFC). *Average financial aid package:* $12,510 (excluding resources awarded to replace EFC). 2% of all full-time undergraduates had no need and received non-need-based gift aid.

GIFT AID (NEED-BASED) *Total amount:* $8,562,580 (25% federal, 10% state, 61% institutional, 4% external sources). *Receiving aid:* Freshmen: 73% (307); all full-time undergraduates: 66% (1,120). *Average award:* Freshmen: $10,521; Undergraduates: $10,996. *Scholarships, grants, and awards:* Federal Pell, FSEOG, state, private, college/university gift aid from institutional funds.

GIFT AID (NON-NEED-BASED) *Total amount:* $3,231,185 (11% federal, 89% institutional). *Receiving aid:* Freshmen: 19% (80). Undergraduates: 17% (288). *Average award:* Freshmen: $714. Undergraduates: $904. *Scholarships, grants, and awards by category: Academic interests/achievement:* general academic interests/achievements. *Creative arts/performance:* art/fine arts, dance, performing arts. *Special achievements/activities:* leadership. *Special characteristics:* local/state students. *Tuition waivers:* Full or partial for employees or children of employees, senior citizens.

LOANS *Student loans:* $9,732,799 (61% need-based, 39% non-need-based). 77% of past graduating class borrowed through all loan programs. *Average indebtedness per student:* $15,206. *Average need-based loan:* Freshmen: $3477. Undergraduates: $4125. *Parent loans:* $9,907,456 (100% need-based). *Programs:* Federal Direct (Subsidized and Unsubsidized Stafford, PLUS).

WORK-STUDY *Federal work-study:* Total amount: $371,055; jobs available. *State or other work-study/employment:* Part-time jobs available.

APPLYING FOR FINANCIAL AID *Required financial aid form:* FAFSA. *Financial aid deadline (priority):* 3/15. *Notification date:* Continuous beginning 3/15. Students must reply by 5/1 or within 2 weeks of notification.

CONTACT Director of Financial Aid, Marymount Manhattan College, 221 East 71st Street, New York, NY 10021, 212-517-0500 or toll-free 800-MARYMOUNT. *Fax:* 212-517-0491.
Website: http://www.mmm.edu/.

MARYMOUNT UNIVERSITY
Arlington, VA

Tuition & fees: $26,430	Average undergraduate aid package: $16,113

ABOUT THE INSTITUTION Independent Roman Catholic Church, coed. *Awards:* certificates, bachelor's, master's, and doctoral degrees. 27 undergraduate majors. *Total enrollment:* 3,702. Undergraduates: 2,470. Freshmen: 375. Both federal and institutional methodology are used as a basis for awarding need-based institutional aid.

UNDERGRADUATE EXPENSES for 2013–2014 *Application fee:* $40. *One-time required fee:* $360. *Comprehensive fee:* $37,980 includes full-time tuition ($26,100), mandatory fees ($330), and room and board ($11,550). Room and board charges vary according to housing facility. *Part-time tuition:* $850 per credit hour.

FRESHMAN FINANCIAL AID (Fall 2012, est.) 325 applied for aid; of those 85% were deemed to have need. 100% of freshmen with need received aid; of those 20% had need fully met. *Average percent of need met:* 70% (excluding resources awarded to replace EFC). *Average financial aid package:* $19,058 (excluding resources awarded to replace EFC). 21% of all full-time freshmen had no need and received non-need-based gift aid.

UNDERGRADUATE FINANCIAL AID (Fall 2012, est.) 1,576 applied for aid; of those 88% were deemed to have need. 100% of undergraduates with need received aid; of those 15% had need fully met. *Average percent of need met:* 59% (excluding resources awarded to replace EFC). *Average financial aid package:* $16,113 (excluding resources awarded to replace EFC). 17% of all full-time undergraduates had no need and received non-need-based gift aid.

GIFT AID (NEED-BASED) *Total amount:* $3,280,594 (86% federal, 1% state, 13% institutional). *Receiving aid:* Freshmen: 33% (124); all full-time undergraduates: 32% (698). *Average award:* Freshmen: $4051; Undergraduates: $4663. *Scholarships, grants, and awards:* Federal Pell, FSEOG, state, private, college/university gift aid from institutional funds.

GIFT AID (NON-NEED-BASED) *Total amount:* $17,902,362 (1% federal, 12% state, 86% institutional, 1% external sources). *Receiving aid:* Freshmen: 74% (276). Undergraduates: 58% (1,260). *Average award:* Freshmen: $12,575. Undergraduates: $12,004. *Scholarships, grants, and awards by category: Academic interests/achievement:* biological sciences, business, general academic interests/achievements, health fields, mathematics, social sciences. *Special achievements/activities:* community service, general special achievements/activities, leadership. *Special characteristics:* children of current students, children of faculty/staff, general special characteristics, international students, religious affiliation, veterans. *Tuition waivers:* Full or partial for employees or children of employees, senior citizens. *ROTC:* Army cooperative.

LOANS *Student loans:* $17,007,715 (32% need-based, 68% non-need-based). 77% of past graduating class borrowed through all loan programs. *Average indebtedness per student:* $25,598. *Average need-based loan:* Freshmen: $3533. Undergraduates: $4565. *Parent loans:* $6,267,830 (100% non-need-based). *Programs:* Federal Direct (Subsidized and Unsubsidized Stafford, PLUS), Perkins.

WORK-STUDY *Federal work-study:* Total amount: $1,333,261; 715 jobs averaging $1873.

APPLYING FOR FINANCIAL AID *Required financial aid form:* FAFSA. *Financial aid deadline (priority):* 3/1. *Notification date:* Continuous beginning 3/15. Students must reply within 2 weeks of notification.

CONTACT Ms. Debbie A. Raines, Director of Financial Aid, Marymount University, 2807 North Glebe Road, Arlington, VA 22207-4299, 703-284-1530 or toll-free 800-548-7638. *Fax:* 703-516-4771. *E-mail:* debbie.raines@marymount.edu. *Website:* http://www.marymount.edu/.

MARYVILLE COLLEGE
Maryville, TN

Tuition & fees: $31,132	Average undergraduate aid package: $29,187

ABOUT THE INSTITUTION Independent Presbyterian, coed. *Awards:* bachelor's degrees. 59 undergraduate majors. *Total enrollment:* 1,093. Undergraduates: 1,093. Freshmen: 313. Federal methodology is used as a basis for awarding need-based institutional aid.

UNDERGRADUATE EXPENSES for 2013–2014 *Comprehensive fee:* $41,022 includes full-time tuition ($30,410), mandatory fees ($722), and room and board ($9890). *College room only:* $4908. Full-time tuition and fees vary according to course load. Room and board charges vary according to board plan and housing facility. *Part-time tuition:* $800 per credit hour. Part-time tuition and fees vary according to course load.

FRESHMAN FINANCIAL AID (Fall 2012, est.) 313 applied for aid; of those 90% were deemed to have need. 100% of freshmen with need received aid; of those 19% had need fully met. *Average financial aid package:* $30,575 (excluding resources awarded to replace EFC). 10% of all full-time freshmen had no need and received non-need-based gift aid.

UNDERGRADUATE FINANCIAL AID (Fall 2012, est.) 1,050 applied for aid; of those 86% were deemed to have need. 100% of undergraduates with need received

aid; of those 25% had need fully met. **Average financial aid package:** $29,187 (excluding resources awarded to replace EFC). 14% of all full-time undergraduates had no need and received non-need-based gift aid.
GIFT AID (NEED-BASED) Total amount: $21,154,238 (10% federal, 3% state, 73% institutional, 14% external sources). **Receiving aid:** Freshmen: 90% (281); all full-time undergraduates: 86% (899). **Average award:** Freshmen: $25,510; Undergraduates: $23,495. **Scholarships, grants, and awards:** Federal Pell, FSEOG, state, private, college/university gift aid from institutional funds.
GIFT AID (NON-NEED-BASED) Total amount: $4,067,924 (83% institutional, 17% external sources). **Receiving aid:** Freshmen: 12% (38). Undergraduates: 12% (131). **Average award:** Freshmen: $18,877. Undergraduates: $16,966. **Scholarships, grants, and awards by category:** Academic interests/achievement: general academic interests/achievements. Creative arts/performance: art/fine arts, music, theater/drama. Special achievements/activities: community service, leadership. Special characteristics: children and siblings of alumni, children of faculty/staff, members of minority groups, religious affiliation, veterans. **Tuition waivers:** Full or partial for employees or children of employees.
LOANS Student loans: $6,561,398 (81% need-based, 19% non-need-based). **Average need-based loan:** Freshmen: $4058. Undergraduates: $5677. **Parent loans:** $1,039,742 (50% need-based, 50% non-need-based). **Programs:** Federal Direct (Subsidized and Unsubsidized Stafford, PLUS), Perkins.
WORK-STUDY Federal work-study: Total amount: $887,113; 550 jobs averaging $1704. **State or other work-study/employment:** Total amount: $109,888 (45% need-based, 55% non-need-based). 66 part-time jobs averaging $1665.
APPLYING FOR FINANCIAL AID Required financial aid form: FAFSA. **Financial aid deadline (priority):** 3/1. **Notification date:** Continuous beginning 3/15. Students must reply within 4 weeks of notification.
CONTACT Mr. Richard Brand, Director of Financial Aid, Maryville College, 502 East Lamar Alexander Parkway, Maryville, TN 37804-5907, 865-981-8100 or toll-free 800-597-2687. Fax: 865-981-8084. E-mail: richard.brand@maryvillecollege.edu. Website: http://www.maryvillecollege.edu/.

MARYVILLE UNIVERSITY OF SAINT LOUIS
St. Louis, MO

Tuition & fees: $23,746	Average undergraduate aid package: $16,507

ABOUT THE INSTITUTION Independent, coed. **Awards:** certificates, bachelor's, master's, and doctoral degrees. 48 undergraduate majors. **Total enrollment:** 4,203. Undergraduates: 2,980. Freshmen: 368. Both federal and institutional methodology are used as a basis for awarding need-based institutional aid.
UNDERGRADUATE EXPENSES for 2013–2014 Application fee: $30. **Comprehensive fee:** $32,988 includes full-time tuition ($22,786), mandatory fees ($960), and room and board ($9242). Full-time tuition and fees vary according to course load. Room and board charges vary according to board plan and housing facility. **Part-time tuition:** $683 per credit hour. **Part-time fees:** $240 per term. Part-time tuition and fees vary according to class time.
FRESHMAN FINANCIAL AID (Fall 2012, est.) 271 applied for aid; of those 90% were deemed to have need. 100% of freshmen with need received aid; of those 20% had need fully met. **Average percent of need met:** 69% (excluding resources awarded to replace EFC. **Average financial aid package:** $19,570 (excluding resources awarded to replace EFC). 18% of all full-time freshmen had no need and received non-need-based gift aid.
UNDERGRADUATE FINANCIAL AID (Fall 2012, est.) 1,380 applied for aid; of those 91% were deemed to have need. 100% of undergraduates with need received aid; of those 16% had need fully met. **Average percent of need met:** 56% (excluding resources awarded to replace EFC). **Average financial aid package:** $16,507 (excluding resources awarded to replace EFC). 19% of all full-time undergraduates had no need and received non-need-based gift aid.
GIFT AID (NEED-BASED) Total amount: $15,955,114 (22% federal, 7% state, 69% institutional, 2% external sources). **Receiving aid:** Freshmen: 70% (244); all full-time undergraduates: 69% (1,184). **Average award:** Freshmen: $16,323; Undergraduates: $10,871. **Scholarships, grants, and awards:** Federal Pell, FSEOG, state, private, college/university gift aid from institutional funds, Academic Competitiveness Grants, National SMART Grants, TEACH Grants.

GIFT AID (NON-NEED-BASED) Total amount: $4,385,473 (1% state, 98% institutional, 1% external sources). **Receiving aid:** Freshmen: 9% (31). Undergraduates: 7% (123). **Average award:** Freshmen: $9300. Undergraduates: $7317. **Scholarships, grants, and awards by category:** Academic interests/achievement: 1,749 awards ($12,630,881 total): biological sciences, business, education, general academic interests/achievements, health fields, international studies. Creative arts/performance: 77 awards ($202,875 total): art/fine arts. Special achievements/activities: 378 awards ($626,190 total): cheerleading/drum major, community service, general special achievements/activities, leadership, religious involvement. Special characteristics: 145 awards ($626,190 total): adult students, children of faculty/staff, ethnic background, general special characteristics, international students, members of minority groups, out-of-state students, parents of current students, veterans. **Tuition waivers:** Full or partial for employees or children of employees, senior citizens. **ROTC:** Army cooperative.
LOANS Student loans: $17,906,492 (76% need-based, 24% non-need-based). 76% of past graduating class borrowed through all loan programs. **Average indebtedness per student:** $21,835. **Average need-based loan:** Freshmen: $6685. Undergraduates: $4794. **Parent loans:** $7,062,915 (42% need-based, 58% non-need-based). **Programs:** Federal Direct (Subsidized and Unsubsidized Stafford, PLUS), Perkins, private loans.
WORK-STUDY Federal work-study: Total amount: $197,900; 273 jobs averaging $658. **State or other work-study/employment:** Total amount: $786,070 (83% need-based, 17% non-need-based). 133 part-time jobs averaging $2435.
ATHLETIC AWARDS Total amount: $1,783,793 (57% need-based, 43% non-need-based).
APPLYING FOR FINANCIAL AID Required financial aid form: FAFSA. **Financial aid deadline (priority):** 3/1. **Notification date:** Continuous beginning 3/15. Students must reply by 5/1 or within 2 weeks of notification.
CONTACT Ms. Martha Harbaugh, Director of Financial Aid, Maryville University of Saint Louis, 650 Maryville University Drive, St. Louis, MO 63141-7299, 800-627-9855 Ext. 9360 or toll-free 800-627-9855. Fax: 314-529-9199. E-mail: fin_aid@maryville.edu. Website: http://www.maryville.edu/.

MARYWOOD UNIVERSITY
Scranton, PA

Tuition & fees: $30,440	Average undergraduate aid package: $20,979

ABOUT THE INSTITUTION Independent Roman Catholic, coed. **Awards:** certificates, bachelor's, master's, and doctoral degrees. 62 undergraduate majors. **Total enrollment:** 3,479. Undergraduates: 2,267. Freshmen: 458. Federal methodology is used as a basis for awarding need-based institutional aid.
UNDERGRADUATE EXPENSES for 2013–2014 Application fee: $35. **Comprehensive fee:** $44,006 includes full-time tuition ($29,340), mandatory fees ($1100), and room and board ($13,566). **College room only:** $7634. Full-time tuition and fees vary according to course load. Room and board charges vary according to board plan and housing facility. Part-time tuition and fees vary according to course load.
FRESHMAN FINANCIAL AID (Fall 2012, est.) 429 applied for aid; of those 92% were deemed to have need. 92% of freshmen with need received aid; of those 2% had need fully met. **Average percent of need met:** 76% (excluding resources awarded to replace EFC). **Average financial aid package:** $21,936 (excluding resources awarded to replace EFC). 12% of all full-time freshmen had no need and received non-need-based gift aid.
UNDERGRADUATE FINANCIAL AID (Fall 2012, est.) 1,873 applied for aid; of those 94% were deemed to have need. 94% of undergraduates with need received aid; of those 5% had need fully met. **Average percent of need met:** 73% (excluding resources awarded to replace EFC). **Average financial aid package:** $20,979 (excluding resources awarded to replace EFC). 12% of all full-time undergraduates had no need and received non-need-based gift aid.
GIFT AID (NEED-BASED) Total amount: $33,162,135 (11% federal, 9% state, 79% institutional, 1% external sources). **Receiving aid:** Freshmen: 76% (344); all full-time undergraduates: 75% (1,555). **Average award:** Freshmen: $19,039; Undergraduates: $17,612. **Scholarships, grants, and awards:** Federal Pell, FSEOG, state, private, college/university gift aid from institutional funds, Federal Nursing, Academic

Competitiveness Grants, National SMART Grants, Scholarships for Disadvantaged Students.

GIFT AID (NON-NEED-BASED) *Total amount:* $3,542,781 (99% institutional, 1% external sources). *Receiving aid:* Freshmen: 1% (6). Undergraduates: 4% (83). *Average award:* Freshmen: $14,609. Undergraduates: $13,271. *Scholarships, grants, and awards by category: Academic interests/achievement:* business, communication, education, foreign languages, general academic interests/achievements, health fields, mathematics, religion/biblical studies. *Creative arts/performance:* art/fine arts, cinema/film/broadcasting, journalism/publications, music, performing arts, theater/drama. *Special achievements/activities:* community service, general special achievements/activities, leadership. *Special characteristics:* adult students, children and siblings of alumni, children of current students, children of faculty/staff, children of workers in trades, ethnic background, general special characteristics, international students, local/state students, religious affiliation, siblings of current students, spouses of current students. *Tuition waivers:* Full or partial for employees or children of employees, senior citizens. **ROTC:** Army cooperative, Air Force cooperative.

LOANS *Student loans:* $17,670,336 (96% need-based, 4% non-need-based). 84% of past graduating class borrowed through all loan programs. *Average indebtedness per student:* $41,198. *Average need-based loan:* Freshmen: $3433. Undergraduates: $4358. *Parent loans:* $3,208,783 (97% need-based, 3% non-need-based). *Programs:* Federal Direct (Subsidized and Unsubsidized Stafford, PLUS), Perkins, private loans.

WORK-STUDY *Federal work-study:* Total amount: $996,500; 502 jobs averaging $1981.

APPLYING FOR FINANCIAL AID *Required financial aid forms:* FAFSA, institution's own form. *Financial aid deadline (priority):* 2/15. *Notification date:* Continuous beginning 2/15. Students must reply by 5/1 or within 3 weeks of notification.

CONTACT Director of Financial Aid, Marywood University, 2300 Adams Avenue, Scranton, PA 18509-1598, 570-348-6225 or toll-free 866-279-9663. *Fax:* 570-961-4739. *E-mail:* skrutski@marywood.edu.
Website: http://www.marywood.edu/.

MASSACHUSETTS COLLEGE OF ART AND DESIGN
Boston, MA

Tuition & fees (MA res): $10,400	Average undergraduate aid package: $9532

ABOUT THE INSTITUTION State-supported, coed. *Awards:* certificates, bachelor's, and master's degrees. 17 undergraduate majors. *Total enrollment:* 2,326. Undergraduates: 2,172. Freshmen: 353. Federal methodology is used as a basis for awarding need-based institutional aid.

UNDERGRADUATE EXPENSES for 2013–2014 *Application fee:* $50. *Tuition, state resident:* full-time $10,400. *Tuition, nonresident:* full-time $27,500. Part-time tuition and fees vary according to course load. *College room and board:* $12,150. Room and board charges vary according to board plan and housing facility.

FRESHMAN FINANCIAL AID (Fall 2012, est.) 312 applied for aid; of those 74% were deemed to have need. 100% of freshmen with need received aid. *Average financial aid package:* $10,463 (excluding resources awarded to replace EFC). 15% of all full-time freshmen had no need and received non-need-based gift aid.

UNDERGRADUATE FINANCIAL AID (Fall 2012, est.) 1,315 applied for aid; of those 79% were deemed to have need. 100% of undergraduates with need received aid. *Average financial aid package:* $9532 (excluding resources awarded to replace EFC). 7% of all full-time undergraduates had no need and received non-need-based gift aid.

GIFT AID (NEED-BASED) *Total amount:* $6,254,953 (38% federal, 11% state, 51% institutional). *Receiving aid:* Freshmen: 46% (163); all full-time undergraduates: 46% (749). *Average award:* Freshmen: $7976; Undergraduates: $7209. *Scholarships, grants, and awards:* Federal Pell, FSEOG, state, private, college/university gift aid from institutional funds.

GIFT AID (NON-NEED-BASED) *Total amount:* $977,852 (52% institutional, 48% external sources). *Receiving aid:* Freshmen: 14% (48). Undergraduates: 7% (116). *Average award:* Freshmen: $3549. Undergraduates: $3974. *Scholarships, grants, and awards by category: Special characteristics:* children of faculty/staff,

children of union members/company employees, veterans. *Tuition waivers:* Full or partial for employees or children of employees, senior citizens.

LOANS *Student loans:* $10,032,306 (42% need-based, 58% non-need-based). 73% of past graduating class borrowed through all loan programs. *Average indebtedness per student:* $25,875. *Average need-based loan:* Freshmen: $3357. Undergraduates: $4284. *Parent loans:* $5,341,684 (100% non-need-based). *Programs:* Federal Direct (Subsidized and Unsubsidized Stafford, PLUS), Perkins, state, alternative loans.

WORK-STUDY *Federal work-study:* Total amount: $160,000; 187 jobs averaging $1420. *State or other work-study/employment:* Total amount: $222,246 (100% non-need-based). Part-time jobs available.

APPLYING FOR FINANCIAL AID *Required financial aid form:* FAFSA. *Financial aid deadline (priority):* 3/1. *Notification date:* Continuous beginning 3/15. Students must reply within 3 weeks of notification.

CONTACT Auelio Ramirez, Director of Student Financial Assistance, Massachusetts College of Art and Design, 621 Huntington Avenue, Boston, MA 02115-5882, 617-879-7850. *Fax:* 617-879-7880. *E-mail:* aurelio.ramirez@massart.edu.
Website: http://www.massart.edu/.

MASSACHUSETTS COLLEGE OF LIBERAL ARTS
North Adams, MA

Tuition & fees (MA res): $8525	Average undergraduate aid package: $14,131

ABOUT THE INSTITUTION State-supported, coed. *Awards:* certificates, bachelor's, and master's degrees. 42 undergraduate majors. *Total enrollment:* 1,799. Undergraduates: 1,600. Freshmen: 313. Federal methodology is used as a basis for awarding need-based institutional aid.

UNDERGRADUATE EXPENSES for 2013–2014 *Application fee:* $40. *Tuition, state resident:* full-time $1030; part-time $42.92 per credit. *Tuition, nonresident:* full-time $9975; part-time $415.63 per credit. *Required fees:* full-time $7495; $253.42 per credit. Part-time tuition and fees vary according to course load. *College room and board:* $9102. Room and board charges vary according to board plan and housing facility.

FRESHMAN FINANCIAL AID (Fall 2012, est.) 297 applied for aid; of those 85% were deemed to have need. 99% of freshmen with need received aid; of those 73% had need fully met. *Average percent of need met:* 80% (excluding resources awarded to replace EFC). *Average financial aid package:* $14,397 (excluding resources awarded to replace EFC). 7% of all full-time freshmen had no need and received non-need-based gift aid.

UNDERGRADUATE FINANCIAL AID (Fall 2012, est.) 1,263 applied for aid; of those 83% were deemed to have need. 99% of undergraduates with need received aid; of those 73% had need fully met. *Average percent of need met:* 84% (excluding resources awarded to replace EFC). *Average financial aid package:* $14,131 (excluding resources awarded to replace EFC). 5% of all full-time undergraduates had no need and received non-need-based gift aid.

GIFT AID (NEED-BASED) *Total amount:* $6,114,745 (50% federal, 13% state, 31% institutional, 6% external sources). *Receiving aid:* Freshmen: 70% (215); all full-time undergraduates: 61% (858). *Average award:* Freshmen: $6832; Undergraduates: $6297. *Scholarships, grants, and awards:* Federal Pell, FSEOG, state, private, college/university gift aid from institutional funds.

GIFT AID (NON-NEED-BASED) *Total amount:* $230,803 (4% state, 66% institutional, 30% external sources). *Receiving aid:* Freshmen: 30% (92). Undergraduates: 14% (198). *Average award:* Freshmen: $4424. Undergraduates: $3390. *Scholarships, grants, and awards by category: Academic interests/ achievement:* biological sciences, business, communication, computer science, education, English, general academic interests/achievements, health fields, humanities, mathematics, physical sciences, social sciences. *Creative arts/performance:* applied art and design, art/fine arts, cinema/film/broadcasting, journalism/publications, music, performing arts, theater/drama. *Special achievements/activities:* general special achievements/activities, leadership, memberships. *Tuition waivers:* Full or partial for employees or children of employees, senior citizens.

LOANS *Student loans:* $8,380,693 (88% need-based, 12% non-need-based). 69% of past graduating class borrowed through all loan programs. *Average indebtedness per student:* $29,534. *Average need-based loan:* Freshmen: $3450. Undergraduates: $4147. *Parent loans:* $903,792 (72% need-based, 28% non-need-based). *Programs:* Federal Direct (Subsidized and Unsubsidized Stafford, PLUS), Perkins, state.

WORK-STUDY *Federal work-study:* Total amount: $278,506; jobs available. *State or other work-study/employment:* Total amount: $646,083 (100% non-need-based). Part-time jobs available.
APPLYING FOR FINANCIAL AID *Required financial aid forms:* FAFSA, institution's own form. *Financial aid deadline (priority):* 3/1. *Notification date:* Continuous beginning 3/1. Students must reply by 5/1 or within 2 weeks of notification.
CONTACT Mrs. Elizabeth M. Petri, Director of Financial Aid, Massachusetts College of Liberal Arts, 375 Church Street, North Adams, MA 01247, 413-662-5219 or toll-free 800-989-MCLA. *Fax:* 413-662-5105. *E-mail:* e.petri@mcla.edu. *Website:* http://www.mcla.edu/.

MASSACHUSETTS COLLEGE OF PHARMACY AND HEALTH SCIENCES
Boston, MA

CONTACT Shannon Gallagher, Director of Student Financial Services, Massachusetts College of Pharmacy and Health Sciences, 179 Longwood Avenue, Boston, MA 02115-5896, 617-879-5932. *Fax:* 617-732-2082. *E-mail:* shannon.gallagher1@mcphs.edu. *Website:* http://www.mcphs.edu/.

MASSACHUSETTS INSTITUTE OF TECHNOLOGY
Cambridge, MA

Tuition & fees: $42,050	Average undergraduate aid package: $38,604

ABOUT THE INSTITUTION Independent, coed. *Awards:* bachelor's, master's, and doctoral degrees. 35 undergraduate majors. *Total enrollment:* 11,189. Undergraduates: 4,503. Freshmen: 1,135. Institutional methodology is used as a basis for awarding need-based institutional aid.
UNDERGRADUATE EXPENSES for 2013–2014 *Application fee:* $75. *Comprehensive fee:* $54,238 includes full-time tuition ($41,770), mandatory fees ($280), and room and board ($12,188). *College room only:* $7554. Room and board charges vary according to board plan and housing facility. *Part-time tuition:* $650 per unit. Part-time tuition and fees vary according to course load.
FRESHMAN FINANCIAL AID (Fall 2011) 887 applied for aid; of those 79% were deemed to have need. 100% of freshmen with need received aid; of those 100% had need fully met. *Average percent of need met:* 100% (excluding resources awarded to replace EFC). *Average financial aid package:* $37,979 (excluding resources awarded to replace EFC).
UNDERGRADUATE FINANCIAL AID (Fall 2011) 3,222 applied for aid; of those 87% were deemed to have need. 100% of undergraduates with need received aid; of those 100% had need fully met. *Average percent of need met:* 100% (excluding resources awarded to replace EFC). *Average financial aid package:* $38,604 (excluding resources awarded to replace EFC).
GIFT AID (NEED-BASED) *Total amount:* $98,112,763 (7% federal, 89% institutional, 4% external sources). *Receiving aid:* Freshmen: 59% (670); all full-time undergraduates: 62% (2,695). *Average award:* Freshmen: $35,719; Undergraduates: $35,993. *Scholarships, grants, and awards:* Federal Pell, FSEOG, state, private, college/university gift aid from institutional funds.
GIFT AID (NON-NEED-BASED) *Total amount:* $6,733,664 (18% federal, 82% external sources). *Receiving aid:* Freshmen: 2% (21). Undergraduates: 2% (76). *Tuition waivers:* Full or partial for employees or children of employees. *ROTC:* Army, Naval, Air Force.
LOANS *Student loans:* $10,861,503 (53% need-based, 47% non-need-based). 41% of past graduating class borrowed through all loan programs. *Average indebtedness per student:* $20,794. *Average need-based loan:* Freshmen: $3159. Undergraduates: $3511. *Parent loans:* $4,142,499 (4% need-based, 96% non-need-based). *Programs:* Federal Direct (Subsidized and Unsubsidized Stafford, PLUS), Perkins, college/university.

WORK-STUDY *Federal work-study:* Total amount: $2,194,466; 849 jobs averaging $2585. *State or other work-study/employment:* Total amount: $3,233,810 (72% need-based, 28% non-need-based). 1,091 part-time jobs averaging $2964.
APPLYING FOR FINANCIAL AID *Required financial aid forms:* FAFSA, CSS Financial Aid PROFILE, noncustodial (divorced/separated) parent's statement, business/farm supplement, federal income tax form(s), W-2 forms. *Financial aid deadline:* 2/15. *Notification date:* 4/1. Students must reply by 5/1.
CONTACT Elizabeth Hicks, Executive Director of Student Financial Services, Massachusetts Institute of Technology, 77 Massachusetts Avenue, Room 11-320, Cambridge, MA 02139-4307, 617-258-8600. *Fax:* 617-258-0700. *E-mail:* sfs@mit.edu. *Website:* http://web.mit.edu/.

MASSACHUSETTS MARITIME ACADEMY
Buzzards Bay, MA

Tuition & fees: N/R	Average undergraduate aid package: $9510

ABOUT THE INSTITUTION State-supported, coed, primarily men. *Awards:* bachelor's and master's degrees. 10 undergraduate majors. *Total enrollment:* 1,415. Undergraduates: 1,312. Freshmen: 305. Federal methodology is used as a basis for awarding need-based institutional aid.
UNDERGRADUATE FINANCIAL AID (Fall 2011) 911 applied for aid; of those 71% were deemed to have need. 100% of undergraduates with need received aid; of those 24% had need fully met. *Average percent of need met:* 70% (excluding resources awarded to replace EFC). *Average financial aid package:* $9510 (excluding resources awarded to replace EFC). 7% of all full-time undergraduates had no need and received non-need-based gift aid.
GIFT AID (NEED-BASED) *Total amount:* $2,323,169 (45% federal, 19% state, 36% institutional). *Receiving aid:* All full-time undergraduates: 37% (473). *Average award:* Undergraduates: $5192. *Scholarships, grants, and awards:* Federal Pell, FSEOG, state, private, college/university gift aid from institutional funds.
GIFT AID (NON-NEED-BASED) *Total amount:* $1,067,727 (16% federal, 5% state, 58% institutional, 21% external sources). *Receiving aid:* Undergraduates: 2% (21). *Average award:* Undergraduates: $3296. *Scholarships, grants, and awards by category:* Academic interests/achievement: 10 awards ($93,975 total): general academic interests/achievements. *Special achievements/activities:* leadership. *Special characteristics:* children and siblings of alumni, children of faculty/staff, veterans. *ROTC:* Army cooperative, Naval.
LOANS *Student loans:* $8,751,656 (28% need-based, 72% non-need-based). 75% of past graduating class borrowed through all loan programs. *Average indebtedness per student:* $32,400. *Average need-based loan:* Undergraduates: $3938. *Parent loans:* $1,675,895 (100% non-need-based). *Programs:* Federal Direct (Subsidized and Unsubsidized Stafford, PLUS).
WORK-STUDY *Federal work-study:* Total amount: $82,625; 115 jobs averaging $1000.
APPLYING FOR FINANCIAL AID *Required financial aid forms:* FAFSA, institution's own form. *Financial aid deadline (priority):* 5/1. *Notification date:* Continuous beginning 3/20.
CONTACT Ms. Catherine Kedski, Director of Financial Aid, Massachusetts Maritime Academy, 101 Academy Drive, Buzzards Bay, MA 02532, 508-830-5042 or toll-free 800-544-3411. *Fax:* 508-830-5077. *E-mail:* ckedski@maritime.edu. *Website:* http://www.maritime.edu/.

THE MASTER'S COLLEGE AND SEMINARY
Santa Clarita, CA

Tuition & fees: $29,480	Average undergraduate aid package: $18,530

ABOUT THE INSTITUTION Independent nondenominational, coed. *Awards:* certificates, bachelor's, master's, and doctoral degrees. 47 undergraduate majors.

Total enrollment: 1,534. Undergraduates: 1,134. Freshmen: 209. Federal methodology is used as a basis for awarding need-based institutional aid.

UNDERGRADUATE EXPENSES for 2013–2014 Application fee: $40. **Comprehensive fee:** $38,840 includes full-time tuition ($28,380), mandatory fees ($1100), and room and board ($9360). Full-time tuition and fees vary according to course load, degree level, and program. Room and board charges vary according to board plan. **Part-time tuition:** $1190 per credit hour. **Part-time fees:** $1190 per credit hour. Part-time tuition and fees vary according to course load, degree level, and program.

FRESHMAN FINANCIAL AID (Fall 2012, est.) 210 applied for aid; of those 85% were deemed to have need. 99% of freshmen with need received aid; of those 11% had need fully met. **Average percent of need met:** 67% (excluding resources awarded to replace EFC). **Average financial aid package:** $19,556 (excluding resources awarded to replace EFC). 19% of all full-time freshmen had no need and received non-need-based gift aid.

UNDERGRADUATE FINANCIAL AID (Fall 2012, est.) 1,014 applied for aid; of those 89% were deemed to have need. 98% of undergraduates with need received aid; of those 11% had need fully met. **Average percent of need met:** 63% (excluding resources awarded to replace EFC). **Average financial aid package:** $18,530 (excluding resources awarded to replace EFC). 15% of all full-time undergraduates had no need and received non-need-based gift aid.

GIFT AID (NEED-BASED) Total amount: $11,700,940 (16% federal, 16% state, 53% institutional, 15% external sources). **Receiving aid:** Freshmen: 65% (174); all full-time undergraduates: 72% (846). **Average award:** Freshmen: $16,174; Undergraduates: $14,911. **Scholarships, grants, and awards:** Federal Pell, FSEOG, state, private, college/university gift aid from institutional funds.

GIFT AID (NON-NEED-BASED) Total amount: $2,362,262 (67% institutional, 33% external sources). **Receiving aid:** Freshmen: 6% (16). Undergraduates: 6% (71). **Average award:** Freshmen: $7659. Undergraduates: $8489. **Scholarships, grants, and awards by category:** Academic interests/achievement: 594 awards ($3,492,842 total): biological sciences, business, education, general academic interests/achievements, mathematics, physical sciences, religion/biblical studies, social sciences. Creative arts/performance: 87 awards ($239,689 total): music. Special achievements/activities: 21 awards ($294,000 total): leadership. Special characteristics: 286 awards ($1,664,149 total): children and siblings of alumni, children of faculty/staff, general special characteristics, international students, relatives of clergy. **Tuition waivers:** Full or partial for employees or children of employees.

LOANS Student loans: $7,797,084 (80% need-based, 20% non-need-based). 40% of past graduating class borrowed through all loan programs. **Average indebtedness per student:** $18,121. **Average need-based loan:** Freshmen: $3318. Undergraduates: $4208. **Parent loans:** $1,878,576 (56% need-based, 44% non-need-based). **Programs:** Perkins, alternative loans.

WORK-STUDY Federal work-study: Total amount: $85,224; 56 jobs averaging $1519. **State or other work-study/employment:** Total amount: $588,776 (75% need-based, 25% non-need-based). 187 part-time jobs averaging $2209.

ATHLETIC AWARDS Total amount: $1,996,419 (57% need-based, 43% non-need-based).

APPLYING FOR FINANCIAL AID Required financial aid forms: FAFSA, institution's own form, state aid form. **Financial aid deadline (priority):** 3/2. **Notification date:** Continuous beginning 2/1. Students must reply by 5/1 or within 2 weeks of notification.

CONTACT Mr. Gary Edwards, Director of Financial Aid, The Master's College and Seminary, 21726 Placerita Canyon Road, Santa Clarita, CA 91321-1200, 661-362-2291 or toll-free 800-568-6248. *Fax:* 661-362-2693. *E-mail:* gedwards@masters.edu. *Website:* http://www.masters.edu/.

MATER ECCLESIAE COLLEGE
Greenville, RI

CONTACT Financial Aid Office, Mater Ecclesiae College, 60 Austin Avenue, Greenville, RI 02828, 401-949-2820.
Website: http://www.mecollege.edu/.

MAYVILLE STATE UNIVERSITY
Mayville, ND

Tuition & fees (ND res): $6193	Average undergraduate aid package: $8207

ABOUT THE INSTITUTION State-supported, coed. **Awards:** associate and bachelor's degrees. 34 undergraduate majors. **Total enrollment:** 1,020. Undergraduates: 990. Freshmen: 157. Federal methodology is used as a basis for awarding need-based institutional aid.

UNDERGRADUATE EXPENSES for 2013–2014 Application fee: $35. **One-time required fee:** $35. **Tuition, state resident:** full-time $4484; part-time $187 per credit hour. **Tuition, nonresident:** full-time $6727; part-time $280 per credit hour. **Required fees:** full-time $1709; $71.22 per credit hour. Full-time tuition and fees vary according to course load and reciprocity agreements. Part-time tuition and fees vary according to course load and reciprocity agreements. **College room and board:** $4854; **Room only:** $1874. Room and board charges vary according to board plan and housing facility.

FRESHMAN FINANCIAL AID (Fall 2012, est.) 131 applied for aid; of those 78% were deemed to have need. 100% of freshmen with need received aid; of those 17% had need fully met. **Average percent of need met:** 2% (excluding resources awarded to replace EFC). **Average financial aid package:** $7996 (excluding resources awarded to replace EFC). 40% of all full-time freshmen had no need and received non-need-based gift aid.

UNDERGRADUATE FINANCIAL AID (Fall 2012, est.) 513 applied for aid; of those 77% were deemed to have need. 99% of undergraduates with need received aid; of those 12% had need fully met. **Average percent of need met:** 1% (excluding resources awarded to replace EFC). **Average financial aid package:** $8207 (excluding resources awarded to replace EFC). 27% of all full-time undergraduates had no need and received non-need-based gift aid.

GIFT AID (NEED-BASED) Total amount: $1,766,686 (72% federal, 14% state, 10% institutional, 4% external sources). **Receiving aid:** Freshmen: 61% (91); all full-time undergraduates: 56% (345). **Average award:** Freshmen: $4093; Undergraduates: $4117. **Scholarships, grants, and awards:** Federal Pell, FSEOG, state, private, college/university gift aid from institutional funds.

GIFT AID (NON-NEED-BASED) Total amount: $40,276 (18% federal, 10% state, 40% institutional, 32% external sources). **Receiving aid:** Freshmen: 4% (6). Undergraduates: 2% (12). **Average award:** Freshmen: $1098. Undergraduates: $1109. **Scholarships, grants, and awards by category:** Academic interests/achievement: 325 awards ($248,091 total): biological sciences, business, communication, computer science, education, English, general academic interests/achievements, health fields, library science, mathematics, physical sciences, premedicine, social sciences. Creative arts/performance: 76 awards ($35,500 total): music, theater/drama. Special characteristics: 107 awards ($194,020 total): children of faculty/staff, international students, local/state students, members of minority groups, out-of-state students. **Tuition waivers:** Full or partial for minority students, employees or children of employees, senior citizens. **ROTC:** Army cooperative, Air Force cooperative.

LOANS Student loans: $3,275,063 (83% need-based, 17% non-need-based). 77% of past graduating class borrowed through all loan programs. **Average indebtedness per student:** $30,351. **Average need-based loan:** Freshmen: $3681. Undergraduates: $4076. **Parent loans:** $599,785 (40% need-based, 60% non-need-based). **Programs:** Federal Direct (Subsidized and Unsubsidized Stafford, PLUS), Perkins, college/university.

WORK-STUDY Federal work-study: Total amount: $51,583; 52 jobs averaging $1000.

ATHLETIC AWARDS Total amount: $178,928 (53% need-based, 47% non-need-based).

APPLYING FOR FINANCIAL AID Required financial aid form: FAFSA. **Financial aid deadline (priority):** 2/15. **Notification date:** Continuous beginning 5/1. Students must reply within 2 weeks of notification.

CONTACT Ms. Shirley Hanson, Director of Financial Aid, Mayville State University, 330 3rd Street NE, Mayville, ND 58257-1299, 701-788-4767 or toll-free 800-437-4104. *Fax:* 701-788-4818. *E-mail:* shirley.hanson@mayvillestate.edu. *Website:* http://www.mayvillestate.edu/.

MCDANIEL COLLEGE
Westminster, MD

Tuition & fees: $36,960	Average undergraduate aid package: $27,184

ABOUT THE INSTITUTION Independent, coed. **Awards:** certificates, bachelor's, and master's degrees. 34 undergraduate majors. **Total enrollment:** 3,284. Undergraduates: 1,650. Freshmen: 437. Both federal and institutional methodology are used as a basis for awarding need-based institutional aid.

UNDERGRADUATE EXPENSES for 2013–2014 Application fee: $50. **Comprehensive fee:** $45,600 includes full-time tuition ($36,960) and room and board ($8640). Full-time tuition and fees vary according to course load. Room and board charges vary according to board plan and housing facility. **Part-time tuition:** $1155 per credit hour. Part-time tuition and fees vary according to course load and reciprocity agreements. **Payment plan:** Tuition prepayment.

FRESHMAN FINANCIAL AID (Fall 2012, est.) 400 applied for aid; of those 90% were deemed to have need. 100% of freshmen with need received aid; of those 25% had need fully met. **Average percent of need met:** 86% (excluding resources awarded to replace EFC). **Average financial aid package:** $29,516 (excluding resources awarded to replace EFC). 16% of all full-time freshmen had no need and received non-need-based gift aid.

UNDERGRADUATE FINANCIAL AID (Fall 2012, est.) 1,301 applied for aid; of those 92% were deemed to have need. 99% of undergraduates with need received aid; of those 30% had need fully met. **Average percent of need met:** 78% (excluding resources awarded to replace EFC). **Average financial aid package:** $27,184 (excluding resources awarded to replace EFC). 26% of all full-time undergraduates had no need and received non-need-based gift aid.

GIFT AID (NEED-BASED) Total amount: $27,872,119 (9% federal, 3% state, 88% institutional). **Receiving aid:** Freshmen: 81% (353); all full-time undergraduates: 71% (1,140). **Average award:** Freshmen: $25,674; Undergraduates: $23,284. **Scholarships, grants, and awards:** Federal Pell, FSEOG, state, private, college/university gift aid from institutional funds.

GIFT AID (NON-NEED-BASED) Total amount: $7,302,437 (4% state, 94% institutional, 2% external sources). **Receiving aid:** Freshmen: 18% (77). Undergraduates: 8% (136). **Average award:** Freshmen: $17,312. Undergraduates: $15,825. **Scholarships, grants, and awards by category:** Academic interests/achievement: 1,159 awards ($18,131,686 total): general academic interests/achievements. Special achievements/activities: 6 awards ($11,000 total): junior miss, leadership. Special characteristics: 262 awards ($620,318 total): general special characteristics, local/state students, previous college experience, siblings of current students, veterans. **Tuition waivers:** Full or partial for employees or children of employees. **ROTC:** Army.

LOANS Student loans: $9,490,040 (45% need-based, 55% non-need-based). 64% of past graduating class borrowed through all loan programs. **Average indebtedness per student:** $31,919. **Average need-based loan:** Freshmen: $4340. Undergraduates: $4773. **Parent loans:** $2,660,799 (100% non-need-based). **Programs:** Federal Direct (Subsidized and Unsubsidized Stafford, PLUS), Perkins, college/university.

WORK-STUDY Federal work-study: Total amount: $355,801; 349 jobs averaging $1019. **State or other work-study/employment:** Total amount: $220,416 (100% non-need-based). 301 part-time jobs averaging $732.

APPLYING FOR FINANCIAL AID Required financial aid forms: FAFSA, institution's own form, federal income tax form(s). **Financial aid deadline (priority):** 3/1. **Notification date:** Continuous beginning 3/1. Students must reply by 5/1 or within 2 weeks of notification.

CONTACT Ms. Ellie Geiman, Financial Aid Office, McDaniel College, 2 College Hill, Westminster, MD 21157-4390, 410-857-2233 or toll-free 800-638-5005. Fax: 410-857-2729. E-mail: finaid@mcdaniel.edu.
Website: http://www.mcdaniel.edu/.

MCKENDREE UNIVERSITY
Lebanon, IL

Tuition & fees: $26,050	Average undergraduate aid package: $17,998

ABOUT THE INSTITUTION Independent United Methodist Church, coed. **Awards:** certificates, associate, bachelor's, master's, and doctoral degrees. 56 undergraduate majors. **Total enrollment:** 3,308. Undergraduates: 2,356. Freshmen: 290. Federal methodology is used as a basis for awarding need-based institutional aid.

UNDERGRADUATE EXPENSES for 2013–2014 Comprehensive fee: $34,740 includes full-time tuition ($25,050), mandatory fees ($1000), and room and board ($8690). **College room only:** $4620. Full-time tuition and fees vary according to course load, degree level, and location. Room and board charges vary according to board plan and housing facility. **Part-time tuition:** $830 per credit hour. Part-time tuition and fees vary according to course load, degree level, and location.

FRESHMAN FINANCIAL AID (Fall 2012, est.) 265 applied for aid; of those 86% were deemed to have need. 100% of freshmen with need received aid; of those 20% had need fully met. **Average percent of need met:** 77% (excluding resources awarded to replace EFC). **Average financial aid package:** $21,182 (excluding resources awarded to replace EFC). 24% of all full-time freshmen had no need and received non-need-based gift aid.

UNDERGRADUATE FINANCIAL AID (Fall 2012, est.) 1,366 applied for aid; of those 91% were deemed to have need. 99% of undergraduates with need received aid; of those 18% had need fully met. **Average percent of need met:** 71% (excluding resources awarded to replace EFC). **Average financial aid package:** $17,998 (excluding resources awarded to replace EFC). 14% of all full-time undergraduates had no need and received non-need-based gift aid.

GIFT AID (NEED-BASED) Total amount: $15,636,503 (19% federal, 14% state, 63% institutional, 4% external sources). **Receiving aid:** Freshmen: 74% (225); all full-time undergraduates: 78% (1,187). **Average award:** Freshmen: $17,974; Undergraduates: $14,459. **Scholarships, grants, and awards:** Federal Pell, FSEOG, state, private, college/university gift aid from institutional funds.

GIFT AID (NON-NEED-BASED) Total amount: $2,668,650 (87% institutional, 13% external sources). **Receiving aid:** Freshmen: 11% (34). Undergraduates: 10% (153). **Average award:** Freshmen: $11,741. Undergraduates: $9033. **Scholarships, grants, and awards by category:** Academic interests/achievement: 876 awards ($5,958,028 total): biological sciences, business, general academic interests/achievements, religion/biblical studies. Creative arts/performance: 158 awards ($624,262 total): dance, debating, music. Special achievements/activities: 48 awards ($120,750 total): cheerleading/drum major, community service, leadership. Special characteristics: 266 awards ($560,136 total): children and siblings of alumni, children of faculty/staff, general special characteristics, international students, religious affiliation, veterans, veterans' children. **Tuition waivers:** Full or partial for children of alumni, employees or children of employees. **ROTC:** Army cooperative, Air Force cooperative.

LOANS Student loans: $10,905,108 (73% need-based, 27% non-need-based). 76% of past graduating class borrowed through all loan programs. **Average indebtedness per student:** $23,005. **Average need-based loan:** Freshmen: $3144. Undergraduates: $4147. **Parent loans:** $3,578,434 (29% need-based, 71% non-need-based). **Programs:** Federal Direct (Subsidized and Unsubsidized Stafford, PLUS), Perkins.

WORK-STUDY Federal work-study: Total amount: $866,117; 767 jobs averaging $1784. **State or other work-study/employment:** Total amount: $110,369 (5% need-based, 95% non-need-based). 99 part-time jobs averaging $1148.

ATHLETIC AWARDS Total amount: $3,761,987 (54% need-based, 46% non-need-based).

APPLYING FOR FINANCIAL AID Required financial aid form: FAFSA. **Financial aid deadline (priority):** 5/31. **Notification date:** Continuous beginning 3/1.

CONTACT Elizabeth L. Juehne, Director of Financial Aid, McKendree University, 701 College Road, Lebanon, IL 62254-1299, 618-537-6532 or toll-free 800-232-7228. Fax: 618-537-6530. E-mail: bjuehne@mckendree.edu.
Website: http://www.mckendree.edu/.

MCMURRY UNIVERSITY
Abilene, TX

Tuition & fees: $23,305	Average undergraduate aid package: $19,228

ABOUT THE INSTITUTION Independent United Methodist, coed. *Awards:* bachelor's and master's degrees. 46 undergraduate majors. *Total enrollment:* 1,368. Undergraduates: 1,365. Freshmen: 303. Federal methodology is used as a basis for awarding need-based institutional aid.

UNDERGRADUATE EXPENSES for 2013–2014 *Application fee:* $25. *One-time required fee:* $175. *Comprehensive fee:* $30,765 includes full-time tuition ($23,305) and room and board ($7460). *College room only:* $3636. Full-time tuition and fees vary according to course load. Room and board charges vary according to board plan and housing facility. *Part-time tuition:* $728 per credit hour. Part-time tuition and fees vary according to course load.

FRESHMAN FINANCIAL AID (Fall 2012, est.) 283 applied for aid; of those 91% were deemed to have need. 100% of freshmen with need received aid; of those 8% had need fully met. *Average percent of need met:* 82% (excluding resources awarded to replace EFC). *Average financial aid package:* $21,519 (excluding resources awarded to replace EFC). 6% of all full-time freshmen had no need and received non-need-based gift aid.

UNDERGRADUATE FINANCIAL AID (Fall 2012, est.) 1,044 applied for aid; of those 91% were deemed to have need. 100% of undergraduates with need received aid; of those 7% had need fully met. *Average percent of need met:* 78% (excluding resources awarded to replace EFC). *Average financial aid package:* $19,228 (excluding resources awarded to replace EFC). 6% of all full-time undergraduates had no need and received non-need-based gift aid.

GIFT AID (NEED-BASED) *Total amount:* $8,922,756 (31% federal, 18% state, 48% institutional, 3% external sources). *Receiving aid:* Freshmen: 77% (233); all full-time undergraduates: 73% (843). *Average award:* Freshmen: $11,285; Undergraduates: $9552. *Scholarships, grants, and awards:* Federal Pell, FSEOG, state, private, college/university gift aid from institutional funds.

GIFT AID (NON-NEED-BASED) *Total amount:* $4,802,763 (2% federal, 12% state, 86% institutional). *Receiving aid:* Freshmen: 48% (145). Undergraduates: 52% (602). *Average award:* Freshmen: $6842. Undergraduates: $6556. *Scholarships, grants, and awards by category: Academic interests/achievement:* 386 awards ($1,036,439 total): biological sciences, business, computer science, education, English, general academic interests/achievements, mathematics, physical sciences, premedicine, religion/biblical studies, social sciences. *Creative arts/performance:* 16 awards ($28,329 total): art/fine arts, music, theater/drama. *Special achievements/activities:* 64 awards ($128,200 total): general special achievements/activities. *Special characteristics:* 331 awards ($2,303,793 total): children of faculty/staff, ethnic background, international students, local/state students, out-of-state students, previous college experience, relatives of clergy, religious affiliation. *Tuition waivers:* Full or partial for employees or children of employees.

LOANS *Student loans:* $7,968,192 (43% need-based, 57% non-need-based). 82% of past graduating class borrowed through all loan programs. *Average indebtedness per student:* $38,921. *Average need-based loan:* Freshmen: $3697. Undergraduates: $4522. *Parent loans:* $590,204 (100% non-need-based). *Programs:* Federal Direct (Subsidized and Unsubsidized Stafford, PLUS), Perkins, state, alternative loans, Bonner Price Loans, United Methodist Student Loans.

WORK-STUDY *Federal work-study:* Total amount: $501,701; 228 jobs averaging $2184. *State or other work-study/employment:* Total amount: $113,064 (31% need-based, 69% non-need-based). 48 part-time jobs averaging $2291.

ATHLETIC AWARDS Total amount: $2,986,350 (100% non-need-based).

APPLYING FOR FINANCIAL AID *Required financial aid form:* FAFSA. *Financial aid deadline (priority):* 3/15. *Notification date:* Continuous beginning 2/1. Students must reply within 3 weeks of notification.

CONTACT Rachel Atkins, Director of Financial Aid, McMurry University, #1 McMurry University Box 908, Abilene, TX 79697, 325-793-4709 or toll-free 800-460-2392. *Fax:* 325-793-4718. *E-mail:* atkinsr@mcmurryadm.mcm.edu. *Website:* http://www.mcm.edu/.

MCNALLY SMITH COLLEGE OF MUSIC
Saint Paul, MN

Tuition & fees: $25,990	Average undergraduate aid package: $7419

ABOUT THE INSTITUTION Proprietary, coed. *Awards:* diplomas, associate, bachelor's, and master's degrees. 9 undergraduate majors. *Total enrollment:* 644. Undergraduates: 629. Freshmen: 120. Federal methodology is used as a basis for awarding need-based institutional aid.

UNDERGRADUATE EXPENSES for 2013–2014 *Application fee:* $75. *Comprehensive fee:* $31,090 includes full-time tuition ($23,790), mandatory fees ($2200), and room and board ($5100). Full-time tuition and fees vary according to course load and degree level. Room and board charges vary according to board plan and housing facility. *Part-time tuition:* $915 per credit hour. *Part-time fees:* $450 per term. Part-time tuition and fees vary according to course load and degree level. *Payment plans:* Guaranteed tuition, tuition prepayment.

FRESHMAN FINANCIAL AID (Fall 2011) 100 applied for aid; of those 93% were deemed to have need. 99% of freshmen with need received aid. *Average percent of need met:* 34% (excluding resources awarded to replace EFC). *Average financial aid package:* $7844 (excluding resources awarded to replace EFC).

UNDERGRADUATE FINANCIAL AID (Fall 2011) 514 applied for aid; of those 91% were deemed to have need. 89% of undergraduates with need received aid. *Average percent of need met:* 32% (excluding resources awarded to replace EFC). *Average financial aid package:* $7419 (excluding resources awarded to replace EFC).

GIFT AID (NEED-BASED) *Total amount:* $1,533,984 (64% federal, 21% state, 15% institutional). *Receiving aid:* Freshmen: 49% (56); all full-time undergraduates: 40% (259). *Average award:* Freshmen: $5590; Undergraduates: $6096. *Scholarships, grants, and awards:* Federal Pell, FSEOG, state, private, college/university gift aid from institutional funds.

GIFT AID (NON-NEED-BASED) *Total amount:* $860,690 (31% federal, 11% state, 46% institutional, 12% external sources). *Receiving aid:* Freshmen: 12% (14). Undergraduates: 6% (38). *Scholarships, grants, and awards by category: Creative arts/performance:* music. *Special characteristics:* children of faculty/staff, veterans, veterans' children. *Tuition waivers:* Full or partial for employees or children of employees.

LOANS *Student loans:* $6,444,088 (32% need-based, 68% non-need-based). *Average need-based loan:* Freshmen: $3343. Undergraduates: $4114. *Parent loans:* $3,233,010 (100% non-need-based). *Programs:* Federal Direct (Subsidized and Unsubsidized Stafford, PLUS), state, college/university, private loans.

WORK-STUDY *Federal work-study:* Total amount: $75,340; 38 jobs averaging $1983. *State or other work-study/employment:* Total amount: $29,720 (100% need-based). 23 part-time jobs averaging $1292.

APPLYING FOR FINANCIAL AID *Required financial aid forms:* FAFSA, institution's own form. *Financial aid deadline:* 8/1 (priority: 3/1). *Notification date:* Continuous beginning 3/15. Students must reply by 5/1 or within 2 weeks of notification.

CONTACT Mr. Paul Haugen, Director of Financial Aid, McNally Smith College of Music, 19 Exchange Street East, Saint Paul, MN 55101-2220, 651-361-3321 or toll-free 800-594-9500. *Fax:* 651-291-0366. *E-mail:* paul.haugen@mcnallysmith.edu. *Website:* http://www.mcnallysmith.edu/.

MCNEESE STATE UNIVERSITY
Lake Charles, LA

Tuition & fees (LA res): $5120	Average undergraduate aid package: N/A

ABOUT THE INSTITUTION State-supported, coed. *Awards:* certificates, associate, bachelor's, and master's degrees. 37 undergraduate majors. *Total enrollment:* 8,588. Undergraduates: 7,711. Freshmen: 1,315. Federal methodology is used as a basis for awarding need-based institutional aid.

UNDERGRADUATE EXPENSES for 2013–2014 *Application fee:* $20. *Tuition, state resident:* full-time $5120. *Tuition, nonresident:* full-time $11,454. Full-time tuition and fees vary according to course load. Part-time tuition and fees vary according to course load. *College room and board:* $7468. Room and board charges vary according to board plan and housing facility.

GIFT AID (NEED-BASED) *Scholarships, grants, and awards:* Federal Pell, FSEOG, state.

GIFT AID (NON-NEED-BASED) *Scholarships, grants, and awards by category:* *Academic interests/achievement:* agriculture, biological sciences, business, communication, computer science, education, engineering/technologies, English, foreign languages, general academic interests/achievements, health fields, home economics, humanities, library science, mathematics, physical sciences, premedicine, social sciences. *Creative arts/performance:* art/fine arts, cinema/film/broadcasting, creative writing, dance, debating, general creative arts/performance, journalism/publications, music, performing arts, theater/drama. *Special achievements/activities:* cheerleading/drum major, community service, general special achievements/activities, leadership, memberships, rodeo. *Special characteristics:* adult students, children and siblings of alumni, children of faculty/staff, children of public servants, children with a deceased or disabled parent, ethnic background, first-generation college students, general special characteristics, handicapped students, international students, local/state students, members of minority groups, out-of-state students, previous college experience, veterans, veterans' children. *Tuition waivers:* Full or partial for employees or children of employees, senior citizens.

LOANS *Programs:* Federal Direct (Subsidized Stafford), Perkins.

APPLYING FOR FINANCIAL AID *Required financial aid forms:* FAFSA, institution's own form. *Financial aid deadline (priority):* 5/1. *Notification date:* Continuous beginning 3/15. Students must reply within 2 weeks of notification.

CONTACT Ms. Taina J. Savoit, Director of Financial Aid, McNeese State University, PO Box 93260, Lake Charles, LA 70609-3260, 337-475-5065 or toll-free 800-622-3352. *Fax:* 337-475-5068. *E-mail:* financialaid@mcneese.edu. *Website:* http://www.mcneese.edu/.

MCPHERSON COLLEGE
McPherson, KS

Tuition & fees: $21,801	Average undergraduate aid package: $21,302

ABOUT THE INSTITUTION Independent Church of the Brethren, coed. *Awards:* bachelor's degrees. 28 undergraduate majors. *Total enrollment:* 620. Undergraduates: 620. Freshmen: 134. Federal methodology is used as a basis for awarding need-based institutional aid.

UNDERGRADUATE EXPENSES for 2013–2014 *Application fee:* $25. *Comprehensive fee:* $29,565 includes full-time tuition ($21,801) and room and board ($7764). *College room only:* $3206. Full-time tuition and fees vary according to course load and program.

FRESHMAN FINANCIAL AID (Fall 2011) 127 applied for aid; of those 89% were deemed to have need. 100% of freshmen with need received aid; of those 20% had need fully met. *Average percent of need met:* 79% (excluding resources awarded to replace EFC). *Average financial aid package:* $20,412 (excluding resources awarded to replace EFC). 14% of all full-time freshmen had no need and received non-need-based gift aid.

UNDERGRADUATE FINANCIAL AID (Fall 2011) 547 applied for aid; of those 90% were deemed to have need. 100% of undergraduates with need received aid; of those 23% had need fully met. *Average percent of need met:* 83% (excluding resources awarded to replace EFC). *Average financial aid package:* $21,302 (excluding resources awarded to replace EFC). 14% of all full-time undergraduates had no need and received non-need-based gift aid.

GIFT AID (NEED-BASED) *Total amount:* $2,731,091 (47% federal, 16% state, 37% institutional). *Receiving aid:* Freshmen: 70% (93); all full-time undergraduates: 70% (413). *Average award:* Freshmen: $6065; Undergraduates: $6328. *Scholarships, grants, and awards:* Federal Pell, FSEOG, state, private, college/university gift aid from institutional funds.

GIFT AID (NON-NEED-BASED) *Total amount:* $4,836,543 (98% institutional, 2% external sources). *Receiving aid:* Freshmen: 83% (110). Undergraduates: 82% (484). *Average award:* Freshmen: $7694. Undergraduates: $8097. *Scholarships, grants, and awards by category:* *Academic interests/achievement:* 664 awards ($2,993,079 total): general academic interests/achievements. *Creative arts/performance:* 50 awards ($122,750 total): art/fine arts, journalism/publications, music, performing arts, theater/drama. *Special achievements/activities:* 40 awards ($88,383 total): cheerleading/drum major, community service, religious involvement. *Special characteristics:* 24 awards ($38,000 total): children and siblings of alumni, religious affiliation. *Tuition waivers:* Full or partial for employees or children of employees.

LOANS *Student loans:* $4,343,878 (100% need-based). 88% of past graduating class borrowed through all loan programs. *Average indebtedness per student:* $27,529. *Average need-based loan:* Freshmen: $6927. Undergraduates: $8194. *Parent loans:* $1,102,619 (100% non-need-based). *Programs:* Federal Direct (Subsidized and Unsubsidized Stafford, PLUS), Perkins.

WORK-STUDY *Federal work-study:* Total amount: $219,416; 300 jobs averaging $978. *State or other work-study/employment:* Part-time jobs available.

ATHLETIC AWARDS Total amount: $1,321,641 (100% non-need-based).

APPLYING FOR FINANCIAL AID *Required financial aid forms:* FAFSA, state aid form. *Financial aid deadline (priority):* 3/1. *Notification date:* Continuous beginning 3/1. Students must reply within 3 weeks of notification.

CONTACT Ms. Brenda Krehbiel, Director of Financial Aid, McPherson College, 1600 East Euclid, McPherson, KS 67460-1402, 620-242-0400 Ext. 2415 or toll-free 800-365-7402. *Fax:* 620-241-8443. *E-mail:* krehbieb2@mcpherson.edu. *Website:* http://www.mcpherson.edu/.

MEDAILLE COLLEGE
Buffalo, NY

ABOUT THE INSTITUTION Independent, coed. *Awards:* certificates, associate, bachelor's, master's, and doctoral degrees. 18 undergraduate majors. *Total enrollment:* 2,634. Undergraduates: 1,844. Freshmen: 400.

GIFT AID (NEED-BASED) *Scholarships, grants, and awards:* Federal Pell, FSEOG, state, private, college/university gift aid from institutional funds.

GIFT AID (NON-NEED-BASED) *Scholarships, grants, and awards by category:* *Academic interests/achievement:* biological sciences, business, communication, education, general academic interests/achievements, mathematics. *Creative arts/performance:* general creative arts/performance. *Special characteristics:* adult students, children of faculty/staff.

LOANS *Programs:* Federal Direct (Subsidized and Unsubsidized Stafford, PLUS), state.

WORK-STUDY *Federal work-study:* Total amount: $339,670; 234 jobs averaging $1451.

APPLYING FOR FINANCIAL AID *Required financial aid forms:* FAFSA, institution's own form, state aid form.

CONTACT Ms. Catherine Buzanski, Director of Financial Aid, Medaille College, 18 Agassiz Circle, Buffalo, NY 14214-2695, 716-880-2179 or toll-free 800-292-1582. *Fax:* 716-884-0291. *E-mail:* cbuzanski@medaille.edu. *Website:* http://www.medaille.edu/.

MEDGAR EVERS COLLEGE OF THE CITY UNIVERSITY OF NEW YORK
Brooklyn, NY

Tuition & fees (NY res): $5432	Average undergraduate aid package: $4040

ABOUT THE INSTITUTION State and locally supported, coed. *Awards:* certificates, associate, and bachelor's degrees. 15 undergraduate majors. *Total enrollment:* 6,966. Undergraduates: 6,966. Freshmen: 1,201. Federal methodology is used as a basis for awarding need-based institutional aid.

UNDERGRADUATE EXPENSES for 2013–2014 *Application fee:* $65. *Tuition, state resident:* full-time $5130; part-time $215 per credit. *Tuition, nonresident:* full-time $13,800; part-time $460 per credit. *Required fees:* full-time $302; $100.85 per term. Full-time tuition and fees vary according to course load. Part-time tuition and fees vary according to course load.

FRESHMAN FINANCIAL AID (Fall 2012, est.) *Average financial aid package:* $3908 (excluding resources awarded to replace EFC).

UNDERGRADUATE FINANCIAL AID (Fall 2012, est.) *Average financial aid package:* $4040 (excluding resources awarded to replace EFC).

GIFT AID (NEED-BASED) *Total amount:* $29,083,984 (69% federal, 31% state). *Receiving aid:* Freshmen: 87% (862); all full-time undergraduates: 84% (3,477). *Average award:* Freshmen: $3738; Undergraduates: $3628. *Scholarships, grants,*

and awards: Federal Pell, FSEOG, state, private, college/university gift aid from institutional funds, Thurgood Marshall Scholarship Fund.
GIFT AID (NON-NEED-BASED) *Scholarships, grants, and awards by category:* Academic interests/achievement: general academic interests/achievements.
LOANS *Average need-based loan:* Freshmen: $1642. Undergraduates: $1814.
Programs: Federal Direct (Subsidized and Unsubsidized Stafford, PLUS), Perkins.
WORK-STUDY *Federal work-study:* Total amount: $400,484; jobs available.
APPLYING FOR FINANCIAL AID *Required financial aid forms:* FAFSA, state aid form, University Financial Aid Information Supplemental Request (FASIR). *Financial aid deadline (priority):* 1/2. *Notification date:* Continuous beginning 4/1. Students must reply within 3 weeks of notification.
CONTACT Conley James, Director of Financial Aid, Medgar Evers College of the City University of New York, 1650 Bedford Avenue, Brooklyn, NY 11225, 718-270-6038. *Fax:* 718-270-6194. *E-mail:* conley@mec.cuny.edu.
Website: http://www.mec.cuny.edu/.

MEDICAL UNIVERSITY OF SOUTH CAROLINA
Charleston, SC

Tuition & fees (SC res): $15,438	Average undergraduate aid package: N/A

ABOUT THE INSTITUTION State-supported, coed. *Awards:* certificates, bachelor's, master's, and doctoral degrees. 2 undergraduate majors. *Total enrollment:* 2,679. Undergraduates: 200. Federal methodology is used as a basis for awarding need-based institutional aid.
UNDERGRADUATE EXPENSES for 2013–2014 *Application fee:* $95. *One-time required fee:* $485. *Tuition, state resident:* full-time $14,298; part-time $647 per semester hour. *Tuition, nonresident:* full-time $24,300; part-time $1124 per semester hour. *Required fees:* full-time $1140; $1296 per unit. Full-time tuition and fees vary according to program. Part-time tuition and fees vary according to course load and program.
GIFT AID (NEED-BASED) *Scholarships, grants, and awards:* Federal Pell, FSEOG, state, private, college/university gift aid from institutional funds, Federal Nursing, Scholarships for Disadvantaged Students (SDS).
GIFT AID (NON-NEED-BASED) *Scholarships, grants, and awards by category:* Academic interests/achievement: general academic interests/achievements, health fields. *Special characteristics:* ethnic background, general special characteristics, local/state students, members of minority groups. *Tuition waivers:* Full or partial for minority students, employees or children of employees, adult students, senior citizens.
ROTC: Air Force cooperative.
LOANS *Programs:* Federal Direct (Subsidized and Unsubsidized Stafford, PLUS), Perkins, Federal Nursing, state, alternative loans, Health Professions Student Loans (HPSL), Loans for Disadvantaged Students program, Primary Care Loans.
WORK-STUDY Federal work-study jobs available.
APPLYING FOR FINANCIAL AID *Required financial aid form:* FAFSA. *Notification date:* Continuous.
CONTACT Mr. Joseph M. DuRant, Director for Financial Aid Services, Medical University of South Carolina, 45 Courtenay Drive, Charleston, SC 29425, 843-792-2536. *Fax:* 843-792-6356. *E-mail:* durantjm@musc.edu.
Website: http://www.musc.edu/.

MEMPHIS COLLEGE OF ART
Memphis, TN

Tuition & fees: $26,250	Average undergraduate aid package: $19,932

ABOUT THE INSTITUTION Independent, coed. *Awards:* bachelor's and master's degrees. 6 undergraduate majors. *Total enrollment:* 433. Undergraduates: 377. Freshmen: 94. Both federal and institutional methodology are used as a basis for awarding need-based institutional aid.
UNDERGRADUATE EXPENSES for 2013–2014 *Application fee:* $25. *Comprehensive fee:* $34,250 includes full-time tuition ($25,600), mandatory fees ($650), and room and board ($8000). *College room only:* $6000. Full-time tuition and fees

vary according to degree level and program. Room and board charges vary according to housing facility. *Part-time tuition:* $1117 per credit. *Part-time fees:* $650 per year. Part-time tuition and fees vary according to course load, degree level, and program.
FRESHMAN FINANCIAL AID (Fall 2011) 106 applied for aid; of those 98% were deemed to have need. 100% of freshmen with need received aid; of those 10% had need fully met. *Average percent of need met:* 69% (excluding resources awarded to replace EFC). *Average financial aid package:* $20,337 (excluding resources awarded to replace EFC). 3% of all full-time freshmen had no need and received non-need-based gift aid.
UNDERGRADUATE FINANCIAL AID (Fall 2011) 322 applied for aid; of those 93% were deemed to have need. 100% of undergraduates with need received aid; of those 9% had need fully met. *Average percent of need met:* 54% (excluding resources awarded to replace EFC). *Average financial aid package:* $19,932 (excluding resources awarded to replace EFC). 14% of all full-time undergraduates had no need and received non-need-based gift aid.
GIFT AID (NEED-BASED) *Total amount:* $4,953,224 (21% federal, 10% state, 68% institutional, 1% external sources). *Receiving aid:* Freshmen: 97% (104); all full-time undergraduates: 86% (298). *Average award:* Freshmen: $17,295; Undergraduates: $15,614. *Scholarships, grants, and awards:* Federal Pell, FSEOG, state, private, college/university gift aid from institutional funds.
GIFT AID (NON-NEED-BASED) *Total amount:* $619,333 (7% state, 92% institutional, 1% external sources). *Receiving aid:* Freshmen: 9% (10). Undergraduates: 5% (16). *Average award:* Freshmen: $13,167. Undergraduates: $10,748. *Scholarships, grants, and awards by category:* Academic interests/achievement: general academic interests/achievements. *Creative arts/performance:* applied art and design, art/fine arts. *Special characteristics:* children of faculty/staff, previous college experience. *Tuition waivers:* Full or partial for employees or children of employees.
LOANS *Student loans:* $2,723,320 (89% need-based, 11% non-need-based). *Average need-based loan:* Freshmen: $3539. Undergraduates: $4502. *Parent loans:* $1,005,196 (58% need-based, 42% non-need-based). *Programs:* Federal Direct (Subsidized and Unsubsidized Stafford, PLUS), college/university.
WORK-STUDY *Federal work-study:* Total amount: $39,271; jobs available. *State or other work-study/employment:* Total amount: $13,165 (17% need-based, 83% non-need-based). Part-time jobs available.
APPLYING FOR FINANCIAL AID *Required financial aid form:* FAFSA. *Financial aid deadline (priority):* 3/1. *Notification date:* Continuous beginning 4/1.
CONTACT Aaron White, Director of Financial Aid, Memphis College of Art, 1930 Poplar Avenue, Overton Park, Memphis, TN 38104, 901-272-5136 or toll-free 800-727-1088. *Fax:* 901-272-5134. *E-mail:* awhite@mca.edu.
Website: http://www.mca.edu/.

MENLO COLLEGE
Atherton, CA

Tuition & fees: $37,100	Average undergraduate aid package: $28,606

ABOUT THE INSTITUTION Independent, coed. *Awards:* bachelor's degrees. 11 undergraduate majors. *Total enrollment:* 681. Undergraduates: 681. Freshmen: 179. Federal methodology is used as a basis for awarding need-based institutional aid.
UNDERGRADUATE EXPENSES for 2013–2014 *Application fee:* $40. *Comprehensive fee:* $49,002 includes full-time tuition ($36,500), mandatory fees ($600), and room and board ($11,902). Room and board charges vary according to housing facility. *Part-time tuition:* $1521 per credit.
FRESHMAN FINANCIAL AID (Fall 2012, est.) 126 applied for aid; of those 90% were deemed to have need. 100% of freshmen with need received aid; of those 11% had need fully met. *Average percent of need met:* 71% (excluding resources awarded to replace EFC). *Average financial aid package:* $29,239 (excluding resources awarded to replace EFC). 38% of all full-time freshmen had no need and received non-need-based gift aid.
UNDERGRADUATE FINANCIAL AID (Fall 2012, est.) 477 applied for aid; of those 93% were deemed to have need. 100% of undergraduates with need received aid; of those 8% had need fully met. *Average percent of need met:* 69% (excluding resources awarded to replace EFC). *Average financial aid package:* $28,606 (excluding resources awarded to replace EFC). 29% of all full-time undergraduates had no need and received non-need-based gift aid.

GIFT AID (NEED-BASED) *Total amount:* $9,484,056 (12% federal, 11% state, 76% institutional, 1% external sources). *Receiving aid:* Freshmen: 58% (114); all full-time undergraduates: 66% (444). *Average award:* Freshmen: $25,859; Undergraduates: $24,443. *Scholarships, grants, and awards:* Federal Pell, FSEOG, state, college/university gift aid from institutional funds.

GIFT AID (NON-NEED-BASED) *Total amount:* $2,606,847 (2% federal, 97% institutional, 1% external sources). *Receiving aid:* Freshmen: 6% (11). Undergraduates: 4% (28). *Average award:* Freshmen: $12,986. Undergraduates: $12,410. *Scholarships, grants, and awards by category:* Academic interests/achievement: 617 awards ($5,967,437 total): general academic interests/achievements. *Tuition waivers:* Full or partial for employees or children of employees. *ROTC:* Army cooperative, Air Force cooperative.

LOANS *Student loans:* $3,548,002 (84% need-based, 16% non-need-based). 43% of past graduating class borrowed through all loan programs. *Average indebtedness per student:* $25,753. *Average need-based loan:* Freshmen: $3090. Undergraduates: $3987. *Parent loans:* $2,092,512 (52% need-based, 48% non-need-based). *Programs:* Federal Direct (Subsidized and Unsubsidized Stafford, PLUS).

WORK-STUDY *Federal work-study:* Total amount: $273,205; 318 jobs averaging $673.

ATHLETIC AWARDS Total amount: $1,887,785 (73% need-based, 27% non-need-based).

APPLYING FOR FINANCIAL AID *Required financial aid forms:* FAFSA, state aid form. *Financial aid deadline (priority):* 3/2. *Notification date:* Continuous beginning 3/15.

CONTACT Anne Heaton-Dunlap, Director of Financial Aid, Menlo College, 1000 El Camino Real, Atherton, CA 94027-4301, 650-543-3880 or toll-free 800-556-3656. *Fax:* 650-543-4103. *E-mail:* financialaid@menlo.edu. *Website:* http://www.menlo.edu/.

MERCER UNIVERSITY
Macon, GA

Tuition & fees: $32,466	Average undergraduate aid package: $29,373

ABOUT THE INSTITUTION Independent Baptist, coed. *Awards:* certificates, bachelor's, master's, and doctoral degrees. 55 undergraduate majors. *Total enrollment:* 6,288. Undergraduates: 2,382. Freshmen: 645. Federal methodology is used as a basis for awarding need-based institutional aid.

UNDERGRADUATE EXPENSES for 2013–2014 *Application fee:* $50. *Comprehensive fee:* $43,163 includes full-time tuition ($32,166), mandatory fees ($300), and room and board ($10,697). *College room only:* $5244. Full-time tuition and fees vary according to class time and location. Room and board charges vary according to board plan, housing facility, and location. *Part-time tuition:* $1072 per credit hour. *Part-time fees:* $10 per credit hour. Part-time tuition and fees vary according to class time, course load, and location.

FRESHMAN FINANCIAL AID (Fall 2012, est.) 645 applied for aid; of those 79% were deemed to have need. 100% of freshmen with need received aid; of those 27% had need fully met. *Average percent of need met:* 83% (excluding resources awarded to replace EFC). *Average financial aid package:* $30,748 (excluding resources awarded to replace EFC). 20% of all full-time freshmen had no need and received non-need-based gift aid.

UNDERGRADUATE FINANCIAL AID (Fall 2012, est.) 2,297 applied for aid; of those 73% were deemed to have need. 100% of undergraduates with need received aid; of those 26% had need fully met. *Average percent of need met:* 79% (excluding resources awarded to replace EFC). *Average financial aid package:* $29,373 (excluding resources awarded to replace EFC). 25% of all full-time undergraduates had no need and received non-need-based gift aid.

GIFT AID (NEED-BASED) *Total amount:* $37,489,805 (9% federal, 10% state, 79% institutional, 2% external sources). *Receiving aid:* Freshmen: 79% (509); all full-time undergraduates: 72% (1,667). *Average award:* Freshmen: $24,913; Undergraduates: $23,528. *Scholarships, grants, and awards:* Federal Pell, FSEOG, state, college/university gift aid from institutional funds, Federal Nursing.

GIFT AID (NON-NEED-BASED) *Total amount:* $15,403,273 (15% state, 84% institutional, 1% external sources). *Receiving aid:* Freshmen: 18% (118). Undergraduates: 16% (380). *Average award:* Freshmen: $19,370. Undergraduates: $18,895. *Scholarships, grants, and awards by category:* Academic interests/achievement: biological sciences, business, education, engineering/technologies,

English, foreign languages, general academic interests/achievements, international studies, military science, religion/biblical studies. *Creative arts/performance:* art/fine arts, debating, music, theater/drama. *Special achievements/activities:* community service, general special achievements/activities, leadership. *Special characteristics:* adult students, children of faculty/staff, children of public servants, general special characteristics, international students, relatives of clergy, siblings of current students. *Tuition waivers:* Full or partial for employees or children of employees. *ROTC:* Army.

LOANS *Student loans:* $12,686,428 (75% need-based, 25% non-need-based). 69% of past graduating class borrowed through all loan programs. *Average indebtedness per student:* $31,488. *Average need-based loan:* Freshmen: $5624. Undergraduates: $6074. *Parent loans:* $2,111,997 (42% need-based, 58% non-need-based). *Programs:* Federal Direct (Subsidized and Unsubsidized Stafford, PLUS), Perkins, Federal Nursing, college/university.

WORK-STUDY *Federal work-study:* Total amount: $365,359; jobs available.

ATHLETIC AWARDS Total amount: $4,176,420 (43% need-based, 57% non-need-based).

APPLYING FOR FINANCIAL AID *Required financial aid forms:* FAFSA, institution's own form, state aid form (GA residents only). *Financial aid deadline (priority):* 4/1. *Notification date:* Continuous. Students must reply within 2 weeks of notification.

CONTACT Ms. Carol Williams, Associate Vice President of Financial Planning, Mercer University, 1400 Coleman Avenue, Macon, GA 31207-0003, 478-301-2670 or toll-free 800-MERCER-U. *Fax:* 478-301-2671. *E-mail:* williams_ck@mercer.edu. *Website:* http://www.mercer.edu/.

MERCY COLLEGE
Dobbs Ferry, NY

Tuition & fees: $17,556	Average undergraduate aid package: $13,245

ABOUT THE INSTITUTION Independent, coed. *Awards:* certificates, bachelor's, master's, and doctoral degrees. 35 undergraduate majors. *Total enrollment:* 11,454. Undergraduates: 8,029. Freshmen: 833. Federal methodology is used as a basis for awarding need-based institutional aid.

UNDERGRADUATE EXPENSES for 2013–2014 *Application fee:* $40. *Comprehensive fee:* $29,740 includes full-time tuition ($16,996), mandatory fees ($560), and room and board ($12,184). *College room only:* $8734. Full-time tuition and fees vary according to course load. Room and board charges vary according to board plan and housing facility. *Part-time tuition:* $715 per credit. *Part-time fees:* $140 per term. Part-time tuition and fees vary according to course load.

FRESHMAN FINANCIAL AID (Fall 2011) 1,140 applied for aid; of those 96% were deemed to have need. 97% of freshmen with need received aid; of those 2% had need fully met. *Average percent of need met:* 58% (excluding resources awarded to replace EFC). *Average financial aid package:* $15,080 (excluding resources awarded to replace EFC). 1% of all full-time freshmen had no need and received non-need-based gift aid.

UNDERGRADUATE FINANCIAL AID (Fall 2011) 5,073 applied for aid; of those 96% were deemed to have need. 96% of undergraduates with need received aid; of those 2% had need fully met. *Average percent of need met:* 53% (excluding resources awarded to replace EFC). *Average financial aid package:* $13,245 (excluding resources awarded to replace EFC). 1% of all full-time undergraduates had no need and received non-need-based gift aid.

GIFT AID (NEED-BASED) *Total amount:* $42,469,505 (42% federal, 23% state, 35% institutional). *Receiving aid:* Freshmen: 85% (999); all full-time undergraduates: 79% (4,282). *Average award:* Freshmen: $11,925; Undergraduates: $9656. *Scholarships, grants, and awards:* Federal Pell, FSEOG, state, private, college/university gift aid from institutional funds.

GIFT AID (NON-NEED-BASED) *Total amount:* $3,755,891 (12% state, 84% institutional, 4% external sources). *Receiving aid:* Freshmen: 32% (370). Undergraduates: 27% (1,467). *Average award:* Freshmen: $3054. Undergraduates: $3036. *Scholarships, grants, and awards by category:* Academic interests/achievement: general academic interests/achievements. *Tuition waivers:* Full or partial for employees or children of employees. *ROTC:* Army cooperative, Air Force cooperative.

LOANS *Student loans:* $36,658,242 (49% need-based, 51% non-need-based). 71% of past graduating class borrowed through all loan programs. *Average indebtedness*

per student: $24,138. **Average need-based loan:** Freshmen: $3228. Undergraduates: $3955. **Parent loans:** $4,921,815 (100% non-need-based). **Programs:** Federal Direct (Subsidized and Unsubsidized Stafford, PLUS), Federal Nursing, state.
WORK-STUDY Federal work-study: Total amount: $678,449; jobs available.
ATHLETIC AWARDS Total amount: $1,007,429 (100% non-need-based).
APPLYING FOR FINANCIAL AID Required financial aid forms: FAFSA, state aid form. **Financial aid deadline (priority):** 2/15. **Notification date:** Continuous beginning 2/20. Students must reply by 5/1 or within 2 weeks of notification.
CONTACT Margaret McGrail, Vice President of Student Services , Mercy College, 555 Broadway, Dobbs Ferry, NY 10522, 888-464-6737 or toll-free 800-MERCY-NY. Fax: 914-375-8582.
Website: http://www.mercy.edu/.

MERCY COLLEGE OF HEALTH SCIENCES
Des Moines, IA

CONTACT Lisa Croat, Financial Aid Assistant Coordinator, Mercy College of Health Sciences, 928 Sixth Avenue, Des Moines, IA 50309, 515-643-6720 or toll-free 800-637-2994. Fax: 515-643-6702. E-mail: lcroat@mercydesmoines.org.
Website: http://www.mchs.edu/.

MERCY COLLEGE OF OHIO
Toledo, OH

Tuition & fees: N/R	Average undergraduate aid package: $8416

ABOUT THE INSTITUTION Independent Roman Catholic Church, coed, primarily women. **Awards:** certificates, associate, and bachelor's degrees. 8 undergraduate majors. **Total enrollment:** 1,206. Undergraduates: 1,205. Freshmen: 49. Federal methodology is used as a basis for awarding need-based institutional aid.
FRESHMAN FINANCIAL AID (Fall 2011) 31 applied for aid; of those 77% were deemed to have need. 100% of freshmen with need received aid. **Average percent of need met:** 40% (excluding resources awarded to replace EFC). **Average financial aid package:** $8858 (excluding resources awarded to replace EFC). 13% of all full-time freshmen had no need and received non-need-based gift aid.
UNDERGRADUATE FINANCIAL AID (Fall 2011) 416 applied for aid; of those 92% were deemed to have need. 100% of undergraduates with need received aid; of those 2% had need fully met. **Average percent of need met:** 36% (excluding resources awarded to replace EFC). **Average financial aid package:** $8416 (excluding resources awarded to replace EFC). 2% of all full-time undergraduates had no need and received non-need-based gift aid.
GIFT AID (NEED-BASED) Total amount: $3,272,395 (79% federal, 16% state, 2% institutional, 3% external sources). **Receiving aid:** Freshmen: 62% (20); all full-time undergraduates: 57% (257). **Average award:** Freshmen: $5236; Undergraduates: $5726. **Scholarships, grants, and awards:** Federal Pell, FSEOG, state, private, college/university gift aid from institutional funds, Federal Nursing.
GIFT AID (NON-NEED-BASED) Total amount: $435,538 (3% state, 33% institutional, 64% external sources). **Receiving aid:** Freshmen: 38% (12). Undergraduates: 15% (66). **Average award:** Freshmen: $1000. Undergraduates: $1000. **Scholarships, grants, and awards by category:** Academic interests/achievement: health fields.
LOANS Student loans: $11,801,870 (39% need-based, 61% non-need-based). 100% of past graduating class borrowed through all loan programs. **Average indebtedness per student:** $24,127. **Average need-based loan:** Freshmen: $3417. Undergraduates: $4600. **Parent loans:** $285,583 (100% need-based). **Programs:** Federal Direct (Subsidized and Unsubsidized Stafford, PLUS), state, college/university.
WORK-STUDY Federal work-study: Total amount: $45,477; 34 jobs averaging $1337.
APPLYING FOR FINANCIAL AID Required financial aid form: FAFSA. **Financial aid deadline:** Continuous. **Notification date:** Continuous beginning 3/1. Students must reply by 8/15.

CONTACT Julie Leslie, Director of Financial Aid, Mercy College of Ohio, 2221 Madison Avenue, Toledo, OH 43604, 419-251-1598 or toll-free 888-80-MERCY. Fax: 419-251-1462. E-mail: julie.leslie@mercycollege.edu.
Website: http://www.mercycollege.edu/.

MERCYHURST UNIVERSITY
Erie, PA

Tuition & fees: $29,037	Average undergraduate aid package: $23,686

ABOUT THE INSTITUTION Independent Roman Catholic, coed. **Awards:** certificates, associate, bachelor's, and master's degrees. 76 undergraduate majors. **Total enrollment:** 3,122. Undergraduates: 2,790. Freshmen: 672. Federal methodology is used as a basis for awarding need-based institutional aid.
UNDERGRADUATE EXPENSES for 2013–2014 Application fee: $30. **Comprehensive fee:** $39,141 includes full-time tuition ($27,150), mandatory fees ($1887), and room and board ($10,104). **College room only:** $5118. Full-time tuition and fees vary according to class time, course load, degree level, location, and program. Room and board charges vary according to board plan, housing facility, and location. **Part-time tuition:** $905 per semester hour. Part-time tuition and fees vary according to class time, course load, degree level, location, and program.
FRESHMAN FINANCIAL AID (Fall 2012, est.) 590 applied for aid; of those 90% were deemed to have need. 100% of freshmen with need received aid; of those 26% had need fully met. **Average percent of need met:** 74% (excluding resources awarded to replace EFC). **Average financial aid package:** $25,960 (excluding resources awarded to replace EFC). 13% of all full-time freshmen had no need and received non-need-based gift aid.
UNDERGRADUATE FINANCIAL AID (Fall 2012, est.) 2,226 applied for aid; of those 91% were deemed to have need. 100% of undergraduates with need received aid; of those 24% had need fully met. **Average percent of need met:** 52% (excluding resources awarded to replace EFC). **Average financial aid package:** $23,686 (excluding resources awarded to replace EFC). 13% of all full-time undergraduates had no need and received non-need-based gift aid.
GIFT AID (NEED-BASED) Total amount: $37,486,874 (12% federal, 7% state, 80% institutional, 1% external sources). **Receiving aid:** Freshmen: 80% (531); all full-time undergraduates: 72% (1,874). **Average award:** Freshmen: $15,285; Undergraduates: $13,134. **Scholarships, grants, and awards:** Federal Pell, FSEOG, state, private, college/university gift aid from institutional funds.
GIFT AID (NON-NEED-BASED) Total amount: $6,305,015 (3% federal, 96% institutional, 1% external sources). **Receiving aid:** Freshmen: 61% (400). Undergraduates: 50% (1,313). **Average award:** Freshmen: $10,301. Undergraduates: $11,284. **Scholarships, grants, and awards by category:** Academic interests/achievement: general academic interests/achievements. Creative arts/performance: applied art and design, art/fine arts, dance, music. Special achievements/activities: community service, general special achievements/activities, leadership, religious involvement. Special characteristics: children and siblings of alumni, children of faculty/staff. **Tuition waivers:** Full or partial for employees or children of employees, adult students. **ROTC:** Army cooperative, Air Force cooperative.
LOANS Student loans: $20,960,383 (92% need-based, 8% non-need-based). 73% of past graduating class borrowed through all loan programs. **Average indebtedness per student:** $26,063. **Average need-based loan:** Freshmen: $2834. Undergraduates: $4078. **Parent loans:** $3,745,018 (92% need-based, 8% non-need-based). **Programs:** Federal Direct (Subsidized and Unsubsidized Stafford, PLUS), Perkins, college/university.
WORK-STUDY Federal work-study: Total amount: $658,800; jobs available. **State or other work-study/employment:** Total amount: $379,892 (56% need-based, 44% non-need-based). Part-time jobs available.
ATHLETIC AWARDS Total amount: $6,765,929 (58% need-based, 42% non-need-based).
APPLYING FOR FINANCIAL AID Required financial aid form: FAFSA. **Financial aid deadline:** 5/1 (priority: 3/1). **Notification date:** Continuous beginning 2/15. Students must reply within 2 weeks of notification.
CONTACT Carrie Newman, Director of Student Financial Services, Mercyhurst University, 501 East 38th Street, Erie, PA 16546, 814-824-2288 or toll-free 800-825-1926. Fax: 814-824-2300. E-mail: sfs@mercyhurst.edu.
Website: http://www.mercyhurst.edu/.

MEREDITH COLLEGE
Raleigh, NC

Tuition & fees: $29,106	Average undergraduate aid package: $20,864

ABOUT THE INSTITUTION Independent, undergraduate: women only; graduate: coed. *Awards:* certificates, bachelor's, and master's degrees. 41 undergraduate majors. *Total enrollment:* 1,980. Undergraduates: 1,707. Freshmen: 398. Federal methodology is used as a basis for awarding need-based institutional aid.

UNDERGRADUATE EXPENSES for 2013–2014 *Application fee:* $40. *Comprehensive fee:* $37,454 includes full-time tuition ($29,106) and room and board ($8348). Full-time tuition and fees vary according to course load. Part-time tuition and fees vary according to course load.

FRESHMAN FINANCIAL AID (Fall 2012, est.) 361 applied for aid; of those 88% were deemed to have need. 100% of freshmen with need received aid; of those 18% had need fully met. *Average percent of need met:* 75% (excluding resources awarded to replace EFC). *Average financial aid package:* $21,961 (excluding resources awarded to replace EFC). 11% of all full-time freshmen had no need and received non-need-based gift aid.

UNDERGRADUATE FINANCIAL AID (Fall 2012, est.) 1,318 applied for aid; of those 90% were deemed to have need. 100% of undergraduates with need received aid; of those 17% had need fully met. *Average percent of need met:* 71% (excluding resources awarded to replace EFC). *Average financial aid package:* $20,864 (excluding resources awarded to replace EFC). 8% of all full-time undergraduates had no need and received non-need-based gift aid.

GIFT AID (NEED-BASED) *Total amount:* $20,110,485 (13% federal, 22% state, 57% institutional, 8% external sources). *Receiving aid:* Freshmen: 78% (319); all full-time undergraduates: 75% (1,178). *Average award:* Freshmen: $18,515; Undergraduates: $17,011. *Scholarships, grants, and awards:* Federal Pell, FSEOG, state, private, college/university gift aid from institutional funds.

GIFT AID (NON-NEED-BASED) *Total amount:* $4,117,999 (4% state, 82% institutional, 14% external sources). *Average award:* Freshmen: $10,711. Undergraduates: $8655. *Scholarships, grants, and awards by category: Academic interests/achievement:* biological sciences, business, computer science, education, English, foreign languages, general academic interests/achievements, mathematics, physical sciences, religion/biblical studies. *Creative arts/performance:* applied art and design, art/fine arts, creative writing, music. *Special achievements/activities:* community service, leadership. *Special characteristics:* adult students, children of faculty/staff, ethnic background, first-generation college students, international students, members of minority groups, out-of-state students, previous college experience, religious affiliation. *Tuition waivers:* Full or partial for employees or children of employees. *ROTC:* Army cooperative, Air Force cooperative.

LOANS *Student loans:* $10,923,228 (92% need-based, 8% non-need-based). 75% of past graduating class borrowed through all loan programs. *Average indebtedness per student:* $33,945. *Average need-based loan:* Freshmen: $3302. Undergraduates: $4253. *Parent loans:* $4,385,098 (42% need-based, 58% non-need-based). *Programs:* Federal Direct (Subsidized and Unsubsidized Stafford, PLUS), Perkins, college/university.

WORK-STUDY *Federal work-study:* Total amount: $171,574; jobs available. *State or other work-study/employment:* Part-time jobs available.

APPLYING FOR FINANCIAL AID *Required financial aid form:* FAFSA. *Financial aid deadline (priority):* 2/15. *Notification date:* Continuous beginning 3/15. Students must reply by 5/1 or within 2 weeks of notification.

CONTACT Mr. Kevin Michaelsen, Director of Financial Assistance, Meredith College, 3800 Hillsborough Street, Raleigh, NC 27607-5298, 919-760-8565 or toll-free 800-MEREDITH. *Fax:* 919-760-2375. *E-mail:* michaelsen@meredith.edu. *Website:* http://www.meredith.edu/.

MERRIMACK COLLEGE
North Andover, MA

Tuition & fees: $33,920	Average undergraduate aid package: $20,669

ABOUT THE INSTITUTION Independent Roman Catholic, coed. *Awards:* certificates, bachelor's, and master's degrees. 58 undergraduate majors. *Total enrollment:* 2,657. Undergraduates: 2,429. Freshmen: 699. Federal methodology is used as a basis for awarding need-based institutional aid.

UNDERGRADUATE EXPENSES for 2013–2014 *Comprehensive fee:* $45,610 includes full-time tuition ($32,720), mandatory fees ($1200), and room and board ($11,690). Room and board charges vary according to board plan and housing facility. Part-time tuition and fees vary according to class time, course level, course load, and degree level.

FRESHMAN FINANCIAL AID (Fall 2012, est.) 584 applied for aid; of those 88% were deemed to have need. 100% of freshmen with need received aid; of those 13% had need fully met. *Average percent of need met:* 63% (excluding resources awarded to replace EFC). *Average financial aid package:* $21,045 (excluding resources awarded to replace EFC). 18% of all full-time freshmen had no need and received non-need-based gift aid.

UNDERGRADUATE FINANCIAL AID (Fall 2012, est.) 1,804 applied for aid; of those 90% were deemed to have need. 100% of undergraduates with need received aid; of those 16% had need fully met. *Average percent of need met:* 64% (excluding resources awarded to replace EFC). *Average financial aid package:* $20,669 (excluding resources awarded to replace EFC). 21% of all full-time undergraduates had no need and received non-need-based gift aid.

GIFT AID (NEED-BASED) *Total amount:* $23,527,602 (11% federal, 3% state, 85% institutional, 1% external sources). *Receiving aid:* Freshmen: 73% (509); all full-time undergraduates: 69% (1,600). *Average award:* Freshmen: $17,965; Undergraduates: $17,029. *Scholarships, grants, and awards:* Federal Pell, FSEOG, state, private, college/university gift aid from institutional funds.

GIFT AID (NON-NEED-BASED) *Total amount:* $5,495,935 (99% institutional, 1% external sources). *Receiving aid:* Freshmen: 6% (42). Undergraduates: 7% (172). *Average award:* Freshmen: $8864. Undergraduates: $9757. *Scholarships, grants, and awards by category: Academic interests/achievement:* general academic interests/achievements. *Special characteristics:* children and siblings of alumni, children of faculty/staff, international students, relatives of clergy, siblings of current students. *Tuition waivers:* Full or partial for employees or children of employees, senior citizens. *ROTC:* Air Force cooperative.

LOANS *Student loans:* $19,560,640 (67% need-based, 33% non-need-based). *Average need-based loan:* Freshmen: $3515. Undergraduates: $4522. *Parent loans:* $5,628,640 (48% need-based, 52% non-need-based). *Programs:* Federal Direct (Subsidized and Unsubsidized Stafford, PLUS), Perkins, state, college/university, alternative loans.

WORK-STUDY *Federal work-study:* Total amount: $113,195; 129 jobs averaging $1239. *State or other work-study/employment:* 488 part-time jobs averaging $915.

ATHLETIC AWARDS Total amount: $5,675,587 (52% need-based, 48% non-need-based).

APPLYING FOR FINANCIAL AID *Required financial aid forms:* FAFSA, noncustodial (divorced/separated) parent's statement, business/farm supplement. *Financial aid deadline:* 2/15. *Notification date:* Continuous beginning 3/15. Students must reply by 5/1 or within 2 weeks of notification.

CONTACT Adrienne Montgomery, Director of Student Financial Aid, Merrimack College, 315 Turnpike Street, North Andover, MA 01845, 978-837-5186. *Fax:* 978-837-5067. *E-mail:* montgomerya@merrimack.edu. *Website:* http://www.merrimack.edu/.

MESIVTA OF EASTERN PARKWAY–YESHIVA ZICHRON MEILECH
Brooklyn, NY

CONTACT Rabbi Joseph Halberstadt, Dean, Mesivta of Eastern Parkway–Yeshiva Zichron Meilech, 510 Dahill Road, Brooklyn, NY 11218-5559, 718-438-1002.

MESIVTA TIFERETH JERUSALEM OF AMERICA
New York, NY

CONTACT Rabbi Dickstein, Director of Financial Aid, Mesivta Tifereth Jerusalem of America, 141 East Broadway, New York, NY 10002-6301, 212-964-2830.

MESIVTA TORAH VODAATH RABBINICAL SEMINARY
Brooklyn, NY

CONTACT Mrs. Kayla Goldring, Director of Financial Aid, Mesivta Torah Vodaath Rabbinical Seminary, 425 East Ninth Street, Brooklyn, NY 11218-5209, 718-941-8000. *Website:* http://www.torahvodaath.org/.

MESSENGER COLLEGE
Euless, TX

ABOUT THE INSTITUTION Independent Pentecostal, coed. 13 undergraduate majors.

GIFT AID (NEED-BASED) Scholarships, grants, and awards: Federal Pell, FSEOG, private, college/university gift aid from institutional funds.

GIFT AID (NON-NEED-BASED) Scholarships, grants, and awards by category: *Academic interests/achievement:* general academic interests/achievements, religion/biblical studies. *Creative arts/performance:* music. *Special achievements/activities:* religious involvement. *Special characteristics:* religious affiliation.

LOANS Programs: Federal Direct (Subsidized and Unsubsidized Stafford, PLUS).

APPLYING FOR FINANCIAL AID Required financial aid form: FAFSA.

CONTACT Patricia J. Pentecost, Director of Financial Aid, Messenger College, 300 East 50th Street, Joplin, MO 64804, 417-624-7070 Ext. 104 or toll-free 800-385-8940. *Fax:* 417-624-5070. *E-mail:* ppentecost@messengercollege.edu. *Website:* http://www.messengercollege.edu/.

MESSIAH COLLEGE
Mechanicsburg, PA

Tuition & fees: $30,470	Average undergraduate aid package: $20,782

ABOUT THE INSTITUTION Independent interdenominational, coed. *Awards:* certificates, bachelor's, and master's degrees. 79 undergraduate majors. *Total enrollment:* 3,017. Undergraduates: 2,798. Freshmen: 708. Federal methodology is used as a basis for awarding need-based institutional aid.

UNDERGRADUATE EXPENSES for 2013–2014 Application fee: $30. *Comprehensive fee:* $39,540 includes full-time tuition ($29,650), mandatory fees ($820), and room and board ($9070). *College room only:* $4800. Room and board charges vary according to board plan, housing facility, and location. *Part-time tuition:* $1235 per credit hour.

FRESHMAN FINANCIAL AID (Fall 2012, est.) 617 applied for aid; of those 88% were deemed to have need. 100% of freshmen with need received aid; of those 17% had need fully met. *Average percent of need met:* 72% (excluding resources awarded to replace EFC). *Average financial aid package:* $21,772 (excluding resources awarded to replace EFC). 23% of all full-time freshmen had no need and received non-need-based gift aid.

UNDERGRADUATE FINANCIAL AID (Fall 2012, est.) 2,254 applied for aid; of those 88% were deemed to have need. 100% of undergraduates with need received aid; of those 18% had need fully met. *Average percent of need met:* 70% (excluding resources awarded to replace EFC). *Average financial aid package:* $20,782 (excluding resources awarded to replace EFC). 25% of all full-time undergraduates had no need and received non-need-based gift aid.

GIFT AID (NEED-BASED) Total amount: $29,778,022 (9% federal, 8% state, 79% institutional, 4% external sources). *Receiving aid:* Freshmen: 76% (539); all full-time undergraduates: 73% (1,971). *Average award:* Freshmen: $16,835; Undergraduates: $15,077. *Scholarships, grants, and awards:* Federal Pell, FSEOG, state, private, college/university gift aid from institutional funds, Federal Nursing.

GIFT AID (NON-NEED-BASED) Total amount: $9,609,385 (3% federal, 93% institutional, 4% external sources). *Receiving aid:* Freshmen: 8% (54). Undergraduates: 7% (188). *Average award:* Freshmen: $12,886. Undergraduates: $11,434. *Scholarships, grants, and awards by category:* *Academic interests/achievement:* 2,201 awards ($18,819,626 total): general academic interests/achievements. *Creative arts/performance:* 109 awards ($758,884 total): art/fine arts, music, theater/drama. *Special achievements/activities:* 399 awards ($5,956,267 total): lead-ership. *Special characteristics:* 192 awards ($1,982,102 total): adult students, children of faculty/staff, local/state students, religious affiliation. *Tuition waivers:* Full or partial for minority students, children of alumni, employees or children of employees, adult students, senior citizens.

LOANS Student loans: $18,233,072 (70% need-based, 30% non-need-based). 74% of past graduating class borrowed through all loan programs. *Average indebtedness per student:* $35,306. *Average need-based loan:* Freshmen: $3727. Undergraduates: $4790. *Parent loans:* $4,786,009 (45% need-based, 55% non-need-based). *Programs:* Federal Direct (Subsidized and Unsubsidized Stafford, PLUS), Perkins, Federal Nursing.

WORK-STUDY Federal work-study: Total amount: $1,809,651; 893 jobs averaging $2087. *State or other work-study/employment:* Total amount: $2,108,158 (25% need-based, 75% non-need-based). 779 part-time jobs averaging $1941.

APPLYING FOR FINANCIAL AID Required financial aid form: FAFSA. *Financial aid deadline (priority):* 4/1. *Notification date:* Continuous beginning 3/15. Students must reply by 5/1 or within 4 weeks of notification.

CONTACT Mr. Michael Strite, Assistant Director of Financial Aid, Messiah College, One College Avenue, Suite 3006, Mechanicsburg, PA 17055, 717-691-6007 or toll-free 800-233-4220. *Fax:* 717-796-4791. *E-mail:* mstrite@messiah.edu. *Website:* http://www.messiah.edu/.

METHODIST UNIVERSITY
Fayetteville, NC

Tuition & fees: N/R	Average undergraduate aid package: $16,879

ABOUT THE INSTITUTION Independent United Methodist, coed. 57 undergraduate majors. Federal methodology is used as a basis for awarding need-based institutional aid.

FRESHMAN FINANCIAL AID (Fall 2011) 443 applied for aid; of those 70% were deemed to have need. 99% of freshmen with need received aid; of those 9% had need fully met. *Average percent of need met:* 61% (excluding resources awarded to replace EFC). *Average financial aid package:* $16,805 (excluding resources awarded to replace EFC). 17% of all full-time freshmen had no need and received non-need-based gift aid.

UNDERGRADUATE FINANCIAL AID (Fall 2011) 1,668 applied for aid; of those 69% were deemed to have need. 99% of undergraduates with need received aid; of those 10% had need fully met. *Average percent of need met:* 62% (excluding resources awarded to replace EFC). *Average financial aid package:* $16,879 (excluding resources awarded to replace EFC). 21% of all full-time undergraduates had no need and received non-need-based gift aid.

GIFT AID (NEED-BASED) Total amount: $14,926,749 (27% federal, 10% state, 63% institutional). *Receiving aid:* Freshmen: 58% (279); all full-time undergraduates: 48% (968). *Average award:* Freshmen: $9930; Undergraduates: $8940. *Scholarships, grants, and awards:* Federal Pell, FSEOG, state, private, college/university gift aid from institutional funds.

GIFT AID (NON-NEED-BASED) Total amount: $16,040,692 (37% federal, 11% state, 39% institutional, 13% external sources). *Receiving aid:* Freshmen: 51% (244). Undergraduates: 48% (968). *Average award:* Freshmen: $5000. Undergraduates: $6787. *Scholarships, grants, and awards by category:* *Academic interests/achievement:* 487 awards ($1,997,988 total): business, English, general academic interests/achievements, international studies, military science. *Creative arts/performance:* 163 awards ($142,675 total): dance, debating, music, theater/drama. *Special achievements/activities:* 49 awards ($33,825 total): cheerleading/drum major, leadership, religious involvement. *Special characteristics:* 810 awards ($2,232,113 total): children and siblings of alumni, children of faculty/staff, ethnic background, local/state students, members of minority groups, relatives of clergy, religious affiliation, siblings of current students, veterans.

LOANS Student loans: $9,712,850 (52% need-based, 48% non-need-based). 99% of past graduating class borrowed through all loan programs. *Average indebtedness per student:* $29,809. *Average need-based loan:* Freshmen: $3121. Undergraduates: $4005. *Parent loans:* $5,396,756 (100% non-need-based). *Programs:* Federal Direct (Subsidized and Unsubsidized Stafford, PLUS), Perkins.

WORK-STUDY Federal work-study: Total amount: $220,273; 587 jobs averaging $375. *State or other work-study/employment:* Total amount: $769,072 (100% non-need-based). 129 part-time jobs averaging $5962.

APPLYING FOR FINANCIAL AID *Required financial aid form:* FAFSA. *Financial aid deadline (priority):* 8/1. *Notification date:* Continuous beginning 3/6. Students must reply within 2 weeks of notification.
CONTACT Bonnie Adamson, Financial Aid Office, Methodist University, 5400 Ramsey Street, Fayetteville, NC 28311-1420, 910-630-7307 or toll-free 800-488-7110 Ext. 7027. *Fax:* 910-630-7285. *E-mail:* adamson@methodist.edu. *Website:* http://www.methodist.edu/.

METROPOLITAN COLLEGE OF NEW YORK
New York, NY

CONTACT Rosibel Gomez, Financial Aid Director, Metropolitan College of New York, 75 Varick Street, New York, NY 10013-1919, 212-343-1234 Ext. 5004 or toll-free 800-33-THINK Ext. 5001. *Fax:* 212-343-7399. *Website:* http://www.metropolitan.edu/.

METROPOLITAN STATE UNIVERSITY
St. Paul, MN

CONTACT Dr. Lois Larson, Director of Financial Aid, Metropolitan State University, Founder's Hall, Room 147A, 700 East 7th Street, St. Paul, MN 55106-5000, 651-793-1411. *Fax:* 651-793-1410. *E-mail:* finaid@metrostate.edu. *Website:* http://www.metrostate.edu/.

METROPOLITAN STATE UNIVERSITY OF DENVER
Denver, CO

Tuition & fees: N/R	Average undergraduate aid package: $7569

ABOUT THE INSTITUTION State-supported, coed. *Awards:* certificates, bachelor's, and master's degrees. 48 undergraduate majors. *Total enrollment:* 23,381. Undergraduates: 23,019. Freshmen: 2,306. Federal methodology is used as a basis for awarding need-based institutional aid.
FRESHMAN FINANCIAL AID (Fall 2011) 1,540 applied for aid; of those 77% were deemed to have need. 91% of freshmen with need received aid; of those 1% had need fully met. *Average percent of need met:* 52% (excluding resources awarded to replace EFC). *Average financial aid package:* $6367 (excluding resources awarded to replace EFC). 16% of all full-time freshmen had no need and received non-need-based gift aid.
UNDERGRADUATE FINANCIAL AID (Fall 2011) 10,533 applied for aid; of those 85% were deemed to have need. 94% of undergraduates with need received aid; of those 2% had need fully met. *Average percent of need met:* 53% (excluding resources awarded to replace EFC). *Average financial aid package:* $7569 (excluding resources awarded to replace EFC). 17% of all full-time undergraduates had no need and received non-need-based gift aid.
GIFT AID (NEED-BASED) *Total amount:* $47,701,512 (70% federal, 18% state, 10% institutional, 2% external sources). *Receiving aid:* Freshmen: 49% (903); all full-time undergraduates: 51% (6,968). *Average award:* Freshmen: $4776; Undergraduates: $4792. *Scholarships, grants, and awards:* Federal Pell, FSEOG, state, private, college/university gift aid from institutional funds.
GIFT AID (NON-NEED-BASED) *Total amount:* $1,991,267 (1% federal, 79% institutional, 20% external sources). *Receiving aid:* Freshmen: 5. Undergraduates: 1% (194). *Average award:* Freshmen: $1447. Undergraduates: $1706. *Scholarships, grants, and awards by category:* Academic interests/achievement: education, general academic interests/achievements. Creative arts/performance: music, performing arts, theater/drama. Special achievements/activities: leadership. Special characteristics: adult students, first-generation college students, local/state students, veterans. ROTC: Army cooperative, Air Force cooperative.

LOANS *Student loans:* $88,766,633 (89% need-based, 11% non-need-based). 60% of past graduating class borrowed through all loan programs. *Average indebtedness per student:* $31,427. *Average need-based loan:* Freshmen: $2965. Undergraduates: $3884. *Parent loans:* $3,452,468 (60% need-based, 40% non-need-based). *Programs:* Federal Direct (Subsidized and Unsubsidized Stafford, PLUS), Perkins.
WORK-STUDY *Federal work-study:* Total amount: $565,635; 4 jobs averaging $4119. *State or other work-study/employment:* Total amount: $1,750,510 (83% need-based, 17% non-need-based). 16 part-time jobs averaging $3460.
ATHLETIC AWARDS Total amount: $1,231,618 (38% need-based, 62% non-need-based).
APPLYING FOR FINANCIAL AID *Required financial aid form:* FAFSA. *Financial aid deadline:* Continuous. *Notification date:* Continuous beginning 3/15.
CONTACT Office of Financial Aid, Metropolitan State University of Denver, PO Box 173362, Denver, CO 80217-3362, 303-556-8593. *Fax:* 303-556-4927. *Website:* http://www.msudenver.edu/.

MIAMI INTERNATIONAL UNIVERSITY OF ART & DESIGN
Miami, FL

CONTACT Financial Aid Office, Miami International University of Art & Design, 1737 Bayshore Drive, Miami, FL 33132, 800-225-9023 Ext. 125 or toll-free 800-225-9023. *Fax:* 305-374-7946.

MIAMI UNIVERSITY
Oxford, OH

Tuition & fees (OH res): $13,595	Average undergraduate aid package: $11,437

ABOUT THE INSTITUTION State-related, coed. *Awards:* certificates, associate, bachelor's, master's, and doctoral degrees. 100 undergraduate majors. *Total enrollment:* 17,683. Undergraduates: 15,081. Freshmen: 3,734. Federal methodology is used as a basis for awarding need-based institutional aid.
UNDERGRADUATE EXPENSES for 2013–2014 *Application fee:* $50. *Tuition, state resident:* full-time $13,067. *Tuition, nonresident:* full-time $28,631. *Required fees:* full-time $528. Full-time tuition and fees vary according to location and program. Part-time tuition and fees vary according to course load, location, and program. *College room and board:* $10,596; *Room only:* $5250. Room and board charges vary according to board plan and housing facility.
FRESHMAN FINANCIAL AID (Fall 2012, est.) 2,762 applied for aid; of those 63% were deemed to have need. 99% of freshmen with need received aid; of those 17% had need fully met. *Average percent of need met:* 53% (excluding resources awarded to replace EFC). *Average financial aid package:* $10,647 (excluding resources awarded to replace EFC). 24% of all full-time freshmen had no need and received non-need-based gift aid.
UNDERGRADUATE FINANCIAL AID (Fall 2012, est.) 8,694 applied for aid; of those 73% were deemed to have need. 99% of undergraduates with need received aid; of those 16% had need fully met. *Average percent of need met:* 56% (excluding resources awarded to replace EFC). *Average financial aid package:* $11,437 (excluding resources awarded to replace EFC). 21% of all full-time undergraduates had no need and received non-need-based gift aid.
GIFT AID (NEED-BASED) *Total amount:* $25,492,225 (48% federal, 5% state, 47% institutional). *Receiving aid:* Freshmen: 32% (1,183); all full-time undergraduates: 29% (4,302). *Average award:* Freshmen: $4439; Undergraduates: $5231. *Scholarships, grants, and awards:* Federal Pell, FSEOG, state, private, college/university gift aid from institutional funds.
GIFT AID (NON-NEED-BASED) *Total amount:* $37,810,979 (92% institutional, 8% external sources). *Receiving aid:* Freshmen: 31% (1,173). Undergraduates: 26% (3,759). *Average award:* Freshmen: $6793. Undergraduates: $5910. *Scholarships, grants, and awards by category:* Academic interests/achievement: architecture, education, engineering/technologies, general academic interests/achievements. Creative arts/performance: art/fine arts, music, theater/drama. Special achievements/activities: general special achievements/activities, leadership. Special characteristics:

children of faculty/staff, local/state students, members of minority groups, out-of-state students. *Tuition waivers:* Full or partial for employees or children of employees. *ROTC:* Army cooperative, Naval, Air Force.

LOANS *Student loans:* $62,456,557 (36% need-based, 64% non-need-based). 55% of past graduating class borrowed through all loan programs. *Average indebtedness per student:* $27,817. *Average need-based loan:* Freshmen: $3479. Undergraduates: $4424. *Parent loans:* $33,476,305 (100% non-need-based). *Programs:* Federal Direct (Subsidized and Unsubsidized Stafford, PLUS), Perkins, Federal Nursing, college/university, private loans.

WORK-STUDY *Federal work-study:* Total amount: $1,621,320; 687 jobs averaging $2360.

ATHLETIC AWARDS Total amount: $8,821,103 (100% non-need-based).

APPLYING FOR FINANCIAL AID *Required financial aid form:* FAFSA. *Financial aid deadline (priority):* 2/15. *Notification date:* Continuous beginning 3/20. Students must reply by 5/1 or within 3 weeks of notification.

CONTACT Mr. Brent Shock, Office of Student Financial Aid, Miami University, Campus Avenue Building, Oxford, OH 45056-3427, 513-529-8734. *Fax:* 513-529-8713. *E-mail:* financialaid@MiamiOH.edu.
Website: http://www.muohio.edu/.

MIAMI UNIVERSITY HAMILTON
Hamilton, OH

CONTACT Financial Aid Office, Miami University Hamilton, 1601 Peck Boulevard, Hamilton, OH 45011-3399, 513-785-3000.
Website: http://www.ham.muohio.edu/.

MICHIGAN JEWISH INSTITUTE
West Bloomfield, MI

CONTACT Financial Aid Office, Michigan Jewish Institute, 6890 Maple Road, West Bloomfield, MI 48322, 248-414-6900 or toll-free 888-INFO-MJI.
Website: http://www.mji.edu/.

MICHIGAN STATE UNIVERSITY
East Lansing, MI

Tuition & fees (MI res): $13,800	Average undergraduate aid package: $11,509

ABOUT THE INSTITUTION State-supported, coed. *Awards:* certificates, bachelor's, master's, and doctoral degrees. 158 undergraduate majors. *Total enrollment:* 48,906. Undergraduates: 37,454. Freshmen: 8,354. Federal methodology is used as a basis for awarding need-based institutional aid.

UNDERGRADUATE EXPENSES for 2013–2014 *Application fee:* $50. *Tuition, state resident:* full-time $13,800; part-time $420.75 per credit hour. *Tuition, nonresident:* full-time $33,608; part-time $1086 per credit hour. Full-time tuition and fees vary according to course load, program, and student level. Part-time tuition and fees vary according to course load, program, and student level. *College room and board:* $8476; *Room only:* $3500. Room and board charges vary according to board plan and housing facility.

FRESHMAN FINANCIAL AID (Fall 2012, est.) 5,608 applied for aid; of those 70% were deemed to have need. 98% of freshmen with need received aid; of those 21% had need fully met. *Average percent of need met:* 63% (excluding resources awarded to replace EFC). *Average financial aid package:* $11,718 (excluding resources awarded to replace EFC). 6% of all full-time freshmen had no need and received non-need-based gift aid.

UNDERGRADUATE FINANCIAL AID (Fall 2012, est.) 21,827 applied for aid; of those 78% were deemed to have need. 99% of undergraduates with need received aid; of those 14% had need fully met. *Average percent of need met:* 61% (excluding resources awarded to replace EFC). *Average financial aid package:* $11,509 (excluding resources awarded to replace EFC). 3% of all full-time undergraduates had no need and received non-need-based gift aid.

GIFT AID (NEED-BASED) *Total amount:* $103,068,040 (38% federal, 62% institutional). *Receiving aid:* Freshmen: 27% (2,253); all full-time undergraduates: 32% (10,784). *Average award:* Freshmen: $9685; Undergraduates: $8949. *Scholarships, grants, and awards:* Federal Pell, FSEOG, state, private, college/university gift aid from institutional funds, United Negro College Fund.

GIFT AID (NON-NEED-BASED) *Total amount:* $67,089,949 (3% federal, 34% state, 31% institutional, 32% external sources). *Receiving aid:* Freshmen: 27% (2,194). Undergraduates: 23% (7,789). *Average award:* Freshmen: $7414. Undergraduates: $10,362. *Scholarships, grants, and awards by category: Academic interests/achievement:* agriculture, biological sciences, business, communication, computer science, education, engineering/technologies, English, foreign languages, general academic interests/achievements, health fields, home economics, international studies, mathematics, military science, physical sciences, social sciences. *Creative arts/performance:* art/fine arts, creative writing, debating, journalism/publications, music, performing arts, theater/drama. *Special achievements/activities:* community service, general special achievements/activities, hobbies/interests, leadership, memberships, rodeo. *Special characteristics:* children and siblings of alumni, children of faculty/staff, children of union members/company employees, first-generation college students, handicapped students, international students, local/state students, out-of-state students, spouses of deceased or disabled public servants, veterans. *Tuition waivers:* Full or partial for employees or children of employees. *ROTC:* Army, Air Force.

LOANS *Student loans:* $151,315,153 (43% need-based, 57% non-need-based). 46% of past graduating class borrowed through all loan programs. *Average indebtedness per student:* $24,987. *Average need-based loan:* Freshmen: $3393. Undergraduates: $4167. *Parent loans:* $78,730,253 (100% non-need-based). *Programs:* Federal Direct (Subsidized and Unsubsidized Stafford, PLUS), Perkins, college/university.

WORK-STUDY *Federal work-study:* Total amount: $2,450,839; jobs available.

ATHLETIC AWARDS Total amount: $11,190,943 (48% need-based, 52% non-need-based).

APPLYING FOR FINANCIAL AID *Required financial aid form:* FAFSA. *Financial aid deadline:* Continuous. *Notification date:* Continuous beginning 3/15. Students must reply within 4 weeks of notification.

CONTACT Mr. Keith Williams, Associate Director, Michigan State University, 252 Student Services Building, East Lansing, MI 48824-1113, 517-353-5940. *Fax:* 517-432-1155. *E-mail:* willi398@msu.edu.
Website: http://www.msu.edu/.

MICHIGAN TECHNOLOGICAL UNIVERSITY
Houghton, MI

Tuition & fees (MI res): $13,353	Average undergraduate aid package: $12,675

ABOUT THE INSTITUTION State-supported, coed. *Awards:* certificates, associate, bachelor's, master's, and doctoral degrees. 88 undergraduate majors. *Total enrollment:* 7,034. Undergraduates: 5,731. Freshmen: 1,161. Federal methodology is used as a basis for awarding need-based institutional aid.

UNDERGRADUATE EXPENSES for 2013–2014 *Tuition, state resident:* full-time $13,095; part-time $436.50 per credit hour. *Tuition, nonresident:* full-time $27,000; part-time $900 per credit hour. *Required fees:* full-time $258; $129 per term. Full-time tuition and fees vary according to course load and program. Part-time tuition and fees vary according to course load and program. *College room and board:* $8865; *Room only:* $4742. Room and board charges vary according to board plan and housing facility.

FRESHMAN FINANCIAL AID (Fall 2011) 1,019 applied for aid; of those 79% were deemed to have need. 100% of freshmen with need received aid; of those 21% had need fully met. *Average percent of need met:* 78% (excluding resources awarded to replace EFC). *Average financial aid package:* $14,114 (excluding resources awarded to replace EFC). 24% of all full-time freshmen had no need and received non-need-based gift aid.

UNDERGRADUATE FINANCIAL AID (Fall 2011) 4,074 applied for aid; of those 83% were deemed to have need. 99% of undergraduates with need received aid; of those 17% had need fully met. *Average percent of need met:* 71% (excluding resources awarded to replace EFC). *Average financial aid package:* $12,675 (excluding resources awarded to replace EFC). 21% of all full-time undergraduates had no need and received non-need-based gift aid.

GIFT AID (NEED-BASED) *Total amount:* $33,052,047 (24% federal, 8% state, 59% institutional, 9% external sources). *Receiving aid:* Freshmen: 59% (679); all full-time undergraduates: 51% (2,626). *Average award:* Freshmen: $7897; Undergraduates: $6299. *Scholarships, grants, and awards:* Federal Pell, FSEOG, state, private, college/university gift aid from institutional funds.

GIFT AID (NON-NEED-BASED) *Total amount:* $6,822,703 (1% state, 89% institutional, 10% external sources). *Receiving aid:* Freshmen: 56% (643). Undergraduates: 44% (2,299). *Average award:* Freshmen: $5594. Undergraduates: $5278. *Scholarships, grants, and awards by category: Academic interests/achievement:* general academic interests/achievements. *Special achievements/activities:* leadership. *Special characteristics:* children and siblings of alumni, local/state students. *Tuition waivers:* Full or partial for children of alumni, employees or children of employees, senior citizens. *ROTC:* Army, Air Force.

LOANS *Student loans:* $37,872,914 (86% need-based, 14% non-need-based). 72% of past graduating class borrowed through all loan programs. *Average indebtedness per student:* $34,938. *Average need-based loan:* Freshmen: $3532. Undergraduates: $4701. *Parent loans:* $6,282,056 (85% need-based, 15% non-need-based). *Programs:* Federal Direct (Subsidized and Unsubsidized Stafford, PLUS), Perkins, college/university.

WORK-STUDY *Federal work-study:* Total amount: $396,822; jobs available. *State or other work-study/employment:* Part-time jobs available.

ATHLETIC AWARDS Total amount: $2,667,814 (42% need-based, 58% non-need-based).

APPLYING FOR FINANCIAL AID *Required financial aid form:* FAFSA. *Financial aid deadline (priority):* 2/16. *Notification date:* Continuous beginning 3/15. Students must reply by 5/1.

CONTACT Mr. William Roberts, Director of Financial Aid, Michigan Technological University, 1400 Townsend Drive, Houghton, MI 49931-1295, 906-487-1742 or toll-free 888-MTU-1885. *Fax:* 906-487-3042. *E-mail:* wrrobert@mtu.edu. *Website:* http://www.mtu.edu/.

MID-AMERICA CHRISTIAN UNIVERSITY
Oklahoma City, OK

CONTACT Mr. Todd Martin, Director of Financial Aid, Mid-America Christian University, 3500 Southwest 119th Street, Oklahoma City, OK 73170-4504, 405-691-3800 or toll-free 888-436-3035. *Fax:* 405-692-3165. *E-mail:* tmartin@mabc.edu. *Website:* http://www.macu.edu/.

MIDAMERICA NAZARENE UNIVERSITY
Olathe, KS

CONTACT Rhonda L. Cole, Director of Student Financial Services, MidAmerica Nazarene University, 2030 East College Way, Olathe, KS 66062-1899, 913-791-3298 or toll-free 800-800-8887. *Fax:* 913-791-3482. *E-mail:* rcole@mnu.edu. *Website:* http://www.mnu.edu/.

MID-ATLANTIC CHRISTIAN UNIVERSITY
Elizabeth City, NC

Tuition & fees: $12,160 — Average undergraduate aid package: $9387

ABOUT THE INSTITUTION Independent Christian, coed. *Awards:* certificates, associate, and bachelor's degrees. 10 undergraduate majors. *Total enrollment:* 165. Undergraduates: 165. Freshmen: 37. Federal methodology is used as a basis for awarding need-based institutional aid.

UNDERGRADUATE EXPENSES for 2013–2014 *Application fee:* $50. *Comprehensive fee:* $19,940 includes full-time tuition ($12,160) and room and board ($7780). Full-time tuition and fees vary according to program. Room and board charges vary according to housing facility. *Part-time tuition:* $380 per credit hour. Part-time tuition and fees vary according to program.

FRESHMAN FINANCIAL AID (Fall 2011) 26 applied for aid; of those 100% were deemed to have need. 100% of freshmen with need received aid. *Average percent of need met:* 49% (excluding resources awarded to replace EFC). *Average financial aid package:* $9047 (excluding resources awarded to replace EFC). 4% of all full-time freshmen had no need and received non-need-based gift aid.

UNDERGRADUATE FINANCIAL AID (Fall 2011) 148 applied for aid; of those 97% were deemed to have need. 100% of undergraduates with need received aid; of those 3% had need fully met. *Average percent of need met:* 52% (excluding resources awarded to replace EFC). *Average financial aid package:* $9387 (excluding resources awarded to replace EFC). 4% of all full-time undergraduates had no need and received non-need-based gift aid.

GIFT AID (NEED-BASED) *Total amount:* $792,495 (57% federal, 1% state, 40% institutional, 2% external sources). *Receiving aid:* Freshmen: 96% (26); all full-time undergraduates: 89% (139). *Average award:* Freshmen: $5800; Undergraduates: $5701. *Scholarships, grants, and awards:* Federal Pell, FSEOG, state, private, college/university gift aid from institutional funds.

GIFT AID (NON-NEED-BASED) *Total amount:* $19,780 (100% institutional). *Receiving aid:* Undergraduates: 1% (1). *Average award:* Freshmen: $8125. Undergraduates: $3064. *Scholarships, grants, and awards by category: Academic interests/achievement:* 23 awards ($74,225 total): general academic interests/achievements, religion/biblical studies. *Special achievements/activities:* 12 awards ($30,376 total): general special achievements/activities, religious involvement. *Special characteristics:* 83 awards ($74,075 total): children and siblings of alumni, children of faculty/staff, general special characteristics, handicapped students, international students, married students, spouses of current students. *Tuition waivers:* Full or partial for children of alumni, employees or children of employees, senior citizens. *ROTC:* Army cooperative.

LOANS *Student loans:* $1,171,793 (91% need-based, 9% non-need-based). 97% of past graduating class borrowed through all loan programs. *Average indebtedness per student:* $37,108. *Average need-based loan:* Freshmen: $3078. Undergraduates: $4158. *Parent loans:* $188,122 (71% need-based, 29% non-need-based). *Programs:* Federal Direct (Subsidized and Unsubsidized Stafford, PLUS), private loans.

WORK-STUDY *Federal work-study:* Total amount: $9890; 12 jobs averaging $824.

APPLYING FOR FINANCIAL AID *Required financial aid forms:* FAFSA, institution's own form. *Financial aid deadline (priority):* 2/1. *Notification date:* Continuous beginning 4/1. Students must reply by 5/1 or within 2 weeks of notification.

CONTACT Lisa W. Pipkin, Financial Aid Administrator, Mid-Atlantic Christian University, 715 North Poindexter Street, Elizabeth City, NC 27909, 252-334-2020 or toll-free 866-996-MACU. *Fax:* 252-334-2064. *E-mail:* lisa.pipkin@macuniversity.edu. *Website:* http://www.macuniversity.edu/.

MID-CONTINENT UNIVERSITY
Mayfield, KY

CONTACT Kent Youngblood, Director of Financial Aid, Mid-Continent University, 99 Powell Road East, Mayfield, KY 42066, 270-251-9400 Ext. 260 or toll-free 866-894-8878. *Fax:* 270-251-9475. *E-mail:* kyoungblood@midcontinent.edu. *Website:* http://www.midcontinent.edu/.

MIDDLEBURY COLLEGE
Middlebury, VT

Tuition & fees: $43,731 — Average undergraduate aid package: $39,079

ABOUT THE INSTITUTION Independent, coed. *Awards:* bachelor's, master's, and doctoral degrees. 47 undergraduate majors. *Total enrollment:* 2,516. Undergraduates: 2,516. Freshmen: 598. Both federal and institutional methodology are used as a basis for awarding need-based institutional aid.

UNDERGRADUATE EXPENSES for 2013–2014 Application fee: $65. **Comprehensive fee:** $55,570 includes full-time tuition ($43,731) and room and board ($11,839). **Payment plan:** Tuition prepayment.

FRESHMAN FINANCIAL AID (Fall 2012, est.) 366 applied for aid; of those 73% were deemed to have need. 100% of freshmen with need received aid; of those 95% had need fully met. **Average percent of need met:** 100% (excluding resources awarded to replace EFC). **Average financial aid package:** $38,670 (excluding resources awarded to replace EFC).

UNDERGRADUATE FINANCIAL AID (Fall 2012, est.) 1,191 applied for aid; of those 85% were deemed to have need. 100% of undergraduates with need received aid; of those 95% had need fully met. **Average percent of need met:** 100% (excluding resources awarded to replace EFC). **Average financial aid package:** $39,079 (excluding resources awarded to replace EFC). 1% of all full-time undergraduates had no need and received non-need-based gift aid.

GIFT AID (NEED-BASED) Total amount: $37,573,969 (5% federal, 93% institutional, 2% external sources). **Receiving aid:** Freshmen: 42% (254); all full-time undergraduates: 39% (968). **Average award:** Freshmen: $36,277; Undergraduates: $36,245. **Scholarships, grants, and awards:** Federal Pell, FSEOG, state, private, college/university gift aid from institutional funds.

GIFT AID (NON-NEED-BASED) Total amount: $5000 (100% institutional). **Receiving aid:** Undergraduates: 2. **Average award:** Undergraduates: $2500. **Tuition waivers:** Full or partial for employees or children of employees. **ROTC:** Army cooperative.

LOANS Student loans: $5,784,290 (48% need-based, 52% non-need-based). 49% of past graduating class borrowed through all loan programs. **Average indebtedness per student:** $17,246. **Average need-based loan:** Freshmen: $3268. Undergraduates: $3904. **Parent loans:** $2,938,448 (100% non-need-based). **Programs:** Federal Direct (Subsidized and Unsubsidized Stafford, PLUS), Perkins.

WORK-STUDY Federal work-study: Total amount: $253,648; jobs available. **State or other work-study/employment:** Total amount: $380,000 (100% need-based). Part-time jobs available.

APPLYING FOR FINANCIAL AID Required financial aid forms: FAFSA, CSS Financial Aid PROFILE, noncustodial (divorced/separated) parent's statement. **Financial aid deadline:** 2/1 (priority: 11/15). **Notification date:** 4/1. Students must reply by 5/1.

CONTACT Marguerite Corbin, Financial Aid Assistant, Middlebury College, Service Building 104, Middlebury, VT 05753, 802-443-5158. E-mail: financialaid@middlebury.edu.
Website: http://www.middlebury.edu/.

MIDDLE GEORGIA STATE COLLEGE
Cochran, GA

CONTACT Financial Aid Office, Middle Georgia State College, 1100 Second Street, SE, Cochran, GA 31014-1599, 478-934-6221.
Website: http://www.mgc.edu/.

MIDDLE TENNESSEE STATE UNIVERSITY
Murfreesboro, TN

Tuition & fees (TN res): $7210	Average undergraduate aid package: $9176

ABOUT THE INSTITUTION State-supported, coed. **Awards:** certificates, bachelor's, master's, and doctoral degrees. 61 undergraduate majors. **Total enrollment:** 25,394. Undergraduates: 22,371. Freshmen: 3,120. Federal methodology is used as a basis for awarding need-based institutional aid.

UNDERGRADUATE EXPENSES for 2013–2014 Application fee: $25. **Tuition, state resident:** full-time $5616; part-time $234 per credit hour. **Tuition, nonresident:** full-time $20,232; part-time $843 per credit hour. **Required fees:** full-time $1594. Full-time tuition and fees vary according to course load. Part-time tuition and fees vary according to course load. **College room and board:** $7532. Room and board charges vary according to board plan and housing facility.

FRESHMAN FINANCIAL AID (Fall 2012, est.) 2,976 applied for aid; of those 79% were deemed to have need. 99% of freshmen with need received aid; of those 15% had need fully met. **Average percent of need met:** 76% (excluding resources awarded to replace EFC). **Average financial aid package:** $10,606 (excluding resources awarded to replace EFC). 8% of all full-time freshmen had no need and received non-need-based gift aid.

UNDERGRADUATE FINANCIAL AID (Fall 2012, est.) 16,349 applied for aid; of those 79% were deemed to have need. 99% of undergraduates with need received aid; of those 13% had need fully met. **Average percent of need met:** 63% (excluding resources awarded to replace EFC). **Average financial aid package:** $9176 (excluding resources awarded to replace EFC). 5% of all full-time undergraduates had no need and received non-need-based gift aid.

GIFT AID (NEED-BASED) Total amount: $50,462,014 (82% federal, 16% state, 2% institutional). **Receiving aid:** Freshmen: 51% (1,570); all full-time undergraduates: 47% (8,729). **Average award:** Freshmen: $6279; Undergraduates: $5168. **Scholarships, grants, and awards:** Federal Pell, FSEOG, state, private, college/university gift aid from institutional funds.

GIFT AID (NON-NEED-BASED) Total amount: $39,901,060 (74% state, 21% institutional, 5% external sources). **Receiving aid:** Freshmen: 76% (2,340). Undergraduates: 41% (7,551). **Average award:** Freshmen: $2495. Undergraduates: $2582. **Scholarships, grants, and awards by category:** Academic interests/achievement: 926 awards ($1,215,620 total): agriculture, area/ethnic studies, biological sciences, business, communication, computer science, education, engineering/technology, English, foreign languages, general academic interests/achievements, health fields, home economics, humanities, international studies, mathematics, military science, physical sciences, premedicine, social sciences. Creative arts/performance: 519 awards ($279,897 total): dance, debating, journalism/publications, music, theater/drama. Special achievements/activities: 2,375 awards ($5,739,476 total): cheerleading/drum major, general special achievements/activities, leadership. Special characteristics: 502 awards ($751,386 total): adult students, first-generation college students, general special characteristics, international students, local/state students, members of minority groups. **ROTC:** Army, Air Force cooperative.

LOANS Student loans: $96,391,326 (46% need-based, 54% non-need-based). 60% of past graduating class borrowed through all loan programs. **Average indebtedness per student:** $22,039. **Average need-based loan:** Freshmen: $3144. Undergraduates: $3963. **Parent loans:** $10,173,388 (100% non-need-based). **Programs:** Federal Direct (Subsidized and Unsubsidized Stafford, PLUS), Perkins, college/university.

WORK-STUDY Federal work-study: Total amount: $661,287; 255 jobs averaging $2524.

ATHLETIC AWARDS Total amount: $5,991,294 (100% non-need-based).

APPLYING FOR FINANCIAL AID Required financial aid form: FAFSA. **Financial aid deadline (priority):** 3/1. **Notification date:** Continuous beginning 4/15. Students must reply by 6/1.

CONTACT Stephen White, Director of Financial Aid, Middle Tennessee State University, 218 Cope Administration Building, Murfreesboro, TN 37132, 615-898-2830 or toll-free 800-331-MTSU. Fax: 615-898-5167.
Website: http://www.mtsu.edu/.

MIDLAND COLLEGE
Midland, TX

CONTACT Latisha Williams, Director, Midland College, 3600 North Garfield, Midland, TX 79705, 432-685-4507. Fax: 432-685-6857. E-mail: lwilliams@midland.edu.
Website: http://www.midland.edu/.

MIDLAND UNIVERSITY
Fremont, NE

CONTACT Penny James, Director of Financial Aid, Midland University, 900 North Clarkson Street, Fremont, NE 68025-4200, 402-721-5480 Ext. 6520 or toll-free 800-642-8382 Ext. 6501. Fax: 402-721-0250. E-mail: finaid@mlc.edu.
Website: http://www.midlandu.edu/.

MIDSTATE COLLEGE
Peoria, IL

CONTACT Financial Aid Office, Midstate College, 411 West Northmoor Road, Peoria, IL 61614, 309-692-4092 or toll-free 800-251-4299. *Website:* http://www.midstate.edu/.

MIDWAY COLLEGE
Midway, KY

CONTACT Katie Conrad, Director of Financial Aid, Midway College, 512 East Stephens Street, Midway, KY 40347-1120, 859-846-5410 or toll-free 800-755-0031. *Fax:* 859-846-5751. *E-mail:* kconrad@midway.edu. *Website:* http://www.midway.edu/.

MIDWESTERN STATE UNIVERSITY
Wichita Falls, TX

Tuition & fees (area res): $7238	Average undergraduate aid package: $9162

ABOUT THE INSTITUTION State-supported, coed. *Awards:* certificates, associate, bachelor's, and master's degrees. 73 undergraduate majors. *Total enrollment:* 5,916. Undergraduates: 5,238. Freshmen: 623. Federal methodology is used as a basis for awarding need-based institutional aid.

UNDERGRADUATE EXPENSES for 2013–2014 *Application fee:* $25. *Tuition, area resident:* full-time $4845. *Tuition, state resident:* full-time $4548; part-time $161.50 per credit. *Tuition, nonresident:* full-time $6795; part-time $226.50 per credit. *Required fees:* full-time $2393; $68.50 per credit or $199 per term. Full-time tuition and fees vary according to course load, location, and program. Part-time tuition and fees vary according to course load, location, and program. *College room and board:* $6350; *Room only:* $3350. Room and board charges vary according to board plan and housing facility.

FRESHMAN FINANCIAL AID (Fall 2011) 545 applied for aid; of those 70% were deemed to have need. 99% of freshmen with need received aid; of those 19% had need fully met. *Average percent of need met:* 74% (excluding resources awarded to replace EFC). *Average financial aid package:* $9990 (excluding resources awarded to replace EFC). 9% of all full-time freshmen had no need and received non-need-based gift aid.

UNDERGRADUATE FINANCIAL AID (Fall 2011) 3,141 applied for aid; of those 73% were deemed to have need. 98% of undergraduates with need received aid; of those 15% had need fully met. *Average percent of need met:* 67% (excluding resources awarded to replace EFC). *Average financial aid package:* $9162 (excluding resources awarded to replace EFC). 8% of all full-time undergraduates had no need and received non-need-based gift aid.

GIFT AID (NEED-BASED) *Total amount:* $13,653,048 (60% federal, 22% state, 15% institutional, 3% external sources). *Receiving aid:* Freshmen: 56% (346); all full-time undergraduates: 38% (1,972). *Average award:* Freshmen: $7517; Undergraduates: $5913. *Scholarships, grants, and awards:* Federal Pell, FSEOG, state, private, college/university gift aid from institutional funds, state nursing scholarships.

GIFT AID (NON-NEED-BASED) *Total amount:* $1,211,602 (1% federal, 2% state, 83% institutional, 14% external sources). *Receiving aid:* Freshmen: 8% (50). Undergraduates: 4% (217). *Average award:* Freshmen: $2510. Undergraduates: $1939. *Scholarships, grants, and awards by category: Academic interests/achievement:* biological sciences, business, communication, computer science, education, engineering/technologies, English, foreign languages, general academic interests/achievements, health fields, humanities, international studies, mathematics, physical sciences, premedicine, social sciences. *Creative arts/performance:* art/fine arts, creative writing, general creative arts/performance, journalism/publications, music, theater/drama. *Special achievements/activities:* cheerleading/drum major, general special achievements/activities, leadership. *Special characteristics:* children and siblings of alumni, children of faculty/staff, children of union members/company employees, children of workers in trades, children with a deceased or disabled parent, first-generation college students, handicapped students, international students, members of minority groups, veterans, veterans' children. *Tuition waivers:* Full or partial for employees or children of employees, senior citizens. *ROTC:* Air Force cooperative.

LOANS *Student loans:* $23,830,839 (81% need-based, 19% non-need-based). 64% of past graduating class borrowed through all loan programs. *Average indebtedness per student:* $22,891. *Average need-based loan:* Freshmen: $5330. Undergraduates: $7223. *Parent loans:* $4,119,512 (44% need-based, 56% non-need-based). *Programs:* Federal Direct (Subsidized and Unsubsidized Stafford, PLUS), Perkins, state, college/university, private loans.

WORK-STUDY *Federal work-study:* Total amount: $106,243; jobs available. *State or other work-study/employment:* Total amount: $37,989 (100% need-based). Part-time jobs available.

ATHLETIC AWARDS Total amount: $1,208,662 (50% need-based, 50% non-need-based).

APPLYING FOR FINANCIAL AID *Required financial aid forms:* FAFSA, institution's own form. *Financial aid deadline (priority):* 3/1. *Notification date:* Continuous beginning 4/15. Students must reply within 4 weeks of notification.

CONTACT Ms. Kathy Pennartz, Director of Financial Aid, Midwestern State University, 3410 Taft Boulevard, Wichita Falls, TX 76308, 940-397-4214 or toll-free 800-842-1922. *Fax:* 940-397-4852. *E-mail:* financial-aid@mwsu.edu. *Website:* http://www.mwsu.edu/.

MIDWIVES COLLEGE OF UTAH
Salt Lake City, UT

CONTACT Financial Aid Office, Midwives College of Utah, 1174 East 2700 South, Suite 2, Salt Lake City, UT 84106, 801-764-9068 or toll-free 866-680-2756. *Website:* http://www.midwifery.edu/.

MILES COLLEGE
Fairfield, AL

CONTACT P. N. Lanier, Financial Aid Administrator, Miles College, PO Box 3800, Birmingham, AL 35208, 205-929-1663 or toll-free 800-445-0708 (out-of-state). *Fax:* 205-929-1668. *E-mail:* pnlani@netscape.net. *Website:* http://www.miles.edu/.

MILLENNIA ATLANTIC UNIVERSITY
Doral, FL

Tuition & fees: N/R	Average undergraduate aid package: N/A

ABOUT THE INSTITUTION Proprietary, coed. Federal methodology is used as a basis for awarding need-based institutional aid.

FRESHMAN FINANCIAL AID (Fall 2012, est.) 26 applied for aid; of those 88% were deemed to have need. 100% of freshmen with need received aid; of those 9% had need fully met. *Average percent of need met:* 900% (excluding resources awarded to replace EFC). *Average financial aid package:* $8500 (excluding resources awarded to replace EFC).

GIFT AID (NEED-BASED) *Total amount:* $66,595 (99% federal, 1% state). *Receiving aid:* Freshmen: 18. *Average award:* Freshmen: $5500. *Scholarships, grants, and awards:* Federal Pell, FSEOG, state, college/university gift aid from institutional funds.

LOANS *Student loans:* $214,026 (100% need-based). *Average need-based loan:* Freshmen: $2000. *Programs:* Federal Direct (Subsidized and Unsubsidized Stafford, PLUS), college/university.

WORK-STUDY *Federal work-study:* Total amount: $5000; 1 job averaging $5000.

APPLYING FOR FINANCIAL AID *Required financial aid forms:* FAFSA, institution's own form. *Financial aid deadline:* Continuous. *Notification date:* Continuous beginning 7/1. Students must reply by 8/1.

CONTACT Mrs. Karen S. Terry, Financial Aid Manager, Millennia Atlantic University, 3801 NW 97th Avenue, Suite 100, Doral, FL 33178, 785-331-1000 Ext. 202. *E-mail:* kterry@maufl.edu. *Website:* http://www.maufl.edu/.

MILLERSVILLE UNIVERSITY OF PENNSYLVANIA
Millersville, PA

Tuition & fees (PA res): $8600

Average undergraduate aid package: $8185

ABOUT THE INSTITUTION State-supported, coed. *Awards:* certificates, associate, bachelor's, and master's degrees. 37 undergraduate majors. *Total enrollment:* 8,368. Undergraduates: 7,424. Freshmen: 1,318. Federal methodology is used as a basis for awarding need-based institutional aid.

UNDERGRADUATE EXPENSES for 2013–2014 *Application fee:* $50. *Tuition, state resident:* full-time $6428; part-time $268 per credit. *Tuition, non-resident:* full-time $16,070; part-time $670 per credit. *Required fees:* full-time $2172; $75.75 per credit or $15 per credit. Part-time tuition and fees vary according to course load. *College room and board:* $9234; *Room only:* $5378. Room and board charges vary according to board plan and housing facility.

FRESHMAN FINANCIAL AID (Fall 2011) 1,175 applied for aid; of those 74% were deemed to have need. 95% of freshmen with need received aid; of those 10% had need fully met. *Average percent of need met:* 67% (excluding resources awarded to replace EFC). *Average financial aid package:* $7570 (excluding resources awarded to replace EFC). 2% of all full-time freshmen had no need and received non-need-based gift aid.

UNDERGRADUATE FINANCIAL AID (Fall 2011) 5,680 applied for aid; of those 80% were deemed to have need. 97% of undergraduates with need received aid; of those 10% had need fully met. *Average percent of need met:* 70% (excluding resources awarded to replace EFC). *Average financial aid package:* $8185 (excluding resources awarded to replace EFC). 2% of all full-time undergraduates had no need and received non-need-based gift aid.

GIFT AID (NEED-BASED) *Total amount:* $17,520,978 (51% federal, 41% state, 4% institutional, 4% external sources). *Receiving aid:* Freshmen: 47% (606); all full-time undergraduates: 45% (3,071). *Average award:* Freshmen: $5451; Undergraduates: $5395. *Scholarships, grants, and awards:* Federal Pell, FSEOG, state, private, college/university gift aid from institutional funds, Schock Scholarships.

GIFT AID (NON-NEED-BASED) *Total amount:* $2,845,930 (2% federal, 11% state, 37% institutional, 50% external sources). *Receiving aid:* Freshmen: 12% (154). Undergraduates: 7% (484). *Average award:* Freshmen: $1924. Undergraduates: $3113. *Scholarships, grants, and awards by category:* Academic interests/achievement: 447 awards ($1,358,847 total): biological sciences, business, communication, computer science, education, English, foreign languages, general academic interests/achievements, health fields, humanities, mathematics, physical sciences, social sciences. *Creative arts/performance:* 24 awards ($29,911 total): art/fine arts, music. *Special achievements/activities:* 3 awards ($2577 total): community service. *Special characteristics:* 163 awards ($736,970 total): children of union members/company employees, international students. *Tuition waivers:* Full or partial for employees or children of employees, senior citizens. *ROTC:* Army.

LOANS *Student loans:* $37,252,784 (48% need-based, 52% non-need-based). 67% of past graduating class borrowed through all loan programs. *Average indebtedness per student:* $30,210. *Average need-based loan:* Freshmen: $3237. Undergraduates: $4236. *Parent loans:* $8,165,600 (100% non-need-based). *Programs:* Federal Direct (Subsidized and Unsubsidized Stafford, PLUS), Perkins, college/university.

WORK-STUDY *Federal work-study:* Total amount: $260,705; 260 jobs averaging $1086. *State or other work-study/employment:* Total amount: $2,755,956 (100% non-need-based). 1,844 part-time jobs averaging $1564.

ATHLETIC AWARDS Total amount: $474,673 (28% need-based, 72% non-need-based).

APPLYING FOR FINANCIAL AID *Required financial aid form:* FAFSA. *Financial aid deadline (priority):* 3/15. *Notification date:* Continuous beginning 3/19. Students must reply within 2 weeks of notification.

CONTACT Mr. Dwight G. Horsey, Director of Financial Aid, Millersville University of Pennsylvania, PO Box 1002, Millersville, PA 17551-0302, 717-872-3026 or toll-free 800-MU-ADMIT. *Fax:* 717-871-2248. *E-mail:* dwight.horsey@millersville.edu. *Website:* http://www.millersville.edu/.

MILLIGAN COLLEGE
Milligan College, TN

Tuition & fees: $26,760

Average undergraduate aid package: $19,698

ABOUT THE INSTITUTION Independent Christian, coed. *Awards:* bachelor's and master's degrees. 27 undergraduate majors. *Total enrollment:* 1,208. Undergraduates: 984. Freshmen: 204. Federal methodology is used as a basis for awarding need-based institutional aid.

UNDERGRADUATE EXPENSES for 2013–2014 *Application fee:* $30. *Comprehensive fee:* $32,610 includes full-time tuition ($25,735), mandatory fees ($1025), and room and board ($5850). *College room only:* $2850. Full-time tuition and fees vary according to course load. Room and board charges vary according to housing facility. Part-time tuition and fees vary according to course load.

FRESHMAN FINANCIAL AID (Fall 2012, est.) 166 applied for aid; of those 86% were deemed to have need. 100% of freshmen with need received aid; of those 30% had need fully met. *Average percent of need met:* 79% (excluding resources awarded to replace EFC). *Average financial aid package:* $20,655 (excluding resources awarded to replace EFC). 15% of all full-time freshmen had no need and received non-need-based gift aid.

UNDERGRADUATE FINANCIAL AID (Fall 2012, est.) 804 applied for aid; of those 89% were deemed to have need. 100% of undergraduates with need received aid; of those 24% had need fully met. *Average percent of need met:* 75% (excluding resources awarded to replace EFC). *Average financial aid package:* $19,698 (excluding resources awarded to replace EFC). 12% of all full-time undergraduates had no need and received non-need-based gift aid.

GIFT AID (NEED-BASED) *Total amount:* $9,707,603 (15% federal, 13% state, 54% institutional, 18% external sources). *Receiving aid:* Freshmen: 83% (142); all full-time undergraduates: 82% (697). *Average award:* Freshmen: $18,298; Undergraduates: $16,561. *Scholarships, grants, and awards:* Federal Pell, FSEOG, state, private, college/university gift aid from institutional funds.

GIFT AID (NON-NEED-BASED) *Total amount:* $1,999,925 (19% state, 57% institutional, 24% external sources). *Receiving aid:* Freshmen: 19% (33). Undergraduates: 16% (134). *Average award:* Freshmen: $8735. Undergraduates: $8560. *Scholarships, grants, and awards by category:* Academic interests/achievement: 597 awards ($5,517,397 total): general academic interests/achievements, religion/biblical studies. *Creative arts/performance:* 55 awards ($169,700 total): art/fine arts, cinema/film/broadcasting, dance, music, theater/drama. *Special achievements/activities:* 90 awards ($251,450 total): cheerleading/drum major, community service. *Special characteristics:* 19 awards ($347,306 total): children of faculty/staff. *Tuition waivers:* Full or partial for employees or children of employees. *ROTC:* Army cooperative.

LOANS *Student loans:* $4,665,449 (75% need-based, 25% non-need-based). 63% of past graduating class borrowed through all loan programs. *Average indebtedness per student:* $27,687. *Average need-based loan:* Freshmen: $3240. Undergraduates: $4451. *Parent loans:* $950,457 (54% need-based, 46% non-need-based). *Programs:* Federal Direct (Subsidized and Unsubsidized Stafford, PLUS), Perkins, alternative loans.

WORK-STUDY *Federal work-study:* Total amount: $195,600; 163 jobs averaging $1200. *State or other work-study/employment:* Total amount: $237,266 (23% need-based, 77% non-need-based). 153 part-time jobs averaging $1551.

ATHLETIC AWARDS Total amount: $2,823,664 (64% need-based, 36% non-need-based).

APPLYING FOR FINANCIAL AID *Required financial aid form:* FAFSA. *Financial aid deadline (priority):* 3/1. *Notification date:* Continuous beginning 3/1. Students must reply within 2 weeks of notification.

CONTACT Diane Keasling, Coordinator of Financial Aid, Milligan College, PO Box 250, Milligan College, TN 37682, 423-461-8968 or toll-free 800-262-8337. *Fax:* 423-929-2368. *E-mail:* dlkeasling@milligan.edu. *Website:* http://www.milligan.edu/.

MILLIKIN UNIVERSITY
Decatur, IL

Tuition & fees: $28,644	Average undergraduate aid package: $22,924

ABOUT THE INSTITUTION Independent Presbyterian Church (U.S.A.), coed. *Awards:* bachelor's and master's degrees. 54 undergraduate majors. *Total enrollment:* 2,347. Undergraduates: 2,264. Freshmen: 532. Federal methodology is used as a basis for awarding need-based institutional aid.

UNDERGRADUATE EXPENSES for 2013–2014 Comprehensive fee: $37,614 includes full-time tuition ($27,852), mandatory fees ($792), and room and board ($8970). *College room only:* $5000. Room and board charges vary according to board plan and housing facility. *Part-time tuition:* $931 per credit hour. *Part-time fees:* $22 per credit hour.

FRESHMAN FINANCIAL AID (Fall 2011) 425 applied for aid; of those 89% were deemed to have need. 100% of freshmen with need received aid; of those 29% had need fully met. *Average percent of need met:* 88% (excluding resources awarded to replace EFC). *Average financial aid package:* $24,330 (excluding resources awarded to replace EFC). 11% of all full-time freshmen had no need and received non-need-based gift aid.

UNDERGRADUATE FINANCIAL AID (Fall 2011) 1,932 applied for aid; of those 89% were deemed to have need. 100% of undergraduates with need received aid; of those 53% had need fully met. *Average percent of need met:* 92% (excluding resources awarded to replace EFC). *Average financial aid package:* $22,924 (excluding resources awarded to replace EFC). 9% of all full-time undergraduates had no need and received non-need-based gift aid.

GIFT AID (NEED-BASED) Total amount: $16,261,883 (23% federal, 25% state, 52% institutional). *Receiving aid:* Freshmen: 86% (373); all full-time undergraduates: 75% (1,589). *Average award:* Freshmen: $10,832; Undergraduates: $9940. *Scholarships, grants, and awards:* Federal Pell, FSEOG, state, private, college/university gift aid from institutional funds.

GIFT AID (NON-NEED-BASED) Total amount: $20,219,477 (1% federal, 96% institutional, 3% external sources). *Receiving aid:* Freshmen: 88% (379). Undergraduates: 75% (1,581). *Average award:* Freshmen: $10,898. Undergraduates: $11,192. *Scholarships, grants, and awards by category:* Academic interests/achievement: 2,105 awards ($18,246,635 total): biological sciences, business, communication, education, English, foreign languages, general academic interests/achievements, health fields, humanities, international studies, mathematics, physical sciences, premedicine. *Creative arts/performance:* 556 awards ($1,240,875 total): art/fine arts, dance, music, theater/drama. *Special achievements/activities:* 10 awards ($19,000 total): community service. *Special characteristics:* 264 awards ($1,320,805 total): children and siblings of alumni, children of faculty/staff, children of union members/company employees, children with a deceased or disabled parent, international students, parents of current students, relatives of clergy, siblings of current students, veterans. *Tuition waivers:* Full or partial for employees or children of employees.

LOANS Student loans: $14,978,007 (45% need-based, 55% non-need-based). 78% of past graduating class borrowed through all loan programs. *Average indebtedness per student:* $29,871. *Average need-based loan:* Freshmen: $3686. Undergraduates: $4520. *Parent loans:* $2,505,878 (100% non-need-based). *Programs:* Federal Direct (Subsidized and Unsubsidized Stafford, PLUS), Perkins, private loans.

WORK-STUDY Federal work-study: Total amount: $591,574; 598 jobs averaging $989. *State or other work-study/employment:* Total amount: $234,334 (100% non-need-based). 300 part-time jobs averaging $781.

APPLYING FOR FINANCIAL AID Required financial aid form: FAFSA. *Financial aid deadline (priority):* 3/1. *Notification date:* Continuous beginning 3/1. Students must reply by 5/1 or within 4 weeks of notification.

CONTACT Cheryl Howerton, Director of Financial Aid, Millikin University, 1184 West Main Street, Decatur, IL 62522-2084, 217-424-6317 or toll-free 800-373-7733. *Fax:* 217-424-5070. *E-mail:* studentservicecenter@millikin.edu. *Website:* http://www.millikin.edu/.

MILLSAPS COLLEGE
Jackson, MS

Tuition & fees: $30,974	Average undergraduate aid package: $27,049

ABOUT THE INSTITUTION Independent United Methodist, coed. *Awards:* bachelor's and master's degrees. 31 undergraduate majors. *Total enrollment:* 915. Undergraduates: 849. Freshmen: 211. Federal methodology is used as a basis for awarding need-based institutional aid.

UNDERGRADUATE EXPENSES for 2013–2014 Comprehensive fee: $41,800 includes full-time tuition ($29,052), mandatory fees ($1922), and room and board ($10,826). *College room only:* $6110. Room and board charges vary according to housing facility. Part-time tuition and fees vary according to course load.

FRESHMAN FINANCIAL AID (Fall 2012, est.) 170 applied for aid; of those 83% were deemed to have need. 100% of freshmen with need received aid; of those 31% had need fully met. *Average percent of need met:* 80% (excluding resources awarded to replace EFC). *Average financial aid package:* $27,094 (excluding resources awarded to replace EFC). 33% of all full-time freshmen had no need and received non-need-based gift aid.

UNDERGRADUATE FINANCIAL AID (Fall 2012, est.) 601 applied for aid; of those 83% were deemed to have need. 100% of undergraduates with need received aid; of those 25% had need fully met. *Average percent of need met:* 81% (excluding resources awarded to replace EFC). *Average financial aid package:* $27,049 (excluding resources awarded to replace EFC). 34% of all full-time undergraduates had no need and received non-need-based gift aid.

GIFT AID (NEED-BASED) Total amount: $10,650,739 (9% federal, 2% state, 88% institutional, 1% external sources). *Receiving aid:* Freshmen: 67% (141); all full-time undergraduates: 58% (479). *Average award:* Freshmen: $22,038; Undergraduates: $21,545. *Scholarships, grants, and awards:* Federal Pell, FSEOG, state, private, college/university gift aid from institutional funds.

GIFT AID (NON-NEED-BASED) Total amount: $6,648,056 (3% state, 96% institutional, 1% external sources). *Receiving aid:* Freshmen: 15% (31). Undergraduates: 12% (99). *Average award:* Freshmen: $21,612. Undergraduates: $18,124. *Scholarships, grants, and awards by category:* Academic interests/achievement: business, general academic interests/achievements. *Creative arts/performance:* art/fine arts, music, theater/drama. *Special achievements/activities:* community service, general special achievements/activities, hobbies/interests, leadership, religious involvement. *Special characteristics:* adult students, children of faculty/staff, ethnic background, first-generation college students, local/state students, religious affiliation. *Tuition waivers:* Full or partial for employees or children of employees. *ROTC:* Army cooperative, Air Force cooperative.

LOANS Student loans: $3,781,789 (63% need-based, 37% non-need-based). 56% of past graduating class borrowed through all loan programs. *Average indebtedness per student:* $28,965. *Average need-based loan:* Freshmen: $3518. Undergraduates: $4840. *Parent loans:* $1,176,647 (26% need-based, 74% non-need-based). *Programs:* Federal Direct (Subsidized and Unsubsidized Stafford, PLUS), Perkins, college/university.

WORK-STUDY Federal work-study: Total amount: $467,495; jobs available.

APPLYING FOR FINANCIAL AID Required financial aid form: FAFSA. *Financial aid deadline (priority):* 3/1. *Notification date:* Continuous beginning 3/15. Students must reply by 5/1 or within 2 weeks of notification.

CONTACT Patrick James, Director of Financial Aid, Millsaps College, 1701 North State Street, Jackson, MS 39210-0001, 601-974-1220 or toll-free 800-352-1050. *Fax:* 601-974-1224. *E-mail:* patrick.james@millsaps.edu. *Website:* http://www.millsaps.edu/.

MILLS COLLEGE
Oakland, CA

Tuition & fees: $41,494	Average undergraduate aid package: $36,185

ABOUT THE INSTITUTION Independent, undergraduate: women only; graduate: coed. *Awards:* certificates, bachelor's, master's, and doctoral degrees. 38 undergraduate majors. *Total enrollment:* 1,533. Undergraduates: 937. Freshmen: 208. Federal methodology is used as a basis for awarding need-based institutional aid.

UNDERGRADUATE EXPENSES for 2013–2014 *Application fee:* $50. *Comprehensive fee:* $54,119 includes full-time tuition ($40,210), mandatory fees ($1284), and room and board ($12,625). *College room only:* $6495. Full-time tuition and fees vary according to course load. Room and board charges vary according to board plan and housing facility. *Part-time tuition:* $6702 per course. *Part-time fees:* $1284 per year. Part-time tuition and fees vary according to course load.

FRESHMAN FINANCIAL AID (Fall 2012, est.) 189 applied for aid; of those 93% were deemed to have need. 100% of freshmen with need received aid; of those 20% had need fully met. *Average percent of need met:* 87% (excluding resources awarded to replace EFC). *Average financial aid package:* $38,795 (excluding resources awarded to replace EFC). 15% of all full-time freshmen had no need and received non-need-based gift aid.

UNDERGRADUATE FINANCIAL AID (Fall 2012, est.) 797 applied for aid; of those 94% were deemed to have need. 99% of undergraduates with need received aid; of those 16% had need fully met. *Average percent of need met:* 80% (excluding resources awarded to replace EFC). *Average financial aid package:* $36,185 (excluding resources awarded to replace EFC). 12% of all full-time undergraduates had no need and received non-need-based gift aid.

GIFT AID (NEED-BASED) *Total amount:* $20,163,180 (10% federal, 13% state, 75% institutional, 2% external sources). *Receiving aid:* Freshmen: 81% (168); all full-time undergraduates: 80% (718). *Average award:* Freshmen: $22,402; Undergraduates: $19,839. *Scholarships, grants, and awards:* Federal Pell, FSEOG, state, private, college/university gift aid from institutional funds.

GIFT AID (NON-NEED-BASED) *Total amount:* $1,844,595 (100% institutional). *Receiving aid:* Freshmen: 6% (12). Undergraduates: 4% (37). *Average award:* Freshmen: $15,101. Undergraduates: $15,326. *Scholarships, grants, and awards by category:* Academic interests/achievement: 117 awards ($1,647,456 total): biological sciences, computer science, general academic interests/achievements, mathematics, physical sciences, premedicine. *Creative arts/performance:* 6 awards ($35,000 total): art/fine arts, music. *Tuition waivers:* Full or partial for employees or children of employees. *ROTC:* Army cooperative.

LOANS *Student loans:* $5,347,219 (98% need-based, 2% non-need-based). 77% of past graduating class borrowed through all loan programs. *Average indebtedness per student:* $27,021. *Average need-based loan:* Freshmen: $5859. Undergraduates: $7688. *Parent loans:* $1,836,665 (100% need-based). *Programs:* Federal Direct (Subsidized and Unsubsidized Stafford, PLUS), Perkins, state, college/university.

WORK-STUDY *Federal work-study:* Total amount: $868,343; 281 jobs averaging $3184. *State or other work-study/employment:* Total amount: $586,639 (94% need-based, 6% non-need-based). 254 part-time jobs averaging $2709.

APPLYING FOR FINANCIAL AID *Required financial aid forms:* FAFSA, institution's own form, noncustodial (divorced/separated) parent's statement. *Financial aid deadline (priority):* 2/15. *Notification date:* Continuous beginning 3/1. Students must reply by 5/1 or within 2 weeks of notification.

CONTACT Miss Shari Keller, The M Center and Office of Financial Aid, Mills College, 5000 MacArthur Boulevard, Oakland, CA 94613, 510-430-2000 or toll-free 800-87-MILLS. *Fax:* 510-430-2003. *E-mail:* mcenter-finaid@mills.edu. *Website:* http://www.mills.edu/.

MILWAUKEE INSTITUTE OF ART AND DESIGN
Milwaukee, WI

CONTACT Carol Masse, Director of Financial Aid, Milwaukee Institute of Art and Design, 273 East Erie Street, Milwaukee, WI 53202-6003, 414-291-3272 or toll-free 888-749-MIAD. *Fax:* 414-291-8077. *E-mail:* carolmasse@miad.edu. *Website:* http://www.miad.edu/.

MILWAUKEE SCHOOL OF ENGINEERING
Milwaukee, WI

Tuition & fees: $34,470	Average undergraduate aid package: $21,818

ABOUT THE INSTITUTION Independent, coed, primarily men. *Awards:* bachelor's and master's degrees. 22 undergraduate majors. *Total enrollment:* 2,564. Undergraduates: 2,378. Freshmen: 490. Federal methodology is used as a basis for awarding need-based institutional aid.

UNDERGRADUATE EXPENSES for 2013–2014 *Comprehensive fee:* $42,741 includes full-time tuition ($32,880), mandatory fees ($1590), and room and board ($8271). *College room only:* $5280. Full-time tuition and fees vary according to course load. Room and board charges vary according to board plan and housing facility. *Part-time tuition:* $570 per credit. Part-time tuition and fees vary according to course load.

FRESHMAN FINANCIAL AID (Fall 2011) 403 applied for aid; of those 92% were deemed to have need. 100% of freshmen with need received aid; of those 10% had need fully met. *Average percent of need met:* 74% (excluding resources awarded to replace EFC). *Average financial aid package:* $23,772 (excluding resources awarded to replace EFC). 14% of all full-time freshmen had no need and received non-need-based gift aid.

UNDERGRADUATE FINANCIAL AID (Fall 2011) 1,946 applied for aid; of those 94% were deemed to have need. 100% of undergraduates with need received aid; of those 13% had need fully met. *Average percent of need met:* 68% (excluding resources awarded to replace EFC). *Average financial aid package:* $21,818 (excluding resources awarded to replace EFC). 13% of all full-time undergraduates had no need and received non-need-based gift aid.

GIFT AID (NEED-BASED) *Total amount:* $33,473,377 (7% federal, 6% state, 81% institutional, 6% external sources). *Receiving aid:* Freshmen: 84% (369); all full-time undergraduates: 86% (1,818). *Average award:* Freshmen: $21,207; Undergraduates: $18,545. *Scholarships, grants, and awards:* Federal Pell, FSEOG, state, private, college/university gift aid from institutional funds.

GIFT AID (NON-NEED-BASED) *Total amount:* $4,577,698 (89% institutional, 11% external sources). *Receiving aid:* Freshmen: 7% (29). Undergraduates: 8% (170). *Average award:* Freshmen: $12,170. Undergraduates: $11,256. *Scholarships, grants, and awards by category:* Academic interests/achievement: 2,025 awards ($21,402,512 total): business, communication, computer science, engineering/technologies, health fields. *Special characteristics:* 25 awards ($659,912 total): children of faculty/staff. *Tuition waivers:* Full or partial for employees or children of employees. *ROTC:* Army cooperative, Naval cooperative, Air Force cooperative.

LOANS *Student loans:* $18,064,258 (71% need-based, 29% non-need-based). 84% of past graduating class borrowed through all loan programs. *Average indebtedness per student:* $38,038. *Average need-based loan:* Freshmen: $2794. Undergraduates: $3608. *Parent loans:* $4,312,458 (69% need-based, 31% non-need-based). *Programs:* Federal Direct (Subsidized and Unsubsidized Stafford, PLUS), Perkins, state, college/university.

WORK-STUDY *Federal work-study:* Total amount: $359,661; 269 jobs averaging $1313.

APPLYING FOR FINANCIAL AID *Required financial aid form:* FAFSA. *Financial aid deadline (priority):* 3/15. *Notification date:* Continuous beginning 3/1. Students must reply within 2 weeks of notification.

CONTACT Steve Midthun, Director of Financial Aid, Milwaukee School of Engineering, 1025 North Broadway, Milwaukee, WI 53202-3109, 414-277-7223 or toll-free 800-332-6763. *Fax:* 414-277-6952. *E-mail:* finaid@msoe.edu. *Website:* http://www.msoe.edu/.

MINNEAPOLIS COLLEGE OF ART AND DESIGN
Minneapolis, MN

Tuition & fees: N/R	Average undergraduate aid package: $19,544

ABOUT THE INSTITUTION Independent, coed. 11 undergraduate majors. Federal methodology is used as a basis for awarding need-based institutional aid.

FRESHMAN FINANCIAL AID (Fall 2012, est.) 123 applied for aid; of those 92% were deemed to have need. 100% of freshmen with need received aid; of those 7% had need fully met. *Average percent of need met:* 67% (excluding resources awarded to replace EFC). *Average financial aid package:* $21,672 (excluding resources awarded to replace EFC). 13% of all full-time freshmen had no need and received non-need-based gift aid.

UNDERGRADUATE FINANCIAL AID (Fall 2012, est.) 565 applied for aid; of those 93% were deemed to have need. 100% of undergraduates with need received aid; of those 10% had need fully met. *Average percent of need met:* 65% (excluding resources awarded to replace EFC). *Average financial aid package:* $19,544 (excluding resources awarded to replace EFC). 11% of all full-time undergraduates had no need and received non-need-based gift aid.

GIFT AID (NEED-BASED) *Total amount:* $7,567,467 (15% federal, 6% state, 75% institutional, 4% external sources). *Receiving aid:* Freshmen: 87% (113); all full-time undergraduates: 80% (509). *Average award:* Freshmen: $17,140; Undergraduates: $14,824. *Scholarships, grants, and awards:* Federal Pell, FSEOG, state, private, college/university gift aid from institutional funds.

GIFT AID (NON-NEED-BASED) *Total amount:* $953,979 (85% institutional, 15% external sources). *Receiving aid:* Freshmen: 5% (7). Undergraduates: 5% (35). *Average award:* Freshmen: $10,047. Undergraduates: $9162. *Scholarships, grants, and awards by category:* Creative arts/performance: applied art and design, art/fine arts, cinema/film/broadcasting, general creative arts/performance.

LOANS *Student loans:* $5,571,970 (80% need-based, 20% non-need-based). 87% of past graduating class borrowed through all loan programs. *Average indebtedness per student:* $43,650. *Average need-based loan:* Freshmen: $3695. Undergraduates: $4533. *Parent loans:* $1,286,621 (59% need-based, 41% non-need-based). *Programs:* Federal Direct (Subsidized and Unsubsidized Stafford, PLUS), Perkins, state.

WORK-STUDY *Federal work-study:* Total amount: $164,292; jobs available. *State or other work-study/employment:* Total amount: $475,148 (66% need-based, 34% non-need-based). Part-time jobs available.

APPLYING FOR FINANCIAL AID *Required financial aid form:* FAFSA. *Financial aid deadline:* 4/1 (priority: 3/1). *Notification date:* Continuous beginning 3/1. Students must reply by 5/1 or within 2 weeks of notification.

CONTACT Ms. Laura Link, Director of Financial Aid, Minneapolis College of Art and Design, 2501 Stevens Avenue South, Minneapolis, MN 55404-4347, 612-874-3733 or toll-free 800-874-6223. *Fax:* 612-874-3701. *E-mail:* laura_link@mead.edu. *Website:* http://www.mcad.edu/.

MINNESOTA SCHOOL OF BUSINESS–BLAINE
Blaine, MN

Tuition & fees: $16,848	Average undergraduate aid package: N/A

ABOUT THE INSTITUTION Proprietary, coed, primarily women. *Awards:* diplomas, associate, and bachelor's degrees. 15 undergraduate majors. *Total enrollment:* 1,012. Undergraduates: 1,012. Freshmen: 96. Both federal and institutional methodology are used as a basis for awarding need-based institutional aid.

UNDERGRADUATE EXPENSES for 2013–2014 *Application fee:* $50. *Tuition:* full-time $15,300; part-time $460 per credit. *Required fees:* full-time $1548; $43 per credit. Full-time tuition and fees vary according to course load, degree level, location, and program. Part-time tuition and fees vary according to course load, degree level, location, and program.

GIFT AID (NEED-BASED) *Scholarships, grants, and awards:* Federal Pell, FSEOG, state, private, college/university gift aid from institutional funds.

GIFT AID (NON-NEED-BASED) *Scholarships, grants, and awards by category:* Academic interests/achievement: business, computer science, engineering/technologies, health fields. Special achievements/activities: community service. Special characteristics: children of faculty/staff, veterans, veterans' children. Tuition waivers: Full or partial for employees or children of employees.

LOANS *Programs:* Federal Direct (Subsidized and Unsubsidized Stafford, PLUS), state, college/university, alternative loans.

APPLYING FOR FINANCIAL AID *Required financial aid forms:* FAFSA, institution's own form. *Financial aid deadline:* Continuous. *Notification date:* Continuous beginning 1/2. Students must reply within 2 weeks of notification.

CONTACT Office of Financial Aid, Minnesota School of Business–Blaine, 3680 Pheasant Ridge Drive NE, Blaine, MN 55449, 763-225-8008. *Fax:* 763-225-8001. *E-mail:* lfourniea@msbcollege.edu. *Website:* http://www.msbcollege.edu/.

MINNESOTA SCHOOL OF BUSINESS–ELK RIVER
Elk River, MN

Tuition & fees: $16,848	Average undergraduate aid package: N/A

ABOUT THE INSTITUTION Proprietary, coed. *Awards:* diplomas, associate, and bachelor's degrees. 13 undergraduate majors. *Total enrollment:* 545. Undergraduates: 545. Freshmen: 79.

UNDERGRADUATE EXPENSES for 2013–2014 *Application fee:* $50. *Tuition:* full-time $15,300; part-time $460 per credit. *Required fees:* full-time $1548; $43 per credit. Full-time tuition and fees vary according to course load, degree level, location, and program. Part-time tuition and fees vary according to course load, degree level, location, and program.

GIFT AID (NEED-BASED) *Scholarships, grants, and awards:* Federal Pell, FSEOG, state, private, college/university gift aid from institutional funds.

GIFT AID (NON-NEED-BASED) *Scholarships, grants, and awards by category:* Academic interests/achievement: business, computer science, engineering/technologies, health fields. Special achievements/activities: community service. Special characteristics: children of faculty/staff, veterans, veterans' children. Tuition waivers: Full or partial for employees or children of employees.

LOANS *Programs:* Federal Direct (Subsidized and Unsubsidized Stafford, PLUS), state, college/university, alternative loans.

APPLYING FOR FINANCIAL AID *Required financial aid forms:* FAFSA, institution's own form. *Financial aid deadline:* Continuous. *Notification date:* Continuous beginning 1/2. Students must reply within 2 weeks of notification.

CONTACT Office of Financial Aid, Minnesota School of Business–Elk River, 11500 193rd Avenue, Elk River, MN 55330, 763-367-7000. *Website:* http://www.msbcollege.edu/.

MINNESOTA SCHOOL OF BUSINESS–LAKEVILLE
Lakeville, MN

Tuition & fees: $16,848	Average undergraduate aid package: N/A

ABOUT THE INSTITUTION Proprietary, coed. *Awards:* diplomas, associate, and bachelor's degrees. 11 undergraduate majors. *Total enrollment:* 255. Undergraduates: 255. Freshmen: 35. Both federal and institutional methodology are used as a basis for awarding need-based institutional aid.

UNDERGRADUATE EXPENSES for 2013–2014 *Application fee:* $50. *Tuition:* full-time $15,300; part-time $460 per credit. *Required fees:* full-time $1548; $43 per credit. Full-time tuition and fees vary according to course load, degree level, location, and program. Part-time tuition and fees vary according to course load, degree level, location, and program.

GIFT AID (NEED-BASED) *Scholarships, grants, and awards:* Federal Pell, FSEOG, state, private, college/university gift aid from institutional funds.

GIFT AID (NON-NEED-BASED) *Scholarships, grants, and awards by category:* Academic interests/achievement: business, computer science, engineering/technologies, health fields. Special achievements/activities: community service. Special characteristics: children of faculty/staff, veterans, veterans' children. Tuition waivers: Full or partial for employees or children of employees.

LOANS *Programs:* Federal Direct (Subsidized and Unsubsidized Stafford, PLUS), state, college/university, alternative loans.

APPLYING FOR FINANCIAL AID *Required financial aid forms:* FAFSA, institution's own form, state aid form. *Financial aid deadline:* Continuous. *Notification date:* Continuous beginning 1/2. Students must reply within 2 weeks of notification.

CONTACT Office of Financial Aid, Minnesota School of Business–Lakeville, 17685 Juniper Path , Lakeville , MN 55044, 952-892-9000. *Fax:* 952-892-9001. *Website:* http://www.msbcollege.edu/.

MINNESOTA SCHOOL OF BUSINESS– MOORHEAD
Moorhead, MN

Tuition & fees: N/R	Average undergraduate aid package: N/A

ABOUT THE INSTITUTION Proprietary, coed. *Awards:* diplomas, associate, and bachelor's degrees. 10 undergraduate majors. *Total enrollment:* 318. Undergraduates: 318. Freshmen: 35. Both federal and institutional methodology are used as a basis for awarding need-based institutional aid.

GIFT AID (NEED-BASED) Scholarships, grants, and awards: Federal Pell, FSEOG, state, private, college/university gift aid from institutional funds.

GIFT AID (NON-NEED-BASED) *Scholarships, grants, and awards by category:* Academic interests/achievement: business, computer science, engineering/technologies, health fields. *Special achievements/activities:* community service. *Special characteristics:* children of faculty/staff, veterans, veterans' children.

LOANS *Programs:* Federal Direct (Subsidized and Unsubsidized Stafford, PLUS), state, college/university, alternative loans.

APPLYING FOR FINANCIAL AID *Required financial aid forms:* FAFSA, institution's own form, state aid form. *Financial aid deadline:* Continuous. *Notification date:* Continuous beginning 1/2. Students must reply within 2 weeks of notification.

CONTACT Office of Financial Aid, Minnesota School of Business–Moorhead, 2777 34th Street South, Moorhead , MN 56560, 218-422-1000. *Fax:* 218-422-1001. *Website:* http://www.msbcollege.edu/.

MINNESOTA SCHOOL OF BUSINESS– ROCHESTER
Rochester, MN

Tuition & fees: $16,848	Average undergraduate aid package: N/A

ABOUT THE INSTITUTION Proprietary, coed. *Awards:* diplomas, associate, bachelor's, and master's degrees. 13 undergraduate majors. *Total enrollment:* 650. Undergraduates: 650. Freshmen: 54. Both federal and institutional methodology are used as a basis for awarding need-based institutional aid.

UNDERGRADUATE EXPENSES for 2013–2014 *Application fee:* $50. *Tuition:* full-time $15,300; part-time $460 per credit. *Required fees:* full-time $1548; $43 per credit. Full-time tuition and fees vary according to course level, course load, degree level, location, and program. Part-time tuition and fees vary according to course level, course load, degree level, location, and program.

GIFT AID (NEED-BASED) Scholarships, grants, and awards: Federal Pell, FSEOG, state, private, college/university gift aid from institutional funds.

GIFT AID (NON-NEED-BASED) *Scholarships, grants, and awards by category:* Academic interests/achievement: business, computer science, engineering/technologies, health fields. *Special achievements/activities:* community service. *Special characteristics:* children of faculty/staff, veterans, veterans' children. *Tuition waivers:* Full or partial for employees or children of employees.

LOANS *Programs:* Federal Direct (Subsidized and Unsubsidized Stafford, PLUS), state, college/university, alternative loans.

APPLYING FOR FINANCIAL AID *Required financial aid forms:* FAFSA, institution's own form, state aid form. *Financial aid deadline:* Continuous. *Notification date:* Continuous beginning 1/2. Students must reply within 2 weeks of notification.

CONTACT Office of Financial Aid, Minnesota School of Business–Rochester, 2521 Pennington Drive NW , Rochester , MN 55901, 507-536-9500 or toll-free 888-662-8772. *Fax:* 507-536-8011. *Website:* http://www.msbcollege.edu/.

MINNESOTA STATE UNIVERSITY MANKATO
Mankato, MN

Tuition & fees (MN res): $8396	Average undergraduate aid package: $9183

ABOUT THE INSTITUTION State-supported, coed. *Awards:* certificates, associate, bachelor's, master's, and doctoral degrees. 109 undergraduate majors. *Total enrollment:* 15,195. Undergraduates: 13,285. Freshmen: 2,311. Federal methodology is used as a basis for awarding need-based institutional aid.

UNDERGRADUATE EXPENSES for 2013–2014 *Application fee:* $20. *Tuition, state resident:* full-time $7532; part-time $262.33 per credit hour. *Tuition, nonresident:* full-time $15,010; part-time $564.04 per credit hour. *Required fees:* full-time $864; $35.91 per credit hour. Full-time tuition and fees vary according to course load, location, and reciprocity agreements. Part-time tuition and fees vary according to course load, location, and reciprocity agreements. *College room and board:* $7053. Room and board charges vary according to board plan and housing facility.

FRESHMAN FINANCIAL AID (Fall 2012, est.) 2,025 applied for aid; of those 69% were deemed to have need. 99% of freshmen with need received aid; of those 37% had need fully met. *Average percent of need met:* 79% (excluding resources awarded to replace EFC). *Average financial aid package:* $9278 (excluding resources awarded to replace EFC). 9% of all full-time freshmen had no need and received non-need-based gift aid.

UNDERGRADUATE FINANCIAL AID (Fall 2012, est.) 9,114 applied for aid; of those 74% were deemed to have need. 99% of undergraduates with need received aid; of those 26% had need fully met. *Average percent of need met:* 80% (excluding resources awarded to replace EFC). *Average financial aid package:* $9183 (excluding resources awarded to replace EFC). 4% of all full-time undergraduates had no need and received non-need-based gift aid.

GIFT AID (NEED-BASED) *Total amount:* $28,088,524 (60% federal, 27% state, 6% institutional, 7% external sources). *Receiving aid:* Freshmen: 49% (1,133); all full-time undergraduates: 44% (4,972). *Average award:* Freshmen: $5290; Undergraduates: $4951. *Scholarships, grants, and awards:* Federal Pell, FSEOG, state, private, college/university gift aid from institutional funds.

GIFT AID (NON-NEED-BASED) *Total amount:* $4,683,852 (11% federal, 7% state, 37% institutional, 45% external sources). *Receiving aid:* Freshmen: 23% (521). Undergraduates: 14% (1,543). *Average award:* Freshmen: $2271. Undergraduates: $3512. *Scholarships, grants, and awards by category:* Academic interests/achievement: general academic interests/achievements. *Creative arts/performance:* art/fine arts, general creative arts/performance. *Special achievements/activities:* leadership. *Special characteristics:* members of minority groups. *Tuition waivers:* Full or partial for employees or children of employees. *ROTC:* Army.

LOANS *Student loans:* $79,425,074 (58% need-based, 42% non-need-based). 75% of past graduating class borrowed through all loan programs. *Average indebtedness per student:* $29,587. *Average need-based loan:* Freshmen: $3619. Undergraduates: $4277. *Parent loans:* $836,250 (51% need-based, 49% non-need-based). *Programs:* Federal Direct (Subsidized and Unsubsidized Stafford, PLUS), Perkins, state, college/university, alternative loans.

WORK-STUDY *Federal work-study:* Total amount: $1,705,386; 385 jobs averaging $3840. *State or other work-study/employment:* Total amount: $4,226,704 (34% need-based, 66% non-need-based). 532 part-time jobs averaging $3840.

ATHLETIC AWARDS Total amount: $2,281,225 (17% need-based, 83% non-need-based).

APPLYING FOR FINANCIAL AID *Required financial aid form:* FAFSA. *Financial aid deadline (priority):* 3/15. *Notification date:* Continuous beginning 3/30.

CONTACT Sandra Loerts, Director of Financial Aid, Minnesota State University Mankato, 120 Wigley Administration Center, Mankato, MN 56001, 507-389-1866 or toll-free 800-722-0544. *Fax:* 507-389-2227. *E-mail:* campushub@mnsu.edu. *Website:* http://www.mnsu.edu/.

MINNESOTA STATE UNIVERSITY MOORHEAD
Moorhead, MN

Tuition & fees (MN res): $7834	Average undergraduate aid package: N/A

ABOUT THE INSTITUTION State-supported, coed. *Awards:* certificates, associate, bachelor's, master's, and doctoral degrees. 64 undergraduate majors. *Total enrollment:* 6,904. Undergraduates: 6,426. Freshmen: 1,098. Federal methodology is used as a basis for awarding need-based institutional aid.

UNDERGRADUATE EXPENSES for 2013–2014 *Application fee:* $20. *Tuition, state resident:* full-time $6898; part-time $222.43 per credit hour. *Tuition, nonresident:* full-time $13,796; part-time $444.86 per credit hour. *Required fees:* full-time $936; $41.74 per credit hour. Full-time tuition and fees vary according to course load, degree level, program, and reciprocity agreements. Part-time tuition and fees vary according to course load, degree level, program, and reciprocity agreements. *College room and board:* $6984; *Room only:* $4310. Room and board charges vary according to board plan and housing facility.

FRESHMAN FINANCIAL AID (Fall 2012, est.) 943 applied for aid; of those 70% were deemed to have need. 100% of freshmen with need received aid.

UNDERGRADUATE FINANCIAL AID (Fall 2012, est.) 4,583 applied for aid; of those 72% were deemed to have need. 100% of undergraduates with need received aid.

GIFT AID (NEED-BASED) *Total amount:* $11,928,663 (70% federal, 28% state, 2% institutional). *Receiving aid:* Freshmen: 40% (427); all full-time undergraduates: 41% (2,178). *Average award:* Freshmen: $4692; Undergraduates: $4591. *Scholarships, grants, and awards:* Federal Pell, FSEOG, state, private, college/university gift aid from institutional funds.

GIFT AID (NON-NEED-BASED) *Total amount:* $1,552,261 (50% institutional, 50% external sources). *Scholarships, grants, and awards by category:* Academic interests/achievement: biological sciences, business, communication, computer science, education, engineering/technologies, English, general academic interests/achievements, health fields, international studies, mathematics, physical sciences, pre-medicine, social sciences. *Creative arts/performance:* art/fine arts, cinema/film/broadcasting, creative writing, music, theater/drama. *Special achievements/activities:* community service, general special achievements/activities. *Special characteristics:* adult students, children of faculty/staff, first-generation college students, members of minority groups, out-of-state students. *Tuition waivers:* Full or partial for employees or children of employees, senior citizens. *ROTC:* Army cooperative, Air Force cooperative.

LOANS *Student loans:* $36,100,486 (39% need-based, 61% non-need-based). 62% of past graduating class borrowed through all loan programs. *Average indebtedness per student:* $25,124. *Average need-based loan:* Freshmen: $3738. Undergraduates: $4229. *Parent loans:* $426,717 (100% non-need-based). *Programs:* Federal Direct (Subsidized and Unsubsidized Stafford, PLUS), Perkins, state, alternative loans.

WORK-STUDY *Federal work-study:* Total amount: $624,586; 332 jobs averaging $2173. *State or other work-study/employment:* Total amount: $3,623,656 (12% need-based, 88% non-need-based). 220 part-time jobs averaging $2197.

ATHLETIC AWARDS Total amount: $528,359 (100% non-need-based).

APPLYING FOR FINANCIAL AID *Required financial aid form:* FAFSA. *Financial aid deadline (priority):* 2/15. *Notification date:* Continuous beginning 6/1. Students must reply within 2 weeks of notification.

CONTACT Ms. Carolyn Zehren, Director of Financial Aid, Minnesota State University Moorhead, 1104 7th Avenue South, Moorhead, MN 56563, 218-477-2251 or toll-free 800-593-7246. *Fax:* 218-477-2058. *E-mail:* finaid@mnstate.edu. *Website:* http://www.mnstate.edu/.

MINOT STATE UNIVERSITY
Minot, ND

Tuition & fees (ND res): $5921	Average undergraduate aid package: $7847

ABOUT THE INSTITUTION State-supported, coed. *Awards:* certificates, associate, bachelor's, and master's degrees. 58 undergraduate majors. *Total enrollment:* 3,560. Undergraduates: 3,298. Freshmen: 398. Federal methodology is used as a basis for awarding need-based institutional aid.

UNDERGRADUATE EXPENSES for 2013–2014 *Application fee:* $35. *Tuition, state resident:* full-time $4702; part-time $246.74 per credit hour. *Tuition, nonresident:* full-time $4702; part-time $246.74 per credit hour. *Required fees:* full-time $1219. Full-time tuition and fees vary according to class time, course load, degree level, location, program, and reciprocity agreements. Part-time tuition and fees vary according to class time, course load, degree level, location, program, and reciprocity agreements. *College room and board:* $4994. Room and board charges vary according to board plan and housing facility.

FRESHMAN FINANCIAL AID (Fall 2011) 278 applied for aid; of those 61% were deemed to have need. 98% of freshmen with need received aid; of those 100% had need fully met. *Average percent of need met:* 57% (excluding resources awarded to replace EFC). *Average financial aid package:* $7694 (excluding resources awarded to replace EFC). 15% of all full-time freshmen had no need and received non-need-based gift aid.

UNDERGRADUATE FINANCIAL AID (Fall 2011) 1,426 applied for aid; of those 72% were deemed to have need. 99% of undergraduates with need received aid; of those 99% had need fully met. *Average percent of need met:* 48% (excluding resources awarded to replace EFC). *Average financial aid package:* $7847 (excluding resources awarded to replace EFC). 14% of all full-time undergraduates had no need and received non-need-based gift aid.

GIFT AID (NEED-BASED) *Total amount:* $5,149,099 (64% federal, 17% state, 6% institutional, 13% external sources). *Receiving aid:* Freshmen: 37% (143); all full-time undergraduates: 42% (879). *Average award:* Freshmen: $4048; Undergraduates: $4154. *Scholarships, grants, and awards:* Federal Pell, FSEOG, state, private, college/university gift aid from institutional funds.

GIFT AID (NON-NEED-BASED) *Total amount:* $93,173 (3% federal, 5% state, 18% institutional, 74% external sources). *Receiving aid:* Freshmen: 1% (5). Undergraduates: 1% (15). *Average award:* Freshmen: $826. Undergraduates: $978. *Scholarships, grants, and awards by category:* Academic interests/achievement: business, communication, computer science, education, English, general academic interests/achievements, health fields, humanities, mathematics, social sciences. *Creative arts/performance:* music, performing arts, theater/drama. *Special characteristics:* children and siblings of alumni, children of faculty/staff, ethnic background, international students, local/state students, members of minority groups, out-of-state students, veterans, veterans' children. *Tuition waivers:* Full or partial for minority students, children of alumni, employees or children of employees, senior citizens.

LOANS *Student loans:* $7,290,703 (79% need-based, 21% non-need-based). 66% of past graduating class borrowed through all loan programs. *Average indebtedness per student:* $25,117. *Average need-based loan:* Freshmen: $3184. Undergraduates: $4160. *Parent loans:* $67,368 (16% need-based, 84% non-need-based). *Programs:* Federal Direct (Subsidized and Unsubsidized Stafford, PLUS), Perkins, Federal Nursing.

WORK-STUDY *Federal work-study:* Total amount: $120,851; jobs available.

ATHLETIC AWARDS Total amount: $254,672 (69% need-based, 31% non-need-based).

APPLYING FOR FINANCIAL AID *Required financial aid form:* FAFSA. *Financial aid deadline (priority):* 4/15. *Notification date:* Continuous beginning 4/15. Students must reply within 2 weeks of notification.

CONTACT Ms. Laurie Weber, Director of Financial Aid, Minot State University, 500 University Avenue, West, Minot, ND 58707-0002, 701-858-3875 or toll-free 800-777-0750 Ext. 3350. *Fax:* 701-858-4310. *E-mail:* laurie.weber@minotstateu.edu. *Website:* http://www.minotstateu.edu/.

MIRRER YESHIVA
Brooklyn, NY

CONTACT Financial Aid Office, Mirrer Yeshiva, 1795 Ocean Parkway, Brooklyn, NY 11223-2010, 718-645-0536.

MISERICORDIA UNIVERSITY
Dallas, PA

Tuition & fees: $27,230	Average undergraduate aid package: $19,070

ABOUT THE INSTITUTION Independent Roman Catholic, coed, primarily women. *Awards:* certificates, bachelor's, master's, and doctoral degrees. 34 undergraduate majors. *Total enrollment:* 3,012. Undergraduates: 2,427. Freshmen: 511. Federal methodology is used as a basis for awarding need-based institutional aid.

UNDERGRADUATE EXPENSES for 2013–2014 *Application fee:* $25. *Comprehensive fee:* $38,420 includes full-time tuition ($25,890), mandatory fees ($1340), and room and board ($11,190). *College room only:* $6530. Room and board charges vary according to board plan and housing facility. *Part-time tuition:* $495 per credit. Part-time tuition and fees vary according to class time, degree level, and location.

FRESHMAN FINANCIAL AID (Fall 2012, est.) 499 applied for aid; of those 83% were deemed to have need. 100% of freshmen with need received aid; of those 23% had need fully met. *Average percent of need met:* 78% (excluding resources awarded to replace EFC). *Average financial aid package:* $19,765 (excluding resources awarded to replace EFC). 16% of all full-time freshmen had no need and received non-need-based gift aid.

UNDERGRADUATE FINANCIAL AID (Fall 2012, est.) 1,656 applied for aid; of those 88% were deemed to have need. 100% of undergraduates with need received aid; of those 21% had need fully met. *Average percent of need met:* 75% (excluding resources awarded to replace EFC). *Average financial aid package:* $19,070 (excluding resources awarded to replace EFC). 11% of all full-time undergraduates had no need and received non-need-based gift aid.

GIFT AID (NEED-BASED) *Total amount:* $20,514,892 (15% federal, 12% state, 72% institutional, 1% external sources). *Receiving aid:* Freshmen: 81% (413); all full-time undergraduates: 82% (1,449). *Average award:* Freshmen: $14,021; Undergraduates: $13,496. *Scholarships, grants, and awards:* Federal Pell, FSEOG, state, private, college/university gift aid from institutional funds, Federal Nursing.

GIFT AID (NON-NEED-BASED) *Total amount:* $3,547,913 (98% institutional, 2% external sources). *Receiving aid:* Freshmen: 15% (75). Undergraduates: 12% (215). *Average award:* Freshmen: $9162. Undergraduates: $8631. *Scholarships, grants, and awards by category:* Academic interests/achievement: 1,376 awards ($10,347,135 total): business, computer science, education, general academic interests/achievements, health fields, physical sciences, social sciences. *Special achievements/activities:* 1,386 awards ($2,777,164 total): community service, general special achievements/activities, leadership. *Special characteristics:* 669 awards ($1,942,260 total): children and siblings of alumni, children of current students, children of faculty/staff, general special characteristics, members of minority groups, out-of-state students, previous college experience, relatives of clergy, siblings of current students. *Tuition waivers:* Full or partial for employees or children of employees. *ROTC:* Army cooperative, Air Force cooperative.

LOANS *Student loans:* $16,899,198 (72% need-based, 28% non-need-based). *Average need-based loan:* Freshmen: $7741. Undergraduates: $8237. *Parent loans:* $5,172,756 (40% need-based, 60% non-need-based). *Programs:* Perkins, Federal Nursing, state.

WORK-STUDY *Federal work-study:* Total amount: $220,804; jobs available.

APPLYING FOR FINANCIAL AID *Required financial aid forms:* FAFSA, institution's own form. *Financial aid deadline (priority):* 3/1. *Notification date:* 3/15. Students must reply within 2 weeks of notification.

CONTACT Jane Dessoye, Executive Director of Enrollment Management, Misericordia University, 301 Lake Street, Dallas, PA 18612-1098, 570-674-6280 or toll-free 866-262-6363. *Fax:* 570-675-2441. *E-mail:* finaid@misericordia.edu. *Website:* http://www.misericordia.edu/.

MISSISSIPPI COLLEGE
Clinton, MS

Tuition & fees: $14,868	Average undergraduate aid package: $16,315

ABOUT THE INSTITUTION Independent Southern Baptist, coed. *Awards:* certificates, bachelor's, master's, and doctoral degrees. 61 undergraduate majors. *Total*
enrollment: 5,070. Undergraduates: 3,042. Freshmen: 482. Federal methodology is used as a basis for awarding need-based institutional aid.

UNDERGRADUATE EXPENSES for 2013–2014 *Application fee:* $25. *Comprehensive fee:* $22,018 includes full-time tuition ($14,120), mandatory fees ($748), and room and board ($7150). Full-time tuition and fees vary according to course load. Room and board charges vary according to housing facility. *Part-time tuition:* $442 per credit hour. *Part-time fees:* $188 per term. Part-time tuition and fees vary according to course load.

FRESHMAN FINANCIAL AID (Fall 2011) 485 applied for aid; of those 62% were deemed to have need. 100% of freshmen with need received aid; of those 29% had need fully met. *Average percent of need met:* 76% (excluding resources awarded to replace EFC). *Average financial aid package:* $15,930 (excluding resources awarded to replace EFC). 38% of all full-time freshmen had no need and received non-need-based gift aid.

UNDERGRADUATE FINANCIAL AID (Fall 2011) 2,617 applied for aid; of those 65% were deemed to have need. 100% of undergraduates with need received aid; of those 24% had need fully met. *Average percent of need met:* 71% (excluding resources awarded to replace EFC). *Average financial aid package:* $16,315 (excluding resources awarded to replace EFC). 32% of all full-time undergraduates had no need and received non-need-based gift aid.

GIFT AID (NEED-BASED) *Total amount:* $14,527,729 (39% federal, 4% state, 53% institutional, 4% external sources). *Receiving aid:* Freshmen: 43% (214); all full-time undergraduates: 48% (1,332). *Average award:* Freshmen: $11,268; Undergraduates: $9161. *Scholarships, grants, and awards:* Federal Pell, FSEOG, state, private, college/university gift aid from institutional funds, Federal Nursing.

GIFT AID (NON-NEED-BASED) *Total amount:* $11,382,475 (8% state, 87% institutional, 5% external sources). *Receiving aid:* Freshmen: 17% (84). Undergraduates: 11% (320). *Average award:* Freshmen: $11,307. Undergraduates: $10,133. *Scholarships, grants, and awards by category:* Academic interests/achievement: 1,729 awards ($9,161,300 total): general academic interests/achievements. *Creative arts/performance:* 99 awards ($153,390 total): applied art and design, art/fine arts, music. *Special achievements/activities:* 1,675 awards ($3,148,177 total): general special achievements/activities, leadership, religious involvement. *Special characteristics:* 857 awards ($1,923,241 total): children and siblings of alumni, children of faculty/staff, general special characteristics, relatives of clergy. *Tuition waivers:* Full or partial for employees or children of employees. *ROTC:* Army, Air Force.

LOANS *Student loans:* $16,539,032 (84% need-based, 16% non-need-based). 53% of past graduating class borrowed through all loan programs. *Average indebtedness per student:* $26,677. *Average need-based loan:* Freshmen: $5533. Undergraduates: $7823. *Parent loans:* $1,231,772 (100% non-need-based). *Programs:* Federal Direct (Subsidized and Unsubsidized Stafford, PLUS), Perkins, Federal Nursing, college/university.

WORK-STUDY *Federal work-study:* Total amount: $264,757; 285 jobs averaging $929.

APPLYING FOR FINANCIAL AID *Required financial aid forms:* FAFSA, state aid form. *Financial aid deadline (priority):* 3/1. *Notification date:* Continuous beginning 3/1. Students must reply by 5/1.

CONTACT Mrs. Karon Q. McMillan, Director of Financial Aid, Mississippi College, Box 4035, 200 South Capitol Street, Clinton, MS 39058-0001, 601-925-3249 or toll-free 800-738-1236. *Fax:* 601-925-3950. *E-mail:* kmcmilla@mc.edu. *Website:* http://www.mc.edu/.

MISSISSIPPI STATE UNIVERSITY
Mississippi State, MS

Tuition & fees (MS res): $6264	Average undergraduate aid package: $12,310

ABOUT THE INSTITUTION State-supported, coed. *Awards:* certificates, associate, bachelor's, master's, and doctoral degrees. 72 undergraduate majors. *Total enrollment:* 20,365. Undergraduates: 16,390. Freshmen: 2,894. Federal methodology is used as a basis for awarding need-based institutional aid.

UNDERGRADUATE EXPENSES for 2013–2014 *Application fee:* $40. *Tuition, state resident:* full-time $6264; part-time $261 per credit hour. *Tuition, nonresident:* full-time $15,828; part-time $659.50 per credit hour. Part-time tuition and fees vary according to course load. *College room and board:* $8486; *Room only:* $4936. Room and board charges vary according to board plan, housing facility, and student level. *Payment plan:* Tuition prepayment.

FRESHMAN FINANCIAL AID (Fall 2011) 2,390 applied for aid; of those 83% were deemed to have need. 99% of freshmen with need received aid; of those 30% had need fully met. *Average percent of need met:* 63% (excluding resources awarded to replace EFC). *Average financial aid package:* $13,045 (excluding resources awarded to replace EFC). 21% of all full-time freshmen had no need and received non-need-based gift aid.
UNDERGRADUATE FINANCIAL AID (Fall 2011) 10,844 applied for aid; of those 86% were deemed to have need. 99% of undergraduates with need received aid; of those 23% had need fully met. *Average percent of need met:* 62% (excluding resources awarded to replace EFC). *Average financial aid package:* $12,310 (excluding resources awarded to replace EFC). 17% of all full-time undergraduates had no need and received non-need-based gift aid.
GIFT AID (NEED-BASED) *Total amount:* $47,054,510 (58% federal, 9% state, 21% institutional, 12% external sources). *Receiving aid:* Freshmen: 63% (1,814); all full-time undergraduates: 55% (8,217). *Average award:* Freshmen: $5440; Undergraduates: $5180. *Scholarships, grants, and awards:* Federal Pell, FSEOG, state, private, college/university gift aid from institutional funds, United Negro College Fund.
GIFT AID (NON-NEED-BASED) *Total amount:* $14,244,723 (21% state, 68% institutional, 11% external sources). *Receiving aid:* Freshmen: 9% (259). Undergraduates: 4% (576). *Average award:* Freshmen: $3161. Undergraduates: $3208. *Scholarships, grants, and awards by category:* Academic interests/achievement: agriculture, architecture, area/ethnic studies, biological sciences, business, communication, computer science, education, engineering/technologies, English, foreign languages, general academic interests/achievements, health fields, home economics, humanities, international studies, library science, mathematics, military science, physical sciences, premedicine, religion/biblical studies, social sciences. *Creative arts/performance:* applied art and design, art/fine arts, cinema/film/broadcasting, creative writing, dance, debating, general creative arts/performance, journalism/publications, music, performing arts, theater/drama. *Special achievements/activities:* cheerleading/drum major, general special achievements/activities, junior miss, leadership, memberships. *Special characteristics:* adult students, children and siblings of alumni, children of educators, children of faculty/staff, children of public servants, first-generation college students, handicapped students, local/state students, out-of-state students, previous college experience, spouses of deceased or disabled public servants. *Tuition waivers:* Full or partial for children of alumni, employees or children of employees, senior citizens. *ROTC:* Army, Air Force.
LOANS *Student loans:* $98,908,266 (84% need-based, 16% non-need-based). 49% of past graduating class borrowed through all loan programs. *Average indebtedness per student:* $26,139. *Average need-based loan:* Freshmen: $3253. Undergraduates: $3944. *Parent loans:* $11,429,362 (62% need-based, 38% non-need-based). *Programs:* Federal Direct (Subsidized and Unsubsidized Stafford, PLUS), Perkins, college/university.
WORK-STUDY *Federal work-study:* Total amount: $2,335,439; 682 jobs averaging $3424.
ATHLETIC AWARDS Total amount: $6,050,847 (100% non-need-based).
APPLYING FOR FINANCIAL AID *Required financial aid forms:* FAFSA, state aid form. *Financial aid deadline (priority):* 3/1. *Notification date:* Continuous beginning 12/1. Students must reply by 5/1.
CONTACT Mr. Kenneth Paul McKinney, Director of Financial Aid, Mississippi State University, PO Box 6035, Mississippi State, MS 39762, 662-325-7428. *Fax:* 662-325-0702. *E-mail:* financialaid@saffairs.msstate.edu.
Website: http://www.msstate.edu/.

MISSISSIPPI UNIVERSITY FOR WOMEN
Columbus, MS

Tuition & fees (MS res): $5316	Average undergraduate aid package: $8810

ABOUT THE INSTITUTION State-supported, coed, primarily women. *Awards:* certificates, associate, bachelor's, master's, and doctoral degrees. 28 undergraduate majors. *Total enrollment:* 2,650. Undergraduates: 2,503. Freshmen: 193. Federal methodology is used as a basis for awarding need-based institutional aid.
UNDERGRADUATE EXPENSES for 2013–2014 *Tuition, state resident:* full-time $5316; part-time $221.50 per credit hour. *Tuition, nonresident:* full-time $14,484; part-time $603.50 per credit hour. Part-time tuition and fees vary according to course load. *College room and board:* $5991; *Room only:* $3454. Room and board charges vary according to housing facility.

FRESHMAN FINANCIAL AID (Fall 2011) 156 applied for aid; of those 90% were deemed to have need. 99% of freshmen with need received aid; of those 40% had need fully met. *Average percent of need met:* 40% (excluding resources awarded to replace EFC). *Average financial aid package:* $10,180 (excluding resources awarded to replace EFC). 18% of all full-time freshmen had no need and received non-need-based gift aid.
UNDERGRADUATE FINANCIAL AID (Fall 2011) 1,664 applied for aid; of those 91% were deemed to have need. 99% of undergraduates with need received aid; of those 69% had need fully met. *Average percent of need met:* 69% (excluding resources awarded to replace EFC). *Average financial aid package:* $8810 (excluding resources awarded to replace EFC). 12% of all full-time undergraduates had no need and received non-need-based gift aid.
GIFT AID (NEED-BASED) *Total amount:* $6,335,034 (99% federal, 1% state). *Receiving aid:* Freshmen: 64% (115); all full-time undergraduates: 61% (1,177). *Average award:* Freshmen: $5337; Undergraduates: $5399. *Scholarships, grants, and awards:* Federal Pell, FSEOG, state, private, college/university gift aid from institutional funds.
GIFT AID (NON-NEED-BASED) *Total amount:* $5,057,318 (14% state, 82% institutional, 4% external sources). *Receiving aid:* Freshmen: 64% (115). Undergraduates: 40% (773). *Average award:* Freshmen: $7418. Undergraduates: $5628. *Scholarships, grants, and awards by category:* Academic interests/achievement: 850 awards ($1,981,244 total): biological sciences, business, communication, computer science, education, English, general academic interests/achievements, health fields, home economics, humanities, mathematics, physical sciences. *Creative arts/performance:* 70 awards ($34,675 total): art/fine arts, journalism/publications, music, performing arts, theater/drama. *Special achievements/activities:* 18 awards ($30,136 total): junior miss, leadership. *Special characteristics:* 249 awards ($1,531,402 total): adult students, children and siblings of alumni, children of faculty/staff, ethnic background, international students, members of minority groups, out-of-state students, parents of current students. *Tuition waivers:* Full or partial for employees or children of employees. *ROTC:* Army cooperative, Air Force cooperative.
LOANS *Student loans:* $11,182,740 (46% need-based, 54% non-need-based). 69% of past graduating class borrowed through all loan programs. *Average indebtedness per student:* $22,398. *Average need-based loan:* Freshmen: $3528. Undergraduates: $4826. *Parent loans:* $545,342 (100% non-need-based). *Programs:* Federal Direct (Subsidized and Unsubsidized Stafford, PLUS), Perkins.
WORK-STUDY *Federal work-study:* Total amount: $92,862; 60 jobs averaging $1958. *State or other work-study/employment:* Total amount: $247,995 (100% non-need-based). 185 part-time jobs averaging $1719.
APPLYING FOR FINANCIAL AID *Required financial aid forms:* FAFSA, institution's own form, state aid form. *Financial aid deadline (priority):* 3/1. *Notification date:* Continuous beginning 4/1. Students must reply within 2 weeks of notification.
CONTACT Ms. Searcy Taylor, Acting Director of Financial Aid, Mississippi University for Women, 1100 College Street, MUW 1614, Columbus, MS 39701-4044, 662-329-7114 or toll-free 877-GO 2 THE W. *Fax:* 662-329-7325. *E-mail:* dmiller@finaid.muw.edu.
Website: http://www.muw.edu/.

MISSISSIPPI VALLEY STATE UNIVERSITY
Itta Bena, MS

CONTACT Margaret Sherrer, Director of Student Financial Aid, Mississippi Valley State University, 14000 Highway 82W #7268, Itta Bena, MS 38941-1400, 662-254-3335 or toll-free 800-844-6885 (in-state). *Fax:* 662-254-7900. *E-mail:* margaret.sherrer@mvsu.edu.
Website: http://www.mvsu.edu/.

MISSOURI BAPTIST UNIVERSITY
St. Louis, MO

Tuition & fees: $20,654	Average undergraduate aid package: $14,435

ABOUT THE INSTITUTION Independent Southern Baptist, coed. **Awards:** certificates, associate, bachelor's, master's, and doctoral degrees. 52 undergraduate majors. **Total enrollment:** 5,212. Undergraduates: 3,850. Freshmen: 242. Federal methodology is used as a basis for awarding need-based institutional aid.

UNDERGRADUATE EXPENSES for 2013–2014 Application fee: $30. **Comprehensive fee:** $28,884 includes full-time tuition ($19,730), mandatory fees ($924), and room and board ($8230). Full-time tuition and fees vary according to course load and location. Room and board charges vary according to board plan and housing facility. **Part-time tuition:** $680 per credit. **Part-time fees:** $22 per credit; $30 per term. Part-time tuition and fees vary according to course load and location.

FRESHMAN FINANCIAL AID (Fall 2012, est.) 223 applied for aid; of those 13% were deemed to have need. 100% of freshmen with need received aid; of those 13% had need fully met. **Average financial aid package:** $20,926 (excluding resources awarded to replace EFC). 46% of all full-time freshmen had no need and received non-need-based gift aid.

UNDERGRADUATE FINANCIAL AID (Fall 2012, est.) 1,266 applied for aid; of those 47% were deemed to have need. 100% of undergraduates with need received aid; of those 12% had need fully met. **Average financial aid package:** $14,435 (excluding resources awarded to replace EFC). 39% of all full-time undergraduates had no need and received non-need-based gift aid.

GIFT AID (NEED-BASED) Total amount: $7,227,845 (51% federal, 18% state, 24% institutional, 7% external sources). **Receiving aid:** Freshmen: 11% (26); all full-time undergraduates: 34% (479). **Average award:** Freshmen: $6502; Undergraduates: $5389. **Scholarships, grants, and awards:** Federal Pell, FSEOG, state, private, college/university gift aid from institutional funds.

GIFT AID (NON-NEED-BASED) Total amount: $55,740 (10% federal, 12% state, 73% institutional, 5% external sources). **Receiving aid:** Freshmen: 12% (29). Undergraduates: 26% (368). **Average award:** Freshmen: $12,262. Undergraduates: $10,456. **Scholarships, grants, and awards by category:** Academic interests/achievement: general academic interests/achievements, religion/biblical studies. Creative arts/performance: music, theater/drama. Special achievements/activities: cheerleading/drum major, memberships, religious involvement. Special characteristics: adult students, children and siblings of alumni, children of current students, children of faculty/staff, first-generation college students, parents of current students, public servants, relatives of clergy, religious affiliation, siblings of current students, spouses of current students, veterans, veterans' children. **Tuition waivers:** Full or partial, for children of alumni, employees or children of employees, senior citizens. **ROTC:** Army cooperative.

LOANS Student loans: $11,099,210 (98% need-based, 2% non-need-based). 89% of past graduating class borrowed through all loan programs. Average indebtedness per student: $21,479. **Average need-based loan:** Freshmen: $3278. Undergraduates: $3890. **Parent loans:** $577,838 (98% need-based, 2% non-need-based). **Programs:** Federal Direct (Subsidized and Unsubsidized Stafford, PLUS).

WORK-STUDY Federal work-study: Total amount: $939,960; 527 jobs averaging $1797. **State or other work-study/employment:** 25 part-time jobs averaging $1359.

ATHLETIC AWARDS Total amount: $4,715,583 (93% need-based, 7% non-need-based).

APPLYING FOR FINANCIAL AID Required financial aid forms: FAFSA, institution's own form. **Financial aid deadline (priority):** 4/1. **Notification date:** Continuous beginning 4/15. Students must reply within 2 weeks of notification.

CONTACT Mr. John Brandt, Director of Student Financial Services, Missouri Baptist University, One College Park Drive, St. Louis, MO 63141, 314-744-7639 or toll-free 877-434-1115 Ext. 2290. Fax: 314-744-5320. E-mail: taphorn@mobap.edu. Website: http://www.mobap.edu/.

MISSOURI SOUTHERN STATE UNIVERSITY
Joplin, MO

Tuition & fees (MO res): $5090	Average undergraduate aid package: $10,790

ABOUT THE INSTITUTION State-supported, coed. **Awards:** certificates, associate, bachelor's, and master's degrees. 38 undergraduate majors. **Total enrollment:** 5,591. Undergraduates: 5,536. Freshmen: 775. Federal methodology is used as a basis for awarding need-based institutional aid.

UNDERGRADUATE EXPENSES for 2013–2014 Application fee: $25. **Tuition, state resident:** full-time $4564; part-time $143 per credit hour. **Tuition, nonresident:** full-time $9128; part-time $297.20 per credit hour. **Required fees:** full-time $526. Full-time tuition and fees vary according to course load. **College room and board:** $5976. Room and board charges vary according to board plan and housing facility.

FRESHMAN FINANCIAL AID (Fall 2012, est.) 547 applied for aid; of those 78% were deemed to have need. 100% of freshmen with need received aid; of those 8% had need fully met. **Average percent of need met:** 45% (excluding resources awarded to replace EFC). **Average financial aid package:** $9275 (excluding resources awarded to replace EFC). 19% of all full-time freshmen had no need and received non-need-based gift aid.

UNDERGRADUATE FINANCIAL AID (Fall 2012, est.) 2,596 applied for aid; of those 85% were deemed to have need. 99% of undergraduates with need received aid; of those 8% had need fully met. **Average percent of need met:** 45% (excluding resources awarded to replace EFC). **Average financial aid package:** $10,790 (excluding resources awarded to replace EFC). 10% of all full-time undergraduates had no need and received non-need-based gift aid.

GIFT AID (NEED-BASED) Total amount: $13,394,810 (91% federal, 9% state). **Receiving aid:** Freshmen: 66% (365); all full-time undergraduates: 70% (1,876). **Average award:** Freshmen: $3971; Undergraduates: $4588. **Scholarships, grants, and awards:** Federal Pell, FSEOG, state, private, college/university gift aid from institutional funds, TEACH Grants.

GIFT AID (NON-NEED-BASED) Total amount: $4,627,669 (2% state, 86% institutional, 12% external sources). **Receiving aid:** Freshmen: 54% (297). Undergraduates: 36% (967). **Average award:** Freshmen: $2841. Undergraduates: $3035. **Scholarships, grants, and awards by category:** Academic interests/achievement: general academic interests/achievements. Creative arts/performance: art/fine arts, debating, journalism/publications, music, theater/drama. Special achievements/activities: general special achievements/activities. Special characteristics: children and siblings of alumni, children of faculty/staff, ethnic background, local/state students, members of minority groups, religious affiliation. **Tuition waivers:** Full or partial for employees or children of employees, senior citizens.

LOANS Student loans: $23,566,471 (51% need-based, 49% non-need-based). 52% of past graduating class borrowed through all loan programs. Average indebtedness per student: $20,005. **Average need-based loan:** Freshmen: $3332. Undergraduates: $4353. **Parent loans:** $261,669 (100% non-need-based). **Programs:** Federal Direct (Subsidized and Unsubsidized Stafford, PLUS), Perkins.

WORK-STUDY Federal work-study: Total amount: $199,868; jobs available. **State or other work-study/employment:** Total amount: $1,033,601 (100% non-need-based). Part-time jobs available.

ATHLETIC AWARDS Total amount: $1,660,201 (100% non-need-based).

APPLYING FOR FINANCIAL AID Required financial aid form: FAFSA. **Financial aid deadline (priority):** 4/1. **Notification date:** Continuous beginning 3/15. Students must reply by 5/1.

CONTACT Becca L. Diskin, Director of Financial Aid, Missouri Southern State University, 3950 East Newman Road, Joplin, MO 64801-1595, 417-625-5422 or toll-free 866-818-MSSU. Fax: 417-659-4474. E-mail: diskin-b@mssu.edu. Website: http://www.mssu.edu/.

MISSOURI STATE UNIVERSITY
Springfield, MO

Tuition & fees (MO res): $6792	Average undergraduate aid package: $7987

ABOUT THE INSTITUTION State-supported, coed. *Awards:* certificates, bachelor's, master's, and doctoral degrees. 97 undergraduate majors. *Total enrollment:* 20,629. Undergraduates: 17,434. Freshmen: 2,566. Federal methodology is used as a basis for awarding need-based institutional aid.

UNDERGRADUATE EXPENSES for 2013–2014 *Application fee:* $35. *Tuition, state resident:* full-time $6014; part-time $200.48 per credit hour. *Tuition, nonresident:* full-time $12,360; part-time $412 per credit hour. *Required fees:* full-time $778. Full-time tuition and fees vary according to course level, course load, and program. Part-time tuition and fees vary according to course level, course load, and program. *College room and board:* $6844. Room and board charges vary according to board plan, housing facility, and location.

FRESHMAN FINANCIAL AID (Fall 2012, est.) 2,125 applied for aid; of those 75% were deemed to have need. 100% of freshmen with need received aid; of those 14% had need fully met. *Average percent of need met:* 87% (excluding resources awarded to replace EFC). *Average financial aid package:* $8164 (excluding resources awarded to replace EFC). 4% of all full-time freshmen had no need and received non-need-based gift aid.

UNDERGRADUATE FINANCIAL AID (Fall 2012, est.) 9,868 applied for aid; of those 81% were deemed to have need. 100% of undergraduates with need received aid; of those 12% had need fully met. *Average percent of need met:* 88% (excluding resources awarded to replace EFC). *Average financial aid package:* $7987 (excluding resources awarded to replace EFC). 5% of all full-time undergraduates had no need and received non-need-based gift aid.

GIFT AID (NEED-BASED) *Total amount:* $40,051,438 (59% federal, 13% state, 24% institutional, 4% external sources). *Receiving aid:* Freshmen: 56% (1,415); all full-time undergraduates: 49% (6,617). *Average award:* Freshmen: $5897; Undergraduates: $5201. *Scholarships, grants, and awards:* Federal Pell, FSEOG, state, private, college/university gift aid from institutional funds.

GIFT AID (NON-NEED-BASED) *Total amount:* $3,392,885 (5% federal, 9% state, 81% institutional, 5% external sources). *Receiving aid:* Freshmen: 11% (278). Undergraduates: 5% (731). *Average award:* Freshmen: $3948. Undergraduates: $4200. *Scholarships, grants, and awards by category:* Academic interests/achievement: general academic interests/achievements. Creative arts/performance: general creative arts/performance. Special achievements/activities: leadership. Special characteristics: children and siblings of alumni, local/state students, members of minority groups. *Tuition waivers:* Full or partial for children of alumni, employees or children of employees, senior citizens. *ROTC:* Army.

LOANS *Student loans:* $67,269,487 (100% need-based). 77% of past graduating class borrowed through all loan programs. *Average indebtedness per student:* $20,545. *Average need-based loan:* Freshmen: $3444. Undergraduates: $4246. *Parent loans:* $8,143,299 (100% need-based). *Programs:* Federal Direct (Subsidized and Unsubsidized Stafford, PLUS), Perkins.

WORK-STUDY *Federal work-study:* Total amount: $454,708; jobs available.

ATHLETIC AWARDS Total amount: $3,211,617 (42% need-based, 58% non-need-based).

APPLYING FOR FINANCIAL AID *Required financial aid form:* FAFSA. *Financial aid deadline (priority):* 3/31. *Notification date:* Continuous beginning 3/31.

CONTACT Vicki Mattocks, Director of Financial Aid, Missouri State University, 901 South National Avenue, Springfield, MO 65804, 417-836-5262 or toll-free 800-492-7900. *E-mail:* financialaid@missouristate.edu. *Website:* http://www.missouristate.edu/.

MISSOURI TECH
St. Charles, MO

Tuition & fees: N/R	Average undergraduate aid package: N/A

ABOUT THE INSTITUTION Proprietary, coed, primarily men. 7 undergraduate majors. Both federal and institutional methodology are used as a basis for awarding need-based institutional aid.

GIFT AID (NEED-BASED) *Scholarships, grants, and awards:* Federal Pell, private, college/university gift aid from institutional funds.
LOANS *Programs:* Federal Direct (Subsidized and Unsubsidized Stafford, PLUS).
APPLYING FOR FINANCIAL AID *Required financial aid forms:* FAFSA, institution's own form. *Financial aid deadline:* Continuous. *Notification date:* Continuous.
CONTACT Mrs. Cindy Ann Sinnott, Director of Financial Aid, Missouri Tech, 1690 Country Club Plaza Drive, St. Charles, MO 63303, 636-573-9300 or toll-free 800-960-TECH. *Fax:* 636-573-9398. *E-mail:* contact@motech.edu: *Website:* http://www.motech.edu/.

MISSOURI UNIVERSITY OF SCIENCE AND TECHNOLOGY
Rolla, MO

Tuition & fees (MO res): $9350	Average undergraduate aid package: $10,235

ABOUT THE INSTITUTION State-supported, coed, primarily men. *Awards:* certificates, bachelor's, master's, and doctoral degrees. 35 undergraduate majors. *Total enrollment:* 7,647. Undergraduates: 5,843. Freshmen: 1,124. Federal methodology is used as a basis for awarding need-based institutional aid.

UNDERGRADUATE EXPENSES for 2013–2014 *Application fee:* $50. *Tuition, state resident:* full-time $8082; part-time $269.40 per credit hour. *Tuition, nonresident:* full-time $22,398; part-time $746.60 per credit hour. *Required fees:* full-time $1268; $269.40 per credit hour. Full-time tuition and fees vary according to course load, degree level, and program. Part-time tuition and fees vary according to course load, degree level, and program. *College room and board:* $8900; *Room only:* $5610. Room and board charges vary according to board plan, housing facility, and location.

FRESHMAN FINANCIAL AID (Fall 2012, est.) 1,001 applied for aid; of those 73% were deemed to have need. 99% of freshmen with need received aid; of those 24% had need fully met. *Average percent of need met:* 74% (excluding resources awarded to replace EFC). *Average financial aid package:* $11,773 (excluding resources awarded to replace EFC). 20% of all full-time freshmen had no need and received non-need-based gift aid.

UNDERGRADUATE FINANCIAL AID (Fall 2012, est.) 4,068 applied for aid; of those 79% were deemed to have need. 98% of undergraduates with need received aid; of those 18% had need fully met. *Average percent of need met:* 64% (excluding resources awarded to replace EFC). *Average financial aid package:* $10,235 (excluding resources awarded to replace EFC). 11% of all full-time undergraduates had no need and received non-need-based gift aid.

GIFT AID (NEED-BASED) *Total amount:* $22,716,935 (28% federal, 11% state, 51% institutional, 10% external sources). *Receiving aid:* Freshmen: 63% (709); all full-time undergraduates: 55% (2,856). *Average award:* Freshmen: $9131; Undergraduates: $6963. *Scholarships, grants, and awards:* Federal Pell, FSEOG, state, private, college/university gift aid from institutional funds, ROTC (Army and Air Force) Scholarships.

GIFT AID (NON-NEED-BASED) *Total amount:* $8,301,395 (10% state, 76% institutional, 14% external sources). *Receiving aid:* Freshmen: 13% (141). Undergraduates: 7% (343). *Average award:* Freshmen: $6300. Undergraduates: $5249. *Scholarships, grants, and awards by category:* Academic interests/achievement: 7,477 awards ($14,680,198 total): biological sciences, business, computer science, education, engineering/technologies, English, general academic interests/achievements, humanities, mathematics, military science, physical sciences, premedicine, social sciences. Creative arts/performance: 2 awards ($2000 total): music, theater/drama. Special characteristics: 1,280 awards ($5,714,842 total): children and siblings of alumni, children of faculty/staff, members of minority groups, out-of-state students. *Tuition waivers:* Full or partial for employees or children of employees. *ROTC:* Army, Naval cooperative, Air Force.

LOANS *Student loans:* $27,608,330 (66% need-based, 34% non-need-based). 73% of past graduating class borrowed through all loan programs. *Average indebtedness per student:* $21,659. *Average need-based loan:* Freshmen: $3584. Undergraduates: $4533. *Parent loans:* $23,352,280 (50% need-based, 50% non-need-based). *Programs:* Federal Direct (Subsidized and Unsubsidized Stafford), Perkins, state, college/university, alternative loans.

WORK-STUDY *Federal work-study:* Total amount: $301,800; 125 jobs averaging $2414. *State or other work-study/employment:* Part-time jobs available.
ATHLETIC AWARDS Total amount: $2,567,866 (74% need-based, 26% non-need-based).
APPLYING FOR FINANCIAL AID *Required financial aid form:* FAFSA. *Financial aid deadline (priority):* 3/1. *Notification date:* Continuous beginning 4/1. Students must reply within 3 weeks of notification.
CONTACT Ms. Bridgette Betz, Director of Student Financial Assistance, Missouri University of Science and Technology, G1 Parker Hall, Rolla, MO 65409, 573-341-4282 or toll-free 800-522-0938. *Fax:* 573-341-4274. *E-mail:* berry@mst.edu.
Website: http://www.mst.edu/.

MISSOURI VALLEY COLLEGE
Marshall, MO

Tuition & fees: N/R	Average undergraduate aid package: $14,500

ABOUT THE INSTITUTION Independent Presbyterian Church, coed. 38 undergraduate majors. Federal methodology is used as a basis for awarding need-based institutional aid.
FRESHMAN FINANCIAL AID (Fall 2011) 366 applied for aid; of those 86% were deemed to have need. 100% of freshmen with need received aid; of those 44% had need fully met. *Average percent of need met:* 86% (excluding resources awarded to replace EFC). *Average financial aid package:* $14,900 (excluding resources awarded to replace EFC). 24% of all full-time freshmen had no need and received non-need-based gift aid.
UNDERGRADUATE FINANCIAL AID (Fall 2011) 1,149 applied for aid; of those 99% were deemed to have need. 100% of undergraduates with need received aid; of those 46% had need fully met. *Average percent of need met:* 83% (excluding resources awarded to replace EFC). *Average financial aid package:* $14,500 (excluding resources awarded to replace EFC). 27% of all full-time undergraduates had no need and received non-need-based gift aid.
GIFT AID (NEED-BASED) *Total amount:* $9,659,234 (37% federal, 11% state, 52% institutional). *Receiving aid:* Freshmen: 75% (313); all full-time undergraduates: 73% (1,136). *Average award:* Freshmen: $11,940; Undergraduates: $11,670. *Scholarships, grants, and awards:* Federal Pell, FSEOG, state, private, college/university gift aid from institutional funds.
GIFT AID (NON-NEED-BASED) *Total amount:* $304,743 (100% external sources). *Receiving aid:* Freshmen: 75% (313). Undergraduates: 73% (1,136). *Average award:* Freshmen: $11,700. Undergraduates: $11,400. *Scholarships, grants, and awards by category: Academic interests/achievement:* 141 awards ($839,078 total): biological sciences, business, communication, computer science, education, English, general academic interests/achievements, health fields, humanities, mathematics, military science, physical sciences, premedicine, social sciences. *Creative arts/performance:* 57 awards ($245,290 total): applied art and design, art/fine arts, cinema/film/broadcasting, dance, journalism/publications, music, performing arts, theater/drama. *Special achievements/activities:* 47 awards ($79,800 total): cheerleading/drum major, community service, general special achievements/activities, hobbies/interests, junior miss, leadership, rodeo. *Special characteristics:* 115 awards ($270,940 total): children and siblings of alumni, children of faculty/staff.
LOANS *Student loans:* $7,579,059 (49% need-based, 51% non-need-based). 79% of past graduating class borrowed through all loan programs. *Average indebtedness per student:* $23,200. *Average need-based loan:* Freshmen: $3050. Undergraduates: $3250. *Parent loans:* $1,062,897 (100% non-need-based). *Programs:* Federal Direct (Subsidized and Unsubsidized Stafford, PLUS), Perkins.
WORK-STUDY *Federal work-study:* Total amount: $120,479; 104 jobs averaging $1860. *State or other work-study/employment:* Total amount: $498,852 (100% non-need-based). 433 part-time jobs averaging $1860.
ATHLETIC AWARDS Total amount: $8,995,750 (100% need-based).
APPLYING FOR FINANCIAL AID *Required financial aid form:* FAFSA. *Financial aid deadline (priority):* 3/15. *Notification date:* Continuous beginning 10/1. Students must reply within 4 weeks of notification.
CONTACT Mrs. Rachel Kimberly Robinson, Director of Financial Aid, Missouri Valley College, 500 East College, Marshall, MO 65340-3197, 660-831-4176. *Fax:* 660-831-4003. *E-mail:* robinsonr@moval.edu.
Website: http://www.moval.edu/.

MISSOURI WESTERN STATE UNIVERSITY
St. Joseph, MO

Tuition & fees (MO res): $6385	Average undergraduate aid package: $7948

ABOUT THE INSTITUTION State-supported, coed. *Awards:* certificates, associate, bachelor's, and master's degrees. 55 undergraduate majors. *Total enrollment:* 6,056. Undergraduates: 5,885. Freshmen: 1,074. Federal methodology is used as a basis for awarding need-based institutional aid.
UNDERGRADUATE EXPENSES for 2013–2014 *Application fee:* $15. *Tuition, state resident:* full-time $5667; part-time $188.91 per credit hour. *Tuition, nonresident:* full-time $11,171; part-time $372.36 per credit hour. *Required fees:* full-time $718. Full-time tuition and fees vary according to location and program. Part-time tuition and fees vary according to location and program. *College room and board:* $6918. Room and board charges vary according to board plan and housing facility.
FRESHMAN FINANCIAL AID (Fall 2012, est.) 868 applied for aid; of those 80% were deemed to have need. 100% of freshmen with need received aid; of those 12% had need fully met. *Average percent of need met:* 63% (excluding resources awarded to replace EFC). *Average financial aid package:* $7467 (excluding resources awarded to replace EFC). 13% of all full-time freshmen had no need and received non-need-based gift aid.
UNDERGRADUATE FINANCIAL AID (Fall 2012, est.) 3,816 applied for aid; of those 82% were deemed to have need. 99% of undergraduates with need received aid; of those 9% had need fully met. *Average percent of need met:* 62% (excluding resources awarded to replace EFC). *Average financial aid package:* $7948 (excluding resources awarded to replace EFC). 9% of all full-time undergraduates had no need and received non-need-based gift aid.
GIFT AID (NEED-BASED) *Receiving aid:* Freshmen: 76% (679); all full-time undergraduates: 69% (2,856). *Average award:* Freshmen: $5385; Undergraduates: $5415. *Scholarships, grants, and awards:* Federal Pell, FSEOG, state, private, college/university gift aid from institutional funds.
GIFT AID (NON-NEED-BASED) *Receiving aid:* Freshmen: 9% (82). Undergraduates: 6% (249). *Average award:* Freshmen: $2612. Undergraduates: $3308. *Scholarships, grants, and awards by category: Academic interests/achievement:* biological sciences, business, communication, computer science, education, engineering/technologies, English, foreign languages, general academic interests/achievements, health fields, humanities, mathematics, military science, physical sciences, religion/biblical studies, social sciences. *Creative arts/performance:* applied art and design, art/fine arts, cinema/film/broadcasting, creative writing, dance, journalism/publications, music, performing arts, theater/drama. *Special achievements/activities:* cheerleading/drum major, community service, general special achievements/activities, hobbies/interests, leadership. *Special characteristics:* adult students, children and siblings of alumni, children of faculty/staff, children of public servants, children of union members/company employees, general special characteristics, handicapped students, international students, local/state students, out-of-state students, previous college experience, religious affiliation. *Tuition waivers:* Full or partial for employees or children of employees, senior citizens. *ROTC:* Army.
LOANS *Student loans:* 70% of past graduating class borrowed through all loan programs. *Average indebtedness per student:* $22,287. *Average need-based loan:* Freshmen: $2720. Undergraduates: $3733. *Programs:* Federal Direct (Subsidized and Unsubsidized Stafford, PLUS), Perkins.
WORK-STUDY *Federal work-study:* 356 jobs averaging $1262. *State or other work-study/employment:* 809 part-time jobs averaging $1612.
APPLYING FOR FINANCIAL AID *Required financial aid forms:* FAFSA, institutional scholarship application form. *Financial aid deadline:* Continuous. *Notification date:* Continuous beginning 4/15. Students must reply within 2 weeks of notification.
CONTACT Marilyn Baker, Director of Financial Aid, Missouri Western State University, 4525 Downs Drive, Saint Joseph, MO 64507-2294, 816-271-5939 or toll-free 800-662-7041. *Fax:* 816-271-5879. *E-mail:* mbaker3@missouriwestern.edu.
Website: http://www.missouriwestern.edu/.

MITCHELL COLLEGE
New London, CT

CONTACT Jacklyn Stoltz, Director of Financial Aid, Mitchell College, 437 Pequot Avenue, New London, CT 06320-4498, 800-443-2811. *Fax:* 860-444-1209. *E-mail:* stoltz_j@mitchell.edu. *Website:* http://www.mitchell.edu/.

MOLLOY COLLEGE
Rockville Centre, NY

Tuition & fees: $24,420	Average undergraduate aid package: $13,818

ABOUT THE INSTITUTION Independent, coed. *Awards:* certificates, associate, bachelor's, master's, and doctoral degrees. 40 undergraduate majors. *Total enrollment:* 4,482. Undergraduates: 3,444. Freshmen: 455. Federal methodology is used as a basis for awarding need-based institutional aid.

UNDERGRADUATE EXPENSES for 2013–2014 Application fee: $30. *Comprehensive fee:* $36,500 includes full-time tuition ($23,410), mandatory fees ($1010), and room and board ($12,080). *College room only:* $9090. Full-time tuition and fees vary according to degree level. Room and board charges vary according to board plan. *Part-time tuition:* $770 per credit hour. Part-time tuition and fees vary according to degree level.

FRESHMAN FINANCIAL AID (Fall 2011) 379 applied for aid; of those 88% were deemed to have need. 100% of freshmen with need received aid; of those 17% had need fully met. *Average percent of need met:* 61% (excluding resources awarded to replace EFC). *Average financial aid package:* $16,610 (excluding resources awarded to replace EFC). 9% of all full-time freshmen had no need and received non-need-based gift aid.

UNDERGRADUATE FINANCIAL AID (Fall 2011) 2,583 applied for aid; of those 90% were deemed to have need. 100% of undergraduates with need received aid; of those 10% had need fully met. *Average percent of need met:* 50% (excluding resources awarded to replace EFC). *Average financial aid package:* $13,818 (excluding resources awarded to replace EFC). 6% of all full-time undergraduates had no need and received non-need-based gift aid.

GIFT AID (NEED-BASED) Total amount: $18,070,555 (29% federal, 18% state, 52% institutional, 1% external sources). *Receiving aid:* Freshmen: 82% (324); all full-time undergraduates: 78% (2,053). *Average award:* Freshmen: $13,214; Undergraduates: $9438. *Scholarships, grants, and awards:* Federal Pell, FSEOG, state, private, college/university gift aid from institutional funds, Federal Nursing, TEACH Grants, TRiO Scholarships.

GIFT AID (NON-NEED-BASED) Total amount: $1,849,086 (1% federal, 3% state, 94% institutional, 2% external sources). *Receiving aid:* Freshmen: 9% (37). Undergraduates: 5% (134). *Average award:* Freshmen: $9076. Undergraduates: $8006. *Scholarships, grants, and awards by category: Academic interests/achievement:* biological sciences, business, communication, education, English, general academic interests/achievements, health fields, international studies, mathematics, social sciences. *Creative arts/performance:* art/fine arts, music, performing arts, theater/drama. *Special achievements/activities:* community service, leadership, memberships, religious involvement. *Special characteristics:* ethnic background, members of minority groups, religious affiliation, siblings of current students. *Tuition waivers:* Full or partial for employees or children of employees. *ROTC:* Army cooperative, Naval cooperative.

LOANS Student loans: $25,610,991 (85% need-based, 15% non-need-based). 77% of past graduating class borrowed through all loan programs. *Average indebtedness per student:* $29,823. *Average need-based loan:* Freshmen: $3651. Undergraduates: $5988. *Parent loans:* $8,156,976 (57% need-based, 43% non-need-based). *Programs:* Federal Direct (Subsidized and Unsubsidized Stafford, PLUS), Perkins, Federal Nursing, state, private loans.

WORK-STUDY Federal work-study: Total amount: $289,500; jobs available.

ATHLETIC AWARDS Total amount: $1,715,567 (71% need-based, 29% non-need-based).

APPLYING FOR FINANCIAL AID Required financial aid forms: FAFSA, state aid form. *Financial aid deadline:* 5/1 (priority: 4/15). *Notification date:* Continuous beginning 2/1. Students must reply within 5 weeks of notification.

CONTACT Ana C. Lockward, Director of Financial Aid, Molloy College, 1000 Hempstead Avenue, Rockville Centre, NY 11571, 516-678-5000 Ext. 6221 or toll-free 888-4MOLLOY. *Fax:* 516-256-2292. *E-mail:* alockward@molloy.edu. *Website:* http://www.molloy.edu/.

MONMOUTH COLLEGE
Monmouth, IL

Tuition & fees: $31,500	Average undergraduate aid package: $27,194

ABOUT THE INSTITUTION Independent Presbyterian Church, coed. *Awards:* bachelor's degrees. 36 undergraduate majors. *Total enrollment:* 1,247. Undergraduates: 1,247. Freshmen: 343. Both federal and institutional methodology are used as a basis for awarding need-based institutional aid.

UNDERGRADUATE EXPENSES for 2013–2014 One-time required fee: $190. *Comprehensive fee:* $39,100 includes full-time tuition ($31,500) and room and board ($7600). Full-time tuition and fees vary according to course load. Room and board charges vary according to board plan and housing facility.

FRESHMAN FINANCIAL AID (Fall 2012, est.) 330 applied for aid; of those 92% were deemed to have need. 100% of freshmen with need received aid; of those 16% had need fully met. *Average percent of need met:* 89% (excluding resources awarded to replace EFC). *Average financial aid package:* $30,251 (excluding resources awarded to replace EFC). 12% of all full-time freshmen had no need and received non-need-based gift aid.

UNDERGRADUATE FINANCIAL AID (Fall 2012, est.) 1,169 applied for aid; of those 92% were deemed to have need. 99% of undergraduates with need received aid; of those 18% had need fully met. *Average percent of need met:* 85% (excluding resources awarded to replace EFC). *Average financial aid package:* $27,194 (excluding resources awarded to replace EFC). 12% of all full-time undergraduates had no need and received non-need-based gift aid.

GIFT AID (NEED-BASED) Total amount: $23,130,156 (11% federal, 12% state, 77% institutional). *Receiving aid:* Freshmen: 88% (303); all full-time undergraduates: 87% (1,068). *Average award:* Freshmen: $25,651; Undergraduates: $21,934. *Scholarships, grants, and awards:* Federal Pell, FSEOG, state, private, college/university gift aid from institutional funds.

GIFT AID (NON-NEED-BASED) Total amount: $3,217,597 (88% institutional, 12% external sources). *Receiving aid:* Freshmen: 9% (32). Undergraduates: 9% (110). *Average award:* Freshmen: $16,210. Undergraduates: $13,824. *Scholarships, grants, and awards by category: Academic interests/achievement:* foreign languages, general academic interests/achievements, military science. *Creative arts/performance:* art/fine arts, debating, music, theater/drama. *Special achievements/activities:* general special achievements/activities, leadership, religious involvement. *Special characteristics:* international students, veterans. *Tuition waivers:* Full or partial for employees or children of employees. *ROTC:* Army cooperative.

LOANS Student loans: $8,207,793 (48% need-based, 52% non-need-based). 82% of past graduating class borrowed through all loan programs. *Average indebtedness per student:* $31,578. *Average need-based loan:* Freshmen: $3683. Undergraduates: $4524. *Parent loans:* $3,085,645 (100% non-need-based). *Programs:* Federal Direct (Subsidized and Unsubsidized Stafford, PLUS), Perkins.

WORK-STUDY Federal work-study: Total amount: $993,031; jobs available. *State or other work-study/employment:* Part-time jobs available.

APPLYING FOR FINANCIAL AID Required financial aid form: FAFSA. *Financial aid deadline (priority):* 2/1. *Notification date:* Continuous beginning 2/15. Students must reply by 5/1.

CONTACT Mrs. Jayne Schreck, Director of Scholarships and Financial Aid, Monmouth College, 700 East Broadway, Monmouth, IL 61462-1998, 309-457-2129 or toll-free 800-747-2687. *Fax:* 309-457-2373. *E-mail:* jayne@monmouthcollege.edu. *Website:* http://www.monm.edu/.

MONMOUTH UNIVERSITY
West Long Branch, NJ

Tuition & fees: $29,710	Average undergraduate aid package: $21,477

ABOUT THE INSTITUTION Independent, coed. *Awards:* certificates, associate, bachelor's, master's, and doctoral degrees. 34 undergraduate majors. *Total enrollment:* 6,472. Undergraduates: 4,738. Freshmen: 1,006. Federal methodology is used as a basis for awarding need-based institutional aid.

UNDERGRADUATE EXPENSES for 2013–2014 *Application fee:* $50. *One-time required fee:* $200. *Comprehensive fee:* $40,512 includes full-time tuition ($29,082), mandatory fees ($628), and room and board ($10,802). *College room only:* $6169. Room and board charges vary according to board plan and housing facility. *Part-time tuition:* $842 per credit hour. *Part-time fees:* $157 per term. Part-time tuition and fees vary according to course load.

FRESHMAN FINANCIAL AID (Fall 2012, est.) 894 applied for aid; of those 81% were deemed to have need. 100% of freshmen with need received aid; of those 18% had need fully met. *Average percent of need met:* 68% (excluding resources awarded to replace EFC). *Average financial aid package:* $21,636 (excluding resources awarded to replace EFC). 27% of all full-time freshmen had no need and received non-need-based gift aid.

UNDERGRADUATE FINANCIAL AID (Fall 2012, est.) 3,616 applied for aid; of those 86% were deemed to have need. 100% of undergraduates with need received aid; of those 16% had need fully met. *Average percent of need met:* 66% (excluding resources awarded to replace EFC). *Average financial aid package:* $21,477 (excluding resources awarded to replace EFC). 27% of all full-time undergraduates had no need and received non-need-based gift aid.

GIFT AID (NEED-BASED) *Total amount:* $17,995,340 (31% federal, 50% state, 9% institutional, 10% external sources). *Receiving aid:* Freshmen: 30% (305); all full-time undergraduates: 28% (1,253). *Average award:* Freshmen: $12,995; Undergraduates: $12,554. *Scholarships, grants, and awards:* Federal Pell, FSEOG, state, private, college/university gift aid from institutional funds, Federal Nursing.

GIFT AID (NON-NEED-BASED) *Total amount:* $32,744,839 (1% federal, 99% institutional). *Receiving aid:* Freshmen: 72% (725). Undergraduates: 64% (2,845). *Average award:* Freshmen: $8704. Undergraduates: $7678. *Scholarships, grants, and awards by category:* Academic interests/achievement: 4,099 awards ($31,216,129 total): business, communication, computer science, education, general academic interests/achievements, health fields, humanities, international studies, mathematics, social sciences. *Special achievements/activities:* 1 award ($2500 total): leadership. *Special characteristics:* 541 awards ($4,703,951 total): adult students, children and siblings of alumni, children of faculty/staff, children of public servants, first-generation college students, general special characteristics, international students, local/state students, members of minority groups, out-of-state students, previous college experience, veterans. *Tuition waivers:* Full or partial for employees or children of employees, senior citizens. *ROTC:* Army cooperative, Air Force cooperative.

LOANS *Student loans:* $40,453,602 (32% need-based, 68% non-need-based). 72% of past graduating class borrowed through all loan programs. *Average indebtedness per student:* $34,810. *Average need-based loan:* Freshmen: $3713. Undergraduates: $4940. *Parent loans:* $9,313,423 (100% non-need-based). *Programs:* Federal Direct (Subsidized and Unsubsidized Stafford, PLUS), Perkins, state, college/university, private loans.

WORK-STUDY *Federal work-study:* Total amount: $1,564,614; 955 jobs averaging $1968.

ATHLETIC AWARDS Total amount: $5,930,402 (100% non-need-based).

APPLYING FOR FINANCIAL AID *Required financial aid form:* FAFSA. *Financial aid deadline:* Continuous. *Notification date:* Continuous beginning 2/1. Students must reply within 2 weeks of notification.

CONTACT Ms. Claire Alasio, Associate Vice President for Enrollment Management and Director of Financial Aid, Monmouth University, 400 Cedar Avenue, West Long Branch, NJ 07764-1898, 732-571-3463 or toll-free 800-543-9671. *Fax:* 732-923-4791. *E-mail:* finaid@monmouth.edu. *Website:* http://www.monmouth.edu/.

MONROE COLLEGE
Bronx, NY

CONTACT Howard Leslie, Dean of Student Financial Services, Monroe College, 434 Main Street, New Rochelle, NY 10468, 718-817-8203 or toll-free 800-55MONROE. *Fax:* 718-365-2363. *E-mail:* hleslie@monroecollege.edu. *Website:* http://www.monroecollege.edu/.

MONROE COLLEGE
New Rochelle, NY

CONTACT James Gathard, Vice President, Student Financial Services, Monroe College, 2501 Jerome Avenue, Bronx, NY 10468, 718-933-6700 Ext. 8236 or toll-free 800-55MONROE. *Fax:* 718-365-2365. *E-mail:* hleslie@monroecollege.edu. *Website:* http://www.monroecollege.edu/.

MONTANA STATE UNIVERSITY
Bozeman, MT

Tuition & fees (MT res): $6749	Average undergraduate aid package: $12,028

ABOUT THE INSTITUTION State-supported, coed. *Awards:* certificates, associate, bachelor's, master's, and doctoral degrees. 59 undergraduate majors. *Total enrollment:* 14,660. Undergraduates: 12,772. Freshmen: 2,710. Federal methodology is used as a basis for awarding need-based institutional aid.

UNDERGRADUATE EXPENSES for 2013–2014 *Application fee:* $30. *Tuition, state resident:* full-time $5330; part-time $222 per credit. *Tuition, non-resident:* full-time $18,599; part-time $779 per credit. *Required fees:* full-time $1419; $106 per credit. Full-time tuition and fees vary according to course load, degree level, and program. Part-time tuition and fees vary according to course load, degree level, and program. *College room and board:* $8070. Room and board charges vary according to board plan and housing facility.

FRESHMAN FINANCIAL AID (Fall 2011) 1,556 applied for aid; of those 74% were deemed to have need. 97% of freshmen with need received aid; of those 6% had need fully met. *Average percent of need met:* 76% (excluding resources awarded to replace EFC). *Average financial aid package:* $11,860 (excluding resources awarded to replace EFC). 4% of all full-time freshmen had no need and received non-need-based gift aid.

UNDERGRADUATE FINANCIAL AID (Fall 2011) 6,744 applied for aid; of those 81% were deemed to have need. 97% of undergraduates with need received aid; of those 4% had need fully met. *Average percent of need met:* 72% (excluding resources awarded to replace EFC). *Average financial aid package:* $12,028 (excluding resources awarded to replace EFC). 3% of all full-time undergraduates had no need and received non-need-based gift aid.

GIFT AID (NEED-BASED) *Total amount:* $24,443,329 (65% federal, 5% state, 11% institutional, 19% external sources). *Receiving aid:* Freshmen: 44% (874); all full-time undergraduates: 41% (4,024). *Average award:* Freshmen: $4957; Undergraduates: $5123. *Scholarships, grants, and awards:* Federal Pell, FSEOG, state, private, college/university gift aid from institutional funds, Federal Nursing.

GIFT AID (NON-NEED-BASED) *Total amount:* $5,401,038 (4% state, 14% institutional, 82% external sources). *Receiving aid:* Freshmen: 2% (48). Undergraduates: 2% (178). *Average award:* Freshmen: $1084. Undergraduates: $1588. *Scholarships, grants, and awards by category:* Academic interests/achievement: agriculture, architecture, area/ethnic studies, biological sciences, business, communication, computer science, education, engineering/technologies, English, foreign languages, general academic interests/achievements, health fields, home economics, humanities, mathematics, military science, physical sciences, social sciences. *Creative arts/performance:* art/fine arts, cinema/film/broadcasting, dance, music, theater/drama. *Special achievements/activities:* general special achievements/activities, leadership. *Special characteristics:* children and siblings of alumni, general special characteristics, local/state students, members of minority groups. *Tuition waivers:* Full or partial for minority students, employees or children of employees, senior citizens. *ROTC:* Army, Air Force.

LOANS *Student loans:* $46,874,154 (81% need-based, 19% non-need-based). 65% of past graduating class borrowed through all loan programs. *Average indebtedness*

per student: $27,320. **Average need-based loan:** Freshmen: $3718. Undergraduates: $4368. **Parent loans:** $13,345,278 (38% need-based, 62% non-need-based). **Programs:** Federal Direct (Subsidized and Unsubsidized Stafford, PLUS), Perkins, Federal Nursing, college/university.
WORK-STUDY Federal work-study: Total amount: $566,368; jobs available. **State or other work-study/employment:** Total amount: $323,077 (100% need-based). Part-time jobs available.
ATHLETIC AWARDS Total amount: $1,542,225 (63% need-based, 37% non-need-based).
APPLYING FOR FINANCIAL AID Required financial aid form: FAFSA. **Financial aid deadline (priority):** 3/1. **Notification date:** Continuous beginning 4/1.
CONTACT Brandi Payne, Director of Financial Aid, Montana State University, PO Box 174160, Bozeman, MT 59717-4160, 406-994-2845 or toll-free 888-MSU-CATS. *Fax:* 406-994-6962. *E-mail:* bpayne@montana.edu.
Website: http://www.montana.edu/.

MONTANA STATE UNIVERSITY BILLINGS
Billings, MT

Tuition & fees (MT res): $5711	Average undergraduate aid package: $9806

ABOUT THE INSTITUTION State-supported, coed. **Awards:** certificates, associate, bachelor's, and master's degrees. 70 undergraduate majors. **Total enrollment:** 5,274. Undergraduates: 4,719. Freshmen: 865. Federal methodology is used as a basis for awarding need-based institutional aid.
UNDERGRADUATE EXPENSES for 2013–2014 Application fee: $30. **Tuition, state resident:** full-time $4397; part-time $158 per credit hour. **Tuition, nonresident:** full-time $16,726; part-time $522 per credit hour. **Required fees:** full-time $1314. Full-time tuition and fees vary according to course load, degree level, and location. Part-time tuition and fees vary according to course load, degree level, and location. **College room and board:** $6320. Room and board charges vary according to board plan and housing facility.
FRESHMAN FINANCIAL AID (Fall 2011) 636 applied for aid; of those 83% were deemed to have need. 96% of freshmen with need received aid; of those 4% had need fully met. **Average percent of need met:** 65% (excluding resources awarded to replace EFC). **Average financial aid package:** $8553 (excluding resources awarded to replace EFC). 2% of all full-time freshmen had no need and received non-need-based gift aid.
UNDERGRADUATE FINANCIAL AID (Fall 2011) 2,698 applied for aid; of those 84% were deemed to have need. 98% of undergraduates with need received aid; of those 4% had need fully met. **Average percent of need met:** 71% (excluding resources awarded to replace EFC). **Average financial aid package:** $9806 (excluding resources awarded to replace EFC). 2% of all full-time undergraduates had no need and received non-need-based gift aid.
GIFT AID (NEED-BASED) Total amount: $10,382,842 (79% federal, 4% state, 12% institutional, 5% external sources). **Receiving aid:** Freshmen: 58% (435); all full-time undergraduates: 53% (1,814). **Average award:** Freshmen: $4831; Undergraduates: $5034. **Scholarships, grants, and awards:** Federal Pell, FSEOG, state, private, college/university gift aid from institutional funds.
GIFT AID (NON-NEED-BASED) Total amount: $535,288 (3% state, 85% institutional, 12% external sources). **Receiving aid:** Freshmen: 2% (16). Undergraduates: 2% (58). **Average award:** Freshmen: $1832. Undergraduates: $2337. **Scholarships, grants, and awards by category:** Academic interests/achievement: biological sciences, business, communication, computer science, education, engineering/technologies, English, foreign languages, general academic interests/achievements, health fields, humanities, mathematics, physical sciences, premedicine, social sciences. Creative arts/performance: art/fine arts, music, theater/drama. Special achievements/activities: cheerleading/drum major, general special achievements/activities. Special characteristics: adult students, children and siblings of alumni, children of faculty/staff, children of union members/company employees, ethnic background, first-generation college students, local/state students, members of minority groups, out-of-state students, veterans. **Tuition waivers:** Full or partial for employees or children of employees, senior citizens. **ROTC:** Army.

LOANS Student loans: $22,367,268 (47% need-based, 53% non-need-based). 73% of past graduating class borrowed through all loan programs. *Average indebtedness per student:* $27,178. **Average need-based loan:** Freshmen: $2794. Undergraduates: $3445. **Parent loans:** $1,121,954 (28% need-based, 72% non-need-based). **Programs:** Federal Direct (Subsidized and Unsubsidized Stafford, PLUS), Perkins.
WORK-STUDY Federal work-study: Total amount: $337,718; 265 jobs averaging $1275. **State or other work-study/employment:** Total amount: $152,537 (87% need-based, 13% non-need-based). 86 part-time jobs averaging $1679.
ATHLETIC AWARDS Total amount: $1,359,263 (54% need-based, 46% non-need-based).
APPLYING FOR FINANCIAL AID Required financial aid form: FAFSA. **Financial aid deadline (priority):** 3/1. **Notification date:** Continuous beginning 4/1. Students must reply within 3 weeks of notification.
CONTACT Ms. Leslie Weldon, Director of Financial Aid, Montana State University Billings, 1500 University Drive, Billings, MT 59101, 406-657-2188 or toll-free 800-565-6782. *Fax:* 406-657-1789. *E-mail:* leslie.weldon@msubillings.edu.
Website: http://www.msubillings.edu/.

MONTANA STATE UNIVERSITY–NORTHERN
Havre, MT

Tuition & fees (MT res): $5070	Average undergraduate aid package: $10,291

ABOUT THE INSTITUTION State-supported, coed. **Awards:** certificates, diplomas, associate, bachelor's, and master's degrees. 27 undergraduate majors. **Total enrollment:** 1,273. Undergraduates: 1,208. Freshmen: 228. Federal methodology is used as a basis for awarding need-based institutional aid.
UNDERGRADUATE EXPENSES for 2013–2014 Application fee: $30. **Tuition, state resident:** full-time $3765; part-time $232 per credit hour. **Tuition, nonresident:** full-time $14,943; part-time $635 per credit hour. **Required fees:** full-time $1305. Full-time tuition and fees vary according to course level, course load, degree level, location, reciprocity agreements, and student level. Part-time tuition and fees vary according to course level, course load, degree level, location, reciprocity agreements, and student level. **College room and board:** $6275; **Room only:** $2147. Room and board charges vary according to board plan.
FRESHMAN FINANCIAL AID (Fall 2012, est.) 162 applied for aid; of those 83% were deemed to have need. 100% of freshmen with need received aid; of those 5% had need fully met. **Average percent of need met:** 59% (excluding resources awarded to replace EFC). **Average financial aid package:** $9054 (excluding resources awarded to replace EFC). 1% of all full-time freshmen had no need and received non-need-based gift aid.
UNDERGRADUATE FINANCIAL AID (Fall 2012, est.) 772 applied for aid; of those 89% were deemed to have need. 99% of undergraduates with need received aid; of those 3% had need fully met. **Average percent of need met:** 60% (excluding resources awarded to replace EFC). **Average financial aid package:** $10,291 (excluding resources awarded to replace EFC). 1% of all full-time undergraduates had no need and received non-need-based gift aid.
GIFT AID (NEED-BASED) Total amount: $3,276,209 (71% federal, 6% state, 1% institutional, 22% external sources). **Receiving aid:** Freshmen: 69% (123); all full-time undergraduates: 66% (596). **Average award:** Freshmen: $4647; Undergraduates: $4826. **Scholarships, grants, and awards:** Federal Pell, FSEOG, state, private, college/university gift aid from institutional funds.
GIFT AID (NON-NEED-BASED) Total amount: $296,507 (4% state, 3% institutional, 93% external sources). **Receiving aid:** Freshmen: 2% (4). Undergraduates: 2% (16). **Average award:** Freshmen: $250. Undergraduates: $715. **Scholarships, grants, and awards by category:** Academic interests/achievement: agriculture, architecture, biological sciences, business, computer science, education, engineering/technologies, English, foreign languages, general academic interests/achievements, health fields, humanities, social sciences. Creative arts/performance: art/fine arts. Special achievements/activities: community service, general special achievements/activities, hobbies/interests, memberships, rodeo. Special characteristics: adult students, children and siblings of alumni, general special characteristics, international students, members of minority groups, out-of-state students, veterans.
LOANS Student loans: $4,513,806 (84% need-based, 16% non-need-based). 76% of past graduating class borrowed through all loan programs. *Average indebtedness*

per student: $21,365. **Average need-based loan:** Freshmen: $2914. Undergraduates: $3522. **Parent loans:** $67,491 (44% need-based, 56% non-need-based). **Programs:** Federal Direct (Subsidized and Unsubsidized Stafford, PLUS), Perkins, Federal Nursing, college/university, alternative loans.

WORK-STUDY *Federal work-study:* Total amount: $84,275; 61 jobs averaging $1382. *State or other work-study/employment:* Total amount: $41,090 (100% need-based). 25 part-time jobs averaging $1644.

ATHLETIC AWARDS Total amount: $84,236 (58% need-based, 42% non-need-based).

APPLYING FOR FINANCIAL AID *Required financial aid form:* FAFSA. *Financial aid deadline (priority):* 4/15. *Notification date:* Continuous beginning 4/1. Students must reply within 3 weeks of notification.

CONTACT Cindy Small, Director of Financial Aid, Montana State University–Northern, PO Box 7751, Havre, MT 59501, 406-265-3787 or toll-free 800-662-6132. *Website:* http://www.msun.edu/.

MONTANA TECH OF THE UNIVERSITY OF MONTANA
Butte, MT

Tuition & fees (MT res): $6693	Average undergraduate aid package: $10,505

ABOUT THE INSTITUTION State-supported, coed. **Awards:** certificates, diplomas, associate, bachelor's, and master's degrees. 36 undergraduate majors. **Total enrollment:** 2,816. Undergraduates: 2,646. Freshmen: 426. Federal methodology is used as a basis for awarding need-based institutional aid.

UNDERGRADUATE EXPENSES for 2013–2014 **Application fee:** $30. **Tuition, state resident:** full-time $5177; part-time $215 per credit. **Tuition, nonresident:** full-time $17,432; part-time $726 per credit. **Required fees:** full-time $1516; $69 per credit hour. Full-time tuition and fees vary according to course load, degree level, location, program, and student level. Part-time tuition and fees vary according to course load, degree level, location, program, and student level. **College room and board:** $7626; **Room only:** $3392. Room and board charges vary according to board plan.

FRESHMAN FINANCIAL AID (Fall 2011) 399 applied for aid; of those 75% were deemed to have need. 100% of freshmen with need received aid; of those 42% had need fully met. **Average percent of need met:** 80% (excluding resources awarded to replace EFC). **Average financial aid package:** $9592 (excluding resources awarded to replace EFC). 13% of all full-time freshmen had no need and received non-need-based gift aid.

UNDERGRADUATE FINANCIAL AID (Fall 2011) 1,625 applied for aid; of those 80% were deemed to have need. 100% of undergraduates with need received aid; of those 34% had need fully met. **Average percent of need met:** 84% (excluding resources awarded to replace EFC). **Average financial aid package:** $10,505 (excluding resources awarded to replace EFC). 12% of all full-time undergraduates had no need and received non-need-based gift aid.

GIFT AID (NEED-BASED) Total amount: $6,430,900 (68% federal, 6% state, 19% institutional, 7% external sources). **Receiving aid:** Freshmen: 58% (268); all full-time undergraduates: 52% (1,136). **Average award:** Freshmen: $5363; Undergraduates: $5285. **Scholarships, grants, and awards:** Federal Pell, FSEOG, state, private, college/university gift aid from institutional funds.

GIFT AID (NON-NEED-BASED) Total amount: $1,376,126 (5% state, 73% institutional, 22% external sources). **Receiving aid:** Freshmen: 7% (31). Undergraduates: 3% (68). **Average award:** Freshmen: $3060. Undergraduates: $3213. **Scholarships, grants, and awards by category:** Academic interests/achievement: business, computer science, engineering/technologies, general academic interests/achievements, health fields, mathematics, physical sciences. Special achievements/activities: community service, general special achievements/activities. Special characteristics: children and siblings of alumni, children of faculty/staff, general special characteristics, local/state students, married students, out-of-state students, veterans. **Tuition waivers:** Full or partial for minority students, employees or children of employees, senior citizens.

LOANS Student loans: $8,837,150 (79% need-based, 21% non-need-based). 55% of past graduating class borrowed through all loan programs. Average indebtedness per student: $25,360. **Average need-based loan:** Freshmen: $3071. Undergraduates: $3825. **Parent loans:** $1,357,892 (29% need-based, 71% non-need-based).

Programs: Federal Direct (Subsidized and Unsubsidized Stafford, PLUS), Perkins, college/university.

WORK-STUDY *Federal work-study:* Total amount: $137,125; jobs available. *State or other work-study/employment:* Total amount: $51,594 (100% need-based). Part-time jobs available.

ATHLETIC AWARDS Total amount: $760,091 (44% need-based, 56% non-need-based).

APPLYING FOR FINANCIAL AID *Required financial aid forms:* FAFSA, institution's own form. *Financial aid deadline (priority):* 3/1. *Notification date:* Continuous beginning 3/15. Students must reply within 2 weeks of notification.

CONTACT Mike Richardson, Director of Financial Aid, Montana Tech of The University of Montana, West Park Street, Butte, MT 59701-8997, 406-496-4256 or toll-free 800-445-TECH. *Fax:* 406-496-4710. *E-mail:* mrichardson@mtech.edu. *Website:* http://www.mtech.edu/.

MONTCLAIR STATE UNIVERSITY
Montclair, NJ

Tuition & fees (NJ res): $11,058	Average undergraduate aid package: $9202

ABOUT THE INSTITUTION State-supported, coed. **Awards:** certificates, bachelor's, master's, and doctoral degrees. 44 undergraduate majors. **Total enrollment:** 18,382. Undergraduates: 14,432. Freshmen: 2,213. Federal methodology is used as a basis for awarding need-based institutional aid.

UNDERGRADUATE EXPENSES for 2013–2014 **Application fee:** $65. **Tuition, state resident:** full-time $7982; part-time $266.07 per credit. **Tuition, nonresident:** full-time $17,060; part-time $568.65 per credit. **Required fees:** full-time $3076; $102.52 per credit. **College room and board:** $13,443; **Room only:** $9543. Room and board charges vary according to board plan, housing facility, and student level.

FRESHMAN FINANCIAL AID (Fall 2011) 2,213 applied for aid; of those 92% were deemed to have need. 96% of freshmen with need received aid; of those 13% had need fully met. **Average percent of need met:** 72% (excluding resources awarded to replace EFC). **Average financial aid package:** $8461 (excluding resources awarded to replace EFC). 2% of all full-time freshmen had no need and received non-need-based gift aid.

UNDERGRADUATE FINANCIAL AID (Fall 2011) 9,977 applied for aid; of those 86% were deemed to have need. 96% of undergraduates with need received aid; of those 10% had need fully met. **Average percent of need met:** 72% (excluding resources awarded to replace EFC). **Average financial aid package:** $9202 (excluding resources awarded to replace EFC). 1% of all full-time undergraduates had no need and received non-need-based gift aid.

GIFT AID (NEED-BASED) Total amount: $42,465,465 (58% federal, 42% state). **Receiving aid:** Freshmen: 81% (1,900); all full-time undergraduates: 56% (7,950). **Average award:** Freshmen: $8868; Undergraduates: $8271. **Scholarships, grants, and awards:** Federal Pell, FSEOG, state, private, college/university gift aid from institutional funds.

GIFT AID (NON-NEED-BASED) Total amount: $7,855,947 (12% state, 69% institutional, 19% external sources). **Receiving aid:** Freshmen: 10% (229). Undergraduates: 7% (1,050). **Average award:** Freshmen: $10,454. Undergraduates: $12,179. **Scholarships, grants, and awards by category:** Academic interests/achievement: biological sciences, business, communication, education, English, foreign languages, general academic interests/achievements, home economics, humanities, international studies, mathematics, physical sciences, religion/biblical studies, social sciences. Creative arts/performance: art/fine arts, cinema/film/broadcasting, dance, music, performing arts, theater/drama. Special achievements/activities: community service, general special achievements/activities, leadership. Special characteristics: children and siblings of alumni, international students. **Tuition waivers:** Full or partial for employees or children of employees, senior citizens. **ROTC:** Army, Naval, Air Force.

LOANS Student loans: $87,963,385 (49% need-based, 51% non-need-based). 71% of past graduating class borrowed through all loan programs. Average indebtedness per student: $28,070. **Average need-based loan:** Freshmen: $3397. Undergraduates: $4534. **Parent loans:** $13,649,774 (100% non-need-based). **Programs:** Federal Direct (Subsidized and Unsubsidized Stafford, PLUS), Perkins, state, private loans.

WORK-STUDY *Federal work-study:* Total amount: $413,559; 399 jobs averaging $1029. *State or other work-study/employment:* Total amount: $5,263,666 (100% non-need-based). Part-time jobs available.
APPLYING FOR FINANCIAL AID *Required financial aid form:* FAFSA. *Financial aid deadline (priority):* 3/1. *Notification date:* Continuous beginning 3/15. Students must reply within 2 weeks of notification.
CONTACT Mr. James T. Anderson, Director of Financial Aid, Montclair State University, College Hall, Room 222, Montclair, NJ 07043, 973-655-7022. *Fax:* 973-655-7712. *E-mail:* financialaid@montclair.edu.
Website: http://www.montclair.edu/.

MONTREAT COLLEGE
Montreat, NC

Tuition & fees: $22,784	Average undergraduate aid package: $17,314

ABOUT THE INSTITUTION Independent Presbyterian Church (U.S.A.), coed. *Awards:* certificates, associate, bachelor's, and master's degrees. 19 undergraduate majors. *Total enrollment:* 889. Undergraduates: 766. Freshmen: 102. Federal methodology is used as a basis for awarding need-based institutional aid.
UNDERGRADUATE EXPENSES for 2013–2014 *Comprehensive fee:* $30,278 includes full-time tuition ($22,684), mandatory fees ($100), and room and board ($7494). Room and board charges vary according to board plan. *Part-time tuition:* $600 per credit hour.
FRESHMAN FINANCIAL AID (Fall 2012, est.) 95 applied for aid; of those 92% were deemed to have need. 100% of freshmen with need received aid; of those 18% had need fully met. *Average percent of need met:* 78% (excluding resources awarded to replace EFC). *Average financial aid package:* $20,129 (excluding resources awarded to replace EFC). 16% of all full-time freshmen had no need and received non-need-based gift aid.
UNDERGRADUATE FINANCIAL AID (Fall 2012, est.) 468 applied for aid; of those 91% were deemed to have need. 100% of undergraduates with need received aid; of those 18% had need fully met. *Average percent of need met:* 74% (excluding resources awarded to replace EFC). *Average financial aid package:* $17,314 (excluding resources awarded to replace EFC). 12% of all full-time undergraduates had no need and received non-need-based gift aid.
GIFT AID (NEED-BASED) *Total amount:* $4,841,267 (25% federal, 18% state, 57% institutional). *Receiving aid:* Freshmen: 83% (86); all full-time undergraduates: 82% (410). *Average award:* Freshmen: $15,905; Undergraduates: $12,932. *Scholarships, grants, and awards:* Federal Pell, FSEOG, state, private, college/university gift aid from institutional funds.
GIFT AID (NON-NEED-BASED) *Total amount:* $195,000 (100% external sources). *Receiving aid:* Freshmen: 10% (10). Undergraduates: 7% (36). *Average award:* Freshmen: $7518. Undergraduates: $7232. *Scholarships, grants, and awards by category:* Academic interests/achievement: 250 awards ($850,000 total): general academic interests/achievements. Creative arts/performance: 11 awards ($90,157 total): music. Special achievements/activities: 14 awards ($71,000 total): leadership. Special characteristics: 13 awards ($154,789 total): children of faculty/staff, first-generation college students, international students, local/state students, relatives of clergy, religious affiliation, veterans, veterans' children.
LOANS *Student loans:* $4,342,579 (54% need-based, 46% non-need-based). 80% of past graduating class borrowed through all loan programs. *Average indebtedness per student:* $18,147. *Average need-based loan:* Freshmen: $3411. Undergraduates: $4113. *Parent loans:* $311,211 (100% non-need-based). *Programs:* Federal Direct (Subsidized and Unsubsidized Stafford, PLUS), Perkins.
WORK-STUDY *Federal work-study:* Total amount: $71,150; 50 jobs averaging $1820. *State or other work-study/employment:* Total amount: $65,633 (100% non-need-based). 30 part-time jobs averaging $870.
ATHLETIC AWARDS Total amount: $597,872 (100% non-need-based).
APPLYING FOR FINANCIAL AID *Required financial aid forms:* FAFSA, state aid form. *Financial aid deadline (priority):* 4/1. *Notification date:* Continuous beginning 4/1. Students must reply within 2 weeks of notification.
CONTACT Lisa Lounsbury, Financial Aid Awarding Specialist, Montreat College, PO Box 1267, Montreat, NC 28757, 828-669-8012 Ext. 3795 or toll-free 800-622-6968. *Fax:* 828-669-0120.
Website: http://www.montreat.edu/.

MONTSERRAT COLLEGE OF ART
Beverly, MA

CONTACT Creda Carney, Director of Financial Aid, Montserrat College of Art, 23 Essex Street, PO Box 26, Beverly, MA 01915, 978-922-8222 Ext. 1155 or toll-free 800-836-0487. *Fax:* 978-922-4268. *E-mail:* finaid@montserrat.edu.
Website: http://www.montserrat.edu/.

MOODY BIBLE INSTITUTE
Chicago, IL

CONTACT Esther Kim, Director of Financial Aid, Moody Bible Institute, 820 North LaSalle Boulevard, Chicago, IL 60610-3284, 312-329-4178 or toll-free 800-967-4MBI. *Fax:* 312-329-4197. *E-mail:* esther.kim@moody.edu.
Website: http://www.moody.edu/.

MOORE COLLEGE OF ART & DESIGN
Philadelphia, PA

CONTACT Kristina Fripps, Director of Financial Aid, Moore College of Art & Design, 20th and the Parkway, Philadelphia, PA 19103-1179, 215-965-4042 or toll-free 800-523-2025. *Fax:* 215-568-1773. *E-mail:* kfripps@moore.edu.
Website: http://www.moore.edu/.

MORAVIAN COLLEGE
Bethlehem, PA

Tuition & fees: $34,484	Average undergraduate aid package: $25,753

ABOUT THE INSTITUTION Independent Moravian Church, coed. *Awards:* certificates, bachelor's, and master's degrees. 55 undergraduate majors. *Total enrollment:* 1,909. Undergraduates: 1,582. Freshmen: 378. Both federal and institutional methodology are used as a basis for awarding need-based institutional aid.
UNDERGRADUATE EXPENSES for 2013–2014 *Application fee:* $40. *Comprehensive fee:* $44,630 includes full-time tuition ($33,919), mandatory fees ($565), and room and board ($10,146). *College room only:* $5676. Room and board charges vary according to board plan and housing facility. *Part-time tuition:* $942.25 per credit hour. Part-time tuition and fees vary according to class time.
FRESHMAN FINANCIAL AID (Fall 2012, est.) 362 applied for aid; of those 92% were deemed to have need. 100% of freshmen with need received aid; of those 11% had need fully met. *Average percent of need met:* 77% (excluding resources awarded to replace EFC). *Average financial aid package:* $26,847 (excluding resources awarded to replace EFC). 11% of all full-time freshmen had no need and received non-need-based gift aid.
UNDERGRADUATE FINANCIAL AID (Fall 2012, est.) 1,321 applied for aid; of those 93% were deemed to have need. 100% of undergraduates with need received aid; of those 12% had need fully met. *Average percent of need met:* 74% (excluding resources awarded to replace EFC). *Average financial aid package:* $25,753 (excluding resources awarded to replace EFC). 12% of all full-time undergraduates had no need and received non-need-based gift aid.
GIFT AID (NEED-BASED) *Total amount:* $23,892,753 (9% federal, 8% state, 80% institutional, 3% external sources). *Receiving aid:* Freshmen: 88% (334); all full-time undergraduates: 85% (1,222). *Average award:* Freshmen: $21,404; Undergraduates: $19,876. *Scholarships, grants, and awards:* Federal Pell, FSEOG, state, private, college/university gift aid from institutional funds.
GIFT AID (NON-NEED-BASED) *Total amount:* $2,700,091 (87% institutional, 13% external sources). *Receiving aid:* Freshmen: 8% (32). Undergraduates: 8% (109). *Average award:* Freshmen: $10,292. Undergraduates: $10,271. *Scholarships, grants, and awards by category:* Academic interests/achievement: biological sciences, business, computer science, foreign languages, general academic interests/achievements, health fields, mathematics, physical sciences, premedicine. Creative arts/performance: 20 awards ($49,275 total): music. Special achievements/activ-

ities: 53 awards ($66,000 total): leadership, religious involvement. *Special characteristics:* 544 awards ($2,096,676 total): adult students, children and siblings of alumni, children of educators, children of faculty/staff, ethnic background, first-generation college students, international students, relatives of clergy, religious affiliation. *Tuition waivers:* Full or partial for employees or children of employees. *ROTC:* Army cooperative.

LOANS *Student loans:* $13,813,105 (70% need-based, 30% non-need-based). *Average need-based loan:* Freshmen: $3814. Undergraduates: $4715. *Parent loans:* $4,741,624 (40% need-based, 60% non-need-based). *Programs:* Federal Direct (Subsidized and Unsubsidized Stafford, PLUS), Perkins.

WORK-STUDY *Federal work-study:* Total amount: $1,966,098; 997 jobs averaging $1858. *State or other work-study/employment:* Total amount: $138,458 (5% need-based, 95% non-need-based). 173 part-time jobs averaging $870.

APPLYING FOR FINANCIAL AID *Required financial aid forms:* FAFSA, institution's own form, state aid form, business/farm supplement. *Financial aid deadline (priority):* 2/14. *Notification date:* 3/31. Students must reply by 5/1 or within 2 weeks of notification.

CONTACT Mrs. Colby T. McCarthy, Director of Financial Aid, Moravian College, 1200 Main Street, Bethlehem, PA 18018-6650, 610-861-1330 or toll-free 800-441-3191. *Fax:* 610-861-1346. *E-mail:* cmccarthy@moravian.edu. *Website:* http://www.moravian.edu/.

MOREHEAD STATE UNIVERSITY
Morehead, KY

Tuition & fees: N/R	Average undergraduate aid package: $10,305

ABOUT THE INSTITUTION State-supported, coed. *Awards:* certificates, associate, bachelor's, master's, and doctoral degrees. 49 undergraduate majors. *Total enrollment:* 11,172. Undergraduates: 9,725. Freshmen: 1,649. Federal methodology is used as a basis for awarding need-based institutional aid.

UNDERGRADUATE EXPENSES for 2013–2014 *Application fee:* $30. *Tuition, area resident:* part-time $276 per credit hour. *Tuition, nonresident:* part-time $690 per credit hour. Full-time tuition and fees vary according to course load, degree level, location, reciprocity agreements, and student level. Part-time tuition and fees vary according to course load, degree level, location, reciprocity agreements, and student level. Room and board charges vary according to board plan and housing facility.

FRESHMAN FINANCIAL AID (Fall 2012, est.) 1,543 applied for aid; of those 85% were deemed to have need. 100% of freshmen with need received aid; of those 25% had need fully met. *Average percent of need met:* 68% (excluding resources awarded to replace EFC). *Average financial aid package:* $10,974 (excluding resources awarded to replace EFC). 15% of all full-time freshmen had no need and received non-need-based gift aid.

UNDERGRADUATE FINANCIAL AID (Fall 2012, est.) 5,152 applied for aid; of those 89% were deemed to have need. 99% of undergraduates with need received aid; of those 22% had need fully met. *Average percent of need met:* 63% (excluding resources awarded to replace EFC). *Average financial aid package:* $10,305 (excluding resources awarded to replace EFC). 13% of all full-time undergraduates had no need and received non-need-based gift aid.

GIFT AID (NEED-BASED) *Total amount:* $17,566,008 (86% federal, 13% state, 1% institutional). *Receiving aid:* Freshmen: 53% (860); all full-time undergraduates: 54% (3,137). *Average award:* Freshmen: $5408; Undergraduates: $4960. *Scholarships, grants, and awards:* Federal Pell, FSEOG, state, private, college/university gift aid from institutional funds.

GIFT AID (NON-NEED-BASED) *Total amount:* $22,040,114 (24% state, 68% institutional, 8% external sources). *Receiving aid:* Freshmen: 75% (1,213). Undergraduates: 51% (2,999). *Average award:* Freshmen: $5697. Undergraduates: $6602. *Scholarships, grants, and awards by category: Academic interests/achievement:* 1,643 awards ($8,332,532 total): agriculture, biological sciences, business, communication, education, engineering/technologies, general academic interests/achievements, health fields, international studies, military science, physical sciences, social sciences. *Creative arts/performance:* 119 awards ($175,555 total): applied art and design, art/fine arts, journalism/publications, music, theater/drama. *Special achievements/activities:* 111 awards ($140,568 total): cheerleading/drum major, community service, general special achievements/activities, junior miss, leadership. *Special characteristics:* 1,364 awards ($6,113,300 total): adult students, children and siblings of alumni, ethnic background, international students, local/state

students, members of minority groups, out-of-state students, veterans, veterans' children. *Tuition waivers:* Full or partial for children of alumni, employees or children of employees, senior citizens. *ROTC:* Army.

LOANS *Student loans:* $36,107,214 (43% need-based, 57% non-need-based). 67% of past graduating class borrowed through all loan programs. *Average indebtedness per student:* $28,768. *Average need-based loan:* Freshmen: $2874. Undergraduates: $3646. *Parent loans:* $1,521,400 (100% non-need-based). *Programs:* Federal Direct (Subsidized and Unsubsidized Stafford, PLUS), Perkins, college/university.

WORK-STUDY *Federal work-study:* Total amount: $893,880; 438 jobs averaging $2048. *State or other work-study/employment:* Total amount: $1,829,844 (100% non-need-based). 731 part-time jobs averaging $2371.

ATHLETIC AWARDS Total amount: $2,288,347 (100% non-need-based).

APPLYING FOR FINANCIAL AID *Required financial aid form:* FAFSA. *Financial aid deadline (priority):* 3/15. *Notification date:* Continuous.

CONTACT Donna King, Director of Financial Aid, Morehead State University, 100 Admissions Center, Morehead, KY 40351, 606-783-2000 or toll-free 800-585-6781. *Fax:* 606-783-2293. *E-mail:* d.king@moreheadstate.edu. *Website:* http://www.moreheadstate.edu/.

MOREHOUSE COLLEGE
Atlanta, GA

Tuition & fees: $24,744	Average undergraduate aid package: $15,450

ABOUT THE INSTITUTION Independent, men only. *Awards:* bachelor's degrees. 30 undergraduate majors. *Total enrollment:* 2,377. Undergraduates: 2,377. Freshmen: 570. Both federal and institutional methodology are used as a basis for awarding need-based institutional aid.

UNDERGRADUATE EXPENSES for 2013–2014 *Application fee:* $50. *Comprehensive fee:* $37,416 includes full-time tuition ($22,482), mandatory fees ($2262), and room and board ($12,672). *College room only:* $7220. Full-time tuition and fees vary according to course load and student level. Room and board charges vary according to board plan. Part-time tuition and fees vary according to course load.

FRESHMAN FINANCIAL AID (Fall 2012, est.) 526 applied for aid; of those 100% were deemed to have need. 100% of freshmen with need received aid; of those 8% had need fully met. *Average percent of need met:* 22% (excluding resources awarded to replace EFC). *Average financial aid package:* $13,450 (excluding resources awarded to replace EFC).

UNDERGRADUATE FINANCIAL AID (Fall 2012, est.) 2,359 applied for aid; of those 100% were deemed to have need. 100% of undergraduates with need received aid; of those 8% had need fully met. *Average percent of need met:* 25% (excluding resources awarded to replace EFC). *Average financial aid package:* $15,450 (excluding resources awarded to replace EFC).

GIFT AID (NEED-BASED) *Total amount:* $6,050,820 (99% federal, 1% state). *Receiving aid:* Freshmen: 62% (340); all full-time undergraduates: 53% (1,273). *Average award:* Freshmen: $7050; Undergraduates: $7050. *Scholarships, grants, and awards:* Federal Pell, FSEOG, state, private, college/university gift aid from institutional funds, United Negro College Fund.

GIFT AID (NON-NEED-BASED) *Total amount:* $13,998,161 (8% state, 83% institutional, 9% external sources). *Receiving aid:* Freshmen: 33% (182). Undergraduates: 34% (804). *Scholarships, grants, and awards by category: Academic interests/achievement:* business, general academic interests/achievements, military science. *Creative arts/performance:* art/fine arts, music. *Special achievements/activities:* community service, leadership, religious involvement. *Special characteristics:* children and siblings of alumni, children of faculty/staff, local/state students. *Tuition waivers:* Full or partial for employees or children of employees. *ROTC:* Army, Naval, Air Force.

LOANS *Student loans:* $17,473,930 (87% need-based, 13% non-need-based). *Average need-based loan:* Freshmen: $3500. Undergraduates: $5500. *Parent loans:* $17,962,186 (100% non-need-based). *Programs:* Federal Direct (Subsidized and Unsubsidized Stafford, PLUS), Perkins, state, college/university.

WORK-STUDY *Federal work-study:* Total amount: $423,033; jobs available. *State or other work-study/employment:* Total amount: $121,735 (100% non-need-based). Part-time jobs available.

ATHLETIC AWARDS Total amount: $1,558,954 (100% non-need-based).

APPLYING FOR FINANCIAL AID *Required financial aid forms:* FAFSA, institution's own form, CSS Financial Aid PROFILE, state aid form. *Financial aid deadline:* 4/1 (priority: 2/15). *Notification date:* Continuous beginning 3/18. Students must reply by 5/1 or within 2 weeks of notification.

CONTACT Sheryl T. Spivey, Interim Director of Financial Aid, Morehouse College, 830 Westview Drive, SW, Atlanta, GA 30314, 404-215-2639 or toll-free 800-851-1254. *Fax:* 404-215-2711. *E-mail:* jstotts@morehouse.edu.
Website: http://www.morehouse.edu/.

MORGAN STATE UNIVERSITY
Baltimore, MD

Tuition & fees: N/R	Average undergraduate aid package: $20,274

ABOUT THE INSTITUTION State-supported, coed. 55 undergraduate majors. Both federal and institutional methodology are used as a basis for awarding need-based institutional aid.

FRESHMAN FINANCIAL AID (Fall 2012, est.) 954 applied for aid; of those 88% were deemed to have need. 100% of freshmen with need received aid; of those 6% had need fully met. *Average percent of need met:* 45% (excluding resources awarded to replace EFC). *Average financial aid package:* $20,994 (excluding resources awarded to replace EFC). 3% of all full-time freshmen had no need and received non-need-based gift aid.

UNDERGRADUATE FINANCIAL AID (Fall 2012, est.) 5,171 applied for aid; of those 91% were deemed to have need. 100% of undergraduates with need received aid; of those 7% had need fully met. *Average percent of need met:* 52% (excluding resources awarded to replace EFC). *Average financial aid package:* $20,274 (excluding resources awarded to replace EFC). 2% of all full-time undergraduates had no need and received non-need-based gift aid.

GIFT AID (NEED-BASED) *Total amount:* $28,013,571 (68% federal, 14% state, 13% institutional, 5% external sources). *Receiving aid:* Freshmen: 72% (695); all full-time undergraduates: 71% (3,887). *Average award:* Freshmen: $6448; Undergraduates: $6407. *Scholarships, grants, and awards:* Federal Pell, FSEOG, state, private, college/university gift aid from institutional funds.

GIFT AID (NON-NEED-BASED) *Total amount:* $5,720,237 (3% federal, 9% state, 88% institutional). *Receiving aid:* Freshmen: 13% (123). Undergraduates: 14% (742). *Average award:* Freshmen: $6227. Undergraduates: $6156. *Scholarships, grants, and awards by category: Academic interests/achievement:* general academic interests/achievements.

LOANS *Student loans:* $44,021,675 (52% need-based, 48% non-need-based). 85% of past graduating class borrowed through all loan programs. *Average indebtedness per student:* $36,086. *Average need-based loan:* Freshmen: $4233. Undergraduates: $5115. *Parent loans:* $6,232,611 (100% non-need-based). *Programs:* Federal Direct (Subsidized and Unsubsidized Stafford, PLUS), Perkins.

WORK-STUDY *Federal work-study:* Total amount: $619,167; 235 jobs averaging $2635. *State or other work-study/employment:* Total amount: $289,325 (100% need-based). 96 part-time jobs averaging $3014.

ATHLETIC AWARDS Total amount: $3,426,535 (100% non-need-based).

APPLYING FOR FINANCIAL AID *Required financial aid forms:* FAFSA, institution's own form, federal income tax form(s). *Financial aid deadline (priority):* 4/1. *Notification date:* Continuous beginning 6/1. Students must reply within 2 weeks of notification.

CONTACT Tanya Wilkerson, Director of Financial Aid, Morgan State University, 1700 East Cold Spring Lane, Baltimore, MD 21251, 443-885-3170 or toll-free 800-332-6674. *Fax:* 443-885-8272.
Website: http://www.morgan.edu/.

MORNINGSIDE COLLEGE
Sioux City, IA

Tuition & fees: $25,000	Average undergraduate aid package: $24,394

ABOUT THE INSTITUTION Independent United Methodist Church, coed. *Awards:* bachelor's and master's degrees. 42 undergraduate majors. *Total*

enrollment: 2,224. Undergraduates: 1,242. Freshmen: 273. Federal methodology is used as a basis for awarding need-based institutional aid.

UNDERGRADUATE EXPENSES for 2013–2014 *Comprehensive fee:* $32,620 includes full-time tuition ($23,780), mandatory fees ($1220), and room and board ($7620). *College room only:* $3900. Room and board charges vary according to housing facility. Part-time tuition and fees vary according to course load.

FRESHMAN FINANCIAL AID (Fall 2012, est.) 259 applied for aid; of those 93% were deemed to have need. 100% of freshmen with need received aid; of those 28% had need fully met. *Average percent of need met:* 85% (excluding resources awarded to replace EFC). *Average financial aid package:* $25,717 (excluding resources awarded to replace EFC). 97% of all full-time freshmen had no need and received non-need-based gift aid.

UNDERGRADUATE FINANCIAL AID (Fall 2012, est.) 1,102 applied for aid; of those 92% were deemed to have need. 100% of undergraduates with need received aid; of those 35% had need fully met. *Average percent of need met:* 82% (excluding resources awarded to replace EFC). *Average financial aid package:* $24,394 (excluding resources awarded to replace EFC). 97% of all full-time undergraduates had no need and received non-need-based gift aid.

GIFT AID (NEED-BASED) *Total amount:* $5,610,593 (37% federal, 33% state, 30% institutional). *Receiving aid:* Freshmen: 72% (196); all full-time undergraduates: 66% (786). *Average award:* Freshmen: $7175; Undergraduates: $7138. *Scholarships, grants, and awards:* Federal Pell, FSEOG, state, private, college/university gift aid from institutional funds.

GIFT AID (NON-NEED-BASED) *Total amount:* $10,638,846 (6% federal, 2% state, 88% institutional, 4% external sources). *Receiving aid:* Freshmen: 88% (240). Undergraduates: 85% (1,012). *Average award:* Freshmen: $8983. Undergraduates: $8200. *Scholarships, grants, and awards by category: Academic interests/achievement:* $4,634,779 total: computer science, general academic interests/achievements. *Creative arts/performance:* $1,390,759 total: art/fine arts, cinema/film/broadcasting, creative writing, dance, journalism/publications, music, theater/drama. *Special achievements/activities:* $873,406 total: cheerleading/drum major, community service, general special achievements/activities, leadership. *Special characteristics:* $2,371,941 total: children and siblings of alumni, children of faculty/staff, international students, local/state students, out-of-state students, religious affiliation. *Tuition waivers:* Full or partial for children of alumni, employees or children of employees, senior citizens. *ROTC:* Army cooperative.

LOANS *Student loans:* $9,112,688 (45% need-based, 55% non-need-based). 87% of past graduating class borrowed through all loan programs. *Average indebtedness per student:* $36,140. *Average need-based loan:* Freshmen: $4412. Undergraduates: $4766. *Parent loans:* $1,465,193 (100% non-need-based). *Programs:* Federal Direct (Subsidized and Unsubsidized Stafford, PLUS), Perkins, college/university, private loans.

WORK-STUDY *Federal work-study:* Total amount: $532,657; 530 jobs averaging $1020. *State or other work-study/employment:* Total amount: $589,242 (100% non-need-based). 341 part-time jobs averaging $1843.

ATHLETIC AWARDS Total amount: $2,473,342 (100% non-need-based).

APPLYING FOR FINANCIAL AID *Required financial aid form:* FAFSA. *Financial aid deadline (priority):* 3/1. *Notification date:* 3/15.

CONTACT Karen Gagnon, Director of Student Financial Planning, Morningside College, 1501 Morningside Avenue, Sioux City, IA 51106, 712-274-5272 or toll-free 800-831-0806 Ext. 5111. *Fax:* 712-274-5605. *E-mail:* gagnon@morningside.edu.
Website: http://www.morningside.edu/.

MORRIS COLLEGE
Sumter, SC

CONTACT Ms. Sandra S. Gibson, Director of Financial Aid, Morris College, 100 West College Street, Sumter, SC 29150-3599, 803-934-3238 or toll-free 866-853-1345. *Fax:* 803-773-3687.
Website: http://www.morris.edu/.

MORRISON UNIVERSITY
Reno, NV

CONTACT Kim Droniak, Financial Aid Administrator, Morrison University, 140 Washington Street, Reno, NV 89503-5600, 775-850-0700 or toll-free 866-381-6050. *Fax:* 775-850-0711.
Website: http://anthem.edu/morrison/.

MORRISVILLE STATE COLLEGE
Morrisville, NY

CONTACT Financial Aid Office, Morrisville State College, PO Box 901, Morrisville, NY 13408-0901, 315-684-6289 or toll-free 800-258-0111. *Fax:* 315-684-6628.
Website: http://www.morrisville.edu/.

MOUNT ALOYSIUS COLLEGE
Cresson, PA

Tuition & fees: N/R	Average undergraduate aid package: $13,250

ABOUT THE INSTITUTION Independent Roman Catholic, coed. *Awards:* certificates, associate, bachelor's, and master's degrees. 25 undergraduate majors. *Total enrollment:* 1,768. Undergraduates: 1,706. Freshmen: 379. Federal methodology is used as a basis for awarding need-based institutional aid.
FRESHMAN FINANCIAL AID (Fall 2012, est.) 372 applied for aid; of those 90% were deemed to have need. 100% of freshmen with need received aid. *Average percent of need met:* 30% (excluding resources awarded to replace EFC). *Average financial aid package:* $14,670 (excluding resources awarded to replace EFC). 10% of all full-time freshmen had no need and received non-need-based gift aid.
UNDERGRADUATE FINANCIAL AID (Fall 2012, est.) 1,240 applied for aid; of those 96% were deemed to have need. 100% of undergraduates with need received aid. *Average percent of need met:* 35% (excluding resources awarded to replace EFC). *Average financial aid package:* $13,250 (excluding resources awarded to replace EFC). 4% of all full-time undergraduates had no need and received non-need-based gift aid.
GIFT AID (NEED-BASED) *Total amount:* $12,441,178 (26% federal, 23% state, 50% institutional, 1% external sources). *Receiving aid:* Freshmen: 90% (334); all full-time undergraduates: 96% (1,194). *Average award:* Freshmen: $4840; Undergraduates: $4300. *Scholarships, grants, and awards:* Federal Pell, FSEOG, state, private, college/university gift aid from institutional funds.
GIFT AID (NON-NEED-BASED) *Receiving aid:* Freshmen: 10% (38). Undergraduates: 4% (46). *Average award:* Freshmen: $4860. Undergraduates: $4370. *Scholarships, grants, and awards by category:* Academic interests/achievement: 1,277 awards ($3,874,795 total): general academic interests/achievements. Creative arts/performance: 14 awards ($14,000 total): music, performing arts. Special achievements/activities: 71 awards ($670,000 total): leadership. Special characteristics: 150 awards ($137,000 total): children of current students, parents of current students, religious affiliation, siblings of current students, spouses of current students, twins.
LOANS *Student loans:* $10,755,813 (100% need-based). 91% of past graduating class borrowed through all loan programs. *Average indebtedness per student:* $33,793. *Average need-based loan:* Freshmen: $3650. Undergraduates: $4030. *Parent loans:* $3,134,769 (100% need-based). *Programs:* Federal Direct (Subsidized and Unsubsidized Stafford, PLUS), Perkins, Federal Nursing, alternative loans.
WORK-STUDY *Federal work-study:* Total amount: $323,438; 253 jobs averaging $1400.
APPLYING FOR FINANCIAL AID *Required financial aid form:* FAFSA. *Financial aid deadline (priority):* 2/15. *Notification date:* Continuous beginning 3/15. Students must reply within 2 weeks of notification.
CONTACT Mrs. Stacy L. Schenk, Director of Financial Aid, Mount Aloysius College, 7373 Admiral Peary Highway, Cresson, PA 16630-1900, 814-886-6357 or toll-free 888-823-2220. *Fax:* 814-886-6463. *E-mail:* sschenk@mtaloy.edu.
Website: http://www.mtaloy.edu/.

MOUNT ANGEL SEMINARY
Saint Benedict, OR

CONTACT Dorene Preis, Director of Student Financial Aid/Registrar, Mount Angel Seminary, 1 Abbey Drive, Saint Benedict, OR 97373, 503-845-3951. *Fax:* 503-845-3126. *E-mail:* dpreis@mtangel.edu.
Website: http://www.mountangelabbey.org/seminary/.

MOUNT CARMEL COLLEGE OF NURSING
Columbus, OH

Tuition & fees: $11,365	Average undergraduate aid package: $13,500

ABOUT THE INSTITUTION Independent, coed, primarily women. *Awards:* certificates, bachelor's, and master's degrees. 1 undergraduate major. *Total enrollment:* 1,056. Undergraduates: 886. Freshmen: 87. Federal methodology is used as a basis for awarding need-based institutional aid.
UNDERGRADUATE EXPENSES for 2013–2014 *Application fee:* $30. *One-time required fee:* $225. *Tuition:* full-time $10,633; part-time $343 per semester hour. *Required fees:* full-time $732; $276 per term. Full-time tuition and fees vary according to course level, course load, and student level. Part-time tuition and fees vary according to course level, course load, and student level.
FRESHMAN FINANCIAL AID (Fall 2012, est.) 61 applied for aid; of those 100% were deemed to have need. 100% of freshmen with need received aid. *Average percent of need met:* 45% (excluding resources awarded to replace EFC). *Average financial aid package:* $7375 (excluding resources awarded to replace EFC). 5% of all full-time freshmen had no need and received non-need-based gift aid.
UNDERGRADUATE FINANCIAL AID (Fall 2012, est.) 722 applied for aid; of those 100% were deemed to have need. 100% of undergraduates with need received aid. *Average percent of need met:* 65% (excluding resources awarded to replace EFC). *Average financial aid package:* $13,500 (excluding resources awarded to replace EFC). 1% of all full-time undergraduates had no need and received non-need-based gift aid.
GIFT AID (NEED-BASED) *Total amount:* $1,263,204 (71% federal, 23% state, 6% external sources). *Receiving aid:* Freshmen: 17% (15); all full-time undergraduates: 30% (235). *Average award:* Freshmen: $1200; Undergraduates: $1700. *Scholarships, grants, and awards:* Federal Pell, FSEOG, state, private, college/university gift aid from institutional funds.
GIFT AID (NON-NEED-BASED) *Total amount:* $551,075 (1% state, 99% institutional). *Receiving aid:* Freshmen: 37% (32). Undergraduates: 20% (157). *Average award:* Freshmen: $1600. Undergraduates: $2300. *Scholarships, grants, and awards by category:* Academic interests/achievement: 147 awards ($305,500 total): general academic interests/achievements. Special achievements/activities: 3 awards ($3000 total): community service. Special characteristics: 4 awards ($4000 total): children of faculty/staff, members of minority groups. *Tuition waivers:* Full or partial for employees or children of employees. *ROTC:* Army cooperative, Naval cooperative, Air Force cooperative.
LOANS *Student loans:* $6,425,443 (41% need-based, 59% non-need-based). 91% of past graduating class borrowed through all loan programs. *Average indebtedness per student:* $8985. *Average need-based loan:* Freshmen: $3500. Undergraduates: $4427. *Parent loans:* $1,369,314 (100% non-need-based). *Programs:* Federal Direct (Subsidized and Unsubsidized Stafford, PLUS), Federal Nursing, college/university.
WORK-STUDY *State or other work-study/employment:* Total amount: $50,987 (100% need-based). Part-time jobs available.
APPLYING FOR FINANCIAL AID *Required financial aid form:* FAFSA. *Financial aid deadline:* Continuous. *Notification date:* Continuous beginning 5/1. Students must reply within 2 weeks of notification.
CONTACT Alynica M. Bowen, PhD, Director of Financial Aid, Mount Carmel College of Nursing, 127 South Davis Avenue, Columbus, OH 43222, 614-234-5800 Ext. 5177 or toll-free 800-556-6942. *Fax:* 614-234-5427. *E-mail:* abowen@mccn.edu.
Website: http://www.mccn.edu/.

MOUNT HOLYOKE COLLEGE
South Hadley, MA

Tuition & fees: $41,456	Average undergraduate aid package: $35,643

ABOUT THE INSTITUTION Independent, women only. *Awards:* certificates, bachelor's, and master's degrees. 50 undergraduate majors. *Total enrollment:* 2,344. Undergraduates: 2,322. Freshmen: 496. Institutional methodology is used as a basis for awarding need-based institutional aid.

UNDERGRADUATE EXPENSES for 2013–2014 *Application fee:* $60. *Comprehensive fee:* $53,596 includes full-time tuition ($41,270), mandatory fees ($186), and room and board ($12,140). *College room only:* $5940. *Part-time tuition:* $1290 per credit hour. *Payment plan:* Tuition prepayment.

FRESHMAN FINANCIAL AID (Fall 2012, est.) 362 applied for aid; of those 83% were deemed to have need. 100% of freshmen with need received aid; of those 100% had need fully met. *Average percent of need met:* 100% (excluding resources awarded to replace EFC). *Average financial aid package:* $31,846 (excluding resources awarded to replace EFC). 16% of all full-time freshmen had no need and received non-need-based gift aid.

UNDERGRADUATE FINANCIAL AID (Fall 2012, est.) 1,774 applied for aid; of those 93% were deemed to have need. 100% of undergraduates with need received aid; of those 100% had need fully met. *Average percent of need met:* 100% (excluding resources awarded to replace EFC). *Average financial aid package:* $35,643 (excluding resources awarded to replace EFC). 13% of all full-time undergraduates had no need and received non-need-based gift aid.

GIFT AID (NEED-BASED) Total amount: $48,216,432 (5% federal, 1% state, 91% institutional, 3% external sources). *Receiving aid:* Freshmen: 59% (294); all full-time undergraduates: 68% (1,609). *Average award:* Freshmen: $28,248; Undergraduates: $30,163. *Scholarships, grants, and awards:* Federal Pell, FSEOG, state, private, college/university gift aid from institutional funds.

GIFT AID (NON-NEED-BASED) Total amount: $6,286,019 (91% institutional, 9% external sources). *Average award:* Freshmen: $15,756. Undergraduates: $16,222. *Scholarships, grants, and awards by category: Academic interests/achievement:* general academic interests/achievements. *Special characteristics:* general special characteristics. *Tuition waivers:* Full or partial for employees or children of employees. *ROTC:* Army cooperative, Air Force cooperative.

LOANS Student loans: $10,200,472 (88% need-based, 12% non-need-based). 65% of past graduating class borrowed through all loan programs. *Average indebtedness per student:* $22,691. *Average need-based loan:* Freshmen: $3580. Undergraduates: $5042. *Parent loans:* $4,652,862 (100% non-need-based). *Programs:* Federal Direct (Subsidized and Unsubsidized Stafford, PLUS), Perkins, college/university.

WORK-STUDY Federal work-study: Total amount: $1,713,846; 912 jobs averaging $1806. *State or other work-study/employment:* Total amount: $810,710 (100% need-based). 432 part-time jobs averaging $1851.

APPLYING FOR FINANCIAL AID *Required financial aid forms:* FAFSA, CSS Financial Aid PROFILE, noncustodial (divorced/separated) parent's statement, federal income tax form(s), W-2 forms. *Financial aid deadline:* 3/1 (priority: 2/15). *Notification date:* 4/1. Students must reply by 5/1.

CONTACT Ms. Kathryn Blaisdell, Director of Student Financial Services, Mount Holyoke College, 50 College Street, South Hadley, MA 01075-1492, 413-538-2291. *Fax:* 413-538-2512. *E-mail:* kblaisde@mtholyoke.edu. *Website:* http://www.mtholyoke.edu/.

MOUNT IDA COLLEGE
Newton, MA

CONTACT David L. Goldman, Director of Financial Aid, Mount Ida College, 777 Dedham Street, Newton, MA 02459-3310, 617-928-4785. *Fax:* 617-332-7869. *E-mail:* finaid@mountida.edu. *Website:* http://www.mountida.edu/.

MOUNT MARTY COLLEGE
Yankton, SD

Tuition & fees: $22,130	Average undergraduate aid package: $22,375

ABOUT THE INSTITUTION Independent Roman Catholic, coed. *Awards:* certificates, associate, bachelor's, and master's degrees. 32 undergraduate majors. *Total enrollment:* 1,178. Undergraduates: 1,036. Freshmen: 116. Federal methodology is used as a basis for awarding need-based institutional aid.

UNDERGRADUATE EXPENSES for 2013–2014 *Application fee:* $35. *Comprehensive fee:* $28,520 includes full-time tuition ($20,300), mandatory fees ($1830), and room and board ($6390). Full-time tuition and fees vary according to location. Room and board charges vary according to board plan. *Part-time tuition:* $325 per credit hour. Part-time tuition and fees vary according to course load and location.

FRESHMAN FINANCIAL AID (Fall 2012, est.) 100 applied for aid; of those 100% were deemed to have need. 100% of freshmen with need received aid; of those 48% had need fully met. *Average percent of need met:* 89% (excluding resources awarded to replace EFC). *Average financial aid package:* $24,523 (excluding resources awarded to replace EFC). 4% of all full-time freshmen had no need and received non-need-based gift aid.

UNDERGRADUATE FINANCIAL AID (Fall 2012, est.) 508 applied for aid; of those 91% were deemed to have need. 99% of undergraduates with need received aid; of those 36% had need fully met. *Average percent of need met:* 85% (excluding resources awarded to replace EFC). *Average financial aid package:* $22,375 (excluding resources awarded to replace EFC). 3% of all full-time undergraduates had no need and received non-need-based gift aid.

GIFT AID (NEED-BASED) Total amount: $5,071,142 (28% federal, 1% state, 67% institutional, 4% external sources). *Receiving aid:* Freshmen: 100% (100); all full-time undergraduates: 84% (457). *Average award:* Freshmen: $6129; Undergraduates: $5741. *Scholarships, grants, and awards:* Federal Pell, FSEOG, state, private, college/university gift aid from institutional funds.

GIFT AID (NON-NEED-BASED) Total amount: $197,250 (2% federal, 3% state, 93% institutional, 2% external sources). *Average award:* Freshmen: $11,400. Undergraduates: $7547. *Scholarships, grants, and awards by category: Academic interests/achievement:* 378 awards ($2,376,159 total): general academic interests/achievements. *Creative arts/performance:* 42 awards ($56,335 total): music, theater/drama. *Special characteristics:* children of current students, children of faculty/staff, international students, parents of current students, religious affiliation, siblings of current students, spouses of current students. *Tuition waivers:* Full or partial for employees or children of employees. *ROTC:* Army cooperative.

LOANS Student loans: $2,730,755 (99% need-based, 1% non-need-based). 88% of past graduating class borrowed through all loan programs. *Average indebtedness per student:* $32,369. *Average need-based loan:* Freshmen: $3704. Undergraduates: $4836. *Parent loans:* $700,699 (94% need-based, 6% non-need-based). *Programs:* Federal Direct (Subsidized and Unsubsidized Stafford, PLUS), Perkins, Federal Nursing, state, college/university.

WORK-STUDY Federal work-study: Total amount: $311,235; 206 jobs averaging $1478. *State or other work-study/employment:* Total amount: $70,500 (72% need-based, 28% non-need-based). 31 part-time jobs averaging $1500.

ATHLETIC AWARDS Total amount: $741,803 (91% need-based, 9% non-need-based).

APPLYING FOR FINANCIAL AID *Required financial aid forms:* FAFSA, institution's own form. *Financial aid deadline (priority):* 3/1. *Notification date:* Continuous beginning 3/15. Students must reply within 2 weeks of notification.

CONTACT Mr. Ken Kocer, Director of Financial Assistance, Mount Marty College, 1105 West 8th Street, Yankton, SD 57078-3724, 605-668-1589 or toll-free 800-658-4552. *Fax:* 605-668-1585. *E-mail:* kkocer@mtmc.edu. *Website:* http://www.mtmc.edu/.

MOUNT MARY COLLEGE
Milwaukee, WI

Tuition & fees: $25,098	Average undergraduate aid package: $19,595

ABOUT THE INSTITUTION Independent Roman Catholic, undergraduate: women only; graduate: coed. *Awards:* certificates, bachelor's, master's, and doctoral degrees. 58 undergraduate majors. *Total enrollment:* 1,640. Undergraduates: 1,054. Freshmen: 95. Federal methodology is used as a basis for awarding need-based institutional aid.

UNDERGRADUATE EXPENSES for 2013–2014 *Comprehensive fee:* $32,836 includes full-time tuition ($24,598), mandatory fees ($500), and room and board ($7738). Full-time tuition and fees vary according to program. Room and board charges vary according to board plan. *Part-time tuition:* $746 per credit. *Part-time fees:* $310 per year. Part-time tuition and fees vary according to course load and program.

FRESHMAN FINANCIAL AID (Fall 2012, est.) 90 applied for aid; of those 98% were deemed to have need. 100% of freshmen with need received aid; of those 15% had need fully met. *Average percent of need met:* 79% (excluding resources awarded to replace EFC). *Average financial aid package:* $23,232 (excluding resources awarded to replace EFC). 6% of all full-time freshmen had no need and received non-need-based gift aid.

UNDERGRADUATE FINANCIAL AID (Fall 2012, est.) 690 applied for aid; of those 96% were deemed to have need. 100% of undergraduates with need received aid; of those 7% had need fully met. *Average percent of need met:* 68% (excluding resources awarded to replace EFC). *Average financial aid package:* $19,595 (excluding resources awarded to replace EFC). 10% of all full-time undergraduates had no need and received non-need-based gift aid.

GIFT AID (NEED-BASED) *Total amount:* $10,187,537 (22% federal, 13% state, 64% institutional, 1% external sources). *Receiving aid:* Freshmen: 93% (88); all full-time undergraduates: 91% (659). *Average award:* Freshmen: $19,701; Undergraduates: $14,767. *Scholarships, grants, and awards:* Federal Pell, FSEOG, state, private, college/university gift aid from institutional funds.

GIFT AID (NON-NEED-BASED) *Total amount:* $825,538 (1% state, 96% institutional, 3% external sources). *Receiving aid:* Freshmen: 9% (9). Undergraduates: 5% (34). *Average award:* Freshmen: $11,099. Undergraduates: $8053. *Scholarships, grants, and awards by category:* Academic interests/achievement: 691 awards ($3,675,607 total): business, communication, education, English, general academic interests/achievements, health fields, home economics, humanities, mathematics, physical sciences, social sciences. Creative arts/performance: 41 awards ($126,075 total): applied art and design, art/fine arts, music. Special achievements/activities: 15 awards ($84,306 total): general special achievements/activities, leadership. Special characteristics: 24 awards ($254,614 total): children of faculty/staff, international students, parents of current students, siblings of current students. *Tuition waivers:* Full or partial for employees or children of employees, senior citizens. *ROTC:* Army cooperative, Naval cooperative.

LOANS *Student loans:* $7,229,392 (88% need-based, 12% non-need-based). 85% of past graduating class borrowed through all loan programs. *Average indebtedness per student:* $29,618. *Average need-based loan:* Freshmen: $3012. Undergraduates: $4620. *Parent loans:* $384,501 (43% need-based, 57% non-need-based). *Programs:* Federal Direct (Subsidized and Unsubsidized Stafford, PLUS), Perkins, state.

WORK-STUDY *Federal work-study:* Total amount: $145,757; 115 jobs averaging $1261. *State or other work-study/employment:* Total amount: $142,943 (100% non-need-based). 72 part-time jobs averaging $1985.

APPLYING FOR FINANCIAL AID *Required financial aid form:* FAFSA. *Financial aid deadline (priority):* 3/1. *Notification date:* Continuous. Students must reply within 2 weeks of notification.

CONTACT Debra Duff, Director of Financial Aid, Mount Mary College, 2900 North Menomonee River Parkway, Milwaukee, WI 53222-4597, 414-256-1258 or toll-free 800-321-6265. *Fax:* 414-443-3602. *E-mail:* finaid@mtmary.edu. *Website:* http://www.mtmary.edu/.

MOUNT MERCY UNIVERSITY
Cedar Rapids, IA

Tuition & fees: $26,310	Average undergraduate aid package: $16,281

ABOUT THE INSTITUTION Independent Roman Catholic, coed. *Awards:* bachelor's and master's degrees. 42 undergraduate majors. *Total enrollment:* 1,810. Undergraduates: 1,513. Freshmen: 158. Federal methodology is used as a basis for awarding need-based institutional aid.

UNDERGRADUATE EXPENSES for 2013–2014 *Comprehensive fee:* $34,385 includes full-time tuition ($26,160), mandatory fees ($150), and room and board ($8075). Full-time tuition and fees vary according to course load. Room and board charges vary according to board plan and housing facility. *Part-time tuition:* $710 per semester hour. *Part-time fees:* $150 per year. Part-time tuition and fees vary according to course load.

FRESHMAN FINANCIAL AID (Fall 2011) 142 applied for aid; of those 92% were deemed to have need. 100% of freshmen with need received aid; of those 19% had need fully met. *Average percent of need met:* 70% (excluding resources awarded to replace EFC). *Average financial aid package:* $18,386 (excluding resources awarded to replace EFC). 14% of all full-time freshmen had no need and received non-need-based gift aid.

UNDERGRADUATE FINANCIAL AID (Fall 2011) 986 applied for aid; of those 92% were deemed to have need. 98% of undergraduates with need received aid; of those 14% had need fully met. *Average percent of need met:* 67% (excluding resources awarded to replace EFC). *Average financial aid package:* $16,281 (excluding resources awarded to replace EFC). 11% of all full-time undergraduates had no need and received non-need-based gift aid.

GIFT AID (NEED-BASED) *Total amount:* $11,898,910 (17% federal, 21% state, 56% institutional, 6% external sources). *Receiving aid:* Freshmen: 85% (131); all full-time undergraduates: 70% (881). *Average award:* Freshmen: $15,180; Undergraduates: $12,207. *Scholarships, grants, and awards:* Federal Pell, FSEOG, state, private, college/university gift aid from institutional funds.

GIFT AID (NON-NEED-BASED) *Total amount:* $1,826,173 (1% federal, 1% state, 88% institutional, 10% external sources). *Receiving aid:* Freshmen: 12% (19). Undergraduates: 7% (93). *Average award:* Freshmen: $9491. Undergraduates: $8708. *Scholarships, grants, and awards by category:* Academic interests/achievement: 1,249 awards ($6,654,499 total): general academic interests/achievements. Creative arts/performance: 53 awards ($63,900 total): art/fine arts, music, theater/drama. Special achievements/activities: 91 awards ($67,750 total): leadership. Special characteristics: 19 awards ($13,250 total): previous college experience. *Tuition waivers:* Full or partial for employees or children of employees.

LOANS *Student loans:* $10,594,345 (78% need-based, 22% non-need-based). 77% of past graduating class borrowed through all loan programs. *Average indebtedness per student:* $28,900. *Average need-based loan:* Freshmen: $3225. Undergraduates: $4451. *Parent loans:* $2,254,745 (50% need-based, 50% non-need-based). *Programs:* Federal Direct (Subsidized and Unsubsidized Stafford, PLUS), Perkins, state, college/university.

WORK-STUDY *Federal work-study:* Total amount: $366,410; 262 jobs averaging $1398. *State or other work-study/employment:* Total amount: $224,549 (100% non-need-based). 225 part-time jobs averaging $998.

ATHLETIC AWARDS Total amount: $890,322 (63% need-based, 37% non-need-based).

APPLYING FOR FINANCIAL AID *Required financial aid form:* FAFSA. *Financial aid deadline (priority):* 3/1. *Notification date:* Continuous beginning 3/15. Students must reply by 5/1 or within 3 weeks of notification.

CONTACT Bethany Rinderknecht, Director of Financial Aid, Mount Mercy University, 1330 Elmhurst Drive NE, Cedar Rapids, IA 52402-4797, 319-368-6467 Ext. 1545 or toll-free 800-248-4504. *Fax:* 319-364-3546. *E-mail:* brinderknecht@mtmercy.edu. *Website:* http://www.mtmercy.edu/.

MOUNT OLIVE COLLEGE
Mount Olive, NC

Tuition & fees: N/R	Average undergraduate aid package: $11,424

ABOUT THE INSTITUTION Independent Free Will Baptist, coed. 24 undergraduate majors. Federal methodology is used as a basis for awarding need-based institutional aid.

FRESHMAN FINANCIAL AID (Fall 2011) 219 applied for aid; of those 90% were deemed to have need. 100% of freshmen with need received aid; of those 14% had need fully met. *Average percent of need met:* 73% (excluding resources awarded to replace EFC). *Average financial aid package:* $14,333 (excluding resources awarded to replace EFC). 2% of all full-time freshmen had no need and received non-need-based gift aid.

UNDERGRADUATE FINANCIAL AID (Fall 2011) 1,486 applied for aid; of those 90% were deemed to have need. 99% of undergraduates with need received aid; of those 10% had need fully met. *Average percent of need met:* 62% (excluding resources awarded to replace EFC). *Average financial aid package:* $11,424 (excluding resources awarded to replace EFC). 1% of all full-time undergraduates had no need and received non-need-based gift aid.

GIFT AID (NEED-BASED) *Total amount:* $15,272,697 (51% federal, 37% state, 1% institutional, 11% external sources). *Receiving aid:* Freshmen: 81% (196); all full-time undergraduates: 74% (1,254). *Average award:* Freshmen: $11,963; Undergraduates: $8846. *Scholarships, grants, and awards:* Federal Pell, FSEOG, state, private, college/university gift aid from institutional funds.

GIFT AID (NON-NEED-BASED) *Total amount:* $1,292,113 (30% state, 4% institutional, 66% external sources). *Receiving aid:* Freshmen: 8% (20). Undergraduates: 5% (86). *Average award:* Freshmen: $2448. Undergraduates: $2077. *Scholarships, grants, and awards by category:* Academic interests/achievement: general academic interests/achievements. *Creative arts/performance:* general creative arts/performance. *Special achievements/activities:* cheerleading/drum major, leadership, religious involvement. *Special characteristics:* children of faculty/staff, religious affiliation, veterans, veterans' children.

LOANS *Student loans:* $22,068,988 (86% need-based, 14% non-need-based). 82% of past graduating class borrowed through all loan programs. *Average indebtedness per student:* $28,201. *Average need-based loan:* Freshmen: $2967. Undergraduates: $3669. *Parent loans:* $549,797 (50% need-based, 50% non-need-based). *Programs:* Federal Direct (Subsidized and Unsubsidized Stafford, PLUS), Perkins, state.

WORK-STUDY *Federal work-study:* Total amount: $122,506; jobs available.

ATHLETIC AWARDS Total amount: $1,204,888 (65% need-based, 35% non-need-based).

APPLYING FOR FINANCIAL AID *Required financial aid forms:* FAFSA, state aid form. *Financial aid deadline:* Continuous. *Notification date:* Continuous beginning 3/1. Students must reply within 2 weeks of notification.

CONTACT Mrs. Katrina K. Lee, Director of Financial Aid, Mount Olive College, 634 Henderson Street, Mount Olive, NC 28365, 919-658-2502 or toll-free 800-653-0854. *Fax:* 919-658-9816. *E-mail:* klee@moc.edu. *Website:* http://www.moc.edu/.

MOUNT SAINT MARY COLLEGE
Newburgh, NY

Tuition & fees: $26,250	Average undergraduate aid package: $15,564

ABOUT THE INSTITUTION Independent, coed. *Awards:* certificates, bachelor's, and master's degrees. 25 undergraduate majors. *Total enrollment:* 2,581. Undergraduates: 2,286. Freshmen: 442. Federal methodology is used as a basis for awarding need-based institutional aid.

UNDERGRADUATE EXPENSES for 2013–2014 *Application fee:* $45. *Comprehensive fee:* $39,540 includes full-time tuition ($25,300), mandatory fees ($950), and room and board ($13,290). *College room only:* $7698. Full-time tuition and fees vary according to class time, location, and program. Room and board charges vary according to board plan and housing facility. *Part-time tuition:* $843 per credit hour. Part-time tuition and fees vary according to class time, location, and program.

FRESHMAN FINANCIAL AID (Fall 2012, est.) 430 applied for aid; of those 88% were deemed to have need. 100% of freshmen with need received aid; of those 20% had need fully met. *Average percent of need met:* 64% (excluding resources awarded to replace EFC). *Average financial aid package:* $16,818 (excluding resources awarded to replace EFC). 15% of all full-time freshmen had no need and received non-need-based gift aid.

UNDERGRADUATE FINANCIAL AID (Fall 2012, est.) 1,705 applied for aid; of those 88% were deemed to have need. 100% of undergraduates with need received aid; of those 18% had need fully met. *Average percent of need met:* 60% (excluding resources awarded to replace EFC). *Average financial aid package:* $15,564 (excluding resources awarded to replace EFC). 12% of all full-time undergraduates had no need and received non-need-based gift aid.

GIFT AID (NEED-BASED) *Total amount:* $17,292,734 (19% federal, 13% state, 65% institutional, 3% external sources). *Receiving aid:* Freshmen: 85% (377); all full-time undergraduates: 78% (1,449). *Average award:* Freshmen: $13,424; Undergraduates: $11,839. *Scholarships, grants, and awards:* Federal Pell, FSEOG, state, private, college/university gift aid from institutional funds, Federal Nursing, Academic Competitiveness Grants, National SMART Grants.

GIFT AID (NON-NEED-BASED) *Total amount:* $2,956,508 (10% state, 85% institutional, 5% external sources). *Receiving aid:* Freshmen: 13% (58). Undergraduates: 9% (162). *Average award:* Freshmen: $7845. Undergraduates: $8243. *Scholarships, grants, and awards by category:* Academic interests/achievement: 1,063 awards ($7,256,074 total): general academic interests/achievements. *Special achievements/activities:* 12 awards ($55,000 total): leadership. *Special characteristics:* 46 awards ($800,309 total): children of faculty/staff. *Tuition waivers:* Full or partial for employees or children of employees. *ROTC:* Army cooperative.

LOANS *Student loans:* $18,466,405 (73% need-based, 27% non-need-based). 81% of past graduating class borrowed through all loan programs. *Average indebtedness per student:* $28,716. *Average need-based loan:* Freshmen: $3193. Undergraduates: $4269. *Parent loans:* $22,141,351 (36% need-based, 64% non-need-based). *Programs:* Federal Direct (Subsidized and Unsubsidized Stafford, PLUS), Perkins, Federal Nursing.

WORK-STUDY *Federal work-study:* Total amount: $506,500; 273 jobs averaging $1396. *State or other work-study/employment:* Part-time jobs available.

APPLYING FOR FINANCIAL AID *Required financial aid form:* FAFSA. *Financial aid deadline:* 3/1 (priority: 2/15). *Notification date:* Continuous beginning 3/15. Students must reply by 5/1.

CONTACT Barbara Winchell, Director of Financial Aid, Mount Saint Mary College, 330 Powell Avenue, Newburgh, NY 12550-3494, 845-561-3298 or toll-free 888-937-6762. *Fax:* 845-569-3302. *E-mail:* barbara.winchell@msmc.edu. *Website:* http://www.msmc.edu/.

MOUNT ST. MARY'S COLLEGE
Los Angeles, CA

Tuition & fees: $33,852	Average undergraduate aid package: $27,615

ABOUT THE INSTITUTION Independent Roman Catholic, coed, primarily women. *Awards:* certificates, associate, bachelor's, master's, and doctoral degrees. 39 undergraduate majors. *Total enrollment:* 3,146. Undergraduates: 2,458. Freshmen: 535. Both federal and institutional methodology are used as a basis for awarding need-based institutional aid.

UNDERGRADUATE EXPENSES for 2013–2014 *Application fee:* $50. *Comprehensive fee:* $44,382 includes full-time tuition ($32,882), mandatory fees ($970), and room and board ($10,530). *College room only:* $6318. Full-time tuition and fees vary according to course load, degree level, and program. Room and board charges vary according to board plan and housing facility. *Part-time tuition:* $1370 per unit. Part-time tuition and fees vary according to course load, degree level, and program.

FRESHMAN FINANCIAL AID (Fall 2011) 517 applied for aid; of those 97% were deemed to have need. 100% of freshmen with need received aid; of those 6% had need fully met. *Average percent of need met:* 73% (excluding resources awarded to replace EFC). *Average financial aid package:* $28,106 (excluding resources awarded to replace EFC). 5% of all full-time freshmen had no need and received non-need-based gift aid.

UNDERGRADUATE FINANCIAL AID (Fall 2011) 1,832 applied for aid; of those 97% were deemed to have need. 99% of undergraduates with need received aid;

of those 5% had need fully met. *Average percent of need met:* 69% (excluding resources awarded to replace EFC). *Average financial aid package:* $27,615 (excluding resources awarded to replace EFC). 2% of all full-time undergraduates had no need and received non-need-based gift aid.

GIFT AID (NEED-BASED) *Total amount:* $37,081,372 (17% federal, 24% state, 59% institutional). *Receiving aid:* Freshmen: 95% (503); all full-time undergraduates: 88% (1,686). *Average award:* Freshmen: $23,110; Undergraduates: $21,066. *Scholarships, grants, and awards:* Federal Pell, FSEOG, state, private, college/university gift aid from institutional funds.

GIFT AID (NON-NEED-BASED) *Total amount:* $443,162 (49% institutional, 51% external sources). *Receiving aid:* Freshmen: 2% (13). Undergraduates: 2% (48). *Average award:* Freshmen: $13,600. Undergraduates: $11,911. *Scholarships, grants, and awards by category: Academic interests/achievement:* general academic interests/achievements. *Creative arts/performance:* music. *Special achievements/activities:* community service, leadership. *Special characteristics:* children and siblings of alumni. *Tuition waivers:* Full or partial for employees or children of employees.

LOANS *Student loans:* $13,343,669 (51% need-based, 49% non-need-based). 83% of past graduating class borrowed through all loan programs. *Average indebtedness per student:* $34,998. *Average need-based loan:* Freshmen: $3012. Undergraduates: $4632. *Parent loans:* $3,424,504 (100% non-need-based). *Programs:* Federal Direct (Subsidized and Unsubsidized Stafford, PLUS), Federal Nursing, college/university.

WORK-STUDY *Federal work-study:* Total amount: $1,140,150; jobs available. *State or other work-study/employment:* Part-time jobs available.

APPLYING FOR FINANCIAL AID *Required financial aid forms:* FAFSA, institution's own form. *Financial aid deadline:* Continuous. *Notification date:* Continuous beginning 3/1. Students must reply by 5/1.

CONTACT La Royce Housley, Director of Financial Aid, Mount St. Mary's College, 12001 Chalon Road, Los Angeles, CA 90049, 310-954-4192 or toll-free 800-999-9893. *Website:* http://www.msmc.la.edu/.

MOUNT ST. MARY'S UNIVERSITY
Emmitsburg, MD

Tuition & fees: $32,954	Average undergraduate aid package: $22,587

ABOUT THE INSTITUTION Independent Roman Catholic, coed. *Awards:* certificates, bachelor's, and master's degrees. 28 undergraduate majors. *Total enrollment:* 2,350. Undergraduates: 1,842. Freshmen: 447. Federal methodology is used as a basis for awarding need-based institutional aid.

UNDERGRADUATE EXPENSES for 2013–2014 *Application fee:* $45. *Comprehensive fee:* $43,972 includes full-time tuition ($32,224), mandatory fees ($730), and room and board ($11,018). *College room only:* $5392. Full-time tuition and fees vary according to location and program. Room and board charges vary according to board plan. *Part-time tuition:* $1076 per credit hour. Part-time tuition and fees vary according to location and program.

FRESHMAN FINANCIAL AID (Fall 2012, est.) 385 applied for aid; of those 86% were deemed to have need. 100% of freshmen with need received aid; of those 28% had need fully met. *Average percent of need met:* 78% (excluding resources awarded to replace EFC). *Average financial aid package:* $23,790 (excluding resources awarded to replace EFC). 25% of all full-time freshmen had no need and received non-need-based gift aid.

UNDERGRADUATE FINANCIAL AID (Fall 2012, est.) 1,406 applied for aid; of those 89% were deemed to have need. 100% of undergraduates with need received aid; of those 22% had need fully met. *Average percent of need met:* 72% (excluding resources awarded to replace EFC). *Average financial aid package:* $22,587 (excluding resources awarded to replace EFC). 25% of all full-time undergraduates had no need and received non-need-based gift aid.

GIFT AID (NEED-BASED) *Total amount:* $20,760,249 (10% federal, 5% state, 82% institutional, 3% external sources). *Receiving aid:* Freshmen: 74% (331); all full-time undergraduates: 71% (1,243). *Average award:* Freshmen: $19,453; Undergraduates: $18,245. *Scholarships, grants, and awards:* Federal Pell, FSEOG, state, private, college/university gift aid from institutional funds.

GIFT AID (NON-NEED-BASED) *Total amount:* $7,609,858 (3% federal, 1% state, 89% institutional, 7% external sources). *Receiving aid:* Freshmen: 15% (69). Undergraduates: 11% (197). *Average award:* Freshmen: $15,073. Undergraduates:

$13,462. *Scholarships, grants, and awards by category: Academic interests/achievement:* 1,571 awards ($18,553,049 total): general academic interests/achievements. *Creative arts/performance:* 22 awards ($43,000 total): art/fine arts. *Special characteristics:* 473 awards ($1,765,304 total): children of educators, children of faculty/staff, members of minority groups, siblings of current students. *Tuition waivers:* Full or partial for employees or children of employees. *ROTC:* Army cooperative.

LOANS *Student loans:* $12,173,693 (65% need-based, 35% non-need-based). 70% of past graduating class borrowed through all loan programs. *Average indebtedness per student:* $32,311. *Average need-based loan:* Freshmen: $4202. Undergraduates: $4571. *Parent loans:* $5,029,882 (38% need-based, 62% non-need-based). *Programs:* Federal Direct (Subsidized and Unsubsidized Stafford, PLUS), Perkins.

WORK-STUDY *Federal work-study:* Total amount: $200,000; 121 jobs averaging $1559. *State or other work-study/employment:* Total amount: $646,728 (83% need-based, 17% non-need-based). 528 part-time jobs averaging $1181.

ATHLETIC AWARDS Total amount: $2,692,324 (58% need-based, 42% non-need-based).

APPLYING FOR FINANCIAL AID *Required financial aid form:* FAFSA. *Financial aid deadline:* 3/1. *Notification date:* Continuous beginning 2/15. Students must reply by 5/1.

CONTACT Mr. David C. Reeder, Director of Financial Aid, Mount St. Mary's University, 16300 Old Emmitsburg Road, Emmitsburg, MD 21727-7799, 301-447-5207 or toll-free 800-448-4347. *Fax:* 301-447-5915. *E-mail:* reeder@msmary.edu. *Website:* http://www.msmary.edu/.

MT. SIERRA COLLEGE
Monrovia, CA

CONTACT Financial Aid Office, Mt. Sierra College, 101 East Huntington Drive, Monrovia, CA 91016, 888-828-8800 or toll-free 888-828-8000. *Website:* http://www.mtsierra.edu/.

MOUNT VERNON NAZARENE UNIVERSITY
Mount Vernon, OH

Tuition & fees: $23,690	Average undergraduate aid package: $18,609

ABOUT THE INSTITUTION Independent Nazarene, coed. *Awards:* associate, bachelor's, and master's degrees. 80 undergraduate majors. *Total enrollment:* 2,267. Undergraduates: 1,756. Freshmen: 290. Federal methodology is used as a basis for awarding need-based institutional aid.

UNDERGRADUATE EXPENSES for 2013–2014 *Application fee:* $25. *Comprehensive fee:* $30,670 includes full-time tuition ($23,690) and room and board ($6980). *College room only:* $3900. *Part-time tuition:* $658 per credit hour.

FRESHMAN FINANCIAL AID (Fall 2012, est.) 290 applied for aid; of those 93% were deemed to have need. 100% of freshmen with need received aid; of those 14% had need fully met. *Average percent of need met:* 67% (excluding resources awarded to replace EFC). *Average financial aid package:* $19,139 (excluding resources awarded to replace EFC). 3% of all full-time freshmen had no need and received non-need-based gift aid.

UNDERGRADUATE FINANCIAL AID (Fall 2012, est.) 1,333 applied for aid; of those 88% were deemed to have need. 100% of undergraduates with need received aid; of those 16% had need fully met. *Average percent of need met:* 68% (excluding resources awarded to replace EFC). *Average financial aid package:* $18,609 (excluding resources awarded to replace EFC). 4% of all full-time undergraduates had no need and received non-need-based gift aid.

GIFT AID (NEED-BASED) *Total amount:* $14,280,474 (21% federal, 6% state, 68% institutional, 5% external sources). *Receiving aid:* Freshmen: 89% (259); all full-time undergraduates: 78% (1,117). *Average award:* Freshmen: $12,604; Undergraduates: $11,449. *Scholarships, grants, and awards:* Federal Pell, FSEOG, state, private, college/university gift aid from institutional funds.

GIFT AID (NON-NEED-BASED) *Total amount:* $1,823,431 (2% federal, 10% state, 86% institutional, 2% external sources). *Receiving aid:* Freshmen: 14% (40). Undergraduates: 15% (222). *Average award:* Freshmen: $8349. Undergraduates:

$7899. *Scholarships, grants, and awards by category: Academic interests/achievement:* 927 awards ($5,196,561 total): general academic interests/achievements. *Creative arts/performance:* 54 awards ($59,530 total): art/fine arts, music. *Special achievements/activities:* 230 awards ($232,463 total): general special achievements/activities, religious involvement. *Special characteristics:* 1,001 awards ($2,751,361 total): children of faculty/staff, international students, members of minority groups, relatives of clergy, religious affiliation. *Tuition waivers:* Full or partial for employees or children of employees, senior citizens.
LOANS *Student loans:* $12,049,783 (93% need-based, 7% non-need-based). 85% of past graduating class borrowed through all loan programs. *Average indebtedness per student:* $25,462. *Average need-based loan:* Freshmen: $3256. Undergraduates: $3970. *Parent loans:* $2,492,680 (47% need-based, 53% non-need-based). *Programs:* Federal Direct (Subsidized and Unsubsidized Stafford, PLUS), Perkins, Federal Nursing, state, Schell Loans.
WORK-STUDY *Federal work-study:* Total amount: $444,895; 254 jobs averaging $1752. *State or other work-study/employment:* Total amount: $548,496 (35% need-based, 65% non-need-based). 326 part-time jobs averaging $1683.
ATHLETIC AWARDS Total amount: $793,909 (63% need-based, 37% non-need-based).
APPLYING FOR FINANCIAL AID *Required financial aid form:* FAFSA. *Financial aid deadline (priority):* 3/15. *Notification date:* Continuous beginning 3/1.
CONTACT Mary V. Cannon, Director of Student Financial Services, Mount Vernon Nazarene University, 800 Martinsburg Road, Mount Vernon, OH 43050-9500, 866-686-8243 or toll-free 866-462-6868. *Fax:* 740-399-8682. *E-mail:* finaid@mvnu.edu. *Website:* http://www.mvnu.edu/.

MUHLENBERG COLLEGE
Allentown, PA

Tuition & fees: $41,510	Average undergraduate aid package: $26,328

ABOUT THE INSTITUTION Independent Lutheran Church, coed. *Awards:* certificates, associate, and bachelor's degrees. 33 undergraduate majors. *Total enrollment:* 2,422. Undergraduates: 2,422. Freshmen: 581. Institutional methodology is used as a basis for awarding need-based institutional aid.
UNDERGRADUATE EXPENSES for 2013–2014 *Application fee:* $50. *Comprehensive fee:* $52,650 includes full-time tuition ($41,225), mandatory fees ($285), and room and board ($11,140). *College room only:* $7175. Room and board charges vary according to board plan, housing facility, and location. Part-time tuition and fees vary according to program.
FRESHMAN FINANCIAL AID (Fall 2012, est.) 417 applied for aid; of those 71% were deemed to have need. 100% of freshmen with need received aid; of those 87% had need fully met. *Average percent of need met:* 92% (excluding resources awarded to replace EFC). *Average financial aid package:* $26,110 (excluding resources awarded to replace EFC). 33% of all full-time freshmen had no need and received non-need-based gift aid.
UNDERGRADUATE FINANCIAL AID (Fall 2012, est.) 1,460 applied for aid; of those 83% were deemed to have need. 95% of undergraduates with need received aid; of those 91% had need fully met. *Average percent of need met:* 93% (excluding resources awarded to replace EFC). *Average financial aid package:* $26,328 (excluding resources awarded to replace EFC). 30% of all full-time undergraduates had no need and received non-need-based gift aid.
GIFT AID (NEED-BASED) *Total amount:* $27,494,187 (5% federal, 2% state, 91% institutional, 2% external sources). *Receiving aid:* Freshmen: 51% (294); all full-time undergraduates: 48% (1,104). *Average award:* Freshmen: $23,105; Undergraduates: $23,328. *Scholarships, grants, and awards:* Federal Pell, FSEOG, state, private, college/university gift aid from institutional funds, United Negro College Fund.
GIFT AID (NON-NEED-BASED) *Total amount:* $9,202,365 (97% institutional, 3% external sources). *Receiving aid:* Freshmen: 14% (81). Undergraduates: 11% (244). *Average award:* Freshmen: $9858. Undergraduates: $10,756. *Scholarships, grants, and awards by category: Academic interests/achievement:* general academic interests/achievements. *Creative arts/performance:* art/fine arts, general creative arts/performance. *Special achievements/activities:* leadership. *Tuition waivers:* Full or partial for employees or children of employees. *ROTC:* Army cooperative.
LOANS *Student loans:* $9,877,522 (52% need-based, 48% non-need-based). 65% of past graduating class borrowed through all loan programs. *Average indebtedness*

per student: $25,858. *Average need-based loan:* Freshmen: $3694. Undergraduates: $4405. *Parent loans:* $3,702,143 (16% need-based, 84% non-need-based). *Programs:* Federal Direct (Subsidized and Unsubsidized Stafford, PLUS), Perkins.
WORK-STUDY *Federal work-study:* Total amount: $220,000; jobs available. *State or other work-study/employment:* Total amount: $175,000 (14% need-based, 86% non-need-based). Part-time jobs available.
APPLYING FOR FINANCIAL AID *Required financial aid forms:* FAFSA, institution's own form, CSS Financial Aid PROFILE, noncustodial (divorced/separated) parent's statement, business/farm supplement. *Financial aid deadline:* 2/15. *Notification date:* 3/20. Students must reply by 5/1.
CONTACT Mr. Greg Mitton, Director of Financial Aid, Muhlenberg College, 2400 Chew Street, Allentown, PA 18104-5586, 484-664-3175. *Fax:* 484-664-3234. *E-mail:* mitton@muhlenberg.edu. *Website:* http://www.muhlenberg.edu/.

MULTNOMAH UNIVERSITY
Portland, OR

CONTACT Mrs. Mary J. McGlothlan, Director of Financial Aid, Multnomah University, 8435 NE Glisan Street, Portland, OR 97220-5898, 503-251-5337 or toll-free 877-251-6560. *Fax:* 503-445-5199. *E-mail:* mmcglothlan@multnomah.edu. *Website:* http://www.multnomah.edu/.

MURRAY STATE UNIVERSITY
Murray, KY

Tuition & fees (KY res): $6840	Average undergraduate aid package: $10,810

ABOUT THE INSTITUTION State-supported, coed. *Awards:* certificates, associate, bachelor's, master's, and doctoral degrees. 67 undergraduate majors. *Total enrollment:* 10,832. Undergraduates: 8,891. Freshmen: 1,626. Federal methodology is used as a basis for awarding need-based institutional aid.
UNDERGRADUATE EXPENSES for 2013–2014 *Application fee:* $30. *Tuition, state resident:* full-time $5880; part-time $285 per credit hour. *Tuition, nonresident:* full-time $7942; part-time $369 per credit hour. *Required fees:* full-time $960. Full-time tuition and fees vary according to reciprocity agreements. Part-time tuition and fees vary according to reciprocity agreements. *College room and board:* $7638; *Room only:* $4430. Room and board charges vary according to board plan and housing facility.
FRESHMAN FINANCIAL AID (Fall 2012, est.) 1,339 applied for aid; of those 81% were deemed to have need. 100% of freshmen with need received aid; of those 23% had need fully met. *Average percent of need met:* 34% (excluding resources awarded to replace EFC). *Average financial aid package:* $11,716 (excluding resources awarded to replace EFC). 9% of all full-time freshmen had no need and received non-need-based gift aid.
UNDERGRADUATE FINANCIAL AID (Fall 2012, est.) 5,318 applied for aid; of those 84% were deemed to have need. 100% of undergraduates with need received aid; of those 18% had need fully met. *Average percent of need met:* 29% (excluding resources awarded to replace EFC). *Average financial aid package:* $10,810 (excluding resources awarded to replace EFC). 3% of all full-time undergraduates had no need and received non-need-based gift aid.
GIFT AID (NEED-BASED) *Total amount:* $22,879,427 (59% federal, 18% state, 18% institutional, 5% external sources). *Receiving aid:* Freshmen: 62% (991); all full-time undergraduates: 55% (3,816). *Average award:* Freshmen: $6253; Undergraduates: $5611. *Scholarships, grants, and awards:* Federal Pell, FSEOG, state, private, college/university gift aid from institutional funds.
GIFT AID (NON-NEED-BASED) *Total amount:* $6,469,879 (2% federal, 47% state, 43% institutional, 8% external sources). *Receiving aid:* Freshmen: 8% (122). Undergraduates: 4% (289). *Average award:* Freshmen: $4713. Undergraduates: $3224. *Scholarships, grants, and awards by category: Academic interests/achievement:* 1,774 awards ($3,331,539 total): agriculture, biological sciences, business, communication, computer science, education, engineering/technologies, English, general academic interests/achievements, health fields, home economics, humanities, international studies, mathematics, military science, physical sciences, pre-medicine. *Creative arts/performance:* 130 awards ($157,322 total): art/fine arts,

dance, journalism/publications, music, theater/drama. *Special achievements/activities:* 235 awards ($713,959 total): memberships, rodeo. *Special characteristics:* 492 awards ($1,354,384 total): adult students, children of faculty/staff, general special characteristics, local/state students, members of minority groups, out-of-state students. *Tuition waivers:* Full or partial for children of alumni, employees or children of employees, senior citizens. *ROTC:* Army.

LOANS *Student loans:* $32,798,195 (81% need-based, 19% non-need-based). 47% of past graduating class borrowed through all loan programs. *Average indebtedness per student:* $20,644. *Average need-based loan:* Freshmen: $5376. Undergraduates: $6671. *Parent loans:* $3,193,904 (29% need-based, 71% non-need-based). *Programs:* Federal Direct (Subsidized and Unsubsidized Stafford, PLUS), Perkins, Federal Nursing, state, college/university.

WORK-STUDY *Federal work-study:* Total amount: $589,122; 264 jobs averaging $2088. *State or other work-study/employment:* Total amount: $2,270,533 (29% need-based, 71% non-need-based). 1,332 part-time jobs averaging $2913.

ATHLETIC AWARDS Total amount: $3,581,040 (48% need-based, 52% non-need-based).

APPLYING FOR FINANCIAL AID *Required financial aid forms:* FAFSA, institution's own form. *Financial aid deadline (priority):* 4/1. *Notification date:* Continuous beginning 4/15.

CONTACT Lori Mitchum, Director of Financial Aid and Scholarships, Murray State University, 500 Sparks Hall, Murray, KY 42071-0009, 270-809-2546 or toll-free 800-272-4678. *Fax:* 270-809-3116. *E-mail:* lmitchum@murraystate.edu. *Website:* http://www.murraystate.edu/.

MUSICIANS INSTITUTE
Hollywood, CA

CONTACT Director of Financial Aid, Musicians Institute, 1655 North McCadden Place, Hollywood, CA 90028, 323-462-1384 or toll-free 800-255-PLAY. *Website:* http://www.mi.edu/.

MUSKINGUM UNIVERSITY
New Concord, OH

ABOUT THE INSTITUTION Independent Presbyterian Church (U.S.A.), coed. 57 undergraduate majors.

GIFT AID (NEED-BASED) *Scholarships, grants, and awards:* Federal Pell, FSEOG, state, private, college/university gift aid from institutional funds.

GIFT AID (NON-NEED-BASED) *Scholarships, grants, and awards by category: Academic interests/achievement:* biological sciences, computer science, engineering/technologies, general academic interests/achievements, mathematics, physical sciences, premedicine. *Creative arts/performance:* art/fine arts, debating, journalism/publications, music, theater/drama. *Special achievements/activities:* community service, junior miss, leadership. *Special characteristics:* children and siblings of alumni, ethnic background, local/state students, members of minority groups, relatives of clergy, religious affiliation, siblings of current students.

LOANS *Programs:* Federal Direct (Subsidized and Unsubsidized Stafford, PLUS), Perkins, Federal Nursing, college/university.

WORK-STUDY *Federal work-study:* Total amount: $112,221; 430 jobs averaging $1000. *State or other work-study/employment:* Total amount: $480,000 (69% need-based, 31% non-need-based). 5 part-time jobs averaging $1000.

APPLYING FOR FINANCIAL AID *Required financial aid form:* FAFSA.

CONTACT Mr. Jeff Zellers, Vice President of Enrollment, Muskingum University, 163 Stormont Street, New Concord, OH 43762, 740-826-8139 or toll-free 800-752-6082. *Fax:* 740-826-8100. *E-mail:* jzellers@muskingum.edu. *Website:* http://www.muskingum.edu/.

NAROPA UNIVERSITY
Boulder, CO

Tuition & fees: $28,790	Average undergraduate aid package: $33,744

ABOUT THE INSTITUTION Independent, coed. *Awards:* bachelor's and master's degrees. 13 undergraduate majors. *Total enrollment:* 1,019. Undergraduates: 403. Freshmen: 27. Federal methodology is used as a basis for awarding need-based institutional aid.

UNDERGRADUATE EXPENSES for 2013–2014 *Application fee:* $50. *Comprehensive fee:* $37,770 includes full-time tuition ($28,620), mandatory fees ($170), and room and board ($8980). Full-time tuition and fees vary according to course load. *Part-time tuition:* $936 per hour. *Part-time fees:* $335 per term. Part-time tuition and fees vary according to course load.

FRESHMAN FINANCIAL AID (Fall 2012, est.) 15 applied for aid; of those 100% were deemed to have need. 100% of freshmen with need received aid; of those 7% had need fully met. *Average percent of need met:* 82% (excluding resources awarded to replace EFC). *Average financial aid package:* $33,234 (excluding resources awarded to replace EFC).

UNDERGRADUATE FINANCIAL AID (Fall 2012, est.) 250 applied for aid; of those 96% were deemed to have need. 100% of undergraduates with need received aid; of those 3% had need fully met. *Average percent of need met:* 86% (excluding resources awarded to replace EFC). *Average financial aid package:* $33,744 (excluding resources awarded to replace EFC). 1% of all full-time undergraduates had no need and received non-need-based gift aid.

GIFT AID (NEED-BASED) *Total amount:* $3,994,578 (24% federal, 3% state, 71% institutional, 2% external sources). *Receiving aid:* Freshmen: 56% (15); all full-time undergraduates: 66% (234). *Average award:* Freshmen: $23,254; Undergraduates: $21,331. *Scholarships, grants, and awards:* Federal Pell, FSEOG, state, private, college/university gift aid from institutional funds.

GIFT AID (NON-NEED-BASED) *Total amount:* $66,050 (100% institutional). *Receiving aid:* Undergraduates: 1% (4). *Average award:* Undergraduates: $4000. *Scholarships, grants, and awards by category: Academic interests/achievement:* 9 awards ($8427 total): general academic interests/achievements. *Tuition waivers:* Full or partial for employees or children of employees.

LOANS *Student loans:* $2,609,894 (97% need-based, 3% non-need-based). 70% of past graduating class borrowed through all loan programs. *Average indebtedness per student:* $26,511. *Average need-based loan:* Freshmen: $7353. Undergraduates: $10,412. *Parent loans:* $851,368 (87% need-based, 13% non-need-based). *Programs:* Federal Direct (Subsidized and Unsubsidized Stafford, PLUS), Perkins.

WORK-STUDY *Federal work-study:* Total amount: $531,170; 177 jobs averaging $3156. *State or other work-study/employment:* Total amount: $30,000 (100% need-based). 17 part-time jobs averaging $2000.

APPLYING FOR FINANCIAL AID *Required financial aid form:* FAFSA. *Financial aid deadline (priority):* 3/1. *Notification date:* Continuous beginning 3/1. Students must reply within 4 weeks of notification.

CONTACT Ms. Nancy Morrell, Assistant Director of Financial Aid, Naropa University, 2130 Arapahoe Avenue, Boulder, CO 80302-6697, 303-546-3534 or toll-free 800-772-6951. *Fax:* 303-546-3536. *E-mail:* finaid@naropa.edu. *Website:* http://www.naropa.edu/.

NATIONAL AMERICAN UNIVERSITY
Colorado Springs, CO

CONTACT Financial Aid Coordinator, National American University, 2577 North Chelton Road, Colorado Springs, CO 80909, 719-471-4205. *Website:* http://www.national.edu/.

NATIONAL AMERICAN UNIVERSITY
Denver, CO

CONTACT Cheryl Schunneman, Director of Financial Aid, National American University, 321 Kansas City Street, Rapid City, SD 57701, 605-394-4800. *Website:* http://www.national.edu/.

NATIONAL AMERICAN UNIVERSITY
Roseville, MN

CONTACT Financial Aid Office, National American University, 1500 West Highway 36, Roseville, MN 55113, 651-644-1265.
Website: http://www.national.edu/.

NATIONAL AMERICAN UNIVERSITY
Kansas City, MO

CONTACT Mary Anderson, Coordinator of Financial Aid, National American University, 4200 Blue Ridge, Kansas City, MO 64133, 816-353-4554. *Fax:* 816-353-1176.
Website: http://www.national.edu/.

NATIONAL AMERICAN UNIVERSITY
Albuquerque, NM

CONTACT Director of Financial Aid, National American University, 321 Kansas City Street, Rapid City, SD 57701, 605-394-4800 or toll-free 800-895-9904.
Website: http://www.national.edu/.

NATIONAL AMERICAN UNIVERSITY
Tulsa, OK

CONTACT Financial Aid Office, National American University, 8040 South Sheridan Road, Tulsa, OK 74133, 918-879-8400.
Website: http://www.national.edu/.

NATIONAL AMERICAN UNIVERSITY
Rapid City, SD

CONTACT Financial Aid Director, National American University, PO Box 1780, Rapid City, SD 57709-1780, 605-721-5213 or toll-free 800-209-0490 (in-state), 800-209-4090 (out-of-state).
Website: http://www.national.edu/.

NATIONAL AMERICAN UNIVERSITY– SIOUX FALLS BRANCH
Sioux Falls, SD

CONTACT Ms. Rhonda Kohnen, Financial Aid Coordinator, National American University–Sioux Falls Branch, 2801 South Kiwanis Avenue, Suite 100, Sioux Falls, SD 57105-4293, 605-334-5430 or toll-free 800-388-5430. *Fax:* 605-334-1575. *E-mail:* rkohnen@national.edu.
Website: http://www.national.edu/.

THE NATIONAL HISPANIC UNIVERSITY
San Jose, CA

CONTACT Takeo Kubo, Director of Financial Aid and Scholarship, The National Hispanic University, 14271 Story Road, San Jose, CA 95127-3823, 408-273-2708. *Fax:* 408-254-1369. *E-mail:* tkubo@nhu.edu.
Website: http://www.nhu.edu/.

NATIONAL LABOR COLLEGE
Silver Spring, MD

CONTACT Financial Aid Office, National Labor College, 10000 New Hampshire Avenue, Silver Spring, MD 20903, 301-431-6400 or toll-free 888-427-8100.
Website: http://www.nlc.edu/.

NATIONAL LOUIS UNIVERSITY
Chicago, IL

Tuition & fees: N/R	Average undergraduate aid package: $12,225

ABOUT THE INSTITUTION Independent, coed. *Awards:* certificates, bachelor's, master's, and doctoral degrees. 17 undergraduate majors. *Total enrollment:* 5,737. Undergraduates: 1,437. Freshmen: 26. Federal methodology is used as a basis for awarding need-based institutional aid.

FRESHMAN FINANCIAL AID (Fall 2011) 21 applied for aid; of those 86% were deemed to have need. 100% of freshmen with need received aid. *Average percent of need met:* 53% (excluding resources awarded to replace EFC). *Average financial aid package:* $18,689 (excluding resources awarded to replace EFC). 22% of all full-time freshmen had no need and received non-need-based gift aid.

UNDERGRADUATE FINANCIAL AID (Fall 2011) 772 applied for aid; of those 95% were deemed to have need. 100% of undergraduates with need received aid; of those 1% had need fully met. *Average percent of need met:* 43% (excluding resources awarded to replace EFC). *Average financial aid package:* $12,225 (excluding resources awarded to replace EFC). 6% of all full-time undergraduates had no need and received non-need-based gift aid.

GIFT AID (NEED-BASED) *Total amount:* $7,133,362 (42% federal, 30% state, 27% institutional, 1% external sources). *Receiving aid:* Freshmen: 56% (18); all full-time undergraduates: 75% (658). *Average award:* Freshmen: $14,990; Undergraduates: $8302. *Scholarships, grants, and awards:* Federal Pell, FSEOG, state, private, college/university gift aid from institutional funds.

GIFT AID (NON-NEED-BASED) *Total amount:* $433,297 (10% state, 87% institutional, 3% external sources). *Receiving aid:* Undergraduates: 2. *Average award:* Freshmen: $8915. Undergraduates: $5605. *Scholarships, grants, and awards by category:* Academic interests/achievement: 159 awards ($374,707 total): general academic interests/achievements.

LOANS *Student loans:* $10,911,076 (93% need-based, 7% non-need-based). 88% of past graduating class borrowed through all loan programs. *Average indebtedness per student:* $29,900. *Average need-based loan:* Freshmen: $3130. Undergraduates: $4426. *Parent loans:* $1,543,333 (59% need-based, 41% non-need-based). *Programs:* Federal Direct (Subsidized and Unsubsidized Stafford, PLUS), Perkins.

WORK-STUDY *Federal work-study:* Total amount: $256,760; 66 jobs averaging $3890. *State or other work-study/employment:* Total amount: $75,066 (72% need-based, 28% non-need-based). Part-time jobs available.

APPLYING FOR FINANCIAL AID *Required financial aid form:* FAFSA. *Financial aid deadline:* Continuous. *Notification date:* Continuous beginning 4/1.

CONTACT Janet Jazwiec, Assistant Director of Student Finance, National Louis University, 1000 Capitol Drive, Wheeling, IL 60090, 847-947-5453 or toll-free 888-658-8632. *Fax:* 847-947-5453. *E-mail:* jjazwiec@nl.edu.
Website: http://www.nl.edu/.

NATIONAL PARALEGAL COLLEGE
Phoenix, AZ

CONTACT Financial Aid Office, National Paralegal College, 6516 N 7th Street, Suite 103, Phoenix, AZ 85014, 845-371-9101 or toll-free 800-371-6105.
Website: http://nationalparalegal.edu/.

NATIONAL UNIVERSITY
La Jolla, CA

Tuition & fees: $14,670	Average undergraduate aid package: $8242

ABOUT THE INSTITUTION Independent, coed. *Awards:* certificates, associate, bachelor's, master's, and doctoral degrees. 72 undergraduate majors. *Total enrollment:* 17,898. Undergraduates: 9,482. Freshmen: 893. Federal methodology is used as a basis for awarding need-based institutional aid.

UNDERGRADUATE EXPENSES for 2013-2014 *Application fee:* $60. *Tuition:* full-time $14,670; part-time $326 per quarter hour. Full-time tuition and fees vary according to location and program. Part-time tuition and fees vary according to location and program.

FRESHMAN FINANCIAL AID (Fall 2011) 1,295 applied for aid; of those 79% were deemed to have need. 96% of freshmen with need received aid; of those 2% had need fully met. *Average percent of need met:* 83% (excluding resources awarded to replace EFC). *Average financial aid package:* $4896 (excluding resources awarded to replace EFC).

UNDERGRADUATE FINANCIAL AID (Fall 2011) 7,341 applied for aid; of those 83% were deemed to have need. 91% of undergraduates with need received aid; of those 1% had need fully met. *Average percent of need met:* 86% (excluding resources awarded to replace EFC). *Average financial aid package:* $8242 (excluding resources awarded to replace EFC).

GIFT AID (NEED-BASED) *Total amount:* $14,781,914 (88% federal, 12% state). *Receiving aid:* Freshmen: 34% (748); all full-time undergraduates: 43% (4,573). *Average award:* Freshmen: $3526; Undergraduates: $4682. *Scholarships, grants, and awards:* Federal Pell, FSEOG, state, college/university gift aid from institutional funds.

GIFT AID (NON-NEED-BASED) *Total amount:* $1,128,129 (36% federal, 64% institutional). *Receiving aid:* Freshmen: 14% (317). Undergraduates: 6% (670). *Scholarships, grants, and awards by category: Academic interests/ achievement:* general academic interests/achievements. *Special achievements/activities:* leadership. *Tuition waivers:* Full or partial for employees or children of employees. *ROTC:* Army cooperative, Air Force cooperative.

LOANS *Student loans:* $45,390,885 (43% need-based, 57% non-need-based). *Average need-based loan:* Freshmen: $7423. Undergraduates: $8468. *Parent loans:* $1,015,397 (100% need-based). *Programs:* Federal Direct (Subsidized and Unsubsidized Stafford, PLUS), Perkins, college/university.

APPLYING FOR FINANCIAL AID *Required financial aid forms:* FAFSA, institution's own form. *Financial aid deadline:* Continuous. *Notification date:* Continuous beginning 6/30.

CONTACT Valerie Ryan, Office of Financial Aid, National University, 11255 North Torrey Pines Road, La Jolla, CA 92037-1011, 858-642-8500 or toll-free 800-NAT-UNIV. *Fax:* 858-642-8720. *E-mail:* vryan@nu.edu. *Website:* http://www.nu.edu/.

NATIONAL UNIVERSITY COLLEGE
Bayamón, PR

Tuition & fees: N/R	Average undergraduate aid package: $4462

ABOUT THE INSTITUTION Private, coed. 17 undergraduate majors. Federal methodology is used as a basis for awarding need-based institutional aid.

FRESHMAN FINANCIAL AID (Fall 2011) 1,032 applied for aid; of those 100% were deemed to have need. 100% of freshmen with need received aid. *Average percent of need met:* 90% (excluding resources awarded to replace EFC). *Average financial aid package:* $5519 (excluding resources awarded to replace EFC).

UNDERGRADUATE FINANCIAL AID (Fall 2011) 5,214 applied for aid; of those 100% were deemed to have need. 100% of undergraduates with need received aid. *Average percent of need met:* 90% (excluding resources awarded to replace EFC). *Average financial aid package:* $4462 (excluding resources awarded to replace EFC).

GIFT AID (NEED-BASED) *Total amount:* $30,345,511 (97% federal, 3% state). *Receiving aid:* Freshmen: 99% (1,032); all full-time undergraduates: 83% (4,540).

Average award: Freshmen: $4744; Undergraduates: $5140. *Scholarships, grants, and awards:* Federal Pell, FSEOG, state.

LOANS *Student loans:* $11,088,090 (89% need-based, 11% non-need-based). 66% of past graduating class borrowed through all loan programs. *Average indebtedness per student:* $4633. *Average need-based loan:* Freshmen: $2648. Undergraduates: $4527. *Parent loans:* $12,678 (100% non-need-based). *Programs:* Federal Direct (Subsidized and Unsubsidized Stafford, PLUS).

WORK-STUDY *Federal work-study:* Total amount: $439,549; 415 jobs averaging $1059.

APPLYING FOR FINANCIAL AID *Required financial aid forms:* FAFSA, commonwealth aid form. *Financial aid deadline:* Continuous. *Notification date:* Continuous beginning 7/1. Students must reply within 2 weeks of notification.

CONTACT Ms. Elizabeth Cruz, Institutional Director of Financial Aid, National University College, PO Box 2036, Bayamon, PR 00961, 787-780-5134 Ext. 4021 or toll-free 800-780-5134. *E-mail:* ecruz@nuc.edu. *Website:* http://www.nuc.edu/.

NATIONAL UNIVERSITY COLLEGE
Ponce, PR

CONTACT Financial Aid Office, National University College, PO Box 801243, Ponce, PR 00716, 787-840-4474. *Website:* http://www.nuc.edu/.

NATIONAL UNIVERSITY COLLEGE
Rio Grande, PR

CONTACT Financial Aid Office, National University College, Carretera #3 Km. 22.1, Bo. Ciénaga Baja, Rio Grande, PR 00745, 787-888-8286 or toll-free 800-981-0812. *Website:* http://www.nuc.edu/.

NAZARENE BIBLE COLLEGE
Colorado Springs, CO

Tuition & fees: $10,800	Average undergraduate aid package: $4500

ABOUT THE INSTITUTION Independent Church of the Nazarene, coed. 6 undergraduate majors. Federal methodology is used as a basis for awarding need-based institutional aid.

UNDERGRADUATE EXPENSES for 2013-2014 *Tuition:* full-time $10,050; part-time $335 per credit hour. *Required fees:* full-time $750; $25 per credit hour.

FRESHMAN FINANCIAL AID (Fall 2011) 1 applied for aid; of those 100% were deemed to have need. 100% of freshmen with need received aid. *Average percent of need met:* 56% (excluding resources awarded to replace EFC). *Average financial aid package:* $7600 (excluding resources awarded to replace EFC).

UNDERGRADUATE FINANCIAL AID (Fall 2011) 112 applied for aid; of those 100% were deemed to have need. 96% of undergraduates with need received aid. *Average percent of need met:* 52% (excluding resources awarded to replace EFC). *Average financial aid package:* $4500 (excluding resources awarded to replace EFC).

GIFT AID (NEED-BASED) *Total amount:* $1,249,240 (93% federal, 7% institutional). *Receiving aid:* Freshmen: 50% (1); all full-time undergraduates: 69% (107). *Average award:* Freshmen: $4100; Undergraduates: $2500. *Scholarships, grants, and awards:* Federal Pell, FSEOG, college/university gift aid from institutional funds.

GIFT AID (NON-NEED-BASED) *Scholarships, grants, and awards by category: Academic interests/achievement:* religion/biblical studies. *Tuition waivers:* Full or partial for employees or children of employees.

LOANS *Student loans:* $2,395,152 (60% need-based, 40% non-need-based). 63% of past graduating class borrowed through all loan programs. *Average indebtedness per student:* $31,757. *Average need-based loan:* Freshmen: $3500. Undergraduates: $4500. *Parent loans:* $11,700 (100% need-based). *Programs:* Federal Direct (Subsidized and Unsubsidized Stafford, PLUS), Perkins, college/university.

WORK-STUDY *Federal work-study:* Total amount: $17,279; 4 jobs averaging $4320.
APPLYING FOR FINANCIAL AID *Required financial aid form:* FAFSA. *Financial aid deadline:* Continuous. *Notification date:* Continuous beginning 2/1.
CONTACT Mr. Malcolm Britton, Director of Financial Aid, Nazarene Bible College, 1111 Academy Park Loop, Colorado Springs, CO 80910-3717, 719-884-5051 or toll-free 800-873-3873. *Fax:* 719-884-5199.
Website: http://www.nbc.edu/.

NAZARETH COLLEGE OF ROCHESTER
Rochester, NY

Tuition & fees: $27,222	Average undergraduate aid package: $23,635

ABOUT THE INSTITUTION Independent, coed. *Awards:* certificates, bachelor's, master's, and doctoral degrees. 73 undergraduate majors. *Total enrollment:* 2,910. Undergraduates: 2,456. Freshmen: 472. Federal methodology is used as a basis for awarding need-based institutional aid.
UNDERGRADUATE EXPENSES for 2013–2014 *Application fee:* $45. *Comprehensive fee:* $38,366 includes full-time tuition ($26,048), mandatory fees ($1174), and room and board ($11,144). Full-time tuition and fees vary according to course load and program. Room and board charges vary according to board plan and housing facility. *Part-time tuition:* $621 per credit hour. *Part-time fees:* $25 per term.
FRESHMAN FINANCIAL AID (Fall 2012, est.) 438 applied for aid; of those 89% were deemed to have need. 100% of freshmen with need received aid; of those 30% had need fully met. *Average percent of need met:* 81% (excluding resources awarded to replace EFC). *Average financial aid package:* $23,507 (excluding resources awarded to replace EFC). 10% of all full-time freshmen had no need and received non-need-based gift aid.
UNDERGRADUATE FINANCIAL AID (Fall 2012, est.) 1,748 applied for aid; of those 91% were deemed to have need. 100% of undergraduates with need received aid; of those 28% had need fully met. *Average percent of need met:* 79% (excluding resources awarded to replace EFC). *Average financial aid package:* $23,635 (excluding resources awarded to replace EFC). 8% of all full-time undergraduates had no need and received non-need-based gift aid.
GIFT AID (NEED-BASED) *Total amount:* $23,206,133 (13% federal, 10% state, 73% institutional, 4% external sources). *Receiving aid:* Freshmen: 83% (391); all full-time undergraduates: 81% (1,587). *Average award:* Freshmen: $15,493; Undergraduates: $14,509. *Scholarships, grants, and awards:* Federal Pell, FSEOG, state, private, college/university gift aid from institutional funds, Federal Nursing.
GIFT AID (NON-NEED-BASED) *Total amount:* $2,266,206 (1% state, 90% institutional, 9% external sources). *Receiving aid:* Freshmen: 32% (151). Undergraduates: 25% (489). *Average award:* Freshmen: $16,793. Undergraduates: $17,470. *Scholarships, grants, and awards by category:* Academic interests/achievement: 1,661 awards ($14,314,389 total): general academic interests/achievements. Creative arts/performance: 233 awards ($618,500 total): art/fine arts, music, theater/drama. Special characteristics: 191 awards ($1,788,500 total): children and siblings of alumni, children of faculty/staff, siblings of current students. *Tuition waivers:* Full or partial for minority students, children of alumni, employees or children of employees. *ROTC:* Army cooperative, Air Force cooperative.
LOANS *Student loans:* $15,799,076 (85% need-based, 15% non-need-based). 94% of past graduating class borrowed through all loan programs. *Average indebtedness per student:* $30,500. *Average need-based loan:* Freshmen: $3596. Undergraduates: $4362. *Parent loans:* $6,019,540 (50% need-based, 50% non-need-based). *Programs:* Federal Direct (Subsidized and Unsubsidized Stafford, PLUS), Perkins, Federal Nursing.
WORK-STUDY *Federal work-study:* Total amount: $2,100,558; 1,008 jobs averaging $2021.
APPLYING FOR FINANCIAL AID *Required financial aid forms:* FAFSA, state aid form. *Financial aid deadline (priority):* 2/15. *Notification date:* Continuous beginning 1/15. Students must reply by 5/1 or within 2 weeks of notification.

CONTACT Samantha Veeder, Director of Financial Aid, Nazareth College of Rochester, 4245 East Avenue, Rochester, NY 14618-3790, 585-389-2310 or toll-free 800-462-3944. *Fax:* 585-389-2317. *E-mail:* sveeder0@naz.edu.
Website: http://www.naz.edu/.

NEBRASKA CHRISTIAN COLLEGE
Papillion, NE

CONTACT Ms. Tina Larsen, Director of Financial Aid, Nebraska Christian College, 12550 South 114th Street, Papillion, NE 68046, 402-935-9400. *Fax:* 402-935-9500. *E-mail:* tlarsen@nechristian.edu.
Website: http://www.nechristian.edu/.

NEBRASKA METHODIST COLLEGE
Omaha, NE

Tuition & fees: $17,067	Average undergraduate aid package: $8564

ABOUT THE INSTITUTION Independent United Methodist Church, coed, primarily women. *Awards:* certificates, associate, bachelor's, and master's degrees. 8 undergraduate majors. *Total enrollment:* 891. Undergraduates: 738. Freshmen: 29. Federal methodology is used as a basis for awarding need-based institutional aid.
UNDERGRADUATE EXPENSES for 2013–2014 *Application fee:* $25. *Tuition:* full-time $15,840; part-time $528 per credit hour. Full-time tuition and fees vary according to degree level and program. Part-time tuition and fees vary according to degree level and program. Room and board charges vary according to housing facility.
FRESHMAN FINANCIAL AID (Fall 2012, est.) 26 applied for aid; of those 77% were deemed to have need. 100% of freshmen with need received aid; of those 20% had need fully met. *Average percent of need met:* 52% (excluding resources awarded to replace EFC). *Average financial aid package:* $9553 (excluding resources awarded to replace EFC). 26% of all full-time freshmen had no need and received non-need-based gift aid.
UNDERGRADUATE FINANCIAL AID (Fall 2012, est.) 413 applied for aid; of those 87% were deemed to have need. 99% of undergraduates with need received aid; of those 8% had need fully met. *Average percent of need met:* 43% (excluding resources awarded to replace EFC). *Average financial aid package:* $8564 (excluding resources awarded to replace EFC). 11% of all full-time undergraduates had no need and received non-need-based gift aid.
GIFT AID (NEED-BASED) *Total amount:* $2,085,133 (45% federal, 6% state, 43% institutional, 6% external sources). *Receiving aid:* Freshmen: 63% (17); all full-time undergraduates: 63% (284). *Average award:* Freshmen: $6950; Undergraduates: $5717. *Scholarships, grants, and awards:* Federal Pell, FSEOG, state, private, college/university gift aid from institutional funds, Federal Nursing.
GIFT AID (NON-NEED-BASED) *Total amount:* $322,300 (85% institutional, 15% external sources). *Receiving aid:* Freshmen: 15% (4). Undergraduates: 4% (16). *Average award:* Freshmen: $3429. Undergraduates: $3819. *Scholarships, grants, and awards by category:* Academic interests/achievement: general academic interests/achievements, health fields. Special characteristics: children of faculty/staff. *Tuition waivers:* Full or partial for employees or children of employees. *ROTC:* Army cooperative, Air Force cooperative.
LOANS *Student loans:* $5,729,912 (79% need-based, 21% non-need-based). 84% of past graduating class borrowed through all loan programs. *Average indebtedness per student:* $39,753. *Average need-based loan:* Freshmen: $3193. Undergraduates: $4244. *Parent loans:* $935,489 (31% need-based, 69% non-need-based). *Programs:* Federal Direct (Subsidized and Unsubsidized Stafford, PLUS), Perkins, Federal Nursing, college/university, private loans.
WORK-STUDY *Federal work-study:* Total amount: $61,751; 25 jobs averaging $1605.
APPLYING FOR FINANCIAL AID *Required financial aid forms:* FAFSA, institution's own form. *Financial aid deadline (priority):* 4/1. *Notification date:* Continuous beginning 3/1. Students must reply within 3 weeks of notification.

CONTACT Ms. Penny James, Director of Financial Aid, Nebraska Methodist College, The Josie Harper Campus, 720 North 87th Street, Omaha, NE 68114-3426, 402-354-7225 or toll-free 800-335-5510. *Fax:* 402-354-7020. *E-mail:* penny.james@methodistcollege.edu.
Website: http://www.methodistcollege.edu/.

NEBRASKA WESLEYAN UNIVERSITY
Lincoln, NE

Tuition & fees: $27,240	Average undergraduate aid package: $17,992

ABOUT THE INSTITUTION Independent United Methodist, coed. *Awards:* certificates, bachelor's, and master's degrees. 43 undergraduate majors. *Total enrollment:* 2,071. Undergraduates: 1,814. Freshmen: 356. Federal methodology is used as a basis for awarding need-based institutional aid.
UNDERGRADUATE EXPENSES for 2013–2014 *Application fee:* $20. *One-time required fee:* $120. *Comprehensive fee:* $34,790 includes full-time tuition ($26,740), mandatory fees ($500), and room and board ($7550). Room and board charges vary according to board plan and housing facility. *Part-time tuition:* $1005 per credit hour. Part-time tuition and fees vary according to class time and location.
FRESHMAN FINANCIAL AID (Fall 2012, est.) 310 applied for aid; of those 83% were deemed to have need. 100% of freshmen with need received aid; of those 20% had need fully met. *Average percent of need met:* 71% (excluding resources awarded to replace EFC). *Average financial aid package:* $18,589 (excluding resources awarded to replace EFC). 26% of all full-time freshmen had no need and received non-need-based gift aid.
UNDERGRADUATE FINANCIAL AID (Fall 2012, est.) 1,172 applied for aid; of those 86% were deemed to have need. 100% of undergraduates with need received aid; of those 18% had need fully met. *Average percent of need met:* 69% (excluding resources awarded to replace EFC). *Average financial aid package:* $17,992 (excluding resources awarded to replace EFC). 29% of all full-time undergraduates had no need and received non-need-based gift aid.
GIFT AID (NEED-BASED) *Total amount:* $13,069,942 (12% federal, 2% state, 83% institutional, 3% external sources). *Receiving aid:* Freshmen: 72% (257); all full-time undergraduates: 70% (999). *Average award:* Freshmen: $14,027; Undergraduates: $13,077. *Scholarships, grants, and awards:* Federal Pell, FSEOG, state, private, college/university gift aid from institutional funds.
GIFT AID (NON-NEED-BASED) *Total amount:* $4,373,621 (96% institutional, 4% external sources). *Receiving aid:* Freshmen: 12% (41). Undergraduates: 9% (123). *Average award:* Freshmen: $10,298. Undergraduates: $8867. *Scholarships, grants, and awards by category: Academic interests/achievement:* general academic interests/achievements. *Creative arts/performance:* art/fine arts, music, theater/drama. *Special characteristics:* children and siblings of alumni, children of educators, children of faculty/staff, international students, relatives of clergy, siblings of current students. *Tuition waivers:* Full or partial for employees or children of employees, senior citizens. *ROTC:* Army cooperative, Air Force cooperative.
LOANS *Student loans:* $8,093,508 (73% need-based, 27% non-need-based). 74% of past graduating class borrowed through all loan programs. *Average indebtedness per student:* $28,077. *Average need-based loan:* Freshmen: $4370. Undergraduates: $4729. *Parent loans:* $3,333,582 (41% need-based, 59% non-need-based). *Programs:* Federal Direct (Subsidized and Unsubsidized Stafford, PLUS), Perkins.
WORK-STUDY *Federal work-study:* Total amount: $112,000; jobs available. *State or other work-study/employment:* Total amount: $680,921 (42% need-based, 58% non-need-based). Part-time jobs available.
APPLYING FOR FINANCIAL AID *Required financial aid form:* FAFSA. *Financial aid deadline:* Continuous. *Notification date:* Continuous beginning 10/1. Students must reply within 3 weeks of notification.
CONTACT Mr. Thomas J. Ochsner, Director of Scholarships and Financial Aid, Nebraska Wesleyan University, 5000 Saint Paul Avenue, Lincoln, NE 68504, 402-465-2212 or toll-free 800-541-3818. *Fax:* 402-465-2194. *E-mail:* tjo@nebrwesleyan.edu.
Website: http://www.nebrwesleyan.edu/.

NER ISRAEL RABBINICAL COLLEGE
Baltimore, MD

CONTACT Mr. Moshe Pelberg, Financial Aid Administrator , Ner Israel Rabbinical College, 400 Mount Wilson Lane, Baltimore, MD 21208, 410-484-7200.

NEUMANN UNIVERSITY
Aston, PA

Tuition & fees: $24,232	Average undergraduate aid package: $20,250

ABOUT THE INSTITUTION Independent Roman Catholic, coed. *Awards:* certificates, associate, bachelor's, master's, and doctoral degrees. 22 undergraduate majors. *Total enrollment:* 3,100. Undergraduates: 2,674. Freshmen: 574. Federal methodology is used as a basis for awarding need-based institutional aid.
UNDERGRADUATE EXPENSES for 2013–2014 *Application fee:* $40. *Comprehensive fee:* $35,302 includes full-time tuition ($23,262), mandatory fees ($970), and room and board ($11,070). *College room only:* $6510. Room and board charges vary according to board plan. *Part-time tuition:* $531 per credit hour. *Part-time fees:* $50 per semester hour.
FRESHMAN FINANCIAL AID (Fall 2011) 541 applied for aid; of those 89% were deemed to have need. 100% of freshmen with need received aid; of those 1% had need fully met. *Average percent of need met:* 70% (excluding resources awarded to replace EFC). *Average financial aid package:* $20,250 (excluding resources awarded to replace EFC). 16% of all full-time freshmen had no need and received non-need-based gift aid.
UNDERGRADUATE FINANCIAL AID (Fall 2011) 1,826 applied for aid; of those 90% were deemed to have need. 100% of undergraduates with need received aid; of those 1% had need fully met. *Average percent of need met:* 70% (excluding resources awarded to replace EFC). *Average financial aid package:* $20,250 (excluding resources awarded to replace EFC). 23% of all full-time undergraduates had no need and received non-need-based gift aid.
GIFT AID (NEED-BASED) *Total amount:* $25,769,584 (17% federal, 10% state, 73% institutional). *Receiving aid:* Freshmen: 84% (481); all full-time undergraduates: 73% (1,560). *Average award:* Freshmen: $3830; Undergraduates: $4300. *Scholarships, grants, and awards:* Federal Pell, FSEOG, state, private, college/university gift aid from institutional funds.
GIFT AID (NON-NEED-BASED) *Total amount:* $16,092,962 (98% institutional, 2% external sources). *Receiving aid:* Freshmen: 84% (481). Undergraduates: 76% (1,639). *Average award:* Freshmen: $7800. Undergraduates: $7400. *Scholarships, grants, and awards by category: Academic interests/achievement:* general academic interests/achievements. *Tuition waivers:* Full or partial for employees or children of employees. *ROTC:* Army cooperative.
LOANS *Student loans:* 95% of past graduating class borrowed through all loan programs. *Average indebtedness per student:* $27,000. *Average need-based loan:* Freshmen: $3500. Undergraduates: $4500. *Parent loans:* $4,608,790 (100% need-based). *Programs:* Federal Direct (Subsidized and Unsubsidized Stafford, PLUS), Perkins.
WORK-STUDY *Federal work-study:* Total amount: $289,468; jobs available. *State or other work-study/employment:* Part-time jobs available.
APPLYING FOR FINANCIAL AID *Required financial aid form:* FAFSA. *Financial aid deadline:* Continuous. *Notification date:* Continuous. Students must reply by 5/1 or within 2 weeks of notification.
CONTACT Deborah Cawley, Director of Financial Aid, Neumann University, One Neumann Drive, Aston, PA 19014-1298, 610-558-5519 or toll-free 800-963-8626. *E-mail:* cawleyd@neumann.edu.
Website: http://www.neumann.edu/.

NEUMONT UNIVERSITY
South Jordan, UT

Tuition & fees: $23,100	Average undergraduate aid package: N/A

ABOUT THE INSTITUTION Proprietary, coed, primarily men. *Awards:* bachelor's and master's degrees. 13 undergraduate majors. *Total enrollment:* 366. Undergraduates: 366. Freshmen: 166. Both federal and institutional methodology are used as a basis for awarding need-based institutional aid.

UNDERGRADUATE EXPENSES for 2013–2014 *Application fee:* $35. *Tuition:* full-time $21,600; part-time $495 per unit.

GIFT AID (NEED-BASED) *Scholarships, grants, and awards:* Federal Pell, FSEOG, college/university gift aid from institutional funds.

GIFT AID (NON-NEED-BASED) *Scholarships, grants, and awards by category: Academic interests/achievement:* computer science. *Tuition waivers:* Full or partial for employees or children of employees.

LOANS *Programs:* Federal Direct (Subsidized and Unsubsidized Stafford, PLUS), college/university.

APPLYING FOR FINANCIAL AID *Required financial aid forms:* FAFSA, institution's own form. *Financial aid deadline (priority):* 4/1. *Notification date:* 5/1. Students must reply by 7/1.

CONTACT Mr. Nate Blanchard, Supervising Financial Aid Officer, Neumont University, 10701 South River Front Parkway, Suite 300, South Jordan, UT 84095, 801-302-2873 or toll-free 888-NEUMONT. *Fax:* 801-302-2834. *E-mail:* nate.blanchard@neumont.edu.
Website: http://www.neumont.edu/.

NEVADA STATE COLLEGE AT HENDERSON
Henderson, NV

CONTACT Financial Aid Office, Nevada State College at Henderson, 1125 Nevada State Drive, Henderson, NV 89015, 702-992-2000.
Website: http://www.nsc.nevada.edu/.

NEWBERRY COLLEGE
Newberry, SC

Tuition & fees: $23,800	Average undergraduate aid package: $19,330

ABOUT THE INSTITUTION Independent Evangelical Lutheran, coed. *Awards:* bachelor's degrees. 27 undergraduate majors. *Total enrollment:* 1,042. Undergraduates: 1,042. Freshmen: 221. Federal methodology is used as a basis for awarding need-based institutional aid.

UNDERGRADUATE EXPENSES for 2013–2014 *Application fee:* $30. *Comprehensive fee:* $32,800 includes full-time tuition ($22,050), mandatory fees ($1750), and room and board ($9000). *College room only:* $4500. Full-time tuition and fees vary according to class time, course load, and student level. Room and board charges vary according to board plan and housing facility. *Part-time tuition:* $525 per hour. Part-time tuition and fees vary according to class time, course load, and student level. *Payment plan:* Guaranteed tuition.

FRESHMAN FINANCIAL AID (Fall 2011) 245 applied for aid; of those 93% were deemed to have need. 100% of freshmen with need received aid; of those 16% had need fully met. *Average percent of need met:* 68% (excluding resources awarded to replace EFC). *Average financial aid package:* $20,509 (excluding resources awarded to replace EFC). 9% of all full-time freshmen had no need and received non-need-based gift aid.

UNDERGRADUATE FINANCIAL AID (Fall 2011) 1,066 applied for aid; of those 93% were deemed to have need. 100% of undergraduates with need received aid; of those 18% had need fully met. *Average percent of need met:* 67% (excluding resources awarded to replace EFC). *Average financial aid package:* $19,330 (excluding resources awarded to replace EFC). 10% of all full-time undergraduates had no need and received non-need-based gift aid.

GIFT AID (NEED-BASED) *Total amount:* $14,626,133 (17% federal, 22% state, 57% institutional, 4% external sources). *Receiving aid:* Freshmen: 80% (224); all full-time undergraduates: 86% (980). *Average award:* Freshmen: $17,870; Undergraduates: $16,323. *Scholarships, grants, and awards:* Federal Pell, FSEOG, state, private, college/university gift aid from institutional funds.

GIFT AID (NON-NEED-BASED) *Total amount:* $2,921,337 (29% state, 63% institutional, 8% external sources). *Receiving aid:* Freshmen: 12% (35). Undergraduates: 14% (166). *Average award:* Freshmen: $10,655. Undergraduates: $11,726. *Scholarships, grants, and awards by category: Academic interests/achievement:* biological sciences, business, communication, education, foreign languages, general academic interests/achievements, humanities, mathematics, physical sciences, religion/biblical studies, social sciences. *Creative arts/performance:* music, theater/drama. *Special achievements/activities:* cheerleading/drum major, religious involvement. *Special characteristics:* children and siblings of alumni, children of faculty/staff, international students, local/state students, relatives of clergy, religious affiliation, siblings of current students. *Tuition waivers:* Full or partial for employees or children of employees. *ROTC:* Army cooperative.

LOANS *Student loans:* $7,326,621 (77% need-based, 23% non-need-based). 83% of past graduating class borrowed through all loan programs. *Average indebtedness per student:* $30,610. *Average need-based loan:* Freshmen: $3801. Undergraduates: $4113. *Parent loans:* $2,649,432 (74% need-based, 26% non-need-based). *Programs:* Federal Direct (Subsidized and Unsubsidized Stafford, PLUS), Perkins, state.

WORK-STUDY *Federal work-study:* Total amount: $50,673; jobs available. *State or other work-study/employment:* Part-time jobs available.

ATHLETIC AWARDS Total amount: $2,221,540 (65% need-based, 35% non-need-based).

APPLYING FOR FINANCIAL AID *Required financial aid forms:* FAFSA, institution's own form, state aid form. *Financial aid deadline (priority):* 3/15. *Notification date:* Continuous beginning 3/15. Students must reply by 8/15 or within 2 weeks of notification.

CONTACT Mrs. Danielle Bell, Interim Director of Financial Aid, Newberry College, 2100 College Street, Newberry, SC 29108, 803-321-5128 or toll-free 800-845-4955. *Fax:* 803-321-5627. *E-mail:* danielle.bell@newberry.edu.
Website: http://www.newberry.edu/.

NEWBURY COLLEGE
Brookline, MA

Tuition & fees: $28,950	Average undergraduate aid package: $12,974

ABOUT THE INSTITUTION Independent, coed. *Awards:* certificates, associate, and bachelor's degrees. 23 undergraduate majors. *Total enrollment:* 1,003. Undergraduates: 1,003. Freshmen: 286. Federal methodology is used as a basis for awarding need-based institutional aid.

UNDERGRADUATE EXPENSES for 2013–2014 *Application fee:* $25. *One-time required fee:* $175. *Comprehensive fee:* $41,850 includes full-time tuition ($27,850), mandatory fees ($1100), and room and board ($12,900). Full-time tuition and fees vary according to program and reciprocity agreements. Room and board charges vary according to housing facility. Part-time tuition and fees vary according to class time, course load, program, and reciprocity agreements.

FRESHMAN FINANCIAL AID (Fall 2012, est.) 240 applied for aid; of those 94% were deemed to have need. 100% of freshmen with need received aid; of those .4% had need fully met. *Average percent of need met:* 58% (excluding resources awarded to replace EFC). *Average financial aid package:* $15,482 (excluding resources awarded to replace EFC). 6% of all full-time freshmen had no need and received non-need-based gift aid.

UNDERGRADUATE FINANCIAL AID (Fall 2012, est.) 826 applied for aid; of those 95% were deemed to have need. 100% of undergraduates with need received aid; of those .1% had need fully met. *Average percent of need met:* 47% (excluding resources awarded to replace EFC). *Average financial aid package:* $12,974 (excluding resources awarded to replace EFC). 4% of all full-time undergraduates had no need and received non-need-based gift aid.

GIFT AID (NEED-BASED) *Total amount:* $7,159,798 (35% federal, 6% state, 59% institutional). *Receiving aid:* Freshmen: 84% (225); all full-time undergraduates: 82% (783). *Average award:* Freshmen: $13,036; Undergraduates: $11,712. *Schol-*

arships, grants, and awards: Federal Pell, FSEOG, state, private, college/university gift aid from institutional funds.

GIFT AID (NON-NEED-BASED) *Total amount:* $5,937,851 (98% institutional, 2% external sources). *Receiving aid:* Freshmen: 75% (203). Undergraduates: 61% (583). *Average award:* Freshmen: $11,734. Undergraduates: $10,313. *Tuition waivers:* Full or partial for employees or children of employees.

LOANS *Student loans:* $8,101,556 (40% need-based, 60% non-need-based). 90% of past graduating class borrowed through all loan programs. *Average indebtedness per student:* $29,530. *Average need-based loan:* Freshmen: $3500. Undergraduates: $4500. *Parent loans:* $2,822,161 (100% need-based). *Programs:* Federal Direct (Subsidized and Unsubsidized Stafford, PLUS), Perkins, alternative loans, MEFA Loans, Signature Loans, Sallie Mae Loans.

WORK-STUDY *Federal work-study:* Total amount: $314,198; 197 jobs averaging $1592.

APPLYING FOR FINANCIAL AID *Required financial aid form:* FAFSA. *Financial aid deadline (priority):* 3/1. *Notification date:* Continuous beginning 10/1.

CONTACT Elreo Campbell, Office of Financial Assistance, Newbury College, 129 Fisher Avenue, Brookline, MA 02445-5796, 617-730-7100 or toll-free 800-NEWBURY. *Fax:* 617-730-7108.

Website: http://www.newbury.edu/.

NEW COLLEGE OF FLORIDA
Sarasota, FL

Tuition & fees (FL res): $6783	Average undergraduate aid package: $12,186

ABOUT THE INSTITUTION State-supported, coed. *Awards:* bachelor's degrees. 42 undergraduate majors. *Total enrollment:* 832. Undergraduates: 832. Freshmen: 223. Federal methodology is used as a basis for awarding need-based institutional aid.

UNDERGRADUATE EXPENSES for 2013–2014 *Application fee:* $30. *Tuition, state resident:* full-time $6783. *Tuition, nonresident:* full-time $29,812. Full-time tuition and fees vary according to course load. *College room and board:* $8856; *Room only:* $6078. Room and board charges vary according to board plan and housing facility.

FRESHMAN FINANCIAL AID (Fall 2012, est.) 213 applied for aid; of those 61% were deemed to have need. 100% of freshmen with need received aid; of those 44% had need fully met. *Average percent of need met:* 87% (excluding resources awarded to replace EFC). *Average financial aid package:* $12,104 (excluding resources awarded to replace EFC). 35% of all full-time freshmen had no need and received non-need-based gift aid.

UNDERGRADUATE FINANCIAL AID (Fall 2012, est.) 745 applied for aid; of those 65% were deemed to have need. 99% of undergraduates with need received aid; of those 28% had need fully met. *Average percent of need met:* 80% (excluding resources awarded to replace EFC). *Average financial aid package:* $12,186 (excluding resources awarded to replace EFC). 25% of all full-time undergraduates had no need and received non-need-based gift aid.

GIFT AID (NEED-BASED) *Total amount:* $3,824,315 (29% federal, 30% state, 40% institutional, 1% external sources). *Receiving aid:* Freshmen: 58% (129); all full-time undergraduates: 58% (480). *Average award:* Freshmen: $9857; Undergraduates: $8819. *Scholarships, grants, and awards:* Federal Pell, FSEOG, state, private, college/university gift aid from institutional funds.

GIFT AID (NON-NEED-BASED) *Total amount:* $1,343,421 (60% state, 39% institutional, 1% external sources). *Receiving aid:* Freshmen: 13% (28). Undergraduates: 8% (67). *Average award:* Freshmen: $2415. Undergraduates: $2282. *Scholarships, grants, and awards by category: Academic interests/achievement:* 782 awards ($2,133,157 total): general academic interests/achievements. *Special achievements/activities:* 127 awards ($367,875 total): general special achievements/activities. *Special characteristics:* 148 awards ($1,187,632 total): out-of-state students.

LOANS *Student loans:* $3,743,819 (53% need-based, 47% non-need-based). 39% of past graduating class borrowed through all loan programs. *Average indebtedness per student:* $16,640. *Average need-based loan:* Freshmen: $2936. Undergraduates: $4176. *Parent loans:* $291,274 (23% need-based, 77% non-need-based). *Programs:* Federal Direct (Subsidized and Unsubsidized Stafford, PLUS), alternative loans.

WORK-STUDY *Federal work-study:* Total amount: $27,804; 12 jobs averaging $2325. *State or other work-study/employment:* Part-time jobs available.

APPLYING FOR FINANCIAL AID *Required financial aid form:* FAFSA. *Financial aid deadline (priority):* 2/15. *Notification date:* Continuous beginning 3/15. Students must reply by 5/1 or within 4 weeks of notification.

CONTACT Tara Karas, Director of Financial Aid, New College of Florida, 5800 Bay Shore Road, Sarasota, FL 34243-2109, 941-487-5000. *Fax:* 941-487-5010. *E-mail:* ncfinaid@ncf.edu.

Website: http://www.ncf.edu/.

NEW ENGLAND COLLEGE
Henniker, NH

Tuition & fees: $31,744	Average undergraduate aid package: $25,290

ABOUT THE INSTITUTION Independent, coed. *Awards:* associate, bachelor's, master's, and doctoral degrees. 40 undergraduate majors. *Total enrollment:* 2,016. Undergraduates: 1,126. Freshmen: 335. Institutional methodology is used as a basis for awarding need-based institutional aid.

UNDERGRADUATE EXPENSES for 2013–2014 *Application fee:* $35. *Comprehensive fee:* $44,178 includes full-time tuition ($31,394), mandatory fees ($350), and room and board ($12,434). *College room only:* $5750. Full-time tuition and fees vary according to class time, course load, degree level, location, program, and reciprocity agreements. Room and board charges vary according to board plan and housing facility. *Part-time tuition:* $385 per credit. Part-time tuition and fees vary according to class time, course load, degree level, location, and program.

FRESHMAN FINANCIAL AID (Fall 2012, est.) 281 applied for aid; of those 95% were deemed to have need. 100% of freshmen with need received aid; of those 13% had need fully met. *Average percent of need met:* 75% (excluding resources awarded to replace EFC). *Average financial aid package:* $26,502 (excluding resources awarded to replace EFC). 12% of all full-time freshmen had no need and received non-need-based gift aid.

UNDERGRADUATE FINANCIAL AID (Fall 2012, est.) 833 applied for aid; of those 95% were deemed to have need. 100% of undergraduates with need received aid; of those 19% had need fully met. *Average percent of need met:* 74% (excluding resources awarded to replace EFC). *Average financial aid package:* $25,290 (excluding resources awarded to replace EFC). 16% of all full-time undergraduates had no need and received non-need-based gift aid.

GIFT AID (NEED-BASED) *Total amount:* $9,213,544 (1% state, 97% institutional, 2% external sources). *Receiving aid:* Freshmen: 81% (262); all full-time undergraduates: 73% (761). *Average award:* Freshmen: $13,229; Undergraduates: $16,485. *Scholarships, grants, and awards:* Federal Pell, FSEOG, state, private, college/university gift aid from institutional funds.

GIFT AID (NON-NEED-BASED) *Total amount:* $425,220 (2% federal, 94% institutional, 4% external sources). *Receiving aid:* Freshmen: 58% (188). Undergraduates: 47% (489). *Average award:* Freshmen: $12,541. Undergraduates: $12,686. *Scholarships, grants, and awards by category: Academic interests/achievement:* 499 awards ($4,216,800 total): biological sciences, business, communication, computer science, education, engineering/technologies, English, general academic interests/achievements, health fields, humanities, international studies, mathematics, social sciences. *Creative arts/performance:* 6 awards ($7500 total): applied art and design, art/fine arts, creative writing, theater/drama. *Special achievements/activities:* 372 awards ($1,641,615 total): community service, leadership. *Special characteristics:* 143 awards ($1,996,981 total): children and siblings of alumni, children of educators, children of faculty/staff, ethnic background, international students, local/state students, parents of current students, siblings of current students. *Tuition waivers:* Full or partial for children of alumni, employees or children of employees, adult students, senior citizens. *ROTC:* Army cooperative, Air Force cooperative.

LOANS *Student loans:* $8,476,253 (95% need-based, 5% non-need-based). 72% of past graduating class borrowed through all loan programs. *Average indebtedness per student:* $33,797. *Average need-based loan:* Freshmen: $4306. Undergraduates: $4865. *Parent loans:* $2,454,792 (95% need-based, 5% non-need-based). *Programs:* Federal Direct (Subsidized and Unsubsidized Stafford, PLUS), Perkins, state.

WORK-STUDY *Federal work-study:* Total amount: $433,588; 247 jobs available. *State or other work-study/employment:* Total amount: $30,340 (38% need-based, 62% non-need-based). Part-time jobs available.

APPLYING FOR FINANCIAL AID *Required financial aid form:* FAFSA. *Financial aid deadline (priority):* 4/1. *Notification date:* Continuous beginning 2/1. Students must reply by 9/7 or within 2 weeks of notification.

CONTACT Kristen Blase, Student Financial Services Director, New England College, 15 Main Street, Henniker, NH 03242-3293, 603-428-2226 or toll-free 800-521-7642. *Fax:* 603-428-2404. *E-mail:* rstein@nec.edu. *Website:* http://www.nec.edu/.

NEW ENGLAND COLLEGE OF BUSINESS AND FINANCE
Boston, MA

CONTACT Financial Aid Office, New England College of Business and Finance, 10 High Street, Suite 204, Boston, MA 02111-2645, 617-951-2350 or toll-free 800-997-1673.
Website: http://necb.edu/.

NEW ENGLAND CONSERVATORY OF MUSIC
Boston, MA

Tuition & fees: $38,455	Average undergraduate aid package: $23,951

ABOUT THE INSTITUTION Independent, coed. *Awards:* certificates, diplomas, bachelor's, master's, and doctoral degrees. 9 undergraduate majors. *Total enrollment:* 814. Undergraduates: 436. Freshmen: 102. Federal methodology is used as a basis for awarding need-based institutional aid.
UNDERGRADUATE EXPENSES for 2013–2014 *Application fee:* $115. *Comprehensive fee:* $50,805 includes full-time tuition ($38,000), mandatory fees ($455), and room and board ($12,350). Room and board charges vary according to board plan. *Part-time tuition:* $1210 per credit.
FRESHMAN FINANCIAL AID (Fall 2011) 64 applied for aid; of those 83% were deemed to have need. 100% of freshmen with need received aid; of those 9% had need fully met. *Average percent of need met:* 56% (excluding resources awarded to replace EFC). *Average financial aid package:* $22,194 (excluding resources awarded to replace EFC). 51% of all full-time freshmen had no need and received non-need-based gift aid.
UNDERGRADUATE FINANCIAL AID (Fall 2011) 261 applied for aid; of those 83% were deemed to have need. 100% of undergraduates with need received aid; of those 16% had need fully met. *Average percent of need met:* 61% (excluding resources awarded to replace EFC). *Average financial aid package:* $23,951 (excluding resources awarded to replace EFC). 45% of all full-time undergraduates had no need and received non-need-based gift aid.
GIFT AID (NEED-BASED) *Total amount:* $3,829,683 (11% federal, 86% institutional, 3% external sources). *Receiving aid:* Freshmen: 52% (53); all full-time undergraduates: 53% (216). *Average award:* Freshmen: $17,098; Undergraduates: $17,843. *Scholarships, grants, and awards:* Federal Pell, FSEOG, state, private, college/university gift aid from institutional funds.
GIFT AID (NON-NEED-BASED) *Total amount:* $3,039,280 (98% institutional, 2% external sources). *Receiving aid:* Freshmen: 2% (2). Undergraduates: 5% (20). *Average award:* Freshmen: $15,423. Undergraduates: $15,922. *Scholarships, grants, and awards by category:* Creative arts/performance: 385 awards ($3,340,260 total): music, theater/drama. *Tuition waivers:* Full or partial for employees or children of employees.
LOANS *Student loans:* $2,628,750 (74% need-based, 26% non-need-based). 49% of past graduating class borrowed through all loan programs. *Average indebtedness per student:* $25,189. *Average need-based loan:* Freshmen: $4939. Undergraduates: $6102. *Parent loans:* $891,797 (56% need-based, 44% non-need-based). *Programs:* Federal Direct (Subsidized and Unsubsidized Stafford, PLUS), Perkins, state.
WORK-STUDY *Federal work-study:* Total amount: $178,131; 103 jobs averaging $1608.
APPLYING FOR FINANCIAL AID *Required financial aid forms:* FAFSA, institution's own form. *Financial aid deadline (priority):* 2/15. *Notification date:* Continuous beginning 4/1. Students must reply by 5/1.

CONTACT Ms. Lauren G. Urbanek, Director of Financial Aid, New England Conservatory of Music, 290 Huntington Avenue, Boston, MA 02115, 617-585-1110. *Fax:* 617-585-1115. *E-mail:* finaid@necmusic.edu. *Website:* http://necmusic.edu/.

THE NEW ENGLAND INSTITUTE OF ART
Brookline, MA

CONTACT Financial Aid Office, The New England Institute of Art, 10 Brookline Place West, Brookline, MA 02445, 617-267-7910 or toll-free 800-903-4425.

NEW ENGLAND INSTITUTE OF TECHNOLOGY
East Greenwich, RI

CONTACT Financial Aid Office, New England Institute of Technology, One New England Tech Boulevard, East Greenwich, RI 02818, 401-467-7744 or toll-free 800-736-7744.
Website: http://www.neit.edu/.

NEW ENGLAND SCHOOL OF COMMUNICATIONS
Bangor, ME

Tuition & fees: $14,104	Average undergraduate aid package: N/A

ABOUT THE INSTITUTION Independent, coed, primarily men. *Awards:* bachelor's degrees. 10 undergraduate majors. *Total enrollment:* 499. Undergraduates: 499. Freshmen: 108. Federal methodology is used as a basis for awarding need-based institutional aid.
UNDERGRADUATE EXPENSES for 2013–2014 *Application fee:* $25. *One-time required fee:* $100. *Comprehensive fee:* $22,410 includes full-time tuition ($13,034), mandatory fees ($1070), and room and board ($8306). *College room only:* $4102.
FRESHMAN FINANCIAL AID (Fall 2012, est.) 102 applied for aid; of those 82% were deemed to have need. 100% of freshmen with need received aid. 4% of all full-time freshmen had no need and received non-need-based gift aid.
UNDERGRADUATE FINANCIAL AID (Fall 2012, est.) 430 applied for aid; of those 86% were deemed to have need. 100% of undergraduates with need received aid. 5% of all full-time undergraduates had no need and received non-need-based gift aid.
GIFT AID (NEED-BASED) *Total amount:* $1,305,857 (72% federal, 15% state, 5% institutional, 8% external sources). *Receiving aid:* Freshmen: 60% (64); all full-time undergraduates: 57% (264). *Average award:* Freshmen: $4610; Undergraduates: $4691. *Scholarships, grants, and awards:* Federal Pell, FSEOG, state, private, college/university gift aid from institutional funds.
GIFT AID (NON-NEED-BASED) *Total amount:* $16,228 (100% institutional). *Receiving aid:* Freshmen: 68% (73). Undergraduates: 23% (105). *Average award:* Freshmen: $437. Undergraduates: $815. *Scholarships, grants, and awards by category:* Academic interests/achievement: communication. Creative arts/performance: cinema/film/broadcasting, journalism/publications, performing arts, theater/drama. Special achievements/activities: general special achievements/activities.
ROTC: Army cooperative.
LOANS *Student loans:* $3,910,051 (41% need-based, 59% non-need-based). 85% of past graduating class borrowed through all loan programs. *Average indebtedness per student:* $34,426. *Average need-based loan:* Freshmen: $3173. Undergraduates: $4193. *Parent loans:* $992,307 (100% non-need-based). *Programs:* Federal Direct (Subsidized and Unsubsidized Stafford, PLUS), alternative loans.
WORK-STUDY *Federal work-study:* Total amount: $34,000; jobs available. *State or other work-study/employment:* Total amount: $52,700 (100% non-need-based). Part-time jobs available.

APPLYING FOR FINANCIAL AID *Required financial aid form:* FAFSA. *Financial aid deadline (priority):* 4/15. *Notification date:* Continuous beginning 5/1. Students must reply within 4 weeks of notification.
CONTACT Mrs. Nicole Vachon, Director of Financial Aid, New England School of Communications, One College Circle, Bangor, ME 04401, 888-877-1876. *Fax:* 207-947-3987. *E-mail:* nikki@nescom.edu.
Website: http://www.nescom.edu/.

NEW HAMPSHIRE INSTITUTE OF ART
Manchester, NH

CONTACT Linda Lavallee, Director of Financial Aid, New Hampshire Institute of Art, 148 Concord Street, Manchester, NH 03104-4858, 603-623-0313 Ext. 577 or toll-free 866-241-4918. *Fax:* 603-647-0658. *E-mail:* llavallee@nhia.edu.
Website: http://www.nhia.edu/.

NEW HOPE CHRISTIAN COLLEGE
Eugene, OR

Tuition & fees: N/R	Average undergraduate aid package: N/A

ABOUT THE INSTITUTION Independent Open Bible Standard Churches, coed. *Awards:* bachelor's degrees. 7 undergraduate majors. *Total enrollment:* 143. Undergraduates: 143. Freshmen: 38. Both federal and institutional methodology are used as a basis for awarding need-based institutional aid.
GIFT AID (NEED-BASED) *Scholarships, grants, and awards:* Federal Pell, FSEOG, private, college/university gift aid from institutional funds.
GIFT AID (NON-NEED-BASED) *Scholarships, grants, and awards by category: Academic interests/achievement:* general academic interests/achievements, religion/biblical studies. *Creative arts/performance:* music. *Special achievements/activities:* community service, general special achievements/activities, hobbies/interests, leadership, religious involvement. *Special characteristics:* general special characteristics, international students, married students, out-of-state students, relatives of clergy, spouses of current students, veterans, veterans' children.
LOANS *Programs:* Federal Direct (Subsidized and Unsubsidized Stafford, PLUS).
WORK-STUDY Federal work-study jobs available. *State or other work-study/employment:* Part-time jobs available.
APPLYING FOR FINANCIAL AID *Required financial aid forms:* FAFSA, institution's own form. *Financial aid deadline:* 9/1 (priority: 3/1). *Notification date:* Continuous beginning 4/1. Students must reply within 4 weeks of notification.
CONTACT Nathan Icenhower, Financial Aid Administrator, New Hope Christian College, 2155 Bailey Hill Road, Eugene, OR 97405-1194, 541-485-1780 Ext. 3106 or toll-free 800-322-2638. *Fax:* 541-343-5801. *E-mail:* finaid@newhope.edu.
Website: http://www.newhope.edu/.

NEW JERSEY CITY UNIVERSITY
Jersey City, NJ

Tuition & fees: N/R	Average undergraduate aid package: $20,515

ABOUT THE INSTITUTION State-supported, coed. *Awards:* certificates, bachelor's, and master's degrees. 29 undergraduate majors. *Total enrollment:* 8,493. Undergraduates: 6,584. Freshmen: 797. Federal methodology is used as a basis for awarding need-based institutional aid.
UNDERGRADUATE EXPENSES for 2013–2014 *Application fee:* $50. *Tuition, state resident:* part-time $245.25 per credit hour. *Tuition, nonresident:* part-time $518.20 per credit hour. Full-time tuition and fees vary according to program. Part-time tuition and fees vary according to course load.
FRESHMAN FINANCIAL AID (Fall 2011) 634 applied for aid; of those 94% were deemed to have need. 97% of freshmen with need received aid; of those 6% had need fully met. *Average percent of need met:* 59% (excluding resources awarded to replace EFC). *Average financial aid package:* $16,616 (excluding resources

awarded to replace EFC). 2% of all full-time freshmen had no need and received non-need-based gift aid.
UNDERGRADUATE FINANCIAL AID (Fall 2011) 4,407 applied for aid; of those 96% were deemed to have need. 97% of undergraduates with need received aid; of those 6% had need fully met. *Average percent of need met:* 59% (excluding resources awarded to replace EFC). *Average financial aid package:* $20,515 (excluding resources awarded to replace EFC). 1% of all full-time undergraduates had no need and received non-need-based gift aid.
GIFT AID (NEED-BASED) *Total amount:* $26,612,521 (62% federal, 38% state). *Receiving aid:* Freshmen: 72% (483); all full-time undergraduates: 67% (3,275). *Average award:* Freshmen: $8702; Undergraduates: $7603. *Scholarships, grants, and awards:* Federal Pell, FSEOG, state, college/university gift aid from institutional funds.
GIFT AID (NON-NEED-BASED) *Total amount:* $1,662,877 (8% state, 92% institutional). *Receiving aid:* Freshmen: 10% (66). Undergraduates: 7% (348). *Average award:* Freshmen: $4995. Undergraduates: $6398. *Tuition waivers:* Full or partial for employees or children of employees, senior citizens.
LOANS *Student loans:* $69,558,605 (57% need-based, 43% non-need-based). 65% of past graduating class borrowed through all loan programs. *Average indebtedness per student:* $19,233. *Average need-based loan:* Freshmen: $9654. Undergraduates: $12,190. *Parent loans:* $29,097,174 (100% non-need-based). *Programs:* Federal Direct (Subsidized and Unsubsidized Stafford, PLUS).
WORK-STUDY *Federal work-study:* Total amount: $604,750; jobs available.
APPLYING FOR FINANCIAL AID *Required financial aid form:* FAFSA. *Financial aid deadline (priority):* 4/15. *Notification date:* 5/15.
CONTACT Mr. Frank Cuozzo, Director of Financial Aid, New Jersey City University, 2039 Kennedy Boulevard, Jersey City, NJ 07305-1597, 201-200-3173 or toll-free 888-441-NJCU.
Website: http://www.njcu.edu/.

NEW JERSEY INSTITUTE OF TECHNOLOGY
Newark, NJ

Tuition & fees (NJ res): $14,740	Average undergraduate aid package: $12,201

ABOUT THE INSTITUTION State-supported, coed. *Awards:* certificates, bachelor's, master's, and doctoral degrees. 34 undergraduate majors. *Total enrollment:* 9,944. Undergraduates: 7,111. Freshmen: 1,020. Federal methodology is used as a basis for awarding need-based institutional aid.
UNDERGRADUATE EXPENSES for 2013–2014 *Application fee:* $70. *Tuition, state resident:* full-time $12,400; part-time $472 per credit. *Tuition, nonresident:* full-time $24,800; part-time $1060 per credit. *Required fees:* full-time $2340; $116 per credit. Full-time tuition and fees vary according to course load and degree level. Part-time tuition and fees vary according to course load and degree level. *College room and board:* $11,750. Room and board charges vary according to board plan and housing facility.
FRESHMAN FINANCIAL AID (Fall 2011) 770 applied for aid; of those 85% were deemed to have need. 94% of freshmen with need received aid; of those 2% had need fully met. *Average percent of need met:* 49% (excluding resources awarded to replace EFC). *Average financial aid package:* $12,163 (excluding resources awarded to replace EFC). 14% of all full-time freshmen had no need and received non-need-based gift aid.
UNDERGRADUATE FINANCIAL AID (Fall 2011) 4,045 applied for aid; of those 91% were deemed to have need. 95% of undergraduates with need received aid; of those 4% had need fully met. *Average percent of need met:* 50% (excluding resources awarded to replace EFC). *Average financial aid package:* $12,201 (excluding resources awarded to replace EFC). 11% of all full-time undergraduates had no need and received non-need-based gift aid.
GIFT AID (NEED-BASED) *Total amount:* $37,949,249 (28% federal, 33% state, 38% institutional, 1% external sources). *Receiving aid:* Freshmen: 46% (411); all full-time undergraduates: 50% (2,583). *Average award:* Freshmen: $11,792; Undergraduates: $10,748. *Scholarships, grants, and awards:* Federal Pell, FSEOG, state, private, college/university gift aid from institutional funds, United Negro College Fund.
GIFT AID (NON-NEED-BASED) *Total amount:* $350,321 (100% state). *Receiving aid:* Freshmen: 11% (95). Undergraduates: 5% (267). *Average award:* Freshmen: $11,296. Undergraduates: $12,252. *Scholarships, grants, and awards*

by category: *Academic interests/achievement:* 2,252 awards ($11,528,586 total): architecture, area/ethnic studies, biological sciences, business, communication, computer science, education, engineering/technologies, general academic interests/achievements, humanities, international studies, mathematics, physical sciences, premedicine. *Creative arts/performance:* 8 awards ($27,872 total): applied art and design, art/fine arts, journalism/publications, performing arts, theater/drama. *Special achievements/activities:* 295 awards ($845,000 total): community service, general special achievements/activities, hobbies/interests, leadership, religious involvement. *Special characteristics:* 75 awards ($750,000 total): adult students, children of faculty/staff, children of union members/company employees, ethnic background, first-generation college students, general special characteristics, handicapped students, international students, local/state students, members of minority groups, out-of-state students, relatives of clergy, religious affiliation, siblings of current students, veterans, veterans' children. *Tuition waivers:* Full or partial for employees or children of employees. **ROTC:** Army cooperative, Air Force.

LOANS *Student loans:* $30,359,132 (38% need-based, 62% non-need-based). 61% of past graduating class borrowed through all loan programs. *Average indebtedness per student:* $34,867. *Average need-based loan:* Freshmen: $3377. Undergraduates: $4344. *Parent loans:* $1,936,929 (100% non-need-based). *Programs:* Federal Direct (Subsidized and Unsubsidized Stafford, PLUS), Perkins, state, college/university, alternative loans.

WORK-STUDY *Federal work-study:* Total amount: $318,059; 264 jobs averaging $1205. *State or other work-study/employment:* Total amount: $1,438,102 (100% non-need-based). 704 part-time jobs averaging $2043.

ATHLETIC AWARDS Total amount: $2,776,046 (100% need-based).

APPLYING FOR FINANCIAL AID *Required financial aid forms:* FAFSA, institution's own form. *Financial aid deadline (priority):* 3/15. *Notification date:* Continuous beginning 1/1. Students must reply by 5/1.

CONTACT Ivon Nunez, Director of Financial Aid Services, New Jersey Institute of Technology, Student Mall, University Heights, Newark, NJ 07102, 973-596-3476 or toll-free 800-925-NJIT. *Fax:* 973-596-6471. *E-mail:* ivon.nunez@njit.edu. *Website:* http://www.njit.edu/.

NEW LIFE THEOLOGICAL SEMINARY
Charlotte, NC

Tuition & fees: N/R	Average undergraduate aid package: N/A

ABOUT THE INSTITUTION Independent Christian, coed. 2 undergraduate majors. Federal methodology is used as a basis for awarding need-based institutional aid.

FRESHMAN FINANCIAL AID (Fall 2011) 11 applied for aid; of those 100% were deemed to have need. 100% of freshmen with need received aid; of those 100% had need fully met. *Average percent of need met:* 100% (excluding resources awarded to replace EFC). *Average financial aid package:* $11,905 (excluding resources awarded to replace EFC).

GIFT AID (NEED-BASED) *Total amount:* $450,762 (91% federal, 9% institutional). *Receiving aid:* Freshmen: 100% (11). *Scholarships, grants, and awards:* Federal Pell, FSEOG, private, college/university gift aid from institutional funds, Veterans Education Benefits (GI Bill).

GIFT AID (NON-NEED-BASED) *Total amount:* $41,382 (100% institutional). *Receiving aid:* Freshmen: 100% (11). *Scholarships, grants, and awards by category:* Academic interests/achievement: education, foreign languages, religion/biblical studies. *Special achievements/activities:* memberships, religious involvement. *Special characteristics:* religious affiliation.

LOANS *Student loans:* $1,600,240 (47% need-based, 53% non-need-based). *Programs:* Federal Direct (Subsidized and Unsubsidized Stafford, PLUS).

WORK-STUDY *Federal work-study:* Total amount: $8387; jobs available.

APPLYING FOR FINANCIAL AID *Required financial aid form:* FAFSA. *Financial aid deadline:* Continuous. *Notification date:* 3/15. Students must reply within 2 weeks of notification.

CONTACT Mr. Kenneth Neal Roach, Financial Aid Officer, New Life Theological Seminary, 3117 Whiting Avenue, PO Box 790106, Charlotte, NC 28206-7901, 704-334-6882 Ext. 114. *Fax:* 704-334-6885. *E-mail:* kroach@nlts.edu. *Website:* http://www.nlts.org/.

NEWMAN UNIVERSITY
Wichita, KS

CONTACT Kara Schwinn, Financial Aid Counselor, Newman University, 3100 McCormick Avenue, Wichita, KS 67213, 316-942-4291 Ext. 2302 or toll-free 877-NEWMANU. *Fax:* 316-942-4483.
Website: http://www.newmanu.edu/.

NEW MEXICO HIGHLANDS UNIVERSITY
Las Vegas, NM

Tuition & fees (NM res): $3504	Average undergraduate aid package: $1747

ABOUT THE INSTITUTION State-supported, coed. *Awards:* certificates, bachelor's, and master's degrees. 44 undergraduate majors. *Total enrollment:* 3,738. Undergraduates: 2,416. Freshmen: 436. Both federal and institutional methodology are used as a basis for awarding need-based institutional aid.

UNDERGRADUATE EXPENSES for 2013–2014 *Tuition, state resident:* full-time $2653; part-time $221.22 per credit hour. *Tuition, nonresident:* full-time $5671; part-time $401.72 per credit hour. *Required fees:* full-time $851. Full-time tuition and fees vary according to course load and location. Part-time tuition and fees vary according to course load and location. *College room and board:* $5920. Room and board charges vary according to board plan and housing facility.

FRESHMAN FINANCIAL AID (Fall 2011) 364 applied for aid; of those 85% were deemed to have need. 99% of freshmen with need received aid; of those 1% had need fully met. *Average financial aid package:* $1472 (excluding resources awarded to replace EFC).

UNDERGRADUATE FINANCIAL AID (Fall 2011) 1,399 applied for aid; of those 89% were deemed to have need. 92% of undergraduates with need received aid; of those 4% had need fully met. *Average financial aid package:* $1747 (excluding resources awarded to replace EFC).

GIFT AID (NEED-BASED) *Total amount:* $6,643,465 (88% federal, 8% state, 4% external sources). *Receiving aid:* Freshmen: 68% (281); all full-time undergraduates: 62% (1,023). *Average award:* Freshmen: $1919; Undergraduates: $1889. *Scholarships, grants, and awards:* Federal Pell, FSEOG, state, private, college/university gift aid from institutional funds.

GIFT AID (NON-NEED-BASED) *Total amount:* $1,703,228 (40% state, 38% institutional, 22% external sources). *Receiving aid:* Freshmen: 60% (247). Undergraduates: 27% (447). *Scholarships, grants, and awards by category:* Academic interests/achievement: biological sciences, business, communication, computer science, education, engineering/technologies, English, foreign languages, general academic interests/achievements, health fields, humanities, mathematics, physical sciences, social sciences. *Creative arts/performance:* art/fine arts, music, performing arts, theater/drama. *Special characteristics:* children and siblings of alumni, children of faculty/staff, children with a deceased or disabled parent, first-generation college students, international students, local/state students. *Tuition waivers:* Full or partial for employees or children of employees, senior citizens.

LOANS *Student loans:* $6,003,059 (61% need-based, 39% non-need-based). *Average need-based loan:* Freshmen: $1605. Undergraduates: $2056. *Parent loans:* $80,551 (100% non-need-based). *Programs:* Federal Direct (Subsidized and Unsubsidized Stafford, PLUS), Perkins.

WORK-STUDY *Federal work-study:* Total amount: $490,672; jobs available. *State or other work-study/employment:* Total amount: $185,605 (98% need-based, 2% non-need-based). Part-time jobs available.

ATHLETIC AWARDS Total amount: $597,114 (100% non-need-based).

APPLYING FOR FINANCIAL AID *Required financial aid form:* FAFSA. *Financial aid deadline:* Continuous. *Notification date:* Continuous beginning 3/15. Students must reply within 2 weeks of notification.

CONTACT Eileen Sedillo, Director of Financial Aid, New Mexico Highlands University, Box 9000, Las Vegas, NM 87701, 505-454-3430 or toll-free 800-338-6648. *Fax:* 505-454-3398. *E-mail:* sedillo_e@nmhu.edu. *Website:* http://www.nmhu.edu/.

NEW MEXICO INSTITUTE OF MINING AND TECHNOLOGY
Socorro, NM

Tuition & fees (NM res): $5496	Average undergraduate aid package: $12,026

ABOUT THE INSTITUTION State-supported, coed. *Awards:* associate, bachelor's, master's, and doctoral degrees. 22 undergraduate majors. *Total enrollment:* 2,105. Undergraduates: 1,565. Freshmen: 348. Federal methodology is used as a basis for awarding need-based institutional aid.
UNDERGRADUATE EXPENSES for 2013–2014 *Application fee:* $15. *Tuition, state resident:* full-time $4828; part-time $201.18 per credit hour. *Tuition, nonresident:* full-time $15,699; part-time $654.12 per credit hour. *Required fees:* full-time $668; $18 per credit hour or $71.50 per term. Full-time tuition and fees vary according to reciprocity agreements. Part-time tuition and fees vary according to course load. *College room and board:* $6304. Room and board charges vary according to board plan and housing facility.
FRESHMAN FINANCIAL AID (Fall 2012, est.) 343 applied for aid; of those 57% were deemed to have need. 98% of freshmen with need received aid; of those 24% had need fully met. *Average percent of need met:* 84% (excluding resources awarded to replace EFC). *Average financial aid package:* $11,261 (excluding resources awarded to replace EFC). 37% of all full-time freshmen had no need and received non-need-based gift aid.
UNDERGRADUATE FINANCIAL AID (Fall 2012, est.) 1,216 applied for aid; of those 59% were deemed to have need. 97% of undergraduates with need received aid; of those 22% had need fully met. *Average percent of need met:* 82% (excluding resources awarded to replace EFC). *Average financial aid package:* $12,026 (excluding resources awarded to replace EFC). 33% of all full-time undergraduates had no need and received non-need-based gift aid.
GIFT AID (NEED-BASED) Total amount: $2,726,045 (82% federal, 15% state, 3% external sources). *Receiving aid:* Freshmen: 30% (110); all full-time undergraduates: 32% (438). *Average award:* Freshmen: $6818; Undergraduates: $6046. *Scholarships, grants, and awards:* Federal Pell, FSEOG, state, private, college/university gift aid from institutional funds.
GIFT AID (NON-NEED-BASED) Total amount: $6,206,448 (45% state, 46% institutional, 9% external sources). *Receiving aid:* Freshmen: 49% (183). Undergraduates: 38% (511). *Average award:* Freshmen: $6953. Undergraduates: $6707. *Scholarships, grants, and awards by category: Academic interests/ achievement:* general academic interests/achievements. *Tuition waivers:* Full or partial for employees or children of employees, senior citizens.
LOANS Student loans: $3,304,875 (48% need-based, 52% non-need-based). 42% of past graduating class borrowed through all loan programs. *Average indebtedness per student:* $18,834. *Average need-based loan:* Freshmen: $2862. Undergraduates: $4293. *Parent loans:* $164,400 (100% need-based). *Programs:* Federal Direct (Subsidized and Unsubsidized Stafford, PLUS), Perkins.
WORK-STUDY Federal work-study: Total amount: $688,486; jobs available. *State or other work-study/employment:* Total amount: $101,465 (44% need-based, 56% non-need-based). Part-time jobs available.
APPLYING FOR FINANCIAL AID *Required financial aid form:* FAFSA. *Financial aid deadline (priority):* 5/1. *Notification date:* Continuous beginning 5/1. Students must reply within 2 weeks of notification.
CONTACT Ms. Annette Kaus, Director of Financial Aid, New Mexico Institute of Mining and Technology, 801 Leroy Place, Socorro, NM 87801, 575-835-5333 or toll-free 800-428-TECH. *Fax:* 575-835-5959. *E-mail:* akaus@admin.nmt.edu. *Website:* http://www.nmt.edu/.

NEW MEXICO STATE UNIVERSITY
Las Cruces, NM

Tuition & fees (NM res): $6040	Average undergraduate aid package: $9715

ABOUT THE INSTITUTION State-supported, coed. *Awards:* certificates, associate, bachelor's, master's, and doctoral degrees. 81 undergraduate majors. *Total enrollment:* 17,651. Undergraduates: 14,276. Freshmen: 2,061. Federal methodology is used as a basis for awarding need-based institutional aid.

UNDERGRADUATE EXPENSES for 2013–2014 *Application fee:* $20. *One-time required fee:* $40. *Tuition, state resident:* full-time $4766; part-time $199 per credit hour. *Tuition, nonresident:* full-time $17,794; part-time $741 per credit hour. *Required fees:* full-time $1274; $53.10 per credit hour. *College room and board:* $7182; *Room only:* $3946. Room and board charges vary according to board plan and housing facility.
FRESHMAN FINANCIAL AID (Fall 2012, est.) 1,879 applied for aid; of those 76% were deemed to have need. 99% of freshmen with need received aid; of those 16% had need fully met. *Average percent of need met:* 70% (excluding resources awarded to replace EFC). *Average financial aid package:* $9442 (excluding resources awarded to replace EFC). 5% of all full-time freshmen had no need and received non-need-based gift aid.
UNDERGRADUATE FINANCIAL AID (Fall 2012, est.) 9,092 applied for aid; of those 85% were deemed to have need. 97% of undergraduates with need received aid; of those 12% had need fully met. *Average percent of need met:* 69% (excluding resources awarded to replace EFC). *Average financial aid package:* $9715 (excluding resources awarded to replace EFC). 5% of all full-time undergraduates had no need and received non-need-based gift aid.
GIFT AID (NEED-BASED) Total amount: $44,391,758 (60% federal, 32% state, 6% institutional, 2% external sources). *Receiving aid:* Freshmen: 69% (1,399); all full-time undergraduates: 61% (7,028). *Average award:* Freshmen: $8310; Undergraduates: $8313. *Scholarships, grants, and awards:* Federal Pell, FSEOG, state, private, college/university gift aid from institutional funds, United Negro College Fund.
GIFT AID (NON-NEED-BASED) Total amount: $12,225,012 (77% state, 14% institutional, 9% external sources). *Receiving aid:* Freshmen: 9% (186). Undergraduates: 6% (649). *Average award:* Freshmen: $678. Undergraduates: $1872. *Scholarships, grants, and awards by category: Academic interests/achievement:* 639 awards ($603,729 total): agriculture, area/ethnic studies, biological sciences, business, communication, computer science, education, engineering/technologies, English, foreign languages, general academic interests/achievements, health fields, home economics, humanities, mathematics, military science, physical sciences, social sciences. *Creative arts/performance:* 60 awards ($44,659 total): applied art and design, art/fine arts, cinema/film/broadcasting, creative writing, dance, general creative arts/performance, journalism/publications, music, performing arts, theater/drama. *Special achievements/activities:* 42 awards ($49,451 total): cheerleading/drum major, general special achievements/activities, hobbies/interests, junior miss, leadership, memberships, rodeo. *Special characteristics:* 475 awards ($767,623 total): adult students, children and siblings of alumni, children of current students, children of faculty/staff, children of public servants, children of union members/company employees, children of workers in trades, children with a deceased or disabled parent, ethnic background, handicapped students, international students, local/state students, married students, members of minority groups, out-of-state students, previous college experience, public servants, spouses of current students, spouses of deceased or disabled public servants, veterans, veterans' children. *Tuition waivers:* Full or partial for employees or children of employees, senior citizens. *ROTC:* Army, Air Force.
LOANS Student loans: $42,764,712 (79% need-based, 21% non-need-based). 54% of past graduating class borrowed through all loan programs. *Average indebtedness per student:* $18,922. *Average need-based loan:* Freshmen: $2986. Undergraduates: $3754. *Parent loans:* $1,137,529 (19% need-based, 81% non-need-based). *Programs:* Federal Direct (Subsidized and Unsubsidized Stafford, PLUS), Perkins, state.
WORK-STUDY Federal work-study: Total amount: $978,443; 330 jobs averaging $3018. *State or other work-study/employment:* Total amount: $971,905 (76% need-based, 24% non-need-based). 314 part-time jobs averaging $3179.
ATHLETIC AWARDS Total amount: $3,187,087 (25% need-based, 75% non-need-based).
APPLYING FOR FINANCIAL AID *Required financial aid forms:* FAFSA, institution's own form. *Financial aid deadline (priority):* 3/1. *Notification date:* Continuous beginning 3/15.
CONTACT Ms. Janie Merchant, Director of Financial Aid, New Mexico State University, Box 30001, Department 5100, Las Cruces, NM 88003-8001, 575-646-4105 or toll-free 800-662-6678. *Fax:* 575-646-7381. *Website:* http://www.nmsu.edu/.

NEW ORLEANS BAPTIST THEOLOGICAL SEMINARY
New Orleans, LA

ABOUT THE INSTITUTION Independent Southern Baptist, coed, primarily men. 4 undergraduate majors.

GIFT AID (NEED-BASED) *Scholarships, grants, and awards:* state, private, college/university gift aid from institutional funds.

LOANS *Programs:* Sallie Mae Signature Loans.

APPLYING FOR FINANCIAL AID *Required financial aid form:* institution's own form.

CONTACT Owen Nease, Financial Aid Office, New Orleans Baptist Theological Seminary, 3939 Gentilly Boulevard, New Orleans, LA 70126-4858, 504-282-4455 Ext. 3348 or toll-free 800-662-8701. *Fax:* 504-816-8437. *E-mail:* financialaid@nobts.edu. *Website:* http://www.nobts.edu/.

NEW SAINT ANDREWS COLLEGE
Moscow, ID

Tuition & fees: $11,200	Average undergraduate aid package: N/A

ABOUT THE INSTITUTION Independent Christian, coed. *Awards:* certificates, associate, bachelor's, and master's degrees. 1 undergraduate major. *Total enrollment:* 175. Undergraduates: 149. Freshmen: 46. Institutional methodology is used as a basis for awarding need-based institutional aid.

UNDERGRADUATE EXPENSES for 2013–2014 *Application fee:* $40. *Tuition:* full-time $11,200; part-time $950 per course. Full-time tuition and fees vary according to program. Part-time tuition and fees vary according to program. *Payment plan:* Guaranteed tuition.

GIFT AID (NEED-BASED) *Total amount:* $134,580 (49% institutional, 51% external sources).

GIFT AID (NON-NEED-BASED) *Total amount:* $104,925 (100% institutional). *Tuition waivers:* Full or partial for employees or children of employees.

APPLYING FOR FINANCIAL AID *Notification date:* Continuous.

CONTACT Brenda Schlect, College Bursars Office, New Saint Andrews College, 405 South Main Street, PO Box 9025, Moscow, ID 83843, 208-882-1566 Ext. 113. *Fax:* 208-882-4297. *E-mail:* bschlect@nsa.edu. *Website:* http://www.nsa.edu/.

THE NEW SCHOOL FOR JAZZ AND CONTEMPORARY MUSIC
New York, NY

Tuition & fees: $38,226	Average undergraduate aid package: N/A

ABOUT THE INSTITUTION Independent, coed. *Awards:* bachelor's degrees. 7 undergraduate majors. *Total enrollment:* 269. Undergraduates: 269. Freshmen: 49. Federal methodology is used as a basis for awarding need-based institutional aid.

UNDERGRADUATE EXPENSES for 2013–2014 *Application fee:* $100. *Comprehensive fee:* $55,526 includes full-time tuition ($37,950), mandatory fees ($276), and room and board ($17,300). *Part-time tuition:* $1245 per credit.

GIFT AID (NEED-BASED) *Scholarships, grants, and awards:* Federal Pell, FSEOG, state, private, college/university gift aid from institutional funds.

GIFT AID (NON-NEED-BASED) *Scholarships, grants, and awards by category: Academic interests/achievement:* general academic interests/achievements. *Creative arts/performance:* music.

LOANS *Programs:* Federal Direct (Subsidized and Unsubsidized Stafford, PLUS), Perkins.

APPLYING FOR FINANCIAL AID *Required financial aid form:* FAFSA. *Financial aid deadline:* Continuous. *Notification date:* Continuous beginning 3/1. Students must reply within 4 weeks of notification.

CONTACT Eileen F. Doyle, Assistant Vice President for Student Financial Services, The New School for Jazz and Contemporary Music, 72 Fifth Avenue, New York, NY 10011, 212-229-8930 or toll-free 800-292-3040. *E-mail:* sfs@newschool.edu. *Website:* http://www.jazz.newschool.edu/.

THE NEW SCHOOL FOR PUBLIC ENGAGEMENT
New York, NY

CONTACT Eileen F. Doyle, Assistant Vice President for Student Financial Services, The New School for Public Engagement, 65 Fifth Avenue, New York, NY 10003, 212-229-8930 or toll-free 800-292-3040. *Fax:* 212-229-5919. *E-mail:* sfs@newschool.edu. *Website:* http://www.newschool.edu/public-engagement/.

NEWSCHOOL OF ARCHITECTURE & DESIGN
San Diego, CA

CONTACT Matt Wakeman, Director of Financial Aid, Newschool of Architecture & Design, 1249 F Street, San Diego, CA 92101-6634, 619-235-4100 Ext. 103 or toll-free 800-490-7081. *Fax:* 619-235-4651. *Website:* http://www.newschoolarch.edu/.

NEW WORLD SCHOOL OF THE ARTS
Miami, FL

CONTACT Financial Aid Office, New World School of the Arts, 300 NE 2nd Avenue, Miami, FL 33132, 305-237-3135. *Website:* http://www.mdc.edu/nwsa/.

NEW YORK CITY COLLEGE OF TECHNOLOGY OF THE CITY UNIVERSITY OF NEW YORK
Brooklyn, NY

Tuition & fees (NY res): $5769	Average undergraduate aid package: $8867

ABOUT THE INSTITUTION State and locally supported, coed. *Awards:* certificates, associate, and bachelor's degrees. 38 undergraduate majors. *Total enrollment:* 16,207. Undergraduates: 16,207. Freshmen: 2,861. Both federal and institutional methodology are used as a basis for awarding need-based institutional aid.

UNDERGRADUATE EXPENSES for 2013–2014 *Application fee:* $65. *Tuition, state resident:* full-time $5430; part-time $230 per credit. *Tuition, nonresident:* full-time $14,550; part-time $485 per credit. *Required fees:* full-time $339; $85.20 per term.

FRESHMAN FINANCIAL AID (Fall 2012, est.) 2,566 applied for aid; of those 90% were deemed to have need. 97% of freshmen with need received aid; of those 10% had need fully met. *Average percent of need met:* 64% (excluding resources awarded to replace EFC). *Average financial aid package:* $8985 (excluding resources awarded to replace EFC). 3% of all full-time freshmen had no need and received non-need-based gift aid.

UNDERGRADUATE FINANCIAL AID (Fall 2012, est.) 8,718 applied for aid; of those 95% were deemed to have need. 98% of undergraduates with need received aid; of those 4% had need fully met. *Average percent of need met:* 57% (excluding resources awarded to replace EFC). *Average financial aid package:* $8867 (excluding resources awarded to replace EFC). 1% of all full-time undergraduates had no need and received non-need-based gift aid.

GIFT AID (NEED-BASED) *Total amount:* $77,921,023 (60% federal, 37% state, 3% external sources). *Receiving aid:* Freshmen: 81% (2,228); all full-time undergraduates: 80% (7,911). *Average award:* Freshmen: $8730; Undergraduates: $8356. *Scholarships, grants, and awards:* Federal Pell, FSEOG, state, private, Federal Nursing.
GIFT AID (NON-NEED-BASED) *Receiving aid:* Freshmen: 70% (1,935). Undergraduates: 68% (6,738). *Average award:* Freshmen: $271. Undergraduates: $233. *Tuition waivers:* Full or partial for employees or children of employees.
LOANS *Student loans:* $7,073,619 (100% need-based). *Average need-based loan:* Freshmen: $3297. Undergraduates: $4267. *Programs:* Federal Direct (Subsidized and Unsubsidized Stafford, PLUS), Perkins, Federal Nursing.
WORK-STUDY *Federal work-study:* Total amount: $2,081,073; jobs available.
APPLYING FOR FINANCIAL AID *Required financial aid forms:* FAFSA, state aid form. *Financial aid deadline (priority):* 3/31. *Notification date:* Continuous.
CONTACT Sandra Higgins, Director of Financial Aid, New York City College of Technology of the City University of New York, 300 Jay Street, Namm Hall, Room G-13, Brooklyn, NY 11201, 718-260-5700. *Fax:* 718-254-8525. *E-mail:* financialaid@citytech.cuny.edu.
Website: http://www.citytech.cuny.edu/.

NEW YORK COLLEGE OF HEALTH PROFESSIONS
Syosset, NY

CONTACT Financial Aid Office, New York College of Health Professions, 6801 Jericho Turnpike, Syosset, NY 11791-4413, 516-364-0808 or toll-free 800-922-7337 Ext. 351.
Website: http://www.nycollege.edu/.

NEW YORK FILM ACADEMY
Los Angeles, CA

CONTACT Financial Aid Office, New York Film Academy, 3801 Barham Boulevard, Los Angeles, CA 90068, 818-733-2600.
Website: http://www.nyfa.com/.

NEW YORK INSTITUTE OF TECHNOLOGY
Old Westbury, NY

Tuition & fees: $28,940	Average undergraduate aid package: $22,693

ABOUT THE INSTITUTION Independent, coed. *Awards:* certificates, associate, bachelor's, master's, and doctoral degrees. 47 undergraduate majors. *Total enrollment:* 7,883. Undergraduates: 4,796. Freshmen: 898. Federal methodology is used as a basis for awarding need-based institutional aid.
UNDERGRADUATE EXPENSES for 2013–2014 *Application fee:* $50. *Comprehensive fee:* $40,590 includes full-time tuition ($28,020), mandatory fees ($920), and room and board ($11,650). *College room only:* $7320. Full-time tuition and fees vary according to course load and program. Room and board charges vary according to board plan, housing facility, and location. *Part-time tuition:* $950 per credit hour. *Part-time fees:* $400 per term. Part-time tuition and fees vary according to course load.
FRESHMAN FINANCIAL AID (Fall 2012, est.) 994 applied for aid; of those 92% were deemed to have need. 99% of freshmen with need received aid. *Average financial aid package:* $18,712 (excluding resources awarded to replace EFC). 14% of all full-time freshmen had no need and received non-need-based gift aid.
UNDERGRADUATE FINANCIAL AID (Fall 2012, est.) 3,124 applied for aid; of those 93% were deemed to have need. 99% of undergraduates with need received aid. *Average financial aid package:* $22,693 (excluding resources awarded to replace EFC). 12% of all full-time undergraduates had no need and received non-need-based gift aid.
GIFT AID (NEED-BASED) *Total amount:* $17,366,718 (44% federal, 27% state, 29% institutional). *Receiving aid:* Freshmen: 56% (647); all full-time undergraduates: 60% (2,260). *Average award:* Freshmen: $5326; Undergraduates: $6468. *Scholarships, grants, and awards:* Federal Pell, FSEOG, state, private, college/university gift aid from institutional funds.
GIFT AID (NON-NEED-BASED) *Total amount:* $28,725,218 (6% federal, 1% state, 90% institutional, 3% external sources). *Receiving aid:* Freshmen: 74% (858). Undergraduates: 67% (2,530). *Average award:* Freshmen: $12,066. Undergraduates: $14,333. *Scholarships, grants, and awards by category: Academic interests/achievement:* general academic interests/achievements. *Special characteristics:* children and siblings of alumni, children of faculty/staff, local/state students, previous college experience, veterans. *Tuition waivers:* Full or partial for employees or children of employees, senior citizens. *ROTC:* Army, Air Force.
LOANS *Student loans:* $25,606,527 (41% need-based, 59% non-need-based). *Average need-based loan:* Freshmen: $3535. Undergraduates: $5375. *Parent loans:* $13,522,398 (100% non-need-based). *Programs:* Federal Direct (Subsidized and Unsubsidized Stafford, PLUS), Perkins, alternative loans.
WORK-STUDY *Federal work-study:* Total amount: $283,676; jobs available. *State or other work-study/employment:* Total amount: $678,601 (100% non-need-based). Part-time jobs available.
ATHLETIC AWARDS Total amount: $2,525,200 (100% non-need-based).
APPLYING FOR FINANCIAL AID *Required financial aid form:* FAFSA. *Financial aid deadline (priority):* 3/1. *Notification date:* Continuous beginning 3/1. Students must reply within 4 weeks of notification.
CONTACT Doreen Meyer, Director of Financial Aid, New York Institute of Technology, PO Box 8000, Old Westbury, NY 11568-8000, 516-686-1083 or toll-free 800-345-NYIT. *Fax:* 516-686-7997. *E-mail:* dmeyer@nyit.edu.
Website: http://www.nyit.edu/.

NEW YORK SCHOOL OF INTERIOR DESIGN
New York, NY

Tuition & fees: $27,894	Average undergraduate aid package: $9590

ABOUT THE INSTITUTION Independent, coed, primarily women. *Awards:* certificates, associate, bachelor's, and master's degrees. 1 undergraduate major. *Total enrollment:* 710. Undergraduates: 556. Freshmen: 40. Federal methodology is used as a basis for awarding need-based institutional aid.
UNDERGRADUATE EXPENSES for 2013–2014 *Application fee:* $60. *Tuition:* full-time $27,324; part-time $828 per credit. *Required fees:* full-time $570; $570 per term. Full-time tuition and fees vary according to course load. Part-time tuition and fees vary according to course load.
FRESHMAN FINANCIAL AID (Fall 2011) 12 applied for aid; of those 100% were deemed to have need. 100% of freshmen with need received aid. *Average percent of need met:* 32% (excluding resources awarded to replace EFC). *Average financial aid package:* $9557 (excluding resources awarded to replace EFC).
UNDERGRADUATE FINANCIAL AID (Fall 2011) 110 applied for aid; of those 96% were deemed to have need. 100% of undergraduates with need received aid; of those 1% had need fully met. *Average percent of need met:* 29% (excluding resources awarded to replace EFC). *Average financial aid package:* $9590 (excluding resources awarded to replace EFC). 5% of all full-time undergraduates had no need and received non-need-based gift aid.
GIFT AID (NEED-BASED) *Total amount:* $861,190 (48% federal, 8% state, 44% institutional). *Receiving aid:* Freshmen: 100% (12); all full-time undergraduates: 73% (84). *Average award:* Freshmen: $6485; Undergraduates: $7394. *Scholarships, grants, and awards:* Federal Pell, FSEOG, state, private, college/university gift aid from institutional funds.
GIFT AID (NON-NEED-BASED) *Total amount:* $90,302 (1% state, 99% institutional). *Receiving aid:* Undergraduates: 1% (1). *Average award:* Undergraduates: $8390. *Tuition waivers:* Full or partial for employees or children of employees.
LOANS *Student loans:* $1,704,731 (88% need-based, 12% non-need-based). 67% of past graduating class borrowed through all loan programs. *Average indebtedness per student:* $35,502. *Average need-based loan:* Freshmen: $3022. Undergrad-

uates: $3825. **Parent loans:** $395,207 (62% need-based, 38% non-need-based). **Programs:** Federal Direct (Subsidized and Unsubsidized Stafford, PLUS).
WORK-STUDY Federal work-study: Total amount: $34,803; 24 jobs averaging $1800.
APPLYING FOR FINANCIAL AID Required financial aid forms: FAFSA, state aid form. **Financial aid deadline (priority):** 8/1. **Notification date:** Continuous beginning 4/15. Students must reply within 2 weeks of notification.
CONTACT Mrs. Rashmi H. Wadhvani, Director of Financial Aid, New York School of Interior Design, 170 East 70th Street, New York, NY 10021-5110, 212-472-1500 Ext. 212 or toll-free 800-336-9743 Ext. 204. Fax: 212-472-1867. E-mail: rwadhvani@nysid.edu.
Website: http://www.nysid.edu/.

NEW YORK UNIVERSITY
New York, NY

Tuition & fees: $43,204	Average undergraduate aid package: $29,367

ABOUT THE INSTITUTION Independent, coed. **Awards:** certificates, associate, bachelor's, master's, and doctoral degrees. 87 undergraduate majors. **Total enrollment:** 44,516. Undergraduates: 22,498. Freshmen: 5,140. Both federal and institutional methodology are used as a basis for awarding need-based institutional aid.
UNDERGRADUATE EXPENSES for 2013–2014 **Application fee:** $70. **Comprehensive fee:** $59,337 includes full-time tuition ($40,878), mandatory fees ($2326), and room and board ($16,133). Full-time tuition and fees vary according to course load and program. Room and board charges vary according to board plan and housing facility. **Part-time tuition:** $1204 per credit. **Part-time fees:** $63 per credit; $434 per term. Part-time tuition and fees vary according to program. **Payment plan:** Tuition prepayment.
FRESHMAN FINANCIAL AID (Fall 2011) 3,216 applied for aid; of those 84% were deemed to have need. 98% of freshmen with need received aid; of those 3% had need fully met. **Average percent of need met:** 59% (excluding resources awarded to replace EFC). **Average financial aid package:** $28,920 (excluding resources awarded to replace EFC). 2% of all full-time freshmen had no need and received non-need-based gift aid.
UNDERGRADUATE FINANCIAL AID (Fall 2011) 13,081 applied for aid; of those 88% were deemed to have need. 98% of undergraduates with need received aid; of those 4% had need fully met. **Average percent of need met:** 55% (excluding resources awarded to replace EFC). **Average financial aid package:** $29,367 (excluding resources awarded to replace EFC). 5% of all full-time undergraduates had no need and received non-need-based gift aid.
GIFT AID (NEED-BASED) Total amount: $213,986,089 (10% federal, 5% state, 82% institutional, 3% external sources). **Receiving aid:** Freshmen: 53% (2,570); all full-time undergraduates: 52% (10,824). **Average award:** Freshmen: $20,882; Undergraduates: $19,497. **Scholarships, grants, and awards:** Federal Pell, FSEOG, state, private, college/university gift aid from institutional funds.
GIFT AID (NON-NEED-BASED) Total amount: $15,079,063 (2% state, 74% institutional, 24% external sources). **Receiving aid:** Freshmen: 2% (74). Undergraduates: 2% (437). **Average award:** Freshmen: $7371. Undergraduates: $7841. **Scholarships, grants, and awards by category:** Academic interests/achievement: 1,432 awards ($10,932,145 total): general academic interests/achievements. Creative arts/performance: general creative arts/performance. **Tuition waivers:** Full or partial for employees or children of employees. **ROTC:** Army cooperative, Air Force cooperative.
LOANS Student loans: $107,143,777 (86% need-based, 14% non-need-based). 53% of past graduating class borrowed through all loan programs. Average indebtedness per student: $35,104. **Average need-based loan:** Freshmen: $5486. Undergraduates: $5555. **Parent loans:** $129,459,875 (59% need-based, 41% non-need-based). **Programs:** Federal Direct (Subsidized and Unsubsidized Stafford, PLUS), Perkins, Federal Nursing, college/university.
WORK-STUDY Federal work-study: Total amount: $19,215,435; 6,625 jobs averaging $2882.
APPLYING FOR FINANCIAL AID Required financial aid forms: FAFSA, CSS Financial Aid PROFILE, state aid form, noncustodial (divorced/separated) parent's statement. **Financial aid deadline:** 2/15. **Notification date:** 4/1. Students must reply by 5/1.

CONTACT Office of Financial Aid, New York University, 25 West Fourth Street, New York, NY 10012-1199, 212-998-4444. Fax: 212-995-4661. E-mail: financial.aid@nyu.edu.
Website: http://www.nyu.edu/.

NIAGARA UNIVERSITY
Niagara Falls, NY

Tuition & fees: $27,230	Average undergraduate aid package: $22,337

ABOUT THE INSTITUTION Independent Roman Catholic Church, coed. **Awards:** certificates, associate, bachelor's, master's, and doctoral degrees. 59 undergraduate majors. **Total enrollment:** 4,045. Undergraduates: 3,175. Freshmen: 641. Federal methodology is used as a basis for awarding need-based institutional aid.
UNDERGRADUATE EXPENSES for 2013–2014 **Application fee:** $30. **Comprehensive fee:** $38,530 includes full-time tuition ($26,100), mandatory fees ($1130), and room and board ($11,300). **Part-time tuition:** $870 per credit hour.
FRESHMAN FINANCIAL AID (Fall 2012, est.) 590 applied for aid; of those 100% were deemed to have need. 92% of freshmen with need received aid; of those 50% had need fully met. **Average percent of need met:** 88% (excluding resources awarded to replace EFC). **Average financial aid package:** $25,251 (excluding resources awarded to replace EFC). 13% of all full-time freshmen had no need and received non-need-based gift aid.
UNDERGRADUATE FINANCIAL AID (Fall 2012, est.) 2,251 applied for aid; of those 93% were deemed to have need. 100% of undergraduates with need received aid; of those 51% had need fully met. **Average percent of need met:** 83% (excluding resources awarded to replace EFC). **Average financial aid package:** $22,337 (excluding resources awarded to replace EFC). 16% of all full-time undergraduates had no need and received non-need-based gift aid.
GIFT AID (NEED-BASED) Total amount: $38,449,120 (14% federal, 8% state, 77% institutional, 1% external sources). **Receiving aid:** Freshmen: 83% (531); all full-time undergraduates: 74% (2,059). **Average award:** Freshmen: $20,935; Undergraduates: $17,961. **Scholarships, grants, and awards:** Federal Pell, FSEOG, state, private, college/university gift aid from institutional funds.
GIFT AID (NON-NEED-BASED) Total amount: $6,301,244 (8% federal, 91% institutional, 1% external sources). **Receiving aid:** Freshmen: 70% (447). Undergraduates: 58% (1,622). **Average award:** Freshmen: $13,011. Undergraduates: $11,523. **Scholarships, grants, and awards by category:** Academic interests/achievement: 2,503 awards ($27,763,674 total): general academic interests/achievements. Creative arts/performance: 70 awards ($353,677 total): theater/drama. Special achievements/activities: 8 awards ($40,000 total): community service. Special characteristics: 82 awards ($2,047,803 total): children of faculty/staff, relatives of clergy. **Tuition waivers:** Full or partial for employees or children of employees, senior citizens. **ROTC:** Army.
LOANS Student loans: $17,780,767 (95% need-based, 5% non-need-based). 79% of past graduating class borrowed through all loan programs. Average indebtedness per student: $32,114. **Average need-based loan:** Freshmen: $4684. Undergraduates: $4819. **Parent loans:** $4,401,515 (94% need-based, 6% non-need-based). **Programs:** Federal Direct (Subsidized and Unsubsidized Stafford, PLUS), Perkins, Federal Nursing, college/university.
WORK-STUDY Federal work-study: Total amount: $1,192,022; 366 jobs averaging $2910. **State or other work-study/employment:** Total amount: $243,219 (100% non-need-based). 41 part-time jobs averaging $5350.
ATHLETIC AWARDS Total amount: $3,407,855 (50% need-based, 50% non-need-based).
APPLYING FOR FINANCIAL AID Required financial aid forms: FAFSA, state aid form. **Financial aid deadline (priority):** 2/15. **Notification date:** Continuous beginning 3/15. Students must reply within 3 weeks of notification.
CONTACT Ms. Katie L. Kocsis, Assistant Director of Financial Aid, Niagara University, Niagara Falls, NY 14109, 716-286-8686 or toll-free 800-462-2111. Fax: 716-286-8678. E-mail: kkocsis@niagara.edu.
Website: http://www.niagara.edu/.

NICHOLLS STATE UNIVERSITY
Thibodaux, LA

Tuition & fees (LA res): $5679	Average undergraduate aid package: $8359

ABOUT THE INSTITUTION State-supported, coed. **Awards:** certificates, associate, bachelor's, and master's degrees. 37 undergraduate majors. **Total enrollment:** 6,606. Undergraduates: 6,012. Freshmen: 1,253. Federal methodology is used as a basis for awarding need-based institutional aid.

UNDERGRADUATE EXPENSES for 2013–2014 Application fee: $20. **Tuition, state resident:** full-time $3924. **Tuition, nonresident:** full-time $12,774. **Required fees:** full-time $1755. Part-time tuition and fees vary according to course load. **College room and board:** $8560; **Room only:** $5670. Room and board charges vary according to board plan, housing facility, and location.

FRESHMAN FINANCIAL AID (Fall 2011) 910 applied for aid; of those 65% were deemed to have need. 99% of freshmen with need received aid; of those 29% had need fully met. **Average percent of need met:** 73% (excluding resources awarded to replace EFC). **Average financial aid package:** $9311 (excluding resources awarded to replace EFC). 14% of all full-time freshmen had no need and received non-need-based gift aid.

UNDERGRADUATE FINANCIAL AID (Fall 2011) 4,140 applied for aid; of those 70% were deemed to have need. 98% of undergraduates with need received aid; of those 19% had need fully met. **Average percent of need met:** 63% (excluding resources awarded to replace EFC). **Average financial aid package:** $8359 (excluding resources awarded to replace EFC). 8% of all full-time undergraduates had no need and received non-need-based gift aid.

GIFT AID (NEED-BASED) Total amount: $16,630,644 (60% federal, 26% state, 9% institutional, 5% external sources). **Receiving aid:** Freshmen: 58% (567); all full-time undergraduates: 53% (2,579). **Average award:** Freshmen: $7059; Undergraduates: $6124. **Scholarships, grants, and awards:** Federal Pell, FSEOG, state, private, college/university gift aid from institutional funds.

GIFT AID (NON-NEED-BASED) Total amount: $6,180,405 (3% federal, 62% state, 28% institutional, 7% external sources). **Receiving aid:** Freshmen: 12% (118). Undergraduates: 7% (327). **Average award:** Freshmen: $3578. Undergraduates: $3873. **Scholarships, grants, and awards by category:** Academic interests/achievement: general academic interests/achievements. Creative arts/performance: dance, music. Special achievements/activities: cheerleading/drum major, leadership. Special characteristics: children of faculty/staff, general special characteristics, local/state students, members of minority groups, out-of-state students, previous college experience, public servants, veterans. **Tuition waivers:** Full or partial for employees or children of employees.

LOANS Student loans: $14,142,818 (65% need-based, 35% non-need-based). 56% of past graduating class borrowed through all loan programs. **Average indebtedness per student:** $27,396. **Average need-based loan:** Freshmen: $2429. Undergraduates: $3172. **Parent loans:** $1,014,314 (45% need-based, 55% non-need-based). **Programs:** Federal Direct (Subsidized and Unsubsidized Stafford, PLUS).

WORK-STUDY Federal work-study: Total amount: $178,207; 102 jobs averaging $1654. **State or other work-study/employment:** Total amount: $236,792 (55% need-based, 45% non-need-based). 667 part-time jobs averaging $1555.

ATHLETIC AWARDS Total amount: $1,685,716 (50% need-based, 50% non-need-based).

APPLYING FOR FINANCIAL AID Required financial aid forms: FAFSA, institution's own form, state aid form, noncustodial (divorced/separated) parent's statement. **Financial aid deadline:** 6/30 (priority: 4/15). **Notification date:** Continuous.

CONTACT Casie Triche, Director of Financial Aid, Nicholls State University, PO Box 2005, Thibodaux, LA 70310, 985-448-4077 or toll-free 877-NICHOLLS. Fax: 985-448-4124. E-mail: finaid@nicholls.edu. Website: http://www.nicholls.edu/.

NICHOLS COLLEGE
Dudley, MA

Tuition & fees: $31,740	Average undergraduate aid package: $21,795

ABOUT THE INSTITUTION Independent, coed. **Awards:** certificates, associate, bachelor's, and master's degrees. 19 undergraduate majors. **Total enrollment:** 1,547. Undergraduates: 1,337. Freshmen: 250. Federal methodology is used as a basis for awarding need-based institutional aid.

UNDERGRADUATE EXPENSES for 2013–2014 Application fee: $25. **Comprehensive fee:** $42,440 includes full-time tuition ($31,440), mandatory fees ($300), and room and board ($10,700). **College room only:** $5800. Room and board charges vary according to housing facility.

FRESHMAN FINANCIAL AID (Fall 2012, est.) 316 applied for aid; of those 98% were deemed to have need. 100% of freshmen with need received aid; of those 6% had need fully met. **Average percent of need met:** 77% (excluding resources awarded to replace EFC). **Average financial aid package:** $21,400 (excluding resources awarded to replace EFC). 6% of all full-time freshmen had no need and received non-need-based gift aid.

UNDERGRADUATE FINANCIAL AID (Fall 2012, est.) 961 applied for aid; of those 99% were deemed to have need. 100% of undergraduates with need received aid; of those 3% had need fully met. **Average percent of need met:** 78% (excluding resources awarded to replace EFC). **Average financial aid package:** $21,795 (excluding resources awarded to replace EFC). 5% of all full-time undergraduates had no need and received non-need-based gift aid.

GIFT AID (NEED-BASED) Total amount: $16,311,751 (11% federal, 3% state, 84% institutional, 2% external sources). **Receiving aid:** Freshmen: 94% (309); all full-time undergraduates: 93% (949). **Average award:** Freshmen: $17,679; Undergraduates: $17,830. **Scholarships, grants, and awards:** Federal Pell, FSEOG, state, private, college/university gift aid from institutional funds.

GIFT AID (NON-NEED-BASED) Total amount: $423,246 (100% institutional). **Receiving aid:** Freshmen: 2% (7). Undergraduates: 1% (12). **Average award:** Freshmen: $9876. Undergraduates: $9984. **Scholarships, grants, and awards by category:** Academic interests/achievement: general academic interests/achievements. Special achievements/activities: community service, general special achievements/activities, leadership. Special characteristics: children and siblings of alumni, children of faculty/staff, siblings of current students. **Tuition waivers:** Full or partial for employees or children of employees. **ROTC:** Army cooperative.

LOANS Student loans: $10,195,591 (97% need-based, 3% non-need-based). 89% of past graduating class borrowed through all loan programs. **Average indebtedness per student:** $30,890. **Average need-based loan:** Freshmen: $3279. Undergraduates: $3940. **Parent loans:** $4,649,004 (100% need-based). **Programs:** Federal Direct (Subsidized and Unsubsidized Stafford, PLUS).

WORK-STUDY Federal work-study: Total amount: $175,270; 387 jobs averaging $1470.

APPLYING FOR FINANCIAL AID Required financial aid form: FAFSA. **Financial aid deadline (priority):** 3/1. **Notification date:** Continuous. Students must reply within 2 weeks of notification.

CONTACT Ms. Denise Brindle, Director of Financial Aid, Nichols College, PO Box 5000, Dudley, MA 01571, 508-213-2372 or toll-free 800-470-3379. Fax: 508-213-2118. E-mail: denise.brindle@nichols.edu. Website: http://www.nichols.edu/.

NORFOLK STATE UNIVERSITY
Norfolk, VA

Tuition & fees (VA res): $6860	Average undergraduate aid package: N/A

ABOUT THE INSTITUTION State-supported, coed. **Awards:** associate, bachelor's, master's, and doctoral degrees. 32 undergraduate majors. **Total enrollment:** 8,343. Undergraduates: 7,455. Freshmen: 1,088. Federal methodology is used as a basis for awarding need-based institutional aid.

UNDERGRADUATE EXPENSES for 2013–2014 Tuition, state resident: full-time $6860; part-time $252 per credit hour. **Tuition, nonresident:** full-time $20,343; part-time $702 per credit hour. Full-time tuition and fees vary according to course load. Part-time tuition and fees vary according to course load. **College room**

and board: $8130. Room and board charges vary according to board plan and housing facility.

GIFT AID (NEED-BASED) *Total amount:* $26,450,851 (69% federal, 26% state, 5% institutional). *Scholarships, grants, and awards:* Federal Pell, FSEOG, state, private, college/university gift aid from institutional funds.

GIFT AID (NON-NEED-BASED) *Scholarships, grants, and awards by category:* Creative arts/performance: music, performing arts. Special achievements/activities: general special achievements/activities. ROTC: Army, Naval.

LOANS *Student loans:* $18,173,273 (100% need-based). *Programs:* Federal Direct (Subsidized and Unsubsidized Stafford), Perkins, state, alternative loans.

WORK-STUDY *Federal work-study:* Total amount: $851,500; jobs available. *State or other work-study/employment:* Total amount: $281,262 (100% need-based). Part-time jobs available.

ATHLETIC AWARDS Total amount: $3,056,657 (100% non-need-based).

APPLYING FOR FINANCIAL AID *Required financial aid form:* FAFSA. *Financial aid deadline:* 5/31. *Notification date:* 6/15. Students must reply within 2 weeks of notification.

CONTACT Mr. Kevin Burns, Director of Financial Aid, Norfolk State University, 700 Park Avenue, Norfolk, VA 23504-3907, 757-823-8381 or toll-free 800-274-1821. *Fax:* 757-823-9059. *E-mail:* kburns@nsu.edu. *Website:* http://www.nsu.edu/.

NORTH AMERICAN COLLEGE
Houston, TX

CONTACT Financial Aid Office, North American College, 3203 North Sam Houston Parkway W., Houston, TX 77038, 832-230-5555. *Website:* http://www.northamerican.edu/.

NORTH CAROLINA AGRICULTURAL AND TECHNICAL STATE UNIVERSITY
Greensboro, NC

Tuition & fees (NC res): $5058	Average undergraduate aid package: $13,599

ABOUT THE INSTITUTION State-supported, coed. *Awards:* bachelor's, master's, and doctoral degrees. 92 undergraduate majors. *Total enrollment:* 10,881. Undergraduates: 9,206. Freshmen: 1,875. Both federal and institutional methodology are used as a basis for awarding need-based institutional aid.

UNDERGRADUATE EXPENSES for 2013–2014 *Application fee:* $45. *Tuition, state resident:* full-time $5058. *Tuition, nonresident:* full-time $15,657. Full-time tuition and fees vary according to course load and student level. Part-time tuition and fees vary according to course load and student level. *College room and board:* $7349. Room and board charges vary according to board plan and housing facility.

FRESHMAN FINANCIAL AID (Fall 2012, est.) 1,800 applied for aid; of those 89% were deemed to have need. 99% of freshmen with need received aid; of those 5% had need fully met. *Average percent of need met:* 80% (excluding resources awarded to replace EFC). *Average financial aid package:* $14,094 (excluding resources awarded to replace EFC). 3% of all full-time freshmen had no need and received non-need-based gift aid.

UNDERGRADUATE FINANCIAL AID (Fall 2012, est.) 7,717 applied for aid; of those 90% were deemed to have need. 100% of undergraduates with need received aid; of those 4% had need fully met. *Average percent of need met:* 80% (excluding resources awarded to replace EFC). *Average financial aid package:* $13,599 (excluding resources awarded to replace EFC). 3% of all full-time undergraduates had no need and received non-need-based gift aid.

GIFT AID (NEED-BASED) *Total amount:* $43,770,998 (54% federal, 25% state, 16% institutional, 5% external sources). *Receiving aid:* Freshmen: 63% (1,168); all full-time undergraduates: 64% (5,137). *Average award:* Freshmen: $5202; Undergraduates: $5023. *Scholarships, grants, and awards:* Federal Pell, FSEOG, state, private, college/university gift aid from institutional funds.

GIFT AID (NON-NEED-BASED) *Total amount:* $3,636,701 (32% federal, 5% state, 48% institutional, 15% external sources). *Receiving aid:* Freshmen: 76%

(1,400). Undergraduates: 71% (5,699). *Average award:* Freshmen: $6143. Undergraduates: $7434. *Scholarships, grants, and awards by category:* Academic interests/achievement: agriculture, business, engineering/technologies, general academic interests/achievements. Creative arts/performance: music. Tuition waivers: Full or partial for employees or children of employees. ROTC: Army, Air Force.

LOANS *Student loans:* $57,631,869 (91% need-based, 9% non-need-based). 70% of past graduating class borrowed through all loan programs. *Average indebtedness per student:* $28,119. *Average need-based loan:* Freshmen: $3405. Undergraduates: $4052. *Parent loans:* $4,495,829 (81% need-based, 19% non-need-based). *Programs:* Federal Direct (Subsidized and Unsubsidized Stafford, PLUS), Perkins.

WORK-STUDY *Federal work-study:* Total amount: $375,503; 350 jobs averaging $1178.

ATHLETIC AWARDS Total amount: $2,183,888 (77% need-based, 23% non-need-based).

APPLYING FOR FINANCIAL AID *Required financial aid form:* FAFSA. *Financial aid deadline (priority):* 3/1. *Notification date:* 4/15. Students must reply within 2 weeks of notification.

CONTACT Mrs. Sherri Avent, Director of Student Financial Aid, North Carolina Agricultural and Technical State University, Dowdy Administration Building, Room 100, 1601 East Market Street, Greensboro, NC 27411, 336-334-7973 or toll-free 800-443-8964 (in-state). *Fax:* 336-334-7954. *E-mail:* avent@ncat.edu. *Website:* http://www.ncat.edu/.

NORTH CAROLINA CENTRAL UNIVERSITY
Durham, NC

Tuition & fees (NC res): $3244	Average undergraduate aid package: $11,956

ABOUT THE INSTITUTION State-supported, coed. *Awards:* bachelor's, master's, and doctoral degrees. 47 undergraduate majors. *Total enrollment:* 8,604. Undergraduates: 6,658. Freshmen: 1,407. Federal methodology is used as a basis for awarding need-based institutional aid.

UNDERGRADUATE EXPENSES for 2013–2014 *Application fee:* $40. *Tuition, state resident:* full-time $3244. *Tuition, nonresident:* full-time $13,817. Part-time tuition and fees vary according to course load. *College room and board:* $9923. *Room only:* $6791. Room and board charges vary according to board plan, housing facility, and location.

FRESHMAN FINANCIAL AID (Fall 2011) 1,230 applied for aid; of those 95% were deemed to have need. 100% of freshmen with need received aid; of those 4% had need fully met. *Average percent of need met:* 64% (excluding resources awarded to replace EFC). *Average financial aid package:* $11,865 (excluding resources awarded to replace EFC). 1% of all full-time freshmen had no need and received non-need-based gift aid.

UNDERGRADUATE FINANCIAL AID (Fall 2011) 5,049 applied for aid; of those 94% were deemed to have need. 100% of undergraduates with need received aid; of those 4% had need fully met. *Average percent of need met:* 61% (excluding resources awarded to replace EFC). *Average financial aid package:* $11,956 (excluding resources awarded to replace EFC). 1% of all full-time undergraduates had no need and received non-need-based gift aid.

GIFT AID (NEED-BASED) *Total amount:* $35,221,466 (56% federal, 26% state, 14% institutional, 4% external sources). *Receiving aid:* Freshmen: 79% (985); all full-time undergraduates: 74% (3,841). *Average award:* Freshmen: $6142; Undergraduates: $6213. *Scholarships, grants, and awards:* Federal Pell, FSEOG, state, private, college/university gift aid from institutional funds, Federal Nursing.

GIFT AID (NON-NEED-BASED) *Total amount:* $844,757 (4% federal, 23% state, 22% institutional, 51% external sources). *Receiving aid:* Freshmen: 81% (1,011). Undergraduates: 69% (3,589). *Average award:* Freshmen: $4265. Undergraduates: $4446. *Scholarships, grants, and awards by category:* Academic interests/achievement: biological sciences, business, computer science, education, English, general academic interests/achievements, library science, physical sciences, social sciences. Creative arts/performance: music, theater/drama. Special characteristics: general special characteristics. Tuition waivers: Full or partial for employees or children of employees. ROTC: Army, Air Force.

LOANS *Student loans:* $41,059,936 (96% need-based, 4% non-need-based). *Average need-based loan:* Freshmen: $3318. Undergraduates: $4034. *Parent*

loans: $11,217,447 (87% need-based, 13% non-need-based). **Programs:** Federal Direct (Subsidized and Unsubsidized Stafford, PLUS), Perkins, Federal Nursing.
WORK-STUDY *Federal work-study:* Total amount: $552,835; jobs available. *State or other work-study/employment:* Total amount: $727,647 (85% need-based, 15% non-need-based). Part-time jobs available.
ATHLETIC AWARDS Total amount: $2,402,464 (77% need-based, 23% non-need-based).
APPLYING FOR FINANCIAL AID *Required financial aid form:* FAFSA. *Financial aid deadline (priority):* 3/1. *Notification date:* Continuous beginning 3/15. Students must reply within 2 weeks of notification.
CONTACT Mrs. Sharon J. Oliver, Director of Scholarships and Student Aid, North Carolina Central University, 106 Student Services Building, Durham, NC 27707-3129, 919-530-5313 or toll-free 877-667-7533. *Fax:* 919-530-7959. *E-mail:* soliver@nccu.edu.
Website: http://www.nccu.edu/.

NORTH CAROLINA STATE UNIVERSITY
Raleigh, NC

Tuition & fees (NC res): $7788	Average undergraduate aid package: $12,652

ABOUT THE INSTITUTION State-supported, coed. **Awards:** certificates, associate, bachelor's, master's, and doctoral degrees. 100 undergraduate majors. **Total enrollment:** 34,340. Undergraduates: 24,833. Freshmen: 4,398. Federal methodology is used as a basis for awarding need-based institutional aid.
UNDERGRADUATE EXPENSES for 2013–2014 *Application fee:* $70. *Tuition, state resident:* full-time $5748. *Tuition, nonresident:* full-time $18,913. *Required fees:* full-time $2040. Full-time tuition and fees vary according to degree level, location, and program. Part-time tuition and fees vary according to course load, degree level, location, and program. *College room and board:* $8414; *Room only:* $5434. Room and board charges vary according to board plan and housing facility.
FRESHMAN FINANCIAL AID (Fall 2012, est.) 3,287 applied for aid; of those 65% were deemed to have need. 98% of freshmen with need received aid; of those 34% had need fully met. *Average percent of need met:* 86% (excluding resources awarded to replace EFC). *Average financial aid package:* $12,846 (excluding resources awarded to replace EFC). 4% of all full-time freshmen had no need and received non-need-based gift aid.
UNDERGRADUATE FINANCIAL AID (Fall 2012, est.) 14,206 applied for aid; of those 76% were deemed to have need. 98% of undergraduates with need received aid; of those 33% had need fully met. *Average percent of need met:* 84% (excluding resources awarded to replace EFC). *Average financial aid package:* $12,652 (excluding resources awarded to replace EFC). 4% of all full-time undergraduates had no need and received non-need-based gift aid.
GIFT AID (NEED-BASED) Total amount: $93,956,202 (24% federal, 25% state, 48% institutional, 3% external sources). **Receiving aid:** Freshmen: 46% (2,006); all full-time undergraduates: 45% (9,815). **Average award:** Freshmen: $9771; Undergraduates: $9360. **Scholarships, grants, and awards:** Federal Pell, FSEOG, state, private, college/university gift aid from institutional funds, United Negro College Fund.
GIFT AID (NON-NEED-BASED) Total amount: $12,733,388 (1% federal, 10% state, 57% institutional, 32% external sources). **Receiving aid:** Freshmen: 12% (538). Undergraduates: 7% (1,605). **Average award:** Freshmen: $5982. Undergraduates: $5587. **Scholarships, grants, and awards by category:** *Academic interests/achievement:* agriculture, biological sciences, business, education, engineering/technologies, general academic interests/achievements, humanities, mathematics, military science, physical sciences, social sciences. *Special achievements/activities:* leadership. *Special characteristics:* children and siblings of alumni, local/state students. **Tuition waivers:** Full or partial for employees or children of employees. **ROTC:** Army, Naval, Air Force.
LOANS Student loans: $81,179,775 (59% need-based, 41% non-need-based). 57% of past graduating class borrowed through all loan programs. *Average indebtedness per student:* $22,626. *Average need-based loan:* Freshmen: $3196. Undergraduates: $3907. *Parent loans:* $10,373,814 (6% need-based, 94% non-need-based). *Programs:* Federal Direct (Subsidized and Unsubsidized Stafford, PLUS), Perkins, state, college/university.

WORK-STUDY *Federal work-study:* Total amount: $1,092,532; jobs available. *State or other work-study/employment:* Total amount: $1,702,338 (30% need-based, 70% non-need-based). Part-time jobs available.
ATHLETIC AWARDS Total amount: $6,924,466 (36% need-based, 64% non-need-based).
APPLYING FOR FINANCIAL AID *Required financial aid form:* FAFSA. *Financial aid deadline (priority):* 3/1. *Notification date:* Continuous beginning 4/1.
CONTACT Ms. Krista Ringler Domnick, Director of Scholarships and Financial Aid, North Carolina State University, 2016 Harris Hall, Box 7302, Raleigh, NC 27695-7302, 919-515-2866. *Fax:* 919-515-8422. *E-mail:* krista_domnick@ncsu.edu. *Website:* http://www.ncsu.edu/.

NORTH CAROLINA WESLEYAN COLLEGE
Rocky Mount, NC

CONTACT Leah Hill, Director of Financial Aid, North Carolina Wesleyan College, 3400 North Wesleyan Boulevard, Rocky Mount, NC 27804, 252-985-5200 or toll-free 800-488-6292. *Fax:* 252-985-5295. *E-mail:* lhill@ncwc.edu. *Website:* http://www.ncwc.edu/.

NORTH CENTRAL COLLEGE
Naperville, IL

Tuition & fees: $31,071	Average undergraduate aid package: $22,061

ABOUT THE INSTITUTION Independent United Methodist, coed. **Awards:** certificates, bachelor's, and master's degrees. 63 undergraduate majors. **Total enrollment:** 3,042. Undergraduates: 2,755. Freshmen: 552. Federal methodology is used as a basis for awarding need-based institutional aid.
UNDERGRADUATE EXPENSES for 2013–2014 *Application fee:* $25. *Comprehensive fee:* $39,954 includes full-time tuition ($30,891), mandatory fees ($180), and room and board ($8883). Room and board charges vary according to housing facility. *Part-time tuition:* $750 per credit hour. *Part-time fees:* $20 per term. Part-time tuition and fees vary according to course load.
FRESHMAN FINANCIAL AID (Fall 2012, est.) 517 applied for aid; of those 86% were deemed to have need. 100% of freshmen with need received aid; of those 22% had need fully met. *Average percent of need met:* 78% (excluding resources awarded to replace EFC). *Average financial aid package:* $23,790 (excluding resources awarded to replace EFC). 18% of all full-time freshmen had no need and received non-need-based gift aid.
UNDERGRADUATE FINANCIAL AID (Fall 2012, est.) 2,179 applied for aid; of those 90% were deemed to have need. 100% of undergraduates with need received aid; of those 20% had need fully met. *Average percent of need met:* 73% (excluding resources awarded to replace EFC). *Average financial aid package:* $22,061 (excluding resources awarded to replace EFC). 21% of all full-time undergraduates had no need and received non-need-based gift aid.
GIFT AID (NEED-BASED) Total amount: $33,464,336 (8% federal, 9% state, 81% institutional, 2% external sources). **Receiving aid:** Freshmen: 80% (442); all full-time undergraduates: 76% (1,939). **Average award:** Freshmen: $19,332; Undergraduates: $16,944. **Scholarships, grants, and awards:** Federal Pell, FSEOG, state, private, college/university gift aid from institutional funds.
GIFT AID (NON-NEED-BASED) Total amount: $8,500,311 (97% institutional, 3% external sources). **Receiving aid:** Freshmen: 11% (59). Undergraduates: 8% (214). **Average award:** Freshmen: $14,595. Undergraduates: $12,632. **Scholarships, grants, and awards by category:** *Academic interests/achievement:* biological sciences, business, communication, computer science, education, English, foreign languages, general academic interests/achievements, humanities, international studies, mathematics, physical sciences, premedicine, religion/biblical studies, social sciences. *Creative arts/performance:* art/fine arts, cinema/film/broadcasting, debating, journalism/publications, music, theater/drama. *Special achievements/activities:* community service, religious involvement. *Special characteristics:* adult students, children of faculty/staff, general special characteristics, international students, relatives of clergy.

Tuition waivers: Full or partial for employees or children of employees, senior citizens. *ROTC:* Army cooperative, Air Force cooperative.
LOANS *Student loans:* $18,398,253 (73% need-based, 27% non-need-based). 77% of past graduating class borrowed through all loan programs. *Average indebtedness per student:* $33,304. *Average need-based loan:* Freshmen: $3675. Undergraduates: $4737. *Parent loans:* $4,425,297 (27% need-based, 73% non-need-based). *Programs:* Federal Direct (Subsidized and Unsubsidized Stafford, PLUS), Perkins, state, college/university.
WORK-STUDY *Federal work-study:* Total amount: $216,031; 163 jobs averaging $1297. *State or other work-study/employment:* Total amount: $468,927 (46% need-based, 54% non-need-based). Part-time jobs available.
APPLYING FOR FINANCIAL AID *Required financial aid forms:* FAFSA, institution's own form, federal income tax form(s). *Financial aid deadline:* Continuous. *Notification date:* Continuous beginning 3/1. Students must reply within 4 weeks of notification.
CONTACT Marty P. Rossman, Director of Financial Aid, North Central College, 30 North Brainard Street, Naperville, IL 60540, 630-637-5600 or toll-free 800-411-1861. *Fax:* 630-637-5608. *E-mail:* mprossman@noctrl.edu. *Website:* http://www.northcentralcollege.edu/.

NORTH CENTRAL UNIVERSITY
Minneapolis, MN

CONTACT Mrs. Donna Jager, Director of Financial Aid, North Central University, 910 Elliot Avenue, Minneapolis, MN 55404-1322, 612-343-4485 or toll-free 800-289-6222. *Fax:* 612-343-8067. *E-mail:* finaid@northcentral.edu. *Website:* http://www.northcentral.edu/.

NORTH DAKOTA STATE UNIVERSITY
Fargo, ND

CONTACT Jeanne Enebo, Director of Financial Aid, North Dakota State University, PO Box 5315, Fargo, ND 58105, 701-231-7537 or toll-free 800-488-NDSU. *Fax:* 701-231-6126. *E-mail:* j.enebo@ndsu.edu. *Website:* http://www.ndsu.edu/.

NORTHEASTERN ILLINOIS UNIVERSITY
Chicago, IL

Tuition & fees (IL res): $9926	Average undergraduate aid package: $8530

ABOUT THE INSTITUTION State-supported, coed. *Awards:* bachelor's and master's degrees. 43 undergraduate majors. *Total enrollment:* 11,149. Undergraduates: 9,140. Freshmen: 1,040. Federal methodology is used as a basis for awarding need-based institutional aid.
UNDERGRADUATE EXPENSES for 2013–2014 *Application fee:* $30. *Tuition, state resident:* full-time $8610; part-time $287 per credit hour. *Tuition, nonresident:* full-time $14,700; part-time $550 per credit hour. *Required fees:* full-time $1316. Full-time tuition and fees vary according to student level. Part-time tuition and fees vary according to student level. *Payment plan:* Guaranteed tuition.
FRESHMAN FINANCIAL AID (Fall 2012, est.) 904 applied for aid; of those 85% were deemed to have need. 93% of freshmen with need received aid; of those 1% had need fully met. *Average percent of need met:* 34% (excluding resources awarded to replace EFC). *Average financial aid package:* $8090 (excluding resources awarded to replace EFC). 2% of all full-time freshmen had no need and received non-need-based gift aid.
UNDERGRADUATE FINANCIAL AID (Fall 2012, est.) 4,429 applied for aid; of those 90% were deemed to have need. 94% of undergraduates with need received aid; of those 2% had need fully met. *Average percent of need met:* 29% (excluding resources awarded to replace EFC). *Average financial aid package:* $8530

(excluding resources awarded to replace EFC). 2% of all full-time undergraduates had no need and received non-need-based gift aid.
GIFT AID (NEED-BASED) *Total amount:* $21,531,663 (63% federal, 35% state, 2% external sources). *Receiving aid:* Freshmen: 66% (655); all full-time undergraduates: 60% (3,238). *Average award:* Freshmen: $7150; Undergraduates: $6505. *Scholarships, grants, and awards:* Federal Pell, FSEOG, state, private, college/university gift aid from institutional funds.
GIFT AID (NON-NEED-BASED) *Total amount:* $1,734,669 (40% state, 40% institutional, 20% external sources). *Receiving aid:* Freshmen: 6% (60). Undergraduates: 9% (484). *Average award:* Freshmen: $1532. Undergraduates: $3195. *Scholarships, grants, and awards by category:* Academic interests/achievement: biological sciences, business, communication, computer science, education, English, foreign languages, general academic interests/achievements, mathematics, physical sciences, social sciences. Creative arts/performance: art/fine arts, creative writing, dance, journalism/publications, music, performing arts, theater/drama. Special achievements/activities: general special achievements/activities, leadership. Special characteristics: adult students, children of faculty/staff, general special characteristics. *Tuition waivers:* Full or partial for employees or children of employees, senior citizens. *ROTC:* Army cooperative, Air Force cooperative.
LOANS *Student loans:* $18,059,939 (43% need-based, 57% non-need-based). 18% of past graduating class borrowed through all loan programs. *Average indebtedness per student:* $11,112. *Average need-based loan:* Freshmen: $3247. Undergraduates: $4571. *Parent loans:* $245,611 (100% non-need-based). *Programs:* Federal Direct (Subsidized and Unsubsidized Stafford, PLUS), Perkins.
WORK-STUDY *Federal work-study:* Total amount: $183,924; jobs available. *State or other work-study/employment:* Total amount: $557,937 (100% non-need-based). Part-time jobs available.
APPLYING FOR FINANCIAL AID *Required financial aid form:* FAFSA. *Financial aid deadline (priority):* 2/15. *Notification date:* Continuous beginning 12/15. Students must reply within 2 weeks of notification.
CONTACT Maureen T. Amos, Office of Financial Aid, Northeastern Illinois University, 5500 North St. Louis Avenue, Chicago, IL 60625, 773-442-5010. *Fax:* 773-442-5040. *E-mail:* financial-aid@neiu.edu. *Website:* http://www.neiu.edu/.

NORTHEASTERN STATE UNIVERSITY
Tahlequah, OK

Tuition & fees (OK res): $4857	Average undergraduate aid package: $11,270

ABOUT THE INSTITUTION State-supported, coed. *Awards:* certificates, bachelor's, master's, and doctoral degrees. 67 undergraduate majors. *Total enrollment:* 9,361. Undergraduates: 8,116. Freshmen: 953. Federal methodology is used as a basis for awarding need-based institutional aid.
UNDERGRADUATE EXPENSES for 2013–2014 *Application fee:* $25. *Tuition, state resident:* full-time $3750; part-time $125 per credit hour. *Tuition, nonresident:* full-time $10,500; part-time $350 per credit hour. *Required fees:* full-time $1107; $36.90 per credit hour. Full-time tuition and fees vary according to course load and program. Part-time tuition and fees vary according to course load and program. *College room and board:* $5914. Room and board charges vary according to board plan and housing facility.
FRESHMAN FINANCIAL AID (Fall 2012, est.) 765 applied for aid; of those 72% were deemed to have need. 99% of freshmen with need received aid; of those 83% had need fully met. *Average percent of need met:* 100% (excluding resources awarded to replace EFC). *Average financial aid package:* $10,210 (excluding resources awarded to replace EFC). 7% of all full-time freshmen had no need and received non-need-based gift aid.
UNDERGRADUATE FINANCIAL AID (Fall 2012, est.) 4,555 applied for aid; of those 80% were deemed to have need. 99% of undergraduates with need received aid; of those 73% had need fully met. *Average percent of need met:* 96% (excluding resources awarded to replace EFC). *Average financial aid package:* $11,270 (excluding resources awarded to replace EFC). 4% of all full-time undergraduates had no need and received non-need-based gift aid.
GIFT AID (NEED-BASED) *Total amount:* $21,756,321 (74% federal, 20% state, 1% institutional, 5% external sources). *Receiving aid:* Freshmen: 60% (515); all full-time undergraduates: 59% (3,161). *Average award:* Freshmen: $6727; Undergrad-

uates: $6082. *Scholarships, grants, and awards:* Federal Pell, FSEOG, state, private, college/university gift aid from institutional funds.
GIFT AID (NON-NEED-BASED) *Total amount:* $2,168,647 (2% federal, 1% state, 30% institutional, 67% external sources). *Receiving aid:* Freshmen: 16% (140). Undergraduates: 10% (508). *Average award:* Freshmen: $2651. Undergraduates: $2692. *Scholarships, grants, and awards by category: Academic interests/ achievement:* biological sciences, business, communication, computer science, education, English, foreign languages, general academic interests/achievements, health fields, home economics, humanities, library science, mathematics, physical sciences, premedicine, social sciences. *Creative arts/performance:* applied art and design, art/ fine arts, dance, debating, journalism/publications, music, performing arts, theater/ drama. *Special achievements/activities:* cheerleading/drum major, community service, junior miss, leadership. *Special characteristics:* children and siblings of alumni, children of faculty/staff, children with a deceased or disabled parent, local/state students, members of minority groups, out-of-state students, religious affiliation, spouses of deceased or disabled public servants. *Tuition waivers:* Full or partial for employees or children of employees, senior citizens. *ROTC:* Army.
LOANS *Student loans:* $35,141,566 (75% need-based, 25% non-need-based). 60% of past graduating class borrowed through all loan programs. *Average indebtedness per student:* $20,503. *Average need-based loan:* Freshmen: $4489. Undergraduates: $6438. *Parent loans:* $1,191,834 (40% need-based, 60% non-need-based). *Programs:* Federal Direct (Subsidized and Unsubsidized Stafford, PLUS), Perkins.
WORK-STUDY *Federal work-study:* Total amount: $639,497; 115 jobs averaging $1179. *State or other work-study/employment:* Total amount: $1,300,000 (100% non-need-based). 550 part-time jobs averaging $1886.
ATHLETIC AWARDS Total amount: $999,640 (13% need-based, 87% non-need-based).
APPLYING FOR FINANCIAL AID *Required financial aid form:* FAFSA. *Financial aid deadline (priority):* 3/1. *Notification date:* Continuous beginning 4/1.
CONTACT Dr. Teri Cochran, Director of Student Financial Services, Northeastern State University, 715 North Grand Avenue, Tahlequah, OK 74464-2399, 918-444-3410 or toll-free 800-722-9614. *Fax:* 918-458-2510. *E-mail:* cochrant@nsuok.edu. *Website:* http://www.nsuok.edu/.

NORTHEASTERN UNIVERSITY
Boston, MA

Tuition & fees: $39,736	Average undergraduate aid package: $22,787

ABOUT THE INSTITUTION Independent, coed. *Awards:* certificates, bachelor's, master's, and doctoral degrees. 62 undergraduate majors. *Total enrollment:* 24,540. Undergraduates: 16,685. Freshmen: 2,664. Both federal and institutional methodology are used as a basis for awarding need-based institutional aid.
UNDERGRADUATE EXPENSES for 2013–2014 *Application fee:* $75. *Comprehensive fee:* $53,356 includes full-time tuition ($39,320), mandatory fees ($416), and room and board ($13,620). *College room only:* $7240. Room and board charges vary according to board plan and housing facility.
FRESHMAN FINANCIAL AID (Fall 2012, est.) 1,866 applied for aid; of those 70% were deemed to have need. 100% of freshmen with need received aid; of those 36% had need fully met. *Average percent of need met:* 89% (excluding resources awarded to replace EFC). *Average financial aid package:* $29,409 (excluding resources awarded to replace EFC). 23% of all full-time freshmen had no need and received non-need-based gift aid.
UNDERGRADUATE FINANCIAL AID (Fall 2012, est.) 9,646 applied for aid; of those 77% were deemed to have need. 98% of undergraduates with need received aid; of those 27% had need fully met. *Average percent of need met:* 70% (excluding resources awarded to replace EFC). *Average financial aid package:* $22,787 (excluding resources awarded to replace EFC). 24% of all full-time undergraduates had no need and received non-need-based gift aid.
GIFT AID (NEED-BASED) *Total amount:* $126,423,460 (10% federal, 2% state, 85% institutional, 3% external sources). *Receiving aid:* Freshmen: 48% (1,273); all full-time undergraduates: 42% (6,943). *Average award:* Freshmen: $24,949; Undergraduates: $18,575. *Scholarships, grants, and awards:* Federal Pell, FSEOG, state, private, college/university gift aid from institutional funds.
GIFT AID (NON-NEED-BASED) *Total amount:* $62,565,128 (1% federal, 92% institutional, 7% external sources). *Receiving aid:* Freshmen: 17% (449). Undergrad-

uates: 12% (1,930). *Average award:* Freshmen: $18,338. Undergraduates: $11,629. *Tuition waivers:* Full or partial for employees or children of employees. *ROTC:* Army, Naval cooperative, Air Force cooperative.
LOANS *Student loans:* $80,680,814 (59% need-based, 41% non-need-based). *Average need-based loan:* Freshmen: $4556. Undergraduates: $4700. *Parent loans:* $18,991,863 (31% need-based, 69% non-need-based). *Programs:* Federal Direct (Subsidized and Unsubsidized Stafford, PLUS), Perkins, Federal Nursing, state, college/university.
WORK-STUDY *Federal work-study:* Total amount: $7,789,341; jobs available.
ATHLETIC AWARDS Total amount: $9,753,804 (30% need-based, 70% non-need-based).
APPLYING FOR FINANCIAL AID *Required financial aid forms:* FAFSA, CSS Financial Aid PROFILE, noncustodial (divorced/separated) parent's statement. *Financial aid deadline (priority):* 2/15. *Notification date:* 4/1. Students must reply by 5/1.
CONTACT Mr. Anthony Erwin, Dean of Financial Aid, Northeastern University, 360 Huntington Avenue, Boston, MA 02115, 617-373-3190. *Fax:* 617-373-8735. *E-mail:* sfs@neu.edu.
Website: http://www.northeastern.edu/.

NORTHERN ARIZONA UNIVERSITY
Flagstaff, AZ

Tuition & fees (AZ res): $9271	Average undergraduate aid package: $9810

ABOUT THE INSTITUTION State-supported, coed. *Awards:* certificates, bachelor's, master's, and doctoral degrees. 67 undergraduate majors. *Total enrollment:* 26,002. Undergraduates: 21,774. Freshmen: 4,254. Federal methodology is used as a basis for awarding need-based institutional aid.
UNDERGRADUATE EXPENSES for 2013–2014 *Application fee:* $25. *Tuition, state resident:* full-time $8453; part-time $363 per credit hour. *Tuition, nonresident:* full-time $20,808; part-time $749 per credit hour. *Required fees:* full-time $818; $6 per credit hour or $322 per term. Full-time tuition and fees vary according to degree level, location, and program. Part-time tuition and fees vary according to course load, degree level, location, and program. *College room and board:* $8784; *Room only:* $4824. Room and board charges vary according to board plan and housing facility. *Payment plan:* Guaranteed tuition.
FRESHMAN FINANCIAL AID (Fall 2011) 2,769 applied for aid; of those 76% were deemed to have need. 97% of freshmen with need received aid; of those 12% had need fully met. *Average percent of need met:* 60% (excluding resources awarded to replace EFC). *Average financial aid package:* $9835 (excluding resources awarded to replace EFC). 14% of all full-time freshmen had no need and received non-need-based gift aid.
UNDERGRADUATE FINANCIAL AID (Fall 2011) 13,629 applied for aid; of those 84% were deemed to have need. 98% of undergraduates with need received aid; of those 9% had need fully met. *Average percent of need met:* 58% (excluding resources awarded to replace EFC). *Average financial aid package:* $9810 (excluding resources awarded to replace EFC). 11% of all full-time undergraduates had no need and received non-need-based gift aid.
GIFT AID (NEED-BASED) *Total amount:* $78,668,225 (47% federal, 2% state, 45% institutional, 6% external sources). *Receiving aid:* Freshmen: 42% (1,364); all full-time undergraduates: 47% (8,316). *Average award:* Freshmen: $6306; Undergraduates: $6019. *Scholarships, grants, and awards:* Federal Pell, FSEOG, state, private, college/university gift aid from institutional funds, Federal Nursing, TEACH Grants, tribal grants, LEAP Grants.
GIFT AID (NON-NEED-BASED) *Total amount:* $12,894,687 (2% federal, 91% institutional, 7% external sources). *Receiving aid:* Freshmen: 35% (1,136). Undergraduates: 27% (4,709). *Average award:* Freshmen: $5098. Undergraduates: $4601. *Scholarships, grants, and awards by category: Academic interests/ achievement:* general academic interests/achievements. *Creative arts/performance:* art/fine arts, music, theater/drama. *Special achievements/activities:* leadership. *Special characteristics:* children and siblings of alumni, local/state students, members of minority groups. *Tuition waivers:* Full or partial for employees or children of employees. *ROTC:* Army, Air Force.
LOANS *Student loans:* $98,195,576 (87% need-based, 13% non-need-based). 58% of past graduating class borrowed through all loan programs. *Average indebtedness per student:* $22,621. *Average need-based loan:* Freshmen: $3300. Undergrad-

uates: $4131. *Parent loans:* $31,422,466 (72% need-based, 28% non-need-based). *Programs:* Federal Direct (Subsidized and Unsubsidized Stafford, PLUS), Perkins, Federal Nursing, state, college/university.

WORK-STUDY *Federal work-study:* Total amount: $930,004; jobs available. *State or other work-study/employment:* Total amount: $9,851,097 (64% need-based, 36% non-need-based). Part-time jobs available.

ATHLETIC AWARDS Total amount: $3,554,085 (46% need-based, 54% non-need-based).

APPLYING FOR FINANCIAL AID *Required financial aid form:* FAFSA. *Financial aid deadline (priority):* 2/14. *Notification date:* Continuous beginning 3/15.

CONTACT Office of Financial Aid, Northern Arizona University, PO Box 4108, Flagstaff, AZ 86011-4108, 928-523-4951 or toll-free 888-MORE-NAU. *Fax:* 928-523-1551. *E-mail:* financial.aid@nau.edu. *Website:* http://www.nau.edu/.

NORTHERN ILLINOIS UNIVERSITY
De Kalb, IL

Tuition & fees (IL res): $13,061	Average undergraduate aid package: $11,698

ABOUT THE INSTITUTION State-supported, coed. *Awards:* bachelor's, master's, and doctoral degrees. 67 undergraduate majors. *Total enrollment:* 21,869. Undergraduates: 16,552. Freshmen: 2,664. Federal methodology is used as a basis for awarding need-based institutional aid.

UNDERGRADUATE EXPENSES for 2013–2014 *Application fee:* $40. *Tuition, state resident:* full-time $11,484. *Tuition, nonresident:* full-time $20,377. *Required fees:* full-time $1577. Full-time tuition and fees vary according to course load, location, and student level. Part-time tuition and fees vary according to course load, location, and student level. *College room and board:* $10,648. Room and board charges vary according to board plan and housing facility. *Payment plan:* Guaranteed tuition.

FRESHMAN FINANCIAL AID (Fall 2011) 2,322 applied for aid; of those 89% were deemed to have need. 99% of freshmen with need received aid; of those 13% had need fully met. *Average percent of need met:* 69% (excluding resources awarded to replace EFC). *Average financial aid package:* $14,059 (excluding resources awarded to replace EFC).

UNDERGRADUATE FINANCIAL AID (Fall 2011) 13,091 applied for aid; of those 88% were deemed to have need. 98% of undergraduates with need received aid; of those 8% had need fully met. *Average percent of need met:* 60% (excluding resources awarded to replace EFC). *Average financial aid package:* $11,698 (excluding resources awarded to replace EFC).

GIFT AID (NEED-BASED) *Total amount:* $70,559,569 (45% federal, 36% state, 16% institutional, 3% external sources). *Receiving aid:* Freshmen: 76% (1,982); all full-time undergraduates: 54% (8,523). *Average award:* Freshmen: $8803; Undergraduates: $7511. *Scholarships, grants, and awards:* Federal Pell, FSEOG, state, private, college/university gift aid from institutional funds, United Negro College Fund, Federal Nursing, TEACH Grants.

GIFT AID (NON-NEED-BASED) *Total amount:* $1,927,606 (100% external sources). *Receiving aid:* Freshmen: 1% (16). Undergraduates: 1% (206). *Scholarships, grants, and awards by category:* Academic interests/achievement: biological sciences, business, communication, computer science, education, engineering/technologies, English, foreign languages, general academic interests/achievements, health fields, humanities, international studies, mathematics, physical sciences, social sciences. *Creative arts/performance:* applied art and design, art/fine arts, creative writing, dance, debating, journalism/publications, music, performing arts, theater/drama. *Special achievements/activities:* leadership. *Special characteristics:* adult students, children of faculty/staff, ethnic background, international students, members of minority groups, veterans. *ROTC:* Army, Air Force cooperative.

LOANS *Student loans:* $103,829,125 (46% need-based, 54% non-need-based). 72% of past graduating class borrowed through all loan programs. *Average indebtedness per student:* $30,521. *Average need-based loan:* Freshmen: $3399. Undergraduates: $4388. *Parent loans:* $15,954,949 (100% non-need-based). *Programs:* Federal Direct (Subsidized and Unsubsidized Stafford, PLUS), Perkins.

WORK-STUDY *Federal work-study:* Total amount: $19,467,309; 6,400 jobs averaging $3042.

ATHLETIC AWARDS Total amount: $6,314,859 (100% need-based).

APPLYING FOR FINANCIAL AID *Required financial aid form:* FAFSA. *Financial aid deadline (priority):* 3/1. *Notification date:* Continuous beginning 3/15. Students must reply within 2 weeks of notification.

CONTACT Ms. Rebecca A. Babel, Director of Student Financial Aid, Northern Illinois University, Swen Parson Hall, Room 245, De Kalb, IL 60115, 815-753-1395 or toll-free 800-892-3050. *Fax:* 815-753-9475. *E-mail:* rbabel@niu.edu. *Website:* http://www.niu.edu/.

NORTHERN KENTUCKY UNIVERSITY
Highland Heights, KY

Tuition & fees (KY res): $8064	Average undergraduate aid package: $8506

ABOUT THE INSTITUTION State-supported, coed. *Awards:* certificates, associate, bachelor's, master's, and doctoral degrees. 73 undergraduate majors. *Total enrollment:* 15,634. Undergraduates: 13,318. Freshmen: 2,107. Federal methodology is used as a basis for awarding need-based institutional aid.

UNDERGRADUATE EXPENSES for 2013–2014 *Application fee:* $40. *Tuition, state resident:* full-time $7872; part-time $328 per credit hour. *Tuition, nonresident:* full-time $15,744; part-time $656 per credit hour. *Required fees:* full-time $192. Full-time tuition and fees vary according to course load and reciprocity agreements. Part-time tuition and fees vary according to course load and reciprocity agreements. *College room and board:* $7430. Room and board charges vary according to board plan and housing facility.

FRESHMAN FINANCIAL AID (Fall 2012, est.) 1,945 applied for aid; of those 80% were deemed to have need. 99% of freshmen with need received aid; of those 15% had need fully met. *Average percent of need met:* 60% (excluding resources awarded to replace EFC). *Average financial aid package:* $8544 (excluding resources awarded to replace EFC). 9% of all full-time freshmen had no need and received non-need-based gift aid.

UNDERGRADUATE FINANCIAL AID (Fall 2012, est.) 7,913 applied for aid; of those 83% were deemed to have need. 98% of undergraduates with need received aid; of those 14% had need fully met. *Average percent of need met:* 53% (excluding resources awarded to replace EFC). *Average financial aid package:* $8506 (excluding resources awarded to replace EFC). 8% of all full-time undergraduates had no need and received non-need-based gift aid.

GIFT AID (NEED-BASED) *Total amount:* $22,197,430 (90% federal, 10% state). *Receiving aid:* Freshmen: 41% (895); all full-time undergraduates: 39% (3,885). *Average award:* Freshmen: $5682; Undergraduates: $5107. *Scholarships, grants, and awards:* Federal Pell, FSEOG, state, private, college/university gift aid from institutional funds.

GIFT AID (NON-NEED-BASED) *Total amount:* $20,117,513 (7% federal, 28% state, 40% institutional, 25% external sources). *Receiving aid:* Freshmen: 52% (1,148). Undergraduates: 32% (3,190). *Average award:* Freshmen: $4330. Undergraduates: $4405. *Scholarships, grants, and awards by category:* Academic interests/achievement: biological sciences, business, communication, computer science, education, engineering/technologies, English, general academic interests/achievements, health fields, mathematics, physical sciences, premedicine, social sciences. *Creative arts/performance:* art/fine arts, music, theater/drama. *Special achievements/activities:* community service, general special achievements/activities, leadership. *Special characteristics:* adult students, children and siblings of alumni, children of faculty/staff, children of public servants, children with a deceased or disabled parent, general special characteristics, handicapped students, local/state students, members of minority groups, spouses of deceased or disabled public servants, veterans, veterans' children. *Tuition waivers:* Full or partial for employees or children of employees, senior citizens. *ROTC:* Army cooperative, Air Force cooperative.

LOANS *Student loans:* $61,835,790 (41% need-based, 59% non-need-based). 73% of past graduating class borrowed through all loan programs. *Average indebtedness per student:* $13,432. *Average need-based loan:* Freshmen: $2834. Undergraduates: $3656. *Parent loans:* $18,458,461 (100% non-need-based). *Programs:* Federal Direct (Subsidized and Unsubsidized Stafford, PLUS), Perkins, private loans.

WORK-STUDY *Federal work-study:* Total amount: $2,743,799; jobs available. *State or other work-study/employment:* Total amount: $2,730,407 (100% non-need-based). Part-time jobs available.

ATHLETIC AWARDS Total amount: $1,720,597 (100% non-need-based).

APPLYING FOR FINANCIAL AID *Required financial aid form:* FAFSA. *Financial aid deadline (priority):* 3/1. *Notification date:* Continuous beginning 4/1.

CONTACT Leah Stewart, Director of Student Financial Assistance, Northern Kentucky University, 416 Administrative Center, Highland Heights, KY 41099, 859-572-5144 or toll-free 800-637-9948. *Fax:* 859-572-6997. *E-mail:* ofa@nku.edu. *Website:* http://www.nku.edu/.

NORTHERN MICHIGAN UNIVERSITY
Marquette, MI

Tuition & fees (MI res): $8710	Average undergraduate aid package: $9094

ABOUT THE INSTITUTION State-supported, coed. *Awards:* certificates, diplomas, associate, bachelor's, and master's degrees. 143 undergraduate majors. *Total enrollment:* 9,089. Undergraduates: 8,451. Freshmen: 1,659. Federal methodology is used as a basis for awarding need-based institutional aid.

UNDERGRADUATE EXPENSES for 2013–2014 *Application fee:* $30. *One-time required fee:* $225. *Tuition, state resident:* full-time $8646; part-time $324 per credit hour. *Tuition, nonresident:* full-time $13,542; part-time $521 per credit hour. *Required fees:* full-time $64. Full-time tuition and fees vary according to program. Part-time tuition and fees vary according to program. *College room and board:* $8404; *Room only:* $4208. Room and board charges vary according to board plan and housing facility.

FRESHMAN FINANCIAL AID (Fall 2011) 1,717 applied for aid; of those 71% were deemed to have need. 97% of freshmen with need received aid; of those 13% had need fully met. *Average percent of need met:* 57% (excluding resources awarded to replace EFC). *Average financial aid package:* $8833 (excluding resources awarded to replace EFC). 8% of all full-time freshmen had no need and received non-need-based gift aid.

UNDERGRADUATE FINANCIAL AID (Fall 2011) 7,336 applied for aid; of those 73% were deemed to have need. 97% of undergraduates with need received aid; of those 11% had need fully met. *Average percent of need met:* 61% (excluding resources awarded to replace EFC). *Average financial aid package:* $9094 (excluding resources awarded to replace EFC). 5% of all full-time undergraduates had no need and received non-need-based gift aid.

GIFT AID (NEED-BASED) *Total amount:* $19,859,082 (75% federal, 3% state, 21% institutional, 1% external sources). *Receiving aid:* Freshmen: 42% (729); all full-time undergraduates: 42% (3,257). *Average award:* Freshmen: $5147; Undergraduates: $5365. *Scholarships, grants, and awards:* Federal Pell, FSEOG, state, private, college/university gift aid from institutional funds.

GIFT AID (NON-NEED-BASED) *Total amount:* $12,804,340 (1% federal, 21% state, 62% institutional, 16% external sources). *Receiving aid:* Freshmen: 31% (547). Undergraduates: 25% (1,940). *Average award:* Freshmen: $3686. Undergraduates: $2868. *Scholarships, grants, and awards by category:* Academic interests/achievement: biological sciences, business, communication, computer science, education, engineering/technologies, English, foreign languages, general academic interests/achievements, health fields, international studies, mathematics, military science, physical sciences, premedicine, social sciences. *Creative arts/performance:* applied art and design, music, theater/drama. *Special achievements/activities:* cheerleading/drum major, leadership, memberships. *Special characteristics:* children of faculty/staff, children of union members/company employees, international students, members of minority groups, out-of-state students. *Tuition waivers:* Full or partial for employees or children of employees, senior citizens. *ROTC:* Army.

LOANS *Student loans:* $45,982,147 (47% need-based, 53% non-need-based). 68% of past graduating class borrowed through all loan programs. *Average indebtedness per student:* $29,371. *Average need-based loan:* Freshmen: $3222. Undergraduates: $4145. *Parent loans:* $4,803,348 (100% non-need-based). *Programs:* Federal Direct (Subsidized and Unsubsidized Stafford, PLUS), Perkins, state, alternative loans.

WORK-STUDY *Federal work-study:* Total amount: $1,032,510; jobs available.

ATHLETIC AWARDS Total amount: $2,405,092 (100% non-need-based).

APPLYING FOR FINANCIAL AID *Required financial aid form:* FAFSA. *Financial aid deadline (priority):* 3/1. *Notification date:* Continuous beginning 4/1. Students must reply within 2 weeks of notification.

CONTACT Michael Rotundo, Director of Financial Aid, Northern Michigan University, 1401 Presque Isle Avenue, Marquette, MI 49855, 906-227-1575 or toll-free 800-682-9797. *Fax:* 906-227-2321. *E-mail:* mrotundo@nmu.edu. *Website:* http://www.nmu.edu/.

NORTHERN STATE UNIVERSITY
Aberdeen, SD

Tuition & fees (SD res): $7269	Average undergraduate aid package: $9974

ABOUT THE INSTITUTION State-supported, coed. *Awards:* certificates, associate, bachelor's, and master's degrees. 46 undergraduate majors. *Total enrollment:* 3,449. Undergraduates: 2,967. Freshmen: 405. Federal methodology is used as a basis for awarding need-based institutional aid.

UNDERGRADUATE EXPENSES for 2013–2014 *Application fee:* $20. *Tuition, state resident:* full-time $3726. *Tuition, nonresident:* full-time $5590. *Required fees:* full-time $3543. Full-time tuition and fees vary according to course level, course load, and reciprocity agreements. Part-time tuition and fees vary according to course level, course load, and reciprocity agreements. *College room and board:* $6147; *Room only:* $2703. Room and board charges vary according to board plan.

FRESHMAN FINANCIAL AID (Fall 2012, est.) 349 applied for aid; of those 76% were deemed to have need. 100% of freshmen with need received aid; of those 25% had need fully met. *Average percent of need met:* 69% (excluding resources awarded to replace EFC). *Average financial aid package:* $9889 (excluding resources awarded to replace EFC). 14% of all full-time freshmen had no need and received non-need-based gift aid.

UNDERGRADUATE FINANCIAL AID (Fall 2012, est.) 1,201 applied for aid; of those 78% were deemed to have need. 100% of undergraduates with need received aid; of those 20% had need fully met. *Average percent of need met:* 69% (excluding resources awarded to replace EFC). *Average financial aid package:* $9974 (excluding resources awarded to replace EFC). 10% of all full-time undergraduates had no need and received non-need-based gift aid.

GIFT AID (NEED-BASED) *Total amount:* $3,805,509 (75% federal, 3% state, 12% institutional, 10% external sources). *Receiving aid:* Freshmen: 59% (223); all full-time undergraduates: 52% (730). *Average award:* Freshmen: $4530; Undergraduates: $4354. *Scholarships, grants, and awards:* Federal Pell, FSEOG, state, private, college/university gift aid from institutional funds, South Dakota Education Access Foundation Grants.

GIFT AID (NON-NEED-BASED) *Total amount:* $778,519 (8% federal, 15% state, 46% institutional, 31% external sources). *Receiving aid:* Freshmen: 6% (23). Undergraduates: 4% (55). *Average award:* Freshmen: $1309. Undergraduates: $1558. *Scholarships, grants, and awards by category:* Academic interests/achievement: 552 awards ($719,247 total): biological sciences, business, communication, computer science, education, English, foreign languages, general academic interests/achievements, humanities, international studies, mathematics, physical sciences, social sciences. *Creative arts/performance:* 113 awards ($90,006 total): art/fine arts, music, theater/drama. *Special achievements/activities:* 11 awards ($6000 total): leadership. *Special characteristics:* 15 awards ($9190 total): adult students, ethnic background, handicapped students, international students, local/state students, members of minority groups.

LOANS *Student loans:* $8,393,694 (69% need-based, 31% non-need-based). 76% of past graduating class borrowed through all loan programs. *Average indebtedness per student:* $27,153. *Average need-based loan:* Freshmen: $5094. Undergraduates: $5158. *Parent loans:* $485,539 (29% need-based, 71% non-need-based). *Programs:* Federal Direct (Subsidized and Unsubsidized Stafford, PLUS), Perkins, college/university, alternative loans.

WORK-STUDY *Federal work-study:* Total amount: $951,853; 301 jobs averaging $1849. *State or other work-study/employment:* Total amount: $484,000 (100% non-need-based). 360 part-time jobs averaging $1345.

ATHLETIC AWARDS Total amount: $947,484 (55% need-based, 45% non-need-based).

APPLYING FOR FINANCIAL AID *Required financial aid form:* FAFSA. *Financial aid deadline (priority):* 3/1. *Notification date:* 4/15. Students must reply within 2 weeks of notification.

CONTACT Ms. Sharon Kienow, Director of Financial Aid, Northern State University, 1200 South Jay Street, Aberdeen, SD 57401-7198, 605-626-2640 or toll-free 800-678-5330. *Fax:* 605-626-2587. *E-mail:* kienows@northern.edu. *Website:* http://www.northern.edu/.

NORTH GREENVILLE UNIVERSITY
Tigerville, SC

CONTACT Mike Jordan, Director of Financial Aid, North Greenville University, PO Box 1892, Tigerville, SC 29688, 864-977-7058 or toll-free 800-468-6642 Ext. 7001. *Fax:* 864-977-7177. *E-mail:* mjordan@ngu.edu. *Website:* http://www.ngu.edu/.

NORTHLAND COLLEGE
Ashland, WI

Tuition & fees: $29,990	Average undergraduate aid package: $32,660

ABOUT THE INSTITUTION Independent United Church of Christ, coed. *Awards:* bachelor's degrees. 27 undergraduate majors. *Total enrollment:* 600. Undergraduates: 590. Freshmen: 183. Federal methodology is used as a basis for awarding need-based institutional aid.
UNDERGRADUATE EXPENSES for 2013–2014 *Comprehensive fee:* $37,500 includes full-time tuition ($29,000), mandatory fees ($990), and room and board ($7510). *College room only:* $3220. Full-time tuition and fees vary according to course load. Room and board charges vary according to board plan and housing facility. *Part-time tuition:* $600 per credit hour. Part-time tuition and fees vary according to course load.
FRESHMAN FINANCIAL AID (Fall 2012, est.) 179 applied for aid; of those 92% were deemed to have need. 100% of freshmen with need received aid; of those 17% had need fully met. *Average percent of need met:* 84% (excluding resources awarded to replace EFC). *Average financial aid package:* $32,590 (excluding resources awarded to replace EFC). 9% of all full-time freshmen had no need and received non-need-based gift aid.
UNDERGRADUATE FINANCIAL AID (Fall 2012, est.) 537 applied for aid; of those 93% were deemed to have need. 100% of undergraduates with need received aid; of those 16% had need fully met. *Average percent of need met:* 80% (excluding resources awarded to replace EFC). *Average financial aid package:* $32,660 (excluding resources awarded to replace EFC). 10% of all full-time undergraduates had no need and received non-need-based gift aid.
GIFT AID (NEED-BASED) *Total amount:* $9,552,434 (14% federal, 5% state, 80% institutional, 1% external sources). *Receiving aid:* Freshmen: 90% (163); all full-time undergraduates: 87% (493). *Average award:* Freshmen: $22,229; Undergraduates: $19,286. *Scholarships, grants, and awards:* Federal Pell, FSEOG, state, private, college/university gift aid from institutional funds, Academic Competitiveness Grants, Bureau of Indian Affairs Grants.
GIFT AID (NON-NEED-BASED) *Total amount:* $855,057 (1% state, 97% institutional, 2% external sources). *Receiving aid:* Freshmen: 18% (33). Undergraduates: 12% (69). *Average award:* Freshmen: $17,527. Undergraduates: $14,097. *Scholarships, grants, and awards by category: Academic interests/achievement:* 381 awards ($4,457,238 total): general academic interests/achievements. *Creative arts/performance:* 29 awards ($47,800 total): art/fine arts, creative writing, music. *Special achievements/activities:* 178 awards ($530,500 total): leadership. *Special characteristics:* 44 awards ($67,507 total): children and siblings of alumni, ethnic background. *Tuition waivers:* Full or partial for employees or children of employees.
LOANS *Student loans:* $3,712,681 (50% need-based, 50% non-need-based). 82% of past graduating class borrowed through all loan programs. *Average indebtedness per student:* $24,374. *Average need-based loan:* Freshmen: $3733. Undergraduates: $4710. *Parent loans:* $482,086 (79% need-based, 21% non-need-based). *Programs:* Federal Direct (Subsidized and Unsubsidized Stafford, PLUS), Perkins, state.
WORK-STUDY *Federal work-study:* Total amount: $539,350; 311 jobs averaging $1734. *State or other work-study/employment:* Total amount: $411,948 (100% non-need-based). 241 part-time jobs averaging $1709.

APPLYING FOR FINANCIAL AID *Required financial aid form:* FAFSA. *Financial aid deadline (priority):* 3/15. *Notification date:* Continuous beginning 3/1. Students must reply by 5/1 or within 4 weeks of notification.
CONTACT Heather Shelly, Director of Financial Aid, Northland College, 1411 Ellis Avenue, Ashland, WI 54806, 715-682-1255 or toll-free 800-753-1840 (in-state), 800-753-1040 (out-of-state). *Fax:* 715-682-1368. *E-mail:* finaid@northland.edu. *Website:* http://www.northland.edu/.

NORTHLAND INTERNATIONAL UNIVERSITY
Dunbar, WI

Tuition & fees: N/R	Average undergraduate aid package: $10,856

ABOUT THE INSTITUTION Independent religious, coed. Federal methodology is used as a basis for awarding need-based institutional aid.
FRESHMAN FINANCIAL AID (Fall 2012, est.) 71 applied for aid; of those 100% were deemed to have need. 99% of freshmen with need received aid; of those 7% had need fully met. *Average percent of need met:* 53% (excluding resources awarded to replace EFC). *Average financial aid package:* $9276 (excluding resources awarded to replace EFC).
UNDERGRADUATE FINANCIAL AID (Fall 2012, est.) 324 applied for aid; of those 100% were deemed to have need. 99% of undergraduates with need received aid; of those 6% had need fully met. *Average percent of need met:* 56% (excluding resources awarded to replace EFC). *Average financial aid package:* $10,856 (excluding resources awarded to replace EFC).
GIFT AID (NEED-BASED) *Total amount:* $2,939,767 (36% federal, 3% state, 60% institutional, 1% external sources). *Receiving aid:* Freshmen: 97% (69); all full-time undergraduates: 98% (318). *Average award:* Freshmen: $7689; Undergraduates: $8752. *Scholarships, grants, and awards:* Federal Pell, FSEOG, state, private, college/university gift aid from institutional funds.
GIFT AID (NON-NEED-BASED) *Total amount:* $57,674 (2% state, 91% institutional, 7% external sources). *Receiving aid:* Freshmen: 7% (5). Undergraduates: 6% (20). *Scholarships, grants, and awards by category: Academic interests/achievement:* 92 awards ($227,937 total): general academic interests/achievements. *Special achievements/activities:* 1 award ($1250 total): leadership. *Special characteristics:* 231 awards ($949,054 total): children of educators, children of faculty/staff, children of public servants, international students, local/state students, out-of-state students, relatives of clergy, spouses of current students.
LOANS *Student loans:* $958,071 (95% need-based, 5% non-need-based). 46% of past graduating class borrowed through all loan programs. *Average indebtedness per student:* $11,482. *Average need-based loan:* Freshmen: $2898. Undergraduates: $3813. *Parent loans:* $128,275 (30% need-based, 70% non-need-based). *Programs:* Federal Direct (Subsidized and Unsubsidized Stafford, PLUS), college/university.
WORK-STUDY *Federal work-study:* Total amount: $23,475; 19 jobs averaging $1598.
APPLYING FOR FINANCIAL AID *Required financial aid forms:* FAFSA, institution's own form. *Financial aid deadline:* 6/1 (priority: 3/1). *Notification date:* Continuous beginning 3/15. Students must reply within 2 weeks of notification.
CONTACT Mrs. Mandy McLain, Financial Aid Director, Northland International University, W10085 Pike Plains Road, Dunbar, WI 54119, 715-324-6900 Ext. 3150. *Fax:* 715-324-4211. *E-mail:* financialaid@ni.edu. *Website:* http://www.ni.edu/.

NORTH PARK UNIVERSITY
Chicago, IL

CONTACT Dr. Lucy Shaker, Director of Financial Aid , North Park University, 3225 West Foster Avenue, Chicago, IL 60625-4895, 773-244-5526 or toll-free 800-888-NPC8. *Fax:* 773-244-4953. *Website:* http://www.northpark.edu/.

NORTHPOINT BIBLE COLLEGE
Haverhill, MA

CONTACT Financial Aid Office, Northpoint Bible College, 320 South Main Street, Haverhill, MA 01835, 978-478-3400 or toll-free 800-356-4014. *Website:* http://northpoint.edu/.

NORTHWEST CHRISTIAN UNIVERSITY
Eugene, OR

Tuition & fees: $24,880	Average undergraduate aid package: $19,056

ABOUT THE INSTITUTION Independent Christian, coed. *Awards:* certificates, associate, bachelor's, and master's degrees. 18 undergraduate majors. *Total enrollment:* 635. Undergraduates: 456. Freshmen: 68. Federal methodology is used as a basis for awarding need-based institutional aid.

UNDERGRADUATE EXPENSES for 2013–2014 *Comprehensive fee:* $32,480 includes full-time tuition ($24,780), mandatory fees ($100), and room and board ($7600). Full-time tuition and fees vary according to course load. Room and board charges vary according to board plan and housing facility. *Part-time tuition:* $825 per credit. *Part-time fees:* $100 per year. Part-time tuition and fees vary according to course load.

FRESHMAN FINANCIAL AID (Fall 2011) 63 applied for aid; of those 92% were deemed to have need. 100% of freshmen with need received aid; of those 19% had need fully met. *Average percent of need met:* 72% (excluding resources awarded to replace EFC). *Average financial aid package:* $19,140 (excluding resources awarded to replace EFC). 8% of all full-time freshmen had no need and received non-need-based gift aid.

UNDERGRADUATE FINANCIAL AID (Fall 2011) 334 applied for aid; of those 92% were deemed to have need. 99% of undergraduates with need received aid; of those 14% had need fully met. *Average percent of need met:* 68% (excluding resources awarded to replace EFC). *Average financial aid package:* $19,056 (excluding resources awarded to replace EFC). 8% of all full-time undergraduates had no need and received non-need-based gift aid.

GIFT AID (NEED-BASED) *Total amount:* $4,203,341 (25% federal, 4% state, 56% institutional, 15% external sources). *Receiving aid:* Freshmen: 91% (58); all full-time undergraduates: 86% (296). *Average award:* Freshmen: $16,614; Undergraduates: $14,917. *Scholarships, grants, and awards:* Federal Pell, FSEOG, state, private, college/university gift aid from institutional funds.

GIFT AID (NON-NEED-BASED) *Total amount:* $282,570 (3% federal, 85% institutional, 12% external sources). *Receiving aid:* Freshmen: 14% (9). Undergraduates: 6% (20). *Average award:* Freshmen: $5887. Undergraduates: $7046. *Scholarships, grants, and awards by category: Academic interests/achievement:* 226 awards ($1,280,632 total): general academic interests/achievements. *Creative arts/performance:* 8 awards ($8000 total): music. *Special achievements/activities:* 201 awards ($253,000 total): community service, leadership, religious involvement. *Special characteristics:* 59 awards ($183,440 total): children of faculty/staff, relatives of clergy, religious affiliation, siblings of current students. *Tuition waivers:* Full or partial for employees or children of employees.

LOANS *Student loans:* $3,332,470 (80% need-based, 20% non-need-based). 68% of past graduating class borrowed through all loan programs. *Average indebtedness per student:* $32,045. *Average need-based loan:* Freshmen: $2950. Undergraduates: $4560. *Parent loans:* $304,968 (82% need-based, 18% non-need-based). *Programs:* Federal Direct (Subsidized and Unsubsidized Stafford, PLUS), Perkins.

WORK-STUDY *Federal work-study:* Total amount: $196,187; 62 jobs averaging $993. *State or other work-study/employment:* Total amount: $2750 (100% non-need-based). 60 part-time jobs averaging $1386.

ATHLETIC AWARDS Total amount: $564,280 (68% need-based, 32% non-need-based).

APPLYING FOR FINANCIAL AID *Required financial aid forms:* FAFSA, merit worksheet. *Financial aid deadline (priority):* 3/1. *Notification date:* Continuous beginning 3/1. Students must reply within 2 weeks of notification.

CONTACT Scott Palmer, Director of Financial Aid, Northwest Christian University, 828 East 11th Avenue, Eugene, OR 97401-3745, 541-684-7291 or toll-free 877-463-6622. *Fax:* 541-684-7300. *E-mail:* spalmer@nwcu.edu. *Website:* http://www.nwcu.edu/.

NORTHWEST COLLEGE OF ART & DESIGN
Poulsbo, WA

ABOUT THE INSTITUTION Proprietary, coed. 2 undergraduate majors.

GIFT AID (NEED-BASED) *Scholarships, grants, and awards:* Federal Pell, state, private, college/university gift aid from institutional funds.

GIFT AID (NON-NEED-BASED) *Scholarships, grants, and awards by category: Creative arts/performance:* applied art and design, art/fine arts.

LOANS *Programs:* Federal Direct (Subsidized and Unsubsidized Stafford, PLUS), alternative loans.

APPLYING FOR FINANCIAL AID *Required financial aid form:* FAFSA.

CONTACT Julie K. Perigard, Financial Aid Officer and Registrar, Northwest College of Art & Design, 16301 Creative Drive NE, Poulsbo, WA 98370, 360-779-9993 or toll-free 800-769-ARTS. *Fax:* 360-779-9933. *E-mail:* jperigard@ncad.edu. *Website:* http://www.ncad.edu/.

NORTHWESTERN COLLEGE
Orange City, IA

CONTACT Mr. Gerry Korver, Director of Financial Aid, Northwestern College, 101 Seventh Street, SW, Orange City, IA 51041-1996, 712-707-7131 or toll-free 800-747-4757. *Fax:* 712-707-7164. *Website:* http://www.nwciowa.edu/.

NORTHWESTERN COLLEGE
St. Paul, MN

Tuition & fees: $26,960	Average undergraduate aid package: $18,390

ABOUT THE INSTITUTION Independent nondenominational, coed. *Awards:* certificates, associate, bachelor's, and master's degrees. 50 undergraduate majors. *Total enrollment:* 3,267. Undergraduates: 3,086. Freshmen: 398. Federal methodology is used as a basis for awarding need-based institutional aid.

UNDERGRADUATE EXPENSES for 2013–2014 *Application fee:* $25. *Comprehensive fee:* $35,170 includes full-time tuition ($26,740), mandatory fees ($220), and room and board ($8210). *College room only:* $4820. Full-time tuition and fees vary according to course load. Room and board charges vary according to board plan and student level. *Part-time tuition:* $1140 per semester hour. *Part-time fees:* $65 per term. Part-time tuition and fees vary according to course load.

FRESHMAN FINANCIAL AID (Fall 2012, est.) 421 applied for aid; of those 90% were deemed to have need. 100% of freshmen with need received aid; of those 8% had need fully met. *Average percent of need met:* 70% (excluding resources awarded to replace EFC). *Average financial aid package:* $19,740 (excluding resources awarded to replace EFC). 16% of all full-time freshmen had no need and received non-need-based gift aid.

UNDERGRADUATE FINANCIAL AID (Fall 2012, est.) 1,661 applied for aid; of those 92% were deemed to have need. 100% of undergraduates with need received aid; of those 11% had need fully met. *Average percent of need met:* 67% (excluding resources awarded to replace EFC). *Average financial aid package:* $18,390 (excluding resources awarded to replace EFC). 15% of all full-time undergraduates had no need and received non-need-based gift aid.

GIFT AID (NEED-BASED) *Total amount:* $20,243,256 (16% federal, 13% state, 67% institutional, 4% external sources). *Receiving aid:* Freshmen: 82% (370); all full-time undergraduates: 80% (1,476). *Average award:* Freshmen: $15,602; Undergraduates: $13,504. *Scholarships, grants, and awards:* Federal Pell, FSEOG, state, private, college/university gift aid from institutional funds.

GIFT AID (NON-NEED-BASED) Total amount: $2,600,993 (94% institutional, 6% external sources). **Receiving aid:** Freshmen: 19% (84). Undergraduates: 20% (368). **Average award:** Freshmen: $8624. Undergraduates: $8213. **Scholarships, grants, and awards by category:** Academic interests/achievement: 658 awards ($3,089,036 total): general academic interests/achievements. Creative arts/performance: 155 awards ($299,225 total): music, theater/drama. Special achievements/activities: 364 awards ($858,236 total): general special achievements/activities, leadership. Special characteristics: 651 awards ($4,199,207 total): children of faculty/staff, ethnic background, international students, relatives of clergy, siblings of current students. **Tuition waivers:** Full or partial for children of alumni, employees or children of employees. **ROTC:** Army cooperative, Air Force cooperative.
LOANS Student loans: $12,800,703 (88% need-based, 12% non-need-based). 80% of past graduating class borrowed through all loan programs. Average indebtedness per student: $24,299. **Average need-based loan:** Freshmen: $3926. Undergraduates: $4468. **Parent loans:** $3,902,383 (65% need-based, 35% non-need-based). **Programs:** Federal Direct (Subsidized and Unsubsidized Stafford, PLUS), Perkins, state.
WORK-STUDY Federal work-study: Total amount: $388,156; 187 jobs averaging $4151. **State or other work-study/employment:** Total amount: $599,559 (100% need-based). 281 part-time jobs averaging $4267.
APPLYING FOR FINANCIAL AID Required financial aid forms: FAFSA, institution's own form. **Financial aid deadline (priority):** 3/1. **Notification date:** Continuous beginning 3/1. Students must reply within 2 weeks of notification.
CONTACT Mr. Richard L. Blatchley, Director of Financial Aid, Northwestern College, 3003 Snelling Avenue North, St. Paul, MN 55113-1598, 651-631-5321 or toll-free 800-827-6827. Fax: 651-628-3332. E-mail: rlb@nwc.edu. Website: http://www.nwc.edu/.

NORTHWESTERN OKLAHOMA STATE UNIVERSITY
Alva, OK

Tuition & fees (OK res): $5198	Average undergraduate aid package: N/A

ABOUT THE INSTITUTION State-supported, coed. **Awards:** bachelor's and master's degrees. 40 undergraduate majors. **Total enrollment:** 2,295. Undergraduates: 2,066. Freshmen: 419. Both federal and institutional methodology are used as a basis for awarding need-based institutional aid.
UNDERGRADUATE EXPENSES for 2013–2014 **Application fee:** $15. **Tuition, state resident:** full-time $4253. **Tuition, nonresident:** full-time $10,185. **Required fees:** full-time $945. Full-time tuition and fees vary according to course load, degree level, location, and program. Part-time tuition and fees vary according to course load, degree level, location, and program. **College room and board:** $3780; **Room only:** $1300. Room and board charges vary according to board plan.
FRESHMAN FINANCIAL AID (Fall 2012, est.) 283 applied for aid; of those 76% were deemed to have need. 99% of freshmen with need received aid.
UNDERGRADUATE FINANCIAL AID (Fall 2012, est.) 1,172 applied for aid; of those 84% were deemed to have need. 98% of undergraduates with need received aid.
GIFT AID (NEED-BASED) Total amount: $5,640,393 (69% federal, 26% state, 5% institutional). **Receiving aid:** Freshmen: 54% (193); all full-time undergraduates: 54% (838). **Scholarships, grants, and awards:** Federal Pell, FSEOG, state, private, college/university gift aid from institutional funds.
GIFT AID (NON-NEED-BASED) Total amount: $1,071,139 (8% state, 30% institutional, 62% external sources). **Scholarships, grants, and awards by category:** Academic interests/achievement: agriculture, biological sciences, business, communication, computer science, education, English, foreign languages, general academic interests/achievements, health fields, library science, mathematics, physical sciences, premedicine, social sciences. Creative arts/performance: art/fine arts, cinema/film/broadcasting, debating, general creative arts/performance, journalism/publications, music, theater/drama. Special achievements/activities: cheerleading/drum major, general special achievements/activities, leadership, memberships, rodeo. Special characteristics: children of faculty/staff. **Tuition waivers:** Full or partial for employees or children of employees, senior citizens.
LOANS Student loans: $5,589,535 (54% need-based, 46% non-need-based). 43% of past graduating class borrowed through all loan programs. Average indebtedness per student: $14,975. **Parent loans:** $106,712 (100% non-need-based). **Programs:** Federal Direct (Subsidized and Unsubsidized Stafford, PLUS).

WORK-STUDY Federal work-study: Total amount: $183,877; 110 jobs averaging $1672. **State or other work-study/employment:** Total amount: $256,049 (100% non-need-based). 190 part-time jobs averaging $1348.
ATHLETIC AWARDS Total amount: $434,851 (84% need-based, 16% non-need-based).
APPLYING FOR FINANCIAL AID Required financial aid forms: FAFSA, institution's own form. **Financial aid deadline:** Continuous. **Notification date:** Continuous beginning 3/1. Students must reply by 8/15.
CONTACT Calleb N. Mosburg, Director of Financial Aid, Northwestern Oklahoma State University, 709 Oklahoma Boulevard, Alva, OK 73717-2799, 580-327-8542. Fax: 580-327-8177. E-mail: cnmosburg@nwosu.edu. Website: http://www.nwosu.edu/.

NORTHWESTERN STATE UNIVERSITY OF LOUISIANA
Natchitoches, LA

Tuition & fees (LA res): $5480	Average undergraduate aid package: $10,000

ABOUT THE INSTITUTION State-supported, coed. **Awards:** certificates, associate, bachelor's, and master's degrees. 34 undergraduate majors. **Total enrollment:** 9,447. Undergraduates: 8,312. Freshmen: 1,369. Federal methodology is used as a basis for awarding need-based institutional aid.
UNDERGRADUATE EXPENSES for 2013–2014 **Application fee:** $20. **Tuition, state resident:** full-time $3938. **Tuition, nonresident:** full-time $13,304. **Required fees:** full-time $1542. Full-time tuition and fees vary according to course load and location. Part-time tuition and fees vary according to course load and location. **College room and board:** $7826; **Room only:** $4896. Room and board charges vary according to board plan, housing facility, and location.
FRESHMAN FINANCIAL AID (Fall 2012, est.) 1,232 applied for aid; of those 84% were deemed to have need. 99% of freshmen with need received aid; of those 5% had need fully met. **Average percent of need met:** 39% (excluding resources awarded to replace EFC). **Average financial aid package:** $11,115 (excluding resources awarded to replace EFC). 15% of all full-time freshmen had no need and received non-need-based gift aid.
UNDERGRADUATE FINANCIAL AID (Fall 2012, est.) 4,793 applied for aid; of those 84% were deemed to have need. 99% of undergraduates with need received aid; of those 3% had need fully met. **Average percent of need met:** 64% (excluding resources awarded to replace EFC). **Average financial aid package:** $10,000 (excluding resources awarded to replace EFC). 8% of all full-time undergraduates had no need and received non-need-based gift aid.
GIFT AID (NEED-BASED) Total amount: $27,403,655 (59% federal, 21% state, 12% institutional, 8% external sources). **Receiving aid:** Freshmen: 50% (646); all full-time undergraduates: 53% (2,798). **Average award:** Freshmen: $8364; Undergraduates: $6483. **Scholarships, grants, and awards:** Federal Pell, state, private, college/university gift aid from institutional funds.
GIFT AID (NON-NEED-BASED) Total amount: $5,604,837 (62% state, 29% institutional, 9% external sources). **Receiving aid:** Freshmen: 33% (428). Undergraduates: 20% (1,056). **Average award:** Freshmen: $3822. Undergraduates: $3170. **Scholarships, grants, and awards by category:** Academic interests/achievement: biological sciences, business, communication, education, engineering/technologies, English, general academic interests/achievements, health fields, humanities, mathematics, military science, social sciences. Creative arts/performance: art/fine arts, cinema/film/broadcasting, creative writing, dance, general creative arts/performance, music, performing arts, theater/drama. Special achievements/activities: cheerleading/drum major, general special achievements/activities, leadership, memberships. Special characteristics: adult students, children of faculty/staff, children of public servants, general special characteristics, international students, married students, out-of-state students, public servants, veterans, veterans' children. **Tuition waivers:** Full or partial for employees or children of employees, senior citizens. **ROTC:** Army, Air Force cooperative.
LOANS Student loans: $33,058,613 (86% need-based, 14% non-need-based). 66% of past graduating class borrowed through all loan programs. Average indebtedness per student: $24,676. **Average need-based loan:** Freshmen: $3097. Undergraduates: $3943. **Parent loans:** $549,868 (38% need-based, 62% non-need-based). **Pro-**

grams: Federal Direct (Subsidized and Unsubsidized Stafford), Perkins, Federal Nursing, state, college/university, alternative loans.
WORK-STUDY *Federal work-study:* Total amount: $405,379; 175 jobs averaging $1074. *State or other work-study/employment:* Total amount: $401,017 (65% need-based, 35% non-need-based). 206 part-time jobs averaging $1021.
ATHLETIC AWARDS Total amount: $3,351,209 (88% need-based, 12% non-need-based).
APPLYING FOR FINANCIAL AID *Required financial aid forms:* FAFSA, institution's own form. *Financial aid deadline (priority):* 5/1. *Notification date:* Continuous beginning 5/1. Students must reply within 4 weeks of notification.
CONTACT Ms. Lauren Jackson, Director of Financial Aid, Northwestern State University of Louisiana, 212 Student Services Center, Natchitoches, LA 71497, 318-357-5961 or toll-free 800-327-1903. *Fax:* 318-357-5488. *E-mail:* nsufinaid@nsula.edu. *Website:* http://www.nsula.edu/.

NORTHWESTERN UNIVERSITY
Evanston, IL

CONTACT Office of Financial Aid, Northwestern University, 1801 Hinman Avenue, Evanston, IL 60204-1270, 847-491-7400. *E-mail:* ug-finaid@u.northwestern.edu. *Website:* http://www.northwestern.edu/.

NORTHWEST MISSOURI STATE UNIVERSITY
Maryville, MO

Tuition & fees (MO res): $7719	Average undergraduate aid package: $8597

ABOUT THE INSTITUTION State-supported, coed. *Awards:* certificates, bachelor's, and master's degrees. 83 undergraduate majors. *Total enrollment:* 6,831. Undergraduates: 6,014. Freshmen: 1,357. Federal methodology is used as a basis for awarding need-based institutional aid.
UNDERGRADUATE EXPENSES for 2013–2014 *Application fee:* $25. *One-time required fee:* $140. *Tuition, state resident:* full-time $5237; part-time $174.56 per credit hour. *Tuition, nonresident:* full-time $11,345; part-time $378.18 per credit hour. *Required fees:* full-time $2482; $82.75 per credit hour. Full-time tuition and fees vary according to course load, location, and reciprocity agreements. Part-time tuition and fees vary according to course load and location. *College room and board:* $8614; *Room only:* $5538. Room and board charges vary according to board plan and housing facility.
FRESHMAN FINANCIAL AID (Fall 2011) 1,489 applied for aid; of those 77% were deemed to have need. 100% of freshmen with need received aid; of those 47% had need fully met. *Average percent of need met:* 69% (excluding resources awarded to replace EFC). *Average financial aid package:* $9208 (excluding resources awarded to replace EFC). 14% of all full-time freshmen had no need and received non-need-based gift aid.
UNDERGRADUATE FINANCIAL AID (Fall 2011) 4,786 applied for aid; of those 80% were deemed to have need. 99% of undergraduates with need received aid; of those 39% had need fully met. *Average percent of need met:* 67% (excluding resources awarded to replace EFC). *Average financial aid package:* $8597 (excluding resources awarded to replace EFC). 9% of all full-time undergraduates had no need and received non-need-based gift aid.
GIFT AID (NEED-BASED) *Total amount:* $14,807,051 (58% federal, 14% state, 26% institutional, 2% external sources). *Receiving aid:* Freshmen: 62% (979); all full-time undergraduates: 54% (3,008). *Average award:* Freshmen: $6587; Undergraduates: $5590. *Scholarships, grants, and awards:* Federal Pell, FSEOG, state, private, college/university gift aid from institutional funds.
GIFT AID (NON-NEED-BASED) *Total amount:* $3,821,585 (4% federal, 3% state, 89% institutional, 4% external sources). *Receiving aid:* Freshmen: 27% (431). Undergraduates: 16% (887). *Average award:* Freshmen: $2275. Undergraduates: $2307. *Scholarships, grants, and awards by category: Academic interests/achievement:* agriculture, biological sciences, business, communication, computer science, education, English, foreign languages, general academic interests/achievements, health fields, home economics, humanities, mathematics, physical sciences, social sciences. *Creative arts/performance:* art/fine arts, cinema/film/broadcasting, dance,

debating, journalism/publications, music, theater/drama. *Special achievements/activities:* cheerleading/drum major, general special achievements/activities, leadership, memberships. *Special characteristics:* children and siblings of alumni, children of faculty/staff, general special characteristics, members of minority groups, out-of-state students, previous college experience. *Tuition waivers:* Full or partial for employees or children of employees, senior citizens. *ROTC:* Army.
LOANS *Student loans:* $32,947,759 (60% need-based, 40% non-need-based). 70% of past graduating class borrowed through all loan programs. *Average indebtedness per student:* $23,400. *Average need-based loan:* Freshmen: $3250. Undergraduates: $3889. *Parent loans:* $7,806,942 (31% need-based, 69% non-need-based). *Programs:* Federal Direct (Subsidized and Unsubsidized Stafford, PLUS), Perkins.
WORK-STUDY *Federal work-study:* Total amount: $488,384; 413 jobs averaging $1183. *State or other work-study/employment:* Total amount: $1,259,806 (37% need-based, 63% non-need-based). 1,055 part-time jobs averaging $1538.
ATHLETIC AWARDS Total amount: $1,879,018 (40% need-based, 60% non-need-based).
APPLYING FOR FINANCIAL AID *Required financial aid form:* FAFSA. *Financial aid deadline:* Continuous. *Notification date:* Continuous beginning 3/15.
CONTACT Mr. Del Morley, Director of Financial Assistance, Northwest Missouri State University, 800 University Drive, Maryville, MO 64468-6001, 660-562-1138 or toll-free 800-633-1175.
Website: http://www.nwmissouri.edu/.

NORTHWEST NAZARENE UNIVERSITY
Nampa, ID

Tuition & fees: $26,550	Average undergraduate aid package: $17,811

ABOUT THE INSTITUTION Independent Church of the Nazarene, coed. *Awards:* certificates, bachelor's, master's, and doctoral degrees. 72 undergraduate majors. *Total enrollment:* 2,232. Undergraduates: 1,477. Freshmen: 243. Federal methodology is used as a basis for awarding need-based institutional aid.
UNDERGRADUATE EXPENSES for 2013–2014 *Application fee:* $25. *Comprehensive fee:* $32,950 includes full-time tuition ($26,150), mandatory fees ($400), and room and board ($6400). Full-time tuition and fees vary according to course load, degree level, program, and reciprocity agreements. Room and board charges vary according to board plan. *Part-time tuition:* $1130 per semester hour. *Payment plan:* Tuition prepayment.
FRESHMAN FINANCIAL AID (Fall 2011) 245 applied for aid; of those 91% were deemed to have need. 100% of freshmen with need received aid; of those 25% had need fully met. *Average percent of need met:* 77% (excluding resources awarded to replace EFC). *Average financial aid package:* $18,853 (excluding resources awarded to replace EFC). 13% of all full-time freshmen had no need and received non-need-based gift aid.
UNDERGRADUATE FINANCIAL AID (Fall 2011) 1,044 applied for aid; of those 92% were deemed to have need. 100% of undergraduates with need received aid; of those 16% had need fully met. *Average percent of need met:* 68% (excluding resources awarded to replace EFC). *Average financial aid package:* $17,811 (excluding resources awarded to replace EFC). 18% of all full-time undergraduates had no need and received non-need-based gift aid.
GIFT AID (NEED-BASED) *Total amount:* $10,846,115 (23% federal, 1% state, 66% institutional, 10% external sources). *Receiving aid:* Freshmen: 87% (222); all full-time undergraduates: 78% (912). *Average award:* Freshmen: $13,457; Undergraduates: $11,653. *Scholarships, grants, and awards:* Federal Pell, FSEOG, state, private, college/university gift aid from institutional funds.
GIFT AID (NON-NEED-BASED) *Total amount:* $2,101,274 (1% state, 78% institutional, 21% external sources). *Receiving aid:* Freshmen: 12% (32). Undergraduates: 6% (72). *Average award:* Freshmen: $9600. Undergraduates: $8263. *Scholarships, grants, and awards by category: Academic interests/achievement:* 744 awards ($4,225,188 total): biological sciences, business, computer science, education, English, general academic interests/achievements, health fields, mathematics, military science, physical sciences, premedicine, religion/biblical studies, social sciences. *Creative arts/performance:* 80 awards ($162,715 total): art/fine arts, debating, general creative arts/performance, journalism/publications, music, performing arts, theater/drama. *Special achievements/activities:* 48 awards ($79,000 total): cheerleading/drum

major, general special achievements/activities, leadership, religious involvement. *Special characteristics:* 627 awards ($3,211,651 total): children and siblings of alumni, children of educators, children of faculty/staff, ethnic background, international students, members of minority groups, out-of-state students, relatives of clergy, religious affiliation, siblings of current students, veterans. *Tuition waivers:* Full or partial for minority students, children of alumni, employees or children of employees. *ROTC:* Army.

LOANS *Student loans:* $8,425,548 (86% need-based, 14% non-need-based). 72% of past graduating class borrowed through all loan programs. *Average indebtedness per student:* $28,872. *Average need-based loan:* Freshmen: $3629. Undergraduates: $4759. *Parent loans:* $1,615,549 (56% need-based, 44% non-need-based). *Programs:* Perkins, college/university.

WORK-STUDY *Federal work-study:* Total amount: $116,173; 151 jobs averaging $769. *State or other work-study/employment:* Part-time jobs available.

ATHLETIC AWARDS Total amount: $1,553,651 (47% need-based, 53% non-need-based).

APPLYING FOR FINANCIAL AID *Required financial aid forms:* FAFSA, institution's own form. *Financial aid deadline (priority):* 3/1. *Notification date:* Continuous beginning 4/1. Students must reply within 3 weeks of notification.

CONTACT Mr. David Klaffke, Director of Financial Aid, Northwest Nazarene University, 623 South University Boulevard, Nampa, ID 83686, 208-467-8422 or toll-free 877-668-4968. *Fax:* 208-467-8375. *E-mail:* dklaffke@nnu.edu. *Website:* http://www.nnu.edu/.

NORTHWEST UNIVERSITY
Kirkland, WA

Tuition & fees: N/R	Average undergraduate aid package: $17,722

ABOUT THE INSTITUTION Independent Assemblies of God, coed. *Awards:* certificates, diplomas, associate, bachelor's, master's, and doctoral degrees. 43 undergraduate majors. *Total enrollment:* 1,612. Undergraduates: 1,355. Freshmen: 215. Federal methodology is used as a basis for awarding need-based institutional aid.

FRESHMAN FINANCIAL AID (Fall 2012, est.) 182 applied for aid; of those 93% were deemed to have need. 100% of freshmen with need received aid; of those 14% had need fully met. *Average percent of need met:* 79% (excluding resources awarded to replace EFC). *Average financial aid package:* $19,612 (excluding resources awarded to replace EFC). 12% of all full-time freshmen had no need and received non-need-based gift aid.

UNDERGRADUATE FINANCIAL AID (Fall 2012, est.) 1,080 applied for aid; of those 90% were deemed to have need. 99% of undergraduates with need received aid; of those 15% had need fully met. *Average percent of need met:* 68% (excluding resources awarded to replace EFC). *Average financial aid package:* $17,722 (excluding resources awarded to replace EFC). 13% of all full-time undergraduates had no need and received non-need-based gift aid.

GIFT AID (NEED-BASED) *Total amount:* $12,676,556 (18% federal, 9% state, 69% institutional, 4% external sources). *Receiving aid:* Freshmen: 82% (165); all full-time undergraduates: 82% (956). *Average award:* Freshmen: $16,135; Undergraduates: $13,790. *Scholarships, grants, and awards:* Federal Pell, FSEOG, state, private, college/university gift aid from institutional funds.

GIFT AID (NON-NEED-BASED) *Total amount:* $1,678,091 (95% institutional, 5% external sources). *Receiving aid:* Freshmen: 9% (18). Undergraduates: 8% (91). *Average award:* Freshmen: $7594. Undergraduates: $7772. *Scholarships, grants, and awards by category:* Academic interests/achievement: general academic interests/achievements. Creative arts/performance: debating, music, performing arts, theater/drama. Special achievements/activities: leadership. Special characteristics: children of current students, children of faculty/staff, general special characteristics, international students, married students, parents of current students, relatives of clergy, religious affiliation, siblings of current students, spouses of current students. *ROTC:* Army cooperative, Air Force cooperative.

LOANS *Student loans:* $8,120,052 (78% need-based, 22% non-need-based). 83% of past graduating class borrowed through all loan programs. *Average indebtedness per student:* $31,691. *Average need-based loan:* Freshmen: $3250. Undergraduates: $3930. *Parent loans:* $1,054,922 (46% need-based, 54% non-need-based). *Programs:* Federal Direct (Subsidized and Unsubsidized Stafford, PLUS), Perkins, state, alternative loans.

WORK-STUDY *Federal work-study:* Total amount: $179,351; 72 jobs averaging $3066. *State or other work-study/employment:* Total amount: $57,942 (92% need-based, 8% non-need-based). 13 part-time jobs averaging $4107.

ATHLETIC AWARDS Total amount: $871,153 (69% need-based, 31% non-need-based).

APPLYING FOR FINANCIAL AID *Required financial aid forms:* FAFSA, institution's own form. *Financial aid deadline:* 8/1 (priority: 2/15). *Notification date:* Continuous beginning 3/1. Students must reply within 4 weeks of notification.

CONTACT Mr. Roger Wilson, Director of Financial Aid, Northwest University, PO Box 579, Kirkland, WA 98083-0579, 425-889-5336 or toll-free 800-669-3781. *Fax:* 425-889-5224. *E-mail:* roger.wilson@northwestu.edu. *Website:* http://www.northwestu.edu/.

NORTHWOOD UNIVERSITY, FLORIDA CAMPUS
West Palm Beach, FL

Tuition & fees: $22,130	Average undergraduate aid package: $21,509

ABOUT THE INSTITUTION Private, coed. *Awards:* bachelor's and master's degrees. 12 undergraduate majors. *Total enrollment:* 537. Undergraduates: 497. Freshmen: 103. Federal methodology is used as a basis for awarding need-based institutional aid.

UNDERGRADUATE EXPENSES for 2013–2014 *Application fee:* $25. *Comprehensive fee:* $32,171 includes full-time tuition ($21,000), mandatory fees ($1130), and room and board ($10,041). *Part-time tuition:* $811 per credit hour.

FRESHMAN FINANCIAL AID (Fall 2012, est.) 69 applied for aid; of those 91% were deemed to have need. 100% of freshmen with need received aid; of those 25% had need fully met. *Average percent of need met:* 66% (excluding resources awarded to replace EFC). *Average financial aid package:* $22,610 (excluding resources awarded to replace EFC). 17% of all full-time freshmen had no need and received non-need-based gift aid.

UNDERGRADUATE FINANCIAL AID (Fall 2012, est.) 247 applied for aid; of those 88% were deemed to have need. 100% of undergraduates with need received aid; of those 18% had need fully met. *Average percent of need met:* 62% (excluding resources awarded to replace EFC). *Average financial aid package:* $21,509 (excluding resources awarded to replace EFC). 19% of all full-time undergraduates had no need and received non-need-based gift aid.

GIFT AID (NEED-BASED) *Total amount:* $3,263,414 (23% federal, 9% state, 68% institutional). *Receiving aid:* Freshmen: 53% (55); all full-time undergraduates: 38% (186). *Average award:* Freshmen: $7779; Undergraduates: $7575. *Scholarships, grants, and awards:* Federal Pell, FSEOG, state, private, college/university gift aid from institutional funds.

GIFT AID (NON-NEED-BASED) *Total amount:* $1,552,020 (4% state, 95% institutional, 1% external sources). *Receiving aid:* Freshmen: 17% (17). Undergraduates: 9% (45). *Average award:* Freshmen: $10,567. Undergraduates: $6890. *Scholarships, grants, and awards by category:* Academic interests/achievement: 421 awards ($2,711,250 total): business, general academic interests/achievements. *Special achievements/activities:* cheerleading/drum major. *Special characteristics:* 11 awards ($20,312 total): children and siblings of alumni, children of faculty/staff, siblings of current students.

LOANS *Student loans:* $1,979,576 (79% need-based, 21% non-need-based). 61% of past graduating class borrowed through all loan programs. *Average indebtedness per student:* $27,505. *Average need-based loan:* Freshmen: $3382. Undergraduates: $4198. *Parent loans:* $366,914 (43% need-based, 57% non-need-based). *Programs:* Federal Direct (Subsidized and Unsubsidized Stafford, PLUS).

WORK-STUDY *Federal work-study:* Total amount: $97,645; 42 jobs averaging $2042.

ATHLETIC AWARDS Total amount: $1,140,433 (34% need-based, 66% non-need-based).

APPLYING FOR FINANCIAL AID *Required financial aid forms:* FAFSA, state aid form. *Financial aid deadline (priority):* 2/1. *Notification date:* Continuous beginning 3/1.

CONTACT Ms. Hollie Crotts, Assistant Director of Financial Aid, Northwood University, Florida Campus, 2600 North Military Trail, West Palm Beach, FL 33409-2911, 561-478-5590 or toll-free 800-622-9000. *Fax:* 561-681-7990. *E-mail:* crottsh@northwood.edu.
Website: http://www.northwood.edu/.

NORTHWOOD UNIVERSITY, MICHIGAN CAMPUS
Midland, MI

Tuition & fees: $20,996	Average undergraduate aid package: $18,858

ABOUT THE INSTITUTION Independent, coed. *Awards:* associate, bachelor's, and master's degrees. 13 undergraduate majors. *Total enrollment:* 1,787. Undergraduates: 1,536. Freshmen: 323. Federal methodology is used as a basis for awarding need-based institutional aid.

UNDERGRADUATE EXPENSES for 2013–2014 *Application fee:* $25. *Comprehensive fee:* $29,766 includes full-time tuition ($20,040), mandatory fees ($956), and room and board ($8770). *College room only:* $4570. Room and board charges vary according to board plan. *Part-time tuition:* $776 per credit hour.

FRESHMAN FINANCIAL AID (Fall 2012, est.) 268 applied for aid; of those 86% were deemed to have need. 100% of freshmen with need received aid; of those 26% had need fully met. *Average percent of need met:* 66% (excluding resources awarded to replace EFC). *Average financial aid package:* $21,185 (excluding resources awarded to replace EFC). 19% of all full-time freshmen had no need and received non-need-based gift aid.

UNDERGRADUATE FINANCIAL AID (Fall 2012, est.) 1,127 applied for aid; of those 89% were deemed to have need. 100% of undergraduates with need received aid; of those 24% had need fully met. *Average percent of need met:* 62% (excluding resources awarded to replace EFC). *Average financial aid package:* $18,858 (excluding resources awarded to replace EFC). 20% of all full-time undergraduates had no need and received non-need-based gift aid.

GIFT AID (NEED-BASED) *Total amount:* $12,657,766 (17% federal, 10% state, 71% institutional, 2% external sources). *Receiving aid:* Freshmen: 70% (210); all full-time undergraduates: 60% (879). *Average award:* Freshmen: $6289; Undergraduates: $5480. *Scholarships, grants, and awards:* Federal Pell, FSEOG, state, private, college/university gift aid from institutional funds.

GIFT AID (NON-NEED-BASED) *Total amount:* $3,608,263 (96% institutional, 4% external sources). *Receiving aid:* Freshmen: 31% (95). Undergraduates: 26% (384). *Average award:* Freshmen: $10,044. Undergraduates: $7197. *Scholarships, grants, and awards by category:* Academic interests/achievement: 1,405 awards ($10,018,769 total): business, general academic interests/achievements. *Special achievements/activities:* 8 awards ($3095 total): cheerleading/drum major. *Special characteristics:* 98 awards ($657,635 total): children and siblings of alumni, children of faculty/staff, siblings of current students. *Tuition waivers:* Full or partial for employees or children of employees.

LOANS *Student loans:* $9,393,303 (71% need-based, 29% non-need-based). 74% of past graduating class borrowed through all loan programs. *Average indebtedness per student:* $32,457. *Average need-based loan:* Freshmen: $3302. Undergraduates: $4243. *Parent loans:* $1,940,322 (37% need-based, 63% non-need-based). *Programs:* Federal Direct (Subsidized and Unsubsidized Stafford, PLUS).

WORK-STUDY *Federal work-study:* Total amount: $145,468; 101 jobs averaging $1612.

ATHLETIC AWARDS Total amount: $2,910,570 (51% need-based, 49% non-need-based).

APPLYING FOR FINANCIAL AID *Required financial aid form:* FAFSA. *Financial aid deadline (priority):* 2/1. *Notification date:* Continuous beginning 3/1.

CONTACT Terri Mieler, Director of Financial Aid, Northwood University, Michigan Campus, 4000 Whiting Drive, Midland, MI 48640-2398, 989-837-4301 or toll-free 800-457-7878. *Fax:* 989-837-4130. *E-mail:* mieler@northwood.edu.
Website: http://www.northwood.edu/.

NORTHWOOD UNIVERSITY, TEXAS CAMPUS
Cedar Hill, TX

Tuition & fees: $20,996	Average undergraduate aid package: $21,625

ABOUT THE INSTITUTION Independent, coed. *Awards:* bachelor's and master's degrees. 3 undergraduate majors. *Total enrollment:* 587. Undergraduates: 534. Freshmen: 172. Federal methodology is used as a basis for awarding need-based institutional aid.

UNDERGRADUATE EXPENSES for 2013–2014 *Application fee:* $25. *Comprehensive fee:* $30,103 includes full-time tuition ($20,040), mandatory fees ($956), and room and board ($9107). *College room only:* $4907. Room and board charges vary according to board plan. *Part-time tuition:* $776 per semester hour.

FRESHMAN FINANCIAL AID (Fall 2012, est.) 160 applied for aid; of those 92% were deemed to have need. 100% of freshmen with need received aid; of those 17% had need fully met. *Average percent of need met:* 71% (excluding resources awarded to replace EFC). *Average financial aid package:* $23,720 (excluding resources awarded to replace EFC). 5% of all full-time freshmen had no need and received non-need-based gift aid.

UNDERGRADUATE FINANCIAL AID (Fall 2012, est.) 437 applied for aid; of those 94% were deemed to have need. 100% of undergraduates with need received aid; of those 16% had need fully met. *Average percent of need met:* 65% (excluding resources awarded to replace EFC). *Average financial aid package:* $21,625 (excluding resources awarded to replace EFC). 10% of all full-time undergraduates had no need and received non-need-based gift aid.

GIFT AID (NEED-BASED) *Total amount:* $6,168,681 (22% federal, 78% institutional). *Receiving aid:* Freshmen: 80% (135); all full-time undergraduates: 73% (365). *Average award:* Freshmen: $8209; Undergraduates: $6995. *Scholarships, grants, and awards:* Federal Pell, FSEOG, state, private, college/university gift aid from institutional funds.

GIFT AID (NON-NEED-BASED) *Total amount:* $1,087,199 (100% institutional). *Receiving aid:* Freshmen: 21% (35). Undergraduates: 18% (91). *Average award:* Freshmen: $9056. Undergraduates: $8340. *Scholarships, grants, and awards by category:* Academic interests/achievement: 507 awards ($3,920,713 total): business, general academic interests/achievements. *Special achievements/activities:* memberships. *Special characteristics:* 27 awards ($46,000 total): children and siblings of alumni, children of faculty/staff, siblings of current students. *Tuition waivers:* Full or partial for employees or children of employees.

LOANS *Student loans:* $3,411,818 (82% need-based, 18% non-need-based). 81% of past graduating class borrowed through all loan programs. *Average indebtedness per student:* $24,254. *Average need-based loan:* Freshmen: $3378. Undergraduates: $4131. *Parent loans:* $354,665 (31% need-based, 69% non-need-based). *Programs:* Federal Direct (Subsidized and Unsubsidized Stafford, PLUS).

WORK-STUDY *Federal work-study:* Total amount: $127,650; 66 jobs averaging $1920.

ATHLETIC AWARDS Total amount: $1,309,735 (59% need-based, 41% non-need-based).

APPLYING FOR FINANCIAL AID *Required financial aid form:* FAFSA. *Financial aid deadline:* Continuous. *Notification date:* Continuous beginning 3/1.

CONTACT Ms. Dawn Shestko, Assistant Director of Financial Aid, Northwood University, Texas Campus, 1114 West FM 1382, Cedar Hill, TX 75104, 972-293-5431 or toll-free 800-927-9663. *Fax:* 972-293-7196. *E-mail:* shestkod@northwood.edu.
Website: http://www.northwood.edu/.

NORWICH UNIVERSITY
Northfield, VT

Tuition & fees: $31,782	Average undergraduate aid package: $25,644

ABOUT THE INSTITUTION Independent, coed, primarily men. *Awards:* certificates, bachelor's, and master's degrees. 28 undergraduate majors. *Total enrollment:* 3,452. Undergraduates: 2,227. Freshmen: 712. Federal methodology is used as a basis for awarding need-based institutional aid.

UNDERGRADUATE EXPENSES for 2013–2014 *Application fee:* $35. *Comprehensive fee:* $42,758 includes full-time tuition ($30,048), mandatory fees ($1734), and room and board ($10,976). Part-time tuition and fees vary according to course load.

FRESHMAN FINANCIAL AID (Fall 2012, est.) 579 applied for aid; of those 90% were deemed to have need. 100% of freshmen with need received aid; of those 17% had need fully met. *Average percent of need met:* 79% (excluding resources awarded to replace EFC). *Average financial aid package:* $27,661 (excluding resources awarded to replace EFC). 15% of all full-time freshmen had no need and received non-need-based gift aid.

UNDERGRADUATE FINANCIAL AID (Fall 2012, est.) 1,876 applied for aid; of those 91% were deemed to have need. 100% of undergraduates with need received aid; of those 21% had need fully met. *Average percent of need met:* 74% (excluding resources awarded to replace EFC). *Average financial aid package:* $25,644 (excluding resources awarded to replace EFC). 20% of all full-time undergraduates had no need and received non-need-based gift aid.

GIFT AID (NEED-BASED) *Total amount:* $36,749,851 (9% federal, 2% state, 75% institutional, 14% external sources). *Receiving aid:* Freshmen: 85% (522); all full-time undergraduates: 77% (1,705). *Average award:* Freshmen: $23,519; Undergraduates: $21,425. *Scholarships, grants, and awards:* Federal Pell, FSEOG, state, private, college/university gift aid from institutional funds.

GIFT AID (NON-NEED-BASED) *Total amount:* $13,998,143 (52% institutional, 48% external sources). *Receiving aid:* Freshmen: 11% (67). Undergraduates: 13% (282). *Average award:* Freshmen: $15,204. Undergraduates: $14,104. *Scholarships, grants, and awards by category:* Academic interests/achievement: 1,439 awards ($17,055,942 total): general academic interests/achievements. Special characteristics: 106 awards ($1,976,522 total): children of faculty/staff. *ROTC:* Army, Naval, Air Force.

LOANS *Student loans:* $14,420,479 (76% need-based, 24% non-need-based). 78% of past graduating class borrowed through all loan programs. *Average indebtedness per student:* $35,310. *Average need-based loan:* Freshmen: $4525. Undergraduates: $4991. *Parent loans:* $9,454,296 (41% need-based, 59% non-need-based). *Programs:* Federal Direct (Subsidized and Unsubsidized Stafford, PLUS), Perkins, private loans.

WORK-STUDY *Federal work-study:* Total amount: $649,755; 760 jobs averaging $1326.

APPLYING FOR FINANCIAL AID *Required financial aid form:* FAFSA. *Financial aid deadline (priority):* 3/1. *Notification date:* Continuous beginning 2/15.

CONTACT Ms. Jana Cox, Director of Student Financial Planning, Norwich University, 158 Harmon Drive, Northfield, VT 05663, 802-485-2015 or toll-free 800-468-6679. *Fax:* 802-485-2024. *E-mail:* jcox1@norwich.edu. *Website:* http://www.norwich.edu/.

NOTRE DAME COLLEGE
South Euclid, OH

CONTACT Ms. Dianna Roberts, Assistant Director of Financial Aid, Notre Dame College, 4545 College Road, South Euclid, OH 44118, 216-373-5213 or toll-free 877-NDC-OHIO. *Fax:* 216-373-5243. *E-mail:* droberts@ndc.edu. *Website:* http://www.notredamecollege.edu/.

NOTRE DAME DE NAMUR UNIVERSITY
Belmont, CA

Tuition & fees: $31,206	Average undergraduate aid package: $22,173

ABOUT THE INSTITUTION Independent Roman Catholic, coed. *Awards:* certificates, bachelor's, master's, and doctoral degrees. 25 undergraduate majors. *Total enrollment:* 2,001. Undergraduates: 1,183. Freshmen: 182. Both federal and institutional methodology are used as a basis for awarding need-based institutional aid.

UNDERGRADUATE EXPENSES for 2013–2014 *Application fee:* $50. *Comprehensive fee:* $43,358 includes full-time tuition ($30,806), mandatory fees ($400), and room and board ($12,152). *College room only:* $7878. Full-time tuition and fees vary according to degree level and program. Room and board charges vary

according to board plan and housing facility. *Part-time tuition:* $994 per unit. Part-time tuition and fees vary according to degree level and program.

FRESHMAN FINANCIAL AID (Fall 2012, est.) 179 applied for aid; of those 93% were deemed to have need. 100% of freshmen with need received aid; of those 4% had need fully met. *Average percent of need met:* 61% (excluding resources awarded to replace EFC). *Average financial aid package:* $25,031 (excluding resources awarded to replace EFC). 6% of all full-time freshmen had no need and received non-need-based gift aid.

UNDERGRADUATE FINANCIAL AID (Fall 2012, est.) 761 applied for aid; of those 95% were deemed to have need. 100% of undergraduates with need received aid; of those 4% had need fully met. *Average percent of need met:* 53% (excluding resources awarded to replace EFC). *Average financial aid package:* $22,173 (excluding resources awarded to replace EFC). 4% of all full-time undergraduates had no need and received non-need-based gift aid.

GIFT AID (NEED-BASED) *Total amount:* $13,515,576 (17% federal, 13% state, 68% institutional, 2% external sources). *Receiving aid:* Freshmen: 91% (166); all full-time undergraduates: 90% (719). *Average award:* Freshmen: $21,692; Undergraduates: $18,050. *Scholarships, grants, and awards:* Federal Pell, FSEOG, state, private, college/university gift aid from institutional funds.

GIFT AID (NON-NEED-BASED) *Total amount:* $328,976 (98% institutional, 2% external sources). *Receiving aid:* Freshmen: 3% (5). Undergraduates: 2% (19). *Average award:* Freshmen: $9268. Undergraduates: $7189. *Scholarships, grants, and awards by category:* Academic interests/achievement: general academic interests/achievements. Creative arts/performance: applied art and design, art/fine arts, creative writing, music, performing arts, theater/drama. Special achievements/activities: community service, general special achievements/activities, leadership. Special characteristics: children and siblings of alumni, children of faculty/staff, general special characteristics, religious affiliation. *Tuition waivers:* Full or partial for employees or children of employees, senior citizens. *ROTC:* Air Force cooperative.

LOANS *Student loans:* $8,705,251 (89% need-based, 11% non-need-based). 73% of past graduating class borrowed through all loan programs. *Average indebtedness per student:* $31,915. *Average need-based loan:* Freshmen: $3478. Undergraduates: $4767. *Parent loans:* $3,882,211 (54% need-based, 46% non-need-based). *Programs:* Federal Direct (Subsidized and Unsubsidized Stafford, PLUS), Perkins.

WORK-STUDY *Federal work-study:* Total amount: $329,500; 167 jobs averaging $1991. *State or other work-study/employment:* Total amount: $142,582 (100% need-based). Part-time jobs available.

ATHLETIC AWARDS Total amount: $418,914 (86% need-based, 14% non-need-based).

APPLYING FOR FINANCIAL AID *Required financial aid form:* FAFSA. *Financial aid deadline (priority):* 3/2. *Notification date:* Continuous. Students must reply within 2 weeks of notification.

CONTACT Wilbert Lleses, Director of Financial Aid, Notre Dame de Namur University, 1500 Ralston Avenue, Belmont, CA 94002, 650-508-3441 or toll-free 800-263-0545. *Fax:* 650-508-3635. *E-mail:* wlleses@ndnu.edu. *Website:* http://www.ndnu.edu/.

NOTRE DAME OF MARYLAND UNIVERSITY
Baltimore, MD

Tuition & fees: $30,850	Average undergraduate aid package: $21,973

ABOUT THE INSTITUTION Independent Roman Catholic, coed, primarily women. *Awards:* certificates, bachelor's, master's, and doctoral degrees (offers coed undergraduate program for adult students). 38 undergraduate majors. *Total enrollment:* 2,731. Undergraduates: 1,296. Freshmen: 137. Federal methodology is used as a basis for awarding need-based institutional aid.

UNDERGRADUATE EXPENSES for 2013–2014 *Application fee:* $45. *Comprehensive fee:* $41,000 includes full-time tuition ($29,850), mandatory fees ($1000), and room and board ($10,150). Room and board charges vary according to board plan.

FRESHMAN FINANCIAL AID (Fall 2012, est.) 120 applied for aid; of those 96% were deemed to have need. 100% of freshmen with need received aid; of those 12% had need fully met. *Average percent of need met:* 70% (excluding resources awarded to replace EFC). *Average financial aid package:* $24,726 (excluding

resources awarded to replace EFC). 9% of all full-time freshmen had no need and received non-need-based gift aid.

UNDERGRADUATE FINANCIAL AID (Fall 2012, est.) 480 applied for aid; of those 96% were deemed to have need. 99% of undergraduates with need received aid; of those 14% had need fully met. *Average percent of need met:* 67% (excluding resources awarded to replace EFC). *Average financial aid package:* $21,973 (excluding resources awarded to replace EFC). 9% of all full-time undergraduates had no need and received non-need-based gift aid.

GIFT AID (NEED-BASED) *Total amount:* $8,367,500 (19% federal, 10% state, 67% institutional, 4% external sources). *Receiving aid:* Freshmen: 90% (115); all full-time undergraduates: 84% (447). *Average award:* Freshmen: $20,722; Undergraduates: $17,844. *Scholarships, grants, and awards:* Federal Pell, FSEOG, state, private, college/university gift aid from institutional funds, TEACH Grants.

GIFT AID (NON-NEED-BASED) *Total amount:* $1,611,326 (1% federal, 63% institutional, 36% external sources). *Receiving aid:* Freshmen: 9% (11). Undergraduates: 9% (47). *Average award:* Freshmen: $15,413. Undergraduates: $13,456. *Scholarships, grants, and awards by category:* Academic interests/achievement: 257 awards ($3,083,231 total): general academic interests/achievements. Creative arts/performance: 8 awards ($52,000 total): art/fine arts, general creative arts/performance. Special achievements/activities: 226 awards ($1,489,900 total): community service, general special achievements/activities, leadership, memberships, religious involvement. Special characteristics: 72 awards ($148,480 total): general special characteristics, international students, siblings of current students. *ROTC:* Army cooperative.

LOANS *Student loans:* $6,404,967 (82% need-based, 18% non-need-based). 81% of past graduating class borrowed through all loan programs. *Average indebtedness per student:* $28,735. *Average need-based loan:* Freshmen: $3694. Undergraduates: $4298. *Parent loans:* $1,433,184 (22% need-based, 78% non-need-based). *Programs:* Federal Direct (Subsidized and Unsubsidized Stafford, PLUS), Perkins.

WORK-STUDY *Federal work-study:* Total amount: $91,801; 95 jobs averaging $966.

APPLYING FOR FINANCIAL AID *Required financial aid form:* FAFSA. *Financial aid deadline (priority):* 2/15. *Notification date:* Continuous beginning 3/1. Students must reply by 5/1.

CONTACT Zhanna Goltser, Director of Financial Aid, Notre Dame of Maryland University, 4701 North Charles Street, Baltimore, MD 21210-2404, 410-532-5369 or toll-free 800-435-0200. *Fax:* 410-532-6287. *E-mail:* finaid@ndm.edu. *Website:* http://www.ndm.edu/.

NOVA SOUTHEASTERN UNIVERSITY
Fort Lauderdale, FL

Tuition & fees: $24,500	Average undergraduate aid package: $23,612

ABOUT THE INSTITUTION Independent, coed. *Awards:* certificates, associate, bachelor's, master's, and doctoral degrees. 43 undergraduate majors. *Total enrollment:* 26,808. Undergraduates: 5,739. Freshmen: 724. Federal methodology is used as a basis for awarding need-based institutional aid.

UNDERGRADUATE EXPENSES for 2013–2014 *Application fee:* $50. *Comprehensive fee:* $34,016 includes full-time tuition ($23,850), mandatory fees ($650), and room and board ($9516). *College room only:* $6916. Full-time tuition and fees vary according to class time and program. Room and board charges vary according to board plan and housing facility. *Part-time tuition:* $795 per credit hour. Part-time tuition and fees vary according to class time, course load, and program.

FRESHMAN FINANCIAL AID (Fall 2012, est.) 550 applied for aid; of those 85% were deemed to have need. 99% of freshmen with need received aid; of those 14% had need fully met. *Average percent of need met:* 71% (excluding resources awarded to replace EFC). *Average financial aid package:* $24,280 (excluding resources awarded to replace EFC). 20% of all full-time freshmen had no need and received non-need-based gift aid.

UNDERGRADUATE FINANCIAL AID (Fall 2012, est.) 3,088 applied for aid; of those 89% were deemed to have need. 100% of undergraduates with need received aid; of those 8% had need fully met. *Average percent of need met:* 58% (excluding resources awarded to replace EFC). *Average financial aid package:* $23,612 (excluding resources awarded to replace EFC). 13% of all full-time undergraduates had no need and received non-need-based gift aid.

GIFT AID (NEED-BASED) *Total amount:* $33,423,351 (39% federal, 26% state, 30% institutional, 5% external sources). *Receiving aid:* Freshmen: 75% (459); all full-time undergraduates: 73% (2,632). *Average award:* Freshmen: $12,430; Undergraduates: $10,231. *Scholarships, grants, and awards:* Federal Pell, FSEOG, state, private, college/university gift aid from institutional funds, United Negro College Fund.

GIFT AID (NON-NEED-BASED) *Total amount:* $4,831,437 (1% federal, 16% state, 69% institutional, 14% external sources). *Receiving aid:* Freshmen: 4% (27). Undergraduates: 3% (92). *Average award:* Freshmen: $6417. Undergraduates: $5839. *Scholarships, grants, and awards by category:* Academic interests/achievement: 2,037 awards ($17,172,859 total): general academic interests/achievements. Creative arts/performance: 36 awards ($73,750 total): music, performing arts. Special achievements/activities: 138 awards ($656,725 total): leadership, memberships. Special characteristics: 84 awards ($447,899 total): children of faculty/staff, veterans. *Tuition waivers:* Full or partial for employees or children of employees.

LOANS *Student loans:* $44,178,156 (96% need-based, 4% non-need-based). 68% of past graduating class borrowed through all loan programs. *Average indebtedness per student:* $31,137. *Average need-based loan:* Freshmen: $2898. Undergraduates: $4180. *Parent loans:* $6,116,108 (91% need-based, 9% non-need-based). *Programs:* Federal Direct (Subsidized and Unsubsidized Stafford, PLUS), Perkins.

WORK-STUDY *Federal work-study:* Total amount: $7,607,363; 1,499 jobs averaging $5075. *State or other work-study/employment:* Total amount: $493,222 (75% need-based, 25% non-need-based). 352 part-time jobs averaging $1401.

ATHLETIC AWARDS Total amount: $4,219,348 (57% need-based, 43% non-need-based).

APPLYING FOR FINANCIAL AID *Required financial aid forms:* FAFSA, state aid form. *Financial aid deadline (priority):* 4/15. *Notification date:* Continuous beginning 2/15.

CONTACT Stephanie G. Brown, EdD, Vice President for Enrollment and Student Services, Nova Southeastern University, 3301 College Avenue, Fort Lauderdale, FL 33314, 954-262-7456 or toll-free 800-541-NOVA. *Fax:* 954-262-3967. *E-mail:* browstep@nova.edu. *Website:* http://www.nova.edu/.

NYACK COLLEGE
Nyack, NY

Tuition & fees: $23,250	Average undergraduate aid package: $18,553

ABOUT THE INSTITUTION Independent The Christian and Missionary Alliance, coed. *Awards:* associate, bachelor's, master's, and doctoral degrees. 35 undergraduate majors. *Total enrollment:* 3,318. Undergraduates: 2,040. Freshmen: 297. Federal methodology is used as a basis for awarding need-based institutional aid.

UNDERGRADUATE EXPENSES for 2013–2014 *Application fee:* $25. *One-time required fee:* $100. *Comprehensive fee:* $31,900 includes full-time tuition ($23,000), mandatory fees ($250), and room and board ($8650). Room and board charges vary according to board plan and housing facility. *Part-time tuition:* $960 per credit hour. *Part-time fees:* $75 per term.

FRESHMAN FINANCIAL AID (Fall 2011) 281 applied for aid; of those 95% were deemed to have need. 100% of freshmen with need received aid; of those 17% had need fully met. *Average percent of need met:* 66% (excluding resources awarded to replace EFC). *Average financial aid package:* $19,138 (excluding resources awarded to replace EFC). 9% of all full-time freshmen had no need and received non-need-based gift aid.

UNDERGRADUATE FINANCIAL AID (Fall 2011) 1,403 applied for aid; of those 96% were deemed to have need. 100% of undergraduates with need received aid; of those 10% had need fully met. *Average percent of need met:* 64% (excluding resources awarded to replace EFC). *Average financial aid package:* $18,553 (excluding resources awarded to replace EFC). 11% of all full-time undergraduates had no need and received non-need-based gift aid.

GIFT AID (NEED-BASED) *Total amount:* $16,403,923 (28% federal, 14% state, 57% institutional, 1% external sources). *Receiving aid:* Freshmen: 91% (267); all full-time undergraduates: 88% (1,337). *Average award:* Freshmen: $15,158; Undergraduates: $13,144. *Scholarships, grants, and awards:* Federal Pell, FSEOG, state, private, college/university gift aid from institutional funds.

GIFT AID (NON-NEED-BASED) *Total amount:* $1,487,949 (97% institutional, 3% external sources). *Receiving aid:* Freshmen: 8% (25). Undergraduates: 5% (71). *Average award:* Freshmen: $8115. Undergraduates: $7668. *Scholarships, grants, and awards by category:* Academic interests/achievement: $1,904,076 total: general academic interests/achievements. Creative arts/performance: $252,800 total:

journalism/publications, music, performing arts, theater/drama. *Special achievements/activities:* $2,080,588 total: cheerleading/drum major, community service, general special achievements/activities, leadership, religious involvement. *Special characteristics:* $2,029,745 total: children and siblings of alumni, children of faculty/staff, general special characteristics, international students, local/state students, out-of-state students, relatives of clergy, religious affiliation, spouses of current students. *Tuition waivers:* Full or partial for employees or children of employees.
LOANS *Student loans:* $13,478,087 (87% need-based, 13% non-need-based). 87% of past graduating class borrowed through all loan programs. *Average indebtedness per student:* $32,003. *Average need-based loan:* Freshmen: $3474. Undergraduates: $4643. *Parent loans:* $2,687,363 (66% need-based, 34% non-need-based). *Programs:* Federal Direct (Subsidized and Unsubsidized Stafford, PLUS), Perkins.
WORK-STUDY *Federal work-study:* Total amount: $204,186; 193 jobs averaging $1084. *State or other work-study/employment:* Total amount: $89,676 (88% need-based, 12% non-need-based). 53 part-time jobs averaging $1692.
ATHLETIC AWARDS Total amount: $1,876,470 (65% need-based, 35% non-need-based).
APPLYING FOR FINANCIAL AID *Required financial aid forms:* FAFSA, state aid form. *Financial aid deadline (priority):* 3/1. *Notification date:* Continuous beginning 3/1. Students must reply by 5/1 or within 4 weeks of notification.
CONTACT Steve Phillips, Director of Student Financial Services, Nyack College, 1 South Boulevard, Nyack, NY 10960-3698, 845-675-4747 or toll-free 800-33-NYACK. *Fax:* 845-358-7016. *E-mail:* nyacksfs@nyack.edu.
Website: http://www.nyack.edu/.

OAK HILLS CHRISTIAN COLLEGE
Bemidji, MN

CONTACT Daniel Hovestol, Financial Aid Director, Oak Hills Christian College, 1600 Oak Hills Road, SW, Bemidji, MN 56601-8832, 218-751-8671 Ext. 1220 or toll-free 888-751-8670 Ext. 1285. *Fax:* 218-444-1311. *E-mail:* ohfinaid@oakhills.edu. *Website:* http://www.oakhills.edu/.

OAKLAND CITY UNIVERSITY
Oakland City, IN

CONTACT Mrs. Caren K. Richeson, Director of Financial Aid, Oakland City University, 138 North Lucretia Street, Oakland City, IN 47660-1099, 812-749-1225 or toll-free 800-737-5125. *Fax:* 812-749-1438. *E-mail:* cricheson@oak.edu. *Website:* http://www.oak.edu/.

OAKLAND UNIVERSITY
Rochester, MI

Tuition & fees (area res): $11,183	Average undergraduate aid package: $12,511

ABOUT THE INSTITUTION State-supported, coed. *Awards:* certificates, bachelor's, master's, and doctoral degrees. 84 undergraduate majors. *Total enrollment:* 19,740. Undergraduates: 16,190. Freshmen: 2,464. Federal methodology is used as a basis for awarding need-based institutional aid.
UNDERGRADUATE EXPENSES for 2013–2014 *Tuition, area resident:* full-time $11,183. *Tuition, state resident:* full-time $11,183; part-time $341 per credit hour. *Tuition, nonresident:* full-time $25,598; part-time $795.75 per credit hour. Full-time tuition and fees vary according to program and student level. Part-time tuition and fees vary according to program and student level. *College room and board:* $8208. Room and board charges vary according to housing facility.
FRESHMAN FINANCIAL AID (Fall 2012, est.) 1,798 applied for aid; of those 82% were deemed to have need. 97% of freshmen with need received aid; of those 7% had need fully met. *Average percent of need met:* 77% (excluding resources awarded to replace EFC). *Average financial aid package:* $12,885 (excluding resources awarded to replace EFC). 16% of all full-time freshmen had no need and received non-need-based gift aid.

UNDERGRADUATE FINANCIAL AID (Fall 2012, est.) 9,192 applied for aid; of those 85% were deemed to have need. 98% of undergraduates with need received aid; of those 7% had need fully met. *Average percent of need met:* 70% (excluding resources awarded to replace EFC). *Average financial aid package:* $12,511 (excluding resources awarded to replace EFC). 10% of all full-time undergraduates had no need and received non-need-based gift aid.
GIFT AID (NEED-BASED) *Total amount:* $27,667,321 (75% federal, 2% state, 23% institutional). *Receiving aid:* Freshmen: 54% (1,173); all full-time undergraduates: 45% (5,486). *Average award:* Freshmen: $5645; Undergraduates: $4552. *Scholarships, grants, and awards:* Federal Pell, FSEOG, state, private, college/university gift aid from institutional funds.
GIFT AID (NON-NEED-BASED) *Total amount:* $18,916,884 (69% institutional, 31% external sources). *Receiving aid:* Freshmen: 58% (1,258). Undergraduates: 28% (3,451). *Average award:* Freshmen: $3764. Undergraduates: $3091. *Scholarships, grants, and awards by category:* Academic interests/achievement: area/ethnic studies, biological sciences, business, education, engineering/technologies, English, foreign languages, general academic interests/achievements, health fields, humanities. Creative arts/performance: dance, music, performing arts. Special characteristics: adult students, ethnic background, out-of-state students. *Tuition waivers:* Full or partial for employees or children of employees, senior citizens. *ROTC:* Air Force cooperative.
LOANS *Student loans:* $66,149,203 (46% need-based, 54% non-need-based). 60% of past graduating class borrowed through all loan programs. *Average indebtedness per student:* $19,697. *Average need-based loan:* Freshmen: $3033. Undergraduates: $4127. *Parent loans:* $10,124,462 (100% need-based). *Programs:* Federal Direct (Subsidized and Unsubsidized Stafford, PLUS), Perkins, private loans.
WORK-STUDY *Federal work-study:* Total amount: $428,698; jobs available. *State or other work-study/employment:* Part-time jobs available.
ATHLETIC AWARDS Total amount: $3,213,200 (100% non-need-based).
APPLYING FOR FINANCIAL AID *Required financial aid form:* FAFSA. *Financial aid deadline (priority):* 3/15. *Notification date:* Continuous beginning 3/15.
CONTACT Ms. Cindy Hermsen, Director of Financial Aid, Oakland University, 120 North Foundation Hall, Rochester, MI 48309-4401, 248-370-2550 or toll-free 800-OAK-UNIV. *E-mail:* finaid@oakland.edu.
Website: http://www.oakland.edu/.

OAKWOOD UNIVERSITY
Huntsville, AL

CONTACT Financial Aid Director, Oakwood University, 7000 Adventist Boulevard, Huntsville, AL 35896, 256-726-7210 or toll-free 800-824-5312.
Website: http://www.oakwood.edu/.

OBERLIN COLLEGE
Oberlin, OH

Tuition & fees: N/R	Average undergraduate aid package: $33,632

ABOUT THE INSTITUTION Independent, coed. 55 undergraduate majors. Both federal and institutional methodology are used as a basis for awarding need-based institutional aid.
FRESHMAN FINANCIAL AID (Fall 2012, est.) 510 applied for aid; of those 83% were deemed to have need. 100% of freshmen with need received aid; of those 100% had need fully met. *Average percent of need met:* 100% (excluding resources awarded to replace EFC). *Average financial aid package:* $31,983 (excluding resources awarded to replace EFC). 32% of all full-time freshmen had no need and received non-need-based gift aid.
UNDERGRADUATE FINANCIAL AID (Fall 2012, est.) 1,786 applied for aid; of those 87% were deemed to have need. 100% of undergraduates with need received aid; of those 100% had need fully met. *Average percent of need met:* 100% (excluding resources awarded to replace EFC). *Average financial aid package:* $33,632 (excluding resources awarded to replace EFC). 32% of all full-time undergraduates had no need and received non-need-based gift aid.

GIFT AID (NEED-BASED) Total amount: $44,426,463 (5% federal, 91% institutional, 4% external sources). **Receiving aid:** Freshmen: 36% (271); all full-time undergraduates: 40% (1,156). **Average award:** Freshmen: $29,351; Undergraduates: $29,082. **Scholarships, grants, and awards:** Federal Pell, FSEOG, state, private, college/university gift aid from institutional funds.

GIFT AID (NON-NEED-BASED) Total amount: $11,937,558 (91% institutional, 9% external sources). **Receiving aid:** Freshmen: 28% (214). Undergraduates: 30% (855). **Average award:** Freshmen: $13,169. Undergraduates: $14,100. **Scholarships, grants, and awards by category:** Academic interests/achievement: 1,650 awards ($19,402,438 total): general academic interests/achievements, physical sciences. Creative arts/performance: 526 awards ($7,356,222 total): music.

LOANS Student loans: $8,687,237 (90% need-based, 10% non-need-based). **Average need-based loan:** Freshmen: $4533. Undergraduates: $5253. **Parent loans:** $2,768,067 (76% need-based, 24% non-need-based). **Programs:** Federal Direct (Subsidized and Unsubsidized Stafford, PLUS), Perkins.

WORK-STUDY Federal work-study: Total amount: $2,074,356; 1,500 jobs averaging $2400. **State or other work-study/employment:** 600 part-time jobs averaging $2400.

APPLYING FOR FINANCIAL AID Required financial aid forms: FAFSA, CSS Financial Aid PROFILE, institution's own non-custodial form. **Financial aid deadline (priority):** 2/15. **Notification date:** 3/25. Students must reply by 5/1.

CONTACT Mr. Robert A. Reddy Jr., Director of Financial Aid, Oberlin College, Carnegie Building #123, 52 West Lorain Street, Oberlin, OH 44074, 440-775-8142 or toll-free 800-622-OBIE. Fax: 440-775-8249. E-mail: financial.aid@oberlin.edu. Website: http://www.oberlin.edu/.

OCCIDENTAL COLLEGE
Los Angeles, CA

Tuition & fees: $46,270	Average undergraduate aid package: $39,160

ABOUT THE INSTITUTION Independent, coed. **Awards:** bachelor's and master's degrees. 33 undergraduate majors. **Total enrollment:** 2,178. Undergraduates: 2,176. Freshmen: 530. Institutional methodology is used as a basis for awarding need-based institutional aid.

UNDERGRADUATE EXPENSES for 2013–2014 Application fee: $60. **Comprehensive fee:** $59,210 includes full-time tuition ($45,190), mandatory fees ($1080), and room and board ($12,940). Room and board charges vary according to board plan. **Payment plan:** Tuition prepayment.

FRESHMAN FINANCIAL AID (Fall 2011) 379 applied for aid; of those 80% were deemed to have need. 100% of freshmen with need received aid; of those 100% had need fully met. **Average percent of need met:** 100% (excluding resources awarded to replace EFC). **Average financial aid package:** $38,084 (excluding resources awarded to replace EFC). 14% of all full-time freshmen had no need and received non-need-based gift aid.

UNDERGRADUATE FINANCIAL AID (Fall 2011) 1,386 applied for aid; of those 87% were deemed to have need. 100% of undergraduates with need received aid; of those 100% had need fully met. **Average percent of need met:** 100% (excluding resources awarded to replace EFC). **Average financial aid package:** $39,160 (excluding resources awarded to replace EFC). 17% of all full-time undergraduates had no need and received non-need-based gift aid.

GIFT AID (NEED-BASED) Total amount: $38,359,306 (6% federal, 8% state, 83% institutional, 3% external sources). **Receiving aid:** Freshmen: 56% (301); all full-time undergraduates: 56% (1,188). **Average award:** Freshmen: $32,282; Undergraduates: $32,146. **Scholarships, grants, and awards:** Federal Pell, FSEOG, state, private, college/university gift aid from institutional funds.

GIFT AID (NON-NEED-BASED) Total amount: $5,289,907 (84% institutional, 16% external sources). **Receiving aid:** Freshmen: 6% (30). Undergraduates: 5% (102). **Average award:** Freshmen: $11,369. Undergraduates: $10,619. **Scholarships, grants, and awards by category:** Academic interests/achievement: 355 awards ($3,652,183 total): general academic interests/achievements. Creative arts/performance: 26 awards ($21,939 total): music. Special achievements/activities: 11 awards ($165,000 total): leadership. Special characteristics: 17 awards ($654,852 total): children of educators, children of faculty/staff. **Tuition waivers:** Full or partial for employees or children of employees. **ROTC:** Army cooperative, Air Force cooperative.

LOANS Student loans: $10,722,263 (72% need-based, 28% non-need-based). 57% of past graduating class borrowed through all loan programs. **Average indebtedness per student:** $28,723. **Average need-based loan:** Freshmen: $4637. Undergraduates: $6145. **Parent loans:** $4,264,009 (16% need-based, 84% non-need-based). **Programs:** Federal Direct (Subsidized and Unsubsidized Stafford, PLUS), Perkins, college/university, alternative loans.

WORK-STUDY Federal work-study: Total amount: $716,099; 601 jobs averaging $1477. **State or other work-study/employment:** Total amount: $1,901,741 (68% need-based, 32% non-need-based). 251 part-time jobs averaging $3254.

APPLYING FOR FINANCIAL AID Required financial aid forms: FAFSA, CSS Financial Aid PROFILE, state aid form, noncustodial (divorced/separated) parent's statement. **Financial aid deadline:** 2/1. **Notification date:** 4/1. Students must reply by 5/1.

CONTACT Maureen McRae, Director of Financial Aid, Occidental College, 1600 Campus Road, Los Angeles, CA 90041, 323-259-2548 or toll-free 800-825-5262. Fax: 323-341-4961. E-mail: finaid@oxy.edu. Website: http://www.oxy.edu/.

OGLALA LAKOTA COLLEGE
Kyle, SD

CONTACT Financial Aid Director, Oglala Lakota College, 490 Piya Wiconi Road, Kyle, SD 57752-0490, 605-455-6000. Website: http://www.olc.edu/.

OGLETHORPE UNIVERSITY
Atlanta, GA

Tuition & fees: $31,280	Average undergraduate aid package: $27,081

ABOUT THE INSTITUTION Independent, coed. **Awards:** bachelor's and master's degrees. 32 undergraduate majors. **Total enrollment:** 1,079. Undergraduates: 1,053. Freshmen: 277. Federal methodology is used as a basis for awarding need-based institutional aid.

UNDERGRADUATE EXPENSES for 2013–2014 Application fee: $40. **Comprehensive fee:** $42,580 includes full-time tuition ($31,000), mandatory fees ($280), and room and board ($11,300). Full-time tuition and fees vary according to degree level. Room and board charges vary according to housing facility and location. **Part-time tuition:** $1260 per credit hour. Part-time tuition and fees vary according to class time, course load, and degree level. **Payment plan:** Tuition prepayment.

FRESHMAN FINANCIAL AID (Fall 2012, est.) 227 applied for aid; of those 88% were deemed to have need. 100% of freshmen with need received aid; of those 14% had need fully met. **Average percent of need met:** 78% (excluding resources awarded to replace EFC). **Average financial aid package:** $28,042 (excluding resources awarded to replace EFC). 21% of all full-time freshmen had no need and received non-need-based gift aid.

UNDERGRADUATE FINANCIAL AID (Fall 2012, est.) 872 applied for aid; of those 93% were deemed to have need. 100% of undergraduates with need received aid; of those 11% had need fully met. **Average percent of need met:** 72% (excluding resources awarded to replace EFC). **Average financial aid package:** $27,081 (excluding resources awarded to replace EFC). 25% of all full-time undergraduates had no need and received non-need-based gift aid.

GIFT AID (NEED-BASED) Total amount: $13,545,959 (17% federal, 9% state, 72% institutional, 2% external sources). **Receiving aid:** Freshmen: 70% (193); all full-time undergraduates: 78% (800). **Average award:** Freshmen: $22,032; Undergraduates: $21,498. **Scholarships, grants, and awards:** Federal Pell, FSEOG, state, private, college/university gift aid from institutional funds.

GIFT AID (NON-NEED-BASED) Total amount: $6,117,584 (7% state, 91% institutional, 2% external sources). **Receiving aid:** Freshmen: 40% (111). Undergraduates: 47% (482). **Average award:** Freshmen: $18,208. Undergraduates: $15,442. **Scholarships, grants, and awards by category:** Academic interests/achievement: general academic interests/achievements. Creative arts/performance: art/fine arts, journalism/publications, music, performing arts, theater/drama. Special achievements/activities: community service, religious involvement. Special character-

istics: children of faculty/staff, siblings of current students. *Tuition waivers:* Full or partial for employees or children of employees. *ROTC:* Air Force cooperative.

LOANS *Student loans:* $6,609,654 (42% need-based, 58% non-need-based). 88% of past graduating class borrowed through all loan programs. *Average indebtedness per student:* $22,692. *Average need-based loan:* Freshmen: $3198. Undergraduates: $4146. *Parent loans:* $1,309,249 (100% non-need-based). *Programs:* Federal Direct (Subsidized and Unsubsidized Stafford, PLUS), Perkins, state.

WORK-STUDY *Federal work-study:* Total amount: $200,000; jobs available.

APPLYING FOR FINANCIAL AID *Required financial aid form:* FAFSA. *Financial aid deadline (priority):* 2/1. *Notification date:* Continuous beginning 3/1. Students must reply by 3/1 or within 3 weeks of notification.

CONTACT Ms. Meg McGinnis, Director of Financial Aid, Oglethorpe University, 4484 Peachtree Road NE, Atlanta, GA 30319, 404-364-8366 or toll-free 800-428-4484. *E-mail:* mmcginnis@oglethorpe.edu. *Website:* http://www.oglethorpe.edu/.

OHIO CHRISTIAN UNIVERSITY
Circleville, OH

CONTACT Michael Fracassa, Assistant Vice President of Finance, Ohio Christian University, 1476 Lancaster Pike, PO Box 458, Circleville, OH 43113-9487, 740-477-7758 or toll-free 877-762-8669. *Fax:* 740-477-5921. *E-mail:* mfracassa@ohiochristian.edu. *Website:* http://www.ohiochristian.edu/.

OHIO DOMINICAN UNIVERSITY
Columbus, OH

CONTACT Ms. Cynthia A. Hahn, Director of Financial Aid, Ohio Dominican University, 1216 Sunbury Road, Columbus, OH 43219, 614-251-4778 or toll-free 800-955-6446. *Fax:* 614-251-4456. *E-mail:* fin-aid@ohiodominican.edu. *Website:* http://www.ohiodominican.edu/.

OHIO MID-WESTERN COLLEGE
Sharonville, OH

CONTACT Financial Aid Office, Ohio Mid-Western College, 19 Triangle Park Drive, Sharonville, OH 45246, 513-772-9888. *Website:* http://omw.edu/.

OHIO NORTHERN UNIVERSITY
Ada, OH

ABOUT THE INSTITUTION Independent United Methodist Church, coed. *Awards:* certificates, bachelor's, master's, and doctoral degrees. 108 undergraduate majors. *Total enrollment:* 3,557. Undergraduates: 2,629. Freshmen: 630.

GIFT AID (NEED-BASED) *Scholarships, grants, and awards:* Federal Pell, FSEOG, state, private, college/university gift aid from institutional funds.

GIFT AID (NON-NEED-BASED) *Scholarships, grants, and awards by category:* Academic interests/achievement: biological sciences, business, communication, computer science, education, engineering/technologies, English, foreign languages, general academic interests/achievements, health fields, humanities, international studies, mathematics, physical sciences, premedicine, religion/biblical studies, social sciences. *Creative arts/performance:* applied art and design, art/fine arts, creative writing, dance, journalism/publications, music, performing arts, theater/drama. *Special achievements/activities:* community service, general special achievements/activities, junior miss, leadership. *Special characteristics:* children and siblings of alumni, children of faculty/staff, ethnic background, international students, out-of-state students, relatives of clergy, religious affiliation, siblings of current students, veterans.

LOANS *Programs:* Federal Direct (Subsidized and Unsubsidized Stafford, PLUS), Perkins, state, college/university.

APPLYING FOR FINANCIAL AID *Required financial aid form:* FAFSA.

CONTACT Melanie Weaver, Director of Financial Aid, Ohio Northern University, 525 South Main Street, Ada, OH 45810, 419-772-2272 or toll-free 888-408-4ONU. *Fax:* 419-772-2313. *E-mail:* m-weaver.2@onu.edu. *Website:* http://www.onu.edu/.

THE OHIO STATE UNIVERSITY
Columbus, OH

Tuition & fees (OH res): $10,037	Average undergraduate aid package: $11,671

ABOUT THE INSTITUTION State-supported, coed. *Awards:* certificates, bachelor's, master's, and doctoral degrees. 171 undergraduate majors. *Total enrollment:* 56,387. Undergraduates: 43,058. Freshmen: 7,215. Federal methodology is used as a basis for awarding need-based institutional aid.

UNDERGRADUATE EXPENSES for 2013–2014 *Application fee:* $60. *Tuition, state resident:* full-time $10,037. *Tuition, nonresident:* full-time $25,445. Full-time tuition and fees vary according to course load, location, program, and reciprocity agreements. Part-time tuition and fees vary according to course load, location, program, and reciprocity agreements. *College room and board:* $10,392. Room and board charges vary according to board plan, housing facility, and location.

FRESHMAN FINANCIAL AID (Fall 2012, est.) 5,787 applied for aid; of those 66% were deemed to have need. 99% of freshmen with need received aid; of those 24% had need fully met. *Average percent of need met:* 69% (excluding resources awarded to replace EFC). *Average financial aid package:* $12,201 (excluding resources awarded to replace EFC). 26% of all full-time freshmen had no need and received non-need-based gift aid.

UNDERGRADUATE FINANCIAL AID (Fall 2012, est.) 26,697 applied for aid; of those 77% were deemed to have need. 99% of undergraduates with need received aid; of those 17% had need fully met. *Average percent of need met:* 64% (excluding resources awarded to replace EFC). *Average financial aid package:* $11,671 (excluding resources awarded to replace EFC). 19% of all full-time undergraduates had no need and received non-need-based gift aid.

GIFT AID (NEED-BASED) *Total amount:* $137,304,056 (30% federal, 5% state, 61% institutional, 4% external sources). *Receiving aid:* Freshmen: 45% (3,262); all full-time undergraduates: 40% (15,609). *Average award:* Freshmen: $9404; Undergraduates: $8795. *Scholarships, grants, and awards:* Federal Pell, FSEOG, state, private, college/university gift aid from institutional funds.

GIFT AID (NON-NEED-BASED) *Total amount:* $47,036,746 (2% state, 93% institutional, 5% external sources). *Receiving aid:* Freshmen: 3% (229). Undergraduates: 2% (654). *Average award:* Freshmen: $6003. Undergraduates: $5336. *Scholarships, grants, and awards by category:* Academic interests/achievement: agriculture, architecture, area/ethnic studies, biological sciences, business, communication, computer science, education, engineering/technologies, English, foreign languages, general academic interests/achievements, health fields, home economics, humanities, international studies, mathematics, military science, physical sciences, premedicine, social sciences. *Creative arts/performance:* creative writing, dance, journalism/publications, music, performing arts, theater/drama. *Special achievements/activities:* cheerleading/drum major, hobbies/interests, leadership, memberships. *Special characteristics:* adult students, children and siblings of alumni, children of faculty/staff, children of public servants, children of union members/company employees, children of workers in trades, ethnic background, handicapped students, members of minority groups, out-of-state students, previous college experience. *Tuition waivers:* Full or partial for employees or children of employees, senior citizens. *ROTC:* Army, Naval, Air Force.

LOANS *Student loans:* $202,790,053 (69% need-based, 31% non-need-based). 59% of past graduating class borrowed through all loan programs. *Average indebtedness per student:* $26,409. *Average need-based loan:* Freshmen: $3599. Undergraduates: $4675. *Parent loans:* $42,824,330 (100% non-need-based). *Programs:* Federal Direct (Subsidized and Unsubsidized Stafford, PLUS), Perkins, Federal Nursing, college/university.

WORK-STUDY *Federal work-study:* Total amount: $9,721,422; 4,321 jobs averaging $2250. *State or other work-study/employment:* Total amount: $402,761 (39% need-based, 61% non-need-based). 172 part-time jobs averaging $2342.

ATHLETIC AWARDS Total amount: $16,339,720 (100% non-need-based).

APPLYING FOR FINANCIAL AID *Required financial aid form:* FAFSA. *Financial aid deadline (priority):* 2/15. *Notification date:* 3/15. Students must reply by 5/1 or within 4 weeks of notification.

CONTACT Ms. Diane Stemper, Director of Student Financial Aid, The Ohio State University, 281 West Lane Avenue, 4th Floor, Columbus, OH 43210, 614-292-3600. *Fax:* 614-292-9264. *E-mail:* scsc@osu.edu. *Website:* http://www.osu.edu/.

OHIO UNIVERSITY
Athens, OH

Tuition & fees (OH res): $10,282	Average undergraduate aid package: $8458

ABOUT THE INSTITUTION State-supported, coed. *Awards:* associate, bachelor's, master's, and doctoral degrees. 121 undergraduate majors. *Total enrollment:* 27,402. Undergraduates: 22,685. Freshmen: 3,886. Federal methodology is used as a basis for awarding need-based institutional aid.

UNDERGRADUATE EXPENSES for 2013–2014 *Application fee:* $45. *Tuition, state resident:* full-time $10,282; part-time $487 per semester hour. *Tuition, nonresident:* full-time $19,246; part-time $929 per semester hour. Full-time tuition and fees vary according to degree level, location, program, and reciprocity agreements. Part-time tuition and fees vary according to course load, degree level, location, program, and reciprocity agreements. *College room and board:* $10,010; *Room only:* $5648. Room and board charges vary according to board plan.

FRESHMAN FINANCIAL AID (Fall 2012, est.) 3,059 applied for aid; of those 76% were deemed to have need. 100% of freshmen with need received aid; of those 13% had need fully met. *Average percent of need met:* 53% (excluding resources awarded to replace EFC). *Average financial aid package:* $8562 (excluding resources awarded to replace EFC). 13% of all full-time freshmen had no need and received non-need-based gift aid.

UNDERGRADUATE FINANCIAL AID (Fall 2012, est.) 11,659 applied for aid; of those 80% were deemed to have need. 100% of undergraduates with need received aid; of those 11% had need fully met. *Average percent of need met:* 53% (excluding resources awarded to replace EFC). *Average financial aid package:* $8458 (excluding resources awarded to replace EFC). 11% of all full-time undergraduates had no need and received non-need-based gift aid.

GIFT AID (NEED-BASED) *Total amount:* $41,529,473 (52% federal, 6% state, 37% institutional, 5% external sources). *Receiving aid:* Freshmen: 47% (1,800); all full-time undergraduates: 38% (6,381). *Average award:* Freshmen; $6187; Undergraduates: $5797. *Scholarships, grants, and awards:* Federal Pell, FSEOG, state, private, college/university gift aid from institutional funds.

GIFT AID (NON-NEED-BASED) *Total amount:* $10,685,505 (1% federal, 2% state, 88% institutional, 9% external sources). *Receiving aid:* Freshmen: 5% (197). Undergraduates: 3% (567). *Average award:* Freshmen: $4145. Undergraduates: $4331. *Scholarships, grants, and awards by category: Academic interests/achievement:* area/ethnic studies, biological sciences, business, communication, computer science, education, engineering/technologies, English, foreign languages, general academic interests/achievements, health fields, home economics, humanities, international studies, mathematics, military science, physical sciences, premedicine, social sciences. *Creative arts/performance:* applied art and design, art/fine arts, cinema/film/broadcasting, dance, debating, journalism/publications, music, performing arts, theater/drama. *Special characteristics:* children and siblings of alumni, children of faculty/staff, first-generation college students, members of minority groups. *Tuition waivers:* Full or partial for employees or children of employees, senior citizens. *ROTC:* Army, Air Force.

LOANS *Student loans:* $112,920,741 (65% need-based, 35% non-need-based). 67% of past graduating class borrowed through all loan programs. *Average indebtedness per student:* $27,060. *Average need-based loan:* Freshmen: $3419. Undergraduates: $4044. *Parent loans:* $29,765,340 (42% need-based, 58% non-need-based). *Programs:* Federal Direct (Subsidized and Unsubsidized Stafford, PLUS), Perkins, state, college/university.

WORK-STUDY *Federal work-study:* Total amount: $1,337,996; 800 jobs averaging $1672. *State or other work-study/employment:* Total amount: $13,726,355 (100% non-need-based). Part-time jobs available.

ATHLETIC AWARDS Total amount: $6,236,963 (40% need-based, 60% non-need-based).

APPLYING FOR FINANCIAL AID *Required financial aid form:* FAFSA. *Financial aid deadline (priority):* 3/15. *Notification date:* 3/15.

CONTACT Ms. Valerie K. Miller, Director of Financial Aid, Ohio University, 020 Chubb Hall, Athens, OH 45701-2979, 740-593-9853. *Fax:* 740-593-4140. *E-mail:* millerv@ohio.edu. *Website:* http://www.ohio.edu/.

OHIO UNIVERSITY–CHILLICOTHE
Chillicothe, OH

Tuition & fees (OH res): $4956	Average undergraduate aid package: $7729

ABOUT THE INSTITUTION State-supported, coed. *Awards:* associate, bachelor's, and master's degrees (offers first 2 years of most bachelor's degree programs available at the main campus in Athens; also offers several bachelor's degree programs that can be completed at this campus and several programs exclusive to this campus; also offers some graduate programs). 22 undergraduate majors. *Total enrollment:* 2,200. Undergraduates: 2,200. Federal methodology is used as a basis for awarding need-based institutional aid.

UNDERGRADUATE EXPENSES for 2013–2014 *Application fee:* $20. *Tuition, state resident:* full-time $4956; part-time $222 per credit hour. *Tuition, nonresident:* full-time $6802; part-time $308 per credit hour. Full-time tuition and fees vary according to course load, location, program, and student level. Part-time tuition and fees vary according to course load, location, program, and student level.

FRESHMAN FINANCIAL AID (Fall 2012, est.) 277 applied for aid; of those 92% were deemed to have need. 100% of freshmen with need received aid; of those 7% had need fully met. *Average percent of need met:* 54% (excluding resources awarded to replace EFC). *Average financial aid package:* $6668 (excluding resources awarded to replace EFC). 1% of all full-time freshmen had no need and received non-need-based gift aid.

UNDERGRADUATE FINANCIAL AID (Fall 2012, est.) 1,149 applied for aid; of those 93% were deemed to have need. 100% of undergraduates with need received aid; of those 4% had need fully met. *Average percent of need met:* 50% (excluding resources awarded to replace EFC). *Average financial aid package:* $7729 (excluding resources awarded to replace EFC). 1% of all full-time undergraduates had no need and received non-need-based gift aid.

GIFT AID (NEED-BASED) *Total amount:* $6,222,672 (91% federal, 7% institutional, 2% external sources). *Receiving aid:* Freshmen: 76% (221); all full-time undergraduates: 76% (929). *Average award:* Freshmen: $4607; Undergraduates: $4979. *Scholarships, grants, and awards:* Federal Pell, FSEOG, state, private, college/university gift aid from institutional funds.

GIFT AID (NON-NEED-BASED) *Total amount:* $83,171 (7% federal, 3% state, 58% institutional, 32% external sources). *Receiving aid:* Freshmen: 3% (10). Undergraduates: 1% (15). *Average award:* Freshmen: $3761. Undergraduates: $4151. *Scholarships, grants, and awards by category: Academic interests/achievement:* area/ethnic studies, biological sciences, business, communication, computer science, education, engineering/technologies, English, foreign languages, general academic interests/achievements, health fields, home economics, humanities, international studies, mathematics, military science, physical sciences, premedicine, social sciences. *Creative arts/performance:* applied art and design, art/fine arts, cinema/film/broadcasting, dance, debating, journalism/publications, music, performing arts, theater/drama. *Special characteristics:* children and siblings of alumni, children of faculty/staff, first-generation college students, members of minority groups. *Tuition waivers:* Full or partial for employees or children of employees, senior citizens.

LOANS *Student loans:* $11,873,988 (92% need-based, 8% non-need-based). 64% of past graduating class borrowed through all loan programs. *Average indebtedness per student:* $27,060. *Average need-based loan:* Freshmen: $2970. Undergraduates: $3614. *Parent loans:* $44,868 (26% need-based, 74% non-need-based). *Programs:* Federal Direct (Subsidized and Unsubsidized Stafford, PLUS), Perkins, state, college/university.

WORK-STUDY *Federal work-study:* Total amount: $35,263; 20 jobs averaging $1763. *State or other work-study/employment:* Part-time jobs available.

APPLYING FOR FINANCIAL AID *Required financial aid form:* FAFSA. *Financial aid deadline (priority):* 3/15. *Notification date:* 3/15.

CONTACT Ms. Valerie K. Miller, Director of Financial Aid, Ohio University–Chillicothe, 020 Chubb Hall, Athens, OH 45701-2979, 740-593-4141 or toll-free 877-462-6824. *Fax:* 740-593-4140. *E-mail:* millerv@ohio.edu. *Website:* http://www.chillicothe.ohiou.edu/.

OHIO UNIVERSITY–EASTERN
St. Clairsville, OH

Tuition & fees: N/R	Average undergraduate aid package: $6460

ABOUT THE INSTITUTION State-supported, coed. 11 undergraduate majors. Federal methodology is used as a basis for awarding need-based institutional aid.

FRESHMAN FINANCIAL AID (Fall 2012, est.) 105 applied for aid; of those 81% were deemed to have need. 100% of freshmen with need received aid; of those 13% had need fully met. *Average percent of need met:* 63% (excluding resources awarded to replace EFC). *Average financial aid package:* $5978 (excluding resources awarded to replace EFC). 12% of all full-time freshmen had no need and received non-need-based gift aid.

UNDERGRADUATE FINANCIAL AID (Fall 2012, est.) 393 applied for aid; of those 86% were deemed to have need. 100% of undergraduates with need received aid; of those 11% had need fully met. *Average percent of need met:* 58% (excluding resources awarded to replace EFC). *Average financial aid package:* $6460 (excluding resources awarded to replace EFC). 6% of all full-time undergraduates had no need and received non-need-based gift aid.

GIFT AID (NEED-BASED) Total amount: $1,368,653 (85% federal, 14% institutional, 1% external sources). *Receiving aid:* Freshmen: 57% (73); all full-time undergraduates: 63% (271). *Average award:* Freshmen: $4273; Undergraduates: $4152. *Scholarships, grants, and awards:* Federal Pell, FSEOG, state, college/university gift aid from institutional funds.

GIFT AID (NON-NEED-BASED) Total amount: $74,016 (5% federal, 3% state, 73% institutional, 19% external sources). *Receiving aid:* Freshmen: 8% (10). Undergraduates: 4% (16). *Average award:* Freshmen: $1535. Undergraduates: $1663. *Scholarships, grants, and awards by category: Academic interests/achievement:* area/ethnic studies, biological sciences, business, communication, computer science, education, engineering/technologies, English, foreign languages, general academic interests/achievements, health fields, home economics, humanities, international studies, mathematics, military science, physical sciences, premedicine, social sciences. *Creative arts/performance:* applied art and design, art/fine arts, cinema/film/broadcasting, dance, debating, journalism/publications, music, performing arts, theater/drama. *Special characteristics:* children of faculty/staff, members of minority groups.

LOANS Student loans: $2,785,121 (80% need-based, 20% non-need-based). 67% of past graduating class borrowed through all loan programs. *Average indebtedness per student:* $27,060. *Average need-based loan:* Freshmen: $2736. Undergraduates: $3344. *Parent loans:* $73,069 (19% need-based, 81% non-need-based). *Programs:* Federal Direct (Subsidized and Unsubsidized Stafford, PLUS), Perkins, state, college/university.

WORK-STUDY Federal work-study: Total amount: $55,168; 30 jobs averaging $1839. *State or other work-study/employment:* Part-time jobs available.

APPLYING FOR FINANCIAL AID Required financial aid form: FAFSA. *Financial aid deadline (priority):* 3/15. *Notification date:* 3/15.

CONTACT Ms. Valerie K. Miller, Director of Financial Aid, Ohio University–Eastern, 020 Chubb Hall, Athens, OH 45701-2979, 740-593-4141 or toll-free 800-648-3331. *Fax:* 740-593-4140. *E-mail:* millerv@ohio.edu. *Website:* http://www.eastern.ohiou.edu/.

OHIO UNIVERSITY–LANCASTER
Lancaster, OH

Tuition & fees: N/R	Average undergraduate aid package: $7110

ABOUT THE INSTITUTION State-supported, coed. 14 undergraduate majors. Federal methodology is used as a basis for awarding need-based institutional aid.

FRESHMAN FINANCIAL AID (Fall 2012, est.) 293 applied for aid; of those 84% were deemed to have need. 100% of freshmen with need received aid; of those 13% had need fully met. *Average percent of need met:* 62% (excluding resources awarded to replace EFC). *Average financial aid package:* $6409 (excluding resources awarded to replace EFC). 8% of all full-time freshmen had no need and received non-need-based gift aid.

UNDERGRADUATE FINANCIAL AID (Fall 2012, est.) 1,018 applied for aid; of those 89% were deemed to have need. 100% of undergraduates with need received aid; of those 9% had need fully met. *Average percent of need met:* 55% (excluding

resources awarded to replace EFC). *Average financial aid package:* $7110 (excluding resources awarded to replace EFC). 3% of all full-time undergraduates had no need and received non-need-based gift aid.

GIFT AID (NEED-BASED) Total amount: $4,775,318 (87% federal, 11% institutional, 2% external sources). *Receiving aid:* Freshmen: 64% (201); all full-time undergraduates: 61% (736). *Average award:* Freshmen: $4552; Undergraduates: $4761. *Scholarships, grants, and awards:* Federal Pell, FSEOG, state, private, college/university gift aid from institutional funds.

GIFT AID (NON-NEED-BASED) Total amount: $254,119 (4% federal, 2% state, 74% institutional, 20% external sources). *Receiving aid:* Freshmen: 8% (24). Undergraduates: 3% (33). *Average award:* Freshmen: $3894. Undergraduates: $3749. *Scholarships, grants, and awards by category: Academic interests/achievement:* area/ethnic studies, biological sciences, business, communication, computer science, education, engineering/technologies, English, foreign languages, general academic interests/achievements, health fields, home economics, humanities, international studies, mathematics, military science, physical sciences, premedicine, social sciences. *Creative arts/performance:* applied art and design, art/fine arts, cinema/film/broadcasting, dance, debating, journalism/publications, music, performing arts, theater/drama. *Special characteristics:* children and siblings of alumni, children of faculty/staff, first-generation college students, members of minority groups.

LOANS Student loans: $9,250,640 (87% need-based, 13% non-need-based). 67% of past graduating class borrowed through all loan programs. *Average indebtedness per student:* $27,060. *Average need-based loan:* Freshmen: $2906. Undergraduates: $3542. *Parent loans:* $142,579 (11% need-based, 89% non-need-based). *Programs:* Federal Direct (Subsidized and Unsubsidized Stafford, PLUS), Perkins, state, college/university.

WORK-STUDY Federal work-study: Total amount: $30,376; 18 jobs averaging $1688. *State or other work-study/employment:* Part-time jobs available.

APPLYING FOR FINANCIAL AID Required financial aid form: FAFSA. *Financial aid deadline (priority):* 3/15. *Notification date:* 3/15.

CONTACT Ms. Valerie K. Miller, Director of Financial Aid, Ohio University–Lancaster, 020 Chubb Hall, Athens, OH 45701-2979, 740-593-4141 or toll-free 888-446-4468. *Fax:* 740-593-4140. *E-mail:* millerv@ohio.edu. *Website:* http://www.ohiou.edu/lancaster/.

OHIO UNIVERSITY–SOUTHERN CAMPUS
Ironton, OH

Tuition & fees: N/R	Average undergraduate aid package: $7801

ABOUT THE INSTITUTION State-supported, coed. 17 undergraduate majors. Federal methodology is used as a basis for awarding need-based institutional aid.

FRESHMAN FINANCIAL AID (Fall 2012, est.) 219 applied for aid; of those 89% were deemed to have need. 100% of freshmen with need received aid; of those 7% had need fully met. *Average percent of need met:* 55% (excluding resources awarded to replace EFC). *Average financial aid package:* $6762 (excluding resources awarded to replace EFC). 7% of all full-time freshmen had no need and received non-need-based gift aid.

UNDERGRADUATE FINANCIAL AID (Fall 2012, est.) 1,003 applied for aid; of those 94% were deemed to have need. 100% of undergraduates with need received aid; of those 5% had need fully met. *Average percent of need met:* 52% (excluding resources awarded to replace EFC). *Average financial aid package:* $7801 (excluding resources awarded to replace EFC). 4% of all full-time undergraduates had no need and received non-need-based gift aid.

GIFT AID (NEED-BASED) Total amount: $5,326,587 (89% federal, 10% institutional, 1% external sources). *Receiving aid:* Freshmen: 79% (183); all full-time undergraduates: 77% (851). *Average award:* Freshmen: $4663; Undergraduates: $4874. *Scholarships, grants, and awards:* Federal Pell, FSEOG, state, private, college/university gift aid from institutional funds.

GIFT AID (NON-NEED-BASED) Total amount: $148,154 (8% federal, 3% state, 75% institutional, 14% external sources). *Receiving aid:* Freshmen: 4% (9). Undergraduates: 2% (23). *Average award:* Freshmen: $2286. Undergraduates: $2193. *Scholarships, grants, and awards by category: Academic interests/achievement:* area/ethnic studies, biological sciences, business, communication, computer science, education, engineering/technologies, English, foreign languages, general

academic interests/achievements, health fields, home economics, humanities, international studies, mathematics, military science, physical sciences, premedicine, social sciences. *Creative arts/performance:* applied art and design, art/fine arts, cinema/film/broadcasting, dance, debating, journalism/publications, music, performing arts, theater/drama. *Special characteristics:* children and siblings of alumni, children of faculty/staff, first-generation college students, members of minority groups.
LOANS *Student loans:* $9,980,917 (91% need-based, 9% non-need-based). 67% of past graduating class borrowed through all loan programs. *Average indebtedness per student:* $27,060. *Average need-based loan:* Freshmen: $2875. Undergraduates: $3663. *Parent loans:* $16,088 (28% need-based, 72% non-need-based). *Programs:* Federal Direct (Subsidized and Unsubsidized Stafford, PLUS), Perkins, state, college/university.
WORK-STUDY *Federal work-study:* Total amount: $40,252; 25 jobs averaging $1610. *State or other work-study/employment:* Part-time jobs available.
APPLYING FOR FINANCIAL AID *Required financial aid form:* FAFSA. *Financial aid deadline (priority):* 3/15. *Notification date:* 3/15.
CONTACT Ms. Valerie K. Miller, Director of Financial Aid, Ohio University–Southern Campus, 020 Chubb Hall, Athens, OH 45701-2979, 740-593-4141 or toll-free 800-626-0513. *Fax:* 740-593-4140. *E-mail:* millerv@ohio.edu. *Website:* http://www.ohiou.edu/.

OHIO UNIVERSITY–ZANESVILLE
Zanesville, OH

Tuition & fees (OH res): $5104	Average undergraduate aid package: $7437

ABOUT THE INSTITUTION State-supported, coed. *Awards:* associate and bachelor's degrees (offers first 2 years of most bachelor's degree programs available at the main campus in Athens; also offers several bachelor's degree programs that can be completed at this campus; also offers some graduate courses). 7 undergraduate majors. *Total enrollment:* 1,972. Undergraduates: 1,972. Freshmen: 290. Federal methodology is used as a basis for awarding need-based institutional aid.
UNDERGRADUATE EXPENSES for 2013–2014 *Application fee:* $20. *Tuition, state resident:* full-time $5038; part-time $219 per semester hour. *Tuition, nonresident:* full-time $6884; part-time $307 per semester hour. *Required fees:* full-time $66.
FRESHMAN FINANCIAL AID (Fall 2012, est.) 229 applied for aid; of those 86% were deemed to have need. 100% of freshmen with need received aid; of those 21% had need fully met. *Average percent of need met:* 66% (excluding resources awarded to replace EFC). *Average financial aid package:* $6596 (excluding resources awarded to replace EFC). 8% of all full-time freshmen had no need and received non-need-based gift aid.
UNDERGRADUATE FINANCIAL AID (Fall 2012, est.) 934 applied for aid; of those 90% were deemed to have need. 100% of undergraduates with need received aid; of those 11% had need fully met. *Average percent of need met:* 57% (excluding resources awarded to replace EFC). *Average financial aid package:* $7437 (excluding resources awarded to replace EFC). 5% of all full-time undergraduates had no need and received non-need-based gift aid.
GIFT AID (NEED-BASED) *Total amount:* $4,392,711 (80% federal, 17% institutional, 3% external sources). *Receiving aid:* Freshmen: 67% (178); all full-time undergraduates: 70% (729). *Average award:* Freshmen: $4662; Undergraduates: $4851. *Scholarships, grants, and awards:* Federal Pell, FSEOG, state, private, college/university gift aid from institutional funds.
GIFT AID (NON-NEED-BASED) *Total amount:* $285,390 (2% federal, 3% state, 78% institutional, 17% external sources). *Receiving aid:* Freshmen: 14% (37). Undergraduates: 5% (56). *Average award:* Freshmen: $3726. Undergraduates: $3288. *Scholarships, grants, and awards by category:* Academic interests/achievement: area/ethnic studies, biological sciences, business, communication, computer science, education, engineering/technologies, English, foreign languages, general academic interests/achievements, health fields, home economics, humanities, international studies, mathematics, military science, physical sciences, premedicine, social sciences. *Creative arts/performance:* applied art and design, art/fine arts, cinema/film/broadcasting, dance, debating, journalism/publications, music, performing arts, theater/drama. *Special characteristics:* children and siblings of alumni, children of faculty/staff, first-generation college students, members of minority groups. *Tuition waivers:* Full or partial for employees or children of employees, senior citizens.
LOANS *Student loans:* $7,898,237 (87% need-based, 13% non-need-based). 67% of past graduating class borrowed through all loan programs. *Average indebtedness*

per student: $27,060. *Average need-based loan:* Freshmen: $2709. Undergraduates: $3555. *Parent loans:* $78,027 (28% need-based, 72% non-need-based). *Programs:* Federal Direct (Subsidized and Unsubsidized Stafford, PLUS), Perkins, state, college/university.
WORK-STUDY *Federal work-study:* Total amount: $25,900; 17 jobs averaging $1524. *State or other work-study/employment:* Part-time jobs available.
APPLYING FOR FINANCIAL AID *Required financial aid form:* FAFSA. *Financial aid deadline (priority):* 3/15. *Notification date:* 3/15.
CONTACT Ms. Valerie K. Miller, Director of Financial Aid, Ohio University–Zanesville, 020 Chubb Hall, Athens, OH 45701-2979, 740-593-4141. *Fax:* 740-593-4140. *E-mail:* millerv@ohio.edu. *Website:* http://www.zanesville.ohiou.edu/.

OHIO VALLEY UNIVERSITY
Vienna, WV

Tuition & fees: $18,750	Average undergraduate aid package: $13,833

ABOUT THE INSTITUTION Independent Church of Christ, coed. *Awards:* certificates, associate, bachelor's, and master's degrees. 16 undergraduate majors. *Total enrollment:* 478. Undergraduates: 436. Freshmen: 100. Federal methodology is used as a basis for awarding need-based institutional aid.
UNDERGRADUATE EXPENSES for 2013–2014 *Comprehensive fee:* $25,650 includes full-time tuition ($17,000), mandatory fees ($1750), and room and board ($6900). *College room only:* $3500. Full-time tuition and fees vary according to course load. Room and board charges vary according to board plan and housing facility. *Part-time tuition:* $475 per credit. *Part-time fees:* $75 per credit. Part-time tuition and fees vary according to course load.
FRESHMAN FINANCIAL AID (Fall 2012, est.) 94 applied for aid; of those 93% were deemed to have need. 100% of freshmen with need received aid; of those 22% had need fully met. *Average percent of need met:* 70% (excluding resources awarded to replace EFC). *Average financial aid package:* $14,010 (excluding resources awarded to replace EFC). 11% of all full-time freshmen had no need and received non-need-based gift aid.
UNDERGRADUATE FINANCIAL AID (Fall 2012, est.) 389 applied for aid; of those 89% were deemed to have need. 98% of undergraduates with need received aid; of those 18% had need fully met. *Average percent of need met:* 67% (excluding resources awarded to replace EFC). *Average financial aid package:* $13,833 (excluding resources awarded to replace EFC). 11% of all full-time undergraduates had no need and received non-need-based gift aid.
GIFT AID (NEED-BASED) *Total amount:* $2,500,196 (35% federal, 8% state, 51% institutional, 6% external sources). *Receiving aid:* Freshmen: 80% (87); all full-time undergraduates: 79% (332). *Average award:* Freshmen: $11,413; Undergraduates: $10,645. *Scholarships, grants, and awards:* Federal Pell, FSEOG, state, private, college/university gift aid from institutional funds.
GIFT AID (NON-NEED-BASED) *Total amount:* $458,712 (9% state, 84% institutional, 7% external sources). *Receiving aid:* Freshmen: 16% (17). Undergraduates: 13% (53). *Average award:* Freshmen: $7055. Undergraduates: $6558. *Scholarships, grants, and awards by category:* Academic interests/achievement: education, English, general academic interests/achievements, religion/biblical studies. *Creative arts/performance:* general creative arts/performance, journalism/publications, music, performing arts, theater/drama. *Special achievements/activities:* community service, general special achievements/activities, leadership, religious involvement. *Special characteristics:* adult students, children of faculty/staff, ethnic background, general special characteristics, international students, local/state students, relatives of clergy, religious affiliation. *Tuition waivers:* Full or partial for employees or children of employees.
LOANS *Student loans:* $2,313,950 (84% need-based, 16% non-need-based). 67% of past graduating class borrowed through all loan programs. *Average indebtedness per student:* $24,868. *Average need-based loan:* Freshmen: $2974. Undergraduates: $3783. *Parent loans:* $508,231 (45% need-based, 55% non-need-based). *Programs:* Federal Direct (Subsidized and Unsubsidized Stafford, PLUS), Perkins.
WORK-STUDY *Federal work-study:* Total amount: $88,540; jobs available. *State or other work-study/employment:* Total amount: $1000 (100% non-need-based). Part-time jobs available.
ATHLETIC AWARDS Total amount: $1,584,929 (69% need-based, 31% non-need-based).

APPLYING FOR FINANCIAL AID *Required financial aid form:* FAFSA. *Financial aid deadline (priority):* 4/15. *Notification date:* Continuous beginning 3/15. Students must reply within 4 weeks of notification.

CONTACT Wes Wilson, Assistant Director of Financial Aid, Ohio Valley University, 1 Campus View Drive, Vienna, WV 26105-8000, 304-865-6207 or toll-free 877-446-8668. *Fax:* 304-865-6001. *E-mail:* wes.wilson@ovu.edu. *Website:* http://www.ovu.edu/.

OHIO WESLEYAN UNIVERSITY
Delaware, OH

Tuition & fees: $39,150	Average undergraduate aid package: $27,376

ABOUT THE INSTITUTION Independent United Methodist, coed. *Awards:* bachelor's degrees. 88 undergraduate majors. *Total enrollment:* 1,821. Undergraduates: 1,821. Freshmen: 537. Both federal and institutional methodology are used as a basis for awarding need-based institutional aid.

UNDERGRADUATE EXPENSES for 2013–2014 *Application fee:* $35. *Comprehensive fee:* $49,460 includes full-time tuition ($38,890), mandatory fees ($260), and room and board ($10,310). *College room only:* $5500. Room and board charges vary according to board plan.

FRESHMAN FINANCIAL AID (Fall 2011) 393 applied for aid; of those 87% were deemed to have need. 100% of freshmen with need received aid; of those 31% had need fully met. *Average percent of need met:* 84% (excluding resources awarded to replace EFC). *Average financial aid package:* $28,940 (excluding resources awarded to replace EFC). 26% of all full-time freshmen had no need and received non-need-based gift aid.

UNDERGRADUATE FINANCIAL AID (Fall 2011) 1,337 applied for aid; of those 89% were deemed to have need. 100% of undergraduates with need received aid; of those 28% had need fully met. *Average percent of need met:* 80% (excluding resources awarded to replace EFC). *Average financial aid package:* $27,376 (excluding resources awarded to replace EFC). 32% of all full-time undergraduates had no need and received non-need-based gift aid.

GIFT AID (NEED-BASED) *Total amount:* $25,263,382 (8% federal, 1% state, 90% institutional, 1% external sources). *Receiving aid:* Freshmen: 71% (341); all full-time undergraduates: 65% (1,173). *Average award:* Freshmen: $25,446; Undergraduates: $28,530. *Scholarships, grants, and awards:* Federal Pell, FSEOG, state, private, college/university gift aid from institutional funds.

GIFT AID (NON-NEED-BASED) *Total amount:* $14,199,105 (98% institutional, 2% external sources). *Receiving aid:* Freshmen: 20% (96). Undergraduates: 16% (295). *Average award:* Freshmen: $20,485. Undergraduates: $19,780. *Scholarships, grants, and awards by category:* Academic interests/achievement: business, education, general academic interests/achievements. Creative arts/performance: applied art and design, art/fine arts, dance, music, performing arts, theater/drama. Special achievements/activities: general special achievements/activities, leadership. Special characteristics: children and siblings of alumni, international students, local/state students, members of minority groups, relatives of clergy, religious affiliation, twins.

LOANS *Student loans:* $7,870,612 (50% need-based, 50% non-need-based). 65% of past graduating class borrowed through all loan programs. *Average indebtedness per student:* $30,900. *Average need-based loan:* Freshmen: $3079. Undergraduates: $4542. *Parent loans:* $3,490,803 (36% need-based, 64% non-need-based). *Programs:* Federal Direct (Subsidized and Unsubsidized Stafford, PLUS), Perkins, college/university.

WORK-STUDY *Federal work-study:* Total amount: $304,146; jobs available. *State or other work-study/employment:* Total amount: $960,524 (9% need-based, 91% non-need-based). Part-time jobs available.

APPLYING FOR FINANCIAL AID *Required financial aid forms:* FAFSA, CSS Financial Aid PROFILE. *Financial aid deadline (priority):* 2/15. *Notification date:* Continuous beginning 2/15. Students must reply by 5/1 or within 2 weeks of notification.

CONTACT Mr. Lee Harrell, Assistant Vice President of Admission and Financial Aid, Ohio Wesleyan University, 61 South Sandusky Street, Delaware, OH 43015, 740-368-3050 or toll-free 800-922-8953. *Fax:* 740-368-3066. *E-mail:* financialaid@owu.edu . *Website:* http://www.owu.edu/.

OHR HAMEIR THEOLOGICAL SEMINARY
Cortlandt Manor, NY

CONTACT Financial Aid Office, Ohr Hameir Theological Seminary, Furnace Woods Road, Peekskill, NY 10566, 914-736-1500.

OHR SOMAYACH/JOSEPH TANENBAUM EDUCATIONAL CENTER
Monsey, NY

CONTACT Financial Aid Office, Ohr Somayach/Joseph Tanenbaum Educational Center, PO Box 334244, Route 306, Monsey, NY 10952-0334, 914-425-1370. *Website:* http://ohr.edu/.

OKLAHOMA BAPTIST UNIVERSITY
Shawnee, OK

Tuition & fees: $20,856	Average undergraduate aid package: $19,333

ABOUT THE INSTITUTION Independent Southern Baptist, coed. *Awards:* associate, bachelor's, and master's degrees. 67 undergraduate majors. *Total enrollment:* 76. Undergraduates: 1,903. Freshmen: 506. Federal methodology is used as a basis for awarding need-based institutional aid.

UNDERGRADUATE EXPENSES for 2013–2014 *One-time required fee:* $50. *Comprehensive fee:* $27,056 includes full-time tuition ($18,954), mandatory fees ($1902), and room and board ($6200). Full-time tuition and fees vary according to course load. Room and board charges vary according to housing facility. *Part-time tuition:* $614 per credit hour. Part-time tuition and fees vary according to course load.

FRESHMAN FINANCIAL AID (Fall 2011) 428 applied for aid; of those 89% were deemed to have need. 100% of freshmen with need received aid; of those 30% had need fully met. *Average percent of need met:* 93% (excluding resources awarded to replace EFC). *Average financial aid package:* $20,451 (excluding resources awarded to replace EFC). 10% of all full-time freshmen had no need and received non-need-based gift aid.

UNDERGRADUATE FINANCIAL AID (Fall 2011) 1,338 applied for aid; of those 93% were deemed to have need. 100% of undergraduates with need received aid; of those 27% had need fully met. *Average percent of need met:* 83% (excluding resources awarded to replace EFC). *Average financial aid package:* $19,333 (excluding resources awarded to replace EFC). 6% of all full-time undergraduates had no need and received non-need-based gift aid.

GIFT AID (NEED-BASED) *Total amount:* $9,324,184 (28% federal, 14% state, 50% institutional, 8% external sources). *Receiving aid:* Freshmen: 70% (329); all full-time undergraduates: 60% (913). *Average award:* Freshmen: $5007; Undergraduates: $4666. *Scholarships, grants, and awards:* Federal Pell, FSEOG, state, private, college/university gift aid from institutional funds, TEACH Grants.

GIFT AID (NON-NEED-BASED) *Total amount:* $1,330,638 (30% federal, 5% state, 59% institutional, 6% external sources). *Receiving aid:* Freshmen: 70% (330). Undergraduates: 53% (799). *Average award:* Freshmen: $6895. Undergraduates: $6285. *Scholarships, grants, and awards by category:* Academic interests/achievement: business, general academic interests/achievements, religion/biblical studies. Creative arts/performance: applied art and design, art/fine arts, music, performing arts, theater/drama. Special achievements/activities: leadership, religious involvement. Special characteristics: children and siblings of alumni, children of faculty/staff, general special characteristics, local/state students, out-of-state students, relatives of clergy, religious affiliation, veterans. *Tuition waivers:* Full or partial for employees or children of employees, senior citizens. *ROTC:* Air Force cooperative.

LOANS *Student loans:* $4,705,139 (95% need-based, 5% non-need-based). 62% of past graduating class borrowed through all loan programs. *Average indebtedness per student:* $23,039. *Average need-based loan:* Freshmen: $3040. Undergraduates: $3921. *Parent loans:* $1,766,533 (53% need-based, 47% non-need-based). *Pro-*

grams: Federal Direct (Subsidized and Unsubsidized Stafford, PLUS), Perkins, college/university.

WORK-STUDY *Federal work-study:* Total amount: $121,307; 204 jobs averaging $1389. *State or other work-study/employment:* Total amount: $346,336 (76% need-based, 24% non-need-based). Part-time jobs available.

ATHLETIC AWARDS Total amount: $1,918,155 (63% need-based, 37% non-need-based).

APPLYING FOR FINANCIAL AID *Required financial aid form:* FAFSA. *Financial aid deadline:* Continuous. *Notification date:* Continuous beginning 2/1.

CONTACT Jonna Raney, Student Financial Services, Oklahoma Baptist University, 500 West University, Shawnee, OK 74804, 405-585-5020 or toll-free 800-654-3285. *Fax:* 405-585-5030. *E-mail:* jonna.raney@okbu.edu. *Website:* http://www.okbu.edu/.

OKLAHOMA CHRISTIAN UNIVERSITY
Oklahoma City, OK

Tuition & fees: $18,800   Average undergraduate aid package: $21,593

ABOUT THE INSTITUTION Independent Church of Christ, coed. *Awards:* bachelor's and master's degrees. 60 undergraduate majors. *Total enrollment:* 2,271. Undergraduates: 1,910. Freshmen: 446. Federal methodology is used as a basis for awarding need-based institutional aid.

UNDERGRADUATE EXPENSES for 2013–2014 *Application fee:* $25. *Comprehensive fee:* $24,975 includes full-time tuition ($18,800) and room and board ($6175). *College room only:* $3575. Full-time tuition and fees vary according to course load. Room and board charges vary according to board plan and housing facility. *Part-time tuition:* $783 per credit hour. Part-time tuition and fees vary according to course load.

FRESHMAN FINANCIAL AID (Fall 2012, est.) 363 applied for aid; of those 78% were deemed to have need. 100% of freshmen with need received aid; of those 47% had need fully met. *Average percent of need met:* 72% (excluding resources awarded to replace EFC). *Average financial aid package:* $21,347 (excluding resources awarded to replace EFC). 25% of all full-time freshmen had no need and received non-need-based gift aid.

UNDERGRADUATE FINANCIAL AID (Fall 2012, est.) 1,364 applied for aid; of those 84% were deemed to have need. 99% of undergraduates with need received aid; of those 45% had need fully met. *Average percent of need met:* 84% (excluding resources awarded to replace EFC). *Average financial aid package:* $21,593 (excluding resources awarded to replace EFC). 22% of all full-time undergraduates had no need and received non-need-based gift aid.

GIFT AID (NEED-BASED) *Total amount:* $12,956,535 (18% federal, 6% state, 70% institutional, 6% external sources). *Receiving aid:* Freshmen: 43% (186); all full-time undergraduates: 36% (717). *Average award:* Freshmen: $3106; Undergraduates: $2951. *Scholarships, grants, and awards:* Federal Pell, FSEOG, state, private, college/university gift aid from institutional funds.

GIFT AID (NON-NEED-BASED) *Total amount:* $8,921,643 (1% state, 82% institutional, 17% external sources). *Receiving aid:* Freshmen: 56% (242). Undergraduates: 45% (891). *Average award:* Freshmen: $4579. Undergraduates: $5492. *Scholarships, grants, and awards by category:* Academic interests/achievement: 1,156 awards ($7,164,399 total): engineering/technologies, general academic interests/achievements, religion/biblical studies. Creative arts/performance: 195 awards ($438,207 total): applied art and design, journalism/publications, music, theater/drama. Special achievements/activities: 14 awards ($18,000 total): cheerleading/drum major. Special characteristics: 166 awards ($1,817,896 total): children of faculty/staff, international students. *Tuition waivers:* Full or partial for employees or children of employees. *ROTC:* Army cooperative, Air Force cooperative.

LOANS *Student loans:* $7,463,945 (75% need-based, 25% non-need-based). 65% of past graduating class borrowed through all loan programs. *Average indebtedness per student:* $29,388. *Average need-based loan:* Freshmen: $2384. Undergraduates: $2246. *Parent loans:* $3,330,659 (23% need-based, 77% non-need-based). *Programs:* Federal Direct (Subsidized and Unsubsidized Stafford, PLUS), Perkins, alternative loans.

WORK-STUDY *Federal work-study:* Total amount: $259,695; 851 jobs averaging $1614.

ATHLETIC AWARDS Total amount: $2,809,194 (10% need-based, 90% non-need-based).

APPLYING FOR FINANCIAL AID *Required financial aid form:* FAFSA. *Financial aid deadline:* 8/31 (priority: 3/15). *Notification date:* Continuous beginning 2/15. Students must reply within 4 weeks of notification.

CONTACT Clint LaRue, Director of Financial Services, Oklahoma Christian University, Box 11000, Oklahoma City, OK 73136-1100, 405-425-5190 or toll-free 800-877-5010 (in-state). *Fax:* 405-425-5197. *E-mail:* clint.larue@oc.edu. *Website:* http://www.oc.edu/.

OKLAHOMA CITY UNIVERSITY
Oklahoma City, OK

Tuition & fees: $28,190   Average undergraduate aid package: $23,737

ABOUT THE INSTITUTION Independent United Methodist, coed. *Awards:* bachelor's, master's, and doctoral degrees. 123 undergraduate majors. Federal methodology is used as a basis for awarding need-based institutional aid.

UNDERGRADUATE EXPENSES for 2013–2014 *Comprehensive fee:* $37,360 includes full-time tuition ($24,740), mandatory fees ($3450), and room and board ($9170). *College room only:* $5090. Room and board charges vary according to board plan and housing facility. *Part-time tuition:* $840 per credit hour. *Payment plan:* Guaranteed tuition.

FRESHMAN FINANCIAL AID (Fall 2012, est.) 277 applied for aid; of those 83% were deemed to have need. 100% of freshmen with need received aid; of those 27% had need fully met. *Average percent of need met:* 79% (excluding resources awarded to replace EFC). *Average financial aid package:* $21,838 (excluding resources awarded to replace EFC). 23% of all full-time freshmen had no need and received non-need-based gift aid.

UNDERGRADUATE FINANCIAL AID (Fall 2012, est.) 1,321 applied for aid; of those 86% were deemed to have need. 100% of undergraduates with need received aid; of those 20% had need fully met. *Average percent of need met:* 78% (excluding resources awarded to replace EFC). *Average financial aid package:* $23,737 (excluding resources awarded to replace EFC). 28% of all full-time undergraduates had no need and received non-need-based gift aid.

GIFT AID (NEED-BASED) *Total amount:* $5,074,129 (36% federal, 16% state, 37% institutional, 11% external sources). *Receiving aid:* Freshmen: 72% (229); all full-time undergraduates: 66% (1,132). *Average award:* Freshmen: $17,377; Undergraduates: $16,100. *Scholarships, grants, and awards:* Federal Pell, FSEOG, state, private, college/university gift aid from institutional funds, United Negro College Fund, Federal Nursing, Native American Grants.

GIFT AID (NON-NEED-BASED) *Total amount:* $367,095 (26% state, 74% external sources). *Receiving aid:* Freshmen: 39% (125). Undergraduates: 23% (387). *Average award:* Freshmen: $12,976. Undergraduates: $12,524. *Scholarships, grants, and awards by category:* Academic interests/achievement: business, communication, education, general academic interests/achievements, health fields, religion/biblical studies. Creative arts/performance: applied art and design, art/fine arts, dance, music, performing arts, theater/drama. Special achievements/activities: cheerleading/drum major, general special achievements/activities, junior miss, leadership, religious involvement. Special characteristics: children of faculty/staff, relatives of clergy, religious affiliation. *Tuition waivers:* Full or partial for employees or children of employees. *ROTC:* Army cooperative, Naval cooperative, Air Force cooperative.

LOANS *Student loans:* $10,979,872 (79% need-based, 21% non-need-based). 46% of past graduating class borrowed through all loan programs. *Average indebtedness per student:* $25,557. *Average need-based loan:* Freshmen: $3968. Undergraduates: $5166. *Parent loans:* $5,948,980 (36% need-based, 64% non-need-based). *Programs:* Federal Direct (Subsidized and Unsubsidized Stafford, PLUS), Perkins, Federal Nursing.

WORK-STUDY *Federal work-study:* Total amount: $501,662; 326 jobs averaging $2196. *State or other work-study/employment:* Total amount: $545,704 (100% non-need-based). 327 part-time jobs averaging $1669.

ATHLETIC AWARDS Total amount: $4,342,302 (44% need-based, 56% non-need-based).

APPLYING FOR FINANCIAL AID *Required financial aid forms:* FAFSA, institution's own form. *Financial aid deadline (priority):* 3/1. *Notification date:* Continuous beginning 3/25. Students must reply within 4 weeks of notification.

CONTACT Denise Flis, Senior Director of Student Financial Services, Oklahoma City University, 2501 North Blackwelder, Oklahoma City, OK 73106-1493, 405-208-5848 or toll-free 800-633-7242. *Fax:* 405-208-5466. *E-mail:* dflis@okcu.edu. *Website:* http://www.okcu.edu/.

OKLAHOMA PANHANDLE STATE UNIVERSITY
Goodwell, OK

ABOUT THE INSTITUTION State-supported, coed. 28 undergraduate majors.
GIFT AID (NEED-BASED) *Scholarships, grants, and awards:* Federal Pell, FSEOG, state, private, college/university gift aid from institutional funds.
GIFT AID (NON-NEED-BASED) *Scholarships, grants, and awards by category: Academic interests/achievement:* agriculture, biological sciences, business, computer science, education, English, general academic interests/achievements, health fields, mathematics, physical sciences. *Creative arts/performance:* art/fine arts, debating, music, performing arts, theater/drama. *Special achievements/activities:* cheerleading/drum major, general special achievements/activities, rodeo. *Special characteristics:* children of faculty/staff, general special characteristics, local/state students, out-of-state students, veterans, veterans' children.
LOANS *Programs:* Perkins.
APPLYING FOR FINANCIAL AID *Required financial aid form:* FAFSA.
CONTACT Ms. Lori Ferguson, Director of Financial Aid, Oklahoma Panhandle State University, PO Box 430, Goodwell, OK 73939-0430, 580-349-1582 or toll-free 800-664-6778. *E-mail:* lorif@opsu.edu. *Website:* http://www.opsu.edu/.

OKLAHOMA STATE UNIVERSITY
Stillwater, OK

Tuition & fees (OK res): $7441	Average undergraduate aid package: $12,601

ABOUT THE INSTITUTION State-supported, coed. *Awards:* certificates, bachelor's, master's, and doctoral degrees. 84 undergraduate majors. *Total enrollment:* 25,544. Undergraduates: 20,130. Freshmen: 4,289. Federal methodology is used as a basis for awarding need-based institutional aid.
UNDERGRADUATE EXPENSES for 2013–2014 *Application fee:* $40. *One-time required fee:* $95. *Tuition, state resident:* full-time $4425; part-time $147.50 per credit hour. *Tuition, nonresident:* full-time $16,440; part-time $548 per credit hour. *Required fees:* full-time $3016; $100.55 per credit hour. Full-time tuition and fees vary according to program and student level. Part-time tuition and fees vary according to program and student level. *College room and board:* $6868; *Room only:* $3710. Room and board charges vary according to board plan and housing facility.
FRESHMAN FINANCIAL AID (Fall 2011) 2,824 applied for aid; of those 71% were deemed to have need. 97% of freshmen with need received aid; of those 17% had need fully met. *Average percent of need met:* 79% (excluding resources awarded to replace EFC). *Average financial aid package:* $12,558 (excluding resources awarded to replace EFC). 29% of all full-time freshmen had no need and received non-need-based gift aid.
UNDERGRADUATE FINANCIAL AID (Fall 2011) 11,159 applied for aid; of those 79% were deemed to have need. 98% of undergraduates with need received aid; of those 13% had need fully met. *Average percent of need met:* 77% (excluding resources awarded to replace EFC). *Average financial aid package:* $12,601 (excluding resources awarded to replace EFC). 26% of all full-time undergraduates had no need and received non-need-based gift aid.
GIFT AID (NEED-BASED) *Total amount:* $48,146,278 (49% federal, 27% state, 19% institutional, 5% external sources). *Receiving aid:* Freshmen: 43% (1,546); all full-time undergraduates: 42% (6,814). *Average award:* Freshmen: $6584; Undergraduates: $6297. *Scholarships, grants, and awards:* Federal Pell, FSEOG, state, private, college/university gift aid from institutional funds, TEACH Grants.
GIFT AID (NON-NEED-BASED) *Total amount:* $11,463,564 (5% federal, 14% state, 46% institutional, 35% external sources). *Receiving aid:* Freshmen: 5% (182). Undergraduates: 3% (507). *Average award:* Freshmen: $6126. Undergraduates:

$5049. *Scholarships, grants, and awards by category: Academic interests/achievement:* agriculture, architecture, area/ethnic studies, biological sciences, business, communication, computer science, education, engineering/technologies, English, foreign languages, general academic interests/achievements, home economics, humanities, international studies, mathematics, military science, physical sciences, pre-medicine, social sciences. *Creative arts/performance:* art/fine arts, creative writing, general creative arts/performance, journalism/publications, music, theater/drama. *Special achievements/activities:* cheerleading/drum major, community service, general special achievements/activities, leadership, memberships, rodeo. *Special characteristics:* adult students, children and siblings of alumni, ethnic background, first-generation college students, general special characteristics, handicapped students, international students, local/state students, out-of-state students, previous college experience. *Tuition waivers:* Full or partial for children of alumni. *ROTC:* Army, Air Force.
LOANS *Student loans:* $60,509,277 (76% need-based, 24% non-need-based). 52% of past graduating class borrowed through all loan programs. *Average indebtedness per student:* $22,736. *Average need-based loan:* Freshmen: $3166. Undergraduates: $4081. *Parent loans:* $28,690,538 (32% need-based, 68% non-need-based). *Programs:* Federal Direct (Subsidized and Unsubsidized Stafford, PLUS), Perkins.
WORK-STUDY *Federal work-study:* Total amount: $977,845; 388 jobs averaging $2410. *State or other work-study/employment:* Total amount: $10,319,669 (100% non-need-based). 3,623 part-time jobs averaging $2647.
ATHLETIC AWARDS Total amount: $4,664,119 (31% need-based, 69% non-need-based).
APPLYING FOR FINANCIAL AID *Required financial aid form:* FAFSA. *Financial aid deadline (priority):* 2/1. *Notification date:* Continuous beginning 4/1. Students must reply by 5/1 or within 2 weeks of notification.
CONTACT Office of Scholarships and Financial Aid, Oklahoma State University, 119 Student Union, Stillwater, OK 74078-5061, 405-744-6604 or toll-free 800-233-5019 Ext. 1 (in-state), 800-852-1255 (out-of-state). *Fax:* 405-744-6438. *E-mail:* finaid@okstate.edu. *Website:* http://www.okstate.edu/.

OKLAHOMA WESLEYAN UNIVERSITY
Bartlesville, OK

Tuition & fees: $21,140	Average undergraduate aid package: $12,544

ABOUT THE INSTITUTION Independent Wesleyan Church, coed. *Awards:* associate, bachelor's, and master's degrees. 40 undergraduate majors. *Total enrollment:* 1,178. Undergraduates: 1,083. Freshmen: 134. Both federal and institutional methodology are used as a basis for awarding need-based institutional aid.
UNDERGRADUATE EXPENSES for 2013–2014 *Application fee:* $25. *Comprehensive fee:* $28,380 includes full-time tuition ($19,940), mandatory fees ($1200), and room and board ($7240). *College room only:* $3820. Full-time tuition and fees vary according to course load. Room and board charges vary according to board plan and housing facility. *Part-time tuition:* $795 per credit hour. *Part-time fees:* $55 per credit hour; $60 per term.
FRESHMAN FINANCIAL AID (Fall 2012, est.) 128 applied for aid; of those 88% were deemed to have need. 100% of freshmen with need received aid; of those 13% had need fully met. *Average percent of need met:* 59% (excluding resources awarded to replace EFC). *Average financial aid package:* $14,016 (excluding resources awarded to replace EFC). 25% of all full-time freshmen had no need and received non-need-based gift aid.
UNDERGRADUATE FINANCIAL AID (Fall 2012, est.) 688 applied for aid; of those 88% were deemed to have need. 100% of undergraduates with need received aid; of those 13% had need fully met. *Average percent of need met:* 59% (excluding resources awarded to replace EFC). *Average financial aid package:* $12,544 (excluding resources awarded to replace EFC). 13% of all full-time undergraduates had no need and received non-need-based gift aid.
GIFT AID (NEED-BASED) *Total amount:* $4,694,226 (38% federal, 9% state, 44% institutional, 9% external sources). *Receiving aid:* Freshmen: 70% (108); all full-time undergraduates: 69% (522). *Average award:* Freshmen: $10,956; Undergraduates: $9809. *Scholarships, grants, and awards:* Federal Pell, FSEOG, state, private, college/university gift aid from institutional funds.
GIFT AID (NON-NEED-BASED) *Total amount:* $660,761 (1% federal, 1% state, 80% institutional, 18% external sources). *Receiving aid:* Freshmen: 6% (9).

Undergraduates: 5% (36). **Average award:** Freshmen: $4301. Undergraduates: $5100. **Scholarships, grants, and awards by category:** Academic interests/achievement: 287 awards ($1,216,820 total): biological sciences, business, computer science, education, general academic interests/achievements, health fields, religion/biblical studies. *Creative arts/performance:* 43 awards ($92,772 total): music. *Special achievements/activities:* 219 awards ($115,439 total): leadership, religious involvement. *Special characteristics:* 320 awards ($641,238 total): children and siblings of alumni, children of educators, children of faculty/staff, international students, relatives of clergy, religious affiliation, siblings of current students. **Tuition waivers:** Full or partial for employees or children of employees, senior citizens.
LOANS Student loans: $7,787,342 (82% need-based, 18% non-need-based). 76% of past graduating class borrowed through all loan programs. *Average indebtedness per student:* $20,060. **Average need-based loan:** Freshmen: $3688. Undergraduates: $4171. **Parent loans:** $1,425,490 (52% need-based, 48% non-need-based). **Programs:** Federal Direct (Subsidized and Unsubsidized Stafford, PLUS), Perkins, college/university.
WORK-STUDY Federal work-study: Total amount: $214,569; 123 jobs averaging $1744. **State or other work-study/employment:** Total amount: $41,615 (43% need-based, 57% non-need-based). 24 part-time jobs averaging $1734.
ATHLETIC AWARDS Total amount: $1,656,430 (61% need-based, 39% non-need-based).
APPLYING FOR FINANCIAL AID Required financial aid forms: FAFSA, institution's own form. **Financial aid deadline (priority):** 3/1. **Notification date:** Continuous beginning 1/15. Students must reply within 1 week of notification.
CONTACT Mrs. Kandi Lyn Molder, Director of Student Financial Services, Oklahoma Wesleyan University, 2201 Silver Lake Road, Bartlesville, OK 74006, 918-335-6282 or toll-free 866-222-8226. *Fax:* 918-335-6811. *E-mail:* financialaid@okwu.edu. *Website:* http://www.okwu.edu/.

OLD DOMINION UNIVERSITY
Norfolk, VA

Tuition & fees (VA res): $8450	Average undergraduate aid package: $9551

ABOUT THE INSTITUTION State-supported, coed. **Awards:** certificates, bachelor's, master's, and doctoral degrees. 52 undergraduate majors. **Total enrollment:** 24,670. Undergraduates: 19,612. Freshmen: 2,702. Federal methodology is used as a basis for awarding need-based institutional aid.
UNDERGRADUATE EXPENSES for 2013–2014 Application fee: $50. **Tuition, state resident:** full-time $8190; part-time $273 per credit hour. **Tuition, nonresident:** full-time $23,070; part-time $769 per credit hour. **Required fees:** full-time $260; $59 per term. **College room and board:** $9066; **Room only:** $5210. Room and board charges vary according to board plan and housing facility.
FRESHMAN FINANCIAL AID (Fall 2012, est.) 2,306 applied for aid; of those 76% were deemed to have need. 94% of freshmen with need received aid; of those 15% had need fully met. **Average percent of need met:** 51% (excluding resources awarded to replace EFC). **Average financial aid package:** $9925 (excluding resources awarded to replace EFC). 7% of all full-time freshmen had no need and received non-need-based gift aid.
UNDERGRADUATE FINANCIAL AID (Fall 2012, est.) 11,362 applied for aid; of those 81% were deemed to have need. 95% of undergraduates with need received aid; of those 14% had need fully met. **Average percent of need met:** 49% (excluding resources awarded to replace EFC). **Average financial aid package:** $9551 (excluding resources awarded to replace EFC). 5% of all full-time undergraduates had no need and received non-need-based gift aid.
GIFT AID (NEED-BASED) Total amount: $44,189,382 (63% federal, 34% state, 2% institutional, 1% external sources). **Receiving aid:** Freshmen: 43% (1,140); all full-time undergraduates: 42% (6,219). **Average award:** Freshmen: $7761; Undergraduates: $6418. **Scholarships, grants, and awards:** Federal Pell, FSEOG, state, private, college/university gift aid from institutional funds, United Negro College Fund, Federal Nursing.
GIFT AID (NON-NEED-BASED) Total amount: $10,546,309 (7% state, 77% institutional, 16% external sources). **Receiving aid:** Freshmen: 21% (566). Undergraduates: 14% (2,052). **Average award:** Freshmen: $1868. Undergraduates: $3681. **Scholarships, grants, and awards by category:** Academic interests/achievement: 1,564 awards ($4,435,654 total): biological sciences, business, engineering/technologies, English, general academic interests/achievements, health fields,

humanities, military science, physical sciences. *Creative arts/performance:* 88 awards ($100,235 total): art/fine arts, dance, music, performing arts, theater/drama. *Special achievements/activities:* 25 awards ($34,235 total): cheerleading/drum major, community service, leadership, memberships. *Special characteristics:* 40 awards ($18,250 total): children of faculty/staff, handicapped students, international students, local/state students, members of minority groups, previous college experience, veterans' children. **Tuition waivers:** Full or partial for employees or children of employees, senior citizens. **ROTC:** Army, Naval.
LOANS Student loans: $85,867,651 (44% need-based, 56% non-need-based). 70% of past graduating class borrowed through all loan programs. *Average indebtedness per student:* $25,585. **Average need-based loan:** Freshmen: $3386. Undergraduates: $4323. **Parent loans:** $9,116,955 (100% non-need-based). **Programs:** Federal Direct (Subsidized and Unsubsidized Stafford, PLUS), Perkins, Federal Nursing, college/university.
WORK-STUDY Federal work-study: Total amount: $1,228,715; 220 jobs averaging $2400.
ATHLETIC AWARDS Total amount: $5,584,082 (100% non-need-based).
APPLYING FOR FINANCIAL AID Required financial aid form: FAFSA. **Financial aid deadline:** 3/15 (priority: 2/15). **Notification date:** Continuous beginning 2/1. Students must reply within 2 weeks of notification.
CONTACT Office of Financial Aid, Old Dominion University, 121 Rollins Hall, Norfolk, VA 23529, 757-683-3683 or toll-free 800-348-7926. *Fax:* 757-683-5920. *E-mail:* finaid@odu.edu.
Website: http://www.odu.edu/.

OLIVET COLLEGE
Olivet, MI

Tuition & fees: N/R	Average undergraduate aid package: $17,446

ABOUT THE INSTITUTION Independent Congregational Christian Church, coed. **Awards:** bachelor's and master's degrees. 43 undergraduate majors. **Total enrollment:** 1,206. Undergraduates: 1,164. Freshmen: 305. Federal methodology is used as a basis for awarding need-based institutional aid.
FRESHMAN FINANCIAL AID (Fall 2011) 215 applied for aid; of those 92% were deemed to have need. 100% of freshmen with need received aid; of those 30% had need fully met. **Average percent of need met:** 79% (excluding resources awarded to replace EFC). **Average financial aid package:** $16,353 (excluding resources awarded to replace EFC). 14% of all full-time freshmen had no need and received non-need-based gift aid.
UNDERGRADUATE FINANCIAL AID (Fall 2011) 1,089 applied for aid; of those 95% were deemed to have need. 100% of undergraduates with need received aid; of those 16% had need fully met. **Average percent of need met:** 81% (excluding resources awarded to replace EFC). **Average financial aid package:** $17,446 (excluding resources awarded to replace EFC). 9% of all full-time undergraduates had no need and received non-need-based gift aid.
GIFT AID (NEED-BASED) Total amount: $11,857,598 (21% federal, 10% state, 67% institutional, 2% external sources). **Receiving aid:** Freshmen: 91% (198); all full-time undergraduates: 89% (1,001). **Average award:** Freshmen: $12,856; Undergraduates: $11,382. **Scholarships, grants, and awards:** Federal Pell, FSEOG, state, private, college/university gift aid from institutional funds.
GIFT AID (NON-NEED-BASED) Total amount: $1,260,645 (95% institutional, 5% external sources). **Receiving aid:** Freshmen: 16% (35). Undergraduates: 9% (97). **Average award:** Freshmen: $8729. Undergraduates: $10,950. **Scholarships, grants, and awards by category:** Academic interests/achievement: 428 awards ($2,311,760 total): business, communication, education, English, foreign languages, general academic interests/achievements. *Creative arts/performance:* art/fine arts, journalism/publications, music. *Special achievements/activities:* 401 awards ($739,200 total): community service, leadership, memberships. *Special characteristics:* 51 awards ($588,828 total): children and siblings of alumni, children of faculty/staff, international students, religious affiliation, siblings of current students. **ROTC:** Air Force cooperative.
LOANS Student loans: $7,408,023 (72% need-based, 28% non-need-based). 88% of past graduating class borrowed through all loan programs. *Average indebtedness per student:* $24,890. **Average need-based loan:** Freshmen: $2725. Undergraduates: $4631. **Parent loans:** $1,675,429 (39% need-based, 61% non-need-based).

Programs: Perkins, state, alternative loans, CitiAssist Loans, Sallie Mae Smart Option Loans.
WORK-STUDY *Federal work-study:* Total amount: $178,105; 201 jobs averaging $886. *State or other work-study/employment:* Part-time jobs available.
APPLYING FOR FINANCIAL AID *Required financial aid form:* FAFSA. *Financial aid deadline:* Continuous. *Notification date:* Continuous beginning 3/1.
CONTACT Ms. Libby M. Jean, Director of Student Services, Olivet College, 320 South Main Street, Olivet, MI 49076-9701, 269-749-7655 Ext. 7655 or toll-free 800-456-7189. *Fax:* 269-749-3821. *E-mail:* ljean@olivetcollege.edu.
Website: http://www.olivetcollege.edu/.

OLIVET NAZARENE UNIVERSITY
Bourbonnais, IL

Tuition & fees: $28,090	Average undergraduate aid package: $21,692

ABOUT THE INSTITUTION Independent Church of the Nazarene, coed. 66 undergraduate majors. Federal methodology is used as a basis for awarding need-based institutional aid.
UNDERGRADUATE EXPENSES for 2013–2014 *Comprehensive fee:* $35,990 includes full-time tuition ($27,250), mandatory fees ($840), and room and board ($7900). Full-time tuition and fees vary according to course load. Room and board charges vary according to board plan. *Part-time tuition:* $1135 per credit hour. Part-time tuition and fees vary according to course load.
FRESHMAN FINANCIAL AID (Fall 2012, est.) 637 applied for aid; of those 88% were deemed to have need. 100% of freshmen with need received aid; of those 27% had need fully met. *Average percent of need met:* 81% (excluding resources awarded to replace EFC). *Average financial aid package:* $22,459 (excluding resources awarded to replace EFC). 11% of all full-time freshmen had no need and received non-need-based gift aid.
UNDERGRADUATE FINANCIAL AID (Fall 2012, est.) 2,345 applied for aid; of those 91% were deemed to have need. 100% of undergraduates with need received aid; of those 26% had need fully met. *Average percent of need met:* 80% (excluding resources awarded to replace EFC). *Average financial aid package:* $21,692 (excluding resources awarded to replace EFC). 15% of all full-time undergraduates had no need and received non-need-based gift aid.
GIFT AID (NEED-BASED) *Total amount:* $35,369,167 (10% federal, 8% state, 78% institutional, 4% external sources). *Receiving aid:* Freshmen: 84% (562); all full-time undergraduates: 81% (2,135). *Average award:* Freshmen: $17,481; Undergraduates: $15,992. *Scholarships, grants, and awards:* Federal Pell, FSEOG, state, private, college/university gift aid from institutional funds.
GIFT AID (NON-NEED-BASED) *Total amount:* $7,562,456 (15% federal, 1% state, 82% institutional, 2% external sources). *Receiving aid:* Freshmen: 17% (111). Undergraduates: 15% (390). *Average award:* Freshmen: $13,290. Undergraduates: $12,326. *Scholarships, grants, and awards by category: Academic interests/achievement:* 2,673 awards ($27,379,878 total): general academic interests/achievements, military science. *Creative arts/performance:* 322 awards ($958,396 total): art/fine arts, music, performing arts, theater/drama. *Special achievements/activities:* 25 awards ($24,500 total): cheerleading/drum major, religious involvement. *Special characteristics:* 993 awards ($10,919,616 total): children of faculty/staff, general special characteristics, relatives of clergy, religious affiliation. *Tuition waivers:* Full or partial for employees or children of employees.
LOANS *Student loans:* $18,813,040 (39% need-based, 61% non-need-based). 79% of past graduating class borrowed through all loan programs. *Average indebtedness per student:* $31,313. *Average need-based loan:* Freshmen: $3522. Undergraduates: $4443. *Parent loans:* $4,442,848 (93% need-based, 7% non-need-based). *Programs:* Federal Direct (Subsidized and Unsubsidized Stafford, PLUS), Perkins, private loans.
WORK-STUDY *Federal work-study:* Total amount: $277,627; 347 jobs averaging $800. *State or other work-study/employment:* Total amount: $1,161,293 (100% non-need-based). 967 part-time jobs averaging $1212.
ATHLETIC AWARDS Total amount: $3,796,952 (73% need-based, 27% non-need-based).
APPLYING FOR FINANCIAL AID *Financial aid deadline (priority):* 3/1. *Notification date:* Continuous beginning 2/1. Students must reply by 5/1.

CONTACT Mr. Greg Bruner, Director of Financial Aid, Olivet Nazarene University, One University Avenue, Bourbonnais, IL 60914, 815-939-5249 or toll-free 800-648-1463. *Fax:* 815-939-5074. *E-mail:* gbruner@olivet.edu.
Website: http://www.olivet.edu/.

O'MORE COLLEGE OF DESIGN
Franklin, TN

CONTACT Office of Financial Aid, O'More College of Design, 423 South Margin Street, Franklin, TN 37064-2816, 615-794-4254 Ext. 30 or toll-free 888-662-1970.
Website: http://www.omorecollege.edu/.

ORAL ROBERTS UNIVERSITY
Tulsa, OK

Tuition & fees: $22,438	Average undergraduate aid package: $18,229

ABOUT THE INSTITUTION Independent interdenominational, coed. *Awards:* bachelor's, master's, and doctoral degrees. 75 undergraduate majors. *Total enrollment:* 3,335. Undergraduates: 480. Freshmen: 480. Federal methodology is used as a basis for awarding need-based institutional aid.
UNDERGRADUATE EXPENSES for 2013–2014 *Application fee:* $35. *Comprehensive fee:* $31,734 includes full-time tuition ($21,696), mandatory fees ($742), and room and board ($9296). *College room only:* $4534. Full-time tuition and fees vary according to degree level. Room and board charges vary according to board plan and housing facility. *Part-time tuition:* $906 per credit hour. Part-time tuition and fees vary according to degree level.
FRESHMAN FINANCIAL AID (Fall 2011) 491 applied for aid; of those 85% were deemed to have need. 100% of freshmen with need received aid; of those 37% had need fully met. *Average percent of need met:* 86% (excluding resources awarded to replace EFC). *Average financial aid package:* $15,320 (excluding resources awarded to replace EFC). 25% of all full-time freshmen had no need and received non-need-based gift aid.
UNDERGRADUATE FINANCIAL AID (Fall 2011) 1,978 applied for aid; of those 88% were deemed to have need. 100% of undergraduates with need received aid; of those 37% had need fully met. *Average percent of need met:* 86% (excluding resources awarded to replace EFC). *Average financial aid package:* $18,229 (excluding resources awarded to replace EFC). 20% of all full-time undergraduates had no need and received non-need-based gift aid.
GIFT AID (NEED-BASED) *Total amount:* $4,670,402 (72% federal, 14% state, 14% institutional). *Receiving aid:* Freshmen: 69% (412); all full-time undergraduates: 67% (1,679). *Average award:* Freshmen: $9759; Undergraduates: $9304. *Scholarships, grants, and awards:* Federal Pell, FSEOG, state, private, college/university gift aid from institutional funds.
GIFT AID (NON-NEED-BASED) *Receiving aid:* Freshmen: 29% (173). Undergraduates: 25% (629). *Average award:* Freshmen: $6871. Undergraduates: $7151. *Scholarships, grants, and awards by category: Academic interests/achievement:* biological sciences, business, communication, education, engineering/technologies, general academic interests/achievements, health fields, religion/biblical studies. *Creative arts/performance:* applied art and design, art/fine arts, cinema/film/broadcasting, journalism/publications, music. *Special achievements/activities:* cheerleading/drum major, community service, general special achievements/activities, leadership, memberships, religious involvement. *Special characteristics:* children and siblings of alumni, children of faculty/staff, general special characteristics, international students, relatives of clergy, siblings of current students. *ROTC:* Air Force cooperative.
LOANS *Student loans:* $20,668,979 (100% need-based). 67% of past graduating class borrowed through all loan programs. *Average indebtedness per student:* $34,555. *Average need-based loan:* Freshmen: $6534. Undergraduates: $10,159. *Parent loans:* $5,718,217 (100% need-based). *Programs:* Perkins.
WORK-STUDY *Federal work-study:* Total amount: $490,900; jobs available. *State or other work-study/employment:* Total amount: $323,702 (100% non-need-based). Part-time jobs available.
ATHLETIC AWARDS Total amount: $3,610,814 (100% non-need-based).

APPLYING FOR FINANCIAL AID *Required financial aid form:* FAFSA. *Financial aid deadline (priority):* 3/15. *Notification date:* Continuous. Students must reply by 7/15.

CONTACT Office of Financial Aid, Oral Roberts University, 7777 South Lewis Avenue, Tulsa, OK 74171, 918-495-6510 or toll-free 800-678-8876. *Fax:* 918-495-6803. *E-mail:* finaid@oru.edu. *Website:* http://www.oru.edu/.

OREGON COLLEGE OF ART & CRAFT
Portland, OR

Tuition & fees: N/R	Average undergraduate aid package: $22,239

ABOUT THE INSTITUTION Independent, coed. *Awards:* certificates and bachelor's degrees. 2 undergraduate majors. *Total enrollment:* 164. Undergraduates: 164. Freshmen: 18. Both federal and institutional methodology are used as a basis for awarding need-based institutional aid.

FRESHMAN FINANCIAL AID (Fall 2012, est.) 16 applied for aid; of those 100% were deemed to have need. 100% of freshmen with need received aid; of those 6% had need fully met. *Average percent of need met:* 68% (excluding resources awarded to replace EFC). *Average financial aid package:* $18,439 (excluding resources awarded to replace EFC). 16% of all full-time freshmen had no need and received non-need-based gift aid.

UNDERGRADUATE FINANCIAL AID (Fall 2012, est.) 116 applied for aid; of those 97% were deemed to have need. 100% of undergraduates with need received aid; of those 7% had need fully met. *Average percent of need met:* 73% (excluding resources awarded to replace EFC). *Average financial aid package:* $22,239 (excluding resources awarded to replace EFC). 11% of all full-time undergraduates had no need and received non-need-based gift aid.

GIFT AID (NEED-BASED) *Total amount:* $1,458,710 (29% federal, 4% state, 64% institutional, 3% external sources). *Receiving aid:* Freshmen: 47% (9); all full-time undergraduates: 61% (81). *Average award:* Freshmen: $5858; Undergraduates: $6986. *Scholarships, grants, and awards:* Federal Pell, FSEOG, state, private, college/university gift aid from institutional funds.

GIFT AID (NON-NEED-BASED) *Total amount:* $155,593 (96% institutional, 4% external sources). *Receiving aid:* Freshmen: 84% (16). Undergraduates: 83% (110). *Average award:* Freshmen: $7667. Undergraduates: $7533. *Scholarships, grants, and awards by category:* Academic interests/achievement: general academic interests/achievements. Creative arts/performance: art/fine arts.

LOANS *Student loans:* $1,438,077 (80% need-based, 20% non-need-based). 66% of past graduating class borrowed through all loan programs. *Average indebtedness per student:* $22,500. *Average need-based loan:* Freshmen: $3250. Undergraduates: $4332. *Parent loans:* $151,050 (82% need-based, 18% non-need-based). *Programs:* Federal Direct (Subsidized and Unsubsidized Stafford, PLUS), private loans.

WORK-STUDY *Federal work-study:* Total amount: $26,126; jobs available. *State or other work-study/employment:* Total amount: $77,529 (43% need-based, 57% non-need-based). Part-time jobs available.

APPLYING FOR FINANCIAL AID *Required financial aid form:* FAFSA. *Financial aid deadline:* Continuous. *Notification date:* Continuous beginning 3/1.

CONTACT Ms. Linda L. Anderson, Director of Financial Aid, Oregon College of Art & Craft, 8245 Southwest Barnes Road, Portland, OR 97225, 971-255-4224 or toll-free 800-390-0632. *Fax:* 503-297-9651. *E-mail:* landerson@ocac.edu. *Website:* http://www.ocac.edu/.

OREGON HEALTH & SCIENCE UNIVERSITY
Portland, OR

Tuition & fees: N/R	Average undergraduate aid package: $9971

ABOUT THE INSTITUTION State-related, coed. *Awards:* certificates, bachelor's, master's, and doctoral degrees. 2 undergraduate majors. *Total*

enrollment: 2,849. Undergraduates: 825. Federal methodology is used as a basis for awarding need-based institutional aid.

UNDERGRADUATE FINANCIAL AID (Fall 2012, est.) 290 applied for aid; of those 97% were deemed to have need. 98% of undergraduates with need received aid; of those 5% had need fully met. *Average percent of need met:* 29% (excluding resources awarded to replace EFC). *Average financial aid package:* $9971 (excluding resources awarded to replace EFC). 1% of all full-time undergraduates had no need and received non-need-based gift aid.

GIFT AID (NEED-BASED) *Total amount:* $2,297,490 (53% federal, 9% state, 13% institutional, 25% external sources). *Receiving aid:* All full-time undergraduates: 53% (164). *Average award:* Undergraduates: $7903. *Scholarships, grants, and awards:* Federal Pell, FSEOG, state, private, college/university gift aid from institutional funds, Health Profession Scholarships.

GIFT AID (NON-NEED-BASED) *Total amount:* $39,886 (8% federal, 74% institutional, 18% external sources). *Receiving aid:* Undergraduates: 1. *Average award:* Undergraduates: $400. *Scholarships, grants, and awards by category:* Academic interests/achievement: 101 awards ($975,714 total): health fields.

LOANS *Student loans:* $14,224,433 (88% need-based, 12% non-need-based). *Average need-based loan:* Undergraduates: $4943. *Parent loans:* $704,689 (61% need-based, 39% non-need-based). *Programs:* Federal Direct (Subsidized and Unsubsidized Stafford, PLUS), Perkins, Federal Nursing, state, college/university, alternative loans.

WORK-STUDY *Federal work-study:* Total amount: $20,500; 15 jobs averaging $1367.

APPLYING FOR FINANCIAL AID *Notification date:* Continuous.

CONTACT Debbie Cox, Administrative Coordinator, Oregon Health & Science University, 3181 SW Sam Jackson Park Road, L-109, Portland, OR 97239-3089, 503-494-7323. *Fax:* 503-494-4629. *E-mail:* finaid@ohsu.edu. *Website:* http://www.ohsu.edu/.

OREGON INSTITUTE OF TECHNOLOGY
Klamath Falls, OR

Tuition & fees: N/R	Average undergraduate aid package: $7722

ABOUT THE INSTITUTION State-supported, coed. *Awards:* certificates, associate, bachelor's, and master's degrees. 19 undergraduate majors. *Total enrollment:* 3,911. Undergraduates: 3,881. Freshmen: 318. Federal methodology is used as a basis for awarding need-based institutional aid.

FRESHMAN FINANCIAL AID (Fall 2011) 248 applied for aid; of those 81% were deemed to have need. 98% of freshmen with need received aid; of those 43% had need fully met. *Average percent of need met:* 21% (excluding resources awarded to replace EFC). *Average financial aid package:* $6832 (excluding resources awarded to replace EFC).

UNDERGRADUATE FINANCIAL AID (Fall 2011) 1,851 applied for aid; of those 89% were deemed to have need. 97% of undergraduates with need received aid; of those 31% had need fully met. *Average percent of need met:* 21% (excluding resources awarded to replace EFC). *Average financial aid package:* $7722 (excluding resources awarded to replace EFC).

GIFT AID (NEED-BASED) *Total amount:* $8,021,354 (74% federal, 13% state, 10% institutional, 3% external sources). *Receiving aid:* Freshmen: 58% (156); all full-time undergraduates: 51% (1,099). *Average award:* Freshmen: $5583; Undergraduates: $5611. *Scholarships, grants, and awards:* Federal Pell, FSEOG, state, private, college/university gift aid from institutional funds.

GIFT AID (NON-NEED-BASED) *Total amount:* $1,322,460 (1% state, 33% institutional, 66% external sources). *Receiving aid:* Freshmen: 38% (102). Undergraduates: 25% (546). *Scholarships, grants, and awards by category:* Academic interests/achievement: general academic interests/achievements. Special achievements/activities: general special achievements/activities, leadership. ROTC: Army cooperative.

LOANS *Student loans:* $15,483,650 (66% need-based, 34% non-need-based). 67% of past graduating class borrowed through all loan programs. *Average indebtedness per student:* $28,546. *Average need-based loan:* Freshmen: $3323. Undergraduates: $4402. *Parent loans:* $5,072,206 (50% need-based, 50% non-need-based). *Programs:* Federal Direct (Subsidized and Unsubsidized Stafford, PLUS), Perkins, college/university.

WORK-STUDY *Federal work-study:* Total amount: $177,937; jobs available. *State or other work-study/employment:* Total amount: $29,645 (100% need-based). Part-time jobs available.

ATHLETIC AWARDS Total amount: $191,742 (26% need-based, 74% non-need-based).

APPLYING FOR FINANCIAL AID *Required financial aid form:* FAFSA. *Financial aid deadline (priority):* 2/1. *Notification date:* Continuous beginning 4/1. Students must reply within 3 weeks of notification.

CONTACT Tracey Lehman, Director of Financial Aid, Oregon Institute of Technology, 3201 Campus Drive, Klamath Falls, OR 97601, 541-885-1280 or toll-free 800-422-2017. *Fax:* 541-885-1024. *E-mail:* tracey.lehman@oit.edu. *Website:* http://www.oit.edu/.

OREGON STATE UNIVERSITY
Corvallis, OR

Tuition & fees (OR res): $8138	Average undergraduate aid package: $10,515

ABOUT THE INSTITUTION State-supported, coed. *Awards:* certificates, bachelor's, master's, and doctoral degrees. 84 undergraduate majors. *Total enrollment:* 26,393. Undergraduates: 21,812. Freshmen: 3,333. Federal methodology is used as a basis for awarding need-based institutional aid.

UNDERGRADUATE EXPENSES for 2013–2014 *Application fee:* $50. *One-time required fee:* $300. *Tuition, state resident:* full-time $6660; part-time $185 per credit hour. *Tuition, nonresident:* full-time $20,844; part-time $579 per credit hour. *Required fees:* full-time $1478; $450.57 per term. Full-time tuition and fees vary according to course load and program. Part-time tuition and fees vary according to course load and program. *College room and board:* $10,563; *Room only:* $7130. Room and board charges vary according to board plan and housing facility.

FRESHMAN FINANCIAL AID (Fall 2012, est.) 2,834 applied for aid; of those 72% were deemed to have need. 97% of freshmen with need received aid; of those 19% had need fully met. *Average percent of need met:* 59% (excluding resources awarded to replace EFC). *Average financial aid package:* $10,651 (excluding resources awarded to replace EFC). 19% of all full-time freshmen had no need and received non-need-based gift aid.

UNDERGRADUATE FINANCIAL AID (Fall 2012, est.) 12,514 applied for aid; of those 82% were deemed to have need. 97% of undergraduates with need received aid; of those 11% had need fully met. *Average percent of need met:* 53% (excluding resources awarded to replace EFC). *Average financial aid package:* $10,515 (excluding resources awarded to replace EFC). 13% of all full-time undergraduates had no need and received non-need-based gift aid.

GIFT AID (NEED-BASED) *Total amount:* $53,658,606 (58% federal, 12% state, 23% institutional, 7% external sources). *Receiving aid:* Freshmen: 52% (1,715); all full-time undergraduates: 46% (8,009). *Average award:* Freshmen: $3041; Undergraduates: $3220. *Scholarships, grants, and awards:* Federal Pell, FSEOG, state, private, college/university gift aid from institutional funds.

GIFT AID (NON-NEED-BASED) *Total amount:* $10,341,273 (2% federal, 81% institutional, 17% external sources). *Receiving aid:* Freshmen: 3% (88). Undergraduates: 1% (218). *Average award:* Freshmen: $3817. Undergraduates: $3568. *Scholarships, grants, and awards by category:* Academic interests/achievement: general academic interests/achievements. *Special achievements/activities:* leadership. *Special characteristics:* children and siblings of alumni, local/state students, members of minority groups. *Tuition waivers:* Full or partial for employees or children of employees. *ROTC:* Army, Naval, Air Force.

LOANS *Student loans:* $92,257,144 (86% need-based, 14% non-need-based). *Average need-based loan:* Freshmen: $2904. Undergraduates: $3750. *Parent loans:* $57,039,439 (59% need-based, 41% non-need-based). *Programs:* Federal Direct (Subsidized and Unsubsidized Stafford, PLUS), Perkins, college/university.

WORK-STUDY *Federal work-study:* Total amount: $2,529,244; jobs available.

ATHLETIC AWARDS Total amount: $8,330,743 (8% need-based, 92% non-need-based).

APPLYING FOR FINANCIAL AID *Required financial aid form:* FAFSA. *Financial aid deadline (priority):* 2/28. *Notification date:* Continuous beginning 4/1. Students must reply within 4 weeks of notification.

CONTACT Doug Severs, Director of Financial Aid and Scholarships, Oregon State University, 218 Kerr Administration Building, Corvallis, OR 97331-2120, 541-737-2241 or toll-free 800-291-4192. *E-mail:* doug.severs@oregonstate.edu. *Website:* http://www.oregonstate.edu/.

OREGON STATE UNIVERSITY– CASCADES
Bend, OR

CONTACT Financial Aid Office, Oregon State University–Cascades, 2600 Northwest College Way, Bend, OR 97701, 541-322-3100. *Website:* http://www.osucascades.edu/.

OTIS COLLEGE OF ART AND DESIGN
Los Angeles, CA

Tuition & fees: N/R	Average undergraduate aid package: $21,771

ABOUT THE INSTITUTION Independent, coed. *Awards:* bachelor's and master's degrees. 10 undergraduate majors. *Total enrollment:* 1,165. Undergraduates: 1,105. Freshmen: 183. Federal methodology is used as a basis for awarding need-based institutional aid.

FRESHMAN FINANCIAL AID (Fall 2012, est.) 140 applied for aid; of those 94% were deemed to have need. 100% of freshmen with need received aid; of those 7% had need fully met. *Average percent of need met:* 58% (excluding resources awarded to replace EFC). *Average financial aid package:* $22,594 (excluding resources awarded to replace EFC). 19% of all full-time freshmen had no need and received non-need-based gift aid.

UNDERGRADUATE FINANCIAL AID (Fall 2012, est.) 803 applied for aid; of those 96% were deemed to have need. 100% of undergraduates with need received aid; of those 4% had need fully met. *Average percent of need met:* 52% (excluding resources awarded to replace EFC). *Average financial aid package:* $21,771 (excluding resources awarded to replace EFC). 15% of all full-time undergraduates had no need and received non-need-based gift aid.

GIFT AID (NEED-BASED) *Total amount:* $14,392,071 (20% federal, 16% state, 63% institutional, 1% external sources). *Receiving aid:* Freshmen: 69% (126); all full-time undergraduates: 70% (756). *Average award:* Freshmen: $19,134; Undergraduates: $16,717. *Scholarships, grants, and awards:* Federal Pell, FSEOG, state, private, college/university gift aid from institutional funds.

GIFT AID (NON-NEED-BASED) *Total amount:* $1,684,564 (98% institutional, 2% external sources). *Receiving aid:* Freshmen: 8% (15). Undergraduates: 4% (39). *Average award:* Freshmen: $12,174. Undergraduates: $10,243. *Scholarships, grants, and awards by category:* Academic interests/achievement: 158 awards ($1,584,767 total): general academic interests/achievements. *Creative arts/performance:* applied art and design, art/fine arts.

LOANS *Student loans:* $7,052,937 (98% need-based, 2% non-need-based). 95% of past graduating class borrowed through all loan programs. *Average indebtedness per student:* $41,842. *Average need-based loan:* Freshmen: $3475. Undergraduates: $4788. *Parent loans:* $4,861,562 (95% need-based, 5% non-need-based). *Programs:* Federal Direct (Subsidized and Unsubsidized Stafford, PLUS), Perkins.

WORK-STUDY *Federal work-study:* Total amount: $126,962; 150 jobs averaging $661. *State or other work-study/employment:* Total amount: $30,000 (100% non-need-based). 4 part-time jobs averaging $309.

APPLYING FOR FINANCIAL AID *Required financial aid form:* FAFSA. *Financial aid deadline (priority):* 2/15. *Notification date:* 3/1.

CONTACT Jessika Huerta, Associate Director of Financial Aid, Otis College of Art and Design, 9045 Lincoln Boulevard, Los Angeles, CA 90045-9785, 310-665-6898 or toll-free 800-527-OTIS. *Fax:* 310-665-6884. *E-mail:* jhuerta@otis.edu. *Website:* http://www.otis.edu/.

OTTAWA UNIVERSITY
Ottawa, KS

CONTACT Financial Aid Coordinator, Ottawa University, 1001 South Cedar, Ottawa, KS 66067-3399, 785-242-5200 or toll-free 800-755-5200. *E-mail:* finaid@ottawa.edu.
Website: http://www.ottawa.edu/.

OTTERBEIN UNIVERSITY
Westerville, OH

ABOUT THE INSTITUTION Independent United Methodist, coed. *Awards:* certificates, bachelor's, master's, and doctoral degrees. 61 undergraduate majors. *Total enrollment:* 2,997. Undergraduates: 2,575. Freshmen: 638.
GIFT AID (NEED-BASED) *Scholarships, grants, and awards:* Federal Pell, FSEOG, state, private, college/university gift aid from institutional funds, Federal Nursing.
GIFT AID (NON-NEED-BASED) *Scholarships, grants, and awards by category: Academic interests/achievement:* general academic interests/achievements. *Creative arts/performance:* art/fine arts, music, theater/drama. *Special achievements/activities:* community service, leadership. *Special characteristics:* children and siblings of alumni, children of faculty/staff, general special characteristics, international students, members of minority groups, previous college experience, relatives of clergy, siblings of current students, veterans.
LOANS *Programs:* Federal Direct (Subsidized and Unsubsidized Stafford, PLUS), Perkins, Federal Nursing, state, college/university.
WORK-STUDY *Federal work-study:* Total amount: $1,447,141; 500 jobs averaging $1000. *State or other work-study/employment:* Total amount: $268,546 (100% non-need-based). 250 part-time jobs averaging $1000.
APPLYING FOR FINANCIAL AID *Required financial aid form:* FAFSA.
CONTACT Mr. Thomas V. Yarnell, Director of Financial Aid, Otterbein University, One Otterbein College, Westerville, OH 43081-2006, 614-823-1502 or toll-free 800-488-8144. *Fax:* 614-823-1200. *E-mail:* tyarnell@otterbein.edu.
Website: http://www.otterbein.edu/.

OUACHITA BAPTIST UNIVERSITY
Arkadelphia, AR

Tuition & fees: $22,340	Average undergraduate aid package: $19,727

ABOUT THE INSTITUTION Independent Baptist, coed. *Awards:* bachelor's degrees. 54 undergraduate majors. *Total enrollment:* 1,532. Undergraduates: 1,532. Freshmen: 363. Both federal and institutional methodology are used as a basis for awarding need-based institutional aid.
UNDERGRADUATE EXPENSES for 2013–2014 *Comprehensive fee:* $28,980 includes full-time tuition ($21,860), mandatory fees ($480), and room and board ($6640). Room and board charges vary according to housing facility. *Part-time tuition:* $605 per semester hour.
FRESHMAN FINANCIAL AID (Fall 2012, est.) 337 applied for aid; of those 78% were deemed to have need. 100% of freshmen with need received aid; of those 30% had need fully met. *Average percent of need met:* 82% (excluding resources awarded to replace EFC). *Average financial aid package:* $19,418 (excluding resources awarded to replace EFC). 28% of all full-time freshmen had no need and received non-need-based gift aid.
UNDERGRADUATE FINANCIAL AID (Fall 2012, est.) 1,128 applied for aid; of those 82% were deemed to have need. 100% of undergraduates with need received aid; of those 34% had need fully met. *Average percent of need met:* 84% (excluding resources awarded to replace EFC). *Average financial aid package:* $19,727 (excluding resources awarded to replace EFC). 35% of all full-time undergraduates had no need and received non-need-based gift aid.
GIFT AID (NEED-BASED) *Total amount:* $11,881,124 (14% federal, 13% state, 69% institutional, 4% external sources). *Receiving aid:* Freshmen: 68% (248); all full-time undergraduates: 59% (877). *Average award:* Freshmen: $13,758; Undergraduates: $13,534. *Scholarships, grants, and awards:* Federal Pell, FSEOG, state, private, college/university gift aid from institutional funds.

GIFT AID (NON-NEED-BASED) *Total amount:* $8,278,762 (1% federal, 25% state, 70% institutional, 4% external sources). *Receiving aid:* Freshmen: 18% (65). Undergraduates: 16% (236). *Average award:* Freshmen: $9338. Undergraduates: $9643. *Scholarships, grants, and awards by category: Academic interests/achievement:* area/ethnic studies, biological sciences, business, communication, computer science, education, engineering/technologies, English, foreign languages, general academic interests/achievements, health fields, home economics, humanities, international studies, mathematics, physical sciences, premedicine, religion/biblical studies, social sciences. *Creative arts/performance:* art/fine arts, journalism/publications, music, performing arts, theater/drama. *Special achievements/activities:* cheerleading/drum major, general special achievements/activities. *Special characteristics:* children and siblings of alumni, children of faculty/staff, ethnic background, first-generation college students, general special characteristics, handicapped students, international students, local/state students, married students, members of minority groups, out-of-state students, previous college experience, relatives of clergy, religious affiliation, twins. *Tuition waivers:* Full or partial for employees or children of employees. **ROTC:** Army.
LOANS *Student loans:* $5,834,846 (59% need-based, 41% non-need-based). 46% of past graduating class borrowed through all loan programs. *Average indebtedness per student:* $24,367. *Average need-based loan:* Freshmen: $3322. Undergraduates: $4191. *Parent loans:* $1,176,343 (29% need-based, 71% non-need-based). *Programs:* Federal Direct (Subsidized and Unsubsidized Stafford, PLUS), Perkins, college/university.
WORK-STUDY *Federal work-study:* Total amount: $533,772; 303 jobs averaging $1800. *State or other work-study/employment:* Total amount: $268,691 (37% need-based, 63% non-need-based). 154 part-time jobs averaging $1730.
ATHLETIC AWARDS Total amount: $2,171,560 (58% need-based, 42% non-need-based).
APPLYING FOR FINANCIAL AID *Required financial aid forms:* FAFSA, state aid form. *Financial aid deadline:* 6/1 (priority: 1/15). *Notification date:* Continuous beginning 11/1. Students must reply by 6/1.
CONTACT Ms. Susan Hurst, Director of Financial Aid, Ouachita Baptist University, PO Box 3774, Arkadelphia, AR 71998-0001, 870-245-5570 or toll-free 800-342-5628. *Fax:* 870-245-5318. *E-mail:* hursts@obu.edu.
Website: http://www.obu.edu/.

OUR LADY OF HOLY CROSS COLLEGE
New Orleans, LA

CONTACT Mrs. Katherine Gonzales, Dean of Admissions and Student Affairs, Our Lady of Holy Cross College, 4123 Woodland Drive, New Orleans, LA 70131-7399, 504-398-2185 or toll-free 800-259-7744. *Fax:* 504-394-1182. *E-mail:* kgonzales@olhcc.edu.
Website: http://www.olhcc.edu/.

OUR LADY OF THE LAKE COLLEGE
Baton Rouge, LA

CONTACT Tiffany D. Magee, Director of Financial Aid, Our Lady of the Lake College, 7434 Perkins Road, Baton Rouge, LA 70808, 225-768-1701. *Fax:* 225-490-1632. *E-mail:* tiffany.magee@ololcollege.edu.
Website: http://www.ololcollege.edu/.

OUR LADY OF THE LAKE UNIVERSITY OF SAN ANTONIO
San Antonio, TX

CONTACT Michael Fuller, Director of Financial Aid, Our Lady of the Lake University of San Antonio, 411 Southwest 24th Street, San Antonio, TX 78207-4689, 210-434-6711 Ext. 2541 or toll-free 800-436-6558. *Fax:* 210-431-3958. *E-mail:* mfuller@lake.ollusa.edu.
Website: http://www.ollusa.edu/.

OZARK CHRISTIAN COLLEGE
Joplin, MO

CONTACT Jill Kaminsky, Application Processor, Ozark Christian College, 1111 North Main Street, Joplin, MO 64801-4804, 417-624-2518 Ext. 2017 or toll-free 800-299-4622. *Fax:* 417-624-0090. *E-mail:* finaid@occ.edu. *Website:* http://www.occ.edu/.

PACE UNIVERSITY
New York, NY

Tuition & fees: $36,564	Average undergraduate aid package: $28,354

ABOUT THE INSTITUTION Independent, coed. *Awards:* certificates, associate, bachelor's, master's, and doctoral degrees. 73 undergraduate majors. *Total enrollment:* 12,772. Undergraduates: 8,336. Freshmen: 1,848. Federal methodology is used as a basis for awarding need-based institutional aid.

UNDERGRADUATE EXPENSES for 2013–2014 Application fee: $50. *Comprehensive fee:* $49,154 includes full-time tuition ($35,320), mandatory fees ($1244), and room and board ($12,590). Room and board charges vary according to board plan, housing facility, location, and student level. *Part-time tuition:* $1013 per credit. Part-time tuition and fees vary according to course load.

FRESHMAN FINANCIAL AID (Fall 2012, est.) 1,612 applied for aid; of those 92% were deemed to have need. 100% of freshmen with need received aid; of those 8% had need fully met. *Average percent of need met:* 74% (excluding resources awarded to replace EFC). *Average financial aid package:* $30,563 (excluding resources awarded to replace EFC). 17% of all full-time freshmen had no need and received non-need-based gift aid.

UNDERGRADUATE FINANCIAL AID (Fall 2012, est.) 5,772 applied for aid; of those 93% were deemed to have need. 100% of undergraduates with need received aid; of those 9% had need fully met. *Average percent of need met:* 70% (excluding resources awarded to replace EFC). *Average financial aid package:* $28,354 (excluding resources awarded to replace EFC). 19% of all full-time undergraduates had no need and received non-need-based gift aid.

GIFT AID (NEED-BASED) Total amount: $122,594,772 (12% federal, 6% state, 80% institutional, 2% external sources). *Receiving aid:* Freshmen: 82% (1,487); all full-time undergraduates: 75% (5,336). *Average award:* Freshmen: $25,057; Undergraduates: $23,746. *Scholarships, grants, and awards:* Federal Pell, FSEOG, state, private, college/university gift aid from institutional funds, Federal Nursing, endowed and restricted scholarships and grants.

GIFT AID (NON-NEED-BASED) Total amount: $19,786,185 (92% institutional, 8% external sources). *Receiving aid:* Freshmen: 5% (98). Undergraduates: 5% (334). *Average award:* Freshmen: $13,054. Undergraduates: $12,438. *Scholarships, grants, and awards by category:* Academic interests/achievement: 6,200 awards ($76,630,062 total): biological sciences, business, communication, computer science, education, English, foreign languages, general academic interests/achievements, health fields, humanities, mathematics, physical sciences, social sciences. *Creative arts/performance:* 26 awards ($37,500 total): performing arts, theater/drama. *Special achievements/activities:* 428 awards ($6,607,842 total): community service, general special achievements/activities, leadership, memberships. *Special characteristics:* 267 awards ($2,759,314 total): adult students, children of faculty/staff, children with a deceased or disabled parent, general special characteristics, international students, parents of current students, previous college experience, spouses of deceased or disabled public servants, veterans. *Tuition waivers:* Full or partial for employees or children of employees, senior citizens. *ROTC:* Army cooperative, Air Force cooperative.

LOANS Student loans: $48,085,876 (83% need-based, 17% non-need-based). 74% of past graduating class borrowed through all loan programs. *Average indebtedness per student:* $35,895. *Average need-based loan:* Freshmen: $4049. Undergraduates: $4644. *Parent loans:* $33,176,362 (53% need-based, 47% non-need-based). *Programs:* Federal Direct (Subsidized and Unsubsidized Stafford, PLUS), Perkins, Federal Nursing.

WORK-STUDY Federal work-study: Total amount: $1,062,922; 1,176 jobs averaging $3623.

ATHLETIC AWARDS Total amount: $3,996,932 (66% need-based, 34% non-need-based).

APPLYING FOR FINANCIAL AID Required financial aid forms: FAFSA, state aid form. *Financial aid deadline (priority):* 2/15. *Notification date:* Continuous beginning 3/1. Students must reply by 5/1 or within 2 weeks of notification.
CONTACT Office of Financial Aid, Pace University, 861 Bedford Road, Pleasantville, NY 10570, 877-672-1830 or toll-free 800-874-7223. *Fax:* 212-346-1750. *Website:* http://www.pace.edu/.

PACIFIC ISLANDS UNIVERSITY
Mangilao, GU

CONTACT Financial Aid Office, Pacific Islands University, 172 Kinney's Road, Mangilao, GU 96913, 671-734-1812. *Website:* http://www.piu.edu/.

PACIFIC LUTHERAN UNIVERSITY
Tacoma, WA

Tuition & fees: $34,740	Average undergraduate aid package: $25,521

ABOUT THE INSTITUTION Independent Evangelical Lutheran Church in America, coed. *Awards:* certificates, bachelor's, and master's degrees. 41 undergraduate majors. *Total enrollment:* 3,473. Undergraduates: 3,166. Freshmen: 633. Federal methodology is used as a basis for awarding need-based institutional aid.

UNDERGRADUATE EXPENSES for 2013–2014 Application fee: $40. *Comprehensive fee:* $44,840 includes full-time tuition ($34,440), mandatory fees ($300), and room and board ($10,100). *College room only:* $4870. Full-time tuition and fees vary according to course load. Room and board charges vary according to board plan and housing facility. *Part-time fees:* $1030 per semester hour. Part-time tuition and fees vary according to course load.

FRESHMAN FINANCIAL AID (Fall 2012, est.) 585 applied for aid; of those 91% were deemed to have need. 99% of freshmen with need received aid; of those 40% had need fully met. *Average percent of need met:* 89% (excluding resources awarded to replace EFC). *Average financial aid package:* $28,009 (excluding resources awarded to replace EFC). 15% of all full-time freshmen had no need and received non-need-based gift aid.

UNDERGRADUATE FINANCIAL AID (Fall 2012, est.) 2,550 applied for aid; of those 89% were deemed to have need. 99% of undergraduates with need received aid; of those 23% had need fully met. *Average percent of need met:* 79% (excluding resources awarded to replace EFC). *Average financial aid package:* $25,521 (excluding resources awarded to replace EFC). 21% of all full-time undergraduates had no need and received non-need-based gift aid.

GIFT AID (NEED-BASED) Total amount: $42,295,643 (11% federal, 8% state, 80% institutional, 1% external sources). *Receiving aid:* Freshmen: 83% (525); all full-time undergraduates: 74% (2,229). *Average award:* Freshmen: $21,829; Undergraduates: $18,471. *Scholarships, grants, and awards:* Federal Pell, FSEOG, state, private, college/university gift aid from institutional funds, Federal Nursing.

GIFT AID (NON-NEED-BASED) Total amount: $12,609,793 (74% institutional, 26% external sources). *Receiving aid:* Freshmen: 67% (424). Undergraduates: 61% (1,815). *Average award:* Freshmen: $15,362. Undergraduates: $14,442. *Scholarships, grants, and awards by category:* Academic interests/achievement: 2,400 awards ($31,586,636 total): general academic interests/achievements. *Creative arts/performance:* 250 awards ($1,456,285 total): art/fine arts, dance, debating, music, theater/drama. *Special achievements/activities:* 132 awards ($220,862 total): leadership. *Special characteristics:* 895 awards ($1,818,628 total): children and siblings of alumni, first-generation college students, international students, out-of-state students, relatives of clergy, religious affiliation. *Tuition waivers:* Full or partial for children of alumni, employees or children of employees. *ROTC:* Army.

LOANS Student loans: $21,886,633 (75% need-based, 25% non-need-based). 73% of past graduating class borrowed through all loan programs. *Average indebtedness per student:* $31,320. *Average need-based loan:* Freshmen: $4197. Undergraduates: $5325. *Parent loans:* $10,877,218 (37% need-based, 63% non-need-based). *Programs:* Federal Direct (Subsidized and Unsubsidized Stafford, PLUS), Perkins, Federal Nursing, state.

WORK-STUDY *Federal work-study:* Total amount: $2,532,834; 752 jobs averaging $3063. *State or other work-study/employment:* Total amount: $1,899,980 (18% need-based, 82% non-need-based). 1,153 part-time jobs averaging $3159.
APPLYING FOR FINANCIAL AID *Required financial aid form:* FAFSA. *Financial aid deadline (priority):* 1/31. *Notification date:* Continuous beginning 3/1. Students must reply by 5/1 or within 3 weeks of notification.
CONTACT Office of Financial Aid, Pacific Lutheran University, Hauge Administration Building Room 130, Tacoma, WA 98447, 253-535-7134 or toll-free 800-274-6758. *Fax:* 253-535-8406. *E-mail:* finaid@plu.edu.
Website: http://www.plu.edu/.

PACIFIC NORTHWEST COLLEGE OF ART
Portland, OR

CONTACT Peggy Burgus, Director of Financial Aid, Pacific Northwest College of Art, 1241 Northwest Johnson Street, Portland, OR 97209, 503-821-8976. *Fax:* 503-821-8978.
Website: http://www.pnca.edu/.

PACIFIC OAKS COLLEGE
Pasadena, CA

CONTACT Rosie Tristan, Financial Aid Specialist, Pacific Oaks College, 5 Westmoreland Place, Pasadena, CA 91103, 626-397-1350 or toll-free 877-314-2380. *Fax:* 626-577-6144. *E-mail:* financial@pacificoaks.edu.
Website: http://www.pacificoaks.edu/.

PACIFIC UNION COLLEGE
Angwin, CA

Tuition & fees: $26,850	Average undergraduate aid package: $21,314

ABOUT THE INSTITUTION Independent Seventh-day Adventist, coed. *Awards:* certificates, associate, bachelor's, and master's degrees. 40 undergraduate majors. *Total enrollment:* 1,564. Undergraduates: 1,564. Freshmen: 292. Federal methodology is used as a basis for awarding need-based institutional aid.
UNDERGRADUATE EXPENSES for 2013–2014 *Comprehensive fee:* $34,335 includes full-time tuition ($26,550), mandatory fees ($300), and room and board ($7485). Full-time tuition and fees vary according to course load. Part-time tuition and fees vary according to course load. *Payment plan:* Guaranteed tuition.
FRESHMAN FINANCIAL AID (Fall 2012, est.) 291 applied for aid; of those 86% were deemed to have need. 100% of freshmen with need received aid; of those 2% had need fully met. *Average percent of need met:* 73% (excluding resources awarded to replace EFC). *Average financial aid package:* $22,470 (excluding resources awarded to replace EFC). 14% of all full-time freshmen had no need and received non-need-based gift aid.
UNDERGRADUATE FINANCIAL AID (Fall 2012, est.) 1,356 applied for aid; of those 80% were deemed to have need. 100% of undergraduates with need received aid; of those .4% had need fully met. *Average percent of need met:* 51% (excluding resources awarded to replace EFC). *Average financial aid package:* $21,314 (excluding resources awarded to replace EFC). 21% of all full-time undergraduates had no need and received non-need-based gift aid.
GIFT AID (NEED-BASED) *Total amount:* $21,931,758 (18% federal, 13% state, 60% institutional, 9% external sources). *Receiving aid:* Freshmen: 86% (250); all full-time undergraduates: 79% (1,083). *Average award:* Freshmen: $20,222; Undergraduates: $19,477. *Scholarships, grants, and awards:* Federal Pell, FSEOG, state, private, college/university gift aid from institutional funds.
GIFT AID (NON-NEED-BASED) *Total amount:* $3,713,371 (63% institutional, 37% external sources). *Receiving aid:* Freshmen: 20% (57). Undergraduates: 29% (390). *Average award:* Freshmen: $9886. Undergraduates: $5428. *Scholarships, grants, and awards by category:* Academic interests/achievement: 53 awards ($155,000 total): education, religion/biblical studies. Creative arts/performance: 18

awards ($54,000 total): art/fine arts, music, theater/drama. *Special achievements/activities:* 38 awards ($76,332 total): community service, general special achievements/activities, leadership, religious involvement. *Special characteristics:* 500 awards ($340,922 total): members of minority groups, religious affiliation, siblings of current students, spouses of current students, veterans. *Tuition waivers:* Full or partial for employees or children of employees, senior citizens.
LOANS *Student loans:* $16,353,894 (37% need-based, 63% non-need-based). 76% of past graduating class borrowed through all loan programs. *Average indebtedness per student:* $33,662. *Average need-based loan:* Freshmen: $3180. Undergraduates: $4421. *Parent loans:* $1,463,926 (60% need-based, 40% non-need-based). *Programs:* Federal Direct (Subsidized and Unsubsidized Stafford, PLUS), Perkins, college/university.
WORK-STUDY *Federal work-study:* Total amount: $395,500; 201 jobs averaging $1964.
ATHLETIC AWARDS Total amount: $82,633 (40% need-based, 60% non-need-based).
APPLYING FOR FINANCIAL AID *Required financial aid forms:* FAFSA, institution's own form. *Financial aid deadline (priority):* 3/2. *Notification date:* Continuous beginning 4/1. Students must reply within 3 weeks of notification.
CONTACT Laurie Wheeler, Director of Student Financial Services, Pacific Union College, One Angwin Avenue, Angwin, CA 94508, 707-965-7321 or toll-free 800-862-7080. *Fax:* 707-965-6595. *E-mail:* llwheeler@puc.edu.
Website: http://www.puc.edu/.

PACIFIC UNIVERSITY
Forest Grove, OR

Tuition & fees: $35,260	Average undergraduate aid package: $27,799

ABOUT THE INSTITUTION Independent, coed. *Awards:* certificates, bachelor's, master's, and doctoral degrees. 50 undergraduate majors. *Total enrollment:* 3,416. Undergraduates: 1,716. Freshmen: 460. Federal methodology is used as a basis for awarding need-based institutional aid.
UNDERGRADUATE EXPENSES for 2013–2014 *Application fee:* $40. *Comprehensive fee:* $45,252 includes full-time tuition ($35,260) and room and board ($9992). Room and board charges vary according to board plan and housing facility. Part-time tuition and fees vary according to course load.
FRESHMAN FINANCIAL AID (Fall 2012, est.) 435 applied for aid; of those 90% were deemed to have need. 100% of freshmen with need received aid; of those 17% had need fully met. *Average percent of need met:* 85% (excluding resources awarded to replace EFC). *Average financial aid package:* $27,564 (excluding resources awarded to replace EFC). 14% of all full-time freshmen had no need and received non-need-based gift aid.
UNDERGRADUATE FINANCIAL AID (Fall 2012, est.) 1,481 applied for aid; of those 92% were deemed to have need. 100% of undergraduates with need received aid; of those 15% had need fully met. *Average percent of need met:* 80% (excluding resources awarded to replace EFC). *Average financial aid package:* $27,799 (excluding resources awarded to replace EFC). 15% of all full-time undergraduates had no need and received non-need-based gift aid.
GIFT AID (NEED-BASED) *Total amount:* $27,870,103 (9% federal, 1% state, 86% institutional, 4% external sources). *Receiving aid:* Freshmen: 83% (383); all full-time undergraduates: 80% (1,324). *Average award:* Freshmen: $21,788; Undergraduates: $21,234. *Scholarships, grants, and awards:* Federal Pell, FSEOG, state, private, college/university gift aid from institutional funds.
GIFT AID (NON-NEED-BASED) *Total amount:* $4,036,566 (97% institutional, 3% external sources). *Receiving aid:* Freshmen: 24% (110). Undergraduates: 22% (359). *Average award:* Freshmen: $16,110. Undergraduates: $12,982. *Scholarships, grants, and awards by category:* Academic interests/achievement: biological sciences, business, communication, education, English, foreign languages, general academic interests/achievements, health fields, humanities, mathematics, physical sciences, premedicine, social sciences. Creative arts/performance: art/fine arts, debating, journalism/publications, music, theater/drama. Special achievements/activities: community service, memberships, religious involvement. Special characteristics: children and siblings of alumni, children of faculty/staff, ethnic background, first-generation college students, general special characteristics, international students, relatives of clergy, veterans. *Tuition waivers:* Full or partial for employees or children of employees. *ROTC:* Army cooperative, Air Force cooperative.

LOANS *Student loans:* $13,686,617 (77% need-based, 23% non-need-based). 74% of past graduating class borrowed through all loan programs. *Average indebtedness per student:* $30,880. *Average need-based loan:* Freshmen: $5671. Undergraduates: $5266. *Parent loans:* $3,671,753 (25% need-based, 75% non-need-based). *Programs:* Federal Direct (Subsidized and Unsubsidized Stafford, PLUS), Perkins, private loans.

WORK-STUDY *Federal work-study:* Total amount: $1,728,013; jobs available. *State or other work-study/employment:* Total amount: $149,341 (6% need-based, 94% non-need-based). Part-time jobs available.

APPLYING FOR FINANCIAL AID *Required financial aid form:* FAFSA. *Financial aid deadline (priority):* 3/1. *Notification date:* Continuous beginning 3/1.

CONTACT Office of Financial Aid, Pacific University, 2043 College Way, Forest Grove, OR 97116-1797, 503-352-2222 or toll-free 877-722-8648. *E-mail:* financialaid@pacificu.edu. *Website:* http://www.pacificu.edu/.

PAIER COLLEGE OF ART, INC.
Hamden, CT

CONTACT Mr. John DeRose, Director of Financial Aid, Paier College of Art, Inc., 20 Gorham Avenue, Hamden, CT 06514-3902, 203-287-3034. *Fax:* 203-287-3021. *E-mail:* paier.art@snet.net. *Website:* http://www.paiercollegeofart.edu/.

PAINE COLLEGE
Augusta, GA

CONTACT Ms. Gerri Bogan, Director of Financial Aid, Paine College, 1235 15th Street, Augusta, GA 30901, 706-821-8262 or toll-free 800-476-7703. *Fax:* 706-821-8691. *E-mail:* bogang@mail.paine.edu. *Website:* http://www.paine.edu/.

PALM BEACH ATLANTIC UNIVERSITY
West Palm Beach, FL

Tuition & fees: $25,532	Average undergraduate aid package: $16,343

ABOUT THE INSTITUTION Independent nondenominational, coed. *Awards:* associate, bachelor's, master's, and doctoral degrees. 48 undergraduate majors. *Total enrollment:* 3,579. Undergraduates: 2,751. Freshmen: 445. Federal methodology is used as a basis for awarding need-based institutional aid.

UNDERGRADUATE EXPENSES for 2013–2014 *Application fee:* $50. *Comprehensive fee:* $33,882 includes full-time tuition ($25,232), mandatory fees ($300), and room and board ($8350). *College room only:* $4700. Full-time tuition and fees vary according to course load, degree level, location, and program. Room and board charges vary according to board plan and housing facility. *Part-time tuition:* $590 per credit. *Part-time fees:* $99 per term. Part-time tuition and fees vary according to course load, degree level, location, and program.

FRESHMAN FINANCIAL AID (Fall 2012, est.) 408 applied for aid; of those 81% were deemed to have need. 100% of freshmen with need received aid; of those 13% had need fully met. *Average percent of need met:* 63% (excluding resources awarded to replace EFC). *Average financial aid package:* $17,836 (excluding resources awarded to replace EFC). 26% of all full-time freshmen had no need and received non-need-based gift aid.

UNDERGRADUATE FINANCIAL AID (Fall 2012, est.) 1,959 applied for aid; of those 86% were deemed to have need. 100% of undergraduates with need received aid; of those 12% had need fully met. *Average percent of need met:* 57% (excluding resources awarded to replace EFC). *Average financial aid package:* $16,343 (excluding resources awarded to replace EFC). 19% of all full-time undergraduates had no need and received non-need-based gift aid.

GIFT AID (NEED-BASED) *Total amount:* $20,845,880 (22% federal, 17% state, 48% institutional, 13% external sources). *Receiving aid:* Freshmen: 74% (329); all full-time undergraduates: 76% (1,674). *Average award:* Freshmen: $15,229; Undergraduates: $12,958. *Scholarships, grants, and awards:* Federal Pell, FSEOG, state, private, college/university gift aid from institutional funds.

GIFT AID (NON-NEED-BASED) *Total amount:* $4,895,427 (18% state, 74% institutional, 8% external sources). *Receiving aid:* Freshmen: 8% (36). Undergraduates: 7% (146). *Average award:* Freshmen: $8285. Undergraduates: $7571. *Scholarships, grants, and awards by category: Academic interests/achievement:* general academic interests/achievements. *Creative arts/performance:* dance, music, theater/drama. *Special achievements/activities:* leadership. *Special characteristics:* adult students, children and siblings of alumni, children of current students, children of educators, children of faculty/staff, international students, out-of-state students, previous college experience, siblings of current students, spouses of current students. *Tuition waivers:* Full or partial for employees or children of employees. *ROTC:* Army cooperative.

LOANS *Student loans:* $13,613,751 (84% need-based, 16% non-need-based). 67% of past graduating class borrowed through all loan programs. *Average indebtedness per student:* $24,749. *Average need-based loan:* Freshmen: $3337. Undergraduates: $4168. *Parent loans:* $3,257,732 (49% need-based, 51% non-need-based). *Programs:* Federal Direct (Subsidized and Unsubsidized Stafford, PLUS), Perkins.

WORK-STUDY *Federal work-study:* Total amount: $410,700; 244 jobs averaging $2460. *State or other work-study/employment:* Total amount: $6000 (100% need-based). 5 part-time jobs averaging $2009.

ATHLETIC AWARDS Total amount: $1,478,915 (48% need-based, 52% non-need-based).

APPLYING FOR FINANCIAL AID *Required financial aid form:* FAFSA. *Financial aid deadline:* 8/1 (priority: 5/1). *Notification date:* Continuous beginning 2/15. Students must reply within 4 weeks of notification.

CONTACT Mr. Todd Martin, Director of Financial Aid, Palm Beach Atlantic University, PO Box 24708, West Palm Beach, FL 33416-4708, 561-803-2000 or toll-free 888-GO-TO-PBA. *Fax:* 561-803-2130. *E-mail:* finaid@pba.edu. *Website:* http://www.pba.edu/.

PALM BEACH STATE COLLEGE
Lake Worth, FL

CONTACT Financial Aid Office, Palm Beach State College, 4200 Congress Avenue, Lake Worth, FL 33461-4796, 561-967-7222. *Website:* http://www.palmbeachstate.edu/.

PALMER COLLEGE OF CHIROPRACTIC
Davenport, IA

CONTACT Ms. Jennifer Randazzo, Senior Director of Financial Planning, Palmer College of Chiropractic, 1000 Brady Street, Davenport, IA 52803, 563-884-5888 or toll-free 800-722-3648. *Fax:* 563-884-5299. *E-mail:* jennifer.randazzo@palmer.edu. *Website:* http://www.palmer.edu/.

PARK UNIVERSITY
Parkville, MO

Tuition & fees: $9900	Average undergraduate aid package: $10,512

ABOUT THE INSTITUTION Independent, coed. *Awards:* certificates, associate, bachelor's, and master's degrees. 44 undergraduate majors. *Total enrollment:* 2,458. Undergraduates: 1,674. Freshmen: 212. Federal methodology is used as a basis for awarding need-based institutional aid.

UNDERGRADUATE EXPENSES for 2013–2014 *Application fee:* $25. *Comprehensive fee:* $17,051 includes full-time tuition ($9800), mandatory fees ($100), and room and board ($7151). *College room only:* $3525. Full-time tuition and fees vary according to course load. Room and board charges vary according to housing facility. *Part-time tuition:* $350 per credit. Part-time tuition and fees vary according to course load.

FRESHMAN FINANCIAL AID (Fall 2011) 139 applied for aid; of those 78% were deemed to have need. 100% of freshmen with need received aid; of those 23% had need fully met. *Average percent of need met:* 71% (excluding resources awarded to replace EFC). *Average financial aid package:* $10,825 (excluding resources awarded to replace EFC). 10% of all full-time freshmen had no need and received non-need-based gift aid.

UNDERGRADUATE FINANCIAL AID (Fall 2011) 756 applied for aid; of those 79% were deemed to have need. 98% of undergraduates with need received aid; of those 16% had need fully met. *Average percent of need met:* 67% (excluding resources awarded to replace EFC). *Average financial aid package:* $10,512 (excluding resources awarded to replace EFC). 15% of all full-time undergraduates had no need and received non-need-based gift aid.

GIFT AID (NEED-BASED) *Total amount:* $17,246,901 (69% federal, 6% state, 9% institutional, 16% external sources). *Receiving aid:* Freshmen: 49% (85); all full-time undergraduates: 42% (423). *Average award:* Freshmen: $4588; Undergraduates: $4659. *Scholarships, grants, and awards:* Federal Pell, FSEOG, state, private, college/university gift aid from institutional funds.

GIFT AID (NON-NEED-BASED) *Total amount:* $7,709,443 (3% federal, 21% institutional, 76% external sources). *Receiving aid:* Freshmen: 48% (83). Undergraduates: 32% (324). *Average award:* Freshmen: $6374. Undergraduates: $8862. *Scholarships, grants, and awards by category:* Academic interests/achievement: 148 awards ($1,482,872 total): general academic interests/achievements. *Special achievements/activities:* 20 awards ($31,200 total): cheerleading/drum major. *Special characteristics:* 52 awards ($275,615 total): children of faculty/staff, religious affiliation, siblings of current students. *Tuition waivers:* Full or partial for employees or children of employees, senior citizens. *ROTC:* Army.

LOANS *Student loans:* $29,341,158 (82% need-based, 18% non-need-based). 35% of past graduating class borrowed through all loan programs. *Average indebtedness per student:* $21,558. *Average need-based loan:* Freshmen: $2921. Undergraduates: $4519. *Parent loans:* $315,477 (3% need-based, 97% non-need-based). *Programs:* Federal Direct (Subsidized and Unsubsidized Stafford, PLUS), Perkins, college/university.

WORK-STUDY *Federal work-study:* Total amount: $261,145; 104 jobs averaging $2496. *State or other work-study/employment:* Total amount: $502,848 (25% need-based, 75% non-need-based). 127 part-time jobs averaging $3306.

ATHLETIC AWARDS Total amount: $873,350 (40% need-based, 60% non-need-based).

APPLYING FOR FINANCIAL AID *Required financial aid forms:* FAFSA, institution's own form. *Financial aid deadline (priority):* 3/15. *Notification date:* Continuous beginning 2/15. Students must reply within 2 weeks of notification.

CONTACT Carla Boren, Director of Financial Aid, Park University, 8700 NW River Park Drive, Parkville, MO 64152, 816-584-6317 or toll-free 800-745-7275. Fax: 816-741-9668. E-mail: finaid@park.edu. *Website:* http://www.park.edu/.

PARSONS THE NEW SCHOOL FOR DESIGN
New York, NY

Tuition & fees: $40,140	Average undergraduate aid package: $25,665

ABOUT THE INSTITUTION Independent, coed. *Awards:* certificates, associate, bachelor's, and master's degrees. 13 undergraduate majors. *Total enrollment:* 4,916. Undergraduates: 717. Freshmen: 717. Federal methodology is used as a basis for awarding need-based institutional aid.

UNDERGRADUATE EXPENSES for 2013–2014 *Application fee:* $50. *Comprehensive fee:* $55,240 includes full-time tuition ($39,280), mandatory fees ($860), and room and board ($15,100). *Part-time tuition:* $1335 per credit hour.

FRESHMAN FINANCIAL AID (Fall 2011) 395 applied for aid; of those 85% were deemed to have need. 94% of freshmen with need received aid; of those 25% had need fully met. *Average percent of need met:* 65% (excluding resources awarded to replace EFC). *Average financial aid package:* $25,252 (excluding resources awarded to replace EFC). 8% of all full-time freshmen had no need and received non-need-based gift aid.

UNDERGRADUATE FINANCIAL AID (Fall 2011) 2,175 applied for aid; of those 91% were deemed to have need. 93% of undergraduates with need received aid; of those 13% had need fully met. *Average percent of need met:* 59% (excluding resources awarded to replace EFC). *Average financial aid package:* $25,665 (excluding resources awarded to replace EFC). 3% of all full-time undergraduates had no need and received non-need-based gift aid.

GIFT AID (NEED-BASED) *Total amount:* $33,075,665 (13% federal, 3% state, 82% institutional, 2% external sources). *Receiving aid:* Freshmen: 43% (304); all full-time undergraduates: 47% (1,788). *Average award:* Freshmen: $17,490; Undergraduates: $16,265. *Scholarships, grants, and awards:* Federal Pell, FSEOG, state, private, college/university gift aid from institutional funds.

GIFT AID (NON-NEED-BASED) *Total amount:* $10,619,380 (96% institutional, 4% external sources). *Receiving aid:* Freshmen: 8% (53). Undergraduates: 4% (144). *Average award:* Freshmen: $9315. Undergraduates: $6695. *Scholarships, grants, and awards by category:* Academic interests/achievement: general academic interests/achievements. Creative arts/performance: general creative arts/performance. Special achievements/activities: leadership. Special characteristics: members of minority groups.

LOANS *Student loans:* $18,577,342 (100% need-based). 56% of past graduating class borrowed through all loan programs. *Average indebtedness per student:* $32,715. *Average need-based loan:* Freshmen: $9495. Undergraduates: $9190. *Parent loans:* $10,334,282 (92% need-based, 8% non-need-based). *Programs:* Federal Direct (Subsidized and Unsubsidized Stafford, PLUS), Perkins.

WORK-STUDY *Federal work-study:* Total amount: $407,304; jobs available. *State or other work-study/employment:* Part-time jobs available.

APPLYING FOR FINANCIAL AID *Required financial aid forms:* FAFSA, state aid form. *Financial aid deadline:* Continuous. *Notification date:* Continuous beginning 4/1. Students must reply within 4 weeks of notification.

CONTACT Office of Student Financial Services, Parsons The New School for Design, 72 Fifth Avenue, New York, NY 10011, 212-229-8930 or toll-free 800-292-3040. E-mail: sfs@newschool.edu. *Website:* http://www.parsons.edu/.

PATRICK HENRY COLLEGE
Purcellville, VA

ABOUT THE INSTITUTION Independent nondenominational, coed. *Awards:* bachelor's degrees. 5 undergraduate majors. *Total enrollment:* 345. Undergraduates: 345. Freshmen: 72.

GIFT AID (NEED-BASED) *Scholarships, grants, and awards:* private, college/university gift aid from institutional funds.

GIFT AID (NON-NEED-BASED) *Scholarships, grants, and awards by category:* Academic interests/achievement: general academic interests/achievements. Creative arts/performance: debating, journalism/publications, music. Special achievements/activities: community service, leadership, memberships, religious involvement. Special characteristics: children of faculty/staff, children of public servants, public servants, relatives of clergy, veterans.

LOANS *Programs:* private loans.

APPLYING FOR FINANCIAL AID *Required financial aid form:* CSS Financial Aid PROFILE.

CONTACT Mrs. Christine W. Guenard, Associate Director of Financial Aid, Patrick Henry College, 10 Patrick Henry Circle, Purcellville, VA 20132, 540-441-8140. Fax: 540-441-8149. E-mail: cwguenard@phc.edu. *Website:* http://www.phc.edu/.

PATTEN UNIVERSITY
Oakland, CA

CONTACT Mr. Robert A. Olivera, Dean of Enrollment Services, Patten University, 2433 Coolidge Avenue, Oakland, CA 94601-2699, 510-261-8500 Ext. 783 or toll-free 877-4PATTEN. Fax: 510-534-8969. E-mail: oliverob@patten.edu. *Website:* http://www.patten.edu/.

PAUL QUINN COLLEGE
Dallas, TX

CONTACT Khaleelah Ali, Assistant Director of Financial Aid, Paul Quinn College, 3837 Simpson Stuart Road, Dallas, TX 75241, 214-302-3530 or toll-free 877-346-1063. *Fax:* 214-302-3535. *E-mail:* kali@pqc.edu. *Website:* http://www.pqc.edu/.

PAUL SMITH'S COLLEGE
Paul Smiths, NY

Tuition & fees: N/R	Average undergraduate aid package: $22,006

ABOUT THE INSTITUTION Independent, coed. 12 undergraduate majors. Federal methodology is used as a basis for awarding need-based institutional aid. **FRESHMAN FINANCIAL AID (Fall 2012, est.)** 283 applied for aid; of those 94% were deemed to have need. 100% of freshmen with need received aid; of those 13% had need fully met. *Average percent of need met:* 77% (excluding resources awarded to replace EFC). *Average financial aid package:* $22,576 (excluding resources awarded to replace EFC). 7% of all full-time freshmen had no need and received non-need-based gift aid. **UNDERGRADUATE FINANCIAL AID (Fall 2012, est.)** 999 applied for aid; of those 94% were deemed to have need. 100% of undergraduates with need received aid; of those 12% had need fully met. *Average percent of need met:* 76% (excluding resources awarded to replace EFC). *Average financial aid package:* $22,006 (excluding resources awarded to replace EFC). 10% of all full-time undergraduates had no need and received non-need-based gift aid. **GIFT AID (NEED-BASED)** *Total amount:* $15,515,739 (13% federal, 8% state, 68% institutional, 11% external sources). *Receiving aid:* Freshmen: 92% (266); all full-time undergraduates: 89% (937). *Average award:* Freshmen: $16,441; Undergraduates: $15,016. *Scholarships, grants, and awards:* Federal Pell, FSEOG, state, private, college/university gift aid from institutional funds. **GIFT AID (NON-NEED-BASED)** *Receiving aid:* Freshmen: 8% (22). Undergraduates: 8% (82). *Average award:* Freshmen: $9078. Undergraduates: $8615. *Scholarships, grants, and awards by category:* Academic interests/achievement: general academic interests/achievements. **LOANS** *Student loans:* $8,639,244 (100% need-based). 91% of past graduating class borrowed through all loan programs. *Average indebtedness per student:* $16,175. *Average need-based loan:* Freshmen: $4446. Undergraduates: $5379. *Parent loans:* $3,580,698 (100% need-based). *Programs:* Federal Direct (Subsidized and Unsubsidized Stafford, PLUS), Perkins. **WORK-STUDY** *Federal work-study:* Total amount: $1,942,104; 828 jobs averaging $2500. *State or other work-study/employment:* Part-time jobs available. **APPLYING FOR FINANCIAL AID** *Required financial aid forms:* FAFSA, state aid form. *Financial aid deadline (priority):* 3/15. *Notification date:* Continuous. Students must reply within 4 weeks of notification. **CONTACT** Mary Ellen Chamberlain, Director of Financial Aid, Paul Smith's College, Routes 86 and 30, Paul Smiths, NY 12970, 518-327-6119 or toll-free 800-421-2605. *Fax:* 518-327-6055. *E-mail:* mchamberlain@paulsmiths.edu. *Website:* http://www.paulsmiths.edu/.

PEABODY CONSERVATORY OF THE JOHNS HOPKINS UNIVERSITY
Baltimore, MD

Tuition & fees: $38,915	Average undergraduate aid package: $16,339

ABOUT THE INSTITUTION Independent, coed. *Awards:* certificates, diplomas, bachelor's, master's, and doctoral degrees. 9 undergraduate majors. *Total enrollment:* 686. Undergraduates: 312. Freshmen: 61. Federal methodology is used as a basis for awarding need-based institutional aid.

UNDERGRADUATE EXPENSES for 2013–2014 *Application fee:* $100. *One-time required fee:* $700. *Comprehensive fee:* $51,595 includes full-time tuition ($38,450), mandatory fees ($465), and room and board ($12,680). Full-time tuition and fees vary according to program. Room and board charges vary according to board plan. *Part-time tuition:* $1097 per semester hour. Part-time tuition and fees vary according to course load. **FRESHMAN FINANCIAL AID (Fall 2012, est.)** 54 applied for aid; of those 83% were deemed to have need. 100% of freshmen with need received aid; of those 18% had need fully met. *Average percent of need met:* 75% (excluding resources awarded to replace EFC). *Average financial aid package:* $18,100 (excluding resources awarded to replace EFC). 16% of all full-time freshmen had no need and received non-need-based gift aid. **UNDERGRADUATE FINANCIAL AID (Fall 2012, est.)** 199 applied for aid; of those 86% were deemed to have need. 97% of undergraduates with need received aid; of those 25% had need fully met. *Average percent of need met:* 74% (excluding resources awarded to replace EFC). *Average financial aid package:* $16,339 (excluding resources awarded to replace EFC). 27% of all full-time undergraduates had no need and received non-need-based gift aid. **GIFT AID (NEED-BASED)** *Total amount:* $3,886,394 (11% federal, 2% state, 85% institutional, 2% external sources). *Receiving aid:* Freshmen: 57% (33); all full-time undergraduates: 50% (150). *Average award:* Freshmen: $15,023; Undergraduates: $12,778. *Scholarships, grants, and awards:* Federal Pell, FSEOG, state, private, college/university gift aid from institutional funds. **GIFT AID (NON-NEED-BASED)** *Total amount:* $1,538,184 (97% institutional, 3% external sources). *Receiving aid:* Freshmen: 14% (8). Undergraduates: 27% (82). *Average award:* Freshmen: $15,930. Undergraduates: $18,524. *Scholarships, grants, and awards by category:* Creative arts/performance: music. **LOANS** *Student loans:* $1,831,190 (89% need-based, 11% non-need-based). 46% of past graduating class borrowed through all loan programs. *Average indebtedness per student:* $33,961. *Average need-based loan:* Freshmen: $4431. Undergraduates: $5478. *Parent loans:* $634,932 (100% need-based). *Programs:* Federal Direct (Subsidized and Unsubsidized Stafford, PLUS), Perkins, college/university. **WORK-STUDY** *Federal work-study:* Total amount: $172,480; 103 jobs averaging $1892. **APPLYING FOR FINANCIAL AID** *Required financial aid form:* FAFSA. *Financial aid deadline (priority):* 3/1. *Notification date:* 4/1. Students must reply by 5/1. **CONTACT** Rebecca Polgar, Director of Financial Aid, Peabody Conservatory of The Johns Hopkins University, 1 East Mount Vernon Place, Baltimore, MD 21202-2397, 410-234-4900 or toll-free 800-368-2521 (out-of-state). *Fax:* 410-783-7785. *E-mail:* finaid@peabody.jhu.edu. *Website:* http://www.peabody.jhu.edu/.

PEIRCE COLLEGE
Philadelphia, PA

Tuition & fees: $16,500	Average undergraduate aid package: $9438

ABOUT THE INSTITUTION Independent, coed, primarily women. *Awards:* certificates, associate, and bachelor's degrees. 10 undergraduate majors. *Total enrollment:* 2,261. Undergraduates: 2,261. Freshmen: 135. Federal methodology is used as a basis for awarding need-based institutional aid. **UNDERGRADUATE EXPENSES** for 2013–2014 *Application fee:* $50. *Tuition:* full-time $15,450; part-time $515 per credit hour. *Required fees:* full-time $1050; $105 per course. **FRESHMAN FINANCIAL AID (Fall 2011)** 23 applied for aid; of those 91% were deemed to have need. 100% of freshmen with need received aid. *Average percent of need met:* 35% (excluding resources awarded to replace EFC). *Average financial aid package:* $7343 (excluding resources awarded to replace EFC). 4% of all full-time freshmen had no need and received non-need-based gift aid. **UNDERGRADUATE FINANCIAL AID (Fall 2011)** 675 applied for aid; of those 98% were deemed to have need. 99% of undergraduates with need received aid; of those 1% had need fully met. *Average percent of need met:* 39% (excluding resources awarded to replace EFC). *Average financial aid package:* $9438 (excluding resources awarded to replace EFC). 4% of all full-time undergraduates had no need and received non-need-based gift aid.

GIFT AID (NEED-BASED) *Total amount:* $5,810,184 (71% federal, 15% state, 13% institutional, 1% external sources). *Receiving aid:* Freshmen: 79% (19); all full-time undergraduates: 83% (591). *Average award:* Freshmen: $3997; Undergraduates: $5026. *Scholarships, grants, and awards:* Federal Pell, FSEOG, state, private, college/university gift aid from institutional funds.
GIFT AID (NON-NEED-BASED) *Total amount:* $151,362 (99% institutional, 1% external sources). *Receiving aid:* Freshmen: 38% (9). Undergraduates: 3. *Average award:* Freshmen: $2599. Undergraduates: $2290. *Scholarships, grants, and awards by category:* Academic interests/achievement: 52 awards ($94,259 total): business, computer science, general academic interests/achievements, health fields. *Special achievements/activities:* 11 awards ($22,546 total): leadership, memberships. *Special characteristics:* 116 awards ($222,022 total): children and siblings of alumni, children of faculty/staff, children of public servants, international students, public servants, siblings of current students, veterans, veterans' children. *Tuition waivers:* Full or partial for children of alumni, employees or children of employees.
LOANS *Student loans:* $16,712,603 (92% need-based, 8% non-need-based). 79% of past graduating class borrowed through all loan programs. *Average need-based loan:* Freshmen: $3983. Undergraduates: $5013. *Parent loans:* $179,660 (85% need-based, 15% non-need-based). *Programs:* Federal Direct (Subsidized and Unsubsidized Stafford, PLUS).
WORK-STUDY *Federal work-study:* Total amount: $133,363; 54 jobs averaging $2626.
APPLYING FOR FINANCIAL AID *Required financial aid form:* FAFSA. *Financial aid deadline:* Continuous. *Notification date:* Continuous beginning 5/1.
CONTACT Chanel Greene, Manager of Financial Aid, Peirce College, 1420 Pine Street, Philadelphia, PA 19102, 215-670-9330 or toll-free 888-467-3472. Fax: 215-545-3671. *E-mail:* cgreen1@peirce.edu. *Website:* http://www.peirce.edu/.

PENN FOSTER COLLEGE
Scottsdale, AZ

CONTACT Financial Aid Office, Penn Foster College, 14300 North Northsight Boulevard, Suite 120, Scottsdale, AZ 85260, 480-947-6644 or toll-free 800-471-3232. *Website:* http://www.pennfostercollege.edu/.

PENN STATE ABINGTON
Abington, PA

Tuition & fees (area res): $13,356	Average undergraduate aid package: $10,042

ABOUT THE INSTITUTION State-related, coed. *Awards:* certificates, associate, and bachelor's degrees (enrollment figures include students enrolled at The Graduate School at Penn State who are taking courses at this location). 118 undergraduate majors. *Total enrollment:* 3,516. Undergraduates: 3,506. Freshmen: 691. Federal methodology is used as a basis for awarding need-based institutional aid.
UNDERGRADUATE EXPENSES for 2013–2014 *Application fee:* $50. *Tuition, area resident:* full-time $12,474; part-time $504 per credit hour. *Tuition, state resident:* full-time $12,474; part-time $504 per credit hour. *Tuition, nonresident:* full-time $19,030; part-time $793 per credit hour. *Required fees:* full-time $882. Full-time tuition and fees vary according to course level, degree level, location, program, and student level. Part-time tuition and fees vary according to course level, course load, degree level, location, program, and student level.
FRESHMAN FINANCIAL AID (Fall 2011) 734 applied for aid; of those 82% were deemed to have need. 98% of freshmen with need received aid; of those 3% had need fully met. *Average percent of need met:* 61% (excluding resources awarded to replace EFC). *Average financial aid package:* $9830 (excluding resources awarded to replace EFC). 4% of all full-time freshmen had no need and received non-need-based gift aid.
UNDERGRADUATE FINANCIAL AID (Fall 2011) 2,305 applied for aid; of those 85% were deemed to have need. 99% of undergraduates with need received aid; of those 3% had need fully met. *Average percent of need met:* 61% (excluding resources awarded to replace EFC). *Average financial aid package:* $10,042

(excluding resources awarded to replace EFC). 3% of all full-time undergraduates had no need and received non-need-based gift aid.
GIFT AID (NEED-BASED) *Total amount:* $12,974,460 (54% federal, 31% state, 12% institutional, 3% external sources). *Receiving aid:* Freshmen: 61% (492); all full-time undergraduates: 58% (1,565). *Average award:* Freshmen: $7794; Undergraduates: $7090. *Scholarships, grants, and awards:* Federal Pell, FSEOG, state, private, college/university gift aid from institutional funds.
GIFT AID (NON-NEED-BASED) *Total amount:* $932,831 (52% federal, 1% state, 23% institutional, 24% external sources). *Receiving aid:* Freshmen: 32% (253). Undergraduates: 16% (417). *Average award:* Freshmen: $1627. Undergraduates: $1645. *Scholarships, grants, and awards by category:* Academic interests/achievement: general academic interests/achievements. *Special characteristics:* children and siblings of alumni, general special characteristics. *Tuition waivers:* Full or partial for employees or children of employees, senior citizens. *ROTC:* Army, Air Force cooperative.
LOANS *Student loans:* $16,556,123 (85% need-based, 15% non-need-based). 66% of past graduating class borrowed through all loan programs. *Average indebtedness per student:* $35,100. *Average need-based loan:* Freshmen: $3257. Undergraduates: $4054. *Parent loans:* $1,957,094 (70% need-based, 30% non-need-based). *Programs:* Federal Direct (Subsidized and Unsubsidized Stafford, PLUS), Perkins, college/university, private loans.
WORK-STUDY *Federal work-study:* Total amount: $80,886; jobs available.
ATHLETIC AWARDS Total amount: $2393 (100% non-need-based).
APPLYING FOR FINANCIAL AID *Required financial aid form:* FAFSA. *Financial aid deadline (priority):* 2/15. *Notification date:* Continuous.
CONTACT Student Aid Office, Penn State Abington, 1600 Woodland Road, Abington, PA 19001-3990, 215-881-7348. *Fax:* 215-881-7655. *Website:* http://www.abington.psu.edu/.

PENN STATE ALTOONA
Altoona, PA

Tuition & fees (area res): $13,900	Average undergraduate aid package: $9636

ABOUT THE INSTITUTION State-related, coed. *Awards:* certificates, associate, and bachelor's degrees (enrollment figures include students enrolled at The Graduate School at Penn State who are taking courses at this location). 125 undergraduate majors. *Total enrollment:* 3,863. Undergraduates: 3,863. Freshmen: 1,379. Federal methodology is used as a basis for awarding need-based institutional aid.
UNDERGRADUATE EXPENSES for 2013–2014 *Application fee:* $50. *Tuition, area resident:* full-time $13,018; part-time $542 per credit hour. *Tuition, state resident:* full-time $13,018; part-time $542 per credit hour. *Tuition, nonresident:* full-time $19,912; part-time $830 per credit hour. *Required fees:* full-time $882. Full-time tuition and fees vary according to course level, degree level, location, program, and student level. Part-time tuition and fees vary according to course level, course load, degree level, location, program, and student level. *College room and board:* $9690; *Room only:* $4910. Room and board charges vary according to board plan, housing facility, and location.
FRESHMAN FINANCIAL AID (Fall 2011) 1,360 applied for aid; of those 80% were deemed to have need. 97% of freshmen with need received aid; of those 5% had need fully met. *Average percent of need met:* 57% (excluding resources awarded to replace EFC). *Average financial aid package:* $8480 (excluding resources awarded to replace EFC). 3% of all full-time freshmen had no need and received non-need-based gift aid.
UNDERGRADUATE FINANCIAL AID (Fall 2011) 3,255 applied for aid; of those 85% were deemed to have need. 98% of undergraduates with need received aid; of those 5% had need fully met. *Average percent of need met:* 60% (excluding resources awarded to replace EFC). *Average financial aid package:* $9636 (excluding resources awarded to replace EFC). 3% of all full-time undergraduates had no need and received non-need-based gift aid.
GIFT AID (NEED-BASED) *Total amount:* $14,201,216 (50% federal, 31% state, 14% institutional, 5% external sources). *Receiving aid:* Freshmen: 42% (658); all full-time undergraduates: 47% (1,816). *Average award:* Freshmen: $6044; Undergraduates: $6001. *Scholarships, grants, and awards:* Federal Pell, FSEOG, state, private, college/university gift aid from institutional funds.
GIFT AID (NON-NEED-BASED) *Total amount:* $918,336 (47% federal, 4% state, 16% institutional, 33% external sources). *Receiving aid:* Freshmen: 22% (344).

Undergraduates: 23% (882). *Average award:* Freshmen: $926. Undergraduates: $1322. *Scholarships, grants, and awards by category: Academic interests/ achievement:* general academic interests/achievements. *Special characteristics:* children and siblings of alumni, general special characteristics. *Tuition waivers:* Full or partial for employees or children of employees. *ROTC:* Army, Air Force.
LOANS *Student loans:* $24,063,324 (88% need-based, 12% non-need-based). 66% of past graduating class borrowed through all loan programs. *Average indebtedness per student:* $35,100. *Average need-based loan:* Freshmen: $3378. Undergraduates: $4015. *Parent loans:* $9,394,799 (86% need-based, 14% non-need-based). *Programs:* Federal Direct (Subsidized and Unsubsidized Stafford, PLUS), Perkins, college/university, private loans.
WORK-STUDY *Federal work-study:* Total amount: $332,658; jobs available.
APPLYING FOR FINANCIAL AID *Required financial aid form:* FAFSA. *Financial aid deadline (priority):* 2/15. *Notification date:* Continuous beginning 3/1.
CONTACT Mr. David Pearlman, Director of Student Aid, Penn State Altoona, W113 Smith Building, Altoona, PA 16601-3760, 814-949-5055 or toll-free 800-848-9843. *Fax:* 814-949-5536. *E-mail:* dpp1@psu.edu.
Website: http://www.aa.psu.edu/.

PENN STATE BERKS
Reading, PA

Tuition & fees (area res): $13,900	Average undergraduate aid package: $9395

ABOUT THE INSTITUTION State-related, coed. *Awards:* certificates, associate, and bachelor's degrees (enrollment figures include students enrolled at The Graduate School at Penn State who are taking courses at this location). 129 undergraduate majors. *Total enrollment:* 2,747. Undergraduates: 2,743. Freshmen: 814. Federal methodology is used as a basis for awarding need-based institutional aid.
UNDERGRADUATE EXPENSES for 2013–2014 *Application fee:* $50. *Tuition, area resident:* full-time $13,018; part-time $542 per credit hour. *Tuition, state resident:* full-time $13,018; part-time $542 per credit hour. *Tuition, nonresident:* full-time $19,912; part-time $830 per credit hour. *Required fees:* full-time $882. Full-time tuition and fees vary according to course level, degree level, location, program, and student level. Part-time tuition and fees vary according to course level, course load, degree level, location, program, and student level. *College room and board:* $10,560; *Room only:* $5780. Room and board charges vary according to board plan, housing facility, and location.
FRESHMAN FINANCIAL AID (Fall 2011) 750 applied for aid; of those 83% were deemed to have need. 95% of freshmen with need received aid; of those 4% had need fully met. *Average percent of need met:* 56% (excluding resources awarded to replace EFC). *Average financial aid package:* $8195 (excluding resources awarded to replace EFC). 2% of all full-time freshmen had no need and received non-need-based gift aid.
UNDERGRADUATE FINANCIAL AID (Fall 2011) 2,118 applied for aid; of those 84% were deemed to have need. 97% of undergraduates with need received aid; of those 4% had need fully met. *Average percent of need met:* 60% (excluding resources awarded to replace EFC). *Average financial aid package:* $9395 (excluding resources awarded to replace EFC). 2% of all full-time undergraduates had no need and received non-need-based gift aid.
GIFT AID (NEED-BASED) *Total amount:* $9,503,029 (48% federal, 33% state, 15% institutional, 4% external sources). *Receiving aid:* Freshmen: 43% (366); all full-time undergraduates: 49% (1,223). *Average award:* Freshmen: $6489; Undergraduates: $6351. *Scholarships, grants, and awards:* Federal Pell, FSEOG, state, private, college/university gift aid from institutional funds.
GIFT AID (NON-NEED-BASED) *Total amount:* $608,281 (56% federal, 1% state, 27% institutional, 16% external sources). *Receiving aid:* Freshmen: 17% (147). Undergraduates: 15% (366). *Average award:* Freshmen: $1839. Undergraduates: $2214. *Scholarships, grants, and awards by category: Academic interests/ achievement:* general academic interests/achievements. *Special characteristics:* children and siblings of alumni. *Tuition waivers:* Full or partial for employees or children of employees. *ROTC:* Army cooperative.
LOANS *Student loans:* $16,319,575 (87% need-based, 13% non-need-based). 66% of past graduating class borrowed through all loan programs. *Average indebtedness per student:* $35,100. *Average need-based loan:* Freshmen: $3332. Undergrad-

uates: $4095. *Parent loans:* $6,087,419 (85% need-based, 15% non-need-based).
Programs: Federal Direct (Subsidized and Unsubsidized Stafford, PLUS), Perkins, college/university, private loans.
WORK-STUDY *Federal work-study:* Total amount: $93,532; jobs available.
APPLYING FOR FINANCIAL AID *Required financial aid form:* FAFSA. *Financial aid deadline (priority):* 2/15. *Notification date:* Continuous beginning 3/1.
CONTACT Judith A. Rile, Financial Aid Coordinator, Penn State Berks, Perkins Student Center, Room 6, Reading, PA 19610-6009, 610-396-6070. *Fax:* 610-396-6316. *E-mail:* jar38@psu.edu.
Website: http://www.bk.psu.edu/.

PENN STATE ERIE, THE BEHREND COLLEGE
Erie, PA

Tuition & fees (area res): $13,900	Average undergraduate aid package: $9771

ABOUT THE INSTITUTION State-related, coed. *Awards:* certificates, associate, bachelor's, and master's degrees. 129 undergraduate majors. *Total enrollment:* 4,149. Undergraduates: 4,065. Freshmen: 1,080. Federal methodology is used as a basis for awarding need-based institutional aid.
UNDERGRADUATE EXPENSES for 2013–2014 *Application fee:* $50. *Tuition, area resident:* full-time $13,018; part-time $542 per credit hour. *Tuition, state resident:* full-time $13,018; part-time $542 per credit hour. *Tuition, nonresident:* full-time $19,912; part-time $830 per credit hour. *Required fees:* full-time $882. Full-time tuition and fees vary according to course level, degree level, location, program, and student level. Part-time tuition and fees vary according to course level, course load, degree level, location, program, and student level. *College room and board:* $9690; *Room only:* $4910. Room and board charges vary according to board plan, housing facility, and location.
FRESHMAN FINANCIAL AID (Fall 2011) 981 applied for aid; of those 82% were deemed to have need. 96% of freshmen with need received aid; of those 4% had need fully met. *Average percent of need met:* 61% (excluding resources awarded to replace EFC). *Average financial aid package:* $8815 (excluding resources awarded to replace EFC). 2% of all full-time freshmen had no need and received non-need-based gift aid.
UNDERGRADUATE FINANCIAL AID (Fall 2011) 3,236 applied for aid; of those 87% were deemed to have need. 98% of undergraduates with need received aid; of those 4% had need fully met. *Average percent of need met:* 61% (excluding resources awarded to replace EFC). *Average financial aid package:* $9771 (excluding resources awarded to replace EFC). 3% of all full-time undergraduates had no need and received non-need-based gift aid.
GIFT AID (NEED-BASED) *Total amount:* $15,598,161 (42% federal, 32% state, 20% institutional, 6% external sources). *Receiving aid:* Freshmen: 48% (519); all full-time undergraduates: 51% (1,895). *Average award:* Freshmen: $6254; Undergraduates: $6129. *Scholarships, grants, and awards:* Federal Pell, FSEOG, state, private, college/university gift aid from institutional funds.
GIFT AID (NON-NEED-BASED) *Total amount:* $791,190 (27% federal, 48% institutional, 25% external sources). *Receiving aid:* Freshmen: 25% (268). Undergraduates: 22% (803). *Average award:* Freshmen: $1752. Undergraduates: $3860. *Scholarships, grants, and awards by category: Academic interests/ achievement:* general academic interests/achievements. *Special characteristics:* children and siblings of alumni. *Tuition waivers:* Full or partial for employees or children of employees. *ROTC:* Army.
LOANS *Student loans:* $26,779,997 (90% need-based, 10% non-need-based). 66% of past graduating class borrowed through all loan programs. *Average indebtedness per student:* $35,100. *Average need-based loan:* Freshmen: $3384. Undergraduates: $4323. *Parent loans:* $10,382,071 (89% need-based, 11% non-need-based). *Programs:* Federal Direct (Subsidized and Unsubsidized Stafford, PLUS), Perkins, college/university, private loans.
WORK-STUDY *Federal work-study:* Total amount: $313,930; jobs available.
APPLYING FOR FINANCIAL AID *Required financial aid form:* FAFSA. *Financial aid deadline (priority):* 2/15. *Notification date:* Continuous beginning 3/1.

CONTACT Ms. Jane Brady, Associate Director of Financial Aid, Penn State Erie, The Behrend College, 4851 College Drive, Metzgar Admissions and Alumni Center, Erie, PA 16563, 814-898-6162 or toll-free 866-374-3378. *Fax:* 814-898-7595. *E-mail:* jub9@psu.edu.
Website: http://www.pserie.psu.edu/.

PENN STATE HARRISBURG
Middletown, PA

Tuition & fees (area res): $13,900	Average undergraduate aid package: $10,542

ABOUT THE INSTITUTION State-related, coed. *Awards:* certificates, associate, bachelor's, master's, and doctoral degrees. 29 undergraduate majors. *Total enrollment:* 4,376. Undergraduates: 3,426. Freshmen: 628. Federal methodology is used as a basis for awarding need-based institutional aid.
UNDERGRADUATE EXPENSES for 2013–2014 *Application fee:* $50. *Tuition, area resident:* full-time $13,018; part-time $542 per credit hour. *Tuition, state resident:* full-time $13,018; part-time $542 per credit hour. *Tuition, nonresident:* full-time $19,912; part-time $830 per credit hour. *Required fees:* full-time $882. Full-time tuition and fees vary according to course level, degree level, location, program, and student level. Part-time tuition and fees vary according to course load, degree level, location, program, and student level. *College room and board:* $11,000; *Room only:* $6220. Room and board charges vary according to board plan, housing facility, and location.
FRESHMAN FINANCIAL AID (Fall 2011) 443 applied for aid; of those 83% were deemed to have need. 97% of freshmen with need received aid; of those 7% had need fully met. *Average percent of need met:* 62% (excluding resources awarded to replace EFC). *Average financial aid package:* $9202 (excluding resources awarded to replace EFC). 2% of all full-time freshmen had no need and received non-need-based gift aid.
UNDERGRADUATE FINANCIAL AID (Fall 2011) 2,128 applied for aid; of those 88% were deemed to have need. 98% of undergraduates with need received aid; of those 6% had need fully met. *Average percent of need met:* 59% (excluding resources awarded to replace EFC). *Average financial aid package:* $10,542 (excluding resources awarded to replace EFC). 2% of all full-time undergraduates had no need and received non-need-based gift aid.
GIFT AID (NEED-BASED) *Total amount:* $11,503,760 (54% federal, 28% state, 13% institutional, 5% external sources). *Receiving aid:* Freshmen: 41% (221); all full-time undergraduates: 47% (1,238). *Average award:* Freshmen: $6820; Undergraduates: $6432. *Scholarships, grants, and awards:* Federal Pell, FSEOG, state, private, college/university gift aid from institutional funds.
GIFT AID (NON-NEED-BASED) *Total amount:* $941,407 (67% federal, 4% state, 11% institutional, 18% external sources). *Receiving aid:* Freshmen: 23% (122). Undergraduates: 19% (499). *Average award:* Freshmen: $1864. Undergraduates: $1522. *Scholarships, grants, and awards by category:* Academic interests/achievement: general academic interests/achievements. *Special characteristics:* children and siblings of alumni, general special characteristics. *Tuition waivers:* Full or partial for employees or children of employees. *ROTC:* Army cooperative.
LOANS *Student loans:* $19,879,236 (90% need-based, 10% non-need-based). 66% of past graduating class borrowed through all loan programs. *Average indebtedness per student:* $35,100. *Average need-based loan:* Freshmen: $3300. Undergraduates: $4505. *Parent loans:* $4,936,902 (88% need-based, 12% non-need-based). *Programs:* Federal Direct (Subsidized and Unsubsidized Stafford, PLUS), Perkins, college/university, private loans.
WORK-STUDY *Federal work-study:* Total amount: $83,797; jobs available.
APPLYING FOR FINANCIAL AID *Required financial aid form:* FAFSA. *Financial aid deadline (priority):* 2/15. *Notification date:* Continuous beginning 3/1.
CONTACT Student Aid Office, Penn State Harrisburg, 777 West Harrisburg Pike, Middletown, PA 17057-4898, 717-948-6307 or toll-free 800-222-2056. *Fax:* 717-948-6008. *E-mail:* hbgfinaid@psu.edu.
Website: http://www.hbg.psu.edu/.

PENN STATE SHENANGO
Sharon, PA

Tuition & fees (PA res): $13,244	Average undergraduate aid package: $12,880

ABOUT THE INSTITUTION State-related, coed. *Awards:* certificates, associate, and bachelor's degrees. 124 undergraduate majors. *Total enrollment:* 578. Undergraduates: 578. Freshmen: 90. Federal methodology is used as a basis for awarding need-based institutional aid.
UNDERGRADUATE EXPENSES for 2013–2014 *Application fee:* $50. *Tuition, state resident:* full-time $12,474; part-time $504 per credit. *Tuition, nonresident:* full-time $19,030; part-time $793 per credit. *Required fees:* full-time $770. Full-time tuition and fees vary according to course level, degree level, location, program, and student level. Part-time tuition and fees vary according to course level, course load, degree level, location, program, and student level.
FRESHMAN FINANCIAL AID (Fall 2011) 91 applied for aid; of those 96% were deemed to have need. 99% of freshmen with need received aid; of those 1% had need fully met. *Average percent of need met:* 63% (excluding resources awarded to replace EFC). *Average financial aid package:* $11,264 (excluding resources awarded to replace EFC). 3% of all full-time freshmen had no need and received non-need-based gift aid.
UNDERGRADUATE FINANCIAL AID (Fall 2011) 354 applied for aid; of those 96% were deemed to have need. 100% of undergraduates with need received aid; of those 3% had need fully met. *Average percent of need met:* 63% (excluding resources awarded to replace EFC). *Average financial aid package:* $12,880 (excluding resources awarded to replace EFC). 3% of all full-time undergraduates had no need and received non-need-based gift aid.
GIFT AID (NEED-BASED) *Total amount:* $3,611,750 (44% federal, 20% state, 30% institutional, 6% external sources). *Receiving aid:* Freshmen: 84% (77); all full-time undergraduates: 83% (304). *Average award:* Freshmen: $6643; Undergraduates: $6864. *Scholarships, grants, and awards:* Federal Pell, FSEOG, state, private, college/university gift aid from institutional funds.
GIFT AID (NON-NEED-BASED) *Total amount:* $90,529 (7% federal, 73% institutional, 20% external sources). *Receiving aid:* Freshmen: 55% (51). Undergraduates: 45% (165). *Average award:* Freshmen: $1740. Undergraduates: $2060. *Scholarships, grants, and awards by category:* Academic interests/achievement: general academic interests/achievements. *Special characteristics:* children and siblings of alumni. *Tuition waivers:* Full or partial for employees or children of employees.
LOANS *Student loans:* $3,948,875 (96% need-based, 4% non-need-based). 66% of past graduating class borrowed through all loan programs. *Average indebtedness per student:* $35,100. *Average need-based loan:* Freshmen: $3392. Undergraduates: $4145. *Parent loans:* $114,710 (81% need-based, 19% non-need-based). *Programs:* Federal Direct (Subsidized and Unsubsidized Stafford, PLUS), Perkins, college/university, private loans.
WORK-STUDY *Federal work-study:* Total amount: $71,268; jobs available. *State or other work-study/employment:* Part-time jobs available.
APPLYING FOR FINANCIAL AID *Required financial aid form:* FAFSA. *Financial aid deadline (priority):* 2/15. *Notification date:* Continuous beginning 3/1.
CONTACT Shawn O'Neill, Financial Aid Coordinator, Penn State Shenango, Lecture Hall, Room 225, 147 Shenango Avenue, Sharon, PA 16146, 724-983-2804. *E-mail:* swo3@psu.edu.
Website: http://www.shenango.psu.edu/.

PENN STATE UNIVERSITY PARK
State College, PA

Tuition & fees (PA res): $16,444	Average undergraduate aid package: $10,552

ABOUT THE INSTITUTION State-related, coed. *Awards:* certificates, associate, bachelor's, master's, and doctoral degrees. 126 undergraduate majors. *Total enrollment:* 45,783. Undergraduates: 39,192. Freshmen: 7,649. Federal methodology is used as a basis for awarding need-based institutional aid.
UNDERGRADUATE EXPENSES for 2013–2014 *Application fee:* $50. *Tuition, state resident:* full-time $15,562; part-time $648 per credit. *Tuition,*

nonresident: full-time $27,864; part-time $1161 per credit. *Required fees:* full-time $882. Full-time tuition and fees vary according to course level, degree level, location, program, and student level. Part-time tuition and fees vary according to course level, course load, degree level, location, program, and student level. *College room and board:* $9690; *Room only:* $4910. Room and board charges vary according to board plan, housing facility, and location.
FRESHMAN FINANCIAL AID (Fall 2011) 5,374 applied for aid; of those 69% were deemed to have need. 93% of freshmen with need received aid; of those 8% had need fully met. *Average percent of need met:* 59% (excluding resources awarded to replace EFC). *Average financial aid package:* $9481 (excluding resources awarded to replace EFC). 7% of all full-time freshmen had no need and received non-need-based gift aid.
UNDERGRADUATE FINANCIAL AID (Fall 2011) 24,671 applied for aid; of those 80% were deemed to have need. 97% of undergraduates with need received aid; of those 8% had need fully met. *Average percent of need met:* 61% (excluding resources awarded to replace EFC). *Average financial aid package:* $10,552 (excluding resources awarded to replace EFC). 8% of all full-time undergraduates had no need and received non-need-based gift aid.
GIFT AID (NEED-BASED) *Total amount:* $103,839,779 (38% federal, 23% state, 31% institutional, 8% external sources). *Receiving aid:* Freshmen: 22% (1,645); all full-time undergraduates: 28% (10,467). *Average award:* Freshmen: $6655; Undergraduates: $6524. *Scholarships, grants, and awards:* Federal Pell, FSEOG, state, private, college/university gift aid from institutional funds.
GIFT AID (NON-NEED-BASED) *Total amount:* $36,322,645 (18% federal, 26% institutional, 56% external sources). *Receiving aid:* Freshmen: 21% (1,526). Undergraduates: 17% (6,496). *Average award:* Freshmen: $3532. Undergraduates: $3153. *Scholarships, grants, and awards by category: Academic interests/achievement:* general academic interests/achievements. *Tuition waivers:* Full or partial for employees or children of employees. *ROTC:* Army, Naval, Air Force.
LOANS *Student loans:* $213,352,818 (85% need-based, 15% non-need-based). 66% of past graduating class borrowed through all loan programs. *Average indebtedness per student:* $35,100. *Average need-based loan:* Freshmen: $3380. Undergraduates: $4693. *Parent loans:* $109,839,343 (83% need-based, 17% non-need-based). *Programs:* Federal Direct (Subsidized and Unsubsidized Stafford, PLUS), Perkins, college/university, private loans.
WORK-STUDY *Federal work-study:* Total amount: $1,683,968; 869 jobs averaging $1911.
ATHLETIC AWARDS Total amount: $12,987,015 (44% need-based, 56% non-need-based).
APPLYING FOR FINANCIAL AID *Required financial aid form:* FAFSA. *Financial aid deadline (priority):* 2/15. *Notification date:* Continuous.
CONTACT Ms. Anna Griswold, Assistant Vice President for Undergraduate Education and Executive Director for Student Aid, Penn State University Park, 311 Shields Building, University Park, PA 16802, 814-863-0507. *Fax:* 814-863-0322. *E-mail:* amg5@psu.edu.
Website: http://www.psu.edu/.

PENNSYLVANIA ACADEMY OF THE FINE ARTS
Philadelphia, PA

CONTACT Financial Aid Office, Pennsylvania Academy of the Fine Arts, 128 North Broad Street, Philadelphia, PA 19102, 215-972-7600.
Website: http://www.pafa.edu/.

PENNSYLVANIA COLLEGE OF ART & DESIGN
Lancaster, PA

CONTACT J. David Hershey, Registrar/Director of Financial Aid, Pennsylvania College of Art & Design, 204 North Prince Street, PO Box 59, Lancaster, PA 17608-0059, 717-396-7833 Ext. 13. *Fax:* 717-396-1339. *E-mail:* finaid@pcad.edu.
Website: http://www.pcad.edu/.

PENNSYLVANIA COLLEGE OF TECHNOLOGY
Williamsport, PA

Tuition & fees (PA res): $14,370 — Average undergraduate aid package: $15,034

ABOUT THE INSTITUTION State-related, coed. *Awards:* certificates, associate, and bachelor's degrees. 76 undergraduate majors. *Total enrollment:* 5,671. Undergraduates: 5,657. Freshmen: 1,235. Federal methodology is used as a basis for awarding need-based institutional aid.
UNDERGRADUATE EXPENSES for 2013–2014 *Application fee:* $50. *Tuition, state resident:* full-time $12,000; part-time $400 per credit hour. *Tuition, nonresident:* full-time $15,630; part-time $521 per credit hour. *Required fees:* full-time $2370; $79 per credit hour. Full-time tuition and fees vary according to course load and program. Part-time tuition and fees vary according to course load and program. *College room and board:* $10,500; *Room only:* $5994. Room and board charges vary according to board plan and housing facility.
FRESHMAN FINANCIAL AID (Fall 2011) 1,240 applied for aid; of those 96% were deemed to have need. 100% of freshmen with need received aid. *Average financial aid package:* $14,358 (excluding resources awarded to replace EFC).
UNDERGRADUATE FINANCIAL AID (Fall 2011) 4,318 applied for aid; of those 100% were deemed to have need. 100% of undergraduates with need received aid. *Average financial aid package:* $15,034 (excluding resources awarded to replace EFC).
GIFT AID (NEED-BASED) *Total amount:* $29,436,681 (36% federal, 25% state, 3% institutional, 36% external sources). *Receiving aid:* Freshmen: 69% (937); all full-time undergraduates: 70% (3,464). *Average award:* Freshmen: $6537; Undergraduates: $7289. *Scholarships, grants, and awards:* Federal Pell, FSEOG, state, private, college/university gift aid from institutional funds.
GIFT AID (NON-NEED-BASED) *Tuition waivers:* Full or partial for employees or children of employees. *ROTC:* Army.
LOANS *Student loans:* $43,847,676 (100% need-based). *Average need-based loan:* Freshmen: $2964. Undergraduates: $3608. *Parent loans:* $14,649,478 (100% need-based). *Programs:* Federal Direct (Subsidized and Unsubsidized Stafford, PLUS).
WORK-STUDY *Federal work-study:* Total amount: $256,086; 141 jobs averaging $1816.
APPLYING FOR FINANCIAL AID *Required financial aid forms:* FAFSA, institution's own form. *Financial aid deadline (priority):* 4/15. *Notification date:* Continuous beginning 6/1. Students must reply within 2 weeks of notification.
CONTACT Candace Baran, Director of Financial Aid, Pennsylvania College of Technology, One College Avenue, Williamsport, PA 17701, 570-326-4766 or toll-free 800-367-9222. *Fax:* 570-321-5552. *E-mail:* cbaran@pct.edu.
Website: http://www.pct.edu/.

PEPPERDINE UNIVERSITY
Malibu, CA

Tuition & fees: $42,772 — Average undergraduate aid package: $39,417

ABOUT THE INSTITUTION Independent Church of Christ, coed. *Awards:* bachelor's, master's, and doctoral degrees. 66 undergraduate majors. *Total enrollment:* 7,319. Undergraduates: 3,488. Freshmen: 777. Federal methodology is used as a basis for awarding need-based institutional aid.
UNDERGRADUATE EXPENSES for 2013–2014 *Application fee:* $65. *Comprehensive fee:* $55,372 includes full-time tuition ($42,520), mandatory fees ($252), and room and board ($12,600). *College room only:* $9600. Room and board charges vary according to board plan and housing facility. *Part-time tuition:* $1330 per credit hour.
FRESHMAN FINANCIAL AID (Fall 2012, est.) 660 applied for aid; of those 77% were deemed to have need. 98% of freshmen with need received aid; of those 33% had need fully met. *Average percent of need met:* 85% (excluding resources awarded to replace EFC). *Average financial aid package:* $40,014 (excluding resources awarded to replace EFC). 13% of all full-time freshmen had no need and received non-need-based gift aid.

UNDERGRADUATE FINANCIAL AID (Fall 2012, est.) 2,416 applied for aid; of those 73% were deemed to have need. 98% of undergraduates with need received aid; of those 28% had need fully met. *Average percent of need met:* 83% (excluding resources awarded to replace EFC). *Average financial aid package:* $39,417 (excluding resources awarded to replace EFC). 15% of all full-time undergraduates had no need and received non-need-based gift aid.

GIFT AID (NEED-BASED) *Total amount:* $57,397,901 (6% federal, 7% state, 84% institutional, 3% external sources). *Receiving aid:* Freshmen: 27% (210); all full-time undergraduates: 26% (789). *Average award:* Freshmen: $42,251; Undergraduates: $40,830. *Scholarships, grants, and awards:* Federal Pell, FSEOG, state, private, college/university gift aid from institutional funds, United Negro College Fund, Academic Competitiveness Grants, National SMART Grants.

GIFT AID (NON-NEED-BASED) *Total amount:* $8,876,388 (1% federal, 94% institutional, 5% external sources). *Receiving aid:* Freshmen: 58% (456). Undergraduates: 53% (1,637). *Average award:* Freshmen: $23,432. Undergraduates: $19,161. *Tuition waivers:* Full or partial for employees or children of employees. *ROTC:* Army cooperative, Air Force cooperative.

LOANS *Student loans:* $15,165,501 (90% need-based, 10% non-need-based). 56% of past graduating class borrowed through all loan programs. *Average indebtedness per student:* $30,101. *Average need-based loan:* Freshmen: $3532. Undergraduates: $4911. *Parent loans:* $13,314,374 (86% need-based, 14% non-need-based). *Programs:* Federal Direct (Subsidized and Unsubsidized Stafford, PLUS), Perkins, college/university.

WORK-STUDY *Federal work-study:* Total amount: $562,474; jobs available. *State or other work-study/employment:* Total amount: $176,421 (74% need-based, 26% non-need-based). Part-time jobs available.

ATHLETIC AWARDS Total amount: $4,845,614 (26% need-based, 74% non-need-based).

APPLYING FOR FINANCIAL AID *Required financial aid form:* FAFSA. *Financial aid deadline (priority):* 2/15. *Notification date:* 4/15. Students must reply by 5/1.

CONTACT Ms. Janet Lockhart, Director of Financial Assistance, Pepperdine University, 24255 Pacific Coast Highway, Malibu, CA 90263-4301, 310-506-4301. *Fax:* 310-506-4746. *E-mail:* janet.lockhart@pepperdine.edu. *Website:* http://www.pepperdine.edu/.

PERELANDRA COLLEGE
La Mesa, CA

CONTACT Financial Aid Office, Perelandra College, 8697-C La Mesa Boulevard, PMB 21, La Mesa, CA 91941, 619-677-3308. *Website:* http://www.perelandra.edu/.

PERU STATE COLLEGE
Peru, NE

CONTACT Diana Lind, Director of Financial Aid, Peru State College, PO Box 10, Peru, NE 68421, 402-872-2228 or toll-free 800-742-4412 (in-state), 800-741-4412 (out-of-state). *Fax:* 402-872-2419. *E-mail:* finaid@oakmail.peru.edu. *Website:* http://www.peru.edu/.

PFEIFFER UNIVERSITY
Misenheimer, NC

CONTACT Amy Brown, Director of Financial Aid, Pfeiffer University, PO Box 960, Misenheimer, NC 28109, 704-463-1360 Ext. 3046 or toll-free 800-338-2060. *Fax:* 704-463-1363. *E-mail:* amy.brown@pfeiffer.edu. *Website:* http://www.pfeiffer.edu/.

PHILADELPHIA UNIVERSITY
Philadelphia, PA

Tuition & fees: $31,874	Average undergraduate aid package: $22,634

ABOUT THE INSTITUTION Independent, coed. *Awards:* certificates, associate, bachelor's, master's, and doctoral degrees. 32 undergraduate majors. *Total enrollment:* 3,540. Undergraduates: 2,888. Freshmen: 604. Federal methodology is used as a basis for awarding need-based institutional aid.

UNDERGRADUATE EXPENSES for 2013–2014 *Application fee:* $40. *Comprehensive fee:* $42,052 includes full-time tuition ($31,874) and room and board ($10,178). *College room only:* $5032. Full-time tuition and fees vary according to degree level and program. Room and board charges vary according to board plan and housing facility. Part-time tuition and fees vary according to class time, course load, degree level, program, and reciprocity agreements.

FRESHMAN FINANCIAL AID (Fall 2012, est.) 529 applied for aid; of those 88% were deemed to have need. 100% of freshmen with need received aid; of those 14% had need fully met. *Average percent of need met:* 74% (excluding resources awarded to replace EFC). *Average financial aid package:* $24,833 (excluding resources awarded to replace EFC). 21% of all full-time freshmen had no need and received non-need-based gift aid.

UNDERGRADUATE FINANCIAL AID (Fall 2012, est.) 2,281 applied for aid; of those 91% were deemed to have need. 100% of undergraduates with need received aid; of those 11% had need fully met. *Average percent of need met:* 67% (excluding resources awarded to replace EFC). *Average financial aid package:* $22,634 (excluding resources awarded to replace EFC). 18% of all full-time undergraduates had no need and received non-need-based gift aid.

GIFT AID (NEED-BASED) *Total amount:* $33,539,164 (13% federal, 6% state, 80% institutional, 1% external sources). *Receiving aid:* Freshmen: 77% (463); all full-time undergraduates: 74% (2,050). *Average award:* Freshmen: $20,708; Undergraduates: $17,799. *Scholarships, grants, and awards:* Federal Pell, FSEOG, state, private, college/university gift aid from institutional funds, university-chosen non-endowed scholarships from outside sources.

GIFT AID (NON-NEED-BASED) *Total amount:* $4,578,132 (4% federal, 94% institutional, 2% external sources). *Receiving aid:* Freshmen: 9% (56). Undergraduates: 5% (141). *Average award:* Freshmen: $8914. Undergraduates: $7835. *Scholarships, grants, and awards by category:* Academic interests/achievement: engineering/technologies, general academic interests/achievements. *Tuition waivers:* Full or partial for employees or children of employees.

LOANS *Student loans:* $21,788,199 (75% need-based, 25% non-need-based). 79% of past graduating class borrowed through all loan programs. *Average indebtedness per student:* $39,938. *Average need-based loan:* Freshmen: $3997. Undergraduates: $4620. *Parent loans:* $10,100,158 (43% need-based, 57% non-need-based). *Programs:* Federal Direct (Subsidized and Unsubsidized Stafford, PLUS), Perkins, private loans.

WORK-STUDY *Federal work-study:* Total amount: $2,528,000; jobs available. *State or other work-study/employment:* Total amount: $540,575 (75% need-based, 25% non-need-based). Part-time jobs available.

ATHLETIC AWARDS Total amount: $2,513,367 (50% need-based, 50% non-need-based).

APPLYING FOR FINANCIAL AID *Required financial aid form:* FAFSA. *Financial aid deadline:* 4/15. *Notification date:* Continuous beginning 2/10. Students must reply by 5/1.

CONTACT Ms. Lisa J. Cooper, Director of Financial Aid, Philadelphia University, School House Lane and Henry Avenue, Philadelphia, PA 19144, 215-951-2940. *Fax:* 215-951-2907. *E-mail:* cooperl@philau.edu. *Website:* http://www.philau.edu/.

PHILANDER SMITH COLLEGE
Little Rock, AR

Tuition & fees: $11,910	Average undergraduate aid package: $11,422

ABOUT THE INSTITUTION Independent United Methodist, coed. *Awards:* bachelor's degrees. 19 undergraduate majors. *Total enrollment:* 732. Undergraduates: 732. Freshmen: 197. Federal methodology is used as a basis for awarding need-based institutional aid.

UNDERGRADUATE EXPENSES for 2013–2014 Application fee: $25. **Comprehensive fee:** $19,510 includes full-time tuition ($11,350), mandatory fees ($560), and room and board ($7600). Full-time tuition and fees vary according to course load, program, and student level. Room and board charges vary according to housing facility. **Part-time tuition:** $400 per credit hour. Part-time tuition and fees vary according to course load, program, and student level.

FRESHMAN FINANCIAL AID (Fall 2011) 180 applied for aid; of those 98% were deemed to have need. 100% of freshmen with need received aid; of those 5% had need fully met. **Average percent of need met:** 57% (excluding resources awarded to replace EFC). **Average financial aid package:** $12,466 (excluding resources awarded to replace EFC). 3% of all full-time freshmen had no need and received non-need-based gift aid.

UNDERGRADUATE FINANCIAL AID (Fall 2011) 695 applied for aid; of those 97% were deemed to have need. 99% of undergraduates with need received aid; of those 5% had need fully met. **Average percent of need met:** 53% (excluding resources awarded to replace EFC). **Average financial aid package:** $11,422 (excluding resources awarded to replace EFC). 5% of all full-time undergraduates had no need and received non-need-based gift aid.

GIFT AID (NEED-BASED) Total amount: $6,039,581 (49% federal, 7% state, 34% institutional, 10% external sources). **Receiving aid:** Freshmen: 92% (175); all full-time undergraduates: 88% (644). **Average award:** Freshmen: $9; Undergraduates: $36. **Scholarships, grants, and awards:** Federal Pell, FSEOG, state, private, college/university gift aid from institutional funds, United Negro College Fund.

GIFT AID (NON-NEED-BASED) Receiving aid: Freshmen: 3% (6). Undergraduates: 3% (22). **Average award:** Freshmen: $10,980. Undergraduates: $10,812. **Scholarships, grants, and awards by category:** Academic interests/achievement: 178 awards ($1,653,954 total): general academic interests/achievements. Creative arts/performance: 34 awards ($40,000 total): music. Special achievements/activities: general special achievements/activities. **Tuition waivers:** Full or partial for employees or children of employees.

LOANS Student loans: $5,483,694 (47% need-based, 53% non-need-based). 96% of past graduating class borrowed through all loan programs. Average indebtedness per student: $37,450. **Average need-based loan:** Freshmen: $3292. Undergraduates: $3635. **Parent loans:** $1,234,293 (100% non-need-based). **Programs:** Federal Direct (Subsidized and Unsubsidized Stafford, PLUS), state.

WORK-STUDY Federal work-study: Total amount: $141,148; 81 jobs averaging $2600.

ATHLETIC AWARDS Total amount: $126,621 (100% need-based).

APPLYING FOR FINANCIAL AID Required financial aid forms: FAFSA, institution's own form. **Financial aid deadline (priority):** 3/1. **Notification date:** Continuous beginning 3/1.

CONTACT David D. Page, Vice President for Enrollment Management/Director of Financial Aid, Philander Smith College, 900 Daisy Bates Drive, Little Rock, AR 72202-3799, 501-370-5270 or toll-free 800-446-6772. E-mail: dpage@philander.edu. Website: http://www.philander.edu/.

PIEDMONT COLLEGE
Demorest, GA

Tuition & fees: $20,730	Average undergraduate aid package: $17,250

ABOUT THE INSTITUTION Independent United Church of Christ, coed. **Awards:** certificates, bachelor's, master's, and doctoral degrees. 32 undergraduate majors. **Total enrollment:** 1,170. Undergraduates: 1,294. Freshmen: 210. Both federal and institutional methodology are used as a basis for awarding need-based institutional aid.

UNDERGRADUATE EXPENSES for 2013–2014 Comprehensive fee: $29,260 includes full-time tuition ($20,730) and room and board ($8530). **College room only:** $4744. Full-time tuition and fees vary according to course load, degree level, location, and program. **Part-time tuition:** $864 per credit. Part-time tuition and fees vary according to course load, degree level, location, and program.

FRESHMAN FINANCIAL AID (Fall 2012, est.) 174 applied for aid; of those 87% were deemed to have need. 100% of freshmen with need received aid; of those 24% had need fully met. **Average percent of need met:** 76% (excluding resources awarded to replace EFC). **Average financial aid package:** $18,849 (excluding

---

resources awarded to replace EFC). 19% of all full-time freshmen had no need and received non-need-based gift aid.

UNDERGRADUATE FINANCIAL AID (Fall 2012, est.) 1,026 applied for aid; of those 92% were deemed to have need. 100% of undergraduates with need received aid; of those 15% had need fully met. **Average percent of need met:** 70% (excluding resources awarded to replace EFC). **Average financial aid package:** $17,250 (excluding resources awarded to replace EFC). 11% of all full-time undergraduates had no need and received non-need-based gift aid.

GIFT AID (NEED-BASED) Total amount: $10,587,901 (28% federal, 20% state, 52% institutional). **Receiving aid:** Freshmen: 80% (152); all full-time undergraduates: 84% (942). **Average award:** Freshmen: $14,771; Undergraduates: $12,208. **Scholarships, grants, and awards:** Federal Pell, FSEOG, state, private, college/university gift aid from institutional funds.

GIFT AID (NON-NEED-BASED) Total amount: $2,585,664 (16% state, 76% institutional, 8% external sources). **Receiving aid:** Freshmen: 33% (62). Undergraduates: 14% (159). **Average award:** Freshmen: $11,878. Undergraduates: $10,628. **Scholarships, grants, and awards by category:** Academic interests/achievement: 736 awards ($5,148,214 total): biological sciences, business, education, English, foreign languages, general academic interests/achievements, health fields, humanities, mathematics, premedicine, religion/biblical studies, social sciences. Creative arts/performance: 117 awards ($189,150 total): art/fine arts, debating, journalism/publications, music, theater/drama. Special achievements/activities: 507 awards ($1,554,151 total): community service, leadership, religious involvement. Special characteristics: 165 awards ($1,383,028 total): adult students, children of faculty/staff, international students, out-of-state students. **Tuition waivers:** Full or partial for employees or children of employees.

LOANS Student loans: $7,351,498 (86% need-based, 14% non-need-based). 74% of past graduating class borrowed through all loan programs. Average indebtedness per student: $18,129. **Average need-based loan:** Freshmen: $3407. Undergraduates: $4486. **Parent loans:** $1,109,668 (35% need-based, 65% non-need-based). **Programs:** Federal Direct (Subsidized and Unsubsidized Stafford, PLUS), state.

WORK-STUDY Federal work-study: Total amount: $161,244; 82 jobs averaging $1966. **State or other work-study/employment:** Total amount: $571,126 (45% need-based, 55% non-need-based). 316 part-time jobs averaging $1910.

APPLYING FOR FINANCIAL AID Required financial aid forms: FAFSA, state aid form. **Financial aid deadline (priority):** 3/1. **Notification date:** Continuous beginning 1/15. Students must reply within 2 weeks of notification.

CONTACT Mr. David Richmond McMillion, Director of Financial Aid, Piedmont College, PO Box 10, Demorest, GA 30535-0010, 706-778-3000 Ext. 1191 or toll-free 800-277-7020. Fax: 706-778-0708. E-mail: dmcmillion@piedmont.edu. Website: http://www.piedmont.edu/.

PIEDMONT INTERNATIONAL UNIVERSITY
Winston-Salem, NC

Tuition & fees: $13,195	Average undergraduate aid package: N/A

ABOUT THE INSTITUTION Independent Baptist, coed. **Awards:** certificates, associate, bachelor's, master's, and doctoral degrees. 15 undergraduate majors. **Total enrollment:** 392. Undergraduates: 274. Freshmen: 39. Federal methodology is used as a basis for awarding need-based institutional aid.

UNDERGRADUATE EXPENSES for 2013–2014 Application fee: $55. **Comprehensive fee:** $19,605 includes full-time tuition ($12,340), mandatory fees ($855), and room and board ($6410). Part-time tuition and fees vary according to course load.

GIFT AID (NEED-BASED) Total amount: $858,731 (74% federal, 26% institutional). **Scholarships, grants, and awards:** Federal Pell, FSEOG.

GIFT AID (NON-NEED-BASED) Total amount: $627,419 (87% institutional, 13% external sources). **Scholarships, grants, and awards by category:** Academic interests/achievement: general academic interests/achievements. Special characteristics: children of faculty/staff, relatives of clergy, spouses of current students, veterans. **Tuition waivers:** Full or partial for employees or children of employees.

LOANS Student loans: $1,046,264 (57% need-based, 43% non-need-based). **Parent loans:** $56,479 (100% non-need-based). **Programs:** Sallie Mae Smart Option Loans.

WORK-STUDY Federal work-study: Total amount: $14,452; jobs available.

APPLYING FOR FINANCIAL AID *Required financial aid forms:* FAFSA, institution's own form. *Financial aid deadline:* 8/31 (priority: 6/1). *Notification date:* Continuous.
CONTACT Angela D. Hoover, Interim Director of Financial Aid, Piedmont International University, 420 South Broad Street, Winston-Salem, NC 27101-5197, 336-714-7927 or toll-free 800-937-5097. *Fax:* 336-714-8094. *E-mail:* hoovera@piedmontu.edu.
Website: http://www.pbc.edu/.

PILLAR COLLEGE
Zarephath, NJ

CONTACT Financial Aid Office, Pillar College, 10 College Way, PO Box 9035, Zarephath, NJ 08890-9035, 732-356-1595 or toll-free 800-234-9305.
Website: http://www.somerset.edu/.

PINE MANOR COLLEGE
Chestnut Hill, MA

Tuition & fees: $24,301	Average undergraduate aid package: $21,650

ABOUT THE INSTITUTION Independent, women only. *Awards:* associate, bachelor's, and master's degrees. 13 undergraduate majors. *Total enrollment:* 28. Undergraduates: 317. Freshmen: 122. Federal methodology is used as a basis for awarding need-based institutional aid.
UNDERGRADUATE EXPENSES for 2013–2014 *Application fee:* $25. *Comprehensive fee:* $37,051 includes full-time tuition ($24,301) and room and board ($12,750). Full-time tuition and fees vary according to course load. Room and board charges vary according to housing facility. *Part-time tuition:* $725 per credit. Part-time tuition and fees vary according to course load.
FRESHMAN FINANCIAL AID (Fall 2012, est.) 78 applied for aid; of those 97% were deemed to have need. 100% of freshmen with need received aid; of those 3% had need fully met. *Average percent of need met:* 74% (excluding resources awarded to replace EFC). *Average financial aid package:* $25,120 (excluding resources awarded to replace EFC). 13% of all full-time freshmen had no need and received non-need-based gift aid.
UNDERGRADUATE FINANCIAL AID (Fall 2012, est.) 241 applied for aid; of those 99% were deemed to have need. 100% of undergraduates with need received aid; of those 2% had need fully met. *Average percent of need met:* 71% (excluding resources awarded to replace EFC). *Average financial aid package:* $21,650 (excluding resources awarded to replace EFC). 8% of all full-time undergraduates had no need and received non-need-based gift aid.
GIFT AID (NEED-BASED) *Total amount:* $4,676,256 (22% federal, 5% state, 70% institutional, 3% external sources). *Receiving aid:* Freshmen: 62% (76); all full-time undergraduates: 77% (236). *Average award:* Freshmen: $20,195; Undergraduates: $16,020. *Scholarships, grants, and awards:* Federal Pell, FSEOG, state, private, college/university gift aid from institutional funds.
GIFT AID (NON-NEED-BASED) *Total amount:* $200,547 (85% institutional, 15% external sources). *Average award:* Freshmen: $9835. Undergraduates: $9746. *Scholarships, grants, and awards by category:* Academic interests/achievement: biological sciences, education, general academic interests/achievements. *Special achievements/activities:* general special achievements/activities, leadership. *Special characteristics:* children and siblings of alumni, members of minority groups, siblings of current students. *Tuition waivers:* Full or partial for children of alumni, employees or children of employees.
LOANS *Student loans:* $1,974,599 (98% need-based, 2% non-need-based). 89% of past graduating class borrowed through all loan programs. *Average indebtedness per student:* $30,808. *Average need-based loan:* Freshmen: $4250. Undergraduates: $5300. *Parent loans:* $463,489 (73% need-based, 27% non-need-based). *Programs:* Federal Direct (Subsidized and Unsubsidized Stafford, PLUS), state, alternative loans.
WORK-STUDY *Federal work-study:* Total amount: $133,765; 160 jobs averaging $800.
APPLYING FOR FINANCIAL AID *Required financial aid form:* FAFSA. *Financial aid deadline (priority):* 5/1. *Notification date:* Continuous beginning 4/1. Students must reply by 5/1 or within 2 weeks of notification.

CONTACT Elizabeth M. Gorra, Director of Financial Aid, Pine Manor College, 400 Heath Street, Chestnut Hill, MA 02467, 617-731-7628 or toll-free 800-762-1357. *Fax:* 617-731-7102. *E-mail:* egorra@pmc.edu.
Website: http://www.pmc.edu/.

PIONEER PACIFIC COLLEGE
Clackamas, OR

CONTACT Financial Aid Office, Pioneer Pacific College, 8800 SE Sunnyside Road, Clackamas, OR 97015 or toll-free 866-772-4636.
Website: http://www.pioneerpacific.edu/.

PIONEER PACIFIC COLLEGE
Wilsonville, OR

CONTACT Financial Aid Office, Pioneer Pacific College, 27501 Southwest Parkway Avenue, Wilsonville, OR 97070, 503-682-3903 or toll-free 866-PPC-INFO.
Website: http://www.pioneerpacific.edu/.

PIONEER PACIFIC COLLEGE–EUGENE/SPRINGFIELD BRANCH
Springfield, OR

CONTACT Financial Aid Office, Pioneer Pacific College–Eugene/Springfield Branch, 3800 Sports Way, Springfield, OR 97477 or toll-free 866-772-4636.
Website: http://www.pioneerpacific.edu/.

PITTSBURG STATE UNIVERSITY
Pittsburg, KS

Tuition & fees (KS res): $5494	Average undergraduate aid package: $8567

ABOUT THE INSTITUTION State-supported, coed. *Awards:* certificates, associate, bachelor's, and master's degrees. 103 undergraduate majors. *Total enrollment:* 7,107. Undergraduates: 5,984. Freshmen: 1,102. Federal methodology is used as a basis for awarding need-based institutional aid.
UNDERGRADUATE EXPENSES for 2013–2014 *Application fee:* $30. *Tuition, state resident:* full-time $5494. *Tuition, nonresident:* full-time $15,050. Part-time tuition and fees vary according to course load. *College room and board:* $6758. Room and board charges vary according to board plan and housing facility.
FRESHMAN FINANCIAL AID (Fall 2011) 935 applied for aid; of those 77% were deemed to have need. 99% of freshmen with need received aid; of those 39% had need fully met. *Average percent of need met:* 94% (excluding resources awarded to replace EFC). *Average financial aid package:* $8367 (excluding resources awarded to replace EFC). 17% of all full-time freshmen had no need and received non-need-based gift aid.
UNDERGRADUATE FINANCIAL AID (Fall 2011) 4,177 applied for aid; of those 81% were deemed to have need. 100% of undergraduates with need received aid; of those 41% had need fully met. *Average percent of need met:* 91% (excluding resources awarded to replace EFC). *Average financial aid package:* $8567 (excluding resources awarded to replace EFC). 9% of all full-time undergraduates had no need and received non-need-based gift aid.
GIFT AID (NEED-BASED) *Total amount:* $13,586,830 (73% federal, 6% state, 13% institutional, 8% external sources). *Receiving aid:* Freshmen: 52% (482); all full-time undergraduates: 52% (2,407). *Average award:* Freshmen: $4505; Undergraduates: $4402. *Scholarships, grants, and awards:* Federal Pell, FSEOG, state, private, college/university gift aid from institutional funds.
GIFT AID (NON-NEED-BASED) *Total amount:* $1,895,878 (1% federal, 3% state, 69% institutional, 27% external sources). *Receiving aid:* Freshmen: 39% (363). Undergraduates: 26% (1,218). *Average award:* Freshmen: $2744. Undergraduates: $2478. *Scholarships, grants, and awards by category:* Academic interests/

achievement: biological sciences, business, communication, computer science, education, engineering/technologies, English, foreign languages, general academic interests/achievements, health fields, home economics, mathematics, military science, physical sciences, social sciences. *Creative arts/performance*: music. *Special characteristics*: children and siblings of alumni, general special characteristics. *Tuition waivers*: Full or partial for employees or children of employees. *ROTC*: Army.
LOANS *Student loans*: $23,008,027 (82% need-based, 18% non-need-based). 36% of past graduating class borrowed through all loan programs. *Average indebtedness per student*: $20,808. *Average need-based loan*: Freshmen: $3198. Undergraduates: $3914. *Parent loans*: $1,407,326 (56% need-based, 44% non-need-based).
Programs: Federal Direct (Subsidized and Unsubsidized Stafford, PLUS), Perkins, Federal Nursing, college/university.
WORK-STUDY *Federal work-study*: Total amount: $509,182; jobs available. *State or other work-study/employment*: Total amount: $1,751,477 (1% need-based, 99% non-need-based). Part-time jobs available.
ATHLETIC AWARDS Total amount: $1,331,101 (60% need-based, 40% non-need-based).
APPLYING FOR FINANCIAL AID *Required financial aid forms*: FAFSA, state aid form. *Financial aid deadline (priority)*: 3/1. *Notification date*: Continuous. Students must reply within 2 weeks of notification.
CONTACT Tammy Higgins, Director of Student Financial Assistance, Pittsburg State University, 1701 South Broadway Street, Pittsburg, KS 66762-7534, 620-235-4238 or toll-free 800-854-7488. *Fax*: 620-235-4078. *E-mail*: thiggins@pittstate.edu. *Website*: http://www.pittstate.edu/.

PITZER COLLEGE
Claremont, CA

Tuition & fees: $43,402	Average undergraduate aid package: $39,231

ABOUT THE INSTITUTION Independent, coed. *Awards*: bachelor's degrees. 37 undergraduate majors. *Total enrollment*: 1,084. Undergraduates: 1,084. Freshmen: 273. Both federal and institutional methodology are used as a basis for awarding need-based institutional aid.
UNDERGRADUATE EXPENSES for 2013–2014 *Application fee*: $60. *Comprehensive fee*: $57,266 includes full-time tuition ($43,136), mandatory fees ($266), and room and board ($13,864). *College room only*: $8028. Full-time tuition and fees vary according to course load. Room and board charges vary according to board plan. *Part-time tuition*: $5392 per course. Part-time tuition and fees vary according to course load.
FRESHMAN FINANCIAL AID (Fall 2012, est.) 120 applied for aid; of those 78% were deemed to have need. 97% of freshmen with need received aid; of those 100% had need fully met. *Average percent of need met*: 100% (excluding resources awarded to replace EFC). *Average financial aid package*: $41,456 (excluding resources awarded to replace EFC). 1% of all full-time freshmen had no need and received non-need-based gift aid.
UNDERGRADUATE FINANCIAL AID (Fall 2012, est.) 464 applied for aid; of those 88% were deemed to have need. 99% of undergraduates with need received aid; of those 100% had need fully met. *Average percent of need met*: 100% (excluding resources awarded to replace EFC). *Average financial aid package*: $39,231 (excluding resources awarded to replace EFC). 1% of all full-time undergraduates had no need and received non-need-based gift aid.
GIFT AID (NEED-BASED) *Total amount*: $13,984,033 (7% federal, 5% state, 86% institutional, 2% external sources). *Receiving aid*: Freshmen: 33% (86); all full-time undergraduates: 37% (385). *Average award*: Freshmen: $38,953; Undergraduates: $35,282. *Scholarships, grants, and awards*: Federal Pell, FSEOG, state, private, college/university gift aid from institutional funds.
GIFT AID (NON-NEED-BASED) *Total amount*: $279,810 (15% institutional, 85% external sources). *Receiving aid*: Freshmen: 1% (3). Undergraduates: 4. *Average award*: Freshmen: $5000. Undergraduates: $6277. *Scholarships, grants, and awards by category*: Academic interests/achievement: general academic interests/achievements. Special achievements/activities: community service, leadership. *Tuition waivers*: Full or partial for employees or children of employees. *ROTC*: Army cooperative, Air Force cooperative.
LOANS *Student loans*: $2,632,939 (68% need-based, 32% non-need-based). 47% of past graduating class borrowed through all loan programs. *Average indebtedness per student*: $20,900. *Average need-based loan*: Freshmen: $2748. Undergrad-

uates: $3657. *Parent loans*: $1,062,566 (47% need-based, 53% non-need-based).
Programs: Federal Direct (Subsidized and Unsubsidized Stafford, PLUS), Perkins, college/university.
WORK-STUDY *Federal work-study*: Total amount: $868,388; jobs available.
APPLYING FOR FINANCIAL AID *Required financial aid forms*: FAFSA, CSS Financial Aid PROFILE, state aid form, noncustodial (divorced/separated) parent's statement. *Financial aid deadline*: 2/1. *Notification date*: 4/1. Students must reply by 5/1.
CONTACT Margaret Carothers, Director of Financial Aid, Pitzer College, 1050 North Mills Avenue, Claremont, CA 91711-6101, 909-621-8208 or toll-free 800-748-9371. *Fax*: 909-607-1205. *E-mail*: margaret_carothers@pitzer.edu. *Website*: http://www.pitzer.edu/.

PLATT COLLEGE
Aurora, CO

Tuition & fees: N/R	Average undergraduate aid package: N/A

ABOUT THE INSTITUTION Proprietary, coed. 2 undergraduate majors. Federal methodology is used as a basis for awarding need-based institutional aid.
GIFT AID (NEED-BASED) *Total amount*: $545,000 (98% federal, 2% external sources). *Scholarships, grants, and awards*: Federal Pell, FSEOG.
LOANS *Student loans*: $2,750,000 (45% need-based, 55% non-need-based). *Parent loans*: $10,000 (100% need-based). *Programs*: Perkins.
APPLYING FOR FINANCIAL AID *Required financial aid forms*: FAFSA, institution's own form. *Financial aid deadline*: Continuous. *Notification date*: Continuous beginning 1/1.
CONTACT Office of Financial Aid, Platt College, 3100 South Parker Road, #200, Aurora, CO 80014, 303-369-5151. *Fax*: 303-745-1433. *Website*: http://www.plattcolorado.edu/.

PLATT COLLEGE SAN DIEGO
San Diego, CA

CONTACT Financial Aid Office, Platt College San Diego, 6250 El Cajon Boulevard, San Diego, CA 92115-3919, 619-265-0107 or toll-free 866-752-8826. *Website*: http://www.platt.edu/.

PLYMOUTH STATE UNIVERSITY
Plymouth, NH

Tuition & fees (NH res): $12,560	Average undergraduate aid package: $9202

ABOUT THE INSTITUTION State-supported, coed. *Awards*: certificates, bachelor's, master's, and doctoral degrees. 52 undergraduate majors. *Total enrollment*: 5,431. Undergraduates: 4,238. Freshmen: 933. Federal methodology is used as a basis for awarding need-based institutional aid.
UNDERGRADUATE EXPENSES for 2013–2014 *Application fee*: $50. *One-time required fee*: $198. *Tuition, state resident*: full-time $10,410; part-time $435 per credit hour. *Tuition, nonresident*: full-time $17,310; part-time $720 per credit hour. *Required fees*: full-time $2150; $92 per credit hour. Full-time tuition and fees vary according to reciprocity agreements. Part-time tuition and fees vary according to reciprocity agreements. *College room and board*: $9440; *Room only*: $6370. Room and board charges vary according to board plan and housing facility.
FRESHMAN FINANCIAL AID (Fall 2011) 958 applied for aid; of those 79% were deemed to have need. 99% of freshmen with need received aid; of those 12% had need fully met. *Average percent of need met*: 52% (excluding resources awarded to replace EFC). *Average financial aid package*: $8874 (excluding resources awarded to replace EFC). 5% of all full-time freshmen had no need and received non-need-based gift aid.

UNDERGRADUATE FINANCIAL AID (Fall 2011) 3,595 applied for aid; of those 80% were deemed to have need. 99% of undergraduates with need received aid; of those 9% had need fully met. *Average percent of need met:* 55% (excluding resources awarded to replace EFC). *Average financial aid package:* $9202 (excluding resources awarded to replace EFC). 6% of all full-time undergraduates had no need and received non-need-based gift aid.

GIFT AID (NEED-BASED) *Total amount:* $10,452,983 (46% federal, 3% state, 51% institutional). *Receiving aid:* Freshmen: 45% (455); all full-time undergraduates: 43% (1,772). *Average award:* Freshmen: $6604; Undergraduates: $5794. *Scholarships, grants, and awards:* Federal Pell, FSEOG, state, college/university gift aid from institutional funds.

GIFT AID (NON-NEED-BASED) *Total amount:* $4,196,570 (82% institutional, 18% external sources). *Receiving aid:* Freshmen: 29% (300). Undergraduates: 22% (899). *Average award:* Freshmen: $4059. Undergraduates: $3503. *Scholarships, grants, and awards by category: Academic interests/achievement:* 635 awards ($2,486,517 total): general academic interests/achievements. *Creative arts/performance:* 43 awards ($64,875 total): creative writing, dance, music, theater/drama. *Special characteristics:* 70 awards ($250,147 total): children of faculty/staff, international students. *Tuition waivers:* Full or partial for employees or children of employees, senior citizens. *ROTC:* Army cooperative, Air Force cooperative.

LOANS *Student loans:* $29,851,518 (39% need-based, 61% non-need-based). 83% of past graduating class borrowed through all loan programs. *Average indebtedness per student:* $31,214. *Average need-based loan:* Freshmen: $3221. Undergraduates: $4189. *Parent loans:* $13,879,267 (100% non-need-based). *Programs:* Federal Direct (Subsidized and Unsubsidized Stafford, PLUS), Perkins.

WORK-STUDY *Federal work-study:* Total amount: $4,179,433; 1,880 jobs averaging $2239.

APPLYING FOR FINANCIAL AID *Required financial aid form:* FAFSA. *Financial aid deadline (priority):* 3/1. *Notification date:* Continuous beginning 3/1. Students must reply by 5/1.

CONTACT June Louise Schlabach, Director of Financial Aid, Plymouth State University, 17 High Street, Plymouth, NH 03264-1595, 603-535-2338 or toll-free 800-842-6900. *Fax:* 603-535-2627. *E-mail:* jlschlabach@plymouth.edu.
Website: http://www.plymouth.edu/.

POINT LOMA NAZARENE UNIVERSITY
San Diego, CA

Tuition & fees: $29,510	Average undergraduate aid package: $20,225

ABOUT THE INSTITUTION Independent Nazarene, coed. *Awards:* certificates, bachelor's, and master's degrees. 59 undergraduate majors. *Total enrollment:* 3,192. Undergraduates: 2,415. Freshmen: 601. Federal methodology is used as a basis for awarding need-based institutional aid.

UNDERGRADUATE EXPENSES for 2013–2014 *Application fee:* $50. *Comprehensive fee:* $39,060 includes full-time tuition ($28,900), mandatory fees ($610), and room and board ($9550). *College room only:* $5440. Full-time tuition and fees vary according to course load. Room and board charges vary according to board plan. *Part-time tuition:* $1205 per credit hour. Part-time tuition and fees vary according to course load.

FRESHMAN FINANCIAL AID (Fall 2012, est.) 499 applied for aid; of those 83% were deemed to have need. 100% of freshmen with need received aid; of those 17% had need fully met. *Average percent of need met:* 65% (excluding resources awarded to replace EFC). *Average financial aid package:* $19,970 (excluding resources awarded to replace EFC). 13% of all full-time freshmen had no need and received non-need-based gift aid.

UNDERGRADUATE FINANCIAL AID (Fall 2012, est.) 1,925 applied for aid; of those 86% were deemed to have need. 100% of undergraduates with need received aid; of those 17% had need fully met. *Average percent of need met:* 63% (excluding resources awarded to replace EFC). *Average financial aid package:* $20,225 (excluding resources awarded to replace EFC). 14% of all full-time undergraduates had no need and received non-need-based gift aid.

GIFT AID (NEED-BASED) *Total amount:* $21,530,516 (14% federal, 19% state, 55% institutional, 12% external sources). *Receiving aid:* Freshmen: 71% (387); all full-time undergraduates: 65% (1,527). *Average award:* Freshmen: $15,899; Undergraduates: $15,237. *Scholarships, grants, and awards:* Federal Pell, FSEOG, state, private, college/university gift aid from institutional funds, Federal Nursing.

GIFT AID (NON-NEED-BASED) *Total amount:* $3,834,553 (80% institutional, 20% external sources). *Receiving aid:* Freshmen: 8% (42). Undergraduates: 5% (123). *Average award:* Freshmen: $8959. Undergraduates: $8049. *Scholarships, grants, and awards by category: Academic interests/achievement:* biological sciences, business, communication, education, engineering/technologies, general academic interests/achievements, health fields, home economics, humanities, mathematics, religion/biblical studies, social sciences. *Creative arts/performance:* art/fine arts, debating, music, theater/drama. *Tuition waivers:* Full or partial for employees or children of employees, senior citizens. *ROTC:* Army cooperative, Naval cooperative, Air Force cooperative.

LOANS *Student loans:* $17,504,007 (71% need-based, 29% non-need-based). 59% of past graduating class borrowed through all loan programs. *Average indebtedness per student:* $31,851. *Average need-based loan:* Freshmen: $3444. Undergraduates: $4608. *Parent loans:* $7,083,556 (45% need-based, 55% non-need-based). *Programs:* Federal Direct (Subsidized and Unsubsidized Stafford, PLUS), Perkins, Federal Nursing.

WORK-STUDY *Federal work-study:* Total amount: $3,260,923; jobs available.

ATHLETIC AWARDS Total amount: $2,043,499 (54% need-based, 46% non-need-based).

APPLYING FOR FINANCIAL AID *Required financial aid form:* FAFSA. *Financial aid deadline (priority):* 3/2. *Notification date:* Continuous beginning 12/15. Students must reply by 5/15.

CONTACT Office of Student Financial Services, Point Loma Nazarene University, 3900 Lomaland Drive, San Diego, CA 92106, 619-849-2538 or toll-free 800-733-7770. *Fax:* 619-849-7078. *E-mail:* sfs@pointloma.edu.
Website: http://www.pointloma.edu/.

POINT PARK UNIVERSITY
Pittsburgh, PA

Tuition & fees: $25,190	Average undergraduate aid package: $18,384

ABOUT THE INSTITUTION Independent, coed. *Awards:* certificates, associate, bachelor's, and master's degrees. 59 undergraduate majors. *Total enrollment:* 3,827. Undergraduates: 3,225. Freshmen: 523. Federal methodology is used as a basis for awarding need-based institutional aid.

UNDERGRADUATE EXPENSES for 2013–2014 *Application fee:* $40. *Comprehensive fee:* $33,190 includes full-time tuition ($24,020), mandatory fees ($1170), and room and board ($8000). *College room only:* $4720. Full-time tuition and fees vary according to program. Room and board charges vary according to board plan and housing facility. Part-time tuition and fees vary according to program.

FRESHMAN FINANCIAL AID (Fall 2012, est.) 484 applied for aid; of those 92% were deemed to have need. 100% of freshmen with need received aid; of those 15% had need fully met. *Average percent of need met:* 73% (excluding resources awarded to replace EFC). *Average financial aid package:* $21,053 (excluding resources awarded to replace EFC). 8% of all full-time freshmen had no need and received non-need-based gift aid.

UNDERGRADUATE FINANCIAL AID (Fall 2012, est.) 2,440 applied for aid; of those 92% were deemed to have need. 100% of undergraduates with need received aid; of those 14% had need fully met. *Average percent of need met:* 67% (excluding resources awarded to replace EFC). *Average financial aid package:* $18,384 (excluding resources awarded to replace EFC). 6% of all full-time undergraduates had no need and received non-need-based gift aid.

GIFT AID (NEED-BASED) *Total amount:* $29,961,497 (19% federal, 12% state, 58% institutional, 11% external sources). *Receiving aid:* Freshmen: 91% (441); all full-time undergraduates: 91% (2,228). *Average award:* Freshmen: $16,030; Undergraduates: $13,081. *Scholarships, grants, and awards:* Federal Pell, FSEOG, state, private, college/university gift aid from institutional funds.

GIFT AID (NON-NEED-BASED) *Total amount:* $2,618,020 (1% federal, 1% state, 75% institutional, 23% external sources). *Receiving aid:* Freshmen: 10% (48). Undergraduates: 9% (209). *Average award:* Freshmen: $10,369. Undergraduates: $8376. *Scholarships, grants, and awards by category: Academic interests/achievement:* 2,029 awards ($9,910,070 total): biological sciences, business, communication, computer science, education, engineering/technologies, English, general academic interests/achievements, health fields, humanities, international studies, mathematics, physical sciences, premedicine, social sciences. *Creative arts/performance:* 590 awards ($5,066,780 total): cinema/film/broadcasting, dance, performing arts, theater/drama. *Special achievements/activities:* 321 awards ($257,750 total):

community service, memberships. *Special characteristics:* 26 awards ($66,250 total): children and siblings of alumni, children of faculty/staff, international students, members of minority groups, previous college experience, siblings of current students. *Tuition waivers:* Full or partial for employees or children of employees. *ROTC:* Army cooperative, Air Force cooperative.

LOANS *Student loans:* $25,711,697 (79% need-based, 21% non-need-based). 79% of past graduating class borrowed through all loan programs. *Average indebtedness per student:* $26,526. *Average need-based loan:* Freshmen: $4311. Undergraduates: $5122. *Parent loans:* $5,093,421 (51% need-based, 49% non-need-based). *Programs:* Federal Direct (Subsidized and Unsubsidized Stafford, PLUS), Perkins.

WORK-STUDY *Federal work-study:* Total amount: $430,816; 235 jobs averaging $1795. *State or other work-study/employment:* Total amount: $2,635,483 (75% need-based, 25% non-need-based). 214 part-time jobs averaging $3180.

ATHLETIC AWARDS Total amount: $1,739,780 (79% need-based, 21% non-need-based).

APPLYING FOR FINANCIAL AID *Required financial aid form:* FAFSA. *Financial aid deadline:* 3/15. *Notification date:* Continuous beginning 2/15. Students must reply within 2 weeks of notification.

CONTACT Sheila Nelson-Hensley, Director of Financial Aid, Point Park University, 201 Wood Street, Pittsburgh, PA 15222-1984, 412-392-3930 or toll-free 800-321-0129. *E-mail:* snelsonhensley@pointpark.edu. *Website:* http://www.pointpark.edu/.

POINT UNIVERSITY
East Point, GA

CONTACT Blair Walker, Director of Financial Aid, Point University, 2605 Ben Hill Road, East Point, GA 30344, 404-761-8861 or toll-free 855-37-POINT. *Fax:* 404-669-2024. *E-mail:* blairw@acc.edu. *Website:* http://point.edu/.

POLK STATE COLLEGE
Winter Haven, FL

CONTACT Lenora Burnett, Financial Aid Supervisor, Polk State College, 999 Avenue H, NE, Winter Haven, FL 33881, 863-297-5269. *E-mail:* lburnett@polk.edu. *Website:* http://www.polk.edu/.

POLYTECHNIC INSTITUTE OF NEW YORK UNIVERSITY
Brooklyn, NY

Tuition & fees: N/R	Average undergraduate aid package: $28,035

ABOUT THE INSTITUTION Independent, coed. *Awards:* certificates, bachelor's, master's, and doctoral degrees. 14 undergraduate majors. *Total enrollment:* 4,652. Undergraduates: 2,071. Freshmen: 495. Federal methodology is used as a basis for awarding need-based institutional aid.

FRESHMAN FINANCIAL AID (Fall 2011) 409 applied for aid; of those 76% were deemed to have need. 98% of freshmen with need received aid; of those 43% had need fully met. *Average percent of need met:* 91% (excluding resources awarded to replace EFC). *Average financial aid package:* $29,625 (excluding resources awarded to replace EFC). 24% of all full-time freshmen had no need and received non-need-based gift aid.

UNDERGRADUATE FINANCIAL AID (Fall 2011) 1,720 applied for aid; of those 81% were deemed to have need. 98% of undergraduates with need received aid; of those 38% had need fully met. *Average percent of need met:* 87% (excluding resources awarded to replace EFC). *Average financial aid package:* $28,035 (excluding resources awarded to replace EFC). 17% of all full-time undergraduates had no need and received non-need-based gift aid.

GIFT AID (NEED-BASED) *Total amount:* $20,174,012 (23% federal, 15% state, 62% institutional). *Receiving aid:* Freshmen: 69% (286); all full-time undergraduates:

70% (1,286). *Average award:* Freshmen: $13,421; Undergraduates: $15,812. *Scholarships, grants, and awards:* Federal Pell, FSEOG, state, private, college/university gift aid from institutional funds, United Negro College Fund.

GIFT AID (NON-NEED-BASED) *Total amount:* $17,085,914 (1% state, 99% institutional). *Receiving aid:* Freshmen: 65% (271). Undergraduates: 45% (816). *Average award:* Freshmen: $14,888. Undergraduates: $16,827. *Scholarships, grants, and awards by category:* Academic interests/achievement: computer science, engineering/technologies, general academic interests/achievements. *Special characteristics:* members of minority groups. *ROTC:* Army cooperative, Air Force cooperative.

LOANS *Student loans:* $10,678,107 (48% need-based, 52% non-need-based). 68% of past graduating class borrowed through all loan programs. *Average indebtedness per student:* $30,560. *Average need-based loan:* Freshmen: $3922. Undergraduates: $4597. *Parent loans:* $3,989,327 (100% non-need-based). *Programs:* Perkins, college/university, alternative loans.

WORK-STUDY *Federal work-study:* Total amount: $257,528; jobs available.

APPLYING FOR FINANCIAL AID *Required financial aid forms:* FAFSA, state aid form. *Financial aid deadline:* Continuous. *Notification date:* Continuous beginning 2/15. Students must reply by 5/1 or within 2 weeks of notification.

CONTACT Ms. Christine Falzerano, Director of Financial Aid, Polytechnic Institute of New York University, 6 Metrotech Center, Brooklyn, NY 11201-2990, 718-260-3025 or toll-free 800-POLYTECH. *Fax:* 718-260-3052. *E-mail:* cfalzera@poly.edu. *Website:* http://www.poly.edu/.

POLYTECHNIC UNIVERSITY OF PUERTO RICO
Hato Rey, PR

Tuition & fees: $7548	Average undergraduate aid package: $10,278

ABOUT THE INSTITUTION Independent, coed, primarily men. *Awards:* bachelor's and master's degrees. 13 undergraduate majors. *Total enrollment:* 4,743. Undergraduates: 4,031. Freshmen: 408. Federal methodology is used as a basis for awarding need-based institutional aid.

UNDERGRADUATE EXPENSES for 2013-2014 *Application fee:* $30. *Tuition:* full-time $6768; part-time $188 per credit. *Required fees:* full-time $780; $260 per term. Full-time tuition and fees vary according to course level, course load, degree level, and program. Part-time tuition and fees vary according to course level, course load, degree level, and program.

FRESHMAN FINANCIAL AID (Fall 2011) 192 applied for aid; of those 97% were deemed to have need. 94% of freshmen with need received aid. *Average percent of need met:* 31% (excluding resources awarded to replace EFC). *Average financial aid package:* $7249 (excluding resources awarded to replace EFC).

UNDERGRADUATE FINANCIAL AID (Fall 2011) 2,410 applied for aid; of those 98% were deemed to have need. 94% of undergraduates with need received aid; of those 1% had need fully met. *Average percent of need met:* 54% (excluding resources awarded to replace EFC). *Average financial aid package:* $10,278 (excluding resources awarded to replace EFC).

GIFT AID (NEED-BASED) *Total amount:* $13,479,875 (95% federal, 4% state, 1% external sources). *Receiving aid:* Freshmen: 37% (174); all full-time undergraduates: 79% (2,224). *Average award:* Freshmen: $4128; Undergraduates: $4250. *Scholarships, grants, and awards:* Federal Pell, FSEOG, state, college/university gift aid from institutional funds.

GIFT AID (NON-NEED-BASED) *Total amount:* $299,140 (100% institutional). *Receiving aid:* Freshmen: 2% (8). Undergraduates: 13% (370). *Average award:* Undergraduates: $903. *Scholarships, grants, and awards by category:* Academic interests/achievement: architecture, business, engineering/technologies. *Tuition waivers:* Full or partial for employees or children of employees. *ROTC:* Army cooperative.

LOANS *Student loans:* $11,142,551 (73% need-based, 27% non-need-based). *Average need-based loan:* Freshmen: $1921. Undergraduates: $3162. *Parent loans:* $92,300 (100% need-based).

WORK-STUDY *Federal work-study:* Total amount: $208,492; jobs available.

ATHLETIC AWARDS Total amount: $269,090 (100% non-need-based).

APPLYING FOR FINANCIAL AID *Required financial aid form:* FAFSA. *Financial aid deadline:* 5/15. *Notification date:* 7/15. Students must reply within 2 weeks of notification.
CONTACT Sergio E. Villoldo, Financial Aid Director, Polytechnic University of Puerto Rico, 377 Ponce de Leon Avenue, Hato Rey, PR 00919, 787-754-8000 Ext. 253. *Fax:* 787-766-1163.
Website: http://www.pupr.edu/.

POLYTECHNIC UNIVERSITY OF PUERTO RICO, MIAMI CAMPUS
Miami, FL

CONTACT Maria Victoria Shehadeh, Administrative Affairs Coordinator/Financial Aid Officer, Polytechnic University of Puerto Rico, Miami Campus, 8180 Northwest 36th Street, Suite 401, Miami, FL 33166, 305-418-8000 Ext. 204 or toll-free 888-729-7659. *E-mail:* mshehadeh@pupr.edu.
Website: http://www.pupr.edu/miami/.

POLYTECHNIC UNIVERSITY OF PUERTO RICO, ORLANDO CAMPUS
Winter Park, FL

CONTACT Mrs. Maria Victoria Shehadeh, Financial Aid Officer, Polytechnic University of Puerto Rico, Orlando Campus, 8180 N.W. 36TH Street, Miami, FL 33166, 305-418-8000 Ext. 204 or toll-free 888-577-POLY. *Fax:* 305-418-4325. *E-mail:* mshehadeh@pupr.edu.
Website: http://www.pupr.edu/orlando/.

POMONA COLLEGE
Claremont, CA

Tuition & fees: $41,438	Average undergraduate aid package: $39,506

ABOUT THE INSTITUTION Independent, coed. *Awards:* bachelor's degrees. 55 undergraduate majors. *Total enrollment:* 1,607. Undergraduates: 1,607. Freshmen: 399. Both federal and institutional methodology are used as a basis for awarding need-based institutional aid.
UNDERGRADUATE EXPENSES for 2013–2014 *Application fee:* $70. *Comprehensive fee:* $54,964 includes full-time tuition ($41,120), mandatory fees ($318), and room and board ($13,526). Room and board charges vary according to board plan.
FRESHMAN FINANCIAL AID (Fall 2011) 269 applied for aid; of those 80% were deemed to have need. 100% of freshmen with need received aid; of those 100% had need fully met. *Average percent of need met:* 100% (excluding resources awarded to replace EFC). *Average financial aid package:* $40,107 (excluding resources awarded to replace EFC).
UNDERGRADUATE FINANCIAL AID (Fall 2011) 1,078 applied for aid; of those 78% were deemed to have need. 100% of undergraduates with need received aid; of those 100% had need fully met. *Average percent of need met:* 100% (excluding resources awarded to replace EFC). *Average financial aid package:* $39,506 (excluding resources awarded to replace EFC).
GIFT AID (NEED-BASED) *Total amount:* $31,812,587 (5% federal, 3% state, 89% institutional, 3% external sources). *Receiving aid:* Freshmen: 55% (216); all full-time undergraduates: 54% (844). *Average award:* Freshmen: $38,475; Undergraduates: $37,611. *Scholarships, grants, and awards:* Federal Pell, FSEOG, state, private, college/university gift aid from institutional funds.
GIFT AID (NON-NEED-BASED) *Total amount:* $873,976 (2% federal, 98% external sources). *Tuition waivers:* Full or partial for employees or children of employees. *ROTC:* Army cooperative, Air Force cooperative.
LOANS *Student loans:* $2,126,524 (100% non-need-based). 32% of past graduating class borrowed through all loan programs. *Average indebtedness per student:* $15,714. *Parent loans:* $838,708 (100% non-need-based). *Programs:* Federal Direct (Subsidized and Unsubsidized Stafford, PLUS), Perkins, college/university.

WORK-STUDY *Federal work-study:* Total amount: $239,684; 175 jobs averaging $1369. *State or other work-study/employment:* Total amount: $1,145,018 (63% need-based, 37% non-need-based). 949 part-time jobs averaging $1188.
APPLYING FOR FINANCIAL AID *Required financial aid forms:* FAFSA, CSS Financial Aid PROFILE, state aid form, noncustodial (divorced/separated) parent's statement, business/farm supplement. *Financial aid deadline:* 2/1. *Notification date:* 4/10. Students must reply by 5/1.
CONTACT Mary Booker, Director of Financial Aid, Pomona College, 550 North College Avenue, Claremont, CA 91711, 909-621-8205. *Fax:* 909-607-7941. *E-mail:* financial_aid@pomadm.pomona.edu.
Website: http://www.pomona.edu/.

PONTIFICAL CATHOLIC UNIVERSITY OF PUERTO RICO
Ponce, PR

CONTACT Mrs. Rosalia Martinez, Director of Financial Aid, Pontifical Catholic University of Puerto Rico, 2250 Las Americas Avenue, Suite 549, Ponce, PR 00717-9777, 787-841-2000 Ext. 1065 or toll-free 800-961-7696. *Fax:* 787-651-2041. *E-mail:* rosalia.martinez@email.pucpr.edu.
Website: http://www.pucpr.edu/.

PONTIFICAL COLLEGE JOSEPHINUM
Columbus, OH

Tuition & fees: N/R	Average undergraduate aid package: $12,382

ABOUT THE INSTITUTION Independent Roman Catholic, men only. 6 undergraduate majors. Federal methodology is used as a basis for awarding need-based institutional aid.
FRESHMAN FINANCIAL AID (Fall 2012, est.) 11 applied for aid; of those 100% were deemed to have need. 82% of freshmen with need received aid; of those 33% had need fully met. *Average percent of need met:* 68% (excluding resources awarded to replace EFC). *Average financial aid package:* $10,817 (excluding resources awarded to replace EFC).
UNDERGRADUATE FINANCIAL AID (Fall 2012, est.) 87 applied for aid; of those 80% were deemed to have need. 51% of undergraduates with need received aid; of those 14% had need fully met. *Average percent of need met:* 70% (excluding resources awarded to replace EFC). *Average financial aid package:* $12,382 (excluding resources awarded to replace EFC).
GIFT AID (NEED-BASED) *Total amount:* $178,959 (47% federal, 8% state, 33% institutional, 12% external sources). *Receiving aid:* Freshmen: 8% (2); all full-time undergraduates: 11% (12). *Average award:* Freshmen: $3600; Undergraduates: $4200. *Scholarships, grants, and awards:* Federal Pell, FSEOG, state, private, college/university gift aid from institutional funds.
GIFT AID (NON-NEED-BASED) *Receiving aid:* Freshmen: 20% (5). Undergraduates: 18% (19). *Scholarships, grants, and awards by category:* Special characteristics: local/state students.
LOANS *Student loans:* $199,277 (61% need-based, 39% non-need-based). 26% of past graduating class borrowed through all loan programs. *Average indebtedness per student:* $15,324. *Parent loans:* $43,535 (100% non-need-based). *Programs:* Federal Direct (Subsidized and Unsubsidized Stafford, PLUS), Perkins.
WORK-STUDY *Federal work-study:* Total amount: $3870; 7 jobs averaging $600.
APPLYING FOR FINANCIAL AID *Required financial aid forms:* FAFSA, institution's own form. *Financial aid deadline (priority):* 9/2. *Notification date:* Continuous. Students must reply within 2 weeks of notification.
CONTACT Marky Leichtnam, Financial Aid Director, Pontifical College Josephinum, 7625 North High Street, Columbus, OH 43235-1498, 614-985-2212 or toll-free 888-252-5812. *Fax:* 614-885-2307. *E-mail:* mleichtnam@pcj.edu.
Website: http://www.pcj.edu/.

PORTLAND STATE UNIVERSITY
Portland, OR

Tuition & fees (OR res): $7653	Average undergraduate aid package: $14,205

ABOUT THE INSTITUTION State-supported, coed. *Awards:* certificates, bachelor's, master's, and doctoral degrees. 77 undergraduate majors. *Total enrollment:* 28,731. Undergraduates: 23,170. Freshmen: 1,418. Federal methodology is used as a basis for awarding need-based institutional aid.

UNDERGRADUATE EXPENSES for 2013–2014 *Application fee:* $50. *One-time required fee:* $300. *Tuition, state resident:* full-time $6390; part-time $142 per credit hour. *Tuition, nonresident:* full-time $21,600; part-time $480 per credit hour. *Required fees:* full-time $1263; $17 per credit hour or $98 per term. Full-time tuition and fees vary according to program and reciprocity agreements. Part-time tuition and fees vary according to program. *College room and board:* $11,019; *Room only:* $7650. Room and board charges vary according to board plan and housing facility.

FRESHMAN FINANCIAL AID (Fall 2011) 1,102 applied for aid; of those 80% were deemed to have need. 98% of freshmen with need received aid; of those 23% had need fully met. *Average percent of need met:* 74% (excluding resources awarded to replace EFC). *Average financial aid package:* $12,894 (excluding resources awarded to replace EFC). 1% of all full-time freshmen had no need and received non-need-based gift aid.

UNDERGRADUATE FINANCIAL AID (Fall 2011) 10,901 applied for aid; of those 90% were deemed to have need. 99% of undergraduates with need received aid; of those 19% had need fully met. *Average percent of need met:* 76% (excluding resources awarded to replace EFC). *Average financial aid package:* $14,205 (excluding resources awarded to replace EFC). 1% of all full-time undergraduates had no need and received non-need-based gift aid.

GIFT AID (NEED-BASED) *Total amount:* $49,412,760 (82% federal, 11% state, 2% institutional, 5% external sources). *Receiving aid:* Freshmen: 56% (683); all full-time undergraduates: 55% (7,655). *Average award:* Freshmen: $5983; Undergraduates: $5412. *Scholarships, grants, and awards:* Federal Pell, FSEOG, state, private, college/university gift aid from institutional funds, United Negro College Fund.

GIFT AID (NON-NEED-BASED) *Total amount:* $652,655 (6% federal, 36% institutional, 58% external sources). *Receiving aid:* Freshmen: 2% (19). Undergraduates: 55. *Average award:* Freshmen: $2000. Undergraduates: $1516. *Scholarships, grants, and awards by category:* Academic interests/achievement: architecture, area/ethnic studies, business, computer science, education, engineering/technologies, foreign languages, general academic interests/achievements, humanities, international studies, physical sciences, social sciences. *Creative arts/performance:* art/fine arts, general creative arts/performance, music, theater/drama. *Special achievements/activities:* community service, general special achievements/activities, leadership, memberships. *Special characteristics:* adult students, ethnic background, handicapped students, international students, members of minority groups, out-of-state students, veterans. *Tuition waivers:* Full or partial for employees or children of employees, senior citizens. *ROTC:* Army, Air Force cooperative.

LOANS *Student loans:* $112,138,153 (87% need-based, 13% non-need-based). 61% of past graduating class borrowed through all loan programs. *Average indebtedness per student:* $26,066. *Average need-based loan:* Freshmen: $6347. Undergraduates: $8817. *Parent loans:* $7,242,156 (45% need-based, 55% non-need-based). *Programs:* Federal Direct (Subsidized and Unsubsidized Stafford, PLUS), Perkins.

WORK-STUDY *Federal work-study:* Total amount: $2,236,169; jobs available. *State or other work-study/employment:* Total amount: $436,503 (55% need-based, 45% non-need-based). Part-time jobs available.

ATHLETIC AWARDS Total amount: $1,271,660 (43% need-based, 57% non-need-based).

APPLYING FOR FINANCIAL AID *Required financial aid form:* FAFSA. *Financial aid deadline:* Continuous. *Notification date:* Continuous. Students must reply within 4 weeks of notification.

CONTACT Phillip Rodgers, Director of Financial Aid, Portland State University, PO Box 851, Portland, OR 97207, 800-547-8887. *Fax:* 503-725-5965. *E-mail:* askfa@pdx.edu.
Website: http://www.pdx.edu/.

POST UNIVERSITY
Waterbury, CT

Tuition & fees: $27,450	Average undergraduate aid package: $19,550

ABOUT THE INSTITUTION Independent, coed. *Awards:* certificates, associate, bachelor's, and master's degrees. 22 undergraduate majors. *Total enrollment:* 722. Undergraduates: 722. Freshmen: 208. Federal methodology is used for awarding need-based institutional aid.

UNDERGRADUATE EXPENSES for 2013–2014 *Application fee:* $40. *Comprehensive fee:* $37,880 includes full-time tuition ($26,250), mandatory fees ($1200), and room and board ($10,430). Full-time tuition and fees vary according to degree level and program. Room and board charges vary according to housing facility. *Part-time tuition:* $875 per credit. Part-time tuition and fees vary according to class time, course load, degree level, and program.

FRESHMAN FINANCIAL AID (Fall 2011) 190 applied for aid; of those 93% were deemed to have need. 100% of freshmen with need received aid; of those 15% had need fully met. *Average percent of need met:* 55% (excluding resources awarded to replace EFC). *Average financial aid package:* $20,135 (excluding resources awarded to replace EFC). 2% of all full-time freshmen had no need and received non-need-based gift aid.

UNDERGRADUATE FINANCIAL AID (Fall 2011) 626 applied for aid; of those 95% were deemed to have need. 99% of undergraduates with need received aid; of those 13% had need fully met. *Average percent of need met:* 54% (excluding resources awarded to replace EFC). *Average financial aid package:* $19,550 (excluding resources awarded to replace EFC). 2% of all full-time undergraduates had no need and received non-need-based gift aid.

GIFT AID (NEED-BASED) *Total amount:* $5,463,967 (39% federal, 55% institutional, 6% external sources). *Receiving aid:* Freshmen: 79% (167); all full-time undergraduates: 78% (544). *Average award:* Freshmen: $16,562; Undergraduates: $15,408. *Scholarships, grants, and awards:* Federal Pell, FSEOG, state, private, college/university gift aid from institutional funds.

GIFT AID (NON-NEED-BASED) *Total amount:* $4,546,835 (97% institutional, 3% external sources). *Receiving aid:* Freshmen: 27% (57). Undergraduates: 28% (198). *Average award:* Freshmen: $10,400. Undergraduates: $8769. *Scholarships, grants, and awards by category:* Academic interests/achievement: agriculture, biological sciences, business, communication, computer science, education, English, general academic interests/achievements, humanities, international studies, social sciences. *Special characteristics:* children and siblings of alumni, local/state students, siblings of current students. *Tuition waivers:* Full or partial for employees or children of employees, senior citizens.

LOANS *Student loans:* $5,506,254 (41% need-based, 59% non-need-based). 90% of past graduating class borrowed through all loan programs. *Average indebtedness per student:* $16,499. *Average need-based loan:* Freshmen: $3456. Undergraduates: $4245. *Parent loans:* $1,859,011 (100% non-need-based). *Programs:* Federal Direct (Subsidized and Unsubsidized Stafford, PLUS), Perkins, college/university.

WORK-STUDY *Federal work-study:* Total amount: $167,967; jobs available. *State or other work-study/employment:* Total amount: $1500 (100% non-need-based). Part-time jobs available.

ATHLETIC AWARDS Total amount: $1,569,928 (100% non-need-based).

APPLYING FOR FINANCIAL AID *Required financial aid form:* FAFSA. *Financial aid deadline (priority):* 3/1. *Notification date:* Continuous beginning 4/1. Students must reply within 2 weeks of notification.

CONTACT Ms. Regina Faulds, Director of Financial Aid, Post University, 800 Country Club Road, Waterbury, CT 06723-2540, 203-596-4528 or toll-free 800-345-2562. *Fax:* 203-596-4599. *E-mail:* rfaulds@post.edu.
Website: http://www.post.edu/.

POTOMAC COLLEGE
Washington, DC

CONTACT Phyllis Crews, Financial Aid Counselor, Potomac College, 4000 Chesapeake Street NW, Washington, DC 20016, 202-686-0876 or toll-free 888-686-0876. *Fax:* 202-686-0818. *E-mail:* pcrews@potomac.edu.
Website: http://www.potomac.edu/.

PRAIRIE VIEW A&M UNIVERSITY
Prairie View, TX

ABOUT THE INSTITUTION State-supported, coed. *Awards:* bachelor's, master's, and doctoral degrees. 43 undergraduate majors. *Total enrollment:* 8,425. Undergraduates: 6,813. Freshmen: 1,689.

GIFT AID (NEED-BASED) *Scholarships, grants, and awards:* Federal Pell, FSEOG, state, private, college/university gift aid from institutional funds, United Negro College Fund, Federal Nursing.

GIFT AID (NON-NEED-BASED) *Scholarships, grants, and awards by category:* Academic interests/achievement: agriculture, architecture, education, general academic interests/achievements, premedicine. *Creative arts/performance:* art/fine arts, music, performing arts.

LOANS *Programs:* Federal Direct (Subsidized and Unsubsidized Stafford, PLUS), state, college/university.

APPLYING FOR FINANCIAL AID *Required financial aid form:* FAFSA.

CONTACT Mr. K. Michael Francois, Director of Student Financial Aid and Scholarships, Prairie View A&M University, PO Box 519, Mail Stop 1005, Prairie View, TX 77446, 936-261-1009. *E-mail:* kmfrancois@pvamu.edu. *Website:* http://www.pvamu.edu/.

PRATT INSTITUTE
Brooklyn, NY

ABOUT THE INSTITUTION Independent, coed. *Awards:* certificates, associate, bachelor's, and master's degrees. 25 undergraduate majors. *Total enrollment:* 4,722. Undergraduates: 3,021. Freshmen: 608.

GIFT AID (NEED-BASED) *Scholarships, grants, and awards:* Federal Pell, FSEOG, state, private.

GIFT AID (NON-NEED-BASED) *Scholarships, grants, and awards by category:* Academic interests/achievement: general academic interests/achievements.

LOANS *Programs:* Federal Direct (Subsidized and Unsubsidized Stafford, PLUS), Perkins.

WORK-STUDY *Federal work-study:* Total amount: $571,969; jobs available. *State or other work-study/employment:* Part-time jobs available.

APPLYING FOR FINANCIAL AID *Required financial aid forms:* FAFSA, state aid form.

CONTACT Savior Wright, Assistant Director of Financial Aid, Pratt Institute, 200 Willoughby Avenue, Myrtle Hall, Room 6E-9, Brooklyn, NY 11205-3899, 718-636-3563 or toll-free 800-331-0834. *Fax:* 718-636-3739. *E-mail:* finaid@pratt.edu. *Website:* http://www.pratt.edu/.

PRESBYTERIAN COLLEGE
Clinton, SC

Tuition & fees: $32,680	Average undergraduate aid package: $31,773

ABOUT THE INSTITUTION Independent Presbyterian Church (U.S.A.), coed. *Awards:* bachelor's and doctoral degrees. 31 undergraduate majors. *Total enrollment:* 1,403. Undergraduates: 1,172. Freshmen: 282. Federal methodology is used as a basis for awarding need-based institutional aid.

UNDERGRADUATE EXPENSES for 2013–2014 *Comprehensive fee:* $41,430 includes full-time tuition ($30,080), mandatory fees ($2600), and room and board ($8750). *College room only:* $4260. Full-time tuition and fees vary according to reciprocity agreements. Room and board charges vary according to board plan and housing facility. Part-time tuition and fees vary according to course load and program.

FRESHMAN FINANCIAL AID (Fall 2012, est.) 262 applied for aid; of those 88% were deemed to have need. 100% of freshmen with need received aid; of those 39% had need fully met. *Average percent of need met:* 90% (excluding resources awarded to replace EFC). *Average financial aid package:* $32,031 (excluding resources awarded to replace EFC). 20% of all full-time freshmen had no need and received non-need-based gift aid.

UNDERGRADUATE FINANCIAL AID (Fall 2012, est.) 986 applied for aid; of those 87% were deemed to have need. 100% of undergraduates with need received aid; of those 44% had need fully met. *Average percent of need met:* 90%

(excluding resources awarded to replace EFC). *Average financial aid package:* $31,773 (excluding resources awarded to replace EFC). 20% of all full-time undergraduates had no need and received non-need-based gift aid.

GIFT AID (NEED-BASED) *Total amount:* $7,474,450 (16% federal, 22% state, 62% institutional). *Receiving aid:* Freshmen: 82% (230); all full-time undergraduates: 76% (853). *Average award:* Freshmen: $31,013; Undergraduates: $31,846. *Scholarships, grants, and awards:* Federal Pell, FSEOG, state, private, college/university gift aid from institutional funds.

GIFT AID (NON-NEED-BASED) *Total amount:* $18,872,782 (16% state, 80% institutional, 4% external sources). *Receiving aid:* Freshmen: 40% (112). Undergraduates: 32% (360). *Average award:* Freshmen: $15,987. Undergraduates: $14,689. *Scholarships, grants, and awards by category:* Academic interests/achievement: general academic interests/achievements. *Creative arts/performance:* music. *Special achievements/activities:* leadership, religious involvement. *Special characteristics:* children of faculty/staff, relatives of clergy, religious affiliation. *Tuition waivers:* Full or partial for employees or children of employees, senior citizens. *ROTC:* Army.

LOANS *Student loans:* $4,626,682 (40% need-based, 60% non-need-based). 48% of past graduating class borrowed through all loan programs. *Average indebtedness per student:* $25,425. *Average need-based loan:* Freshmen: $3068. Undergraduates: $3863. *Parent loans:* $1,846,492 (100% non-need-based). *Programs:* Federal Direct (Subsidized and Unsubsidized Stafford, PLUS), Perkins, state, college/university, private loans.

WORK-STUDY *Federal work-study:* Total amount: $200,000; jobs available. *State or other work-study/employment:* Part-time jobs available.

ATHLETIC AWARDS Total amount: $5,438,620 (100% non-need-based).

APPLYING FOR FINANCIAL AID *Required financial aid form:* FAFSA. *Financial aid deadline:* 6/30 (priority: 3/15). *Notification date:* 3/1. Students must reply by 5/1.

CONTACT Ms. Rebecca D. Pressley, Director of Financial Aid, Presbyterian College, 503 South Broad Street, Clinton, SC 29325, 864-833-8287 or toll-free 800-960-7583 (in-state), 800-930-7583 (out-of-state). *E-mail:* rpressley@presby.edu . *Website:* http://www.presby.edu/.

PRESCOTT COLLEGE
Prescott, AZ

Tuition & fees: $28,019	Average undergraduate aid package: $18,738

ABOUT THE INSTITUTION Independent, coed. *Awards:* certificates, bachelor's, master's, and doctoral degrees. 41 undergraduate majors. *Total enrollment:* 1,065. Undergraduates: 673. Freshmen: 64. Federal methodology is used as a basis for awarding need-based institutional aid.

UNDERGRADUATE EXPENSES for 2013–2014 *Application fee:* $25. *Comprehensive fee:* $33,919 includes full-time tuition ($27,408), mandatory fees ($611), and room and board ($5900). *College room only:* $4230. Full-time tuition and fees vary according to course load, degree level, and reciprocity agreements. Room and board charges vary according to board plan and housing facility. *Part-time tuition:* $1142 per credit. *Part-time fees:* $306 per term. Part-time tuition and fees vary according to course load, degree level, and reciprocity agreements.

FRESHMAN FINANCIAL AID (Fall 2012, est.) 51 applied for aid; of those 98% were deemed to have need. 100% of freshmen with need received aid; of those 10% had need fully met. *Average percent of need met:* 69% (excluding resources awarded to replace EFC). *Average financial aid package:* $22,273 (excluding resources awarded to replace EFC). 14% of all full-time freshmen had no need and received non-need-based gift aid.

UNDERGRADUATE FINANCIAL AID (Fall 2012, est.) 410 applied for aid; of those 92% were deemed to have need. 100% of undergraduates with need received aid; of those 9% had need fully met. *Average percent of need met:* 58% (excluding resources awarded to replace EFC). *Average financial aid package:* $18,738 (excluding resources awarded to replace EFC). 20% of all full-time undergraduates had no need and received non-need-based gift aid.

GIFT AID (NEED-BASED) *Total amount:* $5,443,681 (27% federal, 71% institutional, 2% external sources). *Receiving aid:* Freshmen: 77% (49); all full-time undergraduates: 69% (373). *Average award:* Freshmen: $18,100; Undergraduates: $13,497. *Scholarships, grants, and awards:* Federal Pell, FSEOG, state, private,

college/university gift aid from institutional funds, Academic Competitiveness Grants, National SMART Grants.
GIFT AID (NON-NEED-BASED) *Total amount:* $1,016,033 (1% federal, 97% institutional, 2% external sources). *Receiving aid:* Freshmen: 5% (3). Undergraduates: 3% (14). *Average award:* Freshmen: $8777. Undergraduates: $8232. *Scholarships, grants, and awards by category:* Academic interests/achievement: general academic interests/achievements. *Special achievements/activities:* general special achievements/activities. *Tuition waivers:* Full or partial for employees or children of employees.
LOANS *Student loans:* $5,089,806 (86% need-based, 14% non-need-based). 68% of past graduating class borrowed through all loan programs. *Average indebtedness per student:* $23,476. *Average need-based loan:* Freshmen: $3895. Undergraduates: $5278. *Parent loans:* $730,850 (53% need-based, 47% non-need-based). *Programs:* Federal Direct (Subsidized and Unsubsidized Stafford, PLUS).
WORK-STUDY *Federal work-study:* Total amount: $153,544; 92 jobs averaging $1500. *State or other work-study/employment:* 141 part-time jobs averaging $660.
APPLYING FOR FINANCIAL AID *Required financial aid form:* FAFSA. *Financial aid deadline (priority):* 3/1. *Notification date:* Continuous beginning 3/15. Students must reply within 12 weeks of notification.
CONTACT Mary Frances Causey, Director of Financial Aid, Prescott College, 220 Grove Avenue, Prescott, AZ 86301-2990, 928-350-1111 or toll-free 877-350-2100. *Fax:* 928-350-1120. *E-mail:* finaid@prescott.edu.
Website: http://www.prescott.edu/.

PRESENTATION COLLEGE
Aberdeen, SD

CONTACT Ms. Janel Wagner, Director of Financial Aid, Presentation College, 1500 North Main Street, Aberdeen, SD 57401-1299, 605-229-8427 or toll-free 800-437-6060. *Fax:* 605-229-8537. *E-mail:* janel.wagner@presentation.edu.
Website: http://www.presentation.edu/.

PRINCETON UNIVERSITY
Princeton, NJ

Tuition & fees: $40,715	Average undergraduate aid package: $36,989

ABOUT THE INSTITUTION Independent, coed. *Awards:* bachelor's, master's, and doctoral degrees. 35 undergraduate majors. *Total enrollment:* 8,010. Undergraduates: 5,336. Freshmen: 1,357. Both federal and institutional methodology are used as a basis for awarding need-based institutional aid.
UNDERGRADUATE EXPENSES for 2013–2014 *Application fee:* $65. *Comprehensive fee:* $53,795 includes full-time tuition ($40,170), mandatory fees ($545), and room and board ($13,080). *College room only:* $7220. Room and board charges vary according to board plan.
FRESHMAN FINANCIAL AID (Fall 2011) 933 applied for aid; of those 87% were deemed to have need. 100% of freshmen with need received aid; of those 100% had need fully met. *Average percent of need met:* 100% (excluding resources awarded to replace EFC). *Average financial aid package:* $39,406 (excluding resources awarded to replace EFC).
UNDERGRADUATE FINANCIAL AID (Fall 2011) 3,334 applied for aid; of those 92% were deemed to have need. 100% of undergraduates with need received aid; of those 100% had need fully met. *Average percent of need met:* 100% (excluding resources awarded to replace EFC). *Average financial aid package:* $36,989 (excluding resources awarded to replace EFC).
GIFT AID (NEED-BASED) *Total amount:* $109,559,375 (4% federal, 93% institutional, 3% external sources). *Receiving aid:* Freshmen: 59% (809); all full-time undergraduates: 59% (3,072). *Average award:* Freshmen: $37,926; Undergraduates: $35,664. *Scholarships, grants, and awards:* Federal Pell, FSEOG, state, private, college/university gift aid from institutional funds.
GIFT AID (NON-NEED-BASED) *Tuition waivers:* Full or partial for employees or children of employees. *ROTC:* Army, Naval cooperative.

LOANS *Student loans:* 24% of past graduating class borrowed through all loan programs. *Average indebtedness per student:* $5096. *Parent loans:* $318,785 (100% non-need-based). *Programs:* Federal Direct (Subsidized and Unsubsidized Stafford, PLUS), Perkins, college/university.
WORK-STUDY *Federal work-study:* Total amount: $615,108; 696 jobs averaging $884. *State or other work-study/employment:* Total amount: $2,005,675 (100% need-based). 1,559 part-time jobs averaging $1286.
APPLYING FOR FINANCIAL AID *Required financial aid forms:* FAFSA, institution's own form. *Financial aid deadline (priority):* 2/1. *Notification date:* 4/1. Students must reply by 5/1.
CONTACT Robin Moscato, Director of Financial Aid, Princeton University, PO Box 591, Princeton, NJ 08542, 609-258-3330. *Fax:* 609-258-3558. *E-mail:* moscato@princeton.edu.
Website: http://www.princeton.edu/.

PRINCIPIA COLLEGE
Elsah, IL

Tuition & fees: $25,980	Average undergraduate aid package: $26,856

ABOUT THE INSTITUTION Independent Christian Science, coed. *Awards:* bachelor's degrees. 28 undergraduate majors. *Total enrollment:* 489. Undergraduates: 489. Freshmen: 114. Institutional methodology is used as a basis for awarding need-based institutional aid.
UNDERGRADUATE EXPENSES for 2013–2014 *Comprehensive fee:* $36,480 includes full-time tuition ($25,500), mandatory fees ($480), and room and board ($10,500). *College room only:* $5000. Full-time tuition and fees vary according to course load. Part-time tuition and fees vary according to course load.
FRESHMAN FINANCIAL AID (Fall 2012, est.) 91 applied for aid; of those 97% were deemed to have need. 100% of freshmen with need received aid; of those 44% had need fully met. *Average percent of need met:* 88% (excluding resources awarded to replace EFC). *Average financial aid package:* $25,918 (excluding resources awarded to replace EFC). 23% of all full-time freshmen had no need and received non-need-based gift aid.
UNDERGRADUATE FINANCIAL AID (Fall 2012, est.) 385 applied for aid; of those 97% were deemed to have need. 100% of undergraduates with need received aid; of those 46% had need fully met. *Average percent of need met:* 83% (excluding resources awarded to replace EFC). *Average financial aid package:* $26,856 (excluding resources awarded to replace EFC). 21% of all full-time undergraduates had no need and received non-need-based gift aid.
GIFT AID (NEED-BASED) *Total amount:* $8,534,616 (99% institutional, 1% external sources). *Receiving aid:* Freshmen: 75% (88); all full-time undergraduates: 73% (372). *Average award:* Freshmen: $21,956; Undergraduates: $22,681. *Scholarships, grants, and awards:* private, college/university gift aid from institutional funds.
GIFT AID (NON-NEED-BASED) *Total amount:* $2,006,427 (100% institutional). *Receiving aid:* Freshmen: 32% (38). Undergraduates: 29% (147). *Average award:* Freshmen: $20,930. Undergraduates: $18,408. *Scholarships, grants, and awards by category:* Academic interests/achievement: 93 awards ($1,779,828 total): general academic interests/achievements. *Special achievements/activities:* 138 awards ($1,996,195 total): community service, general special achievements/activities, leadership, religious involvement. *Special characteristics:* 14 awards ($54,000 total): children and siblings of alumni, children of faculty/staff.
LOANS *Student loans:* $1,633,138 (95% need-based, 5% non-need-based). *Average need-based loan:* Freshmen: $5471. Undergraduates: $4566. *Programs:* college/university.
APPLYING FOR FINANCIAL AID *Required financial aid forms:* CSS Financial Aid PROFILE, noncustodial (divorced/separated) parent's statement, federal income tax form(s). *Financial aid deadline (priority):* 3/1. *Notification date:* Continuous beginning 3/1. Students must reply by 5/1 or within 4 weeks of notification.
CONTACT Tami Gavaletz, Director of Financial Aid, Principia College, 1 Maybeck Place, Elsah, IL 62028-9799, 618-374-5187 or toll-free 800-277-4648 Ext. 2804. *Fax:* 618-374-4000. *E-mail:* tami.gavaletz@principia.edu.
Website: http://www.principiacollege.edu/.

PROVIDENCE COLLEGE
Providence, RI

Tuition & fees: $42,206	Average undergraduate aid package: $26,379

ABOUT THE INSTITUTION Independent Roman Catholic, coed. *Awards:* certificates, associate, bachelor's, and master's degrees. 45 undergraduate majors. *Total enrollment:* 4,336. Undergraduates: 3,810. Freshmen: 998. Both federal and institutional methodology are used as a basis for awarding need-based institutional aid.

UNDERGRADUATE EXPENSES for 2013–2014 *Comprehensive fee:* $54,646 includes full-time tuition ($41,350), mandatory fees ($856), and room and board ($12,440). *College room only:* $7170. Full-time tuition and fees vary according to degree level and student level. Room and board charges vary according to board plan and housing facility. *Part-time tuition:* $1477 per credit. Part-time tuition and fees vary according to degree level.

FRESHMAN FINANCIAL AID (Fall 2012, est.) 728 applied for aid; of those 71% were deemed to have need. 100% of freshmen with need received aid; of those 39% had need fully met. *Average percent of need met:* 87% (excluding resources awarded to replace EFC). *Average financial aid package:* $28,357 (excluding resources awarded to replace EFC). 12% of all full-time freshmen had no need and received non-need-based gift aid.

UNDERGRADUATE FINANCIAL AID (Fall 2012, est.) 2,610 applied for aid; of those 81% were deemed to have need. 100% of undergraduates with need received aid; of those 36% had need fully met. *Average percent of need met:* 84% (excluding resources awarded to replace EFC). *Average financial aid package:* $26,379 (excluding resources awarded to replace EFC). 12% of all full-time undergraduates had no need and received non-need-based gift aid.

GIFT AID (NEED-BASED) *Total amount:* $43,147,023 (7% federal, 1% state, 90% institutional, 2% external sources). *Receiving aid:* Freshmen: 51% (504); all full-time undergraduates: 55% (2,116). *Average award:* Freshmen: $23,530; Undergraduates: $22,045. *Scholarships, grants, and awards:* Federal Pell, FSEOG, state, private, college/university gift aid from institutional funds, Academic Competitiveness Grants, National SMART Grants.

GIFT AID (NON-NEED-BASED) *Total amount:* $11,604,717 (97% institutional, 3% external sources). *Receiving aid:* Freshmen: 4% (38). Undergraduates: 6% (233). *Average award:* Freshmen: $15,222. Undergraduates: $19,925. *Scholarships, grants, and awards by category:* Academic interests/achievement: 400 awards ($3,750,000 total): business, general academic interests/achievements, military science, premedicine. Creative arts/performance: 5 awards ($15,000 total): theater/drama. Special achievements/activities: 20 awards ($100,000 total): community service. Special characteristics: 84 awards ($84,000 total): siblings of current students. *Tuition waivers:* Full or partial for employees or children of employees. *ROTC:* Army.

LOANS *Student loans:* $22,203,203 (64% need-based, 36% non-need-based). 70% of past graduating class borrowed through all loan programs. *Average indebtedness per student:* $26,832. *Average need-based loan:* Freshmen: $4890. Undergraduates: $5070. *Parent loans:* $10,709,869 (65% need-based, 35% non-need-based). *Programs:* Federal Direct (Subsidized and Unsubsidized Stafford, PLUS), Perkins.

WORK-STUDY *Federal work-study:* Total amount: $1,077,921; 1,148 jobs averaging $1800. *State or other work-study/employment:* Total amount: $800,000 (100% non-need-based). Part-time jobs available.

ATHLETIC AWARDS Total amount: $6,448,633 (20% need-based, 80% non-need-based).

APPLYING FOR FINANCIAL AID *Required financial aid forms:* FAFSA, CSS Financial Aid PROFILE, federal income tax form(s). *Financial aid deadline:* 2/1 (priority: 2/1). *Notification date:* 3/15. Students must reply by 5/1.

CONTACT Ms. Sandra J. Oliveira, Executive Director of Financial Aid, Providence College, One Cunningham Square, Providence, RI 02918, 401-865-2286 or toll-free 800-721-6444. *Fax:* 401-865-1186. *E-mail:* solivei6@providence.edu. *Website:* http://www.providence.edu/.

PURCHASE COLLEGE, STATE UNIVERSITY OF NEW YORK
Purchase, NY

Tuition & fees (NY res): $7230	Average undergraduate aid package: $10,079

ABOUT THE INSTITUTION State-supported, coed. *Awards:* certificates, bachelor's, and master's degrees. 43 undergraduate majors. *Total enrollment:* 4,267. Undergraduates: 4,155. Freshmen: 694. Federal methodology is used as a basis for awarding need-based institutional aid.

UNDERGRADUATE EXPENSES for 2013–2014 *Application fee:* $40. *One-time required fee:* $200. *Tuition, state resident:* full-time $5570; part-time $232 per credit. *Tuition, nonresident:* full-time $14,820; part-time $618 per credit. *Required fees:* full-time $1660; $68 per credit. Full-time tuition and fees vary according to program. Part-time tuition and fees vary according to course load and program. *College room and board:* $11,566; *Room only:* $7378. Room and board charges vary according to board plan and housing facility.

FRESHMAN FINANCIAL AID (Fall 2012, est.) 597 applied for aid; of those 75% were deemed to have need. 100% of freshmen with need received aid; of those 3% had need fully met. *Average percent of need met:* 50% (excluding resources awarded to replace EFC). *Average financial aid package:* $9124 (excluding resources awarded to replace EFC). 4% of all full-time freshmen had no need and received non-need-based gift aid.

UNDERGRADUATE FINANCIAL AID (Fall 2012, est.) 2,894 applied for aid; of those 80% were deemed to have need. 100% of undergraduates with need received aid; of those 4% had need fully met. *Average percent of need met:* 53% (excluding resources awarded to replace EFC). *Average financial aid package:* $10,079 (excluding resources awarded to replace EFC). 3% of all full-time undergraduates had no need and received non-need-based gift aid.

GIFT AID (NEED-BASED) *Total amount:* $12,100,779 (49% federal, 39% state, 9% institutional, 3% external sources). *Receiving aid:* Freshmen: 53% (369); all full-time undergraduates: 51% (1,919). *Average award:* Freshmen: $6413; Undergraduates: $6305. *Scholarships, grants, and awards:* Federal Pell, FSEOG, state, private, college/university gift aid from institutional funds.

GIFT AID (NON-NEED-BASED) *Total amount:* $510,775 (21% state, 56% institutional, 23% external sources). *Receiving aid:* Freshmen: 1% (5). Undergraduates: 1% (27). *Average award:* Freshmen: $2844. Undergraduates: $2231. *Scholarships, grants, and awards by category:* Academic interests/achievement: area/ethnic studies, biological sciences, computer science, English, general academic interests/achievements, humanities, mathematics, social sciences. Creative arts/performance: art/fine arts, cinema/film/broadcasting, creative writing, dance, general creative arts/performance, music, performing arts, theater/drama. *Tuition waivers:* Full or partial for employees or children of employees.

LOANS *Student loans:* $22,587,042 (75% need-based, 25% non-need-based). 60% of past graduating class borrowed through all loan programs. *Average indebtedness per student:* $26,684. *Average need-based loan:* Freshmen: $3771. Undergraduates: $4714. *Parent loans:* $27,272,084 (34% need-based, 66% non-need-based). *Programs:* Federal Direct (Subsidized and Unsubsidized Stafford, PLUS), Perkins.

WORK-STUDY *Federal work-study:* Total amount: $202,142; jobs available. *State or other work-study/employment:* Total amount: $630,087 (54% need-based, 46% non-need-based). Part-time jobs available.

APPLYING FOR FINANCIAL AID *Required financial aid forms:* FAFSA, state aid form. *Financial aid deadline (priority):* 2/1. *Notification date:* Continuous beginning 3/1.

CONTACT Ms. Corey York, Director of Student Financial Services, Purchase College, State University of New York, 735 Anderson Hill Road, Purchase, NY 10577-1400, 914-251-6085. *Fax:* 914-251-6099. *E-mail:* corey.york@purchase.edu. *Website:* http://www.purchase.edu/.

PURDUE UNIVERSITY
West Lafayette, IN

Tuition & fees (IN res): $10,466	Average undergraduate aid package: $12,300

ABOUT THE INSTITUTION State-supported, coed. **Awards:** certificates, associate, bachelor's, master's, and doctoral degrees. 225 undergraduate majors. **Total enrollment:** 39,256. Undergraduates: 30,147. Freshmen: 6,349. Federal methodology is used as a basis for awarding need-based institutional aid.

UNDERGRADUATE EXPENSES for 2013–2014 Application fee: $50. **Tuition, state resident:** full-time $9900. **Tuition, nonresident:** full-time $28,702. **Required fees:** full-time $566. Full-time tuition and fees vary according to course load and program. Part-time tuition and fees vary according to course load. **College room and board:** $9990; **Room only:** $5196. Room and board charges vary according to board plan and housing facility.

FRESHMAN FINANCIAL AID (Fall 2012, est.) 4,539 applied for aid; of those 74% were deemed to have need. 100% of freshmen with need received aid; of those 44% had need fully met. **Average percent of need met:** 84% (excluding resources awarded to replace EFC). **Average financial aid package:** $12,668 (excluding resources awarded to replace EFC). 9% of all full-time freshmen had no need and received non-need-based gift aid.

UNDERGRADUATE FINANCIAL AID (Fall 2012, est.) 18,211 applied for aid; of those 78% were deemed to have need. 100% of undergraduates with need received aid; of those 35% had need fully met. **Average percent of need met:** 85% (excluding resources awarded to replace EFC). **Average financial aid package:** $12,300 (excluding resources awarded to replace EFC). 8% of all full-time undergraduates had no need and received non-need-based gift aid.

GIFT AID (NEED-BASED) Total amount: $84,531,089 (33% federal, 25% state, 39% institutional, 3% external sources). **Receiving aid:** Freshmen: 33% (2,131); all full-time undergraduates: 32% (9,312). **Average award:** Freshmen: $12,486; Undergraduates: $10,702. **Scholarships, grants, and awards:** Federal Pell, FSEOG, state, private, college/university gift aid from institutional funds.

GIFT AID (NON-NEED-BASED) Total amount: $42,218,598 (20% federal, 5% state, 57% institutional, 18% external sources). **Receiving aid:** Freshmen: 22% (1,443). Undergraduates: 16% (4,763). **Average award:** Freshmen: $7531. Undergraduates: $6321. **Scholarships, grants, and awards by category:** Academic interests/achievement: agriculture, computer science, education, engineering/technologies, general academic interests/achievements, health fields, humanities, mathematics, military science, physical sciences. Creative arts/performance: music. Special achievements/activities: leadership. Special characteristics: children of faculty/staff. **Tuition waivers:** Full or partial for employees or children of employees, senior citizens. **ROTC:** Army, Naval, Air Force.

LOANS Student loans: $135,610,199 (68% need-based, 32% non-need-based). 54% of past graduating class borrowed through all loan programs. **Average indebtedness per student:** $27,798. **Average need-based loan:** Freshmen: $3847. Undergraduates: $4776. **Parent loans:** $139,055,843 (30% need-based, 70% non-need-based). **Programs:** Federal Direct (Subsidized and Unsubsidized Stafford, PLUS), Perkins, college/university.

WORK-STUDY Federal work-study: Total amount: $4,591,940; 1,935 jobs averaging $2373. **State or other work-study/employment:** Total amount: $2,392,129 (40% need-based, 60% non-need-based). Part-time jobs available.

ATHLETIC AWARDS Total amount: $8,868,377 (37% need-based, 63% non-need-based).

APPLYING FOR FINANCIAL AID Required financial aid form: FAFSA. **Financial aid deadline (priority):** 3/1. **Notification date:** 4/15.

CONTACT Theodore E. Malone, Division of Financial Aid, Purdue University, Schleman Hall of Student Services, Room 305, West Lafayette, IN 47907-2050, 765-494-5056. Fax: 765-496-3918.
Website: http://www.purdue.edu/.

PURDUE UNIVERSITY CALUMET
Hammond, IN

Tuition & fees (IN res): $6991	Average undergraduate aid package: $7306

ABOUT THE INSTITUTION State-supported, coed. **Awards:** certificates, associate, bachelor's, and master's degrees. 68 undergraduate majors. **Total enrollment:** 10,054. Undergraduates: 8,912. Freshmen: 994. Federal methodology is used as a basis for awarding need-based institutional aid.

UNDERGRADUATE EXPENSES for 2013–2014 Application fee: $25. **Tuition, state resident:** full-time $6991; part-time $231.95 per credit hour. **Tuition, nonresident:** full-time $15,169; part-time $524 per credit hour. Full-time tuition and fees vary according to course load and program. Part-time tuition and fees vary according to course load and program. **College room and board:** $7717; **Room only:** $5170. Room and board charges vary according to housing facility.

FRESHMAN FINANCIAL AID (Fall 2011) 782 applied for aid; of those 84% were deemed to have need. 93% of freshmen with need received aid; of those 13% had need fully met. **Average percent of need met:** 18% (excluding resources awarded to replace EFC). **Average financial aid package:** $4052 (excluding resources awarded to replace EFC). 4% of all full-time freshmen had no need and received non-need-based gift aid.

UNDERGRADUATE FINANCIAL AID (Fall 2011) 4,882 applied for aid; of those 90% were deemed to have need. 94% of undergraduates with need received aid; of those 8% had need fully met. **Average percent of need met:** 18% (excluding resources awarded to replace EFC). **Average financial aid package:** $7306 (excluding resources awarded to replace EFC). 3% of all full-time undergraduates had no need and received non-need-based gift aid.

GIFT AID (NEED-BASED) Total amount: $18,747,187 (73% federal, 25% state, 2% institutional). **Receiving aid:** Freshmen: 45% (430); all full-time undergraduates: 48% (2,995). **Average award:** Freshmen: $3130; Undergraduates: $5330. **Scholarships, grants, and awards:** Federal Pell, FSEOG, state, private, college/university gift aid from institutional funds.

GIFT AID (NON-NEED-BASED) Total amount: $4,508,261 (1% state, 59% institutional, 40% external sources). **Receiving aid:** Freshmen: 17% (166). Undergraduates: 11% (673). **Average award:** Freshmen: $2392. Undergraduates: $4348. **Scholarships, grants, and awards by category:** Academic interests/achievement: 596 awards ($2,517,581 total): general academic interests/achievements. **Tuition waivers:** Full or partial for employees or children of employees, senior citizens. **ROTC:** Army.

LOANS Student loans: $31,831,809 (98% need-based, 2% non-need-based). 58% of past graduating class borrowed through all loan programs. **Average indebtedness per student:** $26,273. **Average need-based loan:** Freshmen: $1847. Undergraduates: $3469. **Parent loans:** $3,004,435 (100% non-need-based). **Programs:** Federal Direct (Subsidized and Unsubsidized Stafford, PLUS), Perkins.

WORK-STUDY Federal work-study: Total amount: $192,536; 68 jobs averaging $2478.

ATHLETIC AWARDS Total amount: $76,358 (100% non-need-based).

APPLYING FOR FINANCIAL AID Required financial aid form: FAFSA. **Financial aid deadline (priority):** 3/10. **Notification date:** Continuous beginning 4/15. Students must reply within 2 weeks of notification.

CONTACT Ms. Beatriz Contreras, Director of Student Financial Services, Purdue University Calumet, 2200 169th Street, Hammond, IN 46323-2094, 219-989-2301 or toll-free 800-447-8738. Fax: 219-989-2141. E-mail: finaid2@purduecal.edu. Website: http://www.purduecal.edu/.

PURDUE UNIVERSITY NORTH CENTRAL
Westville, IN

Tuition & fees (IN res): $7045	Average undergraduate aid package: $7588

ABOUT THE INSTITUTION State-supported, coed. **Awards:** certificates, associate, bachelor's, and master's degrees. 23 undergraduate majors. **Total enrollment:**

6,048. Undergraduates: 5,982. Freshmen: 655. Federal methodology is used as a basis for awarding need-based institutional aid.

UNDERGRADUATE EXPENSES for 2013–2014 *Tuition, state resident:* full-time $6440; part-time $214.65 per credit hour. *Tuition, nonresident:* full-time $16,164; part-time $538.80 per credit hour. *Required fees:* full-time $605; $20.17 per credit hour. Full-time tuition and fees vary according to reciprocity agreements. Part-time tuition and fees vary according to reciprocity agreements.

FRESHMAN FINANCIAL AID (Fall 2011) 560 applied for aid; of those 73% were deemed to have need. 91% of freshmen with need received aid; of those 3% had need fully met. *Average percent of need met:* 44% (excluding resources awarded to replace EFC). *Average financial aid package:* $6485 (excluding resources awarded to replace EFC). 1% of all full-time freshmen had no need and received non-need-based gift aid.

UNDERGRADUATE FINANCIAL AID (Fall 2011) 2,552 applied for aid; of those 74% were deemed to have need. 94% of undergraduates with need received aid; of those 2% had need fully met. *Average percent of need met:* 48% (excluding resources awarded to replace EFC). *Average financial aid package:* $7588 (excluding resources awarded to replace EFC). 1% of all full-time undergraduates had no need and received non-need-based gift aid.

GIFT AID (NEED-BASED) *Total amount:* $9,574,487 (65% federal, 34% state, 1% institutional). *Receiving aid:* Freshmen: 43% (243); all full-time undergraduates: 49% (1,257). *Average award:* Freshmen: $6435; Undergraduates: $6297. *Scholarships, grants, and awards:* Federal Pell, FSEOG, state, private, college/university gift aid from institutional funds.

GIFT AID (NON-NEED-BASED) *Total amount:* $462,978 (59% institutional, 41% external sources). *Receiving aid:* Freshmen: 13% (73). Undergraduates: 9% (225). *Average award:* Freshmen: $841. Undergraduates: $1728. *Scholarships, grants, and awards by category: Academic interests/achievement:* business, communication, education, engineering/technologies, English, foreign languages, general academic interests/achievements, health fields. *Special achievements/activities:* general special achievements/activities, leadership. *Special characteristics:* children of faculty/staff, veterans' children. *Tuition waivers:* Full or partial for employees or children of employees, senior citizens.

LOANS *Student loans:* $14,665,928 (44% need-based, 56% non-need-based). 66% of past graduating class borrowed through all loan programs. *Average indebtedness per student:* $22,952. *Average need-based loan:* Freshmen: $2846. Undergraduates: $3619. *Parent loans:* $798,106 (100% non-need-based). *Programs:* Federal Direct (Subsidized and Unsubsidized Stafford, PLUS), Perkins.

WORK-STUDY *Federal work-study:* Total amount: $108,956; jobs available. *State or other work-study/employment:* Part-time jobs available.

ATHLETIC AWARDS Total amount: $24,550 (100% non-need-based).

APPLYING FOR FINANCIAL AID *Required financial aid form:* FAFSA. *Financial aid deadline:* 6/30 (priority: 3/10). *Notification date:* Continuous.

CONTACT Brad Remmenga, Director of Financial Aid and Compliance, Purdue University North Central, 1401 South US Highway 421, Westville, IN 46391-9528, 219-785-5749 or toll-free 800-872-1231 (in-state). *Fax:* 219-785-5538. *E-mail:* remmenga@pnc.edu.

Website: http://www.pnc.edu/.

QUEENS COLLEGE OF THE CITY UNIVERSITY OF NEW YORK

Flushing, NY

Tuition & fees (NY res): $5730	Average undergraduate aid package: $8000

ABOUT THE INSTITUTION State and locally supported, coed. *Awards:* certificates, bachelor's, and master's degrees. 58 undergraduate majors. *Total enrollment:* 20,100. Undergraduates: 16,187. Freshmen: 1,449. Federal methodology is used as a basis for awarding need-based institutional aid.

UNDERGRADUATE EXPENSES for 2013–2014 *Application fee:* $65. *Tuition, state resident:* full-time $5730; part-time $245 per credit. *Tuition, nonresident:* full-time $15,300; part-time $510 per credit. Room and board charges vary according to board plan and housing facility.

FRESHMAN FINANCIAL AID (Fall 2012, est.) 1,333 applied for aid; of those 100% were deemed to have need. 94% of freshmen with need received aid; of those 61% had need fully met. *Average percent of need met:* 95% (excluding resources awarded to replace EFC). *Average financial aid package:* $6450 (excluding

resources awarded to replace EFC). 2% of all full-time freshmen had no need and received non-need-based gift aid.

UNDERGRADUATE FINANCIAL AID (Fall 2012, est.) 11,207 applied for aid; of those 77% were deemed to have need. 100% of undergraduates with need received aid; of those 81% had need fully met. *Average percent of need met:* 95% (excluding resources awarded to replace EFC). *Average financial aid package:* $8000 (excluding resources awarded to replace EFC). 2% of all full-time undergraduates had no need and received non-need-based gift aid.

GIFT AID (NEED-BASED) *Total amount:* $48,958,000 (57% federal, 42% state, 1% institutional). *Receiving aid:* Freshmen: 67% (968); all full-time undergraduates: 63% (7,075). *Average award:* Freshmen: $5100; Undergraduates: $4800. *Scholarships, grants, and awards:* Federal Pell, FSEOG, state, college/university gift aid from institutional funds, Peter Vallone Scholarships.

GIFT AID (NON-NEED-BASED) *Total amount:* $1,197,880 (100% institutional). *Receiving aid:* Freshmen: 34% (486). Undergraduates: 12% (1,300). *Average award:* Freshmen: $7800. Undergraduates: $7800. *Scholarships, grants, and awards by category: Academic interests/achievement:* general academic interests/achievements. *Creative arts/performance:* music. *Special achievements/activities:* community service, leadership. *Tuition waivers:* Full or partial for senior citizens. *ROTC:* Army cooperative, Naval cooperative.

LOANS *Student loans:* $20,355,386 (37% need-based, 63% non-need-based). 47% of past graduating class borrowed through all loan programs. *Average indebtedness per student:* $20,624. *Average need-based loan:* Freshmen: $2850. Undergraduates: $4500. *Parent loans:* $586,886 (100% non-need-based). *Programs:* Federal Direct (Subsidized and Unsubsidized Stafford, PLUS), Perkins.

WORK-STUDY *Federal work-study:* Total amount: $471,274; 456 jobs averaging $1033. *State or other work-study/employment:* Part-time jobs available.

ATHLETIC AWARDS Total amount: $626,791 (100% non-need-based).

APPLYING FOR FINANCIAL AID *Required financial aid forms:* FAFSA, institution's own form, state aid form. *Financial aid deadline (priority):* 2/15. *Notification date:* Continuous beginning 5/1. Students must reply within 3 weeks of notification.

CONTACT Rena Smith-Kiawu, Director of Financial Aid, Queens College of the City University of New York, 65-30 Kissena Boulevard, Flushing, NY 11367-1597, 718-997-5100.

Website: http://www.qc.cuny.edu/.

QUEENS UNIVERSITY OF CHARLOTTE

Charlotte, NC

ABOUT THE INSTITUTION Independent Presbyterian, coed. *Awards:* certificates, bachelor's, and master's degrees. 44 undergraduate majors. *Total enrollment:* 2,386. Undergraduates: 1,869. Freshmen: 359.

GIFT AID (NEED-BASED) *Scholarships, grants, and awards:* Federal Pell, FSEOG, state, private, college/university gift aid from institutional funds.

GIFT AID (NON-NEED-BASED) *Scholarships, grants, and awards by category: Academic interests/achievement:* general academic interests/achievements. *Creative arts/performance:* art/fine arts, music, theater/drama. *Special achievements/activities:* community service, general special achievements/activities, leadership, religious involvement. *Special characteristics:* adult students, children of current students, children of faculty/staff, first-generation college students, international students, members of minority groups, relatives of clergy, religious affiliation, siblings of current students.

LOANS *Programs:* Federal Direct (Subsidized and Unsubsidized Stafford, PLUS), Perkins, state.

WORK-STUDY *Federal work-study:* Total amount: $302,411; jobs available. *State or other work-study/employment:* Part-time jobs available.

APPLYING FOR FINANCIAL AID *Required financial aid forms:* FAFSA, state aid form.

CONTACT Trisha Barker, Director of Financial Aid, Queens University of Charlotte, 1900 Selwyn Avenue, Charlotte, NC 28274-0002, 704-337-2368 or toll-free 800-849-0202. *Fax:* 704-337-2416. *E-mail:* barkert@queens.edu.

Website: http://www.queens.edu/.

QUINCY UNIVERSITY
Quincy, IL

Tuition & fees: $25,834	Average undergraduate aid package: $23,101

ABOUT THE INSTITUTION Independent Roman Catholic, coed. *Awards:* associate, bachelor's, and master's degrees. 38 undergraduate majors. *Total enrollment:* 1,632. Undergraduates: 1,226. Freshmen: 262. Federal methodology is used as a basis for awarding need-based institutional aid.

UNDERGRADUATE EXPENSES for 2013–2014 *Application fee:* $25. *Comprehensive fee:* $35,714 includes full-time tuition ($24,974), mandatory fees ($860), and room and board ($9880). *College room only:* $5500. Room and board charges vary according to board plan, housing facility, and student level. *Part-time tuition:* $585 per semester hour. *Part-time fees:* $30 per semester hour. Part-time tuition and fees vary according to course load.

FRESHMAN FINANCIAL AID (Fall 2012, est.) 255 applied for aid; of those 94% were deemed to have need. 100% of freshmen with need received aid; of those 19% had need fully met. *Average percent of need met:* 79% (excluding resources awarded to replace EFC). *Average financial aid package:* $24,534 (excluding resources awarded to replace EFC). 4% of all full-time freshmen had no need and received non-need-based gift aid.

UNDERGRADUATE FINANCIAL AID (Fall 2012, est.) 1,027 applied for aid; of those 94% were deemed to have need. 97% of undergraduates with need received aid; of those 20% had need fully met. *Average percent of need met:* 72% (excluding resources awarded to replace EFC). *Average financial aid package:* $23,101 (excluding resources awarded to replace EFC). 3% of all full-time undergraduates had no need and received non-need-based gift aid.

GIFT AID (NEED-BASED) *Total amount:* $15,345,634 (16% federal, 12% state, 71% institutional, 1% external sources). *Receiving aid:* Freshmen: 92% (240); all full-time undergraduates: 84% (925). *Average award:* Freshmen: $21,038; Undergraduates: $19,152. *Scholarships, grants, and awards:* Federal Pell, FSEOG, state, private, college/university gift aid from institutional funds.

GIFT AID (NON-NEED-BASED) *Total amount:* $1,133,874 (3% federal, 2% state, 92% institutional, 3% external sources). *Receiving aid:* Freshmen: 13% (33). Undergraduates: 11% (117). *Average award:* Freshmen: $12,818. Undergraduates: $11,836. *Scholarships, grants, and awards by category: Academic interests/ achievement:* 1,148 awards ($9,982,662 total): biological sciences, business, communication, computer science, education, English, general academic interests/achievements, health fields, humanities, international studies, mathematics, physical sciences, premedicine, religion/biblical studies, social sciences. *Creative arts/performance:* 54 awards ($89,017 total): art/fine arts, cinema/film/broadcasting, music. *Special achievements/ activities:* 148 awards ($157,040 total): cheerleading/drum major, community service, general special achievements/activities, hobbies/interests, leadership, memberships. *Special characteristics:* 133 awards ($317,725 total): adult students, children and siblings of alumni, children of faculty/staff, first-generation college students, general special characteristics, local/state students, members of minority groups. *Tuition waivers:* Full or partial for employees or children of employees, senior citizens.

LOANS *Student loans:* $7,249,723 (79% need-based, 21% non-need-based). 82% of past graduating class borrowed through all loan programs. *Average indebtedness per student:* $26,080. *Average need-based loan:* Freshmen: $3295. Undergraduates: $4312. *Parent loans:* $981,133 (30% need-based, 70% non-need-based). *Programs:* Federal Direct (Subsidized and Unsubsidized Stafford, PLUS), Perkins.

WORK-STUDY *Federal work-study:* Total amount: $249,000; 410 jobs averaging $2000. *State or other work-study/employment:* Total amount: $143,000 (100% non-need-based). 35 part-time jobs averaging $2000.

ATHLETIC AWARDS Total amount: $3,008,672 (77% need-based, 23% non-need-based).

APPLYING FOR FINANCIAL AID *Required financial aid form:* FAFSA. *Financial aid deadline (priority):* 3/1. *Notification date:* Continuous beginning 3/1. Students must reply by 5/1 or within 2 weeks of notification.

CONTACT Lisa Flack, Director of Financial Aid, Quincy University, 1800 College Avenue, Quincy, IL 62301-2699, 217-228-5260 or toll-free 800-688-4295. *Fax:* 217-228-5635. *E-mail:* financialaid@quincy.edu. *Website:* http://www.quincy.edu/.

QUINNIPIAC UNIVERSITY
Hamden, CT

Tuition & fees: $39,330	Average undergraduate aid package: $22,679

ABOUT THE INSTITUTION Independent, coed. *Awards:* certificates, bachelor's, master's, and doctoral degrees. 68 undergraduate majors. *Total enrollment:* 8,614. Undergraduates: 6,430. Freshmen: 1,781. Both federal and institutional methodology are used as a basis for awarding need-based institutional aid.

UNDERGRADUATE EXPENSES for 2013–2014 *Application fee:* $45. *Comprehensive fee:* $53,580 includes full-time tuition ($37,830), mandatory fees ($1500), and room and board ($14,250). Room and board charges vary according to housing facility. *Part-time tuition:* $900 per credit. *Part-time fees:* $37 per credit. Part-time tuition and fees vary according to class time and course load.

FRESHMAN FINANCIAL AID (Fall 2012, est.) 1,450 applied for aid; of those 82% were deemed to have need. 99% of freshmen with need received aid; of those 12% had need fully met. *Average percent of need met:* 66% (excluding resources awarded to replace EFC). *Average financial aid package:* $23,867 (excluding resources awarded to replace EFC). 18% of all full-time freshmen had no need and received non-need-based gift aid.

UNDERGRADUATE FINANCIAL AID (Fall 2012, est.) 4,658 applied for aid; of those 86% were deemed to have need. 99% of undergraduates with need received aid; of those 12% had need fully met. *Average percent of need met:* 64% (excluding resources awarded to replace EFC). *Average financial aid package:* $22,679 (excluding resources awarded to replace EFC). 16% of all full-time undergraduates had no need and received non-need-based gift aid.

GIFT AID (NEED-BASED) *Total amount:* $43,686,729 (10% federal, 5% state, 80% institutional, 5% external sources). *Receiving aid:* Freshmen: 65% (1,157); all full-time undergraduates: 62% (3,857). *Average award:* Freshmen: $18,911; Undergraduates: $17,162. *Scholarships, grants, and awards:* Federal Pell, FSEOG, state, private, college/university gift aid from institutional funds.

GIFT AID (NON-NEED-BASED) *Total amount:* $33,954,069 (99% institutional, 1% external sources). *Receiving aid:* Freshmen: 39% (702). Undergraduates: 31% (1,929). *Average award:* Freshmen: $13,059. Undergraduates: $12,053. *Scholarships, grants, and awards by category: Academic interests/achievement:* 2,745 awards ($32,431,214 total): general academic interests/achievements. *Special characteristics:* 348 awards ($2,972,842 total): children of faculty/staff, international students, siblings of current students. *Tuition waivers:* Full or partial for employees or children of employees. *ROTC:* Army cooperative, Naval cooperative, Air Force cooperative.

LOANS *Student loans:* $50,278,095 (71% need-based, 29% non-need-based). 67% of past graduating class borrowed through all loan programs. *Average indebtedness per student:* $42,730. *Average need-based loan:* Freshmen: $3582. Undergraduates: $4593. *Parent loans:* $22,951,782 (100% non-need-based). *Programs:* Federal Direct (Subsidized and Unsubsidized Stafford, PLUS), Perkins.

WORK-STUDY *Federal work-study:* Total amount: $3,762,461; 1,829 jobs averaging $2032. *State or other work-study/employment:* Total amount: $42,148 (100% need-based). 27 part-time jobs averaging $1686.

ATHLETIC AWARDS Total amount: $8,849,900 (100% non-need-based).

APPLYING FOR FINANCIAL AID *Required financial aid forms:* FAFSA, CSS Financial Aid PROFILE. *Financial aid deadline (priority):* 3/1. *Notification date:* Continuous beginning 3/1. Students must reply by 5/1 or within 2 weeks of notification.

CONTACT Mr. Dominic Yoia, Associate Vice President and University Director of Financial Aid, Quinnipiac University, 275 Mount Carmel Avenue, Hamden, CT 06518, 203-582-5224 or toll-free 800-462-1944. *Fax:* 203-582-5238. *E-mail:* finaid@quinnipiac.edu. *Website:* http://www.quinnipiac.edu/.

RABBI JACOB JOSEPH SCHOOL
Edison, NJ

CONTACT Financial Aid Office, Rabbi Jacob Joseph School, One Plainfield Ave, Edison, NJ 08817, 908-985-6533.

RABBINICAL ACADEMY MESIVTA RABBI CHAIM BERLIN
Brooklyn, NY

CONTACT Office of Financial Aid, Rabbinical Academy Mesivta Rabbi Chaim Berlin, 1605 Coney Island Avenue, Brooklyn, NY 11230-4715, 718-377-0777.

RABBINICAL COLLEGE BETH SHRAGA
Monsey, NY

CONTACT Financial Aid Office, Rabbinical College Beth Shraga, 28 Saddle River Road, Monsey, NY 10952-3035, 914-356-1980.

RABBINICAL COLLEGE BOBOVER YESHIVA B'NEI ZION
Brooklyn, NY

CONTACT Financial Aid Office, Rabbinical College Bobover Yeshiva B'nei Zion, 1577 48th Street, Brooklyn, NY 11219, 718-438-2018.

RABBINICAL COLLEGE CH'SAN SOFER
Brooklyn, NY

CONTACT Financial Aid Office, Rabbinical College Ch'san Sofer, 1876 50th Street, Brooklyn, NY 11204, 718-236-1171.

RABBINICAL COLLEGE OF AMERICA
Morristown, NJ

CONTACT Financial Aid Office , Rabbinical College of America, 226 Sussex Avenue, Morristown, NJ 07960, 973-267-9404. *Fax:* 973-267-5208. *Website:* http://www.rca.edu/.

RABBINICAL COLLEGE OF LONG ISLAND
Long Beach, NY

CONTACT Rabbi Cone, Financial Aid Administrator, Rabbinical College of Long Island, 201 Magnolia Boulevard, Long Beach, NY 11561-3305, 516-431-7414.

RABBINICAL COLLEGE OF OHR SHIMON YISROEL
Brooklyn, NY

CONTACT Financial Aid Office, Rabbinical College of Ohr Shimon Yisroel, 215-217 Hewes Street, Brooklyn, NY 11211, 718-855-4092.

RABBINICAL COLLEGE OF TELSHE
Wickliffe, OH

CONTACT Financial Aid Office, Rabbinical College of Telshe, 28400 Euclid Avenue, Wickliffe, OH 44092-2523, 216-943-5300.

RABBINICAL SEMINARY ADAS YEREIM
Brooklyn, NY

CONTACT Mr. Israel Weingarten, Financial Aid Administrator , Rabbinical Seminary Adas Yereim, 185 Wilson Street, Brooklyn, NY 11211-7206, 718-388-1751.

RABBINICAL SEMINARY M'KOR CHAIM
Brooklyn, NY

CONTACT Financial Aid Office, Rabbinical Seminary M'kor Chaim, 1571 55th Street, Brooklyn, NY 11219, 718-851-0183.

RABBINICAL SEMINARY OF AMERICA
Flushing, NY

CONTACT Ms. Leah Eisenstein, Director of Financial Aid, Rabbinical Seminary of America, 92-15 69th Avenue, Forest Hills, NY 11375, 718-268-4700. *Fax:* 718-268-4684.

RADFORD UNIVERSITY
Radford, VA

Tuition & fees (VA res): $8590	Average undergraduate aid package: $9198

ABOUT THE INSTITUTION State-supported, coed. *Awards:* certificates, bachelor's, master's, and doctoral degrees. 39 undergraduate majors. *Total enrollment:* 9,573. Undergraduates: 8,610. Freshmen: 2,053. Federal methodology is used as a basis for awarding need-based institutional aid.

UNDERGRADUATE EXPENSES for 2013–2014 *Application fee:* $50. *Tuition, state resident:* full-time $5702; part-time $238 per credit hour. *Tuition, nonresident:* full-time $16,826; part-time $701 per credit hour. *Required fees:* full-time $2888; $121 per credit hour. Part-time tuition and fees vary according to course load. *College room and board:* $7881; *Room only:* $4307. Room and board charges vary according to board plan and housing facility.

FRESHMAN FINANCIAL AID (Fall 2012, est.) 1,614 applied for aid; of those 69% were deemed to have need. 94% of freshmen with need received aid; of those 25% had need fully met. *Average percent of need met:* 81% (excluding resources awarded to replace EFC). *Average financial aid package:* $8601 (excluding resources awarded to replace EFC). 3% of all full-time freshmen had no need and received non-need-based gift aid.

UNDERGRADUATE FINANCIAL AID (Fall 2012, est.) 5,864 applied for aid; of those 75% were deemed to have need. 96% of undergraduates with need received aid; of those 29% had need fully met. *Average percent of need met:* 81% (excluding resources awarded to replace EFC). *Average financial aid package:* $9198 (excluding resources awarded to replace EFC). 3% of all full-time undergraduates had no need and received non-need-based gift aid.

GIFT AID (NEED-BASED) *Total amount:* $21,710,713 (48% federal, 34% state, 15% institutional, 3% external sources). *Receiving aid:* Freshmen: 32% (656); all full-time undergraduates: 33% (2,764). *Average award:* Freshmen: $7174; Undergraduates: $6892. *Scholarships, grants, and awards:* Federal Pell, FSEOG, state, private, college/university gift aid from institutional funds.

GIFT AID (NON-NEED-BASED) *Total amount:* $1,946,733 (25% federal, 3% state, 48% institutional, 24% external sources). *Receiving aid:* Freshmen: 14% (295). Undergraduates: 11% (899). *Average award:* Freshmen: $3138. Undergraduates: $3371. *Tuition waivers:* Full or partial for employees or children of employees, senior citizens. *ROTC:* Army.

LOANS *Student loans:* $41,411,441 (78% need-based, 22% non-need-based). 63% of past graduating class borrowed through all loan programs. *Average indebtedness per student:* $25,241. *Average need-based loan:* Freshmen: $3255. Undergraduates: $4071. *Parent loans:* $8,619,563 (59% need-based, 41% non-need-based).

Programs: Federal Direct (Subsidized and Unsubsidized Stafford, PLUS), Perkins, Federal Nursing, state.

WORK-STUDY *Federal work-study:* Total amount: $751,047; 311 jobs averaging $2267. *State or other work-study/employment:* Total amount: $1,030,098 (50% need-based, 50% non-need-based). 579 part-time jobs averaging $1970.

ATHLETIC AWARDS Total amount: $2,543,221 (41% need-based, 59% non-need-based).

APPLYING FOR FINANCIAL AID *Required financial aid form:* FAFSA. *Financial aid deadline (priority):* 2/15. *Notification date:* 4/15. Students must reply within 4 weeks of notification.

CONTACT Mrs. Barbara Porter, Director of Financial Aid, Radford University, PO Box 6905, Radford, VA 24142, 540-831-5408. *Fax:* 540-831-5138. *E-mail:* bporter@radford.edu.
Website: http://www.radford.edu/.

RAMAPO COLLEGE OF NEW JERSEY
Mahwah, NJ

Tuition & fees (NJ res): $13,144	Average undergraduate aid package: $10,999

ABOUT THE INSTITUTION State-supported, coed. *Awards:* certificates, bachelor's, and master's degrees. 36 undergraduate majors. *Total enrollment:* 5,817. Undergraduates: 5,624. Freshmen: 871. Federal methodology is used as a basis for awarding need-based institutional aid.

UNDERGRADUATE EXPENSES for 2013–2014 *Application fee:* $60. *Tuition, state resident:* full-time $8480; part-time $265 per credit hour. *Tuition, nonresident:* full-time $16,960; part-time $530 per credit hour. *Required fees:* full-time $4664. *College room and board:* $11,370; *Room only:* $1940.

FRESHMAN FINANCIAL AID (Fall 2012, est.) 723 applied for aid; of those 74% were deemed to have need. 94% of freshmen with need received aid; of those 14% had need fully met. *Average percent of need met:* 66% (excluding resources awarded to replace EFC). *Average financial aid package:* $12,742 (excluding resources awarded to replace EFC). 12% of all full-time freshmen had no need and received non-need-based gift aid.

UNDERGRADUATE FINANCIAL AID (Fall 2012, est.) 3,899 applied for aid; of those 77% were deemed to have need. 97% of undergraduates with need received aid; of those 15% had need fully met. *Average percent of need met:* 59% (excluding resources awarded to replace EFC). *Average financial aid package:* $10,999 (excluding resources awarded to replace EFC). 7% of all full-time undergraduates had no need and received non-need-based gift aid.

GIFT AID (NEED-BASED) *Total amount:* $12,549,347 (47% federal, 45% state, 8% institutional). *Receiving aid:* Freshmen: 24% (207); all full-time undergraduates: 28% (1,395). *Average award:* Freshmen: $14,405; Undergraduates: $8902. *Scholarships, grants, and awards:* Federal Pell, FSEOG, state, private, college/university gift aid from institutional funds, Federal Nursing.

GIFT AID (NON-NEED-BASED) *Total amount:* $7,975,217 (4% state, 87% institutional, 9% external sources). *Receiving aid:* Freshmen: 16% (138). Undergraduates: 16% (789). *Average award:* Freshmen: $9756. Undergraduates: $10,272. *Scholarships, grants, and awards by category:* Academic interests/achievement: 878 awards ($7,989,987 total): general academic interests/achievements. *Special characteristics:* 41 awards ($533,779 total): children of faculty/staff, international students, out-of-state students. *ROTC:* Air Force cooperative.

LOANS *Student loans:* $34,467,164 (33% need-based, 67% non-need-based). 67% of past graduating class borrowed through all loan programs. *Average indebtedness per student:* $30,053. *Average need-based loan:* Freshmen: $3248. Undergraduates: $4397. *Parent loans:* $6,439,197 (100% non-need-based). *Programs:* Federal Direct (Subsidized and Unsubsidized Stafford, PLUS), Perkins, state.

WORK-STUDY *Federal work-study:* Total amount: $295,109; 109 jobs averaging $1976. *State or other work-study/employment:* Total amount: $1,502,022 (100% non-need-based). 748 part-time jobs averaging $2008.

APPLYING FOR FINANCIAL AID *Required financial aid form:* FAFSA. *Financial aid deadline (priority):* 3/1. *Notification date:* Continuous beginning 4/1. Students must reply by 5/1 or within 2 weeks of notification.

CONTACT Bernice Mulch, Assistant Director of Financial Aid, Ramapo College of New Jersey, 505 Ramapo Valley Road, Mahwah, NJ 07430-1680, 201-684-7252 or toll-free 800-9RAMAPO. *Fax:* 201-684-7085. *E-mail:* finaid@ramapo.edu.
Website: http://www.ramapo.edu/.

RANDOLPH COLLEGE
Lynchburg, VA

Tuition & fees: $31,540	Average undergraduate aid package: $26,644

ABOUT THE INSTITUTION Independent Methodist, coed. *Awards:* bachelor's and master's degrees. 37 undergraduate majors. *Total enrollment:* 645. Undergraduates: 623. Freshmen: 180. Both federal and institutional methodology are used as a basis for awarding need-based institutional aid.

UNDERGRADUATE EXPENSES for 2013–2014 *Application fee:* $35. *Comprehensive fee:* $42,330 includes full-time tuition ($31,030), mandatory fees ($510), and room and board ($10,790). Part-time tuition and fees vary according to course load.

FRESHMAN FINANCIAL AID (Fall 2012, est.) 144 applied for aid; of those 93% were deemed to have need. 100% of freshmen with need received aid; of those 18% had need fully met. *Average percent of need met:* 80% (excluding resources awarded to replace EFC). *Average financial aid package:* $27,128 (excluding resources awarded to replace EFC). 25% of all full-time freshmen had no need and received non-need-based gift aid.

UNDERGRADUATE FINANCIAL AID (Fall 2012, est.) 477 applied for aid; of those 91% were deemed to have need. 100% of undergraduates with need received aid; of those 21% had need fully met. *Average percent of need met:* 78% (excluding resources awarded to replace EFC). *Average financial aid package:* $26,644 (excluding resources awarded to replace EFC). 27% of all full-time undergraduates had no need and received non-need-based gift aid.

GIFT AID (NEED-BASED) *Total amount:* $9,141,566 (9% federal, 7% state, 83% institutional, 1% external sources). *Receiving aid:* Freshmen: 69% (134); all full-time undergraduates: 69% (433). *Average award:* Freshmen: $22,650; Undergraduates: $21,263. *Scholarships, grants, and awards:* Federal Pell, FSEOG, state, private, college/university gift aid from institutional funds.

GIFT AID (NON-NEED-BASED) *Total amount:* $3,872,556 (6% state, 93% institutional, 1% external sources). *Receiving aid:* Freshmen: 8% (16). Undergraduates: 10% (62). *Average award:* Freshmen: $20,662. Undergraduates: $19,189. *Scholarships, grants, and awards by category:* Academic interests/achievement: biological sciences, education, English, general academic interests/achievements, mathematics, physical sciences, premedicine, social sciences. *Special achievements/activities:* community service, general special achievements/activities, leadership. *Special characteristics:* adult students, children of faculty/staff, international students, local/state students, relatives of clergy, religious affiliation, twins. *Tuition waivers:* Full or partial for employees or children of employees, adult students.

LOANS *Student loans:* $4,165,180 (70% need-based, 30% non-need-based). 73% of past graduating class borrowed through all loan programs. *Average indebtedness per student:* $33,737. *Average need-based loan:* Freshmen: $4349. Undergraduates: $5572. *Parent loans:* $1,432,477 (40% need-based, 60% non-need-based). *Programs:* Federal Direct (Subsidized and Unsubsidized Stafford, PLUS), Perkins, college/university.

WORK-STUDY *Federal work-study:* Total amount: $295,954; jobs available. *State or other work-study/employment:* Total amount: $214,140 (13% need-based, 87% non-need-based). Part-time jobs available.

APPLYING FOR FINANCIAL AID *Required financial aid forms:* FAFSA, noncustodial (divorced/separated) parent's statement. *Financial aid deadline (priority):* 3/1. *Notification date:* Continuous beginning 3/1. Students must reply by 5/1 or within 2 weeks of notification.

CONTACT Michael Farris, Director of Student Financial Services, Randolph College, 2500 Rivermont Avenue, Lynchburg, VA 24503, 434-947-8128 or toll-free 800-745-7692. *Fax:* 434-947-8996. *E-mail:* mfarris@randolphcollege.edu.
Website: http://www.randolphcollege.edu/.

RANDOLPH-MACON COLLEGE
Ashland, VA

Tuition & fees: $33,525	Average undergraduate aid package: $24,819

ABOUT THE INSTITUTION Independent United Methodist, coed. *Awards:* bachelor's degrees. 31 undergraduate majors. *Total enrollment:* 1,312. Undergrad-

uates: 1,312. Freshmen: 411. Federal methodology is used as a basis for awarding need-based institutional aid.

UNDERGRADUATE EXPENSES for 2013–2014 *Application fee:* $30. *One-time required fee:* $100. *Comprehensive fee:* $43,925 includes full-time tuition ($32,625), mandatory fees ($900), and room and board ($10,400). *College room only:* $5755. Full-time tuition and fees vary according to reciprocity agreements. Room and board charges vary according to board plan and housing facility. *Part-time tuition:* $3625 per course. *Part-time fees:* $135 per year.

FRESHMAN FINANCIAL AID (Fall 2012, est.) 378 applied for aid; of those 84% were deemed to have need. 100% of freshmen with need received aid; of those 25% had need fully met. *Average percent of need met:* 79% (excluding resources awarded to replace EFC). *Average financial aid package:* $25,209 (excluding resources awarded to replace EFC). 22% of all full-time freshmen had no need and received non-need-based gift aid.

UNDERGRADUATE FINANCIAL AID (Fall 2012, est.) 1,108 applied for aid; of those 86% were deemed to have need. 100% of undergraduates with need received aid; of those 23% had need fully met. *Average percent of need met:* 78% (excluding resources awarded to replace EFC). *Average financial aid package:* $24,819 (excluding resources awarded to replace EFC). 25% of all full-time undergraduates had no need and received non-need-based gift aid.

GIFT AID (NEED-BASED) *Total amount:* $19,794,740 (7% federal, 9% state, 81% institutional, 3% external sources). *Receiving aid:* Freshmen: 77% (316); all full-time undergraduates: 75% (953). *Average award:* Freshmen: $21,759; Undergraduates: $20,935. *Scholarships, grants, and awards:* Federal Pell, FSEOG, state, private, college/university gift aid from institutional funds.

GIFT AID (NON-NEED-BASED) *Total amount:* $7,048,022 (12% state, 82% institutional, 6% external sources). *Receiving aid:* Freshmen: 17% (68). Undergraduates: 13% (165). *Average award:* Freshmen: $15,275. Undergraduates: $14,834. *Scholarships, grants, and awards by category: Academic interests/achievement:* 686 awards ($9,896,908 total): general academic interests/achievements, religion/biblical studies. *Special achievements/activities:* 565 awards ($5,007,886 total): general special achievements/activities, religious involvement. *Special characteristics:* 627 awards ($2,076,704 total): children and siblings of alumni, children of faculty/staff, ethnic background, out-of-state students, relatives of clergy, siblings of current students, veterans, veterans' children. *Tuition waivers:* Full or partial for employees or children of employees. *ROTC:* Army cooperative.

LOANS *Student loans:* $9,119,396 (66% need-based, 34% non-need-based). 70% of past graduating class borrowed through all loan programs. *Average indebtedness per student:* $31,112. *Average need-based loan:* Freshmen: $3988. Undergraduates: $4496. *Parent loans:* $4,687,989 (32% need-based, 68% non-need-based). *Programs:* Federal Direct (Subsidized and Unsubsidized Stafford, PLUS), Perkins, college/university.

WORK-STUDY *Federal work-study:* Total amount: $236,954; 194 jobs averaging $1301.

APPLYING FOR FINANCIAL AID *Required financial aid forms:* FAFSA, state aid form. *Financial aid deadline (priority):* 2/15. *Notification date:* 3/1. Students must reply by 5/1 or within 2 weeks of notification.

CONTACT Ms. Mary Neal, Director of Financial Aid, Randolph-Macon College, PO Box 5005, Ashland, VA 23005-5505, 804-752-7259 or toll-free 800-888-1762. *Fax:* 804-752-3719. *E-mail:* mneal@rmc.edu. *Website:* http://www.rmc.edu/.

RASMUSSEN COLLEGE APPLETON
Appleton, WI

CONTACT Financial Aid Office, Rasmussen College Appleton, 3500 E. Destination Drive, Appleton, WI 54915, 920-750-5900 or toll-free 888-549-6755. *Website:* http://www.rasmussen.edu/.

RASMUSSEN COLLEGE BLAINE
Blaine, MN

CONTACT Financial Aid Office, Rasmussen College Blaine, 3629 95th Avenue NE, Blaine, MN 55014, 763-795-4720 or toll-free 888-549-6755. *Website:* http://www.rasmussen.edu/.

RASMUSSEN COLLEGE LAND O' LAKES
Land O' Lakes, FL

CONTACT Financial Aid Office, Rasmussen College Land O' Lakes, 18600 Fernview Street, Land O' Lakes, FL 34638, 813-435-3601 or toll-free 888-549-6755. *Website:* http://www.rasmussen.edu/.

RASMUSSEN COLLEGE MOKENA/ TINLEY PARK
Mokena, IL

CONTACT Financial Aid Office, Rasmussen College Mokena/Tinley Park, 8650 West Spring Lake Road, Mokena, IL 60448, 815-534-3300 or toll-free 888-549-6755. *Website:* http://www.rasmussen.edu/.

RASMUSSEN COLLEGE OCALA SCHOOL OF NURSING
Ocala, FL

CONTACT Financial Aid Office, Rasmussen College Ocala School of Nursing, 2100 SW 22nd Place, Ocala, FL 34471, 352-291-8560 or toll-free 888-549-6755. *Website:* http://www.rasmussen.edu/.

RASMUSSEN COLLEGE ROMEOVILLE/ JOLIET
Romeoville, IL

CONTACT Financial Aid Office, Rasmussen College Romeoville/Joliet, 1400 W. Normantown Road, Romeoville, IL 60446, 815-306-2600 or toll-free 888-549-6755. *Website:* http://www.rasmussen.edu/.

RASMUSSEN COLLEGE TAMPA/ BRANDON
Tampa, FL

CONTACT Financial Aid Office, Rasmussen College Tampa/Brandon, 4042 Park Oaks Boulevard, Tampa, FL 33610, 813-246-7600 or toll-free 888-549-6755. *Website:* http://www.rasmussen.edu/.

RASMUSSEN COLLEGE WAUSAU
Wausau, WI

CONTACT Financial Aid Office, Rasmussen College Wausau, 1101 Westwood Drive, Wausau, WI 54401, 715-841-8000 or toll-free 888-549-6755. *Website:* http://www.rasmussen.edu/.

REED COLLEGE
Portland, OR

Tuition & fees: $44,460	Average undergraduate aid package: $36,625

ABOUT THE INSTITUTION Independent, coed. *Awards:* bachelor's and master's degrees. 30 undergraduate majors. *Total enrollment:* 1,455. Undergraduates: 1,432. Freshmen: 320. Both federal and institutional methodology are used as a basis for awarding need-based institutional aid.

UNDERGRADUATE EXPENSES for 2013–2014 *Application fee:* $50. *Comprehensive fee:* $55,920 includes full-time tuition ($44,200), mandatory fees ($260), and room and board ($11,460). *College room only:* $5960. Room and board charges vary according to board plan and housing facility. *Part-time tuition:* $1903 per semester hour. Part-time tuition and fees vary according to course load.

FRESHMAN FINANCIAL AID (Fall 2012, est.) 210 applied for aid; of those 85% were deemed to have need. 100% of freshmen with need received aid; of those 100% had need fully met. *Average percent of need met:* 100% (excluding resources awarded to replace EFC). *Average financial aid package:* $36,132 (excluding resources awarded to replace EFC).

UNDERGRADUATE FINANCIAL AID (Fall 2012, est.) 781 applied for aid; of those 91% were deemed to have need. 100% of undergraduates with need received aid; of those 100% had need fully met. *Average percent of need met:* 100% (excluding resources awarded to replace EFC). *Average financial aid package:* $36,625 (excluding resources awarded to replace EFC).

GIFT AID (NEED-BASED) *Total amount:* $22,637,845 (6% federal, 93% institutional, 1% external sources). *Receiving aid:* Freshmen: 46% (147); all full-time undergraduates: 46% (640). *Average award:* Freshmen: $38,917; Undergraduates: $35,081. *Scholarships, grants, and awards:* Federal Pell, FSEOG, state, private, college/university gift aid from institutional funds.

GIFT AID (NON-NEED-BASED) *Total amount:* $71,973 (100% external sources). *Tuition waivers:* Full or partial for employees or children of employees.

LOANS *Student loans:* $3,426,454 (76% need-based, 24% non-need-based). 57% of past graduating class borrowed through all loan programs. *Average indebtedness per student:* $19,407. *Average need-based loan:* Freshmen: $3217. Undergraduates: $4370. *Parent loans:* $1,181,712 (100% non-need-based). *Programs:* Federal Direct (Subsidized and Unsubsidized Stafford, PLUS), Perkins, college/university.

WORK-STUDY *Federal work-study:* Total amount: $524,511; jobs available. *State or other work-study/employment:* Total amount: $254,365 (100% need-based). Part-time jobs available.

APPLYING FOR FINANCIAL AID *Required financial aid forms:* FAFSA, CSS Financial Aid PROFILE, noncustodial (divorced/separated) parent's statement. *Financial aid deadline:* 2/1. *Notification date:* 4/1. Students must reply by 5/1 or within 2 weeks of notification.

CONTACT Leslie Limper, Director of Financial Aid, Reed College, 3203 Southeast Woodstock Boulevard, Portland, OR 97202-8199, 503-777-7223 or toll-free 800-547-4750. *Fax:* 503-788-6682. *E-mail:* financial.aid@reed.edu. *Website:* http://www.reed.edu/.

REGENT UNIVERSITY
Virginia Beach, VA

Tuition & fees: $15,960	Average undergraduate aid package: $11,462

ABOUT THE INSTITUTION Independent Christian, coed. *Awards:* certificates, associate, bachelor's, master's, and doctoral degrees. 22 undergraduate majors. *Total enrollment:* 5,863. Undergraduates: 2,432. Freshmen: 218. Federal methodology is used as a basis for awarding need-based institutional aid.

UNDERGRADUATE EXPENSES for 2013–2014 *Application fee:* $50. *Comprehensive fee:* $24,390 includes full-time tuition ($15,300), mandatory fees ($660), and room and board ($8430). *College room only:* $5460. Full-time tuition and fees vary according to course level, course load, program, and student level. Room and board charges vary according to housing facility. *Part-time tuition:* $510 per credit hour. *Part-time fees:* $510 per credit hour; $330 per term. Part-time tuition and fees vary according to course level, course load, program, and student level.

FRESHMAN FINANCIAL AID (Fall 2012, est.) 191 applied for aid; of those 92% were deemed to have need. 100% of freshmen with need received aid; of those 9% had need fully met. *Average percent of need met:* 56% (excluding resources awarded to replace EFC). *Average financial aid package:* $11,634 (excluding resources awarded to replace EFC). 11% of all full-time freshmen had no need and received non-need-based gift aid.

UNDERGRADUATE FINANCIAL AID (Fall 2012, est.) 1,192 applied for aid; of those 96% were deemed to have need. 100% of undergraduates with need received aid; of those 3% had need fully met. *Average percent of need met:* 58% (excluding resources awarded to replace EFC). *Average financial aid package:* $11,462 (excluding resources awarded to replace EFC). 13% of all full-time undergraduates had no need and received non-need-based gift aid.

GIFT AID (NEED-BASED) *Total amount:* $10,857,252 (47% federal, 12% state, 39% institutional, 2% external sources). *Receiving aid:* Freshmen: 85% (172); all full-time undergraduates: 75% (1,072). *Average award:* Freshmen: $8368; Undergraduates: $7769. *Scholarships, grants, and awards:* Federal Pell, state, private, college/university gift aid from institutional funds.

GIFT AID (NON-NEED-BASED) *Total amount:* $1,557,111 (18% state, 78% institutional, 4% external sources). *Receiving aid:* Freshmen: 7% (15). Undergraduates: 3% (36). *Average award:* Freshmen: $5521. Undergraduates: $5571. *Scholarships, grants, and awards by category:* Academic interests/achievement: business, communication, education, English, foreign languages, humanities, religion/biblical studies, social sciences. Creative arts/performance: cinema/film/broadcasting, journalism/publications. Special achievements/activities: leadership. Special characteristics: children and siblings of alumni, children of faculty/staff, public servants, siblings of current students. *Tuition waivers:* Full or partial for employees or children of employees. *ROTC:* Army cooperative, Naval cooperative.

LOANS *Student loans:* $21,777,233 (32% need-based, 68% non-need-based). 67% of past graduating class borrowed through all loan programs. *Average indebtedness per student:* $45,326. *Average need-based loan:* Freshmen: $3077. Undergraduates: $4037. *Parent loans:* $7,985,545 (58% need-based, 42% non-need-based). *Programs:* Federal Direct (Subsidized and Unsubsidized Stafford, PLUS).

APPLYING FOR FINANCIAL AID *Required financial aid forms:* FAFSA, institution's own form, state aid form. *Financial aid deadline:* Continuous. *Notification date:* Continuous beginning 3/1. Students must reply within 2 weeks of notification.

CONTACT Mrs. Dorothy Davidson, Director of Central Financial Aid, Regent University, 1000 Regent University Drive, Student Center 251, Virginia Beach, VA 23464, 757-352-4108 or toll-free 800-373-5504. *Fax:* 757-352-4118. *E-mail:* finaid@regent.edu. *Website:* http://www.regent.edu/.

REGIS COLLEGE
Weston, MA

CONTACT Dee J. Ludwick, Director of Financial Aid, Regis College, Box 81, Weston, MA 02493, 781-768-7180 or toll-free 866-438-7344. *Fax:* 781-768-7225. *E-mail:* finaid@regiscollege.edu. *Website:* http://www.regiscollege.edu/.

REGIS UNIVERSITY
Denver, CO

Tuition & fees: $32,424	Average undergraduate aid package: $18,947

ABOUT THE INSTITUTION Independent Roman Catholic (Jesuit), coed. *Awards:* certificates, bachelor's, master's, and doctoral degrees. 41 undergraduate majors. *Total enrollment:* 10,683. Undergraduates: 5,750. Freshmen: 490. Federal methodology is used as a basis for awarding need-based institutional aid.

UNDERGRADUATE EXPENSES for 2013–2014 *Application fee:* $40. *Comprehensive fee:* $41,804 includes full-time tuition ($31,824), mandatory fees ($600), and room and board ($9380). *College room only:* $5200. Full-time tuition and fees vary according to course load, location, program, and reciprocity agreements. Room and board charges vary according to board plan and housing facility. *Part-time* tuition: $995 per credit hour. Part-time tuition and fees vary according to location, program, and reciprocity agreements.

FRESHMAN FINANCIAL AID (Fall 2011) 430 applied for aid; of those 85% were deemed to have need. 100% of freshmen with need received aid; of those 43% had need fully met. *Average percent of need met:* 75% (excluding resources awarded to replace EFC). *Average financial aid package:* $23,723 (excluding resources awarded to replace EFC). 26% of all full-time freshmen had no need and received non-need-based gift aid.

UNDERGRADUATE FINANCIAL AID (Fall 2011) 2,244 applied for aid; of those 77% were deemed to have need. 99% of undergraduates with need received aid; of those 36% had need fully met. *Average percent of need met:* 63% (excluding resources awarded to replace EFC). *Average financial aid package:* $18,947 (excluding resources awarded to replace EFC). 18% of all full-time undergraduates had no need and received non-need-based gift aid.

GIFT AID (NEED-BASED) *Total amount:* $27,972,330 (23% federal, 6% state, 64% institutional, 7% external sources). *Receiving aid:* Freshmen: 70% (358); all full-time undergraduates: 55% (1,362). *Average award:* Freshmen: $19,759; Undergraduates: $12,565. *Scholarships, grants, and awards:* Federal Pell, FSEOG, state, private, college/university gift aid from institutional funds, Academic Competitiveness Grants, National SMART Grants.

GIFT AID (NON-NEED-BASED) *Total amount:* $9,037,506 (95% institutional, 5% external sources). *Receiving aid:* Freshmen: 34% (175). Undergraduates: 21% (535). *Average award:* Freshmen: $11,897. Undergraduates: $12,561. *Scholarships, grants, and awards by category: Academic interests/achievement:* 651 awards ($7,260,416 total): biological sciences, general academic interests/achievements, physical sciences. *Creative arts/performance:* 29 awards ($149,860 total): debating, music. *Special achievements/activities:* 30 awards ($126,000 total): leadership. *Special characteristics:* 59 awards ($301,116 total): adult students, children of faculty/staff, local/state students, public servants. *Tuition waivers:* Full or partial for employees or children of employees. *ROTC:* Army cooperative, Naval cooperative, Air Force cooperative.

LOANS *Student loans:* $94,075,070 (81% need-based, 19% non-need-based). 60% of past graduating class borrowed through all loan programs. *Average indebtedness per student:* $28,127. *Average need-based loan:* Freshmen: $2339. Undergraduates: $4328. *Parent loans:* $11,017,857 (79% need-based, 21% non-need-based). *Programs:* Federal Direct (Subsidized and Unsubsidized Stafford, PLUS), Perkins, Federal Nursing.

WORK-STUDY *Federal work-study:* Total amount: $559,672; 351 jobs averaging $1501. *State or other work-study/employment:* Total amount: $1,312,652 (71% need-based, 29% non-need-based). 554 part-time jobs averaging $1795.

ATHLETIC AWARDS Total amount: $2,730,411 (48% need-based, 52% non-need-based).

APPLYING FOR FINANCIAL AID *Required financial aid form:* FAFSA. *Financial aid deadline (priority):* 4/15. *Notification date:* Continuous beginning 3/15.

CONTACT Ellie Miller, Director of Financial Aid, Regis University, 3333 Regis Boulevard, Denver, CO 80221-1099, 303-964-5758 or toll-free 800-388-2366 Ext. 4900. *Fax:* 303-964-5449. *E-mail:* emiller@regis.edu. *Website:* http://www.regis.edu/.

REINHARDT UNIVERSITY
Waleska, GA

CONTACT Angela D. Harlow, Director of Financial Aid, Reinhardt University, 7300 Reinhardt College Circle, Waleska, GA 30183-2981, 770-720-5603. *Fax:* 770-720-9126.
Website: http://www.reinhardt.edu/.

RENSSELAER POLYTECHNIC INSTITUTE
Troy, NY

| Tuition & fees: $44,475 | Average undergraduate aid package: $30,208 |

ABOUT THE INSTITUTION Independent, coed. *Awards:* bachelor's, master's, and doctoral degrees. 40 undergraduate majors. *Total enrollment:* 6,999. Undergraduates: 5,391. Freshmen: 1,326. Both federal and institutional methodology are used as a basis for awarding need-based institutional aid.

UNDERGRADUATE EXPENSES for 2013-2014 *Application fee:* $70. *Comprehensive fee:* $56,925 includes full-time tuition ($43,350), mandatory fees ($1125), and room and board ($12,450). *College room only:* $7110. Room and board charges vary according to board plan and location. *Part-time tuition:* $1805 per credit hour.

FRESHMAN FINANCIAL AID (Fall 2012, est.) 1,100 applied for aid; of those 83% were deemed to have need. 100% of freshmen with need received aid; of those 37% had need fully met. *Average percent of need met:* 88% (excluding resources awarded to replace EFC). *Average financial aid package:* $34,436 (excluding resources awarded to replace EFC). 26% of all full-time freshmen had no need and received non-need-based gift aid.

UNDERGRADUATE FINANCIAL AID (Fall 2012, est.) 3,834 applied for aid; of those 90% were deemed to have need. 100% of undergraduates with need received aid; of those 25% had need fully met. *Average percent of need met:* 79% (excluding resources awarded to replace EFC). *Average financial aid package:* $30,208 (excluding resources awarded to replace EFC). 29% of all full-time undergraduates had no need and received non-need-based gift aid.

GIFT AID (NEED-BASED) *Total amount:* $84,675,775 (13% federal, 2% state, 83% institutional, 2% external sources). *Receiving aid:* Freshmen: 69% (912); all full-time undergraduates: 65% (3,450). *Average award:* Freshmen: $29,429; Undergraduates: $24,799. *Scholarships, grants, and awards:* Federal Pell, FSEOG, state, private, college/university gift aid from institutional funds, Academic Competitiveness Grants, National SMART Grants, Gates Millennium Scholarships.

GIFT AID (NON-NEED-BASED) *Total amount:* $25,592,082 (4% federal, 1% state, 92% institutional, 3% external sources). *Receiving aid:* Freshmen: 16% (207). Undergraduates: 8% (428). *Average award:* Freshmen: $15,507. Undergraduates: $13,334. *Scholarships, grants, and awards by category: Academic interests/achievement:* general academic interests/achievements, humanities, mathematics, military science. *Creative arts/performance:* general creative arts/performance. *Special achievements/activities:* general special achievements/activities. *Special characteristics:* children and siblings of alumni, children of faculty/staff, ethnic background, general special characteristics, members of minority groups. *Tuition waivers:* Full or partial for employees or children of employees. *ROTC:* Army, Naval, Air Force.

LOANS *Student loans:* $36,717,811 (60% need-based, 40% non-need-based). 68% of past graduating class borrowed through all loan programs. *Average indebtedness per student:* $31,000. *Average need-based loan:* Freshmen: $3955. Undergraduates: $4996. *Parent loans:* $9,411,631 (24% need-based, 76% non-need-based). *Programs:* Federal Direct (Subsidized and Unsubsidized Stafford, PLUS), Perkins, college/university.

WORK-STUDY *Federal work-study:* Total amount: $1,905,349; 1,110 jobs averaging $1917.

ATHLETIC AWARDS Total amount: $2,131,145 (100% non-need-based).

APPLYING FOR FINANCIAL AID *Required financial aid forms:* FAFSA, CSS Financial Aid PROFILE. *Financial aid deadline (priority):* 2/1. *Notification date:* 3/12.

CONTACT Mr. Larry Chambers, Director of Financial Aid, Rensselaer Polytechnic Institute, Academy Hall, Troy, NY 12180-3590, 518-276-6813. *Fax:* 518-276-4797. *E-mail:* financial_aid@rpi.edu. *Website:* http://www.rpi.edu/.

RESEARCH COLLEGE OF NURSING
Kansas City, MO

Tuition & fees: $29,840 — **Average undergraduate aid package: N/A**

ABOUT THE INSTITUTION Independent, coed, primarily women. *Awards:* bachelor's and master's degrees (bachelor's degree offered jointly with Rockhurst College). 1 undergraduate major. *Total enrollment:* 441. Undergraduates: 306. Freshmen: 83. Federal methodology is used as a basis for awarding need-based institutional aid.

UNDERGRADUATE EXPENSES for 2013–2014 *Comprehensive fee:* $38,300 includes full-time tuition ($29,100), mandatory fees ($740), and room and board ($8460). *College room only:* $5060. Room and board charges vary according to board plan, housing facility, and location. *Part-time tuition:* $970 per credit hour. Part-time tuition and fees vary according to class time.

GIFT AID (NEED-BASED) *Total amount:* $1,307,427 (13% federal, 2% state, 85% institutional). *Scholarships, grants, and awards:* Federal Pell, FSEOG, state, private, college/university gift aid from institutional funds.

GIFT AID (NON-NEED-BASED) *Total amount:* $2,845,562 (90% institutional, 10% external sources). *Scholarships, grants, and awards by category: Academic interests/achievement:* general academic interests/achievements, health fields. *Special characteristics:* children and siblings of alumni, children of educators, children of faculty/staff, siblings of current students. *Tuition waivers:* Full or partial for employees or children of employees, senior citizens. *ROTC:* Army cooperative.

LOANS *Student loans:* $1,838,104 (41% need-based, 59% non-need-based). *Programs:* Federal Direct (Subsidized and Unsubsidized Stafford, PLUS), Federal Nursing.

APPLYING FOR FINANCIAL AID *Required financial aid form:* FAFSA. *Financial aid deadline (priority):* 3/15. *Notification date:* Continuous. Students must reply within 2 weeks of notification.

CONTACT Ms. Stacie Withers, Director of Financial Aid, Research College of Nursing, 2525 East Meyer Boulevard, Kansas City, MO 64132, 816-995-2832. *Fax:* 816-995-2833. *E-mail:* stacie.withers@researchcollege.edu. *Website:* http://www.researchcollege.edu/.

RESURRECTION UNIVERSITY
Chicago, IL

Tuition & fees: $11,639 — **Average undergraduate aid package: $15,500**

ABOUT THE INSTITUTION Independent, coed, primarily women. *Awards:* certificates, bachelor's, and master's degrees. 2 undergraduate majors. *Total enrollment:* 515. Undergraduates: 392. Both federal and institutional methodology are used as a basis for awarding need-based institutional aid.

UNDERGRADUATE EXPENSES for 2013–2014 *Application fee:* $50. *Tuition:* full-time $11,349; part-time $769 per credit hour. *Required fees:* full-time $290; $140 per term.

UNDERGRADUATE FINANCIAL AID (Fall 2011) 304 applied for aid; of those 100% were deemed to have need. 100% of undergraduates with need received aid; of those 25% had need fully met. *Average percent of need met:* 85% (excluding resources awarded to replace EFC). *Average financial aid package:* $15,500 (excluding resources awarded to replace EFC). 5% of all full-time undergraduates had no need and received non-need-based gift aid.

GIFT AID (NEED-BASED) *Total amount:* $1,393,551 (31% federal, 20% state, 48% institutional, 1% external sources). *Receiving aid:* All full-time undergraduates: 67% (216). *Average award:* Undergraduates: $3000. *Scholarships, grants, and awards:* Federal Pell, FSEOG, state, private, college/university gift aid from institutional funds.

GIFT AID (NON-NEED-BASED) *Total amount:* $83,865 (53% institutional, 47% external sources). *Receiving aid:* Undergraduates: 32% (103). *Average award:* Undergraduates: $3000. *Tuition waivers:* Full or partial for employees or children of employees.

LOANS *Student loans:* $3,996,918 (72% need-based, 28% non-need-based). *Average need-based loan:* Undergraduates: $5500. *Parent loans:* $301,301 (100% need-based). *Programs:* Federal Direct (Subsidized and Unsubsidized Stafford, PLUS).

WORK-STUDY *Federal work-study:* Total amount: $28,868; 17 jobs averaging $1700.

APPLYING FOR FINANCIAL AID *Notification date:* Continuous.

CONTACT Ms. Shirley Howell, Financial Aid Officer, Resurrection University, 1431 North Claremont Avenue, Chicago, IL 60622, 773-252-5125. *Fax:* 773-227-3838. *E-mail:* shirley.howell@resu.edu. *Website:* http://www.resu.edu/.

RHODE ISLAND COLLEGE
Providence, RI

Tuition & fees (RI res): $7598 — **Average undergraduate aid package: $8874**

ABOUT THE INSTITUTION State-supported, coed. *Awards:* certificates, bachelor's, master's, and doctoral degrees. 75 undergraduate majors. *Total enrollment:* 8,869. Undergraduates: 7,553. Freshmen: 1,071. Institutional methodology is used as a basis for awarding need-based institutional aid.

UNDERGRADUATE EXPENSES for 2013–2014 *Application fee:* $50. *Tuition, state resident:* full-time $6530; part-time $272 per credit. *Tuition, nonresident:* full-time $17,228; part-time $670 per credit. *Required fees:* full-time $1068; $32 per credit or $72 per term. Part-time tuition and fees vary according to course load. *College room and board:* $9534; *Room only:* $5424. Room and board charges vary according to housing facility.

FRESHMAN FINANCIAL AID (Fall 2012, est.) 950 applied for aid; of those 76% were deemed to have need. 97% of freshmen with need received aid; of those 19% had need fully met. *Average percent of need met:* 73% (excluding resources awarded to replace EFC). *Average financial aid package:* $9402 (excluding resources awarded to replace EFC). 4% of all full-time freshmen had no need and received non-need-based gift aid.

UNDERGRADUATE FINANCIAL AID (Fall 2012, est.) 4,550 applied for aid; of those 81% were deemed to have need. 96% of undergraduates with need received aid; of those 24% had need fully met. *Average percent of need met:* 72% (excluding resources awarded to replace EFC). *Average financial aid package:* $8874 (excluding resources awarded to replace EFC). 2% of all full-time undergraduates had no need and received non-need-based gift aid.

GIFT AID (NEED-BASED) *Total amount:* $19,447,212 (63% federal, 10% state, 25% institutional, 2% external sources). *Receiving aid:* Freshmen: 61% (636); all full-time undergraduates: 57% (3,124). *Average award:* Freshmen: $6665; Undergraduates: $5394. *Scholarships, grants, and awards:* Federal Pell, FSEOG, state, private, college/university gift aid from institutional funds.

GIFT AID (NON-NEED-BASED) *Total amount:* $487,955 (75% institutional, 25% external sources). *Receiving aid:* Freshmen: 2% (21). Undergraduates: 2% (84). *Average award:* Freshmen: $1999. Undergraduates: $2013. *Scholarships, grants, and awards by category: Academic interests/achievement:* general academic interests/achievements. *Creative arts/performance:* art/fine arts, cinema/film/broadcasting, dance, journalism/publications, music, theater/drama. *Special characteristics:* children and siblings of alumni. *Tuition waivers:* Full or partial for employees or children of employees. *ROTC:* Army cooperative.

LOANS *Student loans:* $36,496,932 (69% need-based, 31% non-need-based). 79% of past graduating class borrowed through all loan programs. *Average indebtedness per student:* $23,110. *Average need-based loan:* Freshmen: $3351. Undergraduates: $4054. *Parent loans:* $1,096,177 (29% need-based, 71% non-need-based). *Programs:* Federal Direct (Subsidized and Unsubsidized Stafford, PLUS), Perkins, state, private loans.

WORK-STUDY *Federal work-study:* Total amount: $1,905,383; jobs available.

APPLYING FOR FINANCIAL AID *Required financial aid forms:* FAFSA, institution's own form. *Financial aid deadline (priority):* 3/1. *Notification date:* Continuous beginning 3/15. Students must reply by 5/1 or within 3 weeks of notification.

CONTACT Mr. James T. Hanbury, Director of Financial Aid, Rhode Island College, 600 Mount Pleasant Avenue, Providence, RI 02908, 401-456-8033 or toll-free 800-669-5760. *Fax:* 401-456-8686. *E-mail:* jhanbury@ric.edu. *Website:* http://www.ric.edu/.

RHODE ISLAND SCHOOL OF DESIGN
Providence, RI

CONTACT Director of Financial Aid, Rhode Island School of Design, 2 College Street, Providence, RI 02903-2784, 401-454-6661 or toll-free 800-364-7473. *Fax:* 401-454-6412.
Website: http://www.risd.edu/.

RHODES COLLEGE
Memphis, TN

Tuition & fees: $38,092	Average undergraduate aid package: $34,042

ABOUT THE INSTITUTION Independent, coed. *Awards:* bachelor's and master's degrees (master's degree in accounting only). 32 undergraduate majors. *Total enrollment:* 1,927. Undergraduates: 1,916. Freshmen: 554. Institutional methodology is used as a basis for awarding need-based institutional aid.
UNDERGRADUATE EXPENSES for 2013–2014 *Application fee:* $45. *Comprehensive fee:* $47,596 includes full-time tuition ($37,782), mandatory fees ($310), and room and board ($9504). Room and board charges vary according to board plan and housing facility. *Part-time tuition:* $1590 per credit hour.
FRESHMAN FINANCIAL AID (Fall 2012, est.) 462 applied for aid; of those 67% were deemed to have need. 100% of freshmen with need received aid; of those 48% had need fully met. *Average percent of need met:* 93% (excluding resources awarded to replace EFC). *Average financial aid package:* $34,271 (excluding resources awarded to replace EFC). 39% of all full-time freshmen had no need and received non-need-based gift aid.
UNDERGRADUATE FINANCIAL AID (Fall 2012, est.) 1,272 applied for aid; of those 74% were deemed to have need. 100% of undergraduates with need received aid; of those 47% had need fully met. *Average percent of need met:* 90% (excluding resources awarded to replace EFC). *Average financial aid package:* $34,042 (excluding resources awarded to replace EFC). 41% of all full-time undergraduates had no need and received non-need-based gift aid.
GIFT AID (NEED-BASED) *Total amount:* $22,078,157 (7% federal, 5% state, 87% institutional, 1% external sources). *Receiving aid:* Freshmen: 55% (307); all full-time undergraduates: 49% (927). *Average award:* Freshmen: $23,691; Undergraduates: $23,536. *Scholarships, grants, and awards:* Federal Pell, FSEOG, state, private, college/university gift aid from institutional funds.
GIFT AID (NON-NEED-BASED) *Total amount:* $15,946,327 (6% state, 88% institutional, 6% external sources). *Receiving aid:* Freshmen: 22% (123). Undergraduates: 14% (264). *Average award:* Freshmen: $16,832. Undergraduates: $16,385. *Scholarships, grants, and awards by category:* Academic interests/achievement: general academic interests/achievements, physical sciences. Creative arts/performance: art/fine arts, general creative arts/performance, music, theater/drama. Special characteristics: children of faculty/staff, members of minority groups, relatives of clergy, religious affiliation. *Tuition waivers:* Full or partial for employees or children of employees. *ROTC:* Army cooperative, Air Force cooperative.
LOANS Student loans: $6,357,781 (54% need-based, 46% non-need-based). 44% of past graduating class borrowed through all loan programs. *Average indebtedness per student:* $26,372. *Average need-based loan:* Freshmen: $5080. Undergraduates: $6627. *Parent loans:* $1,961,731 (15% need-based, 85% non-need-based). *Programs:* Federal Direct (Subsidized and Unsubsidized Stafford, PLUS), Perkins.
WORK-STUDY Federal work-study: Total amount: $923,083; jobs available. *State or other work-study/employment:* Total amount: $534,570 (6% need-based, 94% non-need-based). Part-time jobs available.
APPLYING FOR FINANCIAL AID Required financial aid forms: FAFSA, CSS Financial Aid PROFILE, noncustodial (divorced/separated) parent's statement. *Financial aid deadline:* 3/1. *Notification date:* 4/15. Students must reply by 5/1.
CONTACT Mrs. Ashley Bianchi, Director of Financial Aid, Rhodes College, 2000 North Parkway, Memphis, TN 38112-1690, 901-843-3808 or toll-free 800-844-5969. *Fax:* 901-843-3435. *E-mail:* bianchia@rhodes.edu.
Website: http://www.rhodes.edu/.

RICE UNIVERSITY
Houston, TX

Tuition & fees: $38,942	Average undergraduate aid package: $33,004

ABOUT THE INSTITUTION Independent, coed. *Awards:* bachelor's, master's, and doctoral degrees. 58 undergraduate majors. *Total enrollment:* 6,484. Undergraduates: 7,866. Freshmen: 4,931. Both federal and institutional methodology are used as a basis for awarding need-based institutional aid.
UNDERGRADUATE EXPENSES for 2013–2014 *Application fee:* $75. *One-time required fee:* $520. *Comprehensive fee:* $51,942 includes full-time tuition ($38,260), mandatory fees ($682), and room and board ($13,000). *College room only:* $8800.
FRESHMAN FINANCIAL AID (Fall 2012, est.) 621 applied for aid; of those 67% were deemed to have need. 100% of freshmen with need received aid; of those 100% had need fully met. *Average percent of need met:* 100% (excluding resources awarded to replace EFC). *Average financial aid package:* $35,549 (excluding resources awarded to replace EFC). 16% of all full-time freshmen had no need and received non-need-based gift aid.
UNDERGRADUATE FINANCIAL AID (Fall 2012, est.) 2,391 applied for aid; of those 67% were deemed to have need. 100% of undergraduates with need received aid; of those 100% had need fully met. *Average percent of need met:* 100% (excluding resources awarded to replace EFC). *Average financial aid package:* $33,004 (excluding resources awarded to replace EFC). 16% of all full-time undergraduates had no need and received non-need-based gift aid.
GIFT AID (NEED-BASED) *Total amount:* $51,385,723 (5% federal, 4% state, 91% institutional). *Receiving aid:* Freshmen: 44% (411); all full-time undergraduates: 42% (1,599). *Average award:* Freshmen: $33,564; Undergraduates: $31,820. *Scholarships, grants, and awards:* Federal Pell, FSEOG, state, private, college/university gift aid from institutional funds.
GIFT AID (NON-NEED-BASED) *Total amount:* $12,120,336 (76% institutional, 24% external sources). *Receiving aid:* Freshmen: 15% (140). Undergraduates: 8% (311). *Average award:* Freshmen: $12,033. Undergraduates: $12,068. *Scholarships, grants, and awards by category:* Academic interests/achievement: engineering/technologies, general academic interests/achievements. Creative arts/performance: art/fine arts, music. Special achievements/activities: general special achievements/activities, leadership. Special characteristics: local/state students, members of minority groups. *Tuition waivers:* Full or partial for employees or children of employees. *ROTC:* Army cooperative, Naval, Air Force cooperative.
LOANS Student loans: $4,217,250 (40% need-based, 60% non-need-based). 25% of past graduating class borrowed through all loan programs. *Average indebtedness per student:* $18,133. *Average need-based loan:* Freshmen: $1340. Undergraduates: $1428. *Parent loans:* $2,663,946 (100% non-need-based). *Programs:* Federal Direct (Subsidized and Unsubsidized Stafford, PLUS), Perkins, state.
WORK-STUDY Federal work-study: Total amount: $2,085,288; jobs available. *State or other work-study/employment:* Total amount: $1,278,450 (100% non-need-based). Part-time jobs available.
ATHLETIC AWARDS Total amount: $10,155,755 (8% need-based, 92% non-need-based).
APPLYING FOR FINANCIAL AID Required financial aid forms: FAFSA, CSS Financial Aid PROFILE, noncustodial (divorced/separated) parent's statement, business/farm supplement, federal income tax form(s), W-2 forms. *Financial aid deadline (priority):* 3/1. *Notification date:* Continuous beginning 4/1. Students must reply by 5/1.
CONTACT Ms. Anne Walker, Director of Student Financial Services, Rice University, 116 Allen Center, MS 12, Houston, TX 77005, 713-348-4958 or toll-free 800-527-OWLS. *Fax:* 713-348-2139. *E-mail:* fina@rice.edu.
Website: http://www.rice.edu/.

THE RICHARD STOCKTON COLLEGE OF NEW JERSEY
Galloway, NJ

Tuition & fees (NJ res): $12,322	Average undergraduate aid package: $15,774

ABOUT THE INSTITUTION State-supported, coed. **Awards:** certificates, bachelor's, master's, and doctoral degrees. 32 undergraduate majors. **Total enrollment:** 8,400. Undergraduates: 7,516. Freshmen: 1,003. Federal methodology is used as a basis for awarding need-based institutional aid.

UNDERGRADUATE EXPENSES for 2013–2014 Application fee: $50. **Tuition, state resident:** full-time $7948; part-time $306 per credit hour. **Tuition, nonresident:** full-time $14,341; part-time $552 per credit hour. **Required fees:** full-time $4374; $168 per credit hour or $70 per term. Part-time tuition and fees vary according to course load. **College room and board:** $10,796; **Room only:** $7381. Room and board charges vary according to board plan and housing facility.

FRESHMAN FINANCIAL AID (Fall 2012, est.) 932 applied for aid; of those 82% were deemed to have need. 96% of freshmen with need received aid; of those 29% had need fully met. **Average percent of need met:** 67% (excluding resources awarded to replace EFC). **Average financial aid package:** $16,163 (excluding resources awarded to replace EFC). 6% of all full-time freshmen had no need and received non-need-based gift aid.

UNDERGRADUATE FINANCIAL AID (Fall 2012, est.) 5,806 applied for aid; of those 87% were deemed to have need. 97% of undergraduates with need received aid; of those 24% had need fully met. **Average percent of need met:** 64% (excluding resources awarded to replace EFC). **Average financial aid package:** $15,774 (excluding resources awarded to replace EFC). 5% of all full-time undergraduates had no need and received non-need-based gift aid.

GIFT AID (NEED-BASED) Total amount: $30,044,350 (41% federal, 33% state, 25% institutional, 1% external sources). **Receiving aid:** Freshmen: 40% (396); all full-time undergraduates: 39% (2,681). **Average award:** Freshmen: $8939; Undergraduates: $8034. **Scholarships, grants, and awards:** Federal Pell, FSEOG, state, private, college/university gift aid from institutional funds.

GIFT AID (NON-NEED-BASED) Total amount: $2,509,895 (6% state, 87% institutional, 7% external sources). **Receiving aid:** Freshmen: 26% (257). Undergraduates: 19% (1,274). **Average award:** Freshmen: $6567. Undergraduates: $6716. **Scholarships, grants, and awards by category:** Academic interests/achievement: area/ethnic studies, biological sciences, business, computer science, education, general academic interests/achievements, health fields, humanities, mathematics, physical sciences, social sciences. **Creative arts/performance:** applied art and design, art/fine arts, creative writing, dance, journalism/publications, music, performing arts, theater/drama. **Special achievements/activities:** community service, general special achievements/activities, leadership. **Special characteristics:** adult students, children of faculty/staff, children of union members/company employees, ethnic background, first-generation college students, general special characteristics, international students, local/state students, members of minority groups, previous college experience. **Tuition waivers:** Full or partial for employees or children of employees, senior citizens. **ROTC:** Army cooperative.

LOANS Student loans: $53,803,206 (89% need-based, 11% non-need-based). 74% of past graduating class borrowed through all loan programs. **Average indebtedness per student:** $34,287. **Average need-based loan:** Freshmen: $3436. Undergraduates: $4586. **Parent loans:** $5,588,893 (81% need-based, 19% non-need-based). **Programs:** Federal Direct (Subsidized and Unsubsidized Stafford, PLUS), Perkins, state.

WORK-STUDY Federal work-study: Total amount: $262,985; 158 jobs averaging $1664. **State or other work-study/employment:** Total amount: $1,265,894 (100% non-need-based). 699 part-time jobs averaging $1677.

APPLYING FOR FINANCIAL AID Required financial aid form: FAFSA. **Financial aid deadline (priority):** 3/1. **Notification date:** Continuous beginning 4/1. Students must reply within 2 weeks of notification.

CONTACT Mrs. Jeanne S. Lewis, Director of Financial Aid, The Richard Stockton College of New Jersey, 101 Vera King Farris Drive, Galloway, NJ 08205-9441, 609-652-4203. *Fax:* 609-626-5517. *E-mail:* jeanne.lewis@stockton.edu. *Website:* http://www.stockton.edu/.

RIDER UNIVERSITY
Lawrenceville, NJ

Tuition & fees: $33,420	Average undergraduate aid package: $22,352

ABOUT THE INSTITUTION Independent, coed. **Awards:** certificates, associate, bachelor's, and master's degrees. 60 undergraduate majors. **Total enrollment:** 5,485. Undergraduates: 4,549. Freshmen: 920. Federal methodology is used as a basis for awarding need-based institutional aid.

UNDERGRADUATE EXPENSES for 2013–2014 Application fee: $50. **Comprehensive fee:** $45,760 includes full-time tuition ($32,820), mandatory fees ($600), and room and board ($12,340). **College room only:** $7770. Full-time tuition and fees vary according to course load and program. Room and board charges vary according to board plan, housing facility, and location. **Part-time tuition:** $596.87 per credit. **Part-time fees:** $35 per course. Part-time tuition and fees vary according to course load and program.

FRESHMAN FINANCIAL AID (Fall 2012, est.) 821 applied for aid; of those 88% were deemed to have need. 100% of freshmen with need received aid; of those 16% had need fully met. **Average percent of need met:** 73% (excluding resources awarded to replace EFC). **Average financial aid package:** $25,177 (excluding resources awarded to replace EFC). 17% of all full-time freshmen had no need and received non-need-based gift aid.

UNDERGRADUATE FINANCIAL AID (Fall 2012, est.) 3,215 applied for aid; of those 87% were deemed to have need. 100% of undergraduates with need received aid; of those 15% had need fully met. **Average percent of need met:** 70% (excluding resources awarded to replace EFC). **Average financial aid package:** $22,352 (excluding resources awarded to replace EFC). 21% of all full-time undergraduates had no need and received non-need-based gift aid.

GIFT AID (NEED-BASED) Total amount: $46,790,816 (13% federal, 16% state, 70% institutional, 1% external sources). **Receiving aid:** Freshmen: 78% (714); all full-time undergraduates: 69% (2,739). **Average award:** Freshmen: $20,455; Undergraduates: $18,157. **Scholarships, grants, and awards:** Federal Pell, state, college/university gift aid from institutional funds.

GIFT AID (NON-NEED-BASED) Total amount: $12,347,735 (2% federal, 97% institutional, 1% external sources). **Receiving aid:** Freshmen: 12% (106). Undergraduates: 10% (395). **Average award:** Freshmen: $13,718. Undergraduates: $12,657. **Scholarships, grants, and awards by category:** Academic interests/achievement: general academic interests/achievements. **Creative arts/performance:** theater/drama. **Special characteristics:** members of minority groups. **Tuition waivers:** Full or partial for employees or children of employees. **ROTC:** Army cooperative.

LOANS Student loans: $37,907,533 (69% need-based, 31% non-need-based). 75% of past graduating class borrowed through all loan programs. **Average indebtedness per student:** $32,718. **Average need-based loan:** Freshmen: $3226. Undergraduates: $3919. **Parent loans:** $9,402,619 (48% need-based, 52% non-need-based). **Programs:** Federal Direct (Subsidized and Unsubsidized Stafford, PLUS), Perkins, state, alternative loans.

WORK-STUDY Federal work-study: Total amount: $4,021,200; jobs available. **State or other work-study/employment:** Part-time jobs available.

ATHLETIC AWARDS Total amount: $3,552,816 (51% need-based, 49% non-need-based).

APPLYING FOR FINANCIAL AID Required financial aid form: FAFSA. **Financial aid deadline (priority):** 3/1. **Notification date:** Continuous beginning 2/20.

CONTACT Dr. Dennis Levy, Director of Financial Aid, Rider University, 2083 Lawrenceville Road, Lawrenceville, NJ 08648-3001, 609-896-5360 or toll-free 800-257-9026. *Fax:* 609-219-4487. *E-mail:* finaid@rider.edu. *Website:* http://www.rider.edu/.

RINGLING COLLEGE OF ART AND DESIGN
Sarasota, FL

Tuition & fees: $35,300   **Average undergraduate aid package:** $17,427

ABOUT THE INSTITUTION Independent, coed. *Awards:* certificates and bachelor's degrees. 13 undergraduate majors. *Total enrollment:* 1,364. Undergraduates: 1,364. Freshmen: 312. Federal methodology is used as a basis for awarding need-based institutional aid.

UNDERGRADUATE EXPENSES for 2013–2014 *Application fee:* $70. *Comprehensive fee:* $47,530 includes full-time tuition ($33,960), mandatory fees ($1340), and room and board ($12,230). *College room only:* $6670. Full-time tuition and fees vary according to course load, program, and student level. Room and board charges vary according to board plan and housing facility. *Part-time tuition:* $1583 per credit hour. Part-time tuition and fees vary according to course load, program, and student level.

FRESHMAN FINANCIAL AID (Fall 2012, est.) 217 applied for aid; of those 88% were deemed to have need. 100% of freshmen with need received aid; of those 2% had need fully met. *Average percent of need met:* 38% (excluding resources awarded to replace EFC). *Average financial aid package:* $16,254 (excluding resources awarded to replace EFC). 16% of all full-time freshmen had no need and received non-need-based gift aid.

UNDERGRADUATE FINANCIAL AID (Fall 2012, est.) 964 applied for aid; of those 90% were deemed to have need. 100% of undergraduates with need received aid; of those 4% had need fully met. *Average percent of need met:* 40% (excluding resources awarded to replace EFC). *Average financial aid package:* $17,427 (excluding resources awarded to replace EFC). 11% of all full-time undergraduates had no need and received non-need-based gift aid.

GIFT AID (NEED-BASED) *Total amount:* $9,056,636 (20% federal, 17% state, 49% institutional, 14% external sources). *Receiving aid:* Freshmen: 76% (180); all full-time undergraduates: 78% (804). *Average award:* Freshmen: $10,136; Undergraduates: $10,881. *Scholarships, grants, and awards:* Federal Pell, FSEOG, state, private, college/university gift aid from institutional funds.

GIFT AID (NON-NEED-BASED) *Total amount:* $3,317,260 (5% state, 89% institutional, 6% external sources). *Receiving aid:* Freshmen: 1% (3). Undergraduates: 2% (21). *Average award:* Freshmen: $12,398. Undergraduates: $16,972. *Scholarships, grants, and awards by category:* Academic interests/achievement: general academic interests/achievements. Creative arts/performance: applied art and design, art/fine arts. Special achievements/activities: community service. *Tuition waivers:* Full or partial for employees or children of employees.

LOANS *Student loans:* $10,328,152 (87% need-based, 13% non-need-based). 73% of past graduating class borrowed through all loan programs. *Average indebtedness per student:* $48,515. *Average need-based loan:* Freshmen: $6887. Undergraduates: $7657. *Parent loans:* $17,403,089 (66% need-based, 34% non-need-based). *Programs:* Federal Direct (Subsidized and Unsubsidized Stafford, PLUS), alternative loans.

WORK-STUDY *Federal work-study:* Total amount: $98,122; 168 jobs averaging $824. *State or other work-study/employment:* Part-time jobs available.

APPLYING FOR FINANCIAL AID *Required financial aid form:* FAFSA. *Financial aid deadline (priority):* 3/1. *Notification date:* Continuous beginning 3/15. Students must reply within 4 weeks of notification.

CONTACT Adam Ghiloni, Assistant Director of Financial Aid, Ringling College of Art and Design, 2700 North Tamiami Trail, Sarasota, FL 34243, 941-359-7533 or toll-free 800-255-7695. *Fax:* 941-359-6107. *E-mail:* finaid@ringling.edu. *Website:* http://www.ringling.edu/.

RIO GRANDE BIBLE INSTITUTE
Edinburg, TX

CONTACT Financial Aid Office, Rio Grande Bible Institute, 4300 S US Hwy 281, Edinburg, TX 78539, 956-380-8100. *Website:* http://www.riogrande.edu/.

RIPON COLLEGE
Ripon, WI

Tuition & fees: $31,602   **Average undergraduate aid package:** $25,418

ABOUT THE INSTITUTION Independent, coed. *Awards:* bachelor's degrees. 38 undergraduate majors. *Total enrollment:* 931. Undergraduates: 931. Freshmen: 205. Federal methodology is used as a basis for awarding need-based institutional aid.

UNDERGRADUATE EXPENSES for 2013–2014 *Application fee:* $30. *Comprehensive fee:* $40,417 includes full-time tuition ($31,327), mandatory fees ($275), and room and board ($8815). *College room only:* $4665.

FRESHMAN FINANCIAL AID (Fall 2012, est.) 188 applied for aid; of those 87% were deemed to have need. 100% of freshmen with need received aid; of those 17% had need fully met. *Average percent of need met:* 86% (excluding resources awarded to replace EFC). *Average financial aid package:* $27,046 (excluding resources awarded to replace EFC). 16% of all full-time freshmen had no need and received non-need-based gift aid.

UNDERGRADUATE FINANCIAL AID (Fall 2012, est.) 840 applied for aid; of those 90% were deemed to have need. 100% of undergraduates with need received aid; of those 18% had need fully met. *Average percent of need met:* 84% (excluding resources awarded to replace EFC). *Average financial aid package:* $25,418 (excluding resources awarded to replace EFC). 13% of all full-time undergraduates had no need and received non-need-based gift aid.

GIFT AID (NEED-BASED) *Total amount:* $16,839,906 (9% federal, 7% state, 69% institutional, 15% external sources). *Receiving aid:* Freshmen: 76% (163); all full-time undergraduates: 81% (752). *Average award:* Freshmen: $21,836; Undergraduates: $19,763. *Scholarships, grants, and awards:* Federal Pell, FSEOG, state, private, college/university gift aid from institutional funds.

GIFT AID (NON-NEED-BASED) *Total amount:* $3,152,584 (1% state, 57% institutional, 42% external sources). *Receiving aid:* Freshmen: 8% (18). Undergraduates: 9% (81). *Average award:* Freshmen: $14,728. Undergraduates: $10,803. *Scholarships, grants, and awards by category:* Academic interests/achievement: 492 awards ($3,899,728 total): biological sciences, business, computer science, education, English, foreign languages, general academic interests/achievements, humanities, mathematics, military science, physical sciences, premedicine, religion/biblical studies, social sciences. Creative arts/performance: 76 awards ($218,750 total): art/fine arts, debating, music, theater/drama. Special achievements/activities: 159 awards ($727,671 total): general special achievements/activities, leadership, memberships. Special characteristics: 385 awards ($2,059,792 total): children and siblings of alumni, children of faculty/staff, ethnic background, first-generation college students, general special characteristics, international students, local/state students, members of minority groups, out-of-state students, previous college experience, religious affiliation, siblings of current students. *Tuition waivers:* Full or partial for employees or children of employees. *ROTC:* Army.

LOANS *Student loans:* $7,881,500 (72% need-based, 28% non-need-based). 81% of past graduating class borrowed through all loan programs. *Average indebtedness per student:* $31,216. *Average need-based loan:* Freshmen: $4477. Undergraduates: $5329. *Parent loans:* $991,528 (26% need-based, 74% non-need-based). *Programs:* Federal Direct (Subsidized and Unsubsidized Stafford, PLUS), Perkins, alternative loans.

WORK-STUDY *Federal work-study:* Total amount: $927,446; 437 jobs averaging $1777. *State or other work-study/employment:* Total amount: $669,964 (8% need-based, 92% non-need-based). 326 part-time jobs averaging $1727.

APPLYING FOR FINANCIAL AID *Required financial aid form:* FAFSA. *Financial aid deadline (priority):* 3/1. *Notification date:* Continuous beginning 3/7. Students must reply within 2 weeks of notification.

CONTACT Mr. Leigh D. Mlodzik, Dean of Admission and Financial Aid, Ripon College, 300 Seward Street, Ripon, WI 54971, 920-748-8704 or toll-free 800-947-4766. *Fax:* 920-748-8335. *E-mail:* financialaid@ripon.edu. *Website:* http://www.ripon.edu/.

RIVIER UNIVERSITY
Nashua, NH

CONTACT Valerie Patnaude, Director of Financial Aid, Rivier University, 420 Main Street, Nashua, NH 03060-5086, 603-897-8533 or toll-free 800-44RIVIER. *Fax:* 603-897-8810. *E-mail:* vpatnaude@rivier.edu.
Website: http://www.rivier.edu/.

ROANOKE COLLEGE
Salem, VA

Tuition & fees: $36,472	Average undergraduate aid package: $26,518

ABOUT THE INSTITUTION Independent Evangelical Lutheran Church in America, coed. *Awards:* bachelor's degrees. 32 undergraduate majors. *Total enrollment:* 2,060. Undergraduates: 2,060. Freshmen: 543. Federal methodology is used as a basis for awarding need-based institutional aid.
UNDERGRADUATE EXPENSES for 2013–2014 *Application fee:* $30. *One-time required fee:* $125. *Comprehensive fee:* $47,996 includes full-time tuition ($35,108), mandatory fees ($1364), and room and board ($11,524). *College room only:* $5310. Full-time tuition and fees vary according to reciprocity agreements. Room and board charges vary according to board plan and housing facility. *Part-time tuition:* $1680 per course. *Part-time fees:* $38 per term. Part-time tuition and fees vary according to course load and reciprocity agreements.
FRESHMAN FINANCIAL AID (Fall 2012, est.) 483 applied for aid; of those 87% were deemed to have need. 100% of freshmen with need received aid; of those 21% had need fully met. *Average percent of need met:* 78% (excluding resources awarded to replace EFC). *Average financial aid package:* $28,401 (excluding resources awarded to replace EFC). 22% of all full-time freshmen had no need and received non-need-based gift aid.
UNDERGRADUATE FINANCIAL AID (Fall 2012, est.) 1,689 applied for aid; of those 89% were deemed to have need. 100% of undergraduates with need received aid; of those 18% had need fully met. *Average percent of need met:* 77% (excluding resources awarded to replace EFC). *Average financial aid package:* $26,518 (excluding resources awarded to replace EFC). 23% of all full-time undergraduates had no need and received non-need-based gift aid.
GIFT AID (NEED-BASED) *Total amount:* $32,649,981 (7% federal, 7% state, 83% institutional, 3% external sources). *Receiving aid:* Freshmen: 76% (412); all full-time undergraduates: 75% (1,479). *Average award:* Freshmen: $24,168; Undergraduates: $21,527. *Scholarships, grants, and awards:* Federal Pell, FSEOG, state, private, college/university gift aid from institutional funds.
GIFT AID (NON-NEED-BASED) *Total amount:* $6,351,022 (9% state, 88% institutional, 3% external sources). *Receiving aid:* Freshmen: 76% (412). Undergraduates: 73% (1,456). *Average award:* Freshmen: $13,196. Undergraduates: $12,711. *Tuition waivers:* Full or partial for employees or children of employees, senior citizens.
LOANS *Student loans:* $13,929,002 (92% need-based, 8% non-need-based). 72% of past graduating class borrowed through all loan programs. *Average indebtedness per student:* $33,004. *Average need-based loan:* Freshmen: $4122. Undergraduates: $4784. *Parent loans:* $3,692,024 (90% need-based, 10% non-need-based). *Programs:* Federal Direct (Subsidized and Unsubsidized Stafford, PLUS), Perkins, college/university, alternative loans.
WORK-STUDY *Federal work-study:* Total amount: $1,802,378; 1,112 jobs averaging $1563.
APPLYING FOR FINANCIAL AID *Required financial aid forms:* FAFSA, state aid form. *Financial aid deadline (priority):* 3/1. *Notification date:* Continuous beginning 10/1. Students must reply within 2 weeks of notification.
CONTACT Mr. Thomas S. Blair Jr., Director of Financial Aid, Roanoke College, 221 College Lane, Salem, VA 24153-3794, 540-375-2235 or toll-free 800-388-2276. *E-mail:* finaid@roanoke.edu.
Website: http://www.roanoke.edu/.

THE ROBERT B. MILLER COLLEGE
Battle Creek, MI

Tuition & fees: N/R	Average undergraduate aid package: $7600

ABOUT THE INSTITUTION Independent, coed. Federal methodology is used as a basis for awarding need-based institutional aid.
UNDERGRADUATE FINANCIAL AID (Fall 2012, est.) 233 applied for aid; of those 80% were deemed to have need. 100% of undergraduates with need received aid. *Average financial aid package:* $7600 (excluding resources awarded to replace EFC). 4% of all full-time undergraduates had no need and received non-need-based gift aid.
GIFT AID (NEED-BASED) *Total amount:* $382,978 (79% federal, 21% state). *Receiving aid:* All full-time undergraduates: 46% (168). *Average award:* Undergraduates: $1260. *Scholarships, grants, and awards:* Federal Pell, FSEOG, state, private, college/university gift aid from institutional funds.
GIFT AID (NON-NEED-BASED) *Total amount:* $27,216 (65% institutional, 35% external sources). *Receiving aid:* Undergraduates: 7% (25). *Average award:* Undergraduates: $1362.
LOANS *Student loans:* $978,942 (46% need-based, 54% non-need-based). *Average need-based loan:* Undergraduates: $2230. *Programs:* Federal Direct (Subsidized and Unsubsidized Stafford, PLUS).
WORK-STUDY *Federal work-study:* Total amount: $5000; 3 jobs averaging $511.
APPLYING FOR FINANCIAL AID *Notification date:* Continuous.
CONTACT Mrs. Kimberly Cvitkovic, Dean of Student Services and Director of Financial Aid, The Robert B. Miller College, 450 North Avenue, Battle Creek, MI 49017, 269-660-8021 Ext. 2926. *Fax:* 269-565-2180. *E-mail:* cvitkovick@ millercollege.edu .
Website: http://www.millercollege.edu/.

ROBERT MORRIS UNIVERSITY
Moon Township, PA

Tuition & fees: $24,064	Average undergraduate aid package: $17,807

ABOUT THE INSTITUTION Independent, coed. *Awards:* certificates, bachelor's, master's, and doctoral degrees. 30 undergraduate majors. *Total enrollment:* 5,181. Undergraduates: 4,144. Freshmen: 853. Federal methodology is used as a basis for awarding need-based institutional aid.
UNDERGRADUATE EXPENSES for 2013–2014 *Application fee:* $30. *Comprehensive fee:* $35,424 includes full-time tuition ($23,410), mandatory fees ($654), and room and board ($11,360). *College room only:* $5370. Full-time tuition and fees vary according to degree level and program. Room and board charges vary according to board plan and housing facility. *Part-time tuition:* $760 per credit hour. *Part-time fees:* $30 per credit hour. Part-time tuition and fees vary according to course load, degree level, and program.
FRESHMAN FINANCIAL AID (Fall 2012, est.) 756 applied for aid; of those 91% were deemed to have need. 100% of freshmen with need received aid; of those 11% had need fully met. *Average percent of need met:* 77% (excluding resources awarded to replace EFC). *Average financial aid package:* $21,703 (excluding resources awarded to replace EFC). 15% of all full-time freshmen had no need and received non-need-based gift aid.
UNDERGRADUATE FINANCIAL AID (Fall 2012, est.) 3,230 applied for aid; of those 90% were deemed to have need. 99% of undergraduates with need received aid; of those 12% had need fully met. *Average percent of need met:* 68% (excluding resources awarded to replace EFC). *Average financial aid package:* $17,807 (excluding resources awarded to replace EFC). 15% of all full-time undergraduates had no need and received non-need-based gift aid.
GIFT AID (NEED-BASED) *Total amount:* $30,374,518 (23% federal, 17% state, 56% institutional, 4% external sources). *Receiving aid:* Freshmen: 80% (682); all full-time undergraduates: 73% (2,761). *Average award:* Freshmen: $15,786; Undergraduates: $11,768. *Scholarships, grants, and awards:* Federal Pell, FSEOG, state, private, college/university gift aid from institutional funds.
GIFT AID (NON-NEED-BASED) *Total amount:* $8,123,229 (15% federal, 2% state, 73% institutional, 10% external sources). *Receiving aid:* Freshmen: 6% (55).

Undergraduates: 6% (218). **Average award:** Freshmen: $11,118. Undergraduates: $9119. **Scholarships, grants, and awards by category:** Academic interests/achievement: general academic interests/achievements. **Tuition waivers:** Full or partial for employees or children of employees. **ROTC:** Army, Air Force cooperative.
LOANS Student loans: $29,819,505 (77% need-based, 23% non-need-based). 73% of past graduating class borrowed through all loan programs. **Average indebtedness per student:** $41,093. **Average need-based loan:** Freshmen: $4398. Undergraduates: $5732. **Parent loans:** $10,914,965 (50% need-based, 50% non-need-based). **Programs:** Federal Direct (Subsidized and Unsubsidized Stafford, PLUS), Perkins, private loans.
WORK-STUDY Federal work-study: Total amount: $4,040,285; jobs available. **State or other work-study/employment:** Part-time jobs available.
ATHLETIC AWARDS Total amount: $3,295,224 (47% need-based, 53% non-need-based).
APPLYING FOR FINANCIAL AID Required financial aid form: FAFSA. **Financial aid deadline:** Continuous. **Notification date:** Continuous beginning 3/1. Students must reply within 2 weeks of notification.
CONTACT Ms. Stephanie Hendershot, Director of Financial Aid, Robert Morris University, 6001 University Boulevard, Moon Township, PA 15108-1189, 412-397-6250 or toll-free 800-762-0097. Fax: 412-397-2200. E-mail: finaid@rmu.edu. Website: http://www.rmu.edu/.

ROBERT MORRIS UNIVERSITY ILLINOIS
Chicago, IL

Tuition & fees: $22,800	Average undergraduate aid package: $14,319

ABOUT THE INSTITUTION Independent, coed. **Awards:** associate, bachelor's, and master's degrees. 15 undergraduate majors. **Total enrollment:** 3,802. Undergraduates: 3,230. Freshmen: 756. Federal methodology is used as a basis for awarding need-based institutional aid.
UNDERGRADUATE EXPENSES for 2013–2014 Application fee: $20. **Comprehensive fee:** $34,554 includes full-time tuition ($22,800) and room and board ($11,754). **College room only:** $10,500. Room and board charges vary according to housing facility. **Part-time tuition:** $633 per credit hour. Part-time tuition and fees vary according to course load.
FRESHMAN FINANCIAL AID (Fall 2012, est.) 862 applied for aid; of those 96% were deemed to have need. 95% of freshmen with need received aid; of those 5% had need fully met. **Average percent of need met:** 47% (excluding resources awarded to replace EFC). **Average financial aid package:** $14,940 (excluding resources awarded to replace EFC). 2% of all full-time freshmen had no need and received non-need-based gift aid.
UNDERGRADUATE FINANCIAL AID (Fall 2012, est.) 3,907 applied for aid; of those 93% were deemed to have need. 97% of undergraduates with need received aid; of those 4% had need fully met. **Average percent of need met:** 47% (excluding resources awarded to replace EFC). **Average financial aid package:** $14,319 (excluding resources awarded to replace EFC). 2% of all full-time undergraduates had no need and received non-need-based gift aid.
GIFT AID (NEED-BASED) Total amount: $23,134,255 (57% federal, 29% state, 14% institutional). **Receiving aid:** Freshmen: 83% (767); all full-time undergraduates: 84% (3,396). **Average award:** Freshmen: $12,487; Undergraduates: $11,372. **Scholarships, grants, and awards:** Federal Pell, FSEOG, state, private, college/university gift aid from institutional funds.
GIFT AID (NON-NEED-BASED) Total amount: $10,526,975 (96% institutional, 4% external sources). **Receiving aid:** Freshmen: 41% (377). Undergraduates: 66% (2,683). **Average award:** Freshmen: $7787. Undergraduates: $9229. **Scholarships, grants, and awards by category:** Academic interests/achievement: architecture, business, computer science, general academic interests/achievements, health fields. **Creative arts/performance:** applied art and design, journalism/publications. **Special achievements/activities:** cheerleading/drum major, community service, general special achievements/activities, leadership. **Special characteristics:** adult students, children of faculty/staff, general special characteristics, local/state students, out-of-state students, veterans. **Tuition waivers:** Full or partial for employees or children of employees. **ROTC:** Army cooperative.
LOANS Student loans: $22,850,176 (92% need-based, 8% non-need-based). 97% of past graduating class borrowed through all loan programs. **Average indebtedness**

per student: $30,133. **Average need-based loan:** Freshmen: $3990. Undergraduates: $4151. **Parent loans:** $4,148,202 (83% need-based, 17% non-need-based). **Programs:** Federal Direct (Subsidized and Unsubsidized Stafford, PLUS), Perkins.
WORK-STUDY Federal work-study: Total amount: $382,303; 148 jobs averaging $1907.
ATHLETIC AWARDS Total amount: $7,468,277 (83% need-based, 17% non-need-based).
APPLYING FOR FINANCIAL AID Required financial aid form: FAFSA. **Financial aid deadline:** Continuous. **Notification date:** Continuous.
CONTACT Leigh Brinson, Vice President of Financial Services, Robert Morris University Illinois, 401 South State Street, Suite 122, Chicago, IL 60605, 312-935-4408 or toll-free 800-RMC-5960. Fax: 312-935-4415. E-mail: lbrinson@robertmorris.edu. Website: http://www.robertmorris.edu/.

ROBERTS WESLEYAN COLLEGE
Rochester, NY

Tuition & fees: $27,464	Average undergraduate aid package: $17,512

ABOUT THE INSTITUTION Independent Free Methodist Church of North America, coed. **Awards:** associate, bachelor's, and master's degrees. 56 undergraduate majors. **Total enrollment:** 1,752. Undergraduates: 1,323. Freshmen: 213. Federal methodology is used as a basis for awarding need-based institutional aid.
UNDERGRADUATE EXPENSES for 2013–2014 Application fee: $35. **One-time required fee:** $375. **Comprehensive fee:** $37,094 includes full-time tuition ($26,352), mandatory fees ($1112), and room and board ($9630). **College room only:** $6166. Room and board charges vary according to board plan and housing facility. Part-time tuition and fees vary according to course load.
FRESHMAN FINANCIAL AID (Fall 2012, est.) 194 applied for aid; of those 97% were deemed to have need. 100% of freshmen with need received aid; of those 18% had need fully met. **Average percent of need met:** 80% (excluding resources awarded to replace EFC). **Average financial aid package:** $23,246 (excluding resources awarded to replace EFC). 12% of all full-time freshmen had no need and received non-need-based gift aid.
UNDERGRADUATE FINANCIAL AID (Fall 2012, est.) 1,323 applied for aid; of those 95% were deemed to have need. 100% of undergraduates with need received aid; of those 11% had need fully met. **Average percent of need met:** 67% (excluding resources awarded to replace EFC). **Average financial aid package:** $17,512 (excluding resources awarded to replace EFC). 11% of all full-time undergraduates had no need and received non-need-based gift aid.
GIFT AID (NEED-BASED) Total amount: $14,926,984 (18% federal, 10% state, 60% institutional, 12% external sources). **Receiving aid:** Freshmen: 86% (188); all full-time undergraduates: 85% (1,232). **Average award:** Freshmen: $18,640; Undergraduates: $12,663. **Scholarships, grants, and awards:** Federal Pell, FSEOG, state, private, college/university gift aid from institutional funds, Academic Competitiveness Grants, National SMART Grants, TEACH Grants.
GIFT AID (NON-NEED-BASED) Total amount: $2,131,591 (1% state, 70% institutional, 29% external sources). **Receiving aid:** Freshmen: 11% (24). Undergraduates: 6% (87). **Average award:** Freshmen: $10,188. Undergraduates: $7025. **Scholarships, grants, and awards by category:** Academic interests/achievement: 408 awards ($3,011,350 total): general academic interests/achievements. **Creative arts/performance:** 125 awards ($304,475 total): art/fine arts, music. **Special achievements/activities:** 366 awards ($1,122,250 total): general special achievements/activities, junior miss. **Special characteristics:** 473 awards ($1,599,145 total): children and siblings of alumni, children of faculty/staff, international students, out-of-state students, relatives of clergy, religious affiliation, siblings of current students. **Tuition waivers:** Full or partial for employees or children of employees, senior citizens. **ROTC:** Army, Air Force cooperative.
LOANS Student loans: $10,931,770 (85% need-based, 15% non-need-based). 88% of past graduating class borrowed through all loan programs. **Average indebtedness per student:** $33,528. **Average need-based loan:** Freshmen: $4217. Undergraduates: $4878. **Parent loans:** $1,925,933 (55% need-based, 45% non-need-based). **Programs:** Federal Direct (Subsidized and Unsubsidized Stafford, PLUS), Perkins.
WORK-STUDY Federal work-study: Total amount: $307,063; 732 jobs averaging $1847. **State or other work-study/employment:** Total amount: $66,700 (100% non-need-based). 37 part-time jobs averaging $1803.

ATHLETIC AWARDS Total amount: $1,260,156 (70% need-based, 30% non-need-based).

APPLYING FOR FINANCIAL AID *Required financial aid forms:* FAFSA, state aid form. *Financial aid deadline (priority):* 3/15. *Notification date:* Continuous beginning 3/15. Students must reply by 5/1 or within 2 weeks of notification.

CONTACT Financial Aid Office, Roberts Wesleyan College, 2301 Westside Drive, Rochester, NY 14624-1997, 585-594-6150 or toll-free 800-777-4RWC. *Fax:* 585-594-6036. *E-mail:* finaid@roberts.edu.
Website: http://www.roberts.edu/.

ROCHESTER COLLEGE
Rochester Hills, MI

Tuition & fees: N/R	Average undergraduate aid package: N/A

ABOUT THE INSTITUTION Independent Church of Christ, coed. 30 undergraduate majors. Both federal and institutional methodology are used as a basis for awarding need-based institutional aid.

GIFT AID (NEED-BASED) *Total amount:* $5,572,100 (33% federal, 13% state, 46% institutional, 8% external sources). *Scholarships, grants, and awards:* Federal Pell, FSEOG, state, private, college/university gift aid from institutional funds.

GIFT AID (NON-NEED-BASED) *Scholarships, grants, and awards by category: Academic interests/achievement:* business, computer science, education, general academic interests/achievements, mathematics, religion/biblical studies. *Creative arts/performance:* journalism/publications, music, theater/drama. *Special achievements/activities:* general special achievements/activities, leadership. *Special characteristics:* adult students, children and siblings of alumni, children of faculty/staff, first-generation college students, general special characteristics, local/state students, out-of-state students, previous college experience, relatives of clergy, religious affiliation, siblings of current students.

LOANS *Student loans:* $6,750,227 (100% need-based). *Parent loans:* $784,866 (100% need-based). *Programs:* Federal Direct (Subsidized and Unsubsidized Stafford, PLUS), Perkins.

WORK-STUDY *Federal work-study:* Total amount: $68,828; jobs available. *State or other work-study/employment:* Part-time jobs available.

ATHLETIC AWARDS Total amount: $115,154 (100% need-based).

APPLYING FOR FINANCIAL AID *Required financial aid form:* FAFSA. *Financial aid deadline:* Continuous. *Notification date:* Continuous beginning 1/1.

CONTACT Student Financial Services, Rochester College, 800 West Avon Road, Rochester Hills, MI 48307, 248-218-2038 or toll-free 800-521-6010. *Fax:* 248-218-2065.
Website: http://www.rc.edu/.

ROCHESTER INSTITUTE OF TECHNOLOGY
Rochester, NY

Tuition & fees: $34,424	Average undergraduate aid package: $23,800

ABOUT THE INSTITUTION Independent, coed. *Awards:* certificates, associate, bachelor's, master's, and doctoral degrees. 117 undergraduate majors. *Total enrollment:* 16,362. Undergraduates: 13,711. Freshmen: 2,736. Both federal and institutional methodology are used as a basis for awarding need-based institutional aid.

UNDERGRADUATE EXPENSES for 2013–2014 *Application fee:* $60. *Comprehensive fee:* $46,164 includes full-time tuition ($33,932), mandatory fees ($492), and room and board ($11,740). *College room only:* $6530. Full-time tuition and fees vary according to course load. Room and board charges vary according to board plan and housing facility. *Part-time tuition:* $1191 per credit. Part-time tuition and fees vary according to class time and course load.

FRESHMAN FINANCIAL AID (Fall 2011) 2,362 applied for aid; of those 88% were deemed to have need. 100% of freshmen with need received aid; of those 82% had need fully met. *Average percent of need met:* 87% (excluding resources

awarded to replace EFC). *Average financial aid package:* $24,000 (excluding resources awarded to replace EFC). 15% of all full-time freshmen had no need and received non-need-based gift aid.

UNDERGRADUATE FINANCIAL AID (Fall 2011) 9,329 applied for aid; of those 91% were deemed to have need. 100% of undergraduates with need received aid; of those 82% had need fully met. *Average percent of need met:* 87% (excluding resources awarded to replace EFC). *Average financial aid package:* $23,800 (excluding resources awarded to replace EFC). 12% of all full-time undergraduates had no need and received non-need-based gift aid.

GIFT AID (NEED-BASED) *Total amount:* $123,803,130 (14% federal, 7% state, 77% institutional, 2% external sources). *Receiving aid:* Freshmen: 74% (1,965); all full-time undergraduates: 64% (7,881). *Average award:* Freshmen: $18,500; Undergraduates: $1800. *Scholarships, grants, and awards:* Federal Pell, FSEOG, state, private, college/university gift aid from institutional funds, NACME Scholarships, National Science Foundation Grants.

GIFT AID (NON-NEED-BASED) *Total amount:* $32,125,670 (7% federal, 23% state, 61% institutional, 9% external sources). *Receiving aid:* Freshmen: 22% (599). Undergraduates: 20% (2,516). *Average award:* Freshmen: $12,000. Undergraduates: $10,000. *Scholarships, grants, and awards by category: Academic interests/achievement:* biological sciences, business, communication, computer science, engineering/technologies, general academic interests/achievements, health fields, international studies, mathematics, military science, physical sciences, premedicine, social sciences. *Creative arts/performance:* applied art and design, art/fine arts, cinema/film/broadcasting. *Special achievements/activities:* community service, leadership. *Special characteristics:* children of faculty/staff, veterans. *Tuition waivers:* Full or partial for employees or children of employees. *ROTC:* Army, Naval cooperative, Air Force.

LOANS *Student loans:* $83,804,360 (56% need-based, 44% non-need-based). *Average need-based loan:* Freshmen: $3500. Undergraduates: $5400. *Parent loans:* $20,463,000 (52% need-based, 48% non-need-based). *Programs:* Federal Direct (Subsidized and Unsubsidized Stafford, PLUS), Perkins, alternative loans.

WORK-STUDY *Federal work-study:* Total amount: $3,915,583; jobs available. *State or other work-study/employment:* Total amount: $9,870,900 (100% non-need-based). Part-time jobs available.

APPLYING FOR FINANCIAL AID *Required financial aid forms:* FAFSA, state aid form. *Financial aid deadline (priority):* 3/1. *Notification date:* Continuous beginning 3/15. Students must reply by 5/1.

CONTACT Mrs. Verna Hazen, Assistant Vice President for Financial Aid and Scholarships, Rochester Institute of Technology, 56 Lomb Memorial Drive, Rochester, NY 14623-5604, 585-475-2186. *Fax:* 585-475-7270. *E-mail:* verna.hazen@rit.edu. *Website:* http://www.rit.edu/.

ROCKFORD COLLEGE
Rockford, IL

Tuition & fees: $26,310	Average undergraduate aid package: $16,725

ABOUT THE INSTITUTION Independent, coed. *Awards:* bachelor's and master's degrees. 47 undergraduate majors. *Total enrollment:* 1,238. Undergraduates: 1,022. Freshmen: 105. Federal methodology is used as a basis for awarding need-based institutional aid.

UNDERGRADUATE EXPENSES for 2013–2014 *Comprehensive fee:* $33,630 includes full-time tuition ($26,210), mandatory fees ($100), and room and board ($7320). *College room only:* $4070. Full-time tuition and fees vary according to course load. Room and board charges vary according to board plan and housing facility. *Part-time tuition:* $715 per credit. *Part-time fees:* $40 per term. Part-time tuition and fees vary according to course load.

FRESHMAN FINANCIAL AID (Fall 2011) 125 applied for aid; of those 96% were deemed to have need. 100% of freshmen with need received aid; of those 9% had need fully met. *Average percent of need met:* 68% (excluding resources awarded to replace EFC). *Average financial aid package:* $17,322 (excluding resources awarded to replace EFC). 7% of all full-time freshmen had no need and received non-need-based gift aid.

UNDERGRADUATE FINANCIAL AID (Fall 2011) 917 applied for aid; of those 95% were deemed to have need. 100% of undergraduates with need received aid; of those 9% had need fully met. *Average percent of need met:* 64% (excluding resources awarded to replace EFC). *Average financial aid package:* $16,725

(excluding resources awarded to replace EFC). 8% of all full-time undergraduates had no need and received non-need-based gift aid.
GIFT AID (NEED-BASED) *Total amount:* $10,884,846 (20% federal, 18% state, 60% institutional, 2% external sources). *Receiving aid:* Freshmen: 91% (118); all full-time undergraduates: 88% (845). *Average award:* Freshmen: $14,276; Undergraduates: $12,342. *Scholarships, grants, and awards:* Federal Pell, FSEOG, state, private, college/university gift aid from institutional funds.
GIFT AID (NON-NEED-BASED) *Total amount:* $1,202,468 (1% state, 80% institutional, 19% external sources). *Receiving aid:* Freshmen: 9% (11). Undergraduates: 8% (75). *Average award:* Freshmen: $9290. Undergraduates: $7404. *Scholarships, grants, and awards by category:* Academic interests/achievement: 886 awards ($5,601,839 total): biological sciences, business, computer science, education, English, foreign languages, general academic interests/achievements, mathematics, physical sciences, premedicine, social sciences. *Creative arts/performance:* 32 awards ($55,625 total): art/fine arts, dance, music, performing arts, theater/drama. *Special achievements/activities:* 11 awards ($20,947 total): community service, leadership. *Special characteristics:* 143 awards ($448,773 total): children and siblings of alumni, children of current students, children of educators, children of faculty/staff, general special characteristics, international students, out-of-state students, parents of current students, siblings of current students. *Tuition waivers:* Full or partial for employees or children of employees. *ROTC:* Army cooperative.
LOANS *Student loans:* $8,764,302 (87% need-based, 13% non-need-based). 100% of past graduating class borrowed through all loan programs. *Average indebtedness per student:* $22,245. *Average need-based loan:* Freshmen: $3252. Undergraduates: $4828. *Parent loans:* $1,354,324 (53% need-based, 47% non-need-based). *Programs:* Federal Direct (Subsidized and Unsubsidized Stafford, PLUS), Perkins, college/university, alternative loans.
WORK-STUDY *Federal work-study:* Total amount: $75,785; 141 jobs averaging $696. *State or other work-study/employment:* Total amount: $153,452 (47% need-based, 53% non-need-based). 206 part-time jobs averaging $745.
APPLYING FOR FINANCIAL AID *Required financial aid form:* FAFSA. *Financial aid deadline (priority):* 3/1. *Notification date:* Continuous beginning 3/15. Students must reply within 4 weeks of notification.
CONTACT Todd M. Free, Assistant Vice President of Student Administrative Services, Rockford College, 5050 East State Street, Rockford, IL 61108, 815-226-3385 or toll-free 800-892-2984. *Fax:* 815-394-5174. *E-mail:* tfree@rockford.edu. *Website:* http://www.rockford.edu/.

ROCKHURST UNIVERSITY
Kansas City, MO

Tuition & fees: $29,840	Average undergraduate aid package: $28,936

ABOUT THE INSTITUTION Independent Roman Catholic (Jesuit), coed. *Awards:* certificates, bachelor's, master's, and doctoral degrees. 30 undergraduate majors. *Total enrollment:* 2,808. Undergraduates: 2,160. Freshmen: 447. Federal methodology is used as a basis for awarding need-based institutional aid.
UNDERGRADUATE EXPENSES for 2013–2014 *Application fee:* $25. *Comprehensive fee:* $37,900 includes full-time tuition ($29,100), mandatory fees ($740), and room and board ($8060). *College room only:* $5060. Full-time tuition and fees vary according to class time and course load. Room and board charges vary according to board plan and housing facility. Part-time tuition and fees vary according to class time and course load.
FRESHMAN FINANCIAL AID (Fall 2012, est.) 417 applied for aid; of those 100% were deemed to have need. 100% of freshmen with need received aid; of those 1% had need fully met. *Average percent of need met:* 90% (excluding resources awarded to replace EFC). *Average financial aid package:* $30,538 (excluding resources awarded to replace EFC). 5% of all full-time freshmen had no need and received non-need-based gift aid.
UNDERGRADUATE FINANCIAL AID (Fall 2012, est.) 1,297 applied for aid; of those 100% were deemed to have need. 97% of undergraduates with need received aid; of those 6% had need fully met. *Average percent of need met:* 85% (excluding resources awarded to replace EFC). *Average financial aid package:* $28,936 (excluding resources awarded to replace EFC). 12% of all full-time undergraduates had no need and received non-need-based gift aid.
GIFT AID (NEED-BASED) *Total amount:* $32,853,932 (5% federal, 3% state, 91% institutional, 1% external sources). *Receiving aid:* Freshmen: 71% (317); all full-time undergraduates: 73% (1,027). *Average award:* Freshmen: $6733; Undergrad-

uates: $7077. *Scholarships, grants, and awards:* Federal Pell, FSEOG, state, private, college/university gift aid from institutional funds, United Negro College Fund.
GIFT AID (NON-NEED-BASED) *Total amount:* $19,759,519 (100% institutional). *Receiving aid:* Freshmen: 93% (415). Undergraduates: 88% (1,237). *Average award:* Freshmen: $16,511. Undergraduates: $15,146. *Scholarships, grants, and awards by category:* Academic interests/achievement: biological sciences, business, communication, English, foreign languages, general academic interests/achievements, health fields, humanities, mathematics, physical sciences, premedicine, religion/biblical studies, social sciences. *Creative arts/performance:* creative writing, music, performing arts, theater/drama. *Special achievements/activities:* community service, leadership. *Special characteristics:* children and siblings of alumni, children of faculty/staff, siblings of current students. *Tuition waivers:* Full or partial for employees or children of employees, senior citizens. *ROTC:* Army cooperative.
LOANS *Student loans:* $8,519,749 (43% need-based, 57% non-need-based). 74% of past graduating class borrowed through all loan programs. *Average indebtedness per student:* $20,003. *Average need-based loan:* Freshmen: $3286. Undergraduates: $3819. *Parent loans:* $1,801,308 (72% need-based, 28% non-need-based). *Programs:* Federal Direct (Subsidized and Unsubsidized Stafford, PLUS), Perkins.
WORK-STUDY *Federal work-study:* Total amount: $250,000; jobs available. *State or other work-study/employment:* Total amount: $62,500 (100% non-need-based). Part-time jobs available.
ATHLETIC AWARDS Total amount: $2,343,499 (33% need-based, 67% non-need-based).
APPLYING FOR FINANCIAL AID *Required financial aid form:* FAFSA. *Financial aid deadline (priority):* 3/1. *Notification date:* Continuous beginning 3/1. Students must reply by 6/1 or within 4 weeks of notification.
CONTACT Maureen McKinnon, Director of Financial Aid, Rockhurst University, 1100 Rockhurst Road, Kansas City, MO 64110-2561, 816-501-4831 or toll-free 800-842-6776. *Fax:* 816-501-3139. *E-mail:* maureen.mckinnon@rockhurst.edu. *Website:* http://www.rockhurst.edu/.

ROCKY MOUNTAIN COLLEGE
Billings, MT

Tuition & fees: $23,718	Average undergraduate aid package: $18,988

ABOUT THE INSTITUTION Independent interdenominational, coed. *Awards:* associate, bachelor's, and master's degrees. 51 undergraduate majors. *Total enrollment:* 1,087. Undergraduates: 1,007. Freshmen: 262. Federal methodology is used as a basis for awarding need-based institutional aid.
UNDERGRADUATE EXPENSES for 2013–2014 *Application fee:* $35. *Comprehensive fee:* $31,148 includes full-time tuition ($23,228), mandatory fees ($490), and room and board ($7430). *College room only:* $3462. Full-time tuition and fees vary according to course load, degree level, and program. Room and board charges vary according to board plan and housing facility. *Part-time tuition:* $968 per credit. Part-time tuition and fees vary according to course load, degree level, and program.
FRESHMAN FINANCIAL AID (Fall 2012, est.) 232 applied for aid; of those 92% were deemed to have need. 100% of freshmen with need received aid; of those 19% had need fully met. *Average percent of need met:* 73% (excluding resources awarded to replace EFC). *Average financial aid package:* $19,420 (excluding resources awarded to replace EFC). 6% of all full-time freshmen had no need and received non-need-based gift aid.
UNDERGRADUATE FINANCIAL AID (Fall 2012, est.) 817 applied for aid; of those 91% were deemed to have need. 100% of undergraduates with need received aid; of those 18% had need fully met. *Average percent of need met:* 71% (excluding resources awarded to replace EFC). *Average financial aid package:* $18,988 (excluding resources awarded to replace EFC). 7% of all full-time undergraduates had no need and received non-need-based gift aid.
GIFT AID (NEED-BASED) *Total amount:* $9,304,205 (19% federal, 76% institutional, 5% external sources). *Receiving aid:* Freshmen: 79% (208); all full-time undergraduates: 74% (720). *Average award:* Freshmen: $15,470; Undergraduates: $14,404. *Scholarships, grants, and awards:* Federal Pell, FSEOG, state, private, college/university gift aid from institutional funds.
GIFT AID (NON-NEED-BASED) *Total amount:* $2,118,719 (93% institutional, 7% external sources). *Receiving aid:* Freshmen: 78% (204). Undergraduates: 72% (698). *Average award:* Freshmen: $10,500. Undergraduates: $9860. *Scholarships, grants, and awards by category:* Special achievements/activities: 12 awards

($17,700 total): cheerleading/drum major. *Special characteristics:* 31 awards ($694,802 total): children and siblings of alumni, children of faculty/staff. *Tuition waivers:* Full or partial for employees or children of employees. *ROTC:* Army.
LOANS *Student loans:* $6,180,740 (78% need-based, 22% non-need-based). 78% of past graduating class borrowed through all loan programs. *Average indebtedness per student:* $30,948. *Average need-based loan:* Freshmen: $3494. Undergraduates: $4590. *Parent loans:* $1,222,702 (39% need-based, 61% non-need-based). *Programs:* Federal Direct (Subsidized and Unsubsidized Stafford, PLUS), Perkins.
WORK-STUDY *Federal work-study:* Total amount: $136,825; 166 jobs averaging $824. *State or other work-study/employment:* Total amount: $181,700 (41% need-based, 59% non-need-based). 81 part-time jobs averaging $920.
ATHLETIC AWARDS Total amount: $2,405,803 (46% need-based, 54% non-need-based).
APPLYING FOR FINANCIAL AID *Required financial aid form:* FAFSA. *Financial aid deadline:* Continuous. *Notification date:* Continuous beginning 2/15. Students must reply within 4 weeks of notification.
CONTACT Jessica Francischetti, Financial Aid Director, Rocky Mountain College, 1511 Poly Drive, Billings, MT 59102-1796, 406-657-1031 or toll-free 800-877-6259. *Fax:* 406-657-1169. *E-mail:* finaid@rocky.edu. *Website:* http://www.rocky.edu/.

ROCKY MOUNTAIN COLLEGE OF ART + DESIGN
Lakewood, CO

Tuition & fees: $27,648	Average undergraduate aid package: $20,977

ABOUT THE INSTITUTION Proprietary, coed. *Awards:* bachelor's and master's degrees. 8 undergraduate majors. *Total enrollment:* 651. Undergraduates: 623. Freshmen: 111. Federal methodology is used as a basis for awarding need-based institutional aid.
UNDERGRADUATE EXPENSES for 2013–2014 *Application fee:* $50. *Tuition:* full-time $27,648; part-time $1152 per credit hour. Full-time tuition and fees vary according to degree level and location. Part-time tuition and fees vary according to course load, degree level, and location. *Payment plan:* Guaranteed tuition.
FRESHMAN FINANCIAL AID (Fall 2012, est.) 99 applied for aid; of those 88% were deemed to have need. 100% of freshmen with need received aid; of those 13% had need fully met. *Average percent of need met:* 74% (excluding resources awarded to replace EFC). *Average financial aid package:* $20,855 (excluding resources awarded to replace EFC). 17% of all full-time freshmen had no need and received non-need-based gift aid.
UNDERGRADUATE FINANCIAL AID (Fall 2012, est.) 439 applied for aid; of those 90% were deemed to have need. 100% of undergraduates with need received aid; of those 10% had need fully met. *Average percent of need met:* 73% (excluding resources awarded to replace EFC). *Average financial aid package:* $20,977 (excluding resources awarded to replace EFC). 19% of all full-time undergraduates had no need and received non-need-based gift aid.
GIFT AID (NEED-BASED) *Total amount:* $4,142,460 (23% federal, 2% state, 74% institutional, 1% external sources). *Receiving aid:* Freshmen: 36% (38); all full-time undergraduates: 37% (195). *Average award:* Freshmen: $5252; Undergraduates: $4682. *Scholarships, grants, and awards:* Federal Pell, FSEOG, state, college/university gift aid from institutional funds.
GIFT AID (NON-NEED-BASED) *Total amount:* $729,914 (100% institutional). *Receiving aid:* Freshmen: 79% (83). Undergraduates: 67% (349). *Average award:* Freshmen: $9647. Undergraduates: $7142. *Scholarships, grants, and awards by category:* Academic interests/achievement: general academic interests/achievements. Creative arts/performance: applied art and design, art/fine arts. Special characteristics: children of faculty/staff. *Tuition waivers:* Full or partial for employees or children of employees.
LOANS *Student loans:* $4,183,891 (86% need-based, 14% non-need-based). 7% of past graduating class borrowed through all loan programs. *Average indebtedness per student:* $30,067. *Average need-based loan:* Freshmen: $3417. Undergraduates: $4346. *Parent loans:* $2,620,605 (67% need-based, 33% non-need-based). *Programs:* Federal Direct (Subsidized and Unsubsidized Stafford, PLUS), alternative loans.

WORK-STUDY *Federal work-study:* Total amount: $59,683; 29 jobs averaging $2417. *State or other work-study/employment:* Total amount: $115,755 (95% need-based, 5% non-need-based). 40 part-time jobs averaging $2767.
APPLYING FOR FINANCIAL AID *Required financial aid form:* FAFSA. *Financial aid deadline (priority):* 3/15. *Notification date:* Continuous beginning 4/1. Students must reply within 2 weeks of notification.
CONTACT Tammy Dybdahl, Director of Financial Aid, Rocky Mountain College of Art + Design, 1600 Pierce Street, Lakewood, CO 80214, 303-225-8551 or toll-free 800-888-ARTS. *Fax:* 303-567-7280. *E-mail:* tdybdahl@rmcad.edu. *Website:* http://www.rmcad.edu/.

ROGERS STATE UNIVERSITY
Claremore, OK

Tuition & fees (OK res): $5047	Average undergraduate aid package: $8723

ABOUT THE INSTITUTION State-supported, coed. *Awards:* associate and bachelor's degrees. 25 undergraduate majors. *Total enrollment:* 4,646. Undergraduates: 4,646. Freshmen: 834. Federal methodology is used as a basis for awarding need-based institutional aid.
UNDERGRADUATE EXPENSES for 2013–2014 *Tuition, state resident:* full-time $3263; part-time $108.75 per hour. *Tuition, nonresident:* full-time $9788; part-time $326.25 per hour. *Required fees:* full-time $1784; $58.45 per hour or $15 per term. Full-time tuition and fees vary according to course level, course load, location, program, and student level. Part-time tuition and fees vary according to course level, course load, location, program, and student level. *College room and board:* $6425. Room and board charges vary according to housing facility.
FRESHMAN FINANCIAL AID (Fall 2012, est.) 608 applied for aid; of those 84% were deemed to have need. 96% of freshmen with need received aid; of those 4% had need fully met. *Average percent of need met:* 42% (excluding resources awarded to replace EFC). *Average financial aid package:* $8324 (excluding resources awarded to replace EFC). 2% of all full-time freshmen had no need and received non-need-based gift aid.
UNDERGRADUATE FINANCIAL AID (Fall 2012, est.) 2,375 applied for aid; of those 86% were deemed to have need. 98% of undergraduates with need received aid; of those 4% had need fully met. *Average percent of need met:* 44% (excluding resources awarded to replace EFC). *Average financial aid package:* $8723 (excluding resources awarded to replace EFC). 2% of all full-time undergraduates had no need and received non-need-based gift aid.
GIFT AID (NEED-BASED) *Total amount:* $14,114,404 (66% federal, 24% state, 3% institutional, 7% external sources). *Receiving aid:* Freshmen: 58% (394); all full-time undergraduates: 58% (1,628). *Average award:* Freshmen: $6073; Undergraduates: $5610. *Scholarships, grants, and awards:* Federal Pell, FSEOG, state, private, college/university gift aid from institutional funds.
GIFT AID (NON-NEED-BASED) *Total amount:* $1,831,474 (69% state, 16% institutional, 15% external sources). *Receiving aid:* Freshmen: 23% (159). Undergraduates: 18% (497). *Average award:* Freshmen: $4804. Undergraduates: $5296. *Scholarships, grants, and awards by category:* Academic interests/achievement: 16 awards ($19,296 total): general academic interests/achievements. Creative arts/performance: 19 awards ($18,358 total): music, theater/drama. Special achievements/activities: 58 awards ($162,351 total): cheerleading/drum major, leadership, rodeo. Special characteristics: 205 awards ($1,018,290 total): adult students, out-of-state students. *Tuition waivers:* Full or partial for employees or children of employees, senior citizens.
LOANS *Student loans:* $14,209,213 (92% need-based, 8% non-need-based). 45% of past graduating class borrowed through all loan programs. *Average indebtedness per student:* $19,019. *Average need-based loan:* Freshmen: $3449. Undergraduates: $4126. *Parent loans:* $122,611 (85% need-based, 15% non-need-based). *Programs:* Federal Direct (Subsidized and Unsubsidized Stafford, PLUS), alternative loans.
WORK-STUDY *Federal work-study:* Total amount: $113,232; 65 jobs averaging $1742. *State or other work-study/employment:* Total amount: $836,250 (47% need-based, 53% non-need-based). 244 part-time jobs averaging $1696.
ATHLETIC AWARDS Total amount: $952,733 (56% need-based, 44% non-need-based).
APPLYING FOR FINANCIAL AID *Required financial aid form:* FAFSA. *Financial aid deadline (priority):* 6/1. *Notification date:* Continuous beginning 4/1. Students must reply within 2 weeks of notification.

CONTACT Ms. Kelly Hicks, Director of Financial Aid, Rogers State University, 1701 West Will Rogers Boulevard, Claremore, OK 74017-3252, 918-343-7553 or toll-free 800-256-7511. *Fax:* 918-343-7598. *E-mail:* finaid@rsu.edu. *Website:* http://www.rsu.edu/.

ROGER WILLIAMS UNIVERSITY
Bristol, RI

| Tuition & fees: $31,668 | Average undergraduate aid package: $18,872 |

ABOUT THE INSTITUTION Independent, coed. *Awards:* certificates, associate, bachelor's, master's, and doctoral degrees. 55 undergraduate majors. *Total enrollment:* 5,274. Undergraduates: 4,391. Freshmen: 997. Institutional methodology is used as a basis for awarding need-based institutional aid.

UNDERGRADUATE EXPENSES for 2013–2014 *Application fee:* $50. *Comprehensive fee:* $45,788 includes full-time tuition ($29,976), mandatory fees ($1692), and room and board ($14,120). *College room only:* $7610. Full-time tuition and fees vary according to class time, course load, and program. Room and board charges vary according to board plan and housing facility. *Part-time tuition:* $939 per course. Part-time tuition and fees vary according to class time. *Payment plan:* Guaranteed tuition.

FRESHMAN FINANCIAL AID (Fall 2012, est.) 774 applied for aid; of those 80% were deemed to have need. 100% of freshmen with need received aid; of those 10% had need fully met. *Average percent of need met:* 86% (excluding resources awarded to replace EFC). *Average financial aid package:* $18,935 (excluding resources awarded to replace EFC). 15% of all full-time freshmen had no need and received non-need-based gift aid.

UNDERGRADUATE FINANCIAL AID (Fall 2012, est.) 2,742 applied for aid; of those 82% were deemed to have need. 99% of undergraduates with need received aid; of those 9% had need fully met. *Average percent of need met:* 76% (excluding resources awarded to replace EFC). *Average financial aid package:* $18,872 (excluding resources awarded to replace EFC). 11% of all full-time undergraduates had no need and received non-need-based gift aid.

GIFT AID (NEED-BASED) *Total amount:* $29,722,956 (8% federal, 1% state, 89% institutional, 2% external sources). *Receiving aid:* Freshmen: 36% (359); all full-time undergraduates: 37% (1,403). *Average award:* Freshmen: $12,615; Undergraduates: $11,872. *Scholarships, grants, and awards:* Federal Pell, FSEOG, state, private, college/university gift aid from institutional funds.

GIFT AID (NON-NEED-BASED) *Total amount:* $4,370,095 (99% institutional, 1% external sources). *Receiving aid:* Freshmen: 47% (469). Undergraduates: 41% (1,552). *Average award:* Freshmen: $11,051. Undergraduates: $10,223. *Scholarships, grants, and awards by category:* Academic interests/achievement: 2,456 awards ($22,357,161 total): general academic interests/achievements. *Tuition waivers:* Full or partial for employees or children of employees. *ROTC:* Army cooperative.

LOANS *Student loans:* $15,570,364 (87% need-based, 13% non-need-based). 66% of past graduating class borrowed through all loan programs. *Average indebtedness per student:* $38,550. *Average need-based loan:* Freshmen: $4078. Undergraduates: $4769. *Parent loans:* $11,164,174 (91% need-based, 9% non-need-based). *Programs:* Federal Direct (Subsidized and Unsubsidized Stafford, PLUS), Perkins, state.

WORK-STUDY *Federal work-study:* Total amount: $481,162; 383 jobs averaging $2222. *State or other work-study/employment:* Part-time jobs available.

APPLYING FOR FINANCIAL AID *Required financial aid forms:* FAFSA, CSS Financial Aid PROFILE. *Financial aid deadline:* 2/1. *Notification date:* Continuous beginning 3/15. Students must reply within 2 weeks of notification.

CONTACT Diane Usher, Associate Director of Student Financial Aid and Planning, Roger Williams University, One Old Ferry Road, Bristol, RI 02809, 800-458-7144 Ext. 3100 or toll-free 800-458-7144. *Fax:* 401-254-3356 . *E-mail:* finaid@rwu.edu . *Website:* http://www.rwu.edu/.

ROLLINS COLLEGE
Winter Park, FL

| Tuition & fees: $39,900 | Average undergraduate aid package: $34,058 |

ABOUT THE INSTITUTION Independent, coed. *Awards:* bachelor's and master's degrees. 32 undergraduate majors. *Total enrollment:* 2,459. Undergraduates: 1,884. Freshmen: 518. Federal methodology is used as a basis for awarding need-based institutional aid.

UNDERGRADUATE EXPENSES for 2013–2014 *Application fee:* $40. *Comprehensive fee:* $52,370 includes full-time tuition ($39,900) and room and board ($12,470). *College room only:* $7340. Room and board charges vary according to housing facility.

FRESHMAN FINANCIAL AID (Fall 2012, est.) 357 applied for aid; of those 77% were deemed to have need. 100% of freshmen with need received aid; of those 62% had need fully met. *Average percent of need met:* 82% (excluding resources awarded to replace EFC). *Average financial aid package:* $33,676 (excluding resources awarded to replace EFC). 30% of all full-time freshmen had no need and received non-need-based gift aid.

UNDERGRADUATE FINANCIAL AID (Fall 2012, est.) 1,289 applied for aid; of those 83% were deemed to have need. 100% of undergraduates with need received aid; of those 24% had need fully met. *Average percent of need met:* 80% (excluding resources awarded to replace EFC). *Average financial aid package:* $34,058 (excluding resources awarded to replace EFC). 23% of all full-time undergraduates had no need and received non-need-based gift aid.

GIFT AID (NEED-BASED) *Total amount:* $27,673,599 (7% federal, 13% state, 79% institutional, 1% external sources). *Receiving aid:* Freshmen: 53% (276); all full-time undergraduates: 56% (1,059). *Average award:* Freshmen: $29,818; Undergraduates: $29,722. *Scholarships, grants, and awards:* Federal Pell, FSEOG, state, private, college/university gift aid from institutional funds.

GIFT AID (NON-NEED-BASED) *Total amount:* $9,389,400 (8% state, 91% institutional, 1% external sources). *Receiving aid:* Freshmen: 15% (77). Undergraduates: 11% (206). *Average award:* Freshmen: $19,727. Undergraduates: $18,325. *Scholarships, grants, and awards by category:* Academic interests/achievement: 72 awards ($485,014 total): computer science, engineering/technologies, general academic interests/achievements, mathematics, physical sciences. *Creative arts/performance:* 66 awards ($361,313 total): art/fine arts, music, theater/drama. *Tuition waivers:* Full or partial for employees or children of employees.

LOANS *Student loans:* $6,712,828 (79% need-based, 21% non-need-based). 46% of past graduating class borrowed through all loan programs. *Average indebtedness per student:* $24,096. *Average need-based loan:* Freshmen: $4045. Undergraduates: $4772. *Parent loans:* $3,409,458 (49% need-based, 51% non-need-based). *Programs:* Federal Direct (Subsidized and Unsubsidized Stafford, PLUS), Perkins.

WORK-STUDY *Federal work-study:* Total amount: $659,035; 347 jobs averaging $1531. *State or other work-study/employment:* Total amount: $6000 (100% need-based). Part-time jobs available.

ATHLETIC AWARDS Total amount: $3,445,434 (30% need-based, 70% non-need-based).

APPLYING FOR FINANCIAL AID *Required financial aid form:* FAFSA. *Financial aid deadline (priority):* 3/1. *Notification date:* Continuous beginning 3/1.

CONTACT Mr. Steve Booker, Director of Financial Aid, Rollins College, 1000 Holt Avenue, #2721, Winter Park, FL 32789-4499, 407-646-2395. *Fax:* 407-646-2173. *E-mail:* sbooker@rollins.edu. *Website:* http://www.rollins.edu/.

ROOSEVELT UNIVERSITY
Chicago, IL

| Tuition & fees: $25,950 | Average undergraduate aid package: $20,970 |

ABOUT THE INSTITUTION Independent, coed. *Awards:* certificates, bachelor's, master's, and doctoral degrees. 57 undergraduate majors. *Total enrollment:* 6,343. Undergraduates: 3,795. Freshmen: 553. Federal methodology is used as a basis for awarding need-based institutional aid.

UNDERGRADUATE EXPENSES for 2013–2014 *Application fee:* $25. *Comprehensive fee:* $38,050 includes full-time tuition ($25,950) and room and board ($12,100). Full-time tuition and fees vary according to course load, program, and reciprocity agreements. Room and board charges vary according to board plan and housing facility. *Part-time tuition:* $699 per credit. Part-time tuition and fees vary according to course load, program, and reciprocity agreements.

FRESHMAN FINANCIAL AID (Fall 2011) 468 applied for aid; of those 88% were deemed to have need. 99% of freshmen with need received aid; of those 21% had need fully met. *Average percent of need met:* 75% (excluding resources awarded to replace EFC). *Average financial aid package:* $23,217 (excluding resources awarded to replace EFC). 17% of all full-time freshmen had no need and received non-need-based gift aid.

UNDERGRADUATE FINANCIAL AID (Fall 2011) 2,675 applied for aid; of those 85% were deemed to have need. 99% of undergraduates with need received aid; of those 8% had need fully met. *Average percent of need met:* 75% (excluding resources awarded to replace EFC). *Average financial aid package:* $20,970 (excluding resources awarded to replace EFC). 19% of all full-time undergraduates had no need and received non-need-based gift aid.

GIFT AID (NEED-BASED) *Total amount:* $18,045,197 (37% federal, 27% state, 36% institutional). *Receiving aid:* Freshmen: 71% (340); all full-time undergraduates: 66% (1,849). *Average award:* Freshmen: $11,743; Undergraduates: $8927. *Scholarships, grants, and awards:* Federal Pell, FSEOG, state, private, college/university gift aid from institutional funds.

GIFT AID (NON-NEED-BASED) *Total amount:* $13,453,648 (98% institutional, 2% external sources). *Receiving aid:* Freshmen: 80% (387). Undergraduates: 73% (2,044). *Average award:* Freshmen: $10,064. Undergraduates: $6718. *Scholarships, grants, and awards by category:* Academic interests/achievement: general academic interests/achievements. Creative arts/performance: music, theater/drama. Special achievements/activities: general special achievements/activities. Special characteristics: general special characteristics. *Tuition waivers:* Full or partial for employees or children of employees.

LOANS *Student loans:* $25,367,890 (100% need-based). *Average need-based loan:* Freshmen: $6716. Undergraduates: $8827. *Parent loans:* $5,208,447 (100% need-based).

WORK-STUDY *Federal work-study:* Total amount: $1,593,565; jobs available.

APPLYING FOR FINANCIAL AID *Required financial aid forms:* FAFSA, institution's own form. *Financial aid deadline (priority):* 3/1. *Notification date:* Continuous beginning 2/15. Students must reply within 3 weeks of notification.

CONTACT Ms. Grace McGinnis, Director of Financial Aid, Roosevelt University, 430 South Michigan Avenue, Chicago, IL 60605-1394, 312-341-2367 or toll-free 877-APPLYRU. *Fax:* 312-341-3545. *E-mail:* gmcginni@roosevelt.edu. *Website:* http://www.roosevelt.edu/.

ROSE-HULMAN INSTITUTE OF TECHNOLOGY
Terre Haute, IN

Tuition & fees: $39,078	Average undergraduate aid package: $26,703

ABOUT THE INSTITUTION Independent, coed, primarily men. *Awards:* bachelor's and master's degrees. 16 undergraduate majors. *Total enrollment:* 2,214. Undergraduates: 2,121. Freshmen: 621. Federal methodology is used as a basis for awarding need-based institutional aid.

UNDERGRADUATE EXPENSES for 2013–2014 *Application fee:* $40. *One-time required fee:* $2400. *Comprehensive fee:* $50,013 includes full-time tuition ($38,313), mandatory fees ($765), and room and board ($10,935). *College room only:* $6705. Full-time tuition and fees vary according to course load. Room and board charges vary according to board plan. *Part-time tuition:* $1118 per credit hour. Part-time tuition and fees vary according to course load. *Payment plan:* Tuition prepayment.

FRESHMAN FINANCIAL AID (Fall 2012, est.) 516 applied for aid; of those 86% were deemed to have need. 100% of freshmen with need received aid; of those 15% had need fully met. *Average percent of need met:* 76% (excluding resources awarded to replace EFC). *Average financial aid package:* $28,031 (excluding resources awarded to replace EFC). 28% of all full-time freshmen had no need and received non-need-based gift aid.

UNDERGRADUATE FINANCIAL AID (Fall 2012, est.) 1,619 applied for aid; of those 89% were deemed to have need. 100% of undergraduates with need received aid; of those 14% had need fully met. *Average percent of need met:* 72% (excluding resources awarded to replace EFC). *Average financial aid package:* $26,703 (excluding resources awarded to replace EFC). 29% of all full-time undergraduates had no need and received non-need-based gift aid.

GIFT AID (NEED-BASED) *Total amount:* $32,636,734 (6% federal, 3% state, 83% institutional, 8% external sources). *Receiving aid:* Freshmen: 71% (444); all full-time undergraduates: 69% (1,444). *Average award:* Freshmen: $23,657; Undergraduates: $21,881. *Scholarships, grants, and awards:* Federal Pell, FSEOG, state, college/university gift aid from institutional funds.

GIFT AID (NON-NEED-BASED) *Total amount:* $8,581,520 (82% institutional, 18% external sources). *Receiving aid:* Freshmen: 12% (72). Undergraduates: 8% (173). *Average award:* Freshmen: $10,527. Undergraduates: $11,441. *Tuition waivers:* Full or partial for employees or children of employees. *ROTC:* Army, Air Force.

LOANS *Student loans:* $13,041,894 (95% need-based, 5% non-need-based). 71% of past graduating class borrowed through all loan programs. *Average indebtedness per student:* $44,965. *Average need-based loan:* Freshmen: $4696. Undergraduates: $5147. *Parent loans:* $8,064,146 (95% need-based, 5% non-need-based). *Programs:* Federal Direct (Subsidized and Unsubsidized Stafford, PLUS), Perkins.

WORK-STUDY *Federal work-study:* Total amount: $547,430; 419 jobs averaging $1297. *State or other work-study/employment:* Total amount: $731,350 (99% need-based, 1% non-need-based). 560 part-time jobs averaging $1300.

APPLYING FOR FINANCIAL AID *Required financial aid form:* FAFSA. *Financial aid deadline (priority):* 3/1. *Notification date:* 3/10. Students must reply by 5/1.

CONTACT Melinda L. Middleton, Director of Financial Aid, Rose-Hulman Institute of Technology, 5500 Wabash Avenue, CM 5, Terre Haute, IN 47803, 812-877-8259 or toll-free 800-248-7448. *Fax:* 812-877-8746. *E-mail:* melinda.middleton@rose-hulman.edu. *Website:* http://www.rose-hulman.edu/.

ROSEMONT COLLEGE
Rosemont, PA

Tuition & fees: $30,950	Average undergraduate aid package: $27,065

ABOUT THE INSTITUTION Independent Roman Catholic, coed. *Awards:* certificates, bachelor's, and master's degrees. 27 undergraduate majors. *Total enrollment:* 908. Undergraduates: 524. Freshmen: 75. Federal methodology is used as a basis for awarding need-based institutional aid.

UNDERGRADUATE EXPENSES for 2013–2014 *Comprehensive fee:* $43,330 includes full-time tuition ($30,000), mandatory fees ($950), and room and board ($12,380). Full-time tuition and fees vary according to course load and program. Room and board charges vary according to board plan and housing facility. *Part-time tuition:* $1140 per credit hour. Part-time tuition and fees vary according to course load and program.

FRESHMAN FINANCIAL AID (Fall 2011) 105 applied for aid; of those 91% were deemed to have need. 100% of freshmen with need received aid; of those 12% had need fully met. *Average percent of need met:* 83% (excluding resources awarded to replace EFC). *Average financial aid package:* $28,011 (excluding resources awarded to replace EFC). 9% of all full-time freshmen had no need and received non-need-based gift aid.

UNDERGRADUATE FINANCIAL AID (Fall 2011) 369 applied for aid; of those 96% were deemed to have need. 100% of undergraduates with need received aid; of those 10% had need fully met. *Average percent of need met:* 75% (excluding resources awarded to replace EFC). *Average financial aid package:* $27,065 (excluding resources awarded to replace EFC). 7% of all full-time undergraduates had no need and received non-need-based gift aid.

GIFT AID (NEED-BASED) *Total amount:* $8,448,249 (15% federal, 10% state, 73% institutional, 2% external sources). *Receiving aid:* Freshmen: 90% (96); all full-time undergraduates: 91% (355). *Average award:* Freshmen: $24,003; Undergraduates: $21,765. *Scholarships, grants, and awards:* Federal Pell, FSEOG, state, private, college/university gift aid from institutional funds, Academic Competitiveness Grants, National SMART Grants.

GIFT AID (NON-NEED-BASED) *Total amount:* $554,409 (95% institutional, 5% external sources). *Receiving aid:* Freshmen: 10% (11). Undergraduates: 7% (27). *Average award:* Freshmen: $12,350. Undergraduates: $13,203. *Scholarships, grants, and awards by category: Academic interests/achievement:* general academic interests/achievements. *Creative arts/performance:* art/fine arts. *Special achievements/activities:* community service, general special achievements/activities, leadership, religious involvement. *Special characteristics:* children and siblings of alumni, children of educators, children of faculty/staff, relatives of clergy, siblings of current students. *Tuition waivers:* Full or partial for employees or children of employees, senior citizens. *ROTC:* Army cooperative.

LOANS *Student loans:* $4,072,652 (88% need-based, 12% non-need-based). 88% of past graduating class borrowed through all loan programs. *Average indebtedness per student:* $22,597. *Average need-based loan:* Freshmen: $3517. Undergraduates: $4682. *Parent loans:* $1,460,097 (59% need-based, 41% non-need-based). *Programs:* Federal Direct (Subsidized and Unsubsidized Stafford, PLUS), Perkins, alternative loans.

WORK-STUDY *Federal work-study:* Total amount: $63,538; 87 jobs averaging $589. *State or other work-study/employment:* Total amount: $14,288 (100% need-based). 65 part-time jobs averaging $190.

APPLYING FOR FINANCIAL AID *Required financial aid form:* FAFSA. *Financial aid deadline (priority):* 2/15. *Notification date:* Continuous beginning 3/15. Students must reply by 5/1 or within 4 weeks of notification.

CONTACT Ms. Laverne Glenn, Director of Financial Aid, Rosemont College, 1400 Montgomery Avenue, Rosemont, PA 19010, 610-527-0200 Ext. 2236 or toll-free 888-2-ROSEMONT. *Fax:* 610-526-2971. *E-mail:* laverne.glenn@rosemont.edu. *Website:* http://www.rosemont.edu/.

ROWAN UNIVERSITY
Glassboro, NJ

Tuition & fees (NJ res): $12,380	Average undergraduate aid package: $9312

ABOUT THE INSTITUTION State-supported, coed. *Awards:* certificates, bachelor's, master's, and doctoral degrees. 58 undergraduate majors. *Total enrollment:* 12,133. Undergraduates: 10,750. Freshmen: 1,484. Both federal and institutional methodology are used as a basis for awarding need-based institutional aid.

UNDERGRADUATE EXPENSES for 2013–2014 *Application fee:* $65. *Tuition, state resident:* full-time $8906; part-time $342 per credit hour. *Tuition, nonresident:* full-time $16,712; part-time $644 per credit hour. *Required fees:* full-time $3474. Full-time tuition and fees vary according to course load, degree level, and program. Part-time tuition and fees vary according to course load, degree level, and program. *College room and board:* $10,972; *Room only:* $6892. Room and board charges vary according to board plan and housing facility.

FRESHMAN FINANCIAL AID (Fall 2011) 1,424 applied for aid; of those 74% were deemed to have need. 92% of freshmen with need received aid; of those 11% had need fully met. *Average percent of need met:* 87% (excluding resources awarded to replace EFC). *Average financial aid package:* $9315 (excluding resources awarded to replace EFC). 11% of all full-time freshmen had no need and received non-need-based gift aid.

UNDERGRADUATE FINANCIAL AID (Fall 2011) 7,350 applied for aid; of those 80% were deemed to have need. 95% of undergraduates with need received aid; of those 7% had need fully met. *Average percent of need met:* 82% (excluding resources awarded to replace EFC). *Average financial aid package:* $9312 (excluding resources awarded to replace EFC). 6% of all full-time undergraduates had no need and received non-need-based gift aid.

GIFT AID (NEED-BASED) *Total amount:* $32,412,809 (40% federal, 40% state, 17% institutional, 3% external sources). *Receiving aid:* Freshmen: 30% (472); all full-time undergraduates: 34% (3,037). *Average award:* Freshmen: $9814; Undergraduates: $8659. *Scholarships, grants, and awards:* Federal Pell, FSEOG, state, private, college/university gift aid from institutional funds.

GIFT AID (NON-NEED-BASED) *Total amount:* $3,494,635 (1% state, 84% institutional, 15% external sources). *Receiving aid:* Freshmen: 21% (332). Undergraduates: 11% (949). *Average award:* Freshmen: $5475. Undergraduates: $5623. *Scholarships, grants, and awards by category: Academic interests/achievement:* general academic interests/achievements. *Creative arts/performance:* general creative arts/performance, music. *Tuition waivers:* Full or partial for employees or children of employees. *ROTC:* Army cooperative.

LOANS *Student loans:* $57,433,297 (94% need-based, 6% non-need-based). 74% of past graduating class borrowed through all loan programs. *Average indebtedness per student:* $35,027. *Average need-based loan:* Freshmen: $3276. Undergraduates: $4347. *Parent loans:* $21,033,897 (78% need-based, 22% non-need-based). *Programs:* Federal Direct (Subsidized and Unsubsidized Stafford, PLUS), state.

WORK-STUDY *Federal work-study:* Total amount: $573,817; 332 jobs averaging $1500. *State or other work-study/employment:* Total amount: $1,588,953 (76% need-based, 24% non-need-based). 341 part-time jobs averaging $1400.

APPLYING FOR FINANCIAL AID *Required financial aid form:* FAFSA. *Financial aid deadline (priority):* 3/16. *Notification date:* Continuous beginning 3/16. Students must reply by 5/1.

CONTACT Luis Tavarez, Director of Financial Aid, Rowan University, 201 Mullica Hill Road, Glassboro, NJ 08028-1701, 856-256-4276 or toll-free 800-447-1165 (in-state), 800-447-1165N (out-of-state). *Fax:* 856-256-4413. *E-mail:* tavarez@rowan.edu. *Website:* http://www.rowan.edu/.

RUSH UNIVERSITY
Chicago, IL

Tuition & fees: N/R	Average undergraduate aid package: $12,254

ABOUT THE INSTITUTION Independent, coed. 3 undergraduate majors. Both federal and institutional methodology are used as a basis for awarding need-based institutional aid.

UNDERGRADUATE FINANCIAL AID (Fall 2011) 71 applied for aid; of those 97% were deemed to have need. 100% of undergraduates with need received aid; of those 20% had need fully met. *Average percent of need met:* 37% (excluding resources awarded to replace EFC). *Average financial aid package:* $12,254 (excluding resources awarded to replace EFC). 5% of all full-time undergraduates had no need and received non-need-based gift aid.

GIFT AID (NEED-BASED) *Total amount:* $418,338 (59% federal, 17% state, 24% institutional). *Receiving aid:* All full-time undergraduates: 49% (37). *Average award:* Undergraduates: $6998. *Scholarships, grants, and awards:* Federal Pell, FSEOG, state, private, college/university gift aid from institutional funds.

GIFT AID (NON-NEED-BASED) *Total amount:* $12,500 (100% institutional). *Receiving aid:* Undergraduates: 29% (22). *Average award:* Undergraduates: $3600. *Scholarships, grants, and awards by category: Academic interests/achievement:* 20 awards ($114,556 total): general academic interests/achievements.

LOANS *Student loans:* $1,270,020 (98% need-based, 2% non-need-based). *Average need-based loan:* Undergraduates: $7168. *Parent loans:* $47,500 (100% need-based). *Programs:* Federal Direct (Subsidized and Unsubsidized Stafford, PLUS), Perkins, credit-based loans.

WORK-STUDY *Federal work-study:* Total amount: $1771; 3 jobs averaging $1005.

APPLYING FOR FINANCIAL AID *Required financial aid forms:* FAFSA, institution's own form. *Financial aid deadline (priority):* 5/1. *Notification date:* Continuous beginning 4/1. Students must reply within 3 weeks of notification.

CONTACT Mike Frechette, Director of Student Financial Aid, Rush University, 600 South Paulina Street, Suite 440, Chicago, IL 60612-3832, 312-942-6256. *Fax:* 312-942-2732. *E-mail:* michael_frechette@rush.edu. *Website:* http://www.rushu.rush.edu/.

RUSSELL SAGE COLLEGE
Troy, NY

Tuition & fees: $28,000	Average undergraduate aid package: N/A

ABOUT THE INSTITUTION Independent, women only. *Awards:* bachelor's degrees. 22 undergraduate majors. *Total enrollment:* 827. Undergraduates: 827. Freshmen: 158. Federal methodology is used as a basis for awarding need-based institutional aid.

UNDERGRADUATE EXPENSES for 2013–2014 *Application fee:* $30. *Comprehensive fee:* $38,995 includes full-time tuition ($27,000), mandatory fees ($1000), and room and board ($10,995). *College room only:* $5795. Room and board charges vary according to board plan. **Part-time tuition:** $900 per credit hour.

FRESHMAN FINANCIAL AID (Fall 2012, est.) 155 applied for aid; of those 96% were deemed to have need. 100% of freshmen with need received aid. 4% of all full-time freshmen had no need and received non-need-based gift aid.

UNDERGRADUATE FINANCIAL AID (Fall 2012, est.) 754 applied for aid; of those 95% were deemed to have need. 99% of undergraduates with need received aid. 4% of all full-time undergraduates had no need and received non-need-based gift aid.

GIFT AID (NEED-BASED) Total amount: $8,235,862 (19% federal, 14% state, 67% institutional). **Receiving aid:** Freshmen: 79% (125); all full-time undergraduates: 74% (578). **Average award:** Freshmen: $16,680; Undergraduates: $13,542. **Scholarships, grants, and awards:** Federal Pell, FSEOG, state, private, college/university gift aid from institutional funds, Federal Nursing.

GIFT AID (NON-NEED-BASED) Total amount: $6,428,821 (1% state, 98% institutional, 1% external sources). **Receiving aid:** Freshmen: 68% (107). Undergraduates: 73% (569). **Average award:** Freshmen: $9833. Undergraduates: $10,479. **Scholarships, grants, and awards by category:** Academic interests/achievement: 607 awards ($5,594,943 total): general academic interests/achievements. Creative arts/performance: 4 awards ($80,300 total): theater/drama. **Special achievements/activities:** community service, general special achievements/activities, leadership. **Special characteristics:** 256 awards ($561,807 total): adult students, children and siblings of alumni, ethnic background, first-generation college students, general special characteristics. **Tuition waivers:** Full or partial for employees or children of employees, senior citizens. **ROTC:** Army cooperative, Air Force cooperative.

LOANS Student loans: $5,107,477 (52% need-based, 48% non-need-based). 88% of past graduating class borrowed through all loan programs. **Average indebtedness per student:** $27,907. **Average need-based loan:** Freshmen: $3075. Undergraduates: $3963. **Parent loans:** $1,008,469 (100% non-need-based). **Programs:** Federal Direct (Subsidized and Unsubsidized Stafford, PLUS), Perkins.

WORK-STUDY Federal work-study: Total amount: $499,667; 258 jobs averaging $1937. **State or other work-study/employment:** Total amount: $100,182 (100% non-need-based). 17 part-time jobs averaging $5893.

APPLYING FOR FINANCIAL AID Required financial aid forms: FAFSA, state aid form. **Financial aid deadline (priority):** 3/1. **Notification date:** Continuous beginning 3/1. Students must reply within 2 weeks of notification.

CONTACT Kelley Robinson, Director of Financial Aid, Russell Sage College, 65 First Street, Troy, NY 12180, 518-244-2062 or toll-free 888-VERY-SAGE (in-state), 888-VERY SAGE (out-of-state). *Fax:* 518-244-2460. *E-mail:* robink3@sage.edu. *Website:* http://www.sage.edu/rsc/.

RUST COLLEGE
Holly Springs, MS

CONTACT Mrs. Helen L. Street, Director of Financial Aid, Rust College, 150 Rust Avenue, Holly Springs, MS 38635, 662-252-8000 Ext. 4061 or toll-free 888-886-8492 Ext. 4065. *Fax:* 662-252-8895.
Website: http://www.rustcollege.edu/.

RUTGERS, THE STATE UNIVERSITY OF NEW JERSEY, CAMDEN
Camden, NJ

Tuition & fees (NJ res): $12,923	Average undergraduate aid package: $11,535

ABOUT THE INSTITUTION State-supported, coed. **Awards:** bachelor's, master's, and doctoral degrees. 33 undergraduate majors. **Total enrollment:** 6,343. Undergraduates: 4,708. Freshmen: 485. Federal methodology is used as a basis for awarding need-based institutional aid.

UNDERGRADUATE EXPENSES for 2013–2014 Application fee: $65. **Tuition, state resident:** full-time $10,356; part-time $333 per credit. **Tuition, nonresident:** full-time $23,232; part-time $754 per credit. **Required fees:** full-time $2567; $1004 per year. Part-time tuition and fees vary according to course load. **College room and board:** $11,206; **Room only:** $7906. Room and board charges vary according to board plan and housing facility.

FRESHMAN FINANCIAL AID (Fall 2012, est.) 445 applied for aid; of those 87% were deemed to have need. 100% of freshmen with need received aid; of those 6% had need fully met. **Average percent of need met:** 57% (excluding resources awarded to replace EFC). **Average financial aid package:** $12,070 (excluding resources awarded to replace EFC). 2% of all full-time freshmen had no need and received non-need-based gift aid.

UNDERGRADUATE FINANCIAL AID (Fall 2012, est.) 3,173 applied for aid; of those 89% were deemed to have need. 100% of undergraduates with need received aid; of those 7% had need fully met. **Average percent of need met:** 55% (excluding resources awarded to replace EFC). **Average financial aid package:** $11,535 (excluding resources awarded to replace EFC). 1% of all full-time undergraduates had no need and received non-need-based gift aid.

GIFT AID (NEED-BASED) Total amount: $21,793,717 (38% federal, 41% state, 21% institutional). **Receiving aid:** Freshmen: 64% (310); all full-time undergraduates: 55% (2,121). **Average award:** Freshmen: $9621; Undergraduates: $9216. **Scholarships, grants, and awards:** Federal Pell, FSEOG, state, private, college/university gift aid from institutional funds, Federal Nursing.

GIFT AID (NON-NEED-BASED) Total amount: $1,617,434 (2% state, 66% institutional, 32% external sources). **Receiving aid:** Freshmen: 13% (63). Undergraduates: 8% (296). **Average award:** Freshmen: $10,129. Undergraduates: $7548. **ROTC:** Army cooperative, Air Force cooperative.

LOANS Student loans: $28,634,651 (42% need-based, 58% non-need-based). 75% of past graduating class borrowed through all loan programs. **Average indebtedness per student:** $27,535. **Average need-based loan:** Freshmen: $3760. Undergraduates: $4473. **Parent loans:** $3,328,260 (100% non-need-based). **Programs:** Federal Direct (Subsidized and Unsubsidized Stafford, PLUS), Perkins, Federal Nursing, state, college/university, alternative loans.

WORK-STUDY Federal work-study: Total amount: $360,704; 254 jobs averaging $1420. **State or other work-study/employment:** Total amount: $1,250,866 (100% non-need-based). 533 part-time jobs averaging $2347.

APPLYING FOR FINANCIAL AID Required financial aid form: FAFSA. **Financial aid deadline (priority):** 3/15. **Notification date:** Continuous beginning 3/1. Students must reply within 2 weeks of notification.

CONTACT Mr. Willie L. Williams, Manager of University Financial Aid Funds Control, Rutgers, The State University of New Jersey, Camden, 620 George Street, New Brunswick, NJ 08901, 848-932-2603. *Fax:* 732-932-0516. *E-mail:* billw@rci.rutgers.edu.
Website: http://www.rutgers.edu/.

RUTGERS, THE STATE UNIVERSITY OF NEW JERSEY, NEWARK
Newark, NJ

Tuition & fees (NJ res): $12,590	Average undergraduate aid package: $12,795

ABOUT THE INSTITUTION State-supported, coed. **Awards:** bachelor's, master's, and doctoral degrees. 50 undergraduate majors. **Total enrollment:** 12,011. Undergraduates: 7,666. Freshmen: 1,052. Federal methodology is used as a basis for awarding need-based institutional aid.

UNDERGRADUATE EXPENSES for 2013–2014 Application fee: $65. **Tuition, state resident:** full-time $10,356; part-time $333 per credit. **Tuition, nonresident:** full-time $23,676; part-time $768 per credit. **Required fees:** full-time $2234; $632 per year. Part-time tuition and fees vary according to course load. **College room and board:** $12,285; **Room only:** $7613. Room and board charges vary according to board plan and housing facility.

FRESHMAN FINANCIAL AID (Fall 2012, est.) 753 applied for aid; of those 91% were deemed to have need. 100% of freshmen with need received aid; of those 98% had need fully met. **Average percent of need met:** 59% (excluding resources awarded to replace EFC). **Average financial aid package:** $13,097 (excluding resources awarded to replace EFC). 1% of all full-time freshmen had no need and received non-need-based gift aid.

UNDERGRADUATE FINANCIAL AID (Fall 2012, est.) 4,672 applied for aid; of those 93% were deemed to have need. 100% of undergraduates with need received aid; of those 99% had need fully met. **Average percent of need met:** 56% (excluding resources awarded to replace EFC). **Average financial aid package:** $12,795 (excluding resources awarded to replace EFC). 1% of all full-time undergraduates had no need and received non-need-based gift aid.

GIFT AID (NEED-BASED) *Total amount:* $39,529,481 (38% federal, 43% state, 19% institutional). *Receiving aid:* Freshmen: 54% (566); all full-time undergraduates: 59% (3,659). *Average award:* Freshmen: $11,011; Undergraduates: $10,206. *Scholarships, grants, and awards:* Federal Pell, FSEOG, state, private, college/university gift aid from institutional funds.

GIFT AID (NON-NEED-BASED) *Total amount:* $2,552,484 (6% state, 76% institutional, 18% external sources). *Receiving aid:* Freshmen: 6% (65). Undergraduates: 6% (395). *Average award:* Freshmen: $10,104. Undergraduates: $9219. *ROTC:* Army, Naval, Air Force.

LOANS *Student loans:* $34,145,709 (48% need-based, 52% non-need-based). 56% of past graduating class borrowed through all loan programs. *Average indebtedness per student:* $24,837. *Average need-based loan:* Freshmen: $3904. Undergraduates: $4605. *Parent loans:* $7,474,503 (100% non-need-based). *Programs:* Federal Direct (Subsidized and Unsubsidized Stafford, PLUS), Perkins, state, college/university, alternative loans.

WORK-STUDY *Federal work-study:* Total amount: $1,318,428; 472 jobs averaging $1355. *State or other work-study/employment:* Total amount: $1,263,754 (29% need-based, 71% non-need-based). 785 part-time jobs averaging $1852.

ATHLETIC AWARDS Total amount: $490,000 (100% non-need-based).

APPLYING FOR FINANCIAL AID *Required financial aid form:* FAFSA. *Financial aid deadline (priority):* 3/15. *Notification date:* Continuous beginning 3/1. Students must reply within 4 weeks of notification.

CONTACT Mr. Willie L. Williams, Manager of University Financial Aid Funds Control, Rutgers, The State University of New Jersey, Newark, 620 George Street, New Brunswick, NJ 08901, 848-932-2603. *Fax:* 732-932-0516. *E-mail:* billw@rci.rutgers.edu.
Website: http://www.rutgers.edu/.

RUTGERS, THE STATE UNIVERSITY OF NEW JERSEY, NEW BRUNSWICK
Piscataway, NJ

Tuition & fees (NJ res): $13,073	Average undergraduate aid package: $12,393

ABOUT THE INSTITUTION State-supported, coed. *Awards:* certificates, bachelor's, master's, and doctoral degrees. 120 undergraduate majors. *Total enrollment:* 40,434. Undergraduates: 31,593. Freshmen: 6,170. Federal methodology is used as a basis for awarding need-based institutional aid.

UNDERGRADUATE EXPENSES for 2013–2014 *Application fee:* $65. *Tuition, state resident:* full-time $10,356; part-time $333 per credit. *Tuition, nonresident:* full-time $23,676; part-time $768 per credit. *Required fees:* full-time $2717; $658 per year. *College room and board:* $11,412; *Room only:* $7042. Room and board charges vary according to board plan and housing facility.

FRESHMAN FINANCIAL AID (Fall 2012, est.) 4,533 applied for aid; of those 83% were deemed to have need. 100% of freshmen with need received aid; of those 8% had need fully met. *Average percent of need met:* 43% (excluding resources awarded to replace EFC). *Average financial aid package:* $12,992 (excluding resources awarded to replace EFC). 2% of all full-time freshmen had no need and received non-need-based gift aid.

UNDERGRADUATE FINANCIAL AID (Fall 2012, est.) 20,240 applied for aid; of those 86% were deemed to have need. 100% of undergraduates with need received aid; of those 8% had need fully met. *Average percent of need met:* 52% (excluding resources awarded to replace EFC). *Average financial aid package:* $12,393 (excluding resources awarded to replace EFC). 2% of all full-time undergraduates had no need and received non-need-based gift aid.

GIFT AID (NEED-BASED) *Total amount:* $155,914,266 (27% federal, 33% state, 40% institutional). *Receiving aid:* Freshmen: 43% (2,660); all full-time undergraduates: 41% (12,264). *Average award:* Freshmen: $10,873; Undergraduates: $10,009. *Scholarships, grants, and awards:* Federal Pell, FSEOG, state, private, college/university gift aid from institutional funds, Federal Nursing.

GIFT AID (NON-NEED-BASED) *Total amount:* $14,756,297 (9% state, 64% institutional, 27% external sources). *Receiving aid:* Freshmen: 11% (702). Undergraduates: 10% (2,882). *Average award:* Freshmen: $7653. Undergraduates: $8901. *Tuition waivers:* Full or partial for employees or children of employees. *ROTC:* Army, Air Force.

LOANS *Student loans:* $165,443,007 (41% need-based, 59% non-need-based). 57% of past graduating class borrowed through all loan programs. *Average indebtedness*

per student: $26,656. *Average need-based loan:* Freshmen: $3927. Undergraduates: $4548. *Parent loans:* $80,627,775 (100% non-need-based). *Programs:* Federal Direct (Subsidized and Unsubsidized Stafford, PLUS), Perkins, Federal Nursing, state, college/university, alternative loans.

WORK-STUDY *Federal work-study:* Total amount: $6,196,597; 2,410 jobs averaging $1240. *State or other work-study/employment:* 6,129 part-time jobs averaging $1929.

ATHLETIC AWARDS Total amount: $9,832,813 (100% non-need-based).

APPLYING FOR FINANCIAL AID *Required financial aid form:* FAFSA. *Financial aid deadline (priority):* 3/15. *Notification date:* Continuous beginning 3/1. Students must reply within 4 weeks of notification.

CONTACT Mr. Willie L. Williams, Manager of University Financial Aid Funds Control, Rutgers, The State University of New Jersey, New Brunswick, 620 George Street, New Brunswick, NJ 08901, 848-932-2603. *Fax:* 732-932-0516. *E-mail:* billw@rci.rutgers.edu.
Website: http://www.rutgers.edu/.

SACRED HEART MAJOR SEMINARY
Detroit, MI

ABOUT THE INSTITUTION Independent Roman Catholic, coed. *Awards:* certificates, diplomas, associate, bachelor's, and master's degrees. 3 undergraduate majors. *Total enrollment:* 466. Undergraduates: 264. Freshmen: 3.

GIFT AID (NEED-BASED) *Scholarships, grants, and awards:* Federal Pell, FSEOG, state, private, college/university gift aid from institutional funds.

GIFT AID (NON-NEED-BASED) *Scholarships, grants, and awards by category:* Academic interests/achievement: religion/biblical studies. Special achievements/activities: religious involvement. Special characteristics: local/state students, religious affiliation.

LOANS *Programs:* Federal Direct (Subsidized and Unsubsidized Stafford).

APPLYING FOR FINANCIAL AID *Required financial aid forms:* FAFSA, institution's own form.

CONTACT Financial Aid Office, Sacred Heart Major Seminary, 2701 Chicago Boulevard, Detroit, MI 48206-1799, 313-883-8534. *Fax:* 313-868-7025. *E-mail:* financialaid@shms.edu.
Website: http://www.shms.edu/.

SACRED HEART UNIVERSITY
Fairfield, CT

Tuition & fees: $34,030	Average undergraduate aid package: $18,184

ABOUT THE INSTITUTION Independent Roman Catholic, coed. *Awards:* certificates, bachelor's, master's, and doctoral degrees (also offers part-time program with significant enrollment not reflected in profile). 46 undergraduate majors. *Total enrollment:* 6,347. Undergraduates: 4,092. Freshmen: 865. Both federal and institutional methodology are used as a basis for awarding need-based institutional aid.

UNDERGRADUATE EXPENSES for 2013–2014 *Application fee:* $70. *Comprehensive fee:* $47,260 includes full-time tuition ($33,780), mandatory fees ($250), and room and board ($13,230). *College room only:* $9380. Full-time tuition and fees vary according to course load, location, and program. Room and board charges vary according to board plan, housing facility, and student level. *Part-time tuition:* $515 per credit. *Part-time fees:* $90 per term. Part-time tuition and fees vary according to location and program.

FRESHMAN FINANCIAL AID (Fall 2011) 916 applied for aid; of those 81% were deemed to have need. 100% of freshmen with need received aid; of those 12% had need fully met. *Average percent of need met:* 56% (excluding resources awarded to replace EFC). *Average financial aid package:* $18,087 (excluding resources awarded to replace EFC). 19% of all full-time freshmen had no need and received non-need-based gift aid.

UNDERGRADUATE FINANCIAL AID (Fall 2011) 3,101 applied for aid; of those 83% were deemed to have need. 99% of undergraduates with need received aid; of those 12% had need fully met. *Average percent of need met:* 58% (excluding resources awarded to replace EFC). *Average financial aid package:* $18,184 (excluding resources awarded to replace EFC). 14% of all full-time undergraduates had no need and received non-need-based gift aid.

GIFT AID (NEED-BASED) *Total amount:* $31,126,104 (11% federal, 7% state, 74% institutional, 8% external sources). *Receiving aid:* Freshmen: 76% (741); all full-time undergraduates: 71% (2,481). *Average award:* Freshmen: $13,596; Undergraduates: $13,958. *Scholarships, grants, and awards:* Federal Pell, FSEOG, state, private, college/university gift aid from institutional funds.

GIFT AID (NON-NEED-BASED) *Total amount:* $4,344,349 (3% federal, 77% institutional, 20% external sources). *Receiving aid:* Freshmen: 7% (67). Undergraduates: 7% (230). *Average award:* Freshmen: $6271. Undergraduates: $5652. *Scholarships, grants, and awards by category: Academic interests/achievement:* 1,686 awards ($10,012,393 total): biological sciences, business, computer science, education, English, general academic interests/achievements, health fields, humanities, mathematics, physical sciences, premedicine. *Creative arts/performance:* 355 awards ($1,024,299 total): applied art and design, art/fine arts, cinema/film/broadcasting, creative writing, dance, music, performing arts, theater/drama. *Special achievements/activities:* 319 awards ($392,623 total): community service, general special achievements/activities, hobbies/interests, leadership, memberships, religious involvement. *Special characteristics:* 821 awards ($3,781,709 total): adult students, children and siblings of alumni, children of current students, children of faculty/staff, children of union members/company employees, ethnic background, general special characteristics, handicapped students, local/state students, members of minority groups, out-of-state students, religious affiliation, siblings of current students, twins, veterans, veterans' children. *Tuition waivers:* Full or partial for minority students, employees or children of employees, adult students, senior citizens. *ROTC:* Army cooperative.

LOANS *Student loans:* $32,735,997 (67% need-based, 33% non-need-based). 74% of past graduating class borrowed through all loan programs. *Average indebtedness per student:* $42,779. *Average need-based loan:* Freshmen: $5019. Undergraduates: $5087. *Parent loans:* $11,689,467 (52% need-based, 48% non-need-based). *Programs:* Federal Direct (Subsidized and Unsubsidized Stafford, PLUS), Perkins, state.

WORK-STUDY *Federal work-study:* Total amount: $406,681; 944 jobs averaging $668. *State or other work-study/employment:* Total amount: $748,050 (36% need-based, 64% non-need-based). 858 part-time jobs averaging $832.

ATHLETIC AWARDS Total amount: $7,685,163 (50% need-based, 50% non-need-based).

APPLYING FOR FINANCIAL AID *Required financial aid forms:* FAFSA, CSS Financial Aid PROFILE, noncustodial (divorced/separated) parent's statement. *Financial aid deadline (priority):* 2/15. *Notification date:* Continuous beginning 3/1. Students must reply within 2 weeks of notification.

CONTACT Ms. Julie B. Savino, Executive Director of University Financial Assistance, Sacred Heart University, 5151 Park Avenue, Fairfield, CT 06825, 203-371-7980. *Fax:* 203-365-7608. *E-mail:* savinoj@sacredheart.edu. *Website:* http://www.sacredheart.edu/.

SAGE COLLEGE OF ALBANY
Albany, NY

Tuition & fees: $28,000	Average undergraduate aid package: N/A

ABOUT THE INSTITUTION Independent, coed. *Awards:* bachelor's degrees. 18 undergraduate majors. *Total enrollment:* 911. Undergraduates: 911. Freshmen: 127. Federal methodology is used as a basis for awarding need-based institutional aid.

UNDERGRADUATE EXPENSES for 2013–2014 *Application fee:* $30. *Comprehensive fee:* $38,995 includes full-time tuition ($27,000), mandatory fees ($1000), and room and board ($10,995). *College room only:* $5795. Room and board charges vary according to board plan. *Part-time tuition:* $900 per credit hour.

FRESHMAN FINANCIAL AID (Fall 2012, est.) 122 applied for aid; of those 96% were deemed to have need. 98% of freshmen with need received aid. 2% of all full-time freshmen had no need and received non-need-based gift aid.

UNDERGRADUATE FINANCIAL AID (Fall 2012, est.) 624 applied for aid; of those 97% were deemed to have need. 99% of undergraduates with need received aid. 1% of all full-time undergraduates had no need and received non-need-based gift aid.

GIFT AID (NEED-BASED) *Total amount:* $8,751,221 (20% federal, 13% state, 67% institutional). *Receiving aid:* Freshmen: 81% (100); all full-time undergraduates: 80% (519). *Average award:* Freshmen: $16,670; Undergraduates: $14,673. *Scholarships, grants, and awards:* Federal Pell, FSEOG, state, private, college/university gift aid from institutional funds.

GIFT AID (NON-NEED-BASED) *Total amount:* $3,888,018 (1% federal, 98% institutional, 1% external sources). *Receiving aid:* Freshmen: 59% (73). Undergraduates: 62% (400). *Average award:* Freshmen: $5000. Undergraduates: $7056. *Scholarships, grants, and awards by category: Academic interests/achievement:* 411 awards ($3,591,601 total): general academic interests/achievements. *Creative arts/performance:* 4 awards ($10,041 total): art/fine arts. *Special achievements/activities:* community service, general special achievements/activities. *Special characteristics:* 59 awards ($85,815 total): children and siblings of alumni, first-generation college students, general special characteristics, siblings of current students. *Tuition waivers:* Full or partial for employees or children of employees. *ROTC:* Army cooperative, Air Force cooperative.

LOANS *Student loans:* $4,409,179 (59% need-based, 41% non-need-based). 88% of past graduating class borrowed through all loan programs. *Average indebtedness per student:* $28,971. *Average need-based loan:* Freshmen: $3319. Undergraduates: $4421. *Parent loans:* $822,682 (100% non-need-based). *Programs:* Federal Direct (Subsidized and Unsubsidized Stafford, PLUS), Perkins, state, alternative loans.

WORK-STUDY *Federal work-study:* Total amount: $506,667; 253 jobs averaging $2003. *State or other work-study/employment:* Total amount: $64,506 (100% non-need-based). 11 part-time jobs averaging $5864.

APPLYING FOR FINANCIAL AID *Required financial aid forms:* FAFSA, state aid form. *Financial aid deadline (priority):* 3/1. *Notification date:* Continuous beginning 3/1. Students must reply within 2 weeks of notification.

CONTACT Kelley Robinson, Director of Financial Aid, Sage College of Albany, 65 1st Street, Troy, NY 12180, 518-244-2062 or toll-free 888-VERY-SAGE. *Fax:* 518-244-2460. *E-mail:* robink3@sage.edu. *Website:* http://www.sage.edu/.

SAGINAW VALLEY STATE UNIVERSITY
University Center, MI

Tuition & fees (MI res): $8120	Average undergraduate aid package: N/A

ABOUT THE INSTITUTION State-supported, coed. *Awards:* certificates, bachelor's, and master's degrees. 64 undergraduate majors. *Total enrollment:* 10,552. Undergraduates: 9,052. Freshmen: 1,653. Federal methodology is used as a basis for awarding need-based institutional aid.

UNDERGRADUATE EXPENSES for 2013–2014 *Application fee:* $30. *Tuition, state resident:* full-time $7682; part-time $256.05 per credit hour. *Tuition, nonresident:* full-time $18,626; part-time $620.85 per credit hour. *Required fees:* full-time $438; $14.60 per credit hour. Full-time tuition and fees vary according to course level, course load, location, and program. Part-time tuition and fees vary according to course level, course load, location, and program. *College room and board:* $8190; *Room only:* $5560. Room and board charges vary according to board plan, housing facility, and student level.

FRESHMAN FINANCIAL AID (Fall 2012, est.) 1,590 applied for aid; of those 77% were deemed to have need. 98% of freshmen with need received aid.

UNDERGRADUATE FINANCIAL AID (Fall 2012, est.) 7,022 applied for aid; of those 78% were deemed to have need. 99% of undergraduates with need received aid.

GIFT AID (NEED-BASED) *Total amount:* $17,908,759 (88% federal, 6% state, 5% institutional, 1% external sources). *Receiving aid:* Freshmen: 67% (1,095); all full-time undergraduates: 67% (5,041). *Scholarships, grants, and awards:* Federal Pell, FSEOG, state, private, college/university gift aid from institutional funds.

GIFT AID (NON-NEED-BASED) *Total amount:* $16,970,475 (3% federal, 1% state, 57% institutional, 39% external sources). *Scholarships, grants, and awards by category: Academic interests/achievement:* biological sciences, business, computer science, education, engineering/technologies, general academic interests/achievements, health fields, mathematics, physical sciences. *Creative arts/performance:* art/fine arts, music, theater/drama. *Special achievements/activities:* community service, leadership. *Special characteristics:* local/state students, members of minority groups. *Tuition waivers:* Full or partial for employees or children of employees.

LOANS *Student loans:* $53,900,591 (92% need-based, 8% non-need-based). *Programs:* Federal Direct (Subsidized and Unsubsidized Stafford, PLUS), CitiAssist Loans, Chase Select loans, Charter One TruFit Student Loans.

WORK-STUDY *Federal work-study:* Total amount: $328,070; jobs available. *State or other work-study/employment:* Part-time jobs available.

APPLYING FOR FINANCIAL AID *Required financial aid form:* FAFSA. *Financial aid deadline (priority):* 2/14. *Notification date:* Continuous beginning 3/20. Students must reply within 10 weeks of notification.

CONTACT Robert Lemuel, Director of Scholarships and Financial Aid, Saginaw Valley State University, 7400 Bay Road, University Center, MI 48710, 989-964-4103 or toll-free 800-968-9500. *Fax:* 989-790-0180. *E-mail:* lemuel@svsu.edu. *Website:* http://www.svsu.edu/.

APPLYING FOR FINANCIAL AID *Required financial aid form:* FAFSA. *Financial aid deadline (priority):* 3/15. *Notification date:* Continuous beginning 2/15. Students must reply within 2 weeks of notification.

CONTACT Ms. Julie Haack, Director of Financial Aid, St. Ambrose University, 518 West Locust Street, Davenport, IA 52803, 563-333-6314 or toll-free 800-383-2627. *Fax:* 563-333-6243. *E-mail:* haackjuliea@sau.edu. *Website:* http://www.sau.edu/.

ST. AMBROSE UNIVERSITY
Davenport, IA

Tuition & fees: $26,740	Average undergraduate aid package: $18,133

ABOUT THE INSTITUTION Independent Roman Catholic, coed. *Awards:* certificates, bachelor's, master's, and doctoral degrees. 71 undergraduate majors. *Total enrollment:* 3,671. Undergraduates: 2,794. Freshmen: 582. Federal methodology is used as a basis for awarding need-based institutional aid.

UNDERGRADUATE EXPENSES for 2013–2014 *Application fee:* $25. *Comprehensive fee:* $35,756 includes full-time tuition ($26,500), mandatory fees ($240), and room and board ($9016). *College room only:* $5500. Full-time tuition and fees vary according to course load, location, program, and reciprocity agreements. Room and board charges vary according to board plan and housing facility. *Part-time tuition:* $820 per credit hour. Part-time tuition and fees vary according to course load and location.

FRESHMAN FINANCIAL AID (Fall 2012, est.) 542 applied for aid; of those 87% were deemed to have need. 100% of freshmen with need received aid; of those 24% had need fully met. *Average percent of need met:* 75% (excluding resources awarded to replace EFC). *Average financial aid package:* $19,228 (excluding resources awarded to replace EFC). 18% of all full-time freshmen had no need and received non-need-based gift aid.

UNDERGRADUATE FINANCIAL AID (Fall 2012, est.) 2,111 applied for aid; of those 89% were deemed to have need. 100% of undergraduates with need received aid; of those 23% had need fully met. *Average percent of need met:* 70% (excluding resources awarded to replace EFC). *Average financial aid package:* $18,133 (excluding resources awarded to replace EFC). 20% of all full-time undergraduates had no need and received non-need-based gift aid.

GIFT AID (NEED-BASED) *Total amount:* $22,684,628 (12% federal, 8% state, 78% institutional, 2% external sources). *Receiving aid:* Freshmen: 81% (470); all full-time undergraduates: 75% (1,818). *Average award:* Freshmen: $13,787; Undergraduates: $12,076. *Scholarships, grants, and awards:* Federal Pell, FSEOG, state, private, college/university gift aid from institutional funds.

GIFT AID (NON-NEED-BASED) *Total amount:* $6,513,442 (98% institutional, 2% external sources). *Receiving aid:* Freshmen: 44% (258). Undergraduates: 4% (88). *Average award:* Freshmen: $11,567. Undergraduates: $10,538. *Scholarships, grants, and awards by category:* Academic interests/achievement: 2,110 awards ($19,047,826 total): biological sciences, communication, engineering/technologies, foreign languages, general academic interests/achievements, health fields, international studies, religion/biblical studies. Creative arts/performance: 103 awards ($202,510 total): art/fine arts, dance, journalism/publications, music, theater/drama. Special achievements/activities: 42 awards ($57,300 total): cheerleading/drum major, leadership. Special characteristics: 289 awards ($2,548,069 total): adult students, children and siblings of alumni, children of educators, children of faculty/staff, international students, members of minority groups, out-of-state students, previous college experience, religious affiliation, veterans. *Tuition waivers:* Full or partial for employees or children of employees, senior citizens.

LOANS *Student loans:* $20,292,007 (91% need-based, 9% non-need-based). 80% of past graduating class borrowed through all loan programs. *Average indebtedness per student:* $37,236. *Average need-based loan:* Freshmen: $3376. Undergraduates: $4284. *Parent loans:* $4,969,199 (91% need-based, 9% non-need-based). *Programs:* Federal Direct (Subsidized and Unsubsidized Stafford, PLUS), Perkins, private loans.

WORK-STUDY *Federal work-study:* Total amount: $995,566; 567 jobs averaging $1850. *State or other work-study/employment:* Total amount: $442,347 (87% need-based, 13% non-need-based). 279 part-time jobs averaging $1850.

ATHLETIC AWARDS Total amount: $2,495,548 (86% need-based, 14% non-need-based).

SAINT ANSELM COLLEGE
Manchester, NH

Tuition & fees: $35,634	Average undergraduate aid package: $25,424

ABOUT THE INSTITUTION Independent Roman Catholic, coed. *Awards:* bachelor's degrees. 40 undergraduate majors. *Total enrollment:* 1,954. Undergraduates: 1,954. Freshmen: 527. Both federal and institutional methodology are used as a basis for awarding need-based institutional aid.

UNDERGRADUATE EXPENSES for 2013–2014 *Application fee:* $55. *Comprehensive fee:* $48,324 includes full-time tuition ($34,084), mandatory fees ($1550), and room and board ($12,690). *College room only:* $7636. Room and board charges vary according to housing facility.

FRESHMAN FINANCIAL AID (Fall 2012, est.) 491 applied for aid; of those 83% were deemed to have need. 100% of freshmen with need received aid; of those 23% had need fully met. *Average percent of need met:* 82% (excluding resources awarded to replace EFC). *Average financial aid package:* $24,629 (excluding resources awarded to replace EFC). 19% of all full-time freshmen had no need and received non-need-based gift aid.

UNDERGRADUATE FINANCIAL AID (Fall 2012, est.) 1,635 applied for aid; of those 88% were deemed to have need. 100% of undergraduates with need received aid; of those 20% had need fully met. *Average percent of need met:* 81% (excluding resources awarded to replace EFC). *Average financial aid package:* $25,424 (excluding resources awarded to replace EFC). 19% of all full-time undergraduates had no need and received non-need-based gift aid.

GIFT AID (NEED-BASED) *Total amount:* $25,613,123 (6% federal, 92% institutional, 2% external sources). *Receiving aid:* Freshmen: 77% (407); all full-time undergraduates: 75% (1,425). *Average award:* Freshmen: $19,744; Undergraduates: $19,351. *Scholarships, grants, and awards:* Federal Pell, FSEOG, state, private, college/university gift aid from institutional funds.

GIFT AID (NON-NEED-BASED) *Total amount:* $4,739,186 (96% institutional, 4% external sources). *Receiving aid:* Freshmen: 13% (66). Undergraduates: 9% (172). *Average award:* Freshmen: $10,208. Undergraduates: $10,366. *Scholarships, grants, and awards by category:* Academic interests/achievement: 1,435 awards ($13,342,125 total): general academic interests/achievements. Creative arts/performance: 89 awards ($1,028,500 total): general creative arts/performance. Special characteristics: 173 awards ($2,440,596 total): children of educators, children of faculty/staff, siblings of current students. *Tuition waivers:* Full or partial for employees or children of employees. *ROTC:* Army cooperative, Air Force cooperative.

LOANS *Student loans:* $15,931,826 (59% need-based, 41% non-need-based). 79% of past graduating class borrowed through all loan programs. *Average indebtedness per student:* $42,631. *Average need-based loan:* Freshmen: $4550. Undergraduates: $5712. *Parent loans:* $4,539,275 (32% need-based, 68% non-need-based). *Programs:* Federal Direct (Subsidized and Unsubsidized Stafford, PLUS), Perkins.

WORK-STUDY *Federal work-study:* Total amount: $1,741,991; 1,180 jobs averaging $1482. *State or other work-study/employment:* Total amount: $18,000 (100% non-need-based). 9 part-time jobs averaging $2000.

ATHLETIC AWARDS Total amount: $1,928,228 (48% need-based, 52% non-need-based).

APPLYING FOR FINANCIAL AID *Required financial aid forms:* FAFSA, CSS Financial Aid PROFILE, noncustodial (divorced/separated) parent's statement. *Financial aid deadline:* 3/15 (priority: 3/15). *Notification date:* Continuous beginning 3/1. Students must reply by 5/1 or within 2 weeks of notification.

CONTACT Elizabeth Keuffel, Director of Financial Aid, Saint Anselm College, 100 Saint Anselm Drive, Manchester, NH 03102-1310, 603-641-7110 or toll-free 888-4ANSELM. *Fax:* 603-656-6015. *E-mail:* financial_aid@anselm.edu. *Website:* http://www.anselm.edu/.

SAINT ANTHONY COLLEGE OF NURSING
Rockford, IL

Tuition & fees: $20,286	Average undergraduate aid package: $15,770

ABOUT THE INSTITUTION Independent Roman Catholic, coed, primarily women. 1 undergraduate major. Federal methodology is used as a basis for awarding need-based institutional aid.

UNDERGRADUATE EXPENSES for 2013–2014 *Tuition:* full-time $20,134; part-time $630 per credit hour. *Required fees:* full-time $152; $30 per term. Full-time tuition and fees vary according to course load and degree level. Part-time tuition and fees vary according to course load and degree level.

UNDERGRADUATE FINANCIAL AID (Fall 2012, est.) 161 applied for aid; of those 96% were deemed to have need. 100% of undergraduates with need received aid. *Average financial aid package:* $15,770 (excluding resources awarded to replace EFC).

GIFT AID (NEED-BASED) *Total amount:* $716,196 (54% federal, 42% state, 2% institutional, 2% external sources). *Receiving aid:* All full-time undergraduates: 55% (99). *Average award:* Undergraduates: $7234. *Scholarships, grants, and awards:* Federal Pell, state, private, college/university gift aid from institutional funds.

GIFT AID (NON-NEED-BASED) *Total amount:* $29,626 (94% state, 6% external sources). *Receiving aid:* Undergraduates: 1% (2).

LOANS *Student loans:* $1,639,641 (47% need-based, 53% non-need-based). *Average need-based loan:* Undergraduates: $5243. *Parent loans:* $214,664 (100% non-need-based). *Programs:* Federal Direct (Subsidized and Unsubsidized Stafford, PLUS), alternative loans.

APPLYING FOR FINANCIAL AID *Notification date:* Continuous.

CONTACT Serrita Woods, Financial Aid Officer, Saint Anthony College of Nursing, 5658 East State Street, Rockford, IL 61108-2468, 815-395-5089. *Fax:* 815-227-2730. *E-mail:* serritawoods@sacn.edu. *Website:* http://www.sacn.edu/.

ST. AUGUSTINE COLLEGE
Chicago, IL

CONTACT Mrs. Maria Zambonino, Director of Financial Aid, St. Augustine College, 1345 W Angyle, Chicago, IL 60640, 773-878-3813. *Fax:* 773-878-9032. *E-mail:* mzambonino@hotmail.com. *Website:* http://www.staugustine.edu/.

SAINT AUGUSTINE'S COLLEGE
Raleigh, NC

Tuition & fees: $17,160	Average undergraduate aid package: $6882

ABOUT THE INSTITUTION Independent Episcopal, coed. *Awards:* bachelor's degrees. 23 undergraduate majors. *Total enrollment:* 1,506. Undergraduates: 1,506. Freshmen: 461. Federal methodology is used as a basis for awarding need-based institutional aid.

UNDERGRADUATE EXPENSES for 2013–2014 *Application fee:* $25. *Comprehensive fee:* $24,722 includes full-time tuition ($12,364), mandatory fees ($4796), and room and board ($7562). *College room only:* $3128. Full-time tuition and fees vary according to course load. Room and board charges vary according to housing facility. *Part-time tuition:* $515 per credit hour. *Part-time fees:* $200 per credit hour. Part-time tuition and fees vary according to course load.

FRESHMAN FINANCIAL AID (Fall 2012, est.) 389 applied for aid; of those 95% were deemed to have need. 100% of freshmen with need received aid; of those 57% had need fully met. *Average percent of need met:* 85% (excluding resources awarded to replace EFC). *Average financial aid package:* $6735 (excluding resources awarded to replace EFC). 8% of all full-time freshmen had no need and received non-need-based gift aid.

UNDERGRADUATE FINANCIAL AID (Fall 2012, est.) 1,279 applied for aid; of those 100% were deemed to have need. 100% of undergraduates with need received aid; of those 87% had need fully met. *Average percent of need met:* 81% (excluding resources awarded to replace EFC). *Average financial aid package:* $6882 (excluding resources awarded to replace EFC). 3% of all full-time undergraduates had no need and received non-need-based gift aid.

GIFT AID (NEED-BASED) *Total amount:* $8,950,126 (67% federal, 33% state). *Receiving aid:* Freshmen: 92% (368); all full-time undergraduates: 94% (1,279). *Average award:* Freshmen: $4530; Undergraduates: $10,563. *Scholarships, grants, and awards:* Federal Pell, FSEOG, state, private, college/university gift aid from institutional funds, United Negro College Fund.

GIFT AID (NON-NEED-BASED) *Total amount:* $2,523,227 (93% institutional, 7% external sources). *Receiving aid:* Freshmen: 92% (368). Undergraduates: 94% (1,279). *Average award:* Freshmen: $5212. Undergraduates: $6527. *Scholarships, grants, and awards by category:* Academic interests/achievement: biological sciences, general academic interests/achievements, military science. Creative arts/performance: music, performing arts. Special characteristics: children of faculty/staff, local/state students. *Tuition waivers:* Full or partial for employees or children of employees. *ROTC:* Army, Air Force cooperative.

LOANS *Student loans:* $11,841,392 (46% need-based, 54% non-need-based). 83% of past graduating class borrowed through all loan programs. *Average indebtedness per student:* $28,960. *Average need-based loan:* Freshmen: $2963. Undergraduates: $4350. *Parent loans:* $2,084,811 (100% non-need-based). *Programs:* Federal Direct (Subsidized and Unsubsidized Stafford, PLUS), Perkins.

WORK-STUDY *Federal work-study:* Total amount: $871,697; 323 jobs averaging $2500. *State or other work-study/employment:* Total amount: $21,250 (100% non-need-based). 9 part-time jobs averaging $2500.

ATHLETIC AWARDS Total amount: $1,902,551 (100% non-need-based).

APPLYING FOR FINANCIAL AID *Required financial aid forms:* FAFSA, institution's own form. *Financial aid deadline (priority):* 3/15. *Notification date:* Continuous beginning 3/1. Students must reply within 2 weeks of notification.

CONTACT Ms. Nadine Y. Ford, Director of Financial Aid, Saint Augustine's College, 1315 Oakwood Avenue, Raleigh, NC 27610-2298, 919-516-4131 or toll-free 800-948-1126. *Fax:* 919-516-4431. *E-mail:* nford@st-aug.edu. *Website:* http://www.st-aug.edu/.

ST. BONAVENTURE UNIVERSITY
St. Bonaventure, NY

Tuition & fees: $28,727	Average undergraduate aid package: $25,378

ABOUT THE INSTITUTION Independent Roman Catholic Church, coed. *Awards:* certificates, bachelor's, and master's degrees. 40 undergraduate majors. *Total enrollment:* 2,329. Undergraduates: 1,908. Freshmen: 486. Federal methodology is used as a basis for awarding need-based institutional aid.

UNDERGRADUATE EXPENSES for 2013–2014 *Comprehensive fee:* $39,431 includes full-time tuition ($27,762), mandatory fees ($965), and room and board ($10,704). *College room only:* $5294. Room and board charges vary according to board plan and housing facility. *Part-time tuition:* $830 per credit hour. Part-time tuition and fees vary according to course load.

FRESHMAN FINANCIAL AID (Fall 2011) 449 applied for aid; of those 84% were deemed to have need. 100% of freshmen with need received aid; of those 20% had need fully met. *Average percent of need met:* 74% (excluding resources awarded to replace EFC). *Average financial aid package:* $24,807 (excluding resources awarded to replace EFC). 21% of all full-time freshmen had no need and received non-need-based gift aid.

UNDERGRADUATE FINANCIAL AID (Fall 2011) 1,609 applied for aid; of those 88% were deemed to have need. 100% of undergraduates with need received aid; of those 18% had need fully met. *Average percent of need met:* 74% (excluding resources awarded to replace EFC). *Average financial aid package:* $25,378 (excluding resources awarded to replace EFC). 22% of all full-time undergraduates had no need and received non-need-based gift aid.

GIFT AID (NEED-BASED) *Total amount:* $22,086,450 (13% federal, 9% state, 77% institutional, 1% external sources). *Receiving aid:* Freshmen: 78% (379); all full-time undergraduates: 76% (1,420). *Average award:* Freshmen: $18,394; Undergraduates: $17,472. *Scholarships, grants, and awards:* Federal Pell, FSEOG, state, private, college/university gift aid from institutional funds.

GIFT AID (NON-NEED-BASED) *Total amount:* $5,571,314 (7% federal, 1% state, 89% institutional, 3% external sources). *Receiving aid:* Freshmen: 73% (356). Undergraduates: 71% (1,335). *Average award:* Freshmen: $13,393. Undergraduates: $11,697. *Scholarships, grants, and awards by category:* Academic interests/achievement: 1,680 awards ($17,145,690 total): business, general academic interests/achievements. *Creative arts/performance:* 67 awards ($56,083 total): journalism/publications, music, performing arts. *Special characteristics:* 562 awards ($2,674,127 total): children of faculty/staff, local/state students, members of minority groups, out-of-state students, relatives of clergy, religious affiliation, siblings of current students. *Tuition waivers:* Full or partial for employees or children of employees, senior citizens. *ROTC:* Army.

LOANS *Student loans:* $13,525,333 (93% need-based, 7% non-need-based). 80% of past graduating class borrowed through all loan programs. *Average indebtedness per student:* $37,102. *Average need-based loan:* Freshmen: $3899. Undergraduates: $4483. *Parent loans:* $5,368,171 (96% need-based, 4% non-need-based). *Programs:* Federal Direct (Subsidized and Unsubsidized Stafford, PLUS), Perkins, college/university.

WORK-STUDY *Federal work-study:* Total amount: $272,297; 313 jobs averaging $834. *State or other work-study/employment:* Total amount: $290,470 (100% non-need-based). 340 part-time jobs averaging $854.

ATHLETIC AWARDS Total amount: $2,668,005 (48% need-based, 52% non-need-based).

APPLYING FOR FINANCIAL AID *Required financial aid forms:* FAFSA, state aid form. *Financial aid deadline (priority):* 2/15. *Notification date:* Continuous beginning 3/1. Students must reply by 5/1 or within 2 weeks of notification.

CONTACT Mr. Troy R. Martin, Director of Financial Aid, St. Bonaventure University, 3261 West State Road, St. Bonaventure, NY 14778-2284, 716-375-2373 or toll-free 800-462-5050. *Fax:* 716-375-2087. *E-mail:* tmartin@sbu.edu. *Website:* http://www.sbu.edu/.

ST. CATHARINE COLLEGE
St. Catharine, KY

CONTACT Financial Aid Office, St. Catharine College, 2735 Bardstown Road, St. Catharine, KY 40061-9499, 859-336-5082 or toll-free 800-599-2000. *Website:* http://www.sccky.edu/.

ST. CATHERINE UNIVERSITY
St. Paul, MN

Tuition & fees: $33,276	Average undergraduate aid package: $27,900

ABOUT THE INSTITUTION Independent Roman Catholic, undergraduate: women only; graduate: coed. *Awards:* certificates, associate, bachelor's, master's, and doctoral degrees. 80 undergraduate majors. *Total enrollment:* 5,227. Undergraduates: 3,826. Freshmen: 463. Federal methodology is used as a basis for awarding need-based institutional aid.

UNDERGRADUATE EXPENSES for 2013–2014 *Comprehensive fee:* $41,564 includes full-time tuition ($32,896), mandatory fees ($380), and room and board ($8288). *College room only:* $4670. Full-time tuition and fees vary according to class time and degree level. Room and board charges vary according to board plan and housing facility. Part-time tuition and fees vary according to class time and degree level.

FRESHMAN FINANCIAL AID (Fall 2012, est.) 386 applied for aid; of those 93% were deemed to have need. 100% of freshmen with need received aid; of those 17% had need fully met. *Average percent of need met:* 88% (excluding resources awarded to replace EFC). *Average financial aid package:* $29,500 (excluding resources awarded to replace EFC). 10% of all full-time freshmen had no need and received non-need-based gift aid.

UNDERGRADUATE FINANCIAL AID (Fall 2012, est.) 1,755 applied for aid; of those 94% were deemed to have need. 100% of undergraduates with need received aid; of those 14% had need fully met. *Average percent of need met:* 84% (excluding resources awarded to replace EFC). *Average financial aid package:* $27,900 (excluding resources awarded to replace EFC). 12% of all full-time undergraduates had no need and received non-need-based gift aid.

GIFT AID (NEED-BASED) *Total amount:* $39,921,308 (18% federal, 10% state, 69% institutional, 3% external sources). *Receiving aid:* Freshmen: 90% (360); all full-time undergraduates: 87% (1,641). *Average award:* Freshmen: $22,000; Undergraduates: $18,270. *Scholarships, grants, and awards:* Federal Pell, FSEOG, state, private, college/university gift aid from institutional funds.

GIFT AID (NON-NEED-BASED) *Total amount:* $570,266 (16% federal, 84% institutional). *Receiving aid:* Freshmen: 1% (4). Undergraduates: 1% (22). *Average award:* Freshmen: $16,980. Undergraduates: $13,230. *Scholarships, grants, and awards by category:* Academic interests/achievement: business, education, English, foreign languages, general academic interests/achievements, health fields, home economics, humanities, mathematics, physical sciences, premedicine, social sciences. *Creative arts/performance:* art/fine arts, music. *Special achievements/activities:* community service, general special achievements/activities, leadership, memberships. *Special characteristics:* adult students, children and siblings of alumni, children of current students, children of educators, children of faculty/staff, ethnic background, general special characteristics, international students, local/state students, out-of-state students, religious affiliation, siblings of current students, spouses of current students. *Tuition waivers:* Full or partial for employees or children of employees, senior citizens. *ROTC:* Army cooperative, Air Force cooperative.

LOANS *Student loans:* $29,951,388 (43% need-based, 57% non-need-based). 85% of past graduating class borrowed through all loan programs. *Average indebtedness per student:* $39,230. *Average need-based loan:* Freshmen: $4100. Undergraduates: $5150. *Parent loans:* $4,569,520 (100% non-need-based). *Programs:* Federal Direct (Subsidized and Unsubsidized Stafford, PLUS), Perkins, Federal Nursing, state, alternative loans.

WORK-STUDY *Federal work-study:* Total amount: $258,575; jobs available. *State or other work-study/employment:* Total amount: $217,714 (100% need-based). Part-time jobs available.

APPLYING FOR FINANCIAL AID *Required financial aid forms:* FAFSA, institution's own form. *Financial aid deadline (priority):* 4/15. *Notification date:* Continuous. Students must reply within 2 weeks of notification.

CONTACT Beth Stevens, Director of Financial Aid, St. Catherine University, 2004 Randolph Avenue, Derham Hall, Suite 208, St. Paul, MN 55105, 651-690-6540 or toll-free 800-945-4599. *Fax:* 651-690-6765. *E-mail:* finaid@stkate.edu. *Website:* http://www.stkate.edu/.

SAINT CHARLES BORROMEO SEMINARY, OVERBROOK
Wynnewood, PA

Tuition & fees: $19,150	Average undergraduate aid package: $20,000

ABOUT THE INSTITUTION Independent Roman Catholic, coed, primarily men. *Awards:* certificates, bachelor's, and master's degrees (also offers coed part-time programs). 1 undergraduate major. *Total enrollment:* 218. Undergraduates: 98. Freshmen: 7. Federal methodology is used as a basis for awarding need-based institutional aid.

UNDERGRADUATE EXPENSES for 2013–2014 *Comprehensive fee:* $31,210 includes full-time tuition ($17,950), mandatory fees ($1200), and room and board ($12,060). *Part-time tuition:* $880 per course.

FRESHMAN FINANCIAL AID (Fall 2012, est.) 5 applied for aid; of those 60% were deemed to have need. 100% of freshmen with need received aid; of those 100% had need fully met. *Average percent of need met:* 80% (excluding resources awarded to replace EFC). *Average financial aid package:* $20,000 (excluding resources awarded to replace EFC).

UNDERGRADUATE FINANCIAL AID (Fall 2012, est.) 22 applied for aid; of those 45% were deemed to have need. 100% of undergraduates with need received aid; of those 60% had need fully met. *Average percent of need met:* 60% (excluding resources awarded to replace EFC). *Average financial aid package:* $20,000 (excluding resources awarded to replace EFC).

GIFT AID (NEED-BASED) *Total amount:* $533,577 (10% federal, 9% state, 75% institutional, 6% external sources). *Receiving aid:* Freshmen: 40% (2); all full-time undergraduates: 18% (8). *Average award:* Freshmen: $5000; Undergraduates: $5000. *Scholarships, grants, and awards:* Federal Pell, FSEOG, state, college/university gift aid from institutional funds.

GIFT AID (NON-NEED-BASED) *Receiving aid:* Freshmen: 60% (3). Undergraduates: 18% (8). *Scholarships, grants, and awards by category:* Academic *interests/achievement:* general academic interests/achievements. ***Tuition waivers:*** Full or partial for employees or children of employees.

LOANS *Student loans:* $400,600 (100% need-based). 50% of past graduating class borrowed through all loan programs. *Average indebtedness per student:* $19,000. *Average need-based loan:* Freshmen: $4500. Undergraduates: $5500. *Parent loans:* $16,400 (100% need-based). *Programs:* Federal Direct (Subsidized and Unsubsidized Stafford, PLUS).

APPLYING FOR FINANCIAL AID *Required financial aid forms:* FAFSA, institution's own form. *Financial aid deadline (priority):* 4/15. *Notification date:* 6/1. Students must reply by 6/15.

CONTACT Ms. Nora M. Downey, Coordinator of Financial Aid, Saint Charles Borromeo Seminary, Overbrook, 100 East Wynnewood Road, Wynnewood, PA 19096-3099, 610-785-6582. *Fax:* 610-667-3971. *E-mail:* ndowney@scs.edu. *Website:* http://www.scs.edu/.

ST. CLOUD STATE UNIVERSITY
St. Cloud, MN

Tuition & fees (MN res): $7439	Average undergraduate aid package: $8939

ABOUT THE INSTITUTION State-supported, coed. *Awards:* certificates, diplomas, associate, bachelor's, master's, and doctoral degrees. 143 undergraduate majors. *Total enrollment:* 17,231. Undergraduates: 15,536. Freshmen: 1,902. Federal methodology is used as a basis for awarding need-based institutional aid.

UNDERGRADUATE EXPENSES for 2013–2014 *Application fee:* $20. *Tuition, state resident:* full-time $6584. *Tuition, nonresident:* full-time $14,226. *Required fees:* full-time $855. Full-time tuition and fees vary according to course load and reciprocity agreements. Part-time tuition and fees vary according to course load and reciprocity agreements. *College room and board:* $6994. Room and board charges vary according to board plan and housing facility.

FRESHMAN FINANCIAL AID (Fall 2012, est.) 1,562 applied for aid; of those 77% were deemed to have need. 100% of freshmen with need received aid; of those 11% had need fully met. *Average percent of need met:* 57% (excluding resources awarded to replace EFC). *Average financial aid package:* $8445 (excluding resources awarded to replace EFC). 18% of all full-time freshmen had no need and received non-need-based gift aid.

UNDERGRADUATE FINANCIAL AID (Fall 2012, est.) 8,023 applied for aid; of those 80% were deemed to have need. 100% of undergraduates with need received aid; of those 13% had need fully met. *Average percent of need met:* 59% (excluding resources awarded to replace EFC). *Average financial aid package:* $8939 (excluding resources awarded to replace EFC). 16% of all full-time undergraduates had no need and received non-need-based gift aid.

GIFT AID (NEED-BASED) *Total amount:* $18,172,159 (73% federal, 26% state, 1% institutional). *Receiving aid:* Freshmen: 47% (875); all full-time undergraduates: 46% (4,710). *Average award:* Freshmen: $4943; Undergraduates: $4765. *Scholarships, grants, and awards:* Federal Pell, FSEOG, state, private, college/university gift aid from institutional funds.

GIFT AID (NON-NEED-BASED) *Total amount:* $7,569,702 (17% federal, 10% state, 52% institutional, 21% external sources). *Receiving aid:* Freshmen: 25% (461). Undergraduates: 16% (1,664). *Average award:* Freshmen: $9460. Undergraduates: $9844. *Scholarships, grants, and awards by category: Academic interests/achievement:* biological sciences, business, communication, computer science, education, engineering/technologies, English, general academic interests/achievements, health fields, international studies, mathematics, physical sciences, social sciences. *Creative arts/performance:* applied art and design, art/fine arts, cinema/film/broadcasting, creative writing, journalism/publications, music, performing arts, theater/drama. *Special achievements/activities:* community service, general special achievements/activities, leadership. *Special characteristics:* children of faculty/staff, children of union members/company employees, out-of-state students. *Tuition waivers:* Full or partial for employees or children of employees, senior citizens. *ROTC:* Army.

LOANS *Student loans:* $56,946,377 (42% need-based, 58% non-need-based). 75% of past graduating class borrowed through all loan programs. *Average indebtedness per student:* $30,990. *Average need-based loan:* Freshmen: $3350. Undergraduates: $4140. *Parent loans:* $599,036 (100% non-need-based). *Programs:* Federal Direct (Subsidized and Unsubsidized Stafford, PLUS), Perkins, state.

WORK-STUDY *Federal work-study:* Total amount: $1,280,599; jobs available. *State or other work-study/employment:* Total amount: $1,282,576 (100% need-based). Part-time jobs available.

ATHLETIC AWARDS Total amount: $1,269,180 (100% non-need-based).

APPLYING FOR FINANCIAL AID *Required financial aid forms:* FAFSA, institution's own form. *Financial aid deadline:* Continuous. *Notification date:* Continuous beginning 6/1.

CONTACT Financial Aid Office, St. Cloud State University, 720 4th Avenue South, AS106, St. Cloud, MN 56301-4498, 320-308-2047 or toll-free 877-654-7278. *Fax:* 320-308-5424. *E-mail:* financialaid@stcloudstate.edu. *Website:* http://www.stcloudstate.edu/.

ST. EDWARD'S UNIVERSITY
Austin, TX

Tuition & fees: $33,720	Average undergraduate aid package: $23,013

ABOUT THE INSTITUTION Independent Roman Catholic, coed. *Awards:* certificates, bachelor's, and master's degrees. 60 undergraduate majors. *Total enrollment:* 5,095. Undergraduates: 4,238. Freshmen: 788. Federal methodology is used as a basis for awarding need-based institutional aid.

UNDERGRADUATE EXPENSES for 2013–2014 *Application fee:* $50. *Comprehensive fee:* $44,674 includes full-time tuition ($33,320), mandatory fees ($400), and room and board ($10,954). *College room only:* $6024. Full-time tuition and fees vary according to course load and degree level. Room and board charges vary according to board plan and housing facility. *Part-time tuition:* $1112 per credit hour. *Part-time fees:* $50 per term. Part-time tuition and fees vary according to course load and degree level.

FRESHMAN FINANCIAL AID (Fall 2012, est.) 622 applied for aid; of those 80% were deemed to have need. 100% of freshmen with need received aid; of those 11% had need fully met. *Average percent of need met:* 71% (excluding resources awarded to replace EFC). *Average financial aid package:* $25,537 (excluding resources awarded to replace EFC). 6% of all full-time freshmen had no need and received non-need-based gift aid.

UNDERGRADUATE FINANCIAL AID (Fall 2012, est.) 2,530 applied for aid; of those 84% were deemed to have need. 99% of undergraduates with need received aid; of those 9% had need fully met. *Average percent of need met:* 63% (excluding resources awarded to replace EFC). *Average financial aid package:* $23,013 (excluding resources awarded to replace EFC). 5% of all full-time undergraduates had no need and received non-need-based gift aid.

GIFT AID (NEED-BASED) *Total amount:* $30,372,716 (20% federal, 13% state, 67% institutional). *Receiving aid:* Freshmen: 56% (432); all full-time undergraduates: 56% (1,916). *Average award:* Freshmen: $16,713; Undergraduates: $13,936. *Scholarships, grants, and awards:* Federal Pell, FSEOG, state, private, college/university gift aid from institutional funds.

GIFT AID (NON-NEED-BASED) *Total amount:* $19,529,537 (12% federal, 83% institutional, 5% external sources). *Receiving aid:* Freshmen: 43% (336). Undergraduates: 41% (1,426). *Average award:* Freshmen: $11,198. Undergraduates: $10,003. *Scholarships, grants, and awards by category: Academic interests/achievement:* 1,888 awards ($15,024,163 total): biological sciences, business, communication, computer science, education, English, foreign languages, general academic interests/achievements, health fields, humanities, international studies, mathematics, military science, physical sciences, premedicine, religion/biblical studies, social sciences. *Creative arts/performance:* 31 awards ($64,411 total): art/fine arts, journalism/publications, theater/drama. *Special achievements/activities:* 62 awards ($118,357 total): cheerleading/drum major, community service, general special achievements/activities, leadership. *Special characteristics:* 76 awards ($1,253,673 total): adult students, children of faculty/staff, religious affiliation, veterans. *Tuition waivers:* Full or partial for employees or children of employees. *ROTC:* Army cooperative, Air Force cooperative.

LOANS *Student loans:* $26,774,213 (37% need-based, 63% non-need-based). 70% of past graduating class borrowed through all loan programs. *Average indebtedness per student:* $34,314. *Average need-based loan:* Freshmen: $3666. Undergraduates: $4590. *Parent loans:* $3,459,280 (100% non-need-based). *Programs:* Federal Direct (Subsidized and Unsubsidized Stafford, PLUS), Perkins, state.

WORK-STUDY *Federal work-study:* Total amount: $457,118; 240 jobs averaging $1905. *State or other work-study/employment:* Total amount: $33,000 (100% need-based). 16 part-time jobs averaging $2063.

ATHLETIC AWARDS Total amount: $2,587,000 (100% non-need-based).

APPLYING FOR FINANCIAL AID *Required financial aid form:* FAFSA. *Financial aid deadline:* 5/1 (priority: 3/1). *Notification date:* Continuous beginning 1/15. Students must reply by 5/1 or within 2 weeks of notification.

CONTACT Office of Student Financial Services, St. Edward's University, 3001 South Congress Avenue, Austin, TX 78704-6489, 512-448-8523 or toll-free 800-555-0164. *Fax:* 512-416-5837. *E-mail:* seu.finaid@stedwards.edu. *Website:* http://www.gotostedwards.com/.

ST. FRANCIS COLLEGE
Brooklyn Heights, NY

CONTACT Joseph Cummings, Director of Student Financial Services, St. Francis College, 180 Remsen Street, Brooklyn Heights, NY 11201-4398, 718-489-5390. *Fax:* 718-522-1274. *E-mail:* jcummings@stfranciscollege.edu. *Website:* http://www.sfc.edu/.

SAINT FRANCIS MEDICAL CENTER COLLEGE OF NURSING
Peoria, IL

Tuition & fees: $16,964 | Average undergraduate aid package: $11,259

ABOUT THE INSTITUTION Independent Roman Catholic, coed, primarily women. *Awards:* certificates, bachelor's, master's, and doctoral degrees. 1 undergraduate major. *Total enrollment:* 638. Undergraduates: 402. Federal methodology is used as a basis for awarding need-based institutional aid.

UNDERGRADUATE EXPENSES for 2013–2014 *Application fee:* $50. *Tuition:* full-time $16,368; part-time $528 per hour. Full-time tuition and fees vary according to course load. Part-time tuition and fees vary according to course load.

UNDERGRADUATE FINANCIAL AID (Fall 2012, est.) 253 applied for aid; of those 83% were deemed to have need. 100% of undergraduates with need received aid; of those 8% had need fully met. *Average percent of need met:* 61% (excluding resources awarded to replace EFC). *Average financial aid package:* $11,259 (excluding resources awarded to replace EFC). 5% of all full-time undergraduates had no need and received non-need-based gift aid.

GIFT AID (NEED-BASED) *Total amount:* $1,385,625 (40% federal, 47% state, 7% institutional, 6% external sources). *Receiving aid:* All full-time undergraduates: 55% (162). *Average award:* Undergraduates: $7558. *Scholarships, grants, and awards:* Federal Pell, state, private, college/university gift aid from institutional funds.

GIFT AID (NON-NEED-BASED) *Total amount:* $46,217 (21% state, 51% institutional, 28% external sources). *Receiving aid:* Undergraduates: 5% (16). *Average award:* Undergraduates: $1737. *Scholarships, grants, and awards by category:* Academic interests/achievement: 14 awards ($16,831 total): general academic interests/achievements, health fields. *Tuition waivers:* Full or partial for employees or children of employees.

LOANS *Student loans:* $2,278,584 (91% need-based, 9% non-need-based). *Average need-based loan:* Undergraduates: $5429. *Parent loans:* $228,386 (43% need-based, 57% non-need-based). *Programs:* Federal Direct (Subsidized and Unsubsidized Stafford, PLUS), college/university.

APPLYING FOR FINANCIAL AID *Required financial aid forms:* FAFSA, institution's own form. *Financial aid deadline (priority):* 3/1. *Notification date:* Continuous beginning 5/1.

CONTACT Ms. Nancy Perryman, Coordinator for Student Finance, Saint Francis Medical Center College of Nursing, 511 Northeast Greenleaf Street, Peoria, IL 61603-3783, 309-655-4119. *Fax:* 309-655-3962. *E-mail:* nancy.s.perryman@osfhealthcare.org. *Website:* http://www.sfmccon.edu/.

SAINT FRANCIS UNIVERSITY
Loretto, PA

Tuition & fees: $28,878 | Average undergraduate aid package: $18,343

ABOUT THE INSTITUTION Independent Roman Catholic, coed. *Awards:* certificates, associate, bachelor's, master's, and doctoral degrees. 69 undergraduate majors. *Total enrollment:* 2,398. Undergraduates: 1,746. Freshmen: 421. Federal methodology is used as a basis for awarding need-based institutional aid.

UNDERGRADUATE EXPENSES for 2013–2014 *Application fee:* $30. *One-time required fee:* $60. *Comprehensive fee:* $38,778 includes full-time tuition ($27,828), mandatory fees ($1050), and room and board ($9900). *College room only:* $4970. Full-time tuition and fees vary according to course load, degree level, program, and student level. Room and board charges vary according to board plan and housing facility. *Part-time tuition:* $874 per credit hour. *Part-time fees:* $412 per credit hour. Part-time tuition and fees vary according to class time, degree level, and program.

FRESHMAN FINANCIAL AID (Fall 2012, est.) 435 applied for aid; of those 90% were deemed to have need. 100% of freshmen with need received aid; of those 16% had need fully met. *Average percent of need met:* 78% (excluding resources awarded to replace EFC). *Average financial aid package:* $22,404 (excluding resources awarded to replace EFC). 9% of all full-time freshmen had no need and received non-need-based gift aid.

UNDERGRADUATE FINANCIAL AID (Fall 2012, est.) 1,502 applied for aid; of those 79% were deemed to have need. 100% of undergraduates with need received aid; of those 13% had need fully met. *Average percent of need met:* 62% (excluding resources awarded to replace EFC). *Average financial aid package:* $18,343 (excluding resources awarded to replace EFC). 8% of all full-time undergraduates had no need and received non-need-based gift aid.

GIFT AID (NEED-BASED) *Total amount:* $17,364,355 (11% federal, 11% state, 77% institutional, 1% external sources). *Receiving aid:* Freshmen: 48% (211); all full-time undergraduates: 47% (727). *Average award:* Freshmen: $10,552; Undergraduates: $15,307. *Scholarships, grants, and awards:* Federal Pell, FSEOG, state, private, college/university gift aid from institutional funds.

GIFT AID (NON-NEED-BASED) *Total amount:* $2,809,781 (99% institutional, 1% external sources). *Receiving aid:* Freshmen: 88% (391). Undergraduates: 76% (1,172). *Average award:* Freshmen: $12,214. Undergraduates: $11,494. *Scholarships, grants, and awards by category:* Academic interests/achievement: 762 awards ($3,157,000 total): biological sciences, business, computer science, education, engineering/technologies, English, general academic interests/achievements, health fields, humanities, mathematics, religion/biblical studies, social sciences. *Creative arts/performance:* 42 awards ($44,700 total): art/fine arts, music. *Special achievements/activities:* 45 awards ($115,252 total): cheerleading/drum major, religious involvement. *Special characteristics:* 733 awards ($3,615,021 total): adult students, children and siblings of alumni, children of current students, children of educators, children of faculty/staff, international students, out-of-state students, previous college experience, religious affiliation, siblings of current students, spouses of current students. *Tuition waivers:* Full or partial for employees or children of employees. *ROTC:* Army.

LOANS *Student loans:* $13,054,663 (94% need-based, 6% non-need-based). 83% of past graduating class borrowed through all loan programs. *Average indebtedness per student:* $9677. *Average need-based loan:* Freshmen: $3539. Undergraduates: $4506. *Parent loans:* $2,861,089 (95% need-based, 5% non-need-based). *Programs:* Federal Direct (Subsidized and Unsubsidized Stafford, PLUS), Perkins, private loans.

WORK-STUDY *Federal work-study:* Total amount: $310,212; 271 jobs averaging $1000. *State or other work-study/employment:* Total amount: $376,500 (96% need-based, 4% non-need-based). 746 part-time jobs averaging $1000.

ATHLETIC AWARDS Total amount: $4,744,225 (86% need-based, 14% non-need-based).

APPLYING FOR FINANCIAL AID *Required financial aid form:* FAFSA. *Financial aid deadline (priority):* 5/1. *Notification date:* Continuous beginning 3/1. Students must reply by 5/1.

CONTACT Mr. Jamie Kosh, Director of Financial Aid, Saint Francis University, PO Box 600, Loretto, PA 15931, 814-472-3010 or toll-free 866-DIAL-SFU. *Fax:* 814-472-3999. *E-mail:* jkosh@francis.edu. *Website:* http://www.francis.edu/.

ST. GREGORY'S UNIVERSITY
Shawnee, OK

CONTACT Matt McCoin, Director of Financial Aid, St. Gregory's University, 1900 West MacArthur Drive, Shawnee, OK 74804, 405-878-5412 or toll-free 888-STGREGS. *Fax:* 405-878-5403. *E-mail:* mdmccoin@stgregorys.edu. *Website:* http://www.stgregorys.edu/.

ST. GREGORY THE GREAT SEMINARY
Seward, NE

CONTACT Financial Aid Office, St. Gregory the Great Seminary, 800 Fletcher Road, Seward, NE 67434, 402-643-4052. *Website:* http://www.stgregoryseminary.edu/.

ST. JOHN FISHER COLLEGE
Rochester, NY

Tuition & fees: $28,430	Average undergraduate aid package: $19,460

ABOUT THE INSTITUTION Independent Roman Catholic Church, coed. *Awards:* certificates, bachelor's, master's, and doctoral degrees. 38 undergraduate majors. *Total enrollment:* 4,008. Undergraduates: 2,960. Freshmen: 578. Federal methodology is used as a basis for awarding need-based institutional aid.

UNDERGRADUATE EXPENSES for 2013–2014 *Application fee:* $30. *Comprehensive fee:* $39,370 includes full-time tuition ($27,870), mandatory fees ($560), and room and board ($10,940). *College room only:* $7090. Room and board charges vary according to board plan. *Part-time tuition:* $730 per credit hour. Part-time tuition and fees vary according to course load.

FRESHMAN FINANCIAL AID (Fall 2012, est.) 559 applied for aid; of those 88% were deemed to have need. 100% of freshmen with need received aid; of those 45% had need fully met. *Average percent of need met:* 82% (excluding resources awarded to replace EFC). *Average financial aid package:* $20,384 (excluding resources awarded to replace EFC). 15% of all full-time freshmen had no need and received non-need-based gift aid.

UNDERGRADUATE FINANCIAL AID (Fall 2012, est.) 2,523 applied for aid; of those 91% were deemed to have need. 100% of undergraduates with need received aid; of those 39% had need fully met. *Average percent of need met:* 78% (excluding resources awarded to replace EFC). *Average financial aid package:* $19,460 (excluding resources awarded to replace EFC). 15% of all full-time undergraduates had no need and received non-need-based gift aid.

GIFT AID (NEED-BASED) Total amount: $32,505,093 (15% federal, 10% state, 73% institutional, 2% external sources). *Receiving aid:* Freshmen: 85% (491); all full-time undergraduates: 83% (2,290). *Average award:* Freshmen: $16,531; Undergraduates: $14,561. *Scholarships, grants, and awards:* Federal Pell, FSEOG, state, private, college/university gift aid from institutional funds, Federal Nursing.

GIFT AID (NON-NEED-BASED) Total amount: $3,997,505 (2% federal, 1% state, 93% institutional, 4% external sources). *Receiving aid:* Freshmen: 58% (334). Undergraduates: 40% (1,100). *Average award:* Freshmen: $10,030. Undergraduates: $9876. *Scholarships, grants, and awards by category:* Academic interests/achievement: 1,261 awards ($13,192,970 total): biological sciences, business, English, foreign languages, general academic interests/achievements, humanities, mathematics, physical sciences. *Special achievements/activities:* 112 awards ($1,004,910 total): community service. *Special characteristics:* 170 awards ($2,637,759 total): children and siblings of alumni, children of faculty/staff, ethnic background, first-generation college students, local/state students, members of minority groups. *Tuition waivers:* Full or partial for employees or children of employees. *ROTC:* Army cooperative, Naval cooperative, Air Force cooperative.

LOANS Student loans: $22,925,643 (94% need-based, 6% non-need-based). 82% of past graduating class borrowed through all loan programs. *Average indebtedness per student:* $32,157. *Average need-based loan:* Freshmen: $3657. Undergraduates: $4704. *Parent loans:* $13,251,630 (87% need-based, 13% non-need-based). *Programs:* Federal Direct (Subsidized and Unsubsidized Stafford, PLUS), Perkins.

WORK-STUDY *Federal work-study:* Total amount: $1,996,593; 1,366 jobs averaging $1448.

APPLYING FOR FINANCIAL AID *Required financial aid forms:* FAFSA, state aid form. *Financial aid deadline (priority):* 2/15. *Notification date:* Continuous beginning 3/21. Students must reply by 5/1 or within 3 weeks of notification.

CONTACT Mrs. Angela Monnat, Director of Financial Aid, St. John Fisher College, 3690 East Avenue, Rochester, NY 14618-3597, 585-385-8042 or toll-free 800-444-4640. *Fax:* 585-385-8044. *E-mail:* amonnat@sjfc.edu. *Website:* http://www.sjfc.edu/.

ST. JOHN'S COLLEGE
Springfield, IL

CONTACT Mary M. Deatherage, Financial Aid Officer, St. John's College, 421 North Ninth Street, Springfield, IL 62702, 217-544-6464 Ext. 44705. *Fax:* 217-757-6870. *E-mail:* mdeather@st-johns.org. *Website:* http://www.stjohnscollegespringfield.edu/.

ST. JOHN'S COLLEGE
Annapolis, MD

Tuition & fees: $45,004	Average undergraduate aid package: $33,665

ABOUT THE INSTITUTION Independent, coed. *Awards:* bachelor's and master's degrees. 1 undergraduate major. *Total enrollment:* 509. Undergraduates: 449. Freshmen: 118. Both federal and institutional methodology are used as a basis for awarding need-based institutional aid.

UNDERGRADUATE EXPENSES for 2013–2014 *Comprehensive fee:* $55,648 includes full-time tuition ($44,554), mandatory fees ($450), and room and board ($10,644). Room and board charges vary according to board plan.

FRESHMAN FINANCIAL AID (Fall 2012, est.) 108 applied for aid; of those 90% were deemed to have need. 100% of freshmen with need received aid; of those 13% had need fully met. *Average financial aid package:* $36,407 (excluding resources awarded to replace EFC). 6% of all full-time freshmen had no need and received non-need-based gift aid.

UNDERGRADUATE FINANCIAL AID (Fall 2012, est.) 356 applied for aid; of those 90% were deemed to have need. 99% of undergraduates with need received aid; of those 10% had need fully met. *Average percent of need met:* 98% (excluding resources awarded to replace EFC). *Average financial aid package:* $33,665 (excluding resources awarded to replace EFC). 4% of all full-time undergraduates had no need and received non-need-based gift aid.

GIFT AID (NEED-BASED) Total amount: $8,676,443 (7% federal, 1% state, 92% institutional). *Receiving aid:* Freshmen: 81% (96); all full-time undergraduates: 69% (310). *Average award:* Freshmen: $31,330; Undergraduates: $28,695. *Scholarships, grants, and awards:* Federal Pell, FSEOG, state, private, college/university gift aid from institutional funds.

GIFT AID (NON-NEED-BASED) Total amount: $911,581 (1% state, 25% institutional, 74% external sources). *Receiving aid:* Freshmen: 3% (4). Undergraduates: 4% (16). *Average award:* Freshmen: $17,804. Undergraduates: $16,340. *Tuition waivers:* Full or partial for employees or children of employees.

LOANS Student loans: $2,224,625 (85% need-based, 15% non-need-based). 69% of past graduating class borrowed through all loan programs. *Average indebtedness per student:* $29,265. *Average need-based loan:* Freshmen: $4272. Undergraduates: $4842. *Parent loans:* $1,519,913 (100% non-need-based). *Programs:* Federal Direct (Subsidized and Unsubsidized Stafford, PLUS), Perkins, college/university.

WORK-STUDY *Federal work-study:* Total amount: $187,533; 99 jobs averaging $1894. *State or other work-study/employment:* Total amount: $182,633 (100% non-need-based). 88 part-time jobs averaging $2075.

APPLYING FOR FINANCIAL AID *Required financial aid forms:* FAFSA, CSS Financial Aid PROFILE, noncustodial (divorced/separated) parent's statement, business/farm supplement. *Financial aid deadline (priority):* 2/15. *Notification date:* Continuous beginning 1/1. Students must reply by 5/1.

ST. JOHN'S COLLEGE

CONTACT Ms. Dana Kennedy, Director of Financial Aid, St. John's College, PO Box 2800, Annapolis, MD 21404, 410-626-2502 or toll-free 800-727-9238. *Fax:* 410-626-2885. *E-mail:* dana.kennedy@sjca.edu.
Website: http://www.stjohnscollege.edu/.

ST. JOHN'S COLLEGE
Santa Fe, NM

Tuition & fees: $45,004	Average undergraduate aid package: $34,220

ABOUT THE INSTITUTION Independent, coed. *Awards:* diplomas, bachelor's, and master's degrees. 3 undergraduate majors. *Total enrollment:* 430. Undergraduates: 349. Freshmen: 99. Both federal and institutional methodology are used as a basis for awarding need-based institutional aid.
UNDERGRADUATE EXPENSES for 2013–2014 *Comprehensive fee:* $54,998 includes full-time tuition ($44,554), mandatory fees ($450), and room and board ($9994). *College room only:* $4997. Room and board charges vary according to board plan. *Part-time tuition:* $1311 per credit hour. *Payment plan:* Tuition prepayment.
FRESHMAN FINANCIAL AID (Fall 2011) 123 applied for aid; of those 98% were deemed to have need. 100% of freshmen with need received aid; of those 95% had need fully met. *Average percent of need met:* 94% (excluding resources awarded to replace EFC). *Average financial aid package:* $35,980 (excluding resources awarded to replace EFC).
UNDERGRADUATE FINANCIAL AID (Fall 2011) 342 applied for aid; of those 94% were deemed to have need. 100% of undergraduates with need received aid; of those 89% had need fully met. *Average percent of need met:* 90% (excluding resources awarded to replace EFC). *Average financial aid package:* $34,220 (excluding resources awarded to replace EFC).
GIFT AID (NEED-BASED) *Total amount:* $8,541,772 (9% federal, 91% institutional). *Receiving aid:* Freshmen: 84% (104); all full-time undergraduates: 81% (317). *Average award:* Freshmen: $27,750; Undergraduates: $25,580. *Scholarships, grants, and awards:* Federal Pell, FSEOG, state, private, college/university gift aid from institutional funds.
GIFT AID (NON-NEED-BASED) *Total amount:* $196,587 (8% federal, 28% institutional, 64% external sources). *Scholarships, grants, and awards by category:* Special characteristics: 8 awards ($169,429 total): children of faculty/staff, veterans. *Tuition waivers:* Full or partial for employees or children of employees.
LOANS *Student loans:* $2,050,345 (72% need-based, 28% non-need-based). 68% of past graduating class borrowed through all loan programs. *Average indebtedness per student:* $28,563. *Average need-based loan:* Freshmen: $4430. Undergraduates: $59,800. *Parent loans:* $994,819 (100% non-need-based). *Programs:* Federal Direct (Subsidized and Unsubsidized Stafford, PLUS), Perkins, college/university.
WORK-STUDY *Federal work-study:* Total amount: $280,929; 121 jobs averaging $2920. *State or other work-study/employment:* Total amount: $23,440 (100% need-based). 8 part-time jobs averaging $2930.
APPLYING FOR FINANCIAL AID *Required financial aid forms:* FAFSA, CSS Financial Aid PROFILE, noncustodial (divorced/separated) parent's statement, business/farm supplement. *Financial aid deadline (priority):* 2/15. *Notification date:* Continuous beginning 12/15. Students must reply by 5/1 or within 2 weeks of notification.
CONTACT Michael R. Rodriguez, Director of Financial Aid, St. John's College, 1160 Camino Cruz Blanca, Santa Fe, NM 87505, 505-984-6058 or toll-free 800-331-5232. *Fax:* 505-984-6164. *E-mail:* mike.rodriguez@sjcsf.edu.
Website: http://www.stjohnscollege.edu/.

SAINT JOHN'S UNIVERSITY
Collegeville, MN

Tuition & fees: $35,486	Average undergraduate aid package: $26,628

ABOUT THE INSTITUTION Independent Roman Catholic, men only. *Awards:* bachelor's and master's degrees (coordinate with College of Saint Benedict for women). 50 undergraduate majors. *Total enrollment:* 1,983. Undergraduates: 1,854. Freshmen: 449. Federal methodology is used as a basis for awarding need-based institutional aid.
UNDERGRADUATE EXPENSES for 2013–2014 *Comprehensive fee:* $44,125 includes full-time tuition ($34,838), mandatory fees ($648), and room and board ($8639). *College room only:* $4350. Room and board charges vary according to board plan and housing facility. *Part-time tuition:* $1452 per credit hour. Part-time tuition and fees vary according to course load.
FRESHMAN FINANCIAL AID (Fall 2012, est.) 365 applied for aid; of those 86% were deemed to have need. 100% of freshmen with need received aid; of those 42% had need fully met. *Average percent of need met:* 92% (excluding resources awarded to replace EFC). *Average financial aid package:* $28,318 (excluding resources awarded to replace EFC). 24% of all full-time freshmen had no need and received non-need-based gift aid.
UNDERGRADUATE FINANCIAL AID (Fall 2012, est.) 1,340 applied for aid; of those 88% were deemed to have need. 100% of undergraduates with need received aid; of those 38% had need fully met. *Average percent of need met:* 87% (excluding resources awarded to replace EFC). *Average financial aid package:* $26,628 (excluding resources awarded to replace EFC). 28% of all full-time undergraduates had no need and received non-need-based gift aid.
GIFT AID (NEED-BASED) *Total amount:* $25,996,715 (7% federal, 6% state, 84% institutional, 3% external sources). *Receiving aid:* Freshmen: 69% (311); all full-time undergraduates: 64% (1,166). *Average award:* Freshmen: $23,415; Undergraduates: $21,605. *Scholarships, grants, and awards:* Federal Pell, FSEOG, state, private, college/university gift aid from institutional funds.
GIFT AID (NON-NEED-BASED) *Total amount:* $10,120,735 (89% institutional, 11% external sources). *Receiving aid:* Freshmen: 68% (305). Undergraduates: 62% (1,121). *Average award:* Freshmen: $14,539. Undergraduates: $13,277. *Scholarships, grants, and awards by category:* Academic interests/achievement: 1,648 awards ($20,368,290 total): general academic interests/achievements. Creative arts/performance: 112 awards ($260,200 total): art/fine arts, music, theater/drama. Special characteristics: 409 awards ($3,150,454 total): international students, out-of-state students. *Tuition waivers:* Full or partial for employees or children of employees. *ROTC:* Army.
LOANS *Student loans:* $10,968,560 (90% need-based, 10% non-need-based). 70% of past graduating class borrowed through all loan programs. *Average indebtedness per student:* $34,889. *Average need-based loan:* Freshmen: $3868. Undergraduates: $4099. *Parent loans:* $1,214,493 (91% need-based, 9% non-need-based). *Programs:* Federal Direct (Subsidized and Unsubsidized Stafford, PLUS), Perkins, state, alternative loans.
WORK-STUDY *Federal work-study:* Total amount: $1,262,728; 465 jobs averaging $2727. *State or other work-study/employment:* Total amount: $1,733,123 (66% need-based, 34% non-need-based). 690 part-time jobs averaging $2752.
APPLYING FOR FINANCIAL AID *Required financial aid forms:* FAFSA, institution's own form, federal income tax form(s). *Financial aid deadline (priority):* 3/15. *Notification date:* Continuous beginning 3/15. Students must reply by 5/1 or within 3 weeks of notification.
CONTACT Ms. Mary Dehler, Senior Associate Director of Financial Aid, Saint John's University, PO Box 5000, Collegeville, MN 56321-5000, 320-363-3664 or toll-free 800-544-1489. *Fax:* 320-363-3102. *E-mail:* mdehler@csbsju.edu.
Website: http://www.csbsju.edu/.

ST. JOHN'S UNIVERSITY
Queens, NY

Tuition & fees: $35,520	Average undergraduate aid package: $23,468

ABOUT THE INSTITUTION Independent Roman Catholic Church, coed. *Awards:* certificates, associate, bachelor's, master's, and doctoral degrees. 70 undergraduate majors. *Total enrollment:* 21,087. Undergraduates: 15,840. Freshmen: 2,792. Federal methodology is used as a basis for awarding need-based institutional aid.
UNDERGRADUATE EXPENSES for 2013–2014 *Application fee:* $50. *Comprehensive fee:* $50,790 includes full-time tuition ($34,750), mandatory fees ($770), and room and board ($15,270). *College room only:* $9550. Full-time tuition and fees vary according to course load, program, and student level. Room and board charges vary according to board plan, housing facility, and location. *Part-time tuition:* $1158 per credit. *Part-time fees:* $287.50 per term. Part-time tuition and fees vary according to course load, program, and student level.

FRESHMAN FINANCIAL AID (Fall 2011) 2,505 applied for aid; of those 94% were deemed to have need. 100% of freshmen with need received aid; of those 12% had need fully met. *Average percent of need met:* 86% (excluding resources awarded to replace EFC). *Average financial aid package:* $27,045 (excluding resources awarded to replace EFC). 5% of all full-time freshmen had no need and received non-need-based gift aid.

UNDERGRADUATE FINANCIAL AID (Fall 2011) 9,814 applied for aid; of those 95% were deemed to have need. 100% of undergraduates with need received aid; of those 10% had need fully met. *Average percent of need met:* 70% (excluding resources awarded to replace EFC). *Average financial aid package:* $23,468 (excluding resources awarded to replace EFC). 3% of all full-time undergraduates had no need and received non-need-based gift aid.

GIFT AID (NEED-BASED) *Total amount:* $105,991,243 (23% federal, 13% state, 64% institutional). *Receiving aid:* Freshmen: 77% (2,121); all full-time undergraduates: 73% (8,284). *Average award:* Freshmen: $14,275; Undergraduates: $13,255. *Scholarships, grants, and awards:* Federal Pell, FSEOG, state, private, college/university gift aid from institutional funds.

GIFT AID (NON-NEED-BASED) *Total amount:* $96,373,678 (1% state, 90% institutional, 9% external sources). *Receiving aid:* Freshmen: 77% (2,122). Undergraduates: 62% (7,006). *Average award:* Freshmen: $12,628. Undergraduates: $12,133. *Scholarships, grants, and awards by category: Academic interests/achievement:* 6,703 awards ($70,418,414 total): biological sciences, business, communication, computer science, education, English, foreign languages, general academic interests/achievements, health fields, humanities, mathematics, military science, physical sciences, premedicine, social sciences. *Creative arts/performance:* 109 awards ($301,972 total): art/fine arts, cinema/film/broadcasting, creative writing, dance, debating, journalism/publications, music. *Special achievements/activities:* 482 awards ($1,057,639 total): cheerleading/drum major, community service, general special achievements/activities, hobbies/interests, leadership, religious involvement. *Special characteristics:* 1,106 awards ($10,341,024 total): children of faculty/staff, general special characteristics, local/state students, relatives of clergy, religious affiliation. *Tuition waivers:* Full or partial for employees or children of employees, senior citizens. *ROTC:* Army.

LOANS *Student loans:* $71,945,984 (44% need-based, 56% non-need-based). 71% of past graduating class borrowed through all loan programs. *Average indebtedness per student:* $29,199. *Average need-based loan:* Freshmen: $3621. Undergraduates: $4682. *Parent loans:* $66,726,792 (100% non-need-based). *Programs:* Federal Direct (Subsidized and Unsubsidized Stafford, PLUS), Perkins, Federal Health Professions Loans.

WORK-STUDY *Federal work-study:* Total amount: $2,117,706; 835 jobs averaging $2512.

ATHLETIC AWARDS Total amount: $6,135,382 (100% non-need-based).

APPLYING FOR FINANCIAL AID *Required financial aid form:* FAFSA. *Financial aid deadline (priority):* 2/1. *Notification date:* Continuous beginning 3/15. Students must reply by 5/1 or within 2 weeks of notification.

CONTACT Mr. Jorge Rodriguez, Associate Vice President for Student Financial Services, St. John's University, 8000 Utopia Parkway, Queens, NY 11439, 718-990-2000 or toll-free 888-9STJOHNS. *Fax:* 718-990-5945. *E-mail:* studentfinancialserv@stjohns.edu. *Website:* http://www.stjohns.edu/.

ST. JOHN VIANNEY COLLEGE SEMINARY
Miami, FL

CONTACT Ms. Bonnie DeAngulo, Director of Financial Aid, St. John Vianney College Seminary, 2900 Southwest 87th Avenue, Miami, FL 33165-3244, 305-223-4561 Ext. 10. *Website:* http://www.sjvcs.edu/.

SAINT JOSEPH'S COLLEGE
Rensselaer, IN

Tuition & fees: $27,350	Average undergraduate aid package: $24,940

ABOUT THE INSTITUTION Independent Roman Catholic, coed. *Awards:* diplomas, associate, bachelor's, and master's degrees. 31 undergraduate majors. *Total enrollment:* 1,084. Undergraduates: 1,074. Freshmen: 235. Federal methodology is used as a basis for awarding need-based institutional aid.

UNDERGRADUATE EXPENSES for 2013–2014 *Application fee:* $25. *Comprehensive fee:* $35,600 includes full-time tuition ($27,160), mandatory fees ($190), and room and board ($8250). *College room only:* $4010. Full-time tuition and fees vary according to reciprocity agreements. Room and board charges vary according to housing facility. *Part-time tuition:* $910 per credit. Part-time tuition and fees vary according to course load and reciprocity agreements.

FRESHMAN FINANCIAL AID (Fall 2011) 263 applied for aid; of those 93% were deemed to have need. 100% of freshmen with need received aid; of those 23% had need fully met. *Average percent of need met:* 79% (excluding resources awarded to replace EFC). *Average financial aid package:* $24,409 (excluding resources awarded to replace EFC). 6% of all full-time freshmen had no need and received non-need-based gift aid.

UNDERGRADUATE FINANCIAL AID (Fall 2011) 800 applied for aid; of those 89% were deemed to have need. 100% of undergraduates with need received aid; of those 28% had need fully met. *Average percent of need met:* 81% (excluding resources awarded to replace EFC). *Average financial aid package:* $24,940 (excluding resources awarded to replace EFC). 10% of all full-time undergraduates had no need and received non-need-based gift aid.

GIFT AID (NEED-BASED) *Total amount:* $10,526,541 (16% federal, 12% state, 70% institutional, 2% external sources). *Receiving aid:* Freshmen: 92% (242); all full-time undergraduates: 87% (695). *Average award:* Freshmen: $18,439; Undergraduates: $17,827. *Scholarships, grants, and awards:* Federal Pell, FSEOG, state, private, college/university gift aid from institutional funds.

GIFT AID (NON-NEED-BASED) *Total amount:* $1,967,192 (97% institutional, 3% external sources). *Receiving aid:* Freshmen: 24% (63). Undergraduates: 23% (187). *Average award:* Freshmen: $16,824. Undergraduates: $14,628. *Scholarships, grants, and awards by category: Academic interests/achievement:* 565 awards ($6,359,113 total): general academic interests/achievements. *Creative arts/performance:* 140 awards ($321,377 total): cinema/film/broadcasting, dance, music, theater/drama. *Special achievements/activities:* 15 awards ($31,800 total): cheerleading/drum major. *Special characteristics:* 99 awards ($306,078 total): children and siblings of alumni, children of faculty/staff, siblings of current students. *Tuition waivers:* Full or partial for minority students, children of alumni, employees or children of employees.

LOANS *Student loans:* $5,190,252 (88% need-based, 12% non-need-based). 81% of past graduating class borrowed through all loan programs. *Average indebtedness per student:* $30,963. *Average need-based loan:* Freshmen: $3846. Undergraduates: $4362. *Parent loans:* $1,504,639 (68% need-based, 32% non-need-based). *Programs:* Federal Direct (Subsidized and Unsubsidized Stafford, PLUS), Perkins.

WORK-STUDY *Federal work-study:* Total amount: $96,948; 107 jobs averaging $935.

ATHLETIC AWARDS Total amount: $2,633,208 (62% need-based, 38% non-need-based).

APPLYING FOR FINANCIAL AID *Required financial aid form:* FAFSA. *Financial aid deadline (priority):* 3/1. *Notification date:* Continuous beginning 3/1. Students must reply by 5/1 or within 2 weeks of notification.

CONTACT Debra Sizemore, Director of Student Financial Services, Saint Joseph's College, 1498 South College Avenue, PO Box 971, Rensselaer, IN 47978, 219-866-6163 or toll-free 800-447-8781. *Fax:* 219-866-6144. *E-mail:* debbie@saintjoe.edu. *Website:* http://www.saintjoe.edu/.

ST. JOSEPH'S COLLEGE, LONG ISLAND CAMPUS
Patchogue, NY

Tuition & fees: $20,125	Average undergraduate aid package: $11,309

ABOUT THE INSTITUTION Independent, coed. *Awards:* certificates, bachelor's, and master's degrees. 36 undergraduate majors. *Total enrollment:* 4,113. Undergraduates: 3,522. Freshmen: 378. Federal methodology is used as a basis for awarding need-based institutional aid.

UNDERGRADUATE EXPENSES for 2013–2014 *Application fee:* $25. *Tuition:* full-time $19,500; part-time $635 per credit hour. Full-time tuition and fees vary according to course load, degree level, and program. Part-time tuition and fees vary according to course load, degree level, and program.

FRESHMAN FINANCIAL AID (Fall 2011) 433 applied for aid; of those 71% were deemed to have need. 99% of freshmen with need received aid; of those 30% had need fully met. *Average percent of need met:* 72% (excluding resources awarded to replace EFC). *Average financial aid package:* $12,118 (excluding resources awarded to replace EFC). 23% of all full-time freshmen had no need and received non-need-based gift aid.

UNDERGRADUATE FINANCIAL AID (Fall 2011) 2,811 applied for aid; of those 75% were deemed to have need. 99% of undergraduates with need received aid; of those 24% had need fully met. *Average percent of need met:* 67% (excluding resources awarded to replace EFC). *Average financial aid package:* $11,309 (excluding resources awarded to replace EFC). 17% of all full-time undergraduates had no need and received non-need-based gift aid.

GIFT AID (NEED-BASED) *Total amount:* $18,137,833 (21% federal, 17% state, 62% institutional). *Receiving aid:* Freshmen: 68% (299); all full-time undergraduates: 66% (1,964). *Average award:* Freshmen: $9001; Undergraduates: $8006. *Scholarships, grants, and awards:* Federal Pell, FSEOG, state, private, college/university gift aid from institutional funds.

GIFT AID (NON-NEED-BASED) *Total amount:* $4,440,058 (4% state, 93% institutional, 3% external sources). *Receiving aid:* Freshmen: 58% (256). Undergraduates: 49% (1,459). *Average award:* Freshmen: $9166. Undergraduates: $7797. *Scholarships, grants, and awards by category:* Academic interests/achievement: 1,920 awards ($13,466,072 total): general academic interests/achievements. Special achievements/activities: 10 awards ($25,000 total): community service, leadership. Special characteristics: 224 awards ($689,539 total): children and siblings of alumni, children of faculty/staff, parents of current students, public servants, siblings of current students, spouses of current students, twins. *Tuition waivers:* Full or partial for employees or children of employees, senior citizens.

LOANS *Student loans:* $18,051,821 (75% need-based, 25% non-need-based). 71% of past graduating class borrowed through all loan programs. *Average indebtedness per student:* $25,137. *Average need-based loan:* Freshmen: $3106. Undergraduates: $4237. *Parent loans:* $5,210,070 (75% need-based, 25% non-need-based). *Programs:* Federal Direct (Subsidized and Unsubsidized Stafford, PLUS), Perkins, state.

WORK-STUDY *Federal work-study:* Total amount: $194,385; 83 jobs averaging $2342. *State or other work-study/employment:* Total amount: $385,189 (68% need-based, 32% non-need-based). 131 part-time jobs averaging $2940.

APPLYING FOR FINANCIAL AID *Required financial aid forms:* FAFSA, state aid form. *Financial aid deadline (priority):* 2/25. *Notification date:* Continuous beginning 3/15. Students must reply by 5/1 or within 2 weeks of notification.

CONTACT Amy Thompson, Director of Financial Aid, St. Joseph's College, Long Island Campus, 155 West Roe Boulevard, Patchogue, NY 11772-2399, 631-687-2611. *Fax:* 631-650-2525. *E-mail:* althompson@sjcny.edu. *Website:* http://www.sjcny.edu/.

ST. JOSEPH'S COLLEGE, NEW YORK
Brooklyn, NY

Tuition & fees: $20,115	Average undergraduate aid package: $13,853

ABOUT THE INSTITUTION Independent, coed. *Awards:* certificates, bachelor's, and master's degrees. 39 undergraduate majors. *Total enrollment:* 1,519. Undergraduates: 1,299. Freshmen: 211. Federal methodology is used as a basis for awarding need-based institutional aid.

UNDERGRADUATE EXPENSES for 2013–2014 *Application fee:* $25. *Tuition:* full-time $19,500; part-time $635 per credit hour. Full-time tuition and fees vary according to course load, degree level, and program. Part-time tuition and fees vary according to course load, degree level, and program.

FRESHMAN FINANCIAL AID (Fall 2011) 193 applied for aid; of those 78% were deemed to have need. 100% of freshmen with need received aid; of those 16% had need fully met. *Average percent of need met:* 72% (excluding resources awarded to replace EFC). *Average financial aid package:* $15,145 (excluding resources awarded to replace EFC). 22% of all full-time freshmen had no need and received non-need-based gift aid.

UNDERGRADUATE FINANCIAL AID (Fall 2011) 880 applied for aid; of those 84% were deemed to have need. 100% of undergraduates with need received aid; of those 15% had need fully met. *Average percent of need met:* 66% (excluding resources awarded to replace EFC). *Average financial aid package:* $13,853 (excluding resources awarded to replace EFC). 16% of all full-time undergraduates had no need and received non-need-based gift aid.

GIFT AID (NEED-BASED) *Total amount:* $8,481,022 (28% federal, 19% state, 53% institutional). *Receiving aid:* Freshmen: 74% (151); all full-time undergraduates: 77% (728). *Average award:* Freshmen: $12,431; Undergraduates: $10,680. *Scholarships, grants, and awards:* Federal Pell, FSEOG, state, private, college/university gift aid from institutional funds.

GIFT AID (NON-NEED-BASED) *Total amount:* $1,495,371 (1% state, 94% institutional, 5% external sources). *Receiving aid:* Freshmen: 67% (138). Undergraduates: 62% (584). *Average award:* Freshmen: $10,180. Undergraduates: $9013. *Scholarships, grants, and awards by category:* Academic interests/achievement: 512 awards ($3,643,642 total): general academic interests/achievements. Special achievements/activities: 4 awards ($10,000 total): community service, leadership. Special characteristics: 82 awards ($218,725 total): children and siblings of alumni, children of faculty/staff, parents of current students, public servants, siblings of current students, spouses of current students, twins. *Tuition waivers:* Full or partial for employees or children of employees, senior citizens.

LOANS *Student loans:* $5,060,241 (86% need-based, 14% non-need-based). 62% of past graduating class borrowed through all loan programs. *Average indebtedness per student:* $25,836. *Average need-based loan:* Freshmen: $2865. Undergraduates: $3742. *Parent loans:* $809,930 (73% need-based, 27% non-need-based). *Programs:* Federal Direct (Subsidized and Unsubsidized Stafford, PLUS), Perkins, state.

WORK-STUDY *Federal work-study:* Total amount: $202,089; 112 jobs averaging $1804. *State or other work-study/employment:* Total amount: $44,607 (67% need-based, 33% non-need-based). 23 part-time jobs averaging $1939.

APPLYING FOR FINANCIAL AID *Required financial aid forms:* FAFSA, state aid form. *Financial aid deadline (priority):* 2/25. *Notification date:* Continuous beginning 3/15. Students must reply by 5/1 or within 2 weeks of notification.

CONTACT Ms. Amy Thompson, Director of Financial Aid, St. Joseph's College, New York, 245 Clinton Avenue, Brooklyn, NY 11205-3688, 718-940-5713. *Fax:* 718-636-6827. *E-mail:* althompson@sjcny.edu. *Website:* http://www.sjcny.edu/.

SAINT JOSEPH'S COLLEGE OF MAINE
Standish, ME

CONTACT Office of Financial Aid, Saint Joseph's College of Maine, 278 Whites Bridge Road, Standish, ME 04084-5263, 800-752-1266 or toll-free 800-338-7057. *Fax:* 207-893-6699. *E-mail:* finaid@sjcme.edu. *Website:* http://www.sjcme.edu/.

SAINT JOSEPH SEMINARY COLLEGE
Saint Benedict, LA

Tuition & fees: $15,140	Average undergraduate aid package: N/A

ABOUT THE INSTITUTION Independent Roman Catholic, coed, primarily men. **Awards:** bachelor's degrees (Religious Studies Institute is coed). 1 undergraduate major. **Total enrollment:** 107. Undergraduates: 107. Freshmen: 11. Federal methodology is used as a basis for awarding need-based institutional aid.

UNDERGRADUATE EXPENSES for 2013–2014 One-time required fee: $150. **Comprehensive fee:** $28,180 includes full-time tuition ($13,500), mandatory fees ($1640), and room and board ($13,040). **College room only:** $6850. **Part-time tuition:** $175 per credit hour.

GIFT AID (NEED-BASED) Total amount: $196,393 (53% federal, 47% state). **Scholarships, grants, and awards:** Federal Pell, state, private, college/university gift aid from institutional funds.

LOANS Student loans: $9160 (100% need-based).

WORK-STUDY Federal work-study jobs available. **State or other work-study/ employment:** Part-time jobs available.

APPLYING FOR FINANCIAL AID Required financial aid form: FAFSA. **Financial aid deadline (priority):** 8/15. **Notification date:** Continuous beginning 7/1. Students must reply within 4 weeks of notification.

CONTACT George J. Binder Jr., Diector of Student Financial Aid, Saint Joseph Seminary College, 75376 River Road, Saint Benedict, LA 70457, 985-867-2248. *Fax:* 985-867-2270. *E-mail:* gbinder@sjasc.edu. *Website:* http://www.sjasc.edu/.

SAINT JOSEPH'S UNIVERSITY
Philadelphia, PA

Tuition & fees: $37,830	Average undergraduate aid package: $22,124

ABOUT THE INSTITUTION Independent Roman Catholic (Jesuit), coed. **Awards:** certificates, associate, bachelor's, master's, and doctoral degrees. 55 undergraduate majors. **Total enrollment:** 8,805. Undergraduates: 5,342. Freshmen: 1,231. Federal methodology is used as a basis for awarding need-based institutional aid.

UNDERGRADUATE EXPENSES for 2013–2014 Application fee: $60. **Comprehensive fee:** $50,630 includes full-time tuition ($37,670), mandatory fees ($160), and room and board ($12,800). **College room only:** $8105. Full-time tuition and fees vary according to course load. Room and board charges vary according to board plan and housing facility. **Part-time tuition:** $500 per credit. **Payment plan:** Tuition prepayment.

FRESHMAN FINANCIAL AID (Fall 2012, est.) 1,029 applied for aid; of those 77% were deemed to have need. 100% of freshmen with need received aid; of those 23% had need fully met. **Average percent of need met:** 77% (excluding resources awarded to replace EFC). **Average financial aid package:** $24,005 (excluding resources awarded to replace EFC). 30% of all full-time freshmen had no need and received non-need-based gift aid.

UNDERGRADUATE FINANCIAL AID (Fall 2012, est.) 3,245 applied for aid; of those 81% were deemed to have need. 100% of undergraduates with need received aid; of those 23% had need fully met. **Average percent of need met:** 76% (excluding resources awarded to replace EFC). **Average financial aid package:** $22,124 (excluding resources awarded to replace EFC). 39% of all full-time undergraduates had no need and received non-need-based gift aid.

GIFT AID (NEED-BASED) Total amount: $45,879,145 (5% federal, 3% state, 90% institutional, 2% external sources). **Receiving aid:** Freshmen: 63% (779); all full-time undergraduates: 58% (2,563). **Average award:** Freshmen: $19,990; Undergraduates: $17,323. **Scholarships, grants, and awards:** Federal Pell, FSEOG, state, private, college/university gift aid from institutional funds.

GIFT AID (NON-NEED-BASED) Total amount: $19,770,272 (98% institutional, 2% external sources). **Receiving aid:** Freshmen: 62% (762). Undergraduates: 55% (2,437). **Average award:** Freshmen: $11,000. Undergraduates: $11,330. **Scholarships, grants, and awards by category:** Academic interests/achievement: general academic interests/achievements. Creative arts/performance: debating, general creative arts/performance, theater/drama. Special achievements/activities: community service, general special achievements/activities. Special characteristics: children and siblings of alumni, children of faculty/staff, first-generation college students, international students, members of minority groups, veterans, veterans' children. **Tuition waivers:** Full or partial for employees or children of employees. **ROTC:** Army cooperative, Naval cooperative, Air Force.

LOANS Student loans: $24,940,960 (85% need-based, 15% non-need-based). **Average need-based loan:** Freshmen: $4500. Undergraduates: $5500. **Parent loans:** $21,319,103 (85% need-based, 15% non-need-based). **Programs:** Federal Direct (Subsidized and Unsubsidized Stafford, PLUS), Perkins.

WORK-STUDY Federal work-study: Total amount: $764,400; jobs available.

ATHLETIC AWARDS Total amount: $5,017,887 (51% need-based, 49% non-need-based).

APPLYING FOR FINANCIAL AID Required financial aid form: FAFSA. **Financial aid deadline (priority):** 2/15. **Notification date:** Continuous beginning 3/31. Students must reply by 5/1.

CONTACT Eileen M. Tucker, Director of Financial Assistance, Saint Joseph's University, 5600 City Avenue, Philadelphia, PA 19131-1395, 610-660-1555 or toll-free 888-BE-A-HAWK (in-state), 800-BE-A-HAWK (out-of-state). *Fax:* 610-660-1342. *E-mail:* finaid@sju.edu. *Website:* http://www.sju.edu/.

ST. LAWRENCE UNIVERSITY
Canton, NY

Tuition & fees: $44,390	Average undergraduate aid package: $38,941

ABOUT THE INSTITUTION Independent, coed. **Awards:** certificates, bachelor's, and master's degrees. 41 undergraduate majors. **Total enrollment:** 2,488. Undergraduates: 2,398. Freshmen: 642. Both federal and institutional methodology are used as a basis for awarding need-based institutional aid.

UNDERGRADUATE EXPENSES for 2013–2014 Application fee: $60. **Comprehensive fee:** $55,825 includes full-time tuition ($44,075), mandatory fees ($315), and room and board ($11,435). **College room only:** $6155. Room and board charges vary according to board plan.

FRESHMAN FINANCIAL AID (Fall 2012, est.) 469 applied for aid; of those 88% were deemed to have need. 100% of freshmen with need received aid; of those 33% had need fully met. **Average percent of need met:** 89% (excluding resources awarded to replace EFC). **Average financial aid package:** $39,811 (excluding resources awarded to replace EFC). 30% of all full-time freshmen had no need and received non-need-based gift aid.

UNDERGRADUATE FINANCIAL AID (Fall 2012, est.) 1,674 applied for aid; of those 90% were deemed to have need. 100% of undergraduates with need received aid; of those 39% had need fully met. **Average percent of need met:** 88% (excluding resources awarded to replace EFC). **Average financial aid package:** $38,941 (excluding resources awarded to replace EFC). 26% of all full-time undergraduates had no need and received non-need-based gift aid.

GIFT AID (NEED-BASED) Total amount: $43,636,789 (5% federal, 4% state, 88% institutional, 3% external sources). **Receiving aid:** Freshmen: 63% (404); all full-time undergraduates: 62% (1,461). **Average award:** Freshmen: $31,089; Undergraduates: $29,285. **Scholarships, grants, and awards:** Federal Pell, FSEOG, state, private, college/university gift aid from institutional funds, TEACH Grants.

GIFT AID (NON-NEED-BASED) Total amount: $11,383,545 (100% institutional). **Receiving aid:** Freshmen: 9% (58). Undergraduates: 9% (202). **Average award:** Freshmen: $17,957. Undergraduates: $18,579. **Scholarships, grants, and awards by category:** Academic interests/achievement: 1,374 awards ($27,998,462 total): general academic interests/achievements. Special achievements/activities: 64 awards ($696,000 total): community service, leadership. Special characteristics: 402 awards ($1,002,010 total): children and siblings of alumni, siblings of current students, veterans' children. **Tuition waivers:** Full or partial for employees or children of employees. **ROTC:** Army cooperative, Air Force cooperative.

LOANS Student loans: $11,277,906 (44% need-based, 56% non-need-based). 61% of past graduating class borrowed through all loan programs. *Average indebtedness per student:* $25,058. **Average need-based loan:** Freshmen: $3279. Undergraduates: $4433. **Parent loans:** $5,322,368 (100% non-need-based). **Programs:** Federal Direct (Subsidized and Unsubsidized Stafford, PLUS), Perkins, college/university.

WORK-STUDY Federal work-study: Total amount: $1,337,482; 844 jobs averaging $1585. **State or other work-study/employment:** Total amount: $529,230 (100% non-need-based). 339 part-time jobs averaging $1561.

ATHLETIC AWARDS Total amount: $1,951,790 (100% non-need-based).
APPLYING FOR FINANCIAL AID *Required financial aid forms:* FAFSA, CSS Financial Aid PROFILE, noncustodial (divorced/separated) parent's statement, business/farm supplement. *Financial aid deadline:* 2/1. *Notification date:* 3/30. Students must reply by 5/1 or within 2 weeks of notification.
CONTACT Mrs. Patricia J.B. Farmer, Director of Financial Aid, St. Lawrence University, Payson Hall, 23 Romoda Drive, Canton, NY 13617-1455, 315-229-5265 or toll-free 800-285-1856. *Fax:* 315-229-7418. *E-mail:* pfarmer@stlawu.edu. *Website:* http://www.stlawu.edu/.

SAINT LEO UNIVERSITY
Saint Leo, FL

ABOUT THE INSTITUTION Independent Roman Catholic, coed. *Awards:* certificates, associate, bachelor's, and master's degrees. 34 undergraduate majors. *Total enrollment:* 5,383. Undergraduates: 2,167. Freshmen: 634.
GIFT AID (NEED-BASED) *Scholarships, grants, and awards:* Federal Pell, FSEOG, state, private, college/university gift aid from institutional funds, United Negro College Fund.
LOANS *Programs:* Federal Direct (Subsidized and Unsubsidized Stafford, PLUS).
WORK-STUDY *Federal work-study:* Total amount: $2,289,463; 711 jobs averaging $3220.
APPLYING FOR FINANCIAL AID *Required financial aid form:* FAFSA.
CONTACT Ms. Christine Gibson, Associate Vice President of Business Affairs, Saint Leo University, PO Box 6665, MC 2228, Saint Leo, FL 33574-6665, 800-240-7658 or toll-free 800-334-5532. *Fax:* 352-588-8403. *E-mail:* finaid@saintleo.edu. *Website:* http://www.saintleo.edu/.

SAINT LOUIS CHRISTIAN COLLEGE
Florissant, MO

Tuition & fees: $8215	Average undergraduate aid package: $18,610

ABOUT THE INSTITUTION Independent Christian, coed. *Awards:* associate and bachelor's degrees. 5 undergraduate majors. *Total enrollment:* 246. Undergraduates: 246. Freshmen: 23. Federal methodology is used as a basis for awarding need-based institutional aid.
UNDERGRADUATE EXPENSES for 2013–2014 *Comprehensive fee:* $12,215 includes full-time tuition ($8215) and room and board ($4000). Room and board charges vary according to housing facility.
FRESHMAN FINANCIAL AID (Fall 2012, est.) 18 applied for aid; of those 89% were deemed to have need. 100% of freshmen with need received aid. *Average percent of need met:* 77% (excluding resources awarded to replace EFC). *Average financial aid package:* $20,737 (excluding resources awarded to replace EFC). 9% of all full-time freshmen had no need and received non-need-based gift aid.
UNDERGRADUATE FINANCIAL AID (Fall 2012, est.) 176 applied for aid; of those 91% were deemed to have need. 100% of undergraduates with need received aid; of those 8% had need fully met. *Average percent of need met:* 74% (excluding resources awarded to replace EFC). *Average financial aid package:* $18,610 (excluding resources awarded to replace EFC). 16% of all full-time undergraduates had no need and received non-need-based gift aid.
GIFT AID (NEED-BASED) *Total amount:* $2,704,784 (25% federal, 72% institutional, 3% external sources). *Receiving aid:* Freshmen: 70% (16); all full-time undergraduates: 77% (161). *Average award:* Freshmen: $17,080; Undergraduates: $15,064. *Scholarships, grants, and awards:* Federal Pell, FSEOG, state, private, college/university gift aid from institutional funds.
GIFT AID (NON-NEED-BASED) *Total amount:* $311,320 (100% institutional). *Average award:* Freshmen: $16,320. Undergraduates: $9127. *Tuition waivers:* Full or partial for employees or children of employees.
LOANS *Student loans:* $1,427,083 (95% need-based, 5% non-need-based). 91% of past graduating class borrowed through all loan programs. *Average indebtedness per student:* $22,586. *Average need-based loan:* Freshmen: $2946. Undergraduates: $3542. *Parent loans:* $50,255 (83% need-based, 17% non-need-based). *Programs:* Federal Direct (Subsidized and Unsubsidized Stafford, PLUS), private loans.

WORK-STUDY *Federal work-study:* Total amount: $23,940; jobs available. *State or other work-study/employment:* Total amount: $130,000 (100% non-need-based). Part-time jobs available.
APPLYING FOR FINANCIAL AID *Required financial aid form:* FAFSA. *Financial aid deadline:* Continuous. *Notification date:* Continuous.
CONTACT Mrs. Catherine Wilhoit, Director of Financial Aid, Saint Louis Christian College, 1360 Grandview Drive, Florissant, MO 63033-6499, 314-837-6777 Ext. 1101 or toll-free 800-887-SLCC. *Fax:* 314-837-8291. *Website:* http://www.slcconline.edu/.

ST. LOUIS COLLEGE OF PHARMACY
St. Louis, MO

Tuition & fees: $26,125	Average undergraduate aid package: $14,171

ABOUT THE INSTITUTION Independent, coed. *Awards:* doctoral degrees. 1 undergraduate major. *Total enrollment:* 1,299. Undergraduates: 714. Freshmen: 247. Federal methodology is used as a basis for awarding need-based institutional aid.
UNDERGRADUATE EXPENSES for 2013–2014 *Application fee:* $50. *Comprehensive fee:* $35,405 includes full-time tuition ($25,800), mandatory fees ($325), and room and board ($9280). *College room only:* $5475. Full-time tuition and fees vary according to student level. Room and board charges vary according to housing facility. *Part-time tuition:* $845 per credit.
FRESHMAN FINANCIAL AID (Fall 2012, est.) 231 applied for aid; of those 85% were deemed to have need. 99% of freshmen with need received aid; of those 14% had need fully met. *Average percent of need met:* 55% (excluding resources awarded to replace EFC). *Average financial aid package:* $14,617 (excluding resources awarded to replace EFC). 20% of all full-time freshmen had no need and received non-need-based gift aid.
UNDERGRADUATE FINANCIAL AID (Fall 2012, est.) 626 applied for aid; of those 90% were deemed to have need. 99% of undergraduates with need received aid; of those 8% had need fully met. *Average percent of need met:* 46% (excluding resources awarded to replace EFC). *Average financial aid package:* $14,171 (excluding resources awarded to replace EFC). 18% of all full-time undergraduates had no need and received non-need-based gift aid.
GIFT AID (NEED-BASED) *Total amount:* $4,402,097 (19% federal, 7% state, 66% institutional, 8% external sources). *Receiving aid:* Freshmen: 80% (195); all full-time undergraduates: 71% (504). *Average award:* Freshmen: $9639; Undergraduates: $9054. *Scholarships, grants, and awards:* Federal Pell, FSEOG, state, private, college/university gift aid from institutional funds.
GIFT AID (NON-NEED-BASED) *Total amount:* $1,064,098 (2% state, 86% institutional, 12% external sources). *Receiving aid:* Freshmen: 8% (19). Undergraduates: 4% (30). *Average award:* Freshmen: $6260. Undergraduates: $6366. *Scholarships, grants, and awards by category:* Academic interests/achievement: 615 awards ($4,024,557 total): general academic interests/achievements. *Special achievements/activities:* 23 awards ($71,000 total): community service, leadership. *Special characteristics:* children of faculty/staff, local/state students. *Tuition waivers:* Full or partial for employees or children of employees. *ROTC:* Army cooperative, Naval cooperative, Air Force cooperative.
LOANS *Student loans:* $7,595,811 (80% need-based, 20% non-need-based). 87% of past graduating class borrowed through all loan programs. *Average indebtedness per student:* $119,711. *Average need-based loan:* Freshmen: $5295. Undergraduates: $5875. *Parent loans:* $2,053,866 (62% need-based, 38% non-need-based). *Programs:* Federal Direct (Subsidized and Unsubsidized Stafford, PLUS), Perkins, Health Professions Student Loans (HPSL).
WORK-STUDY *Federal work-study:* Total amount: $341,985; 366 jobs averaging $767.
ATHLETIC AWARDS Total amount: $128,840 (65% need-based, 35% non-need-based).
APPLYING FOR FINANCIAL AID *Required financial aid forms:* FAFSA, institution's own form. *Financial aid deadline (priority):* 3/15. *Notification date:* Continuous beginning 3/15. Students must reply within 2 weeks of notification.
CONTACT Mr. Dan Stiffler, Director of Financial Aid, St. Louis College of Pharmacy, 4588 Parkview Place, St. Louis, MO 63110, 314-446-8321 or toll-free 800-278-5267 (in-state), 800-278-267 (out-of-state). *Fax:* 314-446-8310. *E-mail:* daniel.stiffler@stlcop.edu. *Website:* http://www.stlcop.edu/.

SAINT LOUIS UNIVERSITY
St. Louis, MO

Tuition & fees: $35,266	Average undergraduate aid package: $25,925

ABOUT THE INSTITUTION Independent Roman Catholic (Jesuit), coed. *Awards:* certificates, bachelor's, master's, and doctoral degrees. 86 undergraduate majors. *Total enrollment:* 13,981. Undergraduates: 8,806. Freshmen: 1,687. Federal methodology is used as a basis for awarding need-based institutional aid.

UNDERGRADUATE EXPENSES for 2013–2014 Comprehensive fee: $44,878 includes full-time tuition ($34,740), mandatory fees ($526), and room and board ($9612). *College room only:* $5444. Full-time tuition and fees vary according to location and program. Room and board charges vary according to board plan, housing facility, and location. *Part-time tuition:* $1215 per credit hour. *Part-time fees:* $153 per term. Part-time tuition and fees vary according to location and program.

FRESHMAN FINANCIAL AID (Fall 2011) 1,427 applied for aid; of those 83% were deemed to have need. 100% of freshmen with need received aid; of those 18% had need fully met. *Average percent of need met:* 71% (excluding resources awarded to replace EFC). *Average financial aid package:* $26,900 (excluding resources awarded to replace EFC). 25% of all full-time freshmen had no need and received non-need-based gift aid.

UNDERGRADUATE FINANCIAL AID (Fall 2011) 5,069 applied for aid; of those 89% were deemed to have need. 100% of undergraduates with need received aid; of those 14% had need fully met. *Average percent of need met:* 65% (excluding resources awarded to replace EFC). *Average financial aid package:* $25,925 (excluding resources awarded to replace EFC). 25% of all full-time undergraduates had no need and received non-need-based gift aid.

GIFT AID (NEED-BASED) Total amount: $85,629,698 (11% federal, 3% state, 84% institutional, 2% external sources). *Receiving aid:* Freshmen: 68% (1,154); all full-time undergraduates: 55% (4,269). *Average award:* Freshmen: $21,349; Undergraduates: $19,167. *Scholarships, grants, and awards:* Federal Pell, FSEOG, state, private, college/university gift aid from institutional funds, Federal Nursing.

GIFT AID (NON-NEED-BASED) Total amount: $21,543,264 (2% state, 89% institutional, 9% external sources). *Receiving aid:* Freshmen: 7% (127). Undergraduates: 5% (357). *Average award:* Freshmen: $13,369. Undergraduates: $12,403. *Scholarships, grants, and awards by category:* Academic interests/achievement: 5,341 awards ($61,192,296 total): area/ethnic studies, biological sciences, business, communication, computer science, education, engineering/technologies, English, foreign languages, general academic interests/achievements, health fields, humanities, international studies, mathematics, military science, physical sciences, pre-medicine, religion/biblical studies, social sciences. *Creative arts/performance:* 137 awards ($132,972 total): art/fine arts, music, performing arts, theater/drama. *Special achievements/activities:* 346 awards ($4,703,032 total): cheerleading/drum major, community service, general special achievements/activities, leadership, memberships, religious involvement. *Special characteristics:* 1,274 awards ($16,981,374 total): children of faculty/staff, first-generation college students, general special characteristics, international students, members of minority groups, previous college experience, religious affiliation, siblings of current students. *Tuition waivers:* Full or partial for children of alumni, employees or children of employees. *ROTC:* Army cooperative, Air Force.

LOANS Student loans: $45,411,335 (41% need-based, 59% non-need-based). 63% of past graduating class borrowed through all loan programs. *Average indebtedness per student:* $36,797. *Average need-based loan:* Freshmen: $3820. Undergraduates: $4743. *Parent loans:* $14,618,583 (100% non-need-based). *Programs:* Federal Direct (Subsidized and Unsubsidized Stafford, PLUS), Perkins, Federal Nursing, college/university.

WORK-STUDY Federal work-study: Total amount: $1,469,553; 846 jobs averaging $1737. *State or other work-study/employment:* Total amount: $95,476 (100% non-need-based). 45 part-time jobs averaging $2122.

ATHLETIC AWARDS Total amount: $3,750,176 (47% need-based, 53% non-need-based).

APPLYING FOR FINANCIAL AID Required financial aid form: FAFSA. *Financial aid deadline (priority):* 3/1. *Notification date:* Continuous beginning 3/1. Students must reply by 5/1 or within 4 weeks of notification.

CONTACT Cari S. Wickliffe, Assistant Vice President and Director of Student Financial Services, Saint Louis University, 221 North Grand Boulevard, DuBourg Hall, Room 121, St. Louis, MO 63103-2097, 314-977-2350 or toll-free 800-758-3678. *Fax:* 314-977-3437. *E-mail:* sfs@slu.edu.
Website: http://www.slu.edu/.

SAINT LUKE'S COLLEGE OF HEALTH SCIENCES
Kansas City, MO

Tuition & fees: N/R	Average undergraduate aid package: $13,000

ABOUT THE INSTITUTION Independent Episcopal, coed, primarily women. 1 undergraduate major. Both federal and institutional methodology are used as a basis for awarding need-based institutional aid.

UNDERGRADUATE FINANCIAL AID (Fall 2012, est.) 277 applied for aid; of those 92% were deemed to have need. 100% of undergraduates with need received aid; of those 5% had need fully met. *Average percent of need met:* 60% (excluding resources awarded to replace EFC). *Average financial aid package:* $13,000 (excluding resources awarded to replace EFC).

GIFT AID (NEED-BASED) Total amount: $696,223 (52% federal, 17% state, 31% institutional). *Receiving aid:* All full-time undergraduates: 61% (177). *Average award:* Undergraduates: $2000. *Scholarships, grants, and awards:* Federal Pell, FSEOG, state, private, college/university gift aid from institutional funds.

GIFT AID (NON-NEED-BASED) Total amount: $162,839 (17% institutional, 83% external sources). *Receiving aid:* Undergraduates: 7% (21).

LOANS Student loans: $2,655,228 (45% need-based, 55% non-need-based). *Average need-based loan:* Undergraduates: $5500. *Parent loans:* $300,946 (100% non-need-based). *Programs:* Federal Direct (Subsidized and Unsubsidized Stafford, PLUS), Perkins, Federal Nursing, college/university.

WORK-STUDY Federal work-study: Total amount: $9250; 6 jobs averaging $1500.

APPLYING FOR FINANCIAL AID Notification date: Continuous.

CONTACT Jennifer Wright, Financial Aid Administrator, Saint Luke's College of Health Sciences, 624 Westport Road, Kansas City, MO 64111, 816-932-6749. *Fax:* 816-932-6760. *E-mail:* jrwright@saintlukescollege.edu.
Website: http://www.saintlukescollege.edu/.

SAINT MARTIN'S UNIVERSITY
Lacey, WA

Tuition & fees: $29,834	Average undergraduate aid package: $19,370

ABOUT THE INSTITUTION Independent Roman Catholic, coed. *Awards:* certificates, bachelor's, and master's degrees. 22 undergraduate majors. *Total enrollment:* 1,823. Undergraduates: 1,479. Freshmen: 228. Federal methodology is used as a basis for awarding need-based institutional aid.

UNDERGRADUATE EXPENSES for 2013–2014 Comprehensive fee: $39,494 includes full-time tuition ($29,500), mandatory fees ($334), and room and board ($9660). *College room only:* $4820. Full-time tuition and fees vary according to degree level, location, and program. Room and board charges vary according to board plan. *Part-time tuition:* $990 per credit. Part-time tuition and fees vary according to course load, degree level, location, and program.

FRESHMAN FINANCIAL AID (Fall 2011) 180 applied for aid; of those 89% were deemed to have need. 100% of freshmen with need received aid; of those 22% had need fully met. *Average percent of need met:* 79% (excluding resources awarded to replace EFC). *Average financial aid package:* $23,893 (excluding resources awarded to replace EFC). 11% of all full-time freshmen had no need and received non-need-based gift aid.

UNDERGRADUATE FINANCIAL AID (Fall 2011) 1,045 applied for aid; of those 92% were deemed to have need. 100% of undergraduates with need received aid; of those 17% had need fully met. *Average percent of need met:* 70% (excluding resources awarded to replace EFC). *Average financial aid package:* $19,370 (excluding resources awarded to replace EFC). 8% of all full-time undergraduates had no need and received non-need-based gift aid.

GIFT AID (NEED-BASED) Total amount: $12,899,196 (17% federal, 16% state, 59% institutional, 8% external sources). *Receiving aid:* Freshmen: 89% (160); all full-time undergraduates: 88% (935). *Average award:* Freshmen: $20,162; Undergraduates: $15,291. *Scholarships, grants, and awards:* Federal Pell, FSEOG, state, private, college/university gift aid from institutional funds.

GIFT AID (NON-NEED-BASED) *Total amount:* $1,289,461 (1% federal, 91% institutional, 8% external sources). *Receiving aid:* Freshmen: 12% (21). Undergraduates: 8% (90). *Average award:* Freshmen: $11,716. Undergraduates: $9420. *Scholarships, grants, and awards by category:* Academic interests/achievement: business, education, engineering/technologies, general academic interests/achievements, humanities, international studies, premedicine. *Creative arts/performance:* music, theater/drama. *Special achievements/activities:* community service, general special achievements/activities, hobbies/interests, leadership, religious involvement. *Special characteristics:* children and siblings of alumni, children of faculty/staff, ethnic background, general special characteristics, international students, local/state students, members of minority groups, out-of-state students, siblings of current students, veterans, veterans' children. *Tuition waivers:* Full or partial for children of alumni, employees or children of employees. *ROTC:* Army cooperative, Air Force cooperative.

LOANS *Student loans:* $9,663,578 (78% need-based, 22% non-need-based). 79% of past graduating class borrowed through all loan programs. *Average indebtedness per student:* $34,235. *Average need-based loan:* Freshmen: $3245. Undergraduates: $4145. *Parent loans:* $1,606,351 (39% need-based, 61% non-need-based). *Programs:* Federal Direct (Subsidized and Unsubsidized Stafford, PLUS), Perkins, state, private loans.

WORK-STUDY *Federal work-study:* Total amount: $399,661; 194 jobs averaging $1935. *State or other work-study/employment:* Total amount: $227,794 (100% need-based). 58 part-time jobs averaging $4854.

ATHLETIC AWARDS Total amount: $1,230,943 (69% need-based, 31% non-need-based).

APPLYING FOR FINANCIAL AID *Required financial aid form:* FAFSA. *Financial aid deadline (priority):* 4/15. *Notification date:* Continuous beginning 2/15. Students must reply within 3 weeks of notification.

CONTACT Ms. Isabelle Mora, Director of Financial Aid, Saint Martin's University, 5000 Abbey Way SE, Lacey, WA 98503-7500, 360-438-4389 or toll-free 800-368-8803. *Fax:* 360-412-6190. *E-mail:* finaid@stmartin.edu. *Website:* http://www.stmartin.edu/.

uates: $8563. *Scholarships, grants, and awards:* Federal Pell, FSEOG, state, private, college/university gift aid from institutional funds.

GIFT AID (NON-NEED-BASED) *Total amount:* $2,256,864 (2% federal, 98% institutional). *Receiving aid:* Freshmen: 38% (26). Undergraduates: 74% (319). *Average award:* Freshmen: $13,425. Undergraduates: $7512. *Scholarships, grants, and awards by category:* Academic interests/achievement: general academic interests/achievements. *Creative arts/performance:* applied art and design, art/fine arts, creative writing, dance, general creative arts/performance, journalism/publications, music, performing arts, theater/drama. *Special achievements/activities:* community service, general special achievements/activities, leadership, memberships, religious involvement. *Special characteristics:* adult students, children and siblings of alumni, children of current students, children of faculty/staff, ethnic background, first-generation college students, general special characteristics, international students, local/state students, members of minority groups, out-of-state students, parents of current students, religious affiliation, siblings of current students, spouses of current students. *Tuition waivers:* Full or partial for employees or children of employees. *ROTC:* Army cooperative, Air Force cooperative.

LOANS *Student loans:* $5,798,550 (50% need-based, 50% non-need-based). 93% of past graduating class borrowed through all loan programs. *Average indebtedness per student:* $18,742. *Average need-based loan:* Freshmen: $3823. Undergraduates: $4503. *Parent loans:* $582,978 (100% non-need-based). *Programs:* Federal Direct (Subsidized and Unsubsidized Stafford, PLUS), Perkins, college/university, private loans.

WORK-STUDY *Federal work-study:* Total amount: $66,231; 80 jobs averaging $827.

ATHLETIC AWARDS Total amount: $446,822 (100% non-need-based).

APPLYING FOR FINANCIAL AID *Required financial aid form:* FAFSA. *Financial aid deadline:* Continuous. *Notification date:* Continuous beginning 3/1. Students must reply by 5/1.

CONTACT Ms. Darla Hopper, Director of Financial Aid, Saint Mary-of-the-Woods College, 226 Guerin Hall, Saint Mary-of-the-Woods, IN 47876, 812-535-5110 or toll-free 800-926-SMWC. *Fax:* 812-535-4900. *E-mail:* dhopper@smwc.edu. *Website:* http://www.smwc.edu/.

SAINT MARY-OF-THE-WOODS COLLEGE
Saint Mary of the Woods, IN

Tuition & fees: $27,672	Average undergraduate aid package: $15,450

ABOUT THE INSTITUTION Independent Roman Catholic, coed, primarily women. *Awards:* certificates, associate, bachelor's, and master's degrees (also offers external degree program with significant enrollment not reflected in profile). 37 undergraduate majors. *Total enrollment:* 956. Undergraduates: 795. Freshmen: 72. Federal methodology is used as a basis for awarding need-based institutional aid.

UNDERGRADUATE EXPENSES for 2013–2014 *Application fee:* $30. *One-time required fee:* $225. *Comprehensive fee:* $37,472 includes full-time tuition ($26,872), mandatory fees ($800), and room and board ($9800). *College room only:* $3826. Full-time tuition and fees vary according to program and student level. Room and board charges vary according to housing facility. *Part-time tuition:* $482 per credit hour. *Part-time fees:* $150 per term. Part-time tuition and fees vary according to course load. *Payment plan:* Guaranteed tuition.

FRESHMAN FINANCIAL AID (Fall 2012, est.) 69 applied for aid; of those 94% were deemed to have need. 100% of freshmen with need received aid; of those 77% had need fully met. *Average percent of need met:* 22% (excluding resources awarded to replace EFC). *Average financial aid package:* $24,813 (excluding resources awarded to replace EFC). 6% of all full-time freshmen had no need and received non-need-based gift aid.

UNDERGRADUATE FINANCIAL AID (Fall 2012, est.) 431 applied for aid; of those 91% were deemed to have need. 100% of undergraduates with need received aid; of those 55% had need fully met. *Average percent of need met:* 27% (excluding resources awarded to replace EFC). *Average financial aid package:* $15,450 (excluding resources awarded to replace EFC). 3% of all full-time undergraduates had no need and received non-need-based gift aid.

GIFT AID (NEED-BASED) *Total amount:* $5,432,503 (32% federal, 23% state, 43% institutional, 2% external sources). *Receiving aid:* Freshmen: 78% (54); all full-time undergraduates: 73% (315). *Average award:* Freshmen: $8049; Undergrad-

SAINT MARY'S COLLEGE
Notre Dame, IN

Tuition & fees: $33,280	Average undergraduate aid package: $27,360

ABOUT THE INSTITUTION Independent Roman Catholic, women only. *Awards:* bachelor's degrees. 37 undergraduate majors. *Total enrollment:* 1,469. Undergraduates: 1,469. Freshmen: 417. Both federal and institutional methodology are used as a basis for awarding need-based institutional aid.

UNDERGRADUATE EXPENSES for 2013–2014 *Comprehensive fee:* $43,420 includes full-time tuition ($32,560), mandatory fees ($720), and room and board ($10,140). *College room only:* $6250. Room and board charges vary according to board plan and housing facility. *Part-time tuition:* $1290 per credit hour. *Part-time fees:* $360 per term.

FRESHMAN FINANCIAL AID (Fall 2012, est.) 349 applied for aid; of those 79% were deemed to have need. 100% of freshmen with need received aid; of those 28% had need fully met. *Average percent of need met:* 85% (excluding resources awarded to replace EFC). *Average financial aid package:* $27,047 (excluding resources awarded to replace EFC). 33% of all full-time freshmen had no need and received non-need-based gift aid.

UNDERGRADUATE FINANCIAL AID (Fall 2012, est.) 1,118 applied for aid; of those 73% were deemed to have need. 100% of undergraduates with need received aid; of those 24% had need fully met. *Average percent of need met:* 84% (excluding resources awarded to replace EFC). *Average financial aid package:* $27,360 (excluding resources awarded to replace EFC). 35% of all full-time undergraduates had no need and received non-need-based gift aid.

GIFT AID (NEED-BASED) *Total amount:* $18,001,853 (8% federal, 3% state, 85% institutional, 4% external sources). *Receiving aid:* Freshmen: 65% (270); all full-time undergraduates: 56% (805). *Average award:* Freshmen: $23,149; Undergraduates: $22,653. *Scholarships, grants, and awards:* Federal Pell, FSEOG, state, private, college/university gift aid from institutional funds.

GIFT AID (NON-NEED-BASED) *Total amount:* $6,537,326 (1% federal, 95% institutional, 4% external sources). *Receiving aid:* Freshmen: 61% (253). Undergraduates: 45% (647). *Average award:* Freshmen: $13,532. Undergraduates: $12,125.

Tuition waivers: Full or partial for employees or children of employees. **ROTC:** Army cooperative, Naval cooperative, Air Force cooperative.

LOANS Student loans: $7,857,127 (77% need-based, 23% non-need-based). 68% of past graduating class borrowed through all loan programs. *Average indebtedness per student:* $31,891. **Average need-based loan:** Freshmen: $3895. Undergraduates: $4753. **Parent loans:** $3,087,115 (71% need-based, 29% non-need-based).

Programs: Federal Direct (Subsidized and Unsubsidized Stafford, PLUS), Perkins.

WORK-STUDY Federal work-study: Total amount: $611,385; jobs available. **State or other work-study/employment:** Total amount: $27,200 (93% need-based, 7% non-need-based). Part-time jobs available.

APPLYING FOR FINANCIAL AID Required financial aid forms: FAFSA, CSS Financial Aid PROFILE, noncustodial (divorced/separated) parent's statement. **Financial aid deadline:** 3/1 (priority: 3/1). **Notification date:** Continuous beginning 3/15. Students must reply within 3 weeks of notification.

CONTACT Kathleen M. Brown, Director of Financial Aid, Saint Mary's College, 141 Le Mans Hall, Notre Dame, IN 46556, 574-284-4557 or toll-free 800-551-7621. *Fax:* 574-284-4818. *E-mail:* kbrown@saintmarys.edu.

Website: http://www.saintmarys.edu/.

SAINT MARY'S COLLEGE OF CALIFORNIA
Moraga, CA

Tuition & fees: $39,890	Average undergraduate aid package: $25,521

ABOUT THE INSTITUTION Independent Roman Catholic, coed. **Awards:** bachelor's, master's, and doctoral degrees. 67 undergraduate majors. **Total enrollment:** 4,228. Undergraduates: 3,035. Entering class: 39. Federal methodology is used as a basis for awarding need-based institutional aid.

UNDERGRADUATE EXPENSES for 2013–2014 Application fee: $55. **Comprehensive fee:** $53,550 includes full-time tuition ($39,740), mandatory fees ($150), and room and board ($13,660). **College room only:** $7450. Room and board charges vary according to board plan and housing facility. **Part-time tuition:** $4972 per course. Part-time tuition and fees vary according to course load and program. **Payment plan:** Tuition prepayment.

UNDERGRADUATE FINANCIAL AID (Fall 2012, est.) 2,248 applied for aid; of those 94% were deemed to have need. 100% of undergraduates with need received aid; of those 7% had need fully met. **Average percent of need met:** 60% (excluding resources awarded to replace EFC). **Average financial aid package:** $25,521 (excluding resources awarded to replace EFC). 8% of all full-time undergraduates had no need and received non-need-based gift aid.

GIFT AID (NEED-BASED) Total amount: $42,750,762 (9% federal, 13% state, 76% institutional, 2% external sources). **Receiving aid:** Entering class: 76% (474); all full-time undergraduates: 73% (2,073). **Average award:** Freshmen: $23,519; Undergraduates: $21,919. **Scholarships, grants, and awards:** Federal Pell, FSEOG, state, private, college/university gift aid from institutional funds.

GIFT AID (NON-NEED-BASED) Total amount: $3,073,714 (98% institutional, 2% external sources). **Receiving aid:** Freshmen: 27% (171). Undergraduates: 26% (742). **Average award:** Freshmen: $13,984. Undergraduates: $16,868. **Scholarships, grants, and awards by category:** Academic interests/achievement: 685 awards ($9,585,439 total): general academic interests/achievements. Creative arts/performance: 54 awards ($667,000 total): dance, debating, music, performing arts, theater/drama. Special achievements/activities: 123 awards ($1,247,439 total): leadership, memberships. Special characteristics: 63 awards ($1,638,421 total): children and siblings of alumni, children of educators, children of faculty/staff, general special characteristics, relatives of clergy, veterans, veterans' children. **Tuition waivers:** Full or partial for employees or children of employees. **ROTC:** Army cooperative, Air Force cooperative.

LOANS Student loans: $18,843,762 (94% need-based, 6% non-need-based). 77% of past graduating class borrowed through all loan programs. *Average indebtedness per student:* $31,828. **Average need-based loan:** Freshmen: $3700. Undergraduates: $4662. **Parent loans:** $10,208,025 (92% need-based, 8% non-need-based).

Programs: Federal Direct (Subsidized and Unsubsidized Stafford, PLUS), Perkins.

WORK-STUDY Federal work-study: Total amount: $665,250; 342 jobs averaging $1970.

ATHLETIC AWARDS Total amount: $5,333,772 (48% need-based, 52% non-need-based).

APPLYING FOR FINANCIAL AID Required financial aid forms: FAFSA, state aid form. **Financial aid deadline (priority):** 2/15. **Notification date:** Continuous beginning 3/15. Students must reply by 5/1 or within 2 weeks of notification.

CONTACT Priscilla Muha, Director of Financial Aid, Saint Mary's College of California, PO Box 4530, Moraga, CA 94575, 925-631-4370 or toll-free 800-800-4SMC. *Fax:* 925-376-2965. *E-mail:* finaid@stmarys-ca.edu.

Website: http://www.stmarys-ca.edu/.

ST. MARY'S COLLEGE OF MARYLAND
St. Mary's City, MD

Tuition & fees (MD res): $14,773	Average undergraduate aid package: $12,652

ABOUT THE INSTITUTION State-supported, coed. **Awards:** bachelor's and master's degrees. 24 undergraduate majors. **Total enrollment:** 1,933. Undergraduates: 1,901. Freshmen: 419. Federal methodology is used as a basis for awarding need-based institutional aid.

UNDERGRADUATE EXPENSES for 2013–2014 Application fee: $50. **Tuition, state resident:** full-time $12,245; part-time $195 per credit hour. **Tuition, nonresident:** full-time $25,045; part-time $195 per credit hour. **Required fees:** full-time $2528. Full-time tuition and fees vary according to course load and degree level. Part-time tuition and fees vary according to course load and degree level. **College room and board:** $11,305; **Room only:** $6385. Room and board charges vary according to board plan and housing facility.

FRESHMAN FINANCIAL AID (Fall 2011) 368 applied for aid; of those 60% were deemed to have need. 95% of freshmen with need received aid; of those 10% had need fully met. **Average percent of need met:** 68% (excluding resources awarded to replace EFC). **Average financial aid package:** $13,646 (excluding resources awarded to replace EFC). 21% of all full-time freshmen had no need and received non-need-based gift aid.

UNDERGRADUATE FINANCIAL AID (Fall 2011) 1,250 applied for aid; of those 67% were deemed to have need. 97% of undergraduates with need received aid; of those 6% had need fully met. **Average percent of need met:** 64% (excluding resources awarded to replace EFC). **Average financial aid package:** $12,652 (excluding resources awarded to replace EFC). 21% of all full-time undergraduates had no need and received non-need-based gift aid.

GIFT AID (NEED-BASED) Total amount: $7,329,206 (18% federal, 21% state, 56% institutional, 5% external sources). **Receiving aid:** Freshmen: 37% (164); all full-time undergraduates: 33% (617). **Average award:** Freshmen: $12,071; Undergraduates: $9345. **Scholarships, grants, and awards:** Federal Pell, FSEOG, state, private, college/university gift aid from institutional funds.

GIFT AID (NON-NEED-BASED) Total amount: $1,991,195 (10% state, 80% institutional, 10% external sources). **Receiving aid:** Freshmen: 24% (106). Undergraduates: 22% (421). **Average award:** Freshmen: $3898. Undergraduates: $3849. **Scholarships, grants, and awards by category:** Academic interests/achievement: 740 awards ($2,861,925 total): general academic interests/achievements. Special characteristics: 16 awards ($183,775 total): children of faculty/staff. **Tuition waivers:** Full or partial for employees or children of employees, senior citizens.

LOANS Student loans: $6,165,407 (70% need-based, 30% non-need-based). 54% of past graduating class borrowed through all loan programs. *Average indebtedness per student:* $23,834. **Average need-based loan:** Freshmen: $3161. Undergraduates: $4363. **Parent loans:** $5,299,523 (63% need-based, 37% non-need-based).

Programs: Federal Direct (Subsidized and Unsubsidized Stafford, PLUS).

WORK-STUDY Federal work-study: Total amount: $64,008; 114 jobs averaging $561.

APPLYING FOR FINANCIAL AID Required financial aid form: FAFSA. **Financial aid deadline (priority):** 2/28. **Notification date:** 4/1. Students must reply by 5/1.

CONTACT Ms. Caroline Bright, Director of Financial Aid, St. Mary's College of Maryland, 18952 East Fisher Road, St. Mary's City, MD 20686-3001, 240-895-3000 or toll-free 800-492-7181. *Fax:* 240-895-4959. *E-mail:* cobright@smcm.edu.

Website: http://www.smcm.edu/.

ST. MARY'S UNIVERSITY
San Antonio, TX

CONTACT Mr. David R. Krause, Director of Financial Assistance, St. Mary's University, One Camino Santa Maria, San Antonio, TX 78228-8541, 210-436-3141 or toll-free 800-FOR-STMU. *Fax:* 210-431-2221. *E-mail:* dkrause@alvin.stmarytx.edu. *Website:* http://www.stmarytx.edu/.

SAINT MARY'S UNIVERSITY OF MINNESOTA
Winona, MN

Tuition & fees: $29,315	Average undergraduate aid package: $20,127

ABOUT THE INSTITUTION Independent Roman Catholic, coed. *Awards:* certificates, diplomas, bachelor's, master's, and doctoral degrees. 57 undergraduate majors. *Total enrollment:* 5,574. Undergraduates: 1,985. Freshmen: 328. Federal methodology is used as a basis for awarding need-based institutional aid.

UNDERGRADUATE EXPENSES for 2013–2014 *Application fee:* $25. *Comprehensive fee:* $37,015 includes full-time tuition ($28,790), mandatory fees ($525), and room and board ($7700). *College room only:* $4310. Full-time tuition and fees vary according to course load. Room and board charges vary according to board plan and housing facility. *Part-time tuition:* $960 per credit. *Part-time fees:* $525 per year. Part-time tuition and fees vary according to course load.

FRESHMAN FINANCIAL AID (Fall 2012, est.) 292 applied for aid; of those 93% were deemed to have need. 100% of freshmen with need received aid; of those 18% had need fully met. *Average percent of need met:* 81% (excluding resources awarded to replace EFC). *Average financial aid package:* $24,135 (excluding resources awarded to replace EFC). 15% of all full-time freshmen had no need and received non-need-based gift aid.

UNDERGRADUATE FINANCIAL AID (Fall 2012, est.) 1,122 applied for aid; of those 92% were deemed to have need. 100% of undergraduates with need received aid; of those 19% had need fully met. *Average percent of need met:* 70% (excluding resources awarded to replace EFC). *Average financial aid package:* $20,127 (excluding resources awarded to replace EFC). 18% of all full-time undergraduates had no need and received non-need-based gift aid.

GIFT AID (NEED-BASED) *Total amount:* $18,928,954 (13% federal, 6% state, 80% institutional, 1% external sources). *Receiving aid:* Freshmen: 83% (271); all full-time undergraduates: 76% (1,001). *Average award:* Freshmen: $19,358; Undergraduates: $16,251. *Scholarships, grants, and awards:* Federal Pell, FSEOG, state, college/university gift aid from institutional funds.

GIFT AID (NON-NEED-BASED) *Average award:* Freshmen: $8982. Undergraduates: $10,611. *Scholarships, grants, and awards by category: Academic interests/achievement:* 716 awards ($5,140,850 total): general academic interests/achievements. *Creative arts/performance:* 123 awards ($173,125 total): art/fine arts, music, theater/drama. *Special achievements/activities:* 87 awards ($240,250 total): leadership. *Special characteristics:* 324 awards ($1,622,111 total): children and siblings of alumni, children of faculty/staff, first-generation college students, international students, members of minority groups. *Tuition waivers:* Full or partial for employees or children of employees. *ROTC:* Army cooperative.

LOANS *Student loans:* $9,381,543 (100% need-based). 77% of past graduating class borrowed through all loan programs. *Average indebtedness per student:* $35,134. *Average need-based loan:* Freshmen: $4175. Undergraduates: $4820. *Parent loans:* $1,428,698 (100% need-based). *Programs:* Federal Direct (Subsidized and Unsubsidized Stafford, PLUS), Perkins, state.

WORK-STUDY *Federal work-study:* Total amount: $293,380; 172 jobs averaging $1630. *State or other work-study/employment:* Total amount: $671,714 (100% need-based). 288 part-time jobs averaging $1731.

APPLYING FOR FINANCIAL AID *Required financial aid form:* FAFSA. *Financial aid deadline (priority):* 3/15. *Notification date:* Continuous beginning 2/1. Students must reply within 3 weeks of notification.

CONTACT Ms. Jayne P. Wobig, Director of Financial Aid, Saint Mary's University of Minnesota, 700 Terrace Heights, #5, Winona, MN 55987-1399, 507-457-1437 or toll-free 800-635-5987. *Fax:* 507-457-6698. *E-mail:* jwobig@smumn.edu. *Website:* http://www.smumn.edu/.

SAINT MICHAEL'S COLLEGE
Colchester, VT

Tuition & fees: $39,015	Average undergraduate aid package: $26,222

ABOUT THE INSTITUTION Independent Roman Catholic, coed. *Awards:* certificates, bachelor's, and master's degrees. 37 undergraduate majors. *Total enrollment:* 2,410. Undergraduates: 1,971. Freshmen: 544. Federal methodology is used as a basis for awarding need-based institutional aid.

UNDERGRADUATE EXPENSES for 2013–2014 *Application fee:* $50. *Comprehensive fee:* $48,740 includes full-time tuition ($38,690), mandatory fees ($325), and room and board ($9725). Full-time tuition and fees vary according to course load. Room and board charges vary according to board plan and housing facility. *Part-time tuition:* $1290 per credit hour. Part-time tuition and fees vary according to course load.

FRESHMAN FINANCIAL AID (Fall 2012, est.) 471 applied for aid; of those 90% were deemed to have need. 100% of freshmen with need received aid; of those 31% had need fully met. *Average percent of need met:* 82% (excluding resources awarded to replace EFC). *Average financial aid package:* $26,539 (excluding resources awarded to replace EFC). 20% of all full-time freshmen had no need and received non-need-based gift aid.

UNDERGRADUATE FINANCIAL AID (Fall 2012, est.) 1,477 applied for aid; of those 88% were deemed to have need. 100% of undergraduates with need received aid; of those 56% had need fully met. *Average percent of need met:* 77% (excluding resources awarded to replace EFC). *Average financial aid package:* $26,222 (excluding resources awarded to replace EFC). 27% of all full-time undergraduates had no need and received non-need-based gift aid.

GIFT AID (NEED-BASED) *Total amount:* $25,221,248 (7% federal, 2% state, 88% institutional, 3% external sources). *Receiving aid:* Freshmen: 77% (420); all full-time undergraduates: 67% (1,284). *Average award:* Freshmen: $21,468; Undergraduates: $20,289. *Scholarships, grants, and awards:* Federal Pell, FSEOG, state, private, college/university gift aid from institutional funds.

GIFT AID (NON-NEED-BASED) *Total amount:* $8,031,867 (97% institutional, 3% external sources). *Receiving aid:* Freshmen: 15% (82). Undergraduates: 12% (225). *Average award:* Freshmen: $12,993. Undergraduates: $12,103. *Scholarships, grants, and awards by category: Academic interests/achievement:* general academic interests/achievements. *Creative arts/performance:* art/fine arts, performing arts, theater/drama. *Special characteristics:* local/state students, members of minority groups, out-of-state students, religious affiliation, siblings of current students. *Tuition waivers:* Full or partial for employees or children of employees. *ROTC:* Army cooperative, Air Force cooperative.

LOANS *Student loans:* $13,733,787 (62% need-based, 38% non-need-based). 71% of past graduating class borrowed through all loan programs. *Average indebtedness per student:* $33,054. *Average need-based loan:* Freshmen: $4922. Undergraduates: $5215. *Parent loans:* $4,041,698 (30% need-based, 70% non-need-based). *Programs:* Federal Direct (Subsidized and Unsubsidized Stafford, PLUS), Perkins.

WORK-STUDY *Federal work-study:* Total amount: $425,250; 232 jobs averaging $1600. *State or other work-study/employment:* Total amount: $425,400 (95% need-based, 5% non-need-based). 224 part-time jobs averaging $1630.

ATHLETIC AWARDS Total amount: $889,340 (92% need-based, 8% non-need-based).

APPLYING FOR FINANCIAL AID *Required financial aid forms:* FAFSA, federal income tax form(s). *Financial aid deadline (priority):* 2/15. *Notification date:* 4/1. Students must reply by 5/1 or within 2 weeks of notification.

CONTACT Mrs. Nelberta B. Lunde, Director of New Student Aid and Scholarships, Saint Michael's College, Winooski Park, Colchester, VT 05439, 802-654-3243 or toll-free 800-762-8000. *Fax:* 802-654-2591. *E-mail:* finaid@smcvt.edu. *Website:* http://www.smcvt.edu/.

ST. NORBERT COLLEGE
De Pere, WI

Tuition & fees: $30,675	Average undergraduate aid package: $25,822

ABOUT THE INSTITUTION Independent Roman Catholic, coed. *Awards:* bachelor's and master's degrees. 32 undergraduate majors. *Total enrollment:* 2,287.

Undergraduates: 2,229. Freshmen: 601. Federal methodology is used as a basis for awarding need-based institutional aid.

UNDERGRADUATE EXPENSES for 2013–2014 *Application fee:* $25. *Comprehensive fee:* $38,488 includes full-time tuition ($30,165), mandatory fees ($510), and room and board ($7813). *College room only:* $4170. Full-time tuition and fees vary according to course load. Room and board charges vary according to board plan, housing facility, and student level. *Part-time tuition:* $943 per credit. Part-time tuition and fees vary according to course load.

FRESHMAN FINANCIAL AID (Fall 2011) 523 applied for aid; of those 84% were deemed to have need. 100% of freshmen with need received aid; of those 25% had need fully met. *Average percent of need met:* 100% (excluding resources awarded to replace EFC). *Average financial aid package:* $25,330 (excluding resources awarded to replace EFC). 24% of all full-time freshmen had no need and received non-need-based gift aid.

UNDERGRADUATE FINANCIAL AID (Fall 2011) 1,696 applied for aid; of those 86% were deemed to have need. 100% of undergraduates with need received aid; of those 30% had need fully met. *Average percent of need met:* 100% (excluding resources awarded to replace EFC). *Average financial aid package:* $25,822 (excluding resources awarded to replace EFC). 26% of all full-time undergraduates had no need and received non-need-based gift aid.

GIFT AID (NEED-BASED) *Total amount:* $24,128,975 (9% federal, 7% state, 80% institutional, 4% external sources). *Receiving aid:* Freshmen: 73% (436); all full-time undergraduates: 67% (1,408). *Average award:* Freshmen: $21,146; Undergraduates: $20,688. *Scholarships, grants, and awards:* Federal Pell, FSEOG, state, private, college/university gift aid from institutional funds.

GIFT AID (NON-NEED-BASED) *Total amount:* $6,201,270 (1% federal, 93% institutional, 6% external sources). *Receiving aid:* Freshmen: 2% (14). Undergraduates: 2% (44). *Average award:* Freshmen: $10,291. Undergraduates: $10,440. *Scholarships, grants, and awards by category:* Academic interests/achievement: general academic interests/achievements. Creative arts/performance: art/fine arts, music, theater/drama. Special characteristics: children of faculty/staff, international students. *Tuition waivers:* Full or partial for employees or children of employees. *ROTC:* Army.

LOANS *Student loans:* $14,540,746 (94% need-based, 6% non-need-based). 67% of past graduating class borrowed through all loan programs. *Average indebtedness per student:* $31,331. *Average need-based loan:* Freshmen: $3759. Undergraduates: $4633. *Parent loans:* $3,387,479 (85% need-based, 15% non-need-based). *Programs:* Federal Direct (Subsidized and Unsubsidized Stafford, PLUS), Perkins, state, college/university.

WORK-STUDY *Federal work-study:* Total amount: $552,568; 282 jobs averaging $1272. *State or other work-study/employment:* Total amount: $1,489,335 (62% need-based, 38% non-need-based). 725 part-time jobs averaging $1253.

APPLYING FOR FINANCIAL AID *Required financial aid form:* FAFSA. *Financial aid deadline (priority):* 3/1. *Notification date:* Continuous beginning 3/15. Students must reply within 2 weeks of notification.

CONTACT Mr. Jeffrey A. Zahn, Director of Financial Aid, St. Norbert College, 100 Grant Street, De Pere, WI 54115-2099, 920-403-3071 or toll-free 800-236-4878. *Fax:* 920-403-3062. *E-mail:* jeff.zahn@snc.edu. *Website:* http://www.snc.edu/.

ST. OLAF COLLEGE
Northfield, MN

Tuition & fees: $39,560	Average undergraduate aid package: $33,967

ABOUT THE INSTITUTION Independent Lutheran, coed. *Awards:* bachelor's degrees. 44 undergraduate majors. *Total enrollment:* 3,176. Undergraduates: 3,176. Freshmen: 864. Both federal and institutional methodology are used as a basis for awarding need-based institutional aid.

UNDERGRADUATE EXPENSES for 2013–2014 *Application fee:* $40. *Comprehensive fee:* $48,650 includes full-time tuition ($39,560) and room and board ($9090). *College room only:* $4260. Full-time tuition and fees vary according to course load. Room and board charges vary according to board plan and housing facility. *Part-time tuition:* $4945 per course. Part-time tuition and fees vary according to course load.

FRESHMAN FINANCIAL AID (Fall 2012, est.) 718 applied for aid; of those 81% were deemed to have need. 100% of freshmen with need received aid; of those 100%

had need fully met. *Average percent of need met:* 100% (excluding resources awarded to replace EFC). *Average financial aid package:* $35,190 (excluding resources awarded to replace EFC). 24% of all full-time freshmen had no need and received non-need-based gift aid.

UNDERGRADUATE FINANCIAL AID (Fall 2012, est.) 2,359 applied for aid; of those 90% were deemed to have need. 100% of undergraduates with need received aid; of those 100% had need fully met. *Average percent of need met:* 100% (excluding resources awarded to replace EFC). *Average financial aid package:* $33,967 (excluding resources awarded to replace EFC). 22% of all full-time undergraduates had no need and received non-need-based gift aid.

GIFT AID (NEED-BASED) *Total amount:* $54,105,887 (4% federal, 3% state, 90% institutional, 3% external sources). *Receiving aid:* Freshmen: 68% (584); all full-time undergraduates: 68% (2,116). *Average award:* Freshmen: $28,491; Undergraduates: $26,194. *Scholarships, grants, and awards:* Federal Pell, FSEOG, state, private, college/university gift aid from institutional funds.

GIFT AID (NON-NEED-BASED) *Total amount:* $8,323,464 (94% institutional, 6% external sources). *Receiving aid:* Freshmen: 31% (268). Undergraduates: 18% (570). *Average award:* Freshmen: $12,670. Undergraduates: $11,438. *Scholarships, grants, and awards by category:* Academic interests/achievement: 556 awards ($6,950,211 total): general academic interests/achievements. Creative arts/performance: 258 awards ($1,760,000 total): art/fine arts, dance, music, theater/drama. Special achievements/activities: 193 awards ($1,302,325 total): community service, religious involvement. Special characteristics: international students. *Tuition waivers:* Full or partial for employees or children of employees, senior citizens.

LOANS *Student loans:* $14,069,822 (45% need-based, 55% non-need-based). 61% of past graduating class borrowed through all loan programs. *Average indebtedness per student:* $27,637. *Average need-based loan:* Freshmen: $3346. Undergraduates: $4694. *Parent loans:* $3,155,568 (100% non-need-based). *Programs:* Federal Direct (Subsidized and Unsubsidized Stafford, PLUS), Perkins, Federal Nursing, state, college/university.

WORK-STUDY *Federal work-study:* Total amount: $1,679,204; 851 jobs averaging $1973. *State or other work-study/employment:* Total amount: $2,343,440 (89% need-based, 11% non-need-based). 1,277 part-time jobs averaging $1828.

APPLYING FOR FINANCIAL AID *Required financial aid forms:* FAFSA, CSS Financial Aid PROFILE, noncustodial (divorced/separated) parent's statement, business/farm supplement. *Financial aid deadline:* 3/1 (priority: 2/1). *Notification date:* 3/22. Students must reply by 5/1.

CONTACT Ms. Sandy Sundstrom, Director of Student Financial Aid, St. Olaf College, 1520 Saint Olaf Avenue, Northfield, MN 55057-1098, 507-786-3019 or toll-free 800-800-3025. *Fax:* 507-786-6688. *E-mail:* sundstro@stolaf.edu. *Website:* http://www.stolaf.edu/.

ST. PETERSBURG COLLEGE
St. Petersburg, FL

CONTACT Financial Aid Office, St. Petersburg College, PO Box 13489, St. Petersburg, FL 33733-3489, 727-341-3600. *Website:* http://www.spcollege.edu/.

SAINT PETER'S UNIVERSITY
Jersey City, NJ

Tuition & fees: $32,230	Average undergraduate aid package: $25,359

ABOUT THE INSTITUTION Independent Roman Catholic (Jesuit), coed. *Awards:* certificates, associate, bachelor's, master's, and doctoral degrees. 47 undergraduate majors. *Total enrollment:* 3,045. Undergraduates: 2,317. Freshmen: 394. Federal methodology is used as a basis for awarding need-based institutional aid.

UNDERGRADUATE EXPENSES for 2013–2014 *Comprehensive fee:* $45,688 includes full-time tuition ($31,230), mandatory fees ($1000), and room and board ($13,458). *College room only:* $8542. Full-time tuition and fees vary according to class time and course load. Room and board charges vary according to board plan, housing facility, and student level. *Part-time tuition:* $990 per credit hour. Part-time tuition and fees vary according to class time and course load.

FRESHMAN FINANCIAL AID (Fall 2012, est.) 389 applied for aid; of those 91% were deemed to have need. 100% of freshmen with need received aid; of those 12% had need fully met. *Average percent of need met:* 77% (excluding resources awarded to replace EFC). *Average financial aid package:* $28,057 (excluding resources awarded to replace EFC). 8% of all full-time freshmen had no need and received non-need-based gift aid.

UNDERGRADUATE FINANCIAL AID (Fall 2012, est.) 1,873 applied for aid; of those 89% were deemed to have need. 100% of undergraduates with need received aid; of those 11% had need fully met. *Average percent of need met:* 73% (excluding resources awarded to replace EFC). *Average financial aid package:* $25,359 (excluding resources awarded to replace EFC). 10% of all full-time undergraduates had no need and received non-need-based gift aid.

GIFT AID (NEED-BASED) *Total amount:* $32,708,166 (17% federal, 26% state, 57% institutional). *Receiving aid:* Freshmen: 90% (350); all full-time undergraduates: 85% (1,616). *Average award:* Freshmen: $22,925; Undergraduates: $20,088. *Scholarships, grants, and awards:* Federal Pell, FSEOG, state, private, college/university gift aid from institutional funds, Federal Nursing.

GIFT AID (NON-NEED-BASED) *Total amount:* $3,537,582 (4% federal, 96% institutional). *Receiving aid:* Freshmen: 6% (25). Undergraduates: 4% (80). *Average award:* Freshmen: $20,139. Undergraduates: $15,134. *Scholarships, grants, and awards by category: Academic interests/achievement:* general academic interests/achievements. *Special achievements/activities:* leadership. *Special characteristics:* children of faculty/staff, general special characteristics, relatives of clergy, religious affiliation. *Tuition waivers:* Full or partial for employees or children of employees. *ROTC:* Army cooperative, Air Force cooperative.

LOANS *Student loans:* $12,467,785 (85% need-based, 15% non-need-based). 76% of past graduating class borrowed through all loan programs. *Average indebtedness per student:* $32,218. *Average need-based loan:* Freshmen: $3077. Undergraduates: $3815. *Parent loans:* $3,405,353 (50% need-based, 50% non-need-based). *Programs:* Federal Direct (Subsidized and Unsubsidized Stafford, PLUS).

WORK-STUDY *Federal work-study:* Total amount: $356,432; jobs available.

ATHLETIC AWARDS Total amount: $3,783,943 (53% need-based, 47% non-need-based).

APPLYING FOR FINANCIAL AID *Required financial aid forms:* FAFSA, noncustodial (divorced/separated) parent's statement. *Financial aid deadline (priority):* 3/15. *Notification date:* Continuous beginning 2/15. Students must reply within 2 weeks of notification.

CONTACT Jennifer Ragsdale, Acting Director of Financial Aid, Saint Peter's University, 2641 Kennedy Boulevard, Jersey City, NJ 07306, 201-761-6071 or toll-free 888-SPC-9933. *Fax:* 201-761-6073. *E-mail:* jragsdale@spc.edu. *Website:* http://www.spcollege.edu/.

ST. THOMAS AQUINAS COLLEGE
Sparkill, NY

ABOUT THE INSTITUTION Independent, coed. *Awards:* certificates, associate, bachelor's, and master's degrees. 38 undergraduate majors. *Total enrollment:* 1,957. Undergraduates: 1,796. Freshmen: 270.

GIFT AID (NEED-BASED) *Scholarships, grants, and awards:* Federal Pell, FSEOG, state, private, college/university gift aid from institutional funds.

GIFT AID (NON-NEED-BASED) *Scholarships, grants, and awards by category: Academic interests/achievement:* business, communication, computer science, education, engineering/technologies, English, foreign languages, general academic interests/achievements, humanities, mathematics, religion/biblical studies, social sciences. *Creative arts/performance:* creative writing. *Special achievements/activities:* community service, leadership. *Special characteristics:* siblings of current students, spouses of current students, twins, veterans.

LOANS *Programs:* Federal Direct (Subsidized and Unsubsidized Stafford, PLUS), Perkins, state, alternative loans.

WORK-STUDY *Federal work-study:* Total amount: $343,450; 200 jobs averaging $1717.

APPLYING FOR FINANCIAL AID *Required financial aid forms:* FAFSA, state aid form.

CONTACT Mrs. Jean Marie Mohr, Director of Financial Aid, St. Thomas Aquinas College, 125 Route 340, Sparkill, NY 10976, 845-398-4098 or toll-free 800-999-STAC. *Fax:* 845-398-4114. *E-mail:* jmohr@stac.edu. *Website:* http://www.stac.edu/.

ST. THOMAS UNIVERSITY
Miami Gardens, FL

Tuition & fees: $25,110	Average undergraduate aid package: N/A

ABOUT THE INSTITUTION Independent Roman Catholic, coed. *Awards:* certificates, bachelor's, master's, and doctoral degrees. 39 undergraduate majors. *Total enrollment:* 2,472. Undergraduates: 1,085. Freshmen: 209. Federal methodology is used as a basis for awarding need-based institutional aid.

UNDERGRADUATE EXPENSES for 2013–2014 *Application fee:* $40. *Comprehensive fee:* $32,250 includes full-time tuition ($25,110) and room and board ($7140). Full-time tuition and fees vary according to program. Room and board charges vary according to board plan and housing facility. *Part-time tuition:* $502 per credit hour. Part-time tuition and fees vary according to program.

FRESHMAN FINANCIAL AID (Fall 2012, est.) 169 applied for aid; of those 95% were deemed to have need. 100% of freshmen with need received aid; of those 42% had need fully met. 22% of all full-time freshmen had no need and received non-need-based gift aid.

UNDERGRADUATE FINANCIAL AID (Fall 2012, est.) 833 applied for aid; of those 90% were deemed to have need. 100% of undergraduates with need received aid; of those 52% had need fully met. 18% of all full-time undergraduates had no need and received non-need-based gift aid.

GIFT AID (NEED-BASED) *Total amount:* $14,392,460 (20% federal, 13% state, 66% institutional, 1% external sources). *Receiving aid:* Freshmen: 60% (124); all full-time undergraduates: 55% (567). *Average award:* Freshmen: $3520; Undergraduates: $3604. *Scholarships, grants, and awards:* Federal Pell, FSEOG, state, private, college/university gift aid from institutional funds.

GIFT AID (NON-NEED-BASED) *Receiving aid:* Freshmen: 77% (161). Undergraduates: 73% (747). *Average award:* Freshmen: $10,373. Undergraduates: $8365. *Scholarships, grants, and awards by category: Academic interests/achievement:* general academic interests/achievements. *Special achievements/activities:* leadership. *Tuition waivers:* Full or partial for employees or children of employees.

LOANS *Student loans:* $5,666,374 (100% need-based). *Average need-based loan:* Freshmen: $3478. Undergraduates: $4295. *Parent loans:* $563,652 (100% need-based). *Programs:* Federal Direct (Subsidized and Unsubsidized Stafford, PLUS), Perkins.

WORK-STUDY *Federal work-study:* Total amount: $354,000; jobs available.

ATHLETIC AWARDS Total amount: $1,050,788 (100% need-based).

APPLYING FOR FINANCIAL AID *Required financial aid form:* FAFSA. *Financial aid deadline (priority):* 4/1. *Notification date:* Continuous beginning 3/1.

CONTACT Ms. Yaidani Rivero, Associate Director of Financial Aid, St. Thomas University, 16401 Northwest 37th Avenue, Miami Gardens, FL 33054, 305-474-6900 or toll-free 800-367-9010. *Fax:* 305-474-6930. *E-mail:* yrivero@stu.edu. *Website:* http://www.stu.edu/.

SAINT VINCENT COLLEGE
Latrobe, PA

CONTACT Kimberly Woodley, Director of Financial Aid, Saint Vincent College, 300 Fraser Purchase Road, Latrobe, PA 15650, 724-805-2500 or toll-free 800-782-5549. *E-mail:* kimberly.woodley@email.stvincent.edu. *Website:* http://www.stvincent.edu/.

SAINT XAVIER UNIVERSITY
Chicago, IL

ABOUT THE INSTITUTION Independent Roman Catholic, coed. *Awards:* certificates, bachelor's, and master's degrees. 39 undergraduate majors. *Total enrollment:* 4,709. Undergraduates: 2,993. Freshmen: 583.

GIFT AID (NEED-BASED) *Scholarships, grants, and awards:* Federal Pell, FSEOG, state, private, college/university gift aid from institutional funds, United Negro College Fund, Federal Nursing.

GIFT AID (NON-NEED-BASED) *Scholarships, grants, and awards by category: Academic interests/achievement:* general academic interests/achievements.

Creative arts/performance: art/fine arts, music. Special achievements/activities: religious involvement. Special characteristics: children of faculty/staff.

LOANS Programs: Federal Direct (Subsidized and Unsubsidized Stafford, PLUS), Perkins.

WORK-STUDY Federal work-study: Total amount: $5,141,838; 1,757 jobs averaging $2377. **State or other work-study/employment:** Total amount: $267,530 (62% need-based, 38% non-need-based). Part-time jobs available.

APPLYING FOR FINANCIAL AID Required financial aid form: FAFSA.

CONTACT Ms. Susan Swisher, Director of Financial Aid, Saint Xavier University, 3700 West 103rd Street, Chicago, IL 60655-3105, 773-298-3073 or toll-free 800-462-9288. Fax: 773-298-3033. E-mail: swisher@sxu.edu.
Website: http://www.sxu.edu/.

SALEM COLLEGE
Winston-Salem, NC

ABOUT THE INSTITUTION Independent Moravian, coed, primarily women. 32 undergraduate majors.

GIFT AID (NEED-BASED) Scholarships, grants, and awards: Federal Pell, FSEOG, state, private, college/university gift aid from institutional funds.

GIFT AID (NON-NEED-BASED) Scholarships, grants, and awards by category: Academic interests/achievement: general academic interests/achievements. Creative arts/performance: music. Special achievements/activities: leadership. Special characteristics: children of educators, children of faculty/staff, relatives of clergy.

LOANS Programs: Federal Direct (Subsidized and Unsubsidized Stafford, PLUS), Perkins.

APPLYING FOR FINANCIAL AID Required financial aid forms: FAFSA, institution's own form.

CONTACT Lori A. Lewis, Director of Financial Aid, Salem College, 601 South Church Street, Winston-Salem, NC 27101, 336-917-5577 or toll-free 800-327-2536. Fax: 336-917-5584. E-mail: lori.lewis@salem.edu.
Website: http://www.salem.edu/.

SALEM INTERNATIONAL UNIVERSITY
Salem, WV

CONTACT Pat Zinsmeister, Vice President for Financial Aid and Compliance, Salem International University, 223 West Main Street, Salem, WV 26426-0500, 304-326-1299 or toll-free 888-235-5024. Fax: 304-326-1509. E-mail: pzinsmeister@salemu.edu.
Website: http://www.salemu.edu/.

SALEM STATE UNIVERSITY
Salem, MA

CONTACT Mary Benda, Director of Financial Aid, Salem State University, 352 Lafayette Street, Salem, MA 01970-5353, 978-542-6139. Fax: 978-542-6876.
Website: http://www.salemstate.edu/.

SALISBURY UNIVERSITY
Salisbury, MD

Tuition & fees (MD res): $7700	Average undergraduate aid package: $7391

ABOUT THE INSTITUTION State-supported, coed. **Awards:** certificates, bachelor's, master's, and doctoral degrees. 41 undergraduate majors. **Total enrollment:** 8,657. Undergraduates: 7,969. Freshmen: 1,232. Federal methodology is used as a basis for awarding need-based institutional aid.

UNDERGRADUATE EXPENSES for 2013–2014 Application fee: $50. **Tuition, state resident:** full-time $5576; part-time $231 per credit hour. **Tuition, nonresident:** full-time $13,922; part-time $578 per credit hour. **Required fees:**

full-time $2124; $77 per credit hour. Full-time tuition and fees vary according to degree level. Part-time tuition and fees vary according to course load and degree level. **College room and board:** $9120; **Room only:** $5250. Room and board charges vary according to board plan and housing facility.

FRESHMAN FINANCIAL AID (Fall 2011) 1,052 applied for aid; of those 57% were deemed to have need. 98% of freshmen with need received aid; of those 16% had need fully met. **Average percent of need met:** 52% (excluding resources awarded to replace EFC). **Average financial aid package:** $7143 (excluding resources awarded to replace EFC). 27% of all full-time freshmen had no need and received non-need-based gift aid.

UNDERGRADUATE FINANCIAL AID (Fall 2011) 5,256 applied for aid; of those 71% were deemed to have need. 96% of undergraduates with need received aid; of those 12% had need fully met. **Average percent of need met:** 50% (excluding resources awarded to replace EFC). **Average financial aid package:** $7391 (excluding resources awarded to replace EFC). 12% of all full-time undergraduates had no need and received non-need-based gift aid.

GIFT AID (NEED-BASED) Total amount: $14,124,003 (50% federal, 27% state, 17% institutional, 6% external sources). **Receiving aid:** Freshmen: 42% (518); all full-time undergraduates: 38% (2,742). **Average award:** Freshmen: $5644; Undergraduates: $5192. **Scholarships, grants, and awards:** Federal Pell, FSEOG, state, private, college/university gift aid from institutional funds.

GIFT AID (NON-NEED-BASED) Total amount: $2,774,699 (17% state, 64% institutional, 19% external sources). **Average award:** Freshmen: $2514. Undergraduates: $2448. **Scholarships, grants, and awards by category:** Academic interests/achievement: 1,786 awards ($3,522,994 total): biological sciences, business, communication, computer science, education, English, foreign languages, general academic interests/achievements, health fields, humanities, mathematics, physical sciences, social sciences. Creative arts/performance: 36 awards ($22,150 total): applied art and design, music, theater/drama. Special characteristics: 10 awards ($12,000 total): children and siblings of alumni, first-generation college students. **Tuition waivers:** Full or partial for employees or children of employees, senior citizens. **ROTC:** Army, Air Force cooperative.

LOANS Student loans: $31,072,164 (74% need-based, 26% non-need-based). 59% of past graduating class borrowed through all loan programs. Average indebtedness per student: $23,159. **Average need-based loan:** Freshmen: $3164. Undergraduates: $4128. **Parent loans:** $15,262,408 (64% need-based, 36% non-need-based). **Programs:** Federal Direct (Subsidized and Unsubsidized Stafford, PLUS), Perkins.

WORK-STUDY Federal work-study: Total amount: $122,702; 65 jobs averaging $1888.

APPLYING FOR FINANCIAL AID Required financial aid form: FAFSA. **Financial aid deadline (priority):** 3/1. **Notification date:** Continuous beginning 3/15. Students must reply by 5/1.

CONTACT Ms. Elizabeth B. Zimmerman, Director of Financial Aid, Salisbury University, 1101 Camden Avenue, Salisbury, MD 21801, 410-543-6165 or toll-free 888-543-0148. Fax: 410-543-6138. E-mail: finaid@salisbury.edu.
Website: http://www.salisbury.edu/.

SALVE REGINA UNIVERSITY
Newport, RI

Tuition & fees: $33,950	Average undergraduate aid package: $22,619

ABOUT THE INSTITUTION Independent Roman Catholic, coed. **Awards:** certificates, associate, bachelor's, master's, and doctoral degrees. 51 undergraduate majors. **Total enrollment:** 2,615. Undergraduates: 2,053. Freshmen: 545. Both federal and institutional methodology are used as a basis for awarding need-based institutional aid.

UNDERGRADUATE EXPENSES for 2013–2014 Application fee: $50. **Comprehensive fee:** $45,850 includes full-time tuition ($33,450), mandatory fees ($500), and room and board ($11,900). Full-time tuition and fees vary according to course load and location. Room and board charges vary according to board plan and housing facility. **Part-time tuition:** $1115 per credit. **Part-time fees:** $40 per term. Part-time tuition and fees vary according to course load and location.

FRESHMAN FINANCIAL AID (Fall 2012, est.) 509 applied for aid; of those 89% were deemed to have need. 99% of freshmen with need received aid; of those 11% had need fully met. **Average percent of need met:** 70% (excluding resources awarded to replace EFC). **Average financial aid package:** $22,520 (excluding resources

awarded to replace EFC). 37% of all full-time freshmen had no need and received non-need-based gift aid.

UNDERGRADUATE FINANCIAL AID (Fall 2012, est.) 1,738 applied for aid; of those 90% were deemed to have need. 97% of undergraduates with need received aid; of those 8% had need fully met. *Average percent of need met:* 65% (excluding resources awarded to replace EFC). *Average financial aid package:* $22,619 (excluding resources awarded to replace EFC). 14% of all full-time undergraduates had no need and received non-need-based gift aid.

GIFT AID (NEED-BASED) *Total amount:* $26,236,867 (9% federal, 1% state, 87% institutional, 3% external sources). *Receiving aid:* Freshmen: 82% (446); all full-time undergraduates: 75% (1,482). *Average award:* Freshmen: $18,814; Undergraduates: $17,824. *Scholarships, grants, and awards:* Federal Pell, FSEOG, state, private, college/university gift aid from institutional funds.

GIFT AID (NON-NEED-BASED) *Total amount:* $3,889,598 (4% federal, 87% institutional, 9% external sources). *Receiving aid:* Freshmen: 7% (36). Undergraduates: 4% (87). *Average award:* Freshmen: $10,630. Undergraduates: $10,358. *Scholarships, grants, and awards by category:* Academic interests/achievement: general academic interests/achievements. *Tuition waivers:* Full or partial for employees or children of employees. *ROTC:* Army cooperative.

LOANS *Student loans:* $16,876,078 (72% need-based, 28% non-need-based). 80% of past graduating class borrowed through all loan programs. *Average indebtedness per student:* $39,996. *Average need-based loan:* Freshmen: $3205. Undergraduates: $4455. *Parent loans:* $5,381,871 (47% need-based, 53% non-need-based). *Programs:* Federal Direct (Subsidized and Unsubsidized Stafford, PLUS), Perkins, Federal Nursing, college/university, alternative loans.

WORK-STUDY *Federal work-study:* Total amount: $282,799; 409 jobs averaging $691. *State or other work-study/employment:* Total amount: $143,088 (100% non-need-based). 111 part-time jobs averaging $1281.

APPLYING FOR FINANCIAL AID *Required financial aid forms:* FAFSA, CSS Financial Aid PROFILE, noncustodial (divorced/separated) parent's statement, business/farm supplement. *Financial aid deadline (priority):* 3/1. *Notification date:* Continuous beginning 12/15. Students must reply by 5/1 or within 2 weeks of notification.

CONTACT Ms. Aida Mirante, Director of Financial Aid, Salve Regina University, 100 Ochre Point Avenue, Newport, RI 02840-4192, 401-341-2901 or toll-free 888-GO SALVE. *Fax:* 401-341-2928. *E-mail:* financial_aid@salve.edu.
Website: http://www.salve.edu/.

time undergraduates: 43% (1,176). *Average award:* Freshmen: $13,739; Undergraduates: $12,884. *Scholarships, grants, and awards:* Federal Pell, FSEOG, state, private, college/university gift aid from institutional funds, United Negro College Fund, Federal Nursing.

GIFT AID (NON-NEED-BASED) *Total amount:* $10,287,500 (1% state, 92% institutional, 7% external sources). *Receiving aid:* Freshmen: 10% (71). Undergraduates: 8% (216). *Average award:* Freshmen: $8668. Undergraduates: $8475. *Scholarships, grants, and awards by category:* Academic interests/achievement: 1,731 awards ($12,416,883 total): biological sciences, business, computer science, education, English, foreign languages, general academic interests/achievements, health fields, international studies, mathematics, physical sciences, premedicine, religion/biblical studies, social sciences. *Creative arts/performance:* 267 awards ($981,735 total): debating, journalism/publications, music, performing arts, theater/drama. *Special achievements/activities:* 430 awards ($978,339 total): cheerleading/drum major, leadership. *Special characteristics:* 175 awards ($2,245,508 total): children of faculty/staff, relatives of clergy, siblings of current students, spouses of current students, veterans. *Tuition waivers:* Full or partial for employees or children of employees. *ROTC:* Army cooperative, Air Force.

LOANS *Student loans:* $13,494,182 (71% need-based, 29% non-need-based). 52% of past graduating class borrowed through all loan programs. *Average indebtedness per student:* $25,252. *Average need-based loan:* Freshmen: $3057. Undergraduates: $3600. *Parent loans:* $19,854,416 (30% need-based, 70% non-need-based). *Programs:* Federal Direct (Subsidized and Unsubsidized Stafford, PLUS), Perkins, Federal Nursing, college/university.

WORK-STUDY *Federal work-study:* Total amount: $662,416; 308 jobs averaging $2151. *State or other work-study/employment:* Total amount: $933,178 (16% need-based, 84% non-need-based). 587 part-time jobs averaging $1599.

ATHLETIC AWARDS Total amount: $6,564,676 (42% need-based, 58% non-need-based).

APPLYING FOR FINANCIAL AID *Required financial aid forms:* FAFSA, state aid form. *Financial aid deadline (priority):* 3/1. *Notification date:* 4/1. Students must reply by 5/1.

CONTACT Lane Smith, Director of Financial Aid, Samford University, 800 Lakeshore Drive, Birmingham, AL 35229, 205-726-2905 or toll-free 800-888-7218. *Fax:* 205-726-2738. *E-mail:* lsmith1@samford.edu.
Website: http://www.samford.edu/.

SAMFORD UNIVERSITY
Birmingham, AL

Tuition & fees: $25,150	Average undergraduate aid package: $16,804

ABOUT THE INSTITUTION Independent Baptist, coed. *Awards:* certificates, bachelor's, master's, and doctoral degrees. 68 undergraduate majors. *Total enrollment:* 4,758. Undergraduates: 2,965. Freshmen: 708. Federal methodology is used as a basis for awarding need-based institutional aid.

UNDERGRADUATE EXPENSES for 2013–2014 *Application fee:* $35. *Comprehensive fee:* $33,400 includes full-time tuition ($24,570), mandatory fees ($580), and room and board ($8250). *College room only:* $4250. Full-time tuition and fees vary according to course load, location, and program. Room and board charges vary according to board plan, housing facility, and location. *Part-time tuition:* $821 per credit hour. *Part-time fees:* $210 per term. Part-time tuition and fees vary according to course load and program.

FRESHMAN FINANCIAL AID (Fall 2011) 478 applied for aid; of those 65% were deemed to have need. 100% of freshmen with need received aid; of those 23% had need fully met. *Average percent of need met:* 73% (excluding resources awarded to replace EFC). *Average financial aid package:* $17,254 (excluding resources awarded to replace EFC). 49% of all full-time freshmen had no need and received non-need-based gift aid.

UNDERGRADUATE FINANCIAL AID (Fall 2011) 1,639 applied for aid; of those 76% were deemed to have need. 100% of undergraduates with need received aid; of those 21% had need fully met. *Average percent of need met:* 68% (excluding resources awarded to replace EFC). *Average financial aid package:* $16,804 (excluding resources awarded to replace EFC). 37% of all full-time undergraduates had no need and received non-need-based gift aid.

GIFT AID (NEED-BASED) *Total amount:* $12,091,458 (16% federal, 2% state, 74% institutional, 8% external sources). *Receiving aid:* Freshmen: 45% (307); all full-

SAM HOUSTON STATE UNIVERSITY
Huntsville, TX

Tuition & fees (TX res): $8120	Average undergraduate aid package: $9572

ABOUT THE INSTITUTION State-supported, coed. *Awards:* bachelor's, master's, and doctoral degrees. 52 undergraduate majors. *Total enrollment:* 18,461. Undergraduates: 15,611. Freshmen: 2,415. Federal methodology is used as a basis for awarding need-based institutional aid.

UNDERGRADUATE EXPENSES for 2013–2014 *Application fee:* $45. *Tuition, state resident:* full-time $5610. *Tuition, nonresident:* full-time $16,140. *Required fees:* full-time $2510. Full-time tuition and fees vary according to course level, course load, location, and program. Part-time tuition and fees vary according to course level, course load, location, and program. *College room and board:* $8092. Room and board charges vary according to board plan and housing facility.

FRESHMAN FINANCIAL AID (Fall 2011) 1,627 applied for aid; of those 78% were deemed to have need. 97% of freshmen with need received aid; of those 9% had need fully met. *Average percent of need met:* 65% (excluding resources awarded to replace EFC). *Average financial aid package:* $10,152 (excluding resources awarded to replace EFC). 11% of all full-time freshmen had no need and received non-need-based gift aid.

UNDERGRADUATE FINANCIAL AID (Fall 2011) 9,139 applied for aid; of those 85% were deemed to have need. 97% of undergraduates with need received aid; of those 4% had need fully met. *Average percent of need met:* 53% (excluding resources awarded to replace EFC). *Average financial aid package:* $9572 (excluding resources awarded to replace EFC). 8% of all full-time undergraduates had no need and received non-need-based gift aid.

GIFT AID (NEED-BASED) *Total amount:* $43,389,230 (57% federal, 33% state, 5% institutional, 5% external sources). *Receiving aid:* Freshmen: 56% (1,084); all full-time undergraduates: 51% (6,281). *Average award:* Freshmen: $7863; Undergraduates: $6314. **Scholarships, grants, and awards:** Federal Pell, FSEOG, state, college/university gift aid from institutional funds.

GIFT AID (NON-NEED-BASED) Total amount: $2,581,933 (1% federal, 61% institutional, 38% external sources). **Receiving aid:** Freshmen: 2% (43). Undergraduates: 1% (90). **Average award:** Freshmen: $2302. Undergraduates: $2281. **Scholarships, grants, and awards by category:** Academic interests/achievement: agriculture, biological sciences, business, communication, computer science, education, engineering/technologies, English, foreign languages, general academic interests/achievements, home economics, humanities, library science, mathematics, military science, physical sciences, social sciences. **Creative arts/performance:** art/fine arts, dance, music. **Special achievements/activities:** cheerleading/drum major, general special achievements/activities, leadership, rodeo. **Special characteristics:** children and siblings of alumni, general special characteristics, handicapped students, local/state students, religious affiliation. **Tuition waivers:** Full or partial for employees or children of employees. **ROTC:** Army.

LOANS Student loans: $67,676,732 (81% need-based, 19% non-need-based). 62% of past graduating class borrowed through all loan programs. Average indebtedness per student: $27,202. **Average need-based loan:** Freshmen: $3138. Undergraduates: $4162. **Parent loans:** $8,740,174 (47% need-based, 53% non-need-based). **Programs:** Federal Direct (Subsidized and Unsubsidized Stafford, PLUS), Perkins, state, college/university.

WORK-STUDY Federal work-study: Total amount: $449,495; jobs available. **State or other work-study/employment:** Total amount: $121,053 (100% need-based). Part-time jobs available.

ATHLETIC AWARDS Total amount: $2,931,981 (47% need-based, 53% non-need-based).

APPLYING FOR FINANCIAL AID Required financial aid form: FAFSA. **Financial aid deadline (priority):** 4/1. **Notification date:** Continuous beginning 3/15. Students must reply within 4 weeks of notification.

CONTACT Lisa Tatom, Director of Financial Aid, Sam Houston State University, 1903 University, Estill 201, Box 2328, Huntsville, TX 77341-2328, 936-294-1774 or toll-free 866-232-7528 Ext. 1828. Fax: 936-294-3668. E-mail: fao.tatom@shsu.edu. Website: http://www.shsu.edu/.

SAMUEL MERRITT UNIVERSITY
Oakland, CA

CONTACT Adel Mareghni, Financial Aid Counselor, Samuel Merritt University, 450 30th Street, Oakland, CA 94609, 510-869-6193 or toll-free 800-607-MERRITT. Fax: 510-869-1529. E-mail: amareghni@samuelmerritt.edu. Website: http://www.samuelmerritt.edu/.

SAN DIEGO CHRISTIAN COLLEGE
El Cajon, CA

Tuition & fees: $25,888	Average undergraduate aid package: $14,346

ABOUT THE INSTITUTION Independent nondenominational, coed. **Awards:** certificates, associate, and bachelor's degrees. 25 undergraduate majors. **Total enrollment:** 752. Undergraduates: 739. Freshmen: 101. Federal methodology is used as a basis for awarding need-based institutional aid.

UNDERGRADUATE EXPENSES for 2013-2014 Application fee: $25. **Comprehensive fee:** $35,166 includes full-time tuition ($24,540), mandatory fees ($1348), and room and board ($9278). Full-time tuition and fees vary according to class time, course load, location, and program. Room and board charges vary according to location. Part-time tuition and fees vary according to class time, course load, and program.

FRESHMAN FINANCIAL AID (Fall 2012, est.) 84 applied for aid; of those 99% were deemed to have need. 100% of freshmen with need received aid; of those 16% had need fully met. **Average percent of need met:** 59% (excluding resources awarded to replace EFC). **Average financial aid package:** $16,232 (excluding resources awarded to replace EFC). 2% of all full-time freshmen had no need and received non-need-based gift aid.

UNDERGRADUATE FINANCIAL AID (Fall 2012, est.) 627 applied for aid; of those 87% were deemed to have need. 100% of undergraduates with need received

aid; of those 12% had need fully met. **Average percent of need met:** 82% (excluding resources awarded to replace EFC). **Average financial aid package:** $14,346 (excluding resources awarded to replace EFC). 1% of all full-time undergraduates had no need and received non-need-based gift aid.

GIFT AID (NEED-BASED) Total amount: $3,493,191 (68% federal, 24% state, 8% institutional). **Receiving aid:** Freshmen: 66% (63); all full-time undergraduates: 62% (409). **Average award:** Freshmen: $8316; Undergraduates: $7114. **Scholarships, grants, and awards:** Federal Pell, FSEOG, state, private, college/university gift aid from institutional funds.

GIFT AID (NON-NEED-BASED) Total amount: $1,612,935 (94% institutional, 6% external sources). **Receiving aid:** Freshmen: 87% (83). Undergraduates: 82% (546). **Average award:** Freshmen: $2941. Undergraduates: $3296. **Scholarships, grants, and awards by category:** Academic interests/achievement: 195 awards ($668,517 total): general academic interests/achievements. Creative arts/performance: 42 awards ($82,675 total): music, performing arts, theater/drama. Special achievements/activities: 75 awards ($308,323 total): leadership, religious involvement. Special characteristics: 88 awards ($392,855 total): children and siblings of alumni, children of faculty/staff, international students, out-of-state students, relatives of clergy, religious affiliation, siblings of current students. **Tuition waivers:** Full or partial for employees or children of employees. **ROTC:** Army cooperative, Air Force cooperative.

LOANS Student loans: $6,937,675 (42% need-based, 58% non-need-based). 72% of past graduating class borrowed through all loan programs. Average indebtedness per student: $23,868. **Average need-based loan:** Freshmen: $3394. Undergraduates: $4229. **Parent loans:** $1,524,294 (100% non-need-based). **Programs:** Federal Direct (Subsidized and Unsubsidized Stafford, PLUS), Perkins.

WORK-STUDY Federal work-study: Total amount: $53,824; 28 jobs averaging $2211. **State or other work-study/employment:** Total amount: $21,000 (100% need-based). 12 part-time jobs averaging $2233.

ATHLETIC AWARDS Total amount: $1,836,765 (100% non-need-based).

APPLYING FOR FINANCIAL AID Required financial aid forms: FAFSA, institution's own form, state aid form. **Financial aid deadline:** 7/15 (priority: 3/2). **Notification date:** Continuous beginning 3/15. Students must reply by 9/1 or within 4 weeks of notification.

CONTACT Erin Neill, Financial Aid Specialist, San Diego Christian College, 2100 Greenfield Drive, El Cajon, CA 92019, 619-201-8731 or toll-free 800-676-2242. Fax: 619-201-8797. E-mail: eneill@sdcc.edu. Website: http://www.sdcc.edu/.

SAN DIEGO STATE UNIVERSITY
San Diego, CA

Tuition & fees (CA res): $6766	Average undergraduate aid package: $11,000

ABOUT THE INSTITUTION State-supported, coed. **Awards:** certificates, bachelor's, master's, and doctoral degrees. 88 undergraduate majors. **Total enrollment:** 31,597. Undergraduates: 22,814. Freshmen: 4,240. Federal methodology is used as a basis for awarding need-based institutional aid.

UNDERGRADUATE EXPENSES for 2013-2014 Application fee: $55. **Tuition, state resident:** full-time $0. **Tuition, nonresident:** full-time $11,160; part-time $372 per unit. **Required fees:** full-time $6766; $2140 per term. Full-time tuition and fees vary according to degree level, location, and program. Part-time tuition and fees vary according to course load, degree level, location, and program. **College room and board:** $13,812. Room and board charges vary according to board plan and housing facility.

FRESHMAN FINANCIAL AID (Fall 2012, est.) 3,160 applied for aid; of those 73% were deemed to have need. 96% of freshmen with need received aid; of those 9% had need fully met. **Average percent of need met:** 69% (excluding resources awarded to replace EFC). **Average financial aid package:** $9000 (excluding resources awarded to replace EFC). 3% of all full-time freshmen had no need and received non-need-based gift aid.

UNDERGRADUATE FINANCIAL AID (Fall 2012, est.) 17,000 applied for aid; of those 84% were deemed to have need. 97% of undergraduates with need received aid; of those 22% had need fully met. **Average percent of need met:** 71% (excluding resources awarded to replace EFC). **Average financial aid package:** $11,000 (excluding resources awarded to replace EFC). 4% of all full-time undergraduates had no need and received non-need-based gift aid.

GIFT AID (NEED-BASED) *Total amount:* $106,266,000 (42% federal, 26% state, 32% institutional). *Receiving aid:* Freshmen: 39% (1,500); all full-time undergraduates: 43% (10,200). *Average award:* Freshmen: $11,000; Undergraduates: $10,100. *Scholarships, grants, and awards:* Federal Pell, FSEOG, state, private, college/university gift aid from institutional funds, Federal Nursing.

GIFT AID (NON-NEED-BASED) *Total amount:* $4,748,000 (1% state, 42% institutional, 57% external sources). *Receiving aid:* Freshmen: 18% (700). Undergraduates: 11% (2,600). *Average award:* Freshmen: $3600. Undergraduates: $1800. *Scholarships, grants, and awards by category: Academic interests/achievement:* area/ethnic studies, biological sciences, business, communication, computer science, education, engineering/technologies, English, foreign languages, general academic interests/achievements, health fields, humanities, international studies, mathematics, military science, physical sciences, religion/biblical studies, social sciences. *Creative arts/performance:* applied art and design, art/fine arts, cinema/film/broadcasting, creative writing, dance, debating, journalism/publications, music, performing arts, theater/drama. *Special achievements/activities:* cheerleading/drum major, hobbies/interests, leadership, memberships. *Special characteristics:* adult students, children and siblings of alumni, children of faculty/staff, children of workers in trades, first-generation college students, handicapped students, local/state students, previous college experience, veterans, veterans' children. *Tuition waivers:* Full or partial for employees or children of employees. *ROTC:* Army, Naval, Air Force.

LOANS *Student loans:* $111,202,000 (71% need-based, 29% non-need-based). 44% of past graduating class borrowed through all loan programs. *Average indebtedness per student:* $17,600. *Average need-based loan:* Freshmen: $3100. Undergraduates: $3900. *Parent loans:* $79,264,000 (20% need-based, 80% non-need-based). *Programs:* Federal Direct (Subsidized and Unsubsidized Stafford, PLUS), Perkins, college/university.

WORK-STUDY *Federal work-study:* Total amount: $1,194,000; 537 jobs averaging $2010.

ATHLETIC AWARDS Total amount: $6,170,000 (100% non-need-based).

APPLYING FOR FINANCIAL AID *Required financial aid forms:* FAFSA, state aid form. *Financial aid deadline:* 3/2 (priority: 4/1). *Notification date:* Continuous beginning 3/4.

CONTACT Mr. Howard Craig Yamamoto, Director of Financial Aid and Scholarships, San Diego State University, 5500 Campanile Drive, SSW-3605, San Diego, CA 92182-7436, 619-594-6323.
Website: http://www.sdsu.edu/.

SANFORD COLLEGE OF NURSING
Bismarck, ND

ABOUT THE INSTITUTION Independent, coed, primarily women. *Awards:* bachelor's degrees. 1 undergraduate major. *Total enrollment:* 109. Undergraduates: 109.

GIFT AID (NEED-BASED) *Scholarships, grants, and awards:* Federal Pell, FSEOG, state, private, college/university gift aid from institutional funds.

GIFT AID (NON-NEED-BASED) *Scholarships, grants, and awards by category: Academic interests/achievement:* general academic interests/achievements, health fields. *Special achievements/activities:* memberships. *Special characteristics:* children and siblings of alumni, general special characteristics, local/state students.

LOANS *Programs:* Federal Direct (Subsidized and Unsubsidized Stafford, PLUS), Perkins, Federal Nursing, college/university.

WORK-STUDY *Federal work-study:* Total amount: $7000; 6 jobs averaging $1200.

CONTACT Ms. Janell Thomas, Financial Aid Director, Sanford College of Nursing, 512 North 7th Street, Bismarck, ND 58501-4494, 701-323-6270. *Fax:* 701-323-6289. *E-mail:* jthomas@mocn.edu.
Website: http://bismarck.sanfordhealth.org/collegeofnursing/index.asp.

SAN FRANCISCO ART INSTITUTE
San Francisco, CA

Tuition & fees: $36,618	Average undergraduate aid package: $16,990

ABOUT THE INSTITUTION Independent, coed. *Awards:* certificates, bachelor's, and master's degrees. 9 undergraduate majors. *Total enrollment:* 670. Undergraduates: 453. Freshmen: 82. Federal methodology is used as a basis for awarding need-based institutional aid.

UNDERGRADUATE EXPENSES for 2013–2014 *Application fee:* $65. *Comprehensive fee:* $50,462 includes full-time tuition ($35,748), mandatory fees ($870), and room and board ($13,844). *College room only:* $9974. Full-time tuition and fees vary according to degree level. Room and board charges vary according to housing facility. *Part-time tuition:* $1566 per credit. Part-time tuition and fees vary according to degree level.

FRESHMAN FINANCIAL AID (Fall 2011) 55 applied for aid; of those 73% were deemed to have need. 100% of freshmen with need received aid. *Average percent of need met:* 49% (excluding resources awarded to replace EFC). *Average financial aid package:* $16,960 (excluding resources awarded to replace EFC). 17% of all full-time freshmen had no need and received non-need-based gift aid.

UNDERGRADUATE FINANCIAL AID (Fall 2011) 161 applied for aid; of those 100% were deemed to have need. 100% of undergraduates with need received aid. *Average percent of need met:* 47% (excluding resources awarded to replace EFC). *Average financial aid package:* $16,990 (excluding resources awarded to replace EFC). 14% of all full-time undergraduates had no need and received non-need-based gift aid.

GIFT AID (NEED-BASED) *Total amount:* $12,173,418 (7% federal, 3% state, 40% institutional, 50% external sources). *Receiving aid:* Freshmen: 46% (40); all full-time undergraduates: 40% (161). *Average award:* Freshmen: $6420; Undergraduates: $7120. *Scholarships, grants, and awards:* Federal Pell, FSEOG, state, private, college/university gift aid from institutional funds.

GIFT AID (NON-NEED-BASED) *Total amount:* $12,173,418 (7% federal, 3% state, 40% institutional, 50% external sources). *Receiving aid:* Freshmen: 18% (16). Undergraduates: 4% (16). *Average award:* Freshmen: $7533. Undergraduates: $5673. *Scholarships, grants, and awards by category: Academic interests/achievement:* general academic interests/achievements. *Creative arts/performance:* art/fine arts. *Tuition waivers:* Full or partial for employees or children of employees.

LOANS *Student loans:* $9,934,342 (50% need-based, 50% non-need-based). 53% of past graduating class borrowed through all loan programs. *Average indebtedness per student:* $29,541. *Average need-based loan:* Freshmen: $3156. Undergraduates: $3720. *Parent loans:* $4,173,494 (50% need-based, 50% non-need-based). *Programs:* Federal Direct (Subsidized and Unsubsidized Stafford, PLUS), state, college/university.

WORK-STUDY *Federal work-study:* Total amount: $153,087; jobs available. *State or other work-study/employment:* Total amount: $711,240 (50% need-based, 50% non-need-based). Part-time jobs available.

APPLYING FOR FINANCIAL AID *Required financial aid forms:* FAFSA, Cal Grant forms, GPA verification form (CA residents only). *Financial aid deadline:* 5/31 (priority: 3/1). *Notification date:* Continuous beginning 4/15. Students must reply within 3 weeks of notification.

CONTACT Larry Blair, Director of Financial Aid, San Francisco Art Institute, 800 Chestnut Street, San Francisco, CA 94133, 415-749-4560 or toll-free 800-345-SFAI. *Fax:* 415-351-3503. *E-mail:* lblair@sfai.edu.
Website: http://www.sfai.edu/.

SAN FRANCISCO CONSERVATORY OF MUSIC
San Francisco, CA

Tuition & fees: $38,140	Average undergraduate aid package: $26,936

ABOUT THE INSTITUTION Independent, coed. *Awards:* certificates, diplomas, bachelor's, and master's degrees. 8 undergraduate majors. *Total enrollment:* 415. Undergraduates: 186. Freshmen: 37. Both federal and institutional methodology are used as a basis for awarding need-based institutional aid.

UNDERGRADUATE EXPENSES for 2013–2014 Tuition: full-time $37,600; part-time $1660 per credit. **Required fees:** full-time $540; $270 per term. Part-time tuition and fees vary according to course load and program.
FRESHMAN FINANCIAL AID (Fall 2012, est.) 26 applied for aid; of those 73% were deemed to have need. 100% of freshmen with need received aid; of those 11% had need fully met. **Average percent of need met:** 62% (excluding resources awarded to replace EFC). **Average financial aid package:** $24,795 (excluding resources awarded to replace EFC). 50% of all full-time freshmen had no need and received non-need-based gift aid.
UNDERGRADUATE FINANCIAL AID (Fall 2012, est.) 134 applied for aid; of those 86% were deemed to have need. 100% of undergraduates with need received aid; of those 10% had need fully met. **Average percent of need met:** 63% (excluding resources awarded to replace EFC). **Average financial aid package:** $26,936 (excluding resources awarded to replace EFC). 37% of all full-time undergraduates had no need and received non-need-based gift aid.
GIFT AID (NEED-BASED) Total amount: $2,909,763 (11% federal, 7% state, 81% institutional, 1% external sources). **Receiving aid:** Freshmen: 48% (19); all full-time undergraduates: 60% (115). **Average award:** Freshmen: $20,914; Undergraduates: $21,546. **Scholarships, grants, and awards:** Federal Pell, FSEOG, state, private, college/university gift aid from institutional funds.
GIFT AID (NON-NEED-BASED) Total amount: $763,112 (99% institutional, 1% external sources). **Receiving aid:** Freshmen: 5% (2). Undergraduates: 4% (8). **Average award:** Freshmen: $16,650. Undergraduates: $15,884. **Scholarships, grants, and awards by category:** Creative arts/performance: music. **Tuition waivers:** Full or partial for employees or children of employees.
LOANS Student loans: $1,080,542 (83% need-based, 17% non-need-based). 61% of past graduating class borrowed through all loan programs. **Average indebtedness per student:** $18,028. **Average need-based loan:** Freshmen: $4338. Undergraduates: $5580. **Parent loans:** $1,967,547 (46% need-based, 54% non-need-based). **Programs:** Federal Direct (Subsidized and Unsubsidized Stafford, PLUS), Perkins.
WORK-STUDY Federal work-study: Total amount: $22,769; 18 jobs averaging $1265. **State or other work-study/employment:** Total amount: $2000 (100% non-need-based). 2 part-time jobs averaging $1000.
APPLYING FOR FINANCIAL AID Required financial aid forms: FAFSA, institution's own form, CSS Financial Aid PROFILE. **Financial aid deadline (priority):** 2/15. **Notification date:** Continuous beginning 4/1. Students must reply by 5/1 or within 2 weeks of notification.
CONTACT Doris Howard, Director of Financial Aid, San Francisco Conservatory of Music, 50 Oak Street, San Francisco, CA 94102-6011, 415-503-6214. Fax: 415-503-6299. E-mail: dbh@sfcm.edu. Website: http://www.sfcm.edu/.

SAN FRANCISCO STATE UNIVERSITY
San Francisco, CA

Tuition & fees (CA res): $6440	Average undergraduate aid package: $11,652

ABOUT THE INSTITUTION State-supported, coed. **Awards:** certificates, bachelor's, master's, and doctoral degrees. 91 undergraduate majors. **Total enrollment:** 30,500. Undergraduates: 26,449. Freshmen: 3,807. Federal methodology is used as a basis for awarding need-based institutional aid.
UNDERGRADUATE EXPENSES for 2013–2014 Application fee: $55. **Tuition, state resident:** full-time $5472. **Tuition, nonresident:** full-time $16,632; part-time $372 per unit. **Required fees:** full-time $968. Full-time tuition and fees vary according to course load. Part-time tuition and fees vary according to course load. **College room and board:** $11,576. Room and board charges vary according to board plan and housing facility.
FRESHMAN FINANCIAL AID (Fall 2012, est.) 3,205 applied for aid; of those 83% were deemed to have need. 96% of freshmen with need received aid; of those 7% had need fully met. **Average percent of need met:** 64% (excluding resources awarded to replace EFC). **Average financial aid package:** $11,932 (excluding resources awarded to replace EFC). 1% of all full-time freshmen had no need and received non-need-based gift aid.
UNDERGRADUATE FINANCIAL AID (Fall 2012, est.) 15,846 applied for aid; of those 90% were deemed to have need. 97% of undergraduates with need received aid; of those 6% had need fully met. **Average percent of need met:** 60% (excluding resources awarded to replace EFC). **Average financial aid package:** $11,652

(excluding resources awarded to replace EFC). 1% of all full-time undergraduates had no need and received non-need-based gift aid.
GIFT AID (NEED-BASED) Total amount: $111,441,024 (45% federal, 53% state, 2% external sources). **Receiving aid:** Freshmen: 51% (1,900); all full-time undergraduates: 48% (10,620). **Average award:** Freshmen: $10,404; Undergraduates: $9436. **Scholarships, grants, and awards:** Federal Pell, FSEOG, state, private, college/university gift aid from institutional funds.
GIFT AID (NON-NEED-BASED) Total amount: $664,952 (24% institutional, 76% external sources). **Receiving aid:** Freshmen: 7% (254). Undergraduates: 4% (885). **Average award:** Freshmen: $2536. Undergraduates: $2526. **Tuition waivers:** Full or partial for employees or children of employees. **ROTC:** Army cooperative, Air Force cooperative.
LOANS Student loans: $72,650,562 (91% need-based, 9% non-need-based). 43% of past graduating class borrowed through all loan programs. **Average indebtedness per student:** $20,493. **Average need-based loan:** Freshmen: $2433. Undergraduates: $3243. **Parent loans:** $26,719,820 (73% need-based, 27% non-need-based). **Programs:** Federal Direct (Subsidized and Unsubsidized Stafford, PLUS), Perkins.
WORK-STUDY Federal work-study: Total amount: $740,919; jobs available.
ATHLETIC AWARDS Total amount: $358,163 (60% need-based, 40% non-need-based).
APPLYING FOR FINANCIAL AID Required financial aid form: FAFSA. **Financial aid deadline (priority):** 3/2. **Notification date:** Continuous beginning 3/30. Students must reply within 2 weeks of notification.
CONTACT Barbara Hubler, Director of Financial Aid, San Francisco State University, 1600 Holloway Avenue, San Francisco, CA 94132-1722; 415-338-7000. Fax: 415-338-0949. E-mail: finaid@sfsu.edu. Website: http://www.sfsu.edu/.

SAN JOSE STATE UNIVERSITY
San Jose, CA

Tuition & fees (CA res): $13,704	Average undergraduate aid package: $16,323

ABOUT THE INSTITUTION State-supported, coed. **Awards:** bachelor's and master's degrees. 89 undergraduate majors. **Total enrollment:** 30,448. Undergraduates: 25,157. Freshmen: 3,384. Federal methodology is used as a basis for awarding need-based institutional aid.
UNDERGRADUATE EXPENSES for 2013–2014 Application fee: $55. **Tuition, state resident:** full-time $6852. **Tuition, nonresident:** full-time $11,160. **Required fees:** full-time $6852. **College room and board:** $11,733; **Room only:** $6633.
FRESHMAN FINANCIAL AID (Fall 2011) 3,003 applied for aid; of those 86% were deemed to have need. 95% of freshmen with need received aid; of those 61% had need fully met. **Average percent of need met:** 83% (excluding resources awarded to replace EFC). **Average financial aid package:** $16,334 (excluding resources awarded to replace EFC). 1% of all full-time freshmen had no need and received non-need-based gift aid.
UNDERGRADUATE FINANCIAL AID (Fall 2011) 14,829 applied for aid; of those 91% were deemed to have need. 96% of undergraduates with need received aid; of those 54% had need fully met. **Average percent of need met:** 87% (excluding resources awarded to replace EFC). **Average financial aid package:** $16,323 (excluding resources awarded to replace EFC). 1% of all full-time undergraduates had no need and received non-need-based gift aid.
GIFT AID (NEED-BASED) Total amount: $92,745,836 (45% federal, 53% state, 2% external sources). **Receiving aid:** Freshmen: 46% (1,761); all full-time undergraduates: 48% (9,551). **Average award:** Freshmen: $14,794; Undergraduates: $7142. **Scholarships, grants, and awards:** Federal Pell, FSEOG, state, private, college/university gift aid from institutional funds.
GIFT AID (NON-NEED-BASED) Total amount: $910,784 (87% institutional, 13% external sources). **Receiving aid:** Freshmen: 1% (42). Undergraduates: 1% (198). **Average award:** Freshmen: $43,626. Undergraduates: $1948. **Scholarships, grants, and awards by category:** Academic interests/achievement: general academic interests/achievements. Creative arts/performance: art/fine arts, general creative arts/performance. Special achievements/activities: leadership. Special characteristics: local/state students. **ROTC:** Army, Air Force.

LOANS *Student loans:* $61,983,805 (91% need-based, 9% non-need-based). 40% of past graduating class borrowed through all loan programs. *Average indebtedness per student:* $16,519. *Average need-based loan:* Freshmen: $3290. Undergraduates: $3823. *Parent loans:* $9,039,549 (72% need-based, 28% non-need-based). *Programs:* Federal Direct (Subsidized and Unsubsidized Stafford, PLUS), Perkins.

WORK-STUDY *Federal work-study:* Total amount: $1,510,248; jobs available.

ATHLETIC AWARDS Total amount: $4,253,730 (76% need-based, 24% non-need-based).

APPLYING FOR FINANCIAL AID *Required financial aid form:* FAFSA. *Financial aid deadline:* 6/15 (priority: 3/2). *Notification date:* Continuous beginning 4/1.

CONTACT Coleetta McElroy, Director of Financial Aid and Scholarship Office, San Jose State University, One Washington Square, San Jose, CA 95192-0036, 408-924-6086. *E-mail:* coleetta.mcelroy@sjsu.edu. *Website:* http://www.sjsu.edu/.

SANTA CLARA UNIVERSITY
Santa Clara, CA

Tuition & fees: $40,572	Average undergraduate aid package: $27,067

ABOUT THE INSTITUTION Independent Roman Catholic (Jesuit), coed. *Awards:* certificates, bachelor's, master's, and doctoral degrees. 47 undergraduate majors. *Total enrollment:* 8,519. Undergraduates: 5,250. Freshmen: 1,278. Both federal and institutional methodology are used as a basis for awarding need-based institutional aid.

UNDERGRADUATE EXPENSES for 2013–2014 *Application fee:* $55. *Comprehensive fee:* $52,848 includes full-time tuition ($40,572) and room and board ($12,276). Room and board charges vary according to board plan, housing facility, location, and student level. *Part-time tuition:* $1127 per unit. Part-time tuition and fees vary according to course load.

FRESHMAN FINANCIAL AID (Fall 2012, est.) 896 applied for aid; of those 71% were deemed to have need. 99% of freshmen with need received aid; of those 38% had need fully met. *Average percent of need met:* 73% (excluding resources awarded to replace EFC). *Average financial aid package:* $26,310 (excluding resources awarded to replace EFC). 28% of all full-time freshmen had no need and received non-need-based gift aid.

UNDERGRADUATE FINANCIAL AID (Fall 2012, est.) 3,400 applied for aid; of those 78% were deemed to have need. 85% of undergraduates with need received aid; of those 36% had need fully met. *Average percent of need met:* 68% (excluding resources awarded to replace EFC). *Average financial aid package:* $27,067 (excluding resources awarded to replace EFC). 28% of all full-time undergraduates had no need and received non-need-based gift aid.

GIFT AID (NEED-BASED) *Total amount:* $49,548,334 (7% federal, 10% state, 81% institutional, 2% external sources). *Receiving aid:* Freshmen: 39% (495); all full-time undergraduates: 35% (1,777). *Average award:* Freshmen: $19,450; Undergraduates: $19,985. *Scholarships, grants, and awards:* Federal Pell, FSEOG, state, private, college/university gift aid from institutional funds.

GIFT AID (NON-NEED-BASED) *Total amount:* $21,306,660 (94% institutional, 6% external sources). *Receiving aid:* Freshmen: 25% (319). Undergraduates: 19% (982). *Average award:* Freshmen: $10,357. Undergraduates: $12,228. *Scholarships, grants, and awards by category:* Academic interests/achievement: 2,402 awards ($30,326,437 total): business, engineering/technologies, general academic interests/achievements, military science. *Creative arts/performance:* 42 awards ($257,400 total): dance, debating, music, theater/drama. *Special characteristics:* 105 awards ($3,459,679 total): children and siblings of alumni, children of faculty/staff, children with a deceased or disabled parent, handicapped students. *Tuition waivers:* Full or partial for employees or children of employees. *ROTC:* Army, Air Force cooperative.

LOANS *Student loans:* $13,167,364 (88% need-based, 12% non-need-based). 46% of past graduating class borrowed through all loan programs. *Average indebtedness per student:* $28,672. *Average need-based loan:* Freshmen: $3459. Undergraduates: $4971. *Parent loans:* $11,659,292 (82% need-based, 18% non-need-based). *Programs:* Federal Direct (Subsidized and Unsubsidized Stafford, PLUS), Perkins, alternative loans.

WORK-STUDY *Federal work-study:* Total amount: $1,214,520; 407 jobs averaging $3015. *State or other work-study/employment:* Total amount: $3,924,699 (69% need-based, 31% non-need-based). Part-time jobs available.

ATHLETIC AWARDS Total amount: $4,848,301 (29% need-based, 71% non-need-based).

APPLYING FOR FINANCIAL AID *Required financial aid forms:* FAFSA, CSS Financial Aid PROFILE. *Financial aid deadline (priority):* 2/1. *Notification date:* 4/1. Students must reply by 5/1 or within 2 weeks of notification.

CONTACT Marta I. Murchison, Associate Director of Systems and Data Analysis, Santa Clara University, 500 El Camino Real, Santa Clara, CA 95053, 408-551-6088. *Fax:* 408-551-6085. *E-mail:* mmurchison@scu.edu. *Website:* http://www.scu.edu/.

SANTA FE COLLEGE
Gainesville, FL

CONTACT Financial Aid Office, Santa Fe College, 3000 Northwest 83rd Street, Gainesville, FL 32606, 352-395-5000. *Website:* http://www.sfcollege.edu/.

SANTA FE UNIVERSITY OF ART AND DESIGN
Santa Fe, NM

CONTACT Amy Kearns, Director of Financial Aid, Santa Fe University of Art and Design, 1600 St. Michael's Drive, Santa Fe, NM 87505-7634, 505-473-6454 or toll-free 800-456-2673. *Fax:* 505-473-6399. *E-mail:* sfs@santafeuniversity.edu. *Website:* http://www.santafeuniversity.edu/.

SARAH LAWRENCE COLLEGE
Bronxville, NY

Tuition & fees: $46,924	Average undergraduate aid package: $36,266

ABOUT THE INSTITUTION Independent, coed. *Awards:* certificates, bachelor's, and master's degrees. 111 undergraduate majors. *Total enrollment:* 1,744. Undergraduates: 1,413. Freshmen: 374. Both federal and institutional methodology are used as a basis for awarding need-based institutional aid.

UNDERGRADUATE EXPENSES for 2013–2014 *Tuition:* full-time $45,900. Full-time tuition and fees vary according to course load. Part-time tuition and fees vary according to course load. Room and board charges vary according to board plan.

FRESHMAN FINANCIAL AID (Fall 2012, est.) 265 applied for aid; of those 83% were deemed to have need. 99% of freshmen with need received aid; of those 53% had need fully met. *Average percent of need met:* 83% (excluding resources awarded to replace EFC). *Average financial aid package:* $30,946 (excluding resources awarded to replace EFC). 10% of all full-time freshmen had no need and received non-need-based gift aid.

UNDERGRADUATE FINANCIAL AID (Fall 2012, est.) 1,061 applied for aid; of those 90% were deemed to have need. 92% of undergraduates with need received aid; of those 65% had need fully met. *Average percent of need met:* 84% (excluding resources awarded to replace EFC). *Average financial aid package:* $36,266 (excluding resources awarded to replace EFC). 8% of all full-time undergraduates had no need and received non-need-based gift aid.

GIFT AID (NEED-BASED) *Total amount:* $27,408,798 (5% federal, 1% state, 92% institutional, 2% external sources). *Receiving aid:* Freshmen: 62% (214); all full-time undergraduates: 63% (835). *Average award:* Freshmen: $29,670; Undergraduates: $32,825. *Scholarships, grants, and awards:* Federal Pell, FSEOG, state, private, college/university gift aid from institutional funds.

GIFT AID (NON-NEED-BASED) *Total amount:* $743,513 (2% federal, 1% state, 92% institutional, 5% external sources). *Receiving aid:* Freshmen: 10% (36). Undergraduates: 8% (109). *Average award:* Freshmen: $12,667. Undergraduates: $6821. *Scholarships, grants, and awards by category:* Academic interests/achievement: 53 awards ($534,077 total): general academic interests/achievements. *Tuition waivers:* Full or partial for employees or children of employees.

LOANS *Student loans:* $3,618,395 (93% need-based, 7% non-need-based). 61% of past graduating class borrowed through all loan programs. *Average indebtedness per*

student: $15,309. **Average need-based loan:** Freshmen: $2811. Undergraduates: $4546. **Parent loans:** $3,949,843 (87% need-based, 13% non-need-based). **Programs:** Federal Direct (Subsidized and Unsubsidized Stafford, PLUS), Perkins, college/university, Sallie Mae Smart Option Loans, CitiAssist Loans.
WORK-STUDY Federal work-study: Total amount: $1,153,905; 686 jobs averaging $1682. **State or other work-study/employment:** Total amount: $104,143 (84% need-based, 16% non-need-based). 46 part-time jobs averaging $1892.
APPLYING FOR FINANCIAL AID Required financial aid forms: FAFSA, CSS Financial Aid PROFILE, state aid form, noncustodial (divorced/separated) parent's statement. **Financial aid deadline:** 2/1. **Notification date:** 4/1. Students must reply by 5/1.
CONTACT Ms. Heather McDonnell, Director of Financial Aid, Sarah Lawrence College, One Mead Way, Bronxville, NY 10708, 914-395-2570 or toll-free 800-888-2858. *Fax:* 914-395-2676. *E-mail:* hmcdonn@sarahlawrence.edu. *Website:* http://www.sarahlawrence.edu/.

SAVANNAH COLLEGE OF ART AND DESIGN
Savannah, GA

Tuition & fees: $32,405	Average undergraduate aid package: $25,296

ABOUT THE INSTITUTION Independent, coed. **Awards:** certificates, bachelor's, and master's degrees. 31 undergraduate majors. **Total enrollment:** 11,415. Undergraduates: 9,182. Freshmen: 1,794. Federal methodology is used as a basis for awarding need-based institutional aid.
UNDERGRADUATE EXPENSES for 2013–2014 Application fee: $35. **Comprehensive fee:** $45,395 includes full-time tuition ($31,905), mandatory fees ($500), and room and board ($12,990). **College room only:** $8220. Full-time tuition and fees vary according to course load and degree level. Room and board charges vary according to board plan, housing facility, and location. **Part-time tuition:** $709 per quarter hour. Part-time tuition and fees vary according to course load and degree level.
FRESHMAN FINANCIAL AID (Fall 2012, est.) 1,256 applied for aid; of those 85% were deemed to have need. 100% of freshmen with need received aid; of those 12% had need fully met. **Average percent of need met:** 16% (excluding resources awarded to replace EFC). **Average financial aid package:** $28,283 (excluding resources awarded to replace EFC). 36% of all full-time freshmen had no need and received non-need-based gift aid.
UNDERGRADUATE FINANCIAL AID (Fall 2012, est.) 5,059 applied for aid; of those 89% were deemed to have need. 100% of undergraduates with need received aid; of those 8% had need fully met. **Average percent of need met:** 20% (excluding resources awarded to replace EFC). **Average financial aid package:** $25,296 (excluding resources awarded to replace EFC). 32% of all full-time undergraduates had no need and received non-need-based gift aid.
GIFT AID (NEED-BASED) Total amount: $22,732,984 (48% federal, 4% state, 37% institutional, 11% external sources). **Receiving aid:** Freshmen: 37% (660); all full-time undergraduates: 39% (2,970). **Average award:** Freshmen: $5556; Undergraduates: $6465. **Scholarships, grants, and awards:** Federal Pell, FSEOG, state, private, college/university gift aid from institutional funds.
GIFT AID (NON-NEED-BASED) Total amount: $66,325,134 (5% state, 95% institutional). **Receiving aid:** Freshmen: 60% (1,049). Undergraduates: 48% (3,720). **Average award:** Freshmen: $10,278. Undergraduates: $9612. **Scholarships, grants, and awards by category:** Academic interests/achievement: architecture, education, general academic interests/achievements. Creative arts/performance: art/fine arts, general creative arts/performance. Special achievements/activities: general special achievements/activities. Special characteristics: general special characteristics. **Tuition waivers:** Full or partial for employees or children of employees. **ROTC:** Army cooperative.
LOANS Student loans: $60,234,940 (90% need-based, 10% non-need-based). 62% of past graduating class borrowed through all loan programs. *Average indebtedness per student:* $37,776. **Average need-based loan:** Freshmen: $2852. Undergraduates: $3975. **Parent loans:** $59,956,695 (85% need-based, 15% non-need-based). **Programs:** Federal Direct (Subsidized and Unsubsidized Stafford, PLUS), state.
WORK-STUDY Federal work-study: Total amount: $535,000; jobs available.
ATHLETIC AWARDS Total amount: $5,068,251 (52% need-based, 48% non-need-based).

APPLYING FOR FINANCIAL AID Required financial aid forms: FAFSA, state aid form. **Financial aid deadline:** Continuous. **Notification date:** Continuous beginning 3/15. Students must reply within 4 weeks of notification.
CONTACT Kim Beveridge, Director of Financial Aid, Savannah College of Art and Design, PO Box 3146, Savannah, GA 31402-3146, 800-859-7223 or toll-free 800-869-7223. *E-mail:* admission@scad.edu. *Website:* http://www.scad.edu/.

SAVANNAH STATE UNIVERSITY
Savannah, GA

ABOUT THE INSTITUTION State-supported, coed. 24 undergraduate majors.
GIFT AID (NEED-BASED) Scholarships, grants, and awards: Federal Pell, FSEOG, state, private, college/university gift aid from institutional funds.
GIFT AID (NON-NEED-BASED) Scholarships, grants, and awards by category: Academic interests/achievement: biological sciences, business, computer science, engineering/technologies, English, general academic interests/achievements, humanities, mathematics, military science, physical sciences, social sciences. Creative arts/performance: music.
LOANS Programs: Federal Direct (Subsidized and Unsubsidized Stafford, PLUS), Perkins, state, college/university.
WORK-STUDY Federal work-study jobs available.
APPLYING FOR FINANCIAL AID Required financial aid form: FAFSA.
CONTACT Adrienne Brown, Director of Financial Aid, Savannah State University, PO Box 20523, Savannah, GA 31404, 912-358-4162 or toll-free 800-788-0478. *Fax:* 912-353-3150. *E-mail:* finaid@savannahstate.edu. *Website:* http://www.savannahstate.edu/.

SCHILLER INTERNATIONAL UNIVERSITY
Largo, FL

CONTACT Financial Aid Office, Schiller International University, 300 East Bay Drive, Largo, FL 33770, 727-736-5082 or toll-free 800-261-9571 (in-state), 800-261-9751 (out-of-state). *Website:* http://www.schiller.edu/.

SCHOOL OF THE ART INSTITUTE OF CHICAGO
Chicago, IL

Tuition & fees: $39,020	Average undergraduate aid package: $33,404

ABOUT THE INSTITUTION Independent, coed. **Awards:** certificates, bachelor's, and master's degrees. 33 undergraduate majors. **Total enrollment:** 3,308. Undergraduates: 2,627. Freshmen: 563. Federal methodology is used as a basis for awarding need-based institutional aid.
UNDERGRADUATE EXPENSES for 2013–2014 Application fee: $65. **One-time required fee:** $150. **Comprehensive fee:** $52,830 includes full-time tuition ($38,340), mandatory fees ($680), and room and board ($13,810). **College room only:** $10,400. Full-time tuition and fees vary according to course load, degree level, and program. Room and board charges vary according to board plan. **Part-time tuition:** $1278 per credit hour. **Part-time fees:** $235 per term. Part-time tuition and fees vary according to course load, degree level, and program.
FRESHMAN FINANCIAL AID (Fall 2011) 277 applied for aid; of those 83% were deemed to have need. 100% of freshmen with need received aid; of those 7% had need fully met. **Average percent of need met:** 76% (excluding resources awarded to replace EFC). **Average financial aid package:** $31,035 (excluding resources awarded to replace EFC). 49% of all full-time freshmen had no need and received non-need-based gift aid.

SCHOOL OF THE ART INSTITUTE OF CHICAGO

UNDERGRADUATE FINANCIAL AID (Fall 2011) 1,418 applied for aid; of those 91% were deemed to have need. 100% of undergraduates with need received aid; of those 5% had need fully met. *Average percent of need met:* 77% (excluding resources awarded to replace EFC). *Average financial aid package:* $33,404 (excluding resources awarded to replace EFC). 38% of all full-time undergraduates had no need and received non-need-based gift aid.
GIFT AID (NEED-BASED) *Total amount:* $20,845,760 (16% federal, 5% state, 78% institutional, 1% external sources). *Receiving aid:* Freshmen: 51% (228); all full-time undergraduates: 55% (1,278). *Average award:* Freshmen: $15,889; Undergraduates: $15,671. *Scholarships, grants, and awards:* Federal Pell, FSEOG, state, private, college/university gift aid from institutional funds.
GIFT AID (NON-NEED-BASED) *Total amount:* $6,481,438 (97% institutional, 3% external sources). *Receiving aid:* Freshmen: 3% (13). Undergraduates: 2% (52). *Average award:* Freshmen: $6719. Undergraduates: $6469. *Scholarships, grants, and awards by category: Academic interests/achievement:* general academic interests/achievements. *Creative arts/performance:* art/fine arts. *Tuition waivers:* Full or partial for employees or children of employees.
LOANS *Student loans:* $14,101,680 (85% need-based, 15% non-need-based). 53% of past graduating class borrowed through all loan programs. *Average indebtedness per student:* $39,914. *Average need-based loan:* Freshmen: $4258. Undergraduates: $4835. *Parent loans:* $8,329,737 (59% need-based, 41% non-need-based). *Programs:* Federal Direct (Subsidized and Unsubsidized Stafford, PLUS), Perkins.
WORK-STUDY *Federal work-study:* Total amount: $922,591; jobs available. *State or other work-study/employment:* Total amount: $604,562 (59% need-based, 41% non-need-based). Part-time jobs available.
APPLYING FOR FINANCIAL AID *Required financial aid form:* FAFSA. *Financial aid deadline (priority):* 3/1. *Notification date:* Continuous beginning 4/1.
CONTACT Mr. Patrick James, Student Financial Services Office, School of the Art Institute of Chicago, 36 South Wabash, Suite 1218, Chicago, IL 60603-3103, 312-629-6600 or toll-free 800-232-SAIC. *Fax:* 312-629-6601. *E-mail:* finaid@saic.edu. *Website:* http://www.saic.edu/.

SCHOOL OF THE MUSEUM OF FINE ARTS, BOSTON
Boston, MA

Tuition & fees: $38,028	Average undergraduate aid package: $20,230

ABOUT THE INSTITUTION Independent, coed. *Awards:* certificates, diplomas, bachelor's, and master's degrees. 19 undergraduate majors. *Total enrollment:* 775. Undergraduates: 594. Freshmen: 94. Federal methodology is used as a basis for awarding need-based institutional aid.
UNDERGRADUATE EXPENSES for 2013–2014 *Application fee:* $65. *Comprehensive fee:* $50,018 includes full-time tuition ($36,828), mandatory fees ($1200), and room and board ($11,990). Full-time tuition and fees vary according to course load, degree level, program, and student level. Room and board charges vary according to board plan and housing facility. *Part-time tuition:* $1370 per unit. Part-time tuition and fees vary according to class time, course load, program, and student level.
FRESHMAN FINANCIAL AID (Fall 2012, est.) 83 applied for aid; of those 89% were deemed to have need. 100% of freshmen with need received aid; of those 3% had need fully met. *Average percent of need met:* 61% (excluding resources awarded to replace EFC). *Average financial aid package:* $17,937 (excluding resources awarded to replace EFC). 20% of all full-time freshmen had no need and received non-need-based gift aid.
UNDERGRADUATE FINANCIAL AID (Fall 2012, est.) 319 applied for aid; of those 92% were deemed to have need. 100% of undergraduates with need received aid; of those 7% had need fully met. *Average percent of need met:* 52% (excluding resources awarded to replace EFC). *Average financial aid package:* $20,230 (excluding resources awarded to replace EFC). 28% of all full-time undergraduates had no need and received non-need-based gift aid.
GIFT AID (NEED-BASED) *Total amount:* $12,529,375 (61% federal, 1% state, 38% institutional). *Receiving aid:* Freshmen: 70% (65); all full-time undergraduates: 69% (278). *Average award:* Freshmen: $12,135; Undergraduates: $12,963. *Scholarships, grants, and awards:* Federal Pell, FSEOG, state, private, college/university gift aid from institutional funds.

GIFT AID (NON-NEED-BASED) *Total amount:* $114,750 (100% institutional). *Receiving aid:* Freshmen: 78% (73). Undergraduates: 4% (16). *Average award:* Freshmen: $7789. Undergraduates: $7682. *Scholarships, grants, and awards by category: Creative arts/performance:* art/fine arts. *Special characteristics:* general special characteristics. *Tuition waivers:* Full or partial for employees or children of employees.
LOANS *Student loans:* $2,768,383 (100% need-based). *Average need-based loan:* Freshmen: $3434. Undergraduates: $4376. *Parent loans:* $2,009,544 (100% need-based). *Programs:* Federal Direct (Subsidized and Unsubsidized Stafford, PLUS), state.
WORK-STUDY *Federal work-study:* Total amount: $83,579; jobs available.
APPLYING FOR FINANCIAL AID *Required financial aid forms:* FAFSA, institution's own form. *Financial aid deadline (priority):* 3/15. *Notification date:* Continuous beginning 4/15. Students must reply by 5/1.
CONTACT Ms. Elizabeth Goreham, Director of Financial Aid, School of the Museum of Fine Arts, Boston, 230 The Fenway, Boston, MA 02115, 617-369-3684 or toll-free 800-643-6078 (in-state). *Fax:* 617-369-3041. *Website:* http://www.smfa.edu/.

SCHOOL OF VISUAL ARTS
New York, NY

Tuition & fees: $31,030	Average undergraduate aid package: $14,898

ABOUT THE INSTITUTION Proprietary, coed. 15 undergraduate majors. Federal methodology is used as a basis for awarding need-based institutional aid.
UNDERGRADUATE EXPENSES for 2013–2014 *Comprehensive fee:* $47,230 includes full-time tuition ($31,030) and room and board ($16,200). *College room only:* $13,200. Room and board charges vary according to housing facility. *Part-time tuition:* $1034 per credit hour.
FRESHMAN FINANCIAL AID (Fall 2012, est.) 401 applied for aid; of those 87% were deemed to have need. 95% of freshmen with need received aid; of those 2% had need fully met. *Average percent of need met:* 39% (excluding resources awarded to replace EFC). *Average financial aid package:* $14,555 (excluding resources awarded to replace EFC). 5% of all full-time freshmen had no need and received non-need-based gift aid.
UNDERGRADUATE FINANCIAL AID (Fall 2012, est.) 1,912 applied for aid; of those 92% were deemed to have need. 98% of undergraduates with need received aid; of those 1% had need fully met. *Average percent of need met:* 35% (excluding resources awarded to replace EFC). *Average financial aid package:* $14,898 (excluding resources awarded to replace EFC). 6% of all full-time undergraduates had no need and received non-need-based gift aid.
GIFT AID (NEED-BASED) *Total amount:* $13,664,144 (34% federal, 10% state, 54% institutional, 2% external sources). *Receiving aid:* Freshmen: 39% (241); all full-time undergraduates: 35% (1,197). *Average award:* Freshmen: $11,295; Undergraduates: $10,782. *Scholarships, grants, and awards:* Federal Pell, FSEOG, state, private, college/university gift aid from institutional funds.
GIFT AID (NON-NEED-BASED) *Total amount:* $2,577,165 (13% federal, 80% institutional, 7% external sources). *Receiving aid:* Freshmen: 15% (92). Undergraduates: 10% (335). *Average award:* Freshmen: $8653. Undergraduates: $10,574. *Scholarships, grants, and awards by category: Creative arts/performance:* art/fine arts. *Tuition waivers:* Full or partial for employees or children of employees.
LOANS *Student loans:* $22,418,046 (93% need-based, 7% non-need-based). 61% of past graduating class borrowed through all loan programs. *Average indebtedness per student:* $29,678. *Average need-based loan:* Freshmen: $3594. Undergraduates: $4603. *Parent loans:* $13,764,876 (93% need-based, 7% non-need-based). *Programs:* Federal Direct (Subsidized and Unsubsidized Stafford, PLUS), Perkins, alternative loans.
WORK-STUDY *Federal work-study:* Total amount: $994,791; jobs available. *State or other work-study/employment:* Total amount: $604,725 (76% need-based, 24% non-need-based). Part-time jobs available.
APPLYING FOR FINANCIAL AID *Required financial aid forms:* FAFSA, state aid form. *Financial aid deadline:* 3/1 (priority: 2/1). *Notification date:* Continuous beginning 2/15. Students must reply within 4 weeks of notification.

CONTACT Mr. William Berrios, Financial Aid Office, School of Visual Arts, 209 East 23rd Street, New York, NY 10010, 212-592-2030 or toll-free 800-436-4204. *Fax:* 212-592-2029. *E-mail:* fa@sva.edu. *Website:* http://www.sva.edu/.

SCHREINER UNIVERSITY
Kerrville, TX

Tuition & fees: $21,540	Average undergraduate aid package: $16,844

ABOUT THE INSTITUTION Independent Presbyterian, coed. *Awards:* certificates, associate, bachelor's, and master's degrees. 36 undergraduate majors. *Total enrollment:* 1,126. Undergraduates: 1,068. Freshmen: 272. Federal methodology is used as a basis for awarding need-based institutional aid.

UNDERGRADUATE EXPENSES for 2013–2014 *Application fee:* $25. *One-time required fee:* $25. *Comprehensive fee:* $31,602 includes full-time tuition ($20,940), mandatory fees ($600), and room and board ($10,062). Room and board charges vary according to board plan and housing facility. *Part-time tuition:* $894 per credit hour. *Part-time fees:* $300 per term.

FRESHMAN FINANCIAL AID (Fall 2011) 265 applied for aid; of those 83% were deemed to have need. 100% of freshmen with need received aid; of those 12% had need fully met. *Average percent of need met:* 73% (excluding resources awarded to replace EFC). *Average financial aid package:* $17,390 (excluding resources awarded to replace EFC). 12% of all full-time freshmen had no need and received non-need-based gift aid.

UNDERGRADUATE FINANCIAL AID (Fall 2011) 874 applied for aid; of those 89% were deemed to have need. 100% of undergraduates with need received aid; of those 10% had need fully met. *Average percent of need met:* 69% (excluding resources awarded to replace EFC). *Average financial aid package:* $16,844 (excluding resources awarded to replace EFC). 9% of all full-time undergraduates had no need and received non-need-based gift aid.

GIFT AID (NEED-BASED) *Total amount:* $10,711,815 (18% federal, 11% state, 54% institutional, 17% external sources). *Receiving aid:* Freshmen: 83% (221); all full-time undergraduates: 89% (779). *Average award:* Freshmen: $14,885; Undergraduates: $13,600. *Scholarships, grants, and awards:* Federal Pell, FSEOG, state, private, college/university gift aid from institutional funds.

GIFT AID (NON-NEED-BASED) *Total amount:* $1,124,706 (1% state, 67% institutional, 32% external sources). *Receiving aid:* Freshmen: 10% (26). Undergraduates: 8% (70). *Average award:* Freshmen: $7575. Undergraduates: $7332. *Scholarships, grants, and awards by category: Academic interests/achievement:* biological sciences, business, education, English, general academic interests/achievements, mathematics, physical sciences, premedicine, religion/biblical studies, social sciences. *Creative arts/performance:* art/fine arts, journalism/publications, music, theater/drama. *Special achievements/activities:* community service, leadership, memberships, religious involvement. *Special characteristics:* children of faculty/staff, general special characteristics, international students, relatives of clergy, religious affiliation, siblings of current students. *Tuition waivers:* Full or partial for employees or children of employees.

LOANS *Student loans:* $6,234,512 (78% need-based, 22% non-need-based). 36% of past graduating class borrowed through all loan programs. *Average indebtedness per student:* $20,900. *Average need-based loan:* Freshmen: $2968. Undergraduates: $3762. *Parent loans:* $1,176,496 (45% need-based, 55% non-need-based). *Programs:* Federal Direct (Subsidized and Unsubsidized Stafford, PLUS), state.

WORK-STUDY *Federal work-study:* Total amount: $53,900; jobs available. *State or other work-study/employment:* Total amount: $203,703 (46% need-based, 54% non-need-based). Part-time jobs available.

APPLYING FOR FINANCIAL AID *Required financial aid form:* FAFSA. *Financial aid deadline (priority):* 5/1. *Notification date:* Continuous beginning 2/15. Students must reply within 2 weeks of notification.

CONTACT Toni Bryant, Director of Financial Aid, Schreiner University, 2100 Memorial Boulevard, Kerrville, TX 78028, 830-792-7217 or toll-free 800-343-4919. *Fax:* 830-792-7226. *E-mail:* finaid@schreiner.edu. *Website:* http://www.schreiner.edu/.

SCRIPPS COLLEGE
Claremont, CA

Tuition & fees: $43,620	Average undergraduate aid package: $39,422

ABOUT THE INSTITUTION Independent, women only. *Awards:* certificates and bachelor's degrees. 62 undergraduate majors. *Total enrollment:* 962. Undergraduates: 945. Freshmen: 235. Both federal and institutional methodology are used as a basis for awarding need-based institutional aid.

UNDERGRADUATE EXPENSES for 2013–2014 *Application fee:* $60. *Comprehensive fee:* $57,088 includes full-time tuition ($43,406), mandatory fees ($214), and room and board ($13,468). *College room only:* $7280. Full-time tuition and fees vary according to course load. Room and board charges vary according to board plan. *Part-time tuition:* $5426 per course. Part-time tuition and fees vary according to course load. *Payment plan:* Tuition prepayment.

FRESHMAN FINANCIAL AID (Fall 2011) 152 applied for aid; of those 63% were deemed to have need. 100% of freshmen with need received aid; of those 100% had need fully met. *Average percent of need met:* 100% (excluding resources awarded to replace EFC). *Average financial aid package:* $36,473 (excluding resources awarded to replace EFC). 13% of all full-time freshmen had no need and received non-need-based gift aid.

UNDERGRADUATE FINANCIAL AID (Fall 2011) 506 applied for aid; of those 78% were deemed to have need. 100% of undergraduates with need received aid; of those 100% had need fully met. *Average percent of need met:* 100% (excluding resources awarded to replace EFC). *Average financial aid package:* $39,422 (excluding resources awarded to replace EFC). 12% of all full-time undergraduates had no need and received non-need-based gift aid.

GIFT AID (NEED-BASED) *Total amount:* $13,403,568 (5% federal, 4% state, 88% institutional, 3% external sources). *Receiving aid:* Freshmen: 37% (96); all full-time undergraduates: 41% (388). *Average award:* Freshmen: $31,408; Undergraduates: $34,296. *Scholarships, grants, and awards:* Federal Pell, FSEOG, state, private, college/university gift aid from institutional funds.

GIFT AID (NON-NEED-BASED) *Total amount:* $2,380,199 (91% institutional, 9% external sources). *Receiving aid:* Freshmen: 4% (10). Undergraduates: 4% (40). *Average award:* Freshmen: $15,030. Undergraduates: $20,557. *Scholarships, grants, and awards by category: Academic interests/achievement:* general academic interests/achievements. *Tuition waivers:* Full or partial for employees or children of employees. *ROTC:* Army cooperative, Air Force cooperative.

LOANS *Student loans:* $2,387,808 (82% need-based, 18% non-need-based). 44% of past graduating class borrowed through all loan programs. *Average indebtedness per student:* $17,487. *Average need-based loan:* Freshmen: $3219. Undergraduates: $3476. *Parent loans:* $1,309,912 (53% need-based, 47% non-need-based). *Programs:* Federal Direct (Subsidized and Unsubsidized Stafford, PLUS), Perkins, college/university.

WORK-STUDY *Federal work-study:* Total amount: $628,342; jobs available. *State or other work-study/employment:* Total amount: $69,961 (87% need-based, 13% non-need-based). Part-time jobs available.

APPLYING FOR FINANCIAL AID *Required financial aid forms:* FAFSA, CSS Financial Aid PROFILE, state aid form, noncustodial (divorced/separated) parent's statement, business/farm supplement. *Financial aid deadline (priority):* 2/1. *Notification date:* 4/1. Students must reply by 5/1.

CONTACT Office of Financial Aid, Scripps College, 1030 Columbia Avenue, Claremont, CA 91711-3948, 909-621-8275 or toll-free 800-770-1333. *Fax:* 909-607-7742. *E-mail:* finaid@scrippscollege.edu. *Website:* http://www.scrippscollege.edu/.

SEATTLE PACIFIC UNIVERSITY
Seattle, WA

Tuition & fees: $32,067	Average undergraduate aid package: $27,783

ABOUT THE INSTITUTION Independent Free Methodist, coed. *Awards:* certificates, bachelor's, master's, and doctoral degrees. 51 undergraduate majors. *Total enrollment:* 4,095. Undergraduates: 3,249. Freshmen: 784. Federal methodology is used as a basis for awarding need-based institutional aid.

UNDERGRADUATE EXPENSES for 2013–2014 *Application fee:* $50. *Comprehensive fee:* $41,559 includes full-time tuition ($31,701), mandatory fees ($366), and room and board ($9492). *College room only:* $5190. Room and board charges vary according to board plan and housing facility. *Part-time tuition:* $881 per credit hour. *Part-time fees:* $122 per term. Part-time tuition and fees vary according to course load.

FRESHMAN FINANCIAL AID (Fall 2012, est.) 704 applied for aid; of those 85% were deemed to have need. 100% of freshmen with need received aid; of those 6% had need fully met. *Average percent of need met:* 82% (excluding resources awarded to replace EFC). *Average financial aid package:* $28,411 (excluding resources awarded to replace EFC). 17% of all full-time freshmen had no need and received non-need-based gift aid.

UNDERGRADUATE FINANCIAL AID (Fall 2012, est.) 2,572 applied for aid; of those 87% were deemed to have need. 100% of undergraduates with need received aid; of those 5% had need fully met. *Average percent of need met:* 77% (excluding resources awarded to replace EFC). *Average financial aid package:* $27,783 (excluding resources awarded to replace EFC). 20% of all full-time undergraduates had no need and received non-need-based gift aid.

GIFT AID (NEED-BASED) *Total amount:* $44,784,920 (11% federal, 8% state, 76% institutional, 5% external sources). *Receiving aid:* Freshmen: 77% (599); all full-time undergraduates: 73% (2,230). *Average award:* Freshmen: $22,292; Undergraduates: $22,786. *Scholarships, grants, and awards:* Federal Pell, FSEOG, state, private, college/university gift aid from institutional funds.

GIFT AID (NON-NEED-BASED) *Total amount:* $10,154,665 (82% institutional, 18% external sources). *Average award:* Freshmen: $18,235. Undergraduates: $16,655. *Scholarships, grants, and awards by category:* Academic interests/achievement: 516 awards ($5,483,823 total): engineering/technologies, general academic interests/achievements. Creative arts/performance: 30 awards ($39,884 total): art/fine arts, performing arts. Special characteristics: 249 awards ($912,558 total): children and siblings of alumni, children of faculty/staff, general special characteristics, international students, relatives of clergy, religious affiliation, veterans. *Tuition waivers:* Full or partial for employees or children of employees, senior citizens. *ROTC:* Army cooperative, Naval cooperative, Air Force cooperative.

LOANS *Student loans:* $18,345,158 (93% need-based, 7% non-need-based). 67% of past graduating class borrowed through all loan programs. *Average indebtedness per student:* $28,263. *Average need-based loan:* Freshmen: $5028. Undergraduates: $5145. *Parent loans:* $7,602,867 (85% need-based, 15% non-need-based). *Programs:* Federal Direct (Subsidized and Unsubsidized Stafford, PLUS), Perkins, Federal Nursing, college/university.

WORK-STUDY *Federal work-study:* Total amount: $540,824; 381 jobs averaging $1419. *State or other work-study/employment:* Total amount: $338,211 (100% need-based). 190 part-time jobs averaging $1780.

ATHLETIC AWARDS Total amount: $1,748,560 (59% need-based, 41% non-need-based).

APPLYING FOR FINANCIAL AID *Required financial aid form:* FAFSA. *Financial aid deadline (priority):* 2/1. *Notification date:* Continuous beginning 3/15. Students must reply by 5/1 or within 4 weeks of notification.

CONTACT Mr. Jordan Grant, Director of Student Financial Services, Seattle Pacific University, 3307 Third Avenue West, Seattle, WA 98119-1997, 206-281-2469 or toll-free 800-366-3344. *E-mail:* grantj@spu.edu. *Website:* http://www.spu.edu/.

SEATTLE UNIVERSITY
Seattle, WA

Tuition & fees: $34,800	Average undergraduate aid package: $29,210

ABOUT THE INSTITUTION Independent Roman Catholic, coed. *Awards:* certificates, bachelor's, master's, and doctoral degrees. 62 undergraduate majors. *Total enrollment:* 7,484. Undergraduates: 4,589. Freshmen: 903. Federal methodology is used as a basis for awarding need-based institutional aid.

UNDERGRADUATE EXPENSES for 2013–2014 *Application fee:* $50. *Comprehensive fee:* $45,096 includes full-time tuition ($34,200), mandatory fees ($600), and room and board ($10,296). Full-time tuition and fees vary according to course load. Room and board charges vary according to board plan and housing facility. *Part-time tuition:* $760 per credit hour. Part-time tuition and fees vary according to course load.

FRESHMAN FINANCIAL AID (Fall 2012, est.) 774 applied for aid; of those 81% were deemed to have need. 100% of freshmen with need received aid; of those 8% had need fully met. *Average percent of need met:* 72% (excluding resources awarded to replace EFC). *Average financial aid package:* $27,375 (excluding resources awarded to replace EFC). 9% of all full-time freshmen had no need and received non-need-based gift aid.

UNDERGRADUATE FINANCIAL AID (Fall 2012, est.) 3,235 applied for aid; of those 85% were deemed to have need. 100% of undergraduates with need received aid; of those 10% had need fully met. *Average percent of need met:* 69% (excluding resources awarded to replace EFC). *Average financial aid package:* $29,210 (excluding resources awarded to replace EFC). 4% of all full-time undergraduates had no need and received non-need-based gift aid.

GIFT AID (NEED-BASED) *Total amount:* $56,383,553 (11% federal, 6% state, 79% institutional, 4% external sources). *Receiving aid:* Freshmen: 62% (556); all full-time undergraduates: 57% (2,465). *Average award:* Freshmen: $13,142; Undergraduates: $15,106. *Scholarships, grants, and awards:* Federal Pell, FSEOG, state, private, college/university gift aid from institutional funds, Federal Nursing.

GIFT AID (NON-NEED-BASED) *Total amount:* $10,448,549 (18% federal, 76% institutional, 6% external sources). *Receiving aid:* Freshmen: 45% (406). Undergraduates: 27% (1,176). *Average award:* Freshmen: $9927. Undergraduates: $9846. *Scholarships, grants, and awards by category:* Academic interests/achievement: general academic interests/achievements. Creative arts/performance: art/fine arts, music, theater/drama. Special achievements/activities: leadership. Special characteristics: children and siblings of alumni, children of educators, children of faculty/staff, members of minority groups, religious affiliation. *Tuition waivers:* Full or partial for employees or children of employees. *ROTC:* Army, Naval cooperative, Air Force cooperative.

LOANS *Student loans:* $26,228,136 (68% need-based, 32% non-need-based). 73% of past graduating class borrowed through all loan programs. *Average indebtedness per student:* $29,498. *Average need-based loan:* Freshmen: $3795. Undergraduates: $4851. *Parent loans:* $8,365,413 (8% need-based, 92% non-need-based). *Programs:* Federal Direct (Subsidized and Unsubsidized Stafford, PLUS), Perkins, Federal Nursing.

WORK-STUDY *Federal work-study:* Total amount: $2,335,747; jobs available. *State or other work-study/employment:* Total amount: $2,294,640 (100% need-based). Part-time jobs available.

ATHLETIC AWARDS Total amount: $4,193,881 (37% need-based, 63% non-need-based).

APPLYING FOR FINANCIAL AID *Required financial aid form:* FAFSA. *Financial aid deadline (priority):* 2/1. *Notification date:* 3/1. Students must reply by 5/1 or within 2 weeks of notification.

CONTACT Ms. Lindy Hall, Interim Director of Student Financial Services, Seattle University, 901 12th Avenue, PO Box 222000, Seattle, WA 98122-1090, 206-296-2000 or toll-free 800-542-0833 (in-state), 800-426-7123 (out-of-state). *Fax:* 206-296-5755. *E-mail:* financial-aid@seattleu.edu. *Website:* http://www.seattleu.edu/.

SELMA UNIVERSITY
Selma, AL

CONTACT Financial Aid Office, Selma University, 1501 Lapsley Street, Selma, AL 36701-5299, 334-872-2533. *Website:* http://www.selmauniversity.org/.

SENTARA COLLEGE OF HEALTH SCIENCES
Chesapeake, VA

CONTACT Financial Aid Office, Sentara College of Health Sciences, 1441 Crossways Boulevard, Crossways I, Suite 105, Chesapeake, VA 23320, 757-388-2900. *Website:* http://www.sentara.edu/.

SETON HALL UNIVERSITY
South Orange, NJ

CONTACT Office of Enrollment Services, Seton Hall University, 400 South Orange Avenue, South Orange, NJ 07079, 973-761-9350 or toll-free 800-THE HALL. *Fax:* 973-275-2040. *E-mail:* thehall@shu.edu.
Website: http://www.shu.edu/.

SETON HILL UNIVERSITY
Greensburg, PA

Tuition & fees: $29,450	Average undergraduate aid package: $23,392

ABOUT THE INSTITUTION Independent Roman Catholic, coed. *Awards:* certificates, bachelor's, and master's degrees. 73 undergraduate majors. *Total enrollment:* 2,091. Undergraduates: 1,673. Freshmen: 350. Federal methodology is used as a basis for awarding need-based institutional aid.

UNDERGRADUATE EXPENSES for 2013–2014 *Application fee:* $35. *Comprehensive fee:* $39,394 includes full-time tuition ($28,350), mandatory fees ($1100), and room and board ($9944). Full-time tuition and fees vary according to course load and program. Room and board charges vary according to board plan and housing facility. *Part-time tuition:* $760 per credit hour. *Part-time fees:* $25 per credit hour; $50 per term. Part-time tuition and fees vary according to course load and program.

FRESHMAN FINANCIAL AID (Fall 2012, est.) 337 applied for aid; of those 94% were deemed to have need. 100% of freshmen with need received aid; of those 19% had need fully met. *Average percent of need met:* 76% (excluding resources awarded to replace EFC). *Average financial aid package:* $24,590 (excluding resources awarded to replace EFC). 10% of all full-time freshmen had no need and received non-need-based gift aid.

UNDERGRADUATE FINANCIAL AID (Fall 2012, est.) 1,258 applied for aid; of those 94% were deemed to have need. 100% of undergraduates with need received aid; of those 17% had need fully met. *Average percent of need met:* 74% (excluding resources awarded to replace EFC). *Average financial aid package:* $23,392 (excluding resources awarded to replace EFC). 10% of all full-time undergraduates had no need and received non-need-based gift aid.

GIFT AID (NEED-BASED) *Total amount:* $19,048,559 (14% federal, 12% state, 72% institutional, 2% external sources). *Receiving aid:* Freshmen: 91% (315); all full-time undergraduates: 86% (1,169). *Average award:* Freshmen: $19,742; Undergraduates: $18,123. *Scholarships, grants, and awards:* Federal Pell, FSEOG, state, private, college/university gift aid from institutional funds.

GIFT AID (NON-NEED-BASED) *Total amount:* $2,133,191 (1% state, 92% institutional, 7% external sources). *Receiving aid:* Freshmen: 13% (45). Undergraduates: 10% (140). *Average award:* Freshmen: $9769. Undergraduates: $10,668. *Scholarships, grants, and awards by category:* Academic interests/achievement: biological sciences, business, communication, computer science, education, English, foreign languages, general academic interests/achievements, home economics, humanities, mathematics, physical sciences, religion/biblical studies, social sciences. Creative arts/performance: applied art and design, art/fine arts, music, performing arts, theater/drama. Special achievements/activities: cheerleading/drum major. Special characteristics: children and siblings of alumni, children of faculty/staff, siblings of current students. Tuition waivers: Full or partial for employees or children of employees. ROTC: Army.

LOANS *Student loans:* $8,440,775 (72% need-based, 28% non-need-based). 90% of past graduating class borrowed through all loan programs. *Average indebtedness per student:* $32,290. *Average need-based loan:* Freshmen: $5069. Undergraduates: $5605. *Parent loans:* $2,180,249 (46% need-based, 54% non-need-based). *Programs:* Federal Direct (Subsidized and Unsubsidized Stafford, PLUS), Perkins, college/university.

WORK-STUDY *Federal work-study:* Total amount: $835,614; jobs available. *State or other work-study/employment:* Total amount: $232,781 (9% need-based, 91% non-need-based). Part-time jobs available.

ATHLETIC AWARDS Total amount: $3,618,748 (61% need-based, 39% non-need-based).

APPLYING FOR FINANCIAL AID *Required financial aid forms:* FAFSA, institution's own form. *Financial aid deadline:* Continuous. *Notification date:* Continuous beginning 11/20. Students must reply by 5/1.
CONTACT Maryann B. Dudas, Director of Financial Aid, Seton Hill University, I Seton Hill Drive, Greensburg, PA 15601, 724-838-4293 or toll-free 800-826-6234. *Fax:* 724-830-1194. *E-mail:* dudas@setonhill.edu.
Website: http://www.setonhill.edu/.

SEWANEE: THE UNIVERSITY OF THE SOUTH
Sewanee, TN

Tuition & fees: $35,756	Average undergraduate aid package: $29,202

ABOUT THE INSTITUTION Independent Episcopal, coed. *Awards:* certificates, bachelor's, master's, and doctoral degrees. 40 undergraduate majors. *Total enrollment:* 1,557. Undergraduates: 1,478. Freshmen: 453. Both federal and institutional methodology are used as a basis for awarding need-based institutional aid.

UNDERGRADUATE EXPENSES for 2013–2014 *Application fee:* $45. *Comprehensive fee:* $45,970 includes full-time tuition ($35,484), mandatory fees ($272), and room and board ($10,214). *College room only:* $5302. Full-time tuition and fees vary according to student level. Room and board charges vary according to student level. *Part-time tuition:* $1250 per credit hour. *Payment plan:* Guaranteed tuition.

FRESHMAN FINANCIAL AID (Fall 2012, est.) 314 applied for aid; of those 75% were deemed to have need. 99% of freshmen with need received aid; of those 64% had need fully met. *Average percent of need met:* 94% (excluding resources awarded to replace EFC). *Average financial aid package:* $33,849 (excluding resources awarded to replace EFC). 21% of all full-time freshmen had no need and received non-need-based gift aid.

UNDERGRADUATE FINANCIAL AID (Fall 2012, est.) 898 applied for aid; of those 95% were deemed to have need. 100% of undergraduates with need received aid; of those 73% had need fully met. *Average percent of need met:* 94% (excluding resources awarded to replace EFC). *Average financial aid package:* $29,202 (excluding resources awarded to replace EFC). 26% of all full-time undergraduates had no need and received non-need-based gift aid.

GIFT AID (NEED-BASED) *Total amount:* $16,197,376 (8% federal, 5% state, 83% institutional, 4% external sources). *Receiving aid:* Freshmen: 51% (231); all full-time undergraduates: 57% (836). *Average award:* Freshmen: $27,066; Undergraduates: $20,795. *Scholarships, grants, and awards:* Federal Pell, FSEOG, state, private, college/university gift aid from institutional funds.

GIFT AID (NON-NEED-BASED) *Total amount:* $5,152,390 (7% state, 81% institutional, 12% external sources). *Receiving aid:* Freshmen: 27% (121). Undergraduates: 31% (450). *Average award:* Freshmen: $9984. Undergraduates: $11,076. *Scholarships, grants, and awards by category:* Academic interests/achievement: 125 awards ($793,454 total): general academic interests/achievements. Special characteristics: 33 awards ($82,500 total): children of faculty/staff, ethnic background, members of minority groups, relatives of clergy, religious affiliation. *Tuition waivers:* Full or partial for employees or children of employees.

LOANS *Student loans:* $2,786,328 (84% need-based, 16% non-need-based). 40% of past graduating class borrowed through all loan programs. *Average indebtedness per student:* $23,721. *Average need-based loan:* Freshmen: $7979. Undergraduates: $9525. *Parent loans:* $1,605,957 (41% need-based, 59% non-need-based). *Programs:* Federal Direct (Subsidized and Unsubsidized Stafford, PLUS), Perkins, state, college/university, private loans.

WORK-STUDY *Federal work-study:* Total amount: $588,295; 60 jobs averaging $1609. *State or other work-study/employment:* Total amount: $147,830 (59% need-based, 41% non-need-based). 26 part-time jobs averaging $1650.

APPLYING FOR FINANCIAL AID *Required financial aid forms:* FAFSA, institution's own form. *Financial aid deadline:* 3/1 (priority: 2/1). *Notification date:* 2/25. Students must reply within 2 weeks of notification.

CONTACT Ms. Beth A. Cragar, Associate Dean of Admission for Financial Aid, Sewanee: The University of the South, 735 University Avenue, Sewanee, TN 37383-1000, 931-598-1312 or toll-free 800-522-2234. *Fax:* 931-598-3273. *E-mail:* finaid@sewanee.edu.
Website: http://www.sewanee.edu/.

SHASTA BIBLE COLLEGE
Redding, CA

CONTACT Linda Iles, Financial Aid Administrator, Shasta Bible College, 2951 Goodwater Avenue, Redding, CA 96002, 530-221-4275 or toll-free 800-800-4SBC. *Fax:* 530-221-6929. *E-mail:* finaid@shasta.edu. *Website:* http://www.shasta.edu/.

SHAWNEE STATE UNIVERSITY
Portsmouth, OH

Tuition & fees (OH res): $6988	Average undergraduate aid package: N/A

ABOUT THE INSTITUTION State-supported, coed. *Awards:* certificates, associate, bachelor's, and master's degrees. 48 undergraduate majors. *Total enrollment:* 4,652. Undergraduates: 4,554. Freshmen: 1,167. Both federal and institutional methodology are used as a basis for awarding need-based financial aid.

UNDERGRADUATE EXPENSES for 2013–2014 *Tuition, state resident:* full-time $5918; part-time $246.60 per credit hour. *Tuition, nonresident:* full-time $10,893; part-time $453.94 per credit hour. *Required fees:* full-time $1070; $44.58 per credit hour. Full-time tuition and fees vary according to course load and reciprocity agreements. Part-time tuition and fees vary according to course load and reciprocity agreements. *College room and board:* $9012; *Room only:* $5478. Room and board charges vary according to board plan and housing facility.

GIFT AID (NEED-BASED) *Scholarships, grants, and awards:* Federal Pell, FSEOG, state, private, college/university gift aid from institutional funds.

GIFT AID (NON-NEED-BASED) *Scholarships, grants, and awards by category:* Academic interests/achievement: general academic interests/achievements. Creative arts/performance: art/fine arts, performing arts. Special achievements/activities: memberships. Special characteristics: ethnic background, first-generation college students, handicapped students, local/state students, members of minority groups, veterans. *Tuition waivers:* Full or partial for employees or children of employees, senior citizens.

LOANS *Programs:* Federal Direct (Subsidized and Unsubsidized Stafford).

APPLYING FOR FINANCIAL AID *Required financial aid form:* FAFSA. *Financial aid deadline:* Continuous. *Notification date:* Continuous beginning 3/15.

CONTACT Nicole Neal, Director of Financial Aid, Shawnee State University, 940 Second Street, Portsmouth, OH 45662-4344, 740-351-3140 or toll-free 800-959-2SSU. *E-mail:* nneal@shawnee.edu. *Website:* http://www.shawnee.edu/.

SHAW UNIVERSITY
Raleigh, NC

CONTACT Rochelle King, Director of Financial Aid, Shaw University, 118 East South Street, Raleigh, NC 27601-2399, 919-546-8565 or toll-free 800-214-6683. *Fax:* 919-546-8356. *E-mail:* rking@shawu.edu. *Website:* http://www.shawu.edu/.

SHENANDOAH UNIVERSITY
Winchester, VA

Tuition & fees: $27,850	Average undergraduate aid package: $19,000

ABOUT THE INSTITUTION Independent United Methodist, coed. *Awards:* certificates, diplomas, bachelor's, master's, and doctoral degrees. 40 undergraduate majors. *Total enrollment:* 4,176. Undergraduates: 2,402. Freshmen: 459. Federal methodology is used as a basis for awarding need-based institutional aid.

UNDERGRADUATE EXPENSES for 2013–2014 *Application fee:* $30. *Comprehensive fee:* $37,090 includes full-time tuition ($27,550), mandatory fees ($300), and room and board ($9240). Full-time tuition and fees vary according to course load, location, program, and student level. Room and board charges vary according to board plan and housing facility. *Part-time tuition:* $800 per credit hour. Part-time tuition and fees vary according to course load, location, program, and student level.

FRESHMAN FINANCIAL AID (Fall 2012, est.) 388 applied for aid; of those 87% were deemed to have need. 100% of freshmen with need received aid; of those 19% had need fully met. *Average percent of need met:* 71% (excluding resources awarded to replace EFC). *Average financial aid package:* $19,000 (excluding resources awarded to replace EFC). 13% of all full-time freshmen had no need and received non-need-based gift aid.

UNDERGRADUATE FINANCIAL AID (Fall 2012, est.) 1,194 applied for aid; of those 94% were deemed to have need. 100% of undergraduates with need received aid; of those 6% had need fully met. *Average percent of need met:* 71% (excluding resources awarded to replace EFC). *Average financial aid package:* $19,000 (excluding resources awarded to replace EFC). 8% of all full-time undergraduates had no need and received non-need-based gift aid.

GIFT AID (NEED-BASED) *Total amount:* $8,766,575 (24% federal, 32% state, 41% institutional, 3% external sources). *Receiving aid:* Freshmen: 74% (338); all full-time undergraduates: 61% (1,122). *Average award:* Freshmen: $8500; Undergraduates: $8000. *Scholarships, grants, and awards:* Federal Pell, FSEOG, state, private, college/university gift aid from institutional funds, Federal Nursing.

GIFT AID (NON-NEED-BASED) *Total amount:* $12,827,463 (100% institutional). *Receiving aid:* Freshmen: 74% (338). Undergraduates: 61% (1,122). *Average award:* Freshmen: $6000. Undergraduates: $5000. *Scholarships, grants, and awards by category:* Academic interests/achievement: 1,679 awards ($10,245,171 total): business, general academic interests/achievements. Creative arts/performance: 157 awards ($1,563,803 total): dance, music, performing arts, theater/drama. Special achievements/activities: 55 awards ($54,522 total): religious involvement. Special characteristics: 49 awards ($651,853 total): children of faculty/staff, local/state students, relatives of clergy, religious affiliation. *Tuition waivers:* Full or partial for employees or children of employees.

LOANS *Student loans:* $15,247,720 (47% need-based, 53% non-need-based). 85% of past graduating class borrowed through all loan programs. *Average indebtedness per student:* $27,000. *Average need-based loan:* Freshmen: $3500. Undergraduates: $4500. *Parent loans:* $6,260,334 (20% need-based, 80% non-need-based). *Programs:* Federal Direct (Subsidized and Unsubsidized Stafford, PLUS), Perkins, Federal Nursing, college/university.

WORK-STUDY *Federal work-study:* Total amount: $1,727,544; 900 jobs averaging $1919. *State or other work-study/employment:* Total amount: $749,220 (11% need-based, 89% non-need-based). 388 part-time jobs averaging $1931.

APPLYING FOR FINANCIAL AID *Required financial aid forms:* FAFSA, state aid form. *Financial aid deadline (priority):* 3/1. *Notification date:* Continuous beginning 3/15. Students must reply within 4 weeks of notification.

CONTACT Nancy Bragg, Director of Financial Aid, Shenandoah University, 1460 University Drive, Winchester, VA 22601-5195, 540-665-4538 or toll-free 800-432-2266. *Fax:* 540-665-4939. *E-mail:* nbragg@su.edu. *Website:* http://www.su.edu/.

SHEPHERDS THEOLOGICAL SEMINARY
Cary, NC

Tuition & fees: N/R	Average undergraduate aid package: N/A

ABOUT THE INSTITUTION Independent religious, coed. Both federal and institutional methodology are used as a basis for awarding need-based institutional aid.

GIFT AID (NEED-BASED) *Total amount:* $8013 (100% federal). *Scholarships, grants, and awards:* Federal Pell, endowment scholarships and grants.

LOANS *Student loans:* $5809 (100% need-based). *Programs:* Federal Direct (Subsidized and Unsubsidized Stafford, PLUS).

APPLYING FOR FINANCIAL AID *Notification date:* Continuous.

CONTACT Lucy Burggraff, Financial Aid Administrator, Shepherds Theological Seminary, 6051 Tryon Road, Cary, NC 27518, 919-573-5350. *E-mail:* lburggraff@shepherds.edu. *Website:* http://shepherds.edu/.

SHEPHERD UNIVERSITY
Shepherdstown, WV

Tuition & fees (WV res): $5834	Average undergraduate aid package: $11,671

ABOUT THE INSTITUTION State-supported, coed. *Awards:* bachelor's and master's degrees. 25 undergraduate majors. *Total enrollment:* 4,326. Undergraduates: 4,170. Freshmen: 756. Federal methodology is used as a basis for awarding need-based institutional aid.

UNDERGRADUATE EXPENSES for 2013–2014 *Application fee:* $45. *Tuition, state resident:* full-time $5834; part-time $237 per credit hour. *Tuition, nonresident:* full-time $15,136; part-time $625 per credit hour. Full-time tuition and fees vary according to program and reciprocity agreements. Part-time tuition and fees vary according to program. *College room and board:* $8424. Room and board charges vary according to board plan and housing facility.

FRESHMAN FINANCIAL AID (Fall 2012, est.) 719 applied for aid; of those 67% were deemed to have need. 98% of freshmen with need received aid; of those 25% had need fully met. *Average percent of need met:* 74% (excluding resources awarded to replace EFC). *Average financial aid package:* $10,971 (excluding resources awarded to replace EFC). 25% of all full-time freshmen had no need and received non-need-based gift aid.

UNDERGRADUATE FINANCIAL AID (Fall 2012, est.) 3,181 applied for aid; of those 68% were deemed to have need. 98% of undergraduates with need received aid; of those 23% had need fully met. *Average percent of need met:* 74% (excluding resources awarded to replace EFC). *Average financial aid package:* $11,671 (excluding resources awarded to replace EFC). 19% of all full-time undergraduates had no need and received non-need-based gift aid.

GIFT AID (NEED-BASED) *Total amount:* $7,960,429 (73% federal, 25% state, 2% institutional). *Receiving aid:* Freshmen: 43% (320); all full-time undergraduates: 43% (1,506). *Average award:* Freshmen: $4992; Undergraduates: $4984. *Scholarships, grants, and awards:* Federal Pell, FSEOG, state, private, college/university gift aid from institutional funds.

GIFT AID (NON-NEED-BASED) *Total amount:* $5,638,938 (42% state, 52% institutional, 6% external sources). *Receiving aid:* Freshmen: 28% (213). Undergraduates: 17% (593). *Average award:* Freshmen: $9945. Undergraduates: $9946. *Scholarships, grants, and awards by category: Academic interests/achievement:* 559 awards ($2,343,373 total): biological sciences, business, communication, computer science, education, engineering/technologies, English, general academic interests/achievements, health fields, home economics, humanities, mathematics, physical sciences, premedicine, social sciences. *Creative arts/performance:* 57 awards ($259,257 total): applied art and design, art/fine arts, music, performing arts, theater/drama. *Special achievements/activities:* 133 awards ($424,100 total): leadership. *Special characteristics:* 122 awards ($328,899 total): ethnic background, handicapped students, local/state students, members of minority groups, out-of-state students, previous college experience. *Tuition waivers:* Full or partial for minority students, employees or children of employees, senior citizens. *ROTC:* Air Force cooperative.

LOANS *Student loans:* $15,582,870 (44% need-based, 56% non-need-based). 69% of past graduating class borrowed through all loan programs. *Average indebtedness per student:* $23,940. *Average need-based loan:* Freshmen: $3273. Undergraduates: $4035. *Parent loans:* $4,426,513 (100% non-need-based). *Programs:* Federal Direct (Subsidized and Unsubsidized Stafford, PLUS), Perkins.

WORK-STUDY *Federal work-study:* Total amount: $201,856; 112 jobs averaging $1340. *State or other work-study/employment:* Total amount: $1,093,033 (100% non-need-based). 484 part-time jobs averaging $2258.

ATHLETIC AWARDS Total amount: $1,158,616 (100% non-need-based).

APPLYING FOR FINANCIAL AID *Required financial aid forms:* FAFSA, state aid form. *Financial aid deadline (priority):* 3/1. *Notification date:* Continuous beginning 3/30. Students must reply within 2 weeks of notification.

CONTACT Ms. Sandra Oerly-Bennett, Director of Financial Aid, Shepherd University, PO Box 5000, Shepherdstown, WV 25443-5000, 304-876-5470 or toll-free 800-344-5231. *Fax:* 304-876-5238. *E-mail:* faoweb@shepherd.edu. *Website:* http://www.shepherd.edu/.

SHIMER COLLEGE
Chicago, IL

Tuition & fees: $31,230	Average undergraduate aid package: $18,207

ABOUT THE INSTITUTION Independent, coed. *Awards:* bachelor's degrees. 7 undergraduate majors. *Total enrollment:* 127. Undergraduates: 127. Freshmen: 16. Both federal and institutional methodology are used as a basis for awarding need-based institutional aid.

UNDERGRADUATE EXPENSES for 2013–2014 *Application fee:* $25. *Comprehensive fee:* $41,856 includes full-time tuition ($26,510), mandatory fees ($4720), and room and board ($10,626). Full-time tuition and fees vary according to class time, course load, and program. Room and board charges vary according to housing facility. Part-time tuition and fees vary according to class time, course load, and program.

FRESHMAN FINANCIAL AID (Fall 2011) 19 applied for aid; of those 74% were deemed to have need. 100% of freshmen with need received aid. *Average percent of need met:* 61% (excluding resources awarded to replace EFC). *Average financial aid package:* $17,741 (excluding resources awarded to replace EFC). 32% of all full-time freshmen had no need and received non-need-based gift aid.

UNDERGRADUATE FINANCIAL AID (Fall 2011) 109 applied for aid; of those 89% were deemed to have need. 100% of undergraduates with need received aid; of those 8% had need fully met. *Average percent of need met:* 55% (excluding resources awarded to replace EFC). *Average financial aid package:* $18,207 (excluding resources awarded to replace EFC). 16% of all full-time undergraduates had no need and received non-need-based gift aid.

GIFT AID (NEED-BASED) *Total amount:* $1,488,710 (18% federal, 6% state, 74% institutional, 2% external sources). *Receiving aid:* Freshmen: 74% (14); all full-time undergraduates: 84% (97). *Average award:* Freshmen: $9399; Undergraduates: $10,802. *Scholarships, grants, and awards:* Federal Pell, FSEOG, state, private, college/university gift aid from institutional funds.

GIFT AID (NON-NEED-BASED) *Total amount:* $209,762 (100% institutional). *Receiving aid:* Freshmen: 58% (11). Undergraduates: 39% (45). *Average award:* Freshmen: $9566. Undergraduates: $9094. *Scholarships, grants, and awards by category: Academic interests/achievement:* general academic interests/achievements. *Special characteristics:* children and siblings of alumni. *Tuition waivers:* Full or partial for employees or children of employees, adult students, senior citizens.

LOANS *Student loans:* $1,037,446 (93% need-based, 7% non-need-based). 100% of past graduating class borrowed through all loan programs. *Average indebtedness per student:* $30,000. *Average need-based loan:* Freshmen: $3071. Undergraduates: $4002. *Parent loans:* $290,750 (84% need-based, 16% non-need-based). *Programs:* Federal Direct (Subsidized and Unsubsidized Stafford, PLUS), Perkins.

WORK-STUDY *Federal work-study:* Total amount: $74,819; jobs available. *State or other work-study/employment:* Total amount: $13,800 (100% non-need-based). Part-time jobs available.

APPLYING FOR FINANCIAL AID *Required financial aid forms:* FAFSA, institution's own form. *Financial aid deadline:* Continuous. *Notification date:* Continuous beginning 3/15. Students must reply by 5/1 or within 3 weeks of notification.

CONTACT Janet Henthorn, Director of Financial Aid, Shimer College, 3424 South State Street, Chicago, IL 60616, 312-235-3507 or toll-free 800-215-7173. *Fax:* 312-235-3502. *E-mail:* j.henthorn@shimer.edu. *Website:* http://www.shimer.edu/.

SHIPPENSBURG UNIVERSITY OF PENNSYLVANIA
Shippensburg, PA

Tuition & fees (PA res): $9154	Average undergraduate aid package: $8168

ABOUT THE INSTITUTION State-supported, coed. *Awards:* certificates, bachelor's, and master's degrees. 36 undergraduate majors. *Total enrollment:* 7,724. Undergraduates: 6,712. Freshmen: 1,485. Federal methodology is used as a basis for awarding need-based institutional aid.

UNDERGRADUATE EXPENSES for 2013–2014 *Application fee:* $30. *Tuition, state resident:* full-time $6428; part-time $268 per credit hour. *Tuition, nonresident:* full-time $14,464; part-time $603 per credit hour. *Required fees:* full-time $2726; $113 per credit hour. *College room and board:* $7910; *Room only:* $4180. Room and board charges vary according to board plan and housing facility.

FRESHMAN FINANCIAL AID (Fall 2012, est.) 1,376 applied for aid; of those 77% were deemed to have need. 98% of freshmen with need received aid; of those 11% had need fully met. *Average percent of need met:* 56% (excluding resources awarded to replace EFC). *Average financial aid package:* $7598 (excluding resources awarded to replace EFC). 7% of all full-time freshmen had no need and received non-need-based gift aid.

UNDERGRADUATE FINANCIAL AID (Fall 2012, est.) 5,349 applied for aid; of those 80% were deemed to have need. 99% of undergraduates with need received aid; of those 13% had need fully met. *Average percent of need met:* 60% (excluding resources awarded to replace EFC). *Average financial aid package:* $8168 (excluding resources awarded to replace EFC). 7% of all full-time undergraduates had no need and received non-need-based gift aid.

GIFT AID (NEED-BASED) *Total amount:* $16,263,047 (52% federal, 38% state, 2% institutional, 8% external sources). *Receiving aid:* Freshmen: 49% (728); all full-time undergraduates: 46% (2,894). *Average award:* Freshmen: $6086; Undergraduates: $5872. *Scholarships, grants, and awards:* Federal Pell, FSEOG, state, private, college/university gift aid from institutional funds.

GIFT AID (NON-NEED-BASED) *Total amount:* $1,336,071 (22% institutional, 78% external sources). *Receiving aid:* Freshmen: 2% (32). Undergraduates: 2% (129). *Average award:* Freshmen: $4352. Undergraduates: $4837. *Scholarships, grants, and awards by category: Academic interests/achievement:* biological sciences, business, communication, computer science, education, English, foreign languages, general academic interests/achievements, humanities, mathematics, physical sciences, social sciences. *Creative arts/performance:* art/fine arts, music, theater/drama. *Special achievements/activities:* community service, general special achievements/activities, leadership. *Special characteristics:* children and siblings of alumni, general special characteristics, handicapped students, local/state students. *Tuition waivers:* Full or partial for employees or children of employees, senior citizens. *ROTC:* Army.

LOANS *Student loans:* $43,978,376 (67% need-based, 33% non-need-based). 78% of past graduating class borrowed through all loan programs. *Average indebtedness per student:* $27,661. *Average need-based loan:* Freshmen: $3339. Undergraduates: $3957. *Parent loans:* $7,505,578 (30% need-based, 70% non-need-based). *Programs:* Federal Direct (Subsidized and Unsubsidized Stafford, PLUS), Perkins, alternative loans.

WORK-STUDY *Federal work-study:* Total amount: $205,398; 122 jobs averaging $1684. *State or other work-study/employment:* Total amount: $1,233,145 (39% need-based, 61% non-need-based). 603 part-time jobs averaging $2045.

ATHLETIC AWARDS Total amount: $675,324 (53% need-based, 47% non-need-based).

APPLYING FOR FINANCIAL AID *Required financial aid form:* FAFSA. *Financial aid deadline (priority):* 3/15. *Notification date:* Continuous. Students must reply within 2 weeks of notification.

CONTACT Dr. Sandra L. Tarbox, Director of Financial Aid and Scholarships, Shippensburg University of Pennsylvania, 1871 Old Main Drive, Shippensburg, PA 17257-2299, 717-477-1131 or toll-free 800-822-8028. *Fax:* 717-477-4028. *E-mail:* finaid@ship.edu.
Website: http://www.ship.edu/.

resources awarded to replace EFC). 12% of all full-time freshmen had no need and received non-need-based gift aid.

UNDERGRADUATE FINANCIAL AID (Fall 2012, est.) 1,198 applied for aid; of those 90% were deemed to have need. 100% of undergraduates with need received aid; of those 18% had need fully met. *Average percent of need met:* 61% (excluding resources awarded to replace EFC). *Average financial aid package:* $16,335 (excluding resources awarded to replace EFC). 9% of all full-time undergraduates had no need and received non-need-based gift aid.

GIFT AID (NEED-BASED) *Total amount:* $9,582,544 (32% federal, 21% state, 44% institutional, 3% external sources). *Receiving aid:* Freshmen: 73% (226); all full-time undergraduates: 82% (1,070). *Average award:* Freshmen: $13,382; Undergraduates: $12,863. *Scholarships, grants, and awards:* Federal Pell, FSEOG, state, private, college/university gift aid from institutional funds.

GIFT AID (NON-NEED-BASED) *Total amount:* $1,679,767 (46% state, 48% institutional, 6% external sources). *Receiving aid:* Freshmen: 13% (39). Undergraduates: 11% (149). *Average award:* Freshmen: $6564. Undergraduates: $5371. *Scholarships, grants, and awards by category: Academic interests/achievement:* English, foreign languages, general academic interests/achievements, religion/biblical studies. *Creative arts/performance:* art/fine arts, music, theater/drama. *Special achievements/activities:* cheerleading/drum major, religious involvement. *Special characteristics:* children of faculty/staff, children of union members/company employees, local/state students, relatives of clergy, religious affiliation, siblings of current students.

LOANS *Student loans:* $8,407,191 (82% need-based, 18% non-need-based). 66% of past graduating class borrowed through all loan programs. *Average indebtedness per student:* $19,625. *Average need-based loan:* Freshmen: $3466. Undergraduates: $4164. *Parent loans:* $2,290,988 (46% need-based, 54% non-need-based). *Programs:* Federal Direct (Subsidized and Unsubsidized Stafford, PLUS), Perkins, state.

WORK-STUDY *Federal work-study:* Total amount: $241,277; jobs available. *State or other work-study/employment:* Total amount: $159,237 (20% need-based, 80% non-need-based). Part-time jobs available.

ATHLETIC AWARDS Total amount: $3,473,648 (56% need-based, 44% non-need-based).

APPLYING FOR FINANCIAL AID *Required financial aid forms:* FAFSA, institution's own form, state aid form. *Financial aid deadline (priority):* 4/1. *Notification date:* Continuous beginning 3/1. Students must reply within 2 weeks of notification.

CONTACT Ms. Tara Jones, Director of Financial Aid, Shorter University, 315 Shorter Avenue, Rome, GA 30165, 706-233-7227 or toll-free 800-868-6980. *Fax:* 706-233-7314. *E-mail:* tjones@shorter.edu.
Website: http://www.shorter.edu/.

SH'OR YOSHUV RABBINICAL COLLEGE
Lawrence, NY

CONTACT Office of Financial Aid, Sh'or Yoshuv Rabbinical College, 1526 Central Avenue, Far Rockaway, NY 11691-4002, 718-327-2048.
Website: http://www.shoryoshuv.org/.

SHORTER UNIVERSITY
Rome, GA

Tuition & fees: N/R	Average undergraduate aid package: $16,335

ABOUT THE INSTITUTION Independent Baptist, coed. *Awards:* associate, bachelor's, and master's degrees. 35 undergraduate majors. *Total enrollment:* 1,696. Undergraduates: 1,642. Freshmen: 405. Federal methodology is used as a basis for awarding need-based institutional aid.

FRESHMAN FINANCIAL AID (Fall 2012, est.) 257 applied for aid; of those 88% were deemed to have need. 100% of freshmen with need received aid; of those 22% had need fully met. *Average percent of need met:* 67% (excluding resources awarded to replace EFC). *Average financial aid package:* $16,164 (excluding

SIENA COLLEGE
Loudonville, NY

Tuition & fees: $31,368	Average undergraduate aid package: $20,000

ABOUT THE INSTITUTION Independent Roman Catholic, coed. *Awards:* certificates, bachelor's, and master's degrees. 28 undergraduate majors. *Total enrollment:* 3,289. Undergraduates: 3,236. Freshmen: 734. Federal methodology is used as a basis for awarding need-based institutional aid.

UNDERGRADUATE EXPENSES for 2013–2014 *Application fee:* $50. *One-time required fee:* $250. *Comprehensive fee:* $43,863 includes full-time tuition ($31,118), mandatory fees ($250), and room and board ($12,495). *College room only:* $7365. Full-time tuition and fees vary according to course load and student level. Room and board charges vary according to board plan and housing facility. **Part-time tuition:** $500 per credit. Part-time tuition and fees vary according to course load and student level.

FRESHMAN FINANCIAL AID (Fall 2012, est.) 687 applied for aid; of those 87% were deemed to have need. 100% of freshmen with need received aid; of those 19% had need fully met. **Average percent of need met:** 71% (excluding resources awarded to replace EFC). **Average financial aid package:** $21,000 (excluding resources awarded to replace EFC). 7% of all full-time freshmen had no need and received non-need-based gift aid.

UNDERGRADUATE FINANCIAL AID (Fall 2012, est.) 2,498 applied for aid; of those 88% were deemed to have need. 100% of undergraduates with need received aid; of those 14% had need fully met. **Average percent of need met:** 68% (excluding resources awarded to replace EFC). **Average financial aid package:** $20,000 (excluding resources awarded to replace EFC). 6% of all full-time undergraduates had no need and received non-need-based gift aid.

GIFT AID (NEED-BASED) Total amount: $34,680,000 (9% federal, 8% state, 83% institutional). **Receiving aid:** Freshmen: 81% (595); all full-time undergraduates: 72% (2,186). **Average award:** Freshmen: $17,000; Undergraduates: $15,000. **Scholarships, grants, and awards:** Federal Pell, FSEOG, state, private, college/university gift aid from institutional funds, Siena Grants, Franciscan Community Grants.

GIFT AID (NON-NEED-BASED) Total amount: $5,720,000 (1% state, 90% institutional, 9% external sources). **Receiving aid:** Freshmen: 78% (572). Undergraduates: 66% (2,022). **Average award:** Freshmen: $9800. Undergraduates: $8600. **Scholarships, grants, and awards by category:** Academic interests/achievement: biological sciences, business, communication, computer science, education, English, foreign languages, general academic interests/achievements, health fields, humanities, international studies, mathematics, military science, physical sciences, premedicine, religion/biblical studies, social sciences. Creative arts/performance: creative writing, general creative arts/performance, journalism/publications, music, performing arts, theater/drama. Special achievements/activities: community service, general special achievements/activities, hobbies/interests, leadership, memberships, religious involvement. Special characteristics: adult students, children and siblings of alumni, children of faculty/staff, children of public servants, children of union members/company employees, children of workers in trades, children with a deceased or disabled parent, ethnic background, general special characteristics, local/state students, out-of-state students, previous college experience, relatives of clergy, religious affiliation, veterans' children. **Tuition waivers:** Full or partial for employees or children of employees. **ROTC:** Army, Naval cooperative, Air Force cooperative.

LOANS Student loans: $15,200,000 (56% need-based, 44% non-need-based). 77% of past graduating class borrowed through all loan programs. **Average indebtedness per student:** $32,000. **Average need-based loan:** Freshmen: $3500. Undergraduates: $4500. **Parent loans:** $8,600,000 (65% need-based, 35% non-need-based). **Programs:** Federal Direct (Subsidized and Unsubsidized Stafford, PLUS), Perkins.

WORK-STUDY Federal work-study: Total amount: $350,000; jobs available.

ATHLETIC AWARDS Total amount: $4,400,000 (64% need-based, 36% non-need-based).

APPLYING FOR FINANCIAL AID Required financial aid forms: FAFSA, state aid form. **Financial aid deadline (priority):** 2/15. **Notification date:** 4/1. Students must reply by 5/1.

CONTACT Financial Aid Office, Siena College, 515 Loudon Road, Loudonville, NY 12211-1462, 518-783-2427 or toll-free 888-AT-SIENA. Fax: 518-783-2410. E-mail: aid@siena.edu. Website: http://www.siena.edu/.

SIENA HEIGHTS UNIVERSITY
Adrian, MI

CONTACT Office of Financial Aid, Siena Heights University, 1247 East Siena Heights Drive, Adrian, MI 49221, 517-264-7130 or toll-free 800-521-0009. Website: http://www.sienaheights.edu/.

SIERRA NEVADA COLLEGE
Incline Village, NV

Tuition & fees: $28,483	Average undergraduate aid package: $20,100

ABOUT THE INSTITUTION Independent, coed. **Awards:** bachelor's and master's degrees. 24 undergraduate majors. **Total enrollment:** 925. Undergraduates: 536. Freshmen: 70. Federal methodology is used as a basis for awarding need-based institutional aid.

UNDERGRADUATE EXPENSES for 2013–2014 Comprehensive fee: $40,255 includes full-time tuition ($27,753), mandatory fees ($730), and room and board ($11,772). **College room only:** $5900. Full-time tuition and fees vary according to degree level and location. Room and board charges vary according to board plan. **Part-time tuition:** $1180 per credit. Part-time tuition and fees vary according to degree level and location.

FRESHMAN FINANCIAL AID (Fall 2012, est.) 48 applied for aid; of those 90% were deemed to have need. 100% of freshmen with need received aid; of those 9% had need fully met. **Average percent of need met:** 55% (excluding resources awarded to replace EFC). **Average financial aid package:** $21,200 (excluding resources awarded to replace EFC). 39% of all full-time freshmen had no need and received non-need-based gift aid.

UNDERGRADUATE FINANCIAL AID (Fall 2012, est.) 363 applied for aid; of those 93% were deemed to have need. 100% of undergraduates with need received aid; of those 5% had need fully met. **Average percent of need met:** 55% (excluding resources awarded to replace EFC). **Average financial aid package:** $20,100 (excluding resources awarded to replace EFC). 36% of all full-time undergraduates had no need and received non-need-based gift aid.

GIFT AID (NEED-BASED) Total amount: $4,803,228 (20% federal, 79% institutional, 1% external sources). **Receiving aid:** Freshmen: 61% (43); all full-time undergraduates: 64% (339). **Average award:** Freshmen: $14,120; Undergraduates: $14,169. **Scholarships, grants, and awards:** Federal Pell, FSEOG, state, private, college/university gift aid from institutional funds.

GIFT AID (NON-NEED-BASED) Receiving aid: Freshmen: 61% (43). Undergraduates: 64% (339). **Average award:** Freshmen: $6500. Undergraduates: $6500. **Scholarships, grants, and awards by category:** Academic interests/achievement: 487 awards ($4,045,553 total): English, general academic interests/achievements. Creative arts/performance: 8 awards ($107,963 total): art/fine arts. Special characteristics: 11 awards ($52,515 total): veterans. **Tuition waivers:** Full or partial for employees or children of employees.

LOANS Student loans: $3,100,000 (77% need-based, 23% non-need-based). 50% of past graduating class borrowed through all loan programs. **Average indebtedness per student:** $27,000. **Average need-based loan:** Freshmen: $4750. Undergraduates: $4750. **Parent loans:** $1,500,000 (75% need-based, 25% non-need-based). **Programs:** Federal Direct (Subsidized and Unsubsidized Stafford, PLUS), alternative loans.

WORK-STUDY Federal work-study: Total amount: $140,000; 248 jobs averaging $410.

ATHLETIC AWARDS Total amount: $368,244 (100% need-based).

APPLYING FOR FINANCIAL AID Required financial aid form: FAFSA. **Financial aid deadline (priority):** 1/1. **Notification date:** Continuous beginning 4/1. Students must reply by 8/20 or within 4 weeks of notification.

CONTACT Nicole D. Ferguson, Director of Financial Aid, Sierra Nevada College, 999 Tahoe Boulevard, Incline Village, NV 89451, 775-831-1314 Ext. 7404. Fax: 775-832-1678 . E-mail: nferguson@sierranevada.edu. Website: http://www.sierranevada.edu/.

SILICON VALLEY UNIVERSITY
San Jose, CA

CONTACT Financial Aid Office, Silicon Valley University, 2160 Lundy Avenue, Suite 110, San Jose, CA 95131, 408-435-8989. Website: http://www.svuca.edu/.

SILVER LAKE COLLEGE OF THE HOLY FAMILY
Manitowoc, WI

ABOUT THE INSTITUTION Independent Roman Catholic, coed. 26 undergraduate majors.

GIFT AID (NEED-BASED) *Scholarships, grants, and awards:* Federal Pell, FSEOG, state, private, college/university gift aid from institutional funds.

GIFT AID (NON-NEED-BASED) *Scholarships, grants, and awards by category: Academic interests/achievement:* general academic interests/achievements. *Creative arts/performance:* applied art and design, art/fine arts, creative writing, music. *Special achievements/activities:* community service. *Special characteristics:* children and siblings of alumni, international students, local/state students, previous college experience, religious affiliation.

LOANS *Programs:* Federal Direct (Subsidized and Unsubsidized Stafford, PLUS), state.

WORK-STUDY *Federal work-study:* Total amount: $204,338; 97 jobs averaging $1429. *State or other work-study/employment:* Total amount: $7350 (100% need-based). 3 part-time jobs averaging $2450.

APPLYING FOR FINANCIAL AID *Required financial aid form:* FAFSA.

CONTACT Ms. Michelle Leider, Associate Director of Financial Aid, Silver Lake College of the Holy Family, 2406 South Alverno Road, Manitowoc, WI 54220-9319, 920-686-6122 or toll-free 800-236-4752 Ext. 175. *Fax:* 920-684-7082. *E-mail:* financialaid@sl.edu. *Website:* http://www.sl.edu/.

SIMMONS COLLEGE
Boston, MA

Tuition & fees: $35,370	Average undergraduate aid package: $24,139

ABOUT THE INSTITUTION Independent, undergraduate: women only; graduate: coed. *Awards:* certificates, bachelor's, master's, and doctoral degrees. 45 undergraduate majors. *Total enrollment:* 4,830. Undergraduates: 1,792. Freshmen: 401. Federal methodology is used as a basis for awarding need-based institutional aid.

UNDERGRADUATE EXPENSES for 2013–2014 *Application fee:* $55. *Comprehensive fee:* $48,770 includes full-time tuition ($34,350), mandatory fees ($1020), and room and board ($13,400). Full-time tuition and fees vary according to course load and program. Room and board charges vary according to board plan. *Part-time tuition:* $1178 per credit hour. Part-time tuition and fees vary according to course load and program.

FRESHMAN FINANCIAL AID (Fall 2012, est.) 349 applied for aid; of those 87% were deemed to have need. 100% of freshmen with need received aid; of those 18% had need fully met. *Average percent of need met:* 76% (excluding resources awarded to replace EFC). *Average financial aid package:* $25,593 (excluding resources awarded to replace EFC). 20% of all full-time freshmen had no need and received non-need-based gift aid.

UNDERGRADUATE FINANCIAL AID (Fall 2012, est.) 1,390 applied for aid; of those 92% were deemed to have need. 99% of undergraduates with need received aid; of those 10% had need fully met. *Average percent of need met:* 66% (excluding resources awarded to replace EFC). *Average financial aid package:* $24,139 (excluding resources awarded to replace EFC). 13% of all full-time undergraduates had no need and received non-need-based gift aid.

GIFT AID (NEED-BASED) *Total amount:* $26,130,756 (9% federal, 2% state, 85% institutional, 4% external sources). *Receiving aid:* Freshmen: 76% (304); all full-time undergraduates: 77% (1,271). *Average award:* Freshmen: $23,723; Undergraduates: $19,947. *Scholarships, grants, and awards:* Federal Pell, FSEOG, state, private, college/university gift aid from institutional funds.

GIFT AID (NON-NEED-BASED) *Total amount:* $3,209,614 (90% institutional, 10% external sources). *Receiving aid:* Freshmen: 7% (28). Undergraduates: 3% (57). *Average award:* Freshmen: $11,238. Undergraduates: $9415. *Scholarships, grants, and awards by category: Academic interests/achievement:* general academic interests/achievements. *Special achievements/activities:* community service, general special achievements/activities. *Special characteristics:* children and siblings of alumni, general special characteristics. *Tuition waivers:* Full or partial for employees or children of employees. *ROTC:* Army cooperative, Naval cooperative.

LOANS *Student loans:* $16,562,504 (35% need-based, 65% non-need-based). *Average need-based loan:* Freshmen: $3410. Undergraduates: $4880. *Parent loans:* $5,040,909 (100% non-need-based). *Programs:* Federal Direct (Subsidized and Unsubsidized Stafford, PLUS), Perkins, college/university.

WORK-STUDY *Federal work-study:* Total amount: $2,120,927; 892 jobs averaging $2327.

APPLYING FOR FINANCIAL AID *Required financial aid forms:* FAFSA, institution's own form. *Financial aid deadline (priority):* 2/15. *Notification date:* Continuous beginning 3/15.

CONTACT Daniel Forster, Director of Student Financial Services, Simmons College, 300 The Fenway, Boston, MA 02115, 617-521-2001 or toll-free 800-345-8468. *Fax:* 617-521-3195. *E-mail:* daniel.forster@simmons.edu. *Website:* http://www.simmons.edu/.

SIMPSON COLLEGE
Indianola, IA

Tuition & fees: $30,999	Average undergraduate aid package: $27,785

ABOUT THE INSTITUTION Independent United Methodist, coed. *Awards:* certificates, bachelor's, and master's degrees. 58 undergraduate majors. *Total enrollment:* 1,897. Undergraduates: 1,844. Freshmen: 415. Federal methodology is used as a basis for awarding need-based institutional aid.

UNDERGRADUATE EXPENSES for 2013–2014 *One-time required fee:* $200. *Comprehensive fee:* $38,962 includes full-time tuition ($30,423), mandatory fees ($576), and room and board ($7963). *College room only:* $3860. Full-time tuition and fees vary according to class time, course load, degree level, and program. Room and board charges vary according to board plan and housing facility. *Part-time tuition:* $355 per credit hour. Part-time tuition and fees vary according to class time, course load, degree level, and program.

FRESHMAN FINANCIAL AID (Fall 2012, est.) 408 applied for aid; of those 87% were deemed to have need. 100% of freshmen with need received aid; of those 28% had need fully met. *Average percent of need met:* 91% (excluding resources awarded to replace EFC). *Average financial aid package:* $29,667 (excluding resources awarded to replace EFC). 13% of all full-time freshmen had no need and received non-need-based gift aid.

UNDERGRADUATE FINANCIAL AID (Fall 2012, est.) 1,419 applied for aid; of those 85% were deemed to have need. 100% of undergraduates with need received aid; of those 27% had need fully met. *Average percent of need met:* 88% (excluding resources awarded to replace EFC). *Average financial aid package:* $27,785 (excluding resources awarded to replace EFC). 14% of all full-time undergraduates had no need and received non-need-based gift aid.

GIFT AID (NEED-BASED) *Total amount:* $23,192,543 (11% federal, 12% state, 74% institutional, 3% external sources). *Receiving aid:* Freshmen: 87% (353); all full-time undergraduates: 85% (1,205). *Average award:* Freshmen: $20,792; Undergraduates: $18,784. *Scholarships, grants, and awards:* Federal Pell, FSEOG, state, private, college/university gift aid from institutional funds.

GIFT AID (NON-NEED-BASED) *Total amount:* $4,627,754 (2% federal, 94% institutional, 4% external sources). *Receiving aid:* Freshmen: 16% (66). Undergraduates: 14% (193). *Average award:* Freshmen: $18,715. Undergraduates: $16,534. *Scholarships, grants, and awards by category: Academic interests/achievement:* $11,790,935 total: general academic interests/achievements. *Creative arts/performance:* $381,409 total: art/fine arts, music, theater/drama. *Special achievements/activities:* $238,750 total: community service, leadership, religious involvement. *Special characteristics:* $2,765,220 total: adult students, children and siblings of alumni, children of educators, children of faculty/staff, ethnic background, international students, members of minority groups, relatives of clergy, religious affiliation, siblings of current students, twins. *Tuition waivers:* Full or partial for children of alumni, employees or children of employees, senior citizens.

LOANS *Student loans:* $12,218,507 (70% need-based, 30% non-need-based). 89% of past graduating class borrowed through all loan programs. *Average indebtedness per student:* $35,228. *Average need-based loan:* Freshmen: $3529. Undergraduates: $3785. *Parent loans:* $1,998,328 (30% need-based, 70% non-need-based). *Programs:* Federal Direct (Subsidized and Unsubsidized Stafford, PLUS), Perkins, state, college/university, alternative loans.

WORK-STUDY *Federal work-study:* Total amount: $351,395; 343 jobs averaging $1079. *State or other work-study/employment:* Total amount: $592,307 (33% need-based, 67% non-need-based). 449 part-time jobs averaging $1372.
APPLYING FOR FINANCIAL AID *Required financial aid form:* FAFSA. *Financial aid deadline:* Continuous. *Notification date:* Continuous beginning 3/15. Students must reply by 5/1 or within 3 weeks of notification.
CONTACT Tracie Lynn Pavon, Assistant Vice President for Enrollment and Financial Assistance, Simpson College, 701 North C Street, Indianola, IA 50125-1297, 515-961-1630 Ext. 1596 or toll-free 800-362-2454. *Fax:* 515-961-1300. *E-mail:* tracie.pavon@ simpson.edu.
Website: http://www.simpson.edu/.

SIMPSON UNIVERSITY
Redding, CA

Tuition & fees: $23,300	Average undergraduate aid package: $19,272

ABOUT THE INSTITUTION Independent The Christian and Missionary Alliance, coed. *Awards:* certificates, associate, bachelor's, and master's degrees. 28 undergraduate majors. *Total enrollment:* 1,297. Undergraduates: 1,033. Freshmen: 147. Federal methodology is used as a basis for awarding need-based institutional aid.
UNDERGRADUATE EXPENSES for 2013–2014 *Application fee:* $25. *Comprehensive fee:* $30,800 includes full-time tuition ($23,300) and room and board ($7500). *College room only:* $4200. Full-time tuition and fees vary according to course load. Room and board charges vary according to board plan. *Part-time tuition:* $975 per credit. Part-time tuition and fees vary according to course load.
FRESHMAN FINANCIAL AID (Fall 2012, est.) 144 applied for aid; of those 94% were deemed to have need. 100% of freshmen with need received aid; of those 5% had need fully met. *Average percent of need met:* 71% (excluding resources awarded to replace EFC). *Average financial aid package:* $19,784 (excluding resources awarded to replace EFC). 4% of all full-time freshmen had no need and received non-need-based gift aid.
UNDERGRADUATE FINANCIAL AID (Fall 2012, est.) 728 applied for aid; of those 92% were deemed to have need. 100% of undergraduates with need received aid; of those 3% had need fully met. *Average percent of need met:* 68% (excluding resources awarded to replace EFC). *Average financial aid package:* $19,272 (excluding resources awarded to replace EFC). 5% of all full-time undergraduates had no need and received non-need-based gift aid.
GIFT AID (NEED-BASED) *Total amount:* $9,228,831 (27% federal, 28% state, 43% institutional, 2% external sources). *Receiving aid:* Freshmen: 78% (115); all full-time undergraduates: 76% (573). *Average award:* Freshmen: $13,660; Undergraduates: $12,752. *Scholarships, grants, and awards:* Federal Pell, FSEOG, state, private, college/university gift aid from institutional funds.
GIFT AID (NON-NEED-BASED) *Total amount:* $432,291 (90% institutional, 10% external sources). *Receiving aid:* Freshmen: 41% (60). Undergraduates: 34% (260). *Average award:* Freshmen: $9667. Undergraduates: $7646. *Scholarships, grants, and awards by category:* Academic interests/achievement: 112 awards ($282,634 total): general academic interests/achievements. Creative arts/performance: 74 awards ($91,000 total): music. Special achievements/activities: 130 awards ($101,860 total): community service, leadership, religious involvement. Special characteristics: 176 awards ($235,777 total): children of faculty/staff, general special characteristics, members of minority groups, out-of-state students, relatives of clergy, religious affiliation, siblings of current students. *Tuition waivers:* Full or partial for employees or children of employees. *ROTC:* Army.
LOANS *Student loans:* $7,903,711 (90% need-based, 10% non-need-based). 70% of past graduating class borrowed through all loan programs. *Average indebtedness per student:* $28,196. *Average need-based loan:* Freshmen: $3508. Undergraduates: $4559. *Parent loans:* $5,391,407 (46% need-based, 54% non-need-based). *Programs:* Federal Direct (Subsidized and Unsubsidized Stafford, PLUS), Perkins, alternative loans.
WORK-STUDY *Federal work-study:* Total amount: $81,123; 184 jobs averaging $549.
ATHLETIC AWARDS Total amount: $2,227,414 (87% need-based, 13% non-need-based).
APPLYING FOR FINANCIAL AID *Required financial aid forms:* FAFSA, institution's own form, state aid form. *Financial aid deadline (priority):* 3/2.

Notification date: Continuous beginning 3/15. Students must reply within 3 weeks of notification.
CONTACT Melissa Hudson, Director of Student Financial Services, Simpson University, 2211 College View Drive, Redding, CA 96003-8606, 530-226-4974 or toll-free 888-9-SIMPSON. *Fax:* 530-226-4855. *E-mail:* financialaid@simpsonu.edu. *Website:* http://www.simpsonu.edu/.

SINTE GLESKA UNIVERSITY
Mission, SD

CONTACT Office of Financial Aid, Sinte Gleska University, PO Box 490, Rosebud, SD 57570-0490, 605-747-4258. *Fax:* 605-747-2098.
Website: http://www.sintegleska.edu/.

SKIDMORE COLLEGE
Saratoga Springs, NY

Tuition & fees: $44,020	Average undergraduate aid package: $37,824

ABOUT THE INSTITUTION Independent, coed. *Awards:* bachelor's and master's degrees. 42 undergraduate majors. *Total enrollment:* 2,689. Undergraduates: 2,663. Freshmen: 647. Both federal and institutional methodology are used as a basis for awarding need-based institutional aid.
UNDERGRADUATE EXPENSES for 2013–2014 *Application fee:* $65. *Comprehensive fee:* $55,764 includes full-time tuition ($43,138), mandatory fees ($882), and room and board ($11,744). *College room only:* $6944. Full-time tuition and fees vary according to course load. Room and board charges vary according to board plan and housing facility. *Part-time tuition:* $1438 per credit. *Part-time fees:* $25 per term. Part-time tuition and fees vary according to course load. *Payment plan:* Tuition prepayment.
FRESHMAN FINANCIAL AID (Fall 2012, est.) 304 applied for aid; of those 98% were deemed to have need. 100% of freshmen with need received aid; of those 100% had need fully met. *Average percent of need met:* 100% (excluding resources awarded to replace EFC). *Average financial aid package:* $37,067 (excluding resources awarded to replace EFC). 1% of all full-time freshmen had no need and received non-need-based gift aid.
UNDERGRADUATE FINANCIAL AID (Fall 2012, est.) 1,269 applied for aid; of those 91% were deemed to have need. 99% of undergraduates with need received aid; of those 89% had need fully met. *Average percent of need met:* 95% (excluding resources awarded to replace EFC). *Average financial aid package:* $37,824 (excluding resources awarded to replace EFC). 1% of all full-time undergraduates had no need and received non-need-based gift aid.
GIFT AID (NEED-BASED) *Total amount:* $38,907,431 (5% federal, 3% state, 92% institutional). *Receiving aid:* Freshmen: 44% (284); all full-time undergraduates: 43% (1,114). *Average award:* Freshmen: $35,770; Undergraduates: $34,926. *Scholarships, grants, and awards:* Federal Pell, FSEOG, state, private, college/university gift aid from institutional funds.
GIFT AID (NON-NEED-BASED) *Total amount:* $1,195,090 (5% state, 46% institutional, 49% external sources). *Receiving aid:* Freshmen: 1% (7). Undergraduates: 1% (33). *Average award:* Freshmen: $12,500. Undergraduates: $11,700. *Scholarships, grants, and awards by category:* Academic interests/achievement: biological sciences, computer science, mathematics, physical sciences. Creative arts/performance: music. Special characteristics: children of faculty/staff. *Tuition waivers:* Full or partial for employees or children of employees, senior citizens. *ROTC:* Army cooperative, Air Force cooperative.
LOANS *Student loans:* $6,974,052 (46% need-based, 54% non-need-based). 42% of past graduating class borrowed through all loan programs. *Average indebtedness per student:* $22,753. *Average need-based loan:* Freshmen: $2347. Undergraduates: $3634. *Parent loans:* $3,000,000 (100% non-need-based). *Programs:* Federal Direct (Subsidized and Unsubsidized Stafford, PLUS), Perkins, state.
WORK-STUDY *Federal work-study:* Total amount: $1,231,942; jobs available. *State or other work-study/employment:* Total amount: $994,612 (100% non-need-based). Part-time jobs available.

APPLYING FOR FINANCIAL AID *Required financial aid forms:* FAFSA, CSS Financial Aid PROFILE, noncustodial (divorced/separated) parent's statement. *Financial aid deadline:* 2/1. *Notification date:* 4/1. Students must reply by 5/1.

CONTACT Ms. Beth A. Post-Lundquist, Director of Financial Aid, Skidmore College, 815 North Broadway, Saratoga Springs, NY 12866-1632, 518-580-5750 or toll-free 800-867-6007. *Fax:* 518-580-5752. *E-mail:* finaid@skidmore.edu. *Website:* http://www.skidmore.edu/.

SKYLINE COLLEGE
Roanoke, VA

ABOUT THE INSTITUTION Proprietary, coed. 10 undergraduate majors.

GIFT AID (NEED-BASED) *Scholarships, grants, and awards:* Federal Pell, FSEOG, state, private, college/university gift aid from institutional funds.

GIFT AID (NON-NEED-BASED) *Scholarships, grants, and awards by category: Academic interests/achievement:* business, computer science, engineering/technologies, health fields. *Special achievements/activities:* community service, general special achievements/activities. *Special characteristics:* adult students, children of faculty/staff, general special characteristics, previous college experience, veterans, veterans' children.

LOANS *Programs:* Federal Direct (Subsidized and Unsubsidized Stafford, PLUS), Perkins, college/university, private loans.

APPLYING FOR FINANCIAL AID *Required financial aid form:* FAFSA.

CONTACT Ms. Amanda Little, Director of Financial Aid, Skyline College, 5234 Airport Road, Roanoke, VA 24012, 540-563-8080 or toll-free 866-708-6178. *E-mail:* alittle@ecpi.edu. *Website:* http://www.skyline.edu/.

SLIPPERY ROCK UNIVERSITY OF PENNSYLVANIA
Slippery Rock, PA

Tuition & fees (PA res): $8747	Average undergraduate aid package: $8598

ABOUT THE INSTITUTION State-supported, coed. *Awards:* certificates, bachelor's, master's, and doctoral degrees. 65 undergraduate majors. *Total enrollment:* 8,559. Undergraduates: 7,860. Freshmen: 1,546. Federal methodology is used as a basis for awarding need-based institutional aid.

UNDERGRADUATE EXPENSES for 2013–2014 *Application fee:* $30. *Tuition, state resident:* full-time $6428; part-time $268 per credit hour. *Tuition, nonresident:* full-time $9642; part-time $536 per credit hour. *Required fees:* full-time $2319; $96.77 per credit hour. Full-time tuition and fees vary according to course load and degree level. Part-time tuition and fees vary according to course load and degree level. *College room and board:* $9364; *Room only:* $6206. Room and board charges vary according to board plan and housing facility.

FRESHMAN FINANCIAL AID (Fall 2012, est.) 1,445 applied for aid; of those 77% were deemed to have need. 100% of freshmen with need received aid; of those 13% had need fully met. *Average percent of need met:* 58% (excluding resources awarded to replace EFC). *Average financial aid package:* $8152 (excluding resources awarded to replace EFC). 7% of all full-time freshmen had no need and received non-need-based gift aid.

UNDERGRADUATE FINANCIAL AID (Fall 2012, est.) 6,345 applied for aid; of those 81% were deemed to have need. 98% of undergraduates with need received aid; of those 13% had need fully met. *Average percent of need met:* 62% (excluding resources awarded to replace EFC). *Average financial aid package:* $8598 (excluding resources awarded to replace EFC). 5% of all full-time undergraduates had no need and received non-need-based gift aid.

GIFT AID (NEED-BASED) *Total amount:* $18,546,675 (55% federal, 40% state, 5% institutional). *Receiving aid:* Freshmen: 47% (720); all full-time undergraduates: 45% (3,305). *Average award:* Freshmen: $5608; Undergraduates: $5443. *Scholarships, grants, and awards:* Federal Pell, FSEOG, state, private, college/university gift aid from institutional funds.

GIFT AID (NON-NEED-BASED) *Total amount:* $4,312,187 (46% institutional, 54% external sources). *Receiving aid:* Freshmen: 26% (400). Undergraduates: 15% (1,106). *Average award:* Freshmen: $2177. Undergraduates: $2674. *Scholarships,*

grants, and awards by category: Academic interests/achievement: biological sciences, business, communication, computer science, education, English, general academic interests/achievements, health fields, physical sciences, social sciences. *Creative arts/performance:* applied art and design, art/fine arts, dance, music, performing arts, theater/drama. *Special achievements/activities:* community service, general special achievements/activities, leadership. *Special characteristics:* children and siblings of alumni, children of faculty/staff, children of union members/company employees, ethnic background, general special characteristics, local/state students, members of minority groups, out-of-state students, previous college experience. *Tuition waivers:* Full or partial for minority students, employees or children of employees, senior citizens. *ROTC:* Army.

LOANS *Student loans:* $49,959,571 (42% need-based, 58% non-need-based). 85% of past graduating class borrowed through all loan programs. *Average indebtedness per student:* $28,959. *Average need-based loan:* Freshmen: $3508. Undergraduates: $4327. *Parent loans:* $8,864,254 (100% non-need-based). *Programs:* Federal Direct (Subsidized and Unsubsidized Stafford, PLUS), Perkins.

WORK-STUDY *Federal work-study:* Total amount: $915,796; 645 jobs averaging $1588. *State or other work-study/employment:* Total amount: $1,517,345 (100% non-need-based). 843 part-time jobs averaging $1869.

ATHLETIC AWARDS Total amount: $1,089,047 (100% non-need-based).

APPLYING FOR FINANCIAL AID *Required financial aid form:* FAFSA. *Financial aid deadline (priority):* 5/1. *Notification date:* Continuous beginning 3/15.

CONTACT Ms. Patty A. Hladio, Director of Financial Aid, Slippery Rock University of Pennsylvania, 1 Morrow Way, Slippery Rock, PA 16057, 724-738-2044 or toll-free 800-SRU-9111. *Fax:* 724-738-2922. *E-mail:* financial.aid@sru.edu. *Website:* http://www.sru.edu/.

SMITH COLLEGE
Northampton, MA

Tuition & fees: $41,460	Average undergraduate aid package: $39,120

ABOUT THE INSTITUTION Independent, undergraduate: women only; graduate: coed. *Awards:* certificates, bachelor's, master's, and doctoral degrees. 53 undergraduate majors. *Total enrollment:* 3,212. Undergraduates: 2,664. Freshmen: 651. Both federal and institutional methodology are used as a basis for awarding need-based institutional aid.

UNDERGRADUATE EXPENSES for 2013–2014 *Application fee:* $60. *Comprehensive fee:* $55,320 includes full-time tuition ($41,190), mandatory fees ($270), and room and board ($13,860). *College room only:* $6940. *Part-time tuition:* $1290 per credit hour. *Payment plan:* Tuition prepayment.

FRESHMAN FINANCIAL AID (Fall 2012, est.) 513 applied for aid; of those 82% were deemed to have need. 100% of freshmen with need received aid; of those 100% had need fully met. *Average percent of need met:* 100% (excluding resources awarded to replace EFC). *Average financial aid package:* $39,440 (excluding resources awarded to replace EFC). 3% of all full-time freshmen had no need and received non-need-based gift aid.

UNDERGRADUATE FINANCIAL AID (Fall 2012, est.) 1,915 applied for aid; of those 87% were deemed to have need. 100% of undergraduates with need received aid; of those 100% had need fully met. *Average percent of need met:* 100% (excluding resources awarded to replace EFC). *Average financial aid package:* $39,120 (excluding resources awarded to replace EFC). 4% of all full-time undergraduates had no need and received non-need-based gift aid.

GIFT AID (NEED-BASED) *Total amount:* $56,123,466 (6% federal, 1% state, 91% institutional, 2% external sources). *Receiving aid:* Freshmen: 62% (404); all full-time undergraduates: 60% (1,578). *Average award:* Freshmen: $36,172; Undergraduates: $34,654. *Scholarships, grants, and awards:* Federal Pell, FSEOG, state, private, college/university gift aid from institutional funds.

GIFT AID (NON-NEED-BASED) *Total amount:* $2,847,137 (1% federal, 71% institutional, 28% external sources). *Receiving aid:* Freshmen: 1% (5). Undergraduates: 12. *Average award:* Freshmen: $16,176. Undergraduates: $17,691. *Scholarships, grants, and awards by category: Academic interests/achievement:* general academic interests/achievements. *Special characteristics:* local/state students. *Tuition waivers:* Full or partial for employees or children of employees. *ROTC:* Army cooperative, Air Force cooperative.

LOANS *Student loans:* $9,836,461 (65% need-based, 35% non-need-based). 67% of past graduating class borrowed through all loan programs. *Average indebtedness per student:* $23,071. *Average need-based loan:* Freshmen: $3247. Undergraduates: $4513. *Parent loans:* $4,058,872 (100% non-need-based). *Programs:* Federal Direct (Subsidized and Unsubsidized Stafford, PLUS), Perkins, college/university. **WORK-STUDY** *Federal work-study:* Total amount: $2,538,307; jobs available. *State or other work-study/employment:* Total amount: $1,241,179 (87% need-based, 13% non-need-based). Part-time jobs available. **APPLYING FOR FINANCIAL AID** *Required financial aid forms:* FAFSA, institution's own form, CSS Financial Aid PROFILE, noncustodial (divorced/separated) parent's statement, federal income tax form(s). *Financial aid deadline:* 2/15. *Notification date:* 4/1. Students must reply by 5/1. **CONTACT** David Belanger, Director of Student Financial Services, Smith College, College Hall, Northampton, MA 01063, 413-585-2530 or toll-free 800-383-3232. *Fax:* 413-585-2566. *E-mail:* sfs@smith.edu. *Website:* http://www.smith.edu/.

SOJOURNER-DOUGLASS COLLEGE
Baltimore, MD

CONTACT Ms. Rebecca Chalk, Financial Aid Director, Sojourner-Douglass College, 200 North Central Avenue, Baltimore, MD 21202, 410-276-0306 Ext. 258. *Fax:* 410-276-0148. *E-mail:* rchalk@host.sdc.edu. *Website:* http://sdc.edu/.

SOKA UNIVERSITY OF AMERICA
Aliso Viejo, CA

Tuition & fees: $28,808	Average undergraduate aid package: $34,091

ABOUT THE INSTITUTION Independent, coed. *Awards:* bachelor's and master's degrees. 1 undergraduate major. *Total enrollment:* 438. Undergraduates: 436. Freshmen: 103. Both federal and institutional methodology are used as a basis for awarding need-based institutional aid. **UNDERGRADUATE EXPENSES** for 2013–2014 *Application fee:* $30. *Comprehensive fee:* $39,724 includes full-time tuition ($27,950), mandatory fees ($858), and room and board ($10,916). Full-time tuition and fees vary according to class time, course load, and program. Room and board charges vary according to board plan. *Part-time tuition:* $1164 per credit. Part-time tuition and fees vary according to class time, course load, and program. **FRESHMAN FINANCIAL AID (Fall 2012, est.)** 103 applied for aid; of those 89% were deemed to have need. 100% of freshmen with need received aid; of those 11% had need fully met. *Average percent of need met:* 80% (excluding resources awarded to replace EFC). *Average financial aid package:* $32,990 (excluding resources awarded to replace EFC). 11% of all full-time freshmen had no need and received non-need-based gift aid. **UNDERGRADUATE FINANCIAL AID (Fall 2012, est.)** 409 applied for aid; of those 97% were deemed to have need. 100% of undergraduates with need received aid; of those 8% had need fully met. *Average percent of need met:* 83% (excluding resources awarded to replace EFC). *Average financial aid package:* $34,091 (excluding resources awarded to replace EFC). 7% of all full-time undergraduates had no need and received non-need-based gift aid. **GIFT AID (NEED-BASED)** *Total amount:* $8,618,073 (7% federal, 9% state, 84% institutional). *Receiving aid:* Freshmen: 88% (92); all full-time undergraduates: 86% (376). *Average award:* Freshmen: $22,356; Undergraduates: $23,032. *Scholarships, grants, and awards:* Federal Pell, FSEOG, state, private, college/university gift aid from institutional funds. **GIFT AID (NON-NEED-BASED)** *Total amount:* $2,928,204 (97% institutional, 3% external sources). *Receiving aid:* Freshmen: 88% (91). Undergraduates: 78% (340). *Average award:* Freshmen: $10,311. Undergraduates: $13,833. *Scholarships, grants, and awards by category:* Special characteristics: children of faculty/staff. *Tuition waivers:* Full or partial for employees or children of employees. **LOANS** *Student loans:* $2,158,419 (100% need-based). 47% of past graduating class borrowed through all loan programs. *Average indebtedness per student:*

$22,387. *Average need-based loan:* Freshmen: $5676. Undergraduates: $5718. *Parent loans:* $2,788,992 (100% need-based). *Programs:* Federal Direct (Subsidized and Unsubsidized Stafford, PLUS), college/university. **WORK-STUDY** *Federal work-study:* Total amount: $16,717; 15 jobs averaging $1114. *State or other work-study/employment:* Total amount: $106,280 (100% non-need-based). 10 part-time jobs averaging $10,628. **ATHLETIC AWARDS** Total amount: $438,463 (100% non-need-based). **APPLYING FOR FINANCIAL AID** *Required financial aid form:* FAFSA. *Financial aid deadline:* 3/2 (priority: 2/15). *Notification date:* Continuous beginning 3/1. Students must reply by 6/1. **CONTACT** Ms. Caterina D'Adamo, Manager of Financial Aid, Soka University of America, 1 University Drive, Aliso Viejo, CA 92656, 949-480-4351 or toll-free 888-600-SOKA. *Fax:* 949-480-4151. *E-mail:* cdadamo@soka.edu. *Website:* http://www.soka.edu/.

SONOMA STATE UNIVERSITY
Rohnert Park, CA

Tuition & fees (CA res): $7396	Average undergraduate aid package: $12,196

ABOUT THE INSTITUTION State-supported, coed. *Awards:* bachelor's and master's degrees. 63 undergraduate majors. *Total enrollment:* 9,021. Undergraduates: 8,122. Freshmen: 1,749. Federal methodology is used as a basis for awarding need-based institutional aid. **UNDERGRADUATE EXPENSES** for 2013–2014 *Application fee:* $55. *Tuition, state resident:* full-time $5970. *Tuition, nonresident:* full-time $10,434; part-time $372 per unit. *Required fees:* full-time $1426. Full-time tuition and fees vary according to course load and degree level. Part-time tuition and fees vary according to course load and degree level. *College room and board:* $11,241. Room and board charges vary according to housing facility. **FRESHMAN FINANCIAL AID (Fall 2012, est.)** 1,022 applied for aid; of those 71% were deemed to have need. 95% of freshmen with need received aid; of those 9% had need fully met. *Average percent of need met:* 81% (excluding resources awarded to replace EFC). *Average financial aid package:* $11,900 (excluding resources awarded to replace EFC). 1% of all full-time freshmen had no need and received non-need-based gift aid. **UNDERGRADUATE FINANCIAL AID (Fall 2012, est.)** 5,368 applied for aid; of those 81% were deemed to have need. 95% of undergraduates with need received aid; of those 7% had need fully met. *Average percent of need met:* 79% (excluding resources awarded to replace EFC). *Average financial aid package:* $12,196 (excluding resources awarded to replace EFC). 1% of all full-time undergraduates had no need and received non-need-based gift aid. **GIFT AID (NEED-BASED)** *Total amount:* $17,155,639 (61% federal, 39% state). *Receiving aid:* Freshmen: 22% (390); all full-time undergraduates: 33% (2,713). *Average award:* Freshmen: $10,006; Undergraduates: $9250. *Scholarships, grants, and awards:* Federal Pell, FSEOG, state, private, college/university gift aid from institutional funds. **GIFT AID (NON-NEED-BASED)** *Total amount:* $1,825,742 (4% federal, 16% state, 33% institutional, 47% external sources). *Receiving aid:* Freshmen: 7% (120). Undergraduates: 7% (551). *Average award:* Freshmen: $1583. Undergraduates: $4268. *Scholarships, grants, and awards by category:* Academic interests/achievement: 114 awards ($158,175 total): area/ethnic studies, biological sciences, business, communication, computer science, education, engineering/technologies, English, foreign languages, general academic interests/achievements, health fields, humanities, mathematics, physical sciences, premedicine, social sciences. *Creative arts/performance:* 64 awards ($123,850 total): applied art and design, art/fine arts, cinema/film/broadcasting, creative writing, dance, journalism/publications, music, performing arts, theater/drama. *Special achievements/activities:* 8 awards ($21,700 total): community service, leadership, memberships. *Special characteristics:* 127 awards ($396,580 total): adult students, children and siblings of alumni, children of educators, children of faculty/staff, children of public servants, children of union members/company employees, children of workers in trades, ethnic background, first-generation college students, general special characteristics, handicapped students, international students, local/state students, married students, members of minority groups, out-of-state students, previous college experience, veterans. *Tuition waivers:* Full or partial for employees or children of employees. *ROTC:* Army cooperative, Air Force cooperative.

LOANS *Student loans:* $21,765,550 (53% need-based, 47% non-need-based). 62% of past graduating class borrowed through all loan programs. *Average indebtedness per student:* $21,206. *Average need-based loan:* Freshmen: $3288. Undergraduates: $4268. *Parent loans:* $10,060,339 (100% non-need-based). *Programs:* Federal Direct (Subsidized and Unsubsidized Stafford, PLUS), Perkins.

WORK-STUDY *Federal work-study:* Total amount: $549,397; 188 jobs averaging $2922. *State or other work-study/employment:* Total amount: $1,600,000 (100% non-need-based). 620 part-time jobs averaging $2580.

ATHLETIC AWARDS Total amount: $559,573 (100% non-need-based).

APPLYING FOR FINANCIAL AID *Required financial aid form:* FAFSA. *Financial aid deadline (priority):* 1/31. *Notification date:* Continuous beginning 3/15. Students must reply within 2 weeks of notification.

CONTACT Susan Gutierrez, Director of Financial Aid, Sonoma State University, 1801 East Cotati Avenue, Rohnert Park, CA 94928-3609, 707-664-2287. *Fax:* 707-664-4242. *E-mail:* susan.gutierrez@sonoma.edu.
Website: http://www.sonoma.edu/.

SOUTH CAROLINA STATE UNIVERSITY
Orangeburg, SC

CONTACT Sandra S. Davis, Director of Financial Aid, South Carolina State University, 300 College Street Northeast, Orangeburg, SC 29117, 803-536-7067 or toll-free 800-260-5956. *Fax:* 803-536-8420. *E-mail:* sdavis@scsu.edu.
Website: http://www.scsu.edu/.

SOUTH COLLEGE
Knoxville, TN

CONTACT Financial Aid Office, South College, 720 North Fifth Avenue, Knoxville, TN 37917, 865-524-3043.
Website: http://www.southcollegetn.edu/.

SOUTH DAKOTA SCHOOL OF MINES AND TECHNOLOGY
Rapid City, SD

Tuition & fees: N/R	Average undergraduate aid package: $13,246

ABOUT THE INSTITUTION State-supported, coed. *Awards:* certificates, associate, bachelor's, master's, and doctoral degrees. 17 undergraduate majors. *Total enrollment:* 2,311. Undergraduates: 2,008. Freshmen: 419. Both federal and institutional methodology are used as a basis for awarding need-based institutional aid.

FRESHMAN FINANCIAL AID (Fall 2012, est.) 427 applied for aid; of those 63% were deemed to have need. 100% of freshmen with need received aid; of those 44% had need fully met. *Average percent of need met:* 81% (excluding resources awarded to replace EFC). *Average financial aid package:* $13,258 (excluding resources awarded to replace EFC). 26% of all full-time freshmen had no need and received non-need-based gift aid.

UNDERGRADUATE FINANCIAL AID (Fall 2012, est.) 1,516 applied for aid; of those 65% were deemed to have need. 100% of undergraduates with need received aid; of those 37% had need fully met. *Average percent of need met:* 78% (excluding resources awarded to replace EFC). *Average financial aid package:* $13,246 (excluding resources awarded to replace EFC). 17% of all full-time undergraduates had no need and received non-need-based gift aid.

GIFT AID (NEED-BASED) *Total amount:* $3,867,480 (58% federal, 21% institutional, 21% external sources). *Receiving aid:* Freshmen: 45% (201); all full-time undergraduates: 37% (632). *Average award:* Freshmen: $4115; Undergraduates: $4246. *Scholarships, grants, and awards:* Federal Pell, FSEOG, state, private, college/university gift aid from institutional funds.

GIFT AID (NON-NEED-BASED) *Total amount:* $1,025,841 (63% institutional, 37% external sources). *Receiving aid:* Freshmen: 37% (166). Undergraduates: 21%

(369). *Average award:* Freshmen: $2799. Undergraduates: $2790. *Scholarships, grants, and awards by category:* Academic interests/achievement: 383 awards ($428,347 total): computer science, engineering/technologies, mathematics, military science, physical sciences. *Special characteristics:* 154 awards ($242,800 total): adult students, ethnic background, international students, local/state students, married students, members of minority groups, out-of-state students. *ROTC:* Army.

LOANS *Student loans:* $7,717,301 (100% need-based). 60% of past graduating class borrowed through all loan programs. *Average indebtedness per student:* $18,331. *Average need-based loan:* Freshmen: $3269. Undergraduates: $4115. *Parent loans:* $1,795,965 (81% need-based, 19% non-need-based). *Programs:* Federal Direct (Subsidized and Unsubsidized Stafford, PLUS), Perkins.

WORK-STUDY *Federal work-study:* Total amount: $187,829; 116 jobs averaging $1810.

ATHLETIC AWARDS Total amount: $628,830 (64% need-based, 36% non-need-based).

APPLYING FOR FINANCIAL AID *Required financial aid form:* FAFSA. *Financial aid deadline:* Continuous. *Notification date:* Continuous beginning 4/15. Students must reply within 3 weeks of notification.

CONTACT David W. Martin, Director of Financial Aid, South Dakota School of Mines and Technology, 501 East Saint Joseph Street, Rapid City, SD 57701-3995, 605-394-2274 or toll-free 800-544-8162. *Fax:* 605-394-1979. *E-mail:* david.martin@sdsmt.edu.
Website: http://www.sdsmt.edu/.

SOUTH DAKOTA STATE UNIVERSITY
Brookings, SD

Tuition & fees (SD res): $7404	Average undergraduate aid package: $9722

ABOUT THE INSTITUTION State-supported, coed. *Awards:* certificates, associate, bachelor's, master's, and doctoral degrees. 78 undergraduate majors. *Total enrollment:* 12,583. Undergraduates: 11,118. Freshmen: 2,223. Federal methodology is used as a basis for awarding need-based institutional aid.

UNDERGRADUATE EXPENSES for 2013–2014 *Application fee:* $20. *Tuition, state resident:* full-time $3897; part-time $129.90 per credit hour. *Tuition, nonresident:* full-time $5843; part-time $194.75 per credit hour. *Required fees:* full-time $3507. Full-time tuition and fees vary according to course level, course load, degree level, location, program, and reciprocity agreements. Part-time tuition and fees vary according to course level, course load, degree level, location, program, and reciprocity agreements. *College room and board:* $5586; *Room only:* $2839. Room and board charges vary according to board plan and housing facility.

FRESHMAN FINANCIAL AID (Fall 2012, est.) 1,752 applied for aid; of those 83% were deemed to have need. 100% of freshmen with need received aid; of those 85% had need fully met. *Average percent of need met:* 92% (excluding resources awarded to replace EFC). *Average financial aid package:* $8791 (excluding resources awarded to replace EFC). 23% of all full-time freshmen had no need and received non-need-based gift aid.

UNDERGRADUATE FINANCIAL AID (Fall 2012, est.) 7,411 applied for aid; of those 87% were deemed to have need. 100% of undergraduates with need received aid; of those 80% had need fully met. *Average percent of need met:* 90% (excluding resources awarded to replace EFC). *Average financial aid package:* $9722 (excluding resources awarded to replace EFC). 19% of all full-time undergraduates had no need and received non-need-based gift aid.

GIFT AID (NEED-BASED) *Total amount:* $20,908,231 (66% federal, 7% state, 18% institutional, 9% external sources). *Receiving aid:* Freshmen: 43% (913); all full-time undergraduates: 47% (4,008). *Average award:* Freshmen: $4876; Undergraduates: $4904. *Scholarships, grants, and awards:* Federal Pell, FSEOG, state, private, college/university gift aid from institutional funds, United Negro College Fund, Federal Nursing, TEACH Grants, TRiO Scholarships, SDEAF.

GIFT AID (NON-NEED-BASED) *Total amount:* $4,442,346 (3% federal, 19% state, 54% institutional, 24% external sources). *Receiving aid:* Freshmen: 49% (1,045). Undergraduates: 63% (5,404). *Average award:* Freshmen: $1674. Undergraduates: $1420. *Scholarships, grants, and awards by category:* Academic interests/achievement: 3,224 awards ($3,968,420 total): agriculture, area/ethnic studies, biological sciences, business, communication, computer science, education, engineering/technologies, English, foreign languages, general academic interests/achievements, health fields, home economics, humanities, international studies, mathematics, military science, physical sciences, premedicine, social sciences. *Creative arts/performance:* 345 awards ($402,484 total): art/fine arts, debating, general creative arts/performance, journalism/publications, music, performing arts, theater/drama. *Special achievements/activities:* 158 awards ($152,166 total): community service, general special achievements/activities, hobbies/interests, junior miss, leadership, memberships, rodeo. *Special characteristics:* 220 awards ($320,160 total): adult students, children of faculty/staff, children of workers in trades, ethnic background, first-generation college students, general special characteristics, handicapped students, international students, members of minority groups, veterans, veterans' children. *Tuition waivers:* Full or partial for employees or children of employees, senior citizens. *ROTC:* Army, Air Force.

LOANS *Student loans:* $45,692,770 (91% need-based, 9% non-need-based). 80% of past graduating class borrowed through all loan programs. *Average indebtedness per student:* $22,735. *Average need-based loan:* Freshmen: $4836. Undergraduates: $5044. *Parent loans:* $3,617,140 (55% need-based, 45% non-need-based). *Programs:* Federal Direct (Subsidized and Unsubsidized Stafford, PLUS), Perkins, Federal Nursing, college/university, alternative loans, Health Professions Student Loans (HPSL).

WORK-STUDY *Federal work-study:* Total amount: $872,310; 490 jobs averaging $1540. *State or other work-study/employment:* Total amount: $1,258,680 (77% need-based, 23% non-need-based). 1,860 part-time jobs averaging $1810.

ATHLETIC AWARDS Total amount: $3,033,424 (51% need-based, 49% non-need-based).

APPLYING FOR FINANCIAL AID *Required financial aid form:* FAFSA. *Financial aid deadline (priority):* 3/15. *Notification date:* Continuous beginning 3/30. Students must reply within 3 weeks of notification.

CONTACT Mr. Jay Larsen, Director of Financial Aid, South Dakota State University, Administration 106, PO Box 2201, Brookings, SD 57007, 605-688-4703 or toll-free 800-952-3541. *Fax:* 605-688-5882. *E-mail:* jay.larsen@sdstate.edu. *Website:* http://www.sdstate.edu/.

SOUTHEASTERN BAPTIST COLLEGE
Laurel, MS

CONTACT Financial Aid Officer, Southeastern Baptist College, 4229 Highway 15 North, Laurel, MS 39440-1096, 601-426-6346. *Website:* http://www.southeasternbaptist.edu/.

SOUTHEASTERN BAPTIST THEOLOGICAL SEMINARY
Wake Forest, NC

CONTACT Financial Aid Office, Southeastern Baptist Theological Seminary, PO Box 1889, Wake Forest, NC 27588-1889, 919-556-3101 or toll-free 800-284-6317. *Website:* http://www.sebts.edu/.

SOUTHEASTERN BIBLE COLLEGE
Birmingham, AL

CONTACT Mr. Jay Powell, Financial Aid Administrator, Southeastern Bible College, 2545 Valleydale Road, Birmingham, AL 35244-2083, 205-970-9216 or toll-free 800-749-8878. *Fax:* 205-970-9207. *E-mail:* finaid@sebc.edu. *Website:* http://www.sebc.edu/.

SOUTHEASTERN LOUISIANA UNIVERSITY
Hammond, LA

Tuition & fees (LA res): $5426	Average undergraduate aid package: $8238

ABOUT THE INSTITUTION State-supported, coed. *Awards:* associate, bachelor's, master's, and doctoral degrees. 39 undergraduate majors. *Total enrollment:* 15,602. Undergraduates: 14,240. Freshmen: 2,471. Federal methodology is used as a basis for awarding need-based institutional aid.

UNDERGRADUATE EXPENSES for 2013–2014 *Application fee:* $20. *Tuition, state resident:* full-time $5426. *Tuition, nonresident:* full-time $16,285. Full-time tuition and fees vary according to course load. Part-time tuition and fees vary according to course load. *College room and board:* $6510; *Room only:* $4260. Room and board charges vary according to board plan and housing facility.

FRESHMAN FINANCIAL AID (Fall 2011) 2,051 applied for aid; of those 69% were deemed to have need. 99% of freshmen with need received aid; of those 33% had need fully met. *Average financial aid package:* $8195 (excluding resources awarded to replace EFC). 10% of all full-time freshmen had no need and received non-need-based gift aid.

UNDERGRADUATE FINANCIAL AID (Fall 2011) 8,373 applied for aid; of those 74% were deemed to have need. 99% of undergraduates with need received aid; of those 37% had need fully met. *Average financial aid package:* $8238 (excluding resources awarded to replace EFC). 10% of all full-time undergraduates had no need and received non-need-based gift aid.

GIFT AID (NEED-BASED) *Total amount:* $21,743,548 (87% federal, 13% state). *Receiving aid:* Freshmen: 40% (913); all full-time undergraduates: 39% (4,170). *Average award:* Freshmen: $5128; Undergraduates: $4823. *Scholarships, grants, and awards:* Federal Pell, FSEOG, state, private, college/university gift aid from institutional funds.

GIFT AID (NON-NEED-BASED) *Total amount:* $24,378,115 (60% state, 37% institutional, 3% external sources). *Receiving aid:* Freshmen: 42% (959). Undergraduates: 27% (2,855). *Average award:* Freshmen: $3476. Undergraduates: $2787. *Scholarships, grants, and awards by category: Academic interests/achievement:* business, communication, computer science, education, English, foreign languages, general academic interests/achievements, humanities, mathematics, physical sciences, premedicine, social sciences. *Creative arts/performance:* art/fine arts, music, theater/drama. *Special achievements/activities:* cheerleading/drum major, leadership, memberships. *Special characteristics:* adult students, children and siblings of alumni, children of faculty/staff, out-of-state students, veterans, veterans' children. *Tuition waivers:* Full or partial for employees or children of employees. *ROTC:* Army cooperative.

LOANS *Student loans:* $35,312,018 (44% need-based, 56% non-need-based). 60% of past graduating class borrowed through all loan programs. *Average indebtedness per student:* $19,661. *Average need-based loan:* Freshmen: $2957. Undergraduates: $3791. *Parent loans:* $1,026,194 (100% non-need-based). *Programs:* Federal Direct (Subsidized and Unsubsidized Stafford, PLUS), Perkins, college/university.

WORK-STUDY *Federal work-study:* Total amount: $278,504; jobs available. *State or other work-study/employment:* Total amount: $2,744,971 (100% non-need-based). Part-time jobs available.

ATHLETIC AWARDS Total amount: $2,984,634 (100% non-need-based).

APPLYING FOR FINANCIAL AID *Required financial aid forms:* FAFSA, institution's own form. *Financial aid deadline (priority):* 5/1. *Notification date:* Continuous beginning 4/1. Students must reply within 2 weeks of notification.

CONTACT Mrs. Mary Lacour, Director of Financial Aid, Southeastern Louisiana University, SLU 10768, Hammond, LA 70402, 985-549-2244 or toll-free 800-222-7358. *Fax:* 985-549-5077. *E-mail:* finaid@selu.edu. *Website:* http://www.selu.edu/.

SOUTHEASTERN OKLAHOMA STATE UNIVERSITY
Durant, OK

Tuition & fees (OK res): $5060	Average undergraduate aid package: $9609

ABOUT THE INSTITUTION State-supported, coed. **Awards:** certificates, bachelor's, and master's degrees. 42 undergraduate majors. **Total enrollment:** 4,120. Undergraduates: 3,676. Freshmen: 600. Federal methodology is used as a basis for awarding need-based institutional aid.

UNDERGRADUATE EXPENSES for 2013–2014 Application fee: $20. **Tuition, state resident:** full-time $4427; part-time $147.55 per credit hour. **Tuition, nonresident:** full-time $12,162; part-time $257.85 per credit hour. **Required fees:** full-time $633; $21.10 per credit hour. Full-time tuition and fees vary according to course level. Part-time tuition and fees vary according to course level and course load. **College room and board:** $4970; **Room only:** $2200. Room and board charges vary according to board plan and housing facility.

FRESHMAN FINANCIAL AID (Fall 2011) 522 applied for aid; of those 89% were deemed to have need. 98% of freshmen with need received aid; of those 19% had need fully met. **Average percent of need met:** 20% (excluding resources awarded to replace EFC). **Average financial aid package:** $9566 (excluding resources awarded to replace EFC).

UNDERGRADUATE FINANCIAL AID (Fall 2011) 2,437 applied for aid; of those 90% were deemed to have need. 98% of undergraduates with need received aid; of those 23% had need fully met. **Average percent of need met:** 29% (excluding resources awarded to replace EFC). **Average financial aid package:** $9609 (excluding resources awarded to replace EFC). 1% of all full-time undergraduates had no need and received non-need-based gift aid.

GIFT AID (NEED-BASED) Total amount: $11,214,514 (75% federal, 25% state). **Receiving aid:** Freshmen: 61% (325); all full-time undergraduates: 60% (1,538). **Average award:** Freshmen: $1764; Undergraduates: $1813. **Scholarships, grants, and awards:** Federal Pell, FSEOG, state, private, college/university gift aid from institutional funds.

GIFT AID (NON-NEED-BASED) Total amount: $2,396,261 (4% state, 11% institutional, 85% external sources). **Receiving aid:** Freshmen: 36% (195). Undergraduates: 26% (668). **Average award:** Undergraduates: $288. **Scholarships, grants, and awards by category:** Academic interests/achievement: 536 awards ($447,838 total): biological sciences, business, communication, computer science, education, engineering/technologies, English, general academic interests/achievements, mathematics, physical sciences, social sciences. Creative arts/performance: 207 awards ($148,320 total): art/fine arts, dance, debating, music, performing arts, theater/drama. Special achievements/activities: 758 awards ($1,256,444 total): cheerleading/drum major, leadership, rodeo. Special characteristics: 2,699 awards ($6,453,517 total): children and siblings of alumni, out-of-state students. **Tuition waivers:** Full or partial for minority students, children of alumni, employees or children of employees, senior citizens.

LOANS Student loans: $12,536,625 (54% need-based, 46% non-need-based). 63% of past graduating class borrowed through all loan programs. Average indebtedness per student: $15,605. **Average need-based loan:** Freshmen: $1381. Undergraduates: $1922. **Parent loans:** $499,454 (100% non-need-based). **Programs:** Federal Direct (Subsidized and Unsubsidized Stafford, PLUS).

WORK-STUDY Federal work-study: Total amount: $1,608,884; 813 jobs averaging $1980. **State or other work-study/employment:** Part-time jobs available.

ATHLETIC AWARDS Total amount: $1,310,063 (100% non-need-based).

APPLYING FOR FINANCIAL AID Required financial aid forms: FAFSA, institution's own form. **Financial aid deadline (priority):** 3/1. **Notification date:** Continuous beginning 4/15. Students must reply within 2 weeks of notification.

CONTACT Tony Lehrling, Director of Student Financial Aid, Southeastern Oklahoma State University, 1405 North 4th Avenue, Durant, OK 74701-0609, 580-745-2186 or toll-free 800-435-1327. Fax: 580-745-7469. E-mail: shudson@se.edu. Website: http://www.se.edu/.

SOUTHEASTERN UNIVERSITY
Lakeland, FL

ABOUT THE INSTITUTION Independent Assemblies of God, coed. **Awards:** associate, bachelor's, and master's degrees. 40 undergraduate majors. **Total enrollment:** 2,703. Undergraduates: 2,448. Freshmen: 592.

GIFT AID (NEED-BASED) Scholarships, grants, and awards: Federal Pell, FSEOG, state, private, college/university gift aid from institutional funds.

GIFT AID (NON-NEED-BASED) Scholarships, grants, and awards by category: Academic interests/achievement: communication, general academic interests/achievements, religion/biblical studies. Creative arts/performance: cinema/film/broadcasting, journalism/publications, music, performing arts, theater/drama. Special achievements/activities: general special achievements/activities, leadership, religious involvement. Special characteristics: children of educators, children of faculty/staff, international students, religious affiliation.

LOANS Programs: Federal Direct (Subsidized and Unsubsidized Stafford, PLUS), Perkins.

WORK-STUDY Federal work-study: Total amount: $126,320; jobs available.

APPLYING FOR FINANCIAL AID Required financial aid forms: FAFSA, institution's own form, state aid form, state aid form (FL residents only).

CONTACT Ms. Carol B. Bradley, Director of Student Financial Services, Southeastern University, 1000 Longfellow Boulevard, Lakeland, FL 33801-6099, 863-667-5000 or toll-free 800-500-8760. Fax: 863-667-5200. E-mail: cbradley@seu.edu. Website: http://www.seu.edu/.

SOUTHEAST MISSOURI STATE UNIVERSITY
Cape Girardeau, MO

Tuition & fees (MO res): $6750	Average undergraduate aid package: $8191

ABOUT THE INSTITUTION State-supported, coed. **Awards:** certificates, associate, bachelor's, and master's degrees. 64 undergraduate majors. **Total enrollment:** 11,729. Undergraduates: 10,541. Freshmen 1,888. Federal methodology is used as a basis for awarding need-based institutional aid.

UNDERGRADUATE EXPENSES for 2013–2014 Application fee: $30. **Tuition, state resident:** full-time $5814; part-time $193.80 per credit hour. **Tuition, nonresident:** full-time $11,049; part-time $368.30 per credit hour. **Required fees:** full-time $936; $31.20 per credit hour. Full-time tuition and fees vary according to course load and location. Part-time tuition and fees vary according to course load and location. **College room and board:** $8110; **Room only:** $5420. Room and board charges vary according to board plan and housing facility.

FRESHMAN FINANCIAL AID (Fall 2011) 1,528 applied for aid; of those 76% were deemed to have need. 99% of freshmen with need received aid; of those 16% had need fully met. **Average percent of need met:** 61% (excluding resources awarded to replace EFC). **Average financial aid package:** $8153 (excluding resources awarded to replace EFC). 20% of all full-time freshmen had no need and received non-need-based gift aid.

UNDERGRADUATE FINANCIAL AID (Fall 2011) 6,288 applied for aid; of those 80% were deemed to have need. 99% of undergraduates with need received aid; of those 14% had need fully met. **Average percent of need met:** 58% (excluding resources awarded to replace EFC). **Average financial aid package:** $8191 (excluding resources awarded to replace EFC). 15% of all full-time undergraduates had no need and received non-need-based gift aid.

GIFT AID (NEED-BASED) Total amount: $24,931,238 (58% federal, 12% state, 27% institutional, 3% external sources). **Receiving aid:** Freshmen: 61% (1,082); all full-time undergraduates: 55% (4,381). **Average award:** Freshmen: $5794; Undergraduates: $5213. **Scholarships, grants, and awards:** Federal Pell, FSEOG, state, private, college/university gift aid from institutional funds.

GIFT AID (NON-NEED-BASED) Total amount: $6,791,647 (2% federal, 5% state, 85% institutional, 8% external sources). **Receiving aid:** Freshmen: 7% (115). Undergraduates: 4% (313). **Average award:** Freshmen: $3790. Undergraduates: $4051. **Scholarships, grants, and awards by category:** Academic interests/achievement: 2,696 awards ($6,229,541 total): agriculture, biological sciences, business, communication, computer science, education, engineering/technologies, English, foreign languages, general academic interests/achievements, health fields, home economics, humanities, international studies, mathematics, military science, physical sciences, premedicine, religion/biblical studies, social sciences. *Creative arts/performance:* 285 awards ($299,465 total): music, performing arts, theater/drama. *Special achievements/activities:* 1,230 awards ($3,281,257 total): cheerleading/drum major, general special achievements/activities, leadership, memberships. *Special characteristics:* 926 awards ($3,016,967 total): children of faculty/staff, first-generation college students, general special characteristics, international students, members of minority groups, out-of-state students, previous college experience, veterans. *Tuition waivers:* Full or partial for employees or children of employees, senior citizens. *ROTC:* Air Force.

LOANS *Student loans:* $36,732,762 (74% need-based, 26% non-need-based). 64% of past graduating class borrowed through all loan programs. *Average indebtedness per student:* $24,398. *Average need-based loan:* Freshmen: $3108. Undergraduates: $4017. *Parent loans:* $5,932,946 (26% need-based, 74% non-need-based). *Programs:* Federal Direct (Subsidized and Unsubsidized Stafford, PLUS), Perkins.

WORK-STUDY *Federal work-study:* Total amount: $301,711; 207 jobs averaging $1473. *State or other work-study/employment:* 1,512 part-time jobs averaging $1883.

ATHLETIC AWARDS Total amount: $2,814,757 (45% need-based, 55% non-need-based).

APPLYING FOR FINANCIAL AID *Required financial aid form:* FAFSA. *Financial aid deadline (priority):* 3/1. *Notification date:* Continuous beginning 4/1. Students must reply within 3 weeks of notification.

CONTACT Office of Student Financial Services, Southeast Missouri State University, One University Plaza, Cape Girardeau, MO 63701, 573-651-2253. *Fax:* 573-651-5006. *E-mail:* sfs@semo.edu. *Website:* http://www.semo.edu/.

SOUTHERN ADVENTIST UNIVERSITY
Collegedale, TN

Tuition & fees: $19,124	Average undergraduate aid package: $217,378

ABOUT THE INSTITUTION Independent Seventh-day Adventist, coed. 71 undergraduate majors. Federal methodology is used as a basis for awarding need-based institutional aid.

UNDERGRADUATE EXPENSES for 2013–2014 *Comprehensive fee:* $24,708 includes full-time tuition ($18,324), mandatory fees ($800), and room and board ($5584). *College room only:* $3484. Room and board charges vary according to housing facility. *Part-time tuition:* $774 per semester hour. Part-time tuition and fees vary according to course load. *Payment plan:* Tuition prepayment.

FRESHMAN FINANCIAL AID (Fall 2012, est.) 464 applied for aid; of those 65% were deemed to have need. 99% of freshmen with need received aid; of those 85% had need fully met. *Average percent of need met:* 84% (excluding resources awarded to replace EFC). *Average financial aid package:* $17,177 (excluding resources awarded to replace EFC). 28% of all full-time freshmen had no need and received non-need-based gift aid.

UNDERGRADUATE FINANCIAL AID (Fall 2012, est.) 1,668 applied for aid; of those 72% were deemed to have need. 100% of undergraduates with need received aid; of those 84% had need fully met. *Average percent of need met:* 83% (excluding resources awarded to replace EFC). *Average financial aid package:* $217,378 (excluding resources awarded to replace EFC). 18% of all full-time undergraduates had no need and received non-need-based gift aid.

GIFT AID (NEED-BASED) *Total amount:* $18,544,643 (26% federal, 4% state, 48% institutional, 22% external sources). *Receiving aid:* Freshmen: 52% (298); all full-time undergraduates: 49% (1,195). *Average award:* Freshmen: $10,665; Undergraduates: $11,536. *Scholarships, grants, and awards:* Federal Pell, FSEOG, state, private, college/university gift aid from institutional funds.

GIFT AID (NON-NEED-BASED) *Total amount:* $3,579,133 (17% state, 48% institutional, 35% external sources). *Receiving aid:* Freshmen: 44% (248). Undergraduates: 28% (675). *Average award:* Freshmen: $7984. Undergraduates: $7161. *Scholarships, grants, and awards by category:* Academic interests/achievement: business, communication, education, English, general academic interests/achievements, health fields, mathematics, religion/biblical studies. *Creative arts/performance:* art/fine arts, journalism/publications, music, theater/drama. *Special achievements/activities:* community service, general special achievements/activities, leadership, religious involvement. *Special characteristics:* children and siblings of alumni, general

special characteristics, international students, local/state students, members of minority groups, out-of-state students, siblings of current students, spouses of current students. *Tuition waivers:* Full or partial for employees or children of employees, senior citizens.

LOANS *Student loans:* $14,942,565 (76% need-based, 24% non-need-based). 65% of past graduating class borrowed through all loan programs. *Average indebtedness per student:* $34,114. *Average need-based loan:* Freshmen: $4177. Undergraduates: $4739. *Parent loans:* $2,306,549 (48% need-based, 52% non-need-based). *Programs:* Federal Direct (Subsidized and Unsubsidized Stafford, PLUS), Perkins, Federal Nursing, college/university.

WORK-STUDY *Federal work-study:* Total amount: $3,078,898; jobs available. *State or other work-study/employment:* Total amount: $251,921 (70% need-based, 30% non-need-based). Part-time jobs available.

APPLYING FOR FINANCIAL AID *Required financial aid form:* FAFSA. *Financial aid deadline (priority):* 3/1. *Notification date:* Continuous. Students must reply within 2 weeks of notification.

CONTACT Mr. Marc Grundy, Vice President of Enrollment Services, Southern Adventist University, PO Box 370, Collegedale, TN 37315-0370, 423-236-2875 or toll-free 800-768-8437. *Fax:* 423-236-1835. *Website:* http://www.southern.edu/.

SOUTHERN ARKANSAS UNIVERSITY–MAGNOLIA
Magnolia, AR

Tuition & fees (AR res): $7346	Average undergraduate aid package: $12,717

ABOUT THE INSTITUTION State-supported, coed. *Awards:* certificates, associate, bachelor's, and master's degrees. 41 undergraduate majors. *Total enrollment:* 3,383. Undergraduates: 2,918. Freshmen: 598. Federal methodology is used as a basis for awarding need-based institutional aid.

UNDERGRADUATE EXPENSES for 2013–2014 *Tuition, state resident:* full-time $5880; part-time $196 per hour. *Tuition, nonresident:* full-time $8910; part-time $297 per hour. *Required fees:* full-time $1466; $39 per hour or $18 per term. Full-time tuition and fees vary according to course load. Part-time tuition and fees vary according to course load. *College room and board:* $4974; *Room only:* $2440. Room and board charges vary according to board plan and housing facility.

FRESHMAN FINANCIAL AID (Fall 2012, est.) 549 applied for aid; of those 85% were deemed to have need. 99% of freshmen with need received aid; of those 34% had need fully met. *Average percent of need met:* 82% (excluding resources awarded to replace EFC). *Average financial aid package:* $12,983 (excluding resources awarded to replace EFC). 13% of all full-time freshmen had no need and received non-need-based gift aid.

UNDERGRADUATE FINANCIAL AID (Fall 2012, est.) 2,093 applied for aid; of those 90% were deemed to have need. 99% of undergraduates with need received aid; of those 30% had need fully met. *Average percent of need met:* 73% (excluding resources awarded to replace EFC). *Average financial aid package:* $12,717 (excluding resources awarded to replace EFC). 11% of all full-time undergraduates had no need and received non-need-based gift aid.

GIFT AID (NEED-BASED) *Total amount:* $6,732,610 (97% federal, 3% state). *Receiving aid:* Freshmen: 59% (346); all full-time undergraduates: 59% (1,416). *Average award:* Freshmen: $4550; Undergraduates: $4426. *Scholarships, grants, and awards:* Federal Pell, FSEOG, state, private, college/university gift aid from institutional funds.

GIFT AID (NON-NEED-BASED) *Total amount:* $10,003,224 (39% state, 51% institutional, 10% external sources). *Receiving aid:* Freshmen: 63% (367). Undergraduates: 42% (1,019). *Average award:* Freshmen: $4824. Undergraduates: $5973. *Scholarships, grants, and awards by category:* Academic interests/achievement: 891 awards ($4,587,267 total): agriculture, biological sciences, business, computer science, education, English, foreign languages, general academic interests/achievements, health fields, library science, mathematics, physical sciences, social sciences. *Creative arts/performance:* 143 awards ($383,956 total): art/fine arts, dance, music, theater/drama. *Special achievements/activities:* 49 awards ($156,302 total): cheerleading/drum major, leadership, rodeo. *Special characteristics:* 529 awards ($1,548,208 total): adult students, children and siblings of alumni, children of faculty/

staff, out-of-state students. *Tuition waivers:* Full or partial for children of alumni, employees or children of employees, senior citizens.

LOANS *Student loans:* $9,146,441 (51% need-based, 49% non-need-based). 56% of past graduating class borrowed through all loan programs. *Average indebtedness per student:* $13,120. *Average need-based loan:* Freshmen: $1432. Undergraduates: $2614. *Parent loans:* $229,999 (100% non-need-based). *Programs:* Federal Direct (Subsidized and Unsubsidized Stafford, PLUS), Perkins.

WORK-STUDY *Federal work-study:* Total amount: $597,683; 482 jobs averaging $1240. *State or other work-study/employment:* Total amount: $176,119 (100% non-need-based). 123 part-time jobs averaging $1432.

ATHLETIC AWARDS Total amount: $469,022 (100% non-need-based).

APPLYING FOR FINANCIAL AID *Required financial aid forms:* FAFSA, state aid form. *Financial aid deadline (priority):* 7/1. *Notification date:* Continuous beginning 4/1. Students must reply within 2 weeks of notification.

CONTACT Ms. Bronwyn C. Sneed, Director of Student Aid, Southern Arkansas University–Magnolia, PO Box 9344, Magnolia, AR 71754-9344, 870-235-4023 or toll-free 800-332-7286. *Fax:* 870-235-4913. *E-mail:* bcsneed@saumag.edu. *Website:* http://www.saumag.edu/.

SOUTHERN BAPTIST THEOLOGICAL SEMINARY
Louisville, KY

CONTACT Mrs. Erin Joiner, Manager of Financial Aid, Southern Baptist Theological Seminary, 2825 Lexington Road, Louisville, KY 40280, 502-897-4206. *Fax:* 502-897-4031. *E-mail:* financialaid@sbts.edu. *Website:* http://www.sbts.edu/.

SOUTHERN CALIFORNIA INSTITUTE OF ARCHITECTURE
Los Angeles, CA

CONTACT Lina Johnson, Financial Aid Director, Southern California Institute of Architecture, 960 East 3rd Street, Los Angeles, CA 90013, 213-613-2200 Ext. 345. *Fax:* 213-613-2260. *E-mail:* financialaid@sciarc.edu. *Website:* http://www.sciarc.edu/.

SOUTHERN CALIFORNIA INSTITUTE OF TECHNOLOGY
Anaheim, CA

CONTACT Financial Aid Office, Southern California Institute of Technology, 525 North Muller Street, Anaheim, CA 92801, 714-520-5552. *Website:* http://www.scitech.edu/.

SOUTHERN CALIFORNIA SEMINARY
El Cajon, CA

CONTACT Financial Aid Office, Southern California Seminary, 2075 East Madison Avenue, El Cajon, CA 92019, 619-442-9841. *Website:* http://www.socalsem.edu/.

SOUTHERN CONNECTICUT STATE UNIVERSITY
New Haven, CT

Tuition & fees (CT res): $8570	Average undergraduate aid package: $13,599

ABOUT THE INSTITUTION State-supported, coed. *Awards:* certificates, bachelor's, master's, and doctoral degrees. 43 undergraduate majors. *Total enrollment:* 11,117. Undergraduates: 8,525. Freshmen: 1,382. Federal methodology is used as a basis for awarding need-based institutional aid.

UNDERGRADUATE EXPENSES for 2013–2014 *Application fee:* $50. *Tuition, state resident:* full-time $4285; part-time $427 per credit hour. *Tuition, nonresident:* full-time $13,866; part-time $441 per credit hour. *Required fees:* full-time $4285; $55 per term. Full-time tuition and fees vary according to course load and reciprocity agreements. Part-time tuition and fees vary according to course load. *College room and board:* $10,641; *Room only:* $5859. Room and board charges vary according to board plan and housing facility.

FRESHMAN FINANCIAL AID (Fall 2012, est.) 1,251 applied for aid; of those 79% were deemed to have need. 93% of freshmen with need received aid; of those 25% had need fully met. *Average percent of need met:* 69% (excluding resources awarded to replace EFC). *Average financial aid package:* $13,274 (excluding resources awarded to replace EFC). 4% of all full-time freshmen had no need and received non-need-based gift aid.

UNDERGRADUATE FINANCIAL AID (Fall 2012, est.) 6,216 applied for aid; of those 81% were deemed to have need. 95% of undergraduates with need received aid; of those 22% had need fully met. *Average percent of need met:* 70% (excluding resources awarded to replace EFC). *Average financial aid package:* $13,599 (excluding resources awarded to replace EFC). 3% of all full-time undergraduates had no need and received non-need-based gift aid.

GIFT AID (NEED-BASED) *Total amount:* $23,382,751 (54% federal, 19% state, 26% institutional, 1% external sources). *Receiving aid:* Freshmen: 47% (643); all full-time undergraduates: 49% (3,597). *Average award:* Freshmen: $5795; Undergraduates: $6191. *Scholarships, grants, and awards:* Federal Pell, FSEOG, state, private, college/university gift aid from institutional funds.

GIFT AID (NON-NEED-BASED) *Total amount:* $2,344,254 (1% state, 66% institutional, 33% external sources). *Receiving aid:* Freshmen: 13% (173). Undergraduates: 8% (577). *Average award:* Freshmen: $4263. Undergraduates: $4575. *Scholarships, grants, and awards by category: Special characteristics:* children of faculty/staff, veterans. *Tuition waivers:* Full or partial for employees or children of employees, senior citizens. *ROTC:* Army cooperative, Air Force cooperative.

LOANS *Student loans:* $42,653,973 (44% need-based, 56% non-need-based). 70% of past graduating class borrowed through all loan programs. *Average indebtedness per student:* $23,663. *Average need-based loan:* Freshmen: $5578. Undergraduates: $4662. *Parent loans:* $11,049,597 (100% need-based). *Programs:* Federal Direct (Subsidized and Unsubsidized Stafford, PLUS).

WORK-STUDY *Federal work-study:* Total amount: $676,942; 170 jobs averaging $3931. *State or other work-study/employment:* Total amount: $279,129 (100% need-based). Part-time jobs available.

ATHLETIC AWARDS Total amount: $1,392,811 (100% non-need-based).

APPLYING FOR FINANCIAL AID *Required financial aid form:* FAFSA. *Financial aid deadline:* 3/9 (priority: 3/5). *Notification date:* Continuous beginning 4/11. Students must reply within 2 weeks of notification.

CONTACT Gloria Lee, Director of Financial Aid, Southern Connecticut State University, Wintergreen Building, New Haven, CT 06515-1355, 203-392-5445. *Fax:* 203-392-5229. *E-mail:* leeg1@southernct.edu. *Website:* http://www.southernct.edu/.

SOUTHERN ILLINOIS UNIVERSITY CARBONDALE
Carbondale, IL

CONTACT Terri R. Harfst, Director of Financial Aid, Southern Illinois University Carbondale, Woody Hall, Third Floor, B-Wing, Carbondale, IL 62901-4702, 618-453-3102. *Fax:* 618-453-4606. *E-mail:* fao@siu.edu. *Website:* http://www.siuc.edu/.

Tuition & fees (IL res): $11,528	Average undergraduate aid package: $12,466

ABOUT THE INSTITUTION State-supported, coed. *Awards:* certificates, associate, bachelor's, master's, and doctoral degrees. 89 undergraduate majors. *Total enrollment:* 18,847. Undergraduates: 14,130. Freshmen: 2,321. Federal methodology is used as a basis for awarding need-based institutional aid.

UNDERGRADUATE EXPENSES for 2013–2014 Application fee: $30. *Tuition, state resident:* full-time $8169; part-time $272 per credit hour. *Tuition, nonresident:* full-time $20,422; part-time $681 per credit hour. *Required fees:* full-time $3359; $156 per credit hour. Full-time tuition and fees vary according to course load, program, and student level. Part-time tuition and fees vary according to course load, program, and student level. *College room and board:* $9126. Room and board charges vary according to board plan and housing facility. *Payment plan:* Guaranteed tuition.

FRESHMAN FINANCIAL AID (Fall 2012, est.) 2,064 applied for aid; of those 87% were deemed to have need. 97% of freshmen with need received aid; of those 5% had need fully met. *Average percent of need met:* 56% (excluding resources awarded to replace EFC). *Average financial aid package:* $14,205 (excluding resources awarded to replace EFC). 3% of all full-time freshmen had no need and received non-need-based gift aid.

UNDERGRADUATE FINANCIAL AID (Fall 2012, est.) 9,944 applied for aid; of those 88% were deemed to have need. 96% of undergraduates with need received aid; of those 3% had need fully met. *Average percent of need met:* 51% (excluding resources awarded to replace EFC). *Average financial aid package:* $12,466 (excluding resources awarded to replace EFC). 1% of all full-time undergraduates had no need and received non-need-based gift aid.

GIFT AID (NEED-BASED) Total amount: $58,483,315 (51% federal, 33% state, 13% institutional, 3% external sources). *Receiving aid:* Freshmen: 58% (1,318); all full-time undergraduates: 49% (6,089). *Average award:* Freshmen: $9029; Undergraduates: $7630. *Scholarships, grants, and awards:* Federal Pell, FSEOG, state, private, college/university gift aid from institutional funds.

GIFT AID (NON-NEED-BASED) Total amount: $9,047,868 (13% federal, 13% state, 27% institutional, 47% external sources). *Receiving aid:* Freshmen: 19% (437). Undergraduates: 18% (2,197). *Average award:* Freshmen: $6559. Undergraduates: $4390. *Scholarships, grants, and awards by category: Academic interests/achievement:* agriculture, architecture, area/ethnic studies, biological sciences, business, communication, computer science, education, engineering/technologies, English, foreign languages, general academic interests/achievements, health fields, home economics, humanities, international studies, mathematics, military science, physical sciences, premedicine, religion/biblical studies, social sciences. *Creative arts/performance:* applied art and design, cinema/film/broadcasting, creative writing, dance, debating, general creative arts/performance, journalism/publications, performing arts. *Special achievements/activities:* cheerleading/drum major, community service, general special achievements/activities, leadership. *Special characteristics:* children and siblings of alumni, children of educators, children of faculty/staff, children of public servants, children with a deceased or disabled parent, general special characteristics, handicapped students, international students, members of minority groups, public servants, spouses of deceased or disabled public servants, veterans. *Tuition waivers:* Full or partial for children of alumni, employees or children of employees, senior citizens. *ROTC:* Army, Air Force.

LOANS Student loans: $74,485,482 (81% need-based, 19% non-need-based). 68% of past graduating class borrowed through all loan programs. *Average indebtedness per student:* $32,652. *Average need-based loan:* Freshmen: $3414. Undergraduates: $4469. *Parent loans:* $11,371,379 (35% need-based, 65% non-need-based). *Programs:* Federal Direct (Subsidized and Unsubsidized Stafford, PLUS), Perkins.

WORK-STUDY Federal work-study: Total amount: $2,174,996; 1,672 jobs averaging $1301. *State or other work-study/employment:* Part-time jobs available.

ATHLETIC AWARDS Total amount: $2,932,686 (37% need-based, 63% non-need-based).

APPLYING FOR FINANCIAL AID Required financial aid form: FAFSA. *Financial aid deadline (priority):* 3/1. *Notification date:* Continuous beginning 3/15.

SOUTHERN ILLINOIS UNIVERSITY EDWARDSVILLE
Edwardsville, IL

Tuition & fees (IL res): $9251	Average undergraduate aid package: $11,214

ABOUT THE INSTITUTION State-supported, coed. *Awards:* certificates, bachelor's, master's, and doctoral degrees. 44 undergraduate majors. *Total enrollment:* 14,055. Undergraduates: 11,341. Freshmen: 2,075. Federal methodology is used as a basis for awarding need-based institutional aid.

UNDERGRADUATE EXPENSES for 2013–2014 Application fee: $30. *Tuition, state resident:* full-time $6948; part-time $231.60 per credit hour. *Tuition, nonresident:* full-time $17,370. *Required fees:* full-time $2303; $272.80 per credit hour. Full-time tuition and fees vary according to course load. Part-time tuition and fees vary according to course load. *College room and board:* $8281. Room and board charges vary according to board plan and housing facility. *Payment plan:* Guaranteed tuition.

FRESHMAN FINANCIAL AID (Fall 2011) 1,841 applied for aid; of those 85% were deemed to have need. 96% of freshmen with need received aid; of those 29% had need fully met. *Average percent of need met:* 58% (excluding resources awarded to replace EFC). *Average financial aid package:* $11,620 (excluding resources awarded to replace EFC). 1% of all full-time freshmen had no need and received non-need-based gift aid.

UNDERGRADUATE FINANCIAL AID (Fall 2011) 7,785 applied for aid; of those 86% were deemed to have need. 96% of undergraduates with need received aid; of those 26% had need fully met. *Average percent of need met:* 54% (excluding resources awarded to replace EFC). *Average financial aid package:* $11,214 (excluding resources awarded to replace EFC). 2% of all full-time undergraduates had no need and received non-need-based gift aid.

GIFT AID (NEED-BASED) Total amount: $32,796,057 (60% federal, 30% state, 7% institutional, 3% external sources). *Receiving aid:* Freshmen: 53% (1,061); all full-time undergraduates: 43% (4,139). *Average award:* Freshmen: $8827; Undergraduates: $8930. *Scholarships, grants, and awards:* Federal Pell, FSEOG, state, private, college/university gift aid from institutional funds, Federal Nursing.

GIFT AID (NON-NEED-BASED) Total amount: $3,749,679 (33% federal, 26% state, 30% institutional, 11% external sources). *Receiving aid:* Freshmen: 21% (422). Undergraduates: 12% (1,136). *Average award:* Freshmen: $10,660. Undergraduates: $7620. *Scholarships, grants, and awards by category: Academic interests/achievement:* business, education, general academic interests/achievements, health fields. *Creative arts/performance:* art/fine arts, dance, music, theater/drama. *Special characteristics:* children of faculty/staff. *Tuition waivers:* Full or partial for employees or children of employees, senior citizens. *ROTC:* Army, Air Force cooperative.

LOANS Student loans: $48,804,564 (82% need-based, 18% non-need-based). 46% of past graduating class borrowed through all loan programs. *Average indebtedness per student:* $25,998. *Average need-based loan:* Freshmen: $3558. Undergraduates: $4499. *Parent loans:* $21,394,054 (32% need-based, 68% non-need-based). *Programs:* Federal Direct (Subsidized and Unsubsidized Stafford, PLUS), Perkins, Federal Nursing, college/university, alternative loans.

WORK-STUDY Federal work-study: Total amount: $5,658,245; jobs available. *State or other work-study/employment:* Part-time jobs available.

ATHLETIC AWARDS Total amount: $846,100 (47% need-based, 53% non-need-based).

APPLYING FOR FINANCIAL AID Required financial aid form: FAFSA. *Financial aid deadline (priority):* 3/1. *Notification date:* Continuous beginning 3/15. Students must reply within 2 weeks of notification.

CONTACT Sharon Berry, Director of Financial Aid, Southern Illinois University Edwardsville, Campus Box 1060, Edwardsville, IL 62026-1060, 618-650-3834 or toll-free 800-447-SIUE. *Fax:* 618-650-3885. *E-mail:* shaberr@siue.edu. *Website:* http://www.siue.edu/.

SOUTHERN METHODIST COLLEGE
Orangeburg, SC

CONTACT Financial Aid Officer, Southern Methodist College, PO Box 1027, 541 Broughton Street, Orangeburg, SC 29116, 803-534-7826 Ext. 1326. *Fax:* 803-534-7827.
Website: http://www.smcollege.edu/.

SOUTHERN METHODIST UNIVERSITY
Dallas, TX

Tuition & fees: $43,800	Average undergraduate aid package: $35,182

ABOUT THE INSTITUTION Independent United Methodist Church, coed. *Awards:* certificates, bachelor's, master's, and doctoral degrees. 67 undergraduate majors. *Total enrollment:* 10,893. Undergraduates: 6,249. Freshmen: 1,426. Both federal and institutional methodology are used as a basis for awarding need-based institutional aid.

UNDERGRADUATE EXPENSES for 2013–2014 *Application fee:* $60. *Comprehensive fee:* $57,755 includes full-time tuition ($38,870), mandatory fees ($4930), and room and board ($13,955). Room and board charges vary according to board plan and housing facility. *Part-time tuition:* $1624 per credit hour. Part-time tuition and fees vary according to course load. *Payment plan:* Tuition prepayment.
FRESHMAN FINANCIAL AID (Fall 2011) 791 applied for aid; of those 77% were deemed to have need. 100% of freshmen with need received aid; of those 36% had need fully met. *Average percent of need met:* 88% (excluding resources awarded to replace EFC). *Average financial aid package:* $35,683 (excluding resources awarded to replace EFC). 32% of all full-time freshmen had no need and received non-need-based gift aid.
UNDERGRADUATE FINANCIAL AID (Fall 2011) 2,841 applied for aid; of those 85% were deemed to have need. 99% of undergraduates with need received aid; of those 33% had need fully met. *Average percent of need met:* 87% (excluding resources awarded to replace EFC). *Average financial aid package:* $35,182 (excluding resources awarded to replace EFC). 31% of all full-time undergraduates had no need and received non-need-based gift aid.
GIFT AID (NEED-BASED) *Total amount:* $59,693,814 (8% federal, 7% state, 83% institutional, 2% external sources). *Receiving aid:* Freshmen: 30% (427); all full-time undergraduates: 31% (1,838). *Average award:* Freshmen: $20,189; Undergraduates: $18,730. *Scholarships, grants, and awards:* Federal Pell, FSEOG, state, private, college/university gift aid from institutional funds.
GIFT AID (NON-NEED-BASED) *Total amount:* $30,767,295 (95% institutional, 5% external sources). *Receiving aid:* Freshmen: 31% (446). Undergraduates: 26% (1,556). *Average award:* Freshmen: $15,674. Undergraduates: $18,300. *Tuition waivers:* Full or partial for employees or children of employees. *ROTC:* Army, Air Force cooperative.
LOANS *Student loans:* $24,060,737 (62% need-based, 38% non-need-based). 35% of past graduating class borrowed through all loan programs. *Average indebtedness per student:* $30,987. *Average need-based loan:* Freshmen: $3487. Undergraduates: $4382. *Parent loans:* $9,803,202 (31% need-based, 69% non-need-based). *Programs:* Federal Direct (Subsidized and Unsubsidized Stafford, PLUS), Perkins, state, college/university.
WORK-STUDY *Federal work-study:* Total amount: $6,674,337; jobs available. *State or other work-study/employment:* Total amount: $288,443 (33% need-based, 67% non-need-based). Part-time jobs available.
ATHLETIC AWARDS Total amount: $13,667,002 (42% need-based, 58% non-need-based).
APPLYING FOR FINANCIAL AID *Required financial aid forms:* FAFSA, CSS Financial Aid PROFILE, noncustodial (divorced/separated) parent's statement, business/farm supplement. *Financial aid deadline (priority):* 2/15. *Notification date:* Continuous beginning 3/15.
CONTACT Marc Peterson, Director of Financial Aid, Southern Methodist University, PO Box 750181, Dallas, TX 75275, 214-768-3417 or toll-free 800-323-0672. *Fax:* 214-768-3878. *E-mail:* enrol_serv@smu.edu.
Website: http://www.smu.edu/.

SOUTHERN NAZARENE UNIVERSITY
Bethany, OK

CONTACT Diana Lee, Director of Financial Assistance, Southern Nazarene University, 6729 Northwest 39th Expressway, Bethany, OK 73008, 405-491-6310 or toll-free 800-648-9899. *Fax:* 405-717-6271. *E-mail:* dlee@snu.edu.
Website: http://www.snu.edu/.

SOUTHERN NEW HAMPSHIRE UNIVERSITY
Manchester, NH

CONTACT Financial Aid Office, Southern New Hampshire University, 2500 North River Road, Manchester, NH 03106, 603-645-9645 or toll-free 888-327-7648. *Fax:* 603-645-9639. *E-mail:* finaid@snhu.edu.
Website: http://www.snhu.edu/.

SOUTHERN OREGON UNIVERSITY
Ashland, OR

CONTACT Enrollment Services Center, Southern Oregon University, 1250 Siskiyou Boulevard, Ashland, OR 97520, 541-552-6600. *Fax:* 541-552-6614. *E-mail:* esc@sou.edu.
Website: http://www.sou.edu/.

SOUTHERN POLYTECHNIC STATE UNIVERSITY
Marietta, GA

Tuition & fees (GA res): $6678	Average undergraduate aid package: $2851

ABOUT THE INSTITUTION State-supported, coed. *Awards:* certificates, associate, bachelor's, and master's degrees. 34 undergraduate majors. *Total enrollment:* 6,202. Undergraduates: 5,402. Freshmen: 790. Federal methodology is used as a basis for awarding need-based institutional aid.
UNDERGRADUATE EXPENSES for 2013–2014 *Application fee:* $40. *Tuition, state resident:* full-time $5256; part-time $175.20 per semester hour. *Tuition, nonresident:* full-time $18,704; part-time $623.47 per semester hour. *Required fees:* full-time $1422; $711 per term. Full-time tuition and fees vary according to course load. Part-time tuition and fees vary according to course load. *College room and board:* $7280; *Room only:* $4020. Room and board charges vary according to board plan and housing facility.
FRESHMAN FINANCIAL AID (Fall 2011) 500 applied for aid; of those 100% were deemed to have need. 97% of freshmen with need received aid; of those 28% had need fully met. *Average percent of need met:* 71% (excluding resources awarded to replace EFC). *Average financial aid package:* $1999 (excluding resources awarded to replace EFC).
UNDERGRADUATE FINANCIAL AID (Fall 2011) 3,871 applied for aid; of those 100% were deemed to have need. 97% of undergraduates with need received aid; of those 15% had need fully met. *Average percent of need met:* 61% (excluding resources awarded to replace EFC). *Average financial aid package:* $2851 (excluding resources awarded to replace EFC).
GIFT AID (NEED-BASED) *Total amount:* $9,308,909 (65% federal, 35% state). *Receiving aid:* Freshmen: 41% (225); all full-time undergraduates: 45% (2,172). *Average award:* Freshmen: $2775; Undergraduates: $2117. *Scholarships, grants, and awards:* Federal Pell, FSEOG, state, private, college/university gift aid from institutional funds.
GIFT AID (NON-NEED-BASED) *Total amount:* $1,586,545 (59% state, 16% institutional, 25% external sources). *Receiving aid:* Freshmen: 64% (353). Undergraduates: 27% (1,300). *Average award:* Undergraduates: $4482. *Scholarships, grants, and awards by category:* Academic interests/achievement: general aca-

demic interests/achievements. *Special characteristics:* members of minority groups. *Tuition waivers:* Full or partial for employees or children of employees, senior citizens. *ROTC:* Army cooperative, Naval cooperative, Air Force cooperative.

LOANS *Student loans:* $22,144,533 (45% need-based, 55% non-need-based). 61% of past graduating class borrowed through all loan programs. *Average indebtedness per student:* $22,250. *Average need-based loan:* Freshmen: $1854. Undergraduates: $2100. *Parent loans:* $1,548,650 (100% non-need-based). *Programs:* Federal Direct (Subsidized and Unsubsidized Stafford, PLUS).

WORK-STUDY *Federal work-study:* Total amount: $150,327; 254 jobs averaging $4000. *State or other work-study/employment:* Total amount: $95,211 (100% non-need-based). Part-time jobs available.

ATHLETIC AWARDS Total amount: $235,400 (100% non-need-based).

APPLYING FOR FINANCIAL AID *Required financial aid form:* FAFSA. *Financial aid deadline (priority):* 3/1. *Notification date:* Continuous beginning 5/1. Students must reply by 8/15.

CONTACT Mr. Gary L. Mann, Director of Financial Aid, Southern Polytechnic State University, 1100 South Marietta Parkway, Marietta, GA 30060-2896, 678-915-7290 or toll-free 800-635-3204. *Fax:* 678-915-4227. *E-mail:* gmann@spsu.edu. *Website:* http://www.spsu.edu/.

SOUTHERN UNIVERSITY AND AGRICULTURAL AND MECHANICAL COLLEGE
Baton Rouge, LA

CONTACT Mr. Phillip Rodgers Sr., Director of Financial Aid, Southern University and Agricultural and Mechanical College, PO Box 9961, Baton Rouge, LA 70813, 225-771-2790. *Fax:* 225-771-5898. *E-mail:* phillip_rodgers@cxs.subr.edu. *Website:* http://www.subr.edu/.

SOUTHERN UNIVERSITY AT NEW ORLEANS
New Orleans, LA

CONTACT Director of Financial Aid, Southern University at New Orleans, 6400 Press Drive, New Orleans, LA 70126, 504-286-5263. *Fax:* 504-286-5213. *Website:* http://www.suno.edu/.

SOUTHERN UTAH UNIVERSITY
Cedar City, UT

Tuition & fees (UT res): $5576	Average undergraduate aid package: $8528

ABOUT THE INSTITUTION State-supported, coed. *Awards:* certificates, diplomas, associate, bachelor's, and master's degrees. 67 undergraduate majors. *Total enrollment:* 8,297. Undergraduates: 7,633. Freshmen: 1,264. Federal methodology is used as a basis for awarding need-based institutional aid.

UNDERGRADUATE EXPENSES for 2013–2014 *Application fee:* $50. *Tuition, state resident:* full-time $4960; part-time $233 per credit hour. *Tuition, nonresident:* full-time $16,368; part-time $773 per credit hour. *Required fees:* full-time $616; $308 per term. Full-time tuition and fees vary according to program. Part-time tuition and fees vary according to course load and program. *Room only:* $2878. Room and board charges vary according to board plan and housing facility.

FRESHMAN FINANCIAL AID (Fall 2011) 842 applied for aid; of those 86% were deemed to have need. 99% of freshmen with need received aid; of those 9% had need fully met. *Average percent of need met:* 49% (excluding resources awarded to replace EFC). *Average financial aid package:* $8008 (excluding resources awarded to replace EFC). 22% of all full-time freshmen had no need and received non-need-based gift aid.

UNDERGRADUATE FINANCIAL AID (Fall 2011) 3,823 applied for aid; of those 98% were deemed to have need. 92% of undergraduates with need received aid; of those 6% had need fully met. *Average percent of need met:* 53% (excluding resources awarded to replace EFC). *Average financial aid package:* $8528 (excluding resources awarded to replace EFC). 15% of all full-time undergraduates had no need and received non-need-based gift aid.

GIFT AID (NEED-BASED) *Total amount:* $13,612,793 (97% federal, 1% state, 1% institutional, 1% external sources). *Receiving aid:* Freshmen: 60% (715); all full-time undergraduates: 67% (3,449). *Average award:* Freshmen: $7936; Undergraduates: $8406. *Scholarships, grants, and awards:* Federal Pell, FSEOG, state, private, college/university gift aid from institutional funds.

GIFT AID (NON-NEED-BASED) *Total amount:* $7,660,002 (89% institutional, 11% external sources). *Receiving aid:* Freshmen: 16% (185). Undergraduates: 9% (442). *Average award:* Freshmen: $4083. Undergraduates: $4359. *Scholarships, grants, and awards by category:* Academic interests/achievement: general academic interests/achievements. Creative arts/performance: art/fine arts, music, theater/drama. Special achievements/activities: general special achievements/activities, leadership. Special characteristics: children and siblings of alumni, local/state students, members of minority groups. *Tuition waivers:* Full or partial for children of alumni, employees or children of employees, senior citizens. *ROTC:* Army.

LOANS *Student loans:* $18,700,847 (66% need-based, 34% non-need-based). 55% of past graduating class borrowed through all loan programs. *Average indebtedness per student:* $13,478. *Average need-based loan:* Freshmen: $2964. Undergraduates: $3076. *Programs:* Federal Direct (Subsidized and Unsubsidized Stafford, PLUS), Perkins.

WORK-STUDY *Federal work-study:* Total amount: $284,348; jobs available. *State or other work-study/employment:* Total amount: $92,453 (100% need-based). Part-time jobs available.

ATHLETIC AWARDS Total amount: $2,587,743 (100% non-need-based).

APPLYING FOR FINANCIAL AID *Required financial aid form:* FAFSA. *Financial aid deadline (priority):* 12/1. *Notification date:* Continuous beginning 11/1. Students must reply within 4 weeks of notification.

CONTACT Jan Carey-McDonald, Director of Financial Aid and Scholarships, Southern Utah University, 351 West University Boulevard, Cedar City, UT 84720-2498, 435-586-7735. *Fax:* 435-586-7736. *E-mail:* careymcdonald@suu.edu. *Website:* http://www.suu.edu/.

SOUTHERN VERMONT COLLEGE
Bennington, VT

Tuition & fees: $21,275	Average undergraduate aid package: $13,589

ABOUT THE INSTITUTION Independent, coed. *Awards:* associate and bachelor's degrees. 14 undergraduate majors. *Total enrollment:* 530. Undergraduates: 530. Freshmen: 157. Federal methodology is used as a basis for awarding need-based institutional aid.

UNDERGRADUATE EXPENSES for 2013–2014 *Application fee:* $30. *Comprehensive fee:* $31,218 includes full-time tuition ($21,000), mandatory fees ($275), and room and board ($9943). *College room only:* $4924. Full-time tuition and fees vary according to program. Room and board charges vary according to board plan and housing facility. *Part-time tuition:* $800 per credit. Part-time tuition and fees vary according to course load and program.

FRESHMAN FINANCIAL AID (Fall 2011) 140 applied for aid; of those 75% were deemed to have need. 100% of freshmen with need received aid; of those 16% had need fully met. *Average percent of need met:* 75% (excluding resources awarded to replace EFC). *Average financial aid package:* $15,254 (excluding resources awarded to replace EFC). 7% of all full-time freshmen had no need and received non-need-based gift aid.

UNDERGRADUATE FINANCIAL AID (Fall 2011) 392 applied for aid; of those 96% were deemed to have need. 97% of undergraduates with need received aid. *Average percent of need met:* 81% (excluding resources awarded to replace EFC). *Average financial aid package:* $13,589 (excluding resources awarded to replace EFC). 4% of all full-time undergraduates had no need and received non-need-based gift aid.

GIFT AID (NEED-BASED) *Total amount:* $4,398,597 (25% federal, 10% state, 57% institutional, 8% external sources). *Receiving aid:* Freshmen: 61% (89); all full-time undergraduates: 66% (351). *Average award:* Freshmen: $9500; Undergraduates: $8250. *Scholarships, grants, and awards:* Federal Pell, FSEOG, state, private, college/university gift aid from institutional funds.

GIFT AID (NON-NEED-BASED) *Total amount:* $702,000 (100% institutional). *Receiving aid:* Freshmen: 4% (6). Undergraduates: 2% (10). *Average award:* Freshmen: $5500. Undergraduates: $4865. *Scholarships, grants, and awards by category:* Academic interests/achievement: 92 awards ($701,950 total): general academic interests/achievements. *Special achievements/activities:* 53 awards ($105,700 total): community service, leadership. *Tuition waivers:* Full or partial for employees or children of employees, senior citizens.

LOANS *Student loans:* $3,199,763 (50% need-based, 50% non-need-based). 88% of past graduating class borrowed through all loan programs. *Average indebtedness per student:* $24,652. *Average need-based loan:* Freshmen: $2625. Undergraduates: $3500. *Parent loans:* $1,288,682 (100% need-based). *Programs:* Federal Direct (Subsidized and Unsubsidized Stafford, PLUS).

WORK-STUDY *Federal work-study:* Total amount: $77,208; 88 jobs averaging $878.

APPLYING FOR FINANCIAL AID *Required financial aid forms:* FAFSA, institution's own form. *Financial aid deadline (priority):* 3/1. *Notification date:* Continuous. Students must reply within 2 weeks of notification.

CONTACT Joel Phelps, Assistant Dean and Director of Financial Aid, Southern Vermont College, 982 Mansion Drive, Bennington, VT 05201, 802-447-6306. *Fax:* 802-447-6313. *E-mail:* financialaid@svc.edu.
Website: http://www.svc.edu/.

SOUTHERN VIRGINIA UNIVERSITY
Buena Vista, VA

CONTACT Darin Hassell, Financial Aid Specialist, Southern Virginia University, One University Hill Drive, Buena Vista, VA 24416, 540-261-4351 or toll-free 800-229-8420. *Fax:* 540-261-8559. *E-mail:* finaid@svu.edu.
Website: http://www.svu.edu/.

SOUTHERN WESLEYAN UNIVERSITY
Central, SC

CONTACT Mrs. Sherri Peters, Financial Aid Associate, Southern Wesleyan University, 907 Wesleyan Drive, Central, SC 29630-1020, 800-289-1292 Ext. 5517 or toll-free 800-CU-AT-SWU. *Fax:* 864-644-5970. *E-mail:* finaid@swu.edu.
Website: http://www.swu.edu/.

SOUTH UNIVERSITY
Montgomery, AL

CONTACT Financial Aid Office, South University, 5355 Vaughn Road, Montgomery, AL 36116-1120, 334-395-8800 or toll-free 866-629-2962.
Website: http://www.southuniversity.edu/montgomery/.

SOUTH UNIVERSITY
Royal Palm Beach, FL

CONTACT Financial Aid Office, South University, University Centre, 9801 Belvedere Road, Royal Palm Beach, FL 33411, 561-697-9200 or toll-free 866-629-2902.

SOUTH UNIVERSITY
Tampa, FL

CONTACT Financial Aid Office, South University, 4401 North Himes Avenue, Suite 175, Tampa, FL 33614, 813-393-3800 or toll-free 800-846-1472.
Website: http://www.southuniversity.edu/tampa/.

SOUTH UNIVERSITY
Savannah, GA

CONTACT Financial Aid Office, South University, 709 Mall Boulevard, Savannah, GA 31406, 912-201-8000 or toll-free 866-629-2901.
Website: http://www.southuniversity.edu/savannah/.

SOUTH UNIVERSITY
Novi, MI

CONTACT Financial Aid Office, South University, 41555 Twelve Mile Road, Novi, MI 48377 or toll-free 877-693-2085.
Website: http://www.southuniversity.edu/novi.aspx.

SOUTH UNIVERSITY
High Point, NC

CONTACT Financial Aid Office, South University, 3975 Premier Drive, High Point, NC 27265, 336-812-7200 or toll-free 855-268-2187.
Website: http://www.southuniversity.edu/high-point.aspx.

SOUTH UNIVERSITY
Cleveland, OH

CONTACT Financial Aid Office, South University, 4743 Richmond Road, Cleveland, OH 44128, 216-755-5000 or toll-free 855-398-9280.
Website: http://www.southuniversity.edu/cleveland.aspx.

SOUTH UNIVERSITY
Columbia, SC

CONTACT Financial Aid Office, South University, 9 Science Court, Columbia, SC 29203, 803-799-9082 or toll-free 866-629-3031.
Website: http://www.southuniversity.edu/columbia/.

SOUTH UNIVERSITY
Austin, TX

CONTACT Financial Aid Office, South University, 810 Hesters Crossing Road, Suite 220, Austin, TX 78681.
Website: http://www.southuniversity.edu/austin.aspx.

SOUTH UNIVERSITY
Glen Allen, VA

CONTACT Financial Aid Office, South University, 2151 Old Brick Road, Glen Allen, VA 23060, 804-727-6800 or toll-free 888-422-5076.
Website: http://www.southuniversity.edu/richmond.

SOUTH UNIVERSITY
Virginia Beach, VA

CONTACT Financial Aid Office, South University, 301 Bendix Road, Suite 100, Virginia Beach, VA 23452, 757-493-6900 or toll-free 877-206-1845.
Website: http://www.southuniversity.edu/virginia-beach.

SOUTHWEST BAPTIST UNIVERSITY
Bolivar, MO

Tuition & fees: $19,150	Average undergraduate aid package: $15,142

ABOUT THE INSTITUTION Independent Southern Baptist, coed. **Awards:** certificates, associate, bachelor's, master's, and doctoral degrees. 56 undergraduate majors. **Total enrollment:** 3,864. Undergraduates: 3,009. Freshmen: 521. Federal methodology is used as a basis for awarding need-based institutional aid.

UNDERGRADUATE EXPENSES for 2013–2014 Application fee: $30. **Comprehensive fee:** $25,500 includes full-time tuition ($18,360), mandatory fees ($790), and room and board ($6350). **College room only:** $3150. Full-time tuition and fees vary according to course load and location. Room and board charges vary according to board plan and housing facility. Part-time tuition and fees vary according to course load and location.

FRESHMAN FINANCIAL AID (Fall 2012, est.) 542 applied for aid; of those 81% were deemed to have need. 99% of freshmen with need received aid; of those 20% had need fully met. **Average percent of need met:** 73% (excluding resources awarded to replace EFC). **Average financial aid package:** $16,742 (excluding resources awarded to replace EFC). 17% of all full-time freshmen had no need and received non-need-based gift aid.

UNDERGRADUATE FINANCIAL AID (Fall 2012, est.) 2,001 applied for aid; of those 81% were deemed to have need. 99% of undergraduates with need received aid; of those 16% had need fully met. **Average percent of need met:** 68% (excluding resources awarded to replace EFC). **Average financial aid package:** $15,142 (excluding resources awarded to replace EFC). 16% of all full-time undergraduates had no need and received non-need-based gift aid.

GIFT AID (NEED-BASED) Total amount: $7,147,796 (78% federal, 22% state). **Receiving aid:** Freshmen: 68% (371); all full-time undergraduates: 68% (1,411). **Average award:** Freshmen: $4864; Undergraduates: $4942. **Scholarships, grants, and awards:** Federal Pell, FSEOG, state, private, college/university gift aid from institutional funds.

GIFT AID (NON-NEED-BASED) Total amount: $13,292,067 (1% state, 94% institutional, 5% external sources). **Receiving aid:** Freshmen: 71% (386). Undergraduates: 62% (1,286). **Average award:** Freshmen: $9195. Undergraduates: $8960. **Scholarships, grants, and awards by category:** Academic interests/achievement: general academic interests/achievements. Creative arts/performance: art/fine arts, debating, general creative arts/performance, music, theater/drama. Special achievements/activities: religious involvement. Special characteristics: general special characteristics, local/state students, relatives of clergy. **Tuition waivers:** Full or partial for employees or children of employees. **ROTC:** Army cooperative.

LOANS Student loans: $14,738,968 (49% need-based, 51% non-need-based). **Average need-based loan:** Freshmen: $3756. Undergraduates: $4171. **Parent loans:** $608,710 (100% non-need-based). **Programs:** Federal Direct (Subsidized and Unsubsidized Stafford, PLUS), Perkins, Federal Nursing, state, alternative loans.

WORK-STUDY Federal work-study: Total amount: $656,175; 351 jobs averaging $1800.

ATHLETIC AWARDS Total amount: $2,510,304 (100% non-need-based).

APPLYING FOR FINANCIAL AID Required financial aid forms: FAFSA, institution's own form. **Financial aid deadline (priority):** 3/15. **Notification date:** Continuous beginning 3/1. Students must reply within 2 weeks of notification.

CONTACT Mr. Brad Gamble, Director of Financial Aid, Southwest Baptist University, 1600 University Avenue, Bolivar, MO 65613-2597, 417-328-1823 or toll-free 800-526-5859. Fax: 417-328-1514. E-mail: bgamble@sbuniv.edu. Website: http://www.sbuniv.edu/.

SOUTHWESTERN ADVENTIST UNIVERSITY
Keene, TX

CONTACT Student Financial Services, Southwestern Adventist University, PO Box 567, Keene, TX 76059, 817-645-3921 Ext. 262 or toll-free 800-433-2240. Fax: 817-556-4744. Website: http://www.swau.edu/.

SOUTHWESTERN ASSEMBLIES OF GOD UNIVERSITY
Waxahachie, TX

CONTACT Financial Aid Office, Southwestern Assemblies of God University, 1200 Sycamore Street, Waxahachie, TX 75165-2397, 972-825-4730 or toll-free 888-937-7248. Fax: 972-937-4001. E-mail: finaid@sagu.edu. Website: http://www.sagu.edu/.

SOUTHWESTERN CHRISTIAN COLLEGE
Terrell, TX

Tuition & fees: N/R	Average undergraduate aid package: N/A

ABOUT THE INSTITUTION Independent Church of Christ, coed. 2 undergraduate majors. Federal methodology is used as a basis for awarding need-based institutional aid.

GIFT AID (NEED-BASED) Total amount: $1,085,942 (78% federal, 8% state, 12% institutional, 2% external sources). **Scholarships, grants, and awards:** FSEOG, state.

GIFT AID (NON-NEED-BASED) Total amount: $17,000 (100% external sources). **Scholarships, grants, and awards by category:** Academic interests/achievement: general academic interests/achievements. Creative arts/performance: music. Special characteristics: children of faculty/staff, local/state students.

LOANS Student loans: $566,448 (63% need-based, 37% non-need-based). **Parent loans:** $12,796 (100% non-need-based).

WORK-STUDY Federal work-study: Total amount: $127,508; jobs available. **State or other work-study/employment:** Total amount: $2005 (100% need-based). Part-time jobs available.

ATHLETIC AWARDS Total amount: $317,559 (100% need-based).

APPLYING FOR FINANCIAL AID Required financial aid form: FAFSA. **Financial aid deadline (priority):** 6/1. **Notification date:** Continuous.

CONTACT Mrs. Tonya Dean, Financial Aid Office, Southwestern Christian College, PO Box 10, 200 Bowser Circle, Terrell, TX 75160, 972-524-3341 Ext. 124. Fax: 972-563-7133. E-mail: tdean@swcc.edu. Website: http://www.swcc.edu/.

SOUTHWESTERN CHRISTIAN UNIVERSITY
Bethany, OK

CONTACT Mrs. Billie Stewart, Financial Aid Director, Southwestern Christian University, PO Box 340, Bethany, OK 73008, 405-789-7661 Ext. 3456. Fax: 405-495-0078. E-mail: billie.stewart@swcu.edu. Website: http://www.swcu.edu/.

SOUTHWESTERN COLLEGE
Winfield, KS

Tuition & fees: $23,886	Average undergraduate aid package: $18,444

ABOUT THE INSTITUTION Independent United Methodist, coed. **Awards:** certificates, bachelor's, and master's degrees. 45 undergraduate majors. **Total enrollment:** 1,637. Undergraduates: 1,304. Freshmen: 148. Federal methodology is used as a basis for awarding need-based institutional aid.

UNDERGRADUATE EXPENSES for 2013–2014 Application fee: $25. **Comprehensive fee:** $30,522 includes full-time tuition ($23,736), mandatory fees ($150), and room and board ($6636). **College room only:** $3000. Full-time tuition and fees

Peterson's How to Get Money for College 2014

www.petersonsbooks.com **535**

vary according to class time, course load, degree level, location, and program. Room and board charges vary according to board plan and housing facility. **Part-time tuition:** $989 per credit hour. Part-time tuition and fees vary according to class time, course load, degree level, location, and program.

FRESHMAN FINANCIAL AID (Fall 2011) 146 applied for aid; of those 90% were deemed to have need. 100% of freshmen with need received aid; of those 12% had need fully met. **Average percent of need met:** 72% (excluding resources awarded to replace EFC). **Average financial aid package:** $19,016 (excluding resources awarded to replace EFC). 18% of all full-time freshmen had no need and received non-need-based gift aid.

UNDERGRADUATE FINANCIAL AID (Fall 2011) 507 applied for aid; of those 92% were deemed to have need. 100% of undergraduates with need received aid; of those 12% had need fully met. **Average percent of need met:** 69% (excluding resources awarded to replace EFC). **Average financial aid package:** $18,444 (excluding resources awarded to replace EFC). 17% of all full-time undergraduates had no need and received non-need-based gift aid.

GIFT AID (NEED-BASED) Total amount: $6,037,011 (33% federal, 10% state, 53% institutional, 4% external sources). **Receiving aid:** Freshmen: 82% (131); all full-time undergraduates: 80% (457). **Average award:** Freshmen: $14,578; Undergraduates: $13,106. **Scholarships, grants, and awards:** Federal Pell, FSEOG, state, private, college/university gift aid from institutional funds.

GIFT AID (NON-NEED-BASED) Total amount: $967,221 (94% institutional, 6% external sources). **Receiving aid:** Freshmen: 6% (9). Undergraduates: 6% (34). **Average award:** Freshmen: $7231. Undergraduates: $8119. **Scholarships, grants, and awards by category:** Academic interests/achievement: $2,713,237 total: biological sciences, business, communication, computer science, general academic interests/achievements, health fields, physical sciences, religion/biblical studies, social sciences. Creative arts/performance: $213,300 total: cinema/film/broadcasting, dance, journalism/publications, music, performing arts, theater/drama. Special achievements/activities: $216,350 total: cheerleading/drum major, community service, general special achievements/activities, leadership, memberships, religious involvement. Special characteristics: $491,752 total: children of faculty/staff, international students, members of minority groups, religious affiliation. **Tuition waivers:** Full or partial for employees or children of employees, senior citizens.

LOANS Student loans: $6,866,102 (89% need-based, 11% non-need-based). 81% of past graduating class borrowed through all loan programs. Average indebtedness per student: $34,056. **Average need-based loan:** Freshmen: $4372. Undergraduates: $5110. **Parent loans:** $1,500,573 (42% need-based, 58% non-need-based). **Programs:** Federal Direct (Subsidized and Unsubsidized Stafford, PLUS), Perkins.

WORK-STUDY Federal work-study: Total amount: $213,073; 177 jobs averaging $1204. **State or other work-study/employment:** Total amount: $160,071 (42% need-based, 58% non-need-based). 140 part-time jobs averaging $1143.

ATHLETIC AWARDS Total amount: $1,081,400 (80% need-based, 20% non-need-based).

APPLYING FOR FINANCIAL AID Required financial aid forms: FAFSA, institution's own form. **Financial aid deadline:** 8/15 (priority: 4/1). **Notification date:** Continuous beginning 2/1. Students must reply within 2 weeks of notification.

CONTACT Mrs. Brenda D. Hicks, Director of Financial Aid, Southwestern College, 100 College Street, Winfield, KS 67156-2499, 620-229-6215 or toll-free 800-846-1543. Fax: 620-229-6363. E-mail: finaid@sckans.edu. Website: http://www.sckans.edu/.

SOUTHWESTERN OKLAHOMA STATE UNIVERSITY
Weatherford, OK

ABOUT THE INSTITUTION State-supported, coed. **Awards:** associate, bachelor's, master's, and doctoral degrees. 53 undergraduate majors. **Total enrollment:** 5,340. Undergraduates: 4,517. Freshmen: 953.

GIFT AID (NEED-BASED) Scholarships, grants, and awards: Federal Pell, FSEOG, state, private, college/university gift aid from institutional funds.

GIFT AID (NON-NEED-BASED) Scholarships, grants, and awards by category: Academic interests/achievement: biological sciences, business, communication, computer science, education, engineering/technologies, English, foreign languages, general academic interests/achievements, health fields, mathematics, physical sciences, social sciences. Creative arts/performance: applied art and design, art/fine arts, music, theater/drama. Special achievements/activities: cheerleading/drum major, leadership, rodeo. Special characteristics: children and siblings of alumni, local/state students, out-of-state students.

LOANS Programs: Federal Direct (Subsidized and Unsubsidized Stafford, PLUS).

WORK-STUDY Federal work-study: Total amount: $2,266,366; jobs available.

APPLYING FOR FINANCIAL AID Required financial aid forms: FAFSA, institution's own form.

CONTACT Mr. Jerome Wichert, Director of Student Financial Services, Southwestern Oklahoma State University, 100 Campus Drive, Weatherford, OK 73096, 580-774-6003. Fax: 580-774-7066. E-mail: jerome.wichert@swosu.edu. Website: http://www.swosu.edu/.

SOUTHWESTERN UNIVERSITY
Georgetown, TX

Tuition & fees: $35,240	Average undergraduate aid package: $30,060

ABOUT THE INSTITUTION Independent Methodist, coed. **Awards:** bachelor's degrees. 37 undergraduate majors. **Total enrollment:** 1,394. Undergraduates: 1,394. Freshmen: 357. Federal methodology is used as a basis for awarding need-based institutional aid.

UNDERGRADUATE EXPENSES for 2013–2014 Comprehensive fee: $46,250 includes full-time tuition ($35,240) and room and board ($11,010). **College room only:** $5650. Room and board charges vary according to board plan and housing facility. **Part-time tuition:** $1470 per credit hour. Part-time tuition and fees vary according to course load.

FRESHMAN FINANCIAL AID (Fall 2012, est.) 290 applied for aid; of those 83% were deemed to have need. 100% of freshmen with need received aid; of those 33% had need fully met. **Average percent of need met:** 92% (excluding resources awarded to replace EFC). **Average financial aid package:** $30,816 (excluding resources awarded to replace EFC). 32% of all full-time freshmen had no need and received non-need-based gift aid.

UNDERGRADUATE FINANCIAL AID (Fall 2012, est.) 971 applied for aid; of those 88% were deemed to have need. 100% of undergraduates with need received aid; of those 33% had need fully met. **Average percent of need met:** 88% (excluding resources awarded to replace EFC). **Average financial aid package:** $30,060 (excluding resources awarded to replace EFC). 34% of all full-time undergraduates had no need and received non-need-based gift aid.

GIFT AID (NEED-BASED) Total amount: $20,697,157 (9% federal, 7% state, 78% institutional, 6% external sources). **Receiving aid:** Freshmen: 67% (239); all full-time undergraduates: 62% (851). **Average award:** Freshmen: $26,235; Undergraduates: $24,309. **Scholarships, grants, and awards:** Federal Pell, FSEOG, state, private, college/university gift aid from institutional funds.

GIFT AID (NON-NEED-BASED) Total amount: $8,434,191 (93% institutional, 7% external sources). **Receiving aid:** Freshmen: 66% (235). Undergraduates: 57% (773). **Average award:** Freshmen: $16,099. Undergraduates: $16,414. **Scholarships, grants, and awards by category:** Academic interests/achievement: $19,703,754 total: business, general academic interests/achievements, humanities, international studies, mathematics, premedicine, social sciences. Creative arts/performance: $511,813 total: art/fine arts, music, theater/drama. Special achievements/activities: $5000 total: leadership. Special characteristics: $1,275,569 total: children of faculty/staff, ethnic background, general special characteristics, relatives of clergy, religious affiliation. **Tuition waivers:** Full or partial for employees or children of employees.

LOANS Student loans: $7,401,860 (91% need-based, 9% non-need-based). 57% of past graduating class borrowed through all loan programs. Average indebtedness per student: $36,299. **Average need-based loan:** Freshmen: $4053. Undergraduates: $4995. **Parent loans:** $3,960,601 (87% need-based, 13% non-need-based). **Programs:** Federal Direct (Subsidized and Unsubsidized Stafford, PLUS), Perkins, state, college/university.

WORK-STUDY Federal work-study: Total amount: $365,112; jobs available. **State or other work-study/employment:** Total amount: $1,264,372 (58% need-based, 42% non-need-based). Part-time jobs available.

APPLYING FOR FINANCIAL AID Required financial aid form: FAFSA. **Financial aid deadline:** 3/1 (priority: 3/1). **Notification date:** Continuous beginning 3/1. Students must reply by 5/1 or within 2 weeks of notification.

CONTACT Mr. James P. Gaeta, Director of Financial Aid, Southwestern University, PO Box 770, Georgetown, TX 78627-0770, 512-863-1259 or toll-free 800-252-3166. *Fax:* 512-863-1507. *E-mail:* gaetaj@southwestern.edu. *Website:* http://www.southwestern.edu/.

SOUTHWEST FLORIDA COLLEGE
Fort Myers, FL

CONTACT Financial Aid Office, Southwest Florida College, 1685 Medical Lane, Fort Myers, FL 33907, 239-939-4766 or toll-free 877-493-5147 (in-state), 877-793-5147 (out-of-state). *Website:* http://www.swfc.edu/.

SOUTHWEST MINNESOTA STATE UNIVERSITY
Marshall, MN

ABOUT THE INSTITUTION State-supported, coed. *Awards:* certificates, associate, bachelor's, and master's degrees. 56 undergraduate majors. *Total enrollment:* 6,588. Undergraduates: 6,160. Freshmen: 408.

GIFT AID (NEED-BASED) *Scholarships, grants, and awards:* Federal Pell, FSEOG, state, private, college/university gift aid from institutional funds.

GIFT AID (NON-NEED-BASED) *Scholarships, grants, and awards by category: Academic interests/achievement:* agriculture, biological sciences, business, communication, computer science, education, English, foreign languages, general academic interests/achievements, mathematics, physical sciences, premedicine, social sciences. *Creative arts/performance:* art/fine arts, creative writing, debating, journalism/publications, music, performing arts, theater/drama. *Special achievements/activities:* general special achievements/activities, hobbies/interests, leadership. *Special characteristics:* children and siblings of alumni, children of union members/company employees, ethnic background, first-generation college students, general special characteristics, handicapped students, international students, local/state students, members of minority groups, previous college experience, veterans, veterans' children.

LOANS *Programs:* Federal Direct (Subsidized and Unsubsidized Stafford, PLUS), Perkins, state, private loans.

WORK-STUDY *Federal work-study:* Total amount: $197,689; 101 jobs averaging $2271. *State or other work-study/employment:* Total amount: $243,670 (100% need-based). 139 part-time jobs averaging $2136.

APPLYING FOR FINANCIAL AID *Required financial aid forms:* FAFSA, institution's own form.

CONTACT Mr. David Vikander, Director of Financial Aid, Southwest Minnesota State University, 1501 State Street, Marshall, MN 56258, 507-537-6281 or toll-free 800-642-0684. *Fax:* 507-537-6275. *E-mail:* vikander@smsu.edu. *Website:* http://www.smsu.edu/.

SOUTHWEST UNIVERSITY
Kenner, LA

CONTACT Financial Aid Office, Southwest University, 2200 Veterans Memorial Boulevard, Kenner, LA 70062, 504-468-2900 or toll-free 800-433-5923. *Website:* http://www.southwest.edu/.

SOUTHWEST UNIVERSITY OF VISUAL ARTS
Tucson, AZ

CONTACT Financial Aid Office, Southwest University of Visual Arts, 2525 North Country Club Road, Tucson, AZ 85716-2505, 520-325-0123 or toll-free 800-825-8753. *Website:* http://www.suva.edu/.

SPALDING UNIVERSITY
Louisville, KY

CONTACT Director of Student Financial Services, Spalding University, 851 South Fourth Street, Louisville, KY 40203, 502-588-7185 or toll-free 800-896-8941. *Fax:* 502-585-7128. *E-mail:* onestop@spalding.edu. *Website:* http://www.spalding.edu/.

SPELMAN COLLEGE
Atlanta, GA

Tuition & fees: $23,794	Average undergraduate aid package: $14,391

ABOUT THE INSTITUTION Independent, women only. *Awards:* bachelor's degrees. 25 undergraduate majors. *Total enrollment:* 2,145. Undergraduates: 2,145. Freshmen: 523. Federal methodology is used as a basis for awarding need-based institutional aid.

UNDERGRADUATE EXPENSES for 2013–2014 *Application fee:* $35. *One-time required fee:* $250. *Comprehensive fee:* $35,335 includes full-time tuition ($20,569), mandatory fees ($3225), and room and board ($11,541). Full-time tuition and fees vary according to course load. Room and board charges vary according to board plan and housing facility. *Part-time tuition:* $860 per credit hour. *Part-time fees:* $1612 per term. Part-time tuition and fees vary according to course load. $1,612.50 per term fees are optional if a student registers for less than six semester hours.

FRESHMAN FINANCIAL AID (Fall 2012, est.) 475 applied for aid; of those 95% were deemed to have need. 99% of freshmen with need received aid; of those 16% had need fully met. *Average percent of need met:* 53% (excluding resources awarded to replace EFC). *Average financial aid package:* $13,904 (excluding resources awarded to replace EFC).

UNDERGRADUATE FINANCIAL AID (Fall 2012, est.) 1,834 applied for aid; of those 94% were deemed to have need. 99% of undergraduates with need received aid; of those 13% had need fully met. *Average percent of need met:* 39% (excluding resources awarded to replace EFC). *Average financial aid package:* $14,391 (excluding resources awarded to replace EFC). 1% of all full-time undergraduates had no need and received non-need-based gift aid.

GIFT AID (NEED-BASED) *Total amount:* $20,242,072 (25% federal, 6% state, 50% institutional, 19% external sources). *Receiving aid:* Freshmen: 82% (434); all full-time undergraduates: 78% (1,630). *Average award:* Freshmen: $12,202; Undergraduates: $12,190. *Scholarships, grants, and awards:* Federal Pell, FSEOG, state, private, college/university gift aid from institutional funds, United Negro College Fund.

GIFT AID (NON-NEED-BASED) *Total amount:* $170,658 (32% institutional, 68% external sources). *Receiving aid:* Undergraduates: 2% (35). *Average award:* Undergraduates: $3429. *Tuition waivers:* Full or partial for employees or children of employees. *ROTC:* Army cooperative, Naval cooperative, Air Force cooperative.

LOANS *Student loans:* $15,668,544 (78% need-based, 22% non-need-based). 74% of past graduating class borrowed through all loan programs. *Average indebtedness per student:* $33,898. *Average need-based loan:* Freshmen: $3324. Undergraduates: $4330. *Parent loans:* $21,442,213 (100% non-need-based). *Programs:* Federal Direct (Subsidized and Unsubsidized Stafford, PLUS), Perkins.

WORK-STUDY *Federal work-study:* Total amount: $125,002; 148 jobs averaging $1470.

APPLYING FOR FINANCIAL AID *Required financial aid forms:* FAFSA, institution's own form. *Financial aid deadline (priority):* 2/1. *Notification date:* Continuous beginning 2/15. Students must reply within 2 weeks of notification.

CONTACT Lenora J. Jackson, Director of Financial Aid, Spelman College, 350 Spelman Lane, SW, Atlanta, GA 30314-4399, 404-270-5212 or toll-free 800-982-2411. *Fax:* 404-270-5220. *E-mail:* lenoraj@spelman.edu. *Website:* http://www.spelman.edu/.

SPRING ARBOR UNIVERSITY
Spring Arbor, MI

Tuition & fees: $22,538	Average undergraduate aid package: $21,113

ABOUT THE INSTITUTION Independent Free Methodist, coed. *Awards:* certificates, associate, bachelor's, and master's degrees. 62 undergraduate majors. *Total enrollment:* 4,125. Undergraduates: 3,058. Freshmen: 314. Federal methodology is used as a basis for awarding need-based institutional aid.

UNDERGRADUATE EXPENSES for 2013–2014 *Application fee:* $30. *Comprehensive fee:* $30,438 includes full-time tuition ($21,998), mandatory fees ($540), and room and board ($7900). *College room only:* $3710. Full-time tuition and fees vary according to course load, degree level, and program. Room and board charges vary according to board plan and housing facility. *Part-time tuition:* $535 per credit hour. *Part-time fees:* $255 per term. Part-time tuition and fees vary according to course load, degree level, program, and reciprocity agreements.

FRESHMAN FINANCIAL AID (Fall 2012, est.) 301 applied for aid; of those 89% were deemed to have need. 100% of freshmen with need received aid; of those 22% had need fully met. *Average percent of need met:* 84% (excluding resources awarded to replace EFC). *Average financial aid package:* $22,408 (excluding resources awarded to replace EFC).

UNDERGRADUATE FINANCIAL AID (Fall 2012, est.) 1,333 applied for aid; of those 93% were deemed to have need. 100% of undergraduates with need received aid; of those 22% had need fully met. *Average percent of need met:* 82% (excluding resources awarded to replace EFC). *Average financial aid package:* $21,113 (excluding resources awarded to replace EFC). 1% of all full-time undergraduates had no need and received non-need-based gift aid.

GIFT AID (NEED-BASED) *Total amount:* $21,595,239 (25% federal, 11% state, 64% institutional). *Receiving aid:* Freshmen: 85% (267); all full-time undergraduates: 86% (1,230). *Average award:* Freshmen: $14,567; Undergraduates: $12,934. *Scholarships, grants, and awards:* Federal Pell, FSEOG, private, college/university gift aid from institutional funds.

GIFT AID (NON-NEED-BASED) *Total amount:* $267,156 (67% state, 33% external sources). *Receiving aid:* Freshmen: 11% (35). Undergraduates: 8% (119). *Average award:* Undergraduates: $1000. *Scholarships, grants, and awards by category:* Academic interests/achievement: general academic interests/achievements. *Creative arts/performance:* art/fine arts. *Special achievements/activities:* junior miss. *Special characteristics:* adult students, children of faculty/staff, general special characteristics, international students, members of minority groups, relatives of clergy, religious affiliation. *Tuition waivers:* Full or partial for employees or children of employees. *ROTC:* Army, Air Force cooperative.

LOANS *Student loans:* $32,108,348 (31% need-based, 69% non-need-based). 87% of past graduating class borrowed through all loan programs. *Average indebtedness per student:* $32,791. *Average need-based loan:* Freshmen: $4357. Undergraduates: $4893. *Parent loans:* $1,913,545 (100% need-based). *Programs:* Federal Direct (Subsidized and Unsubsidized Stafford, PLUS), Perkins.

WORK-STUDY *Federal work-study:* Total amount: $193,097; jobs available.

ATHLETIC AWARDS Total amount: $1,885,596 (100% need-based).

APPLYING FOR FINANCIAL AID *Required financial aid form:* FAFSA. *Financial aid deadline (priority):* 3/1. *Notification date:* Continuous. Students must reply within 2 weeks of notification.

CONTACT Geoff Marsh, Director of Financial Aid, Spring Arbor University, 106 East Main Street, Spring Arbor, MI 49283-9799, 517-750-6468 or toll-free 800-968-0011. *Fax:* 517-750-6620. *E-mail:* geoff.marsh@arbor.edu. *Website:* http://www.arbor.edu/.

SPRINGFIELD COLLEGE
Springfield, MA

CONTACT Ms. Kinser Cancelmo, Assistant Director of Financial Aid, Springfield College, 263 Alden Street, Springfield, MA 01109-3797, 413-748-3108 or toll-free 800-343-1257. *Fax:* 413-748-3462. *E-mail:* finaid@spfldcol.edu. *Website:* http://www.spfldcol.edu/.

SPRING HILL COLLEGE
Mobile, AL

Tuition & fees: $29,450	Average undergraduate aid package: $28,744

ABOUT THE INSTITUTION Independent Roman Catholic (Jesuit), coed. *Awards:* certificates, bachelor's, and master's degrees. 42 undergraduate majors. *Total enrollment:* 1,328. Undergraduates: 1,202. Freshmen: 299. Federal methodology is used as a basis for awarding need-based institutional aid.

UNDERGRADUATE EXPENSES for 2013–2014 *Application fee:* $25. *Comprehensive fee:* $40,746 includes full-time tuition ($27,670), mandatory fees ($1780), and room and board ($11,296). *College room only:* $5900. Room and board charges vary according to housing facility. *Part-time tuition:* $975 per credit hour. *Part-time fees:* $50 per credit hour.

FRESHMAN FINANCIAL AID (Fall 2012, est.) 262 applied for aid; of those 85% were deemed to have need. 100% of freshmen with need received aid; of those 20% had need fully met. *Average percent of need met:* 90% (excluding resources awarded to replace EFC). *Average financial aid package:* $30,933 (excluding resources awarded to replace EFC). 24% of all full-time freshmen had no need and received non-need-based gift aid.

UNDERGRADUATE FINANCIAL AID (Fall 2012, est.) 893 applied for aid; of those 85% were deemed to have need. 100% of undergraduates with need received aid; of those 22% had need fully met. *Average percent of need met:* 86% (excluding resources awarded to replace EFC). *Average financial aid package:* $28,744 (excluding resources awarded to replace EFC). 28% of all full-time undergraduates had no need and received non-need-based gift aid.

GIFT AID (NEED-BASED) *Total amount:* $15,275,949 (11% federal, 1% state, 87% institutional, 1% external sources). *Receiving aid:* Freshmen: 73% (217); all full-time undergraduates: 65% (731). *Average award:* Freshmen: $9864; Undergraduates: $9454. *Scholarships, grants, and awards:* Federal Pell, FSEOG, state, private, college/university gift aid from institutional funds, TEACH Grants.

GIFT AID (NON-NEED-BASED) *Total amount:* $5,591,527 (99% institutional, 1% external sources). *Receiving aid:* Freshmen: 72% (214). Undergraduates: 66% (734). *Average award:* Freshmen: $16,574. Undergraduates: $14,993. *Scholarships, grants, and awards by category:* Academic interests/achievement: general academic interests/achievements. *Special achievements/activities:* community service. *Special characteristics:* children of faculty/staff, siblings of current students. *Tuition waivers:* Full or partial for employees or children of employees. *ROTC:* Army cooperative, Air Force cooperative.

LOANS *Student loans:* $7,546,857 (78% need-based, 22% non-need-based). 71% of past graduating class borrowed through all loan programs. *Average indebtedness per student:* $30,356. *Average need-based loan:* Freshmen: $4666. Undergraduates: $4767. *Parent loans:* $1,487,589 (30% need-based, 70% non-need-based). *Programs:* Federal Direct (Subsidized and Unsubsidized Stafford, PLUS), Perkins, alternative loans.

WORK-STUDY *Federal work-study:* Total amount: $236,800; jobs available. *State or other work-study/employment:* Total amount: $256,010 (28% need-based, 72% non-need-based). Part-time jobs available.

ATHLETIC AWARDS Total amount: $1,624,892 (54% need-based, 46% non-need-based).

APPLYING FOR FINANCIAL AID *Required financial aid forms:* FAFSA, state aid form. *Financial aid deadline (priority):* 3/1. *Notification date:* Continuous beginning 2/15. Students must reply by 5/1 or within 2 weeks of notification.

CONTACT Ms. Ellen F. Foster, Director of Financial Aid, Spring Hill College, 4000 Dauphin Street, Mobile, AL 36608, 251-380-3460 or toll-free 800-SHC-6704. *Fax:* 251-460-2176. *E-mail:* efoster@shc.edu. *Website:* http://www.shc.edu/.

STANFORD UNIVERSITY
Stanford, CA

Tuition & fees: $42,690	Average undergraduate aid package: $42,354

ABOUT THE INSTITUTION Independent, coed. *Awards:* certificates, bachelor's, master's, and doctoral degrees. 79 undergraduate majors. *Total* *enrollment:* 18,217. Undergraduates: 7,063. Freshmen: 1,762. Both federal and institutional methodology are used as a basis for awarding need-based institutional aid.

UNDERGRADUATE EXPENSES for 2013–2014 *Application fee:* $90. *Comprehensive fee:* $55,856 includes full-time tuition ($42,690) and room and board ($13,166). Room and board charges vary according to board plan.

FRESHMAN FINANCIAL AID (Fall 2011) 1,080 applied for aid; of those 83% were deemed to have need. 98% of freshmen with need received aid; of those 92% had need fully met. *Average percent of need met:* 100% (excluding resources awarded to replace EFC). *Average financial aid package:* $41,894 (excluding resources awarded to replace EFC). 1% of all full-time freshmen had no need and received non-need-based gift aid.

UNDERGRADUATE FINANCIAL AID (Fall 2011) 4,008 applied for aid; of those 92% were deemed to have need. 99% of undergraduates with need received aid; of those 88% had need fully met. *Average percent of need met:* 100% (excluding resources awarded to replace EFC). *Average financial aid package:* $42,354 (excluding resources awarded to replace EFC). 1% of all full-time undergraduates had no need and received non-need-based gift aid.

GIFT AID (NEED-BASED) *Total amount:* $141,219,914 (5% federal, 3% state, 89% institutional, 3% external sources). *Receiving aid:* Freshmen: 50% (848); all full-time undergraduates: 51% (3,541). *Average award:* Freshmen: $39,933; Undergraduates: $39,897. *Scholarships, grants, and awards:* Federal Pell, FSEOG, state, private, college/university gift aid from institutional funds.

GIFT AID (NON-NEED-BASED) *Total amount:* $6,203,611 (7% federal, 1% state, 10% institutional, 82% external sources). *Receiving aid:* Freshmen: 1% (15). Undergraduates: 1% (77). *Average award:* Freshmen: $1009. Undergraduates: $14,010. *Tuition waivers:* Full or partial for employees or children of employees. *ROTC:* Army cooperative, Naval cooperative, Air Force cooperative.

LOANS *Student loans:* $7,897,457 (30% need-based, 70% non-need-based). 25% of past graduating class borrowed through all loan programs. *Average indebtedness per student:* $18,833. *Average need-based loan:* Freshmen: $2743. Undergraduates: $2945. *Parent loans:* $6,126,800 (100% non-need-based). *Programs:* Federal Direct (Subsidized and Unsubsidized Stafford, PLUS), Perkins.

WORK-STUDY *Federal work-study:* Total amount: $1,642,241; 707 jobs averaging $2322. *State or other work-study/employment:* Total amount: $3,937,110 (88% need-based, 12% non-need-based). 1,780 part-time jobs averaging $2212.

ATHLETIC AWARDS Total amount: $18,453,205 (19% need-based, 81% non-need-based).

APPLYING FOR FINANCIAL AID *Required financial aid forms:* FAFSA, CSS Financial Aid PROFILE. *Financial aid deadline (priority):* 2/15. *Notification date:* Continuous beginning 4/1. Students must reply by 5/1.

CONTACT Financial Aid Office, Stanford University, Montag Hall, 355 Galvez Street, Stanford, CA 94305-3021, 650-723-3058. *Fax:* 650-725-0540. *E-mail:* financialaid@stanford.edu.
Website: http://www.stanford.edu/.

STATE COLLEGE OF FLORIDA MANATEE-SARASOTA
Bradenton, FL

CONTACT Financial Aid Office, State College of Florida Manatee-Sarasota, 5840 26th Street West, PO Box 1849, Bradenton, FL 34206-7046, 941-752-5000. *Website:* http://www.scf.edu/.

STATE UNIVERSITY OF NEW YORK AT FREDONIA
Fredonia, NY

Tuition & fees (NY res): $7058	Average undergraduate aid package: $9530

ABOUT THE INSTITUTION State-supported, coed. *Awards:* certificates, bachelor's, and master's degrees. 72 undergraduate majors. *Total enrollment:* 5,523. Undergraduates: 5,228. Freshmen: 1,003. Federal methodology is used as a basis for awarding need-based institutional aid.

UNDERGRADUATE EXPENSES for 2013–2014 *Application fee:* $50. *Tuition, state resident:* full-time $5570; part-time $232 per credit hour. *Tuition, nonresident:* full-time $14,820; part-time $618 per credit hour. *Required fees:* full-time $1488; $61.85 per credit. *College room and board:* $11,100; *Room only:* $6550. Room and board charges vary according to board plan and housing facility.

FRESHMAN FINANCIAL AID (Fall 2012, est.) 900 applied for aid; of those 75% were deemed to have need. 95% of freshmen with need received aid; of those 12% had need fully met. *Average percent of need met:* 61% (excluding resources awarded to replace EFC). *Average financial aid package:* $10,364 (excluding resources awarded to replace EFC). 9% of all full-time freshmen had no need and received non-need-based gift aid.

UNDERGRADUATE FINANCIAL AID (Fall 2012, est.) 4,230 applied for aid; of those 81% were deemed to have need. 94% of undergraduates with need received aid; of those 11% had need fully met. *Average percent of need met:* 59% (excluding resources awarded to replace EFC). *Average financial aid package:* $9530 (excluding resources awarded to replace EFC). 6% of all full-time undergraduates had no need and received non-need-based gift aid.

GIFT AID (NEED-BASED) *Total amount:* $16,821,283 (46% federal, 40% state, 10% institutional, 4% external sources). *Receiving aid:* Freshmen: 49% (496); all full-time undergraduates: 50% (2,509). *Average award:* Freshmen: $5358; Undergraduates: $4798. *Scholarships, grants, and awards:* Federal Pell, FSEOG, state, private, college/university gift aid from institutional funds, TEACH Grants.

GIFT AID (NON-NEED-BASED) *Total amount:* $833,000 (100% federal). *Receiving aid:* Freshmen: 16% (162). Undergraduates: 12% (599). *Average award:* Freshmen: $2345. Undergraduates: $2338. *Scholarships, grants, and awards by category:* *Academic interests/achievement:* 317 awards ($278,632 total): biological sciences, business, communication, computer science, education, English, foreign languages, general academic interests/achievements, humanities, international studies, mathematics, physical sciences, social sciences. *Creative arts/performance:* 120 awards ($83,487 total): applied art and design, art/fine arts, dance, music, performing arts, theater/drama. *Special achievements/activities:* 22 awards ($68,450 total): general special achievements/activities, leadership. *Special characteristics:* 132 awards ($335,898 total): children and siblings of alumni, ethnic background, general special characteristics, international students, local/state students, members of minority groups, out-of-state students, parents of current students, previous college experience.

LOANS *Student loans:* $32,914,831 (41% need-based, 59% non-need-based). 87% of past graduating class borrowed through all loan programs. *Average indebtedness per student:* $27,431. *Average need-based loan:* Freshmen: $5227. Undergraduates: $5120. *Parent loans:* $4,157,896 (100% non-need-based). *Programs:* Federal Direct (Subsidized and Unsubsidized Stafford, PLUS), Perkins, alternative loans.

WORK-STUDY *Federal work-study:* Total amount: $345,205; 240 jobs averaging $1704.

APPLYING FOR FINANCIAL AID *Required financial aid forms:* FAFSA, state aid form. *Financial aid deadline:* Continuous. *Notification date:* Continuous beginning 3/1. Students must reply by 5/1.

CONTACT Mr. Jeremy R. Corrente, Assistant Director, State University of New York at Fredonia, 215 Maytum Hall, Fredonia, NY 14063, 716-673-3253 or toll-free 800-252-1212. *Fax:* 716-673-3785. *E-mail:* corrente@fredonia.edu. *Website:* http://www.fredonia.edu/.

STATE UNIVERSITY OF NEW YORK AT NEW PALTZ
New Paltz, NY

Tuition & fees: N/R	Average undergraduate aid package: $9493

ABOUT THE INSTITUTION State-supported, coed. *Awards:* certificates, bachelor's, and master's degrees. 81 undergraduate majors. *Total enrollment:* 1,082. Undergraduates: 6,685. Freshmen: 1,119. Federal methodology is used as a basis for awarding need-based institutional aid.

FRESHMAN FINANCIAL AID (Fall 2012, est.) 998 applied for aid; of those 66% were deemed to have need. 98% of freshmen with need received aid; of those 6% had need fully met. *Average percent of need met:* 54% (excluding resources awarded to replace EFC). *Average financial aid package:* $9493 (excluding resources

awarded to replace EFC). 3% of all full-time freshmen had no need and received non-need-based gift aid.

UNDERGRADUATE FINANCIAL AID (Fall 2012, est.) 4,626 applied for aid; of those 72% were deemed to have need. 99% of undergraduates with need received aid; of those 6% had need fully met. *Average percent of need met:* 55% (excluding resources awarded to replace EFC). *Average financial aid package:* $9493 (excluding resources awarded to replace EFC). 3% of all full-time undergraduates had no need and received non-need-based gift aid.

GIFT AID (NEED-BASED) *Total amount:* $16,326,709 (52% federal, 48% state). *Receiving aid:* Freshmen: 29% (328); all full-time undergraduates: 30% (1,794). *Average award:* Freshmen: $5089; Undergraduates: $4655. *Scholarships, grants, and awards:* Federal Pell, FSEOG, state, private, college/university gift aid from institutional funds.

GIFT AID (NON-NEED-BASED) *Total amount:* $1,202,280 (1% federal, 24% state, 10% institutional, 65% external sources). *Receiving aid:* Freshmen: 2% (27). Undergraduates: 2% (150). *Average award:* Freshmen: $1842. Undergraduates: $1856. *Scholarships, grants, and awards by category: Academic interests/achievement:* 81 awards ($97,000 total): area/ethnic studies, biological sciences, business, communication, education, engineering/technologies, English, foreign languages, general academic interests/achievements, international studies, mathematics, physical sciences. *Creative arts/performance:* 17 awards ($40,000 total): art/fine arts, music, theater/drama. *Special characteristics:* 40 awards ($89,100 total): children of faculty/staff, ethnic background, first-generation college students, local/state students, members of minority groups.

LOANS *Student loans:* $27,004,420 (48% need-based, 52% non-need-based). 63% of past graduating class borrowed through all loan programs. *Average indebtedness per student:* $24,445. *Average need-based loan:* Freshmen: $3490. Undergraduates: $4428. *Parent loans:* $17,805,720 (100% non-need-based). *Programs:* Federal Direct (Subsidized and Unsubsidized Stafford, PLUS), Perkins, state, private loans.

WORK-STUDY *Federal work-study:* Total amount: $1,310,333; 1,166 jobs averaging $1000. *State or other work-study/employment:* Total amount: $735,774 (100% non-need-based). 1,023 part-time jobs averaging $1108.

APPLYING FOR FINANCIAL AID *Required financial aid forms:* FAFSA, state aid form. *Financial aid deadline (priority):* 3/15. *Notification date:* Continuous beginning 4/1. Students must reply within 6 weeks of notification.

CONTACT Mr. Daniel Sistarenik, Director of Financial Aid, State University of New York at New Paltz, 200 Hawk Drive, New Paltz, NY 12561-2437, 845-257-3250. *Fax:* 845-257-3568. *E-mail:* sistared@newpaltz.edu. *Website:* http://www.newpaltz.edu/.

STATE UNIVERSITY OF NEW YORK AT OSWEGO
Oswego, NY

Tuition & fees (NY res): $6841	Average undergraduate aid package: $8138

ABOUT THE INSTITUTION State-supported, coed. *Awards:* certificates, bachelor's, and master's degrees. 66 undergraduate majors. *Total enrollment:* 7,921. Undergraduates: 7,151. Freshmen: 1,271. Federal methodology is used as a basis for awarding need-based institutional aid.

UNDERGRADUATE EXPENSES for 2013–2014 *Application fee:* $50. *Tuition, state resident:* full-time $5570; part-time $232 per credit hour. *Tuition, nonresident:* full-time $14,820; part-time $618 per credit hour. *Required fees:* full-time $1271; $52.96 per credit hour. Full-time tuition and fees vary according to degree level. Part-time tuition and fees vary according to course load and degree level. *College room and board:* $12,510. Room and board charges vary according to board plan and housing facility.

FRESHMAN FINANCIAL AID (Fall 2012, est.) 1,171 applied for aid; of those 75% were deemed to have need. 100% of freshmen with need received aid; of those 9% had need fully met. *Average percent of need met:* 79% (excluding resources awarded to replace EFC). *Average financial aid package:* $7887 (excluding resources awarded to replace EFC). 16% of all full-time freshmen had no need and received non-need-based gift aid.

UNDERGRADUATE FINANCIAL AID (Fall 2012, est.) 5,876 applied for aid; of those 80% were deemed to have need. 100% of undergraduates with need received aid; of those 14% had need fully met. *Average percent of need met:* 81%

(excluding resources awarded to replace EFC). *Average financial aid package:* $8138 (excluding resources awarded to replace EFC). 9% of all full-time undergraduates had no need and received non-need-based gift aid.

GIFT AID (NEED-BASED) *Total amount:* $24,611,941 (48% federal, 39% state, 11% institutional, 2% external sources). *Receiving aid:* Freshmen: 61% (781); all full-time undergraduates: 59% (4,002). *Average award:* Freshmen: $6554; Undergraduates: $6150. *Scholarships, grants, and awards:* Federal Pell, FSEOG, state, private, college/university gift aid from institutional funds.

GIFT AID (NON-NEED-BASED) *Total amount:* $2,212,112 (1% federal, 6% state, 87% institutional, 6% external sources). *Receiving aid:* Freshmen: 29% (364). Undergraduates: 18% (1,203). *Average award:* Freshmen: $2888. Undergraduates: $2999. *Scholarships, grants, and awards by category: Academic interests/achievement:* area/ethnic studies, biological sciences, business, communication, computer science, education, English, foreign languages, general academic interests/achievements, humanities, international studies, mathematics, physical sciences, premedicine, social sciences. *ROTC:* Army cooperative.

LOANS *Student loans:* $39,237,409 (85% need-based, 15% non-need-based). 81% of past graduating class borrowed through all loan programs. *Average indebtedness per student:* $27,004. *Average need-based loan:* Freshmen: $4072. Undergraduates: $4565. *Parent loans:* $13,194,620 (73% need-based, 27% non-need-based). *Programs:* Federal Direct (Subsidized and Unsubsidized Stafford, PLUS), Perkins.

WORK-STUDY *Federal work-study:* Total amount: $527,868; 468 jobs averaging $1136. *State or other work-study/employment:* Total amount: $872,940 (56% need-based, 44% non-need-based). 1,541 part-time jobs averaging $1713.

APPLYING FOR FINANCIAL AID *Required financial aid forms:* FAFSA, state aid form. *Financial aid deadline (priority):* 3/1. *Notification date:* Continuous beginning 2/15. Students must reply by 5/1 or within 3 weeks of notification.

CONTACT Mark C. Humbert, Director of Financial Aid, State University of New York at Oswego, 206 Culkin Hall, Oswego, NY 13126, 315-312-2248. *Fax:* 315-312-3696. *E-mail:* finaid@oswego.edu. *Website:* http://www.oswego.edu/.

STATE UNIVERSITY OF NEW YORK AT PLATTSBURGH
Plattsburgh, NY

Tuition & fees (NY res): $6808	Average undergraduate aid package: $12,058

ABOUT THE INSTITUTION State-supported, coed. *Awards:* certificates, bachelor's, and master's degrees. 61 undergraduate majors. *Total enrollment:* 6,167. Undergraduates: 5,706. Freshmen: 970. Both federal and institutional methodology are used as a basis for awarding need-based institutional aid.

UNDERGRADUATE EXPENSES for 2013–2014 *Application fee:* $50. *Tuition, state resident:* full-time $5570; part-time $232 per credit hour. *Tuition, nonresident:* full-time $14,820; part-time $618 per credit hour. *Required fees:* full-time $1238; $51.40 per credit hour. Part-time tuition and fees vary according to course load. *College room and board:* $10,582; *Room only:* $6682. Room and board charges vary according to board plan and housing facility.

FRESHMAN FINANCIAL AID (Fall 2012, est.) 856 applied for aid; of those 73% were deemed to have need. 98% of freshmen with need received aid; of those 23% had need fully met. *Average percent of need met:* 83% (excluding resources awarded to replace EFC). *Average financial aid package:* $12,018 (excluding resources awarded to replace EFC). 28% of all full-time freshmen had no need and received non-need-based gift aid.

UNDERGRADUATE FINANCIAL AID (Fall 2012, est.) 4,357 applied for aid; of those 80% were deemed to have need. 98% of undergraduates with need received aid; of those 21% had need fully met. *Average percent of need met:* 80% (excluding resources awarded to replace EFC). *Average financial aid package:* $12,058 (excluding resources awarded to replace EFC). 23% of all full-time undergraduates had no need and received non-need-based gift aid.

GIFT AID (NEED-BASED) *Total amount:* $18,790,783 (48% federal, 34% state, 15% institutional, 3% external sources). *Receiving aid:* Freshmen: 57% (554); all full-time undergraduates: 57% (3,016). *Average award:* Freshmen: $7187; Undergraduates: $6230. *Scholarships, grants, and awards:* Federal Pell, FSEOG, state, private, college/university gift aid from institutional funds.

GIFT AID (NON-NEED-BASED) *Total amount:* $2,942,014 (5% federal, 7% state, 85% institutional, 3% external sources). *Receiving aid:* Freshmen: 20% (194).

Undergraduates: 15% (791). *Average award:* Freshmen: $6540. Undergraduates: $6533. *Scholarships, grants, and awards by category: Academic interests/ achievement:* 5,083 awards ($5,187,131 total): area/ethnic studies, biological sciences, business, communication, computer science, education, engineering/technologies, English, general academic interests/achievements, health fields, home economics, humanities, international studies, mathematics, physical sciences, premedicine, social sciences. *Creative arts/performance:* 277 awards ($241,499 total): art/fine arts, journalism/publications, music, theater/drama. *Special achievements/activities:* 13 awards ($21,750 total): community service, general special achievements/activities, leadership. *Special characteristics:* 1,251 awards ($2,200,145 total): international students, out-of-state students. *Tuition waivers:* Full or partial for employees or children of employees. *ROTC:* Army.
LOANS *Student loans:* $27,924,799 (82% need-based, 18% non-need-based). 70% of past graduating class borrowed through all loan programs. *Average indebtedness per student:* $25,297. *Average need-based loan:* Freshmen: $6342. Undergraduates: $7602. *Parent loans:* $4,297,328 (73% need-based, 27% non-need-based). *Programs:* Federal Direct (Subsidized and Unsubsidized Stafford, PLUS), Perkins, Federal Nursing, alternative loans.
WORK-STUDY *Federal work-study:* Total amount: $604,283; 353 jobs averaging $1993. *State or other work-study/employment:* Part-time jobs available.
APPLYING FOR FINANCIAL AID *Required financial aid forms:* FAFSA, state aid form. *Financial aid deadline (priority):* 2/15. *Notification date:* Continuous beginning 3/1. Students must reply within 8 weeks of notification.
CONTACT Mr. Todd Moravec, Director of Financial Aid, State University of New York at Plattsburgh, 101 Broad Street, Plattsburgh, NY 12901-2681, 518-564-2072 or toll-free 888-673-0012. *Fax:* 518-564-4079. *E-mail:* todd.moravec@plattsburgh.edu. *Website:* http://www.plattsburgh.edu/.

STATE UNIVERSITY OF NEW YORK COLLEGE AT CORTLAND
Cortland, NY

Tuition & fees (NY res): $6942	Average undergraduate aid package: $12,801

ABOUT THE INSTITUTION State-supported, coed. *Awards:* certificates, bachelor's, and master's degrees. 57 undergraduate majors. *Total enrollment:* 7,098. Undergraduates: 6,345. Freshmen: 1,210. Federal methodology is used as a basis for awarding need-based institutional aid.
UNDERGRADUATE EXPENSES for 2013–2014 *Application fee:* $50. *Tuition, state resident:* full-time $5570; part-time $232 per credit hour. *Tuition, nonresident:* full-time $14,820; part-time $618 per credit hour. *Required fees:* full-time $1372. Full-time tuition and fees vary according to degree level. Part-time tuition and fees vary according to degree level. *College room and board:* $11,430; *Room only:* $7070. Room and board charges vary according to board plan and housing facility.
FRESHMAN FINANCIAL AID (Fall 2011) 1,115 applied for aid; of those 67% were deemed to have need. 96% of freshmen with need received aid; of those 9% had need fully met. *Average percent of need met:* 70% (excluding resources awarded to replace EFC). *Average financial aid package:* $13,122 (excluding resources awarded to replace EFC). 5% of all full-time freshmen had no need and received non-need-based gift aid.
UNDERGRADUATE FINANCIAL AID (Fall 2011) 5,214 applied for aid; of those 74% were deemed to have need. 97% of undergraduates with need received aid; of those 10% had need fully met. *Average percent of need met:* 69% (excluding resources awarded to replace EFC). *Average financial aid package:* $12,801 (excluding resources awarded to replace EFC). 3% of all full-time undergraduates had no need and received non-need-based gift aid.
GIFT AID (NEED-BASED) *Total amount:* $12,431,281 (53% federal, 47% state). *Receiving aid:* Freshmen: 41% (500); all full-time undergraduates: 45% (2,827). *Average award:* Freshmen: $5117; Undergraduates: $5277. *Scholarships, grants, and awards:* Federal Pell, FSEOG, state, private, college/university gift aid from institutional funds.
GIFT AID (NON-NEED-BASED) *Total amount:* $4,695,071 (37% federal, 29% institutional, 34% external sources). *Receiving aid:* Freshmen: 27% (322). Undergraduates: 17% (1,056). *Average award:* Freshmen: $2413. Undergraduates: $2896. *Scholarships, grants, and awards by category: Academic interests/*

achievement: education, general academic interests/achievements, international studies, mathematics, physical sciences. *Creative arts/performance:* art/fine arts, music. *Special achievements/activities:* community service, general special achievements/activities, hobbies/interests, leadership. *Special characteristics:* adult students, local/state students, members of minority groups. *ROTC:* Army cooperative, Air Force cooperative.
LOANS *Student loans:* $34,126,153 (42% need-based, 58% non-need-based). 79% of past graduating class borrowed through all loan programs. *Average indebtedness per student:* $27,534. *Average need-based loan:* Freshmen: $3528. Undergraduates: $4198. *Parent loans:* $7,295,703 (100% non-need-based). *Programs:* Federal Direct (Subsidized and Unsubsidized Stafford, PLUS), Perkins.
WORK-STUDY *Federal work-study:* Total amount: $352,195; jobs available. *State or other work-study/employment:* Total amount: $883,622 (100% non-need-based). Part-time jobs available.
APPLYING FOR FINANCIAL AID *Required financial aid forms:* FAFSA, state aid form. *Financial aid deadline (priority):* 3/1. *Notification date:* Continuous beginning 3/15. Students must reply by 5/1 or within 4 weeks of notification.
CONTACT Karen Gallagher, Director of Financial Advisement, State University of New York College at Cortland, PO Box 2000, Cortland, NY 13045, 607-753-4717. *Fax:* 607-753-5990. *E-mail:* finaid@cortland.edu. *Website:* http://www.cortland.edu/.

STATE UNIVERSITY OF NEW YORK COLLEGE AT GENESEO
Geneseo, NY

Tuition & fees (NY res): $7095	Average undergraduate aid package: $9144

ABOUT THE INSTITUTION State-supported, coed. *Awards:* bachelor's and master's degrees. 41 undergraduate majors. *Total enrollment:* 5,557. Undergraduates: 5,388. Freshmen: 997. Federal methodology is used as a basis for awarding need-based institutional aid.
UNDERGRADUATE EXPENSES for 2013–2014 *Application fee:* $50. *Tuition, state resident:* full-time $5570. *Tuition, nonresident:* full-time $14,820. *Required fees:* full-time $1525. Part-time tuition and fees vary according to course load. *College room and board:* $10,960; *Room only:* $6950. Room and board charges vary according to board plan and housing facility.
FRESHMAN FINANCIAL AID (Fall 2011) 826 applied for aid; of those 51% were deemed to have need. 91% of freshmen with need received aid; of those 62% had need fully met. *Average percent of need met:* 62% (excluding resources awarded to replace EFC). *Average financial aid package:* $6006 (excluding resources awarded to replace EFC). 1% of all full-time freshmen had no need and received non-need-based gift aid.
UNDERGRADUATE FINANCIAL AID (Fall 2011) 4,028 applied for aid; of those 58% were deemed to have need. 96% of undergraduates with need received aid; of those 68% had need fully met. *Average percent of need met:* 68% (excluding resources awarded to replace EFC). *Average financial aid package:* $9144 (excluding resources awarded to replace EFC). 9% of all full-time undergraduates had no need and received non-need-based gift aid.
GIFT AID (NEED-BASED) *Total amount:* $9,943,864 (52% federal, 48% state). *Receiving aid:* Freshmen: 36% (360); all full-time undergraduates: 39% (2,250). *Average award:* Freshmen: $3821; Undergraduates: $4735. *Scholarships, grants, and awards:* Federal Pell, FSEOG, state.
GIFT AID (NON-NEED-BASED) *Total amount:* $2,856,795 (4% federal, 21% state, 42% institutional, 33% external sources). *Receiving aid:* Freshmen: 7% (71). Undergraduates: 16% (925). *Average award:* Freshmen: $3300. Undergraduates: $2100. *Scholarships, grants, and awards by category: Academic interests/ achievement:* area/ethnic studies, biological sciences, business, communication, computer science, education, English, foreign languages, general academic interests/achievements, humanities, international studies, mathematics, physical sciences, premedicine, social sciences. *Creative arts/performance:* applied art and design, art/fine arts, creative writing, dance, general creative arts/performance, journalism/publications, music, performing arts, theater/drama. *Special achievements/activities:* community service, leadership, memberships. *Special characteristics:* 571 awards ($1,205,760 total): adult students, ethnic background, local/state students, members of minority groups, religious affiliation. *ROTC:* Army cooperative, Air Force cooperative.

LOANS *Student loans:* $20,261,342 (44% need-based, 56% non-need-based). 67% of past graduating class borrowed through all loan programs. *Average indebtedness per student:* $21,000. *Average need-based loan:* Freshmen: $3211. Undergraduates: $4173. *Parent loans:* $6,327,287 (100% non-need-based). *Programs:* Federal Direct (Subsidized and Unsubsidized Stafford, PLUS), Perkins.

WORK-STUDY *Federal work-study:* Total amount: $549,340; 409 jobs averaging $1438. *State or other work-study/employment:* Total amount: $950,142 (100% non-need-based). 906 part-time jobs averaging $1465.

APPLYING FOR FINANCIAL AID *Required financial aid forms:* FAFSA, state aid form. *Financial aid deadline (priority):* 2/15. *Notification date:* Continuous beginning 3/15. Students must reply by 5/1.

CONTACT Archie Cureton, Director of Financial Aid, State University of New York College at Geneseo, 1 College Circle, Erwin Hall 104, Geneseo, NY 14454, 585-245-5731 or toll-free 866-245-5211. *Fax:* 585-245-5717. *E-mail:* finaid@geneseo.edu. *Website:* http://www.geneseo.edu/.

STATE UNIVERSITY OF NEW YORK COLLEGE AT OLD WESTBURY
Old Westbury, NY

Tuition & fees (NY res): $6624	Average undergraduate aid package: $9202

ABOUT THE INSTITUTION State-supported, coed. *Awards:* certificates, bachelor's, and master's degrees. 42 undergraduate majors. *Total enrollment:* 4,422. Undergraduates: 4,217. Freshmen: 414. Both federal and institutional methodology are used as a basis for awarding need-based institutional aid.

UNDERGRADUATE EXPENSES for 2013–2014 *Application fee:* $50. *Tuition, state resident:* full-time $5570; part-time $232 per credit. *Tuition, nonresident:* full-time $14,820; part-time $618 per credit. *Required fees:* full-time $1054; $20.85 per credit or $148 per term. Part-time tuition and fees vary according to course load. *College room and board:* $9700; *Room only:* $6600. Room and board charges vary according to board plan.

FRESHMAN FINANCIAL AID (Fall 2012, est.) 342 applied for aid; of those 100% were deemed to have need. 79% of freshmen with need received aid; of those 126% had need fully met. *Average percent of need met:* 54% (excluding resources awarded to replace EFC). *Average financial aid package:* $9074 (excluding resources awarded to replace EFC).

UNDERGRADUATE FINANCIAL AID (Fall 2012, est.) 2,968 applied for aid; of those 100% were deemed to have need. 84% of undergraduates with need received aid; of those 100% had need fully met. *Average percent of need met:* 54% (excluding resources awarded to replace EFC). *Average financial aid package:* $9202 (excluding resources awarded to replace EFC).

GIFT AID (NEED-BASED) *Total amount:* $16,839,778 (51% federal, 49% state). *Receiving aid:* Freshmen: 66% (259); all full-time undergraduates: 64% (2,276). *Average award:* Freshmen: $7576; Undergraduates: $6169. *Scholarships, grants, and awards:* Federal Pell, FSEOG, state, private, college/university gift aid from institutional funds.

GIFT AID (NON-NEED-BASED) *Total amount:* $293,314 (11% federal, 21% state, 50% institutional, 18% external sources). *Receiving aid:* Freshmen: 5% (21). Undergraduates: 2% (74). *Scholarships, grants, and awards by category:* Academic interests/achievement: biological sciences, health fields, physical sciences. *Tuition waivers:* Full or partial for senior citizens. *ROTC:* Army cooperative, Air Force cooperative.

LOANS *Student loans:* $17,007,141 (69% need-based, 31% non-need-based). 54% of past graduating class borrowed through all loan programs. *Average indebtedness per student:* $18,972. *Average need-based loan:* Freshmen: $3818. Undergraduates: $4695. *Parent loans:* $1,890,456 (46% need-based, 54% non-need-based). *Programs:* Federal Direct (Subsidized and Unsubsidized Stafford, PLUS), Perkins.

WORK-STUDY *Federal work-study:* Total amount: $182,646; jobs available.

APPLYING FOR FINANCIAL AID *Required financial aid forms:* FAFSA, institution's own form, state aid form, verification worksheet. *Financial aid deadline (priority):* 4/15. *Notification date:* Continuous beginning 4/25. Students must reply within 2 weeks of notification.

CONTACT Ms. Dee Darrell, Financial Aid Assistant, State University of New York College at Old Westbury, PO Box 210, Old Westbury, NY 11568-0210, 516-876-3224. *Fax:* 516-876-3008. *E-mail:* finaid@oldwestbury.edu. *Website:* http://www.oldwestbury.edu/.

STATE UNIVERSITY OF NEW YORK COLLEGE AT ONEONTA
Oneonta, NY

Tuition & fees (NY res): $6887	Average undergraduate aid package: $8697

ABOUT THE INSTITUTION State-supported, coed. *Awards:* certificates, bachelor's, and master's degrees. 68 undergraduate majors. *Total enrollment:* 6,023. Undergraduates: 5,852. Freshmen: 1,172. Federal methodology is used as a basis for awarding need-based institutional aid.

UNDERGRADUATE EXPENSES for 2013–2014 *Application fee:* $50. *Tuition, state resident:* full-time $5570; part-time $232 per semester hour. *Tuition, nonresident:* full-time $14,820; part-time $618 per semester hour. *Required fees:* full-time $1317; $37 per semester hour. Part-time tuition and fees vary according to course load. *College room and board:* $10,540; *Room only:* $6740. Room and board charges vary according to housing facility.

FRESHMAN FINANCIAL AID (Fall 2012, est.) 900 applied for aid; of those 74% were deemed to have need. 100% of freshmen with need received aid; of those 4% had need fully met. *Average percent of need met:* 81% (excluding resources awarded to replace EFC). *Average financial aid package:* $8818 (excluding resources awarded to replace EFC). 25% of all full-time freshmen had no need and received non-need-based gift aid.

UNDERGRADUATE FINANCIAL AID (Fall 2012, est.) 4,764 applied for aid; of those 74% were deemed to have need. 96% of undergraduates with need received aid; of those 1% had need fully met. *Average percent of need met:* 73% (excluding resources awarded to replace EFC). *Average financial aid package:* $8697 (excluding resources awarded to replace EFC). 8% of all full-time undergraduates had no need and received non-need-based gift aid.

GIFT AID (NEED-BASED) *Total amount:* $14,952,499 (50% federal, 43% state, 7% institutional). *Receiving aid:* Freshmen: 42% (483); all full-time undergraduates: 59% (3,350). *Average award:* Freshmen: $6510; Undergraduates: $4709. *Scholarships, grants, and awards:* Federal Pell, FSEOG, state, private, college/university gift aid from institutional funds.

GIFT AID (NON-NEED-BASED) *Total amount:* $3,361,653 (5% federal, 31% state, 40% institutional, 24% external sources). *Receiving aid:* Freshmen: 15% (171). Undergraduates: 3% (171). *Average award:* Freshmen: $2840. Undergraduates: $2827. *Scholarships, grants, and awards by category:* Academic interests/achievement: biological sciences, business, computer science, education, English, general academic interests/achievements, home economics, physical sciences, premedicine, social sciences. Creative arts/performance: music, theater/drama. *Special achievements/activities:* community service, general special achievements/activities, leadership. *Special characteristics:* general special characteristics, international students, local/state students. *Tuition waivers:* Full or partial for employees or children of employees.

LOANS *Student loans:* $27,766,265 (48% need-based, 52% non-need-based). 66% of past graduating class borrowed through all loan programs. *Average indebtedness per student:* $15,373. *Average need-based loan:* Freshmen: $3850. Undergraduates: $5666. *Parent loans:* $17,008,610 (100% non-need-based). *Programs:* Federal Direct (Subsidized and Unsubsidized Stafford, PLUS), Perkins.

WORK-STUDY *Federal work-study:* Total amount: $300,000; jobs available. *State or other work-study/employment:* Total amount: $1,002,540 (100% non-need-based). Part-time jobs available.

APPLYING FOR FINANCIAL AID *Required financial aid forms:* FAFSA, noncustodial (divorced/separated) parent's statement. *Financial aid deadline (priority):* 3/1. *Notification date:* Continuous beginning 3/1. Students must reply by 5/1 or within 4 weeks of notification.

CONTACT Mr. Bill Goodhue, Director of Financial Aid, State University of New York College at Oneonta, 108 Ravine Parkway, Oneonta, NY 13820, 607-436-2992 or toll-free 800-SUNY-123. *Fax:* 607-436-2659. *E-mail:* bill.goodhue@oneonta.edu. *Website:* http://www.oneonta.edu/.

STATE UNIVERSITY OF NEW YORK COLLEGE AT POTSDAM
Potsdam, NY

Tuition & fees (NY res): $6842	Average undergraduate aid package: $13,076

ABOUT THE INSTITUTION State-supported, coed. *Awards:* bachelor's and master's degrees. 39 undergraduate majors. *Total enrollment:* 4,224. Undergraduates: 3,868. Freshmen: 888. Federal methodology is used as a basis for awarding need-based institutional aid.

UNDERGRADUATE EXPENSES for 2013–2014 *Application fee:* $50. *Tuition, state resident:* full-time $5570; part-time $232 per credit hour. *Tuition, nonresident:* full-time $14,820; part-time $618 per credit hour. *Required fees:* full-time $1272. *College room and board:* $10,180; *Room only:* $5970. Room and board charges vary according to board plan and housing facility.

FRESHMAN FINANCIAL AID (Fall 2012, est.) 845 applied for aid; of those 80% were deemed to have need. 99% of freshmen with need received aid; of those 47% had need fully met. *Average percent of need met:* 88% (excluding resources awarded to replace EFC). *Average financial aid package:* $13,701 (excluding resources awarded to replace EFC). 9% of all full-time freshmen had no need and received non-need-based gift aid.

UNDERGRADUATE FINANCIAL AID (Fall 2012, est.) 3,441 applied for aid; of those 80% were deemed to have need. 99% of undergraduates with need received aid; of those 47% had need fully met. *Average percent of need met:* 88% (excluding resources awarded to replace EFC). *Average financial aid package:* $13,076 (excluding resources awarded to replace EFC). 8% of all full-time undergraduates had no need and received non-need-based gift aid.

GIFT AID (NEED-BASED) *Total amount:* $16,830,342 (46% federal, 39% state, 13% institutional, 2% external sources). *Receiving aid:* Freshmen: 71% (629); all full-time undergraduates: 65% (2,436). *Average award:* Freshmen: $7175; Undergraduates: $6571. *Scholarships, grants, and awards:* Federal Pell, FSEOG, state, private, college/university gift aid from institutional funds, Academic Competitiveness Grants, National SMART Grants, TEACH Grants, Veterans Benefits.

GIFT AID (NON-NEED-BASED) *Total amount:* $1,184,718 (8% federal, 8% state, 71% institutional, 13% external sources). *Receiving aid:* Freshmen: 32% (279). Undergraduates: 23% (852). *Average award:* Freshmen: $2196. Undergraduates: $2366. *Scholarships, grants, and awards by category: Academic interests/achievement:* 204 awards ($334,035 total): biological sciences, business, communication, computer science, education, engineering/technologies, English, foreign languages, general academic interests/achievements, humanities, mathematics, physical sciences, social sciences. *Creative arts/performance:* 150 awards ($201,613 total): art/fine arts, dance, music, performing arts, theater/drama. *Special achievements/activities:* 759 awards ($1,655,486 total): community service, general special achievements/activities, leadership. *Special characteristics:* 71 awards ($88,308 total): adult students, children and siblings of alumni, children of faculty/staff, ethnic background, handicapped students, local/state students, members of minority groups, previous college experience. *Tuition waivers:* Full or partial for employees or children of employees. *ROTC:* Army cooperative, Air Force cooperative.

LOANS *Student loans:* $22,438,589 (74% need-based, 26% non-need-based). 78% of past graduating class borrowed through all loan programs. *Average indebtedness per student:* $20,734. *Average need-based loan:* Freshmen: $3946. Undergraduates: $4635. *Parent loans:* $10,448,517 (26% need-based, 74% non-need-based). *Programs:* Federal Direct (Subsidized and Unsubsidized Stafford, PLUS), Perkins, alternative loans.

WORK-STUDY *Federal work-study:* Total amount: $311,114; 246 jobs averaging $1090.

APPLYING FOR FINANCIAL AID *Required financial aid forms:* FAFSA, state aid form. *Financial aid deadline:* 5/1 (priority: 3/1). *Notification date:* Continuous beginning 2/1. Students must reply by 5/1 or within 4 weeks of notification.

CONTACT Susan C. Merchant, Director of Financial Aid, State University of New York College at Potsdam, 44 Pierrepont Avenue, Potsdam, NY 13676, 315-267-2162 or toll-free 877-POTSDAM. *Fax:* 315-267-3067. *E-mail:* finaid@potsdam.edu. *Website:* http://www.potsdam.edu/.

STATE UNIVERSITY OF NEW YORK COLLEGE OF AGRICULTURE AND TECHNOLOGY AT COBLESKILL
Cobleskill, NY

Tuition & fees (NY res): $8262	Average undergraduate aid package: $7791

ABOUT THE INSTITUTION State-supported, coed. *Awards:* certificates, associate, and bachelor's degrees. 36 undergraduate majors. *Total enrollment:* 2,519. Undergraduates: 2,492. Freshmen: 758. Federal methodology is used as a basis for awarding need-based institutional aid.

UNDERGRADUATE EXPENSES for 2013–2014 *Application fee:* $50. *One-time required fee:* $55. *Tuition, state resident:* full-time $5570; part-time $232 per credit hour. *Tuition, nonresident:* full-time $14,820; part-time $618 per credit hour. *Required fees:* full-time $2692; $73.32 per credit hour. *College room and board:* $10,866; *Room only:* $6600. Room and board charges vary according to board plan.

FRESHMAN FINANCIAL AID (Fall 2011) 903 applied for aid; of those 88% were deemed to have need. 100% of freshmen with need received aid; of those 2% had need fully met. *Average percent of need met:* 80% (excluding resources awarded to replace EFC). *Average financial aid package:* $8727 (excluding resources awarded to replace EFC). 11% of all full-time freshmen had no need and received non-need-based gift aid.

UNDERGRADUATE FINANCIAL AID (Fall 2011) 2,226 applied for aid; of those 88% were deemed to have need. 99% of undergraduates with need received aid; of those 2% had need fully met. *Average percent of need met:* 68% (excluding resources awarded to replace EFC). *Average financial aid package:* $7791 (excluding resources awarded to replace EFC). 10% of all full-time undergraduates had no need and received non-need-based gift aid.

GIFT AID (NEED-BASED) *Total amount:* $10,061,703 (55% federal, 45% state). *Receiving aid:* Freshmen: 81% (795); all full-time undergraduates: 77% (1,946). *Average award:* Freshmen: $5354; Undergraduates: $4713. *Scholarships, grants, and awards:* Federal Pell, FSEOG, state, private, college/university gift aid from institutional funds.

GIFT AID (NON-NEED-BASED) *Total amount:* $915,481 (40% institutional, 60% external sources). *Receiving aid:* Freshmen: 22% (219). Undergraduates: 16% (417). *Average award:* Freshmen: $383. Undergraduates: $316. *Scholarships, grants, and awards by category: Academic interests/achievement:* general academic interests/achievements. *Special achievements/activities:* leadership. *Special characteristics:* children and siblings of alumni, local/state students, members of minority groups. *Tuition waivers:* Full or partial for employees or children of employees, senior citizens.

LOANS *Student loans:* $12,659,830 (48% need-based, 52% non-need-based). 73% of past graduating class borrowed through all loan programs. *Average indebtedness per student:* $21,195. *Average need-based loan:* Freshmen: $3981. Undergraduates: $3755. *Parent loans:* $4,536,859 (100% need-based). *Programs:* Federal Direct (Subsidized and Unsubsidized Stafford, PLUS), Perkins.

WORK-STUDY *Federal work-study:* Total amount: $95,130; jobs available. *State or other work-study/employment:* Part-time jobs available.

APPLYING FOR FINANCIAL AID *Required financial aid forms:* FAFSA, state aid form. *Financial aid deadline (priority):* 2/15. *Notification date:* 3/15. Students must reply within 2 weeks of notification.

CONTACT Office of Financial Aid, State University of New York College of Agriculture and Technology at Cobleskill, 118B Knapp Hall, Cobleskill, NY 12043, 518-255-5623 or toll-free 800-295-8988. *Fax:* 518-255-5844. *E-mail:* financialaid@cobleskill.edu. *Website:* http://www.cobleskill.edu/.

STATE UNIVERSITY OF NEW YORK COLLEGE OF ENVIRONMENTAL SCIENCE AND FORESTRY
Syracuse, NY

Tuition & fees (NY res): $6593	Average undergraduate aid package: $13,000

ABOUT THE INSTITUTION State-supported, coed. *Awards:* certificates, associate, bachelor's, master's, and doctoral degrees. 48 undergraduate majors. *Total enrollment:* 2,401. Undergraduates: 10,177. Freshmen: 325. Federal methodology is used as a basis for awarding need-based institutional aid.

UNDERGRADUATE EXPENSES for 2013–2014 Application fee: $50. *Tuition, state resident:* full-time $5570; part-time $232 per credit hour. *Tuition, nonresident:* full-time $14,820; part-time $618 per credit hour. *Required fees:* full-time $1023; $43.10 per credit hour. Full-time tuition and fees vary according to location. Part-time tuition and fees vary according to course load and location. *College room and board:* $14,400. Room and board charges vary according to board plan, housing facility, and location.

FRESHMAN FINANCIAL AID (Fall 2012, est.) 300 applied for aid; of those 69% were deemed to have need. 100% of freshmen with need received aid; of those 87% had need fully met. *Average percent of need met:* 90% (excluding resources awarded to replace EFC). *Average financial aid package:* $13,000 (excluding resources awarded to replace EFC). 13% of all full-time freshmen had no need and received non-need-based gift aid.

UNDERGRADUATE FINANCIAL AID (Fall 2012, est.) 1,396 applied for aid; of those 72% were deemed to have need. 100% of undergraduates with need received aid; of those 89% had need fully met. *Average percent of need met:* 90% (excluding resources awarded to replace EFC). *Average financial aid package:* $13,000 (excluding resources awarded to replace EFC). 6% of all full-time undergraduates had no need and received non-need-based gift aid.

GIFT AID (NEED-BASED) Total amount: $6,133,727 (33% federal, 25% state, 38% institutional, 4% external sources). *Receiving aid:* Freshmen: 57% (184); all full-time undergraduates: 59% (991). *Average award:* Freshmen: $3500; Undergraduates: $2500. *Scholarships, grants, and awards:* Federal Pell, FSEOG, state, private, college/university gift aid from institutional funds.

GIFT AID (NON-NEED-BASED) Total amount: $701,263 (15% state, 52% institutional, 33% external sources). *Receiving aid:* Freshmen: 44% (142). Undergraduates: 31% (524). *Average award:* Freshmen: $3874. Undergraduates: $3233. *Scholarships, grants, and awards by category: Academic interests/achievement:* 517 awards ($1,680,913 total): agriculture, architecture, biological sciences, engineering/technologies, general academic interests/achievements, physical sciences, premedicine. *Special achievements/activities:* community service, general special achievements/activities, leadership, memberships. *Special characteristics:* children and siblings of alumni, general special characteristics, international students, local/state students, members of minority groups, out-of-state students. *ROTC:* Army cooperative, Air Force cooperative.

LOANS Student loans: $8,811,627 (41% need-based, 59% non-need-based). 80% of past graduating class borrowed through all loan programs. *Average indebtedness per student:* $26,000. *Average need-based loan:* Freshmen: $4500. Undergraduates: $5500. *Parent loans:* $2,469,575 (32% need-based, 68% non-need-based). *Programs:* Federal Direct (Subsidized and Unsubsidized Stafford, PLUS), Perkins.

WORK-STUDY Federal work-study: Total amount: $330,000; 194 jobs averaging $1625. *State or other work-study/employment:* Total amount: $339,807 (47% need-based, 53% non-need-based). 291 part-time jobs averaging $1168.

APPLYING FOR FINANCIAL AID Required financial aid forms: FAFSA, state aid form. *Financial aid deadline (priority):* 3/1. *Notification date:* Continuous beginning 3/15. Students must reply within 2 weeks of notification.

CONTACT Mr. John E. View, Director of Financial Aid, State University of New York College of Environmental Science and Forestry, One Forestry Drive, Syracuse, NY 13210-2779, 315-470-6671. *Fax:* 315-470-4734. *E-mail:* jeview@esf.edu. *Website:* http://www.esf.edu/.

STATE UNIVERSITY OF NEW YORK COLLEGE OF TECHNOLOGY AT CANTON
Canton, NY

CONTACT Ms. Kerrie Cooper, Director of Financial Aid, State University of New York College of Technology at Canton, Student Service Center, Canton, NY 13617, 315-386-7616 or toll-free 800-388-7123. *Fax:* 315-386-7930. *E-mail:* cooper@canton.edu. *Website:* http://www.canton.edu/.

STATE UNIVERSITY OF NEW YORK COLLEGE OF TECHNOLOGY AT DELHI
Delhi, NY

Tuition & fees (NY res): $7090	Average undergraduate aid package: N/A

ABOUT THE INSTITUTION State-supported, coed. *Awards:* certificates, associate, and bachelor's degrees. 32 undergraduate majors. *Total enrollment:* 3,151. Undergraduates: 3,151. Freshmen: 922. Federal methodology is used as a basis for awarding need-based institutional aid.

UNDERGRADUATE EXPENSES for 2013–2014 Application fee: $50. *Tuition, state resident:* full-time $5570; part-time $232 per credit hour. *Tuition, nonresident:* full-time $9740; part-time $406 per credit hour. *Required fees:* full-time $1520; $76.24 per credit hour or $76.24 per credit hour. Full-time tuition and fees vary according to degree level. Part-time tuition and fees vary according to degree level. *College room and board:* $10,346; *Room only:* $5936. Room and board charges vary according to board plan and housing facility.

FRESHMAN FINANCIAL AID (Fall 2012, est.) 856 applied for aid.

UNDERGRADUATE FINANCIAL AID (Fall 2012, est.) 2,836 applied for aid.

GIFT AID (NEED-BASED) Total amount: $13,163,314 (50% federal, 38% state, 8% institutional, 4% external sources). *Receiving aid:* Freshmen: 78% (720); all full-time undergraduates: 70% (2,204). *Scholarships, grants, and awards:* Federal Pell, FSEOG, state, private, college/university gift aid from institutional funds.

GIFT AID (NON-NEED-BASED) Scholarships, grants, and awards by category: Academic interests/achievement: general academic interests/achievements. *Special achievements/activities:* community service.

LOANS Student loans: $15,672,150 (100% need-based). 87% of past graduating class borrowed through all loan programs. *Parent loans:* $5,675,222 (100% need-based). *Programs:* Federal Direct (Subsidized and Unsubsidized Stafford, PLUS), Perkins.

WORK-STUDY Federal work-study: Total amount: $69,037; 97 jobs averaging $1046. *State or other work-study/employment:* Total amount: $427,376 (100% need-based). Part-time jobs available.

APPLYING FOR FINANCIAL AID Required financial aid forms: FAFSA, state aid form. *Financial aid deadline (priority):* 2/15. *Notification date:* Continuous beginning 3/15.

CONTACT Office of Financial Aid, State University of New York College of Technology at Delhi, 158 Bush Hall, Delhi, NY 13753, 607-746-4570 or toll-free 800-96-DELHI. *Fax:* 607-746-4104. *Website:* http://www.delhi.edu/.

STATE UNIVERSITY OF NEW YORK DOWNSTATE MEDICAL CENTER
Brooklyn, NY

CONTACT Financial Aid Office, State University of New York Downstate Medical Center, 450 Clarkson Avenue, Brooklyn, NY 11203-2098, 718-270-2488. *Fax:* 718-270-7592. *E-mail:* finaid1@downstate.edu. *Website:* http://www.downstate.edu/.

STATE UNIVERSITY OF NEW YORK INSTITUTE OF TECHNOLOGY
Utica, NY

Tuition & fees (NY res): $6764	Average undergraduate aid package: $8626

ABOUT THE INSTITUTION State-supported, coed. *Awards:* certificates, bachelor's, and master's degrees. 16 undergraduate majors. *Total enrollment:* 2,377. Undergraduates: 1,693. Freshmen: 198. Federal methodology is used as a basis for awarding need-based institutional aid.

UNDERGRADUATE EXPENSES for 2013–2014 *Application fee:* $50. *Tuition, state resident:* full-time $5570; part-time $232 per credit hour. *Tuition, nonresident:* full-time $14,820; part-time $618 per credit hour. *Required fees:* full-time $1194; $49.63 per credit hour or $49.63 per credit hour. Part-time tuition and fees vary according to course load. *College room and board:* $10,290. Room and board charges vary according to board plan.

FRESHMAN FINANCIAL AID (Fall 2012, est.) 184 applied for aid; of those 78% were deemed to have need. 100% of freshmen with need received aid; of those 100% had need fully met. *Average financial aid package:* $10,338 (excluding resources awarded to replace EFC). 13% of all full-time freshmen had no need and received non-need-based gift aid.

UNDERGRADUATE FINANCIAL AID (Fall 2012, est.) 1,124 applied for aid; of those 83% were deemed to have need. 100% of undergraduates with need received aid; of those 99% had need fully met. *Average financial aid package:* $8626 (excluding resources awarded to replace EFC). 5% of all full-time undergraduates had no need and received non-need-based gift aid.

GIFT AID (NEED-BASED) *Total amount:* $4,970,433 (52% federal, 34% state, 12% institutional, 2% external sources). *Receiving aid:* Freshmen: 69% (137); all full-time undergraduates: 64% (818). *Average award:* Freshmen: $7990; Undergraduates: $5955. *Scholarships, grants, and awards:* Federal Pell, FSEOG, state, private, college/university gift aid from institutional funds.

GIFT AID (NON-NEED-BASED) *Total amount:* $227,558 (28% state, 40% institutional, 32% external sources). *Receiving aid:* Freshmen: 13% (25). Undergraduates: 5% (70). *Average award:* Freshmen: $1685. Undergraduates: $1370. *Scholarships, grants, and awards by category:* Academic interests/achievement: computer science, engineering/technologies, general academic interests/achievements. *Special characteristics:* local/state students, members of minority groups, previous college experience. *ROTC:* Army cooperative, Air Force cooperative.

LOANS *Student loans:* $6,889,149 (88% need-based, 12% non-need-based). *Average need-based loan:* Freshmen: $3433. Undergraduates: $4157. *Parent loans:* $1,208,039 (73% need-based, 27% non-need-based). *Programs:* Federal Direct (Subsidized and Unsubsidized Stafford, PLUS), Perkins, Federal Nursing.

WORK-STUDY *Federal work-study:* Total amount: $205,254; jobs available. *State or other work-study/employment:* Total amount: $21,150 (100% need-based). Part-time jobs available.

APPLYING FOR FINANCIAL AID *Required financial aid forms:* FAFSA, state aid form. *Financial aid deadline (priority):* 3/1. *Notification date:* Continuous beginning 3/15. Students must reply within 2 weeks of notification.

CONTACT Director of Financial Aid, State University of New York Institute of Technology, 100 Seymour Road, Utica, NY 13502, 315-792-7210 or toll-free 866-2-SUNYIT. *Fax:* 315-792-7220. *E-mail:* finaid@sunyit.edu. *Website:* http://www.sunyit.edu/.

STATE UNIVERSITY OF NEW YORK MARITIME COLLEGE
Throggs Neck, NY

Tuition & fees (NY res): $6782	Average undergraduate aid package: N/A

ABOUT THE INSTITUTION State-supported, coed, primarily men. *Awards:* associate, bachelor's, and master's degrees. 7 undergraduate majors. *Total enrollment:* 1,761. Undergraduates: 1,614. Freshmen: 327. Federal methodology is used as a basis for awarding need-based institutional aid.

UNDERGRADUATE EXPENSES for 2013–2014 *Application fee:* $50. *Tuition, state resident:* full-time $5570; part-time $232 per credit hour. *Tuition,* *nonresident:* full-time $14,820; part-time $618 per credit hour. *Required fees:* full-time $1212; $50.50 per credit hour. Full-time tuition and fees vary according to degree level and program. Part-time tuition and fees vary according to course load, degree level, and program. *College room and board:* $10,444; *Room only:* $6594. Room and board charges vary according to board plan, gender, and housing facility.

UNDERGRADUATE FINANCIAL AID (Fall 2011) 903 applied for aid; of those 95% were deemed to have need. 96% of undergraduates with need received aid. 3% of all full-time undergraduates had no need and received non-need-based gift aid.

GIFT AID (NEED-BASED) *Total amount:* $3,361,673 (58% federal, 35% state, 3% institutional, 4% external sources). *Receiving aid:* All full-time undergraduates: 35% (554). *Scholarships, grants, and awards:* Federal Pell, FSEOG, state, private, college/university gift aid from institutional funds, Educational Opportunity Program (EOP).

GIFT AID (NON-NEED-BASED) *Total amount:* $742,731 (40% federal, 29% state, 13% institutional, 18% external sources). *Average award:* Undergraduates: $1994. *Scholarships, grants, and awards by category:* Academic interests/achievement: general academic interests/achievements. *Tuition waivers:* Full or partial for employees or children of employees. *ROTC:* Army cooperative, Naval.

LOANS *Student loans:* $7,686,555 (68% need-based, 32% non-need-based). *Parent loans:* $3,308,792 (30% need-based, 70% non-need-based). *Programs:* Federal Direct (Subsidized and Unsubsidized Stafford, PLUS), Perkins, alternative loans.

WORK-STUDY *Federal work-study:* Total amount: $19,972; jobs available. *State or other work-study/employment:* Part-time jobs available.

APPLYING FOR FINANCIAL AID *Required financial aid forms:* FAFSA, institution's own form. *Financial aid deadline:* 7/15 (priority: 3/15). *Notification date:* Continuous beginning 3/15.

CONTACT Mr. Paul Bamonte, Director of Enrollment Services and Financial Aid, State University of New York Maritime College, 6 Pennyfield Avenue, Throgs Neck, NY 10465-4198, 718-409-7400. *Fax:* 718-409-7275. *E-mail:* pbamonte@ sunymaritime.edu. *Website:* http://www.sunymaritime.edu/.

STATE UNIVERSITY OF NEW YORK UPSTATE MEDICAL UNIVERSITY
Syracuse, NY

CONTACT Michael Pede, Office of Financial Aid, State University of New York Upstate Medical University, 155 Elizabeth Blackwell Street, Syracuse, NY 13210-2375, 315-464-4329 or toll-free 800-736-2171. *E-mail:* finaid@upstate.edu. *Website:* http://www.upstate.edu/.

STEPHEN F. AUSTIN STATE UNIVERSITY
Nacogdoches, TX

Tuition & fees (TX res): $7928	Average undergraduate aid package: $10,584

ABOUT THE INSTITUTION State-supported, coed. *Awards:* bachelor's, master's, and doctoral degrees. 62 undergraduate majors. *Total enrollment:* 12,999. Undergraduates: 11,298. Freshmen: 2,136. Federal methodology is used as a basis for awarding need-based institutional aid.

UNDERGRADUATE EXPENSES for 2013–2014 *Application fee:* $35. *Tuition, state resident:* full-time $5756; part-time $191.86 per credit hour. *Tuition, nonresident:* full-time $16,286; part-time $542.86 per credit hour. *Required fees:* full-time $2172; $154 per credit hour. Full-time tuition and fees vary according to course load, degree level, and location. Part-time tuition and fees vary according to course load, degree level, and location. *College room and board:* $8476. Room and board charges vary according to board plan and housing facility.

FRESHMAN FINANCIAL AID (Fall 2011) 2,077 applied for aid; of those 83% were deemed to have need. 100% of freshmen with need received aid; of those 8% had need fully met. *Average percent of need met:* 53% (excluding resources awarded to replace EFC). *Average financial aid package:* $10,747 (excluding resources

awarded to replace EFC). 8% of all full-time freshmen had no need and received non-need-based gift aid.

UNDERGRADUATE FINANCIAL AID (Fall 2011) 8,278 applied for aid; of those 85% were deemed to have need. 100% of undergraduates with need received aid; of those 9% had need fully met. *Average percent of need met:* 53% (excluding resources awarded to replace EFC). *Average financial aid package:* $10,584 (excluding resources awarded to replace EFC). 7% of all full-time undergraduates had no need and received non-need-based gift aid.

GIFT AID (NEED-BASED) *Total amount:* $34,138,547 (66% federal, 17% state, 17% institutional). *Receiving aid:* Freshmen: 57% (1,367); all full-time undergraduates: 54% (5,601). *Average award:* Freshmen: $7120; Undergraduates: $5955. *Scholarships, grants, and awards:* Federal Pell, FSEOG, state, private, college/university gift aid from institutional funds, Academic Competitiveness Grants, National SMART Grants, TEACH Grants.

GIFT AID (NON-NEED-BASED) *Total amount:* $11,521,147 (4% federal, 8% state, 65% institutional, 23% external sources). *Receiving aid:* Freshmen: 32% (778). Undergraduates: 21% (2,227). *Average award:* Freshmen: $4735. Undergraduates: $2744. *Scholarships, grants, and awards by category: Academic interests/achievement:* agriculture, biological sciences, business, communication, computer science, education, general academic interests/achievements, health fields, home economics, mathematics, military science, physical sciences, premedicine. *Creative arts/performance:* journalism/publications, music, theater/drama. *Special achievements/activities:* cheerleading/drum major, general special achievements/activities, hobbies/interests, leadership, rodeo. *Special characteristics:* adult students, children and siblings of alumni, children of faculty/staff, children of union members/company employees, first-generation college students, general special characteristics, local/state students, previous college experience. *Tuition waivers:* Full or partial for employees or children of employees, senior citizens. *ROTC:* Army.

LOANS *Student loans:* $73,627,050 (44% need-based, 56% non-need-based). 71% of past graduating class borrowed through all loan programs. *Average indebtedness per student:* $20,858. *Average need-based loan:* Freshmen: $3538. Undergraduates: $4640. *Parent loans:* $17,575,625 (100% non-need-based). *Programs:* Perkins, state, short-term emergency loans.

WORK-STUDY *Federal work-study:* Total amount: $708,919; jobs available. *State or other work-study/employment:* Total amount: $75,070 (100% need-based). Part-time jobs available.

ATHLETIC AWARDS Total amount: $3,407,762 (100% non-need-based).

APPLYING FOR FINANCIAL AID *Required financial aid form:* FAFSA. *Financial aid deadline:* Continuous. *Notification date:* Continuous beginning 4/1.

CONTACT Office of Financial Aid, Stephen F. Austin State University, PO Box 13052, Nacogdoches, TX 75962, 936-468-2403 or toll-free 800-731-2902. *Fax:* 936-468-1048. *E-mail:* finaid@sfasu.edu. *Website:* http://www.sfasu.edu/.

STEPHENS COLLEGE
Columbia, MO

Tuition & fees: $27,210	Average undergraduate aid package: $20,846

ABOUT THE INSTITUTION Independent, coed, primarily women. *Awards:* certificates, associate, bachelor's, and master's degrees. 26 undergraduate majors. *Total enrollment:* 881. Undergraduates: 673. Freshmen: 140. Federal methodology is used as a basis for awarding need-based institutional aid.

UNDERGRADUATE EXPENSES for 2013–2014 *Application fee:* $25. *One-time required fee:* $200. *Comprehensive fee:* $37,510 includes full-time tuition ($27,210) and room and board ($10,300). *College room only:* $6900. Full-time tuition and fees vary according to course load, degree level, program, and reciprocity agreements. Room and board charges vary according to board plan and housing facility. *Part-time tuition:* $700 per credit hour. Part-time tuition and fees vary according to course load, degree level, and program.

FRESHMAN FINANCIAL AID (Fall 2011) 152 applied for aid; of those 82% were deemed to have need. 100% of freshmen with need received aid. *Average percent of need met:* 69% (excluding resources awarded to replace EFC). *Average financial aid package:* $22,765 (excluding resources awarded to replace EFC). 10% of all full-time freshmen had no need and received non-need-based gift aid.

UNDERGRADUATE FINANCIAL AID (Fall 2011) 545 applied for aid; of those 94% were deemed to have need. 100% of undergraduates with need received aid.

Average percent of need met: 73% (excluding resources awarded to replace EFC). *Average financial aid package:* $20,846 (excluding resources awarded to replace EFC). 8% of all full-time undergraduates had no need and received non-need-based gift aid.

GIFT AID (NEED-BASED) *Total amount:* $4,751,641 (26% federal, 8% state, 66% institutional). *Receiving aid:* Freshmen: 81% (125); all full-time undergraduates: 82% (498). *Average award:* Freshmen: $14,854; Undergraduates: $15,787. *Scholarships, grants, and awards:* Federal Pell, FSEOG, state, private, college/university gift aid from institutional funds, Academic Competitiveness Grants, National SMART Grants.

GIFT AID (NON-NEED-BASED) *Total amount:* $3,834,907 (95% institutional, 5% external sources). *Receiving aid:* Freshmen: 76% (117). Undergraduates: 76% (465). *Average award:* Freshmen: $7281. Undergraduates: $8384. *Scholarships, grants, and awards by category: Academic interests/achievement:* 507 awards ($3,237,157 total): English, general academic interests/achievements. *Creative arts/performance:* 47 awards ($68,014 total): dance, performing arts, theater/drama. *Special achievements/activities:* 365 awards ($902,552 total): leadership, memberships. *Special characteristics:* 10 awards ($121,565 total): children of faculty/staff, children of union members/company employees, parents of current students, siblings of current students, veterans, veterans' children. *Tuition waivers:* Full or partial for employees or children of employees. *ROTC:* Army cooperative, Naval cooperative, Air Force cooperative.

LOANS *Student loans:* $4,480,050 (46% need-based, 54% non-need-based). 83% of past graduating class borrowed through all loan programs. *Average indebtedness per student:* $22,293. *Average need-based loan:* Freshmen: $2977. Undergraduates: $3842. *Parent loans:* $1,541,967 (100% non-need-based). *Programs:* Federal Direct (Subsidized and Unsubsidized Stafford, PLUS), Perkins, alternative loans.

WORK-STUDY *Federal work-study:* Total amount: $126,119; 106 jobs averaging $1525. *State or other work-study/employment:* Total amount: $63,208 (100% need-based). 92 part-time jobs averaging $1516.

ATHLETIC AWARDS Total amount: $503,722 (100% non-need-based).

APPLYING FOR FINANCIAL AID *Required financial aid form:* FAFSA. *Financial aid deadline (priority):* 3/1. *Notification date:* Continuous beginning 2/15.

CONTACT Mr. Paul Gordon, Director of Financial Aid, Stephens College, 1200 East Broadway, Columbia, MO 65215-0002, 800-876-7207. *Fax:* 573-876-2320. *E-mail:* finaid@stephens.edu. *Website:* http://www.stephens.edu/.

STERLING COLLEGE
Sterling, KS

CONTACT Ms. Jodi Lightner, Director of Financial Aid, Sterling College, PO Box 98, Sterling, KS 67579-0098, 620-278-4207 or toll-free 800-346-1017. *Fax:* 620-278-4416. *E-mail:* jlightner@sterling.edu. *Website:* http://www.sterling.edu/.

STERLING COLLEGE
Craftsbury Common, VT

Tuition & fees: $28,760	Average undergraduate aid package: $30,382

ABOUT THE INSTITUTION Independent, coed. *Awards:* bachelor's degrees. 11 undergraduate majors. *Total enrollment:* 95. Undergraduates: 95. Freshmen: 16. Both federal and institutional methodology are used as a basis for awarding need-based institutional aid.

UNDERGRADUATE EXPENSES for 2013–2014 *Application fee:* $35. *Comprehensive fee:* $37,092 includes full-time tuition ($28,410), mandatory fees ($350), and room and board ($8332). Full-time tuition and fees vary according to course load. Room and board charges vary according to board plan. *Part-time tuition:* $900 per credit. Part-time tuition and fees vary according to course load.

FRESHMAN FINANCIAL AID (Fall 2011) 15 applied for aid; of those 100% were deemed to have need. 100% of freshmen with need received aid; of those 7% had need fully met. *Average percent of need met:* 90% (excluding resources awarded to replace EFC). *Average financial aid package:* $24,984 (excluding resources

awarded to replace EFC). 25% of all full-time freshmen had no need and received non-need-based gift aid.

UNDERGRADUATE FINANCIAL AID (Fall 2011) 78 applied for aid; of those 100% were deemed to have need. 100% of undergraduates with need received aid; of those 6% had need fully met. *Average percent of need met:* 89% (excluding resources awarded to replace EFC). *Average financial aid package:* $30,382 (excluding resources awarded to replace EFC). 16% of all full-time undergraduates had no need and received non-need-based gift aid.
GIFT AID (NEED-BASED) *Total amount:* $1,622,526 (17% federal, 5% state, 76% institutional, 2% external sources). *Receiving aid:* Freshmen: 70% (14); all full-time undergraduates: 83% (77). *Average award:* Freshmen: $19,137; Undergraduates: $20,832. *Scholarships, grants, and awards:* Federal Pell, FSEOG, state, private, college/university gift aid from institutional funds, Veterans Administration Benefits, Yellow Ribbon Grant Program.
GIFT AID (NON-NEED-BASED) *Total amount:* $69,206 (100% institutional). *Receiving aid:* Freshmen: 25% (5). Undergraduates: 16% (15). *Average award:* Freshmen: $1500. Undergraduates: $4414. *Scholarships, grants, and awards by category: Academic interests/achievement:* general academic interests/achievements. *Special achievements/activities:* general special achievements/activities, leadership. *Special characteristics:* general special characteristics, previous college experience. *Tuition waivers:* Full or partial for employees or children of employees.
LOANS *Student loans:* $535,417 (100% need-based). 60% of past graduating class borrowed through all loan programs. *Average indebtedness per student:* $39,724. *Average need-based loan:* Freshmen: $3311. Undergraduates: $5306. *Parent loans:* $333,312 (78% need-based, 22% non-need-based). *Programs:* Federal Direct (Subsidized and Unsubsidized Stafford, PLUS).
WORK-STUDY *Federal work-study:* Total amount: $132,387; jobs available. *State or other work-study/employment:* Total amount: $25,330 (100% non-need-based). Part-time jobs available.
APPLYING FOR FINANCIAL AID *Required financial aid forms:* FAFSA, institution's own form. *Financial aid deadline:* Continuous. *Notification date:* Continuous.
CONTACT Barbara Stuart, Associate Director of Financial Aid, Sterling College, PO Box 72, Craftsbury Common, VT 05827, 800-648-3591 Ext. 2 or toll-free 800-648-3591 Ext. 100. *Fax:* 802-586-2596. *E-mail:* bstuart@sterlingcollege.edu. *Website:* http://www.sterlingcollege.edu/.

STETSON UNIVERSITY
DeLand, FL

Tuition & fees: $36,644	Average undergraduate aid package: $32,011

ABOUT THE INSTITUTION Independent, coed. *Awards:* certificates, bachelor's, master's, and doctoral degrees. 56 undergraduate majors. *Total enrollment:* 3,961. Undergraduates: 2,516. Freshmen: 818. Federal methodology is used as a basis for awarding need-based institutional aid.
UNDERGRADUATE EXPENSES for 2013–2014 *Application fee:* $50. *Comprehensive fee:* $47,332 includes full-time tuition ($36,344), mandatory fees ($300), and room and board ($10,688). *College room only:* $6088. Room and board charges vary according to board plan and housing facility. *Part-time tuition:* $3785 per course. Part-time tuition and fees vary according to course load, location, and program.
FRESHMAN FINANCIAL AID (Fall 2012, est.) 762 applied for aid; of those 84% were deemed to have need. 100% of freshmen with need received aid; of those 25% had need fully met. *Average percent of need met:* 83% (excluding resources awarded to replace EFC). *Average financial aid package:* $33,011 (excluding resources awarded to replace EFC). 18% of all full-time freshmen had no need and received non-need-based gift aid.
UNDERGRADUATE FINANCIAL AID (Fall 2012, est.) 2,167 applied for aid; of those 86% were deemed to have need. 100% of undergraduates with need received aid; of those 22% had need fully met. *Average percent of need met:* 80% (excluding resources awarded to replace EFC). *Average financial aid package:* $32,011 (excluding resources awarded to replace EFC). 18% of all full-time undergraduates had no need and received non-need-based gift aid.
GIFT AID (NEED-BASED) *Total amount:* $43,940,638 (10% federal, 12% state, 77% institutional, 1% external sources). *Receiving aid:* Freshmen: 78% (636); all full-time undergraduates: 75% (1,852). *Average award:* Freshmen: $26,247; Undergrad-

uates: $24,768. *Scholarships, grants, and awards:* Federal Pell, FSEOG, state, private, college/university gift aid from institutional funds.
GIFT AID (NON-NEED-BASED) *Total amount:* $12,828,803 (14% state, 84% institutional, 2% external sources). *Receiving aid:* Freshmen: 18% (149). Undergraduates: 13% (332). *Average award:* Freshmen: $20,835. Undergraduates: $18,327. *Scholarships, grants, and awards by category: Academic interests/achievement:* area/ethnic studies, biological sciences, business, communication, computer science, education, English, foreign languages, general academic interests/achievements, humanities, mathematics, military science, physical sciences, premedicine, religion/biblical studies, social sciences. *Creative arts/performance:* applied art and design, art/fine arts, music, theater/drama. *Special achievements/activities:* cheerleading/drum major, community service, general special achievements/activities, leadership, religious involvement. *Special characteristics:* children and siblings of alumni, children of faculty/staff, ethnic background, general special characteristics, international students, local/state students, members of minority groups. *Tuition waivers:* Full or partial for employees or children of employees. *ROTC:* Army cooperative.
LOANS *Student loans:* $14,845,380 (78% need-based, 22% non-need-based). 77% of past graduating class borrowed through all loan programs. *Average indebtedness per student:* $32,750. *Average need-based loan:* Freshmen: $4020. Undergraduates: $4824. *Parent loans:* $3,799,100 (46% need-based, 54% non-need-based). *Programs:* Federal Direct (Subsidized and Unsubsidized Stafford, PLUS), Perkins.
WORK-STUDY *Federal work-study:* Total amount: $2,196,174; 1,061 jobs averaging $2070. *State or other work-study/employment:* Total amount: $607,515 (30% need-based, 70% non-need-based). 201 part-time jobs averaging $3032.
ATHLETIC AWARDS Total amount: $4,576,713 (43% need-based, 57% non-need-based).
APPLYING FOR FINANCIAL AID *Required financial aid forms:* FAFSA, institution's own form. *Financial aid deadline (priority):* 3/15. *Notification date:* Continuous beginning 2/15. Students must reply within 2 weeks of notification.
CONTACT Tara Jones, Director of Financial Aid, Stetson University, 421 North Woodland Boulevard, DeLand, FL 32723, 386-822-7120 or toll-free 800-688-0101. *Fax:* 386-822-7126. *E-mail:* finaid@stetson.edu. *Website:* http://www.stetson.edu/.

STEVENS-HENAGER COLLEGE–BOISE
Boise, ID

CONTACT Ms. Jaime L. Davis, Training and Project Development, Stevens-Henager College–Boise, 1444 South Entertainment Avenue, Boise, ID 83709, 208-383-4540 Ext. 1875 or toll-free 800-622-2670 (in-state), 800-622-2640 (out-of-state). *Fax:* 208-345-6999. *E-mail:* jaime.davis@stevenshenager.edu. *Website:* http://www.stevenshenager.edu/.

STEVENS-HENAGER COLLEGE–OGDEN/WEST HAVEN
Ogden, UT

CONTACT Financial Aid Office, Stevens-Henager College–Ogden/West Haven, 1890 South 1350 West, Ogden, UT 84401, 801-394-7791 or toll-free 800-622-2640. *Website:* http://www.stevenshenager.edu/.

STEVENS INSTITUTE OF BUSINESS & ARTS
St. Louis, MO

CONTACT Financial Aid Office, Stevens Institute of Business & Arts, 1521 Washington Avenue, St. Louis, MO 63102, 314-421-0949 or toll-free 800-871-0949. *Website:* http://www.siba.edu/.

STEVENS INSTITUTE OF TECHNOLOGY

STEVENS INSTITUTE OF TECHNOLOGY
Hoboken, NJ

CONTACT Ms. Adrienne Hynek, Associate Director of Financial Aid, Stevens Institute of Technology, Castle Point on Hudson, Hoboken, NJ 07030, 201-216-5555 or toll-free 800-458-5323. *Fax:* 201-216-8050. *E-mail:* ahynek@stevens.edu. *Website:* http://www.stevens.edu/.

STEVENSON UNIVERSITY
Stevenson, MD

Tuition & fees: $25,310	Average undergraduate aid package: $15,500

ABOUT THE INSTITUTION Independent, coed. *Awards:* bachelor's and master's degrees. 21 undergraduate majors. *Total enrollment:* 4,418. Undergraduates: 3,904. Freshmen: 861. Federal methodology is used as a basis for awarding need-based institutional aid.

UNDERGRADUATE EXPENSES for 2013–2014 *Application fee:* $40. *Comprehensive fee:* $37,204 includes full-time tuition ($23,562), mandatory fees ($1748), and room and board ($11,894). *College room only:* $7888. Full-time tuition and fees vary according to degree level. Room and board charges vary according to board plan and housing facility. *Part-time tuition:* $596 per credit hour. *Part-time fees:* $75 per term. Part-time tuition and fees vary according to course load and degree level.

FRESHMAN FINANCIAL AID (Fall 2011) 816 applied for aid; of those 89% were deemed to have need. 100% of freshmen with need received aid; of those 10% had need fully met. *Average percent of need met:* 59% (excluding resources awarded to replace EFC). *Average financial aid package:* $16,803 (excluding resources awarded to replace EFC). 16% of all full-time freshmen had no need and received non-need-based gift aid.

UNDERGRADUATE FINANCIAL AID (Fall 2011) 2,715 applied for aid; of those 89% were deemed to have need. 100% of undergraduates with need received aid; of those 9% had need fully met. *Average percent of need met:* 57% (excluding resources awarded to replace EFC). *Average financial aid package:* $15,500 (excluding resources awarded to replace EFC). 19% of all full-time undergraduates had no need and received non-need-based gift aid.

GIFT AID (NEED-BASED) *Total amount:* $28,697,138 (18% federal, 11% state, 68% institutional, 3% external sources). *Receiving aid:* Freshmen: 83% (718); all full-time undergraduates: 73% (2,328). *Average award:* Freshmen: $13,707; Undergraduates: $12,197. *Scholarships, grants, and awards:* Federal Pell, FSEOG, state, private, college/university gift aid from institutional funds.

GIFT AID (NON-NEED-BASED) *Total amount:* $5,868,135 (2% state, 91% institutional, 7% external sources). *Receiving aid:* Freshmen: 8% (67). Undergraduates: 6% (192). *Average award:* Freshmen: $6868. Undergraduates: $7536. *Scholarships, grants, and awards by category:* Academic interests/achievement: 2,346 awards ($16,503,211 total): general academic interests/achievements. Creative arts/performance: 9 awards ($15,000 total): art/fine arts. *Tuition waivers:* Full or partial for employees or children of employees. *ROTC:* Army cooperative, Air Force cooperative.

LOANS *Student loans:* $21,262,323 (75% need-based, 25% non-need-based). 69% of past graduating class borrowed through all loan programs. *Average indebtedness per student:* $28,032. *Average need-based loan:* Freshmen: $3262. Undergraduates: $4035. *Parent loans:* $14,740,092 (47% need-based, 53% non-need-based). *Programs:* Federal Direct (Subsidized and Unsubsidized Stafford, PLUS), Perkins.

WORK-STUDY *Federal work-study:* Total amount: $274,366; 142 jobs averaging $1932.

APPLYING FOR FINANCIAL AID *Required financial aid form:* FAFSA. *Financial aid deadline (priority):* 2/15. *Notification date:* Continuous beginning 3/15. Students must reply by 5/1 or within 2 weeks of notification.

CONTACT Ms. Barbara L. Miller, Director of Financial Aid, Stevenson University, 100 Campus Circle, Owings Mills, MD 21117, 443-352-4369 or toll-free 877-468-6852 (in-state), 877-468-3852 (out-of-state). *Fax:* 443-352-4370. *E-mail:* blmiller@stevenson.edu. *Website:* http://www.stevenson.edu/.

STILLMAN COLLEGE
Tuscaloosa, AL

ABOUT THE INSTITUTION Independent Presbyterian Church (U.S.A.), coed. *Awards:* bachelor's degrees. 14 undergraduate majors. *Total enrollment:* 1,072. Undergraduates: 1,072. Freshmen: 305.

GIFT AID (NEED-BASED) *Scholarships, grants, and awards:* Federal Pell, FSEOG, state, private, college/university gift aid from institutional funds, United Negro College Fund.

GIFT AID (NON-NEED-BASED) *Scholarships, grants, and awards by category:* Academic interests/achievement: education, general academic interests/achievements. Creative arts/performance: music. *Special characteristics:* children of faculty/staff.

LOANS *Programs:* Federal Direct (Subsidized and Unsubsidized Stafford, PLUS), Perkins.

WORK-STUDY *Federal work-study:* Total amount: $213,000; 169 jobs averaging $1056.

APPLYING FOR FINANCIAL AID *Required financial aid forms:* FAFSA, state aid form.

CONTACT Jacqueline S. Morris, Director of Financial Aid, Stillman College, PO Box 1430, Tuscaloosa, AL 35403, 205-366-8950 or toll-free 800-841-5722. *Fax:* 205-247-8106. *E-mail:* jmorris@stillman.edu. *Website:* http://www.stillman.edu/.

STONEHILL COLLEGE
Easton, MA

Tuition & fees: $36,160	Average undergraduate aid package: $26,199

ABOUT THE INSTITUTION Independent Roman Catholic, coed. *Awards:* bachelor's degrees. 35 undergraduate majors. *Total enrollment:* 2,599. Undergraduates: 2,599. Freshmen: 814. Institutional methodology is used as a basis for awarding need-based institutional aid.

UNDERGRADUATE EXPENSES for 2013–2014 *Application fee:* $60. *Comprehensive fee:* $49,970 includes full-time tuition ($36,160) and room and board ($13,810). Room and board charges vary according to board plan. *Part-time tuition:* $1205 per credit. Part-time tuition and fees vary according to course load. *Payment plan:* Tuition prepayment.

FRESHMAN FINANCIAL AID (Fall 2012, est.) 691 applied for aid; of those 72% were deemed to have need. 100% of freshmen with need received aid; of those 48% had need fully met. *Average percent of need met:* 90% (excluding resources awarded to replace EFC). *Average financial aid package:* $27,392 (excluding resources awarded to replace EFC). 27% of all full-time freshmen had no need and received non-need-based gift aid.

UNDERGRADUATE FINANCIAL AID (Fall 2012, est.) 2,090 applied for aid; of those 72% were deemed to have need. 100% of undergraduates with need received aid; of those 48% had need fully met. *Average percent of need met:* 90% (excluding resources awarded to replace EFC). *Average financial aid package:* $26,199 (excluding resources awarded to replace EFC). 29% of all full-time undergraduates had no need and received non-need-based gift aid.

GIFT AID (NEED-BASED) *Total amount:* $28,037,149 (7% federal, 3% state, 88% institutional, 2% external sources). *Receiving aid:* Freshmen: 50% (409); all full-time undergraduates: 48% (1,231). *Average award:* Freshmen: $22,796; Undergraduates: $20,657. *Scholarships, grants, and awards:* Federal Pell, FSEOG, state, private, college/university gift aid from institutional funds.

GIFT AID (NON-NEED-BASED) *Total amount:* $9,925,170 (3% federal, 95% institutional, 2% external sources). *Receiving aid:* Freshmen: 11% (89). Undergraduates: 10% (261). *Average award:* Freshmen: $12,762. Undergraduates: $10,836. *Scholarships, grants, and awards by category:* Academic interests/achievement: general academic interests/achievements. *Special characteristics:* children of faculty/staff, children of union members/company employees, relatives of clergy, siblings of current students, veterans, veterans' children. *Tuition waivers:* Full or partial for employees or children of employees. *ROTC:* Army.

LOANS *Student loans:* $15,712,255 (49% need-based, 51% non-need-based). 73% of past graduating class borrowed through all loan programs. *Average indebtedness per student:* $27,794. *Average need-based loan:* Freshmen: $4359. Undergraduates: $5002. *Parent loans:* $10,639,047 (11% need-based, 89% non-need-based).

Programs: Federal Direct (Subsidized and Unsubsidized Stafford, PLUS), Perkins, state.
WORK-STUDY *Federal work-study:* Total amount: $1,653,520; jobs available. *State or other work-study/employment:* Total amount: $384,380 (6% need-based, 94% non-need-based). Part-time jobs available.
ATHLETIC AWARDS Total amount: $2,339,759 (12% need-based, 88% non-need-based).
APPLYING FOR FINANCIAL AID *Required financial aid forms:* FAFSA, CSS Financial Aid PROFILE, noncustodial (divorced/separated) parent's statement. *Financial aid deadline (priority):* 2/1. *Notification date:* 4/1. Students must reply by 5/1.
CONTACT Rhonda Nickley, Office Manager, Stonehill College, 320 Washington Street, Easton, MA 02357, 508-565-1088. *Fax:* 508-565-1426. *E-mail:* finaid@stonehill.edu.
Website: http://www.stonehill.edu/.

STONY BROOK UNIVERSITY, STATE UNIVERSITY OF NEW YORK
Stony Brook, NY

Tuition & fees (NY res): $7560	Average undergraduate aid package: $11,473

ABOUT THE INSTITUTION State-supported, coed. *Awards:* certificates, bachelor's, master's, and doctoral degrees. 80 undergraduate majors. *Total enrollment:* 24,149. Undergraduates: 16,003. Freshmen: 2,676. Federal methodology is used as a basis for awarding need-based institutional aid.
UNDERGRADUATE EXPENSES for 2013–2014 *Application fee:* $50. *Tuition, state resident:* full-time $5570; part-time $232 per credit hour. *Tuition, nonresident:* full-time $16,190; part-time $675 per credit hour. *Required fees:* full-time $1990; $97.55 per credit hour. Full-time tuition and fees vary according to course load. Part-time tuition and fees vary according to course load. *College room and board:* $10,934; *Room only:* $6968. Room and board charges vary according to board plan and housing facility.
FRESHMAN FINANCIAL AID (Fall 2012, est.) 2,165 applied for aid; of those 72% were deemed to have need. 100% of freshmen with need received aid; of those 17% had need fully met. *Average percent of need met:* 69% (excluding resources awarded to replace EFC). *Average financial aid package:* $11,359 (excluding resources awarded to replace EFC). 18% of all full-time freshmen had no need and received non-need-based gift aid.
UNDERGRADUATE FINANCIAL AID (Fall 2012, est.) 10,424 applied for aid; of those 83% were deemed to have need. 98% of undergraduates with need received aid; of those 14% had need fully met. *Average percent of need met:* 65% (excluding resources awarded to replace EFC). *Average financial aid package:* $11,473 (excluding resources awarded to replace EFC). 8% of all full-time undergraduates had no need and received non-need-based gift aid.
GIFT AID (NEED-BASED) *Total amount:* $55,086,226 (48% federal, 41% state, 10% institutional, 1% external sources). *Receiving aid:* Freshmen: 53% (1,404); all full-time undergraduates: 52% (7,477). *Average award:* Freshmen: $7344; Undergraduates: $6905. *Scholarships, grants, and awards:* Federal Pell, FSEOG, state, private, college/university gift aid from institutional funds.
GIFT AID (NON-NEED-BASED) *Total amount:* $6,479,720 (4% federal, 4% state, 80% institutional, 12% external sources). *Receiving aid:* Freshmen: 4% (113). Undergraduates: 2% (319). *Average award:* Freshmen: $3935. Undergraduates: $3926. *Scholarships, grants, and awards by category:* Academic interests/achievement: area/ethnic studies, biological sciences, business, computer science, engineering/technologies, English, foreign languages, general academic interests/achievements, health fields, international studies, mathematics, physical sciences, social sciences. *Creative arts/performance:* cinema/film/broadcasting, journalism/publications, music. *Special achievements/activities:* community service, leadership. *Special characteristics:* ethnic background, general special characteristics. *ROTC:* Army, Naval cooperative, Air Force cooperative.
LOANS *Student loans:* $85,150,089 (75% need-based, 25% non-need-based). 59% of past graduating class borrowed through all loan programs. *Average indebtedness per student:* $20,954. *Average need-based loan:* Freshmen: $3585. Undergraduates: $4692. *Parent loans:* $5,824,018 (36% need-based, 64% non-need-based). *Programs:* Federal Direct (Subsidized and Unsubsidized Stafford, PLUS), Perkins.

WORK-STUDY *Federal work-study:* Total amount: $830,793; 392 jobs averaging $2119. *State or other work-study/employment:* Total amount: $5,143,575 (44% need-based, 56% non-need-based). 1,669 part-time jobs averaging $1986.
ATHLETIC AWARDS Total amount: $5,975,871 (42% need-based, 58% non-need-based).
APPLYING FOR FINANCIAL AID *Required financial aid form:* FAFSA. *Financial aid deadline (priority):* 3/1. *Notification date:* Continuous beginning 4/1. Students must reply within 2 weeks of notification.
CONTACT Office of Student Financial Aid and Scholarship Services, Stony Brook University, State University of New York, Administration Building, Room 180, Stony Brook, NY 11794, 631-632-6840. *Fax:* 631-632-9525. *E-mail:* finaid@stonybrook.edu. *Website:* http://www.sunysb.edu/.

STRATFORD UNIVERSITY
Baltimore, MD

CONTACT Kim Wittler, Director, Student Financial Planning, Stratford University, 17 Commerce Street, Baltimore, MD 21202, 410-752-0490 or toll-free 800-624-9926 (in-state), 800-624-9926 Ext. 120 (out-of-state). *Fax:* 410-752-3730.
Website: http://www.stratford.edu/.

STRATFORD UNIVERSITY
Falls Church, VA

Tuition & fees: N/R	Average undergraduate aid package: N/A

ABOUT THE INSTITUTION Proprietary, coed. *Awards:* certificates, diplomas, associate, bachelor's, and master's degrees. 12 undergraduate majors. *Total enrollment:* 955. Undergraduates: 604. Freshmen: 211. Federal methodology is used as a basis for awarding need-based institutional aid.
UNDERGRADUATE EXPENSES for 2013–2014 *Application fee:* $50. *Tuition:* part-time $370 per quarter hour. *Required fees:* $100 per degree program.
FRESHMAN FINANCIAL AID (Fall 2011) 17 applied for aid; of those 100% were deemed to have need. 100% of freshmen with need received aid.
GIFT AID (NEED-BASED) *Total amount:* $3,749,323 (100% federal). *Receiving aid:* Freshmen: 24% (12). *Average award:* Freshmen: $3675. *Scholarships, grants, and awards:* Federal Pell, FSEOG, state, private, college/university gift aid from institutional funds.
GIFT AID (NON-NEED-BASED) *Scholarships, grants, and awards by category:* Academic interests/achievement: 14 awards ($10,571 total): general academic interests/achievements. *Tuition waivers:* Full or partial for employees or children of employees.
LOANS *Student loans:* $12,915,206 (100% need-based). *Parent loans:* $939,544 (100% need-based). *Programs:* Federal Direct (Subsidized and Unsubsidized Stafford, PLUS).
WORK-STUDY *Federal work-study:* Total amount: $42,983; 14 jobs averaging $3070.
APPLYING FOR FINANCIAL AID *Required financial aid form:* FAFSA. *Financial aid deadline:* Continuous. *Notification date:* Continuous beginning 1/1.
CONTACT Ms. Noshuo Rivers, Corporate Financial Director, Stratford University, 3201 Jermantown Road, Suite 500, Fairfax, VA 22030, 703-539-6890 or toll-free 800-444-0804. *Fax:* 703-539-6960. *E-mail:* studentaccounts@stratford.edu. *Website:* http://www.stratford.edu/.

STRATFORD UNIVERSITY
Glen Allen, VA

CONTACT Financial Aid Office, Stratford University, 11104 W. Broad Street, Glen Allen, VA 23060, 804-290-4231 or toll-free 877-373-5173.
Website: http://www.stratford.edu/.

STRATFORD UNIVERSITY
Newport News, VA

CONTACT Financial Aid Office, Stratford University, 836 J. Clyde Morris Boulevard, Newport News, VA 23601, 757-873-4235 or toll-free 855-873-4235.
Website: http://www.stratford.edu/.

STRATFORD UNIVERSITY
Woodbridge, VA

CONTACT Financial Aid Office, Stratford University, 14349 Gideon Drive, Woodbridge, VA 22192 or toll-free 888-546-1250.
Website: http://www.stratford.edu/.

STRAYER UNIVERSITY - AKRON CAMPUS
Akron, OH

CONTACT Financial Aid Office, Strayer University - Akron Campus, 51 Park West Boulevard, Akron, OH 44320, 330-734-6700.
Website: http://www.strayer.edu/campus/akron.

STRAYER UNIVERSITY - ALEXANDRIA CAMPUS
Alexandria, VA

CONTACT Financial Aid Office, Strayer University - Alexandria Campus, 2730 Eisenhower Avenue, Alexandria, VA 22314, 703-317-2626.
Website: http://www.strayer.edu/campus/alexandria.

STRAYER UNIVERSITY - ALLENTOWN CAMPUS
Center Valley, PA

CONTACT Financial Aid Office, Strayer University - Allentown Campus, 3800 Sierra Circle, Suite 300, Center Valley, PA 18034, 484-809-7770.
Website: http://www.strayer.edu/campus/allentown/.

STRAYER UNIVERSITY - ANNE ARUNDEL CAMPUS
Millersville, MD

CONTACT Financial Aid Office, Strayer University - Anne Arundel Campus, 1520 Jabez Run, Millersville, MD 21108, 410-923-4500.
Website: http://www.strayer.edu/campus/anne-arundel.

STRAYER UNIVERSITY - ARLINGTON CAMPUS
Arlington, VA

CONTACT Financial Aid Office, Strayer University - Arlington Campus, 2121 15th Street North, Arlington, VA 22201, 703-892-5100.
Website: http://www.strayer.edu/campus/arlington.

STRAYER UNIVERSITY - AUGUSTA CAMPUS
Augusta, GA

CONTACT Financial Aid Office, Strayer University - Augusta Campus, 1330 Augusta West Parkway, Augusta, GA 30909, 706-855-8233.
Website: http://www.strayer.edu/campus/augusta/.

STRAYER UNIVERSITY - BAYMEADOWS CAMPUS
Jacksonville, FL

CONTACT Financial Aid Office, Strayer University - Baymeadows Campus, 8375 Dix Ellis Trail, Suite 200, Jacksonville, FL 32256, 904-538-1000.
Website: http://www.strayer.edu/campus/baymeadows/.

STRAYER UNIVERSITY - BIRMINGHAM CAMPUS
Birmingham, AL

CONTACT Financial Aid Office, Strayer University - Birmingham Campus, 3570 Grandview Parkway, Suite 200, Birmingham, AL 35243, 205-453-6300.
Website: http://www.strayer.edu/campus/birmingham/.

STRAYER UNIVERSITY - BRICKELL CAMPUS
Miami, FL

CONTACT Financial Aid Office, Strayer University - Brickell Campus, 1201 Brickell Avenue, Suite 700, Miami, FL 33131, 305-507-5800.
Website: http://www.strayer.edu/campus/brickell.

STRAYER UNIVERSITY - CENTER CITY CAMPUS
Philadelphia, PA

CONTACT Financial Aid Office, Strayer University - Center City Campus, 1601 Cherry Street, Suite 100, Philadelphia, PA 19102, 267-256-0200.
Website: http://www.strayer.edu/campus/center-city.

STRAYER UNIVERSITY - CHAMBLEE CAMPUS
Atlanta, GA

CONTACT Financial Aid Office, Strayer University - Chamblee Campus, 3355 Northeast Expressway, Suite 100, Atlanta, GA 30341, 770-454-9270.
Website: http://www.strayer.edu/campus/chamblee/.

STRAYER UNIVERSITY - CHARLESTON CAMPUS

North Charleston, SC

CONTACT Financial Aid Office, Strayer University - Charleston Campus, 5010 Wetland Crossing, North Charleston, SC 29418, 843-746-5100. *Website:* http://www.strayer.edu/campus/charleston/.

STRAYER UNIVERSITY - CHERRY HILL CAMPUS

Cherry Hill, NJ

CONTACT Financial Aid Office, Strayer University - Cherry Hill Campus, 2201 Route 38, Suite 100, Cherry Hill, NJ 08002, 856-482-4200. *Website:* http://www.strayer.edu/campus/cherry-hill/.

STRAYER UNIVERSITY - CHESAPEAKE CAMPUS

Chesapeake, VA

CONTACT Financial Aid Office, Strayer University - Chesapeake Campus, 676 Independence Parkway, Suite 300, Chesapeake, VA 23320, 757-382-9900. *Website:* http://www.strayer.edu/campus/chesapeake/.

STRAYER UNIVERSITY - CHESTERFIELD CAMPUS

Midlothian, VA

CONTACT Financial Aid Office, Strayer University - Chesterfield Campus, 2820 Waterford Lake Drive, Suite 100, Midlothian, VA 23112, 804-763-6300. *Website:* http://www.strayer.edu/campus/chesterfield/.

STRAYER UNIVERSITY - CHRISTIANA CAMPUS

Newark, DE

CONTACT Financial Aid Office, Strayer University - Christiana Campus, 240 Continental Drive, Suite 108, Newark, DE 19713, 302-292-6100. *Website:* http://www.strayer.edu/campus/christiana.

STRAYER UNIVERSITY - COBB COUNTY CAMPUS

Atlanta, GA

CONTACT Financial Aid Office, Strayer University - Cobb County Campus, 3101 Towercreek Parkway, SE, Suite 700, Atlanta, GA 30339-3256, 770-612-2170. *Website:* http://www.strayer.edu/campus/cobb-county/.

STRAYER UNIVERSITY - COLUMBIA CAMPUS

Columbia, SC

CONTACT Financial Aid Office, Strayer University - Columbia Campus, 200 Center Point Circle, Suite 300, Columbia, SC 29210, 803-750-2500. *Website:* http://www.strayer.edu/campus/columbia.

STRAYER UNIVERSITY - COLUMBUS CAMPUS

Columbus, OH

CONTACT Financial Aid Office, Strayer University - Columbus Campus, 8425 Pulsar Place, Suite 400, Columbus, OH 43240, 614-310-6700. *Website:* http://www.strayer.edu/campus/columbus/.

STRAYER UNIVERSITY - CORAL SPRINGS CAMPUS

Coral Springs, FL

CONTACT Financial Aid Office, Strayer University - Coral Springs Campus, 5830 Coral Ridge Drive, Suite 300, Coral Springs, FL 33076, 954-369-0700. *Website:* http://www.strayer.edu/campus/coral-springs/.

STRAYER UNIVERSITY - DELAWARE COUNTY CAMPUS

Springfield, PA

CONTACT Financial Aid Office, Strayer University - Delaware County Campus, 760 West Sproul Road, Suite 200, Springfield, PA 19064-1215, 610-604-7700. *Website:* http://www.strayer.edu/campus/delaware-county.

STRAYER UNIVERSITY - DORAL CAMPUS

Miami, FL

CONTACT Financial Aid Office, Strayer University - Doral Campus, 11430 Northwest 20th Street, Suite 150, Miami, FL 33172, 305-507-5700. *Website:* http://www.strayer.edu/campus/doral.

STRAYER UNIVERSITY - DOUGLASVILLE CAMPUS

Douglasville, GA

CONTACT Financial Aid Office, Strayer University - Douglasville Campus, 4655 Timber Ridge Drive, Douglasville, GA 30135, 678-715-2200. *Website:* http://www.strayer.edu/campus/douglasville/.

STRAYER UNIVERSITY - FAIRVIEW PARK CAMPUS

Fairview Park, OH

CONTACT Financial Aid Office, Strayer University - Fairview Park Campus, 22730 Fairview Center Drive, Suite 150, Fairview Park, OH 44126-3616, 440-471-6400. *Website:* http://www.strayer.edu/campus/fairview-park.

STRAYER UNIVERSITY - FLORENCE CAMPUS

Florence, KY

CONTACT Financial Aid Office, Strayer University - Florence Campus, 7300 Turfway Road, Suite 250, Florence, KY 41042, 859-692-2800. *Website:* http://www.strayer.edu/campus/florence.

STRAYER UNIVERSITY - FORT LAUDERDALE CAMPUS

Fort Lauderdale, FL

CONTACT Financial Aid Office, Strayer University - Fort Lauderdale Campus, 2307 West Broward Boulevard, Suite 100, Fort Lauderdale, FL 33312, 954-745-6960. *Website:* http://www.strayer.edu/campus/fort-lauderdale/.

STRAYER UNIVERSITY - FREDERICKSBURG CAMPUS

Fredericksburg, VA

CONTACT Financial Aid Office, Strayer University - Fredericksburg Campus, 150 Riverside Parkway, Suite 100, Fredericksburg, VA 22406, 540-374-4300. *Website:* http://www.strayer.edu/campus/fredericksburg.

STRAYER UNIVERSITY - GREENSBORO CAMPUS

Greensboro, NC

CONTACT Financial Aid Office, Strayer University - Greensboro Campus, 4900 Koger Boulevard, Suite 400, Greensboro, NC 27407, 336-315.7800. *Website:* http://www.strayer.edu/campus/greensboro.

STRAYER UNIVERSITY - GREENVILLE CAMPUS

Greenville, SC

CONTACT Financial Aid Office, Strayer University - Greenville Campus, 555 North Pleasantburg Drive, Suite 300, Greenville, SC 29607, 864-250-7000. *Website:* http://www.strayer.edu/campus/greenville.

STRAYER UNIVERSITY - HENRICO CAMPUS

Glen Allen, VA

CONTACT Financial Aid Office, Strayer University - Henrico Campus, 11501 Nuckols Road, Glen Allen, VA 23059, 804-527-1000. *Website:* http://www.strayer.edu/campus/henrico.

STRAYER UNIVERSITY - HUNTERSVILLE CAMPUS

Huntersville, NC

CONTACT Financial Aid Office, Strayer University - Huntersville Campus, 13620 Reese Boulevard, Suite 130, Huntersville, NC 28078, 704-379-6800. *Website:* http://www.strayer.edu/campus/huntersville/.

STRAYER UNIVERSITY - HUNTSVILLE CAMPUS

Huntsville, AL

CONTACT Financial Aid Office, Strayer University - Huntsville Campus, 4955 Corporate Drive, NW, Suite 200, Huntsville, AL 35805, 256-665-9800. *Website:* http://www.strayer.edu/campus/huntsville/.

STRAYER UNIVERSITY - IRVING CAMPUS

Irving, TX

CONTACT Financial Aid Office, Strayer University - Irving Campus, 7701 Las Colinas Ridge, Suite 450, Irving, TX 75063, 214-429-3900. *Website:* http://www.strayer.edu/campus/irving.

STRAYER UNIVERSITY - JACKSON CAMPUS

Jackson, MS

CONTACT Financial Aid Office, Strayer University - Jackson Campus, 460 Briarwood Drive, Suite 200, Jackson, MS 39206, 601-718-5900. *Website:* http://www.strayer.edu/campus/jackson.

STRAYER UNIVERSITY - KING OF PRUSSIA CAMPUS

King of Prussia, PA

CONTACT Financial Aid Office, Strayer University - King of Prussia Campus, 234 Mall Boulevard, Suite G-50, King of Prussia, PA 19406, 610-992-1700. *Website:* http://www.strayer.edu/campus/king-prussia.

STRAYER UNIVERSITY - KNOXVILLE CAMPUS

Knoxville, TN

CONTACT Financial Aid Office, Strayer University - Knoxville Campus, 10118 Parkside Drive, Suite 200, Knoxville, TN 37922, 865-288-6000. *Website:* http://www.strayer.edu/campus/knoxville/.

STRAYER UNIVERSITY - LAWRENCEVILLE CAMPUS

Lawrenceville, NJ

CONTACT Financial Aid Office, Strayer University - Lawrenceville Campus, 3150 Brunswick Pike, Suite 100, Lawrenceville, NJ 08648, 609-406-7600. *Website:* http://www.strayer.edu/campus/lawrenceville.

STRAYER UNIVERSITY - LEXINGTON CAMPUS

Lexington, KY

CONTACT Financial Aid Office, Strayer University - Lexington Campus, 220 Lexington Green Circle, Suite 550, Lexington, KY 40503, 859-971-4400. *Website:* http://www.strayer.edu/campus/lexington/.

STRAYER UNIVERSITY - LITHONIA CAMPUS

Lithonia, GA

CONTACT Financial Aid Office, Strayer University - Lithonia Campus, 3120 Stonecrest Boulevard, Suite 200, Lithonia, GA 30038, 678-323-7700. *Website:* http://www.strayer.edu/campus/lithonia/.

STRAYER UNIVERSITY - LITTLE ROCK CAMPUS

Little Rock, AR

CONTACT Financial Aid Office, Strayer University - Little Rock Campus, 10825 Financial Centre Parkway, Suite 131, Little Rock, AR 72211. *Website:* http://www.strayer.edu/campus/little-rock.

STRAYER UNIVERSITY - LOUDOUN CAMPUS

Ashburn, VA

CONTACT Financial Aid Office, Strayer University - Loudoun Campus, 45150 Russell Branch Parkway, Suite 200, Ashburn, VA 20147, 703-729-8800. *Website:* http://www.strayer.edu/campus/loudoun.

STRAYER UNIVERSITY - LOUISVILLE CAMPUS

Louisville, KY

CONTACT Financial Aid Office, Strayer University - Louisville Campus, 2650 Eastpoint Parkway, Suite 100, Louisville, KY 40223, 502-253-5000. *Website:* http://www.strayer.edu/campus/louisville/.

STRAYER UNIVERSITY - LOWER BUCKS COUNTY CAMPUS

Trevose, PA

CONTACT Financial Aid Office, Strayer University - Lower Bucks County Campus, 3800 Horizon Boulevard, Suite 100, Trevose, PA 19053, 215-953-5999. *Website:* http://www.strayer.edu/campus/lower-bucks-county/.

STRAYER UNIVERSITY - MAITLAND CAMPUS

Maitland, FL

CONTACT Financial Aid Office, Strayer University - Maitland Campus, 850 Trafalgar Court, Suite 360, Maitland, FL 32751, 407-618-5900. *Website:* http://www.strayer.edu/campus/maitland/.

STRAYER UNIVERSITY - MANASSAS CAMPUS

Manassas, VA

CONTACT Financial Aid Office, Strayer University - Manassas Campus, 9990 Battleview Parkway, Manassas, VA 20109, 703-330-8400. *Website:* http://www.strayer.edu/campus/manassas.

STRAYER UNIVERSITY - MASON CAMPUS

Mason, OH

CONTACT Financial Aid Office, Strayer University - Mason Campus, 4605 Duke Drive, Suite 700, Mason, OH 45040, 513-234-6450. *Website:* http://www.strayer.edu/campus/mason/.

STRAYER UNIVERSITY - METAIRIE CAMPUS

Metairie, LA

CONTACT Financial Aid Office, Strayer University - Metairie Campus, 111 Veterans Memorial Boulevard, Suite 420, Metairie, LA 70005, 504-799-1700. *Website:* http://www.strayer.edu/campus/metairie.

STRAYER UNIVERSITY - MIRAMAR CAMPUS

Miramar, FL

CONTACT Financial Aid Office, Strayer University - Miramar Campus, 15620 Southwest 29th Street, Miramar, FL 33027, 954-378-2400. *Website:* http://www.strayer.edu/campus/miramar.

STRAYER UNIVERSITY - MORROW CAMPUS

Morrow, GA

CONTACT Financial Aid Office, Strayer University - Morrow Campus, 3000 Corporate Center Drive, Suite 100, Morrow, GA 30260, 678-422-4100. *Website:* http://www.strayer.edu/campus/morrow.

STRAYER UNIVERSITY - NASHVILLE CAMPUS

Nashville, TN

CONTACT Financial Aid Office, Strayer University - Nashville Campus, 1809 Dabbs Avenue, Nashville, TN 37210, 615-871-2260. *Website:* http://www.strayer.edu/campus/nashville.

STRAYER UNIVERSITY - NEWPORT NEWS CAMPUS

Newport News, VA

CONTACT Financial Aid Office, Strayer University - Newport News Campus, 99 Old Oyster Point Road, Unit 1, Newport News, VA 23602, 757-873-3100. *Website:* http://www.strayer.edu/campus/newport-news.

STRAYER UNIVERSITY - NORTH AUSTIN CAMPUS

Austin, TX

CONTACT Financial Aid Office, Strayer University - North Austin Campus, 8501 North Mo-pac Expressway, Suite 100, Austin, TX 78759, 512-568-3300. *Website:* http://www.strayer.edu/campus/north-austin.

STRAYER UNIVERSITY - NORTH CHARLOTTE CAMPUS

Concord, NC

CONTACT Financial Aid Office, Strayer University - North Charlotte Campus, 7870 Commons Park Circle NW, Concord, NC 28027, 704-886-6500. *Website:* http://www.strayer.edu/campus/north-charlotte.

STRAYER UNIVERSITY - NORTH RALEIGH CAMPUS

Raleigh, NC

CONTACT Financial Aid Office, Strayer University - North Raleigh Campus, 8701 Wadford Drive, Raleigh, NC 27616, 919-878-9900. *Website:* http://www.strayer.edu/campus/north-raleigh.

STRAYER UNIVERSITY - NORTHWEST HOUSTON CAMPUS

Houston, TX

CONTACT Financial Aid Office, Strayer University - Northwest Houston Campus, 10940 W. Sam Houston Parkway N., Suite 200, Houston, TX 77064, 281-949-1800. *Website:* http://www.strayer.edu/campus/northwest-houston.

STRAYER UNIVERSITY - ORLANDO EAST CAMPUS

Orlando, FL

CONTACT Financial Aid Office, Strayer University - Orlando East Campus, 2200 North Alafaya Trail, Suite 500, Orlando, FL 32826, 407-926-2000. *Website:* http://www.strayer.edu/campus/orlando-east/.

STRAYER UNIVERSITY - OWINGS MILLS CAMPUS

Owings Mills, MD

CONTACT Financial Aid Office, Strayer University - Owings Mills Campus, 500 Redland Court, Suite 100, Owings Mills, MD 21117, 443-394-3339. *Website:* http://www.strayer.edu/campus/owings-mills.

STRAYER UNIVERSITY - PALM BEACH GARDENS CAMPUS

Palm Beach Gardens, FL

CONTACT Financial Aid Office, Strayer University - Palm Beach Gardens Campus, 11025 RCA Center Drive, Suite 200, Palm Beach Gardens, FL 33410, 561-904-3000. *Website:* http://www.strayer.edu/campus/palm-beach-gardens.

STRAYER UNIVERSITY - PENN CENTER WEST CAMPUS

Pittsburgh, PA

CONTACT Financial Aid Office, Strayer University - Penn Center West Campus, One Penn Center West, Suite 320, Pittsburgh, PA 15276, 412-747-7800. *Website:* http://www.strayer.edu/campus/penn-center-west/.

STRAYER UNIVERSITY - PISCATAWAY CAMPUS
Piscataway, NJ

CONTACT Financial Aid Office, Strayer University - Piscataway Campus, 242 Old New Brunswick Road, Suite 220, Piscataway, NJ 08854, 732-743-3800. *Website:* http://www.strayer.edu/campus/piscataway.

STRAYER UNIVERSITY - PLANO CAMPUS
Plano, TX

CONTACT Financial Aid Office, Strayer University - Plano Campus, 2701 North Dallas Parkway, Suite 300, Plano, TX 75093, 972-535-3700. *Website:* http://www.strayer.edu/campus/plano.

STRAYER UNIVERSITY - PRINCE GEORGE'S CAMPUS
Suitland, MD

CONTACT Financial Aid Office, Strayer University - Prince George's Campus, 4710 Auth Place, First Floor, Suitland, MD 20746, 301-423-3600. *Website:* http://www.strayer.edu/campus/prince-georges.

STRAYER UNIVERSITY - ROCKVILLE CAMPUS
Rockville, MD

CONTACT Financial Aid Office, Strayer University - Rockville Campus, 4 Research Place, Suite 100, Rockville, MD 20850, 301-548-5500. *Website:* http://www.strayer.edu/campus/rockville.

STRAYER UNIVERSITY - ROSWELL CAMPUS
Roswell, GA

CONTACT Financial Aid Office, Strayer University - Roswell Campus, 100 Mansell Court East, Suite 100, Roswell, GA 30076, 770-650-3000. *Website:* http://www.strayer.edu/campus/roswell.

STRAYER UNIVERSITY - RTP CAMPUS
Morrisville, NC

CONTACT Financial Aid Office, Strayer University - RTP Campus, 4 Copley Parkway, Morrisville, NC 27560, 919-466-4400. *Website:* http://www.strayer.edu/campus/rtp.

STRAYER UNIVERSITY - SAND LAKE CAMPUS
Orlando, FL

CONTACT Financial Aid Office, Strayer University - Sand Lake Campus, 8541 South Park Circle, Building 900, Orlando, FL 32819, 407-264-9400. *Website:* http://www.strayer.edu/campus/sand-lake/.

STRAYER UNIVERSITY - SANDY CAMPUS
Sandy, UT

CONTACT Financial Aid Office, Strayer University - Sandy Campus, 9815 South Monroe Street, Suite 200, Sandy, UT 84070, 801-432-5000. *Website:* http://www.strayer.edu/campus/sandy.

STRAYER UNIVERSITY - SAVANNAH CAMPUS
Savannah, GA

CONTACT Financial Aid Office, Strayer University - Savannah Campus, 20 Martin Court, Savannah, GA 31419, 912-921-2900. *Website:* http://www.strayer.edu/campus/savannah/.

STRAYER UNIVERSITY - SHELBY CAMPUS
Memphis, TN

CONTACT Financial Aid Office, Strayer University - Shelby Campus, 7275 Appling Farms Parkway, Memphis, TN 38133, 901-383-6750. *Website:* http://www.strayer.edu/campus/shelby.

STRAYER UNIVERSITY - SOUTH CHARLOTTE CAMPUS
Charlotte, NC

CONTACT Financial Aid Office, Strayer University - South Charlotte Campus, 9101 Kings Parade Boulevard, Suite 200, Charlotte, NC 28273, 704-499-9200. *Website:* http://www.strayer.edu/campus/south-charlotte.

STRAYER UNIVERSITY - SOUTH RALEIGH CAMPUS
Raleigh, NC

CONTACT Financial Aid Office, Strayer University - South Raleigh Campus, 3421 Olympia Drive, Raleigh, NC 27603, 919-890-7500. *Website:* http://www.strayer.edu/campus/south-raleigh.

STRAYER UNIVERSITY - TAKOMA PARK CAMPUS
Washington, DC

CONTACT Financial Aid Office, Strayer University - Takoma Park Campus, 6830 Laurel Street, NW, Washington, DC 20012, 202-722-8100.
Website: http://www.strayer.edu/campus/takoma-park.

STRAYER UNIVERSITY - TAMPA EAST CAMPUS
Tampa, FL

CONTACT Financial Aid Office, Strayer University - Tampa East Campus, 6302 East Martin Luther King Boulevard, Suite 450, Tampa, FL 33619, 813-663-0100.
Website: http://www.strayer.edu/campus/tampa-east.

STRAYER UNIVERSITY - TAMPA WESTSHORE CAMPUS
Tampa, FL

CONTACT Financial Aid Office, Strayer University - Tampa Westshore Campus, 4902 Eisenhower Boulevard, Suite 100, Tampa, FL 33634, 813-882-0100.
Website: http://www.strayer.edu/campus/tampa-westshore.

STRAYER UNIVERSITY - TEAYS VALLEY CAMPUS
Scott Depot, WV

CONTACT Financial Aid Office, Strayer University - Teays Valley Campus, 100 Corporate Center Drive, Scott Depot, WV 25560, 304-760-1700.
Website: http://www.strayer.edu/campus/teays-valley.

STRAYER UNIVERSITY - THOUSAND OAKS CAMPUS
Memphis, TN

CONTACT Financial Aid Office, Strayer University - Thousand Oaks Campus, 2620 Thousand Oaks Boulevard, Suite 1100, Memphis, TN 38118, 901-369-0835.
Website: http://www.strayer.edu/campus/thousand-oaks.

STRAYER UNIVERSITY - VIRGINIA BEACH CAMPUS
Virginia Beach, VA

CONTACT Financial Aid Office, Strayer University - Virginia Beach Campus, 249 Central Park Avenue, Suite 350, Virginia Beach, VA 23462, 757-493-6000.
Website: http://www.strayer.edu/campus/virginia-beach.

STRAYER UNIVERSITY - WARRENDALE CAMPUS
Warrendale, PA

CONTACT Financial Aid Office, Strayer University - Warrendale Campus, 802 Warrendale Village Drive, Warrendale, PA 15086, 724-799-2900.
Website: http://www.strayer.edu/campus/warrendale.

STRAYER UNIVERSITY - WASHINGTON CAMPUS
Washington, DC

CONTACT Financial Aid Office, Strayer University - Washington Campus, 1133 15th Street, NW, Washington, DC 20025, 202-408-2400.
Website: http://www.strayer.edu/campus/washington.

STRAYER UNIVERSITY - WHITE MARSH CAMPUS
Baltimore, MD

CONTACT Financial Aid Office, Strayer University - White Marsh Campus, 9920 Franklin Square Drive, Suite 200, Baltimore, MD 21236, 410-238-9000.
Website: http://www.strayer.edu/campus/white-marsh.

STRAYER UNIVERSITY - WILLINGBORO CAMPUS
Willingboro, NJ

CONTACT Financial Aid Office, Strayer University - Willingboro Campus, 300 Willingboro Parkway, Willingboro Town Center, Suite 125, Willingboro, NJ 08046, 609-835-6000.
Website: http://www.strayer.edu/campus/willingboro.

STRAYER UNIVERSITY - WOODBRIDGE CAMPUS
Woodbridge, VA

CONTACT Financial Aid Office, Strayer University - Woodbridge Campus, 13385 Minnieville Road, Woodbridge, VA 22192, 703-878-2800.
Website: http://www.strayer.edu/campus/woodbridge.

SUFFOLK UNIVERSITY
Boston, MA

Tuition & fees: $30,792	Average undergraduate aid package: $22,115

ABOUT THE INSTITUTION Independent, coed. *Awards:* certificates, diplomas, associate, bachelor's, master's, and doctoral degrees (doctoral degree in law). 85 undergraduate majors. *Total enrollment:* 9,044. Undergraduates: 5,770. Freshmen: 1,240. Both federal and institutional methodology are used as a basis for awarding need-based institutional aid.
UNDERGRADUATE EXPENSES for 2013–2014 *Application fee:* $50. *One-time required fee:* $200. *Comprehensive fee:* $45,522 includes full-time tuition ($30,672), mandatory fees ($120), and room and board ($14,730). *College room*

only: $12,124. Room and board charges vary according to board plan and housing facility. Part-time tuition and fees vary according to course load.

FRESHMAN FINANCIAL AID (Fall 2012, est.) 952 applied for aid; of those 92% were deemed to have need. 100% of freshmen with need received aid; of those 6% had need fully met. *Average percent of need met:* 66% (excluding resources awarded to replace EFC). *Average financial aid package:* $23,479 (excluding resources awarded to replace EFC). 7% of all full-time freshmen had no need and received non-need-based gift aid.

UNDERGRADUATE FINANCIAL AID (Fall 2012, est.) 3,738 applied for aid; of those 93% were deemed to have need. 99% of undergraduates with need received aid; of those 9% had need fully met. *Average percent of need met:* 65% (excluding resources awarded to replace EFC). *Average financial aid package:* $22,115 (excluding resources awarded to replace EFC). 7% of all full-time undergraduates had no need and received non-need-based gift aid.

GIFT AID (NEED-BASED) Total amount: $46,695,608 (17% federal, 4% state, 78% institutional, 1% external sources). *Receiving aid:* Freshmen: 67% (829); all full-time undergraduates: 59% (3,188). *Average award:* Freshmen: $15,882; Undergraduates: $14,463. *Scholarships, grants, and awards:* Federal Pell, FSEOG, state, private, college/university gift aid from institutional funds.

GIFT AID (NON-NEED-BASED) Total amount: $15,224,059 (88% institutional, 12% external sources). *Receiving aid:* Freshmen: 25% (311). Undergraduates: 23% (1,244). *Average award:* Freshmen: $10,522. Undergraduates: $8872. *Scholarships, grants, and awards by category: Academic interests/achievement:* 1,435 awards ($13,318,297 total): engineering/technologies, general academic interests/achievements. *Special achievements/activities:* 3 awards ($15,000 total): community service. *Special characteristics:* 166 awards ($801,702 total): children and siblings of alumni, children of faculty/staff, siblings of current students. *Tuition waivers:* Full or partial for children of alumni, employees or children of employees, senior citizens. *ROTC:* Army cooperative.

LOANS Student loans: $36,867,036 (40% need-based, 60% non-need-based). 77% of past graduating class borrowed through all loan programs. *Average indebtedness per student:* $33,823. *Average need-based loan:* Freshmen: $3887. Undergraduates: $4677. *Parent loans:* $9,628,485 (100% non-need-based). *Programs:* Federal Direct (Subsidized and Unsubsidized Stafford, PLUS), Perkins, state, college/university.

WORK-STUDY Federal work-study: Total amount: $2,642,850; 1,104 jobs averaging $2394. *State or other work-study/employment:* Total amount: $1,337,709 (100% non-need-based). 428 part-time jobs averaging $3125.

APPLYING FOR FINANCIAL AID Required financial aid form: FAFSA. *Financial aid deadline:* 2/15. *Notification date:* Continuous beginning 2/5. Students must reply by 5/1 or within 2 weeks of notification.

CONTACT Ms. Christine A. Perry, Director of Student Financial Services, Suffolk University, 8 Ashburton Place, Boston, MA 02108, 617-573-8470 or toll-free 800-6-SUFFOLK. *Fax:* 617-720-3579. *E-mail:* finaid@suffolk.edu. *Website:* http://www.suffolk.edu/.

SULLIVAN UNIVERSITY
Louisville, KY

CONTACT Charlene Geiser, Financial Planning Office, Sullivan University, 3101 Bardstown Road, Louisville, KY 40205, 502-456-6504 Ext. 311 or toll-free 800-844-1354. *Fax:* 502-456-0040. *E-mail:* cgeiser@sullivan.edu. *Website:* http://www.sullivan.edu/.

SUL ROSS STATE UNIVERSITY
Alpine, TX

ABOUT THE INSTITUTION State-supported, coed. *Awards:* certificates, associate, bachelor's, and master's degrees. 34 undergraduate majors. *Total enrollment:* 1,782. Undergraduates: 1,236. Freshmen: 252.

GIFT AID (NEED-BASED) Scholarships, grants, and awards: Federal Pell, FSEOG, state, private, college/university gift aid from institutional funds.

GIFT AID (NON-NEED-BASED) Scholarships, grants, and awards by category: Academic interests/achievement: agriculture, biological sciences, business, education, English, foreign languages, general academic interests/achievements, health fields. *Creative arts/performance:* art/fine arts, cinema/film/broadcasting, journalism/

publications, music, theater/drama. *Special achievements/activities:* leadership. *Special characteristics:* local/state students.

LOANS Programs: Federal Direct (Subsidized and Unsubsidized Stafford, PLUS), Perkins, state, college/university.

APPLYING FOR FINANCIAL AID Required financial aid forms: FAFSA, institution's own form, business/farm supplement.

CONTACT Mickey Corbett, Director of Financial Aid, Sul Ross State University, Box C-2, Lawrence Hall, Alpine, TX 79832, 432-837-8055 or toll-free 888-722-7778. *Fax:* 432-837-8411. *E-mail:* fa@sulross.edu. *Website:* http://www.sulross.edu/.

SUSQUEHANNA UNIVERSITY
Selinsgrove, PA

ABOUT THE INSTITUTION Independent Evangelical Lutheran Church in America, coed. *Awards:* bachelor's degrees (also offers evening associate degree program limited to local adult students). 43 undergraduate majors. *Total enrollment:* 2,215. Undergraduates: 2,197. Freshmen: 631.

GIFT AID (NEED-BASED) Scholarships, grants, and awards: Federal Pell, FSEOG, state, private, college/university gift aid from institutional funds.

GIFT AID (NON-NEED-BASED) Scholarships, grants, and awards by category: Academic interests/achievement: business, general academic interests/achievements. *Creative arts/performance:* creative writing, music, theater/drama. *Special achievements/activities:* general special achievements/activities, leadership. *Special characteristics:* children and siblings of alumni, children of faculty/staff, members of minority groups, relatives of clergy, veterans.

LOANS Programs: Federal Direct (Subsidized and Unsubsidized Stafford, PLUS), Perkins, college/university.

WORK-STUDY Federal work-study: Total amount: $1,649,733; jobs available. *State or other work-study/employment:* Total amount: $460,561 (51% need-based, 49% non-need-based). Part-time jobs available.

APPLYING FOR FINANCIAL AID Required financial aid forms: FAFSA, CSS Financial Aid PROFILE, business/farm supplement, federal income tax form(s).

CONTACT Ms. Helen S. Nunn, Director of Financial Aid, Susquehanna University, 514 University Avenue, Selinsgrove, PA 17870, 570-372-4453 or toll-free 800-326-9672. *Fax:* 570-372-2722. *E-mail:* nunn@susqu.edu. *Website:* http://www.susqu.edu/.

SWARTHMORE COLLEGE
Swarthmore, PA

Tuition & fees: $43,080	Average undergraduate aid package: $39,255

ABOUT THE INSTITUTION Independent, coed. *Awards:* bachelor's degrees. 48 undergraduate majors. *Total enrollment:* 1,552. Undergraduates: 1,552. Freshmen: 378. Institutional methodology is used as a basis for awarding need-based institutional aid.

UNDERGRADUATE EXPENSES for 2013–2014 Application fee: $60. *Comprehensive fee:* $55,750 includes full-time tuition ($42,744), mandatory fees ($336), and room and board ($12,670). *College room only:* $6500. Room and board charges vary according to board plan.

FRESHMAN FINANCIAL AID (Fall 2012, est.) 251 applied for aid; of those 73% were deemed to have need. 100% of freshmen with need received aid; of those 100% had need fully met. *Average percent of need met:* 100% (excluding resources awarded to replace EFC). *Average financial aid package:* $39,427 (excluding resources awarded to replace EFC). 1% of all full-time freshmen had no need and received non-need-based gift aid.

UNDERGRADUATE FINANCIAL AID (Fall 2012, est.) 890 applied for aid; of those 89% were deemed to have need. 100% of undergraduates with need received aid; of those 100% had need fully met. *Average percent of need met:* 100% (excluding resources awarded to replace EFC). *Average financial aid package:* $39,255 (excluding resources awarded to replace EFC). 1% of all full-time undergraduates had no need and received non-need-based gift aid.

GIFT AID (NEED-BASED) Total amount: $29,549,088 (4% federal, 1% state, 93% institutional, 2% external sources). *Receiving aid:* Freshmen: 49% (184); all full-

time undergraduates: 51% (788). *Average award:* Freshmen: $37,775; Undergraduates: $37,651. *Scholarships, grants, and awards:* Federal Pell, FSEOG, state, private, college/university gift aid from institutional funds.
GIFT AID (NON-NEED-BASED) *Total amount:* $887,724 (58% institutional, 42% external sources). *Average award:* Freshmen: $42,744. Undergraduates: $42,744. *Scholarships, grants, and awards by category:* Academic interests/achievement: general academic interests/achievements. *ROTC:* Army cooperative, Naval cooperative, Air Force cooperative.
LOANS *Student loans:* $2,012,964 (100% non-need-based). 34% of past graduating class borrowed through all loan programs. *Average indebtedness per student:* $20,020. *Parent loans:* $1,573,408 (100% non-need-based). *Programs:* Federal Direct (Subsidized and Unsubsidized Stafford, PLUS), Perkins, college/university.
WORK-STUDY *Federal work-study:* Total amount: $881,811; 707 jobs averaging $1788. *State or other work-study/employment:* Total amount: $612,687 (82% need-based, 18% non-need-based). Part-time jobs available.
APPLYING FOR FINANCIAL AID *Required financial aid forms:* FAFSA, institution's own form, CSS Financial Aid PROFILE, state aid form, noncustodial (divorced/separated) parent's statement, business/farm supplement, federal income tax form(s), W-2 forms, year-end paycheck stub. *Financial aid deadline:* 2/15. *Notification date:* 4/1. Students must reply by 5/1.
CONTACT Laura Talbot, Director of Financial Aid, Swarthmore College, 500 College Avenue, Swarthmore, PA 19081-1397, 610-328-8358 or toll-free 800-667-3110. *Fax:* 610-690-5751. *E-mail:* finaid@swarthmore.edu.
Website: http://www.swarthmore.edu/.

SWEDISH INSTITUTE, COLLEGE OF HEALTH SCIENCES
New York, NY

CONTACT Financial Aid Office, Swedish Institute, College of Health Sciences, 226 West 26th Street, New York, NY 1000J-6700, 212-924-5900.
Website: http://www.swedishinstitute.org/.

SWEET BRIAR COLLEGE
Sweet Briar, VA

Tuition & fees: $32,325	Average undergraduate aid package: $25,289

ABOUT THE INSTITUTION Independent, women only. *Awards:* bachelor's and master's degrees. 37 undergraduate majors. *Total enrollment:* 739. Undergraduates: 723. Freshmen: 176. Federal methodology is used as a basis for awarding need-based institutional aid.
UNDERGRADUATE EXPENSES for 2013–2014 *Application fee:* $40. *Comprehensive fee:* $43,765 includes full-time tuition ($31,850), mandatory fees ($475), and room and board ($11,440). Room and board charges vary according to board plan. *Part-time tuition:* $885 per credit hour.
FRESHMAN FINANCIAL AID (Fall 2011) 185 applied for aid; of those 86% were deemed to have need. 100% of freshmen with need received aid; of those 18% had need fully met. *Average percent of need met:* 80% (excluding resources awarded to replace EFC). *Average financial aid package:* $26,448 (excluding resources awarded to replace EFC). 18% of all full-time freshmen had no need and received non-need-based gift aid.
UNDERGRADUATE FINANCIAL AID (Fall 2011) 501 applied for aid; of those 85% were deemed to have need. 100% of undergraduates with need received aid; of those 17% had need fully met. *Average percent of need met:* 78% (excluding resources awarded to replace EFC). *Average financial aid package:* $25,289 (excluding resources awarded to replace EFC). 26% of all full-time undergraduates had no need and received non-need-based gift aid.
GIFT AID (NEED-BASED) *Total amount:* $8,859,776 (8% federal, 6% state, 81% institutional, 5% external sources). *Receiving aid:* Freshmen: 82% (160); all full-time undergraduates: 70% (426). *Average award:* Freshmen: $22,129; Undergraduates: $20,738. *Scholarships, grants, and awards:* Federal Pell, FSEOG, state, private, college/university gift aid from institutional funds.
GIFT AID (NON-NEED-BASED) *Total amount:* $2,390,765 (12% state, 83% institutional, 5% external sources). *Receiving aid:* Freshmen: 15% (29). Undergrad-

uates: 10% (62). *Average award:* Freshmen: $11,883. Undergraduates: $11,187. *Scholarships, grants, and awards by category:* Academic interests/achievement: general academic interests/achievements, premedicine. *Creative arts/performance:* art/fine arts, general creative arts/performance, music. *Special achievements/activities:* community service. *Special characteristics:* adult students, general special characteristics, international students, local/state students. *Tuition waivers:* Full or partial for employees or children of employees, adult students, senior citizens.
LOANS *Student loans:* $3,022,406 (77% need-based, 23% non-need-based). 63% of past graduating class borrowed through all loan programs. *Average indebtedness per student:* $23,596. *Average need-based loan:* Freshmen: $4101. Undergraduates: $4655. *Parent loans:* $2,989,236 (27% need-based, 73% non-need-based). *Programs:* Federal Direct (Subsidized and Unsubsidized Stafford, PLUS), Perkins, college/university.
WORK-STUDY *Federal work-study:* Total amount: $74,807; 105 jobs averaging $712. *State or other work-study/employment:* Total amount: $115,828 (100% need-based). 124 part-time jobs averaging $934.
APPLYING FOR FINANCIAL AID *Required financial aid forms:* FAFSA, noncustodial (divorced/separated) parent's statement. *Financial aid deadline (priority):* 2/15. *Notification date:* Continuous beginning 3/1. Students must reply by 5/1 or within 2 weeks of notification.
CONTACT Bobbi Carpenter, Director of Financial Aid, Sweet Briar College, Box AS, Sweet Briar, VA 24595, 800-381-6156 or toll-free 800-381-6142. *Fax:* 434-381-6450. *E-mail:* bcarpenter@sbc.edu.
Website: http://www.sbc.edu/.

SYRACUSE UNIVERSITY
Syracuse, NY

Tuition & fees: $39,004	Average undergraduate aid package: $34,000

ABOUT THE INSTITUTION Independent, coed. *Awards:* certificates, bachelor's, master's, and doctoral degrees. 120 undergraduate majors. *Total enrollment:* 21,029. Undergraduates: 14,798. Freshmen: 3,392. Institutional methodology is used as a basis for awarding need-based institutional aid.
UNDERGRADUATE EXPENSES for 2013–2014 *Application fee:* $70. *Comprehensive fee:* $52,696 includes full-time tuition ($37,610), mandatory fees ($1394), and room and board ($13,692). *College room only:* $7212. Full-time tuition and fees vary according to course load. Room and board charges vary according to board plan and housing facility. *Part-time tuition:* $1637 per credit hour. Part-time tuition and fees vary according to course load.
FRESHMAN FINANCIAL AID (Fall 2012, est.) 2,517 applied for aid; of those 79% were deemed to have need. 100% of freshmen with need received aid; of those 70% had need fully met. *Average percent of need met:* 96% (excluding resources awarded to replace EFC). *Average financial aid package:* $35,120 (excluding resources awarded to replace EFC). 10% of all full-time freshmen had no need and received non-need-based gift aid.
UNDERGRADUATE FINANCIAL AID (Fall 2012, est.) 9,666 applied for aid; of those 85% were deemed to have need. 100% of undergraduates with need received aid; of those 60% had need fully met. *Average percent of need met:* 93% (excluding resources awarded to replace EFC). *Average financial aid package:* $34,000 (excluding resources awarded to replace EFC). 10% of all full-time undergraduates had no need and received non-need-based gift aid.
GIFT AID (NEED-BASED) *Total amount:* $222,479,570 (11% federal, 4% state, 83% institutional, 2% external sources). *Receiving aid:* Freshmen: 53% (1,803); all full-time undergraduates: 54% (7,497). *Average award:* Freshmen: $26,000; Undergraduates: $24,740. *Scholarships, grants, and awards:* Federal Pell, FSEOG, state, private, college/university gift aid from institutional funds.
GIFT AID (NON-NEED-BASED) *Total amount:* $13,980,052 (11% federal, 83% institutional, 6% external sources). *Receiving aid:* Freshmen: 4% (142). Undergraduates: 4% (531). *Average award:* Freshmen: $9010. Undergraduates: $9030. *Scholarships, grants, and awards by category:* Academic interests/achievement: general academic interests/achievements. *Creative arts/performance:* music, performing arts. *Tuition waivers:* Full or partial for employees or children of employees. *ROTC:* Army, Air Force.
LOANS *Student loans:* $78,338,814 (93% need-based, 7% non-need-based). 61% of past graduating class borrowed through all loan programs. *Average indebtedness per student:* $33,504. *Average need-based loan:* Freshmen: $6500. Undergrad-

uates: $7300. *Parent loans:* $35,365,647 (86% need-based, 14% non-need-based).
Programs: Federal Direct (Subsidized and Unsubsidized Stafford, PLUS), Perkins.
WORK-STUDY *Federal work-study:* Total amount: $3,923,000; jobs available.
ATHLETIC AWARDS Total amount: $14,305,850 (45% need-based, 55% non-need-based).
APPLYING FOR FINANCIAL AID *Required financial aid forms:* FAFSA, CSS Financial Aid PROFILE, noncustodial (divorced/separated) parent's statement. *Financial aid deadline:* 2/1. *Notification date:* 3/15. Students must reply by 5/1.
CONTACT Office of Financial Aid, Syracuse University, 200 Archbold Gymnasium, Syracuse, NY 13244-1140, 315-443-1513. *E-mail:* finmail@syr.edu. *Website:* http://www.syr.edu/.

TABOR COLLEGE
Hillsboro, KS

CONTACT Mr. Scott Franz, Director of Student Financial Assistance, Tabor College, 400 South Jefferson, Hillsboro, KS 67063, 620-947-3121 Ext. 1726 or toll-free 800-822-6799. *Fax:* 620-947-6276. *E-mail:* scottf@tabor.edu. *Website:* http://www.tabor.edu/.

TALLADEGA COLLEGE
Talladega, AL

CONTACT K. Michael Francois, Director of Financial Aid, Talladega College, 627 West Battle Street, Talladega, AL 35160, 256-761-6341 or toll-free 866-540-3956. *Fax:* 256-761-6462. *Website:* http://www.talladega.edu/.

TALMUDICAL ACADEMY OF NEW JERSEY
Adelphia, NJ

CONTACT Office of Financial Aid, Talmudical Academy of New Jersey, Route 524, Adelphia, NJ 07710, 732-431-1600.

TALMUDICAL INSTITUTE OF UPSTATE NEW YORK
Rochester, NY

CONTACT Mrs. Ella Berenstein, Financial Aid Administrator, Talmudical Institute of Upstate New York, 769 Park Avenue, Rochester, NY 14607-3046, 585-473-2810. *Website:* http://www.tiuny.org/.

TALMUDICAL SEMINARY OHOLEI TORAH
Brooklyn, NY

CONTACT Financial Aid Administrator, Talmudical Seminary Oholei Torah, 667 Eastern Parkway, Brooklyn, NY 11213-3310, 718-774-5050.

TALMUDICAL YESHIVA OF PHILADELPHIA
Philadelphia, PA

CONTACT Director of Student Financial Aid/Registrar, Talmudical Yeshiva of Philadelphia, 6063 Drexel Road, Philadelphia, PA 19131-1296, 215-473-1212.

TALMUDIC COLLEGE OF FLORIDA
Miami Beach, FL

CONTACT Rabbi Ira Hill, Director of Financial Aid, Talmudic College of Florida, 1910 Alton Road, Miami Beach, FL 33139, 305-534-7050. *Fax:* 305-534-8444. *Website:* http://www.talmudicu.edu/.

TARLETON STATE UNIVERSITY
Stephenville, TX

Tuition & fees (TX res): $6939	Average undergraduate aid package: $6985

ABOUT THE INSTITUTION State-supported, coed. *Awards:* associate, bachelor's, master's, and doctoral degrees. 76 undergraduate majors. *Total enrollment:* 10,279. Undergraduates: 8,917. Freshmen: 1,618. Federal methodology is used as a basis for awarding need-based institutional aid.
UNDERGRADUATE EXPENSES for 2013–2014 *Application fee:* $30. *Tuition, state resident:* full-time $4619; part-time $153.97 per credit hour. *Tuition, nonresident:* full-time $15,149; part-time $504.97 per credit hour. *Required fees:* full-time $2320. Full-time tuition and fees vary according to course load and degree level. Part-time tuition and fees vary according to course load and degree level. *College room and board:* $7336; *Room only:* $3972. Room and board charges vary according to board plan and housing facility.
FRESHMAN FINANCIAL AID (Fall 2011) 2,471 applied for aid; of those 97% were deemed to have need. 83% of freshmen with need received aid; of those 39% had need fully met. *Average percent of need met:* 53% (excluding resources awarded to replace EFC). *Average financial aid package:* $7653 (excluding resources awarded to replace EFC). 16% of all full-time freshmen had no need and received non-need-based gift aid.
UNDERGRADUATE FINANCIAL AID (Fall 2011) 12,487 applied for aid; of those 94% were deemed to have need. 93% of undergraduates with need received aid; of those 26% had need fully met. *Average percent of need met:* 44% (excluding resources awarded to replace EFC). *Average financial aid package:* $6985 (excluding resources awarded to replace EFC). 11% of all full-time undergraduates had no need and received non-need-based gift aid.
GIFT AID (NEED-BASED) *Total amount:* $25,718,309 (70% federal, 23% state, 7% institutional). *Receiving aid:* Freshmen: 52% (1,528); all full-time undergraduates: 46% (7,523). *Average award:* Freshmen: $3439; Undergraduates: $3003. *Scholarships, grants, and awards:* Federal Pell, FSEOG, state, college/university gift aid from institutional funds.
GIFT AID (NON-NEED-BASED) *Total amount:* $3,663,942 (100% institutional). *Receiving aid:* Freshmen: 21% (626). Undergraduates: 15% (2,501). *Average award:* Freshmen: $3237. Undergraduates: $4062. *Scholarships, grants, and awards by category:* Academic interests/achievement: general academic interests/achievements. Creative arts/performance: music, theater/drama. *ROTC:* Army.
LOANS *Student loans:* $42,427,544 (46% need-based, 54% non-need-based). 56% of past graduating class borrowed through all loan programs. *Average indebtedness per student:* $15,548. *Average need-based loan:* Freshmen: $1945. Undergraduates: $2451. *Parent loans:* $9,093,836 (100% non-need-based). *Programs:* Federal Direct (Subsidized and Unsubsidized Stafford, PLUS), state.
WORK-STUDY *Federal work-study:* Total amount: $200,983; jobs available. *State or other work-study/employment:* Total amount: $2,530,628 (2% need-based, 98% non-need-based). Part-time jobs available.
ATHLETIC AWARDS Total amount: $1,282,195 (100% non-need-based).

APPLYING FOR FINANCIAL AID *Required financial aid form:* FAFSA. *Financial aid deadline:* 11/1 (priority: 4/1). *Notification date:* Continuous beginning 3/1. Students must reply within 2 weeks of notification.

CONTACT Ms. Betty Murray, Director of Student Financial Aid, Tarleton State University, Box T-0310, Stephenville, TX 76402, 254-968-9070 or toll-free 800-687-8236. *Fax:* 254-968-9600. *E-mail:* finaid@tarleton.edu.

Website: http://www.tarleton.edu/.

TAYLOR UNIVERSITY
Upland, IN

Tuition & fees: $28,088	Average undergraduate aid package: $18,428

ABOUT THE INSTITUTION Independent interdenominational, coed. *Awards:* certificates, diplomas, associate, bachelor's, and master's degrees. 58 undergraduate majors. *Total enrollment:* 2,358. Undergraduates: 2,237. Freshmen: 498. Federal methodology is used as a basis for awarding need-based institutional aid.

UNDERGRADUATE EXPENSES for 2013–2014 *Application fee:* $25. *Comprehensive fee:* $35,845 includes full-time tuition ($27,850), mandatory fees ($238), and room and board ($7757). *College room only:* $4041. Full-time tuition and fees vary according to course load. Room and board charges vary according to board plan and housing facility. *Part-time tuition:* $981 per credit hour. *Part-time fees:* $36.50 per term. Part-time tuition and fees vary according to course load.

FRESHMAN FINANCIAL AID (Fall 2012, est.) 415 applied for aid; of those 84% were deemed to have need. 100% of freshmen with need received aid; of those 22% had need fully met. *Average percent of need met:* 73% (excluding resources awarded to replace EFC). *Average financial aid package:* $19,318 (excluding resources awarded to replace EFC). 22% of all full-time freshmen had no need and received non-need-based gift aid.

UNDERGRADUATE FINANCIAL AID (Fall 2012, est.) 1,335 applied for aid; of those 86% were deemed to have need. 100% of undergraduates with need received aid; of those 22% had need fully met. *Average percent of need met:* 71% (excluding resources awarded to replace EFC). *Average financial aid package:* $18,428 (excluding resources awarded to replace EFC). 26% of all full-time undergraduates had no need and received non-need-based gift aid.

GIFT AID (NEED-BASED) *Total amount:* $13,603,477 (13% federal, 6% state, 74% institutional, 7% external sources). *Receiving aid:* Freshmen: 70% (349); all full-time undergraduates: 61% (1,121). *Average award:* Freshmen: $15,069; Undergraduates: $14,266. *Scholarships, grants, and awards:* Federal Pell, FSEOG, state, private, college/university gift aid from institutional funds, Academic Competitiveness Grants, National SMART Grants.

GIFT AID (NON-NEED-BASED) *Total amount:* $5,546,253 (1% state, 85% institutional, 14% external sources). *Receiving aid:* Freshmen: 12% (58). Undergraduates: 9% (158). *Average award:* Freshmen: $9829. Undergraduates: $8147. *Scholarships, grants, and awards by category:* Academic interests/achievement: 1,029 awards ($6,827,304 total): general academic interests/achievements. *Creative arts/performance:* 96 awards ($257,663 total): music, theater/drama. *Special achievements/activities:* 304 awards ($717,044 total): leadership. *Special characteristics:* 739 awards ($3,247,453 total): children and siblings of alumni, children of faculty/staff, ethnic background, international students, religious affiliation. *Tuition waivers:* Full or partial for employees or children of employees, senior citizens.

LOANS *Student loans:* $10,339,483 (69% need-based, 31% non-need-based). 60% of past graduating class borrowed through all loan programs. *Average indebtedness per student:* $26,003. *Average need-based loan:* Freshmen: $4653. Undergraduates: $4735. *Parent loans:* $19,155,639 (31% need-based, 69% non-need-based). *Programs:* Federal Direct (Subsidized and Unsubsidized Stafford, PLUS), Perkins, college/university.

WORK-STUDY *Federal work-study:* Total amount: $468,527; 831 jobs averaging $564.

ATHLETIC AWARDS Total amount: $2,113,046 (59% need-based, 41% non-need-based).

APPLYING FOR FINANCIAL AID *Required financial aid form:* FAFSA. *Financial aid deadline:* 3/10. *Notification date:* Continuous beginning 3/1. Students must reply by 5/1.

CONTACT Mr. Timothy A. Nace, Director of Financial Aid, Taylor University, 236 West Reade Avenue, Upland, IN 46989-1001, 765-998-5358 or toll-free 800-882-3456. *Fax:* 765-998-4910. *E-mail:* tmnace@taylor.edu.

Website: http://www.taylor.edu/.

TELSHE YESHIVA–CHICAGO
Chicago, IL

CONTACT Office of Financial Aid, Telshe Yeshiva–Chicago, 3535 West Foster Avenue, Chicago, IL 60625-5598, 773-463-7738.

TEMPLE UNIVERSITY
Philadelphia, PA

Tuition & fees (PA res): $13,596	Average undergraduate aid package: $15,957

ABOUT THE INSTITUTION State-related, coed. *Awards:* certificates, diplomas, associate, bachelor's, master's, and doctoral degrees. 121 undergraduate majors. *Total enrollment:* 36,744. Undergraduates: 27,567. Freshmen: 4,132. Federal methodology is used as a basis for awarding need-based institutional aid.

UNDERGRADUATE EXPENSES for 2013–2014 *Application fee:* $55. *Tuition, state resident:* full-time $13,006; part-time $502 per credit hour. *Tuition, nonresident:* full-time $22,832; part-time $813 per credit hour. *Required fees:* full-time $590. Full-time tuition and fees vary according to course load, program, and reciprocity agreements, and student level. Part-time tuition and fees vary according to course load, program, reciprocity agreements, and student level. *College room and board:* $10,276; *Room only:* $6956. Room and board charges vary according to board plan and housing facility.

FRESHMAN FINANCIAL AID (Fall 2011) 3,730 applied for aid; of those 79% were deemed to have need. 98% of freshmen with need received aid; of those 30% had need fully met. *Average percent of need met:* 70% (excluding resources awarded to replace EFC). *Average financial aid package:* $15,332 (excluding resources awarded to replace EFC). 13% of all full-time freshmen had no need and received non-need-based gift aid.

UNDERGRADUATE FINANCIAL AID (Fall 2011) 20,194 applied for aid; of those 86% were deemed to have need. 98% of undergraduates with need received aid; of those 25% had need fully met. *Average percent of need met:* 68% (excluding resources awarded to replace EFC). *Average financial aid package:* $15,957 (excluding resources awarded to replace EFC). 8% of all full-time undergraduates had no need and received non-need-based gift aid.

GIFT AID (NEED-BASED) *Total amount:* $99,790,978 (40% federal, 27% state, 33% institutional). *Receiving aid:* Freshmen: 58% (2,453); all full-time undergraduates: 57% (14,046). *Average award:* Freshmen: $6206; Undergraduates: $6734. *Scholarships, grants, and awards:* Federal Pell, FSEOG, state, private, college/university gift aid from institutional funds, Federal Nursing.

GIFT AID (NON-NEED-BASED) *Total amount:* $33,913,193 (79% institutional, 21% external sources). *Receiving aid:* Freshmen: 36% (1,548). Undergraduates: 24% (5,847). *Average award:* Freshmen: $4604. Undergraduates: $4474. *Scholarships, grants, and awards by category:* Academic interests/achievement: 5,639 awards ($21,531,935 total): general academic interests/achievements. *Creative arts/performance:* 215 awards ($598,900 total): art/fine arts, general creative arts/performance, music, performing arts. *Special achievements/activities:* 202 awards ($305,541 total): cheerleading/drum major. *Special characteristics:* 2,114 awards ($8,025,306 total): children of faculty/staff, general special characteristics, veterans. *Tuition waivers:* Full or partial for employees or children of employees. *ROTC:* Army, Naval cooperative, Air Force cooperative.

LOANS *Student loans:* $181,232,749 (77% need-based, 23% non-need-based). 76% of past graduating class borrowed through all loan programs. *Average indebtedness per student:* $33,500. *Average need-based loan:* Freshmen: $3594. Undergraduates: $4513. *Parent loans:* $37,613,282 (100% non-need-based). *Programs:* Federal Direct (Subsidized and Unsubsidized Stafford, PLUS), Perkins, Federal Nursing, state, college/university.

WORK-STUDY *Federal work-study:* Total amount: $1,951,201; 1,835 jobs averaging $1057.

ATHLETIC AWARDS Total amount: $8,570,557 (100% non-need-based).

APPLYING FOR FINANCIAL AID *Required financial aid form:* FAFSA. *Financial aid deadline (priority):* 3/1. *Notification date:* Continuous beginning 2/15. Students must reply by 5/1 or within 3 weeks of notification.

CONTACT Mr. Craig Fennell, Director of Student Financial Services, Temple University, Conwell Hall, Ground Floor, Philadelphia, PA 19122-6096, 215-204-8760 or toll-free 888-340-2222. *Fax:* 215-204-2016. *E-mail:* craig.fennell@temple.edu.

Website: http://www.temple.edu/.

TENNESSEE STATE UNIVERSITY
Nashville, TN

Tuition & fees: N/R	Average undergraduate aid package: $14,393

ABOUT THE INSTITUTION State-supported, coed. *Awards:* certificates, associate, bachelor's, and master's degrees. 58 undergraduate majors. *Total enrollment:* 8,775. Undergraduates: 6,780. Freshmen: 1,058. Federal methodology is used as a basis for awarding need-based institutional aid.

FRESHMAN FINANCIAL AID (Fall 2012, est.) 994 applied for aid; of those 94% were deemed to have need. 100% of freshmen with need received aid; of those 1% had need fully met. *Average financial aid package:* $14,351 (excluding resources awarded to replace EFC). 3% of all full-time freshmen had no need and received non-need-based gift aid.

UNDERGRADUATE FINANCIAL AID (Fall 2012, est.) 5,094 applied for aid; of those 94% were deemed to have need. 99% of undergraduates with need received aid; of those 1% had need fully met. *Average financial aid package:* $14,393 (excluding resources awarded to replace EFC). 2% of all full-time undergraduates had no need and received non-need-based gift aid.

GIFT AID (NEED-BASED) *Total amount:* $23,204,006 (91% federal, 9% state). *Receiving aid:* Freshmen: 78% (797); all full-time undergraduates: 75% (3,961). *Average award:* Freshmen: $6072; Undergraduates: $5564. *Scholarships, grants, and awards:* Federal Pell, FSEOG, state, private, college/university gift aid from institutional funds.

GIFT AID (NON-NEED-BASED) *Total amount:* $9,188,913 (38% state, 62% institutional). *Receiving aid:* Freshmen: 43% (439). Undergraduates: 34% (1,793). *Average award:* Freshmen: $8008. Undergraduates: $7315. *Scholarships, grants, and awards by category:* Academic interests/achievement: general academic interests/achievements. Creative arts/performance: music. Special achievements/activities: general special achievements/activities. Special characteristics: local/state students, members of minority groups. *ROTC:* Army cooperative, Naval cooperative, Air Force.

LOANS *Student loans:* $41,852,679 (46% need-based, 54% non-need-based). 85% of past graduating class borrowed through all loan programs. *Average indebtedness per student:* $30,477. *Average need-based loan:* Freshmen: $2991. Undergraduates: $3663. *Parent loans:* $4,273,105 (100% non-need-based). *Programs:* Federal Direct (Subsidized and Unsubsidized Stafford, PLUS), Perkins.

WORK-STUDY *Federal work-study:* Total amount: $1,527,990; 715 jobs averaging $2033.

ATHLETIC AWARDS Total amount: $2,435,021 (100% non-need-based).

APPLYING FOR FINANCIAL AID *Required financial aid form:* FAFSA. *Financial aid deadline (priority):* 4/1. *Notification date:* Continuous beginning 4/25. Students must reply within 3 weeks of notification.

CONTACT Amy Wood, Director of Financial Aid, Tennessee State University, 3500 John Merritt Boulevard, Nashville, TN 37209-1561, 615-963-5772. *Fax:* 615-963-7540. *E-mail:* finaid@tnstate.edu.
Website: http://www.tnstate.edu/.

TENNESSEE TECHNOLOGICAL UNIVERSITY
Cookeville, TN

Tuition & fees (TN res): $6724	Average undergraduate aid package: $10,897

ABOUT THE INSTITUTION State-supported, coed. 67 undergraduate majors. Federal methodology is used as a basis for awarding need-based institutional aid.

UNDERGRADUATE EXPENSES for 2013–2014 *Tuition, state resident:* full-time $6724; part-time $310 per credit hour. *Tuition, nonresident:* full-time $20,884; part-time $900 per credit hour. Full-time tuition and fees vary according to course load and program. Part-time tuition and fees vary according to course load and program. *College room and board:* $7642; *Room only:* $3980. Room and board charges vary according to board plan and housing facility.

FRESHMAN FINANCIAL AID (Fall 2012, est.) 1,862 applied for aid; of those 77% were deemed to have need. 100% of freshmen with need received aid; of those 26% had need fully met. *Average percent of need met:* 65% (excluding resources awarded to replace EFC). *Average financial aid package:* $11,945 (excluding resources awarded to replace EFC). 8% of all full-time freshmen had no need and received non-need-based gift aid.

UNDERGRADUATE FINANCIAL AID (Fall 2012, est.) 7,797 applied for aid; of those 79% were deemed to have need. 97% of undergraduates with need received aid; of those 22% had need fully met. *Average percent of need met:* 62% (excluding resources awarded to replace EFC). *Average financial aid package:* $10,897 (excluding resources awarded to replace EFC). 6% of all full-time undergraduates had no need and received non-need-based gift aid.

GIFT AID (NEED-BASED) *Total amount:* $20,138,292 (81% federal, 17% state, 2% institutional). *Receiving aid:* Freshmen: 36% (746); all full-time undergraduates: 39% (3,481). *Average award:* Freshmen: $5112; Undergraduates: $3244. *Scholarships, grants, and awards:* Federal Pell, FSEOG, state, private, college/university gift aid from institutional funds, United Negro College Fund.

GIFT AID (NON-NEED-BASED) *Total amount:* $32,423,272 (71% state, 21% institutional, 8% external sources). *Receiving aid:* Freshmen: 64% (1,308). Undergraduates: 44% (3,951). *Average award:* Freshmen: $2032. Undergraduates: $2008. *Scholarships, grants, and awards by category:* Academic interests/achievement: 3,171 awards ($3,888,375 total): agriculture, biological sciences, business, communication, computer science, education, engineering/technologies, English, foreign languages, general academic interests/achievements, health fields, home economics, humanities, international studies, mathematics, military science, physical sciences, premedicine, social sciences. Creative arts/performance: 11 awards ($8600 total): art/fine arts, debating, music. Special achievements/activities: 304 awards ($1,860,439 total): cheerleading/drum major, general special achievements/activities. Special characteristics: 1,717 awards ($1,530,487 total): children and siblings of alumni, children of educators, children of faculty/staff, children of public servants, ethnic background, first-generation college students, local/state students, members of minority groups, out-of-state students, public servants. *Tuition waivers:* Full or partial for employees or children of employees, senior citizens.

LOANS *Student loans:* $32,817,991 (59% need-based, 41% non-need-based). 60% of past graduating class borrowed through all loan programs. *Average indebtedness per student:* $6432. *Average need-based loan:* Freshmen: $3149. Undergraduates: $3910. *Parent loans:* $2,054,308 (100% non-need-based). *Programs:* Federal Direct (Subsidized and Unsubsidized Stafford, PLUS), Perkins, college/university.

WORK-STUDY *Federal work-study:* Total amount: $554,804; 917 jobs averaging $1471. *State or other work-study/employment:* Part-time jobs available.

ATHLETIC AWARDS Total amount: $3,411,682 (100% non-need-based).

APPLYING FOR FINANCIAL AID *Required financial aid form:* FAFSA. *Financial aid deadline (priority):* 3/15. *Notification date:* Continuous beginning 4/1. Students must reply within 2 weeks of notification.

CONTACT Lester C. McKenzie III, Director of Financial Aid, Tennessee Technological University, PO Box 5076, 1000 North Dixie Avenue, Cookeville, TN 38501, 931-372-3073 or toll-free 800-255-8881. *Fax:* 931-372-6309. *E-mail:* lmckenzie@tntech.edu.
Website: http://www.tntech.edu/.

TENNESSEE TEMPLE UNIVERSITY
Chattanooga, TN

ABOUT THE INSTITUTION Independent Baptist, coed. 28 undergraduate majors.

GIFT AID (NEED-BASED) *Scholarships, grants, and awards:* Federal Pell, FSEOG, state, private, college/university gift aid from institutional funds.

GIFT AID (NON-NEED-BASED) *Scholarships, grants, and awards by category:* Academic interests/achievement: general academic interests/achievements. Creative arts/performance: music. Special achievements/activities: leadership, religious involvement. Special characteristics: children and siblings of alumni, children of faculty/staff, local/state students, siblings of current students, spouses of current students.

LOANS *Programs:* Perkins.

APPLYING FOR FINANCIAL AID *Required financial aid forms:* FAFSA, institution's own form.

CONTACT Jeffrey Davis, Director of Financial Aid, Tennessee Temple University, 1815 Union Avenue, Chattanooga, TN 37404-3587, 423-493-4223 or toll-free 800-553-4050. *Fax:* 423-493-4497. *E-mail:* davisj@tntemple.edu.
Website: http://www.tntemple.edu/.

TENNESSEE WESLEYAN COLLEGE
Athens, TN

Tuition & fees: N/R	Average undergraduate aid package: $15,709

ABOUT THE INSTITUTION Independent United Methodist, coed. **Awards:** bachelor's and master's degrees (profile includes information for both the main and branch campuses). 42 undergraduate majors. **Total enrollment:** 1,116. Undergraduates: 1,106. Freshmen: 220. Federal methodology is used as a basis for awarding need-based institutional aid.

FRESHMAN FINANCIAL AID (Fall 2011) 220 applied for aid; of those 87% were deemed to have need. 97% of freshmen with need received aid; of those 18% had need fully met. **Average percent of need met:** 66% (excluding resources awarded to replace EFC). **Average financial aid package:** $15,700 (excluding resources awarded to replace EFC). 9% of all full-time freshmen had no need and received non-need-based gift aid.

UNDERGRADUATE FINANCIAL AID (Fall 2011) 1,029 applied for aid; of those 90% were deemed to have need. 97% of undergraduates with need received aid; of those 19% had need fully met. **Average percent of need met:** 65% (excluding resources awarded to replace EFC). **Average financial aid package:** $15,709 (excluding resources awarded to replace EFC). 7% of all full-time undergraduates had no need and received non-need-based gift aid.

GIFT AID (NEED-BASED) Total amount: $9,971,562 (22% federal, 24% state, 48% institutional, 6% external sources). **Receiving aid:** Freshmen: 77% (186); all full-time undergraduates: 78% (866). **Average award:** Freshmen: $13,790; Undergraduates: $13,454. **Scholarships, grants, and awards:** Federal Pell, FSEOG, state, private, college/university gift aid from institutional funds.

GIFT AID (NON-NEED-BASED) Total amount: $1,682,687 (32% state, 59% institutional, 9% external sources). **Receiving aid:** Freshmen: 13% (31). Undergraduates: 12% (135). **Average award:** Freshmen: $9847. Undergraduates: $9012. **Scholarships, grants, and awards by category:** Academic interests/achievement: biological sciences, business, communication, computer science, education, English, foreign languages, general academic interests/achievements, health fields, humanities, international studies, mathematics, physical sciences, premedicine, religion/biblical studies, social sciences. Creative arts/performance: music. Special achievements/activities: cheerleading/drum major, general special achievements/activities, junior miss, memberships, religious involvement. Special characteristics: children and siblings of alumni, children of faculty/staff, general special characteristics, international students, members of minority groups, relatives of clergy, religious affiliation.

LOANS Student loans: $5,531,972 (80% need-based, 20% non-need-based). 100% of past graduating class borrowed through all loan programs. Average indebtedness per student: $27,011. **Average need-based loan:** Freshmen: $2759. Undergraduates: $3730. **Parent loans:** $512,545 (39% need-based, 61% non-need-based). **Programs:** Federal Direct (Subsidized and Unsubsidized Stafford, PLUS).

WORK-STUDY Federal work-study: Total amount: $77,705; jobs available. **State or other work-study/employment:** Total amount: $21,572 (100% non-need-based). Part-time jobs available.

ATHLETIC AWARDS Total amount: $2,703,062 (62% need-based, 38% non-need-based).

APPLYING FOR FINANCIAL AID Required financial aid forms: FAFSA, institution's own form. **Financial aid deadline:** Continuous. **Notification date:** Continuous beginning 2/15.

CONTACT Mr. Bob Perry, Director of Financial Aid, Tennessee Wesleyan College, 204 East College Street, Athens, TN 37303, 423-746-5209 or toll-free 800-PICK-TWC. Fax: 423-744-9968. E-mail: rkperry@twcnet.edu. Website: http://www.twcnet.edu/.

TEXAS A&M INTERNATIONAL UNIVERSITY
Laredo, TX

Tuition & fees (TX res): $6838	Average undergraduate aid package: $9669

ABOUT THE INSTITUTION State-supported, coed. **Awards:** bachelor's, master's, and doctoral degrees. 34 undergraduate majors. **Total enrollment:** 7,213. Undergraduates: 6,384. Freshmen: 837. Federal methodology is used as a basis for awarding need-based institutional aid.

UNDERGRADUATE EXPENSES for 2013–2014 Tuition, state resident: full-time $6838. **Tuition, nonresident:** full-time $17,368. Full-time tuition and fees vary according to course load. Part-time tuition and fees vary according to course load and reciprocity agreements. **College room and board:** $6275. Room and board charges vary according to board plan and housing facility.

FRESHMAN FINANCIAL AID (Fall 2012, est.) 808 applied for aid; of those 91% were deemed to have need. 100% of freshmen with need received aid; of those 4% had need fully met. **Average percent of need met:** 67% (excluding resources awarded to replace EFC). **Average financial aid package:** $9816 (excluding resources awarded to replace EFC). 6% of all full-time freshmen had no need and received non-need-based gift aid.

UNDERGRADUATE FINANCIAL AID (Fall 2012, est.) 3,833 applied for aid; of those 91% were deemed to have need. 98% of undergraduates with need received aid; of those 10% had need fully met. **Average percent of need met:** 67% (excluding resources awarded to replace EFC). **Average financial aid package:** $9669 (excluding resources awarded to replace EFC). 5% of all full-time undergraduates had no need and received non-need-based gift aid.

GIFT AID (NEED-BASED) Total amount: $21,575,719 (68% federal, 25% state, 7% institutional). **Receiving aid:** Freshmen: 82% (718); all full-time undergraduates: 86% (3,404). **Average award:** Freshmen: $6645; Undergraduates: $5742. **Scholarships, grants, and awards:** Federal Pell, FSEOG, state, college/university gift aid from institutional funds, Federal Nursing.

GIFT AID (NON-NEED-BASED) Total amount: $3,007,125 (20% state, 67% institutional, 13% external sources). **Receiving aid:** Freshmen: 38% (335). Undergraduates: 33% (1,286). **Average award:** Freshmen: $3336. Undergraduates: $3745. **Scholarships, grants, and awards by category:** Academic interests/achievement: 1,804 awards ($3,827,216 total): business, communication, education, engineering/technologies, English, foreign languages, general academic interests/achievements, health fields, international studies, mathematics, physical sciences, pre-medicine, social sciences. Creative arts/performance: 31 awards ($26,101 total): art/fine arts, dance, music, performing arts. **Tuition waivers:** Full or partial for senior citizens. **ROTC:** Army.

LOANS Student loans: $13,712,925 (66% need-based, 34% non-need-based). 70% of past graduating class borrowed through all loan programs. Average indebtedness per student: $17,644. **Average need-based loan:** Freshmen: $2666. Undergraduates: $3762. **Parent loans:** $65,111 (100% non-need-based). **Programs:** Federal Direct (Subsidized and Unsubsidized Stafford, PLUS), state, college/university, Hinson-Hazelwood Loan Program.

WORK-STUDY Federal work-study: Total amount: $255,602; 113 jobs averaging $2583. **State or other work-study/employment:** Total amount: $56,065 (100% need-based). 17 part-time jobs averaging $3298.

ATHLETIC AWARDS Total amount: $646,410 (100% non-need-based).

APPLYING FOR FINANCIAL AID Required financial aid form: FAFSA. **Financial aid deadline:** 8/1 (priority: 3/15). **Notification date:** Continuous beginning 4/15. Students must reply within 6 weeks of notification.

CONTACT Laura Elizondo, Director of Financial Aid, Texas A&M International University, 5201 University Boulevard, Laredo, TX 78041, 956-326-2225 or toll-free 888-489-2648. Fax: 956-326-2224. E-mail: laura@tamiu.edu. Website: http://www.tamiu.edu/.

TEXAS A&M UNIVERSITY
College Station, TX

Tuition & fees (TX res): $8506	Average undergraduate aid package: $14,938

ABOUT THE INSTITUTION State-supported, coed. **Awards:** certificates, bachelor's, master's, and doctoral degrees. 109 undergraduate majors. **Total enrollment:** 50,227. Undergraduates: 40,103. Freshmen: 8,139. Both federal and institutional methodology are used as a basis for awarding need-based institutional aid.

UNDERGRADUATE EXPENSES for 2013–2014 Application fee: $60. **Tuition, state resident:** full-time $5297; part-time $176.55 per credit hour. **Tuition, nonresident:** full-time $21,827; part-time $727.55 per credit hour. **Required fees:** full-time $3209. Full-time tuition and fees vary according to program. Part-time tuition and fees vary according to program. **College room and board:** $8400. Room and board charges vary according to board plan, housing facility, and location.

FRESHMAN FINANCIAL AID (Fall 2012, est.) 5,591 applied for aid; of those 63% were deemed to have need. 98% of freshmen with need received aid; of those 53% had need fully met. *Average percent of need met:* 78% (excluding resources awarded to replace EFC). *Average financial aid package:* $16,477 (excluding resources awarded to replace EFC). 12% of all full-time freshmen had no need and received non-need-based gift aid.

UNDERGRADUATE FINANCIAL AID (Fall 2012, est.) 21,932 applied for aid; of those 70% were deemed to have need. 97% of undergraduates with need received aid; of those 42% had need fully met. *Average percent of need met:* 70% (excluding resources awarded to replace EFC). *Average financial aid package:* $14,938 (excluding resources awarded to replace EFC). 6% of all full-time undergraduates had no need and received non-need-based gift aid.

GIFT AID (NEED-BASED) *Total amount:* $130,175,712 (28% federal, 24% state, 35% institutional, 13% external sources). *Receiving aid:* Freshmen: 48% (3,421); all full-time undergraduates: 36% (13,165). *Average award:* Freshmen: $11,970; Undergraduates: $9195. *Scholarships, grants, and awards:* Federal Pell, FSEOG, state, private, college/university gift aid from institutional funds.

GIFT AID (NON-NEED-BASED) *Total amount:* $19,263,199 (4% federal, 6% state, 50% institutional, 40% external sources). *Receiving aid:* Freshmen: 8% (555). Undergraduates: 4% (1,420). *Average award:* Freshmen: $4341. Undergraduates: $3673. *Scholarships, grants, and awards by category:* Academic interests/achievement: agriculture, architecture, biological sciences, business, computer science, education, engineering/technologies, general academic interests/achievements, health fields, mathematics, physical sciences. Creative arts/performance: journalism/publications, performing arts, theater/drama. Special achievements/activities: community service, general special achievements/activities, leadership, memberships, rodeo. Special characteristics: children of faculty/staff, first-generation college students, general special characteristics, international students, local/state students, veterans, veterans' children. ROTC: Army, Naval, Air Force.

LOANS *Student loans:* $109,624,813 (60% need-based, 40% non-need-based). 46% of past graduating class borrowed through all loan programs. *Average indebtedness per student:* $22,955. *Average need-based loan:* Freshmen: $4706. Undergraduates: $6693. *Parent loans:* $29,464,284 (16% need-based, 84% non-need-based). *Programs:* Federal Direct (Subsidized and Unsubsidized Stafford, PLUS), Perkins, state, college/university.

WORK-STUDY *Federal work-study:* Total amount: $1,661,410; 640 jobs averaging $2596. *State or other work-study/employment:* Total amount: $402,549 (100% need-based). 201 part-time jobs averaging $2003.

ATHLETIC AWARDS Total amount: $6,083,359 (92% need-based, 8% non-need-based).

APPLYING FOR FINANCIAL AID *Required financial aid forms:* FAFSA, scholarships portion of the ApplyTexas application. *Financial aid deadline (priority):* 3/15. *Notification date:* Continuous beginning 4/1. Students must reply within 4 weeks of notification.

CONTACT Scholarships and Financial Aid Office, Texas A&M University, The Pavilion 200, Spence Street, 1252 TAMU, College Station, TX 77842-3016, 979-845-3236. *Fax:* 979-847-9061. *E-mail:* financialaid@tamu.edu.
Website: http://www.tamu.edu/.

TEXAS A&M UNIVERSITY AT GALVESTON
Galveston, TX

CONTACT Dennis Carlton, Director for Financial Aid, Texas A&M University at Galveston, PO Box 1675, Galveston, TX 77553-1675, 409-740-4500. *Fax:* 409-740-4959. *E-mail:* carltond@tamug.tamu.edu.
Website: http://www.tamug.edu/.

TEXAS A&M UNIVERSITY–COMMERCE
Commerce, TX

Tuition & fees (TX res): $8376	Average undergraduate aid package: $9901

ABOUT THE INSTITUTION State-supported, coed. *Awards:* bachelor's, master's, and doctoral degrees. 77 undergraduate majors. *Total enrollment:* 11,187. Undergraduates: 6,768. Freshmen: 786. Federal methodology is used as a basis for awarding need-based institutional aid.

UNDERGRADUATE EXPENSES for 2013–2014 *Tuition, state resident:* full-time $6583; part-time $159.68 per semester hour. *Tuition, nonresident:* full-time $17,113. *Required fees:* full-time $1793. Full-time tuition and fees vary according to course load. Part-time tuition and fees vary according to course load. *College room and board:* $3627; *Room only:* $2062. Room and board charges vary according to board plan and housing facility.

FRESHMAN FINANCIAL AID (Fall 2011) 705 applied for aid; of those 85% were deemed to have need. 99% of freshmen with need received aid; of those 21% had need fully met. *Average percent of need met:* 71% (excluding resources awarded to replace EFC). *Average financial aid package:* $11,774 (excluding resources awarded to replace EFC). 7% of all full-time freshmen had no need and received non-need-based gift aid.

UNDERGRADUATE FINANCIAL AID (Fall 2011) 4,096 applied for aid; of those 90% were deemed to have need. 99% of undergraduates with need received aid; of those 14% had need fully met. *Average percent of need met:* 58% (excluding resources awarded to replace EFC). *Average financial aid package:* $9901 (excluding resources awarded to replace EFC). 4% of all full-time undergraduates had no need and received non-need-based gift aid.

GIFT AID (NEED-BASED) *Total amount:* $23,797,612 (62% federal, 20% state, 16% institutional, 2% external sources). *Receiving aid:* Freshmen: 75% (579); all full-time undergraduates: 67% (3,383). *Average award:* Freshmen: $9458; Undergraduates: $6995. *Scholarships, grants, and awards:* Federal Pell, FSEOG, state, private, college/university gift aid from institutional funds.

GIFT AID (NON-NEED-BASED) *Total amount:* $1,635,389 (4% federal, 87% institutional, 9% external sources). *Average award:* Freshmen: $2316. Undergraduates: $1762. *Scholarships, grants, and awards by category:* Academic interests/achievement: agriculture, general academic interests/achievements. Creative arts/performance: art/fine arts, journalism/publications, music, theater/drama. Special achievements/activities: cheerleading/drum major, general special achievements/activities, leadership.

LOANS *Student loans:* $33,169,618 (93% need-based, 7% non-need-based). 67% of past graduating class borrowed through all loan programs. *Average indebtedness per student:* $28,839. *Average need-based loan:* Freshmen: $3397. Undergraduates: $4077. *Parent loans:* $1,355,373 (69% need-based, 31% non-need-based). *Programs:* Federal Direct (Subsidized and Unsubsidized Stafford, PLUS), Perkins, state.

WORK-STUDY *Federal work-study:* Total amount: $388,830; jobs available. *State or other work-study/employment:* Total amount: $69,406 (100% need-based). Part-time jobs available.

ATHLETIC AWARDS Total amount: $1,474,115 (65% need-based, 35% non-need-based).

APPLYING FOR FINANCIAL AID *Required financial aid form:* FAFSA. *Financial aid deadline:* Continuous. *Notification date:* Continuous beginning 5/1. Students must reply within 2 weeks of notification.

CONTACT Maria Ramos, Director of Financial Aid, Texas A&M University–Commerce, PO Box 3011, Commerce, TX 75429, 903-886-5091 or toll-free 888-868-2682. *Fax:* 903-886-5098. *E-mail:* maria_ramos@tamu-commerce.edu.
Website: http://www.tamuc.edu/.

TEXAS A&M UNIVERSITY–CORPUS CHRISTI
Corpus Christi, TX

Tuition & fees: N/R | **Average undergraduate aid package:** $9140

ABOUT THE INSTITUTION State-supported, coed. *Awards:* bachelor's, master's, and doctoral degrees. 62 undergraduate majors. *Total enrollment:* 10,162. Undergraduates: 8,275. Freshmen: 1,422. Federal methodology is used as a basis for awarding need-based institutional aid.

FRESHMAN FINANCIAL AID (Fall 2012, est.) 1,292 applied for aid; of those 79% were deemed to have need. 96% of freshmen with need received aid; of those 10% had need fully met. *Average percent of need met:* 59% (excluding resources awarded to replace EFC). *Average financial aid package:* $8997 (excluding resources awarded to replace EFC). 8% of all full-time freshmen had no need and received non-need-based gift aid.

UNDERGRADUATE FINANCIAL AID (Fall 2012, est.) 4,544 applied for aid; of those 84% were deemed to have need. 97% of undergraduates with need received aid; of those 9% had need fully met. *Average percent of need met:* 58% (excluding resources awarded to replace EFC). *Average financial aid package:* $9140 (excluding resources awarded to replace EFC). 9% of all full-time undergraduates had no need and received non-need-based gift aid.

GIFT AID (NEED-BASED) *Total amount:* $23,318,025 (69% federal, 23% state, 8% institutional). *Receiving aid:* Freshmen: 59% (885); all full-time undergraduates: 52% (3,134). *Average award:* Freshmen: $6018; Undergraduates: $5649. *Scholarships, grants, and awards:* Federal Pell, FSEOG, state, college/university gift aid from institutional funds.

GIFT AID (NON-NEED-BASED) *Total amount:* $3,655,294 (76% institutional, 24% external sources). *Receiving aid:* Freshmen: 8% (120). Undergraduates: 9% (541). *Average award:* Freshmen: $2576. Undergraduates: $2087. *Scholarships, grants, and awards by category:* Academic interests/achievement: general academic interests/achievements. Creative arts/performance: art/fine arts, general creative arts/performance. Special characteristics: first-generation college students, international students. ROTC: Army.

LOANS *Student loans:* $36,812,222 (43% need-based, 57% non-need-based). 67% of past graduating class borrowed through all loan programs. *Average indebtedness per student:* $24,168. *Average need-based loan:* Freshmen: $3319. Undergraduates: $4049. *Parent loans:* $9,320,836 (100% non-need-based). *Programs:* Perkins, state, college/university.

WORK-STUDY *Federal work-study:* Total amount: $510,249; 108 jobs averaging $3694. *State or other work-study/employment:* Total amount: $768,881 (100% need-based). 167 part-time jobs averaging $3865.

ATHLETIC AWARDS Total amount: $1,669,346 (100% non-need-based).

APPLYING FOR FINANCIAL AID *Required financial aid form:* FAFSA. *Financial aid deadline (priority):* 3/31. *Notification date:* Continuous beginning 4/1. Students must reply within 2 weeks of notification.

CONTACT Jeannie Gage, Director of Financial Assistance, Texas A&M University–Corpus Christi, 6300 Ocean Drive, Corpus Christi, TX 78412-5503, 361-825-2338 or toll-free 800-482-6822. *Fax:* 361-825-6095. *E-mail:* faoweb@tamucc.edu. *Website:* http://www.tamucc.edu/.

TEXAS A&M UNIVERSITY–KINGSVILLE
Kingsville, TX

CONTACT Ralph Perri, Director, Financial Aid, Texas A&M University–Kingsville, 700 University Boulevard, Kingsville, TX 78363, 361-593-2883 or toll-free 800-687-6000. *Fax:* 361-593-3036. *E-mail:* financial.aid@tamuk.edu. *Website:* http://www.tamuk.edu/.

TEXAS A&M UNIVERSITY–SAN ANTONIO
San Antonio, TX

CONTACT Financial Aid Office, Texas A&M University–San Antonio, One University Way, San Antonio, TX 78224, 210-784-1000. *Website:* http://www.tamusa.tamus.edu/.

TEXAS A&M UNIVERSITY–TEXARKANA
Texarkana, TX

Tuition & fees: N/R | **Average undergraduate aid package:** N/A

ABOUT THE INSTITUTION State-supported, coed. 20 undergraduate majors. Federal methodology is used as a basis for awarding need-based institutional aid.

GIFT AID (NEED-BASED) *Scholarships, grants, and awards:* Federal Pell, FSEOG, state, private, college/university gift aid from institutional funds.

GIFT AID (NON-NEED-BASED) *Scholarships, grants, and awards by category:* Academic interests/achievement: business, education, engineering/technologies, English, general academic interests/achievements, mathematics, social sciences. Special achievements/activities: community service, general special achievements/activities, leadership, memberships.

LOANS *Programs:* Federal Direct (Subsidized and Unsubsidized Stafford, PLUS), college/university.

APPLYING FOR FINANCIAL AID *Required financial aid forms:* FAFSA, institution's own form, state aid form. *Financial aid deadline (priority):* 5/1. *Notification date:* Continuous beginning 7/15. Students must reply within 2 weeks of notification.

CONTACT Alyssa Haley, Director of Financial Aid and Veterans Services, Texas A&M University–Texarkana, 7101 University Avenue, Texarkana, TX 75503, 903-223-3060. *Fax:* 903-223-3140. *E-mail:* ahaley@tamut.edu. *Website:* http://www.tamut.edu/.

TEXAS CHRISTIAN UNIVERSITY
Fort Worth, TX

Tuition & fees: $36,590 | **Average undergraduate aid package:** $21,185

ABOUT THE INSTITUTION Independent Christian Church (Disciples of Christ), coed. *Awards:* certificates, diplomas, bachelor's, master's, and doctoral degrees. 93 undergraduate majors. *Total enrollment:* 9,727. Undergraduates: 8,456. Freshmen: 1,854. Federal methodology is used as a basis for awarding need-based institutional aid.

UNDERGRADUATE EXPENSES for 2013–2014 *Application fee:* $40. *Tuition:* full-time $36,500. Part-time tuition and fees vary according to course load. Room and board charges vary according to board plan and housing facility.

FRESHMAN FINANCIAL AID (Fall 2012, est.) 1,153 applied for aid; of those 65% were deemed to have need. 99% of freshmen with need received aid; of those 31% had need fully met. *Average percent of need met:* 70% (excluding resources awarded to replace EFC). *Average financial aid package:* $21,669 (excluding resources awarded to replace EFC). 27% of all full-time freshmen had no need and received non-need-based gift aid.

UNDERGRADUATE FINANCIAL AID (Fall 2012, est.) 4,352 applied for aid; of those 82% were deemed to have need. 97% of undergraduates with need received aid; of those 24% had need fully met. *Average percent of need met:* 62% (excluding resources awarded to replace EFC). *Average financial aid package:* $21,185 (excluding resources awarded to replace EFC). 23% of all full-time undergraduates had no need and received non-need-based gift aid.

GIFT AID (NEED-BASED) *Total amount:* $53,288,769 (10% federal, 6% state, 81% institutional, 3% external sources). *Receiving aid:* Freshmen: 39% (721); all full-time undergraduates: 40% (3,240). *Average award:* Freshmen: $18,555; Undergraduates: $17,990. *Scholarships, grants, and awards:* Federal Pell, FSEOG, state, private, college/university gift aid from institutional funds.

GIFT AID (NON-NEED-BASED) *Total amount:* $27,481,091 (97% institutional, 3% external sources). *Receiving aid:* Freshmen: 25% (471). Undergraduates: 25% (1,993). *Average award:* Freshmen: $13,166. Undergraduates: $12,263. *Scholarships, grants, and awards by category: Academic interests/achievement:* 3,084 awards ($31,447,753 total): agriculture, biological sciences, business, communication, education, engineering/technologies, English, foreign languages, general academic interests/achievements, health fields, humanities, international studies, mathematics, military science, physical sciences, premedicine, religion/biblical studies, social sciences. *Creative arts/performance:* 417 awards ($2,973,791 total): applied art and design, art/fine arts, cinema/film/broadcasting, creative writing, dance, general creative arts/performance, journalism/publications, music, performing arts, theater/drama. *Special achievements/activities:* 374 awards ($4,243,745 total): general special achievements/activities, leadership, memberships, religious involvement. *Special characteristics:* 673 awards ($13,507,470 total): adult students, children of educators, children of faculty/staff, children of union members/company employees, children of workers in trades, ethnic background, general special characteristics, handicapped students, international students, local/state students, members of minority groups, previous college experience, relatives of clergy, religious affiliation, veterans, veterans' children. *Tuition waivers:* Full or partial for employees or children of employees. **ROTC:** Army, Air Force.

LOANS *Student loans:* $44,318,032 (62% need-based, 38% non-need-based). 41% of past graduating class borrowed through all loan programs. *Average indebtedness per student:* $38,516. *Average need-based loan:* Freshmen: $3555. Undergraduates: $4758. *Parent loans:* $20,722,609 (27% need-based, 73% non-need-based). *Programs:* Federal Direct (Subsidized and Unsubsidized Stafford, PLUS), Perkins, Federal Nursing, state.

WORK-STUDY *Federal work-study:* Total amount: $2,749,760; 1,491 jobs averaging $1761. *State or other work-study/employment:* Total amount: $37,500 (100% need-based). 25 part-time jobs averaging $1729.

ATHLETIC AWARDS Total amount: $12,247,507 (48% need-based, 52% non-need-based).

APPLYING FOR FINANCIAL AID *Required financial aid form:* FAFSA. *Financial aid deadline:* 5/1 (priority: 5/1). *Notification date:* Continuous beginning 3/15. Students must reply by 5/1.

CONTACT Michael Scott, Director of Scholarships and Student Financial Aid, Texas Christian University, PO Box 297012, Fort Worth, TX 76129-0002, 817-257-7858 or toll-free 800-828-3764. *Fax:* 817-257-7462. *E-mail:* m.scott@tcu.edu. *Website:* http://www.tcu.edu/.

TEXAS COLLEGE
Tyler, TX

Tuition & fees: $9686	Average undergraduate aid package: $9329

ABOUT THE INSTITUTION Independent Christian Methodist Episcopal Church, coed. *Awards:* certificates, associate, and bachelor's degrees. 18 undergraduate majors. *Total enrollment:* 883. Undergraduates: 860. Freshmen: 218. Federal methodology is used as a basis for awarding need-based institutional aid.

UNDERGRADUATE EXPENSES for 2013–2014 *Application fee:* $20. *Comprehensive fee:* $16,686 includes full-time tuition ($7996), mandatory fees ($1690), and room and board ($7000). *College room only:* $3600.

FRESHMAN FINANCIAL AID (Fall 2011) 236 applied for aid; of those 97% were deemed to have need. 99% of freshmen with need received aid; of those 1% had need fully met. *Average percent of need met:* 55% (excluding resources awarded to replace EFC). *Average financial aid package:* $8767 (excluding resources awarded to replace EFC). 2% of all full-time freshmen had no need and received non-need-based gift aid.

UNDERGRADUATE FINANCIAL AID (Fall 2011) 928 applied for aid; of those 98% were deemed to have need. 99% of undergraduates with need received aid; of those 3% had need fully met. *Average percent of need met:* 53% (excluding resources awarded to replace EFC). *Average financial aid package:* $9329 (excluding resources awarded to replace EFC). 2% of all full-time undergraduates had no need and received non-need-based gift aid.

GIFT AID (NEED-BASED) *Total amount:* $4,652,975 (82% federal, 18% state). *Receiving aid:* Freshmen: 89% (224); all full-time undergraduates: 91% (869). *Average award:* Freshmen: $6177; Undergraduates: $6285. *Scholarships, grants,*

and awards: Federal Pell, FSEOG, state, private, college/university gift aid from institutional funds, United Negro College Fund.

GIFT AID (NON-NEED-BASED) *Total amount:* $678,262 (14% state, 26% institutional, 60% external sources). *Receiving aid:* Freshmen: 1. Undergraduates: 1% (10). *Average award:* Freshmen: $2000. Undergraduates: $2433. *Scholarships, grants, and awards by category: Academic interests/achievement:* 37 awards ($60,992 total): general academic interests/achievements. *Creative arts/performance:* 73 awards ($77,765 total): dance, music. *Special achievements/activities:* 4 awards ($8215 total): cheerleading/drum major, leadership. *Special characteristics:* 11 awards ($29,106 total): children of faculty/staff, general special characteristics. *Tuition waivers:* Full or partial for employees or children of employees.

LOANS *Student loans:* $5,658,765 (49% need-based, 51% non-need-based). 93% of past graduating class borrowed through all loan programs. *Average indebtedness per student:* $21,147. *Average need-based loan:* Freshmen: $2769. Undergraduates: $3288. *Parent loans:* $604,676 (100% non-need-based). *Programs:* Federal Direct (Subsidized and Unsubsidized Stafford, PLUS), state.

WORK-STUDY *Federal work-study:* Total amount: $211,508; 160 jobs averaging $1320. *State or other work-study/employment:* Total amount: $17,072 (43% need-based, 57% non-need-based). 17 part-time jobs averaging $1010.

ATHLETIC AWARDS Total amount: $341,323 (100% non-need-based).

APPLYING FOR FINANCIAL AID *Required financial aid forms:* FAFSA, institution's own form. *Financial aid deadline (priority):* 6/1. *Notification date:* Continuous. Students must reply within 2 weeks of notification.

CONTACT Ms. Cecelia K. Jones, Director of Financial Aid, Texas College, 2404 North Grand Avenue, Tyler, TX 75702, 903-593-8311 Ext. 2241 or toll-free 800-306-6299. *Fax:* 903-593-9607. *E-mail:* ckjones@texascollege.edu. *Website:* http://www.texascollege.edu/.

TEXAS LUTHERAN UNIVERSITY
Seguin, TX

Tuition & fees: $24,990	Average undergraduate aid package: $20,997

ABOUT THE INSTITUTION Independent Evangelical Lutheran Church, coed. *Awards:* bachelor's and master's degrees. 38 undergraduate majors. *Total enrollment:* 1,318. Undergraduates: 1,311. Freshmen: 355. Federal methodology is used as a basis for awarding need-based institutional aid.

UNDERGRADUATE EXPENSES for 2013–2014 *Application fee:* $40. *Comprehensive fee:* $32,330 includes full-time tuition ($24,860), mandatory fees ($130), and room and board ($7340). *College room only:* $3800. Room and board charges vary according to board plan and housing facility. *Part-time tuition:* $825 per semester hour.

FRESHMAN FINANCIAL AID (Fall 2012, est.) 337 applied for aid; of those 91% were deemed to have need. 100% of freshmen with need received aid; of those 25% had need fully met. *Average percent of need met:* 83% (excluding resources awarded to replace EFC). *Average financial aid package:* $22,417 (excluding resources awarded to replace EFC). 14% of all full-time freshmen had no need and received non-need-based gift aid.

UNDERGRADUATE FINANCIAL AID (Fall 2012, est.) 1,139 applied for aid; of those 90% were deemed to have need. 100% of undergraduates with need received aid; of those 20% had need fully met. *Average percent of need met:* 78% (excluding resources awarded to replace EFC). *Average financial aid package:* $20,997 (excluding resources awarded to replace EFC). 17% of all full-time undergraduates had no need and received non-need-based gift aid.

GIFT AID (NEED-BASED) *Total amount:* $15,419,063 (16% federal, 14% state, 68% institutional, 2% external sources). *Receiving aid:* Freshmen: 86% (306); all full-time undergraduates: 81% (1,013). *Average award:* Freshmen: $17,938; Undergraduates: $15,641. *Scholarships, grants, and awards:* Federal Pell, FSEOG, state, college/university gift aid from institutional funds, TEACH Grants.

GIFT AID (NON-NEED-BASED) *Total amount:* $3,000,443 (1% state, 94% institutional, 5% external sources). *Receiving aid:* Freshmen: 15% (53). Undergraduates: 10% (126). *Average award:* Freshmen: $13,444. Undergraduates: $11,092. *Scholarships, grants, and awards by category: Academic interests/achievement:* biological sciences, business, education, general academic interests/achievements, mathematics, physical sciences, premedicine. *Creative arts/performance:* journalism/publications, music, theater/drama. *Special achievements/activities:*

general special achievements/activities, junior miss, leadership, memberships, religious involvement. *Special characteristics:* 764 awards ($1,548,636 total): children and siblings of alumni, children of faculty/staff, first-generation college students, religious affiliation, veterans, veterans' children. *Tuition waivers:* Full or partial for children of alumni, employees or children of employees. *ROTC:* Army cooperative, Air Force cooperative.

LOANS *Student loans:* $9,887,646 (72% need-based, 28% non-need-based). 75% of past graduating class borrowed through all loan programs. *Average indebtedness per student:* $37,145. *Average need-based loan:* Freshmen: $4089. Undergraduates: $4955. *Parent loans:* $1,288,146 (31% need-based, 69% non-need-based). *Programs:* Federal Direct (Subsidized and Unsubsidized Stafford, PLUS), Perkins, state, alternative loans.

WORK-STUDY *Federal work-study:* Total amount: $1,194,124; 604 jobs averaging $2015. *State or other work-study/employment:* Total amount: $13,521 (78% need-based, 22% non-need-based). 9 part-time jobs averaging $1990.

APPLYING FOR FINANCIAL AID *Required financial aid form:* FAFSA. *Financial aid deadline (priority):* 3/1. *Notification date:* Continuous beginning 3/1. Students must reply by 8/15.

CONTACT Cathleen Wright, Director of Financial Aid, Texas Lutheran University, 1000 West Court Street, Seguin, TX 78155-5999, 830-372-8075 or toll-free 800-771-8521. *Fax:* 830-372-8096. *E-mail:* financialaid@tlu.edu. *Website:* http://www.tlu.edu/.

TEXAS SOUTHERN UNIVERSITY
Houston, TX

Tuition & fees (TX res): $7646	Average undergraduate aid package: $22,266

ABOUT THE INSTITUTION State-supported, coed. *Awards:* bachelor's, master's, and doctoral degrees. 55 undergraduate majors. *Total enrollment:* 9,646. Undergraduates: 7,021. Freshmen: 1,349. Federal methodology is used as a basis for awarding need-based institutional aid.

UNDERGRADUATE EXPENSES for 2013–2014 *Application fee:* $42. *Tuition, state resident:* full-time $7646. *Tuition, nonresident:* full-time $16,946. Full-time tuition and fees vary according to course level, course load, degree level, and program. Part-time tuition and fees vary according to course level, course load, degree level, and program. *College room and board:* $10,566. Room and board charges vary according to board plan, housing facility, and location.

FRESHMAN FINANCIAL AID (Fall 2012, est.) 1,156 applied for aid; of those 98% were deemed to have need. 100% of freshmen with need received aid; of those 100% had need fully met. *Average percent of need met:* 100% (excluding resources awarded to replace EFC). *Average financial aid package:* $17,500 (excluding resources awarded to replace EFC).

UNDERGRADUATE FINANCIAL AID (Fall 2012, est.) 5,498 applied for aid; of those 100% were deemed to have need. 100% of undergraduates with need received aid; of those 85% had need fully met. *Average percent of need met:* 85% (excluding resources awarded to replace EFC). *Average financial aid package:* $22,266 (excluding resources awarded to replace EFC).

GIFT AID (NEED-BASED) *Total amount:* $34,631,168 (58% federal, 20% state, 20% institutional, 2% external sources). *Receiving aid:* Freshmen: 93% (1,134); all full-time undergraduates: 93% (5,483). *Average award:* Freshmen: $11,250; Undergraduates: $15,125. *Scholarships, grants, and awards:* Federal Pell, FSEOG, state, private, college/university gift aid from institutional funds, United Negro College Fund, Federal Nursing.

GIFT AID (NON-NEED-BASED) *Tuition waivers:* Full or partial for minority students, senior citizens. *ROTC:* Army, Naval cooperative, Air Force cooperative.

LOANS *Student loans:* $40,566,300 (100% need-based). 83% of past graduating class borrowed through all loan programs. *Average indebtedness per student:* $39,197. *Average need-based loan:* Freshmen: $3122. Undergraduates: $4099. *Parent loans:* $3,065,784 (100% need-based). *Programs:* Federal Direct (Subsidized and Unsubsidized Stafford, PLUS), Perkins, state, college/university.

WORK-STUDY *Federal work-study:* Total amount: $329,098; 283 jobs averaging $4000. *State or other work-study/employment:* Total amount: $32,968 (100% need-based). 20 part-time jobs averaging $4000.

ATHLETIC AWARDS Total amount: $2,588,191 (100% need-based).

APPLYING FOR FINANCIAL AID *Required financial aid forms:* FAFSA, institution's own form. *Financial aid deadline (priority):* 4/15. *Notification date:* Continuous beginning 4/15.

CONTACT Office of Financial Aid, Texas Southern University, 3100 Cleburne Street, Houston, TX 77004-4584, 713-313-7011. *Fax:* 713-313-1858. *Website:* http://www.tsu.edu/.

TEXAS STATE UNIVERSITY–SAN MARCOS
San Marcos, TX

Tuition & fees (TX res): $8772	Average undergraduate aid package: $12,568

ABOUT THE INSTITUTION State-supported, coed. *Awards:* certificates, bachelor's, master's, and doctoral degrees. 89 undergraduate majors. *Total enrollment:* 34,225. Undergraduates: 29,458. Freshmen: 4,251. Federal methodology is used as a basis for awarding need-based institutional aid.

UNDERGRADUATE EXPENSES for 2013–2014 *Application fee:* $60. *Tuition, state resident:* full-time $6510; part-time $217 per credit hour. *Tuition, nonresident:* full-time $17,040; part-time $568 per credit hour. *Required fees:* full-time $2262; $52 per credit hour or $396 per term. Full-time tuition and fees vary according to course load and degree level. Part-time tuition and fees vary according to course load and degree level. *College room and board:* $7070; *Room only:* $4670. Room and board charges vary according to board plan and housing facility.

FRESHMAN FINANCIAL AID (Fall 2012, est.) 3,704 applied for aid; of those 69% were deemed to have need. 98% of freshmen with need received aid; of those 32% had need fully met. *Average percent of need met:* 72% (excluding resources awarded to replace EFC). *Average financial aid package:* $12,599 (excluding resources awarded to replace EFC). 2% of all full-time freshmen had no need and received non-need-based gift aid.

UNDERGRADUATE FINANCIAL AID (Fall 2012, est.) 19,786 applied for aid; of those 70% were deemed to have need. 99% of undergraduates with need received aid; of those 28% had need fully met. *Average percent of need met:* 72% (excluding resources awarded to replace EFC). *Average financial aid package:* $12,568 (excluding resources awarded to replace EFC). 1% of all full-time undergraduates had no need and received non-need-based gift aid.

GIFT AID (NEED-BASED) *Total amount:* $86,857,230 (52% federal, 43% state, 1% institutional, 4% external sources). *Receiving aid:* Freshmen: 51% (2,144); all full-time undergraduates: 47% (11,484). *Average award:* Freshmen: $7799; Undergraduates: $6689. *Scholarships, grants, and awards:* Federal Pell, FSEOG, state, private, college/university gift aid from institutional funds.

GIFT AID (NON-NEED-BASED) *Total amount:* $3,496,806 (1% federal, 34% institutional, 65% external sources). *Receiving aid:* Freshmen: 2% (79). Undergraduates: 1% (169). *Average award:* Freshmen: $5327. Undergraduates: $3363. *Scholarships, grants, and awards by category:* Academic interests/achievement: agriculture, business, education, English, general academic interests/achievements, home economics, international studies, military science. *Creative arts/performance:* applied art and design, art/fine arts, journalism/publications, music, theater/drama. *Special achievements/activities:* leadership. *Special characteristics:* children and siblings of alumni, first-generation college students, handicapped students, local/state students. *Tuition waivers:* Full or partial for employees or children of employees. *ROTC:* Army, Air Force.

LOANS *Student loans:* $117,915,135 (80% need-based, 20% non-need-based). 62% of past graduating class borrowed through all loan programs. *Average indebtedness per student:* $23,575. *Average need-based loan:* Freshmen: $5247. Undergraduates: $6843. *Parent loans:* $59,008,722 (26% need-based, 74% non-need-based). *Programs:* Federal Direct (Subsidized and Unsubsidized Stafford, PLUS), Perkins, state, college/university, short-term emergency loans.

WORK-STUDY *Federal work-study:* Total amount: $2,881,624; 735 jobs averaging $3920. *State or other work-study/employment:* Total amount: $237,768 (100% need-based). 54 part-time jobs averaging $4403.

ATHLETIC AWARDS Total amount: $3,397,806 (36% need-based, 64% non-need-based).

APPLYING FOR FINANCIAL AID *Required financial aid form:* FAFSA. *Financial aid deadline (priority):* 4/1. *Notification date:* Continuous beginning 5/1. Students must reply within 3 weeks of notification.

CONTACT Mr. Chris Murr, Director of Financial Aid, Texas State University–San Marcos, 601 University Drive, San Marcos, TX 78666-4602, 512-245-2315. *Fax:* 512-245-7920. *E-mail:* cm18@txstate.edu. *Website:* http://www.txstate.edu/.

TEXAS TECH UNIVERSITY
Lubbock, TX

Tuition & fees (TX res): $8942	Average undergraduate aid package: $10,031

ABOUT THE INSTITUTION State-supported, coed. *Awards:* certificates, bachelor's, master's, and doctoral degrees. 88 undergraduate majors. *Total enrollment:* 32,327. Undergraduates: 26,063. Freshmen: 4,464. Federal methodology is used as a basis for awarding need-based institutional aid.

UNDERGRADUATE EXPENSES for 2013–2014 *Application fee:* $60. *Tuition, state resident:* full-time $6077; part-time $203 per credit hour. *Tuition, nonresident:* full-time $16,607; part-time $554 per credit hour. *Required fees:* full-time $2865; $35 per credit hour or $908 per credit hour. Full-time tuition and fees vary according to course load, location, and reciprocity agreements. Part-time tuition and fees vary according to course load, location, and reciprocity agreements. *College room and board:* $8275; *Room only:* $4380. Room and board charges vary according to board plan and housing facility.

FRESHMAN FINANCIAL AID (Fall 2011) 2,890 applied for aid; of those 87% were deemed to have need. 82% of freshmen with need received aid; of those 17% had need fully met. *Average percent of need met:* 53% (excluding resources awarded to replace EFC). *Average financial aid package:* $9907 (excluding resources awarded to replace EFC). 8% of all full-time freshmen had no need and received non-need-based gift aid.

UNDERGRADUATE FINANCIAL AID (Fall 2011) 14,181 applied for aid; of those 96% were deemed to have need. 83% of undergraduates with need received aid; of those 11% had need fully met. *Average percent of need met:* 44% (excluding resources awarded to replace EFC). *Average financial aid package:* $10,031 (excluding resources awarded to replace EFC). 4% of all full-time undergraduates had no need and received non-need-based gift aid.

GIFT AID (NEED-BASED) *Total amount:* $83,617,400 (38% federal, 20% state, 35% institutional, 7% external sources). *Receiving aid:* Freshmen: 39% (1,706); all full-time undergraduates: 40% (9,339). *Average award:* Freshmen: $8197; Undergraduates: $7430. *Scholarships, grants, and awards:* Federal Pell, FSEOG, state, private, college/university gift aid from institutional funds.

GIFT AID (NON-NEED-BASED) *Total amount:* $2,954,570 (70% institutional, 30% external sources). *Receiving aid:* Freshmen: 20% (874). Undergraduates: 12% (2,813). *Average award:* Freshmen: $2335. Undergraduates: $2130. *Scholarships, grants, and awards by category: Academic interests/achievement:* agriculture, architecture, biological sciences, business, communication, computer science, education, engineering/technologies, English, foreign languages, general academic interests/ achievements, home economics, humanities, international studies, mathematics, military science, physical sciences, premedicine, social sciences. *Creative arts/performance:* applied art and design, art/fine arts, dance, journalism/publications, music, performing arts, theater/drama. *Special achievements/activities:* community service, memberships, rodeo. *Special characteristics:* children of faculty/staff, first-generation college students, handicapped students, out-of-state students, veterans, veterans' children. *Tuition waivers:* Full or partial for employees or children of employees, senior citizens. *ROTC:* Army, Air Force.

LOANS *Student loans:* $108,508,932 (84% need-based, 16% non-need-based). 44% of past graduating class borrowed through all loan programs. *Average indebtedness per student:* $18,358. *Average need-based loan:* Freshmen: $3955. Undergraduates: $4425. *Parent loans:* $20,079,182 (75% need-based, 25% non-need-based). *Programs:* Perkins, state, college/university.

WORK-STUDY *Federal work-study:* Total amount: $1,079,710; jobs available. *State or other work-study/employment:* Total amount: $48,780 (100% need-based). Part-time jobs available.

ATHLETIC AWARDS Total amount: $4,405,202 (97% need-based, 3% non-need-based).

APPLYING FOR FINANCIAL AID *Required financial aid form:* FAFSA. *Financial aid deadline (priority):* 4/15. *Notification date:* Continuous. Students must reply within 2 weeks of notification.

CONTACT Becky Wilson, Managing Director of Student Financial Aid, Texas Tech University, PO Box 45011, Lubbock, TX 79409-5011, 806-742-0454. *Fax:* 806-742-0880.
Website: http://www.ttu.edu/.

TEXAS WESLEYAN UNIVERSITY
Fort Worth, TX

Tuition & fees: $20,840	Average undergraduate aid package: $16,198

ABOUT THE INSTITUTION Independent United Methodist, coed. *Awards:* bachelor's, master's, and doctoral degrees. 39 undergraduate majors. *Total enrollment:* 3,204. Undergraduates: 1,794. Freshmen: 282. Federal methodology is used as a basis for awarding need-based institutional aid.

UNDERGRADUATE EXPENSES for 2013–2014 *Comprehensive fee:* $28,310 includes full-time tuition ($18,722), mandatory fees ($2118), and room and board ($7470). *College room only:* $4380. Full-time tuition and fees vary according to course load. Room and board charges vary according to housing facility. *Part-time tuition:* $635 per credit hour. *Part-time fees:* $80 per credit hour. Part-time tuition and fees vary according to course load.

FRESHMAN FINANCIAL AID (Fall 2011) 141 applied for aid; of those 72% were deemed to have need. 100% of freshmen with need received aid; of those 15% had need fully met. *Average percent of need met:* 60% (excluding resources awarded to replace EFC). *Average financial aid package:* $13,598 (excluding resources awarded to replace EFC). 13% of all full-time freshmen had no need and received non-need-based gift aid.

UNDERGRADUATE FINANCIAL AID (Fall 2011) 1,088 applied for aid; of those 99% were deemed to have need. 100% of undergraduates with need received aid; of those 6% had need fully met. *Average percent of need met:* 64% (excluding resources awarded to replace EFC). *Average financial aid package:* $16,198 (excluding resources awarded to replace EFC). 11% of all full-time undergraduates had no need and received non-need-based gift aid.

GIFT AID (NEED-BASED) *Total amount:* $10,954,137 (37% federal, 24% state, 38% institutional, 1% external sources). *Receiving aid:* Freshmen: 63% (102); all full-time undergraduates: 85% (1,013). *Average award:* Freshmen: $12,069; Undergraduates: $10,779. *Scholarships, grants, and awards:* Federal Pell, FSEOG, state, private, college/university gift aid from institutional funds.

GIFT AID (NON-NEED-BASED) *Total amount:* $998,582 (20% federal, 78% institutional, 2% external sources). *Receiving aid:* Freshmen: 2% (4). Undergraduates: 11% (131). *Average award:* Freshmen: $7718. Undergraduates: $6439. *Scholarships, grants, and awards by category: Academic interests/ achievement:* biological sciences, business, communication, education, English, foreign languages, general academic interests/achievements, health fields, humanities, international studies, mathematics, military science, physical sciences, premedicine, religion/ biblical studies, social sciences. *Creative arts/performance:* art/fine arts, creative writing, dance, debating, journalism/publications, music, performing arts, theater/ drama. *Special achievements/activities:* cheerleading/drum major, community service, leadership, memberships, religious involvement. *Special characteristics:* adult students, children and siblings of alumni, children of current students, children of educators, children of faculty/staff, children of public servants, children of union members/ company employees, children with a deceased or disabled parent, ethnic background, first-generation college students, general special characteristics, handicapped students, international students, local/state students, married students, members of minority groups, out-of-state students, parents of current students, previous college experience, public servants, relatives of clergy, religious affiliation, siblings of current students, spouses of current students, spouses of deceased or disabled public servants, twins, veterans, veterans' children. *Tuition waivers:* Full or partial for employees or children of employees. *ROTC:* Army, Air Force cooperative.

LOANS *Student loans:* $13,307,060 (97% need-based, 3% non-need-based). *Average need-based loan:* Freshmen: $3100. Undergraduates: $4129. *Parent loans:* $938,453 (95% need-based, 5% non-need-based). *Programs:* Federal Direct (Subsidized and Unsubsidized Stafford, PLUS), state.

WORK-STUDY Federal work-study jobs available. *State or other work-study/ employment:* Total amount: $216,195 (7% need-based, 93% non-need-based). Part-time jobs available.

ATHLETIC AWARDS Total amount: $1,395,091 (70% need-based, 30% non-need-based).

APPLYING FOR FINANCIAL AID *Required financial aid form:* FAFSA. *Financial aid deadline:* Continuous. *Notification date:* Continuous beginning 3/1. Students must reply by 3/1.

CONTACT Laurie Rosenkrantz, Office of Financial Aid, Texas Wesleyan University, 1201 Wesleyan Street, Fort Worth, TX 76105-1536, 817-531-4420 or toll-free 800-580-8980. *Fax:* 817-531-4231. *E-mail:* financialaid@txwes.edu.
Website: http://www.txwes.edu/.

TEXAS WOMAN'S UNIVERSITY
Denton, TX

Tuition & fees (TX res): $6703 | **Average undergraduate aid package: $8121**

ABOUT THE INSTITUTION State-supported, coed, primarily women. *Awards:* certificates, bachelor's, master's, and doctoral degrees. 38 undergraduate majors. *Total enrollment:* 15,168. Undergraduates: 9,443. Freshmen: 1,159. Both federal and institutional methodology are used as a basis for awarding need-based institutional aid.

UNDERGRADUATE EXPENSES for 2013–2014 *Application fee:* $50. *Tuition, state resident:* full-time $5156; part-time $171.84 per credit hour. *Tuition, nonresident:* full-time $15,685; part-time $522.84 per credit hour. *Required fees:* full-time $1547. Full-time tuition and fees vary according to course load, program, and reciprocity agreements. Part-time tuition and fees vary according to course load, program, and reciprocity agreements. *College room and board:* $6930; *Room only:* $3582. Room and board charges vary according to board plan and housing facility.

FRESHMAN FINANCIAL AID (Fall 2012, est.) 1,059 applied for aid; of those 87% were deemed to have need. 99% of freshmen with need received aid; of those 15% had need fully met. *Average percent of need met:* 74% (excluding resources awarded to replace EFC). *Average financial aid package:* $9331 (excluding resources awarded to replace EFC). 3% of all full-time freshmen had no need and received non-need-based gift aid.

UNDERGRADUATE FINANCIAL AID (Fall 2012, est.) 5,399 applied for aid; of those 88% were deemed to have need. 99% of undergraduates with need received aid; of those 12% had need fully met. *Average percent of need met:* 70% (excluding resources awarded to replace EFC). *Average financial aid package:* $8121 (excluding resources awarded to replace EFC). 1% of all full-time undergraduates had no need and received non-need-based gift aid.

GIFT AID (NEED-BASED) *Total amount:* $31,146,126 (54% federal, 29% state, 13% institutional, 4% external sources). *Receiving aid:* Freshmen: 72% (850); all full-time undergraduates: 62% (4,074). *Average award:* Freshmen: $7931; Undergraduates: $6294. *Scholarships, grants, and awards:* Federal Pell, FSEOG, state, private, college/university gift aid from institutional funds, United Negro College Fund.

GIFT AID (NON-NEED-BASED) *Total amount:* $6,051,102 (100% institutional). *Receiving aid:* Freshmen: 24% (282). Undergraduates: 17% (1,129). *Average award:* Freshmen: $1591. Undergraduates: $1955. *Scholarships, grants, and awards by category: Academic interests/achievement:* biological sciences, business, communication, computer science, education, English, foreign languages, general academic interests/achievements, health fields, home economics, humanities, library science, mathematics, physical sciences, premedicine, social sciences. *Creative arts/performance:* applied art and design, art/fine arts, cinema/film/broadcasting, dance, journalism/publications, music, theater/drama. *Special characteristics:* international students. *Tuition waivers:* Full or partial for senior citizens. *ROTC:* Army cooperative, Air Force cooperative.

LOANS Student loans: $32,505,691 (100% need-based). 71% of past graduating class borrowed through all loan programs. *Average indebtedness per student:* $25,155. *Average need-based loan:* Freshmen: $4573. Undergraduates: $4066. *Parent loans:* $581,493 (100% need-based). *Programs:* Federal Direct (Subsidized and Unsubsidized Stafford, PLUS), Perkins, Federal Nursing, state, college/university, alternative loans.

WORK-STUDY *Federal work-study:* Total amount: $178,084; jobs available. *State or other work-study/employment:* Total amount: $1,861,043 (5% need-based, 95% non-need-based). Part-time jobs available.

ATHLETIC AWARDS Total amount: $533,951 (100% need-based).

APPLYING FOR FINANCIAL AID *Required financial aid form:* FAFSA. *Financial aid deadline (priority):* 4/1. *Notification date:* 5/1.

CONTACT Mr. Governor Jackson, Director of Financial Aid, Texas Woman's University, PO Box 425408, Denton, TX 76204-5408, 940-898-3051 or toll-free 866-809-6130. *Fax:* 940-898-3068. *E-mail:* gjackson@twu.edu. *Website:* http://www.twu.edu/.

THIEL COLLEGE
Greenville, PA

Tuition & fees: $25,988 | **Average undergraduate aid package: $20,877**

ABOUT THE INSTITUTION Independent Evangelical Lutheran Church in America, coed. *Awards:* associate and bachelor's degrees. 43 undergraduate majors. *Total enrollment:* 1,109. Undergraduates: 1,109. Freshmen: 371. Federal methodology is used as a basis for awarding need-based institutional aid.

UNDERGRADUATE EXPENSES for 2013–2014 *Application fee:* $35. *One-time required fee:* $300. *Comprehensive fee:* $36,108 includes full-time tuition ($24,208), mandatory fees ($1780), and room and board ($10,120). *College room only:* $5060. Room and board charges vary according to board plan and housing facility. *Part-time tuition:* $808 per credit. *Part-time fees:* $890 per term. Part-time tuition and fees vary according to course load.

FRESHMAN FINANCIAL AID (Fall 2012, est.) 317 applied for aid; of those 97% were deemed to have need. 100% of freshmen with need received aid; of those 5% had need fully met. *Average percent of need met:* 68% (excluding resources awarded to replace EFC). *Average financial aid package:* $21,360 (excluding resources awarded to replace EFC). 4% of all full-time freshmen had no need and received non-need-based gift aid.

UNDERGRADUATE FINANCIAL AID (Fall 2012, est.) 1,047 applied for aid; of those 96% were deemed to have need. 99% of undergraduates with need received aid; of those 6% had need fully met. *Average percent of need met:* 66% (excluding resources awarded to replace EFC). *Average financial aid package:* $20,877 (excluding resources awarded to replace EFC). 6% of all full-time undergraduates had no need and received non-need-based gift aid.

GIFT AID (NEED-BASED) *Total amount:* $16,630,976 (16% federal, 10% state, 71% institutional, 3% external sources). *Receiving aid:* Freshmen: 83% (308); all full-time undergraduates: 88% (998). *Average award:* Freshmen: $17,743; Undergraduates: $16,660. *Scholarships, grants, and awards:* Federal Pell, FSEOG, state, private, college/university gift aid from institutional funds.

GIFT AID (NON-NEED-BASED) *Total amount:* $2,182,583 (2% federal, 1% state, 45% institutional, 52% external sources). *Receiving aid:* Freshmen: 4% (16). Undergraduates: 5% (61). *Average award:* Freshmen: $8325. Undergraduates: $9508. *Scholarships, grants, and awards by category: Academic interests/achievement:* 1,231 awards ($8,520,478 total): biological sciences, business, computer science, education, English, general academic interests/achievements, mathematics, physical sciences, religion/biblical studies. *Creative arts/performance:* 50 awards ($46,000 total): music. *Special achievements/activities:* 235 awards ($196,775 total): leadership. *Special characteristics:* 200 awards ($694,928 total): children and siblings of alumni, children of faculty/staff, relatives of clergy, religious affiliation, siblings of current students. *Tuition waivers:* Full or partial for employees or children of employees, senior citizens.

LOANS Student loans: $9,152,907 (83% need-based, 17% non-need-based). 83% of past graduating class borrowed through all loan programs. *Average indebtedness per student:* $28,401. *Average need-based loan:* Freshmen: $3823. Undergraduates: $4303. *Parent loans:* $3,472,625 (54% need-based, 46% non-need-based). *Programs:* Federal Direct (Subsidized and Unsubsidized Stafford, PLUS), Perkins, college/university.

WORK-STUDY *Federal work-study:* Total amount: $61,844; 42 jobs averaging $1472. *State or other work-study/employment:* Total amount: $492,885 (65% need-based, 35% non-need-based). 271 part-time jobs averaging $1472.

APPLYING FOR FINANCIAL AID *Required financial aid forms:* FAFSA, state aid form. *Financial aid deadline:* Continuous. *Notification date:* Continuous beginning 2/15. Students must reply within 2 weeks of notification.

CONTACT Ms. Cynthia H. Farrell, Director of Financial Aid, Thiel College, 75 College Avenue, Greenville, PA 16125-2181, 724-589-2178 or toll-free 800-248-4435. *Fax:* 724-589-2850. *E-mail:* cfarrell@thiel.edu. *Website:* http://www.thiel.edu/.

THOMAS AQUINAS COLLEGE
Santa Paula, CA

Tuition & fees: $24,500	Average undergraduate aid package: $21,556

ABOUT THE INSTITUTION Independent Roman Catholic, coed. *Awards:* bachelor's degrees. 1 undergraduate major. *Total enrollment:* 370. Undergraduates: 370. Freshmen: 84. Both federal and institutional methodology are used as a basis for awarding need-based institutional aid.

UNDERGRADUATE EXPENSES for 2013–2014 *Comprehensive fee:* $32,450 includes full-time tuition ($24,500) and room and board ($7950).

FRESHMAN FINANCIAL AID (Fall 2012, est.) 81 applied for aid; of those 98% were deemed to have need. 100% of freshmen with need received aid; of those 100% had need fully met. *Average percent of need met:* 100% (excluding resources awarded to replace EFC). *Average financial aid package:* $22,441 (excluding resources awarded to replace EFC).

UNDERGRADUATE FINANCIAL AID (Fall 2012, est.) 302 applied for aid; of those 99% were deemed to have need. 100% of undergraduates with need received aid; of those 100% had need fully met. *Average percent of need met:* 100% (excluding resources awarded to replace EFC). *Average financial aid package:* $21,556 (excluding resources awarded to replace EFC).

GIFT AID (NEED-BASED) *Total amount:* $4,339,521 (13% federal, 10% state, 76% institutional, 1% external sources). *Receiving aid:* Freshmen: 76% (78); all full-time undergraduates: 76% (280). *Average award:* Freshmen: $16,123; Undergraduates: $15,498. *Scholarships, grants, and awards:* Federal Pell, state, private, college/university gift aid from institutional funds, Canadian Federal and Provincial Grants.

GIFT AID (NON-NEED-BASED) *Total amount:* $26,300 (100% external sources).

LOANS *Student loans:* $1,248,660 (86% need-based, 14% non-need-based). 63% of past graduating class borrowed through all loan programs. *Average indebtedness per student:* $17,820. *Average need-based loan:* Freshmen: $3221. Undergraduates: $3973. *Parent loans:* $280,853 (100% non-need-based). *Programs:* Federal Direct (Subsidized and Unsubsidized Stafford, PLUS), college/university, Canadian federal and provincial loans.

WORK-STUDY *State or other work-study/employment:* Total amount: $1,010,823 (100% need-based). 265 part-time jobs averaging $3814.

APPLYING FOR FINANCIAL AID *Required financial aid forms:* FAFSA, institution's own form, state aid form, federal income tax form(s), W-2 forms, institution's own Non-custodial Parent Statement. *Financial aid deadline:* 3/2. *Notification date:* Continuous beginning 3/1. Students must reply by 5/1 or within 2 weeks of notification.

CONTACT Mr. Gregory Becher, Director of Financial Aid, Thomas Aquinas College, 10,000 Ojai Road, Santa Paula, CA 93060-9980, 805-525-4419 Ext. 5936 or toll-free 800-634-9797. *Fax:* 805-525-9342. *E-mail:* gbecher@thomasaquinas.edu. *Website:* http://www.thomasaquinas.edu/.

THOMAS COLLEGE
Waterville, ME

CONTACT Jeannine Bosse, Associate Director of Student Financial Aid, Thomas College, 180 West River Road, Waterville, ME 04901-5097, 800-339-7001. *Fax:* 207-859-1114. *E-mail:* sfsassistant@thomas.edu. *Website:* http://www.thomas.edu/.

THOMAS EDISON STATE COLLEGE
Trenton, NJ

ABOUT THE INSTITUTION State-supported, coed. *Awards:* certificates, associate, bachelor's, and master's degrees (offers only distance learning degree programs). 74 undergraduate majors. *Total enrollment:* 20,606. Undergraduates: 19,406.

GIFT AID (NEED-BASED) *Scholarships, grants, and awards:* Federal Pell, state, private.

LOANS *Programs:* state, private loans.

APPLYING FOR FINANCIAL AID *Required financial aid forms:* FAFSA, institution's own form.

CONTACT James Owens, Director of Financial Aid, Thomas Edison State College, 101 West State Street, Trenton, NJ 08608, 609-633-9658 or toll-free 888-442-8372. *Fax:* 609-633-6489. *E-mail:* finaid@tesc.edu. *Website:* http://www.tesc.edu/.

THOMAS JEFFERSON UNIVERSITY
Philadelphia, PA

CONTACT Susan McFadden, University Director of Financial Aid, Thomas Jefferson University, 1025 Walnut Street, Philadelphia, PA 19107, 215-955-2867 or toll-free 877-533-3247. *Fax:* 215-955-5186. *E-mail:* financial.aid@jefferson.edu. *Website:* http://www.jefferson.edu/.

THOMAS MORE COLLEGE
Crestview Hills, KY

Tuition & fees: $27,220	Average undergraduate aid package: $19,944

ABOUT THE INSTITUTION Independent Roman Catholic, coed. *Awards:* certificates, associate, bachelor's, and master's degrees. 44 undergraduate majors. *Total enrollment:* 1,761. Undergraduates: 1,652. Freshmen: 266. Federal methodology is used as a basis for awarding need-based institutional aid.

UNDERGRADUATE EXPENSES for 2013–2014 *Application fee:* $25. *Comprehensive fee:* $34,720 includes full-time tuition ($26,500), mandatory fees ($720), and room and board ($7500). *College room only:* $3500. Full-time tuition and fees vary according to student level. Room and board charges vary according to board plan and housing facility. *Part-time tuition:* $590 per credit. *Part-time fees:* $30 per hour; $15 per term. Part-time tuition and fees vary according to student level.

FRESHMAN FINANCIAL AID (Fall 2012, est.) 245 applied for aid; of those 91% were deemed to have need. 100% of freshmen with need received aid; of those 21% had need fully met. *Average percent of need met:* 72% (excluding resources awarded to replace EFC). *Average financial aid package:* $20,662 (excluding resources awarded to replace EFC). 6% of all full-time freshmen had no need and received non-need-based gift aid.

UNDERGRADUATE FINANCIAL AID (Fall 2012, est.) 1,028 applied for aid; of those 68% were deemed to have need. 100% of undergraduates with need received aid; of those 22% had need fully met. *Average percent of need met:* 71% (excluding resources awarded to replace EFC). *Average financial aid package:* $19,944 (excluding resources awarded to replace EFC). 14% of all full-time undergraduates had no need and received non-need-based gift aid.

GIFT AID (NEED-BASED) *Total amount:* $11,612,349 (15% federal, 14% state, 70% institutional, 1% external sources). *Receiving aid:* Freshmen: 85% (224); all full-time undergraduates: 55% (694). *Average award:* Freshmen: $16,519; Undergraduates: $15,461. *Scholarships, grants, and awards:* Federal Pell, FSEOG, state, private, college/university gift aid from institutional funds, Federal Nursing.

GIFT AID (NON-NEED-BASED) *Total amount:* $2,891,600 (5% state, 93% institutional, 2% external sources). *Receiving aid:* Freshmen: 11% (29). Undergraduates: 6% (79). *Average award:* Freshmen: $14,421. Undergraduates: $13,433. *Scholarships, grants, and awards by category:* Academic interests/achievement: 589 awards ($6,400,513 total): biological sciences, business, communication, computer science, education, English, general academic interests/achievements, mathematics, physical sciences, premedicine, religion/biblical studies, social sciences. Creative arts/performance: 15 awards ($25,018 total): art/fine arts, theater/drama. Special achievements/activities: 62 awards ($105,400 total): community service, leadership, memberships, religious involvement. Special characteristics: 529 awards ($2,880,208 total): adult students, children and siblings of alumni, children of faculty/staff, children of union members/company employees, international students, members of minority groups, out-of-state students, religious affiliation, siblings of current students, veterans, veterans' children. *Tuition waivers:* Full or partial for employees or children of employees, senior citizens. *ROTC:* Army cooperative, Air Force cooperative.

LOANS *Student loans:* $6,839,045 (43% need-based, 57% non-need-based). 73% of past graduating class borrowed through all loan programs. *Average indebtedness*

per student: $32,650. **Average need-based loan:** Freshmen: $3388. Undergraduates: $4185. **Parent loans:** $1,646,760 (100% non-need-based). **Programs:** Federal Direct (Subsidized and Unsubsidized Stafford, PLUS), Perkins, Federal Nursing, college/university.

WORK-STUDY Federal work-study: Total amount: $191,250; 125 jobs averaging $1530. **State or other work-study/employment:** Total amount: $32,955 (43% need-based, 57% non-need-based). 169 part-time jobs averaging $195.

APPLYING FOR FINANCIAL AID Required financial aid form: FAFSA. **Financial aid deadline (priority):** 3/15. **Notification date:** Continuous beginning 3/1. Students must reply by 5/1.

CONTACT Ms. Mary Givhan, Director of Financial Aid, Thomas More College, 333 Thomas More Parkway, Crestview Hills, KY 41017-3495, 859-344-3531 or toll-free 800-825-4557. Fax: 859-344-3638. E-mail: mary.givhan@thomasmore.edu. Website: http://www.thomasmore.edu/.

THOMAS MORE COLLEGE OF LIBERAL ARTS
Merrimack, NH

Tuition & fees: N/R	Average undergraduate aid package: $17,808

ABOUT THE INSTITUTION Independent Roman Catholic Church, coed. **Awards:** bachelor's degrees. 1 undergraduate major. **Total enrollment:** 99. Undergraduates: 99. Freshmen: 24. Federal methodology is used as a basis for awarding need-based institutional aid.

FRESHMAN FINANCIAL AID (Fall 2012, est.) 34 applied for aid; of those 91% were deemed to have need. 100% of freshmen with need received aid; of those 3% had need fully met. **Average percent of need met:** 73% (excluding resources awarded to replace EFC). **Average financial aid package:** $16,889 (excluding resources awarded to replace EFC). 8% of all full-time freshmen had no need and received non-need-based gift aid.

UNDERGRADUATE FINANCIAL AID (Fall 2012, est.) 87 applied for aid; of those 90% were deemed to have need. 100% of undergraduates with need received aid; of those 9% had need fully met. **Average percent of need met:** 76% (excluding resources awarded to replace EFC). **Average financial aid package:** $17,808 (excluding resources awarded to replace EFC). 16% of all full-time undergraduates had no need and received non-need-based gift aid.

GIFT AID (NEED-BASED) Total amount: $1,082,577 (17% federal, 2% state, 80% institutional, 1% external sources). **Receiving aid:** Freshmen: 82% (31); all full-time undergraduates: 78% (74). **Average award:** Freshmen: $9974; Undergraduates: $8651. **Scholarships, grants, and awards:** Federal Pell, FSEOG, state, private, college/university gift aid from institutional funds.

GIFT AID (NON-NEED-BASED) Total amount: $72,800 (100% institutional). **Receiving aid:** Freshmen: 47% (18). Undergraduates: 59% (56). **Average award:** Freshmen: $2833. Undergraduates: $4853. **Scholarships, grants, and awards by category:** Academic interests/achievement: general academic interests/achievements.

LOANS Student loans: $455,750 (55% need-based, 45% non-need-based). 70% of past graduating class borrowed through all loan programs. Average indebtedness per student: $20,107. **Average need-based loan:** Freshmen: $3417. Undergraduates: $3713. **Parent loans:** $135,020 (69% need-based, 31% non-need-based). **Programs:** Federal Direct (Subsidized and Unsubsidized Stafford, PLUS).

WORK-STUDY State or other work-study/employment: Total amount: $92,900 (95% need-based, 5% non-need-based). 53 part-time jobs averaging $1425.

APPLYING FOR FINANCIAL AID Required financial aid form: FAFSA. **Financial aid deadline:** Continuous. **Notification date:** Continuous beginning 2/15. Students must reply within 2 weeks of notification.

CONTACT Clinton A. Hanson Jr., Director of Financial Aid, Thomas More College of Liberal Arts, 6 Manchester Street, Merrimack, NH 03054-4818, 603-880-8308 Ext. 23 or toll-free 800-880-8308. Fax: 603-880-9280. E-mail: chanson@thomasmorecollege.edu. Website: http://www.thomasmorecollege.edu/.

THOMAS UNIVERSITY
Thomasville, GA

Tuition & fees: N/R	Average undergraduate aid package: N/A

ABOUT THE INSTITUTION Independent, coed. **Awards:** certificates, associate, bachelor's, and master's degrees. 23 undergraduate majors. **Total enrollment:** 1,124. Undergraduates: 882. Freshmen: 142. Federal methodology is used as a basis for awarding need-based institutional aid.

GIFT AID (NEED-BASED) Scholarships, grants, and awards: Federal Pell, FSEOG, state, private, college/university gift aid from institutional funds.

GIFT AID (NON-NEED-BASED) Scholarships, grants, and awards by category: Academic interests/achievement: biological sciences, business, education, English, general academic interests/achievements, health fields, humanities, international studies, physical sciences, social sciences. Creative arts/performance: art/fine arts, music. Special characteristics: children of faculty/staff, ethnic background, out-of-state students, veterans.

LOANS Programs: Federal Direct (Subsidized and Unsubsidized Stafford, PLUS), state, alternative loans.

WORK-STUDY Federal work-study jobs available.

APPLYING FOR FINANCIAL AID Required financial aid forms: FAFSA, state aid form. **Financial aid deadline (priority):** 5/1. **Notification date:** Continuous.

CONTACT Mr. Michael C. Rayburn, Director of Financial Aid, Thomas University, 1501 Millpond Road, Thomasville, GA 31792-7499, 229-226-1621 Ext. 1023 or toll-free 800-538-9784. Fax: 229-227-6888. E-mail: mrayburn@thomasu.edu. Website: http://www.thomasu.edu/.

TIFFIN UNIVERSITY
Tiffin, OH

Tuition & fees: $20,700	Average undergraduate aid package: $14,571

ABOUT THE INSTITUTION Independent, coed. **Awards:** certificates, associate, bachelor's, and master's degrees. 39 undergraduate majors. **Total enrollment:** 6,920. Undergraduates: 5,728. Freshmen: 1,313. Federal methodology is used as a basis for awarding need-based institutional aid.

UNDERGRADUATE EXPENSES for 2013-2014 Application fee: $20. **Comprehensive fee:** $30,273 includes full-time tuition ($20,700) and room and board ($9573). **College room only:** $4973. Full-time tuition and fees vary according to course load, degree level, location, and program. Room and board charges vary according to board plan and housing facility. **Part-time tuition:** $690 per credit. Part-time tuition and fees vary according to course load, degree level, location, and program.

FRESHMAN FINANCIAL AID (Fall 2012, est.) 480 applied for aid; of those 95% were deemed to have need. 100% of freshmen with need received aid; of those 10% had need fully met. **Average percent of need met:** 65% (excluding resources awarded to replace EFC). **Average financial aid package:** $17,482 (excluding resources awarded to replace EFC).

UNDERGRADUATE FINANCIAL AID (Fall 2012, est.) 2,157 applied for aid; of those 96% were deemed to have need. 100% of undergraduates with need received aid; of those 7% had need fully met. **Average percent of need met:** 56% (excluding resources awarded to replace EFC). **Average financial aid package:** $14,571 (excluding resources awarded to replace EFC).

GIFT AID (NEED-BASED) Total amount: $43,664,892 (34% federal, 5% state, 61% institutional). **Receiving aid:** Freshmen: 65% (454); all full-time undergraduates: 75% (2,052). **Average award:** Freshmen: $11,966; Undergraduates: $10,363. **Scholarships, grants, and awards:** Federal Pell, FSEOG, state, private, college/university gift aid from institutional funds.

GIFT AID (NON-NEED-BASED) Receiving aid: Freshmen: 5% (33). Undergraduates: 3% (82). **Scholarships, grants, and awards by category:** Academic interests/achievement: 1,160 awards ($8,789,126 total): general academic interests/achievements. Creative arts/performance: 195 awards ($420,200 total): music, performing arts, theater/drama. Special achievements/activities: 20 awards ($22,600 total): cheerleading/drum major. Special characteristics: 24 awards ($272,779 total): children of faculty/staff. **Tuition waivers:** Full or partial for employees or children of employees, senior citizens. **ROTC:** Army cooperative, Air Force cooperative.

LOANS *Student loans:* $37,056,024 (100% need-based). 73% of past graduating class borrowed through all loan programs. *Average indebtedness per student:* $30,119. *Average need-based loan:* Freshmen: $4816. Undergraduates: $4807. *Parent loans:* $1,536,521 (100% need-based). *Programs:* Federal Direct (Subsidized and Unsubsidized Stafford, PLUS), Perkins, college/university.

WORK-STUDY *Federal work-study:* Total amount: $1,752,566; 221 jobs averaging $1234.

ATHLETIC AWARDS Total amount: $1,977,091 (100% need-based).

APPLYING FOR FINANCIAL AID *Required financial aid form:* FAFSA. *Financial aid deadline:* Continuous. *Notification date:* Continuous beginning 2/1. Students must reply within 2 weeks of notification.

CONTACT Ms. Cindy Little, Director of Financial Aid Operations, Tiffin University, 155 Miami Street, Tiffin, OH 44883, 419-448-3415 or toll-free 800-968-6446. *Fax:* 419-443-5006. *E-mail:* clittle@tiffin.edu. *Website:* http://www.tiffin.edu/.

TOCCOA FALLS COLLEGE
Toccoa Falls, GA

CONTACT Vince Welch, Director of Financial Aid, Toccoa Falls College, PO Box 800900, Toccoa Falls, GA 30598, 706-886-7299 Ext. 5234. *Fax:* 706-282-6041. *E-mail:* vwelch@tfc.edu. *Website:* http://www.tfc.edu/.

TORAH TEMIMAH TALMUDICAL SEMINARY
Brooklyn, NY

CONTACT Financial Aid Office, Torah Temimah Talmudical Seminary, 507 Ocean Parkway, Brooklyn, NY 11218-5913, 718-853-8500.

TOUGALOO COLLEGE
Tougaloo, MS

CONTACT Director of Financial Aid, Tougaloo College, 500 West County Line Road, Tougaloo, MS 39174, 601-977-6134 or toll-free 888-42GALOO. *Fax:* 601-977-6164. *Website:* http://www.tougaloo.edu/.

TOURO COLLEGE
New York, NY

CONTACT Office of Financial Aid, Touro College, 27 West 23rd Street, New York, NY 10010, 212-463-0400. *Website:* http://www.touro.edu/.

TOURO COLLEGE LOS ANGELES
West Hollywood, CA

CONTACT Financial Aid Office, Touro College Los Angeles, 1317 North Crescent Heights Boulevard, West Hollywood, CA 90046, 323-822-9700. *Website:* http://www.touro.edu/losangeles/.

TOWSON UNIVERSITY
Towson, MD

Tuition & fees (MD res): $8132	Average undergraduate aid package: $9169

ABOUT THE INSTITUTION State-supported, coed. *Awards:* certificates, bachelor's, master's, and doctoral degrees. 58 undergraduate majors. *Total enrollment:* 21,464. Undergraduates: 17,517. Freshmen: 2,543. Federal methodology is used as a basis for awarding need-based institutional aid.

UNDERGRADUATE EXPENSES for 2013–2014 *Application fee:* $45. *Tuition, state resident:* full-time $5660; part-time $246 per credit hour. *Tuition, nonresident:* full-time $17,282; part-time $723 per credit hour. *Required fees:* full-time $2472; $103 per credit hour. Full-time tuition and fees vary according to course load. Part-time tuition and fees vary according to course load. *College room and board:* $10,338; *Room only:* $5910. Room and board charges vary according to board plan and housing facility.

FRESHMAN FINANCIAL AID (Fall 2012, est.) 2,072 applied for aid; of those 68% were deemed to have need. 91% of freshmen with need received aid; of those 13% had need fully met. *Average percent of need met:* 57% (excluding resources awarded to replace EFC). *Average financial aid package:* $9227 (excluding resources awarded to replace EFC). 7% of all full-time freshmen had no need and received non-need-based gift aid.

UNDERGRADUATE FINANCIAL AID (Fall 2012, est.) 11,207 applied for aid; of those 76% were deemed to have need. 95% of undergraduates with need received aid; of those 12% had need fully met. *Average percent of need met:* 60% (excluding resources awarded to replace EFC). *Average financial aid package:* $9169 (excluding resources awarded to replace EFC). 6% of all full-time undergraduates had no need and received non-need-based gift aid.

GIFT AID (NEED-BASED) *Total amount:* $42,933,309 (46% federal, 17% state, 36% institutional, 1% external sources). *Receiving aid:* Freshmen: 29% (721); all full-time undergraduates: 32% (5,025). *Average award:* Freshmen: $8668; Undergraduates: $7816. *Scholarships, grants, and awards:* Federal Pell, FSEOG, state, private, college/university gift aid from institutional funds.

GIFT AID (NON-NEED-BASED) *Total amount:* $10,328,369 (4% federal, 8% state, 69% institutional, 19% external sources). *Receiving aid:* Freshmen: 21% (519). Undergraduates: 14% (2,147). *Average award:* Freshmen: $4935. Undergraduates: $4441. *Scholarships, grants, and awards by category: Academic interests/achievement:* 1,652 awards ($7,527,699 total): biological sciences, business, communication, computer science, education, English, foreign languages, general academic interests/achievements, health fields, mathematics, physical sciences. *Creative arts/performance:* 154 awards ($523,258 total): art/fine arts, cinema/film/broadcasting, dance, debating, music, performing arts, theater/drama. *Special achievements/activities:* 240 awards ($576,205 total): community service, memberships. *Special characteristics:* 583 awards ($1,623,948 total): adult students, children and siblings of alumni, children of faculty/staff, ethnic background, first-generation college students, handicapped students, international students, members of minority groups, out-of-state students, previous college experience, veterans. *Tuition waivers:* Full or partial for employees or children of employees, senior citizens. *ROTC:* Army cooperative, Air Force cooperative.

LOANS *Student loans:* $68,011,015 (47% need-based, 53% non-need-based). 60% of past graduating class borrowed through all loan programs. *Average indebtedness per student:* $23,812. *Average need-based loan:* Freshmen: $3250. Undergraduates: $4051. *Parent loans:* $29,519,914 (1% need-based, 99% non-need-based). *Programs:* Federal Direct (Subsidized and Unsubsidized Stafford, PLUS), Perkins.

WORK-STUDY *Federal work-study:* Total amount: $636,545; 365 jobs averaging $1729.

ATHLETIC AWARDS Total amount: $5,170,449 (3% need-based, 97% non-need-based).

APPLYING FOR FINANCIAL AID *Required financial aid forms:* FAFSA, state aid form. *Financial aid deadline (priority):* 2/15. *Notification date:* Continuous beginning 3/21. Students must reply by 5/1 or within 2 weeks of notification.

CONTACT Mr. David Horne, Director of Financial Aid, Towson University, 8000 York Road, Towson, MD 21252-0001, 410-704-6242. *E-mail:* finaid@towson.edu. *Website:* http://www.towson.edu/.

TRANSYLVANIA UNIVERSITY
Lexington, KY

Tuition & fees: $29,865	Average undergraduate aid package: $24,373

ABOUT THE INSTITUTION Independent Christian Church (Disciples of Christ), coed. *Awards:* bachelor's degrees. 36 undergraduate majors. *Total enrollment:* 1,074. Undergraduates: 1,074. Freshmen: 333. Federal methodology is used as a basis for awarding need-based institutional aid.

UNDERGRADUATE EXPENSES for 2013–2014 *Comprehensive fee:* $38,615 includes full-time tuition ($28,645), mandatory fees ($1220), and room and board ($8750). Room and board charges vary according to board plan, housing facility, and location. *Part-time tuition:* $3175 per course. Part-time tuition and fees vary according to course load.

FRESHMAN FINANCIAL AID (Fall 2012, est.) 288 applied for aid; of those 86% were deemed to have need. 100% of freshmen with need received aid; of those 22% had need fully met. *Average percent of need met:* 84% (excluding resources awarded to replace EFC). *Average financial aid package:* $24,845 (excluding resources awarded to replace EFC). 24% of all full-time freshmen had no need and received non-need-based gift aid.

UNDERGRADUATE FINANCIAL AID (Fall 2012, est.) 816 applied for aid; of those 89% were deemed to have need. 100% of undergraduates with need received aid; of those 21% had need fully met. *Average percent of need met:* 81% (excluding resources awarded to replace EFC). *Average financial aid package:* $24,373 (excluding resources awarded to replace EFC). 30% of all full-time undergraduates had no need and received non-need-based gift aid.

GIFT AID (NEED-BASED) *Total amount:* $14,482,643 (9% federal, 17% state, 72% institutional, 2% external sources). *Receiving aid:* Freshmen: 74% (248); all full-time undergraduates: 68% (726). *Average award:* Freshmen: $20,791; Undergraduates: $20,083. *Scholarships, grants, and awards:* Federal Pell, FSEOG, state, private, college/university gift aid from institutional funds.

GIFT AID (NON-NEED-BASED) *Total amount:* $5,701,821 (11% state, 86% institutional, 3% external sources). *Receiving aid:* Freshmen: 12% (41). Undergraduates: 9% (99). *Average award:* Freshmen: $13,767. Undergraduates: $13,690. *Scholarships, grants, and awards by category: Academic interests/achievement:* $10,726,836 total: computer science, general academic interests/achievements. *Creative arts/performance:* $305,100 total: art/fine arts, music, theater/drama. *Special achievements/activities:* $3,319,308 total: general special achievements/activities, religious involvement. *Special characteristics:* $1,244,069 total: children of faculty/staff, members of minority groups, out-of-state students, relatives of clergy, religious affiliation. *Tuition waivers:* Full or partial for employees or children of employees. *ROTC:* Army cooperative, Air Force cooperative.

LOANS *Student loans:* $5,397,057 (71% need-based, 29% non-need-based). 66% of past graduating class borrowed through all loan programs. *Average indebtedness per student:* $26,604. *Average need-based loan:* Freshmen: $3887. Undergraduates: $4295. *Parent loans:* $1,101,085 (35% need-based, 65% non-need-based). *Programs:* Federal Direct (Subsidized and Unsubsidized Stafford, PLUS), Perkins, college/university.

WORK-STUDY *Federal work-study:* Total amount: $534,858; 430 jobs averaging $1713. *State or other work-study/employment:* Total amount: $344,870 (34% need-based, 66% non-need-based). 48 part-time jobs averaging $7107.

APPLYING FOR FINANCIAL AID *Required financial aid form:* FAFSA. *Financial aid deadline (priority):* 1/15. *Notification date:* Continuous beginning 3/15. Students must reply within 2 weeks of notification.

CONTACT Mr. Dave Cecil, Associate Vice President for Financial Aid, Transylvania University, 300 North Broadway, Lexington, KY 40508-1797, 859-233-8239 or toll-free 800-872-6798. *Fax:* 859-281-3650. *E-mail:* dcecil@transy.edu. *Website:* http://www.transy.edu/.

TREVECCA NAZARENE UNIVERSITY
Nashville, TN

Tuition & fees: $21,290	Average undergraduate aid package: N/A

ABOUT THE INSTITUTION Independent Nazarene, coed. *Awards:* associate, bachelor's, master's, and doctoral degrees. 72 undergraduate majors. *Total* enrollment: 2,472. Undergraduates: 1,467. Freshmen: 239. Federal methodology is used as a basis for awarding need-based institutional aid.

UNDERGRADUATE EXPENSES for 2013–2014 *Application fee:* $25. *Comprehensive fee:* $28,778 includes full-time tuition ($20,790), mandatory fees ($500), and room and board ($7488). *College room only:* $3744. Full-time tuition and fees vary according to course load and program. Room and board charges vary according to board plan. *Part-time tuition:* $803 per credit hour. Part-time tuition and fees vary according to course load and program. *Payment plan:* Tuition prepayment.

GIFT AID (NEED-BASED) *Total amount:* $3,157,024 (92% federal, 8% state). *Scholarships, grants, and awards:* Federal Pell, FSEOG, state, private, college/university gift aid from institutional funds.

GIFT AID (NON-NEED-BASED) *Total amount:* $6,301,474 (23% state, 70% institutional, 7% external sources). *Scholarships, grants, and awards by category: Academic interests/achievement:* biological sciences, business, communication, education, English, general academic interests/achievements, physical sciences, religion/biblical studies, social sciences. *Creative arts/performance:* cinema/film/broadcasting, music. *Special achievements/activities:* general special achievements/activities. *Special characteristics:* children of faculty/staff, general special characteristics, relatives of clergy, religious affiliation. *Tuition waivers:* Full or partial for employees or children of employees, senior citizens. *ROTC:* Army cooperative.

LOANS *Student loans:* $23,165,634 (54% need-based, 46% non-need-based). 74% of past graduating class borrowed through all loan programs. *Parent loans:* $3,638,260 (100% non-need-based). *Programs:* Federal Direct (Subsidized and Unsubsidized Stafford, PLUS), Perkins.

WORK-STUDY *Federal work-study:* Total amount: $148,770; jobs available. *State or other work-study/employment:* Total amount: $430,133 (100% need-based). Part-time jobs available.

ATHLETIC AWARDS Total amount: $1,241,510 (100% non-need-based).

APPLYING FOR FINANCIAL AID *Required financial aid form:* FAFSA. *Financial aid deadline:* 8/1 (priority: 3/1). *Notification date:* Continuous.

CONTACT Eddie White, Director of Financial Aid, Trevecca Nazarene University, 333 Murfreesboro Road, Nashville, TN 37210-2834, 615-248-1242 or toll-free 888-210-4TNU. *Fax:* 615-248-7728. *E-mail:* ewhite@trevecca.edu. *Website:* http://www.trevecca.edu/.

TRIDENT UNIVERSITY INTERNATIONAL
Cypress, CA

ABOUT THE INSTITUTION Independent, coed. *Awards:* certificates, diplomas, bachelor's, master's, and doctoral degrees (offers only online degree programs). 9 undergraduate majors.

GIFT AID (NEED-BASED) *Scholarships, grants, and awards:* Federal Pell.

LOANS *Programs:* Federal Direct (Subsidized and Unsubsidized Stafford, PLUS).

APPLYING FOR FINANCIAL AID *Required financial aid forms:* FAFSA, institution's own form.

CONTACT Taisha Azlin, Director of Financial Aid, Trident University International, 5665 Plaza Drive, Third Floor, Cypress, CA 90630, 800-375-9878 Ext. 1061. *Fax:* 714-484-7621. *E-mail:* financialaid@tuiu.edu. *Website:* http://www.trident.edu/.

TRINE UNIVERSITY
Angola, IN

Tuition & fees: $28,850	Average undergraduate aid package: $21,543

ABOUT THE INSTITUTION Independent, coed. *Awards:* associate, bachelor's, and master's degrees. 35 undergraduate majors. *Total enrollment:* 1,948. Undergraduates: 1,943. Freshmen: 421. Federal methodology is used as a basis for awarding need-based institutional aid.

UNDERGRADUATE EXPENSES for 2013–2014 *Comprehensive fee:* $38,350 includes full-time tuition ($28,700), mandatory fees ($150), and room and board ($9500). Full-time tuition and fees vary according to degree level, location, and program. Room and board charges vary according to board plan and housing facility.

Part-time tuition: $890 per credit hour. Part-time tuition and fees vary according to degree level, location, and program.

FRESHMAN FINANCIAL AID (Fall 2012, est.) 467 applied for aid; of those 84% were deemed to have need. 100% of freshmen with need received aid; of those 23% had need fully met. **Average percent of need met:** 84% (excluding resources awarded to replace EFC). **Average financial aid package:** $23,417 (excluding resources awarded to replace EFC). 5% of all full-time freshmen had no need and received non-need-based gift aid.

UNDERGRADUATE FINANCIAL AID (Fall 2012, est.) 1,449 applied for aid; of those 82% were deemed to have need. 100% of undergraduates with need received aid; of those 31% had need fully met. **Average percent of need met:** 79% (excluding resources awarded to replace EFC). **Average financial aid package:** $21,543 (excluding resources awarded to replace EFC). 5% of all full-time undergraduates had no need and received non-need-based gift aid.

GIFT AID (NEED-BASED) Total amount: $7,045,612 (27% federal, 21% state, 52% institutional). **Receiving aid:** Freshmen: 74% (344); all full-time undergraduates: 55% (846). **Average award:** Freshmen: $4308; Undergraduates: $4306. **Scholarships, grants, and awards:** Federal Pell, FSEOG, state, private, college/university gift aid from institutional funds.

GIFT AID (NON-NEED-BASED) Total amount: $17,511,762 (95% institutional, 5% external sources). **Receiving aid:** Freshmen: 74% (348). Undergraduates: 68% (1,038). **Average award:** Freshmen: $12,050. Undergraduates: $11,251. **Scholarships, grants, and awards by category:** Academic interests/achievement: general academic interests/achievements. **Special characteristics:** children and siblings of alumni, children of faculty/staff, members of minority groups, siblings of current students. **Tuition waivers:** Full or partial for employees or children of employees. **ROTC:** Air Force cooperative.

LOANS Student loans: $7,897,581 (55% need-based, 45% non-need-based). 88% of past graduating class borrowed through all loan programs. **Average indebtedness per student:** $32,662. **Average need-based loan:** Freshmen: $3331. Undergraduates: $4174. **Parent loans:** $4,250,461 (100% non-need-based). **Programs:** alternative loans.

WORK-STUDY Federal work-study: Total amount: $128,388; jobs available. **State or other work-study/employment:** Total amount: $8499 (100% need-based). Part-time jobs available.

APPLYING FOR FINANCIAL AID Required financial aid form: FAFSA. **Financial aid deadline (priority):** 3/10. **Notification date:** Continuous beginning 3/15. Students must reply by 5/1 or within 2 weeks of notification.

CONTACT Kim Bennett, Director of Financial Aid, Trine University, 1 University Avenue, Angola, IN 46703-1764, 260-665-4175 or toll-free 800-347-4TSU. Fax: 260-665-4511. E-mail: admit@trine.edu. Website: http://www.trine.edu/.

TRINITY BAPTIST COLLEGE
Jacksonville, FL

Tuition & fees: $9040	Average undergraduate aid package: N/A

ABOUT THE INSTITUTION Independent Baptist, coed. **Awards:** associate, bachelor's, and master's degrees. 10 undergraduate majors. **Total enrollment:** 280. Undergraduates: 268. Federal methodology is used as a basis for awarding need-based institutional aid.

UNDERGRADUATE EXPENSES for 2013–2014 Application fee: $30. **Comprehensive fee:** $14,550 includes full-time tuition ($7990), mandatory fees ($1050), and room and board ($5510). **College room only:** $2510. Room and board charges vary according to board plan. **Part-time tuition:** $335 per credit hour.

GIFT AID (NEED-BASED) Total amount: $740,835 (93% federal, 7% state). **Scholarships, grants, and awards:** Federal Pell, FSEOG, state, private, college/university gift aid from institutional funds.

GIFT AID (NON-NEED-BASED) Total amount: $541,708 (14% state, 77% institutional, 9% external sources). **Scholarships, grants, and awards by category:** Academic interests/achievement: education, general academic interests/achievements, religion/biblical studies. **Special achievements/activities:** leadership, religious involvement. **Special characteristics:** relatives of clergy, religious affiliation, spouses of current students. **Tuition waivers:** Full or partial for employees or children of employees.

LOANS Student loans: $818,241 (64% need-based, 36% non-need-based). **Parent loans:** $31,215 (100% non-need-based).

APPLYING FOR FINANCIAL AID Required financial aid forms: FAFSA, institution's own form, state aid form. **Financial aid deadline:** 4/15. **Notification date:** Continuous. Students must reply within 2 weeks of notification.

CONTACT Mr. Mark Elkins, Financial Aid Administrator, Trinity Baptist College, 800 Hammond Boulevard, Jacksonville, FL 32221, 904-596-2445 or toll-free 800-786-2206. Fax: 904-596-2531. E-mail: financialaid@tbc.edu. Website: http://www.tbc.edu/.

TRINITY BIBLE COLLEGE
Ellendale, ND

ABOUT THE INSTITUTION Independent Assemblies of God, coed. 12 undergraduate majors.

GIFT AID (NEED-BASED) Scholarships, grants, and awards: Federal Pell, FSEOG, state, private, college/university gift aid from institutional funds.

GIFT AID (NON-NEED-BASED) Scholarships, grants, and awards by category: Academic interests/achievement: business, education, general academic interests/achievements, religion/biblical studies. **Creative arts/performance:** art/fine arts, creative writing, music, theater/drama. **Special achievements/activities:** community service, general special achievements/activities, leadership, religious involvement. **Special characteristics:** children and siblings of alumni, children of current students, children of faculty/staff, general special characteristics, international students, married students, parents of current students, relatives of clergy, siblings of current students, spouses of current students.

LOANS Programs: Perkins, alternative loans.

WORK-STUDY Federal work-study jobs available.

APPLYING FOR FINANCIAL AID Required financial aid form: FAFSA.

CONTACT Nicole R. McIntosh, Director of Financial Aid, Trinity Bible College, 50 South 6th Avenue, Ellendale, ND 58436-7150, 701-349-3621 Ext. 5403 or toll-free 800-523-1603. Fax: 701-349-5786. E-mail: nicolemcintosh@trinitybiblecollege.edu. Website: http://www.trinitybiblecollege.edu/.

TRINITY CHRISTIAN COLLEGE
Palos Heights, IL

Tuition & fees: $23,513	Average undergraduate aid package: $15,289

ABOUT THE INSTITUTION Independent Christian Reformed, coed. **Awards:** bachelor's and master's degrees. 37 undergraduate majors. **Total enrollment:** 1,369. Undergraduates: 1,346. Freshmen: 187. Federal methodology is used as a basis for awarding need-based institutional aid.

UNDERGRADUATE EXPENSES for 2013–2014 Application fee: $20. **Comprehensive fee:** $31,955 includes full-time tuition ($23,098), mandatory fees ($415), and room and board ($8442). Room and board charges vary according to board plan. **Part-time tuition:** $772 per credit hour.

FRESHMAN FINANCIAL AID (Fall 2012, est.) 167 applied for aid; of those 87% were deemed to have need. 100% of freshmen with need received aid; of those 12% had need fully met. **Average percent of need met:** 71% (excluding resources awarded to replace EFC). **Average financial aid package:** $17,373 (excluding resources awarded to replace EFC). 15% of all full-time freshmen had no need and received non-need-based gift aid.

UNDERGRADUATE FINANCIAL AID (Fall 2012, est.) 923 applied for aid; of those 91% were deemed to have need. 100% of undergraduates with need received aid; of those 14% had need fully met. **Average percent of need met:** 66% (excluding resources awarded to replace EFC). **Average financial aid package:** $15,289 (excluding resources awarded to replace EFC). 16% of all full-time undergraduates had no need and received non-need-based gift aid.

GIFT AID (NEED-BASED) Total amount: $8,893,151 (21% federal, 17% state, 61% institutional, 1% external sources). **Receiving aid:** Freshmen: 78% (146); all full-time undergraduates: 80% (816). **Average award:** Freshmen: $14,193; Undergraduates: $11,690. **Scholarships, grants, and awards:** Federal Pell, FSEOG, state, private, college/university gift aid from institutional funds, Federal Nursing.

GIFT AID (NON-NEED-BASED) *Total amount:* $1,090,559 (6% federal, 93% institutional, 1% external sources). *Receiving aid:* Freshmen: 11% (21). Undergraduates: 8% (82). *Average award:* Freshmen: $6384. Undergraduates: $6200. *Scholarships, grants, and awards by category:* Academic interests/achievement: 608 awards ($3,428,963 total): biological sciences, business, communication, computer science, education, engineering/technologies, English, general academic interests/achievements, health fields, humanities, international studies, mathematics, physical sciences, premedicine, religion/biblical studies, social sciences. Creative arts/performance: 118 awards ($205,375 total): applied art and design, art/fine arts, general creative arts/performance, journalism/publications, music, performing arts, theater/drama. Special achievements/activities: 5 awards ($6200 total): community service, general special achievements/activities, leadership, religious involvement. Special characteristics: 482 awards ($1,118,106 total): adult students, children and siblings of alumni, children of faculty/staff, ethnic background, first-generation college students, local/state students, members of minority groups, out-of-state students, religious affiliation, veterans. *Tuition waivers:* Full or partial for employees or children of employees.
LOANS *Student loans:* $9,385,957 (44% need-based, 56% non-need-based). 79% of past graduating class borrowed through all loan programs. *Average indebtedness per student:* $28,124. *Average need-based loan:* Freshmen: $3820. Undergraduates: $4560. *Parent loans:* $1,051,631 (100% non-need-based). *Programs:* Federal Direct (Subsidized and Unsubsidized Stafford, PLUS), Perkins, Federal Nursing.
WORK-STUDY *Federal work-study:* Total amount: $101,508; 98 jobs averaging $1500. *State or other work-study/employment:* Total amount: $585,258 (100% non-need-based). 352 part-time jobs averaging $1895.
ATHLETIC AWARDS Total amount: $1,275,050 (75% need-based, 25% non-need-based).
APPLYING FOR FINANCIAL AID *Required financial aid form:* FAFSA. *Financial aid deadline (priority):* 2/15. *Notification date:* Continuous beginning 3/1. Students must reply by 5/1 or within 2 weeks of notification.
CONTACT Ryan P. Zantingh, Director of Financial Aid, Trinity Christian College, 6601 West College Drive, Palos Heights, IL 60463-0929, 708-239-4872. *E-mail:* financialaid@trnty.edu.
Website: http://www.trnty.edu/.

TRINITY COLLEGE
Hartford, CT

Tuition & fees: $45,730	Average undergraduate aid package: $41,862

ABOUT THE INSTITUTION Independent, coed. *Awards:* bachelor's and master's degrees. 47 undergraduate majors. *Total enrollment:* 2,387. Undergraduates: 2,301. Freshmen: 591. Both federal and institutional methodology are used as a basis for awarding need-based institutional aid.
UNDERGRADUATE EXPENSES for 2013–2014 *Application fee:* $60. *One-time required fee:* $25. *Comprehensive fee:* $57,530 includes full-time tuition ($43,570), mandatory fees ($2160), and room and board ($11,800). *College room only:* $7660. Full-time tuition and fees vary according to course load and program. Room and board charges vary according to board plan. *Part-time tuition:* $4841 per course. Part-time tuition and fees vary according to course load and program.
FRESHMAN FINANCIAL AID (Fall 2012, est.) 262 applied for aid; of those 88% were deemed to have need. 100% of freshmen with need received aid; of those 100% had need fully met. *Average percent of need met:* 100% (excluding resources awarded to replace EFC). *Average financial aid package:* $41,912 (excluding resources awarded to replace EFC). 2% of all full-time freshmen had no need and received non-need-based gift aid.
UNDERGRADUATE FINANCIAL AID (Fall 2012, est.) 940 applied for aid; of those 95% were deemed to have need. 100% of undergraduates with need received aid; of those 100% had need fully met. *Average percent of need met:* 100% (excluding resources awarded to replace EFC). *Average financial aid package:* $41,862 (excluding resources awarded to replace EFC). 1% of all full-time undergraduates had no need and received non-need-based gift aid.
GIFT AID (NEED-BASED) *Total amount:* $34,838,445 (4% federal, 2% state, 92% institutional, 2% external sources). *Receiving aid:* Freshmen: 38% (223); all full-time undergraduates: 39% (849). *Average award:* Freshmen: $39,009; Undergraduates: $39,131. *Scholarships, grants, and awards:* Federal Pell, FSEOG, state, private, college/university gift aid from institutional funds, Academic Competitiveness Grants, National SMART Grants, Yellow Ribbon Grant Program.

GIFT AID (NON-NEED-BASED) *Total amount:* $1,033,613 (2% federal, 91% institutional, 7% external sources). *Receiving aid:* Freshmen: 2% (10). Undergraduates: 1% (23). *Average award:* Freshmen: $26,785. Undergraduates: $32,371. *Scholarships, grants, and awards by category:* Academic interests/achievement: 23 awards ($992,725 total): general academic interests/achievements. Special achievements/activities: 121 awards ($5,404,578 total): leadership. *Tuition waivers:* Full or partial for employees or children of employees, adult students.
ROTC: Army cooperative.
LOANS *Student loans:* $6,471,124 (52% need-based, 48% non-need-based). 41% of past graduating class borrowed through all loan programs. *Average indebtedness per student:* $18,868. *Average need-based loan:* Freshmen: $3595. Undergraduates: $4600. *Parent loans:* $3,392,476 (100% non-need-based). *Programs:* Federal Direct (PLUS), Perkins, college/university, alternative loans.
WORK-STUDY *Federal work-study:* Total amount: $901,516; 739 jobs averaging $1735.
APPLYING FOR FINANCIAL AID *Required financial aid forms:* FAFSA, CSS Financial Aid PROFILE, noncustodial (divorced/separated) parent's statement, business/farm supplement, federal income tax form(s). *Financial aid deadline:* 3/1 (priority: 2/1). *Notification date:* 4/1. Students must reply by 5/1 or within 2 weeks of notification.
CONTACT Ms. Kelly O'Brien, Director of Financial Aid, Trinity College, 300 Summit Street, Hartford, CT 06106-3100, 860-297-2046. *Fax:* 860-987-6296. *Website:* http://www.trincoll.edu/.

TRINITY COLLEGE OF FLORIDA
New Port Richey, FL

Tuition & fees: $13,320	Average undergraduate aid package: $10,078

ABOUT THE INSTITUTION Independent nondenominational, coed. *Awards:* certificates, associate, and bachelor's degrees. 10 undergraduate majors. *Total enrollment:* 219. Undergraduates: 219. Freshmen: 29. Both federal and institutional methodology are used as a basis for awarding need-based institutional aid.
UNDERGRADUATE EXPENSES for 2013–2014 *Application fee:* $25. *Comprehensive fee:* $19,870 includes full-time tuition ($12,520), mandatory fees ($800), and room and board ($6550). *College room only:* $4450. *Part-time tuition:* $522 per credit hour. *Part-time fees:* $400 per term. Part-time tuition and fees vary according to course load.
FRESHMAN FINANCIAL AID (Fall 2012, est.) 25 applied for aid; of those 92% were deemed to have need. 100% of freshmen with need received aid. *Average percent of need met:* 48% (excluding resources awarded to replace EFC). *Average financial aid package:* $9883 (excluding resources awarded to replace EFC). 4% of all full-time freshmen had no need and received non-need-based gift aid.
UNDERGRADUATE FINANCIAL AID (Fall 2012, est.) 158 applied for aid; of those 95% were deemed to have need. 100% of undergraduates with need received aid; of those 3% had need fully met. *Average percent of need met:* 47% (excluding resources awarded to replace EFC). *Average financial aid package:* $10,078 (excluding resources awarded to replace EFC). 2% of all full-time undergraduates had no need and received non-need-based gift aid.
GIFT AID (NEED-BASED) *Total amount:* $921,864 (61% federal, 13% state, 22% institutional, 4% external sources). *Receiving aid:* Freshmen: 85% (23); all full-time undergraduates: 78% (143). *Average award:* Freshmen: $6674; Undergraduates: $6254. *Scholarships, grants, and awards:* Federal Pell, FSEOG, state, private, college/university gift aid from institutional funds.
GIFT AID (NON-NEED-BASED) *Total amount:* $10,240 (56% state, 29% institutional, 15% external sources). *Receiving aid:* Undergraduates: 1% (2). *Average award:* Freshmen: $300. Undergraduates: $733. *Scholarships, grants, and awards by category:* Academic interests/achievement: general academic interests/achievements, religion/biblical studies. Special achievements/activities: community service, leadership, religious involvement. Special characteristics: 8 awards ($4200 total): children of faculty/staff, relatives of clergy, spouses of current students. *Tuition waivers:* Full or partial for employees or children of employees, senior citizens.
LOANS *Student loans:* $1,171,653 (96% need-based, 4% non-need-based). 25% of past graduating class borrowed through all loan programs. *Average indebtedness per student:* $5500. *Average need-based loan:* Freshmen: $3495. Undergraduates: $4015. *Parent loans:* $34,000 (65% need-based, 35% non-need-based). *Programs:* Federal Direct (Subsidized and Unsubsidized Stafford, PLUS).

WORK-STUDY *Federal work-study:* Total amount: $79,982; 28 jobs averaging $2698. *State or other work-study/employment:* Total amount: $3451 (100% need-based). 2 part-time jobs averaging $2420.

APPLYING FOR FINANCIAL AID *Required financial aid forms:* FAFSA, institution's own form. *Financial aid deadline (priority):* 3/15. *Notification date:* Continuous. Students must reply within 6 weeks of notification.

CONTACT Sue Wayne, Director of Financial Aid, Trinity College of Florida, 2430 Welbilt Boulevard, New Port Richey, FL 34655, 727-569-1413 or toll-free 800-388-0869. *Fax:* 727-376-0781. *E-mail:* swayne@trinitycollege.edu. *Website:* http://www.trinitycollege.edu/.

TRINITY COLLEGE OF NURSING AND HEALTH SCIENCES
Rock Island, IL

Tuition & fees: $24,982 — **Average undergraduate aid package: N/A**

ABOUT THE INSTITUTION Independent, coed. *Awards:* associate and bachelor's degrees (general education requirements are taken off campus, usually at Black Hawk College, Eastern Iowa Community College District and Western Illinois University). 8 undergraduate majors. *Total enrollment:* 232. Undergraduates: 232. Federal methodology is used as a basis for awarding need-based institutional aid.

UNDERGRADUATE EXPENSES for 2013–2014 *Application fee:* $50. *Tuition:* full-time $22,680; part-time $648 per credit hour. Full-time tuition and fees vary according to degree level, program, and student level. Part-time tuition and fees vary according to degree level, program, and student level.

UNDERGRADUATE FINANCIAL AID (Fall 2012, est.) 106 applied for aid; of those 100% were deemed to have need. 100% of undergraduates with need received aid.

GIFT AID (NEED-BASED) *Total amount:* $477,337 (60% federal, 10% state, 24% institutional, 6% external sources). *Receiving aid:* All full-time undergraduates: 73% (87). *Scholarships, grants, and awards:* Federal Pell, FSEOG, state, private, college/university gift aid from institutional funds.

LOANS *Student loans:* $1,552,498 (63% need-based, 37% non-need-based). 78% of past graduating class borrowed through all loan programs. *Average indebtedness per student:* $9500. *Parent loans:* $193,665 (100% non-need-based). *Programs:* Federal Direct (Subsidized and Unsubsidized Stafford, PLUS), Federal Nursing.

APPLYING FOR FINANCIAL AID *Required financial aid forms:* FAFSA, institution's own form. *Financial aid deadline:* Continuous. *Notification date:* Continuous beginning 6/1. Students must reply within 8 weeks of notification.

CONTACT Mrs. Christine Carol Christopherson, Financial Aid Specialist, Trinity College of Nursing and Health Sciences, 2122 25th Avenue, Rock Island, IL 61201, 309-779-7740. *Fax:* 309-779-7748. *E-mail:* christcc@ihs.org. *Website:* http://www.trinitycollegeqc.edu/.

TRINITY INTERNATIONAL UNIVERSITY
Deerfield, IL

CONTACT Pat Coles, Interim Director of Financial Aid, Trinity International University, 2065 Half Day Road, Deerfield, IL 60015-1284, 847-317-8060 or toll-free 800-822-3225. *Fax:* 847-317-7081. *E-mail:* finaid@tiu.edu. *Website:* http://www.tiu.edu/.

TRINITY LUTHERAN COLLEGE
Issaquah, WA

ABOUT THE INSTITUTION Independent Lutheran, coed. *Awards:* certificates, associate, and bachelor's degrees. 9 undergraduate majors. *Total enrollment:* 163. Undergraduates: 163.

GIFT AID (NEED-BASED) *Scholarships, grants, and awards:* Federal Pell, FSEOG, college/university gift aid from institutional funds.

GIFT AID (NON-NEED-BASED) *Scholarships, grants, and awards by category:* Academic interests/achievement: business, general academic interests/achievements, religion/biblical studies. Creative arts/performance: general creative arts/performance, music. Special achievements/activities: leadership, religious involvement. Special characteristics: children of faculty/staff, international students, religious affiliation.

LOANS *Programs:* college/university.

APPLYING FOR FINANCIAL AID *Required financial aid forms:* FAFSA, institution's own form.

CONTACT Ms. Shanna Pyzer, Director of Financial Aid, Trinity Lutheran College, 2802 Wetmore Avenue, Everett, WA 98201, 425-249-4800 or toll-free 800-843-5659. *Fax:* 425-249-4801. *E-mail:* fin_aid@tlc.edu. *Website:* http://www.tlc.edu/.

TRINITY UNIVERSITY
San Antonio, TX

Tuition & fees: $33,688 — **Average undergraduate aid package: $28,521**

ABOUT THE INSTITUTION Independent Presbyterian Church, coed. *Awards:* bachelor's and master's degrees. 50 undergraduate majors. *Total enrollment:* 2,525. Undergraduates: 2,353. Freshmen: 580. Federal methodology is used as a basis for awarding need-based institutional aid.

UNDERGRADUATE EXPENSES for 2013–2014 *Application fee:* $50. *Comprehensive fee:* $44,184 includes full-time tuition ($32,578), mandatory fees ($1110), and room and board ($10,496). *College room only:* $6520. Full-time tuition and fees vary according to course load. Room and board charges vary according to board plan. *Part-time tuition:* $1357 per credit hour. Part-time tuition and fees vary according to course load.

FRESHMAN FINANCIAL AID (Fall 2012, est.) 437 applied for aid; of those 77% were deemed to have need. 100% of freshmen with need received aid; of those 37% had need fully met. *Average percent of need met:* 89% (excluding resources awarded to replace EFC). *Average financial aid package:* $29,216 (excluding resources awarded to replace EFC). 35% of all full-time freshmen had no need and received non-need-based gift aid.

UNDERGRADUATE FINANCIAL AID (Fall 2012, est.) 1,340 applied for aid; of those 83% were deemed to have need. 99% of undergraduates with need received aid; of those 35% had need fully met. *Average percent of need met:* 88% (excluding resources awarded to replace EFC). *Average financial aid package:* $28,521 (excluding resources awarded to replace EFC). 39% of all full-time undergraduates had no need and received non-need-based gift aid.

GIFT AID (NEED-BASED) *Total amount:* $23,830,001 (9% federal, 6% state, 82% institutional, 3% external sources). *Receiving aid:* Freshmen: 57% (337); all full-time undergraduates: 48% (1,105). *Average award:* Freshmen: $23,064; Undergraduates: $22,377. *Scholarships, grants, and awards:* Federal Pell, FSEOG, state, private, college/university gift aid from institutional funds.

GIFT AID (NON-NEED-BASED) *Total amount:* $13,650,664 (1% federal, 96% institutional, 3% external sources). *Receiving aid:* Freshmen: 9% (51). Undergraduates: 6% (131). *Average award:* Freshmen: $14,255. Undergraduates: $13,979. *Scholarships, grants, and awards by category:* Academic interests/achievement: general academic interests/achievements. Creative arts/performance: art/fine arts, debating, music, theater/drama. Special achievements/activities: leadership. Special characteristics: first-generation college students. *Tuition waivers:* Full or partial for employees or children of employees. *ROTC:* Air Force cooperative.

LOANS *Student loans:* $7,033,646 (77% need-based, 23% non-need-based). 46% of past graduating class borrowed through all loan programs. *Average indebtedness per student:* $42,987. *Average need-based loan:* Freshmen: $5088. Undergraduates: $6121. *Parent loans:* $4,308,735 (16% need-based, 84% non-need-based). *Programs:* Federal Direct (Subsidized and Unsubsidized Stafford, PLUS), Perkins, state, college/university.

WORK-STUDY *Federal work-study:* Total amount: $1,288,728; jobs available. *State or other work-study/employment:* Part-time jobs available.

APPLYING FOR FINANCIAL AID *Required financial aid form:* FAFSA. *Financial aid deadline (priority):* 2/15. *Notification date:* 4/1. Students must reply by 5/1 or within 3 weeks of notification.

CONTACT Glendi Gaddis, Director of Financial Aid, Trinity University, One Trinity Place, San Antonio, TX 78212-7200, 210-999-8315 or toll-free 800-TRINITY. *Fax:* 210-999-8316. *E-mail:* financialaid@trinity.edu. *Website:* http://www.trinity.edu/.

TRINITY WASHINGTON UNIVERSITY
Washington, DC

CONTACT Catherine H. Geier, Director of Student Financial Services, Trinity Washington University, 125 Michigan Avenue, NE, Washington, DC 20017-1094, 202-884-9530 or toll-free 800-IWANTTC. *Fax:* 202-884-9524. *E-mail:* financialaid@trinitydc.edu. *Website:* http://www.trinitydc.edu/.

TRI-STATE BIBLE COLLEGE
South Point, OH

Tuition & fees: N/R	Average undergraduate aid package: N/A

ABOUT THE INSTITUTION Independent nondenominational, coed. *Awards:* associate, bachelor's, and master's degrees. 3 undergraduate majors. *Total enrollment:* 65. Undergraduates: 65.
GIFT AID (NEED-BASED) *Scholarships, grants, and awards:* Federal Pell.
LOANS *Programs:* Federal Direct (Subsidized and Unsubsidized Stafford, PLUS).
APPLYING FOR FINANCIAL AID *Required financial aid form:* FAFSA. *Notification date:* Continuous.
CONTACT Mrs. Roberta Mercer, Financial Aid Director, Tri-State Bible College, 506 Margaret Street, PO Box 445, South Point, OH 45680, 740-377-2520 Ext. 23. *Fax:* 740-377-0001. *E-mail:* tsbc@zoominternet.net. *Website:* http://www.tsbc.edu/.

TROY UNIVERSITY
Troy, AL

Tuition & fees (AL res): $9070	Average undergraduate aid package: $4528

ABOUT THE INSTITUTION State-supported, coed. *Awards:* certificates, associate, bachelor's, master's, and doctoral degrees. 46 undergraduate majors. *Total enrollment:* 22,554. Undergraduates: 17,915. Freshmen: 2,087. Federal methodology is used as a basis for awarding need-based institutional aid.
UNDERGRADUATE EXPENSES for 2013–2014 *Application fee:* $30. *Tuition, state resident:* full-time $7470; part-time $249 per credit hour. *Tuition, nonresident:* full-time $14,940; part-time $498 per credit hour. *Required fees:* full-time $1600; $32 per credit hour or $50 per term. Full-time tuition and fees vary according to location and program. Part-time tuition and fees vary according to location and program. *College room and board:* $7071; *Room only:* $3686. Room and board charges vary according to board plan and housing facility.
FRESHMAN FINANCIAL AID (Fall 2012, est.) 1,119 applied for aid; of those 100% were deemed to have need. 100% of freshmen with need received aid. *Average financial aid package:* $3678 (excluding resources awarded to replace EFC). 24% of all full-time freshmen had no need and received non-need-based gift aid.
UNDERGRADUATE FINANCIAL AID (Fall 2012, est.) 6,822 applied for aid; of those 100% were deemed to have need. 100% of undergraduates with need received aid. *Average financial aid package:* $4528 (excluding resources awarded to replace EFC). 22% of all full-time undergraduates had no need and received non-need-based gift aid.
GIFT AID (NEED-BASED) *Total amount:* $42,532,897 (100% federal). *Receiving aid:* Freshmen: 48% (689); all full-time undergraduates: 50% (4,790). *Average award:* Freshmen: $4378; Undergraduates: $4485. *Scholarships, grants, and awards:* Federal Pell, FSEOG, state, private, college/university gift aid from institutional funds.
GIFT AID (NON-NEED-BASED) *Total amount:* $32,856,311 (43% institutional, 57% external sources). *Receiving aid:* Freshmen: 40% (580). Undergraduates:

19% (1,870). *Average award:* Freshmen: $4445. Undergraduates: $5259. *Scholarships, grants, and awards by category:* Academic interests/achievement: general academic interests/achievements. Creative arts/performance: music, theater/drama. Special achievements/activities: leadership. Special characteristics: general special characteristics. *Tuition waivers:* Full or partial for employees or children of employees. *ROTC:* Army, Air Force.
LOANS *Student loans:* $167,064,349 (100% need-based). *Average need-based loan:* Freshmen: $3443. Undergraduates: $4586. *Parent loans:* $61,112,596 (100% need-based). *Programs:* Perkins.
WORK-STUDY *Federal work-study:* Total amount: $1,406,725; jobs available.
ATHLETIC AWARDS Total amount: $4,703,183 (100% non-need-based).
APPLYING FOR FINANCIAL AID *Required financial aid forms:* FAFSA, institution's own form. *Financial aid deadline (priority):* 3/1. *Notification date:* Continuous beginning 6/1. Students must reply within 2 weeks of notification.
CONTACT Ms. Carol Ballard, Associate Vice Chancellor of Financial Aid, Troy University, 131 Adams Administration Building, Troy, AL 36082, 334-670-3186 or toll-free 800-551-9716. *Fax:* 334-670-3702. *E-mail:* csupri@troy.edu. *Website:* http://www.troy.edu/.

TRUETT-MCCONNELL COLLEGE
Cleveland, GA

ABOUT THE INSTITUTION Independent Baptist, coed. *Awards:* associate and bachelor's degrees. 12 undergraduate majors. *Total enrollment:* 921. Undergraduates: 921. Freshmen: 179.
GIFT AID (NEED-BASED) *Scholarships, grants, and awards:* Federal Pell, FSEOG, state, private, college/university gift aid from institutional funds.
GIFT AID (NON-NEED-BASED) *Scholarships, grants, and awards by category:* Academic interests/achievement: general academic interests/achievements. Creative arts/performance: music. Special achievements/activities: leadership. Special characteristics: children of current students, children of faculty/staff, international students, married students, parents of current students, relatives of clergy, siblings of current students, spouses of current students.
LOANS *Programs:* Federal Direct (Subsidized and Unsubsidized Stafford, PLUS).
WORK-STUDY *Federal work-study:* Total amount: $28,927; 24 jobs averaging $1205.
APPLYING FOR FINANCIAL AID *Required financial aid forms:* FAFSA, institution's own form, state aid form.
CONTACT Mrs. Becky Moore, Director of Financial Aid, Truett-McConnell College, 100 Alumni Drive, Cleveland, GA 30528, 706-865-2134 Ext. 144 or toll-free 800-226-8621. *Fax:* 706-243-4642. *E-mail:* bmoore@truett.edu. *Website:* http://www.truett.edu/.

TRUMAN STATE UNIVERSITY
Kirksville, MO

Tuition & fees (MO res): $7216	Average undergraduate aid package: $10,707

ABOUT THE INSTITUTION State-supported, coed. *Awards:* bachelor's and master's degrees. 35 undergraduate majors. *Total enrollment:* 6,237. Undergraduates: 5,872. Freshmen: 1,271. Federal methodology is used as a basis for awarding need-based institutional aid.
UNDERGRADUATE EXPENSES for 2013–2014 *One-time required fee:* $315. *Tuition, state resident:* full-time $6978; part-time $291 per credit hour. *Tuition, nonresident:* full-time $12,714; part-time $530 per credit hour. *Required fees:* full-time $238. Full-time tuition and fees vary according to course load and program. Part-time tuition and fees vary according to course load and program. *College room and board:* $7504. Room and board charges vary according to housing facility.
FRESHMAN FINANCIAL AID (Fall 2011) 1,182 applied for aid; of those 67% were deemed to have need. 100% of freshmen with need received aid; of those 38% had need fully met. *Average percent of need met:* 86% (excluding resources awarded to replace EFC). *Average financial aid package:* $11,431 (excluding resources awarded to replace EFC). 40% of all full-time freshmen had no need and received non-need-based gift aid.

UNDERGRADUATE FINANCIAL AID (Fall 2011) 3,950 applied for aid; of those 72% were deemed to have need. 100% of undergraduates with need received aid; of those 34% had need fully met. **Average percent of need met:** 82% (excluding resources awarded to replace EFC). **Average financial aid package:** $10,707 (excluding resources awarded to replace EFC). 35% of all full-time undergraduates had no need and received non-need-based gift aid.
GIFT AID (NEED-BASED) Total amount: $16,977,736 (29% federal, 11% state, 55% institutional, 5% external sources). **Receiving aid:** Freshmen: 57% (787); all full-time undergraduates: 49% (2,647). **Average award:** Freshmen: $7282; Undergraduates: $6520. **Scholarships, grants, and awards:** Federal Pell, FSEOG, state, private, college/university gift aid from institutional funds, TEACH Grants, Nursing Loan Program.
GIFT AID (NON-NEED-BASED) Total amount: $13,929,548 (2% federal, 8% state, 83% institutional, 7% external sources). **Receiving aid:** Freshmen: 55% (759). Undergraduates: 41% (2,223). **Average award:** Freshmen: $4714. Undergraduates: $5334. **Scholarships, grants, and awards by category:** Academic interests/achievement: 8,731 awards ($21,254,107 total): agriculture, biological sciences, business, communication, computer science, education, English, foreign languages, general academic interests/achievements, health fields, humanities, mathematics, military science, physical sciences, premedicine, social sciences. Creative arts/performance: 139 awards ($139,054 total): art/fine arts, debating, music, theater/drama. Special achievements/activities: 426 awards ($2,001,477 total): leadership. Special characteristics: 641 awards ($1,477,123 total): children and siblings of alumni, children of faculty/staff, ethnic background, first-generation college students, international students, out-of-state students, previous college experience. **Tuition waivers:** Full or partial for children of alumni, employees or children of employees, senior citizens. **ROTC:** Army.
LOANS Student loans: $26,165,595 (50% need-based, 50% non-need-based). 52% of past graduating class borrowed through all loan programs. Average indebtedness per student: $22,922. **Average need-based loan:** Freshmen: $3410. Undergraduates: $4182. **Parent loans:** $1,545,949 (16% need-based, 84% non-need-based). **Programs:** Federal Direct (Subsidized and Unsubsidized Stafford, PLUS), Perkins, Federal Nursing, college/university, alternative loans.
WORK-STUDY Federal work-study: Total amount: $851,810; 489 jobs averaging $1742. **State or other work-study/employment:** Total amount: $1,854,877 (1% need-based, 99% non-need-based). 1,493 part-time jobs averaging $1226.
ATHLETIC AWARDS Total amount: $1,395,953 (29% need-based, 71% non-need-based).
APPLYING FOR FINANCIAL AID Required financial aid forms: FAFSA, institution's own form. **Financial aid deadline:** Continuous. **Notification date:** Continuous beginning 3/1.
CONTACT Kathy Elsea, Director of Financial Aid, Truman State University, 103 McClain Hall, Kirksville, MO 63501-4221, 660-785-4130 or toll-free 800-892-7792. Fax: 660-785-7389. E-mail: kelsea@truman.edu.
Website: http://www.truman.edu/.

TUFTS UNIVERSITY
Medford, MA

Tuition & fees: $46,598	Average undergraduate aid package: $34,802

ABOUT THE INSTITUTION Independent, coed. **Awards:** certificates, bachelor's, master's, and doctoral degrees. 72 undergraduate majors. **Total enrollment:** 10,837. Undergraduates: 5,255. Freshmen: 1,307. Both federal and institutional methodology are used as a basis for awarding need-based institutional aid.
UNDERGRADUATE EXPENSES for 2013–2014 Application fee: $70. **Comprehensive fee:** $58,780 includes full-time tuition ($45,590), mandatory fees ($1008), and room and board ($12,182). **College room only:** $6630. Room and board charges vary according to board plan. **Payment plan:** Tuition prepayment.
FRESHMAN FINANCIAL AID (Fall 2012, est.) 667 applied for aid; of those 78% were deemed to have need. 100% of freshmen with need received aid; of those 100% had need fully met. **Average percent of need met:** 100% (excluding resources awarded to replace EFC). **Average financial aid package:** $35,033 (excluding resources awarded to replace EFC). 2% of all full-time freshmen had no need and received non-need-based gift aid.
UNDERGRADUATE FINANCIAL AID (Fall 2012, est.) 2,396 applied for aid; of those 87% were deemed to have need. 99% of undergraduates with need received aid;

of those 100% had need fully met. **Average percent of need met:** 100% (excluding resources awarded to replace EFC). **Average financial aid package:** $34,802 (excluding resources awarded to replace EFC). 2% of all full-time undergraduates had no need and received non-need-based gift aid.
GIFT AID (NEED-BASED) Total amount: $64,446,694 (5% federal, 1% state, 91% institutional, 3% external sources). **Receiving aid:** Freshmen: 37% (486); all full-time undergraduates: 37% (1,915). **Average award:** Freshmen: $33,208; Undergraduates: $31,716. **Scholarships, grants, and awards:** Federal Pell, FSEOG, state, private, college/university gift aid from institutional funds.
GIFT AID (NON-NEED-BASED) Total amount: $686,991 (6% federal, 8% institutional, 86% external sources). **Receiving aid:** Freshmen: 2% (23). Undergraduates: 2% (89). **Average award:** Freshmen: $500. Undergraduates: $500. **Scholarships, grants, and awards by category:** Academic interests/achievement: general academic interests/achievements. **Tuition waivers:** Full or partial for employees or children of employees. **ROTC:** Army cooperative, Naval cooperative, Air Force cooperative.
LOANS Student loans: $12,351,434 (62% need-based, 38% non-need-based). 37% of past graduating class borrowed through all loan programs. Average indebtedness per student: $23,068. **Average need-based loan:** Freshmen: $2964. Undergraduates: $4016. **Parent loans:** $6,515,101 (100% non-need-based). **Programs:** Federal Direct (Subsidized and Unsubsidized Stafford, PLUS), Perkins, college/university.
WORK-STUDY Federal work-study: Total amount: $2,894,307; 1,605 jobs averaging $1803. **State or other work-study/employment:** Total amount: $175,900 (100% need-based). 93 part-time jobs averaging $1891.
APPLYING FOR FINANCIAL AID Required financial aid forms: FAFSA, CSS Financial Aid PROFILE, noncustodial (divorced/separated) parent's statement, federal income tax form(s). **Financial aid deadline:** 2/15. **Notification date:** 4/5. Students must reply by 5/1.
CONTACT Patricia C. Reilly, Director of Financial Aid, Tufts University, Dowling Hall, Medford, MA 02155, 617-627-5912. Fax: 617-627-3987. E-mail: patricia.reilly@tufts.edu.
Website: http://www.tufts.edu/.

TULANE UNIVERSITY
New Orleans, LA

Tuition & fees: $45,240	Average undergraduate aid package: $32,387

ABOUT THE INSTITUTION Independent, coed. **Awards:** certificates, associate, bachelor's, master's, and doctoral degrees. 82 undergraduate majors. **Total enrollment:** 13,486. Undergraduates: 8,423. Freshmen: 1,641. Both federal and institutional methodology are used as a basis for awarding need-based institutional aid.
UNDERGRADUATE EXPENSES for 2013–2014 Comprehensive fee: $56,787 includes full-time tuition ($41,500), mandatory fees ($3740), and room and board ($11,547). **College room only:** $6597. Room and board charges vary according to board plan and housing facility. **Payment plan:** Tuition prepayment.
FRESHMAN FINANCIAL AID (Fall 2011) 1,046 applied for aid; of those 63% were deemed to have need. 99% of freshmen with need received aid; of those 77% had need fully met. **Average percent of need met:** 95% (excluding resources awarded to replace EFC). **Average financial aid package:** $31,130 (excluding resources awarded to replace EFC). 34% of all full-time freshmen had no need and received non-need-based gift aid.
UNDERGRADUATE FINANCIAL AID (Fall 2011) 3,432 applied for aid; of those 77% were deemed to have need. 99% of undergraduates with need received aid; of those 68% had need fully met. **Average percent of need met:** 91% (excluding resources awarded to replace EFC). **Average financial aid package:** $32,387 (excluding resources awarded to replace EFC). 35% of all full-time undergraduates had no need and received non-need-based gift aid.
GIFT AID (NEED-BASED) Total amount: $65,641,926 (8% federal, 2% state, 89% institutional, 1% external sources). **Receiving aid:** Freshmen: 39% (647); all full-time undergraduates: 39% (2,533). **Average award:** Freshmen: $26,426; Undergraduates: $27,164. **Scholarships, grants, and awards:** Federal Pell, FSEOG, state, college/university gift aid from institutional funds.
GIFT AID (NON-NEED-BASED) Total amount: $57,533,338 (1% federal, 4% state, 94% institutional, 1% external sources). **Receiving aid:** Freshmen: 12% (205). Undergraduates: 10% (671). **Average award:** Freshmen: $19,847. Undergraduates: $21,157. **Scholarships, grants, and awards by category:** Creative arts/perfor-

mance: 64 awards ($152,000 total): music. *Special achievements/activities:* 36 awards ($361,436 total): community service. *Tuition waivers:* Full or partial for employees or children of employees. *ROTC:* Army, Naval, Air Force.

LOANS *Student loans:* $37,685,047 (58% need-based, 42% non-need-based). 41% of past graduating class borrowed through all loan programs. *Average indebtedness per student:* $35,100. *Average need-based loan:* Freshmen: $6211. Undergraduates: $7237. *Parent loans:* $9,737,209 (8% need-based, 92% non-need-based). *Programs:* Federal Direct (Subsidized and Unsubsidized Stafford, PLUS), Perkins.

WORK-STUDY *Federal work-study:* Total amount: $2,136,511; 1,372 jobs averaging $2843. *State or other work-study/employment:* Total amount: $1,007,697 (18% need-based, 82% non-need-based). 138 part-time jobs averaging $7328.

ATHLETIC AWARDS Total amount: $10,438,648 (34% need-based, 66% non-need-based).

APPLYING FOR FINANCIAL AID *Required financial aid forms:* FAFSA, CSS Financial Aid PROFILE, noncustodial (divorced/separated) parent's statement, business/farm supplement. *Financial aid deadline (priority):* 2/15. *Notification date:* Continuous beginning 3/15. Students must reply within 2 weeks of notification.

CONTACT Mr. Michael T. Goodman, Director of Financial Aid, Tulane University, 6823 St. Charles Avenue, New Orleans, LA 70118-5669, 504-865-5723 or toll-free 800-873-9283. *Fax:* 504-862-8750. *E-mail:* finaid@tulane.edu. *Website:* http://www.tulane.edu/.

TUSCULUM COLLEGE
Greeneville, TN

ABOUT THE INSTITUTION Independent Presbyterian, coed. *Awards:* bachelor's and master's degrees. 38 undergraduate majors. *Total enrollment:* 2,199. Undergraduates: 1,980. Freshmen: 344.

GIFT AID (NEED-BASED) *Scholarships, grants, and awards:* Federal Pell, FSEOG, state, private, college/university gift aid from institutional funds.

GIFT AID (NON-NEED-BASED) *Scholarships, grants, and awards by category:* Academic interests/achievement: general academic interests/achievements. Creative arts/performance: general creative arts/performance, music. Special achievements/activities: cheerleading/drum major, community service, leadership. Special characteristics: adult students, children of faculty/staff, local/state students.

LOANS *Programs:* Perkins.

APPLYING FOR FINANCIAL AID *Required financial aid form:* FAFSA.

CONTACT Melena Verity, Director of Financial Aid, Tusculum College, PO Box 5049, 60 Shiloh Road, Greeneville, TN 37743-9997, 423-636-7377 or toll-free 800-729-0256. *Fax:* 615-250-4968. *E-mail:* mverity@tusculum.edu. *Website:* http://www.tusculum.edu/.

TUSKEGEE UNIVERSITY
Tuskegee, AL

Tuition & fees: $18,900	Average undergraduate aid package: $19,250

ABOUT THE INSTITUTION Independent, coed. *Awards:* bachelor's, master's, and doctoral degrees. 43 undergraduate majors. *Total enrollment:* 3,152. Undergraduates: 2,684. Freshmen: 819. Federal methodology is used as a basis for awarding need-based institutional aid.

UNDERGRADUATE EXPENSES for 2013–2014 *Application fee:* $25. *One-time required fee:* $500. *Comprehensive fee:* $27,350 includes full-time tuition ($18,100), mandatory fees ($800), and room and board ($8450). *College room only:* $4190. Full-time tuition and fees vary according to course level, course load, degree level, and program. Room and board charges vary according to housing facility. *Part-time tuition:* $750 per hour. *Part-time fees:* $800 per year. Part-time tuition and fees vary according to course level, course load, degree level, and program.

FRESHMAN FINANCIAL AID (Fall 2011) 635 applied for aid; of those 85% were deemed to have need. 94% of freshmen with need received aid; of those 68% had need fully met. *Average percent of need met:* 85% (excluding resources awarded to replace EFC). *Average financial aid package:* $19,250 (excluding resources awarded to replace EFC). 28% of all full-time freshmen had no need and received non-need-based gift aid.

UNDERGRADUATE FINANCIAL AID (Fall 2011) 2,519 applied for aid; of those 85% were deemed to have need. 92% of undergraduates with need received aid; of those 70% had need fully met. *Average percent of need met:* 85% (excluding resources awarded to replace EFC). *Average financial aid package:* $19,250 (excluding resources awarded to replace EFC). 22% of all full-time undergraduates had no need and received non-need-based gift aid.

GIFT AID (NEED-BASED) *Total amount:* $6,122,249 (97% federal, 1% state, 2% institutional). *Receiving aid:* Freshmen: 58% (434); all full-time undergraduates: 61% (1,675). *Average award:* Freshmen: $800; Undergraduates: $800. *Scholarships, grants, and awards:* Federal Pell, FSEOG, state, private, college/university gift aid from institutional funds, United Negro College Fund.

GIFT AID (NON-NEED-BASED) *Total amount:* $3,524,421 (51% institutional, 49% external sources). *Receiving aid:* Freshmen: 38% (284). Undergraduates: 35% (951). *Average award:* Freshmen: $6000. Undergraduates: $6000. *Scholarships, grants, and awards by category:* Academic interests/achievement: 1,714 awards ($1,375,210 total): general academic interests/achievements. Creative arts/performance: 150 awards ($220,000 total): music. Special characteristics: 36 awards ($612,000 total): children of faculty/staff, local/state students. *Tuition waivers:* Full or partial for employees or children of employees. *ROTC:* Army, Air Force.

LOANS *Student loans:* $22,950,330 (47% need-based, 53% non-need-based). 91% of past graduating class borrowed through all loan programs. *Average indebtedness per student:* $28,575. *Average need-based loan:* Freshmen: $5625. Undergraduates: $6006. *Parent loans:* $5,215,525 (100% non-need-based). *Programs:* Federal Direct (Subsidized and Unsubsidized Stafford, PLUS), Perkins.

WORK-STUDY *Federal work-study:* Total amount: $1,009,000; 525 jobs averaging $1879. *State or other work-study/employment:* Total amount: $628,550 (100% non-need-based). 424 part-time jobs averaging $4628.

ATHLETIC AWARDS Total amount: $1,408,216 (100% non-need-based).

APPLYING FOR FINANCIAL AID *Required financial aid forms:* FAFSA, institution's own form. *Financial aid deadline (priority):* 3/31. *Notification date:* Continuous beginning 2/15. Students must reply within 2 weeks of notification.

CONTACT Mr. A. D. James Jr., Executive Director of Student Financial Services, Tuskegee University, Carnegie Hall, 2nd Floor, Tuskegee, AL 36088, 334-727-8088 or toll-free 800-622-6531. *Fax:* 334-724-4078. *E-mail:* jamesad@mytu.tuskegee.edu. *Website:* http://www.tuskegee.edu/.

UNION COLLEGE
Barbourville, KY

Tuition & fees: $20,800	Average undergraduate aid package: $18,963

ABOUT THE INSTITUTION Independent United Methodist, coed. *Awards:* certificates, bachelor's, and master's degrees. 29 undergraduate majors. *Total enrollment:* 1,194. Undergraduates: 781. Freshmen: 214. Federal methodology is used as a basis for awarding need-based institutional aid.

UNDERGRADUATE EXPENSES for 2013–2014 *Application fee:* $10. *Comprehensive fee:* $27,450 includes full-time tuition ($19,900), mandatory fees ($900), and room and board ($6650). *College room only:* $3000. Full-time tuition and fees vary according to course load. Room and board charges vary according to board plan and housing facility. *Part-time tuition:* $325 per credit hour. Part-time tuition and fees vary according to course load.

FRESHMAN FINANCIAL AID (Fall 2012, est.) 200 applied for aid; of those 94% were deemed to have need. 99% of freshmen with need received aid; of those 11% had need fully met. *Average percent of need met:* 68% (excluding resources awarded to replace EFC). *Average financial aid package:* $18,375 (excluding resources awarded to replace EFC). 10% of all full-time freshmen had no need and received non-need-based gift aid.

UNDERGRADUATE FINANCIAL AID (Fall 2012, est.) 725 applied for aid; of those 93% were deemed to have need. 96% of undergraduates with need received aid; of those 11% had need fully met. *Average percent of need met:* 66% (excluding resources awarded to replace EFC). *Average financial aid package:* $18,963 (excluding resources awarded to replace EFC). 9% of all full-time undergraduates had no need and received non-need-based gift aid.

GIFT AID (NEED-BASED) *Total amount:* $6,742,086 (32% federal, 22% state, 44% institutional, 2% external sources). *Receiving aid:* Freshmen: 89% (188); all full-time undergraduates: 85% (650). *Average award:* Freshmen: $15,186; Undergraduates: $14,835. *Scholarships, grants, and awards:* Federal Pell, FSEOG, state, private, college/university gift aid from institutional funds.

GIFT AID (NON-NEED-BASED) *Total amount:* $443,723 (100% state). *Receiving aid:* Freshmen: 9% (20). Undergraduates: 6% (47). *Average award:* Freshmen: $11,234. Undergraduates: $11,626. *Scholarships, grants, and awards by category:* Academic interests/achievement: 380 awards ($2,353,442 total): biological sciences, general academic interests/achievements, health fields, mathematics. Creative arts/performance: 43 awards ($97,400 total): music. *Special achievements/activities:* 70 awards ($387,582 total): cheerleading/drum major, community service, general special achievements/activities, hobbies/interests, leadership, memberships. Special characteristics: 107 awards ($315,162 total): adult students, children and siblings of alumni, children of current students, children of faculty/staff, ethnic background, religious affiliation, siblings of current students, veterans, veterans' children. *Tuition waivers:* Full or partial for employees or children of employees, senior citizens.

LOANS *Student loans:* $4,542,335 (50% need-based, 50% non-need-based). 83% of past graduating class borrowed through all loan programs. *Average indebtedness per student:* $18,843. *Average need-based loan:* Freshmen: $3518. Undergraduates: $4258. *Parent loans:* $807,331 (44% need-based, 56% non-need-based). *Programs:* Federal Direct (Subsidized and Unsubsidized Stafford, PLUS), Perkins, college/university.

WORK-STUDY *Federal work-study:* Total amount: $166,581; 111 jobs averaging $1500. *State or other work-study/employment:* Total amount: $92,001 (100% need-based). 78 part-time jobs averaging $1500.

ATHLETIC AWARDS Total amount: $3,507,695 (100% need-based).

APPLYING FOR FINANCIAL AID *Required financial aid form:* FAFSA. *Financial aid deadline (priority):* 2/1. *Notification date:* Continuous beginning 4/1. Students must reply within 2 weeks of notification.

CONTACT Mrs. Andra Butler, Director of Financial Aid, Union College, 310 College Street, Barbourville, KY 40906-1499, 606-546-1224 or toll-free 800-489-8646. *Fax:* 606-546-1264. *E-mail:* abutler@unionky.edu. *Website:* http://www.unionky.edu/.

UNION COLLEGE
Lincoln, NE

CONTACT Mrs. Elina N. Bascom, Director of Financial Aid, Union College, 3800 South 48th Street, Lincoln, NE 68506-4300, 800-228-4600. *Fax:* 402-486-2952. *E-mail:* sfs@ucollege.edu. *Website:* http://www.ucollege.edu/.

UNION COLLEGE
Schenectady, NY

Tuition & fees: $46,785	Average undergraduate aid package: $36,295

ABOUT THE INSTITUTION Independent, coed. *Awards:* bachelor's degrees. 37 undergraduate majors. *Total enrollment:* 2,241. Undergraduates: 2,241. Freshmen: 591. Both federal and institutional methodology are used as a basis for awarding need-based institutional aid.

UNDERGRADUATE EXPENSES for 2013–2014 *Application fee:* $50. *Comprehensive fee:* $58,248 includes full-time tuition ($46,314), mandatory fees ($471), and room and board ($11,463). *College room only:* $6285.

FRESHMAN FINANCIAL AID (Fall 2012, est.) 378 applied for aid; of those 78% were deemed to have need. 100% of freshmen with need received aid; of those 99% had need fully met. *Average percent of need met:* 99% (excluding resources awarded to replace EFC). *Average financial aid package:* $36,912 (excluding resources awarded to replace EFC). 28% of all full-time freshmen had no need and received non-need-based gift aid.

UNDERGRADUATE FINANCIAL AID (Fall 2012, est.) 1,295 applied for aid; of those 82% were deemed to have need. 99% of undergraduates with need received aid; of those 98% had need fully met. *Average percent of need met:* 98% (excluding resources awarded to replace EFC). *Average financial aid package:* $36,295 (excluding resources awarded to replace EFC). 21% of all full-time undergraduates had no need and received non-need-based gift aid.

GIFT AID (NEED-BASED) *Total amount:* $37,542,128 (6% federal, 2% state, 91% institutional, 1% external sources). *Receiving aid:* Freshmen: 47% (278); all full-time undergraduates: 46% (999). *Average award:* Freshmen: $32,307; Undergraduates: $30,926. *Scholarships, grants, and awards:* Federal Pell, FSEOG, state, private, college/university gift aid from institutional funds.

GIFT AID (NON-NEED-BASED) *Total amount:* $4,635,863 (4% federal, 3% state, 89% institutional, 4% external sources). *Receiving aid:* Freshmen: 12% (73). Undergraduates: 9% (207). *Average award:* Freshmen: $8493. Undergraduates: $9196. *Scholarships, grants, and awards by category:* Academic interests/achievement: 459 awards ($4,290,647 total): general academic interests/achievements. Special characteristics: 34 awards ($1,497,855 total): children of faculty/staff. *Tuition waivers:* Full or partial for employees or children of employees, senior citizens. *ROTC:* Army cooperative, Naval cooperative, Air Force cooperative.

LOANS *Student loans:* $10,915,534 (46% need-based, 54% non-need-based). *Average need-based loan:* Freshmen: $3388. Undergraduates: $5103. *Parent loans:* $3,134,502 (100% non-need-based). *Programs:* Federal Direct (Subsidized and Unsubsidized Stafford, PLUS), Perkins, college/university.

WORK-STUDY *Federal work-study:* Total amount: $678,678; jobs available. *State or other work-study/employment:* Total amount: $270,000 (100% need-based). Part-time jobs available.

APPLYING FOR FINANCIAL AID *Required financial aid forms:* FAFSA, CSS Financial Aid PROFILE, state aid form, noncustodial (divorced/separated) parent's statement, business/farm supplement. *Financial aid deadline:* 2/1 (priority: 2/1). *Notification date:* 3/25. Students must reply by 5/1.

CONTACT Ms. Linda Parker, Director of Financial Aid, Union College, Grant Hall, 807 Union Street, Schenectady, NY 12308-2311, 518-388-6123 or toll-free 888-843-6688. *Fax:* 518-388-8052. *E-mail:* finaid@union.edu. *Website:* http://www.union.edu/.

UNION INSTITUTE & UNIVERSITY
Cincinnati, OH

CONTACT Ms. Lisa Perdomo, Director of Financial Aid, Union Institute & University, 440 East McMillan Street, Cincinnati, OH 45206-1925, 513-861-6400 Ext. 1261 or toll-free 800-486-3116. *Fax:* 513-487-1078. *Website:* http://www.myunion.edu/.

UNION UNIVERSITY
Jackson, TN

Tuition & fees: $25,650	Average undergraduate aid package: $17,674

ABOUT THE INSTITUTION Independent Southern Baptist, coed. *Awards:* certificates, diplomas, associate, bachelor's, master's, and doctoral degrees. 66 undergraduate majors. *Total enrollment:* 3,996. Undergraduates: 2,829. Freshmen: 457. Federal methodology is used as a basis for awarding need-based institutional aid.

UNDERGRADUATE EXPENSES for 2013–2014 *Application fee:* $35. *Comprehensive fee:* $34,080 includes full-time tuition ($24,940), mandatory fees ($710), and room and board ($8430). Full-time tuition and fees vary according to class time, course load, degree level, location, and program. Room and board charges vary according to board plan and housing facility. *Part-time tuition:* $845 per credit hour. *Part-time fees:* $290. Part-time tuition and fees vary according to class time, course load, degree level, location, and program.

FRESHMAN FINANCIAL AID (Fall 2012, est.) 418 applied for aid; of those 85% were deemed to have need. 100% of freshmen with need received aid; of those 26% had need fully met. *Average percent of need met:* 69% (excluding resources awarded to replace EFC). *Average financial aid package:* $22,414 (excluding resources awarded to replace EFC). 19% of all full-time freshmen had no need and received non-need-based gift aid.

UNDERGRADUATE FINANCIAL AID (Fall 2012, est.) 1,950 applied for aid; of those 88% were deemed to have need. 100% of undergraduates with need received aid; of those 16% had need fully met. *Average percent of need met:* 61% (excluding resources awarded to replace EFC). *Average financial aid package:* $17,674 (excluding resources awarded to replace EFC). 19% of all full-time undergraduates had no need and received non-need-based gift aid.

GIFT AID (NEED-BASED) *Total amount:* $7,540,981 (44% federal, 18% state, 38% institutional). *Receiving aid:* Freshmen: 59% (251); all full-time undergraduates: 54% (1,188). *Average award:* Freshmen: $6693; Undergraduates: $5770. *Scholarships, grants, and awards:* Federal Pell, FSEOG, state, private, college/university gift aid from institutional funds, Federal Nursing.

GIFT AID (NON-NEED-BASED) *Total amount:* $21,516,625 (2% federal, 17% state, 76% institutional, 5% external sources). *Receiving aid:* Freshmen: 84% (355). Undergraduates: 60% (1,328). *Average award:* Freshmen: $11,054. Undergraduates: $10,721. *Scholarships, grants, and awards by category: Academic interests/achievement:* $8,902,132 total: business, communication, education, engineering/technologies, general academic interests/achievements, health fields, mathematics, military science, premedicine, religion/biblical studies. *Creative arts/performance:* $654,859 total: art/fine arts, cinema/film/broadcasting, debating, journalism/publications, music, theater/drama. *Special achievements/activities:* $2,108,480 total: cheerleading/drum major, community service, general special achievements/activities, leadership, religious involvement. *Special characteristics:* $3,677,935 total: children and siblings of alumni, children of current students, children of educators, children of faculty/staff, ethnic background, general special characteristics, international students, members of minority groups, relatives of clergy, religious affiliation, siblings of current students, spouses of current students, twins, veterans, veterans' children. *Tuition waivers:* Full or partial for children of alumni, employees or children of employees. *ROTC:* Army cooperative.

LOANS *Student loans:* $14,922,236 (38% need-based, 62% non-need-based). 61% of past graduating class borrowed through all loan programs. *Average indebtedness per student:* $26,936. *Average need-based loan:* Freshmen: $3419. Undergraduates: $4463. *Parent loans:* $1,900,920 (100% non-need-based). *Programs:* Federal Direct (Subsidized and Unsubsidized Stafford, PLUS), Perkins, alternative loans.

WORK-STUDY *Federal work-study:* Total amount: $196,060; 116 jobs averaging $1690. *State or other work-study/employment:* Total amount: $461,776 (100% non-need-based). 225 part-time jobs averaging $2052.

ATHLETIC AWARDS Total amount: $2,281,533 (100% non-need-based).

APPLYING FOR FINANCIAL AID *Required financial aid forms:* FAFSA, institution's own form. *Financial aid deadline (priority):* 2/1. *Notification date:* Continuous beginning 3/1. Students must reply by 5/1 or within 2 weeks of notification.

CONTACT Mr. John Windham, Director of Student Financial Planning, Union University, 1050 Union University Drive, Jackson, TN 38305-3697, 731-661-5015 or toll-free 800-33-UNION. *Fax:* 731-661-5570. *E-mail:* jwindham@uu.edu. *Website:* http://www.uu.edu/.

UNITED STATES SPORTS ACADEMY
Daphne, AL

CONTACT Financial Aid Office, United States Sports Academy, One Academy Drive, Daphne, AL 36526-7055, 251-626-3303 or toll-free 800-223-2668. *Website:* http://www.ussa.edu/.

UNITED STATES UNIVERSITY
Chula Vista, CA

CONTACT Financial Aid Office, United States University, 830 Bay Boulevard, Chula Vista, CA 91911, 619-477-6310 or toll-free 888-422-3381. *Website:* http://www.usuniversity.edu/sd/.

UNITED STATES UNIVERSITY
Cypress, CA

CONTACT Financial Aid Office, United States University, 6251 Katella Avenue, Cypress, CA 90630, 714-252-8592 or toll-free 888-422-3381. *Website:* http://www.usuniversity.edu/oc/.

UNITED TALMUDICAL SEMINARY
Brooklyn, NY

CONTACT Financial Aid Office, United Talmudical Seminary, 82 Lee Avenue, Brooklyn, NY 11211-7900, 718-963-9770 Ext. 309.

UNITY COLLEGE
Unity, ME

Tuition & fees: $24,100	Average undergraduate aid package: $18,120

ABOUT THE INSTITUTION Independent, coed. *Awards:* associate and bachelor's degrees. 14 undergraduate majors. *Total enrollment:* 537. Undergraduates: 537. Freshmen: 120. Federal methodology is used as a basis for awarding need-based institutional aid.

UNDERGRADUATE EXPENSES for 2013–2014 *Application fee:* $25. *Comprehensive fee:* $32,814 includes full-time tuition ($23,000), mandatory fees ($1100), and room and board ($8714). Room and board charges vary according to board plan and housing facility. *Part-time tuition:* $860 per credit hour. Part-time tuition and fees vary according to course load.

FRESHMAN FINANCIAL AID (Fall 2012, est.) 118 applied for aid; of those 86% were deemed to have need. 100% of freshmen with need received aid; of those 10% had need fully met. *Average percent of need met:* 71% (excluding resources awarded to replace EFC). *Average financial aid package:* $18,123 (excluding resources awarded to replace EFC). 14% of all full-time freshmen had no need and received non-need-based gift aid.

UNDERGRADUATE FINANCIAL AID (Fall 2012, est.) 501 applied for aid; of those 90% were deemed to have need. 100% of undergraduates with need received aid; of those 5% had need fully met. *Average percent of need met:* 71% (excluding resources awarded to replace EFC). *Average financial aid package:* $18,120 (excluding resources awarded to replace EFC). 13% of all full-time undergraduates had no need and received non-need-based gift aid.

GIFT AID (NEED-BASED) *Total amount:* $5,325,037 (22% federal, 3% state, 71% institutional, 4% external sources). *Receiving aid:* Freshmen: 85% (102); all full-time undergraduates: 84% (451). *Average award:* Freshmen: $13,411; Undergraduates: $11,784. *Scholarships, grants, and awards:* Federal Pell, FSEOG, state, private, college/university gift aid from institutional funds.

GIFT AID (NON-NEED-BASED) *Total amount:* $331,724 (89% institutional, 11% external sources). *Receiving aid:* Freshmen: 58% (70). Undergraduates: 59% (315). *Average award:* Freshmen: $3352. Undergraduates: $3927. *Scholarships, grants, and awards by category: Academic interests/achievement:* 296 awards ($1,338,905 total): general academic interests/achievements. *Special achievements/activities:* 41 awards ($36,000 total): community service, leadership. *Special characteristics:* 91 awards ($169,500 total): children of educators, general special characteristics, local/state students, members of minority groups. *Tuition waivers:* Full or partial for employees or children of employees. *ROTC:* Army cooperative.

LOANS *Student loans:* $4,702,047 (80% need-based, 20% non-need-based). *Average need-based loan:* Freshmen: $4400. Undergraduates: $5838. *Parent loans:* $1,222,143 (46% need-based, 54% non-need-based). *Programs:* Federal Direct (Subsidized and Unsubsidized Stafford, PLUS), Perkins.

WORK-STUDY *Federal work-study:* Total amount: $522,381; 385 jobs averaging $1354. *State or other work-study/employment:* Total amount: $14,575 (100% non-need-based). 12 part-time jobs averaging $1200.

APPLYING FOR FINANCIAL AID *Required financial aid form:* FAFSA. *Financial aid deadline:* Continuous. *Notification date:* Continuous beginning 3/10. Students must reply within 2 weeks of notification.

CONTACT Mr. Rand E. Newell, Director of Financial Aid, Unity College, 90 Quaker Hill Road, Unity, ME 04988, 207-948-9201. *Fax:* 207-948-9777. *E-mail:* rnewell@unity.edu. *Website:* http://www.unity.edu/.

UNIVERSIDAD ADVENTISTA DE LAS ANTILLAS
Mayagüez, PR

Tuition & fees: $5550	Average undergraduate aid package: $2900

ABOUT THE INSTITUTION Independent Seventh-day Adventist, coed. **Awards:** associate, bachelor's, and master's degrees. 18 undergraduate majors. **Total enrollment:** 1,322. Undergraduates: 1,241. Freshmen: 238. Both federal and institutional methodology are used as a basis for awarding need-based institutional aid.
UNDERGRADUATE EXPENSES for 2013–2014 Application fee: $20. **One-time required fee:** $20. **Comprehensive fee:** $8450 includes full-time tuition ($4950), mandatory fees ($600), and room and board ($2900). **College room only:** $1100. Full-time tuition and fees vary according to course load and program. Room and board charges vary according to board plan and housing facility. **Part-time tuition:** $165 per credit hour. **Part-time fees:** $235 per term. Part-time tuition and fees vary according to course load and program.
FRESHMAN FINANCIAL AID (Fall 2011) 235 applied for aid; of those 100% were deemed to have need. 100% of freshmen with need received aid. **Average percent of need met:** 80% (excluding resources awarded to replace EFC). **Average financial aid package:** $2900 (excluding resources awarded to replace EFC).
UNDERGRADUATE FINANCIAL AID (Fall 2011) 1,142 applied for aid; of those 97% were deemed to have need. 94% of undergraduates with need received aid. **Average percent of need met:** 80% (excluding resources awarded to replace EFC). **Average financial aid package:** $2900 (excluding resources awarded to replace EFC).
GIFT AID (NEED-BASED) Total amount: $5,169,647 (95% federal, 3% state, 2% institutional). **Receiving aid:** Freshmen: 100% (235); all full-time undergraduates: 91% (1,037). **Average award:** Freshmen: $2900; Undergraduates: $2900. **Scholarships, grants, and awards:** Federal Pell, FSEOG, state, college/university gift aid from institutional funds.
GIFT AID (NON-NEED-BASED) Scholarships, grants, and awards by category: Special achievements/activities: community service. Special characteristics: relatives of clergy, veterans. **Tuition waivers:** Full or partial for employees or children of employees.
LOANS Student loans: $2,120,347 (100% need-based). 10% of past graduating class borrowed through all loan programs. **Average need-based loan:** Freshmen: $1900. Undergraduates: $1900. **Parent loans:** $17,450 (100% need-based). **Programs:** Federal Direct (Subsidized and Unsubsidized Stafford, PLUS).
WORK-STUDY Federal work-study: Total amount: $135,433; 164 jobs averaging $826. **State or other work-study/employment:** Total amount: $181,549 (100% need-based). 236 part-time jobs averaging $970.
APPLYING FOR FINANCIAL AID Required financial aid forms: FAFSA, institution's own form. **Financial aid deadline:** Continuous. **Notification date:** Continuous.
CONTACT Mrs. Awilda Matos, Director of Financial Aid, Universidad Adventista de las Antillas, Box 118, Mayaguez, PR 00681-0118, 787-834-9595 Ext. 2263. Fax: 787-834-9597. E-mail: amatos@uaa.edu. Website: http://www.uaa.edu/.

UNIVERSIDAD DEL ESTE
Carolina, PR

Tuition & fees: N/R	Average undergraduate aid package: N/A

ABOUT THE INSTITUTION Independent, coed. 49 undergraduate majors.
LOANS Programs: Federal Direct (Subsidized and Unsubsidized Stafford, PLUS).
APPLYING FOR FINANCIAL AID Required financial aid form: FAFSA. **Financial aid deadline:** Continuous. **Notification date:** Continuous beginning 2/1.
CONTACT Norberto Pagan, Director of Financial Aid , Universidad del Este, Apartado 2010, Carolina, PR 00928, 787-257-7373 Ext. 3301. E-mail: nopagan@suagm.edu. Website: http://www.suagm.edu/une/.

UNIVERSIDAD DEL TURABO
Gurabo, PR

Tuition & fees: $19,512	Average undergraduate aid package: N/A

ABOUT THE INSTITUTION Independent, coed. **Awards:** certificates, associate, bachelor's, master's, and doctoral degrees. 56 undergraduate majors. **Total enrollment:** 17,040. Undergraduates: 14,333. Freshmen: 2,839. Federal methodology is used as a basis for awarding need-based institutional aid.
UNDERGRADUATE EXPENSES for 2013–2014 Application fee: $15. **Comprehensive fee:** $28,112 includes full-time tuition ($19,512) and room and board ($8600). Full-time tuition and fees vary according to course level, course load, and program.
FRESHMAN FINANCIAL AID (Fall 2012, est.) 4,000 applied for aid; of those 100% were deemed to have need. 100% of freshmen with need received aid.
UNDERGRADUATE FINANCIAL AID (Fall 2012, est.) 10,000 applied for aid; of those 100% were deemed to have need. 100% of undergraduates with need received aid.
GIFT AID (NEED-BASED) Total amount: $5750 (100% federal). **Receiving aid:** Freshmen: 100% (4,000); all full-time undergraduates: 100% (10,000). **Scholarships, grants, and awards:** Federal Pell, FSEOG, state, private, college/university gift aid from institutional funds, Federal Nursing.
GIFT AID (NON-NEED-BASED) ROTC: Army cooperative, Air Force cooperative.
LOANS Programs: Federal Direct (Subsidized and Unsubsidized Stafford).
WORK-STUDY Federal work-study jobs available.
APPLYING FOR FINANCIAL AID Required financial aid form: FAFSA. **Financial aid deadline:** 6/30 (priority: 6/15). **Notification date:** 7/15.
CONTACT Ms. Carmen J. Rivera Lopez, Directora de la Oficina de Asistencia Economica, Universidad del Turabo, Apartado 3030, Gurabo, PR 00778-3030, 787-743-7979 Ext. 4352. Fax: 787-746-6777. Website: http://www.suagm.edu/ut/.

UNIVERSIDAD FLET
Miami, FL

CONTACT Financial Aid Office, Universidad FLET, 14540 Southwest 136th Street, Suite 108, Miami, FL 33186, 305-232-5880 or toll-free 888-376-3538. Website: http://www.flet.edu/.

UNIVERSIDAD METROPOLITANA
San Juan, PR

CONTACT Economic Assistant Director, Universidad Metropolitana, Call Box 21150, Rio Piedras, PR 00928-1150, 787-766-1717 Ext. 6586 or toll-free 800-747-8362 (out-of-state). Website: http://www.suagm.edu/umet/.

UNIVERSIDAD PENTECOSTAL MIZPA
San Juan, PR

ABOUT THE INSTITUTION Independent Pentecostal Church, coed. 4 undergraduate majors.
GIFT AID (NEED-BASED) Scholarships, grants, and awards: Federal Pell, FSEOG.
CONTACT Mrs. Myriam Juarbe, Director of Financial Aid, Universidad Pentecostal Mizpa, PO Box 20966, San Juan, PR 00928, 787-720-4476. Fax: 787-720-2012. E-mail: asistenciaeconomica@colmizpa.edu . Website: http://www.mizpa.edu/.

UNIVERSIDAD TEOLGICA DEL CARIBE
St. Just, PR

Tuition & fees: $4448	Average undergraduate aid package: N/A

ABOUT THE INSTITUTION Independent Pentecostal, coed. *Awards:* certificates, diplomas, and bachelor's degrees. 3 undergraduate majors. *Total enrollment:* 172. Undergraduates: 172. Freshmen: 7. Federal methodology is used as a basis for awarding need-based institutional aid.

UNDERGRADUATE EXPENSES for 2013–2014 *Application fee:* $25. *One-time required fee:* $13. *Comprehensive fee:* $6848 includes full-time tuition ($3784), mandatory fees ($664), and room and board ($2400). *College room only:* $1200. Full-time tuition and fees vary according to course load. Room and board charges vary according to board plan. *Part-time tuition:* $18 per credit. *Part-time fees:* $130 per credit; $3004 per term. Part-time tuition and fees vary according to course load.

FRESHMAN FINANCIAL AID (Fall 2012, est.) 10 applied for aid; of those 100% were deemed to have need. 100% of freshmen with need received aid.

UNDERGRADUATE FINANCIAL AID (Fall 2012, est.) 164 applied for aid; of those 100% were deemed to have need. 100% of undergraduates with need received aid.

GIFT AID (NEED-BASED) *Total amount:* $587,936 (100% federal). *Receiving aid:* Freshmen: 100% (10); all full-time undergraduates: 100% (164). *Scholarships, grants, and awards:* Federal Pell, state.

GIFT AID (NON-NEED-BASED) *Tuition waivers:* Full or partial for employees or children of employees.

LOANS *Student loans:* $169,325 (100% need-based). 35% of past graduating class borrowed through all loan programs. *Programs:* Federal Direct (Subsidized and Unsubsidized Stafford).

WORK-STUDY *State or other work-study/employment:* Part-time jobs available.

APPLYING FOR FINANCIAL AID *Required financial aid form:* FAFSA. *Financial aid deadline:* 6/30 (priority: 1/1). *Notification date:* Continuous.

CONTACT Mrs. Sandra I. Barreto, Financial Aid Officer, Universidad Teolgica del Caribe, PO Box 901, Saint Just, PR 00978-0901, 787-761-0640 Ext. 224. *Fax:* 787-748-9220. *E-mail:* aeconomicautc@yahoo.com. *Website:* http://www.utcpr.edu/.

UNIVERSITY AT ALBANY, STATE UNIVERSITY OF NEW YORK
Albany, NY

Tuition & fees (NY res): $7563	Average undergraduate aid package: $9723

ABOUT THE INSTITUTION State-supported, coed. *Awards:* certificates, bachelor's, master's, and doctoral degrees. 57 undergraduate majors. *Total enrollment:* 17,316. Undergraduates: 12,875. Freshmen: 2,568. Federal methodology is used as a basis for awarding need-based institutional aid.

UNDERGRADUATE EXPENSES for 2013–2014 *Application fee:* $50. *Tuition, state resident:* full-time $5570; part-time $232 per credit hour. *Tuition, nonresident:* full-time $14,050; part-time $613 per credit hour. *Required fees:* full-time $1993. Part-time tuition and fees vary according to course load. *College room and board:* $11,276; *Room only:* $6976. Room and board charges vary according to board plan and housing facility.

FRESHMAN FINANCIAL AID (Fall 2012, est.) 2,243 applied for aid; of those 73% were deemed to have need. 97% of freshmen with need received aid; of those 7% had need fully met. *Average percent of need met:* 62% (excluding resources awarded to replace EFC). *Average financial aid package:* $9925 (excluding resources awarded to replace EFC). 7% of all full-time freshmen had no need and received non-need-based gift aid.

UNDERGRADUATE FINANCIAL AID (Fall 2012, est.) 9,606 applied for aid; of those 79% were deemed to have need. 97% of undergraduates with need received aid; of those 7% had need fully met. *Average percent of need met:* 63% (excluding resources awarded to replace EFC). *Average financial aid package:* $9723 (excluding resources awarded to replace EFC). 5% of all full-time undergraduates had no need and received non-need-based gift aid.

GIFT AID (NEED-BASED) *Total amount:* $41,035,454 (51% federal, 38% state, 9% institutional, 2% external sources). *Receiving aid:* Freshmen: 55% (1,408); all full-time undergraduates: 53% (6,343). *Average award:* Freshmen: $6988; Undergraduates: $6424. *Scholarships, grants, and awards:* Federal Pell, FSEOG, state, private, college/university gift aid from institutional funds.

GIFT AID (NON-NEED-BASED) *Total amount:* $3,163,285 (9% federal, 19% state, 60% institutional, 12% external sources). *Receiving aid:* Freshmen: 2% (44). Undergraduates: 1% (117). *Average award:* Freshmen: $3097. Undergraduates: $2821. *Scholarships, grants, and awards by category:* Academic interests/achievement: 1,104 awards ($3,939,433 total): general academic interests/achievements. *ROTC:* Army, Air Force cooperative.

LOANS *Student loans:* $58,248,331 (47% need-based, 53% non-need-based). 69% of past graduating class borrowed through all loan programs. *Average indebtedness per student:* $24,126. *Average need-based loan:* Freshmen: $3792. Undergraduates: $4444. *Parent loans:* $19,280,745 (100% non-need-based). *Programs:* Federal Direct (Subsidized and Unsubsidized Stafford, PLUS), Perkins.

WORK-STUDY *Federal work-study:* Total amount: $1,132,825; 733 jobs averaging $1545. *State or other work-study/employment:* Total amount: $1,435,948 (77% need-based, 23% non-need-based). 215 part-time jobs averaging $6679.

ATHLETIC AWARDS Total amount: $4,421,082 (8% need-based, 92% non-need-based).

APPLYING FOR FINANCIAL AID *Required financial aid form:* FAFSA. *Financial aid deadline (priority):* 3/15. *Notification date:* Continuous beginning 3/20.

CONTACT Diane Corbett, Director of Financial Aid, University at Albany, State University of New York, Student Financial Center, Campus Center G-26, 1400 Washington Avenue, Albany, NY 12222-0001, 518-442-3202. *Fax:* 518-442-5295. *E-mail:* sfc@albany.edu. *Website:* http://www.albany.edu/.

UNIVERSITY AT BUFFALO, THE STATE UNIVERSITY OF NEW YORK
Buffalo, NY

Tuition & fees (NY res): $7989	Average undergraduate aid package: $7261

ABOUT THE INSTITUTION State-supported, coed. *Awards:* certificates, bachelor's, master's, and doctoral degrees. 75 undergraduate majors. *Total enrollment:* 28,952. Undergraduates: 19,505. Freshmen: 3,650. Federal methodology is used as a basis for awarding need-based institutional aid.

UNDERGRADUATE EXPENSES for 2013–2014 *Application fee:* $50. *Tuition, state resident:* full-time $5570; part-time $232 per credit hour. *Tuition, nonresident:* full-time $16,190; part-time $675 per credit hour. *Required fees:* full-time $2419; $94 per credit hour. Part-time tuition and fees vary according to course load. *College room and board:* $11,310; *Room only:* $6540. Room and board charges vary according to board plan and housing facility.

FRESHMAN FINANCIAL AID (Fall 2011) 2,728 applied for aid; of those 74% were deemed to have need. 99% of freshmen with need received aid; of those 99% had need fully met. *Average percent of need met:* 66% (excluding resources awarded to replace EFC). *Average financial aid package:* $9505 (excluding resources awarded to replace EFC). 3% of all full-time freshmen had no need and received non-need-based gift aid.

UNDERGRADUATE FINANCIAL AID (Fall 2011) 15,403 applied for aid; of those 94% were deemed to have need. 76% of undergraduates with need received aid; of those 86% had need fully met. *Average percent of need met:* 65% (excluding resources awarded to replace EFC). *Average financial aid package:* $7261 (excluding resources awarded to replace EFC). 1% of all full-time undergraduates had no need and received non-need-based gift aid.

GIFT AID (NEED-BASED) *Total amount:* $50,350,209 (54% federal, 41% state, 3% institutional, 2% external sources). *Receiving aid:* Freshmen: 62% (1,993); all full-time undergraduates: 53% (9,263). *Average award:* Freshmen: $5770; Undergraduates: $5140. *Scholarships, grants, and awards:* Federal Pell, FSEOG, state, private, college/university gift aid from institutional funds, Federal Nursing.

GIFT AID (NON-NEED-BASED) *Total amount:* $13,682,576 (100% institutional). *Receiving aid:* Freshmen: 14% (459). Undergraduates: 19% (3,393). *Average award:* Freshmen: $6025. Undergraduates: $5474. *Tuition waivers:* Full or partial for minority students. *ROTC:* Army cooperative.

LOANS *Student loans:* $69,053,020 (100% need-based). 45% of past graduating class borrowed through all loan programs. *Average indebtedness per student:* $16,025. *Average need-based loan:* Freshmen: $3544. Undergraduates: $4425. *Parent loans:* $8,647,767 (100% non-need-based). *Programs:* Federal Direct (Subsidized and Unsubsidized Stafford, PLUS), Perkins, Federal Nursing, college/university.

WORK-STUDY *Federal work-study:* Total amount: $1,267,218; 1,070 jobs averaging $1376. *State or other work-study/employment:* Total amount: $12,388,306 (100% non-need-based). 2,300 part-time jobs averaging $3500.

ATHLETIC AWARDS Total amount: $6,176,406 (100% non-need-based).

APPLYING FOR FINANCIAL AID *Required financial aid form:* FAFSA. *Financial aid deadline (priority):* 3/1. *Notification date:* Continuous beginning 2/1. Students must reply by 5/1.

CONTACT Jen Pollard, Director of Financial Aid, University at Buffalo, the State University of New York, 232 Capen Hall, Buffalo, NY 14260, 716-645-2450 or toll-free 888-UB-ADMIT. *Fax:* 716-645-7760. *E-mail:* pollardj@buffalo.edu. *Website:* http://www.buffalo.edu/.

UNIVERSITY OF ADVANCING TECHNOLOGY
Tempe, AZ

ABOUT THE INSTITUTION Proprietary, coed, primarily men. 7 undergraduate majors.

GIFT AID (NEED-BASED) *Scholarships, grants, and awards:* Federal Pell, FSEOG, state, private, college/university gift aid from institutional funds.

GIFT AID (NON-NEED-BASED) *Scholarships, grants, and awards by category:* Academic interests/achievement: computer science, general academic interests/achievements. Special characteristics: children of faculty/staff, local/state students, veterans, veterans' children.

LOANS *Programs:* Federal Direct (Subsidized and Unsubsidized Stafford, PLUS).

APPLYING FOR FINANCIAL AID *Required financial aid form:* FAFSA.

CONTACT Financial Aid Office, University of Advancing Technology, 2625 West Baseline Road, Tempe, AZ 85283-1042, 602-383-8228 or toll-free 800-658-5744. *Fax:* 602-383-8222. *E-mail:* fa@uat.edu. *Website:* http://www.uat.edu/.

THE UNIVERSITY OF AKRON
Akron, OH

Tuition & fees (OH res): $9863	Average undergraduate aid package: $7522

ABOUT THE INSTITUTION State-supported, coed. *Awards:* certificates, associate, bachelor's, master's, and doctoral degrees. 146 undergraduate majors. *Total enrollment:* 26,580. Undergraduates: 22,122. Freshmen: 4,178. Federal methodology is used as a basis for awarding need-based institutional aid.

UNDERGRADUATE EXPENSES for 2013–2014 *Application fee:* $40. *Tuition, state resident:* full-time $8284; part-time $345.15 per credit hour. *Tuition, nonresident:* full-time $16,484; part-time $686.85 per credit hour. *Required fees:* full-time $1579. Full-time tuition and fees vary according to course load, degree level, and location. Part-time tuition and fees vary according to course load, degree level, and location. *College room and board:* $9878; *Room only:* $6306. Room and board charges vary according to board plan and housing facility.

FRESHMAN FINANCIAL AID (Fall 2012, est.) 3,578 applied for aid; of those 83% were deemed to have need. 100% of freshmen with need received aid; of those 8% had need fully met. *Average percent of need met:* 47% (excluding resources awarded to replace EFC). *Average financial aid package:* $7402 (excluding resources awarded to replace EFC). 12% of all full-time freshmen had no need and received non-need-based gift aid.

UNDERGRADUATE FINANCIAL AID (Fall 2012, est.) 14,613 applied for aid; of those 82% were deemed to have need. 100% of undergraduates with need received aid; of those 8% had need fully met. *Average percent of need met:* 49% (excluding resources awarded to replace EFC). *Average financial aid package:* $7522 (excluding resources awarded to replace EFC). 10% of all full-time undergraduates had no need and received non-need-based gift aid.

GIFT AID (NEED-BASED) *Total amount:* $43,164,388 (89% federal, 11% state). *Receiving aid:* Freshmen: 48% (1,877); all full-time undergraduates: 44% (7,369). *Average award:* Freshmen: $4572; Undergraduates: $4697. *Scholarships, grants, and awards:* Federal Pell, FSEOG, state, college/university gift aid from institutional funds.

GIFT AID (NON-NEED-BASED) *Total amount:* $33,356,733 (1% federal, 6% state, 77% institutional, 16% external sources). *Receiving aid:* Freshmen: 45% (1,782). Undergraduates: 38% (6,389). *Average award:* Freshmen: $4522. Undergraduates: $4408. *Scholarships, grants, and awards by category: Academic interests/achievement:* 3,355 awards ($8,855,121 total): biological sciences, business, communication, computer science, education, engineering/technologies, English, foreign languages, general academic interests/achievements, health fields, home economics, humanities, international studies, mathematics, military science, physical sciences, premedicine, social sciences. *Creative arts/performance:* 114 awards ($114,651 total): applied art and design, art/fine arts, creative writing, dance, debating, general creative arts/performance, journalism/publications, music, performing arts, theater/drama. *Special achievements/activities:* 93 awards ($267,310 total): community service, general special achievements/activities, leadership, memberships. *Special characteristics:* 2,896 awards ($10,468,373 total): adult students, general special characteristics, handicapped students, international students, local/state students, members of minority groups, out-of-state students. *Tuition waivers:* Full or partial for employees or children of employees, senior citizens. *ROTC:* Army, Air Force cooperative.

LOANS *Student loans:* $117,847,700 (43% need-based, 57% non-need-based). 73% of past graduating class borrowed through all loan programs. *Average indebtedness per student:* $23,392. *Average need-based loan:* Freshmen: $2481. Undergraduates: $3112. *Parent loans:* $16,328,669 (100% non-need-based). *Programs:* Federal Direct (Subsidized and Unsubsidized Stafford, PLUS), Perkins, Federal Nursing, college/university.

WORK-STUDY *Federal work-study:* Total amount: $1,200,000; jobs available. *State or other work-study/employment:* Total amount: $7,000,000 (100% non-need-based). Part-time jobs available.

ATHLETIC AWARDS Total amount: $4,701,213 (100% non-need-based).

APPLYING FOR FINANCIAL AID *Required financial aid forms:* FAFSA, institution's own form. *Financial aid deadline (priority):* 2/1. *Notification date:* Continuous beginning 4/1. Students must reply within 2 weeks of notification.

CONTACT Ms. Michelle Ellis, Director of Student Financial Aid, The University of Akron, 302 Buchtel Mall, Akron, OH 44325-6211, 330-972-5860 or toll-free 800-655-4884. *Fax:* 330-972-7139. *E-mail:* mellis@uakron.edu. *Website:* http://www.uakron.edu/.

THE UNIVERSITY OF ALABAMA
Tuscaloosa, AL

Tuition & fees (AL res): $9200	Average undergraduate aid package: $10,485

ABOUT THE INSTITUTION State-supported, coed. *Awards:* certificates, bachelor's, master's, and doctoral degrees. 70 undergraduate majors. *Total enrollment:* 33,503. Undergraduates: 28,026. Freshmen: 6,371. Federal methodology is used as a basis for awarding need-based institutional aid.

UNDERGRADUATE EXPENSES for 2013–2014 *Application fee:* $40. *Tuition, state resident:* full-time $9200. *Tuition, nonresident:* full-time $22,950. Full-time tuition and fees vary according to course load. Part-time tuition and fees vary according to course load. *College room and board:* $8650; *Room only:* $5600. Room and board charges vary according to board plan and housing facility.

FRESHMAN FINANCIAL AID (Fall 2011) 3,561 applied for aid; of those 71% were deemed to have need. 97% of freshmen with need received aid; of those 21% had need fully met. *Average percent of need met:* 55% (excluding resources awarded to replace EFC). *Average financial aid package:* $11,479 (excluding resources awarded to replace EFC). 26% of all full-time freshmen had no need and received non-need-based gift aid.

UNDERGRADUATE FINANCIAL AID (Fall 2011) 12,947 applied for aid; of those 78% were deemed to have need. 98% of undergraduates with need received aid; of those 15% had need fully met. *Average percent of need met:* 52% (excluding resources awarded to replace EFC). *Average financial aid package:* $10,485 (excluding resources awarded to replace EFC). 21% of all full-time undergraduates had no need and received non-need-based gift aid.

GIFT AID (NEED-BASED) *Total amount:* $52,877,964 (47% federal, 1% state, 42% institutional, 10% external sources). *Receiving aid:* Freshmen: 34% (1,939); all full-time undergraduates: 31% (7,424). *Average award:* Freshmen: $9420; Undergraduates: $7619. *Scholarships, grants, and awards:* Federal Pell, FSEOG, state, private, college/university gift aid from institutional funds, Federal Nursing.

GIFT AID (NON-NEED-BASED) *Total amount:* $63,876,096 (80% institutional, 20% external sources). *Receiving aid:* Freshmen: 25% (1,401). Undergraduates: 17% (4,093). *Average award:* Freshmen: $10,365. Undergraduates: $9291. *Scholarships, grants, and awards by category:* Academic interests/achievement: area/ethnic studies, biological sciences, business, communication, computer science, education, engineering/technologies, English, foreign languages, general academic interests/achievements, home economics, library science, mathematics, military science, physical sciences, premedicine, social sciences. Creative arts/performance: art/fine arts, cinema/film/broadcasting, creative writing, dance, debating, journalism/publications, music, theater/drama. Special achievements/activities: cheerleading/drum major, community service, general special achievements/activities, hobbies/interests, junior miss. Special characteristics: children of union members/company employees, general special characteristics, international students, out-of-state students, spouses of deceased or disabled public servants. *Tuition waivers:* Full or partial for employees or children of employees. *ROTC:* Army, Air Force.

LOANS *Student loans:* $101,603,456 (72% need-based, 28% non-need-based). 43% of past graduating class borrowed through all loan programs. *Average indebtedness per student:* $27,639. *Average need-based loan:* Freshmen: $3486. Undergraduates: $4313. *Parent loans:* $42,004,870 (45% need-based, 55% non-need-based). *Programs:* Federal Direct (Subsidized and Unsubsidized Stafford, PLUS), Perkins, college/university, private loans.

WORK-STUDY *Federal work-study:* Total amount: $1,323,768; 430 jobs averaging $3014.

ATHLETIC AWARDS Total amount: $9,928,228 (5% need-based, 95% non-need-based).

APPLYING FOR FINANCIAL AID *Required financial aid form:* FAFSA. *Financial aid deadline (priority):* 3/1. *Notification date:* 4/1. Students must reply within 3 weeks of notification.

CONTACT Helen Allen, Director of Financial Aid, The University of Alabama, Box 870162, Tuscaloosa, AL 35487-0162, 205-348-6756 or toll-free 800-933-BAMA. *Fax:* 205-348-2989. *E-mail:* helen.leathers@ua.edu.
Website: http://www.ua.edu/.

GIFT AID (NEED-BASED) *Total amount:* $18,952,650 (98% federal, 1% state, 1% external sources). *Receiving aid:* Freshmen: 37% (586); all full-time undergraduates: 40% (3,268). *Average award:* Freshmen: $5005; Undergraduates: $4709. *Scholarships, grants, and awards:* Federal Pell, FSEOG, state, private, college/university gift aid from institutional funds, United Negro College Fund.

GIFT AID (NON-NEED-BASED) *Total amount:* $14,447,248 (91% institutional, 9% external sources). *Receiving aid:* Freshmen: 34% (537). Undergraduates: 19% (1,509). *Average award:* Freshmen: $5905. Undergraduates: $6094. *Scholarships, grants, and awards by category:* Academic interests/achievement: business, communication, computer science, engineering/technologies, general academic interests/achievements, health fields, mathematics. Creative arts/performance: art/fine arts, music, performing arts, theater/drama. Special achievements/activities: cheerleading/drum major, junior miss, leadership, memberships, religious involvement. Special characteristics: adult students, children and siblings of alumni, children of current students, children of educators, children of faculty/staff, children of public servants, children of union members/company employees, children of workers in trades, children with a deceased or disabled parent, ethnic background, first-generation college students, general special characteristics, handicapped students, married students, members of minority groups, out-of-state students, parents of current students, previous college experience, public servants, relatives of clergy, siblings of current students, spouses of current students, spouses of deceased or disabled public servants, twins, veterans, veterans' children. *Tuition waivers:* Full or partial for employees or children of employees. *ROTC:* Army, Air Force cooperative.

LOANS *Student loans:* $46,372,502 (49% need-based, 51% non-need-based). 47% of past graduating class borrowed through all loan programs. *Average indebtedness per student:* $21,503. *Average need-based loan:* Freshmen: $4023. Undergraduates: $4511. *Parent loans:* $4,384,495 (100% non-need-based). *Programs:* Federal Direct (Subsidized and Unsubsidized Stafford, PLUS), Perkins, state, college/university.

WORK-STUDY *Federal work-study:* Total amount: $2,127,015; jobs available.

ATHLETIC AWARDS Total amount: $5,858,495 (100% non-need-based).

APPLYING FOR FINANCIAL AID *Required financial aid form:* FAFSA. *Financial aid deadline (priority):* 3/1. *Notification date:* Continuous beginning 4/1. Students must reply within 4 weeks of notification.

CONTACT Ms. Janet B. May, Student Financial Aid Director, The University of Alabama at Birmingham, Hill University Center 317, 1530 3rd Avenue South, Birmingham, AL 35294-1150, 205-934-8132 or toll-free 800-421-8743.
Website: http://www.uab.edu/.

THE UNIVERSITY OF ALABAMA AT BIRMINGHAM
Birmingham, AL

Tuition & fees (AL res): $8400	Average undergraduate aid package: $9420

ABOUT THE INSTITUTION State-supported, coed. *Awards:* certificates, bachelor's, master's, and doctoral degrees. 46 undergraduate majors. *Total enrollment:* 17,999. Undergraduates: 11,291. Freshmen: 1,676. Federal methodology is used as a basis for awarding need-based institutional aid.

UNDERGRADUATE EXPENSES for 2013–2014 *Application fee:* $30. *Tuition, state resident:* full-time $8400; part-time $267 per credit hour. *Tuition, nonresident:* full-time $19,230; part-time $628 per credit hour. Full-time tuition and fees vary according to program. Part-time tuition and fees vary according to program. *Room only:* $5400. Room and board charges vary according to board plan and housing facility.

FRESHMAN FINANCIAL AID (Fall 2011) 1,221 applied for aid; of those 76% were deemed to have need. 99% of freshmen with need received aid; of those 16% had need fully met. *Average percent of need met:* 44% (excluding resources awarded to replace EFC). *Average financial aid package:* $10,124 (excluding resources awarded to replace EFC). 25% of all full-time freshmen had no need and received non-need-based gift aid.

UNDERGRADUATE FINANCIAL AID (Fall 2011) 5,805 applied for aid; of those 84% were deemed to have need. 99% of undergraduates with need received aid; of those 11% had need fully met. *Average percent of need met:* 44% (excluding resources awarded to replace EFC). *Average financial aid package:* $9420 (excluding resources awarded to replace EFC). 16% of all full-time undergraduates had no need and received non-need-based gift aid.

THE UNIVERSITY OF ALABAMA IN HUNTSVILLE
Huntsville, AL

Tuition & fees (AL res): $8794	Average undergraduate aid package: $9394

ABOUT THE INSTITUTION State-supported, coed. *Awards:* certificates, bachelor's, master's, and doctoral degrees. 31 undergraduate majors. *Total enrollment:* 7,629. Undergraduates: 5,935. Freshmen: 677. Both federal and institutional methodology are used as a basis for awarding need-based institutional aid.

UNDERGRADUATE EXPENSES for 2013–2014 *Application fee:* $30. *Tuition, state resident:* full-time $8794; part-time $339.26 per credit hour. *Tuition, nonresident:* full-time $21,108; part-time $814.89 per credit hour. Full-time tuition and fees vary according to course load. Part-time tuition and fees vary according to course load. *College room and board:* $8070; *Room only:* $5480. Room and board charges vary according to board plan and housing facility.

FRESHMAN FINANCIAL AID (Fall 2012, est.) 561 applied for aid; of those 60% were deemed to have need. 99% of freshmen with need received aid; of those 17% had need fully met. *Average percent of need met:* 61% (excluding resources awarded to replace EFC). *Average financial aid package:* $10,839 (excluding resources awarded to replace EFC). 27% of all full-time freshmen had no need and received non-need-based gift aid.

UNDERGRADUATE FINANCIAL AID (Fall 2012, est.) 3,582 applied for aid; of those 68% were deemed to have need. 99% of undergraduates with need received aid; of those 10% had need fully met. *Average percent of need met:* 53% (excluding resources awarded to replace EFC). *Average financial aid package:* $9394 (excluding resources awarded to replace EFC). 15% of all full-time undergraduates had no need and received non-need-based gift aid.

GIFT AID (NEED-BASED) *Total amount:* $12,894,791 (68% federal, 28% institutional, 4% external sources). *Receiving aid:* Freshmen: 48% (295); all full-time undergraduates: 43% (1,912). *Average award:* Freshmen: $8042; Undergraduates: $6311. *Scholarships, grants, and awards:* Federal Pell, FSEOG, state, private, college/university gift aid from institutional funds, Federal Nursing.

GIFT AID (NON-NEED-BASED) *Total amount:* $6,090,920 (94% institutional, 6% external sources). *Receiving aid:* Freshmen: 6% (38). Undergraduates: 3% (111). *Average award:* Freshmen: $9540. Undergraduates: $7798. *Scholarships, grants, and awards by category:* Academic interests/achievement: 2,728 awards ($9,599,316 total): biological sciences, business, communication, computer science, education, engineering/technologies, English, foreign languages, general academic interests/achievements, health fields, humanities, mathematics, physical sciences, social sciences. *Creative arts/performance:* 75 awards ($74,850 total): art/fine arts, music. *Special achievements/activities:* 538 awards ($2,483,344 total): cheerleading/drum major, community service, general special achievements/activities, junior miss, leadership. *Special characteristics:* 38 awards ($91,650 total): general special characteristics, local/state students, members of minority groups. *Tuition waivers:* Full or partial for employees or children of employees. *ROTC:* Army cooperative.

LOANS *Student loans:* $25,964,997 (84% need-based, 16% non-need-based). 53% of past graduating class borrowed through all loan programs. *Average indebtedness per student:* $25,437. *Average need-based loan:* Freshmen: $6055. Undergraduates: $7912. *Parent loans:* $1,672,572 (48% need-based, 52% non-need-based). *Programs:* Federal Direct (Subsidized and Unsubsidized Stafford, PLUS).

WORK-STUDY *Federal work-study:* Total amount: $360,034; 72 jobs averaging $4869.

ATHLETIC AWARDS Total amount: $2,423,092 (27% need-based, 73% non-need-based).

APPLYING FOR FINANCIAL AID *Required financial aid form:* FAFSA. *Financial aid deadline:* 7/31 (priority: 4/1). *Notification date:* Continuous beginning 4/1. Students must reply within 2 weeks of notification.

CONTACT Mr. Andrew Weaver, Director of Student Financial Services, The University of Alabama in Huntsville, 301 Sparkman Drive, UC Room 212, Huntsville, AL 35899, 256-824-6241 or toll-free 800-UAH-CALL. *Fax:* 256-824-6212. *E-mail:* finaid@uah.edu. *Website:* http://www.uah.edu/.

UNIVERSITY OF ALASKA ANCHORAGE
Anchorage, AK

Tuition & fees (AK res): $4950	Average undergraduate aid package: $8188

ABOUT THE INSTITUTION State-supported, coed. *Awards:* certificates, associate, bachelor's, master's, and doctoral degrees. 107 undergraduate majors. *Total enrollment:* 18,107. Undergraduates: 17,129. Freshmen: 1,997. Federal methodology is used as a basis for awarding need-based institutional aid.

UNDERGRADUATE EXPENSES for 2013–2014 *Application fee:* $50. *Tuition, state resident:* full-time $4950. *Tuition, nonresident:* full-time $17,400. Full-time tuition and fees vary according to course level and location. Part-time tuition and fees vary according to course level and location. *College room and board:* $9780; *Room only:* $5980. Room and board charges vary according to board plan and housing facility.

FRESHMAN FINANCIAL AID (Fall 2012, est.) 1,211 applied for aid; of those 64% were deemed to have need. 96% of freshmen with need received aid; of those 40% had need fully met. *Average percent of need met:* 78% (excluding resources awarded to replace EFC). *Average financial aid package:* $7681 (excluding resources awarded to replace EFC). 8% of all full-time freshmen had no need and received non-need-based gift aid.

UNDERGRADUATE FINANCIAL AID (Fall 2012, est.) 3,827 applied for aid; of those 80% were deemed to have need. 94% of undergraduates with need received aid; of those 24% had need fully met. *Average percent of need met:* 69% (excluding resources awarded to replace EFC). *Average financial aid package:* $8188 (excluding resources awarded to replace EFC). 6% of all full-time undergraduates had no need and received non-need-based gift aid.

GIFT AID (NEED-BASED) *Total amount:* $26,233,623 (69% federal, 13% state, 10% institutional, 8% external sources). *Receiving aid:* Freshmen: 46% (648); all full-time undergraduates: 38% (2,269). *Average award:* Freshmen: $2818; Undergraduates: $2810. *Scholarships, grants, and awards:* Federal Pell, FSEOG, state, private, college/university gift aid from institutional funds.

GIFT AID (NON-NEED-BASED) *Total amount:* $4,590,732 (36% state, 32% institutional, 32% external sources). *Receiving aid:* Freshmen: 6% (80). Undergraduates: 1% (77). *Average award:* Freshmen: $2755. Undergraduates: $2392. *Scholarships, grants, and awards by category:* Academic interests/achievement: biological sciences, business, communication, computer science, education, engineering/technologies, English, general academic interests/achievements, health fields, humanities, mathematics, social sciences. *Creative arts/performance:* art/fine arts, dance, debating, music, performing arts. *Special achievements/activities:* general special achievements/activities, leadership. *Special characteristics:* children and siblings of alumni, children of current students, children of educators. *ROTC:* Army, Air Force.

LOANS *Student loans:* $47,423,181 (74% need-based, 26% non-need-based). 49% of past graduating class borrowed through all loan programs. *Average indebtedness per student:* $30,363. *Average need-based loan:* Freshmen: $3216. Undergraduates: $4286. *Parent loans:* $19,787,190 (22% need-based, 78% non-need-based). *Programs:* Federal Direct (Subsidized and Unsubsidized Stafford, PLUS), state.

WORK-STUDY *Federal work-study:* Total amount: $524,309; jobs available.

ATHLETIC AWARDS Total amount: $1,072,448 (26% need-based, 74% non-need-based).

APPLYING FOR FINANCIAL AID *Required financial aid form:* FAFSA. *Financial aid deadline:* Continuous. *Notification date:* Continuous beginning 3/15. Students must reply within 4 weeks of notification.

CONTACT Sonya F. Stein, Director of Student Financial Assistance, University of Alaska Anchorage, PO Box 141608, Anchorage, AK 99514-1608, 907-786-1517. *Fax:* 907-786-6122. *E-mail:* sefisher@uaa.alaska.edu. *Website:* http://www.uaa.alaska.edu/.

UNIVERSITY OF ALASKA FAIRBANKS
Fairbanks, AK

Tuition & fees (AK res): $5580	Average undergraduate aid package: $9615

ABOUT THE INSTITUTION State-supported, coed. *Awards:* certificates, associate, bachelor's, master's, and doctoral degrees. 82 undergraduate majors. *Total enrollment:* 9,314. Undergraduates: 8,131. Freshmen: 945. Federal methodology is used as a basis for awarding need-based institutional aid.

UNDERGRADUATE EXPENSES for 2013–2014 *Application fee:* $50. *Tuition, state resident:* full-time $5580; part-time $168 per credit. *Tuition, nonresident:* full-time $18,270; part-time $591 per credit. Full-time tuition and fees vary according to course level, course load, location, and reciprocity agreements. Part-time tuition and fees vary according to course level, course load, location, and reciprocity agreements. *College room and board:* $7200; *Room only:* $3680. Room and board charges vary according to board plan and housing facility.

FRESHMAN FINANCIAL AID (Fall 2011) 755 applied for aid; of those 63% were deemed to have need. 97% of freshmen with need received aid; of those 30% had need fully met. *Average percent of need met:* 66% (excluding resources awarded to replace EFC). *Average financial aid package:* $8812 (excluding resources awarded to replace EFC). 17% of all full-time freshmen had no need and received non-need-based gift aid.

UNDERGRADUATE FINANCIAL AID (Fall 2011) 2,753 applied for aid; of those 72% were deemed to have need. 95% of undergraduates with need received aid; of those 24% had need fully met. *Average percent of need met:* 66% (excluding resources awarded to replace EFC). *Average financial aid package:* $9615 (excluding resources awarded to replace EFC). 15% of all full-time undergraduates had no need and received non-need-based gift aid.

GIFT AID (NEED-BASED) *Total amount:* $11,474,800 (59% federal, 8% state, 18% institutional, 15% external sources). *Receiving aid:* Freshmen: 47% (401); all full-time undergraduates: 42% (1,556). *Average award:* Freshmen: $6315; Undergraduates: $6001. *Scholarships, grants, and awards:* Federal Pell, FSEOG, state, private, college/university gift aid from institutional funds.

GIFT AID (NON-NEED-BASED) *Total amount:* $4,439,387 (16% state, 48% institutional, 36% external sources). *Receiving aid:* Freshmen: 11% (91). Undergraduates: 6% (205). *Average award:* Freshmen: $3497. Undergraduates: $3727. *Scholarships, grants, and awards by category:* Academic interests/achievement:

agriculture, biological sciences, engineering/technologies, general academic interests/ achievements, mathematics, physical sciences. *Creative arts/performance:* applied art and design, art/fine arts, creative writing, music, theater/drama. *Special achievements/ activities:* community service, general special achievements/activities. *Special characteristics:* local/state students. *Tuition waivers:* Full or partial for children of alumni, employees or children of employees, senior citizens. *ROTC:* Army.

LOANS *Student loans:* $32,332,256 (70% need-based, 30% non-need-based). 44% of past graduating class borrowed through all loan programs. *Average indebtedness per student:* $29,762. *Average need-based loan:* Freshmen: $6081. Undergraduates: $7872. *Parent loans:* $4,464,706 (16% need-based, 84% non-need-based). *Programs:* Federal Direct (Subsidized and Unsubsidized Stafford, PLUS), state.

WORK-STUDY *Federal work-study:* Total amount: $73,388; 17 jobs averaging $4317.

ATHLETIC AWARDS Total amount: $435,906 (17% need-based, 83% non-need-based).

APPLYING FOR FINANCIAL AID *Required financial aid form:* FAFSA. *Financial aid deadline:* 7/1 (priority: 2/15). *Notification date:* Continuous beginning 3/1. Students must reply within 2 weeks of notification.

CONTACT Deanna Dieringer, Director of Financial Aid, University of Alaska Fairbanks, PO Box 756360, Fairbanks, AK 99775-6360, 907-474-7256 or toll-free 800-478-1823. *Fax:* 907-474-7065. *E-mail:* financialaid@uaf.edu. *Website:* http://www.uaf.edu/.

UNIVERSITY OF ALASKA SOUTHEAST
Juneau, AK

ABOUT THE INSTITUTION State-supported, coed. 27 undergraduate majors.

GIFT AID (NEED-BASED) *Scholarships, grants, and awards:* Federal Pell, FSEOG, state, private, college/university gift aid from institutional funds.

GIFT AID (NON-NEED-BASED) *Scholarships, grants, and awards by category: Academic interests/achievement:* general academic interests/achievements. *Creative arts/performance:* general creative arts/performance. *Special achievements/ activities:* leadership. *Special characteristics:* local/state students.

LOANS *Programs:* Federal Direct (Subsidized and Unsubsidized Stafford, PLUS), state.

APPLYING FOR FINANCIAL AID *Required financial aid form:* FAFSA.

CONTACT Ms. Corinne Soltis, Director of Financial Aid, University of Alaska Southeast, 11120 Glacier Highway, Juneau, AK 99801-8680, 907-796-6255 or toll-free 877-465-4827. *Fax:* 907-796-6250. *E-mail:* casoltis@uas.alaska.edu. *Website:* http://www.uas.alaska.edu/.

UNIVERSITY OF ANTELOPE VALLEY
Lancaster, CA

CONTACT Financial Aid Office, University of Antelope Valley, 44055 North Sierra Highway, Lancaster, CA 93534, 661-726-1911. *Website:* http://www.uav.edu/.

THE UNIVERSITY OF ARIZONA
Tucson, AZ

Tuition & fees (AZ res): $10,035	Average undergraduate aid package: $12,059

ABOUT THE INSTITUTION State-supported, coed. *Awards:* certificates, bachelor's, master's, and doctoral degrees. 109 undergraduate majors. *Total enrollment:* 40,223. Undergraduates: 31,565. Freshmen: 7,401. Both federal and institutional methodology are used as a basis for awarding need-based institutional aid.

UNDERGRADUATE EXPENSES for 2013–2014 *Application fee:* $50. *Tuition, state resident:* full-time $9114; part-time $651 per credit hour. *Tuition, nonresident:* full-time $25,310; part-time $1055 per credit hour. *Required fees:* full-time $921; $80 per credit hour. Full-time tuition and fees vary according to course level, course load, degree level, location, program, reciprocity agreements, and student level. Part-time tuition and fees vary according to course level, course load, degree

level, location, program, reciprocity agreements, and student level. *College room and board:* $9714; *Room only:* $6784. Room and board charges vary according to board plan and housing facility.

FRESHMAN FINANCIAL AID (Fall 2011) 5,018 applied for aid; of those 75% were deemed to have need. 97% of freshmen with need received aid; of those 13% had need fully met. *Average percent of need met:* 64% (excluding resources awarded to replace EFC). *Average financial aid package:* $12,180 (excluding resources awarded to replace EFC). 26% of all full-time freshmen had no need and received non-need-based gift aid.

UNDERGRADUATE FINANCIAL AID (Fall 2011) 17,357 applied for aid; of those 82% were deemed to have need. 97% of undergraduates with need received aid; of those 11% had need fully met. *Average percent of need met:* 61% (excluding resources awarded to replace EFC). *Average financial aid package:* $12,059 (excluding resources awarded to replace EFC). 20% of all full-time undergraduates had no need and received non-need-based gift aid.

GIFT AID (NEED-BASED) *Total amount:* $137,302,254 (33% federal, 56% institutional, 11% external sources). *Receiving aid:* Freshmen: 51% (3,472); all full-time undergraduates: 46% (12,637). *Average award:* Freshmen: $10,795; Undergraduates: $10,090. *Scholarships, grants, and awards:* Federal Pell, FSEOG, state, private, college/university gift aid from institutional funds, Federal Nursing.

GIFT AID (NON-NEED-BASED) *Total amount:* $54,867,740 (1% federal, 73% institutional, 26% external sources). *Receiving aid:* Freshmen: 6% (444). Undergraduates: 4% (1,101). *Average award:* Freshmen: $7643. Undergraduates: $7160. *Scholarships, grants, and awards by category: Academic interests/ achievement:* agriculture, architecture, biological sciences, business, education, engineering/technologies, general academic interests/achievements, humanities, military science, physical sciences, religion/biblical studies. *Creative arts/performance:* art/fine arts, dance, music, performing arts, theater/drama. *Special characteristics:* children of faculty/staff, ethnic background, international students. *Tuition waivers:* Full or partial for employees or children of employees. *ROTC:* Army, Naval, Air Force.

LOANS *Student loans:* $95,033,616 (84% need-based, 16% non-need-based). 49% of past graduating class borrowed through all loan programs. *Average indebtedness per student:* $22,269. *Average need-based loan:* Freshmen: $3256. Undergraduates: $4196. *Parent loans:* $43,881,229 (72% need-based, 28% non-need-based). *Programs:* Federal Direct (Subsidized and Unsubsidized Stafford, PLUS), Perkins, Federal Nursing, college/university.

WORK-STUDY *Federal work-study:* Total amount: $2,494,948; jobs available. *State or other work-study/employment:* Total amount: $22,885,860 (60% need-based, 40% non-need-based). Part-time jobs available.

ATHLETIC AWARDS Total amount: $7,479,532 (40% need-based, 60% non-need-based).

APPLYING FOR FINANCIAL AID *Required financial aid form:* FAFSA. *Financial aid deadline:* Continuous. *Notification date:* Continuous.

CONTACT John Nametz, Director of Student Financial Aid, The University of Arizona, PO Box 210066, Tucson, AZ 85721-0066, 520-621-5200. *Fax:* 520-621-9473. *E-mail:* askaid@arizona.edu. *Website:* http://www.arizona.edu/.

UNIVERSITY OF ARKANSAS
Fayetteville, AR

Tuition & fees (AR res): $7553	Average undergraduate aid package: $9669

ABOUT THE INSTITUTION State-supported, coed. *Awards:* certificates, bachelor's, master's, and doctoral degrees. 69 undergraduate majors. *Total enrollment:* 23,199. Undergraduates: 19,027. Freshmen: 4,447. Federal methodology is used as a basis for awarding need-based institutional aid.

UNDERGRADUATE EXPENSES for 2013–2014 *Application fee:* $40. *Tuition, state resident:* full-time $6141. *Tuition, nonresident:* full-time $17,022. *Required fees:* full-time $1412. Full-time tuition and fees vary according to course load and program. Part-time tuition and fees vary according to course load and program. *College room and board:* $8672; *Room only:* $5494. Room and board charges vary according to board plan and housing facility.

FRESHMAN FINANCIAL AID (Fall 2012, est.) 3,726 applied for aid; of those 60% were deemed to have need. 98% of freshmen with need received aid; of those 24% had need fully met. *Average percent of need met:* 68% (excluding resources awarded to replace EFC). *Average financial aid package:* $10,004 (excluding

resources awarded to replace EFC). 15% of all full-time freshmen had no need and received non-need-based gift aid.

UNDERGRADUATE FINANCIAL AID (Fall 2012, est.) 11,786 applied for aid; of those 71% were deemed to have need. 97% of undergraduates with need received aid; of those 18% had need fully met. *Average percent of need met:* 60% (excluding resources awarded to replace EFC). *Average financial aid package:* $9669 (excluding resources awarded to replace EFC). 14% of all full-time undergraduates had no need and received non-need-based gift aid.

GIFT AID (NEED-BASED) *Total amount:* $45,717,819 (44% federal, 33% state, 18% institutional, 5% external sources). *Receiving aid:* Freshmen: 41% (1,846); all full-time undergraduates: 37% (6,572). *Average award:* Freshmen: $7547; Undergraduates: $6939. *Scholarships, grants, and awards:* Federal Pell, FSEOG, state, private, college/university gift aid from institutional funds.

GIFT AID (NON-NEED-BASED) *Total amount:* $34,406,376 (53% state, 42% institutional, 5% external sources). *Receiving aid:* Freshmen: 8% (380). Undergraduates: 5% (952). *Average award:* Freshmen: $4494. Undergraduates: $5273. *Scholarships, grants, and awards by category: Academic interests/achievement:* general academic interests/achievements. *Creative arts/performance:* art/fine arts, music, theater/drama. *Special achievements/activities:* community service, general special achievements/activities, leadership. *Special characteristics:* children and siblings of alumni, children of faculty/staff, ethnic background, international students, local/state students, members of minority groups, out-of-state students, previous college experience. *ROTC:* Army, Air Force.

LOANS *Student loans:* $73,244,613 (66% need-based, 34% non-need-based). 45% of past graduating class borrowed through all loan programs. *Average indebtedness per student:* $24,647. *Average need-based loan:* Freshmen: $3555. Undergraduates: $4369. *Parent loans:* $11,361,456 (30% need-based, 70% non-need-based). *Programs:* Federal Direct (Subsidized and Unsubsidized Stafford, PLUS), Perkins, state, college/university, alternative loans.

WORK-STUDY *Federal work-study:* Total amount: $2,605,675; jobs available.

ATHLETIC AWARDS Total amount: $4,985,098 (34% need-based, 66% non-need-based).

APPLYING FOR FINANCIAL AID *Required financial aid form:* FAFSA. *Financial aid deadline (priority):* 3/15. *Notification date:* Continuous beginning 4/1. Students must reply within 4 weeks of notification.

CONTACT Wendy Stouffer, Interim Director of Financial Aid, University of Arkansas, 114 Silas H. Hunt Hall, Fayetteville, AR 72701-1201, 479-575-3078 or toll-free 800-377-8632. *E-mail:* wstouff@uark.edu. *Website:* http://www.uark.edu/.

UNIVERSITY OF ARKANSAS AT LITTLE ROCK
Little Rock, AR

CONTACT Financial Aid Office, University of Arkansas at Little Rock, 2801 South University Avenue, Little Rock, AR 72204-1099, 501-569-3035 or toll-free 800-482-8892. *E-mail:* financialaid@ualr.edu. *Website:* http://www.ualr.edu/.

UNIVERSITY OF ARKANSAS AT MONTICELLO
Monticello, AR

CONTACT Susan Brewer, Director of Financial Aid, University of Arkansas at Monticello, PO Box 3470, Monticello, AR 71656, 870-460-1050 or toll-free 800-844-1826. *Fax:* 870-460-1450. *E-mail:* brewers@uamont.edu. *Website:* http://www.uamont.edu/.

UNIVERSITY OF ARKANSAS AT PINE BLUFF
Pine Bluff, AR

CONTACT Mrs. Carolyn Iverson, Director of Financial Aid, University of Arkansas at Pine Bluff, 1200 North University Drive, PO Box 4985, Pine Bluff, AR 71601, 870-575-8303 or toll-free 800-621-7440. *Fax:* 870-575-4622. *E-mail:* iverson_c@uapb.edu. *Website:* http://www.uapb.edu/.

UNIVERSITY OF ARKANSAS FOR MEDICAL SCIENCES
Little Rock, AR

CONTACT Mr. Paul Carter, Director of Financial Aid, University of Arkansas for Medical Sciences, 4301 West Markham Street, MS 601, Little Rock, AR 72205, 501-686-5451. *Fax:* 501-686-5661. *E-mail:* pvcarter@uams.edu. *Website:* http://www.uams.edu/.

UNIVERSITY OF ARKANSAS–FORT SMITH
Fort Smith, AR

CONTACT Tammy Malone, Interim Financial Aid Director, University of Arkansas–Fort Smith, 5210 Grand Avenue, Fort Smith, AR 72913, 479-788-7099 or toll-free 888-512-5466. *Fax:* 479-788-7095. *E-mail:* tmalone@uafortsmith.edu. *Website:* http://www.uafortsmith.edu/.

UNIVERSITY OF ATLANTA
Atlanta, GA

CONTACT Financial Aid Office, University of Atlanta, 6685 Peachtree Industrial Boulevard, Atlanta, GA 30360, 770-368-8877 or toll-free 800-533-3378. *Website:* http://www.uofa.edu/.

UNIVERSITY OF BALTIMORE
Baltimore, MD

CONTACT Financial Aid Office, University of Baltimore, 1420 North Charles Street, CH 123, Baltimore, MD 21201-5779, 410-837-4763. *Fax:* 410-837-5493. *E-mail:* financial-aid@ubalt.edu. *Website:* http://www.ubalt.edu/.

UNIVERSITY OF BRIDGEPORT
Bridgeport, CT

Tuition & fees: $28,140	Average undergraduate aid package: $24,192

ABOUT THE INSTITUTION Independent, coed. *Awards:* certificates, associate, bachelor's, master's, and doctoral degrees. 38 undergraduate majors. *Total enrollment:* 4,877. Undergraduates: 2,688. Freshmen: 598. Federal methodology is used as a basis for awarding need-based institutional aid.

UNDERGRADUATE EXPENSES for 2013–2014 *Application fee:* $25. *Comprehensive fee:* $40,190 includes full-time tuition ($25,950), mandatory fees ($2190), and room and board ($12,050). Full-time tuition and fees vary according to course load and program. Room and board charges vary according to board plan, housing facility, and student level. **Part-time tuition:** $865 per credit hour. **Part-time fees:** $200 per term. Part-time tuition and fees vary according to course load and program.

FRESHMAN FINANCIAL AID (Fall 2012, est.) 537 applied for aid; of those 97% were deemed to have need. 99% of freshmen with need received aid; of those 5% had need fully met. **Average percent of need met:** 60% (excluding resources awarded to replace EFC). **Average financial aid package:** $25,200 (excluding resources awarded to replace EFC). 8% of all full-time freshmen had no need and received non-need-based gift aid.

UNDERGRADUATE FINANCIAL AID (Fall 2012, est.) 1,556 applied for aid; of those 97% were deemed to have need. 99% of undergraduates with need received aid; of those 4% had need fully met. **Average percent of need met:** 52% (excluding resources awarded to replace EFC). **Average financial aid package:** $24,192 (excluding resources awarded to replace EFC). 13% of all full-time undergraduates had no need and received non-need-based gift aid.

GIFT AID (NEED-BASED) Total amount: $12,703,364 (45% federal, 9% state, 46% institutional). **Receiving aid:** Freshmen: 75% (443); all full-time undergraduates: 71% (1,315). **Average award:** Freshmen: $7908; Undergraduates: $8073. **Scholarships, grants, and awards:** Federal Pell, FSEOG, state, private, college/university gift aid from institutional funds.

GIFT AID (NON-NEED-BASED) Total amount: $16,768,623 (98% institutional, 2% external sources). **Receiving aid:** Freshmen: 84% (495). Undergraduates: 72% (1,330). **Average award:** Freshmen: $11,026. Undergraduates: $9821. **Scholarships, grants, and awards by category:** Academic interests/achievement: general academic interests/achievements. Creative arts/performance: applied art and design, music. Special characteristics: children of faculty/staff, international students, local/state students, previous college experience. **Tuition waivers:** Full or partial for employees or children of employees, senior citizens. **ROTC:** Army.

LOANS Student loans: $17,194,309 (48% need-based, 52% non-need-based). 86% of past graduating class borrowed through all loan programs. **Average indebtedness per student:** $37,136. **Average need-based loan:** Freshmen: $3819. Undergraduates: $3945. **Parent loans:** $4,602,264 (100% non-need-based). **Programs:** Federal Direct (Subsidized and Unsubsidized Stafford, PLUS), Perkins.

WORK-STUDY Federal work-study: Total amount: $382,555; jobs available. **State or other work-study/employment:** Part-time jobs available.

ATHLETIC AWARDS Total amount: $3,646,635 (100% non-need-based).

APPLYING FOR FINANCIAL AID Required financial aid form: FAFSA. **Financial aid deadline (priority):** 3/1. **Notification date:** Continuous beginning 3/1. Students must reply by 5/15 or within 4 weeks of notification.

CONTACT Ms. Christine Falzerano, Director of Financial Aid, University of Bridgeport, 126 Park Avenue, Bridgeport, CT 06604, 203-576-4568 or toll-free 800-EXCEL-UB. Fax: 203-576-4570. E-mail: finaid@bridgeport.edu. Website: http://www.bridgeport.edu/.

UNIVERSITY OF CALIFORNIA, BERKELEY
Berkeley, CA

Tuition & fees (CA res): $12,874	Average undergraduate aid package: $20,242

ABOUT THE INSTITUTION State-supported, coed. **Awards:** bachelor's, master's, and doctoral degrees. 91 undergraduate majors. **Total enrollment:** 35,899. Undergraduates: 25,774. Federal methodology is used as a basis for awarding need-based institutional aid.

UNDERGRADUATE EXPENSES for 2013–2014 Application fee: $70. **Tuition, state resident:** full-time $11,220. **Tuition, nonresident:** full-time $34,098. **Required fees:** full-time $1654. **College room and board:** $15,000. Room and board charges vary according to board plan and housing facility.

FRESHMAN FINANCIAL AID (Fall 2011) 3,834 applied for aid; of those 70% were deemed to have need. 100% of freshmen with need received aid; of those 44% had need fully met. **Average percent of need met:** 79% (excluding resources awarded to replace EFC). **Average financial aid package:** $21,767 (excluding resources awarded to replace EFC). 3% of all full-time freshmen had no need and received non-need-based gift aid.

UNDERGRADUATE FINANCIAL AID (Fall 2011) 17,116 applied for aid; of those 83% were deemed to have need. 100% of undergraduates with need received aid; of those 37% had need fully met. **Average percent of need met:** 81%

(excluding resources awarded to replace EFC). **Average financial aid package:** $20,242 (excluding resources awarded to replace EFC). 1% of all full-time undergraduates had no need and received non-need-based gift aid.

GIFT AID (NEED-BASED) Total amount: $246,834,252 (17% federal, 30% state, 51% institutional, 2% external sources). **Receiving aid:** Freshmen: 61% (2,525); all full-time undergraduates: 53% (13,150). **Average award:** Freshmen: $18,384; Undergraduates: $16,629. **Scholarships, grants, and awards:** Federal Pell, FSEOG, state, private, college/university gift aid from institutional funds.

GIFT AID (NON-NEED-BASED) Total amount: $18,570,582 (1% state, 77% institutional, 22% external sources). **Receiving aid:** Freshmen: 14% (593). Undergraduates: 7% (1,826). **Average award:** Freshmen: $2756. Undergraduates: $2476. **Scholarships, grants, and awards by category:** Academic interests/achievement: general academic interests/achievements. **ROTC:** Army, Naval, Air Force.

LOANS Student loans: $59,670,758 (78% need-based, 22% non-need-based). 40% of past graduating class borrowed through all loan programs. **Average indebtedness per student:** $17,964. **Average need-based loan:** Freshmen: $4181. Undergraduates: $4644. **Parent loans:** $24,922,478 (24% need-based, 76% non-need-based). **Programs:** Federal Direct (Subsidized and Unsubsidized Stafford, PLUS), Perkins.

WORK-STUDY Federal work-study: Total amount: $4,298,732; jobs available. **State or other work-study/employment:** Total amount: $3,468,053 (100% need-based). Part-time jobs available.

ATHLETIC AWARDS Total amount: $12,621,919 (30% need-based, 70% non-need-based).

APPLYING FOR FINANCIAL AID Required financial aid forms: FAFSA, Cal Grant forms, GPA verification form (CA residents only). **Financial aid deadline:** 3/2. **Notification date:** 3/31. Students must reply by 5/1.

CONTACT Kathy Bradley, Administrative Specialist, University of California, Berkeley, 225 Sproul Hall, Berkeley, CA 94720-1960, 510-642-0649. Fax: 510-643-5526. E-mail: kbradley@berkeley.edu. Website: http://www.berkeley.edu/.

UNIVERSITY OF CALIFORNIA, DAVIS
Davis, CA

Tuition & fees (CA res): $15,727	Average undergraduate aid package: $19,658

ABOUT THE INSTITUTION State-supported, coed. **Awards:** certificates, bachelor's, master's, and doctoral degrees. 83 undergraduate majors. **Total enrollment:** 32,354. Undergraduates: 25,759. Freshmen: 5,208. Both federal and institutional methodology are used as a basis for awarding need-based institutional aid.

UNDERGRADUATE EXPENSES for 2013–2014 Application fee: $70. **Tuition, state resident:** full-time $15,727. **Tuition, nonresident:** full-time $38,605. Room and board charges vary according to board plan.

FRESHMAN FINANCIAL AID (Fall 2012, est.) 4,368 applied for aid; of those 77% were deemed to have need. 97% of freshmen with need received aid; of those 14% had need fully met. **Average percent of need met:** 80% (excluding resources awarded to replace EFC). **Average financial aid package:** $21,420 (excluding resources awarded to replace EFC). 5% of all full-time freshmen had no need and received non-need-based gift aid.

UNDERGRADUATE FINANCIAL AID (Fall 2012, est.) 18,969 applied for aid; of those 87% were deemed to have need. 98% of undergraduates with need received aid; of those 15% had need fully met. **Average percent of need met:** 80% (excluding resources awarded to replace EFC). **Average financial aid package:** $19,658 (excluding resources awarded to replace EFC). 3% of all full-time undergraduates had no need and received non-need-based gift aid.

GIFT AID (NEED-BASED) Total amount: $260,600,702 (21% federal, 37% state, 41% institutional, 1% external sources). **Receiving aid:** Freshmen: 61% (3,174); all full-time undergraduates: 63% (15,771). **Average award:** Freshmen: $18,042; Undergraduates: $16,313. **Scholarships, grants, and awards:** Federal Pell, FSEOG, state, private, college/university gift aid from institutional funds.

GIFT AID (NON-NEED-BASED) Total amount: $10,632,048 (13% federal, 50% institutional, 37% external sources). **Receiving aid:** Freshmen: 25. Undergraduates: 101. **Average award:** Freshmen: $4540. Undergraduates: $5675. **Scholarships, grants, and awards by category:** Academic interests/achievement: agriculture, area/ethnic studies, biological sciences, business, communication, computer science, engineering/technologies, English, foreign languages, general academic interests/achievements, health fields, home economics, humanities, international studies, mathematics, premedicine, religion/biblical studies, social sciences. **ROTC:** Army, Naval cooperative, Air Force cooperative.

LOANS *Student loans:* $66,147,829 (86% need-based, 14% non-need-based). 55% of past graduating class borrowed through all loan programs. *Average indebtedness per student:* $19,285. *Average need-based loan:* Freshmen: $5672. Undergraduates: $5625. *Parent loans:* $18,826,846 (18% need-based, 82% non-need-based). *Programs:* Federal Direct (Subsidized and Unsubsidized Stafford, PLUS), Perkins, college/university.

WORK-STUDY *Federal work-study:* Total amount: $1,888,404; jobs available. *State or other work-study/employment:* Total amount: $312,254 (100% need-based). Part-time jobs available.

ATHLETIC AWARDS Total amount: $4,207,117 (7% need-based, 93% non-need-based).

APPLYING FOR FINANCIAL AID *Required financial aid forms:* FAFSA, state aid form. *Financial aid deadline (priority):* 3/2. *Notification date:* Continuous beginning 3/18.

CONTACT Katy Maloney, Director of Financial Aid, University of California, Davis, One Shields Avenue, 2128 Dutton Hall, Davis, CA 95616, 530-752-2396. *Fax:* 530-752-7339. *E-mail:* kamaloney@ucdavis.edu. *Website:* http://www.ucdavis.edu/.

UNIVERSITY OF CALIFORNIA, IRVINE
Irvine, CA

Tuition & fees (CA res): $14,226	Average undergraduate aid package: $20,510

ABOUT THE INSTITUTION State-supported, coed. *Awards:* certificates, bachelor's, master's, and doctoral degrees. 80 undergraduate majors. *Total enrollment:* 27,479. Undergraduates: 22,216. Freshmen: 5,077. Federal methodology is used as a basis for awarding need-based institutional aid.

UNDERGRADUATE EXPENSES for 2013–2014 *Application fee:* $70. *Tuition, state resident:* full-time $11,220. *Tuition, nonresident:* full-time $34,098. *Required fees:* full-time $3006. *College room and board:* $11,735. Room and board charges vary according to board plan and housing facility.

FRESHMAN FINANCIAL AID (Fall 2012, est.) 4,210 applied for aid; of those 85% were deemed to have need. 97% of freshmen with need received aid; of those 39% had need fully met. *Average percent of need met:* 88% (excluding resources awarded to replace EFC). *Average financial aid package:* $22,665 (excluding resources awarded to replace EFC). 5% of all full-time freshmen had no need and received non-need-based gift aid.

UNDERGRADUATE FINANCIAL AID (Fall 2012, est.) 16,988 applied for aid; of those 88% were deemed to have need. 96% of undergraduates with need received aid; of those 31% had need fully met. *Average percent of need met:* 84% (excluding resources awarded to replace EFC). *Average financial aid package:* $20,510 (excluding resources awarded to replace EFC). 3% of all full-time undergraduates had no need and received non-need-based gift aid.

GIFT AID (NEED-BASED) *Total amount:* $229,942,598 (21% federal, 43% state, 35% institutional, 1% external sources). *Receiving aid:* Freshmen: 66% (3,357); all full-time undergraduates: 62% (13,555). *Average award:* Freshmen: $18,260; Undergraduates: $16,918. *Scholarships, grants, and awards:* Federal Pell, FSEOG, state, private, college/university gift aid from institutional funds.

GIFT AID (NON-NEED-BASED) *Total amount:* $8,029,028 (12% federal, 75% institutional, 13% external sources). *Receiving aid:* Freshmen: 1% (33). Undergraduates: 106. *Average award:* Freshmen: $9167. Undergraduates: $10,007. *Scholarships, grants, and awards by category:* Academic interests/achievement: 411 awards ($977,993 total): area/ethnic studies, biological sciences, business, communication, computer science, education, engineering/technologies, English, foreign languages, general academic interests/achievements, health fields, humanities, international studies, mathematics, physical sciences, premedicine, social sciences. *Creative arts/performance:* 49 awards ($152,611 total): art/fine arts, cinema/film/broadcasting, dance, general creative arts/performance, music, performing arts, theater/drama. *Special characteristics:* 173 awards ($1,332,500 total): international students, out-of-state students. *Tuition waivers:* Full or partial for employees or children of employees. **ROTC:** Army, Air Force cooperative.

LOANS *Student loans:* $62,619,533 (82% need-based, 18% non-need-based). 50% of past graduating class borrowed through all loan programs. *Average indebtedness*

per student: $19,828. *Average need-based loan:* Freshmen: $6076. Undergraduates: $6420. *Parent loans:* $34,807,107 (21% need-based, 79% non-need-based). *Programs:* Federal Direct (Subsidized and Unsubsidized Stafford, PLUS), Perkins, college/university, private loans.

WORK-STUDY *Federal work-study:* Total amount: $2,857,179; 2,605 jobs averaging $1425. *State or other work-study/employment:* Total amount: $3,362,573 (100% need-based). 2,305 part-time jobs averaging $1781.

ATHLETIC AWARDS Total amount: $2,923,507 (32% need-based, 68% non-need-based).

APPLYING FOR FINANCIAL AID *Required financial aid forms:* FAFSA, state aid form. *Financial aid deadline:* 6/28 (priority: 3/2). *Notification date:* Continuous beginning 4/1.

CONTACT Ms. Penny Harrell, Associate Director of Student Services, University of California, Irvine, 102 Aldrich Hall, Irvine, CA 92697-2825, 949-824-8262. *Fax:* 949-824-4876. *E-mail:* finaid@uci.edu. *Website:* http://www.uci.edu/.

UNIVERSITY OF CALIFORNIA, LOS ANGELES
Los Angeles, CA

Tuition & fees (area res): $12,692	Average undergraduate aid package: $20,905

ABOUT THE INSTITUTION State-supported, coed. *Awards:* bachelor's, master's, and doctoral degrees. 98 undergraduate majors. *Total enrollment:* 41,341. Undergraduates: 27,948. Freshmen: 5,621. Both federal and institutional methodology are used as a basis for awarding need-based institutional aid.

UNDERGRADUATE EXPENSES for 2013–2014 *Application fee:* $70. *Tuition, area resident:* full-time $11,220. *Tuition, state resident:* full-time $11,220. *Tuition, nonresident:* full-time $34,098. *Required fees:* full-time $1472. *College room and board:* $12,675. Room and board charges vary according to board plan and housing facility.

FRESHMAN FINANCIAL AID (Fall 2012, est.) 3,247 applied for aid; of those 89% were deemed to have need. 100% of freshmen with need received aid; of those 25% had need fully met. *Average percent of need met:* 83% (excluding resources awarded to replace EFC). *Average financial aid package:* $22,560 (excluding resources awarded to replace EFC). 3% of all full-time freshmen had no need and received non-need-based gift aid.

UNDERGRADUATE FINANCIAL AID (Fall 2012, est.) 16,587 applied for aid; of those 92% were deemed to have need. 100% of undergraduates with need received aid; of those 26% had need fully met. *Average percent of need met:* 83% (excluding resources awarded to replace EFC). *Average financial aid package:* $20,905 (excluding resources awarded to replace EFC). 3% of all full-time undergraduates had no need and received non-need-based gift aid.

GIFT AID (NEED-BASED) *Total amount:* $252,339,246 (18% federal, 34% state, 46% institutional, 2% external sources). *Receiving aid:* Freshmen: 49% (2,761); all full-time undergraduates: 53% (14,561). *Average award:* Freshmen: $18,793; Undergraduates: $17,369. *Scholarships, grants, and awards:* Federal Pell, FSEOG, state, private, college/university gift aid from institutional funds, United Negro College Fund, Federal Nursing.

GIFT AID (NON-NEED-BASED) *Total amount:* $5,633,525 (5% federal, 76% institutional, 19% external sources). *Receiving aid:* Freshmen: 1% (37). Undergraduates: 124. *Average award:* Freshmen: $6027. Undergraduates: $5063. *Scholarships, grants, and awards by category:* Academic interests/achievement: general academic interests/achievements. *Special achievements/activities:* general special achievements/activities. **ROTC:** Army, Naval, Air Force.

LOANS *Student loans:* $72,134,612 (82% need-based, 18% non-need-based). 46% of past graduating class borrowed through all loan programs. *Average indebtedness per student:* $20,409. *Average need-based loan:* Freshmen: $6983. Undergraduates: $6818. *Parent loans:* $29,777,958 (22% need-based, 78% non-need-based). *Programs:* Federal Direct (Subsidized and Unsubsidized Stafford, PLUS), Perkins, Federal Nursing, state, college/university.

WORK-STUDY *Federal work-study:* Total amount: $4,402,137; 2,390 jobs averaging $1842. *State or other work-study/employment:* Total amount: $830,549 (100% need-based). 725 part-time jobs averaging $1146.

ATHLETIC AWARDS Total amount: $10,663,140 (26% need-based, 74% non-need-based).

APPLYING FOR FINANCIAL AID *Required financial aid form:* FAFSA. *Financial aid deadline (priority):* 3/2. *Notification date:* Continuous beginning 3/15.

CONTACT Ms. Yolanda Tan, Administrative Assistant for Financial Aid, University of California, Los Angeles, A-129 Murphy Hall, Los Angeles, CA 90095-1435, 310-206-0404. *E-mail:* finaid@saonet.ucla.edu.
Website: http://www.ucla.edu/.

UNIVERSITY OF CALIFORNIA, MERCED
Merced, CA

Tuition & fees (CA res): $13,070	Average undergraduate aid package: $21,320

ABOUT THE INSTITUTION State-supported, coed. *Awards:* bachelor's, master's, and doctoral degrees. 20 undergraduate majors. *Total enrollment:* 5,760. Undergraduates: 5,431. Freshmen: 1,495. Federal methodology is used as a basis for awarding need-based institutional aid.

UNDERGRADUATE EXPENSES for 2013–2014 *Application fee:* $70. *Tuition, state resident:* full-time $13,070. *Tuition, nonresident:* full-time $35,948. *College room and board:* $14,272.

FRESHMAN FINANCIAL AID (Fall 2012, est.) 1,412 applied for aid; of those 93% were deemed to have need. 99% of freshmen with need received aid; of those 38% had need fully met. *Average percent of need met:* 89% (excluding resources awarded to replace EFC). *Average financial aid package:* $24,674 (excluding resources awarded to replace EFC). 1% of all full-time freshmen had no need and received non-need-based gift aid.

UNDERGRADUATE FINANCIAL AID (Fall 2012, est.) 4,886 applied for aid; of those 93% were deemed to have need. 99% of undergraduates with need received aid; of those 37% had need fully met. *Average percent of need met:* 87% (excluding resources awarded to replace EFC). *Average financial aid package:* $21,320 (excluding resources awarded to replace EFC). 1% of all full-time undergraduates had no need and received non-need-based gift aid.

GIFT AID (NEED-BASED) *Total amount:* $74,824,918 (21% federal, 43% state, 35% institutional, 1% external sources). *Receiving aid:* Freshmen: 85% (1,261); all full-time undergraduates: 80% (4,290). *Average award:* Freshmen: $20,321; Undergraduates: $17,369. *Scholarships, grants, and awards:* Federal Pell, FSEOG, state, private, college/university gift aid from institutional funds.

GIFT AID (NON-NEED-BASED) *Total amount:* $342,893 (14% federal, 57% institutional, 29% external sources). *Receiving aid:* Freshmen: 3. Undergraduates: 8. *Average award:* Freshmen: $8293. Undergraduates: $7201. *Scholarships, grants, and awards by category: Academic interests/achievement:* general academic interests/achievements.

LOANS *Student loans:* $18,033,275 (81% need-based, 19% non-need-based). 64% of past graduating class borrowed through all loan programs. *Average indebtedness per student:* $18,786. *Average need-based loan:* Freshmen: $4230. Undergraduates: $5203. *Parent loans:* $6,570,472 (8% need-based, 92% non-need-based). *Programs:* Federal Direct (Subsidized and Unsubsidized Stafford, PLUS), alternative loans.

WORK-STUDY *Federal work-study:* Total amount: $5,732,410; jobs available.

ATHLETIC AWARDS Total amount: $17,400 (100% need-based).

APPLYING FOR FINANCIAL AID *Required financial aid form:* FAFSA. *Financial aid deadline (priority):* 3/2. *Notification date:* Continuous beginning 3/2.

CONTACT Ms. Diana M. Ralls, Director of Financial Aid, University of California, Merced, Kolligian Library Room 122, 5200 North Lake Road, Merced, CA 95343, 209-228-7178. *Fax:* 209-228-7861. *E-mail:* finaid@ucmerced.edu.
Website: http://www.ucmerced.edu/.

UNIVERSITY OF CALIFORNIA, RIVERSIDE
Riverside, CA

Tuition & fees (CA res): $12,960	Average undergraduate aid package: $20,811

ABOUT THE INSTITUTION State-supported, coed. *Awards:* certificates, bachelor's, master's, and doctoral degrees. 56 undergraduate majors. *Total enrollment:* 21,005. Undergraduates: 18,539. Freshmen: 4,034. Federal methodology is used as a basis for awarding need-based institutional aid.

UNDERGRADUATE EXPENSES for 2013–2014 *Application fee:* $70. *Tuition, state resident:* full-time $11,220. *Tuition, nonresident:* full-time $34,098. *Required fees:* full-time $1740. Full-time tuition and fees vary according to course load. Part-time tuition and fees vary according to course load. *College room and board:* $13,200. Room and board charges vary according to board plan and housing facility.

FRESHMAN FINANCIAL AID (Fall 2012, est.) 3,825 applied for aid; of those 83% were deemed to have need. 98% of freshmen with need received aid; of those 32% had need fully met. *Average percent of need met:* 91% (excluding resources awarded to replace EFC). *Average financial aid package:* $23,585 (excluding resources awarded to replace EFC). 4% of all full-time freshmen had no need and received non-need-based gift aid.

UNDERGRADUATE FINANCIAL AID (Fall 2012, est.) 15,526 applied for aid; of those 92% were deemed to have need. 98% of undergraduates with need received aid; of those 27% had need fully met. *Average percent of need met:* 86% (excluding resources awarded to replace EFC). *Average financial aid package:* $20,811 (excluding resources awarded to replace EFC). 2% of all full-time undergraduates had no need and received non-need-based gift aid.

GIFT AID (NEED-BASED) *Total amount:* $228,775,876 (20% federal, 42% state, 37% institutional, 1% external sources). *Receiving aid:* Freshmen: 76% (3,042); all full-time undergraduates: 74% (13,362). *Average award:* Freshmen: $19,826; Undergraduates: $17,035. *Scholarships, grants, and awards:* Federal Pell, FSEOG, state, private, college/university gift aid from institutional funds.

GIFT AID (NON-NEED-BASED) *Total amount:* $5,043,370 (14% federal, 73% institutional, 13% external sources). *Receiving aid:* Freshmen: 1% (34). Undergraduates: 1% (96). *Average award:* Freshmen: $4319. Undergraduates: $7144. *Scholarships, grants, and awards by category: Academic interests/achievement:* agriculture, area/ethnic studies, biological sciences, business, education, engineering/technologies, English, general academic interests/achievements, humanities, mathematics, physical sciences, premedicine, social sciences. *Creative arts/performance:* art/fine arts, creative writing, dance, music, theater/drama. *Special characteristics:* religious affiliation, veterans, veterans' children. *ROTC:* Army cooperative, Air Force cooperative.

LOANS *Student loans:* $64,512,710 (85% need-based, 15% non-need-based). 65% of past graduating class borrowed through all loan programs. *Average indebtedness per student:* $20,613. *Average need-based loan:* Freshmen: $4983. Undergraduates: $5872. *Parent loans:* $17,809,541 (21% need-based, 79% non-need-based). *Programs:* Federal Direct (Subsidized and Unsubsidized Stafford, PLUS), Perkins, college/university.

WORK-STUDY *Federal work-study:* Total amount: $4,929,827; 3,035 jobs averaging $1607. *State or other work-study/employment:* Part-time jobs available.

ATHLETIC AWARDS Total amount: $3,022,446 (45% need-based, 55% non-need-based).

APPLYING FOR FINANCIAL AID *Required financial aid forms:* FAFSA, state aid form. *Financial aid deadline:* 3/2. *Notification date:* Continuous beginning 3/1. Students must reply by 5/15 or within 3 weeks of notification.

CONTACT Mr. Jose A. Aguilar, Director of Financial Aid, University of California, Riverside, 2106 Student Services Building, Riverside, CA 92521-0209, 951-827-7249. *Fax:* 951-827-5619. *E-mail:* finaid@ucr.edu.
Website: http://www.ucr.edu/.

UNIVERSITY OF CALIFORNIA, SAN DIEGO
La Jolla, CA

Tuition & fees (CA res): $13,234	Average undergraduate aid package: $22,229

ABOUT THE INSTITUTION State-supported, coed. 68 undergraduate majors. Both federal and institutional methodology are used as a basis for awarding need-based institutional aid.

UNDERGRADUATE EXPENSES for 2013–2014 *Tuition, state resident:* full-time $12,192. *Tuition, nonresident:* full-time $35,070. *Required fees:* full-time $1042. *College room and board:* $11,924. Room and board charges vary according to board plan and housing facility.

FRESHMAN FINANCIAL AID (Fall 2012, est.) 3,400 applied for aid; of those 74% were deemed to have need. 96% of freshmen with need received aid; of those 41% had need fully met. *Average percent of need met:* 87% (excluding resources awarded to replace EFC). *Average financial aid package:* $22,041 (excluding resources awarded to replace EFC). 2% of all full-time freshmen had no need and received non-need-based gift aid.

UNDERGRADUATE FINANCIAL AID (Fall 2012, est.) 16,105 applied for aid; of those 88% were deemed to have need. 97% of undergraduates with need received aid; of those 36% had need fully met. *Average percent of need met:* 87% (excluding resources awarded to replace EFC). *Average financial aid package:* $22,229 (excluding resources awarded to replace EFC). 2% of all full-time undergraduates had no need and received non-need-based gift aid.

GIFT AID (NEED-BASED) *Total amount:* $234,223,010 (20% federal, 37% state, 41% institutional, 2% external sources). *Receiving aid:* Freshmen: 51% (2,310); all full-time undergraduates: 61% (13,375). *Average award:* Freshmen: $16,799; Undergraduates: $17,257. *Scholarships, grants, and awards:* Federal Pell, FSEOG, state, private, college/university gift aid from institutional funds, TEACH Grants.

GIFT AID (NON-NEED-BASED) *Total amount:* $7,075,363 (15% federal, 1% state, 71% institutional, 13% external sources). *Receiving aid:* Freshmen: 1% (26). Undergraduates: 71. *Average award:* Freshmen: $9961. Undergraduates: $8927. *Scholarships, grants, and awards by category:* Academic interests/achievement: biological sciences, business, communication, computer science, engineering/technologies, general academic interests/achievements, mathematics, physical sciences, premedicine, social sciences. *Creative arts/performance:* applied art and design, cinema/film/broadcasting, dance, journalism/publications, performing arts. *Special achievements/activities:* community service, leadership. *Special characteristics:* ethnic background, first-generation college students, handicapped students, members of minority groups, veterans' children.

LOANS *Student loans:* $68,344,002 (84% need-based, 16% non-need-based). 56% of past graduating class borrowed through all loan programs. *Average indebtedness per student:* $20,474. *Average need-based loan:* Freshmen: $5696. Undergraduates: $5997. *Parent loans:* $13,362,402 (21% need-based, 79% non-need-based). *Programs:* Federal Direct (Subsidized and Unsubsidized Stafford, PLUS), Perkins, college/university, alternative loans.

WORK-STUDY *Federal work-study:* Total amount: $16,266,293; jobs available. *State or other work-study/employment:* Total amount: $777,447 (100% need-based). Part-time jobs available.

ATHLETIC AWARDS Total amount: $250,000 (44% need-based, 56% non-need-based).

APPLYING FOR FINANCIAL AID *Required financial aid forms:* FAFSA, state aid form. *Financial aid deadline (priority):* 3/2. *Notification date:* Continuous beginning 3/15.

CONTACT Ann Klein, Director of Financial Aid, University of California, San Diego, 9500 Gilman Drive, Mail Code 0013, La Jolla, CA 92093-0013, 858-534-4480. *Fax:* 858-534-5459. *E-mail:* aklein@ucsd.edu. *Website:* http://www.ucsd.edu/.

UNIVERSITY OF CALIFORNIA, SANTA BARBARA
Santa Barbara, CA

Tuition & fees (CA res): $15,036	Average undergraduate aid package: $21,738

ABOUT THE INSTITUTION State-supported, coed. *Awards:* certificates, bachelor's, master's, and doctoral degrees. 75 undergraduate majors. *Total enrollment:* 21,927. Undergraduates: 18,977. Freshmen: 4,736. Both federal and institutional methodology are used as a basis for awarding need-based institutional aid.

UNDERGRADUATE EXPENSES for 2013–2014 *Application fee:* $70. *Tuition, state resident:* full-time $12,192. *Tuition, nonresident:* full-time $34,213. *Required fees:* full-time $2844. *College room and board:* $13,275. Room and board charges vary according to board plan and housing facility.

FRESHMAN FINANCIAL AID (Fall 2012, est.) 3,892 applied for aid; of those 80% were deemed to have need. 94% of freshmen with need received aid; of those 23% had need fully met. *Average percent of need met:* 85% (excluding resources awarded to replace EFC). *Average financial aid package:* $23,996 (excluding resources awarded to replace EFC). 1% of all full-time freshmen had no need and received non-need-based gift aid.

UNDERGRADUATE FINANCIAL AID (Fall 2012, est.) 13,570 applied for aid; of those 85% were deemed to have need. 95% of undergraduates with need received aid; of those 23% had need fully met. *Average percent of need met:* 85% (excluding resources awarded to replace EFC). *Average financial aid package:* $21,738 (excluding resources awarded to replace EFC). 2% of all full-time undergraduates had no need and received non-need-based gift aid.

GIFT AID (NEED-BASED) *Total amount:* $178,478,995 (21% federal, 44% state, 34% institutional, 1% external sources). *Receiving aid:* Freshmen: 58% (2,748); all full-time undergraduates: 55% (10,201). *Average award:* Freshmen: $19,295; Undergraduates: $17,484. *Scholarships, grants, and awards:* Federal Pell, FSEOG, state, private, college/university gift aid from institutional funds, endowed and restricted scholarships and grants.

GIFT AID (NON-NEED-BASED) *Total amount:* $5,682,408 (23% federal, 1% state, 65% institutional, 11% external sources). *Receiving aid:* Freshmen: 1% (25). Undergraduates: 85. *Average award:* Freshmen: $10,886. Undergraduates: $10,564. *Scholarships, grants, and awards by category:* Academic interests/achievement: general academic interests/achievements. *ROTC:* Army, Air Force cooperative.

LOANS *Student loans:* $49,818,380 (85% need-based, 15% non-need-based). 53% of past graduating class borrowed through all loan programs. *Average indebtedness per student:* $19,325. *Average need-based loan:* Freshmen: $6438. Undergraduates: $6325. *Parent loans:* $25,590,281 (18% need-based, 82% non-need-based). *Programs:* Federal Direct (Subsidized and Unsubsidized Stafford, PLUS), Perkins.

WORK-STUDY *Federal work-study:* Total amount: $13,112,708; jobs available.

ATHLETIC AWARDS Total amount: $3,512,799 (31% need-based, 69% non-need-based).

APPLYING FOR FINANCIAL AID *Required financial aid form:* FAFSA. *Financial aid deadline (priority):* 3/2. *Notification date:* Continuous beginning 3/15. Students must reply within 2 weeks of notification.

CONTACT Mike Miller, Office of Financial Aid, University of California, Santa Barbara, 2103 SAASB, Santa Barbara, CA 93106-3180, 805-893-2432. *Fax:* 805-893-8793. *Website:* http://www.ucsb.edu/.

UNIVERSITY OF CALIFORNIA, SANTA CRUZ
Santa Cruz, CA

Tuition & fees (CA res): $13,417	Average undergraduate aid package: $22,861

ABOUT THE INSTITUTION State-supported, coed. *Awards:* certificates, bachelor's, master's, and doctoral degrees. 55 undergraduate majors. *Total enrollment:* 17,404. Undergraduates: 15,978. Freshmen: 3,828. Both federal and institutional methodology are used as a basis for awarding need-based institutional aid.

UNDERGRADUATE EXPENSES for 2013–2014 *Application fee:* $70. *Tuition, state resident:* full-time $12,192. *Tuition, nonresident:* full-time $35,070. *Required fees:* full-time $1225. Part-time tuition and fees vary according to course load. *College room and board:* $14,856. Room and board charges vary according to board plan and housing facility.

FRESHMAN FINANCIAL AID (Fall 2012, est.) 3,482 applied for aid; of those 84% were deemed to have need. 97% of freshmen with need received aid; of those 21% had need fully met. *Average percent of need met:* 88% (excluding resources awarded to replace EFC). *Average financial aid package:* $24,719 (excluding resources awarded to replace EFC). 2% of all full-time freshmen had no need and received non-need-based gift aid.

UNDERGRADUATE FINANCIAL AID (Fall 2012, est.) 12,526 applied for aid; of those 86% were deemed to have need. 97% of undergraduates with need received aid; of those 32% had need fully met. *Average percent of need met:* 88% (excluding resources awarded to replace EFC). *Average financial aid package:* $22,861 (excluding resources awarded to replace EFC). 2% of all full-time undergraduates had no need and received non-need-based gift aid.

GIFT AID (NEED-BASED) *Total amount:* $180,378,728 (18% federal, 41% state, 40% institutional, 1% external sources). *Receiving aid:* Freshmen: 70% (2,686); all full-time undergraduates: 64% (9,895). *Average award:* Freshmen: $19,897; Undergraduates: $18,039. *Scholarships, grants, and awards:* Federal Pell, FSEOG, state, private, college/university gift aid from institutional funds.

GIFT AID (NON-NEED-BASED) *Total amount:* $4,492,178 (3% federal, 85% institutional, 12% external sources). *Receiving aid:* Freshmen: 15. Undergraduates: 50. *Average award:* Freshmen: $20,152. Undergraduates: $12,885. *Scholarships, grants, and awards by category: Academic interests/achievement:* 203 awards ($770,092 total): computer science, general academic interests/achievements, humanities, mathematics, physical sciences, social sciences. *Creative arts/performance:* 127 awards ($80,857 total): art/fine arts, cinema/film/broadcasting, creative writing, music, theater/drama. *Special achievements/activities:* 9 awards ($4919 total): leadership. *Special characteristics:* 105 awards ($378,523 total): first-generation college students, international students, out-of-state students, veterans. *ROTC:* Army cooperative, Naval cooperative, Air Force cooperative.

LOANS *Student loans:* $57,712,713 (81% need-based, 19% non-need-based). 56% of past graduating class borrowed through all loan programs. *Average indebtedness per student:* $20,358. *Average need-based loan:* Freshmen: $5883. Undergraduates: $6067. *Parent loans:* $23,661,929 (10% need-based, 90% non-need-based). *Programs:* Federal Direct (Subsidized and Unsubsidized Stafford, PLUS), Perkins.

WORK-STUDY *Federal work-study:* Total amount: $12,144,861; 7,113 jobs averaging $1918. *State or other work-study/employment:* Part-time jobs available.

APPLYING FOR FINANCIAL AID *Required financial aid forms:* FAFSA, state aid form. *Financial aid deadline:* 6/3 (priority: 4/14). *Notification date:* Continuous beginning 4/1. Students must reply within 4 weeks of notification.

CONTACT Michelle Whittingham, Director of Financial Aid, University of California, Santa Cruz, 201 Hahn Student Services Building, Santa Cruz, CA 95064, 831-459-2963. *Fax:* 831-459-4631.
Website: http://www.ucsc.edu/.

UNIVERSITY OF CENTRAL ARKANSAS
Conway, AR

Tuition & fees (AR res): $7333	Average undergraduate aid package: N/A

ABOUT THE INSTITUTION State-supported, coed. *Awards:* certificates, bachelor's, master's, and doctoral degrees. 61 undergraduate majors. *Total enrollment:* 11,107. Undergraduates: 9,604. Freshmen: 2,157. Federal methodology is used as a basis for awarding need-based institutional aid.

UNDERGRADUATE EXPENSES for 2013–2014 *Application fee:* $25. *Tuition, state resident:* full-time $5498; part-time $183.25 per credit hour. *Tuition, nonresident:* full-time $10,995; part-time $366.50 per credit hour. *Required fees:* full-time $1835; $52.72 per credit hour or $126.50 per term. Full-time tuition and fees vary according to course load. Part-time tuition and fees vary according to course load. *College room and board:* $5270; *Room only:* $3030. Room and board charges vary according to board plan and housing facility.

GIFT AID (NEED-BASED) *Scholarships, grants, and awards:* Federal Pell, FSEOG, state, private, college/university gift aid from institutional funds, Federal Nursing.

GIFT AID (NON-NEED-BASED) *Scholarships, grants, and awards by category: Academic interests/achievement:* general academic interests/achievements. *Tuition waivers:* Full or partial for employees or children of employees, senior citizens. *ROTC:* Army.

LOANS *Programs:* Perkins, Federal Nursing, state, alternative loans.

APPLYING FOR FINANCIAL AID *Required financial aid form:* FAFSA. *Financial aid deadline:* 7/1 (priority: 4/15). *Notification date:* Continuous.

CONTACT Cheryl Lyons, Director of Student Aid, University of Central Arkansas, 201 Donaghey Avenue, Conway, AR 72035, 501-450-3140 or toll-free 800-243-8245. *Fax:* 501-450-5168. *E-mail:* clyons@uca.edu. *Website:* http://www.uca.edu/.

UNIVERSITY OF CENTRAL FLORIDA
Orlando, FL

Tuition & fees (FL res): $6247	Average undergraduate aid package: $7028

ABOUT THE INSTITUTION State-supported, coed. *Awards:* certificates, associate, bachelor's, master's, and doctoral degrees. 81 undergraduate majors. *Total enrollment:* 59,767. Undergraduates: 50,968. Freshmen: 6,082. Federal methodology is used as a basis for awarding need-based institutional aid.

UNDERGRADUATE EXPENSES for 2013–2014 *Application fee:* $30. *Tuition, state resident:* full-time $6247; part-time $208.23 per credit hour. *Tuition, nonresident:* full-time $22,345; part-time $744.84 per credit hour. Full-time tuition and fees vary according to course load. Part-time tuition and fees vary according to course load. *College room and board:* $9357; *Room only:* $5400. Room and board charges vary according to board plan and housing facility. *Payment plan:* Tuition prepayment.

FRESHMAN FINANCIAL AID (Fall 2011) 6,025 applied for aid; of those 81% were deemed to have need. 99% of freshmen with need received aid; of those 17% had need fully met. *Average percent of need met:* 58% (excluding resources awarded to replace EFC). *Average financial aid package:* $6816 (excluding resources awarded to replace EFC). 5% of all full-time freshmen had no need and received non-need-based gift aid.

UNDERGRADUATE FINANCIAL AID (Fall 2011) 33,456 applied for aid; of those 87% were deemed to have need. 97% of undergraduates with need received aid; of those 11% had need fully met. *Average percent of need met:* 56% (excluding resources awarded to replace EFC). *Average financial aid package:* $7028 (excluding resources awarded to replace EFC). 2% of all full-time undergraduates had no need and received non-need-based gift aid.

GIFT AID (NEED-BASED) *Total amount:* $102,926,269 (76% federal, 8% state, 16% institutional). *Receiving aid:* Freshmen: 39% (2,403); all full-time undergraduates: 44% (16,324). *Average award:* Freshmen: $4788; Undergraduates: $4846. *Scholarships, grants, and awards:* Federal Pell, FSEOG, state, private, college/university gift aid from institutional funds.

GIFT AID (NON-NEED-BASED) *Total amount:* $65,629,236 (1% federal, 75% state, 16% institutional, 8% external sources). *Receiving aid:* Freshmen: 75% (4,626). Undergraduates: 52% (19,174). *Average award:* Freshmen: $2945. Undergraduates: $2690. *Scholarships, grants, and awards by category: Academic interests/achievement:* general academic interests/achievements. *Creative arts/performance:* cinema/film/broadcasting, music, theater/drama. *Special achievements/activities:* general special achievements/activities, leadership. *Special characteristics:* first-generation college students. *Tuition waivers:* Full or partial for employees or children of employees, senior citizens. *ROTC:* Army, Air Force.

LOANS *Student loans:* $180,802,060 (51% need-based, 49% non-need-based). 46% of past graduating class borrowed through all loan programs. *Average indebtedness per student:* $20,086. *Average need-based loan:* Freshmen: $3419. Undergraduates: $4759. *Parent loans:* $6,879,540 (100% non-need-based). *Programs:* Federal Direct (Subsidized and Unsubsidized Stafford, PLUS), Perkins.

WORK-STUDY *Federal work-study:* Total amount: $1,212,158; 403 jobs averaging $3008. *State or other work-study/employment:* Part-time jobs available.

ATHLETIC AWARDS Total amount: $2,808,214 (100% non-need-based).

APPLYING FOR FINANCIAL AID *Required financial aid form:* FAFSA. *Financial aid deadline:* 6/15 (priority: 3/1). *Notification date:* Continuous beginning 3/15. Students must reply within 3 weeks of notification.

CONTACT Ms. Inez Ford, Associate Director of Student Financial Assistance, University of Central Florida, 4000 Central Florida Boulevard, Orlando, FL 32816-0113, 407-823-2827. *Fax:* 407-823-5241. *E-mail:* inez.ford@ucf.edu. *Website:* http://www.ucf.edu/.

UNIVERSITY OF CENTRAL MISSOURI
Warrensburg, MO

Tuition & fees: N/R	Average undergraduate aid package: $9082

ABOUT THE INSTITUTION State-supported, coed. *Awards:* certificates, associate, bachelor's, and master's degrees. 66 undergraduate majors. *Total enrollment:* 11,637. Undergraduates: 9,466. Freshmen: 1,689. Federal methodology is used as a basis for awarding need-based institutional aid.
FRESHMAN FINANCIAL AID (Fall 2011) 1,586 applied for aid; of those 66% were deemed to have need. 100% of freshmen with need received aid; of those 16% had need fully met. *Average percent of need met:* 65% (excluding resources awarded to replace EFC). *Average financial aid package:* $8149 (excluding resources awarded to replace EFC). 21% of all full-time freshmen had no need and received non-need-based gift aid.
UNDERGRADUATE FINANCIAL AID (Fall 2011) 5,830 applied for aid; of those 64% were deemed to have need. 100% of undergraduates with need received aid; of those 14% had need fully met. *Average percent of need met:* 69% (excluding resources awarded to replace EFC). *Average financial aid package:* $9082 (excluding resources awarded to replace EFC). 14% of all full-time undergraduates had no need and received non-need-based gift aid.
GIFT AID (NEED-BASED) *Total amount:* $23,088,150 (65% federal, 19% state, 16% external sources). *Receiving aid:* Freshmen: 40% (629); all full-time undergraduates: 39% (2,328). *Average award:* Freshmen: $4042; Undergraduates: $4287. *Scholarships, grants, and awards:* Federal Pell, FSEOG, state, private, college/university gift aid from institutional funds.
GIFT AID (NON-NEED-BASED) *Total amount:* $5,470,773 (11% federal, 5% state, 83% institutional, 1% external sources). *Receiving aid:* Freshmen: 65% (1,026). Undergraduates: 59% (3,522). *Average award:* Freshmen: $5213. Undergraduates: $8540. *ROTC:* Army, Air Force cooperative.
LOANS *Student loans:* $44,502,779 (45% need-based, 55% non-need-based). 69% of past graduating class borrowed through all loan programs. *Average indebtedness per student:* $23,766. *Average need-based loan:* Freshmen: $3565. Undergraduates: $4390. *Parent loans:* $9,572,752 (100% non-need-based). *Programs:* Federal Direct (Subsidized and Unsubsidized Stafford, PLUS), Perkins, private loans.
WORK-STUDY *Federal work-study:* Total amount: $362,537; 157 jobs averaging $1294. *State or other work-study/employment:* Total amount: $3,707,498 (37% need-based, 63% non-need-based). 1,282 part-time jobs averaging $1920.
ATHLETIC AWARDS Total amount: $2,097,606 (100% non-need-based).
APPLYING FOR FINANCIAL AID *Required financial aid forms:* FAFSA, institution's own form, CSS Financial Aid PROFILE, state aid form, noncustodial (divorced/separated) parent's statement, business/farm supplement. *Financial aid deadline (priority):* 4/1. *Notification date:* Continuous beginning 3/20. Students must reply within 3 weeks of notification.
CONTACT Ms. Angela Karlin, Director of Student Financial Assistance, University of Central Missouri, Ward Edwards Building 1100, Warrensburg, MO 64093, 660-543-4177 or toll-free 800-729-8266. *Fax:* 660-543-8080. *E-mail:* sfs@ucmo.edu. *Website:* http://www.ucmo.edu/.

UNIVERSITY OF CENTRAL OKLAHOMA
Edmond, OK

ABOUT THE INSTITUTION State-supported, coed. *Awards:* certificates, associate, bachelor's, and master's degrees. 88 undergraduate majors. *Total enrollment:* 17,211. Undergraduates: 15,379. Freshmen: 2,348.
GIFT AID (NEED-BASED) *Scholarships, grants, and awards:* Federal Pell, FSEOG, state, private, college/university gift aid from institutional funds.

GIFT AID (NON-NEED-BASED) *Scholarships, grants, and awards by category:* Academic interests/achievement: biological sciences, business, computer science, education, foreign languages, general academic interests/achievements, health fields, home economics, mathematics, military science, physical sciences, social sciences. *Creative arts/performance:* applied art and design, art/fine arts, journalism/publications, music, theater/drama. *Special achievements/activities:* general special achievements/activities, leadership. *Special characteristics:* ethnic background, members of minority groups.
LOANS *Programs:* Federal Direct (Subsidized and Unsubsidized Stafford, PLUS).
APPLYING FOR FINANCIAL AID *Required financial aid forms:* FAFSA, institution's own form.
CONTACT Ms. Becky Garrett, Assistant Director of Technical Services, University of Central Oklahoma, 100 North University Drive, Edmond, OK 73034-5209, 405-974-5325. *Fax:* 405-340-7658. *E-mail:* osfa@uco.edu. *Website:* http://www.uco.edu/.

UNIVERSITY OF CHARLESTON
Charleston, WV

Tuition & fees: $25,700	Average undergraduate aid package: $20,933

ABOUT THE INSTITUTION Independent, coed. *Awards:* associate, bachelor's, master's, and doctoral degrees. 33 undergraduate majors. *Total enrollment:* 1,427. Undergraduates: 1,026. Freshmen: 241. Both federal and institutional methodology are used as a basis for awarding need-based institutional aid.
UNDERGRADUATE EXPENSES for 2013–2014 *Application fee:* $25. *Comprehensive fee:* $34,700 includes full-time tuition ($25,500), mandatory fees ($200), and room and board ($9000). *College room only:* $4900. Full-time tuition and fees vary according to location and student level. Room and board charges vary according to board plan, housing facility, and location. *Part-time tuition:* $900 per credit hour. Part-time tuition and fees vary according to course load, location, and program.
FRESHMAN FINANCIAL AID (Fall 2012, est.) 237 applied for aid; of those 100% were deemed to have need. 100% of freshmen with need received aid; of those 8% had need fully met. *Average percent of need met:* 65% (excluding resources awarded to replace EFC). *Average financial aid package:* $17,822 (excluding resources awarded to replace EFC). 1% of all full-time freshmen had no need and received non-need-based gift aid.
UNDERGRADUATE FINANCIAL AID (Fall 2012, est.) 881 applied for aid; of those 100% were deemed to have need. 100% of undergraduates with need received aid; of those 12% had need fully met. *Average percent of need met:* 72% (excluding resources awarded to replace EFC). *Average financial aid package:* $20,933 (excluding resources awarded to replace EFC). 9% of all full-time undergraduates had no need and received non-need-based gift aid.
GIFT AID (NEED-BASED) *Total amount:* $8,516,169 (21% federal, 77% institutional, 2% external sources). *Receiving aid:* Freshmen: 84% (202); all full-time undergraduates: 87% (859). *Average award:* Freshmen: $6118; Undergraduates: $9469. *Scholarships, grants, and awards:* Federal Pell, FSEOG, state, private, college/university gift aid from institutional funds.
GIFT AID (NON-NEED-BASED) *Total amount:* $5,678,628 (26% state, 74% institutional). *Receiving aid:* Freshmen: 85% (203). Undergraduates: 86% (854). *Average award:* Undergraduates: $16,333. *Scholarships, grants, and awards by category:* Academic interests/achievement: general academic interests/achievements. *Creative arts/performance:* music. *Special achievements/activities:* community service, general special achievements/activities, leadership. *Special characteristics:* international students. *Tuition waivers:* Full or partial for children of alumni, employees or children of employees, senior citizens. *ROTC:* Army.
LOANS *Student loans:* $6,707,818 (42% need-based, 58% non-need-based). *Average need-based loan:* Freshmen: $3689. Undergraduates: $4672. *Parent loans:* $744,208 (100% non-need-based). *Programs:* Federal Direct (Subsidized and Unsubsidized Stafford, PLUS), Perkins, Federal Nursing, private loans.
WORK-STUDY *Federal work-study:* Total amount: $149,451; jobs available. *State or other work-study/employment:* Part-time jobs available.
ATHLETIC AWARDS Total amount: $3,067,692 (100% non-need-based).
APPLYING FOR FINANCIAL AID *Required financial aid forms:* FAFSA, institution's own form, state aid form. *Financial aid deadline:* 8/15 (priority: 3/1). *Notification date:* Continuous beginning 3/1. Students must reply by 5/1 or within 4 weeks of notification.

CONTACT Ms. Nina Morton, Director of Financial Aid, University of Charleston, 2300 MacCorkle Avenue SE, Charleston, WV 25304-1099, 304-357-4947 or toll-free 800-995-GOUC. *E-mail:* ninamorton@ucwv.edu. *Website:* http://www.ucwv.edu/.

UNIVERSITY OF CHICAGO
Chicago, IL

Tuition & fees: $44,574	Average undergraduate aid package: $40,089

ABOUT THE INSTITUTION Independent, coed. *Awards:* bachelor's, master's, and doctoral degrees. 48 undergraduate majors. *Total enrollment:* 12,508. Undergraduates: 5,590. Freshmen: 1,527. Both federal and institutional methodology are used as a basis for awarding need-based institutional aid.

UNDERGRADUATE EXPENSES for 2013–2014 *Application fee:* $75. *One-time required fee:* $1035. *Comprehensive fee:* $57,711 includes full-time tuition ($43,581), mandatory fees ($993), and room and board ($13,137). Room and board charges vary according to board plan and housing facility. Part-time tuition and fees vary according to course load. *Payment plan:* Tuition prepayment.

FRESHMAN FINANCIAL AID (Fall 2012, est.) 827 applied for aid; of those 76% were deemed to have need. 100% of freshmen with need received aid; of those 100% had need fully met. *Average percent of need met:* 100% (excluding resources awarded to replace EFC). *Average financial aid package:* $38,524 (excluding resources awarded to replace EFC). 16% of all full-time freshmen had no need and received non-need-based gift aid.

UNDERGRADUATE FINANCIAL AID (Fall 2012, est.) 2,866 applied for aid; of those 87% were deemed to have need. 100% of undergraduates with need received aid; of those 100% had need fully met. *Average percent of need met:* 100% (excluding resources awarded to replace EFC). *Average financial aid package:* $40,089 (excluding resources awarded to replace EFC). 12% of all full-time undergraduates had no need and received non-need-based gift aid.

GIFT AID (NEED-BASED) *Total amount:* $89,449,597 (6% federal, 1% state, 90% institutional, 3% external sources). *Receiving aid:* Freshmen: 44% (615); all full-time undergraduates: 46% (2,444). *Average award:* Freshmen: $36,454; Undergraduates: $36,600. *Scholarships, grants, and awards:* Federal Pell, FSEOG, state, private, college/university gift aid from institutional funds.

GIFT AID (NON-NEED-BASED) *Total amount:* $7,591,702 (100% institutional). *Average award:* Freshmen: $10,636. Undergraduates: $11,955. *Scholarships, grants, and awards by category:* Academic interests/achievement: general academic interests/achievements. Special achievements/activities: community service, leadership. *Tuition waivers:* Full or partial for employees or children of employees. *ROTC:* Army cooperative, Air Force cooperative.

LOANS *Student loans:* $8,502,923 (67% need-based, 33% non-need-based). 34% of past graduating class borrowed through all loan programs. *Average indebtedness per student:* $22,663. *Average need-based loan:* Freshmen: $3052. Undergraduates: $4697. *Parent loans:* $7,997,923 (100% non-need-based). *Programs:* Federal Direct (Subsidized and Unsubsidized Stafford, PLUS), Perkins.

WORK-STUDY *Federal work-study:* Total amount: $2,306,878; jobs available. *State or other work-study/employment:* Total amount: $2,068,186 (100% need-based). Part-time jobs available.

APPLYING FOR FINANCIAL AID *Required financial aid forms:* FAFSA, CSS Financial Aid PROFILE, noncustodial (divorced/separated) parent's statement, federal income tax form(s). *Financial aid deadline:* 2/1. *Notification date:* 4/16. Students must reply by 5/1.

CONTACT Office of College Aid, University of Chicago, 1101 East 58th Street, Chicago, IL 60637, 773-702-8655. *Fax:* 773-834-4300. *E-mail:* college-aid@uchicago.edu. *Website:* http://www.uchicago.edu/.

UNIVERSITY OF CINCINNATI
Cincinnati, OH

Tuition & fees (OH res): $10,784	Average undergraduate aid package: $8650

ABOUT THE INSTITUTION State-supported, coed. *Awards:* certificates, associate, bachelor's, master's, and doctoral degrees. 141 undergraduate majors. *Total enrollment:* 33,347. Undergraduates: 23,096. Freshmen: 4,160. Federal methodology is used as a basis for awarding need-based institutional aid.

UNDERGRADUATE EXPENSES for 2013–2014 *Application fee:* $50. *Tuition, state resident:* full-time $9124; part-time $381 per credit hour. *Tuition, nonresident:* full-time $24,156; part-time $1017 per credit hour. *Required fees:* full-time $1660; $69 per credit hour. Full-time tuition and fees vary according to course load, degree level, location, program, and reciprocity agreements. Part-time tuition and fees vary according to course load, degree level, location, program, and reciprocity agreements. *College room and board:* $10,170; *Room only:* $6030. Room and board charges vary according to board plan and housing facility.

FRESHMAN FINANCIAL AID (Fall 2012, est.) 3,182 applied for aid; of those 77% were deemed to have need. 98% of freshmen with need received aid; of those 11% had need fully met. *Average percent of need met:* 48% (excluding resources awarded to replace EFC). *Average financial aid package:* $8656 (excluding resources awarded to replace EFC). 14% of all full-time freshmen had no need and received non-need-based gift aid.

UNDERGRADUATE FINANCIAL AID (Fall 2012, est.) 14,148 applied for aid; of those 83% were deemed to have need. 98% of undergraduates with need received aid; of those 9% had need fully met. *Average percent of need met:* 47% (excluding resources awarded to replace EFC). *Average financial aid package:* $8650 (excluding resources awarded to replace EFC). 12% of all full-time undergraduates had no need and received non-need-based gift aid.

GIFT AID (NEED-BASED) *Total amount:* $52,882,525 (50% federal, 7% state, 35% institutional, 8% external sources). *Receiving aid:* Freshmen: 25% (976); all full-time undergraduates: 27% (5,230). *Average award:* Freshmen: $6292; Undergraduates: $5561. *Scholarships, grants, and awards:* Federal Pell, FSEOG, state, private, college/university gift aid from institutional funds, United Negro College Fund, Federal Nursing, TEACH Grants.

GIFT AID (NON-NEED-BASED) *Total amount:* $15,500,508 (84% institutional, 16% external sources). *Receiving aid:* Freshmen: 30% (1,166). Undergraduates: 20% (3,966). *Average award:* Freshmen: $5281. Undergraduates: $5243. *Tuition waivers:* Full or partial for employees or children of employees. *ROTC:* Army, Air Force.

LOANS *Student loans:* $117,156,408 (52% need-based, 48% non-need-based). 69% of past graduating class borrowed through all loan programs. *Average indebtedness per student:* $30,078. *Average need-based loan:* Freshmen: $3626. Undergraduates: $4387. *Parent loans:* $103,445,034 (27% need-based, 73% non-need-based). *Programs:* Federal Direct (Subsidized and Unsubsidized Stafford, PLUS), Perkins, Federal Nursing, state, college/university.

WORK-STUDY *Federal work-study:* Total amount: $2,902,706; 913 jobs averaging $3169.

ATHLETIC AWARDS Total amount: $6,005,600 (54% need-based, 46% non-need-based).

APPLYING FOR FINANCIAL AID *Required financial aid form:* FAFSA. *Financial aid deadline:* Continuous. *Notification date:* Continuous beginning 3/10. Students must reply within 2 weeks of notification.

CONTACT Mrs. Dana Pawlowicz, Associate Director of Financial Aid, University of Cincinnati, PO Box 210125, Cincinnati, OH 45221-0125, 513-556-2441. *Fax:* 513-556-9171. *E-mail:* financeaid@uc.edu. *Website:* http://www.uc.edu/.

UNIVERSITY OF COLORADO BOULDER
Boulder, CO

Tuition & fees (CO res): $9482	Average undergraduate aid package: $13,912

ABOUT THE INSTITUTION State-supported, coed. *Awards:* certificates, bachelor's, master's, and doctoral degrees. 67 undergraduate majors. *Total enrollment:* 31,725. Undergraduates: 25,805. Freshmen: 5,472. Federal methodology is used as a basis for awarding need-based institutional aid.

UNDERGRADUATE EXPENSES for 2013–2014 *Application fee:* $50. *One-time required fee:* $182. *Tuition, state resident:* full-time $8056. *Tuition, nonresident:* full-time $29,952. *Required fees:* full-time $1426. Full-time tuition and fees vary according to program. Part-time tuition and fees vary according to course load and program. *College room and board:* $11,730. Room and board charges vary according to board plan, housing facility, and location.

FRESHMAN FINANCIAL AID (Fall 2012, est.) 3,671 applied for aid; of those 67% were deemed to have need. 97% of freshmen with need received aid; of those 62% had need fully met. *Average percent of need met:* 87% (excluding resources awarded to replace EFC). *Average financial aid package:* $12,944 (excluding resources awarded to replace EFC). 26% of all full-time freshmen had no need and received non-need-based gift aid.

UNDERGRADUATE FINANCIAL AID (Fall 2012, est.) 12,362 applied for aid; of those 75% were deemed to have need. 96% of undergraduates with need received aid; of those 57% had need fully met. *Average percent of need met:* 87% (excluding resources awarded to replace EFC). *Average financial aid package:* $13,912 (excluding resources awarded to replace EFC). 21% of all full-time undergraduates had no need and received non-need-based gift aid.

GIFT AID (NEED-BASED) *Total amount:* $54,367,680 (36% federal, 8% state, 51% institutional, 5% external sources). *Receiving aid:* Freshmen: 31% (1,683); all full-time undergraduates: 28% (6,559). *Average award:* Freshmen: $7968; Undergraduates: $7994. *Scholarships, grants, and awards:* Federal Pell, FSEOG, state, private, college/university gift aid from institutional funds.

GIFT AID (NON-NEED-BASED) *Total amount:* $11,914,614 (10% federal, 50% institutional, 40% external sources). *Receiving aid:* Freshmen: 1% (56). Undergraduates: 1% (148). *Average award:* Freshmen: $7512. Undergraduates: $7736. *Scholarships, grants, and awards by category:* Academic interests/achievement: architecture, area/ethnic studies, biological sciences, business, communication, computer science, education, engineering/technologies, English, foreign languages, general academic interests/achievements, health fields, humanities, international studies, mathematics, military science, physical sciences, premedicine, social sciences. *Creative arts/performance:* art/fine arts, cinema/film/broadcasting, creative writing, dance, journalism/publications, music, performing arts, theater/drama. *Special achievements/activities:* community service, general special achievements/activities, leadership. *Special characteristics:* first-generation college students, general special characteristics, local/state students. *Tuition waivers:* Full or partial for employees or children of employees, senior citizens. *ROTC:* Army, Naval, Air Force.

LOANS *Student loans:* $90,310,145 (63% need-based, 37% non-need-based). 45% of past graduating class borrowed through all loan programs. *Average indebtedness per student:* $23,413. *Average need-based loan:* Freshmen: $5337. Undergraduates: $6476. *Parent loans:* $168,390,743 (32% need-based, 68% non-need-based). *Programs:* Federal Direct (Subsidized and Unsubsidized Stafford, PLUS), Perkins, college/university, private loans.

WORK-STUDY *Federal work-study:* Total amount: $1,189,675; 778 jobs averaging $1140. *State or other work-study/employment:* Total amount: $1,609,034 (95% need-based, 5% non-need-based). 605 part-time jobs averaging $1113.

ATHLETIC AWARDS Total amount: $7,119,825 (38% need-based, 62% non-need-based).

APPLYING FOR FINANCIAL AID *Required financial aid forms:* FAFSA, federal income tax form(s). *Financial aid deadline (priority):* 4/1. *Notification date:* Continuous beginning 3/15. Students must reply within 3 weeks of notification.

CONTACT Gwen E. Pomper, Director of Financial Aid, University of Colorado Boulder, Office of Financial Aid, 556 UCB, Boulder, CO 80309-0077, 303-492-5091. *Fax:* 303-492-0838. *E-mail:* finaid@colorado.edu. *Website:* http://www.colorado.edu/.

UNIVERSITY OF COLORADO COLORADO SPRINGS
Colorado Springs, CO

Tuition & fees (CO res): $8339	Average undergraduate aid package: $7907

ABOUT THE INSTITUTION State-supported, coed. *Awards:* bachelor's, master's, and doctoral degrees. 30 undergraduate majors. *Total enrollment:* 10,257. Undergraduates: 8,354. Freshmen: 1,442. Federal methodology is used as a basis for awarding need-based institutional aid.

UNDERGRADUATE EXPENSES for 2013–2014 *Application fee:* $50. *Tuition, state resident:* full-time $7051; part-time $297 per credit hour. *Tuition, nonresident:* full-time $16,720; part-time $848 per credit hour. *Required fees:* full-time $1288; $27.85 per contact hour or $242.85 per term. Full-time tuition and fees vary according to course level, course load, degree level, location, program, reciprocity agreements, and student level. Part-time tuition and fees vary according to course level, course load, degree level, location, program, reciprocity agreements, and student level. *College room and board:* $8300; *Room only:* $7250. Room and board charges vary according to board plan and housing facility.

FRESHMAN FINANCIAL AID (Fall 2011) 1,055 applied for aid; of those 69% were deemed to have need. 90% of freshmen with need received aid; of those 6% had need fully met. *Average percent of need met:* 45% (excluding resources awarded to replace EFC). *Average financial aid package:* $6445 (excluding resources awarded to replace EFC). 8% of all full-time freshmen had no need and received non-need-based gift aid.

UNDERGRADUATE FINANCIAL AID (Fall 2011) 4,647 applied for aid; of those 74% were deemed to have need. 94% of undergraduates with need received aid; of those 6% had need fully met. *Average percent of need met:* 47% (excluding resources awarded to replace EFC). *Average financial aid package:* $7907 (excluding resources awarded to replace EFC). 5% of all full-time undergraduates had no need and received non-need-based gift aid.

GIFT AID (NEED-BASED) *Total amount:* $20,552,029 (50% federal, 12% state, 28% institutional, 10% external sources). *Receiving aid:* Freshmen: 39% (449); all full-time undergraduates: 42% (2,326). *Average award:* Freshmen: $5176; Undergraduates: $5515. *Scholarships, grants, and awards:* Federal Pell, FSEOG, state, private, college/university gift aid from institutional funds.

GIFT AID (NON-NEED-BASED) *Receiving aid:* Freshmen: 16% (190). Undergraduates: 10% (571). *Average award:* Freshmen: $2166. Undergraduates: $3638. *Scholarships, grants, and awards by category:* Academic interests/achievement: general academic interests/achievements. *Special achievements/activities:* leadership. *Special characteristics:* children and siblings of alumni. *Tuition waivers:* Full or partial for employees or children of employees. *ROTC:* Army.

LOANS *Student loans:* $29,396,332 (100% need-based). 53% of past graduating class borrowed through all loan programs. *Average indebtedness per student:* $15,447. *Average need-based loan:* Freshmen: $3201. Undergraduates: $4185. *Parent loans:* $7,018,505 (100% need-based). *Programs:* Federal Direct (Subsidized and Unsubsidized Stafford, PLUS), Perkins.

WORK-STUDY *Federal work-study:* Total amount: $224,655; jobs available. *State or other work-study/employment:* Total amount: $694,817 (93% need-based, 7% non-need-based). Part-time jobs available.

ATHLETIC AWARDS Total amount: $706,750 (100% need-based).

APPLYING FOR FINANCIAL AID *Required financial aid form:* FAFSA. *Financial aid deadline (priority):* 3/1. *Notification date:* Continuous beginning 4/15.

CONTACT Jevita Rogers, Director of Financial Aid, University of Colorado Colorado Springs, 1420 Austin Bluffs Parkway, Colorado Springs, CO 80918, 719-255-3460 or toll-free 800-990-8227 Ext. 3383. *Fax:* 719-255-3650. *E-mail:* finaidse@uccs.edu. *Website:* http://www.uccs.edu/.

UNIVERSITY OF COLORADO DENVER
Denver, CO

Tuition & fees (area res): $7494	Average undergraduate aid package: $8529

ABOUT THE INSTITUTION State-supported, coed. *Awards:* certificates, bachelor's, master's, and doctoral degrees. 35 undergraduate majors. *Total enrollment:* 22,396. Undergraduates: 13,103. Freshmen: 1,030. Federal methodology is used as a basis for awarding need-based institutional aid.

UNDERGRADUATE EXPENSES for 2013–2014 *Application fee:* $50. *Tuition, area resident:* full-time $6384; part-time $266 per credit hour. *Tuition, state resident:* full-time $6384; part-time $266 per credit hour. *Tuition, nonresident:* full-time $19,896; part-time $829 per credit hour. *Required fees:* full-time $1110; $266 per credit hour or $550 per term. Full-time tuition and fees vary according to course level, course load, degree level, location, program, reciprocity agreements, and student level. Part-time tuition and fees vary according to course level, course load, degree level, location, program, reciprocity agreements, and student level. *College room and board:* $10,410; *Room only:* $7110. Room and board charges vary according to board plan.

FRESHMAN FINANCIAL AID (Fall 2011) 739 applied for aid; of those 82% were deemed to have need. 95% of freshmen with need received aid; of those 5% had need fully met. *Average percent of need met:* 45% (excluding resources awarded to replace EFC). *Average financial aid package:* $8120 (excluding resources awarded to replace EFC). 8% of all full-time freshmen had no need and received non-need-based gift aid.

UNDERGRADUATE FINANCIAL AID (Fall 2011) 5,205 applied for aid; of those 87% were deemed to have need. 96% of undergraduates with need received aid; of those 5% had need fully met. *Average percent of need met:* 48% (excluding resources awarded to replace EFC). *Average financial aid package:* $8529 (excluding resources awarded to replace EFC). 3% of all full-time undergraduates had no need and received non-need-based gift aid.

GIFT AID (NEED-BASED) *Total amount:* $27,778,211 (49% federal, 13% state, 30% institutional, 8% external sources). *Receiving aid:* Freshmen: 51% (486); all full-time undergraduates: 45% (3,346). *Average award:* Freshmen: $7500; Undergraduates: $6694. *Scholarships, grants, and awards:* Federal Pell, FSEOG, state, private, college/university gift aid from institutional funds, Federal Nursing.

GIFT AID (NON-NEED-BASED) *Total amount:* $920,227 (1% federal, 3% state, 86% institutional, 10% external sources). *Receiving aid:* Freshmen: 3% (24). Undergraduates: 1% (53). *Average award:* Freshmen: $2289. Undergraduates: $2525. *Tuition waivers:* Full or partial for employees or children of employees. *ROTC:* Army cooperative, Air Force cooperative.

LOANS *Student loans:* $41,153,036 (81% need-based, 19% non-need-based). 54% of past graduating class borrowed through all loan programs. *Average indebtedness per student:* $21,285. *Average need-based loan:* Freshmen: $3125. Undergraduates: $4427. *Parent loans:* $6,743,428 (13% need-based, 87% non-need-based). *Programs:* Federal Direct (Subsidized and Unsubsidized Stafford, PLUS), Perkins, Federal Nursing, college/university.

WORK-STUDY *Federal work-study:* Total amount: $900,571; 223 jobs averaging $3221. *State or other work-study/employment:* Total amount: $741,119 (95% need-based, 5% non-need-based). 199 part-time jobs averaging $3699.

APPLYING FOR FINANCIAL AID *Required financial aid form:* FAFSA. *Financial aid deadline (priority):* 4/1. *Notification date:* Continuous beginning 5/1.

CONTACT James Broscheit, Director of Financial Aid, University of Colorado Denver, PO Box 173364, Denver, CO 80217-3364, 303-556-2886. *Fax:* 303-556-2325. *E-mail:* financial.aid@ucdenver.edu. *Website:* http://www.ucdenver.edu/.

---

enrollment: 25,483. Undergraduates: 17,528. Freshmen: 3,114. Federal methodology is used as a basis for awarding need-based institutional aid.

UNDERGRADUATE EXPENSES for 2013–2014 *Application fee:* $70. *Tuition, state resident:* full-time $9256; part-time $386 per credit. *Tuition, nonresident:* full-time $28,204; part-time $1175 per credit. *Required fees:* full-time $2766. Part-time tuition and fees vary according to course load. *College room and board:* $11,722; *Room only:* $6278. Room and board charges vary according to board plan and housing facility.

FRESHMAN FINANCIAL AID (Fall 2012, est.) 2,539 applied for aid; of those 67% were deemed to have need. 98% of freshmen with need received aid; of those 10% had need fully met. *Average percent of need met:* 61% (excluding resources awarded to replace EFC). *Average financial aid package:* $12,086 (excluding resources awarded to replace EFC). 13% of all full-time freshmen had no need and received non-need-based gift aid.

UNDERGRADUATE FINANCIAL AID (Fall 2012, est.) 12,118 applied for aid; of those 78% were deemed to have need. 97% of undergraduates with need received aid; of those 7% had need fully met. *Average percent of need met:* 64% (excluding resources awarded to replace EFC). *Average financial aid package:* $12,870 (excluding resources awarded to replace EFC). 9% of all full-time undergraduates had no need and received non-need-based gift aid.

GIFT AID (NEED-BASED) *Total amount:* $71,711,461 (21% federal, 12% state, 63% institutional, 4% external sources). *Receiving aid:* Freshmen: 39% (1,201); all full-time undergraduates: 43% (7,084). *Average award:* Freshmen: $7299; Undergraduates: $8587. *Scholarships, grants, and awards:* Federal Pell, FSEOG, state, private, college/university gift aid from institutional funds.

GIFT AID (NON-NEED-BASED) *Total amount:* $16,115,005 (87% institutional, 13% external sources). *Receiving aid:* Freshmen: 25% (768). Undergraduates: 16% (2,630). *Average award:* Freshmen: $6737. Undergraduates: $6685. *Scholarships, grants, and awards by category:* Academic interests/achievement: 4,331 awards ($17,767,610 total): agriculture, biological sciences, business, computer science, education, engineering/technologies, English, foreign languages, general academic interests/achievements, health fields, humanities, international studies, mathematics, physical sciences, premedicine, religion/biblical studies, social sciences. Creative arts/performance: 105 awards ($246,903 total): art/fine arts, music, theater/drama. Special achievements/activities: 911 awards ($7,281,738 total): community service, leadership. Special characteristics: 4,597 awards ($25,455,565 total): adult students, children of faculty/staff, children of union members/company employees, local/state students, out-of-state students, spouses of deceased or disabled public servants, veterans. *Tuition waivers:* Full or partial for employees or children of employees, senior citizens. *ROTC:* Army, Air Force.

LOANS *Student loans:* $71,199,393 (88% need-based, 12% non-need-based). 62% of past graduating class borrowed through all loan programs. *Average indebtedness per student:* $24,373. *Average need-based loan:* Freshmen: $3566. Undergraduates: $4326. *Parent loans:* $40,659,954 (38% need-based, 62% non-need-based). *Programs:* Federal Direct (Subsidized and Unsubsidized Stafford, PLUS), Perkins, Federal Nursing, state.

WORK-STUDY *Federal work-study:* Total amount: $1,837,188; 999 jobs averaging $2091. *State or other work-study/employment:* Total amount: $16,271,579 (44% need-based, 56% non-need-based). 3,849 part-time jobs averaging $1845.

ATHLETIC AWARDS Total amount: $9,703,844 (31% need-based, 69% non-need-based).

APPLYING FOR FINANCIAL AID *Required financial aid form:* FAFSA. *Financial aid deadline (priority):* 3/1. *Notification date:* Continuous beginning 3/1. Students must reply within 4 weeks of notification.

CONTACT Mona L. Lucas, Director of Financial Aid, University of Connecticut, 233 Glenbrook Road, Unit 4116, Storrs, CT 06269-4116, 860-486-2819. *Fax:* 860-486-5098. *E-mail:* financialaid@uconn.edu. *Website:* http://www.uconn.edu/.

UNIVERSITY OF CONNECTICUT
Storrs, CT

Tuition & fees (CT res): $12,022	Average undergraduate aid package: $12,870

ABOUT THE INSTITUTION State-supported, coed. *Awards:* certificates, associate, bachelor's, master's, and doctoral degrees. 96 undergraduate majors. *Total*

UNIVERSITY OF DALLAS
Irving, TX

Tuition & fees: $31,070	Average undergraduate aid package: $25,041

ABOUT THE INSTITUTION Independent Roman Catholic, coed. *Awards:* certificates, bachelor's, master's, and doctoral degrees. 33 undergraduate majors. *Total* enrollment: 2,725. Undergraduates: 1,356. Freshmen: 371. Federal methodology is used as a basis for awarding need-based institutional aid.

UNDERGRADUATE EXPENSES for 2013–2014 *Application fee:* $40. *Comprehensive fee:* $40,960 includes full-time tuition ($29,140), mandatory fees ($1930), and room and board ($9890). *College room only:* $5690. Room and board charges vary according to board plan and housing facility. *Part-time tuition:* $1210 per credit. *Part-time fees:* $1930 per year.

FRESHMAN FINANCIAL AID (Fall 2012, est.) 285 applied for aid; of those 85% were deemed to have need. 100% of freshmen with need received aid; of those 18% had need fully met. *Average percent of need met:* 77% (excluding resources awarded to replace EFC). *Average financial aid package:* $26,613 (excluding resources awarded to replace EFC). 32% of all full-time freshmen had no need and received non-need-based gift aid.

UNDERGRADUATE FINANCIAL AID (Fall 2012, est.) 912 applied for aid; of those 89% were deemed to have need. 100% of undergraduates with need received aid; of those 16% had need fully met. *Average percent of need met:* 72% (excluding resources awarded to replace EFC). *Average financial aid package:* $25,041 (excluding resources awarded to replace EFC). 39% of all full-time undergraduates had no need and received non-need-based gift aid.

GIFT AID (NEED-BASED) *Total amount:* $22,515,126 (6% federal, 4% state, 89% institutional, 1% external sources). *Receiving aid:* Freshmen: 68% (239); all full-time undergraduates: 60% (796). *Average award:* Freshmen: $22,328; Undergraduates: $19,741. *Scholarships, grants, and awards:* Federal Pell, FSEOG, state, private, college/university gift aid from institutional funds.

GIFT AID (NON-NEED-BASED) *Total amount:* $39,000 (100% institutional). *Receiving aid:* Freshmen: 38% (133). Undergraduates: 31% (408). *Average award:* Freshmen: $12,160. Undergraduates: $11,506. *Scholarships, grants, and awards by category:* Academic interests/achievement: biological sciences, business, education, foreign languages, general academic interests/achievements, mathematics, physical sciences, premedicine. Creative arts/performance: art/fine arts, theater/drama. Special characteristics: children of faculty/staff, ethnic background, religious affiliation, siblings of current students. *Tuition waivers:* Full or partial for employees or children of employees. *ROTC:* Army cooperative, Air Force cooperative.

LOANS *Student loans:* $7,085,697 (51% need-based, 49% non-need-based). 58% of past graduating class borrowed through all loan programs. *Average indebtedness per student:* $31,466. *Average need-based loan:* Freshmen: $4699. Undergraduates: $5974. *Parent loans:* $1,360,978 (100% non-need-based). *Programs:* Federal Direct (Subsidized and Unsubsidized Stafford, PLUS), Perkins, state.

WORK-STUDY *Federal work-study:* Total amount: $293,402; 185 jobs averaging $1597. *State or other work-study/employment:* Total amount: $97,089 (100% need-based). 55 part-time jobs averaging $1830.

APPLYING FOR FINANCIAL AID *Required financial aid form:* FAFSA. *Financial aid deadline:* Continuous. *Notification date:* Continuous beginning 3/1. Students must reply by 5/1 or within 2 weeks of notification.

CONTACT Mrs. Taryn Anderson, Director of Financial Aid, University of Dallas, 1845 East Northgate Drive, Irving, TX 75062, 972-721-5266 or toll-free 800-628-6999. Fax: 972-721-5017. E-mail: ugadmis@udallas.edu. Website: http://www.udallas.edu/.

UNIVERSITY OF DAYTON
Dayton, OH

Tuition & fees: $33,400	Average undergraduate aid package: $23,137

ABOUT THE INSTITUTION Independent Roman Catholic, coed. *Awards:* certificates, bachelor's, master's, and doctoral degrees. 75 undergraduate majors. *Total enrollment:* 11,159. Undergraduates: 8,042. Freshmen: 2,027. Federal methodology is used as a basis for awarding need-based institutional aid.

UNDERGRADUATE EXPENSES for 2013–2014 *Comprehensive fee:* $43,750 includes full-time tuition ($32,000), mandatory fees ($1400), and room and board ($10,350). *College room only:* $6450. Full-time tuition and fees vary according to program. Room and board charges vary according to board plan and housing facility. *Part-time tuition:* $1067 per credit hour. Part-time tuition and fees vary according to course load and program. *Payment plan:* Tuition prepayment.

FRESHMAN FINANCIAL AID (Fall 2012, est.) 1,747 applied for aid; of those 69% were deemed to have need. 100% of freshmen with need received aid; of those 34% had need fully met. *Average percent of need met:* 80% (excluding resources

awarded to replace EFC). *Average financial aid package:* $22,850 (excluding resources awarded to replace EFC). 35% of all full-time freshmen had no need and received non-need-based gift aid.

UNDERGRADUATE FINANCIAL AID (Fall 2012, est.) 5,325 applied for aid; of those 75% were deemed to have need. 100% of undergraduates with need received aid; of those 34% had need fully met. *Average percent of need met:* 77% (excluding resources awarded to replace EFC). *Average financial aid package:* $23,137 (excluding resources awarded to replace EFC). 38% of all full-time undergraduates had no need and received non-need-based gift aid.

GIFT AID (NEED-BASED) *Total amount:* $58,645,766 (6% federal, 2% state, 89% institutional, 3% external sources). *Receiving aid:* Freshmen: 59% (1,210); all full-time undergraduates: 54% (4,007). *Average award:* Undergraduates: $15,439. *Scholarships, grants, and awards:* Federal Pell, FSEOG, state, private, college/university gift aid from institutional funds.

GIFT AID (NON-NEED-BASED) *Total amount:* $38,242,072 (94% institutional, 6% external sources). *Receiving aid:* Freshmen: 14% (280). Undergraduates: 12% (870). *Average award:* Freshmen: $12,225. Undergraduates: $11,387. *Scholarships, grants, and awards by category:* Academic interests/achievement: 6,463 awards ($74,363,431 total): biological sciences, business, communication, computer science, education, engineering/technologies, English, foreign languages, general academic interests/achievements, health fields, humanities, international studies, mathematics, military science, physical sciences, premedicine, religion/biblical studies, social sciences. Creative arts/performance: 201 awards ($927,410 total): art/fine arts, music. Special characteristics: 262 awards ($8,380,554 total): children of faculty/staff, religious affiliation. *Tuition waivers:* Full or partial for employees or children of employees, adult students, senior citizens. *ROTC:* Army, Air Force cooperative.

LOANS *Student loans:* $49,627,646 (56% need-based, 44% non-need-based). 62% of past graduating class borrowed through all loan programs. *Average indebtedness per student:* $40,628. *Average need-based loan:* Freshmen: $3377. Undergraduates: $4938. *Parent loans:* $14,997,512 (35% need-based, 65% non-need-based). *Programs:* Federal Direct (Subsidized and Unsubsidized Stafford, PLUS), Perkins.

WORK-STUDY *Federal work-study:* Total amount: $3,670,830; 1,430 jobs averaging $2567. *State or other work-study/employment:* Total amount: $9,634,444 (26% need-based, 74% non-need-based). 3,658 part-time jobs averaging $2634.

ATHLETIC AWARDS Total amount: $4,096,533 (23% need-based, 77% non-need-based).

APPLYING FOR FINANCIAL AID *Required financial aid form:* FAFSA. *Financial aid deadline (priority):* 3/1. *Notification date:* Continuous beginning 3/25. Students must reply within 3 weeks of notification.

CONTACT Kathy Harmon, Dean of Admission and Financial Aid, University of Dayton, 300 College Park Drive, Dayton, OH 45469-1305, 937-229-4311 or toll-free 800-837-7433. Fax: 937-229-4338. E-mail: kharmon@udayton.edu. Website: http://www.udayton.edu/.

UNIVERSITY OF DELAWARE
Newark, DE

Tuition & fees (DE res): $11,682	Average undergraduate aid package: $14,442

ABOUT THE INSTITUTION State-related, coed. *Awards:* associate, bachelor's, master's, and doctoral degrees. 123 undergraduate majors. *Total enrollment:* 21,081. Undergraduates: 17,427. Freshmen: 3,817. Federal methodology is used as a basis for awarding need-based institutional aid.

UNDERGRADUATE EXPENSES for 2013–2014 *Application fee:* $75. *Tuition, state resident:* full-time $10,150; part-time $423 per credit hour. *Tuition, nonresident:* full-time $27,240; part-time $1135 per credit hour. *Required fees:* full-time $1532. *College room and board:* $10,758. *Room only:* $6516. Room and board charges vary according to board plan, housing facility, and student level.

FRESHMAN FINANCIAL AID (Fall 2012, est.) 3,503 applied for aid; of those 63% were deemed to have need. 98% of freshmen with need received aid; of those 48% had need fully met. *Average percent of need met:* 75% (excluding resources awarded to replace EFC). *Average financial aid package:* $14,427 (excluding resources awarded to replace EFC). 28% of all full-time freshmen had no need and received non-need-based gift aid.

UNDERGRADUATE FINANCIAL AID (Fall 2012, est.) 11,420 applied for aid; of those 70% were deemed to have need. 97% of undergraduates with need received aid; of those 47% had need fully met. *Average percent of need met:* 73%

(excluding resources awarded to replace EFC). *Average financial aid package:* $14,442 (excluding resources awarded to replace EFC). 19% of all full-time undergraduates had no need and received non-need-based gift aid.

GIFT AID (NEED-BASED) *Total amount:* $46,626,282 (20% federal, 14% state, 59% institutional, 7% external sources). *Receiving aid:* Freshmen: 49% (1,880); all full-time undergraduates: 37% (5,866). *Average award:* Freshmen: $8756; Undergraduates: $7831. *Scholarships, grants, and awards:* Federal Pell, FSEOG, state, private, college/university gift aid from institutional funds.

GIFT AID (NON-NEED-BASED) *Total amount:* $23,600,806 (6% state, 84% institutional, 10% external sources). *Receiving aid:* Freshmen: 29% (1,106). Undergraduates: 14% (2,250). *Average award:* Freshmen: $6408. Undergraduates: $6597. *Scholarships, grants, and awards by category:* Academic interests/achievement: agriculture, biological sciences, business, communication, computer science, education, engineering/technologies, English, foreign languages, general academic interests/achievements, health fields, humanities, international studies, mathematics, military science, physical sciences, premedicine, religion/biblical studies, social sciences. Creative arts/performance: applied art and design, art/fine arts, music, theater/drama. Special achievements/activities: cheerleading/drum major, community service, general special achievements/activities, leadership. Special characteristics: children and siblings of alumni, children of faculty/staff, children of public servants, ethnic background, first-generation college students, general special characteristics, local/state students, members of minority groups. *Tuition waivers:* Full or partial for employees or children of employees, senior citizens. *ROTC:* Army, Air Force.

LOANS *Student loans:* $87,628,530 (59% need-based, 41% non-need-based). 56% of past graduating class borrowed through all loan programs. *Average indebtedness per student:* $33,649. *Average need-based loan:* Freshmen: $6569. Undergraduates: $7773. *Parent loans:* $31,372,855 (34% need-based, 66% non-need-based). *Programs:* Federal Direct (Subsidized and Unsubsidized Stafford, PLUS), Perkins, Federal Nursing.

WORK-STUDY *Federal work-study:* Total amount: $1,140,312; jobs available. *State or other work-study/employment:* Total amount: $454,304 (88% need-based, 12% non-need-based). Part-time jobs available.

ATHLETIC AWARDS Total amount: $9,381,206 (29% need-based, 71% non-need-based).

APPLYING FOR FINANCIAL AID *Required financial aid form:* FAFSA. *Financial aid deadline:* 3/15 (priority: 2/1). *Notification date:* Continuous beginning 3/15. Students must reply by 5/1 or within 3 weeks of notification.

CONTACT Mr. James Holloway, Associate Director of Financial Aid, University of Delaware, 140 University Visitors Center, Newark, DE 19716, 302-831-8081. *Fax:* 302-831-4334. *E-mail:* holloway@udel.edu. *Website:* http://www.udel.edu/.

UNIVERSITY OF DENVER
Denver, CO

Tuition & fees: $40,707	Average undergraduate aid package: $31,160

ABOUT THE INSTITUTION Independent, coed. *Awards:* certificates, bachelor's, master's, and doctoral degrees. 73 undergraduate majors. *Total enrollment:* 11,656. Undergraduates: 5,394. Freshmen: 1,213. Both federal and institutional methodology are used as a basis for awarding need-based institutional aid.

UNDERGRADUATE EXPENSES for 2013–2014 *Application fee:* $60. *Comprehensive fee:* $51,787 includes full-time tuition ($39,744), mandatory fees ($963), and room and board ($11,080). *College room only:* $6780. Full-time tuition and fees vary according to class time, course load, and program. Room and board charges vary according to board plan and housing facility. *Part-time tuition:* $1104 per quarter hour. Part-time tuition and fees vary according to class time, course load, and program.

FRESHMAN FINANCIAL AID (Fall 2012, est.) 803 applied for aid; of those 73% were deemed to have need. 100% of freshmen with need received aid; of those 32% had need fully met. *Average percent of need met:* 83% (excluding resources awarded to replace EFC). *Average financial aid package:* $30,905 (excluding resources awarded to replace EFC). 32% of all full-time freshmen had no need and received non-need-based gift aid.

UNDERGRADUATE FINANCIAL AID (Fall 2012, est.) 2,660 applied for aid; of those 80% were deemed to have need. 100% of undergraduates with need received aid; of those 33% had need fully met. *Average percent of need met:* 83% (excluding resources awarded to replace EFC). *Average financial aid package:*

$31,160 (excluding resources awarded to replace EFC). 38% of all full-time undergraduates had no need and received non-need-based gift aid.

GIFT AID (NEED-BASED) *Total amount:* $52,128,053 (8% federal, 1% state, 85% institutional, 6% external sources). *Receiving aid:* Freshmen: 48% (573); all full-time undergraduates: 42% (2,067). *Average award:* Freshmen: $25,916; Undergraduates: $25,917. *Scholarships, grants, and awards:* Federal Pell, FSEOG, state, private, college/university gift aid from institutional funds.

GIFT AID (NON-NEED-BASED) *Total amount:* $28,681,917 (94% institutional, 6% external sources). *Receiving aid:* Freshmen: 11% (137). Undergraduates: 8% (408). *Average award:* Freshmen: $15,347. Undergraduates: $13,708. *Scholarships, grants, and awards by category:* Academic interests/achievement: biological sciences, business, communication, computer science, engineering/technologies, general academic interests/achievements, humanities, international studies, mathematics, physical sciences, social sciences. Creative arts/performance: art/fine arts, debating, music, theater/drama. Special achievements/activities: community service, leadership. *Tuition waivers:* Full or partial for employees or children of employees, senior citizens. *ROTC:* Army cooperative, Air Force cooperative.

LOANS *Student loans:* $16,657,266 (62% need-based, 38% non-need-based). 43% of past graduating class borrowed through all loan programs. *Average indebtedness per student:* $30,268. *Average need-based loan:* Freshmen: $3385. Undergraduates: $4220. *Parent loans:* $7,679,294 (23% need-based, 77% non-need-based). *Programs:* Federal Direct (Subsidized and Unsubsidized Stafford, PLUS), Perkins, college/university.

WORK-STUDY *Federal work-study:* Total amount: $1,047,997; 377 jobs averaging $2763. *State or other work-study/employment:* Total amount: $519,590 (84% need-based, 16% non-need-based). 177 part-time jobs averaging $2919.

ATHLETIC AWARDS Total amount: $8,635,106 (18% need-based, 82% non-need-based).

APPLYING FOR FINANCIAL AID *Required financial aid forms:* FAFSA, CSS Financial Aid PROFILE, noncustodial (divorced/separated) parent's statement. *Financial aid deadline:* 5/1 (priority: 2/15). *Notification date:* 3/22. Students must reply by 5/1 or within 4 weeks of notification.

CONTACT Mr. Chris George, Director of Financial Aid, University of Denver, University Hall, Room 255, 2197 South University Boulevard, Denver, CO 80208, 303-871-4020 or toll-free 800-525-9495. *Fax:* 303-871-2341. *E-mail:* finaid@du.edu. *Website:* http://www.du.edu/.

UNIVERSITY OF DETROIT MERCY
Detroit, MI

CONTACT Sandy Ross, Director of Financial Aid and Scholarships, University of Detroit Mercy, 4001 West McNichols Road, Detroit, MI 48221-3038, 313-993-3350 or toll-free 800-635-5020. *Fax:* 313-993-3347. *Website:* http://www.udmercy.edu/.

UNIVERSITY OF DUBUQUE
Dubuque, IA

ABOUT THE INSTITUTION Independent Presbyterian, coed. *Awards:* associate, bachelor's, master's, and doctoral degrees. 32 undergraduate majors. *Total enrollment:* 2,003. Undergraduates: 1,674. Freshmen: 406.

GIFT AID (NEED-BASED) *Scholarships, grants, and awards:* Federal Pell, FSEOG, state, private, college/university gift aid from institutional funds.

GIFT AID (NON-NEED-BASED) *Scholarships, grants, and awards by category:* Academic interests/achievement: general academic interests/achievements. Special characteristics: children and siblings of alumni, children of educators, children of faculty/staff, out-of-state students, relatives of clergy, religious affiliation, siblings of current students, spouses of current students.

LOANS *Programs:* Federal Direct (Subsidized and Unsubsidized Stafford, PLUS), Perkins, state, college/university.

WORK-STUDY *Federal work-study:* Total amount: $166,894; 185 jobs averaging $1500. *State or other work-study/employment:* Total amount: $371,500 (100% need-based). 194 part-time jobs averaging $1500.

APPLYING FOR FINANCIAL AID *Required financial aid form:* FAFSA.

CONTACT Mr. Timothy Kremer, Dean of Student Financial Planning, University of Dubuque, 2000 University Avenue, Dubuque, IA 52001-5050, 563-589-3170 or toll-free 800-722-5583. *Fax:* 563-589-3690. *E-mail:* tkremer@dbq.edu. *Website:* http://www.dbq.edu/.

CONTACT Ms. JoAnn E. Laugel, Director of Financial Aid, University of Evansville, 1800 Lincoln Avenue, Evansville, IN 47722, 812-488-2364 or toll-free 800-423-8633 Ext. 2468. *Fax:* 812-488-2028. *E-mail:* financialaid@evansville.edu. *Website:* http://www.evansville.edu/.

UNIVERSITY OF EVANSVILLE
Evansville, IN

Tuition & fees: $30,556
Average undergraduate aid package: $25,232

ABOUT THE INSTITUTION Independent United Methodist Church, coed. *Awards:* associate, bachelor's, master's, and doctoral degrees. 82 undergraduate majors. *Total enrollment:* 2,757. Undergraduates: 2,612. Freshmen: 518. Federal methodology is used as a basis for awarding need-based institutional aid.

UNDERGRADUATE EXPENSES for 2013–2014 *Application fee:* $35. *Comprehensive fee:* $40,566 includes full-time tuition ($29,740), mandatory fees ($816), and room and board ($10,010). *College room only:* $5230. Room and board charges vary according to board plan and housing facility. *Part-time tuition:* $830 per credit hour. *Part-time fees:* $50 per term. Part-time tuition and fees vary according to course load.

FRESHMAN FINANCIAL AID (Fall 2012, est.) 448 applied for aid; of those 90% were deemed to have need. 99% of freshmen with need received aid; of those 32% had need fully met. *Average percent of need met:* 88% (excluding resources awarded to replace EFC). *Average financial aid package:* $26,242 (excluding resources awarded to replace EFC). 16% of all full-time freshmen had no need and received non-need-based gift aid.

UNDERGRADUATE FINANCIAL AID (Fall 2012, est.) 1,964 applied for aid; of those 88% were deemed to have need. 100% of undergraduates with need received aid; of those 27% had need fully met. *Average percent of need met:* 82% (excluding resources awarded to replace EFC). *Average financial aid package:* $25,232 (excluding resources awarded to replace EFC). 20% of all full-time undergraduates had no need and received non-need-based gift aid.

GIFT AID (NEED-BASED) *Total amount:* $35,010,807 (8% federal, 7% state, 80% institutional, 5% external sources). *Receiving aid:* Freshmen: 76% (396); all full-time undergraduates: 70% (1,700). *Average award:* Freshmen: $23,488; Undergraduates: $21,872. *Scholarships, grants, and awards:* Federal Pell, FSEOG, state, college/university gift aid from institutional funds.

GIFT AID (NON-NEED-BASED) *Total amount:* $7,959,632 (93% institutional, 7% external sources). *Receiving aid:* Freshmen: 76% (396). Undergraduates: 66% (1,587). *Average award:* Freshmen: $16,707. Undergraduates: $16,302. *Scholarships, grants, and awards by category: Academic interests/achievement:* 1,319 awards ($17,439,361 total): biological sciences, business, communication, computer science, education, engineering/technologies, English, foreign languages, general academic interests/achievements, health fields, humanities, international studies, mathematics, physical sciences, premedicine, religion/biblical studies, social sciences. *Creative arts/performance:* 155 awards ($1,890,487 total): art/fine arts, music, theater/drama. *Special achievements/activities:* 40 awards ($464,500 total): leadership, memberships. *Special characteristics:* 606 awards ($5,019,844 total): children and siblings of alumni, children of faculty/staff, international students, members of minority groups, religious affiliation, siblings of current students. *Tuition waivers:* Full or partial for minority students, children of alumni, employees or children of employees, adult students, senior citizens. *ROTC:* Army cooperative.

LOANS *Student loans:* $10,636,314 (95% need-based, 5% non-need-based). 73% of past graduating class borrowed through all loan programs. *Average indebtedness per student:* $27,679. *Average need-based loan:* Freshmen: $4049. Undergraduates: $5036. *Parent loans:* $4,330,376 (92% need-based, 8% non-need-based). *Programs:* Federal Direct (Subsidized and Unsubsidized Stafford, PLUS), Perkins, Federal Nursing, college/university.

WORK-STUDY *Federal work-study:* Total amount: $510,611; 389 jobs averaging $1408. *State or other work-study/employment:* Total amount: $16,013 (38% need-based, 62% non-need-based). 32 part-time jobs averaging $1365.

ATHLETIC AWARDS Total amount: $4,271,683 (52% need-based, 48% non-need-based).

APPLYING FOR FINANCIAL AID *Required financial aid form:* FAFSA. *Financial aid deadline (priority):* 3/10. *Notification date:* Continuous beginning 3/20. Students must reply by 5/1.

THE UNIVERSITY OF FINDLAY
Findlay, OH

ABOUT THE INSTITUTION Independent Church of God, coed. *Awards:* certificates, associate, bachelor's, master's, and doctoral degrees. 60 undergraduate majors. *Total enrollment:* 4,955. Undergraduates: 3,898. Freshmen: 575.

GIFT AID (NEED-BASED) *Scholarships, grants, and awards:* Federal Pell, FSEOG, state, college/university gift aid from institutional funds.

GIFT AID (NON-NEED-BASED) *Scholarships, grants, and awards by category: Academic interests/achievement:* general academic interests/achievements. *Creative arts/performance:* music, theater/drama. *Special characteristics:* children of faculty/staff.

LOANS *Programs:* Federal Direct (Subsidized and Unsubsidized Stafford, PLUS), Perkins, college/university.

WORK-STUDY *Federal work-study:* Total amount: $410,000; jobs available. *State or other work-study/employment:* Part-time jobs available.

APPLYING FOR FINANCIAL AID *Required financial aid form:* FAFSA.

CONTACT Mr. Arman Habegger, Director of Financial Aid, The University of Findlay, 1000 North Main Street, Findlay, OH 45840-3695, 419-434-4791 or toll-free 800-548-0932. *Fax:* 419-434-4344. *E-mail:* finaid@findlay.edu. *Website:* http://www.findlay.edu/.

UNIVERSITY OF FLORIDA
Gainesville, FL

Tuition & fees (FL res): $6143
Average undergraduate aid package: $12,218

ABOUT THE INSTITUTION State-supported, coed. *Awards:* bachelor's, master's, and doctoral degrees. 97 undergraduate majors. *Total enrollment:* 49,913. Undergraduates: 32,776. Freshmen: 6,289. Federal methodology is used as a basis for awarding need-based institutional aid.

UNDERGRADUATE EXPENSES for 2013–2014 *Application fee:* $30. *Tuition, state resident:* full-time $6143; part-time $147.49 per credit hour. *Tuition, nonresident:* full-time $28,420; part-time $854.70 per credit hour. *Required fees:* $57.27 per credit hour or $92.63 per credit hour. Full-time tuition and fees vary according to course level, location, program, and reciprocity agreements. Part-time tuition and fees vary according to course level, location, program, and reciprocity agreements. *College room and board:* $9370; *Room only:* $5240. Room and board charges vary according to board plan and housing facility.

FRESHMAN FINANCIAL AID (Fall 2011) 6,198 applied for aid; of those 61% were deemed to have need. 100% of freshmen with need received aid; of those 23% had need fully met. *Average percent of need met:* 74% (excluding resources awarded to replace EFC). *Average financial aid package:* $13,093 (excluding resources awarded to replace EFC). 6% of all full-time freshmen had no need and received non-need-based gift aid.

UNDERGRADUATE FINANCIAL AID (Fall 2011) 29,158 applied for aid; of those 66% were deemed to have need. 99% of undergraduates with need received aid; of those 22% had need fully met. *Average percent of need met:* 72% (excluding resources awarded to replace EFC). *Average financial aid package:* $12,218 (excluding resources awarded to replace EFC). 5% of all full-time undergraduates had no need and received non-need-based gift aid.

GIFT AID (NEED-BASED) *Total amount:* $73,395,577 (63% federal, 10% state, 27% institutional). *Receiving aid:* Freshmen: 39% (2,520); all full-time undergraduates: 35% (11,838). *Average award:* Freshmen: $6298; Undergraduates: $6184. *Scholarships, grants, and awards:* Federal Pell, FSEOG, state, private, college/university gift aid from institutional funds.

GIFT AID (NON-NEED-BASED) *Total amount:* $130,145,010 (1% federal, 50% state, 14% institutional, 35% external sources). *Receiving aid:* Freshmen: 58% (3,727). Undergraduates: 49% (16,219). *Average award:* Freshmen: $2923. Undergraduates: $2230. *Scholarships, grants, and awards by category: Academic

interests/achievement: agriculture, architecture, business, communication, computer science, education, engineering/technologies, general academic interests/achievements, health fields, military science. *Creative arts/performance:* art/fine arts, dance, general creative arts/performance, journalism/publications, music, performing arts, theater/drama. *Special achievements/activities:* community service, general special achievements/activities, leadership. *Special characteristics:* children of faculty/staff, members of minority groups, out-of-state students. *Tuition waivers:* Full or partial for employees or children of employees, senior citizens. *ROTC:* Army, Naval, Air Force.
LOANS *Student loans:* $72,134,440 (55% need-based, 45% non-need-based). 51% of past graduating class borrowed through all loan programs. *Average indebtedness per student:* $19,636. *Average need-based loan:* Freshmen: $3737. Undergraduates: $4742. *Parent loans:* $8,204,904 (100% non-need-based). *Programs:* Federal Direct (Subsidized and Unsubsidized Stafford, PLUS), Perkins, college/university.
WORK-STUDY *Federal work-study:* Total amount: $2,057,623; 964 jobs averaging $1898. *State or other work-study/employment:* Total amount: $9,885,432 (1% need-based, 99% non-need-based). 4,506 part-time jobs averaging $2494.
ATHLETIC AWARDS Total amount: $8,513,364 (100% non-need-based).
APPLYING FOR FINANCIAL AID *Required financial aid form:* FAFSA. *Financial aid deadline (priority):* 3/15. *Notification date:* Continuous beginning 4/15.
CONTACT Mr. Richard D. Wilder, Director of Student Financial Affairs, University of Florida, S-107 Criser Hall, Gainesville, FL 32611-4025, 352-392-1271. *Fax:* 352-392-2861. *E-mail:* rwilder@ufl.edu.
Website: http://www.ufl.edu/.

UNIVERSITY OF FORT LAUDERDALE
Lauderhill, FL

CONTACT Financial Aid Office, University of Fort Lauderdale, 4093 NW 16th Street, Lauderhill, FL 33313, 954-486-7728.
Website: http://uftl.edu/.

UNIVERSITY OF GEORGIA
Athens, GA

Tuition & fees (GA res): $9842	Average undergraduate aid package: $10,797

ABOUT THE INSTITUTION State-supported, coed. *Awards:* certificates, bachelor's, master's, and doctoral degrees. 130 undergraduate majors. *Total enrollment:* 34,519. Undergraduates: 26,259. Freshmen: 4,936. Federal methodology is used as a basis for awarding need-based institutional aid.
UNDERGRADUATE EXPENSES for 2013–2014 *Application fee:* $60. *Tuition, state resident:* full-time $9842. *Tuition, nonresident:* full-time $28,052. Full-time tuition and fees vary according to course load, location, and program. Part-time tuition and fees vary according to course load, location, and program. *College room and board:* $8970; *Room only:* $5088. Room and board charges vary according to board plan and housing facility.
FRESHMAN FINANCIAL AID (Fall 2012, est.) 4,077 applied for aid; of those 46% were deemed to have need. 100% of freshmen with need received aid; of those 24% had need fully met. *Average percent of need met:* 72% (excluding resources awarded to replace EFC). *Average financial aid package:* $12,058 (excluding resources awarded to replace EFC). 6% of all full-time freshmen had no need and received non-need-based gift aid.
UNDERGRADUATE FINANCIAL AID (Fall 2012, est.) 16,376 applied for aid; of those 59% were deemed to have need. 99% of undergraduates with need received aid; of those 19% had need fully met. *Average percent of need met:* 66% (excluding resources awarded to replace EFC). *Average financial aid package:* $10,797 (excluding resources awarded to replace EFC). 6% of all full-time undergraduates had no need and received non-need-based gift aid.
GIFT AID (NEED-BASED) *Total amount:* $70,778,372 (37% federal, 56% state, 3% institutional, 4% external sources). *Receiving aid:* Freshmen: 37% (1,840); all full-time undergraduates: 36% (8,709). *Average award:* Freshmen: $10,061; Undergraduates: $8433. *Scholarships, grants, and awards:* Federal Pell, FSEOG, state, private, college/university gift aid from institutional funds.

GIFT AID (NON-NEED-BASED) *Total amount:* $79,054,616 (1% federal, 92% state, 4% institutional, 3% external sources). *Receiving aid:* Freshmen: 6% (308). Undergraduates: 4% (1,029). *Average award:* Freshmen: $2340. Undergraduates: $1924. *Scholarships, grants, and awards by category:* Academic interests/achievement: 22,940 awards ($122,001,936 total): agriculture, business, education, general academic interests/achievements. *Creative arts/performance:* 93 awards ($110,390 total): music. *Special characteristics:* 214 awards ($300,500 total): local/state students. *Tuition waivers:* Full or partial for senior citizens. *ROTC:* Army, Air Force.
LOANS *Student loans:* $73,806,312 (63% need-based, 37% non-need-based). 44% of past graduating class borrowed through all loan programs. *Average indebtedness per student:* $19,621. *Average need-based loan:* Freshmen: $3305. Undergraduates: $4206. *Parent loans:* $14,303,858 (28% need-based, 72% non-need-based). *Programs:* Federal Direct (Subsidized and Unsubsidized Stafford, PLUS), Perkins, state, college/university.
WORK-STUDY *Federal work-study:* Total amount: $1,125,134; 407 jobs averaging $2764.
ATHLETIC AWARDS Total amount: $8,336,682 (30% need-based, 70% non-need-based).
APPLYING FOR FINANCIAL AID *Required financial aid form:* FAFSA. *Financial aid deadline (priority):* 3/15. *Notification date:* Continuous beginning 4/1. Students must reply within 2 weeks of notification.
CONTACT Ms. Bonnie C. Joerschke, Director of Financial Aid, University of Georgia, 220 Holmes/Hunter Academic Building, Athens, GA 30602-6114, 706-542-6147. *Fax:* 706-542-8217. *E-mail:* osfa@uga.edu.
Website: http://www.uga.edu/.

UNIVERSITY OF GREAT FALLS
Great Falls, MT

Tuition & fees: $20,960	Average undergraduate aid package: $16,581

ABOUT THE INSTITUTION Independent Roman Catholic, coed. *Awards:* certificates, associate, bachelor's, and master's degrees. 73 undergraduate majors. *Total enrollment:* 1,058. Undergraduates: 974. Freshmen: 142. Federal methodology is used as a basis for awarding need-based institutional aid.
UNDERGRADUATE EXPENSES for 2013–2014 *Application fee:* $35. *Comprehensive fee:* $27,760 includes full-time tuition ($19,860), mandatory fees ($1100), and room and board ($6800). *College room only:* $3900. Full-time tuition and fees vary according to course load. Room and board charges vary according to housing facility. *Part-time tuition:* $607 per credit hour. Part-time tuition and fees vary according to course load, location, and program.
FRESHMAN FINANCIAL AID (Fall 2012, est.) 125 applied for aid; of those 89% were deemed to have need. 98% of freshmen with need received aid; of those 7% had need fully met. *Average percent of need met:* 72% (excluding resources awarded to replace EFC). *Average financial aid package:* $17,228 (excluding resources awarded to replace EFC). 12% of all full-time freshmen had no need and received non-need-based gift aid.
UNDERGRADUATE FINANCIAL AID (Fall 2012, est.) 595 applied for aid; of those 92% were deemed to have need. 99% of undergraduates with need received aid; of those 3% had need fully met. *Average percent of need met:* 65% (excluding resources awarded to replace EFC). *Average financial aid package:* $16,581 (excluding resources awarded to replace EFC). 9% of all full-time undergraduates had no need and received non-need-based gift aid.
GIFT AID (NEED-BASED) *Total amount:* $5,780,076 (31% federal, 69% institutional). *Receiving aid:* Freshmen: 73% (99); all full-time undergraduates: 73% (487). *Average award:* Freshmen: $10,524; Undergraduates: $9473. *Scholarships, grants, and awards:* Federal Pell, FSEOG, private, college/university gift aid from institutional funds.
GIFT AID (NON-NEED-BASED) *Total amount:* $701,560 (100% institutional). *Receiving aid:* Freshmen: 3% (4). Undergraduates: 2% (16). *Average award:* Freshmen: $7119. Undergraduates: $7517. *Scholarships, grants, and awards by category:* Academic interests/achievement: biological sciences, business, computer science, education, general academic interests/achievements, humanities, mathematics, physical sciences, premedicine, religion/biblical studies, social sciences. *Creative arts/performance:* art/fine arts, dance, general creative arts/performance. *Special achievements/activities:* cheerleading/drum major, religious involvement. *Special character-*

istics: children and siblings of alumni, children of current students, children of faculty/staff, ethnic background, first-generation college students, international students, local/state students, parents of current students, religious affiliation, siblings of current students, spouses of current students. *Tuition waivers:* Full or partial for employees or children of employees.

LOANS *Student loans:* $5,323,608 (88% need-based, 12% non-need-based). 85% of past graduating class borrowed through all loan programs. *Average indebtedness per student:* $25,690. *Average need-based loan:* Freshmen: $3392. Undergraduates: $4193. *Parent loans:* $1,300,636 (71% need-based, 29% non-need-based). *Programs:* Federal Direct (Subsidized and Unsubsidized Stafford, PLUS), Perkins.

WORK-STUDY *Federal work-study:* Total amount: $63,519; jobs available. *State or other work-study/employment:* Total amount: $147,000 (100% need-based). Part-time jobs available.

ATHLETIC AWARDS Total amount: $2,646,670 (73% need-based, 27% non-need-based).

APPLYING FOR FINANCIAL AID *Required financial aid form:* FAFSA. *Financial aid deadline (priority):* 3/1. *Notification date:* Continuous beginning 3/1.

CONTACT Kelli Engelhardt, Director of Financial Aid, University of Great Falls, 1301 20th Street South, Great Falls, MT 59405, 406-791-5237 or toll-free 800-856-9544. *Fax:* 406-791-5242. *E-mail:* kengelhardt01@ugf.edu. *Website:* http://www.ugf.edu/.

UNIVERSITY OF GUAM
Mangilao, GU

CONTACT Office of Financial Aid, University of Guam, UOG Station, Mangilao, GU 96923, 671-735-2288. *Fax:* 671-734-2907. *Website:* http://www.uog.edu/.

UNIVERSITY OF HARTFORD
West Hartford, CT

Tuition & fees: $33,358	Average undergraduate aid package: $17,551

ABOUT THE INSTITUTION Independent, coed. *Awards:* certificates, diplomas, associate, bachelor's, master's, and doctoral degrees. 87 undergraduate majors. *Total enrollment:* 6,894. Undergraduates: 5,284. Freshmen: 1,289. Federal methodology is used as a basis for awarding need-based institutional aid.

UNDERGRADUATE EXPENSES for 2013–2014 *Application fee:* $40. *Comprehensive fee:* $45,606 includes full-time tuition ($31,804), mandatory fees ($1554), and room and board ($12,248). *College room only:* $7328. Full-time tuition and fees vary according to program. Room and board charges vary according to board plan and housing facility. *Part-time tuition:* $480 per credit. Part-time tuition and fees vary according to course load and program. *Payment plan:* Tuition prepayment.

FRESHMAN FINANCIAL AID (Fall 2011) 1,320 applied for aid; of those 90% were deemed to have need. 100% of freshmen with need received aid; of those 30% had need fully met. *Average percent of need met:* 92% (excluding resources awarded to replace EFC). *Average financial aid package:* $16,846 (excluding resources awarded to replace EFC). 8% of all full-time freshmen had no need and received non-need-based gift aid.

UNDERGRADUATE FINANCIAL AID (Fall 2011) 4,596 applied for aid; of those 82% were deemed to have need. 99% of undergraduates with need received aid; of those 26% had need fully met. *Average percent of need met:* 90% (excluding resources awarded to replace EFC). *Average financial aid package:* $17,551 (excluding resources awarded to replace EFC). 11% of all full-time undergraduates had no need and received non-need-based gift aid.

GIFT AID (NEED-BASED) *Total amount:* $114,576,604 (6% federal, 2% state, 45% institutional, 47% external sources). *Receiving aid:* Freshmen: 81% (1,071); all full-time undergraduates: 65% (3,479). *Average award:* Freshmen: $14,834; Undergraduates: $15,939. *Scholarships, grants, and awards:* Federal Pell, FSEOG, state, private, college/university gift aid from institutional funds.

GIFT AID (NON-NEED-BASED) *Total amount:* $8,817,902 (58% institutional, 42% external sources). *Receiving aid:* Freshmen: 20% (258). Undergraduates: 21%

(1,141). *Average award:* Freshmen: $14,101. Undergraduates: $11,390. *Scholarships, grants, and awards by category: Academic interests/achievement:* engineering/technologies, general academic interests/achievements, health fields, premedicine. *Creative arts/performance:* art/fine arts, dance, music, performing arts, theater/drama. *Special achievements/activities:* community service. *Special characteristics:* adult students, children of current students, children of faculty/staff, children of union members/company employees, children with a deceased or disabled parent, ethnic background, first-generation college students, handicapped students, international students, local/state students, members of minority groups, parents of current students, previous college experience, religious affiliation, siblings of current students, twins. *Tuition waivers:* Full or partial for employees or children of employees, senior citizens. *ROTC:* Army cooperative, Air Force cooperative.

LOANS *Student loans:* $24,724,923 (100% need-based). 77% of past graduating class borrowed through all loan programs. *Average indebtedness per student:* $28,933. *Average need-based loan:* Freshmen: $3038. Undergraduates: $3976. *Parent loans:* $13,832,756 (100% need-based). *Programs:* Federal Direct (Subsidized and Unsubsidized Stafford, PLUS), Perkins.

WORK-STUDY *Federal work-study:* Total amount: $823,185; 131 jobs averaging $1171.

ATHLETIC AWARDS Total amount: $4,735,520 (48% need-based, 52% non-need-based).

APPLYING FOR FINANCIAL AID *Required financial aid form:* FAFSA. *Financial aid deadline (priority):* 2/1. *Notification date:* Continuous beginning 3/1. Students must reply by 5/1 or within 2 weeks of notification.

CONTACT Jennifer Fuhrmann, Office of Financial Aid, University of Hartford, 200 Bloomfield Avenue, West Hartford, CT 06117-1599, 860-768-4296 or toll-free 800-947-4303. *Fax:* 860-768-4961. *E-mail:* finaid@hartford.edu. *Website:* http://www.hartford.edu/.

UNIVERSITY OF HAWAII AT HILO
Hilo, HI

Tuition & fees (HI res): $6496	Average undergraduate aid package: $11,389

ABOUT THE INSTITUTION State-supported, coed. *Awards:* certificates, bachelor's, master's, and doctoral degrees. 30 undergraduate majors. *Total enrollment:* 4,157. Undergraduates: 3,568. Freshmen: 453. Federal methodology is used as a basis for awarding need-based institutional aid.

UNDERGRADUATE EXPENSES for 2013–2014 *Application fee:* $50. *Tuition, state resident:* full-time $6192; part-time $258 per credit. *Tuition, nonresident:* full-time $17,952; part-time $748 per credit. *Required fees:* full-time $304. Full-time tuition and fees vary according to reciprocity agreements. Part-time tuition and fees vary according to course load. Room and board charges vary according to board plan and housing facility.

FRESHMAN FINANCIAL AID (Fall 2012, est.) 400 applied for aid; of those 69% were deemed to have need. 100% of freshmen with need received aid; of those 24% had need fully met. *Average percent of need met:* 74% (excluding resources awarded to replace EFC). *Average financial aid package:* $9721 (excluding resources awarded to replace EFC). 1% of all full-time freshmen had no need and received non-need-based gift aid.

UNDERGRADUATE FINANCIAL AID (Fall 2012, est.) 2,278 applied for aid; of those 78% were deemed to have need. 100% of undergraduates with need received aid; of those 20% had need fully met. *Average percent of need met:* 70% (excluding resources awarded to replace EFC). *Average financial aid package:* $11,389 (excluding resources awarded to replace EFC). 1% of all full-time undergraduates had no need and received non-need-based gift aid.

GIFT AID (NEED-BASED) *Total amount:* $8,107,597 (91% federal, 7% state, 2% institutional). *Receiving aid:* Freshmen: 45% (201); all full-time undergraduates: 49% (1,367). *Average award:* Freshmen: $4888; Undergraduates: $4963. *Scholarships, grants, and awards:* Federal Pell, FSEOG, state, private, college/university gift aid from institutional funds.

GIFT AID (NON-NEED-BASED) *Total amount:* $1,646,425 (30% institutional, 70% external sources). *Receiving aid:* Freshmen: 12% (53). Undergraduates: 13% (352). *Average award:* Freshmen: $1000. Undergraduates: $1870. *Scholarships, grants, and awards by category: Academic interests/achievement:* 112 awards ($223,661 total): business, computer science, English, general academic interests/achievements, health fields, social sciences. *Creative arts/performance:* 13 awards

($13,250 total): art/fine arts, music, performing arts, theater/drama. *Special achievements/activities:* 38 awards ($27,425 total): community service, general special achievements/activities, leadership. *Special characteristics:* 21 awards ($92,374 total): general special characteristics, local/state students.
LOANS *Student loans:* $23,011,248 (27% need-based, 73% non-need-based). 51% of past graduating class borrowed through all loan programs. *Average indebtedness per student:* $13,035. *Average need-based loan:* Freshmen: $3176. Undergraduates: $4273. *Parent loans:* $753,750 (100% non-need-based). *Programs:* Federal Direct (Subsidized and Unsubsidized Stafford, PLUS), Perkins, state.
WORK-STUDY *Federal work-study:* Total amount: $260,981; 160 jobs averaging $1631. *State or other work-study/employment:* Total amount: $1,142,465 (100% non-need-based). 526 part-time jobs averaging $2172.
ATHLETIC AWARDS Total amount: $689,388 (100% non-need-based).
APPLYING FOR FINANCIAL AID *Required financial aid form:* FAFSA. *Financial aid deadline (priority):* 3/1. *Notification date:* Continuous beginning 3/1. Students must reply within 3 weeks of notification.
CONTACT Financial Aid Office, University of Hawaii at Hilo, 200 West Kawili Street, Hilo, HI 96720-4091, 808-974-7324 or toll-free 800-897-4456. *Fax:* 808-933-0861. *E-mail:* uhhfao@hawaii.edu.
Website: http://www.uhh.hawaii.edu/.

UNIVERSITY OF HAWAII AT MANOA
Honolulu, HI

Tuition & fees (area res): $9884	Average undergraduate aid package: $11,498

ABOUT THE INSTITUTION State-supported, coed. *Awards:* certificates, bachelor's, master's, and doctoral degrees. 82 undergraduate majors. *Total enrollment:* 20,426. Undergraduates: 14,655. Freshmen: 1,964. Federal methodology is used as a basis for awarding need-based institutional aid.
UNDERGRADUATE EXPENSES for 2013–2014 *Application fee:* $70. *Tuition, area resident:* full-time $9144. *Tuition, state resident:* full-time $9144; part-time $381 per credit. *Tuition, nonresident:* full-time $26,712; part-time $1113 per credit. *Required fees:* full-time $740. Full-time tuition and fees vary according to class time, course level, course load, degree level, program, reciprocity agreements, and student level. Part-time tuition and fees vary according to class time, course level, course load, degree level, program, reciprocity agreements, and student level. *College room and board:* $10,029; *Room only:* $6820. Room and board charges vary according to board plan and housing facility.
FRESHMAN FINANCIAL AID (Fall 2011) 1,559 applied for aid; of those 67% were deemed to have need. 99% of freshmen with need received aid; of those 28% had need fully met. *Average percent of need met:* 74% (excluding resources awarded to replace EFC). *Average financial aid package:* $11,694 (excluding resources awarded to replace EFC). 23% of all full-time freshmen had no need and received non-need-based gift aid.
UNDERGRADUATE FINANCIAL AID (Fall 2011) 9,105 applied for aid; of those 72% were deemed to have need. 97% of undergraduates with need received aid; of those 25% had need fully met. *Average percent of need met:* 70% (excluding resources awarded to replace EFC). *Average financial aid package:* $11,498 (excluding resources awarded to replace EFC). 18% of all full-time undergraduates had no need and received non-need-based gift aid.
GIFT AID (NEED-BASED) *Total amount:* $39,853,947 (48% federal, 50% institutional, 2% external sources). *Receiving aid:* Freshmen: 57% (1,020); all full-time undergraduates: 50% (6,000). *Average award:* Freshmen: $8170; Undergraduates: $7836. *Scholarships, grants, and awards:* Federal Pell, FSEOG, state, private, college/university gift aid from institutional funds.
GIFT AID (NON-NEED-BASED) *Total amount:* $8,976,762 (77% institutional, 23% external sources). *Receiving aid:* Freshmen: 13% (224). Undergraduates: 8% (1,001). *Average award:* Freshmen: $8322. Undergraduates: $8592. *Scholarships, grants, and awards by category: Academic interests/achievement:* general academic interests/achievements. *Creative arts/performance:* general creative arts/performance. *Special achievements/activities:* general special achievements/activities. *Special characteristics:* general special characteristics. *Tuition waivers:* Full or partial for minority students, employees or children of employees, adult students, senior citizens.
ROTC: Army, Air Force.
LOANS *Student loans:* $40,268,416 (53% need-based, 47% non-need-based). 42% of past graduating class borrowed through all loan programs. *Average indebtedness per student:* $21,405. *Average need-based loan:* Freshmen: $3638. Undergraduates: $4467. *Parent loans:* $19,180,006 (100% non-need-based). *Programs:* Federal Direct (Subsidized and Unsubsidized Stafford, PLUS), Perkins, state.
WORK-STUDY *Federal work-study:* Total amount: $905,645; 419 jobs averaging $2161.
ATHLETIC AWARDS Total amount: $4,011,994 (3% need-based, 97% non-need-based).
APPLYING FOR FINANCIAL AID *Required financial aid form:* FAFSA. *Financial aid deadline (priority):* 3/1. *Notification date:* Continuous beginning 4/1. Students must reply by 5/1 or within 4 weeks of notification.
CONTACT Jodie Kuba, Director of Financial Aid Services, University of Hawaii at Manoa, 2600 Campus Road, Suite 112, Honolulu, HI 96822, 808-956-7251 or toll-free 800-823-9771. *Fax:* 808-956-3985. *E-mail:* finaid@hawaii.edu.
Website: http://manoa.hawaii.edu/.

UNIVERSITY OF HAWAII–WEST OAHU
Pearl City, HI

Tuition & fees (HI res): $5592	Average undergraduate aid package: $8380

ABOUT THE INSTITUTION State-supported, coed. *Awards:* certificates and bachelor's degrees. 21 undergraduate majors. *Total enrollment:* 1,997. Undergraduates: 1,997. Freshmen: 301. Federal methodology is used as a basis for awarding need-based institutional aid.
UNDERGRADUATE EXPENSES for 2013–2014 *Application fee:* $50. *Tuition, state resident:* full-time $5592; part-time $254 per credit hour. *Tuition, nonresident:* full-time $16,656; part-time $734 per credit hour.
FRESHMAN FINANCIAL AID (Fall 2011) 10 applied for aid; of those 100% were deemed to have need. 100% of freshmen with need received aid. *Average percent of need met:* 50% (excluding resources awarded to replace EFC). *Average financial aid package:* $4450 (excluding resources awarded to replace EFC).
UNDERGRADUATE FINANCIAL AID (Fall 2011) 240 applied for aid; of those 100% were deemed to have need. 100% of undergraduates with need received aid. *Average percent of need met:* 50% (excluding resources awarded to replace EFC). *Average financial aid package:* $8380 (excluding resources awarded to replace EFC). 1% of all full-time undergraduates had no need and received non-need-based gift aid.
GIFT AID (NEED-BASED) *Total amount:* $2,440,660 (82% federal, 18% institutional). *Receiving aid:* Freshmen: 27% (4); all full-time undergraduates: 20% (166). *Average award:* Freshmen: $7884; Undergraduates: $5326. *Scholarships, grants, and awards:* Federal Pell, FSEOG, state, private, college/university gift aid from institutional funds.
GIFT AID (NON-NEED-BASED) *Total amount:* $28,576 (20% institutional, 80% external sources). *Receiving aid:* Freshmen: 47% (7). Undergraduates: 3% (23). *Average award:* Undergraduates: $917. *Tuition waivers:* Full or partial for employees or children of employees. *ROTC:* Army cooperative, Air Force cooperative.
LOANS *Student loans:* $3,524,021 (100% need-based). *Average need-based loan:* Freshmen: $3484. Undergraduates: $4346. *Parent loans:* $16,566 (100% need-based). *Programs:* Federal Direct (Subsidized and Unsubsidized Stafford, PLUS).
WORK-STUDY *Federal work-study:* Total amount: $10,156; jobs available. *State or other work-study/employment:* Part-time jobs available.
APPLYING FOR FINANCIAL AID *Required financial aid form:* FAFSA. *Financial aid deadline (priority):* 4/1. *Notification date:* Continuous beginning 4/1. Students must reply within 2 weeks of notification.
CONTACT Lester Ishimoto, Office of Financial Aid, University of Hawaii–West Oahu, 91-1001 Farrington Highway, Kapolei, HI 96707, 808-689-2689 or toll-free 866-299-8656. *Fax:* 808-689-2691. *E-mail:* uhwo-finaid-l@lists.hawaii.edu.
Website: http://www.uhwo.hawaii.edu/.

UNIVERSITY OF HOUSTON
Houston, TX

Tuition & fees (TX res): $9888	Average undergraduate aid package: $13,317

ABOUT THE INSTITUTION State-supported, coed. *Awards:* bachelor's, master's, and doctoral degrees. 84 undergraduate majors. *Total enrollment:* 40,747. Undergraduates: 32,639. Freshmen: 3,492. Federal methodology is used as a basis for awarding need-based institutional aid.

UNDERGRADUATE EXPENSES for 2013–2014 *Application fee:* $50. *Tuition, state resident:* full-time $8970. *Tuition, nonresident:* full-time $19,500. *Required fees:* full-time $918. Full-time tuition and fees vary according to course level, course load, degree level, program, and student level. Part-time tuition and fees vary according to course level, course load, degree level, program, and student level. Room and board charges vary according to board plan and housing facility.

FRESHMAN FINANCIAL AID (Fall 2012, est.) 2,648 applied for aid; of those 82% were deemed to have need. 97% of freshmen with need received aid; of those 23% had need fully met. *Average percent of need met:* 76% (excluding resources awarded to replace EFC). *Average financial aid package:* $13,387 (excluding resources awarded to replace EFC). 8% of all full-time freshmen had no need and received non-need-based gift aid.

UNDERGRADUATE FINANCIAL AID (Fall 2012, est.) 16,598 applied for aid; of those 90% were deemed to have need. 96% of undergraduates with need received aid; of those 19% had need fully met. *Average percent of need met:* 72% (excluding resources awarded to replace EFC). *Average financial aid package:* $13,317 (excluding resources awarded to replace EFC). 2% of all full-time undergraduates had no need and received non-need-based gift aid.

GIFT AID (NEED-BASED) *Total amount:* $106,292,306 (51% federal, 16% state, 29% institutional, 4% external sources). *Receiving aid:* Freshmen: 59% (1,975); all full-time undergraduates: 55% (12,808). *Average award:* Freshmen: $9721; Undergraduates: $7266. *Scholarships, grants, and awards:* Federal Pell, FSEOG, state, private, college/university gift aid from institutional funds.

GIFT AID (NON-NEED-BASED) *Total amount:* $4,134,672 (4% state, 83% institutional, 13% external sources). *Receiving aid:* Freshmen: 6% (195). Undergraduates: 2% (448). *Average award:* Freshmen: $5814. Undergraduates: $5406. *Scholarships, grants, and awards by category:* Academic interests/achievement: general academic interests/achievements. Creative arts/performance: art/fine arts, general creative arts/performance. Special achievements/activities: leadership. Special characteristics: children and siblings of alumni, local/state students. *Tuition waivers:* Full or partial for employees or children of employees. *ROTC:* Army, Naval cooperative, Air Force.

LOANS *Student loans:* $146,278,393 (85% need-based, 15% non-need-based). 47% of past graduating class borrowed through all loan programs. *Average indebtedness per student:* $16,582. *Average need-based loan:* Freshmen: $5295. Undergraduates: $7698. *Parent loans:* $4,297,938 (30% need-based, 70% non-need-based). *Programs:* Federal Direct (Subsidized and Unsubsidized Stafford, PLUS), Perkins, state.

WORK-STUDY *Federal work-study:* Total amount: $1,986,611; jobs available. *State or other work-study/employment:* Total amount: $112,000 (100% need-based). Part-time jobs available.

ATHLETIC AWARDS Total amount: $5,066,588 (80% need-based, 20% non-need-based).

APPLYING FOR FINANCIAL AID *Required financial aid form:* FAFSA. *Financial aid deadline (priority):* 4/1. *Notification date:* Continuous.

CONTACT Office of Scholarships and Financial Aid, University of Houston, 4800 Calhoun Road, Houston, TX 77204, 713-743-1010. *Fax:* 713-743-9098. *Website:* http://www.uh.edu/.

UNIVERSITY OF HOUSTON–CLEAR LAKE
Houston, TX

Tuition & fees (TX res): $6580	Average undergraduate aid package: $7651

ABOUT THE INSTITUTION State-supported, coed. *Awards:* certificates, bachelor's, master's, and doctoral degrees. 34 undergraduate majors. *Total enrollment:* 8,155. Undergraduates: 4,790. Federal methodology is used as a basis for awarding need-based institutional aid.

UNDERGRADUATE EXPENSES for 2013–2014 *Application fee:* $45. *Tuition, state resident:* full-time $5326; part-time $178 per credit hour. *Tuition, nonresident:* full-time $17,110; part-time $572 per credit hour. *Required fees:* full-time $1254; $486 per term. Full-time tuition and fees vary according to course load and program. Part-time tuition and fees vary according to course load and program. *Room only:* $8354. Room and board charges vary according to housing facility.

UNDERGRADUATE FINANCIAL AID (Fall 2012, est.) 1,666 applied for aid; of those 93% were deemed to have need. 97% of undergraduates with need received aid; of those 25% had need fully met. *Average percent of need met:* 44% (excluding resources awarded to replace EFC). *Average financial aid package:* $7651 (excluding resources awarded to replace EFC). 3% of all full-time undergraduates had no need and received non-need-based gift aid.

GIFT AID (NEED-BASED) *Total amount:* $11,288,426 (66% federal, 23% state, 8% institutional, 3% external sources). *Receiving aid:* All full-time undergraduates: 49% (996). *Average award:* Undergraduates: $3154. *Scholarships, grants, and awards:* Federal Pell, FSEOG, state, college/university gift aid from institutional funds.

GIFT AID (NON-NEED-BASED) *Total amount:* $1,489,272 (14% federal, 75% institutional, 11% external sources). *Receiving aid:* Undergraduates: 40% (807). *Average award:* Undergraduates: $755. *Scholarships, grants, and awards by category:* Academic interests/achievement: biological sciences, business, computer science, education, humanities, mathematics, social sciences. Special achievements/activities: community service, general special achievements/activities, leadership. Special characteristics: 250 awards ($809,161 total): veterans, veterans' children. *Tuition waivers:* Full or partial for senior citizens.

LOANS *Student loans:* $16,842,838 (50% need-based, 50% non-need-based). *Average need-based loan:* Undergraduates: $4527. *Parent loans:* $5769 (100% non-need-based). *Programs:* Federal Direct (Subsidized and Unsubsidized Stafford, PLUS), Perkins, state.

WORK-STUDY *Federal work-study:* Total amount: $111,925; 55 jobs averaging $2619. *State or other work-study/employment:* Total amount: $36,746 (100% need-based). 17 part-time jobs averaging $2807.

APPLYING FOR FINANCIAL AID *Required financial aid form:* FAFSA. *Financial aid deadline (priority):* 5/1. *Notification date:* Continuous.

CONTACT Billy Satterfield, Executive Director of Student Financial Aid, University of Houston–Clear Lake, 2700 Bay Area Boulevard, Houston, TX 77058-1098, 281-283-2480. *Fax:* 281-283-2502. *E-mail:* satterfield@cl.uh.edu. *Website:* http://www.uhcl.edu/.

UNIVERSITY OF HOUSTON–DOWNTOWN
Houston, TX

ABOUT THE INSTITUTION State-supported, coed. *Awards:* bachelor's and master's degrees. 36 undergraduate majors. *Total enrollment:* 13,916. Undergraduates: 13,709. Freshmen: 1,442.

GIFT AID (NEED-BASED) *Scholarships, grants, and awards:* Federal Pell, FSEOG, state, private, college/university gift aid from institutional funds.

GIFT AID (NON-NEED-BASED) *Scholarships, grants, and awards by category:* Academic interests/achievement: business, general academic interests/achievements. Special achievements/activities: community service, general special achievements/activities, leadership. Special characteristics: general special characteristics.

LOANS *Programs:* Federal Direct (Subsidized and Unsubsidized Stafford, PLUS), state.
APPLYING FOR FINANCIAL AID *Required financial aid form:* FAFSA.
CONTACT Office of Scholarships and Financial Aid, University of Houston–Downtown, One Main Street, Houston, TX 77002, 713-221-8041. *Fax:* 713-221-8648. *E-mail:* uhdfinaid@uhd.edu.
Website: http://www.uhd.edu/.

UNIVERSITY OF HOUSTON–VICTORIA
Victoria, TX

ABOUT THE INSTITUTION State-supported, coed. *Awards:* certificates, bachelor's, and master's degrees. 18 undergraduate majors. *Total enrollment:* 4,335. Undergraduates: 2,664. Entering class: 14.
GIFT AID (NEED-BASED) *Scholarships, grants, and awards:* Federal Pell, FSEOG, state, private, college/university gift aid from institutional funds.
GIFT AID (NON-NEED-BASED) *Scholarships, grants, and awards by category:* Academic interests/achievement: biological sciences, business, communication, computer science, education, general academic interests/achievements, humanities, mathematics, social sciences. Special achievements/activities: community service, leadership, memberships.
LOANS *Programs:* Federal Direct (Subsidized and Unsubsidized Stafford, PLUS), state, college/university.
APPLYING FOR FINANCIAL AID *Required financial aid forms:* FAFSA, institution's own form.
CONTACT Carolyn Mallory, Financial Aid Director, University of Houston–Victoria, 3007 North Ben Wilson, Victoria, TX 77901-5731, 361-570-4131 or toll-free 877-970-4848 Ext. 110. *Fax:* 361-580-5555. *E-mail:* malloryc@uhv.edu.
Website: http://www.uhv.edu/.

UNIVERSITY OF IDAHO
Moscow, ID

Tuition & fees (ID res): $6212	Average undergraduate aid package: $13,347

ABOUT THE INSTITUTION State-supported, coed. *Awards:* certificates, bachelor's, master's, and doctoral degrees. 98 undergraduate majors. *Total enrollment:* 12,420. Undergraduates: 9,928. Freshmen: 1,617. Federal methodology is used as a basis for awarding need-based institutional aid.
UNDERGRADUATE EXPENSES for 2013–2014 *Application fee:* $50. *Tuition, state resident:* full-time $4230; part-time $253 per credit hour. *Tuition, nonresident:* full-time $17,018; part-time $892 per credit hour. *Required fees:* full-time $1982; $59 per credit hour. Full-time tuition and fees vary according to course load, degree level, program, and reciprocity agreements. Part-time tuition and fees vary according to course load, degree level, and program. *College room and board:* $7682. Room and board charges vary according to board plan and housing facility.
FRESHMAN FINANCIAL AID (Fall 2011) 1,400 applied for aid; of those 80% were deemed to have need. 99% of freshmen with need received aid; of those 36% had need fully met. *Average percent of need met:* 79% (excluding resources awarded to replace EFC). *Average financial aid package:* $13,554 (excluding resources awarded to replace EFC). 19% of all full-time freshmen had no need and received non-need-based gift aid.
UNDERGRADUATE FINANCIAL AID (Fall 2011) 6,857 applied for aid; of those 85% were deemed to have need. 98% of undergraduates with need received aid; of those 27% had need fully met. *Average percent of need met:* 75% (excluding resources awarded to replace EFC). *Average financial aid package:* $13,347 (excluding resources awarded to replace EFC). 18% of all full-time undergraduates had no need and received non-need-based gift aid.
GIFT AID (NEED-BASED) *Total amount:* $21,175,079 (85% federal, 1% state, 14% institutional). *Receiving aid:* Freshmen: 52% (828); all full-time undergraduates: 48% (4,098). *Average award:* Freshmen: $4681; Undergraduates: $4671. *Scholarships, grants, and awards:* Federal Pell, FSEOG, state, private, college/university gift aid from institutional funds.

GIFT AID (NON-NEED-BASED) *Total amount:* $11,153,029 (11% state, 70% institutional, 19% external sources). *Receiving aid:* Freshmen: 64% (1,031). Undergraduates: 58% (4,927). *Average award:* Freshmen: $4420. Undergraduates: $4996. *Scholarships, grants, and awards by category:* Academic interests/achievement: 1,902 awards ($4,704,633 total): agriculture, architecture, biological sciences, business, communication, computer science, education, engineering/technologies, English, foreign languages, general academic interests/achievements, home economics, humanities, library science, mathematics, military science, physical sciences, premedicine, social sciences. Creative arts/performance: 163 awards ($231,008 total): applied art and design, art/fine arts, creative writing, dance, general creative arts/performance, journalism/publications, music, performing arts, theater/drama. Special achievements/activities: 185 awards ($169,880 total): cheerleading/drum major, general special achievements/activities, junior miss, leadership, rodeo. Special characteristics: 3,124 awards ($16,383,948 total): children and siblings of alumni, children of faculty/staff, ethnic background, first-generation college students, general special characteristics, handicapped students, international students, local/state students, members of minority groups, out-of-state students, veterans. *Tuition waivers:* Full or partial for employees or children of employees, senior citizens. *ROTC:* Army, Naval, Air Force cooperative.
LOANS *Student loans:* $46,224,072 (49% need-based, 51% non-need-based). 66% of past graduating class borrowed through all loan programs. *Average indebtedness per student:* $26,809. *Average need-based loan:* Freshmen: $5573. Undergraduates: $7441. *Parent loans:* $9,856,378 (100% non-need-based). *Programs:* Federal Direct (Subsidized and Unsubsidized Stafford, PLUS), Perkins, college/university.
WORK-STUDY *Federal work-study:* Total amount: $684,152; 383 jobs averaging $1786. *State or other work-study/employment:* Total amount: $301,927 (100% need-based). 163 part-time jobs averaging $1852.
ATHLETIC AWARDS Total amount: $5,216,326 (100% non-need-based).
APPLYING FOR FINANCIAL AID *Required financial aid form:* FAFSA. *Financial aid deadline (priority):* 2/15. *Notification date:* Continuous beginning 3/30. Students must reply within 4 weeks of notification.
CONTACT Mr. Dan D. Davenport, Director of Student Financial Aid Services, University of Idaho, 875 Perimeter Drive, MS-4291, Moscow, ID 83844-4291, 208-885-6312 or toll-free 888-884-3246. *Fax:* 208-885-5592. *E-mail:* dand@uidaho.edu.
Website: http://www.uidaho.edu/.

UNIVERSITY OF ILLINOIS AT CHICAGO
Chicago, IL

Tuition & fees (IL res): $13,354	Average undergraduate aid package: $14,016

ABOUT THE INSTITUTION State-supported, coed. *Awards:* certificates, bachelor's, master's, and doctoral degrees. 86 undergraduate majors. *Total enrollment:* 28,875. Undergraduates: 16,678. Freshmen: 3,123. Federal methodology is used as a basis for awarding need-based institutional aid.
UNDERGRADUATE EXPENSES for 2013–2014 *Application fee:* $50. *Tuition, state resident:* full-time $10,406. *Tuition, nonresident:* full-time $22,796. *Required fees:* full-time $2948; $1193 per term. Full-time tuition and fees vary according to degree level and program. Part-time tuition and fees vary according to course load, degree level, and program. *College room and board:* $10,882; *Room only:* $7462. Room and board charges vary according to board plan and housing facility. *Payment plan:* Guaranteed tuition.
FRESHMAN FINANCIAL AID (Fall 2011) 2,772 applied for aid; of those 89% were deemed to have need. 94% of freshmen with need received aid; of those 12% had need fully met. *Average percent of need met:* 61% (excluding resources awarded to replace EFC). *Average financial aid package:* $14,065 (excluding resources awarded to replace EFC). 3% of all full-time freshmen had no need and received non-need-based gift aid.
UNDERGRADUATE FINANCIAL AID (Fall 2011) 12,832 applied for aid; of those 91% were deemed to have need. 96% of undergraduates with need received aid; of those 10% had need fully met. *Average percent of need met:* 63% (excluding resources awarded to replace EFC). *Average financial aid package:* $14,016 (excluding resources awarded to replace EFC). 3% of all full-time undergraduates had no need and received non-need-based gift aid.
GIFT AID (NEED-BASED) *Total amount:* $110,949,440 (33% federal, 28% state, 37% institutional, 2% external sources). *Receiving aid:* Freshmen: 64% (1,970);

all full-time undergraduates: 60% (9,232). *Average award:* Freshmen: $13,019; Undergraduates: $12,474. *Scholarships, grants, and awards:* Federal Pell, FSEOG, state, private, college/university gift aid from institutional funds.

GIFT AID (NON-NEED-BASED) *Total amount:* $1,539,558 (45% state, 34% institutional, 21% external sources). *Receiving aid:* Freshmen: 3% (77). Undergraduates: 1% (225). *Average award:* Freshmen: $2436. Undergraduates: $3800. *Scholarships, grants, and awards by category:* Academic interests/achievement: 1,380 awards ($2,158,871 total): architecture, business, general academic interests/achievements. *Creative arts/performance:* 199 awards ($591,648 total): applied art and design, art/fine arts, music, performing arts, theater/drama. *Tuition waivers:* Full or partial for employees or children of employees, senior citizens. *ROTC:* Army, Naval cooperative, Air Force cooperative.

LOANS *Student loans:* $66,974,113 (90% need-based, 10% non-need-based). 64% of past graduating class borrowed through all loan programs. *Average indebtedness per student:* $22,256. *Average need-based loan:* Freshmen: $3400. Undergraduates: $4568. *Parent loans:* $17,113,811 (83% need-based, 17% non-need-based). *Programs:* Federal Direct (Subsidized and Unsubsidized Stafford, PLUS), Perkins, Federal Nursing, college/university, private loans.

WORK-STUDY *Federal work-study:* Total amount: $1,849,331; 939 jobs averaging $2000. *State or other work-study/employment:* Total amount: $8,155,707 (80% need-based, 20% non-need-based). 2,808 part-time jobs averaging $2700.

ATHLETIC AWARDS Total amount: $3,640,182 (43% need-based, 57% non-need-based).

APPLYING FOR FINANCIAL AID *Required financial aid form:* FAFSA. *Financial aid deadline (priority):* 3/1. *Notification date:* Continuous beginning 3/15. Students must reply by 5/1.

CONTACT Deidre Rush, Associate Director of Financial Aid, University of Illinois at Chicago, 1200 West Harrison-M/C 334, Chicago, IL 60607-7128, 312-996-5563. *Fax:* 312-996-3385. *E-mail:* deidreb@uic.edu. *Website:* http://www.uic.edu/.

UNIVERSITY OF ILLINOIS AT SPRINGFIELD
Springfield, IL

Tuition & fees (IL res): $11,132	Average undergraduate aid package: $11,392

ABOUT THE INSTITUTION State-supported, coed. *Awards:* certificates, bachelor's, master's, and doctoral degrees. 23 undergraduate majors. *Total enrollment:* 5,048. Undergraduates: 3,054. Freshmen: 270. Federal methodology is used as a basis for awarding need-based institutional aid.

UNDERGRADUATE EXPENSES for 2013–2014 *Application fee:* $50. *Tuition, state resident:* full-time $9248; part-time $308.25 per credit hour. *Tuition, nonresident:* full-time $18,398; part-time $613.25 per credit hour. *Required fees:* full-time $1884. Full-time tuition and fees vary according to course load. Part-time tuition and fees vary according to course load. *College room and board:* $10,350; Room only: $7000. Room and board charges vary according to board plan and housing facility. *Payment plan:* Guaranteed tuition.

FRESHMAN FINANCIAL AID (Fall 2011) 220 applied for aid; of those 81% were deemed to have need. 100% of freshmen with need received aid; of those 17% had need fully met. *Average percent of need met:* 73% (excluding resources awarded to replace EFC). *Average financial aid package:* $12,194 (excluding resources awarded to replace EFC). 20% of all full-time freshmen had no need and received non-need-based gift aid.

UNDERGRADUATE FINANCIAL AID (Fall 2011) 1,703 applied for aid; of those 83% were deemed to have need. 99% of undergraduates with need received aid; of those 6% had need fully met. *Average percent of need met:* 66% (excluding resources awarded to replace EFC). *Average financial aid package:* $11,392 (excluding resources awarded to replace EFC). 14% of all full-time undergraduates had no need and received non-need-based gift aid.

GIFT AID (NEED-BASED) *Total amount:* $9,886,696 (44% federal, 35% state, 17% institutional, 4% external sources). *Receiving aid:* Freshmen: 70% (168); all full-time undergraduates: 59% (1,201). *Average award:* Freshmen: $9873; Undergraduates: $8473. *Scholarships, grants, and awards:* Federal Pell, FSEOG, state, private, college/university gift aid from institutional funds.

GIFT AID (NON-NEED-BASED) *Total amount:* $1,751,750 (13% federal, 39% state, 30% institutional, 18% external sources). *Receiving aid:* Freshmen: 16% (38). Undergraduates: 8% (167). *Average award:* Freshmen: $4152. Undergraduates: $5003. *Scholarships, grants, and awards by category:* Academic interests/achievement: general academic interests/achievements. *Creative arts/performance:* art/fine arts, music, theater/drama. *Special achievements/activities:* leadership. *Special characteristics:* children and siblings of alumni, ethnic background. *Tuition waivers:* Full or partial for employees or children of employees, senior citizens.

LOANS *Student loans:* $13,534,078 (89% need-based, 11% non-need-based). 67% of past graduating class borrowed through all loan programs. *Average indebtedness per student:* $21,057. *Average need-based loan:* Freshmen: $3192. Undergraduates: $4362. *Parent loans:* $1,889,100 (74% need-based, 26% non-need-based). *Programs:* Federal Direct (Subsidized and Unsubsidized Stafford, PLUS), Perkins, college/university.

WORK-STUDY *Federal work-study:* Total amount: $167,503; jobs available. *State or other work-study/employment:* Total amount: $1,243,351 (74% need-based, 26% non-need-based). Part-time jobs available.

ATHLETIC AWARDS Total amount: $702,215 (66% need-based, 34% non-need-based).

APPLYING FOR FINANCIAL AID *Required financial aid form:* FAFSA. *Financial aid deadline:* 11/15 (priority: 3/1). *Notification date:* Continuous beginning 1/1. Students must reply within 3 weeks of notification.

CONTACT Mr. Gerard Joseph, Director of Financial Assistance, University of Illinois at Springfield, One University Plaza, MS UHB 1015, Springfield, IL 62703-5407, 217-206-6724 or toll-free 888-977-4847. *Fax:* 217-206-7376. *E-mail:* finaid@uis.edu. *Website:* http://www.uis.edu/.

UNIVERSITY OF ILLINOIS AT URBANA–CHAMPAIGN
Champaign, IL

Tuition & fees (IL res): $15,338	Average undergraduate aid package: $13,533

ABOUT THE INSTITUTION State-supported, coed. *Awards:* certificates, bachelor's, master's, and doctoral degrees. 219 undergraduate majors. *Total enrollment:* 44,520. Undergraduates: 32,281. Freshmen: 6,921. Federal methodology is used as a basis for awarding need-based institutional aid.

UNDERGRADUATE EXPENSES for 2013–2014 *Application fee:* $50. *Tuition, state resident:* full-time $11,834. *Tuition, nonresident:* full-time $26,216. *Required fees:* full-time $3504. Full-time tuition and fees vary according to program and student level. *College room and board:* $10,636. Room and board charges vary according to board plan, housing facility, and location. *Payment plan:* Guaranteed tuition.

FRESHMAN FINANCIAL AID (Fall 2011) 5,173 applied for aid; of those 72% were deemed to have need. 95% of freshmen with need received aid; of those 33% need fully met. *Average percent of need met:* 66% (excluding resources awarded to replace EFC). *Average financial aid package:* $14,647 (excluding resources awarded to replace EFC). 12% of all full-time freshmen had no need and received non-need-based gift aid.

UNDERGRADUATE FINANCIAL AID (Fall 2011) 18,852 applied for aid; of those 79% were deemed to have need. 96% of undergraduates with need received aid; of those 27% had need fully met. *Average percent of need met:* 63% (excluding resources awarded to replace EFC). *Average financial aid package:* $13,533 (excluding resources awarded to replace EFC). 11% of all full-time undergraduates had no need and received non-need-based gift aid.

GIFT AID (NEED-BASED) *Total amount:* $112,487,119 (25% federal, 26% state, 43% institutional, 6% external sources). *Receiving aid:* Freshmen: 39% (2,863); all full-time undergraduates: 37% (11,301). *Average award:* Freshmen: $12,549; Undergraduates: $11,557. *Scholarships, grants, and awards:* Federal Pell, FSEOG, state, private, college/university gift aid from institutional funds, United Negro College Fund.

GIFT AID (NON-NEED-BASED) *Total amount:* $13,207,944 (5% federal, 3% state, 74% institutional, 18% external sources). *Receiving aid:* Freshmen: 8% (611). Undergraduates: 5% (1,411). *Average award:* Freshmen: $3980. Undergraduates: $4073. *Scholarships, grants, and awards by category:* Academic interests/achievement: agriculture, architecture, area/ethnic studies, biological sciences, business, communication, computer science, education, engineering/technologies, English, foreign languages, general academic interests/achievements, health fields, home economics, humanities, international studies, library science, mathematics, military science, physical sciences, premedicine, religion/biblical studies, social sciences. *Creative arts/performance:* applied art and design, art/fine arts, dance, general creative arts/performance, journalism/publications, music, performing arts, theater/drama. *Special achievements/activities:* general special achievements/activities, leadership. *Special characteristics:* children of faculty/staff, first-generation college students, general special characteristics, international students, local/state students, members of minority groups, veterans. **Tuition waivers:** Full or partial for employees or children of employees, senior citizens. **ROTC:** Army, Naval, Air Force.

LOANS *Student loans:* $105,666,069 (85% need-based, 15% non-need-based). 52% of past graduating class borrowed through all loan programs. *Average indebtedness per student:* $24,657. **Average need-based loan:** Freshmen: $4169. Undergraduates: $4588. **Parent loans:** $80,269,341 (78% need-based, 22% non-need-based). **Programs:** Federal Direct (Subsidized and Unsubsidized Stafford, PLUS), Perkins, college/university.

WORK-STUDY *Federal work-study:* Total amount: $2,659,996; jobs available. *State or other work-study/employment:* Total amount: $19,419,987 (56% need-based, 44% non-need-based). Part-time jobs available.

ATHLETIC AWARDS Total amount: $9,235,264 (34% need-based, 66% non-need-based).

APPLYING FOR FINANCIAL AID *Required financial aid form:* FAFSA. *Financial aid deadline (priority):* 3/15. *Notification date:* 3/15. Students must reply by 5/1 or within 3 weeks of notification.

CONTACT Daniel Mann, Director of Student Financial Aid, University of Illinois at Urbana–Champaign, Student Services Arcade Building, 620 East John Street, Champaign, IL 61820-5711, 217-333-0100. *Website:* http://www.illinois.edu/.

UNIVERSITY OF INDIANAPOLIS
Indianapolis, IN

Tuition & fees: $23,830	Average undergraduate aid package: $15,228

ABOUT THE INSTITUTION Independent United Methodist Church, coed. *Awards:* associate, bachelor's, master's, and doctoral degrees. 62 undergraduate majors. **Total enrollment:** 5,417. Undergraduates: 4,205. Freshmen: 794. Federal methodology is used as a basis for awarding need-based institutional aid.

UNDERGRADUATE EXPENSES for 2013–2014 *Application fee:* $25. *Comprehensive fee:* $32,920 includes full-time tuition ($23,590), mandatory fees ($240), and room and board ($9090). *College room only:* $4300. Room and board charges vary according to board plan and housing facility. *Part-time tuition:* $982 per credit hour. Part-time tuition and fees vary according to course load.

FRESHMAN FINANCIAL AID (Fall 2011) 752 applied for aid; of those 89% were deemed to have need. 100% of freshmen with need received aid; of those 11% had need fully met. *Average percent of need met:* 65% (excluding resources awarded to replace EFC). *Average financial aid package:* $16,536 (excluding resources awarded to replace EFC). 13% of all full-time freshmen had no need and received non-need-based gift aid.

UNDERGRADUATE FINANCIAL AID (Fall 2011) 3,493 applied for aid; of those 89% were deemed to have need. 98% of undergraduates with need received aid; of those 10% had need fully met. *Average percent of need met:* 60% (excluding resources awarded to replace EFC). *Average financial aid package:* $15,228 (excluding resources awarded to replace EFC). 12% of all full-time undergraduates had no need and received non-need-based gift aid.

GIFT AID (NEED-BASED) *Total amount:* $15,535,019 (44% federal, 36% state, 20% institutional). *Receiving aid:* Freshmen: 45% (360); all full-time undergraduates: 50% (2,056). *Average award:* Freshmen: $7967; Undergraduates: $7322. *Scholarships, grants, and awards:* Federal Pell, FSEOG, state, private, college/university gift aid from institutional funds.

GIFT AID (NON-NEED-BASED) *Total amount:* $19,832,051 (1% federal, 99% institutional). *Receiving aid:* Freshmen: 83% (661). Undergraduates: 53% (2,176). *Average award:* Freshmen: $9056. Undergraduates: $7746. *Scholarships, grants, and awards by category:* Academic interests/achievement: business, communication, general academic interests/achievements, health fields, physical sciences, religion/biblical studies. *Creative arts/performance:* art/fine arts, debating, music, theater/drama. *Special achievements/activities:* community service, religious involvement. *Special characteristics:* children of faculty/staff, international students, out-of-state students, relatives of clergy, religious affiliation, veterans. **Tuition waivers:** Full or partial for employees or children of employees. **ROTC:** Army cooperative.

LOANS *Student loans:* $42,075,776 (100% need-based). 79% of past graduating class borrowed through all loan programs. *Average indebtedness per student:* $32,495. **Average need-based loan:** Freshmen: $3613. Undergraduates: $4499. **Parent loans:** $7,123,930 (100% non-need-based). **Programs:** Federal Direct (Subsidized and Unsubsidized Stafford, PLUS), Perkins.

WORK-STUDY *Federal work-study:* Total amount: $267,709; jobs available. *State or other work-study/employment:* Total amount: $969,550 (100% need-based). Part-time jobs available.

ATHLETIC AWARDS Total amount: $4,460,252 (100% non-need-based).

APPLYING FOR FINANCIAL AID *Required financial aid forms:* FAFSA, institution's own form. *Financial aid deadline (priority):* 3/10. *Notification date:* Continuous beginning 3/1.

CONTACT Ms. Linda B. Handy, Director of Financial Aid, University of Indianapolis, 1400 East Hanna Avenue, Indianapolis, IN 46227-3697, 317-788-3217 or toll-free 800-232-8634 Ext. 3216. *Fax:* 317-788-6136. *E-mail:* handy@uindy.edu. *Website:* http://www.uindy.edu/.

THE UNIVERSITY OF IOWA
Iowa City, IA

Tuition & fees (IA res): $8061	Average undergraduate aid package: $11,836

ABOUT THE INSTITUTION State-supported, coed. *Awards:* certificates, bachelor's, master's, and doctoral degrees. 129 undergraduate majors. **Total enrollment:** 30,119. Undergraduates: 21,999. Freshmen: 4,470. Federal methodology is used as a basis for awarding need-based institutional aid.

UNDERGRADUATE EXPENSES for 2013–2014 *Application fee:* $40. *Tuition, state resident:* full-time $6678; part-time $279 per semester hour. *Tuition, nonresident:* full-time $25,548; part-time $1064 per semester hour. *Required fees:* full-time $1383; $72 per semester hour. Full-time tuition and fees vary according to course load, program, and student level. Part-time tuition and fees vary according to course load, program, and student level. *College room and board:* $9420. Room and board charges vary according to board plan and housing facility.

FRESHMAN FINANCIAL AID (Fall 2011) 3,355 applied for aid; of those 64% were deemed to have need. 98% of freshmen with need received aid; of those 29% had need fully met. *Average percent of need met:* 63% (excluding resources awarded to replace EFC). *Average financial aid package:* $12,603 (excluding resources awarded to replace EFC). 23% of all full-time freshmen had no need and received non-need-based gift aid.

UNDERGRADUATE FINANCIAL AID (Fall 2011) 12,822 applied for aid; of those 71% were deemed to have need. 99% of undergraduates with need received aid; of those 28% had need fully met. *Average percent of need met:* 63% (excluding resources awarded to replace EFC). *Average financial aid package:* $11,836 (excluding resources awarded to replace EFC). 36% of all full-time undergraduates had no need and received non-need-based gift aid.

GIFT AID (NEED-BASED) *Total amount:* $41,512,029 (37% federal, 4% state, 55% institutional, 4% external sources). *Receiving aid:* Freshmen: 31% (1,412); all full-time undergraduates: 30% (5,834). *Average award:* Freshmen: $6824; Undergraduates: $6568. *Scholarships, grants, and awards:* Federal Pell, FSEOG, state, private, college/university gift aid from institutional funds.

GIFT AID (NON-NEED-BASED) *Total amount:* $43,672,648 (7% federal, 1% state, 86% institutional, 6% external sources). *Receiving aid:* Freshmen: 28% (1,293). Undergraduates: 19% (3,700). *Average award:* Freshmen: $4388. Undergraduates: $4954. *Scholarships, grants, and awards by category:* Academic interests/achievement: business, engineering/technologies, general academic interests/achievements, military science. *Creative arts/performance:* general creative arts/performance, music. *Special achievements/activities:* general special achievements/activities, leadership. *Special characteristics:* children and siblings of alumni, ethnic background, first-generation college students, handicapped students, local/state students, out-of-state students, veterans. **ROTC:** Army, Air Force.

LOANS *Student loans:* $86,884,043 (55% need-based, 45% non-need-based). 55% of past graduating class borrowed through all loan programs. *Average indebtedness*

per student: $28,554. **Average need-based loan:** Freshmen: $4805. Undergraduates: $5474. **Parent loans:** $49,578,370 (100% non-need-based). **Programs:** Federal Direct (Subsidized and Unsubsidized Stafford, PLUS), Perkins, Federal Nursing, college/university.

WORK-STUDY *Federal work-study:* Total amount: $2,413,533; jobs available.

ATHLETIC AWARDS Total amount: $8,605,118 (100% non-need-based).

APPLYING FOR FINANCIAL AID *Required financial aid forms:* FAFSA, institution's own form. **Financial aid deadline:** Continuous. **Notification date:** Continuous beginning 3/15. Students must reply by 5/1 or within 2 weeks of notification.

CONTACT Mark Warner, Director of Student Financial Aid, The University of Iowa, 208 Calvin Hall, Iowa City, IA 52242, 319-335-3127 or toll-free 800-553-4692. *Website:* http://www.uiowa.edu/.

THE UNIVERSITY OF KANSAS
Lawrence, KS

Tuition & fees (KS res): $9678	Average undergraduate aid package: $8844

ABOUT THE INSTITUTION State-supported, coed. **Awards:** certificates, bachelor's, master's, and doctoral degrees (University of Kansas is a single institution with academic programs and facilities at two primary locations: Lawrence and Kansas City). 112 undergraduate majors. **Total enrollment:** 27,135. Undergraduates: 19,169. Freshmen: 3,771. Federal methodology is used as a basis for awarding need-based institutional aid.

UNDERGRADUATE EXPENSES for 2013–2014 Application fee: $30. **Tuition, state resident:** full-time $8790; part-time $293 per credit hour. **Tuition, nonresident:** full-time $22,860; part-time $762 per credit hour. **Required fees:** full-time $888; $74 per credit hour or $74 per credit hour. Full-time tuition and fees vary according to program, reciprocity agreements, and student level. Part-time tuition and fees vary according to program, reciprocity agreements, and student level. **College room and board:** $7258; **Room only:** $3804. Room and board charges vary according to board plan and housing facility. **Payment plan:** Guaranteed tuition.

FRESHMAN FINANCIAL AID (Fall 2011) 2,697 applied for aid; of those 66% were deemed to have need. 95% of freshmen with need received aid; of those 14% had need fully met. **Average percent of need met:** 54% (excluding resources awarded to replace EFC). **Average financial aid package:** $8933 (excluding resources awarded to replace EFC). 16% of all full-time freshmen had no need and received non-need-based gift aid.

UNDERGRADUATE FINANCIAL AID (Fall 2011) 11,283 applied for aid; of those 74% were deemed to have need. 97% of undergraduates with need received aid; of those 12% had need fully met. **Average percent of need met:** 55% (excluding resources awarded to replace EFC). **Average financial aid package:** $8844 (excluding resources awarded to replace EFC). 9% of all full-time undergraduates had no need and received non-need-based gift aid.

GIFT AID (NEED-BASED) Total amount: $28,760,189 (61% federal, 8% state, 31% institutional). **Receiving aid:** Freshmen: 32% (1,114); all full-time undergraduates: 31% (5,411). **Average award:** Freshmen: $5106; Undergraduates: $5013. **Scholarships, grants, and awards:** Federal Pell, FSEOG, state, private, college/university gift aid from institutional funds, Federal Nursing.

GIFT AID (NON-NEED-BASED) Total amount: $16,415,012 (1% state, 75% institutional, 24% external sources). **Receiving aid:** Freshmen: 22% (755). Undergraduates: 14% (2,396). **Average award:** Freshmen: $3470. Undergraduates: $3731. **Scholarships, grants, and awards by category:** *Academic interests/achievement:* architecture, area/ethnic studies, biological sciences, business, communication, computer science, education, engineering/technologies, English, foreign languages, general academic interests/achievements, health fields, humanities, international studies, mathematics, physical sciences, premedicine, religion/biblical studies, social sciences. *Creative arts/performance:* applied art and design, art/fine arts, cinema/film/broadcasting, creative writing, dance, debating, general creative arts/performance, journalism/publications, music, performing arts, theater/drama. *Special achievements/activities:* community service, general special achievements/activities, leadership. *Special characteristics:* adult students, children and siblings of alumni, children of faculty/staff, ethnic background, first-generation college students, general special characteristics, international students, local/state students, married students, members of minority groups, out-of-state students, previous college experience. **Tuition waivers:** Full or partial for employees or children of employees. **ROTC:** Army, Naval, Air Force.

LOANS *Student loans:* $71,147,329 (43% need-based, 57% non-need-based). 51% of past graduating class borrowed through all loan programs. *Average indebtedness per student:* $23,468. **Average need-based loan:** Freshmen: $3394. Undergraduates: $4380. **Parent loans:** $36,940,033 (100% non-need-based). **Programs:** Federal Direct (Subsidized and Unsubsidized Stafford, PLUS), Perkins, Federal Nursing, college/university.

WORK-STUDY *Federal work-study:* Total amount: $1,026,403; 404 jobs averaging $2416. **State or other work-study/employment:** Total amount: $151,801 (100% non-need-based). 40 part-time jobs averaging $3695.

ATHLETIC AWARDS Total amount: $8,241,567 (100% non-need-based).

APPLYING FOR FINANCIAL AID *Required financial aid form:* FAFSA. **Financial aid deadline (priority):** 3/1. **Notification date:** Continuous beginning 4/1. Students must reply within 4 weeks of notification.

CONTACT Ms. Brenda Maigaard, Assistant Vice Provost of Financial Aid and Scholarships, The University of Kansas, Strong Hall, Lawrence, KS 66045-7535, 785-864-4700 or toll-free 888-686-7323 (in-state). *Fax:* 785-864-5469. *E-mail:* financialaid@ku.edu. *Website:* http://www.ku.edu/.

UNIVERSITY OF KENTUCKY
Lexington, KY

ABOUT THE INSTITUTION State-supported, coed. **Awards:** certificates, bachelor's, master's, and doctoral degrees. 90 undergraduate majors. **Total enrollment:** 28,034. Undergraduates: 20,827. Freshmen: 4,647.

GIFT AID (NEED-BASED) Scholarships, grants, and awards: Federal Pell, FSEOG, state, private, college/university gift aid from institutional funds.

GIFT AID (NON-NEED-BASED) Scholarships, grants, and awards by category: *Academic interests/achievement:* agriculture, architecture, area/ethnic studies, biological sciences, business, communication, computer science, education, engineering/technologies, English, foreign languages, general academic interests/achievements, health fields, home economics, international studies, mathematics, military science, physical sciences. *Creative arts/performance:* applied art and design, art/fine arts, cinema/film/broadcasting, creative writing, dance, debating, general creative arts/performance, journalism/publications, music, performing arts, theater/drama. *Special achievements/activities:* cheerleading/drum major, general special achievements/activities, leadership. *Special characteristics:* adult students, children and siblings of alumni, children of educators, children of faculty/staff, children of public servants, children of union members/company employees, children of workers in trades, children with a deceased or disabled parent, ethnic background, first-generation college students, general special characteristics, handicapped students, international students, members of minority groups, public servants, spouses of deceased or disabled public servants, veterans, veterans' children.

LOANS *Programs:* Federal Direct (Subsidized and Unsubsidized Stafford, PLUS), Perkins, college/university.

APPLYING FOR FINANCIAL AID *Required financial aid form:* FAFSA.

CONTACT Ms. Lynda S. George, Director of Financial Aid, University of Kentucky, 128 Funkhouser Building, Lexington, KY 40506-0054, 859-257-3172 Ext. 241 or toll-free 866-900-GO-UK. *Fax:* 859-257-4398. *E-mail:* lgeorge@email.uky.edu. *Website:* http://www.uky.edu/.

UNIVERSITY OF LA VERNE
La Verne, CA

Tuition & fees: $35,000	Average undergraduate aid package: $27,750

ABOUT THE INSTITUTION Independent, coed. **Awards:** certificates, associate, bachelor's, master's, and doctoral degrees (also offers continuing education program with significant enrollment not reflected in profile). 47 undergraduate majors. **Total enrollment:** 4,973. Undergraduates: 2,499. Freshmen: 621. Federal methodology is used as a basis for awarding need-based institutional aid.

UNDERGRADUATE EXPENSES for 2013–2014 Application fee: $50. **Comprehensive fee:** $46,910 includes full-time tuition ($33,628), mandatory fees ($1372), and room and board ($11,910). **College room only:** $6100. Full-time tuition and fees vary according to degree level and location. Room and board charges vary according to board plan and housing facility. *Part-time tuition:* $979 per unit. Part-time tuition and fees vary according to degree level and location.

FRESHMAN FINANCIAL AID (Fall 2012, est.) 577 applied for aid; of those 94% were deemed to have need. 100% of freshmen with need received aid; of those 15% had need fully met. *Average percent of need met:* 39% (excluding resources awarded to replace EFC). *Average financial aid package:* $28,210 (excluding resources awarded to replace EFC). 10% of all full-time freshmen had no need and received non-need-based gift aid.

UNDERGRADUATE FINANCIAL AID (Fall 2012, est.) 2,164 applied for aid; of those 95% were deemed to have need. 100% of undergraduates with need received aid; of those 10% had need fully met. *Average percent of need met:* 49% (excluding resources awarded to replace EFC). *Average financial aid package:* $27,750 (excluding resources awarded to replace EFC). 11% of all full-time undergraduates had no need and received non-need-based gift aid.

GIFT AID (NEED-BASED) Total amount: $48,425,717 (12% federal, 17% state, 71% institutional). *Receiving aid:* Freshmen: 82% (505); all full-time undergraduates: 81% (1,940). *Average award:* Freshmen: $8622; Undergraduates: $11,716. *Scholarships, grants, and awards:* Federal Pell, FSEOG, state, private, college/university gift aid from institutional funds.

GIFT AID (NON-NEED-BASED) Total amount: $3,391,375 (100% institutional). *Receiving aid:* Freshmen: 87% (540). Undergraduates: 82% (1,966). *Average award:* Freshmen: $21,205. Undergraduates: $18,970. *Scholarships, grants, and awards by category: Academic interests/achievement:* general academic interests/achievements. *Creative arts/performance:* art/fine arts, cinema/film/broadcasting, journalism/publications, music, theater/drama. *Special achievements/activities:* community service, leadership. *Special characteristics:* children of faculty/staff, general special characteristics. *Tuition waivers:* Full or partial for employees or children of employees. *ROTC:* Army cooperative.

LOANS Student loans: $16,693,846 (97% need-based, 3% non-need-based). 78% of past graduating class borrowed through all loan programs. *Average indebtedness per student:* $30,566. *Average need-based loan:* Freshmen: $3767. Undergraduates: $4659. *Parent loans:* $4,718,957 (75% need-based, 25% non-need-based). *Programs:* Federal Direct (Subsidized and Unsubsidized Stafford), Perkins, college/university, alternative loans.

WORK-STUDY Federal work-study: Total amount: $489,762; jobs available. *State or other work-study/employment:* Part-time jobs available.

APPLYING FOR FINANCIAL AID Required financial aid forms: FAFSA, state aid form. *Financial aid deadline (priority):* 3/2. *Notification date:* Continuous beginning 4/1. Students must reply within 2 weeks of notification.

CONTACT Diane A. Anchundia , Director of Financial Aid, University of La Verne, 1950 3rd Street, La Verne, CA 91750-4443, 909-593-3511 Ext. 4180 or toll-free 800-876-4858. *Fax:* 909-392-2751. *E-mail:* finaid@laverne.edu. *Website:* http://www.laverne.edu/.

UNIVERSITY OF LOUISIANA AT LAFAYETTE
Lafayette, LA

Tuition & fees (LA res): $5374	Average undergraduate aid package: $7636

ABOUT THE INSTITUTION State-supported, coed. *Awards:* certificates, bachelor's, master's, and doctoral degrees. 60 undergraduate majors. *Total enrollment:* 16,687. Undergraduates: 15,143. Freshmen: 2,728. Federal methodology is used as a basis for awarding need-based institutional aid.

UNDERGRADUATE EXPENSES for 2013–2014 Application fee: $25. *Tuition, state resident:* full-time $3926; part-time $163.60 per credit hour. *Tuition, nonresident:* full-time $12,896; part-time $537.35 per credit hour. *Required fees:* full-time $1448. Full-time tuition and fees vary according to course load. Part-time tuition and fees vary according to course load. *College room and board:* $8102. Room and board charges vary according to board plan and housing facility.

FRESHMAN FINANCIAL AID (Fall 2011) 2,720 applied for aid; of those 65% were deemed to have need. 98% of freshmen with need received aid; of those 12% had need fully met. *Average percent of need met:* 62% (excluding resources awarded to replace EFC). *Average financial aid package:* $8073 (excluding resources awarded to replace EFC). 12% of all full-time freshmen had no need and received non-need-based gift aid.

UNDERGRADUATE FINANCIAL AID (Fall 2011) 10,446 applied for aid; of those 68% were deemed to have need. 97% of undergraduates with need received aid; of those 9% had need fully met. *Average percent of need met:* 55% (excluding resources awarded to replace EFC). *Average financial aid package:* $7636 (excluding resources awarded to replace EFC). 7% of all full-time undergraduates had no need and received non-need-based gift aid.

GIFT AID (NEED-BASED) Total amount: $23,980,351 (90% federal, 10% state). *Receiving aid:* Freshmen: 57% (1,664); all full-time undergraduates: 48% (6,248). *Average award:* Freshmen: $6560; Undergraduates: $5931. *Scholarships, grants, and awards:* Federal Pell, FSEOG, state, college/university gift aid from institutional funds.

GIFT AID (NON-NEED-BASED) Total amount: $25,463,909 (75% state, 22% institutional, 3% external sources). *Receiving aid:* Freshmen: 7% (205). Undergraduates: 5% (593). *Average award:* Freshmen: $2004. Undergraduates: $1851. *Scholarships, grants, and awards by category: Academic interests/achievement:* general academic interests/achievements. *Creative arts/performance:* general creative arts/performance. *Special achievements/activities:* general special achievements/activities. *ROTC:* Army.

LOANS Student loans: $34,861,191 (49% need-based, 51% non-need-based). *Average need-based loan:* Freshmen: $3143. Undergraduates: $3596. *Parent loans:* $2,176,553 (100% non-need-based). *Programs:* Federal Direct (Subsidized and Unsubsidized Stafford, PLUS), Perkins, Federal Nursing.

WORK-STUDY Federal work-study: Total amount: $845,006; jobs available. *State or other work-study/employment:* Total amount: $467,451 (100% non-need-based). Part-time jobs available.

ATHLETIC AWARDS Total amount: $2,754,589 (100% non-need-based).

APPLYING FOR FINANCIAL AID Required financial aid form: FAFSA. *Financial aid deadline (priority):* 5/1. *Notification date:* Continuous. Students must reply within 2 weeks of notification.

CONTACT Cindy S. Perez, Director of Financial Aid, University of Louisiana at Lafayette, PO Box 41206, Lafayette, LA 70504-1206, 337-482-6497 or toll-free 800-752-6553. *Fax:* 337-482-6502. *E-mail:* cperez@louisiana.edu. *Website:* http://www.louisiana.edu/.

UNIVERSITY OF LOUISIANA AT MONROE
Monroe, LA

CONTACT Ms. Teresa Smith, Director, Financial Aid, University of Louisiana at Monroe, 700 University Avenue, Monroe, LA 71209, 318-342-5320 or toll-free 800-372-5127. *Fax:* 318-342-3539. *E-mail:* tsmith@ulm.edu. *Website:* http://www.ulm.edu/.

UNIVERSITY OF LOUISVILLE
Louisville, KY

Tuition & fees (KY res): $9466	Average undergraduate aid package: $10,980

ABOUT THE INSTITUTION State-supported, coed. *Awards:* certificates, associate, bachelor's, master's, and doctoral degrees. 52 undergraduate majors. *Total enrollment:* 21,242. Undergraduates: 15,727. Freshmen: 2,705. Federal methodology is used as a basis for awarding need-based institutional aid.

UNDERGRADUATE EXPENSES for 2013–2014 Application fee: $40. *Tuition, state resident:* full-time $9466; part-time $395 per credit hour. *Tuition, nonresident:* full-time $22,950; part-time $957 per credit hour. Full-time tuition and fees vary according to reciprocity agreements. Part-time tuition and fees vary according to course load and reciprocity agreements. *College room and board:* $7570; *Room only:* $4650. Room and board charges vary according to board plan and housing facility.

FRESHMAN FINANCIAL AID (Fall 2012, est.) 2,283 applied for aid; of those 78% were deemed to have need. 99% of freshmen with need received aid; of those 25% had need fully met. *Average percent of need met:* 63% (excluding resources awarded to replace EFC). *Average financial aid package:* $11,720 (excluding resources awarded to replace EFC). 16% of all full-time freshmen had no need and received non-need-based gift aid.

UNDERGRADUATE FINANCIAL AID (Fall 2012, est.) 9,205 applied for aid; of those 84% were deemed to have need. 97% of undergraduates with need received aid; of those 20% had need fully met. *Average percent of need met:* 61% (excluding resources awarded to replace EFC). *Average financial aid package:* $10,980 (excluding resources awarded to replace EFC). 13% of all full-time undergraduates had no need and received non-need-based gift aid.
GIFT AID (NEED-BASED) *Total amount:* $55,590,066 (35% federal, 18% state, 36% institutional, 11% external sources). *Receiving aid:* Freshmen: 65% (1,711); all full-time undergraduates: 56% (6,767). *Average award:* Freshmen: $8873; Undergraduates: $8382. *Scholarships, grants, and awards:* Federal Pell, FSEOG, state, private, college/university gift aid from institutional funds.
GIFT AID (NON-NEED-BASED) *Total amount:* $24,679,708 (24% state, 61% institutional, 15% external sources). *Receiving aid:* Freshmen: 12% (314). Undergraduates: 7% (828). *Average award:* Freshmen: $7774. Undergraduates: $7569. *Scholarships, grants, and awards by category: Academic interests/ achievement:* biological sciences, business, education, engineering/technologies, English, foreign languages, general academic interests/achievements, health fields, mathematics, military science, premedicine. *Creative arts/performance:* art/fine arts, creative writing, dance, debating, general creative arts/performance, music, theater/drama. *Special achievements/activities:* cheerleading/drum major, community service, general special achievements/activities, hobbies/interests, junior miss, leadership, memberships. *Special characteristics:* adult students, children and siblings of alumni, children of faculty/staff, children of union members/company employees, children with a deceased or disabled parent, ethnic background, general special characteristics, local/state students, members of minority groups, out-of-state students, previous college experience, veterans, veterans' children. *Tuition waivers:* Full or partial for employees or children of employees, senior citizens. *ROTC:* Army, Air Force.
LOANS *Student loans:* $50,557,411 (76% need-based, 24% non-need-based). 53% of past graduating class borrowed through all loan programs. *Average indebtedness per student:* $19,886. *Average need-based loan:* Freshmen: $3328. Undergraduates: $4085. *Parent loans:* $5,694,077 (32% need-based, 68% non-need-based). *Programs:* Federal Direct (Subsidized and Unsubsidized Stafford, PLUS), Perkins, Federal Nursing.
WORK-STUDY *Federal work-study:* Total amount: $1,306,909; 444 jobs averaging $2972.
ATHLETIC AWARDS Total amount: $9,569,248 (37% need-based, 63% non-need-based).
APPLYING FOR FINANCIAL AID *Required financial aid form:* FAFSA. *Financial aid deadline (priority):* 3/15. *Notification date:* Continuous beginning 4/1. Students must reply by 5/1.
CONTACT Ms. Patricia O. Arauz, Director of Financial Aid, University of Louisville, 2301 South Third Street, Louisville, KY 40292-0001, 502-852-6145 or toll-free 800-334-8635. Fax: 502-852-0182. *E-mail:* finaid@louisville.edu. *Website:* http://www.louisville.edu/.

UNIVERSITY OF MAINE
Orono, ME

Tuition & fees (ME res): $10,588	Average undergraduate aid package: $14,973

ABOUT THE INSTITUTION State-supported, coed. *Awards:* certificates, bachelor's, master's, and doctoral degrees. 104 undergraduate majors. *Total enrollment:* 11,168. Undergraduates: 8,911. Freshmen: 1,785. Federal methodology is used as a basis for awarding need-based institutional aid.
UNDERGRADUATE EXPENSES for 2013-2014 *Application fee:* $40. *Tuition, state resident:* full-time $8370; part-time $279 per credit. *Tuition, non-resident:* full-time $24,090; part-time $803 per credit. *Required fees:* full-time $2218. Full-time tuition and fees vary according to course load and program. Part-time tuition and fees vary according to course load and program. *College room and board:* $8644. Room and board charges vary according to board plan and housing facility.
FRESHMAN FINANCIAL AID (Fall 2012, est.) 1,769 applied for aid; of those 83% were deemed to have need. 100% of freshmen with need received aid; of those 14% had need fully met. *Average percent of need met:* 81% (excluding resources awarded to replace EFC). *Average financial aid package:* $15,867 (excluding resources awarded to replace EFC). 9% of all full-time freshmen had no need and received non-need-based gift aid.

UNDERGRADUATE FINANCIAL AID (Fall 2012, est.) 6,258 applied for aid; of those 85% were deemed to have need. 100% of undergraduates with need received aid; of those 14% had need fully met. *Average percent of need met:* 80% (excluding resources awarded to replace EFC). *Average financial aid package:* $14,973 (excluding resources awarded to replace EFC). 5% of all full-time undergraduates had no need and received non-need-based gift aid.
GIFT AID (NEED-BASED) *Total amount:* $35,971,879 (42% federal, 8% state, 43% institutional, 7% external sources). *Receiving aid:* Freshmen: 70% (1,355); all full-time undergraduates: 60% (4,496). *Average award:* Freshmen: $8582; Undergraduates: $7353. *Scholarships, grants, and awards:* Federal Pell, FSEOG, state, private, college/university gift aid from institutional funds, Academic Competitiveness Grants, National SMART Grants.
GIFT AID (NON-NEED-BASED) *Total amount:* $2,994,521 (1% state, 71% institutional, 28% external sources). *Receiving aid:* Freshmen: 4% (85). Undergraduates: 3% (225). *Average award:* Freshmen: $3940. Undergraduates: $4254. *Scholarships, grants, and awards by category: Academic interests/achievement:* general academic interests/achievements. *Creative arts/performance:* art/fine arts, general creative arts/performance. *Special achievements/activities:* leadership. *Special characteristics:* children and siblings of alumni, local/state students, members of minority groups. *Tuition waivers:* Full or partial for employees or children of employees, senior citizens. *ROTC:* Army, Naval cooperative.
LOANS *Student loans:* $54,079,236 (73% need-based, 27% non-need-based). 78% of past graduating class borrowed through all loan programs. *Average indebtedness per student:* $32,438. *Average need-based loan:* Freshmen: $3718. Undergraduates: $4407. *Parent loans:* $5,371,455 (42% need-based, 58% non-need-based). *Programs:* Federal Direct (Subsidized and Unsubsidized Stafford, PLUS), Perkins, state, college/university, private loans.
WORK-STUDY *Federal work-study:* Total amount: $2,600,484; 1,162 jobs averaging $2612.
ATHLETIC AWARDS Total amount: $5,874,168 (92% need-based, 8% non-need-based).
APPLYING FOR FINANCIAL AID *Required financial aid form:* FAFSA. *Financial aid deadline (priority):* 3/1. *Notification date:* Continuous beginning 3/15.
CONTACT Ms. Gianna Marrs, Interim Director of Student Financial Aid, University of Maine, 5781 Wingate Hall, Orono, ME 04469-5781, 207-581-1324 or toll-free 877-486-2364. Fax: 207-581-3261.
Website: http://www.umaine.edu/.

UNIVERSITY OF MAINE AT AUGUSTA
Augusta, ME

Tuition & fees (ME res): $7448	Average undergraduate aid package: $9322

ABOUT THE INSTITUTION State-supported, coed. *Awards:* certificates, associate, and bachelor's degrees (also offers some graduate courses and continuing education programs with significant enrollment not reflected in profile). 21 undergraduate majors. *Total enrollment:* 4,974. Undergraduates: 4,943. Freshmen: 583. Federal methodology is used as a basis for awarding need-based institutional aid.
UNDERGRADUATE EXPENSES for 2013-2014 *Application fee:* $40. *Tuition, state resident:* full-time $6510; part-time $217 per credit hour. *Tuition, nonresident:* full-time $15,750; part-time $525 per credit hour. *Required fees:* full-time $938; $31.25 per credit hour. Full-time tuition and fees vary according to course load, location, program, and reciprocity agreements. Part-time tuition and fees vary according to course load, location, program, and reciprocity agreements.
FRESHMAN FINANCIAL AID (Fall 2012, est.) 301 applied for aid; of those 91% were deemed to have need. 98% of freshmen with need received aid; of those 3% had need fully met. *Average percent of need met:* 59% (excluding resources awarded to replace EFC). *Average financial aid package:* $8026 (excluding resources awarded to replace EFC).
UNDERGRADUATE FINANCIAL AID (Fall 2012, est.) 1,858 applied for aid; of those 94% were deemed to have need. 98% of undergraduates with need received aid; of those 4% had need fully met. *Average percent of need met:* 60% (excluding resources awarded to replace EFC). *Average financial aid package:* $9322 (excluding resources awarded to replace EFC).
GIFT AID (NEED-BASED) *Total amount:* $15,014,101 (79% federal, 13% state, 8% institutional). *Receiving aid:* Freshmen: 73% (237); all full-time undergraduates:

74% (1,494). *Average award:* Freshmen: $5816; Undergraduates: $6091. *Scholarships, grants, and awards:* Federal Pell, FSEOG, state, private, college/university gift aid from institutional funds.

GIFT AID (NON-NEED-BASED) *Receiving aid:* Freshmen: 1. Undergraduates: 1% (12). *Scholarships, grants, and awards by category: Academic interests/ achievement:* biological sciences, business, general academic interests/achievements, mathematics. *Creative arts/performance:* music. *Special achievements/activities:* general special achievements/activities, leadership. *Special characteristics:* children of faculty/staff, ethnic background, international students, local/state students, veterans' children. *Tuition waivers:* Full or partial for minority students, employees or children of employees, senior citizens. *ROTC:* Army cooperative, Naval cooperative, Air Force cooperative.

LOANS *Student loans:* $23,833,615 (86% need-based, 14% non-need-based). 76% of past graduating class borrowed through all loan programs. *Average indebtedness per student:* $24,353. *Average need-based loan:* Freshmen: $6156. Undergraduates: $7187. *Parent loans:* $47,805 (38% need-based, 62% non-need-based). *Programs:* Federal Direct (Subsidized and Unsubsidized Stafford, PLUS), Perkins, Federal Nursing.

WORK-STUDY *Federal work-study:* Total amount: $356,723; jobs available. *State or other work-study/employment:* Total amount: $50,000 (100% non-need-based). Part-time jobs available.

ATHLETIC AWARDS Total amount: $30,365 (72% need-based, 28% non-need-based).

APPLYING FOR FINANCIAL AID *Required financial aid form:* FAFSA. *Financial aid deadline (priority):* 3/1. *Notification date:* Continuous beginning 3/15. Students must reply within 2 weeks of notification.

CONTACT Financial Aid Office, University of Maine at Augusta, 46 University Drive, Augusta, ME 04330-9410, 207-621-3185 or toll-free 877-862-1234 Ext. 3185 (in-state), 877-862-1234 (out-of-state). *Fax:* 207-621-3116. *E-mail:* umafa@maine.edu. *Website:* http://www.uma.maine.edu/.

UNIVERSITY OF MAINE AT FARMINGTON
Farmington, ME

Tuition & fees (ME res): $9137	Average undergraduate aid package: $10,348

ABOUT THE INSTITUTION State-supported, coed. *Awards:* certificates, bachelor's, and master's degrees. 39 undergraduate majors. *Total enrollment:* 2,180. Undergraduates: 2,029. Freshmen: 424. Federal methodology is used as a basis for awarding need-based institutional aid.

UNDERGRADUATE EXPENSES for 2013–2014 *Application fee:* $40. *Tuition, state resident:* full-time $8352; part-time $261 per credit hour. *Tuition, nonresident:* full-time $17,440; part-time $545 per credit hour. *Required fees:* full-time $785. Full-time tuition and fees vary according to course load, reciprocity agreements, and student level. Part-time tuition and fees vary according to course load, reciprocity agreements, and student level. *College room and board:* $8454; *Room only:* $4500. Room and board charges vary according to board plan and housing facility.

FRESHMAN FINANCIAL AID (Fall 2011) 452 applied for aid; of those 90% were deemed to have need. 100% of freshmen with need received aid; of those 7% had need fully met. *Average percent of need met:* 65% (excluding resources awarded to replace EFC). *Average financial aid package:* $10,735 (excluding resources awarded to replace EFC). 6% of all full-time freshmen had no need and received non-need-based gift aid.

UNDERGRADUATE FINANCIAL AID (Fall 2011) 1,751 applied for aid; of those 89% were deemed to have need. 100% of undergraduates with need received aid; of those 9% had need fully met. *Average percent of need met:* 65% (excluding resources awarded to replace EFC). *Average financial aid package:* $10,348 (excluding resources awarded to replace EFC). 3% of all full-time undergraduates had no need and received non-need-based gift aid.

GIFT AID (NEED-BASED) *Total amount:* $8,657,817 (50% federal, 10% state, 30% institutional, 10% external sources). *Receiving aid:* Freshmen: 78% (356); all full-time undergraduates: 72% (1,290). *Average award:* Freshmen: $7806; Undergraduates: $6383. *Scholarships, grants, and awards:* Federal Pell, FSEOG, state, private, college/university gift aid from institutional funds.

GIFT AID (NON-NEED-BASED) *Total amount:* $177,871 (50% institutional, 50% external sources). *Receiving aid:* Freshmen: 54% (246). Undergraduates: 34% (606). *Average award:* Freshmen: $2284. Undergraduates: $2431. *Scholarships, grants, and awards by category: Academic interests/achievement:* general academic interests/achievements. *Special characteristics:* children of faculty/staff, members of minority groups, out-of-state students, veterans' children. *Tuition waivers:* Full or partial for minority students, employees or children of employees, senior citizens.

LOANS *Student loans:* $13,487,055 (83% need-based, 17% non-need-based). 87% of past graduating class borrowed through all loan programs. *Average indebtedness per student:* $26,319. *Average need-based loan:* Freshmen: $5835. Undergraduates: $7275. *Parent loans:* $1,619,854 (60% need-based, 40% non-need-based). *Programs:* Federal Direct (Subsidized and Unsubsidized Stafford, PLUS), Perkins, state, college/university, Educators For Maine Loans.

WORK-STUDY *Federal work-study:* Total amount: $782,543; jobs available. *State or other work-study/employment:* Total amount: $257,401 (83% need-based, 17% non-need-based). Part-time jobs available.

APPLYING FOR FINANCIAL AID *Required financial aid form:* FAFSA. *Financial aid deadline (priority):* 3/1. *Notification date:* Continuous beginning 3/15. Students must reply within 2 weeks of notification.

CONTACT Mr. Ronald P. Milliken, Director of Financial Aid, University of Maine at Farmington, 224 Main Street, Farmington, ME 04938-1990, 207-778-7105. *Fax:* 207-778-8178. *E-mail:* milliken@maine.edu. *Website:* http://www.umf.maine.edu/.

UNIVERSITY OF MAINE AT FORT KENT
Fort Kent, ME

Tuition & fees (ME res): $7575	Average undergraduate aid package: $9636

ABOUT THE INSTITUTION State-supported, coed. *Awards:* certificates, associate, and bachelor's degrees. 25 undergraduate majors. *Total enrollment:* 1,169. Undergraduates: 1,169. Freshmen: 181. Both federal and institutional methodology are used as a basis for awarding need-based institutional aid.

UNDERGRADUATE EXPENSES for 2013–2014 *Application fee:* $40. *Tuition, state resident:* full-time $6600; part-time $220 per credit hour. *Tuition, nonresident:* full-time $16,560; part-time $552 per credit hour. *Required fees:* full-time $975; $32.50 per credit hour. Full-time tuition and fees vary according to course load and reciprocity agreements. Part-time tuition and fees vary according to reciprocity agreements. *College room and board:* $7400; *Room only:* $4000. Room and board charges vary according to board plan and housing facility.

FRESHMAN FINANCIAL AID (Fall 2011) 126 applied for aid; of those 87% were deemed to have need. 100% of freshmen with need received aid; of those 17% had need fully met. *Average percent of need met:* 69% (excluding resources awarded to replace EFC). *Average financial aid package:* $9829 (excluding resources awarded to replace EFC). 6% of all full-time freshmen had no need and received non-need-based gift aid.

UNDERGRADUATE FINANCIAL AID (Fall 2011) 442 applied for aid; of those 91% were deemed to have need. 100% of undergraduates with need received aid; of those 14% had need fully met. *Average percent of need met:* 68% (excluding resources awarded to replace EFC). *Average financial aid package:* $9636 (excluding resources awarded to replace EFC). 4% of all full-time undergraduates had no need and received non-need-based gift aid.

GIFT AID (NEED-BASED) *Total amount:* $2,852,910 (53% federal, 11% state, 31% institutional, 5% external sources). *Receiving aid:* Freshmen: 65% (90); all full-time undergraduates: 74% (357). *Average award:* Freshmen: $7062; Undergraduates: $5958. *Scholarships, grants, and awards:* Federal Pell, FSEOG, state, private, college/university gift aid from institutional funds, Federal Nursing.

GIFT AID (NON-NEED-BASED) *Total amount:* $46,417 (1% state, 65% institutional, 34% external sources). *Receiving aid:* Freshmen: 50% (69). Undergraduates: 35% (169). *Average award:* Freshmen: $2613. Undergraduates: $1865. *Scholarships, grants, and awards by category: Academic interests/achievement:* biological sciences, business, communication, computer science, education, English, foreign languages, general academic interests/achievements, health fields, humanities, mathematics, social sciences. *Creative arts/performance:* general creative arts/performance, performing arts. *Special achievements/activities:* general

special achievements/activities. *Special characteristics:* adult students, children of faculty/staff, general special characteristics, international students, members of minority groups.
LOANS *Student loans:* $3,759,147 (85% need-based, 15% non-need-based). 56% of past graduating class borrowed through all loan programs. *Average indebtedness per student:* $21,911. *Average need-based loan:* Freshmen: $5532. Undergraduates: $7005. *Parent loans:* $130,681 (50% need-based, 50% non-need-based). *Programs:* Federal Direct (Subsidized and Unsubsidized Stafford, PLUS), Perkins, Federal Nursing, state, college/university.
WORK-STUDY *Federal work-study:* Total amount: $274,535; 150 jobs averaging $1700. *State or other work-study/employment:* Part-time jobs available.
APPLYING FOR FINANCIAL AID *Required financial aid forms:* FAFSA, institution's own form, CSS Financial Aid PROFILE, state aid form. *Financial aid deadline (priority):* 3/1. *Notification date:* Continuous beginning 3/1.
CONTACT Elizabeth Violette, Associate Director of Financial Aid, University of Maine at Fort Kent, 23 University Drive, Fort Kent, ME 04743-1292, 207-834-7607 or toll-free 888-TRY-UMFK. *Fax:* 207-834-7841. *E-mail:* elizabeth.r.violette@maine.edu. *Website:* http://www.umfk.maine.edu/.

UNIVERSITY OF MAINE AT MACHIAS
Machias, ME

CONTACT Ms. Stephanie Larrabee, Director of Financial Aid, University of Maine at Machias, 9 O'Brien Avenue, Machias, ME 04654, 207-255-1203 or toll-free 888-GOTOUMM (in-state), 888-468-6866 (out-of-state). *Fax:* 207-255-4864. *Website:* http://umm.maine.edu/.

UNIVERSITY OF MAINE AT PRESQUE ISLE
Presque Isle, ME

Tuition & fees (ME res): $7435	Average undergraduate aid package: $10,832

ABOUT THE INSTITUTION State-supported, coed. *Awards:* certificates, associate, and bachelor's degrees. 26 undergraduate majors. *Total enrollment:* 1,453. Undergraduates: 1,453. Freshmen: 197. Federal methodology is used as a basis for awarding need-based institutional aid.
UNDERGRADUATE EXPENSES for 2013–2014 *Application fee:* $40. *Tuition, state resident:* full-time $6600; part-time $220 per credit. *Tuition, non-resident:* full-time $16,560; part-time $552 per credit. *Required fees:* full-time $835; $18 per credit or $51.25 per term. Full-time tuition and fees vary according to course load, location, and reciprocity agreements. Part-time tuition and fees vary according to course load, location, and reciprocity agreements. *College room and board:* $7422; *Room only:* $4240. Room and board charges vary according to board plan and housing facility.
FRESHMAN FINANCIAL AID (Fall 2012, est.) 164 applied for aid; of those 89% were deemed to have need. 100% of freshmen with need received aid; of those 34% had need fully met. *Average percent of need met:* 83% (excluding resources awarded to replace EFC). *Average financial aid package:* $11,133 (excluding resources awarded to replace EFC). 6% of all full-time freshmen had no need and received non-need-based gift aid.
UNDERGRADUATE FINANCIAL AID (Fall 2012, est.) 645 applied for aid; of those 92% were deemed to have need. 100% of undergraduates with need received aid; of those 29% had need fully met. *Average percent of need met:* 80% (excluding resources awarded to replace EFC). *Average financial aid package:* $10,832 (excluding resources awarded to replace EFC). 4% of all full-time undergraduates had no need and received non-need-based gift aid.
GIFT AID (NEED-BASED) *Total amount:* $4,421,276 (62% federal, 10% state, 18% institutional, 10% external sources). *Receiving aid:* Freshmen: 81% (137); all full-time undergraduates: 81% (559). *Average award:* Freshmen: $7559; Undergraduates: $6428. *Scholarships, grants, and awards:* Federal Pell, FSEOG, state, private, college/university gift aid from institutional funds.
GIFT AID (NON-NEED-BASED) *Total amount:* $130,567 (74% institutional, 26% external sources). *Receiving aid:* Freshmen: 65% (110). Undergraduates: 37%

(257). *Average award:* Freshmen: $2709. Undergraduates: $2740. *Scholarships, grants, and awards by category: Academic interests/achievement:* general academic interests/achievements. *Special achievements/activities:* community service. *Special characteristics:* children of faculty/staff, ethnic background, international students, local/state students, out-of-state students, veterans' children. *Tuition waivers:* Full or partial for minority students, employees or children of employees, senior citizens.
LOANS *Student loans:* $4,045,692 (85% need-based, 15% non-need-based). 75% of past graduating class borrowed through all loan programs. *Average indebtedness per student:* $18,052. *Average need-based loan:* Freshmen: $4674. Undergraduates: $5461. *Parent loans:* $64,935 (38% need-based, 62% non-need-based). *Programs:* Federal Direct (Subsidized and Unsubsidized Stafford, PLUS), Perkins, state, college/university.
WORK-STUDY *Federal work-study:* Total amount: $664,193; 265 jobs averaging $2406.
APPLYING FOR FINANCIAL AID *Required financial aid form:* FAFSA. *Financial aid deadline (priority):* 4/1. *Notification date:* Continuous beginning 3/1. Students must reply within 2 weeks of notification.
CONTACT Christopher A.R. Bell, Director of Financial Aid, University of Maine at Presque Isle, 181 Main Street, Presque Isle, ME 04769-2888, 207-768-9511. *Fax:* 207-768-9509. *E-mail:* chris@maine.edu. *Website:* http://www.umpi.edu/.

UNIVERSITY OF MANAGEMENT AND TECHNOLOGY
Arlington, VA

Tuition & fees: N/R	Average undergraduate aid package: N/A

ABOUT THE INSTITUTION Proprietary, coed. 5 undergraduate majors. Both federal and institutional methodology are used as a basis for awarding need-based institutional aid.
FRESHMAN FINANCIAL AID (Fall 2011) 6 applied for aid; of those 100% were deemed to have need. 100% of freshmen with need received aid; of those 100% had need fully met. *Average percent of need met:* 100% (excluding resources awarded to replace EFC).
UNDERGRADUATE FINANCIAL AID (Fall 2011) 33 applied for aid; of those 100% were deemed to have need. 100% of undergraduates with need received aid; of those 100% had need fully met. *Average percent of need met:* 100% (excluding resources awarded to replace EFC).
GIFT AID (NEED-BASED) *Total amount:* $45,913 (100% federal). *Receiving aid:* Freshmen: 100% (6); all full-time undergraduates: 62% (25). *Scholarships, grants, and awards:* Federal Pell.
GIFT AID (NON-NEED-BASED) *Total amount:* $18,425 (100% federal). *Receiving aid:* Freshmen: 67% (4). Undergraduates: 80% (32).
LOANS *Student loans:* $168,210 (46% need-based, 54% non-need-based). *Programs:* Federal Direct (Subsidized and Unsubsidized Stafford, PLUS).
APPLYING FOR FINANCIAL AID *Required financial aid form:* FAFSA. *Financial aid deadline:* Continuous. *Notification date:* Continuous.
CONTACT Margo Jacobs, Financial Aid Administrator, University of Management and Technology, 1901 North Fort Myer Drive, Arlington, VA 22209, 703-516-0035 Ext. 2014 or toll-free 800-924-4883. *Fax:* 703-516-0985. *E-mail:* info@umtweb.edu. *Website:* http://www.umtweb.edu/.

UNIVERSITY OF MARY
Bismarck, ND

Tuition & fees: $13,600	Average undergraduate aid package: $10,765

ABOUT THE INSTITUTION Independent Roman Catholic, coed. *Awards:* bachelor's, master's, and doctoral degrees. 47 undergraduate majors. *Total enrollment:* 3,135. Undergraduates: 2,130. Freshmen: 374. Federal methodology is used as a basis for awarding need-based institutional aid.

UNDERGRADUATE EXPENSES for 2013–2014 *Application fee:* $25. *Comprehensive fee:* $19,890 includes full-time tuition ($13,600) and room and board ($6290). *College room only:* $3330. Full-time tuition and fees vary according to course load, degree level, and program. Room and board charges vary according to board plan and housing facility. Part-time tuition and fees vary according to course load, degree level, and program.

FRESHMAN FINANCIAL AID (Fall 2011) 335 applied for aid; of those 80% were deemed to have need. 100% of freshmen with need received aid; of those 48% had need fully met. *Average percent of need met:* 84% (excluding resources awarded to replace EFC). *Average financial aid package:* $11,870 (excluding resources awarded to replace EFC). 26% of all full-time freshmen had no need and received non-need-based gift aid.

UNDERGRADUATE FINANCIAL AID (Fall 2011) 1,435 applied for aid; of those 82% were deemed to have need. 100% of undergraduates with need received aid; of those 21% had need fully met. *Average percent of need met:* 66% (excluding resources awarded to replace EFC). *Average financial aid package:* $10,765 (excluding resources awarded to replace EFC). 27% of all full-time undergraduates had no need and received non-need-based gift aid.

GIFT AID (NEED-BASED) *Total amount:* $9,557,976 (26% federal, 10% state, 59% institutional, 5% external sources). *Receiving aid:* Freshmen: 54% (201); all full-time undergraduates: 50% (814). *Average award:* Freshmen: $4124; Undergraduates: $3790. *Scholarships, grants, and awards:* Federal Pell, FSEOG, state, private, college/university gift aid from institutional funds, TEACH Grants.

GIFT AID (NON-NEED-BASED) *Receiving aid:* Freshmen: 72% (266). Undergraduates: 64% (1,052). *Average award:* Freshmen: $4957. Undergraduates: $4079. *Scholarships, grants, and awards by category: Academic interests/achievement:* 1,362 awards ($4,199,156 total): general academic interests/achievements. *Creative arts/performance:* 62 awards ($87,425 total): music. *Special achievements/activities:* 231 awards ($1,807,340 total): general special achievements/activities. *Special characteristics:* 430 awards ($1,320,748 total): children of faculty/staff, general special characteristics, local/state students, religious affiliation, veterans. *Tuition waivers:* Full or partial for employees or children of employees, senior citizens.

LOANS *Student loans:* $12,512,880 (100% need-based). 81% of past graduating class borrowed through all loan programs. *Average indebtedness per student:* $28,970. *Average need-based loan:* Freshmen: $3189. Undergraduates: $4237. *Parent loans:* $419,236 (100% need-based). *Programs:* Federal Direct (Subsidized and Unsubsidized Stafford, PLUS), Perkins, Federal Nursing, private loans.

WORK-STUDY *Federal work-study:* Total amount: $201,033; 77 jobs averaging $1006. *State or other work-study/employment:* Total amount: $90,468 (100% need-based). 9 part-time jobs averaging $581.

ATHLETIC AWARDS Total amount: $1,724,893 (100% need-based).

APPLYING FOR FINANCIAL AID *Financial aid deadline:* Continuous. *Notification date:* Continuous beginning 3/1. Students must reply within 2 weeks of notification.

CONTACT Brenda Zastoupil, Financial Assistance Director, University of Mary, 7500 University Drive, Bismarck, ND 58504-9652, 701-355-8244 or toll-free 800-288-6279. *Fax:* 701-255-7687. *E-mail:* brendaz@umary.edu. *Website:* http://www.umary.edu/.

FRESHMAN FINANCIAL AID (Fall 2012, est.) 539 applied for aid; of those 88% were deemed to have need. 100% of freshmen with need received aid; of those 7% had need fully met. *Average percent of need met:* 64% (excluding resources awarded to replace EFC). *Average financial aid package:* $17,429 (excluding resources awarded to replace EFC). 15% of all full-time freshmen had no need and received non-need-based gift aid.

UNDERGRADUATE FINANCIAL AID (Fall 2012, est.) 2,355 applied for aid; of those 92% were deemed to have need. 100% of undergraduates with need received aid; of those 8% had need fully met. *Average percent of need met:* 58% (excluding resources awarded to replace EFC). *Average financial aid package:* $15,419 (excluding resources awarded to replace EFC). 13% of all full-time undergraduates had no need and received non-need-based gift aid.

GIFT AID (NEED-BASED) *Total amount:* $25,032,811 (21% federal, 14% state, 63% institutional, 2% external sources). *Receiving aid:* Freshmen: 84% (476); all full-time undergraduates: 84% (2,126). *Average award:* Freshmen: $13,895; Undergraduates: $11,412. *Scholarships, grants, and awards:* Federal Pell, FSEOG, state, private, college/university gift aid from institutional funds.

GIFT AID (NON-NEED-BASED) *Total amount:* $2,354,518 (97% institutional, 3% external sources). *Receiving aid:* Freshmen: 3% (16). Undergraduates: 3% (84). *Average award:* Freshmen: $5242. Undergraduates: $5720. *Scholarships, grants, and awards by category: Academic interests/achievement:* biological sciences, business, communication, computer science, education, English, foreign languages, general academic interests/achievements, health fields, humanities, international studies, mathematics, physical sciences, premedicine, religion/biblical studies, social sciences. *Creative arts/performance:* art/fine arts, music. *Special achievements/activities:* cheerleading/drum major, community service, leadership, religious involvement. *Special characteristics:* children and siblings of alumni, children of faculty/staff, ethnic background, handicapped students, international students, local/state students, members of minority groups, out-of-state students, relatives of clergy, religious affiliation. *Tuition waivers:* Full or partial for employees or children of employees. **ROTC:** Army, Air Force cooperative.

LOANS *Student loans:* $19,426,090 (83% need-based, 17% non-need-based). 84% of past graduating class borrowed through all loan programs. *Average indebtedness per student:* $34,655. *Average need-based loan:* Freshmen: $351. Undergraduates: $4520. *Parent loans:* $4,727,308 (39% need-based, 61% non-need-based). *Programs:* Federal Direct (Subsidized and Unsubsidized Stafford, PLUS), Perkins, state.

WORK-STUDY *Federal work-study:* Total amount: $354,143; 210 jobs averaging $2395. *State or other work-study/employment:* Total amount: $779,947 (56% need-based, 44% non-need-based). 349 part-time jobs averaging $2406.

APPLYING FOR FINANCIAL AID *Required financial aid form:* FAFSA. *Financial aid deadline (priority):* 3/1. *Notification date:* Continuous beginning 2/1. Students must reply within 2 weeks of notification.

CONTACT Mr. David Orsag, Associate Director of Financial Aid, University of Mary Hardin-Baylor, PO Box 8080, Belton, TX 76513, 254-295-4517 or toll-free 800-727-8642. *Fax:* 254-295-5049. *E-mail:* dorsag@umhb.edu. *Website:* http://www.umhb.edu/.

UNIVERSITY OF MARY HARDIN-BAYLOR
Belton, TX

Tuition & fees: $24,150	Average undergraduate aid package: $15,419

ABOUT THE INSTITUTION Independent Southern Baptist, coed. *Awards:* bachelor's, master's, and doctoral degrees. 62 undergraduate majors. *Total enrollment:* 3,287. Undergraduates: 2,926. Freshmen: 631. Federal methodology is used as a basis for awarding need-based institutional aid.

UNDERGRADUATE EXPENSES for 2013–2014 *Application fee:* $35. *Comprehensive fee:* $30,770 includes full-time tuition ($21,900), mandatory fees ($2250), and room and board ($6620). Full-time tuition and fees vary according to course load and degree level. Room and board charges vary according to board plan and housing facility. *Part-time tuition:* $765 per credit hour. *Part-time fees:* $75 per credit hour; $50 per term. Part-time tuition and fees vary according to course load and degree level.

UNIVERSITY OF MARYLAND, BALTIMORE COUNTY
Baltimore, MD

Tuition & fees (MD res): $9764	Average undergraduate aid package: $10,436

ABOUT THE INSTITUTION State-supported, coed. *Awards:* certificates, bachelor's, master's, and doctoral degrees. 46 undergraduate majors. *Total enrollment:* 13,637. Undergraduates: 10,953. Freshmen: 1,560. Federal methodology is used as a basis for awarding need-based institutional aid.

UNDERGRADUATE EXPENSES for 2013–2014 *Application fee:* $50. *One-time required fee:* $125. *Tuition, state resident:* full-time $7085; part-time $295 per credit hour. *Tuition, nonresident:* full-time $18,146; part-time $754 per credit hour. *Required fees:* full-time $2679; $115 per credit hour. Full-time tuition and fees vary according to location and program. Part-time tuition and fees vary according to location and program. *College room and board:* $10,142; *Room only:* $6126. Room and board charges vary according to board plan and housing facility.

FRESHMAN FINANCIAL AID (Fall 2012, est.) 1,156 applied for aid; of those 67% were deemed to have need. 93% of freshmen with need received aid; of those 21% had need fully met. *Average percent of need met:* 62% (excluding resources awarded to replace EFC). *Average financial aid package:* $10,915 (excluding resources awarded to replace EFC). 22% of all full-time freshmen had no need and received non-need-based gift aid.

UNDERGRADUATE FINANCIAL AID (Fall 2012, est.) 6,100 applied for aid; of those 80% were deemed to have need. 94% of undergraduates with need received aid; of those 10% had need fully met. *Average percent of need met:* 56% (excluding resources awarded to replace EFC). *Average financial aid package:* $10,436 (excluding resources awarded to replace EFC). 11% of all full-time undergraduates had no need and received non-need-based gift aid.

GIFT AID (NEED-BASED) *Total amount:* $28,109,345 (45% federal, 21% state, 29% institutional, 5% external sources). *Receiving aid:* Freshmen: 39% (605); all full-time undergraduates: 39% (3,636). *Average award:* Freshmen: $8488; Undergraduates: $7396. *Scholarships, grants, and awards:* Federal Pell, FSEOG, state, private, college/university gift aid from institutional funds.

GIFT AID (NON-NEED-BASED) *Total amount:* $10,205,177 (4% state, 88% institutional, 8% external sources). *Receiving aid:* Freshmen: 15% (235). Undergraduates: 5% (479). *Average award:* Freshmen: $8719. Undergraduates: $8443. *Scholarships, grants, and awards by category:* Academic interests/achievement: 2,268 awards ($13,961,450 total): biological sciences, computer science, education, engineering/technologies, English, foreign languages, general academic interests/achievements, humanities, mathematics, physical sciences, social sciences. *Creative arts/performance:* 37 awards ($34,077 total): art/fine arts, cinema/film/broadcasting, creative writing, dance, music, performing arts, theater/drama. *Tuition waivers:* Full or partial for employees or children of employees, senior citizens. *ROTC:* Army cooperative, Air Force cooperative.

LOANS *Student loans:* $39,243,283 (40% need-based, 60% non-need-based). 53% of past graduating class borrowed through all loan programs. *Average indebtedness per student:* $22,601. *Average need-based loan:* Freshmen: $3384. Undergraduates: $4228. *Parent loans:* $4,671,614 (73% need-based, 27% non-need-based). *Programs:* Federal Direct (Subsidized and Unsubsidized Stafford, PLUS), Perkins.

WORK-STUDY *Federal work-study:* Total amount: $194,377; 94 jobs averaging $2089. *State or other work-study/employment:* Total amount: $959,405 (61% need-based, 39% non-need-based). Part-time jobs available.

ATHLETIC AWARDS Total amount: $2,220,105 (39% need-based, 61% non-need-based).

APPLYING FOR FINANCIAL AID *Required financial aid form:* FAFSA. *Financial aid deadline (priority):* 2/15. *Notification date:* Continuous beginning 3/15.

CONTACT Stephanie Johnson, Director, University of Maryland, Baltimore County, 1000 Hilltop Circle, Baltimore, MD 21250, 410-455-2387 or toll-free 800-UMBC-4U2 (in-state), 800-862-2402 (out-of-state). *Fax:* 410-455-1288. *E-mail:* finaid@umbc.edu. *Website:* http://www.umbc.edu/.

awarded to replace EFC). 18% of all full-time freshmen had no need and received non-need-based gift aid.

UNDERGRADUATE FINANCIAL AID (Fall 2011) 14,885 applied for aid; of those 74% were deemed to have need. 96% of undergraduates with need received aid; of those 15% had need fully met. *Average percent of need met:* 63% (excluding resources awarded to replace EFC). *Average financial aid package:* $11,026 (excluding resources awarded to replace EFC). 12% of all full-time undergraduates had no need and received non-need-based gift aid.

GIFT AID (NEED-BASED) *Total amount:* $46,614,695 (45% federal, 24% state, 26% institutional, 5% external sources). *Receiving aid:* Freshmen: 27% (1,095); all full-time undergraduates: 27% (6,636). *Average award:* Freshmen: $6966; Undergraduates: $6840. *Scholarships, grants, and awards:* Federal Pell, FSEOG, state, private, college/university gift aid from institutional funds.

GIFT AID (NON-NEED-BASED) *Total amount:* $42,794,616 (9% state, 75% institutional, 16% external sources). *Receiving aid:* Freshmen: 23% (920). Undergraduates: 17% (4,125). *Average award:* Freshmen: $6395. Undergraduates: $6482. *Scholarships, grants, and awards by category:* Academic interests/achievement: 3,709 awards ($17,283,501 total): agriculture, architecture, biological sciences, business, communication, computer science, education, engineering/technologies, English, foreign languages, general academic interests/achievements, health fields, humanities, international studies, library science, mathematics, military science, physical sciences, premedicine, social sciences. *Creative arts/performance:* 68 awards ($477,102 total): applied art and design, art/fine arts, dance, music, performing arts, theater/drama. *Special achievements/activities:* 93 awards ($370,669 total): cheerleading/drum major. *Special characteristics:* 1,672 awards ($8,376,853 total): adult students, out-of-state students. *Tuition waivers:* Full or partial for employees or children of employees. *ROTC:* Army, Naval cooperative, Air Force.

LOANS *Student loans:* $122,800,027 (38% need-based, 62% non-need-based). 46% of past graduating class borrowed through all loan programs. *Average indebtedness per student:* $25,276. *Average need-based loan:* Freshmen: $3656. Undergraduates: $4691. *Parent loans:* $25,320,292 (45% need-based, 55% non-need-based). *Programs:* Federal Direct (Subsidized and Unsubsidized Stafford, PLUS), Perkins, private loans.

WORK-STUDY *Federal work-study:* Total amount: $4,631,336; 2,130 jobs averaging $2154.

ATHLETIC AWARDS Total amount: $11,117,275 (100% non-need-based).

APPLYING FOR FINANCIAL AID *Required financial aid form:* FAFSA. *Financial aid deadline (priority):* 2/15. *Notification date:* Continuous beginning 4/1.

CONTACT Sarah Bauder, Assistant Vice President for Enrollment Services and Financial Aid, University of Maryland, College Park, 0102 Lee Building, College Park, MD 20742, 301-314-8279 or toll-free 800-422-5867. *Fax:* 301-314-9587. *E-mail:* sbauder@umd.edu.
Website: http://www.maryland.edu/.

UNIVERSITY OF MARYLAND, COLLEGE PARK

College Park, MD

Tuition & fees (MD res): $8909	Average undergraduate aid package: $11,026

ABOUT THE INSTITUTION State-supported, coed. *Awards:* certificates, bachelor's, master's, and doctoral degrees. 90 undergraduate majors. *Total enrollment:* 37,197. Undergraduates: 26,487. Freshmen: 3,903. Federal methodology is used as a basis for awarding need-based institutional aid.

UNDERGRADUATE EXPENSES for 2013–2014 *Application fee:* $65. *Tuition, state resident:* full-time $7175; part-time $299 per credit hour. *Tuition, nonresident:* full-time $25,554; part-time $1065 per credit hour. *Required fees:* full-time $1734; $399.81 per term. Part-time tuition and fees vary according to course load. *College room and board:* $9893; *Room only:* $5918. Room and board charges vary according to board plan and housing facility.

FRESHMAN FINANCIAL AID (Fall 2011) 3,181 applied for aid; of those 58% were deemed to have need. 96% of freshmen with need received aid; of those 21% had need fully met. *Average percent of need met:* 66% (excluding resources awarded to replace EFC). *Average financial aid package:* $11,370 (excluding resources

UNIVERSITY OF MARYLAND EASTERN SHORE

Princess Anne, MD

Tuition & fees (MD res): $6998	Average undergraduate aid package: $9034

ABOUT THE INSTITUTION State-supported, coed. *Awards:* certificates, bachelor's, master's, and doctoral degrees. 51 undergraduate majors. *Total enrollment:* 4,454. Undergraduates: 3,758. Freshmen: 886. Federal methodology is used as a basis for awarding need-based institutional aid.

UNDERGRADUATE EXPENSES for 2013–2014 *Application fee:* $25. *Tuition, state resident:* full-time $4628; part-time $193 per credit hour. *Tuition, nonresident:* full-time $13,134; part-time $484 per credit hour. *Required fees:* full-time $2370. Full-time tuition and fees vary according to course load. Part-time tuition and fees vary according to course load. *College room and board:* $8374; *Room only:* $4324. Room and board charges vary according to board plan and housing facility.

FRESHMAN FINANCIAL AID (Fall 2011) 730 applied for aid; of those 88% were deemed to have need. 98% of freshmen with need received aid. *Average percent of need met:* 48% (excluding resources awarded to replace EFC). *Average financial*

aid package: $9594 (excluding resources awarded to replace EFC). 3% of all full-time freshmen had no need and received non-need-based gift aid.

UNDERGRADUATE FINANCIAL AID (Fall 2011) 3,352 applied for aid; of those 87% were deemed to have need. 97% of undergraduates with need received aid. *Average percent of need met:* 51% (excluding resources awarded to replace EFC). *Average financial aid package:* $9034 (excluding resources awarded to replace EFC). 4% of all full-time undergraduates had no need and received non-need-based gift aid.

GIFT AID (NEED-BASED) *Total amount:* $16,203,706 (61% federal, 26% state, 13% institutional). *Receiving aid:* Freshmen: 66% (497); all full-time undergraduates: 62% (2,182). *Average award:* Freshmen: $7368; Undergraduates: $7174. *Scholarships, grants, and awards:* Federal Pell, FSEOG, state, college/university gift aid from institutional funds.

GIFT AID (NON-NEED-BASED) *Total amount:* $4,248,178 (6% state, 82% institutional, 12% external sources). *Receiving aid:* Freshmen: 31% (231). Undergraduates: 21% (730). *Average award:* Freshmen: $5163. Undergraduates: $12,202. *Scholarships, grants, and awards by category: Academic interests/achievement:* agriculture, business, computer science, education, engineering/technologies, English, general academic interests/achievements, health fields, home economics, mathematics, physical sciences, social sciences. *Creative arts/performance:* art/fine arts, music, performing arts, theater/drama. *Special characteristics:* adult students, children of faculty/staff, first-generation college students, veterans. *Tuition waivers:* Full or partial for employees or children of employees, senior citizens. *ROTC:* Army cooperative.

LOANS *Student loans:* $20,990,338 (47% need-based, 53% non-need-based). 82% of past graduating class borrowed through all loan programs. *Average indebtedness per student:* $27,215. *Average need-based loan:* Freshmen: $3325. Undergraduates: $4031. *Parent loans:* $6,416,749 (100% non-need-based). *Programs:* Federal Direct (Subsidized and Unsubsidized Stafford, PLUS), Perkins.

WORK-STUDY *Federal work-study:* Total amount: $211,699; 80 jobs averaging $2647. *State or other work-study/employment:* Total amount: $1,500,000 (100% non-need-based). Part-time jobs available.

ATHLETIC AWARDS Total amount: $1,551,473 (100% non-need-based).

APPLYING FOR FINANCIAL AID *Required financial aid form:* FAFSA. *Financial aid deadline (priority):* 3/1. *Notification date:* Continuous beginning 4/15.

CONTACT Mr. James W. Kellam, Director of Financial Aid, University of Maryland Eastern Shore, Backbone Road, Princess Anne, MD 21853-1299, 410-651-6172. *Fax:* 410-651-7670. *E-mail:* jwkellam@umes.edu. *Website:* http://www.umes.edu/.

UNIVERSITY OF MARYLAND UNIVERSITY COLLEGE
Adelphi, MD

Tuition & fees (MD res): $6384	Average undergraduate aid package: $7382

ABOUT THE INSTITUTION State-supported, coed. *Awards:* certificates, associate, bachelor's, master's, and doctoral degrees (offers primarily part-time evening and weekend degree programs at more than 30 off-campus locations in Maryland and the Washington, DC area, and more than 180 military communities in Europe and Asia with military enrollment not reflected in this profile; associate of arts program available to military students only). 27 undergraduate majors. *Total enrollment:* 42,268. Undergraduates: 28,273. Freshmen: 1,406. Federal methodology is used as a basis for awarding need-based institutional aid.

UNDERGRADUATE EXPENSES for 2013–2014 *Application fee:* $50. *Tuition, state resident:* full-time $6024; part-time $251 per credit hour. *Tuition, nonresident:* full-time $11,976; part-time $499 per credit hour. *Required fees:* full-time $360; $15 per credit hour.

FRESHMAN FINANCIAL AID (Fall 2011) 135 applied for aid; of those 98% were deemed to have need. 93% of freshmen with need received aid; of those 3% had need fully met. *Average percent of need met:* 26% (excluding resources awarded to replace EFC). *Average financial aid package:* $5564 (excluding resources awarded to replace EFC).

UNDERGRADUATE FINANCIAL AID (Fall 2011) 3,608 applied for aid; of those 95% were deemed to have need. 92% of undergraduates with need received aid; of those 1% had need fully met. *Average percent of need met:* 31% (excluding

resources awarded to replace EFC). *Average financial aid package:* $7382 (excluding resources awarded to replace EFC).

GIFT AID (NEED-BASED) *Total amount:* $25,310,293 (83% federal, 7% state, 9% institutional, 1% external sources). *Receiving aid:* Freshmen: 62% (99); all full-time undergraduates: 38% (2,153). *Average award:* Freshmen: $3248; Undergraduates: $4586. *Scholarships, grants, and awards:* Federal Pell, FSEOG, state, private, college/university gift aid from institutional funds.

GIFT AID (NON-NEED-BASED) *Total amount:* $2,316,236 (4% state, 81% institutional, 15% external sources). *Receiving aid:* Freshmen: 2% (3). Undergraduates: 7% (420). *Scholarships, grants, and awards by category: Academic interests/achievement:* general academic interests/achievements. *Special achievements/activities:* general special achievements/activities. *Tuition waivers:* Full or partial for employees or children of employees, senior citizens.

LOANS *Student loans:* $92,701,144 (40% need-based, 60% non-need-based). *Average need-based loan:* Freshmen: $3115. Undergraduates: $4213. *Parent loans:* $413,991 (100% non-need-based). *Programs:* Federal Direct (Subsidized and Unsubsidized Stafford, PLUS), Perkins.

WORK-STUDY *Federal work-study:* Total amount: $531,387; jobs available. *State or other work-study/employment:* Part-time jobs available.

APPLYING FOR FINANCIAL AID *Required financial aid form:* FAFSA. *Financial aid deadline (priority):* 6/1. *Notification date:* Continuous beginning 5/1. Students must reply within 2 weeks of notification.

CONTACT Cheryl Storie, Associate Vice President of Financial Aid, University of Maryland University College, 3501 University Boulevard East, Adelphi, MD 20783, 301-985-7847 or toll-free 800-888-8682. *Fax:* 301-985-7462. *E-mail:* finaid@umuc.edu. *Website:* http://www.umuc.edu/.

UNIVERSITY OF MARY WASHINGTON
Fredericksburg, VA

Tuition & fees (VA res): $9246	Average undergraduate aid package: $8190

ABOUT THE INSTITUTION State-supported, coed. *Awards:* certificates, bachelor's, and master's degrees. 29 undergraduate majors. *Total enrollment:* 5,093. Undergraduates: 4,515. Freshmen: 955. Federal methodology is used as a basis for awarding need-based institutional aid.

UNDERGRADUATE EXPENSES for 2013–2014 *Application fee:* $50. *One-time required fee:* $60. *Tuition, state resident:* full-time $4686; part-time $200 per credit hour. *Tuition, nonresident:* full-time $17,000; part-time $712 per credit hour. *Required fees:* full-time $4560; $129 per credit hour or $30 per term. Part-time tuition and fees vary according to course load and location. *College room and board:* $10,238; *Room only:* $5384. Room and board charges vary according to board plan and housing facility.

FRESHMAN FINANCIAL AID (Fall 2012, est.) 732 applied for aid; of those 56% were deemed to have need. 90% of freshmen with need received aid; of those 13% had need fully met. *Average percent of need met:* 48% (excluding resources awarded to replace EFC). *Average financial aid package:* $7700 (excluding resources awarded to replace EFC). 11% of all full-time freshmen had no need and received non-need-based gift aid.

UNDERGRADUATE FINANCIAL AID (Fall 2012, est.) 2,371 applied for aid; of those 64% were deemed to have need. 93% of undergraduates with need received aid; of those 12% had need fully met. *Average percent of need met:* 49% (excluding resources awarded to replace EFC). *Average financial aid package:* $8190 (excluding resources awarded to replace EFC). 8% of all full-time undergraduates had no need and received non-need-based gift aid.

GIFT AID (NEED-BASED) *Total amount:* $5,304,000 (52% federal, 32% state, 16% institutional). *Receiving aid:* Freshmen: 18% (167); all full-time undergraduates: 18% (703). *Average award:* Freshmen: $8000; Undergraduates: $7100. *Scholarships, grants, and awards:* Federal Pell, FSEOG, state, private, college/university gift aid from institutional funds.

GIFT AID (NON-NEED-BASED) *Total amount:* $2,070,000 (3% federal, 2% state, 58% institutional, 37% external sources). *Receiving aid:* Freshmen: 15% (136). Undergraduates: 8% (321). *Average award:* Freshmen: $2840. Undergraduates: $3230. *Scholarships, grants, and awards by category: Academic interests/achievement:* 50 awards ($120,000 total): biological sciences, business, computer science, education, English, foreign languages, general academic interests/achievements, humanities, international studies, mathematics, physical sciences, religion/biblical studies, social sciences. *Creative arts/performance:* 60 awards ($120,000 total): art/fine arts, dance, journalism/publications, music, theater/drama. *Special achievements/activities:* 3 awards ($18,000 total): leadership. *Special characteristics:* 15 awards ($3500 total): adult students, children and siblings of alumni, children of faculty/staff, local/state students. **Tuition waivers:** Full or partial for senior citizens. **ROTC:** Army cooperative.

LOANS Student loans: $16,510,000 (35% need-based, 65% non-need-based). 57% of past graduating class borrowed through all loan programs. *Average indebtedness per student:* $21,000. *Average need-based loan:* Freshmen: $3300. Undergraduates: $4220. *Parent loans:* $3,990,000 (100% non-need-based). **Programs:** Federal Direct (Subsidized and Unsubsidized Stafford, PLUS), Perkins.

WORK-STUDY Federal work-study: Total amount: $67,000; 40 jobs averaging $1800. *State or other work-study/employment:* Total amount: $1,260,000 (100% non-need-based). 600 part-time jobs averaging $2200.

APPLYING FOR FINANCIAL AID Required financial aid forms: FAFSA, UMW scholarship application form. *Financial aid deadline:* 5/15 (priority: 3/1). *Notification date:* 4/1. Students must reply by 5/1 or within 2 weeks of notification.

CONTACT Ms. Debra J. Harber, Director of Financial Aid, University of Mary Washington, 1301 College Avenue, Fredericksburg, VA 22401-5358, 540-654-2468 or toll-free 800-468-5614. *Fax:* 540-654-1858. *E-mail:* dharber@umw.edu. *Website:* http://www.umw.edu/.

drama. *Special achievements/activities:* cheerleading/drum major, general special achievements/activities, leadership. *Special characteristics:* children and siblings of alumni, children of faculty/staff, handicapped students, veterans. **Tuition waivers:** Full or partial for employees or children of employees, senior citizens. **ROTC:** Army, Air Force.

LOANS Student loans: $116,797,580 (65% need-based, 35% non-need-based). 71% of past graduating class borrowed through all loan programs. *Average indebtedness per student:* $27,945. *Average need-based loan:* Freshmen: $3698. Undergraduates: $4636. *Parent loans:* $33,808,880 (30% need-based, 70% non-need-based). **Programs:** Federal Direct (Subsidized and Unsubsidized Stafford, PLUS), Perkins.

WORK-STUDY Federal work-study: Total amount: $6,078,896; 3,517 jobs averaging $1733.

ATHLETIC AWARDS Total amount: $7,576,534 (34% need-based, 66% non-need-based).

APPLYING FOR FINANCIAL AID Required financial aid form: FAFSA. *Financial aid deadline (priority):* 3/1. *Notification date:* Continuous beginning 4/1. Students must reply by 5/1.

CONTACT Office of Financial Aid Services, University of Massachusetts Amherst, 255 Whitmore Administration Building, Amherst, MA 01003, 413-545-0801. *Fax:* 413-545-1700.

Website: http://www.umass.edu/.

UNIVERSITY OF MASSACHUSETTS AMHERST
Amherst, MA

Tuition & fees (MA res): $13,415	Average undergraduate aid package: $15,039

ABOUT THE INSTITUTION State-supported, coed. *Awards:* certificates, associate, bachelor's, master's, and doctoral degrees. 86 undergraduate majors. *Total enrollment:* 28,236. Undergraduates: 21,928. Freshmen: 4,679. Federal methodology is used as a basis for awarding need-based institutional aid.

UNDERGRADUATE EXPENSES for 2013–2014 Application fee: $75. *One-time required fee:* $185. *Tuition, state resident:* full-time $1714; part-time $71.50 per credit. *Tuition, nonresident:* full-time $9937; part-time $414 per credit. *Required fees:* full-time $11,701; $671.83 per credit. Full-time tuition and fees vary according to class time, course load, location, program, reciprocity agreements, and student level. Part-time tuition and fees vary according to class time, course load, location, program, reciprocity agreements, and student level. *College room and board:* $10,767; *Room only:* $5563. Room and board charges vary according to board plan and housing facility.

FRESHMAN FINANCIAL AID (Fall 2011) 4,244 applied for aid; of those 68% were deemed to have need. 97% of freshmen with need received aid; of those 13% had need fully met. *Average percent of need met:* 80% (excluding resources awarded to replace EFC). *Average financial aid package:* $13,920 (excluding resources awarded to replace EFC). 11% of all full-time freshmen had no need and received non-need-based gift aid.

UNDERGRADUATE FINANCIAL AID (Fall 2011) 16,780 applied for aid; of those 74% were deemed to have need. 97% of undergraduates with need received aid; of those 17% had need fully met. *Average percent of need met:* 85% (excluding resources awarded to replace EFC). *Average financial aid package:* $15,039 (excluding resources awarded to replace EFC). 7% of all full-time undergraduates had no need and received non-need-based gift aid.

GIFT AID (NEED-BASED) Total amount: $87,482,221 (29% federal, 8% state, 59% institutional, 4% external sources). *Receiving aid:* Freshmen: 53% (2,500); all full-time undergraduates: 51% (10,222). *Average award:* Freshmen: $8520; Undergraduates: $9408. *Scholarships, grants, and awards:* Federal Pell, FSEOG, state, private, college/university gift aid from institutional funds.

GIFT AID (NON-NEED-BASED) Total amount: $7,966,755 (1% federal, 2% state, 72% institutional, 25% external sources). *Receiving aid:* Freshmen: 4% (178). Undergraduates: 3% (601). *Average award:* Freshmen: $4146. Undergraduates: $3531. *Scholarships, grants, and awards by category:* Academic interests/achievement: agriculture, architecture, biological sciences, business, communication, computer science, education, engineering/technologies, English, health fields, humanities, mathematics, military science, physical sciences, premedicine, social sciences. *Creative arts/performance:* art/fine arts, dance, journalism/publications, music, theater/

UNIVERSITY OF MASSACHUSETTS BOSTON
Boston, MA

Tuition & fees (MA res): $11,966	Average undergraduate aid package: $14,889

ABOUT THE INSTITUTION State-supported, coed. *Awards:* certificates, bachelor's, master's, and doctoral degrees. 36 undergraduate majors. *Total enrollment:* 15,874. Undergraduates: 12,124. Freshmen: 1,267. Federal methodology is used as a basis for awarding need-based institutional aid.

UNDERGRADUATE EXPENSES for 2013–2014 Application fee: $40. *Tuition, state resident:* full-time $11,320. *Tuition, nonresident:* full-time $25,504. *Required fees:* full-time $646. Full-time tuition and fees vary according to program. Part-time tuition and fees vary according to program.

FRESHMAN FINANCIAL AID (Fall 2011) 1,010 applied for aid; of those 86% were deemed to have need. 100% of freshmen with need received aid; of those 45% had need fully met. *Average percent of need met:* 91% (excluding resources awarded to replace EFC). *Average financial aid package:* $14,554 (excluding resources awarded to replace EFC). 6% of all full-time freshmen had no need and received non-need-based gift aid.

UNDERGRADUATE FINANCIAL AID (Fall 2011) 6,227 applied for aid; of those 88% were deemed to have need. 100% of undergraduates with need received aid; of those 50% had need fully met. *Average percent of need met:* 91% (excluding resources awarded to replace EFC). *Average financial aid package:* $14,889 (excluding resources awarded to replace EFC). 3% of all full-time undergraduates had no need and received non-need-based gift aid.

GIFT AID (NEED-BASED) Total amount: $44,436,893 (44% federal, 10% state, 43% institutional, 3% external sources). *Receiving aid:* Freshmen: 64% (796); all full-time undergraduates: 60% (4,792). *Average award:* Freshmen: $9847; Undergraduates: $8882. *Scholarships, grants, and awards:* Federal Pell, FSEOG, state, private, college/university gift aid from institutional funds, TEACH Grants.

GIFT AID (NON-NEED-BASED) Total amount: $2,109,486 (1% federal, 2% state, 85% institutional, 12% external sources). *Receiving aid:* Freshmen: 3% (34). Undergraduates: 1% (108). *Average award:* Freshmen: $5096. Undergraduates: $4501. *Scholarships, grants, and awards by category:* Academic interests/achievement: general academic interests/achievements, health fields. *Special achievements/activities:* general special achievements/activities, leadership. *Special characteristics:* adult students, children of faculty/staff, children of union members/company employees, first-generation college students, veterans. **ROTC:** Army cooperative, Naval cooperative, Air Force cooperative.

LOANS Student loans: $55,193,456 (72% need-based, 28% non-need-based). 74% of past graduating class borrowed through all loan programs. *Average indebtedness per student:* $25,499. *Average need-based loan:* Freshmen: $5197. Undergrad-

uates: $6988. **Parent loans:** $3,256,772 (21% need-based, 79% non-need-based).
Programs: Federal Direct (Subsidized and Unsubsidized Stafford, PLUS), Perkins.
WORK-STUDY *Federal work-study:* Total amount: $2,025,121; 547 jobs averaging $3701.
APPLYING FOR FINANCIAL AID *Required financial aid form:* FAFSA.
Financial aid deadline (priority): 3/1. *Notification date:* Continuous beginning 3/26.
CONTACT Judy L. Keyes, Director of Financial Aid Services, University of Massachusetts Boston, 100 Morrissey Boulevard, Boston, MA 02125-3393, 617-287-6300. *Fax:* 617-287-6323. *E-mail:* judy.keyes@umb.edu.
Website: http://www.umb.edu/.

UNIVERSITY OF MASSACHUSETTS DARTMOUTH
North Dartmouth, MA

Tuition & fees (MA res): $11,681	Average undergraduate aid package: $15,281

ABOUT THE INSTITUTION State-supported, coed. **Awards:** certificates, bachelor's, master's, and doctoral degrees. 49 undergraduate majors. **Total enrollment:** 9,210. Undergraduates: 7,562. Freshmen: 1,577. Federal methodology is used as a basis for awarding need-based institutional aid.
UNDERGRADUATE EXPENSES for 2013–2014 *Application fee:* $40. *Tuition, state resident:* full-time $1417. *Tuition, nonresident:* full-time $8099. *Required fees:* full-time $10,264. Full-time tuition and fees vary according to class time, program, and reciprocity agreements. Part-time tuition and fees vary according to class time, course load, program, and reciprocity agreements. Room and board charges vary according to board plan and housing facility.
FRESHMAN FINANCIAL AID (Fall 2012, est.) 1,396 applied for aid; of those 83% were deemed to have need. 100% of freshmen with need received aid; of those 38% had need fully met. *Average percent of need met:* 84% (excluding resources awarded to replace EFC). *Average financial aid package:* $14,665 (excluding resources awarded to replace EFC). 10% of all full-time freshmen had no need and received non-need-based gift aid.
UNDERGRADUATE FINANCIAL AID (Fall 2012, est.) 5,458 applied for aid; of those 85% were deemed to have need. 100% of undergraduates with need received aid; of those 40% had need fully met. *Average percent of need met:* 86% (excluding resources awarded to replace EFC). *Average financial aid package:* $15,281 (excluding resources awarded to replace EFC). 5% of all full-time undergraduates had no need and received non-need-based gift aid.
GIFT AID (NEED-BASED) *Total amount:* $31,700,000 (38% federal, 10% state, 50% institutional, 2% external sources). *Receiving aid:* Freshmen: 66% (1,028); all full-time undergraduates: 60% (3,901). *Average award:* Freshmen: $8602; Undergraduates: $8637. *Scholarships, grants, and awards:* Federal Pell, FSEOG, state, private, college/university gift aid from institutional funds.
GIFT AID (NON-NEED-BASED) *Total amount:* $5,988,000 (97% institutional, 3% external sources). *Receiving aid:* Freshmen: 3% (53). Undergraduates: 2% (154). *Average award:* Freshmen: $4506. Undergraduates: $4377. *Scholarships, grants, and awards by category:* Academic interests/achievement: biological sciences, business, computer science, education, engineering/technologies, foreign languages, general academic interests/achievements, health fields, mathematics, physical sciences, social sciences. *Creative arts/performance:* applied art and design, art/fine arts. *Special achievements/activities:* community service. *Special characteristics:* adult students, children of faculty/staff, children of union members/company employees, children with a deceased or disabled parent, ethnic background, first-generation college students, local/state students, members of minority groups, previous college experience, public servants, veterans. *Tuition waivers:* Full or partial for employees or children of employees, senior citizens. *ROTC:* Army cooperative.
LOANS *Student loans:* $28,000,000 (57% need-based, 43% non-need-based). 76% of past graduating class borrowed through all loan programs. *Average indebtedness per student:* $32,349. *Average need-based loan:* Freshmen: $6910. Undergraduates: $7872. *Parent loans:* $8,900,000 (51% need-based, 49% non-need-based). *Programs:* Federal Direct (Subsidized and Unsubsidized Stafford, PLUS), Perkins, Federal Nursing, state.
WORK-STUDY *Federal work-study:* Total amount: $1,500,000; jobs available. *State or other work-study/employment:* Total amount: $40,000 (100% non-need-based). Part-time jobs available.

APPLYING FOR FINANCIAL AID *Required financial aid form:* FAFSA. *Financial aid deadline (priority):* 3/1. *Notification date:* Continuous beginning 3/25. Students must reply within 3 weeks of notification.
CONTACT Ms. Audra Callahan, Associate Director of Financial Aid, University of Massachusetts Dartmouth, 285 Old Westport Road, North Dartmouth, MA 02747-2300, 508-999-8643. *Fax:* 508-999-8935. *E-mail:* financialaid@umassd.edu.
Website: http://www.umassd.edu/.

UNIVERSITY OF MASSACHUSETTS LOWELL
Lowell, MA

Tuition & fees (MA res): $11,852	Average undergraduate aid package: $13,549

ABOUT THE INSTITUTION State-supported, coed. **Awards:** certificates, associate, bachelor's, master's, and doctoral degrees. 47 undergraduate majors. **Total enrollment:** 15,431. Undergraduates: 11,729. Freshmen: 1,433. Federal methodology is used as a basis for awarding need-based institutional aid.
UNDERGRADUATE EXPENSES for 2013–2014 *Application fee:* $60. *One-time required fee:* $200. *Tuition, state resident:* full-time $1454; part-time $61 per credit. *Tuition, nonresident:* full-time $8567; part-time $357 per credit. *Required fees:* full-time $10,398; $433.05 per credit. Part-time tuition and fees vary according to course load. *College room and board:* $10,282; *Room only:* $6854. Room and board charges vary according to board plan and housing facility.
FRESHMAN FINANCIAL AID (Fall 2011) 1,269 applied for aid; of those 77% were deemed to have need. 100% of freshmen with need received aid; of those 59% had need fully met. *Average percent of need met:* 93% (excluding resources awarded to replace EFC). *Average financial aid package:* $13,872 (excluding resources awarded to replace EFC). 14% of all full-time freshmen had no need and received non-need-based gift aid.
UNDERGRADUATE FINANCIAL AID (Fall 2011) 6,703 applied for aid; of those 79% were deemed to have need. 100% of undergraduates with need received aid; of those 56% had need fully met. *Average percent of need met:* 92% (excluding resources awarded to replace EFC). *Average financial aid package:* $13,549 (excluding resources awarded to replace EFC). 7% of all full-time undergraduates had no need and received non-need-based gift aid.
GIFT AID (NEED-BASED) *Total amount:* $32,018,198 (46% federal, 10% state, 42% institutional, 2% external sources). *Receiving aid:* Freshmen: 63% (893); all full-time undergraduates: 54% (4,552). *Average award:* Freshmen: $8320; Undergraduates: $7398. *Scholarships, grants, and awards:* Federal Pell, FSEOG, state, private, college/university gift aid from institutional funds.
GIFT AID (NON-NEED-BASED) *Total amount:* $4,060,655 (2% federal, 92% institutional, 6% external sources). *Receiving aid:* Freshmen: 4% (64). Undergraduates: 2% (167). *Average award:* Freshmen: $4405. Undergraduates: $3830. *Scholarships, grants, and awards by category:* Academic interests/achievement: biological sciences, business, computer science, education, engineering/technologies, English, general academic interests/achievements, health fields, humanities, mathematics. *Creative arts/performance:* art/fine arts, music. *Special achievements/activities:* community service, general special achievements/activities. *Special characteristics:* children and siblings of alumni, children of faculty/staff, children of public servants, children of union members/company employees, general special characteristics, out-of-state students, veterans. *Tuition waivers:* Full or partial for employees or children of employees, senior citizens. *ROTC:* Army cooperative, Air Force.
LOANS *Student loans:* $57,578,710 (65% need-based, 35% non-need-based). 77% of past graduating class borrowed through all loan programs. *Average indebtedness per student:* $29,212. *Average need-based loan:* Freshmen: $5673. Undergraduates: $7028. *Parent loans:* $6,778,382 (22% need-based, 78% non-need-based). *Programs:* Federal Direct (Subsidized and Unsubsidized Stafford, PLUS), Perkins.
WORK-STUDY *Federal work-study:* Total amount: $429,838; 175 jobs averaging $2450. *State or other work-study/employment:* Total amount: $2,553,773 (99% need-based, 1% non-need-based). 663 part-time jobs averaging $3026.
ATHLETIC AWARDS Total amount: $1,389,216 (43% need-based, 57% non-need-based).
APPLYING FOR FINANCIAL AID *Required financial aid form:* FAFSA. *Financial aid deadline (priority):* 3/1. *Notification date:* Continuous beginning 3/21.

CONTACT Joyce McLaughlin, Associate Dean of Enrollment and Director of Financial Aid, University of Massachusetts Lowell, 883 Broadway Street, Room 102, Lowell, MA 01854, 978-934-4220. *Fax:* 978-934-3009. *E-mail:* joyce_mclaughlin@uml.edu.
Website: http://www.uml.edu/.

UNIVERSITY OF MEDICINE AND DENTISTRY OF NEW JERSEY
Newark, NJ

CONTACT Financial Aid Office, University of Medicine and Dentistry of New Jersey, 65 Bergen Street, PO Box 1709, Newark, NJ 07107-1709, 973-972-4300.
Website: http://www.umdnj.edu/.

UNIVERSITY OF MEMPHIS
Memphis, TN

Tuition & fees (TN res): $8234	Average undergraduate aid package: $8783

ABOUT THE INSTITUTION State-supported, coed. *Awards:* certificates, bachelor's, master's, and doctoral degrees. 66 undergraduate majors. *Total enrollment:* 22,139. Undergraduates: 17,647. Freshmen: 2,252. Federal methodology is used as a basis for awarding need-based institutional aid.
UNDERGRADUATE EXPENSES for 2013–2014 *Application fee:* $25. *Tuition, state resident:* full-time $6978; part-time $277 per credit hour. *Tuition, nonresident:* full-time $22,428; part-time $890 per credit hour. *Required fees:* full-time $1256; $82.50 per credit hour. Full-time tuition and fees vary according to course load, degree level, program, and reciprocity agreements. Part-time tuition and fees vary according to course load, degree level, and program. *College room and board:* $6860. Room and board charges vary according to board plan and housing facility.
FRESHMAN FINANCIAL AID (Fall 2012, est.) 2,076 applied for aid; of those 81% were deemed to have need. 94% of freshmen with need received aid; of those 23% had need fully met. *Average percent of need met:* 84% (excluding resources awarded to replace EFC). *Average financial aid package:* $9433 (excluding resources awarded to replace EFC). 17% of all full-time freshmen had no need and received non-need-based gift aid.
UNDERGRADUATE FINANCIAL AID (Fall 2012, est.) 11,759 applied for aid; of those 85% were deemed to have need. 88% of undergraduates with need received aid; of those 15% had need fully met. *Average percent of need met:* 76% (excluding resources awarded to replace EFC). *Average financial aid package:* $8783 (excluding resources awarded to replace EFC). 10% of all full-time undergraduates had no need and received non-need-based gift aid.
GIFT AID (NEED-BASED) *Total amount:* $44,139,807 (82% federal, 17% state, 1% institutional). *Receiving aid:* Freshmen: 51% (1,120); all full-time undergraduates: 56% (7,052). *Average award:* Freshmen: $6678; Undergraduates: $5351. *Scholarships, grants, and awards:* Federal Pell, FSEOG, state, private, college/university gift aid from institutional funds.
GIFT AID (NON-NEED-BASED) *Total amount:* $32,761,765 (58% state, 39% institutional, 3% external sources). *Receiving aid:* Freshmen: 35% (769). Undergraduates: 43% (5,399). *Average award:* Freshmen: $7927. Undergraduates: $6109. *Scholarships, grants, and awards by category:* Academic interests/achievement: biological sciences, business, communication, education, engineering/technologies, English, general academic interests/achievements, health fields, humanities, international studies, mathematics, military science, physical sciences, premedicine, social sciences. *Creative arts/performance:* art/fine arts, cinema/film/broadcasting, dance, journalism/publications, music. *Special achievements/activities:* cheerleading/drum major, general special achievements/activities, leadership. *Special characteristics:* adult students, children of educators, children of faculty/staff, children of public servants, handicapped students, members of minority groups, public servants. *ROTC:* Army, Naval, Air Force.
LOANS *Student loans:* $86,994,563 (46% need-based, 54% non-need-based). 57% of past graduating class borrowed through all loan programs. *Average indebtedness per student:* $22,214. *Average need-based loan:* Freshmen: $3283. Undergraduates: $3143. *Parent loans:* $3,997,366 (100% non-need-based). *Programs:* Federal Direct (Subsidized and Unsubsidized Stafford, PLUS), Perkins, college/university.
WORK-STUDY *Federal work-study:* Total amount: $451,050; 207 jobs averaging $2348. *State or other work-study/employment:* Total amount: $3,065,277 (100% non-need-based). Part-time jobs available.
ATHLETIC AWARDS Total amount: $4,689,403 (100% non-need-based).
APPLYING FOR FINANCIAL AID *Required financial aid form:* FAFSA. *Financial aid deadline (priority):* 3/1. *Notification date:* Continuous beginning 4/1. Students must reply by 8/1.
CONTACT Richard Ritzman, Director of Student Financial Aid, University of Memphis, Wilder Tower 103, Memphis, TN 38152, 901-678-2832 or toll-free 800-669-2678. *Fax:* 901-678-3590. *E-mail:* rritzman@memphis.edu.
Website: http://www.memphis.edu/.

UNIVERSITY OF MIAMI
Coral Gables, FL

Tuition & fees: $42,852	Average undergraduate aid package: $33,932

ABOUT THE INSTITUTION Independent, coed. *Awards:* certificates, bachelor's, master's, and doctoral degrees. 119 undergraduate majors. *Total enrollment:* 16,172. Undergraduates: 10,590. Freshmen: 2,012. Both federal and institutional methodology are used as a basis for awarding need-based institutional aid.
UNDERGRADUATE EXPENSES for 2013–2014 *Application fee:* $70. *Comprehensive fee:* $55,166 includes full-time tuition ($41,580), mandatory fees ($1272), and room and board ($12,314). *College room only:* $7122. Room and board charges vary according to board plan and housing facility. *Part-time tuition:* $1730 per credit hour. Part-time tuition and fees vary according to course load. *Payment plans:* Guaranteed tuition, tuition prepayment.
FRESHMAN FINANCIAL AID (Fall 2012, est.) 1,371 applied for aid; of those 69% were deemed to have need. 100% of freshmen with need received aid; of those 45% had need fully met. *Average percent of need met:* 83% (excluding resources awarded to replace EFC). *Average financial aid package:* $34,845 (excluding resources awarded to replace EFC). 21% of all full-time freshmen had no need and received non-need-based gift aid.
UNDERGRADUATE FINANCIAL AID (Fall 2012, est.) 6,105 applied for aid; of those 75% were deemed to have need. 100% of undergraduates with need received aid; of those 38% had need fully met. *Average percent of need met:* 80% (excluding resources awarded to replace EFC). *Average financial aid package:* $33,932 (excluding resources awarded to replace EFC). 19% of all full-time undergraduates had no need and received non-need-based gift aid.
GIFT AID (NEED-BASED) *Total amount:* $96,916,690 (11% federal, 9% state, 78% institutional, 2% external sources). *Receiving aid:* Freshmen: 47% (937); all full-time undergraduates: 45% (4,407). *Average award:* Freshmen: $25,561; Undergraduates: $24,812. *Scholarships, grants, and awards:* Federal Pell, FSEOG, state, private, college/university gift aid from institutional funds.
GIFT AID (NON-NEED-BASED) *Total amount:* $57,616,554 (15% state, 82% institutional, 3% external sources). *Receiving aid:* Freshmen: 20% (405). Undergraduates: 16% (1,519). *Average award:* Freshmen: $19,874. Undergraduates: $20,841. *Scholarships, grants, and awards by category:* Academic interests/achievement: general academic interests/achievements, military science. *Creative arts/performance:* music, performing arts, theater/drama. *Special characteristics:* children of faculty/staff, international students, veterans, veterans' children. *Tuition waivers:* Full or partial for employees or children of employees. *ROTC:* Army, Air Force.
LOANS *Student loans:* $55,261,472 (66% need-based, 34% non-need-based). 45% of past graduating class borrowed through all loan programs. *Average indebtedness per student:* $26,786. *Average need-based loan:* Freshmen: $4479. Undergraduates: $6013. *Parent loans:* $17,481,377 (39% need-based, 61% non-need-based). *Programs:* Federal Direct (Subsidized and Unsubsidized Stafford, PLUS), Perkins, Federal Nursing, college/university, private loans.
WORK-STUDY *Federal work-study:* Total amount: $3,384,602; jobs available. *State or other work-study/employment:* Total amount: $2,809,382 (68% need-based, 32% non-need-based). Part-time jobs available.
ATHLETIC AWARDS Total amount: $11,629,566 (45% need-based, 55% non-need-based).

APPLYING FOR FINANCIAL AID *Required financial aid form:* FAFSA. *Financial aid deadline (priority):* 2/1. *Notification date:* Continuous beginning 3/15.
CONTACT Mr. James M. Bauer, Executive Director for Financial Assistance Services and Dean of Enrollment Management, University of Miami, 1204 Dickinson Drive, Rhodes House, 37R, Coral Gables, FL 33146, 305-284-2270. *Fax:* 305-284-8641. *E-mail:* jbauer@miami.edu.
Website: http://www.miami.edu/.

UNIVERSITY OF MICHIGAN
Ann Arbor, MI

Tuition & fees (MI res): $13,819	Average undergraduate aid package: $19,334

ABOUT THE INSTITUTION State-supported, coed. *Awards:* certificates, bachelor's, master's, and doctoral degrees. 122 undergraduate majors. *Total enrollment:* 42,716. Undergraduates: 27,407. Freshmen: 6,236. Both federal and institutional methodology are used as a basis for awarding need-based institutional aid.
UNDERGRADUATE EXPENSES for 2013–2014 *Application fee:* $65. *Tuition, state resident:* full-time $13,625; part-time $504 per credit hour. *Tuition, nonresident:* full-time $40,302; part-time $1592 per credit hour. *Required fees:* full-time $194; $97 per term. Full-time tuition and fees vary according to course load, program, and student level. Part-time tuition and fees vary according to course load, program, and student level. *College room and board:* $9752. Room and board charges vary according to board plan and housing facility.
FRESHMAN FINANCIAL AID (Fall 2011) 3,759 applied for aid; of those 68% were deemed to have need. 100% of freshmen with need received aid; of those 77% had need fully met. *Average percent of need met:* 85% (excluding resources awarded to replace EFC). *Average financial aid package:* $18,230 (excluding resources awarded to replace EFC). 20% of all full-time freshmen had no need and received non-need-based gift aid.
UNDERGRADUATE FINANCIAL AID (Fall 2011) 14,089 applied for aid; of those 76% were deemed to have need. 98% of undergraduates with need received aid; of those 81% had need fully met. *Average percent of need met:* 85% (excluding resources awarded to replace EFC). *Average financial aid package:* $19,334 (excluding resources awarded to replace EFC). 16% of all full-time undergraduates had no need and received non-need-based gift aid.
GIFT AID (NEED-BASED) *Total amount:* $108,355,959 (19% federal, 81% institutional). *Receiving aid:* Freshmen: 30% (1,837); all full-time undergraduates: 29% (7,919). *Average award:* Freshmen: $13,107; Undergraduates: $13,256. *Scholarships, grants, and awards:* Federal Pell, FSEOG, state, private, college/university gift aid from institutional funds, TEACH Grants, Byrd Scholarships.
GIFT AID (NON-NEED-BASED) *Total amount:* $70,778,085 (10% federal, 3% state, 66% institutional, 21% external sources). *Receiving aid:* Freshmen: 24% (1,465). Undergraduates: 22% (6,070). *Average award:* Freshmen: $6816. Undergraduates: $9756. *Scholarships, grants, and awards by category:* Academic interests/achievement: architecture, area/ethnic studies, biological sciences, business, communication, computer science, education, engineering/technologies, English, foreign languages, general academic interests/achievements, health fields, humanities, international studies, library science, mathematics, military science, physical sciences, premedicine, social sciences. Creative arts/performance: art/fine arts, cinema/film/broadcasting, creative writing, dance, journalism/publications, music, performing arts, theater/drama. Special achievements/activities: community service, general special achievements/activities, leadership. Special characteristics: children of faculty/staff, children of workers in trades, handicapped students, international students, local/state students, members of minority groups, out-of-state students. *ROTC:* Army, Naval, Air Force.
LOANS *Student loans:* $95,700,494 (48% need-based, 52% non-need-based). 44% of past graduating class borrowed through all loan programs. *Average indebtedness per student:* $27,815. *Average need-based loan:* Freshmen: $3950. Undergraduates: $5231. *Parent loans:* $29,271,851 (100% non-need-based). *Programs:* Federal Direct (Subsidized and Unsubsidized Stafford, PLUS), Perkins, Federal Nursing, college/university, Health Professions Student Loans (HPSL).
WORK-STUDY *Federal work-study:* Total amount: $13,761,826; 2,982 jobs averaging $1607.
ATHLETIC AWARDS Total amount: $16,012,508 (100% non-need-based).

APPLYING FOR FINANCIAL AID *Required financial aid forms:* FAFSA, CSS Financial Aid PROFILE. *Financial aid deadline:* 5/31 (priority: 4/30). *Notification date:* Continuous beginning 3/15.
CONTACT Office of Financial Aid Counseling and Advising Services, University of Michigan, 2500 Student Activities Building, 515 East Jefferson Street, Ann Arbor, MI 48109-1316, 734-763-6600. *Fax:* 734-647-3081. *E-mail:* financial.aid@umich.edu. *Website:* http://www.umich.edu/.

UNIVERSITY OF MICHIGAN–DEARBORN
Dearborn, MI

Tuition & fees (MI res): $10,482	Average undergraduate aid package: $10,439

ABOUT THE INSTITUTION State-supported, coed. *Awards:* bachelor's, master's, and doctoral degrees. 53 undergraduate majors. *Total enrollment:* 8,790. Undergraduates: 7,328. Freshmen: 871. Federal methodology is used as a basis for awarding need-based institutional aid.
UNDERGRADUATE EXPENSES for 2013–2014 *Application fee:* $30. *Tuition, state resident:* full-time $9876; part-time $391 per credit hour. *Tuition, nonresident:* full-time $22,290; part-time $887 per credit hour. *Required fees:* full-time $606; $245. Full-time tuition and fees vary according to course level, course load, degree level, program, and student level. Part-time tuition and fees vary according to course level, course load, degree level, program, and student level.
FRESHMAN FINANCIAL AID (Fall 2011) 804 applied for aid; of those 74% were deemed to have need. 97% of freshmen with need received aid; of those 3% had need fully met. *Average percent of need met:* 76% (excluding resources awarded to replace EFC). *Average financial aid package:* $10,662 (excluding resources awarded to replace EFC). 17% of all full-time freshmen had no need and received non-need-based gift aid.
UNDERGRADUATE FINANCIAL AID (Fall 2011) 3,805 applied for aid; of those 83% were deemed to have need. 98% of undergraduates with need received aid; of those 2% had need fully met. *Average percent of need met:* 72% (excluding resources awarded to replace EFC). *Average financial aid package:* $10,439 (excluding resources awarded to replace EFC). 11% of all full-time undergraduates had no need and received non-need-based gift aid.
GIFT AID (NEED-BASED) *Total amount:* $15,751,423 (78% federal, 2% state, 18% institutional, 2% external sources). *Receiving aid:* Freshmen: 49% (443); all full-time undergraduates: 50% (2,374). *Average award:* Freshmen: $5644; Undergraduates: $5297. *Scholarships, grants, and awards:* Federal Pell, FSEOG, state, private, college/university gift aid from institutional funds, United Negro College Fund.
GIFT AID (NON-NEED-BASED) *Total amount:* $2,570,339 (1% federal, 1% state, 94% institutional, 4% external sources). *Receiving aid:* Freshmen: 30% (274). Undergraduates: 15% (742). *Average award:* Freshmen: $4350. Undergraduates: $4563. *Scholarships, grants, and awards by category:* Academic interests/achievement: 1,050 awards ($3,425,956 total): biological sciences, business, communication, computer science, education, engineering/technologies, foreign languages, general academic interests/achievements, international studies, mathematics, physical sciences, social sciences. Creative arts/performance: 42 awards ($36,459 total): art/fine arts, cinema/film/broadcasting, creative writing, debating, general creative arts/performance, journalism/publications. Special achievements/activities: 87 awards ($335,590 total): community service, general special achievements/activities, leadership, memberships. Special characteristics: 400 awards ($1,293,085 total): adult students, children and siblings of alumni, children of faculty/staff, ethnic background, general special characteristics, handicapped students, international students, members of minority groups, out-of-state students, previous college experience, public servants. *Tuition waivers:* Full or partial for employees or children of employees, senior citizens. *ROTC:* Army.
LOANS *Student loans:* $30,293,703 (86% need-based, 14% non-need-based). 55% of past graduating class borrowed through all loan programs. *Average indebtedness per student:* $23,437. *Average need-based loan:* Freshmen: $3368. Undergraduates: $4457. *Parent loans:* $2,609,606 (17% need-based, 83% non-need-based). *Programs:* Federal Direct (Subsidized and Unsubsidized Stafford, PLUS), Perkins, college/university, alternative loans.
WORK-STUDY *Federal work-study:* Total amount: $178,787; 146 jobs averaging $1565. *State or other work-study/employment:* Part-time jobs available.

ATHLETIC AWARDS Total amount: $133,050 (58% need-based, 42% non-need-based).
APPLYING FOR FINANCIAL AID *Required financial aid form:* FAFSA. *Financial aid deadline (priority):* 2/15. *Notification date:* Continuous beginning 3/15. Students must reply within 5 weeks of notification.
CONTACT Ms. Katherine M. Allen, Director of Financial Aid and Scholarships, University of Michigan–Dearborn, 4901 Evergreen Road, 1183 UC, Dearborn, MI 48128-2406, 313-593-5300. *Fax:* 313-593-5313. *E-mail:* ask-ofa@umd.umich.edu. *Website:* http://www.umd.umich.edu/.

UNIVERSITY OF MICHIGAN–FLINT
Flint, MI

Tuition & fees (MI res): $9514	Average undergraduate aid package: $11,775

ABOUT THE INSTITUTION State-supported, coed. *Awards:* certificates, bachelor's, master's, and doctoral degrees. 75 undergraduate majors. *Total enrollment:* 8,289. Undergraduates: 6,984. Freshmen: 626. Federal methodology is used as a basis for awarding need-based institutional aid.
UNDERGRADUATE EXPENSES for 2013–2014 *Application fee:* $30. *Tuition, state resident:* full-time $9102; part-time $359 per credit hour. *Tuition, nonresident:* full-time $17,754; part-time $717.25 per credit hour. *Required fees:* full-time $412; $157 per term. Full-time tuition and fees vary according to course level, course load, degree level, program, and student level. Part-time tuition and fees vary according to course level, course load, degree level, program, and student level. *College room and board:* $7506; *Room only:* $4692. Room and board charges vary according to housing facility.
FRESHMAN FINANCIAL AID (Fall 2011) 546 applied for aid; of those 81% were deemed to have need. 95% of freshmen with need received aid; of those 5% had need fully met. *Average percent of need met:* 73% (excluding resources awarded to replace EFC). *Average financial aid package:* $10,187 (excluding resources awarded to replace EFC). 4% of all full-time freshmen had no need and received non-need-based gift aid.
UNDERGRADUATE FINANCIAL AID (Fall 2011) 3,852 applied for aid; of those 89% were deemed to have need. 97% of undergraduates with need received aid; of those 5% had need fully met. *Average percent of need met:* 73% (excluding resources awarded to replace EFC). *Average financial aid package:* $11,775 (excluding resources awarded to replace EFC). 2% of all full-time undergraduates had no need and received non-need-based gift aid.
GIFT AID (NEED-BASED) *Total amount:* $16,720,547 (76% federal, 2% state, 22% institutional). *Receiving aid:* Freshmen: 43% (285); all full-time undergraduates: 55% (2,485). *Average award:* Freshmen: $4883; Undergraduates: $4380. *Scholarships, grants, and awards:* Federal Pell, FSEOG, state, private, college/university gift aid from institutional funds, TEACH Grants.
GIFT AID (NON-NEED-BASED) *Total amount:* $2,998,004 (7% state, 79% institutional, 14% external sources). *Receiving aid:* Freshmen: 36% (236). Undergraduates: 42% (1,872). *Average award:* Freshmen: $3122. Undergraduates: $3268. *Scholarships, grants, and awards by category: Academic interests/achievement:* biological sciences, business, communication, computer science, education, engineering/technologies, English, foreign languages, general academic interests/achievements, health fields, humanities, international studies, mathematics, physical sciences, premedicine, social sciences. *Creative arts/performance:* art/fine arts, journalism/publications, music, performing arts, theater/drama. *Special achievements/activities:* community service, general special achievements/activities, hobbies/interests, leadership. *Special characteristics:* adult students, children and siblings of alumni, children of faculty/staff, children of union members/company employees, first-generation college students, general special characteristics, handicapped students, international students, local/state students, members of minority groups, veterans, veterans' children. *Tuition waivers:* Full or partial for senior citizens. *ROTC:* Army cooperative, Naval cooperative, Air Force cooperative.
LOANS *Student loans:* $37,605,722 (95% need-based, 5% non-need-based). 71% of past graduating class borrowed through all loan programs. *Average indebtedness per student:* $26,899. *Average need-based loan:* Freshmen: $3485. Undergraduates: $4230. *Parent loans:* $1,490,011 (100% non-need-based). *Programs:* Federal Direct (Subsidized and Unsubsidized Stafford, PLUS), Perkins.
WORK-STUDY *Federal work-study:* Total amount: $579,589; 292 jobs averaging $1999.

APPLYING FOR FINANCIAL AID *Required financial aid forms:* FAFSA, institution's own form. *Financial aid deadline (priority):* 3/1. *Notification date:* Continuous beginning 3/15.
CONTACT Lori Vedder, Office of Financial Aid, University of Michigan–Flint, Room 277 Pavilion, 303 East Kearsley Street, Flint, MI 48502-1950, 810-762-3444 or toll-free 800-942-5636. *Fax:* 810-766-6757. *E-mail:* financial_aid@list.flint.umich.edu. *Website:* http://www.umflint.edu/.

UNIVERSITY OF MINNESOTA, CROOKSTON
Crookston, MN

Tuition & fees (MN res): $11,455	Average undergraduate aid package: $11,905

ABOUT THE INSTITUTION State-supported, coed. *Awards:* bachelor's degrees. 42 undergraduate majors. *Total enrollment:* 2,764. Undergraduates: 2,764. Freshmen: 241. Federal methodology is used as a basis for awarding need-based institutional aid.
UNDERGRADUATE EXPENSES for 2013–2014 *Application fee:* $30. *Tuition, state resident:* full-time $10,030; part-time $385.77 per semester hour. *Tuition, nonresident:* full-time $10,030; part-time $385.77 per semester hour. *Required fees:* full-time $1425. Full-time tuition and fees vary according to course load and reciprocity agreements. Part-time tuition and fees vary according to course load and reciprocity agreements. *College room and board:* $7018; *Room only:* $3170. Room and board charges vary according to board plan and housing facility.
FRESHMAN FINANCIAL AID (Fall 2012, est.) 212 applied for aid; of those 83% were deemed to have need. 98% of freshmen with need received aid; of those 27% had need fully met. *Average percent of need met:* 75% (excluding resources awarded to replace EFC). *Average financial aid package:* $13,370 (excluding resources awarded to replace EFC). 12% of all full-time freshmen had no need and received non-need-based gift aid.
UNDERGRADUATE FINANCIAL AID (Fall 2012, est.) 1,092 applied for aid; of those 86% were deemed to have need. 99% of undergraduates with need received aid; of those 23% had need fully met. *Average percent of need met:* 73% (excluding resources awarded to replace EFC). *Average financial aid package:* $11,905 (excluding resources awarded to replace EFC). 7% of all full-time undergraduates had no need and received non-need-based gift aid.
GIFT AID (NEED-BASED) *Total amount:* $7,503,530 (37% federal, 24% state, 31% institutional, 8% external sources). *Receiving aid:* Freshmen: 71% (165); all full-time undergraduates: 64% (846). *Average award:* Freshmen: $9574; Undergraduates: $8019. *Scholarships, grants, and awards:* Federal Pell, FSEOG, state, private, college/university gift aid from institutional funds, Academic Competitiveness Grants, National SMART Grants.
GIFT AID (NON-NEED-BASED) *Total amount:* $417,378 (48% institutional, 52% external sources). *Receiving aid:* Freshmen: 13% (31). Undergraduates: 7% (96). *Average award:* Freshmen: $3640. Undergraduates: $2441. *Scholarships, grants, and awards by category: Academic interests/achievement:* agriculture, biological sciences, general academic interests/achievements. *Creative arts/performance:* general creative arts/performance. *Special achievements/activities:* leadership. *Special characteristics:* children and siblings of alumni, children of faculty/staff, ethnic background, first-generation college students, general special characteristics, local/state students, members of minority groups. *Tuition waivers:* Full or partial for senior citizens. *ROTC:* Air Force cooperative.
LOANS *Student loans:* $8,374,962 (83% need-based, 17% non-need-based). 73% of past graduating class borrowed through all loan programs. *Average indebtedness per student:* $27,608. *Average need-based loan:* Freshmen: $4404. Undergraduates: $4873. *Parent loans:* $988,847 (100% non-need-based). *Programs:* Federal Direct (Subsidized and Unsubsidized Stafford, PLUS), Perkins, state, private loans.
WORK-STUDY *Federal work-study:* Total amount: $66,745; 138 jobs averaging $490. *State or other work-study/employment:* Total amount: $253,251 (100% need-based). 77 part-time jobs averaging $644.
ATHLETIC AWARDS Total amount: $1,079,532 (100% non-need-based).
APPLYING FOR FINANCIAL AID *Required financial aid form:* FAFSA. *Financial aid deadline (priority):* 3/1. *Notification date:* Continuous. Students must reply within 8 weeks of notification.

CONTACT Melissa Dingmann, Director of Financial Aid, University of Minnesota, Crookston, 170 Owen Hall, 2900 University Avenue, Crookston, MN 56716-5001, 218-281-8576 or toll-free 800-862-6466. *Fax:* 218-281-8575. *E-mail:* dingmann@umn.edu.
Website: http://www.umcrookston.edu/.

UNIVERSITY OF MINNESOTA, DULUTH
Duluth, MN

Tuition & fees (MN res): $12,748	Average undergraduate aid package: $10,738

ABOUT THE INSTITUTION State-supported, coed. *Awards:* certificates, bachelor's, master's, and doctoral degrees. 87 undergraduate majors. *Total enrollment:* 11,491. Undergraduates: 10,346. Freshmen: 1,881. Federal methodology is used as a basis for awarding need-based institutional aid.
UNDERGRADUATE EXPENSES for 2013–2014 *Application fee:* $35. *Tuition, state resident:* full-time $11,720; part-time $450.76 per credit. *Tuition, nonresident:* full-time $14,385; part-time $553.26 per credit. *Required fees:* full-time $1028; $108.83 per term. Full-time tuition and fees vary according to course load, program, and reciprocity agreements. Part-time tuition and fees vary according to course load, program, and reciprocity agreements. *College room and board:* $6732. Room and board charges vary according to board plan and housing facility.
FRESHMAN FINANCIAL AID (Fall 2011) 1,849 applied for aid; of those 71% were deemed to have need. 98% of freshmen with need received aid; of those 22% had need fully met. *Average percent of need met:* 68% (excluding resources awarded to replace EFC). *Average financial aid package:* $10,567 (excluding resources awarded to replace EFC). 13% of all full-time freshmen had no need and received non-need-based gift aid.
UNDERGRADUATE FINANCIAL AID (Fall 2011) 7,729 applied for aid; of those 76% were deemed to have need. 98% of undergraduates with need received aid; of those 23% had need fully met. *Average percent of need met:* 69% (excluding resources awarded to replace EFC). *Average financial aid package:* $10,738 (excluding resources awarded to replace EFC). 11% of all full-time undergraduates had no need and received non-need-based gift aid.
GIFT AID (NEED-BASED) *Total amount:* $37,018,269 (29% federal, 25% state, 41% institutional, 5% external sources). *Receiving aid:* Freshmen: 56% (1,177); all full-time undergraduates: 54% (5,076). *Average award:* Freshmen: $7667; Undergraduates: $7304. *Scholarships, grants, and awards:* Federal Pell, FSEOG, state, private, college/university gift aid from institutional funds.
GIFT AID (NON-NEED-BASED) *Total amount:* $2,967,550 (1% state, 76% institutional, 23% external sources). *Receiving aid:* Freshmen: 11% (239). Undergraduates: 10% (904). *Average award:* Freshmen: $3118. Undergraduates: $3222. *Scholarships, grants, and awards by category:* Academic interests/achievement: general academic interests/achievements. *Tuition waivers:* Full or partial for employees or children of employees. *ROTC:* Air Force.
LOANS *Student loans:* $53,305,157 (78% need-based, 22% non-need-based). 74% of past graduating class borrowed through all loan programs. *Average indebtedness per student:* $31,711. *Average need-based loan:* Freshmen: $4139. Undergraduates: $4863. *Parent loans:* $18,489,205 (100% need-based). *Programs:* Federal Direct (Subsidized and Unsubsidized Stafford, PLUS), Perkins, state, college/university.
WORK-STUDY *Federal work-study:* Total amount: $490,790; 205 jobs averaging $2115. *State or other work-study/employment:* Total amount: $791,369 (100% need-based). 347 part-time jobs averaging $2281.
ATHLETIC AWARDS Total amount: $1,353,724 (100% need-based).
APPLYING FOR FINANCIAL AID *Required financial aid form:* FAFSA. *Financial aid deadline:* Continuous. *Notification date:* Continuous beginning 3/20.
CONTACT Ms. Brenda Herzig, Director of Financial Aid, University of Minnesota, Duluth, 10 University Drive, 184 Darland Administration Building, Duluth, MN 55812-2496, 218-726-8000 or toll-free 800-232-1339. *Fax:* 218-726-8219.
Website: http://www.d.umn.edu/.

UNIVERSITY OF MINNESOTA, MORRIS
Morris, MN

Tuition & fees (MN res): $12,550	Average undergraduate aid package: $15,225

ABOUT THE INSTITUTION State-supported, coed. 42 undergraduate majors. Federal methodology is used as a basis for awarding need-based institutional aid.
UNDERGRADUATE EXPENSES for 2013–2014 *Tuition, state resident:* full-time $11,720. *Tuition, nonresident:* full-time $11,720. *Required fees:* full-time $830. Full-time tuition and fees vary according to reciprocity agreements. Part-time tuition and fees vary according to course load and reciprocity agreements. *College room and board:* $7324; *Room only:* $3460. Room and board charges vary according to board plan and housing facility.
FRESHMAN FINANCIAL AID (Fall 2012, est.) 376 applied for aid; of those 76% were deemed to have need. 100% of freshmen with need received aid; of those 42% had need fully met. *Average percent of need met:* 80% (excluding resources awarded to replace EFC). *Average financial aid package:* $15,592 (excluding resources awarded to replace EFC). 19% of all full-time freshmen had no need and received non-need-based gift aid.
UNDERGRADUATE FINANCIAL AID (Fall 2012, est.) 1,382 applied for aid; of those 81% were deemed to have need. 100% of undergraduates with need received aid; of those 40% had need fully met. *Average percent of need met:* 80% (excluding resources awarded to replace EFC). *Average financial aid package:* $15,225 (excluding resources awarded to replace EFC). 16% of all full-time undergraduates had no need and received non-need-based gift aid.
GIFT AID (NEED-BASED) *Total amount:* $9,980,277 (30% federal, 21% state, 41% institutional, 8% external sources). *Receiving aid:* Freshmen: 65% (269); all full-time undergraduates: 61% (1,053). *Average award:* Freshmen: $10,011; Undergraduates: $9195. *Scholarships, grants, and awards:* Federal Pell, FSEOG, state, private, college/university gift aid from institutional funds.
GIFT AID (NON-NEED-BASED) *Total amount:* $1,469,925 (82% institutional, 18% external sources). *Receiving aid:* Freshmen: 23% (94). Undergraduates: 20% (349). *Average award:* Freshmen: $3656. Undergraduates: $3723. *Scholarships, grants, and awards by category:* Academic interests/achievement: general academic interests/achievements. Creative arts/performance: music. Special achievements/activities: general special achievements/activities. Special characteristics: ethnic background, international students, members of minority groups, veterans, veterans' children. *Tuition waivers:* Full or partial for senior citizens.
LOANS *Student loans:* $8,023,139 (79% need-based, 21% non-need-based). 66% of past graduating class borrowed through all loan programs. *Average indebtedness per student:* $25,124. *Average need-based loan:* Freshmen: $7969. Undergraduates: $7960. *Parent loans:* $289,547 (100% non-need-based). *Programs:* Federal Direct (Subsidized and Unsubsidized Stafford, PLUS), Perkins, state.
WORK-STUDY *Federal work-study:* Total amount: $779,266; 310 jobs averaging $1500. *State or other work-study/employment:* Total amount: $153,339 (100% need-based). 633 part-time jobs averaging $1800.
APPLYING FOR FINANCIAL AID *Required financial aid form:* FAFSA. *Financial aid deadline (priority):* 4/15. *Notification date:* Continuous beginning 3/25. Students must reply within 3 weeks of notification.
CONTACT Ms. Jill Beauregard, Director of Financial Aid, University of Minnesota, Morris, 600 East 4th Street, Morris, MN 56267, 320-589-6046 or toll-free 800-992-8863. *Fax:* 320-589-1673. *E-mail:* morrisfa@morris.umn.edu.
Website: http://www.mrs.umn.edu/.

UNIVERSITY OF MINNESOTA, TWIN CITIES CAMPUS
Minneapolis, MN

Tuition & fees (MN res): $13,459	Average undergraduate aid package: $12,756

ABOUT THE INSTITUTION State-supported, coed. *Awards:* certificates, diplomas, bachelor's, master's, and doctoral degrees. 219 undergraduate majors. *Total enrollment:* 51,853. Undergraduates: 34,469. Freshmen: 5,514. Federal methodology is used as a basis for awarding need-based institutional aid.

UNDERGRADUATE EXPENSES for 2013–2014 *Application fee:* $45. *Tuition, state resident:* full-time $12,060; part-time $463.85 per credit. *Tuition, nonresident:* full-time $17,310; part-time $665.77 per credit. *Required fees:* full-time $1399. Full-time tuition and fees vary according to program and reciprocity agreements. Part-time tuition and fees vary according to course load, program, and reciprocity agreements. *College room and board:* $8000; *Room only:* $4548. Room and board charges vary according to board plan, housing facility, and location.

FRESHMAN FINANCIAL AID (Fall 2012, est.) 4,518 applied for aid; of those 65% were deemed to have need. 99% of freshmen with need received aid; of those 30% had need fully met. *Average percent of need met:* 73% (excluding resources awarded to replace EFC). *Average financial aid package:* $12,910 (excluding resources awarded to replace EFC). 15% of all full-time freshmen had no need and received non-need-based gift aid.

UNDERGRADUATE FINANCIAL AID (Fall 2012, est.) 19,887 applied for aid; of those 76% were deemed to have need. 98% of undergraduates with need received aid; of those 26% had need fully met. *Average percent of need met:* 70% (excluding resources awarded to replace EFC). *Average financial aid package:* $12,756 (excluding resources awarded to replace EFC). 12% of all full-time undergraduates had no need and received non-need-based gift aid.

GIFT AID (NEED-BASED) *Total amount:* $108,451,144 (31% federal, 22% state, 44% institutional, 3% external sources). *Receiving aid:* Freshmen: 45% (2,454); all full-time undergraduates: 45% (12,928). *Average award:* Freshmen: $9279; Undergraduates: $8154. *Scholarships, grants, and awards:* Federal Pell, FSEOG, state, private, college/university gift aid from institutional funds, Federal Nursing, ROTC Scholarships, Academic Merit scholarships.

GIFT AID (NON-NEED-BASED) *Total amount:* $19,075,889 (94% institutional, 6% external sources). *Receiving aid:* Freshmen: 7% (399). Undergraduates: 6% (1,620). *Average award:* Freshmen: $5928. Undergraduates: $6276. *Scholarships, grants, and awards by category: Academic interests/achievement:* agriculture, architecture, area/ethnic studies, biological sciences, business, communication, computer science, education, engineering/technologies, English, foreign languages, general academic interests/achievements, health fields, home economics, humanities, international studies, library science, mathematics, military science, physical sciences, premedicine, religion/biblical studies, social sciences. *Creative arts/performance:* general creative arts/performance. *Special achievements/activities:* hobbies/interests, leadership. *Special characteristics:* general special characteristics, local/state students, members of minority groups. *Tuition waivers:* Full or partial for senior citizens. *ROTC:* Army, Naval, Air Force.

LOANS *Student loans:* $129,205,518 (81% need-based, 19% non-need-based). 63% of past graduating class borrowed through all loan programs. *Average indebtedness per student:* $29,702. *Average need-based loan:* Freshmen: $4831. Undergraduates: $5890. *Parent loans:* $44,220,543 (100% non-need-based). *Programs:* Federal Direct (Subsidized and Unsubsidized Stafford, PLUS), Perkins, Federal Nursing, state, college/university, Health Professions Student Loans (HPSL).

WORK-STUDY *Federal work-study:* Total amount: $4,412,663; jobs available. *State or other work-study/employment:* Total amount: $12,687,260 (100% need-based). Part-time jobs available.

ATHLETIC AWARDS Total amount: $16,766 (100% non-need-based).

APPLYING FOR FINANCIAL AID *Required financial aid forms:* FAFSA, institution's own form. *Financial aid deadline (priority):* 3/1. *Notification date:* Continuous beginning 2/15.

CONTACT Office of Student Finance, University of Minnesota, Twin Cities Campus, 200 Fraser Hall, 106 Pleasant Street SE, Minneapolis, MN 55455, 612-624-1111 or toll-free 800-752-1000. *Fax:* 612-624-9584. *E-mail:* onestop@umn.edu. *Website:* http://www.umn.edu/tc/.

UNIVERSITY OF MISSISSIPPI
Oxford, MS

Tuition & fees (MS res): $6282	Average undergraduate aid package: $7583

ABOUT THE INSTITUTION State-supported, coed. *Awards:* certificates, bachelor's, master's, and doctoral degrees. 65 undergraduate majors. *Total enrollment:* 18,794. Undergraduates: 16,060. Freshmen: 3,373. Federal methodology is used as a basis for awarding need-based institutional aid.

UNDERGRADUATE EXPENSES for 2013–2014 *Application fee:* $35. *Tuition, state resident:* full-time $6282; part-time $261.75 per credit hour.

Tuition, nonresident: full-time $16,266; part-time $677.75 per credit hour. Full-time tuition and fees vary according to course load and program. Part-time tuition and fees vary according to course load and program. *College room and board:* $9200. Room and board charges vary according to board plan and housing facility. *Payment plan:* Tuition prepayment.

FRESHMAN FINANCIAL AID (Fall 2011) 2,635 applied for aid; of those 68% were deemed to have need. 97% of freshmen with need received aid; of those 14% had need fully met. *Average percent of need met:* 77% (excluding resources awarded to replace EFC). *Average financial aid package:* $9347 (excluding resources awarded to replace EFC). 24% of all full-time freshmen had no need and received non-need-based gift aid.

UNDERGRADUATE FINANCIAL AID (Fall 2011) 9,799 applied for aid; of those 78% were deemed to have need. 97% of undergraduates with need received aid; of those 11% had need fully met. *Average percent of need met:* 74% (excluding resources awarded to replace EFC). *Average financial aid package:* $7583 (excluding resources awarded to replace EFC). 13% of all full-time undergraduates had no need and received non-need-based gift aid.

GIFT AID (NEED-BASED) *Total amount:* $41,655,706 (52% federal, 7% state, 37% institutional, 4% external sources). *Receiving aid:* Freshmen: 43% (1,533); all full-time undergraduates: 45% (6,505). *Average award:* Freshmen: $7924; Undergraduates: $6857. *Scholarships, grants, and awards:* Federal Pell, FSEOG, state, private, college/university gift aid from institutional funds.

GIFT AID (NON-NEED-BASED) *Total amount:* $21,911,682 (13% state, 81% institutional, 6% external sources). *Receiving aid:* Freshmen: 7% (243). Undergraduates: 4% (640). *Average award:* Freshmen: $6601. Undergraduates: $5747. *Scholarships, grants, and awards by category: Academic interests/achievement:* 9,693 awards ($23,286,926 total): biological sciences, business, communication, computer science, education, engineering/technologies, English, foreign languages, general academic interests/achievements, health fields, humanities, international studies, mathematics, military science, physical sciences, premedicine, religion/biblical studies, social sciences. *Creative arts/performance:* 694 awards ($1,026,980 total): art/fine arts, cinema/film/broadcasting, creative writing, debating, journalism/publications, music, performing arts, theater/drama. *Special achievements/activities:* 4,246 awards ($8,518,084 total): cheerleading/drum major, community service, general special achievements/activities, junior miss, leadership, memberships. *Special characteristics:* 5,909 awards ($13,193,796 total): adult students, children and siblings of alumni, children of faculty/staff, ethnic background, first-generation college students, general special characteristics, handicapped students, international students, local/state students, members of minority groups, out-of-state students, previous college experience, spouses of current students. *Tuition waivers:* Full or partial for children of alumni, employees or children of employees, senior citizens. *ROTC:* Army, Naval, Air Force.

LOANS *Student loans:* $58,038,945 (79% need-based, 21% non-need-based). 47% of past graduating class borrowed through all loan programs. *Average indebtedness per student:* $23,986. *Average need-based loan:* Freshmen: $3740. Undergraduates: $4389. *Parent loans:* $21,986,380 (39% need-based, 61% non-need-based). *Programs:* Federal Direct (Subsidized and Unsubsidized Stafford, PLUS), Perkins, college/university, alternative loans, Health Professions Student Loans (HPSL).

WORK-STUDY *Federal work-study:* Total amount: $593,642; 422 jobs averaging $1325.

ATHLETIC AWARDS Total amount: $5,740,454 (52% need-based, 48% non-need-based).

APPLYING FOR FINANCIAL AID *Required financial aid form:* FAFSA. *Financial aid deadline (priority):* 3/1. *Notification date:* Continuous beginning 4/1. Students must reply within 4 weeks of notification.

CONTACT Ms. Laura Diven-Brown, Director of Financial Aid, University of Mississippi, 257 Martindale Center, University, MS 38677, 662-915-5788 or toll-free 800-653-6477 (in-state). *Fax:* 662-915-1164. *E-mail:* ldivenbr@olemiss.edu. *Website:* http://www.olemiss.edu/.

UNIVERSITY OF MISSISSIPPI MEDICAL CENTER
Jackson, MS

CONTACT Minetta Veazey, Administrative Secretary, University of Mississippi Medical Center, 2500 North State Street, Jackson, MS 39216, 601-984-1117. *Fax:* 601-984-6984. *E-mail:* mveazey@registrar.umsmed.edu. *Website:* http://www.umc.edu/.

UNIVERSITY OF MISSOURI
Columbia, MO

ABOUT THE INSTITUTION State-supported, coed. **Awards:** certificates, bachelor's, master's, and doctoral degrees. 115 undergraduate majors. **Total enrollment:** 34,748. Undergraduates: 26,996. Freshmen: 6,501.

GIFT AID (NEED-BASED) Scholarships, grants, and awards: Federal Pell, FSEOG, state, private, college/university gift aid from institutional funds, Federal Nursing.

GIFT AID (NON-NEED-BASED) Scholarships, grants, and awards by category: Academic interests/achievement: agriculture, area/ethnic studies, biological sciences, business, communication, computer science, education, engineering/technologies, English, foreign languages, general academic interests/achievements, health fields, home economics, humanities, international studies, library science, mathematics, physical sciences, premedicine, religion/biblical studies, social sciences. Creative arts/performance: art/fine arts, cinema/film/broadcasting, creative writing, journalism/publications, music, theater/drama. Special achievements/activities: cheerleading/drum major, general special achievements/activities, memberships. Special characteristics: adult students, children and siblings of alumni, children of faculty/staff, ethnic background, first-generation college students, international students, local/state students, members of minority groups, out-of-state students.

LOANS Programs: Federal Direct (Subsidized and Unsubsidized Stafford, PLUS), Perkins, Federal Nursing, state, college/university, alternative loans.

WORK-STUDY Federal work-study: Total amount: $1,866,119; jobs available.

APPLYING FOR FINANCIAL AID Required financial aid form: FAFSA.

CONTACT Nicholas Prewett, Director of Student Financial Aid, University of Missouri, 11 Jesse Hall, Columbia, MO 65211, 573-882-7506 or toll-free 800-225-6075 (in-state). Fax: 573-884-5335. E-mail: finaidinfo@missouri.edu. Website: http://www.missouri.edu/.

UNIVERSITY OF MISSOURI–KANSAS CITY
Kansas City, MO

Tuition & fees (MO res): $9220	Average undergraduate aid package: $9513

ABOUT THE INSTITUTION State-supported, coed. **Awards:** certificates, bachelor's, master's, and doctoral degrees. 56 undergraduate majors. **Total enrollment:** 16,019. Undergraduates: 10,626. Freshmen: 1,125. Federal methodology is used as a basis for awarding need-based institutional aid.

UNDERGRADUATE EXPENSES for 2013–2014 Application fee: $45. **Tuition, state resident:** full-time $7968; part-time $265.60 per credit hour. **Tuition, nonresident:** full-time $20,502; part-time $683.40 per credit hour. **Required fees:** full-time $1252; $63.51 per credit hour. Full-time tuition and fees vary according to course load and program. Part-time tuition and fees vary according to course load and program. **College room and board:** $11,428. Room and board charges vary according to board plan and housing facility.

FRESHMAN FINANCIAL AID (Fall 2012, est.) 922 applied for aid; of those 84% were deemed to have need. 98% of freshmen with need received aid; of those 9% had need fully met. **Average percent of need met:** 53% (excluding resources awarded to replace EFC). **Average financial aid package:** $10,463 (excluding resources awarded to replace EFC). 18% of all full-time freshmen had no need and received non-need-based gift aid.

UNDERGRADUATE FINANCIAL AID (Fall 2012, est.) 5,338 applied for aid; of those 89% were deemed to have need. 97% of undergraduates with need received aid; of those 6% had need fully met. **Average percent of need met:** 49% (excluding resources awarded to replace EFC). **Average financial aid package:** $9513 (excluding resources awarded to replace EFC). 14% of all full-time undergraduates had no need and received non-need-based gift aid.

GIFT AID (NEED-BASED) Total amount: $26,593,885 (56% federal, 9% state, 30% institutional, 5% external sources). **Receiving aid:** Freshmen: 66% (729); all full-time undergraduates: 59% (4,002). **Average award:** Freshmen: $7401; Undergraduates: $6346. **Scholarships, grants, and awards:** Federal Pell, FSEOG, state, private, college/university gift aid from institutional funds, United Negro College Fund, Federal Nursing.

GIFT AID (NON-NEED-BASED) Total amount: $5,058,387 (4% state, 82% institutional, 14% external sources). **Receiving aid:** Freshmen: 2% (20). Undergrad-

uates: 1% (56). **Average award:** Freshmen: $4306. Undergraduates: $4493. **Scholarships, grants, and awards by category:** Academic interests/achievement: 5,994 awards ($16,826,243 total): general academic interests/achievements. Creative arts/performance: 309 awards ($796,846 total): art/fine arts, debating, general creative arts/performance, music, performing arts. Special achievements/activities: 234 awards ($310,543 total): general special achievements/activities, leadership. Special characteristics: 2,547 awards ($6,965,503 total): children and siblings of alumni, ethnic background, local/state students, members of minority groups, out-of-state students. **Tuition waivers:** Full or partial for employees or children of employees. **ROTC:** Army, Air Force cooperative.

LOANS Student loans: $42,301,167 (89% need-based, 11% non-need-based). 64% of past graduating class borrowed through all loan programs. Average indebtedness per student: $24,326. **Average need-based loan:** Freshmen: $6357. Undergraduates: $8272. **Parent loans:** $10,400,536 (71% need-based, 29% non-need-based). **Programs:** Federal Direct (Subsidized and Unsubsidized Stafford, PLUS), Perkins, Federal Nursing, state, college/university.

WORK-STUDY Federal work-study: Total amount: $2,463,128; 472 jobs averaging $3975.

ATHLETIC AWARDS Total amount: $3,003,689 (35% need-based, 65% non-need-based).

APPLYING FOR FINANCIAL AID Required financial aid form: FAFSA. **Financial aid deadline (priority):** 3/1. **Notification date:** Continuous beginning 4/15. Students must reply within 2 weeks of notification.

CONTACT Nancy Merz, Director of Financial Aid and Scholarships, University of Missouri–Kansas City, 5100 Rockhill Road, Kansas City, MO 64110-2499, 816-235-1154 or toll-free 800-775-8652. Fax: 816-235-5511. E-mail: merzn@umkc.edu. Website: http://www.umkc.edu/.

UNIVERSITY OF MISSOURI–ST. LOUIS
St. Louis, MO

Tuition & fees (MO res): $9474	Average undergraduate aid package: $11,828

ABOUT THE INSTITUTION State-supported, coed. **Awards:** certificates, bachelor's, master's, and doctoral degrees. 63 undergraduate majors. **Total enrollment:** 16,719. Undergraduates: 13,349. Freshmen: 546. Federal methodology is used as a basis for awarding need-based institutional aid.

UNDERGRADUATE EXPENSES for 2013–2014 Application fee: $35. **Tuition, state resident:** full-time $9474; part-time $315.80 per credit hour. **Tuition, nonresident:** full-time $24,429; part-time $814.30 per credit hour. Full-time tuition and fees vary according to course load, program, and reciprocity agreements. Part-time tuition and fees vary according to course load, program, and reciprocity agreements. **College room and board:** $8830; **Room only:** $5200. Room and board charges vary according to board plan and housing facility.

FRESHMAN FINANCIAL AID (Fall 2012, est.) 452 applied for aid; of those 83% were deemed to have need. 99% of freshmen with need received aid; of those 30% had need fully met. **Average percent of need met:** 77% (excluding resources awarded to replace EFC). **Average financial aid package:** $13,960 (excluding resources awarded to replace EFC). 10% of all full-time freshmen had no need and received non-need-based gift aid.

UNDERGRADUATE FINANCIAL AID (Fall 2012, est.) 4,725 applied for aid; of those 89% were deemed to have need. 99% of undergraduates with need received aid; of those 17% had need fully met. **Average percent of need met:** 63% (excluding resources awarded to replace EFC). **Average financial aid package:** $11,828 (excluding resources awarded to replace EFC). 3% of all full-time undergraduates had no need and received non-need-based gift aid.

GIFT AID (NEED-BASED) Total amount: $29,926,654 (55% federal, 7% state, 31% institutional, 7% external sources). **Receiving aid:** Freshmen: 62% (328); all full-time undergraduates: 56% (3,284). **Average award:** Freshmen: $9594; Undergraduates: $6760. **Scholarships, grants, and awards:** Federal Pell, FSEOG, state, private, college/university gift aid from institutional funds, United Negro College Fund, Federal Nursing, TEACH Grants.

GIFT AID (NON-NEED-BASED) Total amount: $1,993,875 (4% federal, 5% state, 75% institutional, 16% external sources). **Receiving aid:** Freshmen: 18% (97). Undergraduates: 9% (521). **Average award:** Freshmen: $4797. Undergraduates: $4341. **Scholarships, grants, and awards by category:** Academic interests/achievement: biological sciences, business, communication, computer science, education, engineering/technologies, English, foreign languages, general academic interests/

achievements, health fields, humanities, international studies, mathematics, physical sciences, premedicine, social sciences. *Creative arts/performance:* applied art and design, art/fine arts, creative writing, dance, music, theater/drama. *Special achievements/activities:* cheerleading/drum major, community service, memberships. *Special characteristics:* adult students, children and siblings of alumni, children of faculty/staff, ethnic background, general special characteristics, international students, local/state students, members of minority groups, out-of-state students, previous college experience, veterans. *Tuition waivers:* Full or partial for employees or children of employees, senior citizens. **ROTC:** Army cooperative, Air Force cooperative.

LOANS *Student loans:* $56,720,699 (87% need-based, 13% non-need-based). 60% of past graduating class borrowed through all loan programs. *Average indebtedness per student:* $24,377. *Average need-based loan:* Freshmen: $3280. Undergraduates: $4533. *Parent loans:* $2,737,139 (34% need-based, 66% non-need-based). *Programs:* Federal Direct (Subsidized and Unsubsidized Stafford, PLUS), Perkins, Federal Nursing, state.

WORK-STUDY *Federal work-study:* Total amount: $222,079; 66 jobs averaging $3365.

ATHLETIC AWARDS Total amount: $1,749,927 (82% need-based, 18% non-need-based).

APPLYING FOR FINANCIAL AID *Required financial aid form:* FAFSA. *Financial aid deadline (priority):* 3/1. *Notification date:* Continuous beginning 4/1. Students must reply within 2 weeks of notification.

CONTACT Ms. Samantha M. Matchefts, Senior Associate Director of Student Financial Aid, University of Missouri–St. Louis, One University Boulevard, 327 Millennium Student Center, St. Louis, MO 63121-4400, 314-516-6893 or toll-free 888-GO2-UMSL (in-state), 888-GO2-USML (out-of-state). *Fax:* 314-516-5408. *E-mail:* samantha.matchefts@umsl.edu. *Website:* http://www.umsl.edu/.

UNIVERSITY OF MOBILE
Mobile, AL

Tuition & fees: $17,680	Average undergraduate aid package: $15,931

ABOUT THE INSTITUTION Independent Southern Baptist, coed. *Awards:* associate, bachelor's, and master's degrees. 30 undergraduate majors. *Total enrollment:* 1,719. Undergraduates: 1,552. Freshmen: 230. Federal methodology is used as a basis for awarding need-based institutional aid.

UNDERGRADUATE EXPENSES for 2013–2014 *Application fee:* $50. *Comprehensive fee:* $26,330 includes full-time tuition ($17,110), mandatory fees ($570), and room and board ($8650). *College room only:* $5100. Full-time tuition and fees vary according to course load. Room and board charges vary according to housing facility. *Part-time tuition:* $609 per credit hour. *Part-time fees:* $346 per year. Part-time tuition and fees vary according to course load.

FRESHMAN FINANCIAL AID (Fall 2012, est.) 196 applied for aid; of those 87% were deemed to have need. 100% of freshmen with need received aid; of those 19% had need fully met. *Average percent of need met:* 75% (excluding resources awarded to replace EFC). *Average financial aid package:* $16,908 (excluding resources awarded to replace EFC). 11% of all full-time freshmen had no need and received non-need-based gift aid.

UNDERGRADUATE FINANCIAL AID (Fall 2012, est.) 902 applied for aid; of those 90% were deemed to have need. 100% of undergraduates with need received aid; of those 17% had need fully met. *Average percent of need met:* 54% (excluding resources awarded to replace EFC). *Average financial aid package:* $15,931 (excluding resources awarded to replace EFC). 7% of all full-time undergraduates had no need and received non-need-based gift aid.

GIFT AID (NEED-BASED) *Total amount:* $10,139,800 (31% federal, 2% state, 61% institutional, 6% external sources). *Receiving aid:* Freshmen: 46% (106); all full-time undergraduates: 40% (512). *Average award:* Freshmen: $4791; Undergraduates: $5189. *Scholarships, grants, and awards:* Federal Pell, FSEOG, state, private, college/university gift aid from institutional funds, Federal Nursing.

GIFT AID (NON-NEED-BASED) *Total amount:* $253,771 (100% external sources). *Receiving aid:* Freshmen: 74% (170). Undergraduates: 59% (758). *Average award:* Freshmen: $5900. Undergraduates: $5200. *Scholarships, grants, and awards by category:* Academic interests/achievement: general academic interests/achievements. *Creative arts/performance:* art/fine arts, music, performing arts. *Special achievements/activities:* religious involvement. *Special characteristics:*

children of faculty/staff, relatives of clergy. *Tuition waivers:* Full or partial for employees or children of employees. **ROTC:** Army cooperative, Air Force cooperative.

LOANS *Student loans:* $12,232,307 (34% need-based, 66% non-need-based). 91% of past graduating class borrowed through all loan programs. *Average indebtedness per student:* $29,474. *Average need-based loan:* Freshmen: $3542. Undergraduates: $4642. *Parent loans:* $662,512 (100% non-need-based). *Programs:* Federal Direct (Subsidized and Unsubsidized Stafford, PLUS), Perkins, Federal Nursing, college/university.

WORK-STUDY *Federal work-study:* Total amount: $134,529; 63 jobs averaging $2175.

ATHLETIC AWARDS Total amount: $2,754,129 (100% non-need-based).

APPLYING FOR FINANCIAL AID *Required financial aid forms:* FAFSA, institution's own form, state aid form. *Financial aid deadline:* Continuous. *Notification date:* Continuous beginning 2/1. Students must reply within 2 weeks of notification.

CONTACT Mrs. Marie Thomas Batson, Associate Vice President for Campus Life and Enrollment Management Services, University of Mobile, 5735 College Parkway, Mobile, AL 36613, 251-442-2370 or toll-free 800-946-7267. *Fax:* 251-442-2498. *E-mail:* mbatson@umobile.edu. *Website:* http://www.umobile.edu/.

THE UNIVERSITY OF MONTANA
Missoula, MT

Tuition & fees (MT res): $6216	Average undergraduate aid package: $7762

ABOUT THE INSTITUTION State-supported, coed. 116 undergraduate majors. Federal methodology is used as a basis for awarding need-based institutional aid.

UNDERGRADUATE EXPENSES for 2013–2014 *Tuition, state resident:* full-time $4604; part-time $192 per credit hour. *Tuition, nonresident:* full-time $20,194; part-time $841 per credit hour. *Required fees:* full-time $1612; $50 per credit hour. Full-time tuition and fees vary according to degree level, location, program, reciprocity agreements, and student level. Part-time tuition and fees vary according to course load, degree level, location, and student level. *College room and board:* $7262; *Room only:* $3170. Room and board charges vary according to board plan and housing facility.

FRESHMAN FINANCIAL AID (Fall 2012, est.) 1,018 applied for aid; of those 66% were deemed to have need. 98% of freshmen with need received aid; of those 12% had need fully met. *Average percent of need met:* 60% (excluding resources awarded to replace EFC). *Average financial aid package:* $8390 (excluding resources awarded to replace EFC). 61% of all full-time freshmen had no need and received non-need-based gift aid.

UNDERGRADUATE FINANCIAL AID (Fall 2012, est.) 7,369 applied for aid; of those 82% were deemed to have need. 98% of undergraduates with need received aid; of those 8% had need fully met. *Average percent of need met:* 52% (excluding resources awarded to replace EFC). *Average financial aid package:* $7762 (excluding resources awarded to replace EFC). 30% of all full-time undergraduates had no need and received non-need-based gift aid.

GIFT AID (NEED-BASED) *Total amount:* $34,894,324 (90% federal, 5% state, 5% institutional). *Receiving aid:* Freshmen: 33% (428); all full-time undergraduates: 42% (4,169). *Average award:* Freshmen: $4684; Undergraduates: $4913. *Scholarships, grants, and awards:* Federal Pell, FSEOG, state, private, college/university gift aid from institutional funds.

GIFT AID (NON-NEED-BASED) *Total amount:* $15,702,971 (88% institutional, 12% external sources). *Receiving aid:* Freshmen: 35% (458). Undergraduates: 16% (1,645). *Average award:* Freshmen: $3300. Undergraduates: $3156. *Scholarships, grants, and awards by category:* Academic interests/achievement: biological sciences, business, computer science, education, English, foreign languages, general academic interests/achievements, health fields, humanities, international studies, mathematics, military science, physical sciences, premedicine, social sciences. *Creative arts/performance:* creative writing, dance, journalism/publications, music, performing arts, theater/drama. *Special achievements/activities:* cheerleading/drum major, leadership, rodeo. *Special characteristics:* children and siblings of alumni, children with a deceased or disabled parent, general special characteristics, international students, local/state students, out-of-state students, veterans. *Tuition waivers:*

Full or partial for minority students, employees or children of employees, senior citizens.

LOANS *Student loans:* $72,895,558 (100% need-based). 56% of past graduating class borrowed through all loan programs. *Average indebtedness per student:* $29,126. *Average need-based loan:* Freshmen: $3707. Undergraduates: $4263. *Parent loans:* $12,567,986 (6% need-based, 94% non-need-based). *Programs:* Federal Direct (Subsidized and Unsubsidized Stafford, PLUS), Perkins.

WORK-STUDY *Federal work-study:* Total amount: $2,690,446; jobs available. *State or other work-study/employment:* Total amount: $1,475,170 (100% need-based). Part-time jobs available.

ATHLETIC AWARDS Total amount: $1,617,395 (100% non-need-based).

APPLYING FOR FINANCIAL AID *Required financial aid forms:* FAFSA, UM Supplemental Information Sheet. *Financial aid deadline (priority):* 2/15. *Notification date:* Continuous beginning 4/1. Students must reply within 4 weeks of notification.

CONTACT Kent McGowan, Director of Financial Aid, The University of Montana, Lommasson Center 218, Missoula, MT 59812, 406-243-5373 or toll-free 800-462-8636. *Fax:* 406-243-4930. *E-mail:* faid@mso.umt.edu.
Website: http://www.umt.edu/.

THE UNIVERSITY OF MONTANA WESTERN
Dillon, MT

Tuition & fees (MT res): $4719	Average undergraduate aid package: $3262

ABOUT THE INSTITUTION State-supported, coed. *Awards:* certificates, associate, and bachelor's degrees. 34 undergraduate majors. *Total enrollment:* 1,483. Undergraduates: 1,483. Freshmen: 290. Federal methodology is used as a basis for awarding need-based institutional aid.

UNDERGRADUATE EXPENSES for 2013–2014 *Application fee:* $30. *Tuition, state resident:* full-time $3699; part-time $153 per credit. *Tuition, nonresident:* full-time $13,532; part-time $562 per credit. *Required fees:* full-time $1020; $134 per credit. Full-time tuition and fees vary according to course load, location, program, reciprocity agreements, and student level. Part-time tuition and fees vary according to course load, location, program, reciprocity agreements, and student level. *College room and board:* $6180; *Room only:* $2310. Room and board charges vary according to housing facility.

FRESHMAN FINANCIAL AID (Fall 2012, est.) 274 applied for aid; of those 83% were deemed to have need. 100% of freshmen with need received aid; of those 6% had need fully met. *Average percent of need met:* 15% (excluding resources awarded to replace EFC). *Average financial aid package:* $2844 (excluding resources awarded to replace EFC). 1% of all full-time freshmen had no need and received non-need-based gift aid.

UNDERGRADUATE FINANCIAL AID (Fall 2012, est.) 1,200 applied for aid; of those 84% were deemed to have need. 100% of undergraduates with need received aid; of those 11% had need fully met. *Average percent of need met:* 17% (excluding resources awarded to replace EFC). *Average financial aid package:* $3262 (excluding resources awarded to replace EFC). 1% of all full-time undergraduates had no need and received non-need-based gift aid.

GIFT AID (NEED-BASED) *Total amount:* $5,252,252 (52% federal, 3% state, 34% institutional, 11% external sources). *Receiving aid:* Freshmen: 68% (190); all full-time undergraduates: 67% (824). *Average award:* Freshmen: $2968; Undergraduates: $3439. *Scholarships, grants, and awards:* Federal Pell, FSEOG, state, private, college/university gift aid from institutional funds, TEACH Grants, Western Undergraduate Exchange (WUE) Scholarships.

GIFT AID (NON-NEED-BASED) *Total amount:* $910,334 (3% state, 81% institutional, 16% external sources). *Receiving aid:* Freshmen: 76% (210). Undergraduates: 72% (893). *Average award:* Freshmen: $3975. Undergraduates: $1840. *Scholarships, grants, and awards by category: Academic interests/achievement:* 27 awards ($38,250 total): biological sciences, business, education, English, general academic interests/achievements, humanities, mathematics, physical sciences, premedicine, social sciences. *Creative arts/performance:* 25 awards ($60,000 total): art/fine arts. *Special achievements/activities:* 50 awards ($196,220 total): general special achievements/activities, rodeo. *Special characteristics:* 53 awards ($109,422 total): children of faculty/staff, first-generation college students, international students, members of minority groups, out-of-state students, veterans. *Tuition*

waivers: Full or partial for minority students, employees or children of employees, senior citizens.

LOANS *Student loans:* $5,997,984 (76% need-based, 24% non-need-based). 74% of past graduating class borrowed through all loan programs. *Average indebtedness per student:* $22,683. *Average need-based loan:* Freshmen: $3424. Undergraduates: $4101. *Parent loans:* $763,898 (76% need-based, 24% non-need-based). *Programs:* Federal Direct (Subsidized and Unsubsidized Stafford, PLUS), Perkins, college/university.

WORK-STUDY *Federal work-study:* Total amount: $247,405; 122 jobs averaging $2310. *State or other work-study/employment:* Total amount: $99,864 (82% need-based, 18% non-need-based). 121 part-time jobs averaging $2120.

APPLYING FOR FINANCIAL AID *Required financial aid form:* FAFSA. *Financial aid deadline (priority):* 3/1. *Notification date:* Continuous beginning 4/1. Students must reply within 4 weeks of notification.

CONTACT Erica L. Jones, Director of Financial Aid, The University of Montana Western, 710 South Atlantic Street, Dillon, MT 59725, 406-683-7511 or toll-free 877-683-7331. *Fax:* 406-683-7510. *E-mail:* e_jones@umwestern.edu.
Website: http://www.umwestern.edu/.

UNIVERSITY OF MONTEVALLO
Montevallo, AL

Tuition & fees (AL res): $9280	Average undergraduate aid package: $9488

ABOUT THE INSTITUTION State-supported, coed. *Awards:* certificates, bachelor's, and master's degrees. 26 undergraduate majors. *Total enrollment:* 3,085. Undergraduates: 2,598. Freshmen: 552. Federal methodology is used as a basis for awarding need-based institutional aid.

UNDERGRADUATE EXPENSES for 2013–2014 *Application fee:* $30. *Tuition, state resident:* full-time $8790; part-time $293 per credit hour. *Tuition, nonresident:* full-time $17,580; part-time $586 per credit hour. *Required fees:* full-time $490. *College room and board:* $5522. Room and board charges vary according to housing facility.

FRESHMAN FINANCIAL AID (Fall 2012, est.) 420 applied for aid; of those 80% were deemed to have need. 99% of freshmen with need received aid; of those 17% had need fully met. *Average percent of need met:* 58% (excluding resources awarded to replace EFC). *Average financial aid package:* $8873 (excluding resources awarded to replace EFC). 28% of all full-time freshmen had no need and received non-need-based gift aid.

UNDERGRADUATE FINANCIAL AID (Fall 2012, est.) 1,713 applied for aid; of those 85% were deemed to have need. 100% of undergraduates with need received aid; of those 17% had need fully met. *Average percent of need met:* 58% (excluding resources awarded to replace EFC). *Average financial aid package:* $9488 (excluding resources awarded to replace EFC). 22% of all full-time undergraduates had no need and received non-need-based gift aid.

GIFT AID (NEED-BASED) *Total amount:* $8,415,667 (57% federal, 6% state, 34% institutional, 3% external sources). *Receiving aid:* Freshmen: 55% (300); all full-time undergraduates: 54% (1,247). *Average award:* Freshmen: $7014; Undergraduates: $6447. *Scholarships, grants, and awards:* Federal Pell, FSEOG, state, private, college/university gift aid from institutional funds.

GIFT AID (NON-NEED-BASED) *Total amount:* $2,682,241 (8% state, 89% institutional, 3% external sources). *Receiving aid:* Freshmen: 12% (66). Undergraduates: 6% (150). *Average award:* Freshmen: $7807. Undergraduates: $8036. *Scholarships, grants, and awards by category: Academic interests/achievement:* 863 awards ($4,852,503 total): biological sciences, business, communication, education, English, foreign languages, general academic interests/achievements, mathematics, physical sciences, social sciences. *Creative arts/performance:* 128 awards ($276,638 total): art/fine arts, cinema/film/broadcasting, creative writing, journalism/publications, music, theater/drama. *Special achievements/activities:* 217 awards ($820,234 total): junior miss, leadership. *Special characteristics:* 252 awards ($1,926,110 total): children of faculty/staff, international students, out-of-state students. *Tuition waivers:* Full or partial for employees or children of employees. *ROTC:* Army cooperative, Air Force cooperative.

LOANS *Student loans:* $12,784,186 (45% need-based, 55% non-need-based). 53% of past graduating class borrowed through all loan programs. *Average indebtedness per student:* $24,723. *Average need-based loan:* Freshmen: $3215. Undergrad-

uates: $4215. **Parent loans:** $713,221 (75% need-based, 25% non-need-based). **Programs:** Federal Direct (Subsidized and Unsubsidized Stafford, PLUS), Perkins.
WORK-STUDY Federal work-study: Total amount: $183,005; 108 jobs averaging $1550.
ATHLETIC AWARDS Total amount: $1,397,417 (43% need-based, 57% non-need-based).
APPLYING FOR FINANCIAL AID Required financial aid form: FAFSA. **Financial aid deadline (priority):** 3/1. **Notification date:** Continuous beginning 3/25. Students must reply within 2 weeks of notification.
CONTACT Ms. Maria Parker, Director of Student Financial Aid, University of Montevallo, Station 6050, Montevallo, AL 35115, 205-665-6050 or toll-free 800-292-4349. *Fax:* 205-665-6047. *E-mail:* finaid@montevallo.edu. *Website:* http://www.montevallo.edu/.

UNIVERSITY OF MOUNT UNION
Alliance, OH

Tuition & fees: $26,650	Average undergraduate aid package: $20,548

ABOUT THE INSTITUTION Independent United Methodist, coed. **Awards:** bachelor's and master's degrees. 56 undergraduate majors. **Total enrollment:** 2,253. Undergraduates: 2,175. Freshmen: 647. Federal methodology is used as a basis for awarding need-based institutional aid.
UNDERGRADUATE EXPENSES for 2013–2014 Comprehensive fee: $35,130 includes full-time tuition ($26,350), mandatory fees ($300), and room and board ($8480). Full-time tuition and fees vary according to course load and degree level. Room and board charges vary according to board plan and housing facility. **Part-time tuition:** $1110 per credit hour. Part-time tuition and fees vary according to course load. **Payment plan:** Tuition prepayment.
FRESHMAN FINANCIAL AID (Fall 2012, est.) 592 applied for aid; of those 90% were deemed to have need. 100% of freshmen with need received aid; of those 13% had need fully met. **Average percent of need met:** 77% (excluding resources awarded to replace EFC). **Average financial aid package:** $21,041 (excluding resources awarded to replace EFC). 15% of all full-time freshmen had no need and received non-need-based gift aid.
UNDERGRADUATE FINANCIAL AID (Fall 2012, est.) 1,911 applied for aid; of those 92% were deemed to have need. 100% of undergraduates with need received aid; of those 11% had need fully met. **Average percent of need met:** 76% (excluding resources awarded to replace EFC). **Average financial aid package:** $20,548 (excluding resources awarded to replace EFC). 16% of all full-time undergraduates had no need and received non-need-based gift aid.
GIFT AID (NEED-BASED) Total amount: $25,359,925 (12% federal, 4% state, 82% institutional, 2% external sources). **Receiving aid:** Freshmen: 77% (535); all full-time undergraduates: 80% (1,752). **Average award:** Freshmen: $15,886; Undergraduates: $14,863. **Scholarships, grants, and awards:** Federal Pell, FSEOG, state, private, college/university gift aid from institutional funds.
GIFT AID (NON-NEED-BASED) Total amount: $3,979,135 (97% institutional, 3% external sources). **Receiving aid:** Freshmen: 8% (55). Undergraduates: 6% (132). **Average award:** Freshmen: $10,412. Undergraduates: $9625. **Scholarships, grants, and awards by category:** Academic interests/achievement: general academic interests/achievements. Creative arts/performance: art/fine arts, cinema/film/broadcasting, journalism/publications, music, theater/drama. Special achievements/activities: 111 awards ($513,095 total). Special characteristics: children and siblings of alumni, children of faculty/staff, ethnic background, international students, members of minority groups, relatives of clergy. **Tuition waivers:** Full or partial for children of alumni, employees or children of employees, senior citizens. **ROTC:** Army, Air Force cooperative.
LOANS Student loans: $17,641,660 (74% need-based, 26% non-need-based). 87% of past graduating class borrowed through all loan programs. *Average indebtedness per student:* $33,568. **Average need-based loan:** Freshmen: $4985. Undergraduates: $5547. **Parent loans:** $4,967,224 (43% need-based, 57% non-need-based). **Programs:** Federal Direct (Subsidized and Unsubsidized Stafford, PLUS), Perkins, private loans.
WORK-STUDY Federal work-study: Total amount: $1,173,434; 1,440 jobs averaging $1304. **State or other work-study/employment:** Total amount: $411,146 (25% need-based, 75% non-need-based). 264 part-time jobs averaging $1568.

APPLYING FOR FINANCIAL AID Required financial aid form: FAFSA. **Financial aid deadline:** Continuous. **Notification date:** Continuous beginning 3/15. Students must reply by 8/27.
CONTACT Mrs. Emily Mattison, Director of Student Financial Services, University of Mount Union, 1972 Clark Avenue, Alliance, OH 44601-3993, 330-823-2674 or toll-free 800-334-6682 (in-state), 800-992-6682 (out-of-state). *Fax:* 330-829-2814. *E-mail:* mattisej@mountunion.edu. *Website:* http://www.mountunion.edu/.

UNIVERSITY OF NEBRASKA AT KEARNEY
Kearney, NE

Tuition & fees (NE res): $6506	Average undergraduate aid package: $10,256

ABOUT THE INSTITUTION State-supported, coed. **Awards:** certificates, bachelor's, and master's degrees. 38 undergraduate majors. **Total enrollment:** 7,199. Undergraduates: 5,648. Freshmen: 1,136. Federal methodology is used as a basis for awarding need-based institutional aid.
UNDERGRADUATE EXPENSES for 2013–2014 Application fee: $45. **Tuition, state resident:** full-time $5235; part-time $174.50 per credit hour. **Tuition, nonresident:** full-time $10,740; part-time $358 per credit hour. **Required fees:** full-time $1271; $25 per credit hour or $263.50 per term. Full-time tuition and fees vary according to course level, course load, degree level, and location. Part-time tuition and fees vary according to course level, course load, degree level, and location. **College room and board:** $8038; **Room only:** $4114. Room and board charges vary according to board plan and housing facility.
FRESHMAN FINANCIAL AID (Fall 2012, est.) 866 applied for aid; of those 83% were deemed to have need. 100% of freshmen with need received aid; of those 47% had need fully met. **Average percent of need met:** 78% (excluding resources awarded to replace EFC). **Average financial aid package:** $10,994 (excluding resources awarded to replace EFC). 7% of all full-time freshmen had no need and received non-need-based gift aid.
UNDERGRADUATE FINANCIAL AID (Fall 2012, est.) 3,434 applied for aid; of those 85% were deemed to have need. 100% of undergraduates with need received aid; of those 35% had need fully met. **Average percent of need met:** 73% (excluding resources awarded to replace EFC). **Average financial aid package:** $10,256 (excluding resources awarded to replace EFC). 4% of all full-time undergraduates had no need and received non-need-based gift aid.
GIFT AID (NEED-BASED) Total amount: $13,156,482 (55% federal, 6% state, 20% institutional, 19% external sources). **Receiving aid:** Freshmen: 42% (474); all full-time undergraduates: 40% (1,939). **Average award:** Freshmen: $6981; Undergraduates: $6322. **Scholarships, grants, and awards:** Federal Pell, FSEOG, state, private, college/university gift aid from institutional funds.
GIFT AID (NON-NEED-BASED) Total amount: $4,056,341 (1% state, 66% institutional, 33% external sources). **Receiving aid:** Freshmen: 34% (381). Undergraduates: 20% (986). **Average award:** Freshmen: $2373. Undergraduates: $2116. **Scholarships, grants, and awards by category:** Academic interests/achievement: communication, general academic interests/achievements. Creative arts/performance: applied art and design, art/fine arts, debating, journalism/publications, music. Special achievements/activities: cheerleading/drum major, leadership. Special characteristics: children and siblings of alumni, children of faculty/staff, ethnic background, first-generation college students, international students, local/state students, members of minority groups, out-of-state students, veterans, veterans' children. **Tuition waivers:** Full or partial for employees or children of employees. **ROTC:** Army.
LOANS Student loans: $23,032,474 (46% need-based, 54% non-need-based). **Average need-based loan:** Freshmen: $3219. Undergraduates: $3938. **Parent loans:** $2,478,895 (100% non-need-based). **Programs:** Federal Direct (Subsidized and Unsubsidized Stafford, PLUS), Perkins, college/university.
WORK-STUDY Federal work-study: Total amount: $1,291,849; jobs available.
ATHLETIC AWARDS Total amount: $1,147,409 (100% non-need-based).
APPLYING FOR FINANCIAL AID Required financial aid forms: FAFSA, institution's own form. **Financial aid deadline (priority):** 4/1. **Notification date:** Continuous beginning 3/15.

CONTACT Financial Aid Office, University of Nebraska at Kearney, Memorial Student Affairs Building, 905 West 25th Street, Kearney, NE 68849-0001, 308-865-8520 or toll-free 800-532-7639. *Fax:* 308-865-8096. *E-mail:* finaid1@unk.edu. *Website:* http://www.unk.edu/.

UNIVERSITY OF NEBRASKA AT OMAHA
Omaha, NE

Tuition & fees (NE res): $6550	Average undergraduate aid package: $8931

ABOUT THE INSTITUTION State-supported, coed. *Awards:* certificates, bachelor's, master's, and doctoral degrees. 88 undergraduate majors. *Total enrollment:* 14,786. Undergraduates: 12,136. Freshmen: 1,761. Federal methodology is used as a basis for awarding need-based institutional aid.
UNDERGRADUATE EXPENSES for 2013–2014 *Application fee:* $45. *Tuition, state resident:* full-time $5180; part-time $196.75 per credit. *Tuition, nonresident:* full-time $15,520; part-time $598 per credit. *Required fees:* full-time $1370. *College room and board:* $8090.
FRESHMAN FINANCIAL AID (Fall 2011) 1,309 applied for aid; of those 81% were deemed to have need. 95% of freshmen with need received aid; of those 30% had need fully met. *Average percent of need met:* 66% (excluding resources awarded to replace EFC). *Average financial aid package:* $8430 (excluding resources awarded to replace EFC). 7% of all full-time freshmen had no need and received non-need-based gift aid.
UNDERGRADUATE FINANCIAL AID (Fall 2011) 6,501 applied for aid; of those 85% were deemed to have need. 93% of undergraduates with need received aid; of those 30% had need fully met. *Average percent of need met:* 68% (excluding resources awarded to replace EFC). *Average financial aid package:* $8931 (excluding resources awarded to replace EFC). 4% of all full-time undergraduates had no need and received non-need-based gift aid.
GIFT AID (NEED-BASED) *Total amount:* $30,472,240 (49% federal, 7% state, 23% institutional, 21% external sources). *Receiving aid:* Freshmen: 37% (609); all full-time undergraduates: 38% (3,441). *Average award:* Freshmen: $5554; Undergraduates: $5266. *Scholarships, grants, and awards:* Federal Pell, FSEOG, state, private, college/university gift aid from institutional funds.
GIFT AID (NON-NEED-BASED) *Receiving aid:* Freshmen: 12% (195). Undergraduates: 9% (797). *Average award:* Freshmen: $1588. Undergraduates: $1642. *Scholarships, grants, and awards by category:* Academic interests/achievement: biological sciences, business, communication, computer science, education, engineering/technologies, English, foreign languages, general academic interests/achievements, home economics, mathematics, physical sciences, premedicine, social sciences. *Creative arts/performance:* art/fine arts, creative writing, debating, journalism/publications, music, performing arts, theater/drama. *Special achievements/activities:* general special achievements/activities, leadership, memberships. *Special characteristics:* adult students, children and siblings of alumni, children of faculty/staff, ethnic background, first-generation college students, handicapped students, international students, members of minority groups, out-of-state students, veterans' children.
ROTC: Army cooperative, Air Force.
LOANS *Student loans:* $39,978,080 (42% need-based, 58% non-need-based). 62% of past graduating class borrowed through all loan programs. *Average indebtedness per student:* $25,145. *Average need-based loan:* Freshmen: $3196. Undergraduates: $3939. *Parent loans:* $5,735,818 (100% non-need-based). *Programs:* Perkins, college/university.
WORK-STUDY *Federal work-study:* Total amount: $333,874; jobs available.
ATHLETIC AWARDS Total amount: $1,199,496 (100% need-based).
APPLYING FOR FINANCIAL AID *Required financial aid form:* FAFSA. *Financial aid deadline (priority):* 4/1. *Notification date:* Continuous beginning 4/15. Students must reply within 2 weeks of notification.
CONTACT Office of Financial Aid, University of Nebraska at Omaha, 103 Eppley Administration Building, Omaha, NE 68182-0187, 402-554-2327 or toll-free 800-858-8648 (in-state). *Fax:* 402-554-3472. *E-mail:* finaid@unomaha.edu. *Website:* http://www.unomaha.edu/.

UNIVERSITY OF NEBRASKA–LINCOLN
Lincoln, NE

Tuition & fees (NE res): $7896	Average undergraduate aid package: $12,087

ABOUT THE INSTITUTION State-supported, coed. *Awards:* certificates, associate, bachelor's, master's, and doctoral degrees. 127 undergraduate majors. *Total enrollment:* 24,207. Undergraduates: 19,103. Freshmen: 3,937. Both federal and institutional methodology are used as a basis for awarding need-based institutional aid.
UNDERGRADUATE EXPENSES for 2013–2014 *Application fee:* $45. *Tuition, state resident:* full-time $6480; part-time $216 per credit hour. *Tuition, nonresident:* full-time $19,230; part-time $641 per credit hour. *Required fees:* full-time $1416; $11.35 per credit hour or $299 per term. Full-time tuition and fees vary according to course load, program, and reciprocity agreements. Part-time tuition and fees vary according to course load, program, and reciprocity agreements. *College room and board:* $9122. Room and board charges vary according to board plan and housing facility.
FRESHMAN FINANCIAL AID (Fall 2011) 3,066 applied for aid; of those 72% were deemed to have need. 98% of freshmen with need received aid; of those 19% had need fully met. *Average percent of need met:* 82% (excluding resources awarded to replace EFC). *Average financial aid package:* $12,466 (excluding resources awarded to replace EFC). 11% of all full-time freshmen had no need and received non-need-based gift aid.
UNDERGRADUATE FINANCIAL AID (Fall 2011) 11,021 applied for aid; of those 77% were deemed to have need. 97% of undergraduates with need received aid; of those 17% had need fully met. *Average percent of need met:* 78% (excluding resources awarded to replace EFC). *Average financial aid package:* $12,087 (excluding resources awarded to replace EFC). 6% of all full-time undergraduates had no need and received non-need-based gift aid.
GIFT AID (NEED-BASED) *Total amount:* $52,613,910 (35% federal, 5% state, 41% institutional, 19% external sources). *Receiving aid:* Freshmen: 43% (1,759); all full-time undergraduates: 34% (6,217). *Average award:* Freshmen: $6834; Undergraduates: $6731. *Scholarships, grants, and awards:* Federal Pell, FSEOG, state, private, college/university gift aid from institutional funds.
GIFT AID (NON-NEED-BASED) *Total amount:* $24,064,591 (1% federal, 89% institutional, 10% external sources). *Receiving aid:* Freshmen: 5% (184). Undergraduates: 3% (472). *Average award:* Freshmen: $4822. Undergraduates: $5059. *Scholarships, grants, and awards by category:* Academic interests/achievement: agriculture, architecture, biological sciences, business, computer science, education, engineering/technologies, English, foreign languages, general academic interests/achievements, health fields, home economics, humanities, international studies, mathematics, physical sciences, premedicine, social sciences. *Creative arts/performance:* art/fine arts, cinema/film/broadcasting, dance, journalism/publications, music, performing arts, theater/drama. *Special achievements/activities:* cheerleading/drum major, community service, leadership. *Special characteristics:* children and siblings of alumni, ethnic background, handicapped students, international students, members of minority groups, out-of-state students, veterans' children. *Tuition waivers:* Full or partial for employees or children of employees. *ROTC:* Army, Naval, Air Force.
LOANS *Student loans:* $57,076,541 (74% need-based, 26% non-need-based). 60% of past graduating class borrowed through all loan programs. *Average indebtedness per student:* $23,280. *Average need-based loan:* Freshmen: $3359. Undergraduates: $4171. *Parent loans:* $30,690,615 (53% need-based, 47% non-need-based). *Programs:* Federal Direct (Subsidized and Unsubsidized Stafford, PLUS), Perkins, college/university.
WORK-STUDY *Federal work-study:* Total amount: $2,357,214; 1,142 jobs averaging $2115.
ATHLETIC AWARDS Total amount: $8,006,325 (100% non-need-based).
APPLYING FOR FINANCIAL AID *Required financial aid form:* FAFSA. *Financial aid deadline (priority):* 4/1. *Notification date:* Continuous beginning 4/1.
CONTACT Ms. Jo Tederman, Assistant Director of Scholarships and Financial Aid, University of Nebraska–Lincoln, 17 Canfield Administration Building, Lincoln, NE 68588-0411, 402-472-2030 or toll-free 800-742-8800. *Fax:* 402-472-9826. *Website:* http://www.unl.edu/.

UNIVERSITY OF NEBRASKA MEDICAL CENTER
Omaha, NE

CONTACT Judy D. Walker, Director of Financial Aid, University of Nebraska Medical Center, 984265 Nebraska Medical Center, Omaha, NE 68198-4265, 402-559-6409 or toll-free 800-626-8431 Ext. 6468. *Fax:* 402-559-6796. *E-mail:* jdwalker@unmc.edu. *Website:* http://www.unmc.edu/.

UNIVERSITY OF NEVADA, LAS VEGAS
Las Vegas, NV

Tuition & fees (NV res): $6585	Average undergraduate aid package: $9320

ABOUT THE INSTITUTION State-supported, coed. *Awards:* certificates, bachelor's, master's, and doctoral degrees. 89 undergraduate majors. *Total enrollment:* 27,402. Undergraduates: 22,432. Freshmen: 3,294. Federal methodology is used as a basis for awarding need-based institutional aid.

UNDERGRADUATE EXPENSES for 2013–2014 *Application fee:* $60. *Tuition, state resident:* full-time $6089; part-time $191.50 per credit hour. *Tuition, nonresident:* full-time $19,999; part-time $402.25 per credit hour. *Required fees:* full-time $496. Full-time tuition and fees vary according to course level, program, and reciprocity agreements. Part-time tuition and fees vary according to course level, program, and reciprocity agreements. *College room and board:* $10,524; *Room only:* $5880. Room and board charges vary according to board plan.

FRESHMAN FINANCIAL AID (Fall 2012, est.) 2,513 applied for aid; of those 82% were deemed to have need. 98% of freshmen with need received aid; of those 14% had need fully met. *Average percent of need met:* 61% (excluding resources awarded to replace EFC). *Average financial aid package:* $8872 (excluding resources awarded to replace EFC). 12% of all full-time freshmen had no need and received non-need-based gift aid.

UNDERGRADUATE FINANCIAL AID (Fall 2012, est.) 11,049 applied for aid; of those 88% were deemed to have need. 97% of undergraduates with need received aid; of those 11% had need fully met. *Average percent of need met:* 59% (excluding resources awarded to replace EFC). *Average financial aid package:* $9320 (excluding resources awarded to replace EFC). 5% of all full-time undergraduates had no need and received non-need-based gift aid.

GIFT AID (NEED-BASED) Total amount: $66,153,271 (49% federal, 20% state, 28% institutional, 3% external sources). *Receiving aid:* Freshmen: 56% (1,668); all full-time undergraduates: 49% (7,795). *Average award:* Freshmen: $4854; Undergraduates: $4735. *Scholarships, grants, and awards:* Federal Pell, FSEOG, state, private, college/university gift aid from institutional funds.

GIFT AID (NON-NEED-BASED) Total amount: $10,499,249 (40% federal, 26% state, 28% institutional, 6% external sources). *Receiving aid:* Freshmen: 50% (1,486). Undergraduates: 27% (4,264). *Average award:* Freshmen: $2838. Undergraduates: $3103. *Scholarships, grants, and awards by category: Academic interests/achievement:* architecture, biological sciences, business, communication, computer science, education, engineering/technologies, English, foreign languages, general academic interests/achievements, health fields, humanities, international studies, mathematics, physical sciences, premedicine, social sciences. *Creative arts/performance:* applied art and design, art/fine arts, cinema/film/broadcasting, creative writing, dance, debating, general creative arts/performance, journalism/publications, music, performing arts, theater/drama. *Special achievements/activities:* cheerleading/drum major, community service, general special achievements/activities, leadership, rodeo. *Special characteristics:* adult students, children and siblings of alumni, children of faculty/staff, children of public servants, children of union members/company employees, children with a deceased or disabled parent, ethnic background, first-generation college students, general special characteristics, handicapped students, international students, local/state students, members of minority groups, out-of-state students, previous college experience, veterans, veterans' children. *Tuition waivers:* Full or partial for employees or children of employees. *ROTC:* Army, Air Force.

LOANS Student loans: $144,218,845 (67% need-based, 33% non-need-based). 40% of past graduating class borrowed through all loan programs. *Average indebtedness per student:* $21,126. *Average need-based loan:* Freshmen: $3294. Undergraduates: $4216. *Programs:* Federal Direct (Subsidized and Unsubsidized Stafford, PLUS), Perkins, Federal Nursing, state, college/university.

WORK-STUDY *Federal work-study:* Total amount: $797,691; jobs available. *State or other work-study/employment:* Total amount: $1,252,580 (99% need-based, 1% non-need-based). Part-time jobs available.

APPLYING FOR FINANCIAL AID *Required financial aid form:* FAFSA. *Financial aid deadline (priority):* 2/1. *Notification date:* Continuous beginning 3/15.

CONTACT Norm Bedford, Director of Financial Aid and Scholarships, University of Nevada, Las Vegas, 4505 South Maryland Parkway, Las Vegas, NV 89154-2016, 702-895-3424. *Fax:* 702-895-1353. *Website:* http://www.unlv.edu/.

UNIVERSITY OF NEVADA, RENO
Reno, NV

Tuition & fees (NV res): $6365	Average undergraduate aid package: $8367

ABOUT THE INSTITUTION State-supported, coed. *Awards:* certificates, associate, bachelor's, master's, and doctoral degrees. 72 undergraduate majors. *Total enrollment:* 18,227. Undergraduates: 15,082. Freshmen: 2,885. Federal methodology is used as a basis for awarding need-based institutional aid.

UNDERGRADUATE EXPENSES for 2013–2014 *Application fee:* $60. *Tuition, state resident:* full-time $5745; part-time $191.50 per credit hour. *Tuition, nonresident:* full-time $19,655; part-time $402.50 per credit hour. *Required fees:* full-time $620. Full-time tuition and fees vary according to course level, course load, degree level, and program. Part-time tuition and fees vary according to course level, course load, degree level, and program. *College room and board:* $9518. Room and board charges vary according to board plan and housing facility.

FRESHMAN FINANCIAL AID (Fall 2011) 2,460 applied for aid; of those 77% were deemed to have need. 83% of freshmen with need received aid; of those 11% had need fully met. *Average percent of need met:* 62% (excluding resources awarded to replace EFC). *Average financial aid package:* $7895 (excluding resources awarded to replace EFC). 21% of all full-time freshmen had no need and received non-need-based gift aid.

UNDERGRADUATE FINANCIAL AID (Fall 2011) 8,623 applied for aid; of those 85% were deemed to have need. 89% of undergraduates with need received aid; of those 10% had need fully met. *Average percent of need met:* 62% (excluding resources awarded to replace EFC). *Average financial aid package:* $8367 (excluding resources awarded to replace EFC). 14% of all full-time undergraduates had no need and received non-need-based gift aid.

GIFT AID (NEED-BASED) Total amount: $32,144,139 (51% federal, 22% state, 23% institutional, 4% external sources). *Receiving aid:* Freshmen: 34% (953); all full-time undergraduates: 34% (4,260). *Average award:* Freshmen: $5440; Undergraduates: $5490. *Scholarships, grants, and awards:* Federal Pell, FSEOG, state, private, college/university gift aid from institutional funds, Federal Nursing.

GIFT AID (NON-NEED-BASED) Total amount: $12,299,009 (52% state, 36% institutional, 12% external sources). *Receiving aid:* Freshmen: 46% (1,300). Undergraduates: 30% (3,731). *Average award:* Freshmen: $1890. Undergraduates: $1843. *Scholarships, grants, and awards by category: Academic interests/achievement:* general academic interests/achievements. *Creative arts/performance:* general creative arts/performance, music, theater/drama. *Special characteristics:* adult students, children and siblings of alumni, ethnic background, first-generation college students, married students. *Tuition waivers:* Full or partial for employees or children of employees. *ROTC:* Army.

LOANS Student loans: $41,657,650 (72% need-based, 28% non-need-based). 41% of past graduating class borrowed through all loan programs. *Average indebtedness per student:* $19,500. *Average need-based loan:* Freshmen: $5450. Undergraduates: $4290. *Parent loans:* $5,720,962 (9% need-based, 91% non-need-based). *Programs:* Federal Direct (Subsidized and Unsubsidized Stafford, PLUS), Perkins, Federal Nursing, college/university, private loans.

WORK-STUDY *Federal work-study:* Total am̲o̲u̲n̲t̲:̲ ̲$̲8̲7̲1̲,̲9̲9̲9̲; jobs available. *State or other work-study/employment:* Tot̲a̲l̲ ̲a̲m̲o̲u̲n̲t̲:̲ ̲$̲_____ (__% need-based). Part-time jobs available.

ATHLETIC AWARDS Total amount: $4,611,067 (__% need-based, __% non-need-based).

APPLYING FOR FINANCIAL AID *Require̲d̲ ̲f̲i̲n̲a̲n̲c̲i̲a̲l̲ ̲a̲i̲d̲ ̲f̲o̲r̲m̲:̲ ̲F̲A̲F̲S̲A̲.̲* *Financial aid deadline (priority):* 3/1. *N̲o̲t̲i̲f̲i̲c̲a̲t̲i̲o̲n̲ ̲d̲a̲t̲e̲:̲* beginning 4/1. Students must reply within 2 weeks ̲o̲f̲ ̲n̲o̲t̲i̲f̲i̲c̲a̲t̲i̲o̲n̲.

CONTACT Tim Wolfe, Director of Student Financial Aid, University of Nevada, Reno, Mail Stop 076, Reno, NV 89557, 775-784-4666 or toll-free 866-263-8232. *Fax:* 775-784-1025. *E-mail:* tawolfe@unr.edu.
Website: http://www.unr.edu/.

UNIVERSITY OF NEW ENGLAND
Biddeford, ME

Tuition & fees: $31,870	Average undergraduate aid package: N/A

ABOUT THE INSTITUTION Independent, coed. *Awards:* certificates, associate, bachelor's, master's, and doctoral degrees. 34 undergraduate majors. *Total enrollment:* 5,666. Undergraduates: 2,637. Freshmen: 633. Federal methodology is used as a basis for awarding need-based institutional aid.
UNDERGRADUATE EXPENSES for 2013–2014 Application fee: $40. *Comprehensive fee:* $44,370 includes full-time tuition ($30,750), mandatory fees ($1120), and room and board ($12,500). Room and board charges vary according to board plan, housing facility, and location. *Part-time tuition:* $1090 per credit hour.
GIFT AID (NEED-BASED) Scholarships, grants, and awards: Federal Pell, FSEOG, state, private, college/university gift aid from institutional funds.
GIFT AID (NON-NEED-BASED) Scholarships, grants, and awards by category: *Academic interests/achievement:* biological sciences, business, communication, education, English, general academic interests/achievements, health fields, humanities, international studies, mathematics, physical sciences, premedicine, social sciences. *Special achievements/activities:* community service, general special achievements/activities, leadership. *Special characteristics:* children and siblings of alumni, ethnic background, members of minority groups, siblings of current students. *Tuition waivers:* Full or partial for children of alumni, employees or children of employees. *ROTC:* Army cooperative.
LOANS Programs: Federal Direct (Subsidized and Unsubsidized Stafford, PLUS), Perkins, Federal Nursing, state, college/university.
WORK-STUDY Federal work-study jobs available. *State or other work-study/employment:* Part-time jobs available.
APPLYING FOR FINANCIAL AID Required financial aid form: FAFSA. *Financial aid deadline (priority):* 5/1. *Notification date:* Continuous.
CONTACT Paul Henderson, Director of Financial Aid, University of New England, 11 Hills Beach Road, Biddeford, ME 04005, 207-602-2342 or toll-free 800-477-4UNE. *Fax:* 207-602-5968. *E-mail:* finaid@une.edu.
Website: http://www.une.edu/.

UNIVERSITY OF NEW HAMPSHIRE
Durham, NH

Tuition & fees (NH res): $16,422	Average undergraduate aid package: $20,939

ABOUT THE INSTITUTION State-supported, coed. *Awards:* certificates, associate, bachelor's, master's, and doctoral degrees. 89 undergraduate majors. *Total enrollment:* 15,301. Undergraduates: 12,811. Freshmen: 2,999. Federal methodology is used as a basis for awarding need-based institutional aid.
UNDERGRADUATE EXPENSES for 2013–2014 Application fee: $50. *Tuition, state resident:* full-time $13,670; part-time $570 per credit hour. *Tuition, nonresident:* full-time $26,130; part-time $1089 per credit hour. *Required fees:* full-time $2752; $688 per term. Full-time tuition and fees vary according to degree level and program. Part-time tuition and fees vary according to course load, degree level, and program. *College room and board:* $9764; *Room only:* $6090. Room and board charges vary according to board plan and housing facility.
FRESHMAN FINANCIAL AID (Fall 2011) 2,455 applied for aid; of those 80% were deemed to have need. 98% of freshmen with need received aid; of those 22% had need fully met. *Average percent of need met:* 80% (excluding resources awarded to replace EFC). *Average financial aid package:* $21,088 (excluding resources awarded to replace EFC). 16% of all full-time freshmen had no need and received non-based gift aid.
RGRADUATE FINANCIAL AID (Fall 2011) 9,462 applied for aid; of were deemed to have need. 99% of undergraduates with need received aid; need fully met. *Average percent of need met:* 78% (excluding

resources awarded to replace EFC). *Average financial aid package:* $20,939 (excluding resources awarded to replace EFC). 17% of all full-time undergraduates had no need and received non-need-based gift aid.
GIFT AID (NEED-BASED) Total amount: $57,168,972 (24% federal, 1% state, 62% institutional, 13% external sources). *Receiving aid:* Freshmen: 48% (1,329); all full-time undergraduates: 44% (5,127). *Average award:* Freshmen: $5249; Undergraduates: $4647. *Scholarships, grants, and awards:* Federal Pell, FSEOG, state, private, college/university gift aid from institutional funds, Veterans Education Benefits (GI Bill).
GIFT AID (NON-NEED-BASED) Total amount: $13,963,651 (100% institutional). *Receiving aid:* Freshmen: 4% (125). Undergraduates: 3% (372). *Average award:* Freshmen: $7296. Undergraduates: $8460. *Scholarships, grants, and awards by category:* *Academic interests/achievement:* agriculture, business, education, engineering/technologies, English, general academic interests/achievements, health fields, humanities, mathematics, military science. *Creative arts/performance:* art/fine arts, dance, music, theater/drama. *Special achievements/activities:* community service. *Special characteristics:* children and siblings of alumni, children of faculty/staff, handicapped students, international students, local/state students. *Tuition waivers:* Full or partial for employees or children of employees. *ROTC:* Army, Air Force.
LOANS Student loans: $102,332,639 (41% need-based, 59% non-need-based). 78% of past graduating class borrowed through all loan programs. *Average indebtedness per student:* $35,168. *Average need-based loan:* Freshmen: $2670. Undergraduates: $3341. *Parent loans:* $27,593,217 (100% non-need-based). *Programs:* Federal Direct (Subsidized and Unsubsidized Stafford, PLUS), Perkins, state, college/university.
WORK-STUDY Federal work-study: Total amount: $14,498,551; 5,358 jobs averaging $2520. *State or other work-study/employment:* Total amount: $6,189,066 (100% non-need-based). 3,851 part-time jobs averaging $1161.
ATHLETIC AWARDS Total amount: $7,916,352 (100% non-need-based).
APPLYING FOR FINANCIAL AID Required financial aid form: FAFSA. *Financial aid deadline (priority):* 3/1. *Notification date:* Continuous beginning 3/1.
CONTACT Susan K. Allen, Director of Financial Aid, University of New Hampshire, 11 Garrison Avenue, Durham, NH 03824, 603-862-3600. *Fax:* 603-862-1947. *E-mail:* financial.aid@unh.edu.
Website: http://www.unh.edu/.

UNIVERSITY OF NEW HAMPSHIRE AT MANCHESTER
Manchester, NH

Tuition & fees (NH res): $13,757	Average undergraduate aid package: $12,051

ABOUT THE INSTITUTION State-supported, coed. *Awards:* certificates, associate, bachelor's, and master's degrees. 13 undergraduate majors. *Total enrollment:* 777. Undergraduates: 777. Freshmen: 76. Federal methodology is used as a basis for awarding need-based institutional aid.
UNDERGRADUATE EXPENSES for 2013–2014 Application fee: $45. *Tuition, state resident:* full-time $13,350; part-time $556 per credit hour. *Tuition, nonresident:* full-time $25,810; part-time $1075 per credit hour. *Required fees:* full-time $407. Full-time tuition and fees vary according to course load and program. Part-time tuition and fees vary according to course load and program.
FRESHMAN FINANCIAL AID (Fall 2011) 91 applied for aid; of those 78% were deemed to have need. 97% of freshmen with need received aid; of those 13% had need fully met. *Average percent of need met:* 69% (excluding resources awarded to replace EFC). *Average financial aid package:* $10,922 (excluding resources awarded to replace EFC). 4% of all full-time freshmen had no need and received non-need-based gift aid.
UNDERGRADUATE FINANCIAL AID (Fall 2011) 655 applied for aid; of those 81% were deemed to have need. 98% of undergraduates with need received aid; of those 11% had need fully met. *Average percent of need met:* 60% (excluding resources awarded to replace EFC). *Average financial aid package:* $12,051 (excluding resources awarded to replace EFC). 1% of all full-time undergraduates had no need and received non-need-based gift aid.
GIFT AID (NEED-BASED) Total amount: $1,407,082 (69% federal, 20% institutional, 11% external sources). *Receiving aid:* Freshmen: 35% (35); all full-time undergraduates: 26% (219). *Average award:* Freshmen: $921; Undergraduates: $864.

Scholarships, grants, and awards: Federal Pell, FSEOG, state, private, college/university gift aid from institutional funds.

GIFT AID (NON-NEED-BASED) Total amount: $104,830 (100% institutional). **Receiving aid:** Freshmen: 4% (4). Undergraduates: 1% (11). **Average award:** Freshmen: $375. Undergraduates: $655. **Scholarships, grants, and awards by category:** Academic interests/achievement: general academic interests/achievements. Special characteristics: children of faculty/staff. **Tuition waivers:** Full or partial for employees or children of employees, senior citizens. **ROTC:** Army cooperative, Air Force cooperative.

LOANS Student loans: $5,327,855 (42% need-based, 58% non-need-based). 81% of past graduating class borrowed through all loan programs. Average indebtedness per student: $25,411. **Average need-based loan:** Freshmen: $2612. Undergraduates: $3856. **Parent loans:** $518,934 (100% non-need-based). **Programs:** Federal Direct (Subsidized and Unsubsidized Stafford, PLUS), Perkins, state, college/university. **WORK-STUDY Federal work-study:** Total amount: $522,073; 229 jobs averaging $2389.

APPLYING FOR FINANCIAL AID Required financial aid form: FAFSA. **Financial aid deadline (priority):** 3/1. **Notification date:** Continuous beginning 4/1.

CONTACT Jodi Abad, Assistant Director of Financial Aid, University of New Hampshire at Manchester, French Hall, Manchester, NH 03101-1113, 603-641-4146. Fax: 603-641-4125.

Website: http://www.unhm.unh.edu/.

UNIVERSITY OF NEW HAVEN
West Haven, CT

Tuition & fees: $32,750	Average undergraduate aid package: $19,727

ABOUT THE INSTITUTION Independent, coed. **Awards:** certificates, associate, bachelor's, master's, and doctoral degrees. 47 undergraduate majors. **Total enrollment:** 6,351. Undergraduates: 4,693. Freshmen: 1,127. Both federal and institutional methodology are used as a basis for awarding need-based institutional aid.

UNDERGRADUATE EXPENSES for 2013–2014 Application fee: $75. **Comprehensive fee:** $46,450 includes full-time tuition ($31,500), mandatory fees ($1250), and room and board ($13,700). Full-time tuition and fees vary according to course load and program. Room and board charges vary according to board plan and housing facility. Part-time tuition and fees vary according to class time, course load, and program.

FRESHMAN FINANCIAL AID (Fall 2012, est.) 989 applied for aid; of those 90% were deemed to have need. 100% of freshmen with need received aid; of those 10% had need fully met. **Average percent of need met:** 59% (excluding resources awarded to replace EFC). **Average financial aid package:** $20,276 (excluding resources awarded to replace EFC). 14% of all full-time freshmen had no need and received non-need-based gift aid.

UNDERGRADUATE FINANCIAL AID (Fall 2012, est.) 3,733 applied for aid; of those 92% were deemed to have need. 100% of undergraduates with need received aid; of those 11% had need fully met. **Average percent of need met:** 59% (excluding resources awarded to replace EFC). **Average financial aid package:** $19,727 (excluding resources awarded to replace EFC). 12% of all full-time undergraduates had no need and received non-need-based gift aid.

GIFT AID (NEED-BASED) Total amount: $51,278,371 (10% federal, 5% state, 83% institutional, 2% external sources). **Receiving aid:** Freshmen: 80% (890); all full-time undergraduates: 80% (3,402). **Average award:** Freshmen: $17,377; Undergraduates: $16,067. **Scholarships, grants, and awards:** Federal Pell, FSEOG, state, private, college/university gift aid from institutional funds.

GIFT AID (NON-NEED-BASED) Total amount: $7,779,642 (100% institutional). **Receiving aid:** Freshmen: 8% (87). Undergraduates: 8% (337). **Average award:** Freshmen: $11,369. Undergraduates: $11,526. **Tuition waivers:** Full or partial for employees or children of employees, senior citizens. **ROTC:** Army, Air Force cooperative.

LOANS Student loans: $43,838,911 (71% need-based, 29% non-need-based). 48% of past graduating class borrowed through all loan programs. Average indebtedness per student: $42,217. **Average need-based loan:** Freshmen: $3357. Undergraduates: $4271. **Parent loans:** $14,843,814 (100% non-need-based). **Programs:** Federal Direct (Subsidized and Unsubsidized Stafford, PLUS), Perkins. **WORK-STUDY Federal work-study:** Total amount: $247,280; jobs available.

ATHLETIC AWARDS Total amount: $2,599,613 (93% need-based, 7% non-need-based).

APPLYING FOR FINANCIAL AID Required financial aid form: FAFSA. **Financial aid deadline (priority):** 3/1. **Notification date:** Continuous beginning 3/1. Students must reply by 5/1 or within 2 weeks of notification.

CONTACT Mrs. Karen Flynn, Associate Vice President for Financial Aid, University of New Haven, 300 Boston Post Road, West Haven, CT 06516-1916, 203-932-7315 or toll-free 800-DIAL-UNH. Fax: 203-931-6050. E-mail: financialaid@newhaven.edu. Website: http://www.newhaven.edu/.

UNIVERSITY OF NEW MEXICO
Albuquerque, NM

ABOUT THE INSTITUTION State-supported, coed. **Awards:** certificates, associate, bachelor's, master's, and doctoral degrees. 81 undergraduate majors.

GIFT AID (NEED-BASED) Scholarships, grants, and awards: Federal Pell, FSEOG, state, private, college/university gift aid from institutional funds, United Negro College Fund, Federal Nursing.

GIFT AID (NON-NEED-BASED) Scholarships, grants, and awards by category: Academic interests/achievement: engineering/technologies, general academic interests/achievements. Creative arts/performance: art/fine arts, music, theater/drama. Special achievements/activities: general special achievements/activities. Special characteristics: children of faculty/staff, children of union members/company employees, members of minority groups, out-of-state students, veterans.

LOANS Programs: Federal Direct (Subsidized and Unsubsidized Stafford, PLUS), Perkins, Federal Nursing, state, college/university.

APPLYING FOR FINANCIAL AID Required financial aid form: FAFSA.

CONTACT Office of Student Financial Aid, University of New Mexico, MSC 11 6315, 1 University of New Mexico, Albuquerque, NM 87131, 505-277-8900 or toll-free 800-CALL-UNM. Fax: 505-277-6326. E-mail: finaid@unm.edu. Website: http://www.unm.edu/.

UNIVERSITY OF NEW ORLEANS
New Orleans, LA

Tuition & fees (LA res): $5922	Average undergraduate aid package: $8174

ABOUT THE INSTITUTION State-supported, coed. **Awards:** bachelor's, master's, and doctoral degrees. 37 undergraduate majors. **Total enrollment:** 10,071. Undergraduates: 7,689. Freshmen: 882. Federal methodology is used as a basis for awarding need-based institutional aid.

UNDERGRADUATE EXPENSES for 2013–2014 Application fee: $20. **Tuition, state resident:** full-time $5164. **Tuition, nonresident:** full-time $17,176. **Required fees:** full-time $758. Full-time tuition and fees vary according to course load, location, and program. Part-time tuition and fees vary according to course load, location, and program. **College room and board:** $8310. Room and board charges vary according to board plan and housing facility.

FRESHMAN FINANCIAL AID (Fall 2012, est.) 803 applied for aid; of those 85% were deemed to have need. 97% of freshmen with need received aid; of those 12% had need fully met. **Average percent of need met:** 56% (excluding resources awarded to replace EFC). **Average financial aid package:** $9030 (excluding resources awarded to replace EFC). 1% of all full-time freshmen had no need and received non-need-based gift aid.

UNDERGRADUATE FINANCIAL AID (Fall 2012, est.) 4,702 applied for aid; of those 88% were deemed to have need. 91% of undergraduates with need received aid; of those 6% had need fully met. **Average percent of need met:** 48% (excluding resources awarded to replace EFC). **Average financial aid package:** $8174 (excluding resources awarded to replace EFC). 1% of all full-time undergraduates had no need and received non-need-based gift aid.

GIFT AID (NEED-BASED) Total amount: $16,224,416 (65% federal, 7% state, 28% institutional). **Receiving aid:** Freshmen: 57% (488); all full-time undergraduates: 46% (2,634). **Average award:** Freshmen: $6081; Undergraduates: $5702. **Scholarships, grants, and awards:** Federal Pell, FSEOG, state, private, college/university gift aid from institutional funds.

GIFT AID (NON-NEED-BASED) *Total amount:* $8,277,495 (1% federal, 92% state, 5% institutional, 2% external sources). *Receiving aid:* Freshmen: 54% (465). Undergraduates: 27% (1,530). *Average award:* Freshmen: $1000. Undergraduates: $1458. *Scholarships, grants, and awards by category: Academic interests/ achievement:* 2,070 awards ($9,984,719 total): biological sciences, business, education, engineering/technologies, English, foreign languages, general academic interests/ achievements, mathematics, physical sciences, social sciences. *Creative arts/performance:* 12 awards ($45,884 total): general creative arts/performance, music, theater/ drama. *Special achievements/activities:* 83 awards ($395,884 total): community service, general special achievements/activities. *Special characteristics:* 1,789 awards ($8,120,790 total): adult students, children and siblings of alumni, children of public servants, children with a deceased or disabled parent, general special characteristics, international students, local/state students, members of minority groups, out-of-state students, public servants. *Tuition waivers:* Full or partial for employees or children of employees, senior citizens. *ROTC:* Army, Naval cooperative, Air Force cooperative.

LOANS *Student loans:* $20,062,385 (47% need-based, 53% non-need-based). 18% of past graduating class borrowed through all loan programs. *Average indebtedness per student:* $18,271. *Average need-based loan:* Freshmen: $3141. Undergraduates: $4120. *Parent loans:* $360,880 (100% non-need-based). *Programs:* Federal Direct (Subsidized and Unsubsidized Stafford, PLUS), Perkins, college/university.

WORK-STUDY *Federal work-study:* Total amount: $354,088; 150 jobs averaging $2361. *State or other work-study/employment:* Total amount: $607,626 (100% non-need-based). 366 part-time jobs averaging $1660.

ATHLETIC AWARDS Total amount: $862,202 (54% need-based, 46% non-need-based).

APPLYING FOR FINANCIAL AID *Required financial aid form:* FAFSA. *Financial aid deadline (priority):* 3/15. *Notification date:* Continuous beginning 4/20. Students must reply within 4 weeks of notification.

CONTACT Mrs. Denise Spellman, Interim Director, University of New Orleans, Administration Building, Room 1005, New Orleans, LA 70148, 504-280-6603 or toll-free 800-256-5866. *Fax:* 504-280-3973. *E-mail:* dspellma@uno.edu. *Website:* http://www.uno.edu/.

UNIVERSITY OF NORTH ALABAMA
Florence, AL

Tuition & fees (AL res): $8148	Average undergraduate aid package: $7637

ABOUT THE INSTITUTION State-supported, coed. *Awards:* certificates, bachelor's, and master's degrees. 35 undergraduate majors. *Total enrollment:* 7,016. Undergraduates: 6,082. Freshmen: 1,078. Federal methodology is used as a basis for awarding need-based institutional aid.

UNDERGRADUATE EXPENSES for 2013–2014 *Application fee:* $25. *Tuition, state resident:* full-time $6660; part-time $222 per credit hour. *Tuition, nonresident:* full-time $13,320; part-time $444 per credit hour. *Required fees:* full-time $1488. Full-time tuition and fees vary according to course load and program. Part-time tuition and fees vary according to course load and program. *College room and board:* $5678. Room and board charges vary according to board plan and housing facility.

FRESHMAN FINANCIAL AID (Fall 2011) 957 applied for aid; of those 90% were deemed to have need. 95% of freshmen with need received aid; of those 50% had need fully met. *Average percent of need met:* 65% (excluding resources awarded to replace EFC). *Average financial aid package:* $6752 (excluding resources awarded to replace EFC). 36% of all full-time freshmen had no need and received non-need-based gift aid.

UNDERGRADUATE FINANCIAL AID (Fall 2011) 3,953 applied for aid; of those 90% were deemed to have need. 96% of undergraduates with need received aid; of those 54% had need fully met. *Average percent of need met:* 63% (excluding resources awarded to replace EFC). *Average financial aid package:* $7637 (excluding resources awarded to replace EFC). 28% of all full-time undergraduates had no need and received non-need-based gift aid.

GIFT AID (NEED-BASED) *Total amount:* $10,110,230 (99% federal, 1% state). *Receiving aid:* Freshmen: 64% (611); all full-time undergraduates: 69% (2,831). *Average award:* Freshmen: $4472; Undergraduates: $4882. *Scholarships, grants, and awards:* Federal Pell, FSEOG, state, private, college/university gift aid from institutional funds, Academic Competitiveness Grants, National SMART Grants.

GIFT AID (NON-NEED-BASED) *Total amount:* $5,721,732 (84% institutional, 16% external sources). *Receiving aid:* Freshmen: 19% (184). Undergraduates: 20% (805). *Average award:* Freshmen: $2122. Undergraduates: $2174. *Scholarships, grants, and awards by category: Academic interests/achievement:* general academic interests/achievements. *Creative arts/performance:* art/fine arts, journalism/ publications, music. *Special achievements/activities:* cheerleading/drum major, general special achievements/activities, leadership. *Special characteristics:* children of faculty/ staff, first-generation college students, general special characteristics, out-of-state students. *Tuition waivers:* Full or partial for employees or children of employees, senior citizens. *ROTC:* Army.

LOANS *Student loans:* $20,045,518 (50% need-based, 50% non-need-based). 72% of past graduating class borrowed through all loan programs. *Average indebtedness per student:* $32,640. *Average need-based loan:* Freshmen: $3224. Undergraduates: $3856. *Parent loans:* $1,150,225 (100% non-need-based). *Programs:* Federal Direct (Subsidized and Unsubsidized Stafford, PLUS).

WORK-STUDY *Federal work-study:* Total amount: $278,576; jobs available. *State or other work-study/employment:* Total amount: $772,723 (100% non-need-based). Part-time jobs available.

ATHLETIC AWARDS Total amount: $1,919,288 (100% non-need-based).

APPLYING FOR FINANCIAL AID *Required financial aid form:* FAFSA. *Financial aid deadline:* 6/1 (priority: 6/1). *Notification date:* 5/15. Students must reply within 2 weeks of notification.

CONTACT Mr. Ben Baker, Director of Student Financial Services, University of North Alabama, UNA Box 5014, Florence, AL 35632-0001, 256-765-4279 or toll-free 800-TALK-UNA. *E-mail:* bjbaker@una.edu. *Website:* http://www.una.edu/.

UNIVERSITY OF NORTH CAROLINA AT ASHEVILLE
Asheville, NC

Tuition & fees (NC res): $5866	Average undergraduate aid package: $11,490

ABOUT THE INSTITUTION State-supported, coed. *Awards:* certificates, bachelor's, and master's degrees. 32 undergraduate majors. *Total enrollment:* 3,751. Undergraduates: 3,693. Freshmen: 553. Federal methodology is used as a basis for awarding need-based institutional aid.

UNDERGRADUATE EXPENSES for 2013–2014 *Application fee:* $50. *Tuition, state resident:* full-time $3476. *Tuition, nonresident:* full-time $17,292. *Required fees:* full-time $2390. Full-time tuition and fees vary according to course load. Part-time tuition and fees vary according to course load. *College room and board:* $7584; *Room only:* $4348. Room and board charges vary according to housing facility.

FRESHMAN FINANCIAL AID (Fall 2011) 438 applied for aid; of those 65% were deemed to have need. 99% of freshmen with need received aid; of those 33% had need fully met. *Average percent of need met:* 82% (excluding resources awarded to replace EFC). *Average financial aid package:* $11,229 (excluding resources awarded to replace EFC). 5% of all full-time freshmen had no need and received non-need-based gift aid.

UNDERGRADUATE FINANCIAL AID (Fall 2011) 2,292 applied for aid; of those 74% were deemed to have need. 99% of undergraduates with need received aid; of those 37% had need fully met. *Average percent of need met:* 79% (excluding resources awarded to replace EFC). *Average financial aid package:* $11,490 (excluding resources awarded to replace EFC). 4% of all full-time undergraduates had no need and received non-need-based gift aid.

GIFT AID (NEED-BASED) *Total amount:* $10,466,726 (46% federal, 29% state, 25% institutional). *Receiving aid:* Freshmen: 49% (266); all full-time undergraduates: 53% (1,598). *Average award:* Freshmen: $6728; Undergraduates: $6096. *Scholarships, grants, and awards:* Federal Pell, FSEOG, state, private, college/university gift aid from institutional funds.

GIFT AID (NON-NEED-BASED) *Total amount:* $717,056 (5% federal, 40% state, 54% institutional, 1% external sources). *Receiving aid:* Freshmen: 6% (30). Undergraduates: 6% (193). *Average award:* Freshmen: $2909. Undergraduates: $2910. *Scholarships, grants, and awards by category: Academic interests/ achievement:* biological sciences, business, communication, computer science, education, engineering/technologies, English, general academic interests/achievements, health fields, mathematics, physical sciences, premedicine, social sciences. *Creative* arts/performance: art/fine arts, general creative arts/performance, music, theater/drama. *Special achievements/activities:* community service, general special achievements/activities, junior miss, leadership. *Special characteristics:* adult students, children and siblings of alumni, children of faculty/staff, ethnic background, first-generation college students, general special characteristics, handicapped students, international students, local/state students, members of minority groups, veterans, veterans' children. *Tuition waivers:* Full or partial for employees or children of employees.

LOANS *Student loans:* $11,095,271 (71% need-based, 29% non-need-based). 58% of past graduating class borrowed through all loan programs. *Average indebtedness per student:* $17,696. *Average need-based loan:* Freshmen: $3663. Undergraduates: $4483. *Parent loans:* $1,246,564 (21% need-based, 79% non-need-based). *Programs:* Federal Direct (Subsidized and Unsubsidized Stafford, PLUS), Perkins, state, college/university.

WORK-STUDY *Federal work-study:* Total amount: $108,273; 46 jobs averaging $2354.

ATHLETIC AWARDS Total amount: $1,527,645 (33% need-based, 67% non-need-based).

APPLYING FOR FINANCIAL AID *Required financial aid form:* FAFSA. *Financial aid deadline (priority):* 3/1. *Notification date:* Continuous beginning 3/15. Students must reply within 2 weeks of notification.

CONTACT Ms. Elizabeth D. Bartlett, Associate Director of Financial Aid, University of North Carolina at Asheville, 1 University Heights, Asheville, NC 28804-8510, 828-232-6535 or toll-free 800-531-9842. *Fax:* 828-251-2294. *E-mail:* bbartlett@unca.edu. *Website:* http://www.unca.edu/.

THE UNIVERSITY OF NORTH CAROLINA AT CHAPEL HILL
Chapel Hill, NC

Tuition & fees (NC res): $7690	Average undergraduate aid package: $15,983

ABOUT THE INSTITUTION State-supported, coed. *Awards:* certificates, bachelor's, master's, and doctoral degrees. 61 undergraduate majors. *Total enrollment:* 29,278. Undergraduates: 18,503. Freshmen: 3,915. Both federal and institutional methodology are used as a basis for awarding need-based institutional aid.

UNDERGRADUATE EXPENSES for 2013–2014 *Application fee:* $80. *Tuition, state resident:* full-time $5823. *Tuition, nonresident:* full-time $26,575. *Required fees:* full-time $1867. Full-time tuition and fees vary according to program. Part-time tuition and fees vary according to course load and program. *College room and board:* $9734; *Room only:* $5630. Room and board charges vary according to board plan, housing facility, and location.

FRESHMAN FINANCIAL AID (Fall 2011) 2,954 applied for aid; of those 58% were deemed to have need. 100% of freshmen with need received aid; of those 78% had need fully met. *Average percent of need met:* 100% (excluding resources awarded to replace EFC). *Average financial aid package:* $15,939 (excluding resources awarded to replace EFC). 3% of all full-time freshmen had no need and received non-need-based gift aid.

UNDERGRADUATE FINANCIAL AID (Fall 2011) 9,941 applied for aid; of those 74% were deemed to have need. 100% of undergraduates with need received aid; of those 81% had need fully met. *Average percent of need met:* 100% (excluding resources awarded to replace EFC). *Average financial aid package:* $15,983 (excluding resources awarded to replace EFC). 4% of all full-time undergraduates had no need and received non-need-based gift aid.

GIFT AID (NEED-BASED) *Total amount:* $93,850,532 (17% federal, 14% state, 63% institutional, 6% external sources). *Receiving aid:* Freshmen: 40% (1,612); all full-time undergraduates: 41% (7,064). *Average award:* Freshmen: $13,982; Undergraduates: $13,222. *Scholarships, grants, and awards:* Federal Pell, FSEOG, state, private, college/university gift aid from institutional funds.

GIFT AID (NON-NEED-BASED) *Total amount:* $16,213,709 (14% state, 32% institutional, 54% external sources). *Receiving aid:* Freshmen: 5% (182). Undergraduates: 3% (473). *Average award:* Freshmen: $6885. Undergraduates: $6249. *Scholarships, grants, and awards by category:* Academic interests/achievement: business, communication, education, English, general academic interests/achievements, health fields, mathematics. *Creative arts/performance:* applied art and design, art/fine arts, journalism/publications, music, theater/drama. *Special achievements/activities:* community service, general special achievements/activities, leadership. *Special charac-*

teristics: children of faculty/staff, international students, out-of-state students, relatives of clergy, religious affiliation. *Tuition waivers:* Full or partial for employees or children of employees. *ROTC:* Army, Naval, Air Force.

LOANS *Student loans:* $38,214,720 (62% need-based, 38% non-need-based). 35% of past graduating class borrowed through all loan programs. *Average indebtedness per student:* $16,983. *Average need-based loan:* Freshmen: $3449. Undergraduates: $4529. *Parent loans:* $7,744,846 (4% need-based, 96% non-need-based). *Programs:* Federal Direct (Subsidized and Unsubsidized Stafford, PLUS), Perkins, state, college/university, alternative loans.

WORK-STUDY *Federal work-study:* Total amount: $3,355,265; 1,800 jobs averaging $1849.

ATHLETIC AWARDS Total amount: $10,292,404 (51% need-based, 49% non-need-based).

APPLYING FOR FINANCIAL AID *Required financial aid forms:* FAFSA, CSS Financial Aid PROFILE. *Financial aid deadline (priority):* 3/1. *Notification date:* Continuous beginning 3/15. Students must reply by 5/1.

CONTACT Ms. Shirley A. Ort, Associate Provost and Director of Scholarships and Student Aid, The University of North Carolina at Chapel Hill, CB # 2300, 111 Pettigrew Hall, Chapel Hill, NC 27599, 919-962-8396. *Fax:* 919-962-2716. *E-mail:* aidinfo@unc.edu. *Website:* http://www.unc.edu/.

THE UNIVERSITY OF NORTH CAROLINA AT CHARLOTTE
Charlotte, NC

ABOUT THE INSTITUTION State-supported, coed. *Awards:* certificates, bachelor's, master's, and doctoral degrees. 64 undergraduate majors. *Total enrollment:* 26,232. Undergraduates: 21,179. Freshmen: 3,541.

GIFT AID (NEED-BASED) *Scholarships, grants, and awards:* Federal Pell, FSEOG, state, private, college/university gift aid from institutional funds.

GIFT AID (NON-NEED-BASED) *Scholarships, grants, and awards by category:* Academic interests/achievement: architecture, business, computer science, education, engineering/technologies, general academic interests/achievements, health fields, humanities, mathematics, military science. *Creative arts/performance:* music, performing arts. *Special characteristics:* adult students.

LOANS *Programs:* Federal Direct (Subsidized and Unsubsidized Stafford, PLUS), Perkins, state, college/university.

APPLYING FOR FINANCIAL AID *Required financial aid form:* FAFSA.

CONTACT Office of Financial Aid, The University of North Carolina at Charlotte, 9201 University City Boulevard, Charlotte, NC 28223-0001, 704-687-2461. *Fax:* 704-687-3132. *Website:* http://www.uncc.edu/.

THE UNIVERSITY OF NORTH CAROLINA AT GREENSBORO
Greensboro, NC

Tuition & fees (NC res): $6229	Average undergraduate aid package: $9827

ABOUT THE INSTITUTION State-supported, coed. *Awards:* certificates, bachelor's, master's, and doctoral degrees. 69 undergraduate majors. *Total enrollment:* 18,172. Undergraduates: 14,674. Freshmen: 2,516. Federal methodology is used as a basis for awarding need-based institutional aid.

UNDERGRADUATE EXPENSES for 2013–2014 *Application fee:* $55. *Tuition, state resident:* full-time $3779; part-time $492 per unit. *Tuition, nonresident:* full-time $17,577; part-time $2216 per unit. *Required fees:* full-time $2450; $91 per hour. Part-time tuition and fees vary according to course load. *College room and board:* $8948; *Room only:* $5950. Room and board charges vary according to board plan and housing facility.

FRESHMAN FINANCIAL AID (Fall 2012, est.) 2,188 applied for aid; of those 91% were deemed to have need. 100% of freshmen with need received aid; of those 21% had need fully met. *Average percent of need met:* 51% (excluding resources awarded to replace EFC). *Average financial aid package:* $9665 (excluding resources awarded to replace EFC). 3% of all full-time freshmen had no need and received non-need-based gift aid.

UNDERGRADUATE FINANCIAL AID (Fall 2012, est.) 10,677 applied for aid; of those 97% were deemed to have need. 100% of undergraduates with need received aid; of those 18% had need fully met. *Average percent of need met:* 54% (excluding resources awarded to replace EFC). *Average financial aid package:* $9827 (excluding resources awarded to replace EFC). 2% of all full-time undergraduates had no need and received non-need-based gift aid.

GIFT AID (NEED-BASED) *Total amount:* $38,607,637 (71% federal, 3% state, 26% institutional). *Receiving aid:* Freshmen: 49% (1,227); all full-time undergraduates: 50% (6,422). *Average award:* Freshmen: $5850; Undergraduates: $5731. *Scholarships, grants, and awards:* Federal Pell, FSEOG, state, private, college/university gift aid from institutional funds.

GIFT AID (NON-NEED-BASED) *Total amount:* $25,665,818 (71% state, 21% institutional, 8% external sources). *Receiving aid:* Freshmen: 64% (1,608). Undergraduates: 59% (7,602). *Average award:* Freshmen: $4601. Undergraduates: $3206. *Scholarships, grants, and awards by category: Academic interests/ achievement:* biological sciences, business, communication, education, English, foreign languages, general academic interests/achievements, health fields, home economics, humanities, library science, mathematics, physical sciences, premedicine, religion/biblical studies, social sciences. *Creative arts/performance:* art/fine arts, cinema/film/ broadcasting, dance, music, performing arts, theater/drama. *Special achievements/ activities:* community service, general special achievements/activities, junior miss, religious involvement. *Special characteristics:* adult students, children and siblings of alumni, children of faculty/staff, ethnic background, general special characteristics, handicapped students, international students, local/state students, out-of-state students, veterans, veterans' children. *Tuition waivers:* Full or partial for employees or children of employees. *ROTC:* Army cooperative, Air Force cooperative.

LOANS *Student loans:* $62,334,708 (48% need-based, 52% non-need-based). 69% of past graduating class borrowed through all loan programs. *Average indebtedness per student:* $24,199. *Average need-based loan:* Freshmen: $3259. Undergraduates: $4088. *Parent loans:* $13,305,631 (100% non-need-based). *Programs:* Federal Direct (Subsidized and Unsubsidized Stafford, PLUS), Perkins, state, college/ university.

WORK-STUDY *Federal work-study:* Total amount: $462,616; jobs available.

ATHLETIC AWARDS Total amount: $2,693,878 (100% non-need-based).

APPLYING FOR FINANCIAL AID *Required financial aid form:* FAFSA. *Financial aid deadline (priority):* 3/1. *Notification date:* Continuous beginning 3/15.

CONTACT Mr. Bruce Cabiness, Associate Director of Financial Aid, The University of North Carolina at Greensboro, PO Box 26170, Greensboro, NC 27402-6170, 336-334-5702. *Fax:* 336-334-3010. *E-mail:* bruce_cabiness@uncg.edu. *Website:* http://www.uncg.edu/.

THE UNIVERSITY OF NORTH CAROLINA AT PEMBROKE
Pembroke, NC

Tuition & fees (NC res): $4857	Average undergraduate aid package: $9676

ABOUT THE INSTITUTION State-supported, coed. *Awards:* bachelor's and master's degrees. 46 undergraduate majors. *Total enrollment:* 6,269. Undergraduates: 5,504. Freshmen: 1,020. Federal methodology is used as a basis for awarding need-based institutional aid.

UNDERGRADUATE EXPENSES for 2013–2014 *Application fee:* $45. *Tuition, state resident:* full-time $3012. *Tuition, nonresident:* full-time $12,219. *Required fees:* full-time $1845. Full-time tuition and fees vary according to course load and location. Part-time tuition and fees vary according to course load and location. *College room and board:* $7010; *Room only:* $5500. Room and board charges vary according to board plan, housing facility, and location.

FRESHMAN FINANCIAL AID (Fall 2012, est.) 914 applied for aid; of those 85% were deemed to have need. 99% of freshmen with need received aid; of those 10% had need fully met. *Average percent of need met:* 69% (excluding resources awarded to replace EFC). *Average financial aid package:* $9121 (excluding resources awarded to replace EFC). 1% of all full-time freshmen had no need and received non-need-based gift aid.

UNDERGRADUATE FINANCIAL AID (Fall 2012, est.) 3,901 applied for aid; of those 89% were deemed to have need. 98% of undergraduates with need received aid; of those 11% had need fully met. *Average percent of need met:* 71% (excluding resources awarded to replace EFC). *Average financial aid package:* $9676 (excluding resources awarded to replace EFC). 1% of all full-time undergraduates had no need and received non-need-based gift aid.

GIFT AID (NEED-BASED) *Total amount:* $21,970,034 (62% federal, 35% state, 1% institutional, 2% external sources). *Receiving aid:* Freshmen: 75% (724); all full-time undergraduates: 71% (3,146). *Average award:* Freshmen: $6329; Undergraduates: $6239. *Scholarships, grants, and awards:* Federal Pell, FSEOG, state, private, college/university gift aid from institutional funds.

GIFT AID (NON-NEED-BASED) *Total amount:* $703,402 (80% federal, 4% institutional, 16% external sources). *Receiving aid:* Freshmen: 14% (137). Undergraduates: 9% (405). *Average award:* Freshmen: $1160. Undergraduates: $737. *Scholarships, grants, and awards by category: Academic interests/ achievement:* 156 awards ($102,581 total): education, general academic interests/ achievements. *Special characteristics:* 1 award ($1000 total): children and siblings of alumni. *Tuition waivers:* Full or partial for employees or children of employees. *ROTC:* Army, Air Force.

LOANS *Student loans:* $24,001,064 (90% need-based, 10% non-need-based). 78% of past graduating class borrowed through all loan programs. *Average indebtedness per student:* $23,760. *Average need-based loan:* Freshmen: $3284. Undergraduates: $4135. *Parent loans:* $1,903,336 (66% need-based, 34% non-need-based). *Programs:* Federal Direct (Subsidized and Unsubsidized Stafford, PLUS), Perkins, college/university.

WORK-STUDY *Federal work-study:* Total amount: $206,348; 118 jobs averaging $1748. *State or other work-study/employment:* Part-time jobs available.

ATHLETIC AWARDS Total amount: $1,531,558 (100% need-based).

APPLYING FOR FINANCIAL AID *Required financial aid form:* FAFSA. *Financial aid deadline (priority):* 3/15. *Notification date:* Continuous beginning 4/15.

CONTACT Mildred Weber, Associate Director of Financial Aid, The University of North Carolina at Pembroke, PO Box 1510, Pembroke, NC 28372, 910-521-6612 or toll-free 800-949-UNCP. *Fax:* 910-775-4159. *E-mail:* mildred.weber@uncp.edu. *Website:* http://www.uncp.edu/.

UNIVERSITY OF NORTH CAROLINA SCHOOL OF THE ARTS
Winston-Salem, NC

CONTACT Jane C. Kamiab, Director of Financial Aid, University of North Carolina School of the Arts, 1533 South Main Street, Winston-Salem, NC 27127, 336-770-3297. *Fax:* 336-770-1489. *Website:* http://www.uncsa.edu/.

THE UNIVERSITY OF NORTH CAROLINA WILMINGTON
Wilmington, NC

Tuition & fees (NC res): $5800	Average undergraduate aid package: $9668

ABOUT THE INSTITUTION State-supported, coed. *Awards:* certificates, bachelor's, master's, and doctoral degrees. 59 undergraduate majors. *Total enrollment:* 13,733. Undergraduates: 12,348. Freshmen: 2,053. Federal methodology is used as a basis for awarding need-based institutional aid.

UNDERGRADUATE EXPENSES for 2013–2014 *Application fee:* $60. *Tuition, state resident:* full-time $3742. *Tuition, nonresident:* full-time $15,845. *Required fees:* full-time $2058. Full-time tuition and fees vary according to course load. Part-time tuition and fees vary according to course load. *College room and board:* $8016; *Room only:* $4620. Room and board charges vary according to board plan and housing facility.

FRESHMAN FINANCIAL AID (Fall 2012, est.) 1,762 applied for aid; of those 62% were deemed to have need. 100% of freshmen with need received aid; of those 27% had need fully met. *Average percent of need met:* 62% (excluding resources awarded to replace EFC). *Average financial aid package:* $8220 (excluding resources awarded to replace EFC). 2% of all full-time freshmen had no need and received non-need-based gift aid.

UNDERGRADUATE FINANCIAL AID (Fall 2012, est.) 8,100 applied for aid; of those 71% were deemed to have need. 100% of undergraduates with need received aid; of those 34% had need fully met. *Average percent of need met:* 70% (excluding resources awarded to replace EFC). *Average financial aid package:* $9668 (excluding resources awarded to replace EFC). 3% of all full-time undergraduates had no need and received non-need-based gift aid.

GIFT AID (NEED-BASED) *Total amount:* $29,136,051 (51% federal, 16% state, 30% institutional, 3% external sources). *Receiving aid:* Freshmen: 53% (1,086); all full-time undergraduates: 51% (5,683). *Average award:* Freshmen: $4534; Undergraduates: $4911. *Scholarships, grants, and awards:* Federal Pell, FSEOG, state, private, college/university gift aid from institutional funds.

GIFT AID (NON-NEED-BASED) *Total amount:* $2,068,501 (2% federal, 28% state, 44% institutional, 26% external sources). *Receiving aid:* Freshmen: 11% (224). Undergraduates: 8% (884). *Average award:* Freshmen: $2026. Undergraduates: $2464. *Scholarships, grants, and awards by category: Academic interests/achievement:* biological sciences, business, communication, computer science, education, engineering/technologies, English, foreign languages, general academic interests/achievements, health fields, humanities, international studies, mathematics, physical sciences, premedicine, social sciences. *Creative arts/performance:* art/fine arts, cinema/film/broadcasting, creative writing, music, theater/drama. *Special achievements/activities:* cheerleading/drum major, general special achievements/activities, leadership. *Special characteristics:* local/state students, married students. *Tuition waivers:* Full or partial for employees or children of employees.

LOANS *Student loans:* $63,892,016 (61% need-based, 39% non-need-based). 58% of past graduating class borrowed through all loan programs. *Average indebtedness per student:* $25,821. *Average need-based loan:* Freshmen: $3332. Undergraduates: $4326. *Parent loans:* $13,458,640 (19% need-based, 81% non-need-based). *Programs:* Federal Direct (Subsidized and Unsubsidized Stafford, PLUS), Perkins, state.

WORK-STUDY *Federal work-study:* Total amount: $481,469; 151 jobs averaging $2310.

ATHLETIC AWARDS Total amount: $2,201,183 (25% need-based, 75% non-need-based).

APPLYING FOR FINANCIAL AID *Required financial aid form:* FAFSA. *Financial aid deadline (priority):* 3/1. *Notification date:* Continuous beginning 3/15. Students must reply within 3 weeks of notification.

CONTACT Dr. Ixchel Baker-Tate, Director of Financial Aid and Veterans Services, The University of North Carolina Wilmington, 601 South College Road, Wilmington, NC 28403-5951, 910-962-3177. *Fax:* 910-962-3851. *E-mail:* finaid@uncw.edu. *Website:* http://www.uncw.edu/.

UNIVERSITY OF NORTH DAKOTA
Grand Forks, ND

ABOUT THE INSTITUTION State-supported, coed. *Awards:* certificates, diplomas, bachelor's, master's, and doctoral degrees. 90 undergraduate majors. *Total enrollment:* 14,697. Undergraduates: 11,522. Freshmen: 2,091.

GIFT AID (NEED-BASED) *Scholarships, grants, and awards:* Federal Pell, FSEOG, state, private, college/university gift aid from institutional funds, Federal Nursing.

GIFT AID (NON-NEED-BASED) *Scholarships, grants, and awards by category: Academic interests/achievement:* biological sciences, business, communication, computer science, education, engineering/technologies, English, foreign languages, general academic interests/achievements, health fields, humanities, international studies, mathematics, military science, physical sciences, premedicine, social sciences. *Creative arts/performance:* art/fine arts, debating, music, theater/drama. *Special achievements/activities:* general special achievements/activities, leadership, memberships. *Special characteristics:* children of faculty/staff, ethnic background, general special characteristics, handicapped students, international students, members of minority groups, veterans' children.

LOANS *Programs:* Federal Direct (Subsidized and Unsubsidized Stafford, PLUS), Perkins, Federal Nursing, alternative loans.

APPLYING FOR FINANCIAL AID *Required financial aid form:* FAFSA.

CONTACT Janelle Kilgore, Interim Director of Student Financial Aid, University of North Dakota, 264 Centennial Drive Stop 8371, Grand Forks, ND 58202, 701-777-3121 or toll-free 800-CALL-UND. *Fax:* 701-777-2040. *E-mail:* janelle.kilgore@und.edu.
Website: http://www.und.nodak.edu/.

UNIVERSITY OF NORTHERN COLORADO
Greeley, CO

Tuition & fees (CO res): $6514	Average undergraduate aid package: $6171

ABOUT THE INSTITUTION State-supported, coed. *Awards:* bachelor's, master's, and doctoral degrees. 43 undergraduate majors. *Total enrollment:* 12,497. Undergraduates: 10,102. Freshmen: 2,218. Federal methodology is used as a basis for awarding need-based institutional aid.

UNDERGRADUATE EXPENSES for 2013–2014 *Application fee:* $45. *One-time required fee:* $225. *Tuition, state resident:* full-time $5214; part-time $217.25 per credit hour. *Tuition, nonresident:* full-time $16,488; part-time $687 per credit hour. *Required fees:* full-time $1300; $62.59 per credit hour. Full-time tuition and fees vary according to course load and program. Part-time tuition and fees vary according to course load and program. *College room and board:* $10,040; *Room only:* $4914. Room and board charges vary according to board plan, housing facility, and student level.

FRESHMAN FINANCIAL AID (Fall 2011) 1,831 applied for aid; of those 88% were deemed to have need. 98% of freshmen with need received aid; of those 44% had need fully met. *Average percent of need met:* 78% (excluding resources awarded to replace EFC). *Average financial aid package:* $6136 (excluding resources awarded to replace EFC). 19% of all full-time freshmen had no need and received non-need-based gift aid.

UNDERGRADUATE FINANCIAL AID (Fall 2011) 7,141 applied for aid; of those 85% were deemed to have need. 97% of undergraduates with need received aid; of those 36% had need fully met. *Average percent of need met:* 75% (excluding resources awarded to replace EFC). *Average financial aid package:* $6171 (excluding resources awarded to replace EFC). 12% of all full-time undergraduates had no need and received non-need-based gift aid.

GIFT AID (NEED-BASED) *Total amount:* $31,954,507 (45% federal, 9% state, 33% institutional, 13% external sources). *Receiving aid:* Freshmen: 60% (1,390); all full-time undergraduates: 56% (4,726). *Average award:* Freshmen: $4154; Undergraduates: $3643. *Scholarships, grants, and awards:* Federal Pell, FSEOG, state, private, college/university gift aid from institutional funds.

GIFT AID (NON-NEED-BASED) *Total amount:* $5,933,605 (5% federal, 49% institutional, 46% external sources). *Receiving aid:* Freshmen: 3% (67). Undergraduates: 2% (167). *Average award:* Freshmen: $299. Undergraduates: $245. *Scholarships, grants, and awards by category: Academic interests/achievement:* biological sciences, business, communication, education, English, general academic interests/achievements, health fields, home economics, mathematics, military science, physical sciences, social sciences. *Creative arts/performance:* dance, music, performing arts, theater/drama. *Special characteristics:* adult students, children of faculty/staff, children of union members/company employees, ethnic background, general special characteristics, handicapped students, international students, out-of-state students, veterans. *Tuition waivers:* Full or partial for employees or children of employees. *ROTC:* Army, Air Force.

LOANS *Student loans:* $46,376,388 (84% need-based, 16% non-need-based). *Average need-based loan:* Freshmen: $3194. Undergraduates: $3971. *Parent loans:* $19,356,616 (77% need-based, 23% non-need-based). *Programs:* Federal Direct (Subsidized and Unsubsidized Stafford, PLUS), Perkins.

WORK-STUDY *Federal work-study:* Total amount: $408,649; jobs available. *State or other work-study/employment:* Total amount: $1,387,820 (92% need-based, 8% non-need-based). Part-time jobs available.

ATHLETIC AWARDS Total amount: $3,028,577 (37% need-based, 63% non-need-based).

APPLYING FOR FINANCIAL AID *Required financial aid form:* FAFSA. *Financial aid deadline (priority):* 3/1. *Notification date:* Continuous beginning 4/15. Students must reply within 4 weeks of notification.

CONTACT Marty Somero, Director of Financial Aid, University of Northern Colorado, Carter Hall 1005, Greeley, CO 80639, 970-351-2502 or toll-free 888-700-4UNC. *Fax:* 970-351-3737. *E-mail:* ofa@unco.edu. *Website:* http://www.unco.edu/.

UNIVERSITY OF NORTHERN IOWA
Cedar Falls, IA

Tuition & fees (IA res): $7635	Average undergraduate aid package: $7828

ABOUT THE INSTITUTION State-supported, coed. *Awards:* bachelor's, master's, and doctoral degrees. 89 undergraduate majors. *Total enrollment:* 12,273. Undergraduates: 10,655. Freshmen: 1,704. Federal methodology is used as a basis for awarding need-based institutional aid.

UNDERGRADUATE EXPENSES for 2013–2014 *Application fee:* $40. *Tuition, state resident:* full-time $6648; part-time $277 per hour. *Tuition, non-resident:* full-time $15,734; part-time $656 per hour. *Required fees:* full-time $987. Full-time tuition and fees vary according to course load and program. Part-time tuition and fees vary according to course load and program. *College room and board:* $7597; *Room only:* $3703. Room and board charges vary according to board plan and housing facility.

FRESHMAN FINANCIAL AID (Fall 2011) 1,645 applied for aid; of those 72% were deemed to have need. 97% of freshmen with need received aid; of those 19% had need fully met. *Average percent of need met:* 69% (excluding resources awarded to replace EFC). *Average financial aid package:* $7708 (excluding resources awarded to replace EFC). 20% of all full-time freshmen had no need and received non-need-based gift aid.

UNDERGRADUATE FINANCIAL AID (Fall 2011) 8,007 applied for aid; of those 81% were deemed to have need. 96% of undergraduates with need received aid; of those 16% had need fully met. *Average percent of need met:* 68% (excluding resources awarded to replace EFC). *Average financial aid package:* $7828 (excluding resources awarded to replace EFC). 9% of all full-time undergraduates had no need and received non-need-based gift aid.

GIFT AID (NEED-BASED) *Total amount:* $26,127,202 (49% federal, 5% state, 39% institutional, 7% external sources). *Receiving aid:* Freshmen: 34% (577); all full-time undergraduates: 35% (3,413). *Average award:* Freshmen: $4749; Undergraduates: $4227. *Scholarships, grants, and awards:* Federal Pell, FSEOG, state, private, college/university gift aid from institutional funds, TEACH Grants.

GIFT AID (NON-NEED-BASED) *Total amount:* $3,010,037 (21% federal, 3% state, 60% institutional, 16% external sources). *Receiving aid:* Freshmen: 46% (767). Undergraduates: 26% (2,495). *Average award:* Freshmen: $3616. Undergraduates: $3473. *Scholarships, grants, and awards by category: Academic interests/achievement:* biological sciences, business, communication, computer science, education, general academic interests/achievements, mathematics, physical sciences, social sciences. *Creative arts/performance:* applied art and design, art/fine arts, debating, music, theater/drama. *Special achievements/activities:* leadership. *Special characteristics:* general special characteristics, members of minority groups, veterans. **ROTC:** Army.

LOANS *Student loans:* $51,335,966 (47% need-based, 53% non-need-based). 77% of past graduating class borrowed through all loan programs. *Average indebtedness per student:* $23,575. *Average need-based loan:* Freshmen: $2839. Undergraduates: $3832. *Parent loans:* $15,574,585 (100% non-need-based). *Programs:* Federal Direct (Subsidized and Unsubsidized Stafford, PLUS), Perkins, private loans.

WORK-STUDY *Federal work-study:* Total amount: $609,813; 433 jobs averaging $1417. *State or other work-study/employment:* Total amount: $9665 (100% non-need-based). Part-time jobs available.

ATHLETIC AWARDS Total amount: $3,122,435 (90% need-based, 10% non-need-based).

APPLYING FOR FINANCIAL AID *Required financial aid form:* FAFSA. *Financial aid deadline:* Continuous. *Notification date:* Continuous beginning 3/15.

CONTACT Heather Soesbe, Associate Director of Student Financial Aid, University of Northern Iowa, 105 Gilchrist Hall, Cedar Falls, IA 50614-0024, 319-273-2700 or toll-free 800-772-2037. *Fax:* 319-273-6950. *E-mail:* heather.soesbe@uni.edu. *Website:* http://www.uni.edu/.

UNIVERSITY OF NORTH FLORIDA
Jacksonville, FL

Tuition & fees (FL res): $6235	Average undergraduate aid package: $7720

ABOUT THE INSTITUTION State-supported, coed. *Awards:* certificates, associate, bachelor's, master's, and doctoral degrees (doctoral degree in education only). 55 undergraduate majors. *Total enrollment:* 16,201. Undergraduates: 14,398. Freshmen: 1,608. Federal methodology is used as a basis for awarding need-based institutional aid.

UNDERGRADUATE EXPENSES for 2013–2014 *Application fee:* $30. *Tuition, state resident:* full-time $4229; part-time $207.83 per credit hour. *Tuition, nonresident:* full-time $17,999; part-time $689.80 per credit hour. *Required fees:* full-time $2006. Full-time tuition and fees vary according to course load. Part-time tuition and fees vary according to course load. *College room and board:* $8190. Room and board charges vary according to board plan and housing facility.

FRESHMAN FINANCIAL AID (Fall 2012, est.) 1,495 applied for aid; of those 65% were deemed to have need. 98% of freshmen with need received aid; of those 16% had need fully met. *Average percent of need met:* 91% (excluding resources awarded to replace EFC). *Average financial aid package:* $8650 (excluding resources awarded to replace EFC). 7% of all full-time freshmen had no need and received non-need-based gift aid.

UNDERGRADUATE FINANCIAL AID (Fall 2012, est.) 8,765 applied for aid; of those 74% were deemed to have need. 96% of undergraduates with need received aid; of those 9% had need fully met. *Average percent of need met:* 90% (excluding resources awarded to replace EFC). *Average financial aid package:* $7720 (excluding resources awarded to replace EFC). 13% of all full-time undergraduates had no need and received non-need-based gift aid.

GIFT AID (NEED-BASED) *Total amount:* $38,471,359 (58% federal, 24% state, 17% institutional, 1% external sources). *Receiving aid:* Freshmen: 34% (544); all full-time undergraduates: 38% (3,850). *Average award:* Freshmen: $6748; Undergraduates: $5370. *Scholarships, grants, and awards:* Federal Pell, FSEOG, state, private, college/university gift aid from institutional funds, 2+2 Scholarships.

GIFT AID (NON-NEED-BASED) *Total amount:* $6,421,402 (65% state, 32% institutional, 3% external sources). *Receiving aid:* Freshmen: 54% (861). Undergraduates: 33% (3,346). *Average award:* Freshmen: $2791. Undergraduates: $2694. *Scholarships, grants, and awards by category: Academic interests/achievement:* 833 awards ($2,423,788 total): business, computer science, education, engineering/technologies, general academic interests/achievements, health fields, international studies. *Creative arts/performance:* 28 awards ($48,350 total): art/fine arts, music. *Special achievements/activities:* 74 awards ($87,667 total): community service, general special achievements/activities, leadership. *Special characteristics:* 29 awards ($47,300 total): first-generation college students, general special characteristics, international students, members of minority groups, out-of-state students. *Tuition waivers:* Full or partial for employees or children of employees, senior citizens. **ROTC:** Army, Naval cooperative.

LOANS *Student loans:* $46,098,468 (88% need-based, 12% non-need-based). 42% of past graduating class borrowed through all loan programs. *Average indebtedness per student:* $17,000. *Average need-based loan:* Freshmen: $3272. Undergraduates: $4506. *Parent loans:* $1,316,831 (75% need-based, 25% non-need-based). *Programs:* Federal Direct (Subsidized and Unsubsidized Stafford, PLUS).

WORK-STUDY *Federal work-study:* Total amount: $527,346; 214 jobs averaging $2814.

ATHLETIC AWARDS Total amount: $1,137,384 (19% need-based, 81% non-need-based).

APPLYING FOR FINANCIAL AID *Required financial aid form:* FAFSA. *Financial aid deadline (priority):* 4/1. *Notification date:* Continuous beginning 3/15. Students must reply within 2 weeks of notification.

CONTACT Ms. Anissa Agne, Director of Financial Aid, University of North Florida, 1 UNF Drive, Jacksonville, FL 32224-7699, 904-620-2604. *E-mail:* anissa.agne@unf.edu. *Website:* http://www.unf.edu/.

UNIVERSITY OF NORTH GEORGIA
Dahlonega, GA

Tuition & fees (GA res): $6570	Average undergraduate aid package: $12,650

ABOUT THE INSTITUTION State-supported, coed. **Awards:** certificates, associate, bachelor's, master's, and doctoral degrees. 35 undergraduate majors. **Total enrollment:** 6,413. Undergraduates: 5,851. Freshmen: 1,125. Federal methodology is used as a basis for awarding need-based institutional aid.

UNDERGRADUATE EXPENSES for 2013–2014 Application fee: $30. **Tuition, state resident:** full-time $4852; part-time $161.74 per credit hour. **Tuition, nonresident:** full-time $17,128; part-time $570.94 per credit hour. **Required fees:** full-time $1718. Part-time tuition and fees vary according to course load. **College room and board:** $8430; **Room only:** $4760. Room and board charges vary according to board plan and housing facility.

FRESHMAN FINANCIAL AID (Fall 2012, est.) 977 applied for aid; of those 64% were deemed to have need. 100% of freshmen with need received aid; of those 28% had need fully met. **Average percent of need met:** 65% (excluding resources awarded to replace EFC). **Average financial aid package:** $8021 (excluding resources awarded to replace EFC). 2% of all full-time freshmen had no need and received non-need-based gift aid.

UNDERGRADUATE FINANCIAL AID (Fall 2012, est.) 4,087 applied for aid; of those 75% were deemed to have need. 100% of undergraduates with need received aid; of those 26% had need fully met. **Average percent of need met:** 62% (excluding resources awarded to replace EFC). **Average financial aid package:** $12,650 (excluding resources awarded to replace EFC). 2% of all full-time undergraduates had no need and received non-need-based gift aid.

GIFT AID (NEED-BASED) Total amount: $16,261,706 (57% federal, 40% state, 1% institutional, 2% external sources). **Receiving aid:** Freshmen: 33% (368); all full-time undergraduates: 36% (1,744). **Average award:** Freshmen: $4100; Undergraduates: $4900. **Scholarships, grants, and awards:** Federal Pell, FSEOG, state, private, college/university gift aid from institutional funds.

GIFT AID (NON-NEED-BASED) Total amount: $8,168,925 (2% federal, 90% state, 4% institutional, 4% external sources). **Receiving aid:** Freshmen: 39% (432). Undergraduates: 41% (1,984). **Average award:** Freshmen: $1172. Undergraduates: $1109. **Scholarships, grants, and awards by category:** Academic interests/achievement: biological sciences, business, education, English, general academic interests/achievements, health fields, humanities, mathematics, military science, physical sciences, premedicine. Creative arts/performance: applied art and design, general creative arts/performance, music. Special achievements/activities: cheerleading/drum major, community service, general special achievements/activities, leadership. Special characteristics: general special characteristics. **Tuition waivers:** Full or partial for employees or children of employees, senior citizens. **ROTC:** Army.

LOANS Student loans: $101,614,479 (14% need-based, 86% non-need-based). 57% of past graduating class borrowed through all loan programs. Average indebtedness per student: $12,166. **Average need-based loan:** Freshmen: $3772. Undergraduates: $5352. **Parent loans:** $1,470,279 (24% need-based, 76% non-need-based). **Programs:** Federal Direct (Subsidized and Unsubsidized Stafford, PLUS), Perkins, state, college/university.

WORK-STUDY Federal work-study: Total amount: $179,650; 95 jobs averaging $2000. **State or other work-study/employment:** Total amount: $550,300 (100% non-need-based). 115 part-time jobs averaging $1500.

ATHLETIC AWARDS Total amount: $998,939 (22% need-based, 78% non-need-based).

APPLYING FOR FINANCIAL AID Required financial aid form: FAFSA. **Financial aid deadline (priority):** 3/17. **Notification date:** Continuous beginning 4/1. Students must reply within 4 weeks of notification.

CONTACT Jill Rayner, Director of Financial Aid, University of North Georgia, 82 College Circle, Dahlonega, GA 30597-1001, 706-864-1688 or toll-free 800-498-9581. Fax: 706-864-1411. E-mail: jprayner@northgeorgia.edu. Website: http://www.ung.edu/.

UNIVERSITY OF NORTH TEXAS
Denton, TX

Tuition & fees (TX res): $9078	Average undergraduate aid package: $11,024

ABOUT THE INSTITUTION State-supported, coed. **Awards:** certificates, bachelor's, master's, and doctoral degrees. 85 undergraduate majors. **Total enrollment:** 35,836. Undergraduates: 28,956. Freshmen: 4,453. Federal methodology is used as a basis for awarding need-based institutional aid.

UNDERGRADUATE EXPENSES for 2013–2014 Application fee: $60. **Tuition, state resident:** full-time $6488. **Tuition, nonresident:** full-time $17,018. **Required fees:** full-time $2590. **College room and board:** $7150. Room and board charges vary according to board plan and housing facility.

FRESHMAN FINANCIAL AID (Fall 2012, est.) 3,572 applied for aid; of those 76% were deemed to have need. 99% of freshmen with need received aid; of those 23% had need fully met. **Average percent of need met:** 76% (excluding resources awarded to replace EFC). **Average financial aid package:** $12,113 (excluding resources awarded to replace EFC). 17% of all full-time freshmen had no need and received non-need-based gift aid.

UNDERGRADUATE FINANCIAL AID (Fall 2012, est.) 16,881 applied for aid; of those 82% were deemed to have need. 96% of undergraduates with need received aid; of those 16% had need fully met. **Average percent of need met:** 64% (excluding resources awarded to replace EFC). **Average financial aid package:** $11,024 (excluding resources awarded to replace EFC). 12% of all full-time undergraduates had no need and received non-need-based gift aid.

GIFT AID (NEED-BASED) Total amount: $108,941,578 (41% federal, 20% state, 30% institutional, 9% external sources). **Receiving aid:** Freshmen: 51% (2,143); all full-time undergraduates: 45% (10,347). **Average award:** Freshmen: $7989; Undergraduates: $7075. **Scholarships, grants, and awards:** Federal Pell, FSEOG, state, private, college/university gift aid from institutional funds.

GIFT AID (NON-NEED-BASED) Total amount: $8,542,798 (40% institutional, 60% external sources). **Receiving aid:** Freshmen: 38% (1,602). Undergraduates: 18% (4,132). **Average award:** Freshmen: $4051. Undergraduates: $4403. **Tuition waivers:** Full or partial for employees or children of employees, senior citizens. **ROTC:** Army, Air Force.

LOANS Student loans: $126,755,145 (85% need-based, 15% non-need-based). **Average need-based loan:** Freshmen: $3247. Undergraduates: $4362. **Parent loans:** $61,334,003 (66% need-based, 34% non-need-based). **Programs:** Federal Direct (Subsidized and Unsubsidized Stafford, PLUS), Perkins, state.

WORK-STUDY Federal work-study: Total amount: $5,526,750; jobs available. **State or other work-study/employment:** Total amount: $469,854 (100% need-based). Part-time jobs available.

ATHLETIC AWARDS Total amount: $3,296,564 (48% need-based, 52% non-need-based).

APPLYING FOR FINANCIAL AID Required financial aid form: FAFSA. **Financial aid deadline (priority):** 3/31. **Notification date:** Continuous beginning 4/1.

CONTACT Mrs. Zelma DeLeon, Director of Student Financial Aid and Scholarships, University of North Texas, 1155 Union Circle #311370, Denton, TX 76203-5017, 940-565-2302 or toll-free 800-868-8211. Fax: 940-565-2738. E-mail: zelma.deleon@unt.edu. Website: http://www.unt.edu/.

UNIVERSITY OF NORTHWESTERN OHIO
Lima, OH

CONTACT Financial Aid Office, University of Northwestern Ohio, 1441 North Cable Road, Lima, OH 45805-1498, 419-227-3141. Website: http://www.unoh.edu/.

UNIVERSITY OF NOTRE DAME
Notre Dame, IN

Tuition & fees: $42,971	Average undergraduate aid package: $38,818

ABOUT THE INSTITUTION Independent Roman Catholic, coed. **Awards:** bachelor's, master's, and doctoral degrees. 57 undergraduate majors. **Total enrollment:** 12,126. Undergraduates: 8,475. Freshmen: 2,014. Both federal and institutional methodology are used as a basis for awarding need-based institutional aid.

UNDERGRADUATE EXPENSES for 2013–2014 Application fee: $75. **Comprehensive fee:** $54,905 includes full-time tuition ($42,464), mandatory fees ($507), and room and board ($11,934). **Part-time tuition:** $1769 per credit hour.

FRESHMAN FINANCIAL AID (Fall 2012, est.) 1,405 applied for aid; of those 74% were deemed to have need. 100% of freshmen with need received aid; of those 100% had need fully met. **Average percent of need met:** 100% (excluding resources awarded to replace EFC). **Average financial aid package:** $38,664 (excluding resources awarded to replace EFC). 3% of all full-time freshmen had no need and received non-need-based gift aid.

UNDERGRADUATE FINANCIAL AID (Fall 2012, est.) 5,150 applied for aid; of those 83% were deemed to have need. 100% of undergraduates with need received aid; of those 100% had need fully met. **Average percent of need met:** 100% (excluding resources awarded to replace EFC). **Average financial aid package:** $38,818 (excluding resources awarded to replace EFC). 5% of all full-time undergraduates had no need and received non-need-based gift aid.

GIFT AID (NEED-BASED) Total amount: $120,504,613 (6% federal, 91% institutional, 3% external sources). **Receiving aid:** Freshmen: 49% (982); all full-time undergraduates: 48% (4,039). **Average award:** Freshmen: $30,722; Undergraduates: $29,440. **Scholarships, grants, and awards:** Federal Pell, FSEOG, state, private, college/university gift aid from institutional funds.

GIFT AID (NON-NEED-BASED) Total amount: $19,373,307 (29% federal, 1% state, 46% institutional, 24% external sources). **Receiving aid:** Freshmen: 26% (526). Undergraduates: 23% (1,955). **Average award:** Freshmen: $14,793. Undergraduates: $10,182. **Scholarships, grants, and awards by category:** Special characteristics: 292 awards ($8,800,866 total): children of faculty/staff. **Tuition waivers:** Full or partial for employees or children of employees. **ROTC:** Army, Naval, Air Force.

LOANS Student loans: $36,512,847 (53% need-based, 47% non-need-based). 51% of past graduating class borrowed through all loan programs. **Average indebtedness per student:** $29,480. **Average need-based loan:** Freshmen: $3971. Undergraduates: $5358. **Parent loans:** $12,326,656 (1% need-based, 99% non-need-based). **Programs:** Federal Direct (Subsidized and Unsubsidized Stafford, PLUS), Perkins, private loans.

WORK-STUDY Federal work-study: Total amount: $3,834,313; 1,677 jobs averaging $2402. **State or other work-study/employment:** Total amount: $9,851,419 (11% need-based, 89% non-need-based). 3,291 part-time jobs averaging $2993.

ATHLETIC AWARDS Total amount: $17,876,948 (17% need-based, 83% non-need-based).

APPLYING FOR FINANCIAL AID Required financial aid forms: FAFSA, CSS Financial Aid PROFILE, noncustodial (divorced/separated) parent's statement, business/farm supplement. **Financial aid deadline (priority):** 2/15. **Notification date:** Continuous beginning 3/28. Students must reply by 5/1.

CONTACT Dr. Thomas Bear, Executive Director of Student Financial Services, University of Notre Dame, 115 Main Building, Notre Dame, IN 46556, 574-631-6436. Fax: 574-631-6899. E-mail: finaid.1@nd.edu. Website: http://www.nd.edu/.

UNIVERSITY OF OKLAHOMA
Norman, OK

Tuition & fees (OK res): $7341	Average undergraduate aid package: $11,896

ABOUT THE INSTITUTION State-supported, coed. **Awards:** certificates, bachelor's, master's, and doctoral degrees. 97 undergraduate majors. **Total enrollment:** 27,507. Undergraduates: 21,109. Freshmen: 4,138. Federal methodology is used as a basis for awarding need-based institutional aid.

UNDERGRADUATE EXPENSES for 2013–2014 Application fee: $40. **Tuition, state resident:** full-time $3957; part-time $131.90 per credit hour.

Tuition, nonresident: full-time $15,594; part-time $519.80 per credit hour. **Required fees:** full-time $3384; $104.35 per credit hour or $126.50 per term. Full-time tuition and fees vary according to course load, location, program, and reciprocity agreements. Part-time tuition and fees vary according to course load, location, program, and reciprocity agreements. **College room and board:** $8382; **Room only:** $4588. Room and board charges vary according to board plan and housing facility. **Payment plan:** Guaranteed tuition.

FRESHMAN FINANCIAL AID (Fall 2011) 2,960 applied for aid; of those 69% were deemed to have need. 97% of freshmen with need received aid; of those 85% had need fully met. **Average percent of need met:** 85% (excluding resources awarded to replace EFC). **Average financial aid package:** $11,837 (excluding resources awarded to replace EFC). 12% of all full-time freshmen had no need and received non-need-based gift aid.

UNDERGRADUATE FINANCIAL AID (Fall 2011) 11,305 applied for aid; of those 79% were deemed to have need. 97% of undergraduates with need received aid; of those 88% had need fully met. **Average percent of need met:** 88% (excluding resources awarded to replace EFC). **Average financial aid package:** $11,896 (excluding resources awarded to replace EFC). 10% of all full-time undergraduates had no need and received non-need-based gift aid.

GIFT AID (NEED-BASED) Total amount: $47,381,085 (48% federal, 27% state, 13% institutional, 12% external sources). **Receiving aid:** Freshmen: 28% (1,102); all full-time undergraduates: 31% (5,412). **Average award:** Freshmen: $6131; Undergraduates: $5522. **Scholarships, grants, and awards:** Federal Pell, FSEOG, state, private, college/university gift aid from institutional funds, United Negro College Fund.

GIFT AID (NON-NEED-BASED) Total amount: $10,907,807 (1% federal, 36% state, 35% institutional, 28% external sources). **Receiving aid:** Freshmen: 31% (1,233). Undergraduates: 23% (4,045). **Average award:** Freshmen: $1871. Undergraduates: $2069. **Scholarships, grants, and awards by category:** Academic interests/achievement: 6,537 awards ($25,139,756 total): architecture, area/ethnic studies, biological sciences, business, communication, computer science, education, engineering/technologies, English, foreign languages, general academic interests/achievements, humanities, international studies, mathematics, military science, physical sciences, social sciences. Creative arts/performance: 256 awards ($1,027,897 total): art/fine arts, dance, debating, journalism/publications, music, performing arts, theater/drama. Special achievements/activities: 212 awards ($346,224 total): leadership. Special characteristics: 498 awards ($406,256 total): children and siblings of alumni, members of minority groups, previous college experience, public servants. **Tuition waivers:** Full or partial for employees or children of employees, senior citizens. **ROTC:** Army, Naval, Air Force.

LOANS Student loans: $73,421,335 (83% need-based, 17% non-need-based). 50% of past graduating class borrowed through all loan programs. **Average indebtedness per student:** $26,005. **Average need-based loan:** Freshmen: $3534. Undergraduates: $4365. **Parent loans:** $17,348,137 (70% need-based, 30% non-need-based). **Programs:** Federal Direct (Subsidized and Unsubsidized Stafford, PLUS), Perkins, college/university, alternative loans.

WORK-STUDY Federal work-study: Total amount: $1,763,046; 531 jobs averaging $3320. **State or other work-study/employment:** Total amount: $745,550 (56% need-based, 44% non-need-based). 111 part-time jobs averaging $7404.

ATHLETIC AWARDS Total amount: $8,695,185 (42% need-based, 58% non-need-based).

APPLYING FOR FINANCIAL AID Required financial aid form: FAFSA. **Financial aid deadline:** Continuous. **Notification date:** Continuous beginning 3/15. Students must reply within 6 weeks of notification.

CONTACT Office of Financial Aid, University of Oklahoma, 1000 Asp Avenue, Room 216, Norman, OK 73019-4078, 405-325-4521 or toll-free 800-234-6868. Fax: 405-325-0819. E-mail: financialaid@ou.edu. Website: http://www.ou.edu/.

UNIVERSITY OF OREGON
Eugene, OR

Tuition & fees (OR res): $9310	Average undergraduate aid package: $9848

ABOUT THE INSTITUTION State-supported, coed. **Awards:** certificates, bachelor's, master's, and doctoral degrees. 77 undergraduate majors. **Total enrollment:** 24,518. Undergraduates: 20,809. Freshmen: 4,031. Federal methodology is used as a basis for awarding need-based institutional aid.

UNDERGRADUATE EXPENSES for 2013–2014 *Application fee:* $50. *One-time required fee:* $347. *Tuition, state resident:* full-time $8010; part-time $178 per credit hour. *Tuition, nonresident:* full-time $27,360; part-time $608 per credit hour. *Required fees:* full-time $1300. Full-time tuition and fees vary according to course load. Part-time tuition and fees vary according to course load. *College room and board:* $10,580. Room and board charges vary according to board plan and housing facility.

FRESHMAN FINANCIAL AID (Fall 2012, est.) 2,704 applied for aid; of those 69% were deemed to have need. 91% of freshmen with need received aid; of those 13% had need fully met. *Average percent of need met:* 41% (excluding resources awarded to replace EFC). *Average financial aid package:* $9763 (excluding resources awarded to replace EFC). 8% of all full-time freshmen had no need and received non-need-based gift aid.

UNDERGRADUATE FINANCIAL AID (Fall 2012, est.) 11,284 applied for aid; of those 78% were deemed to have need. 93% of undergraduates with need received aid; of those 9% had need fully met. *Average percent of need met:* 47% (excluding resources awarded to replace EFC). *Average financial aid package:* $9848 (excluding resources awarded to replace EFC). 4% of all full-time undergraduates had no need and received non-need-based gift aid.

GIFT AID (NEED-BASED) *Total amount:* $31,629,394 (78% federal, 15% state, 7% institutional). *Receiving aid:* Freshmen: 22% (873); all full-time undergraduates: 26% (4,977). *Average award:* Freshmen: $6155; Undergraduates: $5955. *Scholarships, grants, and awards:* Federal Pell, FSEOG, state, private, college/university gift aid from institutional funds.

GIFT AID (NON-NEED-BASED) *Total amount:* $22,033,272 (94% institutional, 6% external sources). *Receiving aid:* Freshmen: 22% (852). Undergraduates: 15% (2,815). *Average award:* Freshmen: $3589. Undergraduates: $3280. *Scholarships, grants, and awards by category:* Academic interests/achievement: 5,995 awards ($19,004,637 total): architecture, biological sciences, business, education, English, foreign languages, general academic interests/achievements, health fields, humanities, international studies, mathematics, military science, physical sciences, pre-medicine, social sciences. *Creative arts/performance:* 270 awards ($595,462 total): applied art and design, art/fine arts, creative writing, dance, debating, journalism/publications, music, performing arts, theater/drama. *Special characteristics:* 435 awards ($2,405,433 total): children of faculty/staff, general special characteristics, international students, local/state students, veterans, veterans' children. *Tuition waivers:* Full or partial for employees or children of employees. *ROTC:* Army, Air Force cooperative.

LOANS *Student loans:* $65,947,115 (48% need-based, 52% non-need-based). 48% of past graduating class borrowed through all loan programs. *Average indebtedness per student:* $24,528. *Average need-based loan:* Freshmen: $4115. Undergraduates: $4742. *Parent loans:* $51,267,965 (42% need-based, 58% non-need-based). *Programs:* Federal Direct (Subsidized and Unsubsidized Stafford, PLUS), Perkins, college/university.

WORK-STUDY *Federal work-study:* Total amount: $4,084,087; 2,771 jobs averaging $1474. *State or other work-study/employment:* Total amount: $333,420 (100% non-need-based). 151 part-time jobs averaging $2208.

ATHLETIC AWARDS Total amount: $8,773,121 (100% non-need-based).

APPLYING FOR FINANCIAL AID *Required financial aid form:* FAFSA. *Financial aid deadline (priority):* 3/1. *Notification date:* Continuous beginning 4/1. Students must reply within 4 weeks of notification.

CONTACT Jim Brooks, Director of Financial Aid and Scholarships, University of Oregon, 1278 University of Oregon, Eugene, OR 97403-1278, 800-760-6953 or toll-free 800-232-3825. *Fax:* 541-346-1175. *E-mail:* financialaid@uoregon.edu. *Website:* http://www.uoregon.edu/.

UNIVERSITY OF PENNSYLVANIA
Philadelphia, PA

Tuition & fees: $43,738	Average undergraduate aid package: $39,011

ABOUT THE INSTITUTION Independent, coed. *Awards:* certificates, associate, bachelor's, master's, and doctoral degrees (also offers evening program with significant enrollment not reflected in profile). 96 undergraduate majors. *Total enrollment:* 21,339. Undergraduates: 9,682. Freshmen: 2,397. Both federal and institutional methodology are used as a basis for awarding need-based institutional aid.

UNDERGRADUATE EXPENSES for 2013–2014 *Application fee:* $75. *Comprehensive fee:* $56,106 includes full-time tuition ($39,088), mandatory fees

($4650), and room and board ($12,368). *College room only:* $7952. Room and board charges vary according to board plan and housing facility. *Part-time tuition:* $4989 per course. *Part-time fees:* $543 per course. Part-time tuition and fees vary according to course load. *Payment plan:* Tuition prepayment.

FRESHMAN FINANCIAL AID (Fall 2011) 1,376 applied for aid; of those 85% were deemed to have need. 100% of freshmen with need received aid; of those 100% had need fully met. *Average percent of need met:* 100% (excluding resources awarded to replace EFC). *Average financial aid package:* $40,582 (excluding resources awarded to replace EFC).

UNDERGRADUATE FINANCIAL AID (Fall 2011) 5,187 applied for aid; of those 90% were deemed to have need. 100% of undergraduates with need received aid; of those 100% had need fully met. *Average percent of need met:* 100% (excluding resources awarded to replace EFC). *Average financial aid package:* $39,011 (excluding resources awarded to replace EFC).

GIFT AID (NEED-BASED) *Total amount:* $164,680,406 (5% federal, 1% state, 91% institutional, 3% external sources). *Receiving aid:* Freshmen: 46% (1,135); all full-time undergraduates: 44% (4,592). *Average award:* Freshmen: $38,414; Undergraduates: $36,048. *Scholarships, grants, and awards:* Federal Pell, FSEOG, state, private, college/university gift aid from institutional funds.

GIFT AID (NON-NEED-BASED) *Total amount:* $6,210,739 (2% federal, 98% external sources). *Tuition waivers:* Full or partial for employees or children of employees. *ROTC:* Army cooperative, Naval, Air Force cooperative.

LOANS *Student loans:* $17,740,663 (11% need-based, 89% non-need-based). 38% of past graduating class borrowed through all loan programs. *Average indebtedness per student:* $21,190. *Average need-based loan:* Freshmen: $212. Undergraduates: $428. *Parent loans:* $10,323,228 (100% non-need-based). *Programs:* Federal Nursing, college/university, supplemental third-party loans (guaranteed by institution).

WORK-STUDY *Federal work-study:* Total amount: $13,580,594; 3,621 jobs averaging $3078. *State or other work-study/employment:* Total amount: $2,197,948 (100% need-based). 654 part-time jobs averaging $2400.

APPLYING FOR FINANCIAL AID *Required financial aid forms:* FAFSA, institution's own form, CSS Financial Aid PROFILE, noncustodial (divorced/separated) parent's statement, business/farm supplement, federal income tax form(s). *Financial aid deadline (priority):* 2/15. *Notification date:* 4/1. Students must reply by 5/1.

CONTACT Mr. Joel Carstens, Director of Financial Aid, University of Pennsylvania, 212 Franklin Building, Philadelphia, PA 19104-6270, 215-898-6784. *Fax:* 215-573-2208. *E-mail:* carstens@sfs.upenn.edu. *Website:* http://www.upenn.edu/.

UNIVERSITY OF PHOENIX–ATLANTA CAMPUS
Sandy Springs, GA

CONTACT ACS/AFS, University of Phoenix–Atlanta Campus, 875 West Elliot Road, Tempe, AZ 85284, 480-735-3000 or toll-free 866-766-0766. *Fax:* 480-940-2060. *Website:* http://www.phoenix.edu/.

UNIVERSITY OF PHOENIX–BAY AREA CAMPUS
San Jose, CA

CONTACT ACS/AFS, University of Phoenix–Bay Area Campus, 875 West Elliot Road, Tempe, AZ 85284, 480-735-3000 or toll-free 866-766-0766. *Fax:* 480-940-2060. *Website:* http://www.phoenix.edu/.

UNIVERSITY OF PHOENIX–BIRMINGHAM CAMPUS
Birmingham, AL

CONTACT Financial Aid Office, University of Phoenix–Birmingham Campus, One Corporate Center, Suite 400, Birmingham, AL 35244 or toll-free 866-766-0766. *Website:* http://www.phoenix.edu/.

UNIVERSITY OF PHOENIX–BOSTON CAMPUS
Braintree, MA

CONTACT ACS/AFS, University of Phoenix–Boston Campus, 875 West Elliot Road, Tempe, AZ 85284, 480-735-3000 or toll-free 866-766-0766. *Fax:* 480-940-2060. *Website:* http://www.phoenix.edu/.

UNIVERSITY OF PHOENIX–CENTRAL FLORIDA CAMPUS
Maitland, FL

CONTACT ACS/AFS, University of Phoenix–Central Florida Campus, 875 West Elliot Road, Tempe, AZ 85284, 480-735-3000 or toll-free 866-766-0766. *Fax:* 480-940-2060. *Website:* http://www.phoenix.edu/.

UNIVERSITY OF PHOENIX–CENTRAL MASSACHUSETTS CAMPUS
Westborough, MA

CONTACT ACS/AFS, University of Phoenix–Central Massachusetts Campus, 875 West Elliot Road, Tempe, AZ 85284, 480-735-3000 or toll-free 866-766-0766. *Fax:* 480-940-2060. *Website:* http://www.phoenix.edu/.

UNIVERSITY OF PHOENIX–CENTRAL VALLEY CAMPUS
Fresno, CA

CONTACT ACS/AFS, University of Phoenix–Central Valley Campus, 875 West Elliot Road, Tempe, AZ 85284, 480-735-3000 or toll-free 866-766-0766. *Fax:* 480-940-2060. *Website:* http://www.phoenix.edu/.

UNIVERSITY OF PHOENIX–CHARLOTTE CAMPUS
Charlotte, NC

CONTACT ACS/AFS, University of Phoenix–Charlotte Campus, 875 West Elliot Road, Tempe, AZ 85284, 480-735-3000 or toll-free 866-766-0766. *Fax:* 480-940-2060. *Website:* http://www.phoenix.edu/.

UNIVERSITY OF PHOENIX–CHICAGO CAMPUS
Schaumburg, IL

Tuition & fees: N/R **Average undergraduate aid package: N/A**

ABOUT THE INSTITUTION Proprietary, coed. 9 undergraduate majors. Federal methodology is used as a basis for awarding need-based institutional aid.

GIFT AID (NEED-BASED) *Total amount:* $3,292,488 (99% federal, 1% institutional). *Scholarships, grants, and awards:* Federal Pell, FSEOG, state, private, college/university gift aid from institutional funds, TEACH Grants.

GIFT AID (NON-NEED-BASED) *Total amount:* $180,740 (1% federal, 68% institutional, 31% external sources).

LOANS *Student loans:* $8,775,483 (43% need-based, 57% non-need-based). *Parent loans:* $184,137 (100% non-need-based). *Programs:* Federal Direct (Subsidized and Unsubsidized Stafford, PLUS), Perkins.

APPLYING FOR FINANCIAL AID *Required financial aid forms:* FAFSA, institution's own form. *Financial aid deadline:* Continuous. *Notification date:* Continuous.

CONTACT Office of Financial Aid, University of Phoenix–Chicago Campus, 1500 McConner Parkway, Suite 700, Schaumburg, IL 60173-4399, 866-766-0766. *Website:* http://www.phoenix.edu/.

UNIVERSITY OF PHOENIX–CINCINNATI CAMPUS
West Chester, OH

CONTACT ACS/AFS, University of Phoenix–Cincinnati Campus, 875 West Elliot Road, Tempe, AZ 85284, 480-735-3000 or toll-free 866-766-0766. *Fax:* 480-940-2060. *Website:* http://www.phoenix.edu/.

UNIVERSITY OF PHOENIX–CLEVELAND CAMPUS
Independence, OH

CONTACT ACS/AFS, University of Phoenix–Cleveland Campus, 875 West Elliot Road, Tempe, AZ 85284, 480-735-3000 or toll-free 866-766-0766. *Fax:* 480-940-2060. *Website:* http://www.phoenix.edu/.

UNIVERSITY OF PHOENIX–COLUMBIA CAMPUS
Columbia, SC

CONTACT Financial Aid Office, University of Phoenix–Columbia Campus, 1001 Pinnacle Point Drive, Suite 200, Columbia, SC 29223, 803-699-5096 or toll-free 866-766-0766. *Website:* http://www.phoenix.edu/.

UNIVERSITY OF PHOENIX–COLUMBUS GEORGIA CAMPUS
Columbus, GA

CONTACT ACS/AFS, University of Phoenix–Columbus Georgia Campus, 875 West Elliot Road, Tempe, AZ 85284, 480-735-3000 or toll-free 866-766-0766. *Fax:* 480-940-2060. *Website:* http://www.phoenix.edu/.

UNIVERSITY OF PHOENIX–COLUMBUS OHIO CAMPUS
Columbus, OH

CONTACT ACS/AFS, University of Phoenix–Columbus Ohio Campus, 875 West Elliot Road, Tempe, AZ 85284, 480-735-3000 or toll-free 866-766-0766. *Fax:* 480-940-2060.
Website: http://www.phoenix.edu/.

UNIVERSITY OF PHOENIX–DALLAS CAMPUS
Dallas, TX

CONTACT ACS/AFS, University of Phoenix–Dallas Campus, 875 West Elliot Road, Tempe, AZ 85284, 480-735-3000 or toll-free 866-766-0766. *Fax:* 480-940-2060.
Website: http://www.phoenix.edu/.

UNIVERSITY OF PHOENIX–DENVER CAMPUS
Lone Tree, CO

CONTACT ACS/AFS, University of Phoenix–Denver Campus, 875 West Elliot Road, Tempe, AZ 85284, 480-735-3000 or toll-free 866-766-0766. *Fax:* 480-940-2060.
Website: http://www.phoenix.edu/.

UNIVERSITY OF PHOENIX–DETROIT CAMPUS
Southfield, MI

CONTACT ACS/AFS, University of Phoenix–Detroit Campus, 875 West Elliot Road, Tempe, AZ 85284, 480-735-3000 or toll-free 866-766-0766. *Fax:* 480-940-2060.
Website: http://www.phoenix.edu/.

UNIVERSITY OF PHOENIX–EASTERN WASHINGTON CAMPUS
Spokane, WA

CONTACT ACS/AFS, University of Phoenix–Eastern Washington Campus, 875 West Elliot Road, Tempe, AZ 85284, 480-735-3000 or toll-free 866-766-0766. *Fax:* 480-940-2060.
Website: http://www.phoenix.edu/.

UNIVERSITY OF PHOENIX–HAWAII CAMPUS
Honolulu, HI

CONTACT ACS/AFS, University of Phoenix–Hawaii Campus, 875 West Elliot Road, Tempe, AZ 85284, 480-735-3000 or toll-free 866-766-0766. *Fax:* 480-940-2060.
Website: http://www.phoenix.edu/.

UNIVERSITY OF PHOENIX–HOUSTON CAMPUS
Houston, TX

CONTACT ACS/AFS, University of Phoenix–Houston Campus, 875 West Elliot Road, Tempe, AZ 85284, 480-735-3000 or toll-free 866-766-0766. *Fax:* 480-940-2060.
Website: http://www.phoenix.edu/.

UNIVERSITY OF PHOENIX–IDAHO CAMPUS
Meridian, ID

CONTACT ACS/AFS, University of Phoenix–Idaho Campus, 875 West Elliot Road, Tempe, AZ 85284, 480-735-3000 or toll-free 866-766-0766. *Fax:* 480-940-2060.
Website: http://www.phoenix.edu/.

UNIVERSITY OF PHOENIX–INDIANAPOLIS CAMPUS
Indianapolis, IN

CONTACT ACS/AFS, University of Phoenix–Indianapolis Campus, 875 West Elliot Road, Tempe, AZ 85284, 480-735-3000 or toll-free 866-766-0766. *Fax:* 480-940-2060.
Website: http://www.phoenix.edu/.

UNIVERSITY OF PHOENIX–KANSAS CITY CAMPUS
Kansas City, MO

CONTACT ACS/AFS, University of Phoenix–Kansas City Campus, 875 West Elliot Road, Tempe, AZ 85284, 480-735-3000 or toll-free 866-766-0766. *Fax:* 480-940-2060.
Website: http://www.phoenix.edu/.

UNIVERSITY OF PHOENIX–LAS VEGAS CAMPUS
Las Vegas, NV

CONTACT ACS/AFS, University of Phoenix–Las Vegas Campus, 875 West Elliot Road, Tempe, AZ 85284, 480-735-3000 or toll-free 866-766-0766. *Fax:* 480-940-2060.
Website: http://www.phoenix.edu/.

UNIVERSITY OF PHOENIX–LITTLE ROCK CAMPUS
Little Rock, AR

CONTACT ACS/AFS, University of Phoenix–Little Rock Campus, 875 West Elliot Road, Tempe, AZ 85284, 480-735-3000 or toll-free 866-766-0766. *Fax:* 480-940-2060.
Website: http://www.phoenix.edu/.

UNIVERSITY OF PHOENIX–LOUISIANA CAMPUS

Metairie, LA

CONTACT ACS/AFS, University of Phoenix–Louisiana Campus, 875 West Elliot Road, Tempe, AZ 85284, 480-735-3000 or toll-free 866-766-0766. *Fax:* 480-940-2060. *Website:* http://www.phoenix.edu/.

UNIVERSITY OF PHOENIX–MARYLAND CAMPUS

Columbia, MD

Tuition & fees: N/R	Average undergraduate aid package: N/A

ABOUT THE INSTITUTION Proprietary, coed. 22 undergraduate majors. Federal methodology is used as a basis for awarding need-based institutional aid.
GIFT AID (NEED-BASED) Total amount: $926,075 (100% federal). **Scholarships, grants, and awards:** Federal Pell, FSEOG, state, private, college/university gift aid from institutional funds, TEACH Grants.
GIFT AID (NON-NEED-BASED) Total amount: $206,905 (25% federal, 4% state, 42% institutional, 29% external sources).
LOANS Student loans: $3,448,169 (40% need-based, 60% non-need-based). **Parent loans:** $14,039 (100% non-need-based). **Programs:** Federal Direct (Subsidized and Unsubsidized Stafford, PLUS), Perkins.
APPLYING FOR FINANCIAL AID Required financial aid forms: FAFSA, institution's own form. **Financial aid deadline:** Continuous. **Notification date:** Continuous.
CONTACT Office of Financial Aid, University of Phoenix–Maryland Campus, 8830 Stanford Boulevard, Suite 100, Columbia, MD 21045-5424, 866-766-0766. *Website:* http://www.phoenix.edu/.

UNIVERSITY OF PHOENIX–METRO DETROIT CAMPUS

Troy, MI

CONTACT ACS/AFS, University of Phoenix–Metro Detroit Campus, 875 West Elliot Road, Suite 116, Tempe, AZ 85284, 480-735-3000 or toll-free 866-766-0766. *Fax:* 480-940-2060. *Website:* http://www.phoenix.edu/.

UNIVERSITY OF PHOENIX–MILWAUKEE CAMPUS

Milwaukee, WI

CONTACT Financial Aid Office, University of Phoenix–Milwaukee Campus, 20075 Watertower Boulevard, Milwaukee, WI 53045, 262-785-0608 or toll-free 866-766-0766. *Website:* http://www.phoenix.edu/.

UNIVERSITY OF PHOENIX–NASHVILLE CAMPUS

Nashville, TN

CONTACT ACS/AFS, University of Phoenix–Nashville Campus, 875 West Elliot Road, Tempe, AZ 85284, 480-735-3000 or toll-free 866-766-0766. *Fax:* 480-940-2060. *Website:* http://www.phoenix.edu/.

UNIVERSITY OF PHOENIX–NEW MEXICO CAMPUS

Albuquerque, NM

CONTACT ACS/AFS, University of Phoenix–New Mexico Campus, 875 West Elliot Road, Tempe, AZ 85284, 480-735-3000 or toll-free 866-766-0766. *Fax:* 480-940-2060. *Website:* http://www.phoenix.edu/.

UNIVERSITY OF PHOENIX–NORTHERN NEVADA CAMPUS

Reno, NV

CONTACT Financial Aid Office, University of Phoenix–Northern Nevada Campus, 10345 Professional Circle, Suite 200, Reno, NV 89521-5862, 775-828-7999 or toll-free 866-766-0766. *Website:* http://www.phoenix.edu/.

UNIVERSITY OF PHOENIX–NORTHERN VIRGINIA CAMPUS

Reston, VA

CONTACT ACS/AFS, University of Phoenix–Northern Virginia Campus, 875 West Elliott Road, Tempe, AZ 85284, 480-735-3000 or toll-free 866-766-0766. *Fax:* 480-940-2060. *Website:* http://www.phoenix.edu/.

UNIVERSITY OF PHOENIX–NORTH FLORIDA CAMPUS

Jacksonville, FL

CONTACT ACS/AFS, University of Phoenix–North Florida Campus, 875 West Elliot Road, Tempe, AZ 85284, 480-735-3000 or toll-free 866-766-0766. *Fax:* 480-940-2060. *Website:* http://www.phoenix.edu/.

UNIVERSITY OF PHOENIX–OKLAHOMA CITY CAMPUS

Oklahoma City, OK

CONTACT ACS/AFS, University of Phoenix–Oklahoma City Campus, 875 West Elliot Road, Tempe, AZ 85284, 480-735-3000 or toll-free 866-766-0766. *Fax:* 480-940-2060. *Website:* http://www.phoenix.edu/.

UNIVERSITY OF PHOENIX–ONLINE CAMPUS

Phoenix, AZ

Tuition & fees: N/R	Average undergraduate aid package: N/A

ABOUT THE INSTITUTION Proprietary, coed. 11 undergraduate majors. Federal methodology is used as a basis for awarding need-based institutional aid.
GIFT AID (NEED-BASED) Total amount: $578,659,544 (96% federal, 2% state, 2% institutional). **Scholarships, grants, and awards:** Federal Pell, FSEOG, state, private, college/university gift aid from institutional funds, TEACH Grants.

GIFT AID (NON-NEED-BASED) *Total amount:* $78,546,381 (30% federal, 2% state, 43% institutional, 25% external sources).
LOANS *Student loans:* $1,381,471,551 (41% need-based, 59% non-need-based). *Parent loans:* $13,755,422 (100% non-need-based). *Programs:* Federal Direct (Subsidized and Unsubsidized Stafford, PLUS), Perkins.
APPLYING FOR FINANCIAL AID *Required financial aid forms:* FAFSA, institution's own form. *Financial aid deadline:* Continuous. *Notification date:* Continuous.
CONTACT Office of Financial Aid, University of Phoenix–Online Campus, 3157 East Elwood Street, Phoenix, AZ 85034-7209, 866-766-0766.
Website: http://www.uopxonline.com/.

UNIVERSITY OF PHOENIX–OREGON CAMPUS
Tigard, OR

CONTACT ACS/AFS, University of Phoenix–Oregon Campus, 875 West Elliot Road, Tempe, AZ 85284, 480-735-3000 or toll-free 866-766-0766. *Fax:* 480-940-2060.
Website: http://www.phoenix.edu/.

UNIVERSITY OF PHOENIX–PHILADELPHIA CAMPUS
Wayne, PA

CONTACT ACS/AFS, University of Phoenix–Philadelphia Campus, 875 West Elliot Road, Tempe, AZ 85284, 480-735-3000 or toll-free 866-766-0766. *Fax:* 480-940-2060.
Website: http://www.phoenix.edu/.

UNIVERSITY OF PHOENIX–PHOENIX MAIN CAMPUS
Tempe, AZ

Tuition & fees: N/R	Average undergraduate aid package: N/A

ABOUT THE INSTITUTION Proprietary, coed. 25 undergraduate majors. Federal methodology is used as a basis for awarding need-based institutional aid.
GIFT AID (NEED-BASED) *Total amount:* $8,091,418 (98% federal, 1% state, 1% institutional). *Scholarships, grants, and awards:* Federal Pell, FSEOG, state, private, college/university gift aid from institutional funds, TEACH Grants.
GIFT AID (NON-NEED-BASED) *Total amount:* $1,400,175 (3% federal, 8% state, 58% institutional, 31% external sources).
LOANS *Student loans:* $25,797,104 (42% need-based, 58% non-need-based). *Parent loans:* $413,967 (100% non-need-based). *Programs:* Federal Direct (Subsidized and Unsubsidized Stafford, PLUS), Perkins.
APPLYING FOR FINANCIAL AID *Required financial aid forms:* FAFSA, institution's own form. *Financial aid deadline:* Continuous. *Notification date:* Continuous.
CONTACT Office of Financial Aid, University of Phoenix–Phoenix Main Campus, 1625 West Fountainhead Parkway, Tempe, AZ 85282-2371, 866-766-0766.
Website: http://www.phoenix.edu/.

UNIVERSITY OF PHOENIX–PITTSBURGH CAMPUS
Pittsburgh, PA

CONTACT ACS/AFS, University of Phoenix–Pittsburgh Campus, 875 West Elliot Road, Tempe, AZ 85284, 480-735-3000 or toll-free 866-766-0766. *Fax:* 480-940-2060.
Website: http://www.phoenix.edu/.

UNIVERSITY OF PHOENIX–PUERTO RICO CAMPUS
Guaynabo, PR

CONTACT ACS/AFS, University of Phoenix–Puerto Rico Campus, 875 West Elliot Road, Tempe, AZ 85284, 480-735-3000 or toll-free 866-766-0766. *Fax:* 480-940-2060.
Website: http://www.phoenix.edu/.

UNIVERSITY OF PHOENIX–RALEIGH CAMPUS
Raleigh, NC

CONTACT ACS/AFS, University of Phoenix–Raleigh Campus, 875 West Elliot Road, Tempe, AZ 85284, 480-735-3000 or toll-free 866-766-0766. *Fax:* 480-940-2060.
Website: http://www.phoenix.edu/.

UNIVERSITY OF PHOENIX–RICHMOND CAMPUS
Richmond, VA

CONTACT ACS/AFS, University of Phoenix–Richmond Campus, 875 West Elliot Road, Tempe, AZ 85284, 480-735-3000 or toll-free 866-766-0766. *Fax:* 480-940-2060.
Website: http://www.phoenix.edu/.

UNIVERSITY OF PHOENIX–SACRAMENTO VALLEY CAMPUS
Sacramento, CA

CONTACT ACS/AFS, University of Phoenix–Sacramento Valley Campus, 875 West Elliot Road, Tempe, AZ 85284, 480-735-3000 or toll-free 866-766-0766. *Fax:* 480-940-2060.
Website: http://www.phoenix.edu/.

UNIVERSITY OF PHOENIX–ST. LOUIS CAMPUS
St. Louis, MO

CONTACT ACS/AFS, University of Phoenix–St. Louis Campus, 875 West Elliot Road, Tempe, AZ 85284, 480-735-3000 or toll-free 866-766-0766. *Fax:* 480-940-2060.
Website: http://www.phoenix.edu/.

UNIVERSITY OF PHOENIX–SAN DIEGO CAMPUS
San Diego, CA

CONTACT ACS/AFS, University of Phoenix–San Diego Campus, 875 West Elliot Road, Tempe, AZ 85284, 480-735-3000 or toll-free 866-766-0766. *Fax:* 480-940-2060.
Website: http://www.phoenix.edu/.

UNIVERSITY OF PHOENIX– SOUTHERN ARIZONA CAMPUS
Tucson, AZ

CONTACT ACS/AFS, University of Phoenix–Southern Arizona Campus, 875 West Elliot Road, Tempe, AZ 85284, 480-735-3000 or toll-free 866-766-0766. *Fax:* 480-940-2060.
Website: http://www.phoenix.edu/.

UNIVERSITY OF PHOENIX– SOUTHERN CALIFORNIA CAMPUS
Costa Mesa, CA

Tuition & fees: N/R	Average undergraduate aid package: N/A

ABOUT THE INSTITUTION Proprietary, coed. 11 undergraduate majors. Federal methodology is used as a basis for awarding need-based institutional aid.

GIFT AID (NEED-BASED) *Total amount:* $24,787,770 (76% federal, 22% state, 2% institutional). *Scholarships, grants, and awards:* Federal Pell, FSEOG, state, private, college/university gift aid from institutional funds, TEACH Grants.

GIFT AID (NON-NEED-BASED) *Total amount:* $2,211,642 (5% federal, 1% state, 70% institutional, 24% external sources).

LOANS *Student loans:* $57,640,878 (42% need-based, 58% non-need-based). *Parent loans:* $2,630,937 (100% non-need-based). *Programs:* Federal Direct (Subsidized and Unsubsidized Stafford, PLUS), Perkins.

APPLYING FOR FINANCIAL AID *Required financial aid forms:* FAFSA, institution's own form. *Financial aid deadline:* Continuous. *Notification date:* Continuous.

CONTACT Office of Financial Aid, University of Phoenix–Southern California Campus, 3150 Bristol Street, Suite 340, Costa Mesa, CA 92626, 866-766-0766.
Website: http://www.phoenix.edu/.

UNIVERSITY OF PHOENIX– SOUTHERN COLORADO CAMPUS
Colorado Springs, CO

CONTACT ACS/AFS, University of Phoenix–Southern Colorado Campus, 875 West Elliot Road, Tempe, AZ 85284, 480-735-3000 or toll-free 866-766-0766. *Fax:* 480-940-2060.
Website: http://www.phoenix.edu/.

UNIVERSITY OF PHOENIX–SOUTH FLORIDA CAMPUS
Fort Lauderdale, FL

CONTACT ACS/AFS, University of Phoenix–South Florida Campus, 875 West Elliot Road, Tempe, AZ 85284, 480-735-3000 or toll-free 866-766-0766. *Fax:* 480-940-2060.
Website: http://www.phoenix.edu/.

UNIVERSITY OF PHOENIX– SPRINGFIELD CAMPUS
Springfield, MO

CONTACT ACS/AFS, University of Phoenix–Springfield Campus, 875 West Elliot Road, Tempe, AZ 85284, 480-735-3000 or toll-free 866-766-0766. *Fax:* 480-940-2060.
Website: http://www.phoenix.edu/.

UNIVERSITY OF PHOENIX–TULSA CAMPUS
Tulsa, OK

CONTACT ACS/AFS, University of Phoenix–Tulsa Campus, 875 West Elliot Road, Tempe, AZ 85284, 480-735-3000 or toll-free 866-766-0766. *Fax:* 480-940-2060.
Website: http://www.phoenix.edu/.

UNIVERSITY OF PHOENIX–UTAH CAMPUS
Salt Lake City, UT

CONTACT ACS/AFS, University of Phoenix–Utah Campus, 875 West Elliot Road, Tempe, AZ 85284, 480-735-3000 or toll-free 866-766-0766. *Fax:* 480-940-2060.
Website: http://www.phoenix.edu/.

UNIVERSITY OF PHOENIX– WASHINGTON CAMPUS
Tukwila, WA

CONTACT ACS/AFS, University of Phoenix–Washington Campus, 875 West Elliot Road, Tempe, AZ 85284, 480-735-3000 or toll-free 866-766-0766. *Fax:* 480-940-2060.
Website: http://www.phoenix.edu/.

UNIVERSITY OF PHOENIX– WASHINGTON D.C. CAMPUS
Washington, DC

CONTACT Financial Aid Office, University of Phoenix–Washington D.C. Campus, 25 Massachusetts Avenue NW, Suite 150, Washington, DC 20001 or toll-free 866-766-0766.
Website: http://www.phoenix.edu/.

UNIVERSITY OF PHOENIX–WEST FLORIDA CAMPUS
Temple Terrace, FL

CONTACT ACS/AFS, University of Phoenix–West Florida Campus, 875 West Elliot Road, Tempe, AZ 85284, 480-735-3000 or toll-free 866-766-0766. *Fax:* 480-940-2060.
Website: http://www.phoenix.edu/.

UNIVERSITY OF PHOENIX–WEST MICHIGAN CAMPUS
Walker, MI

CONTACT ACS/AFS, University of Phoenix–West Michigan Campus, 875 West Elliot Road, Tempe, AZ 85284, 480-735-3000 or toll-free 866-766-0766. *Fax:* 480-940-2060.
Website: http://www.phoenix.edu/.

UNIVERSITY OF PHOENIX–WICHITA CAMPUS
Wichita, KS

CONTACT ACS/AFS, University of Phoenix–Wichita Campus, 875 West Elliot Road, Tempe, AZ 85284, 480-735-3000 or toll-free 866-766-0766. *Fax:* 480-940-2060. *Website:* http://www.phoenix.edu/.

UNIVERSITY OF PIKEVILLE
Pikeville, KY

Tuition & fees: $17,050 — **Average undergraduate aid package:** $19,231

ABOUT THE INSTITUTION Independent Presbyterian Church (U.S.A.), coed. *Awards:* associate, bachelor's, master's, and doctoral degrees. 18 undergraduate majors. *Total enrollment:* 2,031. Undergraduates: 1,620. Freshmen: 368. Federal methodology is used as a basis for awarding need-based institutional aid.
UNDERGRADUATE EXPENSES for 2013–2014 *Comprehensive fee:* $23,750 includes full-time tuition ($17,050) and room and board ($6700). Full-time tuition and fees vary according to course load. Room and board charges vary according to housing facility. *Part-time tuition:* $710 per credit hour. Part-time tuition and fees vary according to course load.
FRESHMAN FINANCIAL AID (Fall 2012, est.) 363 applied for aid; of those 100% were deemed to have need. 100% of freshmen with need received aid; of those 35% had need fully met. *Average percent of need met:* 82% (excluding resources awarded to replace EFC). *Average financial aid package:* $19,261 (excluding resources awarded to replace EFC).
UNDERGRADUATE FINANCIAL AID (Fall 2012, est.) 1,191 applied for aid; of those 99% were deemed to have need. 100% of undergraduates with need received aid; of those 43% had need fully met. *Average percent of need met:* 83% (excluding resources awarded to replace EFC). *Average financial aid package:* $19,231 (excluding resources awarded to replace EFC).
GIFT AID (NEED-BASED) *Total amount:* $16,175,015 (22% federal, 29% state, 47% institutional, 2% external sources). *Receiving aid:* Freshmen: 98% (361); all full-time undergraduates: 96% (1,164). *Average award:* Freshmen: $14,107; Undergraduates: $13,831. *Scholarships, grants, and awards:* Federal Pell, FSEOG, state, private, college/university gift aid from institutional funds.
GIFT AID (NON-NEED-BASED) *Receiving aid:* Freshmen: 56% (205). Undergraduates: 20% (249). *Tuition waivers:* Full or partial for employees or children of employees, senior citizens. *ROTC:* Army.
LOANS *Student loans:* $8,216,672 (100% need-based). 75% of past graduating class borrowed through all loan programs. *Average indebtedness per student:* $24,954. *Average need-based loan:* Freshmen: $3400. Undergraduates: $4062. *Parent loans:* $239,550 (100% need-based). *Programs:* Federal Direct (Subsidized and Unsubsidized Stafford, PLUS), Perkins, college/university.
WORK-STUDY *Federal work-study:* Total amount: $329,794; 190 jobs averaging $1736.
ATHLETIC AWARDS Total amount: $2,273,798 (100% need-based).
APPLYING FOR FINANCIAL AID *Required financial aid form:* FAFSA. *Financial aid deadline (priority):* 2/1. *Notification date:* Continuous. Students must reply by 5/1.
CONTACT Mrs. Judy Vance Bradley, Assistant Dean of Student Financial Services, University of Pikeville, 147 Sycamore Street, Pikeville, KY 41501, 606-218-5254 or toll-free 866-232-7700. *Fax:* 606-218-5255. *E-mail:* judybradley@upike.edu. *Website:* http://www.upike.edu/.

UNIVERSITY OF PITTSBURGH
Pittsburgh, PA

Tuition & fees (PA res): $16,590 — **Average undergraduate aid package:** $12,338

ABOUT THE INSTITUTION State-related, coed. *Awards:* certificates, bachelor's, master's, and doctoral degrees. 90 undergraduate majors. *Total enrollment:* 28,769. Undergraduates: 18,429. Freshmen: 3,640. Federal methodology is used as a basis for awarding need-based institutional aid.
UNDERGRADUATE EXPENSES for 2013–2014 *Application fee:* $45. *Tuition, state resident:* full-time $15,730; part-time $655 per credit. *Tuition, nonresident:* full-time $25,420; part-time $1059 per credit. *Required fees:* full-time $860; $214 per credit. Full-time tuition and fees vary according to location and program. Part-time tuition and fees vary according to location and program. *College room and board:* $9870; *Room only:* $5950. Room and board charges vary according to board plan, housing facility, and location.
FRESHMAN FINANCIAL AID (Fall 2011) 3,034 applied for aid; of those 70% were deemed to have need. 96% of freshmen with need received aid; of those 13% had need fully met. *Average percent of need met:* 60% (excluding resources awarded to replace EFC). *Average financial aid package:* $15,810 (excluding resources awarded to replace EFC). 5% of all full-time freshmen had no need and received non-need-based gift aid.
UNDERGRADUATE FINANCIAL AID (Fall 2011) 12,212 applied for aid; of those 79% were deemed to have need. 97% of undergraduates with need received aid; of those 10% had need fully met. *Average percent of need met:* 56% (excluding resources awarded to replace EFC). *Average financial aid package:* $12,338 (excluding resources awarded to replace EFC). 2% of all full-time undergraduates had no need and received non-need-based gift aid.
GIFT AID (NEED-BASED) *Total amount:* $52,962,684 (25% federal, 21% state, 40% institutional, 14% external sources). *Receiving aid:* Freshmen: 43% (1,589); all full-time undergraduates: 39% (6,705). *Average award:* Freshmen: $8653; Undergraduates: $7774. *Scholarships, grants, and awards:* Federal Pell, FSEOG, state, private, college/university gift aid from institutional funds, Federal Nursing.
GIFT AID (NON-NEED-BASED) *Total amount:* $29,476,140 (75% institutional, 25% external sources). *Receiving aid:* Freshmen: 5% (173). Undergraduates: 3% (522). *Average award:* Freshmen: $11,177. Undergraduates: $11,543. *Scholarships, grants, and awards by category:* Academic interests/achievement: general academic interests/achievements. *Tuition waivers:* Full or partial for employees or children of employees. *ROTC:* Army, Naval cooperative, Air Force.
LOANS *Student loans:* $104,057,709 (69% need-based, 31% non-need-based). 67% of past graduating class borrowed through all loan programs. *Average indebtedness per student:* $33,662. *Average need-based loan:* Freshmen: $4311. Undergraduates: $4855. *Parent loans:* $26,906,594 (38% need-based, 62% non-need-based). *Programs:* Federal Direct (Subsidized and Unsubsidized Stafford, PLUS), Perkins, Federal Nursing, state, college/university.
WORK-STUDY *Federal work-study:* Total amount: $8,229,153; jobs available.
ATHLETIC AWARDS Total amount: $8,216,621 (45% need-based, 55% non-need-based).
APPLYING FOR FINANCIAL AID *Required financial aid form:* FAFSA. *Financial aid deadline (priority):* 3/1. *Notification date:* Continuous beginning 3/15.
CONTACT Mr. Marc L. Harding, Chief Enrollment Officer, University of Pittsburgh, 4227 Fifth Avenue, First Floor, Pittsburgh, PA 15260, 412-624-7488. *Fax:* 412-648-8815. *E-mail:* oafa@pitt.edu. *Website:* http://www.pitt.edu/.

UNIVERSITY OF PITTSBURGH AT BRADFORD
Bradford, PA

Tuition & fees (PA res): $12,810 — **Average undergraduate aid package:** $12,862

ABOUT THE INSTITUTION State-related, coed. *Awards:* associate and bachelor's degrees. 33 undergraduate majors. *Total enrollment:* 1,518. Undergrad-

uates: 1,518. Freshmen: 379. Federal methodology is used as a basis for awarding need-based institutional aid.

UNDERGRADUATE EXPENSES for 2013–2014 *Application fee:* $45. *One-time required fee:* $90. *Tuition, state resident:* full-time $11,970; part-time $498 per credit hour. *Tuition, nonresident:* full-time $22,366; part-time $931 per credit hour. *Required fees:* full-time $840; $135 per term. Full-time tuition and fees vary according to course load and program. Part-time tuition and fees vary according to course load and program. *College room and board:* $7960; *Room only:* $4920. Room and board charges vary according to board plan and housing facility.

FRESHMAN FINANCIAL AID (Fall 2011) 347 applied for aid; of those 90% were deemed to have need. 100% of freshmen with need received aid; of those 22% had need fully met. *Average percent of need met:* 66% (excluding resources awarded to replace EFC). *Average financial aid package:* $12,975 (excluding resources awarded to replace EFC). 10% of all full-time freshmen had no need and received non-need-based gift aid.

UNDERGRADUATE FINANCIAL AID (Fall 2011) 1,309 applied for aid; of those 90% were deemed to have need. 100% of undergraduates with need received aid; of those 27% had need fully met. *Average percent of need met:* 65% (excluding resources awarded to replace EFC). *Average financial aid package:* $12,862 (excluding resources awarded to replace EFC). 11% of all full-time undergraduates had no need and received non-need-based gift aid.

GIFT AID (NEED-BASED) *Total amount:* $9,552,520 (31% federal, 23% state, 39% institutional, 7% external sources). *Receiving aid:* Freshmen: 82% (297); all full-time undergraduates: 76% (1,097). *Average award:* Freshmen: $9313; Undergraduates: $8682. *Scholarships, grants, and awards:* Federal Pell, FSEOG, state, private, college/university gift aid from institutional funds, Academic Competitiveness Grants, National SMART Grants.

GIFT AID (NON-NEED-BASED) *Total amount:* $857,121 (79% institutional, 21% external sources). *Receiving aid:* Freshmen: 21% (75). Undergraduates: 23% (324). *Average award:* Freshmen: $6660. Undergraduates: $6493. *Scholarships, grants, and awards by category:* Academic interests/achievement: 149 awards ($142,735 total): biological sciences, business, communication, computer science, education, engineering/technologies, English, general academic interests/achievements, health fields, humanities, mathematics, physical sciences, premedicine, social sciences. *Creative arts/performance:* 6 awards ($2500 total): cinema/film/broadcasting. *Special characteristics:* 1,332 awards ($4,674,149 total): adult students, children of faculty/staff, children of union members/company employees, local/state students, out-of-state students, veterans. *Tuition waivers:* Full or partial for employees or children of employees. *ROTC:* Army cooperative.

LOANS *Student loans:* $7,926,586 (90% need-based, 10% non-need-based). 91% of past graduating class borrowed through all loan programs. *Average indebtedness per student:* $35,810. *Average need-based loan:* Freshmen: $3464. Undergraduates: $4101. *Parent loans:* $2,365,448 (27% need-based, 73% non-need-based). *Programs:* Federal Direct (Subsidized and Unsubsidized Stafford, PLUS), Perkins.

WORK-STUDY *Federal work-study:* Total amount: $1,345,825; 192 jobs averaging $1740. *State or other work-study/employment:* 1 part-time job averaging $1764.

APPLYING FOR FINANCIAL AID *Required financial aid form:* FAFSA. *Financial aid deadline (priority):* 3/1. *Notification date:* Continuous beginning 4/1. Students must reply within 2 weeks of notification.

CONTACT Melissa Ibanez, Director of Financial Aid, University of Pittsburgh at Bradford, 300 Campus Drive, Bradford, PA 16701-2812, 814-362-7550 or toll-free 800-872-1787. *Fax:* 814-362-7578. *E-mail:* ibanez@pitt.edu. *Website:* http://www.upb.pitt.edu/.

UNIVERSITY OF PITTSBURGH AT GREENSBURG
Greensburg, PA

Tuition & fees (PA res): $12,890	Average undergraduate aid package: $10,212

ABOUT THE INSTITUTION State-related, coed. *Awards:* certificates and bachelor's degrees. 23 undergraduate majors. *Total enrollment:* 1,733. Undergraduates: 1,733. Freshmen: 394. Federal methodology is used as a basis for awarding need-based institutional aid.

UNDERGRADUATE EXPENSES for 2013–2014 *Application fee:* $45. *Tuition, state resident:* full-time $11,970; part-time $498 per credit hour. *Tuition,*

nonresident: full-time $22,366; part-time $931 per credit hour. *Required fees:* full-time $920; $174 per term. *College room and board:* $8730. Room and board charges vary according to board plan and housing facility.

FRESHMAN FINANCIAL AID (Fall 2011) 391 applied for aid; of those 90% were deemed to have need. 100% of freshmen with need received aid; of those 12% had need fully met. *Average percent of need met:* 46% (excluding resources awarded to replace EFC). *Average financial aid package:* $10,716 (excluding resources awarded to replace EFC). 5% of all full-time freshmen had no need and received non-need-based gift aid.

UNDERGRADUATE FINANCIAL AID (Fall 2011) 1,407 applied for aid; of those 90% were deemed to have need. 100% of undergraduates with need received aid; of those 10% had need fully met. *Average percent of need met:* 38% (excluding resources awarded to replace EFC). *Average financial aid package:* $10,212 (excluding resources awarded to replace EFC). 2% of all full-time undergraduates had no need and received non-need-based gift aid.

GIFT AID (NEED-BASED) *Total amount:* $7,025,110 (38% federal, 33% state, 16% institutional, 13% external sources). *Receiving aid:* Freshmen: 73% (301); all full-time undergraduates: 69% (1,024). *Average award:* Freshmen: $7449; Undergraduates: $6411. *Scholarships, grants, and awards:* Federal Pell, FSEOG, state, private, college/university gift aid from institutional funds, United Negro College Fund.

GIFT AID (NON-NEED-BASED) *Total amount:* $302,447 (3% state, 69% institutional, 28% external sources). *Receiving aid:* Freshmen: 4% (16). Undergraduates: 2% (30). *Average award:* Freshmen: $5038. Undergraduates: $4401. *Tuition waivers:* Full or partial for employees or children of employees, senior citizens. *ROTC:* Army cooperative, Air Force cooperative.

LOANS *Student loans:* $11,261,026 (76% need-based, 24% non-need-based). 83% of past graduating class borrowed through all loan programs. *Average indebtedness per student:* $33,095. *Average need-based loan:* Freshmen: $3409. Undergraduates: $4173. *Parent loans:* $1,971,744 (41% need-based, 59% non-need-based). *Programs:* Federal Direct (Subsidized and Unsubsidized Stafford, PLUS), Perkins.

WORK-STUDY *Federal work-study:* Total amount: $565,999; jobs available.

APPLYING FOR FINANCIAL AID *Required financial aid forms:* FAFSA, state aid form. *Financial aid deadline (priority):* 2/15. *Notification date:* Continuous beginning 3/15. Students must reply within 3 weeks of notification.

CONTACT Ms. Brandi S. Darr, Director of Financial Aid, University of Pittsburgh at Greensburg, 150 Finoli Drive, Greensburg, PA 15601-5898, 724-836-7167. *E-mail:* upgfnaid@pitt.edu. *Website:* http://www.greensburg.pitt.edu/.

UNIVERSITY OF PITTSBURGH AT JOHNSTOWN
Johnstown, PA

Tuition & fees (PA res): $12,892	Average undergraduate aid package: $10,544

ABOUT THE INSTITUTION State-related, coed. *Awards:* certificates, associate, and bachelor's degrees. 50 undergraduate majors. *Total enrollment:* 2,957. Undergraduates: 2,957. Freshmen: 738. Federal methodology is used as a basis for awarding need-based institutional aid.

UNDERGRADUATE EXPENSES for 2013–2014 *Application fee:* $45. *Tuition, state resident:* full-time $11,970; part-time $498 per credit hour. *Tuition, nonresident:* full-time $22,366; part-time $931 per credit hour. *Required fees:* full-time $922. Full-time tuition and fees vary according to program. Part-time tuition and fees vary according to program. *College room and board:* $8230; *Room only:* $5180. Room and board charges vary according to board plan and housing facility.

FRESHMAN FINANCIAL AID (Fall 2011) 663 applied for aid; of those 85% were deemed to have need. 99% of freshmen with need received aid; of those 12% had need fully met. *Average percent of need met:* 54% (excluding resources awarded to replace EFC). *Average financial aid package:* $12,754 (excluding resources awarded to replace EFC). 3% of all full-time freshmen had no need and received non-need-based gift aid.

UNDERGRADUATE FINANCIAL AID (Fall 2011) 2,529 applied for aid; of those 86% were deemed to have need. 98% of undergraduates with need received aid; of those 10% had need fully met. *Average percent of need met:* 55% (excluding resources awarded to replace EFC). *Average financial aid package:* $10,544

(excluding resources awarded to replace EFC). 2% of all full-time undergraduates had no need and received non-need-based gift aid.

GIFT AID (NEED-BASED) *Total amount:* $9,098,332 (39% federal, 44% state, 15% institutional, 2% external sources). *Receiving aid:* Freshmen: 51% (370); all full-time undergraduates: 51% (1,438). *Average award:* Freshmen: $6362; Undergraduates: $5248. *Scholarships, grants, and awards:* Federal Pell, FSEOG, state, private, college/university gift aid from institutional funds.

GIFT AID (NON-NEED-BASED) *Total amount:* $1,400,841 (12% state, 67% institutional, 21% external sources). *Receiving aid:* Freshmen: 41% (299). Undergraduates: 32% (920). *Average award:* Freshmen: $4984. Undergraduates: $3844. *Scholarships, grants, and awards by category:* Academic interests/achievement: biological sciences, business, communication, computer science, education, engineering/technologies, English, general academic interests/achievements, health fields, humanities, mathematics, physical sciences, premedicine, social sciences. *Creative arts/performance:* journalism/publications, theater/drama. *Special achievements/activities:* leadership. *Special characteristics:* children of faculty/staff. *Tuition waivers:* Full or partial for employees or children of employees.

LOANS *Student loans:* $19,842,311 (59% need-based, 41% non-need-based). 81% of past graduating class borrowed through all loan programs. *Average indebtedness per student:* $35,090. *Average need-based loan:* Freshmen: $3833. Undergraduates: $4277. *Parent loans:* $5,156,115 (22% need-based, 78% non-need-based). *Programs:* Federal Direct (Subsidized and Unsubsidized Stafford, PLUS), Perkins.

WORK-STUDY *Federal work-study:* Total amount: $359,384; jobs available. *State or other work-study/employment:* Total amount: $719,353 (21% need-based, 79% non-need-based). Part-time jobs available.

ATHLETIC AWARDS Total amount: $655,932 (30% need-based, 70% non-need-based).

APPLYING FOR FINANCIAL AID *Required financial aid forms:* FAFSA, state aid form. *Financial aid deadline (priority):* 4/1. *Notification date:* Continuous beginning 4/1. Students must reply within 2 weeks of notification.

CONTACT Ms. Jeanine M. Lawn, Director of Student Financial Aid, University of Pittsburgh at Johnstown, 125 Biddle Hall, Johnstown, PA 15904-2990, 814-269-7045 or toll-free 800-765-4875. *Fax:* 814-269-7061. *E-mail:* lawn@pitt.edu. *Website:* http://www.upj.pitt.edu/.

UNIVERSITY OF PORTLAND
Portland, OR

Tuition & fees: $35,260	Average undergraduate aid package: $26,238

ABOUT THE INSTITUTION Independent Roman Catholic, coed. *Awards:* certificates, bachelor's, master's, and doctoral degrees. 42 undergraduate majors. *Total enrollment:* 3,981. Undergraduates: 3,402. Freshmen: 874. Federal methodology is used as a basis for awarding need-based institutional aid.

UNDERGRADUATE EXPENSES for 2013–2014 *Application fee:* $50. *Tuition:* full-time $35,120; part-time $1100 per credit hour. Full-time tuition and fees vary according to program. Part-time tuition and fees vary according to course load and program. Room and board charges vary according to board plan and housing facility.

FRESHMAN FINANCIAL AID (Fall 2012, est.) 741 applied for aid; of those 79% were deemed to have need. 100% of freshmen with need received aid; of those 9% had need fully met. *Average percent of need met:* 73% (excluding resources awarded to replace EFC). *Average financial aid package:* $25,780 (excluding resources awarded to replace EFC). 27% of all full-time freshmen had no need and received non-need-based gift aid.

UNDERGRADUATE FINANCIAL AID (Fall 2012, est.) 2,499 applied for aid; of those 85% were deemed to have need. 100% of undergraduates with need received aid; of those 6% had need fully met. *Average percent of need met:* 71% (excluding resources awarded to replace EFC). *Average financial aid package:* $26,238 (excluding resources awarded to replace EFC). 28% of all full-time undergraduates had no need and received non-need-based gift aid.

GIFT AID (NEED-BASED) *Total amount:* $43,929,171 (8% federal, 1% state, 86% institutional, 5% external sources). *Receiving aid:* Freshmen: 56% (488); all full-time undergraduates: 54% (1,777). *Average award:* Freshmen: $22,920; Undergraduates: $20,703. *Scholarships, grants, and awards:* Federal Pell, FSEOG, state, private, college/university gift aid from institutional funds, United Negro College Fund, Federal Nursing.

GIFT AID (NON-NEED-BASED) *Total amount:* $12,575,945 (99% institutional, 1% external sources). *Receiving aid:* Freshmen: 62% (544). Undergraduates: 57% (1,897). *Average award:* Freshmen: $13,285. Undergraduates: $13,281. *Scholarships, grants, and awards by category:* Academic interests/achievement: 2,015 awards ($27,358,105 total): biological sciences, business, communication, computer science, education, engineering/technologies, English, foreign languages, general academic interests/achievements, health fields, humanities, mathematics, military science, physical sciences, premedicine, religion/biblical studies, social sciences. *Creative arts/performance:* 60 awards ($141,460 total): music, performing arts, theater/drama. *Special achievements/activities:* 26 awards ($24,726 total): general special achievements/activities. *Special characteristics:* 40 awards ($1,359,100 total): children of faculty/staff, relatives of clergy, religious affiliation. *Tuition waivers:* Full or partial for employees or children of employees. *ROTC:* Army, Air Force.

LOANS *Student loans:* $16,556,395 (90% need-based, 10% non-need-based). 71% of past graduating class borrowed through all loan programs. *Average indebtedness per student:* $27,544. *Average need-based loan:* Freshmen: $3458. Undergraduates: $4817. *Parent loans:* $19,438,819 (80% need-based, 20% non-need-based). *Programs:* Federal Direct (Subsidized and Unsubsidized Stafford, PLUS), Perkins, Federal Nursing.

WORK-STUDY *Federal work-study:* Total amount: $461,113; 353 jobs averaging $1305. *State or other work-study/employment:* Total amount: $2,500,000 (100% non-need-based). 1,216 part-time jobs averaging $1350.

ATHLETIC AWARDS Total amount: $4,653,553 (28% need-based, 72% non-need-based).

APPLYING FOR FINANCIAL AID *Required financial aid form:* FAFSA. *Financial aid deadline (priority):* 3/1. *Notification date:* Continuous beginning 3/1. Students must reply by 5/1.

CONTACT Ms. Janet Turner, Director of Financial Aid, University of Portland, 5000 North Willamette Boulevard, Portland, OR 97203-5798, 503-943-7311 or toll-free 888-627-5601. *Fax:* 503-943-7508. *E-mail:* turnerj@up.edu. *Website:* http://www.up.edu/.

UNIVERSITY OF PUERTO RICO, AGUADILLA UNIVERSITY COLLEGE
Aguadilla, PR

CONTACT Director of Financial Aid, University of Puerto Rico, Aguadilla University College, PO Box 250-160, Aguadilla, PR 00604-0160, 787-890-2681 Ext. 273. *Website:* http://www.uprag.edu/.

UNIVERSITY OF PUERTO RICO AT ARECIBO
Arecibo, PR

CONTACT Myrta F. Salcedo-Ortiz, Director of Financial Aid, University of Puerto Rico at Arecibo, PO Box 4010, Arecibo, PR 00613, 787-878-2830 Ext. 2008. *E-mail:* myrta.ortiz@upr.edu. *Website:* http://www.upra.edu/.

UNIVERSITY OF PUERTO RICO AT BAYAMÓN
Bayamón, PR

Tuition & fees (PR res): $2212	Average undergraduate aid package: N/A

ABOUT THE INSTITUTION Commonwealth-supported, coed. *Awards:* associate and bachelor's degrees. 16 undergraduate majors. *Total enrollment:* 5,051. Undergraduates: 5,051. Freshmen: 1,288. Federal methodology is used as a basis for awarding need-based institutional aid.

UNDERGRADUATE EXPENSES for 2013–2014 *Application fee:* $25. *Tuition, state resident:* full-time $1870; part-time $55 per credit. *Tuition, non-*

resident: full-time $3910; part-time $115 per credit. **Required fees:** full-time $342. Full-time tuition and fees vary according to class time, course load, program, and student level. Part-time tuition and fees vary according to class time, course load, program, and student level. **Payment plan:** Guaranteed tuition.

GIFT AID (NEED-BASED) Total amount: $17,439,999 (95% federal, 5% state). **Scholarships, grants, and awards:** Federal Pell, FSEOG, state, college/university gift aid from institutional funds.

GIFT AID (NON-NEED-BASED) Scholarships, grants, and awards by category: *Academic interests/achievement:* general academic interests/achievements. *Creative arts/performance:* dance, music, theater/drama. *Special achievements/activities:* cheerleading/drum major. *Special characteristics:* veterans, veterans' children. **Tuition waivers:** Full or partial for employees or children of employees. **ROTC:** Army, Air Force cooperative.

LOANS Student loans: $1,368,000 (100% need-based). **Programs:** Federal Direct (Unsubsidized Stafford, PLUS), Perkins.

WORK-STUDY Federal work-study: Total amount: $373,279; 292 jobs averaging $891.

APPLYING FOR FINANCIAL AID Required financial aid forms: FAFSA, state income tax form(s). **Notification date:** Continuous.

CONTACT Mr. Hector Cuadrado, Financial Aid Director, University of Puerto Rico at Bayamón, Street 174 #170 Minillas Industrial Park, Bayamon, PR 00959-1911, 787-993-8953 Ext. 4033. *E-mail:* hector.cuadrado@upr.edu.
Website: http://www.uprb.edu/.

UNIVERSITY OF PUERTO RICO AT CAROLINA

Carolina, PR

CONTACT Financial Aid Office, University of Puerto Rico at Carolina, PO Box 4800, Carolina, PR 00984-4800, 787-257-0000.
Website: http://uprc.edu/.

UNIVERSITY OF PUERTO RICO AT HUMACAO

Humacao, PR

CONTACT Alfredo Aponte Serrano, Director of Financial Aid, University of Puerto Rico at Humacao, HUC Station, Humacao, PR 00791-4300, 787-850-9362. *E-mail:* alfredo.aponte@upr.edu.
Website: http://www.uprh.edu/.

UNIVERSITY OF PUERTO RICO AT PONCE

Ponce, PR

CONTACT Carmelo Vega Montes, Director of Financial Aid, University of Puerto Rico at Ponce, Box 7186, Ponce, PR 00732-7186, 787-844-8181. *Fax:* 787-840-8108.
Website: http://upr-ponce.upr.edu/.

UNIVERSITY OF PUERTO RICO AT UTUADO

Utuado, PR

CONTACT Edgar Salv, Director of Financial Assistance, University of Puerto Rico at Utuado, PO Box 2500, Utuado, PR 00641, 787-894-2828 Ext. 2603. *Fax:* 787-894-3810. *E-mail:* esalva@uprutuado.edu.
Website: http://www.uprutuado.edu/.

UNIVERSITY OF PUERTO RICO, CAYEY UNIVERSITY COLLEGE

Cayey, PR

CONTACT Mr. Hector Maldonado Otero, Director of Financial Aid, University of Puerto Rico, Cayey University College, Antonio Barcelo, Cayey, PR 00736, 787-738-2161. *Fax:* 787-263-0676.
Website: http://www.cayey.upr.edu/.

UNIVERSITY OF PUERTO RICO, MAYAGÜEZ CAMPUS

Mayagüez, PR

CONTACT Ms. Ana I. Rodríguez, Director of Financial Aid, University of Puerto Rico, Mayagüez Campus, PO Box 9000, Mayagüez, PR 00681-9000, 787-265-3863. *Fax:* 787-265-1920. *E-mail:* a_rodriguez@rumad.uprm.edu.
Website: http://www.uprm.edu/.

UNIVERSITY OF PUERTO RICO, MEDICAL SCIENCES CAMPUS

San Juan, PR

CONTACT Mrs. Zoraida Figueroa, Financial Aid Director, University of Puerto Rico, Medical Sciences Campus, Terreno Centro Medico-Edificio Decanato Farmacia y Estudiantes, San Juan, PR 00936-5067, 787-763-2525. *Fax:* 787-282-7117. *E-mail:* zoraida.figueroa@upr.edu.
Website: http://www.rcm.upr.edu/.

UNIVERSITY OF PUERTO RICO, RÍO PIEDRAS

San Juan, PR

CONTACT Mr. Efraim Williams, EDP Manager, University of Puerto Rico, Río Piedras, PO Box 23300, San Juan, PR 00931-3300, 787-764-0000 Ext. 5573.
Website: http://www.uprrp.edu/.

UNIVERSITY OF PUGET SOUND

Tacoma, WA

Tuition & fees: $41,868	Average undergraduate aid package: $30,235

ABOUT THE INSTITUTION Independent, coed. **Awards:** bachelor's, master's, and doctoral degrees. 40 undergraduate majors. **Total enrollment:** 2,857. Undergraduates: 2,578. Freshmen: 631. Federal methodology is used as a basis for awarding need-based institutional aid.

UNDERGRADUATE EXPENSES for 2013–2014 **Application fee:** $50. **Comprehensive fee:** $52,648 includes full-time tuition ($41,640), mandatory fees ($228), and room and board ($10,780). **College room only:** $5940. Full-time tuition and fees vary according to course load. Room and board charges vary according to board plan and housing facility. **Part-time tuition:** $5250 per unit. Part-time tuition and fees vary according to course load.

FRESHMAN FINANCIAL AID (Fall 2012, est.) 489 applied for aid; of those 79% were deemed to have need. 100% of freshmen with need received aid; of those 19% had need fully met. **Average percent of need met:** 75% (excluding resources awarded to replace EFC). **Average financial aid package:** $28,062 (excluding resources awarded to replace EFC). 34% of all full-time freshmen had no need and received non-need-based gift aid.

UNDERGRADUATE FINANCIAL AID (Fall 2012, est.) 1,857 applied for aid; of those 88% were deemed to have need. 100% of undergraduates with need received aid; of those 17% had need fully met. *Average percent of need met:* 78% (excluding resources awarded to replace EFC). *Average financial aid package:* $30,235 (excluding resources awarded to replace EFC). 30% of all full-time undergraduates had no need and received non-need-based gift aid.

GIFT AID (NEED-BASED) *Total amount:* $38,233,105 (8% federal, 3% state, 86% institutional, 3% external sources). *Receiving aid:* Freshmen: 61% (384); all full-time undergraduates: 63% (1,610). *Average award:* Freshmen: $23,431; Undergraduates: $24,447. *Scholarships, grants, and awards:* Federal Pell, FSEOG, state, private, college/university gift aid from institutional funds.

GIFT AID (NON-NEED-BASED) *Total amount:* $9,936,904 (97% institutional, 3% external sources). *Receiving aid:* Freshmen: 10% (62). Undergraduates: 5% (139). *Average award:* Freshmen: $15,989. Undergraduates: $12,924. *Scholarships, grants, and awards by category:* Academic interests/achievement: 848 awards ($8,841,710 total): biological sciences, business, communication, computer science, English, foreign languages, general academic interests/achievements, humanities, international studies, mathematics, physical sciences, premedicine, social sciences. *Creative arts/performance:* 52 awards ($208,850 total): art/fine arts, debating, music, theater/drama. *Special achievements/activities:* 4 awards ($12,000 total): community service, leadership, religious involvement. *Special characteristics:* 26 awards ($807,055 total): children of faculty/staff, international students. *Tuition waivers:* Full or partial for employees or children of employees. *ROTC:* Army cooperative.

LOANS *Student loans:* $12,690,997 (94% need-based, 6% non-need-based). 58% of past graduating class borrowed through all loan programs. *Average indebtedness per student:* $28,923. *Average need-based loan:* Freshmen: $4805. Undergraduates: $6165. *Parent loans:* $6,538,746 (92% need-based, 8% non-need-based). *Programs:* Federal Direct (Subsidized and Unsubsidized Stafford, PLUS), Perkins.

WORK-STUDY *Federal work-study:* Total amount: $1,564,000; 535 jobs averaging $2923. *State or other work-study/employment:* Total amount: $2,217,576 (100% need-based). 814 part-time jobs averaging $2724.

APPLYING FOR FINANCIAL AID *Required financial aid form:* FAFSA. *Financial aid deadline (priority):* 2/1. *Notification date:* Continuous beginning 3/15. Students must reply by 5/1.

CONTACT Maggie A. Mittuch, Associate Vice President for Student Financial Services, University of Puget Sound, 1500 North Warner Street #1039, Tacoma, WA 98416-1039, 253-879-3214 or toll-free 800-396-7191. *Fax:* 253-879-8508. *E-mail:* mmittuch@pugetsound.edu. *Website:* http://www.pugetsound.edu/.

UNIVERSITY OF REDLANDS
Redlands, CA

Tuition & fees: $39,338	Average undergraduate aid package: $32,719

ABOUT THE INSTITUTION Independent, coed. *Awards:* certificates, bachelor's, master's, and doctoral degrees. 42 undergraduate majors. *Total enrollment:* 4,956. Undergraduates: 3,360. Freshmen: 724. Federal methodology is used as a basis for awarding need-based institutional aid.

UNDERGRADUATE EXPENSES for 2013–2014 *Application fee:* $30. *Comprehensive fee:* $51,262 includes full-time tuition ($39,038), mandatory fees ($300), and room and board ($11,924). Full-time tuition and fees vary according to program. Room and board charges vary according to board plan and housing facility. *Part-time fees:* $150 per term. Part-time tuition and fees vary according to course load and program.

FRESHMAN FINANCIAL AID (Fall 2012, est.) 681 applied for aid; of those 88% were deemed to have need. 100% of freshmen with need received aid; of those 48% had need fully met. *Average percent of need met:* 89% (excluding resources awarded to replace EFC). *Average financial aid package:* $33,263 (excluding resources awarded to replace EFC). 12% of all full-time freshmen had no need and received non-need-based gift aid.

UNDERGRADUATE FINANCIAL AID (Fall 2012, est.) 2,406 applied for aid; of those 89% were deemed to have need. 100% of undergraduates with need received aid; of those 46% had need fully met. *Average percent of need met:* 87% (excluding resources awarded to replace EFC). *Average financial aid package:* $32,719 (excluding resources awarded to replace EFC). 10% of all full-time undergraduates had no need and received non-need-based gift aid.

GIFT AID (NEED-BASED) *Total amount:* $56,017,967 (7% federal, 11% state, 82% institutional). *Receiving aid:* Freshmen: 82% (591); all full-time undergraduates: 82% (2,091). *Average award:* Freshmen: $28,446; Undergraduates: $27,088. *Scholarships, grants, and awards:* Federal Pell, FSEOG, state, private, college/university gift aid from institutional funds.

GIFT AID (NON-NEED-BASED) *Total amount:* $4,673,857 (82% institutional, 18% external sources). *Receiving aid:* Freshmen: 16% (113). Undergraduates: 7% (182). *Average award:* Freshmen: $15,260. Undergraduates: $14,914. *Scholarships, grants, and awards by category:* Academic interests/achievement: general academic interests/achievements. *Creative arts/performance:* art/fine arts, creative writing, debating, music. *Special achievements/activities:* general special achievements/activities. *Special characteristics:* international students. *Tuition waivers:* Full or partial for employees or children of employees. *ROTC:* Army cooperative, Air Force cooperative.

LOANS *Student loans:* $15,586,468 (99% need-based, 1% non-need-based). 68% of past graduating class borrowed through all loan programs. *Average indebtedness per student:* $32,035. *Average need-based loan:* Freshmen: $4268. Undergraduates: $5027. *Parent loans:* $6,187,758 (90% need-based, 10% non-need-based). *Programs:* Perkins, college/university.

WORK-STUDY *Federal work-study:* Total amount: $2,238,500; jobs available. *State or other work-study/employment:* Total amount: $2,055,565 (100% need-based). Part-time jobs available.

APPLYING FOR FINANCIAL AID *Required financial aid forms:* FAFSA, state aid form. *Financial aid deadline (priority):* 2/15. *Notification date:* Continuous beginning 2/28. Students must reply by 5/1.

CONTACT Alisha Aguilar, Director of Financial Aid, University of Redlands, PO Box 3080, Redlands, CA 92373-0999, 909-748-8047 or toll-free 800-455-5064. *Fax:* 909-335-4089. *E-mail:* financialaid@redlands.edu. *Website:* http://www.redlands.edu/.

UNIVERSITY OF RHODE ISLAND
Kingston, RI

Tuition & fees (RI res): $12,450	Average undergraduate aid package: $14,901

ABOUT THE INSTITUTION State-supported, coed. *Awards:* certificates, bachelor's, master's, and doctoral degrees. 76 undergraduate majors. *Total enrollment:* 16,451. Undergraduates: 13,398. Freshmen: 2,994. Federal methodology is used as a basis for awarding need-based institutional aid.

UNDERGRADUATE EXPENSES for 2013–2014 *Application fee:* $65. *Tuition, state resident:* full-time $10,878. *Tuition, nonresident:* full-time $26,444. *Required fees:* full-time $1572. Full-time tuition and fees vary according to course load, location, and reciprocity agreements. Part-time tuition and fees vary according to course load, location, and reciprocity agreements. Room and board charges vary according to board plan and housing facility. .

FRESHMAN FINANCIAL AID (Fall 2012, est.) 2,463 applied for aid; of those 82% were deemed to have need. 92% of freshmen with need received aid; of those 70% had need fully met. *Average percent of need met:* 64% (excluding resources awarded to replace EFC). *Average financial aid package:* $15,701 (excluding resources awarded to replace EFC). 6% of all full-time freshmen had no need and received non-need-based gift aid.

UNDERGRADUATE FINANCIAL AID (Fall 2012, est.) 11,274 applied for aid; of those 86% were deemed to have need. 83% of undergraduates with need received aid; of those 83% had need fully met. *Average percent of need met:* 58% (excluding resources awarded to replace EFC). *Average financial aid package:* $14,901 (excluding resources awarded to replace EFC). 4% of all full-time undergraduates had no need and received non-need-based gift aid.

GIFT AID (NEED-BASED) *Total amount:* $77,413,573 (21% federal, 3% state, 72% institutional, 4% external sources). *Receiving aid:* Freshmen: 59% (1,758); all full-time undergraduates: 65% (7,752). *Average award:* Freshmen: $9665; Undergraduates: $9219. *Scholarships, grants, and awards:* Federal Pell, FSEOG, state, private, college/university gift aid from institutional funds.

GIFT AID (NON-NEED-BASED) *Total amount:* $3,306,739 (89% institutional, 11% external sources). *Receiving aid:* Freshmen: 7% (201). Undergraduates: 5% (623). *Average award:* Freshmen: $5476. Undergraduates: $5793. *Scholarships, grants, and awards by category:* Academic interests/achievement: general aca-

demic interests/achievements. *Creative arts/performance:* art/fine arts, music, theater/drama. *Special characteristics:* children and siblings of alumni. *Tuition waivers:* Full or partial for minority students, employees or children of employees, senior citizens. *ROTC:* Army.
LOANS *Student loans:* $73,442,009 (79% need-based, 21% non-need-based). 77% of past graduating class borrowed through all loan programs. *Average indebtedness per student:* $30,387. *Average need-based loan:* Freshmen: $5174. Undergraduates: $5396. *Parent loans:* $30,339,115 (63% need-based, 37% non-need-based). *Programs:* Federal Direct (Subsidized and Unsubsidized Stafford, PLUS), Perkins, Federal Nursing, college/university.
WORK-STUDY *Federal work-study:* Total amount: $963,610; jobs available.
ATHLETIC AWARDS Total amount: $7,433,156 (94% need-based, 6% non-need-based).
APPLYING FOR FINANCIAL AID *Required financial aid form:* FAFSA. *Financial aid deadline (priority):* 3/1. *Notification date:* Continuous beginning 3/15. Students must reply by 5/1.
CONTACT Office of Enrollment Services, University of Rhode Island, Green Hall, 35 Campus Avenue, Kingston, RI 02881, 401-874-9500.
Website: http://www.uri.edu/.

UNIVERSITY OF RICHMOND
Richmond, VA

Tuition & fees: $45,320	Average undergraduate aid package: $41,836

ABOUT THE INSTITUTION Independent, coed. *Awards:* bachelor's, master's, and doctoral degrees. 50 undergraduate majors. *Total enrollment:* 3,626. Undergraduates: 3,074. Freshmen: 781. Institutional methodology is used as a basis for awarding need-based institutional aid.
UNDERGRADUATE EXPENSES for 2013–2014 *Application fee:* $50. *Comprehensive fee:* $55,590 includes full-time tuition ($45,320) and room and board ($10,270). *College room only:* $4650. Full-time tuition and fees vary according to course load. Room and board charges vary according to board plan and housing facility. *Part-time tuition:* $2266 per credit hour. Part-time tuition and fees vary according to course load.
FRESHMAN FINANCIAL AID (Fall 2012, est.) 495 applied for aid; of those 62% were deemed to have need. 100% of freshmen with need received aid; of those 94% had need fully met. *Average percent of need met:* 100% (excluding resources awarded to replace EFC). *Average financial aid package:* $41,347 (excluding resources awarded to replace EFC). 10% of all full-time freshmen had no need and received non-need-based gift aid.
UNDERGRADUATE FINANCIAL AID (Fall 2012, est.) 1,771 applied for aid; of those 79% were deemed to have need. 100% of undergraduates with need received aid; of those 90% had need fully met. *Average percent of need met:* 100% (excluding resources awarded to replace EFC). *Average financial aid package:* $41,836 (excluding resources awarded to replace EFC). 15% of all full-time undergraduates had no need and received non-need-based gift aid.
GIFT AID (NEED-BASED) *Total amount:* $47,950,482 (5% federal, 2% state, 92% institutional, 1% external sources). *Receiving aid:* Freshmen: 39% (304); all full-time undergraduates: 43% (1,383). *Average award:* Freshmen: $35,334; Undergraduates: $36,703. *Scholarships, grants, and awards:* Federal Pell, FSEOG, state, private, college/university gift aid from institutional funds.
GIFT AID (NON-NEED-BASED) *Total amount:* $14,332,462 (7% federal, 5% state, 82% institutional, 6% external sources). *Receiving aid:* Freshmen: 9% (71). Undergraduates: 6% (201). *Average award:* Freshmen: $40,071. Undergraduates: $23,005. *Scholarships, grants, and awards by category: Academic interests/achievement:* 179 awards ($7,075,875 total): biological sciences, computer science, general academic interests/achievements, mathematics, physical sciences. *Creative arts/performance:* 33 awards ($981,280 total): art/fine arts, dance, music, performing arts, theater/drama. *Special achievements/activities:* 97 awards ($242,500 total): community service. *Tuition waivers:* Full or partial for employees or children of employees. *ROTC:* Army.
LOANS *Student loans:* $11,856,513 (33% need-based, 67% non-need-based). 43% of past graduating class borrowed through all loan programs. *Average indebtedness per student:* $21,825. *Average need-based loan:* Freshmen: $3121. Undergraduates: $3502. *Parent loans:* $4,016,594 (1% need-based, 99% non-need-based). *Programs:* Federal Direct (Subsidized and Unsubsidized Stafford, PLUS), Perkins.

WORK-STUDY *Federal work-study:* Total amount: $697,616; 519 jobs averaging $1434.
ATHLETIC AWARDS Total amount: $9,503,501 (20% need-based, 80% non-need-based).
APPLYING FOR FINANCIAL AID *Required financial aid forms:* FAFSA, CSS Financial Aid PROFILE, noncustodial (divorced/separated) parent's statement, federal income tax form(s). *Financial aid deadline:* 2/15. *Notification date:* 4/1. Students must reply within 4 weeks of notification.
CONTACT Financial Aid Office, University of Richmond, Brunet Hall, 28 Westhampton Way, University of Richmond, VA 23173, 804-289-8438 or toll-free 800-700-1662. *Fax:* 804-484-1650. *E-mail:* finaid@richmond.edu.
Website: http://www.richmond.edu/.

UNIVERSITY OF RIO GRANDE
Rio Grande, OH

Tuition & fees: N/R	Average undergraduate aid package: $6648

ABOUT THE INSTITUTION Independent, coed. *Awards:* certificates, associate, bachelor's, and master's degrees. 71 undergraduate majors. *Total enrollment:* 2,278. Undergraduates: 2,199. Freshmen: 328. Federal methodology is used as a basis for awarding need-based institutional aid.
FRESHMAN FINANCIAL AID (Fall 2011) 300 applied for aid; of those 99% were deemed to have need. 94% of freshmen with need received aid; of those 73% had need fully met. *Average percent of need met:* 44% (excluding resources awarded to replace EFC). *Average financial aid package:* $5159 (excluding resources awarded to replace EFC). 17% of all full-time freshmen had no need and received non-need-based gift aid.
UNDERGRADUATE FINANCIAL AID (Fall 2011) 1,129 applied for aid; of those 100% were deemed to have need. 98% of undergraduates with need received aid; of those 74% had need fully met. *Average percent of need met:* 73% (excluding resources awarded to replace EFC). *Average financial aid package:* $6648 (excluding resources awarded to replace EFC). 7% of all full-time undergraduates had no need and received non-need-based gift aid.
GIFT AID (NEED-BASED) *Total amount:* $7,467,789 (97% federal, 1% state, 2% external sources). *Receiving aid:* Freshmen: 71% (221); all full-time undergraduates: 81% (954). *Average award:* Freshmen: $2777; Undergraduates: $3423. *Scholarships, grants, and awards:* Federal Pell, FSEOG, state, private, college/university gift aid from institutional funds.
GIFT AID (NON-NEED-BASED) *Total amount:* $4,099,839 (6% federal, 8% state, 66% institutional, 20% external sources). *Receiving aid:* Freshmen: 3% (10). Undergraduates: 36% (424). *Average award:* Freshmen: $2080. Undergraduates: $3749. *Scholarships, grants, and awards by category: Academic interests/achievement:* biological sciences, business, communication, computer science, education, English, general academic interests/achievements, health fields, humanities, mathematics, physical sciences, social sciences. *Creative arts/performance:* art/fine arts, music. *Special achievements/activities:* cheerleading/drum major. *Special characteristics:* children and siblings of alumni, children of faculty/staff, local/state students, out-of-state students.
LOANS *Student loans:* $14,473,693 (100% need-based). 78% of past graduating class borrowed through all loan programs. *Average indebtedness per student:* $22,633. *Average need-based loan:* Freshmen: $3632. Undergraduates: $4065. *Parent loans:* $336,114 (100% need-based). *Programs:* Federal Direct (Subsidized and Unsubsidized Stafford, PLUS), Perkins.
WORK-STUDY *Federal work-study:* Total amount: $201,012; jobs available. *State or other work-study/employment:* Total amount: $153,666 (100% need-based). Part-time jobs available.
ATHLETIC AWARDS Total amount: $812,795 (100% non-need-based).
APPLYING FOR FINANCIAL AID *Required financial aid forms:* FAFSA, institution's own form. *Financial aid deadline:* Continuous. *Notification date:* Continuous beginning 1/15. Students must reply within 3 weeks of notification.
CONTACT Ms. Zana Smith, Director of Financial Aid, University of Rio Grande, PO Box 500, 218 North College Avenue, Rio Grande, OH 45674, 740-245-7218 or toll-free 800-282-7201. *Fax:* 740-245-7102.
Website: http://www.rio.edu/.

UNIVERSITY OF ROCHESTER
Rochester, NY

Tuition & fees: $43,666	Average undergraduate aid package: $36,815

ABOUT THE INSTITUTION Independent, coed. **Awards:** certificates, bachelor's, master's, and doctoral degrees. 63 undergraduate majors. **Total enrollment:** 10,510. Undergraduates: 5,785. Freshmen: 1,343. Institutional methodology is used as a basis for awarding need-based institutional aid.

UNDERGRADUATE EXPENSES for 2013–2014 Application fee: $70. **Comprehensive fee:** $56,284 includes full-time tuition ($42,890), mandatory fees ($776), and room and board ($12,618). **College room only:** $7682. Full-time tuition and fees vary according to student level. Room and board charges vary according to board plan. **Part-time tuition:** $1340 per credit hour. Part-time tuition and fees vary according to course load. **Payment plan:** Tuition prepayment.

FRESHMAN FINANCIAL AID (Fall 2012, est.) 886 applied for aid; of those 78% were deemed to have need. 100% of freshmen with need received aid; of those 100% had need fully met. **Average percent of need met:** 100% (excluding resources awarded to replace EFC). **Average financial aid package:** $37,988 (excluding resources awarded to replace EFC). 28% of all full-time freshmen had no need and received non-need-based gift aid.

UNDERGRADUATE FINANCIAL AID (Fall 2012, est.) 3,038 applied for aid; of those 88% were deemed to have need. 100% of undergraduates with need received aid; of those 90% had need fully met. **Average percent of need met:** 90% (excluding resources awarded to replace EFC). **Average financial aid package:** $36,815 (excluding resources awarded to replace EFC). 28% of all full-time undergraduates had no need and received non-need-based gift aid.

GIFT AID (NEED-BASED) Total amount: $78,691,380 (6% federal, 3% state, 89% institutional, 2% external sources). **Receiving aid:** Freshmen: 56% (691); all full-time undergraduates: 54% (2,623). **Average award:** Freshmen: $34,472; Undergraduates: $31,541. **Scholarships, grants, and awards:** Federal Pell, FSEOG, state, college/university gift aid from institutional funds.

GIFT AID (NON-NEED-BASED) Total amount: $20,757,873 (8% federal, 89% institutional, 3% external sources). **Receiving aid:** Freshmen: 12% (152). Undergraduates: 6% (279). **Average award:** Freshmen: $11,669. Undergraduates: $13,001. **Scholarships, grants, and awards by category:** Academic interests/achievement: engineering/technologies, general academic interests/achievements, military science. Creative arts/performance: general creative arts/performance, music, performing arts. Special achievements/activities: general special achievements/activities, leadership. Special characteristics: children and siblings of alumni, children of faculty/staff, general special characteristics, international students, veterans. **Tuition waivers:** Full or partial for employees or children of employees. **ROTC:** Army cooperative, Naval, Air Force cooperative.

LOANS Student loans: $22,270,625 (75% need-based, 25% non-need-based). 53% of past graduating class borrowed through all loan programs. **Average indebtedness per student:** $27,601. **Average need-based loan:** Freshmen: $4083. Undergraduates: $5057. **Parent loans:** $7,506,547 (24% need-based, 76% non-need-based). **Programs:** Federal Direct (Subsidized and Unsubsidized Stafford, PLUS), Perkins, Federal Nursing.

WORK-STUDY Federal work-study: Total amount: $4,093,118; 1,769 jobs averaging $2314. **State or other work-study/employment:** Total amount: $1,301,044 (44% need-based, 56% non-need-based). Part-time jobs available.

APPLYING FOR FINANCIAL AID Required financial aid forms: FAFSA, CSS Financial Aid PROFILE, state aid form, noncustodial (divorced/separated) parent's statement. **Financial aid deadline (priority):** 2/15. **Notification date:** 4/1. Students must reply by 5/1.

CONTACT Charles W. Puls, Director of Financial Aid, University of Rochester, Wallis Hall, PO Box 270261, Rochester, NY 14627-0261, 585-275-3226 or toll-free 888-822-2256. *Fax:* 585-756-7664. *Website:* http://www.rochester.edu/.

UNIVERSITY OF ST. FRANCIS
Joliet, IL

Tuition & fees: $26,824	Average undergraduate aid package: $21,047

ABOUT THE INSTITUTION Independent Roman Catholic, coed. **Awards:** certificates, bachelor's, master's, and doctoral degrees. 51 undergraduate majors. **Total enrollment:** 2,345. Undergraduates: 1,423. Freshmen: 220. Federal methodology is used as a basis for awarding need-based institutional aid.

UNDERGRADUATE EXPENSES for 2013–2014 Application fee: $30. **Comprehensive fee:** $35,092 includes full-time tuition ($26,374), mandatory fees ($450), and room and board ($8268). Full-time tuition and fees vary according to degree level and location. Room and board charges vary according to board plan and housing facility. **Part-time tuition:** $795 per credit hour. Part-time tuition and fees vary according to degree level.

FRESHMAN FINANCIAL AID (Fall 2012, est.) 207 applied for aid; of those 95% were deemed to have need. 100% of freshmen with need received aid; of those 75% had need fully met. **Average percent of need met:** 81% (excluding resources awarded to replace EFC). **Average financial aid package:** $22,081 (excluding resources awarded to replace EFC). 10% of all full-time freshmen had no need and received non-need-based gift aid.

UNDERGRADUATE FINANCIAL AID (Fall 2012, est.) 1,263 applied for aid; of those 92% were deemed to have need. 100% of undergraduates with need received aid; of those 81% had need fully met. **Average percent of need met:** 76% (excluding resources awarded to replace EFC). **Average financial aid package:** $21,047 (excluding resources awarded to replace EFC). 13% of all full-time undergraduates had no need and received non-need-based gift aid.

GIFT AID (NEED-BASED) Total amount: $11,041,841 (22% federal, 22% state, 55% institutional, 1% external sources). **Receiving aid:** Freshmen: 60% (131); all full-time undergraduates: 63% (851). **Average award:** Freshmen: $8937; Undergraduates: $7860. **Scholarships, grants, and awards:** Federal Pell, FSEOG, state, private, college/university gift aid from institutional funds, Federal Nursing.

GIFT AID (NON-NEED-BASED) Total amount: $6,743,027 (6% federal, 92% institutional, 2% external sources). **Receiving aid:** Freshmen: 85% (187). Undergraduates: 82% (1,120). **Average award:** Freshmen: $11,921. Undergraduates: $9058. **Scholarships, grants, and awards by category:** Academic interests/achievement: 1,253 awards ($9,405,912 total): biological sciences, communication, education, general academic interests/achievements, health fields, international studies, social sciences. Creative arts/performance: 15 awards ($17,950 total): applied art and design, art/fine arts, music. Special achievements/activities: 442 awards ($3,759,022 total): cheerleading/drum major, community service, general special achievements/activities, leadership, religious involvement. Special characteristics: 225 awards ($294,495 total): adult students, children and siblings of alumni, children of educators, ethnic background, first-generation college students, religious affiliation, siblings of current students, veterans, veterans' children. **Tuition waivers:** Full or partial for children of alumni, employees or children of employees. **ROTC:** Army cooperative.

LOANS Student loans: $9,804,946 (44% need-based, 56% non-need-based). 91% of past graduating class borrowed through all loan programs. **Average indebtedness per student:** $28,267. **Average need-based loan:** Freshmen: $3656. Undergraduates: $4642. **Parent loans:** $2,905,322 (35% need-based, 65% non-need-based). **Programs:** Federal Direct (Subsidized and Unsubsidized Stafford, PLUS), Perkins, alternative loans.

WORK-STUDY Federal work-study: Total amount: $251,905; 187 jobs averaging $1961. **State or other work-study/employment:** Total amount: $377,906 (100% non-need-based). 249 part-time jobs averaging $1518.

ATHLETIC AWARDS Total amount: $3,548,729 (53% need-based, 47% non-need-based).

APPLYING FOR FINANCIAL AID Required financial aid forms: FAFSA, institution's own form. **Financial aid deadline (priority):** 2/15. **Notification date:** Continuous beginning 2/15. Students must reply within 3 weeks of notification.

CONTACT Mrs. Mary V. Shaw, Director of Financial Aid Services, University of St. Francis, 500 North Wilcox Street, Joliet, IL 60435-6188, 815-740-3403 or toll-free 800-735-7500. *Fax:* 815-740-3822. *E-mail:* mshaw@stfrancis.edu. *Website:* http://www.stfrancis.edu/.

UNIVERSITY OF SAINT FRANCIS
Fort Wayne, IN

CONTACT Office of Financial Aid, University of Saint Francis, 2701 Spring Street, Fort Wayne, IN 46808, 260-399-8003 or toll-free 800-729-4732. *Fax:* 260-399-8162. *E-mail:* finaid@sf.edu.
Website: http://www.sf.edu/.

UNIVERSITY OF SAINT MARY
Leavenworth, KS

CONTACT Mrs. Judy Wiedower, Financial Aid Director, University of Saint Mary, 4100 South Fourth Street, Leavenworth, KS 66048, 913-758-6314 or toll-free 800-752-7043. *Fax:* 913-758-6146. *E-mail:* wiedower@hub.smcks.edu.
Website: http://www.stmary.edu/.

UNIVERSITY OF SAINT JOSEPH
West Hartford, CT

Tuition & fees: $31,826	Average undergraduate aid package: $21,760

ABOUT THE INSTITUTION Independent Roman Catholic, undergraduate: women only; graduate: coed. *Awards:* certificates, bachelor's, master's, and doctoral degrees. 21 undergraduate majors. *Total enrollment:* 2,525. Undergraduates: 1,067. Freshmen: 159. Federal methodology is used as a basis for awarding need-based institutional aid.
UNDERGRADUATE EXPENSES for 2013–2014 *Application fee:* $50. *Comprehensive fee:* $45,424 includes full-time tuition ($30,408), mandatory fees ($1418), and room and board ($13,598). *College room only:* $6274. Full-time tuition and fees vary according to course load, degree level, location, program, and student level. Room and board charges vary according to board plan and housing facility. *Part-time tuition:* $688 per credit. *Part-time fees:* $45 per credit. Part-time tuition and fees vary according to course load, degree level, location, program, and student level.
FRESHMAN FINANCIAL AID (Fall 2012, est.) 152 applied for aid; of those 97% were deemed to have need. 100% of freshmen with need received aid; of those 11% had need fully met. *Average percent of need met:* 70% (excluding resources awarded to replace EFC). *Average financial aid package:* $22,479 (excluding resources awarded to replace EFC). 4% of all full-time freshmen had no need and received non-need-based gift aid.
UNDERGRADUATE FINANCIAL AID (Fall 2012, est.) 800 applied for aid; of those 95% were deemed to have need. 100% of undergraduates with need received aid; of those 9% had need fully met. *Average percent of need met:* 67% (excluding resources awarded to replace EFC). *Average financial aid package:* $21,760 (excluding resources awarded to replace EFC). 9% of all full-time undergraduates had no need and received non-need-based gift aid.
GIFT AID (NEED-BASED) *Total amount:* $12,953,217 (14% federal, 8% state, 69% institutional, 9% external sources). *Receiving aid:* Freshmen: 95% (148); all full-time undergraduates: 89% (749). *Average award:* Freshmen: $18,308; Undergraduates: $16,990. *Scholarships, grants, and awards:* Federal Pell, FSEOG, state, private, college/university gift aid from institutional funds.
GIFT AID (NON-NEED-BASED) *Total amount:* $1,077,121 (92% institutional, 8% external sources). *Receiving aid:* Freshmen: 10% (15). Undergraduates: 6% (48). *Average award:* Freshmen: $12,785. Undergraduates: $9620. *Scholarships, grants, and awards by category:* Academic interests/achievement: general academic interests/achievements. *Tuition waivers:* Full or partial for employees or children of employees.
LOANS *Student loans:* $8,616,066 (78% need-based, 22% non-need-based). 95% of past graduating class borrowed through all loan programs. *Average need-based loan:* Freshmen: $3847. Undergraduates: $5450. *Parent loans:* $2,728,142 (44% need-based, 56% non-need-based). *Programs:* Federal Direct (Subsidized and Unsubsidized Stafford, PLUS), Perkins, state, private loans.
WORK-STUDY *State or other work-study/employment:* Total amount: $216,000 (64% need-based, 36% non-need-based). Part-time jobs available.
APPLYING FOR FINANCIAL AID *Required financial aid form:* FAFSA. *Financial aid deadline (priority):* 2/15. *Notification date:* Continuous beginning 3/1. Students must reply within 2 weeks of notification.
CONTACT Mr. Daniel Shields, Director of Financial Aid, University of Saint Joseph, 1678 Asylum Avenue, West Hartford, CT 06117, 860-231-5319 or toll-free 866-442-8752. *E-mail:* dshields@usj.edu.
Website: http://www.usj.edu/.

UNIVERSITY OF ST. THOMAS
St. Paul, MN

Tuition & fees: $33,787	Average undergraduate aid package: $23,164

ABOUT THE INSTITUTION Independent Roman Catholic, coed. *Awards:* certificates, bachelor's, master's, and doctoral degrees. 59 undergraduate majors. *Total enrollment:* 10,316. Undergraduates: 6,336. Freshmen: 1,447. Federal methodology is used as a basis for awarding need-based institutional aid.
UNDERGRADUATE EXPENSES for 2013–2014 *Comprehensive fee:* $42,565 includes full-time tuition ($33,040), mandatory fees ($747), and room and board ($8778). *College room only:* $5546. Full-time tuition and fees vary according to course load, degree level, and program. Room and board charges vary according to board plan and housing facility. *Part-time tuition:* $1032 per credit hour. Part-time tuition and fees vary according to course load, degree level, and program.
FRESHMAN FINANCIAL AID (Fall 2012, est.) 1,163 applied for aid; of those 80% were deemed to have need. 100% of freshmen with need received aid; of those 18% had need fully met. *Average percent of need met:* 84% (excluding resources awarded to replace EFC). *Average financial aid package:* $23,042 (excluding resources awarded to replace EFC). 15% of all full-time freshmen had no need and received non-need-based gift aid.
UNDERGRADUATE FINANCIAL AID (Fall 2012, est.) 4,358 applied for aid; of those 82% were deemed to have need. 100% of undergraduates with need received aid; of those 16% had need fully met. *Average percent of need met:* 82% (excluding resources awarded to replace EFC). *Average financial aid package:* $23,164 (excluding resources awarded to replace EFC). 10% of all full-time undergraduates had no need and received non-need-based gift aid.
GIFT AID (NEED-BASED) *Total amount:* $59,410,883 (10% federal, 8% state, 80% institutional, 2% external sources). *Receiving aid:* Freshmen: 63% (915); all full-time undergraduates: 57% (3,481). *Average award:* Freshmen: $17,354; Undergraduates: $16,990. *Scholarships, grants, and awards:* Federal Pell, FSEOG, state, private, college/university gift aid from institutional funds.
GIFT AID (NON-NEED-BASED) *Total amount:* $11,609,252 (95% institutional, 5% external sources). *Receiving aid:* Freshmen: 9% (137). Undergraduates: 6% (389). *Average award:* Freshmen: $14,712. Undergraduates: $13,822. *Scholarships, grants, and awards by category:* Academic interests/achievement: 1,975 awards ($26,461,224 total): biological sciences, business, education, English, general academic interests/achievements, humanities, international studies, mathematics, physical sciences, religion/biblical studies, social sciences. *Creative arts/performance:* 39 awards ($91,484 total): journalism/publications, music. *Special characteristics:* 172 awards ($3,089,004 total): children of educators, children of faculty/staff, general special characteristics. *Tuition waivers:* Full or partial for employees or children of employees, senior citizens. *ROTC:* Army cooperative, Naval cooperative, Air Force.
LOANS *Student loans:* $36,204,272 (67% need-based, 33% non-need-based). 69% of past graduating class borrowed through all loan programs. *Average indebtedness per student:* $36,077. *Average need-based loan:* Freshmen: $7279. Undergraduates: $7909. *Parent loans:* $5,578,632 (49% need-based, 51% non-need-based). *Programs:* Federal Direct (Subsidized and Unsubsidized Stafford, PLUS), Perkins, state, alternative loans.
WORK-STUDY *Federal work-study:* Total amount: $4,075,455; 1,430 jobs averaging $2850. *State or other work-study/employment:* Total amount: $3,111,397 (82% need-based, 18% non-need-based). 1,003 part-time jobs averaging $2808.
APPLYING FOR FINANCIAL AID *Required financial aid form:* FAFSA. *Financial aid deadline (priority):* 4/1. *Notification date:* Continuous beginning 3/1. Students must reply within 3 weeks of notification.

CONTACT Ms. Paula Benson, Associate Director of Student Financial Services, University of St. Thomas, 2115 Summit Avenue, AQU 328, St. Paul, MN 55105-1096, 651-962-6547 or toll-free 800-328-6819. *Fax:* 651-962-6599. *E-mail:* paula.benson@stthomas.edu.
Website: http://www.stthomas.edu/.

CONTACT Lynda McKendree, Dean of Scholarships and Financial Aid, University of St. Thomas, 3800 Montrose Boulevard, Houston, TX 77006-4696, 713-525-2170 or toll-free 800-856-8565. *Fax:* 713-525-2142. *E-mail:* finaid@stthom.edu.
Website: http://www.stthom.edu/.

UNIVERSITY OF ST. THOMAS
Houston, TX

Tuition & fees: $26,890 | **Average undergraduate aid package: $17,805**

ABOUT THE INSTITUTION Independent Roman Catholic, coed. *Awards:* diplomas, bachelor's, master's, and doctoral degrees. 32 undergraduate majors. *Total enrollment:* 3,711. Undergraduates: 1,626. Freshmen: 271. Federal methodology is used as a basis for awarding need-based institutional aid.
UNDERGRADUATE EXPENSES for 2013–2014 *Application fee:* $25. *Comprehensive fee:* $34,790 includes full-time tuition ($26,550), mandatory fees ($340), and room and board ($7900). *College room only:* $4800. Full-time tuition and fees vary according to course load. Room and board charges vary according to board plan and housing facility. *Part-time tuition:* $885 per credit hour. Part-time tuition and fees vary according to course load.
FRESHMAN FINANCIAL AID (Fall 2012, est.) 201 applied for aid; of those 86% were deemed to have need. 99% of freshmen with need received aid; of those 15% had need fully met. *Average percent of need met:* 72% (excluding resources awarded to replace EFC). *Average financial aid package:* $19,110 (excluding resources awarded to replace EFC). 33% of all full-time freshmen had no need and received non-need-based gift aid.
UNDERGRADUATE FINANCIAL AID (Fall 2012, est.) 816 applied for aid; of those 91% were deemed to have need. 100% of undergraduates with need received aid; of those 12% had need fully met. *Average percent of need met:* 64% (excluding resources awarded to replace EFC). *Average financial aid package:* $17,805 (excluding resources awarded to replace EFC). 29% of all full-time undergraduates had no need and received non-need-based gift aid.
GIFT AID (NEED-BASED) *Total amount:* $10,944,205 (23% federal, 10% state, 63% institutional, 4% external sources). *Receiving aid:* Freshmen: 65% (172); all full-time undergraduates: 59% (731). *Average award:* Freshmen: $15,966; Undergraduates: $14,135. *Scholarships, grants, and awards:* Federal Pell, FSEOG, state, private, college/university gift aid from institutional funds, Academic Competitiveness Grants, National SMART Grants.
GIFT AID (NON-NEED-BASED) *Total amount:* $3,371,309 (98% institutional, 2% external sources). *Receiving aid:* Freshmen: 8% (21). Undergraduates: 6% (72). *Average award:* Freshmen: $11,234. Undergraduates: $8963. *Scholarships, grants, and awards by category: Academic interests/achievement:* biological sciences, business, communication, computer science, education, English, foreign languages, general academic interests/achievements, health fields, humanities, international studies, mathematics, physical sciences, premedicine, religion/biblical studies, social sciences. *Creative arts/performance:* applied art and design, art/fine arts, general creative arts/performance, music, performing arts, theater/drama. *Special achievements/activities:* general special achievements/activities, leadership, religious involvement. *Special characteristics:* children of faculty/staff, general special characteristics, previous college experience, religious affiliation. *Tuition waivers:* Full or partial for employees or children of employees, senior citizens. *ROTC:* Army cooperative, Air Force cooperative.
LOANS *Student loans:* $5,217,567 (88% need-based, 12% non-need-based). 58% of past graduating class borrowed through all loan programs. *Average indebtedness per student:* $33,936. *Average need-based loan:* Freshmen: $3343. Undergraduates: $4806. *Parent loans:* $1,015,285 (33% need-based, 67% non-need-based). *Programs:* Federal Direct (Subsidized and Unsubsidized Stafford, PLUS), state, private loans.
WORK-STUDY *Federal work-study:* Total amount: $192,148; 50 jobs averaging $3843. *State or other work-study/employment:* Part-time jobs available.
ATHLETIC AWARDS Total amount: $226,917 (28% need-based, 72% non-need-based).
APPLYING FOR FINANCIAL AID *Required financial aid form:* FAFSA. *Financial aid deadline (priority):* 4/15. *Notification date:* Continuous beginning 2/15. Students must reply within 2 weeks of notification.

UNIVERSITY OF SAN DIEGO
San Diego, CA

Tuition & fees: $41,392 | **Average undergraduate aid package: $29,830**

ABOUT THE INSTITUTION Independent Roman Catholic, coed. *Awards:* certificates, bachelor's, master's, and doctoral degrees. 42 undergraduate majors. *Total enrollment:* 8,105. Undergraduates: 5,457. Freshmen: 1,074. Federal methodology is used as a basis for awarding need-based institutional aid.
UNDERGRADUATE EXPENSES for 2013–2014 *Application fee:* $55. *Comprehensive fee:* $53,302 includes full-time tuition ($40,900), mandatory fees ($492), and room and board ($11,910). Room and board charges vary according to board plan and housing facility. *Part-time tuition:* $1410 per unit. Part-time tuition and fees vary according to course load.
FRESHMAN FINANCIAL AID (Fall 2011) 819 applied for aid; of those 79% were deemed to have need. 99% of freshmen with need received aid; of those 13% had need fully met. *Average percent of need met:* 73% (excluding resources awarded to replace EFC). *Average financial aid package:* $29,600 (excluding resources awarded to replace EFC). 20% of all full-time freshmen had no need and received non-need-based gift aid.
UNDERGRADUATE FINANCIAL AID (Fall 2011) 3,263 applied for aid; of those 88% were deemed to have need. 97% of undergraduates with need received aid; of those 15% had need fully met. *Average percent of need met:* 71% (excluding resources awarded to replace EFC). *Average financial aid package:* $29,830 (excluding resources awarded to replace EFC). 15% of all full-time undergraduates had no need and received non-need-based gift aid.
GIFT AID (NEED-BASED) *Total amount:* $59,657,315 (13% federal, 7% state, 78% institutional, 2% external sources). *Receiving aid:* Freshmen: 55% (626); all full-time undergraduates: 51% (2,655). *Average award:* Freshmen: $23,756; Undergraduates: $22,914. *Scholarships, grants, and awards:* Federal Pell, FSEOG, state, private, college/university gift aid from institutional funds, Federal Nursing, TEACH Grants.
GIFT AID (NON-NEED-BASED) *Total amount:* $14,587,782 (17% federal, 80% institutional, 3% external sources). *Receiving aid:* Freshmen: 34% (388). Undergraduates: 23% (1,229). *Average award:* Freshmen: $12,914. Undergraduates: $13,522. *Scholarships, grants, and awards by category: Academic interests/achievement:* 1,642 awards ($21,967,100 total): general academic interests/achievements. *Creative arts/performance:* 12 awards ($106,500 total): music. *Special achievements/activities:* 89 awards: religious involvement. *Special characteristics:* children of faculty/staff. *Tuition waivers:* Full or partial for employees or children of employees. *ROTC:* Army cooperative, Naval, Air Force cooperative.
LOANS *Student loans:* $23,023,122 (92% need-based, 8% non-need-based). 47% of past graduating class borrowed through all loan programs. *Average indebtedness per student:* $29,874. *Average need-based loan:* Freshmen: $6398. Undergraduates: $8109. *Parent loans:* $26,604,629 (48% need-based, 52% non-need-based). *Programs:* Federal Direct (Subsidized and Unsubsidized Stafford, PLUS), Perkins, college/university.
WORK-STUDY *Federal work-study:* Total amount: $1,128,509; 563 jobs averaging $2008. *State or other work-study/employment:* Total amount: $2,496,054 (17% need-based, 83% non-need-based). Part-time jobs available.
ATHLETIC AWARDS Total amount: $6,161,995 (23% need-based, 77% non-need-based).
APPLYING FOR FINANCIAL AID *Required financial aid form:* FAFSA. *Financial aid deadline (priority):* 3/2. *Notification date:* Continuous beginning 3/1. Students must reply by 5/1 or within 3 weeks of notification.

CONTACT Judith Lewis Logue, Director of Financial Aid Services, University of San Diego, 5998 Alcala Park, San Diego, CA 92110-2492, 619-260-2700 or toll-free 800-248-4873. *E-mail:* jllogue@sandiego.edu.
Website: http://www.sandiego.edu/.

UNIVERSITY OF SAN FRANCISCO
San Francisco, CA

CONTACT Ms. Susan Murphy, Director of Financial Aid, University of San Francisco, 2130 Fulton Street, San Francisco, CA 94117-1080, 415-422-2620 or toll-free 800-CALL-USF. *Fax:* 415-422-6084. *E-mail:* murphy@usfca.edu. *Website:* http://www.usfca.edu/.

UNIVERSITY OF SCIENCE AND ARTS OF OKLAHOMA
Chickasha, OK

Tuition & fees (OK res): $5400	Average undergraduate aid package: $9418

ABOUT THE INSTITUTION State-supported, coed. *Awards:* bachelor's degrees. 24 undergraduate majors. *Total enrollment:* 983. Undergraduates: 983. Freshmen: 187. Federal methodology is used as a basis for awarding need-based institutional aid.

UNDERGRADUATE EXPENSES for 2013–2014 *Application fee:* $40. *Tuition, state resident:* full-time $4230; part-time $141 per credit hour. *Tuition, nonresident:* full-time $11,550; part-time $385 per credit hour. *Required fees:* full-time $1170; $39 per credit hour. *College room and board:* $5160; *Room only:* $2680. Room and board charges vary according to board plan and housing facility. *Payment plan:* Guaranteed tuition.

FRESHMAN FINANCIAL AID (Fall 2012, est.) 143 applied for aid; of those 90% were deemed to have need. 97% of freshmen with need received aid; of those 11% had need fully met. *Average percent of need met:* 62% (excluding resources awarded to replace EFC). *Average financial aid package:* $9174 (excluding resources awarded to replace EFC). 4% of all full-time freshmen had no need and received non-need-based gift aid.

UNDERGRADUATE FINANCIAL AID (Fall 2012, est.) 677 applied for aid; of those 91% were deemed to have need. 98% of undergraduates with need received aid; of those 13% had need fully met. *Average percent of need met:* 61% (excluding resources awarded to replace EFC). *Average financial aid package:* $9418 (excluding resources awarded to replace EFC). 9% of all full-time undergraduates had no need and received non-need-based gift aid.

GIFT AID (NEED-BASED) *Total amount:* $3,405,339 (61% federal, 24% state, 9% institutional, 6% external sources). *Receiving aid:* Freshmen: 66% (120); all full-time undergraduates: 64% (548). *Average award:* Freshmen: $7452; Undergraduates: $7467. *Scholarships, grants, and awards:* Federal Pell, FSEOG, state, private, college/university gift aid from institutional funds, USAO Foundation Grants.

GIFT AID (NON-NEED-BASED) *Total amount:* $377,703 (34% state, 48% institutional, 18% external sources). *Receiving aid:* Freshmen: 6% (11). Undergraduates: 5% (41). *Average award:* Freshmen: $1943. Undergraduates: $2129. *Scholarships, grants, and awards by category: Academic interests/achievement:* 386 awards ($793,656 total): general academic interests/achievements. *Creative arts/performance:* 10 awards ($14,450 total): art/fine arts, music, theater/drama. *Special achievements/activities:* 10 awards ($7650 total): cheerleading/drum major. *Special characteristics:* 67 awards ($204,477 total): children of faculty/staff, international students, out-of-state students, previous college experience. *Tuition waivers:* Full or partial for employees or children of employees, senior citizens.

LOANS *Student loans:* $2,925,873 (82% need-based, 18% non-need-based). 58% of past graduating class borrowed through all loan programs. *Average indebtedness per student:* $18,378. *Average need-based loan:* Freshmen: $2843. Undergraduates: $3281. *Parent loans:* $67,296 (20% need-based, 80% non-need-based). *Programs:* Federal Direct (Subsidized and Unsubsidized Stafford, PLUS), Perkins, college/university.

WORK-STUDY *Federal work-study:* Total amount: $256,204; 170 jobs averaging $1732.

ATHLETIC AWARDS Total amount: $1,212,066 (37% need-based, 63% non-need-based).

APPLYING FOR FINANCIAL AID *Required financial aid forms:* FAFSA, institution's own form. *Financial aid deadline (priority):* 3/1. *Notification date:* Continuous beginning 3/15. Students must reply within 4 weeks of notification.

CONTACT Nancy Moats, Director of Financial Aid, University of Science and Arts of Oklahoma, 1727 West Alabama, Chickasha, OK 73018-5322, 405-574-1251 or toll-free 800-933-8726. *Fax:* 405-574-1220. *E-mail:* nmoats@usao.edu. *Website:* http://www.usao.edu/.

THE UNIVERSITY OF SCRANTON
Scranton, PA

Tuition & fees: $37,456	Average undergraduate aid package: $22,996

ABOUT THE INSTITUTION Independent Roman Catholic (Jesuit), coed. *Awards:* certificates, bachelor's, master's, and doctoral degrees. 67 undergraduate majors. *Total enrollment:* 5,898. Undergraduates: 4,041. Freshmen: 961. Federal methodology is used as a basis for awarding need-based institutional aid.

UNDERGRADUATE EXPENSES for 2013–2014 *Comprehensive fee:* $50,260 includes full-time tuition ($37,106), mandatory fees ($350), and room and board ($12,804). *College room only:* $7500. Room and board charges vary according to board plan and housing facility. *Part-time tuition:* $955 per credit.

FRESHMAN FINANCIAL AID (Fall 2011) 945 applied for aid; of those 86% were deemed to have need. 99% of freshmen with need received aid; of those 11% had need fully met. *Average percent of need met:* 66% (excluding resources awarded to replace EFC). *Average financial aid package:* $21,694 (excluding resources awarded to replace EFC). 13% of all full-time freshmen had no need and received non-need-based gift aid.

UNDERGRADUATE FINANCIAL AID (Fall 2011) 3,168 applied for aid; of those 87% were deemed to have need. 100% of undergraduates with need received aid; of those 9% had need fully met. *Average percent of need met:* 68% (excluding resources awarded to replace EFC). *Average financial aid package:* $22,996 (excluding resources awarded to replace EFC). 16% of all full-time undergraduates had no need and received non-need-based gift aid.

GIFT AID (NEED-BASED) *Total amount:* $49,201,098 (8% federal, 5% state, 85% institutional, 2% external sources). *Receiving aid:* Freshmen: 75% (782); all full-time undergraduates: 69% (2,650). *Average award:* Freshmen: $18,787; Undergraduates: $18,902. *Scholarships, grants, and awards:* Federal Pell, FSEOG, state, private, college/university gift aid from institutional funds.

GIFT AID (NON-NEED-BASED) *Total amount:* $9,930,583 (3% federal, 84% institutional, 13% external sources). *Receiving aid:* Freshmen: 7% (70). Undergraduates: 4% (162). *Average award:* Freshmen: $12,481. Undergraduates: $11,531. *Scholarships, grants, and awards by category: Academic interests/achievement:* general academic interests/achievements, military science. *Special characteristics:* children of educators, children of faculty/staff, siblings of current students. *Tuition waivers:* Full or partial for employees or children of employees, senior citizens. *ROTC:* Army, Air Force cooperative.

LOANS *Student loans:* $28,373,942 (70% need-based, 30% non-need-based). 75% of past graduating class borrowed through all loan programs. *Average indebtedness per student:* $38,560. *Average need-based loan:* Freshmen: $6786. Undergraduates: $7884. *Parent loans:* $14,705,470 (39% need-based, 61% non-need-based). *Programs:* Federal Direct (Subsidized and Unsubsidized Stafford, PLUS), Perkins.

WORK-STUDY *Federal work-study:* Total amount: $1,989,430; jobs available. *State or other work-study/employment:* Total amount: $927,351 (54% need-based, 46% non-need-based). Part-time jobs available.

APPLYING FOR FINANCIAL AID *Required financial aid form:* FAFSA. *Financial aid deadline (priority):* 2/15. *Notification date:* Continuous beginning 3/15. Students must reply within 2 weeks of notification.

CONTACT Mr. William R. Burke, Director of Financial Aid, The University of Scranton, St. Thomas Hall 401, Scranton, PA 18510, 570-941-7887 or toll-free 888-SCRANTON. *Fax:* 570-941-4370. *E-mail:* finaid@scranton.edu. *Website:* http://www.scranton.edu/.

UNIVERSITY OF SIOUX FALLS
Sioux Falls, SD

CONTACT Rachel Gunn, Financial Aid Counselor, University of Sioux Falls, 1101 West 22nd Street, Sioux Falls, SD 57105-1699, 605-331-6623 or toll-free 800-888-1047. Fax: 605-331-6615. *E-mail:* rachel.gunn@usiouxfalls.edu. *Website:* http://www.usiouxfalls.edu/.

UNIVERSITY OF SOUTH ALABAMA
Mobile, AL

Tuition & fees (AL res): $7950	Average undergraduate aid package: $9155

ABOUT THE INSTITUTION State-supported, coed. **Awards:** certificates, bachelor's, master's, and doctoral degrees. 49 undergraduate majors. **Total enrollment:** 14,636. Undergraduates: 11,315. Freshmen: 1,944. Federal methodology is used as a basis for awarding need-based institutional aid.
UNDERGRADUATE EXPENSES for 2013–2014 *Application fee:* $35. *Tuition, state resident:* full-time $7950; part-time $265 per hour. *Tuition, non-resident:* full-time $15,900; part-time $530 per hour. Full-time tuition and fees vary according to course load and program. Part-time tuition and fees vary according to course load and program. *College room and board:* $7150; *Room only:* $3900. Room and board charges vary according to board plan and housing facility.
FRESHMAN FINANCIAL AID (Fall 2011) 1,588 applied for aid; of those 77% were deemed to have need. 100% of freshmen with need received aid; of those 14% had need fully met. *Average percent of need met:* 61% (excluding resources awarded to replace EFC). *Average financial aid package:* $9062 (excluding resources awarded to replace EFC). 17% of all full-time freshmen had no need and received non-need-based gift aid.
UNDERGRADUATE FINANCIAL AID (Fall 2011) 6,038 applied for aid; of those 82% were deemed to have need. 100% of undergraduates with need received aid; of those 10% had need fully met. *Average percent of need met:* 57% (excluding resources awarded to replace EFC). *Average financial aid package:* $9155 (excluding resources awarded to replace EFC). 10% of all full-time undergraduates had no need and received non-need-based gift aid.
GIFT AID (NEED-BASED) *Total amount:* $18,019,734 (99% federal, 1% state). *Receiving aid:* Freshmen: 60% (1,091); all full-time undergraduates: 47% (3,994). *Average award:* Freshmen: $6506; Undergraduates: $6223. *Scholarships, grants, and awards:* Federal Pell, FSEOG, state, private, college/university gift aid from institutional funds.
GIFT AID (NON-NEED-BASED) *Total amount:* $10,765,694 (90% institutional, 10% external sources). *Receiving aid:* Freshmen: 60% (1,091). Undergraduates: 47% (3,994). *Average award:* Freshmen: $4645. Undergraduates: $4350. *Scholarships, grants, and awards by category:* Academic interests/achievement: business, computer science, general academic interests/achievements, humanities, international studies, military science. *Creative arts/performance:* art/fine arts, journalism/publications, music, theater/drama. *Special achievements/activities:* general special achievements/activities, hobbies/interests, junior miss, leadership. *Special characteristics:* children and siblings of alumni, children of faculty/staff, members of minority groups. *Tuition waivers:* Full or partial for employees or children of employees. ROTC: Army, Air Force.
LOANS *Student loans:* $94,682,324 (37% need-based, 63% non-need-based). *Average need-based loan:* Freshmen: $3403. Undergraduates: $4282. *Parent loans:* $6,928,402 (100% non-need-based). *Programs:* Federal Direct (Subsidized and Unsubsidized Stafford, PLUS), Perkins.
WORK-STUDY *Federal work-study:* Total amount: $427,892; jobs available. *State or other work-study/employment:* Part-time jobs available.
ATHLETIC AWARDS Total amount: $4,903,152 (100% non-need-based).
APPLYING FOR FINANCIAL AID *Required financial aid forms:* FAFSA, institution's own form. *Financial aid deadline:* Continuous. *Notification date:* Continuous beginning 5/15. Students must reply within 5 weeks of notification.
CONTACT Financial Aid Office, University of South Alabama, Meisler Hall, Suite 1200, Mobile, AL 36688-0002, 251-460-6231 or toll-free 800-872-5247. Fax: 251-460-6079. *E-mail:* finaid@usouthal.edu.
Website: http://www.southalabama.edu/.

UNIVERSITY OF SOUTH CAROLINA
Columbia, SC

Tuition & fees (SC res): $10,488	Average undergraduate aid package: $13,012

ABOUT THE INSTITUTION State-supported, coed. **Awards:** certificates, bachelor's, master's, and doctoral degrees. 76 undergraduate majors. **Total enrollment:** 31,288. Undergraduates: 23,363. Freshmen: 4,625. Federal methodology is used as a basis for awarding need-based institutional aid.
UNDERGRADUATE EXPENSES for 2013–2014 *Application fee:* $50. *Tuition, state resident:* full-time $10,088; part-time $421 per credit hour. *Tuition, nonresident:* full-time $27,244; part-time $1136 per credit hour. *Required fees:* full-time $400. Full-time tuition and fees vary according to program and reciprocity agreements. Part-time tuition and fees vary according to course load. *College room and board:* $8459; *Room only:* $5624. Room and board charges vary according to board plan, housing facility, and location.
FRESHMAN FINANCIAL AID (Fall 2012, est.) 3,658 applied for aid; of those 62% were deemed to have need. 100% of freshmen with need received aid; of those 30% had need fully met. *Average percent of need met:* 75% (excluding resources awarded to replace EFC). *Average financial aid package:* $12,340 (excluding resources awarded to replace EFC). 40% of all full-time freshmen had no need and received non-need-based gift aid.
UNDERGRADUATE FINANCIAL AID (Fall 2012, est.) 14,096 applied for aid; of those 75% were deemed to have need. 100% of undergraduates with need received aid; of those 27% had need fully met. *Average percent of need met:* 74% (excluding resources awarded to replace EFC). *Average financial aid package:* $13,012 (excluding resources awarded to replace EFC). 33% of all full-time undergraduates had no need and received non-need-based gift aid.
GIFT AID (NEED-BASED) *Total amount:* $63,811,681 (37% federal, 41% state, 12% institutional, 10% external sources). *Receiving aid:* Freshmen: 22% (1,004); all full-time undergraduates: 27% (5,409). *Average award:* Freshmen: $4860; Undergraduates: $4862. *Scholarships, grants, and awards:* Federal Pell, FSEOG, state, private, college/university gift aid from institutional funds, United Negro College Fund, Federal Nursing, USC Opportunity Grants, Gamecock Guarantee.
GIFT AID (NON-NEED-BASED) *Total amount:* $46,098,576 (50% state, 26% institutional, 24% external sources). *Receiving aid:* Freshmen: 45% (2,041). Undergraduates: 33% (6,751). *Average award:* Freshmen: $5304. Undergraduates: $6212. *Scholarships, grants, and awards by category:* Academic interests/achievement: 8,860 awards ($18,968,589 total): area/ethnic studies, biological sciences, business, communication, computer science, education, engineering/technologies, English, foreign languages, general academic interests/achievements, health fields, humanities, international studies, library science, mathematics, military science, physical sciences, premedicine, religion/biblical studies, social sciences. *Creative arts/performance:* 37 awards ($292,975 total): art/fine arts, dance, debating, journalism/publications, music, theater/drama. *Special achievements/activities:* 198 awards ($158,300 total): cheerleading/drum major, community service, general special achievements/activities, leadership, memberships, religious involvement. *Special characteristics:* 6,647 awards ($14,137,397 total): adult students, children and siblings of alumni, children of faculty/staff, children of union members/company employees, children of workers in trades, children with a deceased or disabled parent, ethnic background, first-generation college students, general special characteristics, handicapped students, international students, local/state students, members of minority groups, out-of-state students, religious affiliation, spouses of deceased or disabled public servants. *Tuition waivers:* Full or partial for employees or children of employees, senior citizens. ROTC: Army, Naval, Air Force.
LOANS *Student loans:* $91,068,056 (53% need-based, 47% non-need-based). 46% of past graduating class borrowed through all loan programs. *Average indebtedness per student:* $25,022. *Average need-based loan:* Freshmen: $2261. Undergraduates: $3405. *Parent loans:* $24,802,084 (29% need-based, 71% non-need-based). *Programs:* Federal Direct (Subsidized and Unsubsidized Stafford, PLUS), Perkins, Federal Nursing.
WORK-STUDY *Federal work-study:* Total amount: $1,802,758; 554 jobs averaging $2165. *State or other work-study/employment:* Total amount: $6,390,864 (100% non-need-based). 2,948 part-time jobs averaging $1772.
ATHLETIC AWARDS Total amount: $6,410,016 (37% need-based, 63% non-need-based).
APPLYING FOR FINANCIAL AID *Required financial aid form:* FAFSA. *Financial aid deadline (priority):* 4/1. *Notification date:* Continuous beginning 4/1.

CONTACT Dr. Ed Miller, Director of Financial Aid, University of South Carolina, 1714 College Street, Columbia, SC 29208, 803-777-8134 or toll-free 800-868-5872. *Fax:* 803-777-0941. *E-mail:* ewmiller@mailbox.sc.edu. *Website:* http://www.sc.edu/.

CONTACT Mrs. Linda Aubrey-Higgins, Director of Financial Aid, University of South Carolina Aiken, 471 University Parkway, Aiken, SC 29801, 803-641-3476 or toll-free 888-WOW-USCA. *Fax:* 803-641-6840. *E-mail:* lindahi@usca.edu. *Website:* http://www.usca.edu/.

UNIVERSITY OF SOUTH CAROLINA AIKEN
Aiken, SC

Tuition & fees (SC res): $9024	Average undergraduate aid package: $10,767

ABOUT THE INSTITUTION State-supported, coed. *Awards:* bachelor's and master's degrees. 20 undergraduate majors. *Total enrollment:* 3,210. Undergraduates: 3,123. Freshmen: 525. Federal methodology is used as a basis for awarding need-based institutional aid.

UNDERGRADUATE EXPENSES for 2013–2014 *Application fee:* $45. *Tuition, state resident:* full-time $8734; part-time $380 per credit hour. *Tuition, nonresident:* full-time $17,490; part-time $760 per credit hour. *Required fees:* full-time $290; $9 per credit hour or $25 per term. Full-time tuition and fees vary according to reciprocity agreements. Part-time tuition and fees vary according to course load and reciprocity agreements. *College room and board:* $6780. Room and board charges vary according to board plan and housing facility.

FRESHMAN FINANCIAL AID (Fall 2011) 562 applied for aid; of those 76% were deemed to have need. 100% of freshmen with need received aid; of those 27% had need fully met. *Average percent of need met:* 75% (excluding resources awarded to replace EFC). *Average financial aid package:* $10,817 (excluding resources awarded to replace EFC). 19% of all full-time freshmen had no need and received non-need-based gift aid.

UNDERGRADUATE FINANCIAL AID (Fall 2011) 2,372 applied for aid; of those 73% were deemed to have need. 100% of undergraduates with need received aid; of those 25% had need fully met. *Average percent of need met:* 72% (excluding resources awarded to replace EFC). *Average financial aid package:* $10,767 (excluding resources awarded to replace EFC). 18% of all full-time undergraduates had no need and received non-need-based gift aid.

GIFT AID (NEED-BASED) *Total amount:* $11,086,053 (57% federal, 35% state, 6% institutional, 2% external sources). *Receiving aid:* Freshmen: 71% (404); all full-time undergraduates: 59% (1,474). *Average award:* Freshmen: $7235; Undergraduates: $6799. *Scholarships, grants, and awards:* Federal Pell, FSEOG, state, college/university gift aid from institutional funds.

GIFT AID (NON-NEED-BASED) *Total amount:* $3,435,541 (10% federal, 70% state, 14% institutional, 6% external sources). *Receiving aid:* Freshmen: 10% (60). Undergraduates: 6% (139). *Average award:* Freshmen: $5762. Undergraduates: $6557. *Scholarships, grants, and awards by category: Academic interests/achievement:* biological sciences, business, communication, computer science, education, engineering/technologies, English, general academic interests/achievements, humanities, mathematics, physical sciences, social sciences. *Creative arts/performance:* art/fine arts, journalism/publications, music, theater/drama. *Special achievements/activities:* cheerleading/drum major, community service, leadership. *Special characteristics:* adult students, first-generation college students, handicapped students, international students, members of minority groups. *Tuition waivers:* Full or partial for employees or children of employees, senior citizens.

LOANS *Student loans:* $17,949,844 (70% need-based, 30% non-need-based). 85% of past graduating class borrowed through all loan programs. *Average indebtedness per student:* $22,677. *Average need-based loan:* Freshmen: $3188. Undergraduates: $4103. *Parent loans:* $1,867,467 (39% need-based, 61% non-need-based). *Programs:* Federal Direct (Subsidized and Unsubsidized Stafford, PLUS), Perkins.

WORK-STUDY *Federal work-study:* Total amount: $197,428; 141 jobs averaging $2209. *State or other work-study/employment:* Total amount: $749,154 (17% need-based, 83% non-need-based). 372 part-time jobs averaging $1707.

ATHLETIC AWARDS Total amount: $752,554 (34% need-based, 66% non-need-based).

APPLYING FOR FINANCIAL AID *Required financial aid form:* FAFSA. *Financial aid deadline (priority):* 3/15. *Notification date:* Continuous beginning 4/20. Students must reply within 2 weeks of notification.

UNIVERSITY OF SOUTH CAROLINA BEAUFORT
Bluffton, SC

ABOUT THE INSTITUTION State-supported, coed. *Awards:* bachelor's degrees. 16 undergraduate majors. *Total enrollment:* 1,874. Undergraduates: 1,874.

GIFT AID (NEED-BASED) *Scholarships, grants, and awards:* Federal Pell, FSEOG, state, private, college/university gift aid from institutional funds.

LOANS *Programs:* Federal Direct (Subsidized and Unsubsidized Stafford, PLUS).

WORK-STUDY *Federal work-study:* Total amount: $34,044; 23 jobs averaging $2800. *State or other work-study/employment:* Total amount: $57,908 (100% non-need-based). Part-time jobs available.

APPLYING FOR FINANCIAL AID *Required financial aid form:* FAFSA.

CONTACT Jamella Taylor, Financial Aid Administrative Assistant, University of South Carolina Beaufort, 801 Carteret Street, Beaufort, SC 29902, 843-521-3104. *Fax:* 843-521-3194. *E-mail:* uscbfina@uscb.edu. *Website:* http://www.uscb.edu/.

UNIVERSITY OF SOUTH CAROLINA UPSTATE
Spartanburg, SC

Tuition & fees (SC res): $9892	Average undergraduate aid package: $9971

ABOUT THE INSTITUTION State-supported, coed. *Awards:* certificates, bachelor's, and master's degrees. 27 undergraduate majors. *Total enrollment:* 5,561. Undergraduates: 5,427. Freshmen: 805. Federal methodology is used as a basis for awarding need-based institutional aid.

UNDERGRADUATE EXPENSES for 2013–2014 *Application fee:* $40. *Tuition, state resident:* full-time $9442; part-time $403 per semester hour. *Tuition, nonresident:* full-time $19,164; part-time $815 per semester hour. *Required fees:* full-time $450; $165 per term. Full-time tuition and fees vary according to course load and program. Part-time tuition and fees vary according to course load and program. *College room and board:* $7250; *Room only:* $4450. Room and board charges vary according to board plan and housing facility.

FRESHMAN FINANCIAL AID (Fall 2012, est.) 714 applied for aid; of those 86% were deemed to have need. 100% of freshmen with need received aid; of those 13% had need fully met. *Average percent of need met:* 63% (excluding resources awarded to replace EFC). *Average financial aid package:* $11,180 (excluding resources awarded to replace EFC). 3% of all full-time freshmen had no need and received non-need-based gift aid.

UNDERGRADUATE FINANCIAL AID (Fall 2012, est.) 3,750 applied for aid; of those 89% were deemed to have need. 99% of undergraduates with need received aid; of those 11% had need fully met. *Average percent of need met:* 53% (excluding resources awarded to replace EFC). *Average financial aid package:* $9971 (excluding resources awarded to replace EFC). 2% of all full-time undergraduates had no need and received non-need-based gift aid.

GIFT AID (NEED-BASED) *Total amount:* $11,635,591 (90% federal, 10% state). *Receiving aid:* Freshmen: 52% (402); all full-time undergraduates: 52% (2,192). *Average award:* Freshmen: $5146; Undergraduates: $4736. *Scholarships, grants, and awards:* Federal Pell, FSEOG, state, private, college/university gift aid from institutional funds.

GIFT AID (NON-NEED-BASED) *Total amount:* $9,829,234 (88% state, 7% institutional, 5% external sources). *Receiving aid:* Freshmen: 71% (544). Undergraduates: 37% (1,546). *Average award:* Freshmen: $3585. Undergraduates: $5223. *Scholarships, grants, and awards by category: Academic interests/achievement:* 319 awards ($624,089 total): general academic interests/achievements. *Special characteristics:* 46 awards ($31,606 total): first-generation college students. *Tuition waivers:* Full or partial for senior citizens. *ROTC:* Army cooperative.

LOANS *Student loans:* $27,754,974 (45% need-based, 55% non-need-based). 68% of past graduating class borrowed through all loan programs. *Average indebtedness per student:* $25,301. *Average need-based loan:* Freshmen: $3287. Undergraduates: $4093. *Parent loans:* $1,851,752 (100% non-need-based). *Programs:* Perkins, state, private loans.

WORK-STUDY *Federal work-study:* Total amount: $167,348; 89 jobs averaging $1880. *State or other work-study/employment:* Total amount: $653,719 (100% non-need-based). 497 part-time jobs averaging $1318.

ATHLETIC AWARDS Total amount: $1,501,015 (100% non-need-based).

APPLYING FOR FINANCIAL AID *Required financial aid form:* FAFSA. *Financial aid deadline (priority):* 3/1. *Notification date:* Continuous beginning 4/1. Students must reply within 2 weeks of notification.

CONTACT Allison Sullivan, Director of Financial Aid, University of South Carolina Upstate, 800 University Way, Spartanburg, SC 29303, 864-503-5340 or toll-free 800-277-8727. *Fax:* 864-503-5974. *E-mail:* asullivan@uscupstate.edu. *Website:* http://www.uscupstate.edu/.

THE UNIVERSITY OF SOUTH DAKOTA
Vermillion, SD

Tuition & fees (SD res): $7704	Average undergraduate aid package: $6477

ABOUT THE INSTITUTION State-supported, coed. *Awards:* certificates, associate, bachelor's, master's, and doctoral degrees. 60 undergraduate majors. *Total enrollment:* 10,284. Undergraduates: 7,690. Freshmen: 1,353. Federal methodology is used as a basis for awarding need-based institutional aid.

UNDERGRADUATE EXPENSES for 2013–2014 *Application fee:* $20. *Tuition, state resident:* full-time $3897; part-time $129.30 per credit hour. *Tuition, nonresident:* full-time $5842; part-time $194.75 per credit hour. *Required fees:* full-time $3807; $126.90 per credit hour. Full-time tuition and fees vary according to course load. Part-time tuition and fees vary according to course load. *College room and board:* $6648; *Room only:* $3433. Room and board charges vary according to board plan and housing facility.

FRESHMAN FINANCIAL AID (Fall 2011) 1,015 applied for aid; of those 75% were deemed to have need. 90% of freshmen with need received aid; of those 55% had need fully met. *Average percent of need met:* 74% (excluding resources awarded to replace EFC). *Average financial aid package:* $5608 (excluding resources awarded to replace EFC). 24% of all full-time freshmen had no need and received non-need-based gift aid.

UNDERGRADUATE FINANCIAL AID (Fall 2011) 4,328 applied for aid; of those 80% were deemed to have need. 93% of undergraduates with need received aid; of those 55% had need fully met. *Average percent of need met:* 70% (excluding resources awarded to replace EFC). *Average financial aid package:* $6477 (excluding resources awarded to replace EFC). 17% of all full-time undergraduates had no need and received non-need-based gift aid.

GIFT AID (NEED-BASED) *Total amount:* $10,390,385 (100% federal). *Receiving aid:* Freshmen: 32% (361); all full-time undergraduates: 36% (1,831). *Average award:* Freshmen: $4136; Undergraduates: $4096. *Scholarships, grants, and awards:* Federal Pell, FSEOG, private, college/university gift aid from institutional funds, Federal Nursing.

GIFT AID (NON-NEED-BASED) *Total amount:* $8,073,677 (5% federal, 11% state, 46% institutional, 38% external sources). *Receiving aid:* Freshmen: 51% (573). Undergraduates: 35% (1,798). *Average award:* Freshmen: $4698. Undergraduates: $4483. *Scholarships, grants, and awards by category:* Academic interests/achievement: biological sciences, business, communication, computer science, education, English, foreign languages, general academic interests/achievements, humanities, mathematics, military science, premedicine, social sciences. Creative arts/performance: art/fine arts, creative writing, debating, music, theater/drama. Special achievements/activities: leadership. Special characteristics: members of minority groups. *Tuition waivers:* Full or partial for children of alumni, employees or children of employees, senior citizens. ROTC: Army.

LOANS *Student loans:* $33,847,210 (49% need-based, 51% non-need-based). 75% of past graduating class borrowed through all loan programs. *Average indebtedness per student:* $25,033. *Average need-based loan:* Freshmen: $3588. Undergraduates: $4138. *Parent loans:* $5,402,882 (100% non-need-based). *Programs:* Federal Direct (Subsidized and Unsubsidized Stafford, PLUS), Perkins, Federal Nursing, college/university.

WORK-STUDY *Federal work-study:* Total amount: $7,663,678; jobs available.

ATHLETIC AWARDS Total amount: $2,712,913 (100% non-need-based).

APPLYING FOR FINANCIAL AID *Required financial aid form:* FAFSA. *Financial aid deadline (priority):* 3/15. *Notification date:* Continuous beginning 3/1.

CONTACT Julie Pier, Director of Student Financial Aid, The University of South Dakota, Belbas Center, 414 East Clark Street, Vermillion, SD 57069, 605-677-5446 or toll-free 877-269-6837. *Fax:* 605-677-5238. *Website:* http://www.usd.edu/.

UNIVERSITY OF SOUTHERN CALIFORNIA
Los Angeles, CA

CONTACT Thomas McWhorter, Executive Director, University of Southern California, 700 Childs Way, Los Angeles, CA 90089-0914, 213-740-5445. *Fax:* 213-821-3796. *E-mail:* faodir@usc.edu. *Website:* http://www.usc.edu/.

UNIVERSITY OF SOUTHERN INDIANA
Evansville, IN

Tuition & fees (IN res): $6325	Average undergraduate aid package: $8289

ABOUT THE INSTITUTION State-supported, coed. *Awards:* certificates, associate, bachelor's, master's, and doctoral degrees. 56 undergraduate majors. *Total enrollment:* 10,467. Undergraduates: 9,502. Freshmen: 1,880. Federal methodology is used as a basis for awarding need-based institutional aid.

UNDERGRADUATE EXPENSES for 2013–2014 *Application fee:* $40. *One-time required fee:* $100. *Tuition, state resident:* full-time $6085; part-time $202.83 per credit hour. *Tuition, nonresident:* full-time $14,485; part-time $482.83 per credit hour. *Required fees:* full-time $240. Full-time tuition and fees vary according to course load, program, and reciprocity agreements. Part-time tuition and fees vary according to course load, program, and reciprocity agreements. *College room and board:* $7502; *Room only:* $4032. Room and board charges vary according to board plan and housing facility.

FRESHMAN FINANCIAL AID (Fall 2012, est.) 1,814 applied for aid; of those 69% were deemed to have need. 98% of freshmen with need received aid; of those 8% had need fully met. *Average percent of need met:* 60% (excluding resources awarded to replace EFC). *Average financial aid package:* $8226 (excluding resources awarded to replace EFC). 9% of all full-time freshmen had no need and received non-need-based gift aid.

UNDERGRADUATE FINANCIAL AID (Fall 2012, est.) 7,718 applied for aid; of those 65% were deemed to have need. 96% of undergraduates with need received aid; of those 6% had need fully met. *Average percent of need met:* 59% (excluding resources awarded to replace EFC). *Average financial aid package:* $8289 (excluding resources awarded to replace EFC). 9% of all full-time undergraduates had no need and received non-need-based gift aid.

GIFT AID (NEED-BASED) *Total amount:* $25,251,097 (51% federal, 32% state, 15% institutional, 2% external sources). *Receiving aid:* Freshmen: 52% (958); all full-time undergraduates: 15% (1,194). *Average award:* Freshmen: $5404; Undergraduates: $5073. *Scholarships, grants, and awards:* Federal Pell, FSEOG, state, private, college/university gift aid from institutional funds, Federal Nursing.

GIFT AID (NON-NEED-BASED) *Total amount:* $3,390,688 (79% institutional, 21% external sources). *Receiving aid:* Freshmen: 5% (88). Undergraduates: 3% (249). *Average award:* Freshmen: $2906. Undergraduates: $3008. *Scholarships, grants, and awards by category:* Academic interests/achievement: 1,992 awards ($1,419,725 total): biological sciences, business, education, engineering/technologies, general academic interests/achievements, health fields, humanities, mathematics, premedicine, social sciences. Creative arts/performance: 40 awards ($37,407 total): art/fine arts, creative writing, theater/drama. Special achievements/activities: leadership. Special characteristics: 263 awards ($879,829 total): children of faculty/staff, members of minority groups, out-of-state students, spouses of current students, veterans' children. *Tuition waivers:* Full or partial for employees or children of employees. *ROTC:* Army.

LOANS *Student loans:* $47,225,656 (73% need-based, 27% non-need-based). 56% of past graduating class borrowed through all loan programs. *Average indebtedness per student:* $19,429. *Average need-based loan:* Freshmen: $3578. Undergraduates: $4071. *Parent loans:* $3,048,046 (30% need-based, 70% non-need-based). *Programs:* Federal Direct (Subsidized and Unsubsidized Stafford, PLUS).

WORK-STUDY *Federal work-study:* Total amount: $137,309; 78 jobs averaging $2177.

ATHLETIC AWARDS Total amount: $1,063,537 (42% need-based, 58% non-need-based).

APPLYING FOR FINANCIAL AID *Required financial aid forms:* FAFSA, institution's own form. *Financial aid deadline:* 3/1. *Notification date:* Continuous beginning 4/1.

CONTACT Mary Harper, Financial Aid Office, University of Southern Indiana, 8600 University Boulevard, Evansville, IN 47712-3590, 812-464-1767 or toll-free 800-467-1965. *Fax:* 812-465-7154. *E-mail:* finaid@usi.edu. *Website:* http://www.usi.edu/.

UNIVERSITY OF SOUTHERN MAINE
Portland, ME

Tuition & fees (ME res): $8920	Average undergraduate aid package: $1080

ABOUT THE INSTITUTION State-supported, coed. *Awards:* certificates, bachelor's, master's, and doctoral degrees. 48 undergraduate majors. *Total enrollment:* 9,382. Undergraduates: 7,407. Freshmen: 865. Federal methodology is used as a basis for awarding need-based institutional aid.

UNDERGRADUATE EXPENSES for 2013–2014 *Application fee:* $40. *Tuition, state resident:* full-time $7590; part-time $253 per credit hour. *Tuition, nonresident:* full-time $19,950; part-time $665 per credit hour. *Required fees:* full-time $1330. Full-time tuition and fees vary according to course load, degree level, and reciprocity agreements. Part-time tuition and fees vary according to course load, degree level, and reciprocity agreements. *College room and board:* $9130; *Room only:* $4978. Room and board charges vary according to board plan, housing facility, and location.

FRESHMAN FINANCIAL AID (Fall 2011) 614 applied for aid; of those 88% were deemed to have need. 97% of freshmen with need received aid; of those 7% had need fully met. *Average percent of need met:* 51% (excluding resources awarded to replace EFC). *Average financial aid package:* $9120 (excluding resources awarded to replace EFC). 5% of all full-time freshmen had no need and received non-need-based gift aid.

UNDERGRADUATE FINANCIAL AID (Fall 2011) 3,899 applied for aid; of those 91% were deemed to have need. 97% of undergraduates with need received aid; of those 6% had need fully met. *Average percent of need met:* 51% (excluding resources awarded to replace EFC). *Average financial aid package:* $1080 (excluding resources awarded to replace EFC). 3% of all full-time undergraduates had no need and received non-need-based gift aid.

GIFT AID (NEED-BASED) *Total amount:* $19,459,426 (62% federal, 11% state, 16% institutional, 11% external sources). *Receiving aid:* Freshmen: 61% (404); all full-time undergraduates: 60% (2,684). *Average award:* Freshmen: $4921; Undergraduates: $5008. *Scholarships, grants, and awards:* Federal Pell, FSEOG, state, private, college/university gift aid from institutional funds.

GIFT AID (NON-NEED-BASED) *Total amount:* $691,252 (1% state, 43% institutional, 56% external sources). *Receiving aid:* Freshmen: 33% (221). Undergraduates: 20% (912). *Average award:* Freshmen: $3315. Undergraduates: $4070. *Scholarships, grants, and awards by category:* Academic interests/achievement: general academic interests/achievements. *Creative arts/performance:* music, theater/drama. *Special achievements/activities:* community service. *Special characteristics:* children and siblings of alumni, children of faculty/staff, first-generation college students, general special characteristics, local/state students, out-of-state students. *ROTC:* Army cooperative, Air Force cooperative.

LOANS *Student loans:* $38,785,606 (84% need-based, 16% non-need-based). 74% of past graduating class borrowed through all loan programs. *Average need-based loan:* Freshmen: $6326. Undergraduates: $8331. *Parent loans:* $4,472,939 (48% need-based, 52% non-need-based). *Programs:* Federal Direct (Subsidized and Unsubsidized Stafford, PLUS), Perkins, Federal Nursing.

WORK-STUDY *Federal work-study:* Total amount: $3,579,197; jobs available.

APPLYING FOR FINANCIAL AID *Required financial aid form:* FAFSA. *Financial aid deadline (priority):* 2/15. *Notification date:* Continuous beginning 3/15.

CONTACT Mr. Keith P. Dubois, Director of Financial Aid, University of Southern Maine, 37 College Avenue, Gorham, ME 04038, 207-780-5122 or toll-free 800-800-4USM Ext. 5670. *Fax:* 207-780-5143. *E-mail:* dubois@usm.maine.edu. *Website:* http://www.usm.maine.edu/.

UNIVERSITY OF SOUTHERN MISSISSIPPI
Hattiesburg, MS

Tuition & fees (MS res): $6336	Average undergraduate aid package: $9173

ABOUT THE INSTITUTION State-supported, coed. *Awards:* certificates, bachelor's, master's, and doctoral degrees. 65 undergraduate majors. *Total enrollment:* 16,468. Undergraduates: 13,658. Freshmen: 1,945. Federal methodology is used as a basis for awarding need-based institutional aid.

UNDERGRADUATE EXPENSES for 2013–2014 *Application fee:* $35. *Tuition, state resident:* full-time $6336; part-time $264 per credit hour. *Tuition, nonresident:* full-time $14,448; part-time $602 per credit hour. Part-time tuition and fees vary according to course load and degree level. *College room and board:* $6907. Room and board charges vary according to board plan and housing facility.

FRESHMAN FINANCIAL AID (Fall 2011) 1,594 applied for aid; of those 83% were deemed to have need. 98% of freshmen with need received aid; of those 32% had need fully met. *Average percent of need met:* 75% (excluding resources awarded to replace EFC). *Average financial aid package:* $10,446 (excluding resources awarded to replace EFC). 12% of all full-time freshmen had no need and received non-need-based gift aid.

UNDERGRADUATE FINANCIAL AID (Fall 2011) 9,578 applied for aid; of those 89% were deemed to have need. 97% of undergraduates with need received aid; of those 21% had need fully met. *Average percent of need met:* 70% (excluding resources awarded to replace EFC). *Average financial aid package:* $9173 (excluding resources awarded to replace EFC). 6% of all full-time undergraduates had no need and received non-need-based gift aid.

GIFT AID (NEED-BASED) *Total amount:* $35,248,891 (79% federal, 5% state, 13% institutional, 3% external sources). *Receiving aid:* Freshmen: 53% (893); all full-time undergraduates: 52% (5,920). *Average award:* Freshmen: $4505; Undergraduates: $4431. *Scholarships, grants, and awards:* Federal Pell, FSEOG, state, private, college/university gift aid from institutional funds.

GIFT AID (NON-NEED-BASED) *Total amount:* $17,299,427 (17% federal, 17% state, 60% institutional, 6% external sources). *Receiving aid:* Freshmen: 50% (841). Undergraduates: 36% (4,086). *Average award:* Freshmen: $5568. Undergraduates: $4425. *Scholarships, grants, and awards by category:* Academic interests/achievement: general academic interests/achievements. *Creative arts/performance:* art/fine arts, dance, music, theater/drama. *Special achievements/activities:* cheerleading/drum major, leadership. *Special characteristics:* children and siblings of alumni, children of faculty/staff, ethnic background, local/state students, out-of-state students, veterans. *Tuition waivers:* Full or partial for children of alumni, employees or children of employees, senior citizens. *ROTC:* Army cooperative, Air Force.

LOANS *Student loans:* $67,489,945 (46% need-based, 54% non-need-based). 62% of past graduating class borrowed through all loan programs. *Average indebtedness per student:* $29,502. *Average need-based loan:* Freshmen: $3552. Undergraduates: $4306. *Parent loans:* $6,308,102 (47% need-based, 53% non-need-based). *Programs:* Federal Direct (Subsidized and Unsubsidized Stafford, PLUS).

WORK-STUDY *Federal work-study:* Total amount: $432,032; jobs available.

ATHLETIC AWARDS Total amount: $3,717,219 (39% need-based, 61% non-need-based).

APPLYING FOR FINANCIAL AID *Required financial aid forms:* FAFSA, institution's own form. *Financial aid deadline (priority):* 3/15. *Notification date:* Continuous. Students must reply within 2 weeks of notification.

CONTACT Mr. David Williamson, Interim Director of Financial Aid, University of Southern Mississippi, 118 College Drive #5101, Hattiesburg, MS 39406-0001, 601-266-4774. *Fax:* 601-266-5769. *E-mail:* financial.aid@usm.edu. *Website:* http://www.usm.edu/.

UNIVERSITY OF SOUTH FLORIDA
Tampa, FL

ABOUT THE INSTITUTION State-supported, coed. **Awards:** associate, bachelor's, master's, and doctoral degrees. 85 undergraduate majors. **Total enrollment:** 40,111. Undergraduates: 29,289. Freshmen: 3,750.

GIFT AID (NEED-BASED) Scholarships, grants, and awards: Federal Pell, FSEOG, state, private, college/university gift aid from institutional funds.

GIFT AID (NON-NEED-BASED) Scholarships, grants, and awards by category: Academic interests/achievement: architecture, biological sciences, business, communication, computer science, education, engineering/technologies, English, foreign languages, general academic interests/achievements, health fields, humanities, international studies, library science, mathematics, military science, physical sciences, premedicine, religion/biblical studies, social sciences. Creative arts/performance: applied art and design, art/fine arts, cinema/film/broadcasting, creative writing, dance, debating, journalism/publications, music, performing arts, theater/drama. Special achievements/activities: general special achievements/activities. Special characteristics: general special characteristics.

LOANS Programs: Federal Direct (Subsidized and Unsubsidized Stafford, PLUS), Perkins, college/university.

APPLYING FOR FINANCIAL AID Required financial aid form: FAFSA.

CONTACT Ms. Billie Jo Hamilton, Director of Student Financial Aid, University of South Florida, 4202 East Fowler Avenue, SVC 1102, Tampa, FL 33620-6960, 813-974-4700. Fax: 813-974-5144. E-mail: bjhamilton@admin.usf.edu. Website: http://www.usf.edu/.

UNIVERSITY OF SOUTH FLORIDA–ST. PETERSBURG CAMPUS
St. Petersburg, FL

CONTACT Financial Aid Office, University of South Florida–St. Petersburg Campus, 140 Seventh Ave S., St. Petersburg, FL 33701, 727-873-4873. Website: http://www.stpt.usf.edu/.

UNIVERSITY OF SOUTH FLORIDA SARASOTA-MANATEE
Sarasota, FL

CONTACT Financial Aid Office, University of South Florida Sarasota-Manatee, 8350 N Tamiami Trail, Sarasota, FL 34243, 941-359-4200. Website: http://www.sarasota.usf.edu/.

THE UNIVERSITY OF TAMPA
Tampa, FL

Tuition & fees: $25,222	Average undergraduate aid package: $15,742

ABOUT THE INSTITUTION Independent, coed. **Awards:** certificates, associate, bachelor's, and master's degrees. 49 undergraduate majors. **Total enrollment:** 6,912. Undergraduates: 6,143. Freshmen: 1,517. Federal methodology is used as a basis for awarding need-based institutional aid.

UNDERGRADUATE EXPENSES for 2013–2014 Application fee: $40. **One-time required fee:** $85. **Comprehensive fee:** $34,338 includes full-time tuition ($23,520), mandatory fees ($1702), and room and board ($9116). **College room only:** $4852. Full-time tuition and fees vary according to class time. Room and board charges vary according to board plan and housing facility. **Part-time tuition:** $500 per credit hour. **Part-time fees:** $40 per term. Part-time tuition and fees vary according to class time.

FRESHMAN FINANCIAL AID (Fall 2012, est.) 1,215 applied for aid; of those 77% were deemed to have need. 100% of freshmen with need received aid; of those 19% had need fully met. **Average percent of need met:** 62% (excluding resources awarded to replace EFC). **Average financial aid package:** $15,512 (excluding resources awarded to replace EFC). 31% of all full-time freshmen had no need and received non-need-based gift aid.

UNDERGRADUATE FINANCIAL AID (Fall 2012, est.) 4,384 applied for aid; of those 81% were deemed to have need. 100% of undergraduates with need received aid; of those 19% had need fully met. **Average percent of need met:** 61% (excluding resources awarded to replace EFC). **Average financial aid package:** $15,742 (excluding resources awarded to replace EFC). 31% of all full-time undergraduates had no need and received non-need-based gift aid.

GIFT AID (NEED-BASED) Total amount: $41,156,058 (16% federal, 10% state, 72% institutional, 2% external sources). **Receiving aid:** Freshmen: 47% (708); all full-time undergraduates: 54% (3,156). **Average award:** Undergraduates: $12,880. **Scholarships, grants, and awards:** Federal Pell, FSEOG, state, private, college/university gift aid from institutional funds.

GIFT AID (NON-NEED-BASED) Total amount: $5,925,679 (19% state, 80% institutional, 1% external sources). **Receiving aid:** Freshmen: 62% (935). Undergraduates: 60% (3,497). **Average award:** Freshmen: $7284. Undergraduates: $6487. **Scholarships, grants, and awards by category:** Academic interests/achievement: 4,696 awards ($28,419,518 total): biological sciences, English, general academic interests/achievements, international studies, military science, social sciences. Creative arts/performance: 180 awards ($322,700 total): art/fine arts, creative writing, journalism/publications, music, performing arts, theater/drama. Special achievements/activities: 168 awards ($188,000 total): general special achievements/activities, leadership, memberships. Special characteristics: 400 awards ($2,211,356 total): children and siblings of alumni, children of faculty/staff, international students, veterans. Tuition waivers: Full or partial for employees or children of employees. ROTC: Army, Naval cooperative, Air Force cooperative.

LOANS Student loans: $6,088,608 (43% need-based, 57% non-need-based). 59% of past graduating class borrowed through all loan programs. Average indebtedness per student: $31,032. **Average need-based loan:** Freshmen: $3285. Undergraduates: $4315. **Parent loans:** $16,560,120 (82% need-based, 18% non-need-based). **Programs:** Federal Direct (Subsidized and Unsubsidized Stafford, PLUS), Perkins, college/university.

WORK-STUDY Federal work-study: Total amount: $588,763; 358 jobs averaging $2000. **State or other work-study/employment:** Total amount: $4000 (100% need-based). 2 part-time jobs averaging $2000.

ATHLETIC AWARDS Total amount: $1,562,456 (81% need-based, 19% non-need-based).

APPLYING FOR FINANCIAL AID Required financial aid form: FAFSA. **Financial aid deadline:** Continuous. **Notification date:** Continuous beginning 2/1. Students must reply by 5/1.

CONTACT Office of Financial Aid, The University of Tampa, 401 West Kennedy Boulevard, Box E, Tampa, FL 33606-1490, 813-253-6219 or toll-free 888-646-2738 (in-state), 888-MINARET (out-of-state). Fax: 813-258-7439. E-mail: finaid@ut.edu. Website: http://www.ut.edu/.

THE UNIVERSITY OF TENNESSEE
Knoxville, TN

Tuition & fees (TN res): $9092	Average undergraduate aid package: $11,410

ABOUT THE INSTITUTION State-supported, coed. **Awards:** certificates, bachelor's, master's, and doctoral degrees. 76 undergraduate majors. **Total enrollment:** 29,833. Undergraduates: 20,916. Freshmen: 4,207. Federal methodology is used as a basis for awarding need-based institutional aid.

UNDERGRADUATE EXPENSES for 2013–2014 Application fee: $40. **Tuition, state resident:** full-time $7802; part-time $326 per hour. **Tuition, non-resident:** full-time $25,992; part-time $1085 per hour. **Required fees:** full-time $1290; $62 per hour. Full-time tuition and fees vary according to course level, program, and reciprocity agreements. Part-time tuition and fees vary according to course level, program, and reciprocity agreements. **College room and board:** $8752. Room and board charges vary according to board plan and housing facility.

FRESHMAN FINANCIAL AID (Fall 2012, est.) 4,035 applied for aid; of those 63% were deemed to have need. 100% of freshmen with need received aid; of those 27% had need fully met. **Average percent of need met:** 71% (excluding resources awarded to replace EFC). **Average financial aid package:** $12,866 (excluding

resources awarded to replace EFC). 17% of all full-time freshmen had no need and received non-need-based gift aid.

UNDERGRADUATE FINANCIAL AID (Fall 2012, est.) 17,489 applied for aid; of those 66% were deemed to have need. 100% of undergraduates with need received aid; of those 21% had need fully met. *Average percent of need met:* 62% (excluding resources awarded to replace EFC). *Average financial aid package:* $11,410 (excluding resources awarded to replace EFC). 13% of all full-time undergraduates had no need and received non-need-based gift aid.

GIFT AID (NEED-BASED) *Total amount:* $115,033,764 (23% federal, 49% state, 25% institutional, 3% external sources). *Receiving aid:* Freshmen: 59% (2,478); all full-time undergraduates: 54% (10,392). *Average award:* Freshmen: $10,391; Undergraduates: $8182. *Scholarships, grants, and awards:* Federal Pell, FSEOG, state, private, college/university gift aid from institutional funds.

GIFT AID (NON-NEED-BASED) *Average award:* Freshmen: $2783. Undergraduates: $2200. *Scholarships, grants, and awards by category: Academic interests/achievement:* 1,589 awards ($4,105,297 total): agriculture, architecture, business, communication, computer science, education, engineering/technologies, general academic interests/achievements, health fields, humanities, international studies, library science, military science, social sciences. *Creative arts/performance:* 174 awards ($410,750 total): art/fine arts. *Tuition waivers:* Full or partial for employees or children of employees, senior citizens. *ROTC:* Army, Air Force.

LOANS *Student loans:* $67,902,815 (89% need-based, 11% non-need-based). 49% of past graduating class borrowed through all loan programs. *Average indebtedness per student:* $22,860. *Average need-based loan:* Freshmen: $4654. Undergraduates: $6187. *Parent loans:* $12,801,951 (100% need-based). *Programs:* Federal Direct (Subsidized and Unsubsidized Stafford, PLUS), Perkins, state, college/university.

WORK-STUDY *Federal work-study:* Total amount: $1,083,360; 414 jobs averaging $2568.

ATHLETIC AWARDS Total amount: $8,939,928 (100% need-based).

APPLYING FOR FINANCIAL AID *Required financial aid forms:* FAFSA, scholarship application form. *Financial aid deadline (priority):* 2/15. *Notification date:* Continuous beginning 3/15. Students must reply within 3 weeks of notification.

CONTACT Office of Financial Aid and Scholarships, The University of Tennessee, 115 Student Services Building, Knoxville, TN 37996-0210, 865-974-3131. *Fax:* 865-974-2175. *E-mail:* finaid@utk.edu. *Website:* http://www.utk.edu/.

time undergraduates: 53% (4,684). *Average award:* Freshmen: $8649; Undergraduates: $7477. *Scholarships, grants, and awards:* Federal Pell, FSEOG, state, private, college/university gift aid from institutional funds.

GIFT AID (NON-NEED-BASED) *Total amount:* $15,334,768 (67% state, 28% institutional, 5% external sources). *Receiving aid:* Freshmen: 2% (51). Undergraduates: 2% (189). *Average award:* Freshmen: $3575. Undergraduates: $3484. *Scholarships, grants, and awards by category: Academic interests/achievement:* biological sciences, business, communication, education, engineering/technologies, English, general academic interests/achievements, home economics, mathematics, military science, physical sciences. *Creative arts/performance:* art/fine arts, cinema/film/broadcasting, journalism/publications, music, performing arts, theater/drama. *Special achievements/activities:* cheerleading/drum major, community service, memberships, religious involvement. *Special characteristics:* children and siblings of alumni, children of faculty/staff, children of union members/company employees, children with a deceased or disabled parent, ethnic background, handicapped students, religious affiliation. *Tuition waivers:* Full or partial for employees or children of employees, senior citizens. *ROTC:* Army.

LOANS *Student loans:* $47,728,245 (63% need-based, 37% non-need-based). 54% of past graduating class borrowed through all loan programs. *Average indebtedness per student:* $19,836. *Average need-based loan:* Freshmen: $3480. Undergraduates: $4367. *Parent loans:* $2,637,435 (30% need-based, 70% non-need-based). *Programs:* Federal Direct (Subsidized and Unsubsidized Stafford, PLUS), Perkins, private loans.

WORK-STUDY *Federal work-study:* Total amount: $357,606; jobs available. *State or other work-study/employment:* Total amount: $304,501 (9% need-based, 91% non-need-based). Part-time jobs available.

ATHLETIC AWARDS Total amount: $4,122,131 (43% need-based, 57% non-need-based).

APPLYING FOR FINANCIAL AID *Required financial aid forms:* FAFSA, institutional scholarship application form. *Financial aid deadline (priority):* 5/1. *Notification date:* Continuous beginning 3/1. Students must reply within 4 weeks of notification.

CONTACT Dianne Cox, Director of Financial Aid, The University of Tennessee at Chattanooga, 615 McCallie Avenue, Chattanooga, TN 37403-2598, 423-425-4677 or toll-free 800-UTC-MOCS (in-state), 800-UTC.MOCS (out-of-state). *Fax:* 423-425-2292. *E-mail:* dianne-cox@utc.edu. *Website:* http://www.utc.edu/.

THE UNIVERSITY OF TENNESSEE AT CHATTANOOGA
Chattanooga, TN

Tuition & fees (TN res): $7212	Average undergraduate aid package: $7728

ABOUT THE INSTITUTION State-supported, coed. *Awards:* certificates, bachelor's, master's, and doctoral degrees. 47 undergraduate majors. *Total enrollment:* 11,660. Undergraduates: 10,159. Freshmen: 2,290. Federal methodology is used as a basis for awarding need-based institutional aid.

UNDERGRADUATE EXPENSES for 2013–2014 *Application fee:* $30. *Tuition, state resident:* full-time $5722; part-time $238 per credit hour. *Tuition, nonresident:* full-time $20,068; part-time $836 per credit hour. *Required fees:* full-time $1490; $190 per credit hour. *College room and board:* $8300. Room and board charges vary according to board plan and housing facility.

FRESHMAN FINANCIAL AID (Fall 2012, est.) 2,215 applied for aid; of those 66% were deemed to have need. 99% of freshmen with need received aid; of those 25% had need fully met. *Average percent of need met:* 86% (excluding resources awarded to replace EFC). *Average financial aid package:* $8631 (excluding resources awarded to replace EFC). 1% of all full-time freshmen had no need and received non-need-based gift aid.

UNDERGRADUATE FINANCIAL AID (Fall 2012, est.) 8,869 applied for aid; of those 62% were deemed to have need. 98% of undergraduates with need received aid; of those 21% had need fully met. *Average percent of need met:* 79% (excluding resources awarded to replace EFC). *Average financial aid package:* $7728 (excluding resources awarded to replace EFC). 1% of all full-time undergraduates had no need and received non-need-based gift aid.

GIFT AID (NEED-BASED) *Total amount:* $30,109,969 (51% federal, 41% state, 7% institutional, 1% external sources). *Receiving aid:* Freshmen: 61% (1,394); all full-

THE UNIVERSITY OF TENNESSEE AT MARTIN
Martin, TN

Tuition & fees (TN res): $7049	Average undergraduate aid package: $12,615

ABOUT THE INSTITUTION State-supported, coed. *Awards:* bachelor's and master's degrees. 85 undergraduate majors. *Total enrollment:* 7,751. Undergraduates: 7,326. Freshmen: 1,320. Federal methodology is used as a basis for awarding need-based institutional aid.

UNDERGRADUATE EXPENSES for 2013–2014 *Application fee:* $30. *Tuition, state resident:* full-time $5978; part-time $249 per credit hour. *Tuition, nonresident:* full-time $19,134; part-time $798 per credit hour. *Required fees:* full-time $1071; $46 per credit hour. Part-time tuition and fees vary according to course load. *College room and board:* $5593; *Room only:* $2720. Room and board charges vary according to board plan and housing facility.

FRESHMAN FINANCIAL AID (Fall 2012, est.) 1,080 applied for aid; of those 78% were deemed to have need. 85% of freshmen with need received aid; of those 27% had need fully met. *Average percent of need met:* 79% (excluding resources awarded to replace EFC). *Average financial aid package:* $12,826 (excluding resources awarded to replace EFC). 12% of all full-time freshmen had no need and received non-need-based gift aid.

UNDERGRADUATE FINANCIAL AID (Fall 2012, est.) 4,890 applied for aid; of those 74% were deemed to have need. 89% of undergraduates with need received aid; of those 20% had need fully met. *Average percent of need met:* 71% (excluding resources awarded to replace EFC). *Average financial aid package:* $12,615 (excluding resources awarded to replace EFC). 10% of all full-time undergraduates had no need and received non-need-based gift aid.

GIFT AID (NEED-BASED) *Total amount:* $20,831,872 (78% federal, 20% state, 2% institutional). *Receiving aid:* Freshmen: 38% (496); all full-time undergraduates: 37% (2,262). *Average award:* Freshmen: $6579; Undergraduates: $5966. *Scholarships, grants, and awards:* Federal Pell, FSEOG, state, private, college/university gift aid from institutional funds.

GIFT AID (NON-NEED-BASED) *Total amount:* $16,312,628 (71% state, 20% institutional, 9% external sources). *Receiving aid:* Freshmen: 34% (437). Undergraduates: 25% (1,563). *Average award:* Freshmen: $6884. Undergraduates: $6323. *Scholarships, grants, and awards by category:* Academic interests/achievement: 735 awards ($1,339,064 total): agriculture, biological sciences, business, communication, computer science, education, engineering/technologies, English, general academic interests/achievements, health fields, home economics, humanities, mathematics, military science, physical sciences, premedicine, social sciences. *Creative arts/performance:* 150 awards ($119,750 total): art/fine arts, journalism/publications, music, theater/drama. *Special achievements/activities:* 158 awards ($198,545 total): cheerleading/drum major, general special achievements/activities, leadership, rodeo. *Special characteristics:* 1,834 awards ($2,594,416 total): adult students, children and siblings of alumni, children of educators, children of faculty/staff, children of union members/company employees, ethnic background, handicapped students, members of minority groups, out-of-state students. *Tuition waivers:* Full or partial for employees or children of employees, senior citizens. *ROTC:* Army.

LOANS *Student loans:* $29,106,485 (50% need-based, 50% non-need-based). 65% of past graduating class borrowed through all loan programs. *Average indebtedness per student:* $12,436. *Average need-based loan:* Freshmen: $3232. Undergraduates: $4212. *Parent loans:* $1,228,536 (100% non-need-based). *Programs:* Federal Direct (Subsidized and Unsubsidized Stafford, PLUS), Perkins.

WORK-STUDY *Federal work-study:* Total amount: $648,689; 286 jobs averaging $2500.

ATHLETIC AWARDS Total amount: $3,618,976 (100% non-need-based).

APPLYING FOR FINANCIAL AID *Required financial aid form:* FAFSA. *Financial aid deadline (priority):* 2/15. *Notification date:* Continuous beginning 4/1. Students must reply within 2 weeks of notification.

CONTACT Sheryl L. Frazier, Interim Director of Student Financial Assistance, The University of Tennessee at Martin, 205 Administration Building, Martin, TN 38238-1000, 731-881-7040 or toll-free 800-829-8861. *Fax:* 731-881-7036. *E-mail:* sfrazier@utm.edu.

Website: http://www.utm.edu/.

GIFT AID (NEED-BASED) *Total amount:* $96,769,556 (44% federal, 18% state, 33% institutional, 5% external sources). *Receiving aid:* Freshmen: 53% (1,284); all full-time undergraduates: 55% (8,885). *Average award:* Freshmen: $7219; Undergraduates: $6907. *Scholarships, grants, and awards:* Federal Pell, FSEOG, state, private, college/university gift aid from institutional funds, United Negro College Fund.

GIFT AID (NON-NEED-BASED) *Total amount:* $4,799,619 (5% state, 82% institutional, 13% external sources). *Receiving aid:* Freshmen: 36% (876). Undergraduates: 20% (3,304). *Average award:* Freshmen: $5413. Undergraduates: $5179. *Scholarships, grants, and awards by category:* Academic interests/achievement: 3,342 awards ($15,291,971 total): architecture, biological sciences, business, communication, computer science, education, engineering/technologies, English, foreign languages, general academic interests/achievements, health fields, humanities, international studies, mathematics, military science, physical sciences, social sciences. *Creative arts/performance:* journalism/publications, music, theater/drama. *Special achievements/activities:* cheerleading/drum major, community service, general special achievements/activities, leadership. *Special characteristics:* children with a deceased or disabled parent, first-generation college students, general special characteristics, handicapped students, public servants. *Tuition waivers:* Full or partial for employees or children of employees. *ROTC:* Army, Air Force cooperative.

LOANS *Student loans:* $103,800,635 (83% need-based, 17% non-need-based). 63% of past graduating class borrowed through all loan programs. *Average indebtedness per student:* $22,137. *Average need-based loan:* Freshmen: $3286. Undergraduates: $4244. *Parent loans:* $2,979,450 (41% need-based, 59% non-need-based). *Programs:* Federal Direct (Subsidized and Unsubsidized Stafford, PLUS), Perkins, state.

WORK-STUDY *Federal work-study:* Total amount: $5,451,018; 1,605 jobs averaging $2926. *State or other work-study/employment:* Total amount: $270,022 (100% need-based). 272 part-time jobs averaging $982.

ATHLETIC AWARDS Total amount: $2,350,660 (90% need-based, 10% non-need-based).

APPLYING FOR FINANCIAL AID *Required financial aid form:* FAFSA. *Financial aid deadline (priority):* 4/1. *Notification date:* Continuous beginning 4/1. Students must reply within 3 weeks of notification.

CONTACT Karen Krause, Director of Financial Aid, The University of Texas at Arlington, UTA Box 19199, Arlington, TX 76019, 817-272-3561. *Fax:* 817-272-3555. *E-mail:* kkrause@uta.edu.

Website: http://www.uta.edu/.

THE UNIVERSITY OF TEXAS AT ARLINGTON
Arlington, TX

Tuition & fees (TX res): $8878	Average undergraduate aid package: $12,673

ABOUT THE INSTITUTION State-supported, coed. *Awards:* certificates, bachelor's, master's, and doctoral degrees. 64 undergraduate majors. *Total enrollment:* 33,239. Undergraduates: 25,761. Freshmen: 2,473. Federal methodology is used as a basis for awarding need-based institutional aid.

UNDERGRADUATE EXPENSES for 2013–2014 *Application fee:* $50. *Tuition, state resident:* full-time $8878. *Tuition, nonresident:* full-time $19,408. Full-time tuition and fees vary according to course level, course load, and program. Part-time tuition and fees vary according to course level, course load, and program. *College room and board:* $7708; *Room only:* $4028. Room and board charges vary according to board plan and housing facility.

FRESHMAN FINANCIAL AID (Fall 2012, est.) 1,949 applied for aid; of those 86% were deemed to have need. 100% of freshmen with need received aid; of those 21% had need fully met. *Average percent of need met:* 76% (excluding resources awarded to replace EFC). *Average financial aid package:* $12,058 (excluding resources awarded to replace EFC). 5% of all full-time freshmen had no need and received non-need-based gift aid.

UNDERGRADUATE FINANCIAL AID (Fall 2012, est.) 12,158 applied for aid; of those 91% were deemed to have need. 100% of undergraduates with need received aid; of those 11% had need fully met. *Average percent of need met:* 77% (excluding resources awarded to replace EFC). *Average financial aid package:* $12,673 (excluding resources awarded to replace EFC). 1% of all full-time undergraduates had no need and received non-need-based gift aid.

THE UNIVERSITY OF TEXAS AT AUSTIN
Austin, TX

Tuition & fees (TX res): $9792	Average undergraduate aid package: $12,333

ABOUT THE INSTITUTION State-supported, coed. *Awards:* certificates, bachelor's, master's, and doctoral degrees. 100 undergraduate majors. *Total enrollment:* 52,186. Undergraduates: 39,955. Freshmen: 8,092. Federal methodology is used as a basis for awarding need-based institutional aid.

UNDERGRADUATE EXPENSES for 2013–2014 *Application fee:* $75. *Tuition, state resident:* full-time $9792. *Tuition, nonresident:* full-time $33,060. Full-time tuition and fees vary according to course load and program. Part-time tuition and fees vary according to course load and program. *College room and board:* $10,946. Room and board charges vary according to housing facility.

FRESHMAN FINANCIAL AID (Fall 2012, est.) 6,126 applied for aid; of those 63% were deemed to have need. 100% of freshmen with need received aid; of those 32% had need fully met. *Average percent of need met:* 78% (excluding resources awarded to replace EFC). *Average financial aid package:* $13,669 (excluding resources awarded to replace EFC). 1% of all full-time freshmen had no need and received non-need-based gift aid.

UNDERGRADUATE FINANCIAL AID (Fall 2012, est.) 22,837 applied for aid; of those 73% were deemed to have need. 100% of undergraduates with need received aid; of those 20% had need fully met. *Average percent of need met:* 66% (excluding resources awarded to replace EFC). *Average financial aid package:* $12,333 (excluding resources awarded to replace EFC). 1% of all full-time undergraduates had no need and received non-need-based gift aid.

GIFT AID (NEED-BASED) *Total amount:* $143,547,206 (33% federal, 22% state, 37% institutional, 8% external sources). *Receiving aid:* Freshmen: 45% (3,615); all full-time undergraduates: 37% (13,425). *Average award:* Freshmen: $9204; Undergraduates: $8690. *Scholarships, grants, and awards:* Federal Pell, FSEOG, state, private, college/university gift aid from institutional funds.

GIFT AID (NON-NEED-BASED) *Total amount:* $5,928,886 (33% institutional, 67% external sources). *Receiving aid:* Freshmen: 24% (1,902). Undergraduates: 12% (4,443). *Average award:* Freshmen: $6031. Undergraduates: $4306. *Scholarships, grants, and awards by category: Academic interests/achievement:* general academic interests/achievements. *Creative arts/performance:* art/fine arts, general creative arts/performance. *Special achievements/activities:* leadership. *Special characteristics:* local/state students. *Tuition waivers:* Full or partial for employees or children of employees, senior citizens. *ROTC:* Army, Naval, Air Force.

LOANS *Student loans:* $118,913,380 (76% need-based, 24% non-need-based). 50% of past graduating class borrowed through all loan programs. *Average indebtedness per student:* $26,097. *Average need-based loan:* Freshmen: $3601. Undergraduates: $4765. *Parent loans:* $74,974,539 (28% need-based, 72% non-need-based). *Programs:* Federal Direct (Subsidized and Unsubsidized Stafford, PLUS), Perkins, state.

WORK-STUDY *Federal work-study:* Total amount: $3,414,316; jobs available. *State or other work-study/employment:* Part-time jobs available.

APPLYING FOR FINANCIAL AID *Required financial aid forms:* FAFSA, institution's own form. *Financial aid deadline:* Continuous. *Notification date:* Continuous beginning 3/15. Students must reply by 5/1 or within 3 weeks of notification.

CONTACT Tom Melecki, PhD, Director of Student Financial Services, The University of Texas at Austin, PO Box 7758, Student Services Building, Suite 3.214, Austin, TX 78713-7758, 512-475-6203. *Fax:* 512-475-6349. *E-mail:* ask@finaid.utexas.edu. *Website:* http://www.utexas.edu/.

THE UNIVERSITY OF TEXAS AT BROWNSVILLE
Brownsville, TX

Tuition & fees (TX res): $5116	Average undergraduate aid package: $7891

ABOUT THE INSTITUTION State-supported, coed. *Awards:* certificates, associate, bachelor's, master's, and doctoral degrees. 37 undergraduate majors. *Total enrollment:* 13,713. Undergraduates: 12,547. Federal methodology is used as a basis for awarding need-based institutional aid.

UNDERGRADUATE EXPENSES for 2013–2014 *Tuition, state resident:* full-time $3743; part-time $155.95 per credit hour. *Tuition, nonresident:* full-time $12,167; part-time $506.95 per credit hour. *Required fees:* full-time $1373; $469.12 per term. Full-time tuition and fees vary according to class time, course level, course load, location, and program. Part-time tuition and fees vary according to class time, course level, course load, location, and program. *College room and board:* $6602. Room and board charges vary according to board plan.

FRESHMAN FINANCIAL AID (Fall 2012, est.) 1,263 applied for aid; of those 96% were deemed to have need. 99% of freshmen with need received aid. *Average percent of need met:* 49% (excluding resources awarded to replace EFC). *Average financial aid package:* $6967 (excluding resources awarded to replace EFC). 1% of all full-time freshmen had no need and received non-need-based gift aid.

UNDERGRADUATE FINANCIAL AID (Fall 2012, est.) 4,229 applied for aid; of those 95% were deemed to have need. 99% of undergraduates with need received aid. *Average percent of need met:* 44% (excluding resources awarded to replace EFC). *Average financial aid package:* $7891 (excluding resources awarded to replace EFC). 1% of all full-time undergraduates had no need and received non-need-based gift aid.

GIFT AID (NEED-BASED) *Total amount:* $32,185,576 (90% federal, 10% state). *Receiving aid:* Freshmen: 79% (1,107); all full-time undergraduates: 71% (3,613). *Average award:* Freshmen: $4862; Undergraduates: $5268. *Scholarships, grants, and awards:* Federal Pell, FSEOG, state, private, college/university gift aid from institutional funds.

GIFT AID (NON-NEED-BASED) *Total amount:* $3,762,179 (18% state, 63% institutional, 19% external sources). *Receiving aid:* Freshmen: 31% (438). Undergraduates: 32% (1,633). *Average award:* Freshmen: $6222. Undergraduates: $6698.

Scholarships, grants, and awards by category: Academic interests/achievement: biological sciences, business, communication, computer science, education, engineering/technologies, English, foreign languages, general academic interests/achievements, health fields, international studies, mathematics, physical sciences, social sciences. *Creative arts/performance:* art/fine arts, music, performing arts. *Special characteristics:* children of faculty/staff, first-generation college students, general special characteristics, international students. *ROTC:* Army.

LOANS *Student loans:* $30,846,059 (63% need-based, 37% non-need-based). *Average need-based loan:* Freshmen: $3181. Undergraduates: $3773. *Parent loans:* $67,103 (100% non-need-based). *Programs:* Federal Direct (Subsidized and Unsubsidized Stafford, PLUS), state, college/university.

WORK-STUDY *Federal work-study:* Total amount: $524,301; 127 jobs averaging $4128. *State or other work-study/employment:* Total amount: $100,406 (100% need-based). 28 part-time jobs averaging $3586.

ATHLETIC AWARDS Total amount: $446,588 (100% non-need-based).

APPLYING FOR FINANCIAL AID *Required financial aid form:* FAFSA. *Financial aid deadline (priority):* 3/1. *Notification date:* 5/1. Students must reply by 7/1 or within 12 weeks of notification.

CONTACT Mrs. Mary Comerota, Financial Aid Director, The University of Texas at Brownsville, 80 Fort Brown, Brownsville, TX 78520-4991, 956-882-8265 or toll-free 877-UTBTSC1. *Fax:* 956-882-8229. *E-mail:* mary.comerota@utb.edu. *Website:* http://www.utb.edu/.

THE UNIVERSITY OF TEXAS AT DALLAS
Richardson, TX

Tuition & fees (TX res): $11,592	Average undergraduate aid package: $11,620

ABOUT THE INSTITUTION State-supported, coed. *Awards:* certificates, bachelor's, master's, and doctoral degrees. 41 undergraduate majors. *Total enrollment:* 19,727. Undergraduates: 12,029. Freshmen: 1,545. Both federal and institutional methodology are used as a basis for awarding need-based institutional aid.

UNDERGRADUATE EXPENSES for 2013–2014 *Application fee:* $50. *Tuition, state resident:* full-time $11,592; part-time $386.40 per credit hour. *Tuition, nonresident:* full-time $29,266; part-time $975.53 per credit hour. Full-time tuition and fees vary according to course load and degree level. Part-time tuition and fees vary according to course load and degree level. *College room and board:* $9050. Room and board charges vary according to board plan and housing facility. *Payment plan:* Guaranteed tuition.

FRESHMAN FINANCIAL AID (Fall 2011) 1,230 applied for aid; of those 77% were deemed to have need. 98% of freshmen with need received aid; of those 33% had need fully met. *Average percent of need met:* 77% (excluding resources awarded to replace EFC). *Average financial aid package:* $14,694 (excluding resources awarded to replace EFC). 31% of all full-time freshmen had no need and received non-need-based gift aid.

UNDERGRADUATE FINANCIAL AID (Fall 2011) 5,728 applied for aid; of those 87% were deemed to have need. 97% of undergraduates with need received aid; of those 16% had need fully met. *Average percent of need met:* 64% (excluding resources awarded to replace EFC). *Average financial aid package:* $11,620 (excluding resources awarded to replace EFC). 22% of all full-time undergraduates had no need and received non-need-based gift aid.

GIFT AID (NEED-BASED) *Total amount:* $53,480,228 (29% federal, 11% state, 57% institutional, 3% external sources). *Receiving aid:* Freshmen: 49% (858); all full-time undergraduates: 47% (4,257). *Average award:* Freshmen: $11,138; Undergraduates: $7821. *Scholarships, grants, and awards:* Federal Pell, FSEOG, state, private, college/university gift aid from institutional funds.

GIFT AID (NON-NEED-BASED) *Total amount:* $6,616,091 (90% institutional, 10% external sources). *Receiving aid:* Freshmen: 10% (177). Undergraduates: 4% (349). *Average award:* Freshmen: $13,418. Undergraduates: $10,478. *Scholarships, grants, and awards by category: Academic interests/achievement:* biological sciences, business, computer science, engineering/technologies, general academic interests/achievements, mathematics, physical sciences. *Special achievements/activities:* general special achievements/activities, leadership. *Special characteristics:* adult students, children of public servants, general special characteristics, handicapped students, international students, local/state students, members of minority groups, out-of-state students, public servants, veterans, veterans' children.

Tuition waivers: Full or partial for employees or children of employees, senior citizens. *ROTC:* Army cooperative, Air Force cooperative.
LOANS *Student loans:* $46,756,622 (80% need-based, 20% non-need-based). 36% of past graduating class borrowed through all loan programs. *Average indebtedness per student:* $17,516. *Average need-based loan:* Freshmen: $3284. Undergraduates: $4435. *Parent loans:* $18,786,690 (35% need-based, 65% non-need-based). *Programs:* Federal Direct (Subsidized and Unsubsidized Stafford, PLUS), Perkins, state, college/university.
WORK-STUDY *Federal work-study:* Total amount: $1,116,271; 249 jobs averaging $3769. *State or other work-study/employment:* Total amount: $75,024 (100% need-based). 21 part-time jobs averaging $3428.
APPLYING FOR FINANCIAL AID *Required financial aid form:* FAFSA. *Financial aid deadline (priority):* 3/31. *Notification date:* Continuous beginning 3/1. Students must reply within 2 weeks of notification.
CONTACT M. Beth N. Tolan, Director of Financial Aid, The University of Texas at Dallas, 800 West Campbell Road, SS22, Richardson, TX 75080-3021, 972-883-2941 or toll-free 800-889-2443. *Fax:* 972-883-2947. *E-mail:* bnt031000@utdallas.edu. *Website:* http://www.utdallas.edu/.

THE UNIVERSITY OF TEXAS AT EL PASO
El Paso, TX

Tuition & fees: N/R	Average undergraduate aid package: $12,559

ABOUT THE INSTITUTION State-supported, coed. *Awards:* certificates, bachelor's, master's, and doctoral degrees. 61 undergraduate majors. *Total enrollment:* 22,749. Undergraduates: 19,217. Freshmen: 2,722. Federal methodology is used as a basis for awarding need-based institutional aid.
FRESHMAN FINANCIAL AID (Fall 2011) 2,512 applied for aid; of those 87% were deemed to have need. 99% of freshmen with need received aid; of those 14% had need fully met. *Average percent of need met:* 77% (excluding resources awarded to replace EFC). *Average financial aid package:* $12,874 (excluding resources awarded to replace EFC). 4% of all full-time freshmen had no need and received non-need-based gift aid.
UNDERGRADUATE FINANCIAL AID (Fall 2011) 11,448 applied for aid; of those 88% were deemed to have need. 99% of undergraduates with need received aid; of those 10% had need fully met. *Average percent of need met:* 68% (excluding resources awarded to replace EFC). *Average financial aid package:* $12,559 (excluding resources awarded to replace EFC). 5% of all full-time undergraduates had no need and received non-need-based gift aid.
GIFT AID (NEED-BASED) *Total amount:* $81,413,124 (70% federal, 18% state, 12% institutional). *Receiving aid:* Freshmen: 71% (1,918); all full-time undergraduates: 70% (8,868). *Average award:* Freshmen: $9498; Undergraduates: $7276. *Scholarships, grants, and awards:* Federal Pell, FSEOG, state, private, college/university gift aid from institutional funds, United Negro College Fund, Federal Nursing.
GIFT AID (NON-NEED-BASED) *Total amount:* $8,374,609 (10% federal, 17% state, 56% institutional, 17% external sources). *Receiving aid:* Freshmen: 19% (515). Undergraduates: 11% (1,339). *Average award:* Freshmen: $3244. Undergraduates: $3442. *Scholarships, grants, and awards by category: Academic interests/achievement:* biological sciences, business, communication, computer science, education, engineering/technologies, English, general academic interests/achievements, health fields, humanities, international studies, mathematics, military science, physical sciences. *Creative arts/performance:* applied art and design, art/fine arts, journalism/publications, music, performing arts, theater/drama. *Special achievements/activities:* cheerleading/drum major, leadership. *Special characteristics:* ethnic background, international students, local/state students, members of minority groups, out-of-state students. *ROTC:* Army, Air Force.
LOANS *Student loans:* $70,629,092 (99% need-based, 1% non-need-based). 59% of past graduating class borrowed through all loan programs. *Average indebtedness per student:* $20,913. *Average need-based loan:* Freshmen: $4119. Undergraduates: $6186. *Parent loans:* $15,992,156 (100% non-need-based). *Programs:* Federal Direct (Subsidized and Unsubsidized Stafford, PLUS), Perkins, Federal Nursing, state, college/university.

WORK-STUDY *Federal work-study:* Total amount: $6,774,351; 443 jobs averaging $2826. *State or other work-study/employment:* Total amount: $1,515,067 (100% need-based). 168 part-time jobs averaging $1540.
ATHLETIC AWARDS Total amount: $4,462,823 (100% non-need-based).
APPLYING FOR FINANCIAL AID *Required financial aid forms:* FAFSA, institution's own form. *Financial aid deadline (priority):* 3/15. *Notification date:* Continuous beginning 6/30. Students must reply within 2 weeks of notification.
CONTACT Mr. Ron Williams, Interim Director of Financial Aid, The University of Texas at El Paso, 500 West University Avenue, El Paso, TX 79968-0001, 915-747-5204 or toll-free 877-74MINER. *Fax:* 915-747-5631. *E-mail:* rwilliams@utep.edu. *Website:* http://www.utep.edu/.

THE UNIVERSITY OF TEXAS AT SAN ANTONIO
San Antonio, TX

Tuition & fees (TX res): $8419	Average undergraduate aid package: $9388

ABOUT THE INSTITUTION State-supported, coed. *Awards:* bachelor's, master's, and doctoral degrees. 56 undergraduate majors. *Total enrollment:* 30,474. Undergraduates: 25,979. Freshmen: 4,489. Federal methodology is used as a basis for awarding need-based institutional aid.
UNDERGRADUATE EXPENSES for 2013–2014 *Application fee:* $40. *Tuition, state resident:* full-time $5928; part-time $197.60 per hour. *Tuition, nonresident:* full-time $16,458; part-time $548.60 per hour. *Required fees:* full-time $2491. Full-time tuition and fees vary according to course load and degree level. Part-time tuition and fees vary according to course load and degree level. *College room and board:* $9693; *Room only:* $6651. Room and board charges vary according to board plan and housing facility.
FRESHMAN FINANCIAL AID (Fall 2011) 3,922 applied for aid; of those 78% were deemed to have need. 98% of freshmen with need received aid; of those 23% had need fully met. *Average percent of need met:* 61% (excluding resources awarded to replace EFC). *Average financial aid package:* $10,434 (excluding resources awarded to replace EFC). 12% of all full-time freshmen had no need and received non-need-based gift aid.
UNDERGRADUATE FINANCIAL AID (Fall 2011) 16,205 applied for aid; of those 86% were deemed to have need. 97% of undergraduates with need received aid; of those 17% had need fully met. *Average percent of need met:* 52% (excluding resources awarded to replace EFC). *Average financial aid package:* $9388 (excluding resources awarded to replace EFC). 4% of all full-time undergraduates had no need and received non-need-based gift aid.
GIFT AID (NEED-BASED) *Total amount:* $64,132,462 (77% federal, 23% state). *Receiving aid:* Freshmen: 58% (2,832); all full-time undergraduates: 57% (12,067). *Average award:* Freshmen: $7557; Undergraduates: $5935. *Scholarships, grants, and awards:* Federal Pell, FSEOG, state, private, college/university gift aid from institutional funds.
GIFT AID (NON-NEED-BASED) *Total amount:* $24,132,039 (82% institutional, 18% external sources). *Receiving aid:* Freshmen: 24% (1,174). Undergraduates: 14% (3,045). *Average award:* Freshmen: $1518. Undergraduates: $1889. *Scholarships, grants, and awards by category: Academic interests/achievement:* agriculture, architecture, area/ethnic studies, biological sciences, business, communication, computer science, education, engineering/technologies, English, foreign languages, general academic interests/achievements, humanities, international studies, mathematics, physical sciences, social sciences. *Creative arts/performance:* art/fine arts, creative writing, debating, music. *Special achievements/activities:* cheerleading/drum major, general special achievements/activities. *Special characteristics:* ethnic background, first-generation college students, general special characteristics, handicapped students, local/state students, members of minority groups, out-of-state students. *Tuition waivers:* Full or partial for employees or children of employees. *ROTC:* Army, Air Force.
LOANS *Student loans:* $105,733,713 (48% need-based, 52% non-need-based). 65% of past graduating class borrowed through all loan programs. *Average indebtedness per student:* $25,140. *Average need-based loan:* Freshmen: $3207. Undergraduates: $4164. *Parent loans:* $13,254,664 (100% non-need-based). *Programs:* Federal Direct (Subsidized and Unsubsidized Stafford, PLUS), Perkins, state, college/university.

WORK-STUDY *Federal work-study:* Total amount: $921,044; 539 jobs averaging $1725. *State or other work-study/employment:* Total amount: $1,603,317 (100% need-based). 1,101 part-time jobs averaging $1510.

ATHLETIC AWARDS Total amount: $3,737,395 (100% non-need-based).

APPLYING FOR FINANCIAL AID *Required financial aid form:* FAFSA. *Financial aid deadline (priority):* 3/15. *Notification date:* Continuous beginning 4/1. Students must reply within 4 weeks of notification.

CONTACT Kim Canady, Assistant Director of Student Financial Aid, The University of Texas at San Antonio, One UTSA Circle, San Antonio, TX 78249, 210-458-8000 or toll-free 800-669-0919. *Fax:* 210-458-4638. *E-mail:* financialaid@utsa.edu. *Website:* http://www.utsa.edu/.

THE UNIVERSITY OF TEXAS AT TYLER
Tyler, TX

ABOUT THE INSTITUTION State-supported, coed. *Awards:* bachelor's, master's, and doctoral degrees. 38 undergraduate majors. *Total enrollment:* 6,858. Undergraduates: 5,239. Freshmen: 632.

GIFT AID (NEED-BASED) *Scholarships, grants, and awards:* Federal Pell, FSEOG, state, private, college/university gift aid from institutional funds, Texas Grants, Institutional Grants (Education Affordability Program).

GIFT AID (NON-NEED-BASED) *Scholarships, grants, and awards by category: Academic interests/achievement:* communication, engineering/technologies, general academic interests/achievements, health fields. *Creative arts/performance:* art/fine arts, music. *Special characteristics:* children of faculty/staff.

LOANS *Programs:* Federal Direct (Subsidized and Unsubsidized Stafford, PLUS).

APPLYING FOR FINANCIAL AID *Required financial aid forms:* FAFSA, institution's own form.

CONTACT Candice A. Lindsey, Assistant Vice President for Enrollment Management, Marketing and Customer Relations, The University of Texas at Tyler, 3900 University Boulevard, Tyler, TX 75799, 903-566-7221 or toll-free 800-UTTYLER. *Fax:* 903-566-7183. *E-mail:* enroll@uttyler.edu. *Website:* http://www.uttyler.edu/.

THE UNIVERSITY OF TEXAS HEALTH SCIENCE CENTER AT HOUSTON
Houston, TX

Tuition & fees: N/R	Average undergraduate aid package: $9838

ABOUT THE INSTITUTION State-supported, coed. *Awards:* certificates, bachelor's, master's, and doctoral degrees. 2 undergraduate majors. *Total enrollment:* 4,489. Undergraduates: 563. Entering class: 180. Federal methodology is used as a basis for awarding need-based institutional aid.

UNDERGRADUATE FINANCIAL AID (Fall 2011) 325 applied for aid; of those 93% were deemed to have need. 100% of undergraduates with need received aid; of those 33% had need fully met. *Average percent of need met:* 72% (excluding resources awarded to replace EFC). *Average financial aid package:* $9838 (excluding resources awarded to replace EFC). 1% of all full-time undergraduates had no need and received non-need-based gift aid.

GIFT AID (NEED-BASED) *Total amount:* $1,641,997 (37% federal, 59% institutional, 4% external sources). *Receiving aid:* All full-time undergraduates: 36% (200). *Average award:* Undergraduates: $6154. *Scholarships, grants, and awards:* Federal Pell, FSEOG, state, private, college/university gift aid from institutional funds.

GIFT AID (NON-NEED-BASED) *Average award:* Undergraduates: $6751. *Scholarships, grants, and awards by category: Academic interests/achievement:* health fields. *ROTC:* Army cooperative.

LOANS *Student loans:* $5,250,015 (100% need-based). *Average need-based loan:* Undergraduates: $6215. *Parent loans:* $993,761 (100% need-based). *Programs:* Federal Direct (Subsidized and Unsubsidized Stafford, PLUS), Perkins, Federal Nursing, state, college/university, alternative loans.

APPLYING FOR FINANCIAL AID *Notification date:* Continuous.

CONTACT Ms. Wanda Williams, Director of Financial Aid, The University of Texas Health Science Center at Houston, PO Box 20036, Houston, TX 77225, 713-500-3860. *Fax:* 713-500-3863. *E-mail:* wanda.k.williams@uth.tmc.edu. *Website:* http://www.uthouston.edu/.

THE UNIVERSITY OF TEXAS HEALTH SCIENCE CENTER AT SAN ANTONIO
San Antonio, TX

CONTACT Robert T. Lawson, Financial Aid Administrator, The University of Texas Health Science Center at San Antonio, 7703 Floyd Curl Drive, MSC 7708, San Antonio, TX 78284, 210-567-0025. *Fax:* 210-567-6643. *Website:* http://www.uthscsa.edu/.

THE UNIVERSITY OF TEXAS MEDICAL BRANCH
Galveston, TX

CONTACT Mrs. Carol A. Cromie, University Financial Aid Officer, The University of Texas Medical Branch, 301 University Boulevard, Galveston, TX 77555-1305, 409-772-9795. *Fax:* 409-772-4466. *E-mail:* cacromie@umtb.edu. *Website:* http://www.utmb.edu/.

THE UNIVERSITY OF TEXAS OF THE PERMIAN BASIN
Odessa, TX

Tuition & fees (TX res): $6459	Average undergraduate aid package: $10,007

ABOUT THE INSTITUTION State-supported, coed. *Awards:* bachelor's and master's degrees. 31 undergraduate majors. *Total enrollment:* 4,021. Undergraduates: 3,852. Freshmen: 351. Both federal and institutional methodology are used as a basis for awarding need-based institutional aid.

UNDERGRADUATE EXPENSES for 2013–2014 *Tuition, state resident:* full-time $5037; part-time $167.86 per credit hour. *Tuition, nonresident:* full-time $15,566; part-time $518.86 per credit hour. *Required fees:* full-time $1422; $52.44 per credit hour or $576.80 per term. Full-time tuition and fees vary according to course load and location. Part-time tuition and fees vary according to course load and location. *College room and board:* $7616; *Room only:* $4532. Room and board charges vary according to board plan and housing facility.

FRESHMAN FINANCIAL AID (Fall 2011) 273 applied for aid; of those 84% were deemed to have need. 100% of freshmen with need received aid; of those 20% had need fully met. *Average percent of need met:* 80% (excluding resources awarded to replace EFC). *Average financial aid package:* $10,500 (excluding resources awarded to replace EFC). 24% of all full-time freshmen had no need and received non-need-based gift aid.

UNDERGRADUATE FINANCIAL AID (Fall 2011) 1,523 applied for aid; of those 88% were deemed to have need. 100% of undergraduates with need received aid; of those 12% had need fully met. *Average percent of need met:* 71% (excluding resources awarded to replace EFC). *Average financial aid package:* $10,007 (excluding resources awarded to replace EFC). 19% of all full-time undergraduates had no need and received non-need-based gift aid.

GIFT AID (NEED-BASED) *Total amount:* $6,055,650 (71% federal, 16% state, 13% institutional). *Receiving aid:* Freshmen: 52% (166); all full-time undergraduates: 52% (1,057). *Average award:* Freshmen: $4907; Undergraduates: $5630. *Scholarships, grants, and awards:* Federal Pell, FSEOG, state, private, college/university gift aid from institutional funds.

GIFT AID (NON-NEED-BASED) *Total amount:* $4,469,755 (1% federal, 61% institutional, 38% external sources). *Receiving aid:* Freshmen: 63% (199). Undergraduates: 44% (893). *Average award:* Freshmen: $2862. Undergraduates: $2788. *Scholarships, grants, and awards by category: Academic interests/achievement:* general academic interests/achievements. *Creative arts/performance:*

art/fine arts, dance, general creative arts/performance, music, theater/drama. *Special achievements/activities:* cheerleading/drum major, leadership. *Tuition waivers:* Full or partial for employees or children of employees, senior citizens.

LOANS *Student loans:* $4,743,274 (56% need-based, 44% non-need-based). 50% of past graduating class borrowed through all loan programs. *Average indebtedness per student:* $14,629. *Average need-based loan:* Freshmen: $2727. Undergraduates: $3815. *Parent loans:* $140,189 (100% non-need-based). *Programs:* Federal Direct (Subsidized and Unsubsidized Stafford, PLUS), state.

WORK-STUDY *Federal work-study:* Total amount: $57,126; jobs available. *State or other work-study/employment:* Total amount: $21,398 (100% need-based). Part-time jobs available.

ATHLETIC AWARDS Total amount: $583,220 (100% non-need-based).

APPLYING FOR FINANCIAL AID *Required financial aid forms:* FAFSA, institution's own form. *Financial aid deadline (priority):* 3/15. *Notification date:* Continuous beginning 3/15.

CONTACT Joe Sanders, Director of Financial Aid, The University of Texas of the Permian Basin, 4901 East University Boulevard, Odessa, TX 79762, 432-552-2620 or toll-free 866-552-UTPB. *Fax:* 432-552-2621. *E-mail:* finaid@utpb.edu. *Website:* http://www.utpb.edu/.

THE UNIVERSITY OF TEXAS–PAN AMERICAN
Edinburg, TX

Tuition & fees (TX res): $5165	Average undergraduate aid package: $9767

ABOUT THE INSTITUTION State-supported, coed. *Awards:* certificates, bachelor's, master's, and doctoral degrees. 50 undergraduate majors. *Total enrollment:* 19,302. Undergraduates: 16,966. Freshmen: 3,102. Federal methodology is used as a basis for awarding need-based institutional aid.

UNDERGRADUATE EXPENSES for 2013–2014 *Tuition, state resident:* full-time $4168; part-time $173.65 per credit hour. *Tuition, nonresident:* full-time $12,592; part-time $533.60 per credit hour. *Required fees:* full-time $997; $41.53 per credit hour. Full-time tuition and fees vary according to course load and degree level. Part-time tuition and fees vary according to course load and degree level. *College room and board:* $5656; *Room only:* $3400. Room and board charges vary according to board plan and housing facility.

FRESHMAN FINANCIAL AID (Fall 2011) 2,528 applied for aid; of those 95% were deemed to have need. 100% of freshmen with need received aid; of those 6% had need fully met. *Average percent of need met:* 75% (excluding resources awarded to replace EFC). *Average financial aid package:* $10,125 (excluding resources awarded to replace EFC). 2% of all full-time freshmen had no need and received non-need-based gift aid.

UNDERGRADUATE FINANCIAL AID (Fall 2011) 10,294 applied for aid; of those 96% were deemed to have need. 100% of undergraduates with need received aid; of those 4% had need fully met. *Average percent of need met:* 67% (excluding resources awarded to replace EFC). *Average financial aid package:* $9767 (excluding resources awarded to replace EFC). 2% of all full-time undergraduates had no need and received non-need-based gift aid.

GIFT AID (NEED-BASED) *Total amount:* $84,216,744 (57% federal, 30% state, 12% institutional, 1% external sources). *Receiving aid:* Freshmen: 81% (2,342); all full-time undergraduates: 76% (9,553). *Average award:* Freshmen: $10,577; Undergraduates: $10,621. *Scholarships, grants, and awards:* Federal Pell, FSEOG, state, private, college/university gift aid from institutional funds.

GIFT AID (NON-NEED-BASED) *Total amount:* $1,138,838 (2% federal, 6% state, 78% institutional, 14% external sources). *Receiving aid:* Freshmen: 2% (44). Undergraduates: 1% (81). *Average award:* Freshmen: $3673. Undergraduates: $3082. *Scholarships, grants, and awards by category: Academic interests/ achievement:* 1,341 awards ($3,311,079 total): biological sciences, business, communication, computer science, education, engineering/technologies, English, general academic interests/achievements, health fields, mathematics, military science, premedicine, social sciences. *Creative arts/performance:* 115 awards ($74,604 total): art/fine arts, dance, journalism/publications, music, theater/drama. *Special achievements/activities:* 71 awards ($97,600 total): cheerleading/drum major, community service, general special achievements/activities, leadership, memberships. *Special characteristics:* 73 awards ($113,755 total): ethnic background, general special character-

istics, international students, local/state students, out-of-state students, veterans. *ROTC:* Army.

LOANS *Student loans:* $38,971,052 (90% need-based, 10% non-need-based). 62% of past graduating class borrowed through all loan programs. *Average indebtedness per student:* $15,257. *Average need-based loan:* Freshmen: $3125. Undergraduates: $4786. *Parent loans:* $332,378 (11% need-based, 89% non-need-based). *Programs:* Federal Direct (Subsidized and Unsubsidized Stafford, PLUS), Perkins, state.

WORK-STUDY *Federal work-study:* Total amount: $1,900,522; 829 jobs averaging $2293. *State or other work-study/employment:* Total amount: $585,943 (100% need-based). 299 part-time jobs averaging $1960.

ATHLETIC AWARDS Total amount: $1,152,063 (46% need-based, 54% non-need-based).

APPLYING FOR FINANCIAL AID *Required financial aid form:* FAFSA. *Financial aid deadline (priority):* 4/1. *Notification date:* Continuous beginning 4/1. Students must reply within 2 weeks of notification.

CONTACT Mrs. Elaine Rivera, Executive Director of Student Financial Services, The University of Texas–Pan American, 1201 West University Drive, Edinburg, TX 78541, 956-665-5372. *Fax:* 956-665-2396. *E-mail:* eriverall@utpa.edu. *Website:* http://www.utpa.edu/.

THE UNIVERSITY OF THE ARTS
Philadelphia, PA

CONTACT Office of Financial Aid, The University of the Arts, 320 South Broad Street, Philadelphia, PA 19102-4944, 800-616-ARTS Ext. 6170 or toll-free 800-616-ARTS. *E-mail:* finaid@uarts.edu. *Website:* http://www.uarts.edu/.

UNIVERSITY OF THE CUMBERLANDS
Williamsburg, KY

Tuition & fees: $19,640	Average undergraduate aid package: $18,582

ABOUT THE INSTITUTION Independent Kentucky Baptist, coed. *Awards:* certificates, bachelor's, master's, and doctoral degrees. 43 undergraduate majors. *Total enrollment:* 4,297. Undergraduates: 1,864. Freshmen: 459. Federal methodology is used as a basis for awarding need-based institutional aid.

UNDERGRADUATE EXPENSES for 2013–2014 *Application fee:* $30. *Comprehensive fee:* $27,140 includes full-time tuition ($19,640) and room and board ($7500). *Part-time tuition:* $590 per credit. *Part-time fees:* $90 per term. Part-time tuition and fees vary according to course load.

FRESHMAN FINANCIAL AID (Fall 2012, est.) 423 applied for aid; of those 96% were deemed to have need. 100% of freshmen with need received aid; of those 12% had need fully met. *Average percent of need met:* 77% (excluding resources awarded to replace EFC). *Average financial aid package:* $19,519 (excluding resources awarded to replace EFC). 10% of all full-time freshmen had no need and received non-need-based gift aid.

UNDERGRADUATE FINANCIAL AID (Fall 2012, est.) 1,371 applied for aid; of those 94% were deemed to have need. 100% of undergraduates with need received aid; of those 16% had need fully met. *Average percent of need met:* 76% (excluding resources awarded to replace EFC). *Average financial aid package:* $18,582 (excluding resources awarded to replace EFC). 12% of all full-time undergraduates had no need and received non-need-based gift aid.

GIFT AID (NEED-BASED) *Total amount:* $16,316,780 (23% federal, 22% state, 53% institutional, 2% external sources). *Receiving aid:* Freshmen: 89% (406); all full-time undergraduates: 81% (1,284). *Average award:* Freshmen: $15,106; Undergraduates: $14,482. *Scholarships, grants, and awards:* Federal Pell, FSEOG, state, private, college/university gift aid from institutional funds.

GIFT AID (NON-NEED-BASED) *Total amount:* $2,123,269 (8% state, 88% institutional, 4% external sources). *Receiving aid:* Freshmen: 7% (34). Undergraduates: 8% (119). *Average award:* Freshmen: $7105. Undergraduates: $8489. *Scholarships, grants, and awards by category: Academic interests/achievement:* 1,334 awards ($7,044,190 total): general academic interests/achievements. *Creative arts/performance:* 39 awards ($62,008 total): art/fine arts, debating, journalism/publications, music, theater/drama. *Special achievements/activities:* 153 awards ($165,755 total): cheerleading/drum major, community service, leadership, religious involvement. *Special characteristics:* 287 awards ($1,031,595 total): children and siblings of alumni, children of faculty/staff, general special characteristics, local/state students, relatives of clergy, religious affiliation, siblings of current students. *Tuition waivers:* Full or partial for employees or children of employees, senior citizens. *ROTC:* Army.

LOANS *Student loans:* $7,066,355 (82% need-based, 18% non-need-based). 76% of past graduating class borrowed through all loan programs. *Average indebtedness per student:* $20,090. *Average need-based loan:* Freshmen: $3296. Undergraduates: $3780. *Parent loans:* $1,034,439 (30% need-based, 70% non-need-based). *Programs:* Federal Direct (Subsidized and Unsubsidized Stafford, PLUS), Perkins, college/university.

WORK-STUDY *Federal work-study:* Total amount: $1,639,831; 763 jobs averaging $2029. *State or other work-study/employment:* Total amount: $40,743 (6% need-based, 94% non-need-based). 15 part-time jobs averaging $2462.

ATHLETIC AWARDS Total amount: $2,771,455 (67% need-based, 33% non-need-based).

APPLYING FOR FINANCIAL AID *Required financial aid form:* FAFSA. *Financial aid deadline (priority):* 2/1. *Notification date:* Continuous beginning 3/1. Students must reply within 2 weeks of notification.

CONTACT Mr. Steve Allen, Vice President of Student Financial Planning, University of the Cumberlands, 6190 College Station Drive, Williamsburg, KY 40769-1372, 606-549-2200 or toll-free 800-343-1609. *Fax:* 606-539-4515. *E-mail:* finplan@ ucumberlands.edu.
Website: http://www.ucumberlands.edu/.

UNIVERSITY OF THE DISTRICT OF COLUMBIA
Washington, DC

Tuition & fees (DC res): $7255	Average undergraduate aid package: N/A

ABOUT THE INSTITUTION District-supported, coed. *Awards:* associate, bachelor's, and master's degrees. 79 undergraduate majors. *Total enrollment:* 5,110. Undergraduates: 4,857. Freshmen: 607. Federal methodology is used as a basis for awarding need-based institutional aid.

UNDERGRADUATE EXPENSES for 2013–2014 *Application fee:* $35. *Tuition, state resident:* full-time $6635; part-time $276 per credit. *Tuition, nonresident:* full-time $13,915; part-time $580 per credit. *Required fees:* full-time $620; $30 per credit. Full-time tuition and fees vary according to course load. Part-time tuition and fees vary according to course load. *College room and board:* $6600.

GIFT AID (NEED-BASED) *Total amount:* $9,941,818 (100% federal). *Scholarships, grants, and awards:* Federal Pell, FSEOG, state, private, college/university gift aid from institutional funds, foundation scholarships.

GIFT AID (NON-NEED-BASED) *Scholarships, grants, and awards by category:* Academic interests/achievement: general academic interests/achievements. Creative arts/performance: music. *Special characteristics:* children of faculty/staff. *Tuition waivers:* Full or partial for employees or children of employees, senior citizens. *ROTC:* Army cooperative, Air Force cooperative.

LOANS *Student loans:* $6,748,712 (100% need-based). *Programs:* Federal Direct (Subsidized and Unsubsidized Stafford, PLUS), Perkins.

WORK-STUDY Federal work-study jobs available. *State or other work-study/employment:* Part-time jobs available.

APPLYING FOR FINANCIAL AID *Required financial aid forms:* FAFSA, verification worksheet. *Financial aid deadline (priority):* 3/31. *Notification date:* Continuous beginning 4/1. Students must reply within 2 weeks of notification.

CONTACT James Contreras, Office of Financial Aid, University of the District of Columbia, 4200 Connecticut Avenue NW, Washington, DC 20008-1175, 202-274-5618. *Fax:* 202-274-6060. *E-mail:* finaid@udc.edu.
Website: http://www.udc.edu/.

UNIVERSITY OF THE INCARNATE WORD
San Antonio, TX

Tuition & fees: $23,690	Average undergraduate aid package: $17,809

ABOUT THE INSTITUTION Independent Roman Catholic, coed. *Awards:* diplomas, associate, bachelor's, master's, and doctoral degrees. 67 undergraduate majors. *Total enrollment:* 8,442. Undergraduates: 6,404. Freshmen: 1,064. Federal methodology is used as a basis for awarding need-based institutional aid.

UNDERGRADUATE EXPENSES for 2013–2014 *Application fee:* $20. *Comprehensive fee:* $33,784 includes full-time tuition ($22,800), mandatory fees ($890), and room and board ($10,094). *College room only:* $5980. Full-time tuition and fees vary according to course load, degree level, location, program, and reciprocity agreements. Room and board charges vary according to board plan and housing facility. *Part-time tuition:* $755 per credit hour. Part-time tuition and fees vary according to course load, degree level, location, program, and reciprocity agreements.

FRESHMAN FINANCIAL AID (Fall 2011) 925 applied for aid; of those 92% were deemed to have need. 100% of freshmen with need received aid; of those 28% had need fully met. *Average percent of need met:* 70% (excluding resources awarded to replace EFC). *Average financial aid package:* $18,353 (excluding resources awarded to replace EFC). 7% of all full-time freshmen had no need and received non-need-based gift aid.

UNDERGRADUATE FINANCIAL AID (Fall 2011) 3,375 applied for aid; of those 94% were deemed to have need. 100% of undergraduates with need received aid; of those 27% had need fully met. *Average percent of need met:* 66% (excluding resources awarded to replace EFC). *Average financial aid package:* $17,809 (excluding resources awarded to replace EFC). 5% of all full-time undergraduates had no need and received non-need-based gift aid.

GIFT AID (NEED-BASED) *Total amount:* $31,696,439 (35% federal, 17% state, 47% institutional, 1% external sources). *Receiving aid:* Freshmen: 83% (852); all full-time undergraduates: 77% (3,147). *Average award:* Freshmen: $15,071; Undergraduates: $13,415. *Scholarships, grants, and awards:* Federal Pell, FSEOG, state, private, college/university gift aid from institutional funds, United Negro College Fund, Federal Nursing.

GIFT AID (NON-NEED-BASED) *Total amount:* $10,663,131 (90% institutional, 10% external sources). *Receiving aid:* Freshmen: 83% (849). Undergraduates: 76% (3,078). *Average award:* Freshmen: $9218. Undergraduates: $8659. *Scholarships, grants, and awards by category:* Academic interests/achievement: general academic interests/achievements. Creative arts/performance: art/fine arts, music, theater/drama. *Special achievements/activities:* leadership, religious involvement. *Special characteristics:* children and siblings of alumni, children of faculty/staff. *Tuition waivers:* Full or partial for employees or children of employees, senior citizens. *ROTC:* Army cooperative, Air Force cooperative.

LOANS *Student loans:* $32,826,325 (51% need-based, 49% non-need-based). *Average need-based loan:* Freshmen: $3235. Undergraduates: $4200. *Parent loans:* $6,120,421 (85% need-based, 15% non-need-based). *Programs:* Federal Direct (Subsidized and Unsubsidized Stafford, PLUS), Perkins, Federal Nursing, state, alternative loans.

WORK-STUDY *Federal work-study:* Total amount: $769,474; jobs available. *State or other work-study/employment:* Total amount: $73,880 (100% need-based). Part-time jobs available.

ATHLETIC AWARDS Total amount: $2,522,136 (89% need-based, 11% non-need-based).

APPLYING FOR FINANCIAL AID *Required financial aid form:* FAFSA. *Financial aid deadline (priority):* 4/1. *Notification date:* Continuous beginning 2/15. Students must reply within 2 weeks of notification.

CONTACT Ms. Amy Carcanagues, Director of Financial Assistance, University of the Incarnate Word, 4301 Broadway, San Antonio, TX 78209, 210-829-6008 or toll-free 800-749-WORD. *Fax:* 210-283-5053. *E-mail:* finaid@uiwtx.edu.
Website: http://www.uiw.edu/.

UNIVERSITY OF THE OZARKS
Clarksville, AR

Tuition & fees: $23,250	Average undergraduate aid package: N/A

ABOUT THE INSTITUTION Independent Presbyterian, coed. **Awards:** bachelor's degrees. 30 undergraduate majors. **Total enrollment:** 630. Undergraduates: 630. Freshmen: 186. Federal methodology is used as a basis for awarding need-based institutional aid.

UNDERGRADUATE EXPENSES for 2013–2014 **Application fee:** $30. **Comprehensive fee:** $29,950 includes full-time tuition ($22,650), mandatory fees ($600), and room and board ($6700). **College room only:** $3100. Room and board charges vary according to board plan and housing facility. **Part-time tuition:** $950 per credit hour.

GIFT AID (NEED-BASED) **Scholarships, grants, and awards:** Federal Pell, FSEOG, state, private, college/university gift aid from institutional funds, United Negro College Fund, Federal Nursing.

GIFT AID (NON-NEED-BASED) **Scholarships, grants, and awards by category:** Academic interests/achievement: biological sciences, business, communication, education, English, general academic interests/achievements, humanities, mathematics, premedicine, religion/biblical studies, social sciences. Creative arts/performance: art/fine arts, music, theater/drama. Special achievements/activities: leadership. Special characteristics: children and siblings of alumni, children of faculty/staff, ethnic background, general special characteristics, international students, members of minority groups, relatives of clergy, religious affiliation, siblings of current students. **Tuition waivers:** Full or partial for children of alumni, employees or children of employees.

LOANS **Programs:** Federal Direct (Subsidized and Unsubsidized Stafford, PLUS), Perkins, college/university.

APPLYING FOR FINANCIAL AID **Required financial aid form:** FAFSA. **Financial aid deadline (priority):** 2/15. **Notification date:** Continuous beginning 3/1. Students must reply within 2 weeks of notification.

CONTACT Ms. Jana D. Hart, Director of Financial Aid, University of the Ozarks, 415 North College Avenue, Clarksville, AR 72830-2880, 479-979-1221 or toll-free 800-264-8636. *Fax:* 479-979-1417. *E-mail:* jhart@ozarks.edu. *Website:* http://www.ozarks.edu/.

UNIVERSITY OF THE PACIFIC
Stockton, CA

Tuition & fees: $38,320	Average undergraduate aid package: $29,279

ABOUT THE INSTITUTION Independent, coed. **Awards:** bachelor's, master's, and doctoral degrees. 54 undergraduate majors. **Total enrollment:** 6,652. Undergraduates: 3,867. Freshmen: 852. Federal methodology is used as a basis for awarding need-based institutional aid.

UNDERGRADUATE EXPENSES for 2013–2014 **Comprehensive fee:** $50,358 includes full-time tuition ($37,800), mandatory fees ($520), and room and board ($12,038). Room and board charges vary according to board plan and housing facility. Part-time tuition and fees vary according to course load.

FRESHMAN FINANCIAL AID (Fall 2012, est.) 697 applied for aid; of those 85% were deemed to have need. 100% of freshmen with need received aid; of those 10% had need fully met. **Average financial aid package:** $26,896 (excluding resources awarded to replace EFC). 18% of all full-time freshmen had no need and received non-need-based gift aid.

UNDERGRADUATE FINANCIAL AID (Fall 2012, est.) 3,010 applied for aid; of those 92% were deemed to have need. 100% of undergraduates with need received aid; of those 8% had need fully met. **Average financial aid package:** $29,279 (excluding resources awarded to replace EFC). 11% of all full-time undergraduates had no need and received non-need-based gift aid.

GIFT AID (NEED-BASED) **Total amount:** $59,183,662 (12% federal, 20% state, 68% institutional). **Receiving aid:** Freshmen: 69% (585); all full-time undergraduates: 71% (2,673). **Average award:** Freshmen: $20,872; Undergraduates: $21,896. **Scholarships, grants, and awards:** Federal Pell, FSEOG, state, private, college/university gift aid from institutional funds.

GIFT AID (NON-NEED-BASED) **Total amount:** $3,857,659 (100% institutional). **Average award:** Freshmen: $8773. Undergraduates: $9074. **Scholarships,**

grants, and awards by category: Academic interests/achievement: general academic interests/achievements. Creative arts/performance: debating, music. Special achievements/activities: leadership, religious involvement. Special characteristics: religious affiliation. **Tuition waivers:** Full or partial for employees or children of employees. **ROTC:** Air Force cooperative.

LOANS **Student loans:** $21,141,873 (95% need-based, 5% non-need-based). **Average need-based loan:** Freshmen: $5649. Undergraduates: $7561. **Parent loans:** $50,222,760 (85% need-based, 15% non-need-based). **Programs:** Federal Direct (Subsidized and Unsubsidized Stafford, PLUS), Perkins.

WORK-STUDY **Federal work-study:** Total amount: $3,524,579; jobs available.

ATHLETIC AWARDS Total amount: $7,003,356 (32% need-based, 68% non-need-based).

APPLYING FOR FINANCIAL AID **Required financial aid form:** FAFSA. **Financial aid deadline (priority):** 2/15. **Notification date:** Continuous beginning 4/1.

CONTACT Lynn Fox, Director of Financial Aid, University of the Pacific, 3601 Pacific Avenue, Stockton, CA 95211-0197, 209-946-2421. *Website:* http://www.pacific.edu/.

UNIVERSITY OF THE SACRED HEART
San Juan, PR

CONTACT Ms. Maria Torres, Director of Financial Aid, University of the Sacred Heart, PO Box 12383, San Juan, PR 00914-0383, 787-728-1515 Ext. 3605. *Website:* http://www.sagrado.edu/.

UNIVERSITY OF THE SCIENCES
Philadelphia, PA

Tuition & fees: N/R	Average undergraduate aid package: $20,350

ABOUT THE INSTITUTION Independent, coed. **Awards:** certificates, bachelor's, master's, and doctoral degrees. 17 undergraduate majors. **Total enrollment:** 2,770. Undergraduates: 2,436. Freshmen: 483. Federal methodology is used as a basis for awarding need-based institutional aid.

FRESHMAN FINANCIAL AID (Fall 2011) 457 applied for aid; of those 92% were deemed to have need. 100% of freshmen with need received aid; of those 34% had need fully met. **Average percent of need met:** 34% (excluding resources awarded to replace EFC). **Average financial aid package:** $31,256 (excluding resources awarded to replace EFC). 11% of all full-time freshmen had no need and received non-need-based gift aid.

UNDERGRADUATE FINANCIAL AID (Fall 2011) 2,434 applied for aid; of those 95% were deemed to have need. 100% of undergraduates with need received aid; of those 33% had need fully met. **Average percent of need met:** 28% (excluding resources awarded to replace EFC). **Average financial aid package:** $20,350 (excluding resources awarded to replace EFC). 4% of all full-time undergraduates had no need and received non-need-based gift aid.

GIFT AID (NEED-BASED) **Total amount:** $7,989,677 (35% federal, 20% state, 45% institutional). **Receiving aid:** Freshmen: 87% (419); all full-time undergraduates: 56% (1,377). **Average award:** Freshmen: $12,678; Undergraduates: $7907. **Scholarships, grants, and awards:** Federal Pell, FSEOG, state, private, college/university gift aid from institutional funds, Academic Competitiveness Grants, National SMART Grants.

GIFT AID (NON-NEED-BASED) **Total amount:** $22,461,682 (97% institutional, 3% external sources). **Receiving aid:** Freshmen: 83% (402). Undergraduates: 85% (2,078). **Average award:** Freshmen: $10,505. Undergraduates: $7810. **Scholarships, grants, and awards by category:** Academic interests/achievement: general academic interests/achievements. **ROTC:** Army cooperative, Air Force cooperative.

LOANS **Student loans:** $36,510,333 (29% need-based, 71% non-need-based). 82% of past graduating class borrowed through all loan programs. **Average indebtedness per student:** $10,620. **Average need-based loan:** Freshmen: $3627. Undergraduates: $5675. **Parent loans:** $5,488,185 (100% non-need-based). **Programs:** Federal Direct (Subsidized and Unsubsidized Stafford, PLUS), Perkins, college/university.

WORK-STUDY *Federal work-study:* Total amount: $696,119; jobs available. *State or other work-study/employment:* Part-time jobs available.
ATHLETIC AWARDS Total amount: $967,944 (100% non-need-based).
APPLYING FOR FINANCIAL AID *Required financial aid form:* FAFSA. *Financial aid deadline:* 3/15. *Notification date:* Continuous beginning 1/15. Students must reply by 5/1 or within 2 weeks of notification.
CONTACT Ms. Paula Lehrberger, Director of Financial Aid, University of the Sciences, 600 South 43rd Street, Philadelphia, PA 19104, 215-596-8894 or toll-free 888-996-8747. *Fax:* 215-596-8554.
Website: http://www.usciences.edu/.

UNIVERSITY OF THE SOUTHWEST
Hobbs, NM

ABOUT THE INSTITUTION Independent Christian, coed. *Awards:* bachelor's and master's degrees. 21 undergraduate majors. *Total enrollment:* 627. Undergraduates: 322. Freshmen: 98.
GIFT AID (NEED-BASED) *Scholarships, grants, and awards:* Federal Pell, FSEOG, state, private, college/university gift aid from institutional funds.
GIFT AID (NON-NEED-BASED) *Scholarships, grants, and awards by category:* Academic interests/achievement: biological sciences, business, education, English, general academic interests/achievements, humanities, mathematics, physical sciences, premedicine, religion/biblical studies, social sciences. *Creative arts/performance:* debating, music. *Special achievements/activities:* community service, general special achievements/activities, leadership, religious involvement. *Special characteristics:* children of faculty/staff.
LOANS *Programs:* Federal Direct (Subsidized and Unsubsidized Stafford, PLUS).
WORK-STUDY *Federal work-study:* Total amount: $36,603; 22 jobs averaging $1663. *State or other work-study/employment:* Total amount: $31,516 (84% need-based, 16% non-need-based). 18 part-time jobs averaging $1751.
APPLYING FOR FINANCIAL AID *Required financial aid form:* FAFSA.
CONTACT Kerrie Mitchell, Director of Financial Aid, University of the Southwest, 6610 North Lovington Highway, Hobbs, NM 88240-9129, 575-492-2114 or toll-free 800-530-4400. *Fax:* 575-392-6006. *E-mail:* kmitchell@usw.edu.
Website: http://www.usw.edu/.

UNIVERSITY OF THE VIRGIN ISLANDS
Saint Thomas, VI

CONTACT Mavis M. Gilchrist, Director of Financial Aid, University of the Virgin Islands, RR #2, Box 10,000, Kingshill, St. Thomas, VI 00850, 340-692-4186. *Fax:* 340-692-4145. *E-mail:* mgilchr@uvi.edu.
Website: http://www.uvi.edu/.

UNIVERSITY OF THE WEST
Rosemead, CA

CONTACT Jamie Johnston, Financial Aid Officer, University of the West, 1409 Walnut Grove Avenue, Rosemead, CA 91770, 626-571-8811 Ext. 122. *Fax:* 626-571-1413. *E-mail:* jamiej@uwest.edu.
Website: http://www.uwest.edu/.

THE UNIVERSITY OF TOLEDO
Toledo, OH

Tuition & fees (OH res): $9275	Average undergraduate aid package: $10,265

ABOUT THE INSTITUTION State-supported, coed. *Awards:* certificates, bachelor's, master's, and doctoral degrees. 166 undergraduate majors. *Total enrollment:* 21,501. Undergraduates: 16,877. Freshmen: 3,431. Federal methodology is used as a basis for awarding need-based institutional aid.
UNDERGRADUATE EXPENSES for 2013–2014 *Application fee:* $40. *Tuition, state resident:* full-time $7864; part-time $327.66 per credit hour. *Tuition, nonresident:* full-time $16,984; part-time $707.66 per credit hour. *Required fees:* full-time $1411; $57.80 per credit hour. Full-time tuition and fees vary according to course load, program, and reciprocity agreements. Part-time tuition and fees vary according to course load, program, and reciprocity agreements. *College room and board:* $9738; *Room only:* $6338. Room and board charges vary according to board plan and housing facility.
FRESHMAN FINANCIAL AID (Fall 2012, est.) 3,114 applied for aid; of those 84% were deemed to have need. 100% of freshmen with need received aid; of those 14% had need fully met. *Average percent of need met:* 60% (excluding resources awarded to replace EFC). *Average financial aid package:* $10,766 (excluding resources awarded to replace EFC). 19% of all full-time freshmen had no need and received non-need-based gift aid.
UNDERGRADUATE FINANCIAL AID (Fall 2012, est.) 11,435 applied for aid; of those 85% were deemed to have need. 99% of undergraduates with need received aid; of those 12% had need fully met. *Average percent of need met:* 55% (excluding resources awarded to replace EFC). *Average financial aid package:* $10,265 (excluding resources awarded to replace EFC). 18% of all full-time undergraduates had no need and received non-need-based gift aid.
GIFT AID (NEED-BASED) *Total amount:* $65,534,810 (44% federal, 7% state, 46% institutional, 3% external sources). *Receiving aid:* Freshmen: 76% (2,558); all full-time undergraduates: 61% (8,467). *Average award:* Freshmen: $8195; Undergraduates: $7701. *Scholarships, grants, and awards:* Federal Pell, FSEOG, state, private, college/university gift aid from institutional funds, Academic Competitiveness Grants, National SMART Grants, TEACH Grants.
GIFT AID (NON-NEED-BASED) *Total amount:* $19,274,032 (2% federal, 3% state, 83% institutional, 12% external sources). *Receiving aid:* Freshmen: 14% (471). Undergraduates: 9% (1,221). *Average award:* Freshmen: $5760. Undergraduates: $5922. *Scholarships, grants, and awards by category:* Academic interests/achievement: 6,100 awards ($16,965,304 total): biological sciences, business, communication, education, engineering/technologies, English, foreign languages, general academic interests/achievements, health fields, humanities, international studies, library science, mathematics, physical sciences, premedicine, social sciences. *Creative arts/performance:* 52 awards ($43,101 total): art/fine arts, general creative arts/performance, music, performing arts, theater/drama. *Special achievements/activities:* 198 awards ($347,984 total): cheerleading/drum major, community service, general special achievements/activities, hobbies/interests, leadership, memberships, religious involvement. *Special characteristics:* 828 awards ($806,259 total): adult students, children and siblings of alumni, children of faculty/staff, children of public servants, children of union members/company employees, ethnic background, first-generation college students, general special characteristics, handicapped students, international students, members of minority groups, out-of-state students, previous college experience, public servants, religious affiliation, veterans, veterans' children. *Tuition waivers:* Full or partial for employees or children of employees. *ROTC:* Army, Air Force cooperative.
LOANS *Student loans:* $82,787,967 (90% need-based, 10% non-need-based). 77% of past graduating class borrowed through all loan programs. *Average indebtedness per student:* $30,421. *Average need-based loan:* Freshmen: $3526. Undergraduates: $4220. *Parent loans:* $16,496,754 (86% need-based, 14% non-need-based). *Programs:* Federal Direct (Subsidized and Unsubsidized Stafford, PLUS), Perkins, alternative loans.
WORK-STUDY *Federal work-study:* Total amount: $1,492,440; 273 jobs averaging $1748.
ATHLETIC AWARDS Total amount: $5,849,154 (55% need-based, 45% non-need-based).
APPLYING FOR FINANCIAL AID *Required financial aid form:* FAFSA. *Financial aid deadline (priority):* 4/1. *Notification date:* Continuous beginning 4/1. Students must reply within 4 weeks of notification.
CONTACT Carolyn Baumgartner, Director, The University of Toledo, 2801 West Bancroft Street, MS-314, Toledo, OH 43606, 419-530-5812 or toll-free 800-5TOLEDO. *Fax:* 419-530-5835. *E-mail:* cbaumga@utnet.utoledo.edu.
Website: http://www.utoledo.edu/.

UNIVERSITY OF TULSA
Tulsa, OK

Tuition & fees: $34,350	Average undergraduate aid package: $24,613

ABOUT THE INSTITUTION Independent, coed. *Awards:* certificates, bachelor's, master's, and doctoral degrees. 63 undergraduate majors. *Total enrollment:* 4,326. Undergraduates: 3,160. Freshmen: 806. Federal methodology is used as a basis for awarding need-based institutional aid.

UNDERGRADUATE EXPENSES for 2013–2014 *Application fee:* $50. *One-time required fee:* $485. *Comprehensive fee:* $44,826 includes full-time tuition ($34,030), mandatory fees ($320), and room and board ($10,476). *College room only:* $5800. Full-time tuition and fees vary according to course load. Room and board charges vary according to board plan and housing facility. *Part-time tuition:* $1221 per credit. Part-time tuition and fees vary according to course load. *Payment plan:* Tuition prepayment.

FRESHMAN FINANCIAL AID (Fall 2012, est.) 752 applied for aid; of those 49% were deemed to have need. 100% of freshmen with need received aid; of those 61% had need fully met. *Average percent of need met:* 89% (excluding resources awarded to replace EFC). *Average financial aid package:* $25,426 (excluding resources awarded to replace EFC). 44% of all full-time freshmen had no need and received non-need-based gift aid.

UNDERGRADUATE FINANCIAL AID (Fall 2012, est.) 2,635 applied for aid; of those 48% were deemed to have need. 100% of undergraduates with need received aid; of those 48% had need fully met. *Average percent of need met:* 82% (excluding resources awarded to replace EFC). *Average financial aid package:* $24,613 (excluding resources awarded to replace EFC). 42% of all full-time undergraduates had no need and received non-need-based gift aid.

GIFT AID (NEED-BASED) Total amount: $4,216,604 (55% federal, 17% state, 28% institutional). *Receiving aid:* Freshmen: 17% (136); all full-time undergraduates: 20% (600). *Average award:* Freshmen: $8277; Undergraduates: $6826. *Scholarships, grants, and awards:* Federal Pell, FSEOG, state, private, college/university gift aid from institutional funds.

GIFT AID (NON-NEED-BASED) Total amount: $36,545,087 (1% federal, 4% state, 91% institutional, 4% external sources). *Receiving aid:* Freshmen: 46% (369). Undergraduates: 40% (1,206). *Average award:* Freshmen: $15,240. Undergraduates: $15,555. *Scholarships, grants, and awards by category: Academic interests/achievement:* biological sciences, business, communication, computer science, education, engineering/technologies, English, foreign languages, general academic interests/achievements, health fields, international studies, mathematics, physical sciences, premedicine, religion/biblical studies, social sciences. *Creative arts/performance:* art/fine arts, music, performing arts, theater/drama. *Special achievements/activities:* cheerleading/drum major, community service, leadership. *Special characteristics:* children and siblings of alumni, children of faculty/staff, relatives of clergy, religious affiliation, siblings of current students. *Tuition waivers:* Full or partial for employees or children of employees. *ROTC:* Air Force cooperative.

LOANS Student loans: $9,092,033 (48% need-based, 52% non-need-based). 43% of past graduating class borrowed through all loan programs. *Average indebtedness per student:* $34,574. *Average need-based loan:* Freshmen: $5707. Undergraduates: $5888. *Parent loans:* $3,583,712 (100% non-need-based). *Programs:* Federal Direct (Subsidized and Unsubsidized Stafford, PLUS), Perkins.

WORK-STUDY *Federal work-study:* Total amount: $969,642; jobs available. *State or other work-study/employment:* Total amount: $2600 (100% non-need-based). Part-time jobs available.

ATHLETIC AWARDS Total amount: $10,341,139 (100% non-need-based).

APPLYING FOR FINANCIAL AID *Required financial aid form:* FAFSA. *Financial aid deadline (priority):* 3/1. *Notification date:* Continuous. Students must reply by 5/1 or within 2 weeks of notification.

CONTACT Ms. Vicki Hendrickson, Director of Student Financial Services, University of Tulsa, 600 South College, Tulsa, OK 74104, 918-631-2526 or toll-free 800-331-3050. *Fax:* 918-631-5105. *E-mail:* vicki-hendrickson@utulsa.edu. *Website:* http://www.utulsa.edu/.

UNIVERSITY OF UTAH
Salt Lake City, UT

Tuition & fees (UT res): $7138	Average undergraduate aid package: $15,437

ABOUT THE INSTITUTION State-supported, coed. *Awards:* certificates, bachelor's, master's, and doctoral degrees. 100 undergraduate majors. *Total enrollment:* 32,388. Undergraduates: 24,840. Freshmen: 3,494. Federal methodology is used as a basis for awarding need-based institutional aid.

UNDERGRADUATE EXPENSES for 2013–2014 *Application fee:* $45. *Tuition, state resident:* full-time $6200; part-time $174 per credit hour. *Tuition, nonresident:* full-time $21,704; part-time $599 per credit hour. *Required fees:* full-time $938. Full-time tuition and fees vary according to course level, course load, degree level, program, and student level. Part-time tuition and fees vary according to course level, course load, degree level, program, and student level. *College room and board:* $7155; *Room only:* $3719. Room and board charges vary according to board plan, housing facility, and location.

FRESHMAN FINANCIAL AID (Fall 2012, est.) 1,794 applied for aid; of those 73% were deemed to have need. 99% of freshmen with need received aid; of those 14% had need fully met. *Average percent of need met:* 59% (excluding resources awarded to replace EFC). *Average financial aid package:* $14,194 (excluding resources awarded to replace EFC). 7% of all full-time freshmen had no need and received non-need-based gift aid.

UNDERGRADUATE FINANCIAL AID (Fall 2012, est.) 9,340 applied for aid; of those 86% were deemed to have need. 100% of undergraduates with need received aid; of those 9% had need fully met. *Average percent of need met:* 61% (excluding resources awarded to replace EFC). *Average financial aid package:* $15,437 (excluding resources awarded to replace EFC). 4% of all full-time undergraduates had no need and received non-need-based gift aid.

GIFT AID (NEED-BASED) Total amount: $47,490,054 (82% federal, 1% state, 5% institutional, 12% external sources). *Receiving aid:* Freshmen: 34% (1,057); all full-time undergraduates: 39% (6,521). *Average award:* Freshmen: $7065; Undergraduates: $5997. *Scholarships, grants, and awards:* Federal Pell, FSEOG, state, private, college/university gift aid from institutional funds, Federal Nursing, TEACH Grants.

GIFT AID (NON-NEED-BASED) Total amount: $4,652,842 (3% federal, 14% state, 4% institutional, 79% external sources). *Receiving aid:* Freshmen: 3% (87). Undergraduates: 1% (165). *Average award:* Freshmen: $6945. Undergraduates: $5652. *Scholarships, grants, and awards by category: Academic interests/achievement:* architecture, area/ethnic studies, biological sciences, business, communication, computer science, education, engineering/technologies, English, foreign languages, general academic interests/achievements, health fields, humanities, international studies, mathematics, military science, physical sciences, social sciences. *Creative arts/performance:* art/fine arts, cinema/film/broadcasting, creative writing, dance, journalism/publications, music, performing arts, theater/drama. *Special achievements/activities:* cheerleading/drum major, general special achievements/activities, leadership. *Special characteristics:* children of faculty/staff, children of public servants, children with a deceased or disabled parent, ethnic background, first-generation college students, handicapped students, out-of-state students, spouses of deceased or disabled public servants. *Tuition waivers:* Full or partial for employees or children of employees, senior citizens. *ROTC:* Army, Naval, Air Force.

LOANS Student loans: $56,290,681 (56% need-based, 44% non-need-based). 50% of past graduating class borrowed through all loan programs. *Average indebtedness per student:* $20,796. *Average need-based loan:* Freshmen: $3281. Undergraduates: $4403. *Parent loans:* $2,106,767 (44% need-based, 56% non-need-based). *Programs:* Federal Direct (Subsidized and Unsubsidized Stafford, PLUS), Perkins, Federal Nursing, college/university, private loans.

WORK-STUDY *Federal work-study:* Total amount: $1,625,027; 333 jobs averaging $4880.

ATHLETIC AWARDS Total amount: $7,977,577 (29% need-based, 71% non-need-based).

APPLYING FOR FINANCIAL AID *Required financial aid forms:* FAFSA, institution's own form. *Financial aid deadline (priority):* 4/1. *Notification date:* Continuous beginning 4/15. Students must reply within 6 weeks of notification.

CONTACT Amy Capps, Assistant Director, University of Utah, 201 South 1460 East, Room 105, Salt Lake City, UT 84112-9055, 801-581-6211 or toll-free 800-685-8856. *Fax:* 801-585-6350. *E-mail:* fawin1@saff.utah.edu. *Website:* http://www.utah.edu/.

UNIVERSITY OF VERMONT
Burlington, VT

Tuition & fees (VT res): $15,254   **Average undergraduate aid package: $21,229**

ABOUT THE INSTITUTION State-supported, coed. **Awards:** certificates, bachelor's, master's, and doctoral degrees. 100 undergraduate majors. **Total enrollment:** 13,097. Undergraduates: 11,211. Freshmen: 2,372. Federal methodology is used as a basis for awarding need-based institutional aid.

UNDERGRADUATE EXPENSES for 2013–2014 Application fee: $55. **Tuition, state resident:** full-time $13,344. **Tuition, nonresident:** full-time $33,672. **Required fees:** full-time $1910. Part-time tuition and fees vary according to course load. **College room and board:** $10,094. Room and board charges vary according to board plan and housing facility.

FRESHMAN FINANCIAL AID (Fall 2011) 1,875 applied for aid; of those 79% were deemed to have need. 99% of freshmen with need received aid; of those 11% had need fully met. **Average percent of need met:** 67% (excluding resources awarded to replace EFC). **Average financial aid package:** $21,526 (excluding resources awarded to replace EFC). 27% of all full-time freshmen had no need and received non-need-based gift aid.

UNDERGRADUATE FINANCIAL AID (Fall 2011) 7,204 applied for aid; of those 84% were deemed to have need. 99% of undergraduates with need received aid; of those 11% had need fully met. **Average percent of need met:** 65% (excluding resources awarded to replace EFC). **Average financial aid package:** $21,229 (excluding resources awarded to replace EFC). 22% of all full-time undergraduates had no need and received non-need-based gift aid.

GIFT AID (NEED-BASED) Total amount: $82,080,580 (14% federal, 5% state, 78% institutional, 3% external sources). **Receiving aid:** Freshmen: 60% (1,431); all full-time undergraduates: 58% (5,841). **Average award:** Freshmen: $15,554; Undergraduates: $14,081. **Scholarships, grants, and awards:** Federal Pell, FSEOG, state, private, college/university gift aid from institutional funds, Federal Nursing.

GIFT AID (NON-NEED-BASED) Total amount: $8,675,004 (4% state, 82% institutional, 14% external sources). **Receiving aid:** Freshmen: 4% (86). Undergraduates: 2% (243). **Average award:** Freshmen: $6995. Undergraduates: $6643. **Scholarships, grants, and awards by category:** Academic interests/achievement: agriculture, area/ethnic studies, business, computer science, education, engineering/technologies, English, foreign languages, general academic interests/achievements, health fields, home economics, humanities, international studies, mathematics, military science, physical sciences, premedicine, social sciences. **Creative arts/performance:** debating, music, theater/drama. **Special achievements/activities:** community service, leadership, memberships. **Special characteristics:** adult students, ethnic background, first-generation college students. **Tuition waivers:** Full or partial for employees or children of employees. **ROTC:** Army.

LOANS Student loans: $45,135,719 (47% need-based, 53% non-need-based). 59% of past graduating class borrowed through all loan programs. **Average indebtedness per student:** $27,588. **Average need-based loan:** Freshmen: $3676. Undergraduates: $4555. **Parent loans:** $39,682,243 (100% non-need-based). **Programs:** Federal Direct (Subsidized and Unsubsidized Stafford, PLUS), Perkins, Federal Nursing, college/university.

WORK-STUDY Federal work-study: Total amount: $2,110,950; 1,392 jobs averaging $1518.

ATHLETIC AWARDS Total amount: $5,857,032 (29% need-based, 71% non-need-based).

APPLYING FOR FINANCIAL AID Required financial aid form: FAFSA. **Financial aid deadline (priority):** 2/10. **Notification date:** Continuous beginning 3/31. Students must reply within 4 weeks of notification.

CONTACT Office of Student Financial Services, University of Vermont, 223 Waterman Building, Burlington, VT 05405-0160, 802-656-5700. Fax: 802-656-4076. E-mail: sfs@uvm.edu. Website: http://www.uvm.edu/.

UNIVERSITY OF VIRGINIA
Charlottesville, VA

Tuition & fees (VA res): $12,458   **Average undergraduate aid package: $23,008**

ABOUT THE INSTITUTION State-supported, coed. **Awards:** certificates, bachelor's, master's, and doctoral degrees. 48 undergraduate majors. **Total enrollment:** 23,907. Undergraduates: 15,822. Freshmen: 3,397. Federal methodology is used as a basis for awarding need-based institutional aid.

UNDERGRADUATE EXPENSES for 2013–2014 Application fee: $60. **Tuition, state resident:** full-time $10,016. **Tuition, nonresident:** full-time $36,720. **Required fees:** full-time $2442. Full-time tuition and fees vary according to program. **College room and board:** $9717; **Room only:** $5337. Room and board charges vary according to board plan and housing facility.

FRESHMAN FINANCIAL AID (Fall 2012, est.) 2,404 applied for aid; of those 46% were deemed to have need. 99% of freshmen with need received aid; of those 97% had need fully met. **Average percent of need met:** 99% (excluding resources awarded to replace EFC). **Average financial aid package:** $22,824 (excluding resources awarded to replace EFC). 9% of all full-time freshmen had no need and received non-need-based gift aid.

UNDERGRADUATE FINANCIAL AID (Fall 2012, est.) 8,273 applied for aid; of those 56% were deemed to have need. 99% of undergraduates with need received aid; of those 96% had need fully met. **Average percent of need met:** 98% (excluding resources awarded to replace EFC). **Average financial aid package:** $23,008 (excluding resources awarded to replace EFC). 11% of all full-time undergraduates had no need and received non-need-based gift aid.

GIFT AID (NEED-BASED) Total amount: $67,476,480 (13% federal, 7% state, 72% institutional, 8% external sources). **Receiving aid:** Freshmen: 27% (916); all full-time undergraduates: 27% (3,821). **Average award:** Freshmen: $17,576; Undergraduates: $18,345. **Scholarships, grants, and awards:** Federal Pell, FSEOG, state, private, college/university gift aid from institutional funds, Federal Nursing.

GIFT AID (NON-NEED-BASED) Total amount: $16,611,264 (19% institutional, 81% external sources). **Receiving aid:** Freshmen: 4% (135). Undergraduates: 3% (407). **Average award:** Freshmen: $10,479. Undergraduates: $9863. **Scholarships, grants, and awards by category:** Academic interests/achievement: general academic interests/achievements. **Creative arts/performance:** music. **Tuition waivers:** Full or partial for employees or children of employees, senior citizens. **ROTC:** Army, Naval, Air Force.

LOANS Student loans: $31,067,734 (53% need-based, 47% non-need-based). 36% of past graduating class borrowed through all loan programs. **Average indebtedness per student:** $21,591. **Average need-based loan:** Freshmen: $5785. Undergraduates: $6131. **Parent loans:** $8,114,814 (12% need-based, 88% non-need-based). **Programs:** Perkins, Federal Nursing, college/university, private loans.

WORK-STUDY Federal work-study: Total amount: $1,862,120; jobs available.

ATHLETIC AWARDS Total amount: $11,953,245 (33% need-based, 67% non-need-based).

APPLYING FOR FINANCIAL AID Required financial aid forms: FAFSA, institution's own form. **Financial aid deadline (priority):** 3/1. **Notification date:** 4/5. Students must reply by 5/1.

CONTACT Ms. Yvonne B. Hubbard, Director of Student Financial Services, University of Virginia, PO Box 400207, Charlottesville, VA 22904-4207, 434-982-6000. E-mail: faid@virginia.edu. Website: http://www.virginia.edu/.

THE UNIVERSITY OF VIRGINIA'S COLLEGE AT WISE
Wise, VA

Tuition & fees (VA res): $8509   **Average undergraduate aid package: $5176**

ABOUT THE INSTITUTION State-supported, coed. **Awards:** certificates and bachelor's degrees. 25 undergraduate majors. **Total enrollment:** 2,420. Undergraduates: 2,420. Freshmen: 373. Federal methodology is used as a basis for awarding need-based institutional aid.

UNIVERSITY OF WASHINGTON, BOTHELL

UNDERGRADUATE EXPENSES for 2013–2014 *Application fee:* $25. *Tuition, state resident:* full-time $8509; part-time $200 per credit hour. *Tuition, nonresident:* full-time $23,565; part-time $808 per credit hour. *Required fees:* $71 per credit hour. Part-time tuition and fees vary according to course load. *College room and board:* $9440; *Room only:* $5642. Room and board charges vary according to board plan and housing facility.
FRESHMAN FINANCIAL AID (Fall 2012, est.) 343 applied for aid; of those 84% were deemed to have need. 100% of freshmen with need received aid; of those 44% had need fully met. *Average percent of need met:* 96% (excluding resources awarded to replace EFC). *Average financial aid package:* $10,026 (excluding resources awarded to replace EFC). 9% of all full-time freshmen had no need and received non-need-based gift aid.
UNDERGRADUATE FINANCIAL AID (Fall 2012, est.) 1,461 applied for aid; of those 87% were deemed to have need. 100% of undergraduates with need received aid; of those 58% had need fully met. *Average percent of need met:* 88% (excluding resources awarded to replace EFC). *Average financial aid package:* $5176 (excluding resources awarded to replace EFC). 7% of all full-time undergraduates had no need and received non-need-based gift aid.
GIFT AID (NEED-BASED) Total amount: $5,906,323 (62% federal, 38% state). *Receiving aid:* Freshmen: 78% (279); all full-time undergraduates: 83% (1,277). *Average award:* Freshmen: $6933; Undergraduates: $7490. *Scholarships, grants, and awards:* Federal Pell, FSEOG, state, private, college/university gift aid from institutional funds.
GIFT AID (NON-NEED-BASED) Total amount: $2,250,796 (82% institutional, 18% external sources). *Receiving aid:* Freshmen: 65% (231). Undergraduates: 83% (1,277). *Average award:* Freshmen: $3879. Undergraduates: $4029. *Scholarships, grants, and awards by category: Academic interests/achievement:* agriculture, biological sciences, business, computer science, education, English, general academic interests/achievements, health fields, humanities, mathematics, physical sciences, pre-medicine, social sciences. *Creative arts/performance:* creative writing, general creative arts/performance, journalism/publications, music, performing arts, theater/drama. *Special achievements/activities:* community service, religious involvement. *Special characteristics:* children with a deceased or disabled parent, ethnic background, local/state students, veterans, veterans' children. *Tuition waivers:* Full or partial for employees or children of employees, senior citizens. *ROTC:* Army.
LOANS Student loans: $6,133,078 (50% need-based, 50% non-need-based). 66% of past graduating class borrowed through all loan programs. *Average indebtedness per student:* $15,033. *Average need-based loan:* Freshmen: $2365. Undergraduates: $1785. *Parent loans:* $1,190,416 (100% non-need-based). *Programs:* Perkins, state, college/university.
WORK-STUDY Federal work-study: Total amount: $264,522; jobs available.
ATHLETIC AWARDS Total amount: $461,315 (100% non-need-based).
APPLYING FOR FINANCIAL AID Required financial aid form: FAFSA. *Financial aid deadline (priority):* 4/1. *Notification date:* Continuous. Students must reply within 4 weeks of notification.
CONTACT Mrs. Rebecca Huffman, Director of Financial Aid, The University of Virginia's College at Wise, 1 College Avenue, Wise, VA 24293, 276-328-0277 or toll-free 888-282-9324. *Fax:* 276-328-0251. *E-mail:* reg5a@uvawise.edu. *Website:* http://www.uvawise.edu/.

UNIVERSITY OF WASHINGTON
Seattle, WA

Tuition & fees (WA res): $11,305	Average undergraduate aid package: $18,600

ABOUT THE INSTITUTION State-supported, coed. *Awards:* certificates, bachelor's, master's, and doctoral degrees. 147 undergraduate majors. *Total enrollment:* 42,428. Undergraduates: 29,017. Freshmen: 5,788. Federal methodology is used as a basis for awarding need-based institutional aid.
UNDERGRADUATE EXPENSES for 2013–2014 *Application fee:* $60. *Tuition, state resident:* full-time $11,305. *Tuition, nonresident:* full-time $28,860. Full-time tuition and fees vary according to course load. Part-time tuition and fees vary according to course load. Room and board charges vary according to board plan and housing facility.
FRESHMAN FINANCIAL AID (Fall 2012, est.) 3,800 applied for aid; of those 61% were deemed to have need. 100% of freshmen with need received aid; of those 23% had need fully met. *Average percent of need met:* 83% (excluding resources

awarded to replace EFC). *Average financial aid package:* $17,000 (excluding resources awarded to replace EFC). 2% of all full-time freshmen had no need and received non-need-based gift aid.
UNDERGRADUATE FINANCIAL AID (Fall 2012, est.) 14,900 applied for aid; of those 76% were deemed to have need. 100% of undergraduates with need received aid; of those 24% had need fully met. *Average percent of need met:* 82% (excluding resources awarded to replace EFC). *Average financial aid package:* $18,600 (excluding resources awarded to replace EFC). 2% of all full-time undergraduates had no need and received non-need-based gift aid.
GIFT AID (NEED-BASED) Total amount: $135,900,000 (29% federal, 40% state, 29% institutional, 2% external sources). *Receiving aid:* Freshmen: 34% (1,950); all full-time undergraduates: 26% (9,600). *Average award:* Freshmen: $13,500; Undergraduates: $14,000. *Scholarships, grants, and awards:* Federal Pell, FSEOG, state, private, college/university gift aid from institutional funds.
GIFT AID (NON-NEED-BASED) Total amount: $12,440,000 (3% state, 64% institutional, 33% external sources). *Receiving aid:* Freshmen: 5% (300). Undergraduates: 2% (700). *Average award:* Freshmen: $7100. Undergraduates: $6200. *Scholarships, grants, and awards by category: Academic interests/achievement:* architecture, business, computer science, education, engineering/technologies, general academic interests/achievements, health fields. *Creative arts/performance:* art/fine arts, general creative arts/performance, music, performing arts. *Special achievements/activities:* general special achievements/activities, leadership, memberships. *Tuition waivers:* Full or partial for employees or children of employees, senior citizens. *ROTC:* Army, Naval, Air Force.
LOANS Student loans: $76,600,000 (77% need-based, 23% non-need-based). 49% of past graduating class borrowed through all loan programs. *Average indebtedness per student:* $20,800. *Average need-based loan:* Freshmen: $5500. Undergraduates: $7000. *Parent loans:* $44,200,000 (34% need-based, 66% non-need-based). *Programs:* Federal Direct (Subsidized and Unsubsidized Stafford, PLUS), Perkins, Federal Nursing, college/university.
WORK-STUDY Federal work-study: Total amount: $2,500,000; jobs available. *State or other work-study/employment:* Total amount: $300,000 (100% need-based). Part-time jobs available.
ATHLETIC AWARDS Total amount: $4,100,000 (100% non-need-based).
APPLYING FOR FINANCIAL AID Required financial aid form: FAFSA. *Financial aid deadline (priority):* 2/28. *Notification date:* 3/31.
CONTACT Office of Student Financial Aid, University of Washington, PO Box 355880, Seattle, WA 98195-5880, 206-543-6101. *E-mail:* osfa@u.washington.edu. *Website:* http://www.washington.edu/.

UNIVERSITY OF WASHINGTON, BOTHELL
Bothell, WA

Tuition & fees: N/R	Average undergraduate aid package: $15,700

ABOUT THE INSTITUTION State-supported, coed. *Awards:* certificates, bachelor's, and master's degrees. 28 undergraduate majors. *Total enrollment:* 4,159. Undergraduates: 3,637. Freshmen: 546. Federal methodology is used as a basis for awarding need-based institutional aid.
FRESHMAN FINANCIAL AID (Fall 2011) 411 applied for aid; of those 78% were deemed to have need. 95% of freshmen with need received aid; of those 22% had need fully met. *Average percent of need met:* 79% (excluding resources awarded to replace EFC). *Average financial aid package:* $14,200 (excluding resources awarded to replace EFC). 2% of all full-time freshmen had no need and received non-need-based gift aid.
UNDERGRADUATE FINANCIAL AID (Fall 2011) 2,000 applied for aid; of those 88% were deemed to have need. 69% of undergraduates with need received aid; of those 18% had need fully met. *Average percent of need met:* 74% (excluding resources awarded to replace EFC). *Average financial aid package:* $15,700 (excluding resources awarded to replace EFC). 1% of all full-time undergraduates had no need and received non-need-based gift aid.
GIFT AID (NEED-BASED) Total amount: $14,438,000 (38% federal, 38% state, 23% institutional, 1% external sources). *Receiving aid:* Freshmen: 52% (274); all full-time undergraduates: 39% (1,020). *Average award:* Freshmen: $10,700; Undergrad-

Peterson's How to Get Money for College 2014

www.petersonsbooks.com **669**

uates: $11,500. *Scholarships, grants, and awards:* Federal Pell, FSEOG, state, private, college/university gift aid from institutional funds.
GIFT AID (NON-NEED-BASED) *Total amount:* $216,000 (13% state, 6% institutional, 81% external sources). *Receiving aid:* Freshmen: 2% (8). Undergraduates: 1% (15). *Average award:* Freshmen: $2600. Undergraduates: $4200. *Scholarships, grants, and awards by category: Academic interests/achievement:* general academic interests/achievements. *ROTC:* Army cooperative, Naval cooperative, Air Force cooperative.
LOANS *Student loans:* $11,076,000 (82% need-based, 18% non-need-based). 51% of past graduating class borrowed through all loan programs. *Average indebtedness per student:* $18,559. *Average need-based loan:* Freshmen: $5000. Undergraduates: $6500. *Parent loans:* $2,866,000 (37% need-based, 63% non-need-based). *Programs:* Federal Direct (Subsidized and Unsubsidized Stafford, PLUS), Perkins.
WORK-STUDY *Federal work-study:* Total amount: $162,000; jobs available. *State or other work-study/employment:* Total amount: $71,000 (100% need-based). Part-time jobs available.
APPLYING FOR FINANCIAL AID *Required financial aid form:* FAFSA. *Financial aid deadline (priority):* 2/28. *Notification date:* Continuous beginning 3/15.
CONTACT Office of Financial Aid and Scholarships, University of Washington, Bothell, Box 358500, 18115 Campus Way NE, Bothell, WA 98011-8246, 425-352-5240. *Fax:* 425-352-3217. *E-mail:* finaid@uwb.edu.
Website: http://www.uwb.edu/.

UNIVERSITY OF WASHINGTON, TACOMA
Tacoma, WA

Tuition & fees (area res): $11,902	Average undergraduate aid package: $17,800

ABOUT THE INSTITUTION State-supported, coed. *Awards:* certificates, bachelor's, master's, and doctoral degrees. 35 undergraduate majors. *Total enrollment:* 3,906. Undergraduates: 3,361. Freshmen: 341. Federal methodology is used as a basis for awarding need-based institutional aid.
UNDERGRADUATE EXPENSES for 2013–2014 *Application fee:* $60. *Tuition, area resident:* full-time $11,305; part-time $376. *Tuition, nonresident:* full-time $28,860; part-time $962. *Required fees:* full-time $597.
FRESHMAN FINANCIAL AID (Fall 2012, est.) 260 applied for aid; of those 92% were deemed to have need. 100% of freshmen with need received aid; of those 33% had need fully met. *Average percent of need met:* 78% (excluding resources awarded to replace EFC). *Average financial aid package:* $14,800 (excluding resources awarded to replace EFC). 4% of all full-time freshmen had no need and received non-need-based gift aid.
UNDERGRADUATE FINANCIAL AID (Fall 2012, est.) 2,690 applied for aid; of those 93% were deemed to have need. 100% of undergraduates with need received aid; of those 32% had need fully met. *Average percent of need met:* 78% (excluding resources awarded to replace EFC). *Average financial aid package:* $17,800 (excluding resources awarded to replace EFC). 4% of all full-time undergraduates had no need and received non-need-based gift aid.
GIFT AID (NEED-BASED) *Total amount:* $30,210,500 (28% federal, 36% state, 35% institutional, 1% external sources). *Receiving aid:* Freshmen: 64% (210); all full-time undergraduates: 78% (2,200). *Average award:* Freshmen: $14,300; Undergraduates: $13,600. *Scholarships, grants, and awards:* Federal Pell, FSEOG, state, private, college/university gift aid from institutional funds.
GIFT AID (NON-NEED-BASED) *Total amount:* $826,000 (72% institutional, 28% external sources). *Receiving aid:* Freshmen: 11% (35). Undergraduates: 3% (80). *Average award:* Freshmen: $2500. Undergraduates: $1500. *Scholarships, grants, and awards by category: Academic interests/achievement:* general academic interests/achievements. *ROTC:* Army cooperative, Naval cooperative, Air Force cooperative.
LOANS *Student loans:* $15,259,000 (84% need-based, 16% non-need-based). 62% of past graduating class borrowed through all loan programs. *Average indebtedness per student:* $20,700. *Average need-based loan:* Freshmen: $5000. Undergraduates: $6500. *Parent loans:* $2,918,000 (32% need-based, 68% non-need-based). *Programs:* Federal Direct (Subsidized and Unsubsidized Stafford, PLUS), Perkins, Federal Nursing.

WORK-STUDY *Federal work-study:* Total amount: $280,000; 100 jobs averaging $2600. *State or other work-study/employment:* Total amount: $63,000 (100% need-based). 30 part-time jobs averaging $3000.
APPLYING FOR FINANCIAL AID *Required financial aid form:* FAFSA. *Financial aid deadline (priority):* 2/28. *Notification date:* 4/1. Students must reply within 3 weeks of notification.
CONTACT Ms. Shari King, Associate Director of Financial Aid and Veterans Affairs, University of Washington, Tacoma, 1900 Commerce Street, Box 358400, Tacoma, WA 98402-3100, 253-692-4400 or toll-free 800-736-7750. *Fax:* 253-692-4414. *E-mail:* osfatac@uw.edu.
Website: http://www.tacoma.washington.edu/.

THE UNIVERSITY OF WEST ALABAMA
Livingston, AL

Tuition & fees (AL res): $7320	Average undergraduate aid package: $9610

ABOUT THE INSTITUTION State-supported, coed. *Awards:* certificates, associate, bachelor's, and master's degrees. 26 undergraduate majors. *Total enrollment:* 4,943. Undergraduates: 2,108. Freshmen: 207. Federal methodology is used as a basis for awarding need-based institutional aid.
UNDERGRADUATE EXPENSES for 2013–2014 *Application fee:* $35. *Tuition, state resident:* full-time $6170; part-time $263 per credit. *Tuition, nonresident:* full-time $12,340; part-time $526 per credit. *Required fees:* full-time $1150. Full-time tuition and fees vary according to course load, degree level, and program. Part-time tuition and fees vary according to course load, degree level, and program. *College room and board:* $5920; *Room only:* $3640. Room and board charges vary according to board plan and housing facility.
FRESHMAN FINANCIAL AID (Fall 2012, est.) 301 applied for aid; of those 84% were deemed to have need. 100% of freshmen with need received aid; of those 2% had need fully met. *Average percent of need met:* 30% (excluding resources awarded to replace EFC). *Average financial aid package:* $9136 (excluding resources awarded to replace EFC). 10% of all full-time freshmen had no need and received non-need-based gift aid.
UNDERGRADUATE FINANCIAL AID (Fall 2012, est.) 1,585 applied for aid; of those 88% were deemed to have need. 100% of undergraduates with need received aid; of those 1% had need fully met. *Average percent of need met:* 28% (excluding resources awarded to replace EFC). *Average financial aid package:* $9610 (excluding resources awarded to replace EFC). 4% of all full-time undergraduates had no need and received non-need-based gift aid.
GIFT AID (NEED-BASED) *Total amount:* $5,473,761 (99% federal, 1% state). *Receiving aid:* Freshmen: 60% (205); all full-time undergraduates: 66% (1,172). *Average award:* Freshmen: $4980; Undergraduates: $4912. *Scholarships, grants, and awards:* Federal Pell, FSEOG, state, private, college/university gift aid from institutional funds, United Negro College Fund.
GIFT AID (NON-NEED-BASED) *Total amount:* $2,072,260 (87% institutional, 13% external sources). *Receiving aid:* Freshmen: 42% (144). Undergraduates: 28% (501). *Average award:* Freshmen: $3930. Undergraduates: $3750. *Scholarships, grants, and awards by category: Academic interests/achievement:* general academic interests/achievements. *Creative arts/performance:* music. *Special achievements/activities:* cheerleading/drum major, general special achievements/activities, rodeo. *Special characteristics:* children of faculty/staff, first-generation college students. *Tuition waivers:* Full or partial for employees or children of employees. *ROTC:* Army cooperative, Air Force cooperative.
LOANS *Student loans:* $10,429,013 (44% need-based, 56% non-need-based). 78% of past graduating class borrowed through all loan programs. *Average indebtedness per student:* $27,815. *Parent loans:* $1,163,153 (100% non-need-based). *Programs:* Federal Direct (Subsidized and Unsubsidized Stafford, PLUS), Perkins.
WORK-STUDY *Federal work-study:* Total amount: $342,041; 132 jobs averaging $3400. *State or other work-study/employment:* Part-time jobs available.
ATHLETIC AWARDS Total amount: $1,154,866 (100% non-need-based).
APPLYING FOR FINANCIAL AID *Required financial aid form:* FAFSA. *Financial aid deadline (priority):* 3/1. *Notification date:* Continuous beginning 4/15. Students must reply within 2 weeks of notification.

CONTACT Mr. Don Rainer, Director of Financial Aid, The University of West Alabama, Station 3, Livingston, AL 35470, 205-652-3576 or toll-free 800-621-8044. *Fax:* 205-652-3847. *E-mail:* drainer@uwa.edu. *Website:* http://www.uwa.edu/.

UNIVERSITY OF WEST FLORIDA
Pensacola, FL

Tuition & fees (FL res): $7022	Average undergraduate aid package: $8495

ABOUT THE INSTITUTION State-supported, coed. *Awards:* certificates, associate, bachelor's, master's, and doctoral degrees. 56 undergraduate majors. *Total enrollment:* 12,651. Undergraduates: 10,332. Freshmen: 1,450. Federal methodology is used as a basis for awarding need-based institutional aid.
UNDERGRADUATE EXPENSES for 2013–2014 *Application fee:* $30. *Tuition, state resident:* full-time $5072; part-time $207.95 per semester hour. *Tuition, nonresident:* full-time $17,954; part-time $637.34 per semester hour. *Required fees:* full-time $1950; $207.95 per semester hour. Full-time tuition and fees vary according to location and reciprocity agreements. Part-time tuition and fees vary according to location and reciprocity agreements. *College room and board:* $9210. Room and board charges vary according to housing facility. *Payment plan:* Tuition prepayment.
FRESHMAN FINANCIAL AID (Fall 2012, est.) 1,315 applied for aid; of those 74% were deemed to have need. 97% of freshmen with need received aid; of those 15% had need fully met. *Average percent of need met:* 66% (excluding resources awarded to replace EFC). *Average financial aid package:* $8846 (excluding resources awarded to replace EFC). 4% of all full-time freshmen had no need and received non-need-based gift aid.
UNDERGRADUATE FINANCIAL AID (Fall 2012, est.) 5,754 applied for aid; of those 80% were deemed to have need. 98% of undergraduates with need received aid; of those 14% had need fully met. *Average percent of need met:* 62% (excluding resources awarded to replace EFC). *Average financial aid package:* $8495 (excluding resources awarded to replace EFC). 5% of all full-time undergraduates had no need and received non-need-based gift aid.
GIFT AID (NEED-BASED) *Total amount:* $27,689,115 (58% federal, 22% state, 18% institutional, 2% external sources). *Receiving aid:* Freshmen: 50% (737); all full-time undergraduates: 46% (3,433). *Average award:* Freshmen: $6131; Undergraduates: $5375. *Scholarships, grants, and awards:* Federal Pell, FSEOG, state, private, college/university gift aid from institutional funds.
GIFT AID (NON-NEED-BASED) *Total amount:* $4,748,039 (1% federal, 54% state, 29% institutional, 16% external sources). *Receiving aid:* Freshmen: 37% (549). Undergraduates: 27% (2,029). *Average award:* Freshmen: $2101. Undergraduates: $2408. *Scholarships, grants, and awards by category: Academic interests/achievement:* biological sciences, business, communication, computer science, education, engineering/technologies, general academic interests/achievements, mathematics, military science, physical sciences, social sciences. *Creative arts/performance:* applied art and design, art/fine arts, music, theater/drama. *Special achievements/activities:* leadership. *Special characteristics:* children and siblings of alumni, children of faculty/staff, handicapped students, international students, out-of-state students, veterans. *Tuition waivers:* Full or partial for employees or children of employees, senior citizens. *ROTC:* Army, Air Force.
LOANS *Student loans:* $36,932,224 (73% need-based, 27% non-need-based). *Average need-based loan:* Freshmen: $3184. Undergraduates: $4109. *Parent loans:* $1,307,069 (28% need-based, 72% non-need-based). *Programs:* Federal Direct (Subsidized and Unsubsidized Stafford, PLUS), Perkins.
WORK-STUDY *Federal work-study:* Total amount: $418,032; jobs available. *State or other work-study/employment:* Part-time jobs available.
ATHLETIC AWARDS Total amount: $1,706,194 (28% need-based, 72% non-need-based).
APPLYING FOR FINANCIAL AID *Required financial aid form:* FAFSA. *Financial aid deadline:* Continuous. *Notification date:* Continuous beginning 2/1.
CONTACT Ms. Georganne E. Major, Coordinator of Financial Aid, University of West Florida, 11000 University Parkway, Pensacola, FL 32514-5750, 850-474-2397 or toll-free 800-263-1074. *E-mail:* gmajor@uwf.edu. *Website:* http://www.uwf.edu/.

UNIVERSITY OF WEST GEORGIA
Carrollton, GA

Tuition & fees (GA res): $6710	Average undergraduate aid package: $8957

ABOUT THE INSTITUTION State-supported, coed. *Awards:* certificates, bachelor's, master's, and doctoral degrees. 46 undergraduate majors. *Total enrollment:* 11,769. Undergraduates: 9,963. Freshmen: 2,070. Federal methodology is used as a basis for awarding need-based institutional aid.
UNDERGRADUATE EXPENSES for 2013–2014 *Application fee:* $40. *Tuition, state resident:* full-time $4852; part-time $161.74 per semester hour. *Tuition, nonresident:* full-time $17,128; part-time $570.94 per semester hour. *Required fees:* full-time $1858; $46.35 per semester hour or $512 per term. Full-time tuition and fees vary according to course load and location. Part-time tuition and fees vary according to course load and location. *College room and board:* $7482; *Room only:* $4100. Room and board charges vary according to board plan and housing facility.
FRESHMAN FINANCIAL AID (Fall 2012, est.) 1,626 applied for aid; of those 82% were deemed to have need. 99% of freshmen with need received aid; of those 23% had need fully met. *Average percent of need met:* 55% (excluding resources awarded to replace EFC). *Average financial aid package:* $9228 (excluding resources awarded to replace EFC). 3% of all full-time freshmen had no need and received non-need-based gift aid.
UNDERGRADUATE FINANCIAL AID (Fall 2012, est.) 7,056 applied for aid; of those 86% were deemed to have need. 98% of undergraduates with need received aid; of those 30% had need fully met. *Average percent of need met:* 51% (excluding resources awarded to replace EFC). *Average financial aid package:* $8957 (excluding resources awarded to replace EFC). 4% of all full-time undergraduates had no need and received non-need-based gift aid.
GIFT AID (NEED-BASED) *Total amount:* $30,350,720 (72% federal, 26% state, 1% institutional, 1% external sources). *Receiving aid:* Freshmen: 57% (1,174); all full-time undergraduates: 60% (4,920). *Average award:* Freshmen: $6445; Undergraduates: $5700. *Scholarships, grants, and awards:* Federal Pell, FSEOG, state, private, college/university gift aid from institutional funds.
GIFT AID (NON-NEED-BASED) *Total amount:* $4,089,555 (93% state, 4% institutional, 3% external sources). *Receiving aid:* Freshmen: 58% (1,202). Undergraduates: 7% (612). *Average award:* Freshmen: $1745. Undergraduates: $1584. *Scholarships, grants, and awards by category: Academic interests/achievement:* biological sciences, business, communication, computer science, education, English, foreign languages, general academic interests/achievements, health fields, humanities, mathematics, physical sciences, premedicine, social sciences. *Creative arts/performance:* applied art and design, art/fine arts, debating, general creative arts/performance, journalism/publications, music, performing arts, theater/drama. *Special achievements/activities:* community service, leadership, memberships, religious involvement. *Special characteristics:* adult students, children and siblings of alumni, general special characteristics, handicapped students, international students, local/state students, members of minority groups. *Tuition waivers:* Full or partial for employees or children of employees, senior citizens. *ROTC:* Air Force cooperative.
LOANS *Student loans:* $47,149,442 (47% need-based, 53% non-need-based). 65% of past graduating class borrowed through all loan programs. *Average indebtedness per student:* $18,603. *Average need-based loan:* Freshmen: $3417. Undergraduates: $4078. *Parent loans:* $6,379,221 (100% non-need-based). *Programs:* Federal Direct (Subsidized and Unsubsidized Stafford, PLUS), Perkins.
WORK-STUDY *Federal work-study:* Total amount: $278,182; 223 jobs averaging $1455. *State or other work-study/employment:* 1,059 part-time jobs averaging $1230.
ATHLETIC AWARDS Total amount: $885,021 (45% need-based, 55% non-need-based).
APPLYING FOR FINANCIAL AID *Required financial aid form:* FAFSA. *Financial aid deadline (priority):* 4/1. *Notification date:* 5/1.
CONTACT Ms. Sherry Robinson, Interim Director of Financial Aid, University of West Georgia, 1601 Maple Street, Aycock Hall, Carrollton, GA 30118, 678-839-6421. *Fax:* 678-839-6422. *E-mail:* finaid@westga.edu. *Website:* http://www.westga.edu/.

UNIVERSITY OF WISCONSIN–EAU CLAIRE
Eau Claire, WI

Tuition & fees (WI res): $8691 | Average undergraduate aid package: $9224

ABOUT THE INSTITUTION State-supported, coed. *Awards:* certificates, associate, bachelor's, master's, and doctoral degrees. 51 undergraduate majors. *Total enrollment:* 11,046. Undergraduates: 10,499. Freshmen: 2,073. Federal methodology is used as a basis for awarding need-based institutional aid.

UNDERGRADUATE EXPENSES for 2013–2014 *Application fee:* $44. *Tuition, state resident:* full-time $7361; part-time $307 per credit. *Tuition, nonresident:* full-time $14,934; part-time $622 per credit. *Required fees:* full-time $1330; $55 per credit or $3 per term. Full-time tuition and fees vary according to reciprocity agreements. Part-time tuition and fees vary according to reciprocity agreements. *College room and board:* $6300; *Room only:* $3192. Room and board charges vary according to board plan and housing facility.

FRESHMAN FINANCIAL AID (Fall 2011) 1,661 applied for aid; of those 65% were deemed to have need. 98% of freshmen with need received aid; of those 28% had need fully met. *Average percent of need met:* 88% (excluding resources awarded to replace EFC). *Average financial aid package:* $8707 (excluding resources awarded to replace EFC). 6% of all full-time freshmen had no need and received non-need-based gift aid.

UNDERGRADUATE FINANCIAL AID (Fall 2011) 7,269 applied for aid; of those 72% were deemed to have need. 99% of undergraduates with need received aid; of those 33% had need fully met. *Average percent of need met:* 89% (excluding resources awarded to replace EFC). *Average financial aid package:* $9224 (excluding resources awarded to replace EFC). 5% of all full-time undergraduates had no need and received non-need-based gift aid.

GIFT AID (NEED-BASED) *Total amount:* $21,269,754 (54% federal, 24% state, 13% institutional, 9% external sources). *Receiving aid:* Freshmen: 44% (848); all full-time undergraduates: 39% (3,786). *Average award:* Freshmen: $5646; Undergraduates: $5640. *Scholarships, grants, and awards:* Federal Pell, FSEOG, state, private, college/university gift aid from institutional funds, Federal Nursing, Bureau of Indian Affairs Grants, Student Support Services Grants.

GIFT AID (NON-NEED-BASED) *Total amount:* $1,514,506 (9% state, 32% institutional, 59% external sources). *Receiving aid:* Freshmen: 2% (37). Undergraduates: 1% (103). *Average award:* Freshmen: $1327. Undergraduates: $1817. *Scholarships, grants, and awards by category:* Academic interests/achievement: area/ethnic studies, biological sciences, business, communication, computer science, education, English, foreign languages, general academic interests/achievements, health fields, humanities, international studies, library science, mathematics, physical sciences, premedicine, religion/biblical studies, social sciences. *Creative arts/performance:* applied art and design, art/fine arts, debating, journalism/publications, music, theater/drama. *Special achievements/activities:* community service, general special achievements/activities, hobbies/interests, leadership, memberships. *Special characteristics:* adult students, ethnic background, first-generation college students, general special characteristics, international students, local/state students, members of minority groups, previous college experience. *Tuition waivers:* Full or partial for minority students. *ROTC:* Army.

LOANS *Student loans:* $37,780,329 (69% need-based, 31% non-need-based). 70% of past graduating class borrowed through all loan programs. *Average indebtedness per student:* $23,825. *Average need-based loan:* Freshmen: $3536. Undergraduates: $4370. *Parent loans:* $2,494,900 (63% need-based, 37% non-need-based). *Programs:* Federal Direct (Subsidized and Unsubsidized Stafford, PLUS), Perkins, state, college/university, private loans.

WORK-STUDY *Federal work-study:* Total amount: $7,152,498; 3,677 jobs averaging $1666.

APPLYING FOR FINANCIAL AID *Required financial aid form:* FAFSA. *Financial aid deadline (priority):* 4/15. *Notification date:* Continuous beginning 4/15.

CONTACT Ms. Kathleen Sahlhoff, Director of Financial Aid, University of Wisconsin–Eau Claire, 115 Schofield Hall, Eau Claire, WI 54701, 715-836-3373. *Fax:* 715-836-3846. *E-mail:* sahlhoka@uwec.edu. *Website:* http://www.uwec.edu/.

UNIVERSITY OF WISCONSIN–GREEN BAY
Green Bay, WI

Tuition & fees (WI res): $7648 | Average undergraduate aid package: $8919

ABOUT THE INSTITUTION State-supported, coed. *Awards:* associate, bachelor's, and master's degrees. 44 undergraduate majors. *Total enrollment:* 6,790. Undergraduates: 6,611. Freshmen: 921. Federal methodology is used as a basis for awarding need-based institutional aid.

UNDERGRADUATE EXPENSES for 2013–2014 *Application fee:* $44. *One-time required fee:* $200. *Tuition, state resident:* full-time $6298; part-time $262 per credit hour. *Tuition, nonresident:* full-time $13,871; part-time $578 per credit hour. *Required fees:* full-time $1350; $57 per credit hour. Full-time tuition and fees vary according to course load and reciprocity agreements. Part-time tuition and fees vary according to reciprocity agreements. *College room and board:* $7076; *Room only:* $4032. Room and board charges vary according to board plan and housing facility.

FRESHMAN FINANCIAL AID (Fall 2012, est.) 837 applied for aid; of those 79% were deemed to have need. 96% of freshmen with need received aid; of those 32% had need fully met. *Average percent of need met:* 60% (excluding resources awarded to replace EFC). *Average financial aid package:* $8339 (excluding resources awarded to replace EFC). 8% of all full-time freshmen had no need and received non-need-based gift aid.

UNDERGRADUATE FINANCIAL AID (Fall 2012, est.) 3,997 applied for aid; of those 84% were deemed to have need. 97% of undergraduates with need received aid; of those 34% had need fully met. *Average percent of need met:* 64% (excluding resources awarded to replace EFC). *Average financial aid package:* $8919 (excluding resources awarded to replace EFC). 4% of all full-time undergraduates had no need and received non-need-based gift aid.

GIFT AID (NEED-BASED) *Total amount:* $14,323,953 (61% federal, 28% state, 2% institutional, 9% external sources). *Receiving aid:* Freshmen: 44% (395); all full-time undergraduates: 50% (2,296). *Average award:* Freshmen: $6696; Undergraduates: $6620. *Scholarships, grants, and awards:* Federal Pell, FSEOG, state, private, college/university gift aid from institutional funds.

GIFT AID (NON-NEED-BASED) *Total amount:* $1,091,173 (19% state, 15% institutional, 66% external sources). *Receiving aid:* Freshmen: 14% (128). Undergraduates: 8% (379). *Average award:* Freshmen: $2865. Undergraduates: $2776. *Scholarships, grants, and awards by category:* Academic interests/achievement: area/ethnic studies, biological sciences, business, communication, education, engineering/technologies, general academic interests/achievements, health fields, humanities, physical sciences, premedicine, social sciences. *Creative arts/performance:* art/fine arts, dance, journalism/publications, music, theater/drama. *Special achievements/activities:* community service, general special achievements/activities, leadership. *Special characteristics:* adult students, children and siblings of alumni, children of public servants, ethnic background, handicapped students, local/state students, members of minority groups, veterans. *Tuition waivers:* Full or partial for senior citizens. *ROTC:* Army cooperative.

LOANS *Student loans:* $27,517,025 (66% need-based, 34% non-need-based). 70% of past graduating class borrowed through all loan programs. *Average indebtedness per student:* $23,650. *Average need-based loan:* Freshmen: $6406. Undergraduates: $7114. *Parent loans:* $1,546,765 (100% non-need-based). *Programs:* Perkins.

WORK-STUDY *Federal work-study:* Total amount: $432,282; 200 jobs averaging $2000. *State or other work-study/employment:* Part-time jobs available.

ATHLETIC AWARDS Total amount: $2,405,928 (62% need-based, 38% non-need-based).

APPLYING FOR FINANCIAL AID *Required financial aid form:* FAFSA. *Financial aid deadline (priority):* 4/15. *Notification date:* Continuous beginning 1/1. Students must reply within 3 weeks of notification.

CONTACT Mr. James Rohan, Director of Financial Aid, University of Wisconsin–Green Bay, 2420 Nicolet Drive, Green Bay, WI 54311-7001, 920-465-2073. *E-mail:* rohanj@uwgb.edu. *Website:* http://www.uwgb.edu/.

UNIVERSITY OF WISCONSIN–LA CROSSE
La Crosse, WI

Tuition & fees (WI res): $8754	Average undergraduate aid package: $7128

ABOUT THE INSTITUTION State-supported, coed. *Awards:* certificates, associate, bachelor's, master's, and doctoral degrees. 50 undergraduate majors. *Total enrollment:* 10,227. Undergraduates: 9,441. Freshmen: 1,888. Federal methodology is used as a basis for awarding need-based institutional aid.

UNDERGRADUATE EXPENSES for 2013–2014 Application fee: $44. *Tuition, state resident:* full-time $8754. *Tuition, nonresident:* full-time $16,327. Full-time tuition and fees vary according to program and reciprocity agreements. Part-time tuition and fees vary according to course load, program, and reciprocity agreements. *College room and board:* $6000; *Room only:* $3500. Room and board charges vary according to board plan and housing facility.

FRESHMAN FINANCIAL AID (Fall 2011) 1,650 applied for aid; of those 62% were deemed to have need. 99% of freshmen with need received aid; of those 17% had need fully met. *Average percent of need met:* 67% (excluding resources awarded to replace EFC). *Average financial aid package:* $6735 (excluding resources awarded to replace EFC). 3% of all full-time freshmen had no need and received non-need-based gift aid.

UNDERGRADUATE FINANCIAL AID (Fall 2011) 6,342 applied for aid; of those 70% were deemed to have need. 99% of undergraduates with need received aid; of those 17% had need fully met. *Average percent of need met:* 69% (excluding resources awarded to replace EFC). *Average financial aid package:* $7128 (excluding resources awarded to replace EFC). 4% of all full-time undergraduates had no need and received non-need-based gift aid.

GIFT AID (NEED-BASED) Total amount: $12,952,238 (66% federal, 28% state, 2% institutional, 4% external sources). *Receiving aid:* Freshmen: 22% (428); all full-time undergraduates: 27% (2,338). *Average award:* Freshmen: $5634; Undergraduates: $5185. *Scholarships, grants, and awards:* Federal Pell, FSEOG, state, private, college/university gift aid from institutional funds.

GIFT AID (NON-NEED-BASED) Total amount: $3,826,074 (2% federal, 23% state, 23% institutional, 52% external sources). *Receiving aid:* Freshmen: 31% (616). Undergraduates: 15% (1,268). *Average award:* Freshmen: $1729. Undergraduates: $1085. *Scholarships, grants, and awards by category: Academic interests/achievement:* area/ethnic studies, biological sciences, business, communication, computer science, education, English, foreign languages, general academic interests/achievements, health fields, humanities, international studies, mathematics, military science, physical sciences, social sciences. *Creative arts/performance:* art/fine arts, music, theater/drama. *Special achievements/activities:* community service, leadership, memberships. *Special characteristics:* adult students, children and siblings of alumni, children of union members/company employees, ethnic background, first-generation college students, general special characteristics, international students, local/state students, members of minority groups, out-of-state students, veterans, veterans' children. *Tuition waivers:* Full or partial for minority students. *ROTC:* Army.

LOANS Student loans: $39,646,572 (43% need-based, 57% non-need-based). 71% of past graduating class borrowed through all loan programs. *Average indebtedness per student:* $24,863. *Average need-based loan:* Freshmen: $3477. Undergraduates: $4105. *Parent loans:* $5,248,727 (100% non-need-based). *Programs:* Federal Direct (Subsidized and Unsubsidized Stafford, PLUS), Perkins.

WORK-STUDY Federal work-study: Total amount: $420,725; jobs available. *State or other work-study/employment:* Total amount: $3,994,845 (100% non-need-based). Part-time jobs available.

APPLYING FOR FINANCIAL AID Required financial aid form: FAFSA. *Financial aid deadline (priority):* 3/15. *Notification date:* Continuous beginning 4/1.

CONTACT Louise Janke, Director of Financial Aid, University of Wisconsin–La Crosse, 1725 State Street, La Crosse, WI 54601-3742, 608-785-8604. *Fax:* 608-785-8843. *E-mail:* finaid@uwlax.edu. *Website:* http://www.uwlax.edu/.

UNIVERSITY OF WISCONSIN–MADISON
Madison, WI

Tuition & fees (WI res): $10,384	Average undergraduate aid package: $12,862

ABOUT THE INSTITUTION State-supported, coed. *Awards:* certificates, bachelor's, master's, and doctoral degrees. 123 undergraduate majors. *Total enrollment:* 42,820. Undergraduates: 30,863. Freshmen: 6,279. Federal methodology is used as a basis for awarding need-based institutional aid.

UNDERGRADUATE EXPENSES for 2013–2014 Application fee: $44. *Tuition, state resident:* full-time $9273; part-time $386.39 per credit hour. *Tuition, nonresident:* full-time $25,523; part-time $1063.46 per credit hour. *Required fees:* full-time $1111; $49.05 per credit hour. Full-time tuition and fees vary according to program and reciprocity agreements. Part-time tuition and fees vary according to course load, program, and reciprocity agreements. *College room and board:* $8080. Room and board charges vary according to board plan and housing facility.

FRESHMAN FINANCIAL AID (Fall 2012, est.) 4,175 applied for aid; of those 61% were deemed to have need. 94% of freshmen with need received aid; of those 29% had need fully met. *Average percent of need met:* 70% (excluding resources awarded to replace EFC). *Average financial aid package:* $12,279 (excluding resources awarded to replace EFC). 7% of all full-time freshmen had no need and received non-need-based gift aid.

UNDERGRADUATE FINANCIAL AID (Fall 2012, est.) 15,592 applied for aid; of those 73% were deemed to have need. 96% of undergraduates with need received aid; of those 28% had need fully met. *Average percent of need met:* 73% (excluding resources awarded to replace EFC). *Average financial aid package:* $12,862 (excluding resources awarded to replace EFC). 7% of all full-time undergraduates had no need and received non-need-based gift aid.

GIFT AID (NEED-BASED) Total amount: $59,598,802 (33% federal, 14% state, 53% institutional). *Receiving aid:* Freshmen: 25% (1,567); all full-time undergraduates: 28% (7,905). *Average award:* Freshmen: $7132; Undergraduates: $7321. *Scholarships, grants, and awards:* Federal Pell, FSEOG, state, private, college/university gift aid from institutional funds.

GIFT AID (NON-NEED-BASED) Total amount: $31,646,728 (1% federal, 16% state, 57% institutional, 26% external sources). *Receiving aid:* Freshmen: 24% (1,503). Undergraduates: 16% (4,591). *Average award:* Freshmen: $3840. Undergraduates: $3260. *Scholarships, grants, and awards by category: Academic interests/achievement:* general academic interests/achievements. *Creative arts/performance:* general creative arts/performance. *Special achievements/activities:* general special achievements/activities. *Special characteristics:* general special characteristics. *ROTC:* Army, Naval, Air Force.

LOANS Student loans: $95,157,142 (49% need-based, 51% non-need-based). 49% of past graduating class borrowed through all loan programs. *Average indebtedness per student:* $24,700. *Average need-based loan:* Freshmen: $4689. Undergraduates: $5492. *Parent loans:* $15,691,367 (100% non-need-based). *Programs:* Federal Direct (Subsidized and Unsubsidized Stafford, PLUS), Perkins.

WORK-STUDY Federal work-study: Total amount: $8,651,009; jobs available. *State or other work-study/employment:* Part-time jobs available.

ATHLETIC AWARDS Total amount: $10,523,491 (100% non-need-based).

APPLYING FOR FINANCIAL AID Required financial aid form: FAFSA. *Financial aid deadline:* Continuous. *Notification date:* Continuous beginning 4/1. Students must reply within 3 weeks of notification.

CONTACT Office of Student Financial Aid, University of Wisconsin–Madison, 333 East Campus Mall #9701, Madison, WI 53715-1382, 608-262-3060. *Fax:* 608-262-9068. *E-mail:* finaid@finaid.wisc.edu. *Website:* http://www.wisc.edu/.

UNIVERSITY OF WISCONSIN–MILWAUKEE
Milwaukee, WI

Tuition & fees (WI res): $9187	Average undergraduate aid package: $7939

ABOUT THE INSTITUTION State-supported, coed. *Awards:* certificates, bachelor's, master's, and doctoral degrees. 79 undergraduate majors. *Total enrollment:* 29,114. Undergraduates: 24,175. Freshmen: 3,492. Federal methodology is used as a basis for awarding need-based institutional aid.

UNDERGRADUATE EXPENSES for 2013–2014 *Application fee:* $44. *Tuition, state resident:* full-time $8091; part-time $337.13 per credit. *Tuition, nonresident:* full-time $17,819; part-time $742.18 per credit. *Required fees:* full-time $1096. Full-time tuition and fees vary according to course load, degree level, location, program, and reciprocity agreements. Part-time tuition and fees vary according to course load, degree level, location, program, and reciprocity agreements. *College room and board:* $7945; *Room only:* $4983. Room and board charges vary according to board plan, housing facility, and location.

FRESHMAN FINANCIAL AID (Fall 2012, est.) 2,818 applied for aid; of those 84% were deemed to have need. 95% of freshmen with need received aid; of those 18% had need fully met. *Average percent of need met:* 39% (excluding resources awarded to replace EFC). *Average financial aid package:* $7224 (excluding resources awarded to replace EFC). 1% of all full-time freshmen had no need and received non-need-based gift aid.

UNDERGRADUATE FINANCIAL AID (Fall 2012, est.) 17,408 applied for aid; of those 89% were deemed to have need. 84% of undergraduates with need received aid; of those 16% had need fully met. *Average percent of need met:* 43% (excluding resources awarded to replace EFC). *Average financial aid package:* $7939 (excluding resources awarded to replace EFC). 1% of all full-time undergraduates had no need and received non-need-based gift aid.

GIFT AID (NEED-BASED) *Total amount:* $54,438,920 (69% federal, 25% state, 4% institutional, 2% external sources). *Receiving aid:* Freshmen: 39% (1,276); all full-time undergraduates: 41% (7,981). *Average award:* Freshmen: $6054; Undergraduates: $5811. *Scholarships, grants, and awards:* Federal Pell, FSEOG, state, private, college/university gift aid from institutional funds, Federal Nursing.

GIFT AID (NON-NEED-BASED) *Total amount:* $12,146,306 (45% federal, 28% state, 11% institutional, 16% external sources). *Receiving aid:* Freshmen: 4% (143). Undergraduates: 10% (2,033). *Average award:* Freshmen: $2644. Undergraduates: $2803. *Scholarships, grants, and awards by category:* Academic interests/achievement: general academic interests/achievements. Creative arts/performance: general creative arts/performance. Special achievements/activities: general special achievements/activities. Special characteristics: general special characteristics. *Tuition waivers:* Full or partial for senior citizens. *ROTC:* Army cooperative, Naval cooperative, Air Force cooperative.

LOANS *Student loans:* $118,339,493 (47% need-based, 53% non-need-based). 72% of past graduating class borrowed through all loan programs. *Average indebtedness per student:* $32,371. *Average need-based loan:* Freshmen: $3688. Undergraduates: $4413. *Parent loans:* $9,930,333 (100% non-need-based). *Programs:* Federal Direct (Subsidized and Unsubsidized Stafford, PLUS), Perkins, Federal Nursing, state, alternative loans.

WORK-STUDY *Federal work-study:* Total amount: $254,963; jobs available.

ATHLETIC AWARDS Total amount: $565,718 (100% non-need-based).

APPLYING FOR FINANCIAL AID *Required financial aid form:* FAFSA. *Financial aid deadline (priority):* 3/1. *Notification date:* Continuous beginning 3/10. Students must reply within 2 weeks of notification.

CONTACT Ms. Jane Hojan-Clark, Director of Financial Aid and Student Employment Services, University of Wisconsin–Milwaukee, Mellencamp Hall 162, Milwaukee, WI 53201, 414-229-6300. *E-mail:* jhojan@uwm.edu. *Website:* http://www.uwm.edu/.

UNIVERSITY OF WISCONSIN–OSHKOSH
Oshkosh, WI

ABOUT THE INSTITUTION State-supported, coed. 56 undergraduate majors.

GIFT AID (NEED-BASED) *Scholarships, grants, and awards:* Federal Pell, FSEOG, state, private, college/university gift aid from institutional funds, United Negro College Fund, Federal Nursing.

GIFT AID (NON-NEED-BASED) *Scholarships, grants, and awards by category:* Academic interests/achievement: general academic interests/achievements. Creative arts/performance: art/fine arts, general creative arts/performance. Special achievements/activities: leadership. Special characteristics: local/state students, members of minority groups.

LOANS *Programs:* Federal Direct (Subsidized and Unsubsidized Stafford, PLUS), Perkins, Federal Nursing, state, college/university.

WORK-STUDY *Federal work-study:* Total amount: $700,000; jobs available. *State or other work-study/employment:* Total amount: $1,500,000 (100% non-need-based). Part-time jobs available.

APPLYING FOR FINANCIAL AID *Required financial aid form:* FAFSA.

CONTACT Ms. Stacy Drews, Financial Aid Counselor, University of Wisconsin–Oshkosh, 800 Algoma Boulevard, Oshkosh, WI 54901, 920-424-3379. *E-mail:* drewss@uwosh.edu. *Website:* http://www.uwosh.edu/.

UNIVERSITY OF WISCONSIN–PARKSIDE
Kenosha, WI

Tuition & fees (WI res): $7287	Average undergraduate aid package: N/A

ABOUT THE INSTITUTION State-supported, coed. *Awards:* certificates, bachelor's, and master's degrees. 37 undergraduate majors. *Total enrollment:* 4,769. Undergraduates: 4,601. Freshmen: 712. Federal methodology is used as a basis for awarding need-based institutional aid.

UNDERGRADUATE EXPENSES for 2013–2014 *Application fee:* $44. *Tuition, state resident:* full-time $6298; part-time $262 per credit. *Tuition, nonresident:* full-time $13,871; part-time $578 per credit. *Required fees:* full-time $989. *College room and board:* $7082; *Room only:* $4152. Room and board charges vary according to board plan.

FRESHMAN FINANCIAL AID (Fall 2011) 527 applied for aid; of those 84% were deemed to have need. 94% of freshmen with need received aid.

UNDERGRADUATE FINANCIAL AID (Fall 2011) 2,601 applied for aid; of those 85% were deemed to have need. 95% of undergraduates with need received aid.

GIFT AID (NEED-BASED) *Total amount:* $12,884,279 (68% federal, 29% state, 1% institutional, 2% external sources). *Receiving aid:* Freshmen: 46% (310); all full-time undergraduates: 46% (1,541). *Average award:* Freshmen: $6483; Undergraduates: $6411. *Scholarships, grants, and awards:* Federal Pell, FSEOG, state, private, college/university gift aid from institutional funds.

GIFT AID (NON-NEED-BASED) *Total amount:* $466,113 (26% state, 74% external sources). *Receiving aid:* Freshmen: 13% (90). Undergraduates: 9% (296). *Scholarships, grants, and awards by category:* Academic interests/achievement: biological sciences, business, communication, education, engineering/technologies, English, foreign languages, general academic interests/achievements, health fields, mathematics, physical sciences, premedicine. Creative arts/performance: applied art and design, art/fine arts, music, theater/drama. Special achievements/activities: community service, leadership. Special characteristics: adult students, children of union members/company employees, children of workers in trades, ethnic background, general special characteristics, international students, local/state students, members of minority groups. *ROTC:* Army cooperative.

LOANS *Student loans:* $20,073,030 (47% need-based, 53% non-need-based). *Parent loans:* $1,648,772 (100% non-need-based). *Programs:* Federal Direct (Subsidized and Unsubsidized Stafford, PLUS), Perkins.

WORK-STUDY *Federal work-study:* Total amount: $124,090; jobs available.

ATHLETIC AWARDS Total amount: $298,129 (100% non-need-based).

APPLYING FOR FINANCIAL AID *Required financial aid form:* FAFSA. *Financial aid deadline (priority):* 3/15. *Notification date:* Continuous beginning 3/15.

CONTACT Dr. Randall McCready, Director of Student Financial Aid, University of Wisconsin–Parkside, 900 Wood Road, Kenosha, WI 53141-2000, 262-595-2004. *Fax:* 262-595-2216. *E-mail:* randall.mccready@uwp.edu. *Website:* http://www.uwp.edu/.

UNIVERSITY OF WISCONSIN–PLATTEVILLE
Platteville, WI

CONTACT Elizabeth Tucker, Director of Financial Aid, University of Wisconsin–Platteville, 1 University Plaza, Platteville, WI 53818-3099, 608-342-1836 or toll-free 800-362-5515. *Fax:* 608-342-1281. *E-mail:* tucker@uwplatt.edu. *Website:* http://www.uwplatt.edu/.

UNIVERSITY OF WISCONSIN–RIVER FALLS
River Falls, WI

Tuition & fees (WI res): $7700	Average undergraduate aid package: $6929

ABOUT THE INSTITUTION State-supported, coed. **Awards:** certificates, bachelor's, and master's degrees. 95 undergraduate majors. **Total enrollment:** 6,455. Undergraduates: 6,061. Freshmen: 1,106. Federal methodology is used as a basis for awarding need-based institutional aid.

UNDERGRADUATE EXPENSES for 2013–2014 Application fee: $44. **Tuition, state resident:** full-time $6428; part-time $262.43 per credit. **Tuition, nonresident:** full-time $14,001; part-time $577.97 per credit. **Required fees:** full-time $1272. Full-time tuition and fees vary according to course load, degree level, and reciprocity agreements. Part-time tuition and fees vary according to course load, degree level, and reciprocity agreements. **College room and board:** $6902. Room and board charges vary according to board plan and housing facility.

FRESHMAN FINANCIAL AID (Fall 2012, est.) 1,112 applied for aid; of those 75% were deemed to have need. 91% of freshmen with need received aid; of those 1% had need fully met. **Average percent of need met:** 53% (excluding resources awarded to replace EFC). **Average financial aid package:** $6159 (excluding resources awarded to replace EFC). 2% of all full-time freshmen had no need and received non-need-based gift aid.

UNDERGRADUATE FINANCIAL AID (Fall 2012, est.) 4,921 applied for aid; of those 78% were deemed to have need. 91% of undergraduates with need received aid; of those 2% had need fully met. **Average percent of need met:** 58% (excluding resources awarded to replace EFC). **Average financial aid package:** $6929 (excluding resources awarded to replace EFC). 1% of all full-time undergraduates had no need and received non-need-based gift aid.

GIFT AID (NEED-BASED) Total amount: $11,896,082 (76% federal, 22% state, 2% external sources). **Receiving aid:** Freshmen: 39% (459); all full-time undergraduates: 37% (2,104). **Average award:** Freshmen: $4416; Undergraduates: $4805. **Scholarships, grants, and awards:** Federal Pell, FSEOG, state, private, college/university gift aid from institutional funds.

GIFT AID (NON-NEED-BASED) Total amount: $580,235 (15% state, 85% institutional). **Receiving aid:** Freshmen: 4% (48). Undergraduates: 6% (329). **Average award:** Freshmen: $1677. Undergraduates: $1386. **Scholarships, grants, and awards by category:** *Academic interests/achievement:* agriculture, area/ethnic studies, biological sciences, business, communication, computer science, education, English, foreign languages, general academic interests/achievements, health fields, humanities, international studies, mathematics, physical sciences, premedicine, social sciences. *Creative arts/performance:* art/fine arts, music, theater/drama. *Special achievements/activities:* leadership. *Special characteristics:* local/state students, members of minority groups. *ROTC:* Army.

LOANS Student loans: $34,708,799 (93% need-based, 7% non-need-based). 74% of past graduating class borrowed through all loan programs. *Average indebtedness per student:* $25,557. **Average need-based loan:** Freshmen: $3646. Undergraduates: $6406. **Parent loans:** $1,433,398 (100% need-based). **Programs:** Federal Direct (Subsidized and Unsubsidized Stafford, PLUS), Perkins, state, alternative loans.

WORK-STUDY Federal work-study: Total amount: $492,877; 404 jobs averaging $677. **State or other work-study/employment:** Part-time jobs available.

APPLYING FOR FINANCIAL AID Required financial aid form: FAFSA. **Financial aid deadline:** Continuous. **Notification date:** Continuous beginning 4/15.

CONTACT Ms. Barbara J. Stinson, Director of Financial Aid, University of Wisconsin–River Falls, 410 South Third Street, River Falls, WI 54022-5001, 715-425-4111. *Fax:* 715-425-0708. *Website:* http://www.uwrf.edu/.

UNIVERSITY OF WISCONSIN–STEVENS POINT
Stevens Point, WI

Tuition & fees (WI res): $7505	Average undergraduate aid package: $8213

ABOUT THE INSTITUTION State-supported, coed. **Awards:** associate, bachelor's, master's, and doctoral degrees. 69 undergraduate majors. **Total enrollment:** 9,677. Undergraduates: 9,296. Freshmen: 1,637. Federal methodology is used as a basis for awarding need-based institutional aid.

UNDERGRADUATE EXPENSES for 2013–2014 Application fee: $44. **Tuition, state resident:** full-time $6298. **Tuition, nonresident:** full-time $13,871. **Required fees:** full-time $1207. Full-time tuition and fees vary according to course load, program, and reciprocity agreements. Part-time tuition and fees vary according to course load, program, and reciprocity agreements. **College room and board:** $6538; **Room only:** $3788. Room and board charges vary according to board plan and housing facility.

FRESHMAN FINANCIAL AID (Fall 2011) 1,417 applied for aid; of those 69% were deemed to have need. 96% of freshmen with need received aid; of those 58% had need fully met. **Average percent of need met:** 73% (excluding resources awarded to replace EFC). **Average financial aid package:** $6571 (excluding resources awarded to replace EFC). 5% of all full-time freshmen had no need and received non-need-based gift aid.

UNDERGRADUATE FINANCIAL AID (Fall 2011) 7,159 applied for aid; of those 77% were deemed to have need. 97% of undergraduates with need received aid; of those 62% had need fully met. **Average percent of need met:** 69% (excluding resources awarded to replace EFC). **Average financial aid package:** $8213 (excluding resources awarded to replace EFC). 5% of all full-time undergraduates had no need and received non-need-based gift aid.

GIFT AID (NEED-BASED) Total amount: $18,464,412 (70% federal, 24% state, 2% institutional, 4% external sources). **Receiving aid:** Freshmen: 31% (497); all full-time undergraduates: 34% (3,040). **Average award:** Freshmen: $5406; Undergraduates: $5727. **Scholarships, grants, and awards:** Federal Pell, FSEOG, state, private, college/university gift aid from institutional funds.

GIFT AID (NON-NEED-BASED) Total amount: $1,907,476 (1% state, 39% institutional, 60% external sources). **Receiving aid:** Freshmen: 4% (71). Undergraduates: 6% (526). **Average award:** Freshmen: $2237. Undergraduates: $2152. **Scholarships, grants, and awards by category:** *Academic interests/achievement:* agriculture, architecture, biological sciences, business, communication, computer science, education, engineering/technologies, English, foreign languages, general academic interests/achievements, health fields, home economics, humanities, international studies, mathematics, military science, physical sciences, premedicine, social sciences. *Creative arts/performance:* applied art and design, creative writing, dance, music, performing arts, theater/drama. *Special achievements/activities:* general special achievements/activities, leadership. *Special characteristics:* adult students, ethnic background, general special characteristics, international students, members of minority groups, out-of-state students, veterans. *ROTC:* Army.

LOANS Student loans: $42,266,987 (64% need-based, 36% non-need-based). 75% of past graduating class borrowed through all loan programs. *Average indebtedness per student:* $24,054. **Average need-based loan:** Freshmen: $3960. Undergraduates: $5251. **Parent loans:** $6,168,598 (19% need-based, 81% non-need-based). **Programs:** Federal Direct (Subsidized and Unsubsidized Stafford, PLUS), Perkins.

WORK-STUDY Federal work-study: Total amount: $1,007,453; jobs available. **State or other work-study/employment:** Part-time jobs available.

APPLYING FOR FINANCIAL AID Required financial aid form: FAFSA. **Financial aid deadline:** 5/1 (priority: 3/15). **Notification date:** Continuous beginning 3/1. Students must reply within 4 weeks of notification.

CONTACT Mr. Paul Watson, Director of Financial Aid, University of Wisconsin–Stevens Point, 106 Student Services Center, Stevens Point, WI 54481-3897, 715-346-4771. *Fax:* 715-346-3526. *E-mail:* finaid@uwsp.edu. *Website:* http://www.uwsp.edu/.

UNIVERSITY OF WISCONSIN–STOUT
Menomonie, WI

Tuition & fees (WI res): $8944	Average undergraduate aid package: $10,590

ABOUT THE INSTITUTION State-supported, coed. *Awards:* certificates, bachelor's, and master's degrees. 40 undergraduate majors. *Total enrollment:* 9,247. Undergraduates: 8,270. Freshmen: 1,473. Federal methodology is used as a basis for awarding need-based institutional aid.

UNDERGRADUATE EXPENSES for 2013–2014 *Application fee:* $44. *Tuition, state resident:* full-time $7014; part-time $234 per credit hour. *Tuition, nonresident:* full-time $14,760; part-time $492 per credit hour. *Required fees:* full-time $1930. Full-time tuition and fees vary according to degree level and reciprocity agreements. Part-time tuition and fees vary according to degree level and reciprocity agreements. *College room and board:* $6054; *Room only:* $3600. Room and board charges vary according to board plan and housing facility.

FRESHMAN FINANCIAL AID (Fall 2012, est.) 1,247 applied for aid; of those 71% were deemed to have need. 100% of freshmen with need received aid; of those 40% had need fully met. *Average percent of need met:* 81% (excluding resources awarded to replace EFC). *Average financial aid package:* $10,193 (excluding resources awarded to replace EFC). 2% of all full-time freshmen had no need and received non-need-based gift aid.

UNDERGRADUATE FINANCIAL AID (Fall 2012, est.) 5,483 applied for aid; of those 77% were deemed to have need. 99% of undergraduates with need received aid; of those 42% had need fully met. *Average percent of need met:* 83% (excluding resources awarded to replace EFC). *Average financial aid package:* $10,590 (excluding resources awarded to replace EFC). 1% of all full-time undergraduates had no need and received non-need-based gift aid.

GIFT AID (NEED-BASED) *Total amount:* $13,865,986 (72% federal, 23% state, 1% institutional, 4% external sources). *Receiving aid:* Freshmen: 21% (312); all full-time undergraduates: 24% (1,602). *Average award:* Freshmen: $2289; Undergraduates: $2465. *Scholarships, grants, and awards:* Federal Pell, FSEOG, state, private, college/university gift aid from institutional funds, Bureau of Indian Affairs Grants, GEAR UP Grants.

GIFT AID (NON-NEED-BASED) *Total amount:* $2,982,635 (2% federal, 14% state, 50% institutional, 34% external sources). *Receiving aid:* Freshmen: 24% (356). Undergraduates: 11% (774). *Average award:* Freshmen: $3233. Undergraduates: $2334. *Scholarships, grants, and awards by category: Academic interests/achievement:* 208 awards ($297,350 total): business, computer science, education, engineering/technologies, general academic interests/achievements, home economics, international studies, mathematics, physical sciences. *Creative arts/performance:* 11 awards ($10,350 total): applied art and design, art/fine arts, music. *Special achievements/activities:* 37 awards ($39,350 total): community service, general special achievements/activities, leadership, memberships, religious involvement. *Special characteristics:* 39 awards ($31,850 total): adult students, first-generation college students, handicapped students, international students, local/state students, members of minority groups, out-of-state students, previous college experience, veterans, veterans' children. *ROTC:* Army, Air Force cooperative.

LOANS *Student loans:* $43,853,640 (42% need-based, 58% non-need-based). 68% of past graduating class borrowed through all loan programs. *Average indebtedness per student:* $29,879. *Average need-based loan:* Freshmen: $3759. Undergraduates: $4450. *Parent loans:* $2,084,885 (100% non-need-based). *Programs:* Federal Direct (Subsidized and Unsubsidized Stafford, PLUS), Perkins, alternative loans.

WORK-STUDY *Federal work-study:* Total amount: $2,497,439; 1,627 jobs averaging $1441.

APPLYING FOR FINANCIAL AID *Required financial aid form:* FAFSA. *Financial aid deadline (priority):* 3/15. *Notification date:* Continuous beginning 4/1. Students must reply within 4 weeks of notification.

CONTACT Beth M. Boisen, Director of Financial Aid, University of Wisconsin–Stout, 210 Bowman Hall, Menomonie, WI 54751, 715-232-1363 or toll-free 800-HI-STOUT. *Fax:* 715-232-5246. *E-mail:* boisenb@uwstout.edu. *Website:* http://www.uwstout.edu/.

UNIVERSITY OF WISCONSIN–SUPERIOR
Superior, WI

Tuition & fees (WI res): $7904	Average undergraduate aid package: $17,266

ABOUT THE INSTITUTION State-supported, coed. *Awards:* certificates, associate, bachelor's, and master's degrees. 67 undergraduate majors. *Total enrollment:* 2,700. Undergraduates: 2,550. Freshmen: 366. Federal methodology is used as a basis for awarding need-based institutional aid.

UNDERGRADUATE EXPENSES for 2013–2014 *Application fee:* $44. *Tuition, state resident:* full-time $6535; part-time $472 per credit hour. *Tuition, nonresident:* full-time $14,108; part-time $776 per credit hour. *Required fees:* full-time $1369. Full-time tuition and fees vary according to course load and reciprocity agreements. Part-time tuition and fees vary according to course load and reciprocity agreements. *College room and board:* $5992; *Room only:* $3232. Room and board charges vary according to board plan, housing facility, and student level.

FRESHMAN FINANCIAL AID (Fall 2012, est.) 310 applied for aid; of those 80% were deemed to have need. 97% of freshmen with need received aid; of those 25% had need fully met. *Average financial aid package:* $11,422 (excluding resources awarded to replace EFC). 3% of all full-time freshmen had no need and received non-need-based gift aid.

UNDERGRADUATE FINANCIAL AID (Fall 2012, est.) 1,646 applied for aid; of those 86% were deemed to have need. 99% of undergraduates with need received aid; of those 19% had need fully met. *Average financial aid package:* $17,266 (excluding resources awarded to replace EFC). 1% of all full-time undergraduates had no need and received non-need-based gift aid.

GIFT AID (NEED-BASED) *Total amount:* $5,738,458 (77% federal, 22% state, 1% external sources). *Receiving aid:* Freshmen: 37% (135); all full-time undergraduates: 47% (952). *Average award:* Freshmen: $5271; Undergraduates: $4817. *Scholarships, grants, and awards:* Federal Pell, FSEOG, state, private, college/university gift aid from institutional funds.

GIFT AID (NON-NEED-BASED) *Total amount:* $1,245,727 (6% state, 58% institutional, 36% external sources). *Receiving aid:* Freshmen: 28% (102). Undergraduates: 19% (375). *Average award:* Freshmen: $2685. Undergraduates: $1060. *Scholarships, grants, and awards by category: Academic interests/achievement:* biological sciences, business, communication, computer science, education, English, general academic interests/achievements, health fields, humanities, mathematics, physical sciences, social sciences. *Creative arts/performance:* general creative arts/performance. *Special characteristics:* general special characteristics, international students, members of minority groups, veterans. *ROTC:* Air Force cooperative.

LOANS *Student loans:* $13,639,532 (44% need-based, 56% non-need-based). 76% of past graduating class borrowed through all loan programs. *Average indebtedness per student:* $26,486. *Average need-based loan:* Freshmen: $3395. Undergraduates: $4039. *Parent loans:* $438,370 (100% non-need-based). *Programs:* Federal Direct (Subsidized and Unsubsidized Stafford, PLUS), Perkins, state, college/university.

WORK-STUDY *Federal work-study:* Total amount: $275,602; jobs available. *State or other work-study/employment:* Total amount: $1,209,743 (100% non-need-based). Part-time jobs available.

APPLYING FOR FINANCIAL AID *Required financial aid form:* FAFSA. *Financial aid deadline (priority):* 4/1. *Notification date:* Continuous beginning 4/1. Students must reply by 5/1 or within 4 weeks of notification.

CONTACT Jennifer Fuchs, Financial Aid Information Manager, University of Wisconsin–Superior, Belknap and Catlin, Old Main 110, PO Box 2000, Superior, WI 54880, 715-394-8200. *Fax:* 715-394-8027. *E-mail:* finaid@uwsuper.edu. *Website:* http://www.uwsuper.edu/.

UNIVERSITY OF WISCONSIN– WHITEWATER
Whitewater, WI

Tuition & fees (WI res): $7528	Average undergraduate aid package: $7884

ABOUT THE INSTITUTION State-supported, coed. **Awards:** associate, bachelor's, and master's degrees. 56 undergraduate majors. **Total enrollment:** 11,629. Undergraduates: 10,214. Freshmen: 2,006. Federal methodology is used as a basis for awarding need-based institutional aid.

UNDERGRADUATE EXPENSES for 2013–2014 Application fee: $44. **Tuition, state resident:** full-time $6519; part-time $271.62 per credit hour. **Tuition, nonresident:** full-time $14,092; part-time $587.16 per credit hour. **Required fees:** full-time $1009. Full-time tuition and fees vary according to degree level and reciprocity agreements. **College room and board:** $5736. Room and board charges vary according to board plan.

FRESHMAN FINANCIAL AID (Fall 2012, est.) 2,125 applied for aid; of those 75% were deemed to have need. 95% of freshmen with need received aid; of those 56% had need fully met. **Average percent of need met:** 57% (excluding resources awarded to replace EFC). **Average financial aid package:** $6926 (excluding resources awarded to replace EFC). 6% of all full-time freshmen had no need and received non-need-based gift aid.

UNDERGRADUATE FINANCIAL AID (Fall 2012, est.) 7,715 applied for aid; of those 80% were deemed to have need. 97% of undergraduates with need received aid; of those 58% had need fully met. **Average percent of need met:** 63% (excluding resources awarded to replace EFC). **Average financial aid package:** $7884 (excluding resources awarded to replace EFC). 4% of all full-time undergraduates had no need and received non-need-based gift aid.

GIFT AID (NEED-BASED) Total amount: $19,880,000 (68% federal, 29% state, 3% external sources). **Receiving aid:** Freshmen: 42% (902); all full-time undergraduates: 37% (3,590). **Average award:** Freshmen: $5203; Undergraduates: $5253. **Scholarships, grants, and awards:** Federal Pell, FSEOG, state, private, college/university gift aid from institutional funds.

GIFT AID (NON-NEED-BASED) Total amount: $4,964,000 (1% federal, 2% state, 26% institutional, 71% external sources). **Receiving aid:** Freshmen: 20% (421). Undergraduates: 10% (950). **Average award:** Freshmen: $1536. Undergraduates: $1854. **Scholarships, grants, and awards by category:** Academic interests/achievement: biological sciences, business, communication, computer science, education, English, foreign languages, general academic interests/achievements, humanities, mathematics, physical sciences, premedicine, social sciences. Creative arts/performance: art/fine arts, cinema/film/broadcasting, creative writing, journalism/publications, music, theater/drama. Special achievements/activities: leadership. Special characteristics: adult students, ethnic background, handicapped students, international students, local/state students, members of minority groups, out-of-state students. **Tuition waivers:** Full or partial for children of alumni, senior citizens. **ROTC:** Army, Air Force.

LOANS Student loans: $58,500,000 (41% need-based, 59% non-need-based). 72% of past graduating class borrowed through all loan programs. Average indebtedness per student: $25,147. **Average need-based loan:** Freshmen: $3415. Undergraduates: $4252. **Parent loans:** $10,000,000 (100% non-need-based). **Programs:** Federal Direct (Subsidized and Unsubsidized Stafford, PLUS), Perkins.

WORK-STUDY Federal work-study: Total amount: $610,000; 702 jobs averaging $870. **State or other work-study/employment:** Total amount: $4,000,000 (100% non-need-based). 1,989 part-time jobs averaging $2011.

APPLYING FOR FINANCIAL AID Required financial aid form: FAFSA. **Financial aid deadline (priority):** 3/15. **Notification date:** Continuous beginning 4/1. Students must reply within 3 weeks of notification.

CONTACT Ms. Carol Miller, Director of Financial Aid, University of Wisconsin–Whitewater, 800 West Main Street, Whitewater, WI 53190-1790, 262-472-1130. *Fax:* 262-472-5655.
Website: http://www.uww.edu/.

UNIVERSITY OF WYOMING
Laramie, WY

Tuition & fees (WY res): $4278	Average undergraduate aid package: $9117

ABOUT THE INSTITUTION State-supported, coed. **Awards:** certificates, bachelor's, master's, and doctoral degrees. 80 undergraduate majors. **Total enrollment:** 12,903. Undergraduates: 10,194. Freshmen: 1,584. Federal methodology is used as a basis for awarding need-based institutional aid.

UNDERGRADUATE EXPENSES for 2013–2014 Application fee: $40. **One-time required fee:** $40. **Tuition, state resident:** full-time $3180; part-time $106 per credit hour. **Tuition, nonresident:** full-time $12,330; part-time $411 per credit hour. **Required fees:** full-time $1098; $262 per term. Full-time tuition and fees vary according to course load, location, and reciprocity agreements. Part-time tuition and fees vary according to course load, location, and reciprocity agreements. **College room and board:** $9084; **Room only:** $3901. Room and board charges vary according to board plan and housing facility.

FRESHMAN FINANCIAL AID (Fall 2011) 1,214 applied for aid; of those 64% were deemed to have need. 98% of freshmen with need received aid; of those 26% had need fully met. **Average percent of need met:** 67% (excluding resources awarded to replace EFC). **Average financial aid package:** $9259 (excluding resources awarded to replace EFC). 11% of all full-time freshmen had no need and received non-need-based gift aid.

UNDERGRADUATE FINANCIAL AID (Fall 2011) 5,537 applied for aid; of those 72% were deemed to have need. 98% of undergraduates with need received aid; of those 17% had need fully met. **Average percent of need met:** 62% (excluding resources awarded to replace EFC). **Average financial aid package:** $9117 (excluding resources awarded to replace EFC). 10% of all full-time undergraduates had no need and received non-need-based gift aid.

GIFT AID (NEED-BASED) Total amount: $16,709,764 (61% federal, 30% state, 5% institutional, 4% external sources). **Receiving aid:** Freshmen: 31% (478); all full-time undergraduates: 33% (2,758). **Average award:** Freshmen: $4660; Undergraduates: $4743. **Scholarships, grants, and awards:** Federal Pell, FSEOG, state, private, college/university gift aid from institutional funds.

GIFT AID (NON-NEED-BASED) Total amount: $26,697,557 (76% state, 16% institutional, 8% external sources). **Receiving aid:** Freshmen: 43% (659). Undergraduates: 31% (2,598). **Average award:** Freshmen: $1936. Undergraduates: $2827. **Scholarships, grants, and awards by category:** Academic interests/achievement: agriculture, business, communication, computer science, education, engineering/technologies, English, foreign languages, general academic interests/achievements, health fields, home economics, international studies, mathematics, military science, physical sciences, social sciences. Creative arts/performance: art/fine arts, dance, debating, journalism/publications, music, theater/drama. Special achievements/activities: cheerleading/drum major, junior miss, leadership, rodeo. Special characteristics: adult students, children and siblings of alumni, ethnic background, first-generation college students, handicapped students, international students, local/state students, out-of-state students, veterans. **Tuition waivers:** Full or partial for children of alumni, employees or children of employees, senior citizens. **ROTC:** Army, Air Force.

LOANS Student loans: $30,181,242 (41% need-based, 59% non-need-based). 47% of past graduating class borrowed through all loan programs. Average indebtedness per student: $21,241. **Average need-based loan:** Freshmen: $2940. Undergraduates: $4173. **Parent loans:** $2,718,162 (100% non-need-based). **Programs:** Federal Direct (Subsidized and Unsubsidized Stafford, PLUS), Perkins.

WORK-STUDY Federal work-study: Total amount: $496,230; jobs available.

ATHLETIC AWARDS Total amount: $4,224,873 (100% non-need-based).

APPLYING FOR FINANCIAL AID Required financial aid form: FAFSA. **Financial aid deadline (priority):** 3/1. **Notification date:** Continuous beginning 3/22. Students must reply within 3 weeks of notification.

CONTACT Joanna Carter, Director of Student Financial Aid, University of Wyoming, Department 3335, 1000 East University Avenue, Laramie, WY 82071, 307-766-2116 or toll-free 800-342-5996. *Fax:* 307-766-3800. *E-mail:* finaid@uwyo.edu.
Website: http://www.uwyo.edu/.

Peterson's How to Get Money for College 2014

www.petersonsbooks.com   **677**

UPPER IOWA UNIVERSITY
Fayette, IA

Tuition & fees: $24,400 | Average undergraduate aid package: $8015

ABOUT THE INSTITUTION Independent, coed. *Awards:* certificates, associate, bachelor's, and master's degrees (enrollment figures include extended learning centers and online and distance education programs). 39 undergraduate majors. *Total enrollment:* 5,178. Undergraduates: 4,645. Freshmen: 230. Federal methodology is used as a basis for awarding need-based institutional aid.

UNDERGRADUATE EXPENSES for 2013–2014 *Comprehensive fee:* $31,910 includes full-time tuition ($24,400) and room and board ($7510). *College room only:* $3028. Full-time tuition and fees vary according to degree level, location, and program. Room and board charges vary according to board plan, housing facility, and location.

FRESHMAN FINANCIAL AID (Fall 2012, est.) 195 applied for aid; of those 100% were deemed to have need. 100% of freshmen with need received aid. *Average percent of need met:* 37% (excluding resources awarded to replace EFC). *Average financial aid package:* $9041 (excluding resources awarded to replace EFC). 25% of all full-time freshmen had no need and received non-need-based gift aid.

UNDERGRADUATE FINANCIAL AID (Fall 2012, est.) 742 applied for aid; of those 100% were deemed to have need. 100% of undergraduates with need received aid. *Average percent of need met:* 33% (excluding resources awarded to replace EFC). *Average financial aid package:* $8015 (excluding resources awarded to replace EFC). 7% of all full-time undergraduates had no need and received non-need-based gift aid.

GIFT AID (NEED-BASED) *Total amount:* $23,230,016 (48% federal, 16% state, 36% institutional). *Receiving aid:* Freshmen: 55% (126); all full-time undergraduates: 18% (507). *Average award:* Freshmen: $6260; Undergraduates: $6819. *Scholarships, grants, and awards:* Federal Pell, FSEOG, state, private, college/university gift aid from institutional funds.

GIFT AID (NON-NEED-BASED) *Total amount:* $134,722 (100% external sources). *Receiving aid:* Freshmen: 85% (195). Undergraduates: 27% (742). *Average award:* Freshmen: $7900. Undergraduates: $6100. *Scholarships, grants, and awards by category:* Academic interests/achievement: 737 awards ($6,528,339 total): general academic interests/achievements. *Special achievements/activities:* 179 awards ($2,304,407 total): general special achievements/activities. *Special characteristics:* 17 awards ($11,313 total): children and siblings of alumni, children of current students, parents of current students, religious affiliation, spouses of current students. *Tuition waivers:* Full or partial for employees or children of employees.

LOANS *Student loans:* $36,790,873 (31% need-based, 69% non-need-based). 91% of past graduating class borrowed through all loan programs. *Average indebtedness per student:* $27,361. *Average need-based loan:* Freshmen: $2851. Undergraduates: $3800. *Parent loans:* $2,180,904 (100% non-need-based). *Programs:* Federal Direct (Subsidized and Unsubsidized Stafford, PLUS), Perkins, college/university, alternative loans.

WORK-STUDY *Federal work-study:* Total amount: $482,703; 228 jobs averaging $1860. *State or other work-study/employment:* Part-time jobs available.

ATHLETIC AWARDS Total amount: $2,266,047 (100% need-based).

APPLYING FOR FINANCIAL AID *Required financial aid form:* FAFSA. *Financial aid deadline (priority):* 3/1. *Notification date:* Continuous beginning 3/1. Students must reply within 3 weeks of notification.

CONTACT Jeannie Barness, Director of Financial Aid, Upper Iowa University, Garbee Hall, Box 1859, Fayette, IA 52142-1859, 563-425-5276 or toll-free 800-553-4150. *Fax:* 563-425-5277. *E-mail:* barnessj@uiu.edu. *Website:* http://www.uiu.edu/.

URBANA UNIVERSITY
Urbana, OH

CONTACT Mrs. Amy M. Barnhart, Director of Financial Aid, Urbana University, 579 College Way, Urbana, OH 43078-2091, 937-484-1359 or toll-free 800-7-URBANA. *Fax:* 937-652-6870. *E-mail:* abarnhart@urbana.edu. *Website:* http://www.urbana.edu/.

URSINUS COLLEGE
Collegeville, PA

Tuition & fees: N/R | Average undergraduate aid package: $32,404

ABOUT THE INSTITUTION Independent, coed. 34 undergraduate majors. Both federal and institutional methodology are used as a basis for awarding need-based institutional aid.

FRESHMAN FINANCIAL AID (Fall 2012, est.) 386 applied for aid; of those 82% were deemed to have need. 100% of freshmen with need received aid; of those 21% had need fully met. *Average percent of need met:* 79% (excluding resources awarded to replace EFC). *Average financial aid package:* $32,460 (excluding resources awarded to replace EFC). 28% of all full-time freshmen had no need and received non-need-based gift aid.

UNDERGRADUATE FINANCIAL AID (Fall 2012, est.) 1,373 applied for aid; of those 87% were deemed to have need. 100% of undergraduates with need received aid; of those 18% had need fully met. *Average percent of need met:* 79% (excluding resources awarded to replace EFC). *Average financial aid package:* $32,404 (excluding resources awarded to replace EFC). 24% of all full-time undergraduates had no need and received non-need-based gift aid.

GIFT AID (NEED-BASED) *Total amount:* $33,096,236 (6% federal, 4% state, 87% institutional, 3% external sources). *Receiving aid:* Freshmen: 69% (314); all full-time undergraduates: 74% (1,189). *Average award:* Freshmen: $28,840; Undergraduates: $27,812. *Scholarships, grants, and awards:* Federal Pell, FSEOG, state, private, college/university gift aid from institutional funds, Academic Competitiveness Grants, National SMART Grants.

GIFT AID (NON-NEED-BASED) *Total amount:* $8,149,083 (82% institutional, 18% external sources). *Receiving aid:* Freshmen: 11% (48). Undergraduates: 9% (142). *Average award:* Freshmen: $14,794. Undergraduates: $14,491. *Scholarships, grants, and awards by category:* Academic interests/achievement: general academic interests/achievements. *Creative arts/performance:* creative writing. *Special achievements/activities:* general special achievements/activities, leadership. *Special characteristics:* children and siblings of alumni, children of faculty/staff, general special characteristics, international students, siblings of current students.

LOANS *Student loans:* $11,679,355 (69% need-based, 31% non-need-based). 74% of past graduating class borrowed through all loan programs. *Average indebtedness per student:* $40,652. *Average need-based loan:* Freshmen: $3106. Undergraduates: $4336. *Parent loans:* $4,610,282 (31% need-based, 69% non-need-based). *Programs:* Federal Direct (Subsidized and Unsubsidized Stafford, PLUS), Perkins.

WORK-STUDY *Federal work-study:* Total amount: $1,135,607; jobs available. *State or other work-study/employment:* Part-time jobs available.

APPLYING FOR FINANCIAL AID *Required financial aid forms:* FAFSA, institution's own form, CSS Financial Aid PROFILE. *Financial aid deadline:* 2/15. *Notification date:* 4/1. Students must reply by 5/1.

CONTACT Mr. Andrew Sturgill, Assistant Director of Student Financial Services, Ursinus College, 601 East Main Street, Collegeville, PA 19426-1000, 610-409-3389 Ext. 2242. *Fax:* 610-409-3362. *E-mail:* asturgill@ursinus.edu. *Website:* http://www.ursinus.edu/.

URSULINE COLLEGE
Pepper Pike, OH

Tuition & fees: $26,760 | Average undergraduate aid package: $15,930

ABOUT THE INSTITUTION Independent Roman Catholic, coed, primarily women. *Awards:* certificates, bachelor's, master's, and doctoral degrees (applications from men are also accepted). 41 undergraduate majors. *Total enrollment:* 1,496. Undergraduates: 879. Freshmen: 90. Federal methodology is used as a basis for awarding need-based institutional aid.

UNDERGRADUATE EXPENSES for 2013–2014 *Application fee:* $25. *Comprehensive fee:* $35,660 includes full-time tuition ($26,490), mandatory fees ($270), and room and board ($8900). *College room only:* $4546. Full-time tuition and fees vary according to location. Room and board charges vary according to board plan and housing facility. *Part-time tuition:* $546 per credit. *Part-time fees:* $90 per term. Part-time tuition and fees vary according to location.

FRESHMAN FINANCIAL AID (Fall 2011) 75 applied for aid; of those 99% were deemed to have need. 100% of freshmen with need received aid; of those 9% had need fully met. *Average percent of need met:* 83% (excluding resources awarded to replace EFC). *Average financial aid package:* $23,278 (excluding resources awarded to replace EFC). 1% of all full-time freshmen had no need and received non-need-based gift aid.

UNDERGRADUATE FINANCIAL AID (Fall 2011) 663 applied for aid; of those 96% were deemed to have need. 98% of undergraduates with need received aid; of those 6% had need fully met. *Average percent of need met:* 63% (excluding resources awarded to replace EFC). *Average financial aid package:* $15,930 (excluding resources awarded to replace EFC). 5% of all full-time undergraduates had no need and received non-need-based gift aid.

GIFT AID (NEED-BASED) *Total amount:* $6,818,657 (30% federal, 9% state, 57% institutional, 4% external sources). *Receiving aid:* Freshmen: 95% (74); all full-time undergraduates: 79% (555). *Average award:* Freshmen: $19,330; Undergraduates: $12,092. *Scholarships, grants, and awards:* Federal Pell, FSEOG, state, private, college/university gift aid from institutional funds, United Negro College Fund.

GIFT AID (NON-NEED-BASED) *Total amount:* $290,443 (2% federal, 4% state, 91% institutional, 3% external sources). *Receiving aid:* Freshmen: 9% (7). Undergraduates: 4% (27). *Average award:* Freshmen: $12,500. Undergraduates: $5611. *Scholarships, grants, and awards by category: Academic interests/ achievement:* general academic interests/achievements. *Special achievements/activities:* community service, leadership. *Special characteristics:* children and siblings of alumni, children of faculty/staff, relatives of clergy, religious affiliation, siblings of current students, veterans. *Tuition waivers:* Full or partial for employees or children of employees. *ROTC:* Army cooperative.

LOANS *Student loans:* $9,484,858 (87% need-based, 13% non-need-based). 89% of past graduating class borrowed through all loan programs. *Average indebtedness per student:* $25,963. *Average need-based loan:* Freshmen: $3845. Undergraduates: $5366. *Parent loans:* $491,441 (50% need-based, 50% non-need-based). *Programs:* Federal Direct (Subsidized and Unsubsidized Stafford, PLUS), Perkins, state, college/university.

WORK-STUDY *Federal work-study:* Total amount: $104,704; jobs available.

ATHLETIC AWARDS Total amount: $860,081 (75% need-based, 25% non-need-based).

APPLYING FOR FINANCIAL AID *Required financial aid form:* FAFSA. *Financial aid deadline:* Continuous. *Notification date:* Continuous beginning 3/1. Students must reply within 3 weeks of notification.

CONTACT Ms. Mary Lynn Perri, Director of Financial Aid and Enrollment Services, Ursuline College, 2550 Lander Road, Pepper Pike, OH 44124-4398, 440-646-8330 or toll-free 888-URSULINE. *Fax:* 440-684-6114. *E-mail:* mperri@ursuline.edu. *Website:* http://www.ursuline.edu/.

UTAH STATE UNIVERSITY
Logan, UT

Tuition & fees (UT res): $6183	Average undergraduate aid package: $8063

ABOUT THE INSTITUTION State-supported, coed. *Awards:* certificates, associate, bachelor's, master's, and doctoral degrees. 115 undergraduate majors. *Total enrollment:* 28,786. Undergraduates: 25,445. Freshmen: 3,824. Federal methodology is used as a basis for awarding need-based institutional aid.

UNDERGRADUATE EXPENSES for 2013–2014 *Application fee:* $40. *Tuition, state resident:* full-time $5273. *Tuition, nonresident:* full-time $16,976. *Required fees:* full-time $910. Full-time tuition and fees vary according to course load, location, program, and reciprocity agreements. Part-time tuition and fees vary according to course load, location, program, and reciprocity agreements. *College room and board:* $5620; *Room only:* $1920. Room and board charges vary according to board plan and housing facility.

FRESHMAN FINANCIAL AID (Fall 2012, est.) 2,100 applied for aid; of those 84% were deemed to have need. 98% of freshmen with need received aid; of those 15% had need fully met. *Average percent of need met:* 47% (excluding resources awarded to replace EFC). *Average financial aid package:* $8137 (excluding resources awarded to replace EFC). 6% of all full-time freshmen had no need and received non-need-based gift aid.

UNDERGRADUATE FINANCIAL AID (Fall 2012, est.) 9,933 applied for aid; of those 91% were deemed to have need. 98% of undergraduates with need received aid;

of those 10% had need fully met. *Average percent of need met:* 46% (excluding resources awarded to replace EFC). *Average financial aid package:* $8063 (excluding resources awarded to replace EFC). 5% of all full-time undergraduates had no need and received non-need-based gift aid.

GIFT AID (NEED-BASED) *Total amount:* $38,835,240 (100% federal). *Receiving aid:* Freshmen: 44% (1,486); all full-time undergraduates: 50% (7,620). *Average award:* Freshmen: $7295; Undergraduates: $6538. *Scholarships, grants, and awards:* Federal Pell, FSEOG, state, private, college/university gift aid from institutional funds.

GIFT AID (NON-NEED-BASED) *Total amount:* $13,146,187 (9% state, 54% institutional, 37% external sources). *Receiving aid:* Freshmen: 28% (952). Undergraduates: 22% (3,316). *Average award:* Freshmen: $1876. Undergraduates: $1997. *Scholarships, grants, and awards by category: Academic interests/ achievement:* agriculture, architecture, biological sciences, business, communication, computer science, education, engineering/technologies, English, foreign languages, general academic interests/achievements, health fields, home economics, humanities, international studies, library science, mathematics, physical sciences, premedicine, social sciences. *Creative arts/performance:* applied art and design, art/fine arts, general creative arts/performance, journalism/publications, music, performing arts, theater/ drama. *Special characteristics:* children and siblings of alumni, children of faculty/staff, international students. *Tuition waivers:* Full or partial for minority students, children of alumni, employees or children of employees, adult students, senior citizens. *ROTC:* Army, Air Force.

LOANS *Student loans:* $46,427,302 (60% need-based, 40% non-need-based). 47% of past graduating class borrowed through all loan programs. *Average indebtedness per student:* $18,900. *Average need-based loan:* Freshmen: $3466. Undergraduates: $4370. *Parent loans:* $1,027,911 (100% non-need-based). *Programs:* Federal Direct (Subsidized and Unsubsidized Stafford, PLUS), Perkins, college/university.

WORK-STUDY *Federal work-study:* Total amount: $610,000; jobs available. *State or other work-study/employment:* Total amount: $915,126 (100% need-based). Part-time jobs available.

ATHLETIC AWARDS Total amount: $5,036,795 (100% non-need-based).

APPLYING FOR FINANCIAL AID *Required financial aid form:* FAFSA. *Financial aid deadline:* Continuous. *Notification date:* Continuous beginning 4/1. Students must reply within 4 weeks of notification.

CONTACT Tamara Allen, Associate Director of Financial Aid, Utah State University, Old Main Hill, Logan, UT 84322-1800, 435-797-3369 or toll-free 800-488-8108. *Fax:* 435-797-0654. *E-mail:* tamara.allen@usu.edu. *Website:* http://www.usu.edu/.

UTAH VALLEY UNIVERSITY
Orem, UT

Tuition & fees (area res) $4786	Average undergraduate aid package: $3806

ABOUT THE INSTITUTION State-supported, coed. *Awards:* certificates, diplomas, associate, bachelor's, and master's degrees. 84 undergraduate majors. *Total enrollment:* 31,562. Undergraduates: 31,405. Freshmen: 3,479. Federal methodology is used as a basis for awarding need-based institutional aid.

UNDERGRADUATE EXPENSES for 2013–2014 *Application fee:* $35. *Tuition, area resident:* full-time $4122; part-time $137.40 per credit. *Tuition, state resident:* full-time $4122; part-time $137.40 per credit. *Tuition, nonresident:* full-time $12,854; part-time $428.47 per credit. *Required fees:* full-time $664; $28.86 per credit or $332 per term.

FRESHMAN FINANCIAL AID (Fall 2012, est.) 2,121 applied for aid; of those 67% were deemed to have need. 95% of freshmen with need received aid; of those 8% had need fully met. *Average percent of need met:* 52% (excluding resources awarded to replace EFC). *Average financial aid package:* $4126 (excluding resources awarded to replace EFC). 21% of all full-time freshmen had no need and received non-need-based gift aid.

UNDERGRADUATE FINANCIAL AID (Fall 2012, est.) 13,627 applied for aid; of those 82% were deemed to have need. 97% of undergraduates with need received aid; of those 4% had need fully met. *Average percent of need met:* 51% (excluding resources awarded to replace EFC). *Average financial aid package:* $3806 (excluding resources awarded to replace EFC). 9% of all full-time undergraduates had no need and received non-need-based gift aid.

GIFT AID (NEED-BASED) *Total amount:* $64,705,840 (87% federal, 1% state, 3% institutional, 9% external sources). *Receiving aid:* Freshmen: 44% (1,161); all full-time undergraduates: 58% (9,276). *Average award:* Freshmen: $4937; Undergraduates: $4858. *Scholarships, grants, and awards:* Federal Pell, FSEOG, state, private, college/university gift aid from institutional funds.
GIFT AID (NON-NEED-BASED) *Total amount:* $5441 (100% institutional). *Receiving aid:* Freshmen: 1. Undergraduates: 5. *Average award:* Freshmen: $4048. Undergraduates: $3854. *Tuition waivers:* Full or partial for employees or children of employees. *ROTC:* Army, Air Force cooperative.
LOANS *Student loans:* $90,841,194 (100% need-based). 70% of past graduating class borrowed through all loan programs. *Average indebtedness per student:* $14,288. *Average need-based loan:* Freshmen: $1667. Undergraduates: $2539. *Parent loans:* $466,975 (100% need-based). *Programs:* Federal Direct (Subsidized and Unsubsidized Stafford, PLUS), Perkins, state, college/university.
WORK-STUDY *Federal work-study:* Total amount: $933,309; jobs available. *State or other work-study/employment:* Total amount: $695,324 (100% need-based). Part-time jobs available.
ATHLETIC AWARDS Total amount: $1,597,360 (98% need-based, 2% non-need-based).
APPLYING FOR FINANCIAL AID *Required financial aid forms:* FAFSA, institution's own form. *Financial aid deadline:* Continuous. *Notification date:* Continuous beginning 1/1. Students must reply by 6/15.
CONTACT Trish Howard, Director of Financial Aid and Scholarships, Utah Valley University, 800 West University Parkway, Orem, UT 84058, 801-863-8442. *Fax:* 801-863-8448. *E-mail:* howardpa@uvu.edu. *Website:* http://www.uvu.edu/.

U.T.A. MESIVTA OF KIRYAS JOEL
Monroe, NY

CONTACT Financial Aid Office, U.T.A. Mesivta of Kiryas Joel, 9 Nickelsburg Road, Unit 312, Monroe, NY 10950, 845-873-9901.

UTICA COLLEGE
Utica, NY

Tuition & fees: N/R	Average undergraduate aid package: $24,203

ABOUT THE INSTITUTION Independent, coed. *Awards:* certificates, bachelor's, master's, and doctoral degrees. 46 undergraduate majors. *Total enrollment:* 3,839. Undergraduates: 2,768. Freshmen: 505. Federal methodology is used as a basis for awarding need-based institutional aid.
FRESHMAN FINANCIAL AID (Fall 2012, est.) 475 applied for aid; of those 96% were deemed to have need. 100% of freshmen with need received aid; of those 9% had need fully met. *Average percent of need met:* 76% (excluding resources awarded to replace EFC). *Average financial aid package:* $28,269 (excluding resources awarded to replace EFC). 4% of all full-time freshmen had no need and received non-need-based gift aid.
UNDERGRADUATE FINANCIAL AID (Fall 2012, est.) 1,952 applied for aid; of those 95% were deemed to have need. 100% of undergraduates with need received aid; of those 9% had need fully met. *Average percent of need met:* 69% (excluding resources awarded to replace EFC). *Average financial aid package:* $24,203 (excluding resources awarded to replace EFC). 5% of all full-time undergraduates had no need and received non-need-based gift aid.
GIFT AID (NEED-BASED) *Total amount:* $35,727,074 (14% federal, 9% state, 76% institutional, 1% external sources). *Receiving aid:* Freshmen: 95% (455); all full-time undergraduates: 91% (1,845). *Average award:* Freshmen: $9107; Undergraduates: $6793. *Scholarships, grants, and awards:* Federal Pell, FSEOG, state, private, college/university gift aid from institutional funds.
GIFT AID (NON-NEED-BASED) *Total amount:* $2,611,950 (1% federal, 1% state, 95% institutional, 3% external sources). *Receiving aid:* Freshmen: 4% (20). Undergraduates: 4% (77). *Average award:* Freshmen: $1624. Undergraduates: $12,857. *Scholarships, grants, and awards by category:* Academic interests/achievement: general academic interests/achievements. *ROTC:* Army, Air Force cooperative.

LOANS *Student loans:* $22,260,513 (94% need-based, 6% non-need-based). 83% of past graduating class borrowed through all loan programs. *Average indebtedness per student:* $42,303. *Average need-based loan:* Freshmen: $3419. Undergraduates: $4403. *Parent loans:* $4,977,852 (99% need-based, 1% non-need-based). *Programs:* Federal Direct (Subsidized and Unsubsidized Stafford, PLUS), Perkins.
WORK-STUDY *Federal work-study:* Total amount: $1,049,850; jobs available. *State or other work-study/employment:* Part-time jobs available.
APPLYING FOR FINANCIAL AID *Required financial aid form:* FAFSA. *Financial aid deadline (priority):* 2/15. *Notification date:* Continuous. Students must reply by 5/1 or within 4 weeks of notification.
CONTACT Laura Bedford, Director of Student Financial Services, Utica College, 1600 Burrstone Road, Utica, NY 13502-4892, 315-792-3179 or toll-free 800-782-8884. *Fax:* 315-792-3368. *E-mail:* lbedford@utica.edu. *Website:* http://www.utica.edu/.

VALDOSTA STATE UNIVERSITY
Valdosta, GA

Tuition & fees (GA res): $5792	Average undergraduate aid package: $14,321

ABOUT THE INSTITUTION State-supported, coed. *Awards:* certificates, associate, bachelor's, master's, and doctoral degrees. 56 undergraduate majors. *Total enrollment:* 12,515. Undergraduates: 10,290. Freshmen: 1,918. Federal methodology is used as a basis for awarding need-based institutional aid.
UNDERGRADUATE EXPENSES for 2013–2014 *Application fee:* $40. *Tuition, state resident:* full-time $3882; part-time $161.74 per credit hour. *Tuition, nonresident:* full-time $13,703; part-time $570.94 per credit hour. *Required fees:* full-time $1910; $955 per term. Full-time tuition and fees vary according to course load, location, program, and reciprocity agreements. Part-time tuition and fees vary according to course load, location, program, and reciprocity agreements. *College room and board:* $7070; *Room only:* $3560. Room and board charges vary according to board plan and housing facility.
FRESHMAN FINANCIAL AID (Fall 2012, est.) 1,846 applied for aid; of those 81% were deemed to have need. 98% of freshmen with need received aid; of those 27% had need fully met. *Average percent of need met:* 85% (excluding resources awarded to replace EFC). *Average financial aid package:* $15,329 (excluding resources awarded to replace EFC). 1% of all full-time freshmen had no need and received non-need-based gift aid.
UNDERGRADUATE FINANCIAL AID (Fall 2012, est.) 8,487 applied for aid; of those 87% were deemed to have need. 100% of undergraduates with need received aid; of those 25% had need fully met. *Average percent of need met:* 83% (excluding resources awarded to replace EFC). *Average financial aid package:* $14,321 (excluding resources awarded to replace EFC). 1% of all full-time undergraduates had no need and received non-need-based gift aid.
GIFT AID (NEED-BASED) *Total amount:* $34,192,224 (65% federal, 32% state, 1% institutional, 2% external sources). *Receiving aid:* Freshmen: 69% (1,289); all full-time undergraduates: 67% (5,935). *Average award:* Freshmen: $6402; Undergraduates: $5975. *Scholarships, grants, and awards:* Federal Pell, FSEOG, state, private, college/university gift aid from institutional funds, United Negro College Fund.
GIFT AID (NON-NEED-BASED) *Total amount:* $5,207,008 (90% state, 4% institutional, 6% external sources). *Receiving aid:* Freshmen: 6% (105). Undergraduates: 3% (277). *Average award:* Freshmen: $1745. Undergraduates: $1933. *Scholarships, grants, and awards by category:* Academic interests/achievement: 55 awards ($74,411 total): biological sciences, communication, education, general academic interests/achievements, health fields, library science, mathematics, physical sciences, social sciences. Creative arts/performance: 58 awards ($77,700 total): art/fine arts, general creative arts/performance, journalism/publications, music, performing arts, theater/drama. Special achievements/activities: 20 awards ($25,000 total): general special achievements/activities, leadership, religious involvement. Special characteristics: 14 awards ($20,000 total): children and siblings of alumni, general special characteristics, members of minority groups. *Tuition waivers:* Full or partial for employees or children of employees, senior citizens. *ROTC:* Air Force.
LOANS *Student loans:* $65,159,389 (80% need-based, 20% non-need-based). 70% of past graduating class borrowed through all loan programs. *Average indebtedness per student:* $23,826. *Average need-based loan:* Freshmen: $3391. Undergraduates: $4352. *Parent loans:* $50,184,178 (33% need-based, 67% non-need-based).

Programs: Federal Direct (Subsidized and Unsubsidized Stafford, PLUS), state, college/university.
WORK-STUDY *Federal work-study:* Total amount: $450,994; 157 jobs averaging $3067.
ATHLETIC AWARDS Total amount: $1,166,250 (54% need-based, 46% non-need-based).
APPLYING FOR FINANCIAL AID *Required financial aid form:* FAFSA. *Financial aid deadline (priority):* 4/1. *Notification date:* Continuous beginning 4/15.
CONTACT Mr. Douglas R. Tanner, Director of Financial Aid, Valdosta State University, 1500 North Patterson Street, Valdosta, GA 31698, 229-333-5935 or toll-free 800-618-1878. *Fax:* 229-333-5430.
Website: http://www.valdosta.edu/.

VALENCIA COLLEGE
Orlando, FL

CONTACT College Answer Center Specialists, Valencia College, PO Box 3028, Orlando, FL 32802-3028, 407-299-5000.
Website: http://valenciacollege.edu/.

VALLEY CITY STATE UNIVERSITY
Valley City, ND

Tuition & fees (ND res): $6324	Average undergraduate aid package: $8178

ABOUT THE INSTITUTION State-supported, coed. *Awards:* bachelor's and master's degrees. 43 undergraduate majors. *Total enrollment:* 1,362. Undergraduates: 1,214. Freshmen: 190. Federal methodology is used as a basis for awarding need-based institutional aid.
UNDERGRADUATE EXPENSES for 2013–2014 *Application fee:* $35. *Tuition, state resident:* full-time $4657; part-time $155.24 per semester hour. *Tuition, nonresident:* full-time $12,435; part-time $155.24 per semester hour. *Required fees:* full-time $1667. Full-time tuition and fees vary according to course load, location, program, and reciprocity agreements. Part-time tuition and fees vary according to course load, location, program, and reciprocity agreements. *College room and board:* $5480; *Room only:* $2040. Room and board charges vary according to board plan and housing facility.
FRESHMAN FINANCIAL AID (Fall 2012, est.) 168 applied for aid; of those 76% were deemed to have need. 98% of freshmen with need received aid; of those 100% had need fully met. *Average percent of need met:* 85% (excluding resources awarded to replace EFC). *Average financial aid package:* $9962 (excluding resources awarded to replace EFC). 30% of all full-time freshmen had no need and received non-need-based gift aid.
UNDERGRADUATE FINANCIAL AID (Fall 2012, est.) 635 applied for aid; of those 80% were deemed to have need. 98% of undergraduates with need received aid; of those 22% had need fully met. *Average percent of need met:* 61% (excluding resources awarded to replace EFC). *Average financial aid package:* $8178 (excluding resources awarded to replace EFC). 12% of all full-time undergraduates had no need and received non-need-based gift aid.
GIFT AID (NEED-BASED) *Total amount:* $2,210,705 (58% federal, 17% state, 18% institutional, 7% external sources). *Receiving aid:* Freshmen: 69% (122); all full-time undergraduates: 60% (454). *Average award:* Freshmen: $5441; Undergraduates: $4357. *Scholarships, grants, and awards:* Federal Pell, FSEOG, state, private, college/university gift aid from institutional funds.
GIFT AID (NON-NEED-BASED) *Total amount:* $356,477 (1% federal, 11% state, 62% institutional, 26% external sources). *Receiving aid:* Freshmen: 30% (52). Undergraduates: 18% (133). *Average award:* Freshmen: $3351. Undergraduates: $1693. *Scholarships, grants, and awards by category: Academic interests/ achievement:* biological sciences, business, communication, computer science, education, English, general academic interests/achievements, humanities, library science, mathematics, physical sciences, social sciences. *Creative arts/performance:* applied art and design, art/fine arts, journalism/publications, music, theater/drama. *Special achievements/activities:* general special achievements/activities. *Special characteristics:* children and siblings of alumni, children of faculty/staff, ethnic background, general

special characteristics, international students, members of minority groups. *Tuition waivers:* Full or partial for employees or children of employees.
LOANS *Student loans:* $3,130,041 (75% need-based, 25% non-need-based). 78% of past graduating class borrowed through all loan programs. *Average indebtedness per student:* $27,884. *Average need-based loan:* Freshmen: $3294. Undergraduates: $3693. *Parent loans:* $37,325 (10% need-based, 90% non-need-based). *Programs:* Federal Direct (Subsidized and Unsubsidized Stafford, PLUS), Perkins.
WORK-STUDY *Federal work-study:* Total amount: $102,287; 53 jobs averaging $1921. *State or other work-study/employment:* Part-time jobs available.
ATHLETIC AWARDS Total amount: $209,853 (68% need-based, 32% non-need-based).
APPLYING FOR FINANCIAL AID *Required financial aid form:* FAFSA. *Financial aid deadline (priority):* 3/15. *Notification date:* Continuous beginning 2/15. Students must reply within 4 weeks of notification.
CONTACT Ms. Betty Kuss Schumacher, Director of Student Financial Aid, Valley City State University, 101 College Street SW, Valley City, ND 58072, 701-845-7412 or toll-free 800-532-8641 Ext. 7101. *Fax:* 701-845-7410. *E-mail:* betty.schumacher@vcsu.edu.
Website: http://www.vcsu.edu/.

VALLEY FORGE CHRISTIAN COLLEGE
Phoenixville, PA

Tuition & fees: N/R	Average undergraduate aid package: $11,203

ABOUT THE INSTITUTION Independent Assemblies of God, coed. 18 undergraduate majors. Federal methodology is used as a basis for awarding need-based institutional aid.
FRESHMAN FINANCIAL AID (Fall 2012, est.) 161 applied for aid; of those 91% were deemed to have need. 98% of freshmen with need received aid; of those 7% had need fully met. *Average percent of need met:* 49% (excluding resources awarded to replace EFC). *Average financial aid package:* $10,943 (excluding resources awarded to replace EFC). 19% of all full-time freshmen had no need and received non-need-based gift aid.
UNDERGRADUATE FINANCIAL AID (Fall 2012, est.) 708 applied for aid; of those 92% were deemed to have need. 99% of undergraduates with need received aid; of those 9% had need fully met. *Average percent of need met:* 50% (excluding resources awarded to replace EFC). *Average financial aid package:* $11,203 (excluding resources awarded to replace EFC). 9% of all full-time undergraduates had no need and received non-need-based gift aid.
GIFT AID (NEED-BASED) *Total amount:* $5,027,327. (33% federal, 13% state, 47% institutional, 7% external sources). *Receiving aid:* Freshmen: 77% (141); all full-time undergraduates: 85% (624). *Average award:* Freshmen: $8120; Undergraduates: $7800. *Scholarships, grants, and awards:* Federal Pell, FSEOG, state, private, college/university gift aid from institutional funds.
GIFT AID (NON-NEED-BASED) *Total amount:* $558,430 (92% institutional, 8% external sources). *Receiving aid:* Freshmen: 4% (7). Undergraduates: 5% (35). *Average award:* Freshmen: $6070. Undergraduates: $5185. *Scholarships, grants, and awards by category: Academic interests/achievement:* $548,255 total: general academic interests/achievements. *Creative arts/performance:* $953,766 total: art/fine arts, music. *Special achievements/activities:* $284,639 total: community service, general special achievements/activities, leadership, religious involvement. *Special characteristics:* $1,197,948 total: children of current students, children of faculty/staff, general special characteristics, local/state students, married students, parents of current students, relatives of clergy, siblings of current students, spouses of current students.
LOANS *Student loans:* $6,353,467 (84% need-based, 16% non-need-based). 92% of past graduating class borrowed through all loan programs. *Average indebtedness per student:* $36,136. *Average need-based loan:* Freshmen: $3332. Undergraduates: $4088. *Parent loans:* $2,021,759 (62% need-based, 38% non-need-based). *Programs:* Federal Direct (Subsidized and Unsubsidized Stafford, PLUS), Perkins.
WORK-STUDY *Federal work-study:* Total amount: $51,627; 27 jobs averaging $1912.
APPLYING FOR FINANCIAL AID *Required financial aid form:* FAFSA. *Financial aid deadline (priority):* 5/1. *Notification date:* Continuous beginning 3/1. Students must reply within 3 weeks of notification.

CONTACT Mrs. Linda Stein, Director of Financial Aid, Valley Forge Christian College, 1401 Charlestown Road, Phoenixville, PA 19460-2399, 610-917-1416 or toll-free 800-432-8322. *Fax:* 610-917-2069. *E-mail:* listein@vfcc.edu. *Website:* http://www.vfcc.edu/.

VALLEY FORGE CHRISTIAN COLLEGE WOODBRIDGE CAMPUS
Woodbridge, VA

CONTACT Christiana Bruwaa-Frimpong, Student Accounts/Financial Aid Counselor, Valley Forge Christian College Woodbridge Campus, 13909 Smoketown Road, Woodbridge, VA 22192, 703-580-4810 Ext. 172 or toll-free 800-432-8322. *Fax:* 703-580-4806. *Website:* http://www.vfcc.edu/woodbridge/.

VALPARAISO UNIVERSITY
Valparaiso, IN

Tuition & fees: $32,250	Average undergraduate aid package: $22,150

ABOUT THE INSTITUTION Independent Lutheran Church, coed. *Awards:* certificates, associate, bachelor's, master's, and doctoral degrees. 84 undergraduate majors. *Total enrollment:* 4,078. Undergraduates: 2,980. Freshmen: 772. Federal methodology is used as a basis for awarding need-based institutional aid.
UNDERGRADUATE EXPENSES for 2013–2014 *Comprehensive fee:* $41,414 includes full-time tuition ($31,170), mandatory fees ($1080), and room and board ($9164). *College room only:* $5564. Full-time tuition and fees vary according to course load and program. Room and board charges vary according to housing facility and student level. *Part-time tuition:* $1400 per credit hour. *Part-time fees:* $96 per term. Part-time tuition and fees vary according to course load and program. *Payment plan:* Tuition prepayment.
FRESHMAN FINANCIAL AID (Fall 2011) 632 applied for aid; of those 90% were deemed to have need. 100% of freshmen with need received aid; of those 26% had need fully met. *Average percent of need met:* 80% (excluding resources awarded to replace EFC). *Average financial aid package:* $24,998 (excluding resources awarded to replace EFC). 16% of all full-time freshmen had no need and received non-need-based gift aid.
UNDERGRADUATE FINANCIAL AID (Fall 2011) 2,245 applied for aid; of those 91% were deemed to have need. 100% of undergraduates with need received aid; of those 24% had need fully met. *Average percent of need met:* 77% (excluding resources awarded to replace EFC). *Average financial aid package:* $22,150 (excluding resources awarded to replace EFC). 20% of all full-time undergraduates had no need and received non-need-based gift aid.
GIFT AID (NEED-BASED) *Total amount:* $32,112,093 (15% federal, 5% state, 77% institutional, 3% external sources). *Receiving aid:* Freshmen: 82% (569); all full-time undergraduates: 76% (2,032). *Average award:* Freshmen: $21,795; Undergraduates: $19,174. *Scholarships, grants, and awards:* Federal Pell, FSEOG, state, private, college/university gift aid from institutional funds.
GIFT AID (NON-NEED-BASED) *Total amount:* $11,409,625 (4% federal, 89% institutional, 7% external sources). *Receiving aid:* Freshmen: 15% (106). Undergraduates: 21% (561). *Average award:* Freshmen: $15,226. Undergraduates: $13,880. *Scholarships, grants, and awards by category:* Academic interests/achievement: business, engineering/technologies, foreign languages, general academic interests/achievements, health fields, physical sciences, religion/biblical studies. *Creative arts/performance:* art/fine arts, music, performing arts, theater/drama. *Special characteristics:* children and siblings of alumni, children of faculty/staff, international students, relatives of clergy, religious affiliation. *Tuition waivers:* Full or partial for employees or children of employees. *ROTC:* Army cooperative, Air Force cooperative.
LOANS *Student loans:* $17,538,516 (84% need-based, 16% non-need-based). 72% of past graduating class borrowed through all loan programs. *Average indebtedness per student:* $31,957. *Average need-based loan:* Freshmen: $4587. Undergraduates: $5133. *Parent loans:* $5,989,778 (38% need-based, 62% non-need-based). *Programs:* Federal Direct (Subsidized and Unsubsidized Stafford, PLUS), Perkins, college/university, private loans.

WORK-STUDY *Federal work-study:* Total amount: $644,909; jobs available. *State or other work-study/employment:* Total amount: $1,173,264 (71% need-based, 29% non-need-based). Part-time jobs available.
ATHLETIC AWARDS Total amount: $3,642,365 (38% need-based, 62% non-need-based).
APPLYING FOR FINANCIAL AID *Required financial aid form:* FAFSA. *Financial aid deadline (priority):* 3/1. *Notification date:* Continuous beginning 3/1.
CONTACT Mr. David Fevig, Executive Director of Financial Aid and Enrollment Planning, Valparaiso University, 1700 Chapel Drive, Valparaiso, IN 46383-6493, 219-464-5015 or toll-free 888-GO-VALPO. *Fax:* 219-464-5012. *E-mail:* david.fevig@valpo.edu. *Website:* http://www.valpo.edu/.

VANDERBILT UNIVERSITY
Nashville, TN

Tuition & fees: $42,118	Average undergraduate aid package: $43,794

ABOUT THE INSTITUTION Independent, coed. *Awards:* bachelor's, master's, and doctoral degrees. 65 undergraduate majors. *Total enrollment:* 12,710. Undergraduates: 6,796. Freshmen: 1,608. Both federal and institutional methodology are used as a basis for awarding need-based institutional aid.
UNDERGRADUATE EXPENSES for 2013–2014 *Application fee:* $50. *Comprehensive fee:* $55,936 includes full-time tuition ($41,088), mandatory fees ($1030), and room and board ($13,818). *College room only:* $9028. Room and board charges vary according to board plan. *Payment plan:* Tuition prepayment.
FRESHMAN FINANCIAL AID (Fall 2012, est.) 975 applied for aid; of those 85% were deemed to have need. 100% of freshmen with need received aid; of those 100% had need fully met. *Average percent of need met:* 100% (excluding resources awarded to replace EFC). *Average financial aid package:* $44,416 (excluding resources awarded to replace EFC). 8% of all full-time freshmen had no need and received non-need-based gift aid.
UNDERGRADUATE FINANCIAL AID (Fall 2012, est.) 3,631 applied for aid; of those 89% were deemed to have need. 100% of undergraduates with need received aid; of those 100% had need fully met. *Average percent of need met:* 100% (excluding resources awarded to replace EFC). *Average financial aid package:* $43,794 (excluding resources awarded to replace EFC). 10% of all full-time undergraduates had no need and received non-need-based gift aid.
GIFT AID (NEED-BASED) *Total amount:* $129,587,739 (4% federal, 2% state, 93% institutional, 1% external sources). *Receiving aid:* Freshmen: 45% (729); all full-time undergraduates: 44% (2,991). *Average award:* Freshmen: $39,892; Undergraduates: $38,577. *Scholarships, grants, and awards:* Federal Pell, FSEOG, state, private, college/university gift aid from institutional funds.
GIFT AID (NON-NEED-BASED) *Total amount:* $20,958,220 (9% federal, 4% state, 82% institutional, 5% external sources). *Receiving aid:* Freshmen: 27% (429). Undergraduates: 20% (1,330). *Average award:* Freshmen: $20,968. Undergraduates: $24,788. *Scholarships, grants, and awards by category:* Academic interests/achievement: general academic interests/achievements. *Creative arts/performance:* general creative arts/performance. *Special achievements/activities:* community service, general special achievements/activities, leadership. *Special characteristics:* general special characteristics, local/state students, members of minority groups. *Tuition waivers:* Full or partial for employees or children of employees. *ROTC:* Army, Naval, Air Force cooperative.
LOANS *Student loans:* $7,492,630 (13% need-based, 87% non-need-based). 34% of past graduating class borrowed through all loan programs. *Average indebtedness per student:* $17,349. *Average need-based loan:* Freshmen: $2955. Undergraduates: $3225. *Parent loans:* $5,905,076 (100% non-need-based). *Programs:* Federal Direct (Subsidized and Unsubsidized Stafford, PLUS), Perkins, Federal Nursing, college/university.
WORK-STUDY *Federal work-study:* Total amount: $3,531,539; 1,388 jobs averaging $2342. *State or other work-study/employment:* Total amount: $860,504 (100% need-based). Part-time jobs available.
ATHLETIC AWARDS Total amount: $10,758,513 (29% need-based, 71% non-need-based).
APPLYING FOR FINANCIAL AID *Required financial aid forms:* FAFSA, CSS Financial Aid PROFILE. *Financial aid deadline (priority):* 2/5. *Notification date:* 4/1. Students must reply by 5/1.

CONTACT David Mohning, Executive Director of Student Financial Aid, Vanderbilt University, 2309 West End Avenue, Nashville, TN 37203, 615-343-5931 or toll-free 800-288-0432. *Fax:* 615-343-8512. *E-mail:* finaid@vanderbilt.edu. *Website:* http://www.vanderbilt.edu/.

VANDERCOOK COLLEGE OF MUSIC
Chicago, IL

CONTACT Ms. D. Denny, Director of Financial Aid, VanderCook College of Music, 3140 South Federal Street, Chicago, IL 60616-3731, 312-225-6288 Ext. 233. *Fax:* 312-225-5211. *E-mail:* ddenny@vandercook.edu. *Website:* http://www.vandercook.edu/.

VANGUARD UNIVERSITY OF SOUTHERN CALIFORNIA
Costa Mesa, CA

CONTACT Undergraduate Admissions Office, Vanguard University of Southern California, 55 Fair Drive, Costa Mesa, CA 92626-6597, 800-722-6279. *Fax:* 714-966-5471. *E-mail:* admissions@vanguard.edu. *Website:* http://www.vanguard.edu/.

VASSAR COLLEGE
Poughkeepsie, NY

Tuition & fees: $46,270	Average undergraduate aid package: $44,285

ABOUT THE INSTITUTION Independent, coed. *Awards:* bachelor's and master's degrees. 50 undergraduate majors. *Total enrollment:* 2,406. Undergraduates: 2,406. Freshmen: 658. Institutional methodology is used as a basis for awarding need-based institutional aid.

UNDERGRADUATE EXPENSES for 2013–2014 *Application fee:* $70. *One-time required fee:* $75. *Comprehensive fee:* $57,070 includes full-time tuition ($45,580), mandatory fees ($690), and room and board ($10,800). *College room only:* $5860. Room and board charges vary according to board plan and housing facility. *Part-time tuition:* $5410 per unit. Part-time tuition and fees vary according to course load.

FRESHMAN FINANCIAL AID (Fall 2012, est.) 464 applied for aid; of those 84% were deemed to have need. 100% of freshmen with need received aid; of those 100% had need fully met. *Average percent of need met:* 100% (excluding resources awarded to replace EFC). *Average financial aid package:* $45,236 (excluding resources awarded to replace EFC).

UNDERGRADUATE FINANCIAL AID (Fall 2012, est.) 1,729 applied for aid; of those 90% were deemed to have need. 100% of undergraduates with need received aid; of those 100% had need fully met. *Average percent of need met:* 100% (excluding resources awarded to replace EFC). *Average financial aid package:* $44,285 (excluding resources awarded to replace EFC).

GIFT AID (NEED-BASED) Total amount: $61,967,699 (5% federal, 1% state, 92% institutional, 2% external sources). *Receiving aid:* Freshmen: 59% (389); all full-time undergraduates: 60% (1,552). *Average award:* Freshmen: $42,101; Undergraduates: $40,045. *Scholarships, grants, and awards:* Federal Pell, FSEOG, state, private, college/university gift aid from institutional funds.

GIFT AID (NON-NEED-BASED) Total amount: $205,441 (4% federal, 6% state, 90% external sources). *Tuition waivers:* Full or partial for employees or children of employees.

LOANS *Student loans:* $2,906,691 (100% non-need-based). 48% of past graduating class borrowed through all loan programs. *Average indebtedness per student:* $17,234. *Average need-based loan:* Freshmen: $1630. Undergraduates: $2544. *Parent loans:* $3,554,656 (100% non-need-based). *Programs:* Federal Direct (Subsidized and Unsubsidized Stafford, PLUS), Perkins.

WORK-STUDY *Federal work-study:* Total amount: $1,839,373; 1,186 jobs averaging $1733. *State or other work-study/employment:* Total amount: $779,352 (100% need-based). 490 part-time jobs averaging $1754.

APPLYING FOR FINANCIAL AID *Required financial aid forms:* FAFSA, CSS Financial Aid PROFILE, noncustodial (divorced/separated) parent's statement. *Financial aid deadline:* 2/15. *Notification date:* 4/1. Students must reply by 5/1.

CONTACT Ms. Jessica L. Bernier, Director of Financial Aid, Vassar College, 124 Raymond Avenue, Poughkeepsie, NY 12604, 845-437-5320 or toll-free 800-827-7270. *Fax:* 845-437-5325. *E-mail:* mafraher@vassar.edu. *Website:* http://www.vassar.edu/.

VAUGHN COLLEGE OF AERONAUTICS AND TECHNOLOGY
Flushing, NY

CONTACT Dorothy Martin, Director of Financial Aid, Vaughn College of Aeronautics and Technology, 86-01 23rd Avenue, Flushing, NY 11369, 718-429-6600 Ext. 187 or toll-free 866-6VAUGHN. *Fax:* 718-779-2231. *E-mail:* dorothy.martin@vaughn.edu. *Website:* http://www.vaughn.edu/.

VERMONT TECHNICAL COLLEGE
Randolph Center, VT

Tuition & fees (VT res): $12,544	Average undergraduate aid package: $11,261

ABOUT THE INSTITUTION State-supported, coed. *Awards:* certificates, associate, and bachelor's degrees. 24 undergraduate majors. *Total enrollment:* 1,645. Undergraduates: 1,645. Freshmen: 220. Federal methodology is used as a basis for awarding need-based institutional aid.

UNDERGRADUATE EXPENSES for 2013–2014 *Application fee:* $40. *Tuition, state resident:* full-time $11,088; part-time $480 per credit hour. *Tuition, nonresident:* full-time $21,192; part-time $918 per credit hour. *Required fees:* full-time $1456. Full-time tuition and fees vary according to course load and program. Part-time tuition and fees vary according to program. *College room and board:* $8786; *Room only:* $5232. Room and board charges vary according to board plan.

FRESHMAN FINANCIAL AID (Fall 2012, est.) 200 applied for aid; of those 90% were deemed to have need. 99% of freshmen with need received aid; of those 9% had need fully met. *Average percent of need met:* 53% (excluding resources awarded to replace EFC). *Average financial aid package:* $10,617 (excluding resources awarded to replace EFC).

UNDERGRADUATE FINANCIAL AID (Fall 2012, est.) 990 applied for aid; of those 91% were deemed to have need. 98% of undergraduates with need received aid; of those 9% had need fully met. *Average percent of need met:* 54% (excluding resources awarded to replace EFC). *Average financial aid package:* $11,261 (excluding resources awarded to replace EFC).

GIFT AID (NEED-BASED) Total amount: $5,635,841 (50% federal, 24% state, 13% institutional, 13% external sources). *Receiving aid:* Freshmen: 75% (161); all full-time undergraduates: 65% (744). *Average award:* Freshmen: $6207; Undergraduates: $6375. *Scholarships, grants, and awards:* Federal Pell, FSEOG, state, private, college/university gift aid from institutional funds.

GIFT AID (NON-NEED-BASED) Total amount: $616,875 (80% institutional, 20% external sources). *Receiving aid:* Freshmen: 5% (11). Undergraduates: 3% (36). *Scholarships, grants, and awards by category:* Academic interests/achievement: agriculture, general academic interests/achievements. *Tuition waivers:* Full or partial for employees or children of employees. *ROTC:* Army cooperative.

LOANS *Student loans:* $10,275,671 (77% need-based, 23% non-need-based). 77% of past graduating class borrowed through all loan programs. *Average indebtedness per student:* $22,380. *Average need-based loan:* Freshmen: $3363. Undergraduates: $3899. *Parent loans:* $1,939,507 (90% need-based, 10% non-need-based). *Programs:* Federal Direct (Subsidized and Unsubsidized Stafford, PLUS), Perkins.

WORK-STUDY *Federal work-study:* Total amount: $173,475; jobs available.

APPLYING FOR FINANCIAL AID *Required financial aid forms:* FAFSA, state aid form. *Financial aid deadline (priority):* 3/1. *Notification date:* Continuous beginning 3/15.
CONTACT Catherine R. McCullough, Director of Financial Aid, Vermont Technical College, PO Box 500, Randolph Center, VT 05061-0500, 802-728-1248 or toll-free 800-442-VTC1. *Fax:* 802-728-1390.
Website: http://www.vtc.edu/.

VICTORY UNIVERSITY
Memphis, TN

CONTACT Ms. LaTonya Branch, Financial Aid Director, Victory University, 255 North Highland Street, Memphis, TN 38111, 901-320-9787 Ext. 1032 or toll-free 800-960-9777. *Fax:* 901-320-9724. *E-mail:* lbranch@victory.edu.
Website: http://www.victory.edu/.

VILLA MARIA COLLEGE OF BUFFALO
Buffalo, NY

Tuition & fees: $18,010	Average undergraduate aid package: $9317

ABOUT THE INSTITUTION Independent Roman Catholic Church, coed. *Awards:* certificates, associate, and bachelor's degrees. 17 undergraduate majors. *Total enrollment:* 411. Undergraduates: 470. Freshmen: 75. Federal methodology is used as a basis for awarding need-based institutional aid.
UNDERGRADUATE EXPENSES for 2013–2014 *Tuition:* full-time $17,640. *Required fees:* full-time $370; $590 or $280. Full-time tuition and fees vary according to program. Part-time tuition and fees vary according to course load and program.
FRESHMAN FINANCIAL AID (Fall 2011) 68 applied for aid; of those 97% were deemed to have need. 100% of freshmen with need received aid; of those 12% had need fully met. *Average percent of need met:* 41% (excluding resources awarded to replace EFC). *Average financial aid package:* $10,528 (excluding resources awarded to replace EFC). 3% of all full-time freshmen had no need and received non-need-based gift aid.
UNDERGRADUATE FINANCIAL AID (Fall 2011) 308 applied for aid; of those 94% were deemed to have need. 100% of undergraduates with need received aid; of those 7% had need fully met. *Average percent of need met:* 56% (excluding resources awarded to replace EFC). *Average financial aid package:* $9317 (excluding resources awarded to replace EFC). 3% of all full-time undergraduates had no need and received non-need-based gift aid.
GIFT AID (NEED-BASED) *Total amount:* $2,092,930 (60% federal, 35% state, 1% institutional, 4% external sources). *Receiving aid:* Freshmen: 93% (65); all full-time undergraduates: 90% (286). *Average award:* Freshmen: $5846; Undergraduates: $4694. *Scholarships, grants, and awards:* Federal Pell, FSEOG, state, private, college/university gift aid from institutional funds.
GIFT AID (NON-NEED-BASED) *Total amount:* $267,795 (48% federal, 3% state, 49% institutional). *Receiving aid:* Freshmen: 61% (43). Undergraduates: 51% (164). *Average award:* Freshmen: $2250. Undergraduates: $857. *Scholarships, grants, and awards by category: Academic interests/achievement:* 95 awards ($200,400 total). *Creative arts/performance:* 2 awards ($4000 total). *Special characteristics:* 3 awards ($17,120 total). *Tuition waivers:* Full or partial for employees or children of employees.
LOANS *Student loans:* $2,526,274 (100% need-based). 84% of past graduating class borrowed through all loan programs. *Average indebtedness per student:* $24,408. *Average need-based loan:* Freshmen: $2593. Undergraduates: $3209. *Parent loans:* $412,124 (100% need-based). *Programs:* Federal Direct (Subsidized and Unsubsidized Stafford, PLUS), private loans.
WORK-STUDY *Federal work-study:* Total amount: $32,007; 75 jobs averaging $441. *State or other work-study/employment:* Part-time jobs available.
APPLYING FOR FINANCIAL AID *Required financial aid forms:* FAFSA, state aid form. *Financial aid deadline:* Continuous. *Notification date:* Continuous beginning 5/1. Students must reply within 2 weeks of notification.

CONTACT Laura Fitzgerald, Director of Financial Aid, Villa Maria College of Buffalo, 240 Pine Ridge Road, Buffalo, NY 14225, 716-961-1828. *Fax:* 716-896-0705. *E-mail:* fitzgeraldl@villa.edu.
Website: http://www.villa.edu/.

VILLANOVA UNIVERSITY
Villanova, PA

Tuition & fees: $42,740	Average undergraduate aid package: $31,592

ABOUT THE INSTITUTION Independent Roman Catholic, coed. *Awards:* certificates, bachelor's, master's, and doctoral degrees. 52 undergraduate majors. *Total enrollment:* 10,661. Undergraduates: 7,111. Freshmen: 1,644. Both federal and institutional methodology are used as a basis for awarding need-based institutional aid.
UNDERGRADUATE EXPENSES for 2013–2014 *Application fee:* $80. *Comprehensive fee:* $54,110 includes full-time tuition ($42,150), mandatory fees ($590), and room and board ($11,370). *College room only:* $6020. Room and board charges vary according to board plan and housing facility. *Part-time tuition:* $1760 per credit. *Part-time fees:* $30 per year. Part-time tuition and fees vary according to class time and program.
FRESHMAN FINANCIAL AID (Fall 2012, est.) 1,158 applied for aid; of those 73% were deemed to have need. 99% of freshmen with need received aid; of those 17% had need fully met. *Average percent of need met:* 82% (excluding resources awarded to replace EFC). *Average financial aid package:* $33,169 (excluding resources awarded to replace EFC). 6% of all full-time freshmen had no need and received non-need-based gift aid.
UNDERGRADUATE FINANCIAL AID (Fall 2012, est.) 3,906 applied for aid; of those 82% were deemed to have need. 98% of undergraduates with need received aid; of those 16% had need fully met. *Average percent of need met:* 80% (excluding resources awarded to replace EFC). *Average financial aid package:* $31,592 (excluding resources awarded to replace EFC). 7% of all full-time undergraduates had no need and received non-need-based gift aid.
GIFT AID (NEED-BASED) *Total amount:* $73,239,027 (9% federal, 2% state, 87% institutional, 2% external sources). *Receiving aid:* Freshmen: 47% (772); all full-time undergraduates: 43% (2,807). *Average award:* Freshmen: $27,851; Undergraduates: $25,860. *Scholarships, grants, and awards:* Federal Pell, FSEOG, state, private, college/university gift aid from institutional funds, endowed and restricted scholarships and grants.
GIFT AID (NON-NEED-BASED) *Total amount:* $9,386,668 (27% federal, 63% institutional, 10% external sources). *Receiving aid:* Freshmen: 13% (216). Undergraduates: 14% (909). *Average award:* Freshmen: $13,622. Undergraduates: $12,489. *Scholarships, grants, and awards by category: Academic interests/achievement:* 936 awards ($8,662,313 total): general academic interests/achievements, international studies, military science. *Special achievements/activities:* 24 awards ($25,500 total): general special achievements/activities. *Special characteristics:* 321 awards ($9,260,231 total): children of educators, children of faculty/staff, general special characteristics, religious affiliation. *Tuition waivers:* Full or partial for employees or children of employees, senior citizens. *ROTC:* Army, Naval, Air Force cooperative.
LOANS *Student loans:* $31,497,426 (84% need-based, 16% non-need-based). 53% of past graduating class borrowed through all loan programs. *Average indebtedness per student:* $35,297. *Average need-based loan:* Freshmen: $3393. Undergraduates: $4498. *Parent loans:* $12,032,651 (73% need-based, 27% non-need-based). *Programs:* Federal Direct (Subsidized and Unsubsidized Stafford, PLUS), Perkins, Federal Nursing, alternative loans.
WORK-STUDY *Federal work-study:* Total amount: $7,631,889; 2,273 jobs averaging $2807. *State or other work-study/employment:* 31 part-time jobs averaging $2903.
ATHLETIC AWARDS Total amount: $10,241,342 (32% need-based, 68% non-need-based).
APPLYING FOR FINANCIAL AID *Required financial aid forms:* FAFSA, CSS Financial Aid PROFILE, noncustodial (divorced/separated) parent's statement, federal income tax form(s), W-2 forms. *Financial aid deadline:* 2/7 (priority: 2/7). *Notification date:* 4/1. Students must reply by 5/1.

CONTACT Bonnie Lee Behm, Director of Financial Assistance, Villanova University, 800 Lancaster Avenue, Villanova, PA 19085-1699, 610-519-4010. *Fax:* 610-519-7599. *E-mail:* bonnie.behm@villanova.edu. *Website:* http://www.villanova.edu/.

VIRGINIA COLLEGE IN BIRMINGHAM
Birmingham, AL

CONTACT Vice President, Campus Administration, Virginia College in Birmingham, 65 Bagby Drive, Birmingham, AL 35209, 205-802-1200. *Fax:* 205-271-8273. *Website:* http://www.vc.edu/.

VIRGINIA COMMONWEALTH UNIVERSITY
Richmond, VA

Tuition & fees (VA res): $9885	Average undergraduate aid package: $9956

ABOUT THE INSTITUTION State-supported, coed. *Awards:* certificates, bachelor's, master's, and doctoral degrees. 60 undergraduate majors. *Total enrollment:* 31,752. Undergraduates: 23,951. Freshmen: 3,617. Federal methodology is used as a basis for awarding need-based institutional aid.

UNDERGRADUATE EXPENSES for 2013–2014 *Application fee:* $40. *Tuition, state resident:* full-time $7860; part-time $327.50 per credit hour. *Tuition, nonresident:* full-time $21,275; part-time $886.46 per credit hour. *Required fees:* full-time $2025; $77.67 per credit hour. *College room and board:* $8748. Room and board charges vary according to board plan and housing facility.

FRESHMAN FINANCIAL AID (Fall 2011) 2,955 applied for aid; of those 77% were deemed to have need. 97% of freshmen with need received aid; of those 10% had need fully met. *Average percent of need met:* 59% (excluding resources awarded to replace EFC). *Average financial aid package:* $11,277 (excluding resources awarded to replace EFC). 9% of all full-time freshmen had no need and received non-need-based gift aid.

UNDERGRADUATE FINANCIAL AID (Fall 2011) 13,931 applied for aid; of those 80% were deemed to have need. 100% of undergraduates with need received aid; of those 8% had need fully met. *Average percent of need met:* 51% (excluding resources awarded to replace EFC). *Average financial aid package:* $9956 (excluding resources awarded to replace EFC). 7% of all full-time undergraduates had no need and received non-need-based gift aid.

GIFT AID (NEED-BASED) *Total amount:* $59,684,568 (52% federal, 33% state, 3% institutional, 12% external sources). *Receiving aid:* Freshmen: 47% (1,765); all full-time undergraduates: 42% (8,153). *Average award:* Freshmen: $6400; Undergraduates: $5930. *Scholarships, grants, and awards:* Federal Pell, FSEOG, state, private, college/university gift aid from institutional funds, United Negro College Fund.

GIFT AID (NON-NEED-BASED) *Total amount:* $11,910,413 (7% federal, 2% state, 15% institutional, 76% external sources). *Receiving aid:* Freshmen: 17% (655). Undergraduates: 10% (1,933). *Average award:* Freshmen: $5525. Undergraduates: $7921. *Scholarships, grants, and awards by category:* Academic interests/achievement: 5,051 awards ($1,690,696 total): biological sciences, business, computer science, education, engineering/technologies, foreign languages, general academic interests/achievements, health fields, humanities, mathematics, military science, physical sciences. *Creative arts/performance:* 141 awards ($230,083 total): art/fine arts, dance, music, performing arts, theater/drama. *Special characteristics:* veterans' children. *Tuition waivers:* Full or partial for employees or children of employees, senior citizens. *ROTC:* Army cooperative.

LOANS *Student loans:* $108,493,764 (85% need-based, 15% non-need-based). 63% of past graduating class borrowed through all loan programs. *Average indebtedness per student:* $28,889. *Average need-based loan:* Freshmen: $3533. Undergraduates: $4340. *Parent loans:* $17,025,078 (81% need-based, 19% non-need-based). *Programs:* Federal Direct (Subsidized and Unsubsidized Stafford, PLUS), Perkins, Federal Nursing, college/university.

WORK-STUDY *Federal work-study:* Total amount: $1,422,598; 820 jobs averaging $1735. *State or other work-study/employment:* Part-time jobs available.

ATHLETIC AWARDS Total amount: $10,968,762 (3% need-based, 97% non-need-based).

APPLYING FOR FINANCIAL AID *Required financial aid form:* FAFSA. *Financial aid deadline (priority):* 3/1. *Notification date:* Continuous beginning 4/1. Students must reply within 2 weeks of notification.

CONTACT Brenda Burke, Director for Financial Aid, Virginia Commonwealth University, PO Box 843026, Richmond, VA 23284-3026, 804-828-6669 or toll-free 800-841-3638. *Fax:* 804-827-0060. *E-mail:* faidmail@vcu.edu. *Website:* http://www.vcu.edu/.

VIRGINIA INTERMONT COLLEGE
Bristol, VA

Tuition & fees: $24,642	Average undergraduate aid package: $17,904

ABOUT THE INSTITUTION Independent religious, coed. *Awards:* bachelor's degrees. 49 undergraduate majors. *Total enrollment:* 496. Undergraduates: 496. Freshmen: 82. Federal methodology is used as a basis for awarding need-based institutional aid.

UNDERGRADUATE EXPENSES for 2013–2014 *Comprehensive fee:* $32,411 includes full-time tuition ($24,542), mandatory fees ($100), and room and board ($7769). *College room only:* $3760. Full-time tuition and fees vary according to course level, course load, program, and reciprocity agreements. Room and board charges vary according to board plan and housing facility. *Part-time tuition:* $491 per credit hour. Part-time tuition and fees vary according to course level, course load, program, and reciprocity agreements.

FRESHMAN FINANCIAL AID (Fall 2012, est.) 70 applied for aid; of those 93% were deemed to have need. 98% of freshmen with need received aid; of those 16% had need fully met. *Average percent of need met:* 64% (excluding resources awarded to replace EFC). *Average financial aid package:* $19,642 (excluding resources awarded to replace EFC). 9% of all full-time freshmen had no need and received non-need-based gift aid.

UNDERGRADUATE FINANCIAL AID (Fall 2012, est.) 407 applied for aid; of those 94% were deemed to have need. 99% of undergraduates with need received aid; of those 10% had need fully met. *Average percent of need met:* 62% (excluding resources awarded to replace EFC). *Average financial aid package:* $17,904 (excluding resources awarded to replace EFC). 10% of all full-time undergraduates had no need and received non-need-based gift aid.

GIFT AID (NEED-BASED) *Total amount:* $3,697,352 (29% federal, 14% state, 49% institutional, 8% external sources). *Receiving aid:* Freshmen: 80% (64); all full-time undergraduates: 84% (367). *Average award:* Freshmen: $16,355; Undergraduates: $13,939. *Scholarships, grants, and awards:* Federal Pell, FSEOG, state, private, college/university gift aid from institutional funds.

GIFT AID (NON-NEED-BASED) *Total amount:* $644,770 (11% state, 79% institutional, 10% external sources). *Receiving aid:* Freshmen: 12% (10). Undergraduates: 7% (30). *Average award:* Freshmen: $10,091. Undergraduates: $9096. *Scholarships, grants, and awards by category:* Academic interests/achievement: general academic interests/achievements. *Creative arts/performance:* applied art and design, art/fine arts, general creative arts/performance, music, performing arts, theater/drama. *Special achievements/activities:* religious involvement. *Special characteristics:* children of faculty/staff, first-generation college students. *Tuition waivers:* Full or partial for employees or children of employees, senior citizens.

LOANS *Student loans:* $3,472,008 (88% need-based, 12% non-need-based). 72% of past graduating class borrowed through all loan programs. *Average indebtedness per student:* $18,335. *Average need-based loan:* Freshmen: $3674. Undergraduates: $4633. *Parent loans:* $564,030 (64% need-based, 36% non-need-based). *Programs:* Federal Direct (Subsidized and Unsubsidized Stafford, PLUS), Perkins, alternative loans.

WORK-STUDY *Federal work-study:* Total amount: $146,528; jobs available.

ATHLETIC AWARDS Total amount: $1,837,281 (73% need-based, 27% non-need-based).

APPLYING FOR FINANCIAL AID *Required financial aid forms:* FAFSA, state aid form. *Financial aid deadline:* Continuous. *Notification date:* Continuous beginning 3/1. Students must reply within 2 weeks of notification.

CONTACT Dr. Richard Carroll, Dean of Admissions/Director of Financial Aid, Virginia Intermont College, 1013 Moore Street, Bristol, VA 24201-4298, 276-466-7851 or toll-free 800-451-1842. *Fax:* 276-466-7855. *E-mail:* richardcarroll@vic.edu. *Website:* http://www.vic.edu/.

VIRGINIA INTERNATIONAL UNIVERSITY
Fairfax, VA

CONTACT Financial Aid Office, Virginia International University, 11200 Waples Mill Road, Fairfax, VA 22030, 703-591-7042 or toll-free 800-514-6848. *Website:* http://www.viu.edu/.

VIRGINIA MILITARY INSTITUTE
Lexington, VA

Tuition & fees (VA res): $13,835	Average undergraduate aid package: $13,285

ABOUT THE INSTITUTION State-supported, coed, primarily men. 14 undergraduate majors. Federal methodology is used as a basis for awarding need-based institutional aid.
UNDERGRADUATE EXPENSES for 2013–2014 Tuition, state resident: full-time $6880. **Tuition, nonresident:** full-time $26,856. **Required fees:** full-time $6955. **College room and board:** $7733.
FRESHMAN FINANCIAL AID (Fall 2011) 372 applied for aid; of those 70% were deemed to have need. 98% of freshmen with need received aid; of those 48% had need fully met. **Average percent of need met:** 92% (excluding resources awarded to replace EFC). **Average financial aid package:** $14,050 (excluding resources awarded to replace EFC). 11% of all full-time freshmen had no need and received non-need-based gift aid.
UNDERGRADUATE FINANCIAL AID (Fall 2011) 1,205 applied for aid; of those 77% were deemed to have need. 91% of undergraduates with need received aid; of those 52% had need fully met. **Average percent of need met:** 93% (excluding resources awarded to replace EFC). **Average financial aid package:** $13,285 (excluding resources awarded to replace EFC). 15% of all full-time undergraduates had no need and received non-need-based gift aid.
GIFT AID (NEED-BASED) Total amount: $7,476,280 (16% federal, 11% state, 67% institutional, 6% external sources). **Receiving aid:** Freshmen: 46% (224); all full-time undergraduates: 45% (735). **Average award:** Freshmen: $13,000; Undergraduates: $12,043. **Scholarships, grants, and awards:** Federal Pell, FSEOG, state, private, college/university gift aid from institutional funds.
GIFT AID (NON-NEED-BASED) Total amount: $8,607,841 (81% federal, 2% state, 12% institutional, 5% external sources). **Receiving aid:** Freshmen: 19% (91). Undergraduates: 25% (406). **Average award:** Freshmen: $4000. Undergraduates: $4118. **Scholarships, grants, and awards by category:** Academic interests/achievement: 150 awards ($800,000 total): biological sciences, business, computer science, engineering/technologies, English, foreign languages, general academic interests/achievements, humanities, international studies, mathematics, military science, physical sciences, premedicine. *Creative arts/performance:* 16 awards ($9000 total): music. *Special achievements/activities:* 20 awards ($5000 total): general special achievements/activities, leadership. *Special characteristics:* 65 awards ($211,288 total): children and siblings of alumni, children of faculty/staff, general special characteristics, local/state students, out-of-state students.
LOANS Student loans: $6,407,693 (35% need-based, 65% non-need-based). 54% of past graduating class borrowed through all loan programs. *Average indebtedness per student:* $22,259. **Average need-based loan:** Freshmen: $4060. Undergraduates: $4356. **Parent loans:** $2,183,754 (100% non-need-based). **Programs:** Federal Direct (Subsidized and Unsubsidized Stafford, PLUS), Perkins.
ATHLETIC AWARDS Total amount: $3,248,775 (42% need-based, 58% non-need-based).
APPLYING FOR FINANCIAL AID Required financial aid forms: FAFSA, institution's own form. **Financial aid deadline (priority):** 3/1. **Notification date:** Continuous beginning 3/1. Students must reply by 5/1.

CONTACT Col. Timothy P. Golden, Director of Financial Aid, Virginia Military Institute, 306 Carroll Hall, Lexington, VA 24450, 540-464-7208 or toll-free 800-767-4207. *Fax:* 540-464-7629. *E-mail:* goldentp@vmi.edu. *Website:* http://www.vmi.edu/.

VIRGINIA POLYTECHNIC INSTITUTE AND STATE UNIVERSITY
Blacksburg, VA

Tuition & fees (VA res): $9187	Average undergraduate aid package: $16,279

ABOUT THE INSTITUTION State-supported, coed. **Awards:** certificates, associate, bachelor's, master's, and doctoral degrees. 67 undergraduate majors. **Total enrollment:** 31,087. Undergraduates: 23,859. Freshmen: 5,487. Federal methodology is used as a basis for awarding need-based institutional aid.
UNDERGRADUATE EXPENSES for 2013–2014 Application fee: $60. **Tuition, state resident:** full-time $9187. **Tuition, nonresident:** full-time $23,575. **College room and board:** $7406; **Room only:** $4190. Room and board charges vary according to board plan.
FRESHMAN FINANCIAL AID (Fall 2011) 4,035 applied for aid; of those 59% were deemed to have need. 94% of freshmen with need received aid; of those 16% had need fully met. **Average percent of need met:** 65% (excluding resources awarded to replace EFC). **Average financial aid package:** $16,600 (excluding resources awarded to replace EFC). 10% of all full-time freshmen had no need and received non-need-based gift aid.
UNDERGRADUATE FINANCIAL AID (Fall 2011) 15,440 applied for aid; of those 67% were deemed to have need. 97% of undergraduates with need received aid; of those 17% had need fully met. **Average percent of need met:** 69% (excluding resources awarded to replace EFC). **Average financial aid package:** $16,279 (excluding resources awarded to replace EFC). 12% of all full-time undergraduates had no need and received non-need-based gift aid.
GIFT AID (NEED-BASED) Total amount: $34,702,297 (50% federal, 41% state, 9% institutional). **Receiving aid:** Freshmen: 29% (1,536); all full-time undergraduates: 31% (7,158). **Average award:** Freshmen: $7178; Undergraduates: $6594. **Scholarships, grants, and awards:** Federal Pell, FSEOG, state, private, college/university gift aid from institutional funds, United Negro College Fund.
GIFT AID (NON-NEED-BASED) Total amount: $59,569,509 (16% institutional, 84% external sources). **Receiving aid:** Freshmen: 22% (1,154). Undergraduates: 16% (3,691). **Average award:** Freshmen: $5170. Undergraduates: $4714. **Scholarships, grants, and awards by category:** Academic interests/achievement: general academic interests/achievements, library science. *Creative arts/performance:* applied art and design, art/fine arts, cinema/film/broadcasting, creative writing, journalism/publications, music, performing arts, theater/drama. *Special achievements/activities:* cheerleading/drum major, community service, general special achievements/activities, leadership, memberships, religious involvement. *Special characteristics:* children of faculty/staff, first-generation college students, local/state students, members of minority groups, out-of-state students, twins, veterans' children. **Tuition waivers:** Full or partial for employees or children of employees, senior citizens. **ROTC:** Army, Naval, Air Force.
LOANS Student loans: $92,963,452 (40% need-based, 60% non-need-based). 54% of past graduating class borrowed through all loan programs. *Average indebtedness per student:* $25,759. **Average need-based loan:** Freshmen: $4067. Undergraduates: $4797. **Parent loans:** $26,067,462 (100% non-need-based). **Programs:** Federal Direct (Subsidized and Unsubsidized Stafford, PLUS), Perkins, state, college/university.
WORK-STUDY Federal work-study: Total amount: $654,103; 583 jobs averaging $1122. **State or other work-study/employment:** Total amount: $9,828,470 (100% non-need-based). Part-time jobs available.
ATHLETIC AWARDS Total amount: $8,318,208 (100% non-need-based).
APPLYING FOR FINANCIAL AID Required financial aid forms: FAFSA, general scholarship application form. **Financial aid deadline (priority):** 3/1. **Notification date:** 4/1. Students must reply by 5/1 or within 4 weeks of notification.
CONTACT Dr. Barry Simmons, Director of Student Financial Services, Virginia Polytechnic Institute and State University, 300 Student Service Building, Blacksburg, VA 24061, 540-231-5179. *Fax:* 540-231-9139. *E-mail:* simmonsb@vt.edu. *Website:* http://www.vt.edu/.

VIRGINIA STATE UNIVERSITY
Petersburg, VA

Tuition & fees (VA res): $7420	Average undergraduate aid package: $12,401

ABOUT THE INSTITUTION State-supported, coed. *Awards:* certificates, associate, bachelor's, master's, and doctoral degrees. 35 undergraduate majors. *Total enrollment:* 6,208. Undergraduates: 5,570. Freshmen: 1,244. Federal methodology is used as a basis for awarding need-based institutional aid.

UNDERGRADUATE EXPENSES for 2013–2014 *Application fee:* $25. *Tuition, state resident:* full-time $4550; part-time $311 per credit hour. *Tuition, nonresident:* full-time $12,988; part-time $663 per credit hour. *Required fees:* full-time $2870; $10 per credit hour. Full-time tuition and fees vary according to course load and program. Part-time tuition and fees vary according to course load and program. *College room and board:* $9680; *Room only:* $5816. Room and board charges vary according to board plan and housing facility.

FRESHMAN FINANCIAL AID (Fall 2012, est.) 1,191 applied for aid; of those 100% were deemed to have need. 100% of freshmen with need received aid; of those 34% had need fully met. *Average percent of need met:* 70% (excluding resources awarded to replace EFC). *Average financial aid package:* $11,696 (excluding resources awarded to replace EFC). 16% of all full-time freshmen had no need and received non-need-based gift aid.

UNDERGRADUATE FINANCIAL AID (Fall 2012, est.) 5,217 applied for aid; of those 100% were deemed to have need. 100% of undergraduates with need received aid; of those 15% had need fully met. *Average percent of need met:* 65% (excluding resources awarded to replace EFC). *Average financial aid package:* $12,401 (excluding resources awarded to replace EFC). 10% of all full-time undergraduates had no need and received non-need-based gift aid.

GIFT AID (NEED-BASED) Total amount: $25,963,650 (64% federal, 22% state, 14% institutional). *Receiving aid:* Freshmen: 74% (952); all full-time undergraduates: 72% (4,174). *Average award:* Freshmen: $7196; Undergraduates: $8196. *Scholarships, grants, and awards:* Federal Pell, FSEOG, state, private, college/university gift aid from institutional funds.

GIFT AID (NON-NEED-BASED) Total amount: $6,941,041 (31% state, 57% institutional, 12% external sources). *Receiving aid:* Freshmen: 20% (262). Undergraduates: 20% (1,147). *Average award:* Freshmen: $500. Undergraduates: $1000. *Scholarships, grants, and awards by category:* Academic interests/achievement: 150 awards ($300,000 total): agriculture, architecture, area/ethnic studies, biological sciences, business, communication, computer science, education, engineering/technologies, English, general academic interests/achievements, health fields, home economics, humanities, mathematics, military science, physical sciences, premedicine, social sciences. *Creative arts/performance:* 65 awards ($92,000 total): applied art and design, art/fine arts, dance, music, performing arts. *Special achievements/activities:* 31 awards ($116,240 total): cheerleading/drum major, community service, hobbies/interests, leadership, religious involvement. *Tuition waivers:* Full or partial for senior citizens. *ROTC:* Army.

LOANS Student loans: $47,088,952 (94% need-based, 6% non-need-based). 92% of past graduating class borrowed through all loan programs. *Average indebtedness per student:* $28,250. *Average need-based loan:* Freshmen: $3500. Undergraduates: $5500. *Parent loans:* $8,065,332 (100% non-need-based). *Programs:* Federal Direct (Subsidized and Unsubsidized Stafford, PLUS), Perkins, college/university.

WORK-STUDY Federal work-study: Total amount: $538,000; 300 jobs averaging $2000.

ATHLETIC AWARDS Total amount: $1,141,388 (100% non-need-based).

APPLYING FOR FINANCIAL AID *Required financial aid forms:* FAFSA, institution's own form. *Financial aid deadline (priority):* 3/31. *Notification date:* Continuous beginning 3/1. Students must reply within 2 weeks of notification.

CONTACT Myra Phillips, Director of Financial Aid, Virginia State University, PO Box 9031, Petersburg, VA 23806-2096, 804-524-5352 or toll-free 800-871-7611. *Fax:* 804-524-6818. *E-mail:* mhphilli@vsu.edu. *Website:* http://www.vsu.edu/.

VIRGINIA UNION UNIVERSITY
Richmond, VA

Tuition & fees: $14,630	Average undergraduate aid package: $12,070

ABOUT THE INSTITUTION Independent Baptist, coed. *Awards:* bachelor's, master's, and doctoral degrees. 23 undergraduate majors. *Total enrollment:* 1,710. Undergraduates: 1,333. Freshmen: 418. Federal methodology is used as a basis for awarding need-based institutional aid.

UNDERGRADUATE EXPENSES for 2013–2014 *Application fee:* $25. *Comprehensive fee:* $22,302 includes full-time tuition ($13,314), mandatory fees ($1316), and room and board ($7672). *College room only:* $3600. Full-time tuition and fees vary according to course level and course load. Room and board charges vary according to housing facility. *Part-time tuition:* $422 per credit hour. *Part-time fees:* $40 per credit hour. Part-time tuition and fees vary according to course level and course load.

FRESHMAN FINANCIAL AID (Fall 2012, est.) 376 applied for aid; of those 95% were deemed to have need. 99% of freshmen with need received aid; of those 5% had need fully met. *Average percent of need met:* 50% (excluding resources awarded to replace EFC). *Average financial aid package:* $11,765 (excluding resources awarded to replace EFC). 4% of all full-time freshmen had no need and received non-need-based gift aid.

UNDERGRADUATE FINANCIAL AID (Fall 2012, est.) 1,275 applied for aid; of those 95% were deemed to have need. 99% of undergraduates with need received aid; of those 7% had need fully met. *Average percent of need met:* 53% (excluding resources awarded to replace EFC). *Average financial aid package:* $12,070 (excluding resources awarded to replace EFC). 3% of all full-time undergraduates had no need and received non-need-based gift aid.

GIFT AID (NEED-BASED) Total amount: $7,983,882 (57% federal, 17% state, 24% institutional, 2% external sources). *Receiving aid:* Freshmen: 78% (338); all full-time undergraduates: 83% (1,116). *Average award:* Freshmen: $8305; Undergraduates: $8384. *Scholarships, grants, and awards:* Federal Pell, FSEOG, state, private, college/university gift aid from institutional funds.

GIFT AID (NON-NEED-BASED) Total amount: $329,629 (28% state, 63% institutional, 9% external sources). *Receiving aid:* Freshmen: 1% (6). Undergraduates: 2% (26). *Average award:* Freshmen: $4741. Undergraduates: $5340. *Scholarships, grants, and awards by category:* Academic interests/achievement: 169 awards ($775,084 total): general academic interests/achievements. *Creative arts/performance:* 49 awards ($57,940 total): music. *Special characteristics:* 5 awards ($29,957 total): children of faculty/staff. *Tuition waivers:* Full or partial for employees or children of employees. *ROTC:* Army cooperative.

LOANS Student loans: $9,009,338 (100% need-based). 98% of past graduating class borrowed through all loan programs. *Average indebtedness per student:* $31,153. *Average need-based loan:* Freshmen: $3380. Undergraduates: $4143. *Parent loans:* $4,125,746 (75% need-based, 25% non-need-based). *Programs:* Federal Direct (Subsidized and Unsubsidized Stafford).

WORK-STUDY Federal work-study: Total amount: $506,035; 205 jobs averaging $1860.

ATHLETIC AWARDS Total amount: $1,213,345 (89% need-based, 11% non-need-based).

APPLYING FOR FINANCIAL AID *Required financial aid forms:* FAFSA, state aid form. *Financial aid deadline (priority):* 5/1. *Notification date:* Continuous. Students must reply within 2 weeks of notification.

CONTACT Mrs. Karen Gee, Director of Financial Aid, Virginia Union University, 1500 North Lombardy Street, Richmond, VA 23220-1170, 804-257-5882 or toll-free 800-368-3227. *E-mail:* klgee@vuu.edu. *Website:* http://www.vuu.edu/.

VIRGINIA UNIVERSITY OF LYNCHBURG
Lynchburg, VA

CONTACT Mrs. Charlene P. Scruggs, Financial Aid Director, Virginia University of Lynchburg, 2058 Garfield Avenue, Lynchburg, VA 24572, 434-528-5276. *Fax:* 434-455-5958. *E-mail:* cscruggs@vul.edu. *Website:* http://www.vul.edu/.

VIRGINIA WESLEYAN COLLEGE
Norfolk, VA

Tuition & fees: $32,182	Average undergraduate aid package: $20,169

ABOUT THE INSTITUTION Independent United Methodist, coed. *Awards:* bachelor's degrees. 48 undergraduate majors. *Total enrollment:* 1,431. Undergraduates: 1,431. Freshmen: 435. Federal methodology is used as a basis for awarding need-based institutional aid.

UNDERGRADUATE EXPENSES for 2013–2014 *Application fee:* $40. *One-time required fee:* $300. *Comprehensive fee:* $40,690 includes full-time tuition ($31,532), mandatory fees ($650), and room and board ($8508). Full-time tuition and fees vary according to course load. Room and board charges vary according to board plan and housing facility. *Part-time tuition:* $1314 per credit hour. Part-time tuition and fees vary according to course load.

FRESHMAN FINANCIAL AID (Fall 2011) 435 applied for aid; of those 87% were deemed to have need. 100% of freshmen with need received aid; of those 11% had need fully met. *Average percent of need met:* 70% (excluding resources awarded to replace EFC). *Average financial aid package:* $21,910 (excluding resources awarded to replace EFC). 13% of all full-time freshmen had no need and received non-need-based gift aid.

UNDERGRADUATE FINANCIAL AID (Fall 2011) 1,231 applied for aid; of those 82% were deemed to have need. 100% of undergraduates with need received aid; of those 11% had need fully met. *Average percent of need met:* 65% (excluding resources awarded to replace EFC). *Average financial aid package:* $20,169 (excluding resources awarded to replace EFC). 17% of all full-time undergraduates had no need and received non-need-based gift aid.

GIFT AID (NEED-BASED) *Total amount:* $16,956,622 (18% federal, 10% state, 70% institutional, 2% external sources). *Receiving aid:* Freshmen: 86% (376); all full-time undergraduates: 81% (1,005). *Average award:* Freshmen: $18,342; Undergraduates: $16,700. *Scholarships, grants, and awards:* Federal Pell, FSEOG, state, private, college/university gift aid from institutional funds, United Negro College Fund.

GIFT AID (NON-NEED-BASED) *Total amount:* $3,884,816 (32% federal, 11% state, 55% institutional, 2% external sources). *Receiving aid:* Freshmen: 15% (68). Undergraduates: 13% (165). *Average award:* Freshmen: $17,492. Undergraduates: $15,876. *Scholarships, grants, and awards by category: Academic interests/achievement:* general academic interests/achievements. *Creative arts/performance:* art/fine arts, music, theater/drama. *Special achievements/activities:* community service, leadership, religious involvement. *Special characteristics:* 27 awards ($568,270 total): children of faculty/staff, relatives of clergy, religious affiliation. *Tuition waivers:* Full or partial for employees or children of employees, adult students, senior citizens. *ROTC:* Army cooperative.

LOANS *Student loans:* $8,393,195 (80% need-based, 20% non-need-based). 85% of past graduating class borrowed through all loan programs. *Average indebtedness per student:* $36,445. *Average need-based loan:* Freshmen: $6241. Undergraduates: $7187. *Parent loans:* $4,364,625 (62% need-based, 38% non-need-based). *Programs:* Federal Direct (Subsidized and Unsubsidized Stafford, PLUS), Perkins, alternative loans.

WORK-STUDY *Federal work-study:* Total amount: $165,776; 182 jobs averaging $911.

APPLYING FOR FINANCIAL AID *Required financial aid forms:* FAFSA, state aid form. *Financial aid deadline (priority):* 3/1. *Notification date:* Continuous beginning 2/15. Students must reply by 5/1 or within 2 weeks of notification.

CONTACT Mrs. Teresa Rhyne, Director of Financial Aid, Virginia Wesleyan College, 1584 Wesleyan Drive, Norfolk, VA 23502-5599, 757-455-3345 or toll-free 800-737-8684. *Fax:* 757-455-6779. *E-mail:* finaid@vwc.edu. *Website:* http://www.vwc.edu/.

VISIBLE MUSIC COLLEGE
Memphis, TN

CONTACT Financial Aid Office, Visible Music College, 200 Madison Avenue, Memphis, TN 38103, 901-381-3939. *Website:* http://visible.edu/.

VITERBO UNIVERSITY
La Crosse, WI

CONTACT Ms. Terry Norman, Director of Financial Aid, Viterbo University, 900 Viterbo Drive, La Crosse, WI 54601-4797, 608-796-3900 or toll-free 800-VITERBO. *Fax:* 608-796-3050. *E-mail:* twnorman@viterbo.edu. *Website:* http://www.viterbo.edu/.

VOORHEES COLLEGE
Denmark, SC

CONTACT Augusta L. Kitchen, Director of Financial Aid, Voorhees College, PO Box 678, Denmark, SC 29042, 803-703-7109 Ext. 7106 or toll-free 866-685-9904. *Fax:* 803-793-0831. *E-mail:* akitchen@voorhees.edu. *Website:* http://www.voorhees.edu/.

WABASH COLLEGE
Crawfordsville, IN

Tuition & fees: $35,650	Average undergraduate aid package: $29,423

ABOUT THE INSTITUTION Independent, men only. *Awards:* bachelor's degrees. 25 undergraduate majors. *Total enrollment:* 906. Undergraduates: 906. Freshmen: 252. Both federal and institutional methodology are used as a basis for awarding need-based institutional aid.

UNDERGRADUATE EXPENSES for 2013–2014 *Application fee:* $40. *Comprehensive fee:* $44,160 includes full-time tuition ($35,000), mandatory fees ($650), and room and board ($8510). *College room only:* $4310. Room and board charges vary according to board plan and housing facility. *Part-time tuition:* $5833 per course. *Payment plan:* Tuition prepayment.

FRESHMAN FINANCIAL AID (Fall 2012, est.) 242 applied for aid; of those 87% were deemed to have need. 100% of freshmen with need received aid; of those 73% had need fully met. *Average percent of need met:* 98% (excluding resources awarded to replace EFC). *Average financial aid package:* $31,769 (excluding resources awarded to replace EFC). 10% of all full-time freshmen had no need and received non-need-based gift aid.

UNDERGRADUATE FINANCIAL AID (Fall 2012, est.) 805 applied for aid; of those 91% were deemed to have need. 100% of undergraduates with need received aid; of those 82% had need fully met. *Average percent of need met:* 97% (excluding resources awarded to replace EFC). *Average financial aid package:* $29,423 (excluding resources awarded to replace EFC). 14% of all full-time undergraduates had no need and received non-need-based gift aid.

GIFT AID (NEED-BASED) *Total amount:* $13,920,324 (6% federal, 6% state, 84% institutional, 4% external sources). *Receiving aid:* Freshmen: 83% (208); all full-time undergraduates: 79% (712). *Average award:* Freshmen: $20,169; Undergraduates: $17,749. *Scholarships, grants, and awards:* Federal Pell, state, private, college/university gift aid from institutional funds.

GIFT AID (NON-NEED-BASED) *Total amount:* $3,172,627 (89% institutional, 11% external sources). *Receiving aid:* Freshmen: 14% (35). Undergraduates: 13% (120). *Average award:* Freshmen: $14,804. Undergraduates: $16,274. *Scholarships, grants, and awards by category: Academic interests/achievement:* 1,089 awards ($9,043,643 total): general academic interests/achievements. *Creative arts/performance:* 58 awards ($263,500 total): art/fine arts, creative writing, journalism/publications, music, theater/drama. *Special achievements/activities:* 87 awards ($670,969 total): community service, leadership. *Special characteristics:* 16 awards ($503,504 total): children of faculty/staff. *Tuition waivers:* Full or partial for employees or children of employees.

LOANS *Student loans:* $6,094,259 (65% need-based, 35% non-need-based). 76% of past graduating class borrowed through all loan programs. *Average indebtedness per student:* $28,919. *Average need-based loan:* Freshmen: $5274. Undergraduates: $5426. *Parent loans:* $1,759,183 (100% non-need-based). *Programs:* Federal Direct (Subsidized and Unsubsidized Stafford, PLUS), college/university.

WORK-STUDY *State or other work-study/employment:* Total amount: $2,537,204 (89% need-based, 11% non-need-based). 784 part-time jobs averaging $3227.

APPLYING FOR FINANCIAL AID *Required financial aid forms:* FAFSA, CSS Financial Aid PROFILE, noncustodial (divorced/separated) parent's statement, business/farm supplement, federal income tax form(s), W-2 forms. *Financial aid deadline:* 3/1 (priority: 2/15). *Notification date:* 3/31. Students must reply by 5/1 or within 2 weeks of notification.

CONTACT Mr. Clint Gasaway, Director of Financial Aid, Wabash College, PO Box 352, Crawfordsville, IN 47933-0352, 800-718-9746 or toll-free 800-345-5385. *Fax:* 765-361-6166. *E-mail:* financialaid@wabash.edu.
Website: http://www.wabash.edu/.

WAGNER COLLEGE
Staten Island, NY

Tuition & fees: $39,220	Average undergraduate aid package: $24,303

ABOUT THE INSTITUTION Independent, coed. *Awards:* certificates, bachelor's, and master's degrees. 38 undergraduate majors. *Total enrollment:* 2,208. Undergraduates: 1,821. Freshmen: 426. Federal methodology is used as a basis for awarding need-based institutional aid.

UNDERGRADUATE EXPENSES for 2013–2014 *Comprehensive fee:* $50,880 includes full-time tuition ($38,920), mandatory fees ($300), and room and board ($11,660). *Part-time tuition:* $4865 per unit.

FRESHMAN FINANCIAL AID (Fall 2012, est.) 372 applied for aid; of those 87% were deemed to have need. 100% of freshmen with need received aid; of those 25% had need fully met. *Average percent of need met:* 76% (excluding resources awarded to replace EFC). *Average financial aid package:* $26,233 (excluding resources awarded to replace EFC). 16% of all full-time freshmen had no need and received non-need-based gift aid.

UNDERGRADUATE FINANCIAL AID (Fall 2012, est.) 1,347 applied for aid; of those 86% were deemed to have need. 99% of undergraduates with need received aid; of those 22% had need fully met. *Average percent of need met:* 70% (excluding resources awarded to replace EFC). *Average financial aid package:* $24,303 (excluding resources awarded to replace EFC). 14% of all full-time undergraduates had no need and received non-need-based gift aid.

GIFT AID (NEED-BASED) *Total amount:* $18,757,414 (8% federal, 5% state, 86% institutional, 1% external sources). *Receiving aid:* Freshmen: 76% (323); all full-time undergraduates: 66% (1,145). *Average award:* Freshmen: $16,613; Undergraduates: $19,209. *Scholarships, grants, and awards:* Federal Pell, FSEOG, state, private, college/university gift aid from institutional funds.

GIFT AID (NON-NEED-BASED) *Total amount:* $8,012,901 (1% state, 99% institutional). *Average award:* Freshmen: $15,507. Undergraduates: $13,042. *Scholarships, grants, and awards by category:* Academic interests/ achievement: general academic interests/achievements. Creative arts/performance: music, theater/drama. Special characteristics: children of faculty/staff, siblings of current students. *Tuition waivers:* Full or partial for employees or children of employees. *ROTC:* Army cooperative.

LOANS *Student loans:* $13,714,197 (86% need-based, 14% non-need-based). *Average need-based loan:* Freshmen: $3624. Undergraduates: $4915. *Parent loans:* $5,154,117 (85% need-based, 15% non-need-based). *Programs:* Federal Direct (Subsidized and Unsubsidized Stafford, PLUS), Perkins, Federal Nursing, alternative loans.

WORK-STUDY *Federal work-study:* Total amount: $807,128; jobs available.

ATHLETIC AWARDS Total amount: $6,058,404 (46% need-based, 54% non-need-based).

APPLYING FOR FINANCIAL AID *Required financial aid forms:* FAFSA, state aid form. *Financial aid deadline:* 4/15 (priority: 2/15). *Notification date:* 3/1. Students must reply within 3 weeks of notification.

CONTACT Ms. Theresa Weimer, Director of Financial Aid, Wagner College, One Campus Road, Staten Island, NY 10301, 718-390-3122 or toll-free 800-221-1010. *Fax:* 718-390-3203. *E-mail:* tweimer@wagner.edu.
Website: http://www.wagner.edu/.

WAKE FOREST UNIVERSITY
Winston-Salem, NC

Tuition & fees: $44,742	Average undergraduate aid package: $32,015

ABOUT THE INSTITUTION Independent, coed. *Awards:* bachelor's, master's, and doctoral degrees. 38 undergraduate majors. *Total enrollment:* 7,432. Undergraduates: 4,815. Freshmen: 1,234. Institutional methodology is used as a basis for awarding need-based institutional aid.

UNDERGRADUATE EXPENSES for 2013–2014 *Application fee:* $50. *Comprehensive fee:* $56,742 includes full-time tuition ($44,200), mandatory fees ($542), and room and board ($12,000). *College room only:* $8000. *Part-time tuition:* $1832 per credit hour.

FRESHMAN FINANCIAL AID (Fall 2012, est.) 556 applied for aid; of those 89% were deemed to have need. 98% of freshmen with need received aid; of those 89% had need fully met. *Average percent of need met:* 99% (excluding resources awarded to replace EFC). *Average financial aid package:* $34,647 (excluding resources awarded to replace EFC). 4% of all full-time freshmen had no need and received non-need-based gift aid.

UNDERGRADUATE FINANCIAL AID (Fall 2012, est.) 2,146 applied for aid; of those 90% were deemed to have need. 99% of undergraduates with need received aid; of those 67% had need fully met. *Average percent of need met:* 99% (excluding resources awarded to replace EFC). *Average financial aid package:* $32,015 (excluding resources awarded to replace EFC). 11% of all full-time undergraduates had no need and received non-need-based gift aid.

GIFT AID (NEED-BASED) *Total amount:* $49,680,184 (8% federal, 3% state, 85% institutional, 4% external sources). *Receiving aid:* Freshmen: 33% (409); all full-time undergraduates: 38% (1,789). *Average award:* Freshmen: $32,846; Undergraduates: $29,732. *Scholarships, grants, and awards:* Federal Pell, FSEOG, state, private, college/university gift aid from institutional funds.

GIFT AID (NON-NEED-BASED) *Total amount:* $7,177,100 (18% federal, 1% state, 63% institutional, 18% external sources). *Receiving aid:* Freshmen: 20% (241). Undergraduates: 28% (1,335). *Average award:* Freshmen: $17,809. Undergraduates: $16,702. *Scholarships, grants, and awards by category:* Academic interests/ achievement: general academic interests/achievements. Creative arts/performance: general creative arts/performance. Special achievements/activities: leadership. Special characteristics: children and siblings of alumni, local/state students, religious affiliation. *ROTC:* Army.

LOANS *Student loans:* $22,496,011 (85% need-based, 15% non-need-based). 38% of past graduating class borrowed through all loan programs. *Average indebtedness per student:* $33,262. *Average need-based loan:* Freshmen: $5629. Undergraduates: $7476. *Parent loans:* $8,082,948 (89% need-based, 11% non-need-based). *Programs:* Federal Direct (Subsidized and Unsubsidized Stafford, PLUS), Perkins, state, college/university.

WORK-STUDY *Federal work-study:* Total amount: $2,403,512; jobs available. *State or other work-study/employment:* Part-time jobs available.

ATHLETIC AWARDS Total amount: $10,916,064 (40% need-based, 60% non-need-based).

APPLYING FOR FINANCIAL AID *Required financial aid forms:* FAFSA, CSS Financial Aid PROFILE, state aid form, noncustodial (divorced/separated) parent's statement. *Financial aid deadline:* 3/1 (priority: 2/15). *Notification date:* Continuous beginning 4/1. Students must reply by 5/1 or within 4 weeks of notification.

CONTACT Adam Holyfield, Associate Director of Student Financial Aid, Wake Forest University, PO Box 7246, Winston-Salem, NC 27109-7246, 336-758-5154. *Fax:* 336-758-4924. *E-mail:* financial-aid@wfu.edu.
Website: http://www.wfu.edu/.

WALDEN UNIVERSITY
Minneapolis, MN

CONTACT Office of Financial Aid, Walden University, 100 Washington South, Minneapolis, MN 55401, 800-444-6795 or toll-free 866-492-5336. *Fax:* 410-843-6211. *E-mail:* finaid@waldenu.edu.
Website: http://www.waldenu.edu/.

WALDORF COLLEGE
Forest City, IA

Tuition & fees: $20,316	Average undergraduate aid package: $12,176

ABOUT THE INSTITUTION Independent Lutheran, coed. *Awards:* associate and bachelor's degrees. 22 undergraduate majors. *Total enrollment:* 1,105. Undergraduates: 1,105. Freshmen: 155. Federal methodology is used as a basis for awarding need-based institutional aid.
UNDERGRADUATE EXPENSES for 2013–2014 *Comprehensive fee:* $27,172 includes full-time tuition ($19,266), mandatory fees ($1050), and room and board ($6856). Full-time tuition and fees vary according to class time, course load, and program. Room and board charges vary according to board plan and housing facility.
FRESHMAN FINANCIAL AID (Fall 2012, est.) 159 applied for aid; of those 89% were deemed to have need. 99% of freshmen with need received aid; of those 16% had need fully met. *Average percent of need met:* 68% (excluding resources awarded to replace EFC). *Average financial aid package:* $14,074 (excluding resources awarded to replace EFC). 11% of all full-time freshmen had no need and received non-need-based gift aid.
UNDERGRADUATE FINANCIAL AID (Fall 2012, est.) 987 applied for aid; of those 85% were deemed to have need. 99% of undergraduates with need received aid; of those 13% had need fully met. *Average percent of need met:* 67% (excluding resources awarded to replace EFC). *Average financial aid package:* $12,176 (excluding resources awarded to replace EFC). 7% of all full-time undergraduates had no need and received non-need-based gift aid.
GIFT AID (NEED-BASED) *Total amount:* $5,090,905 (42% federal, 4% state, 48% institutional, 6% external sources). *Receiving aid:* Freshmen: 73% (122); all full-time undergraduates: 70% (721). *Average award:* Freshmen: $10,319; Undergraduates: $9134. *Scholarships, grants, and awards:* Federal Pell, FSEOG, state, private, college/university gift aid from institutional funds.
GIFT AID (NON-NEED-BASED) *Total amount:* $506,683 (2% federal, 1% state, 77% institutional, 20% external sources). *Receiving aid:* Freshmen: 8% (14). Undergraduates: 3% (31). *Average award:* Freshmen: $5924. Undergraduates: $4726. *Scholarships, grants, and awards by category:* Academic interests/achievement: communication, general academic interests/achievements. *Creative arts/performance:* music, theater/drama. *Special achievements/activities:* cheerleading/drum major, junior miss, leadership. *Special characteristics:* children of faculty/staff, religious affiliation. *Tuition waivers:* Full or partial for employees or children of employees.
LOANS *Student loans:* $7,446,748 (77% need-based, 23% non-need-based). 99% of past graduating class borrowed through all loan programs. *Average indebtedness per student:* $36,966. *Average need-based loan:* Freshmen: $3676. *Parent loans:* $2,554,801 (33% need-based, 67% non-need-based). *Programs:* Federal Direct (Subsidized and Unsubsidized Stafford, PLUS), Perkins, state, alternative loans.
WORK-STUDY *Federal work-study:* Total amount: $428,267; jobs available. *State or other work-study/employment:* Part-time jobs available.
ATHLETIC AWARDS Total amount: $1,883,191 (85% need-based, 15% non-need-based).
APPLYING FOR FINANCIAL AID *Required financial aid form:* FAFSA. *Financial aid deadline (priority):* 3/1. *Notification date:* Continuous beginning 3/1. Students must reply within 2 weeks of notification.
CONTACT Duane Polsdofer, Director of Financial Aid, Waldorf College, 106 South 6th Street, Forest City, IA 50436, 641-585-8120 or toll-free 800-292-1903. *Fax:* 641-585-8125. *E-mail:* polsdofed@waldorf.edu.
Website: http://www.waldorf.edu/.

WALLA WALLA UNIVERSITY
College Place, WA

ABOUT THE INSTITUTION Independent Seventh-day Adventist, coed. *Awards:* diplomas, associate, bachelor's, and master's degrees. 80 undergraduate majors. *Total enrollment:* 1,940. Undergraduates: 1,710. Freshmen: 396.
GIFT AID (NEED-BASED) *Scholarships, grants, and awards:* Federal Pell, FSEOG, state, private, college/university gift aid from institutional funds, Federal Nursing.
GIFT AID (NON-NEED-BASED) *Scholarships, grants, and awards by category:* Academic interests/achievement: biological sciences, business, communication, education, engineering/technologies, English, foreign languages, general academic interests/achievements, humanities, mathematics, religion/biblical studies. *Creative arts/performance:* general creative arts/performance, music, theater/drama. *Special achievements/activities:* leadership. *Special characteristics:* children of faculty/staff, veterans.
LOANS *Programs:* Federal Direct (Subsidized and Unsubsidized Stafford, PLUS), Perkins, Federal Nursing, college/university.
APPLYING FOR FINANCIAL AID *Required financial aid forms:* FAFSA, institution's own form.
CONTACT Ms. Cassie Ragenovich, Director of Student Financial Services, Walla Walla University, 204 South College Avenue, College Place, WA 99324-1198, 509-527-2315 or toll-free 800-541-8900. *Fax:* 509-527-2556. *E-mail:* financial.aid@wallawalla.edu.
Website: http://www.wallawalla.edu/.

WALSH COLLEGE OF ACCOUNTANCY AND BUSINESS ADMINISTRATION
Troy, MI

CONTACT Howard Thomas, Director of Student Financial Resources, Walsh College of Accountancy and Business Administration, 3838 Livernois Road, PO Box 7006, Troy, MI 48007-7006, 248-823-1285 or toll-free 800-925-7401. *Fax:* 248-524-2520. *E-mail:* hthomas@walshcollege.edu.
Website: http://www.walshcollege.edu/.

WALSH UNIVERSITY
North Canton, OH

CONTACT Holly Van Gilder, Director of Financial Aid, Walsh University, 2020 East Maple NW, North Canton, OH 44720-3396, 330-490-7147 or toll-free 800-362-9846 (in-state), 800-362-8846 (out-of-state). *Fax:* 330-490-7372. *E-mail:* hvangilder@walsh.edu.
Website: http://www.walsh.edu/.

WARNER PACIFIC COLLEGE
Portland, OR

Tuition & fees: N/R	Average undergraduate aid package: $15,617

ABOUT THE INSTITUTION Independent Church of God, coed. *Awards:* certificates, associate, bachelor's, and master's degrees. 30 undergraduate majors. *Total enrollment:* 1,333. Undergraduates: 1,181. Freshmen: 101. Federal methodology is used as a basis for awarding need-based institutional aid.
FRESHMAN FINANCIAL AID (Fall 2012, est.) 85 applied for aid; of those 95% were deemed to have need. 100% of freshmen with need received aid; of those 7% had need fully met. *Average percent of need met:* 64% (excluding resources awarded to replace EFC). *Average financial aid package:* $16,122 (excluding resources awarded to replace EFC). 6% of all full-time freshmen had no need and received non-need-based gift aid.

UNDERGRADUATE FINANCIAL AID (Fall 2012, est.) 500 applied for aid; of those 93% were deemed to have need. 100% of undergraduates with need received aid; of those 12% had need fully met. *Average percent of need met:* 65% (excluding resources awarded to replace EFC). *Average financial aid package:* $15,617 (excluding resources awarded to replace EFC). 10% of all full-time undergraduates had no need and received non-need-based gift aid.

GIFT AID (NEED-BASED) *Total amount:* $4,150,502 (35% federal, 6% state, 53% institutional, 6% external sources). *Receiving aid:* Freshmen: 86% (74); all full-time undergraduates: 79% (413). *Average award:* Freshmen: $5342; Undergraduates: $5118. *Scholarships, grants, and awards:* Federal Pell, FSEOG, state, private, college/university gift aid from institutional funds.

GIFT AID (NON-NEED-BASED) *Total amount:* $143,527 (83% institutional, 17% external sources). *Receiving aid:* Freshmen: 88% (76). Undergraduates: 78% (411). *Average award:* Freshmen: $4000. Undergraduates: $5434. *Scholarships, grants, and awards by category: Academic interests/achievement:* 432 awards ($838,510 total): area/ethnic studies, biological sciences, business, communication, education, English, general academic interests/achievements, health fields, humanities, mathematics, physical sciences, religion/biblical studies, social sciences. *Creative arts/performance:* 55 awards ($105,950 total): music, theater/drama. *Special achievements/activities:* 41 awards ($39,000 total): leadership. *Special characteristics:* 278 awards ($200,025 total): children and siblings of alumni, international students, local/state students, members of minority groups, religious affiliation. *ROTC:* Air Force cooperative.

LOANS *Student loans:* $3,809,036 (85% need-based, 15% non-need-based). 91% of past graduating class borrowed through all loan programs. *Average indebtedness per student:* $33,035. *Average need-based loan:* Freshmen: $3775. Undergraduates: $4502. *Parent loans:* $838,711 (45% need-based, 55% non-need-based). *Programs:* Federal Direct (Subsidized and Unsubsidized Stafford, PLUS), Perkins.

WORK-STUDY *Federal work-study:* Total amount: $810,465; 391 jobs averaging $1987.

ATHLETIC AWARDS Total amount: $617,350 (82% need-based, 18% non-need-based).

APPLYING FOR FINANCIAL AID *Required financial aid form:* FAFSA. *Financial aid deadline:* Continuous. *Notification date:* Continuous beginning 3/1. Students must reply within 2 weeks of notification.

CONTACT Katrina L. Sartin Matano, Director of Student Financial Services and Financial Aid, Warner Pacific College, 2219 Southeast 68th Avenue, Portland, OR 97215-4099, 503-517-1018 or toll-free 800-804-1510. *Fax:* 503-517-1352. *E-mail:* ksartinmatano@warnerpacific.edu. *Website:* http://www.warnerpacific.edu/.

WARNER UNIVERSITY
Lake Wales, FL

CONTACT Student Financial Services, Warner University, 13895 Highway 27, Lake Wales, FL 33859, 863-638-7202 or toll-free 800-309-9563. *Fax:* 863-638-7603. *E-mail:* financialaid@warner.edu. *Website:* http://www.warner.edu/.

WARREN WILSON COLLEGE
Swannanoa, NC

Tuition & fees: $29,540	Average undergraduate aid package: $23,653

ABOUT THE INSTITUTION Independent Presbyterian Church (U.S.A.), coed. *Awards:* bachelor's and master's degrees. 20 undergraduate majors. *Total enrollment:* 924. Undergraduates: 852. Freshmen: 214. Both federal and institutional methodology are used as a basis for awarding need-based institutional aid.

UNDERGRADUATE EXPENSES for 2013–2014 *Comprehensive fee:* $38,336 includes full-time tuition ($29,150), mandatory fees ($390), and room and board ($8796). *College room only:* $4398. Full-time tuition and fees vary according to course load. Room and board charges vary according to board plan. *Part-time tuition:* $1215 per credit hour. Part-time tuition and fees vary according to course load.

FRESHMAN FINANCIAL AID (Fall 2012, est.) 173 applied for aid; of those 87% were deemed to have need. 100% of freshmen with need received aid; of those 16% had need fully met. *Average percent of need met:* 70% (excluding resources awarded to replace EFC). *Average financial aid package:* $26,074 (excluding resources awarded to replace EFC). 14% of all full-time freshmen had no need and received non-need-based gift aid.

UNDERGRADUATE FINANCIAL AID (Fall 2012, est.) 657 applied for aid; of those 90% were deemed to have need. 100% of undergraduates with need received aid; of those 11% had need fully met. *Average percent of need met:* 71% (excluding resources awarded to replace EFC). *Average financial aid package:* $23,653 (excluding resources awarded to replace EFC). 14% of all full-time undergraduates had no need and received non-need-based gift aid.

GIFT AID (NEED-BASED) *Total amount:* $9,008,704 (14% federal, 5% state, 77% institutional, 4% external sources). *Receiving aid:* Freshmen: 65% (146); all full-time undergraduates: 63% (561). *Average award:* Freshmen: $19,614; Undergraduates: $16,189. *Scholarships, grants, and awards:* Federal Pell, FSEOG, state, college/university gift aid from institutional funds, Academic Competitiveness Grants, National SMART Grants.

GIFT AID (NON-NEED-BASED) *Total amount:* $938,957 (81% institutional, 19% external sources). *Receiving aid:* Freshmen: 14% (32). Undergraduates: 17% (151). *Average award:* Freshmen: $6781. Undergraduates: $6234. *Scholarships, grants, and awards by category: Academic interests/achievement:* 209 awards ($800,951 total): general academic interests/achievements. *Creative arts/performance:* 5 awards ($8000 total): art/fine arts, creative writing. *Special achievements/activities:* 53 awards ($134,000 total): community service, leadership. *Special characteristics:* 119 awards ($534,139 total): children of faculty/staff, general special characteristics, local/state students, previous college experience, relatives of clergy, religious affiliation. *Tuition waivers:* Full or partial for employees or children of employees.

LOANS *Student loans:* $3,518,166 (95% need-based, 5% non-need-based). 59% of past graduating class borrowed through all loan programs. *Average indebtedness per student:* $23,239. *Average need-based loan:* Freshmen: $2973. Undergraduates: $4020. *Parent loans:* $1,094,383 (81% need-based, 19% non-need-based). *Programs:* Federal Direct (Subsidized and Unsubsidized Stafford, PLUS), Perkins.

WORK-STUDY *Federal work-study:* Total amount: $1,671,617; 538 jobs averaging $3480. *State or other work-study/employment:* Total amount: $1,325,000 (26% need-based, 74% non-need-based). 400 part-time jobs averaging $3480.

ATHLETIC AWARDS Total amount: $77,500 (86% need-based, 14% non-need-based).

APPLYING FOR FINANCIAL AID *Required financial aid forms:* FAFSA, institution's own form, state aid form. *Financial aid deadline (priority):* 4/1. *Notification date:* Continuous beginning 2/15. Students must reply by 5/1 or within 3 weeks of notification.

CONTACT Admissions Office, Warren Wilson College, PO Box 9000, Asheville, NC 28815-9000, 800-934-3536. *Fax:* 828-298-1440. *Website:* http://www.warren-wilson.edu/.

WARTBURG COLLEGE
Waverly, IA

Tuition & fees: $34,250	Average undergraduate aid package: $23,882

ABOUT THE INSTITUTION Independent Lutheran, coed. *Awards:* bachelor's degrees. 57 undergraduate majors. *Total enrollment:* 1,747. Undergraduates: 1,747. Freshmen: 484. Federal methodology is used as a basis for awarding need-based institutional aid.

UNDERGRADUATE EXPENSES for 2013–2014 *Tuition:* full-time $33,400. Room and board charges vary according to board plan.

FRESHMAN FINANCIAL AID (Fall 2012, est.) 455 applied for aid; of those 89% were deemed to have need. 100% of freshmen with need received aid; of those 24% had need fully met. *Average percent of need met:* 84% (excluding resources awarded to replace EFC). *Average financial aid package:* $25,294 (excluding resources awarded to replace EFC). 21% of all full-time freshmen had no need and received non-need-based gift aid.

UNDERGRADUATE FINANCIAL AID (Fall 2012, est.) 1,509 applied for aid; of those 89% were deemed to have need. 100% of undergraduates with need received aid; of those 23% had need fully met. *Average percent of need met:* 80% (excluding resources awarded to replace EFC). *Average financial aid package:*

$23,882 (excluding resources awarded to replace EFC). 22% of all full-time undergraduates had no need and received non-need-based gift aid.
GIFT AID (NEED-BASED) *Total amount:* $25,392,438 (8% federal, 9% state, 74% institutional, 9% external sources). *Receiving aid:* Freshmen: 78% (402); all full-time undergraduates: 77% (1,334). *Average award:* Freshmen: $20,558; Undergraduates: $18,984. *Scholarships, grants, and awards:* Federal Pell, FSEOG, state, private, college/university gift aid from institutional funds.
GIFT AID (NON-NEED-BASED) *Total amount:* $9,566,154 (82% institutional, 18% external sources). *Receiving aid:* Freshmen: 13% (65). Undergraduates: 12% (201). *Average award:* Freshmen: $17,594. Undergraduates: $15,836. *Scholarships, grants, and awards by category: Academic interests/achievement:* 1,591 awards ($16,264,242 total): biological sciences, business, communication, computer science, education, engineering/technologies, English, foreign languages, general academic interests/achievements, humanities, mathematics, physical sciences, premedicine, religion/biblical studies, social sciences. *Creative arts/performance:* 411 awards ($1,141,935 total): art/fine arts, cinema/film/broadcasting, journalism/publications, music, performing arts, theater/drama. *Special achievements/activities:* 30 awards ($30,000 total): junior miss, leadership. *Special characteristics:* 941 awards ($4,678,630 total): children and siblings of alumni, children of faculty/staff, international students, previous college experience, religious affiliation, siblings of current students. *Tuition waivers:* Full or partial for minority students, children of alumni, employees or children of employees.
LOANS *Student loans:* $11,988,947 (65% need-based, 35% non-need-based). 76% of past graduating class borrowed through all loan programs. *Average indebtedness per student:* $36,567. *Average need-based loan:* Freshmen: $4262. Undergraduates: $4986. *Parent loans:* $1,581,685 (62% need-based, 38% non-need-based). *Programs:* Federal Direct (Subsidized and Unsubsidized Stafford, PLUS), Perkins, college/university, private loans.
WORK-STUDY *Federal work-study:* Total amount: $508,356; 408 jobs averaging $1246. *State or other work-study/employment:* 905 part-time jobs averaging $1549.
APPLYING FOR FINANCIAL AID *Required financial aid form:* FAFSA. *Financial aid deadline (priority):* 3/1. *Notification date:* Continuous beginning 3/1. Students must reply within 2 weeks of notification.
CONTACT Ms. Jennifer Sassman, Director of Financial Aid, Wartburg College, 100 Wartburg Boulevard, PO Box 1003, Waverly, IA 50677-0903, 319-352-8262 or toll-free 800-772-2085. *Fax:* 319-352-8514. *E-mail:* jennifer.sassman@wartburg.edu. *Website:* http://www.wartburg.edu/.

WASHBURN UNIVERSITY
Topeka, KS

Tuition & fees (KS res): $5486	Average undergraduate aid package: $9315

ABOUT THE INSTITUTION City-supported, coed. *Awards:* certificates, associate, bachelor's, master's, and doctoral degrees. 92 undergraduate majors. *Total enrollment:* 7,204. Undergraduates: 6,389. Freshmen: 876. Federal methodology is used as a basis for awarding need-based institutional aid.
UNDERGRADUATE EXPENSES for 2013–2014 *Application fee:* $20. *Tuition, state resident:* full-time $5400; part-time $225 per credit hour. *Tuition, nonresident:* full-time $12,216; part-time $509 per credit hour. *Required fees:* full-time $86; $21 per term. Full-time tuition and fees vary according to program. Part-time tuition and fees vary according to program. *College room and board:* $6216; *Room only:* $3501. Room and board charges vary according to board plan and housing facility.
FRESHMAN FINANCIAL AID (Fall 2012, est.) 743 applied for aid; of those 68% were deemed to have need. 100% of freshmen with need received aid; of those 16% had need fully met. *Average percent of need met:* 42% (excluding resources awarded to replace EFC). *Average financial aid package:* $9288 (excluding resources awarded to replace EFC). 21% of all full-time freshmen had no need and received non-need-based gift aid.
UNDERGRADUATE FINANCIAL AID (Fall 2012, est.) 3,732 applied for aid; of those 70% were deemed to have need. 100% of undergraduates with need received aid; of those 15% had need fully met. *Average percent of need met:* 43% (excluding resources awarded to replace EFC). *Average financial aid package:* $9315 (excluding resources awarded to replace EFC). 14% of all full-time undergraduates had no need and received non-need-based gift aid.

GIFT AID (NEED-BASED) *Total amount:* $13,114,470 (81% federal, 4% state, 12% institutional, 3% external sources). *Receiving aid:* Freshmen: 40% (323); all full-time undergraduates: 41% (1,684). *Average award:* Freshmen: $5022; Undergraduates: $4884. *Scholarships, grants, and awards:* Federal Pell, FSEOG, state, private, college/university gift aid from institutional funds.
GIFT AID (NON-NEED-BASED) *Total amount:* $2,820,406 (1% federal, 2% state, 70% institutional, 27% external sources). *Receiving aid:* Freshmen: 38% (307). Undergraduates: 30% (1,217). *Average award:* Freshmen: $2589. Undergraduates: $2371. *Scholarships, grants, and awards by category: Academic interests/achievement:* 2,246 awards ($2,908,122 total): biological sciences, business, communication, computer science, education, engineering/technologies, English, foreign languages, general academic interests/achievements, health fields, humanities, international studies, mathematics, physical sciences, premedicine, religion/biblical studies, social sciences. *Creative arts/performance:* 216 awards ($246,497 total): art/fine arts, cinema/film/broadcasting, debating, journalism/publications, music, performing arts, theater/drama. *Special achievements/activities:* 699 awards ($1,581,762 total): cheerleading/drum major, community service, general special achievements/activities, leadership. *Special characteristics:* 151 awards ($189,355 total): adult students, children and siblings of alumni, children of faculty/staff, ethnic background, international students, local/state students. *Tuition waivers:* Full or partial for employees or children of employees, senior citizens. *ROTC:* Army, Naval cooperative, Air Force cooperative.
LOANS *Student loans:* $30,168,621 (59% need-based, 41% non-need-based). 61% of past graduating class borrowed through all loan programs. *Average indebtedness per student:* $17,995. *Average need-based loan:* Freshmen: $3490. Undergraduates: $4354. *Parent loans:* $7,234,063 (59% need-based, 41% non-need-based). *Programs:* Federal Direct (Subsidized and Unsubsidized Stafford, PLUS), Perkins, college/university, private loans.
WORK-STUDY *Federal work-study:* Total amount: $840,954; 348 jobs averaging $2417. *State or other work-study/employment:* Total amount: $34,103 (100% need-based). 13 part-time jobs averaging $2623.
ATHLETIC AWARDS Total amount: $1,442,783 (65% need-based, 35% non-need-based).
APPLYING FOR FINANCIAL AID *Required financial aid forms:* FAFSA, institution's own form. *Financial aid deadline (priority):* 2/15. *Notification date:* Continuous beginning 3/15. Students must reply within 2 weeks of notification.
CONTACT Gail Palmer, Director of Financial Aid, Washburn University, 1700 SW College Avenue, Topeka, KS 66621, 785-670-1151 or toll-free 800-332-0291. *Fax:* 785-670-1079. *E-mail:* gail.palmer@washburn.edu. *Website:* http://www.washburn.edu/.

WASHINGTON ADVENTIST UNIVERSITY
Takoma Park, MD

Tuition & fees: $20,220	Average undergraduate aid package: $10,442

ABOUT THE INSTITUTION Independent Seventh-day Adventist, coed. *Awards:* certificates, associate, bachelor's, and master's degrees. 33 undergraduate majors. *Total enrollment:* 1,493. Undergraduates: 1,327. Freshmen: 164. Both federal and institutional methodology are used as a basis for awarding need-based institutional aid.
UNDERGRADUATE EXPENSES for 2013–2014 *Application fee:* $25. *Comprehensive fee:* $27,820 includes full-time tuition ($18,900), mandatory fees ($1320), and room and board ($7600). Room and board charges vary according to housing facility. *Part-time tuition:* $760 per credit hour. *Part-time fees:* $432.50 per term. Part-time tuition and fees vary according to class time and course load.
FRESHMAN FINANCIAL AID (Fall 2012, est.) 131 applied for aid; of those 100% were deemed to have need. 100% of freshmen with need received aid; of those 20% had need fully met. *Average percent of need met:* 38% (excluding resources awarded to replace EFC). *Average financial aid package:* $10,442 (excluding resources awarded to replace EFC). 2% of all full-time freshmen had no need and received non-need-based gift aid.
UNDERGRADUATE FINANCIAL AID (Fall 2012, est.) 916 applied for aid; of those 98% were deemed to have need. 100% of undergraduates with need received aid; of those 20% had need fully met. *Average percent of need met:* 38% (excluding resources awarded to replace EFC). *Average financial aid package:*

$10,442 (excluding resources awarded to replace EFC). 3% of all full-time undergraduates had no need and received non-need-based gift aid.

GIFT AID (NEED-BASED) *Total amount:* $8,777,352 (40% federal, 10% state, 37% institutional, 13% external sources). *Receiving aid:* Freshmen: 98% (131); all full-time undergraduates: 95% (900). *Average award:* Freshmen: $8000; Undergraduates: $8000. *Scholarships, grants, and awards:* Federal Pell, FSEOG, state, private, college/university gift aid from institutional funds.

GIFT AID (NON-NEED-BASED) *Total amount:* $2,700,190 (8% federal, 92% institutional). *Receiving aid:* Freshmen: 83% (111). Undergraduates: 81% (765). *Average award:* Freshmen: $7000. Undergraduates: $7000. *Scholarships, grants, and awards by category:* Academic interests/achievement: 308 awards ($1,656,300 total): general academic interests/achievements. Creative arts/performance: 73 awards ($294,850 total): music. Special achievements/activities: 16 awards ($17,500 total): leadership. Special characteristics: 44 awards ($682,884 total): children of faculty/staff, veterans, veterans' children. *Tuition waivers:* Full or partial for employees or children of employees, senior citizens.

LOANS *Student loans:* $9,637,759 (43% need-based, 57% non-need-based). *Parent loans:* $1,028,598 (100% need-based). *Programs:* Federal Direct (Subsidized and Unsubsidized Stafford, PLUS), Perkins, alternative loans.

WORK-STUDY *Federal work-study:* Total amount: $80,092; 28 jobs averaging $3000.

ATHLETIC AWARDS Total amount: $361,397 (100% non-need-based).

APPLYING FOR FINANCIAL AID *Required financial aid form:* FAFSA. *Financial aid deadline (priority):* 3/1. *Notification date:* Continuous beginning 4/1.

CONTACT Sharon Conway, Director of Student Financial Services, Washington Adventist University, 7600 Flower Avenue, Takoma Park, MD 20912, 301-891-4005 or toll-free 800-835-4212. *Fax:* 301-891-4167. *E-mail:* sconway@wau.edu. *Website:* http://www.wau.edu/.

WASHINGTON & JEFFERSON COLLEGE
Washington, PA

Tuition & fees: $38,310	Average undergraduate aid package: $27,800

ABOUT THE INSTITUTION Independent, coed. *Awards:* bachelor's degrees. 30 undergraduate majors. *Total enrollment:* 1,429. Undergraduates: 1,429. Freshmen: 376. Both federal and institutional methodology are used as a basis for awarding need-based institutional aid.

UNDERGRADUATE EXPENSES for 2013–2014 *Application fee:* $25. *Comprehensive fee:* $48,270 includes full-time tuition ($37,850), mandatory fees ($460), and room and board ($9960). *College room only:* $5970. Full-time tuition and fees vary according to reciprocity agreements. Room and board charges vary according to board plan and housing facility. *Part-time tuition:* $950 per credit hour. Part-time tuition and fees vary according to course load.

FRESHMAN FINANCIAL AID (Fall 2012, est.) 335 applied for aid; of those 89% were deemed to have need. 100% of freshmen with need received aid; of those 17% had need fully met. *Average percent of need met:* 79% (excluding resources awarded to replace EFC). *Average financial aid package:* $28,300 (excluding resources awarded to replace EFC). 20% of all full-time freshmen had no need and received non-need-based gift aid.

UNDERGRADUATE FINANCIAL AID (Fall 2012, est.) 1,174 applied for aid; of those 91% were deemed to have need. 100% of undergraduates with need received aid; of those 18% had need fully met. *Average percent of need met:* 76% (excluding resources awarded to replace EFC). *Average financial aid package:* $27,800 (excluding resources awarded to replace EFC). 21% of all full-time undergraduates had no need and received non-need-based gift aid.

GIFT AID (NEED-BASED) *Total amount:* $22,972,173 (7% federal, 7% state, 84% institutional, 2% external sources). *Receiving aid:* Freshmen: 68% (255); all full-time undergraduates: 66% (912). *Average award:* Freshmen: $11,116; Undergraduates: $11,206. *Scholarships, grants, and awards:* Federal Pell, FSEOG, state, private, college/university gift aid from institutional funds.

GIFT AID (NON-NEED-BASED) *Total amount:* $4,129,831 (96% institutional, 4% external sources). *Receiving aid:* Freshmen: 76% (285). Undergraduates: 67% (933). *Average award:* Freshmen: $13,327. Undergraduates: $13,238. Scholar-

ships, grants, and awards by category: Academic interests/achievement: 1,252 awards ($16,137,860 total): business, education, English, general academic interests/achievements, humanities, mathematics, physical sciences, premedicine, social sciences. Special achievements/activities: 3 awards ($10,500 total): community service. Special characteristics: 59 awards ($1,443,797 total): children and siblings of alumni, children of faculty/staff, ethnic background, international students, members of minority groups, veterans, veterans' children. *Tuition waivers:* Full or partial for employees or children of employees. *ROTC:* Army, Air Force cooperative.

LOANS *Student loans:* $11,673,328 (71% need-based, 29% non-need-based). 78% of past graduating class borrowed through all loan programs. *Average need-based loan:* Freshmen: $3514. Undergraduates: $4553. *Parent loans:* $4,385,840 (67% need-based, 33% non-need-based). *Programs:* Federal Direct (Subsidized and Unsubsidized Stafford, PLUS), Perkins, college/university.

WORK-STUDY *Federal work-study:* Total amount: $1,059,435; 608 jobs averaging $1700. *State or other work-study/employment:* Total amount: $230,000 (100% non-need-based). 200 part-time jobs averaging $800.

APPLYING FOR FINANCIAL AID *Required financial aid form:* FAFSA. *Financial aid deadline (priority):* 2/15. *Notification date:* Continuous beginning 3/1. Students must reply by 5/1.

CONTACT Ms. Michelle Anderson, Director of Financial Aid, Washington & Jefferson College, 60 South Lincoln Street, Washington, PA 15301-4801, 724-503-1001 Ext. 6019 or toll-free 888-WANDJAY. *Fax:* 724-250-3340. *E-mail:* manderson@washjeff.edu. *Website:* http://www.washjeff.edu/.

WASHINGTON AND LEE UNIVERSITY
Lexington, VA

Tuition & fees: $43,362	Average undergraduate aid package: $44,800

ABOUT THE INSTITUTION Independent, coed. *Awards:* bachelor's, master's, and doctoral degrees. 35 undergraduate majors. *Total enrollment:* 2,302. Undergraduates: 1,838. Freshmen: 479. Both federal and institutional methodology are used as a basis for awarding need-based institutional aid.

UNDERGRADUATE EXPENSES for 2013–2014 *Application fee:* $50. *Comprehensive fee:* $52,812 includes full-time tuition ($42,425), mandatory fees ($937), and room and board ($9450). *College room only:* $3840. Room and board charges vary according to board plan and housing facility. *Part-time tuition:* $1515 per credit hour.

FRESHMAN FINANCIAL AID (Fall 2012, est.) 251 applied for aid; of those 85% were deemed to have need. 100% of freshmen with need received aid; of those 100% had need fully met. *Average percent of need met:* 100% (excluding resources awarded to replace EFC). *Average financial aid package:* $44,349 (excluding resources awarded to replace EFC). 5% of all full-time freshmen had no need and received non-need-based gift aid.

UNDERGRADUATE FINANCIAL AID (Fall 2012, est.) 846 applied for aid; of those 91% were deemed to have need. 100% of undergraduates with need received aid; of those 100% had need fully met. *Average percent of need met:* 100% (excluding resources awarded to replace EFC). *Average financial aid package:* $44,800 (excluding resources awarded to replace EFC). 8% of all full-time undergraduates had no need and received non-need-based gift aid.

GIFT AID (NEED-BASED) *Total amount:* $29,471,173 (3% federal, 1% state, 95% institutional, 1% external sources). *Receiving aid:* Freshmen: 44% (213); all full-time undergraduates: 41% (765). *Average award:* Freshmen: $39,120; Undergraduates: $38,375. *Scholarships, grants, and awards:* Federal Pell, FSEOG, state, private, college/university gift aid from institutional funds.

GIFT AID (NON-NEED-BASED) *Total amount:* $8,860,432 (6% federal, 5% state, 85% institutional, 4% external sources). *Receiving aid:* Freshmen: 11% (53). Undergraduates: 14% (263). *Average award:* Freshmen: $44,427. Undergraduates: $35,249. *Scholarships, grants, and awards by category:* Academic interests/achievement: 74 awards ($3,683,969 total): general academic interests/achievements. *Tuition waivers:* Full or partial for employees or children of employees. *ROTC:* Army cooperative.

LOANS *Student loans:* $3,336,334 (35% need-based, 65% non-need-based). 31% of past graduating class borrowed through all loan programs. *Average indebtedness per student:* $23,409. *Average need-based loan:* Freshmen: $2440. Undergrad-

uates: $1180. **Parent loans:** $4,118,175 (100% non-need-based). **Programs:** Federal Direct (Subsidized and Unsubsidized Stafford, PLUS), Perkins, college/university.

WORK-STUDY *Federal work-study:* Total amount: $465,808; 237 jobs averaging $2000. **State or other work-study/employment:** Total amount: $743,221 (42% need-based, 58% non-need-based). 381 part-time jobs averaging $2000.

APPLYING FOR FINANCIAL AID *Required financial aid forms:* FAFSA, CSS Financial Aid PROFILE, noncustodial (divorced/separated) parent's statement, federal income tax form(s). **Financial aid deadline:** 2/15. **Notification date:** 4/1. Students must reply by 5/1.

CONTACT James D. Kaster, Director of Financial Aid, Washington and Lee University, 204 West Washington Street, Lexington, VA 24450, 540-458-8720. *Fax:* 540-458-8614. *E-mail:* financialaid@wlu.edu. *Website:* http://www.wlu.edu/.

WASHINGTON COLLEGE
Chestertown, MD

Tuition & fees: $39,944	Average undergraduate aid package: $29,564

ABOUT THE INSTITUTION Independent, coed. **Awards:** bachelor's and master's degrees. 34 undergraduate majors. **Total enrollment:** 1,607. Undergraduates: 1,562. Freshmen: 447. Both federal and institutional methodology are used as a basis for awarding need-based institutional aid.

UNDERGRADUATE EXPENSES for 2013–2014 *Application fee:* $50. **Comprehensive fee:** $48,768 includes full-time tuition ($39,208), mandatory fees ($736), and room and board ($8824). **College room only:** $4482. Room and board charges vary according to board plan, housing facility, and location. **Part-time tuition:** $1578 per credit hour. Part-time tuition and fees vary according to course load. **Payment plan:** Tuition prepayment.

FRESHMAN FINANCIAL AID (Fall 2012, est.) 295 applied for aid; of those 84% were deemed to have need. 100% of freshmen with need received aid; of those 66% had need fully met. **Average percent of need met:** 95% (excluding resources awarded to replace EFC). **Average financial aid package:** $31,111 (excluding resources awarded to replace EFC). 29% of all full-time freshmen had no need and received non-need-based gift aid.

UNDERGRADUATE FINANCIAL AID (Fall 2012, est.) 1,019 applied for aid; of those 86% were deemed to have need. 100% of undergraduates with need received aid; of those 50% had need fully met. **Average percent of need met:** 89% (excluding resources awarded to replace EFC). **Average financial aid package:** $29,564 (excluding resources awarded to replace EFC). 29% of all full-time undergraduates had no need and received non-need-based gift aid.

GIFT AID (NEED-BASED) *Total amount:* $18,720,558 (5% federal, 5% state, 86% institutional, 4% external sources). **Receiving aid:** Freshmen: 63% (249); all full-time undergraduates: 60% (860). **Average award:** Freshmen: $25,047; Undergraduates: $22,865. **Scholarships, grants, and awards:** Federal Pell, FSEOG, state, private, college/university gift aid from institutional funds.

GIFT AID (NON-NEED-BASED) *Total amount:* $6,667,232 (95% institutional, 5% external sources). **Receiving aid:** Freshmen: 20% (80). Undergraduates: 10% (148). **Average award:** Freshmen: $15,782. Undergraduates: $15,034. **Scholarships, grants, and awards by category:** Academic interests/achievement: general academic interests/achievements. Special characteristics: children of faculty/staff. **Tuition waivers:** Full or partial for employees or children of employees.

LOANS *Student loans:* $9,719,881 (36% need-based, 64% non-need-based). 66% of past graduating class borrowed through all loan programs. *Average indebtedness per student:* $34,208. **Average need-based loan:** Freshmen: $3413. Undergraduates: $4543. **Parent loans:** $5,061,497 (100% non-need-based). **Programs:** Federal Direct (Subsidized and Unsubsidized Stafford, PLUS), Perkins.

WORK-STUDY *Federal work-study:* Total amount: $195,650; jobs available.

APPLYING FOR FINANCIAL AID *Required financial aid forms:* FAFSA, institution's own form. **Financial aid deadline (priority):** 2/15. **Notification date:** Continuous beginning 2/15. Students must reply by 5/1.

CONTACT Ms. Jeani M. Narcum, Director of Financial Aid, Washington College, 300 Washington Avenue, Chestertown, MD 21620-1197, 410-778-7214 or toll-free 800-422-1782. *Fax:* 410-778-7287. *E-mail:* jnarcum2@washcoll.edu. *Website:* http://www.washcoll.edu/.

WASHINGTON STATE UNIVERSITY
Pullman, WA

Tuition & fees (WA res): $12,300	Average undergraduate aid package: $16,761

ABOUT THE INSTITUTION State-supported, coed. **Awards:** certificates, bachelor's, master's, and doctoral degrees. 137 undergraduate majors. **Total enrollment:** 27,679. Undergraduates: 23,135. Freshmen: 4,388. Federal methodology is used as a basis for awarding need-based institutional aid.

UNDERGRADUATE EXPENSES for 2013–2014 *Application fee:* $50. **Tuition, state resident:** full-time $10,874; part-time $569 per credit hour. **Tuition, nonresident:** full-time $23,956; part-time $1141 per credit hour. **Required fees:** full-time $1426. Full-time tuition and fees vary according to location and reciprocity agreements. Part-time tuition and fees vary according to course load, location, and reciprocity agreements. **College room and board:** $10,524; **Room only:** $6626. Room and board charges vary according to board plan, housing facility, and location.

FRESHMAN FINANCIAL AID (Fall 2011) 3,569 applied for aid; of those 73% were deemed to have need. 96% of freshmen with need received aid; of those 30% had need fully met. **Average percent of need met:** 92% (excluding resources awarded to replace EFC). **Average financial aid package:** $16,695 (excluding resources awarded to replace EFC). 17% of all full-time freshmen had no need and received non-need-based gift aid.

UNDERGRADUATE FINANCIAL AID (Fall 2011) 14,442 applied for aid; of those 81% were deemed to have need. 95% of undergraduates with need received aid; of those 37% had need fully met. **Average percent of need met:** 91% (excluding resources awarded to replace EFC). **Average financial aid package:** $16,761 (excluding resources awarded to replace EFC). 11% of all full-time undergraduates had no need and received non-need-based gift aid.

GIFT AID (NEED-BASED) *Total amount:* $48,045,651 (48% federal, 37% state, 15% institutional). **Receiving aid:** Freshmen: 37% (1,622); all full-time undergraduates: 39% (7,641). **Average award:** Freshmen: $9776; Undergraduates: $9339. **Scholarships, grants, and awards:** Federal Pell, FSEOG, state, private, college/university gift aid from institutional funds, United Negro College Fund, Federal Nursing.

GIFT AID (NON-NEED-BASED) *Total amount:* $10,810,358 (6% state, 47% institutional, 47% external sources). **Receiving aid:** Freshmen: 31% (1,385). Undergraduates: 20% (3,964). **Average award:** Freshmen: $4136. Undergraduates: $4173. **Scholarships, grants, and awards by category:** Academic interests/achievement: agriculture, architecture, area/ethnic studies, biological sciences, business, communication, computer science, education, engineering/technologies, English, foreign languages, general academic interests/achievements, health fields, home economics, humanities, international studies, mathematics, military science, physical sciences, premedicine, social sciences. Creative arts/performance: applied art and design, art/fine arts, cinema/film/broadcasting, creative writing, general creative arts/performance, journalism/publications, music, performing arts, theater/drama. Special achievements/activities: community service, general special achievements/activities, junior miss, leadership, memberships, religious involvement, rodeo. Special characteristics: children and siblings of alumni, children of faculty/staff, children of public servants, children with a deceased or disabled parent, first-generation college students, handicapped students, international students, out-of-state students, public servants, religious affiliation, veterans, veterans' children. **Tuition waivers:** Full or partial for employees or children of employees, senior citizens. **ROTC:** Army, Naval cooperative, Air Force.

LOANS *Student loans:* $60,638,176 (47% need-based, 53% non-need-based). 57% of past graduating class borrowed through all loan programs. *Average indebtedness per student:* $23,433. **Average need-based loan:** Freshmen: $3494. Undergraduates: $4442. **Parent loans:** $21,496,464 (100% non-need-based). **Programs:** Federal Direct (Subsidized and Unsubsidized Stafford, PLUS), Perkins, Federal Nursing, alternative loans.

WORK-STUDY *Federal work-study:* Total amount: $1,999,919; jobs available. **State or other work-study/employment:** Total amount: $1,399,274 (100% need-based). Part-time jobs available.

ATHLETIC AWARDS Total amount: $5,422,098 (100% non-need-based).

APPLYING FOR FINANCIAL AID *Required financial aid form:* FAFSA. **Financial aid deadline (priority):** 2/15. **Notification date:** Continuous beginning 4/15.

CONTACT Office of Financial Aid and Scholarships, Washington State University, PO Box 641068, Pullman, WA 99164-1068, 509-335-9711 or toll-free 888-468-6978. *Fax:* 509-335-1385. *E-mail:* finaid@wsu.edu. *Website:* http://www.wsu.edu/.

WASHINGTON UNIVERSITY IN ST. LOUIS
St. Louis, MO

Tuition & fees: $44,841	Average undergraduate aid package: $34,558

ABOUT THE INSTITUTION Independent, coed. *Awards:* certificates, bachelor's, master's, and doctoral degrees. 168 undergraduate majors. *Total enrollment:* 13,952. Undergraduates: 7,259. Freshmen: 1,637. Institutional methodology is used as a basis for awarding need-based institutional aid.

UNDERGRADUATE EXPENSES for 2013–2014 *Application fee:* $75. *Comprehensive fee:* $58,818 includes full-time tuition ($44,100), mandatory fees ($741), and room and board ($13,977). *College room only:* $9437. Room and board charges vary according to board plan and housing facility. *Payment plan:* Tuition prepayment.

FRESHMAN FINANCIAL AID (Fall 2012, est.) 1,059 applied for aid; of those 64% were deemed to have need. 97% of freshmen with need received aid; of those 100% had need fully met. *Average percent of need met:* 100% (excluding resources awarded to replace EFC). *Average financial aid package:* $35,508 (excluding resources awarded to replace EFC). 14% of all full-time freshmen had no need and received non-need-based gift aid.

UNDERGRADUATE FINANCIAL AID (Fall 2012, est.) 4,285 applied for aid; of those 60% were deemed to have need. 99% of undergraduates with need received aid; of those 96% had need fully met. *Average percent of need met:* 100% (excluding resources awarded to replace EFC). *Average financial aid package:* $34,558 (excluding resources awarded to replace EFC). 13% of all full-time undergraduates had no need and received non-need-based gift aid.

GIFT AID (NEED-BASED) *Total amount:* $77,360,673 (3% federal, 1% state, 92% institutional, 4% external sources). *Receiving aid:* Freshmen: 39% (634); all full-time undergraduates: 39% (2,472). *Average award:* Freshmen: $32,644; Undergraduates: $31,295. *Scholarships, grants, and awards:* Federal Pell, FSEOG, state, private, college/university gift aid from institutional funds.

GIFT AID (NON-NEED-BASED) *Total amount:* $4,991,450 (7% state, 69% institutional, 24% external sources). *Receiving aid:* Freshmen: 5% (79). Undergraduates: 3% (184). *Average award:* Freshmen: $10,143. Undergraduates: $6072. *Scholarships, grants, and awards by category:* Academic interests/achievement: architecture, biological sciences, business, communication, computer science, education, engineering/technologies, English, foreign languages, general academic interests/achievements, health fields, humanities, international studies, mathematics, military science, physical sciences, premedicine, religion/biblical studies, social sciences. *Creative arts/performance:* applied art and design, art/fine arts, cinema/film/broadcasting, creative writing, dance, music, performing arts, theater/drama. *Tuition waivers:* Full or partial for employees or children of employees. *ROTC:* Army, Air Force cooperative.

LOANS *Student loans:* $11,725,487 (89% need-based, 11% non-need-based). 35% of past graduating class borrowed through all loan programs. *Average need-based loan:* Freshmen: $5458. Undergraduates: $6229. *Parent loans:* $1,459,169 (71% need-based, 29% non-need-based). *Programs:* Federal Direct (Subsidized and Unsubsidized Stafford, PLUS), Perkins, state, college/university.

WORK-STUDY *Federal work-study:* Total amount: $2,286,900; 1,121 jobs averaging $2040.

APPLYING FOR FINANCIAL AID *Required financial aid forms:* FAFSA, CSS Financial Aid PROFILE, noncustodial (divorced/separated) parent's statement. *Financial aid deadline:* 2/1. *Notification date:* 4/1. Students must reply by 5/1.

CONTACT Mr. Michael Runiewicz, Director of Financial Aid, Washington University in St. Louis, Campus Box 1041, St. Louis, MO 63130-4899, 314-935-5900 or toll-free 800-638-0700. *Fax:* 314-935-4037. *E-mail:* financial@wustl.edu. *Website:* http://www.wustl.edu/.

WATKINS COLLEGE OF ART, DESIGN, & FILM
Nashville, TN

CONTACT Lyle Jones, Financial Aid Coordinator, Watkins College of Art, Design, & Film, 2298 Rosa L. Parks Boulevard, Nashville, TN 37228, 615-383-4848 Ext. 7421. *Fax:* 615-383-4849. *E-mail:* financialaid@watkins.edu. *Website:* http://www.watkins.edu/.

WAYLAND BAPTIST UNIVERSITY
Plainview, TX

Tuition & fees: $14,630	Average undergraduate aid package: $12,153

ABOUT THE INSTITUTION Independent Baptist, coed. *Awards:* associate, bachelor's, and master's degrees (branch locations in Anchorage, AK; Amarillo, TX; Luke Air Force Base, AZ; Glorieta, NM; Aiea, HI; Lubbock, TX; San Antonio, TX; Wichita Falls, TX). 44 undergraduate majors. *Total enrollment:* 1,824. Undergraduates: 1,385. Freshmen: 366. Federal methodology is used as a basis for awarding need-based institutional aid.

UNDERGRADUATE EXPENSES for 2013–2014 *Application fee:* $35. *Comprehensive fee:* $18,787 includes full-time tuition ($13,650), mandatory fees ($980), and room and board ($4157). *College room only:* $1368. Full-time tuition and fees vary according to course load and location. Room and board charges vary according to board plan and housing facility. *Part-time tuition:* $455 per credit hour. *Part-time fees:* $110 per term. Part-time tuition and fees vary according to course load and location.

FRESHMAN FINANCIAL AID (Fall 2012, est.) 250 applied for aid; of those 88% were deemed to have need. 100% of freshmen with need received aid; of those 7% had need fully met. *Average percent of need met:* 62% (excluding resources awarded to replace EFC). *Average financial aid package:* $11,665 (excluding resources awarded to replace EFC). 11% of all full-time freshmen had no need and received non-need-based gift aid.

UNDERGRADUATE FINANCIAL AID (Fall 2012, est.) 874 applied for aid; of those 89% were deemed to have need. 100% of undergraduates with need received aid; of those 10% had need fully met. *Average percent of need met:* 63% (excluding resources awarded to replace EFC). *Average financial aid package:* $12,153 (excluding resources awarded to replace EFC). 15% of all full-time undergraduates had no need and received non-need-based gift aid.

GIFT AID (NEED-BASED) *Total amount:* $7,447,863 (40% federal, 15% state, 43% institutional, 2% external sources). *Receiving aid:* Freshmen: 60% (217); all full-time undergraduates: 75% (759). *Average award:* Freshmen: $9244; Undergraduates: $9176. *Scholarships, grants, and awards:* Federal Pell, FSEOG, state, private, college/university gift aid from institutional funds.

GIFT AID (NON-NEED-BASED) *Total amount:* $1,805,492 (1% federal, 1% state, 93% institutional, 5% external sources). *Receiving aid:* Freshmen: 4% (13). Undergraduates: 6% (61). *Average award:* Freshmen: $6407. Undergraduates: $8214. *Scholarships, grants, and awards by category:* Academic interests/achievement: 604 awards ($1,332,539 total): biological sciences, business, communication, education, English, general academic interests/achievements, mathematics, physical sciences, religion/biblical studies, social sciences. *Creative arts/performance:* 38 awards ($54,516 total): art/fine arts, journalism/publications, music, theater/drama. *Special achievements/activities:* 122 awards ($147,032 total): cheerleading/drum major, leadership, memberships, religious involvement. *Special characteristics:* 134 awards ($259,914 total): children and siblings of alumni, children of faculty/staff, ethnic background, general special characteristics, international students, local/state students, members of minority groups, relatives of clergy, religious affiliation. *Tuition waivers:* Full or partial for employees or children of employees. *ROTC:* Army cooperative, Air Force cooperative.

LOANS *Student loans:* $5,683,998 (85% need-based, 15% non-need-based). 58% of past graduating class borrowed through all loan programs. *Average indebtedness per student:* $21,981. *Average need-based loan:* Freshmen: $3082. Undergraduates: $3649. *Parent loans:* $220,427 (100% non-need-based). *Programs:* Federal Direct (Subsidized and Unsubsidized Stafford, PLUS), Perkins, state, private loans.

WORK-STUDY *Federal work-study:* Total amount: $202,021; 142 jobs averaging $1539. *State or other work-study/employment:* Total amount: $145,956 (100% non-need-based). 126 part-time jobs averaging $1688.
ATHLETIC AWARDS Total amount: $2,026,990 (100% non-need-based).
APPLYING FOR FINANCIAL AID *Required financial aid forms:* FAFSA, institution's own form. *Financial aid deadline (priority):* 5/1. *Notification date:* Continuous beginning 1/1. Students must reply within 3 weeks of notification.
CONTACT Karen LaQuey, Director of Financial Aid, Wayland Baptist University, 1900 West 7th Street, Plainview, TX 79072-6998, 806-291-3520 or toll-free 800-588-1928. *Fax:* 806-291-1956. *E-mail:* laquey@wbu.edu.
Website: http://www.wbu.edu/.

WAYNESBURG UNIVERSITY
Waynesburg, PA

Tuition & fees: $19,810	Average undergraduate aid package: $15,052

ABOUT THE INSTITUTION Independent Presbyterian Church (U.S.A.), coed. *Awards:* bachelor's, master's, and doctoral degrees. 49 undergraduate majors. *Total enrollment:* 2,270. Undergraduates: 1,630. Freshmen: 352. Federal methodology is used as a basis for awarding need-based institutional aid.
UNDERGRADUATE EXPENSES for 2013–2014 *Application fee:* $20. *Comprehensive fee:* $28,060 includes full-time tuition ($19,450), mandatory fees ($360), and room and board ($8250). *College room only:* $4170. Full-time tuition and fees vary according to class time. Room and board charges vary according to board plan. *Part-time tuition:* $820 per credit hour. *Part-time fees:* $16 per credit hour. Part-time tuition and fees vary according to class time, course load, and location.
FRESHMAN FINANCIAL AID (Fall 2012, est.) 338 applied for aid; of those 90% were deemed to have need. 100% of freshmen with need received aid; of those 31% had need fully met. *Average percent of need met:* 79% (excluding resources awarded to replace EFC). *Average financial aid package:* $15,863 (excluding resources awarded to replace EFC). 7% of all full-time freshmen had no need and received non-need-based gift aid.
UNDERGRADUATE FINANCIAL AID (Fall 2012, est.) 1,360 applied for aid; of those 90% were deemed to have need. 100% of undergraduates with need received aid; of those 27% had need fully met. *Average percent of need met:* 75% (excluding resources awarded to replace EFC). *Average financial aid package:* $15,052 (excluding resources awarded to replace EFC). 9% of all full-time undergraduates had no need and received non-need-based gift aid.
GIFT AID (NEED-BASED) *Total amount:* $12,995,605 (17% federal, 16% state, 60% institutional, 7% external sources). *Receiving aid:* Freshmen: 44% (303); all full-time undergraduates: 67% (1,184). *Average award:* Freshmen: $11,898; Undergraduates: $10,937. *Scholarships, grants, and awards:* Federal Pell, FSEOG, state, private, college/university gift aid from institutional funds, United Negro College Fund.
GIFT AID (NON-NEED-BASED) *Total amount:* $2,062,766 (87% institutional, 13% external sources). *Receiving aid:* Freshmen: 5% (38). Undergraduates: 6% (112). *Average award:* Freshmen: $9401. Undergraduates: $8250. *Scholarships, grants, and awards by category: Academic interests/achievement:* biological sciences, business, communication, computer science, education, English, general academic interests/achievements, health fields, humanities, international studies, mathematics, physical sciences, religion/biblical studies, social sciences. *Creative arts/performance:* art/fine arts, music, theater/drama. *Special achievements/activities:* community service. *Special characteristics:* 75 awards ($500,000 total): children of faculty/staff. *Tuition waivers:* Full or partial for employees or children of employees. *ROTC:* Army cooperative.
LOANS *Student loans:* $11,610,364 (61% need-based, 39% non-need-based). 93% of past graduating class borrowed through all loan programs. *Average indebtedness per student:* $29,000. *Average need-based loan:* Freshmen: $3881. Undergraduates: $4623. *Parent loans:* $2,976,189 (60% need-based, 40% non-need-based). *Programs:* Federal Direct (Subsidized and Unsubsidized Stafford, PLUS), Perkins, Federal Nursing, college/university.
WORK-STUDY *Federal work-study:* Total amount: $158,000; 300 jobs averaging $1200.
APPLYING FOR FINANCIAL AID *Required financial aid form:* FAFSA. *Financial aid deadline:* Continuous. *Notification date:* Continuous beginning 2/15. Students must reply within 2 weeks of notification.

CONTACT Matthew C. Stokan, Director of Financial Aid, Waynesburg University, 51 West College Street, Waynesburg, PA 15370-1222, 724-852-3208 or toll-free 800-225-7393. *Fax:* 724-852-3269. *E-mail:* mstokan@waynesburg.edu.
Website: http://www.waynesburg.edu/.

WAYNE STATE COLLEGE
Wayne, NE

Tuition & fees (NE res): $5520	Average undergraduate aid package: $8179

ABOUT THE INSTITUTION State-supported, coed. *Awards:* certificates, bachelor's, and master's degrees. 53 undergraduate majors. *Total enrollment:* 3,555. Undergraduates: 3,020. Freshmen: 695. Federal methodology is used as a basis for awarding need-based institutional aid.
UNDERGRADUATE EXPENSES for 2013–2014 *Tuition, state resident:* full-time $4200; part-time $140 per credit hour. *Tuition, nonresident:* full-time $8400; part-time $280 per credit hour. *Required fees:* full-time $1320; $52.25 per credit hour. Full-time tuition and fees vary according to course level and course load. Part-time tuition and fees vary according to course level and course load. *College room and board:* $5960; *Room only:* $2880. Room and board charges vary according to board plan and housing facility.
FRESHMAN FINANCIAL AID (Fall 2012, est.) 617 applied for aid; of those 76% were deemed to have need. 98% of freshmen with need received aid; of those 40% had need fully met. *Average percent of need met:* 54% (excluding resources awarded to replace EFC). *Average financial aid package:* $8647 (excluding resources awarded to replace EFC). 13% of all full-time freshmen had no need and received non-need-based gift aid.
UNDERGRADUATE FINANCIAL AID (Fall 2012, est.) 2,448 applied for aid; of those 80% were deemed to have need. 96% of undergraduates with need received aid; of those 45% had need fully met. *Average percent of need met:* 61% (excluding resources awarded to replace EFC). *Average financial aid package:* $8179 (excluding resources awarded to replace EFC). 8% of all full-time undergraduates had no need and received non-need-based gift aid.
GIFT AID (NEED-BASED) *Total amount:* $7,480,278 (64% federal, 10% state, 26% institutional). *Receiving aid:* Freshmen: 49% (343); all full-time undergraduates: 48% (1,334). *Average award:* Freshmen: $4079; Undergraduates: $4049. *Scholarships, grants, and awards:* Federal Pell, FSEOG, state, private, college/university gift aid from institutional funds.
GIFT AID (NON-NEED-BASED) *Total amount:* $742,114 (4% federal, 11% institutional, 85% external sources). *Receiving aid:* Freshmen: 46% (319). Undergraduates: 41% (1,142). *Average award:* Freshmen: $1191. Undergraduates: $3508. *Scholarships, grants, and awards by category: Academic interests/achievement:* biological sciences, business, communication, computer science, education, English, foreign languages, general academic interests/achievements, health fields, home economics, humanities, mathematics, physical sciences, premedicine, social sciences. *Creative arts/performance:* applied art and design, art/fine arts, creative writing, general creative arts/performance, journalism/publications, music, performing arts, theater/drama. *Special achievements/activities:* general special achievements/activities, leadership. *Special characteristics:* children of faculty/staff, ethnic background, general special characteristics, local/state students, members of minority groups, out-of-state students, veterans, veterans' children. *Tuition waivers:* Full or partial for employees or children of employees. *ROTC:* Army.
LOANS *Student loans:* $12,012,969 (48% need-based, 52% non-need-based). *Average need-based loan:* Freshmen: $3149. Undergraduates: $3895. *Parent loans:* $768,266 (100% non-need-based). *Programs:* Federal Direct (Subsidized and Unsubsidized Stafford, PLUS), Perkins.
WORK-STUDY *Federal work-study:* Total amount: $147,120; jobs available.
ATHLETIC AWARDS Total amount: $376,582 (100% non-need-based).
APPLYING FOR FINANCIAL AID *Required financial aid form:* FAFSA. *Financial aid deadline (priority):* 4/1. *Notification date:* Continuous beginning 3/1. Students must reply within 4 weeks of notification.
CONTACT Kyle M. Rose, Director of Financial Aid, Wayne State College, 1111 Main Street, Wayne, NE 68787, 402-375-7230 or toll-free 866-WSC-CATS. *Fax:* 402-375-7067. *E-mail:* kyrose1@wsc.edu.
Website: http://www.wsc.edu/.

WAYNE STATE UNIVERSITY
Detroit, MI

Tuition & fees: N/R	Average undergraduate aid package: $13,683

ABOUT THE INSTITUTION State-supported, coed. **Awards:** certificates, bachelor's, master's, and doctoral degrees. 88 undergraduate majors. **Total enrollment:** 28,938. Undergraduates: 19,342. Freshmen: 2,338. Federal methodology is used as a basis for awarding need-based institutional aid.

UNDERGRADUATE EXPENSES for 2013–2014 Tuition, state resident: part-time $324.90 per credit hour. **Tuition, nonresident:** part-time $745.75 per credit hour. Full-time tuition and fees vary according to course load, program, reciprocity agreements, and student level. Part-time tuition and fees vary according to course load, program, reciprocity agreements, and student level. **College room and board:** $8504; **Room only:** $5384. Room and board charges vary according to board plan and housing facility.

FRESHMAN FINANCIAL AID (Fall 2011) 1,964 applied for aid; of those 86% were deemed to have need. 99% of freshmen with need received aid; of those 6% had need fully met. **Average percent of need met:** 72% (excluding resources awarded to replace EFC). **Average financial aid package:** $12,954 (excluding resources awarded to replace EFC). 11% of all full-time freshmen had no need and received non-need-based gift aid.

UNDERGRADUATE FINANCIAL AID (Fall 2011) 10,553 applied for aid; of those 92% were deemed to have need. 98% of undergraduates with need received aid; of those 2% had need fully met. **Average percent of need met:** 67% (excluding resources awarded to replace EFC). **Average financial aid package:** $13,683 (excluding resources awarded to replace EFC). 8% of all full-time undergraduates had no need and received non-need-based gift aid.

GIFT AID (NEED-BASED) Total amount: $57,196,734 (73% federal, 27% institutional). **Receiving aid:** Freshmen: 57% (1,269); all full-time undergraduates: 60% (7,655). **Average award:** Freshmen: $6334; Undergraduates: $5949. **Scholarships, grants, and awards:** Federal Pell, FSEOG, state, private, college/university gift aid from institutional funds, United Negro College Fund.

GIFT AID (NON-NEED-BASED) Total amount: $19,784,369 (1% federal, 4% state, 89% institutional, 6% external sources). **Receiving aid:** Freshmen: 38% (837). Undergraduates: 27% (3,421). **Average award:** Freshmen: $6618. Undergraduates: $6195. **Scholarships, grants, and awards by category:** Academic interests/achievement: 2,028 awards ($5,602,300 total): area/ethnic studies, biological sciences, business, communication, computer science, education, engineering/technologies, English, foreign languages, general academic interests/achievements, health fields, humanities, international studies, library science, mathematics, military science, physical sciences, premedicine, social sciences. Creative arts/performance: 460 awards ($1,177,881 total): art/fine arts, dance, debating, general creative arts/performance, journalism/publications, music, theater/drama. Special achievements/activities: 35 awards ($17,700 total): leadership. Special characteristics: 192 awards ($838,454 total): children of faculty/staff. **Tuition waivers:** Full or partial for employees or children of employees, senior citizens. **ROTC:** Army, Naval cooperative, Air Force cooperative.

LOANS Student loans: $89,916,141 (96% need-based, 4% non-need-based). 55% of past graduating class borrowed through all loan programs. *Average indebtedness per student:* $24,316. **Average need-based loan:** Freshmen: $3341. Undergraduates: $4056. **Parent loans:** $11,411,605 (100% non-need-based). **Programs:** Federal Direct (Subsidized and Unsubsidized Stafford, PLUS), Perkins, Federal Nursing, college/university.

WORK-STUDY Federal work-study: Total amount: $717,014; 314 jobs averaging $2283. **State or other work-study/employment:** Part-time jobs available.

ATHLETIC AWARDS Total amount: $2,832,142 (100% non-need-based).

APPLYING FOR FINANCIAL AID Required financial aid forms: FAFSA, federal income tax form(s), W-2 forms. **Financial aid deadline:** 5/31 (priority: 2/15). **Notification date:** Continuous beginning 3/1.

CONTACT Gabriela Garfield, Acting Senior Director of Financial Aid, Wayne State University, 3W HNJ Student Services Building, Detroit, MI 48202, 313-577-3378 or toll-free 877-WSU-INFO. *Fax:* 313-577-6648. *E-mail:* financialaid@wayne.edu. *Website:* http://www.wayne.edu/.

WEBBER INTERNATIONAL UNIVERSITY
Babson Park, FL

Tuition & fees: $20,418	Average undergraduate aid package: $13,062

ABOUT THE INSTITUTION Independent, coed. **Awards:** associate, bachelor's, and master's degrees. 11 undergraduate majors. **Total enrollment:** 717. Undergraduates: 655. Freshmen: 183. Federal methodology is used as a basis for awarding need-based institutional aid.

UNDERGRADUATE EXPENSES for 2013–2014 Application fee: $35. **Comprehensive fee:** $28,318 includes full-time tuition ($20,418) and room and board ($7900). **College room only:** $5072. Full-time tuition and fees vary according to class time and course load. Room and board charges vary according to board plan, gender, and housing facility. **Part-time tuition:** $294 per credit hour. Part-time tuition and fees vary according to course load.

FRESHMAN FINANCIAL AID (Fall 2012, est.) 140 applied for aid; of those 69% were deemed to have need. 100% of freshmen with need received aid; of those 6% had need fully met. **Average percent of need met:** 55% (excluding resources awarded to replace EFC). **Average financial aid package:** $16,603 (excluding resources awarded to replace EFC). 31% of all full-time freshmen had no need and received non-need-based gift aid.

UNDERGRADUATE FINANCIAL AID (Fall 2012, est.) 628 applied for aid; of those 61% were deemed to have need. 100% of undergraduates with need received aid; of those 10% had need fully met. **Average percent of need met:** 58% (excluding resources awarded to replace EFC). **Average financial aid package:** $13,062 (excluding resources awarded to replace EFC). 33% of all full-time undergraduates had no need and received non-need-based gift aid.

GIFT AID (NEED-BASED) Total amount: $3,281,309 (43% federal, 32% state, 23% institutional, 2% external sources). **Receiving aid:** Freshmen: 69% (96); all full-time undergraduates: 43% (267). **Average award:** Freshmen: $2846; Undergraduates: $3185. **Scholarships, grants, and awards:** Federal Pell, FSEOG, state, private, college/university gift aid from institutional funds.

GIFT AID (NON-NEED-BASED) Total amount: $1,869,031 (12% state, 86% institutional, 2% external sources). **Receiving aid:** Freshmen: 69% (96). Undergraduates: 33% (208). **Average award:** Freshmen: $8602. Undergraduates: $8021. **Scholarships, grants, and awards by category:** Academic interests/achievement: 385 awards: business, general academic interests/achievements. Creative arts/performance: 36 awards: general creative arts/performance, journalism/publications. Special achievements/activities: 580 awards: cheerleading/drum major, community service, general special achievements/activities, leadership, memberships. Special characteristics: 125 awards: children and siblings of alumni, children of faculty/staff, first-generation college students, general special characteristics, international students, local/state students, out-of-state students, siblings of current students. **Tuition waivers:** Full or partial for children of alumni, employees or children of employees, adult students, senior citizens.

LOANS Student loans: $3,235,775 (91% need-based, 9% non-need-based). *Average need-based loan:* Freshmen: $3837. Undergraduates: $4396. **Parent loans:** $1,164,576 (90% need-based, 10% non-need-based). **Programs:** Federal Direct (Subsidized and Unsubsidized Stafford, PLUS), Perkins.

WORK-STUDY Federal work-study: Total amount: $36,292; jobs available. **State or other work-study/employment:** Total amount: $37,379 (28% need-based, 72% non-need-based). Part-time jobs available.

ATHLETIC AWARDS Total amount: $3,014,681 (68% need-based, 32% non-need-based).

APPLYING FOR FINANCIAL AID Required financial aid forms: FAFSA, state aid form. **Financial aid deadline:** 8/1 (priority: 5/1). **Notification date:** Continuous beginning 3/1.

CONTACT Ms. Kathleen Wilson, Director of Financial Aid, Webber International University, PO Box 96, 1201 Scenic Highway, Babson Park, FL 33827-0096, 863-638-2930 or toll-free 800-741-1844. *Fax:* 863-638-1317. *E-mail:* wilsonka@webber.edu. *Website:* http://www.webber.edu/.

WEBB INSTITUTE
Glen Cove, NY

Tuition & fees:	Average undergraduate aid package: $4500

ABOUT THE INSTITUTION Independent, coed. *Awards:* bachelor's degrees. 1 undergraduate major. *Total enrollment:* 79. Undergraduates: 79. Freshmen: 22. Federal methodology is used as a basis for awarding need-based institutional aid.

UNDERGRADUATE EXPENSES for 2013–2014 *Application fee:* $25. Full-tuition scholarship covering all four years are awarded to all accepted students who are U.S. citizens or Green Card holders.

FRESHMAN FINANCIAL AID (Fall 2012, est.) 6 applied for aid; of those 100% were deemed to have need. 100% of freshmen with need received aid. *Average financial aid package:* $4500 (excluding resources awarded to replace EFC).

UNDERGRADUATE FINANCIAL AID (Fall 2012, est.) 19 applied for aid; of those 100% were deemed to have need. 100% of undergraduates with need received aid. *Average financial aid package:* $4500 (excluding resources awarded to replace EFC).

GIFT AID (NEED-BASED) *Total amount:* $120,450 (20% federal, 3% state, 33% institutional, 44% external sources). *Receiving aid:* Freshmen: 11% (2); all full-time undergraduates: 8% (6). *Average award:* Freshmen: $5500; Undergraduates: $5500. *Scholarships, grants, and awards:* Federal Pell, state, private, college/university gift aid from institutional funds.

LOANS *Student loans:* $112,250 (100% need-based). 33% of past graduating class borrowed through all loan programs. *Average indebtedness per student:* $4500. *Parent loans:* $27,600 (100% need-based). *Programs:* Federal Direct (Subsidized and Unsubsidized Stafford, PLUS).

APPLYING FOR FINANCIAL AID *Required financial aid form:* FAFSA. *Financial aid deadline (priority):* 7/1. *Notification date:* Continuous beginning 5/1. Students must reply by 7/1.

CONTACT William G. Murray, Director of Enrollment Management , Webb Institute, 298 Crescent Beach Road, Glen Cove, NY 11542-1398, 516-671-2213 Ext. 104. *Fax:* 516-674-9838. *E-mail:* bmurray@webb-institute.edu. *Website:* http://www.webb-institute.edu/.

WEBER STATE UNIVERSITY
Ogden, UT

CONTACT Mr. Richard O. Effiong, Financial Aid Director, Weber State University, 120 Student Service Center, 1136 University Circle, Ogden, UT 84408-1136, 801-626-7569 or toll-free 800-848-7700 (in-state), 800-848-7770 (out-of-state). *E-mail:* finaid@weber.edu. *Website:* http://www.weber.edu/.

WEBSTER UNIVERSITY
St. Louis, MO

Tuition & fees: $23,010	Average undergraduate aid package: $11,677

ABOUT THE INSTITUTION Independent, coed. *Awards:* certificates, bachelor's, master's, and doctoral degrees. 73 undergraduate majors. *Total enrollment:* 5,119. Undergraduates: 2,995. Freshmen: 415. Federal methodology is used as a basis for awarding need-based institutional aid.

UNDERGRADUATE EXPENSES for 2013–2014 *Application fee:* $35. *Comprehensive fee:* $32,960 includes full-time tuition ($23,010) and room and board ($9950). *College room only:* $5520. Full-time tuition and fees vary according to program. Room and board charges vary according to board plan, housing facility, and location. *Part-time tuition:* $590 per credit hour. Part-time tuition and fees vary according to location.

FRESHMAN FINANCIAL AID (Fall 2012, est.) 384 applied for aid; of those 85% were deemed to have need. 100% of freshmen with need received aid; of those 1% had need fully met. *Average percent of need met:* 34% (excluding resources awarded to replace EFC). *Average financial aid package:* $15,170 (excluding resources awarded to replace EFC). 12% of all full-time freshmen had no need and received non-need-based gift aid.

UNDERGRADUATE FINANCIAL AID (Fall 2012, est.) 2,111 applied for aid; of those 81% were deemed to have need. 100% of undergraduates with need received aid; of those .1% had need fully met. *Average percent of need met:* 32% (excluding resources awarded to replace EFC). *Average financial aid package:* $11,677 (excluding resources awarded to replace EFC). 4% of all full-time undergraduates had no need and received non-need-based gift aid.

GIFT AID (NEED-BASED) *Total amount:* $40,583,783 (14% federal, 9% state, 75% institutional, 2% external sources). *Receiving aid:* Freshmen: 70% (294); all full-time undergraduates: 65% (1,574). *Average award:* Freshmen: $4030; Undergraduates: $6462. *Scholarships, grants, and awards:* Federal Pell, FSEOG, state, private, college/university gift aid from institutional funds.

GIFT AID (NON-NEED-BASED) *Total amount:* $13,490,608 (1% state, 95% institutional, 4% external sources). *Receiving aid:* Freshmen: 23% (98). Undergraduates: 27% (659). *Average award:* Freshmen: $4591. Undergraduates: $5474. *Scholarships, grants, and awards by category: Academic interests/achievement:* 1,822 awards ($15,363,806 total): biological sciences, business, communication, computer science, education, English, foreign languages, general academic interests/achievements, humanities, international studies. *Creative arts/performance:* 48 awards ($98,430 total): art/fine arts, creative writing, debating, music, theater/drama. *Special achievements/activities:* 10 awards ($19,000 total); leadership. *Special characteristics:* 134 awards ($971,351 total): children and siblings of alumni, children of faculty/staff, ethnic background, international students, members of minority groups, out-of-state students. *Tuition waivers:* Full or partial for employees or children of employees. *ROTC:* Army cooperative, Air Force cooperative.

LOANS *Student loans:* $20,370,692 (75% need-based, 25% non-need-based). 51% of past graduating class borrowed through all loan programs. *Average indebtedness per student:* $29,723. *Average need-based loan:* Freshmen: $3079. Undergraduates: $4136. *Parent loans:* $2,207,621 (70% need-based, 30% non-need-based). *Programs:* Federal Direct (Subsidized and Unsubsidized Stafford, PLUS), Perkins.

WORK-STUDY *Federal work-study:* Total amount: $2,019,985; 966 jobs averaging $2216. *State or other work-study/employment:* Total amount: $68,700 (43% need-based, 57% non-need-based). 838 part-time jobs averaging $1086.

APPLYING FOR FINANCIAL AID *Required financial aid forms:* FAFSA, institution's own form. *Financial aid deadline (priority):* 4/1. *Notification date:* Continuous beginning 2/1.

CONTACT Marilynn Shelton, Financial Aid Counselor, Webster University, 470 East Lockwood Avenue, St. Louis, MO 63119, 314-968-6992 Ext. 7671 or toll-free 800-75-ENROL. *Fax:* 314-968-7125. *E-mail:* sheltoma@webster.edu. *Website:* http://www.webster.edu/.

WELCH COLLEGE
Nashville, TN

ABOUT THE INSTITUTION Independent Free Will Baptist, coed. *Awards:* associate and bachelor's degrees. 30 undergraduate majors. *Total enrollment:* 291. Undergraduates: 291. Freshmen: 58.

GIFT AID (NEED-BASED) *Scholarships, grants, and awards:* Federal Pell, FSEOG, state, private, college/university gift aid from institutional funds.

GIFT AID (NON-NEED-BASED) *Scholarships, grants, and awards by category: Special characteristics:* children of faculty/staff, international students, married students, relatives of clergy, veterans, veterans' children.

LOANS *Programs:* Federal Direct (Subsidized and Unsubsidized Stafford, PLUS), alternative loans.

WORK-STUDY *Federal work-study:* Total amount: $13,098; 7 jobs averaging $1871. *State or other work-study/employment:* 101 part-time jobs averaging $1960.

APPLYING FOR FINANCIAL AID *Required financial aid forms:* FAFSA, institution's own form.

CONTACT Angie Edgmon, Financial Aid Coordinator, Welch College, 3606 West End Avenue, Nashville, TN 37205, 615-844-5000 Ext. 5249 or toll-free 800-763-9222. *Fax:* 615-269-6028. *E-mail:* finaid@fwbbc.edu. *Website:* http://www.fwbbc.edu/.

WELLESLEY COLLEGE
Wellesley, MA

Tuition & fees: $43,554	Average undergraduate aid package: $40,236

ABOUT THE INSTITUTION Independent, women only. *Awards:* bachelor's degrees (double bachelor's degree with Massachusetts Institute of Technology). 58 undergraduate majors. *Total enrollment:* 2,481. Undergraduates: 2,483. Freshmen: 585. Both federal and institutional methodology are used as a basis for awarding need-based institutional aid.

UNDERGRADUATE EXPENSES for 2013–2014 *Application fee:* $50. *Comprehensive fee:* $57,042 includes full-time tuition ($43,288), mandatory fees ($266), and room and board ($13,488). *College room only:* $6846. *Part-time tuition:* $1352 per credit hour. Part-time tuition and fees vary according to course load. *Payment plan:* Tuition prepayment.

FRESHMAN FINANCIAL AID (Fall 2012, est.) 493 applied for aid; of those 73% were deemed to have need. 100% of freshmen with need received aid; of those 100% had need fully met. *Average percent of need met:* 100% (excluding resources awarded to replace EFC). *Average financial aid package:* $39,937 (excluding resources awarded to replace EFC).

UNDERGRADUATE FINANCIAL AID (Fall 2012, est.) 1,629 applied for aid; of those 87% were deemed to have need. 100% of undergraduates with need received aid; of those 100% had need fully met. *Average percent of need met:* 100% (excluding resources awarded to replace EFC). *Average financial aid package:* $40,236 (excluding resources awarded to replace EFC).

GIFT AID (NEED-BASED) *Total amount:* $52,790,825 (5% federal, 93% institutional, 2% external sources). *Receiving aid:* Freshmen: 59% (343); all full-time undergraduates: 58% (1,375). *Average award:* Freshmen: $39,528; Undergraduates: $38,393. *Scholarships, grants, and awards:* Federal Pell, FSEOG, state, college/university gift aid from institutional funds.

GIFT AID (NON-NEED-BASED) *Total amount:* $489,452 (100% external sources). *Tuition waivers:* Full or partial for employees or children of employees. *ROTC:* Army cooperative, Air Force cooperative.

LOANS *Student loans:* $4,128,937 (67% need-based, 33% non-need-based). 54% of past graduating class borrowed through all loan programs. *Average indebtedness per student:* $14,189. *Average need-based loan:* Freshmen: $2505. Undergraduates: $3298. *Parent loans:* $2,548,829 (100% non-need-based). *Programs:* Federal Direct (Subsidized and Unsubsidized Stafford, PLUS), Perkins, state, college/university.

WORK-STUDY *Federal work-study:* Total amount: $973,285; jobs available. *State or other work-study/employment:* Total amount: $483,063 (100% need-based). Part-time jobs available.

APPLYING FOR FINANCIAL AID *Required financial aid forms:* FAFSA, CSS Financial Aid PROFILE, noncustodial (divorced/separated) parent's statement, federal income tax form(s), W-2 forms. *Financial aid deadline (priority):* 1/15. *Notification date:* 4/1. Students must reply by 5/1.

CONTACT Mr. Scott J. Juedes, Director of Student Financial Services, Wellesley College, 106 Central Street, Wellesley, MA 02481-8203, 781-283-2360. *Fax:* 781-283-3946. *E-mail:* sfs@wellesley.edu. *Website:* http://www.wellesley.edu/.

WELLS COLLEGE
Aurora, NY

Tuition & fees: $34,700	Average undergraduate aid package: $32,524

ABOUT THE INSTITUTION Independent, coed, primarily women. *Awards:* bachelor's degrees. 38 undergraduate majors. *Total enrollment:* 532. Undergraduates: 532. Freshmen: 224. Federal methodology is used as a basis for awarding need-based institutional aid.

UNDERGRADUATE EXPENSES for 2013–2014 *Application fee:* $40. *Comprehensive fee:* $46,600 includes full-time tuition ($33,200), mandatory fees ($1500), and room and board ($11,900).

FRESHMAN FINANCIAL AID (Fall 2012, est.) 191 applied for aid; of those 97% were deemed to have need. 100% of freshmen with need received aid; of those 19% had need fully met. *Average percent of need met:* 84% (excluding resources awarded to replace EFC). *Average financial aid package:* $34,198 (excluding resources awarded to replace EFC). 5% of all full-time freshmen had no need and received non-need-based gift aid.

UNDERGRADUATE FINANCIAL AID (Fall 2012, est.) 486 applied for aid; of those 97% were deemed to have need. 100% of undergraduates with need received aid; of those 20% had need fully met. *Average percent of need met:* 81% (excluding resources awarded to replace EFC). *Average financial aid package:* $32,524 (excluding resources awarded to replace EFC). 8% of all full-time undergraduates had no need and received non-need-based gift aid.

GIFT AID (NEED-BASED) *Total amount:* $12,230,245 (10% federal, 6% state, 81% institutional, 3% external sources). *Receiving aid:* Freshmen: 94% (185); all full-time undergraduates: 91% (469). *Average award:* Freshmen: $29,388; Undergraduates: $26,844. *Scholarships, grants, and awards:* Federal Pell, FSEOG, state, private, college/university gift aid from institutional funds.

GIFT AID (NON-NEED-BASED) *Total amount:* $690,460 (98% institutional, 2% external sources). *Receiving aid:* Freshmen: 79% (155). Undergraduates: 70% (363). *Average award:* Freshmen: $21,550. Undergraduates: $16,455. *Scholarships, grants, and awards by category:* Academic interests/achievement: 300 awards ($4,543,350 total): general academic interests/achievements. Special achievements/activities: 150 awards ($1,860,000 total): leadership. Special characteristics: 23 awards ($55,000 total): children and siblings of alumni, international students. *Tuition waivers:* Full or partial for employees or children of employees, senior citizens. *ROTC:* Army cooperative, Air Force cooperative.

LOANS *Student loans:* $4,239,114 (45% need-based, 55% non-need-based). 82% of past graduating class borrowed through all loan programs. *Average indebtedness per student:* $30,933. *Average need-based loan:* Freshmen: $3246. Undergraduates: $4151. *Parent loans:* $1,257,731 (100% non-need-based). *Programs:* Federal Direct (Subsidized and Unsubsidized Stafford, PLUS), Perkins, state.

WORK-STUDY *Federal work-study:* Total amount: $100,000; 63 jobs averaging $1600. *State or other work-study/employment:* Total amount: $682,382 (96% need-based, 4% non-need-based). 232 part-time jobs averaging $1600.

APPLYING FOR FINANCIAL AID *Required financial aid form:* FAFSA. *Financial aid deadline (priority):* 2/15. *Notification date:* 3/1. Students must reply by 5/1.

CONTACT Ms. Cathleen A. Patella, Director of Financial Aid, Wells College, Route 90, Aurora, NY 13026, 315-364-3289 or toll-free 800-952-9355. *Fax:* 315-364-3227. *E-mail:* cpatella@wells.edu. *Website:* http://www.wells.edu/.

WENTWORTH INSTITUTE OF TECHNOLOGY
Boston, MA

Tuition & fees: $27,950	Average undergraduate aid package: $19,041

ABOUT THE INSTITUTION Independent, coed. *Awards:* associate, bachelor's, and master's degrees. 29 undergraduate majors. *Total enrollment:* 4,155. Undergraduates: 4,003. Freshmen: 1,068. Federal methodology is used as a basis for awarding need-based institutional aid.

UNDERGRADUATE EXPENSES for 2013–2014 *Application fee:* $50. *Comprehensive fee:* $40,476 includes full-time tuition ($27,950) and room and board ($12,526). *College room only:* $11,384. Room and board charges vary according to board plan and housing facility. *Part-time tuition:* $875 per credit hour. *Part-time fees:* $440 per credit hour. Part-time tuition and fees vary according to course load and degree level.

FRESHMAN FINANCIAL AID (Fall 2012, est.) 930 applied for aid; of those 90% were deemed to have need. 100% of freshmen with need received aid; of those 31% had need fully met. *Average percent of need met:* 26% (excluding resources awarded to replace EFC). *Average financial aid package:* $18,897 (excluding resources awarded to replace EFC). 17% of all full-time freshmen had no need and received non-need-based gift aid.

UNDERGRADUATE FINANCIAL AID (Fall 2012, est.) 2,986 applied for aid; of those 92% were deemed to have need. 100% of undergraduates with need received aid; of those 34% had need fully met. *Average percent of need met:* 27% (excluding resources awarded to replace EFC). *Average financial aid package:*

$19,041 (excluding resources awarded to replace EFC). 18% of all full-time undergraduates had no need and received non-need-based gift aid.
GIFT AID (NEED-BASED) *Total amount:* $10,639,043 (49% federal, 10% state, 41% institutional). *Receiving aid:* Freshmen: 58% (598); all full-time undergraduates: 48% (1,735). *Average award:* Freshmen: $6046; Undergraduates: $5931. *Scholarships, grants, and awards:* Federal Pell, FSEOG, state, private, college/university gift aid from institutional funds.
GIFT AID (NON-NEED-BASED) *Total amount:* $26,697,223 (97% institutional, 3% external sources). *Receiving aid:* Freshmen: 82% (840). Undergraduates: 71% (2,556). *Average award:* Freshmen: $8180. Undergraduates: $7466. *Tuition waivers:* Full or partial for employees or children of employees. *ROTC:* Army cooperative, Air Force cooperative.
LOANS *Student loans:* $31,590,498 (39% need-based, 61% non-need-based). 79% of past graduating class borrowed through all loan programs. *Average indebtedness per student:* $24,747. *Average need-based loan:* Freshmen: $3649. Undergraduates: $4616. *Parent loans:* $11,517,344 (100% non-need-based). *Programs:* Federal Direct (Subsidized and Unsubsidized Stafford, PLUS), Perkins, state.
WORK-STUDY *Federal work-study:* Total amount: $733,400; jobs available. *State or other work-study/employment:* Total amount: $2,269,767 (100% need-based). Part-time jobs available.
APPLYING FOR FINANCIAL AID *Required financial aid form:* FAFSA. *Financial aid deadline (priority):* 3/1. *Notification date:* Continuous beginning 3/15. Students must reply within 2 weeks of notification.
CONTACT Anne-Marie Caruso, Director of Financial Aid, Wentworth Institute of Technology, 550 Huntington Avenue, Boston, MA 02115-5998, 617-989-4174 or toll-free 800-556-0610. *Fax:* 617-989-4201. *E-mail:* carusoa@wit.edu.
Website: http://www.wit.edu/.

WESLEYAN COLLEGE
Macon, GA

Tuition & fees: $19,000	Average undergraduate aid package: $17,573

ABOUT THE INSTITUTION Independent United Methodist, undergraduate: women only; graduate: coed. *Awards:* bachelor's and master's degrees. 29 undergraduate majors. *Total enrollment:* 710. Undergraduates: 648. Freshmen: 121. Federal methodology is used as a basis for awarding need-based institutional aid.
UNDERGRADUATE EXPENSES for 2013–2014 *Application fee:* $30. *Comprehensive fee:* $27,400 includes full-time tuition ($19,000) and room and board ($8400). Full-time tuition and fees vary according to degree level, program, and reciprocity agreements. Room and board charges vary according to board plan and housing facility. Part-time tuition and fees vary according to degree level, program, and reciprocity agreements.
FRESHMAN FINANCIAL AID (Fall 2012, est.) 98 applied for aid; of those 92% were deemed to have need. 100% of freshmen with need received aid; of those 16% had need fully met. *Average percent of need met:* 73% (excluding resources awarded to replace EFC). *Average financial aid package:* $17,583 (excluding resources awarded to replace EFC). 34% of all full-time freshmen had no need and received non-need-based gift aid.
UNDERGRADUATE FINANCIAL AID (Fall 2012, est.) 340 applied for aid; of those 93% were deemed to have need. 99% of undergraduates with need received aid; of those 13% had need fully met. *Average percent of need met:* 73% (excluding resources awarded to replace EFC). *Average financial aid package:* $17,573 (excluding resources awarded to replace EFC). 28% of all full-time undergraduates had no need and received non-need-based gift aid.
GIFT AID (NEED-BASED) *Total amount:* $4,386,704 (29% federal, 11% state, 57% institutional, 3% external sources). *Receiving aid:* Freshmen: 59% (90); all full-time undergraduates: 66% (310). *Average award:* Freshmen: $14,636; Undergraduates: $13,911. *Scholarships, grants, and awards:* Federal Pell, FSEOG, state, private, college/university gift aid from institutional funds.
GIFT AID (NON-NEED-BASED) *Total amount:* $1,893,177 (1% federal, 8% state, 89% institutional, 2% external sources). *Receiving aid:* Freshmen: 8% (12). Undergraduates: 8% (37). *Average award:* Freshmen: $11,547. Undergraduates: $12,088. *Scholarships, grants, and awards by category:* Academic interests/achievement: biological sciences, business, communication, education, engineering/technologies, English, foreign languages, general academic interests/achievements, humanities, mathematics, premedicine, religion/biblical studies, social sciences. *Creative arts/performance:* art/fine arts, music, theater/drama. *Special achievements/activities:*

community service, general special achievements/activities, leadership, memberships, religious involvement. *Special characteristics:* adult students, children and siblings of alumni, children of current students, children of faculty/staff, ethnic background, first-generation college students, general special characteristics, handicapped students, international students, parents of current students, relatives of clergy, religious affiliation, siblings of current students, spouses of current students, veterans. *Tuition waivers:* Full or partial for employees or children of employees, senior citizens. *ROTC:* Army cooperative.
LOANS *Student loans:* $2,847,483 (88% need-based, 12% non-need-based). 71% of past graduating class borrowed through all loan programs. *Average indebtedness per student:* $34,368. *Average need-based loan:* Freshmen: $3480. Undergraduates: $4438. *Parent loans:* $276,026 (45% need-based, 55% non-need-based). *Programs:* Federal Direct (Subsidized and Unsubsidized Stafford, PLUS), Perkins, college/university, alternative loans.
WORK-STUDY *Federal work-study:* Total amount: $40,115; jobs available. *State or other work-study/employment:* Total amount: $108,937 (34% need-based, 66% non-need-based). Part-time jobs available.
APPLYING FOR FINANCIAL AID *Required financial aid forms:* FAFSA, institution's own form, state aid form. *Financial aid deadline (priority):* 2/15. *Notification date:* Continuous beginning 3/1. Students must reply by 5/1 or within 3 weeks of notification.
CONTACT Kizzy K. Holmes, Director of Financial Aid, Wesleyan College, 4760 Forsyth Road, Macon, GA 31210-4462, 478-757-5205 or toll-free 800-447-6610. *Fax:* 478-757-3780. *E-mail:* financialaid@wesleyancollege.edu.
Website: http://www.wesleyancollege.edu/.

WESLEYAN UNIVERSITY
Middletown, CT

Tuition & fees: $45,628	Average undergraduate aid package: $42,653

ABOUT THE INSTITUTION Independent, coed. *Awards:* certificates, bachelor's, master's, and doctoral degrees. 47 undergraduate majors. *Total enrollment:* 3,262. Undergraduates: 2,940. Freshmen: 752. Institutional methodology is used as a basis for awarding need-based institutional aid.
UNDERGRADUATE EXPENSES for 2013–2014 *Application fee:* $55. *One-time required fee:* $300. *Comprehensive fee:* $58,202 includes full-time tuition ($45,358), mandatory fees ($270), and room and board ($12,574). Room and board charges vary according to board plan and housing facility.
FRESHMAN FINANCIAL AID (Fall 2012, est.) 402 applied for aid; of those 89% were deemed to have need. 100% of freshmen with need received aid; of those 100% had need fully met. *Average percent of need met:* 100% (excluding resources awarded to replace EFC). *Average financial aid package:* $42,088 (excluding resources awarded to replace EFC). 1% of all full-time freshmen had no need and received non-need-based gift aid.
UNDERGRADUATE FINANCIAL AID (Fall 2012, est.) 1,517 applied for aid; of those 94% were deemed to have need. 100% of undergraduates with need received aid; of those 100% had need fully met. *Average percent of need met:* 100% (excluding resources awarded to replace EFC). *Average financial aid package:* $42,653 (excluding resources awarded to replace EFC). 1% of all full-time undergraduates had no need and received non-need-based gift aid.
GIFT AID (NEED-BASED) *Total amount:* $52,575,560 (6% federal, 1% state, 91% institutional, 2% external sources). *Receiving aid:* Freshmen: 44% (333); all full-time undergraduates: 46% (1,340). *Average award:* Freshmen: $39,761; Undergraduates: $39,026. *Scholarships, grants, and awards:* Federal Pell, FSEOG, state, private, college/university gift aid from institutional funds.
GIFT AID (NON-NEED-BASED) *Total amount:* $1,073,788 (100% institutional). *Average award:* Freshmen: $45,928. Undergraduates: $44,741. *Scholarships, grants, and awards by category:* Special characteristics: international students. *ROTC:* Air Force cooperative.
LOANS *Student loans:* $5,453,871 (100% need-based). 45% of past graduating class borrowed through all loan programs. *Average indebtedness per student:* $20,966. *Average need-based loan:* Freshmen: $3280. Undergraduates: $4470. *Programs:* Federal Direct (Subsidized and Unsubsidized Stafford, PLUS), Perkins, college/university.

WORK-STUDY *Federal work-study:* Total amount: $2,841,500; 1,200 jobs averaging $2400. *State or other work-study/employment:* Total amount: $304,202 (100% need-based). 100 part-time jobs averaging $2400.
APPLYING FOR FINANCIAL AID *Required financial aid forms:* FAFSA, CSS Financial Aid PROFILE, noncustodial (divorced/separated) parent's statement. *Financial aid deadline:* 2/15. *Notification date:* 4/1. Students must reply by 5/1.
CONTACT John Gudvangen, Director of Financial Aid, Wesleyan University, 237 High Street, Middletown, CT 06459-0260, 860-685-2800. *Fax:* 860-685-2801. *E-mail:* finaid@wesleyan.edu.
Website: http://www.wesleyan.edu/.

WESLEY COLLEGE
Dover, DE

Tuition & fees: $22,392	Average undergraduate aid package: $13,896

ABOUT THE INSTITUTION Independent United Methodist, coed. *Awards:* certificates, associate, bachelor's, and master's degrees. 20 undergraduate majors. *Total enrollment:* 1,770. Undergraduates: 1,661. Freshmen: 553. Federal methodology is used as a basis for awarding need-based institutional aid.
UNDERGRADUATE EXPENSES for 2013–2014 *Application fee:* $25. *Comprehensive fee:* $32,830 includes full-time tuition ($21,512), mandatory fees ($880), and room and board ($10,438). *College room only:* $5096. Full-time tuition and fees vary according to class time. Room and board charges vary according to board plan and housing facility.
FRESHMAN FINANCIAL AID (Fall 2011) 468 applied for aid; of those 100% were deemed to have need. 100% of freshmen with need received aid. *Average percent of need met:* 41% (excluding resources awarded to replace EFC). *Average financial aid package:* $14,765 (excluding resources awarded to replace EFC).
UNDERGRADUATE FINANCIAL AID (Fall 2011) 1,265 applied for aid; of those 100% were deemed to have need. 100% of undergraduates with need received aid; of those .2% had need fully met. *Average percent of need met:* 39% (excluding resources awarded to replace EFC). *Average financial aid package:* $13,896 (excluding resources awarded to replace EFC).
GIFT AID (NEED-BASED) *Total amount:* $13,518,576 (20% federal, 1% state, 79% institutional). *Receiving aid:* Freshmen: 80% (468); all full-time undergraduates: 73% (1,265). *Average award:* Freshmen: $14,765; Undergraduates: $13,896. *Scholarships, grants, and awards:* Federal Pell, FSEOG, state, private, college/university gift aid from institutional funds.
GIFT AID (NON-NEED-BASED) *Scholarships, grants, and awards by category:* Academic interests/achievement: general academic interests/achievements. *Special achievements/activities:* community service, general special achievements/activities, leadership, religious involvement. *Tuition waivers:* Full or partial for employees or children of employees, senior citizens. *ROTC:* Army cooperative.
LOANS *Student loans:* $8,084,030 (100% need-based). *Average need-based loan:* Freshmen: $1653. Undergraduates: $1858. *Parent loans:* $5,277,625 (100% need-based). *Programs:* Federal Direct (Subsidized and Unsubsidized Stafford, PLUS), Perkins, state, college/university.
WORK-STUDY Federal work-study jobs available. *State or other work-study/employment:* Part-time jobs available.
APPLYING FOR FINANCIAL AID *Required financial aid forms:* FAFSA, institution's own form. *Financial aid deadline (priority):* 4/15. *Notification date:* Continuous. Students must reply within 2 weeks of notification.
CONTACT Mr. Michael Hall, Director of Student Financial Planning, Wesley College, 120 North State Street, Dover, DE 19901-3875, 302-736-2334 or toll-free 800-937-5398. *Fax:* 302-736-2594. *E-mail:* halljmic@wesley.edu.
Website: http://www.wesley.edu/.

WEST CHESTER UNIVERSITY OF PENNSYLVANIA
West Chester, PA

Tuition & fees (PA res): $8620	Average undergraduate aid package: $7235

ABOUT THE INSTITUTION State-supported, coed. *Awards:* certificates, bachelor's, and master's degrees. 52 undergraduate majors. *Total enrollment:* 15,411. Undergraduates: 13,297. Freshmen: 2,334. Federal methodology is used as a basis for awarding need-based institutional aid.
UNDERGRADUATE EXPENSES for 2013–2014 *Application fee:* $45. *Tuition, state resident:* full-time $6428; part-time $268 per credit hour. *Tuition, nonresident:* full-time $16,070; part-time $670 per credit hour. *Required fees:* full-time $2192; $80.33 per credit hour or $11.08 per credit hour. Full-time tuition and fees vary according to course load. Part-time tuition and fees vary according to course load. *College room and board:* $6786; *Room only:* $4848. Room and board charges vary according to board plan and housing facility.
FRESHMAN FINANCIAL AID (Fall 2012, est.) 2,087 applied for aid; of those 74% were deemed to have need. 100% of freshmen with need received aid; of those 6% had need fully met. *Average percent of need met:* 40% (excluding resources awarded to replace EFC). *Average financial aid package:* $6137 (excluding resources awarded to replace EFC). 2% of all full-time freshmen had no need and received non-need-based gift aid.
UNDERGRADUATE FINANCIAL AID (Fall 2012, est.) 9,473 applied for aid; of those 79% were deemed to have need. 100% of undergraduates with need received aid; of those 8% had need fully met. *Average percent of need met:* 48% (excluding resources awarded to replace EFC). *Average financial aid package:* $7235 (excluding resources awarded to replace EFC). 1% of all full-time undergraduates had no need and received non-need-based gift aid.
GIFT AID (NEED-BASED) *Total amount:* $25,399,954 (51% federal, 33% state, 8% institutional, 8% external sources). *Receiving aid:* Freshmen: 31% (714); all full-time undergraduates: 33% (3,952). *Average award:* Freshmen: $5182; Undergraduates: $5300. *Scholarships, grants, and awards:* Federal Pell, FSEOG, state, private, college/university gift aid from institutional funds.
GIFT AID (NON-NEED-BASED) *Total amount:* $1,616,881 (2% state, 42% institutional, 56% external sources). *Receiving aid:* Freshmen: 12% (282). Undergraduates: 8% (978). *Average award:* Freshmen: $3591. Undergraduates: $3941. *Scholarships, grants, and awards by category:* Academic interests/achievement: business, general academic interests/achievements, mathematics, social sciences. Creative arts/performance: music, theater/drama. Special characteristics: children of faculty/staff. *Tuition waivers:* Full or partial for employees or children of employees, senior citizens. *ROTC:* Army, Air Force cooperative.
LOANS *Student loans:* $88,508,337 (81% need-based, 19% non-need-based). 71% of past graduating class borrowed through all loan programs. *Average indebtedness per student:* $30,345. *Average need-based loan:* Freshmen: $3386. Undergraduates: $4183. *Parent loans:* $14,811,560 (100% non-need-based). *Programs:* Federal Direct (Subsidized and Unsubsidized Stafford, PLUS), Perkins, Federal Nursing.
WORK-STUDY *Federal work-study:* Total amount: $446,739; jobs available. *State or other work-study/employment:* Part-time jobs available.
ATHLETIC AWARDS Total amount: $950,290 (75% need-based, 25% non-need-based).
APPLYING FOR FINANCIAL AID *Required financial aid form:* FAFSA. *Financial aid deadline (priority):* 3/1. *Notification date:* Continuous. Students must reply within 4 weeks of notification.
CONTACT Mr. Dana Parker, Financial Aid Office, West Chester University of Pennsylvania, 25 University Avenue, Suite #030, West Chester, PA 19383, 610-436-2627 or toll-free 877-315-2165 (in-state). *Fax:* 610-436-2574. *E-mail:* finaid@wcupa.edu.
Website: http://www.wcupa.edu/.

WEST COAST UNIVERSITY
Anaheim, CA

CONTACT Financial Aid Office, West Coast University, 1477 S. Manchester Avenue, Anaheim, CA 92802, 714-782-1700.
Website: http://westcoastuniversity.edu/.

WEST COAST UNIVERSITY
North Hollywood, CA

CONTACT Financial Aid Office, West Coast University, 12215 Victory Boulevard, North Hollywood, CA 91606, 323-315-5207 or toll-free 866-508-2684. *Website:* http://www.westcoastuniversity.edu/.

WEST COAST UNIVERSITY
Ontario, CA

CONTACT Financial Aid Office, West Coast University, 2855 E. Guasti Road, Ontario, CA 91761, 909-467-6100. *Website:* http://westcoastuniversity.edu/.

WESTERN CAROLINA UNIVERSITY
Cullowhee, NC

Tuition & fees (NC res): $6479	Average undergraduate aid package: $9207

ABOUT THE INSTITUTION State-supported, coed. *Awards:* certificates, bachelor's, master's, and doctoral degrees. 68 undergraduate majors. *Total enrollment:* 9,608. Undergraduates: 7,979. Freshmen: 1,560. Federal methodology is used as a basis for awarding need-based institutional aid.

UNDERGRADUATE EXPENSES for 2013–2014 *Application fee:* $55. *Tuition, state resident:* full-time $3669. *Tuition, nonresident:* full-time $13,266. *Required fees:* full-time $2810. Full-time tuition and fees vary according to degree level. Part-time tuition and fees vary according to course load and degree level. *College room and board:* $7477; *Room only:* $4429. Room and board charges vary according to board plan and housing facility.

FRESHMAN FINANCIAL AID (Fall 2012, est.) 1,365 applied for aid; of those 76% were deemed to have need. 99% of freshmen with need received aid; of those 14% had need fully met. *Average percent of need met:* 68% (excluding resources awarded to replace EFC). *Average financial aid package:* $8551 (excluding resources awarded to replace EFC). 2% of all full-time freshmen had no need and received non-need-based gift aid.

UNDERGRADUATE FINANCIAL AID (Fall 2012, est.) 5,641 applied for aid; of those 81% were deemed to have need. 98% of undergraduates with need received aid; of those 18% had need fully met. *Average percent of need met:* 71% (excluding resources awarded to replace EFC). *Average financial aid package:* $9207 (excluding resources awarded to replace EFC). 3% of all full-time undergraduates had no need and received non-need-based gift aid.

GIFT AID (NEED-BASED) *Total amount:* $27,427,183 (46% federal, 34% state, 16% institutional, 4% external sources). *Receiving aid:* Freshmen: 65% (1,005); all full-time undergraduates: 64% (4,321). *Average award:* Freshmen: $6214; Undergraduates: $6181. *Scholarships, grants, and awards:* Federal Pell, FSEOG, state, private, college/university gift aid from institutional funds.

GIFT AID (NON-NEED-BASED) *Total amount:* $1,689,768 (34% state, 33% institutional, 33% external sources). *Receiving aid:* Freshmen: 2% (32). Undergraduates: 2% (142). *Average award:* Freshmen: $3071. Undergraduates: $2127. *Scholarships, grants, and awards by category:* Academic interests/achievement: biological sciences, business, communication, education, English, general academic interests/achievements, mathematics. Creative arts/performance: art/fine arts, music, theater/drama. Special characteristics: ethnic background, handicapped students, local/state students, members of minority groups.

LOANS *Student loans:* $30,560,335 (74% need-based, 26% non-need-based). 71% of past graduating class borrowed through all loan programs. *Average indebtedness per student:* $18,483. *Average need-based loan:* Freshmen: $3344. Undergraduates: $3728. *Parent loans:* $9,276,037 (45% need-based, 55% non-need-based). *Programs:* Federal Direct (Subsidized and Unsubsidized Stafford, PLUS), Perkins.

WORK-STUDY *Federal work-study:* Total amount: $568,104; 409 jobs averaging $2047.

ATHLETIC AWARDS Total amount: $2,623,617 (59% need-based, 41% non-need-based).

APPLYING FOR FINANCIAL AID *Required financial aid forms:* FAFSA, institution's own form. *Financial aid deadline (priority):* 3/15. *Notification date:* Continuous beginning 4/1.

CONTACT Ms. Trina F. Orr, Director of Financial Aid, Western Carolina University, 123 Killian Annex, Cullowhee, NC 28723, 828-227-7292 or toll-free 877-WCU4YOU. *Fax:* 828-227-7042. *E-mail:* torr@email.wcu.edu. *Website:* http://www.wcu.edu/.

WESTERN CONNECTICUT STATE UNIVERSITY
Danbury, CT

Tuition & fees (CT res): $8893	Average undergraduate aid package: $7767

ABOUT THE INSTITUTION State-supported, coed. *Awards:* certificates, associate, bachelor's, master's, and doctoral degrees. 37 undergraduate majors. *Total enrollment:* 6,176. Undergraduates: 5,583. Freshmen: 836. Federal methodology is used as a basis for awarding need-based institutional aid.

UNDERGRADUATE EXPENSES for 2013–2014 *Application fee:* $50. *Tuition, state resident:* full-time $4510; part-time $188 per credit. *Tuition, nonresident:* full-time $14,594; part-time $192 per credit. *Required fees:* full-time $4383; $222 per credit. Full-time tuition and fees vary according to course load, program, and reciprocity agreements. *College room and board:* $10,907; *Room only:* $6445. Room and board charges vary according to board plan and housing facility.

FRESHMAN FINANCIAL AID (Fall 2011) 777 applied for aid; of those 81% were deemed to have need. 97% of freshmen with need received aid; of those 3% had need fully met. *Average percent of need met:* 68% (excluding resources awarded to replace EFC). *Average financial aid package:* $7920 (excluding resources awarded to replace EFC). 1% of all full-time freshmen had no need and received non-need-based gift aid.

UNDERGRADUATE FINANCIAL AID (Fall 2011) 3,793 applied for aid; of those 80% were deemed to have need. 96% of undergraduates with need received aid; of those 2% had need fully met. *Average percent of need met:* 63% (excluding resources awarded to replace EFC). *Average financial aid package:* $7767 (excluding resources awarded to replace EFC). 1% of all full-time undergraduates had no need and received non-need-based gift aid.

GIFT AID (NEED-BASED) *Total amount:* $12,492,795 (50% federal, 42% state, 3% institutional, 5% external sources). *Receiving aid:* Freshmen: 63% (544); all full-time undergraduates: 55% (2,622). *Average award:* Freshmen: $5560; Undergraduates: $4556. *Scholarships, grants, and awards:* Federal Pell, FSEOG, state, private, college/university gift aid from institutional funds.

GIFT AID (NON-NEED-BASED) *Total amount:* $976,688 (1% state, 21% institutional, 78% external sources). *Receiving aid:* Freshmen: 13% (113). Undergraduates: 7% (319). *Average award:* Freshmen: $8104. Undergraduates: $7289. *Scholarships, grants, and awards by category:* Academic interests/achievement: general academic interests/achievements. *Tuition waivers:* Full or partial for employees or children of employees, senior citizens. *ROTC:* Army cooperative, Air Force cooperative.

LOANS *Student loans:* $45,920,292 (46% need-based, 54% non-need-based). 74% of past graduating class borrowed through all loan programs. *Average indebtedness per student:* $22,505. *Average need-based loan:* Freshmen: $3363. Undergraduates: $4099. *Parent loans:* $4,223,996 (80% need-based, 20% non-need-based). *Programs:* Federal Direct (Subsidized and Unsubsidized Stafford, PLUS), Perkins.

WORK-STUDY *Federal work-study:* Total amount: $251,193; 112 jobs averaging $2059. *State or other work-study/employment:* Total amount: $45,985 (100% need-based). 23 part-time jobs averaging $1999.

APPLYING FOR FINANCIAL AID *Required financial aid forms:* FAFSA, institution's own form. *Financial aid deadline:* 4/15. *Notification date:* Continuous beginning 4/15. Students must reply by 5/1.

CONTACT Nancy Barton, Director of Student Financial Services, Western Connecticut State University, 181 White Street, Danbury, CT 06810-6860, 203-837-8588 or toll-free 877-837-WCSU. *Fax:* 203-837-8528. *E-mail:* bartonn@wcsu.edu. *Website:* http://www.wcsu.edu/.

WESTERN GOVERNORS UNIVERSITY
Salt Lake City, UT

Tuition & fees: N/R	Average undergraduate aid package: $6174

ABOUT THE INSTITUTION Independent, coed. 7 undergraduate majors. Federal methodology is used as a basis for awarding need-based institutional aid.

FRESHMAN FINANCIAL AID (Fall 2011) 45 applied for aid; of those 91% were deemed to have need. 100% of freshmen with need received aid; of those 12% had need fully met. *Average percent of need met:* 50% (excluding resources awarded to replace EFC). *Average financial aid package:* $6313 (excluding resources awarded to replace EFC). 9% of all full-time freshmen had no need and received non-need-based gift aid.

UNDERGRADUATE FINANCIAL AID (Fall 2011) 17,935 applied for aid; of those 90% were deemed to have need. 100% of undergraduates with need received aid. *Average percent of need met:* 46% (excluding resources awarded to replace EFC). *Average financial aid package:* $6174 (excluding resources awarded to replace EFC). 10% of all full-time undergraduates had no need and received non-need-based gift aid.

GIFT AID (NEED-BASED) *Total amount:* $51,900,170 (95% federal, 2% state, 2% institutional, 1% external sources). *Receiving aid:* Freshmen: 60% (27); all full-time undergraduates: 64% (11,504). *Average award:* Freshmen: $5067; Undergraduates: $4238. *Scholarships, grants, and awards:* Federal Pell, private, college/university gift aid from institutional funds.

GIFT AID (NON-NEED-BASED) *Receiving aid:* Undergraduates: 1% (199).

LOANS *Student loans:* $155,104,948 (39% need-based, 61% non-need-based). 73% of past graduating class borrowed through all loan programs. *Average indebtedness per student:* $35,327. *Average need-based loan:* Freshmen: $3328. Undergraduates: $4183. *Parent loans:* $58,022 (100% non-need-based). *Programs:* Federal Direct (Subsidized and Unsubsidized Stafford, PLUS).

APPLYING FOR FINANCIAL AID *Required financial aid forms:* FAFSA, institution's own form. *Financial aid deadline:* Continuous. *Notification date:* Continuous.

CONTACT Jenny Allen Ryan, Director of Financial Aid, Western Governors University, 4001 South 700 East, Suite 700, Salt Lake City, UT 84107, 877-435-7948 Ext. 5731 or toll-free 866-225-5948. *Fax:* 801-907-7727. *E-mail:* jallenryan@wgu.edu. *Website:* http://www.wgu.edu/.

WESTERN ILLINOIS UNIVERSITY
Macomb, IL

Tuition & fees (IL res): $9955	Average undergraduate aid package: $9985

ABOUT THE INSTITUTION State-supported, coed. *Awards:* certificates, bachelor's, master's, and doctoral degrees. 64 undergraduate majors. *Total enrollment:* 12,205. Undergraduates: 10,263. Freshmen: 1,754. Federal methodology is used as a basis for awarding need-based institutional aid.

UNDERGRADUATE EXPENSES for 2013–2014 *Application fee:* $30. *Tuition, state resident:* full-time $8010. *Tuition, nonresident:* full-time $12,018. *Required fees:* full-time $1945. Full-time tuition and fees vary according to course load and student level. Part-time tuition and fees vary according to course load and student level. *College room and board:* $8820; *Room only:* $5370. Room and board charges vary according to board plan, housing facility, and student level. *Payment plan:* Guaranteed tuition.

FRESHMAN FINANCIAL AID (Fall 2012, est.) 1,534 applied for aid; of those 86% were deemed to have need. 97% of freshmen with need received aid; of those 25% had need fully met. *Average percent of need met:* 52% (excluding resources awarded to replace EFC). *Average financial aid package:* $10,146 (excluding resources awarded to replace EFC). 2% of all full-time freshmen had no need and received non-need-based gift aid.

UNDERGRADUATE FINANCIAL AID (Fall 2012, est.) 7,694 applied for aid; of those 87% were deemed to have need. 97% of undergraduates with need received aid; of those 30% had need fully met. *Average percent of need met:* 55% (excluding resources awarded to replace EFC). *Average financial aid package:* $9985 (excluding resources awarded to replace EFC). 3% of all full-time undergraduates had no need and received non-need-based gift aid.

GIFT AID (NEED-BASED) *Total amount:* $36,610,419 (52% federal, 38% state, 8% institutional, 2% external sources). *Receiving aid:* Freshmen: 61% (1,059); all full-time undergraduates: 53% (4,834). *Average award:* Freshmen: $8269; Undergraduates: $7737. *Scholarships, grants, and awards:* Federal Pell, FSEOG, state, private, college/university gift aid from institutional funds.

GIFT AID (NON-NEED-BASED) *Total amount:* $2,506,550 (1% federal, 36% state, 49% institutional, 14% external sources). *Average award:* Freshmen: $3290. Undergraduates: $3205. *Scholarships, grants, and awards by category:* Academic interests/achievement: 2,407 awards ($3,103,664 total): agriculture, area/ethnic studies, biological sciences, business, communication, computer science, education, engineering/technologies, English, foreign languages, general academic interests/achievements, health fields, home economics, international studies, library science, mathematics, military science, physical sciences, religion/biblical studies, social sciences. Creative arts/performance: 616 awards ($779,924 total): applied art and design, art/fine arts, cinema/film/broadcasting, creative writing, dance, debating, general creative arts/performance, journalism/publications, music, performing arts, theater/drama. Special achievements/activities: 530 awards ($465,940 total): community service, general special achievements/activities, leadership. Special characteristics: 1,600 awards ($2,759,413 total): children of faculty/staff, general special characteristics, international students, members of minority groups, veterans' children. *Tuition waivers:* Full or partial for employees or children of employees, senior citizens. *ROTC:* Army.

LOANS *Student loans:* $64,815,550 (50% need-based, 50% non-need-based). 73% of past graduating class borrowed through all loan programs. *Average indebtedness per student:* $24,993. *Average need-based loan:* Freshmen: $3483. Undergraduates: $4327. *Parent loans:* $13,210,485 (78% need-based, 22% non-need-based). *Programs:* Federal Direct (Subsidized and Unsubsidized Stafford, PLUS), Perkins, college/university.

WORK-STUDY *Federal work-study:* Total amount: $383,028; 140 jobs averaging $2736. *State or other work-study/employment:* Total amount: $1,702,434 (76% need-based, 24% non-need-based). 1,523 part-time jobs averaging $1117.

ATHLETIC AWARDS Total amount: $3,444,502 (47% need-based, 53% non-need-based).

APPLYING FOR FINANCIAL AID *Required financial aid form:* FAFSA. *Financial aid deadline (priority):* 2/15. *Notification date:* Continuous beginning 1/15.

CONTACT Office of Financial Aid, Western Illinois University, 1 University Circle, Macomb, IL 61455-1390, 309-298-2446 or toll-free 877-742-5948. *Fax:* 309-298-2353. *E-mail:* finaid@wiu.edu. *Website:* http://www.wiu.edu/.

WESTERN INTERNATIONAL UNIVERSITY
Phoenix, AZ

CONTACT Ms. Ella Owen, Compliance Officer, Western International University, 9215 North Black Canyon Highway, Phoenix, AZ 85021, 602-429-1056. *Fax:* 602-383-9812. *E-mail:* ella.owen@west.edu. *Website:* http://www.west.edu/.

WESTERN KENTUCKY UNIVERSITY
Bowling Green, KY

Tuition & fees (KY res): $8472	Average undergraduate aid package: $13,194

ABOUT THE INSTITUTION State-supported, coed. *Awards:* certificates, associate, bachelor's, master's, and doctoral degrees. 98 undergraduate majors. *Total enrollment:* 21,110. Undergraduates: 18,101. Freshmen: 3,375. Federal methodology is used as a basis for awarding need-based institutional aid.

UNDERGRADUATE EXPENSES for 2013–2014 *Application fee:* $40. *Tuition, state resident:* full-time $8472; part-time $353 per credit hour. *Tuition, nonresident:* full-time $21,000; part-time $875 per credit hour. Full-time tuition and fees vary according to course load, location, program, and reciprocity agreements. Part-time tuition and fees vary according to course load, location, program, and reciprocity agreements. **College room and board:** $7320; **Room only:** $4170. Room and board charges vary according to board plan and housing facility.

FRESHMAN FINANCIAL AID (Fall 2011) 2,881 applied for aid; of those 80% were deemed to have need. 99% of freshmen with need received aid; of those 30% had need fully met. **Average percent of need met:** 30% (excluding resources awarded to replace EFC). **Average financial aid package:** $12,766 (excluding resources awarded to replace EFC). 9% of all full-time freshmen had no need and received non-need-based gift aid.

UNDERGRADUATE FINANCIAL AID (Fall 2011) 11,413 applied for aid; of those 82% were deemed to have need. 99% of undergraduates with need received aid; of those 30% had need fully met. **Average percent of need met:** 30% (excluding resources awarded to replace EFC). **Average financial aid package:** $13,194 (excluding resources awarded to replace EFC). 9% of all full-time undergraduates had no need and received non-need-based gift aid.

GIFT AID (NEED-BASED) Total amount: $37,254,906 (79% federal, 14% state, 7% institutional). **Receiving aid:** Freshmen: 49% (1,609); all full-time undergraduates: 48% (6,614). **Average award:** Freshmen: $5109; Undergraduates: $4856. **Scholarships, grants, and awards:** Federal Pell, FSEOG, state, private, college/university gift aid from institutional funds, United Negro College Fund.

GIFT AID (NON-NEED-BASED) Total amount: $30,574,642 (9% federal, 36% state, 48% institutional, 7% external sources). **Receiving aid:** Freshmen: 60% (1,960). Undergraduates: 40% (5,573). **Average award:** Freshmen: $5422. Undergraduates: $4927. **Scholarships, grants, and awards by category:** Academic interests/achievement: 2,445 awards ($10,748,341 total): agriculture, biological sciences, business, communication, education, engineering/technologies, English, foreign languages, general academic interests/achievements, health fields, home economics, library science, mathematics, military science, physical sciences, premedicine, religion/biblical studies, social sciences. Creative arts/performance: 484 awards ($1,304,506 total): art/fine arts, cinema/film/broadcasting, dance, debating, general creative arts/performance, journalism/publications, music, theater/drama. Special achievements/activities: 587 awards ($835,878 total): general special achievements/activities, leadership, memberships. Special characteristics: 2,883 awards ($4,010,799 total): adult students, children of union members/company employees, ethnic background, general special characteristics, handicapped students, international students, local/state students, members of minority groups, out-of-state students, religious affiliation, veterans, veterans' children. **Tuition waivers:** Full or partial for children of alumni, employees or children of employees, senior citizens. **ROTC:** Army, Air Force cooperative.

LOANS Student loans: $72,881,746 (43% need-based, 57% non-need-based). 59% of past graduating class borrowed through all loan programs. **Average indebtedness per student:** $26,110. **Average need-based loan:** Freshmen: $3035. Undergraduates: $3822. **Parent loans:** $14,444,203 (100% non-need-based). **Programs:** Federal Direct (Subsidized and Unsubsidized Stafford, PLUS), Perkins.

WORK-STUDY Federal work-study: Total amount: $1,974,625; 820 jobs averaging $2408. **State or other work-study/employment:** Total amount: $3,589,122 (100% non-need-based). 1,649 part-time jobs averaging $2677.

ATHLETIC AWARDS Total amount: $5,110,545 (100% non-need-based).

APPLYING FOR FINANCIAL AID Required financial aid form: FAFSA. **Financial aid deadline (priority):** 2/15. **Notification date:** Continuous beginning 3/1.

CONTACT Cindy Burnette, Director of Student Financial Assistance, Western Kentucky University, Potter Hall, Room 317, Bowling Green, KY 42101-1018, 270-745-2758 or toll-free 800-495-8463. Fax: 270-745-6586. E-mail: cindy.burnette@wku.edu. Website: http://www.wku.edu/.

WESTERN MICHIGAN UNIVERSITY
Kalamazoo, MI

Tuition & fees (MI res): $9982	Average undergraduate aid package: $14,685

ABOUT THE INSTITUTION State-supported, coed. **Awards:** certificates, bachelor's, master's, and doctoral degrees. 142 undergraduate majors. **Total enrollment:** 24,598. Undergraduates: 19,478. Freshmen: 3,026. Federal methodology is used as a basis for awarding need-based institutional aid.

UNDERGRADUATE EXPENSES for 2013–2014 Application fee: $35. **One-time required fee:** $300. **Tuition, state resident:** full-time $9138; part-time $316.03 per credit hour. **Tuition, nonresident:** full-time $22,418; part-time $775.28 per credit hour. **Required fees:** full-time $844; $228.25 per term. Full-time tuition and fees vary according to course load, location, program, and student level. Part-time

---

tuition and fees vary according to course load, location, program, and student level. **College room and board:** $8414; **Room only:** $4340. Room and board charges vary according to board plan.

FRESHMAN FINANCIAL AID (Fall 2011) 2,690 applied for aid; of those 83% were deemed to have need. 100% of freshmen with need received aid; of those 24% had need fully met. **Average percent of need met:** 80% (excluding resources awarded to replace EFC). **Average financial aid package:** $15,353 (excluding resources awarded to replace EFC). 8% of all full-time freshmen had no need and received non-need-based gift aid.

UNDERGRADUATE FINANCIAL AID (Fall 2011) 14,698 applied for aid; of those 85% were deemed to have need. 99% of undergraduates with need received aid; of those 20% had need fully met. **Average percent of need met:** 77% (excluding resources awarded to replace EFC). **Average financial aid package:** $14,685 (excluding resources awarded to replace EFC). 10% of all full-time undergraduates had no need and received non-need-based gift aid.

GIFT AID (NEED-BASED) Total amount: $47,846,317 (66% federal, 2% state, 32% institutional). **Receiving aid:** Freshmen: 46% (1,512); all full-time undergraduates: 50% (8,486). **Average award:** Freshmen: $5604; Undergraduates: $5256. **Scholarships, grants, and awards:** Federal Pell, FSEOG, state, private, college/university gift aid from institutional funds.

GIFT AID (NON-NEED-BASED) Total amount: $20,228,818 (68% institutional, 32% external sources). **Receiving aid:** Freshmen: 30% (975). Undergraduates: 25% (4,180). **Average award:** Freshmen: $4278. Undergraduates: $3817. **Scholarships, grants, and awards by category:** Academic interests/achievement: general academic interests/achievements. Creative arts/performance: general creative arts/performance. Special characteristics: children of faculty/staff, veterans. **Tuition waivers:** Full or partial for employees or children of employees, senior citizens. **ROTC:** Army.

LOANS Student loans: $120,075,469 (57% need-based, 43% non-need-based). 62% of past graduating class borrowed through all loan programs. **Average indebtedness per student:** $30,867. **Average need-based loan:** Freshmen: $2727. Undergraduates: $3855. **Parent loans:** $25,356,154 (50% need-based, 50% non-need-based). **Programs:** Federal Direct (Subsidized and Unsubsidized Stafford, PLUS), Perkins, alternative loans.

WORK-STUDY Federal work-study: Total amount: $1,197,064; jobs available. **State or other work-study/employment:** Part-time jobs available.

ATHLETIC AWARDS Total amount: $6,586,974 (100% non-need-based).

APPLYING FOR FINANCIAL AID Required financial aid form: FAFSA. **Financial aid deadline (priority):** 3/1. **Notification date:** Continuous beginning 3/15.

CONTACT Mr. Mark Delorey, Director of Financial Aid, Western Michigan University, Faunce Student Services Building, Room 3306, 1903 West Michigan Avenue, Kalamazoo, MI 49008-5337, 269-387-6000. E-mail: finaid-info@wmich.edu. Website: http://www.wmich.edu/.

WESTERN NEW ENGLAND UNIVERSITY
Springfield, MA

Tuition & fees: $31,912	Average undergraduate aid package: $21,920

ABOUT THE INSTITUTION Independent, coed. **Awards:** associate, bachelor's, master's, and doctoral degrees. 39 undergraduate majors. **Total enrollment:** 3,729. Undergraduates: 2,673. Freshmen: 786. Federal methodology is used as a basis for awarding need-based institutional aid.

UNDERGRADUATE EXPENSES for 2013–2014 Application fee: $40. **Comprehensive fee:** $44,056 includes full-time tuition ($29,738), mandatory fees ($2174), and room and board ($12,144). Full-time tuition and fees vary according to program. Room and board charges vary according to board plan and housing facility. **Part-time tuition:** $560 per credit hour. Part-time tuition and fees vary according to location and program. **Payment plan:** Tuition prepayment.

FRESHMAN FINANCIAL AID (Fall 2012, est.) 731 applied for aid; of those 90% were deemed to have need. 100% of freshmen with need received aid; of those 10% had need fully met. **Average percent of need met:** 72% (excluding resources awarded to replace EFC). **Average financial aid package:** $23,697 (excluding resources awarded to replace EFC). 14% of all full-time freshmen had no need and received non-need-based gift aid.

UNDERGRADUATE FINANCIAL AID (Fall 2012, est.) 2,256 applied for aid; of those 88% were deemed to have need. 100% of undergraduates with need received aid; of those 11% had need fully met. *Average percent of need met:* 69% (excluding resources awarded to replace EFC). *Average financial aid package:* $21,920 (excluding resources awarded to replace EFC). 15% of all full-time undergraduates had no need and received non-need-based gift aid.

GIFT AID (NEED-BASED) *Total amount:* $31,794,867 (11% federal, 2% state, 85% institutional, 2% external sources). *Receiving aid:* Freshmen: 83% (660); all full-time undergraduates: 78% (1,974). *Average award:* Freshmen: $18,651; Undergraduates: $16,656. *Scholarships, grants, and awards:* Federal Pell, FSEOG, state, private, college/university gift aid from institutional funds.

GIFT AID (NON-NEED-BASED) *Total amount:* $5,139,607 (5% federal, 93% institutional, 2% external sources). *Receiving aid:* Freshmen: 6% (51). Undergraduates: 5% (131). *Average award:* Freshmen: $11,466. Undergraduates: $11,226. *Scholarships, grants, and awards by category: Academic interests/achievement:* general academic interests/achievements. *Creative arts/performance:* music. *Special achievements/activities:* community service, leadership. *Special characteristics:* children of faculty/staff, children of union members/company employees, international students, local/state students, members of minority groups, out-of-state students, siblings of current students, veterans. *Tuition waivers:* Full or partial for employees or children of employees, senior citizens. *ROTC:* Army, Air Force cooperative.

LOANS *Student loans:* $14,426,391 (58% need-based, 42% non-need-based). *Average need-based loan:* Freshmen: $3480. Undergraduates: $4159. *Parent loans:* $9,427,868 (100% non-need-based). *Programs:* Federal Direct (Subsidized and Unsubsidized Stafford, PLUS), Perkins.

WORK-STUDY *Federal work-study:* Total amount: $2,194,623; jobs available. *State or other work-study/employment:* Total amount: $700,000 (100% non-need-based). Part-time jobs available.

APPLYING FOR FINANCIAL AID *Required financial aid forms:* FAFSA, federal income tax form(s), W-2 forms. *Financial aid deadline:* 4/15 (priority: 4/15). *Notification date:* Continuous beginning 3/1. Students must reply by 5/1 or within 2 weeks of notification.

CONTACT Mrs. Kathy M. Chambers, Associate Director of Student Administrative Services, Western New England University, 1215 Wilbraham Road, Springfield, MA 01119-2684, 413-796-2080 or toll-free 800-325-1122 Ext. 1321. *Fax:* 413-796-2081. *E-mail:* finaid@wne.edu.
Website: http://www.wne.edu/.

WESTERN NEW MEXICO UNIVERSITY
Silver City, NM

ABOUT THE INSTITUTION State-supported, coed. 58 undergraduate majors.

GIFT AID (NEED-BASED) *Scholarships, grants, and awards:* Federal Pell, FSEOG, state, private, college/university gift aid from institutional funds.

GIFT AID (NON-NEED-BASED) *Scholarships, grants, and awards by category: Academic interests/achievement:* general academic interests/achievements. *Creative arts/performance:* performing arts. *Special achievements/activities:* general special achievements/activities. *Special characteristics:* general special characteristics, veterans.

LOANS *Programs:* Federal Direct (Subsidized and Unsubsidized Stafford, PLUS), Perkins, state, college/university.

APPLYING FOR FINANCIAL AID *Required financial aid forms:* FAFSA, institution's own form.

CONTACT Debra Reyes, Assistant Director, Western New Mexico University, PO Box 680, Silver City, NM 88062, 575-538-6173 or toll-free 800-872-WNMU. *Fax:* 575-538-6189. *E-mail:* reyesd@wnmu.edu.
Website: http://www.wnmu.edu/.

WESTERN OREGON UNIVERSITY
Monmouth, OR

Tuition & fees (OR res): $8529	Average undergraduate aid package: $9078

ABOUT THE INSTITUTION State-supported, coed. *Awards:* certificates, bachelor's, and master's degrees. 35 undergraduate majors. *Total enrollment:* 6,187. Undergraduates: 5,497. Freshmen: 1,031. Federal methodology is used as a basis for awarding need-based institutional aid.

UNDERGRADUATE EXPENSES for 2013–2014 *Application fee:* $50. *Tuition, state resident:* full-time $8529. *Tuition, nonresident:* full-time $21,114. Room and board charges vary according to board plan and housing facility. *Payment plan:* Guaranteed tuition.

FRESHMAN FINANCIAL AID (Fall 2012, est.) 816 applied for aid; of those 87% were deemed to have need. 100% of freshmen with need received aid; of those 8% had need fully met. *Average percent of need met:* 58% (excluding resources awarded to replace EFC). *Average financial aid package:* $9480 (excluding resources awarded to replace EFC). 6% of all full-time freshmen had no need and received non-need-based gift aid.

UNDERGRADUATE FINANCIAL AID (Fall 2012, est.) 3,994 applied for aid; of those 87% were deemed to have need. 100% of undergraduates with need received aid; of those 9% had need fully met. *Average percent of need met:* 57% (excluding resources awarded to replace EFC). *Average financial aid package:* $9078 (excluding resources awarded to replace EFC). 5% of all full-time undergraduates had no need and received non-need-based gift aid.

GIFT AID (NEED-BASED) *Total amount:* $16,508,246 (65% federal, 15% state, 7% institutional, 13% external sources). *Receiving aid:* Freshmen: 73% (612); all full-time undergraduates: 69% (2,846). *Average award:* Freshmen: $7118; Undergraduates: $6363. *Scholarships, grants, and awards:* Federal Pell, FSEOG, state, private, college/university gift aid from institutional funds, TEACH Grants.

GIFT AID (NON-NEED-BASED) *Total amount:* $858,527 (3% federal, 60% institutional, 37% external sources). *Receiving aid:* Freshmen: 3% (22). Undergraduates: 2% (78). *Average award:* Freshmen: $1896. Undergraduates: $2486. *Scholarships, grants, and awards by category: Academic interests/achievement:* 929 awards ($1,887,171 total): biological sciences, business, computer science, education, English, foreign languages, general academic interests/achievements, humanities, mathematics, physical sciences, premedicine, social sciences. *Creative arts/performance:* 99 awards ($110,374 total): art/fine arts, dance, music, performing arts, theater/drama. *Special achievements/activities:* 74 awards ($336,485 total): community service, general special achievements/activities, leadership. *Special characteristics:* 73 awards ($366,485 total): adult students, children of workers in trades, ethnic background, handicapped students, international students, local/state students, veterans, veterans' children. *ROTC:* Army, Naval cooperative.

LOANS *Student loans:* $28,271,368 (82% need-based, 18% non-need-based). 55% of past graduating class borrowed through all loan programs. *Average indebtedness per student:* $28,774. *Average need-based loan:* Freshmen: $3343. Undergraduates: $4009. *Parent loans:* $6,814,982 (33% need-based, 67% non-need-based). *Programs:* Federal Direct (Subsidized and Unsubsidized Stafford, PLUS), Perkins, college/university.

WORK-STUDY *Federal work-study:* Total amount: $225,000; 963 jobs averaging $908.

ATHLETIC AWARDS Total amount: $533,975 (64% need-based, 36% non-need-based).

APPLYING FOR FINANCIAL AID *Required financial aid form:* FAFSA. *Financial aid deadline (priority):* 2/1. *Notification date:* Continuous beginning 3/15. Students must reply within 3 weeks of notification.

CONTACT Ms. Donna Kirk, Director of Financial Aid, Western Oregon University, 345 North Monmouth Avenue, Monmouth, OR 97361, 503-838-8475 or toll-free 877-877-1593. *Fax:* 503-838-8200. *E-mail:* finaid@wou.edu.
Website: http://www.wou.edu/.

WESTERN STATE COLORADO UNIVERSITY
Gunnison, CO

Tuition & fees (CO res): $7343   **Average undergraduate aid package: $9437**

ABOUT THE INSTITUTION State-supported, coed. *Awards:* certificates, bachelor's, and master's degrees. 70 undergraduate majors. *Total enrollment:* 2,301. Undergraduates: 2,105. Freshmen: 450. Federal methodology is used as a basis for awarding need-based institutional aid.

UNDERGRADUATE EXPENSES for 2013–2014 *Application fee:* $30. *Tuition, state resident:* full-time $5275; part-time $219.80 per credit hour. *Tuition, nonresident:* full-time $15,216; part-time $634 per credit hour. *Required fees:* full-time $2068. Full-time tuition and fees vary according to course load and reciprocity agreements. Part-time tuition and fees vary according to course load and reciprocity agreements. *College room and board:* $8792; *Room only:* $4700. Room and board charges vary according to board plan and housing facility.

FRESHMAN FINANCIAL AID (Fall 2012, est.) 378 applied for aid; of those 75% were deemed to have need. 85% of freshmen with need received aid; of those 22% had need fully met. *Average percent of need met:* 55% (excluding resources awarded to replace EFC). *Average financial aid package:* $9280 (excluding resources awarded to replace EFC). 37% of all full-time freshmen had no need and received non-need-based gift aid.

UNDERGRADUATE FINANCIAL AID (Fall 2012, est.) 1,367 applied for aid; of those 79% were deemed to have need. 99% of undergraduates with need received aid; of those 16% had need fully met. *Average percent of need met:* 50% (excluding resources awarded to replace EFC). *Average financial aid package:* $9437 (excluding resources awarded to replace EFC). 41% of all full-time undergraduates had no need and received non-need-based gift aid.

GIFT AID (NEED-BASED) Total amount: $6,770,689 (41% federal, 7% state, 44% institutional, 8% external sources). *Receiving aid:* Freshmen: 54% (242); all full-time undergraduates: 52% (963). *Average award:* Freshmen: $5480; Undergraduates: $5113. *Scholarships, grants, and awards:* Federal Pell, FSEOG, state, private, college/university gift aid from institutional funds.

GIFT AID (NON-NEED-BASED) Total amount: $52,801 (100% institutional). *Average award:* Freshmen: $1320. Undergraduates: $1209. *Scholarships, grants, and awards by category: Academic interests/achievement:* general academic interests/achievements. *Creative arts/performance:* art/fine arts, music, performing arts. *Special achievements/activities:* leadership. *Special characteristics:* children and siblings of alumni. *Tuition waivers:* Full or partial for senior citizens.

LOANS Student loans: $7,220,571 (100% need-based). 62% of past graduating class borrowed through all loan programs. *Average indebtedness per student:* $18,558. *Average need-based loan:* Freshmen: $3463. Undergraduates: $3720. *Parent loans:* $2,059,595 (100% need-based). *Programs:* Federal Direct (Subsidized and Unsubsidized Stafford, PLUS), Perkins.

WORK-STUDY Federal work-study: Total amount: $249,711; 222 jobs averaging $709. *State or other work-study/employment:* Total amount: $222,308 (100% need-based). 245 part-time jobs averaging $707.

ATHLETIC AWARDS Total amount: $1,037,848 (90% need-based, 10% non-need-based).

APPLYING FOR FINANCIAL AID Required financial aid form: FAFSA. *Financial aid deadline (priority):* 3/1. *Notification date:* Continuous beginning 3/1. Students must reply within 3 weeks of notification.

CONTACT Jerry Martinez, Director of Financial Aid, Western State Colorado University, Taylor Hall, Gunnison, CO 81231, 970-943-3026 or toll-free 800-876-5309. *Fax:* 970-943-3086. *E-mail:* jmartinez@western.edu. *Website:* http://www.western.edu/.

WESTERN WASHINGTON UNIVERSITY
Bellingham, WA

Tuition & fees (WA res): $8805   **Average undergraduate aid package: $13,469**

ABOUT THE INSTITUTION State-supported, coed. *Awards:* certificates, bachelor's, and master's degrees. 112 undergraduate majors. *Total enrollment:* 14,833. Undergraduates: 13,902. Freshmen: 2,688. Federal methodology is used as a basis for awarding need-based institutional aid.

UNDERGRADUATE EXPENSES for 2013–2014 *Application fee:* $55. *Tuition, state resident:* full-time $8022; part-time $267 per credit hour. *Tuition, nonresident:* full-time $18,369; part-time $612 per credit hour. *Required fees:* full-time $783; $26 per credit hour. Full-time tuition and fees vary according to course load, location, and reciprocity agreements. Part-time tuition and fees vary according to course load, location, and reciprocity agreements. *College room and board:* $9372. Room and board charges vary according to board plan, housing facility, and location.

FRESHMAN FINANCIAL AID (Fall 2012, est.) 2,191 applied for aid; of those 64% were deemed to have need. 96% of freshmen with need received aid; of those 20% had need fully met. *Average percent of need met:* 85% (excluding resources awarded to replace EFC). *Average financial aid package:* $13,143 (excluding resources awarded to replace EFC). 2% of all full-time freshmen had no need and received non-need-based gift aid.

UNDERGRADUATE FINANCIAL AID (Fall 2012, est.) 8,581 applied for aid; of those 75% were deemed to have need. 97% of undergraduates with need received aid; of those 17% had need fully met. *Average percent of need met:* 85% (excluding resources awarded to replace EFC). *Average financial aid package:* $13,469 (excluding resources awarded to replace EFC). 2% of all full-time undergraduates had no need and received non-need-based gift aid.

GIFT AID (NEED-BASED) Total amount: $36,888,731 (42% federal, 42% state, 11% institutional, 5% external sources). *Receiving aid:* Freshmen: 41% (1,093); all full-time undergraduates: 37% (4,717). *Average award:* Freshmen: $8828; Undergraduates: $8831. *Scholarships, grants, and awards:* Federal Pell, FSEOG, state, private, college/university gift aid from institutional funds.

GIFT AID (NON-NEED-BASED) Total amount: $1,630,186 (8% federal, 2% state, 33% institutional, 57% external sources). *Receiving aid:* Freshmen: 2% (61). Undergraduates: 1% (139). *Average award:* Freshmen: $1923. Undergraduates: $1907. *Scholarships, grants, and awards by category: Academic interests/achievement:* biological sciences, business, communication, computer science, education, engineering/technologies, English, foreign languages, general academic interests/achievements, health fields, humanities, library science, mathematics, physical sciences, premedicine, social sciences. *Creative arts/performance:* applied art and design, art/fine arts, cinema/film/broadcasting, creative writing, dance, general creative arts/performance, journalism/publications, music, performing arts, theater/drama. *Special achievements/activities:* community service, leadership, memberships. *Special characteristics:* children of public servants, children of union members/company employees, ethnic background, general special characteristics, international students, local/state students, members of minority groups, previous college experience, veterans. *Tuition waivers:* Full or partial for minority students, employees or children of employees.

LOANS Student loans: $48,442,735 (69% need-based, 31% non-need-based). 55% of past graduating class borrowed through all loan programs. *Average indebtedness per student:* $20,473. *Average need-based loan:* Freshmen: $3685. Undergraduates: $4457. *Parent loans:* $36,189,603 (23% need-based, 77% non-need-based). *Programs:* Federal Direct (Subsidized and Unsubsidized Stafford, PLUS), Perkins, college/university, alternative loans.

WORK-STUDY Federal work-study: Total amount: $658,442; 207 jobs averaging $3181. *State or other work-study/employment:* Total amount: $1,578,587 (100% need-based). 488 part-time jobs averaging $3235.

ATHLETIC AWARDS Total amount: $1,372,394 (30% need-based, 70% non-need-based).

APPLYING FOR FINANCIAL AID Required financial aid form: FAFSA. *Financial aid deadline (priority):* 2/15. *Notification date:* Continuous beginning 3/15. Students must reply within 3 weeks of notification.

CONTACT Ms. Barbara Luton, Office Support Supervisor for Financial Aid, Western Washington University, Old Main 255, MS 9006, 516 High Street, Bellingham, WA 98225-9006, 360-650-3470. *E-mail:* financialaid@wwu.edu. *Website:* http://www.wwu.edu/.

WESTFIELD STATE UNIVERSITY
Westfield, MA

Tuition & fees (MA res): $8297	Average undergraduate aid package: $7666

ABOUT THE INSTITUTION State-supported, coed. **Awards:** certificates, bachelor's, and master's degrees. 33 undergraduate majors. **Total enrollment:** 6,079. Undergraduates: 5,368. Freshmen: 997. Federal methodology is used as a basis for awarding need-based institutional aid.

UNDERGRADUATE EXPENSES for 2013–2014 Application fee: $50. **Tuition, state resident:** full-time $970; part-time $260 per credit hour. **Tuition, nonresident:** full-time $7050; part-time $260 per credit hour. **Required fees:** full-time $7327; $75 per term. Full-time tuition and fees vary according to program and reciprocity agreements. Part-time tuition and fees vary according to course load. **College room and board:** $9233. Room and board charges vary according to board plan and housing facility.

FRESHMAN FINANCIAL AID (Fall 2011) 1,067 applied for aid; of those 70% were deemed to have need. 97% of freshmen with need received aid; of those 9% had need fully met. **Average percent of need met:** 65% (excluding resources awarded to replace EFC). **Average financial aid package:** $7807 (excluding resources awarded to replace EFC). 1% of all full-time freshmen had no need and received non-need-based gift aid.

UNDERGRADUATE FINANCIAL AID (Fall 2011) 4,144 applied for aid; of those 72% were deemed to have need. 98% of undergraduates with need received aid; of those 14% had need fully met. **Average percent of need met:** 68% (excluding resources awarded to replace EFC). **Average financial aid package:** $7666 (excluding resources awarded to replace EFC). 1% of all full-time undergraduates had no need and received non-need-based gift aid.

GIFT AID (NEED-BASED) Total amount: $11,564,717 (55% federal, 25% state, 15% institutional, 5% external sources). **Receiving aid:** Freshmen: 41% (462); all full-time undergraduates: 38% (1,861). **Average award:** Freshmen: $5808; Undergraduates: $5279. **Scholarships, grants, and awards:** Federal Pell, FSEOG, state, private, college/university gift aid from institutional funds.

GIFT AID (NON-NEED-BASED) Total amount: $561,500 (30% state, 27% institutional, 43% external sources). **Receiving aid:** Freshmen: 20% (227). Undergraduates: 9% (435). **Average award:** Freshmen: $4190. Undergraduates: $4289. **Scholarships, grants, and awards by category:** Academic interests/achievement: general academic interests/achievements. **Tuition waivers:** Full or partial for employees or children of employees, senior citizens. **ROTC:** Army cooperative, Air Force cooperative.

LOANS Student loans: $27,922,091 (65% need-based, 35% non-need-based). 76% of past graduating class borrowed through all loan programs. **Average indebtedness per student:** $24,825. **Average need-based loan:** Freshmen: $3256. Undergraduates: $4062. **Parent loans:** $4,720,573 (18% need-based, 82% non-need-based). **Programs:** Federal Direct (Subsidized and Unsubsidized Stafford, PLUS), Perkins.

WORK-STUDY Federal work-study: Total amount: $478,326; 307 jobs averaging $1558.

APPLYING FOR FINANCIAL AID Required financial aid form: FAFSA. **Financial aid deadline (priority):** 3/1. **Notification date:** 4/15.

CONTACT Catherine Ryan, Director of Financial Aid, Westfield State University, 333 Western Avenue, Westfield, MA 01086, 413-572-5218. *Website:* http://www.wsc.ma.edu/.

WEST LIBERTY UNIVERSITY
West Liberty, WV

ABOUT THE INSTITUTION State-supported, coed. **Awards:** associate, bachelor's, and master's degrees. 36 undergraduate majors. **Total enrollment:** 2,804. Undergraduates: 2,718. Freshmen: 526.

GIFT AID (NEED-BASED) Scholarships, grants, and awards: Federal Pell, FSEOG, state, private, college/university gift aid from institutional funds.

GIFT AID (NON-NEED-BASED) Scholarships, grants, and awards by category: Academic interests/achievement: business, communication, education, English, general academic interests/achievements, health fields, mathematics, physical sciences. Creative arts/performance: art/fine arts, music, theater/drama. Special achievements/

activities: cheerleading/drum major. Special characteristics: children and siblings of alumni, children of faculty/staff.

LOANS Programs: Federal Direct (Subsidized and Unsubsidized Stafford, PLUS), Perkins, Federal Nursing, alternative loans.

APPLYING FOR FINANCIAL AID Required financial aid form: FAFSA.

CONTACT Christ Taskalines, Financial Aid Manager, West Liberty University, PO Box 295, West Liberty, WV 26074-0295, 304-336-8016 or toll-free 800-732-6204 (in-state), 866-WESTLIB (out-of-state). Fax: 304-336-8088. *E-mail:* taskalic@westliberty.edu.
Website: http://www.westliberty.edu/.

WESTMINSTER COLLEGE
Fulton, MO

Tuition & fees: $20,850	Average undergraduate aid package: $18,710

ABOUT THE INSTITUTION Independent Presbyterian Church, coed. **Awards:** bachelor's degrees. 30 undergraduate majors. **Total enrollment:** 1,084. Undergraduates: 1,084. Freshmen: 260. Federal methodology is used as a basis for awarding need-based institutional aid.

UNDERGRADUATE EXPENSES for 2013–2014 Comprehensive fee: $29,300 includes full-time tuition ($19,750), mandatory fees ($1100), and room and board ($8450). **College room only:** $4500. Room and board charges vary according to board plan and housing facility. **Part-time tuition:** $800 per credit hour.

FRESHMAN FINANCIAL AID (Fall 2012, est.) 200 applied for aid; of those 78% were deemed to have need. 100% of freshmen with need received aid; of those 41% had need fully met. **Average percent of need met:** 82% (excluding resources awarded to replace EFC). **Average financial aid package:** $20,155 (excluding resources awarded to replace EFC). 39% of all full-time freshmen had no need and received non-need-based gift aid.

UNDERGRADUATE FINANCIAL AID (Fall 2012, est.) 824 applied for aid; of those 80% were deemed to have need. 100% of undergraduates with need received aid; of those 45% had need fully met. **Average percent of need met:** 80% (excluding resources awarded to replace EFC). **Average financial aid package:** $18,710 (excluding resources awarded to replace EFC). 39% of all full-time undergraduates had no need and received non-need-based gift aid.

GIFT AID (NEED-BASED) Total amount: $15,195,266 (8% federal, 5% state, 69% institutional, 18% external sources). **Receiving aid:** Freshmen: 57% (155); all full-time undergraduates: 61% (656). **Average award:** Freshmen: $15,940; Undergraduates: $13,812. **Scholarships, grants, and awards:** Federal Pell, FSEOG, state, private, college/university gift aid from institutional funds.

GIFT AID (NON-NEED-BASED) Total amount: $194,678 (100% federal). **Average award:** Freshmen: $11,509. Undergraduates: $10,431. **Scholarships, grants, and awards by category:** Academic interests/achievement: 478 awards ($3,864,024 total): general academic interests/achievements. Creative arts/performance: 13 awards ($24,250 total): music. Special achievements/activities: 493 awards ($1,428,880 total): general special achievements/activities, leadership. Special characteristics: 307 awards ($2,252,457 total): children and siblings of alumni, children of faculty/staff, ethnic background, international students, local/state students, relatives of clergy, religious affiliation, siblings of current students, twins. **Tuition waivers:** Full or partial for children of alumni, employees or children of employees. **ROTC:** Army cooperative, Air Force cooperative.

LOANS Student loans: $5,996,510 (39% need-based, 61% non-need-based). 64% of past graduating class borrowed through all loan programs. **Average indebtedness per student:** $26,723. **Average need-based loan:** Freshmen: $3286. Undergraduates: $4061. **Parent loans:** $1,217,315 (100% non-need-based). **Programs:** Federal Direct (Subsidized and Unsubsidized Stafford, PLUS), Perkins.

WORK-STUDY Federal work-study: Total amount: $707,377; 658 jobs averaging $1408. **State or other work-study/employment:** Total amount: $497,885 (100% non-need-based). 259 part-time jobs averaging $2042.

APPLYING FOR FINANCIAL AID Required financial aid form: FAFSA. **Financial aid deadline (priority):** 2/15. **Notification date:** Continuous beginning 3/15. Students must reply within 3 weeks of notification.

CONTACT Ms. Aimee Bristow, Director of Financial Aid, Westminster College, 501 Westminster Avenue, Fulton, MO 65251-1299, 800-475-3361. Fax: 573-592-5255. *E-mail:* aimee.bristow@westminster-mo.edu.
Website: http://www.westminster-mo.edu/.

WESTMINSTER COLLEGE
New Wilmington, PA

Tuition & fees: $31,410	Average undergraduate aid package: $25,130

ABOUT THE INSTITUTION Independent Presbyterian Church (U.S.A.), coed. **Awards:** bachelor's and master's degrees. 52 undergraduate majors. **Total enrollment:** 1,608. Undergraduates: 1,566. Freshmen: 360. Federal methodology is used as a basis for awarding need-based institutional aid.

UNDERGRADUATE EXPENSES for 2013–2014 Application fee: $35. **Comprehensive fee:** $40,980 includes full-time tuition ($30,320), mandatory fees ($1090), and room and board ($9570). Room and board charges vary according to board plan and housing facility. **Part-time tuition:** $970 per credit hour.

FRESHMAN FINANCIAL AID (Fall 2011) 311 applied for aid; of those 91% were deemed to have need. 100% of freshmen with need received aid; of those 20% had need fully met. **Average percent of need met:** 80% (excluding resources awarded to replace EFC). **Average financial aid package:** $25,141 (excluding resources awarded to replace EFC). 14% of all full-time freshmen had no need and received non-need-based gift aid.

UNDERGRADUATE FINANCIAL AID (Fall 2011) 1,238 applied for aid; of those 93% were deemed to have need. 100% of undergraduates with need received aid; of those 17% had need fully met. **Average percent of need met:** 80% (excluding resources awarded to replace EFC). **Average financial aid package:** $25,130 (excluding resources awarded to replace EFC). 17% of all full-time undergraduates had no need and received non-need-based gift aid.

GIFT AID (NEED-BASED) Total amount: $24,259,297 (9% federal, 8% state, 79% institutional, 4% external sources). **Receiving aid:** Freshmen: 79% (283); all full-time undergraduates: 83% (1,143). **Average award:** Freshmen: $21,568; Undergraduates: $20,443. **Scholarships, grants, and awards:** Federal Pell, FSEOG, state, private, college/university gift aid from institutional funds.

GIFT AID (NON-NEED-BASED) Total amount: $4,015,108 (2% federal, 97% institutional, 1% external sources). **Receiving aid:** Freshmen: 78% (280). Undergraduates: 81% (1,121). **Average award:** Freshmen: $16,138. Undergraduates: $15,671. **Scholarships, grants, and awards by category:** Academic interests/achievement: 1,327 awards ($16,886,725 total): general academic interests/achievements. Creative arts/performance: 136 awards ($115,722 total): cinema/film/broadcasting, general creative arts/performance, music, theater/drama. Special characteristics: 627 awards ($5,079,664 total): children and siblings of alumni, general special characteristics, international students, religious affiliation. **Tuition waivers:** Full or partial for employees or children of employees. **ROTC:** Army cooperative.

LOANS Student loans: $10,781,965 (95% need-based, 5% non-need-based). 84% of past graduating class borrowed through all loan programs. **Average indebtedness per student:** $32,753. **Average need-based loan:** Freshmen: $3718. Undergraduates: $4513. **Parent loans:** $3,457,032 (92% need-based, 8% non-need-based). **Programs:** Federal Direct (Subsidized and Unsubsidized Stafford, PLUS), Perkins, alternative loans.

WORK-STUDY Federal work-study: Total amount: $665,947; 392 jobs averaging $1699. **State or other work-study/employment:** Total amount: $96,698 (59% need-based, 41% non-need-based). 68 part-time jobs averaging $1449.

APPLYING FOR FINANCIAL AID Required financial aid forms: FAFSA, institution's own form, W-2 forms. **Financial aid deadline (priority):** 5/1. **Notification date:** Continuous beginning 3/1. Students must reply by 5/1 or within 3 weeks of notification.

CONTACT Mrs. Cheryl A. Gerber, Director of Financial Aid, Westminster College, 319 South Market Street, New Wilmington, PA 16172-0001, 724-946-7102 or toll-free 800-942-8033. Fax: 724-946-6171. E-mail: gerberca@westminster.edu. Website: http://www.westminster.edu/.

WESTMINSTER COLLEGE
Salt Lake City, UT

Tuition & fees: $28,210	Average undergraduate aid package: $22,336

ABOUT THE INSTITUTION Independent, coed. **Awards:** certificates, bachelor's, and master's degrees. 36 undergraduate majors. **Total enrollment:** 3,301.

Undergraduates: 2,526. Freshmen: 501. Federal methodology is used as a basis for awarding need-based institutional aid.

UNDERGRADUATE EXPENSES for 2013–2014 Application fee: $50. **Comprehensive fee:** $36,100 includes full-time tuition ($27,720), mandatory fees ($490), and room and board ($7890). Full-time tuition and fees vary according to course load and program. Room and board charges vary according to board plan. **Part-time tuition:** $1155 per credit hour. Part-time tuition and fees vary according to course load and program.

FRESHMAN FINANCIAL AID (Fall 2012, est.) 393 applied for aid; of those 84% were deemed to have need. 100% of freshmen with need received aid; of those 22% had need fully met. **Average percent of need met:** 80% (excluding resources awarded to replace EFC). **Average financial aid package:** $23,150 (excluding resources awarded to replace EFC). 27% of all full-time freshmen had no need and received non-need-based gift aid.

UNDERGRADUATE FINANCIAL AID (Fall 2012, est.) 1,534 applied for aid; of those 87% were deemed to have need. 100% of undergraduates with need received aid; of those 21% had need fully met. **Average percent of need met:** 76% (excluding resources awarded to replace EFC). **Average financial aid package:** $22,336 (excluding resources awarded to replace EFC). 31% of all full-time undergraduates had no need and received non-need-based gift aid.

GIFT AID (NEED-BASED) Total amount: $20,330,202 (15% federal, 80% institutional, 5% external sources). **Receiving aid:** Freshmen: 66% (329); all full-time undergraduates: 57% (1,280). **Average award:** Freshmen: $18,070; Undergraduates: $17,206. **Scholarships, grants, and awards:** Federal Pell, FSEOG, state, private, college/university gift aid from institutional funds.

GIFT AID (NON-NEED-BASED) Total amount: $9,272,356 (1% state, 86% institutional, 13% external sources). **Receiving aid:** Freshmen: 3% (17). Undergraduates: 6% (129). **Average award:** Freshmen: $12,539. Undergraduates: $12,920. **Tuition waivers:** Full or partial for employees or children of employees. **ROTC:** Army cooperative, Naval cooperative, Air Force cooperative.

LOANS Student loans: $13,724,963 (80% need-based, 20% non-need-based). 54% of past graduating class borrowed through all loan programs. **Average indebtedness per student:** $28,323. **Average need-based loan:** Freshmen: $3991. Undergraduates: $4736. **Parent loans:** $1,383,002 (82% need-based, 18% non-need-based). **Programs:** Federal Direct (Subsidized and Unsubsidized Stafford, PLUS), Perkins.

WORK-STUDY Federal work-study: Total amount: $1,464,972; 497 jobs averaging $2452. **State or other work-study/employment:** Total amount: $716,329 (16% need-based, 84% non-need-based). 217 part-time jobs averaging $2434.

ATHLETIC AWARDS Total amount: $714,057 (59% need-based, 41% non-need-based).

APPLYING FOR FINANCIAL AID Required financial aid form: FAFSA. **Financial aid deadline:** Continuous. **Notification date:** Continuous beginning 3/1. Students must reply within 3 weeks of notification.

CONTACT Kimberly Sharratt, Associate Director of Financial Aid, Westminster College, 1840 South 1300 East, Salt Lake City, UT 84105, 801-832-2500 or toll-free 800-748-4753. Fax: 801-832-2501. E-mail: ksharratt@westminstercollege.edu. Website: http://www.westminstercollege.edu/.

WESTMONT COLLEGE
Santa Barbara, CA

Tuition & fees: N/R	Average undergraduate aid package: $26,738

ABOUT THE INSTITUTION Independent nondenominational, coed. 43 undergraduate majors. Federal methodology is used as a basis for awarding need-based institutional aid.

FRESHMAN FINANCIAL AID (Fall 2012, est.) 265 applied for aid; of those 80% were deemed to have need. 100% of freshmen with need received aid; of those 21% had need fully met. **Average percent of need met:** 78% (excluding resources awarded to replace EFC). **Average financial aid package:** $26,504 (excluding resources awarded to replace EFC). 24% of all full-time freshmen had no need and received non-need-based gift aid.

UNDERGRADUATE FINANCIAL AID (Fall 2012, est.) 1,036 applied for aid; of those 86% were deemed to have need. 100% of undergraduates with need received aid; of those 21% had need fully met. **Average percent of need met:** 77% (excluding resources awarded to replace EFC). **Average financial aid package:** $26,738 (excluding resources awarded to replace EFC). 30% of all full-time undergraduates had no need and received non-need-based gift aid.

GIFT AID (NEED-BASED) Total amount: $17,227,064 (8% federal, 10% state, 79% institutional, 3% external sources). **Receiving aid:** Freshmen: 63% (213); all full-time undergraduates: 65% (885). **Average award:** Freshmen: $21,831; Undergraduates: $21,276. **Scholarships, grants, and awards:** Federal Pell, FSEOG, state, private, college/university gift aid from institutional funds.

GIFT AID (NON-NEED-BASED) Total amount: $5,502,151 (1% state, 95% institutional, 4% external sources). **Receiving aid:** Freshmen: 10% (34). Undergraduates: 11% (145). **Average award:** Freshmen: $11,627. Undergraduates: $11,584. **Scholarships, grants, and awards by category:** Academic interests/achievement: general academic interests/achievements. Creative arts/performance: art/fine arts, music, theater/drama. Special achievements/activities: general special achievements/activities, leadership. Special characteristics: children of faculty/staff, ethnic background, international students.

LOANS Student loans: $9,583,062 (67% need-based, 33% non-need-based). 64% of past graduating class borrowed through all loan programs. Average indebtedness per student: $31,277. **Average need-based loan:** Freshmen: $3901. Undergraduates: $5625. **Parent loans:** $3,174,013 (30% need-based, 70% non-need-based). **Programs:** Federal Direct (Subsidized and Unsubsidized Stafford, PLUS), Perkins, college/university, alternative loans.

WORK-STUDY Federal work-study: Total amount: $515,986; 258 jobs averaging $2000.

ATHLETIC AWARDS Total amount: $1,921,020 (46% need-based, 54% non-need-based).

APPLYING FOR FINANCIAL AID Required financial aid forms: FAFSA, institution's own form. **Financial aid deadline (priority):** 3/1. **Notification date:** 4/1. Students must reply by 5/1 or within 2 weeks of notification.

CONTACT Mr. Sean Smith, Director of Financial Aid, Westmont College, 955 La Paz Road, Santa Barbara, CA 93108, 805-565-6063 or toll-free 800-777-9011. Fax: 805-565-7157. E-mail: finaid@westmont.edu.
Website: http://www.westmont.edu/.

WEST TEXAS A&M UNIVERSITY
Canyon, TX

Tuition & fees (TX res): $6790	Average undergraduate aid package: $10,451

ABOUT THE INSTITUTION State-supported, coed. **Awards:** bachelor's, master's, and doctoral degrees. 68 undergraduate majors. **Total enrollment:** 7,909. Undergraduates: 6,588. Freshmen: 1,205. Federal methodology is used as a basis for awarding need-based institutional aid.

UNDERGRADUATE EXPENSES for 2013–2014 Application fee: $25. **Tuition, state resident:** full-time $4730; part-time $165 per credit hour. **Tuition, nonresident:** full-time $5630; part-time $195 per credit hour. **Required fees:** full-time $2060; $66 per credit hour or $182 per credit hour. Full-time tuition and fees vary according to course load. Part-time tuition and fees vary according to course load. **College room and board:** $5000. Room and board charges vary according to board plan and housing facility.

FRESHMAN FINANCIAL AID (Fall 2011) 1,005 applied for aid; of those 83% were deemed to have need. 85% of freshmen with need received aid; of those 19% had need fully met. **Average percent of need met:** 80% (excluding resources awarded to replace EFC). **Average financial aid package:** $11,426 (excluding resources awarded to replace EFC). 8% of all full-time freshmen had no need and received non-need-based gift aid.

UNDERGRADUATE FINANCIAL AID (Fall 2011) 3,908 applied for aid; of those 87% were deemed to have need. 87% of undergraduates with need received aid; of those 16% had need fully met. **Average percent of need met:** 70% (excluding resources awarded to replace EFC). **Average financial aid package:** $10,451 (excluding resources awarded to replace EFC). 4% of all full-time undergraduates had no need and received non-need-based gift aid.

GIFT AID (NEED-BASED) Total amount: $16,842,841 (65% federal, 26% state, 9% institutional). **Receiving aid:** Freshmen: 53% (635); all full-time undergraduates: 49% (2,566). **Average award:** Freshmen: $9629; Undergraduates: $7857. **Scholarships, grants, and awards:** Federal Pell, FSEOG, state, private, college/university gift aid from institutional funds.

GIFT AID (NON-NEED-BASED) Total amount: $4,216,382 (10% state, 54% institutional, 36% external sources). **Receiving aid:** Freshmen: 38% (454). Undergraduates: 24% (1,276). **Average award:** Freshmen: $2017. Undergraduates: $3227.

Scholarships, grants, and awards by category: Academic interests/achievement: 3,172 awards ($1,469,934 total): agriculture, business, communication, computer science, education, engineering/technologies, English, general academic interests/achievements, health fields, humanities, mathematics, physical sciences, pre-medicine, social sciences. Creative arts/performance: 550 awards ($218,676 total): art/fine arts, cinema/film/broadcasting, dance, debating, journalism/publications, music, theater/drama. Special achievements/activities: 429 awards ($191,372 total): cheerleading/drum major, community service, hobbies/interests, leadership, memberships, rodeo. Special characteristics: 640 awards ($362,399 total): children and siblings of alumni, children of faculty/staff, children of union members/company employees, children of workers in trades, first-generation college students, handicapped students, local/state students, out-of-state students, public servants, religious affiliation, veterans, veterans' children. **Tuition waivers:** Full or partial for employees or children of employees.

LOANS Student loans: $33,040,669 (50% need-based, 50% non-need-based). 63% of past graduating class borrowed through all loan programs. Average indebtedness per student: $19,774. **Average need-based loan:** Freshmen: $3966. Undergraduates: $5180. **Parent loans:** $1,101,439 (100% non-need-based). **Programs:** Federal Direct (Subsidized and Unsubsidized Stafford, PLUS), state.

WORK-STUDY Federal work-study: Total amount: $572,742; 152 jobs averaging $1287. **State or other work-study/employment:** Total amount: $45,933 (100% need-based). 30 part-time jobs averaging $1148.

ATHLETIC AWARDS Total amount: $1,456,876 (31% need-based, 69% non-need-based).

APPLYING FOR FINANCIAL AID Required financial aid form: FAFSA. **Financial aid deadline:** Continuous. **Notification date:** Continuous beginning 3/1. Students must reply within 2 weeks of notification.

CONTACT Mr. Jim Reed, Director of Financial Aid, West Texas A&M University, WTAMU Box 60939, Canyon, TX 79016-0001, 806-651-2055 or toll-free 800-99-WTAMU. Fax: 806-651-2924. E-mail: jreed@mail.wtamu.edu.
Website: http://www.wtamu.edu/.

WEST VIRGINIA STATE UNIVERSITY
Institute, WV

Tuition & fees (WV res): $5442	Average undergraduate aid package: N/A

ABOUT THE INSTITUTION State-supported, coed. **Awards:** bachelor's and master's degrees. 31 undergraduate majors. **Total enrollment:** 2,644. Undergraduates: 2,561. Federal methodology is used as a basis for awarding need-based institutional aid.

UNDERGRADUATE EXPENSES for 2013–2014 Tuition, state resident: full-time $5442; part-time $222 per credit hour. **Tuition, nonresident:** full-time $12,720; part-time $525 per credit hour. Full-time tuition and fees vary according to course load and program. Part-time tuition and fees vary according to course load and program. **College room and board:** $6698; **Room only:** $3382. Room and board charges vary according to board plan and housing facility.

GIFT AID (NEED-BASED) Scholarships, grants, and awards: Federal Pell, FSEOG, state, private, college/university gift aid from institutional funds.

GIFT AID (NON-NEED-BASED) Scholarships, grants, and awards by category: Academic interests/achievement: biological sciences, business, communication, English, foreign languages, general academic interests/achievements, mathematics, military science. Creative arts/performance: art/fine arts, music. Special achievements/activities: general special achievements/activities, leadership. Special characteristics: ethnic background, general special characteristics. **ROTC:** Army.

LOANS Programs: Federal Direct (Subsidized and Unsubsidized Stafford, PLUS), Perkins.

APPLYING FOR FINANCIAL AID Required financial aid form: FAFSA. **Financial aid deadline:** 6/15 (priority: 4/1). **Notification date:** Continuous.

CONTACT Mrs. JoAnn L. Ross, Director of Student Financial Assistance, West Virginia State University, PO Box 1000, Ferrell Hall 324, Institute, WV 25112-1000, 304-204-4361 or toll-free 800-987-2112.
Website: http://www.wvstateu.edu/.

WEST VIRGINIA UNIVERSITY
Morgantown, WV

Tuition & fees (WV res): $6090	Average undergraduate aid package: $6270

ABOUT THE INSTITUTION State-supported, coed. **Awards:** bachelor's, master's, and doctoral degrees. 63 undergraduate majors. **Total enrollment:** 29,707. Undergraduates: 22,827. Freshmen: 5,135. Federal methodology is used as a basis for awarding need-based institutional aid.

UNDERGRADUATE EXPENSES for 2013–2014 Application fee: $45. **Tuition, state resident:** full-time $6090; part-time $254 per credit hour. **Tuition, nonresident:** full-time $18,868; part-time $786 per credit hour. Full-time tuition and fees vary according to location, program, and reciprocity agreements. Part-time tuition and fees vary according to course load, location, program, and reciprocity agreements. **College room and board:** $8782. Room and board charges vary according to board plan, housing facility, and location.

FRESHMAN FINANCIAL AID (Fall 2012, est.) 4,176 applied for aid; of those 85% were deemed to have need. 97% of freshmen with need received aid; of those 30% had need fully met. **Average percent of need met:** 72% (excluding resources awarded to replace EFC). **Average financial aid package:** $5361 (excluding resources awarded to replace EFC). 36% of all full-time freshmen had no need and received non-need-based gift aid.

UNDERGRADUATE FINANCIAL AID (Fall 2012, est.) 19,743 applied for aid; of those 85% were deemed to have need. 84% of undergraduates with need received aid; of those 30% had need fully met. **Average percent of need met:** 75% (excluding resources awarded to replace EFC). **Average financial aid package:** $6270 (excluding resources awarded to replace EFC). 22% of all full-time undergraduates had no need and received non-need-based gift aid.

GIFT AID (NEED-BASED) Total amount: $39,785,896 (69% federal, 22% state, 9% institutional). **Receiving aid:** Freshmen: 42% (1,859); all full-time undergraduates: 35% (8,042). **Average award:** Freshmen: $4561; Undergraduates: $4748. **Scholarships, grants, and awards:** Federal Pell, FSEOG, state, private, college/university gift aid from institutional funds.

GIFT AID (NON-NEED-BASED) Total amount: $36,873,952 (1% federal, 59% state, 33% institutional, 7% external sources). **Receiving aid:** Freshmen: 64% (2,821). Undergraduates: 40% (9,170). **Average award:** Freshmen: $1940. Undergraduates: $2418. **Scholarships, grants, and awards by category:** Academic interests/achievement: 3,108 awards ($9,029,644 total): agriculture, architecture, area/ethnic studies, biological sciences, business, communication, computer science, education, engineering/technologies, English, foreign languages, general academic interests/achievements, health fields, home economics, humanities, international studies, library science, mathematics, military science, physical sciences, premedicine, religion/biblical studies, social sciences. Creative arts/performance: 104 awards ($1,509,507 total): art/fine arts, debating, music, theater/drama. Special achievements/activities: 7 awards ($65,505 total): general special achievements/activities, leadership. Special characteristics: 404 awards ($2,063,734 total): children of faculty/staff, children of union members/company employees, children of workers in trades, ethnic background, general special characteristics, international students, local/state students, members of minority groups. **Tuition waivers:** Full or partial for employees or children of employees, senior citizens. **ROTC:** Army, Air Force.

LOANS Student loans: $179,123,838 (22% need-based, 78% non-need-based). 42% of past graduating class borrowed through all loan programs. **Average indebtedness per student:** $27,511. **Average need-based loan:** Freshmen: $3535. Undergraduates: $4375. **Parent loans:** $52,747,570 (100% non-need-based). **Programs:** Federal Direct (Subsidized and Unsubsidized Stafford, PLUS), Perkins, Federal Nursing, college/university.

WORK-STUDY Federal work-study: Total amount: $1,603,340; 876 jobs averaging $1974. **State or other work-study/employment:** Total amount: $4,237,570 (100% non-need-based). 1,155 part-time jobs averaging $2449.

ATHLETIC AWARDS Total amount: $5,463,438 (100% non-need-based).

APPLYING FOR FINANCIAL AID Required financial aid forms: FAFSA, state aid form. **Financial aid deadline:** 3/1. **Notification date:** Continuous beginning 3/15. Students must reply within 4 weeks of notification.

CONTACT Tresa Weimer, Interim Director of Financial Aid, West Virginia University, PO Box 6004, Morgantown, WV 26506-6004, 304-293-5242 or toll-free 800-344-9881. Fax: 304-293-4890. E-mail: tresa.weimer@mail.wvu.edu. Website: http://www.wvu.edu/.

WEST VIRGINIA UNIVERSITY INSTITUTE OF TECHNOLOGY
Montgomery, WV

Tuition & fees (WV res): $5558	Average undergraduate aid package: $7249

ABOUT THE INSTITUTION State-supported, coed. **Awards:** certificates and bachelor's degrees. 25 undergraduate majors. **Total enrollment:** 1,107. Undergraduates: 1,107. Freshmen: 199. Federal methodology is used as a basis for awarding need-based institutional aid.

UNDERGRADUATE EXPENSES for 2013–2014 Tuition, state resident: full-time $5558. **Tuition, nonresident:** full-time $13,980. Full-time tuition and fees vary according to program. Part-time tuition and fees vary according to course load and program. **College room and board:** $8414; **Room only:** $4968. Room and board charges vary according to board plan and housing facility.

FRESHMAN FINANCIAL AID (Fall 2012, est.) 170 applied for aid; of those 85% were deemed to have need. 94% of freshmen with need received aid; of those 33% had need fully met. **Average percent of need met:** 72% (excluding resources awarded to replace EFC). **Average financial aid package:** $6970 (excluding resources awarded to replace EFC). 19% of all full-time freshmen had no need and received non-need-based gift aid.

UNDERGRADUATE FINANCIAL AID (Fall 2012, est.) 746 applied for aid; of those 85% were deemed to have need. 98% of undergraduates with need received aid; of those 30% had need fully met. **Average percent of need met:** 75% (excluding resources awarded to replace EFC). **Average financial aid package:** $7249 (excluding resources awarded to replace EFC). 15% of all full-time undergraduates had no need and received non-need-based gift aid.

GIFT AID (NEED-BASED) Total amount: $2,657,142 (74% federal, 26% state). **Receiving aid:** Freshmen: 73% (125); all full-time undergraduates: 64% (493). **Average award:** Freshmen: $5099; Undergraduates: $5159. **Scholarships, grants, and awards:** Federal Pell, FSEOG, state, Federal Nursing.

GIFT AID (NON-NEED-BASED) Total amount: $1,056,917 (69% state, 23% institutional, 8% external sources). **Receiving aid:** Freshmen: 51% (88). Undergraduates: 37% (288). **Average award:** Freshmen: $1887. Undergraduates: $2040. **Scholarships, grants, and awards by category:** Academic interests/achievement: 292 awards ($329,295 total): general academic interests/achievements. Special achievements/activities: 9 awards ($4500 total): cheerleading/drum major. Special characteristics: 21 awards ($21,000 total): first-generation college students. **Tuition waivers:** Full or partial for senior citizens. **ROTC:** Army.

LOANS Student loans: $4,119,198 (42% need-based, 58% non-need-based). 69% of past graduating class borrowed through all loan programs. **Average indebtedness per student:** $13,184. **Average need-based loan:** Freshmen: $3751. Undergraduates: $4271. **Parent loans:** $419,352 (100% non-need-based). **Programs:** Federal Direct (Subsidized and Unsubsidized Stafford, PLUS), Perkins, college/university.

WORK-STUDY Federal work-study: Total amount: $143,000; 22 jobs averaging $1514. **State or other work-study/employment:** Total amount: $166,854 (100% non-need-based). 139 part-time jobs averaging $1339.

ATHLETIC AWARDS Total amount: $786,025 (100% non-need-based).

APPLYING FOR FINANCIAL AID Required financial aid form: FAFSA. **Financial aid deadline (priority):** 3/1. **Notification date:** Continuous beginning 4/1. Students must reply within 4 weeks of notification.

CONTACT Mr. Michael A. White, Director of Financial Aid Services, West Virginia University Institute of Technology, 405 Fayette Pike, Old Main, Room 206, Box 40, Montgomery, WV 25136, 304-442-3140 or toll-free 888-554-8324. Fax: 304-442-3053. E-mail: michael.white@mail.wvu.edu. Website: http://www.wvutech.edu/.

WEST VIRGINIA WESLEYAN COLLEGE
Buckhannon, WV

Tuition & fees: $26,794	Average undergraduate aid package: $24,216

ABOUT THE INSTITUTION Independent United Methodist Church, coed. **Awards:** bachelor's and master's degrees. 62 undergraduate majors. **Total**

enrollment: 1,394. Undergraduates: 1,315. Freshmen: 405. Federal methodology is used as a basis for awarding need-based institutional aid.

UNDERGRADUATE EXPENSES for 2013–2014 *Application fee:* $35. *Comprehensive fee:* $34,534 includes full-time tuition ($25,650), mandatory fees ($1144), and room and board ($7740). Full-time tuition and fees vary according to course load. Room and board charges vary according to board plan and housing facility. Part-time tuition and fees vary according to course load.

FRESHMAN FINANCIAL AID (Fall 2012, est.) 387 applied for aid; of those 89% were deemed to have need. 100% of freshmen with need received aid; of those 32% had need fully met. *Average percent of need met:* 85% (excluding resources awarded to replace EFC). *Average financial aid package:* $23,523 (excluding resources awarded to replace EFC). 15% of all full-time freshmen had no need and received non-need-based gift aid.

UNDERGRADUATE FINANCIAL AID (Fall 2012, est.) 1,132 applied for aid; of those 90% were deemed to have need. 100% of undergraduates with need received aid; of those 32% had need fully met. *Average percent of need met:* 86% (excluding resources awarded to replace EFC). *Average financial aid package:* $24,216 (excluding resources awarded to replace EFC). 21% of all full-time undergraduates had no need and received non-need-based gift aid.

GIFT AID (NEED-BASED) *Total amount:* $18,363,080 (12% federal, 5% state, 80% institutional, 3% external sources). *Receiving aid:* Freshmen: 85% (344); all full-time undergraduates: 79% (1,016). *Average award:* Freshmen: $20,198; Undergraduates: $18,074. *Scholarships, grants, and awards:* Federal Pell, FSEOG, state, private, college/university gift aid from institutional funds, Federal Nursing.

GIFT AID (NON-NEED-BASED) *Total amount:* $5,545,281 (32% state, 67% institutional, 1% external sources). *Receiving aid:* Freshmen: 16% (63). Undergraduates: 14% (183). *Average award:* Freshmen: $13,269. Undergraduates: $14,102. *Scholarships, grants, and awards by category: Academic interests/achievement:* English, general academic interests/achievements, physical sciences. *Creative arts/performance:* art/fine arts, music, performing arts, theater/drama. *Special achievements/activities:* community service, leadership, religious involvement. *Special characteristics:* children and siblings of alumni, children of faculty/staff, general special characteristics, international students, relatives of clergy, religious affiliation. *Tuition waivers:* Full or partial for employees or children of employees.

LOANS *Student loans:* $7,284,577 (60% need-based, 40% non-need-based). 68% of past graduating class borrowed through all loan programs. *Average indebtedness per student:* $25,655. *Average need-based loan:* Freshmen: $3637. Undergraduates: $4450. *Parent loans:* $1,266,801 (100% non-need-based). *Programs:* Federal Direct (Subsidized and Unsubsidized Stafford, PLUS), Perkins, Federal Nursing.

WORK-STUDY *Federal work-study:* Total amount: $305,347; jobs available. *State or other work-study/employment:* Total amount: $82,789 (17% need-based, 83% non-need-based). Part-time jobs available.

ATHLETIC AWARDS Total amount: $2,770,067 (63% need-based, 37% non-need-based).

APPLYING FOR FINANCIAL AID *Required financial aid form:* FAFSA. *Financial aid deadline (priority):* 2/15. *Notification date:* Continuous beginning 3/1.

CONTACT Susan George, Director of Financial Aid, West Virginia Wesleyan College, 59 College Avenue, Buckhannon, WV 26201, 304-473-8080 or toll-free 800-722-9933. *E-mail:* george_s@wvwc.edu.
Website: http://www.wvwc.edu/.

WESTWOOD COLLEGE–ANAHEIM
Anaheim, CA

CONTACT Financial Aid Office, Westwood College–Anaheim, 1551 South Douglass Road, Anaheim, CA 92806, 714-704-2721 or toll-free 877-840-8999.
Website: http://www.westwood.edu/.

WESTWOOD COLLEGE–ANNANDALE CAMPUS
Annandale, VA

CONTACT Financial Aid Office, Westwood College–Annandale Campus, 7619 Little River Turnpike, 5th Floor, Annandale, VA 22003, 706-642-3633 or toll-free 877-305-0049.
Website: http://www.westwood.edu/.

WESTWOOD COLLEGE–ARLINGTON BALLSTON CAMPUS
Arlington, VA

CONTACT Financial Aid Office, Westwood College–Arlington Ballston Campus, 4420 North Fairfax Drive, Arlington, VA 22203, 703-243-1662 or toll-free 877-268-5278.
Website: http://www.westwood.edu/.

WESTWOOD COLLEGE–ATLANTA MIDTOWN
Atlanta, GA

CONTACT Financial Aid Office, Westwood College–Atlanta Midtown, 1100 Spring Street, Suite 102, Atlanta, GA 30309, 404-745-9862 or toll-free 800-613-4595.
Website: http://www.westwood.edu/.

WESTWOOD COLLEGE–ATLANTA NORTHLAKE
Atlanta, GA

CONTACT Financial Aid Office, Westwood College–Atlanta Northlake, 2309 Parklake Drive, NE, Building 10, Atlanta, GA 30345, 404-962-2998 or toll-free 866-821-6145.
Website: http://www.westwood.edu/.

WESTWOOD COLLEGE–CHICAGO DU PAGE
Woodridge, IL

CONTACT Patty Zavala, Senior Student Finance Specialist, Westwood College–Chicago Du Page, 7155 Janes Avenue, Woodridge, IL 60517, 630-434-8244 or toll-free 866-721-7647.
Website: http://www.westwood.edu/.

WESTWOOD COLLEGE–CHICAGO LOOP CAMPUS
Chicago, IL

CONTACT Financial Aid Office, Westwood College–Chicago Loop Campus, 1 North State Street, Suite 1000, Chicago, IL 60602, 312-739-0890 or toll-free 800-693-5411.
Website: http://www.westwood.edu/.

WESTWOOD COLLEGE–CHICAGO O'HARE AIRPORT
Chicago, IL

CONTACT Financial Aid Office, Westwood College–Chicago O'Hare Airport, 8501 West Higgins Road, Suite 100, Chicago, IL 60631, 773-380-6801 or toll-free 866-235-2457.
Website: http://www.westwood.edu/.

WESTWOOD COLLEGE–CHICAGO RIVER OAKS
Calumet City, IL

CONTACT Financial Aid Office, Westwood College–Chicago River Oaks, 80 River Oaks Drive, Suite 111, Calumet City, IL 60409, 708-832-9760 or toll-free 888-549-4960.
Website: http://www.westwood.edu/.

WESTWOOD COLLEGE–DENVER NORTH
Denver, CO

CONTACT Admissions Office, Westwood College–Denver North, 7350 North Broadway, Denver, CO 80221, 800-875-6050 or toll-free 800-281-2978.
Website: http://www.westwood.edu/.

WESTWOOD COLLEGE–DENVER SOUTH
Denver, CO

CONTACT Financial Aid Office, Westwood College–Denver South, 3150 South Sheridan Boulevard, Denver, CO 80227, 303-934-1122 or toll-free 800-281-2978.
Website: http://www.westwood.edu/.

WESTWOOD COLLEGE–INLAND EMPIRE
Upland, CA

CONTACT Financial Aid Office, Westwood College–Inland Empire, 20 West 7th Street, Upland, CA 91786, 909-931-7599 or toll-free 866-221-5632.
Website: http://www.westwood.edu/.

WESTWOOD COLLEGE–LOS ANGELES
Los Angeles, CA

CONTACT Financial Aid Office, Westwood College–Los Angeles, 3250 Wilshire Boulevard, 4th Floor, Los Angeles, CA 90010, 213-382-2328 or toll-free 866-930-9256.
Website: http://www.westwood.edu/.

WESTWOOD COLLEGE–SOUTH BAY CAMPUS
Torrance, CA

CONTACT Financial Aid Office, Westwood College–South Bay Campus, 19700 South Vermont Avenue, Suite 100, Torrance, CA 90502, 310-522-2088 or toll-free 888-403-3308.
Website: http://www.westwood.edu/.

WHEATON COLLEGE
Wheaton, IL

Tuition & fees: $30,120	Average undergraduate aid package: $22,384

ABOUT THE INSTITUTION Independent nondenominational, coed. *Awards:* certificates, bachelor's, master's, and doctoral degrees. 37 undergraduate majors. *Total enrollment:* 3,034. Undergraduates: 2,508. Freshmen: 598. Both federal and institutional methodology are used as a basis for awarding need-based institutional aid.

UNDERGRADUATE EXPENSES for 2013–2014 *Application fee:* $50. *Comprehensive fee:* $38,680 includes full-time tuition ($30,120) and room and board ($8560). *College room only:* $5050. Room and board charges vary according to board plan and housing facility. *Part-time tuition:* $1255 per credit hour. Part-time tuition and fees vary according to course load.

FRESHMAN FINANCIAL AID (Fall 2011) 447 applied for aid; of those 74% were deemed to have need. 100% of freshmen with need received aid; of those 15% had need fully met. *Average percent of need met:* 88% (excluding resources awarded to replace EFC). *Average financial aid package:* $22,466 (excluding resources awarded to replace EFC). 15% of all full-time freshmen had no need and received non-need-based gift aid.

UNDERGRADUATE FINANCIAL AID (Fall 2011) 1,638 applied for aid; of those 80% were deemed to have need. 100% of undergraduates with need received aid; of those 23% had need fully met. *Average percent of need met:* 88% (excluding resources awarded to replace EFC). *Average financial aid package:* $22,384 (excluding resources awarded to replace EFC). 13% of all full-time undergraduates had no need and received non-need-based gift aid.

GIFT AID (NEED-BASED) *Total amount:* $24,760,457 (11% federal, 2% state, 82% institutional, 5% external sources). *Receiving aid:* Freshmen: 55% (328); all full-time undergraduates: 53% (1,290). *Average award:* Freshmen: $18,569; Undergraduates: $18,382. *Scholarships, grants, and awards:* Federal Pell, FSEOG, state, college/university gift aid from institutional funds.

GIFT AID (NON-NEED-BASED) *Total amount:* $2,460,006 (68% institutional, 32% external sources). *Receiving aid:* Freshmen: 19% (116). Undergraduates: 17% (413). *Average award:* Freshmen: $5464. Undergraduates: $5068. *Scholarships, grants, and awards by category:* Academic interests/achievement: 731 awards ($1,926,920 total): biological sciences, business, computer science, education, foreign languages, general academic interests/achievements, health fields, humanities, mathematics, military science, physical sciences, premedicine, religion/biblical studies, social sciences. Creative arts/performance: 93 awards ($276,266 total): art/fine arts, music. Special achievements/activities: 41 awards ($185,661 total): general special achievements/activities. Special characteristics: 117 awards ($1,189,610 total): ethnic background, general special characteristics, handicapped students. *ROTC:* Army, Air Force cooperative.

LOANS *Student loans:* $9,642,830 (88% need-based, 12% non-need-based). 59% of past graduating class borrowed through all loan programs. *Average indebtedness per student:* $24,067. *Average need-based loan:* Freshmen: $4840. Undergraduates: $4848. *Parent loans:* $3,013,390 (75% need-based, 25% non-need-based). *Programs:* Federal Direct (Subsidized and Unsubsidized Stafford, PLUS), Perkins.

WORK-STUDY *Federal work-study:* Total amount: $228,839; 172 jobs averaging $1331.

APPLYING FOR FINANCIAL AID *Required financial aid forms:* FAFSA, institution's own form. *Financial aid deadline (priority):* 2/15. *Notification date:* Continuous beginning 3/10.

CONTACT Ms. Karen Belling, Director of Financial Aid, Wheaton College, 501 College Avenue, Wheaton, IL 60187-5593, 630-752-5021 or toll-free 800-222-2419. *E-mail:* finaid@wheaton.edu.
Website: http://www.wheaton.edu/.

WHEATON COLLEGE
Norton, MA

Tuition & fees: $45,074	Average undergraduate aid package: $34,888

ABOUT THE INSTITUTION Independent, coed. *Awards:* bachelor's degrees. 41 undergraduate majors. *Total enrollment:* 1,616. Undergraduates: 1,619. Freshmen: 466. Institutional methodology is used as a basis for awarding need-based institutional aid.

UNDERGRADUATE EXPENSES for 2013–2014 *Application fee:* $50. *One-time required fee:* $50. *Comprehensive fee:* $56,574 includes full-time tuition ($44,780), mandatory fees ($294), and room and board ($11,500). *College room only:* $6140. *Payment plan:* Tuition prepayment.

FRESHMAN FINANCIAL AID (Fall 2012, est.) 365 applied for aid; of those 88% were deemed to have need. 100% of freshmen with need received aid; of those 52% had need fully met. *Average percent of need met:* 94% (excluding resources awarded to replace EFC). *Average financial aid package:* $33,378 (excluding resources awarded to replace EFC). 25% of all full-time freshmen had no need and received non-need-based gift aid.

UNDERGRADUATE FINANCIAL AID (Fall 2012, est.) 1,156 applied for aid; of those 91% were deemed to have need. 100% of undergraduates with need received aid; of those 41% had need fully met. *Average percent of need met:* 94% (excluding resources awarded to replace EFC). *Average financial aid package:* $34,888 (excluding resources awarded to replace EFC). 19% of all full-time undergraduates had no need and received non-need-based gift aid.

GIFT AID (NEED-BASED) *Total amount:* $30,873,497 (6% federal, 2% state, 90% institutional, 2% external sources). *Receiving aid:* Freshmen: 65% (301); all full-time undergraduates: 60% (970). *Average award:* Freshmen: $27,905; Undergraduates: $28,526. *Scholarships, grants, and awards:* Federal Pell, FSEOG, state, private, college/university gift aid from institutional funds.

GIFT AID (NON-NEED-BASED) *Total amount:* $3,983,510 (91% institutional, 9% external sources). *Receiving aid:* Freshmen: 4% (19). Undergraduates: 2% (29). *Average award:* Freshmen: $11,008. Undergraduates: $12,097. *Scholarships, grants, and awards by category: Academic interests/achievement:* 574 awards ($7,749,266 total): general academic interests/achievements. *Tuition waivers:* Full or partial for employees or children of employees. *ROTC:* Army cooperative.

LOANS *Student loans:* $8,425,106 (76% need-based, 24% non-need-based). 61% of past graduating class borrowed through all loan programs. *Average indebtedness per student:* $27,520. *Average need-based loan:* Freshmen: $3562. Undergraduates: $4432. *Parent loans:* $4,431,452 (100% non-need-based). *Programs:* Federal Direct (Subsidized and Unsubsidized Stafford, PLUS), Perkins, private loans, MEFA Loans.

WORK-STUDY *Federal work-study:* Total amount: $1,371,458; 818 jobs averaging $1677. *State or other work-study/employment:* Total amount: $560,690 (56% need-based, 44% non-need-based). 311 part-time jobs averaging $1802.

APPLYING FOR FINANCIAL AID *Required financial aid forms:* FAFSA, CSS Financial Aid PROFILE, business/farm supplement, federal income tax form(s). *Financial aid deadline:* 2/1. *Notification date:* 4/1. Students must reply by 5/1.

CONTACT Ms. Susan Beard, Director of Financial Aid Programs, Wheaton College, 26 East Main Street, Norton, MA 02766, 508-286-8232 or toll-free 800-394-6003. *Fax:* 508-286-3787. *E-mail:* sfs@wheatonma.edu. *Website:* http://www.wheatoncollege.edu/.

WHEELING JESUIT UNIVERSITY
Wheeling, WV

Tuition & fees: $25,640	Average undergraduate aid package: $22,696

ABOUT THE INSTITUTION Independent Roman Catholic (Jesuit), coed. *Awards:* certificates, bachelor's, master's, and doctoral degrees. 68 undergraduate majors. *Total enrollment:* 1,563. Undergraduates: 1,173. Freshmen: 268. Federal methodology is used as a basis for awarding need-based institutional aid.

UNDERGRADUATE EXPENSES for 2013–2014 *Application fee:* $25. *Comprehensive fee:* $30,640 includes full-time tuition ($24,650), mandatory fees ($990),

and room and board ($5000). Room and board charges vary according to board plan and housing facility. *Part-time tuition:* $675 per credit hour.

FRESHMAN FINANCIAL AID (Fall 2012, est.) 241 applied for aid; of those 91% were deemed to have need. 100% of freshmen with need received aid; of those 37% had need fully met. *Average percent of need met:* 97% (excluding resources awarded to replace EFC). *Average financial aid package:* $21,386 (excluding resources awarded to replace EFC). 18% of all full-time freshmen had no need and received non-need-based gift aid.

UNDERGRADUATE FINANCIAL AID (Fall 2012, est.) 766 applied for aid; of those 89% were deemed to have need. 100% of undergraduates with need received aid; of those 35% had need fully met. *Average percent of need met:* 95% (excluding resources awarded to replace EFC). *Average financial aid package:* $22,696 (excluding resources awarded to replace EFC). 21% of all full-time undergraduates had no need and received non-need-based gift aid.

GIFT AID (NEED-BASED) *Total amount:* $2,899,248 (48% federal, 10% state, 42% institutional). *Receiving aid:* Freshmen: 54% (145); all full-time undergraduates: 53% (467). *Average award:* Freshmen: $6143; Undergraduates: $6017. *Scholarships, grants, and awards:* Federal Pell, FSEOG, state, private, college/university gift aid from institutional funds, Federal Nursing.

GIFT AID (NON-NEED-BASED) *Total amount:* $8,952,374 (1% federal, 7% state, 88% institutional, 4% external sources). *Receiving aid:* Freshmen: 68% (181). Undergraduates: 71% (616). *Average award:* Freshmen: $10,040. Undergraduates: $12,197. *Scholarships, grants, and awards by category: Academic interests/achievement:* 659 awards ($6,806,297 total): general academic interests/achievements, premedicine. *Creative arts/performance:* 35 awards ($74,000 total): music. *Special achievements/activities:* 63 awards ($272,775 total): community service, general special achievements/activities. *Special characteristics:* 169 awards ($955,917 total): children and siblings of alumni, children of faculty/staff, general special characteristics, religious affiliation. *Tuition waivers:* Full or partial for employees or children of employees.

LOANS *Student loans:* $10,680,295 (29% need-based, 71% non-need-based). 79% of past graduating class borrowed through all loan programs. *Average indebtedness per student:* $30,516. *Average need-based loan:* Freshmen: $4275. Undergraduates: $4818. *Parent loans:* $694,724 (100% non-need-based). *Programs:* Federal Direct (Subsidized and Unsubsidized Stafford, PLUS), Perkins, Federal Nursing, alternative loans.

WORK-STUDY *Federal work-study:* Total amount: $184,005; 148 jobs averaging $2200. *State or other work-study/employment:* Total amount: $334,172 (100% non-need-based). 159 part-time jobs averaging $2200.

ATHLETIC AWARDS Total amount: $1,527,128 (100% non-need-based).

APPLYING FOR FINANCIAL AID *Required financial aid forms:* FAFSA, institution's own form. *Financial aid deadline (priority):* 3/1. *Notification date:* Continuous beginning 3/15. Students must reply within 2 weeks of notification.

CONTACT Christie Tomczyk, Director of Financial Aid, Wheeling Jesuit University, 316 Washington Avenue, Wheeling, WV 26003-6295, 304-243-2304 or toll-free 800-624-6992 Ext. 2359. *Fax:* 304-243-4397. *E-mail:* finaid@wju.edu. *Website:* http://www.wju.edu/.

WHEELOCK COLLEGE
Boston, MA

Tuition & fees: $30,955	Average undergraduate aid package: $20,934

ABOUT THE INSTITUTION Independent, coed, primarily women. *Awards:* certificates, bachelor's, and master's degrees. 16 undergraduate majors. *Total enrollment:* 1,308. Undergraduates: 916. Freshmen: 230. Federal methodology is used as a basis for awarding need-based institutional aid.

UNDERGRADUATE EXPENSES for 2013–2014 *Application fee:* $15. *Comprehensive fee:* $43,755 includes full-time tuition ($29,860), mandatory fees ($1095), and room and board ($12,800). Full-time tuition and fees vary according to course load. *Part-time tuition:* $935 per credit hour. *Part-time fees:* $62 per credit. Part-time tuition and fees vary according to course load.

FRESHMAN FINANCIAL AID (Fall 2012, est.) 189 applied for aid; of those 92% were deemed to have need. 99% of freshmen with need received aid; of those 17% had need fully met. *Average percent of need met:* 64% (excluding resources awarded to replace EFC). *Average financial aid package:* $20,524 (excluding resources

awarded to replace EFC). 13% of all full-time freshmen had no need and received non-need-based gift aid.

UNDERGRADUATE FINANCIAL AID (Fall 2012, est.) 752 applied for aid; of those 94% were deemed to have need. 99% of undergraduates with need received aid; of those 12% had need fully met. *Average percent of need met:* 62% (excluding resources awarded to replace EFC). *Average financial aid package:* $20,934 (excluding resources awarded to replace EFC). 13% of all full-time undergraduates had no need and received non-need-based gift aid.

GIFT AID (NEED-BASED) *Total amount:* $11,657,313 (13% federal, 4% state, 80% institutional, 3% external sources). *Receiving aid:* Freshmen: 86% (173); all full-time undergraduates: 84% (695). *Average award:* Freshmen: $17,447; Undergraduates: $16,565. *Scholarships, grants, and awards:* Federal Pell, FSEOG, state, private, college/university gift aid from institutional funds.

GIFT AID (NON-NEED-BASED) *Total amount:* $1,782,343 (96% institutional, 4% external sources). *Receiving aid:* Freshmen: 10% (21). Undergraduates: 7% (61). *Average award:* Freshmen: $13,592. Undergraduates: $12,901. *Scholarships, grants, and awards by category: Academic interests/achievement:* general academic interests/achievements. *Tuition waivers:* Full or partial for employees or children of employees.

LOANS *Student loans:* $8,423,087 (76% need-based, 24% non-need-based). 82% of past graduating class borrowed through all loan programs. *Average indebtedness per student:* $49,439. *Average need-based loan:* Freshmen: $3292. Undergraduates: $4683. *Parent loans:* $2,460,993 (53% need-based, 47% non-need-based). *Programs:* Federal Direct (Subsidized and Unsubsidized Stafford, PLUS), Perkins, college/university.

WORK-STUDY *Federal work-study:* Total amount: $236,707; 160 jobs averaging $1800.

APPLYING FOR FINANCIAL AID *Required financial aid form:* FAFSA. *Financial aid deadline (priority):* 2/15. *Notification date:* Continuous beginning 3/15. Students must reply by 5/1.

CONTACT Roxanne Dumas, Director of Financial Aid, Wheelock College, 200 The Riverway, Boston, MA 02215-4176, 617-879-2443 or toll-free 800-734-5212. *Fax:* 617-879-2470. *E-mail:* finaid@wheelock.edu. *Website:* http://www.wheelock.edu/.

WHITMAN COLLEGE
Walla Walla, WA

Tuition & fees: $42,106	Average undergraduate aid package: $32,267

ABOUT THE INSTITUTION Independent, coed. *Awards:* bachelor's degrees. 41 undergraduate majors. *Total enrollment:* 1,539. Undergraduates: 1,539. Freshmen: 381. Both federal and institutional methodology are used as a basis for awarding need-based institutional aid.

UNDERGRADUATE EXPENSES for 2013–2014 *Application fee:* $50. *Comprehensive fee:* $52,666 includes full-time tuition ($41,790), mandatory fees ($316), and room and board ($10,560). *College room only:* $4880. Room and board charges vary according to board plan and housing facility. *Part-time tuition:* $1741 per credit.

FRESHMAN FINANCIAL AID (Fall 2012, est.) 245 applied for aid; of those 67% were deemed to have need. 100% of freshmen with need received aid; of those 52% had need fully met. *Average percent of need met:* 93% (excluding resources awarded to replace EFC). *Average financial aid package:* $31,278 (excluding resources awarded to replace EFC). 32% of all full-time freshmen had no need and received non-need-based gift aid.

UNDERGRADUATE FINANCIAL AID (Fall 2012, est.) 871 applied for aid; of those 83% were deemed to have need. 100% of undergraduates with need received aid; of those 53% had need fully met. *Average percent of need met:* 97% (excluding resources awarded to replace EFC). *Average financial aid package:* $32,267 (excluding resources awarded to replace EFC). 29% of all full-time undergraduates had no need and received non-need-based gift aid.

GIFT AID (NEED-BASED) *Total amount:* $17,474,656 (4% federal, 3% state, 93% institutional). *Receiving aid:* Freshmen: 43% (165); all full-time undergraduates: 46% (724). *Average award:* Freshmen: $26,170; Undergraduates: $26,076. *Scholarships, grants, and awards:* Federal Pell, FSEOG, state, private, college/university gift aid from institutional funds.

GIFT AID (NON-NEED-BASED) *Total amount:* $6,663,796 (2% state, 84% institutional, 14% external sources). *Receiving aid:* Freshmen: 22% (83). Undergrad-

uates: 15% (232). *Average award:* Freshmen: $9028. Undergraduates: $8745. *Scholarships, grants, and awards by category: Academic interests/achievement:* general academic interests/achievements. *Creative arts/performance:* art/fine arts, debating, music, theater/drama. *Special characteristics:* ethnic background, first-generation college students, international students, veterans, veterans' children. *Tuition waivers:* Full or partial for employees or children of employees.

LOANS *Student loans:* $4,932,333 (74% need-based, 26% non-need-based). 48% of past graduating class borrowed through all loan programs. *Average indebtedness per student:* $16,797. *Average need-based loan:* Freshmen: $4308. Undergraduates: $5025. *Parent loans:* $1,400,165 (100% non-need-based). *Programs:* Federal Direct (Subsidized and Unsubsidized Stafford, PLUS), Perkins, alternative loans.

WORK-STUDY *Federal work-study:* Total amount: $907,739; 480 jobs averaging $1891. *State or other work-study/employment:* Total amount: $134,888 (66% need-based, 34% non-need-based). 162 part-time jobs averaging $1600.

APPLYING FOR FINANCIAL AID *Required financial aid forms:* FAFSA, CSS Financial Aid PROFILE. *Financial aid deadline:* 2/1 (priority: 11/15). *Notification date:* Continuous beginning 12/18. Students must reply within 2 weeks of notification.

CONTACT Tyson Harlow, Assistant Director, Whitman College, 345 Boyer Avenue, Walla Walla, WA 99362-2046, 509-527-5178 or toll-free 877-462-9448. *Fax:* 509-527-4967. *Website:* http://www.whitman.edu/.

WHITTIER COLLEGE
Whittier, CA

Tuition & fees: $40,096	Average undergraduate aid package: $30,737

ABOUT THE INSTITUTION Independent, coed. *Awards:* bachelor's, master's, and doctoral degrees. 25 undergraduate majors. *Total enrollment:* 2,448. Undergraduates: 1,670. Freshmen: 418. Federal methodology is used as a basis for awarding need-based institutional aid.

UNDERGRADUATE EXPENSES for 2013–2014 *Application fee:* $50. *One-time required fee:* $200. *Comprehensive fee:* $51,590 includes full-time tuition ($39,736), mandatory fees ($360), and room and board ($11,494). *College room only:* $6412. Room and board charges vary according to board plan. *Part-time tuition:* $1610 per unit.

FRESHMAN FINANCIAL AID (Fall 2012, est.) 354 applied for aid; of those 93% were deemed to have need. 100% of freshmen with need received aid; of those 12% had need fully met. *Average percent of need met:* 72% (excluding resources awarded to replace EFC). *Average financial aid package:* $30,802 (excluding resources awarded to replace EFC). 15% of all full-time freshmen had no need and received non-need-based gift aid.

UNDERGRADUATE FINANCIAL AID (Fall 2012, est.) 1,374 applied for aid; of those 93% were deemed to have need. 100% of undergraduates with need received aid; of those 11% had need fully met. *Average percent of need met:* 72% (excluding resources awarded to replace EFC). *Average financial aid package:* $30,737 (excluding resources awarded to replace EFC). 16% of all full-time undergraduates had no need and received non-need-based gift aid.

GIFT AID (NEED-BASED) *Total amount:* $26,359,697 (11% federal, 13% state, 75% institutional, 1% external sources). *Receiving aid:* Freshmen: 74% (301); all full-time undergraduates: 73% (1,168). *Average award:* Freshmen: $29,652; Undergraduates: $27,547. *Scholarships, grants, and awards:* Federal Pell, FSEOG, state, private, college/university gift aid from institutional funds.

GIFT AID (NON-NEED-BASED) *Total amount:* $9,436,917 (1% state, 98% institutional, 1% external sources). *Receiving aid:* Freshmen: 7% (28). Undergraduates: 6% (97). *Average award:* Freshmen: $17,849. Undergraduates: $18,250. *Scholarships, grants, and awards by category: Academic interests/achievement:* general academic interests/achievements. *Creative arts/performance:* art/fine arts, music, theater/drama. *Special characteristics:* children and siblings of alumni, children of faculty/staff, international students. *Tuition waivers:* Full or partial for children of alumni, employees or children of employees. *ROTC:* Army cooperative, Air Force cooperative.

LOANS *Student loans:* $11,651,546 (70% need-based, 30% non-need-based). 74% of past graduating class borrowed through all loan programs. *Average indebtedness per student:* $25,212. *Average need-based loan:* Freshmen: $4586. Undergraduates: $6043. *Parent loans:* $3,898,242 (75% need-based, 25% non-need-based).

Programs: Federal Direct (Subsidized and Unsubsidized Stafford, PLUS), Perkins, alternative loans.

WORK-STUDY *Federal work-study:* Total amount: $959,735; jobs available. *State or other work-study/employment:* Total amount: $718,640 (33% need-based, 67% non-need-based). Part-time jobs available.

APPLYING FOR FINANCIAL AID *Required financial aid form:* FAFSA. *Financial aid deadline:* 6/30 (priority: 3/1). *Notification date:* Continuous beginning 2/15. Students must reply within 2 weeks of notification.

CONTACT Mr. David Carnevale, Director of Student Financing, Whittier College, 13406 East Philadelphia Street, Whittier, CA 90608-0634, 562-907-4285. *Fax:* 562-464-4560. *E-mail:* dcarneva@whittier.edu.
Website: http://www.whittier.edu/.

WHITWORTH UNIVERSITY
Spokane, WA

Tuition & fees: $34,346	Average undergraduate aid package: $27,969

ABOUT THE INSTITUTION Independent Presbyterian, coed. *Awards:* certificates, bachelor's, and master's degrees. 44 undergraduate majors. *Total enrollment:* 2,568. Undergraduates: 2,348. Freshmen: 631. Federal methodology is used as a basis for awarding need-based institutional aid.

UNDERGRADUATE EXPENSES for 2013–2014 *Comprehensive fee:* $43,710 includes full-time tuition ($33,676), mandatory fees ($670), and room and board ($9364). *College room only:* $5076. Room and board charges vary according to board plan and housing facility. *Part-time tuition:* $1403 per credit.

FRESHMAN FINANCIAL AID (Fall 2012, est.) 549 applied for aid; of those 84% were deemed to have need. 100% of freshmen with need received aid; of those 20% had need fully met. *Average percent of need met:* 83% (excluding resources awarded to replace EFC). *Average financial aid package:* $29,994 (excluding resources awarded to replace EFC). 25% of all full-time freshmen had no need and received non-need-based gift aid.

UNDERGRADUATE FINANCIAL AID (Fall 2012, est.) 1,797 applied for aid; of those 89% were deemed to have need. 100% of undergraduates with need received aid; of those 19% had need fully met. *Average percent of need met:* 81% (excluding resources awarded to replace EFC). *Average financial aid package:* $27,969 (excluding resources awarded to replace EFC). 25% of all full-time undergraduates had no need and received non-need-based gift aid.

GIFT AID (NEED-BASED) *Total amount:* $31,654,045 (9% federal, 8% state, 80% institutional, 3% external sources). *Receiving aid:* Freshmen: 73% (459); all full-time undergraduates: 69% (1,579). *Average award:* Freshmen: $21,734; Undergraduates: $19,928. *Scholarships, grants, and awards:* Federal Pell, FSEOG, state, private, college/university gift aid from institutional funds.

GIFT AID (NON-NEED-BASED) *Total amount:* $9,654,389 (4% federal, 91% institutional, 5% external sources). *Receiving aid:* Freshmen: 10% (61). Undergraduates: 7% (156). *Average award:* Freshmen: $16,155. Undergraduates: $13,715. *Scholarships, grants, and awards by category:* Academic interests/achievement: 1,847 awards ($21,369,276 total): general academic interests/achievements, military science. *Creative arts/performance:* 210 awards ($632,218 total): art/fine arts, journalism/publications, music, theater/drama. *Special characteristics:* 372 awards ($912,206 total): children and siblings of alumni, ethnic background, international students, members of minority groups. *Tuition waivers:* Full or partial for employees or children of employees, senior citizens. *ROTC:* Army cooperative.

LOANS *Student loans:* $11,664,122 (80% need-based, 20% non-need-based). 64% of past graduating class borrowed through all loan programs. *Average indebtedness per student:* $23,636. *Average need-based loan:* Freshmen: $4188. Undergraduates: $4836. *Parent loans:* $4,611,627 (40% need-based, 60% non-need-based). *Programs:* Federal Direct (Subsidized and Unsubsidized Stafford, PLUS), Perkins.

WORK-STUDY *Federal work-study:* Total amount: $1,809,510; 749 jobs averaging $2318. *State or other work-study/employment:* Total amount: $267,633 (99% need-based, 1% non-need-based). 89 part-time jobs averaging $2953.

APPLYING FOR FINANCIAL AID *Required financial aid form:* FAFSA. *Financial aid deadline (priority):* 3/1. *Notification date:* Continuous beginning 3/15.

CONTACT Ms. Wendy Z. Olson, Director of Financial Aid, Whitworth University, 300 West Hawthorne Road, Spokane, WA 99251-0001, 509-777-4306 or toll-free 800-533-4668. *Fax:* 509-777-4601. *E-mail:* wolson@whitworth.edu.
Website: http://www.whitworth.edu/.

WICHITA STATE UNIVERSITY
Wichita, KS

Tuition & fees (KS res): $6442	Average undergraduate aid package: $7926

ABOUT THE INSTITUTION State-supported, coed. *Awards:* certificates, associate, bachelor's, master's, and doctoral degrees. 59 undergraduate majors. *Total enrollment:* 14,893. Undergraduates: 12,192. Freshmen: 1,359. Federal methodology is used as a basis for awarding need-based institutional aid.

UNDERGRADUATE EXPENSES for 2013–2014 *Application fee:* $30. *Tuition, state resident:* full-time $5205; part-time $173.50 per credit hour. *Tuition, nonresident:* full-time $13,239; part-time $441.30 per credit hour. *Required fees:* full-time $1237. Full-time tuition and fees vary according to course load, degree level, and student level. Part-time tuition and fees vary according to course load, degree level, and student level. *College room and board:* $6460. Room and board charges vary according to board plan and housing facility.

FRESHMAN FINANCIAL AID (Fall 2011) 1,079 applied for aid; of those 48% were deemed to have need. 98% of freshmen with need received aid; of those 72% had need fully met. *Average percent of need met:* 65% (excluding resources awarded to replace EFC). *Average financial aid package:* $4231 (excluding resources awarded to replace EFC). 36% of all full-time freshmen had no need and received non-need-based gift aid.

UNDERGRADUATE FINANCIAL AID (Fall 2011) 7,040 applied for aid; of those 59% were deemed to have need. 93% of undergraduates with need received aid; of those 68% had need fully met. *Average percent of need met:* 63% (excluding resources awarded to replace EFC). *Average financial aid package:* $7926 (excluding resources awarded to replace EFC). 16% of all full-time undergraduates had no need and received non-need-based gift aid.

GIFT AID (NEED-BASED) *Total amount:* $18,542,068 (96% federal, 3% state, 1% external sources). *Receiving aid:* Freshmen: 33% (378); all full-time undergraduates: 34% (2,648). *Average award:* Freshmen: $3947; Undergraduates: $4136. *Scholarships, grants, and awards:* Federal Pell, FSEOG, state, private, college/university gift aid from institutional funds, Bureau of Indian Affairs Grants.

GIFT AID (NON-NEED-BASED) *Total amount:* $10,149,917 (1% state, 89% institutional, 10% external sources). *Receiving aid:* Freshmen: 26% (297). Undergraduates: 17% (1,375). *Average award:* Freshmen: $2842. Undergraduates: $2014. *Scholarships, grants, and awards by category:* Academic interests/achievement: area/ethnic studies, biological sciences, business, communication, computer science, education, engineering/technologies, English, foreign languages, general academic interests/achievements, health fields, humanities, international studies, mathematics, physical sciences, premedicine, social sciences. *Creative arts/performance:* applied art and design, art/fine arts, creative writing, dance, debating, journalism/publications, music, performing arts, theater/drama. *Special achievements/activities:* cheerleading/drum major, general special achievements/activities, leadership, memberships. *Special characteristics:* adult students, children of faculty/staff, first-generation college students, international students, members of minority groups. *Tuition waivers:* Full or partial for employees or children of employees, senior citizens.

LOANS *Student loans:* $48,428,187 (47% need-based, 53% non-need-based). 53% of past graduating class borrowed through all loan programs. *Average indebtedness per student:* $21,068. *Average need-based loan:* Freshmen: $3203. Undergraduates: $4690. *Parent loans:* $930,135 (100% non-need-based). *Programs:* Federal Direct (Subsidized and Unsubsidized Stafford, PLUS), Perkins.

WORK-STUDY *Federal work-study:* Total amount: $297,792; 112 jobs averaging $3144. *State or other work-study/employment:* Total amount: $93,145 (100% need-based). Part-time jobs available.

ATHLETIC AWARDS Total amount: $1,737,101 (100% non-need-based).

APPLYING FOR FINANCIAL AID *Required financial aid forms:* FAFSA, institution's own form. *Financial aid deadline (priority):* 3/1. *Notification date:* Continuous beginning 3/15. Students must reply within 2 weeks of notification.

CONTACT Deborah D. Byers, Director of Financial Aid, Wichita State University, 1845 Fairmount Street, Wichita, KS 67260-0024, 316-978-3430 or toll-free 800-362-2594. *Fax:* 316-978-3396. *E-mail:* deb.byers@wichita.edu. *Website:* http://www.wichita.edu/.

WIDENER UNIVERSITY
Chester, PA

Tuition & fees: $36,382	Average undergraduate aid package: $26,380

ABOUT THE INSTITUTION Independent, coed. *Awards:* associate, bachelor's, master's, and doctoral degrees. 74 undergraduate majors. *Total enrollment:* 6,238. Undergraduates: 3,298. Freshmen: 717. Both federal and institutional methodology are used as a basis for awarding need-based institutional aid.

UNDERGRADUATE EXPENSES for 2013–2014 *Application fee:* $35. *Comprehensive fee:* $48,630 includes full-time tuition ($35,764), mandatory fees ($618), and room and board ($12,248). *College room only:* $6300. Full-time tuition and fees vary according to class time, course load, and program. Room and board charges vary according to board plan and housing facility. *Part-time tuition:* $1190 per credit hour.

FRESHMAN FINANCIAL AID (Fall 2012, est.) 673 applied for aid; of those 93% were deemed to have need. 100% of freshmen with need received aid; of those 20% had need fully met. *Average percent of need met:* 79% (excluding resources awarded to replace EFC). *Average financial aid package:* $28,530 (excluding resources awarded to replace EFC). 6% of all full-time freshmen had no need and received non-need-based gift aid.

UNDERGRADUATE FINANCIAL AID (Fall 2012, est.) 2,427 applied for aid; of those 93% were deemed to have need. 100% of undergraduates with need received aid; of those 17% had need fully met. *Average percent of need met:* 73% (excluding resources awarded to replace EFC). *Average financial aid package:* $26,380 (excluding resources awarded to replace EFC). 11% of all full-time undergraduates had no need and received non-need-based gift aid.

GIFT AID (NEED-BASED) *Total amount:* $44,466,410 (9% federal, 6% state, 83% institutional, 2% external sources). *Receiving aid:* Freshmen: 67% (473); all full-time undergraduates: 65% (1,773). *Average award:* Freshmen: $8920; Undergraduates: $8490. *Scholarships, grants, and awards:* Federal Pell, FSEOG, state, private, college/university gift aid from institutional funds, Federal Nursing.

GIFT AID (NON-NEED-BASED) *Total amount:* $5,525,665 (9% federal, 88% institutional, 3% external sources). *Receiving aid:* Freshmen: 79% (558). Undergraduates: 70% (1,912). *Average award:* Freshmen: $19,150. Undergraduates: $15,500. *Scholarships, grants, and awards by category:* Academic interests/achievement: 2,201 awards ($32,911,940 total): biological sciences, business, communication, computer science, education, engineering/technologies, English, foreign languages, general academic interests/achievements, health fields, humanities, international studies, mathematics, military science, physical sciences, premedicine, social sciences. *Creative arts/performance:* 59 awards ($223,000 total): dance, music. *Special achievements/activities:* 58 awards ($287,500 total): community service, general special achievements/activities, leadership. *Special characteristics:* 88 awards ($2,402,000 total): adult students, children of faculty/staff, ethnic background, international students. *Tuition waivers:* Full or partial for employees or children of employees, senior citizens. *ROTC:* Army, Naval cooperative, Air Force cooperative.

LOANS *Student loans:* $27,258,020 (95% need-based, 5% non-need-based). 88% of past graduating class borrowed through all loan programs. *Average indebtedness per student:* $40,460. *Average need-based loan:* Freshmen: $3650. Undergraduates: $4640. *Parent loans:* $8,128,370 (94% need-based, 6% non-need-based). *Programs:* Federal Direct (Subsidized and Unsubsidized Stafford, PLUS), Perkins.

WORK-STUDY *Federal work-study:* Total amount: $2,405,540; 1,617 jobs averaging $1480. *State or other work-study/employment:* Total amount: $416,320 (81% need-based, 19% non-need-based). Part-time jobs available.

APPLYING FOR FINANCIAL AID *Required financial aid form:* FAFSA. *Financial aid deadline (priority):* 2/15. *Notification date:* Continuous beginning 3/15. Students must reply within 4 weeks of notification.

CONTACT Thomas K. Malloy, Director of Student Financial Services, Widener University, One University Place, Chester, PA 19013-5792, 610-499-4161 or toll-free 888-WIDENER. *Fax:* 610-499-4687. *E-mail:* finaidmc@mail.widener.edu. *Website:* http://www.widener.edu/.

WILBERFORCE UNIVERSITY
Wilberforce, OH

CONTACT Director of Financial Aid, Wilberforce University, 1055 North Bickett Road, Wilberforce, OH 45384, 937-708-5727 or toll-free 800-367-8568. *Fax:* 937-376-4752. *Website:* http://www.wilberforce.edu/.

WILEY COLLEGE
Marshall, TX

ABOUT THE INSTITUTION Independent United Methodist Church, coed. 28 undergraduate majors.

GIFT AID (NEED-BASED) *Scholarships, grants, and awards:* Federal Pell, FSEOG, state, private, college/university gift aid from institutional funds, United Negro College Fund.

GIFT AID (NON-NEED-BASED) *Scholarships, grants, and awards by category:* Academic interests/achievement: biological sciences, business, communication, computer science, education, English, general academic interests/achievements, humanities, mathematics, physical sciences, religion/biblical studies, social sciences. *Creative arts/performance:* music. *Special characteristics:* children of faculty/staff, relatives of clergy, religious affiliation.

LOANS *Programs:* Federal Direct (Subsidized and Unsubsidized Stafford, PLUS), Perkins.

WORK-STUDY *Federal work-study:* Total amount: $264,321; 237 jobs averaging $1800. *State or other work-study/employment:* Total amount: $5553 (100% need-based). 5 part-time jobs averaging $1800.

APPLYING FOR FINANCIAL AID *Required financial aid forms:* FAFSA, institution's own form.

CONTACT Mr. Alan D. Jackson Jr., Director of Financial Aid, Wiley College, 711 Wiley Avenue, Marshall, TX 75670-5199, 903-927-3217 or toll-free 800-658-6889. *E-mail:* adjackson2@wileyc.edu. *Website:* http://www.wileyc.edu/.

WILKES UNIVERSITY
Wilkes-Barre, PA

Tuition & fees: $29,326	Average undergraduate aid package: $21,066

ABOUT THE INSTITUTION Independent, coed. *Awards:* bachelor's, master's, and doctoral degrees. 36 undergraduate majors. *Total enrollment:* 5,030. Undergraduates: 2,302. Freshmen: 596. Federal methodology is used as a basis for awarding need-based institutional aid.

UNDERGRADUATE EXPENSES for 2013–2014 *Application fee:* $40. *Comprehensive fee:* $41,360 includes full-time tuition ($27,908), mandatory fees ($1418), and room and board ($12,034). *College room only:* $7228. Room and board charges vary according to board plan and housing facility. *Part-time tuition:* $775 per credit hour. *Part-time fees:* $64 per credit hour.

FRESHMAN FINANCIAL AID (Fall 2012, est.) 553 applied for aid; of those 92% were deemed to have need. 100% of freshmen with need received aid; of those 10% had need fully met. *Average percent of need met:* 69% (excluding resources awarded to replace EFC). *Average financial aid package:* $20,936 (excluding resources awarded to replace EFC). 9% of all full-time freshmen had no need and received non-need-based gift aid.

UNDERGRADUATE FINANCIAL AID (Fall 2012, est.) 1,829 applied for aid; of those 93% were deemed to have need. 99% of undergraduates with need received aid; of those 11% had need fully met. *Average percent of need met:* 69% (excluding resources awarded to replace EFC). *Average financial aid package:* $21,066 (excluding resources awarded to replace EFC). 11% of all full-time undergraduates had no need and received non-need-based gift aid.

GIFT AID (NEED-BASED) *Total amount:* $28,856,974 (12% federal, 10% state, 77% institutional, 1% external sources). *Receiving aid:* Freshmen: 85% (502); all full-time undergraduates: 78% (1,627). *Average award:* Freshmen: $17,736; Undergraduates: $17,400. *Scholarships, grants, and awards:* Federal Pell, FSEOG, state, private, college/university gift aid from institutional funds.

GIFT AID (NON-NEED-BASED) *Total amount:* $2,643,787 (1% state, 94% institutional, 5% external sources). *Receiving aid:* Freshmen: 71% (421). Undergraduates: 66% (1,374). *Average award:* Freshmen: $11,223. Undergraduates: $10,670. *Scholarships, grants, and awards by category: Academic interests/achievement:* general academic interests/achievements. *Creative arts/performance:* performing arts, theater/drama. *Special achievements/activities:* general special achievements/activities, leadership. *Special characteristics:* children of faculty/staff. *Tuition waivers:* Full or partial for employees or children of employees. *ROTC:* Army cooperative, Air Force.

LOANS *Student loans:* $16,940,606 (91% need-based, 9% non-need-based). 86% of past graduating class borrowed through all loan programs. *Average indebtedness per student:* $38,442. *Average need-based loan:* Freshmen: $3445. Undergraduates: $4306. *Parent loans:* $4,346,232 (79% need-based, 21% non-need-based). *Programs:* Federal Direct (Subsidized and Unsubsidized Stafford, PLUS), Perkins, Federal Nursing, state, college/university, Gulf Oil Loan Fund, Rulison Evans Loan Fund. **WORK-STUDY** *Federal work-study:* Total amount: $259,270; jobs available. *State or other work-study/employment:* Part-time jobs available.

APPLYING FOR FINANCIAL AID *Required financial aid form:* FAFSA. *Financial aid deadline (priority):* 3/1. *Notification date:* Continuous.

CONTACT Melanie Wade, Vice President of Enrollment Services, Wilkes University, 84 West South Street, Wilkes-Barre, PA 18766, 570-408-4000 or toll-free 800-945-5378 Ext. 4400. *Fax:* 570-408-3000. *E-mail:* melanie.wade@wilkes.edu. *Website:* http://www.wilkes.edu/.

WILLAMETTE UNIVERSITY
Salem, OR

Tuition & fees: $40,874	Average undergraduate aid package: $32,296

ABOUT THE INSTITUTION Independent United Methodist, coed. *Awards:* bachelor's, master's, and doctoral degrees. 41 undergraduate majors. *Total enrollment:* 2,933. Undergraduates: 2,103. Freshmen: 525. Federal methodology is used as a basis for awarding need-based institutional aid.

UNDERGRADUATE EXPENSES for 2013–2014 *Application fee:* $50. *Comprehensive fee:* $50,694 includes full-time tuition ($40,560), mandatory fees ($314), and room and board ($9820). Full-time tuition and fees vary according to course load. Room and board charges vary according to board plan and housing facility. *Part-time tuition:* $5070 per course. Part-time tuition and fees vary according to course load. *Payment plan:* Tuition prepayment.

FRESHMAN FINANCIAL AID (Fall 2012, est.) 454 applied for aid; of those 81% were deemed to have need. 100% of freshmen with need received aid; of those 44% had need fully met. *Average percent of need met:* 86% (excluding resources awarded to replace EFC). *Average financial aid package:* $29,552 (excluding resources awarded to replace EFC). 30% of all full-time freshmen had no need and received non-need-based gift aid.

UNDERGRADUATE FINANCIAL AID (Fall 2012, est.) 1,465 applied for aid; of those 87% were deemed to have need. 100% of undergraduates with need received aid; of those 42% had need fully met. *Average percent of need met:* 87% (excluding resources awarded to replace EFC). *Average financial aid package:* $32,296 (excluding resources awarded to replace EFC). 31% of all full-time undergraduates had no need and received non-need-based gift aid.

GIFT AID (NEED-BASED) *Total amount:* $33,677,382 (7% federal, 1% state, 88% institutional, 4% external sources). *Receiving aid:* Freshmen: 69% (363); all full-time undergraduates: 65% (1,268). *Average award:* Freshmen: $23,699; Undergraduates: $25,099. *Scholarships, grants, and awards:* Federal Pell, FSEOG, state, private, college/university gift aid from institutional funds.

GIFT AID (NON-NEED-BASED) *Total amount:* $9,261,532 (98% institutional, 2% external sources). *Receiving aid:* Freshmen: 19% (98). Undergraduates: 13% (249). *Average award:* Freshmen: $16,032. Undergraduates: $15,128. *Scholarships, grants, and awards by category: Academic interests/achievement:* general academic interests/achievements. *Creative arts/performance:* general creative arts/performance. *Special achievements/activities:* general special achievements/activities. *Special characteristics:* general special characteristics. *Tuition waivers:* Full or partial for employees or children of employees. *ROTC:* Army cooperative, Air Force cooperative.

LOANS *Student loans:* $11,605,497 (89% need-based, 11% non-need-based). 61% of past graduating class borrowed through all loan programs. *Average indebtedness per student:* $26,740. *Average need-based loan:* Freshmen: $4152. Undergraduates: $5203. *Parent loans:* $3,116,731 (88% need-based, 12% non-need-based). *Programs:* Federal Direct (Subsidized and Unsubsidized Stafford, PLUS), Perkins. **WORK-STUDY** *Federal work-study:* Total amount: $1,758,664; jobs available. *State or other work-study/employment:* Part-time jobs available.

APPLYING FOR FINANCIAL AID *Required financial aid form:* FAFSA. *Financial aid deadline (priority):* 2/1. *Notification date:* Continuous beginning 4/1. Students must reply by 5/1 or within 2 weeks of notification.

CONTACT Patty Hoban, Director of Financial Aid, Willamette University, 900 State Street, Salem, OR 97301-3931, 503-370-6273 or toll-free 877-542-2787. *Fax:* 503-370-6588. *E-mail:* phoban@willamette.edu. *Website:* http://www.willamette.edu/.

WILLIAM CAREY UNIVERSITY
Hattiesburg, MS

CONTACT Ms. Brenda Pittman, Associate Director of Financial Aid, William Carey University, 498 Tuscan Avenue, Hattiesburg, MS 39401-5499, 601-318-6153 or toll-free 800-962-5991. *Website:* http://www.wmcarey.edu/.

WILLIAM JESSUP UNIVERSITY
Rocklin, CA

Tuition & fees: $22,900	Average undergraduate aid package: $18,852

ABOUT THE INSTITUTION Independent nondenominational, coed. *Awards:* certificates, associate, and bachelor's degrees. 13 undergraduate majors. *Total enrollment:* 896. Undergraduates: 869. Freshmen: 121. Federal methodology is used as a basis for awarding need-based institutional aid.

UNDERGRADUATE EXPENSES for 2013–2014 *Application fee:* $45. *Comprehensive fee:* $31,970 includes full-time tuition ($22,900) and room and board ($9070). Full-time tuition and fees vary according to course load. Room and board charges vary according to board plan and housing facility. *Part-time tuition:* $970 per credit hour. Part-time tuition and fees vary according to course load.

FRESHMAN FINANCIAL AID (Fall 2012, est.) 129 applied for aid; of those 91% were deemed to have need. 100% of freshmen with need received aid; of those 13% had need fully met. *Average percent of need met:* 73% (excluding resources awarded to replace EFC). *Average financial aid package:* $20,164 (excluding resources awarded to replace EFC). 11% of all full-time freshmen had no need and received non-need-based gift aid.

UNDERGRADUATE FINANCIAL AID (Fall 2012, est.) 724 applied for aid; of those 92% were deemed to have need. 100% of undergraduates with need received aid; of those 11% had need fully met. *Average percent of need met:* 66% (excluding resources awarded to replace EFC). *Average financial aid package:* $18,852 (excluding resources awarded to replace EFC). 13% of all full-time undergraduates had no need and received non-need-based gift aid.

GIFT AID (NEED-BASED) *Total amount:* $9,695,871 (20% federal, 26% state, 48% institutional, 6% external sources). *Receiving aid:* Freshmen: 87% (117); all full-time undergraduates: 83% (659). *Average award:* Freshmen: $17,433; Undergraduates: $15,258. *Scholarships, grants, and awards:* Federal Pell, FSEOG, state, private, college/university gift aid from institutional funds.

GIFT AID (NON-NEED-BASED) *Total amount:* $956,139 (71% institutional, 29% external sources). *Receiving aid:* Freshmen: 9% (12). Undergraduates: 6% (45). *Average award:* Freshmen: $4503. Undergraduates: $5775. *Scholarships, grants, and awards by category: Academic interests/achievement:* 497 awards ($1,837,566 total): area/ethnic studies, biological sciences, business, education, English, general academic interests/achievements, humanities, international studies, mathematics, religion/biblical studies, social sciences. *Creative arts/performance:* 138 awards ($357,131 total): art/fine arts, music, theater/drama. *Special achievements/activities:* 339 awards ($1,025,770 total): leadership, religious involvement. *Special characteristics:* 449 awards ($1,233,418 total): adult students, children of faculty/staff, ethnic background, international students, out-of-state students, previous college experience, relatives of clergy, siblings of current students, veterans, veterans' children. *Tuition waivers:* Full or partial for employees or children of employees.

LOANS *Student loans:* $6,018,654 (51% need-based, 49% non-need-based). 70% of past graduating class borrowed through all loan programs. *Average indebtedness per student:* $21,057. *Average need-based loan:* Freshmen: $3371. Undergraduates: $4527. *Parent loans:* $776,996 (37% need-based, 63% non-need-based). *Programs:* Federal Direct (Subsidized and Unsubsidized Stafford, PLUS).

WORK-STUDY *Federal work-study:* Total amount: $100,000; 65 jobs averaging $2591. *State or other work-study/employment:* Total amount: $100,000 (100% non-need-based). 30 part-time jobs averaging $1580.

ATHLETIC AWARDS Total amount: $1,273,764 (79% need-based, 21% non-need-based).

APPLYING FOR FINANCIAL AID *Required financial aid form:* FAFSA. *Financial aid deadline (priority):* 3/2. *Notification date:* Continuous beginning 3/2. Students must reply within 3 weeks of notification.

CONTACT Korey Compaan, Director of Financial Aid, William Jessup University, 333 Sunset Boulevard, Rocklin, CA 95765, 916-577-2231 or toll-free 800-355-7522. *Fax:* 916-577-2230. *E-mail:* kcompaan@jessup.edu.
Website: http://www.jessup.edu/.

WILLIAM JEWELL COLLEGE
Liberty, MO

Tuition & fees: $31,100	Average undergraduate aid package: $22,308

ABOUT THE INSTITUTION Independent, coed. *Awards:* bachelor's degrees (also offers evening program with significant enrollment not reflected in profile). 46 undergraduate majors. *Total enrollment:* 1,052. Undergraduates: 1,052. Freshmen: 305. Federal methodology is used as a basis for awarding need-based institutional aid.

UNDERGRADUATE EXPENSES for 2013–2014 *Application fee:* $25. *Comprehensive fee:* $39,120 includes full-time tuition ($30,800), mandatory fees ($300), and room and board ($8020). Full-time tuition and fees vary according to class time, course load, program, and student level. Room and board charges vary according to board plan and housing facility. *Part-time tuition:* $890 per credit.

FRESHMAN FINANCIAL AID (Fall 2012, est.) 245 applied for aid; of those 100% were deemed to have need. 100% of freshmen with need received aid; of those 18% had need fully met. *Average percent of need met:* 78% (excluding resources awarded to replace EFC). *Average financial aid package:* $25,089 (excluding resources awarded to replace EFC). 18% of all full-time freshmen had no need and received non-need-based gift aid.

UNDERGRADUATE FINANCIAL AID (Fall 2012, est.) 784 applied for aid; of those 100% were deemed to have need. 100% of undergraduates with need received aid; of those 20% had need fully met. *Average percent of need met:* 71% (excluding resources awarded to replace EFC). *Average financial aid package:* $22,308 (excluding resources awarded to replace EFC). 21% of all full-time undergraduates had no need and received non-need-based gift aid.

GIFT AID (NEED-BASED) *Total amount:* $12,229,547 (13% federal, 5% state, 79% institutional, 3% external sources). *Receiving aid:* Freshmen: 80% (245); all full-time undergraduates: 73% (738). *Average award:* Freshmen: $22,300; Undergraduates: $20,311. *Scholarships, grants, and awards:* Federal Pell, FSEOG, state, college/university gift aid from institutional funds.

GIFT AID (NON-NEED-BASED) *Total amount:* $3,161,975 (94% institutional, 6% external sources). *Receiving aid:* Freshmen: 80% (245). Undergraduates: 73% (735). *Average award:* Freshmen: $13,504. Undergraduates: $13,634. *Scholarships, grants, and awards by category:* Academic interests/achievement: 749 awards ($9,066,800 total): general academic interests/achievements. Creative arts/performance: 119 awards ($383,000 total): debating, journalism/publications, music, theater/drama. Special achievements/activities: 30 awards ($67,000 total): cheerleading/drum major, religious involvement. Special characteristics: 131 awards ($796,300 total): children and siblings of alumni, children of faculty/staff, siblings of current students. *Tuition waivers:* Full or partial for employees or children of employees. *ROTC:* Army cooperative.

LOANS *Student loans:* $6,946,912 (44% need-based, 56% non-need-based). 70% of past graduating class borrowed through all loan programs. *Average indebtedness per student:* $31,324. *Average need-based loan:* Freshmen: $4037. Undergraduates: $4955. *Parent loans:* $1,728,947 (90% need-based, 10% non-need-based).

Programs: Federal Direct (Subsidized and Unsubsidized Stafford, PLUS), Perkins, Federal Nursing, alternative loans.

WORK-STUDY *Federal work-study:* Total amount: $847,489; 541 jobs averaging $1565. *State or other work-study/employment:* Total amount: $67,260 (100% non-need-based). Part-time jobs available.

ATHLETIC AWARDS Total amount: $3,707,390 (73% need-based, 27% non-need-based).

APPLYING FOR FINANCIAL AID *Required financial aid form:* FAFSA. *Financial aid deadline (priority):* 3/1. *Notification date:* Continuous. Students must reply within 2 weeks of notification.

CONTACT Mrs. Sue Karnes, Director of Financial Aid and Scholarship Services, William Jewell College, 500 College Hill, Liberty, MO 64068, 816-415-5973 or toll-free 888-2JEWELL. *Fax:* 816-415-5006. *E-mail:* karness@william.jewell.edu.
Website: http://www.jewell.edu/.

WILLIAM PATERSON UNIVERSITY OF NEW JERSEY
Wayne, NJ

ABOUT THE INSTITUTION State-supported, coed. *Awards:* certificates, bachelor's, master's, and doctoral degrees. 67 undergraduate majors. *Total enrollment:* 11,423. Undergraduates: 10,089. Freshmen: 1,240.

GIFT AID (NEED-BASED) *Scholarships, grants, and awards:* Federal Pell, FSEOG, state, private, college/university gift aid from institutional funds.

LOANS *Programs:* Federal Direct (Subsidized and Unsubsidized Stafford, PLUS), Perkins, Federal Nursing, state.

WORK-STUDY *Federal work-study:* Total amount: $358,000; jobs available. *State or other work-study/employment:* Total amount: $278,000 (100% non-need-based). Part-time jobs available.

APPLYING FOR FINANCIAL AID *Required financial aid form:* FAFSA.

CONTACT Elizabeth Riquez, Director of Financial Aid, William Paterson University of New Jersey, 300 Pompton Road, Wayne, NJ 07470, 973-720-2928 or toll-free 877-WPU-EXCEL. *Fax:* 973-720-3133. *E-mail:* riqueze@wpunj.edu.
Website: http://www.wpunj.edu/.

WILLIAM PEACE UNIVERSITY
Raleigh, NC

Tuition & fees: $23,900	Average undergraduate aid package: $20,637

ABOUT THE INSTITUTION Independent Presbyterian Church (U.S.A.), coed. *Awards:* bachelor's degrees. 15 undergraduate majors. *Total enrollment:* 791. Undergraduates: 791. Freshmen: 232. Federal methodology is used as a basis for awarding need-based institutional aid.

UNDERGRADUATE EXPENSES for 2013–2014 *Application fee:* $25. *Comprehensive fee:* $33,041 includes full-time tuition ($23,700), mandatory fees ($200), and room and board ($9141). *College room only:* $6186. Full-time tuition and fees vary according to class time, course load, and program. Room and board charges vary according to board plan and housing facility. *Part-time tuition:* $790 per credit. Part-time tuition and fees vary according to class time, course load, and program.

FRESHMAN FINANCIAL AID (Fall 2012, est.) 221 applied for aid; of those 95% were deemed to have need. 100% of freshmen with need received aid; of those 7% had need fully met. *Average percent of need met:* 74% (excluding resources awarded to replace EFC). *Average financial aid package:* $23,939 (excluding resources awarded to replace EFC). 10% of all full-time freshmen had no need and received non-need-based gift aid.

UNDERGRADUATE FINANCIAL AID (Fall 2012, est.) 673 applied for aid; of those 93% were deemed to have need. 100% of undergraduates with need received aid; of those 10% had need fully met. *Average percent of need met:* 71% (excluding resources awarded to replace EFC). *Average financial aid package:* $20,637 (excluding resources awarded to replace EFC). 11% of all full-time undergraduates had no need and received non-need-based gift aid.

GIFT AID (NEED-BASED) *Total amount:* $20,957,740 (11% federal, 9% state, 30% institutional, 50% external sources). *Receiving aid:* Freshmen: 91% (210); all full-time undergraduates: 83% (607). *Average award:* Freshmen: $20,850; Undergraduates: $17,217. *Scholarships, grants, and awards:* Federal Pell, FSEOG, state, private, college/university gift aid from institutional funds.

GIFT AID (NON-NEED-BASED) *Total amount:* $1,789,338 (46% institutional, 54% external sources). *Receiving aid:* Freshmen: 4% (9). Undergraduates: 5% (38). *Average award:* Freshmen: $6666. Undergraduates: $8192. *Scholarships, grants, and awards by category:* Academic interests/achievement: 613 awards ($3,423,000 total): general academic interests/achievements. *Creative arts/performance:* 16 awards ($24,500 total): art/fine arts, music, theater/drama. *Special achievements/activities:* 86 awards ($294,000 total): leadership. *Special characteristics:* 10 awards ($61,996 total): children of faculty/staff, relatives of clergy, siblings of current students. *Tuition waivers:* Full or partial for employees or children of employees, senior citizens. *ROTC:* Army cooperative, Naval cooperative, Air Force cooperative.

LOANS *Student loans:* $5,428,645 (86% need-based, 14% non-need-based). 71% of past graduating class borrowed through all loan programs. *Average indebtedness per student:* $33,147. *Average need-based loan:* Freshmen: $3308. Undergraduates: $4189. *Parent loans:* $1,400,718 (39% need-based, 61% non-need-based). *Programs:* Federal Direct (Subsidized and Unsubsidized Stafford, PLUS), alternative loans.

WORK-STUDY *Federal work-study:* Total amount: $133,010; 75 jobs averaging $1790. *State or other work-study/employment:* Total amount: $5,561,655 (87% need-based, 13% non-need-based). 1 part-time job averaging $3000.

APPLYING FOR FINANCIAL AID *Required financial aid form:* FAFSA. *Financial aid deadline (priority):* 3/15. *Notification date:* Continuous beginning 3/1. Students must reply within 4 weeks of notification.

CONTACT Ms. Shawn Henderson, Director of Financial Aid, William Peace University, 15 East Peace Street, Raleigh, NC 27604, 919-508-2260 or toll-free 800-PEACE-47. *Fax:* 919-508-2325. *E-mail:* akirkley@peace.edu. *Website:* http://www.peace.edu/.

WILLIAM PENN UNIVERSITY
Oskaloosa, IA

CONTACT Cyndi Peiffer, Director of Financial Aid, William Penn University, 201 Trueblood Avenue, Oskaloosa, IA 52577-1799, 641-673-1060 or toll-free 800-779-7366. *Fax:* 641-673-1115. *E-mail:* peifferc@wmpenn.edu. *Website:* http://www.wmpenn.edu/.

WILLIAMS BAPTIST COLLEGE
Walnut Ridge, AR

Tuition & fees: N/R	Average undergraduate aid package: $14,541

ABOUT THE INSTITUTION Independent Southern Baptist, coed. *Awards:* associate and bachelor's degrees. 26 undergraduate majors. *Total enrollment:* 619. Undergraduates: 619. Federal methodology is used as a basis for awarding need-based institutional aid.

FRESHMAN FINANCIAL AID (Fall 2011) 120 applied for aid; of those 82% were deemed to have need. 100% of freshmen with need received aid. *Average financial aid package:* $14,862 (excluding resources awarded to replace EFC).

UNDERGRADUATE FINANCIAL AID (Fall 2011) 433 applied for aid; of those 86% were deemed to have need. 100% of undergraduates with need received aid. *Average financial aid package:* $14,541 (excluding resources awarded to replace EFC).

GIFT AID (NEED-BASED) *Total amount:* $1,407,399 (96% federal, 4% state). *Receiving aid:* Freshmen: 60% (84); all full-time undergraduates: 59% (305). *Average award:* Freshmen: $4567; Undergraduates: $4491. *Scholarships, grants, and awards:* Federal Pell, FSEOG, state, private, college/university gift aid from institutional funds.

GIFT AID (NON-NEED-BASED) *Total amount:* $4,553,157 (30% state, 37% institutional, 33% external sources). *Receiving aid:* Freshmen: 71% (99). Undergraduates: 72% (372). *Scholarships, grants, and awards by category:* Academic interests/achievement: 473 awards ($1,651,308 total): biological sciences, business, education, general academic interests/achievements, humanities, religion/biblical studies. *Creative arts/performance:* 52 awards ($49,700 total): art/fine arts, music,

theater/drama. *Special achievements/activities:* 13 awards ($4881 total): cheerleading/drum major. *Special characteristics:* 112 awards ($163,301 total): children of faculty/staff, international students, members of minority groups, relatives of clergy, religious affiliation. *ROTC:* Army cooperative.

LOANS *Student loans:* $2,019,525 (56% need-based, 44% non-need-based). 79% of past graduating class borrowed through all loan programs. *Average indebtedness per student:* $18,720. *Average need-based loan:* Freshmen: $2901. Undergraduates: $3664. *Parent loans:* $139,237 (100% non-need-based). *Programs:* Federal Direct (Subsidized and Unsubsidized Stafford, PLUS).

WORK-STUDY *Federal work-study:* Total amount: $252,546; 188 jobs averaging $1329. *State or other work-study/employment:* Total amount: $46,021 (100% non-need-based). 32 part-time jobs averaging $1438.

ATHLETIC AWARDS Total amount: $904,748 (100% non-need-based).

APPLYING FOR FINANCIAL AID *Required financial aid form:* FAFSA. *Financial aid deadline:* Continuous. *Notification date:* Continuous beginning 4/1. Students must reply within 2 weeks of notification.

CONTACT Mrs. Barbara Turner, Director of Financial Aid, Williams Baptist College, 60 West Fulbright Avenue, Walnut Ridge, AR 72476, 870-759-4112 or toll-free 800-722-4434. *Fax:* 870-759-4209. *E-mail:* bturner@wbcoll.edu. *Website:* http://www.wbcoll.edu/.

WILLIAMS COLLEGE
Williamstown, MA

Tuition & fees: $43,190	Average undergraduate aid package: $43,747

ABOUT THE INSTITUTION Independent, coed. *Awards:* bachelor's and master's degrees. 37 undergraduate majors. *Total enrollment:* 2,106. Undergraduates: 2,052. Freshmen: 547. Institutional methodology is used as a basis for awarding need-based institutional aid.

UNDERGRADUATE EXPENSES for 2013–2014 *Application fee:* $65. *Comprehensive fee:* $54,560 includes full-time tuition ($42,938), mandatory fees ($252), and room and board ($11,370). *College room only:* $5780. Room and board charges vary according to board plan.

FRESHMAN FINANCIAL AID (Fall 2012, est.) 358 applied for aid; of those 81% were deemed to have need. 100% of freshmen with need received aid; of those 100% had need fully met. *Average percent of need met:* 100% (excluding resources awarded to replace EFC). *Average financial aid package:* $44,508 (excluding resources awarded to replace EFC).

UNDERGRADUATE FINANCIAL AID (Fall 2012, est.) 1,204 applied for aid; of those 89% were deemed to have need. 100% of undergraduates with need received aid; of those 100% had need fully met. *Average percent of need met:* 100% (excluding resources awarded to replace EFC). *Average financial aid package:* $43,747 (excluding resources awarded to replace EFC).

GIFT AID (NEED-BASED) *Total amount:* $44,387,889 (5% federal, 92% institutional, 3% external sources). *Receiving aid:* Freshmen: 53% (289); all full-time undergraduates: 53% (1,068). *Average award:* Freshmen: $39,679; Undergraduates: $40,511. *Scholarships, grants, and awards:* Federal Pell, FSEOG, state, private, college/university gift aid from institutional funds.

GIFT AID (NON-NEED-BASED) *Total amount:* $892,787 (1% federal, 99% external sources). *ROTC:* Air Force cooperative.

LOANS *Student loans:* $2,196,127 (31% need-based, 69% non-need-based). 31% of past graduating class borrowed through all loan programs. *Average indebtedness per student:* $12,749. *Average need-based loan:* Freshmen: $2678. Undergraduates: $2745. *Parent loans:* $2,370,684 (100% non-need-based). *Programs:* Federal Direct (Subsidized and Unsubsidized Stafford, PLUS), Perkins, college/university.

WORK-STUDY *Federal work-study:* Total amount: $957,484; jobs available. *State or other work-study/employment:* Total amount: $1,012,902 (73% need-based, 27% non-need-based). Part-time jobs available.

APPLYING FOR FINANCIAL AID *Required financial aid forms:* FAFSA, CSS Financial Aid PROFILE, noncustodial (divorced/separated) parent's statement. *Financial aid deadline:* 2/1. *Notification date:* 4/1. Students must reply by 5/1.

CONTACT Paul J. Boyer, Director of Financial Aid, Williams College, PO Box 37, Williamstown, MA 01267, 413-597-4181. *Fax:* 413-597-2999. *E-mail:* paul.j.boyer@williams.edu. *Website:* http://www.williams.edu/.

WILLIAMSON CHRISTIAN COLLEGE
Franklin, TN

CONTACT Jeanie Maguire, Director of Financial Aid, Williamson Christian College, 200 Seaboard Lane, Franklin, TN 37067, 615-771-7821. *Fax:* 615-771-7810. *E-mail:* info@williamsoncc.edu.
Website: http://www.williamsoncc.edu/.

WILLIAM WOODS UNIVERSITY
Fulton, MO

ABOUT THE INSTITUTION Independent Christian Church (Disciples of Christ), coed. *Awards:* certificates, associate, bachelor's, and master's degrees. 47 undergraduate majors. *Total enrollment:* 2,020. Undergraduates: 1,036. Freshmen: 182.
GIFT AID (NEED-BASED) *Scholarships, grants, and awards:* Federal Pell, FSEOG, state, private, college/university gift aid from institutional funds.
GIFT AID (NON-NEED-BASED) *Scholarships, grants, and awards by category:* Academic interests/achievement: general academic interests/achievements, health fields. *Creative arts/performance:* art/fine arts, journalism/publications, performing arts, theater/drama. *Special achievements/activities:* general special achievements/activities, leadership. *Special characteristics:* children and siblings of alumni, children of faculty/staff, relatives of clergy, religious affiliation, siblings of current students.
LOANS *Programs:* Federal Direct (Subsidized and Unsubsidized Stafford, PLUS), Perkins, college/university.
WORK-STUDY *Federal work-study:* Total amount: $419,889; jobs available. *State or other work-study/employment:* Total amount: $152,375 (4% need-based, 96% non-need-based). Part-time jobs available.
APPLYING FOR FINANCIAL AID *Required financial aid forms:* FAFSA, institution's own form.
CONTACT Deana Ready, Director of Student Financial Services, William Woods University, One University Avenue, Fulton, MO 65251, 573-592-4232 or toll-free 800-995-3159 Ext. 4221. *Fax:* 573-592-1180. *E-mail:* deana.ready@williamwoods.edu.
Website: http://www.williamwoods.edu/.

WILMINGTON COLLEGE
Wilmington, OH

CONTACT Donna Barton, Coordinator of Financial Aid, Wilmington College, Pyle Center Box 1184, Wilmington, OH 45177, 937-382-6661 Ext. 466 or toll-free 800-341-9318. *Fax:* 937-383-8564.
Website: http://www.wilmington.edu/.

WILMINGTON UNIVERSITY
New Castle, DE

CONTACT J. Lynn Iocono, Director of Financial Aid, Wilmington University, 320 DuPont Highway, New Castle, DE 19720, 302-328-9437 or toll-free 877-967-5464. *Fax:* 302-328-5902.
Website: http://www.wilmu.edu/.

WILSON COLLEGE
Chambersburg, PA

Tuition & fees: N/R	Average undergraduate aid package: N/A

ABOUT THE INSTITUTION Independent Presbyterian Church (U.S.A.), coed, primarily women. *Awards:* associate, bachelor's, and master's degrees. 29 undergraduate majors. *Total enrollment:* 746. Undergraduates: 698. Federal methodology is used as a basis for awarding need-based institutional aid.
GIFT AID (NEED-BASED) *Scholarships, grants, and awards:* Federal Pell, FSEOG, state, private, college/university gift aid from institutional funds.
GIFT AID (NON-NEED-BASED) *Scholarships, grants, and awards by category:* Academic interests/achievement: biological sciences, business, communication, computer science, education, English, foreign languages, general academic interests/achievements, humanities, international studies, mathematics, physical sciences, premedicine, religion/biblical studies, social sciences. *Creative arts/performance:* music. *Special achievements/activities:* community service, general special achievements/activities, leadership. *Special characteristics:* adult students, children and siblings of alumni, children of current students, children of faculty/staff, international students, local/state students, relatives of clergy, religious affiliation, veterans, veterans' children. *ROTC:* Army cooperative.

LOANS *Student loans:* 73% of past graduating class borrowed through all loan programs. *Average indebtedness per student:* $32,565. **Programs:** Federal Direct (Subsidized and Unsubsidized Stafford, PLUS), Perkins.

WORK-STUDY Federal work-study jobs available. *State or other work-study/ employment:* Part-time jobs available.

APPLYING FOR FINANCIAL AID *Required financial aid forms:* FAFSA, institution's own form. *Financial aid deadline (priority):* 4/30. *Notification date:* Continuous beginning 9/15.

CONTACT Ms. Linda Brittain, Dean of Financial Aid and Senior Enrollment Associate, Wilson College, 1015 Philadelphia Avenue, Chambersburg, PA 17201-1285, 717-262-2002 or toll-free 800-421-8402. *Fax:* 717-262-2530. *E-mail:* finaid@ wilson.edu.

Website: http://www.wilson.edu/.

WINGATE UNIVERSITY
Wingate, NC

ABOUT THE INSTITUTION Independent Baptist, coed. *Awards:* certificates, bachelor's, master's, and doctoral degrees. 34 undergraduate majors. *Total enrollment:* 2,648. Undergraduates: 1,773. Freshmen: 548.

GIFT AID (NEED-BASED) *Scholarships, grants, and awards:* Federal Pell, FSEOG, state, private, college/university gift aid from institutional funds.

GIFT AID (NON-NEED-BASED) *Scholarships, grants, and awards by category:* Academic interests/achievement: general academic interests/achievements. Creative arts/performance: art/fine arts, music, theater/drama. Special characteristics: children and siblings of alumni, relatives of clergy.

LOANS *Programs:* Federal Direct (Subsidized and Unsubsidized Stafford, PLUS).

WORK-STUDY *Federal work-study:* Total amount: $256,610; 293 jobs averaging $900. *State or other work-study/employment:* Total amount: $336,175 (100% non-need-based). 330 part-time jobs averaging $1019.

APPLYING FOR FINANCIAL AID *Required financial aid forms:* FAFSA, state aid form.

CONTACT Teresa G. Williams, Director of Student Financial Planning, Wingate University, Campus Box 3001, Wingate, NC 28174, 704-233-8209 or toll-free 800-755-5550. *Fax:* 704-233-9396. *E-mail:* tgwilliam@wingate.edu.

Website: http://www.wingate.edu/.

WINONA STATE UNIVERSITY
Winona, MN

Tuition & fees (area res): $8930	Average undergraduate aid package: $7280

ABOUT THE INSTITUTION State-supported, coed. *Awards:* certificates, associate, bachelor's, master's, and doctoral degrees. 108 undergraduate majors. *Total enrollment:* 8,890. Undergraduates: 8,369. Freshmen: 1,808. Federal methodology is used as a basis for awarding need-based institutional aid.

UNDERGRADUATE EXPENSES for 2013–2014 *Application fee:* $20. *Tuition, area resident:* full-time $7080. *Tuition, state resident:* full-time $7080; part-time $236 per credit. *Tuition, nonresident:* full-time $12,740; part-time $425 per credit. *Required fees:* full-time $1850. Full-time tuition and fees vary according to location and reciprocity agreements. Part-time tuition and fees vary according to course load, location, and reciprocity agreements. *College room and board:* $7800. Room and board charges vary according to board plan, housing facility, and location.

FRESHMAN FINANCIAL AID (Fall 2011) 1,619 applied for aid; of those 71% were deemed to have need. 98% of freshmen with need received aid; of those 12% had need fully met. *Average percent of need met:* 48% (excluding resources awarded to replace EFC). *Average financial aid package:* $6591 (excluding resources awarded to replace EFC). 18% of all full-time freshmen had no need and received non-need-based gift aid.

UNDERGRADUATE FINANCIAL AID (Fall 2011) 6,019 applied for aid; of those 75% were deemed to have need. 98% of undergraduates with need received aid; of those 11% had need fully met. *Average percent of need met:* 50% (excluding resources awarded to replace EFC). *Average financial aid package:* $7280

(excluding resources awarded to replace EFC). 11% of all full-time undergraduates had no need and received non-need-based gift aid.

GIFT AID (NEED-BASED) *Total amount:* $12,460,472 (67% federal, 32% state, 1% institutional). *Receiving aid:* Freshmen: 32% (607); all full-time undergraduates: 34% (2,534). *Average award:* Freshmen: $4665; Undergraduates: $4593. *Scholarships, grants, and awards:* Federal Pell, FSEOG, state, private, college/university gift aid from institutional funds.

GIFT AID (NON-NEED-BASED) *Total amount:* $5,878,144 (14% federal, 50% institutional, 36% external sources). *Receiving aid:* Freshmen: 34% (628). Undergraduates: 19% (1,470). *Average award:* Freshmen: $2095. Undergraduates: $2748. *Scholarships, grants, and awards by category:* Academic interests/ achievement: general academic interests/achievements. Creative arts/performance: art/fine arts, debating, music, theater/drama. Special characteristics: children and siblings of alumni, children of faculty/staff, local/state students, members of minority groups, out-of-state students. *Tuition waivers:* Full or partial for employees or children of employees. *ROTC:* Army cooperative.

LOANS *Student loans:* $49,900,863 (34% need-based, 66% non-need-based). 75% of past graduating class borrowed through all loan programs. *Average indebtedness per student:* $32,576. *Average need-based loan:* Freshmen: $3245. Undergraduates: $4076. *Parent loans:* $4,134,825 (100% non-need-based). *Programs:* Federal Direct (Subsidized and Unsubsidized Stafford, PLUS), Perkins, state, college/university.

WORK-STUDY *Federal work-study:* Total amount: $352,522; 183 jobs averaging $1926. *State or other work-study/employment:* Total amount: $624,221 (100% need-based). 308 part-time jobs averaging $2027.

ATHLETIC AWARDS Total amount: $854,160 (100% non-need-based).

APPLYING FOR FINANCIAL AID *Required financial aid form:* FAFSA. *Financial aid deadline:* Continuous. *Notification date:* 5/1. Students must reply within 3 weeks of notification.

CONTACT Cindy Groth, Counselor, Winona State University, PO Box 5838, Winona, MN 55987-5838, 507-457-5090 Ext. 5561 or toll-free 800-DIAL WSU. *Website:* http://www.winona.edu/.

WINSTON-SALEM STATE UNIVERSITY
Winston-Salem, NC

CONTACT Raymond Solomon, Director of Financial Aid Office, Winston-Salem State University, 601 Martin Luther King Jr. Drive, PO Box 19524, Winston-Salem, NC 27110-0003, 336-750-3299 or toll-free 800-257-4052. *Fax:* 336-750-3297. *Website:* http://www.wssu.edu/.

WINTHROP UNIVERSITY
Rock Hill, SC

Tuition & fees (SC res): $13,026	Average undergraduate aid package: $11,532

ABOUT THE INSTITUTION State-supported, coed. *Awards:* certificates, bachelor's, and master's degrees. 28 undergraduate majors. *Total enrollment:* 6,170. Undergraduates: 5,029. Freshmen: 1,143. Federal methodology is used as a basis for awarding need-based institutional aid.

UNDERGRADUATE EXPENSES for 2013–2014 *Application fee:* $40. *Tuition, state resident:* full-time $13,026; part-time $543 per credit hour. *Tuition, nonresident:* full-time $24,476; part-time $1020 per credit hour. Full-time tuition and fees vary according to degree level and reciprocity agreements. Part-time tuition and fees vary according to degree level. *College room and board:* $7464; *Room only:* $4674. Room and board charges vary according to board plan and housing facility.

FRESHMAN FINANCIAL AID (Fall 2012, est.) 1,060 applied for aid; of those 85% were deemed to have need. 100% of freshmen with need received aid; of those 18% had need fully met. *Average percent of need met:* 67% (excluding resources awarded to replace EFC). *Average financial aid package:* $13,298 (excluding resources awarded to replace EFC). 11% of all full-time freshmen had no need and received non-need-based gift aid.

UNDERGRADUATE FINANCIAL AID (Fall 2012, est.) 3,737 applied for aid; of those 86% were deemed to have need. 99% of undergraduates with need received aid; of those 13% had need fully met. *Average percent of need met:* 60% (excluding resources awarded to replace EFC). **Average financial aid package:** $11,532 (excluding resources awarded to replace EFC). 11% of all full-time undergraduates had no need and received non-need-based gift aid.

GIFT AID (NEED-BASED) Total amount: $23,048,078 (39% federal, 39% state, 18% institutional, 4% external sources). **Receiving aid:** Freshmen: 78% (885); all full-time undergraduates: 64% (2,837). **Average award:** Freshmen: $9179; Undergraduates: $7767. **Scholarships, grants, and awards:** Federal Pell, FSEOG, state, private, college/university gift aid from institutional funds, TEACH Grants.

GIFT AID (NON-NEED-BASED) Total amount: $8,142,915 (1% federal, 48% state, 47% institutional, 4% external sources). **Receiving aid:** Freshmen: 12% (140). Undergraduates: 7% (305). **Average award:** Freshmen: $4262. Undergraduates: $3270. **Scholarships, grants, and awards by category:** Academic interests/achievement: general academic interests/achievements. Creative arts/performance: art/fine arts, dance, music, performing arts, theater/drama. Special characteristics: children of faculty/staff. Tuition waivers: Full or partial for employees or children of employees, senior citizens. ROTC: Army cooperative, Air Force cooperative.

LOANS Student loans: $89,407,857 (26% need-based, 74% non-need-based). 67% of past graduating class borrowed through all loan programs. **Average indebtedness per student:** $22,521. **Average need-based loan:** Freshmen: $3472. Undergraduates: $4187. **Parent loans:** $3,645,938 (48% need-based, 52% non-need-based). **Programs:** Federal Direct (Subsidized and Unsubsidized Stafford, PLUS), Perkins.

WORK-STUDY Federal work-study: Total amount: $263,769; 233 jobs averaging $742. **State or other work-study/employment:** Part-time jobs available.

ATHLETIC AWARDS Total amount: $1,914,814 (33% need-based, 67% non-need-based).

APPLYING FOR FINANCIAL AID Required financial aid form: FAFSA. **Financial aid deadline (priority):** 3/1. **Notification date:** Continuous beginning 3/26. Students must reply within 2 weeks of notification.

CONTACT Michelle K. Hare, Director of Financial Aid, Winthrop University, Sykes House, 638 Oakland Avenue, Rock Hill, SC 29733, 803-323-2189 or toll-free 800-763-0230. Fax: 803-323-2557. E-mail: finaid@winthrop.edu. Website: http://www.winthrop.edu/.

WISCONSIN LUTHERAN COLLEGE
Milwaukee, WI

Tuition & fees: $23,620	Average undergraduate aid package: $18,647

ABOUT THE INSTITUTION Independent Wisconsin Evangelical Lutheran Synod, coed. 29 undergraduate majors. Federal methodology is used as a basis for awarding need-based institutional aid.

UNDERGRADUATE EXPENSES for 2013–2014 Comprehensive fee: $32,150 includes full-time tuition ($23,470), mandatory fees ($150), and room and board ($8530). **College room only:** $4600. Full-time tuition and fees vary according to degree level and program. Room and board charges vary according to board plan, housing facility, and student level. **Part-time tuition:** $680 per credit. Part-time tuition and fees vary according to degree level and program.

FRESHMAN FINANCIAL AID (Fall 2012, est.) 226 applied for aid; of those 91% were deemed to have need. 100% of freshmen with need received aid; of those 14% had need fully met. **Average percent of need met:** 81% (excluding resources awarded to replace EFC). **Average financial aid package:** $20,605 (excluding resources awarded to replace EFC). 15% of all full-time freshmen had no need and received non-need-based gift aid.

UNDERGRADUATE FINANCIAL AID (Fall 2012, est.) 855 applied for aid; of those 92% were deemed to have need. 100% of undergraduates with need received aid; of those 16% had need fully met. **Average percent of need met:** 78% (excluding resources awarded to replace EFC). **Average financial aid package:** $18,647 (excluding resources awarded to replace EFC). 15% of all full-time undergraduates had no need and received non-need-based gift aid.

GIFT AID (NEED-BASED) Total amount: $11,208,969 (13% federal, 8% state, 77% institutional, 2% external sources). **Receiving aid:** Freshmen: 85% (205); all full-time undergraduates: 79% (767). **Average award:** Freshmen: $16,745; Undergraduates: $14,636. **Scholarships, grants, and awards:** Federal Pell, FSEOG, state, private, college/university gift aid from institutional funds.

GIFT AID (NON-NEED-BASED) Total amount: $1,453,259 (1% state, 96% institutional, 3% external sources). **Receiving aid:** Freshmen: 7% (16). Undergraduates: 7% (69). **Average award:** Freshmen: $8062. Undergraduates: $7982. **Schol-

arships, grants, and awards by category:** Academic interests/achievement: biological sciences, business, communication, computer science, education, general academic interests/achievements, health fields, international studies, mathematics, physical sciences, religion/biblical studies, social sciences. Creative arts/performance: art/fine arts, music, theater/drama. Special achievements/activities: general special achievements/activities, leadership. Special characteristics: adult students, children of faculty/staff, ethnic background, first-generation college students, international students, members of minority groups, out-of-state students, religious affiliation. **Tuition waivers:** Full or partial for employees or children of employees.

LOANS Student loans: $6,712,223 (74% need-based, 26% non-need-based). 80% of past graduating class borrowed through all loan programs. **Average indebtedness per student:** $25,368. **Average need-based loan:** Freshmen: $3269. Undergraduates: $4012. **Parent loans:** $1,584,462 (24% need-based, 76% non-need-based). **Programs:** Federal Direct (Subsidized and Unsubsidized Stafford, PLUS), private loans.

WORK-STUDY Federal work-study: Total amount: $449,775; 245 jobs averaging $1754. **State or other work-study/employment:** Total amount: $256,475 (50% need-based, 50% non-need-based). 28 part-time jobs averaging $1884.

APPLYING FOR FINANCIAL AID Required financial aid forms: FAFSA, institution's own form. **Financial aid deadline (priority):** 3/1. **Notification date:** Continuous beginning 3/15. Students must reply within 2 weeks of notification.

CONTACT Mrs. Linda Loeffel, Director of Financial Aid, Wisconsin Lutheran College, 8800 West Bluemound Road, Milwaukee, WI 53226-4699, 414-443-8856. Fax: 414-443-8514. E-mail: linda.loeffel@wlc.edu. Website: http://www.wlc.edu/.

WITTENBERG UNIVERSITY
Springfield, OH

Tuition & fees: $38,030	Average undergraduate aid package: $30,154

ABOUT THE INSTITUTION Independent Evangelical Lutheran Church, coed. **Awards:** bachelor's and master's degrees. 32 undergraduate majors. **Total enrollment:** 1,894. Undergraduates: 1,881. Freshmen: 489. Federal methodology is used as a basis for awarding need-based institutional aid.

UNDERGRADUATE EXPENSES for 2013–2014 Application fee: $40. **Comprehensive fee:** $47,766 includes full-time tuition ($37,230), mandatory fees ($800), and room and board ($9736). **College room only:** $5056. Room and board charges vary according to board plan and housing facility. **Part-time tuition:** $1241 per credit. Part-time tuition and fees vary according to course load.

FRESHMAN FINANCIAL AID (Fall 2012, est.) 453 applied for aid; of those 89% were deemed to have need. 100% of freshmen with need received aid; of those 1% had need fully met. **Average percent of need met:** 81% (excluding resources awarded to replace EFC). **Average financial aid package:** $30,942 (excluding resources awarded to replace EFC). 17% of all full-time freshmen had no need and received non-need-based gift aid.

UNDERGRADUATE FINANCIAL AID (Fall 2012, est.) 1,581 applied for aid; of those 89% were deemed to have need. 100% of undergraduates with need received aid; of those 2% had need fully met. **Average percent of need met:** 80% (excluding resources awarded to replace EFC). **Average financial aid package:** $30,154 (excluding resources awarded to replace EFC). 20% of all full-time undergraduates had no need and received non-need-based gift aid.

GIFT AID (NEED-BASED) Total amount: $33,616,341 (7% federal, 2% state, 89% institutional, 2% external sources). **Receiving aid:** Freshmen: 83% (405); all full-time undergraduates: 79% (1,404). **Average award:** Freshmen: $26,028; Undergraduates: $24,927. **Scholarships, grants, and awards:** Federal Pell, FSEOG, state, private, college/university gift aid from institutional funds.

GIFT AID (NON-NEED-BASED) Total amount: $5,781,435 (97% institutional, 3% external sources). **Average award:** Freshmen: $16,914. Undergraduates: $15,668. **Scholarships, grants, and awards by category:** Academic interests/achievement: general academic interests/achievements. Creative arts/performance: art/fine arts, dance, music, theater/drama. Special achievements/activities: community service, general special achievements/activities. Special characteristics: adult students, children and siblings of alumni, children of faculty/staff, ethnic background, international students, members of minority groups, relatives of clergy, religious affiliation. **Tuition waivers:** Full or partial for minority students, children of alumni, employees or

children of employees, adult students, senior citizens. *ROTC:* Army cooperative, Air Force cooperative.
LOANS *Student loans:* $12,645,037 (91% need-based, 9% non-need-based). 71% of past graduating class borrowed through all loan programs. *Average indebtedness per student:* $31,712. *Average need-based loan:* Freshmen: $3708. Undergraduates: $4521. *Parent loans:* $5,853,227 (93% need-based, 7% non-need-based). *Programs:* Federal Direct (Subsidized and Unsubsidized Stafford, PLUS), Perkins, college/university.
WORK-STUDY *Federal work-study:* Total amount: $1,391,765; jobs available. *State or other work-study/employment:* Total amount: $1,187,534 (73% need-based, 27% non-need-based). Part-time jobs available.
APPLYING FOR FINANCIAL AID *Required financial aid form:* FAFSA. *Financial aid deadline (priority):* 3/1. *Notification date:* Continuous beginning 3/1. Students must reply by 5/1 or within 2 weeks of notification.
CONTACT Mr. J. Randy Green, Executive Director of Financial Aid, Wittenberg University, PO Box 720, Springfield, OH 45501-0720, 937-327-7321 or toll-free 800-677-7558 Ext. 6314. *Fax:* 937-327-6379. *E-mail:* jgreen@wittenberg.edu.
Website: http://www.wittenberg.edu/.

WOFFORD COLLEGE
Spartanburg, SC

Tuition & fees: $35,515	Average undergraduate aid package: $27,803

ABOUT THE INSTITUTION Independent United Methodist Church, coed. *Awards:* bachelor's degrees. 30 undergraduate majors. *Total enrollment:* 1,588. Undergraduates: 1,588. Freshmen: 439. Federal methodology is used as a basis for awarding need-based institutional aid.
UNDERGRADUATE EXPENSES for 2013–2014 *Application fee:* $35. *Comprehensive fee:* $45,795 includes full-time tuition ($35,515) and room and board ($10,280).
FRESHMAN FINANCIAL AID (Fall 2012, est.) 360 applied for aid; of those 80% were deemed to have need. 100% of freshmen with need received aid; of those 43% had need fully met. *Average percent of need met:* 82% (excluding resources awarded to replace EFC). *Average financial aid package:* $27,554 (excluding resources awarded to replace EFC). 22% of all full-time freshmen had no need and received non-need-based gift aid.
UNDERGRADUATE FINANCIAL AID (Fall 2012, est.) 1,127 applied for aid; of those 85% were deemed to have need. 100% of undergraduates with need received aid; of those 44% had need fully met. *Average percent of need met:* 83% (excluding resources awarded to replace EFC). *Average financial aid package:* $27,803 (excluding resources awarded to replace EFC). 25% of all full-time undergraduates had no need and received non-need-based gift aid.
GIFT AID (NEED-BASED) *Total amount:* $21,819,045 (7% federal, 19% state, 70% institutional, 4% external sources). *Receiving aid:* Freshmen: 60% (264); all full-time undergraduates: 38% (601). *Average award:* Freshmen: $28,588; Undergraduates: $28,915. *Scholarships, grants, and awards:* Federal Pell, FSEOG, state, private, college/university gift aid from institutional funds.
GIFT AID (NON-NEED-BASED) *Total amount:* $10,330,928 (22% state, 68% institutional, 10% external sources). *Receiving aid:* Freshmen: 19% (85). Undergraduates: 19% (296). *Average award:* Freshmen: $14,314. Undergraduates: $14,769. *Scholarships, grants, and awards by category:* Academic interests/achievement: general academic interests/achievements. Creative arts/performance: music. Special achievements/activities: leadership. Special characteristics: 401 awards: children of faculty/staff, general special characteristics, relatives of clergy. *Tuition waivers:* Full or partial for employees or children of employees. *ROTC:* Army.
LOANS *Student loans:* $5,381,877 (72% need-based, 28% non-need-based). 50% of past graduating class borrowed through all loan programs. *Average indebtedness per student:* $22,118. *Average need-based loan:* Freshmen: $3330. Undergraduates: $4251. *Parent loans:* $2,195,952 (43% need-based, 57% non-need-based). *Programs:* Federal Direct (Subsidized and Unsubsidized Stafford, PLUS).
WORK-STUDY *Federal work-study:* Total amount: $145,475; jobs available.
ATHLETIC AWARDS Total amount: $4,790,664 (50% need-based, 50% non-need-based).
APPLYING FOR FINANCIAL AID *Required financial aid form:* FAFSA. *Financial aid deadline (priority):* 3/15. *Notification date:* Continuous beginning 3/31. Students must reply by 5/1.
CONTACT Carolyn B. Sparks, Director of Financial Aid, Wofford College, 429 North Church Street, Spartanburg, SC 29303-3663, 864-597-4160. *Fax:* 864-597-4149. *E-mail:* finaid@wofford.edu.
Website: http://www.wofford.edu/.

WOODBURY UNIVERSITY
Burbank, CA

Tuition & fees: $31,444	Average undergraduate aid package: $20,007

ABOUT THE INSTITUTION Independent, coed. *Awards:* bachelor's and master's degrees. 17 undergraduate majors. *Total enrollment:* 1,771. Undergraduates: 1,488. Freshmen: 180. Federal methodology is used as a basis for awarding need-based institutional aid.
UNDERGRADUATE EXPENSES for 2013–2014 *Application fee:* $50. *Comprehensive fee:* $41,396 includes full-time tuition ($31,054), mandatory fees ($390), and room and board ($9952). *College room only:* $6200. Full-time tuition and fees vary according to course load, degree level, and program. Room and board charges vary according to board plan, housing facility, and location. Part-time tuition and fees vary according to course load, degree level, and program.
FRESHMAN FINANCIAL AID (Fall 2012, est.) 148 applied for aid; of those 91% were deemed to have need. 100% of freshmen with need received aid; of those 4% had need fully met. *Average percent of need met:* 56% (excluding resources awarded to replace EFC). *Average financial aid package:* $20,798 (excluding resources awarded to replace EFC). 15% of all full-time freshmen had no need and received non-need-based gift aid.
UNDERGRADUATE FINANCIAL AID (Fall 2012, est.) 984 applied for aid; of those 95% were deemed to have need. 100% of undergraduates with need received aid; of those 2% had need fully met. *Average percent of need met:* 51% (excluding resources awarded to replace EFC). *Average financial aid package:* $20,007 (excluding resources awarded to replace EFC). 9% of all full-time undergraduates had no need and received non-need-based gift aid.
GIFT AID (NEED-BASED) *Total amount:* $15,538,329 (22% federal, 19% state, 58% institutional, 1% external sources). *Receiving aid:* Freshmen: 77% (133); all full-time undergraduates: 88% (927). *Average award:* Freshmen: $18,042; Undergraduates: $15,923. *Scholarships, grants, and awards:* Federal Pell, FSEOG, state, private, college/university gift aid from institutional funds.
GIFT AID (NON-NEED-BASED) *Total amount:* $1,078,950 (87% institutional, 13% external sources). *Receiving aid:* Freshmen: 2% (3). Undergraduates: 2% (16). *Average award:* Freshmen: $8666. Undergraduates: $9706. *Scholarships, grants, and awards by category:* Academic interests/achievement: 667 awards ($5,780,525 total): architecture, business, general academic interests/achievements. *Tuition waivers:* Full or partial for employees or children of employees.
LOANS *Student loans:* $9,982,715 (93% need-based, 7% non-need-based). 84% of past graduating class borrowed through all loan programs. *Average indebtedness per student:* $37,856. *Average need-based loan:* Freshmen: $3354. Undergraduates: $4469. *Parent loans:* $5,307,377 (71% need-based, 29% non-need-based). *Programs:* Federal Direct (Subsidized and Unsubsidized Stafford, PLUS), Perkins, alternative loans.
WORK-STUDY *Federal work-study:* Total amount: $99,865; jobs available.
APPLYING FOR FINANCIAL AID *Required financial aid form:* FAFSA. *Financial aid deadline:* Continuous. *Notification date:* Continuous beginning 3/15. Students must reply within 2 weeks of notification.
CONTACT Celeastia Williams, Director of Enrollment Services, Woodbury University, 7500 Glenoaks Boulevard, Burbank, CA 91510, 818-767-0888 Ext. 273 or toll-free 800-784-WOOD. *Fax:* 818-767-4816.
Website: http://www.woodbury.edu/.

WORCESTER POLYTECHNIC INSTITUTE
Worcester, MA

Tuition & fees: $42,778	Average undergraduate aid package: $30,954

ABOUT THE INSTITUTION Independent, coed. *Awards:* bachelor's, master's, and doctoral degrees. 51 undergraduate majors. *Total enrollment:* 5,957. Undergraduates: 3,952. Freshmen: 951. Both federal and institutional methodology are used as a basis for awarding need-based institutional aid.

UNDERGRADUATE EXPENSES for 2013–2014 *Application fee:* $60. *One-time required fee:* $200. *Comprehensive fee:* $55,860 includes full-time tuition ($42,178), mandatory fees ($600), and room and board ($13,082). *College room only:* $7466. Room and board charges vary according to board plan and housing facility. *Part-time tuition:* $1172 per credit hour. Part-time tuition and fees vary according to course load. *Payment plan:* Tuition prepayment.

FRESHMAN FINANCIAL AID (Fall 2011) 879 applied for aid; of those 83% were deemed to have need. 100% of freshmen with need received aid; of those 46% had need fully met. *Average percent of need met:* 71% (excluding resources awarded to replace EFC). *Average financial aid package:* $31,426 (excluding resources awarded to replace EFC). 24% of all full-time freshmen had no need and received non-need-based gift aid.

UNDERGRADUATE FINANCIAL AID (Fall 2011) 2,862 applied for aid; of those 90% were deemed to have need. 99% of undergraduates with need received aid; of those 37% had need fully met. *Average percent of need met:* 72% (excluding resources awarded to replace EFC). *Average financial aid package:* $30,954 (excluding resources awarded to replace EFC). 28% of all full-time undergraduates had no need and received non-need-based gift aid.

GIFT AID (NEED-BASED) *Total amount:* $50,905,062 (5% federal, 2% state, 87% institutional, 6% external sources). *Receiving aid:* Freshmen: 72% (722); all full-time undergraduates: 67% (2,445). *Average award:* Freshmen: $20,547; Undergraduates: $19,699. *Scholarships, grants, and awards:* Federal Pell, FSEOG, state, private, college/university gift aid from institutional funds.

GIFT AID (NON-NEED-BASED) *Total amount:* $18,965,717 (81% institutional, 19% external sources). *Receiving aid:* Freshmen: 30% (305). Undergraduates: 22% (786). *Average award:* Freshmen: $12,858. Undergraduates: $15,854. *Scholarships, grants, and awards by category:* Academic interests/achievement: 2,960 awards ($37,150,966 total): general academic interests/achievements, premedicine. *Special achievements/activities:* leadership. *Special characteristics:* 20 awards ($110,475 total): children of workers in trades. *Tuition waivers:* Full or partial for employees or children of employees. *ROTC:* Army, Naval cooperative, Air Force.

LOANS *Student loans:* $28,781,270 (45% need-based, 55% non-need-based). *Average need-based loan:* Freshmen: $2712. Undergraduates: $2746. *Parent loans:* $9,550,504 (100% non-need-based). *Programs:* Federal Direct (Subsidized and Unsubsidized Stafford, PLUS), Perkins, state, college/university.

WORK-STUDY *Federal work-study:* Total amount: $715,984; 749 jobs averaging $956.

APPLYING FOR FINANCIAL AID *Required financial aid forms:* FAFSA, CSS Financial Aid PROFILE, noncustodial (divorced/separated) parent's statement. *Financial aid deadline (priority):* 2/1. *Notification date:* 4/1. Students must reply by 5/1.

CONTACT Office of Financial Aid, Worcester Polytechnic Institute, 100 Institute Road, Worcester, MA 01609-2280, 508-831-5469. *Fax:* 508-831-5039. *E-mail:* finaid@wpi.edu. *Website:* http://www.wpi.edu/.

WORCESTER STATE UNIVERSITY
Worcester, MA

Tuition & fees (MA res): $8157	Average undergraduate aid package: $11,002

ABOUT THE INSTITUTION State-supported, coed. *Awards:* certificates, bachelor's, and master's degrees. 28 undergraduate majors. *Total enrollment:* 6,221. Undergraduates: 5,307. Freshmen: 784. Federal methodology is used as a basis for awarding need-based institutional aid.

UNDERGRADUATE EXPENSES for 2013–2014 *Application fee:* $40. *Tuition, state resident:* full-time $970; part-time $40.42 per credit. *Tuition, nonresident:* full-time $7050; part-time $293.75 per credit. *Required fees:* full-time $7187; $278.45 per credit. Full-time tuition and fees vary according to class time, course load, degree level, and reciprocity agreements. Part-time tuition and fees vary according to class time, course load, degree level, and reciprocity agreements. *College room and board:* $10,500; *Room only:* $7380. Room and board charges vary according to board plan and housing facility.

FRESHMAN FINANCIAL AID (Fall 2011) 733 applied for aid; of those 70% were deemed to have need. 98% of freshmen with need received aid; of those 42% had need fully met. *Average percent of need met:* 82% (excluding resources awarded to replace EFC). *Average financial aid package:* $11,983 (excluding resources awarded to replace EFC). 2% of all full-time freshmen had no need and received non-need-based gift aid.

UNDERGRADUATE FINANCIAL AID (Fall 2011) 3,213 applied for aid; of those 69% were deemed to have need. 98% of undergraduates with need received aid; of those 46% had need fully met. *Average percent of need met:* 83% (excluding resources awarded to replace EFC). *Average financial aid package:* $11,002 (excluding resources awarded to replace EFC). 1% of all full-time undergraduates had no need and received non-need-based gift aid.

GIFT AID (NEED-BASED) *Total amount:* $8,175,955 (65% federal, 21% state, 14% institutional). *Receiving aid:* Freshmen: 58% (459); all full-time undergraduates: 45% (1,745). *Average award:* Freshmen: $4759; Undergraduates: $4596. *Scholarships, grants, and awards:* Federal Pell, FSEOG, state, private, college/university gift aid from institutional funds.

GIFT AID (NON-NEED-BASED) *Total amount:* $1,345,686 (4% state, 62% institutional, 34% external sources). *Receiving aid:* Freshmen: 30% (235). Undergraduates: 17% (649). *Average award:* Freshmen: $1760. Undergraduates: $2268. *Tuition waivers:* Full or partial for employees or children of employees, senior citizens. *ROTC:* Army cooperative, Naval cooperative, Air Force cooperative.

LOANS *Student loans:* $19,966,399 (36% need-based, 64% non-need-based). 74% of past graduating class borrowed through all loan programs. *Average indebtedness per student:* $20,449. *Average need-based loan:* Freshmen: $2732. Undergraduates: $3077. *Parent loans:* $1,626,241 (100% non-need-based). *Programs:* Federal Direct (Subsidized and Unsubsidized Stafford, PLUS), Perkins, state.

WORK-STUDY *Federal work-study:* Total amount: $172,369; 200 jobs averaging $1500.

APPLYING FOR FINANCIAL AID *Required financial aid form:* FAFSA. *Financial aid deadline:* 5/1 (priority: 3/1). *Notification date:* Continuous beginning 3/1. Students must reply within 2 weeks of notification.

CONTACT Ms. Jayne McGinn, Director of Financial Aid, Worcester State University, 486 Chandler Street, Worcester, MA 01602, 508-929-8058 or toll-free 866-WSC-CALL. *Fax:* 508-929-8194. *E-mail:* jayne.mcginn@worcester.edu. *Website:* http://www.worcester.edu/.

WRIGHT STATE UNIVERSITY
Dayton, OH

Tuition & fees (OH res): $8354	Average undergraduate aid package: $10,186

ABOUT THE INSTITUTION State-supported, coed. *Awards:* certificates, associate, bachelor's, master's, and doctoral degrees. 101 undergraduate majors. *Total enrollment:* 16,780. Undergraduates: 13,143. Freshmen: 2,311. Federal methodology is used as a basis for awarding need-based institutional aid.

UNDERGRADUATE EXPENSES for 2013–2014 *Application fee:* $30. *Tuition, state resident:* full-time $8354; part-time $378 per credit hour. *Tuition, nonresident:* full-time $16,182; part-time $738 per credit hour. Full-time tuition and fees vary according to course load. Part-time tuition and fees vary according to course load. *College room and board:* $8629; *Room only:* $5689. Room and board charges vary according to housing facility and location.

FRESHMAN FINANCIAL AID (Fall 2012, est.) 1,990 applied for aid; of those 82% were deemed to have need. 99% of freshmen with need received aid; of those 12% had need fully met. *Average percent of need met:* 60% (excluding resources awarded to replace EFC). *Average financial aid package:* $9693 (excluding resources awarded to replace EFC). 10% of all full-time freshmen had no need and received non-need-based gift aid.

UNDERGRADUATE FINANCIAL AID (Fall 2012, est.) 8,236 applied for aid; of those 87% were deemed to have need. 99% of undergraduates with need received aid;

of those 10% had need fully met. *Average percent of need met:* 57% (excluding resources awarded to replace EFC). *Average financial aid package:* $10,186 (excluding resources awarded to replace EFC). 8% of all full-time undergraduates had no need and received non-need-based gift aid.

GIFT AID (NEED-BASED) *Total amount:* $39,234,881 (63% federal, 13% state, 22% institutional, 2% external sources). *Receiving aid:* Freshmen: 62% (1,399); all full-time undergraduates: 55% (5,658). *Average award:* Freshmen: $5937; Undergraduates: $5995. *Scholarships, grants, and awards:* Federal Pell, FSEOG, state, private, college/university gift aid from institutional funds, United Negro College Fund, Federal Nursing, Choose Ohio First scholarships.

GIFT AID (NON-NEED-BASED) *Total amount:* $5,548,642 (23% state, 70% institutional, 7% external sources). *Receiving aid:* Freshmen: 4% (90). Undergraduates: 3% (279). *Average award:* Freshmen: $3132. Undergraduates: $3997. *Scholarships, grants, and awards by category:* Academic interests/achievement: 2,447 awards ($6,541,613 total): area/ethnic studies, biological sciences, business, communication, computer science, education, engineering/technologies, English, foreign languages, general academic interests/achievements, health fields, humanities, international studies, mathematics, military science, physical sciences, premedicine, religion/biblical studies, social sciences. *Creative arts/performance:* 187 awards ($258,805 total): applied art and design, art/fine arts, cinema/film/broadcasting, creative writing, dance, general creative arts/performance, music, performing arts, theater/drama. *Special achievements/activities:* 794 awards ($3,628,861 total): cheerleading/drum major, community service, general special achievements/activities, leadership, memberships. *Special characteristics:* 799 awards ($2,874,347 total): adult students, children and siblings of alumni, children of educators, children of faculty/staff, ethnic background, first-generation college students, handicapped students, international students, members of minority groups, out-of-state students. *Tuition waivers:* Full or partial for employees or children of employees, senior citizens. *ROTC:* Army, Air Force.

LOANS *Student loans:* $87,963,676 (82% need-based, 18% non-need-based). 83% of past graduating class borrowed through all loan programs. *Average indebtedness per student:* $28,349. *Average need-based loan:* Freshmen: $3743. Undergraduates: $4584. *Parent loans:* $4,162,763 (42% need-based, 58% non-need-based). *Programs:* Federal Direct (Subsidized and Unsubsidized Stafford, PLUS), Perkins, Federal Nursing, state, college/university, private loans.

WORK-STUDY *Federal work-study:* Total amount: $4,491,766; 1,247 jobs averaging $3553.

ATHLETIC AWARDS Total amount: $2,554,131 (35% need-based, 65% non-need-based).

APPLYING FOR FINANCIAL AID *Required financial aid form:* FAFSA. *Financial aid deadline (priority):* 3/1. *Notification date:* Continuous beginning 3/15.

CONTACT Office of Financial Aid, Wright State University, Raider Connect, 3640 Colonel Glenn Highway, Dayton, OH 45435, 937-775-4000 or toll-free 800-247-1770. *Fax:* 937-775-4410. *E-mail:* raiderconnect@wright.edu. *Website:* http://www.wright.edu/.

XAVIER UNIVERSITY
Cincinnati, OH

Tuition & fees: $33,000	Average undergraduate aid package: $20,355

ABOUT THE INSTITUTION Independent Roman Catholic, coed. *Awards:* certificates, associate, bachelor's, master's, and doctoral degrees. 66 undergraduate majors. *Total enrollment:* 6,650. Undergraduates: 4,485. Freshmen: 1,066. Federal methodology is used as a basis for awarding need-based institutional aid.

UNDERGRADUATE EXPENSES for 2013–2014 *Application fee:* $35. *Comprehensive fee:* $43,740 includes full-time tuition ($32,070), mandatory fees ($930), and room and board ($10,740). *College room only:* $5940. Full-time tuition and fees vary according to class time, course load, degree level, location, and program. Room and board charges vary according to board plan and housing facility. Part-time tuition and fees vary according to class time, course load, degree level, location, and program.

FRESHMAN FINANCIAL AID (Fall 2012, est.) 881 applied for aid; of those 79% were deemed to have need. 100% of freshmen with need received aid; of those 22% had need fully met. *Average percent of need met:* 74% (excluding resources awarded to replace EFC). *Average financial aid package:* $19,737 (excluding resources awarded to replace EFC). 32% of all full-time freshmen had no need and received non-need-based gift aid.

UNDERGRADUATE FINANCIAL AID (Fall 2012, est.) 2,926 applied for aid; of those 83% were deemed to have need. 100% of undergraduates with need received aid; of those 19% had need fully met. *Average percent of need met:* 72% (excluding resources awarded to replace EFC). *Average financial aid package:* $20,355 (excluding resources awarded to replace EFC). 35% of all full-time undergraduates had no need and received non-need-based gift aid.

GIFT AID (NEED-BASED) *Total amount:* $36,288,982 (10% federal, 2% state, 84% institutional, 4% external sources). *Receiving aid:* Freshmen: 64% (678); all full-time undergraduates: 57% (2,335). *Average award:* Freshmen: $15,051; Undergraduates: $15,307. *Scholarships, grants, and awards:* Federal Pell, FSEOG, state, private, college/university gift aid from institutional funds.

GIFT AID (NON-NEED-BASED) *Total amount:* $21,688,215 (93% institutional, 7% external sources). *Receiving aid:* Freshmen: 11% (113). Undergraduates: 8% (308). *Average award:* Freshmen: $14,178. Undergraduates: $12,836. *Scholarships, grants, and awards by category:* Academic interests/achievement: foreign languages, general academic interests/achievements, mathematics, military science, physical sciences, social sciences. *Creative arts/performance:* art/fine arts, music, performing arts, theater/drama. *Special characteristics:* children and siblings of alumni, international students, members of minority groups, siblings of current students. *Tuition waivers:* Full or partial for employees or children of employees, senior citizens. *ROTC:* Army, Air Force cooperative.

LOANS *Student loans:* $25,736,663 (67% need-based, 33% non-need-based). 70% of past graduating class borrowed through all loan programs. *Average indebtedness per student:* $32,155. *Average need-based loan:* Freshmen: $2876. Undergraduates: $3509. *Parent loans:* $7,804,514 (42% need-based, 58% non-need-based). *Programs:* Federal Direct (Subsidized and Unsubsidized Stafford, PLUS), Perkins.

WORK-STUDY *Federal work-study:* Total amount: $1,764,818; 630 jobs averaging $2225. *State or other work-study/employment:* 25 part-time jobs averaging $1900.

ATHLETIC AWARDS Total amount: $3,242,963 (38% need-based, 62% non-need-based).

APPLYING FOR FINANCIAL AID *Required financial aid form:* FAFSA. *Financial aid deadline (priority):* 2/15. *Notification date:* Continuous beginning 2/15. Students must reply by 5/1.

CONTACT Office of Financial Aid, Xavier University, 3800 Victory Parkway, Cincinnati, OH 45207-5111, 513-745-3142 or toll-free 877-XUADMIT. *Fax:* 513-745-2806. *Website:* http://www.xu.edu/.

XAVIER UNIVERSITY OF LOUISIANA
New Orleans, LA

Tuition & fees: $18,700	Average undergraduate aid package: $18,268

ABOUT THE INSTITUTION Independent Roman Catholic, coed. *Awards:* bachelor's, master's, and doctoral degrees. 49 undergraduate majors. *Total enrollment:* 3,178. Undergraduates: 2,525. Freshmen: 661. Federal methodology is used as a basis for awarding need-based institutional aid.

UNDERGRADUATE EXPENSES for 2013–2014 *Application fee:* $25. *Comprehensive fee:* $26,300 includes full-time tuition ($17,700), mandatory fees ($1000), and room and board ($7600). Room and board charges vary according to housing facility. *Part-time tuition:* $775 per credit hour. Part-time tuition and fees vary according to course load.

FRESHMAN FINANCIAL AID (Fall 2012, est.) 636 applied for aid; of those 89% were deemed to have need. 100% of freshmen with need received aid; of those .2% had need fully met. *Average percent of need met:* 13% (excluding resources awarded to replace EFC). *Average financial aid package:* $18,572 (excluding resources awarded to replace EFC). 7% of all full-time freshmen had no need and received non-need-based gift aid.

UNDERGRADUATE FINANCIAL AID (Fall 2012, est.) 2,277 applied for aid; of those 90% were deemed to have need. 100% of undergraduates with need received aid; of those .4% had need fully met. *Average percent of need met:* 13% (excluding resources awarded to replace EFC). *Average financial aid package:* $18,268 (excluding resources awarded to replace EFC). 4% of all full-time undergraduates had no need and received non-need-based gift aid.

GIFT AID (NEED-BASED) *Total amount:* $4,245,528 (91% federal, 9% state). *Receiving aid:* Freshmen: 60% (397); all full-time undergraduates: 59% (1,424).

Average award: Freshmen: $5445; Undergraduates: $5469. *Scholarships, grants, and awards:* Federal Pell, FSEOG, state, private, college/university gift aid from institutional funds, United Negro College Fund.

GIFT AID (NON-NEED-BASED) *Total amount:* $6,670,272 (19% state, 81% institutional). *Receiving aid:* Freshmen: 78% (513). Undergraduates: 67% (1,599). *Average award:* Freshmen: $12,462. Undergraduates: $11,899. *Scholarships, grants, and awards by category: Academic interests/achievement:* biological sciences, business, communication, computer science, education, engineering/technologies, English, foreign languages, general academic interests/achievements, health fields, humanities, mathematics, physical sciences, premedicine, religion/biblical studies, social sciences. *Creative arts/performance:* art/fine arts, music. *Special characteristics:* children of faculty/staff, spouses of current students. *Tuition waivers:* Full or partial for employees or children of employees. *ROTC:* Army cooperative, Naval cooperative, Air Force cooperative.

LOANS *Student loans:* $9,128,271 (88% need-based, 12% non-need-based). 87% of past graduating class borrowed through all loan programs. *Average indebtedness per student:* $25,566. *Average need-based loan:* Freshmen: $3624. Undergraduates: $4806. *Parent loans:* $3,401,167 (100% non-need-based). *Programs:* Federal Direct (Subsidized and Unsubsidized Stafford, PLUS), Perkins.

WORK-STUDY *Federal work-study:* Total amount: $302,737; 367 jobs averaging $1827.

ATHLETIC AWARDS Total amount: $755,981 (100% non-need-based).

APPLYING FOR FINANCIAL AID *Required financial aid form:* FAFSA. *Financial aid deadline (priority):* 1/1. *Notification date:* Continuous beginning 4/1. Students must reply within 2 weeks of notification.

CONTACT Mrs. Emily Jones, Financial Aid Director, Xavier University of Louisiana, One Drexel Drive, New Orleans, LA 70125-1098, 504-520-7517 or toll-free 877-XAVIERU. *E-mail:* ejones@xula.edu.
Website: http://www.xula.edu/.

YALE UNIVERSITY
New Haven, CT

Tuition & fees: $44,000	Average undergraduate aid package: $45,425

ABOUT THE INSTITUTION Independent, coed. *Awards:* certificates, bachelor's, master's, and doctoral degrees. 64 undergraduate majors. *Total enrollment:* 11,906. Undergraduates: 5,405. Freshmen: 1,355. Both federal and institutional methodology are used as a basis for awarding need-based institutional aid.

UNDERGRADUATE EXPENSES for 2013–2014 *Application fee:* $75. *Comprehensive fee:* $57,500 includes full-time tuition ($44,000) and room and board ($13,500). Room and board charges vary according to board plan.

FRESHMAN FINANCIAL AID (Fall 2012, est.) 744 applied for aid; of those 93% were deemed to have need. 100% of freshmen with need received aid; of those 100% had need fully met. *Average percent of need met:* 100% (excluding resources awarded to replace EFC). *Average financial aid package:* $46,331 (excluding resources awarded to replace EFC).

UNDERGRADUATE FINANCIAL AID (Fall 2012, est.) 3,058 applied for aid; of those 95% were deemed to have need. 100% of undergraduates with need received aid; of those 100% had need fully met. *Average percent of need met:* 100% (excluding resources awarded to replace EFC). *Average financial aid package:* $45,425 (excluding resources awarded to replace EFC).

GIFT AID (NEED-BASED) *Total amount:* $125,380,592 (4% federal, 93% institutional, 3% external sources). *Receiving aid:* Freshmen: 51% (691); all full-time undergraduates: 54% (2,910). *Average award:* Freshmen: $44,872; Undergraduates: $43,115. *Scholarships, grants, and awards:* Federal Pell, FSEOG, state, private, college/university gift aid from institutional funds, United Negro College Fund, Federal Nursing.

GIFT AID (NON-NEED-BASED) *Total amount:* $262,241 (100% external sources). *ROTC:* Army cooperative, Naval, Air Force.

LOANS *Student loans:* $2,636,105 (42% need-based, 58% non-need-based). 17% of past graduating class borrowed through all loan programs. *Average indebtedness per student:* $10,742. *Average need-based loan:* Freshmen: $2079. Undergraduates: $2734. *Parent loans:* $2,408,580 (100% non-need-based). *Programs:* Federal Direct (Subsidized and Unsubsidized Stafford, PLUS), Perkins, state, college/university.

WORK-STUDY *Federal work-study:* Total amount: $1,547,283; 618 jobs averaging $2507. *State or other work-study/employment:* Total amount: $4,200,301 (100% need-based). 1,589 part-time jobs averaging $2651.

APPLYING FOR FINANCIAL AID *Required financial aid forms:* FAFSA, CSS Financial Aid PROFILE, noncustodial (divorced/separated) parent's statement, business/farm supplement, federal income tax form(s). *Financial aid deadline:* 3/1. *Notification date:* 4/1. Students must reply by 5/1 or within 1 week of notification.

CONTACT Mr. Caesar T. Storlazzi, University Director of Financial Aid, Yale University, PO Box 208288, New Haven, CT 06520-8288, 203-432-0371. *Fax:* 203-777-6100. *E-mail:* sfs@yale.edu.
Website: http://www.yale.edu/.

YESHIVA AND KOLEL BAIS MEDRASH ELYON
Monsey, NY

CONTACT Financial Aid Office, Yeshiva and Kolel Bais Medrash Elyon, 73 Main Street, Monsey, NY 10952, 845-356-7064.

YESHIVA AND KOLLEL HARBOTZAS TORAH
Brooklyn, NY

CONTACT Financial Aid Office, Yeshiva and Kollel Harbotzas Torah, 1049 East 15th Street, Brooklyn, NY 11230, 718-692-0208.

YESHIVA BETH MOSHE
Scranton, PA

CONTACT Financial Aid Office, Yeshiva Beth Moshe, 930 Hickory Street, Scranton, PA 18505-2124, 717-346-1747.

YESHIVA COLLEGE OF THE NATION'S CAPITAL
Silver Spring, MD

CONTACT Financial Aid Office, Yeshiva College of the Nation's Capital, 1216 Arcola Avenue, Silver Spring, MD 20902, 301-593-2534.
Website: http://www.yeshiva.edu/.

YESHIVA DERECH CHAIM
Brooklyn, NY

CONTACT Financial Aid Office, Yeshiva Derech Chaim, 1573 39th Street, Brooklyn, NY 11218, 718-438-5426.

YESHIVA D'MONSEY RABBINICAL COLLEGE
Monsey, NY

CONTACT Financial Aid Office, Yeshiva D'Monsey Rabbinical College, 2 Roman Boulevard, Monsey, NY 10952, 914-352-5852.

YESHIVA GEDOLAH IMREI YOSEF D'SPINKA
Brooklyn, NY

CONTACT Financial Aid Office, Yeshiva Gedolah Imrei Yosef D'Spinka, 1466 56th Street, Brooklyn, NY 11219, 718-851-8721.

YESHIVA GEDOLAH OF GREATER DETROIT
Oak Park, MI

CONTACT Rabbi P. Rushnawitz, Executive Administrator , Yeshiva Gedolah of Greater Detroit, 24600 Greenfield Road, Oak Park, MI 48237-1544, 810-968-3360. *Fax:* 810-968-8613.

YESHIVA GEDOLAH RABBINICAL COLLEGE
Miami Beach, FL

CONTACT Financial Aid Office, Yeshiva Gedolah Rabbinical College, 1140 Alton Road, Miami Beach, FL 33139, 305-673-5664.

YESHIVA KARLIN STOLIN RABBINICAL INSTITUTE
Brooklyn, NY

CONTACT Mr. Daniel Ross, Financial Aid Administrator, Yeshiva Karlin Stolin Rabbinical Institute, 1818 Fifty-fourth Street, Brooklyn, NY 11204, 718-232-7800 Ext. 116. *Fax:* 718-331-4833.

YESHIVA OF NITRA RABBINICAL COLLEGE
Mount Kisco, NY

CONTACT Mr. Yosef Rosen, Financial Aid Administrator , Yeshiva of Nitra Rabbinical College, 194 Division Avenue, Mount Kisco, NY 10549, 718-384-5460. *Fax:* 718-387-9400.

YESHIVA OF THE TELSHE ALUMNI
Riverdale, NY

CONTACT Financial Aid Office, Yeshiva of the Telshe Alumni, 4904 Independence Avenue, Riverdale, NY 10471, 718-601-3523.

YESHIVA OHR ELCHONON CHABAD/ WEST COAST TALMUDICAL SEMINARY
Los Angeles, CA

CONTACT Ms. Hendy Tauber, Director of Financial Aid , Yeshiva Ohr Elchonon Chabad/West Coast Talmudical Seminary, 7215 Waring Avenue, Los Angeles, CA 90046-7660, 213-937-3763. *Fax:* 213-937-9456. *Website:* http://www.yoec.edu/.

YESHIVA SHAAREI TORAH OF ROCKLAND
Suffern, NY

CONTACT Financial Aid Office, Yeshiva Shaarei Torah of Rockland, 91 West Carlton Road, Suffern, NY 10901, 845-352-3431.

YESHIVA SHAAR HATORAH TALMUDIC RESEARCH INSTITUTE
Kew Gardens, NY

CONTACT Mr. Yoel Yankelewitz, Executive Director, Financial Aid, Yeshiva Shaar Hatorah Talmudic Research Institute, 117-06 84th Avenue, Kew Gardens, NY 11418-1469, 718-846-1940.

YESHIVAS NOVOMINSK
Brooklyn, NY

CONTACT Financial Aid Office, Yeshivas Novominsk, 1569 47th Street, Brooklyn, NY 11219, 718-438-2727.

YESHIVATH VIZNITZ
Monsey, NY

CONTACT Financial Aid Office, Yeshivath Viznitz, Phyllis Terrace, PO Box 446, Monsey, NY 10952, 914-356-1010.

YESHIVATH ZICHRON MOSHE
South Fallsburg, NY

CONTACT Ms. Miryom R. Miller, Director of Financial Aid , Yeshivath Zichron Moshe, Laurel Park Road, South Fallsburg, NY 12779, 914-434-5240. *Fax:* 914-434-1009. *E-mail:* lehus@aol.com.

YESHIVAT MIKDASH MELECH
Brooklyn, NY

CONTACT Financial Aid Office, Yeshivat Mikdash Melech, 1326 Ocean Parkway, Brooklyn, NY 11230-5601, 718-339-1090.

YESHIVA TORAS CHAIM TALMUDICAL SEMINARY
Denver, CO

CONTACT Office of Financial Aid, Yeshiva Toras Chaim Talmudical Seminary, 1400 Quitman Street, Denver, CO 80204-1415, 303-629-8200.

YESHIVA UNIVERSITY
New York, NY

Tuition & fees: $37,600	Average undergraduate aid package: $30,650

ABOUT THE INSTITUTION Independent, coed. *Awards:* certificates, associate, bachelor's, master's, and doctoral degrees (Yeshiva College and Stern College for Women are coordinate undergraduate colleges of arts and sciences for men and women, respectively. Sy Syms School of Business offers programs at both campuses). 36 undergraduate majors. *Total enrollment:* 6,753. Undergraduates: 2,869. Freshmen: 939. Both federal and institutional methodology are used as a basis for awarding need-based institutional aid.

UNDERGRADUATE EXPENSES for 2013–2014 *Application fee:* $65. *Comprehensive fee:* $48,750 includes full-time tuition ($36,600), mandatory fees ($1000), and room and board ($11,150). Full-time tuition and fees vary according to student level. *Part-time tuition:* $1240 per credit hour.

FRESHMAN FINANCIAL AID (Fall 2011) 667 applied for aid; of those 84% were deemed to have need. 100% of freshmen with need received aid; of those 29% had need fully met. *Average percent of need met:* 92% (excluding resources awarded to replace EFC). *Average financial aid package:* $32,031 (excluding resources awarded to replace EFC).

UNDERGRADUATE FINANCIAL AID (Fall 2011) 1,924 applied for aid; of those 83% were deemed to have need. 94% of undergraduates with need received aid; of those 25% had need fully met. *Average percent of need met:* 89% (excluding resources awarded to replace EFC). *Average financial aid package:* $30,650 (excluding resources awarded to replace EFC).

GIFT AID (NEED-BASED) *Total amount:* $36,008,431 (7% federal, 1% state, 92% institutional). *Receiving aid:* Freshmen: 61% (558); all full-time undergraduates: 50% (1,423). *Average award:* Freshmen: $28,366; Undergraduates: $26,206. *Scholarships, grants, and awards:* Federal Pell, FSEOG, state, college/university gift aid from institutional funds.

GIFT AID (NON-NEED-BASED) *Total amount:* $9,048,355 (99% institutional, 1% external sources). *Receiving aid:* Freshmen: 1% (10). Undergraduates: 2% (64). *Average award:* Freshmen: $26,763. Undergraduates: $21,511. *Scholarships, grants, and awards by category: Academic interests/achievement:* general academic interests/achievements. *Tuition waivers:* Full or partial for employees or children of employees.

LOANS *Student loans:* $6,568,912 (96% need-based, 4% non-need-based). 47% of past graduating class borrowed through all loan programs. *Average indebtedness per student:* $22,705. *Average need-based loan:* Freshmen: $5500. Undergraduates: $6222. *Parent loans:* $1,547,709 (81% need-based, 19% non-need-based). *Programs:* Federal Direct (Subsidized and Unsubsidized Stafford, PLUS), Perkins, college/university.

WORK-STUDY *Federal work-study:* Total amount: $550,438; jobs available. *State or other work-study/employment:* Part-time jobs available.

APPLYING FOR FINANCIAL AID *Required financial aid form:* FAFSA. *Financial aid deadline (priority):* 2/1. *Notification date:* Continuous beginning 3/15.

CONTACT Marianela Cabral, Director of Student Aid Operations, Yeshiva University, 500 West 185th Street, Room 121, New York, NY 10033, 212-960-5399. *Fax:* 212-960-0037. *E-mail:* mcabral@yu.edu. *Website:* http://www.yu.edu/.

YORK COLLEGE
York, NE

ABOUT THE INSTITUTION Independent Church of Christ, coed. 38 undergraduate majors.

GIFT AID (NEED-BASED) *Scholarships, grants, and awards:* Federal Pell, FSEOG, state, private, college/university gift aid from institutional funds.

GIFT AID (NON-NEED-BASED) *Scholarships, grants, and awards by category: Academic interests/achievement:* biological sciences, business, communication, computer science, education, English, general academic interests/achievements, mathematics, premedicine, religion/biblical studies. *Creative arts/performance:* music, theater/drama. *Special achievements/activities:* leadership, religious involvement. *Special characteristics:* children of faculty/staff, previous college experience, siblings of current students.

LOANS *Programs:* Federal Direct (Subsidized and Unsubsidized Stafford, PLUS), Perkins, college/university, alternative loans.

WORK-STUDY *Federal work-study:* Total amount: $78,744; 78 jobs averaging $1160. *State or other work-study/employment:* Total amount: $325,576 (89% need-based, 11% non-need-based). 190 part-time jobs averaging $1322.

APPLYING FOR FINANCIAL AID *Required financial aid form:* FAFSA.

CONTACT Brien Alley, Director of Financial Aid, York College, 1125 East 8th Street, York, NE 68467, 402-363-5624 or toll-free 800-950-9675. *Fax:* 402-363-5623. *E-mail:* balley@york.edu. *Website:* http://www.york.edu/.

YORK COLLEGE OF PENNSYLVANIA
York, PA

Tuition & fees: $17,010	Average undergraduate aid package: $12,134

ABOUT THE INSTITUTION Independent, coed. *Awards:* certificates, bachelor's, master's, and doctoral degrees. 55 undergraduate majors. *Total enrollment:* 5,439. Undergraduates: 5,182. Freshmen: 1,142. Federal methodology is used as a basis for awarding need-based institutional aid.

UNDERGRADUATE EXPENSES for 2013–2014 *Comprehensive fee:* $26,590 includes full-time tuition ($15,350), mandatory fees ($1660), and room and board ($9580). *College room only:* $5380. Full-time tuition and fees vary according to program. Room and board charges vary according to board plan and housing facility. *Part-time tuition:* $475 per credit. *Part-time fees:* $360 per term.

FRESHMAN FINANCIAL AID (Fall 2012, est.) 1,063 applied for aid; of those 77% were deemed to have need. 100% of freshmen with need received aid; of those 26% had need fully met. *Average percent of need met:* 64% (excluding resources awarded to replace EFC). *Average financial aid package:* $11,676 (excluding resources awarded to replace EFC). 27% of all full-time freshmen had no need and received non-need-based gift aid.

UNDERGRADUATE FINANCIAL AID (Fall 2012, est.) 3,921 applied for aid; of those 80% were deemed to have need. 99% of undergraduates with need received aid; of those 23% had need fully met. *Average percent of need met:* 65% (excluding resources awarded to replace EFC). *Average financial aid package:* $12,134 (excluding resources awarded to replace EFC). 21% of all full-time undergraduates had no need and received non-need-based gift aid.

GIFT AID (NEED-BASED) *Total amount:* $19,522,255 (28% federal, 16% state, 53% institutional, 3% external sources). *Receiving aid:* Freshmen: 46% (518); all full-time undergraduates: 48% (2,193). *Average award:* Freshmen: $4242; Undergraduates: $5098. *Scholarships, grants, and awards:* Federal Pell, FSEOG, state, private, college/university gift aid from institutional funds.

GIFT AID (NON-NEED-BASED) *Total amount:* $3,447,691 (1% state, 95% institutional, 4% external sources). *Receiving aid:* Freshmen: 70% (800). Undergraduates: 46% (2,086). *Average award:* Freshmen: $4243. Undergraduates: $3593. *Scholarships, grants, and awards by category: Academic interests/achievement:* 2,786 awards ($16,197,926 total): engineering/technologies, general academic interests/achievements. *Creative arts/performance:* 14 awards ($22,362 total): music. *Special characteristics:* 28 awards ($55,456 total): children and siblings of alumni, children of union members/company employees, international students, members of minority groups. *Tuition waivers:* Full or partial for employees or children of employees. *ROTC:* Army cooperative.

YOUNGSTOWN STATE UNIVERSITY

LOANS *Student loans:* $25,169,264 (46% need-based, 54% non-need-based). 77% of past graduating class borrowed through all loan programs. *Average indebtedness per student:* $35,297. *Average need-based loan:* Freshmen: $5813. Undergraduates: $6658. *Parent loans:* $6,930,182 (79% need-based, 21% non-need-based). *Programs:* Federal Direct (Subsidized and Unsubsidized Stafford, PLUS), Perkins, Federal Nursing, college/university.

WORK-STUDY *Federal work-study:* Total amount: $570,450; 311 jobs averaging $1989. *State or other work-study/employment:* Total amount: $20,900 (100% non-need-based). 10 part-time jobs averaging $1980.

APPLYING FOR FINANCIAL AID *Required financial aid form:* FAFSA. *Financial aid deadline:* Continuous. *Notification date:* Continuous beginning 3/1. Students must reply within 4 weeks of notification.

CONTACT Calvin Williams, Director of Financial Aid, York College of Pennsylvania, 441 Country Club Road, York, PA 17403, 717-849-1682 or toll-free 800-455-8018. *Fax:* 717-849-1685. *E-mail:* financialaid@ycp.edu. *Website:* http://www.ycp.edu/.

YORK COLLEGE OF THE CITY UNIVERSITY OF NEW YORK
Jamaica, NY

ABOUT THE INSTITUTION State and locally supported, coed. *Awards:* bachelor's and master's degrees. 46 undergraduate majors. *Total enrollment:* 8,389. Undergraduates: 8,350. Freshmen: 1,110.

GIFT AID (NEED-BASED) *Scholarships, grants, and awards:* Federal Pell, FSEOG, state, private, college/university gift aid from institutional funds, United Negro College Fund.

LOANS *Programs:* Federal Direct (Subsidized and Unsubsidized Stafford, PLUS), Perkins.

WORK-STUDY *Federal work-study:* Total amount: $1,999,571; 1,737 jobs averaging $1160.

APPLYING FOR FINANCIAL AID *Required financial aid forms:* FAFSA, state aid form.

CONTACT Ms. Cathy Michaels, Director of Student Financial Services, York College of the City University of New York, 94-20 Guy R. Brewer Boulevard, Jamaica, NY 11451-0001, 718-262-2238. *E-mail:* cmichaels@york.cuny.edu. *Website:* http://www.york.cuny.edu/.

YOUNG HARRIS COLLEGE
Young Harris, GA

Tuition & fees: $25,280	Average undergraduate aid package: $18,612

ABOUT THE INSTITUTION Independent United Methodist, coed. *Awards:* bachelor's degrees. 30 undergraduate majors. *Total enrollment:* 1,034. Undergraduates: 1,034. Freshmen: 388. Federal methodology is used as a basis for awarding need-based institutional aid.

UNDERGRADUATE EXPENSES for 2013–2014 *Comprehensive fee:* $34,940 includes full-time tuition ($24,500), mandatory fees ($780), and room and board ($9660). Full-time tuition and fees vary according to course load. Room and board charges vary according to housing facility. *Part-time tuition:* $675 per credit hour. Part-time tuition and fees vary according to course load.

FRESHMAN FINANCIAL AID (Fall 2011) 278 applied for aid; of those 82% were deemed to have need. 100% of freshmen with need received aid; of those 29% had need fully met. *Average percent of need met:* 80% (excluding resources awarded to replace EFC). *Average financial aid package:* $19,132 (excluding resources awarded to replace EFC). 32% of all full-time freshmen had no need and received non-need-based gift aid.

UNDERGRADUATE FINANCIAL AID (Fall 2011) 727 applied for aid; of those 88% were deemed to have need. 100% of undergraduates with need received aid; of those 22% had need fully met. *Average percent of need met:* 79% (excluding resources awarded to replace EFC). *Average financial aid package:* $18,612 (excluding resources awarded to replace EFC). 28% of all full-time undergraduates had no need and received non-need-based gift aid.

GIFT AID (NEED-BASED) *Total amount:* $10,052,483 (16% federal, 13% state, 70% institutional, 1% external sources). *Receiving aid:* Freshmen: 66% (229); all full-time undergraduates: 70% (638). *Average award:* Freshmen: $16,603; Undergraduates: $15,554. *Scholarships, grants, and awards:* Federal Pell, FSEOG, state, private, college/university gift aid from institutional funds.

GIFT AID (NON-NEED-BASED) *Total amount:* $5,159,384 (12% state, 85% institutional, 3% external sources). *Receiving aid:* Freshmen: 18% (64). Undergraduates: 14% (126). *Average award:* Freshmen: $13,836. Undergraduates: $15,018. *Scholarships, grants, and awards by category:* Creative arts/performance: art/fine arts, music, performing arts, theater/drama. *Special characteristics:* children of faculty/staff. *Tuition waivers:* Full or partial for employees or children of employees.

LOANS *Student loans:* $3,823,402 (74% need-based, 26% non-need-based). 72% of past graduating class borrowed through all loan programs. *Average indebtedness per student:* $25,158. *Average need-based loan:* Freshmen: $3375. Undergraduates: $3783. *Parent loans:* $1,163,292 (44% need-based, 56% non-need-based). *Programs:* Federal Direct (Subsidized and Unsubsidized Stafford, PLUS), college/university.

WORK-STUDY *Federal work-study:* Total amount: $35,311; jobs available. *State or other work-study/employment:* Total amount: $311,335 (43% need-based, 57% non-need-based). Part-time jobs available.

APPLYING FOR FINANCIAL AID *Required financial aid forms:* FAFSA, state aid form. *Financial aid deadline (priority):* 5/1. *Notification date:* Continuous. Students must reply within 2 weeks of notification.

CONTACT Linda Adams, Director of Financial Aid, Young Harris College, 1 College Street, Young Harris, GA 30582, 706-379-5188 or toll-free 800-241-3754 (in-state). *Fax:* 706-379-4594. *E-mail:* leadams@yhc.edu. *Website:* http://www.yhc.edu/.

YOUNGSTOWN STATE UNIVERSITY
Youngstown, OH

Tuition & fees (OH res): $7712	Average undergraduate aid package: $8522

ABOUT THE INSTITUTION State-supported, coed. *Awards:* certificates, diplomas, associate, bachelor's, master's, and doctoral degrees. 123 undergraduate majors. *Total enrollment:* 13,799. Undergraduates: 12,644. Freshmen: 2,220. Federal methodology is used as a basis for awarding need-based institutional aid.

UNDERGRADUATE EXPENSES for 2013–2014 *Application fee:* $40. *Tuition, state resident:* full-time $7483; part-time $312 per credit hour. *Tuition, nonresident:* full-time $13,440; part-time $560 per credit hour. *Required fees:* full-time $229; $10 per credit hour. Full-time tuition and fees vary according to course load. Part-time tuition and fees vary according to course load. *College room and board:* $8150. Room and board charges vary according to board plan and housing facility.

FRESHMAN FINANCIAL AID (Fall 2011) 2,178 applied for aid; of those 89% were deemed to have need. 100% of freshmen with need received aid; of those 9% had need fully met. *Average percent of need met:* 31% (excluding resources awarded to replace EFC). *Average financial aid package:* $8151 (excluding resources awarded to replace EFC). 7% of all full-time freshmen had no need and received non-need-based gift aid.

UNDERGRADUATE FINANCIAL AID (Fall 2011) 9,097 applied for aid; of those 89% were deemed to have need. 100% of undergraduates with need received aid; of those 7% had need fully met. *Average percent of need met:* 29% (excluding resources awarded to replace EFC). *Average financial aid package:* $8522 (excluding resources awarded to replace EFC). 6% of all full-time undergraduates had no need and received non-need-based gift aid.

GIFT AID (NEED-BASED) *Total amount:* $40,236,483 (82% federal, 9% state, 3% institutional, 6% external sources). *Receiving aid:* Freshmen: 67% (1,588); all full-time undergraduates: 62% (6,331). *Average award:* Freshmen: $5135; Undergraduates: $5163. *Scholarships, grants, and awards:* Federal Pell, FSEOG, state, private, college/university gift aid from institutional funds, Advanced Education Nursing Scholarships.

GIFT AID (NON-NEED-BASED) *Total amount:* $7,892,052 (4% federal, 15% state, 17% institutional, 64% external sources). *Receiving aid:* Freshmen: 21% (493). Undergraduates: 20% (2,052). *Average award:* Freshmen: $3139. Undergraduates: $2841. *Scholarships, grants, and awards by category:* Academic interests/achievement: biological sciences, business, communication, computer science, edu-

Peterson's How to Get Money for College 2014

Peterson's How to Get Money for College 2014

www.petersonsbooks.com **729**

YOUNGSTOWN STATE UNIVERSITY

cation, engineering/technologies, English, foreign languages, general academic interests/achievements, health fields, humanities, mathematics, military science, physical sciences, premedicine, religion/biblical studies, social sciences. *Creative arts/performance:* art/fine arts, creative writing, journalism/publications, music, performing arts, theater/drama. *Special achievements/activities:* cheerleading/drum major, community service, leadership, memberships, religious involvement. *Special characteristics:* adult students, children and siblings of alumni, children of faculty/staff, children of union members/company employees, children of workers in trades, children with a deceased or disabled parent, ethnic background, handicapped students, international students, local/state students, members of minority groups, out-of-state students, public servants, religious affiliation, spouses of deceased or disabled public servants, veterans, veterans' children. **Tuition waivers:** Full or partial for employees or children of employees, senior citizens. **ROTC:** Army, Air Force cooperative.

LOANS *Student loans:* $80,872,028 (44% need-based, 56% non-need-based). 72% of past graduating class borrowed through all loan programs. *Average indebtedness per student:* $24,209. **Average need-based loan:** Freshmen: $3285. Undergraduates: $3865. **Parent loans:** $41,798,439 (100% non-need-based). **Programs:** Federal Direct (Subsidized and Unsubsidized Stafford, PLUS), Perkins, Charles E. Schell Foundation loans, George W. Wright Student Aid loans, Rogers student loans.

WORK-STUDY *Federal work-study:* Total amount: $912,051; jobs available. *State or other work-study/employment:* Total amount: $3,515,735 (100% non-need-based). Part-time jobs available.

ATHLETIC AWARDS Total amount: $3,787,113 (100% non-need-based).

APPLYING FOR FINANCIAL AID *Required financial aid forms:* FAFSA, institution's own form. *Financial aid deadline (priority):* 2/15. **Notification date:** Continuous beginning 4/1. Students must reply within 4 weeks of notification.

CONTACT Barbara Greene, Manager of Financial Analysis and Reporting, Youngstown State University, One University Plaza, Youngstown, OH 44555, 330-941-3504 or toll-free 877-468-6978. *Fax:* 330-941-1659. *E-mail:* bgreene@ysu.edu. *Website:* http://www.ysu.edu/.

Appendix

State Scholarship and Grant Programs

E ach state government has established one or more state-administered financial aid programs for qualified students. In many instances, these state programs are restricted to legal residents of the state. However, they often are available to out-of-state students who will be or are attending colleges or universities within the state. In addition to residential status, other qualifications frequently exist.

Gift aid and forgivable loan programs open to under-graduate students for all states and the District of Columbia are described on the following pages. They are arranged in alphabetical order, first by state name, then by program name. The annotation for each program provides information about the program, eligibility, and the contact addresses for applications or further information. Unless otherwise stated, this information refers to awards for 2012–13. Information is provided by the state-sponsoring agency in response to *Peterson's Annual Survey of Non-institutional Aid*, which was conducted between January 2013 and April 2013. Information is accurate when Peterson's receives it. However, it is always advisable to check with the sponsor to ascertain that the information remains correct.

You should write to the address given for each program to request that award details for 2014–15 be sent to you as soon as they are available. Descriptive information, brochures, and application forms for state scholarship programs are usually available from the financial aid offices of public colleges or universities within the specific state. High school guidance offices often have information and relevant forms for awards for which high school seniors may be eligible. Increasingly, state government agencies are putting state scholarship information on state government agency websites. In searching state government websites, however, you should be aware that the higher education agency in many states is separate from the state's general education office, which is often responsible only for elementary and secondary education. Also, the page at public university websites that provides information about student financial aid frequently has a list of state-sponsored scholarships and financial aid programs.

Names of scholarship programs are frequently used inconsistently or become abbreviated in popular usage. Many programs have variant names by which they are known. The program's sponsor has approved the title of the program that Peterson's uses in this guide, yet this name may differ from the program's official name or from its most commonly used name.

In addition to the grant aid and forgivable loan programs listed on the following pages, states may also offer internship or work-study programs, graduate fellowships and grants, or low-interest loans. If you are interested in learning more about these other kinds of programs, the state education office that supplies information or applications for the undergraduate scholarship programs listed here should be able to provide information about other kinds of higher education financial aid programs that are sponsored by the state.

ALABAMA

Air Force ROTC College Scholarship. Scholarship program provides three- and four-year scholarships in three different types to high school seniors. All scholarship cadets receive a nontaxable monthly allowance (stipend) during the academic year. For more details refer to web site http://www.afrotc.com/scholarships/hsschol/types.php. *Award:* Scholarship for use in freshman, sophomore, junior, or senior years; renewable. *Award amount:* $9000–$15,000. *Number of awards:* 2000–4000. *Eligibility Requirements:* Applicant must be age 17-30 and enrolled or expecting to enroll full-time at a two-year or four-year institution or university. Applicant must have 3.0 GPA or higher. Available to U.S. citizens. Applicant or parent must meet one or more of the following requirements: Air Force experience; retired from active duty; disabled or killed as a result of military service; prisoner of war; or missing in action. *Application Requirements:* Application form, interview, test scores, transcript. **Deadline:** December 1.

Contact Ty Christian, Chief Air Force ROTC Advertising Manager, Air Force Reserve Officer Training Corps, 551 East Maxwell Boulevard, Maxwell Air Force Base, AL 36112-6106. *E-mail:* ty.christian@maxwell.af.mil. *Phone:* 334-953-2278. *Fax:* 334-953-4384. *Website:* http://www.afrotc.com/.

Alabama G.I. Dependents Scholarship Program. Full scholarship for dependents of Alabama disabled, prisoner-of-war, or missing-in-action veterans. Child or stepchild must initiate training before 26th birthday; age 30 deadline may apply in certain situations. No age deadline for spouses or widows. *Award:* Scholarship for use in freshman, sophomore, junior, or senior years; renewable. *Eligibility Requirements:* Applicant must be enrolled or expecting to enroll full- or part-time at a four-year institution or university; resident of Alabama and studying in Alabama. Available to U.S. and non-U.S. citizens. Applicant or parent must meet one or more of the following requirements: general military experience; retired from active duty; disabled or killed as a result of military service; prisoner of war; or missing in action. *Application Requirements:* Application form. **Deadline:** varies.

Contact Willie Moore, Scholarship Administrator, Alabama Department of Veterans Affairs, PO Box 1509, Montgomery, AL 36102-1509. *E-mail:* wmoore@va.state.al.us. *Phone:* 334-242-5077. *Fax:* 334-242-5102. *Website:* http://www.va.alabama.gov/.

Alabama National Guard Educational Assistance Program. Renewable award aids Alabama residents who are members of the Alabama National Guard and are enrolled in a nationally recognized accredited college in Alabama. Forms must be signed by a representative of the Alabama Military Department and financial aid officer. Recipient must be in a degree-seeking program. *Award:* Scholarship for use in freshman, sophomore, junior, senior, or graduate years; renewable. *Award amount:* $25–$1000. *Number of awards:* up to 800. *Eligibility Requirements:* Applicant must be enrolled or expecting to enroll full- or part-time at a two-year or four-year or technical institution or university; resident of Alabama and studying in Alabama. Available to U.S. citizens. Applicant must have national guard experience. *Application Requirements:* Application form. **Deadline:** continuous.

Contact Cheryl Newton, Grants Coordinator. *E-mail:* cheryl.newton@ache.alabama.gov. *Phone:* 334-242-2273. *Fax:* 334-242-2269. *Website:* http://www.ache.alabama.gov/.

Alabama Student Assistance Program. Scholarship award of $300 to $5000 per academic year given to undergraduate students residing in the state of Alabama and attending a college or university in Alabama. *Award:* Grant for use in freshman, sophomore, junior, or senior years; not renewable. *Award amount:* $300–$5000. *Eligibility Requirements:* Applicant must be enrolled or expecting to enroll full- or part-time at a two-year or four-year or technical institution or university; resident of Alabama and studying in Alabama. Available to U.S. citizens. *Application Requirements:* Application form. **Deadline:** continuous.

Contact Cheryl Newton, Grants Coordinator. *E-mail:* cheryl.newton@ache.alabama.gov. *Phone:* 334-242-2273. *Fax:* 334-242-2269. *Website:* http://www.ache.alabama.gov/.

Alabama Student Grant Program. Nonrenewable awards available to Alabama residents for undergraduate study at certain independent colleges within the state. Both full and half-time students are eligible. Deadlines: September 15, January 15, and February 15. *Award:* Grant for use in freshman, sophomore, junior, or senior years; not renewable. *Award amount:* up to $1200. *Number of awards:* up to 1200. *Eligibility*

Requirements: Applicant must be enrolled or expecting to enroll full- or part-time at a four-year institution or university; resident of Alabama and studying in Alabama. Available to U.S. citizens. *Application Requirements:* 5 proofs of Alabama residency, application form.

Contact Cheryl Newton, Grants Coordinator. *E-mail:* cheryl.newton@ache.alabama.gov. *Phone:* 334-242-2273. *Fax:* 334-242-2269. *Website:* http://www.ache.alabama.gov/.

Police Officers and Firefighters Survivors Education Assistance Program-Alabama. Provides tuition, fees, books, and supplies to dependents of full-time police officers and firefighters killed or totally disabled in the line of duty. Must attend an Alabama public college as an undergraduate. Must be Alabama resident. *Award:* Scholarship for use in freshman, sophomore, junior, or senior years; renewable. *Award amount:* $1600–$12,000. *Number of awards:* 15-30. *Eligibility Requirements:* Applicant must be enrolled or expecting to enroll full- or part-time at a two-year or four-year or technical institution or university; single; resident of Alabama and studying in Alabama. Available to U.S. citizens. *Application Requirements:* Application form, birth certificate, marriage license, death certificate, letter from medical doctor, transcript. **Deadline:** continuous.

Contact Cheryl Newton, Grants Coordinator. *E-mail:* cheryl.newton@ache.alabama.gov. *Phone:* 334-242-2273. *Fax:* 334-242-2269. *Website:* http://www.ache.alabama.gov/.

ALASKA

AlaskAdvantage Education Grant. The Alaska legislature created the AlaskAdvantage Education Grant Program (AEG) to provide need-based financial assistance to eligible Alaska students attending qualifying postsecondary educational institutions in Alaska. Students apply by completing the FAFSA annually. *Award:* Grant for use in freshman, sophomore, junior, or senior years; not renewable. *Award amount:* $500–$3000. *Eligibility Requirements:* Applicant must be enrolled or expecting to enroll full- or part-time at a two-year or four-year institution or university; resident of Alaska and studying in Alaska. Available to U.S. citizens. *Application Requirements:* Completed FAFSA.

Contact Adam Weed, Special Programs Coordinator. *E-mail:* customer_service@acpe.state.ak.us. *Phone:* 907-

465-6685. *Website:* http://www.acpe.alaska.gov.

Alaska Performance Scholarship. To qualify, students must take a specific, rigorous high school curriculum; earn a minimum 2.5 GPA; and do well on college or career readiness exam. Students apply by completing the FAFSA by the annual deadline. Awards can be used at any regionally accredited college or university in Alaska, or for approved career and technical education programs in the state. Students must use scholarship within 6 years of high school graduation. Students cannot receive award for more than 8 semesters. *Award:* Scholarship for use in freshman, sophomore, junior, senior, graduate, or postgraduate years; not renewable. *Award amount:* $500–$4755. *Eligibility Requirements:* Applicant must be enrolled or expecting to enroll full- or part-time at a two-year or four-year or technical institution or university; resident of Alaska and studying in Alaska. Applicant must have 2.5 GPA or higher. Available to U.S. citizens. *Application Requirements:* FAFSA.

Contact Adam Weed, Special Programs Coordinator. *E-mail:* customer_service@acpe.state.ak.us. *Phone:* 907-465-6685. *Website:* http://www.acpe.alaska.gov.

ARIZONA

Leveraging Educational Assistance Partnership. Grants to financially needy students, who enroll in and attend postsecondary education or training in Arizona schools. Program was formerly known as the State Student Incentive Grant or SSIG Program. *Award:* Grant for use in freshman, sophomore, junior, senior, or graduate years; not renewable. *Award amount:* $100–$2500. *Eligibility Requirements:* Applicant must be enrolled or expecting to enroll full- or part-time at a two-year or four-year or technical institution or university; resident of Arizona and studying in Arizona. Available to U.S. citizens. *Application Requirements:* Application form, financial need analysis, transcript. **Deadline:** April 30.

Contact Mila Zaporteza, Business Manager and LEAP Financial Aid Manager, Arizona Commission for Postsecondary Education, 2020 North Central Avenue, Suite 650, Phoenix, AZ 85004-4503. *E-mail:* mila@azhighered.gov. *Phone:* 602-258-2435 Ext. 102. *Fax:* 602-258-2483. *Website:* http://www.azhighered.gov/.

ARKANSAS

Arkansas Academic Challenge Scholarship Program. Awards for Arkansas residents who are graduating high school seniors, currently enrolled college students and nontraditional students to study at an approved Arkansas institution. Must have at least a 2.5 GPA or 19 ACT composite score (or the equivalent). Renewable up to three additional years. *Award:* Scholarship for use in freshman, sophomore, junior, or senior years; renewable. *Award amount:* $1250–$4500. *Number of awards:* 30,000–35,000. *Eligibility Requirements:* Applicant must be enrolled or expecting to enroll full- or part-time at a two-year or four-year institution or university; resident of Arkansas and studying in Arkansas. Applicant must have 2.5 GPA or higher. Available to U.S. citizens. *Application Requirements:* Application form, application form may be submitted online (http://www.adhe.edu), financial need analysis, test scores, transcript. **Deadline:** June 1.

Contact Philip Axelroth, Financial Aid Program Coordinator. *Phone:* 501-371-2000. *Website:* http://www.adhe.edu/.

Arkansas Governor's Scholars Program. Awards for outstanding Arkansas high school seniors. Must be an Arkansas resident and have a high school GPA of at least 3.5 or have scored at least 27 on the ACT. Award is $4000 per year for four years of full-time undergraduate study. Applicants who attain 32 or above on ACT, 1410 or above on SAT and have an academic 3.5 GPA, or are selected as National Merit or National Achievement finalists may receive an award equal to tuition, mandatory fees, room, and board up to $10,000 per year at any Arkansas institution. *Award:* Scholarship for use in freshman, sophomore, junior, senior, or graduate years; renewable. *Award amount:* $4000–$10,000. *Number of awards:* 75–375. *Eligibility Requirements:* Applicant must be high school student; planning to enroll or expecting to enroll full-time at a two-year or four-year institution or university; resident of Arkansas and studying in Arkansas. Applicant must have 3.5 GPA or higher. Available to U.S. citizens. *Application Requirements:* Application form, application form may be submitted online (http://www.adhe.edu), community service, test scores, transcript. **Deadline:** February 1.

Contact Philip Axelroth, Financial Aid Program Coordinator. *Phone:* 501-371-2000. *Website:* http://www.adhe.edu/.

Arkansas Single Parent Scholarship. Scholarships are awarded to economically disadvantaged single parents who reside in Arkansas. Applicants must have custodial care of at least one minor child and have not already received a 4-year degree. Some scholarships may be awarded to single parents enrolled in a Masters of Arts in Teaching program. Application forms, award values, deadlines, and other requirements vary by county. Visit http://www.aspsf.org for more information. *Award:* Scholarship for use in freshman, sophomore, junior, senior, or graduate years; not renewable. *Award amount:* $200–$1800. *Number of awards:* up to 2600. *Eligibility Requirements:* Applicant must be enrolled or expecting to enroll full- or part-time at a two-year or four-year or technical institution or university; single and resident of Arkansas. Available to U.S. and non-U.S. citizens. *Application Requirements:* Application form, application form may be submitted online (http://www.aspsf.org), essay, FAFSA Student Aid Report (SAR), financial need analysis, interview, recommendations or references, transcript. **Deadline:** varies.

Contact Ruthanne Hill, Executive Director. *E-mail:* rhill@aspsf.org. *Phone:* 479-927-1402 Ext. 11. *Website:* http://www.aspsf.org/.

Law Enforcement Officers' Dependents Scholarship–Arkansas. Scholarship for dependents, under 23 years old, of Arkansas law-enforcement officers killed or permanently disabled in the line of duty. Renewable award is a waiver of tuition, fees, and room, at two- or four-year Arkansas institution. Submit birth certificate, death certificate, and claims commission report of findings of fact. Proof of disability from State Claims Commission may also be submitted. *Award:* Scholarship for use in freshman, sophomore, junior, or senior years; renewable. *Number of awards:* 27–32. *Eligibility Requirements:* Applicant must be enrolled or expecting to enroll full- or part-time at a two-year or four-year or technical institution or university; resident of Arkansas and studying in Arkansas. Available to U.S. citizens. *Application Requirements:* Application form. **Deadline:** continuous.

Contact Tara Smith, Director of Financial Aid, Arkansas Department of Higher Education, 114 East Capitol Avenue, Little Rock, AR 72201-3818. *E-mail:* taras@adhe.edu. *Phone:* 501-371-2000. *Fax:* 501-371-2001. *Website:* http://www.adhe.edu/.

Military Dependent's Scholarship Program. Renewable waiver of tuition, fees, room and board undergraduate students seeking a bachelor's degree or certificate of completion at any public college, university or technical school in Arkansas who qualify as a spouse or dependent child of an Arkansas resident who has been declared to be missing in action, killed in action, a POW, or killed on ordnance delivery, or a veteran who has been declared to be 100 percent totally and permanently disabled during, or as a result of, active military service. *Award:* Scholarship for use in freshman, sophomore, junior, or senior years; renewable. *Number of awards:* 1–60. *Eligibility Requirements:* Applicant must be enrolled or expecting to enroll full-time at a two-year or four-year or technical institution or university; resident of Arkansas and studying in Arkansas. Available to U. S. citizens. Applicant or parent must meet one or more of the following requirements: general military experience; retired from active duty; disabled or killed as a result of military service; prisoner of war; or missing in action. *Application Requirements:* Application form, recommendations or references, report of casualty. **Deadline:** June 1.

Contact Tara Smith, Director of Financial Aid, Arkansas Department of Higher Education, 114 East Capitol Avenue, Little Rock, AR 72201-3818. *E-mail:* taras@adhe.edu. *Phone:* 501-371-2000. *Fax:* 501-371-2001. *Website:* http://www.adhe.edu/.

Second Effort Scholarship. Awarded to those scholars who achieved one of the 10 highest scores on the Arkansas High School Diploma Test (GED). Must be at least age 18 and not have graduated from high school. Students do not apply for this award, they are contacted by the Arkansas Department of Higher Education. *Award:* Scholarship for use in freshman, sophomore, junior, or senior years; renewable. *Award amount:* up to $1000. *Number of awards:* 10. *Eligibility Requirements:* Applicant must be enrolled or expecting to enroll full- or part-time at a two-year or four-year institution or university; resident of Arkansas and studying in Arkansas. Available to U.S. citizens. *Application Requirements:* Application form, application form may be submitted online (http://www.adhe.edu). **Deadline:** varies.

Contact Philip Axelroth, Financial Aid Program Coordinator. *Phone:* 501-371-2000. *Website:* http://www.adhe.edu/.

CALIFORNIA

Cal Grant C. Award for California residents who are enrolled in a short-term vocational training program. Program must lead to a recognized degree or certificate. Course length must be a minimum of 4 months and no longer than 24 months. Students must be attending an approved California institution and show financial need. *Award:* Grant for use in freshman or sophomore years; renewable. *Award amount:* $576–$3168. *Number of awards:* up to 7761. *Eligibility Requirements:* Applicant must be enrolled or expecting to enroll full- or part-time at a two-year or technical institution; resident of California and studying in California. Available to U.S. citizens. *Application Requirements:* Application form, financial need analysis, GPA verification. **Deadline:** March 2.

Contact Catalina Mistler, Chief, Program Administration and Services Division, California Student Aid Commission, PO Box 419026, Rancho Cordova, CA 95741-9026. *E-mail:* studentsupport@csac.ca.gov. *Phone:* 916-526-7268. *Fax:* 916-526-8002. *Website:* http://www.csac.ca.gov/.

Child Development Teacher and Supervisor Grant Program. Award is for those students pursuing an approved course of study leading to a Child Development Permit issued by the California Commission on Teacher Credentialing. In exchange for each year funding is received, recipients agree to provide one year of service in a licensed childcare center. Child and Family Studies; Education. *Award:* Grant for use in freshman, sophomore, junior, senior, or graduate years; renewable. *Award amount:* $1000–$2000. *Number of awards:* up to 300. *Eligibility Requirements:* Applicant must be enrolled or expecting to enroll full- or part-time at a two-year or four-year institution or university; resident of California and studying in California. Applicant or parent of applicant must have employment or volunteer experience in teaching/education. Available to U.S. citizens. *Application Requirements:* Application, financial need analysis, GPA verification, recommendations or references. **Deadline:** April 16.

Contact Catalina Mistler, Chief, Program Administration and Services Division, California Student Aid Commission, PO Box 419026, Rancho Cordova, CA 95741-9026. *E-mail:* studentsupport@csac.ca.gov. *Phone:* 916-526-7268. *Fax:* 916-526-8002. *Website:* http://www.csac.ca.gov/.

Competitive Cal Grant A. Award for California residents who are not recent high school graduates attending an approved college or university within the state. Must show financial need and meet minimum 3.00 GPA requirement. *Award:* Grant for use in freshman, sophomore, junior, or senior years; renewable. *Award amount:* $5472–$12,192. *Number of awards:* 1000–2000. *Eligibility Requirements:* Applicant must be enrolled or expecting to enroll full- or part-time at a two-year or four-year institution or university; resident of California and studying in California. Applicant must have 3.0 GPA or higher. Available to U.S. citizens. *Application Requirements:* Application form, financial need analysis, GPA verification. **Deadline:** March 2.

Contact Catalina Mistler, Chief, Program Administration and Services Division, California Student Aid Commission, PO Box 419026, Rancho Cordova, CA 95741-9026. *E-mail:* studentsupport@csac.ca.gov. *Phone:* 916-526-7268. *Fax:* 916-526-8002. *Website:* http://www.csac.ca.gov/.

Cooperative Agencies Resources for Education Program. Renewable award available to California resident enrolled as a full-time student at a two-year California community college. Must currently receive CalWORKs/TANF and have at least one child under fourteen years of age at time of acceptance into CARE program. Must be in EOPS, a single head of household, and age 18 or older. Contact local college EOPS-CARE office for application and more information. To locate nearest campus, see http://www.icanaffordcollege.com/applications/homepage2.cfm. *Award:* Grant for use in freshman or sophomore years; renewable. *Number of awards:* 10,000–11,000. *Eligibility Requirements:* Applicant must be enrolled or expecting to enroll full-time at a two-year institution; single; resident of California and studying in California. Available to U.S. citizens. *Application Requirements:* Application form, financial need analysis, test scores, transcript. **Deadline:** continuous.

Entitlement Cal Grant B. Provide grant funds for access costs for low-income students in an amount not to exceed $1473 and tuition/fee expenses of up to $12192. Must be California residents and enroll in an undergraduate academic program of not less than one academic year at a qualifying postsecondary institution. Must show financial need and meet the minimum 2.00 GPA requirement. *Award:* Grant for use in freshman, sophomore, junior, or senior years; renewable. *Award amount:* $700–$13,665. *Number of awards:* 56,200. *Eligibility Requirements:* Applicant must be enrolled or expecting to enroll full- or part-time at a two-year or four-year or technical institution or university; resident of California and studying in California. Available to U.S. citizens. *Application Requirements:* Application form, financial need analysis. **Deadline:** March 2.

Contact Catalina Mistler, Chief, Program Administration and Services Division, California Student Aid Commission, PO Box 419026, Rancho Cordova, CA 95741-9026. *E-mail:* studentsupport@csac.ca.gov. *Phone:* 916-526-7268. *Fax:* 916-526-8002. *Website:* http://www.csac.ca.gov/.

Law Enforcement Personnel Dependents Scholarship. Provides college grants to needy dependents of California law enforcement officers, officers and employees of the Department of Corrections and Department of Youth Authority, and firefighters killed or disabled in the line of duty. *Award:* Grant for use in freshman, sophomore, junior, or senior years; renewable. *Award amount:* $100–$13,665. *Eligibility Requirements:* Applicant must be enrolled or expecting to enroll full- or part-time at a two-year or four-year institution or university; resident of California and studying in California. Applicant or parent of applicant must have employment or volunteer experience in police/firefighting. Available to U.S. citizens. *Application Requirements:* Application form, birth certificate, death certificate of parents or spouse, police report, financial need analysis, transcript. **Deadline:** continuous.

Contact Catalina Mistler, Chief, Program Administration and Services Division, California Student Aid Commission, PO Box 419026, Rancho Cordova, CA 95741-9026. *E-mail:* studentsupport@csac.ca.gov. *Phone:* 916-526-7268. *Fax:* 916-526-8002. *Website:* http://www.csac.ca.gov/.

COLORADO

American Legion Auxiliary Department of Colorado Department President's Scholarship for Junior Member. Open to children, spouses, grandchildren, and great-grandchildren of veterans, and veterans who served in the Armed Forces during eligibility dates for membership in the American Legion. Applicants must be Colorado residents who have been accepted by an accredited school in Colorado. *Award:* Scholarship for use in freshman year; not renewable. *Award amount:* up to $500. *Number of awards:* 1–2. *Eligibility Requirements:* Applicant must be high school student; planning to enroll or expecting to enroll full- or part-time at a four-year institution or university; resident of Colorado and studying in Colorado. Available to U.S. citizens. Applicant or parent must meet one or more of the following requirements: general military experience; retired from active duty; disabled or killed as a result of military service; prisoner of war; or missing in action. *Application Requirements:* Application form, essay, recommendations or references, transcript. **Deadline:** April 15.

Contact Lynn Cody, Department Secretary and Treasurer, American Legion Auxiliary Department of Colorado, 7465 East First Avenue, Suite D, Denver, CO 80230. *E-mail:* www.dept-sec@alacolorado.com. *Phone:* 303-367-5388. *Fax:* 303-367-5388. *Website:* http://www.alacolorado.com.

American Legion Auxiliary Department of Colorado Past Presidents' Parley Nurses Scholarship. Open to children, spouses, grandchildren, and great-grandchildren of American Legion veterans, and veterans who served in the armed forces during eligibility dates for membership in the American Legion. Must be Colorado residents who have been accepted by an accredited school of nursing in Colorado. Nursing. *Award:* Scholarship for use in freshman, sophomore, junior, senior, or graduate years; not renewable. *Award amount:* up to $500. *Number of awards:* 3–5. *Eligibility Requirements:* Applicant must be enrolled or expecting to enroll full- or part-time at a four-year institution or university; resident of Colorado and studying in Colorado. Applicant or parent of applicant must be member of American Legion or Auxiliary. Available to U.S. citizens. Applicant or parent must meet one or more of the following requirements: general military experience; retired from active duty; disabled or killed as a result of military service; prisoner of war; or missing in action. *Application Requirements:* Application form, essay, financial need analysis, recommendations or references. **Deadline:** April 1.

Contact Lynn Cody, Department Secretary-Treasurer, American Legion Auxiliary Department of Colorado, 7465 East First Avenue, Suite D, Denver, CO 80230. *E-mail:* www.dept-sec@alacolorado.com. *Phone:* 303-367-5388. *Fax:* 303-367-5388. *Website:* http://www.alacolorado.com.

Colorado Student Grant. Grants for Colorado residents attending eligible public, private, or vocational institutions within the state. Students must complete a Free Application for Federal Student Aid (FAFSA) and qualify at 150% of Pell eligibility. Application deadlines vary by institution. Renewable award for undergraduates. Contact the financial aid office at the college/institution for application and more information. *Award:* Grant for use in freshman, sophomore, junior, or senior years; not renewable. *Award amount:* $850–$5000. *Number of awards:* up to 69,602. *Eligibility Requirements:* Applicant must be enrolled or expecting to enroll full- or part-time at a two-year or four-year or technical institution or university; resident of Colorado and studying in Colorado. Available to U.S. citizens. *Application Requirements:* Application form, financial need analysis, student must have an active FAFSA on file at the institution. **Deadline:** continuous.

Contact Celina Duran, Financial Aid Administrator, Colorado Commission on Higher Education, 1560 Broadway, Suite 1600, Denver, CO 80202. *E-mail:* celina.duran@dhe.state.co.us. *Phone:* 303-866-2723. *Website:* http://www.highered.colorado.gov/dhedefault.html.

CONNECTICUT

AIFS-HACU Scholarships. Scholarships to outstanding Hispanic students to study abroad with AIFS. Available to students attending HACU member schools. Students will receive scholarships of up to 50 percent of the full program fee. Students must meet all standard AIFS eligibility requirements. Deadlines: April 15 for fall, October 1 for spring, and March 15 for summer. *Award:* Scholarship for use in freshman, sophomore, junior, or senior years; not renewable. *Award amount:* $6000–$8000. *Eligibility Requirements:* Applicant must be Hispanic; enrolled or expecting to enroll full-time at a two-year or four-year institution or university and must have an interest in international exchange. Applicant must have 3.0 GPA or higher. Available to U.S. and non-U.S. citizens. *Application Requirements:* Application form, essay, personal photograph, recommendations or references, transcript. *Fee:* $95. **Deadline:** varies.

Contact David Mauro, Admissions Counselor, American Institute for Foreign Study, River Plaza, 9 West Broad Street,

Stamford, CT 06902-3788. *E-mail:* dmauro@aifs.com. *Phone:* 800-727-2437 Ext. 5163. *Fax:* 203-399-5463. *Website:* http://www.aifsabroad.com/.

Capitol Scholarship Program. Award for Connecticut residents attending eligible institutions in Connecticut or in a state with reciprocity with Connecticut (Massachusetts, Pennsylvania, Rhode Island, Vermont, or Washington, D.C). Must be U.S. citizen or permanent resident alien who is a high school senior or graduate. Must rank in top 20% of class or score at least 1800 on SAT or score at least 27 on the ACT. Students must also demonstrate financial need as a result of filing the FAFSA. *Award:* Scholarship for use in freshman, sophomore, junior, or senior years; renewable. *Award amount:* $350–$2000. *Number of awards:* 2500–3500. *Eligibility Requirements:* Applicant must be enrolled or expecting to enroll full- or part-time at a two-year or four-year or technical institution or university; resident of Connecticut and studying in Connecticut, District of Columbia, Massachusetts, Pennsylvania, Rhode Island, Vermont. Available to U.S. citizens. *Application Requirements:* Application form, FAFSA, financial need analysis, test scores. **Deadline:** February 15.

Contact Mrs. Linda Diamond, Senior Associate, Connecticut Office of Higher Education, 61 Woodland Street, Hartford, CT 06105. *E-mail:* csp@ctohe.org. *Phone:* 860-947-1855. *Fax:* 860-947-1313. *Website:* http://www.ctohe.org.

Connecticut Aid to Public College Students Grant. Award for Connecticut residents attending public colleges or universities within the state. Renewable awards based on financial need. Application deadline varies by institution. Apply at college financial aid office. *Award:* Grant for use in freshman, sophomore, junior, or senior years; renewable. *Eligibility Requirements:* Applicant must be enrolled or expecting to enroll full- or part-time at a two-year or four-year institution or university; resident of Connecticut and studying in Connecticut. Available to U.S. citizens. *Application Requirements:* FAFSA, financial need analysis. **Deadline:** continuous.

Contact Ms. Lynne Little, Executive Assistant, Connecticut Office of Higher Education, 61 Woodland Street, Hartford, CT 06105. *E-mail:* caps@ctohe.org. *Phone:* 860-947-1855. *Fax:* 860-947-1838. *Website:* http://www.ctohe.org.

Connecticut Army National Guard 100% Tuition Waiver. Program is for any active member of the Connecticut Army National Guard in good standing. Must be a resident of Connecticut attending any Connecticut state (public) university, community-technical college or regional vocational-technical school. The total number of available awards is unlimited. *Award:* Scholarship for use in freshman, sophomore, junior, or senior years; not renewable. *Award amount:* $16,000. *Eligibility Requirements:* Applicant must be age 17-65; enrolled or expecting to enroll full- or part-time at a two-year or four-year or technical institution or university; resident of Connecticut and studying in Connecticut. Available to U.S. and non-U.S. citizens. Applicant or parent must meet one or more of the following requirements: national guard experience; retired from active duty; disabled or killed as a result of military service; prisoner of war; or missing in action. *Application Requirements:* Application form. **Deadline:** July 1.

Contact Capt. Jeremy Lingenfelser, Education Services Officer, Connecticut Army National Guard, 360 Broad Street, Hartford, CT 06105-3795. *E-mail:* education@ct.ngb.army.mil. *Phone:* 860-524-4816. *Fax:* 860-524-4904. *Website:* http://www.ct.ngb.army.mil/.

Connecticut Independent College Student Grants. Award for Connecticut residents attending a not for profit independent college or university within the state on at least a half-time basis. Renewable awards based on financial need. Application deadline varies by institution. Apply at college financial aid office. *Award:* Grant for use in freshman, sophomore, junior, or senior years; renewable. *Award amount:* $250–$8166. *Eligibility Requirements:* Applicant must be enrolled or expecting to enroll full- or part-time at a two-year or four-year institution or university; resident of Connecticut and studying in Connecticut. Available to U.S. citizens. *Application Requirements:* FAFSA, financial need analysis. **Deadline:** continuous.

Contact Ms. Lynne Little, Executive Assistant, Connecticut Office of Higher Education, 61 Woodland Street, Hartford, CT 06105. *E-mail:* cics@ctohe.org. *Phone:* 860-947-1855. *Fax:* 860-947-1838. *Website:* http://www.ctohe.org.

Minority Teacher Incentive Grant Program. Program provides up to $5000 a year for two years of full-time study in a teacher preparation program for the junior or senior year at a Connecticut college or university. Applicant must be African-American, Hispanic/Latino, Asian American or Native American heritage and be nominated by the Education Dean. Program graduates who teach in Connecticut public schools may be eligible for loan reimbursement stipends up to $2,500 per year for up to four years. Education. *Award:* Grant for use in junior or senior years; renewable. *Award amount:* $2500–$5000. *Number of awards:* 71. *Eligibility Requirements:* Applicant must be American Indian/Alaska Native, Asian/Pacific Islander, Black (non-Hispanic), Hispanic; enrolled or expecting to enroll full-time at a four-year institution or university and studying in Connecticut. Available to U.S. citizens. *Application Requirements:* Application form. **Deadline:** October 1.

Contact Ms. Lynne Little, Executive Assistant, Connecticut Office of Higher Education, 61 Woodland Street, Hartford, CT 06105. *E-mail:* mtip@ctohe.org. *Phone:* 860-947-1855. *Fax:* 860-947-1838. *Website:* http://www.ctohe.org.

DELAWARE

Delaware Solid Waste Authority John P. "Pat" Healy Scholarship. Award for legal residents of Delaware who are U.S. citizens or eligible non-citizens. Must be high school seniors or full-time college students in their freshman or sophomore years. Must major in either environmental engineering or environmental sciences at a Delaware college. Selection based on financial need, academic performance, community and school involvement, and leadership ability. Engineering-Related Technologies; Environmental Science. *Award:* Scholarship for use in freshman or sophomore years; renewable. *Award amount:* $2000. *Number of awards:* 1. *Eligibility Requirements:* Applicant must be enrolled or expecting to enroll full-time at a two-year or four-year institution or university; resident of Delaware; studying in Delaware and must have an interest in leadership. Applicant or parent of applicant must have employment or volunteer experience in community service. Applicant must have 3.0 GPA or higher. Available to U.S. citizens. *Application Requirements:* Application form, FAFSA, Student Aid Report (SAR), financial need analysis. **Deadline:** March 14.

Contact Carylin Brinkley, Program Administrator. *E-mail:* cbrinkley@doe.k12.de.us. *Phone:* 302-735-4120. *Fax:* 302-739-5894. *Website:* http://www.doe.k12.de.us.

Diamond State Scholarship. Award for legal residents of Delaware who are U.S. citizens or eligible non-citizens. Must be enrolled as a full-time student in a degree program at a nonprofit, regionally accredited institution. Minimum 3.0 GPA required. High school seniors should rank in upper quarter of class and have a combined score of at least 1800 on the SAT. *Award:* Scholarship for use in freshman year; renewable. *Award amount:* $1250. *Number of awards:* 50. *Eligibility Requirements:* Applicant must be high school student; planning to enroll or expecting to enroll full-time at a four-year institution or university and resident of Delaware. Applicant must have 3.0 GPA or higher. Available to U.S. citizens. *Application Requirements:* Application form, application form may be submitted online (http://www.doe.k12.de.us/infosuites/students_family/dheo/how_to_apply/financial_aid/FA_webpages/diamond_scholarship.shtml), essay, test scores, transcript. **Deadline:** March 22.

Contact Carylin Brinkley, Program Administrator. *E-mail:* cbrinkley@doe.k12.de.us. *Phone:* 302-735-4120. *Fax:* 302-739-5894. *Website:* http://www.doe.k12.de.us.

Educational Benefits for Children of Deceased Veterans. Award for children between the ages of 16 and 24 of deceased/MIA/POW veterans or state police officers. Must have been a resident of Delaware for 3 or more years prior to the date of application. If the applicant's parent is a member of the armed forces, the parent must have been a resident of Delaware at the time of death or declaration of missing in action or prisoner of war status. Award will not exceed tuition and fees at a Delaware public college. *Award:* Grant for use in freshman, sophomore, junior, or senior years; renewable. *Eligibility Requirements:* Applicant must be age 16-24; enrolled or expecting to enroll full-time at a two-year or four-year institution or university and resident of Delaware. Applicant or parent of applicant must have employment or volunteer experience in police/firefighting. Available to U.S. citizens. Applicant or parent must meet one or more of the following requirements: general military experience; retired from active duty; disabled or killed as a result of military service; prisoner of war; or missing in action. *Application Requirements:* Application form, verification of service-related death. **Deadline:** continuous.

Contact Carylin Brinkley, Program Administrator. *E-mail:* cbrinkley@doe.k12.de.us. *Phone:* 302-735-4120. *Fax:*

302-739-5894. *Website:* http://www.doe.k12.de.us.

Governor's Workforce Development Grant. Grants for part-time undergraduate students attending Delaware College of Art and Design, Delaware State University, Delaware Technical and Community College, Goldey-Beacom College, University of Delaware, Wesley College, Widener University (Delaware Campus), or Wilmington College. Must be at least 18 years old, a resident of Delaware, and employed by a company in Delaware that contributes to the Blue Collar Training Fund Program. *Award:* Grant for use in freshman, sophomore, junior, or senior years; renewable. *Award amount:* $2000. *Number of awards:* 40. *Eligibility Requirements:* Applicant must be enrolled or expecting to enroll full- or part-time at a two-year or four-year institution or university; resident of Delaware and studying in Delaware. Available to U.S. and non-U.S. citizens. *Application Requirements:* Application form. **Deadline:** varies.

Contact Carylin Brinkley, Program Administrator. *E-mail:* cbrinkley@doe.k12.de.us. *Phone:* 302-735-4120. *Fax:* 302-739-5894. *Website:* http://www.doe.k12.de.us.

Legislative Essay Scholarship. Award for legal residents of Delaware who are U.S. citizens or eligible non-citizens. Must be high school seniors in public or private schools or in home school programs who plans to enroll full-time at a nonprofit, regionally accredited college. Must submit an essay on topic: "Pluribus Unum: Is this motto adopted in 1782 relevant to our country today?". *Award:* Prize for use in freshman year; not renewable. *Award amount:* $1000–$10,000. *Number of awards:* up to 62. *Eligibility Requirements:* Applicant must be high school student; planning to enroll or expecting to enroll full- or part-time at a two-year or four-year or technical institution or university and resident of Delaware. Available to U.S. citizens. *Application Requirements:* Application form, entry in a contest, essay. **Deadline:** November 30.

Contact Carylin Brinkley, Program Administrator. *E-mail:* cbrinkley@doe.k12.de.us. *Phone:* 302-735-4120. *Fax:* 302-739-5894. *Website:* http://www.doe.k12.de.us.

Scholarship Incentive Program (ScIP). Award for legal residents of Delaware who are U.S. citizens or eligible non-citizens. Must demonstrate substantial financial need and enroll full-time

in an undergraduate degree program at a nonprofit, regionally accredited institution in Delaware or Pennsylvania. Minimum 2.5 GPA required. *Award:* Grant for use in freshman, sophomore, junior, senior, or graduate years; not renewable. *Award amount:* $700–$2200. *Number of awards:* 1000–1253. *Eligibility Requirements:* Applicant must be enrolled or expecting to enroll full-time at a two-year or four-year institution or university; resident of Delaware and studying in Delaware, Pennsylvania. Applicant must have 2.5 GPA or higher. Available to U.S. citizens. *Application Requirements:* Application form, FAFSA, financial need analysis, transcript. **Deadline:** April 15.

Contact Carylin Brinkley, Program Administrator. *E-mail:* cbrinkley@doe.k12.de.us. *Phone:* 302-735-4120. *Fax:* 302-739-5894. *Website:* http://www.doe.k12.de.us.

State Tuition Assistance. You must enlist in the Delaware National Guard to be eligible for this scholarship award. Award providing tuition assistance for any member of the Air or Army National Guard attending a Delaware two-year or four-year college. Awards are renewable. Applicant's minimum GPA must be 2.0. *Award:* Scholarship for use in freshman, sophomore, junior, or senior years; renewable. *Award amount:* up to $10,000. *Number of awards:* 1–200. *Eligibility Requirements:* Applicant must be enrolled or expecting to enroll full- or part-time at a two-year or four-year institution or university and studying in Delaware. Available to U.S. citizens. Applicant or parent must meet one or more of the following requirements: national guard experience; retired from active duty; disabled or killed as a result of military service; prisoner of war; or missing in action. *Application Requirements:* Application form, transcript.

Contact Robert Csizmadia, State Tuition Assistance Manager, Delaware National Guard, 1st Regiment Road, Wilmington, DE 19808-2191. *E-mail:* robert.csizmadia@us.army.mil. *Phone:* 302-326-7012. *Fax:* 302-326-7029. *Website:* http://www.delawarenationalguard.com/.

DISTRICT OF COLUMBIA

American Council of the Blind Scholarships. Merit-based award available to undergraduate students who are legally blind in both eyes. Submit certificate of legal blindness and proof of acceptance at an accredited postsecondary institution. *Award:* Scholarship for use in freshman, sophomore, junior, or senior years; renewable. *Award amount:* $1000–$2500. *Number of awards:* 16–20. *Eligibility Requirements:* Applicant must be visually impaired and enrolled or expecting to enroll full- or part-time at a four-year institution or university. Applicant must be visually impaired. Applicant must have 3.5 GPA or higher. Available to U.S. citizens. *Application Requirements:* Application form, driver's license, essay, evidence of legal blindness, proof of post-secondary school acceptance, recommendations or references, transcript. **Deadline:** March 1.

Contact Tatricia Castillo, Scholarship Coordinator, American Council of the Blind, 1155 15th Street, NW, Suite 1004, Washington, DC 20005. *E-mail:* tcastillo@acp.org. *Phone:* 202-467-5081. *Fax:* 202-467-5085. *Website:* http://www.acb.org/.

Bureau of Indian Education Grant Program. Grants are provided to supplement financial assistance to eligible American Indian/Alaska Native students entering college seeking a baccalaureate degree. A student must be a member of, or at least one-quarter degree Indian blood descendent of a member of an American Indian tribe who are eligible for the special programs and services provided by the United States through the Bureau of Indian Affairs to Indians because of their status as Indians. *Award:* Grant for use in freshman year; not renewable. *Eligibility Requirements:* Applicant must be American Indian/Alaska Native; high school student and planning to enroll or expecting to enroll full-time at a two-year or four-year institution or university. Available to U.S. citizens. *Application Requirements:* Application form, recommendations or references, test scores, transcript. **Deadline:** varies.

Contact Paulina Bell, Office Automation Assistant. *Phone:* 202-208-6123. *Fax:* 202-208-3312. *Website:* http://www.bie.edu/.

Central Intelligence Agency Undergraduate Scholarship Program. Need and merit-based award for students with minimum 3.0 GPA, who are interested in working for the Central Intelligence Agency upon graduation. Renewable for four years of undergraduate study. Must apply in senior year of high school or sophomore year in college. For further information refer to web site http://www.cia.gov. Accounting; Business/Consumer Services; Computer Science/Data Processing; Economics; Electrical Engineering/Electronics;

Foreign Language; Geography; Graphics/Graphic Arts/Printing; International Studies; Political Science; Surveying, Surveying Technology, Cartography, or Geographic Information Science. *Award:* Scholarship for use in freshman, sophomore, junior, or senior years; renewable. *Award amount:* up to $18,000. *Eligibility Requirements:* Applicant must be enrolled or expecting to enroll full-time at a four-year institution or university. Applicant must have 3.0 GPA or higher. Available to U.S. citizens. *Application Requirements:* Application form, financial need analysis, recommendations or references, resume, test scores, transcript. **Deadline:** November 1.

Contact Van Patrick, Chief, College Relations. *E-mail:* ivanilp0@ucia.gov. *Phone:* 703-613-8388. *Fax:* 703-613-7676. *Website:* http://www.cia.gov/.

Costas G. Lemonopoulos Scholarship. Scholarships to children of NALC members attending public, four-year colleges or universities supported by the state of Florida or St. Petersburg Junior College. Scholarships are renewable one time. *Award:* Scholarship for use in freshman, sophomore, junior, or senior years; renewable. *Number of awards:* 1–20. *Eligibility Requirements:* Applicant must be enrolled or expecting to enroll full-time at a two-year or four-year institution or university and studying in Florida. Applicant or parent of applicant must be member of National Association of Letter Carriers. Available to U.S. citizens. *Application Requirements:* Application form, recommendations or references, transcript. **Deadline:** June 1.

Contact Ann Porch, Membership Committee. *E-mail:* nalcinf@nalc.org. *Phone:* 202-393-4695. *Website:* http://www.nalc.org/.

Harry S. Truman Scholarship. Scholarships for U.S. citizens or U.S. nationals who are college or university students with junior-level academic standing and who wish to attend professional or graduate school to prepare for careers in government or the nonprofit and advocacy sectors. Candidates must be nominated by their institution. Public service and leadership record considered. Visit web site http://www.truman.gov for further information and application. Political Science; Public Policy and Administration. *Award:* Scholarship for use in junior year; renewable. *Award amount:* $30,000. *Number of awards:* 65. *Eligibility Requirements:* Applicant must be enrolled or expecting to enroll full-

time at a four-year institution or university and must have an interest in leadership. Available to U.S. citizens. *Application Requirements:* Application form, interview, policy proposal, recommendations or references. **Deadline:** February 5.

Contact Tonji Wade, Program Officer, Harry S. Truman Scholarship Foundation, 712 Jackson Place, NW, Washington, DC 20006. *E-mail:* office@truman.gov. *Phone:* 202-395-4831. *Fax:* 202-395-6995. *Website:* http://www.truman.gov/.

Montgomery GI Bill (Active Duty) Chapter 30. Award provides up to thirty-six months of education benefits to eligible veterans for college, business school, technical courses, vocational courses, correspondence courses, apprenticeships/job training, or flight training. Must be an eligible veteran with an Honorable Discharge and have high school diploma or GED before applying for benefits. *Award:* Scholarship for use in freshman, sophomore, junior, senior, or graduate years; renewable. *Eligibility Requirements:* Applicant must be enrolled or expecting to enroll full- or part-time at a two-year or four-year or technical institution or university. Available to U.S. citizens. Applicant or parent must meet one or more of the following requirements: general military experience; retired from active duty; disabled or killed as a result of military service; prisoner of war; or missing in action. *Application Requirements:* Application form, proof of active military service of at least 2 years. **Deadline:** continuous.

Contact Keith Wilson, Director, Education Service. *Phone:* 888-442-4551. *Website:* http://www.gibill.va.gov/.

Montgomery GI Bill (Selected Reserve). Educational assistance program for members of the selected reserve of the Army, Navy, Air Force, Marine Corps and Coast Guard, as well as the Army and Air National Guard. Available to all reservists and National Guard personnel who commit to a six-year obligation, and remain in the Reserve or Guard during the six years. Award is renewable. Monthly benefit is $309 for up to thirty-six months for full-time. *Award:* Scholarship for use in freshman, sophomore, junior, senior, or postgraduate years; renewable. *Eligibility Requirements:* Applicant must be enrolled or expecting to enroll full- or part-time at a two-year or four-year or technical institution or university. Available to U.S. citizens. Applicant or parent must meet one or more of the following requirements:

general military experience; retired from active duty; disabled or killed as a result of military service; prisoner of war; or missing in action. *Application Requirements:* Application form, proof of military service of six years in the reserve or guard. **Deadline:** continuous.

Contact Keith Wilson, Director, Education Service. *Phone:* 888-442-4551. *Website:* http://www.gibill.va.gov/.

Reserve Education Assistance Program. The program provides educational assistance to members of National Guard and reserve components. Selected Reserve and Individual Ready Reserve (IRR) who are called or ordered to active duty service in response to a war or national emergency as declared by the president or Congress are eligible. For further information see web site http:// www.GIBILL.va.gov. *Award:* Scholarship for use in freshman, sophomore, junior, senior, graduate, or postgraduate years; renewable. *Eligibility Requirements:* Applicant must be enrolled or expecting to enroll full- or part-time at a two-year or four-year or technical institution or university. Available to U.S. citizens. Applicant or parent must meet one or more of the following requirements: general military experience; retired from active duty; disabled or killed as a result of military service; prisoner of war; or missing in action. *Application Requirements:* Application form. **Deadline:** continuous.

Contact Keith Wilson, Director, Education Service. *Phone:* 888-442-4551. *Website:* http://www.gibill.va.gov/.

Survivors and Dependents Educational Assistance (Chapter 35)-VA. Monthly $860 benefits for up to 45 months. Must be spouses or children under age 26 of current veterans missing in action or of deceased or totally and permanently disabled (service-related) service persons. For more information visit the following web site http://www. gibill.va.gov. *Award:* Scholarship for use in freshman, sophomore, junior, or senior years; renewable. *Eligibility Requirements:* Applicant must be enrolled or expecting to enroll full- or part-time at a two-year or four-year or technical institution or university. Available to U.S. and non-U.S. citizens. Applicant or parent must meet one or more of the following requirements: general military experience; retired from active duty; disabled or killed as a result of military service; prisoner of war; or missing in action. *Application Requirements:* Application form, proof of parent or spouse's qualifying service. **Deadline:** continuous.

Contact Keith Wilson, Director, Education Service. *Phone:* 888-442-4551. *Website:* http://www.gibill.va.gov/.

FLORIDA

Access to Better Learning and Education Grant. Grant program provides tuition assistance to Florida undergraduate students enrolled in degree programs at eligible private Florida colleges or universities. Must be a U.S. citizen or eligible non-citizen and must meet Florida residency requirements. The participating institution determines application procedures, deadlines, and student eligibility. An eligible student must complete and submit the FAFSA in order to receive program funding.

For more details, visit the website at http://www.FloridaStudentFinancialAid. org/SSFAD/home/uamain.htm. *Award:* Grant for use in freshman, sophomore, junior, or senior years; renewable. *Award amount:* up to $803. *Eligibility Requirements:* Applicant must be enrolled or expecting to enroll full-time at a four-year institution or university; resident of Florida and studying in Florida. Available to U.S. citizens.

First Generation Matching Grant Program. Need-based grants to Florida resident undergraduate students who are enrolled in state universities and community colleges in Florida and whose parents have not earned baccalaureate degrees. Available state funds are contingent upon matching contributions from private sources on a dollar-for-dollar basis. Institutions determine application procedures, deadlines, and student eligibility.

For more details, visit the website at http://www.FloridaStudentFinancialAid. org/SSFAD/home/uamain.htm. *Award:* Grant for use in freshman, sophomore, junior, or senior years; renewable. *Eligibility Requirements:* Applicant must be enrolled or expecting to enroll full- or part-time at a two-year or four-year institution or university; resident of Florida and studying in Florida. Available to U.S. citizens. *Application Requirements:* Application form, financial need analysis.

Florida Bright Futures Scholarship Program. Three lottery-funded scholarships reward Florida high school graduates for high academic achievement. Program is comprised of the following three awards: Florida Academic Scholars Award, Florida Medallion Scholars Award and Florida Gold Seal Vocational Scholars Award. An eligible student must

complete and submit the FAFSA in order to receive program funding.

For more details, visit the website at http://www.FloridaStudentFinancialAid. org/SSFAD/home/uamain.htm. *Award:* Scholarship for use in freshman, sophomore, junior, or senior years; renewable. *Eligibility Requirements:* Applicant must be high school student; planning to enroll or expecting to enroll full- or part-time at a two-year or four-year or technical institution or university; resident of Florida and studying in Florida. Applicant must have 3.0 GPA or higher. Available to U.S. citizens. *Application Requirements:* Application form, community service, test scores, transcript.

Florida Postsecondary Student Assistance Grant. Scholarships to degree-seeking, resident, undergraduate students who demonstrate substantial financial need and are enrolled in eligible degree-granting private colleges and universities not eligible under the Florida Private Student Assistance Grant. FSAG is a decentralized program, and each participating institution determines application procedures, deadlines and student eligibility. Number of awards varies.

For more details, visit the website at http://www.FloridaStudentFinancialAid. org/SSFAD/home/uamain.htm. *Award:* Grant for use in freshman, sophomore, junior, or senior years; renewable. *Award amount:* $200–$2534. *Eligibility Requirements:* Applicant must be enrolled or expecting to enroll full-time at a two-year or four-year institution or university; resident of Florida and studying in Florida. Available to U.S. citizens. *Application Requirements:* Application form, financial need analysis.

Florida Private Student Assistance Grant. Grants for Florida residents who are U.S. citizens or eligible non-citizens attending eligible private, nonprofit, four-year colleges and universities in Florida. Must be a full-time student and demonstrate substantial financial need.

For renewal, must have earned a minimum cumulative GPA of 2.0 at the last institution attended. For more details, visit the website at http://www. FloridaStudentFinancialAid.org/SSFAD/ home/uamain.htm. *Award:* Grant for use in freshman, sophomore, junior, or senior years; renewable. *Award amount:* $200– $2534. *Eligibility Requirements:* Applicant must be enrolled or expecting to enroll full-time at a four-year institution or university; resident of Florida and studying in Florida. Available to U.S. citizens. *Application*

Requirements: Application form, financial need analysis.

Florida Public Student Assistance Grant. Grants for Florida residents, U.S. citizens or eligible non-citizens who attend state universities and public community colleges and demonstrate substantial financial need. For renewal, must have earned a minimum cumulative GPA of 2.0 at the last institution attended.

For more details, visit the website at http://www.FloridaStudentFinancialAid.org/SSFAD/home/uamain.htm. *Award:* Grant for use in freshman, sophomore, junior, or senior years; renewable. *Award amount:* $200–$2534. *Eligibility Requirements:* Applicant must be enrolled or expecting to enroll full- or part-time at a two-year or four-year institution or university; resident of Florida and studying in Florida. Available to U.S. citizens. *Application Requirements:* Application form, financial need analysis.

Florida Space Research Program. Grants for faculty researchers from Florida public and private universities and community colleges. One-time award for aerospace and technology research. Submit research proposal with budget. Aviation/Aerospace; Earth Science; Materials Science, Engineering, and Metallurgy; Mathematics; Mechanical Engineering. *Award:* Grant for use in junior, senior, graduate, or postgraduate years; not renewable. *Award amount:* $12,500–$25,000. *Number of awards:* 13–15. *Eligibility Requirements:* Applicant must be enrolled or expecting to enroll full- or part-time at a two-year or four-year institution or university; resident of Florida and studying in Florida. Available to U.S. citizens. *Application Requirements:* Application form, application form may be submitted online (http://www.floridaspacegrant.org/programs/florida-space-research-program-fsrp/), proposal with budget. **Deadline:** May 30.

Contact Dr. Jaydeep Mukherjee, FSGC Director, NASA Florida Space Grant Consortium, PO Box 160650, 12354 Research Parkway, Room 218, Orlando, FL 32826. *E-mail:* fsgc@ucf.edu. *Phone:* 407-823-6177. *Website:* http://www.floridaspacegrant.org/.

Florida Student Assistance Grant-Career Education. Need-based grant program available to Florida residents enrolled in certificate programs of 450 or more clock hours at participating community colleges or career centers operated by district school boards. FSAG-CE is a decentralized state of Florida program,

which means that each participating institution determines application procedures, deadlines, student eligibility, and award amounts.

For more details, visit the website at http://www.FloridaStudentFinancialAid.org/SSFAD/home/uamain.htm. *Award:* Grant for use in freshman, sophomore, junior, or senior years; renewable. *Award amount:* $200–$2534. *Eligibility Requirements:* Applicant must be enrolled or expecting to enroll full- or part-time at a two-year or technical institution; resident of Florida and studying in Florida. Available to U.S. citizens. *Application Requirements:* Application form, financial need analysis.

Florida Work Experience Program. Need-based program providing eligible Florida residents work experiences that will complement and reinforce their educational and career goals. Must maintain GPA of 2.0. Postsecondary institution will determine applicant's eligibility, number of hours to be worked per week, and the award amount.

For more details, visit the website at http://www.FloridaStudentFinancialAid.org/SSFAD/home/uamain.htm. *Award:* Grant for use in freshman, sophomore, junior, or senior years; renewable. *Eligibility Requirements:* Applicant must be enrolled or expecting to enroll full- or part-time at a two-year or four-year institution or university; resident of Florida and studying in Florida. Available to U.S. citizens. *Application Requirements:* Application form, financial need analysis.

Jose Marti Scholarship Challenge Grant Fund. Award available to Hispanic-American students who were born in, or whose parent was born in a Hispanic country. Must be a Florida resident, be enrolled full-time in Florida at an eligible school, and have a GPA of 3.0 or above. Must be U.S. citizen or eligible non-citizen. FAFSA must be processed by May 15.

For more details, visit the website at http://www.FloridaStudentFinancialAid.org/SSFAD/home/uamain.htm. *Award:* Scholarship for use in freshman, sophomore, junior, or senior years; renewable. *Award amount:* $2000. *Eligibility Requirements:* Applicant must be of Hispanic heritage; high school student; planning to enroll or expecting to enroll full-time at a two-year or four-year institution or university; resident of Florida and studying in Florida. Applicant must have 3.0 GPA or higher. Available to U.S. citizens. *Application Requirements:*

Application form, financial need analysis. **Deadline:** April 1.

Mary McLeod Bethune Scholarship. Renewable award to Florida residents with a GPA of 3.0 or above, who will attend Bethune-Cookman University, Edward Waters College, Florida A&M University, or Florida Memorial University. Must not have previously received a baccalaureate degree. Must demonstrate financial need as specified by the institution.

For more details, visit the website at http://www.FloridaStudentFinancialAid.org/SSFAD/home/uamain.htm. *Award:* Scholarship for use in freshman, sophomore, junior, or senior years; renewable. *Award amount:* $3000. *Eligibility Requirements:* Applicant must be enrolled or expecting to enroll full-time at a four-year institution or university; resident of Florida and studying in Florida. Applicant must have 3.0 GPA or higher. Available to U.S. citizens. *Application Requirements:* Application form, financial need analysis.

Rosewood Family Scholarship Fund. Renewable award for eligible direct descendants of African-American Rosewood families affected by the incident of January 1923. Must not have previously received a baccalaureate degree.

For more details, visit the website at http://www.FloridaStudentFinancialAid.org/SSFAD/home/uamain.htm. *Award:* Scholarship for use in freshman, sophomore, junior, or senior years; renewable. *Award amount:* up to $4000. *Number of awards:* up to 25. *Eligibility Requirements:* Applicant must be enrolled or expecting to enroll full-time at a two-year or four-year or technical institution or university and studying in Florida. Available to U.S. citizens. *Application Requirements:* Application form, documentation of Rosewood ancestry, financial need analysis. **Deadline:** April 1.

Scholarships for Children & Spouses of Deceased or Disabled Veterans . Renewable scholarships for children and spouses of deceased or disabled veterans. Children must be between the ages of 16 and 22, and attend an eligible Florida postsecondary institution and enrolled at least part-time. Must ensure that the Florida Department of Veterans Affairs certifies the applicant's eligibility. Must maintain GPA of 2.0.

For more details, visit the website at http://www.FloridaStudentFinancialAid.org/SSFAD/home/uamain.htm. *Award:*

Scholarship for use in freshman, sophomore, junior, or senior years; renewable. *Eligibility Requirements:* Applicant must be age 16-22; enrolled or expecting to enroll full- or part-time at a two-year or four-year or technical institution or university; resident of Florida and studying in Florida. Available to U.S. citizens. Applicant or parent must meet one or more of the following requirements: general military experience; retired from active duty; disabled or killed as a result of military service; prisoner of war; or missing in action. *Application Requirements:* Application form. **Deadline:** April 1.

William L. Boyd IV Florida Resident Access Grant. Renewable awards to Florida undergraduate residents attending an eligible private, nonprofit Florida college or university. Postsecondary institution will determine applicant's eligibility. Renewal applicant must have earned a minimum institutional GPA of 2.0. An eligible student must complete and submit the FAFSA in order to receive program funding.

For more details, visit the website at http://www.FloridaStudentFinancialAid.org/SSFAD/home/uamain.htm. *Award:* Grant for use in freshman, sophomore, junior, or senior years; renewable. *Award amount:* up to $2150. *Eligibility Requirements:* Applicant must be enrolled or expecting to enroll full-time at a four-year institution or university; resident of Florida and studying in Florida. Available to U.S. citizens. *Application Requirements:* Application form.

GEORGIA

American Indian Nurse Scholarship Awards. Renewable award of $500 to $1000. Currently able to fund between 10 and 15 students. Intended originally to benefit females only, the program has expanded to include males and the career goals now include not only nursing careers, but jobs in health care and health education, as well. Health Administration; Nursing. *Award:* Scholarship for use in freshman, sophomore, junior, senior, graduate, or postgraduate years; renewable. *Award amount:* $500–$1000. *Number of awards:* 10–15. *Eligibility Requirements:* Applicant must be American Indian/Alaska Native and enrolled or expecting to enroll full-time at a two-year or four-year or technical institution or university. Applicant must have 2.5 GPA or higher. Available to U.S. citizens. *Application Requirements:* Appli-

cation form, driver's license, financial need analysis, personal photograph, recommendations or references, transcript. **Deadline:** continuous.

Contact Mrs. Joe Calvin, Scholarship Awards Consultant, National Society of The Colonial Dames of America, Nine Cross Creek Drive, Birmingham, AL 35213. *E-mail:* info@nscda.org. *Phone:* 205-871-4072. *Website:* http://www.nscda.org/.

Georgia HOPE Scholarship Program. Scholarship and Grant program for Georgia residents who are college undergraduates to attend an accredited two or four-year Georgia institution. Pays a percentage of actual undergraduate tuition charged at public postsecondary institutions. Percentage paid will vary from year to year. At private postsecondary institutions in Georgia, students may receive up to $3600 per year for full-time study or $1800 per year for part-time. Minimum 3.0 GPA required. Renewable if student maintains grades. See www.GAcollege411.org for full details. *Award:* Scholarship for use in freshman, sophomore, junior, or senior years; renewable. *Award amount:* up to $6000. *Number of awards:* 200,000–230,000. *Eligibility Requirements:* Applicant must be enrolled or expecting to enroll full- or part-time at a two-year or four-year institution or university; resident of Georgia and studying in Georgia. Applicant must have 3.0 GPA or higher. Available to U.S. citizens. *Application Requirements:* Application form, high schools must report transcripts to GSFC. **Deadline:** continuous.

Contact Tracy Ireland, Vice President, Georgia Student Finance Commission, 2082 East Exchange Place, Suite 100, Tucker, GA 30084. *E-mail:* tracyi@gsfc.org. *Phone:* 800-505-4732. *Website:* http://www.GAcollege411.org/.

Georgia Public Safety Memorial Grant. Award for children of Georgia Public Safety Officers, prison guards, fire fighters, law enforcement officers or emergency medical technicians killed or permanently disabled in the line of duty. Must attend an accredited postsecondary Georgia school. Complete the Public Safety Memorial Grant application. *Award:* Grant for use in freshman, sophomore, junior, or senior years; not renewable. *Award amount:* $2000. *Number of awards:* 20–40. *Eligibility Requirements:* Applicant must be enrolled or expecting to enroll full-time at a two-year or four-year or technical institution or university; resident of Georgia and

studying in Georgia. Available to U.S. citizens. *Application Requirements:* Application form, selective service registration. **Deadline:** continuous.

Contact Caylee French, Division Director, Georgia Student Finance Commission, 2082 East Exchange Place, Suite 100, Tucker, GA 30084. *E-mail:* cayleef@gsfc.org. *Phone:* 770-724-9244. *Website:* http://www.GAcollege411.org/.

Georgia Tuition Equalization Grant (GTEG). Award for Georgia residents pursuing undergraduate study at an accredited two- or four-year Georgia private postsecondary institution. *Award:* Grant for use in freshman, sophomore, junior, or senior years; not renewable. *Number of awards:* 1–35,000. *Eligibility Requirements:* Applicant must be learning disabled; Hispanic; enrolled or expecting to enroll full-time at a two-year or four-year institution or university; resident of Georgia and studying in Georgia. Applicant must be learning disabled. Available to U.S. citizens. *Application Requirements:* Application form, application form may be submitted online (http://www.gacollege411.org), social security number.

Contact Ms. Caylee French, Director, Student Aid Services, Georgia Student Finance Commission, 2082 East Exchange Place, Suite 100, Tucker, GA 30084. *E-mail:* cayleef@gsfc.org. *Phone:* 770-724-9244. *Fax:* 770-724-9249. *Website:* http://www.GAcollege411.org/.

HAWAII

Hawaii State Student Incentive Grant. Grants are given to residents of Hawaii who are enrolled in a participating Hawaiian state school. Funds are for undergraduate tuition only. Applicants must submit a financial need analysis. *Award:* Grant for use in freshman, sophomore, junior, or senior years; renewable. *Award amount:* $200–$2000. *Number of awards:* 470. *Eligibility Requirements:* Applicant must be enrolled or expecting to enroll full- or part-time at a two-year or four-year or technical institution or university; resident of Hawaii and studying in Hawaii. Available to U.S. citizens. *Application Requirements:* Application form, financial need analysis. **Deadline:** continuous.

Contact Janine Oyama, Financial Aid Specialist, Hawaii State Postsecondary Education Commission, University of Hawaii, Honolulu, HI 96822. *Phone:* 808-956-6066.

IDAHO

Freedom Scholarship. Waiver of scholastic fees up to $500 per semester for books in addition to on-campus housing and subsistence for children of Idaho citizens determined by the federal government to have been prisoners of war, missing in action, or killed in action or died of injuries or wounds sustained in action in southeast Asia, including Korea, or who shall become so hereafter, in any area of armed conflicts in which the United States is a party.

For additional information, see web site http://www.boardofed.idaho.gov/scholarship/freedom.asp. *Award:* Scholarship for use in freshman, sophomore, junior, or senior years; not renewable. *Award amount:* up to $500. *Eligibility Requirements:* Applicant must be enrolled or expecting to enroll full- or part-time at a two-year or four-year or technical institution or university; resident of Idaho and studying in Idaho. Available to U.S. citizens. Applicant or parent must meet one or more of the following requirements: general military experience; retired from active duty; disabled or killed as a result of military service; prisoner of war; or missing in action. *Application Requirements:* Application form. **Deadline:** February 15.

Public Safety Officer Dependent Scholarship. Scholarship for dependents of full-time Idaho public safety officers who were killed or disabled in the line of duty. Recipients will attend an Idaho postsecondary institution with a full waiver of fees, on-campus housing and campus meal plan, and up to $500 per semester for books and supplies.

For complete information, see web site http://www.boardofed.idaho.gov/scholarship/pub_safety.asp. *Award:* Scholarship for use in freshman year; renewable. *Eligibility Requirements:* Applicant must be enrolled or expecting to enroll full- or part-time at a two-year or four-year institution or university; resident of Idaho and studying in Idaho. Applicant or parent of applicant must have employment or volunteer experience in police/firefighting. Available to U.S. citizens. *Application Requirements:* Application form. **Deadline:** February 15.

ILLINOIS

Golden Apple Scholars of Illinois. Applicants must be between the ages of 16 and 21 and maintain a GPA of 2.5. Eligible applicants must be residents of Illinois studying in Illinois. Recipients must agree to teach in high-need Illinois schools. Education. *Award:* Scholarship for use in freshman, sophomore, junior, or senior years; renewable. *Award amount:* $23,000. *Number of awards:* 100–150. *Eligibility Requirements:* Applicant must be age 16-21; enrolled or expecting to enroll full-time at a four-year institution or university; resident of Illinois and studying in Illinois. Available to U.S. citizens. *Application Requirements:* Application form, essay, interview, personal photograph, recommendations or references, social security card, test scores, transcript. **Deadline:** November 15.

Contact Ms. Patricia Kilduff, Director of Recruitment and Placement. *E-mail:* kilduff@goldenapple.org. *Phone:* 312-407-0006 Ext. 105. *Website:* http://www.goldenapple.org/.

Grant Program for Dependents of Police, Fire, or Correctional Officers. Awards available to Illinois residents who are dependents of police, fire, and correctional officers killed or disabled in line of duty. Provides for tuition and fees at approved Illinois institutions. Number of grants and individual dollar amount awarded vary. *Award:* Grant for use in freshman, sophomore, junior, senior, graduate, or postgraduate years; renewable. *Eligibility Requirements:* Applicant must be enrolled or expecting to enroll full- or part-time at a two-year or four-year or technical institution or university; resident of Illinois and studying in Illinois. Available to U.S. citizens. *Application Requirements:* Application form, proof of status. **Deadline:** varies.

Higher Education License Plate Program-HELP. Grants for students who attend Illinois colleges for which the special collegiate license plates are available. The Illinois Secretary of State issues the license plates, and part of the proceeds are used for grants for undergraduate students attending these colleges, to pay tuition and mandatory fees. *Award:* Grant for use in freshman, sophomore, junior, or senior years; not renewable. *Eligibility Requirements:* Applicant must be enrolled or expecting to enroll full- or part-time at a two-year or four-year institution or university; resident of Illinois and studying in Illinois. Available to U.S. citizens. *Application Requirements:* Application form, financial need analysis. **Deadline:** varies.

Illinois College Savings Bond Bonus Incentive Grant Program. Program offers Illinois college savings bond holders a grant for each year of bond maturity payable upon bond redemption if at least 70 percent of proceeds are used to attend college in Illinois. The amount of grant will depend on the amount of the bond, ranging from a $40 to $440 grant per $5000 of the bond. Applications are accepted between August 1 and May 30 of the academic year in which the bonds matured, or in the academic year immediately following maturity. *Award:* Grant for use in freshman, sophomore, junior, senior, graduate, or postgraduate years; not renewable. *Eligibility Requirements:* Applicant must be enrolled or expecting to enroll full- or part-time at a two-year or four-year or technical institution or university and studying in Illinois. Available to U.S. citizens. *Application Requirements:* Application form. **Deadline:** varies.

Illinois Future Teachers Corps Program. Scholarships are available for students planning to become teachers in Illinois. Students must be Illinois residents, enrolled or accepted as a junior or above in a Teacher Education Program at an Illinois college or university. By receiving the award, students agree to teach for five years at either a public, private, or parochial Illinois preschool, or at a public elementary or secondary school. Education. *Award:* Scholarship for use in junior, senior, or graduate years; renewable. *Award amount:* $5000–$10,000. *Eligibility Requirements:* Applicant must be enrolled or expecting to enroll full- or part-time at a four-year institution or university; resident of Illinois and studying in Illinois. Available to U.S. citizens. *Application Requirements:* Application form, FAFSA, financial need analysis. **Deadline:** March 1.

Illinois Monetary Award Program. Awards to Illinois residents enrolled in a minimum of 3 hours per term in a degree program at an approved Illinois institution. See web site for complete list of participating schools. Must demonstrate financial need, based on the information provided on the Free Application for Federal Student Aid. Number of grants and the individual dollar amount awarded vary. Deadline: As soon as possible after January 1 of the year in which the student will enter college. *Award:* Grant for use in freshman, sophomore, junior, or senior years; renewable. *Award amount:* $2599. *Eligibility Requirements:* Applicant must be enrolled or expecting to enroll full- or part-time at a two-year or four-year or technical institution or university; resident of Illinois and studying in Illinois. Available to U.S. citizens. *Application Requirements:* FAFSA online, financial need analysis. **Deadline:** varies.

Illinois National Guard Grant Program. Active duty members of the Illinois National Guard, or who are within 12 months of discharge, and who have completed one full year of service are eligible. May be used for study at Illinois two- or four-year public colleges for a maximum of the equivalent of four academic years of full-time enrollment. Deadlines: October 1 of the academic year for full year, March 1 for second/third term, or June 15 for the summer term. *Award:* Grant for use in freshman, sophomore, junior, senior, or graduate years; renewable. *Eligibility Requirements:* Applicant must be enrolled or expecting to enroll full- or part-time at a two-year or four-year institution or university; resident of Illinois and studying in Illinois. Available to U.S. citizens. Applicant or parent must meet one or more of the following requirements: national guard experience; retired from active duty; disabled or killed as a result of military service; prisoner of war; or missing in action. *Application Requirements:* Application form, documentation of service. **Deadline:** varies.

Illinois Special Education Teacher Tuition Waiver. Teachers or students who are pursuing a career in special education as public, private or parochial preschool, elementary or secondary school teachers in Illinois may be eligible for this program. This program will exempt such individuals from paying tuition and mandatory fees at an eligible institution, for up to four years. The individual dollar amount awarded are subject to sufficient annual appropriations by the Illinois General Assembly. Special Education. *Award:* Scholarship for use in freshman, sophomore, junior, senior, or graduate years; renewable. *Eligibility Requirements:* Applicant must be enrolled or expecting to enroll full- or part-time at a four-year institution or university; resident of Illinois and studying in Illinois. Available to U.S. citizens. *Application Requirements:* Application form. **Deadline:** March 1.

Illinois Student-to-Student Program of Matching Grants. Matching grant is available to undergraduates at participating state-supported colleges. Number of grants and the individual dollar amount awarded vary. Contact financial aid office at institution. *Award:* Grant for use in freshman, sophomore, junior, or senior years; not renewable. *Award amount:* $300–$1000. *Eligibility Requirements:* Applicant must be enrolled or expecting to enroll full- or part-time at a two-year or four-year institution or university; resident of Illinois and studying in Illinois. Available to U.S. citizens. *Application Requirements:* Application form, financial need analysis. **Deadline:** varies.

Illinois Veteran Grant Program-IVG. Awards qualified veterans and pays eligible tuition and fees for study in Illinois public universities or community colleges. Program eligibility units are based on the enrolled hours for a particular term, not the dollar amount of the benefits paid. Applications are available at college financial aid office and can be submitted any time during the academic year for which assistance is being requested. *Award:* Grant for use in freshman, sophomore, junior, senior, or graduate years; renewable. *Eligibility Requirements:* Applicant must be enrolled or expecting to enroll full- or part-time at a two-year or four-year institution or university; resident of Illinois and studying in Illinois. Available to U.S. citizens. Applicant or parent must meet one or more of the following requirements: general military experience; retired from active duty; disabled or killed as a result of military service; prisoner of war; or missing in action. *Application Requirements:* Application form. **Deadline:** continuous.

ITW Scholarship. Renewable award of $2500 for women pursuing ABET-accredited baccalaureate programs in preparation for careers in engineering, engineering technology, and computer science in the United States and Mexico. Underrepresented groups and UIC preferred. Must be a U.S. citizen and be willing to intern. Computer Science/Data Processing; Electrical Engineering/Electronics; Engineering/Technology; Mechanical Engineering. *Award:* Scholarship for use in junior year; not renewable. *Award amount:* $2500. *Number of awards:* 2. *Eligibility Requirements:* Applicant must be enrolled or expecting to enroll full-time at a four-year institution or university and female. Available to U.S. citizens. *Application Requirements:* Application form, recommendations or references. **Deadline:** February 15.

Jill S. Tietjen P.E. Scholarship. $1500 award for a woman pursuing an ABET-accredited baccalaureate or graduate program in preparation for a career in engineering, engineering technology, and computer science in the United States and Mexico. Must be a U.S. citizen. Chemical Engineering; Civil Engineering; Computer Science/Data Processing; Electrical Engineering/Electronics; Energy and Power Engineering; Engineering/Technology; Marine/Ocean Engineering; Materials Science, Engineering, and Metallurgy; Mechanical Engineering; Paper and Pulp Engineering. *Award:* Scholarship for use in sophomore, junior, senior, or graduate years; not renewable. *Award amount:* $1500. *Number of awards:* 1. *Eligibility Requirements:* Applicant must be enrolled or expecting to enroll full-time at a four-year institution or university and female. Available to U.S. citizens. *Application Requirements:* Application form, recommendations or references. **Deadline:** February 15.

MIA/POW Scholarships. One-time award for spouse, child, or step-child of veterans who are missing in action or were a prisoner of war. Must be enrolled at a state-supported school in Illinois. Candidate must be U.S. citizen. Must apply and be accepted before beginning of school. Also for children and spouses of veterans who are determined to be 100 percent disabled as established by the Veterans Administration. Scholarship value and the number of awards granted varies. *Award:* Scholarship for use in freshman, sophomore, junior, or senior years; renewable. *Eligibility Requirements:* Applicant must be enrolled or expecting to enroll full- or part-time at a two-year or four-year institution or university; resident of Illinois and studying in Illinois. Available to U.S. citizens. Applicant or parent must meet one or more of the following requirements: general military experience; retired from active duty; disabled or killed as a result of military service; prisoner of war; or missing in action. *Application Requirements:* Application form. **Deadline:** continuous.

Contact Ms. Tracy Smith, Grants Section, Illinois Department of Veterans' Affairs, 833 South Spring Street, Springfield, IL 62794-9432. *Phone:* 217-782-3564. *Fax:* 217-782-4161. *Website:* http://www.state.il.us/agency/dva.

Minority Teachers of Illinois Scholarship Program. Award for minority students intending to become school teachers; teaching commitment attached to receipt. Number of scholarships and the individual dollar amounts vary. Education; Special Education. *Award:* Scholarship for use in freshman, sophomore, junior, senior, graduate, or postgraduate years; renewable. *Award amount:* up to $5000. *Eligibility Requirements:* Applicant must be American Indian/ Alaska Native, Asian/Pacific Islander, Black (non-Hispanic), Hispanic; enrolled or expecting to enroll full- or part-time at a two-year or four-year institution or university; resident of Illinois and studying in Illinois. Available to U.S. citizens. *Application Requirements:* Application form, transcript. **Deadline:** March 1.

SWE Baltimore-Washington Section Scholarship. One $1500 award for a woman pursuing an ABET-accredited baccalaureate or graduate program in preparation for a career in engineering, engineering technology, or computer science in the United States and Mexico. For use at a school in DC, MD, or VA. U. S. citizenship and SWE membership required. Chemical Engineering; Civil Engineering; Construction Engineering/ Management; Electrical Engineering/ Electronics; Energy and Power Engineering; Engineering/Technology; Marine/Ocean Engineering; Materials Science, Engineering, and Metallurgy; Mechanical Engineering; Paper and Pulp Engineering. *Award:* Scholarship for use in sophomore, junior, senior, or graduate years; not renewable. *Award amount:* $1500. *Number of awards:* 1. *Eligibility Requirements:* Applicant must be enrolled or expecting to enroll full-time at a four-year institution or university; female and studying in District of Columbia, Maryland, Virginia. Applicant or parent of applicant must be member of Society of Women Engineers. Available to U.S. citizens. *Application Requirements:* Application form, recommendations or references. **Deadline:** February 15.

SWE Central New Mexico Pioneers Scholarship. Renewable $1250 scholarship for a woman pursuing an ABET-accredited baccalaureate program in preparation for a career in engineering, engineering technology, or computer science in the United States and Mexico. Must attend a NM university or 4-year engineering/technology school. US citizenship and SWE membership required. Renewable up to three years. Chemical Engineering; Civil Engineering; Construction Engineering/Management; Electrical Engineering/Electronics; Energy and Power Engineering; Engineering/ Technology; Marine/Ocean Engineering; Materials Science, Engineering, and Metallurgy; Mechanical Engineering; Paper and Pulp Engineering. *Award:* Scholarship for use in sophomore, junior, or senior years; renewable. *Award amount:*

$1250. *Number of awards:* 1. *Eligibility Requirements:* Applicant must be enrolled or expecting to enroll full-time at an institution or university; female and studying in New Mexico. Applicant or parent of applicant must be member of Society of Women Engineers. Available to U.S. citizens. *Application Requirements:* Application form, recommendations or references. **Deadline:** February 15.

Veterans' Children Educational Opportunities. $250 award for each child aged 10 to 18 of a veteran who died or became totally disabled as a result of service during World War I, World War II, Korean, or Vietnam War. Must be Illinois resident studying in Illinois. Death must be service-connected. Disability must be rated 100 percent for two or more years. *Award:* Grant for use in freshman year; not renewable. *Award amount:* $250. *Eligibility Requirements:* Applicant must be age 10-18; enrolled or expecting to enroll full- or part-time at a two-year or four-year institution or university; resident of Illinois and studying in Illinois. Available to U.S. citizens. Applicant or parent must meet one or more of the following requirements: general military experience; retired from active duty; disabled or killed as a result of military service; prisoner of war; or missing in action. *Application Requirements:* Application form. **Deadline:** June 30.

Contact Tracy Smith, Grants Section, Illinois Department of Veterans' Affairs, 833 South Spring Street, Springfield, IL 62794-9432. *Phone:* 217-782-3564. *Fax:* 217-782-4161. *Website:* http://www.state. il.us/agency/dva.

INDIANA

Child of Disabled Veteran Grant or Purple Heart Recipient Grant. Free tuition at Indiana state-supported colleges or universities for children of disabled veterans or Purple Heart recipients. Must submit form DD214 or service record. Covers tuition and mandatory fees. *Award:* Grant for use in freshman, sophomore, junior, senior, graduate, or postgraduate years; renewable. *Eligibility Requirements:* Applicant must be enrolled or expecting to enroll full- or part-time at a two-year or four-year institution or university; resident of Indiana and studying in Indiana. Available to U.S. citizens. Applicant or parent must meet one or more of the following requirements: general military experience; retired from active duty; disabled or killed as a result of military service; prisoner of war; or

missing in action. *Application Requirements:* Application form, FAFSA. **Deadline:** continuous.

Contact Jon Brinkley, State Service Officer, Indiana Department of Veterans Affairs, 302 West Washington Street, Room E-120, Indianapolis, IN 46204-2738. *E-mail:* jbrinkley@dva.in.gov. *Phone:* 317-232-3910. *Fax:* 317-232-7721. *Website:* http://www.in.gov/dva.

Department of Veterans Affairs Free Tuition for Children of POW/ MIA's in Vietnam. Renewable award for residents of Indiana who are the children of veterans declared missing in action or prisoner-of-war after January 1, 1960. Provides tuition at Indiana state-supported institutions for undergraduate study. *Award:* Grant for use in freshman, sophomore, junior, senior, graduate, or postgraduate years; renewable. *Eligibility Requirements:* Applicant must be enrolled or expecting to enroll full- or part-time at a two-year or four-year institution or university; resident of Indiana and studying in Indiana. Available to U.S. citizens. Applicant or parent must meet one or more of the following requirements: general military experience; retired from active duty; disabled or killed as a result of military service; prisoner of war; or missing in action. *Application Requirements:* Application form. **Deadline:** continuous.

Contact Jon Brinkley, State Service Officer, Indiana Department of Veterans Affairs, 302 West Washington Street, Room E-120, Indianapolis, IN 46204-2738. *E-mail:* jbrinkley@dva.in.gov. *Phone:* 317-232-3910. *Fax:* 317-232-7721. *Website:* http://www.in.gov/dva.

Frank O'Bannon Grant Program. A need-based, tuition-restricted program for students attending Indiana public, private, or proprietary institutions seeking a first undergraduate degree. Students (and parents of dependent students) who are U. S. citizens and Indiana residents must file the FAFSA yearly by the March 10 deadline. *Award:* Grant for use in freshman, sophomore, junior, or senior years; not renewable. *Award amount:* $200–$10,992. *Number of awards:* 48,408–70,239. *Eligibility Requirements:* Applicant must be enrolled or expecting to enroll full-time at a two-year or four-year or technical institution or university; resident of Indiana and studying in Indiana. Available to U.S. citizens. *Application Requirements:* Application form, FAFSA, financial need analysis. **Deadline:** March 10.

Hoosier Scholar Award. A $500 non-renewable award. Based on the size of the senior class, one to three scholars are selected by the guidance counselors of each accredited high school in Indiana. The award is based on academic merit and may be used for any educational expense at an eligible Indiana institution of higher education. *Award:* Scholarship for use in freshman year; not renewable. *Award amount:* $500. *Number of awards:* 666–840. *Eligibility Requirements:* Applicant must be high school student; planning to enroll or expecting to enroll full-time at a two-year or four-year institution or university; resident of Indiana and studying in Indiana. Applicant must have 3.5 GPA or higher. Available to U.S. citizens. *Application Requirements:* Application form, recommendations or references. **Deadline:** March 10.

Contact Ada Sparkman, Program Coordinator, State Student Assistance Commission of Indiana (SSACI), 150 West Market Street, Suite 500, Indianapolis, IN 46204-2805. *Phone:* 317-232-2350. *Fax:* 317-232-3260. *Website:* http://www.in.gov/ssaci.

Indiana National Guard Supplemental Grant. The award is a supplement to the Indiana Higher Education Grant program. Applicants must be members of the Indiana National Guard. All Guard paperwork must be completed prior to the start of each semester. The FAFSA must be received by March 10. Award covers certain tuition and fees at select public colleges. *Award:* Grant for use in freshman, sophomore, junior, or senior years; not renewable. *Award amount:* $20–$7110. *Number of awards:* 503–925. *Eligibility Requirements:* Applicant must be enrolled or expecting to enroll full- or part-time at a two-year or four-year institution or university; resident of Indiana and studying in Indiana. Available to U.S. citizens. Applicant or parent must meet one or more of the following requirements: national guard experience; retired from active duty; disabled or killed as a result of military service; prisoner of war; or missing in action. *Application Requirements:* Application form. **Deadline:** March 10.

Contact Kathryn Moore, Grants Counselor, State Student Assistance Commission of Indiana (SSACI), 150 West Market Street, Suite 500, Indianapolis, IN 46204-2805. *E-mail:* kmoore@ssaci.in.gov. *Phone:* 317-232-2350. *Fax:* 317-232-2360. *Website:* http://www.in.gov/ssaci.

Indiana Nursing Scholarship Fund. Need-based tuition funding for nursing students enrolled full- or part-time at an eligible Indiana institution. Must be a U.S. citizen and an Indiana resident and have a minimum 2.0 GPA or meet the minimum requirements for the nursing program. Upon graduation, recipients must practice as a nurse in an Indiana health care setting for two years. Nursing. *Award:* Scholarship for use in freshman, sophomore, junior, or senior years; not renewable. *Award amount:* $200–$5000. *Number of awards:* 490–690. *Eligibility Requirements:* Applicant must be enrolled or expecting to enroll full- or part-time at a two-year or four-year institution or university; resident of Indiana and studying in Indiana. Available to U.S. citizens. *Application Requirements:* Application form, FAFSA, financial need analysis. **Deadline:** continuous.

Contact Yvonne Heflin, Director, Special Programs, State Student Assistance Commission of Indiana (SSACI), 150 West Market Street, Suite 500, Indianapolis, IN 46204-2805. *Phone:* 317-232-2350. *Fax:* 317-232-3260. *Website:* http://www.in.gov/ssaci.

National Guard Scholarship Extension Program. A scholarship extension applicant is eligible for a tuition scholarship under Indiana Code 21-13-5-4 for a period not to exceed the period of scholarship extension the applicant served on active duty as a member of the National Guard (mobilized and deployed). Must apply not later than one (1) year after the applicant ceases to be a member of the Indiana National Guard. Applicant should apply through the education officer of their last unit of assignment. *Award:* Grant for use in freshman, sophomore, junior, or senior years; renewable. *Eligibility Requirements:* Applicant must be enrolled or expecting to enroll full- or part-time at a two-year or four-year or technical institution or university and studying in Indiana. Available to U.S. citizens. Applicant must have national guard experience. *Application Requirements:* Application form. **Deadline:** continuous.

Contact Pamela Moody, National Guard Education Officer, Indiana Department of Veterans Affairs, 302 West Washington Street, Suite E120, Indianapolis, IN 46204. *E-mail:* pamela.moody@in.ngb.army.mil. *Phone:* 317-964-7017. *Fax:* 317-232-7721. *Website:* http://www.in.gov/dva.

National Guard Tuition Supplement Program. Applicant must be a member of the Indiana National Guard, in active drilling status, who has not been AWOL during the last 12 months, does not possess a bachelor's degree, possesses the requisite academic qualifications, meets the requirements of the state-supported college or university, and meets all National Guard requirements. *Award:* Grant for use in freshman, sophomore, junior, or senior years; renewable. *Eligibility Requirements:* Applicant must be enrolled or expecting to enroll full- or part-time at a two-year or four-year or technical institution or university and studying in Indiana. Available to U.S. citizens. Applicant must have national guard experience. *Application Requirements:* Application form, FAFSA. **Deadline:** continuous.

Contact Jon Brinkley, State Service Officer. *E-mail:* jbrinkley@dva.in.gov. *Phone:* 317-232-3910. *Fax:* 317-232-7721. *Website:* http://www.in.gov/dva.

Part-Time Grant Program. Program is designed to encourage part-time undergraduates to start and complete their associate or baccalaureate degrees or certificates by subsidizing part-time tuition costs. It is a term-based award that is based on need. State residency requirements must be met and a FAFSA must be filed. Eligibility is determined at the institutional level subject to approval by SSACI. *Award:* Grant for use in freshman, sophomore, junior, or senior years; not renewable. *Award amount:* $20–$4000. *Number of awards:* 4680–6700. *Eligibility Requirements:* Applicant must be enrolled or expecting to enroll part-time at a two-year or four-year or technical institution or university; resident of Indiana and studying in Indiana. Available to U.S. citizens. *Application Requirements:* Application form, financial need analysis. **Deadline:** continuous.

Resident Tuition for Active Duty Military Personnel. Applicant must be a nonresident of Indiana serving on active duty and stationed in Indiana and attending any state-supported college or university. Dependents remain eligible for the duration of their enrollment, even if the active duty person is no longer in Indiana. Entitlement is to the resident tuition rate. *Award:* Grant for use in freshman, sophomore, junior, senior, graduate, or postgraduate years; renewable. *Eligibility Requirements:* Applicant must be enrolled or expecting to enroll full- or part-time at a two-year or four-year or technical institution or university and studying in Indiana. Available to U.S. citizens. Applicant or parent must meet one or more of the following requirements: Air Force, Army, Marine Corps, or Navy experience; retired from active duty; disabled or killed as a result of military service; prisoner of war; or missing in action. *Application Requirements:* Application form. **Deadline:** continuous.

Contact Jon Brinkley, State Service Officer. *E-mail:* jbrinkley@dva.in.gov. *Phone:* 317-232-3910. *Fax:* 317-232-7721. *Website:* http://www.in.gov/dva.

Tuition and Fee Remission for Children and Spouses of National Guard Members. Award to an individual whose father, mother or spouse was a member of the Indiana National Guard and suffered a service-connected death while serving on state active duty (which includes mobilized and deployed for federal active duty). The student must be eligible to pay the resident tuition rate at the state-supported college or university and must possess the requisite academic qualifications. *Award:* Grant for use in freshman, sophomore, junior, or senior years; renewable. *Eligibility Requirements:* Applicant must be enrolled or expecting to enroll full- or part-time at a two-year or four-year or technical institution or university and studying in Indiana. Available to U.S. citizens. Applicant or parent must meet one or more of the following requirements: national guard experience; retired from active duty; disabled or killed as a result of military service; prisoner of war; or missing in action. *Application Requirements:* Application form, FAFSA. **Deadline:** continuous.

Contact R. Martin Umbarger, Adjutant General, Indiana Department of Veterans Affairs, 2002 South Holt Road, Indianapolis, IN 46241. *E-mail:* r.martin.umbarger@in.ngb.army.mil. *Phone:* 317-247-3559. *Fax:* 317-247-3540. *Website:* http://www.in.gov/dva.

Twenty-first Century Scholars Gear Up Summer Scholarship. Grant of up to $3000 that pays for summer school tuition and regularly assessed course fees (does not cover other costs such as textbooks or room and board). *Award:* Scholarship for use in freshman, sophomore, junior, or senior years; not renewable. *Award amount:* up to $3000. *Number of awards:* 1. *Eligibility Requirements:* Applicant must be enrolled or expecting to enroll full-time at a two-year or four-year institution or university; resident of Indiana and studying in Indiana. Available to U.S. citizens. *Application Requirements:* Application form, must be in twenty-first century scholars program, high school diploma. **Deadline:** varies.

IOWA

All Iowa Opportunity Scholarship. Students attending eligible Iowa colleges and universities may receive awards of up to $6420. Minimum 2.5 GPA. Priority will be given to students who participated in the Federal TRIO Programs or graduated from alternative high schools or alternative high school programs. Applicant must enroll within two academic years of graduating from high school. Maximum individual awards cannot exceed more than the resident tuition and fee rate at Iowa Regent Universities. *Award:* Scholarship for use in freshman or sophomore years; not renewable. *Number of awards:* 200–800. *Eligibility Requirements:* Applicant must be enrolled or expecting to enroll full- or part-time at a two-year or four-year or technical institution or university; resident of Iowa and studying in Iowa. Applicant must have 2.5 GPA or higher. Available to U.S. citizens. *Application Requirements:* Application form, application form may be submitted online (http://www.iowacollegeaid.gov), financial need analysis. **Deadline:** March 1.

Contact Todd Brown, Director, Scholarships, Grants, and Loan Forgiveness, Iowa College Student Aid Commission, 603 East 12th Street, 5th Floor, Des Moines, IA 50319. *E-mail:* grants@iowacollegeaid.gov. *Phone:* 877-272-4456. *Fax:* 515-725-3401. *Website:* http://www.iowacollegeaid.gov/.

Iowa Grants. Statewide need-based program to assist high-need Iowa residents. Recipients must demonstrate a high level of financial need to receive awards ranging from $100 to $1000. Awards are prorated for students enrolled for less than full-time. Awards must be used at Iowa postsecondary institutions. *Award:* Grant for use in freshman, sophomore, junior, or senior years; not renewable. *Award amount:* $100–$1000. *Number of awards:* 1000–3000. *Eligibility Requirements:* Applicant must be enrolled or expecting to enroll full- or part-time at a two-year or four-year or technical institution or university; resident of Iowa and studying in Iowa. Available to U.S. citizens. *Application Requirements:* Application form, application form may be submitted online (http://www.fafsa.gov), financial need analysis. **Deadline:** continuous.

Contact Todd Brown, Director, Scholarships, Grants, and Loan Forgiveness, Iowa College Student Aid Commission, 603 East 12th Street, 5th Floor, Des Moines, IA 50319. *E-mail:* grants@iowacollegeaid.gov. *Phone:* 877-

272-4456. *Fax:* 515-725-3401. *Website:* http://www.iowacollegeaid.gov/.

Iowa National Guard Education Assistance Program. Program provides postsecondary tuition assistance to members of Iowa National Guard Units. Must study at a postsecondary institution in Iowa. Contact the office for additional information. *Award:* Grant for use in freshman, sophomore, junior, or senior years; not renewable. *Number of awards:* 700–1500. *Eligibility Requirements:* Applicant must be enrolled or expecting to enroll full- or part-time at a two-year or four-year or technical institution or university; resident of Iowa and studying in Iowa. Available to U.S. citizens. Applicant must have national guard experience. *Application Requirements:* Application form, application form may be submitted online (http://www.iowacollegeaid.gov). **Deadline:** continuous.

Contact Todd Brown, Director, Scholarships, Grants, and Loan Forgiveness, Iowa College Student Aid Commission, 603 East 12th Street, 5th Floor, Des Moines, IA 50319. *E-mail:* todd.brown@iowa.gov. *Phone:* 877-272-4456. *Fax:* 515-725-3401. *Website:* http://www.iowacollegeaid.gov/.

Iowa Tuition Grant Program. Program assists students who attend independent postsecondary institutions in Iowa. Iowa residents currently enrolled, or planning to enroll, for at least 3 semester hours at one of the eligible Iowa postsecondary institutions may apply. Awards currently range from $100 to $4000. Grants may not exceed the difference between independent college and university tuition fees and the average tuition fees at the three public Regent universities. *Award:* Grant for use in freshman, sophomore, junior, or senior years; not renewable. *Award amount:* $100–$4000. *Number of awards:* 16,500–19,000. *Eligibility Requirements:* Applicant must be enrolled or expecting to enroll full- or part-time at a two-year or four-year institution or university; resident of Iowa and studying in Iowa. Available to U.S. citizens. *Application Requirements:* Application form, application form may be submitted online (http://www.fafsa.gov), financial need analysis. **Deadline:** July 1.

Contact Todd Brown, Director, Scholarships, Grants, and Loan Forgiveness, Iowa College Student Aid Commission, 603 East 12th Street, 5th Floor, Des Moines, IA 50319. *E-mail:* todd.brown@iowa.gov. *Phone:* 877-272-

4456. *Fax:* 515-725-3401. *Website:* http://www.iowacollegeaid.gov/.

Iowa Vocational-Technical Tuition Grant Program. Program provides need-based financial assistance to Iowa residents enrolled in career education (vocational-technical), and career option programs at Iowa area community colleges. Grants range from $150 to $1200, depending on the length of the program, financial need, and available funds. *Award:* Grant for use in freshman or sophomore years; not renewable. *Award amount:* $150–$1200. *Number of awards:* 2500–3500. *Eligibility Requirements:* Applicant must be enrolled or expecting to enroll full- or part-time at a two-year or technical institution; resident of Iowa and studying in Iowa. Available to U.S. citizens. *Application Requirements:* Application form, application form may be submitted online (http://www.fafsa.gov), financial need analysis. **Deadline:** July 1.

Contact Todd Brown, Director, Program Administration, Iowa College Student Aid Commission, 603 East 12th Street, 5th Floor, Des Moines, IA 50319. *E-mail:* todd.brown@iowa.gov. *Phone:* 515-725-3405. *Fax:* 515-725-3401. *Website:* http://www.iowacollegeaid.gov/.

KANSAS

Kansas Educational Benefits for Children of MIA, POW, and Deceased Veterans of the Vietnam War. Scholarship awarded to students who are children of veterans. Must show proof of parent's status as missing in action, prisoner-of-war, or killed in action in the Vietnam War. Kansas residence required of veteran at time of entry to service. Must attend a state-supported postsecondary school. *Award:* Scholarship for use in freshman, sophomore, junior, or senior years; not renewable. *Number of awards:* 1. *Eligibility Requirements:* Applicant must be enrolled or expecting to enroll full-time at a two-year or four-year or technical institution or university and studying in Kansas. Available to U.S. citizens. Applicant or parent must meet one or more of the following requirements: general military experience; retired from active duty; disabled or killed as a result of military service; prisoner of war; or missing in action. *Application Requirements:* Application form, birth certificate, school acceptance letter, military discharge of veteran. **Deadline:** varies.

Contact Wayne Bollig, Program Director. *E-mail:* wbollig@kcva.org.

Phone: 785-296-3976. *Fax:* 785-296-1462. *Website:* http://www.kcva.org/.

Kansas Ethnic Minority Scholarship. Scholarship program designed to assist financially needy, academically competitive students who are identified as members of any of the following ethnic/racial groups: African-American, American Indian or Alaskan Native, Asian or Pacific Islander, or Hispanic. Priority is given to applicants who are freshmen. Students must be Kansas residents attending postsecondary institutions in Kansas. For more details refer to web site http://www.kansasregents.org/financial_aid/minority.html. *Award:* Scholarship for use in freshman, sophomore, junior, or senior years; renewable. *Award amount:* up to $1850. *Eligibility Requirements:* Applicant must be American Indian/Alaska Native, Asian/Pacific Islander, Black (non-Hispanic), Hispanic; enrolled or expecting to enroll full-time at a two-year or four-year institution or university; resident of Kansas and studying in Kansas. Applicant must have 3.0 GPA or higher. Available to U.S. citizens. *Application Requirements:* Application form, financial need analysis, test scores. *Fee:* $12. **Deadline:** May 1.

Contact Diane Lindeman, Director of Student Financial Assistance, Kansas Board of Regents, 1000 SW Jackson, Suite 520, Topeka, KS 66612. *E-mail:* dlindeman@ksbor.org. *Phone:* 785-296-3517. *Fax:* 785-296-0983. *Website:* http://www.kansasregents.org/.

Kansas Nursing Service Scholarship Program. This is a service scholarship loan program available to students attending two-year or four-year public and private postsecondary institutions as well as vocational technical schools with nursing education programs. Students can be pursuing either LPN or RN licensure. This is a service obligation scholarship, therefore students must agree to work in the field of nursing one year for each year they have received the scholarship or must repay the amount of the scholarship award that they received plus interest. Students must be Kansas residents attending a postsecondary institution in Kansas. Nursing. *Award:* Scholarship for use in freshman, sophomore, junior, or senior years; renewable. *Award amount:* $2500–$3500. *Eligibility Requirements:* Applicant must be enrolled or expecting to enroll full-time at a two-year or four-year or technical institution or university. Available to U.S. citizens. *Application Requirements:* Application form, financial need analysis. *Fee:* $12. **Deadline:** May 1.

Contact Diane Lindeman, Director of Student Financial Assistance, Kansas Board of Regents, 1000 SW Jackson, Suite 520, Topeka, KS 66612. *E-mail:* dlindeman@ksbor.org. *Phone:* 785-296-3517. *Fax:* 785-296-0983. *Website:* http://www.kansasregents.org/.

Kansas Teacher Service Scholarship. Scholarship to encourage talented students to enter the teaching profession and teach in Kansas in specific curriculum areas or in underserved areas of Kansas. Students must be Kansas residents attending a postsecondary institution in Kansas. For more details, refer to web site http://www.kansasregents.org. Education. *Award:* Scholarship for use in junior, senior, or graduate years; renewable. *Award amount:* $2206–$5514. *Eligibility Requirements:* Applicant must be enrolled or expecting to enroll full- or part-time at a four-year institution or university. Applicant must have 3.0 GPA or higher. Available to U.S. citizens. *Application Requirements:* Application form, essay, financial need analysis, recommendations or references, resume, test scores, transcript. *Fee:* $12. **Deadline:** May 1.

Contact Diane Lindeman, Director of Student Financial Assistance, Kansas Board of Regents, 1000 SW Jackson, Suite 520, Topeka, KS 66612. *E-mail:* dlindeman@ksbor.org. *Phone:* 785-296-3517. *Fax:* 785-296-0983. *Website:* http://www.kansasregents.org/.

Ted and Nora Anderson Scholarships. Scholarship of $250 for each semester (one year only) given to the children of American Legion members or Auxiliary members who are holding membership for the past three consecutive years. Children of a deceased member can also apply. Parent of the applicant must be a veteran. Must be high school seniors or college freshmen or sophomores in a Kansas institution. Scholarship for use at an approved college, university, or trade school in Kansas. Must maintain a C average in college. *Award:* Scholarship for use in freshman or sophomore years; not renewable. *Award amount:* $250–$500. *Number of awards:* 4. *Eligibility Requirements:* Applicant must be enrolled or expecting to enroll full-time at a two-year or four-year or technical institution or university; resident of Kansas and studying in Kansas. Applicant or parent of applicant must be member of American Legion or Auxiliary. Available to U.S. citizens. Applicant or parent must meet one or more of the following requirements: general military experience; retired from active duty; disabled or killed as a result of military service; prisoner of war; or missing in action. *Application Requirements:* Application form, essay, financial need analysis, personal photograph, recommendations or references, transcript. **Deadline:** February 15.

Contact Jim Gravenstein, Chairman, Scholarship Committee, American Legion Department of Kansas, 1314 Topeka Boulevard, SW, Topeka, KS 66612. *Phone:* 785-232-9315. *Fax:* 785-232-1399. *Website:* http://www.ksamlegion.org/.

KENTUCKY

College Access Program (CAP) Grant. Award for U.S. citizens and Kentucky residents seeking their first undergraduate degree. Applicants enrolled in sectarian institutions are not eligible. Must submit Free Application for Federal Student Aid to demonstrate financial need. Funding is limited. Awards are made on a first-come, first-serve basis. *Award:* Grant for use in freshman, sophomore, junior, or senior years; not renewable. *Award amount:* up to $1900. *Number of awards:* 35,000–45,000. *Eligibility Requirements:* Applicant must be enrolled or expecting to enroll full- or part-time at a two-year or four-year or technical institution or university; resident of Kentucky and studying in Kentucky. Available to U.S. citizens. *Application Requirements:* Application form may be submitted online (http://www.fafsa.ed.gov), FAFSA. **Deadline:** continuous.

Contact Sheila Roe, Program Coordinator, Kentucky Higher Education Assistance Authority (KHEAA), PO Box 798, Frankfort, KY 40602-0798. *E-mail:* sroe@kheaa.com. *Phone:* 800-928-8926 Ext. 67393. *Fax:* 502-696-7373. *Website:* http://www.kheaa.com/.

Department of Veterans Affairs Tuition Waiver-KY KRS 164-507. Scholarship available to college students who are residents of Kentucky under the age of 26. *Award:* Scholarship for use in freshman, sophomore, junior, or senior years; not renewable. *Number of awards:* 400. *Eligibility Requirements:* Applicant must be enrolled or expecting to enroll full- or part-time at a two-year or four-year institution or university and resident of Kentucky. Available to U.S. citizens. *Application Requirements:* Application form. **Deadline:** varies.

Contact Barbara Sipek, Tuition Waiver Coordinator. *E-mail:* barbaraa.sipek@ky.gov. *Phone:* 502-595-4447. *Website:* http://www.veterans.ky.gov/.

Early Childhood Development Scholarship. Awards scholarship with conditional service commitment for part-time students currently employed by participating ECD facility or providing training in ECD for an approved organization. For more information, visit web site at http://www.kheaa.com. Child and Family Studies; Education. *Award:* Scholarship for use in freshman, sophomore, junior, or senior years; not renewable. *Award amount:* up to $1800. *Number of awards:* 800–1200. *Eligibility Requirements:* Applicant must be enrolled or expecting to enroll part-time at a two-year or four-year institution or university; resident of Kentucky and studying in Kentucky. Available to U.S. citizens. *Application Requirements:* Application form, application form may be submitted online (http://www.kheaa.com), FAFSA, financial need analysis. **Deadline:** continuous.

Contact David Lawhorn, Program Coordinator, Kentucky Higher Education Assistance Authority (KHEAA), PO Box 798, Frankfort, KY 40602-0798. *E-mail:* dlawhorn@kheaa.com. *Phone:* 800-928-8926 Ext. 67383. *Fax:* 502-696-7373. *Website:* http://www.kheaa.com/.

Environmental Protection Scholarship. Renewable awards for college juniors, seniors, and graduate students for in-state tuition, fees, room and board, and a book allowance at a Kentucky public university. Minimum 3.0 GPA required. Must work full-time for the Kentucky Department for Environmental Protection upon graduation (six months for each semester of scholarship support received). Interview required. Program not generally appropriate for non-residents. Biology; Chemical Engineering; Civil Engineering; Earth Science; Environmental Science; Hydrology; Mechanical Engineering; Natural Sciences. *Award:* Scholarship for use in junior, senior, or graduate years; renewable. *Award amount:* $15,000–$30,000. *Number of awards:* 1–2. *Eligibility Requirements:* Applicant must be enrolled or expecting to enroll full-time at a four-year institution or university and studying in Kentucky. Applicant must have 3.0 GPA or higher. Available to U.S. and non-U.S. citizens. *Application Requirements:* Application form, essay, interview, recommendations or references, transcript, valid work permit for non-citizens. **Deadline:** February 15.

Contact James Kipp, Scholarship Program Coordinator, Kentucky Energy and Environment Cabinet, 233 Mining/Mineral Resources Building, Lexington,

KY 40506-0107. *E-mail:* kipp@uky.edu. *Phone:* 859-257-1299. *Fax:* 859-323-1049. *Website:* http://www.eec.ky.gov/.

Go Higher Grant. Need-based grant for adult students pursuing their first undergraduate degree. Completion of the FAFSA is required. *Award:* Grant for use in freshman, sophomore, junior, or senior years; not renewable. *Award amount:* up to $1000. *Number of awards:* 100–300. *Eligibility Requirements:* Applicant must be enrolled or expecting to enroll full- or part-time at a two-year or four-year or technical institution or university; resident of Kentucky and studying in Kentucky. Available to U.S. citizens. *Application Requirements:* Application form, application form may be submitted online (http://www.fafsa.ed.gov), FAFSA. **Deadline:** continuous.

Contact Sheila Roe, Grant Program Coordinator, Kentucky Higher Education Assistance Authority (KHEAA), PO Box 798, Frankfort, KY 40206-0798. *E-mail:* sroe@kheaa.com. *Phone:* 800-928-8926 Ext. 67393. *Website:* http://www.kheaa.com/.

Kentucky Educational Excellence Scholarship (KEES). Annual award based on yearly high school GPA and highest ACT or SAT score received by high school graduation. Awards are renewable, if required cumulative GPA is maintained at a Kentucky postsecondary school. Must be a Kentucky resident, and a graduate of a Kentucky high school. *Award:* Scholarship for use in freshman, sophomore, junior, or senior years; renewable. *Award amount:* $125–$2500. *Number of awards:* 65,000–70,000. *Eligibility Requirements:* Applicant must be enrolled or expecting to enroll full- or part-time at a two-year or four-year or technical institution or university; resident of Kentucky and studying in Kentucky. Available to U.S. citizens. *Application Requirements:* Data submitted by KY high schools, test scores. **Deadline:** continuous.

Contact Megan Cummins, KEES Coordinator, Kentucky Higher Education Assistance Authority (KHEAA), PO Box 798, Frankfort, KY 40602. *E-mail:* mcummins@kheaa.com. *Phone:* 800-928-8926 Ext. 67397. *Fax:* 502-696-7373. *Website:* http://www.kheaa.com/.

Kentucky Office of Vocational Rehabilitation. Grant provides services necessary to secure employment. Eligible individual must possess physical or mental impairment that results in a substantial impediment to employment; benefit from vocational rehabilitation services in terms of an employment outcome; and require vocational rehabilitation services to prepare for, enter, or retain employment. *Award:* Grant for use in freshman, sophomore, junior, senior, graduate, or postgraduate years; renewable. *Eligibility Requirements:* Applicant must be enrolled or expecting to enroll full- or part-time at a two-year or four-year or technical institution or university. *Application Requirements:* Application form, eligibility for OVR services and in proper priority category, financial need analysis, interview, transcript. **Deadline:** continuous.

Contact Charles Puckett, Program Administrator, Kentucky Office of Vocational Rehabilitation, 600 West Cedar Street, Suite 2E, Louisville, KY 40202. *E-mail:* marianu.spencer@mail. state.ky.us. *Phone:* 502-595-4173. *Fax:* 502-564-2358. *Website:* http://www.ovr. ky.gov/.

Kentucky Transportation Cabinet Civil Engineering Scholarship Program. Scholarships awarded to qualified Kentucky residents who wish to study civil engineering at University of Kentucky, Western Kentucky University, University of Louisville or Kentucky State University. Applicant should be a graduate of an accredited Kentucky high school or a Kentucky resident. Scholarship recipients are given opportunities to work for the Cabinet during summers and job opportunities upon graduation within the state of KY. Civil Engineering. *Award:* Scholarship for use in freshman, sophomore, junior, or senior years; renewable. *Award amount:* $10,600–$44,000. *Number of awards:* 15–25. *Eligibility Requirements:* Applicant must be enrolled or expecting to enroll full-time at a four-year institution or university; resident of Kentucky and studying in Kentucky. Applicant must have 3.0 GPA or higher. Available to U.S. and non-U.S. citizens. *Application Requirements:* Application form, essay, interview, recommendations or references, test scores, transcript. **Deadline:** March 1.

Contact Cherie Mertz, Scholarship Program Coordinator, Kentucky Transportation Cabinet, 200 Mero Street, 6th Floor West, Frankfort, KY 40622. *E-mail:* Cherie.Mertz@ky.gov. *Website:* http://transportation.ky.gov/Education/Pages/Scholarships.aspx.

Kentucky Tuition Grant (KTG). Grants available to Kentucky residents who are full-time undergraduates at an independent college within the state. Based on financial need. Must submit FAFSA. *Award:* Grant for use in freshman, sophomore, junior, or senior years; not renewable. *Award amount:* $200–$3000. *Number of awards:* 11,500–12,500. *Eligibility Requirements:* Applicant must be enrolled or expecting to enroll full-time at a two-year or four-year institution or university; resident of Kentucky and studying in Kentucky. Available to U.S. citizens. *Application Requirements:* Application form may be submitted online (http://www.fafsa.ed. gov), FAFSA. **Deadline:** continuous.

Contact Sheila Roe, Grant Program Coordinator, Kentucky Higher Education Assistance Authority (KHEAA), PO Box 798, Frankfort, KY 40602-0798. *E-mail:* sroe@kheaa.com. *Phone:* 800-928-8926 Ext. 67393. *Fax:* 502-696-7373. *Website:* http://www.kheaa.com/.

Touchstone Energy All "A" Classic Scholarship. Award of $1000 for senior student in good standing at a Kentucky high school which is a member of the All Classic. Applicant must be a U.S. citizen and must plan to attend a postsecondary institution in Kentucky in the upcoming year as a full-time student and be drug free. *Award:* Scholarship for use in freshman year; not renewable. *Award amount:* $1000. *Number of awards:* 12. *Eligibility Requirements:* Applicant must be high school student; planning to enroll or expecting to enroll full-time at a two-year or four-year or technical institution or university; resident of Kentucky and studying in Kentucky. Available to U.S. citizens. *Application Requirements:* Application form, essay, personal photograph, recommendations or references, transcript. **Deadline:** December 3.

Contact David Cowden, Chairperson, Scholarship Committee, Kentucky Touchstone Energy Cooperatives, 1320 Lincoln Road, Lewisport, KY 42351. *E-mail:* allaclassic@alltel.net. *Phone:* 859-744-4812. *Website:* http://www.ekpc. coop.

LOUISIANA

Hemophilia Federation of America Educational Scholarship. One-time scholarship for persons with hemophilia, attending either full-time or part-time in any accredited two- or four-year college, university, or vocation/technical school in the United States. *Award:* Scholarship for use in freshman, sophomore, junior, or senior years; not renewable. *Award amount:* $1500. *Number of awards:* 1–3. *Eligibility Requirements:* Applicant must be physically disabled and enrolled or expecting to enroll full- or part-time at a two-year or four-year or technical insti-

tution or university. Applicant must be physically disabled. Available to U.S. citizens. *Application Requirements:* Application form, essay, financial need analysis, recommendations or references. **Deadline:** April 30.

Louisiana National Guard State Tuition Exemption Program. Renewable award for college undergraduates to receive tuition exemption upon satisfactory performance in the Louisiana National Guard. Applicant must attend a state-funded institution in Louisiana, be a resident and registered voter in Louisiana, meet the academic and residency requirements of the university attended, and provide documentation of Louisiana National Guard enlistment. The exemption can be used for up to 15 semesters. Minimum 2.5 GPA required. *Award:* Scholarship for use in freshman, sophomore, junior, or senior years; renewable. *Eligibility Requirements:* Applicant must be enrolled or expecting to enroll full- or part-time at a two-year or four-year or technical institution or university; resident of Louisiana and studying in Louisiana. Applicant must have 2.5 GPA or higher. Available to U.S. citizens. Applicant or parent must meet one or more of the following requirements: national guard experience; retired from active duty; disabled or killed as a result of military service; prisoner of war; or missing in action. *Application Requirements:* Application form, test scores, transcript. **Deadline:** continuous.

Contact Jona Hughes, Education Services Officer, Louisiana National Guard, Joint Task Force LA, Building 35, Jackson Barracks, JI-PD, New Orleans, LA 70146-0330. *E-mail:* hughesj@la-arng.ngb.army.mil. *Phone:* 504-278-8531 Ext. 8304. *Fax:* 504-278-8025. *Website:* http://geauxguard.com/.

Rockefeller State Wildlife Scholarship. For college undergraduates with a minimum of 60 credit hours who are majoring in Forestry, Wildlife, or Marine Science, and for college graduate students who are majoring in Forestry, Wildlife, or Marine Science. College undergraduates must have a grade point average of at least 2.50 to apply. College graduate students must have a grade point average of at least 3.00 in order to apply. Renewable up to three years as an undergraduate and two years as a graduate student. Biology; Marine Biology; Marine/Ocean Engineering; Natural Resources; Oceanography. *Award:* Scholarship for use in freshman, sophomore, junior, senior, graduate, or postgraduate years; renewable. *Award amount:* $2000–$3000.

Number of awards: 20–30. *Eligibility Requirements:* Applicant must be enrolled or expecting to enroll full-time at a four-year institution or university; resident of Louisiana and studying in Louisiana. Applicant must have 2.5 GPA or higher. Available to U.S. citizens. *Application Requirements:* Application form, application form may be submitted online (http://www.fafsa.ed.gov), FAFSA, test scores, transcript. **Deadline:** July 1.

Contact Bonnie Lavergne, Public Information, Louisiana Office of Student Financial Assistance, PO Box 91202, Baton Rouge, LA 70821-9202. *E-mail:* custserv@osfa.la.gov. *Phone:* 800-259-5626 Ext. 7714. *Fax:* 225-612-6508. *Website:* http://www.osfa.la.gov/.

Taylor Opportunity Program for Students Honors Level. Program awards 8 semesters or 12 terms of tuition to any Louisiana State postsecondary institution plus $400 stipend per semester. Program awards 8 semesters or 12 terms of an amount equal to the weighted average public tuition to students attending a LAICU (Louisiana Association of Independent Colleges and Universities) institution plus $400 stipend per semester. Program awards 8 semesters or 12 terms of an amount equal to the weighted average public tuition to two out-of-state Institutions for Hearing Impaired Students: Gallaudet University and Rochester Institute of Technology plus $400 stipend per semester. Program awards $1520 per year to Approved Proprietary and Cosmetology schools plus a stipend of $800 per year. When you submit the FAFSA, you have automatically applied for all four levels of TOPS, for Federal Pell Grants and Go Grants and for Federal Student Loans. Please do not send separate letters of application to the TOPS office. *Award:* Scholarship for use in freshman, sophomore, junior, or senior years; renewable. *Award amount:* $780–$6131. *Number of awards:* 8781. *Eligibility Requirements:* Applicant must be enrolled or expecting to enroll full-time at a two-year or four-year or technical institution or university; resident of Louisiana and studying in Louisiana. Applicant must have 3.0 GPA or higher. Available to U.S. citizens. *Application Requirements:* Application form, application form may be submitted online (http://www.fafsa.ed.gov), FAFSA, test scores, transcript. **Deadline:** July 1.

Taylor Opportunity Program for Students Opportunity Level. Program awards 8 semesters or 12 terms of tuition to any Louisiana State postsec-

ondary institution. Program awards 8 semesters or 12 terms of an amount equal to the weighted average public tuition to students attending a LAICU (Louisiana Association of Independent Colleges and Universities) institution. Program awards 8 semesters or 12 terms of an amount equal to the weighted average public tuition to two out-of-state Institutions for Hearing Impaired Students: Gallaudet University and Rochester Institute of Technology. Program awards $1520 per year to Approved Proprietary and Cosmetology schools. When you submit the FAFSA, you have automatically applied for all four levels of TOPS, and for Federal Pell Grants and Go Grants. Please do not send separate letters of application to the TOPS office. *Award:* Scholarship for use in freshman, sophomore, junior, or senior years; renewable. *Award amount:* $380–$5331. *Number of awards:* 23,870. *Eligibility Requirements:* Applicant must be enrolled or expecting to enroll full-time at a two-year or four-year or technical institution or university; resident of Louisiana and studying in Louisiana. Applicant must have 2.5 GPA or higher. Available to U.S. citizens. *Application Requirements:* Application form, application form may be submitted online (http://www.fafsa.ed.gov), FAFSA, test scores, transcript. **Deadline:** July 1.

Taylor Opportunity Program for Students Performance Level. Program awards 8 semesters or 12 terms of tuition to any Louisiana State postsecondary institution plus $200 stipend per semester. Program awards 8 semesters or 12 terms of an amount equal to the weighted average public tuition to students attending a LAICU (Louisiana Association of Independent Colleges and Universities) institution plus $200 stipend per semester. Program awards 8 semesters or 12 terms of an amount equal to the weighted average public tuition to two out-of-state Institutions for Hearing Impaired Students: Gallaudet University and Rochester Institute of Technology plus $200 stipend per semester. Program awards $1520 plus $400 per year to Approved Proprietary and Cosmetology schools. When you submit the FAFSA, you have automatically applied for all four levels of TOPS, for Federal Pell Grants and Go Grants and for Federal Student Loans. Please do not send separate letters of application to the TOPS office. *Award:* Scholarship for use in freshman, sophomore, junior, or senior years; renewable. *Award amount:* $580–$5731. *Number of awards:* 10,938. *Eligi-

bility Requirements:* Applicant must be enrolled or expecting to enroll full-time at a two-year or four-year or technical institution or university; resident of Louisiana and studying in Louisiana. Applicant must have 3.0 GPA or higher. Available to U.S. citizens. *Application Requirements:* Application form, application form may be submitted online (http://www.fafsa.ed.gov), FAFSA, test scores, transcript. **Deadline:** July 1.

Taylor Opportunity Program for Students Tech Level. Program awards an amount equal to tuition for up to 4 semesters and two summers of technical training at a Louisiana postsecondary institution that offers a vocational or technical education certificate or diploma program, or a non-academic degree program; or up to $1520 to an approved Proprietary or Cosmetology school. Must have completed the TOPS Opportunity core curriculum or the TOPS Tech core curriculum, must have achieved a 2.50 grade point average over the core curriculum only, and must have achieved an ACT score of 17 or an SAT score of 810. Program awards an amount equal to the weighted average public tuition for technical programs to students attending a LAICU private institution for technical training. When you submit the FAFSA, you have automatically applied for all four levels of TOPS, for Federal Pell Grants and Go Grants and Federal Student Loans. Please do not send separate letters of application to the TOPS office. *Award:* Scholarship for use in freshman or sophomore years; renewable. *Award amount:* $380–$3556. *Number of awards:* 1242. *Eligibility Requirements:* Applicant must be enrolled or expecting to enroll full-time at a technical institution; resident of Louisiana and studying in Louisiana. Applicant must have 2.5 GPA or higher. Available to U.S. citizens. *Application Requirements:* Application form, application form may be submitted online (http://www.fafsa.ed.gov), FAFSA, test scores, transcript. **Deadline:** July 1.

MAINE

American Legion Auxiliary Department of Maine Daniel E. Lambert Memorial Scholarship. Scholarships to assist young men and women in continuing their education beyond high school. Must demonstrate financial need, must be a resident of the State of Maine, U.S. citizen, and parent must be a veteran. *Award:* Scholarship for use in freshman year; not renewable.

Award amount: $1000. *Number of awards:* up to 2. *Eligibility Requirements:* Applicant must be high school student; planning to enroll or expecting to enroll full-time at a four-year institution or university and resident of Maine. Available to U.S. citizens. Applicant or parent must meet one or more of the following requirements: general military experience; retired from active duty; disabled or killed as a result of military service; prisoner of war; or missing in action. *Application Requirements:* Application form, financial need analysis. **Deadline:** May 1.

Contact Mary Wells, Education Chairman. *E-mail:* aladeptsecme@verizon.net. *Phone:* 207-532-6007. *Website:* http://www.mainelegion.org/.

American Legion Auxiliary Department of Maine National President's Scholarship. Scholarships to children of veterans who served in the Armed Forces during the eligibility dates for The American Legion. One $2500, one $2000, and one $1000 scholarship will be awarded. Applicant must complete 50 hours of community service during his/her high school years. *Award:* Scholarship for use in freshman year; not renewable. *Award amount:* $1000–$2500. *Number of awards:* 3. *Eligibility Requirements:* Applicant must be high school student; planning to enroll or expecting to enroll full-time at a four-year institution or university and resident of Maine. Applicant or parent of applicant must have employment or volunteer experience in community service. Available to U.S. citizens. Applicant or parent must meet one or more of the following requirements: general military experience; retired from active duty; disabled or killed as a result of military service; prisoner of war; or missing in action. *Application Requirements:* Application form, essay, recommendations or references, test scores, transcript. **Deadline:** March 1.

Contact Mary Wells, Education Chairman. *E-mail:* aladeptsecme@verizon.net. *Phone:* 207-532-6007. *Website:* http://www.mainelegion.org/.

American Legion Auxiliary Department of Maine Past Presidents' Parley Nurses Scholarship. One-time award for child, grandchild, sister, or brother of veteran. Must be resident of Maine and wishing to continue education at accredited school in medical field. Must submit photo, doctor's statement, and evidence of civic activity. Minimum 3.5 GPA required. Health and Medical Sciences; Nursing. *Award:* Scholarship for use in freshman, soph-

omore, junior, or senior years; not renewable. *Award amount:* $300. *Number of awards:* 1. *Eligibility Requirements:* Applicant must be enrolled or expecting to enroll full-time at a two-year or four-year or technical institution or university and resident of Maine. Applicant or parent of applicant must have employment or volunteer experience in community service. Applicant must have 2.5 GPA or higher. Available to U.S. citizens. Applicant or parent must meet one or more of the following requirements: general military experience; retired from active duty; disabled or killed as a result of military service; prisoner of war; or missing in action. *Application Requirements:* Application form, doctor's statement, personal photograph, recommendations or references, transcript. **Deadline:** March 31.

Contact Mary Wells, Education Chairman. *E-mail:* aladeptsecme@verizon.net. *Phone:* 207-532-6007. *Website:* http://www.mainelegion.org/.

Early College for ME. Scholarship for high school students who in their junior year have not made plans for college but are academically capable of success in college. Recipients are selected by their school principal or Guidance Director. Students must be entering a Maine Community College. Refer to web site http://www.mccs.me.edu/scholarships.html. *Award:* Scholarship for use in freshman or sophomore years; renewable. *Award amount:* $2000. *Number of awards:* 250–500. *Eligibility Requirements:* Applicant must be high school student; planning to enroll or expecting to enroll full-time at a two-year institution; resident of Maine and studying in Maine. Available to U.S. citizens. *Application Requirements:* Application form, financial need analysis, recommendations or references, transcript. **Deadline:** varies.

Contact Charles Collins, State Director, Center for Career Development, Maine Community College System, 6 Fundy Road, Falmouth, ME 04105. *E-mail:* ccollins@mccs.me.edu. *Phone:* 207-767-5210 Ext. 4897. *Fax:* 207-781-0986. *Website:* http://www.mccs.me.edu/.

Maine Rural Rehabilitation Fund Scholarship Program. One-time scholarship open to Maine residents enrolled in or accepted by any school, college, or university. Must be full time and demonstrate financial need. Those opting for a Maine institution given preference. Major must lead to an agricultural career. Minimum 3.0 GPA required. Agribusiness; Agriculture ; Animal/Veterinary Sciences. *Award:* Scholarship for

use in freshman, sophomore, junior, senior, graduate, or postgraduate years; not renewable. *Award amount:* $800–$2000. *Number of awards:* 10–20. *Eligibility Requirements:* Applicant must be enrolled or expecting to enroll full-time at a two-year or four-year or technical institution or university and resident of Maine. Applicant must have 3.0 GPA or higher. Available to U.S. citizens. *Application Requirements:* Application form, driver's license, financial need analysis, transcript. **Deadline:** June 15.

Contact Jane Aiudi, Director of Marketing. *E-mail:* jane.aiudi@maine.gov. *Phone:* 207-287-7628. *Fax:* 207-287-5576. *Website:* http://www.maine.gov/agriculture.

State of Maine Grant Program. Scholarship for residents of Maine, attending an eligible school in Connecticut, Maine, Massachusetts, New Hampshire, Pennsylvania, Rhode Island, Washington, D.C., or Vermont. Award based on need. Must apply annually. Complete free application for Federal Student Aid to apply. One-time award for undergraduate study. For further information see web site http://www.famemaine.com. *Award:* Grant for use in freshman, sophomore, junior, or senior years; not renewable. *Award amount:* $250–$1250. *Number of awards:* up to 32,295. *Eligibility Requirements:* Applicant must be enrolled or expecting to enroll full- or part-time at a two-year or four-year or technical institution or university; resident of Maine and studying in Connecticut, District of Columbia, Maine, Massachusetts, New Hampshire, Pennsylvania, Rhode Island, Vermont. Available to U.S. citizens. *Application Requirements:* Application form, FAFSA, financial need analysis. **Deadline:** May 1.

Contact Claude Roy, Education Services Officer. *E-mail:* education@famemaine.com. *Phone:* 207-620-3507. *Website:* http://www.famemaine.com/.

Tuition Waiver Programs. Provides tuition waivers for children and spouses of EMS personnel, firefighters, and law enforcement officers who have been killed in the line of duty and for students who were foster children under the custody of the Department of Human Services when they graduated from high school. Waivers valid at the University of Maine System, the Maine Technical College System, and Maine Maritime Academy. Applicant must reside and study in Maine. *Award:* Grant for use in freshman, sophomore, junior, or senior years; renewable. *Number of awards:* up to 30. *Eligibility Requirements:* Applicant must be enrolled or expecting to enroll full- or part-time at a four-year institution or university; resident of Maine and studying in Maine. Applicant or parent of applicant must have employment or volunteer experience in police/firefighting. Available to U.S. citizens. *Application Requirements:* Application form, letter from the Department of Human Services documenting that applicant is in their custody and residing in foster care at the time of graduation from high school or its equivalent. **Deadline:** continuous.

Contact Claude Roy, Education Services Officer. *E-mail:* education@ famemaine.com. *Phone:* 207-620-3507. *Website:* http://www.famemaine.com/.

Veterans Dependents Educational Benefits-Maine. Tuition waiver award for dependent children who have not reached their 22nd birthday or spouses of veterans permanently and totally disabled resulting from service-connected disability; died from a service-connected disability; at time of death was totally and permanently disabled due to service-connected disability, but whose death was not related to the service-connected disability; or member of the Armed Forces on active duty who has been listed for more than 90 days as missing in action, captured or forcibly detained or interned in the line of duty. Benefits apply only to the University of Maine System, Maine community colleges and Maine Maritime Academy. Must be high school graduate. Must submit with application proof of veteran's VA disability along with dependent verification paperwork such as birth, marriage, or adoption certificate and proof of enrollment in degree program. *Award:* Scholarship for use in freshman, sophomore, junior, or senior years; not renewable. *Eligibility Requirements:* Applicant must be enrolled or expecting to enroll full- or part-time at a two-year or four-year institution or university; resident of Maine and studying in Maine. Available to U.S. citizens. Applicant or parent must meet one or more of the following requirements: general military experience; retired from active duty; disabled or killed as a result of military service; prisoner of war; or missing in action. *Application Requirements:* Application form,.

Contact Mrs. Paula Gagnon, Office Associate II, Maine Division of Veterans Services, State House Station 117, Augusta, ME 04333-0117. *E-mail:* mainebvs@maine.gov. *Phone:* 207-430-

6035. *Fax:* 207-626-4471. *Website:* http://www.maine.gov/dvem/bvs.

MARYLAND

Charles W. Riley Fire and Emergency Medical Services Tuition Reimbursement Program. Award intended to reimburse members of rescue organizations serving Maryland communities for tuition costs of course work towards a degree or certificate in fire service or medical technology. Must attend a two- or four-year school in Maryland. Minimum 2.0 GPA. The scholarship is worth up to $6500. Fire Sciences; Health and Medical Sciences; Trade/Technical Specialties. *Award:* Scholarship for use in freshman, sophomore, junior, or senior years; not renewable. *Award amount:* up to $6500. *Number of awards:* up to 150. *Eligibility Requirements:* Applicant must be enrolled or expecting to enroll full- or part-time at a two-year or four-year institution or university; resident of Maryland and studying in Maryland. Applicant or parent of applicant must have employment or volunteer experience in police/firefighting. Available to U.S. citizens. *Application Requirements:* Application form, transcript, tuition receipt, proof of enrollment. **Deadline:** July 1.

Contact Maura Sappington, Office of Student Financial Assistance, Maryland State Higher Education Commission, 839 Bestgate Road, Suite 400, Annapolis, MD 21401-3013. *E-mail:* msapping@mhec.state.md.us. *Phone:* 410-260-4569. *Fax:* 410-260-3203. *Website:* http://www.mhec.state.md.us/.

Delegate Scholarship Program-Maryland. Delegate scholarships help Maryland residents attending Maryland degree-granting institutions, certain career schools, or nursing diploma schools. May attend out-of-state institution if Maryland Higher Education Commission deems major to be unique and not offered at a Maryland institution. Free Application for Federal Student Aid may be required. Students interested in this program should apply by contacting their legislative district delegate. *Award:* Scholarship for use in freshman, sophomore, junior, or senior years; not renewable. *Award amount:* $200–$8650. *Number of awards:* up to 3500. *Eligibility Requirements:* Applicant must be enrolled or expecting to enroll full- or part-time at a two-year or four-year or technical institution or university; resident of Maryland and studying in Maryland. Available to U.S. citizens.

Application Requirements: Application form, FAFSA. **Deadline:** continuous.

Contact Monica Wheatley, Office of Student Financial Assistance, Maryland State Higher Education Commission, 839 Bestgate Road, Suite 400, Annapolis, MD 21401-3013. *E-mail:* osfamail@mhec.state.md.us. *Phone:* 800-974-1024. *Fax:* 410-260-3200. *Website:* http://www.mhec.state.md.us/.

Distinguished Scholar Award-Maryland. Renewable award for Maryland students enrolled full-time at Maryland institutions. National Merit Scholar Finalists automatically offered award. Others may qualify for the award in satisfying criteria of a minimum 3.7 GPA or in combination with high test scores, or for Talent in Arts competition in categories of music, drama, dance, or visual arts. Must maintain annual 3.0 GPA in college for award to be renewed. *Award:* Scholarship for use in freshman, sophomore, junior, or senior years; renewable. *Award amount:* up to $3000. *Number of awards:* up to 1400. *Eligibility Requirements:* Applicant must be high school student; planning to enroll or expecting to enroll full-time at a two-year or four-year institution or university; resident of Maryland and studying in Maryland. Available to U.S. citizens. *Application Requirements:* Application form, test scores, transcript.

Contact Tamika McKelvin, Program Administrator, Maryland State Higher Education Commission, 839 Bestgate Road, Suite 400, Annapolis, MD 21401-3013. *E-mail:* tmckelvi@mhec.state.md.us. *Phone:* 410-260-4546. *Fax:* 410-260-3200. *Website:* http://www.mhec.state.md.us/.

Distinguished Scholar Community College Transfer Program. Scholarship available for Maryland residents who have completed 60 credit hours or an associate degree at a Maryland community college and are transferring to a Maryland four-year institution. *Award:* Scholarship for use in freshman or sophomore years; renewable. *Award amount:* $3000. *Number of awards:* 127. *Eligibility Requirements:* Applicant must be enrolled or expecting to enroll full-time at a two-year institution; resident of Maryland and studying in Maryland. Available to U.S. citizens. *Application Requirements:* Application form, transcript. **Deadline:** March 1.

Contact Maura Sappington, Program Manager, Maryland State Higher Education Commission, 839 Bestgate Road, Suite 400, Annapolis, MD 21401-

3013. *E-mail:* msapping@mhec.state.md.us. *Phone:* 410-260-4569. *Fax:* 410-260-3203. *Website:* http://www.mhec.state.md.us/.

Edward T. Conroy Memorial Scholarship Program. Scholarship for dependents of deceased or 100 percent disabled U.S. Armed Forces personnel; the son, daughter, or surviving spouse of a victim of the September 11, 2001 terrorist attacks who died as a result of the attacks on the World Trade Center in New York City, the attack on the Pentagon in Virginia, or the crash of United Airlines Flight 93 in Pennsylvania; a POW/MIA of the Vietnam Conflict or his/her son or daughter; the son, daughter or surviving spouse (who has not remarried) of a state or local public safety employee or volunteer who died in the line of duty; or a state or local public safety employee or volunteer who was 100 percent disabled in the line of duty. Must be Maryland resident at time of disability. Submit applicable VA certification. Must be at least 16 years of age and attend Maryland institution. *Award:* Scholarship for use in freshman, sophomore, junior, or senior years; renewable. *Award amount:* $7200–$9000. *Number of awards:* up to 121. *Eligibility Requirements:* Applicant must be age 16-24; enrolled or expecting to enroll full- or part-time at a two-year or four-year institution or university; resident of Maryland and studying in Maryland. Applicant or parent of applicant must have employment or volunteer experience in police/firefighting. Available to U.S. citizens. Applicant or parent must meet one or more of the following requirements: general military experience; retired from active duty; disabled or killed as a result of military service; prisoner of war; or missing in action. *Application Requirements:* Application form, birth and death certificate, disability papers. **Deadline:** July 15.

Contact Linda Asplin, Office of Student Financial Assistance, Maryland State Higher Education Commission, 839 Bestgate Road, Suite 400, Annapolis, MD 21401-3013. *E-mail:* lasplin@mhec.state.md.us. *Phone:* 410-260-4563. *Fax:* 410-260-3203. *Website:* http://www.mhec.state.md.us/.

Graduate and Professional Scholarship Program-Maryland. Graduate and professional scholarships provide need-based financial assistance to students attending a Maryland school of medicine, dentistry, law, pharmacy, social work, or nursing. Funds are provided to specific Maryland colleges and universities. Students must demonstrate financial need and be Maryland residents. Contact institution financial aid office for more information. Dental Health/Services; Health and Medical Sciences; Law/Legal Services; Nursing; Social Services. *Award:* Scholarship for use in freshman, sophomore, junior, or senior years; renewable. *Award amount:* $1000–$5000. *Number of awards:* up to 584. *Eligibility Requirements:* Applicant must be enrolled or expecting to enroll full- or part-time at a four-year institution or university; resident of Maryland and studying in Maryland. Available to U.S. citizens. *Application Requirements:* Application form, contact institution financial aid office, financial need analysis. **Deadline:** March 1.

Contact Monica Wheatley, Program Manager, Maryland State Higher Education Commission, 839 Bestgate Road, Suite 400, Annapolis, MD 21401. *E-mail:* mwheatle@mhec.state.md.us. *Phone:* 410-260-4560. *Fax:* 410-260-3202. *Website:* http://www.mhec.state.md.us/.

Howard P. Rawlings Educational Excellence Awards Educational Assistance Grant. Award for Maryland residents accepted or enrolled in a full-time undergraduate degree or certificate program at a Maryland institution or hospital nursing school. Must submit financial aid form by March 1. Must earn 2.0 GPA in college to maintain award. *Award:* Grant for use in freshman, sophomore, junior, or senior years; renewable. *Award amount:* $400–$2700. *Number of awards:* 15,000–30,000. *Eligibility Requirements:* Applicant must be enrolled or expecting to enroll full-time at a two-year or four-year institution or university; resident of Maryland and studying in Maryland. Available to U.S. citizens. *Application Requirements:* Application form, financial need analysis. **Deadline:** March 1.

Howard P. Rawlings Educational Excellence Awards Guaranteed Access Grant. Award for Maryland resident enrolling full-time in an undergraduate program at a Maryland institution. Must be under 21 at time of first award and begin college within one year of completing high school in Maryland with a minimum 2.5 GPA. Must have an annual family income less than 130 percent of the federal poverty level guideline. *Award:* Grant for use in freshman, sophomore, junior, or senior years; renewable. *Award amount:* $400–$14,800. *Number of awards:* up to 1000. *Eligibility Requirements:* Applicant must be enrolled or expecting to enroll full-time at a two-year or four-year institution or university; resident of Maryland and studying in Maryland. Applicant must have 3.5 GPA or higher. Available to U.S. citizens. *Application Requirements:* Application form, financial need analysis, transcript. **Deadline:** March 1.

Contact Theresa Lowe, Office of Student Financial Assistance, Maryland State Higher Education Commission, 839 Bestgate Road, Suite 400, Annapolis, MD 21401-3013. *E-mail:* osfamail@mhec.state.md.us. *Phone:* 410-260-4555. *Fax:* 410-260-3200. *Website:* http://www.mhec.state.md.us/.

Janet L. Hoffmann Loan Assistance Repayment Program. Provides assistance for repayment of loan debt to Maryland residents working full-time in nonprofit organizations and state or local governments. Must submit Employment Verification Form and Lender Verification Form. Education; Law/Legal Services; Nursing; Social Services; Therapy/Rehabilitation. *Award:* Grant for use in freshman, sophomore, junior, or senior years; not renewable. *Award amount:* $1500–$10,000. *Number of awards:* up to 700. *Eligibility Requirements:* Applicant must be enrolled or expecting to enroll full-time at a four-year institution or university; resident of Maryland and studying in Maryland. Applicant or parent of applicant must have employment or volunteer experience in government/politics. Available to U.S. citizens. *Application Requirements:* Application form, IRS 1040 form, transcript. **Deadline:** September 30.

Contact Tamika McKelvin, Office of Student Financial Assistance, Maryland State Higher Education Commission, 839 Bestgate Road, Suite 400, Annapolis, MD 21401. *E-mail:* tmckelvil@mhec.state.md.us. *Phone:* 410-260-4546. *Fax:* 410-260-3203. *Website:* http://www.mhec.state.md.us/.

J.F. Tolbert Memorial Student Grant Program. Awards of $500 granted to Maryland residents attending a private career school in Maryland. The scholarship deadline continues. *Award:* Grant for use in freshman or sophomore years; not renewable. *Award amount:* $500. *Number of awards:* 522. *Eligibility Requirements:* Applicant must be enrolled or expecting to enroll full-time at a technical institution; resident of Maryland and studying in Maryland. Available to U.S. citizens. *Application Requirements:* Application form, financial need analysis. **Deadline:** continuous.

Contact Glenda Hamlet, Office of Student Financial Assistance, Maryland

State Higher Education Commission, 839 Bestgate Road, Suite 400, Annapolis, MD 21401-3013. *E-mail:* osfamail@mhec. state.md.us. *Phone:* 800-974-1024. *Fax:* 410-260-3200. *Website:* http://www. mhec.state.md.us/.

Part-Time Grant Program-Maryland. Funds provided to Maryland colleges and universities. Eligible students must be enrolled on a part-time basis (6 to 11 credits) in an undergraduate degree program. Must demonstrate financial need and also be Maryland resident. Contact financial aid office at institution for more information. *Award:* Grant for use in freshman, sophomore, junior, or senior years; renewable. *Award amount:* $200–$1500. *Number of awards:* 1800–9000. *Eligibility Requirements:* Applicant must be enrolled or expecting to enroll part-time at a two-year or four-year institution or university; resident of Maryland and studying in Maryland. Available to U. S. citizens. *Application Requirements:* Application form, financial need analysis. **Deadline:** March 1.

Contact Monica Wheatley, Program Manager, Maryland State Higher Education Commission, 839 Bestgate Road, Suite 400, Annapolis, MD 21401. *E-mail:* mwheatle@mhec.state.md.us. *Phone:* 410-260-4560. *Fax:* 410-260-3202. *Website:* http://www.mhec.state. md.us/.

Senatorial Scholarships-Maryland. Renewable award for Maryland residents attending a Maryland degree-granting institution, nursing diploma school, or certain private career schools. May be used out-of-state only if Maryland Higher Education Commission deems major to be unique and not offered at Maryland institution. The scholarship value is $400 to $7000. *Award:* Scholarship for use in freshman, sophomore, junior, or senior years; renewable. *Award amount:* $400–$7000. *Number of awards:* up to 7000. *Eligibility Requirements:* Applicant must be enrolled or expecting to enroll full- or part-time at a two-year or four-year or technical institution or university; resident of Maryland and studying in Maryland. Available to U.S. citizens. *Application Requirements:* Application form, financial need analysis, test scores. **Deadline:** March 1.

Contact Monica Wheatley, Office of Student Financial Assistance, Maryland State Higher Education Commission, 839 Bestgate Road, Suite 400, Annapolis, MD 21401-3013. *E-mail:* osfamail@mhec. state.md.us. *Phone:* 800-974-1024. *Fax:*

410-260-3200. *Website:* http://www. mhec.state.md.us/.

Tuition Reduction for Non-Resident Nursing Students. Available to nonresidents of Maryland who attend a two-year or four-year public institution in Maryland. It is renewable provided student maintains academic requirements designated by institution attended. Recipient must agree to serve as a full-time nurse in a hospital or related institution for two to four years. Nursing. *Award:* Scholarship for use in freshman, sophomore, junior, or senior years; renewable. *Eligibility Requirements:* Applicant must be enrolled or expecting to enroll full- or part-time at a two-year or four-year institution and studying in Maryland. Available to U.S. citizens. *Application Requirements:* Application form. **Deadline:** varies.

Contact Robert Parker, Director. *E-mail:* rparker@mhec.state.md.us. *Phone:* 410-260-4558. *Website:* http://www.mhec.state.md.us/.

Tuition Waiver for Foster Care Recipients. Applicant must be a high school graduate or GED recipient and under the age of 21. Must either have resided in a foster care home in Maryland at the time of high school graduation or GED reception, or until 14th birthday, and been adopted after 14th birthday. Applicant, if status approved, will be exempt from paying tuition and mandatory fees at a public college in Maryland. *Award:* Grant for use in freshman, sophomore, junior, senior, or graduate years; renewable. *Eligibility Requirements:* Applicant must be enrolled or expecting to enroll full- or part-time at a two-year or four-year institution or university; resident of Maryland and studying in Maryland. Available to U.S. citizens. *Application Requirements:* Application form, financial need analysis, must inquire at financial aid office of schools. **Deadline:** March 1.

Contact Robert Parker, Director. *E-mail:* rparker@mhec.state.md.us. *Phone:* 410-260-4558. *Website:* http://www.mhec.state.md.us/.

Veterans of the Afghanistan and Iraq Conflicts Scholarship Program. Provides financial assistance to Maryland resident U.S. Armed Forces personnel who served in Afghanistan or Iraq Conflicts and their children or spouses who are attending Maryland institutions. *Award:* Scholarship for use in freshman, sophomore, junior, or senior years; renewable. *Award amount:* $8850. *Number of awards:* 123. *Eligibility*

Requirements: Applicant must be enrolled or expecting to enroll full- or part-time at a two-year or four-year institution or university; resident of Maryland and studying in Maryland. Available to U.S. citizens. Applicant or parent must meet one or more of the following requirements: general military experience; retired from active duty; disabled or killed as a result of military service; prisoner of war; or missing in action. *Application Requirements:* Application form, birth certificate/marriage certificate, documentation of military order, financial need analysis. **Deadline:** March 1.

Contact Linda Asplin, Program Administrator, Maryland State Higher Education Commission, 839 Bestgate Road, Suite 400, Annapolis, MD 21401-3013. *E-mail:* lasplin@mhec.state.md.us. *Phone:* 410-260-4563. *Fax:* 410-260-3203. *Website:* http://www.mhec.state. md.us/.

Workforce Shortage Student Assistance Grant Program. Scholarship of $4000 available to students who will be required to major in specific areas and will be obligated to serve in the state of Maryland after completion of degree. *Award:* Scholarship for use in freshman, sophomore, junior, or senior years; renewable. *Award amount:* $4000. *Number of awards:* 1300. *Eligibility Requirements:* Applicant must be enrolled or expecting to enroll full- or part-time at a two-year or four-year institution or university; resident of Maryland and studying in Maryland. Available to U.S. citizens. *Application Requirements:* Application form, certain majors require additional documentation, essay, financial need analysis, recommendations or references, resume, transcript. **Deadline:** July 1.

Contact Maura Sappington, Program Manager, Maryland State Higher Education Commission, 839 Bestgate Road, Suite 400, Annapolis, MD 21401-3013. *E-mail:* msapping@mhec.state.md. us. *Phone:* 410-260-4569. *Fax:* 410-260-3203. *Website:* http://www.mhec.state. md.us/.

MASSACHUSETTS

Agnes M. Lindsay Scholarship. Scholarships for students with demonstrated financial need who are from rural areas of Massachusetts and attend public institutions of higher education in Massachusetts. Deadline varies. *Award:* Scholarship for use in freshman, sophomore, junior, or senior years; not renewable. *Eli-*

gibility Requirements: Applicant must be enrolled or expecting to enroll full-time at a two-year or four-year institution or university; resident of Massachusetts and studying in Massachusetts. Available to U.S. citizens. *Application Requirements:* Application form, financial need analysis. **Deadline:** varies.

Contact Robert Brun, Director of Scholarships and Grants. *E-mail:* osfa@ osfa.mass.edu. *Phone:* 617-727-9420. *Fax:* 617-727-0667. *Website:* http://www. osfa.mass.edu/.

Christian A. Herter Memorial Scholarship. Renewable award for Massachusetts residents who are in the tenth and eleventh grades, and whose socio-economic backgrounds and environment may inhibit their ability to attain educational goals. Must exhibit severe personal or family-related difficulties, medical problems, or have overcome a personal obstacle. Provides up to 50 percent of the student's calculated need, as determined by federal methodology, at the college of their choice within the continental United States. *Award:* Scholarship for use in freshman, sophomore, junior, or senior years; renewable. *Award amount:* up to $15,000. *Number of awards:* 25. *Eligibility Requirements:* Applicant must be high school student; planning to enroll or expecting to enroll full-time at a two-year or four-year or technical institution or university and resident of Massachusetts. Applicant must have 2.5 GPA or higher. Available to U.S. citizens. *Application Requirements:* Application form, community service, financial need analysis, interview, recommendations or references. **Deadline:** February 1.

Contact Robert Brun, Director of Scholarships and Grants. *E-mail:* osfa@ osfa.mass.edu. *Phone:* 617-727-9420. *Fax:* 617-727-0667. *Website:* http://www. osfa.mass.edu/.

DSS Adopted Children Tuition Waiver. Need-based tuition waiver for Massachusetts residents who are full-time undergraduate students. Must attend a Massachusetts public institution of higher education and be under 24 years of age. File the FAFSA after January 1. Contact school financial aid office for more information. *Award:* Scholarship for use in freshman, sophomore, junior, or senior years; renewable. *Eligibility Requirements:* Applicant must be enrolled or expecting to enroll full-time at a two-year or four-year institution and resident of Massachusetts. Available to U.S. and non-Canadian citizens. *Application Requirements:* Application form, FAFSA,

financial need analysis. **Deadline:** varies.

Contact Robert Brun, Director of Scholarships and Grants. *E-mail:* osfa@ osfa.mass.edu. *Phone:* 617-727-9420. *Fax:* 617-727-0667. *Website:* http://www. osfa.mass.edu/.

Early Childhood Educators Scholarship Program. Scholarship to provide financial assistance for currently employed early childhood educators and providers who enroll in an associate or bachelor degree program in Early Childhood Education or related programs. Awards are not based on financial need. Individuals taking their first college-level ECE course are eligible for 100 percent tuition, while subsequent ECE courses are awarded at 50 percent tuition. Can be used for one class each semester. Education. *Award:* Scholarship for use in freshman, sophomore, junior, or senior years; not renewable. *Award amount:* $150–$3600. *Eligibility Requirements:* Applicant must be enrolled or expecting to enroll full- or part-time at a four-year institution or university. Available to U.S. citizens. *Application Requirements:* Application form. **Deadline:** July 1.

Contact Robert Brun, Director of Scholarships and Grants. *E-mail:* osfa@ osfa.mass.edu. *Phone:* 617-727-9420. *Fax:* 617-727-0667. *Website:* http://www. osfa.mass.edu/.

John and Abigail Adams Scholarship. Scholarship to reward and inspire student achievement, attract more high-performing students to Massachusetts public higher education, and provide families of college-bound students with financial assistance. Must be a U.S. citizen or an eligible non-citizen. There is no application process for the scholarship. Students who are eligible will be notified in the fall of their senior year in high school. *Award:* Scholarship for use in freshman year; not renewable. *Eligibility Requirements:* Applicant must be high school student; planning to enroll or expecting to enroll full-time at a two-year or four-year institution or university; resident of Massachusetts and studying in Massachusetts. Applicant must have 3.0 GPA or higher. Available to U.S. citizens. *Application Requirements:* **Deadline:** varies.

Contact Robert Brun, Director of Scholarships and Grants. *E-mail:* osfa@ osfa.mass.edu. *Phone:* 617-727-9420. *Fax:* 617-727-0667. *Website:* http://www. osfa.mass.edu/.

Massachusetts Assistance for Student Success Program. Provides

need-based financial assistance to Massachusetts residents to attend undergraduate postsecondary institutions in Connecticut, Maine, Massachusetts, New Hampshire, Pennsylvania, Rhode Island, Vermont, and District of Columbia. High school seniors may apply. Expected Family Contribution (EFC) should be $3850. Timely filing of FAFSA required. *Award:* Grant for use in freshman, sophomore, junior, or senior years; not renewable. *Award amount:* $300–$1600. *Number of awards:* 50,000–57,000. *Eligibility Requirements:* Applicant must be enrolled or expecting to enroll full-time at a two-year or four-year or technical institution or university; resident of Massachusetts and studying in Connecticut, District of Columbia, Maine, Massachusetts, New Hampshire, Pennsylvania, Rhode Island, Vermont. Available to U.S. citizens. *Application Requirements:* FAFSA, financial need analysis. **Deadline:** May 1.

Contact Robert Brun, Director of Scholarships and Grants. *E-mail:* osfa@ osfa.mass.edu. *Phone:* 617-727-9420. *Fax:* 617-727-0667. *Website:* http://www. osfa.mass.edu/.

Massachusetts Cash Grant Program. A need-based grant to assist with mandatory fees and non-state supported tuition. This supplemental award is available to Massachusetts residents, who are undergraduates at public two-year, four-year colleges and universities in Massachusetts. Must file FAFSA before May 1. Contact college financial aid office for information. *Award:* Grant for use in freshman, sophomore, junior, or senior years; not renewable. *Eligibility Requirements:* Applicant must be enrolled or expecting to enroll full-time at a two-year or four-year institution or university and resident of Massachusetts. Available to U.S. citizens. *Application Requirements:* Application form, FAFSA, financial need analysis. **Deadline:** continuous.

Contact Robert Brun, Director of Scholarships and Grants. *E-mail:* osfa@ osfa.mass.edu. *Phone:* 617-727-9420. *Fax:* 617-727-0667. *Website:* http://www. osfa.mass.edu/.

Massachusetts Gilbert Matching Student Grant Program. Grants for permanent Massachusetts residents attending an independent, regionally accredited Massachusetts school or school of nursing full time. Must be U.S. citizen and permanent legal resident of Massachusetts. File the Free Application for Federal Student Aid after January 1. Contact college financial aid office for complete details and deadlines. *Award:* Grant for use in freshman, sophomore, junior, or senior years; not renewable. *Award amount:* $200–$2500. *Eligibility Requirements:* Applicant must be enrolled or expecting to enroll full-time at a four-year institution or university; resident of Massachusetts and studying in Massachusetts. Available to U.S. citizens. *Application Requirements:* FAFSA, financial need analysis. **Deadline:** varies.

Contact Robert Brun, Director of Scholarships and Grants, Massachusetts Office of Student Financial Assistance, 454 Broadway, Suite 200, Revere, MA 02151. *E-mail:* rbrun@osfa.mass.edu. *Phone:* 617-727-9420. *Fax:* 617-727-0667. *Website:* http://www.osfa.mass.edu/

Massachusetts Part-Time Grant Program. Award for permanent Massachusetts residents who have enrolled part-time for at least one year in a state-approved postsecondary school. The recipient must not have a bachelor's degree. FAFSA must be filed before May 1. Contact college financial aid office for further information. *Award:* Grant for use in freshman, sophomore, junior, or senior years; not renewable. *Award amount:* $200–$1150. *Number of awards:* 200. *Eligibility Requirements:* Applicant must be enrolled or expecting to enroll part-time at a two-year or four-year or technical institution or university and resident of Massachusetts. Available to U.S. citizens. *Application Requirements:* Application form, FAFSA, financial need analysis. **Deadline:** varies.

Contact Robert Brun, Director of Scholarships and Grants. *E-mail:* osfa@osfa.mass.edu. *Phone:* 617-727-9420. *Fax:* 617-727-0667. *Website:* http://www.osfa.mass.edu/.

Massachusetts Public Service Grant Program. Scholarships for children and/or spouses of deceased members of fire, police, and corrections departments, who were killed in the line of duty. Awards Massachusetts residents attending Massachusetts institutions. Applicant should have not received a prior bachelor's degree or its equivalent. *Award:* Grant for use in freshman, sophomore, junior, or senior years; not renewable. *Award amount:* $910–$1714. *Eligibility Requirements:* Applicant must be enrolled or expecting to enroll full-time at a four-year institution or university; resident of Massachusetts and studying in Massachusetts. Applicant or parent of applicant must have employment or volunteer experience in police/firefighting. Available to U.S. citizens. Applicant must have general military experience. *Application Requirements:* Application form, copy of birth certificate, copy of veteran's death certificate, financial need analysis. **Deadline:** May 1.

New England Regional Student Program-Tuition Break. Tuition discount for residents of six New England states (Connecticut, Maine, Massachusetts, New Hampshire, Rhode Island, Vermont). Students pay reduced out-of-state tuition at public colleges or universities in other New England states when enrolling in certain majors not offered at public institutions in home state. Details are available at http://www.nebhe.org/tuitionbreak. *Award:* Scholarship for use in freshman, sophomore, junior, senior, or graduate years; renewable. *Eligibility Requirements:* Applicant must be enrolled or expecting to enroll full- or part-time at a two-year or four-year institution or university; resident of Connecticut, Maine, Massachusetts, New Hampshire, Rhode Island, Vermont and studying in Connecticut, Maine, Massachusetts, New Hampshire, Rhode Island, Vermont. Available to U.S. citizens. *Application Requirements:* College application for admission. **Deadline:** continuous.

Contact Wendy Lindsay, Senior Director of Regional Student Program, New England Board of Higher Education, 45 Temple Place, Boston, MA 02111. *E-mail:* tuitionbreak@nebhe.org. *Phone:* 617-357-9620 Ext. 111. *Fax:* 617-338-1577. *Website:* http://www.nebhe.org/.

Paraprofessional Teacher Preparation Grant. Grant providing financial aid assistance to Massachusetts residents, who are currently employed as paraprofessionals in Massachusetts public schools and wish to obtain higher education and become certified as full-time teachers. Education. *Award:* Grant for use in freshman, sophomore, junior, or senior years; not renewable. *Award amount:* $250–$7500. *Eligibility Requirements:* Applicant must be enrolled or expecting to enroll full- or part-time at a two-year or four-year institution or university and resident of Massachusetts. Available to U.S. citizens. *Application Requirements:* Application form, FAFSA. **Deadline:** August 1.

Contact Robert Brun, Director of Scholarships and Grants. *E-mail:* osfa@osfa.mass.edu. *Phone:* 617-727-9420. *Fax:* 617-727-0667. *Website:* http://www.osfa.mass.edu/.

MICHIGAN

American Legion Auxiliary Department of Michigan Medical Career Scholarship. Award for training in Michigan as registered nurse, licensed practical nurse, physical therapist, respiratory therapist, or in any medical career. Must be child, grandchild, great-grandchild, wife, or widow of honorably discharged or deceased veteran who has served during the eligibility dates for American Legion membership. Must be Michigan resident attending a Michigan school. Health and Medical Sciences; Nursing; Therapy/Rehabilitation. *Award:* Scholarship for use in freshman year; not renewable. *Award amount:* $500. *Number of awards:* 10–20. *Eligibility Requirements:* Applicant must be high school student; planning to enroll or expecting to enroll full-time at a two-year or four-year or technical institution or university; resident of Michigan and studying in Michigan. Available to U.S. citizens. Applicant must have general military experience. *Application Requirements:* Application form, financial need analysis, recommendations or references, transcript, veteran's discharge papers, copy of pages 1 and 2 of federal income tax return. **Deadline:** March 15.

American Legion Auxiliary Department of Michigan Memorial Scholarship. Scholarship for daughter, granddaughter, and great-granddaughter of any honorably discharged or deceased veteran of U.S. wars or conflicts. Must be Michigan resident for minimum of one year, female between 16 and 21 years, and attend college in Michigan. Must include copy of military discharge and copy of parent or guardian's IRS 1040 form. *Award:* Scholarship for use in freshman or sophomore years; not renewable. *Award amount:* $500. *Number of awards:* 10–20. *Eligibility Requirements:* Applicant must be age 16-21; enrolled or expecting to enroll full-time at a two-year or four-year or technical institution or university; female; resident of Michigan and studying in Michigan. Available to U.S. citizens. Applicant must have general military experience. *Application Requirements:* Application form, discharge papers, financial need analysis, recommendations or references, transcript. **Deadline:** March 15.

American Legion Auxiliary Department of Michigan Scholarship for Non-Traditional Student. Applicant must be a dependent of a veteran. Must be one of the following:

nontraditional student returning to classroom after some period of time in which their education was interrupted, student over the age of 22 attending college for the first time to pursue a degree, or student over the age of 22 attending a trade or vocational school. Applicants must be Michigan residents only and attend Michigan institution. Judging based on need, character/leadership, scholastic standing, and initiative/goal. *Award:* Scholarship for use in freshman, sophomore, junior, or senior years; renewable. *Award amount:* $500. *Number of awards:* 1. *Eligibility Requirements:* Applicant must be age 23–99; enrolled or expecting to enroll full- or part-time at a two-year or four-year or technical institution or university; resident of Michigan and studying in Michigan. Available to U.S. citizens. Applicant must have general military experience. *Application Requirements:* Application form, copy of veteran's discharge papers, financial need analysis, transcript. **Deadline:** March 15.

Michigan Competitive Scholarship. Renewable awards for Michigan resident to pursue undergraduate study at a Michigan institution. Awards limited to tuition. Must maintain at least a 2.0 grade point average and meet the college's academic progress requirements. Must file Free Application for Federal Student Aid. *Award:* Scholarship for use in freshman, sophomore, junior, or senior years; renewable. *Award amount:* $575–$575. *Eligibility Requirements:* Applicant must be enrolled or expecting to enroll full- or part-time at a two-year or four-year institution or university; resident of Michigan and studying in Michigan. Available to U. S. citizens. *Application Requirements:* Application form, financial need analysis, test scores. **Deadline:** March 1.

Michigan Tuition Grant. Need-based program. Students must be Michigan residents and attend a Michigan private, non-profit, degree-granting college. Must file the Free Application for Federal Student Aid and meet the college's academic progress requirements. *Award:* Grant for use in freshman, sophomore, junior, or senior years; renewable. *Award amount:* $1512–$1512. *Eligibility Requirements:* Applicant must be enrolled or expecting to enroll full- or part-time at a four-year institution or university; resident of Michigan and studying in Michigan. Available to U.S. citizens. *Application Requirements:* Financial need analysis. **Deadline:** July 1.

Tuition Incentive Program. Award for Michigan residents who receive or have received Michigan Medicaid for required period of time through the Department of Human Services. Scholarship provides two years tuition towards an associate degree at a Michigan college or university and $2000 total assistance for third and fourth years. Must apply before graduating from high school or earning a general education development diploma and before age 20. *Award:* Grant for use in freshman, sophomore, junior, or senior years; renewable. *Eligibility Requirements:* Applicant must be enrolled or expecting to enroll full- or part-time at a two-year or four-year institution or university; resident of Michigan and studying in Michigan. Available to U.S. citizens. *Application Requirements:* Application form, Medicaid eligibility for specified period of time. **Deadline:** continuous.

MINNESOTA

Leadership, Excellence, and Dedicated Service Scholarship. Scholarship provides a maximum of thirty $1000 to selected high school seniors who become a member of the Minnesota National Guard and complete the application process. The award recognizes demonstrated leadership, community services and potential for success in the Minnesota National Guard. *Award:* Scholarship for use in freshman year; not renewable. *Award amount:* $1000. *Number of awards:* up to 30. *Eligibility Requirements:* Applicant must be high school student; planning to enroll or expecting to enroll full- or part-time at a two-year or four-year or technical institution or university; resident of Minnesota and must have an interest in leadership. Applicant or parent of applicant must have employment or volunteer experience in community service. Available to U.S. citizens. Applicant or parent must meet one or more of the following requirements: national guard experience; retired from active duty; disabled or killed as a result of military service; prisoner of war; or missing in action. *Application Requirements:* Essay, recommendations or references, resume, transcript. **Deadline:** March 15.

Contact Barbara O'Reilly, Education Services Officer. *E-mail:* barbara. oreilly@mn.ngb.army.mil. *Phone:* 651-282-4508. *Website:* http://www. minnesotanationalguard.org/.

Minnesota GI Bill Program. Provides financial assistance to eligible Minnesota veterans and non-veterans who have

served 5 or more years cumulatively as a member of the National Guard or Reserves, and served on or after September 11, 2001. Surviving spouses and children of service members who have died or have a total and permanent disability and who served on or after September 11, 2001, may also be eligible. Full-time students may receive up to $1000 per term, and part-time students up to $500 per term up to $3,000 per year. Maximum lifetime benefit is $10,000. *Award:* Scholarship for use in freshman, sophomore, junior, senior, graduate, or postgraduate years; not renewable. *Award amount:* up to $3000. *Eligibility Requirements:* Applicant must be enrolled or expecting to enroll full- or part-time at a two-year or four-year or technical institution or university; resident of Minnesota and studying in Minnesota. Available to U.S. citizens. Applicant or parent must meet one or more of the following requirements: general military experience; retired from active duty; disabled or killed as a result of military service; prisoner of war; or missing in action. *Application Requirements:* Application form, application form may be submitted online (http://www.getreadyforcollege. org), financial need analysis, military records. **Deadline:** continuous.

Minnesota Indian Scholarship. Scholarship for Minnesota residents who are one-fourth or more American Indian ancestry and attending an eligible Minnesota postsecondary institution. Maximum award is $4000 for undergraduate students and $6000 for graduate students. Scholarships are limited to 3 years for certificate or AA/AS programs, 5 years for bachelor's degree programs, and 5 years for graduate programs. Applicants must maintain satisfactory academic progress, not be in default on student loans, and be eligible to receive Pell or State Grant and have remaining need. Undergraduates must be enrolled on a least a 3/4-time basis. *Award:* Scholarship for use in freshman, sophomore, junior, senior, graduate, or postgraduate years; not renewable. *Award amount:* up to $6000. *Number of awards:* 500–600. *Eligibility Requirements:* Applicant must be American Indian/Alaska Native; enrolled or expecting to enroll full- or part-time at a two-year or four-year or technical institution or university; resident of Minnesota and studying in Minnesota. Available to U.S. citizens. *Application Requirements:* American Indian ancestry documentation, application form, financial need analysis. **Deadline:** continuous.

Minnesota Reciprocal Agreement. Renewable tuition waiver for Minnesota residents. Waives all or part of non-resident tuition surcharge at public institutions in Illinois, Indiana, Iowa, Kansas, Michigan, Missouri, Nebraska, North Dakota, South Dakota, Wisconsin and Manitoba. Deadline: last day of academic term. *Award:* Scholarship for use in freshman, sophomore, junior, senior, graduate, or postgraduate years; renewable. *Award amount:* up to $10,000. *Eligibility Requirements:* Applicant must be enrolled or expecting to enroll full- or part-time at a two-year or four-year or technical institution or university; resident of Minnesota and studying in Illinois, Indiana, Iowa, Kansas, Manitoba, Michigan, Missouri, Nebraska, North Dakota, South Dakota, Wisconsin. Available to U.S. citizens. *Application Requirements:* Application form, application form may be submitted online (http://www.getreadyforcollege.org). **Deadline:** continuous.

Contact Jodi Rouland, Program Assistant. *E-mail:* jodi.rouland@state.mn. us. *Phone:* 651-355-0614. *Fax:* 651-642-0675. *Website:* http://www. getreadyforcollege.org/.

Minnesota State Grant Program. Need-based grant program available for Minnesota residents attending Minnesota colleges. Student covers 46% of cost with remainder covered by Pell Grant, parent contribution and state grant. Students apply with FAFSA and colleges administer the program on campus. *Award:* Grant for use in freshman, sophomore, junior, or senior years; not renewable. *Award amount:* $100–$9620. *Number of awards:* 71,000–105,000. *Eligibility Requirements:* Applicant must be enrolled or expecting to enroll full- or part-time at a two-year or four-year or technical institution or university; resident of Minnesota and studying in Minnesota. Available to U.S. citizens. *Application Requirements:* Application form, application form may be submitted online (http://www.fafsa. gov), financial need analysis. **Deadline:** continuous.

Minnesota State Veterans' Dependents Assistance Program. Tuition assistance to dependents of persons considered to be prisoner-of-war or missing in action after August 1, 1958. Must be Minnesota resident attending Minnesota two- or four-year school. *Award:* Scholarship for use in freshman, sophomore, junior, or senior years; renewable. *Award amount:* up to $250. *Eligibility Requirements:* Applicant must be enrolled or

expecting to enroll full- or part-time at a two-year or four-year institution; resident of Minnesota and studying in Minnesota. Available to U.S. citizens. Applicant or parent must meet one or more of the following requirements: general military experience; retired from active duty; disabled or killed as a result of military service; prisoner of war; or missing in action. *Application Requirements:* Application form. **Deadline:** continuous.

Contact Ginny Dodds, Manager. *E-mail:* ginny.dodds@state.mn.us. *Phone:* 651-355-0610. *Website:* http://www.getreadyforcollege.org/.

Postsecondary Child Care Grant Program-Minnesota. Grant available for students not receiving MFIP. Based on financial need. Cannot exceed actual child care costs or maximum award chart (based on income). Must be Minnesota resident. For use at Minnesota two- or four-year school, including public technical colleges. Available until student has attended college for the equivalent of four full-time academic years. *Award:* Grant for use in freshman, sophomore, junior, or senior years; not renewable. *Award amount:* $100–$2800. *Number of awards:* 2500–3000. *Eligibility Requirements:* Applicant must be enrolled or expecting to enroll full- or part-time at a two-year or four-year or technical institution or university; resident of Minnesota and studying in Minnesota. Available to U.S. citizens. *Application Requirements:* Application form, financial need analysis. **Deadline:** continuous.

Contact Brenda Larter, Program Administrator, Minnesota Office of Higher Education, 1450 Energy Park Drive, Suite 350, St. Paul, MN 55108-5227. *E-mail:* brenda.larter@state.mn.us. *Phone:* 651-355-0612. *Fax:* 651-642-0675. *Website:* http://www. getreadyforcollege.org/.

Safety Officers' Survivor Grant Program. Grant for eligible survivors of Minnesota public safety officers killed in the line of duty. Safety officers who have been permanently or totally disabled in the line of duty are also eligible. Must be used at a Minnesota institution participating in State Grant Program. Write for details. Must submit proof of death or disability and Public Safety Officers Benefit Fund Certificate. Must apply for renewal each year. Five-year limit on awards. *Award:* Grant for use in freshman, sophomore, junior, senior, or graduate years; not renewable. *Award amount:* up to $10,488. *Number of awards:* 1. *Eligibility Requirements:* Applicant must be enrolled

or expecting to enroll full- or part-time at a two-year or four-year or technical institution or university; resident of Minnesota and studying in Minnesota. Applicant or parent of applicant must have employment or volunteer experience in police/firefighting. Available to U.S. citizens. *Application Requirements:* Application form, proof of death or disability. **Deadline:** continuous.

Contact Brenda Larter, Program Administrator. *E-mail:* brenda.larter@ state.mn.us. *Phone:* 651-355-0612. *Fax:* 651-642-0675. *Website:* http://www. getreadyforcollege.org/.

MISSISSIPPI

Higher Education Legislative Plan (HELP). Eligible applicant must be resident of Mississippi and apply for the first time as a freshman and/or sophomore student who graduated from high school within the immediate past two years. Must demonstrate need as determined by the results of the FAFSA, documenting an average family adjusted gross income of $36,500 or less over the prior two years. Must be enrolled full-time at a Mississippi college or university, have a GPA of 2.5, have completed a specific high school core curriculum, and have scored 20 on the ACT. *Award:* Scholarship for use in freshman, sophomore, junior, or senior years; not renewable. *Award amount:* $721–$5835. *Eligibility Requirements:* Applicant must be enrolled or expecting to enroll full-time at a two-year or four-year institution or university; resident of Mississippi and studying in Mississippi. Applicant must have 2.5 GPA or higher. Available to U.S. citizens. *Application Requirements:* Application form, application form may be submitted online (http://www.mississippi.edu/financialaid), FAFSA, specific high school curriculum, residency documentation, financial need analysis, test scores, transcript. **Deadline:** March 31.

Contact Mrs. Jennifer Rogers, Director of Student Financial Aid. *E-mail:* sfa@ mississippi.edu. *Phone:* 601-432-6997. *Website:* http://www.mississippi.edu/ financialaid.

Law Enforcement Officers/Firemen Scholarship. Financial assistance to dependent children and spouses of any Mississippi law enforcement officer, full-time fire fighter or volunteer fire fighter who has suffered fatal injuries or wounds or become permanently and totally disabled as a result of injuries or wounds which occurred in the performance of the official and appointed duties of his or her office. This financial assistance is offered as an eight semester tuition and room scholarship at any state-supported college or university in Mississippi. *Award:* Scholarship for use in freshman, sophomore, junior, or senior years; not renewable. *Award amount:* $1705–$12,707. *Eligibility Requirements:* Applicant must be enrolled or expecting to enroll full-time at a four-year institution or university; resident of Mississippi and studying in Mississippi. Applicant or parent of applicant must have employment or volunteer experience in police/firefighting. Available to U.S. citizens. *Application Requirements:* Application form, application form may be submitted online (http://www.mississippi.edu/financialaid), residency documentation, documentation of parent's death/disability in line of duty. **Deadline:** continuous.

Contact Mrs. Jennifer Rogers, Director of Student Financial Aid. *E-mail:* sfa@mississippi.edu. *Phone:* 601-432-6997. *Website:* http://www.mississippi.edu/financialaid.

Mississippi Eminent Scholars Grant. Award for an entering freshmen or as a renewal for sophomore, junior or senior, who are residents of Mississippi. Applicants must achieve a GPA of 3.5 and must have scored 29 on the ACT. Must enroll full-time at an eligible Mississippi college or university. *Award:* Grant for use in freshman, sophomore, junior, or senior years; not renewable. *Award amount:* $392–$2500. *Eligibility Requirements:* Applicant must be enrolled or expecting to enroll full-time at a two-year or four-year institution or university; resident of Mississippi and studying in Mississippi. Applicant must have 3.5 GPA or higher. Available to U.S. citizens. *Application Requirements:* Application form, application form may be submitted online (http://www.mississippi.edu/financialaid), residency documentation, test scores, transcript. **Deadline:** September 15.

Contact Mrs. Jennifer Rogers, Director of Student Financial Aid. *E-mail:* sfa@mississippi.edu. *Phone:* 601-432-6997. *Website:* http://www.mississippi.edu/financialaid.

Mississippi Resident Tuition Assistance Grant. Must be a resident of Mississippi enrolled full-time at an eligible Mississippi college or university. Must maintain a minimum 2.5 GPA each semester. MTAG awards may be up to $500 per academic year for freshman and sophomores and $1000 per academic year

for juniors and seniors. *Award:* Grant for use in freshman, sophomore, junior, or senior years; not renewable. *Award amount:* $17–$1000. *Eligibility Requirements:* Applicant must be enrolled or expecting to enroll full-time at a two-year or four-year institution or university; resident of Mississippi and studying in Mississippi. Applicant must have 2.5 GPA or higher. Available to U.S. citizens. *Application Requirements:* Application form, application form may be submitted online (http://www.mississippi.edu/financialaid), residency documentation, test scores, transcript. **Deadline:** September 15.

Contact Mrs. Jennifer Rogers, Director of Student Financial Aid. *E-mail:* sfa@mississippi.edu. *Phone:* 601-432-6997. *Website:* http://www.mississippi.edu/financialaid.

MISSOURI

Access Missouri Financial Assistance Program. Need-based program that provides awards to students who are enrolled full time and have an expected family contribution (EFC) of $12,000 or less based on their Free Application for Federal Student Aid (FAFSA). Awards vary depending on EFC and the type of postsecondary school. *Award:* Grant for use in freshman, sophomore, junior, or senior years; not renewable. *Eligibility Requirements:* Applicant must be enrolled or expecting to enroll full-time at a two-year or technical institution or university; resident of Missouri and studying in Missouri. Applicant must have 2.5 GPA or higher. Available to U.S. citizens. *Application Requirements:* FAFSA on file by April 1.

Environmental Education Scholarship Program (EESP). Scholarship to minority and other underrepresented students pursuing a bachelor's or master's degree in an environmental course of study. Must be a Missouri resident having a cumulative high school GPA of 3.0 or if enrolled in college, must have cumulative GPA of 2.5. Environmental Science. *Award:* Scholarship for use in freshman, sophomore, junior, senior, or graduate years; renewable. *Award amount:* $2000. *Number of awards:* 16. *Eligibility Requirements:* Applicant must be American Indian/Alaska Native, Asian/Pacific Islander, Black (non-Hispanic), Hispanic; enrolled or expecting to enroll full-time at a four-year institution or university and resident of Missouri. Applicant must have 3.0 GPA or higher. Available to U.S. citizens. *Application*

Requirements: Application form, community service, essay, recommendations or references, transcript. **Deadline:** June 1.

Contact Dana Muessig, Executive. *E-mail:* danamuessig@dnr.mo.gov. *Phone:* 800-361-4827. *Fax:* 573-526-3878. *Website:* http://www.dnr.mo.gov/.

Lillie Lois Ford Scholarship Fund. Two awards of $1000 each are given each year to one boy and one girl. Applicant must have attended a full session of Missouri Boys/Girls State or Missouri Cadet Patrol Academy. Must be a Missouri resident below age 21, attending an accredited college/university as a full-time student. Must be an unmarried descendant of a veteran having served at least 90 days on active duty in the Army, Air Force, Navy, Marine Corps, or Coast Guard of the United States. *Award:* Scholarship for use in freshman year; not renewable. *Award amount:* $1000. *Number of awards:* 2. *Eligibility Requirements:* Applicant must be high school student; planning to enroll or expecting to enroll full-time at a two-year or four-year institution or university; single and resident of Missouri. Available to U.S. citizens. Applicant or parent must meet one or more of the following requirements: general military experience; retired from active duty; disabled or killed as a result of military service; prisoner of war; or missing in action. *Application Requirements:* Application form, copy of the veteran's discharge certificate, financial need analysis, test scores. **Deadline:** April 20.

Contact John Doane, Chairman, Education and Scholarship Committee, American Legion Department of Missouri, PO Box 179, Jefferson City, MO 65102-0179. *Phone:* 417-924-8186. *Website:* http://www.missourilegion.org/.

Marguerite Ross Barnett Memorial Scholarship. Scholarship was established for students who are employed while attending school part-time. Must be enrolled at least half-time but less than full-time at a participating Missouri postsecondary school, be employed and compensated for at least 20 hours per week, be 18 years of age, be a Missouri resident and a U.S. citizen or a permanent resident. *Award:* Scholarship for use in freshman, sophomore, junior, or senior years; renewable. *Eligibility Requirements:* Applicant must be enrolled or expecting to enroll part-time at a two-year or four-year or technical institution or university; resident of Missouri and studying in Missouri. Applicant must have 2.5 GPA or higher. Available to U.S. citizens. *Appli-*

cation Requirements: FAFSA on file by August 1. **Deadline:** August 1.

Missouri Higher Education Academic Scholarship (Bright Flight). Program encourages top-ranked high school seniors to attend approved Missouri postsecondary schools. Must be a Missouri resident and a U.S. citizen or permanent resident. Must have a composite score on the ACT or SAT in the top 5 percent of all Missouri students taking those tests. Students with scores in the top 3 percent are eligible for an annual award of up to $3000 (up to $1500 each semester). Students with scores in the top 4% and 5% are eligible for an annual award of up to $1000 (up to $500 each semester). Award amounts, and the availability of the award for students in the 4% and 5%, are subject to change based on the amount of funding allocated for the program in the legislative session. *Award:* Scholarship for use in freshman, sophomore, junior, or senior years; renewable. *Award amount:* $1000–$3000. *Eligibility Requirements:* Applicant must be enrolled or expecting to enroll full-time at a two-year or four-year or technical institution or university; resident of Missouri and studying in Missouri. Applicant must have 2.5 GPA or higher. Available to U.S. citizens. *Application Requirements:* Test scores.

MONTANA

Montana Higher Education Opportunity Grant. This grant is awarded based on need to undergraduate students attending either part-time or full-time who are residents of Montana and attending participating Montana schools. Awards are limited to the most needy students. A specific major or program of study is not required. This grant does not need to be repaid, and students may apply each year. Apply by filing FAFSA by March 1 and contacting the financial aid office at the admitting college. *Award:* Grant for use in freshman, sophomore, junior, or senior years; not renewable. *Award amount:* $400–$600. *Number of awards:* up to 800. *Eligibility Requirements:* Applicant must be enrolled or expecting to enroll full- or part-time at a two-year or four-year institution or university; resident of Montana and studying in Montana. Available to U.S. citizens. *Application Requirements:* Application form, FAFSA, financial need analysis, resume. **Deadline:** March 1.

Contact Jamie Dushin, Budget Analyst, Montana University System, Office of Commissioner of Higher Education, PO Box 203101, Helena, MT 59620-3101. *E-mail:* jdushin@mgslp.state.mt.us. *Phone:* 406-444-0638. *Fax:* 406-444-1869. *Website:* http://www.scholarship.mt.gov/.

Montana Tuition Assistance Program-Baker Grant. Need-based grant for Montana residents attending participating Montana schools who have earned at least $2575 during the previous calendar year. Must be enrolled full time. Grant does not need to be repaid. Award covers the first undergraduate degree or certificate. Apply by filing FAFSA by March 1 and contacting the financial aid office at the admitting college. *Award:* Grant for use in freshman, sophomore, junior, or senior years; not renewable. *Award amount:* $100–$1000. *Number of awards:* 1000–3000. *Eligibility Requirements:* Applicant must be enrolled or expecting to enroll full-time at a two-year or four-year institution or university; resident of Montana and studying in Montana. Available to U.S. citizens. *Application Requirements:* Application form, FAFSA, financial need analysis, resume. **Deadline:** March 1.

Contact Jamie Dushin, Budget Analyst, Montana University System, Office of Commissioner of Higher Education, PO Box 203101, Helena, MT 59620-3101. *E-mail:* jdushin@mgslp.state.mt.us. *Phone:* 406-444-0638. *Fax:* 406-444-1869. *Website:* http://www.scholarship.mt.gov/.

Montana University System Honor Scholarship. Scholarship will be awarded annually to high school seniors graduating from accredited Montana high schools. The MUS Honor Scholarship is a four year renewable scholarship that waives the tuition and registration fee at one of the Montana University System campuses or one of the three community colleges (Flathead Valley in Kalispell, Miles in Miles City or Dawson in Glendive). The scholarship must be used within 9 months after high school graduation. Applicant must have a minimum GPA of 3.4. *Award:* Scholarship for use in freshman, sophomore, junior, or senior years; renewable. *Award amount:* $4000–$6000. *Number of awards:* up to 200. *Eligibility Requirements:* Applicant must be high school student; planning to enroll or expecting to enroll full-time at a two-year or four-year institution or university; resident of Montana and studying in Montana. Applicant must have 3.5 GPA or higher. Available to U.S. citizens. *Application Requirements:* Application form, college acceptance letter, test scores, transcript. **Deadline:** March 15.

Contact Sheila Newlun, Grants and Scholarship Coordinator. *E-mail:* snewlun@montana.edu. *Phone:* 406-444-0638. *Fax:* 406-444-1869. *Website:* http://www.scholarship.mt.gov/.

NEBRASKA

Nebraska Opportunity Grant. Available to undergraduates attending a participating postsecondary institution in Nebraska. Must demonstrate financial need. Nebraska residency required. Awards determined by each participating institution. Student must complete the Free Application for Federal Student Aid (FAFSA) to apply. Contact financial aid office at institution for additional information. *Award:* Grant for use in freshman, sophomore, junior, or senior years; not renewable. *Award amount:* $100–$3600. *Eligibility Requirements:* Applicant must be enrolled or expecting to enroll full- or part-time at a two-year or four-year or technical institution or university; resident of Nebraska and studying in Nebraska. Available to U.S. citizens. *Application Requirements:* Application form, application form may be submitted online (http://www.fafsa.ed.gov), financial analysis. **Deadline:** continuous.

Contact Mr. J. Ritchie Morrow, Financial Aid Coordinator, Nebraska's Coordinating Commission for Postsecondary Education, 140 North 8th Street, Suite 300, PO Box 95005, Lincoln, NE 68509-5005. *E-mail:* Ritchie.Morrow@nebraska.gov. *Phone:* 402-471-2847. *Fax:* 402-471-2886. *Website:* http://www.ccpe.state.ne.us/.

NEVADA

Governor Guinn Millennium Scholarship. Scholarship for Nevada residents. Student must graduate from a public or private high school within Nevada with a minimum GPA of 3.25. Must complete core curriculum. Maximum award is $10,000. Student must acknowledge award and use it within 6 years of high school graduation. *Award:* Scholarship for use in freshman, sophomore, junior, or senior years; renewable. *Award amount:* $1–$10,000. *Number of awards:* 1. *Eligibility Requirements:* Applicant must be enrolled or expecting to enroll full-time at a two-year or four-year institution or university; resident of Nevada and studying in Nevada. Available to U.S. citizens. *Application Requirements:* Application form may be submitted online (http://nevadatreasurer. gov). High schools determine eligibility. Student must accept award. **Deadline:** varies.

Contact Linda English, Executive Director. *E-mail:* info@nevadatreasurer. gov. *Phone:* 702-486-3889. *Fax:* 702-486-3246. *Website:* http://www. nevadatreasurer.gov/.

NEW HAMPSHIRE

Scholarships for Orphans of Veterans-New Hampshire. Scholarship to provide financial assistance (room, board, books and supplies) to children of parents) who served in World War II, Korean Conflict, Vietnam (Southeast Asian Conflict) or the Gulf Wars, or any other operation for which the armed forces expeditionary medal or theater of operations service medal was awarded to the veteran. *Award:* Scholarship for use in freshman, sophomore, junior, or senior years; renewable. *Award amount:* up to $2500. *Number of awards:* 1–10. *Eligibility Requirements:* Applicant must be age 16-25; enrolled or expecting to enroll full-time at a two-year or four-year institution or university; resident of New Hampshire and studying in New Hampshire. Available to U.S. citizens. Applicant or parent must meet one or more of the following requirements: general military experience; retired from active duty; disabled or killed as a result of military service; prisoner of war; or missing in action. *Application Requirements:* Application form. **Deadline:** varies.

Contact Ms. Cynthia Capodestria, Student Financial Aid Administrator. *E-mail:* cynthia.capodestria@pec.state. nh.us. *Phone:* 603-271-2555 Ext. 360. *Website:* http://www.nh.gov/ postsecondary.

NEW JERSEY

Dana Christmas Scholarship for Heroism. Honors young New Jersey residents for acts of heroism. Scholarship is a nonrenewable award of up to $10,000 for 5 students. This scholarship may be used for undergraduate or graduate study. Deadline varies. *Award:* Scholarship for use in freshman, sophomore, junior, or senior years; not renewable. *Award amount:* up to $10,000. *Number of awards:* up to 5. *Eligibility Requirements:* Applicant must be enrolled or expecting to enroll full- or part-time at a two-year or four-year or technical institution or university and resident of New Jersey. Available to U.S. citizens. *Application*

Requirements: Application form. **Deadline:** varies.

Contact Gisele Joachim, Director, Financial Aid Services, New Jersey Higher Education Student Assistance Authority, 4 Quakerbridge Plaza, PO Box 540, Trenton, NJ 08625. *E-mail:* gjoachim@hesaa.org. *Phone:* 800-792-8670 Ext. 2349. *Fax:* 609-588-7389. *Website:* http://www.hesaa.org/.

Law Enforcement Officer Memorial Scholarship. Scholarships for full-time undergraduate study at approved New Jersey institutions for the dependent children of New Jersey law enforcement officers killed in the line of duty. Value of scholarship will be established annually. Deadline varies. *Award:* Scholarship for use in freshman, sophomore, junior, or senior years; renewable. *Eligibility Requirements:* Applicant must be enrolled or expecting to enroll full-time at a four-year institution or university; resident of New Jersey and studying in New Jersey. Applicant or parent of applicant must have employment or volunteer experience in police/firefighting. Available to U.S. citizens. *Application Requirements:* Application form. **Deadline:** varies.

Contact Carol Muka, Assistant Director of Grants and Scholarships, New Jersey Higher Education Student Assistance Authority, PO Box 540, Trenton, NJ 08625. *E-mail:* cmuka@ hesaa.org. *Phone:* 800-792-8670 Ext. 3266. *Fax:* 609-588-2228. *Website:* http://www.hesaa.org/.

New Jersey Student Tuition Assistance Reward Scholarship II. Earn an associate degree from the home New Jersey county college as an NJ STARS recipient and graduate with a cumulative GPA of 3.25 or higher. Family income (taxable and untaxed income) must be less than $250,000 as derived from the FAFSA. NJ STARS II students may receive up to $1,250 per semester, paid completely by the State, after all other sources of federal and State grants and scholarships are applied to tuition charges. *Award:* Scholarship for use in freshman year; renewable. *Award amount:* up to $2500. *Number of awards:* 2500–2500. *Eligibility Requirements:* Applicant must be enrolled or expecting to enroll full-time at a four-year institution or university; resident of New Jersey and studying in New Jersey. Applicant must have 3.0 GPA or higher. Available to U.S. citizens. *Application Requirements:* Application form, FAFSA. **Deadline:** varies.

Contact Mr. Andre Maglione, Acting Director of Client Services and

Marketing, New Jersey Higher Education Student Assistance Authority, PO Box 071, Trenton, NJ 08625. *E-mail:* amaglione@hesaa.org. *Phone:* 609-584-4486. *Fax:* 609-588-7389. *Website:* http://www.hesaa.org/.

New Jersey War Orphans Tuition Assistance. $500 scholarship to children of those service personnel who died while in the military or due to service-connected disabilities, or who are officially listed as missing in action by the U.S. Department of Defense. Must be a resident of New Jersey for at least one year immediately preceding the filing of the application and be between the ages of 16 and 21 at the time of application. *Award:* Scholarship for use in freshman, sophomore, junior, or senior years; renewable. *Award amount:* $500. *Eligibility Requirements:* Applicant must be age 16-21; enrolled or expecting to enroll full-time at a four-year institution or university and resident of New Jersey. Available to U.S. citizens. Applicant or parent must meet one or more of the following requirements: general military experience; retired from active duty; disabled or killed as a result of military service; prisoner of war; or missing in action. *Application Requirements:* Application form, transcript. **Deadline:** varies.

Contact Patricia Richter, Grants Manager, New Jersey Department of Military and Veterans Affairs, PO Box 340, Trenton, NJ 08625-0340. *E-mail:* patricia.richter@njdmava.state.nj.us. *Phone:* 609-530-6854. *Fax:* 609-530-6970. *Website:* http://www.state.nj.us/ military.

New Jersey World Trade Center Scholarship. Scholarship was established by the legislature to aid the dependent children and surviving spouses of New Jersey residents who were killed in the terrorist attacks, or who are missing and officially presumed dead as a direct result of the attacks; applies to instate and out-of-state institutions for students seeking undergraduate degrees. Deadlines: March 1 for fall, October 1 for spring. *Award:* Scholarship for use in freshman, sophomore, junior, or senior years; renewable. *Award amount:* up to $6500. *Eligibility Requirements:* Applicant must be enrolled or expecting to enroll full-time at a four-year institution or university and resident of New Jersey. Available to U.S. citizens. *Application Requirements:* Application form. **Deadline:** varies.

Contact Giselle Joachim, Director of Financial Aid Services, New Jersey Higher Education Student Assistance

Authority, PO Box 540, Trenton, NJ 08625. *E-mail:* gjoachim@hesaa.org. *Phone:* 800-792-8670 Ext. 2349. *Fax:* 609-588-7389. *Website:* http://www.hesaa.org/.

NJ Student Tuition Assistance Reward Scholarship. Scholarship for students who graduate in the top 15 percent of their high school class. Recipients may be awarded up to five semesters of tuition (up to 15 credits per term) at one of New Jersey's nineteen county colleges. *Award:* Scholarship for use in freshman, sophomore, junior, or senior years; renewable. *Award amount:* $500–$2600. *Eligibility Requirements:* Applicant must be enrolled or expecting to enroll full-time at a two-year or four-year institution or university; resident of New Jersey and studying in New Jersey. Applicant must have 3.0 GPA or higher. Available to U.S. citizens. *Application Requirements:* Application form, transcript. **Deadline:** varies.

Contact Carol Muka, Assistant Director of Grants and Scholarships, New Jersey Higher Education Student Assistance Authority, PO Box 540, Trenton, NJ 08625. *E-mail:* cmuka@hessa.org. *Phone:* 800-792-8670 Ext. 3266. *Fax:* 609-588-2228. *Website:* http://www.hesaa.org/.

Part-Time Tuition Aid Grant (TAG) for County Colleges. Provides financial aid to eligible part-time undergraduate students enrolled for 9 to 11 credits at participating New Jersey community colleges. Deadlines are March 1 for spring and October 1 for fall. *Award:* Grant for use in freshman, sophomore, junior, or senior years; not renewable. *Award amount:* $419–$628. *Eligibility Requirements:* Applicant must be enrolled or expecting to enroll part-time at a two-year or four-year institution or university; resident of New Jersey and studying in New Jersey. Available to U.S. citizens. *Application Requirements:* Application form, financial need analysis. **Deadline:** varies.

Contact Sherri Fox, Acting Director of Grants and Scholarships, New Jersey Higher Education Student Assistance Authority, PO Box 540, Trenton, NJ 08625. *Phone:* 800-792-8670. *Fax:* 609-588-2228. *Website:* http://www.hesaa.org/

POW-MIA Tuition Benefit Program. Free undergraduate college tuition provided to any child born or adopted before or during the period of time his or her parent was officially declared a prisoner of war or person missing in action after January 1, 1960. The POW-MIA must have been a New Jersey resident at the time he or she entered the service. Child of veteran must attend either a public or private institution in New Jersey. A copy of DD 1300 must be furnished with the application. Minimum 2.5 GPA required. *Award:* Scholarship for use in freshman, sophomore, junior, or senior years; renewable. *Eligibility Requirements:* Applicant must be enrolled or expecting to enroll full-time at a two-year or four-year or technical institution or university; resident of New Jersey and studying in New Jersey. Applicant must have 2.5 GPA or higher. Available to U.S. citizens. Applicant or parent must meet one or more of the following requirements: general military experience; retired from active duty; disabled or killed as a result of military service; prisoner of war; or missing in action. *Application Requirements:* Application form, copy of DD 1300, transcript. **Deadline:** varies.

Contact Patricia Richter, Grants Manager, New Jersey Department of Military and Veterans Affairs, PO Box 340, Trenton, NJ 08625-0340. *E-mail:* patricia.richter@njdmava.state.nj.us. *Phone:* 609-530-6854. *Fax:* 609-530-6970. *Website:* http://www.state.nj.us/military.

Survivor Tuition Benefits Program. The scholarship provides tuition fees for spouses and dependents of law enforcement officers, fire, or emergency services personnel killed in the line of duty. Eligible recipients may attend any independent institution in the state; however, the annual value of the grant cannot exceed the highest tuition charged at a New Jersey public institution. *Award:* Scholarship for use in freshman, sophomore, junior, or senior years; renewable. *Award amount:* up to $99,999. *Number of awards:* up to 99,999. *Eligibility Requirements:* Applicant must be enrolled or expecting to enroll full- or part-time at a two-year or four-year institution or university; resident of New Jersey and studying in New Jersey. Applicant or parent of applicant must have employment or volunteer experience in police/firefighting. Available to U.S. citizens. *Application Requirements:* Application form. **Deadline:** varies.

Contact Carol Muka, Scholarship Coordinator, New Jersey Higher Education Student Assistance Authority, PO Box 540, Trenton, NJ 08625. *E-mail:* cmuka@hesaa.org. *Phone:* 800-792-8670 Ext. 3266. *Fax:* 609-588-2228. *Website:* http://www.hesaa.org/.

Tuition Aid Grant. The program provides tuition fees to eligible undergraduate students attending participating in-state institutions. Deadlines are March 1 for fall and October 1 for spring. *Award:* Grant for use in freshman, sophomore, junior, or senior years; not renewable. *Award amount:* $868–$7272. *Eligibility Requirements:* Applicant must be enrolled or expecting to enroll full-time at a two-year or four-year institution or university; resident of New Jersey and studying in New Jersey. Available to U.S. citizens. *Application Requirements:* Application form, financial need analysis. **Deadline:** varies.

Contact Sherri Fox, Acting Director of Grants and Scholarships, New Jersey Higher Education Student Assistance Authority, PO Box 540, Trenton, NJ 08625. *Phone:* 800-792-8670. *Fax:* 609-588-2228. *Website:* http://www.hesaa.org/

Veterans Tuition Credit Program-New Jersey. Award for New Jersey resident veterans who served in the armed forces between December 31, 1960, and May 7, 1975. Must have been a New Jersey resident at time of induction or discharge or for two years immediately prior to application. *Award:* Scholarship for use in freshman, sophomore, junior, or senior years; renewable. *Award amount:* $200–$400. *Eligibility Requirements:* Applicant must be enrolled or expecting to enroll full- or part-time at a two-year or four-year or technical institution or university and resident of New Jersey. Available to U.S. citizens. Applicant or parent must meet one or more of the following requirements: general military experience; retired from active duty; disabled or killed as a result of military service; prisoner of war; or missing in action. *Application Requirements:* Application form. **Deadline:** varies.

Contact Patricia Richter, Grants Manager, New Jersey Department of Military and Veterans Affairs, PO Box 340, Trenton, NJ 08625-0340. *E-mail:* patricia.richter@njdmava.state.nj.us. *Phone:* 609-530-6854. *Fax:* 609-530-6970. *Website:* http://www.state.nj.us/military.

NEW MEXICO

Children of Deceased Veterans Scholarship-New Mexico. Award for New Mexico residents who are children of veterans killed or disabled as a result of service, prisoner of war, or veterans missing in action. Must be between ages

16 and 26. For use at New Mexico schools for undergraduate study. Must submit parent's death certificate and DD form 214. *Award:* Scholarship for use in freshman, sophomore, junior, or senior years; renewable. *Award amount:* $300. *Eligibility Requirements:* Applicant must be age 16-26; enrolled or expecting to enroll full- or part-time at a two-year or four-year institution or university; resident of New Mexico and studying in New Mexico. Available to U.S. citizens. Applicant or parent must meet one or more of the following requirements: general military experience; retired from active duty; disabled or killed as a result of military service; prisoner of war; or missing in action. *Application Requirements:* Application form, death certificate or notice of casualty, DD form 214, transcript. **Deadline:** continuous.

Contact Alan Martinez, Deputy Secretary. *E-mail:* alan.martinez@state. nm.us. *Phone:* 505-827-6300. *Website:* http://www.dvs.state.nm.us/.

College Affordability Grant. Grant available to New Mexico students with financial need who do not qualify for other state grants and scholarships to attend and complete educational programs at a New Mexico public college or university. Student must have unmet need after all other financial aid has been awarded. Student may not be receiving any other state grants or scholarships. Renewable upon satisfactory academic progress. *Award:* Grant for use in freshman, sophomore, junior, or senior years; renewable. *Award amount:* up to $1000. *Number of awards:* 1. *Eligibility Requirements:* Applicant must be enrolled or expecting to enroll full- or part-time at a two-year or four-year institution or university; resident of New Mexico and studying in New Mexico. Available to U. S. citizens. *Application Requirements:* Application form, FAFSA, financial need analysis. **Deadline:** continuous.

Contact Tashina Acker, Director of Financial Aid, New Mexico Commission on Higher Education, 1068 Cerrillos Road, Santa Fe, NM 87505-1650. *E-mail:* tashina.banks-moore@state.nm.us. *Phone:* 505-476-6549. *Fax:* 505-476-6511. *Website:* http://www.hed.state.nm. us/.

Legislative Endowment Scholarships. Renewable scholarships to provide aid for undergraduate students with substantial financial need who are attending public postsecondary institutions in New Mexico. Four-year schools may award up to $2500 per academic year, two-year schools may award up to $1000 per academic year. Deadlines varies. *Award:* Scholarship for use in freshman, sophomore, junior, or senior years; renewable. *Award amount:* $1000–$2500. *Number of awards:* 1. *Eligibility Requirements:* Applicant must be enrolled or expecting to enroll full- or part-time at a two-year or four-year institution or university; resident of New Mexico and studying in New Mexico. Available to U. S. citizens. *Application Requirements:* Application form, FAFSA, financial need analysis. **Deadline:** varies.

Contact Tashina Moore, Director of Financial Aid, New Mexico Commission on Higher Education, 1068 Cerrillos Road, Santa Fe, NM 87505-1650. *E-mail:* tashina.banks-moore@state.nm.us. *Phone:* 505-475-6549. *Fax:* 505-476-6511. *Website:* http://www.hed.state.nm. us/.

Legislative Lottery Scholarship. Renewable Scholarship for New Mexico high school graduates or GED recipients who plan to attend an eligible New Mexico public college or university. Must be enrolled full-time and maintain 2.5 GPA. *Award:* Scholarship for use in freshman year; renewable. *Number of awards:* 1. *Eligibility Requirements:* Applicant must be high school student; planning to enroll or expecting to enroll full-time at a four-year institution or university; resident of New Mexico and studying in New Mexico. Applicant must have 3.5 GPA or higher. Available to U.S. citizens. *Application Requirements:* Application form, FAFSA. **Deadline:** varies.

Contact Tashina Moore, Director of Financial Aid, New Mexico Commission on Higher Education, 1068 Cerrillos Road, Santa Fe, NM 87505. *E-mail:* tashina.banks-moore@state.nm.us. *Phone:* 505-476-6549. *Fax:* 505-476-6511. *Website:* http://www.hed.state.nm. us/.

New Mexico Competitive Scholarship. Scholarships for non-residents or non-citizens of the United States to encourage out-of-state students who have demonstrated high academic achievement in high school to enroll in public four-year universities in New Mexico. Renewable for up to four years. For details visit http://fin.hed.state.nm.us. *Award:* Scholarship for use in freshman year; renewable. *Eligibility Requirements:* Applicant must be high school student; planning to enroll or expecting to enroll full-time at a four-year institution or university and studying in New Mexico. Available to Canadian and non-U.S. citizens. *Application Requirements:* Application form, essay, recom-

mendations or references, test scores. **Deadline:** varies.

Contact Tashina Moore, Director of Financial Aid, New Mexico Commission on Higher Education, 1068 Cerrillos Road, Santa Fe, NM 87505. *E-mail:* tashina.banks-moore@state.nm.us. *Phone:* 505-476-6549. *Fax:* 505-476-6511. *Website:* http://www.hed.state.nm. us/.

New Mexico Scholars' Program. Renewable award program created to encourage New Mexico high school students to attend public postsecondary institutions or the following private colleges in New Mexico: College of Santa Fe, St. John's College, College of the Southwest. For details visit http://fin.hed.state.nm.us. *Award:* Scholarship for use in freshman year; renewable. *Number of awards:* 1. *Eligibility Requirements:* Applicant must be high school student; planning to enroll or expecting to enroll full-time at a two-year or four-year institution; resident of New Mexico and studying in New Mexico. Available to U.S. citizens. *Application Requirements:* Application form, FAFSA, financial need analysis, test scores. **Deadline:** varies.

Contact Tashina Moore, Director of Financial Aid, New Mexico Commission on Higher Education, 1068 Cerrillos Road, Santa Fe, NM 87505-1650. *E-mail:* tashina.banks-moore@state.nm.us. *Phone:* 505-476-6549. *Fax:* 505-476-6511. *Website:* http://www.hed.state.nm. us/.

New Mexico Student Incentive Grant. Grant created to provide aid for undergraduate students with substantial financial need who are attending public colleges or universities or the following eligible colleges in New Mexico: College of Santa Fe, St. John's College, College of the Southwest, Institute of American Indian Art, Crownpoint Institute of Technology, Dine College and Southwestern Indian Polytechnic Institute. Part-time students are eligible for pro-rated awards. *Award:* Grant for use in freshman, sophomore, junior, or senior years; not renewable. *Award amount:* $200–$2500. *Number of awards:* 1. *Eligibility Requirements:* Applicant must be enrolled or expecting to enroll full- or part-time at a two-year or four-year or technical institution or university; resident of New Mexico and studying in New Mexico. Available to U.S. citizens. *Application Requirements:* Application form, FAFSA, financial need analysis. **Deadline:** varies.

Contact Tashina Moore, Director of Financial Aid, New Mexico Commission on Higher Education, 1068 Cerrillos Road, Santa Fe, NM 87505-1650. *E-mail:* tashina.banks-moore@state.nm.us. *Phone:* 505-476-6549. *Fax:* 505-476-6511. *Website:* http://www.hed.state.nm.us/.

New Mexico Vietnam Veteran Scholarship. Award for Vietnam veterans who have been New Mexico residents for a minimum of ten years and are attending state-funded postsecondary schools. Must have been awarded the Vietnam Campaign medal. Must submit DD 214 and discharge papers. *Award:* Scholarship for use in freshman, sophomore, junior, or senior years; renewable. *Award amount:* $3500–$4000. *Number of awards:* 100. *Eligibility Requirements:* Applicant must be enrolled or expecting to enroll full- or part-time at a two-year or four-year or technical institution or university; resident of New Mexico and studying in New Mexico. Available to U.S. citizens. Applicant or parent must meet one or more of the following requirements: general military experience; retired from active duty; disabled or killed as a result of military service; prisoner of war; or missing in action. *Application Requirements:* Application form, copy of DD Form 214. **Deadline:** continuous.

Contact Alan Martinez, Deputy Secretary. *E-mail:* alan.martinez@state.nm.us. *Phone:* 505-827-6300. *Website:* http://www.dvs.state.nm.us/.

Vietnam Veterans' Scholarship Program. Renewable scholarship program created to provide aid for Vietnam veterans who are undergraduate and graduate students attending public postsecondary institutions or select private colleges in New Mexico. Private colleges include: College of Santa Fe, St. John's College and College of the Southwest. *Award:* Scholarship for use in freshman, sophomore, junior, or senior years; renewable. *Number of awards:* 1. *Eligibility Requirements:* Applicant must be enrolled or expecting to enroll full-time at a two-year or four-year institution; resident of New Mexico and studying in New Mexico. Available to U.S. citizens. Applicant or parent must meet one or more of the following requirements: general military experience; retired from active duty; disabled or killed as a result of military service; prisoner of war; or missing in action. *Application Requirements:* Application form, certification by the NM Veteran's commission. **Deadline:** varies.

Contact Tashina Moore, Director of Financial Aid, New Mexico Commission on Higher Education, 1068 Cerrillos Road, Santa Fe, NM 87505-1650. *E-mail:* tashina.banks-moore@state.nm.us. *Phone:* 505-476-6549. *Fax:* 505-476-6511. *Website:* http://www.hed.state.nm.us/.

NEW YORK

DAAD University Summer Course Grant. Scholarships are awarded to full-time degree students of Canadian or US colleges, sophomore/2nd year and higher, for the pursuit of summer courses at universities in Germany. It is open to applicants of any major but there is a prerequisite of at least two years of college level German or the equivalent German language fluency. Courses are three to four weeks in duration, take place at many locations in Germany (universities), are taught in German, and topics include German language, literature, current affairs, political science, history, culture, arts, film and media, economics, linguistics, law, translation and interpretation, and test prep for German language proficiency examinations. The scholarship is approximately €850 to cover course fees, and room and board in whole or in part, with an additional international travel reimbursement ranging from €300 to €450. Accommodations are arranged by the host institution. Foreign Language. *Award:* Grant for use in sophomore, junior, senior, or graduate years; not renewable. *Eligibility Requirements:* Applicant must be enrolled or expecting to enroll full-time at a four-year institution or university and must have an interest in German language/culture. Available to U.S. and non-U.S. citizens. *Application Requirements:* Application form, application form may be submitted online (http://www.daad.org/?p=summercourse), essay, recommendations or references, resume, transcript. **Deadline:** December 15.

Contact Jane Fu, Information Officer. *E-mail:* daadny@daad.org. *Phone:* 212-758-3223. *Website:* http://www.daad.org/.

Japan-U.S. Friendship Commission Prize for the Translation of Japanese Literature. Annual prize for the best translation into English of a modern work of literature or for the best classical literary translation, or the prize is divided between a classical and a modern work. To qualify, works must be book-length translations of Japanese literary works: novels, collections of short stories, literary essays, memoirs, drama or poetry. Foreign Language. *Award:* Prize for use in freshman, sophomore, junior, or senior years; not renewable. *Award amount:* $3000. *Number of awards:* 2. *Eligibility Requirements:* Applicant must be enrolled or expecting to enroll full- or part-time at a two-year or four-year or technical institution or university. Available to U.S. citizens. *Application Requirements:* Application form, entry in a contest, resume, unpublished manuscripts. **Deadline:** February 29.

Contact Kia Cheleen, Assistant Director. *E-mail:* donald-keene-center@columbia.edu. *Phone:* 212-854-5036. *Website:* http://www.donaldkeenecenter.org/.

New York Aid for Part-Time Study (APTS). Renewable scholarship provides tuition assistance to part-time undergraduate students who are New York residents, meet income eligibility requirements and are attending New York accredited institutions. Deadline varies. Must be U.S. citizen. *Award:* Grant for use in freshman, sophomore, junior, or senior years; renewable. *Award amount:* up to $2000. *Eligibility Requirements:* Applicant must be enrolled or expecting to enroll part-time at a two-year or four-year institution or university; resident of New York and studying in New York. Available to U.S. citizens. *Application Requirements:* Application form, financial need analysis. **Deadline:** varies.

New York Memorial Scholarships for Families of Deceased Police Officers, Fire Fighters, and Peace Officers. Renewable scholarship for children, spouses and financial dependents of deceased fire fighters, volunteer firefighters, police officers, peace officers and emergency medical service workers who died in the line of duty. Provides up to the cost of SUNY educational expenses. *Award:* Scholarship for use in freshman, sophomore, junior, or senior years; renewable. *Eligibility Requirements:* Applicant must be enrolled or expecting to enroll full-time at a four-year institution or university; resident of New York and studying in New York. Available to U.S. citizens. *Application Requirements:* Application form, financial need analysis, transcript. **Deadline:** May 1.

New York State Aid to Native Americans. Award for enrolled members of a New York State tribe and their children who are attending or planning to attend a New York State college and who are New York State residents. Deadlines: July 15 for the fall semester, December 31 for the spring semester, and May 20 for summer session. *Award:* Scholarship for use in freshman, sophomore, junior, or senior years; renewable. *Award amount:* $85–$2000. *Eligibility Requirements:* Applicant must be American Indian/Alaska Native; enrolled or expecting to enroll full- or part-time at a two-year or four-year or technical institution or university; resident of New York and studying in New York. Available to U.S. citizens. *Application Requirements:* Application form, financial need analysis, recommendations or references, transcript. **Deadline:** varies.

New York State Tuition Assistance Program. Award for New York state residents attending a New York postsecondary institution. Must be full-time student in approved program with tuition over $200 per year. Must show financial need and not be in default in any other state program. Renewable award of $500 to $5000 dependent on family income and tuition charged. *Award:* Grant for use in freshman, sophomore, junior, or senior years; renewable. *Award amount:* $500–$5000. *Number of awards:* 350,000–360,000. *Eligibility Requirements:* Applicant must be enrolled or expecting to enroll full-time at a two-year or four-year institution or university; resident of New York and studying in New York. Available to U.S. citizens. *Application Requirements:* Application form, financial need analysis. **Deadline:** May 1.

New York Vietnam/Persian Gulf/Afghanistan Veterans Tuition Awards. Scholarship for veterans who served in Vietnam, the Persian Gulf, or Afghanistan. Must be a New York resident attending a New York institution. Must establish eligibility by September 1. *Award:* Scholarship for use in freshman, sophomore, junior, or senior years; renewable. *Eligibility Requirements:* Applicant must be enrolled or expecting to enroll full- or part-time at a two-year or four-year or technical institution or university; resident of New York and studying in New York. Available to U.S. citizens. Applicant or parent must meet one or more of the following requirements: general military experience; retired from active duty; disabled or killed as a result of military service; prisoner of war; or missing in action. *Application Requirements:* Application form, financial need analysis. **Deadline:** May 1.

Regents Award for Child of Veteran. Award for students whose parent, as a result of service in U.S. Armed Forces during war or national emergency, died; suffered a 40 percent or more disability; or is classified as missing in action or a prisoner of war. Veteran must be current New York State resident or have been so at time of death. Student must be a New York resident, attending, or planning to attend, college in New York State. Must establish eligibility before applying for payment. *Award:* Scholarship for use in freshman, sophomore, junior, or senior years; not renewable. *Award amount:* up to $450. *Eligibility Requirements:* Applicant must be enrolled or expecting to enroll full-time at a two-year or four-year institution or university; resident of New York and studying in New York. Available to U.S. citizens. Applicant or parent must meet one or more of the following requirements: general military experience; retired from active duty; disabled or killed as a result of military service; prisoner of war; or missing in action. *Application Requirements:* Application form, proof of eligibility. **Deadline:** May 1.

Contact Rita McGivern, Student Information, New York State Higher Education Services Corporation, 99 Washington Avenue, Room 1320, Albany, NY 12255. *E-mail:* rmcgivern@hesc.com. *Website:* http://www.hesc.com/.

Scholarship for Academic Excellence. Renewable award for New York residents. Scholarship winners must attend a college or university in New York. 2000 scholarships are for $1500 and 6000 are for $500. The selection criteria used are based on Regents test scores or rank in class or local exam. Must be U.S. citizen or permanent resident. *Award:* Scholarship for use in freshman year; renewable. *Award amount:* $500–$1500. *Number of awards:* up to 8000. *Eligibility Requirements:* Applicant must be high school student; planning to enroll or expecting to enroll full-time at a two-year or four-year institution or university; resident of New York and studying in New York. Available to U.S. citizens. *Application Requirements:* Application form. **Deadline:** December 19.

Contact Lewis Hall, Supervisor. *E-mail:* scholar@mail.nysed.gov. *Phone:* 518-486-1319. *Fax:* 518-486-5346. *Website:* http://www.highered.nysed.gov/.

Scholarships for Academic Excellence. Renewable awards of up to $1500 for academically outstanding New York State high school graduates planning to attend an approved postsecondary institution in New York State. For full-time study only. Contact high school guidance counselor to apply. *Award:* Scholarship for use in freshman, sophomore, junior, or senior years; renewable. *Award amount:* $500–$1500. *Number of awards:* up to 8000. *Eligibility Requirements:* Applicant must be high school student; planning to enroll or expecting to enroll full-time at a four-year institution or university; resident of New York and studying in New York. Available to U.S. citizens. *Application Requirements:* Application form. **Deadline:** varies.

Contact Rita McGivern, Student Information, New York State Higher Education Services Corporation, 99 Washington Avenue, Room 1320, Albany, NY 12255. *E-mail:* scholarship@hesc.com. *Website:* http://www.hesc.com/.

World Trade Center Memorial Scholarship. Renewable awards of up to the cost of educational expenses at a State University of New York four-year college. Available to the children, spouses and financial dependents of victims who died or were severely disabled as a result of the September 11, 2001 terrorist attacks on the U.S. and the rescue and recovery efforts. *Award:* Scholarship for use in freshman, sophomore, junior, or senior years; renewable. *Eligibility Requirements:* Applicant must be enrolled or expecting to enroll full-time at a four-year institution or university and studying in New York. Available to U.S. and non-U.S. citizens. *Application Requirements:* Application form, financial need analysis, recommendations or references, transcript. **Deadline:** May 1.

NORTH CAROLINA

North Carolina Community College Grant Program. Grants are available to North Carolina residents who demonstrate financial need and are enrolled at NC community colleges. The applicant must be a NC resident for tuition purposes, enroll for at least six credit hours per semester in a curriculum program, and meet the Satisfactory Academic Progress requirements of the institution. Eligibility is determined based on the same criteria as the Federal Pell Grant; students not eligible for the Federal Pell Grant may be considered for the grant based on the expected family contribution (EFC). Student who have earned a bachelor's (four-year) degree already are ineligible. Applicants must complete the Free Application for Federal Student Aid (FAFSA). Consideration is AUTOMATIC once the FAFSA is filed. Please contact the financial aid office at the local community college for more specific information regarding institutional processes. *Award:* Grant for use in freshman or sophomore years; not renewable. *Award amount:* $150–$950. *Number of awards:* 25,000. *Eligibility Requirements:* Applicant must be enrolled or expecting to enroll full- or part-time at a two-year or technical institution; resident of North Carolina and studying in North Carolina. Available to U.S. citizens. *Application Requirements:* Application form may be submitted online (http://www.CFNC.org/NCCCG), FAFSA, financial need analysis. **Deadline:** varies.

Contact Trae Brookins, Scholarship and Grant Manager, North Carolina State Education Assistance Authority, PO Box 13663, Research Triangle Park, NC 27709-3663. *E-mail:* tbrookins@ncseaa. edu. *Phone:* 919-248-4650. *Fax:* 919-248-6650. *Website:* http://www.ncseaa. edu/.

North Carolina Division of Services for the Blind Rehabilitation Services. Financial assistance is available for North Carolina residents who are blind or visually impaired and who require vocational rehabilitation to help find employment. Tuition and other assistance provided based on need. Open to U.S. citizens and legal residents of United States. Applicants goal must be to work after receiving vocational services. To apply, contact the local DSB office and apply for vocational rehabilitation services. *Award:* Scholarship for use in freshman, sophomore, junior, or senior years; renewable. *Eligibility Requirements:* Applicant must be visually impaired; enrolled or expecting to enroll full-time at a two-year or four-year or technical institution or university and resident of North Carolina. Applicant must be visually impaired. Available to U.S. citizens. *Application Requirements:* Application form, financial need analysis, interview, proof of eligibility. **Deadline:** continuous.

Contact JoAnn Strader, Chief of Rehabilitation Field Services, North Carolina Division of Services for the Blind, 2601 Mail Service Center, Raleigh, NC 27699-2601. *E-mail:* joann.strader@ ncmail.net. *Phone:* 919-733-9700. *Fax:* 919-715-8771. *Website:* http://www. ncdhhs.gov/.

North Carolina National Guard Tuition Assistance Program. Scholarship for members of the North Carolina Air and Army National Guard who will remain in the service for two years following the period for which assistance is provided. Must reapply for each academic period. For use at approved North Carolina institutions. *Award:* Grant for use in freshman, sophomore, junior, senior, or graduate years; not renewable. *Award amount:* up to $2000. *Eligibility Requirements:* Applicant must be enrolled or expecting to enroll full- or part-time at a two-year or four-year or technical institution or university; resident of North Carolina and studying in North Carolina. Available to U.S. citizens. Applicant or parent must meet one or more of the following requirements: national guard experience; retired from active duty; disabled or killed as a result of military service; prisoner of war; or missing in action. *Application Requirements:* Application form. **Deadline:** varies.

Contact Anne Gildhouse, Education Services Officer. *E-mail:* anne. gildhouse@nc.ngb.army.mil. *Phone:* 919-664-6000. *Fax:* 919-664-6520. *Website:* http://www.nc.ngb.army.mil/.

North Carolina Sheriffs' Association Undergraduate Criminal Justice Scholarships. One-time award for full-time North Carolina resident undergraduate students majoring in criminal justice at a University of North Carolina school. Priority given to child of any North Carolina law enforcement officer. Letter of recommendation from county sheriff required. Criminal Justice/ Criminology; Law Enforcement/Police Administration. *Award:* Scholarship for use in freshman, sophomore, junior, or senior years; not renewable. *Award amount:* $1000–$2000. *Number of awards:* up to 10. *Eligibility Requirements:* Applicant must be enrolled or expecting to enroll full-time at a four-year institution or university; resident of North Carolina and studying in North Carolina. Applicant or parent of applicant must have employment or volunteer experience in police/firefighting. Available to U.S. citizens. *Application Requirements:* Application form, financial need analysis, recommendations or references, statement of career goals, transcript. **Deadline:** continuous.

Contact Nolita Goldston, Assistant, Scholarship and Grant Division, North Carolina State Education Assistance Authority, PO Box 13663, Research Triangle Park, NC 27709. *E-mail:* ngoldston@ncseaa.edu. *Phone:* 919-549-8614. *Fax:* 919-248-4687. *Website:* http:// www.ncseaa.edu/.

North Carolina Veterans Scholarships Class I-A. Scholarships for children of certain deceased, disabled or POW/MIA veterans. Award value is $4500 per nine-month academic year in private colleges and junior colleges. No limit on number awarded each year. *Award:* Scholarship for use in freshman, sophomore, junior, or senior years; renewable. *Award amount:* $4500. *Eligibility Requirements:* Applicant must be enrolled or expecting to enroll full-time at a two-year or four-year or technical institution or university; resident of North Carolina and studying in North Carolina. Available to U.S. citizens. Applicant or parent must meet one or more of the following requirements: general military experience; retired from active duty; disabled or killed as a result of military service; prisoner of war; or missing in action. *Application Requirements:* Application form, financial need analysis, interview, transcript. **Deadline:** continuous.

Contact Charles Smith, Assistant Secretary. *E-mail:* charlie.smith@ncmail. net. *Phone:* 919-733-3851. *Fax:* 919-733-2834. *Website:* http://www.doa.state.nc. us/vets/va.htm.

North Carolina Veterans Scholarships Class I-B. Awards for children of veterans rated by USDVA as 100 percent disabled due to wartime service as defined in the law, and currently or at time of death drawing compensation for such disability. Parent must have been a North Carolina resident at time of entry into service. Duration of the scholarship is four academic years (8 semesters) if used within 8 years. No limit on number awarded each year. *Award:* Scholarship for use in freshman, sophomore, junior, or senior years; renewable. *Award amount:* $1500. *Eligibility Requirements:* Applicant must be enrolled or expecting to enroll full- or part-time at a two-year or four-year or technical institution or university; resident of North Carolina and studying in North Carolina. Available to U.S. citizens. Applicant or parent must meet one or more of the following requirements: general military experience; retired from active duty; disabled or killed as a result of military service; prisoner of war; or missing in action. *Application Requirements:* Application form, financial need analysis, interview, transcript. **Deadline:** continuous.

Contact Charles Smith, Assistant Secretary. *E-mail:* charlie.smith@ncmail. net. *Phone:* 919-733-3851. *Fax:* 919-733-2834. *Website:* http://www.doa.state.nc. us/vets/va.htm.

North Carolina Veterans Scholarships Class II. Awards for children of veterans rated by USDVA as much as 20 percent but less than 100 percent disabled due to wartime service as defined in the law, or awarded Purple Heart Medal for wounds received. Parent must have been a North Carolina resident at time of entry into service. Duration of the scholarship is four academic years (8 semesters) if used within 8 years. Free tuition and exemption from certain mandatory fees as set forth in the law in Public, Community and Technical Colleges. *Award:* Scholarship for use in freshman, sophomore, junior, or senior years; renewable. *Award amount:* $4500. *Number of awards:* up to 100. *Eligibility Requirements:* Applicant must be enrolled or expecting to enroll full- or part-time at a two-year or four-year or technical institution or university; resident of North Carolina and studying in North Carolina. Available to U.S. citizens. Applicant or parent must meet one or more of the following requirements: general military experience; retired from active duty; disabled or killed as a result of military service; prisoner of war; or missing in action. *Application Requirements:* Application form, financial need analysis, interview, transcript. **Deadline:** March 1.

Contact Charles Smith, Assistant Secretary. *E-mail:* charlie.smith@ncmail. net. *Phone:* 919-733-3851. *Fax:* 919-733-2834. *Website:* http://www.doa.state.nc. us/vets/va.htm.

North Carolina Veterans Scholarships Class III. Awards for children of a deceased war veteran, who was honorably discharged and who does not qualify under any other provision within this synopsis or veteran who served in a combat zone or waters adjacent to a combat zone and received a campaign badge or medal and who does not qualify under any other provision within this synopsis. Duration of the scholarship is four academic years (8 semesters) if used within 8 years. *Award:* Scholarship for use in freshman, sophomore, junior, or senior years; renewable. *Award amount:* $4500. *Number of awards:* up to 100. *Eligibility Requirements:* Applicant must be enrolled or expecting to enroll full- or part-time at a two-year or four-year or technical institution or university; resident of North Carolina and studying in North Carolina. Available to U.S. citizens. Applicant or parent must meet one or more of the following requirements: general military experience; retired from active duty; disabled or killed as a result of military service; prisoner of war; or missing in action. *Application Requirements:* Application form, financial need analysis, interview, transcript. **Deadline:** March 1.

Contact Charles Smith, Assistant Secretary. *E-mail:* charlie.smith@ncmail. net. *Phone:* 919-733-3851. *Fax:* 919-733-2834. *Website:* http://www.doa.state.nc. us/vets/va.htm.

North Carolina Veterans Scholarships Class IV. Awards for children of veterans, who were prisoner of war or missing in action. Duration of the scholarship is four academic years (8 semesters) if used within 8 years. No limit on number awarded each year. Award value is $4500 per nine-month academic year in private colleges and junior colleges. *Award:* Scholarship for use in freshman, sophomore, junior, or senior years; renewable. *Award amount:* $4500. *Eligibility Requirements:* Applicant must be enrolled or expecting to enroll full- or part-time at a two-year or four-year or technical institution or university; resident of North Carolina and studying in North Carolina. Available to U.S. citizens. Applicant or parent must meet one or more of the following requirements: general military experience; retired from active duty; disabled or killed as a result of military service; prisoner of war; or missing in action. *Application Requirements:* Application form, financial need analysis, interview, transcript. **Deadline:** continuous.

Contact Charles Smith, Assistant Secretary. *E-mail:* charlie.smith@ncmail. net. *Phone:* 919-733-3851. *Fax:* 919-733-2834. *Website:* http://www.doa.state.nc. us/vets/va.htm.

Teacher Assistant Scholarship Fund. Funding to attend a public or private four-year college or university in North Carolina with an approved teacher education program. Applicant must be employed full-time as a teacher assistant in an instructional area while pursuing licensure and maintain employment to remain eligible. Must have at least 3.0 cumulative GPA. Refer to web site for further details http://www.ncseaa.edu/tas. htm. Education. *Award:* Scholarship for use in freshman, sophomore, junior, or senior years; renewable. *Award amount:* $600–$3600. *Eligibility Requirements:* Applicant must be enrolled or expecting to enroll full- or part-time at a four-year institution or university; resident of North Carolina and studying in North Carolina. Applicant or parent of applicant must have employment or volunteer experience in teaching/education. Applicant must have 3.0 GPA or higher. Available to U.S. citizens. *Application Requirements:* Application form, FAFSA, financial need analysis, transcript. **Deadline:** March 31.

Contact Rashonn Albritton, Processing Assistant, North Carolina State Education Assistance Authority, PO Box 13663, Research Triangle Park, NC 27709. *E-mail:* ralbritton@ncseaa.edu. *Phone:* 919-549-8614. *Fax:* 919-248-4687. *Website:* http://www.ncseaa.edu/.

Training Support for Youth with Disabilities. Public service program that helps persons with disabilities obtain competitive employment. To qualify, student must have a mental, physical, or learning disability that is an impediment to employment. A Rehabilitation Counselor along with the eligible student individually develops a rehabilitation program to achieve an employment outcome which requires post secondary training. Financial assistance is based on NC Division of Vocational Rehabilitation demonstrated financial need and type of program in which the student enrolls. *Award:* Grant for use in freshman, sophomore, junior, or senior years; renewable. *Eligibility Requirements:* Applicant must be hearing impaired, learning disabled, physically disabled, or visually impaired; enrolled or expecting to enroll full- or part-time at a two-year or four-year or technical institution or university and resident of North Carolina. Applicant must be hearing impaired, learning disabled, physically disabled, or visually impaired. Available to U.S. citizens. *Application Requirements:* Application form, financial need analysis, interview, medical and psychological records, must be under an Individualized Plan for Employment, test scores, transcript. **Deadline:** continuous.

Contact Alice Farrar, Program Specialist for Transition. *E-mail:* alice. farrar@dhhs.nc.gov. *Phone:* 919-855-3572. *Website:* http://www.dhhs.state.nc. us/.

University of North Carolina Need-Based Grant. Applicants must be enrolled in at least 6 credit hours at one of sixteen UNC system universities. Eligibility based on need; award varies, consideration for grant automatic when FAFSA is filed. Late applications may be denied due to insufficient funds. *Award:* Grant for use in freshman, sophomore, junior, or senior years; renewable. *Eligibility Requirements:* Applicant must be enrolled or expecting to enroll full- or part-time at an institution or university; resident of North Carolina and studying in North Carolina. Available to U.S. citizens. *Application Requirements:* Application form, FAFSA, financial need analysis. **Deadline:** varies.

Contact Bill Carswell, Manager of Scholarship and Grant Division, North Carolina State Education Assistance Authority, PO Box 13663, Research Triangle Park, NC 27709. *E-mail:* carswellb@ncseaa.edu. *Phone:* 919-549-8614. *Fax:* 919-248-4687. *Website:* http://www.ncseaa.edu/.

University of North Carolina Need-Based Grant. Grants available for eligible students attending one of the 16 campuses of the University of North Carolina. Students must be enrolled in at least 6 credit hours at one of the 16 constituent institutions of The University of North Carolina. Award amounts vary based on legislative appropriations. *Award:* Grant for use in freshman, sophomore, junior, or senior years; not renewable. *Eligibility Requirements:* Applicant must be enrolled or expecting to enroll full- or part-time at a four-year institution or university; resident of North Carolina and studying in North Carolina. Available to U.S. citizens. *Application Requirements:* Financial need analysis. **Deadline:** continuous.

NORTH DAKOTA

North Dakota Academic Scholarship. The ND Academic Scholarships goal is to reward students for taking rigorous high school courses and to retain students in ND. The scholarship has an ACT test score and GPA requirement, and requires students to complete specific high school courses. The scholarship is jointly administered with the Department of Public Instruction (DPI). DPI verifies eligibility, and the ND University System disburses funds and verifies continued eligibility. Students must be enrolled full-time and must maintain a cumulative GPA of 2.75 or higher. *Award:* Scholarship for use in freshman, sophomore, junior, or senior years; renewable. *Award amount:* $6000. *Number of awards:* up to 10,000. *Eligibility Requirements:* Applicant must be high school student; planning to enroll or expecting to enroll full-time at a two-year or four-year institution or university; resident of North Dakota and studying in North Dakota. Applicant must have 3.0 GPA or higher. Available to U.S. citizens. *Application Requirements:* Application form, application form may be submitted online(https://www.dpi.state.nd.us/DPI/Scholarship/Login.aspx?ReturnUrl=%2fdpi%2fScholarship%2flogin.aspx%2f), test scores, transcript. **Deadline:** June 7.

Contact Gina Padilla, Assistant Director of Financial Aid, North Dakota University System, 1815 Schafer Street, Suite 202, Bismarck, ND 58501. *E-mail:* ndfinaid@ndus.edu. *Phone:* 701-224-2647. *Website:* http://www.ndus.edu/.

North Dakota Career and Technical Education Scholarship. The ND Career and Technical Education Scholarship's goal is to reward students taking rigorous courses in high school, to increase awareness of career and technical programs, and to retain students in ND. The scholarship has an ACT or WorkKeys exam score requirement, a GPA requirement, and a specific high school course list that must be completed to qualify. The scholarships are jointly administered with the Department of Public Instruction (DPI). DPI verifies eligibility requirements, and the ND University System disburses funds and verifies continued eligibility. Students must be enrolled full-time and cumulative GPA must be 2.75 or higher. *Award:* Scholarship for use in freshman, sophomore, junior, or senior years; renewable. *Award amount:* $6000. *Number of awards:* up to 10,000. *Eligibility Requirements:* Applicant must be high school student; planning to enroll or expecting to enroll full-time at a two-year or four-year institution or university; resident of North Dakota and studying in North Dakota. Applicant must have 3.0 GPA or higher. Available to U.S. citizens. *Application Requirements:* Application form, application form may be submitted online(https://www.dpi.state.nd.us/DPI/Scholarship/Login.aspx?ReturnUrl=%2fdpi%2fScholarship%2flogin.aspx%2f), test scores, transcript. **Deadline:** June 7.

Contact Gina Padilla, Assistant Director of Financial Aid, North Dakota University System, 1815 Schafer Street, Suite 202, Bismarck, ND 58501. *E-mail:* ndfinaid@ndus.edu. *Phone:* 701-224-2647. *Website:* http://www.ndus.edu/.

North Dakota Indian Scholarship Program. Award of $800 to $2000 per year to assist American Indian students who are North Dakota residents in obtaining a college education. Must have been accepted for admission at an institution of higher learning or state vocational education program within North Dakota. Based upon scholastic ability and unmet financial need. Minimum 2.0 GPA required. *Award:* Scholarship for use in freshman, sophomore, junior, senior, graduate, or postgraduate years; renewable. *Award amount:* $800–$2000. *Number of awards:* 175–230. *Eligibility Requirements:* Applicant must be American Indian/Alaska Native; enrolled or expecting to enroll full- or part-time at a two-year or four-year or technical institution or university; resident of North Dakota and studying in North Dakota. Available to U.S. citizens. *Application Requirements:* Application form, financial need analysis, proof of tribal enrollment, budget, transcript. **Deadline:** July 15.

North Dakota Scholars Program. Provides scholarships equal to cost of tuition at the public colleges in North Dakota for North Dakota residents. To be eligible for consideration for a ND Scholars scholarship, a high school junior must take the ACT Assessment between October and June of their junior year and score in the upper five percentile of all ND ACT test takers. The numeric sum of the English, Math, reading and science reasoning scores will be used as a second selection criteria. The numeric sum of a student's English and mathematics scores will be used as selection criteria if a tie-breaker is needed. *Award:* Scholarship for use in freshman, sophomore, junior, or senior years; renewable. *Award amount:* $4588–$8135. *Number of awards:* 45–50. *Eligibility Requirements:* Applicant must be high school student; planning to enroll or expecting to enroll full-time at a two-year or four-year institution or university; resident of North Dakota and studying in North Dakota. Available to U.S. citizens. *Application Requirements:* No application required, test scores.

North Dakota State Student Incentive Grant Program. The North Dakota State Grant supports North Dakota residents attending an approved college or university in North Dakota. Must be enrolled in a program of at least nine months in length. Must be a U.S. citizen. Completing the FAFSA is the only application required. *Award:* Grant for use in freshman, sophomore, junior, or senior years; not renewable. *Award amount:* $750–$1500. *Number of awards:* 7500–8500. *Eligibility Requirements:* Applicant must be enrolled or expecting to enroll full-time at a two-year or four-year institution or university; resident of North Dakota and studying in North Dakota. Available to U.S. citizens. *Application Requirements:* Financial need analysis, submit a FAFSA. **Deadline:** April 15.

OHIO

Ohio College Opportunity Grant. OCOG provides grant money to Ohio residents who demonstrate the highest levels of financial need (as determined by the results of the FAFSA) who are enrolled at Ohio public university main campuses (not regional campuses or community colleges), Ohio private, non-profit colleges or universities, Ohio private, for-profit institutions or eligible Pennsylvania institutions. *Award:* Grant for use in freshman, sophomore, junior, or senior years; not renewable. *Award amount:* up to $2280. *Eligibility Requirements:* Applicant must be enrolled or expecting to enroll full- or part-time at a two-year or four-year institution or university; resident of Ohio and studying in Ohio, Pennsylvania. Available to U.S. citizens. *Application Requirements:* Application form may be submitted online (http://www.fafsa.ed.gov/), FAFSA. **Deadline:** October 1.

Contact Tamika Braswell, Program Manager, Ohio Board of Regents, Ohio Board of Regents, 25 South Front Street, Columbus, OH 43215. *E-mail:* ocog_admin@regents.state.oh.us. *Phone:* 614-728-8862. *Fax:* 614-752-5903. *Website:* http://www.ohiohighered.org.

Ohio Environmental Science & Engineering Scholarships. Merit-based, non-renewable, tuition-only scholarships awarded to undergraduate students admitted to Ohio state or private colleges and universities. Must be able to demonstrate knowledge of, and commitment to, careers in environmental sciences or environmental engineering. Environmental Science. *Award:* Scholarship for use in senior year; not renewable. *Award amount:* $1250–$2500. *Number of awards:* 18. *Eligibility Requirements:* Applicant must be enrolled or expecting to enroll full- or part-time at a two-year or four-year institution or university and studying in Ohio. Applicant must have 3.0 GPA or higher. Available to U.S. citizens. *Application Requirements:* Application form, community service, essay, recommendations or references, resume, self-addressed stamped envelope with application, transcript. **Deadline:** June 1.

Contact Dr. Lynn Elfner, Chief Executive Officer, Ohio Academy of Science/Ohio Environmental Education Fund, 1500 West Third Avenue, Suite 228, Columbus, OH 43212-2817. *E-mail:* oas@iwaynet.net. *Phone:* 614-488-2228. *Fax:* 614-488-7629. *Website:* http://www.ohiosci.org/.

Ohio National Guard Scholarship Program. Scholarships are for undergraduate studies at an approved Ohio post-secondary institution. Applicants must enlist for six or three years of Selective Service Reserve Duty in the Ohio National Guard. Scholarship pays 100% instructional and general fees for public institutions and an average of cost of public universities is available for private schools. May reapply up to four years of studies (12 quarters or 8 semesters) for six year enlistment and two years of studies (6 quarters or 4 semesters) for three year enlistment. Deadlines: July 1 (fall), November 1 (winter quarter/spring semester), February 1 (spring quarter), April 1 (summer). *Award:* Scholarship for use in freshman, sophomore, junior, or senior years; not renewable. *Award amount:* up to $4006. *Number of awards:* up to 3500. *Eligibility Requirements:* Applicant must be enrolled or expecting to enroll full- or part-time at a two-year or four-year or technical institution or university; resident of Ohio and studying in Ohio. Available to U.S. citizens. Applicant must have national guard experience. *Application Requirements:* Application form. **Deadline:** varies.

Contact Mrs. Toni Davis, Grants Administrator, Ohio National Guard, 2825 West Dublin Granville Road, ONGSP, Columbus, OH 43235-2789. *E-mail:* toni.davis7@us.army.mil. *Phone:* 614-336-7143. *Fax:* 614-336-7318. *Website:* http://www.ongsp.org/.

Ohio Safety Officers College Memorial Fund. Renewable award covering up to full tuition is available to children and surviving spouses of peace officers, other safety officers and fire fighters killed in the line of duty in any state. Children must be under 26 years of age. Dollar value of each award varies. Must be an Ohio resident and enroll full-time or part-time at an Ohio college or university. Any spouse/child of a member of the armed services of the U.S., who has been killed in the line duty during Operation Enduring Freedom, Operation Iraqi Freedom or a combat zone designated by the President of the United States. Dollar value of each award varies. *Award:* Scholarship for use in freshman, sophomore, junior, or senior years; renewable. *Eligibility Requirements:* Applicant must be enrolled or expecting to enroll full- or part-time at a two-year or four-year institution or university; resident of Ohio and studying in Ohio. Available to U.S. citizens. *Application Requirements:* **Deadline:** continuous.

Contact Barbara Thoma, Assistant Director, Ohio Board of Regents, 30 East Broad Street, 36th Floor, Columbus, OH 43215. *E-mail:* osom_admin@regents.state.oh.us. *Phone:* 614-752-9535. *Fax:* 614-752-5903. *Website:* http://www.ohiohighered.org.

Ohio War Orphans Scholarship. Aids Ohio residents attending an eligible college in Ohio. Must be between the ages of 16 and 25, the child of a disabled or deceased veteran, and enrolled full-time. Renewable up to five years. Amount of award varies. Must include Form DD214. *Award:* Scholarship for use in freshman, sophomore, junior, or senior years; renewable. *Eligibility Requirements:* Applicant must be age 16-25; enrolled or expecting to enroll full-time at a two-year or four-year institution or university; resident of Ohio and studying in Ohio. Available to U.S. citizens. Applicant or parent must meet one or more of the following requirements: general military experience; retired from active duty; disabled or killed as a result of military service; prisoner of war; or missing in action. *Application Requirements:* Application form, Form DD214. **Deadline:** July 1.

Contact Amber Brady, Program Manager, Ohio Board of Regents, Ohio Board of Regents, 25 South Front Street, Columbus, OH 43215. *E-mail:* wo_admin@regents.state.oh.us. *Phone:* 614-752-9528. *Fax:* 614-752-5903. *Website:* http://www.ohiohighered.org.

T.E.A.C.H. Early Childhood OHIO Scholarships. Award for early childhood professionals working in Ohio. AAS Scholarships available. Must earn under $15/hr and work 30 hours per week with children in licensed child care or preschool. Child and Family Studies; Education. *Award:* Scholarship for use in freshman, sophomore, junior, or senior years; renewable. *Eligibility Requirements:* Applicant must be enrolled or expecting to enroll full- or part-time at a two-year or four-year institution; resident of Ohio and studying in Ohio. Available to U.S. citizens. *Application Requirements:* Application form.

Contact Greg Yorker, Director. *E-mail:* teach@occrra.org. *Website:* http://www.occrra.org/.

OKLAHOMA

Academic Scholars Program. Awards for students of high academic ability to attend institutions in Oklahoma. Renewable up to four years. ACT or SAT scores must fall between 99.5 and 100th percentiles, or applicant must be designated as a National Merit scholar or finalist. Oklahoma public institutions can also select institutional nominees. *Award:* Scholarship for use in freshman, sophomore, junior, senior, or graduate years; renewable. *Award amount:* $1800–5500. *Eligibility Requirements:* Applicant must be high school student; planning to enroll or expecting to enroll full-time at a two-year or four-year institution or university and studying in Oklahoma. Available to U.S. citizens. *Application Requirements:* Application form, test scores, transcript. **Deadline:** continuous.

Future Teacher Scholarship-Oklahoma. Open to outstanding Oklahoma high school graduates who agree to teach in shortage areas. Must rank in top 15 percent of graduating class or score above 85th percentile on ACT or similar test, or be accepted in an educational program. Students nominated by institution. Reapply to renew. Must attend college/university in Oklahoma. Education. *Award:* Scholarship for use in freshman, sophomore, junior, senior, or graduate years; not renewable. *Award amount:* $500–$1500. *Eligibility Requirements:* Applicant must be enrolled or expecting to enroll full- or part-time at a two-year or four-year institution or university; resident of Oklahoma and studying in Oklahoma. Available to U.S. citizens. *Application Requirements:* Application form, essay, test scores, transcript. **Deadline:** varies.

Oklahoma Tuition Aid Grant. Award for Oklahoma residents enrolled at an Oklahoma institution at least part time each semester in a degree program. May be enrolled in two- or four-year or approved vocational-technical institution. Award for students attending public institutions or private colleges. Application is made through FAFSA. *Award:* Grant for use in freshman, sophomore, junior, or senior years; not renewable. *Award amount:* $1000–$1300. *Eligibility Requirements:* Applicant must be enrolled or expecting to enroll full- or part-time at a two-year or four-year or technical institution or university; resident of Oklahoma and studying in Oklahoma. Available to U.S. citizens. *Application Requirements:* Application form, FAFSA, financial need analysis. **Deadline:** varies.

Contact Mr. Chris Wadsworth, Scholarship Programs Coordinator. *E-mail:* cwadsworth@osrhe.edu. *Phone:* 405-225-9131. *Website:* http://www.okhighered.org/.

Regional University Baccalaureate Scholarship. Renewable award for Oklahoma residents attending one of 11 participating Oklahoma public universities. Must have an ACT composite score of at least 30 or be a National Merit semi-

finalist or commended student. In addition to the award amount, each recipient will receive a resident tuition waiver from the institution. Must maintain a 3.25 GPA. Deadlines vary depending upon the institution attended. *Award:* Scholarship for use in freshman, sophomore, junior, or senior years; renewable. *Award amount:* $3000. *Eligibility Requirements:* Applicant must be enrolled or expecting to enroll full-time at an institution or university; resident of Oklahoma and studying in Oklahoma. Available to U.S. citizens. *Application Requirements:* Application form. **Deadline:** varies.

OREGON

American Legion Auxiliary Department of Oregon Department Grants. One-time award for educational use in the state of Oregon. Must be a resident of Oregon who is the child or widow of a veteran or the wife of a disabled veteran. *Award:* Grant for use in freshman, sophomore, junior, or senior years; not renewable. *Award amount:* $1000. *Number of awards:* 2. *Eligibility Requirements:* Applicant must be enrolled or expecting to enroll full- or part-time at a two-year or four-year or technical institution or university and resident of Oregon. Available to U.S. citizens. Applicant or parent must meet one or more of the following requirements: general military experience; retired from active duty; disabled or killed as a result of military service; prisoner of war; or missing in action. *Application Requirements:* Application form, essay, financial need analysis, interview, recommendations or references, test scores, transcript. **Deadline:** March 10.

Contact Virginia Biddle, Secretary/Treasurer, American Legion Auxiliary Department of Oregon, PO Box 1730, Wilsonville, OR 97070. *E-mail:* alaor@pcez.com. *Phone:* 503-682-3162. *Fax:* 503-685-5008. *Website:* http://www.alaoregon.org/.

American Legion Auxiliary Department of Oregon Nurses Scholarship. One-time award for Oregon residents who are in their senior year of High School, who are the children of veterans who served during eligibility dates for American Legion membership. Must enroll in a nursing program. Contact local units for application. Nursing. *Award:* Scholarship for use in freshman year; not renewable. *Award amount:* $1500. *Number of awards:* 1. *Eligibility*

Requirements: Applicant must be high school student; planning to cnroll or expecting to enroll full- or part-time at a four-year institution or university and resident of Oregon. Available to U.S. citizens. Applicant or parent must meet one or more of the following requirements: general military experience; retired from active duty; disabled or killed as a result of military service; prisoner of war; or missing in action. *Application Requirements:* Application form, essay, financial need analysis, interview, transcript. **Deadline:** May 15.

Contact Virginia Biddle, Secretary/Treasurer, American Legion Auxiliary Department of Oregon, PO Box 1730, Wilsonville, OR 97070. *E-mail:* alaor@pcez.com. *Phone:* 503-682-3162. *Fax:* 503-685-5008. *Website:* http://www.alaoregon.org/.

Better A Life Scholarship. Scholarship award available to single parents age 17-25. High schools seniors must have at least 3.0 GPA and college students must have at least a 2.5 GPA. For use at Oregon public and nonprofit colleges and universities. Applicants may not already possess a bachelor's degree. May reapply for one additional year of funding. *Award:* Scholarship for use in freshman, sophomore, junior, or senior years; not renewable. *Eligibility Requirements:* Applicant must be age 17-25; enrolled or expecting to enroll full- or part-time at a two-year or four-year institution or university; single and studying in Oregon. Available to U.S. citizens. *Application Requirements:* Application form, FAFSA, transcript. **Deadline:** March 1.

Dorothy Campbell Memorial Scholarship. Renewable award for female Oregon high school graduates with a minimum 2.75 GPA. Must submit essay describing strong, continuing interest in golf and the contribution that sport has made to applicant's development. Must have played on high school golf team (including intramural), if available. *Award:* Scholarship for use in freshman, sophomore, junior, or senior years; renewable. *Eligibility Requirements:* Applicant must be enrolled or expecting to enroll full-time at a four-year institution; female; resident of Oregon; studying in Oregon and must have an interest in golf. Available to U.S. citizens. *Application Requirements:* Application form, essay, financial need analysis, transcript. **Deadline:** March 1.

Glenn Jackson Scholars Scholarships. Renewable award for Oregon graduating high school seniors who are dependents of employees or retirees of Oregon Department of Transportation or Parks and Recreation Department. Employees must have worked in their department at least three years as of the March 1 scholarship deadline. *Award:* Scholarship for use in freshman, sophomore, junior, or senior years; renewable. *Eligibility Requirements:* Applicant must be high school student; planning to enroll or expecting to enroll full- or part-time at a two-year or four-year institution or university and resident of Oregon. Applicant or parent of applicant must be affiliated with Oregon Department of Transportation Parks and Recreation. Available to U.S. citizens. *Application Requirements:* Activity chart, application form, essay, financial need analysis, recommendations or references, transcript. **Deadline:** March 1.

Laurence R. Foster Memorial Scholarship. One-time award to students enrolled or planning to enroll in a public health degree program. First preference given to those working in the public health field and those pursuing a graduate degree in public health. Undergraduates entering junior or senior year health programs may apply if seeking a public health career, and not private practice. Applicants from diverse cultures preferred. Additional essays required. Public Health. *Award:* Scholarship for use in freshman, sophomore, junior, or senior years; renewable. *Eligibility Requirements:* Applicant must be enrolled or expecting to enroll full- or part-time at a four-year institution. Available to U.S. citizens. *Application Requirements:* Activity chart, application form, essay, financial need analysis, recommendations or references, transcript. **Deadline:** March 1.

Oregon Scholarship Fund Community College Student Award. Scholarship open to students enrolled or planning to enroll at least half time in Oregon community college programs. Recipients may reapply for one additional year. FAFSA is required. *Award:* Scholarship for use in freshman or sophomore years; not renewable. *Eligibility Requirements:* Applicant must be enrolled or expecting to enroll full- or part-time at a two-year institution and studying in Oregon. Available to U.S. citizens. *Application Requirements:* Activity chart, FAFSA, application form, essay, financial need analysis, transcript. **Deadline:** March 1.

Oregon Scholarship Fund Transfer Student Award. Award open to Oregon residents who are currently enrolled in their second year at an Oregon community college and are planning to transfer to a four-year college in Oregon. Prior recipients may apply for one additional year. Must enroll at least half-time. FAFSA is required. *Award:* Scholarship for use in junior or senior years; not renewable. *Eligibility Requirements:* Applicant must be enrolled or expecting to enroll full- or part-time at a four-year institution or university; resident of Oregon and studying in Oregon. Available to U.S. citizens. *Application Requirements:* Activity chart, FAFSA, application form, essay, financial need analysis, transcript. **Deadline:** March 1.

Oregon Trucking Association Safety Management Council Scholarship. One-time award available to a child of an Oregon Trucking Association member, or child of an employee of OTA member. Applicants must be graduating high school seniors from an Oregon high school planning to attend a public or non-profit college or university. Oregon residency is not required. *Award:* Scholarship for use in freshman year; not renewable. *Eligibility Requirements:* Applicant must be high school student and planning to enroll or expecting to enroll full-time at a four-year institution. Applicant or parent of applicant must be affiliated with Oregon Trucking Association. Available to U.S. citizens. *Application Requirements:* Activity chart, application form, essay, financial need analysis, recommendations or references, transcript. **Deadline:** March 1.

Oregon Veterans' Education Aid. To be eligible, veteran must have actively served in U.S. armed forces 90 days and been discharged under honorable conditions. Must be U.S. citizen and Oregon resident. Korean War veteran or received campaign or expeditionary medal or ribbon awarded by U.S. armed forces for services after June 30, 1958. Full-time students receive up to $150 per month, and part-time students receive up to $100 per month for a maximum of 36 months. Length of benefits depend on length of service. Payments contingent upon available funding. *Award:* Grant for use in freshman, sophomore, junior, senior, graduate, or postgraduate years; not renewable. *Award amount:* $3600–$5400. *Number of awards:* 1–200. *Eligibility Requirements:* Applicant must be enrolled or expecting to enroll full- or part-time at a two-year or four-year or technical institution or university; resident of Oregon and studying in Oregon. Available to U.S. citizens. Applicant must have general military experience. *Application Require-*

ments: Application form, certified copy of DD Form 214. **Deadline:** continuous.

Contact Loriann Sheridan, Veterans Programs Consultant, Oregon Department of Veterans' Affairs, 700 Summer Street, NE, Salem, OR 97301-1289. *E-mail:* sheridl@odva.state.or.us. *Phone:* 503-373-2264. *Fax:* 503-373-2393. *Website:* http://www.oregon.gov/odva.

Peter Connacher Memorial Scholarship. Renewable award for American prisoners-of-war and their descendants. Written proof of prisoner-of-war status and discharge papers from the U.S. Armed Forces must accompany application. Statement of relationship between applicant and former prisoner-of-war is required. Oregon residency preferred but not required. *Award:* Scholarship for use in freshman, sophomore, junior, senior, or graduate years; renewable. *Eligibility Requirements:* Applicant must be enrolled or expecting to enroll full-time at a two-year or four-year institution. Available to U.S. citizens. Applicant or parent must meet one or more of the following requirements: general military experience; retired from active duty; disabled or killed as a result of military service; prisoner of war; or missing in action. *Application Requirements:* Application form, essay, financial need analysis, military discharge papers, documentation of POW status , transcript. **Deadline:** March 1.

PENNSYLVANIA

Pennsylvania State Grant. Award for Pennsylvania residents attending an approved postsecondary institution as undergraduates in a program of at least two years duration. Renewable for up to eight semesters if applicants show continued need and academic progress. Must submit FAFSA. Number of awards granted varies annually. Scholarship value is $200 to $4348. Deadlines: May 1 and August 1. *Award:* Grant for use in freshman, sophomore, junior, or senior years; renewable. *Award amount:* $200–$4348. *Eligibility Requirements:* Applicant must be enrolled or expecting to enroll full- or part-time at a two-year or four-year or technical institution or university and resident of Pennsylvania. Available to U.S. citizens. *Application Requirements:* Application form, application form may be submitted online (http://pheaa.org/funding-opportunities/state-grant-program/index.shtml), FAFSA, financial need analysis. **Deadline:** varies.

Contact Keith New, Director of Public Relations, Pennsylvania Higher Education Assistance Agency, 1200 North Seventh Street, Harrisburg, PA 17102-1444. *Phone:* 717-720-2509. *Fax:* 717-720-3903. *Website:* http://www.pheaa.org/.

Postsecondary Education Gratuity Program. The program offers waiver of tuition and fees for children of Pennsylvania police officers, firefighters, rescue or ambulance squad members, corrections facility employees, or National Guard members who died in line of duty after January 1, 1976. *Award:* Grant for use in freshman, sophomore, junior, or senior years; renewable. *Eligibility Requirements:* Applicant must be enrolled or expecting to enroll full-time at a two-year or four-year institution or university; resident of Pennsylvania and studying in Pennsylvania. Available to U.S. citizens. Applicant or parent must meet one or more of the following requirements: national guard experience; retired from active duty; disabled or killed as a result of military service; prisoner of war; or missing in action. *Application Requirements:* Application form. **Deadline:** August 1.

Contact Keith New, Director of Public Relations. *E-mail:* knew@pheaa.org. *Phone:* 717-720-2509. *Website:* http://www.pheaa.org/.

RHODE ISLAND

Rhode Island State Grant Program. Grants for residents of Rhode Island attending an accredited, Title-IV approved post secondary undergraduate program in the United States, Canada, or Mexico. Based on need as reported by the student and his or her family on the Free Application for Federal Student Aid (FAFSA). Renewable for up to four years if in good academic standing and student continues to meet financial need requirements. *Award:* Grant for use in freshman, sophomore, junior, or senior years; not renewable. *Award amount:* $250–$700. *Number of awards:* 10,000–20,000. *Eligibility Requirements:* Applicant must be enrolled or expecting to enroll full- or part-time at a two-year or four-year or technical institution or university and resident of Rhode Island. Available to U.S. citizens. *Application Requirements:* Application form, application form may be submitted online (http://www.fafsa.edu.gov), financial need analysis. **Deadline:** March 1.

Contact Mr. Michael Joyce, Director of Program Administration, Rhode Island

Higher Education Assistance Authority, 560 Jefferson Boulevard, Suite 100, Warwick, RI 02886. *E-mail:* grants@riheaa.org. *Phone:* 401-736-1170. *Fax:* 401-736-1178. *Website:* http://www.riheaa.org/.

SOUTH CAROLINA

Educational Assistance for Certain War Veterans Dependents Scholarship-South Carolina. Free tuition for South Carolina residents whose parent is a resident, wartime veteran, and meets one of these criteria; awarded Purple Heart or Congressional Medal of Honor; permanently and totally disabled or killed as a result of military service; prisoner of war; or missing in action. Must be age 18?26 and enrolled or expecting to enroll full or part-time at a two-year or four-year technical institution or university in South Carolina. Complete information and qualifications for this award are on web site http://www.govoepp.state.sc.us. *Award:* Scholarship for use in freshman, sophomore, junior, or senior years; not renewable. *Eligibility Requirements:* Applicant must be age 18-26; enrolled or expecting to enroll full- or part-time at a two-year or four-year or technical institution or university; resident of South Carolina and studying in South Carolina. Available to U.S. citizens. Applicant or parent must meet one or more of the following requirements: general military experience; retired from active duty; disabled or killed as a result of military service; prisoner of war; or missing in action. *Application Requirements:* Application form, proof of qualification of veteran, transcript. **Deadline:** continuous.

Contact Dianne Coley, Free Tuition Program Assistant. *E-mail:* va@oepp.sc.gov. *Phone:* 803-647-2434. *Website:* http://www.govoepp.state.sc.us/vetaff.htm.

Palmetto Fellows Scholarship Program. Renewable award for qualified high school seniors in South Carolina to attend a four-year South Carolina institution. The scholarship must be applied directly towards the cost of attendance, less any other gift aid received. *Award:* Scholarship for use in freshman year; renewable. *Award amount:* $6700–$7500. *Number of awards:* 4846. *Eligibility Requirements:* Applicant must be high school student; planning to enroll or expecting to enroll full-time at a four-year institution or university; resident of South Carolina and studying in South Carolina. Applicant must have 3.5 GPA or higher.

Available to U.S. citizens. *Application Requirements:* Application form, test scores, transcript. **Deadline:** December 15.

Contact Dr. Karen Woodfaulk, Director of Student Services, South Carolina Commission on Higher Education, 1333 Main Street, Suite 200, Columbia, SC 29201. *E-mail:* kwoodfaulk@che.sc.gov. *Phone:* 803-737-2244. *Fax:* 803-737-3610. *Website:* http://www.che.sc.gov/.

Robert C. Byrd Honors Scholarship-South Carolina. Renewable award for a graduating high school senior from South Carolina, who will be attending a two- or four-year institution. Applicants should be superior students who demonstrate academic achievement and show promise of continued success at a postsecondary institution. Interested applicants should contact their high school counselors after the first week of December for an application. *Award:* Scholarship for use in freshman year; renewable. *Eligibility Requirements:* Applicant must be high school student; planning to enroll or expecting to enroll full-time at a two-year or four-year institution or university and resident of South Carolina. Available to U.S. citizens. *Application Requirements:* ACT or SAT scores, application form, test scores. **Deadline:** varies.

Contact Beth Cope, Program Coordinator, South Carolina Department of Education, 1424 Senate Street, Columbia, SC 29201. *E-mail:* bcope@sde.state.sc.us. *Phone:* 803-734-8116. *Fax:* 803-734-4387. *Website:* http://www.ed.sc.gov/.

South Carolina HOPE Scholarship. A merit-based scholarship for eligible first-time entering freshman attending a four-year South Carolina institution. Minimum GPA of 3.0 required. Must be a resident of South Carolina. *Award:* Scholarship for use in freshman year; not renewable. *Award amount:* $2800. *Number of awards:* 2605. *Eligibility Requirements:* Applicant must be high school student; planning to enroll or expecting to enroll full-time at a four-year institution or university; resident of South Carolina and studying in South Carolina. Applicant must have 3.0 GPA or higher. Available to U.S. citizens. *Application Requirements:* Transcript. **Deadline:** continuous.

Contact Gerrick Hampton, Scholarship Coordinator, South Carolina Commission on Higher Education, 1333 Main Street, Suite 200, Columbia, SC 29201. *E-mail:*

ghampton@che.sc.gov. *Phone:* 803-737-4544. *Fax:* 803-737-3610. *Website:* http://www.che.sc.gov/.

South Carolina Need-Based Grants Program. Award based on FAFSA. A student may receive up to $2500 annually for full-time and up to $1250 annually for part-time study. The grant must be applied directly towards the cost of college attendance for a maximum of eight full-time equivalent terms. *Award:* Grant for use in freshman, sophomore, junior, senior, or graduate years; renewable. *Award amount:* $1250–$2500. *Number of awards:* 1–26,730. *Eligibility Requirements:* Applicant must be enrolled or expecting to enroll full- or part-time at a two-year or four-year or technical institution or university; resident of South Carolina and studying in South Carolina. Available to U.S. citizens. *Application Requirements:* Application form, financial need analysis. **Deadline:** continuous.

Contact Dr. Karen Woodfaulk, Director of Student Service, South Carolina Commission on Higher Education, 1333 Main Street, Suite 200, Columbia, SC 29201. *E-mail:* kwoodfaulk@che.sc.gov. *Phone:* 803-737-2244. *Fax:* 803-737-2297. *Website:* http://www.che.sc.gov/.

South Carolina Tuition Grants Program. Need-based grant set aside for 21 eligible independent colleges in South Carolina. Student must be a South Carolina resident. Must apply annually by submitting the Free Application for Federal Student Aid (FAFSA). Freshmen must graduate in top 75% of high school class OR score 900 on SAT/19 on ACT OR graduate with at least 2.0 on SC Uniform Grading Scale. Upperclassmen must pass a minimum of 24 credit hours annually. *Award:* Grant for use in freshman, sophomore, junior, or senior years; not renewable. *Award amount:* $100–$2600. *Eligibility Requirements:* Applicant must be enrolled or expecting to enroll full-time at a two-year or four-year institution or university; resident of South Carolina and studying in South Carolina. Available to U.S. citizens. *Application Requirements:* Application form, FAFSA. **Deadline:** June 30.

Contact Toni Cave, Financial Aid Counselor, South Carolina Tuition Grants Commission, 800 Dutch Square Boulevard, Suite 260A, Columbia, SC 29210. *E-mail:* toni@sctuitiongrants.org. *Phone:* 803-896-1120. *Fax:* 803-896-1126. *Website:* http://www.sctuitiongrants.com/.

SOUTH DAKOTA

South Dakota Opportunity Scholarship. Renewable scholarship may be worth up to $5000 over four years to students who take a rigorous college-prep curriculum while in high school and stay in the state for their postsecondary education. *Award:* Scholarship for use in freshman, sophomore, junior, or senior years; renewable. *Award amount:* $1000. *Number of awards:* 1000. *Eligibility Requirements:* Applicant must be high school student; planning to enroll or expecting to enroll full-time at a two-year or four-year or technical institution or university; resident of South Dakota and studying in South Dakota. Applicant must have 3.0 GPA or higher. Available to U.S. citizens. *Application Requirements:* Application form, test scores, transcript. **Deadline:** September 1.

Contact Janelle Toman, Scholarship Committee, South Dakota Board of Regents, 306 East Capitol, Suite 200, Pierre, SD 57501-2545. *E-mail:* info@sdbor.edu. *Phone:* 605-773-3455. *Fax:* 605-773-2422. *Website:* http://www.sdbor.edu/.

TENNESSEE

Christa McAuliffe Scholarship Program. Scholarship to assist and support Tennessee students who have demonstrated a commitment to a career in educating the youth of Tennessee. Offered to college seniors for a period of one academic year. Must have a minimum college GPA of 3.5. Must have attained scores on either the ACT or SAT which meet or exceed the national norms. Award is made on a periodic basis as funding becomes available. Education. *Award:* Scholarship for use in senior year; not renewable. *Award amount:* up to $500. *Number of awards:* up to 1. *Eligibility Requirements:* Applicant must be enrolled or expecting to enroll full-time at a four-year institution or university; resident of Tennessee and studying in Tennessee. Applicant must have 3.5 GPA or higher. Available to U.S. citizens. *Application Requirements:* Application form, application form may be submitted online (http://www.tn.gov/collegepays), essay. **Deadline:** April 1.

Contact Ms. Kathy Stripling, Scholarship Administrator, Tennessee Student Assistance Corporation, Parkway Towers, 404 James Robertson Parkway, Suite 1510, Nashville, TN 37243-0820. *E-mail:* kathy.stripling@tn.gov. *Phone:* 615-253-7480. *Fax:* 615-741-6101. *Website:* http://www.tn.gov/collegepays.

Dependent Children Scholarship Program. Scholarship for Tennessee residents who are dependent children of a Tennessee law enforcement officer, fireman, or an emergency medical service technician who have been killed or totally and permanently disabled while performing duties within the scope of such employment. The scholarship is awarded to full-time undergraduate students for a maximum of four academic years or the period required for the completion of the program of study. *Award:* Scholarship for use in freshman, sophomore, junior, or senior years; renewable. *Eligibility Requirements:* Applicant must be enrolled or expecting to enroll full-time at a two-year or four-year institution or university; resident of Tennessee and studying in Tennessee. Available to U.S. citizens. *Application Requirements:* Application form, application form may be submitted online (http://www.tn.gov/collegepays), FAFSA. **Deadline:** July 15.

Contact Ms. Naomi Derryberry, Director of Grant and Scholarship Programs, Tennessee Student Assistance Corporation, Parkway Towers, 404 James Robertson Parkway, Suite 1510, Nashville, TN 37243-0820. *E-mail:* naomi.derryberry@tn.gov. *Phone:* 615-253-7478. *Fax:* 615-741-6101. *Website:* http://www.tn.gov/collegepays.

Helping Heroes Grant. Provides assistance to Tennessee veterans who have been awarded the Iraq Campaign Medal, Afghanistan Campaign Medal, or Global War on Terrorism Expeditionary Medal (on or after 9/11/01) and who meet eligibility requirements for the program. Award is up to $2,000 per year. For more information, visit http://www.TN.gov/collegepays. *Award:* Grant for use in freshman, sophomore, junior, or senior years; not renewable. *Award amount:* up to $2000. *Eligibility Requirements:* Applicant must be enrolled or expecting to enroll full- or part-time at a two-year or four-year institution or university. Available to U.S. citizens. Applicant must have general military experience. *Application Requirements:* Application form, application form may be submitted online (http://www.tn.gov/collegepays), DD-214. **Deadline:** September 1.

Contact Mr. Robert Biggers, Director of Lottery Programs, Tennessee Student Assistance Corporation, Parkway Towers, Suite 1510, 404 James Robertson Parkway, Nashville, TN 37243. *E-mail:* robert.biggers@tn.gov. *Phone:* 615-253-7453. *Fax:* 615-741-6101. *Website:* http://www.tn.gov/collegepays.

HOPE with ASPIRE. HOPE Scholarship of $2000 per semester (four-year institution) or $1000 per semester (two-year institution) with $750 supplement per semester. Must meet Tennessee HOPE Scholarship requirements and Adjusted Gross Income (AGI) attributable to the student must be $36,000 or less. *Award:* Scholarship for use in freshman, sophomore, junior, or senior years; renewable. *Award amount:* up to $5500. *Eligibility Requirements:* Applicant must be enrolled or expecting to enroll full- or part-time at a two-year or four-year institution or university; resident of Tennessee and studying in Tennessee. Applicant must have 3.0 GPA or higher. Available to U.S. citizens. *Application Requirements:* Application form, application form may be submitted online (http://www.fafsa.gov), financial need analysis. **Deadline:** September 1.

Contact Mr. Robert Biggers, Director of Lottery Scholarship Programs, Tennessee Student Assistance Corporation, Parkway Towers, 404 James Robertson Parkway, Suite 1510, Nashville, TN 37243-0820. *E-mail:* robert.biggers@tn.gov. *Phone:* 615-253-7453. *Fax:* 615-741-6101. *Website:* http://www.tn.gov/collegepays.

Ned McWherter Scholars Program. Award for Tennessee high school seniors with high academic ability. Must have minimum high school GPA of 3.5 and a score of 29 on the ACT or SAT equivalent. Must attend a college or university in Tennessee and be a permanent U.S. citizen. For more information, visit web site http://tn.gov/collegepays. *Award:* Scholarship for use in freshman, sophomore, junior, or senior years; renewable. *Award amount:* up to $3000. *Number of awards:* up to 200. *Eligibility Requirements:* Applicant must be enrolled or expecting to enroll full-time at a two-year or four-year or technical institution or university; resident of Tennessee and studying in Tennessee. Applicant must have 3.5 GPA or higher. Available to U.S. citizens. *Application Requirements:* Application form, application form may be submitted online (http://www.tn.gov/collegepays), test scores, transcript. **Deadline:** February 15.

Contact Mrs. Kathy Stripling, Scholarship Administrator, Tennessee Student Assistance Corporation, 404 James Robertson Parkway, Suite 1510, Parkway Towers, Nashville, TN 37243-0820. *E-mail:* kathy.stripling@tn.gov. *Phone:* 615-253-7480. *Fax:* 615-741-

6101. *Website:* http://www.tn.gov/collegepays.

Tennessee Dual Enrollment Grant. Grant for study at an eligible Tennessee postsecondary institution awarded to juniors and seniors in a Tennessee high school who have been admitted to undergraduate study while still pursuing a high school diploma. For more information, visit web site http://www.tn.gov/collegepays. *Award:* Grant for use in freshman year; renewable. *Award amount:* up to $1200. *Eligibility Requirements:* Applicant must be high school student; planning to enroll or expecting to enroll part-time at a two-year or four-year or technical institution or university; resident of Tennessee and studying in Tennessee. Available to U.S. citizens. *Application Requirements:* Application form, application form may be submitted online (http://www.tn.gov/collegepays). **Deadline:** September 1.

Contact Mr. Robert Biggers, Director of Lottery Scholarship Program, Tennessee Student Assistance Corporation, Parkway Towers, 404 James Robertson Parkway, Suite 1510, Nashville, TN 37243-0820. *E-mail:* robert.biggers@tn.gov. *Phone:* 615-253-7453. *Fax:* 615-741-1601. *Website:* http://www.tn.gov/collegepays.

Tennessee Education Lottery Scholarship Program HOPE Access Grant. Non-renewable award of $2750 for students at four-year colleges or $1750 for students at two-year colleges. Entering freshmen must have a minimum GPA of 2.75, ACT score of 18-20 (or SAT equivalent), and adjusted gross income attributable to the student must be $36,000 or less. Recipients will become eligible for Tennessee HOPE Scholarship by meeting HOPE Scholarship renewal criteria. *Award:* Scholarship for use in freshman, sophomore, junior, or senior years; not renewable. *Award amount:* up to $2750. *Eligibility Requirements:* Applicant must be enrolled or expecting to enroll full- or part-time at a two-year or four-year institution or university; resident of Tennessee and studying in Tennessee. Available to U.S. citizens. *Application Requirements:* Application form, application form may be submitted online (http://www.fafsa.gov), financial need analysis. **Deadline:** September 1.

Contact Mr. Robert Biggers, Director of Lottery Scholarship Programs, Tennessee Student Assistance Corporation, Parkway Towers, 404 James Robertson Parkway, Suite 1510, Nashville, TN 37243-0820. *E-mail:*

robert.biggers@tn.gov. *Phone:* 615-253-7453. *Fax:* 615-741-6101. *Website:* http://www.tn.gov/collegepays.

Tennessee Education Lottery Scholarship Program-HOPE with General Assembly Merit Scholarship (GAMS). HOPE Scholarship of $2000 per semester (four-year institution) or $1000 per semester (two-year institution) with supplemental award of $500 per semester. Entering freshmen must have 3.75 GPA and 29 ACT (1280 SAT). Must be a U.S. citizen and a resident of Tennessee. *Award:* Scholarship for use in freshman, sophomore, junior, or senior years; renewable. *Award amount:* up to $5000. *Eligibility Requirements:* Applicant must be enrolled or expecting to enroll full- or part-time at a two-year or four-year institution or university; resident of Tennessee and studying in Tennessee. Available to U.S. citizens. *Application Requirements:* Application form, application form may be submitted online (http://www.fafsa.gov). **Deadline:** September 1.

Contact Mr. Robert Biggers, Director of Lottery Scholarship Programs, Tennessee Student Assistance Corporation, Parkway Towers, 404 James Robertson Parkway, Suite 1510, Nashville, TN 37243-0820. *E-mail:* robert.biggers@tn.gov. *Phone:* 615-253-7453. *Fax:* 615-741-6101. *Website:* http://www.tn.gov/collegepays.

Tennessee Education Lottery Scholarship Program Tennessee HOPE Scholarship. Award amount is $2000 for per semester at four-year institutions and $1000 per semester at two-year institutions. Must be a Tennessee resident attending an eligible postsecondary institution in Tennessee. For more information, visit http://www.TN.gov/CollegePays. *Award:* Scholarship for use in freshman, sophomore, junior, or senior years; renewable. *Award amount:* $2000–$6000. *Eligibility Requirements:* Applicant must be enrolled or expecting to enroll full- or part-time at a two-year or four-year institution or university; resident of Tennessee and studying in Tennessee. Applicant must have 3.0 GPA or higher. Available to U.S. citizens. *Application Requirements:* Application form, application form may be submitted online (http://www.fafsa.gov). **Deadline:** September 1.

Contact Mr. Robert Biggers, Director of Lottery Scholarship Programs, Tennessee Student Assistance Corporation, Parkway Towers, 404 James Robertson Parkway, Suite 1510, Nashville, TN 37243-0820. *E-mail:*

robert.biggers@tn.gov. *Phone:* 615-253-7453. *Fax:* 615-741-6101. *Website:* http://www.tn.gov/collegepays.

Tennessee Education Lottery Scholarship Program Wilder-Naifeh Technical Skills Grant. Award up to $2000 for students enrolled in a certificate or diploma program at a Tennessee Technology Center. Cannot be prior recipient of Tennessee HOPE Scholarship. For more information, visit http://www.TN.gov/CollegePays. *Award:* Grant for use in freshman or sophomore years; renewable. *Award amount:* up to $2000. *Eligibility Requirements:* Applicant must be enrolled or expecting to enroll full- or part-time at a technical institution; resident of Tennessee and studying in Tennessee. Available to U.S. citizens. *Application Requirements:* Application form, application form may be submitted online (http://www.fafsa.gov). **Deadline:** November 1.

Contact Mr. Robert Biggers, Director of Lottery Scholarship Programs, Tennessee Student Assistance Corporation, Parkway Towers, 404 James Robertson Parkway, Suite 1510, Nashville, TN 37243-0820. *E-mail:* robert.biggers@tn.gov. *Phone:* 615-253-7453. *Fax:* 615-741-6101. *Website:* http://www.tn.gov/collegepays.

Tennessee HOPE Foster Child Tuition Grant. Renewable tuition award available for recipients of the HOPE Scholarship or HOPE Access Grant. Student must have been in Tennessee state custody as a foster child for at least one year after reaching age 14. Award amount varies and shall not exceed the tuition and mandatory fees at an eligible Tennessee public postsecondary institution. For additional information, visit web site http://www.tn.gov/collegepays. *Award:* Scholarship for use in freshman, sophomore, junior, or senior years; renewable. *Eligibility Requirements:* Applicant must be enrolled or expecting to enroll full- or part-time at a two-year or four-year institution or university; resident of Tennessee and studying in Tennessee. Applicant must have 3.0 GPA or higher. Available to U.S. citizens. *Application Requirements:* Application form, application form may be submitted online (http://www.fafsa.gov). **Deadline:** September 1.

Contact Mr. Robert Biggers, Director of Lottery Scholarship Programs, Tennessee Student Assistance Corporation, Parkway Towers, 404 James Robertson Parkway, Suite 1510, Nashville, TN 37243-0820. *E-mail:* robert.biggers@tn.gov. *Phone:* 615-253-

7453. *Fax:* 615-741-6101. *Website:* http://www.tn.gov/collegepays.

Tennessee Student Assistance Award. Award to assist financially-needy Tennessee residents attending an approved college or university within the state. Complete a Free Application for Federal Student Aid form. FAFSA must be processed as soon as possible after January 1 for priority consideration. To apply, go to http://www.fafsa.gov. For more information, go to www.tn.gov/collegepays *Award:* Grant for use in freshman, sophomore, junior, or senior years; not renewable. *Award amount:* $100–$4000. *Number of awards:* 30,000–35,000. *Eligibility Requirements:* Applicant must be enrolled or expecting to enroll full- or part-time at a two-year or four-year or technical institution or university; resident of Tennessee and studying in Tennessee. Available to U.S. citizens. *Application Requirements:* Application form, application form may be submitted online (http://www.fafsa.gov), financial need analysis.

Contact Ms. Naomi Derryberry, Director of Grants and Scholarship Programs, Tennessee Student Assistance Corporation, Parkway Towers, 404 James Robertson Parkway, Suite 1510, Nashville, TN 37243-0820. *E-mail:* naomi.derryberry@tn.gov. *Phone:* 615-253-7478. *Fax:* 615-741-6101. *Website:* http://www.tn.gov/collegepays.

TEXAS

Conditional Grant Program. Renewable award to students who are considered economically disadvantaged based on federal guidelines. The maximum amount awarded per semester is $3000 not to exceed $6000 per academic year. Students already enrolled in an undergraduate program should have minimum GPA 2.5 and students newly enrolling should have minimum GPA 3.0. Civil Engineering; Computer Science/Data Processing; Occupational Safety and Health. *Award:* Grant for use in freshman, sophomore, junior, or senior years; renewable. *Award amount:* up to $6000. *Eligibility Requirements:* Applicant must be enrolled or expecting to enroll full-time at a four-year institution or university; resident of Texas and studying in Texas. Available to U.S. citizens. *Application Requirements:* Application form, essay, interview, recommendations or references, test scores, transcript. **Deadline:** March 1.

Contact Minnie Brown, Program Coordinator, Texas Department of

Transportation, 125 East 11th Street, Austin, TX 78701-2483. *E-mail:* mbrown2@dot.state.tx.us. *Phone:* 512-416-4979. *Fax:* 512-416-4980. *Website:* http://www.txdot.gov/.

Texas National Guard Tuition Assistance Program. Provides exemption from the payment of tuition to certain members of the Texas National Guard, Texas Air Guard or the State Guard. Must be Texas resident and attend school in Texas. Deadline varies. *Award:* Scholarship for use in freshman, sophomore, junior, or senior years; renewable. *Eligibility Requirements:* Applicant must be enrolled or expecting to enroll full- or part-time at a four-year institution or university; resident of Texas and studying in Texas. Available to U.S. citizens. Applicant or parent must meet one or more of the following requirements: national guard experience; retired from active duty; disabled or killed as a result of military service; prisoner of war; or missing in action. *Application Requirements:* Application form. **Deadline:** varies.

Texas Professional Nursing Scholarships. Award to provide financial assistance to encourage students to become Professional Nurses. Only in-state (Texas) colleges or universities may participate in the program. Both public and private, non-profit colleges or universities with professional nursing programs may participate in the programs. Nursing. *Award:* Scholarship for use in freshman, sophomore, junior, or senior years; not renewable. *Award amount:* $2500. *Eligibility Requirements:* Applicant must be enrolled or expecting to enroll at a two-year or four-year or technical institution; resident of Texas and studying in Texas. *Application Requirements:* Application form, financial need analysis.

Texas Vocational Nursing Scholarships. Awards to encourage individuals to pursue vocational nursing. Both public and private, non-profit colleges or universities with vocational nursing programs may participate in the programs. No individual award may be more than the student's financial need. The maximum award is $1500. Nursing. *Award:* Scholarship for use in freshman or sophomore years; not renewable. *Award amount:* $1500. *Eligibility Requirements:* Applicant must be enrolled or expecting to enroll at a two-year or technical institution; resident of Texas and studying in Texas. *Application Requirements:* Application form, financial need analysis.

Toward EXcellence Access and Success (TEXAS Grant). Renewable aid for students enrolled in public colleges or universities in Texas. Must be a resident of Texas and have completed the Recommended High School Curriculum or Distinguished Achievement Curriculum in high school. For renewal awards, must maintain a minimum GPA of 2.5. Based on need. Amount of award is determined by the financial aid office of each school. Deadlines vary. Contact the college/university financial aid office for application information. *Award:* Grant for use in freshman, sophomore, junior, or senior years; renewable. *Award amount:* $2680–$6080. *Eligibility Requirements:* Applicant must be enrolled or expecting to enroll full- or part-time at a two-year or four-year or technical institution or university; resident of Texas and studying in Texas. Available to U.S. citizens. *Application Requirements:* Financial need analysis, transcript.

Tuition Equalization Grant (TEG) Program. Renewable award for Texas residents enrolled full-time at an independent college or university within the state. Based on financial need. Renewal awards require the student to maintain an overall college GPA of at least 2.5. Deadlines vary by institution. Must not be receiving athletic scholarship. Contact college/university financial aid office for application information. Nonresidents who are National Merit Finalists may also receive awards. *Award:* Grant for use in freshman, sophomore, junior, or senior years; renewable. *Award amount:* $3808–$5712. *Eligibility Requirements:* Applicant must be enrolled or expecting to enroll full-time at a two-year or four-year institution or university; resident of Texas and studying in Texas. Available to U.S. citizens. *Application Requirements:* FAFSA, financial need analysis.

Vanessa Rudloff Scholarship Program. Scholarships of $1000 awarded to qualified TWLE members and their dependents who are entering or continuing students at an accredited college or university. For details refer to web site, http://www.twle.net/. *Award:* Scholarship for use in freshman, sophomore, junior, senior, graduate, or postgraduate years; not renewable. *Award amount:* $1000. *Number of awards:* 4. *Eligibility Requirements:* Applicant must be enrolled or expecting to enroll full- or part-time at a two-year or four-year or technical institution or university. Applicant or parent of applicant must be member of Texas Women in Law Enforcement. Applicant

must have 3.0 GPA or higher. Available to U.S. and non-U.S. citizens. *Application Requirements:* Application form, essay, recommendations or references. **Deadline:** April 15.

Contact Glenda Baker, Scholarship Awards Chairperson, Texas Women in Law Enforcement, 12605 Rhea Court, Austin, TX 78727. *E-mail:* gbakerab@aol.com.

UTAH

Higher Education Success Stipend Program. Award available to students with substantial financial need for use at any of the participating Utah institutions. The student must be a Utah resident. Contact the financial aid office of the participating institution for requirements and deadlines. *Award:* Grant for use in freshman, sophomore, junior, or senior years; not renewable. *Award amount:* $300–$5000. *Number of awards:* 422–7028. *Eligibility Requirements:* Applicant must be enrolled or expecting to enroll full- or part-time at a two-year or four-year or technical institution or university; resident of Utah and studying in Utah. Available to U.S. citizens. *Application Requirements:* FAFSA, financial need analysis. **Deadline:** continuous.

Contact Mr. David Hughes, Manager of Student Aid Partnerships. *E-mail:* dhughes@utahsbr.edu. *Phone:* 801-321-7220. *Fax:* 801-321-7168. *Website:* http://www.uheaa.org/.

New Century Scholarship Program. The New Century Scholarship is for Utah high school students who complete the requirements for an Associate's Degree by the date they graduate from high school with a minimum cumulative GPA of 3.5. Recipients receive an award of $1250 per eligible semester at eligible institutions in Utah for up to the shortest of 4 terms, 60 credit hours or completion of a bachelors degree. recipients must complete a minimum of 12 credit hours for each semester of payment with a minimum 3.0 semester GPA. *Award:* Scholarship for use in junior or senior years; renewable. *Award amount:* $1250. *Number of awards:* 2300. *Eligibility Requirements:* Applicant must be enrolled or expecting to enroll full-time at a four-year institution or university; resident of Utah and studying in Utah. Applicant must have 3.0 GPA or higher. Available to U.S. citizens. *Application Requirements:* Application form, GPA/copy of enrollment verification from an eligible Utah 4-year institution, verification from

registrar of completion of requirements for associate's degree, transcript. **Deadline:** February 1.

Contact David Hughes, Manager of Student Aid Partnerships, Utah State Board of Regents, Board of Regents Building, The Gateway, 60 South 400 West, Salt Lake City, UT 84101-1284. *E-mail:* dhughes@utahsbr.edu. *Phone:* 801-321-7220. *Fax:* 801-321-7168. *Website:* http://www.higheredutah.org.

Utah Leveraging Educational Assistance Partnership. Award available to Utah resident students with substantial financial need for use at any of the participating Utah institutions. Contact the financial aid office of the participating institution for requirements and deadlines. This is a State Federal matching program. All State funds were rolled into the Higher Education Success Stipend Program (HESSP). *Award:* Grant for use in freshman, sophomore, junior, or senior years; not renewable. *Award amount:* $300–$2500. *Eligibility Requirements:* Applicant must be enrolled or expecting to enroll full- or part-time at a two-year or four-year or technical institution or university; resident of Utah and studying in Utah. Available to U.S. citizens. *Application Requirements:* FAFSA, financial need analysis. **Deadline:** continuous.

Contact Mr. David Hughes, Manager of Student Aid Partnerships. *E-mail:* dhughes@utahsbr.edu. *Phone:* 801-321-7220. *Fax:* 801-321-7168. *Website:* http://www.uheaa.org/.

VERMONT

Vermont Incentive Grants. Renewable grants for Vermont residents based on financial need. Must meet needs test. Must be college undergraduate or graduate student enrolled full-time at an approved post secondary institution. Only available to Vermont residents. *Award:* Grant for use in freshman, sophomore, junior, or senior years; renewable. *Award amount:* $500–$10,800. *Eligibility Requirements:* Applicant must be enrolled or expecting to enroll full-time at a two-year or four-year or technical institution or university and resident of Vermont. Available to U.S. citizens. *Application Requirements:* Application form, FAFSA, financial need analysis. **Deadline:** continuous.

Vermont Non-Degree Student Grant Program. Need-based, renewable grants for Vermont residents enrolled in non-degree programs in a college, vocational school, or high school adult program, that will improve employability or encourage further study. Award amounts vary. *Award:* Grant for use in freshman, sophomore, junior, or senior years; renewable. *Eligibility Requirements:* Applicant must be enrolled or expecting to enroll full- or part-time at a two-year or four-year or technical institution or university and resident of Vermont. Available to U.S. citizens. *Application Requirements:* Application form, financial need analysis. **Deadline:** continuous.

Vermont Part-Time Student Grants. For undergraduates carrying less than twelve credits per semester who have not received a bachelor's degree. Must be Vermont resident. Based on financial need. Complete Vermont Financial Aid Packet to apply. May be used at any approved post-secondary institution. *Award:* Grant for use in freshman, sophomore, junior, or senior years; renewable. *Award amount:* $250–$8100. *Eligibility Requirements:* Applicant must be enrolled or expecting to enroll part-time at a four-year institution or university and resident of Vermont. Available to U.S. citizens. *Application Requirements:* Application form, financial need analysis. **Deadline:** continuous.

VIRGINIA

Mary Marshall Practical Nursing Scholarship (LPN). The Mary Marshall Nursing Scholarship Program as authorized by Sections 23-35.9 through 23-35.13 and § 32.1-122.6:01 of the Code of Virginia provides annual nursing scholarships from the Nursing Scholarship and Loan Repayment Fund pursuant to § 54.1-3011.1 and § 54.1-3011.2 of the Virginia Code for part time and full- time students that are residents of Virginia and enrolled in a Licensed Practical Nurse (LPN) nursing program. This revolving Nursing Scholarship and Loan Repayment Fund is maintained by fees authorized by Virginia Code section § 54.1-2400 that charges one dollar for every practical nurse and registered nurse obtaining a licensure or renewal in Virginia pursuant to § 54.1-3011.1. This fund also includes any funds appropriated by the General Assembly for the purposes of the fund; and any gifts, grants, or bequests received from any private person or organization. All scholarship awards vary from year to year and are made by an Advisory Committee appointed by the Virginia State Board of Health. The Virginia Department of Health (VDH)-Office of Minority Health and Health Equity (OMHHE)-Health Workforce serves as

the staff element to the Advisory Committee and plays no role in the determination of scholarship recipients. The Advisory Committee recommends to the State Commissioner of Health the award selection with due regard given to scholastic attainment, financial need, character, and adaptability to the nursing profession. Recipient must agree to work in Virginia after graduation as a LPN within a certain amount of time until their service obligation is fulfilled. The recipient service obligation is one month for every $100 received. Nursing. *Award:* Scholarship for use in freshman, sophomore, junior, or senior years; not renewable. *Award amount:* $150–$500. *Number of awards:* 50–150. *Eligibility Requirements:* Applicant must be enrolled or expecting to enroll full- or part-time at a two-year or four-year or technical institution or university; resident of Virginia and studying in Virginia. Applicant must have 2.5 GPA or higher. Available to U.S. citizens. *Application Requirements:* Application form, driver's license, essay, financial need analysis, recommendations or references, transcript. **Deadline:** June 30.

Contact Mrs. Dena Schall, Healthcare Workforce Manager/Program Specialist, Virginia Department of Health, Office of Minority Health and Health Equity, PO Box 2448, 109 Governor Street, Suite 1016-E, Richmond, VA 23218-2448. *E-mail:* IncentivePrograms@vdh.virginia.gov. *Phone:* 804-864-7435. *Fax:* 804-864-7440. *Website:* http://www.vdh.virginia.gov/.

Mary Marshall Registered Nursing Scholarships. The Mary Marshall Nursing Scholarship Program as authorized by Section 23-35.9 through 23-35.13 and § 32.1-122.6:01 of the Code of Virginia (hereinafter referred to as Program) provides annual nursing scholarships from the Nursing Scholarship and Loan Repayment Fund pursuant to § 54.1-3011.1 and § 54.1-3011.2 of the Virginia Code for part time and full time students that are residents of Virginia and enrolled in an undergraduate Registered Nurse (RN) nursing program. Undergraduate nursing programs are defined as those leading to an associate degree, diploma, or baccalaureate degree in nursing. This revolving Nursing Scholarship and Loan Repayment Fund is maintained by fees authorized by Virginia Code section § 54.1-2400 that charges one dollar for every practical nurse and registered nurse obtaining a licensure or renewal in Virginia pursuant to § 54.1-3011.1. This fund also includes any funds

appropriated by the General Assembly for the purposes of the fund; and any gifts, grants, or bequests received from any private person or organization. All scholarship awards are made by an Advisory Committee appointed by the Virginia State Board of Health. The Virginia Department of Health (VDH)-Office of Minority Health and Health Equity (OMHHE)-Health Workforce serves as the staff element to the Advisory Committee and plays no role in the determination of scholarship recipients. The Advisory Committee recommends to the State Commissioner of Health the award selection with due regard given to scholastic attainment, financial need, character, and adaptability to the nursing profession. Recipients are required to start employment as a RN in Virginia within a certain amount of time as a service obligation. The service obligation is one month for every $100 received. Nursing. *Award:* Scholarship for use in freshman, sophomore, junior, or senior years; not renewable. *Award amount:* $150–$2000. *Number of awards:* up to 150. *Eligibility Requirements:* Applicant must be enrolled or expecting to enroll full- or part-time at a two-year or four-year institution or university; resident of Virginia and studying in Virginia. Applicant must have 2.5 GPA or higher. Available to U.S. citizens. *Application Requirements:* Application form, driver's license, essay, financial need analysis, recommendations or references, transcript. **Deadline:** June 30.

Contact Mrs. Dena Schall, Healthcare Workforce Manager/Program Specialist, Virginia Department of Health, Office of Minority Health and Health Equity, PO Box 2448, 109 Governor Street, Suite 1016-E, Richmond, VA 23218-2448. *E-mail:* IncentivePrograms@vdh.virginia.gov. *Phone:* 804-864-7435. *Fax:* 804-864-7440. *Website:* http://www.vdh.virginia.gov/.

MCCA Lloyd M. Johnson Jr. Scholarship. Scholarship support for newly entering first year law students pursuing a Juris Doctor (non-LL.M.) degree. Must be a U.S. citizen and have a minimum undergraduate 3.2 GPA. Should an interest in corporate law, including working in a corporate law department and/or law firm. Must be financially disadvantaged and have completed the FAFSA and provide additional documents as requested, and demonstrate community service and leadership qualities. Law/Legal Services. *Award:* Scholarship for use in senior or graduate years; not renewable. *Award amount:* up to $10,000. *Eligibility Requirements:* Applicant must be Black (non-Hispanic); enrolled or expecting to enroll full-time at a four-year institution or university and must have an interest in leadership. Available to U.S. citizens. *Application Requirements:* Application form, community service, essay, FAFSA, financial need analysis, resume, transcript. **Deadline:** May 30.

NRA Youth Educational Summit (YES) Scholarships. Awards for Youth Educational Summit participants based on the initial application, on-site debate, and degree of participation during the week-long event. Must be graduating high school seniors enrolled in undergraduate program. Must have a minimum GPA of 3.0. *Award:* Scholarship for use in freshman, sophomore, or junior years; not renewable. *Award amount:* $1000–$10,000. *Number of awards:* 1–6. *Eligibility Requirements:* Applicant must be high school student and planning to enroll or expecting to enroll full- or part-time at a two-year or four-year or technical institution or university. Applicant must have 3.0 GPA or higher. Available to U.S. citizens. *Application Requirements:* Application form, entry in a contest, essay, recommendations or references, transcript. **Deadline:** February 1.

Pennsylvania State Employees Scholarship (SECA). Scholarships for UNCF students from Pennsylvania. Funds may be used for tuition, room and board, books, or to repay federal student loans. Minimum 2.5 GPA required. Prospective applicants should complete the Student Profile found at web site http://www.uncf.org. *Award:* Scholarship for use in freshman, sophomore, junior, or senior years; not renewable. *Award amount:* up to $4000. *Eligibility Requirements:* Applicant must be Black (non-Hispanic); enrolled or expecting to enroll full-time at a four-year institution or university and resident of Pennsylvania. Applicant must have 2.5 GPA or higher. Available to U.S. citizens. *Application Requirements:* Application form, financial need analysis, student profile. **Deadline:** July 14.

State Department Federal Credit Union Annual Scholarship Program. Scholarships available to members who are currently enrolled in a degree program and have completed 12 credit hours of coursework at an accredited college or university. Must have own account in good standing with SDFCU, have a minimum 2.5 GPA, submit official cumulative transcripts, and describe need for financial assistance to continue their education. Scholarship only open to members of State Department

Federal Credit Union. *Award:* Scholarship for use in sophomore, junior, senior, or graduate years; not renewable. *Award amount:* $2500. *Eligibility Requirements:* Applicant must be enrolled or expecting to enroll full-time at a four-year institution or university. Applicant must have 2.5 GPA or higher. Available to U.S. and non-U.S. citizens. *Application Requirements:* Application form, entry in a contest, financial need analysis, personal statement, transcript. **Deadline:** April 29.

Virginia Commonwealth Award. Need-based award for undergraduate or graduate study at a Virginia public two- or four-year college, or university. Undergraduates must be Virginia residents. The application and awards process are administered by the financial aid office at the Virginia public institution where student is enrolled. Dollar value of each award varies. Contact financial aid office for application and deadlines. *Award:* Grant for use in freshman, sophomore, junior, or senior years; not renewable. *Eligibility Requirements:* Applicant must be enrolled or expecting to enroll full- or part-time at a two-year or four-year institution or university; resident of Virginia and studying in Virginia. Available to U.S. citizens. *Application Requirements:* Financial need analysis.

Virginia Guaranteed Assistance Program. Awards to undergraduate students proportional to their need, up to full tuition, fees and book allowance. Must be a graduate of a Virginia high school. High school GPA of 2.5 required. Must be enrolled full-time in a public Virginia two- or four-year institution and demonstrate financial need. Must maintain minimum college GPA of 2.0 for renewal awards. *Award:* Grant for use in freshman, sophomore, junior, or senior years; not renewable. *Eligibility Requirements:* Applicant must be enrolled or expecting to enroll full-time at a two-year or four-year institution or university; resident of Virginia and studying in Virginia. Available to U.S. citizens. *Application Requirements:* Financial need analysis, transcript.

Virginia Military Survivors and Dependents Education Program. Scholarships for post-secondary students between ages 16 and 29 to attend Virginia state-supported institutions. Must be child or surviving spouse of veteran who has either been permanently or totally disabled due to war or other armed conflict; died as a result of war or other armed conflict; or been listed as a POW or MIA.

Parent must also meet Virginia residency requirements. *Award:* Scholarship for use in freshman, sophomore, junior, senior, or graduate years; renewable. *Eligibility Requirements:* Applicant must be age 16-29; enrolled or expecting to enroll full-time at a two-year or four-year or technical institution or university; resident of Virginia and studying in Virginia. Available to U.S. citizens. Applicant or parent must meet one or more of the following requirements: general military experience; retired from active duty; disabled or killed as a result of military service; prisoner of war; or missing in action. *Application Requirements:* Application form, DD214 of service member, birth certificate of applicant, marriage certificate, acceptance letter from institution. **Deadline:** varies.

Contact Mrs. Doris Sullivan, Coordinator, Virginia Department of Veterans Services, 1351 Hershberger Road, Suite 220, Roanoke, VA 24012. *Phone:* 540-561-6625. *Fax:* 540-857-7573. *Website:* http://www.dvs.virginia.gov/.

Virginia Tuition Assistance Grant Program (Private Institutions). Awards for undergraduate students. Also available to graduate and first professional degree students pursuing a health-related degree program. Not to be used for religious study. Must be US citizen or eligible non-citizen, Virginia domiciled, and enrolled full-time at an approved private, nonprofit college within Virginia. Information and application available from participating Virginia colleges financial aid office. Visit http://www.schev.edu and click on Financial Aid. *Award:* Grant for use in freshman, sophomore, junior, senior, or graduate years; renewable. *Award amount:* up to $2850. *Number of awards:* 22,000. *Eligibility Requirements:* Applicant must be enrolled or expecting to enroll full-time at a four-year institution or university; resident of Virginia and studying in Virginia. Available to U.S. citizens. *Application Requirements:* Application form. **Deadline:** July 31.

WASHINGTON

American Indian Endowed Scholarship. Awarded to financially needy undergraduate and graduate students with close social and cultural ties with a Native-American community. Must be Washington resident and enrolled full-time at Washington public or private school. Must be committed to use education to return service to the state's American Indian community. *Award:* Scholarship for use in freshman, sophomore, junior, senior, graduate, or postgraduate years; not renewable. *Award amount:* $500–$2000. *Number of awards:* 11–20. *Eligibility Requirements:* Applicant must be American Indian/ Alaska Native; enrolled or expecting to enroll full-time at a two-year or four-year or technical institution or university; resident of Washington and studying in Washington. Available to U.S. citizens. *Application Requirements:* 2 written personal statements, one describing one's social and cultural ties to the American Indian community in WA state; and the other describing how one will use one's education to serve the American Indian community within the state of Washington, application form, recommendations or references, transcript. **Deadline:** February 1.

Contact Ann Voyles, Program Manager, Washington State Higher Education Coordinating Board, 917 Lakeridge Way, PO Box 43430, Olympia, WA 98504-3430. *E-mail:* annv@wsac. wa.gov. *Phone:* 360-753-7843. *Fax:* 360-704-6243. *Website:* http://www.hecb.wa. gov/.

Passport to College Promise Scholarship. Scholarship to encourage Washington residents to prepare for and succeed in college. Recipients must have spent at least one year in foster care after their 16th birthday and emancipated from care in Washington state. *Award:* Scholarship for use in freshman, sophomore, junior, or senior years; renewable. *Award amount:* $1–$4500. *Number of awards:* 1–400. *Eligibility Requirements:* Applicant must be age 18-26; enrolled or expecting to enroll full- or part-time at a two-year or four-year or technical institution or university; resident of Washington and studying in Washington. Available to U.S. citizens. *Application Requirements:* Application form, application form may be submitted online (http://www.wsac.wa.gov/sites/default/ files/PassportConsentForm-2012.pdf), consent form, financial need analysis. **Deadline:** continuous.

Contact Ms. Dawn Cypriano-McAferty, Program Manager, Washington State Higher Education Coordinating Board, 917 Lakeridge Way SW, PO Box 43430, Olympia, WA 98504-3430. *E-mail:* passporttocollege@hecb.wa.gov. *Phone:* 888-535-0747 Ext. 5. *Fax:* 360-704-6246. *Website:* http://www.hecb.wa. gov/.

Washington Award for Vocational Excellence (WAVE). Award to honor vocational students from the legislative districts of Washington. Grants for up to two years of undergraduate resident tuition. Must be enrolled in Washington high school, skills center, or community or technical college at time of application. To be eligible to apply student must complete 360 hours in single vocational program in high school or one year at technical college. Contact principal, guidance counselor, or on-campus WAVE coordinator for more information. No new monetary scholarships awarded for 2011 and 2012 cohorts due to state budget cuts. Payments made during current fiscal year fulfill monetary commitments to cohorts awarded in 2010 and prior. *Award:* Scholarship for use in freshman, sophomore, junior, or senior years; renewable. *Number of awards:* 147. *Eligibility Requirements:* Applicant must be enrolled or expecting to enroll full- or part-time at a two-year or four-year or technical institution or university; resident of Washington and studying in Washington. Available to U.S. citizens. *Application Requirements:* Application form, recommendations or references.

Contact Terri Colbert, Program Specialist, Washington State Higher Education Coordinating Board, Workforce Training and Education Coordinating Board, PO Box 43105, Olympia, WA 98504-3105. *E-mail:* tcolbert@wtb.wa.gov. *Phone:* 360-709-4623. *Fax:* 360-586-5862. *Website:* http:// www.hecb.wa.gov/.

Washington Scholars Program. Awards high school students from the legislative districts of Washington. Must enroll in college or university in Washington. Scholarships up to four years of full-time resident undergraduate tuition and fees. Student must not pursue a degree in theology. Contact principal or guidance counselor for more information. Requires nomination by high school principal and rank within the top 1 percent of his or her graduating senior class. Awards for new recipients selected for the 2011-2013 biennium are honorary recognition-only certificates. The monetary scholarship benefit has been suspended for new Washington Scholars during those years due to state budget cuts. Available funding is obligated to honoring residual, pre-existing monetary benefits awarded to scholarship-eligible recipients selected in 2010 and earlier. *Award:* Scholarship for use in freshman, sophomore, junior, or senior years; renewable. *Number of awards:* 147. *Eligibility Requirements:*

Applicant must be high school student; planning to enroll or expecting to enroll full- or part-time at a two-year or four-year institution or university; resident of Washington and studying in Washington. Available to U.S. citizens. *Application Requirements:* Application form, community service, leadership activities, test scores, transcript. **Deadline:** January 22.

Contact Ann Voyles, Program Manager, Washington State Higher Education Coordinating Board, 917 Lakeridge Way, PO Box 43430, Olympia, WA 98504-3430. *E-mail:* annv@wsac. wa.gov. *Phone:* 360-753-7843. *Fax:* 360-704-6243. *Website:* http://www.hecb.wa. gov/.

Washington State Need Grant Program. The program helps Washington's lowest-income undergraduate students to pursue degrees, hone skills, or retrain for new careers. Students with family incomes equal to or less than 50 percent of the state median are eligible for up to 100 percent of the maximum grant. Students with incomes between 51-70% of the state median are prorated dependent on income. All grants are subject to funding. *Award:* Grant for use in freshman, sophomore, junior, or senior years; not renewable. *Award amount:* $176–$10,868. *Number of awards:* 74,000. *Eligibility Requirements:* Applicant must be enrolled or expecting to enroll full- or part-time at a two-year or four-year or technical institution or university; resident of Washington and studying in Washington. Available to U.S. citizens. *Application Requirements:* Application form, FAFSA, financial need analysis. **Deadline:** continuous.

WEST VIRGINIA

Underwood-Smith Teacher Scholarship Program. Award for West Virginia residents at West Virginia institutions pursuing teaching careers. Must have a 3.25 GPA after completion of two years of course work. Must teach two years in West Virginia public schools for each year the award is received. Recipients will be required to sign an agreement acknowledging an understanding of the program's requirements and their willingness to repay the award if appropriate teaching service is not rendered. Education. *Award:* Scholarship for use in junior, senior, graduate, or postgraduate years; renewable. *Award amount:* $2500–$5000. *Number of awards:* 30–60. *Eligibility Requirements:* Applicant must be enrolled or expecting to enroll full-time at a four-year institution or university; resident of West Virginia and studying in West Virginia. Applicant must have 3.0 GPA or higher. Available to U.S. citizens. *Application Requirements:* Application form, essay, recommendations or references. **Deadline:** March 1.

Contact Jan Ruge, Scholarship Coordinator, West Virginia Higher Education Policy Commission-Student Services, 1018 Kanawha Boulevard East, Suite 700, Charleston, WV 25301. *E-mail:* jruge@hepc.wvnet.edu. *Phone:* 304-558-4618. *Fax:* 304-558-4622. *Website:* http://www.wvhepcnew.wvnet. edu/.

West Virginia Engineering, Science and Technology Scholarship Program. Award for full-time students attending West Virginia institutions, pursuing a degree in engineering, science, or technology. Must be a resident of West Virginia. Must have a 3.0 GPA, and after graduation, must work in the fields of engineering, science, or technology in West Virginia one year for each year the award was received. Electrical Engineering/Electronics; Engineering-Related Technologies; Engineering/Technology; Science, Technology, and Society. *Award:* Scholarship for use in freshman, sophomore, junior, or senior years; renewable. *Award amount:* $1500–$3000. *Number of awards:* 200–300. *Eligibility Requirements:* Applicant must be enrolled or expecting to enroll full-time at a two-year or four-year or technical institution or university; resident of West Virginia and studying in West Virginia. Applicant must have 3.0 GPA or higher. Available to U.S. citizens. *Application Requirements:* Application form, essay, test scores, transcript. **Deadline:** March 1.

Contact Jan Ruge, Scholarship Coordinator. *E-mail:* jruge@hepc.wvnet. edu. *Phone:* 304-558-4618. *Fax:* 304-558-4266. *Website:* http://www. wvhepcnew.wvnet.edu/.

West Virginia Higher Education Grant Program. Award available for West Virginia resident for one year immediately preceding the date of application, high school graduate or the equivalent, demonstrate financial need, and enroll as a full-time undergraduate at an approved university or college located in West Virginia or Pennsylvania. *Award:* Grant for use in freshman, sophomore, junior, or senior years; not renewable. *Award amount:* $300–$2500. *Number of awards:* 19,000–21,152. *Eligibility Requirements:* Applicant must be enrolled or expecting to enroll full-time at a two-year or four-year institution or university; resident of

West Virginia and studying in Pennsylvania, West Virginia. Available to U.S. citizens. *Application Requirements:* FAFSA, financial need analysis. **Deadline:** April 15.

Contact Judy Smith, Senior Project Coordinator, West Virginia Higher Education Policy Commission-Student Services, 1018 Kanawha Boulevard East, Suite 700, Charleston, WV 25301-2827. *E-mail:* kee@hepc.wvnet.edu. *Phone:* 304-558-4618. *Fax:* 304-558-4622. *Website:* http://www.wvhepcnew.wvnet. edu/.

WISCONSIN

Handicapped Student Grant-Wisconsin. One-time award available to residents of Wisconsin who have severe or profound hearing or visual impairment. Must be enrolled at least half-time at a nonprofit institution. If the handicap prevents the student from attending a Wisconsin school, the award may be used out-of-state in a specialized college. Refer to web site for further details http://www. heab.state.wi.us. *Award:* Grant for use in freshman, sophomore, junior, or senior years; not renewable. *Award amount:* $250–$1800. *Eligibility Requirements:* Applicant must be hearing impaired or visually impaired; enrolled or expecting to enroll full- or part-time at a four-year institution or university and resident of Wisconsin. Applicant must be hearing impaired or visually impaired. Available to U.S. citizens. *Application Requirements:* Application form, financial need analysis. **Deadline:** continuous.

Contact Sandy Thomas, Program Coordinator, Wisconsin Higher Educational Aid Board, PO Box 7885, Madison, WI 53707-7885. *E-mail:* sandy. thomas@wi.gov. *Phone:* 608-266-0888. *Fax:* 608-267-2808. *Website:* http://www. heab.wi.gov/.

Menominee Indian Tribe Adult Vocational Training Program. Renewable award for enrolled Menominee tribal members to use at vocational or technical schools. Must be at least 1/4 Menominee and show proof of Indian blood. Must complete financial aid form. *Award:* Grant for use in freshman or sophomore years; renewable. *Award amount:* $100–$2200. *Number of awards:* 50–70. *Eligibility Requirements:* Applicant must be American Indian/Alaska Native and enrolled or expecting to enroll full- or part-time at a technical institution. Available to U.S. citizens. *Application Requirements:* Application

form, financial need analysis, proof of Indian blood. **Deadline:** varies.

Contact Virginia Nuske, Education Director, Menominee Indian Tribe of Wisconsin, PO Box 910, Keshena, WI 54135. *E-mail:* vnuske@mitw.org. *Phone:* 715-799-5110. *Fax:* 715-799-5102. *Website:* http://www.menominee-nsn.gov/.

Minority Undergraduate Retention Grant-Wisconsin. The grant provides financial assistance to African-American, Native-American, Hispanic, and former citizens of Laos, Vietnam, and Cambodia, for study in Wisconsin. Must be Wisconsin resident, enrolled at least half-time in Wisconsin Technical College System schools, non-profit independent colleges and universities, and tribal colleges. Refer to web site for further details http://www. heab.state.wi.us. *Award:* Grant for use in sophomore, junior, or senior years; not renewable. *Award amount:* $250–$2500. *Eligibility Requirements:* Applicant must be American Indian/Alaska Native, Asian/Pacific Islander, Black (non-Hispanic), Hispanic; enrolled or expecting to enroll full- or part-time at a two-year or four-year or technical institution or university; resident of Wisconsin and studying in Wisconsin. Available to U.S. and non-U.S. citizens. *Application Requirements:* Application form, financial need analysis. **Deadline:** continuous.

Contact Mary Lou Kuzdas, Program Coordinator, Wisconsin Higher Educational Aid Board, PO Box 7885, Madison, WI 53707-7885. *E-mail:* mary. kuzdas@wi.gov. *Phone:* 608-267-2212. *Fax:* 608-267-2808. *Website:* http://www. heab.wi.gov/.

Talent Incentive Program Grant. Grant assists residents of Wisconsin who are attending a nonprofit institution in Wisconsin, and who have substantial financial need. Must meet income criteria, be considered economically and educationally disadvantaged, and be enrolled at least half-time. Refer to web site for further details http://www.heab.state.wi. us. *Award:* Grant for use in freshman, sophomore, junior, or senior years; renewable. *Award amount:* $250–$1800. *Eligibility Requirements:* Applicant must be enrolled or expecting to enroll full- or part-time at a two-year or four-year or technical institution or university; resident of Wisconsin and studying in Wisconsin. Available to U.S. citizens. *Application Requirements:* Application form, financial need analysis, nomination by financial aid office. **Deadline:** continuous.

Contact Colette Brown, Program Coordinator, Wisconsin Higher Educational Aid Board, PO Box 7885, Madison, WI 53707-7885. *E-mail:* colette.brown@wi.gov. *Phone:* 608-266-1665. *Fax:* 608-267-2808. *Website:* http://www.heab.wi.gov/.

Veterans Education (VetEd) Reimbursement Grant. The grant is for eligible Wisconsin veterans enrolled at approved schools who have not yet earned a BS/BA. Reimburses up to 120 credits or eight semesters at the UW Madison rate for the same number of credits taken in one semester or term. The number of credits or semesters is based on length of time serving on active duty in the armed forces (active duty for training does not apply). Application is due no later than 60 days after the course start date. The student must earn a 2.0 or better for the semester. An eligible veteran will have entered active duty as a Wisconsin resident or lived in state for twelve consecutive months since entering active duty. *Award:* Grant for use in freshman, sophomore, junior, or senior years; renewable. *Award amount:* up to $4000. *Number of awards:* up to 350. *Eligibility Requirements:* Applicant must be enrolled or expecting to enroll full- or part-time at a two-year or four-year or technical institution or university; resident of Wisconsin and studying in Minnesota, Wisconsin. Available to U.S. citizens. Applicant must have served in the Air Force, Army, Coast Guard, Marine Corps, or Navy. *Application Requirements:* Application form, certified Wisconsin veteran. **Deadline:** continuous.

Contact Mrs. Leslie Busby-Amegashie, Analyst, Wisconsin Department of Veterans Affairs (WDVA), PO Box 7843, Madison, WI 53707-7843. *E-mail:* leslie.busby-amegashie@dva.wisconsin.gov. *Phone:* 800-947-8387. *Fax:* 608-267-0403. *Website:* http://www.dva.state.wi.us/.

Wisconsin Academic Excellence Scholarship. Renewable award for high school seniors with the highest GPA in graduating class. Must be a Wisconsin resident attending a nonprofit Wisconsin institution full-time. Scholarship value is $2250 toward tuition each year for up to four years. Must maintain 3.0 GPA for renewal. Refer to your high school counselor for more details. *Award:* Scholarship for use in freshman year; renewable. *Award amount:* up to $2250. *Eligibility Requirements:* Applicant must be high school student; planning to enroll or expecting to enroll full-time at a two-year or four-year or technical institution or university; resident of Wisconsin and studying in Wisconsin. Applicant must have 3.0 GPA or higher. Available to U.S. citizens. *Application Requirements:* Application form, test scores, transcript. **Deadline:** continuous.

Contact Nancy Wilkison, Program Coordinator, Wisconsin Higher Educational Aid Board, PO Box 7885, Madison, WI 53707-7885. *E-mail:* nancy.wilkison@wi.gov. *Phone:* 608-267-2213. *Fax:* 608-267-2808. *Website:* http://www.heab.wi.gov/.

Wisconsin Higher Education Grants (WHEG). Grants for residents of Wisconsin enrolled at least half-time in degree or certificate programs at a University of Wisconsin Institution, Wisconsin Technical College or an approved Tribal College. Must show financial need. Refer to web site for further details http://www.heab.wi.gov. *Award:* Grant for use in freshman, sophomore, junior, or senior years; not renewable. *Award amount:* $250–$3000. *Eligibility Requirements:* Applicant must be enrolled or expecting to enroll full- or part-time at a two-year or four-year or technical institution or university; resident of Wisconsin and studying in Wisconsin. Available to U.S. citizens. *Application Requirements:* Application form, financial need analysis. **Deadline:** continuous.

Contact Sandra Thomas, Program Coordinator, Wisconsin Higher Educational Aid Board, PO Box 7885, Madison, WI 53707-7885. *E-mail:* sandy.thomas@heab.state.wi.us. *Phone:* 608-266-0888. *Fax:* 608-267-2808. *Website:* http://www.heab.wi.gov/.

Wisconsin League for Nursing, Inc. Scholarship. One-time award for Wisconsin residents who have completed half of an accredited Wisconsin school of nursing program. Financial need of student must be demonstrated. Scholarship applications are mailed by WLN office ONLY to Wisconsin nursing schools in January for distribution to students. Students interested in obtaining an application must contact their nursing school and submit completed applications to their school. Applications sent directly to WLN office will be returned to applicant. For further information visit web site http://www.wisconsinwln.org/Scholarships.htm. Nursing. *Award:* Scholarship for use in junior or senior years; not renewable. *Award amount:* $500–$1000. *Number of awards:* 11–35. *Eligibility Requirements:* Applicant must be enrolled or expecting to enroll full-time at a two-year or four-year or technical institution or university; resident of Wisconsin and studying in Wisconsin. Available to U.S. citizens. *Application Requirements:* Application form, essay, financial need analysis. **Deadline:** March 1.

Contact Mary Ann Tanner, Administrative Secretary. *E-mail:* wln@wisconsinwln.org. *Phone:* 888-755-3329. *Website:* http://www.wisconsinwln.org/.

Wisconsin Native American/Indian Student Assistance Grant. Grants for Wisconsin residents who are at least one-quarter American Indian. Must be attending a college or university within the state. Refer to web site for further details, http://www.heab.state.wi.us. *Award:* Grant for use in freshman, sophomore, junior, or senior years; not renewable. *Award amount:* $250–$1100. *Eligibility Requirements:* Applicant must be American Indian/Alaska Native; enrolled or expecting to enroll full- or part-time at a two-year or four-year or technical institution or university; resident of Wisconsin and studying in Wisconsin. Available to U.S. citizens. *Application Requirements:* Application form, financial need analysis. **Deadline:** continuous.

Contact Sandra Thomas, Program Coordinator, Wisconsin Higher Educational Aid Board, PO Box 7885, Madison, WI 53707-7885. *E-mail:* sandy.thomas@wi.gov. *Phone:* 608-266-0888. *Fax:* 608-267-2808. *Website:* http://www.heab.wi.gov/.

WYOMING

Douvas Memorial Scholarship. Available to Wyoming residents who are first-generation Americans. Must be between 18 and 22 years old. Must be used at any Wyoming public institution of higher education for study in freshman year. *Award:* Scholarship for use in freshman year; not renewable. *Award amount:* $500. *Number of awards:* 2. *Eligibility Requirements:* Applicant must be age 18-22; enrolled or expecting to enroll full- or part-time at a two-year or four-year institution or university; resident of Wyoming and studying in Wyoming. Available to U.S. citizens. *Application Requirements:* Application form. **Deadline:** April 30.

Contact Stephanie Brady, Social Studies Consultant, Wyoming Department of Education, 2300 Capitol Avenue, Hathaway Building, 2nd Floor, Cheyenne, WY 82002. *E-mail:* stephanie.brady@wyo.gov. *Phone:* 307-777-3793. *Fax:*

307-777-6234. *Website:* http://edu.wyoming.gov/.

Hathaway Scholarship. Scholarship for Wyoming students to pursue postsecondary education within the state. Award ranges from $800 to $1600 per semester. Deadline varies. *Award:* Scholarship for use in freshman, sophomore, junior, senior, or graduate years; renewable. *Award amount:* $800–$1600. *Eligibility Requirements:* Applicant must be enrolled or expecting to enroll full- or part-time at a two-year or four-year institution or university; resident of Wyoming and studying in Wyoming. Applicant must have 2.5 GPA or higher. Available to U.S. citizens. *Application Requirements:* Application form, test scores, transcript. **Deadline:** varies.

Contact Lori Kimbrough, Hathaway Scholarship Consultant, Wyoming Department of Education, 2300 Capitol Avenue, Hathaway Building, 2nd Floor, Cheyenne, WY 82002. *E-mail:* lori.kimbrough@wyo.gov. *Phone:* 307-777-8979. *Fax:* 307-777-6234. *Website:* http://edu.wyoming.gov/.

Superior Student in Education Scholarship-Wyoming. Scholarship available each year to sixteen Wyoming high school graduates who plan to teach in Wyoming. The award covers costs of undergraduate tuition at the University of Wyoming or any Wyoming community college. Education. *Award:* Scholarship for use in freshman, sophomore, junior, or senior years; renewable. *Award amount:* $1000. *Number of awards:* 16. *Eligibility Requirements:* Applicant must be high school student; planning to enroll or expecting to enroll full-time at a two-year or four-year institution or university; resident of Wyoming and studying in Wyoming. Applicant must have 3.0 GPA or higher. Available to U.S. citizens. *Application Requirements:* Application form, recommendations or references, test scores, transcript. **Deadline:** October 31.

Contact Tammy Mack, Assistant Director, Scholarships, State of Wyoming, Administered by University of Wyoming, Department 3335, 1000 East University Avenue, Laramie, WY 82071. *E-mail:* westmack@uwyo.edu. *Phone:* 307-766-2412. *Fax:* 307-766-3800. *Website:* http://www.uwyo.edu/scholarships.

Vietnam Veterans Award-Wyoming. Scholarship available to Wyoming residents who served in the armed forces between August 5, 1964 and May 7, 1975, and received a Vietnam service medal. *Award:* Scholarship for use in freshman, sophomore, junior, or senior years; renewable. *Eligibility Requirements:* Applicant must be enrolled or expecting to enroll full- or part-time at a two-year or four-year institution or university and resident of Wyoming. Available to U.S. citizens. Applicant or parent must meet one or more of the following requirements: general military experience; retired from active duty; disabled or killed as a result of military service; prisoner of war; or missing in action. *Application Requirements:* Application form. **Deadline:** continuous.

Contact Tammy Mack, Assistant Director, Scholarships, State of Wyoming, Administered by University of Wyoming, Department 3335, 1000 East University Avenue, Laramie, WY 82071. *E-mail:* westmack@uwyo.edu. *Phone:* 307-766-2412. *Fax:* 307-766-3800. *Website:* http://www.uwyo.edu/scholarships.

Indexes

Non-Need Scholarships for Undergraduates

Academic Interests/Achievements

Agriculture

Abilene Christian University, TX
Angelo State University, TX
Arkansas State University, AR
Auburn University, AL
Austin Peay State University, TN
Berry College, GA
California Polytechnic State University, San Luis Obispo, CA
California State Polytechnic University, Pomona, CA
California State University, Bakersfield, CA
California State University, Chico, CA
California State University, Fresno, CA
California State University, Stanislaus, CA
Cameron University, OK
Clemson University, SC
Dordt College, IA
Eastern Michigan University, MI
Eastern New Mexico University, NM
Ferris State University, MI
Florida Agricultural and Mechanical University, FL
Florida Southern College, FL
Fort Hays State University, KS
Fort Lewis College, CO
Fort Valley State University, GA
Illinois State University, IL
Iowa State University of Science and Technology, IA
Kentucky State University, KY
Keystone College, PA
Lincoln University, MO
Louisiana State University and Agricultural and Mechanical College, LA
Louisiana Tech University, LA
Lubbock Christian University, TX
McNeese State University, LA
Michigan State University, MI
Middle Tennessee State University, TN
Mississippi State University, MS
Montana State University, MT
Montana State University–Northern, MT
Morehead State University, KY
Murray State University, KY
New Mexico State University, NM
North Carolina Agricultural and Technical State University, NC
North Carolina State University, NC
Northwestern Oklahoma State University, OK
Northwest Missouri State University, MO
The Ohio State University, OH
Oklahoma State University, OK
Post University, CT
Purdue University, IN
Sam Houston State University, TX
South Dakota State University, SD
Southeast Missouri State University, MO
Southern Arkansas University–Magnolia, AR
Southern Illinois University Carbondale, IL

State University of New York College of Environmental Science and Forestry, NY
Stephen F. Austin State University, TX
Tennessee Technological University, TN
Texas A&M University, TX
Texas A&M University–Commerce, TX
Texas Christian University, TX
Texas State University–San Marcos, TX
Texas Tech University, TX
Truman State University, MO
University of Alaska Fairbanks, AK
The University of Arizona, AZ
University of California, Davis, CA
University of California, Riverside, CA
University of Connecticut, CT
University of Delaware, DE
University of Florida, FL
University of Georgia, GA
University of Idaho, ID
University of Illinois at Urbana–Champaign, IL
University of Maryland, College Park, MD
University of Maryland Eastern Shore, MD
University of Massachusetts Amherst, MA
University of Minnesota, Crookston, MN
University of Minnesota, Twin Cities Campus, MN
University of Nebraska–Lincoln, NE
University of New Hampshire, NH
The University of Tennessee, TN
The University of Tennessee at Martin, TN
The University of Texas at San Antonio, TX
University of Vermont, VT
The University of Virginia's College at Wise, VA
University of Wisconsin–River Falls, WI
University of Wisconsin–Stevens Point, WI
University of Wyoming, WY
Utah State University, UT
Vermont Technical College, VT
Virginia State University, VA
Washington State University, WA
Western Illinois University, IL
Western Kentucky University, KY
West Texas A&M University, TX
West Virginia University, WV

Architecture

Auburn University, AL
Ball State University, IN
Boston Architectural College, MA
California Polytechnic State University, San Luis Obispo, CA
California State Polytechnic University, Pomona, CA
California State University, Bakersfield, CA
Calvin College, MI
City College of the City University of New York, NY
Clemson University, SC
College of Staten Island of the City University of New York, NY
Cooper Union for the Advancement of Science and Art, NY

Drury University, MO
Eastern Michigan University, MI
Fairmont State University, WV
Ferris State University, MI
Florida Agricultural and Mechanical University, FL
Florida International University, FL
Georgia Institute of Technology, GA
Hampton University, VA
Howard University, DC
Illinois Institute of Technology, IL
Iowa State University of Science and Technology, IA
James Madison University, VA
Kent State University, OH
Lawrence Technological University, MI
Louisiana State University and Agricultural and Mechanical College, LA
Louisiana Tech University, LA
Miami University, OH
Mississippi State University, MS
Montana State University, MT
Montana State University–Northern, MT
New Jersey Institute of Technology, NJ
The Ohio State University, OH
Oklahoma State University, OK
Polytechnic University of Puerto Rico, PR
Portland State University, OR
Robert Morris University Illinois, IL
Savannah College of Art and Design, GA
Southern Illinois University Carbondale, IL
State University of New York College of Environmental Science and Forestry, NY
Texas A&M University, TX
Texas Tech University, TX
The University of Arizona, AZ
University of Colorado Boulder, CO
University of Florida, FL
University of Idaho, ID
University of Illinois at Chicago, IL
University of Illinois at Urbana–Champaign, IL
The University of Kansas, KS
University of Maryland, College Park, MD
University of Massachusetts Amherst, MA
University of Michigan, MI
University of Minnesota, Twin Cities Campus, MN
University of Nebraska–Lincoln, NE
University of Nevada, Las Vegas, NV
University of Oklahoma, OK
University of Oregon, OR
The University of Tennessee, TN
The University of Texas at Arlington, TX
The University of Texas at San Antonio, TX
University of Utah, UT
University of Washington, WA
University of Wisconsin–Stevens Point, WI
Utah State University, UT
Virginia State University, VA
Washington State University, WA
Washington University in St. Louis, MO
West Virginia University, WV
Woodbury University, CA

Area/Ethnic Studies

Arkansas State University, AR
Augustana College, IL
Binghamton University, State University of New York, NY
California State University, Chico, CA
California State University, Fresno, CA
California State University, Fullerton, CA
California State University, Stanislaus, CA
Calvin College, MI
City College of the City University of New York, NY
The College of New Rochelle, NY
College of Staten Island of the City University of New York, NY
Eastern Connecticut State University, CT
Eastern Washington University, WA
Edgewood College, WI
Florida Agricultural and Mechanical University, FL
Fort Hays State University, KS
Fort Lewis College, CO
Furman University, SC
Indiana University of Pennsylvania, PA
Iowa State University of Science and Technology, IA
Kean University, NJ
Kent State University, OH
Middle Tennessee State University, TN
Mississippi State University, MS
Montana State University, MT
New Jersey Institute of Technology, NJ
New Mexico State University, NM
Oakland University, MI
The Ohio State University, OH
Ohio University, OH
Ohio University–Chillicothe, OH
Ohio University–Eastern, OH
Ohio University–Lancaster, OH
Ohio University–Southern Campus, OH
Ohio University–Zanesville, OH
Oklahoma State University, OK
Ouachita Baptist University, AR
Portland State University, OR
Purchase College, State University of New York, NY
The Richard Stockton College of New Jersey, NJ
Saint Louis University, MO
San Diego State University, CA
Sonoma State University, CA
South Dakota State University, SD
Southern Illinois University Carbondale, IL
State University of New York at New Paltz, NY
State University of New York at Oswego, NY
State University of New York at Plattsburgh, NY
State University of New York College at Geneseo, NY
Stetson University, FL
Stony Brook University, State University of New York, NY
The University of Alabama, AL
University of California, Davis, CA
University of California, Irvine, CA
University of California, Riverside, CA
University of Colorado Boulder, CO
University of Illinois at Urbana–Champaign, IL
The University of Kansas, KS
University of Michigan, MI
University of Minnesota, Twin Cities Campus, MN
University of Oklahoma, OK

University of South Carolina, SC
The University of Texas at San Antonio, TX
University of Utah, UT
University of Vermont, VT
University of Wisconsin–Eau Claire, WI
University of Wisconsin–Green Bay, WI
University of Wisconsin–La Crosse, WI
University of Wisconsin–River Falls, WI
Virginia State University, VA
Warner Pacific College, OR
Washington State University, WA
Wayne State University, MI
Western Illinois University, IL
West Virginia University, WV
Wichita State University, KS
William Jessup University, CA
Wright State University, OH

Biological Sciences

Abilene Christian University, TX
Alaska Pacific University, AK
Alfred University, NY
Angelo State University, TX
Arkansas State University, AR
Arkansas Tech University, AR
Armstrong Atlantic State University, GA
Auburn University, AL
Augustana College, IL
Augustana College, SD
Austin Peay State University, TN
Averett University, VA
Ball State University, IN
Bard College, NY
Barton College, NC
Belhaven University, MS
Bellarmine University, KY
Bethel College, IN
Bethel College, KS
Binghamton University, State University of New York, NY
Biola University, CA
Bloomfield College, NJ
Bloomsburg University of Pennsylvania, PA
Blue Mountain College, MS
Boise State University, ID
Bowie State University, MD
Bowling Green State University, OH
Brenau University, GA
Briar Cliff University, IA
Buena Vista University, IA
Butler University, IN
Caldwell College, NJ
California Lutheran University, CA
California Polytechnic State University, San Luis Obispo, CA
California State Polytechnic University, Pomona, CA
California State University, Bakersfield, CA
California State University, Chico, CA
California State University, Fresno, CA
California State University, Fullerton, CA
California State University, Los Angeles, CA
California State University, San Bernardino, CA
California State University, Stanislaus, CA
Calvin College, MI
Cameron University, OK
Campbellsville University, KY
Carroll University, WI
Carson-Newman University, TN
Case Western Reserve University, OH
Centenary College of Louisiana, LA
Central College, IA
Central Methodist University, MO
Central Michigan University, MI
Chapman University, CA

Christopher Newport University, VA
The Citadel, The Military College of South Carolina, SC
City College of the City University of New York, NY
Clarkson University, NY
Clemson University, SC
Cleveland State University, OH
Coastal Carolina University, SC
Coe College, IA
The College at Brockport, State University of New York, NY
College of Charleston, SC
The College of Idaho, ID
The College of New Rochelle, NY
College of Saint Mary, NE
College of Staten Island of the City University of New York, NY
The Colorado College, CO
Colorado Mesa University, CO
Columbia College, MO
Columbus State University, GA
Concordia University, Nebraska, NE
Concordia University Texas, TX
Dakota Wesleyan University, SD
Dallas Baptist University, TX
Davidson College, NC
Defiance College, OH
Denison University, OH
DeSales University, PA
Dordt College, IA
Drury University, MO
D'Youville College, NY
East Carolina University, NC
Eastern Connecticut State University, CT
Eastern Michigan University, MI
Eastern New Mexico University, NM
Eastern Washington University, WA
East Texas Baptist University, TX
Edinboro University of Pennsylvania, PA
Elizabethtown College, PA
Elmhurst College, IL
Elon University, NC
Emmanuel College, MA
Emporia State University, KS
Evangel University, MO
Fairmont State University, WV
Ferris State University, MI
Florida Agricultural and Mechanical University, FL
Florida Gulf Coast University, FL
Florida International University, FL
Florida Southern College, FL
Fort Hays State University, KS
Fort Lewis College, CO
Framingham State University, MA
Francis Marion University, SC
Frostburg State University, MD
Furman University, SC
Gannon University, PA
Gardner-Webb University, NC
George Fox University, OR
Georgia College & State University, GA
Georgia Institute of Technology, GA
Georgian Court University, NJ
Georgia Southern University, GA
Glenville State College, WV
Greenville College, IL
Grove City College, PA
Guilford College, NC
Hamline University, MN
Hampden-Sydney College, VA
Hampshire College, MA
Hampton University, VA
Hardin-Simmons University, TX

Harrisburg University of Science and Technology, PA
Hawai`i Pacific University, HI
Henderson State University, AR
Hillsdale College, MI
Howard Payne University, TX
Howard University, DC
Huntingdon College, AL
Huntington University, IN
Idaho State University, ID
Illinois State University, IL
Indiana University of Pennsylvania, PA
Indiana Wesleyan University, IN
Iona College, NY
Iowa State University of Science and Technology, IA
Jacksonville State University, AL
James Madison University, VA
Jefferson College of Health Sciences, VA
John Carroll University, OH
Juniata College, PA
Kean University, NJ
Kennesaw State University, GA
Kent State University, OH
King's College, PA
Kutztown University of Pennsylvania, PA
Lake Erie College, OH
Lake Forest College, IL
Lakeland College, WI
Lebanon Valley College, PA
Lees-McRae College, NC
Lee University, TN
Lewis-Clark State College, ID
Liberty University, VA
Limestone College, SC
Lindenwood University, MO
Lindsey Wilson College, KY
Lipscomb University, TN
Lock Haven University of Pennsylvania, PA
Long Island University–C. W. Post Campus, NY
Longwood University, VA
Louisiana State University and Agricultural and Mechanical College, LA
Louisiana Tech University, LA
Loyola Marymount University, CA
Lycoming College, PA
Maine Maritime Academy, ME
Malone University, OH
Manhattan College, NY
Mansfield University of Pennsylvania, PA
Marquette University, WI
Marymount University, VA
Maryville University of Saint Louis, MO
Massachusetts College of Liberal Arts, MA
The Master's College and Seminary, CA
Mayville State University, ND
McKendree University, IL
McMurry University, TX
McNeese State University, LA
Mercer University, GA
Meredith College, NC
Michigan State University, MI
Middle Tennessee State University, TN
Midwestern State University, TX
Millersville University of Pennsylvania, PA
Millikin University, IL
Mills College, CA
Minnesota State University Moorhead, MN
Mississippi State University, MS
Mississippi University for Women, MS
Missouri University of Science and Technology, MO
Missouri Valley College, MO
Missouri Western State University, MO

Molloy College, NY
Montana State University, MT
Montana State University Billings, MT
Montana State University–Northern, MT
Montclair State University, NJ
Moravian College, PA
Morehead State University, KY
Murray State University, KY
Newberry College, SC
New England College, NH
New Jersey Institute of Technology, NJ
New Mexico Highlands University, NM
New Mexico State University, NM
North Carolina Central University, NC
North Carolina State University, NC
North Central College, IL
Northeastern Illinois University, IL
Northeastern State University, OK
Northern Illinois University, IL
Northern Kentucky University, KY
Northern Michigan University, MI
Northern State University, SD
Northwestern Oklahoma State University, OK
Northwestern State University of Louisiana, LA
Northwest Missouri State University, MO
Northwest Nazarene University, ID
Oakland University, MI
The Ohio State University, OH
Ohio University, OH
Ohio University–Chillicothe, OH
Ohio University–Eastern, OH
Ohio University–Lancaster, OH
Ohio University–Southern Campus, OH
Ohio University–Zanesville, OH
Oklahoma State University, OK
Oklahoma Wesleyan University, OK
Old Dominion University, VA
Oral Roberts University, OK
Ouachita Baptist University, AR
Pace University, NY
Pacific University, OR
Piedmont College, GA
Pine Manor College, MA
Pittsburg State University, KS
Point Loma Nazarene University, CA
Point Park University, PA
Post University, CT
Purchase College, State University of New York, NY
Quincy University, IL
Randolph College, VA
Regis University, CO
The Richard Stockton College of New Jersey, NJ
Ripon College, WI
Rochester Institute of Technology, NY
Rockford College, IL
Rockhurst University, MO
Sacred Heart University, CT
Saginaw Valley State University, MI
St. Ambrose University, IA
Saint Augustine's College, NC
St. Cloud State University, MN
St. Edward's University, TX
Saint Francis University, PA
St. John Fisher College, NY
St. John's University, NY
Saint Louis University, MO
Salisbury University, MD
Samford University, AL
Sam Houston State University, TX
San Diego State University, CA
Schreiner University, TX

Seton Hill University, PA
Shepherd University, WV
Shippensburg University of Pennsylvania, PA
Siena College, NY
Skidmore College, NY
Slippery Rock University of Pennsylvania, PA
Sonoma State University, CA
South Dakota State University, SD
Southeastern Oklahoma State University, OK
Southeast Missouri State University, MO
Southern Arkansas University–Magnolia, AR
Southern Illinois University Carbondale, IL
Southwestern College, KS
State University of New York at Fredonia, NY
State University of New York at New Paltz, NY
State University of New York at Oswego, NY
State University of New York at Plattsburgh, NY
State University of New York College at Geneseo, NY
State University of New York College at Old Westbury, NY
State University of New York College at Oneonta, NY
State University of New York College at Potsdam, NY
State University of New York College of Environmental Science and Forestry, NY
Stephen F. Austin State University, TX
Stetson University, FL
Stony Brook University, State University of New York, NY
Tennessee Technological University, TN
Tennessee Wesleyan College, TN
Texas A&M University, TX
Texas Christian University, TX
Texas Lutheran University, TX
Texas Tech University, TX
Texas Wesleyan University, TX
Texas Woman's University, TX
Thiel College, PA
Thomas More College, KY
Thomas University, GA
Towson University, MD
Trevecca Nazarene University, TN
Trinity Christian College, IL
Truman State University, MO
Union College, KY
The University of Akron, OH
The University of Alabama, AL
The University of Alabama in Huntsville, AL
University of Alaska Anchorage, AK
University of Alaska Fairbanks, AK
The University of Arizona, AZ
University of California, Davis, CA
University of California, Irvine, CA
University of California, Riverside, CA
University of California, San Diego, CA
University of Colorado Boulder, CO
University of Connecticut, CT
University of Dallas, TX
University of Dayton, OH
University of Delaware, DE
University of Denver, CO
University of Evansville, IN
University of Great Falls, MT
University of Houston–Clear Lake, TX

University of Idaho, ID
University of Illinois at Urbana–Champaign, IL
The University of Kansas, KS
University of Louisville, KY
University of Maine at Augusta, ME
University of Maine at Fort Kent, ME
University of Mary Hardin-Baylor, TX
University of Maryland, Baltimore County, MD
University of Maryland, College Park, MD
University of Mary Washington, VA
University of Massachusetts Amherst, MA
University of Massachusetts Dartmouth, MA
University of Massachusetts Lowell, MA
University of Memphis, TN
University of Michigan, MI
University of Michigan–Dearborn, MI
University of Michigan–Flint, MI
University of Minnesota, Crookston, MN
University of Minnesota, Twin Cities Campus, MN
University of Mississippi, MS
University of Missouri–St. Louis, MO
The University of Montana, MT
The University of Montana Western, MT
University of Montevallo, AL
University of Nebraska at Omaha, NE
University of Nebraska–Lincoln, NE
University of Nevada, Las Vegas, NV
University of New England, ME
University of New Orleans, LA
University of North Carolina at Asheville, NC
The University of North Carolina at Greensboro, NC
The University of North Carolina Wilmington, NC
University of Northern Colorado, CO
University of Northern Iowa, IA
University of North Georgia, GA
University of Oklahoma, OK
University of Oregon, OR
University of Pittsburgh at Bradford, PA
University of Pittsburgh at Johnstown, PA
University of Portland, OR
University of Puget Sound, WA
University of Richmond, VA
University of Rio Grande, OH
University of St. Francis, IL
University of St. Thomas, MN
University of St. Thomas, TX
University of South Carolina, SC
University of South Carolina Aiken, SC
The University of South Dakota, SD
University of Southern Indiana, IN
The University of Tampa, FL
The University of Tennessee at Chattanooga, TN
The University of Tennessee at Martin, TN
The University of Texas at Arlington, TX
The University of Texas at Brownsville, TX
The University of Texas at Dallas, TX
The University of Texas at El Paso, TX
The University of Texas at San Antonio, TX
The University of Texas–Pan American, TX
University of the Ozarks, AR
The University of Toledo, OH
University of Tulsa, OK
University of Utah, UT
The University of Virginia's College at Wise, VA
University of West Florida, FL
University of West Georgia, GA
University of Wisconsin–Eau Claire, WI
University of Wisconsin–Green Bay, WI

University of Wisconsin–La Crosse, WI
University of Wisconsin–Parkside, WI
University of Wisconsin–River Falls, WI
University of Wisconsin–Stevens Point, WI
University of Wisconsin–Superior, WI
University of Wisconsin–Whitewater, WI
Utah State University, UT
Valdosta State University, GA
Valley City State University, ND
Virginia Commonwealth University, VA
Virginia Military Institute, VA
Virginia State University, VA
Warner Pacific College, OR
Wartburg College, IA
Washburn University, KS
Washington State University, WA
Washington University in St. Louis, MO
Wayland Baptist University, TX
Waynesburg University, PA
Wayne State College, NE
Wayne State University, MI
Webster University, MO
Wesleyan College, GA
Western Carolina University, NC
Western Illinois University, IL
Western Kentucky University, KY
Western Oregon University, OR
Western Washington University, WA
West Virginia State University, WV
West Virginia University, WV
Wheaton College, IL
Wichita State University, KS
Widener University, PA
William Jessup University, CA
Williams Baptist College, AR
Wilson College, PA
Wisconsin Lutheran College, WI
Wright State University, OH
Xavier University of Louisiana, LA
Youngstown State University, OH

Business
Abilene Christian University, TX
Adelphi University, NY
Adrian College, MI
Alaska Pacific University, AK
Albion College, MI
Alfred University, NY
Alliant International University, CA
American Jewish University, CA
Anderson University, SC
Angelo State University, TX
Arkansas State University, AR
Arkansas Tech University, AR
Auburn University, AL
Augustana College, IL
Augustana College, SD
Aurora University, IL
Austin Peay State University, TN
Averett University, VA
Ball State University, IN
Baptist University of the Americas, TX
Barton College, NC
Baylor University, TX
Belhaven University, MS
Bellarmine University, KY
Berry College, GA
Bethel College, IN
Binghamton University, State University of New York, NY
Bloomfield College, NJ
Bloomsburg University of Pennsylvania, PA
Blue Mountain College, MS
Boise State University, ID
Bowie State University, MD
Bowling Green State University, OH

Brenau University, GA
Briar Cliff University, IA
Broadview University–Boise, ID
Broadview University–Layton, UT
Broadview University–Orem, UT
Broadview University–West Jordan, UT
Bucknell University, PA
Buena Vista University, IA
Butler University, IN
California Lutheran University, CA
California Polytechnic State University, San Luis Obispo, CA
California State Polytechnic University, Pomona, CA
California State University, Bakersfield, CA
California State University, Chico, CA
California State University, Fresno, CA
California State University, Fullerton, CA
California State University, Los Angeles, CA
California State University, Monterey Bay, CA
California State University, Northridge, CA
California State University, San Bernardino, CA
California State University, Stanislaus, CA
Calvin College, MI
Cameron University, OK
Campbellsville University, KY
Carroll University, WI
Carson-Newman University, TN
Case Western Reserve University, OH
Cedar Crest College, PA
Centenary College of Louisiana, LA
Central College, IA
Central Methodist University, MO
Central Michigan University, MI
Champlain College, VT
Christopher Newport University, VA
The Citadel, The Military College of South Carolina, SC
Clarkson University, NY
Clearwater Christian College, FL
Cleary University, MI
Clemson University, SC
Cleveland State University, OH
Coastal Carolina University, SC
Coe College, IA
The College at Brockport, State University of New York, NY
College of Charleston, SC
The College of Idaho, ID
The College of New Rochelle, NY
The College of Saint Rose, NY
College of Staten Island of the City University of New York, NY
Colorado Mesa University, CO
Colorado School of Mines, CO
Columbia College, MO
Columbia International University, SC
Columbus State University, GA
Concordia University Ann Arbor, MI
Concordia University, Nebraska, NE
Concordia University Texas, TX
Cornerstone University, MI
Creighton University, NE
Dakota State University, SD
Dakota Wesleyan University, SD
Dallas Baptist University, TX
Daniel Webster College, NH
Davidson College, NC
Defiance College, OH
DeSales University, PA
Dordt College, IA
Drury University, MO
D'Youville College, NY
East Carolina University, NC

Eastern Connecticut State University, CT
Eastern Michigan University, MI
Eastern New Mexico University, NM
Eastern Washington University, WA
East Texas Baptist University, TX
Edinboro University of Pennsylvania, PA
Elizabethtown College, PA
Elmhurst College, IL
Elon University, NC
Emmanuel College, GA
Emory University, GA
Emporia State University, KS
Endicott College, MA
Evangel University, MO
Fairmont State University, WV
Felician College, NJ
Ferris State University, MI
Flagler College, FL
Florida Agricultural and Mechanical University, FL
Florida Atlantic University, FL
Florida Gulf Coast University, FL
Florida International University, FL
Florida Southern College, FL
Fort Hays State University, KS
Fort Lewis College, CO
Fort Valley State University, GA
Francis Marion University, SC
Fresno Pacific University, CA
Frostburg State University, MD
Furman University, SC
Gannon University, PA
Gardner-Webb University, NC
George Fox University, OR
Georgia College & State University, GA
Georgian Court University, NJ
Georgia Southern University, GA
Glenville State College, WV
Globe University–Appleton, WI
Globe University–Eau Claire, WI
Globe University–Green Bay, WI
Globe University–La Crosse, WI
Globe University–Madison East, WI
Globe University–Madison West, WI
Globe University–Minneapolis, MN
Globe University–Sioux Falls, SD
Globe University–Wausau, WI
Globe University–Woodbury, MN
Goldey-Beacom College, DE
Gonzaga University, WA
Goshen College, IN
Grand Valley State University, MI
Greenville College, IL
Grove City College, PA
Hamline University, MN
Hampton University, VA
Hardin-Simmons University, TX
Harrisburg University of Science and Technology, PA
Hawai`i Pacific University, HI
Hillsdale College, MI
Hillsdale Free Will Baptist College, OK
Hope International University, CA
Howard Payne University, TX
Howard University, DC
Huntington University, IN
Husson University, ME
Idaho State University, ID
Illinois Institute of Technology, IL
Illinois State University, IL
Indiana Tech, IN
Indiana University of Pennsylvania, PA
Indiana Wesleyan University, IN
Iona College, NY

Iowa State University of Science and Technology, IA
Iowa Wesleyan College, IA
Jacksonville State University, AL
James Madison University, VA
John Carroll University, OH
Johnson State College, VT
Juniata College, PA
Kean University, NJ
Kennesaw State University, GA
Kent State University, OH
Kettering University, MI
King's College, PA
Kutztown University of Pennsylvania, PA
Lake Erie College, OH
Lakeland College, WI
Lawrence Technological University, MI
Lee University, TN
Lehigh University, PA
Lewis-Clark State College, ID
Liberty University, VA
Limestone College, SC
Lindenwood University, MO
Lindsey Wilson College, KY
Lipscomb University, TN
Lock Haven University of Pennsylvania, PA
Long Island University–C. W. Post Campus, NY
Longwood University, VA
Louisiana College, LA
Louisiana State University and Agricultural and Mechanical College, LA
Louisiana Tech University, LA
Loyola Marymount University, CA
Lubbock Christian University, TX
Lycoming College, PA
Lynn University, FL
Lyon College, AR
Maine Maritime Academy, ME
Malone University, OH
Manchester University, IN
Manhattan College, NY
Marquette University, WI
Marymount University, VA
Maryville University of Saint Louis, MO
Marywood University, PA
Massachusetts College of Liberal Arts, MA
The Master's College and Seminary, CA
Mayville State University, ND
McKendree University, IL
McMurry University, TX
McNeese State University, LA
Mercer University, GA
Meredith College, NC
Methodist University, NC
Michigan State University, MI
Middle Tennessee State University, TN
Midwestern State University, TX
Millersville University of Pennsylvania, PA
Millikin University, IL
Millsaps College, MS
Milwaukee School of Engineering, WI
Minnesota School of Business–Blaine, MN
Minnesota School of Business–Elk River, MN
Minnesota School of Business–Lakeville, MN
Minnesota School of Business–Moorhead, MN
Minnesota School of Business–Rochester, MN
Minnesota State University Moorhead, MN
Minot State University, ND
Misericordia University, PA
Mississippi State University, MS

Mississippi University for Women, MS
Missouri University of Science and Technology, MO
Missouri Valley College, MO
Missouri Western State University, MO
Molloy College, NY
Monmouth University, NJ
Montana State University, MT
Montana State University Billings, MT
Montana State University–Northern, MT
Montana Tech of The University of Montana, MT
Montclair State University, NJ
Moravian College, PA
Morehead State University, KY
Morehouse College, GA
Mount Mary College, WI
Murray State University, KY
Newberry College, SC
New England College, NH
New Jersey Institute of Technology, NJ
New Mexico Highlands University, NM
New Mexico State University, NM
North Carolina Agricultural and Technical State University, NC
North Carolina Central University, NC
North Carolina State University, NC
North Central College, IL
Northeastern Illinois University, IL
Northeastern State University, OK
Northern Illinois University, IL
Northern Kentucky University, KY
Northern Michigan University, MI
Northern State University, SD
Northwestern Oklahoma State University, OK
Northwestern State University of Louisiana, LA
Northwest Missouri State University, MO
Northwest Nazarene University, ID
Northwood University, Florida Campus, FL
Northwood University, Michigan Campus, MI
Northwood University, Texas Campus, TX
Oakland University, MI
The Ohio State University, OH
Ohio University, OH
Ohio University–Chillicothe, OH
Ohio University–Eastern, OH
Ohio University–Lancaster, OH
Ohio University–Southern Campus, OH
Ohio University–Zanesville, OH
Ohio Wesleyan University, OH
Oklahoma Baptist University, OK
Oklahoma City University, OK
Oklahoma State University, OK
Oklahoma Wesleyan University, OK
Old Dominion University, VA
Olivet College, MI
Oral Roberts University, OK
Ouachita Baptist University, AR
Pace University, NY
Pacific University, OR
Peirce College, PA
Piedmont College, GA
Pittsburg State University, KS
Point Loma Nazarene University, CA
Point Park University, PA
Polytechnic University of Puerto Rico, PR
Portland State University, OR
Post University, CT
Providence College, RI
Purdue University North Central, IN
Quincy University, IL
Regent University, VA

The Richard Stockton College of New Jersey, NJ
Ripon College, WI
Robert Morris University Illinois, IL
Rochester College, MI
Rochester Institute of Technology, NY
Rockford College, IL
Rockhurst University, MO
Sacred Heart University, CT
Saginaw Valley State University, MI
St. Bonaventure University, NY
St. Catherine University, MN
St. Cloud State University, MN
St. Edward's University, TX
Saint Francis University, PA
St. John Fisher College, NY
St. John's University, NY
Saint Louis University, MO
Saint Martin's University, WA
Salisbury University, MD
Samford University, AL
Sam Houston State University, TX
San Diego State University, CA
Santa Clara University, CA
Schreiner University, TX
Seton Hill University, PA
Shenandoah University, VA
Shepherd University, WV
Shippensburg University of Pennsylvania, PA
Siena College, NY
Slippery Rock University of Pennsylvania, PA
Sonoma State University, CA
South Dakota State University, SD
Southeastern Louisiana University, LA
Southeastern Oklahoma State University, OK
Southeast Missouri State University, MO
Southern Adventist University, TN
Southern Arkansas University–Magnolia, AR
Southern Illinois University Carbondale, IL
Southern Illinois University Edwardsville, IL
Southwestern College, KS
Southwestern University, TX
State University of New York at Fredonia, NY
State University of New York at New Paltz, NY
State University of New York at Oswego, NY
State University of New York at Plattsburgh, NY
State University of New York College at Geneseo, NY
State University of New York College at Oneonta, NY
State University of New York College at Potsdam, NY
Stephen F. Austin State University, TX
Stetson University, FL
Stony Brook University, State University of New York, NY
Tennessee Technological University, TN
Tennessee Wesleyan College, TN
Texas A&M International University, TX
Texas A&M University, TX
Texas A&M University–Texarkana, TX
Texas Christian University, TX
Texas Lutheran University, TX
Texas State University–San Marcos, TX
Texas Tech University, TX
Texas Wesleyan University, TX
Texas Woman's University, TX

Thiel College, PA
Thomas More College, KY
Thomas University, GA
Towson University, MD
Trevecca Nazarene University, TN
Trinity Christian College, IL
Truman State University, MO
Union University, TN
The University of Akron, OH
The University of Alabama, AL
The University of Alabama at Birmingham, AL
The University of Alabama in Huntsville, AL
University of Alaska Anchorage, AK
The University of Arizona, AZ
University of California, Davis, CA
University of California, Irvine, CA
University of California, Riverside, CA
University of California, San Diego, CA
University of Colorado Boulder, CO
University of Connecticut, CT
University of Dallas, TX
University of Dayton, OH
University of Delaware, DE
University of Denver, CO
University of Evansville, IN
University of Florida, FL
University of Georgia, GA
University of Great Falls, MT
University of Hawaii at Hilo, HI
University of Houston–Clear Lake, TX
University of Idaho, ID
University of Illinois at Chicago, IL
University of Illinois at Urbana–Champaign, IL
University of Indianapolis, IN
The University of Iowa, IA
The University of Kansas, KS
University of Louisville, KY
University of Maine at Augusta, ME
University of Maine at Fort Kent, ME
University of Mary Hardin-Baylor, TX
University of Maryland, College Park, MD
University of Maryland Eastern Shore, MD
University of Mary Washington, VA
University of Massachusetts Amherst, MA
University of Massachusetts Dartmouth, MA
University of Massachusetts Lowell, MA
University of Memphis, TN
University of Michigan, MI
University of Michigan–Dearborn, MI
University of Michigan–Flint, MI
University of Minnesota, Twin Cities Campus, MN
University of Mississippi, MS
University of Missouri–St. Louis, MO
The University of Montana, MT
The University of Montana Western, MT
University of Montevallo, AL
University of Nebraska at Omaha, NE
University of Nebraska–Lincoln, NE
University of Nevada, Las Vegas, NV
University of New England, ME
University of New Hampshire, NH
University of New Orleans, LA
University of North Carolina at Asheville, NC
The University of North Carolina at Chapel Hill, NC
The University of North Carolina at Greensboro, NC
The University of North Carolina Wilmington, NC
University of Northern Colorado, CO
University of Northern Iowa, IA

University of North Florida, FL
University of North Georgia, GA
University of Oklahoma, OK
University of Oregon, OR
University of Pittsburgh at Bradford, PA
University of Pittsburgh at Johnstown, PA
University of Portland, OR
University of Puget Sound, WA
University of Rio Grande, OH
University of St. Thomas, MN
University of St. Thomas, TX
University of South Alabama, AL
University of South Carolina, SC
University of South Carolina Aiken, SC
The University of South Dakota, SD
University of Southern Indiana, IN
The University of Tennessee, TN
The University of Tennessee at Chattanooga, TN
The University of Tennessee at Martin, TN
The University of Texas at Arlington, TX
The University of Texas at Brownsville, TX
The University of Texas at Dallas, TX
The University of Texas at El Paso, TX
The University of Texas at San Antonio, TX
The University of Texas–Pan American, TX
University of the Ozarks, AR
The University of Toledo, OH
University of Tulsa, OK
University of Utah, UT
University of Vermont, VT
The University of Virginia's College at Wise, VA
University of Washington, WA
University of West Florida, FL
University of West Georgia, GA
University of Wisconsin–Eau Claire, WI
University of Wisconsin–Green Bay, WI
University of Wisconsin–La Crosse, WI
University of Wisconsin–Parkside, WI
University of Wisconsin–River Falls, WI
University of Wisconsin–Stevens Point, WI
University of Wisconsin–Stout, WI
University of Wisconsin–Superior, WI
University of Wisconsin–Whitewater, WI
University of Wyoming, WY
Utah State University, UT
Valley City State University, ND
Valparaiso University, IN
Virginia Commonwealth University, VA
Virginia Military Institute, VA
Virginia State University, VA
Warner Pacific College, OR
Wartburg College, IA
Washburn University, KS
Washington & Jefferson College, PA
Washington State University, WA
Washington University in St. Louis, MO
Wayland Baptist University, TX
Waynesburg University, PA
Wayne State College, NE
Wayne State University, MI
Webber International University, FL
Webster University, MO
Wesleyan College, GA
West Chester University of Pennsylvania, PA
Western Carolina University, NC
Western Illinois University, IL
Western Kentucky University, KY
Western Oregon University, OR
Western Washington University, WA
West Texas A&M University, TX
West Virginia State University, WV
West Virginia University, WV
Wheaton College, IL
Wichita State University, KS

Widener University, PA
William Jessup University, CA
Williams Baptist College, AR
Wilson College, PA
Wisconsin Lutheran College, WI
Woodbury University, CA
Wright State University, OH
Xavier University of Louisiana, LA
Youngstown State University, OH

Communication

Abilene Christian University, TX
Adelphi University, NY
Alaska Pacific University, AK
Albion College, MI
Alfred University, NY
Alliant International University, CA
Angelo State University, TX
Arkansas State University, AR
Auburn University, AL
Augustana College, IL
Augustana College, SD
Austin Peay State University, TN
Ball State University, IN
Barton College, NC
Baylor University, TX
Belhaven University, MS
Berry College, GA
Bethel College, IN
Bethel College, KS
Biola University, CA
Bloomsburg University of Pennsylvania, PA
Boise State University, ID
Bowie State University, MD
Bowling Green State University, OH
Brenau University, GA
Briar Cliff University, IA
Butler University, IN
California Lutheran University, CA
California Polytechnic State University, San Luis Obispo, CA
California State University, Bakersfield, CA
California State University, Chico, CA
California State University, Fresno, CA
California State University, Fullerton, CA
California State University, Los Angeles, CA
California State University, Northridge, CA
California State University, Stanislaus, CA
Calvin College, MI
Cameron University, OK
Campbellsville University, KY
Case Western Reserve University, OH
Cedar Crest College, PA
Centenary College of Louisiana, LA
Central College, IA
Central Methodist University, MO
Central Michigan University, MI
Champlain College, VT
Christopher Newport University, VA
City College of the City University of New York, NY
Clarkson University, NY
Clemson University, SC
Cleveland State University, OH
The College at Brockport, State University of New York, NY
College of Charleston, SC
The College of New Rochelle, NY
The College of Saint Rose, NY
College of Staten Island of the City University of New York, NY
Colorado Mesa University, CO
Columbia International University, SC
Columbus State University, GA
Concordia University, Nebraska, NE

Concordia University Texas, TX
Cornerstone University, MI
Dakota State University, SD
Dallas Baptist University, TX
Defiance College, OH
DeSales University, PA
Dordt College, IA
Drury University, MO
East Carolina University, NC
Eastern Connecticut State University, CT
Eastern Michigan University, MI
Eastern New Mexico University, NM
Eastern Washington University, WA
East Texas Baptist University, TX
Edinboro University of Pennsylvania, PA
Elizabethtown College, PA
Elmhurst College, IL
Elon University, NC
Emmanuel College, GA
Emporia State University, KS
Evangel University, MO
Ferris State University, MI
Flagler College, FL
Florida Agricultural and Mechanical University, FL
Florida International University, FL
Florida Southern College, FL
Fort Hays State University, KS
Fort Lewis College, CO
Franklin Pierce University, NH
Frostburg State University, MD
Furman University, SC
Gardner-Webb University, NC
George Fox University, OR
Georgia Southern University, GA
Goshen College, IN
Grand Valley State University, MI
Grove City College, PA
Hamline University, MN
Hampton University, VA
Harding University, AR
Hardin-Simmons University, TX
Hastings College, NE
Hawai'i Pacific University, HI
Hofstra University, NY
Howard Payne University, TX
Howard University, DC
Huntington University, IN
Idaho State University, ID
Illinois State University, IL
Indiana University of Pennsylvania, PA
Indiana Wesleyan University, IN
Iona College, NY
Iowa State University of Science and Technology, IA
Ithaca College, NY
Jacksonville State University, AL
John Carroll University, OH
Juniata College, PA
Kean University, NJ
Kennesaw State University, GA
Kent State University, OH
King's College, PA
Kutztown University of Pennsylvania, PA
Lake Erie College, OH
Lee University, TN
Lehigh University, PA
Liberty University, VA
Limestone College, SC
Lindenwood University, MO
Lipscomb University, TN
Lock Haven University of Pennsylvania, PA
Long Island University–Brooklyn Campus, NY

Louisiana State University and Agricultural and Mechanical College, LA
Loyola Marymount University, CA
Lubbock Christian University, TX
Lycoming College, PA
Lynn University, FL
Malone University, OH
Mansfield University of Pennsylvania, PA
Marquette University, WI
Marywood University, PA
Massachusetts College of Liberal Arts, MA
Mayville State University, ND
McNeese State University, LA
Michigan State University, MI
Middle Tennessee State University, TN
Midwestern State University, TX
Millersville University of Pennsylvania, PA
Millikin University, IL
Milwaukee School of Engineering, WI
Minnesota State University Moorhead, MN
Minot State University, ND
Mississippi State University, MS
Mississippi University for Women, MS
Missouri Valley College, MO
Missouri Western State University, MO
Molloy College, NY
Monmouth University, NJ
Montana State University, MT
Montana State University Billings, MT
Montclair State University, NJ
Morehead State University, KY
Mount Mary College, WI
Murray State University, KY
Newberry College, SC
New England College, NH
New England School of Communications, ME
New Jersey Institute of Technology, NJ
New Mexico Highlands University, NM
New Mexico State University, NM
North Central College, IL
Northeastern Illinois University, IL
Northeastern State University, OK
Northern Illinois University, IL
Northern Kentucky University, KY
Northern Michigan University, MI
Northern State University, SD
Northwestern Oklahoma State University, OK
Northwestern State University of Louisiana, LA
Northwest Missouri State University, MO
The Ohio State University, OH
Ohio University, OH
Ohio University–Chillicothe, OH
Ohio University–Eastern, OH
Ohio University–Lancaster, OH
Ohio University–Southern Campus, OH
Ohio University–Zanesville, OH
Oklahoma City University, OK
Oklahoma State University, OK
Olivet College, MI
Oral Roberts University, OK
Ouachita Baptist University, AR
Pace University, NY
Pacific University, OR
Pittsburg State University, KS
Point Loma Nazarene University, CA
Point Park University, PA
Post University, CT
Purdue University North Central, IN
Quincy University, IL
Regent University, VA
Rochester Institute of Technology, NY
Rockhurst University, MO

St. Ambrose University, IA
St. Cloud State University, MN
St. Edward's University, TX
St. John's University, NY
Saint Louis University, MO
Salisbury University, MD
Sam Houston State University, TX
San Diego State University, CA
Seton Hill University, PA
Shepherd University, WV
Shippensburg University of Pennsylvania, PA
Siena College, NY
Slippery Rock University of Pennsylvania, PA
Sonoma State University, CA
South Dakota State University, SD
Southeastern Louisiana University, LA
Southeastern Oklahoma State University, OK
Southeast Missouri State University, MO
Southern Adventist University, TN
Southern Illinois University Carbondale, IL
Southwestern College, KS
State University of New York at Fredonia, NY
State University of New York at New Paltz, NY
State University of New York at Oswego, NY
State University of New York at Plattsburgh, NY
State University of New York College at Geneseo, NY
State University of New York College at Potsdam, NY
Stephen F. Austin State University, TX
Stetson University, FL
Tennessee Technological University, TN
Tennessee Wesleyan College, TN
Texas A&M International University, TX
Texas Christian University, TX
Texas Tech University, TX
Texas Wesleyan University, TX
Texas Woman's University, TX
Thomas More College, KY
Towson University, MD
Trevecca Nazarene University, TN
Trinity Christian College, IL
Truman State University, MO
Union University, TN
The University of Akron, OH
The University of Alabama, AL
The University of Alabama at Birmingham, AL
The University of Alabama in Huntsville, AL
University of Alaska Anchorage, AK
University of California, Davis, CA
University of California, Irvine, CA
University of California, San Diego, CA
University of Colorado Boulder, CO
University of Dayton, OH
University of Delaware, DE
University of Denver, CO
University of Evansville, IN
University of Florida, FL
University of Idaho, ID
University of Illinois at Urbana–Champaign, IL
University of Indianapolis, IN
The University of Kansas, KS
University of Maine at Fort Kent, ME
University of Mary Hardin-Baylor, TX
University of Maryland, College Park, MD
University of Massachusetts Amherst, MA

University of Memphis, TN
University of Michigan, MI
University of Michigan–Dearborn, MI
University of Michigan–Flint, MI
University of Minnesota, Twin Cities Campus, MN
University of Mississippi, MS
University of Missouri–St. Louis, MO
University of Montevallo, AL
University of Nebraska at Kearney, NE
University of Nebraska at Omaha, NE
University of Nevada, Las Vegas, NV
University of New England, ME
University of North Carolina at Asheville, NC
The University of North Carolina at Chapel Hill, NC
The University of North Carolina at Greensboro, NC
The University of North Carolina Wilmington, NC
University of Northern Colorado, CO
University of Northern Iowa, IA
University of Oklahoma, OK
University of Pittsburgh at Bradford, PA
University of Pittsburgh at Johnstown, PA
University of Portland, OR
University of Puget Sound, WA
University of Rio Grande, OH
University of St. Francis, IL
University of St. Thomas, TX
University of South Carolina, SC
University of South Carolina Aiken, SC
The University of South Dakota, SD
The University of Tennessee, TN
The University of Tennessee at Chattanooga, TN
The University of Tennessee at Martin, TN
The University of Texas at Arlington, TX
The University of Texas at Brownsville, TX
The University of Texas at El Paso, TX
The University of Texas at San Antonio, TX
The University of Texas–Pan American, TX
University of the Ozarks, AR
The University of Toledo, OH
University of Tulsa, OK
University of Utah, UT
University of West Florida, FL
University of West Georgia, GA
University of Wisconsin–Eau Claire, WI
University of Wisconsin–Green Bay, WI
University of Wisconsin–La Crosse, WI
University of Wisconsin–Parkside, WI
University of Wisconsin–River Falls, WI
University of Wisconsin–Stevens Point, WI
University of Wisconsin–Superior, WI
University of Wisconsin–Whitewater, WI
University of Wyoming, WY
Utah State University, UT
Valdosta State University, GA
Valley City State University, ND
Virginia State University, VA
Waldorf College, IA
Warner Pacific College, OR
Wartburg College, IA
Washburn University, KS
Washington State University, WA
Washington University in St. Louis, MO
Wayland Baptist University, TX
Waynesburg University, PA
Wayne State College, NE
Wayne State University, MI
Webster University, MO
Wesleyan College, GA
Western Carolina University, NC
Western Illinois University, IL

Western Kentucky University, KY
Western Washington University, WA
West Texas A&M University, TX
West Virginia State University, WV
West Virginia University, WV
Wichita State University, KS
Widener University, PA
Wilson College, PA
Wisconsin Lutheran College, WI
Wright State University, OH
Xavier University of Louisiana, LA
Youngstown State University, OH

Computer Science
Adelphi University, NY
Alliant International University, CA
Angelo State University, TX
Arkansas State University, AR
Arkansas Tech University, AR
Armstrong Atlantic State University, GA
Auburn University, AL
Augustana College, IL
Augustana College, SD
Austin Peay State University, TN
Bard College, NY
Barton College, NC
Baylor University, TX
Binghamton University, State University of New York, NY
Bloomfield College, NJ
Bloomsburg University of Pennsylvania, PA
Boise State University, ID
Bowie State University, MD
Bowling Green State University, OH
Briar Cliff University, IA
Broadview University–Boise, ID
Broadview University–Layton, UT
Broadview University–Orem, UT
Broadview University–West Jordan, UT
Buena Vista University, IA
Butler University, IN
California Lutheran University, CA
California Polytechnic State University, San Luis Obispo, CA
California State Polytechnic University, Pomona, CA
California State University, Chico, CA
California State University, Fullerton, CA
California State University, Los Angeles, CA
California State University, Northridge, CA
California State University, San Bernardino, CA
California State University, Stanislaus, CA
Calvin College, MI
Cameron University, OK
Campbellsville University, KY
Carroll University, WI
Case Western Reserve University, OH
Central College, IA
Central Methodist University, MO
Central Michigan University, MI
Champlain College, VT
Christopher Newport University, VA
City College of the City University of New York, NY
Clarke University, IA
Clarkson University, NY
Cleary University, MI
Clemson University, SC
Cleveland State University, OH
The College at Brockport, State University of New York, NY
College of Charleston, SC
College of Saint Benedict, MN
College of Staten Island of the City University of New York, NY

Colorado Mesa University, CO
Colorado School of Mines, CO
Columbus State University, GA
Concordia University, Nebraska, NE
Concordia University Texas, TX
Cornerstone University, MI
Dakota State University, SD
Dallas Baptist University, TX
Daniel Webster College, NH
Defiance College, OH
DeSales University, PA
DigiPen Institute of Technology, WA
Dordt College, IA
Drury University, MO
Eastern Connecticut State University, CT
Eastern Michigan University, MI
Eastern New Mexico University, NM
Eastern Washington University, WA
Edinboro University of Pennsylvania, PA
Elizabeth City State University, NC
Elizabethtown College, PA
Elmhurst College, IL
Elon University, NC
Emporia State University, KS
Evangel University, MO
Fairmont State University, WV
Ferris State University, MI
Florida Agricultural and Mechanical University, FL
Florida International University, FL
Fort Hays State University, KS
Fort Lewis College, CO
Francis Marion University, SC
Frostburg State University, MD
Furman University, SC
Gardner-Webb University, NC
George Fox University, OR
Georgia College & State University, GA
Georgia Institute of Technology, GA
Georgia Southern University, GA
Globe University–Appleton, WI
Globe University–Eau Claire, WI
Globe University–Green Bay, WI
Globe University–La Crosse, WI
Globe University–Madison East, WI
Globe University–Madison West, WI
Globe University–Minneapolis, MN
Globe University–Sioux Falls, SD
Globe University–Wausau, WI
Globe University–Woodbury, MN
Graceland University, IA
Grand Valley State University, MI
Hampton University, VA
Harding University, AR
Hardin-Simmons University, TX
Harrisburg University of Science and Technology, PA
Howard University, DC
Huntingdon College, AL
Huntington University, IN
Husson University, ME
Idaho State University, ID
Illinois State University, IL
Indiana Tech, IN
Indiana University of Pennsylvania, PA
Indiana Wesleyan University, IN
Iona College, NY
Iowa State University of Science and Technology, IA
Jacksonville State University, AL
James Madison University, VA
John Carroll University, OH
Juniata College, PA
Kean University, NJ
Kennesaw State University, GA

Kent State University, OH
Kettering University, MI
Keystone College, PA
King's College, PA
Kutztown University of Pennsylvania, PA
Lake Forest College, IL
Lawrence Technological University, MI
Liberty University, VA
Limestone College, SC
Lindenwood University, MO
Lock Haven University of Pennsylvania, PA
Long Island University–C. W. Post Campus, NY
Longwood University, VA
Louisiana State University and Agricultural and Mechanical College, LA
Louisiana Tech University, LA
Lubbock Christian University, TX
Lycoming College, PA
Malone University, OH
Manhattan College, NY
Massachusetts College of Liberal Arts, MA
Mayville State University, ND
McMurry University, TX
McNeese State University, LA
Meredith College, NC
Michigan State University, MI
Middle Tennessee State University, TN
Midwestern State University, TX
Millersville University of Pennsylvania, PA
Mills College, CA
Milwaukee School of Engineering, WI
Minnesota School of Business–Blaine, MN
Minnesota School of Business–Elk River, MN
Minnesota School of Business–Lakeville, MN
Minnesota School of Business–Moorhead, MN
Minnesota School of Business–Rochester, MN
Minnesota State University Moorhead, MN
Minot State University, ND
Misericordia University, PA
Mississippi State University, MS
Mississippi University for Women, MS
Missouri University of Science and Technology, MO
Missouri Valley College, MO
Missouri Western State University, MO
Monmouth University, NJ
Montana State University, MT
Montana State University Billings, MT
Montana State University–Northern, MT
Montana Tech of The University of Montana, MT
Moravian College, PA
Morningside College, IA
Murray State University, KY
Neumont University, UT
New England College, NH
New Jersey Institute of Technology, NJ
New Mexico Highlands University, NM
New Mexico State University, NM
North Carolina Central University, NC
North Central College, IL
Northeastern Illinois University, IL
Northeastern State University, OK
Northern Illinois University, IL
Northern Kentucky University, KY
Northern Michigan University, MI
Northern State University, SD
Northwestern Oklahoma State University, OK
Northwest Missouri State University, MO

Northwest Nazarene University, ID
The Ohio State University, OH
Ohio University, OH
Ohio University–Chillicothe, OH
Ohio University–Eastern, OH
Ohio University–Lancaster, OH
Ohio University–Southern Campus, OH
Ohio University–Zanesville, OH
Oklahoma State University, OK
Oklahoma Wesleyan University, OK
Ouachita Baptist University, AR
Pace University, NY
Peirce College, PA
Pittsburg State University, KS
Point Park University, PA
Polytechnic Institute of New York University, NY
Portland State University, OR
Post University, CT
Purchase College, State University of New York, NY
Purdue University, IN
Quincy University, IL
The Richard Stockton College of New Jersey, NJ
Ripon College, WI
Robert Morris University Illinois, IL
Rochester College, MI
Rochester Institute of Technology, NY
Rockford College, IL
Rollins College, FL
Sacred Heart University, CT
Saginaw Valley State University, MI
St. Cloud State University, MN
St. Edward's University, TX
Saint Francis University, PA
St. John's University, NY
Saint Louis University, MO
Salisbury University, MD
Samford University, AL
Sam Houston State University, TX
San Diego State University, CA
Seton Hill University, PA
Shepherd University, WV
Shippensburg University of Pennsylvania, PA
Siena College, NY
Skidmore College, NY
Slippery Rock University of Pennsylvania, PA
Sonoma State University, CA
South Dakota School of Mines and Technology, SD
South Dakota State University, SD
Southeastern Louisiana University, LA
Southeastern Oklahoma State University, OK
Southeast Missouri State University, MO
Southern Arkansas University–Magnolia, AR
Southern Illinois University Carbondale, IL
Southwestern College, KS
State University of New York at Fredonia, NY
State University of New York at Oswego, NY
State University of New York at Plattsburgh, NY
State University of New York College at Geneseo, NY
State University of New York College at Oneonta, NY
State University of New York College at Potsdam, NY

State University of New York Institute of
Technology, NY
Stephen F. Austin State University, TX
Stetson University, FL
Stony Brook University, State University of
New York, NY
Tennessee Technological University, TN
Tennessee Wesleyan College, TN
Texas A&M University, TX
Texas Tech University, TX
Texas Woman's University, TX
Thiel College, PA
Thomas More College, KY
Towson University, MD
Transylvania University, KY
Trinity Christian College, IL
Truman State University, MO
The University of Akron, OH
The University of Alabama, AL
The University of Alabama at Birmingham,
AL
The University of Alabama in Huntsville,
AL
University of Alaska Anchorage, AK
University of California, Davis, CA
University of California, Irvine, CA
University of California, San Diego, CA
University of California, Santa Cruz, CA
University of Colorado Boulder, CO
University of Connecticut, CT
University of Dayton, OH
University of Delaware, DE
University of Denver, CO
University of Evansville, IN
University of Florida, FL
University of Great Falls, MT
University of Hawaii at Hilo, HI
University of Houston–Clear Lake, TX
University of Idaho, ID
University of Illinois at Urbana–Champaign,
IL
The University of Kansas, KS
University of Maine at Fort Kent, ME
University of Mary Hardin-Baylor, TX
University of Maryland, Baltimore County,
MD
University of Maryland, College Park, MD
University of Maryland Eastern Shore, MD
University of Mary Washington, VA
University of Massachusetts Amherst, MA
University of Massachusetts Dartmouth, MA
University of Massachusetts Lowell, MA
University of Michigan, MI
University of Michigan–Dearborn, MI
University of Michigan–Flint, MI
University of Minnesota, Twin Cities
Campus, MN
University of Mississippi, MS
University of Missouri–St. Louis, MO
The University of Montana, MT
University of Nebraska at Omaha, NE
University of Nebraska–Lincoln, NE
University of Nevada, Las Vegas, NV
University of North Carolina at Asheville,
NC
The University of North Carolina
Wilmington, NC
University of Northern Iowa, IA
University of North Florida, FL
University of Oklahoma, OK
University of Pittsburgh at Bradford, PA
University of Pittsburgh at Johnstown, PA
University of Portland, OR
University of Puget Sound, WA
University of Richmond, VA
University of Rio Grande, OH

University of St. Thomas, TX
University of South Alabama, AL
University of South Carolina, SC
University of South Carolina Aiken, SC
The University of South Dakota, SD
The University of Tennessee, TN
The University of Tennessee at Martin, TN
The University of Texas at Arlington, TX
The University of Texas at Brownsville, TX
The University of Texas at Dallas, TX
The University of Texas at El Paso, TX
The University of Texas at San Antonio, TX
The University of Texas–Pan American, TX
University of Tulsa, OK
University of Utah, UT
University of Vermont, VT
The University of Virginia's College at Wise,
VA
University of Washington, WA
University of West Florida, FL
University of West Georgia, GA
University of Wisconsin–Eau Claire, WI
University of Wisconsin–La Crosse, WI
University of Wisconsin–River Falls, WI
University of Wisconsin–Stevens Point, WI
University of Wisconsin–Stout, WI
University of Wisconsin–Superior, WI
University of Wisconsin–Whitewater, WI
University of Wyoming, WY
Utah State University, UT
Valley City State University, ND
Virginia Commonwealth University, VA
Virginia Military Institute, VA
Virginia State University, VA
Wartburg College, IA
Washburn University, KS
Washington State University, WA
Washington University in St. Louis, MO
Waynesburg University, PA
Wayne State College, NE
Wayne State University, MI
Webster University, MO
Western Illinois University, IL
Western Oregon University, OR
Western Washington University, WA
West Texas A&M University, TX
West Virginia University, WV
Wheaton College, IL
Wichita State University, KS
Widener University, PA
Wilson College, PA
Wisconsin Lutheran College, WI
Wright State University, OH
Xavier University of Louisiana, LA
Youngstown State University, OH

Education

Abilene Christian University, TX
Alaska Pacific University, AK
Alfred University, NY
Alliant International University, CA
Anderson University, SC
Angelo State University, TX
Antioch University Midwest, OH
Arkansas State University, AR
Arkansas Tech University, AR
Armstrong Atlantic State University, GA
Auburn University, AL
Augustana College, IL
Augustana College, SD
Aurora University, IL
Austin Peay State University, TN
Averett University, VA
Ball State University, IN
Baptist Bible College of Pennsylvania, PA
The Baptist College of Florida, FL

Barton College, NC
Baylor University, TX
Belhaven University, MS
Bellarmine University, KY
Berry College, GA
Bethel College, IN
Binghamton University, State University of
New York, NY
Bloomfield College, NJ
Bloomsburg University of Pennsylvania, PA
Blue Mountain College, MS
Boise State University, ID
Boston University, MA
Bowling Green State University, OH
Brenau University, GA
Briar Cliff University, IA
Buena Vista University, IA
Butler University, IN
California Lutheran University, CA
California Polytechnic State University, San
Luis Obispo, CA
California State Polytechnic University,
Pomona, CA
California State University, Bakersfield, CA
California State University, Chico, CA
California State University, Fresno, CA
California State University, Fullerton, CA
California State University, Los Angeles, CA
California State University, Northridge, CA
California State University, San Bernardino,
CA
California State University, Stanislaus, CA
Calvin College, MI
Cameron University, OK
Campbellsville University, KY
Carroll University, WI
Carson-Newman University, TN
Case Western Reserve University, OH
Catawba College, NC
Centenary College of Louisiana, LA
Central College, IA
Central Methodist University, MO
Central Michigan University, MI
Champlain College, VT
Christopher Newport University, VA
Cincinnati Christian University, OH
City College of the City University of New
York, NY
Clearwater Christian College, FL
Clemson University, SC
Cleveland State University, OH
Coastal Carolina University, SC
The College at Brockport, State University
of New York, NY
College of Charleston, SC
The College of Idaho, ID
The College of New Rochelle, NY
College of Saint Mary, NE
The College of Saint Rose, NY
College of Staten Island of the City
University of New York, NY
Colorado Mesa University, CO
Columbia College, MO
Columbia International University, SC
Columbus State University, GA
Concordia University Ann Arbor, MI
Concordia University, Nebraska, NE
Concordia University Texas, TX
Cornerstone University, MI
Creighton University, NE
Dakota State University, SD
Dakota Wesleyan University, SD
Dallas Baptist University, TX
Davidson College, NC
Defiance College, OH
DeSales University, PA

Dominican College, NY
Dordt College, IA
Drury University, MO
D'Youville College, NY
East Carolina University, NC
Eastern Connecticut State University, CT
Eastern Michigan University, MI
Eastern New Mexico University, NM
Eastern Washington University, WA
East Texas Baptist University, TX
Edinboro University of Pennsylvania, PA
Elizabeth City State University, NC
Elizabethtown College, PA
Elmhurst College, IL
Elon University, NC
Emmanuel College, GA
Emmanuel College, MA
Emporia State University, KS
Endicott College, MA
Evangel University, MO
Fairmont State University, WV
Felician College, NJ
Ferris State University, MI
Flagler College, FL
Florida Agricultural and Mechanical University, FL
Florida Gulf Coast University, FL
Florida International University, FL
Florida Southern College, FL
Fort Hays State University, KS
Fort Lewis College, CO
Framingham State University, MA
Francis Marion University, SC
Frostburg State University, MD
Furman University, SC
Gannon University, PA
Gardner-Webb University, NC
George Fox University, OR
Georgia College & State University, GA
Georgia Southern University, GA
Glenville State College, WV
Goshen College, IN
Grand Valley State University, MI
Greenville College, IL
Grove City College, PA
Hamline University, MN
Hampden-Sydney College, VA
Hampton University, VA
Hardin-Simmons University, TX
Henderson State University, AR
Hillsdale College, MI
Hillsdale Free Will Baptist College, OK
Howard Payne University, TX
Howard University, DC
Huntington University, IN
Husson University, ME
Idaho State University, ID
Illinois State University, IL
Indiana University of Pennsylvania, PA
Indiana Wesleyan University, IN
Iona College, NY
Iowa State University of Science and Technology, IA
Iowa Wesleyan College, IA
Jacksonville State University, AL
James Madison University, VA
John Carroll University, OH
Johnson State College, VT
Juniata College, PA
Kean University, NJ
Kennesaw State University, GA
Kent State University, OH
King's College, PA
Kutztown University of Pennsylvania, PA
LaGrange College, GA

Lake Erie College, OH
Lawrence Technological University, MI
Lees-McRae College, NC
Lee University, TN
Lewis-Clark State College, ID
Liberty University, VA
Limestone College, SC
Lindenwood University, MO
Lindsey Wilson College, KY
Lipscomb University, TN
Lock Haven University of Pennsylvania, PA
Long Island University–Brooklyn Campus, NY
Long Island University–C. W. Post Campus, NY
Longwood University, VA
Louisiana State University and Agricultural and Mechanical College, LA
Louisiana Tech University, LA
Loyola Marymount University, CA
Lubbock Christian University, TX
Lycoming College, PA
Malone University, OH
Mansfield University of Pennsylvania, PA
Marquette University, WI
Maryville University of Saint Louis, MO
Marywood University, PA
Massachusetts College of Liberal Arts, MA
The Master's College and Seminary, CA
Mayville State University, ND
McMurry University, TX
McNeese State University, LA
Mercer University, GA
Meredith College, NC
Metropolitan State University of Denver, CO
Miami University, OH
Michigan State University, MI
Middle Tennessee State University, TN
Midwestern State University, TX
Millersville University of Pennsylvania, PA
Millikin University, IL
Minnesota State University Moorhead, MN
Minot State University, ND
Misericordia University, PA
Mississippi State University, MS
Mississippi University for Women, MS
Missouri University of Science and Technology, MO
Missouri Valley College, MO
Missouri Western State University, MO
Molloy College, NY
Monmouth University, NJ
Montana State University, MT
Montana State University Billings, MT
Montana State University–Northern, MT
Montclair State University, NJ
Morehead State University, KY
Mount Mary College, WI
Murray State University, KY
Newberry College, SC
New England College, NH
New Jersey Institute of Technology, NJ
New Life Theological Seminary, NC
New Mexico Highlands University, NM
New Mexico State University, NM
North Carolina Central University, NC
North Carolina State University, NC
North Central College, IL
Northeastern Illinois University, IL
Northeastern State University, OK
Northern Illinois University, IL
Northern Kentucky University, KY
Northern Michigan University, MI
Northern State University, SD

Northwestern Oklahoma State University, OK
Northwestern State University of Louisiana, LA
Northwest Missouri State University, MO
Northwest Nazarene University, ID
Oakland University, MI
The Ohio State University, OH
Ohio University, OH
Ohio University–Chillicothe, OH
Ohio University–Eastern, OH
Ohio University–Lancaster, OH
Ohio University–Southern Campus, OH
Ohio University–Zanesville, OH
Ohio Valley University, WV
Ohio Wesleyan University, OH
Oklahoma City University, OK
Oklahoma State University, OK
Oklahoma Wesleyan University, OK
Olivet College, MI
Oral Roberts University, OK
Ouachita Baptist University, AR
Pace University, NY
Pacific Union College, CA
Pacific University, OR
Piedmont College, GA
Pine Manor College, MA
Pittsburg State University, KS
Point Loma Nazarene University, CA
Point Park University, PA
Portland State University, OR
Post University, CT
Purdue University, IN
Purdue University North Central, IN
Quincy University, IL
Randolph College, VA
Regent University, VA
The Richard Stockton College of New Jersey, NJ
Ripon College, WI
Rochester College, MI
Rockford College, IL
Sacred Heart University, CT
Saginaw Valley State University, MI
St. Catherine University, MN
St. Cloud State University, MN
St. Edward's University, TX
Saint Francis University, PA
St. John's University, NY
Saint Louis University, MO
Saint Martin's University, WA
Salisbury University, MD
Samford University, AL
Sam Houston State University, TX
San Diego State University, CA
Savannah College of Art and Design, GA
Schreiner University, TX
Seton Hill University, PA
Shepherd University, WV
Shippensburg University of Pennsylvania, PA
Siena College, NY
Slippery Rock University of Pennsylvania, PA
Sonoma State University, CA
South Dakota State University, SD
Southeastern Louisiana University, LA
Southeastern Oklahoma State University, OK
Southeast Missouri State University, MO
Southern Adventist University, TN
Southern Arkansas University–Magnolia, AR
Southern Illinois University Carbondale, IL

Southern Illinois University Edwardsville, IL
State University of New York at Fredonia, NY
State University of New York at New Paltz, NY
State University of New York at Oswego, NY
State University of New York at Plattsburgh, NY
State University of New York College at Cortland, NY
State University of New York College at Geneseo, NY
State University of New York College at Oneonta, NY
State University of New York College at Potsdam, NY
Stephen F. Austin State University, TX
Stetson University, FL
Tennessee Technological University, TN
Tennessee Wesleyan College, TN
Texas A&M International University, TX
Texas A&M University, TX
Texas A&M University–Texarkana, TX
Texas Christian University, TX
Texas Lutheran University, TX
Texas State University–San Marcos, TX
Texas Tech University, TX
Texas Wesleyan University, TX
Texas Woman's University, TX
Thiel College, PA
Thomas More College, KY
Thomas University, GA
Towson University, MD
Trevecca Nazarene University, TN
Trinity Baptist College, FL
Trinity Christian College, IL
Truman State University, MO
Union University, TN
The University of Akron, OH
The University of Alabama, AL
The University of Alabama in Huntsville, AL
University of Alaska Anchorage, AK
The University of Arizona, AZ
University of California, Irvine, CA
University of California, Riverside, CA
University of Colorado Boulder, CO
University of Connecticut, CT
University of Dallas, TX
University of Dayton, OH
University of Delaware, DE
University of Evansville, IN
University of Florida, FL
University of Georgia, GA
University of Great Falls, MT
University of Houston–Clear Lake, TX
University of Idaho, ID
University of Illinois at Urbana–Champaign, IL
The University of Kansas, KS
University of Louisville, KY
University of Maine at Fort Kent, ME
University of Mary Hardin-Baylor, TX
University of Maryland, Baltimore County, MD
University of Maryland, College Park, MD
University of Maryland Eastern Shore, MD
University of Mary Washington, VA
University of Massachusetts Amherst, MA
University of Massachusetts Dartmouth, MA
University of Massachusetts Lowell, MA
University of Memphis, TN
University of Michigan, MI
University of Michigan–Dearborn, MI

University of Michigan–Flint, MI
University of Minnesota, Twin Cities Campus, MN
University of Mississippi, MS
University of Missouri–St. Louis, MO
The University of Montana, MT
The University of Montana Western, MT
University of Montevallo, AL
University of Nebraska at Omaha, NE
University of Nebraska–Lincoln, NE
University of Nevada, Las Vegas, NV
University of New England, ME
University of New Hampshire, NH
University of New Orleans, LA
University of North Carolina at Asheville, NC
The University of North Carolina at Chapel Hill, NC
The University of North Carolina at Greensboro, NC
The University of North Carolina at Pembroke, NC
The University of North Carolina Wilmington, NC
University of Northern Colorado, CO
University of Northern Iowa, IA
University of North Florida, FL
University of North Georgia, GA
University of Oklahoma, OK
University of Oregon, OR
University of Pittsburgh at Bradford, PA
University of Pittsburgh at Johnstown, PA
University of Portland, OR
University of Rio Grande, OH
University of St. Francis, IL
University of St. Thomas, MN
University of St. Thomas, TX
University of South Carolina, SC
University of South Carolina Aiken, SC
The University of South Dakota, SD
University of Southern Indiana, IN
The University of Tennessee, TN
The University of Tennessee at Chattanooga, TN
The University of Tennessee at Martin, TN
The University of Texas at Arlington, TX
The University of Texas at Brownsville, TX
The University of Texas at El Paso, TX
The University of Texas at San Antonio, TX
The University of Texas–Pan American, TX
University of the Ozarks, AR
The University of Toledo, OH
University of Tulsa, OK
University of Utah, UT
University of Vermont, VT
The University of Virginia's College at Wise, VA
University of Washington, WA
University of West Florida, FL
University of West Georgia, GA
University of Wisconsin–Eau Claire, WI
University of Wisconsin–Green Bay, WI
University of Wisconsin–La Crosse, WI
University of Wisconsin–Parkside, WI
University of Wisconsin–River Falls, WI
University of Wisconsin–Stevens Point, WI
University of Wisconsin–Stout, WI
University of Wisconsin–Superior, WI
University of Wisconsin–Whitewater, WI
University of Wyoming, WY
Utah State University, UT
Valdosta State University, GA
Valley City State University, ND
Virginia Commonwealth University, VA
Virginia State University, VA
Warner Pacific College, OR

Wartburg College, IA
Washburn University, KS
Washington & Jefferson College, PA
Washington State University, WA
Washington University in St. Louis, MO
Wayland Baptist University, TX
Waynesburg University, PA
Wayne State College, NE
Wayne State University, MI
Webster University, MO
Wesleyan College, GA
Western Carolina University, NC
Western Illinois University, IL
Western Kentucky University, KY
Western Oregon University, OR
Western Washington University, WA
West Texas A&M University, TX
West Virginia University, WV
Wheaton College, IL
Wichita State University, KS
Widener University, PA
William Jessup University, CA
Williams Baptist College, AR
Wilson College, PA
Wisconsin Lutheran College, WI
Wright State University, OH
Xavier University of Louisiana, LA
Youngstown State University, OH

Engineering/Technologies
Alfred University, NY
Arkansas State University, AR
Arkansas Tech University, AR
Armstrong Atlantic State University, GA
Auburn University, AL
Averett University, VA
Ball State University, IN
Baylor University, TX
Binghamton University, State University of New York, NY
Bluefield State College, WV
Boise State University, ID
Boston University, MA
Bowie State University, MD
Bowling Green State University, OH
Broadview University–Boise, ID
Broadview University–Layton, UT
Broadview University–Orem, UT
Broadview University–West Jordan, UT
Bucknell University, PA
Butler University, IN
California Polytechnic State University, San Luis Obispo, CA
California State Polytechnic University, Pomona, CA
California State University, Chico, CA
California State University, Fresno, CA
California State University, Fullerton, CA
California State University, Los Angeles, CA
California State University, Northridge, CA
Calvin College, MI
Cameron University, OK
Case Western Reserve University, OH
Centenary College of Louisiana, LA
Central Michigan University, MI
Champlain College, VT
Christian Brothers University, TN
Christopher Newport University, VA
The Citadel, The Military College of South Carolina, SC
City College of the City University of New York, NY
Clarkson University, NY
Clemson University, SC
Cleveland State University, OH
College of Charleston, SC

College of Saint Benedict, MN
The College of Saint Rose, NY
College of Staten Island of the City University of New York, NY
Colorado Mesa University, CO
Colorado School of Mines, CO
Cooper Union for the Advancement of Science and Art, NY
Daniel Webster College, NH
Dordt College, IA
East Carolina University, NC
Eastern Michigan University, MI
Eastern New Mexico University, NM
Eastern Washington University, WA
Edinboro University of Pennsylvania, PA
Elizabethtown College, PA
Elon University, NC
Emmanuel College, MA
Emporia State University, KS
Evangel University, MO
Fairmont State University, WV
Ferris State University, MI
Florida Agricultural and Mechanical University, FL
Florida Atlantic University, FL
Florida Gulf Coast University, FL
Florida International University, FL
Fort Hays State University, KS
Framingham State University, MA
Frostburg State University, MD
Furman University, SC
Gannon University, PA
Geneva College, PA
George Fox University, OR
Georgia Institute of Technology, GA
Georgia Southern University, GA
Globe University–Appleton, WI
Globe University–Eau Claire, WI
Globe University–Green Bay, WI
Globe University–La Crosse, WI
Globe University–Madison East, WI
Globe University–Madison West, WI
Globe University–Minneapolis, MN
Globe University–Sioux Falls, SD
Globe University–Wausau, WI
Globe University–Woodbury, MN
Gonzaga University, WA
Graceland University, IA
Grand Valley State University, MI
Greenville College, IL
Grove City College, PA
Hampton University, VA
Harding University, AR
Hofstra University, NY
Howard University, DC
Idaho State University, ID
Illinois Institute of Technology, IL
Illinois State University, IL
Indiana Tech, IN
Indiana University of Pennsylvania, PA
Iowa State University of Science and Technology, IA
James Madison University, VA
The Johns Hopkins University, MD
Kean University, NJ
Kent State University, OH
Kettering University, MI
Lakeland College, WI
Lawrence Technological University, MI
Lehigh University, PA
Liberty University, VA
Lindenwood University, MO
Lipscomb University, TN
Loras College, IA

Louisiana State University and Agricultural and Mechanical College, LA
Louisiana Tech University, LA
Loyola Marymount University, CA
Maine Maritime Academy, ME
Marquette University, WI
McNeese State University, LA
Mercer University, GA
Miami University, OH
Michigan State University, MI
Middle Tennessee State University, TN
Midwestern State University, TX
Milwaukee School of Engineering, WI
Minnesota School of Business–Blaine, MN
Minnesota School of Business–Elk River, MN
Minnesota School of Business–Lakeville, MN
Minnesota School of Business–Moorhead, MN
Minnesota School of Business–Rochester, MN
Minnesota State University Moorhead, MN
Mississippi State University, MS
Missouri University of Science and Technology, MO
Missouri Western State University, MO
Montana State University, MT
Montana State University Billings, MT
Montana State University–Northern, MT
Montana Tech of The University of Montana, MT
Morehead State University, KY
Murray State University, KY
New England College, NH
New Jersey Institute of Technology, NJ
New Mexico Highlands University, NM
New Mexico State University, NM
North Carolina Agricultural and Technical State University, NC
North Carolina State University, NC
Northern Illinois University, IL
Northern Kentucky University, KY
Northern Michigan University, MI
Northwestern State University of Louisiana, LA
Oakland University, MI
The Ohio State University, OH
Ohio University, OH
Ohio University–Chillicothe, OH
Ohio University–Eastern, OH
Ohio University–Lancaster, OH
Ohio University–Southern Campus, OH
Ohio University–Zanesville, OH
Oklahoma Christian University, OK
Oklahoma State University, OK
Old Dominion University, VA
Oral Roberts University, OK
Ouachita Baptist University, AR
Philadelphia University, PA
Pittsburg State University, KS
Point Loma Nazarene University, CA
Point Park University, PA
Polytechnic Institute of New York University, NY
Polytechnic University of Puerto Rico, PR
Portland State University, OR
Purdue University, IN
Purdue University North Central, IN
Rice University, TX
Rochester Institute of Technology, NY
Rollins College, FL
Saginaw Valley State University, MI
St. Ambrose University, IA
St. Cloud State University, MN

Saint Francis University, PA
Saint Louis University, MO
Saint Martin's University, WA
Sam Houston State University, TX
San Diego State University, CA
Santa Clara University, CA
Seattle Pacific University, WA
Shepherd University, WV
Sonoma State University, CA
South Dakota School of Mines and Technology, SD
South Dakota State University, SD
Southeastern Oklahoma State University, OK
Southeast Missouri State University, MO
Southern Illinois University Carbondale, IL
State University of New York at New Paltz, NY
State University of New York at Plattsburgh, NY
State University of New York College at Potsdam, NY
State University of New York College of Environmental Science and Forestry, NY
State University of New York Institute of Technology, NY
Stony Brook University, State University of New York, NY
Suffolk University, MA
Tennessee Technological University, TN
Texas A&M International University, TX
Texas A&M University, TX
Texas A&M University–Texarkana, TX
Texas Christian University, TX
Texas Tech University, TX
Trinity Christian College, IL
Union University, TN
The University of Akron, OH
The University of Alabama, AL
The University of Alabama at Birmingham, AL
The University of Alabama in Huntsville, AL
University of Alaska Anchorage, AK
University of Alaska Fairbanks, AK
The University of Arizona, AZ
University of California, Davis, CA
University of California, Irvine, CA
University of California, Riverside, CA
University of California, San Diego, CA
University of Colorado Boulder, CO
University of Connecticut, CT
University of Dayton, OH
University of Delaware, DE
University of Denver, CO
University of Evansville, IN
University of Florida, FL
University of Hartford, CT
University of Idaho, ID
University of Illinois at Urbana–Champaign, IL
The University of Iowa, IA
The University of Kansas, KS
University of Louisville, KY
University of Maryland, Baltimore County, MD
University of Maryland, College Park, MD
University of Maryland Eastern Shore, MD
University of Massachusetts Amherst, MA
University of Massachusetts Dartmouth, MA
University of Massachusetts Lowell, MA
University of Memphis, TN
University of Michigan, MI
University of Michigan–Dearborn, MI
University of Michigan–Flint, MI

University of Minnesota, Twin Cities Campus, MN
University of Mississippi, MS
University of Missouri–St. Louis, MO
University of Nebraska at Omaha, NE
University of Nebraska–Lincoln, NE
University of Nevada, Las Vegas, NV
University of New Hampshire, NH
University of New Orleans, LA
University of North Carolina at Asheville, NC
The University of North Carolina Wilmington, NC
University of North Florida, FL
University of Oklahoma, OK
University of Pittsburgh at Bradford, PA
University of Pittsburgh at Johnstown, PA
University of Portland, OR
University of Rochester, NY
University of South Carolina, SC
University of South Carolina Aiken, SC
University of Southern Indiana, IN
The University of Tennessee, TN
The University of Tennessee at Chattanooga, TN
The University of Tennessee at Martin, TN
The University of Texas at Arlington, TX
The University of Texas at Brownsville, TX
The University of Texas at Dallas, TX
The University of Texas at El Paso, TX
The University of Texas at San Antonio, TX
The University of Texas–Pan American, TX
The University of Toledo, OH
University of Tulsa, OK
University of Utah, UT
University of Vermont, VT
University of Washington, WA
University of West Florida, FL
University of Wisconsin–Green Bay, WI
University of Wisconsin–Parkside, WI
University of Wisconsin–Stevens Point, WI
University of Wisconsin–Stout, WI
University of Wyoming, WY
Utah State University, UT
Valparaiso University, IN
Virginia Commonwealth University, VA
Virginia Military Institute, VA
Virginia State University, VA
Wartburg College, IA
Washburn University, KS
Washington State University, WA
Washington University in St. Louis, MO
Wayne State University, MI
Wesleyan College, GA
Western Illinois University, IL
Western Kentucky University, KY
Western Washington University, WA
West Texas A&M University, TX
West Virginia University, WV
Wichita State University, KS
Widener University, PA
Wright State University, OH
Xavier University of Louisiana, LA
York College of Pennsylvania, PA
Youngstown State University, OH

English
Abilene Christian University, TX
Alfred University, NY
Alliant International University, CA
Angelo State University, TX
Arkansas State University, AR
Armstrong Atlantic State University, GA
Auburn University, AL
Augustana College, IL
Augustana College, SD

Austin Peay State University, TN
Averett University, VA
Ball State University, IN
Barton College, NC
Baylor University, TX
Belhaven University, MS
Berry College, GA
Bethel College, IN
Binghamton University, State University of New York, NY
Bloomfield College, NJ
Bloomsburg University of Pennsylvania, PA
Blue Mountain College, MS
Boise State University, ID
Bowling Green State University, OH
Brenau University, GA
Briar Cliff University, IA
Butler University, IN
California Lutheran University, CA
California Polytechnic State University, San Luis Obispo, CA
California State University, Chico, CA
California State University, Fresno, CA
California State University, Fullerton, CA
California State University, Los Angeles, CA
California State University, Northridge, CA
California State University, Stanislaus, CA
Calvin College, MI
Cameron University, OK
Campbellsville University, KY
Case Western Reserve University, OH
Cedar Crest College, PA
Centenary College of Louisiana, LA
Central Methodist University, MO
Central Michigan University, MI
Christopher Newport University, VA
City College of the City University of New York, NY
Clemson University, SC
Cleveland State University, OH
Coe College, IA
The College at Brockport, State University of New York, NY
College of Charleston, SC
The College of Idaho, ID
The College of New Rochelle, NY
College of Saint Mary Magdalen, NH
The College of Saint Rose, NY
College of Staten Island of the City University of New York, NY
Colorado Mesa University, CO
Columbia College, MO
Columbia International University, SC
Columbus State University, GA
Concordia University, Nebraska, NE
Concordia University Texas, TX
Cornerstone University, MI
Dakota State University, SD
Dallas Baptist University, TX
Defiance College, OH
Denison University, OH
DeSales University, PA
Dordt College, IA
Drury University, MO
D'Youville College, NY
East Carolina University, NC
Eastern Connecticut State University, CT
Eastern Michigan University, MI
Eastern New Mexico University, NM
Eastern Washington University, WA
East Texas Baptist University, TX
Edinboro University of Pennsylvania, PA
Elizabethtown College, PA
Elmhurst College, IL
Emmanuel College, GA
Emporia State University, KS

Evangel University, MO
Fairmont State University, WV
Felician College, NJ
Flagler College, FL
Florida Agricultural and Mechanical University, FL
Florida International University, FL
Fort Hays State University, KS
Fort Lewis College, CO
Framingham State University, MA
Francis Marion University, SC
Frostburg State University, MD
Furman University, SC
Gannon University, PA
Gardner-Webb University, NC
George Fox University, OR
Georgian Court University, NJ
Georgia Southern University, GA
Glenville State College, WV
Goldey-Beacom College, DE
Graceland University, IA
Grand Valley State University, MI
Grove City College, PA
Hamline University, MN
Hampshire College, MA
Harding University, AR
Hardin-Simmons University, TX
Hillsdale College, MI
Hillsdale Free Will Baptist College, OK
Howard Payne University, TX
Howard University, DC
Huntington University, IN
Idaho State University, ID
Illinois State University, IL
Indiana University of Pennsylvania, PA
Indiana Wesleyan University, IN
Iona College, NY
Iowa State University of Science and Technology, IA
Iowa Wesleyan College, IA
Jacksonville State University, AL
James Madison University, VA
John Carroll University, OH
Kean University, NJ
Kennesaw State University, GA
Kent State University, OH
King's College, PA
Kutztown University of Pennsylvania, PA
Lake Erie College, OH
Lake Forest College, IL
Lakeland College, WI
Lebanon Valley College, PA
Lewis-Clark State College, ID
Liberty University, VA
Limestone College, SC
Lindenwood University, MO
Lindsey Wilson College, KY
Lipscomb University, TN
Lock Haven University of Pennsylvania, PA
Longwood University, VA
Louisiana State University and Agricultural and Mechanical College, LA
Louisiana Tech University, LA
Loyola Marymount University, CA
Lubbock Christian University, TX
Lycoming College, PA
Malone University, OH
Manchester University, IN
Marquette University, WI
Massachusetts College of Liberal Arts, MA
Mayville State University, ND
McMurry University, TX
McNeese State University, LA
Mercer University, GA
Meredith College, NC
Methodist University, NC

Michigan State University, MI
Middle Tennessee State University, TN
Midwestern State University, TX
Millersville University of Pennsylvania, PA
Millikin University, IL
Minnesota State University Moorhead, MN
Minot State University, ND
Mississippi State University, MS
Mississippi University for Women, MS
Missouri University of Science and Technology, MO
Missouri Valley College, MO
Missouri Western State University, MO
Molloy College, NY
Montana State University, MT
Montana State University Billings, MT
Montana State University–Northern, MT
Montclair State University, NJ
Mount Mary College, WI
Murray State University, KY
New England College, NH
New Mexico Highlands University, NM
New Mexico State University, NM
North Carolina Central University, NC
North Central College, IL
Northeastern Illinois University, IL
Northeastern State University, OK
Northern Illinois University, IL
Northern Kentucky University, KY
Northern Michigan University, MI
Northern State University, SD
Northwestern Oklahoma State University, OK
Northwestern State University of Louisiana, LA
Northwest Missouri State University, MO
Northwest Nazarene University, ID
Oakland University, MI
The Ohio State University, OH
Ohio University, OH
Ohio University–Chillicothe, OH
Ohio University–Eastern, OH
Ohio University–Lancaster, OH
Ohio University–Southern Campus, OH
Ohio University–Zanesville, OH
Ohio Valley University, WV
Oklahoma State University, OK
Old Dominion University, VA
Olivet College, MI
Ouachita Baptist University, AR
Pace University, NY
Pacific University, OR
Piedmont College, GA
Pittsburg State University, KS
Point Park University, PA
Post University, CT
Purchase College, State University of New York, NY
Purdue University North Central, IN
Quincy University, IL
Randolph College, VA
Regent University, VA
Ripon College, WI
Rockford College, IL
Rockhurst University, MO
Sacred Heart University, CT
St. Catherine University, MN
St. Cloud State University, MN
St. Edward's University, TX
Saint Francis University, PA
St. John Fisher College, NY
St. John's University, NY
Saint Louis University, MO
Salisbury University, MD
Samford University, AL

Sam Houston State University, TX
San Diego State University, CA
Schreiner University, TX
Seton Hill University, PA
Shepherd University, WV
Shippensburg University of Pennsylvania, PA
Shorter University, GA
Siena College, NY
Sierra Nevada College, NV
Slippery Rock University of Pennsylvania, PA
Sonoma State University, CA
South Dakota State University, SD
Southeastern Louisiana University, LA
Southeastern Oklahoma State University, OK
Southeast Missouri State University, MO
Southern Adventist University, TN
Southern Arkansas University–Magnolia, AR
Southern Illinois University Carbondale, IL
State University of New York at Fredonia, NY
State University of New York at New Paltz, NY
State University of New York at Oswego, NY
State University of New York at Plattsburgh, NY
State University of New York College at Geneseo, NY
State University of New York College at Oneonta, NY
State University of New York College at Potsdam, NY
Stephens College, MO
Stetson University, FL
Stony Brook University, State University of New York, NY
Tennessee Technological University, TN
Tennessee Wesleyan College, TN
Texas A&M International University, TX
Texas A&M University–Texarkana, TX
Texas Christian University, TX
Texas State University–San Marcos, TX
Texas Tech University, TX
Texas Wesleyan University, TX
Texas Woman's University, TX
Thiel College, PA
Thomas More College, KY
Thomas University, GA
Towson University, MD
Trevecca Nazarene University, TN
Trinity Christian College, IL
Truman State University, MO
The University of Akron, OH
The University of Alabama, AL
The University of Alabama in Huntsville, AL
University of Alaska Anchorage, AK
University of California, Davis, CA
University of California, Irvine, CA
University of California, Riverside, CA
University of Colorado Boulder, CO
University of Connecticut, CT
University of Dayton, OH
University of Delaware, DE
University of Evansville, IN
University of Hawaii at Hilo, HI
University of Idaho, ID
University of Illinois at Urbana–Champaign, IL
The University of Kansas, KS
University of Louisville, KY

University of Maine at Fort Kent, ME
University of Mary Hardin-Baylor, TX
University of Maryland, Baltimore County, MD
University of Maryland, College Park, MD
University of Maryland Eastern Shore, MD
University of Mary Washington, VA
University of Massachusetts Amherst, MA
University of Massachusetts Lowell, MA
University of Memphis, TN
University of Michigan, MI
University of Michigan–Flint, MI
University of Minnesota, Twin Cities Campus, MN
University of Mississippi, MS
University of Missouri–St. Louis, MO
The University of Montana, MT
The University of Montana Western, MT
University of Montevallo, AL
University of Nebraska at Omaha, NE
University of Nebraska–Lincoln, NE
University of Nevada, Las Vegas, NV
University of New England, ME
University of New Hampshire, NH
University of New Orleans, LA
University of North Carolina at Asheville, NC
The University of North Carolina at Chapel Hill, NC
The University of North Carolina at Greensboro, NC
The University of North Carolina Wilmington, NC
University of Northern Colorado, CO
University of North Georgia, GA
University of Oklahoma, OK
University of Oregon, OR
University of Pittsburgh at Bradford, PA
University of Pittsburgh at Johnstown, PA
University of Portland, OR
University of Puget Sound, WA
University of Rio Grande, OH
University of St. Thomas, MN
University of St. Thomas, TX
University of South Carolina, SC
University of South Carolina Aiken, SC
The University of South Dakota, SD
The University of Tampa, FL
The University of Tennessee at Chattanooga, TN
The University of Tennessee at Martin, TN
The University of Texas at Arlington, TX
The University of Texas at Brownsville, TX
The University of Texas at El Paso, TX
The University of Texas at San Antonio, TX
The University of Texas–Pan American, TX
University of the Ozarks, AR
The University of Toledo, OH
University of Tulsa, OK
University of Utah, UT
University of Vermont, VT
The University of Virginia's College at Wise, VA
University of West Georgia, GA
University of Wisconsin–Eau Claire, WI
University of Wisconsin–La Crosse, WI
University of Wisconsin–Parkside, WI
University of Wisconsin–River Falls, WI
University of Wisconsin–Stevens Point, WI
University of Wisconsin–Superior, WI
University of Wisconsin–Whitewater, WI
University of Wyoming, WY
Utah State University, UT
Valley City State University, ND
Virginia Military Institute, VA

Virginia State University, VA
Warner Pacific College, OR
Wartburg College, IA
Washburn University, KS
Washington & Jefferson College, PA
Washington State University, WA
Washington University in St. Louis, MO
Wayland Baptist University, TX
Waynesburg University, PA
Wayne State College, NE
Wayne State University, MI
Webster University, MO
Wesleyan College, GA
Western Carolina University, NC
Western Illinois University, IL
Western Kentucky University, KY
Western Oregon University, OR
Western Washington University, WA
West Texas A&M University, TX
West Virginia State University, WV
West Virginia University, WV
West Virginia Wesleyan College, WV
Wichita State University, KS
Widener University, PA
William Jessup University, CA
Wilson College, PA
Wright State University, OH
Xavier University of Louisiana, LA
Youngstown State University, OH

Foreign Languages

Abilene Christian University, TX
Adelphi University, NY
Alfred University, NY
Alliant International University, CA
Angelo State University, TX
Armstrong Atlantic State University, GA
Auburn University, AL
Augustana College, IL
Augustana College, SD
Austin Peay State University, TN
Averett University, VA
Ball State University, IN
Baylor University, TX
Belhaven University, MS
Binghamton University, State University of New York, NY
Bloomsburg University of Pennsylvania, PA
Boise State University, ID
Boston University, MA
Bowling Green State University, OH
Briar Cliff University, IA
Butler University, IN
California Lutheran University, CA
California Polytechnic State University, San Luis Obispo, CA
California State University, Bakersfield, CA
California State University, Chico, CA
California State University, Fresno, CA
California State University, Fullerton, CA
California State University, Los Angeles, CA
California State University, San Bernardino, CA
California State University, Stanislaus, CA
Calvin College, MI
Cameron University, OK
Case Western Reserve University, OH
Centenary College of Louisiana, LA
Central College, IA
Central Methodist University, MO
Central Michigan University, MI
Centre College, KY
Christopher Newport University, VA
City College of the City University of New York, NY
Clarke University, IA

Clemson University, SC
Coe College, IA
The College at Brockport, State University of New York, NY
College of Charleston, SC
The College of Idaho, ID
The College of New Rochelle, NY
College of Saint Mary Magdalen, NH
The College of Saint Rose, NY
College of Staten Island of the City University of New York, NY
Colorado Mesa University, CO
Concordia University Texas, TX
Cornerstone University, MI
Davidson College, NC
Denison University, OH
DeSales University, PA
Dordt College, IA
Drury University, MO
East Carolina University, NC
Eastern Connecticut State University, CT
Eastern Michigan University, MI
Eastern New Mexico University, NM
Eastern Washington University, WA
Edgewood College, WI
Edinboro University of Pennsylvania, PA
Elizabethtown College, PA
Elmhurst College, IL
Emmanuel College, MA
Emporia State University, KS
Evangel University, MO
Flagler College, FL
Florida Agricultural and Mechanical University, FL
Florida International University, FL
Fort Hays State University, KS
Frostburg State University, MD
Furman University, SC
Gannon University, PA
Gardner-Webb University, NC
George Fox University, OR
Georgian Court University, NJ
Georgia Southern University, GA
Grand Valley State University, MI
Grove City College, PA
Hamline University, MN
Hardin-Simmons University, TX
Hillsdale College, MI
Howard University, DC
Idaho State University, ID
Illinois Institute of Technology, IL
Illinois State University, IL
Indiana University of Pennsylvania, PA
Indiana Wesleyan University, IN
Iona College, NY
Iowa State University of Science and Technology, IA
John Carroll University, OH
Juniata College, PA
Kean University, NJ
Kennesaw State University, GA
Kent State University, OH
King's College, PA
Kutztown University of Pennsylvania, PA
Lake Erie College, OH
Lake Forest College, IL
Lindenwood University, MO
Lock Haven University of Pennsylvania, PA
Louisiana State University and Agricultural and Mechanical College, LA
Louisiana Tech University, LA
Loyola Marymount University, CA
Lubbock Christian University, TX
Lycoming College, PA
Malone University, OH
Manchester University, IN

Manhattan College, NY
Marquette University, WI
Marywood University, PA
McNeese State University, LA
Mercer University, GA
Meredith College, NC
Michigan State University, MI
Middle Tennessee State University, TN
Midwestern State University, TX
Millersville University of Pennsylvania, PA
Millikin University, IL
Mississippi State University, MS
Missouri Western State University, MO
Monmouth College, IL
Montana State University, MT
Montana State University Billings, MT
Montana State University–Northern, MT
Montclair State University, NJ
Moravian College, PA
Newberry College, SC
New Life Theological Seminary, NC
New Mexico Highlands University, NM
New Mexico State University, NM
North Central College, IL
Northeastern Illinois University, IL
Northeastern State University, OK
Northern Illinois University, IL
Northern Michigan University, MI
Northern State University, SD
Northwestern Oklahoma State University, OK
Northwest Missouri State University, MO
Oakland University, MI
The Ohio State University, OH
Ohio University, OH
Ohio University–Chillicothe, OH
Ohio University–Eastern, OH
Ohio University–Lancaster, OH
Ohio University–Southern Campus, OH
Ohio University–Zanesville, OH
Oklahoma State University, OK
Olivet College, MI
Ouachita Baptist University, AR
Pace University, NY
Pacific University, OR
Piedmont College, GA
Pittsburg State University, KS
Portland State University, OR
Purdue University North Central, IN
Regent University, VA
Ripon College, WI
Rockford College, IL
Rockhurst University, MO
St. Ambrose University, IA
St. Catherine University, MN
St. Edward's University, TX
St. John Fisher College, NY
St. John's University, NY
Saint Louis University, MO
Salisbury University, MD
Samford University, AL
Sam Houston State University, TX
San Diego State University, CA
Seton Hill University, PA
Shippensburg University of Pennsylvania, PA
Shorter University, GA
Siena College, NY
Sonoma State University, CA
South Dakota State University, SD
Southeastern Louisiana University, LA
Southeast Missouri State University, MO
Southern Arkansas University–Magnolia, AR
Southern Illinois University Carbondale, IL

State University of New York at Fredonia, NY

State University of New York at New Paltz, NY

State University of New York at Oswego, NY

State University of New York College at Geneseo, NY

State University of New York College at Potsdam, NY

Stetson University, FL

Stony Brook University, State University of New York, NY

Tennessee Technological University, TN

Tennessee Wesleyan College, TN

Texas A&M International University, TX

Texas Christian University, TX

Texas Tech University, TX

Texas Wesleyan University, TX

Texas Woman's University, TX

Towson University, MD

Truman State University, MO

The University of Akron, OH

The University of Alabama, AL

The University of Alabama in Huntsville, AL

University of California, Davis, CA

University of California, Irvine, CA

University of Colorado Boulder, CO

University of Connecticut, CT

University of Dallas, TX

University of Dayton, OH

University of Delaware, DE

University of Evansville, IN

University of Idaho, ID

University of Illinois at Urbana–Champaign, IL

The University of Kansas, KS

University of Louisville, KY

University of Maine at Fort Kent, ME

University of Mary Hardin-Baylor, TX

University of Maryland, Baltimore County, MD

University of Maryland, College Park, MD

University of Mary Washington, VA

University of Massachusetts Dartmouth, MA

University of Michigan, MI

University of Michigan–Dearborn, MI

University of Michigan–Flint, MI

University of Minnesota, Twin Cities Campus, MN

University of Mississippi, MS

University of Missouri–St. Louis, MO

The University of Montana, MT

University of Montevallo, AL

University of Nebraska at Omaha, NE

University of Nebraska–Lincoln, NE

University of Nevada, Las Vegas, NV

University of New Orleans, LA

The University of North Carolina at Greensboro, NC

The University of North Carolina Wilmington, NC

University of Oklahoma, OK

University of Oregon, OR

University of Portland, OR

University of Puget Sound, WA

University of St. Thomas, TX

University of South Carolina, SC

The University of South Dakota, SD

The University of Texas at Arlington, TX

The University of Texas at Brownsville, TX

The University of Texas at San Antonio, TX

The University of Toledo, OH

University of Tulsa, OK

University of Utah, UT

University of Vermont, VT

University of West Georgia, GA

University of Wisconsin–Eau Claire, WI

University of Wisconsin–La Crosse, WI

University of Wisconsin–Parkside, WI

University of Wisconsin–River Falls, WI

University of Wisconsin–Stevens Point, WI

University of Wisconsin–Whitewater, WI

University of Wyoming, WY

Utah State University, UT

Valparaiso University, IN

Virginia Commonwealth University, VA

Virginia Military Institute, VA

Wartburg College, IA

Washburn University, KS

Washington State University, WA

Washington University in St. Louis, MO

Wayne State College, NE

Wayne State University, MI

Webster University, MO

Wesleyan College, GA

Western Illinois University, IL

Western Kentucky University, KY

Western Oregon University, OR

Western Washington University, WA

West Virginia State University, WV

West Virginia University, WV

Wheaton College, IL

Wichita State University, KS

Widener University, PA

Wilson College, PA

Wright State University, OH

Xavier University, OH

Xavier University of Louisiana, LA

Youngstown State University, OH

Health Fields

Alaska Pacific University, AK

Allen College, IA

Antioch University Midwest, OH

Arkansas State University, AR

Arkansas Tech University, AR

Armstrong Atlantic State University, GA

Auburn University, AL

Augustana College, SD

Austin Peay State University, TN

Averett University, VA

Ball State University, IN

Barton College, NC

Bastyr University, WA

Baylor University, TX

Bellarmine University, KY

Bethel College, IN

Binghamton University, State University of New York, NY

Bloomfield College, NJ

Bloomsburg University of Pennsylvania, PA

Blue Mountain College, MS

Boise State University, ID

Bowling Green State University, OH

Brenau University, GA

Briar Cliff University, IA

Broadview University–Boise, ID

Broadview University–Layton, UT

Broadview University–Orem, UT

Broadview University–West Jordan, UT

Butler University, IN

Caldwell College, NJ

California Polytechnic State University, San Luis Obispo, CA

California State University, Bakersfield, CA

California State University, Chico, CA

California State University, Fresno, CA

California State University, Fullerton, CA

California State University, Los Angeles, CA

California State University, San Bernardino, CA

California State University, Stanislaus, CA

Calvin College, MI

Cameron University, OK

Campbellsville University, KY

Carroll University, WI

Case Western Reserve University, OH

Centenary College of Louisiana, LA

Central College, IA

Central Methodist University, MO

Central Michigan University, MI

Chamberlain College of Nursing, MO

Champlain College, VT

Christian Brothers University, TN

Clemson University, SC

Cleveland State University, OH

The College at Brockport, State University of New York, NY

College of Charleston, SC

The College of New Rochelle, NY

College of Staten Island of the City University of New York, NY

Colorado Mesa University, CO

Columbus State University, GA

Concordia University, Nebraska, NE

Concordia University Texas, TX

Dakota Wesleyan University, SD

Defiance College, OH

DeSales University, PA

Dominican College, NY

Drury University, MO

D'Youville College, NY

East Carolina University, NC

Eastern Michigan University, MI

Eastern New Mexico University, NM

Eastern Washington University, WA

East Texas Baptist University, TX

Edinboro University of Pennsylvania, PA

Elizabethtown College, PA

Elmhurst College, IL

Emmanuel College, GA

Emmanuel College, MA

Emporia State University, KS

Endicott College, MA

Evangel University, MO

Fairmont State University, WV

Farmingdale State College, NY

Felician College, NJ

Ferris State University, MI

Florida Agricultural and Mechanical University, FL

Florida Gulf Coast University, FL

Florida International University, FL

Florida Southern College, FL

Fort Hays State University, KS

Francis Marion University, SC

Frostburg State University, MD

Furman University, SC

Gardner-Webb University, NC

George Fox University, OR

Georgia Southern University, GA

Globe University–Appleton, WI

Globe University–Eau Claire, WI

Globe University–Green Bay, WI

Globe University–La Crosse, WI

Globe University–Madison East, WI

Globe University–Madison West, WI

Globe University–Minneapolis, MN

Globe University–Sioux Falls, SD

Globe University–Wausau, WI

Globe University–Woodbury, MN

Grand Valley State University, MI

Hamline University, MN

Hampden-Sydney College, VA
Hampton University, VA
Harding University, AR
Hardin-Simmons University, TX
Hawai'i Pacific University, HI
Hillsdale College, MI
Houston Baptist University, TX
Howard University, DC
Huntington University, IN
Husson University, ME
Idaho State University, ID
Illinois Institute of Technology, IL
Illinois State University, IL
Indiana University of Pennsylvania, PA
Indiana Wesleyan University, IN
Iowa State University of Science and
    Technology, IA
Iowa Wesleyan College, IA
Jacksonville State University, AL
James Madison University, VA
Jefferson College of Health Sciences, VA
John Carroll University, OH
Juniata College, PA
Kean University, NJ
Kennesaw State University, GA
Kent State University, OH
Kentucky State University, KY
Keystone College, PA
King's College, PA
LaGrange College, GA
Lakeview College of Nursing, IL
Lewis-Clark State College, ID
Limestone College, SC
Lindenwood University, MO
Lock Haven University of Pennsylvania, PA
Long Island University–Brooklyn Campus,
    NY
Long Island University–C. W. Post Campus,
    NY
Louisiana College, LA
Louisiana Tech University, LA
Lycoming College, PA
Malone University, OH
Mansfield University of Pennsylvania, PA
Marquette University, WI
Marymount University, VA
Maryville University of Saint Louis, MO
Marywood University, PA
Massachusetts College of Liberal Arts, MA
Mayville State University, ND
McNeese State University, LA
Medical University of South Carolina, SC
Mercy College of Ohio, OH
Michigan State University, MI
Middle Tennessee State University, TN
Midwestern State University, TX
Millersville University of Pennsylvania, PA
Millikin University, IL
Milwaukee School of Engineering, WI
Minnesota School of Business–Blaine, MN
Minnesota School of Business–Elk River,
    MN
Minnesota School of Business–Lakeville,
    MN
Minnesota School of Business–Moorhead,
    MN
Minnesota School of Business–Rochester,
    MN
Minnesota State University Moorhead, MN
Minot State University, ND
Misericordia University, PA
Mississippi State University, MS
Mississippi University for Women, MS
Missouri Valley College, MO
Missouri Western State University, MO
Molloy College, NY

Monmouth University, NJ
Montana State University, MT
Montana State University Billings, MT
Montana State University–Northern, MT
Montana Tech of The University of
    Montana, MT
Moravian College, PA
Morehead State University, KY
Mount Mary College, WI
Murray State University, KY
Nebraska Methodist College, NE
New England College, NH
New Mexico Highlands University, NM
New Mexico State University, NM
Northeastern State University, OK
Northern Illinois University, IL
Northern Kentucky University, KY
Northern Michigan University, MI
Northwestern Oklahoma State University,
    OK
Northwestern State University of Louisiana,
    LA
Northwest Missouri State University, MO
Northwest Nazarene University, ID
Oakland University, MI
The Ohio State University, OH
Ohio University, OH
Ohio University–Chillicothe, OH
Ohio University–Eastern, OH
Ohio University–Lancaster, OH
Ohio University–Southern Campus, OH
Ohio University–Zanesville, OH
Oklahoma City University, OK
Oklahoma Wesleyan University, OK
Old Dominion University, VA
Oral Roberts University, OK
Oregon Health & Science University, OR
Ouachita Baptist University, AR
Pace University, NY
Pacific University, OR
Peirce College, PA
Piedmont College, GA
Pittsburg State University, KS
Point Loma Nazarene University, CA
Point Park University, PA
Purdue University, IN
Purdue University North Central, IN
Quincy University, IL
Research College of Nursing, MO
The Richard Stockton College of New
    Jersey, NJ
Robert Morris University Illinois, IL
Rochester Institute of Technology, NY
Rockhurst University, MO
Sacred Heart University, CT
Saginaw Valley State University, MI
St. Ambrose University, IA
St. Catherine University, MN
St. Cloud State University, MN
St. Edward's University, TX
Saint Francis Medical Center College of
    Nursing, IL
Saint Francis University, PA
St. John's University, NY
Saint Louis University, MO
Salisbury University, MD
Samford University, AL
San Diego State University, CA
Shepherd University, WV
Siena College, NY
Slippery Rock University of Pennsylvania,
    PA
Sonoma State University, CA
South Dakota State University, SD
Southeast Missouri State University, MO
Southern Adventist University, TN

Southern Arkansas University–Magnolia,
    AR
Southern Illinois University Carbondale, IL
Southern Illinois University Edwardsville,
    IL
Southwestern College, KS
State University of New York at Plattsburgh,
    NY
State University of New York College at Old
    Westbury, NY
Stephen F. Austin State University, TX
Stony Brook University, State University of
    New York, NY
Tennessee Technological University, TN
Tennessee Wesleyan College, TN
Texas A&M International University, TX
Texas A&M University, TX
Texas Christian University, TX
Texas Wesleyan University, TX
Texas Woman's University, TX
Thomas University, GA
Towson University, MD
Trinity Christian College, IL
Truman State University, MO
Union College, KY
Union University, TN
The University of Akron, OH
The University of Alabama at Birmingham,
    AL
The University of Alabama in Huntsville,
    AL
University of Alaska Anchorage, AK
University of California, Davis, CA
University of California, Irvine, CA
University of Colorado Boulder, CO
University of Connecticut, CT
University of Dayton, OH
University of Delaware, DE
University of Evansville, IN
University of Florida, FL
University of Hartford, CT
University of Hawaii at Hilo, HI
University of Illinois at Urbana–Champaign,
    IL
University of Indianapolis, IN
The University of Kansas, KS
University of Louisville, KY
University of Maine at Fort Kent, ME
University of Mary Hardin-Baylor, TX
University of Maryland, College Park, MD
University of Maryland Eastern Shore, MD
University of Massachusetts Amherst, MA
University of Massachusetts Boston, MA
University of Massachusetts Dartmouth, MA
University of Massachusetts Lowell, MA
University of Memphis, TN
University of Michigan, MI
University of Michigan–Flint, MI
University of Minnesota, Twin Cities
    Campus, MN
University of Mississippi, MS
University of Missouri–St. Louis, MO
The University of Montana, MT
University of Nebraska–Lincoln, NE
University of Nevada, Las Vegas, NV
University of New England, ME
University of New Hampshire, NH
University of North Carolina at Asheville,
    NC
The University of North Carolina at Chapel
    Hill, NC
The University of North Carolina at
    Greensboro, NC
The University of North Carolina
    Wilmington, NC
University of Northern Colorado, CO

University of North Florida, FL
University of North Georgia, GA
University of Oregon, OR
University of Pittsburgh at Bradford, PA
University of Pittsburgh at Johnstown, PA
University of Portland, OR
University of Rio Grande, OH
University of St. Francis, IL
University of St. Thomas, TX
University of South Carolina, SC
University of Southern Indiana, IN
The University of Tennessee, TN
The University of Tennessee at Martin, TN
The University of Texas at Arlington, TX
The University of Texas at Brownsville, TX
The University of Texas at El Paso, TX
The University of Texas Health Science Center at Houston, TX
The University of Texas–Pan American, TX
The University of Toledo, OH
University of Tulsa, OK
University of Utah, UT
University of Vermont, VT
The University of Virginia's College at Wise, VA
University of Washington, WA
University of West Georgia, GA
University of Wisconsin–Eau Claire, WI
University of Wisconsin–Green Bay, WI
University of Wisconsin–La Crosse, WI
University of Wisconsin–Parkside, WI
University of Wisconsin–River Falls, WI
University of Wisconsin–Stevens Point, WI
University of Wisconsin–Superior, WI
University of Wyoming, WY
Utah State University, UT
Valdosta State University, GA
Valparaiso University, IN
Virginia Commonwealth University, VA
Virginia State University, VA
Warner Pacific College, OR
Washburn University, KS
Washington State University, WA
Washington University in St. Louis, MO
Waynesburg University, PA
Wayne State College, NE
Wayne State University, MI
Western Illinois University, IL
Western Kentucky University, KY
Western Washington University, WA
West Texas A&M University, TX
West Virginia University, WV
Wheaton College, IL
Wichita State University, KS
Widener University, PA
Wisconsin Lutheran College, WI
Wright State University, OH
Xavier University of Louisiana, LA
Youngstown State University, OH

Home Economics
Auburn University, AL
Averett University, VA
Baylor University, TX
Bowling Green State University, OH
California Polytechnic State University, San Luis Obispo, CA
Carson-Newman University, TN
Central Michigan University, MI
College of Staten Island of the City University of New York, NY
East Carolina University, NC
Eastern Michigan University, MI
Eastern New Mexico University, NM
Fort Hays State University, KS

Fort Valley State University, GA
Framingham State University, MA
George Fox University, OR
Idaho State University, ID
Illinois State University, IL
Indiana University of Pennsylvania, PA
Iowa State University of Science and Technology, IA
Jacksonville State University, AL
Lipscomb University, TN
Louisiana State University and Agricultural and Mechanical College, LA
Louisiana Tech University, LA
McNeese State University, LA
Michigan State University, MI
Middle Tennessee State University, TN
Mississippi State University, MS
Mississippi University for Women, MS
Montana State University, MT
Montclair State University, NJ
Mount Mary College, WI
Murray State University, KY
New Mexico State University, NM
Northeastern State University, OK
Northwest Missouri State University, MO
The Ohio State University, OH
Ohio University, OH
Ohio University–Chillicothe, OH
Ohio University–Eastern, OH
Ohio University–Lancaster, OH
Ohio University–Southern Campus, OH
Ohio University–Zanesville, OH
Oklahoma State University, OK
Ouachita Baptist University, AR
Pittsburg State University, KS
Point Loma Nazarene University, CA
St. Catherine University, MN
Sam Houston State University, TX
Seton Hill University, PA
Shepherd University, WV
South Dakota State University, SD
Southeast Missouri State University, MO
Southern Illinois University Carbondale, IL
State University of New York at Plattsburgh, NY
State University of New York College at Oneonta, NY
Stephen F. Austin State University, TX
Tennessee Technological University, TN
Texas State University–San Marcos, TX
Texas Tech University, TX
Texas Woman's University, TX
The University of Akron, OH
The University of Alabama, AL
University of California, Davis, CA
University of Idaho, ID
University of Illinois at Urbana–Champaign, IL
University of Maryland Eastern Shore, MD
University of Minnesota, Twin Cities Campus, MN
University of Nebraska at Omaha, NE
University of Nebraska–Lincoln, NE
The University of North Carolina at Greensboro, NC
University of Northern Colorado, CO
The University of Tennessee at Chattanooga, TN
The University of Tennessee at Martin, TN
University of Vermont, VT
University of Wisconsin–Stevens Point, WI
University of Wisconsin–Stout, WI
University of Wyoming, WY
Utah State University, UT
Virginia State University, VA

Washington State University, WA
Wayne State College, NE
Western Illinois University, IL
Western Kentucky University, KY
West Virginia University, WV

Humanities
Alaska Pacific University, AK
Alfred University, NY
Alliant International University, CA
Angelo State University, TX
Arkansas State University, AR
Arkansas Tech University, AR
Armstrong Atlantic State University, GA
Auburn University, AL
Augustana College, IL
Augustana College, SD
Austin Peay State University, TN
Averett University, VA
Ball State University, IN
Baptist University of the Americas, TX
Barton College, NC
Baylor University, TX
Belhaven University, MS
Berry College, GA
Binghamton University, State University of New York, NY
Bloomfield College, NJ
Bloomsburg University of Pennsylvania, PA
Blue Mountain College, MS
Boise State University, ID
Bowling Green State University, OH
Brenau University, GA
Briar Cliff University, IA
Buena Vista University, IA
Butler University, IN
California Lutheran University, CA
California Polytechnic State University, San Luis Obispo, CA
California State Polytechnic University, Pomona, CA
California State University, Bakersfield, CA
California State University, Chico, CA
California State University, Fresno, CA
California State University, Fullerton, CA
California State University, Stanislaus, CA
Calvin College, MI
Campbellsville University, KY
Carroll University, WI
Case Western Reserve University, OH
Centenary College of Louisiana, LA
Central College, IA
Central Methodist University, MO
Central Michigan University, MI
Christopher Newport University, VA
The Citadel, The Military College of South Carolina, SC
City College of the City University of New York, NY
Clarkson University, NY
Clemson University, SC
Cleveland State University, OH
Coastal Carolina University, SC
The College at Brockport, State University of New York, NY
College of Charleston, SC
The College of Idaho, ID
The College of New Rochelle, NY
College of Saint Mary Magdalen, NH
The College of Saint Rose, NY
College of Staten Island of the City University of New York, NY
College of the Holy Cross, MA
Colorado Mesa University, CO
Columbia College, MO

Columbus State University, GA
Concordia University, Nebraska, NE
Cornerstone University, MI
Dallas Baptist University, TX
Defiance College, OH
DeSales University, PA
Dordt College, IA
Drury University, MO
D'Youville College, NY
East Carolina University, NC
Eastern Connecticut State University, CT
Eastern Michigan University, MI
Eastern New Mexico University, NM
Eastern Washington University, WA
East Texas Baptist University, TX
Edinboro University of Pennsylvania, PA
Elizabethtown College, PA
Elmhurst College, IL
Emmanuel College, MA
Emory University, GA
Emporia State University, KS
Evangel University, MO
Fairmont State University, WV
Flagler College, FL
Florida Agricultural and Mechanical
    University, FL
Florida Gulf Coast University, FL
Florida International University, FL
Fort Hays State University, KS
Fort Lewis College, CO
Francis Marion University, SC
Fresno Pacific University, CA
Frostburg State University, MD
Furman University, SC
Gannon University, PA
Gardner-Webb University, NC
George Fox University, OR
Georgia College & State University, GA
Georgia Southern University, GA
Grand Valley State University, MI
Hamline University, MN
Hampshire College, MA
Hardin-Simmons University, TX
Hillsdale College, MI
Howard University, DC
Idaho State University, ID
Illinois State University, IL
Indiana University of Pennsylvania, PA
Iona College, NY
Iowa State University of Science and
    Technology, IA
Jacksonville State University, AL
James Madison University, VA
Juniata College, PA
Kean University, NJ
Kennesaw State University, GA
Kent State University, OH
King's College, PA
Kutztown University of Pennsylvania, PA
Lake Erie College, OH
Lawrence Technological University, MI
Lewis-Clark State College, ID
Limestone College, SC
Lindenwood University, MO
Longwood University, VA
Louisiana State University and Agricultural
    and Mechanical College, LA
Loyola Marymount University, CA
Lubbock Christian University, TX
Lycoming College, PA
Malone University, OH
Manchester University, IN
Massachusetts College of Liberal Arts, MA
McNeese State University, LA
Middle Tennessee State University, TN
Midwestern State University, TX

Millersville University of Pennsylvania, PA
Millikin University, IL
Minot State University, ND
Mississippi State University, MS
Mississippi University for Women, MS
Missouri University of Science and
    Technology, MO
Missouri Valley College, MO
Missouri Western State University, MO
Monmouth University, NJ
Montana State University, MT
Montana State University Billings, MT
Montana State University–Northern, MT
Montclair State University, NJ
Mount Mary College, WI
Murray State University, KY
Newberry College, SC
New England College, NH
New Jersey Institute of Technology, NJ
New Mexico Highlands University, NM
New Mexico State University, NM
North Carolina State University, NC
North Central College, IL
Northeastern State University, OK
Northern Illinois University, IL
Northern State University, SD
Northwestern State University of Louisiana,
    LA
Northwest Missouri State University, MO
Oakland University, MI
The Ohio State University, OH
Ohio University, OH
Ohio University–Chillicothe, OH
Ohio University–Eastern, OH
Ohio University–Lancaster, OH
Ohio University–Southern Campus, OH
Ohio University–Zanesville, OH
Oklahoma State University, OK
Old Dominion University, VA
Ouachita Baptist University, AR
Pace University, NY
Pacific University, OR
Piedmont College, GA
Point Loma Nazarene University, CA
Point Park University, PA
Portland State University, OR
Post University, CT
Purchase College, State University of New
    York, NY
Purdue University, IN
Quincy University, IL
Regent University, VA
Rensselaer Polytechnic Institute, NY
The Richard Stockton College of New
    Jersey, NJ
Ripon College, WI
Rockhurst University, MO
Sacred Heart University, CT
St. Catherine University, MN
St. Edward's University, TX
Saint Francis University, PA
St. John Fisher College, NY
St. John's University, NY
Saint Louis University, MO
Saint Martin's University, WA
Salisbury University, MD
Sam Houston State University, TX
San Diego State University, CA
Seton Hill University, PA
Shepherd University, WV
Shippensburg University of Pennsylvania,
    PA
Siena College, NY
Sonoma State University, CA
South Dakota State University, SD
Southeastern Louisiana University, LA

Southeast Missouri State University, MO
Southern Illinois University Carbondale, IL
Southwestern University, TX
State University of New York at Fredonia,
    NY
State University of New York at Oswego,
    NY
State University of New York at Plattsburgh,
    NY
State University of New York College at
    Geneseo, NY
State University of New York College at
    Potsdam, NY
Stetson University, FL
Tennessee Technological University, TN
Tennessee Wesleyan College, TN
Texas Christian University, TX
Texas Tech University, TX
Texas Wesleyan University, TX
Texas Woman's University, TX
Thomas University, GA
Trinity Christian College, IL
Truman State University, MO
The University of Akron, OH
The University of Alabama in Huntsville,
    AL
University of Alaska Anchorage, AK
The University of Arizona, AZ
University of California, Davis, CA
University of California, Irvine, CA
University of California, Riverside, CA
University of California, Santa Cruz, CA
University of Colorado Boulder, CO
University of Connecticut, CT
University of Dayton, OH
University of Delaware, DE
University of Denver, CO
University of Evansville, IN
University of Great Falls, MT
University of Houston–Clear Lake, TX
University of Idaho, ID
University of Illinois at Urbana–Champaign,
    IL
The University of Kansas, KS
University of Maine at Fort Kent, ME
University of Mary Hardin-Baylor, TX
University of Maryland, Baltimore County,
    MD
University of Maryland, College Park, MD
University of Mary Washington, VA
University of Massachusetts Amherst, MA
University of Massachusetts Lowell, MA
University of Memphis, TN
University of Michigan, MI
University of Michigan–Flint, MI
University of Minnesota, Twin Cities
    Campus, MN
University of Mississippi, MS
University of Missouri–St. Louis, MO
The University of Montana, MT
The University of Montana Western, MT
University of Nebraska–Lincoln, NE
University of Nevada, Las Vegas, NV
University of New England, ME
University of New Hampshire, NH
The University of North Carolina at
    Greensboro, NC
The University of North Carolina
    Wilmington, NC
University of North Georgia, GA
University of Oklahoma, OK
University of Oregon, OR
University of Pittsburgh at Bradford, PA
University of Pittsburgh at Johnstown, PA
University of Portland, OR
University of Puget Sound, WA

University of Rio Grande, OH
University of St. Thomas, MN
University of St. Thomas, TX
University of South Alabama, AL
University of South Carolina, SC
University of South Carolina Aiken, SC
The University of South Dakota, SD
University of Southern Indiana, IN
The University of Tennessee, TN
The University of Tennessee at Martin, TN
The University of Texas at Arlington, TX
The University of Texas at El Paso, TX
The University of Texas at San Antonio, TX
University of the Ozarks, AR
The University of Toledo, OH
University of Utah, UT
University of Vermont, VT
The University of Virginia's College at Wise, VA
University of West Georgia, GA
University of Wisconsin–Eau Claire, WI
University of Wisconsin–Green Bay, WI
University of Wisconsin–La Crosse, WI
University of Wisconsin–River Falls, WI
University of Wisconsin–Stevens Point, WI
University of Wisconsin–Superior, WI
University of Wisconsin–Whitewater, WI
Utah State University, UT
Valley City State University, ND
Virginia Commonwealth University, VA
Virginia Military Institute, VA
Virginia State University, VA
Warner Pacific College, OR
Wartburg College, IA
Washburn University, KS
Washington & Jefferson College, PA
Washington State University, WA
Washington University in St. Louis, MO
Waynesburg University, PA
Wayne State College, NE
Wayne State University, MI
Webster University, MO
Wesleyan College, GA
Western Oregon University, OR
Western Washington University, WA
West Texas A&M University, TX
West Virginia University, WV
Wheaton College, IL
Wichita State University, KS
Widener University, PA
William Jessup University, CA
Williams Baptist College, AR
Wilson College, PA
Wright State University, OH
Xavier University of Louisiana, LA
Youngstown State University, OH

International Studies

Alfred University, NY
Alliant International University, CA
Angelo State University, TX
Armstrong Atlantic State University, GA
Augustana College, SD
Austin Peay State University, TN
Ball State University, IN
Barton College, NC
Baylor University, TX
Belhaven University, MS
Binghamton University, State University of New York, NY
Bloomsburg University of Pennsylvania, PA
Boise State University, ID
Bowling Green State University, OH
Buena Vista University, IA
Butler University, IN

California Lutheran University, CA
California Polytechnic State University, San Luis Obispo, CA
California State University, Chico, CA
California State University, San Bernardino, CA
California State University, Stanislaus, CA
Calvin College, MI
Carroll University, WI
Case Western Reserve University, OH
Central College, IA
Central Michigan University, MI
City College of the City University of New York, NY
Clemson University, SC
The College at Brockport, State University of New York, NY
College of Staten Island of the City University of New York, NY
Columbia International University, SC
Columbus State University, GA
Concordia University Texas, TX
Davidson College, NC
Defiance College, OH
D'Youville College, NY
East Carolina University, NC
Eastern Washington University, WA
Elizabethtown College, PA
Elmhurst College, IL
Evangel University, MO
Fairmont State University, WV
Fort Hays State University, KS
Frostburg State University, MD
Furman University, SC
Gannon University, PA
George Fox University, OR
Georgia College & State University, GA
Georgia Southern University, GA
Grand Valley State University, MI
Hamline University, MN
Hampden-Sydney College, VA
Hampshire College, MA
Henderson State University, AR
Heritage Christian University, AL
Hillsdale College, MI
Howard University, DC
Idaho State University, ID
Illinois State University, IL
Indiana University of Pennsylvania, PA
Indiana Wesleyan University, IN
Iowa State University of Science and Technology, IA
James Madison University, VA
Juniata College, PA
Kean University, NJ
Kennesaw State University, GA
Kent State University, OH
Keuka College, NY
Kutztown University of Pennsylvania, PA
Lake Erie College, OH
Lawrence Technological University, MI
Lehigh University, PA
Lindenwood University, MO
Lock Haven University of Pennsylvania, PA
Longwood University, VA
Louisiana Tech University, LA
Loyola Marymount University, CA
Lycoming College, PA
Lynn University, FL
Malone University, OH
Maryville University of Saint Louis, MO
Mercer University, GA
Methodist University, NC
Michigan State University, MI
Middle Tennessee State University, TN

Midwestern State University, TX
Millikin University, IL
Minnesota State University Moorhead, MN
Mississippi State University, MS
Molloy College, NY
Monmouth University, NJ
Montclair State University, NJ
Morehead State University, KY
Murray State University, KY
New England College, NH
New Jersey Institute of Technology, NJ
North Central College, IL
Northern Illinois University, IL
Northern Michigan University, MI
Northern State University, SD
The Ohio State University, OH
Ohio University, OH
Ohio University–Chillicothe, OH
Ohio University–Eastern, OH
Ohio University–Lancaster, OH
Ohio University–Southern Campus, OH
Ohio University–Zanesville, OH
Oklahoma State University, OK
Ouachita Baptist University, AR
Point Park University, PA
Portland State University, OR
Post University, CT
Quincy University, IL
Rochester Institute of Technology, NY
St. Ambrose University, IA
St. Cloud State University, MN
St. Edward's University, TX
Saint Louis University, MO
Saint Martin's University, WA
Samford University, AL
San Diego State University, CA
Siena College, NY
South Dakota State University, SD
Southeast Missouri State University, MO
Southern Illinois University Carbondale, IL
Southwestern University, TX
State University of New York at Fredonia, NY
State University of New York at New Paltz, NY
State University of New York at Oswego, NY
State University of New York at Plattsburgh, NY
State University of New York College at Cortland, NY
State University of New York College at Geneseo, NY
Stony Brook University, State University of New York, NY
Tennessee Technological University, TN
Tennessee Wesleyan College, TN
Texas A&M International University, TX
Texas Christian University, TX
Texas State University–San Marcos, TX
Texas Tech University, TX
Texas Wesleyan University, TX
Thomas University, GA
Trinity Christian College, IL
The University of Akron, OH
University of California, Davis, CA
University of California, Irvine, CA
University of Colorado Boulder, CO
University of Connecticut, CT
University of Dayton, OH
University of Delaware, DE
University of Denver, CO
University of Evansville, IN
University of Illinois at Urbana–Champaign, IL

The University of Kansas, KS
University of Mary Hardin-Baylor, TX
University of Maryland, College Park, MD
University of Mary Washington, VA
University of Memphis, TN
University of Michigan, MI
University of Michigan–Dearborn, MI
University of Michigan–Flint, MI
University of Minnesota, Twin Cities Campus, MN
University of Mississippi, MS
University of Missouri–St. Louis, MO
The University of Montana, MT
University of Nebraska–Lincoln, NE
University of Nevada, Las Vegas, NV
University of New England, ME
The University of North Carolina Wilmington, NC
University of North Florida, FL
University of Oklahoma, OK
University of Oregon, OR
University of Puget Sound, WA
University of St. Francis, IL
University of St. Thomas, MN
University of St. Thomas, TX
University of South Alabama, AL
University of South Carolina, SC
The University of Tampa, FL
The University of Tennessee, TN
The University of Texas at Arlington, TX
The University of Texas at Brownsville, TX
The University of Texas at El Paso, TX
The University of Texas at San Antonio, TX
The University of Toledo, OH
University of Tulsa, OK
University of Utah, UT
University of Vermont, VT
University of Wisconsin–Eau Claire, WI
University of Wisconsin–La Crosse, WI
University of Wisconsin–River Falls, WI
University of Wisconsin–Stevens Point, WI
University of Wisconsin–Stout, WI
University of Wyoming, WY
Utah State University, UT
Villanova University, PA
Virginia Military Institute, VA
Washburn University, KS
Washington State University, WA
Washington University in St. Louis, MO
Waynesburg University, PA
Wayne State University, MI
Webster University, MO
Western Illinois University, IL
West Virginia University, WV
Wichita State University, KS
Widener University, PA
William Jessup University, CA
Wilson College, PA
Wisconsin Lutheran College, WI
Wright State University, OH

Library Science
Arkansas State University, AR
Blue Mountain College, MS
California Polytechnic State University, San Luis Obispo, CA
College of Staten Island of the City University of New York, NY
Emporia State University, KS
Illinois State University, IL
Iowa State University of Science and Technology, IA
Kent State University, OH
Kutztown University of Pennsylvania, PA
Lindenwood University, MO
Lock Haven University of Pennsylvania, PA

Mayville State University, ND
McNeese State University, LA
Mississippi State University, MS
North Carolina Central University, NC
Northeastern State University, OK
Northwestern Oklahoma State University, OK
Sam Houston State University, TX
Southern Arkansas University–Magnolia, AR
Texas Woman's University, TX
The University of Alabama, AL
University of Idaho, ID
University of Illinois at Urbana–Champaign, IL
University of Maryland, College Park, MD
University of Michigan, MI
University of Minnesota, Twin Cities Campus, MN
The University of North Carolina at Greensboro, NC
University of South Carolina, SC
The University of Tennessee, TN
The University of Toledo, OH
University of Wisconsin–Eau Claire, WI
Utah State University, UT
Valdosta State University, GA
Valley City State University, ND
Virginia Polytechnic Institute and State University, VA
Wayne State University, MI
Western Illinois University, IL
Western Kentucky University, KY
Western Washington University, WA
West Virginia University, WV

Mathematics
Abilene Christian University, TX
Adelphi University, NY
Alaska Pacific University, AK
Albion College, MI
Alfred University, NY
Angelo State University, TX
Arkansas State University, AR
Armstrong Atlantic State University, GA
Ashland University, OH
Auburn University, AL
Augustana College, IL
Augustana College, SD
Austin Peay State University, TN
Averett University, VA
Ball State University, IN
Bard College, NY
Barton College, NC
Baylor University, TX
Belhaven University, MS
Bethel College, IN
Binghamton University, State University of New York, NY
Bloomfield College, NJ
Bloomsburg University of Pennsylvania, PA
Blue Mountain College, MS
Boise State University, ID
Bowie State University, MD
Bowling Green State University, OH
Briar Cliff University, IA
Bucknell University, PA
Buena Vista University, IA
Butler University, IN
California Lutheran University, CA
California Polytechnic State University, San Luis Obispo, CA
California State Polytechnic University, Pomona, CA
California State University, Bakersfield, CA
California State University, Chico, CA

California State University, Fresno, CA
California State University, Fullerton, CA
California State University, Los Angeles, CA
California State University, Northridge, CA
California State University, San Bernardino, CA
California State University, San Marcos, CA
California State University, Stanislaus, CA
Calvin College, MI
Cameron University, OK
Campbellsville University, KY
Carroll University, WI
Carson-Newman University, TN
Case Western Reserve University, OH
Centenary College of Louisiana, LA
Central College, IA
Central Methodist University, MO
Central Michigan University, MI
Christopher Newport University, VA
City College of the City University of New York, NY
Clarkson University, NY
Clemson University, SC
Cleveland State University, OH
Coastal Carolina University, SC
Coe College, IA
The College at Brockport, State University of New York, NY
College of Charleston, SC
The College of Idaho, ID
The College of New Rochelle, NY
College of Saint Benedict, MN
College of Saint Mary, NE
The College of Saint Rose, NY
College of Staten Island of the City University of New York, NY
The Colorado College, CO
Colorado Mesa University, CO
Colorado School of Mines, CO
Columbia College, MO
Columbus State University, GA
Concordia University, Nebraska, NE
Concordia University, St. Paul, MN
Concordia University Texas, TX
Cornerstone University, MI
Dakota State University, SD
Dakota Wesleyan University, SD
Dallas Baptist University, TX
Davidson College, NC
Defiance College, OH
Denison University, OH
DeSales University, PA
Dordt College, IA
Drury University, MO
Duke University, NC
D'Youville College, NY
East Carolina University, NC
Eastern Connecticut State University, CT
Eastern Michigan University, MI
Eastern New Mexico University, NM
Eastern Washington University, WA
East Texas Baptist University, TX
Edinboro University of Pennsylvania, PA
Elizabeth City State University, NC
Elizabethtown College, PA
Elmhurst College, IL
Elon University, NC
Emmanuel College, MA
Emporia State University, KS
Evangel University, MO
Fairmont State University, WV
Ferris State University, MI
Florida Agricultural and Mechanical University, FL
Florida Gulf Coast University, FL
Florida International University, FL

Fort Hays State University, KS
Fort Lewis College, CO
Framingham State University, MA
Francis Marion University, SC
Frostburg State University, MD
Furman University, SC
Gannon University, PA
Gardner-Webb University, NC
George Fox University, OR
Georgian Court University, NJ
Georgia Southern University, GA
Glenville State College, WV
Grand Valley State University, MI
Greenville College, IL
Grove City College, PA
Hamline University, MN
Hampshire College, MA
Hardin-Simmons University, TX
Henderson State University, AR
Hillsdale College, MI
Hillsdale Free Will Baptist College, OK
Howard Payne University, TX
Howard University, DC
Huntingdon College, AL
Huntington University, IN
Idaho State University, ID
Illinois State University, IL
Indiana University of Pennsylvania, PA
Indiana Wesleyan University, IN
Iona College, NY
Iowa State University of Science and Technology, IA
Jacksonville State University, AL
James Madison University, VA
John Carroll University, OH
Johnson State College, VT
Juniata College, PA
Kean University, NJ
Kennesaw State University, GA
Kent State University, OH
Kettering University, MI
King's College, PA
Knox College, IL
Kutztown University of Pennsylvania, PA
Lake Erie College, OH
Lake Forest College, IL
Lawrence Technological University, MI
Lebanon Valley College, PA
Lees-McRae College, NC
Lewis-Clark State College, ID
Liberty University, VA
Limestone College, SC
Lindenwood University, MO
Lindsey Wilson College, KY
Lipscomb University, TN
Lock Haven University of Pennsylvania, PA
Long Island University–C. W. Post Campus, NY
Longwood University, VA
Louisiana State University and Agricultural and Mechanical College, LA
Louisiana Tech University, LA
Loyola Marymount University, CA
Lycoming College, PA
Malone University, OH
Manhattan College, NY
Manhattanville College, NY
Mansfield University of Pennsylvania, PA
Marquette University, WI
Marymount University, VA
Marywood University, PA
Massachusetts College of Liberal Arts, MA
The Master's College and Seminary, CA
Mayville State University, ND
McMurry University, TX

McNeese State University, LA
Meredith College, NC
Michigan State University, MI
Middle Tennessee State University, TN
Midwestern State University, TX
Millersville University of Pennsylvania, PA
Millikin University, IL
Mills College, CA
Minnesota State University Moorhead, MN
Minot State University, ND
Mississippi State University, MS
Mississippi University for Women, MS
Missouri University of Science and Technology, MO
Missouri Valley College, MO
Missouri Western State University, MO
Molloy College, NY
Monmouth University, NJ
Montana State University, MT
Montana State University Billings, MT
Montana Tech of The University of Montana, MT
Montclair State University, NJ
Moravian College, PA
Mount Mary College, WI
Murray State University, KY
Newberry College, SC
New England College, NH
New Jersey Institute of Technology, NJ
New Mexico Highlands University, NM
New Mexico State University, NM
North Carolina State University, NC
North Central College, IL
Northeastern Illinois University, IL
Northeastern State University, OK
Northern Illinois University, IL
Northern Kentucky University, KY
Northern Michigan University, MI
Northern State University, SD
Northwestern Oklahoma State University, OK
Northwestern State University of Louisiana, LA
Northwest Missouri State University, MO
Northwest Nazarene University, ID
The Ohio State University, OH
Ohio University, OH
Ohio University–Chillicothe, OH
Ohio University–Eastern, OH
Ohio University–Lancaster, OH
Ohio University–Southern Campus, OH
Ohio University–Zanesville, OH
Oklahoma State University, OK
Ouachita Baptist University, AR
Pace University, NY
Pacific University, OR
Piedmont College, GA
Pittsburg State University, KS
Point Loma Nazarene University, CA
Point Park University, PA
Purchase College, State University of New York, NY
Purdue University, IN
Quincy University, IL
Randolph College, VA
Rensselaer Polytechnic Institute, NY
The Richard Stockton College of New Jersey, NJ
Ripon College, WI
Rochester College, MI
Rochester Institute of Technology, NY
Rockford College, IL
Rockhurst University, MO
Rollins College, FL
Sacred Heart University, CT

Saginaw Valley State University, MI
St. Catherine University, MN
St. Cloud State University, MN
St. Edward's University, TX
Saint Francis University, PA
St. John Fisher College, NY
St. John's University, NY
Saint Louis University, MO
Salisbury University, MD
Samford University, AL
Sam Houston State University, TX
San Diego State University, CA
Schreiner University, TX
Seton Hill University, PA
Shepherd University, WV
Shippensburg University of Pennsylvania, PA
Siena College, NY
Skidmore College, NY
Sonoma State University, CA
South Dakota School of Mines and Technology, SD
South Dakota State University, SD
Southeastern Louisiana University, LA
Southeastern Oklahoma State University, OK
Southeast Missouri State University, MO
Southern Adventist University, TN
Southern Arkansas University–Magnolia, AR
Southern Illinois University Carbondale, IL
Southwestern University, TX
State University of New York at Fredonia, NY
State University of New York at New Paltz, NY
State University of New York at Oswego, NY
State University of New York at Plattsburgh, NY
State University of New York College at Cortland, NY
State University of New York College at Geneseo, NY
State University of New York College at Potsdam, NY
Stephen F. Austin State University, TX
Stetson University, FL
Stony Brook University, State University of New York, NY
Tennessee Technological University, TN
Tennessee Wesleyan College, TN
Texas A&M International University, TX
Texas A&M University, TX
Texas A&M University–Texarkana, TX
Texas Christian University, TX
Texas Lutheran University, TX
Texas Tech University, TX
Texas Wesleyan University, TX
Texas Woman's University, TX
Thiel College, PA
Thomas More College, KY
Towson University, MD
Trinity Christian College, IL
Truman State University, MO
Union College, KY
Union University, TN
The University of Akron, OH
The University of Alabama, AL
The University of Alabama at Birmingham, AL
The University of Alabama in Huntsville, AL
University of Alaska Anchorage, AK
University of Alaska Fairbanks, AK

University of California, Davis, CA
University of California, Irvine, CA
University of California, Riverside, CA
University of California, San Diego, CA
University of California, Santa Cruz, CA
University of Colorado Boulder, CO
University of Connecticut, CT
University of Dallas, TX
University of Dayton, OH
University of Delaware, DE
University of Denver, CO
University of Evansville, IN
University of Great Falls, MT
University of Houston–Clear Lake, TX
University of Idaho, ID
University of Illinois at Urbana–Champaign, IL
The University of Kansas, KS
University of Louisville, KY
University of Maine at Augusta, ME
University of Maine at Fort Kent, ME
University of Mary Hardin-Baylor, TX
University of Maryland, Baltimore County, MD
University of Maryland, College Park, MD
University of Maryland Eastern Shore, MD
University of Mary Washington, VA
University of Massachusetts Amherst, MA
University of Massachusetts Dartmouth, MA
University of Massachusetts Lowell, MA
University of Memphis, TN
University of Michigan, MI
University of Michigan–Dearborn, MI
University of Michigan–Flint, MI
University of Minnesota, Twin Cities Campus, MN
University of Mississippi, MS
University of Missouri–St. Louis, MO
The University of Montana, MT
The University of Montana Western, MT
University of Montevallo, AL
University of Nebraska at Omaha, NE
University of Nebraska–Lincoln, NE
University of Nevada, Las Vegas, NV
University of New England, ME
University of New Hampshire, NH
University of New Orleans, LA
University of North Carolina at Asheville, NC
The University of North Carolina at Chapel Hill, NC
The University of North Carolina at Greensboro, NC
The University of North Carolina Wilmington, NC
University of Northern Colorado, CO
University of Northern Iowa, IA
University of North Georgia, GA
University of Oklahoma, OK
University of Oregon, OR
University of Pittsburgh at Bradford, PA
University of Pittsburgh at Johnstown, PA
University of Portland, OR
University of Puget Sound, WA
University of Richmond, VA
University of Rio Grande, OH
University of St. Thomas, MN
University of St. Thomas, TX
University of South Carolina, SC
University of South Carolina Aiken, SC
The University of South Dakota, SD
University of Southern Indiana, IN
The University of Tennessee at Chattanooga, TN
The University of Tennessee at Martin, TN
The University of Texas at Arlington, TX

The University of Texas at Brownsville, TX
The University of Texas at Dallas, TX
The University of Texas at El Paso, TX
The University of Texas at San Antonio, TX
The University of Texas–Pan American, TX
University of the Ozarks, AR
The University of Toledo, OH
University of Tulsa, OK
University of Utah, UT
University of Vermont, VT
The University of Virginia's College at Wise, VA
University of West Florida, FL
University of West Georgia, GA
University of Wisconsin–Eau Claire, WI
University of Wisconsin–La Crosse, WI
University of Wisconsin–Parkside, WI
University of Wisconsin–River Falls, WI
University of Wisconsin–Stevens Point, WI
University of Wisconsin–Stout, WI
University of Wisconsin–Superior, WI
University of Wisconsin–Whitewater, WI
University of Wyoming, WY
Utah State University, UT
Valdosta State University, GA
Valley City State University, ND
Virginia Commonwealth University, VA
Virginia Military Institute, VA
Virginia State University, VA
Warner Pacific College, OR
Wartburg College, IA
Washburn University, KS
Washington & Jefferson College, PA
Washington State University, WA
Washington University in St. Louis, MO
Wayland Baptist University, TX
Waynesburg University, PA
Wayne State College, NE
Wayne State University, MI
Wesleyan College, GA
West Chester University of Pennsylvania, PA
Western Carolina University, NC
Western Illinois University, IL
Western Kentucky University, KY
Western Oregon University, OR
Western Washington University, WA
West Texas A&M University, TX
West Virginia State University, WV
West Virginia University, WV
Wheaton College, IL
Wichita State University, KS
Widener University, PA
William Jessup University, CA
Wilson College, PA
Wisconsin Lutheran College, WI
Wright State University, OH
Xavier University, OH
Xavier University of Louisiana, LA
Youngstown State University, OH

Military Science
Alfred University, NY
Angelo State University, TX
Arkansas State University, AR
Arkansas Tech University, AR
Armstrong Atlantic State University, GA
Austin Peay State University, TN
Ball State University, IN
Baylor University, TX
Boise State University, ID
Boston College, MA
Bowie State University, MD
Bowling Green State University, OH
California Polytechnic State University, San Luis Obispo, CA
California State University, Fullerton, CA

Cameron University, OK
Carson-Newman University, TN
Central Michigan University, MI
Christopher Newport University, VA
The Citadel, The Military College of South Carolina, SC
Claremont McKenna College, CA
Clarkson University, NY
Clemson University, SC
The College at Brockport, State University of New York, NY
College of Saint Benedict, MN
College of the Holy Cross, MA
Colorado School of Mines, CO
Columbus State University, GA
Creighton University, NE
Dickinson College, PA
East Carolina University, NC
Eastern New Mexico University, NM
Eastern Washington University, WA
Edinboro University of Pennsylvania, PA
Elizabeth City State University, NC
Elon University, NC
Florida Agricultural and Mechanical University, FL
Florida Institute of Technology, FL
Fort Hays State University, KS
Fort Valley State University, GA
Furman University, SC
Georgia Southern University, GA
Gonzaga University, WA
Howard University, DC
Idaho State University, ID
Illinois State University, IL
Iowa State University of Science and Technology, IA
Jacksonville State University, AL
James Madison University, VA
John Carroll University, OH
Kent State University, OH
Lawrence Technological University, MI
Lehigh University, PA
Lincoln University, MO
Lindenwood University, MO
Longwood University, VA
Louisiana State University and Agricultural and Mechanical College, LA
Louisiana Tech University, LA
Manhattan College, NY
Mercer University, GA
Methodist University, NC
Michigan State University, MI
Middle Tennessee State University, TN
Mississippi State University, MS
Missouri University of Science and Technology, MO
Missouri Valley College, MO
Missouri Western State University, MO
Monmouth College, IL
Montana State University, MT
Morehead State University, KY
Morehouse College, GA
Murray State University, KY
New Mexico State University, NM
North Carolina State University, NC
Northern Michigan University, MI
Northwestern State University of Louisiana, LA
Northwest Nazarene University, ID
The Ohio State University, OH
Ohio University, OH
Ohio University–Chillicothe, OH
Ohio University–Eastern, OH
Ohio University–Lancaster, OH
Ohio University–Southern Campus, OH
Ohio University–Zanesville, OH

Oklahoma State University, OK
Old Dominion University, VA
Olivet Nazarene University, IL
Pittsburg State University, KS
Providence College, RI
Purdue University, IN
Rensselaer Polytechnic Institute, NY
Ripon College, WI
Rochester Institute of Technology, NY
Saint Augustine's College, NC
St. Edward's University, TX
St. John's University, NY
Saint Louis University, MO
Sam Houston State University, TX
San Diego State University, CA
Santa Clara University, CA
Siena College, NY
South Dakota School of Mines and
    Technology, SD
South Dakota State University, SD
Southeast Missouri State University, MO
Southern Illinois University Carbondale, IL
Stephen F. Austin State University, TX
Stetson University, FL
Tennessee Technological University, TN
Texas Christian University, TX
Texas State University–San Marcos, TX
Texas Tech University, TX
Texas Wesleyan University, TX
Truman State University, MO
Union University, TN
The University of Akron, OH
The University of Alabama, AL
The University of Arizona, AZ
University of Colorado Boulder, CO
University of Dayton, OH
University of Delaware, DE
University of Florida, FL
University of Idaho, ID
University of Illinois at Urbana–Champaign,
    IL
The University of Iowa, IA
University of Louisville, KY
University of Maryland, College Park, MD
University of Massachusetts Amherst, MA
University of Memphis, TN
University of Miami, FL
University of Michigan, MI
University of Minnesota, Twin Cities
    Campus, MN
University of Mississippi, MS
The University of Montana, MT
University of New Hampshire, NH
University of Northern Colorado, CO
University of North Georgia, GA
University of Oklahoma, OK
University of Oregon, OR
University of Portland, OR
University of Rochester, NY
The University of Scranton, PA
University of South Alabama, AL
University of South Carolina, SC
The University of South Dakota, SD
The University of Tampa, FL
The University of Tennessee, TN
The University of Tennessee at Chattanooga,
    TN
The University of Tennessee at Martin, TN
The University of Texas at Arlington, TX
The University of Texas at El Paso, TX
The University of Texas–Pan American, TX
University of Utah, UT
University of Vermont, VT
University of West Florida, FL
University of Wisconsin–La Crosse, WI

University of Wisconsin–Stevens Point, WI
University of Wyoming, WY
Villanova University, PA
Virginia Commonwealth University, VA
Virginia Military Institute, VA
Virginia State University, VA
Washington State University, WA
Washington University in St. Louis, MO
Wayne State University, MI
Western Illinois University, IL
Western Kentucky University, KY
West Virginia State University, WV
West Virginia University, WV
Wheaton College, IL
Whitworth University, WA
Widener University, PA
Wright State University, OH
Xavier University, OH
Youngstown State University, OH

Physical Sciences
Abilene Christian University, TX
Adelphi University, NY
Alaska Pacific University, AK
Alfred University, NY
Angelo State University, TX
Arkansas State University, AR
Arkansas Tech University, AR
Armstrong Atlantic State University, GA
Ashland University, OH
Auburn University, AL
Augustana College, IL
Augustana College, SD
Austin Peay State University, TN
Averett University, VA
Ball State University, IN
Bard College, NY
Barton College, NC
Baylor University, TX
Bethel College, IN
Binghamton University, State University of
    New York, NY
Bloomfield College, NJ
Bloomsburg University of Pennsylvania, PA
Blue Mountain College, MS
Boise State University, ID
Bowling Green State University, OH
Briar Cliff University, IA
Bucknell University, PA
Butler University, IN
California Lutheran University, CA
California Polytechnic State University, San
    Luis Obispo, CA
California State Polytechnic University,
    Pomona, CA
California State University, Bakersfield, CA
California State University, Chico, CA
California State University, Fresno, CA
California State University, Fullerton, CA
California State University, Los Angeles, CA
California State University, San Bernardino,
    CA
California State University, Stanislaus, CA
Calvin College, MI
Cameron University, OK
Campbellsville University, KY
Carroll University, WI
Case Western Reserve University, OH
Centenary College of Louisiana, LA
Central College, IA
Central Methodist University, MO
Central Michigan University, MI
Chapman University, CA
Chicago State University, IL
Clarkson University, NY

Clemson University, SC
Cleveland State University, OH
Coe College, IA
The College at Brockport, State University
    of New York, NY
College of Charleston, SC
The College of Idaho, ID
The College of New Rochelle, NY
College of Saint Benedict, MN
College of Staten Island of the City
    University of New York, NY
The Colorado College, CO
Colorado Mesa University, CO
Colorado School of Mines, CO
Columbia College, MO
Columbus State University, GA
Concordia University, Nebraska, NE
Concordia University, St. Paul, MN
Concordia University Texas, TX
Cornerstone University, MI
Dallas Baptist University, TX
Davidson College, NC
Defiance College, OH
Denison University, OH
DeSales University, PA
Dordt College, IA
Drury University, MO
East Carolina University, NC
Eastern Connecticut State University, CT
Eastern Michigan University, MI
Eastern New Mexico University, NM
Eastern Washington University, WA
East Texas Baptist University, TX
Edinboro University of Pennsylvania, PA
Elizabethtown College, PA
Elmhurst College, IL
Elon University, NC
Emmanuel College, MA
Emory University, GA
Emporia State University, KS
Evangel University, MO
Fairmont State University, WV
Florida Agricultural and Mechanical
    University, FL
Florida Atlantic University, FL
Florida Gulf Coast University, FL
Florida International University, FL
Florida Southern College, FL
Fort Hays State University, KS
Fort Lewis College, CO
Framingham State University, MA
Frostburg State University, MD
Furman University, SC
Gardner-Webb University, NC
George Fox University, OR
Georgia College & State University, GA
Georgia Institute of Technology, GA
Georgian Court University, NJ
Graceland University, IA
Grand Valley State University, MI
Greenville College, IL
Grove City College, PA
Hamline University, MN
Hampshire College, MA
Hampton University, VA
Hardin-Simmons University, TX
Harrisburg University of Science and
    Technology, PA
Hillsdale College, MI
Howard Payne University, TX
Howard University, DC
Idaho State University, ID
Illinois State University, IL
Indiana University of Pennsylvania, PA
Indiana Wesleyan University, IN

Iowa State University of Science and Technology, IA
Jacksonville State University, AL
James Madison University, VA
John Carroll University, OH
Juniata College, PA
Kean University, NJ
Kennesaw State University, GA
Kent State University, OH
Kettering University, MI
King's College, PA
Kutztown University of Pennsylvania, PA
Lake Erie College, OH
Lake Forest College, IL
Lakeland College, WI
Lawrence Technological University, MI
Lebanon Valley College, PA
Lewis-Clark State College, ID
Limestone College, SC
Lindenwood University, MO
Lock Haven University of Pennsylvania, PA
Loras College, IA
Louisiana State University and Agricultural and Mechanical College, LA
Louisiana Tech University, LA
Loyola Marymount University, CA
Lubbock Christian University, TX
Lycoming College, PA
Malone University, OH
Mansfield University of Pennsylvania, PA
Marietta College, OH
Marquette University, WI
Massachusetts College of Liberal Arts, MA
The Master's College and Seminary, CA
Mayville State University, ND
McMurry University, TX
McNeese State University, LA
Meredith College, NC
Michigan State University, MI
Middle Tennessee State University, TN
Midwestern State University, TX
Millersville University of Pennsylvania, PA
Millikin University, IL
Mills College, CA
Minnesota State University Moorhead, MN
Misericordia University, PA
Mississippi State University, MS
Mississippi University for Women, MS
Missouri University of Science and Technology, MO
Missouri Valley College, MO
Missouri Western State University, MO
Montana State University, MT
Montana State University Billings, MT
Montana Tech of The University of Montana, MT
Montclair State University, NJ
Moravian College, PA
Morehead State University, KY
Mount Mary College, WI
Murray State University, KY
Newberry College, SC
New Jersey Institute of Technology, NJ
New Mexico Highlands University, NM
New Mexico State University, NM
North Carolina Central University, NC
North Carolina State University, NC
North Central College, IL
Northeastern Illinois University, IL
Northeastern State University, OK
Northern Illinois University, IL
Northern Kentucky University, KY
Northern Michigan University, MI
Northern State University, SD
Northwestern Oklahoma State University, OK

Northwest Missouri State University, MO
Northwest Nazarene University, ID
Oberlin College, OH
The Ohio State University, OH
Ohio University, OH
Ohio University–Chillicothe, OH
Ohio University–Eastern, OH
Ohio University–Lancaster, OH
Ohio University–Southern Campus, OH
Ohio University–Zanesville, OH
Oklahoma State University, OK
Old Dominion University, VA
Ouachita Baptist University, AR
Pace University, NY
Pacific University, OR
Pittsburg State University, KS
Point Park University, PA
Portland State University, OR
Purdue University, IN
Quincy University, IL
Randolph College, VA
Regis University, CO
Rhodes College, TN
The Richard Stockton College of New Jersey, NJ
Ripon College, WI
Rochester Institute of Technology, NY
Rockford College, IL
Rockhurst University, MO
Rollins College, FL
Sacred Heart University, CT
Saginaw Valley State University, MI
St. Catherine University, MN
St. Cloud State University, MN
St. Edward's University, TX
St. John Fisher College, NY
St. John's University, NY
Saint Louis University, MO
Salisbury University, MD
Samford University, AL
Sam Houston State University, TX
San Diego State University, CA
Schreiner University, TX
Seton Hill University, PA
Shepherd University, WV
Shippensburg University of Pennsylvania, PA
Siena College, NY
Skidmore College, NY
Slippery Rock University of Pennsylvania, PA
Sonoma State University, CA
South Dakota School of Mines and Technology, SD
South Dakota State University, SD
Southeastern Louisiana University, LA
Southeastern Oklahoma State University, OK
Southeast Missouri State University, MO
Southern Arkansas University–Magnolia, AR
Southern Illinois University Carbondale, IL
Southwestern College, KS
State University of New York at Fredonia, NY
State University of New York at New Paltz, NY
State University of New York at Oswego, NY
State University of New York at Plattsburgh, NY
State University of New York College at Cortland, NY
State University of New York College at Geneseo, NY

State University of New York College at Old Westbury, NY
State University of New York College at Oneonta, NY
State University of New York College at Potsdam, NY
State University of New York College of Environmental Science and Forestry, NY
Stephen F. Austin State University, TX
Stetson University, FL
Stony Brook University, State University of New York, NY
Tennessee Technological University, TN
Tennessee Wesleyan College, TN
Texas A&M International University, TX
Texas A&M University, TX
Texas Christian University, TX
Texas Lutheran University, TX
Texas Tech University, TX
Texas Wesleyan University, TX
Texas Woman's University, TX
Thiel College, PA
Thomas More College, KY
Thomas University, GA
Towson University, MD
Trevecca Nazarene University, TN
Trinity Christian College, IL
Truman State University, MO
The University of Akron, OH
The University of Alabama, AL
The University of Alabama in Huntsville, AL
University of Alaska Fairbanks, AK
The University of Arizona, AZ
University of California, Irvine, CA
University of California, Riverside, CA
University of California, San Diego, CA
University of California, Santa Cruz, CA
University of Colorado Boulder, CO
University of Connecticut, CT
University of Dallas, TX
University of Dayton, OH
University of Delaware, DE
University of Denver, CO
University of Evansville, IN
University of Great Falls, MT
University of Idaho, ID
University of Illinois at Urbana–Champaign, IL
University of Indianapolis, IN
The University of Kansas, KS
University of Mary Hardin-Baylor, TX
University of Maryland, Baltimore County, MD
University of Maryland, College Park, MD
University of Maryland Eastern Shore, MD
University of Mary Washington, VA
University of Massachusetts Amherst, MA
University of Massachusetts Dartmouth, MA
University of Memphis, TN
University of Michigan, MI
University of Michigan–Dearborn, MI
University of Michigan–Flint, MI
University of Minnesota, Twin Cities Campus, MN
University of Mississippi, MS
University of Missouri–St. Louis, MO
The University of Montana, MT
The University of Montana Western, MT
University of Montevallo, AL
University of Nebraska at Omaha, NE
University of Nebraska–Lincoln, NE
University of Nevada, Las Vegas, NV
University of New England, ME
University of New Orleans, LA

University of North Carolina at Asheville, NC

The University of North Carolina at Greensboro, NC

The University of North Carolina Wilmington, NC

University of Northern Colorado, CO

University of Northern Iowa, IA

University of North Georgia, GA

University of Oklahoma, OK

University of Oregon, OR

University of Pittsburgh at Bradford, PA

University of Pittsburgh at Johnstown, PA

University of Portland, OR

University of Puget Sound, WA

University of Richmond, VA

University of Rio Grande, OH

University of St. Thomas, MN

University of St. Thomas, TX

University of South Carolina, SC

University of South Carolina Aiken, SC

The University of Tennessee at Chattanooga, TN

The University of Tennessee at Martin, TN

The University of Texas at Arlington, TX

The University of Texas at Brownsville, TX

The University of Texas at Dallas, TX

The University of Texas at El Paso, TX

The University of Texas at San Antonio, TX

The University of Toledo, OH

University of Tulsa, OK

University of Utah, UT

University of Vermont, VT

The University of Virginia's College at Wise, VA

University of West Florida, FL

University of West Georgia, GA

University of Wisconsin–Eau Claire, WI

University of Wisconsin–Green Bay, WI

University of Wisconsin–La Crosse, WI

University of Wisconsin–Parkside, WI

University of Wisconsin–River Falls, WI

University of Wisconsin–Stevens Point, WI

University of Wisconsin–Stout, WI

University of Wisconsin–Superior, WI

University of Wisconsin–Whitewater, WI

University of Wyoming, WY

Utah State University, UT

Valdosta State University, GA

Valley City State University, ND

Valparaiso University, IN

Virginia Commonwealth University, VA

Virginia Military Institute, VA

Virginia State University, VA

Warner Pacific College, OR

Wartburg College, IA

Washburn University, KS

Washington & Jefferson College, PA

Washington State University, WA

Washington University in St. Louis, MO

Wayland Baptist University, TX

Waynesburg University, PA

Wayne State College, NE

Wayne State University, MI

Western Illinois University, IL

Western Kentucky University, KY

Western Oregon University, OR

Western Washington University, WA

West Texas A&M University, TX

West Virginia University, WV

West Virginia Wesleyan College, WV

Wheaton College, IL

Wichita State University, KS

Widener University, PA

Wilson College, PA

Wisconsin Lutheran College, WI

Wright State University, OH

Xavier University, OH

Xavier University of Louisiana, LA

Youngstown State University, OH

Premedicine

Alfred University, NY

American Jewish University, CA

Angelo State University, TX

Arkansas State University, AR

Auburn University, AL

Augustana College, SD

Averett University, VA

Baylor University, TX

Belhaven University, MS

Bethel College, IN

Binghamton University, State University of New York, NY

Blue Mountain College, MS

Boise State University, ID

Butler University, IN

California State University, Bakersfield, CA

California State University, Stanislaus, CA

Calvin College, MI

Campbellsville University, KY

Carroll University, WI

Case Western Reserve University, OH

Centenary College of Louisiana, LA

Central College, IA

Central Methodist University, MO

Central Michigan University, MI

City College of the City University of New York, NY

Clearwater Christian College, FL

Clemson University, SC

Cleveland State University, OH

Coe College, IA

The College at Brockport, State University of New York, NY

College of Charleston, SC

The College of Idaho, ID

The College of New Rochelle, NY

The College of Saint Rose, NY

College of Staten Island of the City University of New York, NY

Concordia University, Nebraska, NE

Dakota Wesleyan University, SD

Dallas Baptist University, TX

Davidson College, NC

Defiance College, OH

DeSales University, PA

Dordt College, IA

Drury University, MO

D'Youville College, NY

Eastern New Mexico University, NM

Eastern Washington University, WA

Edinboro University of Pennsylvania, PA

Elizabethtown College, PA

Elmhurst College, IL

Elon University, NC

Emory & Henry College, VA

Emporia State University, KS

Evangel University, MO

Florida Agricultural and Mechanical University, FL

Fort Hays State University, KS

Fort Valley State University, GA

Francis Marion University, SC

Frostburg State University, MD

Furman University, SC

Gannon University, PA

Gardner-Webb University, NC

Grand Valley State University, MI

Hamline University, MN

Hampden-Sydney College, VA

Hardin-Simmons University, TX

Hillsdale College, MI

Hobart and William Smith Colleges, NY

Howard Payne University, TX

Howard University, DC

Idaho State University, ID

Illinois State University, IL

Indiana State University, IN

Indiana University of Pennsylvania, PA

Indiana Wesleyan University, IN

Iowa State University of Science and Technology, IA

James Madison University, VA

John Carroll University, OH

Juniata College, PA

Kennesaw State University, GA

Kent State University, OH

King's College, PA

Liberty University, VA

Limestone College, SC

Lindenwood University, MO

Lindsey Wilson College, KY

Lipscomb University, TN

Lock Haven University of Pennsylvania, PA

Louisiana State University and Agricultural and Mechanical College, LA

Lycoming College, PA

Malone University, OH

Mayville State University, ND

McMurry University, TX

McNeese State University, LA

Middle Tennessee State University, TN

Midwestern State University, TX

Millikin University, IL

Mills College, CA

Minnesota State University Moorhead, MN

Mississippi State University, MS

Missouri University of Science and Technology, MO

Missouri Valley College, MO

Montana State University Billings, MT

Moravian College, PA

Murray State University, KY

New Jersey Institute of Technology, NJ

North Central College, IL

Northeastern State University, OK

Northern Kentucky University, KY

Northern Michigan University, MI

Northwestern Oklahoma State University, OK

Northwest Nazarene University, ID

The Ohio State University, OH

Ohio University, OH

Ohio University–Chillicothe, OH

Ohio University–Eastern, OH

Ohio University–Lancaster, OH

Ohio University–Southern Campus, OH

Ohio University–Zanesville, OH

Oklahoma State University, OK

Ouachita Baptist University, AR

Pacific University, OR

Piedmont College, GA

Point Park University, PA

Providence College, RI

Quincy University, IL

Randolph College, VA

Ripon College, WI

Rochester Institute of Technology, NY

Rockford College, IL

Rockhurst University, MO

Sacred Heart University, CT

St. Catherine University, MN

St. Edward's University, TX

St. John's University, NY

Saint Louis University, MO
Saint Martin's University, WA
Samford University, AL
Schreiner University, TX
Shepherd University, WV
Siena College, NY
Sonoma State University, CA
South Dakota State University, SD
Southeastern Louisiana University, LA
Southeast Missouri State University, MO
Southern Illinois University Carbondale, IL
Southwestern University, TX
State University of New York at Oswego, NY
State University of New York at Plattsburgh, NY
State University of New York College at Geneseo, NY
State University of New York College at Oneonta, NY
State University of New York College of Environmental Science and Forestry, NY
Stephen F. Austin State University, TX
Stetson University, FL
Sweet Briar College, VA
Tennessee Technological University, TN
Tennessee Wesleyan College, TN
Texas A&M International University, TX
Texas Christian University, TX
Texas Lutheran University, TX
Texas Tech University, TX
Texas Wesleyan University, TX
Texas Woman's University, TX
Thomas More College, KY
Trinity Christian College, IL
Truman State University, MO
Union University, TN
The University of Akron, OH
The University of Alabama, AL
University of California, Davis, CA
University of California, Irvine, CA
University of California, Riverside, CA
University of California, San Diego, CA
University of Colorado Boulder, CO
University of Connecticut, CT
University of Dallas, TX
University of Dayton, OH
University of Delaware, DE
University of Evansville, IN
University of Great Falls, MT
University of Hartford, CT
University of Idaho, ID
University of Illinois at Urbana–Champaign, IL
The University of Kansas, KS
University of Louisville, KY
University of Mary Hardin-Baylor, TX
University of Maryland, College Park, MD
University of Massachusetts Amherst, MA
University of Memphis, TN
University of Michigan, MI
University of Michigan–Flint, MI
University of Minnesota, Twin Cities Campus, MN
University of Mississippi, MS
University of Missouri–St. Louis, MO
The University of Montana, MT
The University of Montana Western, MT
University of Nebraska at Omaha, NE
University of Nebraska–Lincoln, NE
University of Nevada, Las Vegas, NV
University of New England, ME
University of North Carolina at Asheville, NC
The University of North Carolina at Greensboro, NC

The University of North Carolina Wilmington, NC
University of North Georgia, GA
University of Oregon, OR
University of Pittsburgh at Bradford, PA
University of Pittsburgh at Johnstown, PA
University of Portland, OR
University of Puget Sound, WA
University of St. Thomas, TX
University of South Carolina, SC
The University of South Dakota, SD
University of Southern Indiana, IN
The University of Tennessee at Martin, TN
The University of Texas–Pan American, TX
University of the Ozarks, AR
The University of Toledo, OH
University of Tulsa, OK
University of Vermont, VT
The University of Virginia's College at Wise, VA
University of West Georgia, GA
University of Wisconsin–Eau Claire, WI
University of Wisconsin–Green Bay, WI
University of Wisconsin–Parkside, WI
University of Wisconsin–River Falls, WI
University of Wisconsin–Stevens Point, WI
University of Wisconsin–Whitewater, WI
Utah State University, UT
Virginia Military Institute, VA
Virginia State University, VA
Wartburg College, IA
Washburn University, KS
Washington & Jefferson College, PA
Washington State University, WA
Washington University in St. Louis, MO
Wayne State College, NE
Wayne State University, MI
Wesleyan College, GA
Western Kentucky University, KY
Western Oregon University, OR
Western Washington University, WA
West Texas A&M University, TX
West Virginia University, WV
Wheaton College, IL
Wheeling Jesuit University, WV
Wichita State University, KS
Widener University, PA
Wilson College, PA
Worcester Polytechnic Institute, MA
Wright State University, OH
Xavier University of Louisiana, LA
Youngstown State University, OH

Religion/Biblical Studies

Abilene Christian University, TX
Alaska Bible College, AK
Alaska Pacific University, AK
Anderson University, SC
Augustana College, IL
Augustana College, SD
Averett University, VA
Baptist Bible College of Pennsylvania, PA
The Baptist College of Florida, FL
Baptist University of the Americas, TX
Barton College, NC
Baylor University, TX
Belhaven University, MS
Belmont University, TN
Berry College, GA
Bethel College, IN
Bloomfield College, NJ
Bloomsburg University of Pennsylvania, PA
Blue Mountain College, MS
Briar Cliff University, IA
Butler University, IN
California Baptist University, CA

California Lutheran University, CA
California State University, Bakersfield, CA
California State University, Fullerton, CA
Calvin College, MI
Campbellsville University, KY
Carson-Newman University, TN
Case Western Reserve University, OH
Centenary College of Louisiana, LA
Central Christian College of the Bible, MO
Central College, IA
Central Methodist University, MO
Central Michigan University, MI
Christopher Newport University, VA
Cincinnati Christian University, OH
The Citadel, The Military College of South Carolina, SC
Clearwater Christian College, FL
The College of Idaho, ID
The College of New Rochelle, NY
College of Saint Mary Magdalen, NH
Columbia College, MO
Columbia International University, SC
Concordia University, OR
Concordia University Ann Arbor, MI
Concordia University, Nebraska, NE
Concordia University, St. Paul, MN
Concordia University Texas, TX
Concordia University Wisconsin, WI
Cornerstone University, MI
Crossroads Bible College, IN
Dallas Baptist University, TX
Davidson College, NC
Defiance College, OH
DeSales University, PA
Dordt College, IA
Eastern Michigan University, MI
Eastern New Mexico University, NM
East Texas Baptist University, TX
Edinboro University of Pennsylvania, PA
Elizabethtown College, PA
Elmhurst College, IL
Elon University, NC
Emmanuel College, GA
Emmanuel College, MA
Emory & Henry College, VA
Evangel University, MO
Faulkner University, AL
Felician College, NJ
Flagler College, FL
Florida Gulf Coast University, FL
Florida Southern College, FL
Fort Hays State University, KS
Furman University, SC
Gannon University, PA
Gardner-Webb University, NC
Geneva College, PA
George Fox University, OR
Greenville College, IL
Grove City College, PA
Hamline University, MN
Hampden-Sydney College, VA
Harding University, AR
Hardin-Simmons University, TX
Hastings College, NE
Heritage Christian University, AL
Hillsdale College, MI
Hillsdale Free Will Baptist College, OK
Houston Baptist University, TX
Howard Payne University, TX
Howard University, DC
Idaho State University, ID
Indiana Wesleyan University, IN
Iona College, NY
James Madison University, VA
John Carroll University, OH
Kent State University, OH

King's College, PA
Lakeland College, WI
Lebanon Valley College, PA
Lee University, TN
Liberty University, VA
Limestone College, SC
Lindenwood University, MO
Lindsey Wilson College, KY
Lipscomb University, TN
Louisiana College, LA
Loyola Marymount University, CA
Lubbock Christian University, TX
Lycoming College, PA
Malone University, OH
Marywood University, PA
The Master's College and Seminary, CA
McKendree University, IL
McMurry University, TX
Mercer University, GA
Meredith College, NC
Mid-Atlantic Christian University, NC
Milligan College, TN
Mississippi State University, MS
Missouri Baptist University, MO
Missouri Western State University, MO
Montclair State University, NJ
Nazarene Bible College, CO
Newberry College, SC
New Hope Christian College, OR
New Life Theological Seminary, NC
North Central College, IL
Northwest Nazarene University, ID
Ohio Valley University, WV
Oklahoma Baptist University, OK
Oklahoma Christian University, OK
Oklahoma City University, OK
Oklahoma Wesleyan University, OK
Oral Roberts University, OK
Ouachita Baptist University, AR
Pacific Union College, CA
Piedmont College, GA
Point Loma Nazarene University, CA
Quincy University, IL
Randolph-Macon College, VA
Regent University, VA
Ripon College, WI
Rochester College, MI
Rockhurst University, MO
St. Ambrose University, IA
St. Edward's University, TX
Saint Francis University, PA
Saint Louis University, MO
Samford University, AL
San Diego State University, CA
Schreiner University, TX
Seton Hill University, PA
Shorter University, GA
Siena College, NY
Southeast Missouri State University, MO
Southern Adventist University, TN
Southern Illinois University Carbondale, IL
Southwestern College, KS
Stetson University, FL
Tennessee Wesleyan College, TN
Texas Christian University, TX
Texas Wesleyan University, TX
Thiel College, PA
Thomas More College, KY
Trevecca Nazarene University, TN
Trinity Baptist College, FL
Trinity Christian College, IL
Trinity College of Florida, FL
Union University, TN
The University of Arizona, AZ
University of California, Davis, CA

University of Connecticut, CT
University of Dayton, OH
University of Delaware, DE
University of Evansville, IN
University of Great Falls, MT
University of Illinois at Urbana–Champaign, IL
University of Indianapolis, IN
The University of Kansas, KS
University of Mary Hardin-Baylor, TX
University of Mary Washington, VA
University of Minnesota, Twin Cities Campus, MN
University of Mississippi, MS
The University of North Carolina at Greensboro, NC
University of Portland, OR
University of St. Thomas, MN
University of St. Thomas, TX
University of South Carolina, SC
University of the Ozarks, AR
University of Tulsa, OK
University of Wisconsin–Eau Claire, WI
Valparaiso University, IN
Warner Pacific College, OR
Wartburg College, IA
Washburn University, KS
Washington University in St. Louis, MO
Wayland Baptist University, TX
Waynesburg University, PA
Wesleyan College, GA
Western Illinois University, IL
Western Kentucky University, KY
West Virginia University, WV
Wheaton College, IL
William Jessup University, CA
Williams Baptist College, AR
Wilson College, PA
Wisconsin Lutheran College, WI
Wright State University, OH
Xavier University of Louisiana, LA
Youngstown State University, OH

Social Sciences

Abilene Christian University, TX
Alaska Pacific University, AK
Alfred University, NY
Alliant International University, CA
Angelo State University, TX
Arkansas State University, AR
Arkansas Tech University, AR
Ashland University, OH
Auburn University, AL
Augustana College, IL
Augustana College, SD
Austin Peay State University, TN
Ball State University, IN
Barton College, NC
Baylor University, TX
Belhaven University, MS
Bethel College, IN
Bethel College, KS
Binghamton University, State University of New York, NY
Bloomfield College, NJ
Bloomsburg University of Pennsylvania, PA
Blue Mountain College, MS
Boise State University, ID
Bowling Green State University, OH
Briar Cliff University, IA
Butler University, IN
California Lutheran University, CA
California Polytechnic State University, San Luis Obispo, CA

California State Polytechnic University, Pomona, CA
California State University, Bakersfield, CA
California State University, Chico, CA
California State University, Fresno, CA
California State University, Fullerton, CA
California State University, Los Angeles, CA
California State University, Northridge, CA
California State University, San Bernardino, CA
California State University, Stanislaus, CA
Calvin College, MI
Cameron University, OK
Campbellsville University, KY
Carlos Albizu University, PR
Carroll University, WI
Case Western Reserve University, OH
Centenary College of Louisiana, LA
Central College, IA
Central Methodist University, MO
Central Michigan University, MI
Champlain College, VT
City College of the City University of New York, NY
Clarkson University, NY
Clemson University, SC
Cleveland State University, OH
The College at Brockport, State University of New York, NY
College of Charleston, SC
The College of Idaho, ID
The College of New Rochelle, NY
The College of Saint Rose, NY
College of Staten Island of the City University of New York, NY
Colorado Mesa University, CO
Columbia College, MO
Concordia University, Nebraska, NE
Concordia University Texas, TX
Cornerstone University, MI
Dallas Baptist University, TX
Davidson College, NC
Defiance College, OH
DeSales University, PA
Dordt College, IA
Drury University, MO
D'Youville College, NY
Eastern Connecticut State University, CT
Eastern Michigan University, MI
Eastern New Mexico University, NM
Eastern Washington University, WA
East Texas Baptist University, TX
Edinboro University of Pennsylvania, PA
Elizabethtown College, PA
Elmhurst College, IL
Elon University, NC
Emmanuel College, MA
Emporia State University, KS
Evangel University, MO
Fairmont State University, WV
Flagler College, FL
Florida Agricultural and Mechanical University, FL
Florida Atlantic University, FL
Florida Gulf Coast University, FL
Florida International University, FL
Florida Southern College, FL
Fort Hays State University, KS
Fort Lewis College, CO
Fort Valley State University, GA
Francis Marion University, SC
Fresno Pacific University, CA
Frostburg State University, MD
Furman University, SC
Gannon University, PA

Gardner-Webb University, NC
George Fox University, OR
Georgia College & State University, GA
Georgia Southern University, GA
Glenville State College, WV
Goldey-Beacom College, DE
Grand Valley State University, MI
Grove City College, PA
Hamline University, MN
Hampshire College, MA
Hardin-Simmons University, TX
Hawai`i Pacific University, HI
Hillsdale College, MI
Howard Payne University, TX
Howard University, DC
Idaho State University, ID
Illinois State University, IL
Indiana University of Pennsylvania, PA
Indiana Wesleyan University, IN
Iowa State University of Science and
    Technology, IA
Iowa Wesleyan College, IA
Jacksonville State University, AL
James Madison University, VA
John Carroll University, OH
Juniata College, PA
Kean University, NJ
Kennesaw State University, GA
Kent State University, OH
King's College, PA
Lake Erie College, OH
Lake Forest College, IL
Lebanon Valley College, PA
Lewis-Clark State College, ID
Limestone College, SC
Lindenwood University, MO
Lock Haven University of Pennsylvania, PA
Longwood University, VA
Louisiana Tech University, LA
Loyola Marymount University, CA
Lubbock Christian University, TX
Lycoming College, PA
Malone University, OH
Marymount University, VA
Massachusetts College of Liberal Arts, MA
The Master's College and Seminary, CA
Mayville State University, ND
McMurry University, TX
McNeese State University, LA
Michigan State University, MI
Middle Tennessee State University, TN
Midwestern State University, TX
Millersville University of Pennsylvania, PA
Minnesota State University Moorhead, MN
Minot State University, ND
Misericordia University, PA
Mississippi State University, MS
Missouri University of Science and
    Technology, MO
Missouri Valley College, MO
Missouri Western State University, MO
Molloy College, NY
Monmouth University, NJ
Montana State University, MT
Montana State University Billings, MT
Montana State University–Northern, MT
Montclair State University, NJ
Morehead State University, KY
Mount Mary College, WI
Newberry College, SC
New England College, NH
New Mexico Highlands University, NM
New Mexico State University, NM
North Carolina Central University, NC
North Carolina State University, NC
North Central College, IL

Northeastern Illinois University, IL
Northeastern State University, OK
Northern Illinois University, IL
Northern Kentucky University, KY
Northern Michigan University, MI
Northern State University, SD
Northwestern Oklahoma State University,
    OK
Northwestern State University of Louisiana,
    LA
Northwest Missouri State University, MO
Northwest Nazarene University, ID
The Ohio State University, OH
Ohio University, OH
Ohio University–Chillicothe, OH
Ohio University–Eastern, OH
Ohio University–Lancaster, OH
Ohio University–Southern Campus, OH
Ohio University–Zanesville, OH
Oklahoma State University, OK
Ouachita Baptist University, AR
Pace University, NY
Pacific University, OR
Piedmont College, GA
Pittsburg State University, KS
Point Loma Nazarene University, CA
Point Park University, PA
Portland State University, OR
Post University, CT
Purchase College, State University of New
    York, NY
Quincy University, IL
Randolph College, VA
Regent University, VA
The Richard Stockton College of New
    Jersey, NJ
Ripon College, WI
Rochester Institute of Technology, NY
Rockford College, IL
Rockhurst University, MO
St. Catherine University, MN
St. Cloud State University, MN
St. Edward's University, TX
Saint Francis University, PA
St. John's University, NY
Saint Louis University, MO
Salisbury University, MD
Samford University, AL
Sam Houston State University, TX
San Diego State University, CA
Schreiner University, TX
Seton Hill University, PA
Shepherd University, WV
Shippensburg University of Pennsylvania,
    PA
Siena College, NY
Slippery Rock University of Pennsylvania,
    PA
Sonoma State University, CA
South Dakota State University, SD
Southeastern Louisiana University, LA
Southeastern Oklahoma State University,
    OK
Southeast Missouri State University, MO
Southern Arkansas University–Magnolia,
    AR
Southern Illinois University Carbondale, IL
Southwestern College, KS
Southwestern University, TX
State University of New York at Fredonia,
    NY
State University of New York at Oswego,
    NY
State University of New York at Plattsburgh,
    NY

State University of New York College at
    Geneseo, NY
State University of New York College at
    Oneonta, NY
State University of New York College at
    Potsdam, NY
Stetson University, FL
Stony Brook University, State University of
    New York, NY
Tennessee Technological University, TN
Tennessee Wesleyan College, TN
Texas A&M International University, TX
Texas A&M University–Texarkana, TX
Texas Christian University, TX
Texas Tech University, TX
Texas Wesleyan University, TX
Texas Woman's University, TX
Thomas More College, KY
Thomas University, GA
Trevecca Nazarene University, TN
Trinity Christian College, IL
Truman State University, MO
The University of Akron, OH
The University of Alabama, AL
The University of Alabama in Huntsville,
    AL
University of Alaska Anchorage, AK
University of California, Davis, CA
University of California, Irvine, CA
University of California, Riverside, CA
University of California, San Diego, CA
University of California, Santa Cruz, CA
University of Colorado Boulder, CO
University of Connecticut, CT
University of Dayton, OH
University of Delaware, DE
University of Denver, CO
University of Evansville, IN
University of Great Falls, MT
University of Hawaii at Hilo, HI
University of Houston–Clear Lake, TX
University of Idaho, ID
University of Illinois at Urbana–Champaign,
    IL
The University of Kansas, KS
University of Maine at Fort Kent, ME
University of Mary Hardin-Baylor, TX
University of Maryland, Baltimore County,
    MD
University of Maryland, College Park, MD
University of Maryland Eastern Shore, MD
University of Mary Washington, VA
University of Massachusetts Amherst, MA
University of Massachusetts Dartmouth, MA
University of Memphis, TN
University of Michigan, MI
University of Michigan–Dearborn, MI
University of Michigan–Flint, MI
University of Minnesota, Twin Cities
    Campus, MN
University of Mississippi, MS
University of Missouri–St. Louis, MO
The University of Montana, MT
The University of Montana Western, MT
University of Montevallo, AL
University of Nebraska at Omaha, NE
University of Nebraska–Lincoln, NE
University of Nevada, Las Vegas, NV
University of New England, ME
University of New Orleans, LA
University of North Carolina at Asheville,
    NC
The University of North Carolina at
    Greensboro, NC
The University of North Carolina
    Wilmington, NC

University of Northern Colorado, CO
University of Northern Iowa, IA
University of Oklahoma, OK
University of Oregon, OR
University of Pittsburgh at Bradford, PA
University of Pittsburgh at Johnstown, PA
University of Portland, OR
University of Puget Sound, WA
University of Rio Grande, OH
University of St. Francis, IL
University of St. Thomas, MN
University of St. Thomas, TX
University of South Carolina, SC
University of South Carolina Aiken, SC
The University of South Dakota, SD
University of Southern Indiana, IN
The University of Tampa, FL
The University of Tennessee, TN
The University of Tennessee at Martin, TN
The University of Texas at Arlington, TX
The University of Texas at Brownsville, TX
The University of Texas at San Antonio, TX
The University of Texas–Pan American, TX
University of the Ozarks, AR
The University of Toledo, OH
University of Tulsa, OK
University of Utah, UT
University of Vermont, VT
The University of Virginia's College at Wise, VA
University of West Florida, FL
University of West Georgia, GA
University of Wisconsin–Eau Claire, WI
University of Wisconsin–Green Bay, WI
University of Wisconsin–La Crosse, WI
University of Wisconsin–River Falls, WI
University of Wisconsin–Stevens Point, WI
University of Wisconsin–Superior, WI
University of Wisconsin–Whitewater, WI
University of Wyoming, WY
Utah State University, UT
Valdosta State University, GA
Valley City State University, ND
Virginia State University, VA
Warner Pacific College, OR
Wartburg College, IA
Washburn University, KS
Washington & Jefferson College, PA
Washington State University, WA
Washington University in St. Louis, MO
Wayland Baptist University, TX
Waynesburg University, PA
Wayne State College, NE
Wayne State University, MI
Wesleyan College, GA
West Chester University of Pennsylvania, PA
Western Illinois University, IL
Western Kentucky University, KY
Western Oregon University, OR
Western Washington University, WA
West Texas A&M University, TX
West Virginia University, WV
Wheaton College, IL
Wichita State University, KS
Widener University, PA
William Jessup University, CA
Wilson College, PA
Wisconsin Lutheran College, WI
Wright State University, OH
Xavier University, OH
Xavier University of Louisiana, LA
Youngstown State University, OH

Creative Arts/Performance

Applied Art and Design
Arcadia University, PA
Auburn University, AL
Belhaven University, MS
Bloomfield College, NJ
Bowie State University, MD
Brenau University, GA
Brooks Institute, CA
Butler University, IN
California Polytechnic State University, San Luis Obispo, CA
California State University, Chico, CA
Central Michigan University, MI
Chatham University, PA
City College of the City University of New York, NY
Clemson University, SC
The College of New Rochelle, NY
College of Staten Island of the City University of New York, NY
Concordia University, Nebraska, NE
Converse College, SC
Corcoran College of Art and Design, DC
Defiance College, OH
Dominican University, IL
East Carolina University, NC
Eastern Michigan University, MI
Eastern New Mexico University, NM
Emmanuel College, GA
The Evergreen State College, WA
Fashion Institute of Technology, NY
Ferris State University, MI
Flagler College, FL
Florida Agricultural and Mechanical University, FL
Fort Hays State University, KS
Graceland University, IA
Grand Valley State University, MI
Greenville College, IL
Hardin-Simmons University, TX
Hofstra University, NY
Howard University, DC
Huntington University, IN
Illinois State University, IL
Indiana University of Pennsylvania, PA
Iowa State University of Science and Technology, IA
Kean University, NJ
Keene State College, NH
Kent State University, OH
Kutztown University of Pennsylvania, PA
Lafayette College, PA
Laguna College of Art & Design, CA
Lindenwood University, MO
Lindsey Wilson College, KY
Louisiana State University and Agricultural and Mechanical College, LA
Louisiana Tech University, LA
Loyola Marymount University, CA
Massachusetts College of Liberal Arts, MA
Memphis College of Art, TN
Mercyhurst University, PA
Meredith College, NC
Minneapolis College of Art and Design, MN
Mississippi College, MS
Mississippi State University, MS
Missouri Valley College, MO
Missouri Western State University, MO
Morehead State University, KY
Mount Mary College, WI
New England College, NH
New Jersey Institute of Technology, NJ
New Mexico State University, NM

Northeastern State University, OK
Northern Illinois University, IL
Northern Michigan University, MI
Notre Dame de Namur University, CA
Ohio University, OH
Ohio University–Chillicothe, OH
Ohio University–Eastern, OH
Ohio University–Lancaster, OH
Ohio University–Southern Campus, OH
Ohio University–Zanesville, OH
Ohio Wesleyan University, OH
Oklahoma Baptist University, OK
Oklahoma Christian University, OK
Oklahoma City University, OK
Oral Roberts University, OK
Otis College of Art and Design, CA
The Richard Stockton College of New Jersey, NJ
Ringling College of Art and Design, FL
Robert Morris University Illinois, IL
Rochester Institute of Technology, NY
Rocky Mountain College of Art + Design, CO
Sacred Heart University, CT
St. Cloud State University, MN
Saint Mary-of-the-Woods College, IN
Salisbury University, MD
San Diego State University, CA
Seton Hill University, PA
Shepherd University, WV
Slippery Rock University of Pennsylvania, PA
Sonoma State University, CA
Southern Illinois University Carbondale, IL
State University of New York at Fredonia, NY
State University of New York College at Geneseo, NY
Stetson University, FL
Texas Christian University, TX
Texas State University–San Marcos, TX
Texas Tech University, TX
Texas Woman's University, TX
Trinity Christian College, IL
The University of Akron, OH
University of Alaska Fairbanks, AK
University of Bridgeport, CT
University of California, San Diego, CA
University of Delaware, DE
University of Idaho, ID
University of Illinois at Chicago, IL
University of Illinois at Urbana–Champaign, IL
The University of Kansas, KS
University of Maryland, College Park, MD
University of Massachusetts Dartmouth, MA
University of Missouri–St. Louis, MO
University of Nebraska at Kearney, NE
University of Nevada, Las Vegas, NV
The University of North Carolina at Chapel Hill, NC
University of Northern Iowa, IA
University of North Georgia, GA
University of Oregon, OR
University of St. Francis, IL
University of St. Thomas, TX
The University of Texas at El Paso, TX
University of West Florida, FL
University of West Georgia, GA
University of Wisconsin–Eau Claire, WI
University of Wisconsin–Parkside, WI
University of Wisconsin–Stevens Point, WI
University of Wisconsin–Stout, WI
Utah State University, UT
Valley City State University, ND

Virginia Intermont College, VA
Virginia Polytechnic Institute and State
    University, VA
Virginia State University, VA
Washington State University, WA
Washington University in St. Louis, MO
Wayne State College, NE
Western Illinois University, IL
Western Washington University, WA
Wichita State University, KS
Wright State University, OH

Art/Fine Arts
Abilene Christian University, TX
Adelphi University, NY
Adrian College, MI
Alaska Pacific University, AK
Albion College, MI
Albright College, PA
Alfred University, NY
Alma College, MI
Alverno College, WI
Anderson University, IN
Anderson University, SC
Angelo State University, TX
Arcadia University, PA
Arizona State University, AZ
Arkansas State University, AR
Armstrong Atlantic State University, GA
Ashland University, OH
Auburn University, AL
Augustana College, IL
Augustana College, SD
Aurora University, IL
Austin Peay State University, TN
Averett University, VA
Ball State University, IN
Barton College, NC
Baylor University, TX
Belhaven University, MS
Bellarmine University, KY
Berry College, GA
Bethany Lutheran College, MN
Bethel College, IN
Bethel College, KS
Bethel University, MN
Binghamton University, State University of
    New York, NY
Biola University, CA
Bloomfield College, NJ
Bluefield College, VA
Blue Mountain College, MS
Bluffton University, OH
Boise State University, ID
Boston University, MA
Bowie State University, MD
Bowling Green State University, OH
Bradley University, IL
Brenau University, GA
Brevard College, NC
Briar Cliff University, IA
Brigham Young University, UT
Brooks Institute, CA
Bucknell University, PA
Buena Vista University, IA
Butler University, IN
Caldwell College, NJ
California Baptist University, CA
California Lutheran University, CA
California Polytechnic State University, San
    Luis Obispo, CA
California State University, Bakersfield, CA
California State University, Chico, CA
California State University, Fresno, CA
California State University, Fullerton, CA
California State University, Los Angeles, CA

California State University, San Bernardino,
    CA
California State University, Stanislaus, CA
Calumet College of Saint Joseph, IN
Calvin College, MI
Cameron University, OK
Campbellsville University, KY
Campbell University, NC
Canisius College, NY
Cardinal Stritch University, WI
Carnegie Mellon University, PA
Carroll College, MT
Carroll University, WI
Carson-Newman University, TN
Case Western Reserve University, OH
Cedar Crest College, PA
Centenary College of Louisiana, LA
Central College, IA
Central Michigan University, MI
Chapman University, CA
Chatham University, PA
Chicago State University, IL
Christopher Newport University, VA
City College of the City University of New
    York, NY
Clarion University of Pennsylvania, PA
Clarke University, IA
Clemson University, SC
Cleveland Institute of Art, OH
Cleveland State University, OH
Coastal Carolina University, SC
Coe College, IA
Coker College, SC
The College at Brockport, State University
    of New York, NY
College of Charleston, SC
The College of Idaho, ID
College of Mount St. Joseph, OH
The College of New Jersey, NJ
The College of New Rochelle, NY
College of Saint Benedict, MN
College of Saint Mary, NE
The College of Saint Rose, NY
College of Staten Island of the City
    University of New York, NY
Colorado Mesa University, CO
Colorado State University, CO
Columbia College, MO
Columbus College of Art & Design, OH
Columbus State University, GA
Concordia College, MN
Concordia University Ann Arbor, MI
Concordia University, Nebraska, NE
Concordia University, St. Paul, MN
Cooper Union for the Advancement of
    Science and Art, NY
Cornell College, IA
Creighton University, NE
Culver-Stockton College, MO
Dallas Baptist University, TX
Davidson College, NC
Defiance College, OH
DePaul University, IL
Dillard University, LA
Doane College, NE
Dominican University, IL
Drake University, IA
Drury University, MO
East Carolina University, NC
Eastern Michigan University, MI
Eastern New Mexico University, NM
Eastern Oregon University, OR
Eastern Washington University, WA
Eckerd College, FL
Edgewood College, WI
Edinboro University of Pennsylvania, PA

Elizabethtown College, PA
Elmhurst College, IL
Elon University, NC
Emmanuel College, GA
Emory & Henry College, VA
Emory University, GA
Emporia State University, KS
Endicott College, MA
Eureka College, IL
Evangel University, MO
The Evergreen State College, WA
Fairmont State University, WV
Ferris State University, MI
Finlandia University, MI
Flagler College, FL
Florida Agricultural and Mechanical
    University, FL
Florida Gulf Coast University, FL
Florida International University, FL
Florida Southern College, FL
Fort Hays State University, KS
Fort Lewis College, CO
Francis Marion University, SC
Franklin College, IN
Frostburg State University, MD
Furman University, SC
Gardner-Webb University, NC
George Fox University, OR
Georgetown College, KY
Georgia College & State University, GA
Georgian Court University, NJ
Georgia Southern University, GA
Georgia Southwestern State University, GA
Gordon College, MA
Goucher College, MD
Grand Valley State University, MI
Grand View University, IA
Green Mountain College, VT
Greenville College, IL
Gustavus Adolphus College, MN
Hamline University, MN
Hanover College, IN
Harding University, AR
Hardin-Simmons University, TX
Hartwick College, NY
Hastings College, NE
Henderson State University, AR
Hendrix College, AR
Hillsdale College, MI
Hobart and William Smith Colleges, NY
Hofstra University, NY
Hollins University, VA
Hope College, MI
Houghton College, NY
Houston Baptist University, TX
Howard Payne University, TX
Howard University, DC
Huntington University, IN
Idaho State University, ID
Illinois College, IL
Illinois State University, IL
Indiana State University, IN
Indiana University of Pennsylvania, PA
Indiana University–Purdue University Fort
    Wayne, IN
Indiana Wesleyan University, IN
Iowa State University of Science and
    Technology, IA
Iowa Wesleyan College, IA
Jacksonville State University, AL
Jacksonville University, FL
James Madison University, VA
John Brown University, AR
Johnson State College, VT
Juniata College, PA
Kansas City Art Institute, MO

Kean University, NJ
Keene State College, NH
Kent State University, OH
Kentucky State University, KY
Kentucky Wesleyan College, KY
Kenyon College, OH
Knox College, IL
Kutztown University of Pennsylvania, PA
Lafayette College, PA
Laguna College of Art & Design, CA
Lake Erie College, OH
Lake Forest College, IL
Lakeland College, WI
Lesley University, MA
Lewis-Clark State College, ID
Lewis University, IL
Limestone College, SC
Lincoln University, MO
Lindenwood University, MO
Lipscomb University, TN
Lock Haven University of Pennsylvania, PA
Long Island University–Brooklyn Campus, NY
Long Island University–C. W. Post Campus, NY
Longwood University, VA
Louisiana Tech University, LA
Lourdes University, OH
Loyola Marymount University, CA
Loyola University Chicago, IL
Lubbock Christian University, TX
Lycoming College, PA
Lyme Academy College of Fine Arts, CT
Lynchburg College, VA
Lyon College, AR
Mansfield University of Pennsylvania, PA
Marietta College, OH
Marshall University, WV
Marymount Manhattan College, NY
Maryville College, TN
Maryville University of Saint Louis, MO
Marywood University, PA
Massachusetts College of Liberal Arts, MA
McMurry University, TX
McNeese State University, LA
McPherson College, KS
Memphis College of Art, TN
Mercer University, GA
Mercyhurst University, PA
Meredith College, NC
Messiah College, PA
Miami University, OH
Michigan State University, MI
Midwestern State University, TX
Millersville University of Pennsylvania, PA
Milligan College, TN
Millikin University, IL
Millsaps College, MS
Mills College, CA
Minneapolis College of Art and Design, MN
Minnesota State University Mankato, MN
Minnesota State University Moorhead, MN
Mississippi College, MS
Mississippi State University, MS
Mississippi University for Women, MS
Missouri Southern State University, MO
Missouri Valley College, MO
Missouri Western State University, MO
Molloy College, NY
Monmouth College, IL
Montana State University, MT
Montana State University Billings, MT
Montana State University–Northern, MT
Montclair State University, NJ
Morehead State University, KY

Morehouse College, GA
Morningside College, IA
Mount Mary College, WI
Mount Mercy University, IA
Mount St. Mary's University, MD
Mount Vernon Nazarene University, OH
Muhlenberg College, PA
Murray State University, KY
Nazareth College of Rochester, NY
Nebraska Wesleyan University, NE
New England College, NH
New Jersey Institute of Technology, NJ
New Mexico Highlands University, NM
New Mexico State University, NM
North Central College, IL
Northeastern Illinois University, IL
Northeastern State University, OK
Northern Arizona University, AZ
Northern Illinois University, IL
Northern Kentucky University, KY
Northern State University, SD
Northland College, WI
Northwestern Oklahoma State University, OK
Northwestern State University of Louisiana, LA
Northwest Missouri State University, MO
Northwest Nazarene University, ID
Notre Dame de Namur University, CA
Notre Dame of Maryland University, MD
Oglethorpe University, GA
Ohio University, OH
Ohio University–Chillicothe, OH
Ohio University–Eastern, OH
Ohio University–Lancaster, OH
Ohio University–Southern Campus, OH
Ohio University–Zanesville, OH
Ohio Wesleyan University, OH
Oklahoma Baptist University, OK
Oklahoma City University, OK
Oklahoma State University, OK
Old Dominion University, VA
Olivet College, MI
Olivet Nazarene University, IL
Oral Roberts University, OK
Oregon College of Art & Craft, OR
Otis College of Art and Design, CA
Ouachita Baptist University, AR
Pacific Lutheran University, WA
Pacific Union College, CA
Pacific University, OR
Piedmont College, GA
Point Loma Nazarene University, CA
Portland State University, OR
Purchase College, State University of New York, NY
Quincy University, IL
Rhode Island College, RI
Rhodes College, TN
Rice University, TX
The Richard Stockton College of New Jersey, NJ
Ringling College of Art and Design, FL
Ripon College, WI
Roberts Wesleyan College, NY
Rochester Institute of Technology, NY
Rockford College, IL
Rocky Mountain College of Art + Design, CO
Rollins College, FL
Rosemont College, PA
Sacred Heart University, CT
Sage College of Albany, NY
Saginaw Valley State University, MI
St. Ambrose University, IA

St. Catherine University, MN
St. Cloud State University, MN
St. Edward's University, TX
Saint Francis University, PA
Saint John's University, MN
St. John's University, NY
Saint Louis University, MO
Saint Mary-of-the-Woods College, IN
Saint Mary's University of Minnesota, MN
Saint Michael's College, VT
St. Norbert College, WI
St. Olaf College, MN
Sam Houston State University, TX
San Diego State University, CA
San Francisco Art Institute, CA
San Jose State University, CA
Savannah College of Art and Design, GA
School of the Art Institute of Chicago, IL
School of the Museum of Fine Arts, Boston, MA
School of Visual Arts, NY
Schreiner University, TX
Seattle Pacific University, WA
Seattle University, WA
Seton Hill University, PA
Shawnee State University, OH
Shepherd University, WV
Shippensburg University of Pennsylvania, PA
Shorter University, GA
Sierra Nevada College, NV
Simpson College, IA
Slippery Rock University of Pennsylvania, PA
Sonoma State University, CA
South Dakota State University, SD
Southeastern Louisiana University, LA
Southeastern Oklahoma State University, OK
Southern Adventist University, TN
Southern Arkansas University–Magnolia, AR
Southern Illinois University Edwardsville, IL
Southern Utah University, UT
Southwest Baptist University, MO
Southwestern University, TX
Spring Arbor University, MI
State University of New York at Fredonia, NY
State University of New York at New Paltz, NY
State University of New York at Plattsburgh, NY
State University of New York College at Cortland, NY
State University of New York College at Geneseo, NY
State University of New York College at Potsdam, NY
Stetson University, FL
Stevenson University, MD
Sweet Briar College, VA
Temple University, PA
Tennessee Technological University, TN
Texas A&M International University, TX
Texas A&M University–Commerce, TX
Texas A&M University–Corpus Christi, TX
Texas Christian University, TX
Texas State University–San Marcos, TX
Texas Tech University, TX
Texas Wesleyan University, TX
Texas Woman's University, TX
Thomas More College, KY
Thomas University, GA

Towson University, MD
Transylvania University, KY
Trinity Christian College, IL
Trinity University, TX
Truman State University, MO
Union University, TN
The University of Akron, OH
The University of Alabama, AL
The University of Alabama at Birmingham, AL
The University of Alabama in Huntsville, AL
University of Alaska Anchorage, AK
University of Alaska Fairbanks, AK
The University of Arizona, AZ
University of Arkansas, AR
University of California, Irvine, CA
University of California, Riverside, CA
University of California, Santa Cruz, CA
University of Colorado Boulder, CO
University of Connecticut, CT
University of Dallas, TX
University of Dayton, OH
University of Delaware, DE
University of Denver, CO
University of Evansville, IN
University of Florida, FL
University of Great Falls, MT
University of Hartford, CT
University of Hawaii at Hilo, HI
University of Houston, TX
University of Idaho, ID
University of Illinois at Chicago, IL
University of Illinois at Springfield, IL
University of Illinois at Urbana–Champaign, IL
University of Indianapolis, IN
The University of Kansas, KS
University of La Verne, CA
University of Louisville, KY
University of Maine, ME
University of Mary Hardin-Baylor, TX
University of Maryland, Baltimore County, MD
University of Maryland, College Park, MD
University of Maryland Eastern Shore, MD
University of Mary Washington, VA
University of Massachusetts Amherst, MA
University of Massachusetts Dartmouth, MA
University of Massachusetts Lowell, MA
University of Memphis, TN
University of Michigan, MI
University of Michigan–Dearborn, MI
University of Michigan–Flint, MI
University of Mississippi, MS
University of Missouri–Kansas City, MO
University of Missouri–St. Louis, MO
University of Mobile, AL
The University of Montana Western, MT
University of Montevallo, AL
University of Mount Union, OH
University of Nebraska at Kearney, NE
University of Nebraska at Omaha, NE
University of Nebraska–Lincoln, NE
University of Nevada, Las Vegas, NV
University of New Hampshire, NH
University of North Alabama, AL
University of North Carolina at Asheville, NC
The University of North Carolina at Chapel Hill, NC
The University of North Carolina at Greensboro, NC
The University of North Carolina Wilmington, NC
University of Northern Iowa, IA

University of North Florida, FL
University of Oklahoma, OK
University of Oregon, OR
University of Puget Sound, WA
University of Redlands, CA
University of Rhode Island, RI
University of Richmond, VA
University of Rio Grande, OH
University of St. Francis, IL
University of St. Thomas, TX
University of Science and Arts of Oklahoma, OK
University of South Alabama, AL
University of South Carolina, SC
University of South Carolina Aiken, SC
The University of South Dakota, SD
University of Southern Indiana, IN
University of Southern Mississippi, MS
The University of Tampa, FL
The University of Tennessee, TN
The University of Tennessee at Chattanooga, TN
The University of Tennessee at Martin, TN
The University of Texas at Austin, TX
The University of Texas at Brownsville, TX
The University of Texas at El Paso, TX
The University of Texas at San Antonio, TX
The University of Texas of the Permian Basin, TX
The University of Texas–Pan American, TX
University of the Cumberlands, KY
University of the Incarnate Word, TX
University of the Ozarks, AR
The University of Toledo, OH
University of Tulsa, OK
University of Utah, UT
University of Washington, WA
University of West Florida, FL
University of West Georgia, GA
University of Wisconsin–Eau Claire, WI
University of Wisconsin–Green Bay, WI
University of Wisconsin–La Crosse, WI
University of Wisconsin–Parkside, WI
University of Wisconsin–River Falls, WI
University of Wisconsin–Stout, WI
University of Wisconsin–Whitewater, WI
University of Wyoming, WY
Utah State University, UT
Valdosta State University, GA
Valley City State University, ND
Valley Forge Christian College, PA
Valparaiso University, IN
Virginia Commonwealth University, VA
Virginia Intermont College, VA
Virginia Polytechnic Institute and State University, VA
Virginia State University, VA
Virginia Wesleyan College, VA
Wabash College, IN
Warren Wilson College, NC
Wartburg College, IA
Washburn University, KS
Washington State University, WA
Washington University in St. Louis, MO
Wayland Baptist University, TX
Waynesburg University, PA
Wayne State College, NE
Wayne State University, MI
Webster University, MO
Wesleyan College, GA
Western Carolina University, NC
Western Illinois University, IL
Western Kentucky University, KY
Western Oregon University, OR
Western State Colorado University, CO
Western Washington University, WA

Westmont College, CA
West Texas A&M University, TX
West Virginia State University, WV
West Virginia University, WV
West Virginia Wesleyan College, WV
Wheaton College, IL
Whitman College, WA
Whittier College, CA
Whitworth University, WA
Wichita State University, KS
William Jessup University, CA
William Peace University, NC
Williams Baptist College, AR
Winona State University, MN
Winthrop University, SC
Wisconsin Lutheran College, WI
Wittenberg University, OH
Wright State University, OH
Xavier University, OH
Xavier University of Louisiana, LA
Young Harris College, GA
Youngstown State University, OH

Cinema/Film/Broadcasting
Adelphi University, NY
Arkansas State University, AR
Arkansas Tech University, AR
Auburn University, AL
Ball State University, IN
Baylor University, TX
Binghamton University, State University of New York, NY
Biola University, CA
Bloomfield College, NJ
Bowling Green State University, OH
Brenau University, GA
Brooks Institute, CA
Butler University, IN
California Polytechnic State University, San Luis Obispo, CA
California State University, Chico, CA
California State University, Fullerton, CA
Cameron University, OK
Central Michigan University, MI
Chapman University, CA
City College of the City University of New York, NY
The College at Brockport, State University of New York, NY
The College of New Rochelle, NY
College of Staten Island of the City University of New York, NY
DeSales University, PA
Eastern Michigan University, MI
Eastern New Mexico University, NM
Eastern Washington University, WA
Edinboro University of Pennsylvania, PA
Emory University, GA
Flagler College, FL
Florida Agricultural and Mechanical University, FL
Florida State University, FL
Fort Hays State University, KS
George Fox University, OR
Georgia Southern University, GA
Grand Valley State University, MI
Harding University, AR
Henderson State University, AR
Hofstra University, NY
Howard University, DC
Huntington University, IN
Illinois State University, IL
Ithaca College, NY
James Madison University, VA
Kean University, NJ
Keene State College, NH

Kent State University, OH
Lafayette College, PA
Liberty University, VA
Lindenwood University, MO
Long Island University–Brooklyn Campus, NY
Long Island University–C. W. Post Campus, NY
Loyola Marymount University, CA
Marywood University, PA
Massachusetts College of Liberal Arts, MA
McNeese State University, LA
Milligan College, TN
Minneapolis College of Art and Design, MN
Minnesota State University Moorhead, MN
Mississippi State University, MS
Missouri Valley College, MO
Missouri Western State University, MO
Montana State University, MT
Montclair State University, NJ
Morningside College, IA
New England School of Communications, ME
New Mexico State University, NM
North Central College, IL
Northwestern Oklahoma State University, OK
Northwestern State University of Louisiana, LA
Northwest Missouri State University, MO
Ohio University, OH
Ohio University–Chillicothe, OH
Ohio University–Eastern, OH
Ohio University–Lancaster, OH
Ohio University–Southern Campus, OH
Ohio University–Zanesville, OH
Oral Roberts University, OK
Point Park University, PA
Purchase College, State University of New York, NY
Quincy University, IL
Regent University, VA
Rhode Island College, RI
Rochester Institute of Technology, NY
Sacred Heart University, CT
St. Cloud State University, MN
St. John's University, NY
Saint Joseph's College, IN
San Diego State University, CA
Sonoma State University, CA
Southern Illinois University Carbondale, IL
Southwestern College, KS
Stony Brook University, State University of New York, NY
Texas Christian University, TX
Texas Woman's University, TX
Towson University, MD
Trevecca Nazarene University, TN
Union University, TN
The University of Alabama, AL
University of California, Irvine, CA
University of California, San Diego, CA
University of California, Santa Cruz, CA
University of Central Florida, FL
University of Colorado Boulder, CO
The University of Kansas, KS
University of La Verne, CA
University of Maryland, Baltimore County, MD
University of Memphis, TN
University of Michigan, MI
University of Michigan–Dearborn, MI
University of Mississippi, MS
University of Montevallo, AL
University of Mount Union, OH

University of Nebraska–Lincoln, NE
University of Nevada, Las Vegas, NV
The University of North Carolina at Greensboro, NC
The University of North Carolina Wilmington, NC
University of Pittsburgh at Bradford, PA
The University of Tennessee at Chattanooga, TN
University of Utah, UT
University of Wisconsin–Whitewater, WI
Virginia Polytechnic Institute and State University, VA
Wartburg College, IA
Washburn University, KS
Washington State University, WA
Washington University in St. Louis, MO
Western Illinois University, IL
Western Kentucky University, KY
Western Washington University, WA
Westminster College, PA
West Texas A&M University, TX
Wright State University, OH

Creative Writing

Alfred University, NY
Arkansas Tech University, AR
Auburn University, AL
Augustana College, IL
Augustana College, SD
Austin Peay State University, TN
Belhaven University, MS
Binghamton University, State University of New York, NY
Bowling Green State University, OH
Brenau University, GA
Bucknell University, PA
California Institute of Integral Studies, CA
California Lutheran University, CA
California Polytechnic State University, San Luis Obispo, CA
California State University, Chico, CA
Cameron University, OK
Campbell University, NC
Carroll College, MT
Case Western Reserve University, OH
Central College, IA
Central Michigan University, MI
Chapman University, CA
City College of the City University of New York, NY
Cleveland State University, OH
Coe College, IA
Coker College, SC
The College at Brockport, State University of New York, NY
The College of New Rochelle, NY
College of Staten Island of the City University of New York, NY
Colorado Mesa University, CO
Colorado State University, CO
Columbia College, MO
Creighton University, NE
Davidson College, NC
Drury University, MO
Duke University, NC
Eastern Michigan University, MI
Eastern New Mexico University, NM
Eastern Washington University, WA
Eckerd College, FL
Edgewood College, WI
Emmanuel College, GA
Emporia State University, KS
The Evergreen State College, WA
Fairmont State University, WV

Florida Agricultural and Mechanical University, FL
Fort Hays State University, KS
Frostburg State University, MD
Furman University, SC
Georgian Court University, NJ
Graceland University, IA
Green Mountain College, VT
Grove City College, PA
Hamline University, MN
Hampshire College, MA
Hardin-Simmons University, TX
Hobart and William Smith Colleges, NY
Hollins University, VA
Hope College, MI
Huntington University, IN
Illinois State University, IL
Kent State University, OH
Kentucky Wesleyan College, KY
Kenyon College, OH
Knox College, IL
Lafayette College, PA
Lake Forest College, IL
Lakeland College, WI
Lewis-Clark State College, ID
Louisiana Tech University, LA
Loyola Marymount University, CA
Lycoming College, PA
McNeese State University, LA
Meredith College, NC
Michigan State University, MI
Midwestern State University, TX
Minnesota State University Moorhead, MN
Mississippi State University, MS
Missouri Western State University, MO
Morningside College, IA
New England College, NH
New Mexico State University, NM
Northeastern Illinois University, IL
Northern Illinois University, IL
Northland College, WI
Northwestern State University of Louisiana, LA
Notre Dame de Namur University, CA
The Ohio State University, OH
Oklahoma State University, OK
Plymouth State University, NH
Purchase College, State University of New York, NY
The Richard Stockton College of New Jersey, NJ
Rockhurst University, MO
Sacred Heart University, CT
St. Cloud State University, MN
St. John's University, NY
Saint Mary-of-the-Woods College, IN
San Diego State University, CA
Siena College, NY
Sonoma State University, CA
Southern Illinois University Carbondale, IL
State University of New York College at Geneseo, NY
Texas Christian University, TX
Texas Wesleyan University, TX
The University of Akron, OH
The University of Alabama, AL
University of Alaska Fairbanks, AK
University of California, Riverside, CA
University of California, Santa Cruz, CA
University of Colorado Boulder, CO
University of Idaho, ID
The University of Kansas, KS
University of Louisville, KY
University of Maryland, Baltimore County, MD

University of Michigan, MI
University of Michigan–Dearborn, MI
University of Mississippi, MS
University of Missouri–St. Louis, MO
The University of Montana, MT
University of Montevallo, AL
University of Nebraska at Omaha, NE
University of Nevada, Las Vegas, NV
The University of North Carolina
    Wilmington, NC
University of Oregon, OR
University of Redlands, CA
The University of South Dakota, SD
University of Southern Indiana, IN
The University of Tampa, FL
The University of Texas at San Antonio, TX
University of Utah, UT
The University of Virginia's College at Wise,
    VA
University of Wisconsin–Stevens Point, WI
University of Wisconsin–Whitewater, WI
Ursinus College, PA
Virginia Polytechnic Institute and State
    University, VA
Wabash College, IN
Warren Wilson College, NC
Washington State University, WA
Washington University in St. Louis, MO
Wayne State College, NE
Webster University, MO
Western Illinois University, IL
Western Washington University, WA
Wichita State University, KS
Wright State University, OH
Youngstown State University, OH

Dance
Adelphi University, NY
Albion College, MI
Alma College, MI
Angelo State University, TX
Arizona State University, AZ
Ball State University, IN
Belhaven University, MS
Binghamton University, State University of
    New York, NY
Boise State University, ID
Bowling Green State University, OH
Brenau University, GA
Bucknell University, PA
Butler University, IN
California Polytechnic State University, San
    Luis Obispo, CA
California State University, Bakersfield, CA
California State University, Chico, CA
California State University, Fullerton, CA
Canisius College, NY
Case Western Reserve University, OH
Cedar Crest College, PA
Centenary College of Louisiana, LA
Central Michigan University, MI
Chapman University, CA
Cleveland State University, OH
Coker College, SC
The College at Brockport, State University
    of New York, NY
The College of New Rochelle, NY
College of Staten Island of the City
    University of New York, NY
The College of Wooster, OH
Colorado Mesa University, CO
Colorado State University, CO
Columbus State University, GA
Concordia University, Nebraska, NE
Creighton University, NE
DeSales University, PA

Duquesne University, PA
East Carolina University, NC
Eastern Michigan University, MI
Eastern New Mexico University, NM
Emmanuel College, GA
Florida Agricultural and Mechanical
    University, FL
Florida International University, FL
Florida State University, FL
Fort Hays State University, KS
Goucher College, MD
Graceland University, IA
Grand Valley State University, MI
Grand View University, IA
Gustavus Adolphus College, MN
Hastings College, NE
Hawai`i Pacific University, HI
Henderson State University, AR
Hendrix College, AR
Hobart and William Smith Colleges, NY
Hofstra University, NY
Hollins University, VA
Hope College, MI
Howard University, DC
Huntingdon College, AL
Idaho State University, ID
Indiana University of Pennsylvania, PA
Ithaca College, NY
James Madison University, VA
Johnson State College, VT
The Juilliard School, NY
Keene State College, NH
Kent State University, OH
Knox College, IL
Kutztown University of Pennsylvania, PA
Lafayette College, PA
Lake Erie College, OH
Lakeland College, WI
Lees-McRae College, NC
Lindenwood University, MO
Long Island University–Brooklyn Campus,
    NY
Long Island University–C. W. Post Campus,
    NY
Manhattanville College, NY
Marymount Manhattan College, NY
McKendree University, IL
McNeese State University, LA
Mercyhurst University, PA
Methodist University, NC
Middle Tennessee State University, TN
Milligan College, TN
Millikin University, IL
Mississippi State University, MS
Missouri Valley College, MO
Missouri Western State University, MO
Montana State University, MT
Montclair State University, NJ
Morningside College, IA
Murray State University, KY
New Mexico State University, NM
Nicholls State University, LA
Northeastern Illinois University, IL
Northeastern State University, OK
Northern Illinois University, IL
Northwestern State University of Louisiana,
    LA
Northwest Missouri State University, MO
Oakland University, MI
The Ohio State University, OH
Ohio University, OH
Ohio University–Chillicothe, OH
Ohio University–Eastern, OH
Ohio University–Lancaster, OH
Ohio University–Southern Campus, OH
Ohio University–Zanesville, OH

Ohio Wesleyan University, OH
Oklahoma City University, OK
Old Dominion University, VA
Pacific Lutheran University, WA
Palm Beach Atlantic University, FL
Plymouth State University, NH
Point Park University, PA
Purchase College, State University of New
    York, NY
Rhode Island College, RI
The Richard Stockton College of New
    Jersey, NJ
Rockford College, IL
Sacred Heart University, CT
St. Ambrose University, IA
St. John's University, NY
Saint Joseph's College, IN
Saint Mary-of-the-Woods College, IN
Saint Mary's College of California, CA
St. Olaf College, MN
Sam Houston State University, TX
San Diego State University, CA
Santa Clara University, CA
Shenandoah University, VA
Slippery Rock University of Pennsylvania,
    PA
Sonoma State University, CA
Southeastern Oklahoma State University,
    OK
Southern Arkansas University–Magnolia,
    AR
Southern Illinois University Carbondale, IL
Southern Illinois University Edwardsville,
    IL
Southwestern College, KS
State University of New York at Fredonia,
    NY
State University of New York College at
    Geneseo, NY
State University of New York College at
    Potsdam, NY
Stephens College, MO
Texas A&M International University, TX
Texas Christian University, TX
Texas College, TX
Texas Tech University, TX
Texas Wesleyan University, TX
Texas Woman's University, TX
Towson University, MD
The University of Akron, OH
The University of Alabama, AL
University of Alaska Anchorage, AK
The University of Arizona, AZ
University of California, Irvine, CA
University of California, Riverside, CA
University of California, San Diego, CA
University of Colorado Boulder, CO
University of Florida, FL
University of Great Falls, MT
University of Hartford, CT
University of Idaho, ID
University of Illinois at Urbana–Champaign,
    IL
The University of Kansas, KS
University of Louisville, KY
University of Maryland, Baltimore County,
    MD
University of Maryland, College Park, MD
University of Mary Washington, VA
University of Massachusetts Amherst, MA
University of Memphis, TN
University of Michigan, MI
University of Missouri–St. Louis, MO
The University of Montana, MT
University of Nebraska–Lincoln, NE
University of Nevada, Las Vegas, NV

University of New Hampshire, NH
The University of North Carolina at
Greensboro, NC
University of Northern Colorado, CO
University of Oklahoma, OK
University of Oregon, OR
University of Puerto Rico at Bayamón, PR
University of Richmond, VA
University of South Carolina, SC
University of Southern Mississippi, MS
The University of Texas of the Permian
Basin, TX
The University of Texas–Pan American, TX
University of Utah, UT
University of Wisconsin–Green Bay, WI
University of Wisconsin–Stevens Point, WI
University of Wyoming, WY
Virginia Commonwealth University, VA
Virginia State University, VA
Washington University in St. Louis, MO
Wayne State University, MI
Western Illinois University, IL
Western Kentucky University, KY
Western Oregon University, OR
Western Washington University, WA
West Texas A&M University, TX
Wichita State University, KS
Widener University, PA
Winthrop University, SC
Wittenberg University, OH
Wright State University, OH

Debating

Abilene Christian University, TX
Arkansas State University, AR
Augustana College, IL
Austin Peay State University, TN
Ball State University, IN
Baylor University, TX
Berry College, GA
Bethany Lutheran College, MN
Bethel College, KS
Bethel University, MN
Boise State University, ID
Bowling Green State University, OH
California Polytechnic State University, San
Luis Obispo, CA
California State University, Chico, CA
Cameron University, OK
Carroll College, MT
Carson-Newman University, TN
Cedarville University, OH
The College of Idaho, ID
The College of New Rochelle, NY
College of Saint Mary, NE
College of Staten Island of the City
University of New York, NY
Concordia College, MN
Concordia University, CA
Concordia University, Nebraska, NE
Creighton University, NE
Culver-Stockton College, MO
Doane College, NE
Drury University, MO
Eastern Michigan University, MI
Eastern New Mexico University, NM
Emory University, GA
Emporia State University, KS
Evangel University, MO
Fairmont State University, WV
Ferris State University, MI
Fort Hays State University, KS
George Fox University, OR
Gonzaga University, WA
Gustavus Adolphus College, MN

Harding University, AR
Hastings College, NE
Henderson State University, AR
Hillsdale College, MI
Idaho State University, ID
Illinois State University, IL
Lakeland College, WI
Lewis & Clark College, OR
Lewis-Clark State College, ID
Liberty University, VA
Lindenwood University, MO
Linfield College, OR
Louisiana Tech University, LA
Loyola University Chicago, IL
Malone University, OH
Marist College, NY
McKendree University, IL
McNeese State University, LA
Mercer University, GA
Methodist University, NC
Michigan State University, MI
Middle Tennessee State University, TN
Mississippi State University, MS
Missouri Southern State University, MO
Monmouth College, IL
North Central College, IL
Northeastern State University, OK
Northern Illinois University, IL
Northwestern Oklahoma State University,
OK
Northwest Missouri State University, MO
Northwest Nazarene University, ID
Northwest University, WA
Ohio University, OH
Ohio University–Chillicothe, OH
Ohio University–Eastern, OH
Ohio University–Lancaster, OH
Ohio University–Southern Campus, OH
Ohio University–Zanesville, OH
Pacific Lutheran University, WA
Pacific University, OR
Piedmont College, GA
Point Loma Nazarene University, CA
Regis University, CO
Ripon College, WI
St. John's University, NY
Saint Joseph's University, PA
Saint Mary's College of California, CA
Samford University, AL
San Diego State University, CA
Santa Clara University, CA
South Dakota State University, SD
Southeastern Oklahoma State University,
OK
Southern Illinois University Carbondale, IL
Southwest Baptist University, MO
Tennessee Technological University, TN
Texas Wesleyan University, TX
Towson University, MD
Trinity University, TX
Truman State University, MO
Union University, TN
The University of Akron, OH
The University of Alabama, AL
University of Alaska Anchorage, AK
University of Denver, CO
University of Indianapolis, IN
The University of Kansas, KS
University of Louisville, KY
University of Michigan–Dearborn, MI
University of Mississippi, MS
University of Missouri–Kansas City, MO
University of Nebraska at Kearney, NE
University of Nebraska at Omaha, NE
University of Nevada, Las Vegas, NV

University of Northern Iowa, IA
University of Oklahoma, OK
University of Oregon, OR
University of Puget Sound, WA
University of Redlands, CA
University of South Carolina, SC
The University of South Dakota, SD
The University of Texas at San Antonio, TX
University of the Cumberlands, KY
University of the Pacific, CA
University of Vermont, VT
University of West Georgia, GA
University of Wisconsin–Eau Claire, WI
University of Wyoming, WY
Washburn University, KS
Wayne State University, MI
Webster University, MO
Western Illinois University, IL
Western Kentucky University, KY
West Texas A&M University, TX
West Virginia University, WV
Whitman College, WA
Wichita State University, KS
William Jewell College, MO
Winona State University, MN

Journalism/Publications

Abilene Christian University, TX
Alaska Pacific University, AK
Albright College, PA
Angelo State University, TX
Arkansas State University, AR
Arkansas Tech University, AR
Auburn University, AL
Augustana College, SD
Austin Peay State University, TN
Averett University, VA
Ball State University, IN
Baylor University, TX
Belhaven University, MS
Berry College, GA
Bethany Lutheran College, MN
Bethel College, IN
Binghamton University, State University of
New York, NY
Biola University, CA
Boise State University, ID
Bowling Green State University, OH
Brenau University, GA
Brooks Institute, CA
Butler University, IN
California Lutheran University, CA
California Polytechnic State University, San
Luis Obispo, CA
California State University, Chico, CA
California State University, Fresno, CA
California State University, Fullerton, CA
California State University, Los Angeles, CA
California State University, Northridge, CA
California State University, San Bernardino,
CA
Cameron University, OK
Campbellsville University, KY
Campbell University, NC
Carroll University, WI
Carson-Newman University, TN
Central Michigan University, MI
Chicago State University, IL
The Citadel, The Military College of South
Carolina, SC
Cleveland State University, OH
The College at Brockport, State University
of New York, NY
The College of New Rochelle, NY

College of Staten Island of the City
    University of New York, NY
Colorado Mesa University, CO
Creighton University, NE
Dordt College, IA
Eastern New Mexico University, NM
Eastern Washington University, WA
Edinboro University of Pennsylvania, PA
Elon University, NC
Emmanuel College, GA
Emory & Henry College, VA
Fairmont State University, WV
Faulkner University, AL
Ferris State University, MI
Florida Agricultural and Mechanical
    University, FL
Florida International University, FL
Fort Hays State University, KS
Fort Valley State University, GA
Franklin College, IN
Frostburg State University, MD
Georgia College & State University, GA
Glenville State College, WV
Grand Valley State University, MI
Hamline University, MN
Harding University, AR
Hardin-Simmons University, TX
Hastings College, NE
Hawai`i Pacific University, HI
Henderson State University, AR
Hillsdale College, MI
Hofstra University, NY
Howard University, DC
Huntington University, IN
Indiana University of Pennsylvania, PA
Iowa State University of Science and
    Technology, IA
Ithaca College, NY
Jacksonville State University, AL
James Madison University, VA
John Brown University, AR
Kent State University, OH
Lakeland College, WI
Lees-McRae College, NC
Lehigh University, PA
LeMoyne-Owen College, TN
Liberty University, VA
Lincoln University, MO
Lipscomb University, TN
Lock Haven University of Pennsylvania, PA
Long Island University–C. W. Post Campus,
    NY
Louisiana State University and Agricultural
    and Mechanical College, LA
Louisiana Tech University, LA
Loyola Marymount University, CA
Loyola University Chicago, IL
Lubbock Christian University, TX
Malone University, OH
Mansfield University of Pennsylvania, PA
Marywood University, PA
Massachusetts College of Liberal Arts, MA
McNeese State University, LA
McPherson College, KS
Michigan State University, MI
Middle Tennessee State University, TN
Midwestern State University, TX
Mississippi State University, MS
Mississippi University for Women, MS
Missouri Southern State University, MO
Missouri Valley College, MO
Missouri Western State University, MO
Morehead State University, KY
Morningside College, IA
Murray State University, KY

New England School of Communications,
    ME
New Jersey Institute of Technology, NJ
New Mexico State University, NM
North Central College, IL
Northeastern Illinois University, IL
Northeastern State University, OK
Northern Illinois University, IL
Northwestern Oklahoma State University,
    OK
Northwest Missouri State University, MO
Northwest Nazarene University, ID
Nyack College, NY
Oglethorpe University, GA
The Ohio State University, OH
Ohio University, OH
Ohio University–Chillicothe, OH
Ohio University–Eastern, OH
Ohio University–Lancaster, OH
Ohio University–Southern Campus, OH
Ohio University–Zanesville, OH
Ohio Valley University, WV
Oklahoma Christian University, OK
Oklahoma State University, OK
Olivet College, MI
Oral Roberts University, OK
Ouachita Baptist University, AR
Pacific University, OR
Piedmont College, GA
Regent University, VA
Rhode Island College, RI
The Richard Stockton College of New
    Jersey, NJ
Robert Morris University Illinois, IL
Rochester College, MI
St. Ambrose University, IA
St. Bonaventure University, NY
St. Cloud State University, MN
St. Edward's University, TX
St. John's University, NY
Saint Mary-of-the-Woods College, IN
Samford University, AL
San Diego State University, CA
Schreiner University, TX
Siena College, NY
Sonoma State University, CA
South Dakota State University, SD
Southern Adventist University, TN
Southern Illinois University Carbondale, IL
Southwestern College, KS
State University of New York at Plattsburgh,
    NY
State University of New York College at
    Geneseo, NY
Stephen F. Austin State University, TX
Stony Brook University, State University of
    New York, NY
Texas A&M University, TX
Texas A&M University–Commerce, TX
Texas Christian University, TX
Texas Lutheran University, TX
Texas State University–San Marcos, TX
Texas Tech University, TX
Texas Wesleyan University, TX
Texas Woman's University, TX
Trinity Christian College, IL
Union University, TN
The University of Akron, OH
The University of Alabama, AL
University of California, San Diego, CA
University of Colorado Boulder, CO
University of Florida, FL
University of Idaho, ID
University of Illinois at Urbana–Champaign,
    IL
The University of Kansas, KS

University of La Verne, CA
University of Mary Washington, VA
University of Massachusetts Amherst, MA
University of Memphis, TN
University of Michigan, MI
University of Michigan–Dearborn, MI
University of Michigan–Flint, MI
University of Mississippi, MS
The University of Montana, MT
University of Montevallo, AL
University of Mount Union, OH
University of Nebraska at Kearney, NE
University of Nebraska at Omaha, NE
University of Nebraska–Lincoln, NE
University of Nevada, Las Vegas, NV
University of North Alabama, AL
The University of North Carolina at Chapel
    Hill, NC
University of Oklahoma, OK
University of Oregon, OR
University of Pittsburgh at Johnstown, PA
University of St. Thomas, MN
University of South Alabama, AL
University of South Carolina, SC
University of South Carolina Aiken, SC
The University of Tampa, FL
The University of Tennessee at Chattanooga,
    TN
The University of Tennessee at Martin, TN
The University of Texas at Arlington, TX
The University of Texas at El Paso, TX
The University of Texas–Pan American, TX
University of the Cumberlands, KY
University of Utah, UT
The University of Virginia's College at Wise,
    VA
University of West Georgia, GA
University of Wisconsin–Eau Claire, WI
University of Wisconsin–Green Bay, WI
University of Wisconsin–Whitewater, WI
University of Wyoming, WY
Utah State University, UT
Valdosta State University, GA
Valley City State University, ND
Virginia Polytechnic Institute and State
    University, VA
Wabash College, IN
Wartburg College, IA
Washburn University, KS
Washington State University, WA
Wayland Baptist University, TX
Wayne State College, NE
Wayne State University, MI
Webber International University, FL
Western Illinois University, IL
Western Kentucky University, KY
Western Washington University, WA
West Texas A&M University, TX
Whitworth University, WA
Wichita State University, KS
William Jewell College, MO
Youngstown State University, OH

Music
Abilene Christian University, TX
Adelphi University, NY
Adrian College, MI
Alabama State University, AL
Alaska Bible College, AK
Alaska Pacific University, AK
Albion College, MI
Albright College, PA
Alcorn State University, MS
Alma College, MI
Alverno College, WI
Anderson University, IN

Anderson University, SC
Andrews University, MI
Angelo State University, TX
Anna Maria College, MA
Arizona State University, AZ
Arkansas State University, AR
Armstrong Atlantic State University, GA
Asbury University, KY
Ashland University, OH
Auburn University, AL
Augustana College, IL
Augustana College, SD
Aurora University, IL
Austin Peay State University, TN
Averett University, VA
Baldwin Wallace University, OH
Ball State University, IN
Baptist Bible College of Pennsylvania, PA
The Baptist College of Florida, FL
Barton College, NC
Baylor University, TX
Belhaven University, MS
Bellarmine University, KY
Belmont University, TN
Beloit College, WI
Benedict College, SC
Benedictine College, KS
Benedictine University, IL
Berry College, GA
Bethany Lutheran College, MN
Bethel College, IN
Bethel College, KS
Bethel University, MN
Binghamton University, State University of New York, NY
Biola University, CA
Bluefield College, VA
Blue Mountain College, MS
Bluffton University, OH
Boise State University, ID
Boston University, MA
Bowie State University, MD
Bowling Green State University, OH
Bradley University, IL
Brenau University, GA
Brevard College, NC
Briar Cliff University, IA
Bridgewater College, VA
Brigham Young University, UT
Bucknell University, PA
Buena Vista University, IA
Butler University, IN
Cairn University, PA
Caldwell College, NJ
California Baptist University, CA
California Lutheran University, CA
California Polytechnic State University, San Luis Obispo, CA
California State University, Bakersfield, CA
California State University, Chico, CA
California State University, East Bay, CA
California State University, Fresno, CA
California State University, Fullerton, CA
California State University, Los Angeles, CA
California State University, Northridge, CA
California State University, San Bernardino, CA
California State University, Stanislaus, CA
Calvin College, MI
Cameron University, OK
Campbellsville University, KY
Campbell University, NC
Canisius College, NY
Capital University, OH
Cardinal Stritch University, WI

Carleton College, MN
Carnegie Mellon University, PA
Carroll College, MT
Carroll University, WI
Carson-Newman University, TN
Case Western Reserve University, OH
Catawba College, NC
The Catholic University of America, DC
Cedarville University, OH
Centenary College of Louisiana, LA
Central College, IA
Central Methodist University, MO
Central Michigan University, MI
Centre College, KY
Chapman University, CA
Chatham University, PA
Chestnut Hill College, PA
Chicago State University, IL
Chowan University, NC
Christopher Newport University, VA
Cincinnati Christian University, OH
The Citadel, The Military College of South Carolina, SC
City College of the City University of New York, NY
Clarke University, IA
Clear Creek Baptist Bible College, KY
Clearwater Christian College, FL
Cleveland Institute of Music, OH
Cleveland State University, OH
Coastal Carolina University, SC
Coe College, IA
Coker College, SC
The College at Brockport, State University of New York, NY
College of Charleston, SC
The College of Idaho, ID
College of Mount St. Joseph, OH
The College of New Jersey, NJ
The College of New Rochelle, NY
College of Saint Benedict, MN
College of Saint Mary, NE
The College of Saint Rose, NY
The College of St. Scholastica, MN
College of Staten Island of the City University of New York, NY
College of the Holy Cross, MA
The College of William and Mary, VA
The College of Wooster, OH
Colorado Mesa University, CO
Colorado State University, CO
Columbia College, MO
Columbia International University, SC
Columbus State University, GA
Concordia College, MN
Concordia University, CA
Concordia University, OR
Concordia University Ann Arbor, MI
Concordia University, Nebraska, NE
Concordia University, St. Paul, MN
Concordia University Texas, TX
Concordia University Wisconsin, WI
Converse College, SC
Corban University, OR
Cornell College, IA
Cornerstone University, MI
Covenant College, GA
Creighton University, NE
Crown College, MN
Culver-Stockton College, MO
Dakota State University, SD
Dakota Wesleyan University, SD
Dallas Baptist University, TX
Davidson College, NC
Defiance College, OH

DePaul University, IL
Dillard University, LA
Doane College, NE
Dominican University of California, CA
Dordt College, IA
Drake University, IA
Drury University, MO
Duquesne University, PA
East Carolina University, NC
Eastern Kentucky University, KY
Eastern Michigan University, MI
Eastern New Mexico University, NM
Eastern Washington University, WA
East Texas Baptist University, TX
Eckerd College, FL
Edgewood College, WI
Edinboro University of Pennsylvania, PA
Elizabeth City State University, NC
Elizabethtown College, PA
Elmhurst College, IL
Elon University, NC
Emmanuel College, GA
Emory & Henry College, VA
Emory University, GA
Emporia State University, KS
Endicott College, MA
Eureka College, IL
Evangel University, MO
Fairmont State University, WV
Faulkner University, AL
Fayetteville State University, NC
Ferris State University, MI
Florida Agricultural and Mechanical University, FL
Florida Atlantic University, FL
Florida Gulf Coast University, FL
Florida Institute of Technology, FL
Florida International University, FL
Florida Southern College, FL
Florida State University, FL
Fort Hays State University, KS
Fort Lewis College, CO
Fort Valley State University, GA
Francis Marion University, SC
Franklin & Marshall College, PA
Franklin College, IN
Fresno Pacific University, CA
Frostburg State University, MD
Furman University, SC
Gannon University, PA
Gardner-Webb University, NC
Geneva College, PA
George Fox University, OR
Georgetown College, KY
Georgia College & State University, GA
Georgian Court University, NJ
Georgia Southern University, GA
Georgia Southwestern State University, GA
Gettysburg College, PA
Glenville State College, WV
Gonzaga University, WA
Gordon College, MA
Goshen College, IN
Goucher College, MD
Grace Bible College, MI
Graceland University, IA
Grand Valley State University, MI
Grand View University, IA
Green Mountain College, VT
Greenville College, IL
Grove City College, PA
Guilford College, NC
Gustavus Adolphus College, MN
Hamline University, MN
Hampden-Sydney College, VA

Hampton University, VA
Hanover College, IN
Harding University, AR
Hardin-Simmons University, TX
Hartwick College, NY
Hastings College, NE
Hawai`i Pacific University, HI
Heidelberg University, OH
Henderson State University, AR
Hendrix College, AR
Hillsdale College, MI
Hillsdale Free Will Baptist College, OK
Hobart and William Smith Colleges, NY
Hofstra University, NY
Hollins University, VA
Hood College, MD
Hope College, MI
Houghton College, NY
Houston Baptist University, TX
Howard Payne University, TX
Howard University, DC
Huntingdon College, AL
Huntington University, IN
Idaho State University, ID
Illinois College, IL
Illinois State University, IL
Illinois Wesleyan University, IL
Indiana University of Pennsylvania, PA
Indiana University–Purdue University Fort
    Wayne, IN
Indiana Wesleyan University, IN
Iona College, NY
Iowa State University of Science and
    Technology, IA
Iowa Wesleyan College, IA
Ithaca College, NY
Jackson State University, MS
Jacksonville State University, AL
Jacksonville University, FL
James Madison University, VA
John Brown University, AR
Johnson C. Smith University, NC
Johnson State College, VT
The Juilliard School, NY
Juniata College, PA
Kean University, NJ
Keene State College, NH
Kennesaw State University, GA
Kent State University, OH
Kentucky State University, KY
Kentucky Wesleyan College, KY
Kenyon College, OH
King College, TN
Knox College, IL
Kutztown University of Pennsylvania, PA
Kuyper College, MI
Lafayette College, PA
LaGrange College, GA
Lake Erie College, OH
Lake Forest College, IL
Lakeland College, WI
Lancaster Bible College, PA
La Sierra University, CA
Lawrence University, WI
Lebanon Valley College, PA
Lee University, TN
Lehigh University, PA
Le Moyne College, NY
LeMoyne-Owen College, TN
Lewis & Clark College, OR
Lewis-Clark State College, ID
Lewis University, IL
Liberty University, VA
Limestone College, SC
Lincoln University, MO
Lindenwood University, MO

Lindsey Wilson College, KY
Linfield College, OR
Lipscomb University, TN
Lock Haven University of Pennsylvania, PA
Long Island University–Brooklyn Campus,
    NY
Long Island University–C. W. Post Campus,
    NY
Longwood University, VA
Loras College, IA
Louisiana College, LA
Louisiana State University and Agricultural
    and Mechanical College, LA
Louisiana Tech University, LA
Loyola Marymount University, CA
Loyola University Chicago, IL
Lubbock Christian University, TX
Luther College, IA
Lycoming College, PA
Lynchburg College, VA
Lynn University, FL
Lyon College, AR
Malone University, OH
Manchester University, IN
Manhattan College, NY
Mannes College The New School for Music,
    NY
Mansfield University of Pennsylvania, PA
Marian University, WI
Marietta College, OH
Marist College, NY
Maryville College, TN
Marywood University, PA
Massachusetts College of Liberal Arts, MA
The Master's College and Seminary, CA
Mayville State University, ND
McKendree University, IL
McMurry University, TX
McNally Smith College of Music, MN
McNeese State University, LA
McPherson College, KS
Mercer University, GA
Mercyhurst University, PA
Meredith College, NC
Messiah College, PA
Methodist University, NC
Metropolitan State University of Denver, CO
Miami University, OH
Michigan State University, MI
Middle Tennessee State University, TN
Midwestern State University, TX
Millersville University of Pennsylvania, PA
Milligan College, TN
Millikin University, IL
Millsaps College, MS
Mills College, CA
Minnesota State University Moorhead, MN
Minot State University, ND
Mississippi College, MS
Mississippi State University, MS
Mississippi University for Women, MS
Missouri Baptist University, MO
Missouri Southern State University, MO
Missouri University of Science and
    Technology, MO
Missouri Valley College, MO
Missouri Western State University, MO
Molloy College, NY
Monmouth College, IL
Montana State University, MT
Montana State University Billings, MT
Montclair State University, NJ
Montreat College, NC
Moravian College, PA
Morehead State University, KY
Morehouse College, GA

Morningside College, IA
Mount Aloysius College, PA
Mount Marty College, SD
Mount Mary College, WI
Mount Mercy University, IA
Mount St. Mary's College, CA
Mount Vernon Nazarene University, OH
Murray State University, KY
Nazareth College of Rochester, NY
Nebraska Wesleyan University, NE
Newberry College, SC
New England Conservatory of Music, MA
New Hope Christian College, OR
New Mexico Highlands University, NM
New Mexico State University, NM
The New School for Jazz and Contemporary
    Music, NY
Nicholls State University, LA
Norfolk State University, VA
North Carolina Agricultural and Technical
    State University, NC
North Carolina Central University, NC
North Central College, IL
Northeastern Illinois University, IL
Northeastern State University, OK
Northern Arizona University, AZ
Northern Illinois University, IL
Northern Kentucky University, KY
Northern Michigan University, MI
Northern State University, SD
Northland College, WI
Northwest Christian University, OR
Northwestern College, MN
Northwestern Oklahoma State University,
    OK
Northwestern State University of Louisiana,
    LA
Northwest Missouri State University, MO
Northwest Nazarene University, ID
Northwest University, WA
Notre Dame de Namur University, CA
Nova Southeastern University, FL
Nyack College, NY
Oakland University, MI
Oberlin College, OH
Occidental College, CA
Oglethorpe University, GA
The Ohio State University, OH
Ohio University, OH
Ohio University–Chillicothe, OH
Ohio University–Eastern, OH
Ohio University–Lancaster, OH
Ohio University–Southern Campus, OH
Ohio University–Zanesville, OH
Ohio Valley University, WV
Ohio Wesleyan University, OH
Oklahoma Baptist University, OK
Oklahoma Christian University, OK
Oklahoma City University, OK
Oklahoma State University, OK
Oklahoma Wesleyan University, OK
Old Dominion University, VA
Olivet College, MI
Olivet Nazarene University, IL
Oral Roberts University, OK
Ouachita Baptist University, AR
Pacific Lutheran University, WA
Pacific Union College, CA
Pacific University, OR
Palm Beach Atlantic University, FL
Peabody Conservatory of The Johns Hopkins
    University, MD
Philander Smith College, AR
Piedmont College, GA
Pittsburg State University, KS
Plymouth State University, NH

Point Loma Nazarene University, CA
Portland State University, OR
Presbyterian College, SC
Purchase College, State University of New York, NY
Purdue University, IN
Queens College of the City University of New York, NY
Quincy University, IL
Regis University, CO
Rhode Island College, RI
Rhodes College, TN
Rice University, TX
The Richard Stockton College of New Jersey, NJ
Ripon College, WI
Roberts Wesleyan College, NY
Rochester College, MI
Rockford College, IL
Rockhurst University, MO
Rogers State University, OK
Rollins College, FL
Roosevelt University, IL
Rowan University, NJ
Sacred Heart University, CT
Saginaw Valley State University, MI
St. Ambrose University, IA
Saint Augustine's College, NC
St. Bonaventure University, NY
St. Catherine University, MN
St. Cloud State University, MN
Saint Francis University, PA
Saint John's University, MN
St. John's University, NY
Saint Joseph's College, IN
Saint Louis University, MO
Saint Martin's University, WA
Saint Mary-of-the-Woods College, IN
Saint Mary's College of California, CA
Saint Mary's University of Minnesota, MN
St. Norbert College, WI
St. Olaf College, MN
Salisbury University, MD
Samford University, AL
Sam Houston State University, TX
San Diego Christian College, CA
San Diego State University, CA
San Francisco Conservatory of Music, CA
Santa Clara University, CA
Schreiner University, TX
Seattle University, WA
Seton Hill University, PA
Shenandoah University, VA
Shepherd University, WV
Shippensburg University of Pennsylvania, PA
Shorter University, GA
Siena College, NY
Simpson College, IA
Simpson University, CA
Skidmore College, NY
Slippery Rock University of Pennsylvania, PA
Sonoma State University, CA
South Dakota State University, SD
Southeastern Louisiana University, LA
Southeastern Oklahoma State University, OK
Southeast Missouri State University, MO
Southern Adventist University, TN
Southern Arkansas University–Magnolia, AR
Southern Illinois University Edwardsville, IL
Southern Utah University, UT

Southwest Baptist University, MO
Southwestern Christian College, TX
Southwestern College, KS
Southwestern University, TX
State University of New York at Fredonia, NY
State University of New York at New Paltz, NY
State University of New York at Plattsburgh, NY
State University of New York College at Cortland, NY
State University of New York College at Geneseo, NY
State University of New York College at Oneonta, NY
State University of New York College at Potsdam, NY
Stephen F. Austin State University, TX
Stetson University, FL
Stony Brook University, State University of New York, NY
Sweet Briar College, VA
Syracuse University, NY
Tarleton State University, TX
Taylor University, IN
Temple University, PA
Tennessee State University, TN
Tennessee Technological University, TN
Tennessee Wesleyan College, TN
Texas A&M International University, TX
Texas A&M University–Commerce, TX
Texas Christian University, TX
Texas College, TX
Texas Lutheran University, TX
Texas State University–San Marcos, TX
Texas Tech University, TX
Texas Wesleyan University, TX
Texas Woman's University, TX
Thiel College, PA
Thomas University, GA
Tiffin University, OH
Towson University, MD
Transylvania University, KY
Trevecca Nazarene University, TN
Trinity Christian College, IL
Trinity University, TX
Troy University, AL
Truman State University, MO
Tulane University, LA
Tuskegee University, AL
Union College, KY
Union University, TN
The University of Akron, OH
The University of Alabama, AL
The University of Alabama at Birmingham, AL
The University of Alabama in Huntsville, AL
University of Alaska Anchorage, AK
University of Alaska Fairbanks, AK
The University of Arizona, AZ
University of Arkansas, AR
University of Bridgeport, CT
University of California, Irvine, CA
University of California, Riverside, CA
University of California, Santa Cruz, CA
University of Central Florida, FL
University of Charleston, WV
University of Colorado Boulder, CO
University of Connecticut, CT
University of Dayton, OH
University of Delaware, DE
University of Denver, CO
University of Evansville, IN

University of Florida, FL
University of Georgia, GA
University of Hartford, CT
University of Hawaii at Hilo, HI
University of Idaho, ID
University of Illinois at Chicago, IL
University of Illinois at Springfield, IL
University of Illinois at Urbana–Champaign, IL
University of Indianapolis, IN
The University of Iowa, IA
The University of Kansas, KS
University of La Verne, CA
University of Louisville, KY
University of Maine at Augusta, ME
University of Mary, ND
University of Mary Hardin-Baylor, TX
University of Maryland, Baltimore County, MD
University of Maryland, College Park, MD
University of Maryland Eastern Shore, MD
University of Mary Washington, VA
University of Massachusetts Amherst, MA
University of Massachusetts Lowell, MA
University of Memphis, TN
University of Miami, FL
University of Michigan, MI
University of Michigan–Flint, MI
University of Minnesota, Morris, MN
University of Mississippi, MS
University of Missouri–Kansas City, MO
University of Missouri–St. Louis, MO
University of Mobile, AL
The University of Montana, MT
University of Montevallo, AL
University of Mount Union, OH
University of Nebraska at Kearney, NE
University of Nebraska at Omaha, NE
University of Nebraska–Lincoln, NE
University of Nevada, Las Vegas, NV
University of Nevada, Reno, NV
University of New Hampshire, NH
University of New Orleans, LA
University of North Alabama, AL
University of North Carolina at Asheville, NC
The University of North Carolina at Chapel Hill, NC
The University of North Carolina at Greensboro, NC
The University of North Carolina Wilmington, NC
University of Northern Colorado, CO
University of Northern Iowa, IA
University of North Florida, FL
University of North Georgia, GA
University of Oklahoma, OK
University of Oregon, OR
University of Portland, OR
University of Puerto Rico at Bayamón, PR
University of Puget Sound, WA
University of Redlands, CA
University of Rhode Island, RI
University of Richmond, VA
University of Rio Grande, OH
University of Rochester, NY
University of St. Francis, IL
University of St. Thomas, MN
University of St. Thomas, TX
University of San Diego, CA
University of Science and Arts of Oklahoma, OK
University of South Alabama, AL
University of South Carolina, SC
University of South Carolina Aiken, SC

The University of South Dakota, SD
University of Southern Maine, ME
University of Southern Mississippi, MS
The University of Tampa, FL
The University of Tennessee at Chattanooga, TN
The University of Tennessee at Martin, TN
The University of Texas at Arlington, TX
The University of Texas at Brownsville, TX
The University of Texas at El Paso, TX
The University of Texas at San Antonio, TX
The University of Texas of the Permian Basin, TX
The University of Texas–Pan American, TX
University of the Cumberlands, KY
University of the District of Columbia, DC
University of the Incarnate Word, TX
University of the Ozarks, AR
University of the Pacific, CA
The University of Toledo, OH
University of Tulsa, OK
University of Utah, UT
University of Vermont, VT
University of Virginia, VA
The University of Virginia's College at Wise, VA
University of Washington, WA
The University of West Alabama, AL
University of West Florida, FL
University of West Georgia, GA
University of Wisconsin–Eau Claire, WI
University of Wisconsin–Green Bay, WI
University of Wisconsin–La Crosse, WI
University of Wisconsin–Parkside, WI
University of Wisconsin–River Falls, WI
University of Wisconsin–Stevens Point, WI
University of Wisconsin–Stout, WI
University of Wisconsin–Whitewater, WI
University of Wyoming, WY
Utah State University, UT
Valdosta State University, GA
Valley City State University, ND
Valley Forge Christian College, PA
Valparaiso University, IN
Virginia Commonwealth University, VA
Virginia Intermont College, VA
Virginia Military Institute, VA
Virginia Polytechnic Institute and State University, VA
Virginia State University, VA
Virginia Union University, VA
Virginia Wesleyan College, VA
Wabash College, IN
Wagner College, NY
Waldorf College, IA
Warner Pacific College, OR
Wartburg College, IA
Washburn University, KS
Washington Adventist University, MD
Washington State University, WA
Washington University in St. Louis, MO
Wayland Baptist University, TX
Waynesburg University, PA
Wayne State College, NE
Wayne State University, MI
Webster University, MO
Wesleyan College, GA
West Chester University of Pennsylvania, PA
Western Carolina University, NC
Western Illinois University, IL
Western Kentucky University, KY
Western New England University, MA
Western Oregon University, OR
Western State Colorado University, CO
Western Washington University, WA
Westminster College, MO

Westminster College, PA
Westmont College, CA
West Texas A&M University, TX
West Virginia State University, WV
West Virginia University, WV
West Virginia Wesleyan College, WV
Wheaton College, IL
Wheeling Jesuit University, WV
Whitman College, WA
Whittier College, CA
Whitworth University, WA
Wichita State University, KS
Widener University, PA
William Jessup University, CA
William Jewell College, MO
William Peace University, NC
Williams Baptist College, AR
Wilson College, PA
Winona State University, MN
Winthrop University, SC
Wisconsin Lutheran College, WI
Wittenberg University, OH
Wofford College, SC
Wright State University, OH
Xavier University, OH
Xavier University of Louisiana, LA
York College of Pennsylvania, PA
Young Harris College, GA
Youngstown State University, OH

Performing Arts
Adelphi University, NY
Albion College, MI
Alfred University, NY
Alma College, MI
Anderson University, SC
Angelo State University, TX
Arkansas State University, AR
Auburn University, AL
Augustana College, SD
Austin Peay State University, TN
Ball State University, IN
Belhaven University, MS
Binghamton University, State University of New York, NY
Bloomfield College, NJ
Bluefield College, VA
Boise State University, ID
Bowling Green State University, OH
Brenau University, GA
Bucknell University, PA
Butler University, IN
California Lutheran University, CA
California Polytechnic State University, San Luis Obispo, CA
California State University, Chico, CA
California State University, Fullerton, CA
Calvin College, MI
Cameron University, OK
Capital University, OH
Carroll College, MT
Carroll University, WI
Case Western Reserve University, OH
Cedar Crest College, PA
Centenary College of Louisiana, LA
Central Michigan University, MI
Chapman University, CA
Christian Brothers University, TN
City College of the City University of New York, NY
Clemson University, SC
Cleveland State University, OH
Coe College, IA
The College at Brockport, State University of New York, NY
College of Charleston, SC

The College of Idaho, ID
The College of New Rochelle, NY
College of Staten Island of the City University of New York, NY
Colorado Mesa University, CO
Columbus State University, GA
Concordia University Ann Arbor, MI
Corban University, OR
Cornell College, IA
Creighton University, NE
Davidson College, NC
DePaul University, IL
DeSales University, PA
Doane College, NE
East Carolina University, NC
Eastern Michigan University, MI
Eastern New Mexico University, NM
Edgewood College, WI
Elizabeth City State University, NC
Elizabethtown College, PA
Elon University, NC
Emerson College, MA
Emmanuel College, GA
Endicott College, MA
Eureka College, IL
Flagler College, FL
Florida Agricultural and Mechanical University, FL
Florida Atlantic University, FL
Florida International University, FL
Fort Hays State University, KS
Fort Lewis College, CO
Franklin College, IN
Franklin Pierce University, NH
Fresno Pacific University, CA
Frostburg State University, MD
Gannon University, PA
Georgetown College, KY
Goucher College, MD
Green Mountain College, VT
Greenville College, IL
Hamline University, MN
Hardin-Simmons University, TX
Hastings College, NE
Heidelberg University, OH
Henderson State University, AR
Hobart and William Smith Colleges, NY
Hofstra University, NY
Houghton College, NY
Howard University, DC
Huntingdon College, AL
Idaho State University, ID
Illinois State University, IL
Indiana State University, IN
Indiana University of Pennsylvania, PA
Ithaca College, NY
Johnson State College, VT
The Juilliard School, NY
Juniata College, PA
Kean University, NJ
Kennesaw State University, GA
Kent State University, OH
Kentucky State University, KY
Kentucky Wesleyan College, KY
King College, TN
Lafayette College, PA
Lake Erie College, OH
Lakeland College, WI
Lees-McRae College, NC
Lehigh University, PA
Liberty University, VA
Limestone College, SC
Lincoln University, MO
Lindenwood University, MO
Lock Haven University of Pennsylvania, PA
Louisiana College, LA

Louisiana State University and Agricultural and Mechanical College, LA
Louisiana Tech University, LA
Loyola Marymount University, CA
Lubbock Christian University, TX
Manhattanville College, NY
Mannes College The New School for Music, NY
Marietta College, OH
Marymount Manhattan College, NY
Marywood University, PA
Massachusetts College of Liberal Arts, MA
McNeese State University, LA
McPherson College, KS
Metropolitan State University of Denver, CO
Michigan State University, MI
Minot State University, ND
Mississippi State University, MS
Mississippi University for Women, MS
Missouri Valley College, MO
Missouri Western State University, MO
Molloy College, NY
Montclair State University, NJ
Mount Aloysius College, PA
New England School of Communications, ME
New Jersey Institute of Technology, NJ
New Mexico Highlands University, NM
New Mexico State University, NM
Norfolk State University, VA
Northeastern Illinois University, IL
Northeastern State University, OK
Northern Illinois University, IL
Northwestern State University of Louisiana, LA
Northwest Nazarene University, ID
Northwest University, WA
Notre Dame de Namur University, CA
Nova Southeastern University, FL
Nyack College, NY
Oakland University, MI
Oglethorpe University, GA
The Ohio State University, OH
Ohio University, OH
Ohio University–Chillicothe, OH
Ohio University–Eastern, OH
Ohio University–Lancaster, OH
Ohio University–Southern Campus, OH
Ohio University–Zanesville, OH
Ohio Valley University, WV
Ohio Wesleyan University, OH
Oklahoma Baptist University, OK
Oklahoma City University, OK
Old Dominion University, VA
Olivet Nazarene University, IL
Ouachita Baptist University, AR
Pace University, NY
Point Park University, PA
Purchase College, State University of New York, NY
The Richard Stockton College of New Jersey, NJ
Rockford College, IL
Rockhurst University, MO
Sacred Heart University, CT
Saint Augustine's College, NC
St. Bonaventure University, NY
St. Cloud State University, MN
Saint Louis University, MO
Saint Mary-of-the-Woods College, IN
Saint Mary's College of California, CA
Saint Michael's College, VT
Samford University, AL
San Diego Christian College, CA
San Diego State University, CA

Seattle Pacific University, WA
Seton Hill University, PA
Shawnee State University, OH
Shenandoah University, VA
Shepherd University, WV
Siena College, NY
Slippery Rock University of Pennsylvania, PA
Sonoma State University, CA
South Dakota State University, SD
Southeastern Oklahoma State University, OK
Southeast Missouri State University, MO
Southern Illinois University Carbondale, IL
Southwestern College, KS
State University of New York at Fredonia, NY
State University of New York College at Geneseo, NY
State University of New York College at Potsdam, NY
Stephens College, MO
Syracuse University, NY
Temple University, PA
Texas A&M International University, TX
Texas A&M University, TX
Texas Christian University, TX
Texas Tech University, TX
Texas Wesleyan University, TX
Tiffin University, OH
Towson University, MD
Trinity Christian College, IL
The University of Akron, OH
The University of Alabama at Birmingham, AL
University of Alaska Anchorage, AK
The University of Arizona, AZ
University of California, Irvine, CA
University of California, San Diego, CA
University of Colorado Boulder, CO
University of Florida, FL
University of Hartford, CT
University of Hawaii at Hilo, HI
University of Idaho, ID
University of Illinois at Chicago, IL
University of Illinois at Urbana–Champaign, IL
The University of Kansas, KS
University of Maine at Fort Kent, ME
University of Maryland, Baltimore County, MD
University of Maryland, College Park, MD
University of Maryland Eastern Shore, MD
University of Miami, FL
University of Michigan, MI
University of Michigan–Flint, MI
University of Mississippi, MS
University of Missouri–Kansas City, MO
University of Mobile, AL
The University of Montana, MT
University of Nebraska at Omaha, NE
University of Nebraska–Lincoln, NE
University of Nevada, Las Vegas, NV
The University of North Carolina at Greensboro, NC
University of Northern Colorado, CO
University of Oklahoma, OK
University of Oregon, OR
University of Portland, OR
University of Richmond, VA
University of Rochester, NY
University of St. Thomas, TX
The University of Tampa, FL
The University of Tennessee at Chattanooga, TN

The University of Texas at Brownsville, TX
The University of Texas at El Paso, TX
The University of Toledo, OH
University of Tulsa, OK
University of Utah, UT
The University of Virginia's College at Wise, VA
University of Washington, WA
University of West Georgia, GA
University of Wisconsin–Stevens Point, WI
Utah State University, UT
Valdosta State University, GA
Valparaiso University, IN
Virginia Commonwealth University, VA
Virginia Intermont College, VA
Virginia Polytechnic Institute and State University, VA
Virginia State University, VA
Wartburg College, IA
Washburn University, KS
Washington State University, WA
Washington University in St. Louis, MO
Wayne State College, NE
Western Illinois University, IL
Western Oregon University, OR
Western State Colorado University, CO
Western Washington University, WA
West Virginia Wesleyan College, WV
Wichita State University, KS
Wilkes University, PA
Winthrop University, SC
Wright State University, OH
Xavier University, OH
Young Harris College, GA
Youngstown State University, OH

Theater/Drama

Abilene Christian University, TX
Adelphi University, NY
Adrian College, MI
Alabama State University, AL
Alaska Pacific University, AK
Albion College, MI
Albright College, PA
Alma College, MI
Anderson University, SC
Angelo State University, TX
Arcadia University, PA
Arizona State University, AZ
Arkansas State University, AR
Arkansas Tech University, AR
Ashland University, OH
Auburn University, AL
Augustana College, IL
Augustana College, SD
Aurora University, IL
Austin Peay State University, TN
Averett University, VA
Ball State University, IN
Barton College, NC
Baylor University, TX
Belhaven University, MS
Belmont Abbey College, NC
Benedictine College, KS
Berry College, GA
Bethany Lutheran College, MN
Bethel College, IN
Bethel College, KS
Bethel University, MN
Binghamton University, State University of New York, NY
Biola University, CA
Bloomfield College, NJ
Bluefield College, VA
Blue Mountain College, MS

Boise State University, ID
Boston University, MA
Bowling Green State University, OH
Bradley University, IL
Brenau University, GA
Brevard College, NC
Briar Cliff University, IA
Brigham Young University, UT
Bucknell University, PA
Buena Vista University, IA
Butler University, IN
California Baptist University, CA
California Lutheran University, CA
California Polytechnic State University, San
    Luis Obispo, CA
California State University, Bakersfield, CA
California State University, Chico, CA
California State University, Fresno, CA
California State University, Fullerton, CA
California State University, Los Angeles, CA
California State University, San Bernardino,
    CA
Calumet College of Saint Joseph, IN
Calvin College, MI
Cameron University, OK
Campbellsville University, KY
Campbell University, NC
Cardinal Stritch University, WI
Carroll College, MT
Carroll University, WI
Case Western Reserve University, OH
Catawba College, NC
The Catholic University of America, DC
Cedar Crest College, PA
Centenary College of Louisiana, LA
Central College, IA
Central Methodist University, MO
Central Michigan University, MI
Centre College, KY
Chapman University, CA
Christopher Newport University, VA
Clarke University, IA
Clemson University, SC
Cleveland State University, OH
Coastal Carolina University, SC
Coe College, IA
Coker College, SC
The College at Brockport, State University
    of New York, NY
College of Charleston, SC
The College of Idaho, ID
The College of New Rochelle, NY
College of Saint Benedict, MN
College of Staten Island of the City
    University of New York, NY
The College of William and Mary, VA
The College of Wooster, OH
Colorado Mesa University, CO
Colorado State University, CO
Columbus State University, GA
Concordia College, MN
Concordia University, CA
Concordia University Ann Arbor, MI
Concordia University, Nebraska, NE
Concordia University, St. Paul, MN
Converse College, SC
Cornell College, IA
Creighton University, NE
Culver-Stockton College, MO
Dakota Wesleyan University, SD
Davidson College, NC
DePaul University, IL
DeSales University, PA
Dillard University, LA
Doane College, NE
Dordt College, IA

Drake University, IA
Drury University, MO
Eastern Michigan University, MI
Eastern New Mexico University, NM
Eastern Washington University, WA
East Texas Baptist University, TX
Eckerd College, FL
Edgewood College, WI
Elizabethtown College, PA
Elmhurst College, IL
Elon University, NC
Emmanuel College, GA
Emory & Henry College, VA
Emory University, GA
Emporia State University, KS
Eureka College, IL
Evangel University, MO
Fairmont State University, WV
Faulkner University, AL
Ferris State University, MI
Flagler College, FL
Florida Agricultural and Mechanical
    University, FL
Florida International University, FL
Florida Southern College, FL
Florida State University, FL
Fort Hays State University, KS
Fort Lewis College, CO
Francis Marion University, SC
Franklin College, IN
Franklin Pierce University, NH
Fresno Pacific University, CA
Frostburg State University, MD
Furman University, SC
Gannon University, PA
Gardner-Webb University, NC
George Fox University, OR
Georgetown College, KY
Georgia Southern University, GA
Gordon College, MA
Goshen College, IN
Goucher College, MD
Graceland University, IA
Grand Valley State University, MI
Grand View University, IA
Green Mountain College, VT
Guilford College, NC
Gustavus Adolphus College, MN
Hamline University, MN
Hanover College, IN
Hardin-Simmons University, TX
Hastings College, NE
Henderson State University, AR
Hendrix College, AR
Hillsdale College, MI
Hofstra University, NY
Hope College, MI
Howard Payne University, TX
Howard University, DC
Huntington University, IN
Idaho State University, ID
Illinois College, IL
Illinois State University, IL
Illinois Wesleyan University, IL
Indiana University of Pennsylvania, PA
Indiana University–Purdue University Fort
    Wayne, IN
Indiana Wesleyan University, IN
Iowa State University of Science and
    Technology, IA
Ithaca College, NY
Jacksonville State University, AL
Jacksonville University, FL
James Madison University, VA
John Brown University, AR
Johnson State College, VT

The Juilliard School, NY
Juniata College, PA
Kean University, NJ
Keene State College, NH
Kennesaw State University, GA
Kent State University, OH
King College, TN
Knox College, IL
Lafayette College, PA
LaGrange College, GA
Lake Erie College, OH
Lake Forest College, IL
La Sierra University, CA
Lees-McRae College, NC
Lee University, TN
Lehigh University, PA
Lewis-Clark State College, ID
Lewis University, IL
Limestone College, SC
Lincoln University, MO
Lindenwood University, MO
Linfield College, OR
Lipscomb University, TN
Long Island University–Brooklyn Campus,
    NY
Long Island University–C. W. Post Campus,
    NY
Longwood University, VA
Louisiana College, LA
Louisiana State University and Agricultural
    and Mechanical College, LA
Louisiana Tech University, LA
Lourdes University, OH
Loyola Marymount University, CA
Loyola University Chicago, IL
Lubbock Christian University, TX
Lycoming College, PA
Lynchburg College, VA
Lyon College, AR
Malone University, OH
Manchester University, IN
Marietta College, OH
Marquette University, WI
Maryville College, TN
Marywood University, PA
Massachusetts College of Liberal Arts, MA
Mayville State University, ND
McMurry University, TX
McNeese State University, LA
McPherson College, KS
Mercer University, GA
Messiah College, PA
Methodist University, NC
Metropolitan State University of Denver, CO
Miami University, OH
Michigan State University, MI
Middle Tennessee State University, TN
Midwestern State University, TX
Milligan College, TN
Millikin University, IL
Millsaps College, MS
Minnesota State University Moorhead, MN
Minot State University, ND
Mississippi State University, MS
Mississippi University for Women, MS
Missouri Baptist University, MO
Missouri Southern State University, MO
Missouri University of Science and
    Technology, MO
Missouri Valley College, MO
Missouri Western State University, MO
Molloy College, NY
Monmouth College, IL
Montana State University, MT
Montana State University Billings, MT
Montclair State University, NJ

Morehead State University, KY
Morningside College, IA
Mount Marty College, SD
Mount Mercy University, IA
Murray State University, KY
Nazareth College of Rochester, NY
Nebraska Wesleyan University, NE
Newberry College, SC
New England College, NH
New England Conservatory of Music, MA
New England School of Communications, ME
New Jersey Institute of Technology, NJ
New Mexico Highlands University, NM
New Mexico State University, NM
Niagara University, NY
North Carolina Central University, NC
North Central College, IL
Northeastern Illinois University, IL
Northeastern State University, OK
Northern Arizona University, AZ
Northern Illinois University, IL
Northern Kentucky University, KY
Northern Michigan University, MI
Northern State University, SD
Northwestern College, MN
Northwestern Oklahoma State University, OK
Northwestern State University of Louisiana, LA
Northwest Missouri State University, MO
Northwest Nazarene University, ID
Northwest University, WA
Notre Dame de Namur University, CA
Nyack College, NY
Oglethorpe University, GA
The Ohio State University, OH
Ohio University, OH
Ohio University–Chillicothe, OH
Ohio University–Eastern, OH
Ohio University–Lancaster, OH
Ohio University–Southern Campus, OH
Ohio University–Zanesville, OH
Ohio Valley University, WV
Ohio Wesleyan University, OH
Oklahoma Baptist University, OK
Oklahoma Christian University, OK
Oklahoma City University, OK
Oklahoma State University, OK
Old Dominion University, VA
Olivet Nazarene University, IL
Ouachita Baptist University, AR
Pace University, NY
Pacific Lutheran University, WA
Pacific Union College, CA
Pacific University, OR
Palm Beach Atlantic University, FL
Piedmont College, GA
Plymouth State University, NH
Point Loma Nazarene University, CA
Point Park University, PA
Portland State University, OR
Providence College, RI
Purchase College, State University of New York, NY
Rhode Island College, RI
Rhodes College, TN
The Richard Stockton College of New Jersey, NJ
Rider University, NJ
Ripon College, WI
Rochester College, MI
Rockford College, IL
Rockhurst University, MO
Rogers State University, OK

Rollins College, FL
Roosevelt University, IL
Russell Sage College, NY
Sacred Heart University, CT
Saginaw Valley State University, MI
St. Ambrose University, IA
St. Cloud State University, MN
St. Edward's University, TX
Saint John's University, MN
Saint Joseph's College, IN
Saint Joseph's University, PA
Saint Louis University, MO
Saint Martin's University, WA
Saint Mary-of-the-Woods College, IN
Saint Mary's College of California, CA
Saint Mary's University of Minnesota, MN
Saint Michael's College, VT
St. Norbert College, WI
St. Olaf College, MN
Salisbury University, MD
Samford University, AL
San Diego Christian College, CA
San Diego State University, CA
Santa Clara University, CA
Schreiner University, TX
Seattle University, WA
Seton Hill University, PA
Shenandoah University, VA
Shepherd University, WV
Shippensburg University of Pennsylvania, PA
Shorter University, GA
Siena College, NY
Simpson College, IA
Slippery Rock University of Pennsylvania, PA
Sonoma State University, CA
South Dakota State University, SD
Southeastern Louisiana University, LA
Southeastern Oklahoma State University, OK
Southeast Missouri State University, MO
Southern Adventist University, TN
Southern Arkansas University–Magnolia, AR
Southern Illinois University Edwardsville, IL
Southern Utah University, UT
Southwest Baptist University, MO
Southwestern College, KS
Southwestern University, TX
State University of New York at Fredonia, NY
State University of New York at New Paltz, NY
State University of New York at Plattsburgh, NY
State University of New York College at Geneseo, NY
State University of New York College at Oneonta, NY
State University of New York College at Potsdam, NY
Stephen F. Austin State University, TX
Stephens College, MO
Stetson University, FL
Tarleton State University, TX
Taylor University, IN
Texas A&M University, TX
Texas A&M University–Commerce, TX
Texas Christian University, TX
Texas Lutheran University, TX
Texas State University–San Marcos, TX
Texas Tech University, TX
Texas Wesleyan University, TX

Texas Woman's University, TX
Thomas More College, KY
Tiffin University, OH
Towson University, MD
Transylvania University, KY
Trinity Christian College, IL
Trinity University, TX
Troy University, AL
Truman State University, MO
Union University, TN
The University of Akron, OH
The University of Alabama, AL
The University of Alabama at Birmingham, AL
University of Alaska Fairbanks, AK
The University of Arizona, AZ
University of Arkansas, AR
University of California, Irvine, CA
University of California, Riverside, CA
University of California, Santa Cruz, CA
University of Central Florida, FL
University of Colorado Boulder, CO
University of Connecticut, CT
University of Dallas, TX
University of Delaware, DE
University of Denver, CO
University of Evansville, IN
University of Florida, FL
University of Hartford, CT
University of Hawaii at Hilo, HI
University of Idaho, ID
University of Illinois at Chicago, IL
University of Illinois at Springfield, IL
University of Illinois at Urbana–Champaign, IL
University of Indianapolis, IN
The University of Kansas, KS
University of La Verne, CA
University of Louisville, KY
University of Maryland, Baltimore County, MD
University of Maryland, College Park, MD
University of Maryland Eastern Shore, MD
University of Mary Washington, VA
University of Massachusetts Amherst, MA
University of Miami, FL
University of Michigan, MI
University of Michigan–Flint, MI
University of Mississippi, MS
University of Missouri–St. Louis, MO
The University of Montana, MT
University of Montevallo, AL
University of Mount Union, OH
University of Nebraska at Omaha, NE
University of Nebraska–Lincoln, NE
University of Nevada, Las Vegas, NV
University of Nevada, Reno, NV
University of New Hampshire, NH
University of New Orleans, LA
University of North Carolina at Asheville, NC
The University of North Carolina at Chapel Hill, NC
The University of North Carolina at Greensboro, NC
The University of North Carolina Wilmington, NC
University of Northern Colorado, CO
University of Northern Iowa, IA
University of Oklahoma, OK
University of Oregon, OR
University of Pittsburgh at Johnstown, PA
University of Portland, OR
University of Puerto Rico at Bayamón, PR
University of Puget Sound, WA

University of Rhode Island, RI
University of Richmond, VA
University of St. Thomas, TX
University of Science and Arts of Oklahoma, OK
University of South Alabama, AL
University of South Carolina, SC
University of South Carolina Aiken, SC
The University of South Dakota, SD
University of Southern Indiana, IN
University of Southern Maine, ME
University of Southern Mississippi, MS
The University of Tampa, FL
The University of Tennessee at Chattanooga, TN
The University of Tennessee at Martin, TN
The University of Texas at Arlington, TX
The University of Texas at El Paso, TX
The University of Texas of the Permian Basin, TX
The University of Texas–Pan American, TX
University of the Cumberlands, KY
University of the Incarnate Word, TX
University of the Ozarks, AR
The University of Toledo, OH
University of Tulsa, OK
University of Utah, UT
University of Vermont, VT
The University of Virginia's College at Wise, VA
University of West Florida, FL
University of West Georgia, GA
University of Wisconsin–Eau Claire, WI
University of Wisconsin–Green Bay, WI
University of Wisconsin–La Crosse, WI
University of Wisconsin–Parkside, WI
University of Wisconsin–River Falls, WI
University of Wisconsin–Stevens Point, WI
University of Wisconsin–Whitewater, WI
University of Wyoming, WY
Utah State University, UT
Valdosta State University, GA
Valley City State University, ND
Valparaiso University, IN
Virginia Commonwealth University, VA
Virginia Intermont College, VA
Virginia Polytechnic Institute and State University, VA
Virginia Wesleyan College, VA
Wabash College, IN
Wagner College, NY
Waldorf College, IA
Warner Pacific College, OR
Wartburg College, IA
Washburn University, KS
Washington State University, WA
Washington University in St. Louis, MO
Wayland Baptist University, TX
Waynesburg University, PA
Wayne State College, NE
Wayne State University, MI
Webster University, MO
Wesleyan College, GA
West Chester University of Pennsylvania, PA
Western Carolina University, NC
Western Illinois University, IL
Western Kentucky University, KY
Western Oregon University, OR
Western Washington University, WA
Westminster College, PA
Westmont College, CA
West Texas A&M University, TX
West Virginia University, WV
West Virginia Wesleyan College, WV
Whitman College, WA
Whittier College, CA

Whitworth University, WA
Wichita State University, KS
Wilkes University, PA
William Jessup University, CA
William Jewell College, MO
William Peace University, NC
Williams Baptist College, AR
Winona State University, MN
Winthrop University, SC
Wisconsin Lutheran College, WI
Wittenberg University, OH
Wright State University, OH
Xavier University, OH
Young Harris College, GA
Youngstown State University, OH

Special Achievements/Activities

Cheerleading/Drum Major

Abilene Christian University, TX
Anderson University, SC
Angelo State University, TX
Arkansas State University, AR
Ashland University, OH
Auburn University, AL
Belhaven University, MS
Bellarmine University, KY
Bethel College, IN
Bethel College, KS
Bluefield College, VA
Bluefield State College, WV
Boise State University, ID
Brenau University, GA
Brevard College, NC
California Baptist University, CA
Cameron University, OK
Campbellsville University, KY
Campbell University, NC
Carroll College, MT
Central Methodist University, MO
Cleveland State University, OH
Coastal Carolina University, SC
Columbus State University, GA
Culver-Stockton College, MO
Dakota Wesleyan University, SD
Drury University, MO
Eastern Kentucky University, KY
Emmanuel College, GA
Evangel University, MO
Fairmont State University, WV
Faulkner University, AL
Florida Agricultural and Mechanical University, FL
Florida Institute of Technology, FL
Fort Hays State University, KS
Francis Marion University, SC
Gardner-Webb University, NC
Georgia Institute of Technology, GA
Georgia Southern University, GA
Glenville State College, WV
Graceland University, IA
Grand View University, IA
Harding University, AR
Hastings College, NE
Hawai`i Pacific University, HI
Henderson State University, AR
Houston Baptist University, TX
Howard University, DC
Huntingdon College, AL
Huntington University, IN
Idaho State University, ID
Indiana Wesleyan University, IN
James Madison University, VA
Kentucky State University, KY
Lees-McRae College, NC

Lee University, TN
Lewis University, IL
Liberty University, VA
Limestone College, SC
Lincoln University, MO
Lindenwood University, MO
Lindsey Wilson College, KY
Lipscomb University, TN
Long Island University–Brooklyn Campus, NY
Louisiana Tech University, LA
Lubbock Christian University, TX
Lyon College, AR
Maryville University of Saint Louis, MO
McKendree University, IL
McNeese State University, LA
McPherson College, KS
Methodist University, NC
Middle Tennessee State University, TN
Midwestern State University, TX
Milligan College, TN
Mississippi State University, MS
Missouri Baptist University, MO
Missouri Valley College, MO
Missouri Western State University, MO
Montana State University Billings, MT
Morehead State University, KY
Morningside College, IA
Mount Olive College, NC
Newberry College, SC
New Mexico State University, NM
Nicholls State University, LA
Northeastern State University, OK
Northern Michigan University, MI
Northwestern Oklahoma State University, OK
Northwestern State University of Louisiana, LA
Northwest Missouri State University, MO
Northwest Nazarene University, ID
Northwood University, Florida Campus, FL
Northwood University, Michigan Campus, MI
Nyack College, NY
The Ohio State University, OH
Oklahoma Christian University, OK
Oklahoma City University, OK
Oklahoma State University, OK
Old Dominion University, VA
Olivet Nazarene University, IL
Oral Roberts University, OK
Ouachita Baptist University, AR
Park University, MO
Quincy University, IL
Robert Morris University Illinois, IL
Rocky Mountain College, MT
Rogers State University, OK
St. Ambrose University, IA
St. Edward's University, TX
Saint Francis University, PA
St. John's University, NY
Saint Joseph's College, IN
Saint Louis University, MO
Samford University, AL
Sam Houston State University, TX
San Diego State University, CA
Seton Hill University, PA
Shorter University, GA
Southeastern Louisiana University, LA
Southeastern Oklahoma State University, OK
Southeast Missouri State University, MO
Southern Arkansas University–Magnolia, AR
Southern Illinois University Carbondale, IL
Southwestern College, KS

Stephen F. Austin State University, TX
Stetson University, FL
Temple University, PA
Tennessee Technological University, TN
Tennessee Wesleyan College, TN
Texas A&M University–Commerce, TX
Texas College, TX
Texas Wesleyan University, TX
Tiffin University, OH
Union College, KY
Union University, TN
The University of Alabama, AL
The University of Alabama at Birmingham, AL
The University of Alabama in Huntsville, AL
University of Delaware, DE
University of Great Falls, MT
University of Idaho, ID
University of Louisville, KY
University of Mary Hardin-Baylor, TX
University of Maryland, College Park, MD
University of Massachusetts Amherst, MA
University of Memphis, TN
University of Mississippi, MS
University of Missouri–St. Louis, MO
The University of Montana, MT
University of Nebraska at Kearney, NE
University of Nebraska–Lincoln, NE
University of Nevada, Las Vegas, NV
University of North Alabama, AL
The University of North Carolina Wilmington, NC
University of North Georgia, GA
University of Puerto Rico at Bayamón, PR
University of Rio Grande, OH
University of St. Francis, IL
University of Science and Arts of Oklahoma, OK
University of South Carolina, SC
University of South Carolina Aiken, SC
University of Southern Mississippi, MS
The University of Tennessee at Chattanooga, TN
The University of Tennessee at Martin, TN
The University of Texas at Arlington, TX
The University of Texas at El Paso, TX
The University of Texas at San Antonio, TX
The University of Texas of the Permian Basin, TX
The University of Texas–Pan American, TX
University of the Cumberlands, KY
The University of Toledo, OH
University of Tulsa, OK
University of Utah, UT
The University of West Alabama, AL
University of Wyoming, WY
Virginia Polytechnic Institute and State University, VA
Virginia State University, VA
Waldorf College, IA
Washburn University, KS
Wayland Baptist University, TX
Webber International University, FL
West Texas A&M University, TX
West Virginia University Institute of Technology, WV
Wichita State University, KS
William Jewell College, MO
Williams Baptist College, AR
Wright State University, OH
Youngstown State University, OH

Community Service
Adelphi University, NY

Alaska Pacific University, AK
Allen College, IA
Alliant International University, CA
Alverno College, WI
Arcadia University, PA
Arkansas State University, AR
Armstrong Atlantic State University, GA
Ball State University, IN
Baylor University, TX
Bellarmine University, KY
Beloit College, WI
Benedictine University, IL
Bentley University, MA
Berry College, GA
Bethel University, MN
Binghamton University, State University of New York, NY
Biola University, CA
Bloomfield College, NJ
Boise State University, ID
Bradley University, IL
Brenau University, GA
Brevard College, NC
Broadview University–Boise, ID
Broadview University–Layton, UT
Broadview University–Orem, UT
Broadview University–Salt Lake City, UT
Broadview University–West Jordan, UT
Burlington College, VT
Caldwell College, NJ
California Institute of Integral Studies, CA
California Lutheran University, CA
California Polytechnic State University, San Luis Obispo, CA
California State University, Bakersfield, CA
California State University, Chico, CA
California State University, Fresno, CA
California State University, Los Angeles, CA
California State University, San Bernardino, CA
California State University, Stanislaus, CA
Calvin College, MI
Cardinal Stritch University, WI
Cedar Crest College, PA
Centenary College of Louisiana, LA
Central College, IA
Centre College, KY
The Citadel, The Military College of South Carolina, SC
City College of the City University of New York, NY
Clarke University, IA
Clark University, MA
Clemson University, SC
Coe College, IA
The College at Brockport, State University of New York, NY
College of Mount St. Joseph, OH
The College of New Rochelle, NY
College of Saint Elizabeth, NJ
College of Saint Mary, NE
The College of Saint Rose, NY
College of Staten Island of the City University of New York, NY
The College of Wooster, OH
Columbus State University, GA
Cornell College, IA
Dallas Baptist University, TX
Davidson College, NC
Defiance College, OH
DePaul University, IL
DePauw University, IN
DeSales University, PA
Dominican University of California, CA
Eastern Connecticut State University, CT

Eastern New Mexico University, NM
Edgewood College, WI
Elon University, NC
Emmanuel College, MA
Endicott College, MA
Eureka College, IL
The Evergreen State College, WA
Finlandia University, MI
Florida Agricultural and Mechanical University, FL
Florida Gulf Coast University, FL
Florida Southern College, FL
Frostburg State University, MD
Furman University, SC
Gannon University, PA
Georgia Southern University, GA
Globe University–Appleton, WI
Globe University–Eau Claire, WI
Globe University–Green Bay, WI
Globe University–La Crosse, WI
Globe University–Madison East, WI
Globe University–Madison West, WI
Globe University–Minneapolis, MN
Globe University–Sioux Falls, SD
Globe University–Wausau, WI
Globe University–Woodbury, MN
Goshen College, IN
Grand View University, IA
Green Mountain College, VT
Hamline University, MN
Hampshire College, MA
Hawai`i Pacific University, HI
Hendrix College, AR
Hillsdale College, MI
Hollins University, VA
Houston Baptist University, TX
Howard Payne University, TX
Huntingdon College, AL
Illinois Institute of Technology, IL
Illinois State University, IL
Indiana University of Pennsylvania, PA
Indiana Wesleyan University, IN
Iona College, NY
Iowa State University of Science and Technology, IA
John Carroll University, OH
Johnson State College, VT
Juniata College, PA
Kennesaw State University, GA
Kent State University, OH
Keuka College, NY
King's College, PA
Knox College, IL
Kutztown University of Pennsylvania, PA
Lake Erie College, OH
Lakeland College, WI
La Salle University, PA
Lasell College, MA
Lawrence University, WI
Lewis & Clark College, OR
Lewis-Clark State College, ID
Lewis University, IL
Lindenwood University, MO
Linfield College, OR
Lipscomb University, TN
Lock Haven University of Pennsylvania, PA
Longwood University, VA
Loyola Marymount University, CA
Loyola University Chicago, IL
Lycoming College, PA
Malone University, OH
Manhattan College, NY
Manhattanville College, NY
Marymount University, VA
Maryville College, TN

Maryville University of Saint Louis, MO
Marywood University, PA
McKendree University, IL
McNeese State University, LA
McPherson College, KS
Mercer University, GA
Mercyhurst University, PA
Meredith College, NC
Michigan State University, MI
Millersville University of Pennsylvania, PA
Milligan College, TN
Millikin University, IL
Millsaps College, MS
Minnesota School of Business–Blaine, MN
Minnesota School of Business–Elk River, MN
Minnesota School of Business–Lakeville, MN
Minnesota School of Business–Moorhead, MN
Minnesota School of Business–Rochester, MN
Minnesota State University Moorhead, MN
Misericordia University, PA
Missouri Valley College, MO
Missouri Western State University, MO
Molloy College, NY
Montana State University–Northern, MT
Montana Tech of The University of Montana, MT
Montclair State University, NJ
Morehead State University, KY
Morehouse College, GA
Morningside College, IA
Mount Carmel College of Nursing, OH
Mount St. Mary's College, CA
New England College, NH
New Hope Christian College, OR
New Jersey Institute of Technology, NJ
Niagara University, NY
Nichols College, MA
North Central College, IL
Northeastern State University, OK
Northern Kentucky University, KY
Northwest Christian University, OR
Notre Dame de Namur University, CA
Notre Dame of Maryland University, MD
Nyack College, NY
Oglethorpe University, GA
Ohio Valley University, WV
Oklahoma State University, OK
Old Dominion University, VA
Olivet College, MI
Oral Roberts University, OK
Pace University, NY
Pacific Union College, CA
Pacific University, OR
Piedmont College, GA
Pitzer College, CA
Point Park University, PA
Portland State University, OR
Principia College, IL
Providence College, RI
Queens College of the City University of New York, NY
Quincy University, IL
Randolph College, VA
The Richard Stockton College of New Jersey, NJ
Ringling College of Art and Design, FL
Robert Morris University Illinois, IL
Rochester Institute of Technology, NY
Rockford College, IL
Rockhurst University, MO
Rosemont College, PA
Russell Sage College, NY

Sacred Heart University, CT
Sage College of Albany, NY
Saginaw Valley State University, MI
St. Catherine University, MN
St. Cloud State University, MN
St. Edward's University, TX
St. John Fisher College, NY
St. John's University, NY
St. Joseph's College, Long Island Campus, NY
St. Joseph's College, New York, NY
Saint Joseph's University, PA
St. Lawrence University, NY
St. Louis College of Pharmacy, MO
Saint Louis University, MO
Saint Martin's University, WA
Saint Mary-of-the-Woods College, IN
St. Olaf College, MN
Schreiner University, TX
Shippensburg University of Pennsylvania, PA
Siena College, NY
Simmons College, MA
Simpson College, IA
Simpson University, CA
Slippery Rock University of Pennsylvania, PA
Sonoma State University, CA
South Dakota State University, SD
Southern Adventist University, TN
Southern Illinois University Carbondale, IL
Southern Vermont College, VT
Southwestern College, KS
Spring Hill College, AL
State University of New York at Plattsburgh, NY
State University of New York College at Cortland, NY
State University of New York College at Geneseo, NY
State University of New York College at Oneonta, NY
State University of New York College at Potsdam, NY
State University of New York College of Environmental Science and Forestry, NY
State University of New York College of Technology at Delhi, NY
Stetson University, FL
Stony Brook University, State University of New York, NY
Suffolk University, MA
Sweet Briar College, VA
Texas A&M University, TX
Texas A&M University–Texarkana, TX
Texas Tech University, TX
Texas Wesleyan University, TX
Thomas More College, KY
Towson University, MD
Trinity Christian College, IL
Trinity College of Florida, FL
Tulane University, LA
Union College, KY
Union University, TN
Unity College, ME
Universidad Adventista de las Antillas, PR
The University of Akron, OH
The University of Alabama, AL
The University of Alabama in Huntsville, AL
University of Alaska Fairbanks, AK
University of Arkansas, AR
University of California, San Diego, CA
University of Charleston, WV
University of Chicago, IL
University of Colorado Boulder, CO

University of Connecticut, CT
University of Delaware, DE
University of Denver, CO
University of Florida, FL
University of Hartford, CT
University of Hawaii at Hilo, HI
University of Houston–Clear Lake, TX
University of Indianapolis, IN
The University of Kansas, KS
University of La Verne, CA
University of Louisville, KY
University of Maine at Presque Isle, ME
University of Mary Hardin-Baylor, TX
University of Massachusetts Dartmouth, MA
University of Massachusetts Lowell, MA
University of Michigan, MI
University of Michigan–Dearborn, MI
University of Michigan–Flint, MI
University of Mississippi, MS
University of Missouri–St. Louis, MO
University of Nebraska–Lincoln, NE
University of Nevada, Las Vegas, NV
University of New England, ME
University of New Hampshire, NH
University of New Orleans, LA
University of North Carolina at Asheville, NC
The University of North Carolina at Chapel Hill, NC
The University of North Carolina at Greensboro, NC
University of North Florida, FL
University of North Georgia, GA
University of Puget Sound, WA
University of Richmond, VA
University of St. Francis, IL
University of South Carolina, SC
University of South Carolina Aiken, SC
University of Southern Maine, ME
The University of Tennessee at Chattanooga, TN
The University of Texas at Arlington, TX
The University of Texas–Pan American, TX
University of the Cumberlands, KY
The University of Toledo, OH
University of Tulsa, OK
University of Vermont, VT
The University of Virginia's College at Wise, VA
University of West Georgia, GA
University of Wisconsin–Eau Claire, WI
University of Wisconsin–Green Bay, WI
University of Wisconsin–La Crosse, WI
University of Wisconsin–Parkside, WI
University of Wisconsin–Stout, WI
Ursuline College, OH
Valley Forge Christian College, PA
Vanderbilt University, TN
Virginia Polytechnic Institute and State University, VA
Virginia State University, VA
Virginia Wesleyan College, VA
Wabash College, IN
Warren Wilson College, NC
Washburn University, KS
Washington & Jefferson College, PA
Washington State University, WA
Waynesburg University, PA
Webber International University, FL
Wesleyan College, GA
Wesley College, DE
Western Illinois University, IL
Western New England University, MA
Western Oregon University, OR
Western Washington University, WA
West Texas A&M University, TX

West Virginia Wesleyan College, WV
Wheeling Jesuit University, WV
Widener University, PA
Wilson College, PA
Wittenberg University, OH
Wright State University, OH
Youngstown State University, OH

Hobbies/Interests
Angelo State University, TX
Arkansas Tech University, AR
California State Polytechnic University, Pomona, CA
California State University, Chico, CA
California State University, San Bernardino, CA
Capital University, OH
Centenary College of Louisiana, LA
The College at Brockport, State University of New York, NY
The College of New Rochelle, NY
College of Staten Island of the City University of New York, NY
Colorado Mesa University, CO
Corban University, OR
Eastern Nazarene College, MA
Eastern New Mexico University, NM
Emmanuel College, GA
Florida Institute of Technology, FL
Hawai`i Pacific University, HI
Hollins University, VA
Illinois Institute of Technology, IL
Indiana University of Pennsylvania, PA
Indiana Wesleyan University, IN
Lake Erie College, OH
Michigan State University, MI
Millsaps College, MS
Missouri Valley College, MO
Missouri Western State University, MO
Montana State University–Northern, MT
New Hope Christian College, OR
New Jersey Institute of Technology, NJ
New Mexico State University, NM
The Ohio State University, OH
Quincy University, IL
Sacred Heart University, CT
St. John's University, NY
Saint Martin's University, WA
San Diego State University, CA
Siena College, NY
South Dakota State University, SD
State University of New York College at Cortland, NY
Stephen F. Austin State University, TX
Union College, KY
The University of Alabama, AL
University of Louisville, KY
University of Michigan–Flint, MI
University of Minnesota, Twin Cities Campus, MN
University of South Alabama, AL
The University of Toledo, OH
University of Wisconsin–Eau Claire, WI
Virginia State University, VA
West Texas A&M University, TX

Junior Miss
Arkansas Tech University, AR
Belhaven University, MS
Bethel University, MN
Bluefield State College, WV
Campbellsville University, KY
Carroll University, WI
Cedar Crest College, PA
Concordia University Texas, TX
Georgetown College, KY

Georgia Southern University, GA
Goshen College, IN
Grand View University, IA
Gustavus Adolphus College, MN
Hawai`i Pacific University, HI
Huntingdon College, AL
Idaho State University, ID
Kentucky Wesleyan College, KY
Lewis-Clark State College, ID
Lindenwood University, MO
Lindsey Wilson College, KY
Louisiana Tech University, LA
McDaniel College, MD
Mississippi State University, MS
Mississippi University for Women, MS
Missouri Valley College, MO
Morehead State University, KY
New Mexico State University, NM
Northeastern State University, OK
Oklahoma City University, OK
Roberts Wesleyan College, NY
South Dakota State University, SD
Spring Arbor University, MI
Tennessee Wesleyan College, TN
Texas Lutheran University, TX
The University of Alabama, AL
The University of Alabama at Birmingham, AL
The University of Alabama in Huntsville, AL
University of Idaho, ID
University of Louisville, KY
University of Mississippi, MS
University of Montevallo, AL
University of North Carolina at Asheville, NC
The University of North Carolina at Greensboro, NC
University of South Alabama, AL
University of Wyoming, WY
Waldorf College, IA
Wartburg College, IA
Washington State University, WA

Leadership
Abilene Christian University, TX
Adelphi University, NY
Alabama State University, AL
Alaska Pacific University, AK
Alcorn State University, MS
Alfred University, NY
Allen College, IA
Alliant International University, CA
American Jewish University, CA
American University, DC
Anderson University, IN
Anderson University, SC
Andrews University, MI
Angelo State University, TX
Arcadia University, PA
Arizona State University, AZ
Arkansas State University, AR
Arkansas Tech University, AR
Asbury University, KY
Ashland University, OH
Auburn University, AL
Augustana College, SD
Austin Peay State University, TN
Averett University, VA
Azusa Pacific University, CA
Babson College, MA
Baldwin Wallace University, OH
Ball State University, IN
Baptist Bible College of Pennsylvania, PA
Bard College, NY

Barton College, NC
Baylor University, TX
Becker College, MA
Belhaven University, MS
Bellarmine University, KY
Beloit College, WI
Benedictine University, IL
Berry College, GA
Bethel College, IN
Bethel University, MN
Binghamton University, State University of New York, NY
Biola University, CA
Bloomfield College, NJ
Bluefield State College, WV
Blue Mountain College, MS
Boise State University, ID
Boston Architectural College, MA
Boston University, MA
Bowdoin College, ME
Bowling Green State University, OH
Bradley University, IL
Brenau University, GA
Brevard College, NC
Briar Cliff University, IA
Brigham Young University, UT
Bryn Mawr College, PA
Bucknell University, PA
Buena Vista University, IA
Burlington College, VT
California Institute of Integral Studies, CA
California Lutheran University, CA
California Polytechnic State University, San Luis Obispo, CA
California State Polytechnic University, Pomona, CA
California State University, Bakersfield, CA
California State University, Chico, CA
California State University, Fresno, CA
California State University, Fullerton, CA
California State University, Monterey Bay, CA
California State University, Northridge, CA
California State University, San Marcos, CA
California State University, Stanislaus, CA
Calumet College of Saint Joseph, IN
Calvin College, MI
Cameron University, OK
Campbellsville University, KY
Capital University, OH
Carnegie Mellon University, PA
Carroll College, MT
Carroll University, WI
Carson-Newman University, TN
Case Western Reserve University, OH
Catawba College, NC
Cedar Crest College, PA
Cedarville University, OH
Central Methodist University, MO
Central Michigan University, MI
Chatham University, PA
Chicago State University, IL
Chowan University, NC
Christian Brothers University, TN
Christopher Newport University, VA
Cincinnati Christian University, OH
The Citadel, The Military College of South Carolina, SC
City College of the City University of New York, NY
Claremont McKenna College, CA
Clarion University of Pennsylvania, PA
Clarke University, IA
Clarkson University, NY
Clearwater Christian College, FL

Clemson University, SC
Coker College, SC
The College at Brockport, State University
of New York, NY
The College of Idaho, ID
College of Mount St. Joseph, OH
The College of New Rochelle, NY
College of Saint Elizabeth, NJ
College of Saint Mary, NE
College of Staten Island of the City
University of New York, NY
Colorado Mesa University, CO
Columbia College, MO
Columbia International University, SC
Columbus State University, GA
Concordia University, OR
Concordia University Texas, TX
Corban University, OR
Cornell College, IA
Cornerstone University, MI
Covenant College, GA
Creighton University, NE
Crown College, MN
Culver-Stockton College, MO
Dallas Baptist University, TX
Daniel Webster College, NH
Davidson College, NC
Defiance College, OH
DePaul University, IL
Dominican University of California, CA
Dordt College, IA
Drury University, MO
Duke University, NC
Eastern Connecticut State University, CT
Eastern Michigan University, MI
Eastern Nazarene College, MA
Eastern New Mexico University, NM
Eastern Oregon University, OR
East Texas Baptist University, TX
Elmira College, NY
Elon University, NC
Embry-Riddle Aeronautical University–
Daytona, FL
Embry-Riddle Aeronautical University–
Prescott, AZ
Embry-Riddle Aeronautical University–
Worldwide, FL
Emerson College, MA
Emmanuel College, GA
Emmanuel College, MA
Emory University, GA
Emporia State University, KS
Endicott College, MA
Eugene Lang College The New School for
Liberal Arts, NY
Eureka College, IL
Evangel University, MO
Fairfield University, CT
Fairmont State University, WV
Faulkner University, AL
Finlandia University, MI
Flagler College, FL
Florida Agricultural and Mechanical
University, FL
Florida Gulf Coast University, FL
Florida Institute of Technology, FL
Florida Southern College, FL
Fort Hays State University, KS
Fort Lewis College, CO
Franklin Pierce University, NH
Frostburg State University, MD
Furman University, SC
Gallaudet University, DC
Gannon University, PA
George Fox University, OR
Georgetown College, KY

Georgia Institute of Technology, GA
Georgia Southern University, GA
Georgia Southwestern State University, GA
Gonzaga University, WA
Gordon College, MA
Graceland University, IA
Green Mountain College, VT
Greenville College, IL
Grove City College, PA
Hamline University, MN
Hampden-Sydney College, VA
Hampshire College, MA
Hampton University, VA
Harding University, AR
Hawai`i Pacific University, HI
Henderson State University, AR
Hendrix College, AR
Hilbert College, NY
Hillsdale College, MI
Hobart and William Smith Colleges, NY
Hofstra University, NY
Hollins University, VA
Hope International University, CA
Houghton College, NY
Houston Baptist University, TX
Howard Payne University, TX
Howard University, DC
Husson University, ME
Idaho State University, ID
Illinois Institute of Technology, IL
Illinois State University, IL
Indiana University of Pennsylvania, PA
Indiana University–Purdue University Fort
Wayne, IN
Iowa State University of Science and
Technology, IA
Ithaca College, NY
Jackson State University, MS
Jacksonville University, FL
James Madison University, VA
John Carroll University, OH
Johnson State College, VT
Juniata College, PA
Keene State College, NH
Kennesaw State University, GA
Kent State University, OH
Kettering University, MI
Keuka College, NY
King's College, PA
Kutztown University of Pennsylvania, PA
Kuyper College, MI
LaGrange College, GA
Lake Forest College, IL
Lakeland College, WI
Lancaster Bible College, PA
Lasell College, MA
La Sierra University, CA
Lee University, TN
Le Moyne College, NY
LeTourneau University, TX
Lewis & Clark College, OR
Lewis-Clark State College, ID
Liberty University, VA
Limestone College, SC
Lindenwood University, MO
Lindsey Wilson College, KY
Linfield College, OR
Lipscomb University, TN
Lock Haven University of Pennsylvania, PA
Long Island University–Brooklyn Campus,
NY
Long Island University–C. W. Post Campus,
NY
Longwood University, VA
Louisiana College, LA
Lourdes University, OH

Loyola Marymount University, CA
Loyola University Chicago, IL
Lubbock Christian University, TX
Lycoming College, PA
Lynn University, FL
MacMurray College, IL
Malone University, OH
Manchester University, IN
Manhattan College, NY
Manhattanville College, NY
Mannes College The New School for Music,
NY
Mansfield University of Pennsylvania, PA
Marlboro College, VT
Mary Baldwin College, VA
Marymount Manhattan College, NY
Marymount University, VA
Maryville College, TN
Maryville University of Saint Louis, MO
Marywood University, PA
Massachusetts College of Liberal Arts, MA
Massachusetts Maritime Academy, MA
The Master's College and Seminary, CA
McDaniel College, MD
McKendree University, IL
McNeese State University, LA
Mercer University, GA
Mercyhurst University, PA
Meredith College, NC
Messiah College, PA
Methodist University, NC
Metropolitan State University of Denver, CO
Miami University, OH
Michigan State University, MI
Michigan Technological University, MI
Middle Tennessee State University, TN
Midwestern State University, TX
Millsaps College, MS
Minnesota State University Mankato, MN
Misericordia University, PA
Mississippi College, MS
Mississippi State University, MS
Mississippi University for Women, MS
Missouri State University, MO
Missouri Valley College, MO
Missouri Western State University, MO
Molloy College, NY
Monmouth College, IL
Monmouth University, NJ
Montana State University, MT
Montclair State University, NJ
Montreat College, NC
Moravian College, PA
Morehead State University, KY
Morehouse College, GA
Morningside College, IA
Mount Aloysius College, PA
Mount Mary College, WI
Mount Mercy University, IA
Mount Olive College, NC
Mount Saint Mary College, NY
Mount St. Mary's College, CA
Muhlenberg College, PA
National University, CA
New England College, NH
New Hope Christian College, OR
New Jersey Institute of Technology, NJ
New Mexico State University, NM
Nicholls State University, LA
Nichols College, MA
North Carolina State University, NC
Northeastern Illinois University, IL
Northeastern State University, OK
Northern Arizona University, AZ
Northern Illinois University, IL
Northern Kentucky University, KY

Northern Michigan University, MI
Northern State University, SD
Northland College, WI
Northland International University, WI
Northwest Christian University, OR
Northwestern College, MN
Northwestern Oklahoma State University, OK
Northwestern State University of Louisiana, LA
Northwest Missouri State University, MO
Northwest Nazarene University, ID
Northwest University, WA
Notre Dame de Namur University, CA
Notre Dame of Maryland University, MD
Nova Southeastern University, FL
Nyack College, NY
Occidental College, CA
The Ohio State University, OH
Ohio Valley University, WV
Ohio Wesleyan University, OH
Oklahoma Baptist University, OK
Oklahoma City University, OK
Oklahoma State University, OK
Oklahoma Wesleyan University, OK
Old Dominion University, VA
Olivet College, MI
Oral Roberts University, OK
Oregon Institute of Technology, OR
Oregon State University, OR
Pace University, NY
Pacific Lutheran University, WA
Pacific Union College, CA
Palm Beach Atlantic University, FL
Parsons The New School for Design, NY
Peirce College, PA
Piedmont College, GA
Pine Manor College, MA
Pitzer College, CA
Portland State University, OR
Presbyterian College, SC
Principia College, IL
Purdue University, IN
Purdue University North Central, IN
Queens College of the City University of New York, NY
Quincy University, IL
Randolph College, VA
Regent University, VA
Regis University, CO
Rice University, TX
The Richard Stockton College of New Jersey, NJ
Ripon College, WI
Robert Morris University Illinois, IL
Rochester College, MI
Rochester Institute of Technology, NY
Rockford College, IL
Rockhurst University, MO
Rogers State University, OK
Rosemont College, PA
Russell Sage College, NY
Sacred Heart University, CT
Saginaw Valley State University, MI
St. Ambrose University, IA
St. Catherine University, MN
St. Cloud State University, MN
St. Edward's University, TX
St. John's University, NY
St. Joseph's College, Long Island Campus, NY
St. Joseph's College, New York, NY
St. Lawrence University, NY
St. Louis College of Pharmacy, MO
Saint Louis University, MO

Saint Martin's University, WA
Saint Mary-of-the-Woods College, IN
Saint Mary's College of California, CA
Saint Mary's University of Minnesota, MN
Saint Peter's University, NJ
St. Thomas University, FL
Samford University, AL
Sam Houston State University, TX
San Diego Christian College, CA
San Diego State University, CA
San Jose State University, CA
Schreiner University, TX
Seattle University, WA
Shepherd University, WV
Shippensburg University of Pennsylvania, PA
Siena College, NY
Simpson College, IA
Simpson University, CA
Slippery Rock University of Pennsylvania, PA
Sonoma State University, CA
South Dakota State University, SD
Southeastern Louisiana University, LA
Southeastern Oklahoma State University, OK
Southeast Missouri State University, MO
Southern Adventist University, TN
Southern Arkansas University–Magnolia, AR
Southern Illinois University Carbondale, IL
Southern Utah University, UT
Southern Vermont College, VT
Southwestern College, KS
Southwestern University, TX
State University of New York at Fredonia, NY
State University of New York at Plattsburgh, NY
State University of New York College at Cortland, NY
State University of New York College at Geneseo, NY
State University of New York College at Oneonta, NY
State University of New York College at Potsdam, NY
State University of New York College of Agriculture and Technology at Cobleskill, NY
State University of New York College of Environmental Science and Forestry, NY
Stephen F. Austin State University, TX
Stephens College, MO
Sterling College, VT
Stetson University, FL
Stony Brook University, State University of New York, NY
Taylor University, IN
Texas A&M University, TX
Texas A&M University–Commerce, TX
Texas A&M University–Texarkana, TX
Texas Christian University, TX
Texas College, TX
Texas Lutheran University, TX
Texas State University–San Marcos, TX
Texas Wesleyan University, TX
Thiel College, PA
Thomas More College, KY
Trinity Baptist College, FL
Trinity Christian College, IL
Trinity College, CT
Trinity College of Florida, FL
Trinity University, TX
Troy University, AL

Truman State University, MO
Union College, KY
Union University, TN
Unity College, ME
The University of Akron, OH
The University of Alabama at Birmingham, AL
The University of Alabama in Huntsville, AL
University of Alaska Anchorage, AK
University of Arkansas, AR
University of California, San Diego, CA
University of California, Santa Cruz, CA
University of Central Florida, FL
University of Charleston, WV
University of Chicago, IL
University of Colorado Boulder, CO
University of Colorado Colorado Springs, CO
University of Connecticut, CT
University of Delaware, DE
University of Denver, CO
University of Evansville, IN
University of Florida, FL
University of Hawaii at Hilo, HI
University of Houston, TX
University of Houston–Clear Lake, TX
University of Idaho, ID
University of Illinois at Springfield, IL
University of Illinois at Urbana–Champaign, IL
The University of Iowa, IA
The University of Kansas, KS
University of La Verne, CA
University of Louisville, KY
University of Maine, ME
University of Maine at Augusta, ME
University of Mary Hardin-Baylor, TX
University of Mary Washington, VA
University of Massachusetts Amherst, MA
University of Massachusetts Boston, MA
University of Memphis, TN
University of Michigan, MI
University of Michigan–Dearborn, MI
University of Michigan–Flint, MI
University of Minnesota, Crookston, MN
University of Minnesota, Twin Cities Campus, MN
University of Mississippi, MS
University of Missouri–Kansas City, MO
The University of Montana, MT
University of Montevallo, AL
University of Nebraska at Kearney, NE
University of Nebraska at Omaha, NE
University of Nebraska–Lincoln, NE
University of Nevada, Las Vegas, NV
University of New England, ME
University of North Alabama, AL
University of North Carolina at Asheville, NC
The University of North Carolina at Chapel Hill, NC
The University of North Carolina Wilmington, NC
University of Northern Iowa, IA
University of North Florida, FL
University of North Georgia, GA
University of Oklahoma, OK
University of Pittsburgh at Johnstown, PA
University of Puget Sound, WA
University of Rochester, NY
University of St. Francis, IL
University of St. Thomas, TX
University of South Alabama, AL
University of South Carolina, SC

University of South Carolina Aiken, SC
The University of South Dakota, SD
University of Southern Indiana, IN
University of Southern Mississippi, MS
The University of Tampa, FL
The University of Tennessee at Martin, TN
The University of Texas at Arlington, TX
The University of Texas at Austin, TX
The University of Texas at Dallas, TX
The University of Texas at El Paso, TX
The University of Texas of the Permian
    Basin, TX
The University of Texas–Pan American, TX
University of the Cumberlands, KY
University of the Incarnate Word, TX
University of the Ozarks, AR
University of the Pacific, CA
The University of Toledo, OH
University of Tulsa, OK
University of Utah, UT
University of Vermont, VT
University of Washington, WA
University of West Florida, FL
University of West Georgia, GA
University of Wisconsin–Eau Claire, WI
University of Wisconsin–Green Bay, WI
University of Wisconsin–La Crosse, WI
University of Wisconsin–Parkside, WI
University of Wisconsin–River Falls, WI
University of Wisconsin–Stevens Point, WI
University of Wisconsin–Stout, WI
University of Wisconsin–Whitewater, WI
University of Wyoming, WY
Ursinus College, PA
Ursuline College, OH
Valdosta State University, GA
Valley Forge Christian College, PA
Vanderbilt University, TN
Virginia Military Institute, VA
Virginia Polytechnic Institute and State
    University, VA
Virginia State University, VA
Virginia Wesleyan College, VA
Wabash College, IN
Wake Forest University, NC
Waldorf College, IA
Warner Pacific College, OR
Warren Wilson College, NC
Wartburg College, IA
Washburn University, KS
Washington Adventist University, MD
Washington State University, WA
Wayland Baptist University, TX
Wayne State College, NE
Wayne State University, MI
Webber International University, FL
Webster University, MO
Wells College, NY
Wesleyan College, GA
Wesley College, DE
Western Illinois University, IL
Western Kentucky University, KY
Western New England University, MA
Western Oregon University, OR
Western State Colorado University, CO
Western Washington University, WA
Westminster College, MO
Westmont College, CA
West Texas A&M University, TX
West Virginia State University, WV
West Virginia University, WV
West Virginia Wesleyan College, WV
Wichita State University, KS
Widener University, PA
Wilkes University, PA
William Jessup University, CA

William Peace University, NC
Wilson College, PA
Wisconsin Lutheran College, WI
Wofford College, SC
Worcester Polytechnic Institute, MA
Wright State University, OH
Youngstown State University, OH

Memberships
Adelphi University, NY
Albright College, PA
American University, DC
Anderson University, SC
Angelo State University, TX
Arcadia University, PA
Arkansas Tech University, AR
Auburn University, AL
Austin Peay State University, TN
Averett University, VA
Benedictine University, IL
Blue Mountain College, MS
Boston University, MA
California State University, Chico, CA
California State University, San Bernardino,
    CA
California State University, Stanislaus, CA
Carroll University, WI
Carson-Newman University, TN
Cedar Crest College, PA
The College of New Rochelle, NY
Corban University, OR
Dallas Baptist University, TX
Davenport University, MI
Eastern Connecticut State University, CT
Eastern Michigan University, MI
Eastern New Mexico University, NM
Emmanuel College, GA
Emporia State University, KS
Ferris State University, MI
Flagler College, FL
Florida Institute of Technology, FL
Georgia Southern University, GA
Gonzaga University, WA
Greenville College, IL
Grove City College, PA
Hamline University, MN
Hawai`i Pacific University, HI
Howard University, DC
Idaho State University, ID
Illinois Institute of Technology, IL
Johnson State College, VT
Kennesaw State University, GA
Kettering University, MI
Lewis University, IL
LIM College, NY
Lock Haven University of Pennsylvania, PA
Longwood University, VA
Loyola Marymount University, CA
Loyola University Chicago, IL
MacMurray College, IL
Massachusetts College of Liberal Arts, MA
McNeese State University, LA
Michigan State University, MI
Mississippi State University, MS
Missouri Baptist University, MO
Molloy College, NY
Montana State University–Northern, MT
Murray State University, KY
New Life Theological Seminary, NC
New Mexico State University, NM
Northern Michigan University, MI
Northwestern Oklahoma State University,
    OK
Northwestern State University of Louisiana,
    LA
Northwest Missouri State University, MO

Northwood University, Texas Campus, TX
Notre Dame of Maryland University, MD
Nova Southeastern University, FL
The Ohio State University, OH
Oklahoma State University, OK
Old Dominion University, VA
Olivet College, MI
Oral Roberts University, OK
Pace University, NY
Pacific University, OR
Peirce College, PA
Point Park University, PA
Portland State University, OR
Quincy University, IL
Ripon College, WI
Sacred Heart University, CT
St. Catherine University, MN
Saint Louis University, MO
Saint Mary-of-the-Woods College, IN
Saint Mary's College of California, CA
San Diego State University, CA
Schreiner University, TX
Shawnee State University, OH
Siena College, NY
Sonoma State University, CA
South Dakota State University, SD
Southeastern Louisiana University, LA
Southeast Missouri State University, MO
Southwestern College, KS
State University of New York College at
    Geneseo, NY
State University of New York College of
    Environmental Science and Forestry, NY
Stephens College, MO
Tennessee Wesleyan College, TN
Texas A&M University, TX
Texas A&M University–Texarkana, TX
Texas Christian University, TX
Texas Lutheran University, TX
Texas Tech University, TX
Texas Wesleyan University, TX
Thomas More College, KY
Towson University, MD
Union College, KY
The University of Akron, OH
The University of Alabama at Birmingham,
    AL
University of Evansville, IN
University of Louisville, KY
University of Michigan–Dearborn, MI
University of Mississippi, MS
University of Missouri–St. Louis, MO
University of Nebraska at Omaha, NE
University of South Carolina, SC
The University of Tampa, FL
The University of Tennessee at Chattanooga,
    TN
The University of Texas–Pan American, TX
The University of Toledo, OH
University of Vermont, VT
University of Washington, WA
University of West Georgia, GA
University of Wisconsin–Eau Claire, WI
University of Wisconsin–La Crosse, WI
University of Wisconsin–Stout, WI
Virginia Polytechnic Institute and State
    University, VA
Washington State University, WA
Wayland Baptist University, TX
Webber International University, FL
Wesleyan College, GA
Western Kentucky University, KY
Western Washington University, WA
West Texas A&M University, TX
Wichita State University, KS

Wright State University, OH
Youngstown State University, OH

Religious Involvement
Adrian College, MI
Alaska Bible College, AK
Alaska Pacific University, AK
Albright College, PA
Alma College, MI
Amridge University, AL
Andrews University, MI
Anna Maria College, MA
Ashland University, OH
Aurora University, IL
Averett University, VA
Baptist Bible College of Pennsylvania, PA
Barton College, NC
Baylor University, TX
Bellarmine University, KY
Berry College, GA
Bethel College, IN
Bethel University, MN
Blue Mountain College, MS
Briar Cliff University, IA
Brigham Young University, UT
Caldwell College, NJ
California Lutheran University, CA
Calvary Bible College and Theological
    Seminary, MO
Calvin College, MI
Campbellsville University, KY
Campbell University, NC
Canisius College, NY
Capital University, OH
Carroll College, MT
Carroll University, WI
Cedar Crest College, PA
Centenary College of Louisiana, LA
Central College, IA
Central Methodist University, MO
Cincinnati Christian University, OH
The Citadel, The Military College of South
    Carolina, SC
The College at Brockport, State University
    of New York, NY
The College of New Rochelle, NY
College of Saint Mary, NE
The College of Wooster, OH
Columbia International University, SC
Concordia University, OR
Concordia University Texas, TX
Corban University, OR
Cornell College, IA
Crossroads Bible College, IN
Dallas Baptist University, TX
Davidson College, NC
Defiance College, OH
Drury University, MO
Earlham College, IN
Eastern Michigan University, MI
Eastern Nazarene College, MA
East Texas Baptist University, TX
Elizabethtown College, PA
Elon University, NC
Emmanuel College, GA
Endicott College, MA
Eureka College, IL
Evangel University, MO
Faulkner University, AL
Ferrum College, VA
Finlandia University, MI
Flagler College, FL
Furman University, SC
Gardner-Webb University, NC
George Fox University, OR

Georgetown College, KY
Georgia Southern University, GA
Graceland University, IA
Grand View University, IA
Green Mountain College, VT
Greenville College, IL
Grove City College, PA
Guilford College, NC
Harding University, AR
Hawai'i Pacific University, HI
Hendrix College, AR
Heritage Christian University, AL
Hillsdale Free Will Baptist College, OK
Houston Baptist University, TX
Howard Payne University, TX
Howard University, DC
Huntington University, IN
Indiana Wesleyan University, IN
Kutztown University of Pennsylvania, PA
Kuyper College, MI
Lakeland College, WI
Lancaster Bible College, PA
Lee University, TN
Limestone College, SC
Lindsey Wilson College, KY
Lipscomb University, TN
Loyola Marymount University, CA
MacMurray College, IL
Malone University, OH
Maryville University of Saint Louis, MO
McPherson College, KS
Mercyhurst University, PA
Methodist University, NC
Mid-Atlantic Christian University, NC
Millsaps College, MS
Mississippi College, MS
Missouri Baptist University, MO
Molloy College, NY
Monmouth College, IL
Moravian College, PA
Morehouse College, GA
Mount Olive College, NC
Mount Vernon Nazarene University, OH
Newberry College, SC
New Hope Christian College, OR
New Jersey Institute of Technology, NJ
New Life Theological Seminary, NC
North Central College, IL
Northwest Christian University, OR
Northwest Nazarene University, ID
Notre Dame of Maryland University, MD
Nyack College, NY
Oglethorpe University, GA
Ohio Valley University, WV
Oklahoma Baptist University, OK
Oklahoma City University, OK
Oklahoma Wesleyan University, OK
Olivet Nazarene University, IL
Oral Roberts University, OK
Pacific Union College, CA
Pacific University, OR
Piedmont College, GA
Presbyterian College, SC
Principia College, IL
Randolph-Macon College, VA
Rosemont College, PA
Sacred Heart University, CT
Saint Francis University, PA
St. John's University, NY
Saint Louis University, MO
Saint Martin's University, WA
Saint Mary-of-the-Woods College, IN
St. Olaf College, MN
San Diego Christian College, CA
Schreiner University, TX

Shenandoah University, VA
Shorter University, GA
Siena College, NY
Simpson College, IA
Simpson University, CA
Southern Adventist University, TN
Southwest Baptist University, MO
Southwestern College, KS
Stetson University, FL
Tennessee Wesleyan College, TN
Texas Christian University, TX
Texas Lutheran University, TX
Texas Wesleyan University, TX
Thomas More College, KY
Transylvania University, KY
Trinity Baptist College, FL
Trinity Christian College, IL
Trinity College of Florida, FL
Union University, TN
The University of Alabama at Birmingham,
    AL
University of Great Falls, MT
University of Indianapolis, IN
University of Mary Hardin-Baylor, TX
University of Mobile, AL
The University of North Carolina at
    Greensboro, NC
University of Puget Sound, WA
University of St. Francis, IL
University of St. Thomas, TX
University of San Diego, CA
University of South Carolina, SC
The University of Tennessee at Chattanooga,
    TN
University of the Cumberlands, KY
University of the Incarnate Word, TX
University of the Pacific, CA
The University of Toledo, OH
The University of Virginia's College at Wise,
    VA
University of West Georgia, GA
University of Wisconsin–Stout, WI
Valdosta State University, GA
Valley Forge Christian College, PA
Virginia Intermont College, VA
Virginia Polytechnic Institute and State
    University, VA
Virginia State University, VA
Virginia Wesleyan College, VA
Washington State University, WA
Wayland Baptist University, TX
Wesleyan College, GA
Wesley College, DE
West Virginia Wesleyan College, WV
William Jessup University, CA
William Jewell College, MO
Youngstown State University, OH

Rodeo
Angelo State University, TX
Boise State University, ID
California Polytechnic State University, San
    Luis Obispo, CA
Eastern New Mexico University, NM
Fort Hays State University, KS
Hastings College, NE
Idaho State University, ID
Iowa State University of Science and
    Technology, IA
Lewis-Clark State College, ID
McNeese State University, LA
Michigan State University, MI
Missouri Valley College, MO
Montana State University–Northern, MT
Murray State University, KY

New Mexico State University, NM
Northwestern Oklahoma State University, OK
Oklahoma State University, OK
Rogers State University, OK
Sam Houston State University, TX
South Dakota State University, SD
Southeastern Oklahoma State University, OK
Southern Arkansas University–Magnolia, AR
Stephen F. Austin State University, TX
Texas A&M University, TX
Texas Tech University, TX
University of Idaho, ID
The University of Montana, MT
The University of Montana Western, MT
University of Nevada, Las Vegas, NV
The University of Tennessee at Martin, TN
The University of West Alabama, AL
University of Wyoming, WY
Washington State University, WA
West Texas A&M University, TX

Special Characteristics

Adult Students

Allegheny College, PA
American University, DC
Anderson University, IN
Arkansas State University, AR
Averett University, VA
Ball State University, IN
Barton College, NC
Bay Path College, MA
Bellarmine University, KY
Berry College, GA
Bethel College, IN
Binghamton University, State University of New York, NY
Biola University, CA
Bloomfield College, NJ
Bluefield College, VA
California Baptist University, CA
California Lutheran University, CA
California State University, Chico, CA
Calvin College, MI
Campbellsville University, KY
Carroll University, WI
Cedar Crest College, PA
Coe College, IA
College of Mount St. Joseph, OH
College of Saint Elizabeth, NJ
The College of Saint Rose, NY
College of Staten Island of the City University of New York, NY
Colorado Mesa University, CO
Concordia University Texas, TX
Dominican University of California, CA
East Carolina University, NC
Eastern Washington University, WA
Edinboro University of Pennsylvania, PA
Elon University, NC
Emmanuel College, GA
Evangel University, MO
The Evergreen State College, WA
Fairmont State University, WV
Faulkner University, AL
Ferris State University, MI
Florida Gulf Coast University, FL
Fort Hays State University, KS
Francis Marion University, SC
Franklin Pierce University, NH
Frostburg State University, MD
Gannon University, PA

Georgia College & State University, GA
Georgia Southern University, GA
Grand Valley State University, MI
Hampton University, VA
Hastings College, NE
Hollins University, VA
Houghton College, NY
Howard University, DC
Indiana University of Pennsylvania, PA
Inter American University of Puerto Rico, Barranquitas Campus, PR
Iowa State University of Science and Technology, IA
Kent State University, OH
Kentucky State University, KY
Lancaster Bible College, PA
La Sierra University, CA
Lincoln University, MO
Lipscomb University, TN
Lock Haven University of Pennsylvania, PA
Long Island University–C. W. Post Campus, NY
Lourdes University, OH
Loyola Marymount University, CA
Loyola University Chicago, IL
Maryville University of Saint Louis, MO
Marywood University, PA
McNeese State University, LA
Mercer University, GA
Meredith College, NC
Messiah College, PA
Metropolitan State University of Denver, CO
Middle Tennessee State University, TN
Millsaps College, MS
Minnesota State University Moorhead, MN
Mississippi State University, MS
Mississippi University for Women, MS
Missouri Baptist University, MO
Missouri Western State University, MO
Monmouth University, NJ
Montana State University Billings, MT
Montana State University–Northern, MT
Moravian College, PA
Morehead State University, KY
Murray State University, KY
New Jersey Institute of Technology, NJ
New Mexico State University, NM
North Central College, IL
Northeastern Illinois University, IL
Northern Illinois University, IL
Northern Kentucky University, KY
Northern State University, SD
Northwestern State University of Louisiana, LA
Oakland University, MI
The Ohio State University, OH
Ohio Valley University, WV
Oklahoma State University, OK
Pace University, NY
Palm Beach Atlantic University, FL
Piedmont College, GA
Portland State University, OR
Quincy University, IL
Randolph College, VA
Regis University, CO
The Richard Stockton College of New Jersey, NJ
Robert Morris University Illinois, IL
Rochester College, MI
Rogers State University, OK
Russell Sage College, NY
Sacred Heart University, CT
St. Ambrose University, IA
St. Catherine University, MN
St. Edward's University, TX
Saint Francis University, PA

Saint Mary-of-the-Woods College, IN
San Diego State University, CA
Siena College, NY
Simpson College, IA
Sonoma State University, CA
South Dakota School of Mines and Technology, SD
South Dakota State University, SD
Southeastern Louisiana University, LA
Southern Arkansas University–Magnolia, AR
Spring Arbor University, MI
State University of New York College at Cortland, NY
State University of New York College at Geneseo, NY
State University of New York College at Potsdam, NY
Stephen F. Austin State University, TX
Sweet Briar College, VA
Texas Christian University, TX
Texas Wesleyan University, TX
Thomas More College, KY
Towson University, MD
Trinity Christian College, IL
Union College, KY
The University of Akron, OH
The University of Alabama at Birmingham, AL
University of Connecticut, CT
University of Hartford, CT
The University of Kansas, KS
University of Louisville, KY
University of Maine at Fort Kent, ME
University of Maryland, College Park, MD
University of Maryland Eastern Shore, MD
University of Mary Washington, VA
University of Massachusetts Boston, MA
University of Massachusetts Dartmouth, MA
University of Memphis, TN
University of Michigan–Dearborn, MI
University of Michigan–Flint, MI
University of Mississippi, MS
University of Missouri–St. Louis, MO
University of Nebraska at Omaha, NE
University of Nevada, Las Vegas, NV
University of Nevada, Reno, NV
University of New Orleans, LA
University of North Carolina at Asheville, NC
The University of North Carolina at Greensboro, NC
University of Northern Colorado, CO
University of Pittsburgh at Bradford, PA
University of St. Francis, IL
University of South Carolina, SC
University of South Carolina Aiken, SC
The University of Tennessee at Martin, TN
The University of Texas at Dallas, TX
The University of Toledo, OH
University of Vermont, VT
University of West Georgia, GA
University of Wisconsin–Eau Claire, WI
University of Wisconsin–Green Bay, WI
University of Wisconsin–La Crosse, WI
University of Wisconsin–Parkside, WI
University of Wisconsin–Stevens Point, WI
University of Wisconsin–Stout, WI
University of Wisconsin–Whitewater, WI
University of Wyoming, WY
Washburn University, KS
Wesleyan College, GA
Western Kentucky University, KY
Western Oregon University, OR
Wichita State University, KS
Widener University, PA

William Jessup University, CA
Wilson College, PA
Wisconsin Lutheran College, WI
Wittenberg University, OH
Wright State University, OH
Youngstown State University, OH

Children and Siblings of Alumni

Adelphi University, NY
Adrian College, MI
Alaska Pacific University, AK
Albion College, MI
Albright College, PA
Alliant International University, CA
Alma College, MI
American University, DC
Arcadia University, PA
Arkansas State University, AR
Asbury University, KY
Ashland University, OH
Auburn University, AL
Augustana College, IL
Augustana College, SD
Aurora University, IL
Averett University, VA
Baldwin Wallace University, OH
Ball State University, IN
Barton College, NC
Bellarmine University, KY
Bemidji State University, MN
Benedictine University, IL
Bethel College, KS
Bethel University, MN
Biola University, CA
Bloomfield College, NJ
Blue Mountain College, MS
Boston University, MA
Bowling Green State University, OH
Bradley University, IL
Briar Cliff University, IA
Cabrini College, PA
California Lutheran University, CA
California Polytechnic State University, San
    Luis Obispo, CA
California State Polytechnic University,
    Pomona, CA
California State University, Monterey Bay,
    CA
Calumet College of Saint Joseph, IN
Calvary Bible College and Theological
    Seminary, MO
Calvin College, MI
Canisius College, NY
Capital University, OH
Cardinal Stritch University, WI
Carroll University, WI
Carson-Newman University, TN
The Catholic University of America, DC
Cedar Crest College, PA
Cedarville University, OH
Centenary College of Louisiana, LA
Central College, IA
Central Methodist University, MO
Central Michigan University, MI
Centre College, KY
Chapman University, CA
Chatham University, PA
Christian Brothers University, TN
The Citadel, The Military College of South
    Carolina, SC
City College of the City University of New
    York, NY
Clarion University of Pennsylvania, PA
Clarke University, IA
Clarkson University, NY

Clearwater Christian College, FL
Coe College, IA
Coker College, SC
The College at Brockport, State University
    of New York, NY
The College of Idaho, ID
College of Mount St. Joseph, OH
The College of New Rochelle, NY
College of Saint Elizabeth, NJ
The College of Saint Rose, NY
The College of St. Scholastica, MN
College of Staten Island of the City
    University of New York, NY
Columbia College, MO
Columbia International University, SC
Concordia University Ann Arbor, MI
Concordia University, Nebraska, NE
Concordia University Texas, TX
Converse College, SC
Crown College, MN
Culver-Stockton College, MO
Defiance College, OH
DePauw University, IN
Dickinson College, PA
Doane College, NE
Dominican University, IL
Dominican University of California, CA
Dordt College, IA
Drake University, IA
Drury University, MO
Duke University, NC
Duquesne University, PA
D'Youville College, NY
East Carolina University, NC
Eastern Kentucky University, KY
Eastern Michigan University, MI
Eastern Nazarene College, MA
Eastern New Mexico University, NM
Eastern Washington University, WA
East Texas Baptist University, TX
Edinboro University of Pennsylvania, PA
Elmhurst College, IL
Embry-Riddle Aeronautical University–
    Daytona, FL
Embry-Riddle Aeronautical University–
    Prescott, AZ
Emmanuel College, MA
Emporia State University, KS
Endicott College, MA
Eureka College, IL
Evangel University, MO
Fairfield University, CT
Fairmont State University, WV
Farmingdale State College, NY
Faulkner University, AL
Ferris State University, MI
Florida Institute of Technology, FL
Florida Southern College, FL
Fort Hays State University, KS
Fort Lewis College, CO
Francis Marion University, SC
Franklin College, IN
Franklin Pierce University, NH
George Fox University, OR
Georgetown College, KY
Georgia Southern University, GA
Gonzaga University, WA
Gordon College, MA
Graceland University, IA
Grand Valley State University, MI
Grand View University, IA
Green Mountain College, VT
Greenville College, IL
Gustavus Adolphus College, MN
Gwynedd-Mercy College, PA

Hamline University, MN
Hanover College, IN
Hardin-Simmons University, TX
Hartwick College, NY
Hastings College, NE
Henderson State University, AR
Heritage Christian University, AL
Hilbert College, NY
Hillsdale Free Will Baptist College, OK
Hofstra University, NY
Hollins University, VA
Hood College, MD
Houghton College, NY
Howard Payne University, TX
Huntingdon College, AL
Huntington University, IN
Idaho State University, ID
Illinois Institute of Technology, IL
Indiana State University, IN
Indiana University–Purdue University Fort
    Wayne, IN
Indiana Wesleyan University, IN
Iona College, NY
Iowa State University of Science and
    Technology, IA
Ithaca College, NY
James Madison University, VA
Kalamazoo College, MI
Kennesaw State University, GA
Kent State University, OH
Keuka College, NY
Keystone College, PA
King's College, PA
Lake Forest College, IL
Lakeland College, WI
Lancaster Bible College, PA
Lasell College, MA
Lawrence University, WI
Lebanon Valley College, PA
Le Moyne College, NY
LeTourneau University, TX
Lewis-Clark State College, ID
Lewis University, IL
Lindenwood University, MO
Lindsey Wilson College, KY
Lipscomb University, TN
Long Island University–Brooklyn Campus,
    NY
Long Island University–C. W. Post Campus,
    NY
Longwood University, VA
Louisiana Tech University, LA
Loyola Marymount University, CA
Luther College, IA
Lynn University, FL
MacMurray College, IL
Malone University, OH
Manchester University, IN
Marietta College, OH
Marshall University, WV
Maryville College, TN
Marywood University, PA
Massachusetts Maritime Academy, MA
The Master's College and Seminary, CA
McKendree University, IL
McNeese State University, LA
McPherson College, KS
Mercyhurst University, PA
Merrimack College, MA
Methodist University, NC
Michigan State University, MI
Michigan Technological University, MI
Mid-Atlantic Christian University, NC
Midwestern State University, TX
Millikin University, IL

Minot State University, ND
Misericordia University, PA
Mississippi College, MS
Mississippi State University, MS
Mississippi University for Women, MS
Missouri Baptist University, MO
Missouri Southern State University, MO
Missouri State University, MO
Missouri University of Science and
    Technology, MO
Missouri Valley College, MO
Missouri Western State University, MO
Monmouth University, NJ
Montana State University, MT
Montana State University Billings, MT
Montana State University–Northern, MT
Montana Tech of The University of
    Montana, MT
Montclair State University, NJ
Moravian College, PA
Morehead State University, KY
Morehouse College, GA
Morningside College, IA
Mount St. Mary's College, CA
Nazareth College of Rochester, NY
Nebraska Wesleyan University, NE
Newberry College, SC
New England College, NH
New Mexico Highlands University, NM
New Mexico State University, NM
New York Institute of Technology, NY
Nichols College, MA
North Carolina State University, NC
Northeastern State University, OK
Northern Arizona University, AZ
Northern Kentucky University, KY
Northland College, WI
Northwest Missouri State University, MO
Northwest Nazarene University, ID
Northwood University, Florida Campus, FL
Northwood University, Michigan Campus,
    MI
Northwood University, Texas Campus, TX
Notre Dame de Namur University, CA
Nyack College, NY
The Ohio State University, OH
Ohio University, OH
Ohio University–Chillicothe, OH
Ohio University–Lancaster, OH
Ohio University–Southern Campus, OH
Ohio University–Zanesville, OH
Ohio Wesleyan University, OH
Oklahoma Baptist University, OK
Oklahoma State University, OK
Oklahoma Wesleyan University, OK
Olivet College, MI
Oral Roberts University, OK
Oregon State University, OR
Ouachita Baptist University, AR
Pacific Lutheran University, WA
Pacific University, OR
Palm Beach Atlantic University, FL
Peirce College, PA
Penn State Abington, PA
Penn State Altoona, PA
Penn State Berks, PA
Penn State Erie, The Behrend College, PA
Penn State Harrisburg, PA
Penn State Shenango, PA
Pine Manor College, MA
Pittsburg State University, KS
Point Park University, PA
Post University, CT
Principia College, IL
Quincy University, IL
Randolph-Macon College, VA

Regent University, VA
Rensselaer Polytechnic Institute, NY
Research College of Nursing, MO
Rhode Island College, RI
Ripon College, WI
Roberts Wesleyan College, NY
Rochester College, MI
Rockford College, IL
Rockhurst University, MO
Rocky Mountain College, MT
Rosemont College, PA
Russell Sage College, NY
Sacred Heart University, CT
Sage College of Albany, NY
St. Ambrose University, IA
St. Catherine University, MN
Saint Francis University, PA
St. John Fisher College, NY
Saint Joseph's College, IN
St. Joseph's College, Long Island Campus,
    NY
St. Joseph's College, New York, NY
Saint Joseph's University, PA
St. Lawrence University, NY
Saint Martin's University, WA
Saint Mary-of-the-Woods College, IN
Saint Mary's College of California, CA
Saint Mary's University of Minnesota, MN
Salisbury University, MD
Sam Houston State University, TX
San Diego Christian College, CA
San Diego State University, CA
Santa Clara University, CA
Seattle Pacific University, WA
Seattle University, WA
Seton Hill University, PA
Shimer College, IL
Shippensburg University of Pennsylvania,
    PA
Siena College, NY
Simmons College, MA
Simpson College, IA
Slippery Rock University of Pennsylvania,
    PA
Sonoma State University, CA
Southeastern Louisiana University, LA
Southeastern Oklahoma State University,
    OK
Southern Adventist University, TN
Southern Arkansas University–Magnolia,
    AR
Southern Illinois University–Carbondale, IL
Southern Utah University, UT
State University of New York at Fredonia,
    NY
State University of New York College at
    Potsdam, NY
State University of New York College of
    Agriculture and Technology at
    Cobleskill, NY
State University of New York College of
    Environmental Science and Forestry, NY
Stephen F. Austin State University, TX
Stetson University, FL
Suffolk University, MA
Taylor University, IN
Tennessee Technological University, TN
Tennessee Wesleyan College, TN
Texas Lutheran University, TX
Texas State University–San Marcos, TX
Texas Wesleyan University, TX
Thiel College, PA
Thomas More College, KY
Towson University, MD
Trine University, IN
Trinity Christian College, IL

Truman State University, MO
Union College, KY
Union University, TN
The University of Alabama at Birmingham,
    AL
University of Alaska Anchorage, AK
University of Arkansas, AR
University of Colorado Colorado Springs,
    CO
University of Delaware, DE
University of Evansville, IN
University of Great Falls, MT
University of Houston, TX
University of Idaho, ID
University of Illinois at Springfield, IL
The University of Iowa, IA
The University of Kansas, KS
University of Louisville, KY
University of Maine, ME
University of Mary Hardin-Baylor, TX
University of Mary Washington, VA
University of Massachusetts Amherst, MA
University of Massachusetts Lowell, MA
University of Michigan–Dearborn, MI
University of Michigan–Flint, MI
University of Minnesota, Crookston, MN
University of Mississippi, MS
University of Missouri–Kansas City, MO
University of Missouri–St. Louis, MO
The University of Montana, MT
University of Mount Union, OH
University of Nebraska at Kearney, NE
University of Nebraska at Omaha, NE
University of Nebraska–Lincoln, NE
University of Nevada, Las Vegas, NV
University of Nevada, Reno, NV
University of New England, ME
University of New Hampshire, NH
University of New Orleans, LA
University of North Carolina at Asheville,
    NC
The University of North Carolina at
    Greensboro, NC
The University of North Carolina at
    Pembroke, NC
University of Oklahoma, OK
University of Rhode Island, RI
University of Rio Grande, OH
University of Rochester, NY
University of St. Francis, IL
University of South Alabama, AL
University of South Carolina, SC
University of Southern Maine, ME
University of Southern Mississippi, MS
The University of Tampa, FL
The University of Tennessee at Chattanooga,
    TN
The University of Tennessee at Martin, TN
University of the Cumberlands, KY
University of the Incarnate Word, TX
University of the Ozarks, AR
The University of Toledo, OH
University of Tulsa, OK
University of West Florida, FL
University of West Georgia, GA
University of Wisconsin–Green Bay, WI
University of Wisconsin–La Crosse, WI
University of Wyoming, WY
Upper Iowa University, IA
Ursinus College, PA
Ursuline College, OH
Utah State University, UT
Valdosta State University, GA
Valley City State University, ND
Valparaiso University, IN
Virginia Military Institute, VA

Wake Forest University, NC
Warner Pacific College, OR
Wartburg College, IA
Washburn University, KS
Washington & Jefferson College, PA
Washington State University, WA
Wayland Baptist University, TX
Webber International University, FL
Webster University, MO
Wells College, NY
Wesleyan College, GA
Western State Colorado University, CO
Westminster College, MO
Westminster College, PA
West Texas A&M University, TX
West Virginia Wesleyan College, WV
Wheeling Jesuit University, WV
Whittier College, CA
Whitworth University, WA
William Jewell College, MO
Wilson College, PA
Winona State University, MN
Wittenberg University, OH
Wright State University, OH
Xavier University, OH
York College of Pennsylvania, PA
Youngstown State University, OH

Children of Current Students

Alliant International University, CA
Alma College, MI
Augustana College, SD
Bethel College, KS
Bloomfield College, NJ
Blue Mountain College, MS
Caldwell College, NJ
California State Polytechnic University, Pomona, CA
Cardinal Stritch University, WI
Carroll University, WI
Central College, IA
Columbia College, MO
Elmhurst College, IL
Emmanuel College, GA
Finlandia University, MI
Franklin Pierce University, NH
Green Mountain College, VT
Huntington University, IN
Lancaster Bible College, PA
Marymount University, VA
Marywood University, PA
Misericordia University, PA
Missouri Baptist University, MO
Mount Aloysius College, PA
Mount Marty College, SD
New Mexico State University, NM
Northwest University, WA
Palm Beach Atlantic University, FL
Rockford College, IL
Sacred Heart University, CT
St. Catherine University, MN
Saint Francis University, PA
Saint Mary-of-the-Woods College, IN
Texas Wesleyan University, TX
Union College, KY
Union University, TN
The University of Alabama at Birmingham, AL
University of Alaska Anchorage, AK
University of Great Falls, MT
University of Hartford, CT
Upper Iowa University, IA
Valley Forge Christian College, PA
Wesleyan College, GA
Wilson College, PA

Children of Educators

Alfred University, NY
Allegheny College, PA
Amridge University, AL
Austin Peay State University, TN
Bard College, NY
Benedictine College, KS
Bennington College, VT
Bridgewater College, VA
Calvary Bible College and Theological Seminary, MO
Campbellsville University, KY
Canisius College, NY
Centenary College of Louisiana, LA
Chowan University, NC
Coe College, IA
The College of Idaho, ID
The College of Wooster, OH
Columbia College, MO
Columbus College of Art & Design, OH
Concordia University, Nebraska, NE
Cornell College, IA
Emmanuel College, GA
Emmanuel College, MA
Emory & Henry College, VA
Endicott College, MA
Evangel University, MO
Flagler College, FL
Franklin Pierce University, NH
Goshen College, IN
Grand View University, IA
Hampden-Sydney College, VA
Hardin-Simmons University, TX
Hastings College, NE
Hendrix College, AR
Heritage Christian University, AL
Hillsdale Free Will Baptist College, OK
Jacksonville University, FL
John Carroll University, OH
King's College, PA
Lees-McRae College, NC
Lipscomb University, TN
Lycoming College, PA
Lynn University, FL
Mary Baldwin College, VA
Mississippi State University, MS
Moravian College, PA
Mount St. Mary's University, MD
Nebraska Wesleyan University, NE
New England College, NH
Northland International University, WI
Northwest Nazarene University, ID
Occidental College, CA
Oklahoma Wesleyan University, OK
Palm Beach Atlantic University, FL
Research College of Nursing, MO
Rockford College, IL
Rosemont College, PA
St. Ambrose University, IA
Saint Anselm College, NH
St. Catherine University, MN
Saint Francis University, PA
Saint Mary's College of California, CA
Seattle University, WA
Simpson College, IA
Sonoma State University, CA
Southern Illinois University Carbondale, IL
Tennessee Technological University, TN
Texas Christian University, TX
Texas Wesleyan University, TX
Union University, TN
Unity College, ME
The University of Alabama at Birmingham, AL
University of Alaska Anchorage, AK

University of Memphis, TN
University of St. Francis, IL
University of St. Thomas, MN
The University of Scranton, PA
The University of Tennessee at Martin, TN
Villanova University, PA
Wright State University, OH

Children of Faculty/Staff

Abilene Christian University, TX
Adelphi University, NY
Adrian College, MI
Alaska Bible College, AK
Alaska Pacific University, AK
Alcorn State University, MS
Alfred University, NY
Allegheny College, PA
Allen College, IA
Alliant International University, CA
Alverno College, WI
American International College, MA
American University, DC
Amridge University, AL
Anderson University, IN
Anderson University, SC
Andrews University, MI
Anna Maria College, MA
Arizona State University, AZ
Arkansas State University, AR
Arkansas Tech University, AR
Asbury University, KY
Ashland University, OH
Auburn University, AL
Augustana College, IL
Augustana College, SD
Aurora University, IL
Austin Peay State University, TN
Ball State University, IN
Baptist Bible College of Pennsylvania, PA
Bard College, NY
Barton College, NC
Baylor University, TX
Bay Path College, MA
Becker College, MA
Belhaven University, MS
Bellarmine University, KY
Belmont Abbey College, NC
Belmont University, TN
Bemidji State University, MN
Benedictine University, IL
Bennington College, VT
Berry College, GA
Bethany Lutheran College, MN
Bethel College, IN
Bethel College, KS
Bethel University, MN
Binghamton University, State University of New York, NY
Biola University, CA
Bloomsburg University of Pennsylvania, PA
Bluefield College, VA
Blue Mountain College, MS
Bluffton University, OH
Bowdoin College, ME
Bowling Green State University, OH
Bradley University, IL
Brenau University, GA
Brevard College, NC
Bridgewater College, VA
Broadview University–Boise, ID
Broadview University–Layton, UT
Broadview University–Orem, UT
Broadview University–Salt Lake City, UT
Broadview University–West Jordan, UT
Buena Vista University, IA

Cairn University, PA
Caldwell College, NJ
California Baptist University, CA
California Lutheran University, CA
California State University, Bakersfield, CA
California State University, Chico, CA
California State University, Stanislaus, CA
Calumet College of Saint Joseph, IN
Calvary Bible College and Theological
  Seminary, MO
Calvin College, MI
Campbellsville University, KY
Campbell University, NC
Canisius College, NY
Capital University, OH
Carroll College, MT
Carroll University, WI
Case Western Reserve University, OH
The Catholic University of America, DC
Cedarville University, OH
Centenary College of Louisiana, LA
Central College, IA
Central Methodist University, MO
Central Michigan University, MI
Centre College, KY
Chowan University, NC
Cincinnati Christian University, OH
Clarke University, IA
Clarkson University, NY
Cleary University, MI
Clemson University, SC
Cleveland Institute of Music, OH
Cleveland State University, OH
Coe College, IA
Coker College, SC
The College of Idaho, ID
College of Mount St. Joseph, OH
The College of New Rochelle, NY
College of Saint Mary, NE
The College of Saint Rose, NY
The College of St. Scholastica, MN
College of Staten Island of the City
  University of New York, NY
College of the Holy Cross, MA
The College of Wooster, OH
The Colorado College, CO
Colorado State University, CO
Columbia College, MO
Columbia International University, SC
Columbus College of Art & Design, OH
Concordia University, CA
Concordia University, OR
Concordia University Ann Arbor, MI
Concordia University, Nebraska, NE
Concordia University, St. Paul, MN
Concordia University Texas, TX
Converse College, SC
Corban University, OR
Cornell College, IA
Cornerstone University, MI
Covenant College, GA
Creighton University, NE
Crossroads Bible College, IN
Crown College, MN
Culver-Stockton College, MO
Dakota Wesleyan University, SD
Dallas Baptist University, TX
Defiance College, OH
Denison University, OH
DePaul University, IL
Dickinson College, PA
Dillard University, LA
Doane College, NE
Dominican College, NY
Dominican University, IL
Dominican University of California, CA

Dordt College, IA
Drury University, MO
Duquesne University, PA
D'Youville College, NY
East Carolina University, NC
Eastern Connecticut State University, CT
Eastern Kentucky University, KY
Eastern Nazarene College, MA
East Texas Baptist University, TX
Eckerd College, FL
Edgewood College, WI
Edinboro University of Pennsylvania, PA
Elizabethtown College, PA
Elmira College, NY
Elon University, NC
Embry-Riddle Aeronautical University–
  Daytona, FL
Embry-Riddle Aeronautical University–
  Prescott, AZ
Embry-Riddle Aeronautical University–
  Worldwide, FL
Emmanuel College, GA
Emmanuel College, MA
Emory & Henry College, VA
Emory University, GA
Emporia State University, KS
Eureka College, IL
Evangel University, MO
Fairfield University, CT
Fairmont State University, WV
Faulkner University, AL
Felician College, NJ
Ferrum College, VA
Finlandia University, MI
Flagler College, FL
Florida Institute of Technology, FL
Florida Southern College, FL
Fort Hays State University, KS
Fort Lewis College, CO
Framingham State University, MA
Francis Marion University, SC
Franklin College, IN
Franklin Pierce University, NH
Fresno Pacific University, CA
Furman University, SC
Gardner-Webb University, NC
Geneva College, PA
George Fox University, OR
Georgetown College, KY
Georgetown University, DC
Georgia College & State University, GA
Georgian Court University, NJ
Glenville State College, WV
Globe University–Appleton, WI
Globe University–Eau Claire, WI
Globe University–Green Bay, WI
Globe University–La Crosse, WI
Globe University–Madison East, WI
Globe University–Madison West, WI
Globe University–Minneapolis, MN
Globe University–Sioux Falls, SD
Globe University–Wausau, WI
Globe University–Woodbury, MN
Gonzaga University, WA
Goshen College, IN
Grace Bible College, MI
Graceland University, IA
Grand Valley State University, MI
Grand View University, IA
Greenville College, IL
Guilford College, NC
Hampden-Sydney College, VA
Hampshire College, MA
Hampton University, VA
Hanover College, IN
Harding University, AR

Hardin-Simmons University, TX
Hartwick College, NY
Hastings College, NE
Heidelberg University, OH
Henderson State University, AR
Hendrix College, AR
Heritage Christian University, AL
Hillsdale College, MI
Hillsdale Free Will Baptist College, OK
Hollins University, VA
Hood College, MD
Hope International University, CA
Houghton College, NY
Houston Baptist University, TX
Howard Payne University, TX
Huntingdon College, AL
Huntington University, IN
Idaho State University, ID
Illinois College, IL
Illinois Institute of Technology, IL
Illinois State University, IL
Illinois Wesleyan University, IL
Indiana State University, IN
Indiana Tech, IN
Indiana University of Pennsylvania, PA
Indiana Wesleyan University, IN
Iona College, NY
Iowa Wesleyan College, IA
Ithaca College, NY
Jackson State University, MS
Jacksonville University, FL
James Madison University, VA
John Carroll University, OH
The Johns Hopkins University, MD
Johnson C. Smith University, NC
Juniata College, PA
Kent State University, OH
Kentucky State University, KY
Kentucky Wesleyan College, KY
Kettering University, MI
Keuka College, NY
King College, TN
King's College, PA
Kutztown University of Pennsylvania, PA
Kuyper College, MI
LaGrange College, GA
Lake Erie College, OH
Lakeland College, WI
Lancaster Bible College, PA
La Salle University, PA
Lasell College, MA
La Sierra University, CA
Lawrence Technological University, MI
Lebanon Valley College, PA
Lees-McRae College, NC
Lee University, TN
Lehigh University, PA
LeMoyne-Owen College, TN
Lewis & Clark College, OR
Lewis University, IL
Liberty University, VA
Limestone College, SC
Lincoln University, MO
Lindenwood University, MO
Lindsey Wilson College, KY
Linfield College, OR
Lipscomb University, TN
Long Island University–Brooklyn Campus,
  NY
Long Island University–C. W. Post Campus,
  NY
Louisiana College, LA
Louisiana Tech University, LA
Loyola Marymount University, CA
Loyola University New Orleans, LA
Lubbock Christian University, TX

Lycoming College, PA
Lynn University, FL
Lyon College, AR
MacMurray College, IL
Maine Maritime Academy, ME
Malone University, OH
Manhattan College, NY
Marian University, WI
Marquette University, WI
Marshall University, WV
Mary Baldwin College, VA
Marymount University, VA
Maryville College, TN
Maryville University of Saint Louis, MO
Marywood University, PA
Massachusetts College of Art and Design, MA
Massachusetts Maritime Academy, MA
The Master's College and Seminary, CA
Mayville State University, ND
McKendree University, IL
McMurry University, TX
McNally Smith College of Music, MN
McNeese State University, LA
Memphis College of Art, TN
Mercer University, GA
Mercyhurst University, PA
Meredith College, NC
Merrimack College, MA
Messiah College, PA
Methodist University, NC
Miami University, OH
Michigan State University, MI
Mid-Atlantic Christian University, NC
Midwestern State University, TX
Milligan College, TN
Millikin University, IL
Millsaps College, MS
Milwaukee School of Engineering, WI
Minnesota School of Business–Blaine, MN
Minnesota School of Business–Elk River, MN
Minnesota School of Business–Lakeville, MN
Minnesota School of Business–Moorhead, MN
Minnesota School of Business–Rochester, MN
Minnesota State University Moorhead, MN
Minot State University, ND
Misericordia University, PA
Mississippi College, MS
Mississippi State University, MS
Mississippi University for Women, MS
Missouri Baptist University, MO
Missouri Southern State University, MO
Missouri University of Science and Technology, MO
Missouri Valley College, MO
Missouri Western State University, MO
Monmouth University, NJ
Montana State University Billings, MT
Montana Tech of The University of Montana, MT
Montreat College, NC
Moravian College, PA
Morehouse College, GA
Morningside College, IA
Mount Carmel College of Nursing, OH
Mount Marty College, SD
Mount Mary College, WI
Mount Olive College, NC
Mount Saint Mary College, NY
Mount St. Mary's University, MD
Mount Vernon Nazarene University, OH

Murray State University, KY
Nazareth College of Rochester, NY
Nebraska Methodist College, NE
Nebraska Wesleyan University, NE
Newberry College, SC
New England College, NH
New Jersey Institute of Technology, NJ
New Mexico Highlands University, NM
New Mexico State University, NM
New York Institute of Technology, NY
Niagara University, NY
Nicholls State University, LA
Nichols College, MA
North Central College, IL
Northeastern Illinois University, IL
Northeastern State University, OK
Northern Illinois University, IL
Northern Kentucky University, KY
Northern Michigan University, MI
Northland International University, WI
Northwest Christian University, OR
Northwestern College, MN
Northwestern Oklahoma State University, OK
Northwestern State University of Louisiana, LA
Northwest Missouri State University, MO
Northwest Nazarene University, ID
Northwest University, WA
Northwood University, Florida Campus, FL
Northwood University, Michigan Campus, MI
Northwood University, Texas Campus, TX
Norwich University, VT
Notre Dame de Namur University, CA
Nova Southeastern University, FL
Nyack College, NY
Occidental College, CA
Oglethorpe University, GA
The Ohio State University, OH
Ohio University, OH
Ohio University–Chillicothe, OH
Ohio University–Eastern, OH
Ohio University–Lancaster, OH
Ohio University–Southern Campus, OH
Ohio University–Zanesville, OH
Ohio Valley University, WV
Oklahoma Baptist University, OK
Oklahoma Christian University, OK
Oklahoma City University, OK
Oklahoma Wesleyan University, OK
Old Dominion University, VA
Olivet College, MI
Olivet Nazarene University, IL
Oral Roberts University, OK
Ouachita Baptist University, AR
Pace University, NY
Pacific University, OR
Palm Beach Atlantic University, FL
Park University, MO
Peirce College, PA
Piedmont College, GA
Piedmont International University, NC
Plymouth State University, NH
Point Park University, PA
Presbyterian College, SC
Principia College, IL
Purdue University, IN
Purdue University North Central, IN
Quincy University, IL
Quinnipiac University, CT
Ramapo College of New Jersey, NJ
Randolph College, VA
Randolph-Macon College, VA
Regent University, VA

Regis University, CO
Rensselaer Polytechnic Institute, NY
Research College of Nursing, MO
Rhodes College, TN
The Richard Stockton College of New Jersey, NJ
Ripon College, WI
Robert Morris University Illinois, IL
Roberts Wesleyan College, NY
Rochester College, MI
Rochester Institute of Technology, NY
Rockford College, IL
Rockhurst University, MO
Rocky Mountain College, MT
Rocky Mountain College of Art + Design, CO
Rosemont College, PA
Sacred Heart University, CT
St. Ambrose University, IA
Saint Anselm College, NH
Saint Augustine's College, NC
St. Bonaventure University, NY
St. Catherine University, MN
St. Cloud State University, MN
St. Edward's University, TX
Saint Francis University, PA
St. John Fisher College, NY
St. John's College, NM
St. John's University, NY
Saint Joseph's College, IN
St. Joseph's College, Long Island Campus, NY
St. Joseph's College, New York, NY
Saint Joseph's University, PA
St. Louis College of Pharmacy, MO
Saint Louis University, MO
Saint Martin's University, WA
Saint Mary-of-the-Woods College, IN
Saint Mary's College of California, CA
St. Mary's College of Maryland, MD
Saint Mary's University of Minnesota, MN
St. Norbert College, WI
Saint Peter's University, NJ
Samford University, AL
San Diego Christian College, CA
San Diego State University, CA
Santa Clara University, CA
Schreiner University, TX
Seattle Pacific University, WA
Seattle University, WA
Seton Hill University, PA
Sewanee: The University of the South, TN
Shenandoah University, VA
Shorter University, GA
Siena College, NY
Simpson College, IA
Simpson University, CA
Skidmore College, NY
Slippery Rock University of Pennsylvania, PA
Soka University of America, CA
Sonoma State University, CA
South Dakota State University, SD
Southeastern Louisiana University, LA
Southeast Missouri State University, MO
Southern Arkansas University–Magnolia, AR
Southern Connecticut State University, CT
Southern Illinois University Carbondale, IL
Southern Illinois University Edwardsville, IL
Southwestern Christian College, TX
Southwestern College, KS
Southwestern University, TX
Spring Arbor University, MI

Spring Hill College, AL
State University of New York at New Paltz, NY
State University of New York College at Potsdam, NY
Stephen F. Austin State University, TX
Stephens College, MO
Stetson University, FL
Stonehill College, MA
Suffolk University, MA
Taylor University, IN
Temple University, PA
Tennessee Technological University, TN
Tennessee Wesleyan College, TN
Texas A&M University, TX
Texas Christian University, TX
Texas College, TX
Texas Lutheran University, TX
Texas Tech University, TX
Texas Wesleyan University, TX
Thiel College, PA
Thomas More College, KY
Thomas University, GA
Tiffin University, OH
Towson University, MD
Transylvania University, KY
Trevecca Nazarene University, TN
Trine University, IN
Trinity Christian College, IL
Trinity College of Florida, FL
Truman State University, MO
Tuskegee University, AL
Union College, KY
Union College, NY
Union University, TN
The University of Alabama at Birmingham, AL
The University of Arizona, AZ
University of Arkansas, AR
University of Bridgeport, CT
University of Connecticut, CT
University of Dallas, TX
University of Dayton, OH
University of Delaware, DE
University of Evansville, IN
University of Florida, FL
University of Great Falls, MT
University of Hartford, CT
University of Idaho, ID
University of Illinois at Urbana–Champaign, IL
University of Indianapolis, IN
The University of Kansas, KS
University of La Verne, CA
University of Louisville, KY
University of Maine at Augusta, ME
University of Maine at Farmington, ME
University of Maine at Fort Kent, ME
University of Maine at Presque Isle, ME
University of Mary, ND
University of Mary Hardin-Baylor, TX
University of Maryland Eastern Shore, MD
University of Mary Washington, VA
University of Massachusetts Amherst, MA
University of Massachusetts Boston, MA
University of Massachusetts Dartmouth, MA
University of Massachusetts Lowell, MA
University of Memphis, TN
University of Miami, FL
University of Michigan, MI
University of Michigan–Dearborn, MI
University of Michigan–Flint, MI
University of Minnesota, Crookston, MN
University of Mississippi, MS
University of Missouri–St. Louis, MO
University of Mobile, AL

The University of Montana Western, MT
University of Montevallo, AL
University of Mount Union, OH
University of Nebraska at Kearney, NE
University of Nebraska at Omaha, NE
University of Nevada, Las Vegas, NV
University of New Hampshire, NH
University of New Hampshire at Manchester, NH
University of North Alabama, AL
University of North Carolina at Asheville, NC
The University of North Carolina at Chapel Hill, NC
The University of North Carolina at Greensboro, NC
University of Northern Colorado, CO
University of Notre Dame, IN
University of Oregon, OR
University of Pittsburgh at Bradford, PA
University of Pittsburgh at Johnstown, PA
University of Portland, OR
University of Puget Sound, WA
University of Rio Grande, OH
University of Rochester, NY
University of St. Thomas, MN
University of St. Thomas, TX
University of San Diego, CA
University of Science and Arts of Oklahoma, OK
The University of Scranton, PA
University of South Alabama, AL
University of South Carolina, SC
University of Southern Indiana, IN
University of Southern Maine, ME
University of Southern Mississippi, MS
The University of Tampa, FL
The University of Tennessee at Chattanooga, TN
The University of Tennessee at Martin, TN
The University of Texas at Brownsville, TX
University of the Cumberlands, KY
University of the District of Columbia, DC
University of the Incarnate Word, TX
University of the Ozarks, AR
The University of Toledo, OH
University of Tulsa, OK
University of Utah, UT
The University of West Alabama, AL
University of West Florida, FL
Ursinus College, PA
Ursuline College, OH
Utah State University, UT
Valley City State University, ND
Valley Forge Christian College, PA
Valparaiso University, IN
Villanova University, PA
Virginia Intermont College, VA
Virginia Military Institute, VA
Virginia Polytechnic Institute and State University, VA
Virginia Union University, VA
Virginia Wesleyan College, VA
Wabash College, IN
Wagner College, NY
Waldorf College, IA
Warren Wilson College, NC
Wartburg College, IA
Washburn University, KS
Washington Adventist University, MD
Washington & Jefferson College, PA
Washington College, MD
Washington State University, WA
Wayland Baptist University, TX
Waynesburg University, PA
Wayne State College, NE

Wayne State University, MI
Webber International University, FL
Webster University, MO
Wesleyan College, GA
West Chester University of Pennsylvania, PA
Western Illinois University, IL
Western Michigan University, MI
Western New England University, MA
Westminster College, MO
Westmont College, CA
West Texas A&M University, TX
West Virginia University, WV
West Virginia Wesleyan College, WV
Wheeling Jesuit University, WV
Whittier College, CA
Wichita State University, KS
Widener University, PA
Wilkes University, PA
William Jessup University, CA
William Jewell College, MO
William Peace University, NC
Williams Baptist College, AR
Wilson College, PA
Winona State University, MN
Winthrop University, SC
Wisconsin Lutheran College, WI
Wittenberg University, OH
Wofford College, SC
Wright State University, OH
Xavier University of Louisiana, LA
Young Harris College, GA
Youngstown State University, OH

Children of Public Servants
American International College, MA
California State University, San Bernardino, CA
Chowan University, NC
Framingham State University, MA
Georgia Southern University, GA
Illinois Institute of Technology, IL
Louisiana Tech University, LA
McNeese State University, LA
Mercer University, GA
Mississippi State University, MS
Missouri Western State University, MO
Monmouth University, NJ
New Mexico State University, NM
Northern Kentucky University, KY
Northland International University, WI
Northwestern State University of Louisiana, LA
The Ohio State University, OH
Peirce College, PA
Siena College, NY
Sonoma State University, CA
Southern Illinois University Carbondale, IL
Tennessee Technological University, TN
Texas Wesleyan University, TX
The University of Alabama at Birmingham, AL
University of Delaware, DE
University of Massachusetts Lowell, MA
University of Memphis, TN
University of Nevada, Las Vegas, NV
University of New Orleans, LA
The University of Texas at Dallas, TX
The University of Toledo, OH
University of Utah, UT
University of Wisconsin–Green Bay, WI
Washington State University, WA
Western Washington University, WA

Children of Union Members/Company Employees
Adrian College, MI
Auburn University, AL
Averett University, VA

California State University, Bakersfield, CA
Calvin College, MI
Carroll College, MT
Chowan University, NC
The College of New Rochelle, NY
The College of Saint Rose, NY
Eastern Connecticut State University, CT
Eastern Washington University, WA
Edinboro University of Pennsylvania, PA
Emmanuel College, MA
Emporia State University, KS
Framingham State University, MA
Francis Marion University, SC
Frostburg State University, MD
Grand Valley State University, MI
Hofstra University, NY
Husson University, ME
Illinois State University, IL
Kennesaw State University, GA
Kent State University, OH
Kutztown University of Pennsylvania, PA
Marian University, WI
Massachusetts College of Art and Design, MA
Michigan State University, MI
Midwestern State University, TX
Millersville University of Pennsylvania, PA
Millikin University, IL
Missouri Western State University, MO
Montana State University Billings, MT
New Jersey Institute of Technology, NJ
New Mexico State University, NM
Northern Michigan University, MI
The Ohio State University, OH
The Richard Stockton College of New Jersey, NJ
Sacred Heart University, CT
St. Cloud State University, MN
Shorter University, GA
Siena College, NY
Slippery Rock University of Pennsylvania, PA
Sonoma State University, CA
Stephen F. Austin State University, TX
Stephens College, MO
Stonehill College, MA
Texas Christian University, TX
Texas Wesleyan University, TX
Thomas More College, KY
The University of Alabama, AL
The University of Alabama at Birmingham, AL
University of Connecticut, CT
University of Hartford, CT
University of Louisville, KY
University of Massachusetts Boston, MA
University of Massachusetts Dartmouth, MA
University of Massachusetts Lowell, MA
University of Michigan–Flint, MI
University of Nevada, Las Vegas, NV
University of Northern Colorado, CO
University of Pittsburgh at Bradford, PA
University of South Carolina, SC
The University of Tennessee at Chattanooga, TN
The University of Tennessee at Martin, TN
The University of Toledo, OH
University of Wisconsin–La Crosse, WI
University of Wisconsin–Parkside, WI
Western Kentucky University, KY
Western New England University, MA
Western Washington University, WA
West Texas A&M University, TX
West Virginia University, WV
York College of Pennsylvania, PA

Youngstown State University, OH

Children of Workers in Trades
Calvin College, MI
The College of New Rochelle, NY
Grand Valley State University, MI
Huntingdon College, AL
Kennesaw State University, GA
Marywood University, PA
Midwestern State University, TX
New Mexico State University, NM
The Ohio State University, OH
San Diego State University, CA
Siena College, NY
Sonoma State University, CA
South Dakota State University, SD
Texas Christian University, TX
The University of Alabama at Birmingham, AL
University of Michigan, MI
University of South Carolina, SC
University of Wisconsin–Parkside, WI
Western Oregon University, OR
West Texas A&M University, TX
West Virginia University, WV
Worcester Polytechnic Institute, MA
Youngstown State University, OH

Children with a Deceased or Disabled Parent
The Baptist College of Florida, FL
Bay Path College, MA
California State University, San Bernardino, CA
Calvin College, MI
The Citadel, The Military College of South Carolina, SC
The College of New Jersey, NJ
College of Staten Island of the City University of New York, NY
Edinboro University of Pennsylvania, PA
Elmhurst College, IL
Harding University, AR
Illinois State University, IL
Kentucky State University, KY
Lees-McRae College, NC
Lipscomb University, TN
Louisiana State University and Agricultural and Mechanical College, LA
Marian University, WI
McNeese State University, LA
Midwestern State University, TX
Millikin University, IL
New Mexico Highlands University, NM
New Mexico State University, NM
Northeastern State University, OK
Northern Kentucky University, KY
Pace University, NY
Santa Clara University, CA
Siena College, NY
Southern Illinois University Carbondale, IL
Texas Wesleyan University, TX
The University of Alabama at Birmingham, AL
University of Hartford, CT
University of Louisville, KY
University of Massachusetts Dartmouth, MA
The University of Montana, MT
University of Nevada, Las Vegas, NV
University of New Orleans, LA
University of South Carolina, SC
The University of Tennessee at Chattanooga, TN
The University of Texas at Arlington, TX
University of Utah, UT
The University of Virginia's College at Wise, VA

Washington State University, WA
Youngstown State University, OH

Ethnic Background
Abilene Christian University, TX
Alaska Pacific University, AK
Albright College, PA
American University, DC
Arkansas State University, AR
Armstrong Atlantic State University, GA
Asbury University, KY
Ashland University, OH
Auburn University, AL
Augustana College, IL
Augustana College, SD
Austin Peay State University, TN
Ball State University, IN
Bellarmine University, KY
Benedictine College, KS
Berry College, GA
Bethel College, KS
Bethel University, MN
Binghamton University, State University of New York, NY
Biola University, CA
Bluefield College, VA
Boise State University, ID
Buena Vista University, IA
California Institute of Integral Studies, CA
California State University, Bakersfield, CA
California State University, Chico, CA
Calvin College, MI
Capital University, OH
Cedarville University, OH
Centenary College of Louisiana, LA
Central Michigan University, MI
Centre College, KY
Clearwater Christian College, FL
Clemson University, SC
Coe College, IA
The College at Brockport, State University of New York, NY
The College of Saint Rose, NY
The College of St. Scholastica, MN
College of Staten Island of the City University of New York, NY
Columbia International University, SC
Concordia University Ann Arbor, MI
Cornell College, IA
DigiPen Institute of Technology, WA
Drury University, MO
Duke University, NC
Duquesne University, PA
Earlham College, IN
East Carolina University, NC
Eastern Michigan University, MI
Eastern New Mexico University, NM
Eastern Washington University, WA
Elizabeth City State University, NC
Elmhurst College, IL
Elon University, NC
Emmanuel College, MA
Fairfield University, CT
Fairmont State University, WV
Ferris State University, MI
Flagler College, FL
Florida Agricultural and Mechanical University, FL
Florida Gulf Coast University, FL
Fort Lewis College, CO
Franklin College, IN
Furman University, SC
Gannon University, PA
George Fox University, OR
Grove City College, PA

Gustavus Adolphus College, MN
Hamline University, MN
Hampden-Sydney College, VA
Hardin-Simmons University, TX
Hawai`i Pacific University, HI
Hope College, MI
Howard University, DC
Huntington University, IN
Idaho State University, ID
Illinois Institute of Technology, IL
Indiana University of Pennsylvania, PA
Iowa State University of Science and
  Technology, IA
Johnson C. Smith University, NC
Juniata College, PA
Kennesaw State University, GA
Kent State University, OH
Kentucky State University, KY
Kenyon College, OH
LaGrange College, GA
Lawrence University, WI
Lebanon Valley College, PA
Lesley University, MA
Lewis-Clark State College, ID
Lock Haven University of Pennsylvania, PA
Long Island University–Brooklyn Campus,
  NY
Lourdes University, OH
Loyola Marymount University, CA
Lyon College, AR
Macalester College, MN
Manchester University, IN
Marietta College, OH
Maryville University of Saint Louis, MO
Marywood University, PA
McMurry University, TX
McNeese State University, LA
Medical University of South Carolina, SC
Meredith College, NC
Methodist University, NC
Millsaps College, MS
Minot State University, ND
Mississippi University for Women, MS
Missouri Southern State University, MO
Molloy College, NY
Montana State University Billings, MT
Moravian College, PA
Morehead State University, KY
New England College, NH
New Jersey Institute of Technology, NJ
New Mexico State University, NM
Northern Illinois University, IL
Northern State University, SD
Northland College, WI
Northwestern College, MN
Northwest Nazarene University, ID
Oakland University, MI
The Ohio State University, OH
Ohio Valley University, WV
Oklahoma State University, OK
Ouachita Baptist University, AR
Pacific University, OR
Portland State University, OR
Randolph-Macon College, VA
Rensselaer Polytechnic Institute, NY
The Richard Stockton College of New
  Jersey, NJ
Ripon College, WI
Russell Sage College, NY
Sacred Heart University, CT
St. Catherine University, MN
St. John Fisher College, NY
Saint Martin's University, WA
Saint Mary-of-the-Woods College, IN
Sewanee: The University of the South, TN
Shawnee State University, OH

Shepherd University, WV
Siena College, NY
Simpson College, IA
Slippery Rock University of Pennsylvania,
  PA
Sonoma State University, CA
South Dakota School of Mines and
  Technology, SD
South Dakota State University, SD
Southwestern University, TX
State University of New York at Fredonia,
  NY
State University of New York at New Paltz,
  NY
State University of New York College at
  Geneseo, NY
State University of New York College at
  Potsdam, NY
Stetson University, FL
Stony Brook University, State University of
  New York, NY
Taylor University, IN
Tennessee Technological University, TN
Texas Christian University, TX
Texas Wesleyan University, TX
Thomas University, GA
Towson University, MD
Trinity Christian College, IL
Truman State University, MO
Union College, KY
Union University, TN
The University of Alabama at Birmingham,
  AL
The University of Arizona, AZ
University of Arkansas, AR
University of California, San Diego, CA
University of Dallas, TX
University of Delaware, DE
University of Great Falls, MT
University of Hartford, CT
University of Idaho, ID
University of Illinois at Springfield, IL
The University of Iowa, IA
The University of Kansas, KS
University of Louisville, KY
University of Maine at Augusta, ME
University of Maine at Presque Isle, ME
University of Mary Hardin-Baylor, TX
University of Massachusetts Dartmouth, MA
University of Michigan–Dearborn, MI
University of Minnesota, Crookston, MN
University of Minnesota, Morris, MN
University of Mississippi, MS
University of Missouri–Kansas City, MO
University of Missouri–St. Louis, MO
University of Mount Union, OH
University of Nebraska at Kearney, NE
University of Nebraska at Omaha, NE
University of Nebraska–Lincoln, NE
University of Nevada, Las Vegas, NV
University of Nevada, Reno, NV
University of New England, ME
University of North Carolina at Asheville,
  NC
The University of North Carolina at
  Greensboro, NC
University of Northern Colorado, CO
University of St. Francis, IL
University of South Carolina, SC
University of Southern Mississippi, MS
The University of Tennessee at Chattanooga,
  TN
The University of Tennessee at Martin, TN
The University of Texas at El Paso, TX
The University of Texas at San Antonio, TX
The University of Texas–Pan American, TX

University of the Ozarks, AR
The University of Toledo, OH
University of Utah, UT
University of Vermont, VT
The University of Virginia's College at Wise,
  VA
University of Wisconsin–Eau Claire, WI
University of Wisconsin–Green Bay, WI
University of Wisconsin–La Crosse, WI
University of Wisconsin–Parkside, WI
University of Wisconsin–Stevens Point, WI
University of Wisconsin–Whitewater, WI
University of Wyoming, WY
Valley City State University, ND
Washburn University, KS
Washington & Jefferson College, PA
Wayland Baptist University, TX
Wayne State College, NE
Webster University, MO
Wesleyan College, GA
Western Carolina University, NC
Western Kentucky University, KY
Western Oregon University, OR
Western Washington University, WA
Westminster College, MO
Westmont College, CA
West Virginia State University, WV
West Virginia University, WV
Wheaton College, IL
Whitman College, WA
Whitworth University, WA
Widener University, PA
William Jessup University, CA
Wisconsin Lutheran College, WI
Wittenberg University, OH
Wright State University, OH
Youngstown State University, OH

First-Generation College Students
Abilene Christian University, TX
Adrian College, MI
American International College, MA
American University, DC
Angelo State University, TX
Appalachian State University, NC
Arkansas State University, AR
Averett University, VA
Berry College, GA
Binghamton University, State University of
  New York, NY
Bluefield College, VA
Boise State University, ID
Bowie State University, MD
Brenau University, GA
Briar Cliff University, IA
Cabarrus College of Health Sciences, NC
California State University, Bakersfield, CA
California State University, Chico, CA
California State University, San Bernardino,
  CA
California State University, Stanislaus, CA
Calvin College, MI
Centenary College of Louisiana, LA
Centre College, KY
Champlain College, VT
Chowan University, NC
The College at Brockport, State University
  of New York, NY
The College of Idaho, ID
College of Saint Mary, NE
College of Staten Island of the City
  University of New York, NY
Colorado Mesa University, CO
Colorado State University, CO
Columbia College, MO
Concordia University, CA

Creighton University, NE
Eastern New Mexico University, NM
Eastern Washington University, WA
Edinboro University of Pennsylvania, PA
Elon University, NC
Emmanuel College, GA
The Evergreen State College, WA
Fairfield University, CT
Fairmont State University, WV
Finlandia University, MI
Flagler College, FL
Florida Agricultural and Mechanical University, FL
Florida International University, FL
Fort Lewis College, CO
Georgia Southern University, GA
Glenville State College, WV
Graceland University, IA
Guilford College, NC
Gustavus Adolphus College, MN
Howard University, DC
Idaho State University, ID
Illinois State University, IL
Iowa State University of Science and Technology, IA
Kent State University, OH
Kenyon College, OH
Kutztown University of Pennsylvania, PA
LaGrange College, GA
Lewis-Clark State College, ID
Long Island University–Brooklyn Campus, NY
Loyola Marymount University, CA
Lyon College, AR
McNeese State University, LA
Meredith College, NC
Metropolitan State University of Denver, CO
Michigan State University, MI
Middle Tennessee State University, TN
Midwestern State University, TX
Millsaps College, MS
Minnesota State University Moorhead, MN
Mississippi State University, MS
Missouri Baptist University, MO
Monmouth University, NJ
Montana State University Billings, MT
Montreat College, NC
Moravian College, PA
New Jersey Institute of Technology, NJ
New Mexico Highlands University, NM
Ohio University, OH
Ohio University–Chillicothe, OH
Ohio University–Lancaster, OH
Ohio University–Southern Campus, OH
Ohio University–Zanesville, OH
Oklahoma State University, OK
Ouachita Baptist University, AR
Pacific Lutheran University, WA
Pacific University, OR
Quincy University, IL
The Richard Stockton College of New Jersey, NJ
Ripon College, WI
Rochester College, MI
Russell Sage College, NY
Sage College of Albany, NY
St. John Fisher College, NY
Saint Joseph's University, PA
Saint Louis University, MO
Saint Mary-of-the-Woods College, IN
Saint Mary's University of Minnesota, MN
Salisbury University, MD
San Diego State University, CA
Shawnee State University, OH
Sonoma State University, CA

South Dakota State University, SD
Southeast Missouri State University, MO
State University of New York at New Paltz, NY
Stephen F. Austin State University, TX
Tennessee Technological University, TN
Texas A&M University, TX
Texas A&M University–Corpus Christi, TX
Texas Lutheran University, TX
Texas State University–San Marcos, TX
Texas Tech University, TX
Texas Wesleyan University, TX
Towson University, MD
Trinity Christian College, IL
Trinity University, TX
Truman State University, MO
The University of Alabama at Birmingham, AL
University of California, San Diego, CA
University of California, Santa Cruz, CA
University of Central Florida, FL
University of Colorado Boulder, CO
University of Delaware, DE
University of Great Falls, MT
University of Hartford, CT
University of Idaho, ID
University of Illinois at Urbana–Champaign, IL
The University of Iowa, IA
The University of Kansas, KS
University of Maryland Eastern Shore, MD
University of Massachusetts Boston, MA
University of Massachusetts Dartmouth, MA
University of Michigan–Flint, MI
University of Minnesota, Crookston, MN
University of Mississippi, MS
The University of Montana Western, MT
University of Nebraska at Kearney, NE
University of Nebraska at Omaha, NE
University of Nevada, Las Vegas, NV
University of Nevada, Reno, NV
University of North Alabama, AL
University of North Carolina at Asheville, NC
University of North Florida, FL
University of St. Francis, IL
University of South Carolina, SC
University of South Carolina Aiken, SC
University of South Carolina Upstate, SC
University of Southern Maine, ME
The University of Texas at Arlington, TX
The University of Texas at Brownsville, TX
The University of Texas at San Antonio, TX
The University of Toledo, OH
University of Utah, UT
University of Vermont, VT
The University of West Alabama, AL
University of Wisconsin–Eau Claire, WI
University of Wisconsin–La Crosse, WI
University of Wisconsin–Stout, WI
University of Wyoming, WY
Virginia Intermont College, VA
Virginia Polytechnic Institute and State University, VA
Washington State University, WA
Webber International University, FL
Wesleyan College, GA
West Texas A&M University, TX
West Virginia University Institute of Technology, WV
Whitman College, WA
Wichita State University, KS
Wisconsin Lutheran College, WI
Wright State University, OH

Handicapped Students
Appalachian State University, NC
Arkansas State University, AR
Binghamton University, State University of New York, NY
Boise State University, ID
California State University, Chico, CA
California State University, Fresno, CA
California State University, San Bernardino, CA
Calvin College, MI
Central College, IA
Chowan University, NC
Clear Creek Baptist Bible College, KY
The College of St. Scholastica, MN
College of Staten Island of the City University of New York, NY
Dordt College, IA
East Carolina University, NC
Eastern Washington University, WA
Edinboro University of Pennsylvania, PA
Elizabeth City State University, NC
Emmanuel College, MA
Emporia State University, KS
Fairmont State University, WV
Florida Gulf Coast University, FL
Fort Lewis College, CO
Fort Valley State University, GA
Francis Marion University, SC
Gardner-Webb University, NC
Georgia Southern University, GA
Grand Valley State University, MI
Grove City College, PA
Hamline University, MN
Hardin-Simmons University, TX
Hofstra University, NY
Howard University, DC
Idaho State University, ID
James Madison University, VA
Kennesaw State University, GA
Kent State University, OH
Kutztown University of Pennsylvania, PA
Louisiana Tech University, LA
Loyola Marymount University, CA
McNeese State University, LA
Michigan State University, MI
Mid-Atlantic Christian University, NC
Midwestern State University, TX
Mississippi State University, MS
Missouri Western State University, MO
New Jersey Institute of Technology, NJ
New Mexico State University, NM
Northern Kentucky University, KY
Northern State University, SD
The Ohio State University, OH
Oklahoma State University, OK
Old Dominion University, VA
Ouachita Baptist University, AR
Portland State University, OR
Sacred Heart University, CT
Sam Houston State University, TX
San Diego State University, CA
Santa Clara University, CA
Shawnee State University, OH
Shepherd University, WV
Shippensburg University of Pennsylvania, PA
Sonoma State University, CA
South Dakota State University, SD
Southern Illinois University Carbondale, IL
State University of New York College at Potsdam, NY
Texas Christian University, TX
Texas State University–San Marcos, TX
Texas Tech University, TX

Texas Wesleyan University, TX
Towson University, MD
The University of Akron, OH
The University of Alabama at Birmingham, AL
University of California, San Diego, CA
University of Hartford, CT
University of Idaho, ID
The University of Iowa, IA
University of Mary Hardin-Baylor, TX
University of Massachusetts Amherst, MA
University of Memphis, TN
University of Michigan, MI
University of Michigan–Dearborn, MI
University of Michigan–Flint, MI
University of Mississippi, MS
University of Nebraska at Omaha, NE
University of Nebraska–Lincoln, NE
University of Nevada, Las Vegas, NV
University of New Hampshire, NH
University of North Carolina at Asheville, NC
The University of North Carolina at Greensboro, NC
University of Northern Colorado, CO
University of South Carolina, SC
University of South Carolina Aiken, SC
The University of Tennessee at Chattanooga, TN
The University of Tennessee at Martin, TN
The University of Texas at Arlington, TX
The University of Texas at Dallas, TX
The University of Texas at San Antonio, TX
The University of Toledo, OH
University of Utah, UT
University of West Florida, FL
University of West Georgia, GA
University of Wisconsin–Green Bay, WI
University of Wisconsin–Stout, WI
University of Wisconsin–Whitewater, WI
University of Wyoming, WY
Washington State University, WA
Wesleyan College, GA
Western Carolina University, NC
Western Kentucky University, KY
Western Oregon University, OR
West Texas A&M University, TX
Wheaton College, IL
Wright State University, OH
Youngstown State University, OH

International Students
Adrian College, MI
Alaska Pacific University, AK
Alfred University, NY
Allegheny College, PA
Alliant International University, CA
Alverno College, WI
Anderson University, IN
Anderson University, SC
Andrews University, MI
Arizona State University, AZ
Armstrong Atlantic State University, GA
Asbury University, KY
Ashland University, OH
Augustana College, IL
Augustana College, SD
Averett University, VA
Ball State University, IN
Barton College, NC
Bay Path College, MA
Belhaven University, MS
Bellarmine University, KY
Bemidji State University, MN
Benedictine College, KS
Benedictine University, IL

Bentley University, MA
Berry College, GA
Bethel College, IN
Bethel College, KS
Bethel University, MN
Binghamton University, State University of New York, NY
Biola University, CA
Bloomfield College, NJ
Bloomsburg University of Pennsylvania, PA
Bluffton University, OH
Boise State University, ID
Bowling Green State University, OH
Brenau University, GA
Brevard College, NC
Briar Cliff University, IA
Bridgewater College, VA
Bryant University, RI
Buena Vista University, IA
California Baptist University, CA
California Institute of Integral Studies, CA
California Lutheran University, CA
California State University, Chico, CA
Calvin College, MI
Cameron University, OK
Campbellsville University, KY
Canisius College, NY
Capital University, OH
Carroll College, MT
Carroll University, WI
Centenary College of Louisiana, LA
Central College, IA
Central Methodist University, MO
Central Michigan University, MI
Champlain College, VT
Chowan University, NC
Cincinnati Christian University, OH
Clarkson University, NY
Clear Creek Baptist Bible College, KY
Coastal Carolina University, SC
Coe College, IA
Coker College, SC
The College at Brockport, State University of New York, NY
The College of Idaho, ID
College of Saint Benedict, MN
College of Saint Mary, NE
The College of St. Scholastica, MN
College of Staten Island of the City University of New York, NY
The Colorado College, CO
Colorado Mesa University, CO
Colorado State University, CO
Columbia International University, SC
Concordia College, MN
Concordia University, Nebraska, NE
Corban University, OR
Cornell College, IA
Covenant College, GA
Crown College, MN
Culver-Stockton College, MO
Defiance College, OH
Dominican University of California, CA
Dordt College, IA
Drake University, IA
Drury University, MO
Duquesne University, PA
Eastern Connecticut State University, CT
Eastern Michigan University, MI
Eastern Nazarene College, MA
Eastern New Mexico University, NM
East Texas Baptist University, TX
Eckerd College, FL
Edinboro University of Pennsylvania, PA
Elizabeth City State University, NC
Elizabethtown College, PA

Elmira College, NY
Elon University, NC
Emmanuel College, GA
Emmanuel College, MA
Emporia State University, KS
Endicott College, MA
Fairmont State University, WV
Ferris State University, MI
Ferrum College, VA
Finlandia University, MI
Florida Gulf Coast University, FL
Florida Institute of Technology, FL
Fort Hays State University, KS
Fort Lewis College, CO
Fort Valley State University, GA
Francis Marion University, SC
Franklin Pierce University, NH
Frostburg State University, MD
Furman University, SC
Gannon University, PA
George Fox University, OR
Gonzaga University, WA
Goshen College, IN
Graceland University, IA
Grand Valley State University, MI
Green Mountain College, VT
Greenville College, IL
Gustavus Adolphus College, MN
Hamline University, MN
Hampden-Sydney College, VA
Hampton University, VA
Hanover College, IN
Harding University, AR
Hartwick College, NY
Harvey Mudd College, CA
Hastings College, NE
Hawai`i Pacific University, HI
Heidelberg University, OH
Henderson State University, AR
Hendrix College, AR
Heritage Christian University, AL
Hillsdale College, MI
Hollins University, VA
Hood College, MD
Hope International University, CA
Houghton College, NY
Howard University, DC
Huntingdon College, AL
Huntington University, IN
Idaho State University, ID
Illinois College, IL
Illinois Institute of Technology, IL
Illinois Wesleyan University, IL
Indiana University of Pennsylvania, PA
Iowa State University of Science and Technology, IA
Iowa Wesleyan College, IA
Jacksonville University, FL
James Madison University, VA
Johnson State College, VT
Juniata College, PA
Kennesaw State University, GA
Kent State University, OH
Keuka College, NY
Keystone College, PA
King's College, PA
Kuyper College, MI
Lancaster Bible College, PA
Lawrence University, WI
Lebanon Valley College, PA
Lees-McRae College, NC
Liberty University, VA
Life University, GA
Lincoln University, MO
Lipscomb University, TN

Long Island University–Brooklyn Campus, NY
Long Island University–C. W. Post Campus, NY
Louisiana Tech University, LA
Loyola Marymount University, CA
Malone University, OH
Manchester University, IN
Mannes College The New School for Music, NY
Marymount University, VA
Maryville University of Saint Louis, MO
Marywood University, PA
The Master's College and Seminary, CA
Mayville State University, ND
McKendree University, IL
McMurry University, TX
McNeese State University, LA
Mercer University, GA
Meredith College, NC
Merrimack College, MA
Michigan State University, MI
Mid-Atlantic Christian University, NC
Middle Tennessee State University, TN
Midwestern State University, TX
Millersville University of Pennsylvania, PA
Millikin University, IL
Minot State University, ND
Mississippi University for Women, MS
Missouri Western State University, MO
Monmouth College, IL
Monmouth University, NJ
Montana State University–Northern, MT
Montclair State University, NJ
Montreat College, NC
Moravian College, PA
Morehead State University, KY
Morningside College, IA
Mount Marty College, SD
Mount Mary College, WI
Mount Vernon Nazarene University, OH
Nebraska Wesleyan University, NE
Newberry College, SC
New England College, NH
New Hope Christian College, OR
New Jersey Institute of Technology, NJ
New Mexico Highlands University, NM
New Mexico State University, NM
North Central College, IL
Northern Illinois University, IL
Northern Michigan University, MI
Northern State University, SD
Northland International University, WI
Northwestern College, MN
Northwestern State University of Louisiana, LA
Northwest Nazarene University, ID
Northwest University, WA
Notre Dame of Maryland University, MD
Nyack College, NY
Ohio Valley University, WV
Ohio Wesleyan University, OH
Oklahoma Christian University, OK
Oklahoma State University, OK
Oklahoma Wesleyan University, OK
Old Dominion University, VA
Olivet College, MI
Oral Roberts University, OK
Ouachita Baptist University, AR
Pace University, NY
Pacific Lutheran University, WA
Pacific University, OR
Palm Beach Atlantic University, FL
Peirce College, PA
Piedmont College, GA

Plymouth State University, NH
Point Park University, PA
Portland State University, OR
Quinnipiac University, CT
Ramapo College of New Jersey, NJ
Randolph College, VA
The Richard Stockton College of New Jersey, NJ
Ripon College, WI
Roberts Wesleyan College, NY
Rockford College, IL
St. Ambrose University, IA
St. Catherine University, MN
Saint Francis University, PA
Saint John's University, MN
Saint Joseph's University, PA
Saint Louis University, MO
Saint Martin's University, WA
Saint Mary-of-the-Woods College, IN
Saint Mary's University of Minnesota, MN
St. Norbert College, WI
St. Olaf College, MN
San Diego Christian College, CA
Schreiner University, TX
Seattle Pacific University, WA
Simpson College, IA
Sonoma State University, CA
South Dakota School of Mines and Technology, SD
South Dakota State University, SD
Southeast Missouri State University, MO
Southern Adventist University, TN
Southern Illinois University Carbondale, IL
Southwestern College, KS
Spring Arbor University, MI
State University of New York at Fredonia, NY
State University of New York at Plattsburgh, NY
State University of New York College at Oneonta, NY
State University of New York College of Environmental Science and Forestry, NY
Stetson University, FL
Sweet Briar College, VA
Taylor University, IN
Tennessee Wesleyan College, TN
Texas A&M University, TX
Texas A&M University–Corpus Christi, TX
Texas Christian University, TX
Texas Wesleyan University, TX
Texas Woman's University, TX
Thomas More College, KY
Towson University, MD
Truman State University, MO
Union University, TN
The University of Akron, OH
The University of Alabama, AL
The University of Arizona, AZ
University of Arkansas, AR
University of Bridgeport, CT
University of California, Irvine, CA
University of California, Santa Cruz, CA
University of Charleston, WV
University of Evansville, IN
University of Great Falls, MT
University of Hartford, CT
University of Idaho, ID
University of Illinois at Urbana–Champaign, IL
University of Indianapolis, IN
The University of Kansas, KS
University of Maine at Augusta, ME
University of Maine at Fort Kent, ME
University of Maine at Presque Isle, ME

University of Mary Hardin-Baylor, TX
University of Miami, FL
University of Michigan, MI
University of Michigan–Dearborn, MI
University of Michigan–Flint, MI
University of Minnesota, Morris, MN
University of Mississippi, MS
University of Missouri–St. Louis, MO
The University of Montana, MT
The University of Montana Western, MT
University of Montevallo, AL
University of Mount Union, OH
University of Nebraska at Kearney, NE
University of Nebraska at Omaha, NE
University of Nebraska–Lincoln, NE
University of Nevada, Las Vegas, NV
University of New Hampshire, NH
University of New Orleans, LA
University of North Carolina at Asheville, NC
The University of North Carolina at Chapel Hill, NC
The University of North Carolina at Greensboro, NC
University of Northern Colorado, CO
University of North Florida, FL
University of Oregon, OR
University of Puget Sound, WA
University of Redlands, CA
University of Rochester, NY
University of Science and Arts of Oklahoma, OK
University of South Carolina, SC
University of South Carolina Aiken, SC
The University of Tampa, FL
The University of Texas at Brownsville, TX
The University of Texas at Dallas, TX
The University of Texas at El Paso, TX
The University of Texas–Pan American, TX
University of the Ozarks, AR
The University of Toledo, OH
University of West Florida, FL
University of West Georgia, GA
University of Wisconsin–Eau Claire, WI
University of Wisconsin–La Crosse, WI
University of Wisconsin–Parkside, WI
University of Wisconsin–Stevens Point, WI
University of Wisconsin–Stout, WI
University of Wisconsin–Superior, WI
University of Wisconsin–Whitewater, WI
University of Wyoming, WY
Ursinus College, PA
Utah State University, UT
Valley City State University, ND
Valparaiso University, IN
Warner Pacific College, OR
Wartburg College, IA
Washburn University, KS
Washington & Jefferson College, PA
Washington State University, WA
Wayland Baptist University, TX
Webber International University, FL
Webster University, MO
Wells College, NY
Wesleyan College, GA
Wesleyan University, CT
Western Illinois University, IL
Western Kentucky University, KY
Western New England University, MA
Western Oregon University, OR
Western Washington University, WA
Westminster College, MO
Westminster College, PA
Westmont College, CA
West Virginia University, WV

West Virginia Wesleyan College, WV
Whitman College, WA
Whittier College, CA
Whitworth University, WA
Wichita State University, KS
Widener University, PA
William Jessup University, CA
Williams Baptist College, AR
Wilson College, PA
Wisconsin Lutheran College, WI
Wittenberg University, OH
Wright State University, OH
Xavier University, OH
York College of Pennsylvania, PA
Youngstown State University, OH

Local/State Students

Abilene Christian University, TX
Alaska Bible College, AK
Alaska Pacific University, AK
Allen College, IA
Alliant International University, CA
American University, DC
Angelo State University, TX
Anna Maria College, MA
Arizona State University, AZ
Arkansas State University, AR
Auburn University, AL
Augustana College, SD
Averett University, VA
Ball State University, IN
Barton College, NC
Belhaven University, MS
Bellarmine University, KY
Benedictine College, KS
Berry College, GA
Bethel College, KS
Binghamton University, State University of
    New York, NY
Bluefield College, VA
Boise State University, ID
Boston University, MA
Brevard College, NC
Bridgewater State University, MA
Brigham Young University, UT
California Polytechnic State University, San
    Luis Obispo, CA
California State University, Bakersfield, CA
California State University, Chico, CA
California State University, Fresno, CA
California State University, Monterey Bay,
    CA
California State University, San Marcos, CA
California State University, Stanislaus, CA
Carnegie Mellon University, PA
Catawba College, NC
Centenary College of Louisiana, LA
Central College, IA
Central Michigan University, MI
Chowan University, NC
Christopher Newport University, VA
The Citadel, The Military College of South
    Carolina, SC
City College of the City University of New
    York, NY
Clarion University of Pennsylvania, PA
Clarke University, IA
Clarkson University, NY
Clemson University, SC
Coastal Carolina University, SC
The College at Brockport, State University
    of New York, NY
The College of Idaho, ID
College of Staten Island of the City
    University of New York, NY
Colorado Mesa University, CO

Colorado Mountain College, CO
Columbia College, MO
Columbia International University, SC
Columbus College of Art & Design, OH
Concordia University, Nebraska, NE
Cornell College, IA
Creighton University, NE
Culver-Stockton College, MO
Davidson College, NC
DePaul University, IL
Dordt College, IA
Duke University, NC
Eastern Connecticut State University, CT
Eastern Oregon University, OR
Eastern Washington University, WA
Eckerd College, FL
Edinboro University of Pennsylvania, PA
Elizabethtown College, PA
Elmira College, NY
Emmanuel College, GA
Emmanuel College, MA
Emory University, GA
Endicott College, MA
Eugene Lang College The New School for
    Liberal Arts, NY
The Evergreen State College, WA
Fairmont State University, WV
Faulkner University, AL
Fayetteville State University, NC
Ferris State University, MI
Ferrum College, VA
Flagler College, FL
Florida Agricultural and Mechanical
    University, FL
Florida Gulf Coast University, FL
Florida Southern College, FL
Florida State University, FL
Fort Lewis College, CO
Franklin Pierce University, NH
Frostburg State University, MD
Furman University, SC
Gardner-Webb University, NC
Georgetown College, KY
Georgia College & State University, GA
Georgia Institute of Technology, GA
Graceland University, IA
Grand Valley State University, MI
Greenville College, IL
Guilford College, NC
Hamline University, MN
Hawai`i Pacific University, HI
Hollins University, VA
Houghton College, NY
Howard Payne University, TX
Howard University, DC
Huntingdon College, AL
Huntington University, IN
Idaho State University, ID
Illinois Institute of Technology, IL
Indiana University–Purdue University Fort
    Wayne, IN
Iowa State University of Science and
    Technology, IA
James Madison University, VA
Jefferson College of Health Sciences, VA
John Carroll University, OH
The Johns Hopkins University, MD
Johnson State College, VT
Juniata College, PA
Kennesaw State University, GA
Kent State University, OH
Kentucky State University, KY
Kettering University, MI
Kutztown University of Pennsylvania, PA
Lake Forest College, IL
Lees-McRae College, NC

Lee University, TN
Lesley University, MA
LeTourneau University, TX
Liberty University, VA
LIM College, NY
Limestone College, SC
Lock Haven University of Pennsylvania, PA
Longwood University, VA
Lourdes University, OH
Loyola Marymount University, CA
Lyon College, AR
Manchester University, IN
Mannes College The New School for Music,
    NY
Marian University, WI
Marist College, NY
Marshall University, WV
Marymount Manhattan College, NY
Marywood University, PA
Mayville State University, ND
McDaniel College, MD
McMurry University, TX
McNeese State University, LA
Medical University of South Carolina, SC
Messiah College, PA
Methodist University, NC
Metropolitan State University of Denver, CO
Miami University, OH
Michigan State University, MI
Michigan Technological University, MI
Middle Tennessee State University, TN
Millsaps College, MS
Minot State University, ND
Mississippi State University, MS
Missouri Southern State University, MO
Missouri State University, MO
Missouri Western State University, MO
Monmouth University, NJ
Montana State University, MT
Montana State University Billings, MT
Montana Tech of The University of
    Montana, MT
Montreat College, NC
Morehead State University, KY
Morehouse College, GA
Morningside College, IA
Murray State University, KY
Newberry College, SC
New England College, NH
New Jersey Institute of Technology, NJ
New Mexico Highlands University, NM
New Mexico State University, NM
New York Institute of Technology, NY
Nicholls State University, LA
North Carolina State University, NC
Northeastern State University, OK
Northern Arizona University, AZ
Northern Kentucky University, KY
Northern State University, SD
Northland International University, WI
Nyack College, NY
Ohio Valley University, WV
Ohio Wesleyan University, OH
Oklahoma Baptist University, OK
Oklahoma State University, OK
Old Dominion University, VA
Oregon State University, OR
Ouachita Baptist University, AR
Pontifical College Josephinum, OH
Post University, CT
Quincy University, IL
Randolph College, VA
Regis University, CO
Rice University, TX
The Richard Stockton College of New
    Jersey, NJ

Ripon College, WI
Robert Morris University Illinois, IL
Rochester College, MI
Sacred Heart University, CT
Saginaw Valley State University, MI
Saint Augustine's College, NC
St. Bonaventure University, NY
St. Catherine University, MN
St. John Fisher College, NY
St. John's University, NY
St. Louis College of Pharmacy, MO
Saint Martin's University, WA
Saint Mary-of-the-Woods College, IN
Saint Michael's College, VT
Sam Houston State University, TX
San Diego State University, CA
San Jose State University, CA
Shawnee State University, OH
Shenandoah University, VA
Shepherd University, WV
Shippensburg University of Pennsylvania, PA
Shorter University, GA
Siena College, NY
Slippery Rock University of Pennsylvania, PA
Smith College, MA
Sonoma State University, CA
South Dakota School of Mines and Technology, SD
Southern Adventist University, TN
Southern Utah University, UT
Southwest Baptist University, MO
Southwestern Christian College, TX
State University of New York at Fredonia, NY
State University of New York at New Paltz, NY
State University of New York College at Cortland, NY
State University of New York College at Geneseo, NY
State University of New York College at Oneonta, NY
State University of New York College at Potsdam, NY
State University of New York College of Agriculture and Technology at Cobleskill, NY
State University of New York College of Environmental Science and Forestry, NY
State University of New York Institute of Technology, NY
Stephen F. Austin State University, TX
Stetson University, FL
Sweet Briar College, VA
Tennessee State University, TN
Tennessee Technological University, TN
Texas A&M University, TX
Texas Christian University, TX
Texas State University–San Marcos, TX
Texas Wesleyan University, TX
Trinity Christian College, IL
Tuskegee University, AL
Unity College, ME
The University of Akron, OH
The University of Alabama in Huntsville, AL
University of Alaska Fairbanks, AK
University of Arkansas, AR
University of Bridgeport, CT
University of Colorado Boulder, CO
University of Connecticut, CT
University of Delaware, DE
University of Georgia, GA

University of Great Falls, MT
University of Hartford, CT
University of Hawaii at Hilo, HI
University of Houston, TX
University of Idaho, ID
University of Illinois at Urbana–Champaign, IL
The University of Iowa, IA
The University of Kansas, KS
University of Louisville, KY
University of Maine, ME
University of Maine at Augusta, ME
University of Maine at Presque Isle, ME
University of Mary, ND
University of Mary Hardin-Baylor, TX
University of Mary Washington, VA
University of Massachusetts Dartmouth, MA
University of Michigan, MI
University of Michigan–Flint, MI
University of Minnesota, Crookston, MN
University of Minnesota, Twin Cities Campus, MN
University of Mississippi, MS
University of Missouri–Kansas City, MO
University of Missouri–St. Louis, MO
The University of Montana, MT
University of Nebraska at Kearney, NE
University of Nevada, Las Vegas, NV
University of New Hampshire, NH
University of New Orleans, LA
University of North Carolina at Asheville, NC
The University of North Carolina at Greensboro, NC
The University of North Carolina Wilmington, NC
University of Oregon, OR
University of Pittsburgh at Bradford, PA
University of Rio Grande, OH
University of South Carolina, SC
University of Southern Maine, ME
University of Southern Mississippi, MS
The University of Texas at Austin, TX
The University of Texas at Dallas, TX
The University of Texas at El Paso, TX
The University of Texas at San Antonio, TX
The University of Texas–Pan American, TX
University of the Cumberlands, KY
The University of Virginia's College at Wise, VA
University of West Georgia, GA
University of Wisconsin–Eau Claire, WI
University of Wisconsin–Green Bay, WI
University of Wisconsin–La Crosse, WI
University of Wisconsin–Parkside, WI
University of Wisconsin–River Falls, WI
University of Wisconsin–Stout, WI
University of Wisconsin–Whitewater, WI
University of Wyoming, WY
Valley Forge Christian College, PA
Vanderbilt University, TN
Virginia Military Institute, VA
Virginia Polytechnic Institute and State University, VA
Wake Forest University, NC
Warner Pacific College, OR
Warren Wilson College, NC
Washburn University, KS
Wayland Baptist University, TX
Wayne State College, NE
Webber International University, FL
Western Carolina University, NC
Western Kentucky University, KY
Western New England University, MA
Western Oregon University, OR

Western Washington University, WA
Westminster College, MO
West Texas A&M University, TX
West Virginia University, WV
Wilson College, PA
Winona State University, MN
Youngstown State University, OH

Married Students
Alaska Bible College, AK
Auburn University, AL
Baptist Bible College of Pennsylvania, PA
Binghamton University, State University of New York, NY
Blue Mountain College, MS
California State University, Chico, CA
Cincinnati Christian University, OH
The College at Brockport, State University of New York, NY
The College of Idaho, ID
Crossroads Bible College, IN
Eastern Washington University, WA
Emmanuel College, GA
Franklin Pierce University, NH
Georgia Southern University, GA
Heritage Christian University, AL
Howard University, DC
Lancaster Bible College, PA
Lock Haven University of Pennsylvania, PA
Mid-Atlantic Christian University, NC
Montana Tech of The University of Montana, MT
New Hope Christian College, OR
New Mexico State University, NM
Northwestern State University of Louisiana, LA
Northwest University, WA
Ouachita Baptist University, AR
Sonoma State University, CA
South Dakota School of Mines and Technology, SD
Texas Wesleyan University, TX
The University of Alabama at Birmingham, AL
The University of Kansas, KS
University of Nevada, Reno, NV
The University of North Carolina Wilmington, NC
Valley Forge Christian College, PA

Members of Minorities
Abilene Christian University, TX
Alabama State University, AL
Alaska Pacific University, AK
Allen College, IA
American University, DC
Anderson University, SC
Appalachian State University, NC
Arkansas State University, AR
Ashland University, OH
Assumption College, MA
Augustana College, IL
Augustana College, SD
Austin Peay State University, TN
Azusa Pacific University, CA
Baldwin Wallace University, OH
Ball State University, IN
Bellarmine University, KY
Beloit College, WI
Benedictine College, KS
Bentley University, MA
Berry College, GA
Bethel College, IN
Bethel University, MN
Binghamton University, State University of New York, NY

Bluefield College, VA
Bluffton University, OH
Boise State University, ID
Bowling Green State University, OH
Briar Cliff University, IA
Bridgewater College, VA
Bridgewater State University, MA
Brigham Young University, UT
Bryant University, RI
California State Polytechnic University, Pomona, CA
California State University, Chico, CA
Calvin College, MI
Cameron University, OK
Capital University, OH
Carnegie Mellon University, PA
Carson-Newman University, TN
Centenary College of Louisiana, LA
Central College, IA
Central Connecticut State University, CT
Champlain College, VT
Cincinnati Christian University, OH
Clarion University of Pennsylvania, PA
Clarkson University, NY
Clemson University, SC
Coe College, IA
The College at Brockport, State University of New York, NY
The College of Idaho, ID
The College of New Jersey, NJ
The College of Saint Rose, NY
The College of St. Scholastica, MN
College of Staten Island of the City University of New York, NY
The College of Wooster, OH
Colorado Mesa University, CO
Columbia International University, SC
Concordia University, Nebraska, NE
Cornell College, IA
Covenant College, GA
Creighton University, NE
Crown College, MN
Defiance College, OH
DigiPen Institute of Technology, WA
Dominican University of California, CA
Dordt College, IA
Drew University, NJ
Drury University, MO
Duquesne University, PA
Eastern Connecticut State University, CT
Eastern Kentucky University, KY
Eastern Michigan University, MI
Eastern New Mexico University, NM
Eastern Oregon University, OR
Edinboro University of Pennsylvania, PA
Elizabeth City State University, NC
Elizabethtown College, PA
Elmhurst College, IL
Elon University, NC
Embry-Riddle Aeronautical University–Daytona, FL
Emporia State University, KS
Eugene Lang College The New School for Liberal Arts, NY
Fairmont State University, WV
Ferris State University, MI
Flagler College, FL
Florida Gulf Coast University, FL
Franklin College, IN
Fresno Pacific University, CA
Gallaudet University, DC
Gannon University, PA
Gardner-Webb University, NC
George Fox University, OR
Georgia Institute of Technology, GA
Georgia Southern University, GA

Gonzaga University, WA
Goshen College, IN
Graceland University, IA
Grove City College, PA
Gustavus Adolphus College, MN
Hamline University, MN
Hampden-Sydney College, VA
Hampton University, VA
Hanover College, IN
Hilbert College, NY
Howard University, DC
Idaho State University, ID
Illinois Institute of Technology, IL
Illinois State University, IL
Indiana State University, IN
Iowa State University of Science and Technology, IA
Ithaca College, NY
James Madison University, VA
Johnson State College, VT
Kennesaw State University, GA
Kent State University, OH
Kettering University, MI
King College, TN
King's College, PA
Kuyper College, MI
Lawrence Technological University, MI
Lehigh University, PA
Le Moyne College, NY
Lesley University, MA
LeTourneau University, TX
Lewis-Clark State College, ID
Lipscomb University, TN
Lock Haven University of Pennsylvania, PA
Louisiana Tech University, LA
Lourdes University, OH
Loyola Marymount University, CA
Luther College, IA
Lyon College, AR
Manchester University, IN
Mannes College The New School for Music, NY
Marietta College, OH
Marshall University, WV
Maryville College, TN
Maryville University of Saint Louis, MO
Mayville State University, ND
McNeese State University, LA
Medical University of South Carolina, SC
Meredith College, NC
Methodist University, NC
Miami University, OH
Middle Tennessee State University, TN
Midwestern State University, TX
Minnesota State University Mankato, MN
Minnesota State University Moorhead, MN
Minot State University, ND
Misericordia University, PA
Mississippi University for Women, MS
Missouri Southern State University, MO
Missouri State University, MO
Missouri University of Science and Technology, MO
Molloy College, NY
Monmouth University, NJ
Montana State University, MT
Montana State University Billings, MT
Montana State University–Northern, MT
Morehead State University, KY
Mount Carmel College of Nursing, OH
Mount St. Mary's University, MD
Mount Vernon Nazarene University, OH
Murray State University, KY
New Jersey Institute of Technology, NJ
New Mexico State University, NM
Nicholls State University, LA

Northeastern State University, OK
Northern Arizona University, AZ
Northern Illinois University, IL
Northern Kentucky University, KY
Northern Michigan University, MI
Northern State University, SD
Northwest Missouri State University, MO
Northwest Nazarene University, ID
The Ohio State University, OH
Ohio University, OH
Ohio University–Chillicothe, OH
Ohio University–Eastern, OH
Ohio University–Lancaster, OH
Ohio University–Southern Campus, OH
Ohio University–Zanesville, OH
Ohio Wesleyan University, OH
Old Dominion University, VA
Oregon State University, OR
Ouachita Baptist University, AR
Pacific Union College, CA
Parsons The New School for Design, NY
Pine Manor College, MA
Point Park University, PA
Polytechnic Institute of New York University, NY
Portland State University, OR
Quincy University, IL
Rensselaer Polytechnic Institute, NY
Rhodes College, TN
Rice University, TX
The Richard Stockton College of New Jersey, NJ
Rider University, NJ
Ripon College, WI
Sacred Heart University, CT
Saginaw Valley State University, MI
St. Ambrose University, IA
St. Bonaventure University, NY
St. John Fisher College, NY
Saint Joseph's University, PA
Saint Louis University, MO
Saint Martin's University, WA
Saint Mary-of-the-Woods College, IN
Saint Mary's University of Minnesota, MN
Saint Michael's College, VT
Seattle University, WA
Sewanee: The University of the South, TN
Shawnee State University, OH
Shepherd University, WV
Simpson College, IA
Simpson University, CA
Slippery Rock University of Pennsylvania, PA
Sonoma State University, CA
South Dakota School of Mines and Technology, SD
South Dakota State University, SD
Southeast Missouri State University, MO
Southern Adventist University, TN
Southern Illinois University Carbondale, IL
Southern Polytechnic State University, GA
Southern Utah University, UT
Southwestern College, KS
Spring Arbor University, MI
State University of New York at Fredonia, NY
State University of New York at New Paltz, NY
State University of New York College at Cortland, NY
State University of New York College at Geneseo, NY
State University of New York College at Potsdam, NY

State University of New York College of Agriculture and Technology at Cobleskill, NY
State University of New York College of Environmental Science and Forestry, NY
State University of New York Institute of Technology, NY
Stetson University, FL
Tennessee State University, TN
Tennessee Technological University, TN
Tennessee Wesleyan College, TN
Texas Christian University, TX
Texas Wesleyan University, TX
Thomas More College, KY
Towson University, MD
Transylvania University, KY
Trine University, IN
Trinity Christian College, IL
Union University, TN
Unity College, ME
The University of Akron, OH
The University of Alabama at Birmingham, AL
The University of Alabama in Huntsville, AL
University of Arkansas, AR
University of California, San Diego, CA
University of Delaware, DE
University of Evansville, IN
University of Florida, FL
University of Hartford, CT
University of Idaho, ID
University of Illinois at Urbana–Champaign, IL
The University of Kansas, KS
University of Louisville, KY
University of Maine, ME
University of Maine at Farmington, ME
University of Maine at Fort Kent, ME
University of Mary Hardin-Baylor, TX
University of Massachusetts Dartmouth, MA
University of Memphis, TN
University of Michigan, MI
University of Michigan–Dearborn, MI
University of Michigan–Flint, MI
University of Minnesota, Crookston, MN
University of Minnesota, Morris, MN
University of Minnesota, Twin Cities Campus, MN
University of Mississippi, MS
University of Missouri–Kansas City, MO
University of Missouri–St. Louis, MO
The University of Montana Western, MT
University of Mount Union, OH
University of Nebraska at Kearney, NE
University of Nebraska at Omaha, NE
University of Nebraska–Lincoln, NE
University of Nevada, Las Vegas, NV
University of New England, ME
University of New Orleans, LA
University of North Carolina at Asheville, NC
University of Northern Iowa, IA
University of North Florida, FL
University of Oklahoma, OK
University of South Alabama, AL
University of South Carolina, SC
University of South Carolina Aiken, SC
The University of South Dakota, SD
University of Southern Indiana, IN
The University of Tennessee at Martin, TN
The University of Texas at Dallas, TX
The University of Texas at El Paso, TX
The University of Texas at San Antonio, TX
University of the Ozarks, AR

The University of Toledo, OH
University of West Georgia, GA
University of Wisconsin–Eau Claire, WI
University of Wisconsin–Green Bay, WI
University of Wisconsin–La Crosse, WI
University of Wisconsin–Parkside, WI
University of Wisconsin–River Falls, WI
University of Wisconsin–Stevens Point, WI
University of Wisconsin–Stout, WI
University of Wisconsin–Superior, WI
University of Wisconsin–Whitewater, WI
Valdosta State University, GA
Valley City State University, ND
Vanderbilt University, TN
Virginia Polytechnic Institute and State University, VA
Warner Pacific College, OR
Washington & Jefferson College, PA
Wayland Baptist University, TX
Wayne State College, NE
Webster University, MO
Western Carolina University, NC
Western Illinois University, IL
Western Kentucky University, KY
Western New England University, MA
Western Washington University, WA
West Virginia University, WV
Whitworth University, WA
Wichita State University, KS
Williams Baptist College, AR
Winona State University, MN
Wisconsin Lutheran College, WI
Wittenberg University, OH
Wright State University, OH
Xavier University, OH
York College of Pennsylvania, PA
Youngstown State University, OH

Out-of-State Students
Abilene Christian University, TX
Alaska Pacific University, AK
Allen College, IA
Anderson University, SC
Appalachian State University, NC
Arizona State University, AZ
Arkansas State University, AR
Arkansas Tech University, AR
Asbury University, KY
Ashland University, OH
Auburn University, AL
Aurora University, IL
Averett University, VA
Ball State University, IN
Bellarmine University, KY
Bemidji State University, MN
Benedictine College, KS
Benedictine University, IL
Berry College, GA
Bethel University, MN
Binghamton University, State University of New York, NY
Bloomfield College, NJ
Bluefield College, VA
Bluffton University, OH
Boise State University, ID
Buena Vista University, IA
Cabrini College, PA
California State University, Chico, CA
Calvin College, MI
Cameron University, OK
Capital University, OH
Carnegie Mellon University, PA
Centenary College of Louisiana, LA
Central College, IA
Central Michigan University, MI

Chowan University, NC
The Citadel, The Military College of South Carolina, SC
Cleveland State University, OH
Coastal Carolina University, SC
The College at Brockport, State University of New York, NY
The College of Idaho, ID
The College of New Rochelle, NY
College of Saint Benedict, MN
The College of Saint Rose, NY
Colorado Mesa University, CO
Concordia University Ann Arbor, MI
Concordia University Wisconsin, WI
Davidson College, NC
Defiance College, OH
Dordt College, IA
Eastern Michigan University, MI
Eastern New Mexico University, NM
Edinboro University of Pennsylvania, PA
Elmira College, NY
Emory & Henry College, VA
Evangel University, MO
Fairmont State University, WV
Faulkner University, AL
Flagler College, FL
Florida Agricultural and Mechanical University, FL
Florida Gulf Coast University, FL
Florida Southern College, FL
Fort Lewis College, CO
Fort Valley State University, GA
Francis Marion University, SC
Franklin College, IN
Frostburg State University, MD
Gardner-Webb University, NC
George Fox University, OR
Georgetown College, KY
Georgia College & State University, GA
Glenville State College, WV
Grand Valley State University, MI
Greenville College, IL
Gustavus Adolphus College, MN
Hampden-Sydney College, VA
Hanover College, IN
Hardin-Simmons University, TX
Hawai`i Pacific University, HI
Heidelberg University, OH
Henderson State University, AR
Hollins University, VA
Idaho State University, ID
Iowa State University of Science and Technology, IA
James Madison University, VA
Kent State University, OH
Kentucky Wesleyan College, KY
Lakeland College, WI
Lewis-Clark State College, ID
Limestone College, SC
Lincoln University, MO
Louisiana Tech University, LA
Lourdes University, OH
Loyola Marymount University, CA
Lynn University, FL
Marian University, WI
Maryville University of Saint Louis, MO
Mayville State University, ND
McMurry University, TX
McNeese State University, LA
Meredith College, NC
Miami University, OH
Michigan State University, MI
Minnesota State University Moorhead, MN
Minot State University, ND
Misericordia University, PA

Mississippi State University, MS
Mississippi University for Women, MS
Missouri University of Science and
    Technology, MO
Missouri Western State University, MO
Monmouth University, NJ
Montana State University Billings, MT
Montana State University–Northern, MT
Montana Tech of The University of
    Montana, MT
Morehead State University, KY
Morningside College, IA
Murray State University, KY
New College of Florida, FL
New Hope Christian College, OR
New Jersey Institute of Technology, NJ
New Mexico State University, NM
Nicholls State University, LA
Northeastern State University, OK
Northern Michigan University, MI
Northland International University, WI
Northwestern State University of Louisiana,
    LA
Northwest Missouri State University, MO
Northwest Nazarene University, ID
Nyack College, NY
Oakland University, MI
The Ohio State University, OH
Oklahoma Baptist University, OK
Oklahoma State University, OK
Ouachita Baptist University, AR
Pacific Lutheran University, WA
Palm Beach Atlantic University, FL
Piedmont College, GA
Portland State University, OR
Ramapo College of New Jersey, NJ
Randolph-Macon College, VA
Ripon College, WI
Robert Morris University Illinois, IL
Roberts Wesleyan College, NY
Rochester College, MI
Rockford College, IL
Rogers State University, OK
Sacred Heart University, CT
St. Ambrose University, IA
St. Bonaventure University, NY
St. Catherine University, MN
St. Cloud State University, MN
Saint Francis University, PA
Saint John's University, MN
Saint Martin's University, WA
Saint Mary-of-the-Woods College, IN
Saint Michael's College, VT
San Diego Christian College, CA
Shepherd University, WV
Siena College, NY
Simpson University, CA
Slippery Rock University of Pennsylvania,
    PA
Sonoma State University, CA
South Dakota School of Mines and
    Technology, SD
Southeastern Louisiana University, LA
Southeastern Oklahoma State University,
    OK
Southeast Missouri State University, MO
Southern Adventist University, TN
Southern Arkansas University–Magnolia,
    AR
State University of New York at Fredonia,
    NY
State University of New York at Plattsburgh,
    NY
State University of New York College of
    Environmental Science and Forestry, NY
Tennessee Technological University, TN

Texas Tech University, TX
Texas Wesleyan University, TX
Thomas More College, KY
Thomas University, GA
Towson University, MD
Transylvania University, KY
Trinity Christian College, IL
Truman State University, MO
The University of Akron, OH
The University of Alabama, AL
The University of Alabama at Birmingham,
    AL
University of Arkansas, AR
University of California, Irvine, CA
University of California, Santa Cruz, CA
University of Connecticut, CT
University of Florida, FL
University of Idaho, ID
University of Indianapolis, IN
The University of Iowa, IA
The University of Kansas, KS
University of Louisville, KY
University of Maine at Farmington, ME
University of Maine at Presque Isle, ME
University of Mary Hardin-Baylor, TX
University of Maryland, College Park, MD
University of Massachusetts Lowell, MA
University of Michigan, MI
University of Michigan–Dearborn, MI
University of Mississippi, MS
University of Missouri–Kansas City, MO
University of Missouri–St. Louis, MO
The University of Montana, MT
The University of Montana Western, MT
University of Montevallo, AL
University of Nebraska at Kearney, NE
University of Nebraska at Omaha, NE
University of Nebraska–Lincoln, NE
University of Nevada, Las Vegas, NV
University of New Orleans, LA
University of North Alabama, AL
The University of North Carolina at Chapel
    Hill, NC
The University of North Carolina at
    Greensboro, NC
University of Northern Colorado, CO
University of North Florida, FL
University of Pittsburgh at Bradford, PA
University of Rio Grande, OH
University of Science and Arts of Oklahoma,
    OK
University of South Carolina, SC
University of Southern Indiana, IN
University of Southern Maine, ME
University of Southern Mississippi, MS
The University of Tennessee at Martin, TN
The University of Texas at Dallas, TX
The University of Texas at El Paso, TX
The University of Texas at San Antonio, TX
The University of Texas–Pan American, TX
The University of Toledo, OH
University of Utah, UT
University of West Florida, FL
University of Wisconsin–La Crosse, WI
University of Wisconsin–Stevens Point, WI
University of Wisconsin–Stout, WI
University of Wisconsin–Whitewater, WI
University of Wyoming, WY
Virginia Military Institute, VA
Virginia Polytechnic Institute and State
    University, VA
Washington State University, WA
Wayne State College, NE
Webber International University, FL
Webster University, MO
Western Kentucky University, KY

Western New England University, MA
West Texas A&M University, TX
William Jessup University, CA
Winona State University, MN
Wisconsin Lutheran College, WI
Wright State University, OH
Youngstown State University, OH

Parents of Current Students
Aurora University, IL
Blue Mountain College, MS
Caldwell College, NJ
Cincinnati Christian University, OH
The College of New Rochelle, NY
Columbia College, MO
Emmanuel College, GA
Franklin Pierce University, NH
Green Mountain College, VT
Huntington University, IN
Malone University, OH
Maryville University of Saint Louis, MO
Millikin University, IL
Mississippi University for Women, MS
Missouri Baptist University, MO
Mount Aloysius College, PA
Mount Marty College, SD
Mount Mary College, WI
New England College, NH
Northwest University, WA
Pace University, NY
Rockford College, IL
St. Joseph's College, Long Island Campus,
    NY
St. Joseph's College, New York, NY
Saint Mary-of-the-Woods College, IN
State University of New York at Fredonia,
    NY
Stephens College, MO
Texas Wesleyan University, TX
The University of Alabama at Birmingham,
    AL
University of Great Falls, MT
University of Hartford, CT
Upper Iowa University, IA
Valley Forge Christian College, PA
Wesleyan College, GA

Previous College Experience
Abilene Christian University, TX
Alaska Pacific University, AK
American International College, MA
American University, DC
Anna Maria College, MA
Bellarmine University, KY
Bethel College, KS
Boise State University, ID
Brevard College, NC
Bridgewater College, VA
Calumet College of Saint Joseph, IN
Cedar Crest College, PA
Central College, IA
Coker College, SC
The College at Brockport, State University
    of New York, NY
The College of New Rochelle, NY
The College of St. Scholastica, MN
College of Staten Island of the City
    University of New York, NY
Columbia College, MO
Eastern Connecticut State University, CT
Eastern Michigan University, MI
Elmira College, NY
Fairmont State University, WV
Ferris State University, MI
Florida Institute of Technology, FL
Gardner-Webb University, NC
Hamline University, MN

Hawai'i Pacific University, HI
Hendrix College, AR
Hollins University, VA
Howard University, DC
Huntington University, IN
Idaho State University, ID
Illinois College, IL
Illinois Institute of Technology, IL
Illinois State University, IL
Indiana State University, IN
Kent State University, OH
Lake Forest College, IL
Lancaster Bible College, PA
Lees-McRae College, NC
Lewis-Clark State College, ID
Limestone College, SC
Lock Haven University of Pennsylvania, PA
Lourdes University, OH
Loyola Marymount University, CA
Manchester University, IN
Manhattanville College, NY
McDaniel College, MD
McMurry University, TX
McNeese State University, LA
Memphis College of Art, TN
Meredith College, NC
Misericordia University, PA
Mississippi State University, MS
Missouri Western State University, MO
Monmouth University, NJ
Mount Mercy University, IA
New Mexico State University, NM
New York Institute of Technology, NY
Nicholls State University, LA
Northwest Missouri State University, MO
The Ohio State University, OH
Oklahoma State University, OK
Old Dominion University, VA
Ouachita Baptist University, AR
Pace University, NY
Palm Beach Atlantic University, FL
Point Park University, PA
The Richard Stockton College of New Jersey, NJ
Ripon College, WI
Rochester College, MI
St. Ambrose University, IA
Saint Francis University, PA
Saint Louis University, MO
San Diego State University, CA
Shepherd University, WV
Siena College, NY
Slippery Rock University of Pennsylvania, PA
Sonoma State University, CA
Southeast Missouri State University, MO
State University of New York at Fredonia, NY
State University of New York College at Potsdam, NY
State University of New York Institute of Technology, NY
Stephen F. Austin State University, TX
Sterling College, VT
Texas Christian University, TX
Texas Wesleyan University, TX
Towson University, MD
Truman State University, MO
The University of Alabama at Birmingham, AL
University of Arkansas, AR
University of Bridgeport, CT
University of Hartford, CT
The University of Kansas, KS
University of Louisville, KY

University of Massachusetts Dartmouth, MA
University of Michigan–Dearborn, MI
University of Mississippi, MS
University of Missouri–St. Louis, MO
University of Nevada, Las Vegas, NV
University of Oklahoma, OK
University of St. Thomas, TX
University of Science and Arts of Oklahoma, OK
The University of Toledo, OH
University of Wisconsin–Eau Claire, WI
University of Wisconsin–Stout, WI
Warren Wilson College, NC
Wartburg College, IA
Western Washington University, WA
William Jessup University, CA

Public Servants
Arkansas Tech University, AR
Caldwell College, NJ
California Institute of Integral Studies, CA
Chowan University, NC
College of Staten Island of the City University of New York, NY
Georgia College & State University, GA
Grand Valley State University, MI
Hardin-Simmons University, TX
Hofstra University, NY
Lindenwood University, MO
Missouri Baptist University, MO
New Mexico State University, NM
Nicholls State University, LA
Northwestern State University of Louisiana, LA
Peirce College, PA
Regent University, VA
Regis University, CO
St. Joseph's College, Long Island Campus, NY
St. Joseph's College, New York, NY
Southern Illinois University Carbondale, IL
Tennessee Technological University, TN
Texas Wesleyan University, TX
The University of Alabama at Birmingham, AL
University of Massachusetts Dartmouth, MA
University of Memphis, TN
University of Michigan–Dearborn, MI
University of New Orleans, LA
University of Oklahoma, OK
The University of Texas at Arlington, TX
The University of Texas at Dallas, TX
The University of Toledo, OH
Washington State University, WA
West Texas A&M University, TX
Youngstown State University, OH

Relatives of Clergy
Abilene Christian University, TX
Albion College, MI
American University, DC
Anderson University, IN
Arcadia University, PA
Asbury University, KY
Ashland University, OH
Averett University, VA
Barton College, NC
Benedictine University, IL
Bethel College, IN
Bethel College, KS
Bethel University, MN
Biola University, CA
Boston University, MA
Cairn University, PA
Caldwell College, NJ
California Baptist University, CA

California Lutheran University, CA
Calvary Bible College and Theological Seminary, MO
Campbellsville University, KY
Capital University, OH
Carson-Newman University, TN
Cedar Crest College, PA
Centenary College of Louisiana, LA
Central Methodist University, MO
Chowan University, NC
Clarke University, IA
Columbia International University, SC
Concordia University, OR
Corban University, OR
Cornell College, IA
Crown College, MN
Dallas Baptist University, TX
Davidson College, NC
Dominican College, NY
Drury University, MO
Duquesne University, PA
Elon University, NC
Emmanuel College, GA
Eureka College, IL
Evangel University, MO
Faulkner University, AL
Ferrum College, VA
Florida Southern College, FL
Fresno Pacific University, CA
Furman University, SC
Gardner-Webb University, NC
George Fox University, OR
Georgetown College, KY
Gordon College, MA
Grace Bible College, MI
Green Mountain College, VT
Greenville College, IL
Hamline University, MN
Harding University, AR
Hardin-Simmons University, TX
Hawai'i Pacific University, HI
Heidelberg University, OH
Hendrix College, AR
Heritage Christian University, AL
Hillsdale Free Will Baptist College, OK
Houghton College, NY
Houston Baptist University, TX
Howard Payne University, TX
Huntington University, IN
Indiana Wesleyan University, IN
Iona College, NY
Kentucky Wesleyan College, KY
King College, TN
King's College, PA
LaGrange College, GA
Lancaster Bible College, PA
La Salle University, PA
La Sierra University, CA
Lees-McRae College, NC
Lindsey Wilson College, KY
Lipscomb University, TN
Lycoming College, PA
Malone University, OH
The Master's College and Seminary, CA
McMurry University, TX
Mercer University, GA
Merrimack College, MA
Methodist University, NC
Millikin University, IL
Misericordia University, PA
Mississippi College, MS
Missouri Baptist University, MO
Montreat College, NC
Moravian College, PA
Mount Vernon Nazarene University, OH

Nebraska Wesleyan University, NE
Newberry College, SC
New Hope Christian College, OR
New Jersey Institute of Technology, NJ
Niagara University, NY
North Central College, IL
Northland International University, WI
Northwest Christian University, OR
Northwestern College, MN
Northwest Nazarene University, ID
Northwest University, WA
Nyack College, NY
Ohio Valley University, WV
Ohio Wesleyan University, OH
Oklahoma Baptist University, OK
Oklahoma City University, OK
Oklahoma Wesleyan University, OK
Olivet Nazarene University, IL
Oral Roberts University, OK
Ouachita Baptist University, AR
Pacific Lutheran University, WA
Pacific University, OR
Piedmont International University, NC
Presbyterian College, SC
Randolph College, VA
Randolph-Macon College, VA
Rhodes College, TN
Roberts Wesleyan College, NY
Rochester College, MI
Rosemont College, PA
St. Bonaventure University, NY
St. John's University, NY
Saint Mary's College of California, CA
Saint Peter's University, NJ
Samford University, AL
San Diego Christian College, CA
Schreiner University, TX
Seattle Pacific University, WA
Sewanee: The University of the South, TN
Shenandoah University, VA
Shorter University, GA
Siena College, NY
Simpson College, IA
Simpson University, CA
Southwest Baptist University, MO
Southwestern University, TX
Spring Arbor University, MI
Stonehill College, MA
Tennessee Wesleyan College, TN
Texas Christian University, TX
Texas Wesleyan University, TX
Thiel College, PA
Transylvania University, KY
Trevecca Nazarene University, TN
Trinity Baptist College, FL
Trinity College of Florida, FL
Union University, TN
Universidad Adventista de las Antillas, PR
The University of Alabama at Birmingham, AL
University of Indianapolis, IN
University of Mary Hardin-Baylor, TX
University of Mobile, AL
University of Mount Union, OH
The University of North Carolina at Chapel Hill, NC
University of Portland, OR
University of the Cumberlands, KY
University of the Ozarks, AR
University of Tulsa, OK
Ursuline College, OH
Valley Forge Christian College, PA
Valparaiso University, IN
Virginia Wesleyan College, VA
Warren Wilson College, NC
Wayland Baptist University, TX

Wesleyan College, GA
Westminster College, MO
West Virginia Wesleyan College, WV
William Jessup University, CA
William Peace University, NC
Williams Baptist College, AR
Wilson College, PA
Wittenberg University, OH
Wofford College, SC

Religious Affiliation
Abilene Christian University, TX
Adrian College, MI
Alaska Bible College, AK
Alaska Pacific University, AK
Anderson University, SC
Arcadia University, PA
Armstrong Atlantic State University, GA
Ashland University, OH
Augustana College, IL
Augustana College, SD
Aurora University, IL
Averett University, VA
Azusa Pacific University, CA
Baldwin Wallace University, OH
The Baptist College of Florida, FL
Barton College, NC
Bellarmine University, KY
Benedictine College, KS
Bethel College, IN
Bethel College, KS
Bethel University, MN
Bluefield College, VA
Blue Mountain College, MS
Bluffton University, OH
Boston University, MA
Bridgewater College, VA
Brigham Young University, UT
Buena Vista University, IA
Caldwell College, NJ
California Baptist University, CA
California Lutheran University, CA
Calvary Bible College and Theological Seminary, MO
Calvin College, MI
Campbellsville University, KY
Canisius College, NY
Capital University, OH
Cardinal Stritch University, WI
Carroll College, MT
The Catholic University of America, DC
Cedarville University, OH
Centenary College of Louisiana, LA
Central College, IA
Central Methodist University, MO
Chowan University, NC
Christian Brothers University, TN
Clarke University, IA
Clearwater Christian College, FL
Coe College, IA
The College at Brockport, State University of New York, NY
The College of St. Scholastica, MN
Columbia College, MO
Columbia International University, SC
Concordia University, CA
Concordia University, OR
Concordia University Ann Arbor, MI
Concordia University, Nebraska, NE
Concordia University, St. Paul, MN
Concordia University Texas, TX
Cornell College, IA
Covenant College, GA
Creighton University, NE
Culver-Stockton College, MO
Dakota Wesleyan University, SD

Dallas Baptist University, TX
Defiance College, OH
Doane College, NE
Dordt College, IA
Drury University, MO
Duquesne University, PA
Eastern Michigan University, MI
Eastern Nazarene College, MA
East Texas Baptist University, TX
Eckerd College, FL
Edinboro University of Pennsylvania, PA
Elizabethtown College, PA
Elmhurst College, IL
Emmanuel College, GA
Emmanuel College, MA
Emory University, GA
Emporia State University, KS
Endicott College, MA
Eureka College, IL
Evangel University, MO
Faulkner University, AL
Ferrum College, VA
Finlandia University, MI
Florida Southern College, FL
Franklin College, IN
Fresno Pacific University, CA
Furman University, SC
Gannon University, PA
Geneva College, PA
George Fox University, OR
Georgetown College, KY
Georgian Court University, NJ
Georgia Southern University, GA
Graceland University, IA
Green Mountain College, VT
Greenville College, IL
Hamline University, MN
Hampden-Sydney College, VA
Hanover College, IN
Hardin-Simmons University, TX
Hastings College, NE
Hawai'i Pacific University, HI
Heidelberg University, OH
Hillsdale Free Will Baptist College, OK
Houghton College, NY
Howard Payne University, TX
Howard University, DC
Huntingdon College, AL
Huntington University, IN
Indiana Wesleyan University, IN
Iona College, NY
Kennesaw State University, GA
Kentucky Wesleyan College, KY
LaGrange College, GA
Lakeland College, WI
Lancaster Bible College, PA
La Sierra University, CA
Lees-McRae College, NC
LeTourneau University, TX
Lewis University, IL
Liberty University, VA
Lindsey Wilson College, KY
Lourdes University, OH
Loyola Marymount University, CA
Loyola University Chicago, IL
Luther College, IA
Lyon College, AR
Malone University, OH
Manchester University, IN
Marymount University, VA
Maryville College, TN
Marywood University, PA
McKendree University, IL
McMurry University, TX
McPherson College, KS
Meredith College, NC

Messiah College, PA
Methodist University, NC
Millsaps College, MS
Missouri Baptist University, MO
Missouri Southern State University, MO
Missouri Western State University, MO
Molloy College, NY
Montreat College, NC
Moravian College, PA
Morningside College, IA
Mount Aloysius College, PA
Mount Marty College, SD
Mount Olive College, NC
Mount Vernon Nazarene University, OH
Newberry College, SC
New Jersey Institute of Technology, NJ
New Life Theological Seminary, NC
Northeastern State University, OK
Northwest Christian University, OR
Northwest Nazarene University, ID
Northwest University, WA
Notre Dame de Namur University, CA
Nyack College, NY
Ohio Valley University, WV
Ohio Wesleyan University, OH
Oklahoma Baptist University, OK
Oklahoma City University, OK
Oklahoma Wesleyan University, OK
Olivet College, MI
Olivet Nazarene University, IL
Ouachita Baptist University, AR
Pacific Lutheran University, WA
Pacific Union College, CA
Park University, MO
Presbyterian College, SC
Randolph College, VA
Rhodes College, TN
Ripon College, WI
Roberts Wesleyan College, NY
Rochester College, MI
Sacred Heart University, CT
St. Ambrose University, IA
St. Bonaventure University, NY
St. Catherine University, MN
St. Edward's University, TX
Saint Francis University, PA
St. John's University, NY
Saint Louis University, MO
Saint Mary-of-the-Woods College, IN
Saint Michael's College, VT
Saint Peter's University, NJ
Sam Houston State University, TX
San Diego Christian College, CA
Schreiner University, TX
Seattle Pacific University, WA
Seattle University, WA
Sewanee: The University of the South, TN
Shenandoah University, VA
Shorter University, GA
Siena College, NY
Simpson College, IA
Simpson University, CA
Southwestern College, KS
Southwestern University, TX
Spring Arbor University, MI
State University of New York College at
    Geneseo, NY
Taylor University, IN
Tennessee Wesleyan College, TN
Texas Christian University, TX
Texas Lutheran University, TX
Texas Wesleyan University, TX
Thiel College, PA
Thomas More College, KY
Transylvania University, KY

Trevecca Nazarene University, TN
Trinity Baptist College, FL
Trinity Christian College, IL
Union College, KY
Union University, TN
University of California, Riverside, CA
University of Dallas, TX
University of Dayton, OH
University of Evansville, IN
University of Great Falls, MT
University of Hartford, CT
University of Indianapolis, IN
University of Mary, ND
University of Mary Hardin-Baylor, TX
The University of North Carolina at Chapel
    Hill, NC
University of Portland, OR
University of St. Francis, IL
University of St. Thomas, TX
University of South Carolina, SC
The University of Tennessee at Chattanooga,
    TN
University of the Cumberlands, KY
University of the Ozarks, AR
University of the Pacific, CA
The University of Toledo, OH
University of Tulsa, OK
Upper Iowa University, IA
Ursuline College, OH
Valparaiso University, IN
Villanova University, PA
Virginia Wesleyan College, VA
Wake Forest University, NC
Waldorf College, IA
Warner Pacific College, OR
Warren Wilson College, NC
Wartburg College, IA
Washington State University, WA
Wayland Baptist University, TX
Wesleyan College, GA
Western Kentucky University, KY
Westminster College, MO
Westminster College, PA
West Texas A&M University, TX
West Virginia Wesleyan College, WV
Wheeling Jesuit University, WV
Williams Baptist College, AR
Wilson College, PA
Wisconsin Lutheran College, WI
Wittenberg University, OH
Youngstown State University, OH

Siblings of Current Students

Albright College, PA
Alliant International University, CA
Asbury University, KY
Ashland University, OH
Augustana College, IL
Augustana College, SD
Aurora University, IL
Baldwin Wallace University, OH
Barton College, NC
Bay Path College, MA
Becker College, MA
Beloit College, WI
Benedictine University, IL
Bethel College, IN
Bethel College, KS
Bloomfield College, NJ
Blue Mountain College, MS
Bryant University, RI
Buena Vista University, IA
Cabrini College, PA
Caldwell College, NJ
California Baptist University, CA

Calvary Bible College and Theological
    Seminary, MO
Capital University, OH
Cardinal Stritch University, WI
Carroll College, MT
Carroll University, WI
Carson-Newman University, TN
The Catholic University of America, DC
Cedar Crest College, PA
Centenary College of Louisiana, LA
Central College, IA
Central Methodist University, MO
Chatham University, PA
Cincinnati Christian University, OH
Clarke University, IA
Clearwater Christian College, FL
Coe College, IA
The College of Idaho, ID
The College of New Rochelle, NY
The College of Saint Rose, NY
The College of St. Scholastica, MN
Columbia College, MO
Concordia University Ann Arbor, MI
Corban University, OR
Creighton University, NE
Crossroads Bible College, IN
Crown College, MN
Doane College, NE
Dominican University, IL
Elizabethtown College, PA
Elmhurst College, IL
Elmira College, NY
Emmanuel College, GA
Emmanuel College, MA
Eureka College, IL
Faulkner University, AL
Felician College, NJ
Finlandia University, MI
Florida Institute of Technology, FL
Florida Southern College, FL
Franklin College, IN
Franklin Pierce University, NH
Gonzaga University, WA
Green Mountain College, VT
Greenville College, IL
Gustavus Adolphus College, MN
Gwynedd-Mercy College, PA
Hanover College, IN
Harding University, AR
Hardin-Simmons University, TX
Hartwick College, NY
Hastings College, NE
Hilbert College, NY
Hood College, MD
Houghton College, NY
Huntington University, IN
Indiana Tech, IN
Indiana Wesleyan University, IN
Iona College, NY
Ithaca College, NY
James Madison University, VA
Johnson C. Smith University, NC
Kettering University, MI
Keuka College, NY
Keystone College, PA
King's College, PA
Lakeland College, WI
Lancaster Bible College, PA
Lasell College, MA
La Sierra University, CA
Lawrence University, WI
Lee University, TN
Limestone College, SC
Long Island University–C. W. Post Campus,
    NY

Lynn University, FL
MacMurray College, IL
Malone University, OH
Marian University, WI
Marywood University, PA
McDaniel College, MD
Mercer University, GA
Merrimack College, MA
Methodist University, NC
Millikin University, IL
Misericordia University, PA
Missouri Baptist University, MO
Molloy College, NY
Mount Aloysius College, PA
Mount Marty College, SD
Mount Mary College, WI
Mount St. Mary's University, MD
Nazareth College of Rochester, NY
Nebraska Wesleyan University, NE
Newberry College, SC
New England College, NH
New Jersey Institute of Technology, NJ
Nichols College, MA
Northwest Christian University, OR
Northwestern College, MN
Northwest Nazarene University, ID
Northwest University, WA
Northwood University, Florida Campus, FL
Northwood University, Michigan Campus, MI
Northwood University, Texas Campus, TX
Notre Dame of Maryland University, MD
Oglethorpe University, GA
Oklahoma Wesleyan University, OK
Olivet College, MI
Oral Roberts University, OK
Pacific Union College, CA
Palm Beach Atlantic University, FL
Park University, MO
Peirce College, PA
Pine Manor College, MA
Point Park University, PA
Post University, CT
Providence College, RI
Quinnipiac University, CT
Randolph-Macon College, VA
Regent University, VA
Research College of Nursing, MO
Ripon College, WI
Roberts Wesleyan College, NY
Rochester College, MI
Rockford College, IL
Rockhurst University, MO
Rosemont College, PA
Sacred Heart University, CT
Sage College of Albany, NY
Saint Anselm College, NH
St. Bonaventure University, NY
St. Catherine University, MN
Saint Francis University, PA
Saint Joseph's College, IN
St. Joseph's College, Long Island Campus, NY
St. Joseph's College, New York, NY
St. Lawrence University, NY
Saint Louis University, MO
Saint Martin's University, WA
Saint Mary-of-the-Woods College, IN
Saint Michael's College, VT
Samford University, AL
San Diego Christian College, CA
Schreiner University, TX
Seton Hill University, PA
Shorter University, GA
Simpson College, IA
Simpson University, CA

Southern Adventist University, TN
Spring Hill College, AL
Stephens College, MO
Stonehill College, MA
Suffolk University, MA
Texas Wesleyan University, TX
Thiel College, PA
Thomas More College, KY
Trine University, IN
Union College, KY
Union University, TN
The University of Alabama at Birmingham, AL
University of Dallas, TX
University of Evansville, IN
University of Great Falls, MT
University of Hartford, CT
University of New England, ME
University of St. Francis, IL
The University of Scranton, PA
University of the Cumberlands, KY
University of the Ozarks, AR
University of Tulsa, OK
Ursinus College, PA
Ursuline College, OH
Valley Forge Christian College, PA
Wagner College, NY
Wartburg College, IA
Webber International University, FL
Wesleyan College, GA
Western New England University, MA
Westminster College, MO
William Jessup University, CA
William Jewell College, MO
William Peace University, NC
Xavier University, OH

Spouses of Current Students
Alaska Bible College, AK
Alliant International University, CA
American University, DC
Augustana College, SD
The Baptist College of Florida, FL
Bethel College, IN
Bethel College, KS
Bloomfield College, NJ
Blue Mountain College, MS
Boise State University, ID
Caldwell College, NJ
Calvary Bible College and Theological Seminary, MO
Cardinal Stritch University, WI
Carroll College, MT
Carroll University, WI
Central Methodist University, MO
Clarke University, IA
The College of New Rochelle, NY
The College of St. Scholastica, MN
Columbia College, MO
Columbia International University, SC
Crossroads Bible College, IN
Elmhurst College, IL
Emmanuel College, GA
Finlandia University, MI
Fort Hays State University, KS
Franklin Pierce University, NH
Fresno Pacific University, CA
Georgian Court University, NJ
Hastings College, NE
Heritage Christian University, AL
Hope International University, CA
Huntingdon College, AL
Huntington University, IN
Lancaster Bible College, PA
Lee University, TN
Malone University, OH

Marywood University, PA
Mid-Atlantic Christian University, NC
Missouri Baptist University, MO
Mount Aloysius College, PA
Mount Marty College, SD
New Hope Christian College, OR
New Mexico State University, NM
Northland International University, WI
Northwest University, WA
Nyack College, NY
Pacific Union College, CA
Palm Beach Atlantic University, FL
Piedmont International University, NC
St. Catherine University, MN
Saint Francis University, PA
St. Joseph's College, Long Island Campus, NY
St. Joseph's College, New York, NY
Saint Mary-of-the-Woods College, IN
Samford University, AL
Southern Adventist University, TN
Texas Wesleyan University, TX
Trinity Baptist College, FL
Trinity College of Florida, FL
Union University, TN
The University of Alabama at Birmingham, AL
University of Great Falls, MT
University of Mississippi, MS
University of Southern Indiana, IN
Upper Iowa University, IA
Valley Forge Christian College, PA
Wesleyan College, GA
Xavier University of Louisiana, LA

Spouses of Deceased or Disabled Public Servants
The College of New Rochelle, NY
College of Staten Island of the City University of New York, NY
Eastern Washington University, WA
Francis Marion University, SC
Grand Valley State University, MI
Louisiana Tech University, LA
Michigan State University, MI
Mississippi State University, MS
New Mexico State University, NM
Northeastern State University, OK
Northern Kentucky University, KY
Pace University, NY
Southern Illinois University Carbondale, IL
Texas Wesleyan University, TX
The University of Alabama, AL
The University of Alabama at Birmingham, AL
University of Connecticut, CT
University of South Carolina, SC
University of Utah, UT
Youngstown State University, OH

Twins
Becker College, MA
Blue Mountain College, MS
Caldwell College, NJ
Calvin College, MI
The Catholic University of America, DC
Central College, IA
The College of Saint Rose, NY
Emmanuel College, GA
Finlandia University, MI
Lake Erie College, OH
Mount Aloysius College, PA
Ohio Wesleyan University, OH
Ouachita Baptist University, AR
Randolph College, VA
Sacred Heart University, CT
St. Joseph's College, Long Island Campus, NY

St. Joseph's College, New York, NY
Simpson College, IA
Texas Wesleyan University, TX
Union University, TN
The University of Alabama at Birmingham, AL
University of Hartford, CT
Virginia Polytechnic Institute and State University, VA
Westminster College, MO

Veterans
Adelphi University, NY
Adrian College, MI
Alliant International University, CA
Amridge University, AL
Appalachian State University, NC
Arkansas State University, AR
Ashland University, OH
Augustana College, SD
Aurora University, IL
Austin Peay State University, TN
Babson College, MA
Ball State University, IN
Barton College, NC
Benedictine University, IL
Bennington College, VT
Berry College, GA
Bluefield College, VA
Boise State University, ID
Broadview University–Boise, ID
Broadview University–Layton, UT
Broadview University–Orem, UT
Broadview University–Salt Lake City, UT
Broadview University–West Jordan, UT
Brown University, RI
Caldwell College, NJ
California Baptist University, CA
California Institute of Integral Studies, CA
California Lutheran University, CA
California State University, Bakersfield, CA
California State University, San Bernardino, CA
Campbellsville University, KY
Carroll College, MT
The Catholic University of America, DC
Cedarville University, OH
Central College, IA
Chowan University, NC
Christian Brothers University, TN
Clarkson University, NY
Cleary University, MI
Clemson University, SC
Coe College, IA
The College at Brockport, State University of New York, NY
The College of New Rochelle, NY
College of Staten Island of the City University of New York, NY
Columbia College, MO
Columbia International University, SC
Concordia University, Nebraska, NE
Concordia University, St. Paul, MN
Concordia University Texas, TX
Culver-Stockton College, MO
Dallas Baptist University, TX
Defiance College, OH
Denison University, OH
DigiPen Institute of Technology, WA
Dominican University of California, CA
Drury University, MO
D'Youville College, NY
Eastern Connecticut State University, CT
Eastern Nazarene College, MA
Eastern New Mexico University, NM

Eastern Washington University, WA
Edinboro University of Pennsylvania, PA
EDP University of Puerto Rico, PR
EDP University of Puerto Rico–San Sebastian, PR
Elizabeth City State University, NC
Elmhurst College, IL
Elmira College, NY
Emory University, GA
Emporia State University, KS
The Evergreen State College, WA
Fairfield University, CT
Fairmont State University, WV
Ferris State University, MI
Florida International University, FL
Fort Hays State University, KS
Framingham State University, MA
Francis Marion University, SC
Frostburg State University, MD
Furman University, SC
Gannon University, PA
Georgian Court University, NJ
Glenville State College, WV
Globe University–Appleton, WI
Globe University–Eau Claire, WI
Globe University–Green Bay, WI
Globe University–La Crosse, WI
Globe University–Madison East, WI
Globe University–Madison West, WI
Globe University–Minneapolis, MN
Globe University–Sioux Falls, SD
Globe University–Wausau, WI
Globe University–Woodbury, MN
Grand Valley State University, MI
Grand View University, IA
Hamline University, MN
Hampden-Sydney College, VA
Hampton University, VA
Hardin-Simmons University, TX
Hartwick College, NY
Hofstra University, NY
Hollins University, VA
Houghton College, NY
Huntingdon College, AL
Huntington University, IN
Illinois Institute of Technology, IL
Indiana State University, IN
Indiana Wesleyan University, IN
Inter American University of Puerto Rico, Barranquitas Campus, PR
John Carroll University, OH
Kentucky Wesleyan College, KY
King's College, PA
Lake Erie College, OH
La Salle University, PA
Lasell College, MA
Lawrence University, WI
Lebanon Valley College, PA
Lees-McRae College, NC
Lewis University, IL
Liberty University, VA
Lindenwood University, MO
Louisiana Tech University, LA
Loyola Marymount University, CA
MacMurray College, IL
Malone University, OH
Marian University, WI
Marymount University, VA
Maryville College, TN
Maryville University of Saint Louis, MO
Massachusetts College of Art and Design, MA
Massachusetts Maritime Academy, MA
McDaniel College, MD
McKendree University, IL

McNally Smith College of Music, MN
McNeese State University, LA
Methodist University, NC
Metropolitan State University of Denver, CO
Michigan State University, MI
Midwestern State University, TX
Millikin University, IL
Minnesota School of Business–Blaine, MN
Minnesota School of Business–Elk River, MN
Minnesota School of Business–Lakeville, MN
Minnesota School of Business–Moorhead, MN
Minnesota School of Business Rochester, MN
Minot State University, ND
Missouri Baptist University, MO
Monmouth College, IL
Monmouth University, NJ
Montana State University Billings, MT
Montana State University–Northern, MT
Montana Tech of The University of Montana, MT
Montreat College, NC
Morehead State University, KY
Mount Olive College, NC
New Hope Christian College, OR
New Jersey Institute of Technology, NJ
New Mexico State University, NM
New York Institute of Technology, NY
Nicholls State University, LA
Northern Illinois University, IL
Northern Kentucky University, KY
Northwestern State University of Louisiana, LA
Northwest Nazarene University, ID
Nova Southeastern University, FL
Oklahoma Baptist University, OK
Pace University, NY
Pacific Union College, CA
Pacific University, OR
Peirce College, PA
Piedmont International University, NC
Portland State University, OR
Randolph-Macon College, VA
Robert Morris University Illinois, IL
Rochester Institute of Technology, NY
Sacred Heart University, CT
St. Ambrose University, IA
St. Edward's University, TX
St. John's College, NM
Saint Joseph's University, PA
Saint Martin's University, WA
Saint Mary's College of California, CA
Samford University, AL
San Diego State University, CA
Seattle Pacific University, WA
Shawnee State University, OH
Sierra Nevada College, NV
Sonoma State University, CA
South Dakota State University, SD
Southeastern Louisiana University, LA
Southeast Missouri State University, MO
Southern Connecticut State University, CT
Southern Illinois University Carbondale, IL
Stephens College, MO
Stonehill College, MA
Temple University, PA
Texas A&M University, TX
Texas Christian University, TX
Texas Lutheran University, TX
Texas Tech University, TX
Texas Wesleyan University, TX
Thomas More College, KY

Thomas University, GA
Towson University, MD
Trinity Christian College, IL
Union College, KY
Union University, TN
Universidad Adventista de las Antillas, PR
The University of Alabama at Birmingham, AL
University of California, Riverside, CA
University of California, Santa Cruz, CA
University of Connecticut, CT
University of Houston–Clear Lake, TX
University of Idaho, ID
University of Illinois at Urbana–Champaign, IL
University of Indianapolis, IN
The University of Iowa, IA
University of Louisville, KY
University of Mary, ND
University of Maryland Eastern Shore, MD
University of Massachusetts Amherst, MA
University of Massachusetts Boston, MA
University of Massachusetts Dartmouth, MA
University of Massachusetts Lowell, MA
University of Miami, FL
University of Michigan–Flint, MI
University of Minnesota, Morris, MN
University of Missouri–St. Louis, MO
The University of Montana, MT
The University of Montana Western, MT
University of Nebraska at Kearney, NE
University of Nevada, Las Vegas, NV
University of North Carolina at Asheville, NC
The University of North Carolina at Greensboro, NC
University of Northern Colorado, CO
University of Northern Iowa, IA
University of Oregon, OR
University of Pittsburgh at Bradford, PA
University of Puerto Rico at Bayamón, PR
University of Rochester, NY
University of St. Francis, IL
University of Southern Mississippi, MS
The University of Tampa, FL
The University of Texas at Dallas, TX
The University of Texas–Pan American, TX
The University of Toledo, OH
The University of Virginia's College at Wise, VA
University of West Florida, FL
University of Wisconsin–Green Bay, WI
University of Wisconsin–La Crosse, WI
University of Wisconsin–Stevens Point, WI
University of Wisconsin–Stout, WI
University of Wisconsin–Superior, WI
University of Wyoming, WY
Ursuline College, OH
Washington Adventist University, MD
Washington & Jefferson College, PA
Washington State University, WA
Wayne State College, NE
Wesleyan College, GA
Western Kentucky University, KY
Western Michigan University, MI
Western New England University, MA
Western Oregon University, OR
Western Washington University, WA
West Texas A&M University, TX
Whitman College, WA
William Jessup University, CA
Wilson College, PA
Youngstown State University, OH

VeteransChildren'
Adrian College, MI

Appalachian State University, NC
Arkansas State University, AR
Aurora University, IL
Ball State University, IN
Benedictine College, KS
Benedictine University, IL
Bennington College, VT
Berry College, GA
Bluefield College, VA
Boise State University, ID
Brevard College, NC
Broadview University–Boise, ID
Broadview University–Layton, UT
Broadview University–Orem, UT
Broadview University–Salt Lake City, UT
Broadview University–West Jordan, UT
Brown University, RI
California Institute of Integral Studies, CA
California Lutheran University, CA
California State University, San Bernardino, CA
The Catholic University of America, DC
Central College, IA
Chowan University, NC
Christian Brothers University, TN
Coastal Carolina University, SC
Coe College, IA
The College of Idaho, ID
The College of New Rochelle, NY
College of Staten Island of the City University of New York, NY
Columbia International University, SC
Concordia University, Nebraska, NE
Concordia University, St. Paul, MN
Concordia University Texas, TX
Culver-Stockton College, MO
Dallas Baptist University, TX
Defiance College, OH
Dominican University of California, CA
Eastern Washington University, WA
Edinboro University of Pennsylvania, PA
EDP University of Puerto Rico, PR
EDP University of Puerto Rico–San Sebastian, PR
Elizabeth City State University, NC
Elmhurst College, IL
Emory University, GA
Emporia State University, KS
The Evergreen State College, WA
Fairmont State University, WV
Florida International University, FL
Fort Hays State University, KS
Fort Lewis College, CO
Francis Marion University, SC
Frostburg State University, MD
Glenville State College, WV
Globe University–Appleton, WI
Globe University–Eau Claire, WI
Globe University–Green Bay, WI
Globe University–La Crosse, WI
Globe University–Madison East, WI
Globe University–Madison West, WI
Globe University–Minneapolis, MN
Globe University–Sioux Falls, SD
Globe University–Wausau, WI
Globe University–Woodbury, MN
Grand Valley State University, MI
Hampden-Sydney College, VA
Hampton University, VA
Hardin-Simmons University, TX
Huntingdon College, AL
Huntington University, IN
Illinois Institute of Technology, IL
John Carroll University, OH
Kennesaw State University, GA
Lake Erie College, OH

Lasell College, MA
Lawrence University, WI
Lewis University, IL
Lindenwood University, MO
Louisiana Tech University, LA
McKendree University, IL
McNally Smith College of Music, MN
McNeese State University, LA
Midwestern State University, TX
Minnesota School of Business–Blaine, MN
Minnesota School of Business–Elk River, MN
Minnesota School of Business–Lakeville, MN
Minnesota School of Business–Moorhead, MN
Minnesota School of Business–Rochester, MN
Minot State University, ND
Missouri Baptist University, MO
Montreat College, NC
Morehead State University, KY
Mount Olive College, NC
New Hope Christian College, OR
New Jersey Institute of Technology, NJ
New Mexico State University, NM
Northern Kentucky University, KY
Northwestern State University of Louisiana, LA
Old Dominion University, VA
Peirce College, PA
Purdue University North Central, IN
Randolph-Macon College, VA
Sacred Heart University, CT
Saint Joseph's University, PA
St. Lawrence University, NY
Saint Martin's University, WA
Saint Mary's College of California, CA
San Diego State University, CA
Siena College, NY
South Dakota State University, SD
Southeastern Louisiana University, LA
Stephens College, MO
Stonehill College, MA
Texas A&M University, TX
Texas Christian University, TX
Texas Lutheran University, TX
Texas Tech University, TX
Texas Wesleyan University, TX
Thomas More College, KY
Union College, KY
Union University, TN
The University of Alabama at Birmingham, AL
University of California, Riverside, CA
University of California, San Diego, CA
University of Houston–Clear Lake, TX
University of Louisville, KY
University of Maine at Augusta, ME
University of Maine at Farmington, ME
University of Maine at Presque Isle, ME
University of Miami, FL
University of Michigan–Flint, MI
University of Minnesota, Morris, MN
University of Nebraska at Kearney, NE
University of Nebraska at Omaha, NE
University of Nebraska–Lincoln, NE
University of Nevada, Las Vegas, NV
University of North Carolina at Asheville, NC
The University of North Carolina at Greensboro, NC
University of Oregon, OR
University of Puerto Rico at Bayamón, PR
University of St. Francis, IL
University of Southern Indiana, IN

The University of Texas at Dallas, TX
The University of Toledo, OH
The University of Virginia's College at Wise, VA
University of Wisconsin–La Crosse, WI
University of Wisconsin–Stout, WI
Virginia Commonwealth University, VA

Virginia Polytechnic Institute and State University, VA
Washington Adventist University, MD
Washington & Jefferson College, PA
Washington State University, WA
Wayne State College, NE
Western Illinois University, IL

Western Kentucky University, KY
Western Oregon University, OR
West Texas A&M University, TX
Whitman College, WA
William Jessup University, CA
Wilson College, PA
Youngstown State University, OH

Athletic Grants for Undergraduates

Archery
Texas A&M University, TX — W
University of the Cumberlands, KY — M,W

Baseball
Abilene Christian University, TX — M
Academy of Art University, CA — M
Adams State University, CO — M
Adelphi University, NY — M
Alabama State University, AL — M
Alcorn State University, MS — M
Anderson University, SC — M
Angelo State University, TX — M
Appalachian State University, NC — M
Arizona State University, AZ — M
Arkansas State University, AR — M
Arkansas Tech University, AR — M
Armstrong Atlantic State University, GA — M
Asbury University, KY — M
Ashland University, OH — M
Auburn University, AL — M
Auburn University at Montgomery, AL — M
Augustana College, SD — M
Austin Peay State University, TN — M
Azusa Pacific University, CA — M
Ball State University, IN — M
Barry University, FL — M
Barton College, NC — M
Baylor University, TX — M
Belhaven University, MS — M
Bellarmine University, KY — M
Belmont Abbey College, NC — M
Belmont University, TN — M
Bemidji State University, MN — M
Benedictine College, KS — M
Bethel College, IN — M
Bethune-Cookman University, FL — M
Binghamton University, State University of New York, NY — M
Biola University, CA — M
Bloomfield College, NJ — M
Bloomsburg University of Pennsylvania, PA — M
Bluefield College, VA — M
Bluefield State College, WV — M
Blue Mountain College, MS — M
Boston College, MA — M
Bowling Green State University, OH — M,W
Bradley University, IL — M
Brevard College, NC — M
Brigham Young University, UT — M
Bryant University, RI — M
Butler University, IN — M
Caldwell College, NJ — M
California Baptist University, CA — M
California Polytechnic State University, San Luis Obispo, CA — M
California State Polytechnic University, Pomona, CA — M
California State University, Chico, CA — M
California State University, Dominguez Hills, CA — M
California State University, Fresno, CA — M
California State University, Fullerton, CA — M
California State University, Los Angeles, CA — M
California State University, Monterey Bay, CA — M
California State University, Northridge, CA — M
California State University, San Bernardino, CA — M
Calumet College of Saint Joseph, IN — M
Cameron University, OK — M
Campbellsville University, KY — M
Canisius College, NY — M
Carson-Newman University, TN — M
Catawba College, NC — M
Cedarville University, OH — M
Central Connecticut State University, CT — M
Central Methodist University, MO — M
Central Michigan University, MI — M
Chestnut Hill College, PA — M
Chicago State University, IL — M
Chowan University, NC — M
Christian Brothers University, TN — M
The Citadel, The Military College of South Carolina, SC — M
Clarion University of Pennsylvania, PA — M
Clarke University, IA — M
Coastal Carolina University, SC — M
Coker College, SC — M
College of Charleston, SC — M
The College of Idaho, ID — M
The College of Saint Rose, NY — M
College of the Ozarks, MO — M
The College of William and Mary, VA — M
Colorado Mesa University, CO — M
Colorado School of Mines, CO — M
Columbus State University, GA — M
Concordia University, CA — M
Concordia University, OR — M
Concordia University, Nebraska, NE — M
Concordia University, St. Paul, MN — M
Corban University, OR — M
Cornerstone University, MI — M
Creighton University, NE — M
Culver-Stockton College, MO — M
Dakota State University, SD — M
Dakota Wesleyan University, SD — M
Dallas Baptist University, TX — M
Davenport University, MI — M
Davidson College, NC — M
Doane College, NE — M
Dominican College, NY — M
Dordt College, IA — M
Drury University, MO — M
East Carolina University, NC — M
Eastern Illinois University, IL — M
Eastern Michigan University, MI — M
Eastern New Mexico University, NM — M
Eckerd College, FL — M
Elizabeth City State University, NC — M
Elon University, NC — M
Embry-Riddle Aeronautical University–Daytona, FL — M
Emmanuel College, GA — M
Emporia State University, KS — M
Evangel University, MO — M
Fairfield University, CT — M
Fairmont State University, WV — M
Faulkner University, AL — M
Felician College, NJ — M
Flagler College, FL — M
Florida Agricultural and Mechanical University, FL — M
Florida Atlantic University, FL — M
Florida Gulf Coast University, FL — M
Florida Institute of Technology, FL — M
Florida International University, FL — M
Florida Southern College, FL — M
Florida State University, FL — M
Francis Marion University, SC — M
Franklin Pierce University, NH — M
Freed-Hardeman University, TN — M
Furman University, SC — M
Gannon University, PA — M
Gardner-Webb University, NC — M
George Mason University, VA — M
Georgetown College, KY — M
Georgetown University, DC — M
The George Washington University, DC — M
Georgia College & State University, GA — M
Georgia Institute of Technology, GA — M
Georgia Southern University, GA — M
Georgia Southwestern State University, GA — M
Georgia State University, GA — M
Gonzaga University, WA — M
Goshen College, IN — M
Graceland University, IA — M
Grand Valley State University, MI — M
Grand View University, IA — M
Harding University, AR — M
Hawai`i Pacific University, HI — M
Henderson State University, AR — M
Hillsdale College, MI — M
Hofstra University, NY — M
Houston Baptist University, TX — M
Huntington University, IN — M
Illinois Institute of Technology, IL — M
Illinois State University, IL — M
Indiana State University, IN — M
Indiana Tech, IN — M
Indiana University Bloomington, IN — M
Indiana University of Pennsylvania, PA — M
Indiana University–Purdue University Fort Wayne, IN — M

College	
Indiana Wesleyan University, IN	M
Inter American University of Puerto Rico, Bayamón Campus, PR	M
Iona College, NY	M
Jacksonville State University, AL	M
Jacksonville University, FL	M
James Madison University, VA	M
Kansas State University, KS	M
Kennesaw State University, GA	M
Kent State University, OH	M
Kentucky State University, KY	M
Kentucky Wesleyan College, KY	M
King College, TN	M
Kutztown University of Pennsylvania, PA	M
Lake Erie College, OH	M
Lamar University, TX	M
Lane College, TN	M
La Salle University, PA	M
Lee University, TN	M
Le Moyne College, NY	M
Lewis-Clark State College, ID	M
Lewis University, IL	M
Liberty University, VA	M
Limestone College, SC	M
Lincoln University, MO	M
Lindenwood University, MO	M
Lindsey Wilson College, KY	M
Lipscomb University, TN	M
Lock Haven University of Pennsylvania, PA	M
Long Island University–Brooklyn Campus, NY	M
Long Island University–C. W. Post Campus, NY	M
Longwood University, VA	M
Louisiana State University and Agricultural and Mechanical College, LA	M
Louisiana Tech University, LA	M
Lourdes University, OH	M
Loyola Marymount University, CA	M
Lubbock Christian University, TX	M
Lynn University, FL	M
Lyon College, AR	M
Malone University, OH	M
Manhattan College, NY	M
Mansfield University of Pennsylvania, PA	M
Marist College, NY	M
Marshall University, WV	M
Maryville University of Saint Louis, MO	M
The Master's College and Seminary, CA	M
Mayville State University, ND	M
McKendree University, IL	M
McNeese State University, LA	M
Menlo College, CA	M
Mercer University, GA	M
Mercy College, NY	M
Mercyhurst University, PA	M
Merrimack College, MA	M
Metropolitan State University of Denver, CO	M
Miami University, OH	M
Michigan State University, MI	M
Middle Tennessee State University, TN	M
Millersville University of Pennsylvania, PA	M
Minnesota State University Mankato, MN	M
Minot State University, ND	M
Mississippi State University, MS	M
Missouri Baptist University, MO	M
Missouri State University, MO	M
Missouri University of Science and Technology, MO	M
Missouri Western State University, MO	M
Molloy College, NY	M
Monmouth University, NJ	M
Montreat College, NC	M
Morehead State University, KY	M
Morehouse College, GA	M
Morningside College, IA	M
Mount Marty College, SD	M
Mount Mercy University, IA	M
Mount St. Mary's University, MD	M
Mount Vernon Nazarene University, OH	M
Murray State University, KY	M
Newberry College, SC	M
New Jersey Institute of Technology, NJ	M
New Mexico Highlands University, NM	M
New Mexico State University, NM	M
New York Institute of Technology, NY	M
Niagara University, NY	M
Nicholls State University, LA	M
Norfolk State University, VA	M
North Carolina Central University, NC	M
North Carolina State University, NC	M
Northeastern University, MA	M
Northern Illinois University, IL	M
Northern Kentucky University, KY	M
Northern State University, SD	M
Northwestern Oklahoma State University, OK	M
Northwestern State University of Louisiana, LA	M
Northwest Missouri State University, MO	M
Northwest Nazarene University, ID	M
Northwood University, Florida Campus, FL	M
Northwood University, Michigan Campus, MI	M
Northwood University, Texas Campus, TX	M
Nova Southeastern University, FL	M
Nyack College, NY	M
Oakland University, MI	M
The Ohio State University, OH	M
Ohio University, OH	M
Ohio Valley University, WV	M
Oklahoma Baptist University, OK	M
Oklahoma Christian University, OK	M
Oklahoma City University, OK	M
Oklahoma State University, OK	M
Old Dominion University, VA	M
Oral Roberts University, OK	M
Oregon State University, OR	M
Ouachita Baptist University, AR	M
Pace University, NY	M
Palm Beach Atlantic University, FL	M
Park University, MO	M
Penn State University Park, PA	M
Pepperdine University, CA	M
Philadelphia University, PA	M
Pittsburg State University, KS	M
Point Loma Nazarene University, CA	M
Point Park University, PA	M
Post University, CT	M
Presbyterian College, SC	M
Purdue University, IN	M
Purdue University North Central, IN	M
Queens College of the City University of New York, NY	M
Quincy University, IL	M
Quinnipiac University, CT	M
Radford University, VA	M
Regis University, CO	M
Research College of Nursing, MO	M
Rice University, TX	M
Rider University, NJ	M
Robert Morris University Illinois, IL	M
Rockhurst University, MO	M
Rogers State University, OK	M
Rollins College, FL	M
Sacred Heart University, CT	M
Saginaw Valley State University, MI	M
St. Ambrose University, IA	M
Saint Anselm College, NH	M
St. Bonaventure University, NY	M
St. Edward's University, TX	M
St. John's University, NY	M
Saint Joseph's College, IN	M
Saint Joseph's University, PA	M
Saint Louis University, MO	M
Saint Martin's University, WA	M
Saint Mary's College of California, CA	M
Saint Peter's University, NJ	M
St. Thomas University, FL	M
Samford University, AL	M
Sam Houston State University, TX	M
San Diego Christian College, CA	M
San Diego State University, CA	M
San Francisco State University, CA	M
San Jose State University, CA	M
Santa Clara University, CA	M
Seton Hill University, PA	M
Shawnee State University, OH	M
Shepherd University, WV	M
Shippensburg University of Pennsylvania, PA	M
Siena College, NY	M
Simpson University, CA	M
Slippery Rock University of Pennsylvania, PA	M
Sonoma State University, CA	M
South Dakota State University, SD	M
Southeastern Louisiana University, LA	M
Southeastern Oklahoma State University, OK	M
Southeast Missouri State University, MO	M
Southern Arkansas University–Magnolia, AR	M
Southern Connecticut State University, CT	M
Southern Illinois University Carbondale, IL	M
Southern Illinois University Edwardsville, IL	M
Southern Polytechnic State University, GA	M
Southwest Baptist University, MO	M
Spring Arbor University, MI	M
Spring Hill College, AL	M
Stanford University, CA	M

BASEBALL

Stephen F. Austin State University, TX	M
Stetson University, FL	M
Stonehill College, MA	M
Stony Brook University, State University of New York, NY	M
Tarleton State University, TX	M
Taylor University, IN	M
Temple University, PA	M
Tennessee Wesleyan College, TN	M
Texas A&M International University, TX	M
Texas A&M University, TX	M
Texas Christian University, TX	M
Texas Southern University, TX	M
Texas State University–San Marcos, TX	M
Texas Wesleyan University, TX	M
Thomas University, GA	M
Tiffin University, OH	M
Trevecca Nazarene University, TN	M
Trinity Christian College, IL	M
Troy University, AL	M
Truman State University, MO	M
Tulane University, LA	M
Tuskegee University, AL	M
Union College, KY	M
Union University, TN	M
University at Albany, State University of New York, NY	M
University at Buffalo, the State University of New York, NY	M
The University of Akron, OH	M
The University of Alabama, AL	M
The University of Alabama at Birmingham, AL	M
The University of Arizona, AZ	M
University of Bridgeport, CT	M
University of California, Davis, CA	M
University of California, Irvine, CA	M
University of California, Los Angeles, CA	M
University of California, Riverside, CA	M
University of California, Santa Barbara, CA	M
University of Central Arkansas, AR	M
University of Central Florida, FL	M
University of Charleston, WV	M
University of Cincinnati, OH	M
University of Connecticut, CT	M
University of Dayton, OH	M
University of Delaware, DE	M
University of Evansville, IN	M
University of Florida, FL	M
University of Georgia, GA	M
University of Hartford, CT	M
University of Hawaii at Hilo, HI	M
University of Hawaii at Manoa, HI	M
University of Houston, TX	M
University of Illinois at Chicago, IL	M
University of Illinois at Springfield, IL	M
University of Illinois at Urbana–Champaign, IL	M
The University of Iowa, IA	M
The University of Kansas, KS	M
University of Louisiana at Lafayette, LA	M
University of Louisville, KY	M
University of Maryland, Baltimore County, MD	M
University of Maryland, College Park, MD	M
University of Maryland Eastern Shore, MD	M
University of Massachusetts Amherst, MA	M
University of Memphis, TN	M
University of Miami, FL	M
University of Michigan, MI	M
University of Minnesota, Crookston, MN	M
University of Minnesota, Duluth, MN	M
University of Minnesota, Twin Cities Campus, MN	M
University of Mississippi, MS	M
University of Missouri–St. Louis, MO	M
University of Mobile, AL	M
University of Montevallo, AL	M
University of Nebraska at Kearney, NE	M
University of Nebraska at Omaha, NE	M
University of Nebraska–Lincoln, NE	M
University of Nevada, Las Vegas, NV	M
University of Nevada, Reno, NV	M
University of New Haven, CT	M
University of New Orleans, LA	M
University of North Alabama, AL	M
University of North Carolina at Asheville, NC	M
The University of North Carolina at Chapel Hill, NC	M
The University of North Carolina at Greensboro, NC	M
The University of North Carolina at Pembroke, NC	M
The University of North Carolina Wilmington, NC	M
University of Northern Colorado, CO	M
University of North Florida, FL	M
University of North Georgia, GA	M
University of Notre Dame, IN	M
University of Oklahoma, OK	M
University of Oregon, OR	M
University of Pikeville, KY	M
University of Pittsburgh, PA	M
University of Portland, OR	M
University of Puerto Rico at Bayamón, PR	M
University of Rhode Island, RI	M
University of Richmond, VA	M
University of Rio Grande, OH	M
University of St. Francis, IL	M
University of San Diego, CA	M
University of Science and Arts of Oklahoma, OK	M
University of South Alabama, AL	M
University of South Carolina, SC	M
University of South Carolina Aiken, SC	M
University of South Carolina Upstate, SC	M
University of Southern Indiana, IN	M
University of Southern Mississippi, MS	M
The University of Tampa, FL	M
The University of Tennessee, TN	M
The University of Tennessee at Martin, TN	M
The University of Texas at Arlington, TX	M
The University of Texas at Austin, TX	M
The University of Texas at San Antonio, TX	M
The University of Texas of the Permian Basin, TX	M
The University of Texas–Pan American, TX	M
University of the Cumberlands, KY	M
University of the Incarnate Word, TX	M
University of the Pacific, CA	M
University of the Sciences, PA	M
The University of Toledo, OH	M
University of Utah, UT	M
University of Virginia, VA	M
The University of Virginia's College at Wise, VA	M
The University of West Alabama, AL	M
University of West Florida, FL	M
University of West Georgia, GA	M
University of Wisconsin–Milwaukee, WI	M
University of Wisconsin–Parkside, WI	M
Upper Iowa University, IA	M
Utah Valley University, UT	M
Valdosta State University, GA	M
Valley City State University, ND	M
Valparaiso University, IN	M
Vanderbilt University, TN	M
Villanova University, PA	M
Virginia Commonwealth University, VA	M
Virginia Intermont College, VA	M
Virginia State University, VA	M
Wagner College, NY	M
Wake Forest University, NC	M
Waldorf College, IA	M
Washburn University, KS	M
Washington State University, WA	M
Wayland Baptist University, TX	M
Wayne State College, NE	M
Wayne State University, MI	M
Webber International University, FL	M
West Chester University of Pennsylvania, PA	M
Western Carolina University, NC	M
Western Illinois University, IL	M
Western Kentucky University, KY	M
Western Michigan University, MI	M
Western Oregon University, OR	M
West Texas A&M University, TX	M
West Virginia University, WV	M
West Virginia University Institute of Technology, WV	M
West Virginia Wesleyan College, WV	M
Wheeling Jesuit University, WV	M
Wichita State University, KS	M
William Jewell College, MO	M
Winona State University, MN	M
Winthrop University, SC	M
Wofford College, SC	M
Wright State University, OH	M
Xavier University, OH	M
Young Harris College, GA	M
Youngstown State University, OH	M

Basketball

Abilene Christian University, TX	M,W
Academy of Art University, CA	M,W
Adams State University, CO	M,W
Adelphi University, NY	M,W
Alabama State University, AL	M,W
Alcorn State University, MS	M,W

American University, DC	M,W
Anderson University, SC	M,W
Angelo State University, TX	M,W
Appalachian State University, NC	M,W
Arizona State University, AZ	M,W
Arkansas State University, AR	M,W
Arkansas Tech University, AR	M,W
Armstrong Atlantic State University, GA	M,W
Asbury University, KY	M,W
Ashland University, OH	M,W
Assumption College, MA	M,W
Auburn University, AL	M,W
Auburn University at Montgomery, AL	M,W
Augustana College, SD	M,W
Austin Peay State University, TN	M,W
Azusa Pacific University, CA	M,W
Ball State University, IN	M,W
Barry University, FL	M,W
Barton College, NC	M,W
Baylor University, TX	M,W
Belhaven University, MS	M,W
Bellarmine University, KY	M,W
Belmont Abbey College, NC	M,W
Belmont University, TN	M,W
Bemidji State University, MN	M,W
Benedictine College, KS	M,W
Bentley University, MA	M,W
Bethel College, IN	M,W
Bethel College, KS	M,W
Bethune-Cookman University, FL	M,W
Binghamton University, State University of New York, NY	M,W
Biola University, CA	M,W
Bloomfield College, NJ	M,W
Bloomsburg University of Pennsylvania, PA	M,W
Bluefield College, VA	M,W
Bluefield State College, WV	M,W
Blue Mountain College, MS	M,W
Boise State University, ID	M,W
Boston College, MA	M,W
Boston University, MA	M,W
Bowie State University, MD	M,W
Bowling Green State University, OH	M,W
Bradley University, IL	M,W
Brevard College, NC	M,W
Brigham Young University, UT	M,W
Bryant University, RI	M,W
Bucknell University, PA	M,W
Butler University, IN	M,W
Caldwell College, NJ	M,W
California Baptist University, CA	M,W
California Polytechnic State University, San Luis Obispo, CA	M,W
California State Polytechnic University, Pomona, CA	M,W
California State University, Chico, CA	M,W
California State University, Dominguez Hills, CA	M,W
California State University, Fresno, CA	M,W
California State University, Fullerton, CA	M,W
California State University, Long Beach, CA	M,W
California State University, Los Angeles, CA	M,W
California State University, Monterey Bay, CA	M,W
California State University, Northridge, CA	M,W
California State University, San Bernardino, CA	M,W
Calumet College of Saint Joseph, IN	M,W
Cameron University, OK	M,W
Campbellsville University, KY	M,W
Canisius College, NY	M,W
Carroll College, MT	M,W
Carson-Newman University, TN	M,W
Catawba College, NC	M,W
Cedarville University, OH	M,W
Central Connecticut State University, CT	M,W
Central Methodist University, MO	M,W
Central Michigan University, MI	M,W
Chestnut Hill College, PA	M,W
Chicago State University, IL	M,W
Chowan University, NC	M,W
Christian Brothers University, TN	M,W
Cincinnati Christian University, OH	M,W
The Citadel, The Military College of South Carolina, SC	M
Clarion University of Pennsylvania, PA	M,W
Clarke University, IA	M,W
Clayton State University, GA	M,W
Clemson University, SC	M,W
Cleveland State University, OH	M,W
Coastal Carolina University, SC	M,W
Coker College, SC	M,W
Colgate University, NY	M,W
College of Charleston, SC	M,W
The College of Idaho, ID	M,W
College of Saint Mary, NE	W
The College of Saint Rose, NY	M,W
College of the Holy Cross, MA	M,W
College of the Ozarks, MO	M,W
The College of William and Mary, VA	M,W
Colorado Mesa University, CO	M,W
Colorado School of Mines, CO	M,W
Colorado State University, CO	M,W
Columbia College, MO	M,W
Columbus State University, GA	M,W
Concordia University, CA	M,W
Concordia University, OR	M,W
Concordia University, Nebraska, NE	M,W
Concordia University, St. Paul, MN	M,W
Converse College, SC	W
Corban University, OR	M,W
Cornerstone University, MI	M,W
Creighton University, NE	M,W
Culver-Stockton College, MO	M,W
Dakota State University, SD	M,W
Dakota Wesleyan University, SD	M,W
Dallas Baptist University, TX	M
Davenport University, MI	M,W
Davidson College, NC	M,W
DePaul University, IL	M,W
Dillard University, LA	M,W
Doane College, NE	M,W
Dominican College, NY	M,W
Dordt College, IA	M,W
Drake University, IA	M,W
Drury University, MO	M,W
Duquesne University, PA	M,W
East Carolina University, NC	M,W
Eastern Illinois University, IL	M,W
Eastern Michigan University, MI	M,W
Eastern New Mexico University, NM	M,W
Eastern Washington University, WA	M,W
Eckerd College, FL	M,W
Edinboro University of Pennsylvania, PA	M,W
Elizabeth City State University, NC	M,W
Elon University, NC	M,W
Embry-Riddle Aeronautical University–Daytona, FL	M
Emmanuel College, GA	M,W
Emporia State University, KS	M,W
Evangel University, MO	M,W
The Evergreen State College, WA	M,W
Fairfield University, CT	M,W
Fairmont State University, WV	M,W
Faulkner University, AL	M,W
Fayetteville State University, NC	M,W
Felician College, NJ	M,W
Ferris State University, MI	M,W
Flagler College, FL	M,W
Florida Agricultural and Mechanical University, FL	M,W
Florida Atlantic University, FL	M,W
Florida Gulf Coast University, FL	M,W
Florida Institute of Technology, FL	M,W
Florida International University, FL	M,W
Florida Southern College, FL	M,W
Florida State University, FL	M,W
Fort Lewis College, CO	M,W
Francis Marion University, SC	M,W
Franklin Pierce University, NH	M,W
Freed-Hardeman University, TN	M,W
Furman University, SC	M,W
Gannon University, PA	M,W
Gardner-Webb University, NC	M,W
George Mason University, VA	M,W
Georgetown College, KY	M,W
Georgetown University, DC	M,W
The George Washington University, DC	M,W
Georgia College & State University, GA	M,W
Georgia Institute of Technology, GA	M,W
Georgia Southern University, GA	M,W
Georgia Southwestern State University, GA	M,W
Georgia State University, GA	M,W
Goldey-Beacom College, DE	M,W
Gonzaga University, WA	M,W
Goshen College, IN	M,W
Graceland University, IA	M,W
Grand Valley State University, MI	M,W
Grand View University, IA	M,W
Hampton University, VA	M,W
Harding University, AR	M,W
Hawai`i Pacific University, HI	M,W
Henderson State University, AR	M,W
Hillsdale College, MI	M,W
Hofstra University, NY	M,W
Hope International University, CA	M,W
Houston Baptist University, TX	M,W
Huntington University, IN	M,W
Idaho State University, ID	M,W
Illinois State University, IL	M,W
Indiana State University, IN	M,W
Indiana Tech, IN	M,W
Indiana University Bloomington, IN	M,W
Indiana University of Pennsylvania, PA	M,W
Indiana University–Purdue University Fort Wayne, IN	M,W
Indiana University–Purdue University Indianapolis, IN	M,W
Indiana University South Bend, IN	M,W
Indiana University Southeast, IN	M,W
Indiana Wesleyan University, IN	M,W

College	
Inter American University of Puerto Rico, Bayamón Campus, PR	M,W
Inter American University of Puerto Rico, Ponce Campus, PR	M,W
Iona College, NY	M,W
Iowa State University of Science and Technology, IA	M,W
Jacksonville State University, AL	M,W
Jacksonville University, FL	M,W
James Madison University, VA	M,W
John Brown University, AR	M,W
Johnson C. Smith University, NC	M,W
Kansas State University, KS	M,W
Kennesaw State University, GA	M,W
Kent State University, OH	M,W
Kentucky State University, KY	M,W
Kentucky Wesleyan College, KY	M,W
King College, TN	M,W
Kutztown University of Pennsylvania, PA	M,W
Lake Erie College, OH	M,W
Lake Superior State University, MI	M,W
Lamar University, TX	M,W
Lane College, TN	M,W
La Salle University, PA	M,W
Lawrence Technological University, MI	M,W
Lees-McRae College, NC	M,W
Lee University, TN	M,W
Lehigh University, PA	M,W
Le Moyne College, NY	M,W
Lewis-Clark State College, ID	M,W
Lewis University, IL	M,W
Liberty University, VA	M,W
Limestone College, SC	M,W
Lincoln University, MO	M,W
Lindenwood University, MO	M,W
Lindsey Wilson College, KY	M,W
Lipscomb University, TN	M,W
Lock Haven University of Pennsylvania, PA	M,W
Long Island University– Brooklyn Campus, NY	M,W
Long Island University–C. W. Post Campus, NY	M,W
Longwood University, VA	M,W
Louisiana State University and Agricultural and Mechanical College, LA	M,W
Louisiana Tech University, LA	M,W
Lourdes University, OH	M,W
Loyola Marymount University, CA	M,W
Loyola University Chicago, IL	M,W
Loyola University Maryland, MD	M,W
Loyola University New Orleans, LA	M,W
Lubbock Christian University, TX	M,W
Lynn University, FL	M,W
Lyon College, AR	M,W
Malone University, OH	M,W
Manhattan College, NY	M,W
Mansfield University of Pennsylvania, PA	M,W
Marist College, NY	M,W
Marquette University, WI	M,W
Marshall University, WV	M,W
Maryville University of Saint Louis, MO	M,W
The Master's College and Seminary, CA	M,W
Mayville State University, ND	M,W
McKendree University, IL	M,W
McNeese State University, LA	M,W
Menlo College, CA	M,W
Mercer University, GA	M,W
Mercy College, NY	M,W
Mercyhurst University, PA	M,W
Merrimack College, MA	M,W
Metropolitan State University of Denver, CO	M,W
Miami University, OH	M,W
Michigan State University, MI	M,W
Middle Tennessee State University, TN	M,W
Midwestern State University, TX	M,W
Millersville University of Pennsylvania, PA	M,W
Minnesota State University Mankato, MN	M,W
Minot State University, ND	M,W
Mississippi State University, MS	M,W
Missouri Baptist University, MO	M,W
Missouri State University, MO	M,W
Missouri University of Science and Technology, MO	M,W
Missouri Western State University, MO	M,W
Molloy College, NY	M,W
Monmouth University, NJ	M,W
Montana State University, MT	M,W
Montana Tech of The University of Montana, MT	M,W
Montreat College, NC	M,W
Morehead State University, KY	M,W
Morehouse College, GA	M
Morningside College, IA	M,W
Mount Marty College, SD	M,W
Mount Mercy University, IA	M,W
Mount St. Mary's University, MD	M,W
Mount Vernon Nazarene University, OH	M,W
Murray State University, KY	M,W
Newberry College, SC	M,W
New Jersey Institute of Technology, NJ	M,W
New Mexico Highlands University, NM	M,W
New Mexico State University, NM	M,W
New York Institute of Technology, NY	M,W
Niagara University, NY	M,W
Nicholls State University, LA	M,W
Norfolk State University, VA	M,W
North Carolina Central University, NC	M,W
North Carolina State University, NC	M,W
Northeastern University, MA	M,W
Northern Arizona University, AZ	M,W
Northern Illinois University, IL	M,W
Northern Kentucky University, KY	M,W
Northern Michigan University, MI	M,W
Northern State University, SD	M,W
Northwest Christian University, OR	M,W
Northwestern Oklahoma State University, OK	M,W
Northwestern State University of Louisiana, LA	M,W
Northwest Missouri State University, MO	M,W
Northwest Nazarene University, ID	M,W
Northwest University, WA	M,W
Northwood University, Michigan Campus, MI	M,W
Notre Dame de Namur University, CA	M,W
Nova Southeastern University, FL	M,W
Nyack College, NY	M,W
Oakland University, MI	M,W
The Ohio State University, OH	M,W
Ohio University, OH	M,W
Ohio Valley University, WV	M,W
Oklahoma Baptist University, OK	M,W
Oklahoma Christian University, OK	M,W
Oklahoma City University, OK	M,W
Oklahoma State University, OK	M,W
Old Dominion University, VA	M,W
Oral Roberts University, OK	M,W
Oregon State University, OR	M,W
Ouachita Baptist University, AR	M,W
Pace University, NY	M,W
Palm Beach Atlantic University, FL	M,W
Park University, MO	M,W
Penn State University Park, PA	M,W
Pepperdine University, CA	M,W
Philadelphia University, PA	M,W
Pittsburg State University, KS	M,W
Point Loma Nazarene University, CA	M,W
Point Park University, PA	M,W
Polytechnic University of Puerto Rico, PR	M
Post University, CT	M,W
Presbyterian College, SC	M,W
Providence College, RI	M,W
Purdue University, IN	M,W
Purdue University Calumet, IN	M,W
Purdue University North Central, IN	M
Queens College of the City University of New York, NY	M,W
Quincy University, IL	M,W
Quinnipiac University, CT	M,W
Radford University, VA	M,W
Regis University, CO	M,W
Research College of Nursing, MO	M,W
Rice University, TX	M,W
Rider University, NJ	M,W
Robert Morris University, PA	M,W
Robert Morris University Illinois, IL	M,W
Roberts Wesleyan College, NY	M,W
Rockhurst University, MO	M,W
Rocky Mountain College, MT	M,W
Rogers State University, OK	M,W
Rollins College, FL	M,W
Sacred Heart University, CT	M,W
Saginaw Valley State University, MI	M,W
St. Ambrose University, IA	M,W
Saint Anselm College, NH	M,W
St. Bonaventure University, NY	M,W
St. Edward's University, TX	M,W
St. John's University, NY	M,W
Saint Joseph's College, IN	M,W
Saint Joseph's University, PA	M,W
Saint Louis University, MO	M,W
Saint Martin's University, WA	M,W
Saint Mary-of-the-Woods College, IN	W
Saint Mary's College of California, CA	M,W
Saint Michael's College, VT	M,W
Saint Peter's University, NJ	M,W
Samford University, AL	M,W
Sam Houston State University, TX	M,W
San Diego Christian College, CA	M,W
San Diego State University, CA	M,W
San Francisco State University, CA	M,W
San Jose State University, CA	M,W
Santa Clara University, CA	M,W
Seattle Pacific University, WA	M,W
Seattle University, WA	M,W
Seton Hill University, PA	M,W
Shawnee State University, OH	M,W
Shepherd University, WV	M,W

Shippensburg University of Pennsylvania, PA	M,W
Siena College, NY	M,W
Simpson University, CA	M,W
Slippery Rock University of Pennsylvania, PA	M,W
Sonoma State University, CA	M,W
South Dakota State University, SD	M,W
Southeastern Louisiana University, LA	M,W
Southeastern Oklahoma State University, OK	M,W
Southeast Missouri State University, MO	M,W
Southern Arkansas University–Magnolia, AR	M,W
Southern Connecticut State University, CT	M,W
Southern Illinois University Carbondale, IL	M,W
Southern Illinois University Edwardsville, IL	M,W
Southern Methodist University, TX	M,W
Southern Polytechnic State University, GA	M,W
Southern Utah University, UT	M,W
Southwest Baptist University, MO	M,W
Southwestern College, KS	M,W
Spring Arbor University, MI	M,W
Spring Hill College, AL	M,W
Stanford University, CA	M,W
Stephen F. Austin State University, TX	M,W
Stephens College, MO	W
Stetson University, FL	M,W
Stonehill College, MA	M,W
Stony Brook University, State University of New York, NY	M,W
Syracuse University, NY	M,W
Tarleton State University, TX	M,W
Taylor University, IN	M,W
Temple University, PA	M,W
Tennessee State University, TN	M,W
Tennessee Wesleyan College, TN	M,W
Texas A&M International University, TX	M,W
Texas A&M University, TX	M,W
Texas A&M University–Commerce, TX	M,W
Texas Christian University, TX	M,W
Texas Southern University, TX	M,W
Texas State University–San Marcos, TX	M,W
Texas Wesleyan University, TX	M,W
Texas Woman's University, TX	W
Tiffin University, OH	M,W
Trevecca Nazarene University, TN	M,W
Trinity Christian College, IL	M,W
Troy University, AL	M,W
Truman State University, MO	M,W
Tulane University, LA	M,W
Tuskegee University, AL	M,W
Union College, KY	M,W
Union University, TN	M,W
University at Albany, State University of New York, NY	M,W
University at Buffalo, the State University of New York, NY	M,W
The University of Akron, OH	M,W
The University of Alabama, AL	M,W
The University of Alabama at Birmingham, AL	M,W
University of Alaska Anchorage, AK	M,W
University of Alaska Fairbanks, AK	M,W
The University of Arizona, AZ	M,W
University of Bridgeport, CT	M,W
University of California, Davis, CA	M,W
University of California, Irvine, CA	M,W
University of California, Los Angeles, CA	M,W
University of California, Riverside, CA	M,W
University of California, Santa Barbara, CA	M,W
University of Central Arkansas, AR	M,W
University of Central Florida, FL	M,W
University of Charleston, WV	M,W
University of Cincinnati, OH	M,W
University of Colorado Boulder, CO	M,W
University of Colorado Colorado Springs, CO	M,W
University of Connecticut, CT	M,W
University of Dayton, OH	M,W
University of Delaware, DE	M,W
University of Denver, CO	M,W
University of Evansville, IN	M,W
University of Florida, FL	M,W
University of Georgia, GA	M,W
University of Great Falls, MT	M,W
University of Hartford, CT	M,W
University of Hawaii at Hilo, HI	M
University of Hawaii at Manoa, HI	M,W
University of Houston, TX	M,W
University of Idaho, ID	M,W
University of Illinois at Chicago, IL	M,W
University of Illinois at Springfield, IL	M,W
University of Illinois at Urbana–Champaign, IL	M,W
The University of Iowa, IA	M,W
The University of Kansas, KS	M,W
University of Louisiana at Lafayette, LA	M,W
University of Louisville, KY	M,W
University of Maryland, Baltimore County, MD	M,W
University of Maryland, College Park, MD	M,W
University of Maryland Eastern Shore, MD	M,W
University of Massachusetts Amherst, MA	M,W
University of Memphis, TN	M,W
University of Miami, FL	M,W
University of Michigan, MI	M,W
University of Michigan–Dearborn, MI	M,W
University of Minnesota, Crookston, MN	M,W
University of Minnesota, Duluth, MN	M,W
University of Minnesota, Twin Cities Campus, MN	M,W
University of Mississippi, MS	M,W
University of Missouri–Kansas City, MO	M,W
University of Missouri–St. Louis, MO	M,W
University of Mobile, AL	M,W
The University of Montana Western, MT	M,W
University of Montevallo, AL	M,W
University of Nebraska at Kearney, NE	M,W
University of Nebraska at Omaha, NE	M,W
University of Nebraska–Lincoln, NE	M,W
University of Nevada, Las Vegas, NV	M,W
University of Nevada, Reno, NV	M,W
University of New Hampshire, NH	M,W
University of New Haven, CT	M,W
University of New Orleans, LA	M,W
University of North Alabama, AL	M,W
University of North Carolina at Asheville, NC	M,W
The University of North Carolina at Chapel Hill, NC	M,W
The University of North Carolina at Greensboro, NC	M,W
The University of North Carolina at Pembroke, NC	M,W
The University of North Carolina Wilmington, NC	M,W
University of Northern Colorado, CO	M,W
University of Northern Iowa, IA	M,W
University of North Florida, FL	M,W
University of North Georgia, GA	M,W
University of North Texas, TX	M,W
University of Notre Dame, IN	M,W
University of Oklahoma, OK	M,W
University of Oregon, OR	M,W
University of Pikeville, KY	M,W
University of Pittsburgh, PA	M,W
University of Portland, OR	M,W
University of Puerto Rico at Bayamón, PR	M,W
University of Rhode Island, RI	M
University of Richmond, VA	M,W
University of Rio Grande, OH	M,W
University of St. Francis, IL	M,W
University of St. Thomas, TX	M,W
University of San Diego, CA	M,W
University of Science and Arts of Oklahoma, OK	M,W
University of South Alabama, AL	M,W
University of South Carolina, SC	M,W
University of South Carolina Aiken, SC	M,W
University of South Carolina Upstate, SC	M,W
The University of South Dakota, SD	M,W
University of Southern Indiana, IN	M,W
University of Southern Mississippi, MS	M,W
The University of Tampa, FL	M,W
The University of Tennessee, TN	M,W
The University of Tennessee at Chattanooga, TN	M,W
The University of Tennessee at Martin, TN	M,W
The University of Texas at Arlington, TX	M,W
The University of Texas at Austin, TX	M,W
The University of Texas at El Paso, TX	M,W
The University of Texas at San Antonio, TX	M,W
The University of Texas of the Permian Basin, TX	M,W
The University of Texas–Pan American, TX	M,W
University of the Cumberlands, KY	M,W
University of the Incarnate Word, TX	M,W
University of the Pacific, CA	M,W
University of the Sciences, PA	M,W
The University of Toledo, OH	M,W

University of Tulsa, OK	M,W	Bellarmine University, KY	W	Davenport University, MI	W
University of Utah, UT	M,W	Bethune-Cookman University, FL	W	Doane College, NE	W
University of Vermont, VT	M,W	Calumet College of Saint Joseph,		Drake University, IA	M,W
University of Virginia, VA	M,W	IN	M,W	Drury University, MO	M,W
The University of Virginia's		Campbellsville University, KY	M,W	Eastern New Mexico University, NM	M,W
College at Wise, VA	M,W	Clarke University, IA	M,W	Emmanuel College, GA	W
The University of West Alabama, AL	M,W	Davenport University, MI	M,W	Emporia State University, KS	M,W
University of West Florida, FL	M,W	Elizabeth City State University,		Faulkner University, AL	M,W
University of West Georgia, GA	M,W	NC	W	Freed-Hardeman University, TN	W
University of Wisconsin–		Florida Agricultural and		Gardner-Webb University, NC	M,W
Green Bay, WI	M,W	Mechanical University, FL	W	George Mason University, VA	M,W
University of Wisconsin–		Grand View University, IA	M,W	Georgetown College, KY	W
Madison, WI	M,W	Hampton University, VA	W	Georgia Institute of Technology,	
University of Wisconsin–		Huntington University, IN	M,W	GA	M,W
Milwaukee, WI	M,W	Indiana Tech, IN	M,W	Graceland University, IA	M,W
University of Wisconsin–		Johnson C. Smith University, NC	W	Grand View University, IA	W
Parkside, WI	M,W	Kutztown University of		Hawai`i Pacific University, HI	M,W
University of Wyoming, WY	M,W	Pennsylvania, PA	W	Hofstra University, NY	M,W
Upper Iowa University, IA	M,W	Lawrence Technological		Houston Baptist University, TX	M,W
Ursuline College, OH	W	University, MI	M	Indiana Tech, IN	M,W
Utah State University, UT	M,W	Lindenwood University, MO	M,W	Indiana Wesleyan University, IN	M,W
Utah Valley University, UT	M,W	Lindsey Wilson College, KY	M,W	John Brown University, AR	M,W
Valdosta State University, GA	M,W	McKendree University, IL	W	Kentucky State University, KY	W
Valley City State University, ND	M,W	Missouri Baptist University, MO	M,W	King College, TN	M,W
Valparaiso University, IN	M,W	Monmouth University, NJ	W	Lee University, TN	M,W
Vanderbilt University, TN	M,W	North Carolina Central		Lewis University, IL	W
Villanova University, PA	M,W	University, NC	W	Liberty University, VA	M,W
Virginia Commonwealth		Robert Morris University		Limestone College, SC	M,W
University, VA	M,W	Illinois, IL	M,W	Lincoln University, MO	W
Virginia Intermont College, VA	M,W	Sacred Heart University, CT	W	Lindenwood University, MO	M,W
Virginia State University, VA	M,W	Saginaw Valley State University,		Lindsey Wilson College, KY	M,W
Virginia Union University, VA	M,W	MI	M	Lourdes University, OH	M,W
Wagner College, NY	M,W	St. Ambrose University, IA	M,W	Maryville University of Saint	
Wake Forest University, NC	M,W	Sam Houston State University, TX	W	Louis, MO	M,W
Waldorf College, IA	M,W	Stephen F. Austin State		McKendree University, IL	W
Warner Pacific College, OR	M,W	University, TX	W	Menlo College, CA	M,W
Washburn University, KS	M,W	Texas Southern University, TX	W	Middle Tennessee State	
Washington State University, WA	M,W	Union College, KY	M,W	University, TN	M,W
Wayland Baptist University, TX	M,W	University of Nebraska–		Midwestern State University, TX	M,W
Wayne State College, NE	M,W	Lincoln, NE	W	Mississippi State University, MS	M,W
Wayne State University, MI	M,W	University of Pikeville, KY	M,W	Missouri Baptist University, MO	M,W
Webber International University,		University of the Cumberlands, KY	M,W	Montana State University, MT	M,W
FL	M,W	Ursuline College, OH	W	Newberry College, SC	M,W
West Chester University of		Valparaiso University, IN	W	North Carolina State University,	
Pennsylvania, PA	M,W	Vanderbilt University, TN	W	NC	M,W
Western Carolina University, NC	M,W	Virginia State University, VA	W	Northern State University, SD	W
Western Illinois University, IL	M,W	Webber International University,		Northwestern Oklahoma State	
Western Kentucky University, KY	M,W	FL	M,W	University, OK	M,W
Western Michigan University, MI	M,W	West Texas A&M University, TX	M,W	Northwest Missouri State	
Western Oregon University, OR	M,W	Wichita State University, KS	M,W	University, MO	M,W
Western State Colorado				Northwood University, Michigan	
University, CO	M,W	**Cheerleading**		Campus, MI	M,W
Western Washington University, WA	M,W	Adelphi University, NY	W	Nyack College, NY	M,W
Westminster College, UT	M,W	Alabama State University, AL	M,W	Oklahoma City University, OK	M,W
West Texas A&M University, TX	M,W	Anderson University, SC	W	Old Dominion University, VA	W
West Virginia State University, WV	M,W	Arkansas Tech University, AR	M,W	Penn State University Park, PA	M,W
West Virginia University, WV	M,W	Ashland University, OH	W	Pittsburg State University, KS	M,W
West Virginia University		Auburn University at Montgomery,		Presbyterian College, SC	M,W
Institute of Technology, WV	M,W	AL	M,W	Robert Morris University	
West Virginia Wesleyan College, WV	M,W	Austin Peay State University, TN	M,W	Illinois, IL	M,W
Wheeling Jesuit University, WV	M,W	Baylor University, TX	M,W	Rocky Mountain College, MT	W
Wichita State University, KS	M,W	Benedictine College, KS	M,W	Rogers State University, OK	M,W
William Jewell College, MO	M,W	Bethel College, IN	M,W	St. Ambrose University, IA	M,W
Winona State University, MN	M,W	Brevard College, NC	W	St. Edward's University, TX	M,W
Winthrop University, SC	M,W	Brigham Young University, UT	M,W	Saint Joseph's College, IN	M,W
Wofford College, SC	M,W	California Baptist University, CA	M,W	Southeastern Louisiana	
Wright State University, OH	M,W	Cameron University, OK	M,W	University, LA	M,W
Xavier University, OH	M,W	Campbellsville University, KY	M,W	Southeast Missouri State	
Xavier University of Louisiana, LA	M,W	Carroll College, MT	M,W	University, MO	M,W
Young Harris College, GA	M,W	Catawba College, NC	M,W	Southern Arkansas	
Youngstown State University, OH	M,W	Clayton State University, GA	W	University–Magnolia, AR	M,W
		Columbus State University, GA	M,W	Southern Methodist University, TX	M,W
Bowling		Concordia University, CA	M,W	Southern Utah University, UT	M,W
Adelphi University, NY	W	Cornerstone University, MI	W	Southwestern College, KS	M,W
Alabama State University, AL	W	Culver-Stockton College, MO	M,W	Tarleton State University, TX	M,W
Arkansas State University, AR		Dakota Wesleyan University, SD	M,W	Temple University, PA	M,W

Tennessee Wesleyan College, TN	M,W
Texas A&M University–Commerce, TX	M,W
Texas Wesleyan University, TX	M,W
Tiffin University, OH	M,W
Union College, KY	M,W
Union University, TN	W
The University of Alabama, AL	M,W
University of Central Arkansas, AR	M,W
University of Central Florida, FL	M,W
University of Charleston, WV	W
University of Delaware, DE	M,W
University of Florida, FL	M,W
University of Great Falls, MT	M,W
University of Hawaii at Manoa, HI	M,W
University of Maryland, College Park, MD	W
University of Memphis, TN	M,W
University of Mississippi, MS	M,W
University of Mobile, AL	W
University of Nevada, Las Vegas, NV	M,W
University of North Alabama, AL	M,W
The University of North Carolina Wilmington, NC	W
University of Oklahoma, OK	M,W
University of Pikeville, KY	M,W
University of Puerto Rico at Bayamón, PR	M,W
University of Rhode Island, RI	M,W
University of St. Francis, IL	W
University of Science and Arts of Oklahoma, OK	M,W
University of South Carolina, SC	M,W
University of South Carolina Upstate, SC	M,W
The University of Tennessee at Martin, TN	W
The University of Texas of the Permian Basin, TX	M,W
University of the Cumberlands, KY	M,W
University of the Incarnate Word, TX	W
University of Utah, UT	M,W
University of West Georgia, GA	M,W
University of Wyoming, WY	M,W
Waldorf College, IA	W
Washburn University, KS	M,W
Wayland Baptist University, TX	M,W
Webber International University, FL	M,W
West Virginia University Institute of Technology, WV	M,W
William Jewell College, MO	M,W
Young Harris College, GA	M,W

Crew

Barry University, FL	W
Boston College, MA	W
Boston University, MA	M,W
Clemson University, SC	W
Creighton University, NE	W
Duquesne University, PA	W
Eastern Michigan University, MI	W
Fairfield University, CT	M,W
Florida Institute of Technology, FL	M,W
George Mason University, VA	W
The George Washington University, DC	M,W
Gonzaga University, WA	W
Indiana University Bloomington, IN	W
Jacksonville University, FL	M,W
Kansas State University, KS	W
La Salle University, PA	M,W

Lehigh University, PA	W
Loyola Marymount University, CA	W
Loyola University Maryland, MD	M,W
Marist College, NY	W
Mercyhurst University, PA	M,W
Merrimack College, MA	W
Michigan State University, MI	W
Northeastern University, MA	M,W
Nova Southeastern University, FL	W
Oklahoma City University, OK	M,W
Old Dominion University, VA	W
Robert Morris University, PA	W
Saint Joseph's University, PA	M,W
Saint Mary's College of California, CA	W
San Diego State University, CA	W
Seattle Pacific University, WA	W
Southern Methodist University, TX	W
Stanford University, CA	M,W
Stetson University, FL	W
Syracuse University, NY	M,W
Temple University, PA	M,W
University at Buffalo, the State University of New York, NY	W
The University of Alabama, AL	W
University of California, Los Angeles, CA	W
University of Central Florida, FL	W
University of Charleston, WV	M,W
University of Delaware, DE	W
The University of Iowa, IA	W
The University of Kansas, KS	W
University of Louisville, KY	W
University of Massachusetts Amherst, MA	W
University of Miami, FL	W
The University of North Carolina at Chapel Hill, NC	W
University of Notre Dame, IN	W
University of Oklahoma, OK	W
University of Rhode Island, RI	M
University of San Diego, CA	W
The University of Tampa, FL	W
The University of Tennessee, TN	W
The University of Texas at Austin, TX	W
University of Tulsa, OK	W
University of Virginia, VA	W
Washington State University, WA	W
Western Washington University, WA	M,W
West Virginia University, WV	W

Cross-country running

Abilene Christian University, TX	M,W
Academy of Art University, CA	M,W
Adams State University, CO	M,W
Adelphi University, NY	M,W
Alabama State University, AL	M,W
Alcorn State University, MS	M,W
American University, DC	M,W
Anderson University, SC	M,W
Angelo State University, TX	M,W
Appalachian State University, NC	M,W
Arizona State University, AZ	M,W
Arkansas State University, AR	M,W
Arkansas Tech University, AR	W
Armstrong Atlantic State University, GA	M
Asbury University, KY	M,W
Ashland University, OH	M,W
Auburn University, AL	M,W
Auburn University at Montgomery, AL	M,W
Augustana College, SD	M,W

Austin Peay State University, TN	M,W
Azusa Pacific University, CA	M,W
Ball State University, IN	W
Barton College, NC	M,W
Baylor University, TX	M,W
Belhaven University, MS	M,W
Bellarmine University, KY	M,W
Belmont Abbey College, NC	M,W
Belmont University, TN	M,W
Bemidji State University, MN	W
Benedictine College, KS	M,W
Bethel College, IN	M,W
Bethel College, KS	M,W
Bethune-Cookman University, FL	M,W
Binghamton University, State University of New York, NY	M,W
Biola University, CA	M,W
Bloomfield College, NJ	M,W
Bloomsburg University of Pennsylvania, PA	M,W
Bluefield College, VA	M,W
Bluefield State College, WV	M,W
Blue Mountain College, MS	M,W
Boise State University, ID	M,W
Boston College, MA	M,W
Boston University, MA	M,W
Bowie State University, MD	M,W
Bowling Green State University, OH	M,W
Bradley University, IL	M,W
Brevard College, NC	M,W
Brigham Young University, UT	M,W
Bryant University, RI	M,W
Bucknell University, PA	W
Butler University, IN	W
Caldwell College, NJ	W
California Baptist University, CA	M,W
California Polytechnic State University, San Luis Obispo, CA	M,W
California State Polytechnic University, Pomona, CA	M,W
California State University, Chico, CA	
California State University, Fresno, CA	M,W
California State University, Fullerton, CA	M,W
California State University, Long Beach, CA	M,W
California State University, Los Angeles, CA	W
California State University, Monterey Bay, CA	M,W
California State University, Northridge, CA	M,W
Calumet College of Saint Joseph, IN	M,W
Cameron University, OK	M
Campbellsville University, KY	M,W
Canisius College, NY	M,W
Carroll College, MT	M,W
Carson-Newman University, TN	M,W
Catawba College, NC	M,W
Cedarville University, OH	M,W
Central Connecticut State University, CT	M,W
Central Methodist University, MO	M,W
Central Michigan University, MI	M,W
Chestnut Hill College, PA	M,W
Chicago State University, IL	M,W
Chowan University, NC	M,W
Christian Brothers University, TN	M,W
Cincinnati Christian University, OH	M,W
The Citadel, The Military College of South Carolina, SC	M,W

Clarion University of Pennsylvania, PA	W	Gannon University, PA	M,W	Limestone College, SC	M,W
Clarke University, IA	M,W	Gardner-Webb University, NC	M,W	Lincoln University, MO	W
Clayton State University, GA	M,W	George Mason University, VA	M,W	Lindenwood University, MO	M,W
Cleary University, MI	M,W	Georgetown College, KY	M,W	Lindsey Wilson College, KY	M,W
Clemson University, SC	M,W	Georgetown University, DC	M,W	Lipscomb University, TN	M,W
Cleveland State University, OH	W	The George Washington University, DC	M,W	Lock Haven University of Pennsylvania, PA	M,W
Coastal Carolina University, SC	M,W	Georgia College & State University, GA	M,W	Long Island University–Brooklyn Campus, NY	M,W
Coker College, SC	M,W	Georgia Institute of Technology, GA	M,W	Long Island University–C. W. Post Campus, NY	M,W
College of Charleston, SC	M,W	Georgia Southern University, GA	W	Longwood University, VA	M,W
The College of Idaho, ID	M,W	Georgia Southwestern State University, GA	W	Louisiana State University and Agricultural and Mechanical College, LA	M,W
College of Saint Mary, NE	W	Georgia State University, GA	M,W	Louisiana Tech University, LA	M,W
The College of William and Mary, VA	M,W	Goldey-Beacom College, DE	M,W	Lourdes University, OH	M,W
Colorado Mesa University, CO	M,W	Gonzaga University, WA	M,W	Loyola Marymount University, CA	M,W
Colorado School of Mines, CO	M,W	Goshen College, IN	M,W	Loyola University Chicago, IL	M,W
Colorado State University, CO	M,W	Graceland University, IA	M,W	Loyola University Maryland, MD	M,W
Columbia College, MO	M,W	Grand Valley State University, MI	M,W	Lubbock Christian University, TX	M,W
Columbus State University, GA	M,W	Grand View University, IA	M,W	Lynn University, FL	M,W
Concordia University, CA	M,W	Hampton University, VA	M,W	Lyon College, AR	M,W
Concordia University, OR	M,W	Harding University, AR	M,W	Malone University, OH	M,W
Concordia University, Nebraska, NE	M,W	Hawai`i Pacific University, HI	M,W	Manhattan College, NY	M,W
Concordia University, St. Paul, MN	M,W	Henderson State University, AR	W	Mansfield University of Pennsylvania, PA	M,W
Converse College, SC	W	Hillsdale College, MI	M,W	Marist College, NY	M,W
Corban University, OR	M,W	Hofstra University, NY	M,W	Marquette University, WI	M,W
Cornerstone University, MI	M,W	Hope International University, CA	M,W	Marshall University, WV	M,W
Creighton University, NE	M,W	Houston Baptist University, TX	M,W	Maryville University of Saint Louis, MO	M,W
Culver-Stockton College, MO	M,W	Huntington University, IN	M,W	The Master's College and Seminary, CA	M,W
Dakota State University, SD	M,W	Idaho State University, ID	M,W	McKendree University, IL	M,W
Dakota Wesleyan University, SD	M,W	Illinois Institute of Technology, IL	M,W	McNeese State University, LA	M,W
Dallas Baptist University, TX	W	Illinois State University, IL	M,W	Menlo College, CA	M,W
Davenport University, MI	M,W	Indiana State University, IN	M,W	Mercer University, GA	M,W
Davidson College, NC	M,W	Indiana Tech, IN	M,W	Mercyhurst University, PA	M,W
DePaul University, IL	M,W	Indiana University Bloomington, IN	M,W	Merrimack College, MA	M,W
Dillard University, LA	M,W	Indiana University of Pennsylvania, PA	M,W	Miami University, OH	M,W
Doane College, NE	M,W	Indiana University–Purdue University Fort Wayne, IN	M,W	Michigan State University, MI	M,W
Dominican College, NY	W	Indiana University–Purdue University Indianapolis, IN	M,W	Middle Tennessee State University, TN	M,W
Dordt College, IA	M,W	Indiana Wesleyan University, IN	M,W	Midwestern State University, TX	W
Drake University, IA	M,W	Inter American University of Puerto Rico, Bayamón Campus, PR	M,W	Millersville University of Pennsylvania, PA	M,W
Drury University, MO	M,W	Inter American University of Puerto Rico, Ponce Campus, PR	M,W	Minnesota State University Mankato, MN	M,W
Duquesne University, PA	M,W	Iona College, NY	M,W	Minot State University, ND	M,W
East Carolina University, NC	M,W	Iowa State University of Science and Technology, IA	M,W	Mississippi State University, MS	M,W
Eastern Illinois University, IL	M,W	Jacksonville State University, AL	M,W	Missouri Baptist University, MO	M,W
Eastern Michigan University, MI	M,W	Jacksonville University, FL	W	Missouri State University, MO	W
Eastern New Mexico University, NM	M,W	James Madison University, VA	W	Missouri University of Science and Technology, MO	M,W
Eastern Washington University, WA	M,W	John Brown University, AR	M,W	Molloy College, NY	M,W
Edinboro University of Pennsylvania, PA	M,W	Johnson C. Smith University, NC	M,W	Monmouth University, NJ	M,W
Elon University, NC	M,W	Kansas State University, KS	M,W	Montana State University, MT	M,W
Embry-Riddle Aeronautical University–Daytona, FL	M,W	Kennesaw State University, GA	M,W	Montreat College, NC	M,W
Embry-Riddle Aeronautical University–Prescott, AZ	M,W	Kent State University, OH	M,W	Morehead State University, KY	M,W
Emmanuel College, GA	M,W	Kentucky State University, KY	M,W	Morehouse College, GA	M
Emporia State University, KS	M,W	Kentucky Wesleyan College, KY	M,W	Morningside College, IA	M,W
Evangel University, MO	M,W	King College, TN	M,W	Mount Marty College, SD	M,W
The Evergreen State College, WA	M,W	Kutztown University of Pennsylvania, PA	M,W	Mount Mercy University, IA	M,W
Fairfield University, CT	M,W	Lake Erie College, OH	M,W	Mount St. Mary's University, MD	M,W
Fairmont State University, WV	M,W	Lake Superior State University, MI	M,W	Mount Vernon Nazarene University, OH	M,W
Fayetteville State University, NC	M,W	Lamar University, TX	M,W	Murray State University, KY	W
Felician College, NJ	M,W	Lane College, TN	M,W	Newberry College, SC	M,W
Ferris State University, MI	M,W	La Salle University, PA	M,W	New Jersey Institute of Technology, NJ	M,W
Flagler College, FL	M,W	Lees-McRae College, NC	M,W	New Mexico Highlands University, NM	M,W
Florida Agricultural and Mechanical University, FL	M,W	Lee University, TN	M,W	New Mexico State University, NM	M,W
Florida Gulf Coast University, FL	M,W	Lehigh University, PA	M,W		
Florida Institute of Technology, FL	M,W	Le Moyne College, NY	M,W		
Florida International University, FL	M,W	Lewis-Clark State College, ID	M,W		
Florida Southern College, FL	M,W	Lewis University, IL	M,W		
Florida State University, FL	M,W	Liberty University, VA	M,W		
Fort Lewis College, CO	M,W				
Francis Marion University, SC	M,W				
Freed-Hardeman University, TN	M,W				
Furman University, SC	M,W				

New York Institute of Technology, NY	M,W	Saint Louis University, MO	M,W	Tiffin University, OH	M,W
Niagara University, NY	M,W	Saint Martin's University, WA	M,W	Trinity Christian College, IL	M,W
Nicholls State University, LA	M,W	Saint Mary-of-the-Woods College, IN	W	Troy University, AL	M,W
North Carolina Central University, NC	M,W	Saint Mary's College of California, CA	M,W	Truman State University, MO	M,W
North Carolina State University, NC	M,W	Saint Peter's University, NJ	M,W	Tulane University, LA	M,W
Northeastern University, MA	M,W	St. Thomas University, FL	M,W	Union College, KY	M,W
Northern Arizona University, AZ	M,W	Samford University, AL	M,W	Union University, TN	W
Northern Kentucky University, KY	M,W	Sam Houston State University, TX	M,W	University at Albany, State University of New York, NY	M,W
Northern Michigan University, MI	W	San Diego Christian College, CA	M,W	University at Buffalo, the State University of New York, NY	M,W
Northern State University, SD	M,W	San Diego State University, CA	W	The University of Akron, OH	M,W
Northwest Christian University, OR	M,W	San Francisco State University, CA	M,W	The University of Alabama, AL	M,W
Northwestern Oklahoma State University, OK	M,W	San Jose State University, CA	M,W	The University of Alabama at Birmingham, AL	W
Northwestern State University of Louisiana, LA	M,W	Santa Clara University, CA	M,W	University of Alaska Anchorage, AK	M
Northwest Missouri State University, MO	M,W	Savannah College of Art and Design, GA	M,W	University of Alaska Fairbanks, AK	M,W
Northwest Nazarene University, ID	M,W	Seattle Pacific University, WA	M,W	The University of Arizona, AZ	M,W
Northwest University, WA	M,W	Seattle University, WA	M,W	University of Bridgeport, CT	M,W
Northwood University, Michigan Campus, MI	M,W	Seton Hill University, PA	M,W	University of California, Davis, CA	M,W
Northwood University, Texas Campus, TX	M,W	Shawnee State University, OH	M,W	University of California, Irvine, CA	M,W
Notre Dame de Namur University, CA	M,W	Shippensburg University of Pennsylvania, PA	M,W	University of California, Los Angeles, CA	M,W
Nova Southeastern University, FL	M,W	Siena College, NY	M,W	University of California, Riverside, CA	M,W
Nyack College, NY	M,W	Simpson University, CA	M,W	University of California, Santa Barbara, CA	M,W
Oakland University, MI	M,W	Slippery Rock University of Pennsylvania, PA	M,W	University of Central Arkansas, AR	M,W
The Ohio State University, OH	M,W	Soka University of America, CA	M,W	University of Central Florida, FL	W
Ohio University, OH	M,W	Sonoma State University, CA	M	University of Charleston, WV	W
Ohio Valley University, WV	M,W	South Dakota State University, SD	M,W	University of Cincinnati, OH	M,W
Oklahoma Baptist University, OK	M,W	Southeastern Louisiana University, LA	M,W	University of Colorado Boulder, CO	M,W
Oklahoma Christian University, OK	M,W	Southeastern Oklahoma State University, OK	W	University of Colorado Colorado Springs, CO	M,W
Oklahoma State University, OK	M,W	Southeast Missouri State University, MO	M,W	University of Connecticut, CT	M,W
Oral Roberts University, OK	M,W	Southern Arkansas University–Magnolia, AR	M,W	University of Dayton, OH	M,W
Ouachita Baptist University, AR	W	Southern Connecticut State University, CT	M,W	University of Evansville, IN	M,W
Pace University, NY	M,W	Southern Illinois University Carbondale, IL	M,W	University of Florida, FL	M,W
Palm Beach Atlantic University, FL	W	Southern Illinois University Edwardsville, IL	M,W	University of Georgia, GA	M,W
Park University, MO	M,W	Southern Methodist University, TX	W	University of Hartford, CT	M,W
Penn State University Park, PA	M,W	Southern Utah University, UT	M,W	University of Hawaii at Hilo, HI	M,W
Pepperdine University, CA	M,W	Southwest Baptist University, MO	M,W	University of Hawaii at Manoa, HI	W
Pittsburg State University, KS	M,W	Southwestern College, KS	M,W	University of Houston, TX	M,W
Point Loma Nazarene University, CA	M,W	Spring Arbor University, MI	M,W	University of Idaho, ID	M,W
Point Park University, PA	M,W	Spring Hill College, AL	M,W	University of Illinois at Chicago, IL	M,W
Polytechnic University of Puerto Rico, PR	M,W	Stanford University, CA	M,W	University of Illinois at Urbana–Champaign, IL	M,W
Post University, CT	M,W	Stephen F. Austin State University, TX	M,W	The University of Iowa, IA	M,W
Presbyterian College, SC	M,W	Stephens College, MO	W	The University of Kansas, KS	M,W
Providence College, RI	M,W	Stetson University, FL	M,W	University of Louisiana at Lafayette, LA	M,W
Purdue University, IN	M,W	Stonehill College, MA	M,W	University of Louisville, KY	M,W
Queens College of the City University of New York, NY	M,W	Stony Brook University, State University of New York, NY	M,W	University of Maryland, Baltimore County, MD	M,W
Quincy University, IL	M,W	Syracuse University, NY	M,W	University of Maryland, College Park, MD	W
Quinnipiac University, CT	M,W	Tarleton State University, TX	M,W	University of Massachusetts Amherst, MA	M,W
Radford University, VA	M,W	Taylor University, IN	M,W	University of Memphis, TN	M,W
Regis University, CO	M,W	Temple University, PA	M,W	University of Miami, FL	M,W
Rice University, TX	M,W	Tennessee State University, TN	M,W	University of Michigan, MI	M,W
Rider University, NJ	M,W	Tennessee Wesleyan College, TN	M,W	University of Minnesota, Duluth, MN	M,W
Robert Morris University Illinois, IL	M,W	Texas A&M International University, TX	M,W	University of Minnesota, Twin Cities Campus, MN	M,W
Roberts Wesleyan College, NY	M,W	Texas A&M University, TX	M,W	University of Mississippi, MS	M,W
Rocky Mountain College, MT	M,W	Texas A&M University–Commerce, TX	M,W	University of Missouri–Kansas City, MO	M,W
Rogers State University, OK	M,W	Texas Christian University, TX	M,W	University of Mobile, AL	M,W
Sacred Heart University, CT	M,W	Texas Southern University, TX	M,W	University of Nebraska at Kearney, NE	M,W
Saginaw Valley State University, MI	M,W	Texas State University–San Marcos, TX	M,W		
St. Ambrose University, IA	M,W	Texas Wesleyan University, TX	M,W		
Saint Anselm College, NH	M,W				
St. Bonaventure University, NY	M,W				
St. John's University, NY	W				
Saint Joseph's College, IN	M,W				
Saint Joseph's University, PA	M,W				

University of Nebraska–Lincoln, NE	M,W
University of Nevada, Las Vegas, NV	W
University of Nevada, Reno, NV	W
University of New Hampshire, NH	M,W
University of New Haven, CT	M,W
University of New Orleans, LA	M,W
University of North Alabama, AL	M,W
University of North Carolina at Asheville, NC	M,W
The University of North Carolina at Chapel Hill, NC	M,W
The University of North Carolina at Greensboro, NC	M,W
The University of North Carolina at Pembroke, NC	M,W
The University of North Carolina Wilmington, NC	M,W
University of Northern Colorado, CO	W
University of Northern Iowa, IA	M,W
University of North Florida, FL	M,W
University of North Georgia, GA	W
University of North Texas, TX	M,W
University of Notre Dame, IN	M,W
University of Oklahoma, OK	M,W
University of Oregon, OR	M,W
University of Pikeville, KY	M,W
University of Pittsburgh, PA	M,W
University of Portland, OR	M,W
University of Puerto Rico at Bayamón, PR	M,W
University of Rhode Island, RI	M,W
University of Richmond, VA	M,W
University of Rio Grande, OH	M,W
University of St. Francis, IL	M,W
University of San Diego, CA	M,W
University of South Alabama, AL	M,W
University of South Carolina, SC	W
University of South Carolina Aiken, SC	W
University of South Carolina Upstate, SC	M,W
The University of South Dakota, SD	M,W
University of Southern Indiana, IN	M,W
University of Southern Mississippi, MS	W
The University of Tampa, FL	M,W
The University of Tennessee at Chattanooga, TN	M,W
The University of Tennessee at Martin, TN	M,W
The University of Texas at Austin, TX	M,W
The University of Texas at Brownsville, TX	M,W
The University of Texas at El Paso, TX	M,W
The University of Texas at San Antonio, TX	M,W
The University of Texas of the Permian Basin, TX	M,W
The University of Texas–Pan American, TX	M,W
University of the Cumberlands, KY	M,W
University of the Incarnate Word, TX	M,W
University of the Pacific, CA	W
The University of Toledo, OH	M,W
University of Tulsa, OK	M,W
University of Utah, UT	W
University of Vermont, VT	M,W
University of Virginia, VA	M,W
The University of Virginia's College at Wise, VA	M,W

The University of West Alabama, AL	M,W
University of West Florida, FL	M,W
University of West Georgia, GA	M,W
University of Wisconsin–Green Bay, WI	M,W
University of Wisconsin–Madison, WI	M,W
University of Wisconsin–Milwaukee, WI	M,W
University of Wisconsin–Parkside, WI	M,W
University of Wyoming, WY	M,W
Ursuline College, OH	W
Utah State University, UT	M,W
Utah Valley University, UT	M,W
Valdosta State University, GA	M,W
Valley City State University, ND	M,W
Valparaiso University, IN	M,W
Vanderbilt University, TN	M,W
Villanova University, PA	M,W
Virginia Commonwealth University, VA	M,W
Virginia State University, VA	M,W
Virginia Union University, VA	M,W
Wagner College, NY	M,W
Wake Forest University, NC	M,W
Waldorf College, IA	M,W
Warner Pacific College, OR	M,W
Washington State University, WA	M,W
Wayland Baptist University, TX	M,W
Wayne State College, NE	M,W
Wayne State University, MI	M,W
Webber International University, FL	M,W
Western Carolina University, NC	M,W
Western Illinois University, IL	M,W
Western Kentucky University, KY	M,W
Western Michigan University, MI	W
Western Oregon University, OR	M,W
Western State Colorado University, CO	M,W
Western Washington University, WA	M,W
Westminster College, UT	M,W
West Texas A&M University, TX	M,W
West Virginia University, WV	W
West Virginia University Institute of Technology, WV	M,W
West Virginia Wesleyan College, WV	M,W
Wheeling Jesuit University, WV	M,W
Wichita State University, KS	M,W
William Jewell College, MO	M,W
Winona State University, MN	W
Winthrop University, SC	M,W
Wofford College, SC	M,W
Wright State University, OH	M,W
Xavier University, OH	M,W
Young Harris College, GA	M,W
Youngstown State University, OH	M,W

Equestrian sports

Auburn University, AL	W
Baylor University, TX	W
California State University, Fresno, CA	W
Converse College, SC	W
Maryville College, TN	M,W
Oklahoma State University, OK	W
Post University, CT	M,W
Saint Mary-of-the-Woods College, IN	W
Savannah College of Art and Design, GA	M,W
Seton Hill University, PA	W
Southern Methodist University, TX	W
Texas A&M University, TX	W
Texas Christian University, TX	W

Tiffin University, OH	M,W
University of Georgia, GA	W
University of Great Falls, MT	M,W
University of Minnesota, Crookston, MN	W
The University of Montana Western, MT	M,W
University of South Carolina, SC	W
The University of Tennessee at Martin, TN	W
Virginia Intermont College, VA	M,W
West Texas A&M University, TX	W

Fencing

Cleveland State University, OH	M,W
New Jersey Institute of Technology, NJ	M,W
The Ohio State University, OH	M,W
Penn State University Park, PA	M,W
Queens College of the City University of New York, NY	W
St. John's University, NY	M,W
Stanford University, CA	M,W
Temple University, PA	W
University of Notre Dame, IN	M,W
Wayne State University, MI	M,W

Field hockey

Adelphi University, NY	W
American University, DC	W
Appalachian State University, NC	W
Ball State University, IN	W
Bellarmine University, KY	W
Bloomsburg University of Pennsylvania, PA	W
Boston College, MA	W
Boston University, MA	W
Bryant University, RI	W
Central Michigan University, MI	W
Colgate University, NY	W
College of the Holy Cross, MA	W
The College of William and Mary, VA	W
Davidson College, NC	W
Fairfield University, CT	W
Franklin Pierce University, NH	W
Hofstra University, NY	W
Indiana University of Pennsylvania, PA	W
James Madison University, VA	W
Kent State University, OH	W
Kutztown University of Pennsylvania, PA	W
La Salle University, PA	W
Lehigh University, PA	W
Liberty University, VA	W
Limestone College, SC	W
Lindenwood University, MO	W
Lock Haven University of Pennsylvania, PA	W
Long Island University–C. W. Post Campus, NY	W
Longwood University, VA	W
Mansfield University of Pennsylvania, PA	W
Mercy College, NY	W
Mercyhurst University, PA	W
Merrimack College, MA	W
Miami University, OH	W
Michigan State University, MI	W
Millersville University of Pennsylvania, PA	W
Missouri State University, MO	W
Monmouth University, NJ	W
Northeastern University, MA	W
The Ohio State University, OH	W
Ohio University, OH	W

Old Dominion University, VA	W
Penn State University Park, PA	W
Philadelphia University, PA	W
Providence College, RI	W
Quinnipiac University, CT	W
Radford University, VA	W
Rider University, NJ	W
Robert Morris University, PA	W
Robert Morris University Illinois, IL	W
Sacred Heart University, CT	W
Saint Anselm College, NH	W
Saint Joseph's University, PA	W
Saint Louis University, MO	W
Seton Hill University, PA	W
Shippensburg University of Pennsylvania, PA	W
Siena College, NY	W
Slippery Rock University of Pennsylvania, PA	W
Southern Connecticut State University, CT	W
Stanford University, CA	W
Stonehill College, MA	W
Syracuse University, NY	W
Temple University, PA	W
University at Albany, State University of New York, NY	W
University of California, Davis, CA	W
University of Connecticut, CT	W
University of Delaware, DE	W
The University of Iowa, IA	W
University of Louisville, KY	W
University of Maryland, College Park, MD	W
University of Massachusetts Amherst, MA	W
University of Michigan, MI	W
University of New Hampshire, NH	W
The University of North Carolina at Chapel Hill, NC	W
University of Richmond, VA	W
University of the Pacific, CA	W
University of Vermont, VT	W
University of Virginia, VA	W
Villanova University, PA	W
Virginia Commonwealth University, VA	W
Wake Forest University, NC	W
West Chester University of Pennsylvania, PA	W

Football

Abilene Christian University, TX	M
Adams State University, CO	M
Alabama State University, AL	M
Alcorn State University, MS	M
Angelo State University, TX	M
Appalachian State University, NC	M
Arizona State University, AZ	M
Arkansas State University, AR	M
Arkansas Tech University, AR	M
Ashland University, OH	M
Auburn University, AL	M
Augustana College, SD	M
Austin Peay State University, TN	M
Azusa Pacific University, CA	M
Ball State University, IN	M
Baylor University, TX	M
Belhaven University, MS	M
Bemidji State University, MN	M
Benedictine College, KS	M
Bethel College, KS	M

Bethune-Cookman University, FL	M
Bloomsburg University of Pennsylvania, PA	M
Bluefield College, VA	M
Boise State University, ID	M
Boston College, MA	M
Bowie State University, MD	M
Bowling Green State University, OH	M
Brevard College, NC	M
Brigham Young University, UT	M
Bryant University, RI	M
California Polytechnic State University, San Luis Obispo, CA	M
California State University, Fresno, CA	M
California State University, Northridge, CA	M
Campbellsville University, KY	M
Carroll College, MT	M
Carson-Newman University, TN	M
Catawba College, NC	M
Central Methodist University, MO	M
Central Michigan University, MI	M
Chowan University, NC	M
The Citadel, The Military College of South Carolina, SC	M
Clarion University of Pennsylvania, PA	M
Clemson University, SC	M
Coastal Carolina University, SC	M
Colgate University, NY	M
The College of William and Mary, VA	M
Colorado Mesa University, CO	M
Colorado School of Mines, CO	M
Colorado State University, CO	M
Concordia University, Nebraska, NE	M
Concordia University, St. Paul, MN	M
Culver-Stockton College, MO	M
Dakota State University, SD	M
Dakota Wesleyan University, SD	M
Davidson College, NC	M
Doane College, NE	M
Dordt College, IA	M
Duquesne University, PA	M
East Carolina University, NC	M
Eastern Illinois University, IL	M
Eastern Michigan University, MI	M
Eastern New Mexico University, NM	M
Eastern Washington University, WA	M
Edinboro University of Pennsylvania, PA	M
Elizabeth City State University, NC	M
Elon University, NC	M
Emporia State University, KS	M
Evangel University, MO	M
Fairmont State University, WV	M
Faulkner University, AL	M
Fayetteville State University, NC	M
Ferris State University, MI	M
Florida Agricultural and Mechanical University, FL	M
Florida Atlantic University, FL	M
Florida International University, FL	M
Florida State University, FL	M
Fort Lewis College, CO	M
Furman University, SC	M
Gannon University, PA	M
Gardner-Webb University, NC	M
Georgetown College, KY	M
Georgetown University, DC	M
Georgia Institute of Technology, GA	M

Georgia Southern University, GA	M
Georgia State University, GA	M
Graceland University, IA	M
Grand Valley State University, MI	M
Grand View University, IA	M
Hampton University, VA	M
Harding University, AR	M
Henderson State University, AR	M
Hillsdale College, MI	M
Houston Baptist University, TX	M
Idaho State University, ID	M
Illinois State University, IL	M
Indiana State University, IN	M
Indiana University Bloomington, IN	M
Indiana University of Pennsylvania, PA	M
Iowa State University of Science and Technology, IA	M
Jacksonville State University, AL	M
James Madison University, VA	M
Johnson C. Smith University, NC	M
Kansas State University, KS	M
Kent State University, OH	M
Kentucky State University, KY	M
Kentucky Wesleyan College, KY	M
Kutztown University of Pennsylvania, PA	M
Lake Erie College, OH	M
Lamar University, TX	M
Lane College, TN	M
Lehigh University, PA	M
Liberty University, VA	M
Lincoln University, MO	M
Lindenwood University, MO	M
Lindsey Wilson College, KY	M,W
Lock Haven University of Pennsylvania, PA	M
Long Island University–C. W. Post Campus, NY	M,W
Louisiana State University and Agricultural and Mechanical College, LA	M
Louisiana Tech University, LA	M
Malone University, OH	M
Marshall University, WV	M
Mayville State University, ND	M
McKendree University, IL	M
McNeese State University, LA	M
Menlo College, CA	M
Mercyhurst University, PA	M
Merrimack College, MA	M
Miami University, OH	M
Michigan State University, MI	M
Middle Tennessee State University, TN	M
Midwestern State University, TX	M
Millersville University of Pennsylvania, PA	M
Minnesota State University Mankato, MN	M
Minot State University, ND	M
Mississippi State University, MS	M
Missouri State University, MO	M
Missouri University of Science and Technology, MO	M
Missouri Western State University, MO	M
Monmouth University, NJ	M
Montana State University, MT	M
Montana Tech of The University of Montana, MT	M
Morehouse College, GA	M
Morningside College, IA	M
Murray State University, KY	M
Newberry College, SC	M

College	
New Mexico Highlands University, NM	M
New Mexico State University, NM	M
Nicholls State University, LA	M
Norfolk State University, VA	M
North Carolina Central University, NC	M
North Carolina State University, NC	M
Northern Arizona University, AZ	M
Northern Illinois University, IL	M
Northern Michigan University, MI	M
Northern State University, SD	M
Northwestern Oklahoma State University, OK	M
Northwestern State University of Louisiana, LA	M
Northwest Missouri State University, MO	M
Northwood University, Michigan Campus, MI	M
The Ohio State University, OH	M
Ohio University, OH	M
Oklahoma Baptist University, OK	M
Oklahoma State University, OK	M
Old Dominion University, VA	M
Oregon State University, OR	M
Ouachita Baptist University, AR	M
Pace University, NY	M
Penn State University Park, PA	M
Pittsburg State University, KS	M
Presbyterian College, SC	M
Purdue University, IN	M
Quincy University, IL	M
Rice University, TX	M
Robert Morris University, PA	M
Robert Morris University Illinois, IL	M
Rocky Mountain College, MT	M
Sacred Heart University, CT	M
Saginaw Valley State University, MI	M
St. Ambrose University, IA	M
Saint Anselm College, NH	M
Saint Joseph's College, IN	M
Samford University, AL	M
Sam Houston State University, TX	M
San Diego State University, CA	M
San Jose State University, CA	M
Seton Hill University, PA	M
Shepherd University, WV	M
Shippensburg University of Pennsylvania, PA	M
Slippery Rock University of Pennsylvania, PA	M
South Dakota State University, SD	M
Southeastern Louisiana University, LA	M
Southeastern Oklahoma State University, OK	M
Southeast Missouri State University, MO	M
Southern Arkansas University–Magnolia, AR	M
Southern Connecticut State University, CT	M
Southern Illinois University Carbondale, IL	M
Southern Methodist University, TX	M
Southern Utah University, UT	M
Southwest Baptist University, MO	M
Southwestern College, KS	M
Stanford University, CA	M
Stephen F. Austin State University, TX	M
Stonehill College, MA	M
Stony Brook University, State University of New York, NY	M
Syracuse University, NY	M
Tarleton State University, TX	M
Taylor University, IN	M
Temple University, PA	M
Tennessee State University, TN	M
Texas A&M University, TX	M
Texas A&M University–Commerce, TX	M
Texas Christian University, TX	M
Texas Southern University, TX	M
Texas State University–San Marcos, TX	M
Tiffin University, OH	M
Troy University, AL	M
Truman State University, MO	M
Tulane University, LA	M
Tuskegee University, AL	M
Union College, KY	M
University at Albany, State University of New York, NY	M
University at Buffalo, the State University of New York, NY	M
The University of Akron, OH	M
The University of Alabama, AL	M
The University of Alabama at Birmingham, AL	M
The University of Arizona, AZ	M
University of California, Davis, CA	M
University of California, Los Angeles, CA	M
University of Central Arkansas, AR	M
University of Central Florida, FL	M
University of Charleston, WV	M
University of Cincinnati, OH	M
University of Colorado Boulder, CO	M
University of Connecticut, CT	M
University of Delaware, DE	M
University of Florida, FL	M
University of Georgia, GA	M
University of Hawaii at Manoa, HI	M
University of Houston, TX	M
University of Idaho, ID	M
University of Illinois at Urbana–Champaign, IL	M
The University of Iowa, IA	M
The University of Kansas, KS	M
University of Louisiana at Lafayette, LA	M
University of Louisville, KY	M
University of Maryland, College Park, MD	M
University of Massachusetts Amherst, MA	M
University of Memphis, TN	M
University of Miami, FL	M
University of Michigan, MI	M
University of Minnesota, Crookston, MN	M
University of Minnesota, Duluth, MN	M
University of Minnesota, Twin Cities Campus, MN	M
University of Mississippi, MS	M
The University of Montana Western, MT	M
University of Nebraska at Kearney, NE	M
University of Nebraska–Lincoln, NE	M
University of Nevada, Las Vegas, NV	M
University of Nevada, Reno, NV	M
University of New Hampshire, NH	M
University of New Haven, CT	M
University of North Alabama, AL	M
The University of North Carolina at Chapel Hill, NC	M
The University of North Carolina at Pembroke, NC	M
University of Northern Colorado, CO	M
University of Northern Iowa, IA	M
University of North Texas, TX	M
University of Notre Dame, IN	M
University of Oklahoma, OK	M
University of Oregon, OR	M
University of Pikeville, KY	M
University of Pittsburgh, PA	M
University of Rhode Island, RI	M
University of Richmond, VA	M
University of St. Francis, IL	M
University of South Alabama, AL	M
University of South Carolina, SC	M
The University of South Dakota, SD	M
University of Southern Mississippi, MS	M,W
The University of Tennessee, TN	M
The University of Tennessee at Chattanooga, TN	M
The University of Tennessee at Martin, TN	M
The University of Texas at Austin, TX	M
The University of Texas at El Paso, TX	M
The University of Texas at San Antonio, TX	M
University of the Cumberlands, KY	M
University of the Incarnate Word, TX	M
The University of Toledo, OH	M
University of Tulsa, OK	M
University of Utah, UT	M
University of Virginia, VA	M
The University of Virginia's College at Wise, VA	M
The University of West Alabama, AL	M
University of West Georgia, GA	M
University of Wisconsin–Madison, WI	M
University of Wyoming, WY	M
Upper Iowa University, IA	M
Utah State University, UT	M
Valdosta State University, GA	M
Valley City State University, ND	M
Vanderbilt University, TN	M
Villanova University, PA	M
Virginia Polytechnic Institute and State University, VA	M
Virginia State University, VA	M
Virginia Union University, VA	M
Wagner College, NY	M
Wake Forest University, NC	M
Waldorf College, IA	M
Washburn University, KS	M
Washington State University, WA	M
Wayland Baptist University, TX	M
Wayne State College, NE	M
Wayne State University, MI	M
Webber International University, FL	M
West Chester University of Pennsylvania, PA	M
Western Carolina University, NC	M
Western Illinois University, IL	M
Western Kentucky University, KY	M
Western Michigan University, MI	M
Western Oregon University, OR	M

College	
Western State Colorado University, CO	M
West Texas A&M University, TX	M
West Virginia State University, WV	M
West Virginia University, WV	M
West Virginia Wesleyan College, WV	M
William Jewell College, MO	M
Winona State University, MN	M
Wofford College, SC	M
Youngstown State University, OH	M

Golf

College	
Abilene Christian University, TX	M
Academy of Art University, CA	M,W
Adams State University, CO	M,W
Adelphi University, NY	M
Alabama State University, AL	M,W
Alcorn State University, MS	M,W
Anderson University, SC	M,W
Angelo State University, TX	W
Appalachian State University, NC	M,W
Arizona State University, AZ	M,W
Arkansas State University, AR	M,W
Arkansas Tech University, AR	M,W
Armstrong Atlantic State University, GA	M,W
Asbury University, KY	M,W
Ashland University, OH	M,W
Auburn University, AL	M,W
Augustana College, SD	M,W
Austin Peay State University, TN	M,W
Ball State University, IN	M,W
Barry University, FL	M,W
Barton College, NC	M,W
Baylor University, TX	M,W
Belhaven University, MS	M,W
Bellarmine University, KY	M,W
Belmont Abbey College, NC	M,W
Belmont University, TN	M,W
Bemidji State University, MN	M,W
Bethel College, IN	M,W
Bethel College, KS	M,W
Bethune-Cookman University, FL	M,W
Binghamton University, State University of New York, NY	M
Biola University, CA	M,W
Bluefield College, VA	M
Bluefield State College, WV	M
Blue Mountain College, MS	M,W
Boise State University, ID	M,W
Boston College, MA	M,W
Bowling Green State University, OH	M,W
Bradley University, IL	M,W
Brevard College, NC	M,W
Brigham Young University, UT	M,W
Bryant University, RI	M
Butler University, IN	M,W
California Baptist University, CA	M,W
California Polytechnic State University, San Luis Obispo, CA	M,W
California State University, Chico, CA	M,W
California State University, Dominguez Hills, CA	M
California State University, Fresno, CA	M,W
California State University, Fullerton, CA	M,W
California State University, Monterey Bay, CA	M,W
California State University, Northridge, CA	M
California State University, San Bernardino, CA	M

College	
Calumet College of Saint Joseph, IN	M
Cameron University, OK	M,W
Campbellsville University, KY	M,W
Canisius College, NY	M
Carroll College, MT	M,W
Carson-Newman University, TN	M
Catawba College, NC	M,W
Cedarville University, OH	M
Central Connecticut State University, CT	M,W
Chestnut Hill College, PA	M
Chicago State University, IL	M,W
Chowan University, NC	M
Christian Brothers University, TN	M,W
Cincinnati Christian University, OH	M
The Citadel, The Military College of South Carolina, SC	W
Clarion University of Pennsylvania, PA	M,W
Clarke University, IA	M,W
Clayton State University, GA	M
Cleary University, MI	M,W
Clemson University, SC	M
Cleveland State University, OH	M
Coastal Carolina University, SC	M,W
Coker College, SC	M,W
College of Charleston, SC	M,W
The College of Idaho, ID	M,W
College of Saint Mary, NE	W
The College of William and Mary, VA	M,W
Colorado Mesa University, CO	M,W
Colorado State University, CO	M,W
Columbia College, MO	M,W
Columbus State University, GA	M,W
Concordia University, OR	M,W
Concordia University, Nebraska, NE	M,W
Concordia University, St. Paul, MN	M,W
Converse College, SC	W
Corban University, OR	M,W
Cornerstone University, MI	M
Creighton University, NE	M,W
Culver-Stockton College, MO	M,W
Dakota Wesleyan University, SD	M,W
Dallas Baptist University, TX	W
Davenport University, MI	M,W
Davidson College, NC	M
DePaul University, IL	M
Doane College, NE	M,W
Dominican College, NY	M
Dordt College, IA	M,W
Drake University, IA	M
Drury University, MO	M,W
East Carolina University, NC	M,W
Eastern Illinois University, IL	M,W
Eastern Michigan University, MI	M,W
Eastern Washington University, WA	W
Eckerd College, FL	M,W
Elizabeth City State University, NC	M
Elon University, NC	M,W
Embry-Riddle Aeronautical University–Daytona, FL	M,W
Embry-Riddle Aeronautical University–Prescott, AZ	M,W
Emmanuel College, GA	M,W
Evangel University, MO	M,W
Fairfield University, CT	M,W
Fairmont State University, WV	M,W
Faulkner University, AL	M,W
Fayetteville State University, NC	M
Felician College, NJ	M
Ferris State University, MI	M,W

College	
Flagler College, FL	M,W
Florida Agricultural and Mechanical University, FL	M,W
Florida Atlantic University, FL	M,W
Florida Gulf Coast University, FL	M,W
Florida Institute of Technology, FL	M,W
Florida International University, FL	W
Florida Southern College, FL	M,W
Florida State University, FL	M,W
Fort Lewis College, CO	M
Francis Marion University, SC	M
Furman University, SC	M,W
Gannon University, PA	M,W
Gardner-Webb University, NC	M,W
George Mason University, VA	M
Georgetown College, KY	M,W
Georgetown University, DC	M
The George Washington University, DC	M
Georgia College & State University, GA	M
Georgia Institute of Technology, GA	M
Georgia Southern University, GA	M
Georgia Southwestern State University, GA	M
Georgia State University, GA	M,W
Goldey-Beacom College, DE	M
Goshen College, IN	M,W
Graceland University, IA	M,W
Grand Valley State University, MI	M,W
Grand View University, IA	M,W
Hampton University, VA	M,W
Harding University, AR	M,W
Hawai`i Pacific University, HI	M
Henderson State University, AR	M,W
Hofstra University, NY	M,W
Houston Baptist University, TX	M,W
Huntington University, IN	M
Idaho State University, ID	W
Illinois State University, IL	M,W
Indiana State University, IN	W
Indiana Tech, IN	M,W
Indiana University Bloomington, IN	M,W
Indiana University of Pennsylvania, PA	M
Indiana University–Purdue University Fort Wayne, IN	M,W
Indiana University–Purdue University Indianapolis, IN	M,W
Indiana Wesleyan University, IN	M,W
Iona College, NY	M
Iowa State University of Science and Technology, IA	M,W
Jacksonville State University, AL	M,W
Jacksonville University, FL	M,W
James Madison University, VA	M,W
John Brown University, AR	M
Johnson C. Smith University, NC	M
Kansas State University, KS	M,W
Kennesaw State University, GA	M,W
Kent State University, OH	M,W
Kentucky State University, KY	M
Kentucky Wesleyan College, KY	M,W
King College, TN	M,W
Kutztown University of Pennsylvania, PA	W
Lake Erie College, OH	M,W
Lake Superior State University, MI	M,W
Lamar University, TX	M,W
La Salle University, PA	M,W
Lee University, TN	M,W
Lehigh University, PA	M,W

Le Moyne College, NY	M,W	Northern State University, SD	M,W	San Diego State University, CA	M,W
Lewis-Clark State College, ID	M,W	Northwest Christian University, OR	M,W	San Jose State University, CA	M,W
Lewis University, IL	M,W	Northwestern Oklahoma State University, OK	M,W	Santa Clara University, CA	M,W
Liberty University, VA	M			Savannah College of Art and Design, GA	M,W
Limestone College, SC	M,W	Northwest Missouri State University, MO	W	Seattle University, WA	M,W
Lincoln University, MO	M,W	Northwest Nazarene University, ID	M,W	Seton Hill University, PA	W
Lindenwood University, MO	M,W	Northwood University, Florida Campus, FL	M,W	Shawnee State University, OH	M
Lindsey Wilson College, KY	M,W			Shepherd University, WV	M
Lipscomb University, TN	M,W	Northwood University, Michigan Campus, MI	M,W	Siena College, NY	M,W
Long Island University–Brooklyn Campus, NY	M,W	Northwood University, Texas Campus, TX	M,W	Simpson University, CA	M,W
Longwood University, VA	M,W	Notre Dame de Namur University, CA	M	South Dakota State University, SD	M,W
Louisiana State University and Agricultural and Mechanical College, LA	M,W	Nova Southeastern University, FL	M,W	Southeastern Louisiana University, LA	M
Louisiana Tech University, LA	M	Nyack College, NY	M	Southeastern Oklahoma State University, OK	M
Lourdes University, OH	M,W	Oakland University, MI	M,W		
Loyola Marymount University, CA	M	The Ohio State University, OH	M,W	Southern Illinois University Carbondale, IL	M,W
Loyola University Chicago, IL	M,W	Ohio University, OH	M,W	Southern Illinois University Edwardsville, IL	M,W
Loyola University Maryland, MD	M	Ohio Valley University, WV	M,W		
Lubbock Christian University, TX	M,W	Oklahoma Baptist University, OK	M,W	Southern Methodist University, TX	M,W
Lynn University, FL	M,W	Oklahoma Christian University, OK	M	Southern Utah University, UT	M,W
Lyon College, AR	M,W	Oklahoma City University, OK	M,W	Southwest Baptist University, MO	M,W
Malone University, OH	M,W	Oklahoma State University, OK	M,W	Southwestern College, KS	M,W
Manhattan College, NY	M	Old Dominion University, VA	M,W	Spring Arbor University, MI	M,W
Marquette University, WI	M	Oral Roberts University, OK	M,W	Spring Hill College, AL	M,W
Marshall University, WV	M,W	Oregon State University, OR	M,W	Stanford University, CA	M,W
Maryville University of Saint Louis, MO	M,W	Ouachita Baptist University, AR	M,W	Stephen F. Austin State University, TX	M,W
The Master's College and Seminary, CA	M	Park University, MO	W	Stephens College, MO	W
		Penn State University Park, PA	M,W	Stetson University, FL	M,W
McKendree University, IL	M,W	Pepperdine University, CA	M,W	Tarleton State University, TX	W
McNeese State University, LA	M,W	Philadelphia University, PA	M	Taylor University, IN	M,W
Menlo College, CA	M,W	Pittsburg State University, KS	M	Temple University, PA	M
Mercer University, GA	M,W	Point Loma Nazarene University, CA	M	Tennessee State University, TN	M
Mercyhurst University, PA	M,W	Point Park University, PA	M,W	Tennessee Wesleyan College, TN	M,W
Merrimack College, MA	W	Post University, CT	M	Texas A&M International University, TX	M,W
Miami University, OH	M	Presbyterian College, SC	M,W		
Michigan State University, MI	M,W	Purdue University, IN	M,W	Texas A&M University, TX	M,W
Middle Tennessee State University, TN	M	Purdue University North Central, IN	M	Texas A&M University–Commerce, TX	M,W
Midwestern State University, TX	M,W	Quincy University, IL	M,W	Texas Christian University, TX	M,W
Millersville University of Pennsylvania, PA	M	Quinnipiac University, CT	W	Texas Southern University, TX	M,W
		Radford University, VA	M,W	Texas State University–San Marcos, TX	M,W
Minnesota State University Mankato, MN	M,W	Regis University, CO	M,W		
		Research College of Nursing, MO	M,W	Texas Wesleyan University, TX	M,W
Mississippi State University, MS	M,W	Rice University, TX	M	Thomas University, GA	M
Missouri Baptist University, MO	M,W	Rider University, NJ	M	Tiffin University, OH	M,W
Missouri State University, MO	M,W	Robert Morris University, PA	M,W	Trevecca Nazarene University, TN	M,W
Missouri Western State University, MO	M,W	Robert Morris University Illinois, IL	M,W	Trinity Christian College, IL	M
				Troy University, AL	M,W
Monmouth University, NJ	M,W	Roberts Wesleyan College, NY	M	Truman State University, MO	W
Montana State University, MT	W	Rockhurst University, MO	M,W	Tulane University, LA	W
Montana Tech of The University of Montana, MT	M,W	Rocky Mountain College, MT	M,W	Tuskegee University, AL	M
		Rogers State University, OK	M,W	Union College, KY	M,W
Montreat College, NC	M	Rollins College, FL	M,W	Union University, TN	M
Morehead State University, KY	M	Sacred Heart University, CT	M,W	University at Albany, State University of New York, NY	W
Morehouse College, GA	M	Saginaw Valley State University, MI	M		
Morningside College, IA	M,W	St. Ambrose University, IA	M,W	The University of Akron, OH	M,W
Mount Marty College, SD	M,W	Saint Anselm College, NH	M	The University of Alabama, AL	M,W
Mount Mercy University, IA	M,W	St. Bonaventure University, NY	M	The University of Alabama at Birmingham, AL	M,W
Mount Vernon Nazarene University, OH	M,W	St. Edward's University, TX	M,W		
		St. John's University, NY	M,W	The University of Arizona, AZ	M,W
Murray State University, KY	M,W	Saint Joseph's College, IN	M,W	University of California, Davis, CA	M,W
Newberry College, SC	M,W	Saint Joseph's University, PA	M		
New Mexico State University, NM	M,W			University of California, Irvine, CA	M,W
Niagara University, NY	M,W	Saint Martin's University, WA	M,W	University of California, Los Angeles, CA	M,W
Nicholls State University, LA	M,W	Saint Mary-of-the-Woods College, IN	W		
North Carolina Central University, NC	M	Saint Mary's College of California, CA	M	University of California, Riverside, CA	M
North Carolina State University, NC	M,W	Saint Peter's University, NJ	M	University of California, Santa Barbara, CA	M
Northern Arizona University, AZ	W	St. Thomas University, FL	M,W	University of Central Arkansas, AR	M,W
Northern Illinois University, IL	M,W	Samford University, AL	M,W	University of Central Florida, FL	M,W
Northern Kentucky University, KY	M,W	Sam Houston State University, TX	M,W	University of Charleston, WV	M,W
Northern Michigan University, MI	M				

University of Cincinnati, OH	M,W
University of Colorado Boulder, CO	M,W
University of Colorado Colorado Springs, CO	M
University of Connecticut, CT	M
University of Dayton, OH	M
University of Denver, CO	M,W
University of Evansville, IN	M,W
University of Florida, FL	M,W
University of Georgia, GA	M,W
University of Great Falls, MT	M,W
University of Hartford, CT	M,W
University of Hawaii at Hilo, HI	M
University of Hawaii at Manoa, HI	M,W
University of Houston, TX	M,W
University of Idaho, ID	M,W
University of Illinois at Springfield, IL	M,W
University of Illinois at Urbana–Champaign, IL	M,W
The University of Iowa, IA	M,W
The University of Kansas, KS	M,W
University of Louisiana at Lafayette, LA	M
University of Louisville, KY	M,W
University of Maryland, College Park, MD	M,W
University of Memphis, TN	M,W
University of Miami, FL	W
University of Michigan, MI	M,W
University of Minnesota, Crookston, MN	M,W
University of Minnesota, Twin Cities Campus, MN	M,W
University of Mississippi, MS	M,W
University of Missouri–Kansas City, MO	M,W
University of Missouri–St. Louis, MO	M,W
University of Mobile, AL	M,W
University of Montevallo, AL	M,W
University of Nebraska at Kearney, NE	M,W
University of Nebraska at Omaha, NE	M,W
University of Nebraska–Lincoln, NE	M,W
University of Nevada, Las Vegas, NV	M
University of Nevada, Reno, NV	M,W
University of New Orleans, LA	M,W
University of North Alabama, AL	M
The University of North Carolina at Chapel Hill, NC	M,W
The University of North Carolina at Greensboro, NC	M,W
The University of North Carolina at Pembroke, NC	M,W
The University of North Carolina Wilmington, NC	M,W
University of Northern Colorado, CO	M,W
University of Northern Iowa, IA	M,W
University of North Florida, FL	M
University of North Georgia, GA	M,W
University of North Texas, TX	M,W
University of Notre Dame, IN	M,W
University of Oklahoma, OK	M,W
University of Oregon, OR	M,W
University of Pikeville, KY	M,W
University of Rhode Island, RI	M
University of Richmond, VA	M,W
University of St. Francis, IL	M,W
University of St. Thomas, TX	M,W
University of San Diego, CA	M

University of South Carolina, SC	M,W
University of South Carolina Aiken, SC	M
University of South Carolina Upstate, SC	M,W
The University of South Dakota, SD	W
University of Southern Indiana, IN	M,W
University of Southern Mississippi, MS	M,W
The University of Tampa, FL	M,W
The University of Tennessee, TN	M,W
The University of Tennessee at Chattanooga, TN	M,W
The University of Tennessee at Martin, TN	M
The University of Texas at Austin, TX	M,W
The University of Texas at Brownsville, TX	M,W
The University of Texas at El Paso, TX	M
The University of Texas at San Antonio, TX	M,W
The University of Texas–Pan American, TX	M,W
University of the Cumberlands, KY	M,W
University of the District of Columbia, DC	M
University of the Incarnate Word, TX	M,W
University of the Pacific, CA	M
The University of Toledo, OH	M,W
University of Tulsa, OK	M,W
University of Utah, UT	M
University of Virginia, VA	M,W
University of West Florida, FL	M,W
University of West Georgia, GA	M,W
University of Wisconsin–Green Bay, WI	M,W
University of Wisconsin–Madison, WI	M,W
University of Wisconsin–Parkside, WI	M
University of Wyoming, WY	M,W
Upper Iowa University, IA	M,W
Ursuline College, OH	W
Utah State University, UT	M
Utah Valley University, UT	M,W
Valdosta State University, GA	M
Valley City State University, ND	M,W
Valparaiso University, IN	M,W
Vanderbilt University, TN	M,W
Virginia Commonwealth University, VA	M
Virginia Intermont College, VA	M
Virginia Polytechnic Institute and State University, VA	M
Virginia State University, VA	M,W
Virginia Union University, VA	M
Wagner College, NY	M,W
Wake Forest University, NC	M,W
Waldorf College, IA	M,W
Warner Pacific College, OR	M,W
Washburn University, KS	M
Washington State University, WA	M,W
Wayland Baptist University, TX	M,W
Wayne State College, NE	M,W
Wayne State University, MI	M
Webber International University, FL	M,W
West Chester University of Pennsylvania, PA	M,W
Western Carolina University, NC	M,W
Western Illinois University, IL	M
Western Kentucky University, KY	M,W

Western Michigan University, MI	W
Western Washington University, WA	M,W
Westminster College, UT	M,W
West Texas A&M University, TX	M,W
West Virginia University Institute of Technology, WV	M
West Virginia Wesleyan College, WV	M,W
Wheeling Jesuit University, WV	M,W
Wichita State University, KS	M,W
William Jewell College, MO	M,W
Winona State University, MN	M,W
Winthrop University, SC	M,W
Wofford College, SC	M,W
Wright State University, OH	M
Xavier University, OH	M,W
Young Harris College, GA	M,W
Youngstown State University, OH	M,W

Gymnastics

Arizona State University, AZ	W
Auburn University, AL	W
Azusa Pacific University, CA	W
Ball State University, IN	W
Boise State University, ID	W
Bowling Green State University, OH	W
Brigham Young University, UT	W
California State University, Fullerton, CA	W
Central Michigan University, MI	W
The College of William and Mary, VA	M,W
Eastern Michigan University, MI	W
The George Washington University, DC	W
Illinois State University, IL	W
Iowa State University of Science and Technology, IA	W
Kent State University, OH	W
Lindenwood University, MO	W
Louisiana State University and Agricultural and Mechanical College, LA	W
Michigan State University, MI	W
North Carolina State University, NC	W
Northern Illinois University, IL	W
The Ohio State University, OH	M,W
Oregon State University, OR	W
Penn State University Park, PA	M,W
Quinnipiac University, CT	W
San Jose State University, CA	W
Seattle Pacific University, WA	W
Southeast Missouri State University, MO	W
Southern Connecticut State University, CT	W
Southern Utah University, UT	W
Stanford University, CA	M,W
Temple University, PA	M,W
Texas Woman's University, TX	W
The University of Alabama, AL	W
University of Alaska Anchorage, AK	W
The University of Arizona, AZ	W
University of Bridgeport, CT	W
University of California, Davis, CA	W
University of California, Los Angeles, CA	W
University of California, Santa Barbara, CA	M,W
University of Denver, CO	W
University of Florida, FL	W
University of Georgia, GA	W
University of Illinois at Chicago, IL	M,W

University of Illinois at Urbana–Champaign, IL	M,W
The University of Iowa, IA	M,W
University of Michigan, MI	M,W
University of Minnesota, Twin Cities Campus, MN	M,W
University of Nebraska–Lincoln, NE	M,W
University of New Hampshire, NH	W
The University of North Carolina at Chapel Hill, NC	W
University of Oklahoma, OK	M,W
University of Pittsburgh, PA	W
University of Utah, UT	W
Utah State University, UT	W
West Chester University of Pennsylvania, PA	W
Western Michigan University, MI	W
West Virginia University, WV	W

Ice hockey

Bemidji State University, MN	M,W
Bentley University, MA	M
Boston College, MA	M,W
Boston University, MA	M,W
Bowling Green State University, OH	M
Canisius College, NY	M
Clarkson University, NY	M,W
Colgate University, NY	M,W
College of the Holy Cross, MA	M
The Colorado College, CO	M
Davenport University, MI	M,W
Dordt College, IA	M
Ferris State University, MI	M
Lake Superior State University, MI	M
Lindenwood University, MO	M,W
Mercyhurst University, PA	M,W
Merrimack College, MA	M,W
Miami University, OH	M
Michigan State University, MI	M
Minnesota State University Mankato, MN	M,W
Niagara University, NY	M
Northeastern University, MA	M,W
Northern Michigan University, MI	M
The Ohio State University, OH	M,W
Penn State University Park, PA	M,W
Providence College, RI	M,W
Quinnipiac University, CT	M,W
Rensselaer Polytechnic Institute, NY	M,W
Robert Morris University, PA	M,W
Sacred Heart University, CT	M,W
St. Lawrence University, NY	M,W
Syracuse University, NY	W
University of Alaska Anchorage, AK	M
University of Alaska Fairbanks, AK	M
University of Connecticut, CT	M,W
University of Denver, CO	M
University of Massachusetts Amherst, MA	M
University of Michigan, MI	M
University of Minnesota, Duluth, MN	M,W
University of Minnesota, Twin Cities Campus, MN	M,W
University of Nebraska at Omaha, NE	M
University of New Hampshire, NH	M,W
University of Notre Dame, IN	M
University of Vermont, VT	M,W
University of Wisconsin–Madison, WI	M,W
Waldorf College, IA	M
Western Michigan University, MI	M

Lacrosse

Adams State University, CO	M,W
Adelphi University, NY	M,W
American University, DC	W
Bellarmine University, KY	M
Belmont Abbey College, NC	M,W
Binghamton University, State University of New York, NY	M,W
Bloomsburg University of Pennsylvania, PA	W
Boston College, MA	W
Boston University, MA	W
Brevard College, NC	M
Bryant University, RI	M,W
Bucknell University, PA	M,W
California State University, Fresno, CA	W
Canisius College, NY	M,W
Catawba College, NC	M,W
Central Connecticut State University, CT	W
Chestnut Hill College, PA	M,W
Chowan University, NC	W
Coastal Carolina University, SC	W
Colgate University, NY	M,W
The College of Saint Rose, NY	M
The College of William and Mary, VA	W
Colorado Mesa University, CO	M,W
Concordia University, CA	M
Converse College, SC	W
Davenport University, MI	M,W
Davidson College, NC	W
Dominican College, NY	M,W
Duquesne University, PA	W
Edinboro University of Pennsylvania, PA	W
Elon University, NC	W
Emmanuel College, GA	M,W
Fairfield University, CT	M,W
Florida Southern College, FL	M,W
Fort Lewis College, CO	W
Gannon University, PA	W
George Mason University, VA	W
Georgetown College, KY	W
Georgetown University, DC	M,W
Hofstra University, NY	M,W
Indiana Tech, IN	M,W
Indiana University of Pennsylvania, PA	W
Iona College, NY	W
Jacksonville University, FL	M,W
James Madison University, VA	W
The Johns Hopkins University, MD	M,W
Kutztown University of Pennsylvania, PA	W
Lake Erie College, OH	M,W
La Salle University, PA	W
Lawrence Technological University, MI	M
Lees-McRae College, NC	M,W
Lehigh University, PA	M,W
Le Moyne College, NY	M,W
Liberty University, VA	W
Limestone College, SC	M,W
Lindenwood University, MO	M,W
Lock Haven University of Pennsylvania, PA	W
Long Island University–Brooklyn Campus, NY	W
Long Island University–C. W. Post Campus, NY	M,W
Longwood University, VA	W
Lourdes University, OH	M,W
Loyola University Maryland, MD	M,W
Manhattan College, NY	M,W

Marist College, NY	M,W
Marquette University, WI	M,W
McKendree University, IL	W
Mercer University, GA	M
Mercy College, NY	M,W
Mercyhurst University, PA	M,W
Merrimack College, MA	M,W
Millersville University of Pennsylvania, PA	W
Missouri Baptist University, MO	M,W
Molloy College, NY	M,W
Monmouth University, NJ	M,W
Mount St. Mary's University, MD	M,W
Newberry College, SC	W
New York Institute of Technology, NY	M
Niagara University, NY	W
Notre Dame de Namur University, CA	M
Nyack College, NY	W
The Ohio State University, OH	M,W
Ohio Valley University, WV	M
Old Dominion University, VA	W
Pace University, NY	M
Penn State University Park, PA	M,W
Philadelphia University, PA	W
Post University, CT	M,W
Presbyterian College, SC	W
Providence College, RI	M
Queens College of the City University of New York, NY	W
Quinnipiac University, CT	M,W
Regis University, CO	W
Robert Morris University, PA	M,W
Robert Morris University Illinois, IL	M,W
Sacred Heart University, CT	M,W
St. Ambrose University, IA	M
Saint Anselm College, NH	M,W
St. Bonaventure University, NY	W
St. John's University, NY	M
Saint Joseph's University, PA	M,W
Saint Mary's College of California, CA	W
Savannah College of Art and Design, GA	M,W
Seton Hill University, PA	M,W
Shepherd University, WV	W
Shippensburg University of Pennsylvania, PA	W
Siena College, NY	M,W
Slippery Rock University of Pennsylvania, PA	W
Southern Connecticut State University, CT	W
Stanford University, CA	W
Stetson University, FL	W
Stonehill College, MA	W
Stony Brook University, State University of New York, NY	M,W
Syracuse University, NY	M,W
Temple University, PA	W
Tennessee Wesleyan College, TN	M
Tiffin University, OH	W
University at Albany, State University of New York, NY	M,W
University of Bridgeport, CT	W
University of California, Davis, CA	W
University of Cincinnati, OH	W
University of Colorado Boulder, CO	W
University of Delaware, DE	M,W
University of Denver, CO	M,W
University of Florida, FL	W
University of Hartford, CT	M

University of Louisville, KY	W
University of Maryland, Baltimore County, MD	M,W
University of Maryland, College Park, MD	M,W
University of Massachusetts Amherst, MA	M,W
University of Minnesota, Duluth, MN	M
University of New Hampshire, NH	W
University of New Haven, CT	W
The University of North Carolina at Chapel Hill, NC	M,W
University of Notre Dame, IN	M,W
University of Oregon, OR	W
University of Pikeville, KY	W
University of Richmond, VA	M,W
The University of Tampa, FL	M
University of Vermont, VT	M,W
University of Virginia, VA	M,W
Ursuline College, OH	W
Vanderbilt University, TN	W
Villanova University, PA	M,W
Virginia Polytechnic Institute and State University, VA	W
Wagner College, NY	M,W
West Chester University of Pennsylvania, PA	W
Westminster College, UT	M
West Virginia Wesleyan College, WV	W
Wheeling Jesuit University, WV	M,W
Young Harris College, GA	M,W

Riflery

The Citadel, The Military College of South Carolina, SC	M,W
Columbus State University, GA	M,W
Emmanuel College, GA	M,W
Hillsdale College, MI	M,W
Jacksonville State University, AL	M,W
Lindenwood University, MO	M,W
Morehead State University, KY	M,W
Murray State University, KY	M,W
North Carolina State University, NC	M,W
Texas Christian University, TX	W
The University of Akron, OH	W
University of Alaska Fairbanks, AK	M,W
University of Memphis, TN	M,W
University of Mississippi, MS	W
University of Nebraska–Lincoln, NE	W
University of Nevada, Reno, NV	M,W
University of North Georgia, GA	M,W
The University of Tennessee at Martin, TN	M,W
West Virginia University, WV	M,W

Rugby

Davenport University, MI	M,W
Eastern Illinois University, IL	W
Lee University, TN	M,W
Lindenwood University, MO	M,W
Quinnipiac University, CT	W
The University of North Carolina at Pembroke, NC	M
West Chester University of Pennsylvania, PA	W
Wheeling Jesuit University, WV	M

Sailing

Hampton University, VA	M,W

Skiing (cross-country)

Montana State University, MT	M,W
Northern Michigan University, MI	M,W

University of Alaska Anchorage, AK	M,W
University of Alaska Fairbanks, AK	M,W
University of Colorado Boulder, CO	M,W
University of Denver, CO	M,W
University of New Hampshire, NH	M,W
University of Utah, UT	M,W
University of Vermont, VT	M,W
University of Wisconsin–Green Bay, WI	M,W

Skiing (downhill)

The College of Idaho, ID	M,W
Montana State University, MT	M,W
Rocky Mountain College, MT	M,W
Saint Anselm College, NH	M,W
Sierra Nevada College, NV	M,W
University of Alaska Anchorage, AK	M,W
University of Colorado Boulder, CO	M,W
University of Denver, CO	M,W
University of New Hampshire, NH	M,W
University of Utah, UT	M,W
University of Vermont, VT	M,W
Westminster College, UT	M,W

Soccer

Abilene Christian University, TX	W
Academy of Art University, CA	M,W
Adams State University, CO	M,W
Adelphi University, NY	M,W
Alabama State University, AL	W
Alcorn State University, MS	W
American University, DC	M,W
Anderson University, SC	M,W
Angelo State University, TX	W
Appalachian State University, NC	M,W
Arizona State University, AZ	W
Arkansas State University, AR	W
Asbury University, KY	M,W
Ashland University, OH	M,W
Auburn University, AL	W
Auburn University at Montgomery, AL	M,W
Augustana College, SD	W
Austin Peay State University, TN	W
Azusa Pacific University, CA	M,W
Ball State University, IN	W
Barry University, FL	M,W
Barton College, NC	M,W
Baylor University, TX	W
Belhaven University, MS	M,W
Bellarmine University, KY	M,W
Belmont Abbey College, NC	M,W
Belmont University, TN	M,W
Bemidji State University, MN	W
Benedictine College, KS	M,W
Bethel College, IN	M,W
Bethel College, KS	M,W
Binghamton University, State University of New York, NY	M,W
Biola University, CA	M,W
Bloomfield College, NJ	M,W
Bloomsburg University of Pennsylvania, PA	M,W
Bluefield College, VA	M,W
Boise State University, ID	W
Boston College, MA	M,W
Boston University, MA	M,W
Bowling Green State University, OH	M,W
Bradley University, IL	M
Brevard College, NC	M,W
Brigham Young University, UT	W
Bryant University, RI	M,W
Bucknell University, PA	M,W
Butler University, IN	M,W
Caldwell College, NJ	M,W
California Baptist University, CA	M,W

California Polytechnic State University, San Luis Obispo, CA	M,W
California State Polytechnic University, Pomona, CA	M,W
California State University, Chico, CA	M,W
California State University, Dominguez Hills, CA	M,W
California State University, Fresno, CA	W
California State University, Fullerton, CA	M,W
California State University, Long Beach, CA	W
California State University, Los Angeles, CA	M,W
California State University, Monterey Bay, CA	M,W
California State University, Northridge, CA	M
California State University, San Bernardino, CA	M,W
Calumet College of Saint Joseph, IN	M,W
Campbellsville University, KY	M,W
Canisius College, NY	M,W
Carroll College, MT	W
Carson-Newman University, TN	M,W
Catawba College, NC	M,W
Cedarville University, OH	M,W
Central Connecticut State University, CT	M,W
Central Methodist University, MO	M,W
Central Michigan University, MI	W
Chestnut Hill College, PA	M,W
Chowan University, NC	M,W
Christian Brothers University, TN	M,W
Cincinnati Christian University, OH	M,W
The Citadel, The Military College of South Carolina, SC	W
Clarion University of Pennsylvania, PA	W
Clarke University, IA	M,W
Clayton State University, GA	M,W
Clemson University, SC	M,W
Cleveland State University, OH	M
Coastal Carolina University, SC	M,W
Coker College, SC	M,W
Colgate University, NY	M,W
College of Charleston, SC	M,W
The College of Idaho, ID	M,W
College of Saint Mary, NE	W
The College of Saint Rose, NY	M,W
College of the Holy Cross, MA	M,W
The College of William and Mary, VA	M,W
The Colorado College, CO	W
Colorado Mesa University, CO	M,W
Colorado School of Mines, CO	M,W
Colorado State University, CO	W
Columbia College, MO	M,W
Columbia International University, SC	W
Columbus State University, GA	W
Concordia University, CA	M,W
Concordia University, OR	M,W
Concordia University, Nebraska, NE	M,W
Concordia University, St. Paul, MN	W
Converse College, SC	W
Corban University, OR	M,W
Cornerstone University, MI	M,W
Creighton University, NE	M,W
Culver-Stockton College, MO	M,W
Dallas Baptist University, TX	W

Davenport University, MI	M,W	Indiana University of		Midwestern State University, TX	M,W
Davidson College, NC	M,W	Pennsylvania, PA	W	Millersville University of	
DePaul University, IL	M,W	Indiana University–Purdue		Pennsylvania, PA	M,W
Doane College, NE	M,W	University Fort Wayne, IN	M,W	Minnesota State University	
Dominican College, NY	M,W	Indiana University–Purdue		Mankato, MN	W
Dordt College, IA	M,W	University Indianapolis, IN	M,W	Mississippi State University, MS	W
Drake University, IA	M,W	Indiana Wesleyan University, IN	M,W	Missouri Baptist University, MO	M,W
Drury University, MO	M,W	Inter American University of		Missouri State University, MO	M,W
Duquesne University, PA	M,W	Puerto Rico, Ponce Campus, PR	M,W	Missouri University of Science	
East Carolina University, NC	M,W	Iona College, NY	M,W	and Technology, MO	M,W
Eastern Illinois University, IL	M,W	Iowa State University of Science		Missouri Western State	
Eastern Michigan University, MI	W	and Technology, IA	W	University, MO	W
Eastern New Mexico University, NM	M,W	Jacksonville State University, AL	W	Molloy College, NY	M,W
Eastern Washington University, WA	W	Jacksonville University, FL	M,W	Monmouth University, NJ	M,W
Eckerd College, FL	M,W	James Madison University, VA	M,W	Montreat College, NC	M,W
Edinboro University of		John Brown University, AR	M,W	Morehead State University, KY	W
Pennsylvania, PA	W	Kennesaw State University, GA	W	Morningside College, IA	M,W
Elon University, NC	M,W	Kent State University, OH	W	Mount Marty College, SD	M,W
Embry-Riddle Aeronautical		Kentucky Wesleyan College, KY	M,W	Mount Mercy University, IA	M,W
University–Daytona, FL	M,W	King College, TN	M,W	Mount St. Mary's	
Embry-Riddle Aeronautical		Kutztown University of		University, MD	W
University–Prescott, AZ	M,W	Pennsylvania, PA	W	Mount Vernon Nazarene	
Emmanuel College, GA	M,W	Lake Erie College, OH	M,W	University, OH	M,W
Emporia State University, KS	W	Lamar University, TX	W	Murray State University, KY	W
The Evergreen State College, WA	M,W	La Salle University, PA	M,W	Newberry College, SC	M,W
Fairfield University, CT	M,W	Lawrence Technological		New Jersey Institute of	
Faulkner University, AL	M,W	University, MI	M,W	Technology, NJ	M,W
Felician College, NJ	M,W	Lees-McRae College, NC	M,W	New Mexico Highlands University,	
Ferris State University, MI	W	Lee University, TN	M,W	NM	W
Flagler College, FL	M,W	Le Moyne College, NY	M,W	New York Institute of	
Florida Gulf Coast University, FL	M,W	Lewis University, IL	M,W	Technology, NY	M,W
Florida Institute of Technology,		Liberty University, VA	M,W	Niagara University, NY	M,W
FL	M,W	Limestone College, SC	M,W	Nicholls State University, LA	W
Florida International		Lindenwood University, MO	M,W	North Carolina State University,	
University, FL	M,W	Lindsey Wilson College, KY	M,W	NC	M,W
Florida Southern College, FL	M,W	Lipscomb University, TN	M,W	Northeastern University, MA	M,W
Florida State University, FL	W	Lock Haven University of		Northern Arizona University, AZ	W
Fort Lewis College, CO	M,W	Pennsylvania, PA	M,W	Northern Illinois University, IL	M,W
Francis Marion University, SC	M,W	Long Island University–		Northern Kentucky University, KY	M,W
Franklin Pierce University, NH	M,W	Brooklyn Campus, NY	M,W	Northern Michigan University, MI	W
Freed-Hardeman University, TN	M,W	Long Island University–C. W.		Northern State University, SD	W
Furman University, SC	M,W	Post Campus, NY	M,W	Northwest Christian University, OR	M,W
Gannon University, PA	M,W	Longwood University, VA	M,W	Northwestern Oklahoma State	
Gardner-Webb University, NC	M,W	Louisiana State University and		University, OK	W
George Mason University, VA	M,W	Agricultural and Mechanical		Northwestern State University of	
Georgetown College, KY	M,W	College, LA	W	Louisiana, LA	W
Georgetown University, DC	M,W	Loyola Marymount University, CA	M,W	Northwest Missouri State	
The George Washington		Loyola University Chicago, IL	M,W	University, MO	W
University, DC	M,W	Loyola University Maryland, MD	M,W	Northwest Nazarene University, ID	W
Georgia College & State		Lubbock Christian University, TX	M,W	Northwest University, WA	M,W
University, GA	W	Lynn University, FL	M,W	Northwood University, Florida	
Georgia Southern University, GA	M,W	Lyon College, AR	M,W	Campus, FL	M,W
Georgia Southwestern State		Malone University, OH	M,W	Northwood University, Michigan	
University, GA	M,W	Manhattan College, NY	M,W	Campus, MI	M,W
Georgia State University, GA	M,W	Mansfield University of		Northwood University, Texas	
Goldey-Beacom College, DE	M,W	Pennsylvania, PA	W	Campus, TX	M,W
Gonzaga University, WA	M,W	Marist College, NY	M,W	Notre Dame de Namur University, CA	M,W
Goshen College, IN	M,W	Marquette University, WI	M,W	Nova Southeastern University, FL	M,W
Graceland University, IA	M,W	Marshall University, WV	M,W	Nyack College, NY	M,W
Grand Valley State University, MI	W	Maryville University of Saint		Oakland University, MI	M,W
Grand View University, IA	M,W	Louis, MO	M,W	The Ohio State University, OH	M,W
Harding University, AR	M,W	The Master's College and		Ohio University, OH	W
Hartwick College, NY	M	Seminary, CA	M,W	Ohio Valley University, WV	M,W
Hawai`i Pacific University, HI	M,W	McKendree University, IL	M,W	Oklahoma Christian University, OK	M,W
Hofstra University, NY	M,W	McNeese State University, LA	W	Oklahoma City University, OK	M,W
Hope International University, CA	M,W	Menlo College, CA	M,W	Oklahoma State University, OK	W
Houston Baptist University, TX	M,W	Mercer University, GA	M,W	Old Dominion University, VA	M,W
Huntington University, IN	M,W	Mercy College, NY	M,W	Oral Roberts University, OK	M,W
Idaho State University, ID	W	Mercyhurst University, PA	M,W	Oregon State University, OR	M,W
Illinois Institute of		Merrimack College, MA	M,W	Ouachita Baptist University, AR	M,W
Technology, IL	M,W	Metropolitan State University of		Pace University, NY	W
Illinois State University, IL	W	Denver, CO	M,W	Palm Beach Atlantic University, FL	M,W
Indiana State University, IN	W	Miami University, OH	W	Park University, MO	M,W
Indiana Tech, IN	M,W	Michigan State University, MI	M,W	Penn State University Park, PA	M,W
Indiana University Bloomington, IN	M,W	Middle Tennessee State		Pepperdine University, CA	W
		University, TN	W	Philadelphia University, PA	M,W

College	
Point Loma Nazarene University, CA	M,W
Point Park University, PA	M,W
Post University, CT	M,W
Presbyterian College, SC	M,W
Providence College, RI	M,W
Purdue University, IN	W
Queens College of the City University of New York, NY	M,W
Quincy University, IL	M,W
Quinnipiac University, CT	M,W
Radford University, VA	M,W
Regis University, CO	M,W
Research College of Nursing, MO	M,W
Rice University, TX	W
Rider University, NJ	M,W
Robert Morris University, PA	M,W
Robert Morris University Illinois, IL	M,W
Roberts Wesleyan College, NY	M,W
Rockhurst University, MO	M,W
Rocky Mountain College, MT	M,W
Rogers State University, OK	M,W
Rollins College, FL	M,W
Sacred Heart University, CT	M,W
Saginaw Valley State University, MI	M,W
St. Ambrose University, IA	M,W
Saint Anselm College, NH	M,W
St. Bonaventure University, NY	M,W
St. Edward's University, TX	M,W
St. John's University, NY	M,W
Saint Joseph's College, IN	M,W
Saint Joseph's University, PA	M,W
Saint Louis University, MO	M,W
Saint Martin's University, WA	W
Saint Mary-of-the-Woods College, IN	W
Saint Mary's College of California, CA	M,W
Saint Peter's University, NJ	M,W
St. Thomas University, FL	M,W
Samford University, AL	W
Sam Houston State University, TX	W
San Diego Christian College, CA	M,W
San Diego State University, CA	M,W
San Francisco State University, CA	M,W
San Jose State University, CA	M,W
Santa Clara University, CA	M,W
Savannah College of Art and Design, GA	M,W
Seattle Pacific University, WA	M,W
Seattle University, WA	M,W
Seton Hill University, PA	M,W
Shawnee State University, OH	M,W
Shepherd University, WV	M,W
Shippensburg University of Pennsylvania, PA	M,W
Siena College, NY	M,W
Simpson University, CA	M,W
Slippery Rock University of Pennsylvania, PA	M,W
Soka University of America, CA	M,W
Sonoma State University, CA	M,W
South Dakota State University, SD	W
Southeastern Louisiana University, LA	W
Southeast Missouri State University, MO	W
Southern Connecticut State University, CT	M,W
Southern Illinois University Edwardsville, IL	M,W
Southern Methodist University, TX	M,W

College	
Southern Polytechnic State University, GA	M
Southern Utah University, UT	W
Southwest Baptist University, MO	W
Southwestern College, KS	M,W
Spring Arbor University, MI	M,W
Spring Hill College, AL	M,W
Stanford University, CA	M,W
Stephen F. Austin State University, TX	W
Stephens College, MO	W
Stetson University, FL	M,W
Stonehill College, MA	M,W
Stony Brook University, State University of New York, NY	M,W
Syracuse University, NY	M,W
Taylor University, IN	M,W
Temple University, PA	M,W
Tennessee Wesleyan College, TN	M,W
Texas A&M International University, TX	M,W
Texas A&M University, TX	W
Texas A&M University–Commerce, TX	W
Texas Christian University, TX	W
Texas Southern University, TX	W
Texas State University–San Marcos, TX	W
Texas Wesleyan University, TX	M,W
Texas Woman's University, TX	W
Thomas University, GA	M,W
Tiffin University, OH	M,W
Trevecca Nazarene University, TN	M,W
Trinity Christian College, IL	M,W
Troy University, AL	W
Truman State University, MO	M,W
Tulane University, LA	W
Union College, KY	M,W
Union University, TN	M,W
University at Albany, State University of New York, NY	M,W
University at Buffalo, the State University of New York, NY	M,W
The University of Akron, OH	M,W
The University of Alabama, AL	W
The University of Alabama at Birmingham, AL	M,W
The University of Arizona, AZ	W
University of Bridgeport, CT	M,W
University of California, Davis, CA	M,W
University of California, Irvine, CA	M,W
University of California, Los Angeles, CA	M,W
University of California, Riverside, CA	M,W
University of California, Santa Barbara, CA	M,W
University of Central Arkansas, AR	M,W
University of Central Florida, FL	M,W
University of Charleston, WV	M,W
University of Cincinnati, OH	M,W
University of Colorado Boulder, CO	W
University of Colorado Colorado Springs, CO	M,W
University of Connecticut, CT	M,W
University of Dayton, OH	M,W
University of Delaware, DE	M,W
University of Denver, CO	M,W
University of Evansville, IN	M,W
University of Florida, FL	W
University of Georgia, GA	W
University of Great Falls, MT	M,W
University of Hartford, CT	M,W

College	
University of Hawaii at Manoa, HI	W
University of Houston, TX	W
University of Idaho, ID	W
University of Illinois at Chicago, IL	M
University of Illinois at Springfield, IL	M,W
University of Illinois at Urbana–Champaign, IL	W
The University of Iowa, IA	W
The University of Kansas, KS	W
University of Louisville, KY	M,W
University of Maryland, Baltimore County, MD	M,W
University of Maryland, College Park, MD	M,W
University of Massachusetts Amherst, MA	M,W
University of Memphis, TN	M,W
University of Miami, FL	W
University of Michigan, MI	M,W
University of Minnesota, Crookston, MN	W
University of Minnesota, Duluth, MN	W
University of Minnesota, Twin Cities Campus, MN	W
University of Mississippi, MS	W
University of Missouri–Kansas City, MO	M,W
University of Missouri–St. Louis, MO	M,W
University of Mobile, AL	M,W
University of Montevallo, AL	M,W
University of Nebraska at Omaha, NE	M,W
University of Nebraska–Lincoln, NE	W
University of Nevada, Las Vegas, NV	M,W
University of Nevada, Reno, NV	W
University of New Hampshire, NH	M,W
University of New Haven, CT	M,W
University of North Alabama, AL	W
University of North Carolina at Asheville, NC	M,W
The University of North Carolina at Chapel Hill, NC	M,W
The University of North Carolina at Greensboro, NC	M,W
The University of North Carolina at Pembroke, NC	M,W
The University of North Carolina Wilmington, NC	M,W
University of Northern Colorado, CO	W
University of Northern Iowa, IA	W
University of North Florida, FL	M,W
University of North Georgia, GA	M,W
University of North Texas, TX	W
University of Notre Dame, IN	M,W
University of Oklahoma, OK	W
University of Oregon, OR	W
University of Pikeville, KY	M,W
University of Pittsburgh, PA	M,W
University of Portland, OR	M,W
University of Rhode Island, RI	M,W
University of Richmond, VA	W
University of Rio Grande, OH	M
University of St. Francis, IL	M,W
University of St. Thomas, TX	M
University of San Diego, CA	M,W
University of Science and Arts of Oklahoma, OK	M,W
University of South Alabama, AL	W

University of South Carolina, SC	M,W
University of South Carolina Aiken, SC	M,W
University of South Carolina Upstate, SC	M,W
The University of South Dakota, SD	W
University of Southern Indiana, IN	M,W
University of Southern Mississippi, MS	W
The University of Tampa, FL	M,W
The University of Tennessee, TN	W
The University of Tennessee at Chattanooga, TN	W
The University of Tennessee at Martin, TN	W
The University of Texas at Austin, TX	W
The University of Texas at Brownsville, TX	M,W
The University of Texas at San Antonio, TX	W
The University of Texas of the Permian Basin, TX	M,W
University of the Cumberlands, KY	M,W
University of the District of Columbia, DC	M
University of the Incarnate Word, TX	M,W
University of the Pacific, CA	W
The University of Toledo, OH	W
University of Tulsa, OK	M,W
University of Utah, UT	W
University of Vermont, VT	M,W
University of Virginia, VA	M,W
The University of West Alabama, AL	M,W
University of West Florida, FL	M,W
University of West Georgia, GA	W
University of Wisconsin–Green Bay, WI	M,W
University of Wisconsin–Madison, WI	M,W
University of Wisconsin–Milwaukee, WI	M,W
University of Wisconsin–Parkside, WI	M,W
University of Wyoming, WY	W
Upper Iowa University, IA	M,W
Ursuline College, OH	W
Utah State University, UT	W
Utah Valley University, UT	W
Valdosta State University, GA	W
Valparaiso University, IN	M,W
Vanderbilt University, TN	W
Villanova University, PA	M,W
Virginia Commonwealth University, VA	M,W
Virginia Intermont College, VA	M,W
Virginia Polytechnic Institute and State University, VA	M,W
Wagner College, NY	W
Wake Forest University, NC	M,W
Waldorf College, IA	M,W
Warner Pacific College, OR	M,W
Washburn University, KS	W
Washington State University, WA	W
Wayland Baptist University, TX	M,W
Wayne State College, NE	W
Webber International University, FL	M,W
West Chester University of Pennsylvania, PA	M,W
Western Carolina University, NC	W
Western Illinois University, IL	M,W
Western Michigan University, MI	M,W
Western Oregon University, OR	W
Western State Colorado University, CO	W
Western Washington University, WA	M,W
Westminster College, UT	M,W
West Texas A&M University, TX	M,W
West Virginia University, WV	M,W
West Virginia University Institute of Technology, WV	M,W
West Virginia Wesleyan College, WV	M,W
Wheeling Jesuit University, WV	M,W
William Jewell College, MO	M,W
Winona State University, MN	W
Winthrop University, SC	M,W
Wofford College, SC	M,W
Wright State University, OH	M,W
Xavier University, OH	M,W
Young Harris College, GA	M,W
Youngstown State University, OH	W

Softball

Abilene Christian University, TX	W
Academy of Art University, CA	W
Adams State University, CO	W
Adelphi University, NY	W
Alabama State University, AL	W
Alcorn State University, MS	W
Anderson University, SC	W
Angelo State University, TX	W
Appalachian State University, NC	W
Arizona State University, AZ	W
Arkansas Tech University, AR	W
Armstrong Atlantic State University, GA	W
Asbury University, KY	W
Ashland University, OH	W
Auburn University, AL	W
Auburn University at Montgomery, AL	W
Augustana College, SD	W
Austin Peay State University, TN	W
Azusa Pacific University, CA	W
Ball State University, IN	W
Barry University, FL	W
Barton College, NC	W
Baylor University, TX	W
Belhaven University, MS	W
Bellarmine University, KY	W
Belmont Abbey College, NC	W
Belmont University, TN	W
Bemidji State University, MN	W
Benedictine College, KS	W
Bethel College, IN	W
Bethune-Cookman University, FL	W
Binghamton University, State University of New York, NY	W
Biola University, CA	W
Bloomfield College, NJ	W
Bloomsburg University of Pennsylvania, PA	W
Bluefield College, VA	W
Bluefield State College, WV	W
Blue Mountain College, MS	W
Boise State University, ID	W
Boston College, MA	W
Boston University, MA	W
Bowie State University, MD	W
Bowling Green State University, OH	W
Bradley University, IL	W
Brevard College, NC	W
Brigham Young University, UT	W
Bryant University, RI	W
Butler University, IN	W
Caldwell College, NJ	W
California Baptist University, CA	W
California Polytechnic State University, San Luis Obispo, CA	W
California State University, Chico, CA	W
California State University, Dominguez Hills, CA	W
California State University, Fresno, CA	W
California State University, Fullerton, CA	W
California State University, Long Beach, CA	W
California State University, Monterey Bay, CA	W
California State University, Northridge, CA	W
California State University, San Bernardino, CA	W
Calumet College of Saint Joseph, IN	W
Cameron University, OK	W
Campbellsville University, KY	W
Canisius College, NY	W
Carson-Newman University, TN	W
Catawba College, NC	W
Cedarville University, OH	W
Central Connecticut State University, CT	W
Central Methodist University, MO	W
Central Michigan University, MI	W
Chestnut Hill College, PA	W
Chowan University, NC	W
Christian Brothers University, TN	W
Clarion University of Pennsylvania, PA	W
Clarke University, IA	W
Cleveland State University, OH	W
Coastal Carolina University, SC	W
Coker College, SC	W
Colgate University, NY	W
The College of Idaho, ID	W
College of Saint Mary, NE	W
The College of Saint Rose, NY	W
Colorado Mesa University, CO	W
Colorado School of Mines, CO	W
Colorado State University, CO	W
Columbia College, MO	W
Columbus State University, GA	W
Concordia University, CA	W
Concordia University, OR	W
Concordia University, Nebraska, NE	W
Concordia University, St. Paul, MN	W
Corban University, OR	W
Cornerstone University, MI	W
Creighton University, NE	W
Culver-Stockton College, MO	W
Dakota State University, SD	W
Dakota Wesleyan University, SD	W
Davenport University, MI	M,W
DePaul University, IL	W
Doane College, NE	W
Dominican College, NY	W
Dordt College, IA	W
Drake University, IA	W
Drury University, MO	W
East Carolina University, NC	W
Eastern Illinois University, IL	W
Eastern Michigan University, MI	W
Eastern New Mexico University, NM	W
Eckerd College, FL	W
Edinboro University of Pennsylvania, PA	W
Elizabeth City State University, NC	W
Elon University, NC	W
Embry-Riddle Aeronautical University–Daytona, FL	W

Embry-Riddle Aeronautical University–Prescott, AZ	W
Emmanuel College, GA	W
Emporia State University, KS	W
Evangel University, MO	W
Fairfield University, CT	W
Fairmont State University, WV	W
Faulkner University, AL	W
Fayetteville State University, NC	W
Felician College, NJ	W
Ferris State University, MI	W
Flagler College, FL	W
Florida Agricultural and Mechanical University, FL	W
Florida Atlantic University, FL	W
Florida Gulf Coast University, FL	W
Florida Institute of Technology, FL	W
Florida International University, FL	W
Florida Southern College, FL	W
Florida State University, FL	W
Fort Lewis College, CO	W
Francis Marion University, SC	W
Franklin Pierce University, NH	W
Freed-Hardeman University, TN	W
Furman University, SC	W
Gannon University, PA	W
Gardner-Webb University, NC	W
George Mason University, VA	W
Georgetown College, KY	W
Georgetown University, DC	W
Georgia College & State University, GA	W
Georgia Institute of Technology, GA	W
Georgia Southern University, GA	W
Georgia Southwestern State University, GA	W
Georgia State University, GA	W
Goldey-Beacom College, DE	W
Goshen College, IN	W
Graceland University, IA	W
Grand Valley State University, MI	W
Grand View University, IA	W
Hampton University, VA	W
Hawai'i Pacific University, HI	W
Henderson State University, AR	W
Hillsdale College, MI	W
Hofstra University, NY	W
Hope International University, CA	W
Houston Baptist University, TX	W
Huntington University, IN	W
Idaho State University, ID	W
Illinois State University, IL	W
Indiana State University, IN	W
Indiana Tech, IN	W
Indiana University Bloomington, IN	W
Indiana University of Pennsylvania, PA	W
Indiana University–Purdue University Fort Wayne, IN	W
Indiana University–Purdue University Indianapolis, IN	W
Indiana Wesleyan University, IN	W
Inter American University of Puerto Rico, Bayamón Campus, PR	M,W
Inter American University of Puerto Rico, Ponce Campus, PR	M,W
Iona College, NY	W
Iowa State University of Science and Technology, IA	W
Jacksonville State University, AL	W
Jacksonville University, FL	W
James Madison University, VA	W

Johnson C. Smith University, NC	W
Kennesaw State University, GA	W
Kent State University, OH	W
Kentucky State University, KY	W
Kentucky Wesleyan College, KY	W
King College, TN	W
Kutztown University of Pennsylvania, PA	W
Lake Erie College, OH	W
Lake Superior State University, MI	W
Lane College, TN	W
La Salle University, PA	W
Lees-McRae College, NC	W
Lee University, TN	W
Lehigh University, PA	W
Le Moyne College, NY	W
Lewis University, IL	W
Liberty University, VA	W
Limestone College, SC	W
Lincoln University, MO	W
Lindenwood University, MO	W
Lindsey Wilson College, KY	W
Lipscomb University, TN	W
Lock Haven University of Pennsylvania, PA	W
Long Island University–Brooklyn Campus, NY	W
Long Island University–C. W. Post Campus, NY	W
Longwood University, VA	W
Louisiana State University and Agricultural and Mechanical College, LA	W
Louisiana Tech University, LA	W
Lourdes University, OH	W
Loyola Marymount University, CA	W
Loyola University Chicago, IL	W
Lubbock Christian University, TX	W
Lynn University, FL	W
Lyon College, AR	W
Malone University, OH	W
Manhattan College, NY	W
Mansfield University of Pennsylvania, PA	W
Marist College, NY	W
Marshall University, WV	W
Maryville University of Saint Louis, MO	W
Mayville State University, ND	W
McKendree University, IL	W
McNeese State University, LA	W
Menlo College, CA	W
Mercer University, GA	W
Mercy College, NY	W
Mercyhurst University, PA	W
Merrimack College, MA	W
Metropolitan State University of Denver, CO	W
Miami University, OH	W
Michigan State University, MI	W
Middle Tennessee State University, TN	W
Midwestern State University, TX	W
Millersville University of Pennsylvania, PA	W
Minnesota State University Mankato, MN	W
Minot State University, ND	W
Mississippi State University, MS	W
Missouri Baptist University, MO	W
Missouri State University, MO	W
Missouri University of Science and Technology, MO	W
Missouri Western State University, MO	W

Molloy College, NY	W
Monmouth University, NJ	W
Montreat College, NC	W
Morehead State University, KY	W
Morningside College, IA	W
Mount Marty College, SD	W
Mount Mercy University, IA	W
Mount St. Mary's University, MD	W
Mount Vernon Nazarene University, OH	W
Murray State University, KY	W
Newberry College, SC	W
New Mexico Highlands University, NM	W
New Mexico State University, NM	W
New York Institute of Technology, NY	W
Niagara University, NY	W
Nicholls State University, LA	W
Norfolk State University, VA	M
North Carolina Central University, NC	W
North Carolina State University, NC	W
Northern Illinois University, IL	W
Northern Kentucky University, KY	W
Northern State University, SD	W
Northwest Christian University, OR	W
Northwestern Oklahoma State University, OK	W
Northwestern State University of Louisiana, LA	W
Northwest Missouri State University, MO	W
Northwest Nazarene University, ID	W
Northwood University, Florida Campus, FL	W
Northwood University, Michigan Campus, MI	W
Northwood University, Texas Campus, TX	W
Notre Dame de Namur University, CA	W
Nova Southeastern University, FL	W
Nyack College, NY	W
Oakland University, MI	W
The Ohio State University, OH	W
Ohio University, OH	W
Ohio Valley University, WV	W
Oklahoma Baptist University, OK	W
Oklahoma Christian University, OK	W
Oklahoma City University, OK	W
Oklahoma State University, OK	W
Oregon State University, OR	W
Ouachita Baptist University, AR	W
Pace University, NY	W
Palm Beach Atlantic University, FL	W
Park University, MO	W
Penn State University Park, PA	W
Philadelphia University, PA	W
Pittsburg State University, KS	W
Point Park University, PA	W
Post University, CT	W
Presbyterian College, SC	W
Providence College, RI	W
Purdue University, IN	W
Purdue University North Central, IN	W
Queens College of the City University of New York, NY	W
Quincy University, IL	W
Quinnipiac University, CT	W
Radford University, VA	W
Regis University, CO	W
Research College of Nursing, MO	W

Rider University, NJ	W
Robert Morris University, PA	W
Robert Morris University Illinois, IL	W
Rockhurst University, MO	W
Rogers State University, OK	W
Rollins College, FL	W
Sacred Heart University, CT	W
Saginaw Valley State University, MI	W
St. Ambrose University, IA	W
Saint Anselm College, NH	W
St. Bonaventure University, NY	W
St. Edward's University, TX	W
St. John's University, NY	W
Saint Joseph's College, IN	W
Saint Joseph's University, PA	W
Saint Louis University, MO	W
Saint Martin's University, WA	W
Saint Mary-of-the-Woods College, IN	W
Saint Mary's College of California, CA	W
Saint Peter's University, NJ	W
St. Thomas University, FL	W
Samford University, AL	W
Sam Houston State University, TX	W
San Diego State University, CA	W
San Francisco State University, CA	W
Santa Clara University, CA	W
Seattle University, WA	W
Seton Hill University, PA	W
Shawnee State University, OH	M
Shepherd University, WV	W
Shippensburg University of Pennsylvania, PA	W
Siena College, NY	W
Simpson University, CA	W
Slippery Rock University of Pennsylvania, PA	W
Sonoma State University, CA	W
South Dakota State University, SD	W
Southeastern Louisiana University, LA	W
Southeastern Oklahoma State University, OK	W
Southeast Missouri State University, MO	W
Southern Arkansas University–Magnolia, AR	W
Southern Connecticut State University, CT	W
Southern Illinois University Carbondale, IL	W
Southern Illinois University Edwardsville, IL	W
Southern Utah University, UT	W
Southwest Baptist University, MO	W
Southwestern College, KS	W
Spring Arbor University, MI	W
Spring Hill College, AL	W
Stanford University, CA	W
Stephen F. Austin State University, TX	W
Stephens College, MO	W
Stetson University, FL	W
Stonehill College, MA	W
Stony Brook University, State University of New York, NY	W
Syracuse University, NY	W
Tarleton State University, TX	W
Taylor University, IN	W
Temple University, PA	W
Tennessee Wesleyan College, TN	W
Texas A&M International University, TX	W
Texas A&M University, TX	W
Texas Southern University, TX	W
Texas State University–San Marcos, TX	W
Texas Wesleyan University, TX	W
Texas Woman's University, TX	W
Thomas University, GA	W
Tiffin University, OH	W
Trevecca Nazarene University, TN	W
Trinity Christian College, IL	W
Troy University, AL	W
Truman State University, MO	W
Union College, KY	W
Union University, TN	W
University at Albany, State University of New York, NY	W
University at Buffalo, the State University of New York, NY	W
The University of Akron, OH	W
The University of Alabama, AL	W
The University of Alabama at Birmingham, AL	W
The University of Arizona, AZ	W
University of Bridgeport, CT	W
University of California, Davis, CA	W
University of California, Los Angeles, CA	W
University of California, Riverside, CA	W
University of California, Santa Barbara, CA	W
University of Central Arkansas, AR	W
University of Central Florida, FL	W
University of Charleston, WV	W
University of Colorado Colorado Springs, CO	W
University of Connecticut, CT	W
University of Dayton, OH	W
University of Delaware, DE	W
University of Evansville, IN	W
University of Florida, FL	W
University of Georgia, GA	W
University of Hartford, CT	W
University of Hawaii at Hilo, HI	W
University of Hawaii at Manoa, HI	W
University of Houston, TX	W
University of Illinois at Chicago, IL	W
University of Illinois at Springfield, IL	W
University of Illinois at Urbana–Champaign, IL	W
The University of Iowa, IA	W
The University of Kansas, KS	W
University of Louisiana at Lafayette, LA	W
University of Louisville, KY	W
University of Maryland, Baltimore County, MD	W
University of Maryland, College Park, MD	W
University of Massachusetts Amherst, MA	W
University of Michigan, MI	W
University of Michigan–Dearborn, MI	
University of Minnesota, Crookston, MN	W
University of Minnesota, Duluth, MN	W
University of Minnesota, Twin Cities Campus, MN	W
University of Mississippi, MS	W
University of Missouri–Kansas City, MO	W
University of Missouri–St. Louis, MO	W
University of Mobile, AL	W
University of Nebraska at Kearney, NE	W
University of Nebraska at Omaha, NE	W
University of Nebraska–Lincoln, NE	W
University of Nevada, Las Vegas, NV	W
University of Nevada, Reno, NV	W
University of New Haven, CT	W
University of North Alabama, AL	W
The University of North Carolina at Chapel Hill, NC	W
The University of North Carolina at Greensboro, NC	W
The University of North Carolina at Pembroke, NC	W
The University of North Carolina Wilmington, NC	W
University of Northern Colorado, CO	W
University of Northern Iowa, IA	W
University of North Florida, FL	W
University of North Georgia, GA	W
University of North Texas, TX	W
University of Notre Dame, IN	W
University of Oklahoma, OK	W
University of Oregon, OR	W
University of Pikeville, KY	W
University of Pittsburgh, PA	W
University of Puerto Rico at Bayamón, PR	M,W
University of Rhode Island, RI	W
University of Rio Grande, OH	W
University of St. Francis, IL	W
University of San Diego, CA	W
University of Science and Arts of Oklahoma, OK	W
University of South Carolina, SC	W
University of South Carolina Aiken, SC	W
University of South Carolina Upstate, SC	W
The University of South Dakota, SD	W
University of Southern Indiana, IN	W
University of Southern Mississippi, MS	W
The University of Tampa, FL	W
The University of Tennessee, TN	W
The University of Tennessee at Chattanooga, TN	W
The University of Tennessee at Martin, TN	W
The University of Texas at Arlington, TX	W
The University of Texas at Austin, TX	W
The University of Texas at San Antonio, TX	W
The University of Texas of the Permian Basin, TX	W
University of the Cumberlands, KY	W
University of the Incarnate Word, TX	W
University of the Pacific, CA	W
University of the Sciences, PA	W
The University of Toledo, OH	W
University of Tulsa, OK	W
University of Utah, UT	W
University of Virginia, VA	W

The University of Virginia's College at Wise, VA	W
The University of West Alabama, AL	W
University of West Florida, FL	W
University of West Georgia, GA	W
University of Wisconsin–Green Bay, WI	W
University of Wisconsin–Madison, WI	W
University of Wisconsin–Parkside, WI	W
Upper Iowa University, IA	W
Ursuline College, OH	W
Utah State University, UT	W
Utah Valley University, UT	W
Valdosta State University, GA	W
Valley City State University, ND	W
Valparaiso University, IN	W
Villanova University, PA	W
Virginia Intermont College, VA	W
Virginia State University, VA	W
Virginia Union University, VA	W
Wagner College, NY	W
Waldorf College, IA	W
Washburn University, KS	W
Wayne State College, NE	W
Wayne State University, MI	W
Webber International University, FL	W
West Chester University of Pennsylvania, PA	W
Western Carolina University, NC	W
Western Illinois University, IL	W
Western Kentucky University, KY	W
Western Michigan University, MI	W
Western Oregon University, OR	W
Western Washington University, WA	W
West Texas A&M University, TX	W
West Virginia State University, WV	W
West Virginia University Institute of Technology, WV	W
West Virginia Wesleyan College, WV	W
Wheeling Jesuit University, WV	W
Wichita State University, KS	W
William Jewell College, MO	W
Winona State University, MN	W
Winthrop University, SC	W
Wright State University, OH	W
Young Harris College, GA	W
Youngstown State University, OH	W

Squash

University of Great Falls, MT	W

Swimming and diving

Adams State University, CO	M,W
Adelphi University, NY	M,W
Arizona State University, AZ	M,W
Asbury University, KY	M,W
Ashland University, OH	M,W
Auburn University, AL	M,W
Azusa Pacific University, CA	M,W
Ball State University, IN	M,W
Binghamton University, State University of New York, NY	M,W
Biola University, CA	M,W
Bloomsburg University of Pennsylvania, PA	M,W
Boise State University, ID	W
Boston College, MA	M,W
Boston University, MA	M,W
Bowling Green State University, OH	W
Brigham Young University, UT	M,W
Bryant University, RI	M,W
Bucknell University, PA	M,W
California Baptist University, CA	M,W

California Polytechnic State University, San Luis Obispo, CA	M,W
California State University, Fresno, CA	W
California State University, Northridge, CA	M,W
California State University, San Bernardino, CA	M,W
Campbellsville University, KY	M,W
Canisius College, NY	M,W
Catawba College, NC	M,W
Central Connecticut State University, CT	W
Clarion University of Pennsylvania, PA	M,W
Cleveland State University, OH	M,W
College of Charleston, SC	M,W
The College of Idaho, ID	M,W
College of Saint Mary, NE	W
The College of Saint Rose, NY	M,W
Colorado Mesa University, CO	M,W
Colorado State University, CO	W
Concordia University, CA	M,W
Converse College, SC	W
Davidson College, NC	M,W
Drury University, MO	M,W
Duquesne University, PA	W
East Carolina University, NC	M,W
Eastern Illinois University, IL	M,W
Eastern Michigan University, MI	M,W
Edinboro University of Pennsylvania, PA	M,W
Fairfield University, CT	M,W
Fairmont State University, WV	M,W
Florida Agricultural and Mechanical University, FL	M,W
Florida Gulf Coast University, FL	W
Florida Institute of Technology, FL	M,W
Florida International University, FL	W
Florida Southern College, FL	M,W
Florida State University, FL	M,W
Gannon University, PA	M,W
Gardner-Webb University, NC	M,W
George Mason University, VA	M,W
The George Washington University, DC	M,W
Georgia Institute of Technology, GA	M,W
Georgia Southern University, GA	W
Grand Valley State University, MI	M,W
Henderson State University, AR	M,W
Hillsdale College, MI	W
Illinois Institute of Technology, IL	M,W
Illinois State University, IL	W
Indiana University Bloomington, IN	M,W
Indiana University of Pennsylvania, PA	M,W
Indiana University–Purdue University Indianapolis, IN	M,W
Inter American University of Puerto Rico, Bayamón Campus, PR	M,W
Iona College, NY	M,W
Iowa State University of Science and Technology, IA	M,W
James Madison University, VA	W
King College, TN	M,W
Kutztown University of Pennsylvania, PA	W
Lake Erie College, OH	M,W
La Salle University, PA	M,W
Lehigh University, PA	M,W
Le Moyne College, NY	M,W

Lewis University, IL	M,W
Liberty University, VA	W
Limestone College, SC	M,W
Lindenwood University, MO	M,W
Lindsey Wilson College, KY	M,W
Lock Haven University of Pennsylvania, PA	W
Long Island University–C. W. Post Campus, NY	W
Louisiana State University and Agricultural and Mechanical College, LA	M,W
Loyola Marymount University, CA	W
Loyola University Maryland, MD	M,W
Lynn University, FL	W
Malone University, OH	W
Manhattan College, NY	M,W
Marist College, NY	M,W
Marshall University, WV	W
Merrimack College, MA	W
Miami University, OH	M,W
Michigan State University, MI	M,W
Millersville University of Pennsylvania, PA	W
Minnesota State University Mankato, MN	W
Missouri State University, MO	M,W
Missouri University of Science and Technology, MO	M
Morningside College, IA	M,W
Mount St. Mary's University, MD	W
New Jersey Institute of Technology, NJ	M,W
New Mexico State University, NM	W
Niagara University, NY	M,W
North Carolina State University, NC	M,W
Northeastern University, MA	W
Northern Arizona University, AZ	W
Northern Illinois University, IL	M,W
Northern Michigan University, MI	W
Northern State University, SD	W
Nova Southeastern University, FL	M,W
Oakland University, MI	M,W
The Ohio State University, OH	M,W
Ohio University, OH	W
Old Dominion University, VA	M,W
Oregon State University, OR	W
Ouachita Baptist University, AR	M,W
Pace University, NY	M,W
Penn State University Park, PA	M,W
Pepperdine University, CA	W
Post University, CT	M,W
Providence College, RI	M,W
Purdue University, IN	M,W
Queens College of the City University of New York, NY	M,W
Radford University, VA	W
Rice University, TX	W
Rider University, NJ	M,W
Robert Morris University Illinois, IL	W
Sacred Heart University, CT	W
St. Bonaventure University, NY	M,W
Saint Louis University, MO	M,W
Saint Peter's University, NJ	M,W
San Diego State University, CA	W
San Jose State University, CA	W
Savannah College of Art and Design, GA	M,W
Seattle University, WA	M,W
Shippensburg University of Pennsylvania, PA	M,W
Siena College, NY	W

Soka University of America, CA	M,W	University of Notre Dame, IN	M,W	Armstrong Atlantic State University, GA	M,W
South Dakota State University, SD	M,W	University of Pittsburgh, PA	M,W	Asbury University, KY	M,W
Southern Connecticut State University, CT	M,W	University of Rhode Island, RI	W	Auburn University, AL	M,W
		University of Richmond, VA	W	Auburn University at Montgomery, AL	M,W
Southern Illinois University Carbondale, IL	M,W	University of San Diego, CA	W	Augustana College, SD	M,W
		University of South Carolina, SC	M,W	Austin Peay State University, TN	M,W
Southern Methodist University, TX	M,W	The University of South Dakota, SD	M,W	Azusa Pacific University, CA	M,W
Stanford University, CA	M,W	The University of Tampa, FL	M,W	Ball State University, IN	M,W
Stony Brook University, State University of New York, NY	W	The University of Tennessee, TN	M,W	Barry University, FL	M,W
		The University of Texas at Austin, TX	M,W	Barton College, NC	M,W
Texas A&M University, TX	M,W			Baylor University, TX	M,W
Texas Christian University, TX	M,W	The University of Texas of the Permian Basin, TX	M,W	Belhaven University, MS	M,W
Tiffin University, OH	M,W	University of the Cumberlands, KY	M,W	Bellarmine University, KY	M,W
Truman State University, MO	W	University of the Incarnate Word, TX	M,W	Belmont Abbey College, NC	M,W
Tulane University, LA	W			Belmont University, TN	M,W
Union College, KY	M,W	University of the Pacific, CA	M,W	Bemidji State University, MN	W
University at Buffalo, the State University of New York, NY	M,W	The University of Toledo, OH	W	Bethel College, IN	M,W
		University of Utah, UT	M,W	Bethel College, KS	M,W
The University of Akron, OH	W	University of Vermont, VT	W	Bethune-Cookman University, FL	M,W
The University of Alabama, AL	M,W	University of Virginia, VA	M,W	Binghamton University, State University of New York, NY	M,W
University of Alaska Fairbanks, AK	W	University of Wisconsin–Green Bay, WI	M,W		
The University of Arizona, AZ	M,W			Biola University, CA	M,W
University of Bridgeport, CT	M,W	University of Wisconsin–Madison, WI	M,W	Bloomfield College, NJ	M
University of California, Davis, CA	W			Bloomsburg University of Pennsylvania, PA	M,W
		University of Wisconsin–Milwaukee, WI	M,W		
University of California, Los Angeles, CA	W	University of Wyoming, WY	M,W	Bluefield College, VA	M,W
		Ursuline College, OH	W	Bluefield State College, WV	M,W
University of California, Santa Barbara, CA	M,W	Valparaiso University, IN	M,W	Boise State University, ID	M,W
		Vanderbilt University, TN	W	Boston College, MA	M,W
University of Charleston, WV	M,W	Villanova University, PA	W	Boston University, MA	W
University of Cincinnati, OH	M,W	Virginia Polytechnic Institute and State University, VA	M,W	Bowie State University, MD	W
University of Connecticut, CT	M,W			Bowling Green State University, OH	W
University of Delaware, DE	W	Wagner College, NY	W	Bradley University, IL	M,W
University of Denver, CO	M,W	Washington State University, WA	W	Brevard College, NC	M,W
University of Evansville, IN	M,W	Wayne State University, MI	M,W	Brigham Young University, UT	M,W
University of Florida, FL	M,W	West Chester University of Pennsylvania, PA	M,W	Bryant University, RI	M,W
University of Georgia, GA	M,W			Butler University, IN	M,W
University of Hawaii at Manoa, HI	M,W	Western Illinois University, IL	M,W	Caldwell College, NJ	M,W
University of Houston, TX	W	Western Kentucky University, KY	M,W	California Polytechnic State University, San Luis Obispo, CA	M,W
University of Idaho, ID	W	Western State Colorado University, CO	W		
University of Illinois at Chicago, IL	M,W			California State Polytechnic University, Pomona, CA	M,W
		West Virginia University, WV	M,W		
University of Illinois at Urbana–Champaign, IL	W	West Virginia University Institute of Technology, WV	M	California State University, Fresno, CA	M,W
The University of Iowa, IA	M,W	West Virginia Wesleyan College, WV	M,W	California State University, Fullerton, CA	W
The University of Kansas, KS	W	Wheeling Jesuit University, WV	M,W		
University of Louisville, KY	M,W	William Jewell College, MO	M,W	California State University, Long Beach, CA	W
University of Maryland, Baltimore County, MD	M,W	Wright State University, OH	M,W	California State University, Los Angeles, CA	W
		Xavier University, OH	M,W		
University of Massachusetts Amherst, MA	M,W	Youngstown State University, OH	W	California State University, Northridge, CA	W
University of Miami, FL	M,W	**Table tennis**		Calumet College of Saint Joseph, IN	M,W
University of Michigan, MI	M,W	Inter American University of Puerto Rico, Bayamón Campus, PR	M,W	Cameron University, OK	M,W
University of Minnesota, Twin Cities Campus, MN	M,W			Campbellsville University, KY	M,W
		Inter American University of Puerto Rico, Ponce Campus, PR	M,W	Carson-Newman University, TN	M,W
University of Nebraska at Kearney, NE	W			Catawba College, NC	M,W
		Lindenwood University, MO	M,W	Cedarville University, OH	M,W
University of Nebraska at Omaha, NE	W	Polytechnic University of Puerto Rico, PR	M	Chestnut Hill College, PA	M,W
University of Nebraska–Lincoln, NE	W	Texas Wesleyan University, TX	M,W	Chicago State University, IL	M,W
		University of Puerto Rico at Bayamón, PR	M,W	Chowan University, NC	M,W
University of Nevada, Las Vegas, NV	M,W			Christian Brothers University, TN	M,W
University of Nevada, Reno, NV	W	**Tennis**		The Citadel, The Military College of South Carolina, SC	M
University of New Hampshire, NH	W	Abilene Christian University, TX	M,W		
University of North Carolina at Asheville, NC	W	Academy of Art University, CA	W	Clarion University of Pennsylvania, PA	W
		Adelphi University, NY	M,W	Clarke University, IA	W
The University of North Carolina at Chapel Hill, NC	M,W	Alabama State University, AL	M,W	Clayton State University, GA	W
		Alcorn State University, MS	M,W	Clemson University, SC	M,W
The University of North Carolina Wilmington, NC	M,W	Anderson University, SC	M,W	Cleveland State University, OH	W
		Appalachian State University, NC	M,W	Coastal Carolina University, SC	M,W
University of Northern Colorado, CO	W	Arizona State University, AZ	W	Coker College, SC	M,W
University of Northern Iowa, IA	W	Arkansas State University, AR	W	College of Charleston, SC	M,W
University of North Florida, FL	W	Arkansas Tech University, AR	W		
University of North Texas, TX	W				

The College of Idaho, ID	W	Idaho State University, ID	M,W	Mississippi State University, MS	M,W
The College of William and Mary, VA	M,W	Illinois State University, IL	M,W	Missouri Baptist University, MO	M,W
Colorado Mesa University, CO	M,W	Indiana Tech, IN	M,W	Missouri Western State University, MO	W
Colorado State University, CO	W	Indiana University Bloomington, IN	M,W	Molloy College, NY	W
Columbus State University, GA	M,W	Indiana University of Pennsylvania, PA	W	Monmouth University, NJ	M,W
Concordia University, CA	M,W	Indiana University–Purdue University Fort Wayne, IN	M,W	Montana State University, MT	M,W
Concordia University, Nebraska, NE	M,W			Montreat College, NC	M,W
Converse College, SC	W	Indiana University–Purdue University Indianapolis, IN	M,W	Morehead State University, KY	M,W
Creighton University, NE	M,W	Indiana Wesleyan University, IN	M,W	Morehouse College, GA	M
Dallas Baptist University, TX	W	Iowa State University of Science and Technology, IA	W	Morningside College, IA	M,W
Davenport University, MI	M,W	Jacksonville State University, AL	M,W	Mount Marty College, SD	W
Davidson College, NC	M,W	James Madison University, VA	M,W	Mount St. Mary's University, MD	M,W
DePaul University, IL	M,W	John Brown University, AR	M,W	Murray State University, KY	M,W
Drake University, IA	M,W	Johnson C. Smith University, NC	M,W	Newberry College, SC	M,W
Drury University, MO	M,W	Kansas State University, KS	W	New Jersey Institute of Technology, NJ	M,W
Duquesne University, PA	M,W	Kennesaw State University, GA	M,W	New Mexico State University, NM	M,W
East Carolina University, NC	M,W	Kentucky Wesleyan College, KY	W	New York Institute of Technology, NY	M,W
Eastern Illinois University, IL	M,W	King College, TN	M,W	Niagara University, NY	M,W
Eastern Michigan University, MI	W	Kutztown University of Pennsylvania, PA	M,W	Nicholls State University, LA	W
Eastern Washington University, WA	M,W	Lake Erie College, OH	M,W	Norfolk State University, VA	M,W
Eckerd College, FL	M,W	Lake Superior State University, MI	M,W	North Carolina Central University, NC	M,W
Elizabeth City State University, NC	W	Lamar University, TX	M,W	North Carolina State University, NC	M,W
Elon University, NC	M,W	Lane College, TN	M,W		
Embry-Riddle Aeronautical University–Daytona, FL	M,W	La Salle University, PA	M,W	Northern Arizona University, AZ	M,W
		Lees-McRae College, NC	M,W	Northern Illinois University, IL	M,W
Emmanuel College, GA	M,W	Lee University, TN	M,W	Northern Kentucky University, KY	M,W
Emporia State University, KS	M,W	Lehigh University, PA	M,W	Northern State University, SD	W
Evangel University, MO	M,W	Le Moyne College, NY	M,W	Northwestern State University of Louisiana, LA	W
Fairfield University, CT	M,W	Lewis-Clark State College, ID	M,W		
Fairmont State University, WV	M,W	Lewis University, IL	M,W	Northwest Missouri State University, MO	M,W
Fayetteville State University, NC	W	Liberty University, VA	M,W		
Ferris State University, MI	M,W	Limestone College, SC	M,W	Northwood University, Florida Campus, FL	M,W
Flagler College, FL	M,W	Lincoln University, MO	W		
Florida Agricultural and Mechanical University, FL	M,W	Lindenwood University, MO	M,W	Northwood University, Michigan Campus, MI	M,W
		Lindsey Wilson College, KY	M,W		
Florida Gulf Coast University, FL	M,W	Lipscomb University, TN	M,W	Notre Dame de Namur University, CA	W
Florida Institute of Technology, FL	M,W	Long Island University–Brooklyn Campus, NY	W	Nova Southeastern University, FL	W
				Oakland University, MI	W
Florida International University, FL	W	Long Island University–C. W. Post Campus, NY	W	The Ohio State University, OH	M,W
Florida Southern College, FL	M,W	Longwood University, VA	M,W	Oklahoma Baptist University, OK	M,W
Florida State University, FL	M,W	Louisiana State University and Agricultural and Mechanical College, LA	M,W	Oklahoma Christian University, OK	M,W
Francis Marion University, SC	M,W			Oklahoma State University, OK	M,W
Franklin Pierce University, NH	M,W			Old Dominion University, VA	M,W
Furman University, SC	M,W	Louisiana Tech University, LA	W	Oral Roberts University, OK	M,W
Gardner-Webb University, NC	M,W	Loyola Marymount University, CA	M,W	Ouachita Baptist University, AR	M,W
George Mason University, VA	M,W	Loyola University Maryland, MD	M,W	Palm Beach Atlantic University, FL	M,W
Georgetown College, KY	M,W	Lynn University, FL	M,W	Penn State University Park, PA	M,W
Georgetown University, DC	W	Malone University, OH	M,W	Pepperdine University, CA	M,W
The George Washington University, DC	M,W	Manhattan College, NY	W	Philadelphia University, PA	M,W
		Marist College, NY	M,W	Point Loma Nazarene University, CA	M,W
Georgia College & State University, GA	M,W	Marquette University, WI	M,W	Polytechnic University of Puerto Rico, PR	M,W
		Marshall University, WV	W		
Georgia Institute of Technology, GA	M,W	Maryville University of Saint Louis, MO	M,W	Post University, CT	M,W
				Presbyterian College, SC	M,W
Georgia Southern University, GA	M,W	McKendree University, IL	M,W	Providence College, RI	W
Georgia Southwestern State University, GA	M,W	McNeese State University, LA	W	Purdue University, IN	M,W
		Mercer University, GA	M,W	Queens College of the City University of New York, NY	
Georgia State University, GA	M,W	Mercyhurst University, PA	M,W		
Goldey-Beacom College, DE	W	Merrimack College, MA	M,W	Quincy University, IL	M,W
Gonzaga University, WA	M,W	Metropolitan State University of Denver, CO	M,W	Quinnipiac University, CT	M,W
Goshen College, IN	M,W			Radford University, VA	M,W
Graceland University, IA	M,W	Miami University, OH	W	Research College of Nursing, MO	M,W
Grand Valley State University, MI	M,W	Michigan State University, MI	M,W	Rice University, TX	M,W
Grand View University, IA	M,W	Middle Tennessee State University, TN	M,W	Rider University, NJ	M,W
Hampton University, VA	M,W			Robert Morris University, PA	M,W
Harding University, AR	M,W	Midwestern State University, TX	M,W	Robert Morris University Illinois, IL	W
Hawai'i Pacific University, HI	M,W	Millersville University of Pennsylvania, PA	M,W		
Henderson State University, AR	M,W			Roberts Wesleyan College, NY	M,W
Hillsdale College, MI	W	Minnesota State University Mankato, MN	M,W	Rockhurst University, MO	M,W
Hofstra University, NY	M,W			Rollins College, FL	M,W
Hope International University, CA	M,W				
Huntington University, IN	M,W				

Sacred Heart University, CT	M,W	University at Albany, State		University of New Orleans, LA	M,W
Saginaw Valley State University, MI	W	University of New York, NY	W	University of North Alabama, AL	M,W
St. Ambrose University, IA	M,W	University at Buffalo, the State University of New York, NY	M,W	University of North Carolina at Asheville, NC	M,W
Saint Anselm College, NH	M,W	The University of Akron, OH	W	The University of North Carolina at Chapel Hill, NC	M,W
St. Bonaventure University, NY	M,W	The University of Alabama, AL	M,W		
St. Edward's University, TX	M,W	The University of Alabama at Birmingham, AL	M,W	The University of North Carolina at Greensboro, NC	M,W
St. John's University, NY	M,W	The University of Arizona, AZ	M,W		
Saint Joseph's College, IN	M,W	University of California, Davis, CA	M,W	The University of North Carolina at Pembroke, NC	W
Saint Joseph's University, PA	M,W	University of California, Irvine, CA	M,W	The University of North Carolina Wilmington, NC	M,W
Saint Louis University, MO	M,W	University of California, Los Angeles, CA	M,W	University of Northern Colorado, CO	M,W
Saint Mary's College of California, CA	M,W	University of California, Santa Barbara, CA	M,W	University of Northern Iowa, IA	W
Saint Peter's University, NJ	M,W	University of Central Arkansas, AR	W	University of North Florida, FL	M,W
St. Thomas University, FL	M,W	University of Central Florida, FL	M,W	University of North Georgia, GA	M,W
Samford University, AL	M,W	University of Charleston, WV	M,W	University of Notre Dame, IN	M,W
Sam Houston State University, TX	W	University of Cincinnati, OH	W	University of Oklahoma, OK	M,W
San Diego State University, CA	M,W	University of Colorado Boulder, CO	W	University of Oregon, OR	M,W
San Jose State University, CA	W	University of Connecticut, CT	M,W	University of Pikeville, KY	M,W
Santa Clara University, CA	M,W	University of Dayton, OH	M,W	University of Pittsburgh, PA	W
Savannah College of Art and Design, GA	M,W	University of Denver, CO	M,W	University of Portland, OR	M,W
Seton Hill University, PA	W	University of Evansville, IN	W	University of Puerto Rico at Bayamón, PR	M,W
Shawnee State University, OH	M,W	University of Florida, FL	M,W		
Shepherd University, WV	M,W	University of Georgia, GA	M,W	University of Rhode Island, RI	W
Shippensburg University of Pennsylvania, PA	W	University of Hartford, CT	M,W	University of Richmond, VA	M,W
		University of Hawaii at Hilo, HI	M,W	University of St. Francis, IL	M,W
Siena College, NY	M,W	University of Hawaii at Manoa, HI	M,W	University of San Diego, CA	M,W
Slippery Rock University of Pennsylvania, PA	W	University of Houston, TX	W	University of South Alabama, AL	M,W
Sonoma State University, CA	M,W	University of Idaho, ID	M,W	University of South Carolina, SC	M,W
South Dakota State University, SD	M,W	University of Illinois at Chicago, IL	M,W	University of South Carolina Aiken, SC	M,W
Southeastern Louisiana University, LA	W	University of Illinois at Springfield, IL	M,W	University of South Carolina Upstate, SC	M,W
Southeastern Oklahoma State University, OK	M,W	University of Illinois at Urbana–Champaign, IL	M,W	The University of South Dakota, SD	W
Southeast Missouri State University, MO	W	The University of Iowa, IA	M,W	University of Southern Indiana, IN	M,W
		The University of Kansas, KS	W	University of Southern Mississippi, MS	M,W
Southern Arkansas University–Magnolia, AR	W	University of Louisiana at Lafayette, LA	M,W	The University of Tampa, FL	W
Southern Illinois University Carbondale, IL	M,W	University of Louisville, KY	M,W	The University of Tennessee, TN	M,W
		University of Maryland, Baltimore County, MD	M,W	The University of Tennessee at Chattanooga, TN	M,W
Southern Illinois University Edwardsville, IL	M,W	University of Maryland Eastern Shore, MD	M	The University of Tennessee at Martin, TN	W
Southern Methodist University, TX	M,W	University of Massachusetts Amherst, MA	W	The University of Texas at Arlington, TX	M,W
Southern Utah University, UT	M,W				
Southwest Baptist University, MO	M,W	University of Memphis, TN	M,W	The University of Texas at Austin, TX	M,W
Southwestern College, KS	M,W	University of Miami, FL	M,W	The University of Texas at El Paso, TX	W
Spring Arbor University, MI	M,W	University of Michigan, MI	M,W		
Spring Hill College, AL	M,W	University of Minnesota, Crookston, MN	W	The University of Texas at San Antonio, TX	M,W
Stanford University, CA	M,W	University of Minnesota, Duluth, MN	W	The University of Texas– Pan American, TX	M,W
Stephen F. Austin State University, TX	W	University of Minnesota, Twin Cities Campus, MN	M,W	University of the Cumberlands, KY	M,W
Stephens College, MO	W	University of Mississippi, MS	M,W	University of the District of Columbia, DC	M,W
Stetson University, FL	M,W	University of Missouri– Kansas City, MO	M,W		
Stonehill College, MA	M,W			University of the Incarnate Word, TX	M,W
Stony Brook University, State University of New York, NY	M,W	University of Missouri–St. Louis, MO	M,W	University of the Pacific, CA	M,W
Syracuse University, NY	W	University of Mobile, AL	M,W	The University of Toledo, OH	M,W
Tarleton State University, TX	W	University of Montevallo, AL	W	University of Tulsa, OK	M,W
Taylor University, IN	M,W	University of Nebraska at Kearney, NE	M,W	University of Utah, UT	M,W
Temple University, PA	M,W			University of Virginia, VA	M,W
Tennessee State University, TN	M,W	University of Nebraska at Omaha, NE	M,W	The University of Virginia's College at Wise, VA	M,W
Tennessee Wesleyan College, TN	M,W	University of Nebraska– Lincoln, NE	M,W	The University of West Alabama, AL	M,W
Texas A&M University, TX	M,W			University of West Florida, FL	M,W
Texas Christian University, TX	M,W	University of Nevada, Las Vegas, NV	M,W	University of West Georgia, GA	W
Texas Southern University, TX	M,W	University of Nevada, Reno, NV	M,W	University of Wisconsin– Green Bay, WI	M,W
Texas State University–San Marcos, TX	W	University of New Haven, CT	W		
Thomas University, GA	W			University of Wisconsin– Madison, WI	M,W
Tiffin University, OH	M,W				
Troy University, AL	M,W			University of Wisconsin– Milwaukee, WI	W
Truman State University, MO	M,W				
Tulane University, LA	M,W				
Tuskegee University, AL	M,W				

University of Wyoming, WY	W	Bowie State University, MD	M,W	Eastern Illinois University, IL	M,W
Ursuline College, OH	W	Bowling Green State University, OH	W	Eastern Michigan University, MI	M,W
Utah State University, UT	M,W	Bradley University, IL	M,W	Eastern New Mexico University, NM	M,W
Valdosta State University, GA	M,W	Brevard College, NC	M,W	Eastern Washington University, WA	M,W
Valparaiso University, IN	M,W	Brigham Young University, UT	M,W	Edinboro University of	
Vanderbilt University, TN	M,W	Bryant University, RI	M,W	Pennsylvania, PA	M,W
Virginia Commonwealth		Caldwell College, NJ	W	Elon University, NC	W
University, VA	M,W	California Baptist University, CA	M,W	Embry-Riddle Aeronautical	
Virginia Polytechnic Institute		California Polytechnic State		University–Daytona, FL	M,W
and State University, VA	M,W	University, San Luis Obispo, CA	M,W	Emmanuel College, GA	M,W
Virginia State University, VA	M,W	California State Polytechnic		Emporia State University, KS	M,W
Virginia Union University, VA	M	University, Pomona, CA	M,W	Evangel University, MO	M,W
Wagner College, NY	M,W	California State University,		The Evergreen State College, WA	M,W
Wake Forest University, NC	M,W	Chico, CA	M,W	Fayetteville State University, NC	W
Washburn University, KS	M,W	California State University,		Ferris State University, MI	M,W
Washington State University, WA	W	Dominguez Hills, CA	W	Florida Agricultural and	
Wayne State University, MI	M,W	California State University,		Mechanical University, FL	M,W
Webber International University,		Fresno, CA	M,W	Florida Institute of Technology,	
FL	M,W	California State University,		FL	M,W
West Chester University of		Fullerton, CA	M,W	Florida International	
Pennsylvania, PA	M,W	California State University,		University, FL	M,W
Western Carolina University, NC	W	Long Beach, CA	M,W	Florida Southern College, FL	M,W
Western Illinois University, IL	M,W	California State University, Los		Florida State University, FL	M,W
Western Kentucky University, KY	M,W	Angeles, CA	M,W	Furman University, SC	M,W
Western Michigan University, MI	M,W	California State University,		Gardner-Webb University, NC	M,W
West Virginia University, WV	W	Northridge, CA	M,W	George Mason University, VA	M,W
West Virginia Wesleyan College, WV	M,W	Calumet College of Saint Joseph,		Georgetown College, KY	M,W
Wichita State University, KS	M,W	IN	M,W	Georgetown University, DC	M,W
William Jewell College, MO	M,W	Campbellsville University, KY	M,W	Georgia Institute of Technology,	
Winona State University, MN	M,W	Carroll College, MT	M,W	GA	M,W
Winthrop University, SC	M,W	Carson-Newman University, TN	M,W	Georgia Southern University, GA	W
Wofford College, SC	M,W	Cedarville University, OH	M,W	Georgia State University, GA	M,W
Wright State University, OH	M,W	Central Connecticut State		Gonzaga University, WA	M,W
Xavier University, OH	M,W	University, CT	M,W	Goshen College, IN	M,W
Xavier University of Louisiana, LA	M,W	Central Methodist University, MO	M,W	Graceland University, IA	M,W
Young Harris College, GA	M,W	Central Michigan University, MI	M,W	Grand Valley State University, MI	M,W
Youngstown State University, OH	M,W	Chicago State University, IL	M,W	Grand View University, IA	M,W
		The Citadel, The Military		Hampton University, VA	M,W
Track and field		College of South Carolina, SC	M,W	Harding University, AR	M,W
Abilene Christian University, TX	M,W	Clarion University of		Hillsdale College, MI	M,W
Academy of Art University, CA	M,W	Pennsylvania, PA	W	Houston Baptist University, TX	M,W
Adams State University, CO	M,W	Clarke University, IA	M,W	Huntington University, IN	M,W
Adelphi University, NY	M,W	Clayton State University, GA	M,W	Idaho State University, ID	M,W
Alabama State University, AL	M,W	Clemson University, SC	M,W	Illinois State University, IL	M,W
Alcorn State University, MS	M,W	Cleveland State University, OH	W	Indiana State University, IN	M,W
American University, DC	M,W	Coastal Carolina University, SC	M,W	Indiana Tech, IN	M,W
Anderson University, SC	M,W	The College of Idaho, ID	M,W	Indiana University Bloomington, IN	M,W
Angelo State University, TX	M,W	The College of Saint Rose, NY	M,W	Indiana University of	
Appalachian State University, NC	M,W	The College of William and Mary,		Pennsylvania, PA	M,W
Arizona State University, AZ	M,W	VA	M,W	Indiana University–Purdue	
Arkansas State University, AR	M,W	Colorado Mesa University, CO	M,W	University Fort Wayne, IN	W
Ashland University, OH	M,W	Colorado School of Mines, CO	M,W	Indiana Wesleyan University, IN	M,W
Auburn University, AL	M,W	Colorado State University, CO	M,W	Inter American University of	
Augustana College, SD	M,W	Concordia University, CA	M,W	Puerto Rico, Bayamón Campus, PR	M,W
Austin Peay State University, TN	W	Concordia University, OR	M,W	Inter American University of	
Azusa Pacific University, CA	M,W	Concordia University, Nebraska, NE	M,W	Puerto Rico, Ponce Campus, PR	M,W
Ball State University, IN	W	Concordia University, St. Paul, MN	M,W	Iona College, NY	M,W
Barton College, NC	M,W	Converse College, SC	W	Iowa State University of Science	
Baylor University, TX	M,W	Corban University, OR	M,W	and Technology, IA	M,W
Bellarmine University, KY	M,W	Cornerstone University, MI	M,W	Jacksonville University, FL	W
Belmont Abbey College, NC	M,W	Culver-Stockton College, MO	M,W	James Madison University, VA	W
Belmont University, TN	M,W	Dakota State University, SD	M,W	Johnson C. Smith University, NC	M,W
Bemidji State University, MN	W	Dakota Wesleyan University, SD	M,W	Kansas State University, KS	M,W
Benedictine College, KS	M,W	Dallas Baptist University, TX	W	Kennesaw State University, GA	M,W
Bethel College, IN	M,W	Davenport University, MI	M,W	Kent State University, OH	M,W
Bethel College, KS	M,W	Davidson College, NC	M,W	Kentucky State University, KY	M,W
Bethune-Cookman University, FL	M,W	DePaul University, IL	M,W	Kentucky Wesleyan College, KY	M,W
Binghamton University, State		Dillard University, LA	M,W	King College, TN	M,W
University of New York, NY	M,W	Doane College, NE	M,W	Kutztown University of	
Biola University, CA	M,W	Dominican College, NY	W	Pennsylvania, PA	M,W
Bloomsburg University of		Dordt College, IA	M,W	Lake Erie College, OH	M,W
Pennsylvania, PA	M,W	Drake University, IA	M,W	Lake Superior State University, MI	M,W
Boise State University, ID	M,W	Drury University, MO	M,W	Lamar University, TX	M,W
Boston College, MA	M,W	Duquesne University, PA	M,W	Lane College, TN	M,W
Boston University, MA	M,W	East Carolina University, NC	M,W	La Salle University, PA	M,W

Lees-McRae College, NC	M,W
Lee University, TN	M,W
Lehigh University, PA	M,W
Lewis University, IL	M,W
Liberty University, VA	M,W
Limestone College, SC	M,W
Lincoln University, MO	M,W
Lindenwood University, MO	M,W
Lindsey Wilson College, KY	M,W
Lipscomb University, TN	M,W
Lock Haven University of Pennsylvania, PA	M,W
Long Island University–Brooklyn Campus, NY	M,W
Louisiana State University and Agricultural and Mechanical College, LA	M,W
Louisiana Tech University, LA	M,W
Loyola University Chicago, IL	M,W
Loyola University Maryland, MD	W
Malone University, OH	M,W
Manhattan College, NY	M,W
Mansfield University of Pennsylvania, PA	M,W
Marist College, NY	M,W
Marquette University, WI	M,W
Marshall University, WV	M,W
Maryville University of Saint Louis, MO	M,W
The Master's College and Seminary, CA	M,W
McKendree University, IL	M,W
McNeese State University, LA	M,W
Merrimack College, MA	M,W
Miami University, OH	M,W
Michigan State University, MI	M,W
Middle Tennessee State University, TN	M,W
Millersville University of Pennsylvania, PA	M,W
Minnesota State University Mankato, MN	M,W
Minot State University, ND	M,W
Mississippi State University, MS	M,W
Missouri Baptist University, MO	M,W
Missouri State University, MO	W
Missouri University of Science and Technology, MO	M,W
Molloy College, NY	M,W
Monmouth University, NJ	M,W
Montana State University, MT	M,W
Montreat College, NC	M,W
Morehead State University, KY	M,W
Morehouse College, GA	M
Morningside College, IA	M,W
Mount Marty College, SD	M,W
Mount Mercy University, IA	M,W
Mount St. Mary's University, MD	M,W
Murray State University, KY	W
New Mexico State University, NM	W
Niagara University, NY	W
Nicholls State University, LA	M,W
Norfolk State University, VA	M,W
North Carolina Central University, NC	M,W
North Carolina State University, NC	M,W
Northeastern University, MA	M,W
Northern Arizona University, AZ	M,W
Northern Michigan University, MI	W
Northern State University, SD	M,W
Northwest Christian University, OR	M,W
Northwestern State University of Louisiana, LA	M,W

Northwest Missouri State University, MO	M,W
Northwest Nazarene University, ID	M,W
Northwest University, WA	M,W
Northwood University, Michigan Campus, MI	M,W
Northwood University, Texas Campus, TX	M,W
Nova Southeastern University, FL	M,W
The Ohio State University, OH	M,W
Ohio University, OH	W
Oklahoma Baptist University, OK	M,W
Oklahoma Christian University, OK	M,W
Oklahoma City University, OK	M,W
Oklahoma State University, OK	M,W
Oral Roberts University, OK	M,W
Park University, MO	M,W
Penn State University Park, PA	M,W
Pittsburg State University, KS	M,W
Point Loma Nazarene University, CA	M,W
Polytechnic University of Puerto Rico, PR	M,W
Providence College, RI	M,W
Purdue University, IN	M,W
Queens College of the City University of New York, NY	M,W
Quinnipiac University, CT	W
Radford University, VA	M,W
Rice University, TX	M,W
Rider University, NJ	M,W
Robert Morris University, PA	M,W
Robert Morris University Illinois, IL	W
Roberts Wesleyan College, NY	M,W
Sacred Heart University, CT	M,W
Saginaw Valley State University, MI	M,W
St. Ambrose University, IA	M,W
St. John's University, NY	W
Saint Joseph's College, IN	M,W
Saint Joseph's University, PA	M,W
Saint Louis University, MO	M,W
Saint Martin's University, WA	M,W
Saint Mary's College of California, CA	M,W
Saint Peter's University, NJ	M,W
Samford University, AL	M,W
Sam Houston State University, TX	M,W
San Diego State University, CA	W
San Francisco State University, CA	W
Santa Clara University, CA	M,W
Savannah College of Art and Design, GA	M,W
Seattle Pacific University, WA	M,W
Seattle University, WA	M,W
Seton Hill University, PA	M,W
Shippensburg University of Pennsylvania, PA	M,W
Slippery Rock University of Pennsylvania, PA	M,W
Soka University of America, CA	M,W
South Dakota State University, SD	M,W
Southeastern Louisiana University, LA	M,W
Southeast Missouri State University, MO	M,W
Southern Arkansas University–Magnolia, AR	M,W
Southern Connecticut State University, CT	M,W
Southern Illinois University Carbondale, IL	M,W
Southern Illinois University Edwardsville, IL	M,W

Southern Utah University, UT	M,W
Southwest Baptist University, MO	M,W
Southwestern College, KS	M,W
Spring Arbor University, MI	M,W
Spring Hill College, AL	M,W
Stanford University, CA	M,W
Stephen F. Austin State University, TX	M,W
Stonehill College, MA	M,W
Stony Brook University, State University of New York, NY	M,W
Syracuse University, NY	M,W
Tarleton State University, TX	M,W
Taylor University, IN	M,W
Temple University, PA	M,W
Tennessee State University, TN	M,W
Tennessee Wesleyan College, TN	M,W
Texas A&M University, TX	M,W
Texas A&M University–Commerce, TX	M,W
Texas Christian University, TX	M,W
Texas Southern University, TX	M,W
Texas State University–San Marcos, TX	M,W
Texas Wesleyan University, TX	M,W
Tiffin University, OH	M,W
Trevecca Nazarene University, TN	M,W
Trinity Christian College, IL	M,W
Troy University, AL	M,W
Truman State University, MO	M,W
Tulane University, LA	W
Tuskegee University, AL	M,W
Union College, KY	M,W
University at Albany, State University of New York, NY	M,W
University at Buffalo, the State University of New York, NY	M,W
The University of Akron, OH	M,W
The University of Alabama, AL	M,W
The University of Alabama at Birmingham, AL	W
The University of Arizona, AZ	M,W
University of California, Davis, CA	M,W
University of California, Irvine, CA	M,W
University of California, Los Angeles, CA	M,W
University of California, Santa Barbara, CA	M,W
University of Central Arkansas, AR	M,W
University of Central Florida, FL	W
University of Charleston, WV	M,W
University of Cincinnati, OH	M,W
University of Colorado Boulder, CO	M,W
University of Colorado Colorado Springs, CO	M,W
University of Connecticut, CT	M,W
University of Dayton, OH	W
University of Delaware, DE	W
University of Florida, FL	M,W
University of Georgia, GA	M,W
University of Great Falls, MT	M,W
University of Hawaii at Manoa, HI	W
University of Houston, TX	M,W
University of Idaho, ID	M,W
University of Illinois at Chicago, IL	M,W
University of Illinois at Urbana–Champaign, IL	M,W
The University of Iowa, IA	M,W
The University of Kansas, KS	M,W
University of Louisiana at Lafayette, LA	M,W
University of Louisville, KY	M,W

University of Maryland, Baltimore County, MD	M,W
University of Maryland, College Park, MD	W
University of Massachusetts Amherst, MA	M,W
University of Memphis, TN	M,W
University of Miami, FL	M,W
University of Michigan, MI	M,W
University of Minnesota, Duluth, MN	M,W
University of Minnesota, Twin Cities Campus, MN	M,W
University of Mississippi, MS	M,W
University of Missouri–Kansas City, MO	M,W
University of Mobile, AL	M,W
University of Nebraska at Kearney, NE	M,W
University of Nebraska–Lincoln, NE	M,W
University of Nevada, Las Vegas, NV	W
University of Nevada, Reno, NV	W
University of New Hampshire, NH	M,W
University of New Haven, CT	M,W
University of New Orleans, LA	M,W
University of North Carolina at Asheville, NC	M,W
The University of North Carolina at Chapel Hill, NC	M,W
The University of North Carolina at Greensboro, NC	M,W
The University of North Carolina at Pembroke, NC	M,W
The University of North Carolina Wilmington, NC	M,W
University of Northern Colorado, CO	M,W
University of Northern Iowa, IA	M,W
University of North Florida, FL	M,W
University of North Texas, TX	M,W
University of Notre Dame, IN	M,W
University of Oklahoma, OK	M,W
University of Oregon, OR	M,W
University of Pikeville, KY	M,W
University of Pittsburgh, PA	M,W
University of Portland, OR	M,W
University of Puerto Rico at Bayamón, PR	M,W
University of Rhode Island, RI	M,W
University of Richmond, VA	W
University of Rio Grande, OH	M,W
University of St. Francis, IL	M,W
University of San Diego, CA	W
University of South Alabama, AL	M,W
University of South Carolina, SC	M,W
University of South Carolina Upstate, SC	M,W
The University of South Dakota, SD	M,W
University of Southern Mississippi, MS	M,W
The University of Tennessee, TN	M,W
The University of Tennessee at Chattanooga, TN	M,W
The University of Texas at Arlington, TX	M,W
The University of Texas at Austin, TX	M,W
The University of Texas at El Paso, TX	M,W
The University of Texas at San Antonio, TX	M,W
The University of Texas–Pan American, TX	M,W

University of the Cumberlands, KY	M,W
University of the District of Columbia, DC	M,W
University of the Incarnate Word, TX	M,W
The University of Toledo, OH	W
University of Tulsa, OK	M,W
University of Utah, UT	W
University of Vermont, VT	M,W
University of Virginia, VA	M,W
University of West Georgia, GA	W
University of Wisconsin–Madison, WI	M,W
University of Wisconsin–Milwaukee, WI	M,W
University of Wisconsin–Parkside, WI	M,W
University of Wyoming, WY	M,W
Ursuline College, OH	W
Utah State University, UT	M,W
Utah Valley University, UT	M,W
Valley City State University, ND	M,W
Valparaiso University, IN	M,W
Vanderbilt University, TN	W
Villanova University, PA	M,W
Virginia Commonwealth University, VA	M,W
Virginia Polytechnic Institute and State University, VA	M,W
Virginia State University, VA	M,W
Virginia Union University, VA	M,W
Wagner College, NY	M,W
Wake Forest University, NC	M,W
Warner Pacific College, OR	M,W
Washington State University, WA	M,W
Wayland Baptist University, TX	M,W
Wayne State College, NE	M,W
Webber International University, FL	M,W
West Chester University of Pennsylvania, PA	M,W
Western Carolina University, NC	M,W
Western Illinois University, IL	M,W
Western Kentucky University, KY	M,W
Western Michigan University, MI	W
Western Oregon University, OR	M,W
Western State Colorado University, CO	M,W
Western Washington University, WA	M,W
Westminster College, UT	M,W
West Texas A&M University, TX	M,W
West Virginia University, WV	W
West Virginia Wesleyan College, WV	M,W
Wheeling Jesuit University, WV	M,W
Wichita State University, KS	M,W
William Jewell College, MO	M,W
Winona State University, MN	W
Winthrop University, SC	M,W
Wofford College, SC	M,W
Wright State University, OH	W
Xavier University, OH	M,W
Youngstown State University, OH	M,W

Volleyball

Abilene Christian University, TX	W
Academy of Art University, CA	W
Adams State University, CO	W
Adelphi University, NY	W
Alabama State University, AL	W
Alcorn State University, MS	W
American University, DC	W
Anderson University, SC	W
Angelo State University, TX	W
Appalachian State University, NC	W
Arizona State University, AZ	W

Arkansas State University, AR	W
Arkansas Tech University, AR	W
Armstrong Atlantic State University, GA	W
Asbury University, KY	W
Ashland University, OH	W
Auburn University, AL	W
Augustana College, SD	W
Austin Peay State University, TN	W
Azusa Pacific University, CA	W
Ball State University, IN	M,W
Barry University, FL	W
Barton College, NC	M,W
Baylor University, TX	W
Belhaven University, MS	W
Bellarmine University, KY	W
Belmont Abbey College, NC	M,W
Belmont University, TN	W
Bemidji State University, MN	W
Benedictine College, KS	W
Bethel College, IN	W
Bethel College, KS	W
Bethune-Cookman University, FL	W
Binghamton University, State University of New York, NY	W
Biola University, CA	W
Bloomfield College, NJ	W
Bluefield College, VA	W
Boise State University, ID	W
Boston College, MA	W
Bowie State University, MD	W
Bowling Green State University, OH	W
Bradley University, IL	W
Brevard College, NC	W
Brigham Young University, UT	M,W
Bryant University, RI	W
Butler University, IN	W
Caldwell College, NJ	W
California Baptist University, CA	M,W
California Polytechnic State University, San Luis Obispo, CA	W
California State Polytechnic University, Pomona, CA	W
California State University, Chico, CA	W
California State University, Dominguez Hills, CA	W
California State University, Fresno, CA	W
California State University, Fullerton, CA	W
California State University, Long Beach, CA	M,W
California State University, Los Angeles, CA	W
California State University, Monterey Bay, CA	W
California State University, Northridge, CA	M,W
California State University, San Bernardino, CA	W
Calumet College of Saint Joseph, IN	W
Cameron University, OK	W
Campbellsville University, KY	W
Canisius College, NY	W
Carroll College, MT	W
Carson-Newman University, TN	W
Catawba College, NC	W
Cedarville University, OH	W
Central Connecticut State University, CT	W
Central Methodist University, MO	W
Central Michigan University, MI	W
Chestnut Hill College, PA	W

College	
Chicago State University, IL	W
Chowan University, NC	W
Christian Brothers University, TN	W
Cincinnati Christian University, OH	M,W
The Citadel, The Military College of South Carolina, SC	W
Clarion University of Pennsylvania, PA	W
Clarke University, IA	M,W
Clemson University, SC	W
Cleveland State University, OH	W
Coastal Carolina University, SC	W
Coker College, SC	W
Colgate University, NY	W
College of Charleston, SC	W
The College of Idaho, ID	W
College of Saint Mary, NE	W
The College of Saint Rose, NY	W
College of the Ozarks, MO	W
The College of William and Mary, VA	W
Colorado Mesa University, CO	W
Colorado School of Mines, CO	W
Colorado State University, CO	W
Columbia College, MO	W
Columbus State University, GA	W
Concordia University, CA	M,W
Concordia University, OR	W
Concordia University, Nebraska, NE	W
Concordia University, St. Paul, MN	W
Converse College, SC	W
Corban University, OR	W
Cornerstone University, MI	W
Creighton University, NE	W
Culver-Stockton College, MO	W
Dakota State University, SD	W
Dakota Wesleyan University, SD	W
Dallas Baptist University, TX	W
Davenport University, MI	W
Davidson College, NC	W
DePaul University, IL	W
Dillard University, LA	W
Doane College, NE	W
Dominican College, NY	W
Dordt College, IA	W
Drake University, IA	W
Drury University, MO	W
Duquesne University, PA	W
East Carolina University, NC	W
Eastern Illinois University, IL	W
Eastern Michigan University, MI	W
Eastern New Mexico University, NM	W
Eastern Washington University, WA	W
Eckerd College, FL	W
Edinboro University of Pennsylvania, PA	W
Elizabeth City State University, NC	W
Elon University, NC	W
Embry-Riddle Aeronautical University–Daytona, FL	W
Embry-Riddle Aeronautical University–Prescott, AZ	W
Emmanuel College, GA	M,W
Emporia State University, KS	W
Evangel University, MO	W
The Evergreen State College, WA	W
Fairfield University, CT	W
Fairmont State University, WV	W
Faulkner University, AL	W
Fayetteville State University, NC	W
Felician College, NJ	W
Ferris State University, MI	W
Flagler College, FL	W
Florida Agricultural and Mechanical University, FL	W
Florida Atlantic University, FL	W
Florida Gulf Coast University, FL	W
Florida Institute of Technology, FL	W
Florida International University, FL	W
Florida Southern College, FL	W
Florida State University, FL	W
Fort Lewis College, CO	W
Francis Marion University, SC	W
Franklin Pierce University, NH	W
Freed-Hardeman University, TN	W
Furman University, SC	W
Gannon University, PA	W
Gardner-Webb University, NC	W
George Mason University, VA	M,W
Georgetown College, KY	W
Georgetown University, DC	W
The George Washington University, DC	W
Georgia Institute of Technology, GA	W
Georgia Southern University, GA	W
Georgia State University, GA	W
Goldey-Beacom College, DE	W
Gonzaga University, WA	W
Goshen College, IN	W
Graceland University, IA	M,W
Grand Valley State University, MI	W
Grand View University, IA	M,W
Hampton University, VA	W
Harding University, AR	W
Hawai`i Pacific University, HI	W
Henderson State University, AR	W
Hillsdale College, MI	W
Hofstra University, NY	W
Hope International University, CA	M,W
Houston Baptist University, TX	W
Huntington University, IN	W
Idaho State University, ID	W
Illinois Institute of Technology, IL	W
Illinois State University, IL	W
Indiana State University, IN	W
Indiana Tech, IN	W
Indiana University Bloomington, IN	W
Indiana University of Pennsylvania, PA	W
Indiana University–Purdue University Fort Wayne, IN	M,W
Indiana University–Purdue University Indianapolis, IN	W
Indiana University Southeast, IN	W
Indiana Wesleyan University, IN	W
Inter American University of Puerto Rico, Bayamón Campus, PR	M,W
Inter American University of Puerto Rico, Ponce Campus, PR	M,W
Iona College, NY	W
Iowa State University of Science and Technology, IA	W
Jacksonville State University, AL	W
Jacksonville University, FL	W
James Madison University, VA	W
John Brown University, AR	W
Johnson C. Smith University, NC	W
Kansas State University, KS	W
Kennesaw State University, GA	W
Kent State University, OH	W
Kentucky State University, KY	W
Kentucky Wesleyan College, KY	W
King College, TN	M,W
Kutztown University of Pennsylvania, PA	W
Lake Erie College, OH	W
Lake Superior State University, MI	W
Lamar University, TX	W
Lane College, TN	W
La Salle University, PA	W
Lawrence Technological University, MI	W
Lees-McRae College, NC	M,W
Lee University, TN	W
Lehigh University, PA	W
Le Moyne College, NY	W
Lewis-Clark State College, ID	W
Lewis University, IL	M,W
Liberty University, VA	W
Limestone College, SC	M,W
Lindenwood University, MO	M,W
Lindsey Wilson College, KY	W
Lipscomb University, TN	W
Lock Haven University of Pennsylvania, PA	W
Long Island University–Brooklyn Campus, NY	W
Long Island University–C. W. Post Campus, NY	W
Louisiana State University and Agricultural and Mechanical College, LA	W
Louisiana Tech University, LA	W
Lourdes University, OH	M,W
Loyola Marymount University, CA	W
Loyola University Chicago, IL	M,W
Loyola University Maryland, MD	W
Lubbock Christian University, TX	W
Lynn University, FL	W
Lyon College, AR	W
Malone University, OH	W
Manhattan College, NY	W
Marist College, NY	W
Marquette University, WI	W
Marshall University, WV	W
Maryville University of Saint Louis, MO	W
The Master's College and Seminary, CA	W
Mayville State University, ND	W
McKendree University, IL	M,W
McNeese State University, LA	W
Menlo College, CA	W
Mercer University, GA	W
Mercy College, NY	W
Mercyhurst University, PA	W
Merrimack College, MA	W
Metropolitan State University of Denver, CO	W
Miami University, OH	W
Michigan State University, MI	W
Middle Tennessee State University, TN	W
Midwestern State University, TX	W
Millersville University of Pennsylvania, PA	W
Minnesota State University Mankato, MN	W
Minot State University, ND	W
Mississippi State University, MS	W
Missouri Baptist University, MO	M,W
Missouri State University, MO	W
Missouri University of Science and Technology, MO	W
Missouri Western State University, MO	W
Molloy College, NY	W
Montana State University, MT	W
Montana Tech of The University of Montana, MT	W
Montreat College, NC	W

Peterson's How to Get Money for College 2014

Morehead State University, KY	W
Morningside College, IA	W
Mount Marty College, SD	W
Mount Mercy University, IA	W
Mount Vernon Nazarene University, OH	W
Murray State University, KY	W
Newberry College, SC	W
New Jersey Institute of Technology, NJ	M,W
New Mexico Highlands University, NM	W
New Mexico State University, NM	W
New York Institute of Technology, NY	W
Niagara University, NY	W
Nicholls State University, LA	W
Norfolk State University, VA	W
North Carolina Central University, NC	W
North Carolina State University, NC	W
Northeastern University, MA	W
Northern Arizona University, AZ	W
Northern Illinois University, IL	W
Northern Kentucky University, KY	W
Northern Michigan University, MI	W
Northern State University, SD	W
Northwest Christian University, OR	W
Northwestern Oklahoma State University, OK	W
Northwestern State University of Louisiana, LA	W
Northwest Missouri State University, MO	W
Northwest Nazarene University, ID	W
Northwest University, WA	W
Northwood University, Florida Campus, FL	W
Northwood University, Michigan Campus, MI	W
Notre Dame de Namur University, CA	W
Nova Southeastern University, FL	W
Nyack College, NY	W
Oakland University, MI	W
The Ohio State University, OH	M,W
Ohio University, OH	W
Ohio Valley University, WV	W
Oklahoma City University, OK	W
Oral Roberts University, OK	W
Oregon State University, OR	W
Ouachita Baptist University, AR	W
Pace University, NY	W
Palm Beach Atlantic University, FL	W
Park University, MO	M,W
Penn State University Park, PA	M,W
Pepperdine University, CA	M,W
Philadelphia University, PA	W
Pittsburg State University, KS	W
Point Loma Nazarene University, CA	W
Point Park University, PA	W
Polytechnic University of Puerto Rico, PR	M,W
Post University, CT	W
Presbyterian College, SC	W
Providence College, RI	W
Purdue University, IN	W
Purdue University North Central, IN	W
Queens College of the City University of New York, NY	W
Quincy University, IL	M,W
Quinnipiac University, CT	W
Radford University, VA	W
Regis University, CO	W
Research College of Nursing, MO	W
Rice University, TX	W
Rider University, NJ	W
Robert Morris University, PA	W
Robert Morris University Illinois, IL	M,W
Roberts Wesleyan College, NY	W
Rockhurst University, MO	W
Rocky Mountain College, MT	W
Rollins College, FL	W
Sacred Heart University, CT	W
Saginaw Valley State University, MI	W
St. Ambrose University, IA	M,W
Saint Anselm College, NH	W
St. Edward's University, TX	W
St. John's University, NY	W
Saint Joseph's College, IN	W
Saint Louis University, MO	W
Saint Martin's University, WA	W
Saint Mary's College of California, CA	W
Saint Peter's University, NJ	W
St. Thomas University, FL	W
Samford University, AL	W
Sam Houston State University, TX	W
San Diego Christian College, CA	W
San Diego State University, CA	W
San Francisco State University, CA	W
San Jose State University, CA	W
Santa Clara University, CA	W
Seattle Pacific University, WA	W
Seattle University, WA	W
Seton Hill University, PA	W
Shawnee State University, OH	M,W
Shepherd University, WV	W
Shippensburg University of Pennsylvania, PA	W
Siena College, NY	W
Simpson University, CA	W
Slippery Rock University of Pennsylvania, PA	W
Sonoma State University, CA	W
South Dakota State University, SD	W
Southeastern Louisiana University, LA	W
Southeastern Oklahoma State University, OK	W
Southeast Missouri State University, MO	W
Southern Arkansas University–Magnolia, AR	W
Southern Connecticut State University, CT	W
Southern Illinois University Carbondale, IL	W
Southern Illinois University Edwardsville, IL	W
Southern Methodist University, TX	W
Southern Utah University, UT	W
Southwest Baptist University, MO	W
Southwestern College, KS	W
Spring Arbor University, MI	W
Spring Hill College, AL	W
Stanford University, CA	M,W
Stephen F. Austin State University, TX	W
Stephens College, MO	W
Stetson University, FL	W
Stonehill College, MA	W
Stony Brook University, State University of New York, NY	W
Syracuse University, NY	W
Tarleton State University, TX	W
Taylor University, IN	W
Temple University, PA	W
Tennessee Wesleyan College, TN	W
Texas A&M International University, TX	W
Texas A&M University, TX	W
Texas A&M University–Commerce, TX	W
Texas Christian University, TX	W
Texas Southern University, TX	W
Texas State University–San Marcos, TX	W
Texas Wesleyan University, TX	W
Texas Woman's University, TX	W
Tiffin University, OH	W
Trevecca Nazarene University, TN	W
Trinity Christian College, IL	W
Troy University, AL	W
Truman State University, MO	W
Tulane University, LA	W
Tuskegee University, AL	W
Union College, KY	W
Union University, TN	W
University at Albany, State University of New York, NY	W
University at Buffalo, the State University of New York, NY	W
The University of Akron, OH	W
The University of Alabama, AL	W
The University of Alabama at Birmingham, AL	W
University of Alaska Anchorage, AK	W
University of Alaska Fairbanks, AK	W
The University of Arizona, AZ	W
University of Bridgeport, CT	W
University of California, Davis, CA	W
University of California, Irvine, CA	M,W
University of California, Los Angeles, CA	M,W
University of California, Riverside, CA	W
University of California, Santa Barbara, CA	M,W
University of Central Arkansas, AR	W
University of Central Florida, FL	W
University of Charleston, WV	W
University of Cincinnati, OH	W
University of Colorado Boulder, CO	W
University of Colorado Colorado Springs, CO	W
University of Connecticut, CT	W
University of Dayton, OH	W
University of Delaware, DE	W
University of Denver, CO	W
University of Evansville, IN	W
University of Florida, FL	W
University of Georgia, GA	W
University of Great Falls, MT	W
University of Hartford, CT	W
University of Hawaii at Hilo, HI	W
University of Hawaii at Manoa, HI	M,W
University of Houston, TX	W
University of Idaho, ID	W
University of Illinois at Chicago, IL	W
University of Illinois at Springfield, IL	W
University of Illinois at Urbana–Champaign, IL	W
The University of Iowa, IA	W
The University of Kansas, KS	W
University of Louisiana at Lafayette, LA	W

University of Louisville, KY — W
University of Maryland, Baltimore County, MD — W
University of Maryland, College Park, MD — W
University of Memphis, TN — W
University of Miami, FL — W
University of Michigan, MI — W
University of Michigan–Dearborn, MI — W
University of Minnesota, Crookston, MN — W
University of Minnesota, Duluth, MN — W
University of Minnesota, Twin Cities Campus, MN — W
University of Mississippi, MS — W
University of Missouri–Kansas City, MO — W
University of Missouri–St. Louis, MO — W
University of Mobile, AL — W
The University of Montana Western, MT — W
University of Montevallo, AL — W
University of Nebraska at Kearney, NE — W
University of Nebraska at Omaha, NE — W
University of Nebraska–Lincoln, NE — W
University of Nevada, Las Vegas, NV — W
University of Nevada, Reno, NV — W
University of New Hampshire, NH — W
University of New Haven, CT — W
University of New Orleans, LA — W
University of North Alabama, AL — W
University of North Carolina at Asheville, NC — W
The University of North Carolina at Chapel Hill, NC — W
The University of North Carolina at Greensboro, NC — W
The University of North Carolina at Pembroke, NC — W
The University of North Carolina Wilmington, NC — W
University of Northern Colorado, CO — W
University of Northern Iowa, IA — W
University of North Florida, FL — W
University of North Texas, TX — W
University of Notre Dame, IN — W
University of Oklahoma, OK — W
University of Oregon, OR — W
University of Pikeville, KY — W
University of Pittsburgh, PA — W
University of Portland, OR — W
University of Puerto Rico at Bayamón, PR — M,W
University of Rhode Island, RI — W
University of Rio Grande, OH — W
University of St. Francis, IL — W
University of St. Thomas, TX — W
University of San Diego, CA — W
University of South Alabama, AL — W
University of South Carolina, SC — W
University of South Carolina Aiken, SC — W
University of South Carolina Upstate, SC — W
The University of South Dakota, SD — W
University of Southern Indiana, IN — W
University of Southern Mississippi, MS — W

The University of Tampa, FL — W
The University of Tennessee, TN — W
The University of Tennessee at Chattanooga, TN — W
The University of Tennessee at Martin, TN — W
The University of Texas at Arlington, TX — W
The University of Texas at Austin, TX — W
The University of Texas at Brownsville, TX — W
The University of Texas at El Paso, TX — W
The University of Texas at San Antonio, TX — W
The University of Texas of the Permian Basin, TX — W
The University of Texas–Pan American, TX — W
University of the Cumberlands, KY — W
University of the District of Columbia, DC — W
University of the Incarnate Word, TX — W
University of the Pacific, CA — M,W
University of the Sciences, PA — W
The University of Toledo, OH — W
University of Tulsa, OK — W
University of Utah, UT — W
University of Virginia, VA — W
The University of Virginia's College at Wise, VA — W
The University of West Alabama, AL — W
University of West Georgia, GA — W
University of Wisconsin–Green Bay, WI — W
University of Wisconsin–Madison, WI — W
University of Wisconsin–Milwaukee, WI — W
University of Wisconsin–Parkside, WI — W
University of Wyoming, WY — W
Upper Iowa University, IA — W
Ursuline College, OH — W
Utah State University, UT — W
Utah Valley University, UT — W
Valdosta State University, GA — W
Valley City State University, ND — W
Valparaiso University, IN — W
Villanova University, PA — W
Virginia Commonwealth University, VA — W
Virginia Intermont College, VA — W
Virginia State University, VA — W
Virginia Union University, VA — W
Wake Forest University, NC — W
Waldorf College, IA — W
Warner Pacific College, OR — W
Washburn University, KS — W
Washington State University, WA — W
Wayland Baptist University, TX — W
Wayne State College, NE — W
Wayne State University, MI — W
Webber International University, FL — M,W
West Chester University of Pennsylvania, PA — W
Western Carolina University, NC — W
Western Illinois University, IL — W
Western Kentucky University, KY — W
Western Michigan University, MI — W
Western Oregon University, OR — W
Western State Colorado University, CO — W

Western Washington University, WA — W
Westminster College, UT — W
West Texas A&M University, TX — W
West Virginia University, WV — W
West Virginia University Institute of Technology, WV — W
West Virginia Wesleyan College, WV — W
Wheeling Jesuit University, WV — W
Wichita State University, KS — W
William Jewell College, MO — W
Winona State University, MN — W
Winthrop University, SC — W
Wofford College, SC — W
Wright State University, OH — W
Xavier University, OH — W
Youngstown State University, OH — W

Water polo

Arizona State University, AZ — W
California Baptist University, CA — M,W
California State University, Long Beach, CA — M,W
California State University, Monterey Bay, CA — W
Concordia University, CA — M,W
Gannon University, PA — M,W
The George Washington University, DC — M
Hartwick College, NY — W
Indiana University Bloomington, IN — W
Iona College, NY — W
Lindenwood University, MO — M,W
Loyola Marymount University, CA — M,W
Marist College, NY — W
Mercyhurst University, PA — M,W
Pepperdine University, CA — M
San Diego State University, CA — W
San Jose State University, CA — W
Santa Clara University, CA — M,W
Siena College, NY — W
Stanford University, CA — M,W
University of California, Davis, CA — M,W
University of California, Irvine, CA — M,W
University of California, Los Angeles, CA — M,W
University of California, Santa Barbara, CA — M,W
University of Hawaii at Manoa, HI — W
University of Maryland, College Park, MD — W
University of Michigan, MI — W
University of the Pacific, CA — M,W
Wagner College, NY — W

Weight lifting

Inter American University of Puerto Rico, Bayamón Campus, PR — M
Inter American University of Puerto Rico, Ponce Campus, PR — M
Lindenwood University, MO — M,W
University of Puerto Rico at Bayamón, PR — M,W

Wrestling

Adams State University, CO — M
American University, DC — M
Anderson University, SC — M
Appalachian State University, NC — M
Arizona State University, AZ — M
Ashland University, OH — M
Augustana College, SD — M
Belmont Abbey College, NC — M
Benedictine College, KS — M
Binghamton University, State University of New York, NY — M

Bloomsburg University of Pennsylvania, PA	M
Boise State University, ID	M
Boston University, MA	M
Bucknell University, PA	M
California Baptist University, CA	M
California Polytechnic State University, San Luis Obispo, CA	M
Calumet College of Saint Joseph, IN	M
Campbellsville University, KY	M,W
Carson-Newman University, TN	M
Central Michigan University, MI	M
The Citadel, The Military College of South Carolina, SC	M
Clarion University of Pennsylvania, PA	M
Cleveland State University, OH	M
Colorado Mesa University, CO	M
Colorado School of Mines, CO	M
Concordia University, Nebraska, NE	M
Dakota Wesleyan University, SD	M
Davidson College, NC	M
Eastern Michigan University, MI	M
Edinboro University of Pennsylvania, PA	M
Embry-Riddle Aeronautical University–Prescott, AZ	M
Gannon University, PA	M
Gardner-Webb University, NC	M
George Mason University, VA	M
Grand View University, IA	M
Hofstra University, NY	M
Indiana Tech, IN	M
Indiana University Bloomington, IN	M
Inter American University of Puerto Rico, Ponce Campus, PR	M,W
Iowa State University of Science and Technology, IA	M
Kent State University, OH	M
King College, TN	M,W
Kutztown University of Pennsylvania, PA	M
Lake Erie College, OH	M
Lehigh University, PA	M
Limestone College, SC	M
Lindenwood University, MO	M,W
Lindsey Wilson College, KY	M
Lock Haven University of Pennsylvania, PA	M
Maryville University of Saint Louis, MO	M
McKendree University, IL	M
Menlo College, CA	M,W
Mercyhurst University, PA	M
Michigan State University, MI	M
Millersville University of Pennsylvania, PA	M
Minnesota State University Mankato, MN	M
Missouri Baptist University, MO	M,W
Morningside College, IA	M
Newberry College, SC	M
North Carolina State University, NC	M
Northern Illinois University, IL	M
Northern State University, SD	M
The Ohio State University, OH	M
Ohio University, OH	M
Ohio Valley University, WV	M
Oklahoma City University, OK	M,W
Oklahoma State University, OK	M
Old Dominion University, VA	M
Oregon State University, OR	M
Ouachita Baptist University, AR	M
Penn State University Park, PA	M
Polytechnic University of Puerto Rico, PR	M
Purdue University, IN	M
Rider University, NJ	M
Sacred Heart University, CT	M
San Francisco State University, CA	M
Seton Hill University, PA	M
Shippensburg University of Pennsylvania, PA	M
Simpson University, CA	M
South Dakota State University, SD	M
Southern Illinois University Edwardsville, IL	M
Stanford University, CA	M
Tiffin University, OH	M
Truman State University, MO	M
University at Buffalo, the State University of New York, NY	M
University of Great Falls, MT	M
University of Illinois at Urbana–Champaign, IL	M
The University of Iowa, IA	M
University of Maryland, College Park, MD	M
University of Michigan, MI	M
University of Minnesota, Twin Cities Campus, MN	M
University of Nebraska at Kearney, NE	M
University of Nebraska–Lincoln, NE	M
The University of North Carolina at Chapel Hill, NC	M
The University of North Carolina at Pembroke, NC	M
University of Northern Colorado, CO	M
University of Northern Iowa, IA	M
University of Oklahoma, OK	M
University of Pittsburgh, PA	M
University of Puerto Rico at Bayamón, PR	M
The University of Tennessee at Chattanooga, TN	M
University of the Cumberlands, KY	M,W
University of Virginia, VA	M
University of Wisconsin–Madison, WI	M
University of Wisconsin–Parkside, WI	M
University of Wyoming, WY	M
Utah Valley University, UT	M
Waldorf College, IA	M,W
Wayland Baptist University, TX	M,W
Western State Colorado University, CO	M
West Virginia University, WV	M
West Virginia University Institute of Technology, WV	M
Wheeling Jesuit University, WV	M

Co-Op Programs

Adelphi University, NY
Alabama State University, AL
Alcorn State University, MS
Alfred University, NY
Allen College, IA
American Jewish University, CA
American University, DC
Anderson University, SC
Andrews University, MI
Antioch University Midwest, OH
Arcadia University, PA
Arizona State University, AZ
Armstrong Atlantic State University, GA
Ashland University, OH
Athens State University, AL
Auburn University, AL
Auburn University at Montgomery, AL
Augustana College, SD
Austin Peay State University, TN
Averett University, VA
Azusa Pacific University, CA
Ball State University, IN
Barton College, NC
Bastyr University, WA
Bay Path College, MA
Becker College, MA
Belmont Abbey College, NC
Belmont University, TN
Benedictine College, KS
Bethany Lutheran College, MN
Bethune-Cookman University, FL
Biola University, CA
Bloomsburg University of Pennsylvania, PA
Bluefield College, VA
Boise State University, ID
Boston University, MA
Bowie State University, MD
Bowling Green State University, OH
Bradley University, IL
Buffalo State College, State University of New York, NY
Butler University, IN
Cabrini College, PA
Caldwell College, NJ
California College of the Arts, CA
California Institute of Technology, CA
California Lutheran University, CA
California Polytechnic State University, San Luis Obispo, CA
California State Polytechnic University, Pomona, CA
California State University, Chico, CA
California State University, Dominguez Hills, CA
California State University, East Bay, CA
California State University, Fresno, CA
California State University, Fullerton, CA
California State University, Los Angeles, CA
California State University, Monterey Bay, CA
California State University, San Bernardino, CA
California State University, Stanislaus, CA
Calumet College of Saint Joseph, IN
Canisius College, NY
Capital University, OH
Cardinal Stritch University, WI
Carlos Albizu University, PR
Carnegie Mellon University, PA
Carroll College, MT

Case Western Reserve University, OH
The Catholic University of America, DC
Central College, IA
Central Connecticut State University, CT
Centre College, KY
Champlain College, VT
Chatham University, PA
Chicago State University, IL
Chowan University, NC
Christendom College, VA
Cincinnati Christian University, OH
The Citadel, The Military College of South Carolina, SC
Clarion University of Pennsylvania, PA
Clarke University, IA
Clarkson University, NY
Clayton State University, GA
Cleary University, MI
Clemson University, SC
Cleveland State University, OH
Coastal Carolina University, SC
The College at Brockport, State University of New York, NY
College of Charleston, SC
The College of Idaho, ID
College of Mount St. Joseph, OH
The College of New Rochelle, NY
College of Staten Island of the City University of New York, NY
College of the Atlantic, ME
Colorado Mountain College, CO
Colorado School of Mines, CO
Colorado State University, CO
Columbia College, MO
Columbia International University, SC
Columbus State University, GA
Concordia College, MN
Converse College, SC
Corban University, OR
Dakota State University, SD
Dakota Wesleyan University, SD
Davenport University, MI
Defiance College, OH
DePaul University, IL
DeSales University, PA
Dillard University, LA
Doane College, NE
Dominican College, NY
Drake University, IA
Drury University, MO
East Carolina University, NC
Eastern Connecticut State University, CT
Eastern Illinois University, IL
Eastern Michigan University, MI
Eastern New Mexico University, NM
Eastern Washington University, WA
East-West University, IL
Edgewood College, WI
EDP University of Puerto Rico, PR
Elizabeth City State University, NC
Elmhurst College, IL
Embry-Riddle Aeronautical University–Daytona, FL
Embry-Riddle Aeronautical University–Prescott, AZ
Embry-Riddle Aeronautical University–Worldwide, FL
Emory & Henry College, VA
Emporia State University, KS
Endicott College, MA

Fairmont State University, WV
Fayetteville State University, NC
Felician College, NJ
Ferris State University, MI
Florida Agricultural and Mechanical University, FL
Florida Atlantic University, FL
Florida Gulf Coast University, FL
Florida Institute of Technology, FL
Florida International University, FL
Florida National University, FL
Florida State University, FL
Framingham State University, MA
Franklin College, IN
Freed-Hardeman University, TN
Frostburg State University, MD
Gannon University, PA
Gardner-Webb University, NC
Geneva College, PA
George Mason University, VA
Georgetown College, KY
The George Washington University, DC
Georgia Institute of Technology, GA
Georgia Southern University, GA
Georgia State University, GA
Goldey-Beacom College, DE
Gordon College, MA
Graceland University, IA
Grand Valley State University, MI
Grand View University, IA
Greenville College, IL
Guilford College, NC
Gustavus Adolphus College, MN
Hampton University, VA
Hanover College, IN
Harding University, AR
Hawai`i Pacific University, HI
Hendrix College, AR
Hilbert College, NY
Hodges University, FL
Husson University, ME
Idaho State University, ID
Illinois Institute of Technology, IL
Illinois State University, IL
Indiana State University, IN
Indiana Tech, IN
Indiana University Bloomington, IN
Indiana University East, IN
Indiana University Northwest, IN
Indiana University of Pennsylvania, PA
Indiana University–Purdue University Fort Wayne, IN
Indiana University–Purdue University Indianapolis, IN
Inter American University of Puerto Rico, Bayamón Campus, PR
Inter American University of Puerto Rico, Ponce Campus, PR
Iowa State University of Science and Technology, IA
Iowa Wesleyan College, IA
Jacksonville State University, AL
Jacksonville University, FL
John Carroll University, OH
John Jay College of Criminal Justice of the City University of New York, NY
Johnson C. Smith University, NC
Johnson State College, VT
Kansas State University, KS
Kean University, NJ

Keene State College, NH
Kennesaw State University, GA
Kent State University, OH
Kentucky State University, KY
Kentucky Wesleyan College, KY
Keuka College, NY
Keystone College, PA
King College, TN
Kuyper College, MI
Lake Superior State University, MI
Lamar University, TX
Lane College, TN
La Salle University, PA
Lasell College, MA
Lawrence Technological University, MI
Lees-McRae College, NC
Lee University, TN
Lehigh University, PA
Lehman College of the City University of
    New York, NY
Liberty University, VA
LIM College, NY
Lindsey Wilson College, KY
Lock Haven University of Pennsylvania, PA
Long Island University–Brooklyn Campus,
    NY
Long Island University–C. W. Post Campus,
    NY
Louisiana College, LA
Louisiana State University and Agricultural
    and Mechanical College, LA
Loyola Marymount University, CA
Loyola University Chicago, IL
Loyola University Maryland, MD
Loyola University New Orleans, LA
Lynn University, FL
Maine Maritime Academy, ME
Manhattan College, NY
Marian University, WI
Marist College, NY
Marquette University, WI
Marshall University, WV
Maryville University of Saint Louis, MO
Massachusetts College of Liberal Arts, MA
Massachusetts Institute of Technology, MA
Massachusetts Maritime Academy, MA
The Master's College and Seminary, CA
Mayville State University, ND
McKendree University, IL
McNally Smith College of Music, MN
McNeese State University, LA
Menlo College, CA
Mercer University, GA
Mercy College, NY
Mercyhurst University, PA
Merrimack College, MA
Messiah College, PA
Metropolitan State University of Denver, CO
Miami University, OH
Michigan State University, MI
Millersville University of Pennsylvania, PA
Minnesota State University Mankato, MN
Minot State University, ND
Misericordia University, PA
Mississippi College, MS
Mississippi State University, MS
Missouri State University, MO
Missouri University of Science and
    Technology, MO
Monmouth University, NJ
Montana Tech of The University of
    Montana, MT
Montclair State University, NJ
Moravian College, PA
Morehead State University, KY
Morehouse College, GA

Mount Holyoke College, MA
Mount Marty College, SD
Mount Saint Mary College, NY
Murray State University, KY
Naropa University, CO
Nazareth College of Rochester, NY
Neumann University, PA
Newbury College, MA
New College of Florida, FL
New England School of Communications,
    ME
New Jersey City University, NJ
New Jersey Institute of Technology, NJ
New Mexico Highlands University, NM
New Mexico Institute of Mining and
    Technology, NM
New Mexico State University, NM
New York Institute of Technology, NY
Niagara University, NY
Nicholls State University, LA
North Carolina Central University, NC
North Carolina State University, NC
Northeastern Illinois University, IL
Northeastern University, MA
Northern Arizona University, AZ
Northern Illinois University, IL
Northern Kentucky University, KY
Northern State University, SD
Northland College, WI
Northwestern Oklahoma State University,
    OK
Northwestern State University of Louisiana,
    LA
Northwest Nazarene University, ID
Northwest University, WA
Northwood University, Michigan Campus,
    MI
Norwich University, VT
Notre Dame de Namur University, CA
Oakland University, MI
Oglethorpe University, GA
The Ohio State University, OH
Ohio University, OH
Ohio Valley University, WV
Oklahoma Baptist University, OK
Old Dominion University, VA
Olivet College, MI
Oregon State University, OR
Otis College of Art and Design, CA
Ouachita Baptist University, AR
Pace University, NY
Pacific Lutheran University, WA
Pacific Union College, CA
Parsons The New School for Design, NY
Peirce College, PA
Penn State University Park, PA
Pennsylvania College of Technology, PA
Piedmont College, GA
Pittsburg State University, KS
Pitzer College, CA
Point Park University, PA
Polytechnic Institute of New York
    University, NY
Portland State University, OR
Post University, CT
Providence College, RI
Purdue University, IN
Purdue University Calumet, IN
Ramapo College of New Jersey, NJ
Reed College, OR
Regis University, CO
Rensselaer Polytechnic Institute, NY
Rhodes College, TN
Rider University, NJ
Robert Morris University, PA
Roberts Wesleyan College, NY

Rochester Institute of Technology, NY
Rockhurst University, MO
Rocky Mountain College of Art + Design,
    CO
Rogers State University, OK
Roger Williams University, RI
Rose-Hulman Institute of Technology, IN
Rowan University, NJ
Russell Sage College, NY
Rutgers, The State University of New Jersey,
    Camden, NJ
Rutgers, The State University of New Jersey,
    Newark, NJ
Rutgers, The State University of New Jersey,
    New Brunswick, NJ
Sacred Heart University, CT
Sage College of Albany, NY
Saginaw Valley State University, MI
St. Ambrose University, IA
St. Joseph's College, Long Island Campus,
    NY
St. Joseph's College, New York, NY
Saint Joseph's University, PA
Saint Louis University, MO
Saint Martin's University, WA
Saint Mary's College, IN
St. Mary's College of Maryland, MD
Saint Mary's University of Minnesota, MN
Saint Peter's University, NJ
Salisbury University, MD
Samford University, AL
San Francisco State University, CA
Santa Clara University, CA
School of the Art Institute of Chicago, IL
Schreiner University, TX
Shenandoah University, VA
Shepherd University, WV
Shimer College, IL
Shippensburg University of Pennsylvania,
    PA
Sierra Nevada College, NV
Simmons College, MA
Simpson College, IA
Soka University of America, CA
Sonoma State University, CA
South Dakota State University, SD
Southern Connecticut State University, CT
Southern Illinois University Carbondale, IL
Southern Illinois University Edwardsville,
    IL
Southern Methodist University, TX
Southern Polytechnic State University, GA
Southern Utah University, UT
Southwest Baptist University, MO
State University of New York at New Paltz,
    NY
State University of New York at Oswego,
    NY
State University of New York at Plattsburgh,
    NY
State University of New York College of
    Agriculture and Technology at
    Cobleskill, NY
State University of New York College of
    Environmental Science and Forestry, NY
State University of New York Institute of
    Technology, NY
State University of New York Maritime
    College, NY
Stephen F. Austin State University, TX
Stephens College, MO
Stevenson University, MD
Stony Brook University, State University of
    New York, NY
Stratford University, VA
Suffolk University, MA

Swarthmore College, PA
Sweet Briar College, VA
Syracuse University, NY
Tarleton State University, TX
Taylor University, IN
Temple University, PA
Tennessee State University, TN
Texas A&M University, TX
Texas A&M University–Commerce, TX
Texas Southern University, TX
Texas Woman's University, TX
Thomas Aquinas College, CA
Thomas More College, KY
Thomas University, GA
Trine University, IN
Trinity Christian College, IL
Trinity College of Florida, FL
Truman State University, MO
Tulane University, LA
Tuskegee University, AL
Union University, TN
Unity College, ME
Universidad Adventista de las Antillas, PR
University at Buffalo, the State University of New York, NY
The University of Akron, OH
The University of Alabama, AL
The University of Alabama at Birmingham, AL
University of Alaska Anchorage, AK
University of Alaska Fairbanks, AK
The University of Arizona, AZ
University of Bridgeport, CT
University of California, Santa Barbara, CA
University of California, Santa Cruz, CA
University of Central Arkansas, AR
University of Central Florida, FL
University of Charleston, WV
University of Cincinnati, OH
University of Colorado Boulder, CO
University of Colorado Colorado Springs, CO
University of Colorado Denver, CO
University of Connecticut, CT
University of Dayton, OH
University of Denver, CO
University of Evansville, IN
University of Florida, FL
University of Georgia, GA
University of Hartford, CT
University of Hawaii at Manoa, HI
University of Houston, TX
University of Houston–Clear Lake, TX
University of Idaho, ID
University of Illinois at Chicago, IL
University of Illinois at Springfield, IL
University of Illinois at Urbana–Champaign, IL
The University of Iowa, IA
The University of Kansas, KS
University of Louisiana at Lafayette, LA
University of Louisville, KY
University of Maine at Fort Kent, ME
University of Maryland, Baltimore County, MD
University of Maryland, College Park, MD
University of Maryland University College, MD
University of Mary Washington, VA
University of Massachusetts Amherst, MA
University of Massachusetts Boston, MA

University of Massachusetts Dartmouth, MA
University of Memphis, TN
University of Miami, FL
University of Michigan, MI
University of Michigan–Flint, MI
University of Minnesota, Duluth, MN
University of Minnesota, Twin Cities Campus, MN
University of Mississippi, MS
University of Missouri–Kansas City, MO
University of Missouri–St. Louis, MO
The University of Montana Western, MT
University of Mount Union, OH
University of Nebraska at Omaha, NE
University of Nebraska Lincoln, NE
University of Nevada, Las Vegas, NV
University of New England, ME
University of New Hampshire, NH
University of New Haven, CT
University of New Orleans, LA
University of North Alabama, AL
The University of North Carolina at Pembroke, NC
The University of North Carolina Wilmington, NC
University of Northern Colorado, CO
University of Northern Iowa, IA
University of North Florida, FL
University of North Georgia, GA
University of North Texas, TX
University of Oklahoma, OK
University of Oregon, OR
University of Pennsylvania, PA
University of Pittsburgh, PA
University of Puerto Rico at Bayamón, PR
University of Puget Sound, WA
University of Rhode Island, RI
University of Rio Grande, OH
University of Rochester, NY
University of South Alabama, AL
University of South Carolina, SC
University of South Carolina Aiken, SC
University of South Carolina Upstate, SC
The University of South Dakota, SD
University of Southern Indiana, IN
University of Southern Maine, ME
University of Southern Mississippi, MS
The University of Tampa, FL
The University of Tennessee, TN
The University of Tennessee at Chattanooga, TN
The University of Tennessee at Martin, TN
The University of Texas at Arlington, TX
The University of Texas at Austin, TX
The University of Texas at Brownsville, TX
The University of Texas at Dallas, TX
The University of Texas at El Paso, TX
The University of Texas at San Antonio, TX
The University of Texas–Pan American, TX
University of the Cumberlands, KY
University of the District of Columbia, DC
University of the Incarnate Word, TX
University of the Pacific, CA
University of the Sciences, PA
The University of Toledo, OH
University of Utah, UT
University of Vermont, VT
University of Virginia, VA
The University of Virginia's College at Wise, VA
University of Washington, Bothell, WA

University of Washington, Tacoma, WA
The University of West Alabama, AL
University of West Florida, FL
University of West Georgia, GA
University of Wisconsin–Eau Claire, WI
University of Wisconsin–La Crosse, WI
University of Wisconsin–Madison, WI
University of Wisconsin–Milwaukee, WI
University of Wisconsin–Stevens Point, WI
University of Wisconsin–Stout, WI
University of Wisconsin–Superior, WI
Upper Iowa University, IA
Ursuline College, OH
Utah State University, UT
Utah Valley University, UT
Valdosta State University, GA
Valley City State University, ND
Valparaiso University, IN
Vanderbilt University, TN
Vassar College, NY
Vermont Technical College, VT
Villa Maria College of Buffalo, NY
Villanova University, PA
Virginia Commonwealth University, VA
Virginia Polytechnic Institute and State University, VA
Virginia State University, VA
Virginia Union University, VA
Waldorf College, IA
Warner Pacific College, OR
Warren Wilson College, NC
Washburn University, KS
Washington State University, WA
Washington University in St. Louis, MO
Wayne State College, NE
Wayne State University, MI
Webber International University, FL
Webb Institute, NY
Webster University, MO
Wentworth Institute of Technology, MA
Wesleyan College, GA
Wesley College, DE
Western Carolina University, NC
Western Connecticut State University, CT
Western Kentucky University, KY
Western Michigan University, MI
Western Washington University, WA
Westfield State University, MA
Westminster College, MO
Westminster College, UT
West Texas A&M University, TX
West Virginia State University, WV
West Virginia University Institute of Technology, WV
Whitman College, WA
Whitworth University, WA
Wichita State University, KS
Widener University, PA
Wilkes University, PA
William Jewell College, MO
Winthrop University, SC
Wittenberg University, OH
Worcester Polytechnic Institute, MA
Wright State University, OH
Xavier University, OH
Xavier University of Louisiana, LA
York College of Pennsylvania, PA
Young Harris College, GA
Youngstown State University, OH

ROTC Programs

Air Force

Adelphi University, NY*
Adventist University of Health Sciences, FL*
Alabama State University, AL
Alaska Pacific University, AK*
Alverno College, WI*
American University, DC*
Amherst College, MA*
Anderson University, SC*
Angelo State University, TX
Arizona State University, AZ
Asbury University, KY*
Ashland University, OH*
Assumption College, MA*
Auburn University, AL
Auburn University at Montgomery, AL*
Augustana College, SD*
Austin Peay State University, TN*
Azusa Pacific University, CA*
Babson College, MA*
Baldwin Wallace University, OH*
Baptist Bible College of Pennsylvania, PA*
Barry University, FL*
Baylor University, TX
Bay Path College, MA*
Belhaven University, MS*
Bellarmine University, KY*
Belmont Abbey College, NC*
Belmont University, TN*
Bentley University, MA*
Bethel College, IN*
Bethel University, MN*
Bethune-Cookman University, FL*
Binghamton University, State University of New York, NY*
Biola University, CA*
Bloomsburg University of Pennsylvania, PA*
Boston College, MA*
Boston University, MA
Bowling Green State University, OH
Brandeis University, MA*
Bridgewater State University, MA*
Brigham Young University, UT
Bryn Mawr College, PA*
Butler University, IN*
Cabrini College, PA*
Cairn University, PA*
California Baptist University, CA*
California Institute of Technology, CA*
California Lutheran University, CA*
California State University, Dominguez Hills, CA*
California State University, Fresno, CA
California State University, Los Angeles, CA*
California State University, Northridge, CA*
California State University, San Bernardino, CA
California State University, San Marcos, CA*
Capital University, OH*
Carnegie Mellon University, PA
Carson-Newman University, TN*
Case Western Reserve University, OH*
Catawba College, NC*
The Catholic University of America, DC*
Cedarville University, OH*
Central Connecticut State University, CT*
Central Methodist University, MO*
Central Michigan University, MI*
Centre College, KY*

Chapman University, CA*
Chatham University, PA*
Chicago State University, IL*
Christian Brothers University, TN*
The Citadel, The Military College of South Carolina, SC
Claremont McKenna College, CA*
Clarkson University, NY
Clark University, MA*
Clayton State University, GA*
Clearwater Christian College, FL*
Clemson University, SC
Cleveland State University, OH*
Coe College, IA*
The College at Brockport, State University of New York, NY*
College of Charleston, SC*
College of Mount St. Joseph, OH*
The College of New Jersey, NJ*
College of Saint Mary, NE*
The College of Saint Rose, NY*
The College of St. Scholastica, MN*
College of the Holy Cross, MA*
Colorado School of Mines, CO
Colorado State University, CO
Columbia College, MO*
Columbia University, NY*
Columbia University, School of General Studies, NY*
Concordia College, MN*
Concordia University, OR*
Concordia University, Nebraska, NE*
Concordia University, St. Paul, MN*
Concordia University Texas, TX*
Corban University, OR*
Creighton University, NE*
Dakota State University, SD*
Dallas Baptist University, TX*
Daniel Webster College, NH*
Davidson College, NC*
DePauw University, IN*
Dillard University, LA*
Doane College, NE*
Drake University, IA*
Duquesne University, PA*
East Carolina University, NC
Eastern Connecticut State University, CT*
Eastern Michigan University, MI*
Eckerd College, FL*
Edgewood College, WI*
Elmhurst College, IL*
Elmira College, NY*
Elon University, NC*
Embry-Riddle Aeronautical University–Daytona, FL
Embry-Riddle Aeronautical University–Prescott, AZ
Emmanuel College, MA*
Fairfield University, CT*
Fairmont State University, WV*
Farmingdale State College, NY*
Faulkner University, AL*
Fayetteville State University, NC
Florida Agricultural and Mechanical University, FL*
Florida Atlantic University, FL*
Florida International University, FL
Florida Southern College, FL*
Florida State University, FL
Franklin Pierce University, NH*

Gardner-Webb University, NC*
George Fox University, OR*
George Mason University, VA*
Georgetown College, KY*
Georgetown University, DC*
The George Washington University, DC*
Georgia Institute of Technology, GA
Georgia State University, GA*
Goucher College, MD*
Grand View University, IA*
Hamilton College, NY*
Hamline University, MN*
Harvard University, MA*
Harvey Mudd College, CA
Hawai`i Pacific University, HI*
Hobart and William Smith Colleges, NY*
Houston Baptist University, TX*
Huntingdon College, AL*
Illinois Institute of Technology, IL
Indiana State University, IN
Indiana University Bloomington, IN
Indiana University–Purdue University Indianapolis, IN*
Indiana University South Bend, IN*
Indiana University Southeast, IN*
Iona College, NY*
Iowa State University of Science and Technology, IA
Ithaca College, NY*
James Madison University, VA*
John Brown University, AR*
The Johns Hopkins University, MD*
Johnson C. Smith University, NC*
Kansas State University, KS
Kean University, NJ*
Keene State College, NH*
Kennesaw State University, GA*
Kent State University, OH
Kent State University at Geauga, OH*
Kent State University at Stark, OH*
Kentucky State University, KY*
Keystone College, PA*
King's College, PA*
La Roche College, PA*
La Salle University, PA*
Lawrence Technological University, MI*
Le Moyne College, NY*
Lewis-Clark State College, ID*
Lewis University, IL*
Liberty University, VA*
Lincoln University, MO*
Linfield College, OR*
Lipscomb University, TN*
Louisiana State University and Agricultural and Mechanical College, LA
Louisiana Tech University, LA
Lourdes University, OH*
Loyola Marymount University, CA
Loyola University Chicago, IL*
Loyola University Maryland, MD*
Loyola University New Orleans, LA*
Lubbock Christian University, TX*
Lynn University, FL*
Macalester College, MN*
Malone University, OH*
Manhattan College, NY
Marquette University, WI
Mary Baldwin College, VA*
Marywood University, PA*
Massachusetts Institute of Technology, MA

---

* program is offered at another college's campus

Mayville State University, ND*
McKendree University, IL*
Menlo College, CA*
Mercy College, NY*
Mercyhurst University, PA*
Merrimack College, MA*
Metropolitan State University of Denver, CO*
Miami University, OH
Michigan State University, MI
Middle Tennessee State University, TN*
Midwestern State University, TX*
Millsaps College, MS*
Milwaukee School of Engineering, WI*
Minnesota State University Moorhead, MN*
Misericordia University, PA*
Mississippi College, MS
Mississippi State University, MS
Mississippi University for Women, MS*
Missouri University of Science and Technology, MO
Monmouth University, NJ*
Montana State University, MT
Montclair State University, NJ
Morehouse College, GA
Mount Carmel College of Nursing, OH*
Mount Holyoke College, MA*
National University, CA*
Nazareth College of Rochester, NY*
Nebraska Methodist College, NE*
Nebraska Wesleyan University, NE*
New England College, NH*
New Jersey Institute of Technology, NJ
New Mexico State University, NM
New York Institute of Technology, NY
New York University, NY*
North Carolina Central University, NC
North Carolina State University, NC
North Central College, IL*
Northeastern Illinois University, IL*
Northeastern University, MA*
Northern Arizona University, AZ
Northern Illinois University, IL*
Northern Kentucky University, KY*
Northwestern College, MN*
Northwestern State University of Louisiana, LA*
Northwest University, WA*
Norwich University, VT
Notre Dame de Namur University, CA*
Oakland University, MI*
Occidental College, CA*
Oglethorpe University, GA*
The Ohio State University, OH
Ohio University, OH
Oklahoma Baptist University, OK*
Oklahoma Christian University, OK*
Oklahoma City University, OK*
Oklahoma State University, OK
Olivet College, MI*
Oral Roberts University, OK*
Oregon State University, OR
Pace University, NY*
Pacific University, OR*
Penn State Abington, PA*
Penn State Altoona, PA
Penn State University Park, PA
Pepperdine University, CA*
Pitzer College, CA*
Plymouth State University, NH*
Point Loma Nazarene University, CA*
Point Park University, PA*
Polytechnic Institute of New York University, NY*
Pomona College, CA*

Portland State University, OR*
Purdue University, IN
Quinnipiac University, CT*
Ramapo College of New Jersey, NJ*
Regis University, CO*
Rensselaer Polytechnic Institute, NY
Rhodes College, TN*
Rice University, TX*
Robert Morris University, PA*
Roberts Wesleyan College, NY*
Rochester Institute of Technology, NY
Rose-Hulman Institute of Technology, IN
Russell Sage College, NY*
Rutgers, The State University of New Jersey, Camden, NJ*
Rutgers, The State University of New Jersey, Newark, NJ
Rutgers, The State University of New Jersey, New Brunswick, NJ
Sage College of Albany, NY*
Saint Anselm College, NH*
St. Edward's University, TX*
St. John Fisher College, NY*
Saint Joseph's University, PA
St. Lawrence University, NY*
St. Louis College of Pharmacy, MO*
Saint Louis University, MO
Saint Martin's University, WA*
Saint Mary-of-the-Woods College, IN*
Saint Mary's College, IN*
Saint Mary's College of California, CA*
Saint Michael's College, VT*
Saint Peter's University, NJ*
Salisbury University, MD*
Samford University, AL
San Diego Christian College, CA*
San Diego State University, CA
San Francisco State University, CA*
San Jose State University, CA
Santa Clara University, CA*
Scripps College, CA*
Seattle Pacific University, WA*
Seattle University, WA*
Shepherd University, WV*
Siena College, NY*
Skidmore College, NY*
Smith College, MA*
Sonoma State University, CA*
South Dakota State University, SD
Southeast Missouri State University, MO
Southern Connecticut State University, CT*
Southern Illinois University Carbondale, IL
Southern Illinois University Edwardsville, IL*
Southern Methodist University, TX*
Southern Polytechnic State University, GA*
Spelman College, GA*
Spring Arbor University, MI*
Spring Hill College, AL*
Stanford University, CA*
State University of New York College at Cortland, NY*
State University of New York College at Geneseo, NY*
State University of New York College at Old Westbury, NY*
State University of New York College at Potsdam, NY*
State University of New York College of Environmental Science and Forestry, NY*
State University of New York Institute of Technology, NY*
Stephens College, MO*
Stevenson University, MD*

Stony Brook University, State University of New York, NY*
Swarthmore College, PA*
Syracuse University, NY
Temple University, PA*
Tennessee State University, TN
Texas A&M University, TX
Texas Christian University, TX
Texas Lutheran University, TX*
Texas Southern University, TX*
Texas State University–San Marcos, TX
Texas Wesleyan University, TX*
Texas Woman's University, TX*
Thomas More College, KY*
Tiffin University, OH*
Transylvania University, KY*
Trine University, IN*
Trinity University, TX*
Troy University, AL
Tufts University, MA*
Tulane University, LA
Tuskegee University, AL
Union College, NY*
Universidad del Turabo, PR*
University at Albany, State University of New York, NY*
The University of Akron, OH*
The University of Alabama, AL
The University of Alabama at Birmingham, AL*
University of Alaska Anchorage, AK
The University of Arizona, AZ
University of California, Berkeley, CA
University of California, Davis, CA*
University of California, Irvine, CA*
University of California, Los Angeles, CA
University of California, Riverside, CA*
University of California, Santa Barbara, CA*
University of California, Santa Cruz, CA*
University of Central Florida, FL
University of Chicago, IL*
University of Cincinnati, OH
University of Colorado Boulder, CO
University of Colorado Denver, CO*
University of Connecticut, CT
University of Dallas, TX*
University of Dayton, OH*
University of Delaware, DE
University of Denver, CO*
University of Florida, FL
University of Georgia, GA
University of Hartford, CT*
University of Hawaii at Manoa, HI
University of Hawaii–West Oahu, HI*
University of Houston, TX
University of Idaho, ID*
University of Illinois at Chicago, IL*
University of Illinois at Urbana–Champaign, IL
The University of Iowa, IA
The University of Kansas, KS
University of Louisville, KY
University of Mary Hardin-Baylor, TX*
University of Maryland, Baltimore County, MD*
University of Maryland, College Park, MD
University of Massachusetts Amherst, MA
University of Massachusetts Boston, MA*
University of Memphis, TN
University of Miami, FL
University of Michigan, MI
University of Michigan–Flint, MI*
University of Minnesota, Crookston, MN*
University of Minnesota, Duluth, MN

* program is offered at another college's campus

Peterson's How to Get Money for College 2014

University of Minnesota, Twin Cities
  Campus, MN
University of Mississippi, MS
University of Missouri–Kansas City, MO*
University of Missouri–St. Louis, MO*
University of Mobile, AL*
University of Montevallo, AL*
University of Mount Union, OH*
University of Nebraska at Omaha, NE
University of Nebraska–Lincoln, NE
University of Nevada, Las Vegas, NV
University of New Hampshire, NH
University of New Hampshire at Manchester,
  NH*
University of New Haven, CT*
University of New Orleans, LA*
The University of North Carolina at Chapel
  Hill, NC
The University of North Carolina at
  Greensboro, NC*
The University of North Carolina at
  Pembroke, NC
University of Northern Colorado, CO
University of North Texas, TX
University of Notre Dame, IN
University of Oklahoma, OK
University of Oregon, OR*
University of Pennsylvania, PA*
University of Pittsburgh, PA
University of Pittsburgh at Greensburg, PA*
University of Portland, OR
University of Puerto Rico at Bayamón, PR*
University of Redlands, CA*
University of Rochester, NY*
University of St. Thomas, MN
University of St. Thomas, TX*
University of San Diego, CA*
The University of Scranton, PA*
University of South Alabama, AL
University of South Carolina, SC
University of Southern Maine, ME*
University of Southern Mississippi, MS
The University of Tampa, FL*
The University of Tennessee, TN
The University of Texas at Arlington, TX*
The University of Texas at Austin, TX
The University of Texas at Dallas, TX*
The University of Texas at El Paso, TX
The University of Texas at San Antonio, TX
University of the District of Columbia, DC*
University of the Incarnate Word, TX*
University of the Pacific, CA*
University of the Sciences, PA*
The University of Toledo, OH*
University of Tulsa, OK*
University of Utah, UT
University of Virginia, VA
University of Washington, Bothell, WA*
University of Washington, Tacoma, WA*
The University of West Alabama, AL*
University of West Florida, FL
University of West Georgia, GA*
University of Wisconsin–Madison, WI
University of Wisconsin–Milwaukee, WI*
University of Wisconsin–Stout, WI*
University of Wisconsin–Superior, WI*
University of Wyoming, WY
Utah State University, UT
Utah Valley University, UT*
Utica College, NY*
Valdosta State University, GA
Valparaiso University, IN*
Vanderbilt University, TN*
Villanova University, PA*
Virginia Polytechnic Institute and State
  University, VA

Warner Pacific College, OR*
Washburn University, KS*
Washington & Jefferson College, PA*
Washington State University, WA
Washington University in St. Louis, MO*
Wayland Baptist University, TX*
Wayne State University, MI*
Webster University, MO*
Wellesley College, MA*
Wells College, NY*
Wentworth Institute of Technology, MA*
Wesleyan University, CT*
West Chester University of Pennsylvania,
  PA*
Western Connecticut State University, CT*
Western Kentucky University, KY*
Westfield State University, MA*
Westminster College, MO*
Westminster College, UT*
West Virginia University, WV
Wheaton College, IL*
Whittier College, CA*
Widener University, PA*
Wilkes University, PA
Willamette University, OR*
William Peace University, NC*
Williams College, MA*
Winthrop University, SC*
Wittenberg University, OH*
Worcester Polytechnic Institute, MA
Worcester State University, MA*
Wright State University, OH
Xavier University, OH*
Xavier University of Louisiana, LA*
Yale University, CT
Youngstown State University, OH*

Army
Adelphi University, NY*
Alabama State University, AL*
Alaska Pacific University, AK*
Albright College, PA*
Alcorn State University, MS
Alfred University, NY*
Allen College, IA*
Alma College, MI*
Alverno College, WI*
American University, DC*
Amherst College, MA*
Anderson University, SC*
Appalachian State University, NC
Arizona State University, AZ
Arkansas State University, AR
Arkansas Tech University, AR*
Armstrong Atlantic State University, GA
Asbury University, KY*
Ashland University, OH*
Assumption College, MA*
Auburn University, AL
Auburn University at Montgomery, AL
Augustana College, SD*
Aurora University, IL*
Austin Peay State University, TN
Azusa Pacific University, CA
Babson College, MA*
Baldwin Wallace University, OH*
Ball State University, IN
Baptist Bible College of Pennsylvania, PA*
Barry University, FL*
Baylor University, TX
Bay Path College, MA*
Becker College, MA*
Belhaven University, MS*
Bellarmine University, KY*
Belmont Abbey College, NC*
Belmont University, TN*

Benedictine College, KS*
Benedictine University, IL*
Bentley University, MA*
Bethany Lutheran College, MN*
Bethel College, IN*
Bethel University, MN*
Bethune-Cookman University, FL*
Binghamton University, State University of
  New York, NY*
Biola University, CA*
Bloomfield College, NJ*
Bloomsburg University of Pennsylvania, PA
Boise State University, ID
Boston College, MA*
Boston University, MA
Bowie State University, MD
Bowling Green State University, OH
Bradley University, IL
Brandeis University, MA*
Bridgewater State University, MA*
Brigham Young University, UT
Brown University, RI*
Bryant University, RI
Bucknell University, PA
Buena Vista University, IA
Buffalo State College, State University of
  New York, NY*
Butler University, IN
Cabrini College, PA*
Caldwell College, NJ*
California Baptist University, CA
California Institute of Technology, CA*
California Lutheran University, CA*
California Polytechnic State University, San
  Luis Obispo, CA
California State Polytechnic University,
  Pomona, CA
California State University, Dominguez Hills,
  CA
California State University, Fresno, CA
California State University, Fullerton, CA
California State University, Long Beach, CA
California State University, Los Angeles,
  CA*
California State University, Northridge, CA*
California State University, San Bernardino,
  CA
California State University, San Marcos, CA*
Calvin College, MI*
Cameron University, OK
Campbellsville University, KY*
Canisius College, NY
Capital University, OH
Carnegie Mellon University, PA
Carroll College, MT
Carson-Newman University, TN
Case Western Reserve University, OH
Catawba College, NC*
The Catholic University of America, DC*
Cedar Crest College, PA*
Cedarville University, OH*
Central Connecticut State University, CT*
Central Methodist University, MO*
Central Michigan University, MI
Centre College, KY*
Champlain College, VT*
Chapman University, CA*
Chatham University, PA*
Chicago State University, IL
Christian Brothers University, TN*
Christopher Newport University, VA
The Citadel, The Military College of South
  Carolina, SC
City College of the City University of New
  York, NY
Claremont McKenna College, CA

* program is offered at another college's campus

Clarion University of Pennsylvania, PA*
Clarke University, IA*
Clarkson University, NY
Clark University, MA*
Clayton State University, GA
Clearwater Christian College, FL*
Clemson University, SC
Cleveland State University, OH*
Coastal Carolina University, SC
Coe College, IA
Colby College, ME*
Colgate University, NY*
The College at Brockport, State University of New York, NY
The College of Idaho, ID*
College of Mount St. Joseph, OH*
The College of New Jersey, NJ*
College of Saint Benedict, MN*
College of Saint Mary, NE*
The College of Saint Rose, NY*
The College of Saints John Fisher & Thomas More, TX*
College of the Holy Cross, MA*
College of the Ozarks, MO
The College of William and Mary, VA
The Colorado College, CO*
Colorado School of Mines, CO
Colorado State University, CO
Columbia College, MO*
Columbia University, NY*
Columbia University, School of General Studies, NY*
Columbus State University, GA
Concordia College, MN*
Concordia University, Nebraska, NE*
Concordia University, St. Paul, MN*
Concordia University Texas, TX*
Converse College, SC*
Corban University, OR*
Cornerstone University, MI*
Covenant College, GA*
Creighton University, NE
Crown College, MN*
Curry College, MA*
Dakota Wesleyan University, SD
Dallas Baptist University, TX*
Daniel Webster College, NH*
Dartmouth College, NH*
Davidson College, NC
DePaul University, IL
DePauw University, IN*
DeSales University, PA*
DeVry University, OH
Dickinson College, PA
Dillard University, LA*
Doane College, NE*
Drake University, IA
Drury University, MO*
Duquesne University, PA
East Carolina University, NC
Eastern Connecticut State University, CT*
Eastern Illinois University, IL
Eastern Michigan University, MI
Eastern Washington University, WA
Eckerd College, FL*
Edgewood College, WI*
Edinboro University of Pennsylvania, PA
Elizabeth City State University, NC
Elmhurst College, IL*
Elmira College, NY
Elon University, NC
Embry-Riddle Aeronautical University–Daytona, FL
Embry-Riddle Aeronautical University–Prescott, AZ

Emmanuel College, MA*
Endicott College, MA*
Evangel University, MO*
Fairfield University, CT*
Fairmont State University, WV
Farmingdale State College, NY*
Faulkner University, AL*
Fayetteville State University, NC*
Ferris State University, MI*
Fisher College, MA*
Florida Agricultural and Mechanical University, FL
Florida Atlantic University, FL
Florida Institute of Technology, FL
Florida International University, FL
Florida Southern College, FL
Florida State University, FL
Francis Marion University, SC
Franklin & Marshall College, PA*
Franklin College, IN*
Franklin Pierce University, NH*
Furman University, SC
Gannon University, PA
Gardner-Webb University, NC
Geneva College, PA*
George Mason University, VA
Georgetown College, KY*
Georgetown University, DC
The George Washington University, DC*
Georgia College & State University, GA*
Georgia Institute of Technology, GA
Georgia Southern University, GA
Georgia State University, GA
Gettysburg College, PA*
Gonzaga University, WA
Gordon College, MA*
Goucher College, MD*
Grand View University, IA*
Grove City College, PA*
Gustavus Adolphus College, MN*
Hamilton College, NY*
Hamline University, MN*
Hampden-Sydney College, VA*
Hampshire College, MA*
Hampton University, VA
Harvard University, MA*
Harvey Mudd College, CA*
Hawai`i Pacific University, HI*
Henderson State University, AR*
Hendrix College, AR*
Hilbert College, NY*
Hobart and William Smith Colleges, NY*
Hofstra University, NY
Hood College, MD
Hope College, MI*
Hope International University, CA*
Houghton College, NY*
Houston Baptist University, TX*
Huntingdon College, AL*
Husson University, ME
Idaho State University, ID
Illinois Institute of Technology, IL
Illinois State University, IL
Illinois Wesleyan University, IL*
Indiana State University, IN
Indiana Tech, IN*
Indiana University Bloomington, IN
Indiana University Kokomo, IN
Indiana University Northwest, IN
Indiana University of Pennsylvania, PA
Indiana University–Purdue University Fort Wayne, IN
Indiana University–Purdue University Indianapolis, IN
Indiana University South Bend, IN*

Indiana University Southeast, IN*
Indiana Wesleyan University, IN
Inter American University of Puerto Rico, Bayamón Campus, PR*
Iona College, NY*
Iowa State University of Science and Technology, IA
Ithaca College, NY*
Jacksonville State University, AL
Jacksonville University, FL
James Madison University, VA
John Brown University, AR*
John Carroll University, OH
The Johns Hopkins University, MD
Johnson C. Smith University, NC
Johnson State College, VT*
Kalamazoo College, MI*
Kansas State University, KS
Kean University, NJ*
Keene State College, NH*
Kennesaw State University, GA*
Kent State University, OH
Kent State University at Geauga, OH*
Kent State University at Stark, OH*
Kentucky State University, KY*
Kentucky Wesleyan College, KY*
Keystone College, PA*
King College, TN*
King's College, PA
Kutztown University of Pennsylvania, PA*
Kuyper College, MI*
Lafayette College, PA*
La Roche College, PA*
La Salle University, PA*
Lehigh University, PA
Lehman College of the City University of New York, NY*
Le Moyne College, NY*
Lewis-Clark State College, ID*
Lewis University, IL*
Liberty University, VA
Limestone College, SC*
Lincoln University, MO
Lindenwood University, MO
Lipscomb University, TN*
Lock Haven University of Pennsylvania, PA
Long Island University–C. W. Post Campus, NY*
Longwood University, VA
Louisiana College, LA
Louisiana State University and Agricultural and Mechanical College, LA
Louisiana Tech University, LA*
Lourdes University, OH*
Loyola Marymount University, CA*
Loyola University Chicago, IL*
Loyola University Maryland, MD
Loyola University New Orleans, LA*
Lubbock Christian University, TX*
Lycoming College, PA*
Macalester College, MN*
Maine Maritime Academy, ME*
Malone University, OH*
Manhattan College, NY*
Mansfield University of Pennsylvania, PA*
Marian University, WI
Marist College, NY
Marquette University, WI
Marshall University, WV
Mary Baldwin College, VA
Marymount University, VA*
Maryville University of Saint Louis, MO*
Marywood University, PA*
Massachusetts Institute of Technology, MA
Massachusetts Maritime Academy, MA*

---

* program is offered at another college's campus

Peterson's How to Get Money for College 2014

Mayville State University, ND*
McDaniel College, MD
McKendree University, IL*
Menlo College, CA*
Mercer University, GA
Mercy College, NY*
Mercyhurst University, PA*
Metropolitan State University of Denver, CO*
Miami University, OH*
Michigan State University, MI
Mid-Atlantic Christian University, NC*
Middlebury College, VT*
Middle Tennessee State University, TN
Millersville University of Pennsylvania, PA
Millsaps College, MS*
Mills College, CA*
Milwaukee School of Engineering, WI*
Minnesota State University Mankato, MN
Minnesota State University Moorhead, MN*
Misericordia University, PA*
Mississippi College, MS
Mississippi State University, MS
Mississippi University for Women, MS*
Missouri Baptist University, MO*
Missouri State University, MO
Missouri University of Science and Technology, MO
Missouri Western State University, MO
Molloy College, NY*
Monmouth College, IL*
Monmouth University, NJ*
Montana State University, MT
Montclair State University, NJ
Moravian College, PA*
Morehead State University, KY
Morehouse College, GA
Morningside College, IA*
Mount Carmel College of Nursing, OH*
Mount Holyoke College, MA*
Mount Marty College, SD*
Mount Mary College, WI*
Mount Saint Mary College, NY*
Mount St. Mary's University, MD*
Muhlenberg College, PA*
Murray State University, KY
National University, CA*
Nazareth College of Rochester, NY*
Nebraska Methodist College, NE*
Nebraska Wesleyan University, NE*
Neumann University, PA*
Newberry College, SC*
New England College, NH*
New England School of Communications, ME*
New Jersey Institute of Technology, NJ*
New Mexico State University, NM
New York Institute of Technology, NY
New York University, NY*
Niagara University, NY
Norfolk State University, VA
North Carolina Central University, NC
North Carolina State University, NC
North Central College, IL*
Northeastern Illinois University, IL*
Northeastern University, MA
Northern Arizona University, AZ
Northern Illinois University, IL
Northern Kentucky University, KY*
Northern Michigan University, MI
Northwestern College, MN*
Northwestern State University of Louisiana, LA
Northwest Missouri State University, MO
Northwest Nazarene University, ID

Northwest University, WA*
Norwich University, VT
Occidental College, CA*
The Ohio State University, OH
Ohio University, OH
Oklahoma Christian University, OK*
Oklahoma City University, OK*
Oklahoma State University, OK
Old Dominion University, VA
Oregon State University, OR
Ouachita Baptist University, AR
Pace University, NY*
Pacific Lutheran University, WA
Pacific University, OR*
Palm Beach Atlantic University, FL*
Park University, MO
Penn State Abington, PA
Penn State Altoona, PA
Penn State Berks, PA*
Penn State Erie, The Behrend College, PA
Penn State Harrisburg, PA*
Penn State University Park, PA
Pennsylvania College of Technology, PA
Pepperdine University, CA*
Pittsburg State University, KS
Pitzer College, CA*
Plymouth State University, NH*
Point Loma Nazarene University, CA*
Point Park University, PA*
Polytechnic Institute of New York University, NY*
Polytechnic University of Puerto Rico, PR*
Pomona College, CA*
Portland State University, OR
Presbyterian College, SC
Princeton University, NJ
Providence College, RI
Purdue University, IN
Purdue University Calumet, IN
Queens College of the City University of New York, NY*
Quinnipiac University, CT*
Radford University, VA
Randolph-Macon College, VA*
Regent University, VA*
Regis University, CO*
Rensselaer Polytechnic Institute, NY
Research College of Nursing, MO*
Rhode Island College, RI*
Rhodes College, TN*
Rice University, TX*
The Richard Stockton College of New Jersey, NJ*
Rider University, NJ*
Ripon College, WI
Robert Morris University, PA
Robert Morris University Illinois, IL*
Roberts Wesleyan College, NY
Rochester Institute of Technology, NY
Rockford College, IL*
Rockhurst University, MO*
Rocky Mountain College, MT
Roger Williams University, RI*
Rose-Hulman Institute of Technology, IN
Rosemont College, PA*
Rowan University, NJ*
Russell Sage College, NY*
Rutgers, The State University of New Jersey, Camden, NJ*
Rutgers, The State University of New Jersey, Newark, NJ
Rutgers, The State University of New Jersey, New Brunswick, NJ
Sacred Heart University, CT*
Sage College of Albany, NY*

Saint Anselm College, NH*
St. Bonaventure University, NY
St. Edward's University, TX*
St. John Fisher College, NY*
Saint John's University, MN
St. John's University, NY
Saint Joseph's University, PA*
St. Lawrence University, NY*
St. Louis College of Pharmacy, MO*
Saint Louis University, MO*
Saint Martin's University, WA*
Saint Mary-of-the-Woods College, IN*
Saint Mary's College, IN*
Saint Mary's College of California, CA*
Saint Mary's University of Minnesota, MN*
Saint Michael's College, VT*
St. Norbert College, WI
Saint Peter's University, NJ*
Salisbury University, MD
Salve Regina University, RI*
Samford University, AL*
Sam Houston State University, TX
San Diego Christian College, CA*
San Diego State University, CA
San Francisco State University, CA*
San Jose State University, CA
Santa Clara University, CA
Savannah College of Art and Design, GA*
Scripps College, CA*
Seattle Pacific University, WA*
Seattle University, WA
Seton Hill University, PA
Shippensburg University of Pennsylvania, PA
Siena College, NY
Simmons College, MA*
Simpson University, CA
Skidmore College, NY*
Slippery Rock University of Pennsylvania, PA
Smith College, MA*
Sonoma State University, CA*
South Dakota State University, SD
Southeastern Louisiana University, LA*
Southern Connecticut State University, CT*
Southern Illinois University Carbondale, IL
Southern Illinois University Edwardsville, IL
Southern Methodist University, TX
Southern Polytechnic State University, GA*
Southern Utah University, UT
Southwest Baptist University, MO*
Spelman College, GA*
Spring Arbor University, MI
Spring Hill College, AL*
Stanford University, CA*
State University of New York at Oswego, NY*
State University of New York at Plattsburgh, NY
State University of New York College at Cortland, NY*
State University of New York College at Geneseo, NY*
State University of New York College at Old Westbury, NY*
State University of New York College at Potsdam, NY*
State University of New York College of Environmental Science and Forestry, NY*
State University of New York Institute of Technology, NY*
State University of New York Maritime College, NY*
Stephen F. Austin State University, TX
Stephens College, MO*
Stetson University, FL*

* program is offered at another college's campus

Stevenson University, MD*
Stonehill College, MA
Stony Brook University, State University of New York, NY
Suffolk University, MA*
Swarthmore College, PA*
Syracuse University, NY
Tarleton State University, TX
Temple University, PA
Tennessee State University, TN*
Texas A&M International University, TX
Texas A&M University, TX
Texas Christian University, TX
Texas Lutheran University, TX*
Texas Southern University, TX
Texas State University–San Marcos, TX
Texas Wesleyan University, TX
Texas Woman's University, TX*
Thomas More College, KY*
Tiffin University, OH*
Transylvania University, KY*
Trevecca Nazarene University, TN*
Trinity College, CT*
Troy University, AL
Truman State University, MO
Tufts University, MA*
Tulane University, LA
Tuskegee University, AL
Union College, NY*
Union University, TN*
Unity College, ME*
Universidad del Turabo, PR*
University at Albany, State University of New York, NY
University at Buffalo, the State University of New York, NY*
The University of Akron, OH
The University of Alabama, AL
The University of Alabama at Birmingham, AL
University of Alaska Anchorage, AK
University of Alaska Fairbanks, AK
The University of Arizona, AZ
University of Bridgeport, CT
University of California, Berkeley, CA
University of California, Davis, CA
University of California, Irvine, CA
University of California, Los Angeles, CA
University of California, Riverside, CA*
University of California, Santa Barbara, CA
University of California, Santa Cruz, CA*
University of Central Arkansas, AR
University of Central Florida, FL
University of Charleston, WV
University of Chicago, IL*
University of Cincinnati, OH
University of Colorado Boulder, CO
University of Colorado Colorado Springs, CO
University of Colorado Denver, CO*
University of Connecticut, CT
University of Dallas, TX*
University of Dayton, OH
University of Delaware, DE
University of Denver, CO*
University of Evansville, IN*
University of Florida, FL
University of Georgia, GA
University of Hartford, CT*
University of Hawaii at Manoa, HI
University of Hawaii–West Oahu, HI*
University of Houston, TX
University of Idaho, ID
University of Illinois at Chicago, IL
University of Illinois at Urbana–Champaign, IL

The University of Iowa, IA
The University of Kansas, KS
University of La Verne, CA*
University of Louisiana at Lafayette, LA
University of Louisville, KY
University of Mary Hardin-Baylor, TX
University of Maryland, Baltimore County, MD*
University of Maryland, College Park, MD
University of Maryland Eastern Shore, MD*
University of Mary Washington, VA*
University of Massachusetts Amherst, MA
University of Massachusetts Boston, MA*
University of Massachusetts Dartmouth, MA*
University of Memphis, TN
University of Miami, FL
University of Michigan, MI
University of Michigan–Dearborn, MI
University of Michigan–Flint, MI*
University of Minnesota, Twin Cities Campus, MN
University of Mississippi, MS
University of Missouri–Kansas City, MO
University of Missouri–St. Louis, MO*
University of Mobile, AL*
University of Montevallo, AL*
University of Mount Union, OH
University of Nebraska at Kearney, NE
University of Nebraska at Omaha, NE*
University of Nebraska–Lincoln, NE
University of Nevada, Las Vegas, NV
University of Nevada, Reno, NV
University of New England, ME*
University of New Hampshire, NH
University of New Hampshire at Manchester, NH*
University of New Haven, CT
University of New Orleans, LA
University of North Alabama, AL
The University of North Carolina at Chapel Hill, NC
The University of North Carolina at Greensboro, NC*
The University of North Carolina at Pembroke, NC
University of Northern Colorado, CO
University of Northern Iowa, IA
University of North Florida, FL
University of North Georgia, GA
University of North Texas, TX
University of Notre Dame, IN
University of Oklahoma, OK
University of Oregon, OR
University of Pennsylvania, PA*
University of Pikeville, KY
University of Pittsburgh, PA
University of Pittsburgh at Bradford, PA*
University of Pittsburgh at Greensburg, PA*
University of Portland, OR
University of Puerto Rico at Bayamón, PR
University of Puget Sound, WA*
University of Redlands, CA*
University of Rhode Island, RI
University of Richmond, VA
University of Rochester, NY*
University of St. Francis, IL*
University of St. Thomas, MN*
University of St. Thomas, TX*
University of San Diego, CA*
The University of Scranton, PA
University of South Alabama, AL
University of South Carolina, SC
University of South Carolina Upstate, SC*
The University of South Dakota, SD

University of Southern Indiana, IN
University of Southern Maine, ME*
University of Southern Mississippi, MS*
The University of Tampa, FL
The University of Tennessee, TN
The University of Tennessee at Chattanooga, TN
The University of Tennessee at Martin, TN
The University of Texas at Arlington, TX
The University of Texas at Austin, TX
The University of Texas at Brownsville, TX
The University of Texas at Dallas, TX*
The University of Texas at El Paso, TX
The University of Texas at San Antonio, TX
The University of Texas Health Science Center at Houston, TX*
The University of Texas–Pan American, TX
University of the Cumberlands, KY
University of the District of Columbia, DC*
University of the Incarnate Word, TX*
University of the Sciences, PA*
The University of Toledo, OH
University of Utah, UT
University of Vermont, VT
University of Virginia, VA
The University of Virginia's College at Wise, VA
University of Washington, Bothell, WA*
University of Washington, Tacoma, WA*
The University of West Alabama, AL*
University of West Florida, FL
University of Wisconsin–Eau Claire, WI
University of Wisconsin–Green Bay, WI*
University of Wisconsin–La Crosse, WI
University of Wisconsin–Madison, WI
University of Wisconsin–Milwaukee, WI*
University of Wisconsin–Parkside, WI*
University of Wisconsin–River Falls, WI
University of Wisconsin–Stevens Point, WI
University of Wisconsin–Stout, WI
University of Wyoming, WY
Ursuline College, OH*
Utah State University, UT
Utah Valley University, UT
Utica College, NY
Valparaiso University, IN*
Vanderbilt University, TN
Vermont Technical College, VT*
Villanova University, PA
Virginia Commonwealth University, VA*
Virginia Polytechnic Institute and State University, VA
Virginia State University, VA
Virginia Union University, VA*
Virginia Wesleyan College, VA*
Wagner College, NY*
Wake Forest University, NC
Washburn University, KS
Washington & Jefferson College, PA
Washington and Lee University, VA*
Washington State University, WA
Washington University in St. Louis, MO
Wayland Baptist University, TX*
Waynesburg University, PA*
Wayne State College, NE
Wayne State University, MI
Webster University, MO*
Wellesley College, MA*
Wells College, NY*
Wentworth Institute of Technology, MA*
Wesleyan College, GA*
Wesley College, DE*
West Chester University of Pennsylvania, PA
Western Connecticut State University, CT*
Western Illinois University, IL

---

* program is offered at another college's campus

Western Kentucky University, KY
Western Michigan University, MI
Western Oregon University, OR
Westfield State University, MA*
Westminster College, MO*
Westminster College, UT*
West Virginia State University, WV
West Virginia University, WV
West Virginia University Institute of
    Technology, WV
Wheaton College, IL
Wheaton College, MA*
Whittier College, CA*
Whitworth University, WA*
Widener University, PA
Wilkes University, PA*
Willamette University, OR*
William Jewell College, MO*
William Peace University, NC*
Winona State University, MN*
Winthrop University, SC*
Wittenberg University, OH*
Wofford College, SC
Worcester Polytechnic Institute, MA
Worcester State University, MA*
Wright State University, OH
Xavier University, OH
Xavier University of Louisiana, LA*
Yale University, CT*
York College of Pennsylvania, PA*
Youngstown State University, OH

Naval
Arizona State University, AZ
Armstrong Atlantic State University, GA*
Auburn University, AL
Babson College, MA*
Baptist Bible College of Pennsylvania, PA*
Belmont University, TN*
Boston College, MA*
Boston University, MA
California State University, San Marcos, CA*
Carnegie Mellon University, PA
The Catholic University of America, DC*
Chatham University, PA*
Chicago State University, IL*
Christian Brothers University, TN*
The Citadel, The Military College of South
    Carolina, SC
Clark University, MA*
Clayton State University, GA*
Clearwater Christian College, FL*
The College at Brockport, State University of
    New York, NY*
The College of Saint Rose, NY*
College of the Holy Cross, MA
Columbia College, MO*
Columbia University, NY
Columbia University, School of General
    Studies, NY
Duquesne University, PA*
Eastern Michigan University, MI*
Edgewood College, WI*
Embry-Riddle Aeronautical University–
    Daytona, FL
Farmingdale State College, NY*
Florida Agricultural and Mechanical
    University, FL
Florida State University, FL*
Georgetown University, DC*

The George Washington University, DC
Georgia Institute of Technology, GA
Georgia State University, GA*
Hampton University, VA
Harvard University, MA
Houston Baptist University, TX*
Husson University, ME*
Illinois Institute of Technology, IL
Indiana University South Bend, IN*
Iowa State University of Science and
    Technology, IA
Jacksonville University, FL
Kent State University at Stark, OH*
Lewis-Clark State College, ID*
Lincoln University, MO*
Louisiana State University and Agricultural
    and Mechanical College, LA*
Loyola Marymount University, CA*
Loyola University Chicago, IL*
Loyola University New Orleans, LA*
Macalester College, MN*
Maine Maritime Academy, ME
Marquette University, WI
Mary Baldwin College, VA*
Massachusetts Institute of Technology, MA
Massachusetts Maritime Academy, MA
Miami University, OH
Milwaukee School of Engineering, WI*
Missouri University of Science and
    Technology, MO*
Molloy College, NY*
Montclair State University, NJ
Morehouse College, GA
Mount Carmel College of Nursing, OH*
Mount Mary College, WI*
Norfolk State University, VA
North Carolina State University, NC
Northeastern University, MA*
Norwich University, VT
The Ohio State University, OH
Oklahoma City University, OK*
Old Dominion University, VA
Oregon State University, OR
Penn State University Park, PA
Point Loma Nazarene University, CA*
Princeton University, NJ*
Purdue University, IN
Queens College of the City University of
    New York, NY*
Quinnipiac University, CT*
Regent University, VA*
Regis University, CO*
Rensselaer Polytechnic Institute, NY
Rice University, TX
Rochester Institute of Technology, NY*
Rutgers, The State University of New Jersey,
    Newark, NJ
St. John Fisher College, NY*
Saint Joseph's University, PA*
St. Louis College of Pharmacy, MO*
Saint Mary's College, IN*
San Diego State University, CA
Seattle Pacific University, WA*
Seattle University, WA*
Siena College, NY*
Simmons College, MA*
Southern Polytechnic State University, GA*
Spelman College, GA*
Stanford University, CA*

State University of New York Maritime
    College, NY
Stephens College, MO*
Stony Brook University, State University of
    New York, NY*
Swarthmore College, PA*
Temple University, PA*
Tennessee State University, TN*
Texas A&M University, TX
Texas Southern University, TX*
Tufts University, MA*
Tulane University, LA
Union College, NY*
The University of Arizona, AZ
University of California, Berkeley, CA
University of California, Davis, CA*
University of California, Los Angeles, CA
University of California, Santa Cruz, CA*
University of Colorado Boulder, CO
University of Florida, FL
University of Houston, TX*
University of Idaho, ID
University of Illinois at Chicago, IL*
University of Illinois at Urbana–Champaign,
    IL
The University of Kansas, KS
University of Maryland, College Park, MD*
University of Massachusetts Boston, MA*
University of Memphis, TN
University of Michigan, MI
University of Michigan–Flint, MI*
University of Minnesota, Twin Cities
    Campus, MN
University of Mississippi, MS
University of Nebraska–Lincoln, NE
University of New Orleans, LA*
The University of North Carolina at Chapel
    Hill, NC
University of North Florida, FL*
University of Notre Dame, IN
University of Oklahoma, OK
University of Pennsylvania, PA
University of Pittsburgh, PA*
University of Rochester, NY
University of St. Thomas, MN*
University of San Diego, CA
University of South Carolina, SC
The University of Tampa, FL*
The University of Texas at Austin, TX
University of Utah, UT
University of Virginia, VA
University of Washington, Bothell, WA*
University of Washington, Tacoma, WA*
University of Wisconsin–Madison, WI
University of Wisconsin–Milwaukee, WI*
Vanderbilt University, TN
Villanova University, PA
Virginia Polytechnic Institute and State
    University, VA
Washburn University, KS*
Washington State University, WA*
Wayne State University, MI*
Western Oregon University, OR*
Westminster College, UT*
Widener University, PA*
William Peace University, NC*
Worcester Polytechnic Institute, MA*
Worcester State University, MA*
Xavier University of Louisiana, LA*
Yale University, CT

* program is offered at another college's campus

Tuition Waivers

Adult Students
Albright College, PA
Barton College, NC
Bluefield State College, WV
Briar Cliff University, IA
Caldwell College, NJ
Campbellsville University, KY
Centre College, KY
Clarke University, IA
Coe College, IA
Creighton University, NE
DeSales University, PA
Faulkner University, AL
Goucher College, MD
Hilbert College, NY
Lane College, TN
Lewis University, IL
Lipscomb University, TN
Lynchburg College, VA
MacMurray College, IL
Marist College, NY
Medical University of South Carolina, SC
Mercyhurst University, PA
Messiah College, PA
New England College, NH
Randolph College, VA
Sacred Heart University, CT
Shimer College, IL
Sweet Briar College, VA
Trinity College, CT
University of Dayton, OH
University of Evansville, IN
University of Hawaii at Manoa, HI
Utah State University, UT
Virginia Wesleyan College, VA
Webber International University, FL
Wittenberg University, OH
Xavier University, OH

Children of Alumni
Adelphi University, NY
Ashland University, OH
Baldwin Wallace University, OH
Barton College, NC
Cabrini College, PA
Caldwell College, NJ
Calumet College of Saint Joseph, IN
Cedar Crest College, PA
Central Methodist University, MO
Central Michigan University, MI
Clarke University, IA
College of Saint Elizabeth, NJ
Columbia College, MO
Columbus College of Art & Design, OH
Curry College, MA
Dixie State College of Utah, UT
Drake University, IA
Drury University, MO
D'Youville College, NY
Florida Southern College, FL
Goldey-Beacom College, DE
Grand View University, IA
Henderson State University, AR
Hilbert College, NY
Hillsdale College, MI
Hillsdale Free Will Baptist College, OK
Huntingdon College, AL
Huntington University, IN
Iona College, NY
Ithaca College, NY

Johnson C. Smith University, NC
Kentucky State University, KY
Kentucky Wesleyan College, KY
Lake Superior State University, MI
Lasell College, MA
Lewis University, IL
MacMurray College, IL
McKendree University, IL
Messiah College, PA
Michigan Technological University, MI
Mid-Atlantic Christian University, NC
Minot State University, ND
Mississippi State University, MS
Missouri Baptist University, MO
Missouri State University, MO
Morehead State University, KY
Morningside College, IA
Murray State University, KY
Nazareth College of Rochester, NY
New England College, NH
Northwestern College, MN
Northwest Nazarene University, ID
Oklahoma State University, OK
Pacific Lutheran University, WA
Peirce College, PA
Pine Manor College, MA
Saint Joseph's College, IN
Saint Louis University, MO
Saint Martin's University, WA
Simpson College, IA
Southeastern Oklahoma State University, OK
Southern Arkansas University–Magnolia, AR
Southern Illinois University Carbondale, IL
Southern Utah University, UT
Suffolk University, MA
Texas Lutheran University, TX
Truman State University, MO
Union University, TN
University of Alaska Fairbanks, AK
University of Charleston, WV
University of Evansville, IN
University of Mississippi, MS
University of Mount Union, OH
University of New England, ME
University of St. Francis, IL
The University of South Dakota, SD
University of Southern Mississippi, MS
University of the Ozarks, AR
University of Wisconsin–Whitewater, WI
University of Wyoming, WY
Utah State University, UT
Wartburg College, IA
Webber International University, FL
Western Kentucky University, KY
Westminster College, MO
Whittier College, CA
Wittenberg University, OH

Minority Students
Bloomsburg University of Pennsylvania, PA
Drury University, MO
Edinboro University of Pennsylvania, PA
Fort Lewis College, CO
Hilbert College, NY
Huntington University, IN
Illinois State University, IL
Lake Superior State University, MI
Lock Haven University of Pennsylvania, PA

Mayville State University, ND
Medical University of South Carolina, SC
Messiah College, PA
Minot State University, ND
Montana State University, MT
Montana Tech of The University of Montana, MT
Nazareth College of Rochester, NY
Northwest Nazarene University, ID
Sacred Heart University, CT
Saint Joseph's College, IN
Shepherd University, WV
Simpson College, IA
Slippery Rock University of Pennsylvania, PA
Southeastern Oklahoma State University, OK
Texas Southern University, TX
University at Buffalo, the State University of New York, NY
University of Evansville, IN
University of Hawaii at Manoa, HI
University of Maine at Augusta, ME
University of Maine at Farmington, ME
University of Maine at Presque Isle, ME
The University of Montana, MT
The University of Montana Western, MT
University of Rhode Island, RI
University of Wisconsin–Eau Claire, WI
University of Wisconsin–La Crosse, WI
Utah State University, UT
Wartburg College, IA
Western Washington University, WA
Wittenberg University, OH

Senior Citizens
Adams State University, CO
Adelphi University, NY
Albright College, PA
Andrews University, MI
Angelo State University, TX
Arkansas State University, AR
Arkansas Tech University, AR
Armstrong Atlantic State University, GA
Asbury University, KY
Ashland University, OH
Athens State University, AL
Aurora University, IL
Austin Peay State University, TN
Averett University, VA
Ball State University, IN
Barton College, NC
Baruch College of the City University of New York, NY
Becker College, MA
Bellarmine University, KY
Belmont Abbey College, NC
Belmont University, TN
Bemidji State University, MN
Benedictine College, KS
Berry College, GA
Bethany Lutheran College, MN
Bloomfield College, NJ
Bloomsburg University of Pennsylvania, PA
Bluefield College, VA
Bluefield State College, WV
Bob Jones University, SC
Boise State University, ID
Bowie State University, MD
Bowling Green State University, OH

Bradley University, IL
Brevard College, NC
Briar Cliff University, IA
Bridgewater College, VA
Bridgewater State University, MA
Cabrini College, PA
Caldwell College, NJ
California State University, Chico, CA
California State University, Dominguez Hills, CA
California State University, Fullerton, CA
California State University, Long Beach, CA
California State University, Monterey Bay, CA
California State University, Northridge, CA
California State University, San Bernardino, CA
California State University, San Marcos, CA
Calumet College of Saint Joseph, IN
Campbellsville University, KY
Capital University, OH
Carroll College, MT
Carson-Newman University, TN
Cedarville University, OH
Central Connecticut State University, CT
Central Michigan University, MI
Centre College, KY
Chestnut Hill College, PA
Chowan University, NC
Christopher Newport University, VA
The Citadel, The Military College of South Carolina, SC
City College of the City University of New York, NY
Clarion University of Pennsylvania, PA
Clarke University, IA
Clayton State University, GA
Clemson University, SC
Cleveland State University, OH
Coastal Carolina University, SC
Coe College, IA
The College at Brockport, State University of New York, NY
College of Charleston, SC
College of Mount St. Joseph, OH
The College of New Jersey, NJ
College of Saint Elizabeth, NJ
College of Saint Mary, NE
The College of St. Scholastica, MN
College of Staten Island of the City University of New York, NY
The College of William and Mary, VA
Colorado Mountain College, CO
Columbia College, MO
Corban University, OR
Covenant College, GA
Culver-Stockton College, MO
Dakota State University, SD
Dakota Wesleyan University, SD
Defiance College, OH
DeSales University, PA
Dickinson College, PA
Dixie State College of Utah, UT
Doane College, NE
Dominican College, NY
Dordt College, IA
Drake University, IA
Drew University, NJ
Duquesne University, PA
D'Youville College, NY
East Carolina University, NC
Eastern Illinois University, IL
Eastern New Mexico University, NM
Edinboro University of Pennsylvania, PA
Elmhurst College, IL
Emmanuel College, GA

Emporia State University, KS
The Evergreen State College, WA
Fashion Institute of Technology, NY
Faulkner University, AL
Fayetteville State University, NC
Florida Agricultural and Mechanical University, FL
Florida Atlantic University, FL
Florida Institute of Technology, FL
Florida International University, FL
Florida State University, FL
Framingham State University, MA
Francis Marion University, SC
Franklin College, IN
Franklin Pierce University, NH
Frostburg State University, MD
Gannon University, PA
George Fox University, OR
George Mason University, VA
Georgia College & State University, GA
Georgia Southern University, GA
Georgia State University, GA
Glenville State College, WV
Goucher College, MD
Graceland University, IA
Grand View University, IA
Greenville College, IL
Hanover College, IN
Harding University, AR
Henderson State University, AR
Hilbert College, NY
Hillsdale Free Will Baptist College, OK
Hofstra University, NY
Husson University, ME
Idaho State University, ID
Illinois State University, IL
Indiana State University, IN
Indiana University of Pennsylvania, PA
Indiana University–Purdue University Fort Wayne, IN
Iona College, NY
John Carroll University, OH
John Jay College of Criminal Justice of the City University of New York, NY
Juniata College, PA
Kean University, NJ
Keene State College, NH
Kennesaw State University, GA
Kent State University, OH
Kent State University at Geauga, OH
Kent State University at Stark, OH
Kentucky State University, KY
Kentucky Wesleyan College, KY
Keystone College, PA
King College, TN
King's College, PA
Kutztown University of Pennsylvania, PA
LaGrange College, GA
Lake Erie College, OH
Lakeland College, WI
Lake Superior State University, MI
Lamar University, TX
La Roche College, PA
Lebanon Valley College, PA
Lee University, TN
Lewis-Clark State College, ID
Lindenwood University, MO
Lindsey Wilson College, KY
Linfield College, OR
Lock Haven University of Pennsylvania, PA
Longwood University, VA
Lourdes University, OH
Loyola University Chicago, IL
Loyola University New Orleans, LA
Lynchburg College, VA
MacMurray College, IL

Malone University, OH
Manhattanville College, NY
Mansfield University of Pennsylvania, PA
Marian University, WI
Marlboro College, VT
Marquette University, WI
Marshall University, WV
Marymount Manhattan College, NY
Marymount University, VA
Maryville University of Saint Louis, MO
Marywood University, PA
Massachusetts College of Art and Design, MA
Massachusetts College of Liberal Arts, MA
Mayville State University, ND
McNeese State University, LA
Medical University of South Carolina, SC
Merrimack College, MA
Messiah College, PA
Michigan Technological University, MI
Mid-Atlantic Christian University, NC
Midwestern State University, TX
Millersville University of Pennsylvania, PA
Minnesota State University Moorhead, MN
Minot State University, ND
Mississippi State University, MS
Missouri Baptist University, MO
Missouri Southern State University, MO
Missouri State University, MO
Missouri Western State University, MO
Monmouth University, NJ
Montana State University, MT
Montana State University Billings, MT
Montana Tech of The University of Montana, MT
Montclair State University, NJ
Morehead State University, KY
Morningside College, IA
Mount Mary College, WI
Mount Vernon Nazarene University, OH
Murray State University, KY
Nebraska Wesleyan University, NE
New England College, NH
New Jersey City University, NJ
New Mexico Highlands University, NM
New Mexico Institute of Mining and Technology, NM
New Mexico State University, NM
New York Institute of Technology, NY
Niagara University, NY
North Central College, IL
Northeastern Illinois University, IL
Northeastern State University, OK
Northern Kentucky University, KY
Northern Michigan University, MI
Northwestern Oklahoma State University, OK
Northwestern State University of Louisiana, LA
Northwest Missouri State University, MO
Notre Dame de Namur University, CA
Oakland University, MI
The Ohio State University, OH
Ohio University, OH
Ohio University–Chillicothe, OH
Ohio University–Zanesville, OH
Oklahoma Baptist University, OK
Oklahoma Wesleyan University, OK
Old Dominion University, VA
Pace University, NY
Pacific Union College, CA
Park University, MO
Penn State Abington, PA
Plymouth State University, NH
Point Loma Nazarene University, CA
Portland State University, OR

Post University, CT
Presbyterian College, SC
Purdue University, IN
Purdue University Calumet, IN
Purdue University North Central, IN
Queens College of the City University of New York, NY
Quincy University, IL
Radford University, VA
Research College of Nursing, MO
The Richard Stockton College of New Jersey, NJ
Roanoke College, VA
Roberts Wesleyan College, NY
Rockhurst University, MO
Rogers State University, OK
Rosemont College, PA
Russell Sage College, NY
Sacred Heart University, CT
St. Ambrose University, IA
St. Bonaventure University, NY
St. Catherine University, MN
St. Cloud State University, MN
St. John's University, NY
St. Joseph's College, Long Island Campus, NY
St. Joseph's College, New York, NY
St. Mary's College of Maryland, MD
St. Olaf College, MN
Salisbury University, MD
Seattle Pacific University, WA
Shawnee State University, OH
Shepherd University, WV
Shimer College, IL
Shippensburg University of Pennsylvania, PA
Simpson College, IA
Skidmore College, NY
Slippery Rock University of Pennsylvania, PA
South Dakota State University, SD
Southeastern Oklahoma State University, OK
Southeast Missouri State University, MO
Southern Adventist University, TN
Southern Arkansas University–Magnolia, AR
Southern Connecticut State University, CT
Southern Illinois University Carbondale, IL
Southern Illinois University Edwardsville, IL
Southern Polytechnic State University, GA
Southern Utah University, UT
Southern Vermont College, VT
Southwestern College, KS
State University of New York College at Old Westbury, NY
State University of New York College of Agriculture and Technology at Cobleskill, NY
Stephen F. Austin State University, TX
Suffolk University, MA
Sweet Briar College, VA
Taylor University, IN
Tennessee Technological University, TN
Texas A&M International University, TX
Texas Southern University, TX
Texas Tech University, TX
Texas Woman's University, TX
Thiel College, PA

Thomas More College, KY
Tiffin University, OH
Towson University, MD
Trevecca Nazarene University, TN
Trinity College of Florida, FL
Truman State University, MO
Union College, KY
Union College, NY
The University of Akron, OH
University of Alaska Fairbanks, AK
University of Bridgeport, CT
University of Central Arkansas, AR
University of Central Florida, FL
University of Charleston, WV
University of Colorado Boulder, CO
University of Connecticut, CT
University of Dayton, OH
University of Delaware, DE
University of Denver, CO
University of Evansville, IN
University of Florida, FL
University of Georgia, GA
University of Hartford, CT
University of Hawaii at Manoa, HI
University of Houston–Clear Lake, TX
University of Idaho, ID
University of Illinois at Chicago, IL
University of Illinois at Springfield, IL
University of Illinois at Urbana–Champaign, IL
University of Louisville, KY
University of Maine, ME
University of Maine at Augusta, ME
University of Maine at Farmington, ME
University of Maine at Presque Isle, ME
University of Mary, ND
University of Maryland, Baltimore County, MD
University of Maryland Eastern Shore, MD
University of Maryland University College, MD
University of Mary Washington, VA
University of Massachusetts Amherst, MA
University of Massachusetts Dartmouth, MA
University of Massachusetts Lowell, MA
University of Michigan–Dearborn, MI
University of Michigan–Flint, MI
University of Minnesota, Crookston, MN
University of Minnesota, Morris, MN
University of Minnesota, Twin Cities Campus, MN
University of Mississippi, MS
University of Missouri–St. Louis, MO
The University of Montana, MT
The University of Montana Western, MT
University of Mount Union, OH
University of New Hampshire at Manchester, NH
University of New Haven, CT
University of New Orleans, LA
University of North Alabama, AL
University of North Florida, FL
University of North Georgia, GA
University of North Texas, TX
University of Oklahoma, OK
University of Pikeville, KY
University of Pittsburgh at Greensburg, PA
University of Rhode Island, RI
University of St. Thomas, MN
University of St. Thomas, TX

University of Science and Arts of Oklahoma, OK
The University of Scranton, PA
University of South Carolina, SC
University of South Carolina Aiken, SC
University of South Carolina Upstate, SC
The University of South Dakota, SD
University of Southern Mississippi, MS
The University of Tennessee, TN
The University of Tennessee at Chattanooga, TN
The University of Tennessee at Martin, TN
The University of Texas at Austin, TX
The University of Texas at Dallas, TX
The University of Texas of the Permian Basin, TX
University of the Cumberlands, KY
University of the District of Columbia, DC
University of the Incarnate Word, TX
University of Utah, UT
University of Virginia, VA
The University of Virginia's College at Wise, VA
University of Washington, WA
University of West Florida, FL
University of West Georgia, GA
University of Wisconsin–Green Bay, WI
University of Wisconsin–Milwaukee, WI
University of Wisconsin–Whitewater, WI
University of Wyoming, WY
Utah State University, UT
Valdosta State University, GA
Villanova University, PA
Virginia Commonwealth University, VA
Virginia Intermont College, VA
Virginia Polytechnic Institute and State University, VA
Virginia State University, VA
Virginia Wesleyan College, VA
Washburn University, KS
Washington Adventist University, MD
Washington State University, WA
Wayne State University, MI
Webber International University, FL
Wells College, NY
Wesleyan College, GA
Wesley College, DE
West Chester University of Pennsylvania, PA
Western Connecticut State University, CT
Western Illinois University, IL
Western Kentucky University, KY
Western Michigan University, MI
Western New England University, MA
Western State Colorado University, CO
Westfield State University, MA
West Virginia University, WV
West Virginia University Institute of Technology, WV
Whitworth University, WA
Wichita State University, KS
Widener University, PA
William Peace University, NC
Winthrop University, SC
Wittenberg University, OH
Worcester State University, MA
Wright State University, OH
Xavier University, OH
Youngstown State University, OH

Tuition Payment Alternatives

College/University	Code
Abilene Christian University, TX	I,P
Academy of Art University, CA	I
Adams State University, CO	D,I
Adelphi University, NY	D,I,P
Alabama State University, AL	D
Alaska Bible College, AK	
Alaska Pacific University, AK	D,I
Albany College of Pharmacy and Health Sciences, NY	I
Albion College, MI	D,I
Albright College, PA	I
Alcorn State University, MS	I
Alfred University, NY	D,I,P
Allegheny College, PA	I
Allen College, IA	D
Alliant International University, CA	I
Alma College, MI	D,I
Alverno College, WI	D,I
American Baptist College of American Baptist Theological Seminary, TN	I
American Indian College of the Assemblies of God, Inc., AZ	I
American International College, MA	I,P
American Jewish University, CA	I
American University, DC	I,P
Amherst College, MA	D,I
Anderson University, IN	I
Anderson University, SC	I
Andrews University, MI	I
Angelo State University, TX	I
Appalachian State University, NC	I
Arizona State University, AZ	I
Arkansas State University, AR	I
Arkansas Tech University, AR	D,I
Asbury University, KY	I
Ashland University, OH	I
Auburn University, AL	I
Auburn University at Montgomery, AL	I
Augustana College, IL	I,P
Augustana College, SD	I
Aurora University, IL	D,I
Austin Peay State University, TN	I
Averett University, VA	I
Azusa Pacific University, CA	I
Baldwin Wallace University, OH	D,I
Ball State University, IN	I
Baptist Bible College of Pennsylvania, PA	I
Baptist University of the Americas, TX	I
Bard College, NY	I,P
Barnard College, NY	D,I,P
Barton College, NC	I
Baruch College of the City University of New York, NY	D,I
Bates College, ME	I,P
Baylor University, TX	I
Bay Path College, MA	I
Becker College, MA	I
Belhaven University, MS	I
Bellarmine University, KY	I
Belmont Abbey College, NC	D,I
Belmont University, TN	D,I
Beloit College, WI	I
Bemidji State University, MN	I
Benedict College, SC	I
Benedictine College, KS	I
Benedictine University, IL	D,I
Bennington College, VT	I
Bentley University, MA	I
Berry College, GA	I
Bethany Lutheran College, MN	I
Bethel College, IN	I
Bethel University, MN	I,P
Bethune-Cookman University, FL	I
Binghamton University, State University of New York, NY	I
Biola University, CA	I
Bloomfield College, NJ	D,I
Bloomsburg University of Pennsylvania, PA	I
Bluefield College, VA	I
Bluefield State College, WV	I
Blue Mountain College, MS	D,I
Bluffton University, OH	I
Bob Jones University, SC	I
Boise State University, ID	I
Boston College, MA	I
Boston University, MA	I,P
Bowdoin College, ME	D,I
Bowie State University, MD	D,I
Bowling Green State University, OH	I
Bradley University, IL	D,I
Brandeis University, MA	I,P
Brenau University, GA	I
Brevard College, NC	I
Briar Cliff University, IA	D,I
Bridgewater College, VA	I
Bridgewater State University, MA	I
Broadview University–Boise, ID	I
Broadview University–Layton, UT	I
Broadview University–Orem, UT	I
Broadview University–Salt Lake City, UT	I
Broadview University–West Jordan, UT	I
Brown University, RI	I
Bryant University, RI	I
Bucknell University, PA	I,P
Buena Vista University, IA	G,I
Buffalo State College, State University of New York, NY	I
Burlington College, VT	I
Butler University, IN	I
Cabrini College, PA	I
Cairn University, PA	I
Caldwell College, NJ	I
California Baptist University, CA	I
California Christian College, CA	I
California College of the Arts, CA	I
California Institute of Technology, CA	D,I
California Polytechnic State University, San Luis Obispo, CA	I
California State Polytechnic University, Pomona, CA	D,I
California State University, Chico, CA	D,I
California State University, Dominguez Hills, CA	I
California State University, Fresno, CA	I
California State University, Fullerton, CA	D,I
California State University, Long Beach, CA	I
California State University, Los Angeles, CA	I
California State University, Monterey Bay, CA	I
California State University, Northridge, CA	I
California State University, San Bernardino, CA	I
Calumet College of Saint Joseph, IN	D
Calvary Bible College and Theological Seminary, MO	G,I
Calvin College, MI	I,P
Cameron University, OK	I
Campbellsville University, KY	I
Canisius College, NY	D,I
Capital University, OH	I
Cardinal Stritch University, WI	D,I
Carleton College, MN	I,P
Carlos Albizu University, PR	D
Carolina Christian College, NC	I
Carroll College, MT	I
Carson-Newman University, TN	D,I
Case Western Reserve University, OH	I
Catawba College, NC	I
The Catholic University of America, DC	I
Cazenovia College, NY	I
Cedar Crest College, PA	D,I
Cedarville University, OH	I
Centenary College of Louisiana, LA	D,I
Central College, IA	I
Central Connecticut State University, CT	I
Central Methodist University, MO	I
Central Michigan University, MI	I
Centre College, KY	I
Champlain College, VT	I
Chapman University, CA	D,I,P
Chatham University, PA	I
Chestnut Hill College, PA	D,I
Chicago State University, IL	G,P
Chowan University, NC	I
Christendom College, VA	I
Christopher Newport University, VA	I
Cincinnati Christian University, OH	I
City College of the City University of New York, NY	D
Claremont McKenna College, CA	I
Clarion University of Pennsylvania, PA	I
Clarke University, IA	D,I
Clarkson University, NY	I,P
Clark University, MA	I,P
Clearwater Christian College, FL	G,I
Clemson University, SC	I
Cleveland Institute of Art, OH	I
Cleveland State University, OH	I
Coastal Carolina University, SC	I
Coe College, IA	I
Colby College, ME	I
Colgate University, NY	D,I,P
The College at Brockport, State University of New York, NY	D,I
College of Charleston, SC	I
The College of Idaho, ID	D,I
College of Mount St. Joseph, OH	D,I
The College of New Jersey, NJ	I
The College of New Rochelle, NY	I
College of Saint Benedict, MN	I
College of Saint Elizabeth, NJ	I
College of Saint Mary, NE	D,I
The College of Saint Rose, NY	I
The College of St. Scholastica, MN	I
College of Staten Island of the City University of New York, NY	I
College of the Atlantic, ME	I
College of the Holy Cross, MA	I
College of the Ozarks, MO	I
The College of William and Mary, VA	I
The College of Wooster, OH	I
The Colorado College, CO	I
Colorado Mesa University, CO	I

D = deferred payment system; G = guaranteed tuition rate; I = installment payments; P = prepayment locks in tuition rate

Colorado Mountain College, CO	I	Emory & Henry College, VA	D,I	Hanover College, IN	I
Columbia College, MO	D,G,I	Emory University, GA	I	Harding University, AR	I,P
Columbia International University, SC	I	Emporia State University, KS	D,I	Hardin-Simmons University, TX	G,I
Columbia University, NY	I	Endicott College, MA	I,P	Harrisburg University of Science and Technology, PA	D,I
Columbia University, School of General Studies, NY	I,P	Evangel University, MO	I	Hartwick College, NY	I
Columbus College of Art & Design, OH	D,I	Excelsior College, NY	I	Harvard University, MA	I,P
Concordia College, MN	I	Fairfield University, CT	I	Harvey Mudd College, CA	I
Concordia University, CA	I	Fairmont State University, WV	I	Haverford College, PA	I,P
Concordia University Ann Arbor, MI	I	Farmingdale State College, NY	I	Hawai'i Pacific University, HI	I
Concordia University, Nebraska, NE	I	Fashion Institute of Technology, NY	I	Heidelberg University, OH	I
Concordia University, St. Paul, MN	I	Faulkner University, AL	I	Hendrix College, AR	I
Concordia University Texas, TX	I	Fayetteville State University, NC	I	Heritage Christian University, AL	I
Converse College, SC	I	Felician College, NJ	I	Hilbert College, NY	I
Corban University, OR	I	Ferris State University, MI	D	Hillsdale College, MI	I,P
Corcoran College of Art and Design, DC	I	Fisher College, MA	I	Hillsdale Free Will Baptist College, OK	I
Cornell College, IA	I	Florida Agricultural and Mechanical University, FL	P	Hobart and William Smith Colleges, NY	I,P
Cornell University, NY	I	Florida Atlantic University, FL	D,I,P	Hodges University, FL	I
Cornerstone University, MI	I	Florida Institute of Technology, FL	I	Hofstra University, NY	G,I
Covenant College, GA	I	Florida International University, FL	I	Hollins University, VA	I,P
Creighton University, NE	I	Florida National University, FL	G,I,P	Hood College, MD	I
Crossroads Bible College, IN	I	Florida Southern College, FL	I	Hope College, MI	I
Crown College, MN	I	Florida State University, FL	I,P	Hope International University, CA	I
Culver-Stockton College, MO	I	Fort Lewis College, CO	I	Houghton College, NY	I
Curry College, MA	I	Framingham State University, MA	I,P	Houston Baptist University, TX	I
Dakota State University, SD	D,I	Francis Marion University, SC	I	Howard Payne University, TX	I
Dallas Baptist University, TX	D,I	Franklin & Marshall College, PA	D,I	Hunter College of the City University of New York, NY	I
Daniel Webster College, NH	I	Franklin College, IN	I	
Dartmouth College, NH	I,P	Franklin Pierce University, NH	I	Huntingdon College, AL	D,G
Davenport University, MI	I	Franklin W. Olin College of Engineering, MA	I	Huntington University, IN	I
Defiance College, OH	I			Husson University, ME	I,P
Denison University, OH	I	Freed-Hardeman University, TN	I	Idaho State University, ID	D
DePaul University, IL	D,I	Frostburg State University, MD	D,I	Illinois College, IL	D,I
DePauw University, IN	I	Furman University, SC	I	Illinois Institute of Technology, IL	I
DeSales University, PA	D,I	Gallaudet University, DC	D,I	Illinois State University, IL	G,I
Dickinson College, PA	I	Gannon University, PA	D,I	Illinois Wesleyan University, IL	I
DigiPen Institute of Technology, WA	I	Gardner-Webb University, NC	I	Indiana State University, IN	D,I
Dillard University, LA	I	Geneva College, PA	I	Indiana Tech, IN	I
Dixie State College of Utah, UT	I	George Fox University, OR	I	Indiana University Bloomington, IN	D
Doane College, NE	I	George Mason University, VA	I	Indiana University East, IN	D
Dominican College, NY	D,I	Georgetown College, KY	I	Indiana University Kokomo, IN	D
Dominican University, IL	D	Georgetown University, DC	I	Indiana University Northwest, IN	D,I
Dominican University of California, CA	I	The George Washington University, DC	G,I	Indiana University of Pennsylvania, PA	D,I
Dordt College, IA	I	Georgia College & State University, GA	I	Indiana University–Purdue University Fort Wayne, IN	D,I
Drake University, IA	I	Georgia Institute of Technology, GA	D	
Drew University, NJ	D,I,P	Georgian Court University, NJ	I	Indiana University–Purdue University Indianapolis, IN	D,I
Drury University, MO	D,I,P	Glenville State College, WV	I	
Duquesne University, PA	D,I	Globe University–Appleton, WI	I	Indiana University South Bend, IN	D
D'Youville College, NY	D,G,I	Globe University–Eau Claire, WI	I	Indiana University Southeast, IN	D
Earlham College, IN	D,I,P	Globe University–Green Bay, WI	I	Indiana Wesleyan University, IN	I
East Carolina University, NC	D,I	Globe University–La Crosse, WI	I	Inter American University of Puerto Rico, Bayamón Campus, PR	D
Eastern Illinois University, IL	G,I	Globe University–Madison East, WI	I	
Eastern Michigan University, MI	I	Globe University–Madison West, WI	I	Inter American University of Puerto Rico, Guayama Campus, PR	D
Eastern New Mexico University, NM	I	Globe University–Minneapolis, MN	I	
Eastern Washington University, WA	I	Globe University–Sioux Falls, SD	I	Inter American University of Puerto Rico, Ponce Campus, PR	D
East Texas Baptist University, TX	I	Globe University–Wausau, WI	I	
Eckerd College, FL	I	Globe University–Woodbury, MN	I	Iona College, NY	I
Edgewood College, WI	I	Goldey-Beacom College, DE	D,I	Iowa State University of Science and Technology, IA	D,I
Edinboro University of Pennsylvania, PA	I	Gonzaga University, WA	D,I	
EDP University of Puerto Rico, PR	I	Gordon College, MA	I	Iowa Wesleyan College, IA	D,I
EDP University of Puerto Rico–San Sebastian, PR	I	Goucher College, MD	I,P	Ithaca College, NY	I
		Grace Bible College, MI	I	Jacksonville State University, AL	I
Elizabeth City State University, NC	I	Graceland University, IA	I	Jacksonville University, FL	D
Elizabethtown College, PA	I	Grand Valley State University, MI	D,I	James Madison University, VA	I,P
Elmhurst College, IL	I	Grand View University, IA	I	John Brown University, AR	I
Elmira College, NY	I,P	Grinnell College, IA	I	John Carroll University, OH	D,I
Elon University, NC	I	Grove City College, PA	I	John Jay College of Criminal Justice of the City University of New York, NY	I
Embry-Riddle Aeronautical University–Daytona, FL	D	Guilford College, NC	I	
		Gustavus Adolphus College, MN	I,P	The Johns Hopkins University, MD	I
Embry-Riddle Aeronautical University–Prescott, AZ	D,I	Gwynedd-Mercy College, PA	I	Johnson C. Smith University, NC	I
		Hamilton College, NY	I	Johnson State College, VT	I
Emerson College, MA	I	Hamline University, MN	I	Juniata College, PA	I
Emmanuel College, GA	I	Hampden-Sydney College, VA	I	Kalamazoo College, MI	I
Emmanuel College, MA	I	Hampshire College, MA	I	Kansas State University, KS	D,I
		Hampton University, VA	D		

D = deferred payment system; *G* = guaranteed tuition rate; *I* = installment payments; *P* = prepayment locks in tuition rate

College	Code
Kean University, NJ	I
Keene State College, NH	I
Kent State University, OH	D,I
Kent State University at Geauga, OH	D,I
Kent State University at Stark, OH	D,I
Kentucky State University, KY	D
Kentucky Wesleyan College, KY	D,I
Kenyon College, OH	I
Kettering University, MI	G,I
Keuka College, NY	I
Keystone College, PA	D,I
King College, TN	I
The King's College, NY	D,I
King's College, PA	I
Knox College, IL	I
Kutztown University of Pennsylvania, PA	D,I
Lafayette College, PA	I,P
LaGrange College, GA	I
Lake Erie College, OH	I
Lake Forest College, IL	I
Lakeland College, WI	D,G,I,P
Lake Superior State University, MI	D,I
Lamar University, TX	I
Lane College, TN	D,I
La Roche College, PA	I
La Salle University, PA	D,I
Lasell College, MA	I
La Sierra University, CA	I
Lawrence Technological University, MI	I
Lawrence University, WI	I,P
Lebanon Valley College, PA	I,P
Lees-McRae College, NC	I
Lee University, TN	D
Lehigh University, PA	I,P
Lehman College of the City University of New York, NY	I
Le Moyne College, NY	D,I
Lesley University, MA	I
LeTourneau University, TX	I
Lewis & Clark College, OR	I
Lewis-Clark State College, ID	D
Lewis University, IL	I
Liberty University, VA	I
Life University, GA	I
Limestone College, SC	I
Lincoln University, MO	D,I
Lindenwood University, MO	D,I
Lindsey Wilson College, KY	I
Linfield College, OR	I
Lipscomb University, TN	I
Lock Haven University of Pennsylvania, PA	I
Long Island University–Brooklyn Campus, NY	I
Long Island University–C. W. Post Campus, NY	I
Longwood University, VA	I
Loras College, IA	I
Louisiana College, LA	I
Louisiana State University and Agricultural and Mechanical College, LA	D
Lourdes University, OH	D,I
Loyola Marymount University, CA	D,I
Loyola University Chicago, IL	D,I
Loyola University Maryland, MD	I
Loyola University New Orleans, LA	I
Lubbock Christian University, TX	I
Luther College, IA	I
Lycoming College, PA	I
Lyme Academy College of Fine Arts, CT	I
Lynchburg College, VA	I,P
Lynn University, FL	D,I
Lyon College, AR	I
Macalester College, MN	I
MacMurray College, IL	D,I
Maine Maritime Academy, ME	I
Malone University, OH	I
Manchester University, IN	I
Manhattan College, NY	D,I
Manhattanville College, NY	D,I
Mansfield University of Pennsylvania, PA	D,I
Marian University, WI	I
Marist College, NY	I
Marlboro College, VT	I
Marquette University, WI	I
Marshall University, WV	I
Mary Baldwin College, VA	I
Marymount Manhattan College, NY	I
Marymount University, VA	I
Maryville College, TN	I
Maryville University of Saint Louis, MO	D,I
Marywood University, PA	D,I
Massachusetts College of Art and Design, MA	I
Massachusetts College of Liberal Arts, MA	I
Massachusetts Institute of Technology, MA	I
The Master's College and Seminary, CA	I
Mayville State University, ND	I
McDaniel College, MD	I,P
McKendree University, IL	D,I
McMurry University, TX	I
McNally Smith College of Music, MN	D,G,I,P
McPherson College, KS	I
Medgar Evers College of the City University of New York, NY	D,I
Medical University of South Carolina, SC	I
Memphis College of Art, TN	I
Menlo College, CA	I
Mercer University, GA	I
Mercy College, NY	I
Mercyhurst University, PA	I
Merrimack College, MA	I
Messiah College, PA	I
Miami University, OH	I
Michigan State University, MI	D
Michigan Technological University, MI	D,I
Mid-Atlantic Christian University, NC	D
Middlebury College, VT	P
Midwestern State University, TX	I
Millersville University of Pennsylvania, PA	I
Milligan College, TN	I
Millikin University, IL	I
Millsaps College, MS	I
Mills College, CA	I
Milwaukee School of Engineering, WI	I
Minnesota School of Business–Blaine, MN	I
Minnesota School of Business–Elk River, MN	I
Minnesota School of Business–Lakeville, MN	I
Minnesota School of Business–Rochester, MN	I
Minnesota State University Mankato, MN	I
Minnesota State University Moorhead, MN	I
Minot State University, ND	I
Misericordia University, PA	D,I
Mississippi College, MS	I
Mississippi State University, MS	I,P
Mississippi University for Women, MS	I
Missouri Baptist University, MO	I
Missouri State University, MO	D
Missouri University of Science and Technology, MO	I
Missouri Western State University, MO	I
Molloy College, NY	I
Monmouth College, IL	I
Monmouth University, NJ	I
Montana State University, MT	D,I
Montana State University Billings, MT	I
Montana Tech of The University of Montana, MT	I
Montclair State University, NJ	I
Moravian College, PA	I
Morehead State University, KY	I
Morningside College, IA	I
Mount Carmel College of Nursing, OH	I
Mount Holyoke College, MA	I,P
Mount Marty College, SD	I
Mount Mary College, WI	I
Mount Mercy University, IA	I
Mount Saint Mary College, NY	I
Mount St. Mary's College, CA	I
Mount St. Mary's University, MD	I
Mount Vernon Nazarene University, OH	I
Muhlenberg College, PA	I
Murray State University, KY	I
Naropa University, CO	I
Nazarene Bible College, CO	I
Nazareth College of Rochester, NY	I
Nebraska Methodist College, NE	I
Nebraska Wesleyan University, NE	I
Neumann University, PA	I
Neumont University, UT	I
Newberry College, SC	G,I
Newbury College, MA	I
New College of Florida, FL	I
New England College, NH	I
New Jersey City University, NJ	D
New Jersey Institute of Technology, NJ	D,I
New Mexico Highlands University, NM	I
New Mexico State University, NM	D,I
New Saint Andrews College, ID	G,I
New York City College of Technology of the City University of New York, NY	I
New York Institute of Technology, NY	I
New York School of Interior Design, NY	I
New York University, NY	D,I,P
Niagara University, NY	D,I
Nicholls State University, LA	D,I
Nichols College, MA	I
North Carolina Central University, NC	I
North Carolina State University, NC	I
North Central College, IL	I
Northeastern Illinois University, IL	D,G
Northeastern University, MA	I
Northern Arizona University, AZ	G,I
Northern Illinois University, IL	G
Northern Kentucky University, KY	I
Northern Michigan University, MI	D,I
Northern State University, SD	I
Northland College, WI	I
Northwest Christian University, OR	D,I
Northwestern College, MN	I
Northwestern Oklahoma State University, OK	I
Northwestern State University of Louisiana, LA	I
Northwest Missouri State University, MO	D,I
Northwest Nazarene University, ID	I,P
Northwood University, Michigan Campus, MI	I

D = deferred payment system; *G* = guaranteed tuition rate; *I* = installment payments; *P* = prepayment locks in tuition rate

Northwood University, Texas Campus, TX	I
Notre Dame de Namur University, CA	I
Nova Southeastern University, FL	D,I
Nyack College, NY	I
Oakland University, MI	D,I
Occidental College, CA	I,P
Oglethorpe University, GA	I,P
The Ohio State University, OH	I
Ohio University, OH	I
Ohio University–Chillicothe, OH	I
Ohio University–Zanesville, OH	I
Ohio Valley University, WV	I
Ohio Wesleyan University, OH	I
Oklahoma Baptist University, OK	I
Oklahoma Christian University, OK	I
Oklahoma City University, OK	D,G,I
Oklahoma State University, OK	I
Oklahoma Wesleyan University, OK	D,I
Old Dominion University, VA	D,I
Olivet Nazarene University, IL	I
Ouachita Baptist University, AR	D,I
Pace University, NY	I
Pacific Lutheran University, WA	I
Pacific Union College, CA	G,I
Pacific University, OR	D,I
Palm Beach Atlantic University, FL	I
Peabody Conservatory of The Johns Hopkins University, MD	I
Peirce College, PA	I
Penn State Abington, PA	D,I
Penn State Altoona, PA	D,I
Penn State Berks, PA	D,I
Penn State Erie, The Behrend College, PA	D,I
Penn State Harrisburg, PA	D,I
Penn State Shenango, PA	D,I
Penn State University Park, PA	D,I
Pennsylvania College of Technology, PA	D
Pepperdine University, CA	I
Philadelphia University, PA	D,I
Philander Smith College, AR	D,I
Piedmont College, GA	I
Piedmont International University, NC	I
Pine Manor College, MA	I
Pittsburg State University, KS	I
Pitzer College, CA	D,I
Plymouth State University, NH	I
Point Loma Nazarene University, CA	I
Point Park University, PA	D,I
Polytechnic University of Puerto Rico, PR	D
Pomona College, CA	I
Portland State University, OR	I
Post University, CT	I
Presbyterian College, SC	I
Prescott College, AZ	D,I
Princeton University, NJ	D,I
Principia College, IL	I
Providence College, RI	I
Purchase College, State University of New York, NY	I
Purdue University, IN	I
Purdue University Calumet, IN	D
Purdue University North Central, IN	D,I
Queens College of the City University of New York, NY	I
Quincy University, IL	I
Quinnipiac University, CT	I
Radford University, VA	I
Randolph College, VA	I
Randolph-Macon College, VA	I
Reed College, OR	I
Regent University, VA	I
Regis University, CO	D,I
Rensselaer Polytechnic Institute, NY	I
Research College of Nursing, MO	D,I
Resurrection University, IL	D,I
Rhode Island College, RI	I
Rhodes College, TN	I
Rice University, TX	I
The Richard Stockton College of New Jersey, NJ	D,I
Rider University, NJ	I
Ringling College of Art and Design, FL	I
Ripon College, WI	I
Roanoke College, VA	I
Robert Morris University, PA	D,I
Robert Morris University Illinois, IL	I
Roberts Wesleyan College, NY	I
Rochester Institute of Technology, NY	D,I
Rockford College, IL	I
Rockhurst University, MO	D,I
Rocky Mountain College, MT	I
Rocky Mountain College of Art + Design, CO	G,I
Rogers State University, OK	I
Roger Williams University, RI	D,G,I
Rollins College, FL	I
Roosevelt University, IL	I
Rose-Hulman Institute of Technology, IN	I,P
Rosemont College, PA	I
Rowan University, NJ	D
Russell Sage College, NY	D,I
Rutgers, The State University of New Jersey, Newark, NJ	I
Rutgers, The State University of New Jersey, New Brunswick, NJ	I
Sacred Heart University, CT	I
Sage College of Albany, NY	D,I
Saginaw Valley State University, MI	I
St. Ambrose University, IA	I
Saint Anselm College, NH	I
Saint Anthony College of Nursing, IL	D,I
Saint Augustine's College, NC	D
St. Catherine University, MN	I
Saint Charles Borromeo Seminary, Overbrook, PA	I
St. Cloud State University, MN	I
St. Edward's University, TX	D,I
Saint Francis Medical Center College of Nursing, IL	I
St. John Fisher College, NY	D,I
St. John's College, MD	I
St. John's College, NM	I,P
Saint John's University, MN	I
St. John's University, NY	I
Saint Joseph's College, IN	I
St. Joseph's College, Long Island Campus, NY	D,I
St. Joseph's College, New York, NY	D,I
Saint Joseph's University, PA	I,P
St. Lawrence University, NY	I
St. Louis College of Pharmacy, MO	I
Saint Louis University, MO	I
Saint Martin's University, WA	I
Saint Mary-of-the-Woods College, IN	G,I
Saint Mary's College, IN	I
Saint Mary's College of California, CA	I,P
St. Mary's College of Maryland, MD	I
Saint Mary's University of Minnesota, MN	I
Saint Michael's College, VT	I
St. Norbert College, WI	D,I
St. Olaf College, MN	I
Saint Peter's University, NJ	I
St. Thomas University, FL	I
Salisbury University, MD	I
Salve Regina University, RI	I
Sam Houston State University, TX	I
San Diego Christian College, CA	I
San Diego State University, CA	I
San Francisco Art Institute, CA	I
San Francisco Conservatory of Music, CA	I
San Francisco State University, CA	I
Santa Clara University, CA	I
Sarah Lawrence College, NY	I
Savannah College of Art and Design, GA	I
School of the Art Institute of Chicago, IL	I
School of the Museum of Fine Arts, Boston, MA	I
School of Visual Arts, NY	I
Schreiner University, TX	I
Scripps College, CA	I,P
Seattle Pacific University, WA	D,I
Seattle University, WA	D,I
Seton Hill University, PA	I
Sewanee: The University of the South, TN	D,G,I
Shawnee State University, OH	I
Shenandoah University, VA	I
Shepherd University, WV	I
Shimer College, IL	I
Shippensburg University of Pennsylvania, PA	I
Siena College, NY	I
Sierra Nevada College, NV	I
Simmons College, MA	I
Simpson College, IA	I
Simpson University, CA	D
Skidmore College, NY	I,P
Slippery Rock University of Pennsylvania, PA	I
Smith College, MA	I,P
Soka University of America, CA	D,I
Sonoma State University, CA	I
South Dakota State University, SD	D,I
Southeastern Oklahoma State University, OK	I
Southeast Missouri State University, MO	D,I
Southern Adventist University, TN	D,I,P
Southern Arkansas University–Magnolia, AR	I
Southern Connecticut State University, CT	D,I
Southern Illinois University Carbondale, IL	G,I
Southern Illinois University Edwardsville, IL	G,I
Southern Methodist University, TX	I,P
Southern Utah University, UT	I
Southern Vermont College, VT	I
Southwest Baptist University, MO	I
Southwestern College, KS	I
Southwestern University, TX	I
Spelman College, GA	D,I
Spring Arbor University, MI	I
Spring Hill College, AL	I
State University of New York at Fredonia, NY	I
State University of New York at Oswego, NY	I
State University of New York at Plattsburgh, NY	D,I
State University of New York College at Cortland, NY	I
State University of New York College at Geneseo, NY	D,I
State University of New York College at Old Westbury, NY	I
State University of New York College at Oneonta, NY	I
State University of New York College at Potsdam, NY	I

D = deferred payment system; *G* = guaranteed tuition rate; *I* = installment payments; *P* = prepayment locks in tuition rate

State University of New York College of Agriculture and Technology at Cobleskill, NY — D,I

State University of New York College of Environmental Science and Forestry, NY — D,I

State University of New York College of Technology at Delhi, NY — I

State University of New York Institute of Technology, NY — I

State University of New York Maritime College, NY — I

Stephen F. Austin State University, TX — I

Stephens College, MO — I

Sterling College, VT — I

Stetson University, FL — I

Stevenson University, MD — D,I

Stonehill College, MA — I,P

Stony Brook University, State University of New York, NY — I

Stratford University, VA — I

Suffolk University, MA — D,I

Swarthmore College, PA — I

Sweet Briar College, VA — I

Syracuse University, NY — I

Tarleton State University, TX — I

Taylor University, IN — I

Temple University, PA — I

Tennessee Technological University, TN — D

Texas A&M International University, TX — I

Texas A&M University, TX — I

Texas Christian University, TX — I

Texas College, TX — I

Texas Lutheran University, TX — I

Texas Southern University, TX — D,I

Texas State University–San Marcos, TX — I

Texas Tech University, TX — I

Texas Wesleyan University, TX — D,I

Texas Woman's University, TX — I

Thiel College, PA — I

Thomas Aquinas College, CA — I

Thomas More College, KY — D,I

Tiffin University, OH — D,I

Towson University, MD — I

Transylvania University, KY — I

Trevecca Nazarene University, TN — I,P

Trine University, IN — I

Trinity Baptist College, FL — I

Trinity Christian College, IL — I

Trinity College, CT — I

Trinity College of Florida, FL — I

Trinity College of Nursing and Health Sciences, IL — I

Trinity University, TX — I

Troy University, AL — I

Truman State University, MO — I

Tufts University, MA — I,P

Tulane University, LA — I,P

Tuskegee University, AL — I

Union College, KY — I

Union College, NY — I

Union University, TN — D,I

Unity College, ME — I

Universidad Adventista de las Antillas, PR — I

Universidad Teolgica del Caribe, PR — D

University at Buffalo, the State University of New York, NY — I

The University of Akron, OH — I

The University of Alabama, AL — D,I

The University of Alabama at Birmingham, AL — I

The University of Alabama in Huntsville, AL — I

University of Alaska Fairbanks, AK — D,I

The University of Arizona, AZ — I

University of Bridgeport, CT — D,I

University of California, Berkeley, CA — I

University of California, Davis, CA — D

University of California, Irvine, CA — I

University of California, Riverside, CA — D

University of California, Santa Barbara, CA — I

University of California, Santa Cruz, CA — I

University of Central Arkansas, AR — I

University of Central Florida, FL — D,P

University of Charleston, WV — I

University of Chicago, IL — I,P

University of Cincinnati, OH — I

University of Colorado Boulder, CO — D

University of Colorado Colorado Springs, CO — I

University of Colorado Denver, CO — D,I

University of Connecticut, CT — D,I

University of Dallas, TX — I

University of Dayton, OH — D,I,P

University of Delaware, DE — I

University of Denver, CO — D,I

University of Evansville, IN — I

University of Florida, FL — D

University of Great Falls, MT — I

University of Hartford, CT — I,P

University of Hawaii at Manoa, HI — I

University of Hawaii–West Oahu, HI — I

University of Houston, TX — D,I

University of Houston–Clear Lake, TX — D,I

University of Idaho, ID — D,I

University of Illinois at Chicago, IL — G,I

University of Illinois at Springfield, IL — G,I

University of Illinois at Urbana–Champaign, IL — G,I

The University of Iowa, IA — I

The University of Kansas, KS — G,I

University of La Verne, CA — D,I

University of Louisville, KY — I

University of Maine, ME — I

University of Maine at Augusta, ME — I

University of Maine at Farmington, ME — I

University of Maine at Fort Kent, ME — I

University of Maine at Presque Isle, ME — D,I

University of Mary, ND — I

University of Mary Hardin-Baylor, TX — I

University of Maryland, Baltimore County, MD — I

University of Maryland, College Park, MD — D,I

University of Maryland Eastern Shore, MD — D,I

University of Maryland University College, MD — I

University of Mary Washington, VA — I

University of Massachusetts Amherst, MA — I

University of Massachusetts Dartmouth, MA — I

University of Massachusetts Lowell, MA — I

University of Miami, FL — G,I,P

University of Michigan, MI — I

University of Michigan–Dearborn, MI — I

University of Michigan–Flint, MI — I

University of Minnesota, Crookston, MN — I

University of Minnesota, Duluth, MN — I

University of Minnesota, Twin Cities Campus, MN — I

University of Mississippi, MS — P

University of Missouri–Kansas City, MO — I

University of Missouri–St. Louis, MO — I

University of Mobile, AL — I

The University of Montana, MT — I

The University of Montana Western, MT — D,I

University of Mount Union, OH — I,P

University of Nebraska at Kearney, NE — I

University of Nebraska–Lincoln, NE — I

University of Nevada, Las Vegas, NV — D

University of New England, ME — I

University of New Hampshire, NH — I

University of New Hampshire at Manchester, NH — I

University of New Haven, CT — I

University of New Orleans, LA — I

University of North Alabama, AL — I

University of North Carolina at Asheville, NC — I

The University of North Carolina at Chapel Hill, NC — I

The University of North Carolina at Greensboro, NC — I

The University of North Carolina at Pembroke, NC — I

The University of North Carolina Wilmington, NC — I

University of Northern Colorado, CO — D

University of Northern Iowa, IA — I

University of North Florida, FL — I

University of North Texas, TX — I

University of Notre Dame, IN — I

University of Oklahoma, OK — G,I

University of Oregon, OR — I

University of Pennsylvania, PA — I,P

University of Pikeville, KY — I

University of Pittsburgh, PA — D,I

University of Pittsburgh at Bradford, PA — I

University of Pittsburgh at Greensburg, PA — I

University of Pittsburgh at Johnstown, PA — I

University of Portland, OR — D,I

University of Puerto Rico at Bayamón, PR — D,G

University of Puget Sound, WA — D,I

University of Redlands, CA — I

University of Rhode Island, RI — I

University of Richmond, VA — I

University of Rochester, NY — I,P

University of St. Francis, IL — D,I

University of Saint Joseph, CT — I

University of St. Thomas, TX — D,I

University of San Diego, CA — I

University of Science and Arts of Oklahoma, OK — G,I

The University of Scranton, PA — I

University of South Alabama, AL — I

University of South Carolina, SC — D

University of South Carolina Aiken, SC — D

University of South Carolina Upstate, SC — D

The University of South Dakota, SD — D

University of Southern Indiana, IN — I

University of Southern Maine, ME — I

University of Southern Mississippi, MS — I

The University of Tampa, FL — I

The University of Tennessee, TN — I

The University of Tennessee at Chattanooga, TN — I

The University of Tennessee at Martin, TN — D

The University of Texas at Arlington, TX — I

The University of Texas at Austin, TX — I

The University of Texas at Brownsville, TX — I

The University of Texas at Dallas, TX — G,I

The University of Texas at San Antonio, TX — D,I

D = deferred payment system; *G* = guaranteed tuition rate; *I* = installment payments; *P* = prepayment locks in tuition rate

Peterson's How to Get Money for College 2014